How to use the dictionary

atlas ['æt·ləs] <-es> *n* atlante *m*
ATM [,eɪ·tiː·'em] *n abbr of* **automated teller machine** ≈ Bancomat® *m inv*
atmosphere ['æt·məs·fɪr] *n* **1.** *a.* PHYS atmosfera *f* **2.** *fig* atmosfera *f*

build [bɪld] **I.** *vt* <built, built> **1.** (*make: house*) costruire; (*fire*) fare; (*car*) fabbricare ...
  ◆**build in** *vt* incassare
  ◆**build on** *vt* basare su; **to build sth on sth** basare qc su qc

console[1] [kən·'soʊl] *vt* (*comfort*) consolare
console[2] ['kɑːn·soʊl] *n* (*switch panel*) console *f*

decimate ['de·sɪ·meɪt] *vt* decimare

eat [iːt] **I.** <ate, eaten> *vt* mangiare; ...
empty ['emp·ti] **I.** <-ier, -iest> *adj* **1.** ...

gossip ['gɑː·səp] **I.** *n* **1.** (*rumor*) pettegolezzi *mpl*, gossip *m inv*; **idle ~** pettegolezzi; **~ columnist** cronista *mf* mondano, -a **2.** (*person*) pettegolo, -a *m, f* **II.** *vi* **1.** (*spread rumors*) spettegolare; **to ~ about sb** spettegolare su qu **2.** (*chatter*) chiacchierare

hot [hɑːt] **I.** *adj* **1.** (*very warm*) caldo, -a; **it's ~** fa caldo **2.** (*spicy*) piccante **3.** *inf* (*skillful*) bravo, -a; ... **8.** *sl*(*stolen*) **to be ~** scottare ▶**to be all ~ and** bothered essere agitato **II.** *n* **he has the ~s for her** gli piace un sacco ...

absolute ['æb·sə·luːt] **I.** *adj* **1.** (*total, not relative*) *a.* POL assoluto, -a; (*denial*) categorico, -a; ... **2.** CHEM assoluto, -a **II.** *n* **the ~** PHILOS l'assoluto

joyless ['dʒɔɪ·ləs] *adj* (*marriage*) infelice; (*expression*) triste

Discovery Day *n Can:* anniversario della scoperta dell'America

mishap ['mɪs·hæp] *n form* incidente *m;* **a series of ~s** una serie di incidenti

polytechnic [,pɑː·lɪ·'tek·nɪk] *n* istituto *m* tecnico universitario

September [sep·'tem·bəʳ] *n* settembre *m; s.a.* **April**

All **entries** (including words, abbreviations, compounds, variant spellings and cross-references) appear in alphabetical order and are printed in bold type. Abbreviations are followed by their full form.

English phrasal verbs come directly after the base verb and are marked with a diamond (◆).

Superscript, or raised numbers, indicate identically spelled words with different meanings (so-called **homographs**).

The International Phonetic Alphabet is used for all phonetic transcriptions.
Transcriptions of English are divided into syllables by means of centered dots.

Irregular plural forms and **forms of English irregular verbs and adjectives** are given in angle brackets.

Italian feminine forms are shown unless they are identical to the masculine form. Italian nouns are followed by their gender.
Roman numerals are used for the **parts of speech** of a word, and Arabic numerals for **sense divisions.**

The **swung dash** represents the entry word in examples and idioms. The ▶ sign introduces **a block of set expressions, idioms and proverbs**. Key words are underlined as a guide.

Various kinds of **meaning indicators** are used to guide users to the required translation:

- **subject labels (which indicate areas of specialization)**

- **definitions** or **synonyms,** typical **subjects** or **objects** of verbs, typical **nouns** used with adjectives, etc.
- **Regional vocabulary and variants** are shown both as headwords and translations
- **Usage Labels** (which indicate restriction to a particular level or style of usage)

When a word or expression has no direct translation, an explanation or approximate equivalent is given (≈). Where a translation may be ambiguous, it is followed by an explanation in parentheses.

v. a. (vedi anche) or *s. a. (see also)* invites the reader to consult a **model entry** for further information.

W9-BXL-679

With the aid of the alphabetical thumb index overleaf (at the edge of the page) you can quickly locate the letter you need to find in the Italian-English and English-Italian dictionary.

Once you have located the letter you need on the thumb index, simply flip to the correspondingly marked part of the dictionary.

If you are left-handed, you can use the thumb index at the end of this book.

Con l'aiuto dell'indice alfabetico a bordo pagina è possibile selezionare rapidamente la lettera di cui si ha bisogno nelle sezioni Italiano-Inglese e Inglese-Italiano del dizionario.

Dopo aver scelto la lettera nell'indice, aprire il dizionario alla sezione voluta.

Gli utenti mancini possono servirsi dell'indice che si trova alla fine del dizionario.

ITALIAN–ENGLISH

Dictionary

Dizionario
ITALIANO–INGLESE

ITALIAN–ENGLISH
Dictionary

Dizionario
ITALIANO–INGLESE

BARRON'S Foreign Language Guides
Italian-English Dictionary
Dizionario Italiano-Inglese

First edition for the United States and Canada © Copyright 2007 by Barron's Educational Series, Inc.
Original edition © Copyright 2007 by Ernst Klett Sprachen GmbH, Stuttgart, Federal Republic of Germany.

Editorial management:
Roberta Martignon-Burgholte
Dr. Andreas Cyffka

Contributors: Richard Alderman, Gabriella Bacchelli, Silvia Brattoli Pavesi, Roberta Colombo, A. Stella Giusto Franetzki, Tim Gutteridge, Simone Heinold, Helen Hyde, Francesca Logi, Stefano Longo, Debora Mazza, Roberta Martignon-Burgholte, Liz Potter, Delia Prosperi, Loredana Riu, Anna Maria Rubino, Donald Watt, Carla Zipoli

Typesetting: Dörr + Schiller, Stuttgart
Data Processing: Andreas Lang, conTEXT AG für Informatik und Kommunikation, Zürich

All inquiries should be addressed to:
Barron's Educational Series, Inc.
250 Wireless Boulevard
Hauppauge, NY 11788
http://www.barronseduc.com

ISBN-13: 978-0-7641-3764-8
ISBN-10: 0-7641-3764-6
Library of Congress Control Number 2007925333

Printed in China
9 8 7

Indice

Contents

Introduction

This is a new bilingual dictionary designed to meet the needs of people in a time of ever-expanding communication among English and Italian speakers. It has been written and edited by a large team of native speakers of both languages so that it constitutes an updated, comprehensive, and most useful linguistic tool.

This dictionary provides accurate coverage of current vocabulary in English and Italian, as well as abundant examples of words used in context to illustrate idiomatic usage. To facilitate self-expression, pronunciation is provided in both languages, so that the users may express themselves correctly and idiomatically – both orally and in writing.

A unique characteristic is the possibility of downloading this dictionary into your home computer, laptop, and nearly all PDAs and smartphones. In addition, attention is given to small but meaningful features that include alphabet tabs for ease of use, maps and cultural boxes to enrich the process of language acquisition, and useful explanatory sections.

Introduzione

Il Barron's Italian – English Dictionary (Dizionario Italiano – Inglese) è un nuovo dizionario bilingue concepito per far fronte alle crescenti necessità di comunicazione tra i parlanti in inglese e in italiano. Compilato e rivisto da un'équipe di redattori di entrambe le lingue, costituisce un utile strumento linguistico, aggiornato e completo.

Il dizionario include il vocabolario dell'inglese e dell'italiano correnti ed è ricco di esempi contestualizzati che illustrano l'uso idiomatico delle parole. Per facilitare l'espressione autonoma è stata fornita la pronuncia inglese e italiana, in modo da consentire a tutti di esprimersi in modo corretto e idiomatico sia oralmente che per iscritto.

Una peculiarità del dizionario è quella di poter essere scaricato sul proprio PC di casa, sui portatili e anche su quasi tutti i computer palmari e i cellulari smartphone. Grande attenzione è stata data a piccoli ma importanti dettagli come gli identificatori alfabetici che agevolano la consultazione, le cartine e le voci di approfondimento culturale che arricchiscono il processo di acquisizione della lingua, e le utili sezioni esplicative.

La trascrizione fonetica dell'italiano –
Italian phonetic symbols

Vocali/Vowels

[a]	baco
[e]	mela
[ɛ]	elica
[i]	dito
[o]	onda
[ɔ]	oasi
[u]	muro

Dittonghi/Diphtongs

[ja]	piatto
[je]	pieno
[jo]	fionda
[ju]	fiume
[wa]	guaio
[wo]	fuorilegge
[wɔ]	fuori

Consonanti/Consonants

[b]	bello
[d]	dama
[dʒ]	giorno, gelo
[dz]	zeta
[f]	fune
[g]	gola, ghiro
[k]	come, chino, che
[l]	loro
[ʎ]	aglio
[m]	mercato
[ŋ]	natura
[ŋŋ]	degno
[p]	pagina
[r]	regola
[s]	sale
[ʃ]	sciare
[t]	timbro
[ts]	zio
[tʃ]	cinese, cera
[v]	vapore
[z]	slegare

A

A, a [a] <-> *f* A, a; **dall'~ alla zeta** from A to Z; **~ come Ancona** A as in Apple

a *abbr di* **anno** yr.

a [a] <al, allo, all', alla, ai, agli, alle> *prep* **1.** (*stato in luogo*) at; **al mare** at the beach; **al mercato** at the market; **sono ~ casa** I am at home; **~ Trieste** in Trieste; **~ 20 chilometri da Torino** 20 kilometers from Turin; **~ pagina cinque** on page five; **alla televisione** on television **2.** (*moto a luogo*) to; **andare al mare** to go to the beach; **andare al mercato** to go to the market; **andare ~ Trieste** to go to Trieste **3.** (*tempo*) at; (*riferito a mese, stagione*) in; (*fino*) till; **~ mezzogiorno** at noon; **alle sette** at seven; **~ marzo** in March; **~ domani** see you tomorrow; **al venerdì** on Fridays; **due volte al giorno** twice a day; **dall'oggi al domani** from one day to the next **4.** (*con prezzo*) at; **~ 2 euro al chilo** (at) 2 euros a kilo **5.** (*complemento di termine*) to; **lo regalo ~ Giuseppe** I'm giving it to Giuseppe **6.** (*età*) **~ vent'anni** at the age of twenty **7.** (*proposizione finale*) **andare ~ sciare** to go skiing **8.** (*modo*) **fatto ~ mano** handmade; **gnocchi alla romana** gnocchi Roman-style **9.** (*mezzo*) **~ cavallo** on horseback; **~ piedi** on foot **10.** (*velocità*) **viaggiare ~ 120 chilometri l'ora** to travel at 120 kilometers an hour **11.** MATH **due al quadrato** two squared **12.** (*loc*) **~ uno ~ uno** one by one; **~ due ~ due** in pairs

A 1. *abbr di* **Austria** A **2.** *abbr di* **autostrada** M **3.** *abbr di* **ampère** A

AAST *abbr di* **Azienda Autonoma di Soggiorno e Turismo** Local Convention and Visitors Bureau

AA.VV. *abbr di* **Autori Vari** various authors

abate [a·'ba:·te] *m* abbot

abat-jour [a·ba·'ʒu:r] <-> *m* **1.** (*paralume*) lampshade **2.** (*lampada*) lamp

abbacchiato [ab·ba·k'kia:·to] *agg* depressed

abbacinamento [ab·ba·tʃi·na·'men·to] *m fig* (*inganno, illusione*) deception

abbacinare [ab·ba·tʃi·'na:·re] *vt* **1.** (*abbagliare*) to dazzle **2.** *fig* (*illudere*) to deceive

abbagliamento [ab·ba·ʎʎa·'men·to] *m fig* (*sbaglio*) deception

abbagliante [ab·ba·ʎ'ʎan·te] *agg* (*luce*) dazzling

abbaglianti [ab·ba·ʎ'ʎan·ti] *mpl* AUTO high beams

abbagliare [ab·ba·ʎ'ʎa:·re] *vt essere* **1.** (*luce*) to dazzle **2.** *fig* (*ingannare*) to deceive

abbaglio [ab·'ba·ʎʎo] <-gli> *m* blunder; **prendere un ~** to blunder

abbaiare [ab·ba·'ia:·re] *vi* to bark

abbaino [ab·ba·'i:no] *m* dormer; (*soffitta*) attic

abbandonare [ab·ban·do·'na:·re] **I.** *vt* **1.** (*las-ciare: famiglia, paese*) to abandon; (*non aiutare: amico*) to let down **2.** (*trascurare: casa, giardino*) to neglect **3.** (*rinunciare a: progetto, speranza*) to give up **4.** (*reclinare: capo*) to drop **5.** (*allentare*) **~ la presa** to let go **II.** *vr:* **-rsi** *a. fig* to let oneself go; **-rsi a un vizio** to indulge a bad habit

abbandonato, -a [ab·ban·do·'na:·to] *agg* (*bambino*) abandoned; (*trascurato: casa*) neglected; **~ a se stesso** left to one's own resources

abbandono [ab·ban·'do:·no] *m* **1.** (*di famiglia, coniuge*) abandonment **2.** (*trascuratezza*) neglect; **cadere in ~** (*casa*) to become dilapidated; (*giardino*) to become overgrown **3.** (*rinuncia: a progetto*) giving up; (*a gara*) withdrawal **4.** (*rilassamento*) abandon

abbarbicarsi [ab·bar·bi·'ka:r·si] *vr* **~ a** to cling to

abbassamento [ab·bas·sa·'men·to] *m* **1.** (*di prezzi*) reduction **2.** (*di temperatura, pressione*) drop **3.** (*d'intensità*) lowering; **avere un ~ di voce** to have a croaky voice

abbassare [ab·bas·'sa:·re] **I.** *vt* **1.** (*mettere più in basso*) to lower; (*finestrino dell'auto*) to wind down **2.** (*prezzo, temperatura*) to reduce; (*voce*) to keep down; (*radio*) to turn down; (*tasto*) to push down; (*bandiera*) lower; **~ i fari** to dim the headlights; **~ gli occhi** to lower one's eyes; **~ le armi** *fig* to lay down one's arms; **~ la cresta** *fig* to back down **II.** *vr:* **-rsi 1.** (*chinarsi*) to bend down **2.** *fig* (*umiliarsi*) to demean oneself **3.** (*calare: barometro, temperatura*) to drop; (*sole*) to go down

abbasso [ab·'bas·so] *avv* **~ qc!** down with sth!

abbastanza [ab·bas·'tan·tsa] **I.** *avv* **1.** (*a sufficienza*) enough; **averne ~ di qu/qc** to be fed up with sb/sth **2.** (*alquanto*) pretty **II.** <inv> *agg* (*a sufficienza*) enough; **non ho ~ tempo** I do not have enough time

abbattere [ab·'bat·te·re] **I.** *vt* **1.** (*alberi*) to cut down; (*muri*) to pull down **2.** (*uccidere*) to kill; (*bestie al macello*) to slaughter; (*selvaggina*) to shoot **3.** (*aereo*) to down **4.** *fig* (*prostrare*) to depress; (*soggetto: malattia*) to lay low **5.** *fig* (*rovesciare: governo*) to overthrow **II.** *vr:* **-rsi 1.** (*cadere di schianto*) **~ su qu/qc** to hit sb/sth **2.** *fig* (*deprimersi*) to get depressed

abbattimento [ab·bat·ti·'men·to] *m* **1.** (*di alberi*) felling; (*di case*) demolition **2.** (*di bestie al macello*) slaughter; (*di selvaggina*) shooting **3.** (*di aereo*) downing **4.** *fig* (*prostrazione*) depression; (*da malattia*) exhaustion **5.** *fig* (*di governo*) overthrow

abbazia [ab·ba·'tsi:a] <-ie> *f* abbey

abbellimento [ab·bel·li·'men·to] *m* **1.** (*ornamento*) embellishment **2.** MUS grace note

abbellire [ab·bel·'li:·re] <abbellisco> **I.** *vt* **1.** (*rendere più bello*) to make more attractive **2.** (*stanza*) to decorate **3.** (*racconto*) to embellish **II.** *vr:* **-rsi** to become more attractive

abbeverare [ab·be·ve·'ra:·re] I. *vt* to water II. *vr:* -**rsi** to drink

abbeveratoio [ab·be·ve·ra·'to:·io] <-oi> *m* drinking trough

abbia ['ab·bia] *1., 2. e 3. pers sing conj pr di* **avere**[1]

abbiccì [ab·bit·'tʃi] <-> *m* 1.(*alfabeto*) ABC 2.(*sillabario*) ABC book 3. *fig* (*primi elementi*) ABCs

abbiente [ab·'biɛn·te] I. *agg* well-off II. *mf* **gli** -**i** the well-to-do; **i non** -**i** the needy

abbigliamento [ab·bi·ʎʎa·'men·to] *m* clothing; (*indumenti*) clothes

abbigliare [ab·bi·ʎʎa:·re] I. *vt* to dress up II. *vr:* -**rsi** to dress up

abbinamento [ab·bi·na·'men·to] *m* (*di colori, abiti*) combination

abbinare [ab·bi·'na:·re] *vt* (*unire*) to join; (*colori, abiti*) to match; **un vino da ~ ai dolci** a wine to be served with desserts; **una giacca da ~ a questi pantaloni** a jacket to go with these pants

abbindolare [ab·bin·do·'la:·re] *vt* to trick

abbioccato, -a [ab·biok·'ka:·to] *agg* sleepy

abbiocco [ab·'biɔk·ko] <-cchi> *m inf* **avere l'~** to feel dozy

abbisognare [ab·bi·zo·ɲ'ɲa:·re] *vi* ~ **di qc** to need sth

abboccamento [ab·bok·ka·'men·to] *m* meeting

abboccare [ab·bok·'ka:·re] I. *vt* TEC to join II. *vi* 1. *a. fig* (*pesce*) to bite 2. TEC (*combaciare*) to fit together III. *vr:* -**rsi** to have a meeting

abboccato, -a [ab·bok·'ka:·to] *agg* (*vino*) medium sweet

abboccatura [ab·bok·ka·'tu:·ra] *f* (*di recipienti*) opening

abbonamento [ab·bo·na·'men·to] *m* 1.(*a giornale*) subscription; (*a teatro*) season ticket; **fare l'~ a qc** (*giornale*) to subscribe to sth; (*teatro*) to buy a season ticket for sth 2.(*ferroviario, tranviario*) season pass

abbonare [ab·bo·'na:·re] I. *vt* 1.(*debito*) ~ **qc a qu** to let sb off sth 2. *fig* (*perdonare*) ~ **qc a qu** to forgive sb sth 3. (*fare un abbonamento*) ~ **qu a qc** to take out a subscription to sth for sb II. *vr* -**rsi a un giornale** to subscribe to a newspaper

abbonato, -a [ab·bo·'na:·to] I. *agg* **essere ~** (*a giornale*) to be a subscriber; (*alla televisione*) to be a license holder; (*all'autobus*) to be a season pass holder II. *m, f* (*a teatro*) season ticket holder; (*al telefono*) subscriber; (*alla televisione*) license holder

abbondante [ab·bon·'dan·te] *agg* (*pasto*) generous; (*vestito*) large; **tre metri** -**i** well over three meters

abbondanza [ab·bon·'dan·tsa] *f* abundance; **abbiamo verdura in ~** we have plenty of vegetables

abbondare [ab·bon·'da:·re] *vi* 1.(*essere in grande quantità*) to be plentiful 2.(*eccedere*)

~ in generosità to be very generous; **~ di** to be full of

abbordabile [ab·bor·'da:·bi·le] *agg* 1.(*spesa*) affordable 2.(*persona*) approachable

abbordaggio [ab·bor·'dad·dʒo] <-ggi> *m* 1. NAUT boarding 2. *fig* (*approccio: di persona*) hooking up

abbordare [ab·bor·'da:·re] *vt* 1. NAUT to board 2. *inf* (*persona*) to hook up with 3. *fig* (*affrontare: problema*) to tackle

abbordo [ab·'bor·do] *m* NAUT boarding

abborracciare [ab·bor·rat·'tʃa:·re] *vt* to botch up

abbottonare [ab·bot·to·'na:·re] I. *vt* to button up II. *vr:* -**rsi** *fig, inf* to clam up

abbottonatura [ab·bot·to·na·'tu:·ra] *f* 1.(*chiusura*) fastening 2.(*serie di bottoni*) buttons

abbozzare [ab·bot·'tsa:·re] *vt* 1.(*disegno, romanzo*) to sketch 2. *fig* (*accennare: sorriso*) to give a hint of

abbozzo [ab·'bɔt·tso] *m* sketch; **~ di legge** JUR draft bill

abbracciare [ab·brat·'tʃa:·re] I. *vt* 1.(*con le braccia*) to hug 2. *fig* (*contenere: paesaggio, periodo*) to include II. *vr:* -**rsi** to hug

abbraccio [ab·'brat·tʃo] <-cci> *m* hug

abbrancare [ab·braŋ·'ka:·re] I. *vt* to grab II. *vr* -**rsi a qc** to cling to sth

abbreviare [ab·bre·'via:·re] *vt* 1.(*percorso*) to shorten 2.(*parola*) to abbreviate

abbreviazione [ab·bre·viat·'tsio:·ne] *f* (*di parola*) abbreviation

abbronzante [ab·bron·'dzan·te] I. *agg* tanning II. *m* suntan lotion

abbronzare [ab·bron·'dza:·re] I. *vt* (*epidermide*) to tan II. *vr:* -**rsi** to tan

abbronzato, -a [ab·bron·'dza:·to] *agg* tan

abbronzatura [ab·bron·dza·'tu:·ra] *f* tan

abbrustolire [ab·brus·to·'li:·re] <abbrustolisco> I. *vt* (*pane*) to toast; (*verdure*) to broil II. *vr:* -**rsi** *scherz* ~ **al sole** to roast in the sun

abbrutimento [ab·bru·ti·'men·to] *m* mindless state; **l'~ causato dalla televisione** the stupefying effect of television

abbruttire [ab·brut·'ti:·re] <abbruttisco> I. *vt* avere to make ugly II. *vi* essere to become ugly

abbuffarsi [ab·buf·'far·si] *vr inf* to stuff oneself (with food)

abbuffata [ab·buf·'fa:·ta] *f* **fare un'~** to stuff oneself (with food)

abbuiare [ab·bu·'ia:·re] I. *vt* 1.(*lampada*) to dim; (*strada*) to make dark 2. *fig* (*fatto, motivo*) to obscure II. *vr:* -**rsi** to get dark

abbuonare [ab·buo·'na:·re] *v.* abbonare

abbuono [ab·'buɔ:·no] *m* (*di prezzo*) discount

abdicare [ab·di·'ka:·re] *vi* to abdicate

abdicazione [ab·di·kat·'tsio:·ne] *f* abdication

aberrazione [ab·ber·rat·'tsio:·ne] *f* aberration; **~ mentale** MED mental aberration

abete [a·'be:·te] *m* fir; **~ bianco** silver fir; **~ rosso** spruce

abietto, -a [a·'biɛt·to] *agg* despicable

abiezione [abiet·'tsio:·ne] *f* vileness
abile ['a:bi·le] *agg* **1.** (*idoneo*) MIL fit; **essere ~ al lavoro** to be fit for work **2.** (*esperto*) skillful; **un ~ oratore** a skillful communicator **3.** (*accorto*) clever; **~ negli affari** with a good business sense
abilità [abi·li·'ta] <-> *f* **1.** (*idoneità*) fitness; **~ al lavoro** fitness for work **2.** (*capacità*) skill **3.** (*accortezza*) cleverness
abilitante [abi·li·'tan·te] *agg* qualifying; **esame ~** qualifying examination
abilitare [abi·li·'ta:·re] **I.** *vt* to qualify **II.** *vr:* **-rsi** to qualify
abilitato, -a [abi·li·'ta:·to] **I.** *agg* qualified **II.** *m*, *f* qualified teacher
abilitazione [abi·li·tat·'tsio:·ne] *f* qualification; **~ all'insegnamento** qualification to teach
abissale [abis·'sa:·le] *agg* **1.** (*degli abissi marini*) deep-sea **2.** *fig* (*profondo: differenza*) profound
abisso [a'bis·so] *m a. fig* abyss
abitabile [abi·'ta:·bi·le] *agg* habitable
abitabilità <-> *f* habitability; **permesso di ~** certificate of occupancy
abitacolo [abi·'ta:·ko·lo] *m* (*di auto*) interior; (*di camion*) driver's cab; (*di aereo*) cockpit
abitante [abi·'tan·te] *mf* (*di paese*) inhabitant; (*di casa, appartamento*) occupant
abitare [abi·'ta:·re] **I.** *vt* (*paese, mondo*) to inhabit; (*casa, appartamento*) to live in **II.** *vi* to live; **~ a Firenze** to live in Florence; **~ in campagna** to live in the country
abitato [abi·'ta:·to] *m* built-up area
abitato, -a *agg* inhabited; (*popolato*) populated
abitatore, -trice [abi·ta·'to:·re] *m*, *f* inhabitant
abitazione [abi·tat·'tsio:·ne] *f* (*appartamento*) apartment; (*casa*) house; **~ popolare** public housing unit; **~ di proprietà** owner-occupied apartment
abito ['a:bi·to] *m* **1.** (*da donna*) dress; (*da uomo*) suit; **~ da cerimonia** formal dress **2.** *pl* (*vestiti*) clothes *pl*; **in -i borghesi** in civilian clothes **3.** **l'~ non fa il monaco** *prov* you can't judge a book by its cover *prov*
abituale [abi·tu'a:·le] *agg* usual; **cliente ~** regular customer
abitualmente [abi·tual·'men·te] *avv* usually
abituare [abi·tu·'a:re] **I.** *vt* **~ qu a qc** to get sb used to sth **II.** *vr* **-rsi a qc** to get used to sth
abituato, -a [abi·tu·'a:to] *agg* **essere ~ a qc** to be used to sth
abitudinario, -a [abi·tu·di·'na:·rio] <-i, -ie> **I.** *agg* of habit **II.** *m*, *f* creature of habit; (*cliente*) regular customer
abitudine [abi·'tu:·di·ne] *f* **1.** (*consuetudine*) habit; **d'~** usually **2.** (*assuefazione*) **fare l'~ a qc** to get used to sth
abiura [a·'biu:·ra] *f* **1.** (*rinuncia*) renunciation **2.** (*ritrattazione*) recantation
abiurare [a·biu·'ra:·re] *vt* **~ qc** to renounce sth
ablativo [ab·la·'ti:·vo] *m* LING ablative
ablazione [ab·lat·'tsio:·ne] *f* **1.** MED removal **2.** GEOL ablation

abnegazione [ab·ne·gat·'tsio:·ne] *f* self-denial
abnorme [ab·'nɔr·me] *agg* abnormal
abolire [a·bo·'li:·re] <abolisco> *vt* to abolish
abolizione [a·bo·lit·'tsio:·ne] *f* abolition
abominevole [a·bo·mi·'ne:·vo·le] *agg* **1.** (*mostro*) appalling **2.** (*esecrabile: azione*) dreadful
abominio [a·bo·'mi:·nio] <-i> *m* **1.** (*disprezzo*) revulsion **2.** (*cosa, atto*) dreadful thing
aborigeno, -a [a·bo·'ri:·dʒe·no] **I.** *agg* aboriginal **II.** *m*, *f* Aboriginal
aborrire [a·bor·'ri:·re] <aborrisco *o* aborro> **I.** *vt* to abhor **II.** *vi* to be disgusted; **~ da qc** to be disgusted by sth
abortire [a·bor·'ti:·re] <abortisco> *vi* **1.** *avere* MED to have an abortion; (*involontariamente*) to have a miscarriage **2.** *essere fig* (*fallire*) to fail
abortista [a·bor·'tis·ta] <-i, -e> **I.** *mf* abortionist **II.** *agg* pro-abortion
aborto [a·'bɔr·to] *m* **1.** (*procurato*) abortion **2.** (*spontaneo*) miscarriage **3.** *fig* (*persona*) freak; (*opera d'arte*) monstrosity
abrasione [a·bra·'zio:·ne] *f* **1.** *a.* GEOG abrasion **2.** TEC grinding
abrasivo [a·bra·'zi:·vo] *m* abrasive
abrogare [ab·ro·'ga:·re] *vt* to abrogate
abrogazione [ab·ro·gat·'tsio:·ne] *f* abrogation
abruzzese [a·brut·'tse:·se] **I.** *agg* from the Abruzzi **II.** *mf* (*abitante*) inhabitant of the Abruzzi **III.** *m* (*dialetto*) dialect of the Abruzzi
Abruzzi [a·'brut·tsi] *pl* Abruzzo
ABS *m abbr di* **Antiblockiersystem** ABS
abside ['ab·si·de] *f* ARCH apse
abusare [a·bu·'za:·re] *vi* **~ di** (*sessualmente*) to abuse; (*approfittare*) to take advantage of; **~ di alcolici** to drink too much
abusivismo [a·bu·zi·'viz·mo] *m* illegal activity; **~ edilizio** illegal building
abusivista [a·bu·zi·'vis·ta] <-i, -e> *mf person who engages in unauthorized activities*
abusivo, -a [a·bu·'zi:·vo] **I.** *agg* illegal **II.** *m*, *f person who engages in unauthorized activities*
abuso [a·'bu:·zo] *m* abuse; **~ di autorità** abuse of power; **fare ~ di alcolici** to drink too much; **~ di sostanze stupefacenti** drug abuse
a.C. *abbr di* **avanti Cristo** BC
acacia [a·'ka:·tʃa] <-cie> *f* acacia
acattolico, -a [a·kat·'tɔ:·li·ko] <-ci, -che> **I.** *agg* non-Catholic **II.** *m*, *f* non Catholic
acca ['ak·ka] <-> *f* **1.** (*lettera*) letter H **2.** *fig, inf* **non ... un'~** not ... a thing
accaddi [ak·'kad·di] *1. pers sing pass rem di* **accadere**
accademia [ak·ka·'dɛ:·mia] <-ie> *f* academy; **~ di Belle Arti** art school; **~ musicale** conservatory of music

i The **Accademia della Crusca** (Crusca Academy – *crusca* means "bran") was founded in Florence in 1583 with the aim of compiling a dictionary of pure Italian. Various editions of the Crusca Dictionary were published over the centuries, the first being printed in Venice in 1612. These dictionaries have helped to set the standard for written Italian.

accademico, -a [ak·ka·'dɛ:·mi·ko] <-ci, -che> I. *agg* academic II. *m, f* academic

accademismo [ak·ka·de·'miz·mo] *m* academicism

accademista [ak·ka·de·'mi·sta] <-i , -e> *mf* MIL cadet

accadere [ak·ka·'de:·re] <irr> *vi essere* to happen; **accada quel che accada** whatever happens

accaduto [ak·ka·'du:·to] *m* event

accagliare [ak·ka·ʎ'ʎa:·re] I. *vt* to curdle II. *vr:* **-rsi** to curdle

accalappiacani [ak·ka·lap·pia·'ka:·ni] <-> *m* dogcatcher

accalappiare [ak·ka·lap·'pia:·re] *vt* (*catturare*) to catch

accalappiatore, -trice [ak·ka·lap·pia·'to:·re] *m, f* 1.(*accalappiacani*) dogcatcher 2.*fig* ~ **di clienti** person touting for business

accalcare [ak·kal·'ka:·re] I. *vt* to crowd II. *vr:* **-rsi** to crowd

accaldarsi [ak·kal·'dar·si] *vr* 1.(*riscaldarsi*) to get hot 2. *fig* (*infervorarsi*) to get heated

accalorarsi [ak·ka·lo·'rar·si] *vr* to get heated

accampamento [ak·kam·pa·'men·to] *m* camp

accampare [ak·kam·'pa:·re] I. *vt* 1.MIL to encamp 2.*fig* (*ragioni*) to put forward; (*diritti*) to assert; ~ **scuse** to make excuses II. *vr:* **-rsi** (*in tende*) to camp; MIL to pitch camp

accanimento [ak·ka·ni·'men·to] *m* (*tenacia*) tenacity; (*odio*) ferocity

accanirsi [ak·ka·'nir·si] <mi accanisco> *vr* 1.(*infierire*) ~ (**contro qu/qc**) to rage (against sb/sth) 2.(*ostinarsi*) ~ (**in qc**) to persist (in doing sth)

accanito, -a [ak·ka·'ni:·to] *agg* 1.(*discussione*) heated 2.(*lavoratore*) tireless; (*sostenitore, lettore*) keen; (*giocatore*) hardened; **fumatore** ~ chain smoker

accanto [ak·'kan·to] I. *avv* nearby; **abitano qui** ~ they live next door II. *prep* ~ **a** next to III. <inv> *agg* next

accantonare [ak·kan·to·'na:·re] *vt* 1.(*merci*) to put aside 2.COM (*utili*) to set aside 3.MIL (*truppe*) to billet 4.*fig* (*progetto*) to shelve

accaparramento [ak·ka·par·ra·'men·to] *m* (*di merce*) buying up; (*di generi razionati*) stockpiling

accaparrare [ak·ka·par·'ra:·re] I. *vt* (*merce*) to buy up; (*generi razionati*) to stockpile II. *vr* 1.**-rsi qc** (*merce*) to buy sth up; (*generi razionati*) to stockpile sth; (*biglietto, posto*) to

grab sth 2.**-rsi la fiducia di qu** to gain sb's trust

accapigliarsi [ak·ka·pi·ʎ'ʎar·si] *vr* to come to blows

accapo [ak·'ka:·po] *avv* **andare** ~ to begin a new paragraph

accappatoio [ak·kap·pa·'to:·io] <-oi> *m* bathrobe

ac·cap·po·na·re [akkappo'na:re] *vt* **mi fa accapponare la pelle** it makes my flesh creep; **mi si accappona la pelle** I get goose bumps

accarezzare [ak·ka·re·'tsa:·re] *vt* 1.(*con la mano*) to stroke 2.*fig* ~ **qu con lo sguardo** to look at sb fondly 3.*fig* (*progetto, idea*) to toy with; (*speranza*) to cherish

accartocciare [ak·kar·tot·'tʃa:·re] I. *vt* to crumple up II. *vr:* **-rsi** to curl up

accasare [ak·ka·'sa:·re] I. *vt* to marry off II. *vr:* **-rsi** to get married

accasciamento [ak·kaʃ·ʃa·'men·to] *m* (*fisico*) exhaustion; (*morale*) downheartedness

accasciarsi [ak·kaʃ·'ʃa:r·si] *vr* 1.(*lasciarsi cadere*) to collapse 2.*fig* (*avvilirsi*) to become disheartened

accasciato, -a [ak·kaʃ·'ʃa:·to] *agg* 1.(*spossato*) exhausted 2.*fig* (*demoralizzato*) disheartened

accatastabile [ak·ka·tas·'ta:·bi·le] *agg* 1.(*ammucchiabile*) stackable 2.(*registrabile al catasto*) **bene** ~ property that can be registered at the land office

accatastamento [ak·ka·tas·ta·'men·to] *m* 1.(*l'ammucchiare*) stacking 2.(*pila*) stack 3.(*registrazione al catasto*) registering at the land office

accatastare [ak·ka·tas·'ta:·re] *vt* 1.(*disporre a catasta*) to stack 2.*fig* (*ammucchiare*) to accumulate 3.(*registrare al catasto*) to register at the land office

accattivante [ak·kat·ti·'van·te] *agg* captivating; **un sorriso** ~ a captivating smile; **una proposta** ~ an attractive proposal

accattivare [ak·kat·ti·'va:·re] *vt, vr:* **-rsi** (*pubblico*) to captivate; (*attenzione*) to capture; (*fiducia*) to gain

accattonaggio [ak·kat·to·'nad·dʒo] <-ggi> *m* begging

accavallamento [ak·ka·val·la·'men·to] *m* (*di fasi, fotogrammi*) overlapping

accavallare [ak·ka·val·'la:·re] I. *vt* (*gambe*) to cross II. *vr:* **-rsi** *fig* (*pensieri, avvenimenti*) to overlap

accecamento [at·tʃe·ka·'men·to] *m* 1.(*perdita della vista*) loss of sight 2.*fig* (*offuscamento*) blindness

accecare [at·tʃe·'ka:·re] I. *vt avere* 1. *a. fig* (*persone*) to blind 2.(*finestre*) to brick up 3.(*abbagliare*) to dazzle II. *vi essere* to become blind

accedere [at·'tʃɛ:·de·re] <accedo, accedei *o* accedetti, accesso> *vi* 1. *essere* ~ **a qc** (*arrivare*) to get to sth; (*entrare*) to enter sth

2. *avere fig* ~ **a qc** (*università*) to be admitted to sth; (*partito, servizio diplomatico*) to join sth **3.** (*aderire a*) to accede to

acceleramento [at·tʃe·le·ra·'men·to] *m* acceleration

accelerare [at·tʃe·le·'ra:·re] I. *vt* to accelerate II. *vi* to speed up

accelerato [at·tʃe·le·'ra:·to] *m* FERR slow train

accelerato, -a *agg* (*polso, passo, ritmo*) quick

acceleratore [at·tʃe·le·ra·'to:·re] *m* MOT, PHYS accelerator

accelerazione [at·tʃe·le·rat·'tsio:·ne] *f* acceleration

accendere [at·'tʃɛn·de·re] <accendo, accesi, acceso> I. *vt* **1.** (*fuoco, sigaretta*) to light; **mi fai** [*o* **hai da**] **~?** do you have a light? **2.** (*conto*) to open; (*ipoteca*) to take out **3.** (*apparecchio, luce*) to switch on; (*gas*) to turn on; (*motore*) to start **4.** *fig* (*animo, cuore*) to arouse; (*sentimenti*) to inflame II. *vr:* **-rsi 1.** (*prender fuoco*) to catch fire **2.** (*luce, stufa*) to come on **3.** *fig* (*discussione*) to flare up

accendigas [at·tʃen·di·'gas] <-> *m* kitchen lighter

accendino [at·tʃen·'di:·no] *m* lighter

accennare [at·tʃen·'na:·re] I. *vt* **1.** (*canzone*) to sing a few notes of; (*melodia*) to play a few notes of **2.** (*sorriso, smorfia*) to give a hint of; **~ un saluto con la mano** to give half a wave II. *vi* **1.** (*fare un cenno*) to make a sign; **~ di sì** to nod **2.** (*dare indizio*) to make as if; **accennò ad alzarsi** he made as if to get up; **accennava a nevicare** it looked as if it was going to snow; **non accennava a finire** it showed no signs of letting up **3.** (*alludere*) **~ a qc** to mention sth

accenno [at·'tʃen·no] *m* **1.** (*cenno, indizio*) hint **2.** (*allusione*) **fare ~ a qc** to mention sth

accensione [at·tʃen·'sio:·ne] *f* **1.** (*avvio*) switching on **2.** (*di motore*) ignition

accentare [at·tʃen·'ta:·re] *vt* (*parlando*) to stress; (*scrivendo*) to put an accent on

accento [at·'tʃɛn·to] *m* **1.** LING accent, stress; **~ acuto** acute accent; **~ circonflesso** circumflex accent; **~ grave** grave accent; **porre l'~ su qc** *fig* to stress sth **2.** (*intonazione*) accent

accentramento [at·tʃen·tra·'men·to] *m* **1.** (*concentrazione*) concentration **2.** POL (*centralizzazione*) centralization

accentrare [at·tʃen·'tra:·re] *vt* **1.** (*riunire*) to concentrate **2.** POL to centralize **3.** *fig* (*accumulare*) to accumulate **4.** *fig* (*attirare*) to attract

accentuare [at·tʃen·tu·'a:re] I. *vt* **1.** (*dare rilievo*) to stress **2.** (*aumentare: disagio*) to make worse II. *vr:* **-rsi 1.** (*aumentare*) to increase **2.** (*peggiorare*) to get worse; **la crisi si è accentuata** the crisis has got worse

accentuazione [at·tʃen·tu·at·'tsio:·ne] *f* **1.** (*messa in rilievo*) emphasis **2.** (*recrudescenza*) worsening

accerchiamento [at·tʃer·kia·'men·to] *m* **1.** (*assedio*) encirclement **2.** *a. fig* surrounding

accerchiare [at·tʃer·'kia:·re] *vt* **1.** (*assediare*) to encircle **2.** *a. fig* to surround

accertabilità [at·tʃer·ta·bi·li·'ta] <-> *f* verifiability

accertamento [at·tʃer·ta·'men·to] *m* **1.** (*verifica*) check **2.** DIR investigation; **~ fiscale** tax investigation

accertare [at·tʃer·'ta:·re] I. *vt* **1.** (*verificare*) to check **2.** DIR to assess II. *vr:* **-rsi** to make sure

accesi [at·'tʃe:·si] *1. pers sing pass rem di* **accendere**

acceso, -a [at·'tʃe:·so] I. *pp di* **accendere** II. *agg* **1.** (*fuoco*) lit **2.** (*luce, gas*) on; (*motore*) running **3.** (*colore*) bright; **rosso ~** bright red **4.** *fig* heated; **~ d'ira** enraged

accessibile [at·tʃes·'si:·bi·le] *agg* **1.** (*raggiungibile: luogo*) accessible **2.** (*comprensibile: testo*) comprehensible **3.** (*alla mano: persona*) approachable **4.** (*prezzo*) affordable

accessibilità [at·tʃes·si·bi·li·'ta] <-> *f* **1.** (*l'essere accessibile*) accessibility **2.** (*comprensibilità: di testo*) comprehensibility **3.** *fig* (*di persone*) approachability **4.** *fig* (*di prezzi*) affordability

accessione [at·tʃes·'sio:·ne] *f* **1.** POL accession **2.** (*in biblioteca*) acquisition; **recenti -i** recent accessions

accesso¹ [at·'tʃɛs·so] *pp di* **accedere**

accesso² *m* **1.** (*possibilità di entrare*) access; **divieto di ~** no admittance **2.** (*porta*) entrance **3.** MED fit; **~ di tosse** coughing fit **4.** *fig* fit of rage **5.** COMPUT access; **~ a Internet** Internet access

accessori [at·tʃes·'sɔ:·ri] *mpl* accessories

accessoriato, -a [at·tʃes·so·'ria:·to] *agg* with optional extras; **automobile perfettamente -a** fully-loaded car

accessorio, -a <-i, -ie> *agg* (*secondario*) secondary; **spese ~** incidental expenses

accessoristica [at·tʃes·so·'ri·sti·ka] <-che> *f* **1.** (*insieme degli accessori*) accessories; AUTO automotive components **2.** (*industria*) accessories industry; AUTO automotive supply industry

accetta [at·'tʃet·ta] *f* hatchet; **tagliato con l'~** *fig* uncouth; **darsi l'~ sui piedi** *fig* to cut off one's nose to spite one's face *prov*

accettabile [at·tʃet·'ta:·bi·le] *agg* acceptable

accettare [at·tʃet·'ta:·re] *vt* to accept; **~ una scommessa** to accept a bet; **~ una sfida** to accept a challenge

accettazione [at·tʃet·tat·'tsio:·ne] *f* **1.** (*di proposta, persona*) JUR acceptance **2.** (*ufficio*) reception **3.** (*presa in consegna*) receipt; **~ merci** goods inward; **~ bagagli** check-in

accetto, -a [at·'tʃɛt·to] *agg* welcome; **persona ben -a** well-liked person

accezione [at·tʃet·'tsio:·ne] *f* meaning

acchiappafarfalle [ak·kiap·pa·far·'fal·le] <-> *m* butterfly net

acchiappamosche [ak·kiap·pa·'mos·ke] <-> *m* **1.** (*per mosche*) flytrap; (*schiacciamosche*) fly swatter **2.** *fig* (*fannullone*) lazybones

acchiappare [ak·kiap·'pa:·re] *vt* to catch

acchito [ak·'ki:·to] *m fig* **di primo ~** offhand

acciaccare [at·tʃak·'ka:·re] *vt* **1.**(*ammaccare*) to dent **2.**(*schiacciare*) to crush **3.** *inf* (*debilitare*) to weaken

acciaccato, -a [at·tʃak·'ka:·to] *agg* **1.**(*ammaccato: cappello*) battered **2.** *inf* (*indebolito*) full of aches and pains

acciaccatura [at·tʃak·ka·'tu:·ra] *f* **1.**(*ammaccatura*) dent **2.**(*contusione*) bruise

acciacco [at·'tʃak·ko] <-cchi> *m* ailment; **piena di -chi** full of aches and pains

acciaieria [at·tʃa·ie·'ri:·a] <-ie> *f* steelworks

acciaio [at·'tʃa:·io] <-ai> *m* steel; **avere nervi d'~** to have nerves of steel; **occhi d'~** steely glare; **una tempra d'~** *fig* an iron constitution

accidempoli [at·tʃi·'dɛm·po·li] *int inf* damn (it)!

accidentaccio [at·tʃi·den·'tak·kio] **I.** *int* goddamn **II.**<-> *m* mess; **un ~ di situazione** a goddamn awful situation

accidentale [at·tʃi·den·'ta:·le] *agg* **1.**(*casuale*) accidental **2.**(*accessorio*) secondary

accidentalità [at·tʃi·den·ta·li·'ta] <-> *f* **1.**(*casualità*) accidental nature **2.**(*del terreno*) bumpiness

accidentato, -a [at·tʃi·den·'ta:·to] *agg* (*terreno, strada*) bumpy

accidente [at·tʃi·'dɛn·te] *m* **1.**(*evento fortuito*) accident **2.**(*disgrazia*) mishap; **gli venisse un ~!** *inf* damn him! **3.** MED stroke **4.**(*loc*) **non ... un ~** *inf* not a damn; **non m'importa un ~** *inf* I don't give a damn!; **-i!** *inf* damn it!

acciderba [at·tʃi·'dɛr·ba] *int inf* damn it!

accigliarsi [at·tʃiʎ·'ʎar·si] *vr* to frown

accingersi [at·'tʃin·dʒer·si] <irr> *vr* **~ a fare qc** to get ready to do sth

acciottolato [at·tʃiot·to·'la:·to] *m* cobbles *pl*

accipicchia [at·tʃi·'pik·kia] *int inf* shoot!

acciuffare [at·tʃuf·'fa:·re] **I.** *vt* to catch **II.** *vr:* -rsi to come to blows

acciuga [at·'tʃu:·ga] <-ghe> *f* **1.**(*alice*) anchovy; **stare pigiati come -ghe** to be packed like sardines in a can **2.** *fig* (*persona magra*) skinny person; **secco come un'~** as thin as a rail

acclamare [ak·kla·'ma:·re] **I.** *vt* **1.**(*applaudire*) to applaud; **~ qu** to applaud sb **2.**(*eleggere*) to acclaim **II.** *vi* **~ a** to applaud

acclimatarsi [ak·kli·ma·'ta:r·si] *vr* to become acclimated

acclimatazione [ak·kli·ma·tat·'tsio:·ne] *f* acclimation

accludere [ak·'klu:·de·re] <accludo, acclusi, accluso> *vt* to enclose

accluso, -a [ak·'klu:·zo] *agg* enclosed; **~ alla lettera invio ...** please find enclosed ...

accoccolarsi [ak·kok·ko·'lar·si] *vr* to crouch down

accodare [ak·ko·'da:·re] **I.** *vt* to line up **II.** *vr:* -rsi **1.**(*disporsi in fila*) to line up **2.** *fig* (*seguire passivamente*) -rsi a, to follow

accogliente [ak·koʎ·'ʎɛn·te] *agg* (*casa, gesto*) welcoming

accoglienza [ak·koʎ·'ʎɛn·tsa] *f* welcome

accogliere [ak·'kɔʎ·ʎe·re] <irr> *vt* **1.**(*persone*) to welcome **2.**(*consiglio, richiesta*) to accept **3.**(*contenere*) to hold

accollare [ak·kol·'la:·re] **I.** *vt* **~ qc a qu** *fig* to saddle sb with sth **II.** *vr:* -rsi to shoulder

accollato, -a [ak·kol·'la:·to] *agg* (*abito*) high-necked; (*scarpe*) high-fronted

accolsi [ak·'kɔl·si] *1.pers sing pass rem di* **accogliere**

accolta [ak·'kɔl·ta] *f* gathering

accoltellare [ak·kol·tel·'la:·re] *vt* to stab

accolto [ak·'kɔl·to] *pp di* **accogliere**

accomandante [ak·ko·man·'dan·te] *m* JUR, COM limited partner

accomandatario [ak·ko·man·da·'ta:·rio] <-i> *m fully liable partner in a limited partnership*

accomandita [ak·ko·'man·di·ta] *f* limited partnership

accomiatare [ak·ko·mia·'ta:·re] **I.** *vt* to see off **II.** *vr:* -rsi to say goodbye

accomodamento [ak·ko·mo·da·'men·to] *m* JUR settlement; **venire** [*o* **giungere**] **ad un ~** to reach a settlement

accomodante [ak·ko·mo·'dan·te] *agg* accommodating

accomodare [ak·ko·mo·'da:·re] **I.** *vt* **1.**(*aggiustare*) to fix **2.**(*riordinare*) to arrange **3.** *fig* (*debito, lite*) to settle **II.** *vr:* -rsi **1.**(*mettersi a proprio agio*) to settle down; (*sedersi*) to sit down; **prego, si accomodi!** (*si sieda*) please take a seat!; (*entri*) come in! **2.**(*accordarsi*) to reach a settlement

accompagnamento [ak·kom·paɲ·ɲa·'men·to] *m* **1.**(*seguito*) company **2.**(*aggiunta*) lettera di ~ cover letter **3.** JUR ordine di ~ production warrant **4.** MUS musica d'~ accompaniment **5.** ADM (*pensione*) indennità d'~ home care benefit

accompagnare [ak·kom·pa·'ɲa:·re] **I.** *vt* **1.**(*andare insieme*) to go with; **~ un bambino a scuola** to take a child to school; **~ qu alla porta** to see sb off; **essere accompagnato da qu** to have sb with one **2.**(*seguire*) **~ qu con lo sguardo** to follow sb with one's eyes **3.**(*unire*) to enclose; **il curriculum che accompagnava la sua lettera** the résumé enclosed with his letter **4.** MUS **~ qu al** [*o* **con il**] **violino** to accompany sb on the violin **II.** *vr:* -rsi **1.** MUS to accompany oneself **2.**(*armonizzare*) **questo vino si accompagna ai dolci** this wine goes well with desserts **3.**(*prendere come compagno*) **-rsi a qu** to associate with sb

accompagnatore, -trice [ak·kom·pa·ɲa·'to:·re] *m, f* **1.**(*corteggiatore*) companion; **~ turistico** courier **2.**(*call-girl, gigolo*) escort **3.** MUS accompanist

accompagnatoria [ak·kom·pa·ɲa·'tɔ:·ria] <-ie> *f* ADM cover letter

accompagnatorio, -a [ak·kom·pa·ɲa·'tɔ:·rio] <-i, -ie> *agg* accompanying

accompagnatrice *f v.* **accompagnatore**

accomunare [ak·ko·mu·'na:·re] *vt* to unite

acconciare [ak·kon·'tʃaː·re] *vt* (*capelli*) to do sb's hair

acconciatura [ak·kon·tʃa·'tuː·ra] *f* **1.** (*pettinatura*) hairstyle **2.** (*ornamento*) headdress

accondiscendere [ak·kon·diʃ·'ʃen·de·re] <irr> *vi* ~ **a qc** to consent to sth

acconsentimento [ak·kon·sen·ti·'men·to] *m* agreement

acconsentire [ak·kon·sen·'tiː·re] *vi* ~ (**a qc**) to agree (to sth); ~ **a un progetto** to approve a plan

acconsenziente [ak·kon·sen·'tsiɛn·te] *agg* ~ (**a qc**) in agreement with sth

accontentare [ak·kon·ten·'taː·re] **I.** *vt* to please **II.** *vr:* -**rsi** to be content with what one has; -**rsi di qc** to content oneself with sth

acconto [ak·'kon·to] *m* deposit; **ritenuta d'**~ advance tax deduction; **in** ~ as a deposit

accoppare [ak·kop·'paː·re] **I.** *vt* to do in **II.** *vr:* -**rsi** *inf* to do oneself in

accoppiamento [ak·kop·pia·'men·to] *m* **1.** (*di colori, abiti*) combination **2.** TEC coupling **3.** (*tra persone*) sexual intercourse; (*tra animali*) mating

accoppiare [ak·kop·'piaː·re] **I.** *vt* **1.** (*accostare*) to combine **2.** *fig* TEC to couple up **3.** (*animali*) to mate **II.** *vr:* -**rsi** (*unirsi in coppia*) to pair off; (*animali*) to mate

accoppiato, -a [ak·kop·'piaː·to] *agg* TEC coupling; **quei due sono bene -i** those two are a good match

accorato, -a [ak·ko·'raː·to] *agg* heartfelt

accorciamento [ak·kor·tʃa·'men·to] *m* shortening

accorciare [ak·kor·'tʃaː·re] **I.** *vt* to shorten **II.** *vr:* -**rsi** (*giornate*) to grow shorter; (*abito*) to shrink

accordare [ak·kor·'daː·re] **I.** *vt* **1.** (*concedere*) to grant **2.** (*mettere d'accordo*) to reconcile **3.** *fig* (*armonizzare*) to harmonize; (*colori*) to match **4.** MUS to tune **II.** *vr:* -**rsi 1.** (*persone*) to come to an agreement **2.** *fig* (*colori*) to match

accordo [ak·'kɔr·do] *m* **1.** agreement; **andare d'**~ to get on well; **come d'**~ as agreed; **d'**~! OK!; **di comune** ~ by mutual consent; **essere d'**~ to agree; **mettersi d'**~ to reach an agreement; **venire a un** ~ to reach an agreement **2.** MUS chord

accorgersi [ak·'kɔr·dʒer·si] <mi accorgo, mi accorsi, accorto> *vr* ~ **di qc** to notice sth

accorgimento [ak·kor·dʒi·'men·to] *m* (*espediente*) trick

accorpamento [ak·kor·pa·'men·to] *m* ADM putting together

accorpare [ak·kor·'paː·re] *vt* ADM to put together

accorrere [ak·'kor·re·re] <irr> *vi essere* to rush up

accorsi [ak·'kɔr·si] *1. pers sing pass rem di* accorgersi

accortezza [ak·kor·'tet·tsa] *f* good sense

accorto, -a [ak·'kɔr·to] **I.** *pp di* accorgersi **II.** *agg* (*prudente*) cautious; (*astuto*) smart

accostamento [ak·ko·sta·'men·to] *m* (*di colori*) combination

accostare [ak·kos·'taː·re] **I.** *vt* (*mettere vicino*) to move nearer; **lasciare la porta accostata** to leave the door ajar; ~ **qu** to approach sb **II.** *vr:* -**rsi 1.** (*avvicinarsi*) -**rsi a qu** to go closer to sb; -**rsi a qc** (*auto*) to draw up to sth **2.** *fig* -**rsi a qc** to turn to sth; -**rsi ai Sacramenti** to receive the sacrament

account [ə·'kaunt] *m* COMPUT user account

account executive [ə·'kaunt ig·'ze·kju·tiv] <o accounts executive> *mf* account executive

accovacciarsi [ak·ko·vat·'tʃar·si] *vr* to crouch down

accozzaglia [ak·kot·'tsaʎ·ʎa] <-glie> *f* (*di cose*) hodgepodge

accozzamento [ak·kot·tsa·'men·to] *m* (*di cose*) hodgepodge

accozzare [ak·kot·'tsaː·re] *vt* to throw together

accrebbi [ak·'kreb·bi] *1. pers sing pass rem di* accrescere

accreditamento [ak·kre·di·ta·'men·to] *m* **1.** COM crediting; ~ **in conto** crediting to an account **2.** (*di diplomatico*) accreditation **3.** (*avvaloramento: di ipotesi*) confirmation

accreditare [ak·kre·di·'taː·re] *vt* **1.** COM to credit **2.** (*diplomatico*) to accredit **3.** (*ipotesi*) to confirm

accredito [ak·'kre·di·to] *m* credit

accrescere [ak·'kreʃ·ʃe·re] <irr> *vt* to increase

accrescimento [ak·kreʃ·ʃi·'men·to] *m* **1.** (*aumento*) increase **2.** BIOL (*crescita, sviluppo*) growth

accrescitivo [ak·kreʃ·ʃi·'tiː·vo] *m* LING augmentative

accrescitivo, -a *agg* augmentative

accresciuto [ak·kreʃ·'ʃuː·to] *pp di* accrescere

accudire [ak·ku·'diː·re] <accudisco> **I.** *vt* (*anziano*) to take care of; (*bambino*) to look after **II.** *vi* ~ **a qc** to attend to sth

acculturare [ak·kul·tu·'raː·re] **I.** *vt* to help adjust to a new culture **II.** *vr:* -**rsi** to adjust to a new culture

accumulare [ak·ku·mu·'laː·re] **I.** *vt* (*soldi, punti*) to accumulate; (*energia*) to store **II.** *vr:* -**rsi** to accumulate

accumulatore [ak·ku·mu·la·'toː·re] *m* accumulator

accumulazione [ak·ku·mu·lat·'tsio·ne] *f* accumulation

accumulo [ak·'ku:·mu·lo] *m* accumulation

accuratezza [ak·ku·ra·'tet·tsa] *f* accuracy

accurato, -a [ak·ku·'raː·to] *agg* **1.** (*lavoro, traduzione, controllo*) accurate **2.** (*artigiano*) careful

accusa [ak·'kuː·za] *f* **1.** (*attribuzione di colpa*) accusation **2.** JUR charge **3.** JUR prosecution; **pubblica** ~ the prosecution

accusare [ak·ku·'zaː·re] *vt* **1.** (*incolpare*) to accuse; ~ **qu di qc** to accuse sb of sth **2.** JUR to charge; ~ **qu di qc** to charge sb with sth **3.** (*dolore*) to complain of; (*fatica*) to show sings of; ~ **mal di testa** to have a headache **4.** ADM to confirm

accusativo [ak·ku·za·'ti:·vo] *m* LING accusative

accusato, -a [ak·ku·'za:·to] **I.** *agg* accused **II.** *m, f* accused

accusatore, -trice [ak·ku·za·'to:·re] *m, f* **1.** (*chi accusa*) accuser **2.** JUR prosecutor

acerbo, -a [a·'tʃɛr·bo] *agg* **1.** (*immaturo*) unripe **2.** (*aspro*) sour

acero ['a:tʃe·ro] *m* maple

acetato [a·tʃe·'ta:·to] *m* acetate

acetilene [a·tʃe·ti·'lɛː·ne] *m* CHEM acetylene

aceto [a·'tʃe:·to] *m* vinegar; **cetriolini sott'~** pickled gherkins; **mettere sott'~** to pickle

acetone [a·tʃe·'to:·ne] *m* nail polish remover

acetosa [a·tʃe·'to:·sa] *f* sorrel

acetosella [a·tʃe·to·'sɛl·la] *f* wood sorrel

acetoso, -a [a·tʃe·'to:·so] *agg* sour

ACI ['a:·tʃi] *m* **1.** *abbr di* **Automobile Club d'Italia** ≈ AAA **2.** *abbr di* **Azione Cattolica Italiana** Italian Catholic Action

acidificare [a·tʃi·di·fi·'ka:·re] **I.** *vt* to acidify **II.** *vi* to acidify

acidificazione [a·tʃi·di·fi·kat·'tsio:·ne] *f* acidification

acidità [a·tʃi·di·'ta] <-> *f* **1.** *a.* CHEM (*asprezza*) acidity **2.** *fig* (*mordacità*) sharpness **3.** MED ~ **di stomaco** heartburn

acido ['a:·tʃi·do] *m* acid; **resistente agli -i** acid-resistant

acido, -a *agg* **1.** (*aspro*) sour **2.** *fig* (*mordace*) sharp

acidulo, -a [a·'tʃi:·du·lo] *agg* slightly sour

acino ['a:·tʃi·no] *m* (*chicco d'uva*) grape

acme ['ak·me] *f fig* MED crisis

acne ['ak·ne] *f* MED acne

aconfessionale [a·kon·fes·sio·'na:·le] *agg* nondenominational

acostituzionale [a·kos·ti·tut·tsio·'na:·le] *agg* unconstitutional

acqua ['ak·kua] *f* **1.** water; ~ **alta** high tide; ~ **benedetta** holy water; ~ **corrente** running water; ~ **dolce** fresh water; ~ **minerale** mineral water; ~ **morta** stagnant water; ~ **ossigenata** hydrogen peroxide; ~ **potabile** drinking water; ~ **salata** salt water; ~ **tonica** tonic water; ~ **da bere** drinking water; ~ **di Colonia** eau de Cologne; ~ **e sapone** *fig* natural **2.** *pl* (*massa*) waters; (*termale*) the waters; **-e bianche** rainwater; **-e nere** sewage; **-e territoriali** territorial waters; **fare la cura delle -e** to take the waters; **intorbidare le -e** *fig* to muddy the waters; **navigare in cattive -e** *fig* to be hard up **3.** *fig* **calmare le -e** to calm things down; **fare un buco nell'~** to draw a blank; **tirare l'~ al proprio mulino** to feather one's nest; ~ **in bocca!** don't say a word!; **è ~ passata** it's all water under the bridge; **sentirsi come un pesce fuor d'~** to feel like a fish out of water; **fare ~ da tutte le parti** (*barca*) to be leaky; *fig* (*argomento*) to be full of holes **4.** *prov* ~ **cheta rovina i ponti** still waters run deep *prov*

acquacoltura [ak·kua·kol·'tu:·ra] *f* aquaculture

acquaforte [ak·kua·'fɔr·te] <acqueforti> *f* etching

acquaio [ak·'kua:·io] <-quai> *m* (kitchen) sink

acquamarina [ak·kua·ma·'ri:·na] <acquemarine> *f* aquamarine

acquapark [ak·kua·'park] <-> *m* water park

acquaplano [ak·kua·'pla:·no] *m* aquaplane

acquaragia [ak·kua·'ra:·dʒa] <-ge> *f* turpentine

acquario [ak·'kua:·rio] <-i> *m* **1.** (*edificio*) aquarium **2.** ASTR Aquarius; **sono (dell' [o un]) Acquario** I am an Aquarius

acquasanta [ak·kua·'san·ta] *f* holy water; **essere come il diavolo e l'~** to be like oil and water

acquasantiera [ak·kua·ʃan·'tiɛː·ra] *f* stoup

acquascivolo [ak·kua·'ʃi:·vo·lo] *m* waterslide

acquatico, -a [ak·'kua:·ti·ko] <-ci, -che> *agg* aquatic

acquattarsi [ak·kuat·'tar·si] *vr* to crouch down

acquavite [ak·kua'vi:·te] *f* spirit; ~ **di vino** ≈ brandy; ~ **di mele** apple brandy

acquazzone [ak·kuat·'tso:·ne] *m* cloudburst

acquedotto [ak·kue·'dɔt·to] *m* aqueduct

acqueforti *pl di* **acquaforte**

acquemarine *pl di* **acquamarina**

acqueo, -a ['ak·kueo] <-ei, -ee> *agg* aqueous; **vapore ~** steam

acquerello [ak·kuer·'rɛl·lo] *m* watercolor

acquiescente [ak·kuieʃ·'ʃɛn·te] *agg* acquiescent

acquiescenza [ak·kuieʃ·'ʃɛn·tsa] *f* acquiescence

acquietare [ak·kuie·'ta:·re] **I.** *vt* (*dolore, ira*) to soothe; (*desiderio*) to appease **II.** *vr:* **-rsi** to calm down

acquifero, -a [ak·'kui:·fe·ro] *agg* aquiferous; **falda -a** aquifer

acquirente [ak·kui·'rɛn·te] *mf* buyer

acquisire [ak·kui·'zi:·re] <acquisisco> *vt* to acquire

acquisito, -a [ak·kui·'zi:·to] *agg* **1.** (*diritto*) acquired **2.** (*parente*) related by marriage

acquisizione [ak·kui·zit·'tsio:·ne] *f* acquisition; ~ **ostile** hostile takeover

acquistare [ak·kuis·'ta:·re] **I.** *vt* **1.** COM to buy **2.** *fig* (*diritto*) to acquire **II.** *vi* ~ **in qc** to improve in sth; ~ **in bellezza** to become more beautiful

acquistato, -a [ak·kuis·'ta:·to] *agg* (*oggetto, prodotto*) bought

acquisto [ak·'kuis·to] *m* **1.** COM purchase; ~ **in contanti** cash purchase; ~ **a rate** purchase on installments; **fare -i** to shop; **potere d'~** purchasing power **2.** *fig* (*persona*) new entrant

acquitrino [ak·kui·'tri:·no] *m* swamp

acquitrinoso, -a [ak·kui·tri·'no:·so] *agg* swampy

acquolina [ak·kuo·'li:·na] *f* **far venire a qu l'~ in bocca** to make sb's mouth water; **mi viene l'~ in bocca** my mouth is watering

A

acquoso, -a [ak·'kuo:·so] *agg* watery

acre ['a:k·re] <più acre, acerrimo> *agg* 1. (*sapore, odore*) pungent; (*fumo*) acrid 2. *fig* (*critica*) harsh

acredine [a·'krɛ:·di·ne] *f* 1. (*asprezza*) acridity 2. *fig* (*di critica*) harshness

acrilico, -a [a·'kri:·li·ko] <-ci, -che> *agg* acrylic

acrimonia [a·kri·'mɔ:·nia] <-ie> *f* acrimony

acrimonioso, -a [a·kri·mo·'nio:·so] *agg* acrimonious

acriticità [a·kri·ti·tʃi·'ta] <-> *f* uncritical attitude

acritico, -a [a·'kri:·ti·ko] <-ci, -che> *agg* uncritical

acrobata [a·'krɔ:·ba·ta] <-i , -e> *mf* acrobat

acrobatico, -a [a·kro·'ba:·ti·ko] <-ci, -che> *agg* acrobatic; **volo ~** acrobatic flight

acrobatismo [a·kro·ba·'tiz·mo] *m* acrobatics

acrobazia [a·kro·bat·'tsi:a] <-ie> *f* 1. (*ginnastica*) acrobatic feat 2. *fig* (*espediente*) acrobatics

action movie ['æk·ʃən 'mu:·vi] <- *o* action movies> *m* action movie

acuire [a·ku·'i:re] <acuisco> I. *vt* 1. (*crisi*) to make worse 2. *a. fig* (*ingegno*) to sharpen II. *vr:* **-rsi** (*situazione, dolore*) to become worse

aculeo [a·'ku:·leo] *m* 1. ZOO sting 2. BOT prickle

acume [a·'ku:·me] *m* perspicacity

acustica [a·'kus·ti·ka] <-che> *f* acoustics

acustico, -a [a·'kus·ti·ko] <-ci, -che> *agg* 1. PHYS acoustic 2. ANAT **apparecchio ~** hearing aid; **nervo ~** auditory nerve

acustoelettricità [a·kus·to·e·let·tri·tʃi·'ta] *f* electroacoustics

acutangolo [a·ku·'taŋ·go·lo] *agg* acute-angled

acutezza [a·ku·'tet·tsa] *f* 1. (*di problema*) acuteness 2. (*di suono*) shrillness; **~ visiva** keenness of sight 3. *fig* (*perspicacia*) (mental) sharpness

acuto [a·'ku:·to] *m* MUS high note

acuto, -a *agg* 1. (*punta*) sharp 2. (*dolore, accento, angolo*) acute 3. (*vista, udito*) keen; (*suono*) shrill 4. (*intelligenza*) keen; (*osservazione*) acute 5. (*freddo*) sharp; (*odore*) pungent 6. (*desiderio, rimorso*) strong 7. ARCH **arco a sesto ~** Gothic arch

ad [ad] *prep* = **a** *davanti a vocale; v.* **a**

adagiare [a·da·'dʒa:·re] I. *vt* to lay down II. *vr:* **-rsi** 1. (*distendersi*) to lie down 2. *fig* to take things easy; **-rsi in qc** (*ozio*) to give oneself up to sth; (*routine*) to fall into sth

adagio[1] [a·'da:·dʒo] *avv* 1. (*lentamente*) slowly 2. (*con cautela*) gently 3. MUS adagio

adagio[2] <-gi> *m* MUS adagio

adattabile [a·dat·'ta:·bi·le] *agg* adaptable

adattabilità [a·dat·ta·bi·li·'ta] <-> *f* adaptability

adattamento [a·dat·ta·'men·to] *m* 1. BIOL, THEAT adaptation 2. (*di edificio*) conversion 3. *fig* (*adeguamento*) **spirito di ~** adaptability

adattare [a·dat·'ta:·re] I. *vt* 1. (*modificare: comportamento, metodo, opera teatrale*) to

adapt; **~ un abito a qu** to alter a dress to fit sb 2. (*edificio*) to convert 3. (*applicare*) to fit; **~ una presa a qc** to fit a plug to sth II. *vr:* **-rsi** 1. (*stare bene*) to suit; **si adatta molto a lei** it suits her beautifully 2. (*adeguarsi*) **-rsi (a qc)** to adapt (to sth)

adattatore *m* COMPUT adaptor

adatto, -a [a·'dat·to] *agg* (*giusto*) right; (*appropriato*) suitable; **essere ~ per qu** to be suitable for sb

addebitamento [ad·de·bi·ta·'men·to] *m* debiting

addebitare [ad·de·bi·'ta:·re] *vt* 1. COM **~ qc in conto a qu** to debit sb's account with sth 2. *fig* (*incolpare*) **~ qc a qu** to blame sb for sth

addebito [ad·'de:·bi·to] *m* 1. COM debit; **nota di ~** debit note 2. *fig* (*accusa*) blame

addendo [ad·'dɛn·do] *m* MATH addend

addensamento [ad·den·sa·'men·to] *m* (*di salsa*) thickening; (*di nuvole*) gathering

addensare [ad·den·'sa:·re] I. *vt* (*rendere denso: salsa*) to thicken II. *vr:* **-rsi** 1. (*salsa*) to thicken 2. (*folla, nubi*) to gather

addentare [ad·den·'ta:·re] *vt* (*cibo*) to bite into

addentellato [ad·den·tel·'la:·to] *m fig* (*nesso*) link

addentrarsi [ad·den·'trar·si] *vr* 1. (*inoltrarsi: nel bosco*) to go into 2. *fig* (*in materia, discussione*) to go into in more depth

addentro [ad·'den·tro] *avv* deeply; **essere ~ in qc** *fig* to be well-versed in sth

addestramento [ad·des·tra·'men·to] *m* (*di persone, animali*) training; (*di cavalli*) dressage

addestrare [ad·des·'tra:·re] I. *vt* to train II. *vr:* **-rsi -rsi in qc** to practice sth

addestrativo, -a [ad·des·tra·'ti:·vo] *agg* training; **corso ~** training course

addestratore, -trice [ad·des·tra·'to:·re] *m*, *f* trainer

addetto, -a [ad·'det·to] I. *agg* (*responsabile*) responsible; **essere ~ a qc** to be in charge of II. *m*, *f* 1. (*responsabile*) person in charge; **'vietato l'ingresso ai non -i ai lavori'** 'authorized personnel only'; **gli -i alla manutenzione** the maintenance crew; **~ alle vendite** salesperson; **~ alla reception** receptionist; **~ stampa** press officer 2. (*di corpo diplomatico*) attaché; **~ culturale/militare** commercial/military attaché

addice 3. *pers sing pr di* **addirsi**

addietro [ad·'diɛ:·tro] *avv* (*tempo*) before; **anni ~** years before; **tempo ~** previously

addio[1] [ad·'di:o] *int* goodbye; *fig;* **~ serata tranquilla!** you can say goodbye to a quiet evening!

addio[2] <-ii> *m* goodbye; **dare l'ultimo ~ a qu** to pay one's last respects to sb

addirittura [ad·di·rit·'tu:·ra] *avv* 1. (*perfino*) even 2. (*veramente*) **~!** really!

addirsi [ad·'dir·si] <si addice> *vr* **qc si addice a qu** sth suits sb; **un comportamento**

del genere non si addice a giovanotto such behavior hardly suits a young man

additare [ad·di·'ta:·re] *vt* (*mostrare con il dito*) to point at

additivare [ad·di·ti·'va:·re] *vt* to put additives into

additivazione [ad·di·ti·vat·'tsio:·ne] *f* addition of additives

additivo [ad·di·'ti:·vo] *m* CHEM additive

additivo, -a *agg* additive

addizionale [ad·dit·tsio·'na:·le] *agg* additional

addizionare [ad·dit·tsio·'na:·re] *vt* to add

addizione [ad·dit·'tsio:·ne] *f* addition

addobbare [ad·dob·'ba:·re] *vt* to decorate

addobbo [ad·'dɔ·bo] *m* decoration; **-i natalizi** Christmas decorations

addolcire [ad·dol·'tʃi:·re] <addolcisco> I. *vt* 1. (*caffè*) to sweeten 2. (*acciaio*) to temper 3. *a. fig* (*acqua*) to soften II. *vr:* **-rsi** 1. (*carattere*) to soften 2. (*tempo*) to become milder

addolcitore [ad·dol·tʃi·'to:·re] *m* water softener

addolorare [ad·do·lo·'ra:·re] I. *vt* to sadden II. *vr* **-rsi per qc** to be saddened by sth

addome [ad·'dɔ:·me] *m* abdomen

addomesticare [ad·do·mes·ti·'ka:·re] *vt* to tame

addomesticato, -a [ad·do·mes·ti·'ka:·to] *agg* (*animale*) tame

addominale [ad·do·mi·'na:·le] *agg* abdominal

addormentare [ad·dor·men·'ta:·re] I. *vt* 1. *a.* MED (*far dormire*) to put to sleep 2. *fig* (*intorpidire*) to send to sleep II. *vr:* **-rsi** to fall asleep; **mi si è addormentata la mano** my arm has gone to sleep; **-rsi in piedi** *fig* to be dead tired

addormentato, -a [ad·dor·men·'ta:·to] *agg* 1. (*immerso nel sonno*) asleep 2. MED (*con narcotico*) drugged 3. *fig* (*sonnacchioso*) dopey 4. *fig* (*gambe, braccia*) numb

addossare [ad·dos·'sa:·re] I. *vt* 1. (*accostare*) **~ qc a qc** to move sth nearer to sth; (*appoggiare*) to lean sth against sth 2. *fig* **~ qc a qu** (*debiti*) to encumber sb with sth; (*colpa*) to put the blame for sth onto sb II. *vr:* **-rsi** 1. (*appoggiarsi*) **-rsi a qc** to lean against sth 2. (*accalcarsi*) to crowd together 3. *fig* (*accollarsi*) **-rsi la colpa di qc** to take the blame for sth; **-rsi le spese di qc** to take on the cost of sth

addosso [ad·'dɔs·so] I. *avv* on; **avere ~** (*vestito*) to be wearing; (*denaro, carta d'identità*) to carry; **mettere ~** to put on; **avere il diavolo ~** *fig* to be fidgety; **piangersi ~** to feel sorry for oneself; **farsela ~** *vulg* to shit oneself; **levarsi qu d'~** *fig* to get sb off one's back II. *prep* (*sopra*) on; (*contro*) against; (*vicino*) very close to; **mettere le mani ~ a qu** to lay hands on sb; **dare ~ a qu** *fig* to jump down someone's throat; **stare ~ a qu** *fig* to be one someone's back; **tagliare i panni ~ a qu** *fig* to speak ill of sb

addurre [ad·'dur·re] <adduco, addussi,

addotto> *vt* (*scuse, motivazioni*) to put forward

adeguamento [a·de·gua·'men·to] *m* adjustment

adeguare [a·de·'gua:·re] I. *vt* to bring sth into line; **~ gli stipendi al costo della vita** to adjust salaries to the cost of living II. *vr:* **-rsi -rsi a qc** to adapt to sth; **non capisco ma mi adeguo** I do not understand but I go along with it

adeguato, -a [a·de·'gua:·to] *agg* (*stipendio*) adequate; (*momento*) appropriate; (*sistemazione*) suitable

adempiere [a·'dem·pie·re] <adempio *o* adempisco, adempii, adempiuto *o* adempito> I. *vt* (*dovere, desiderio*) to fulfill; (*promessa*) to keep II. *vi* **~ a** (*dovere, desiderio*) to fulfill III. *vr:* **-rsi** to come true

adempimento [a·dem·pi·'men·to] *m* fulfillment

adempire [a·dem·'pi:·re] *v.* **adempiere**

adenotomia [a·de·no·to·'mi:·a] <-ie> *f* removal of adenoids

adepto, -a [a·'dɛp·to] *m, f* follower

aderente [a·de·'rɛn·te] I. *agg* (*vestito*) close-fitting II. *mf* supporter

aderenza [a·de·'rɛn·tsa] *f* 1. TEC, MED adhesion; (*di pneumatico*) grip 2. *gener al pl* (*conoscenze*) connections

aderire [a·de·'ri:·re] <aderisco> *vi* 1. **~ a** (*rimanere a contatto*) to stick to; **~ alla strada** (*pneumatico*) to grip the road; (*automobile*) to hold the road 2. **~ a** *fig* (*proposta, richiesta*) to agree to; (*iniziativa*) to support 3. **~ a** *fig* (*partito*) to join

adescare [a·desk·'ka:·re] *vt a. fig* (*pesci, uccelli*) to lure

adesione [a·de·'zio:·ne] *f* 1. PHYS adhesion 2. *fig* (*a richiesta*) agreement; (*a iniziativa*) support 3. (*a partito*) membership

adesività [a·de·zi·vi·'ta] <-> *f* adhesiveness

adesivo [a·de·'zi:·vo] *m* 1. (*collante*) glue 2. (*autoadesivo*) sticker

adesivo, -a *agg* sticky; **nastro ~** adhesive tape

adesso [a·'dɛs·so] *avv* 1. (*in questo momento, ora*) now 2. (*poco fa*) just now 3. (*tra poco*) any minute now

ad honorem [ad o·'nɔ:·rem] *avv* honorary; **laurea ~** honorary degree

adiacente [a·dia·'tʃɛn·te] *agg* adjacent

adiacenze [a·dia·'tʃɛn·tse] *fpl* vicinity; **nelle ~ dello stabilimento** in the vicinity of the factory

adibire [a·di·'bi:·re] <adibisco> *vt* 1. (*usare*) **~ qc a qc** to use sth as sth; **~ una stanza a ufficio** to use a room as an office 2. (*destinare*) **~ qu a qc** to assign sb to sth

Adige ['a:·di·dʒe] *m* **l'~** the Adige; **Alto ~** South Tyrol

adiposità [a·di·po·si·'ta] <-> *f* adiposity

adiposo, -a [a·di·'po:·so] *agg* adipose; **tessuto ~** adipose tissue

adirarsi [a·di·'rar·si] *vr* **~ con qu** to get angry with sb

adirato, -a [a·di·'ra:·to] *agg* angry
adire [a·'di:·re] <adisco> *vt* (*tribunale*) to lodge a claim with; (*eredità*) to claim; ~ **le vie legali** to take legal action
adito ['a:·di·to] *m fig* **dare** ~ **a qc** to give rise to sth
adocchiare [ad·dok·'kia:·re] *vt* 1. (*trovare*) to spot 2. (*con compiacenza, desiderio*) to eye
adolescente [a·do·leʃ·'ʃɛn·te] I. *agg* teenage II. *mf* teenager
adolescenza [a·do·leʃ·'ʃɛn·tsa] *f* adolescence; **ha trascorso l'~ in Italia** she spent her teenage years in Italy
adolescenziale [a·do·leʃ·ʃen·'tsia:·le] *agg* **problemi -i** teenage [*o* adolescent] problems
adombrare [a·dom·'bra:·re] I. *vt* 1. (*oscurare*) to veil 2. (*ombreggiare*) to shade II. *vr:* **-rsi** (*aversene a male*) to feel resentful
adone [a·'do:·ne] *m* Adonis
adontarsi [a·don·'tar·si] *vr* to be offended
adop(e)rabile [a·do·'pra:·bi·le (a·do·pe·'ra:·bi·le)] *agg* usable
adop(e)rare [a·do·'pra:·re (a·do·pe·'ra:·re)] I. *vt* to use; ~ **le mani** to be ready with one's fists II. *vr* **-rsi per qu** to give sb a hand
adorabile [a·do·'ra:·bi·le] *agg* adorable
adorare [a·do·'ra:·re] *vt* 1. (*divinità*) to worship 2. (*persona*) to adore 3. (*arte, cibo*) to love
adoratore, -trice [a·do·ra·'to:·re] *m, f* 1. (*di divinità, persona*) worshipper 2. (*ammiratore*) admirer
adorazione [a·do·rat·'tsio:·ne] *f* 1. (*di divinità*) worship 2. (*amore*) adoration
adornare [a·dor·'na:·re] I. *vt* ~ (**di qc**) to adorn (with sth) II. *vr:* **-rsi** ~ (**di qc**) to adorn oneself (with sth)
adorno, -a [a·'dor·no] *agg* ~ (**di qc**) adorned (with sth)
adottare [a·dot·'ta:·re] *vt* to adopt; ~ **provvedimenti contro** to take measures against; ~ **un nuovo stile di vita** to embark on a new lifestyle
adottivo, -a [a·dot·'ti:·vo] *agg* 1. (*figlio, padre*) adoptive 2. *fig* (*patria*) adopted
adozione [a·dot·'tsio:·ne] *f* adoption; **patria di** ~ country of adoption; **onde evitare l'~ di provvedimenti** in order to avoid taking measures
adrenalina [a·dre·na·'li:·na] *f* adrenalin
Adriatico [a·dri·'a:·ti·ko] *m* l'~ the Adriatic
adriatico, -a <-ci, -che> *agg* Adriatic; **il Mare Adriatico** the Adriatic Sea
adroterapia [a·dro·te·ra·'pi·a] *f* MED hadrotherapy
ADSL *abbr di* **Asymmetric Digital Subscriber Line** ADSL
adulare [a·du·'la:·re] *vt* to flatter
adulatore, -trice [a·du·la·'to:·re] *m, f* flatterer
adulterare [a·dul·te·'ra:·re] *vt* 1. (*vino, cibo*) to adulterate 2. *fig* (*realtà*) to misrepresent
adulterino, -a [a·dul·te·'ri:·no] *agg* JUR (*relazione*) adulterous; (*figlio*) illegitimate

adulterio [a·dul·'tɛ:·rio] <-i> *m* adultery
adultero, -a [a·'dul·te·ro] I. *agg* adulterous II. *m, f* adulterer, adulteress
adulto, -a [a·'dul·to] I. *agg* 1. (*persona*) adult 2. (*animale*) fully-grown 3. *fig* (*maturo*) mature II. *m, f* adult
adunanza [a·du·'nan·tsa] *f* assembly
adunare [a·du·'na:·re] I. *vt* to assemble II. *vr:* **-rsi** to assemble
adunata [a·du·'na:·ta] *f* 1. MIL muster 2. (*persone riunite*) gathering
adunco, -a [a·'duŋ·ko] <-chi, -che> *agg* (*becco*) curved; (*naso*) hooked
adunghiare [a·duŋ·'gia:·re] *vt* ~ qc (*animale*) to dig its claws into sth; (*persona*) to claw at sth
advertising, advertizing [æd·və·'tai·ziŋ/ad·ver·'tai·zin(g)] *m* advertising
aerare [a·e·'ra:·re] *vt* to air
aerazione [a·e·rat·'tsio:·ne] *f* ventilation
aereo [a·'ɛ:·re·o] <-ei> *m* 1. (*aeroplano*) airplane 2. (*antenna*) aerial
aereo, -a <-ei, -ee> *agg* 1. air; **biglietto** ~ plane ticket; **foto -a** aerial photograph; **linea -a** AERO airline; EL, TEL overhead cable; **rotta -a** flight path; **spazio** ~ airspace; **per via -a** by airmail 2. *fig* (*leggero*) ethereal
aeriforme [a·e·ri·'for·me] *agg* gaseous
aeroacustica [a·e·ro·a·'kus·ti·ka] *f* aeroacoustics
aerobico, -a [a·e·'rɔ:·bi·ko] <-ci, -che> *agg* aerobic; **ginnastica -a** aerobics
aerobus ['a:·e·ro·bus] <-> *m* airbus
aerocisterna [a·e·ro·tʃis·'tɛr·na] *f* air tanker
aeroclub [a·e·ro·'klub] <-> *m* flying club
aerodinamica [a·e·ro·di·'na:·mi·ka] *f* aerodynamics
aerodinamico, -a [a·e·ro·di·'na:·mi·ko] <-ci, -che> *agg* aerodynamic; (*carrozzeria*) streamlined; **linea -a** streamlined design; **resistenza -a** air resistance
aerodromo [a·e·'rɔ:·dro·mo] *m* airfield
aerofotografia [a·e·ro·fo·to·gra·'fi:·a] *f* aerial photograph
aerografo [a·e·'rɔ:·gra·fo] *m* airbrush
aerogramma [a·e·ro·'gram·ma] <-i> *m* airmail letter
aerolinea [a·e·ro·'li:·nea] *f* airline
aeromobile [a·e·ro·'mɔ:·bi·le] *m* aircraft
aeromodello [a·e·ro·mo·'dɛl·lo] *m* model aircraft
aeromoto [a·e·ro·'mɔ:·to] *m* shock wave
aeronautica [a·e·ro·'na:·u·ti·ka] *f* aeronautics; ~ **civile** civil aviation; ~ **militare** air force
aeronautico, -a [a·e·ro·'na:·u·ti·ko] <-ci, -che> *agg* aeronautical
aeroplano [a·e·ro·'pla:·no] *m* airplane; ~ **da caccia** fighter; ~ **da ricognizione** reconnaissance plane; ~ **da turismo** private plane
aeroporto [a·e·ro·'pɔr·to] *m* airport
aeroportuale [a·e·ro·por·tu·'a:·le] I. *mf* airport staff II. *agg* airport; **tassa** ~ airport tax
aeropostale [a·e·ro·pos·'ta:·le] I. *agg* air mail

II. *m* mail plane

aeroscivolante [a·e·ro·ʃi·vo·'lan·te] *m* hover-craft

aerosoccorso [a·e·ro·sok·'kor·so] *m* air ambulance

aerosol [a·e·ro·'sɔl] <-> *m* **1.** (*sistema*) aerosol **2.** (*contenitore*) inhaler

aerospaziale [a·e·ro·spat·'tsia·le] *agg* aerospace

aerospazio [a·e·ro·'spat·tsio] <-zi> *m* airspace

aerostatico, -a [a·e·ro·'sta:·ti·ko] <-ci, -che> *agg* aerostatic; **pallone ~** (hot-air) balloon

aerostato [a·e·'rɔ·sta·to] *m* (hot-air) balloon; (*fisso*) captive balloon; (*dirigibile*) airship

aerostazione [a·e·ro·stat·'tsio:·ne] *f* (airport) terminal

aerotermo [a·e·ro·'tɛr·mo] *m* hot air heating

aerotrasporto [a·e·ro·tras·'pɔr·to] *m* air transportation

afa ['a:·fa] *f* mugginess; **c'è ~** it's muggy

affabile [af·'fa:·bile] *agg* friendly

affabilità [af·fa·bi·li·'ta] <-> *f* friendliness

affabulare [af·fa·bu·'la:·re] *vt* to invent [o make up] stories

affaccendarsi [af·fat·tʃen·'dar·si] *vr* **~ a fare qc** to be busy doing sth

affaccendato, -a [af·fat·tʃen·'da:·to] *agg* busy

affacciarsi [af·fat·'tʃa:r·si] *vr* **~ alla finestra** to look out of the window; **~ alla mente** *fig* to come to one's mind

affamare [af·fa·'ma:·re] *vt* to starve

affamato, -a [af·fa·'ma:·to] I. *agg a. fig* hungry; **essere ~ di qc** to be hungry for sth II. *m, f* hungry person

affannare [af·fan·'na:·re] I. *vt* **1.** (*dare affanno*) to make breathless **2.** *fig* (*procurare pena*) to worry II. *vr:* **-rsi 1.** (*provare affanno*) to pant **2.** *fig* (*affaticarsi*) **-rsi a fare qc** to go to the trouble of doing sth **3.** *fig* (*preoccuparsi*) to worry

affannato, -a [af·fan·'na:·to] *agg* short of breath

affanno [af·'fan·no] *m* **1.** (*difficoltà di respiro*) breathlessness **2.** *fig* (*preoccupazione*) worry

affannoso, -a [af·fan·'no:·so] *agg* **1.** (*respiro*) labored **2.** *fig* frantic

affare [af·'fa:·re] *m* **1.** (*faccenda*) business, matter; **~ da nulla** trivial matter; **bell'~ hai combinato!** you've really made a mess there!; **non è ~ tuo!** it's none of your business!; **~ di stato** affair of state; **ne ha fatto un ~ di stato** he made a great issue of it; **sono -i miei** it's my business **2.** COM deal; **concludere un ~ con qu** to make a deal with sb; **essere in -i con qu** to be doing business with sb; **parlare d'-i** to talk business; **uomo d'-i** businessman; **viaggio d'-i** business trip **3.** occasione, bargain; **fare un ~** to get a bargain **4.** JUR case **5.** *inf* (*cosa, utensile*) thing majig **6.** *pl* affairs; **Ministero degli Affari esteri** Department of State

affarismo [af·fa·'riz·mo] *m* wheeling and dealing

affarista [af·fa·'ris·ta] <-i , -e> *mf pej* wheeler-dealer

affarone [af·fa·'ro:·ne] *m inf* very good deal

affascinante [af·faʃ·ʃi·'nan·te] *agg* attractive

affascinare [af·faʃ·ʃi·'na:·re] *vt* (*attrarre, sedurre*) to charm

affaticamento [af·fa·ti·ka·'men·to] *m* tiredness

affaticare [af·fa·ti·'ka:·re] I. *vt* to tire II. *vr:* **-rsi** to tire oneself out

affatto [af·'fat·to] *avv* **niente** [*o* **non**] **~** not at all

afferire [af·fe·'ri:·re] <afferisco> *vi form* JUR, ADM (*concernere*) **~ (a qc)** to pertain (to sth)

affermare [af·fer·'ma:·re] I. *vt* **1.** (*dire di sì*) to answer in the affirmative **2.** (*sostenere*) to claim **3.** JUR (*innocenza*) to protest; (*diritto*) to assert II. *vr:* **-rsi** (*persona*) to establish oneself; (*moda*) to become popular

affermativo, -a [af·fer·ma·'ti:·vo] *agg* affirmative

affermazione [af·fer·mat·'tsio:·ne] *f* **1.** (*sì*) **rispondere con un'~** to answer in the affirmative **2.** (*asserzione*) statement **3.** (*conferma*) confirmation **4.** (*di diritti*) assertion **5.** (*di persona, squadra*) success; (*di moda*) establishment

afferrare [af·fer·'ra:·re] I. *vt* **1.** (*prendere*) to grab **2.** *fig* (*occasione*) to seize **3.** *fig* (*senso, idea*) to grasp II. *vr:* **-rsi** *a. fig* **-rsi a qc** to cling to sth

Aff. Est. *abbr di* (**Ministero degli**) **Affari Esteri** *Department of State*

affettare [af·fet·'ta:·re] *vt* **1.** (*tagliare a fette*) to slice **2.** (*ostentare*) to affect

affettato [af·fet·'ta:·to] *m* cold cuts

affettato, -a *agg* affected

affettatrice [af·fet·ta·'tri:·tʃe] *f* slicer

affettazione [af·fet·tat·'tsio:·ne] *f pej* affectation

affettivo, -a [af·fet·'ti:·vo] *agg* emotional; **ha solo valore ~** it's only of sentimental value

affetto [af·'fɛt·to] *m* fondness; **provare ~ per qu** to be fond of sb; **'con ~'** (*nelle lettere*) 'with love'

affetto, -a *agg* **essere ~ da qc** to suffer from sth

affettuoso, -a [af·fet·tu·'o:·so] *agg* (*persona*) affectionate; (*parole*) fond; **'un saluto ~'** (*nelle lettere*) 'love'

affezionarsi [af·fet·tsio·'na:r·si] *vr* **~ a qu** to grow fond of sb; **~ a qc** to take a liking to sth

affezionato, -a [af·fe·zio·'na:·to] *agg* **1.** **essere ~ a qu** to be fond of sb **2.** (*cliente*) regular

affezione [af·fet·'tsio:·ne] *f* **1.** (*sentimento*) affection **2.** MED ailment

affiancare [af·fiaŋ·'ka:·re] I. *vt* **1.** (*mettere a lato*) to place side by side **2.** MIL to flank **3.** *fig* (*sostenere*) to support II. *vr* **-rsi a qu** to draw level with sb

affiatamento [af·fia·ta·'men·to] *m* understanding; (*nello sport*) team spirit; **non c'è ~**

tra di noi we don't get on well

affiatare [af·fia·'ta:·re] I. *vt* (*creare accordo tra: gruppo, squadra*) to bind together II. *vr:* -rsi (*coppia, gruppo*) to get on well together; (*squadra*) to play well together

affibbiare [af·fib·'bia:·re] *vt* ~ qc a qu (*compito*) to saddle sb with sth; (*nomignolo, colpa*) to pin sth on sb; (*multa*) to slap sth on sb; ~ un colpo a qu to give sb a slap

affidabile *agg* reliable; è una persona ~ he's/ she's very reliable

affidabilità [af·fi·da·bi·li·'ta] <-> *f* reliability

affidamento [af·fi·da·'men·to] *m* 1.(*fiducia*) trust; dare ~ to seem reliable; fare ~ su qu to rely on sb 2. JUR (*di minori*) fostering; ottenere l'~ di un minore to foster a child

affidare [af·fi·'da:·re] I. *vt* ~ qc a qu (*bambino, casa, cane*) to entrust sth to sb; (*incarico, compito, mansione*) to entrust sb with sth II. *vr:* -rsi -rsi a qu to put oneself in sb's hands

affido [af·'fi:·do] *m* fostering; dare un bambino in ~ to give a child to a foster family; prendere un bambino in ~ to foster a child

affievolire [af·fie·vo·'li:·re] <affievolisco> I. *vt* (*interesse, slancio*) to weaken II. *vr:* -rsi (*fuoco*) to die down; (*luce, suono, ricordo, speranza*) to fade

affiggere [af·'fid·dʒe·re] <affiggo, affissi, affisso> *vt* (*manifesti, cartelloni*) to stick up

affilare [af·fi·'la:·re] I. *vt* 1.(*coltello, lama*) to sharpen 2. *fig* (*lineamenti*) to make thinner II. *vr:* -rsi (*dimagrire*) to get thinner

affilato, -a [af·fi·'la:·to] *agg* 1.(*coltello, lama*) sharp 2. *fig* (*lingua*) sharp 3.(*naso*) pointed; (*volto, lineamenti*) thin

affiliare [af·fi·'lia:·re] I. *vt* (*associare*) to link; ~ a qc to link to sth II. *vr:* -rsi -rsi a qc to join sth

affiliata *f* FIN (*società*) affiliated

affiliazione [af·fi·li·at'tsio:·ne] *f* (*ad associazione, sindacato*) affiliation

affinare [af·fi·'na:·re] I. *vt* 1.(*perfezionare: tecnica*) to polish 2.(*far maturare: vino*) to mature 3. *fig* (*migliorare: gusto*) to refine 4. *fig* (*aguzzare: vista, ingegno*) to sharpen II. *vr:* -rsi 1.(*perfezionarsi: tecnica*) to become polished 2.(*maturare: vino*) to mature 3. *fig* (*migliorare: gusto*) to become refined

affinché [af·fiŋ·'ke] *cong* so that

affine [af·'fi:·ne] I. *agg* (*prodotto, pianta*) related; (*materia, popolazioni*) similar; (*lingua*) cognate II. *mf* (*parente del coniuge*) in-law

affinità [af·fi·ni·'ta] <-> *f a.* CHEM (*somiglianza*) affinity; ~ elettiva attraction

affioramento [af·fio·ra·'men·to] *m* 1.(*l'affiorare*) surfacing 2. GEOL outcrop

affiorare [af·fio·'ra:·re] *vi essere* 1.(*spuntare, emergere*) ~ da to stick (up) out of; ~ in superficie (*subacqueo*) to surface; (*balena, petrolio*) to come to the surface 2. GEOL to crop out 3. *fig* (*problema, dettaglio*) to emerge; ~ alla mente (*dubbio, pensiero, ricordo*) to come to mind

affissi [af·'fis·si] *1. pers sing pass rem di* **affiggere**

affissionale [af·fis·sio·'na:·le] *agg* pubblicità ~ street advertising

affissione [af·fis·'sio:·ne] *f* (*di manifesti, cartelli*) billposting; divieto d'~ post no bills

affisso[1] [af·'fis·so] *pp di* **affiggere**

affisso[2] *m* 1.(*avviso*) notice 2. LING affix

affittabile [af·fit·'ta:·bi·le] *agg* rentable

affittacamere [af·fit·ta·'ka:·me·re] <-> *mf* landlord, landlady

affittare [af·fit·'ta:·re] *vt* 1.(*dare in affitto*) to rent (out); "affittasi alloggio ammobiliato" "furnished house for rent" 2.(*prendere in affitto*) to rent

affitto [af·'fit·to] *m* rental; dare in ~ to rent (out); prendere in ~ to rent

affittuario, -a [af·fit·tu·'a:·ri·o] <-i, -ie> *m, f* (*di immobile*) tenant; (*di terreno*) tenant farmer

affliggere [af·'flid·dʒe·re] <affliggo, afflissi, afflitto> I. *vt* to trouble II. *vr:* -rsi to worry

afflizione [af·flit·'tsio:·ne] *f* 1.(*tristezza*) sadness 2.(*tristezza*) trouble

afflosciare [af·floʃ·'ʃa:·re] I. *vt* (*render floscio: muscolo*) to make flabby II. *vr:* -rsi (*sgonfiarsi*) 1.(*vela, tessuto*) to become limp; (*pallone*) to go down; (*muscolo*) to become flabby; (*sformato, torta*) to collapse; (*fiore*) to wilt 2.(*persona, animale, capanna*) to collapse

affluente [af·flu·'ɛn·te] *m* tributary

affluenza [af·flu·'ɛn·tsa] *f* (*di persone*) influx; (*di traffico, di liquidi*) flow; ~ alle urne turnout; grande ~ di pubblico per la prima della Scala there was a capacity audience for the first night at La Scala

affluire [af·flu·'i:·re] <affluisco> *vi essere* 1.(*persone*) to pour in 2.(*liquidi, gas, merci*) to flow

afflusso [af·'flus·so] *m* 1.(*di persone*) influx 2.(*di liquidi*) flow

affogare [af·fo·'ga:·re] I. *vt avere* to drown; ~ i dispiaceri nell'alcol to drown one's sorrows II. *vi essere* to drown; ~ in un bicchier d'acqua *fig* to be unable to cope with the smallest problem; ~ nell'oro *fig* to be filthy rich III. *vr:* -rsi to drown oneself

affogato, -a [af·fo·'ga:·to] I. *agg* 1.(*annegato*) drowned; morire ~ to drown 2. CULIN gelato ~ al caffè hot coffee with ice cream; uova -e poached eggs II. *m, f* body of a drowned person

affollamento [af·fol·la·'men·to] *m* crowding

affollare [af·fol·'la:·re] I. *vt* 1.(*gremire: sala, teatro*) to crowd 2. *fig* (*opprimere*) to crowd; ~ la mente (*pensieri, problemi*) to crowd sb's mind II. *vr:* -rsi (*accalcarsi*) to crowd around

affollato, -a *agg* (*cinema, spiaggia, strada*) crowded

affondare [af·fon·'da:·re] I. *vt avere* 1.(*nave*) to sink 2.(*nella neve, nell'acqua*) ~ qc in qc to plunge sth into sth II. *vi essere* 1.(*nave*) to sink 2. ~ in qc (*nella neve, nell'acqua*) to sink into sth

affossamento [af·fos·sa·'men·to] *m* (*fosso*) dip

affossato, -a [af·fos·'sa:·to] *agg fig* (*accantonato: progetto*) killed off

affrancare [af·fraŋ·'ka:·re] I. *vt* 1. (*posta*) to frank 2. (*liberare: schiavo*) to free II. *vr:* -**rsi** -**rsi dalla schiavitù** to free oneself from slavery; *fig;* -**rsi dalla schiavitù di qc** (*fumo, droga, gioco*) to free oneself from dependence on sth

affrancatura [af·fraŋ·ka·'tu:·ra] *f* 1. (*operazione*) franking 2. (*tassa*) postage

affranto, -a [af·'fran·to] *agg* 1. (*prostrato dal dolore*) overcome 2. (*spossato, logorato*) exhausted

affratellare [af·fra·tel·'la:·re] *vr:* -**rsi** to unite

affrescare [af·fres·'ka:·re] *vt* to decorate with frescoes

affreschista [af·fres·'kis·ta] <-i , -e> *mf* artist who works in fresco

affresco [af·'fres·ko] <-schi> *m* fresco

affrettare [af·fret·'ta:·re] I. *vt* 1. (*sveltire*) ~ **il passo** to hurry up 2. (*anticipare: arrivo, partenza*) to bring forward; ~ **i tempi** to hurry things along II. *vr:* -**rsi** to hurry (up); -**rsi a fare qc** to hurry to do sth

affrettato, -a [af·fret·'ta:·to] *agg* 1. (*veloce: passo*) quick 2. *pej* (*mal fatto: lavoro*) rushed 3. (*frettoloso: decisione*) hasty

affrontare [af·fron·'ta:·re] I. *vt* 1. (*andare incontro a: pericolo, morte, nemico, avversario*) to face; ~ **il pubblico** to face the public; (*paura, disgrazia*) to confront; (*situazione*) to face up to 2. (*discutere: problema, questione*) to tackle 3. (*sostenere: spesa*) to incur 4. (*iniziare: salita*) to embark on II. *vr:* -**rsi** 1. (*scontrarsi: eserciti*) to clash 2. SPORT (*pugili, squadre*) to face up to one another

affronto [af·'fron·to] *m* (*offesa*) insult; **fare un** ~ **a qu** to offend sb

affumicare [af·fu·mi·'ka:·re] *vt* 1. (*riempire di fumo: ambiente*) to fill with smoke 2. (*pesce, carne, prosciutto*) to smoke

affumicato, -a [af·fu·mi·'ka:·to] *agg* 1. (*pieno fumo: ambiente*) smoky 2. (*pesce, carne, prosciutto*) smoked 3. (*colorato di bruno: vetri, lenti, occhiali*) tinted

affusolato, -a [af·fu·so·'la:·to/af·fu·zo·'la:·to] *agg* 1. (*magro: dita, mano, gambe*) slender 2. (*pantaloni*) tapered; (*corpo, forma*) tapering

Afganistan [af·ga·nis·'tan] *m* l'~ Afghanistan

afgano, -a [af·'ga:·no] I. *agg* Afghan II. *m, f* Afghan

afoso, -a [a·'fo:·so] *agg* (*tempo, giornata, pomeriggio*) muggy

Africa ['a:·fri·ka] *f* Africa

africano, -a [a·fri·'ka:·no] I. *agg* African II. *m, f* African

afrodisiaco [a·fro·di·'zi:a·ko] <-ci> *m* aphrodisiac

afta ['af·ta] *f* MED (mouth) ulcer; ~ **epizootica** foot-and-mouth disease

afterhour [a:ftɐ·'aʊɐ] *m* late night club

aftershave <-> *m* aftershave

agata ['a:·ga·ta] *f* agate

agenda [a·'dʒɛn·da] *f* 1. (*libretto*) diary 2. (*elenco di argomenti*) agenda 3. COMPUT ~ **elettronica** personal organizer

agente [a·'dʒɛn·te] I. *mf* 1. *a.* COM agent; ~ **segreto** secret agent; ~ **di assicurazione** insurance agent; ~ **di cambio** stockbroker; ~ **di commercio** sales representative; ~ **immobiliare** realtor 2. (*guardia*) (police) officer; ~ **di pubblica sicurezza** police officer; ~ **investigativo** detective II. *m* 1. MED, LING, CHEM agent; -**i cancerogeni** carcinogens; ~ **inquinante** pollutant 2. *pl* METEO -**i atmosferici** weather

agenzia [a·dʒen·'tsi:·a] <-ie> 1. (*ufficio*) agency; ~ **di cambio** bureau de change; ~ **d'investigazione** detective agency; ~ **di stampa** press agency; ~ (**di**) **viaggi** travel agency 2. (*filiale*) branch 3. (*comunicato*) agency dispatch

agevolare [a·dʒe·vo·'la:·re] *vt* 1. (*render facile: compito, lavoro, lettura*) to facilitate 2. (*favorire: commercio, investimenti*) to make easier 3. (*aiutare: utenti, investitori*) to help

agevolazione [a·dʒe·vo·lat·'tsio:·ne] *f* -**i** special terms; -**i bancarie** credit facilities; -**i fiscali** tax relief

agevole [a·'dʒe:·vo·le] *agg* 1. (*comodo: strada*) smooth 2. (*facile: lavoro, viaggio*) easy

agganciare [ag·gan·'tʃa:·re] *vt* 1. (*unire: vagone, rimorchio*) to couple 2. (*riappendere: telefono*) to hang up 3. *fig* (*per parlare: persona*) to get talking to

aggancio [ag·'gan·tʃo] <-ci> *m* 1. (*collegamento*) attachment 2. *fig* (*conoscenze*) contact; **avere degli** -**i** to have contacts

aggeggio [ad·'dʒed·dʒo] <-ggi> *m* (*cosa sconosciuta*) thing(amajig)

aggettivo [ad·dʒet·'ti:·vo] *m* LING adjective

agghiacciante [ag·giat·'tʃa:n·te] *agg* (*scena, film, racconto*) chilling; (*urlo, lamento*) blood-curdling

agghiacciare [ag·giat·'tʃa:·re] I. *vt* avere *fig* (*far inorridire: storia, scena*) to make sb's blood run cold II. *vr:* -**rsi** to freeze

agghindare [ag·gin·'da:·re] I. *vt* (*vestire con cura: persona*) to dress up II. *vr:* -**rsi** (*vestirsi con troppa cura*) to get dressed up

aggio ['ad·dʒo] <-ggi> *m* 1. FIN premium 2. (*compenso*) remuneration

aggiogare [ad·dʒo·'ga:·re] *vt fig* (*soggiogare*) to subjugate

aggiornamento [ad·dʒor·na·'men·to] *m* 1. (*perfezionamento: di docenti*) in-service training; **corsi di** ~ refresher courses 2. (*revisione: di testo, sito internet, programma*) updating; ~ **dati** data updating 3. (*rinvio: di seduta, processo*) adjournment 4. (*appendice di un'enciclopedia*) supplement

aggiornare [ad·dʒor·'na:·re] I. *vt avere* 1. (*attualizzare: testo, sito internet, pro-*

gramma) to update **2.** (*adeguare: prezzi*) to revise **3.** (*mettere al corrente: persona*) to bring up to date **4.** (*rinviare: seduta, processo*) to adjourn **II.** *vr:* **-rsi** (*mettersi al corrente*) to keep up to date; **ci aggiorniamo?** (*ci risentiamo*) let's keep in touch

aggirare [ad·dʒi·'ra:·re] **I.** *vt* **1.** (*circondare*) to go around **2.** MIL (*nemico*) to outflank **3.** *fig* (*evitare: ostacolo*) to get around **4.** *fig* (*ingannare*) to con **II.** *vr:* **-rsi 1.** (*andare in giro*) to wander around **2.** (*approsimarsi*) to be around; **-rsi intorno a** [*o* su] qc to be around sth; **il prezzo s'aggira intorno ai duemila euro** the price is around two thousand euros

aggiudicare [ad·dʒu·di·'ka:·re] **I.** *vt* **1.** (*assegnare: premio, appalto*) to award; **~ qc** (**a qu**) to award sth (to sb) **2.** (*nelle aste: quadro*) to sell **II.** *vr:* **-rsi 1.** (*ottenere: premio, posto, appalto*) to win **2.** (*nelle aste: quadro*) to buy

aggiudicazione [ad·dʒu·di·kat·'tsio:·ne] *f* **1.** (*in gara d'appalto: di lavori, forniture, licenze*) assignment **2.** (*nelle aste: di oggetti*) sale

aggiungere [ad·'dʒun·dʒe·re] <irr> **I.** *vt* **1.** **~ qc a qc** to add sth to sth **2.** (*soggiungere*) to add **II.** *vr:* **-rsi** (*unirsi*) to be added

aggiunta [ad·'dʒun·ta] *f* **1.** (*aumento*) addition; **con l'~ di qc** with added sth; **senza ~ di qc** without added sth **2.** (*in libri*) **-e al testo** additions to the text

aggiuntare [ad·dʒun·'ta:·re] *vt* (*congiungere*) to splice

aggiuntatura [ad·dʒun·ta·'tu:·ra] *f* (*attaccatura, giuntura*) splice

aggiunto, -a [ad·'dʒun·to] **I.** *pp di* **aggiungere II.** *agg* (*personale, medico, insegnante*) assistant **III.** *m, f* (*sostituto*) assistant; **~ giudiziario** magistrate who is at the first stage of a judicial career

aggiustamento [ad·dʒus·ta·'men·to] *m* **1.** (*adeguamento: di dati, prezzi, dose di medicina*) adjustment **2.** *fig* (*accomodamento: di malinteso*) settlement **3.** *fig* (*pareggio*) settling; **~ di conti** settling of accounts

aggiustare [ad·dʒus·'ta:·re] **I.** *vt* **1.** (*riparare: motore, televisione*) to repair; (*vestito*) to alter **2.** (*mettere in ordine: capelli*) to tidy; (*abiti*) to straighten **3.** MIL (*regolare bene: mira*) to adjust; **~ il tiro** *fig* to cover a mistake **4.** *pej* FIN (*conti*) to fiddle **5.** (*loc*) **~ qu per le feste** *fig* to beat sb up **II.** *vr:* **-rsi** *inf* (*adattarsi*) to get by

aggiustatura [ad·dʒus·ta·'tu:·ra] *f* (*riparazione*) repair

agglomerato [ag·glo·me·'ra:·to] *m* **1.** (*centro abitato*) built-up area **2.** GEOL agglomerate

aggradare [ag·gra·'da:·re] *vi poet* to please

aggrapparsi [ag·grap·'pa:r·si] *vr* **-rsi** (**a qu/ qc**) **1.** *a. fig* (*salvagente, muro*) to hold onto **2.** (*illusione, speranza, ricordo*) to cling onto

aggravamento [ag·gra·va·'men·to] *m* **1.** (*peggioramento: di malattia, di crisi*) worsening **2.** JUR **~ della pena** increase in the sentence

aggravante [ag·gra·'van·te] **I.** *agg* JUR **circostanza ~** aggravating circumstance **II.** *f* JUR aggravating circumstance

aggravare [ag·gra·'va:·re] **I.** *vt* JUR (*pena*) to increase **II.** *vr:* **-rsi** (*malattia, crisi*) to get worse

aggravio [ag·'gra:·vio] <-i> *m* increase; **~ fiscale** tax increase

aggraziato, -a [ag·gra·'tsia:·to] *agg* **1.** (*grazioso: corpo, viso, forme*) graceful **2.** (*gentile: modi*) pleasing; (*gesto*) gracious

aggredire [ag·gre·'di:·re] <aggredisco> *vt* **1.** (*persona, organi, mercato*) to attack **2.** (*affrontare: problema*) to tackle

aggreditrice *f v.* **aggressore**

aggregare [ag·gre·'ga:·re] **I.** *vt* (*riunire: gruppo, comunità*) to get together **II.** *vr* (*unirsi*) **-rsi a qu/qc** to join sb/sth

aggregato [ag·gre·'ga:·to] *m* **1.** (*complesso*) grouping **2.** MAT, GEOL aggregate

aggregato, -a *agg* **1.** (*aggiunto: socio*) associate **2.** (*distaccato provvisoriamente: giudice, funzionario*) attached

aggressione [ag·gres·'sio:·ne] *f* **1.** (*assalto*) assault; **~ a mano armata** armed assault **2.** MIL aggression; **patto di non ~** non-aggression pact

aggressive [ə·'gre·siv] *agg sl* (*terapia, formula*) aggressive

aggressività [ag·gres·si·vi·'ta] <-> *f* aggressiveness

aggressivo [ag·gres·'si:·vo] *m* **~ chimico** chemical weapon

aggressivo, -a *agg* **1.** (*violento*) aggressive **2.** (*scattante: auto, linee, modo di sciare*) dynamic **3.** (*che attacca: squadra*) attacking; (*pugile*) aggressive; (*sciatore*) daring **4.** CHEM (*corrosivo: prodotto*) corrosive

aggressore, aggreditrice [ag·gres·'so:·re, ag·gre·di·'tri:·tʃe] **I.** *agg* aggressor; **stato ~** aggressor state **II.** *m, f* attacker

aggrinzire [ag·grin·'tsi:·re] **I.** *vt* (*pelle*) to wrinkle **II.** *vr:* **-rsi** (*pelle*) to wrinkle (up)

aggrottare [ag·grot·'ta:·re] *vt* **~ la fronte** to frown, to knit one's (eye)brows

aggrovigliamento [ag·gro·viʎ·ʎa·'men·to] *m* (*di fili, cavi, tubi*) tangle

aggrovigliare [ag·gro·viʎ·'ʎa:·re] **I.** *vt* (*fili, cavi, tubi*) to tangle **II.** *vr:* **-rsi 1.** (*fili, cavi, tubi*) to become tangled **2.** *fig* (*situazione*) to become complicated; (*pensieri*) to become confused

aggrumarsi [ag·gru·'mar·si] *vr* (*sangue*) to clot

agguantare [ag·guan·'ta:·re] **I.** *vt* **1.** (*afferrare: ladro, preda*) to catch **2.** (*raggiungere: vittoria, risultato*) to grasp **II.** *vr:* **-rsi** (*aggrapparsi*) **-rsi a qc** to grab (hold of)

agguato [ag·'gua:·to] *m* ambush; **stare in ~** to lie in wait; **tendere un ~ a qu** to set a trap for sb

agguerrire [ag·guer·'ri:·re] <agguerrisco> **I.** *vt fig* (*temprare*) to toughen (up) **II.** *vr:* **-rsi** (*temprarsi*) **~ contro qc** to become hardened against sth

aghiforme [a·gi·'for·me] *agg* needle-shaped

agiatezza [a·dʒa·'tet·tsa] *f* 1.(*ricchezza: finanziaria, economica*) prosperity; **vivere nell'**~ to be prosperous 2.(*comodità*) comfort

agiato, -a [a·'dʒa··to] *agg* 1.(*benestante*) well-off 2.(*vita, casa, situazione*) comfortable

agibile [a·'dʒi··bi·le] *agg* (*edificio*) habitable; (*strada*) passable

agile ['a··dʒi·le] *agg* 1. *a. fig* (*persona, animale, ingegno*) agile 2.(*veloce: corsa, gioco, movimento*) speedy 3.(*semplice: libro*) easy-to-read

agilità [a·dʒi·li·'ta] <-> *f a. fig* (*di persona, animale*) agility

agio ['a··dʒo] <-gi> *m* 1.(*comodo*) comfort; **trovarsi a proprio** ~ to feel comfortable; **mettiti a tuo** ~! make yourself comfortable! 2.(*opportunità*) chance; **dare** ~ **a qu di fare qc** to enable sb to do sth 3. *pl* (*comodità del vivere*) comforts

AGIP ['a··dʒip] *f acro di* **Azienda Generale Italiana Petroli** *Italian Gas Company*

agire [a·'dʒi··re] <agisco> *vi* 1.(*operare*) to act 2.(*avere effetto: veleno, medicina*) to act 3.(*comportarsi*) to behave; ~ **bene/male** to behave well/badly 4.JUR ~ (**contro qu**) to take action (against sb)

agitare [a·dʒi·'ta··re] I. *vt* 1.(*scuotere: bottiglia*) to shake; (*braccia, fazzoletto*) to wave; (*coda*) to wag; ~ **prima dell'uso** shake before use 2. *fig* (*eccitare: animo, gente*) to agitate 3.(*loc*) ~ **le acque** *fig* to stir things up II. *vr:* **-rsi** 1.(*rigirarsi*) to toss and turn 2.(*mare*) to get rough 3. *fig* (*turbarsi*) to get upset 4.POL (*entrare in lotta*) to agitate

agitato, -a [a·dʒi·'ta··to] *agg* 1.(*mare*) rough 2.(*discussione*) animated 3.(*eccitato, turbato: persona*) worried

agitazione [a·dʒi·tat·'tsio··ne] *f* 1.(*turbamento*) unrest; **mettere in** ~ to upset 2.POL (*protesta*) protest; **essere in** ~ to protest; **stato di** ~ **sindacale** industrial action

agli ['aʎ·ʎi] *prep* = **a** + **gli** *v.* **a**

aglio ['aʎ·ʎo] <-gli> *m* garlic

agnello [aɲ·'ɲɛl·lo] *m* lamb; ~ **arrosto** roast lamb

agnolotti [aɲ·ɲo·'lɔt·ti] *mpl* type of round or square filled pasta

ago ['a··go] <-ghi> *m* needle; (*di bilancia*) pointer; (*da maglia*) (knitting) needle; **cercare un** ~ **in un pagliaio** *fig* to look for a needle in a haystack

agonia [a·go·'ni··a] <-ie> *f* 1.MED death throes 2. *fig* (*angoscia*) torture

agonismo [a·go·'niz·mo] *m* competitiveness

agonistico, -a [a·go·'nis·ti·ko] <-ci, -che> *agg* SPORT (*stagione, attività, calendario*) competitive; **spirito** ~ competitive spirit

agonizzare [a·go·nid·'dza··re] *vi* 1.(*essere in agonia*) to be dying 2. *fig* (*languire*) to be in a bad way

agopressione [a·go·pres·'sio··ne] *f* acupres-

sure

agopuntura [a·go·pun·'tu:·ra] *f* acupuncture

agorafobia [a·go·ra·fo·'bi:·a] *f* agoraphobia

agosto [a·'gos·to] *m* August; *v.a.* **aprile**

agraria [a·'gra:·ria] *f* agriculture

agrario, -a [a·'gra:·rio] <-i, -ie> *agg* agricultural

agretto *m* BOT garden cress

agricolo, -a [a·'gri:·ko·lo] *agg* (*azienda, macchina, attrezzi, prodotto*) agricultural

agricoltore [a·gri·kol·'to:·re] *m* farmer

agricoltura [a·gri·kol·'tu:·ra] *f* agriculture

agrifoglio [a·gri·'fɔʎ·ʎo] *m* holly

Agrigentino (*zona*) Agrigento area; **nell'** ~ in the Agrigento area

agrigentino, -a [a·gri·dʒen·'ti:·no] I. *agg* from Agrigento II. *m, f* (*abitante*) person from Agrigento

Agrigento *f* Agrigento, *city in Sicily*

agrimensore [a·gri·men·'so:·re] *m* land surveyor

agrimensura [a·gri·men·'su:·ra] *f* land surveying

agriturismo [a·gri·tu·'riz·mo] *m* 1.(*attività*) agritourism 2.(*azienda*) agritourism farm

agriturista [a·gri·tu·'ris·ta] <-i , -e> *mf* agritourist

agrituristico, -a [a·gri·tu·'ris·ti·ko] <-ci, -che> *agg* (*ristorante, centro, operatore*) agritourist; **azienda -a** *agritourist business*

agro ['a:·gro] *m* 1.(*sapore aspro*) sharpness; **all'**~ CULIN with lemon or vinegar 2.(*campagna*) countryside

agro, -a ['a:·gro] *agg* 1.(*sapore*) sharp; **in** ~ CULIN with lemon or vinegar 2. *fig* (*pungente: parole*) bitter

agroalimentare [a·gro·a·li·men·'ta:·re] *agg* (*azienda, settore, prodotto*) food and agriculture

agrobiologo, -a [a·gro·'biɔ:·lo·go] <-gi, -ghe> *m, f* agrobiologist

agrochimico, -a [a·gro·'ki:·mi·ko] <-ci, -che> *m, f* agrochemist

agrodolce [a·gro·'dol·tʃe] *agg* bittersweet; **in** ~ CULIN (*petti di pollo, carote*) sweet-and-sour

agroindustria *f* (*industria agroalimentare*) agribusiness

agronica [a·'grɔ:·ni·ka] *f* AGR agro electronics

agronomia [a·gro·no·'mi:·a] <-ie> *f* agronomy

agronomo, -a [a·'grɔ:·no·mo] *m, f* 1.(*esperto*) agronomist 2.(*laureato*) person with a degree in agronomy

agrosistema [a·gro·sis·'tɛ:·ma] <-i> *m* system of agriculture

agrotecnico, -a [a·gro·'tɛk·ni·ko] <-ci, -che> I. *agg* (*cultura, personale*) agro-technical II. *m, f* agricultural technician

agrume [a·'gru:·me] *m* 1.(*frutto*) citrus fruit 2.(*pianta*) citrus

aguzzare [a·gut·'tsa:·re] *vt a. fig* (*rendere appuntito, affilare*) to sharpen; ~ **l'ingegno** to sharpen one's wits; ~ **le orecchie** to listen carefully; ~ **la vista** to look carefully

aguzzino [a·gud·'dzi:·no] *m fig* (*tormentatore*) torturer

aguzzo, -a [a·'gut·tso] *agg* 1.(*acuminato: denti*) sharp 2.(*a punta: naso, mento*) pointed 3.*fig* (*intenso, penetrante: occhi, sguardo*) piercing

ah [a] *int* oh

ahi ['a:i] *int* ow

ahia ['a·ia] *int* ow

ahimè [ai·'mɛ] *int* alas; ~ **non c'è più niente da fare!** unfortunately there's nothing more we can do

ai ['a:i] *prep* = **a + i** *v.* **a**

aia ['a:·ia] <aie> *f* farmyard; **menare il can per l'**~ *fig* to beat around the bush

AIDO *f acro di* **Associazione Italiana Donatori Organi** *Italian Association of Organ Donors*

AIDS *m acro di* **Acquired Immune Deficiency Syndrome** AIDS

aie *pl di* **aia**

AIG ['a:ig] *f acro di* **Associazione Italiana Alberghi per la Gioventù** *Italian Association of Youth Hostels*

AIIP *f acro di* **Associazione Italiana Internet Providers** *Italian Association of Internet Providers*

aiola [a·'iɔ:·la] *f* (*mista, fiorita, erbosa*) flowerbed; ~ **spartitraffico** traffic island

air bag [ɛə bæg] <~ *o* air bags> *m* MOT air bag; ~ **laterale** side airbag

airbus ['ɛə·bʌs] <-> *m* AERO Airbus®

AIRC *f abbr di* **Associazione Italiana per la Ricerca sul Cancro** *Italian Association for Cancer Research*

airone [ai·'ro:·ne] *m* heron

air-show [er·'ʃo] <-> *m* air show

AISM *f abbr di* **Associazione Italiana per la Sclerosi Multipla** *Italian Multiple Sclerosis Association*

aitante [ai·'tan·te] *agg* (*atletico: giovanotto, uomo*) vigorous

aiuola [a·'iu·ɔ:·la] *v.* **aiola**

aiutante [a·iu·'tan·te] *mf* 1.(*collaboratore*) assistant 2. MIL adjutant

aiutare [a·iu·'ta:·re] I. *vt* 1.(*assistere*) ~ **qu** (**a fare qc**) to help sb (do sth) 2.(*favorire*) to aid II. *vr:* -**rsi** to try hard; **aiutati che Dio** [*o* il ciel] **t'aiuta** *prov* God helps those who help themselves *prov*

aiuto [a·'iu:·to] *m* 1.(*assistenza, soccorso*) help; ~! help!; **correre in** ~ **a qu** to go to sb's aid; **essere di** ~ **a qu** to help sb; **invocare** ~ to cry for help 2.(*collaboratore*) assistant; ~ **medico** ≈ resident (*relatively junior hospital doctor*); ~ **regista** assistant director 3. *pl* aid

aizzare [ait·'tsa:·re] *vt* (*folla*) to incite; ~ **i cani contro qu** to set the dogs on sb

al [al] = **a + il** *v.* **a**

ala ['a:·la] <-i> *f a.* ARCH, SPORT (*di uccello, aereo*) wing; ~ **destra/sinistra** right/left wing; **in un batter d'-i** *fig* as quick as a flash;

sotto le -**i di qu** *fig* under sb's wing; **mettere le** -**i ai piedi** *fig* to shake a leg; **tarpare le** -**i a qu** *fig* to clip sb's wings

alabastro [a·la·'bas·tro] *m* alabaster

à la coque [a la 'kɔk] <inv> *agg* **uovo** ~ soft-boiled egg

alacre ['a:·lak·re] *agg* 1.(*sollecito: impiegato, scrittore*) eager 2.*fig* (*fervido: mente, fantasia*) lively

alacrità [a·lak·ri·'ta] <-> *f* 1.(*sveltezza: di impiegato, scrittore*) speed 2.*fig* (*vivacità: di mente*) liveliness

alambicco [a·lam·'bik·ko] <-cchi> *m* still

alano [a·'la:·no] *m* Great Dane

alare [a·'la:·re] *agg* (*carico, profilo*) wing; **apertura** ~ wingspan

alato, -a [a·'la:·to] *agg* 1.(*fornito di ali: cavallo, leone, drago*) winged; **formiche** -**e** flying ants 2.*fig* (*sublime, elevato: parole, vittorie*) sublime

alba ['al·ba] *f* dawn; **all'**~ at dawn

albanese [al·ba·'ne:·se] I. *agg* Albanian II. *mf* Albanian

Albania [al·ba·'ni:·a] *f* Albania

albatro ['al·bat·ro] *m* albatross

albeggiare [al·bed·'dʒa:·re] <albeggia> *vi essere* to dawn; **stava albeggiando** dawn was breaking

alberato, -a [al·be·'ra:·to] *agg* (*viale, piazza, zona*) tree-lined

alberatura [al·be·ra·'tu:·ra] *f* NAUT masts

albergare [al·ber·'ga:·re] I. *vt* 1.(*alloggiare*) to stay 2.*fig* (*sentimenti*) to nurse II. *vi* to stay

albergatore, -trice [al·ber·ga·'to:·re] *m*, *f* hotel owner

alberghiero, -a [al·ber·'giɛ:·ro] *agg* (*istituto, settore*) hotel; **l'industria** -**a** the hotel industry

albergo [al·'bɛr·go] <-ghi> *m* (*hotel*) hotel; ~ **per la gioventù** youth hostel; ~ **diurno** *public baths that offer various services*

albero ['al·be·ro] *m* 1. BOT tree; ~ **di Natale** Christmas tree 2. NAUT mast 3. TEC shaft; ~ **motore** crankshaft 4.(*loc*) ~ **della cuccagna** *greased pole with prizes at the top;* ~ **genealogico** family tree

albicocca [al·bi·'kɔk·ka] <-cche> *f* apricot

albicocco [al·bi·'kɔk·ko] <-cchi> *m* apricot (tree)

albinismo [al·bi·'niz·mo] *m* albinism

albino, -a [al·'bi:·no] I. *agg* albino II. *m*, *f* albino

albo ['al·bo] *m* 1.(*bacheca*) bulletin board 2.(*registro*) register; ~ **dei medici** medical register; **l'**~ **d'oro** honor roll 3.(*libro illustrato*) album

albori [al·'bo:·ri] *mpl* dawn

album ['al·bum] <-> *m* album

albume [al·'bu:·me] *m* egg white

albumina [al·bu·'mi:·na] *f* albumin

alcalino, -a [al·ca·'li:·no] *agg* (*sostanza, soluzione, batteria*) alkaline

alce ['al·tʃe] *f* moose

alchimia [al·'ki:·mia/al·ki·'mi:·a] <-ie> *f* alchemy

alchimista [al·ki·'mis·ta] *mf* alchemist

alco(o)l ['al·kol ('alkool)] <-> *m a.* CHEM alcohol

alco(o)lico [al·'kɔ:·li·ko (alko'ɔ:liko)] <-ci> *m* (*bevanda*) alcohol; **"non si servono -ci"** "we do not serve alcohol"

alco(o)lico, -a <-ci, -che> *agg* (*bevanda, sostanza*) alcoholic

alco(o)lismo [al·ko·'liz·mo (al·ko·'ɔ·liz·mo)] *m* alcoholism

alco(o)lizzare [al·ko·lid·'dza:·re (al·ko·ɔ·lid·'dza:·re)] I. *vt* to get drunk II. *vr:* **-rsi** to drink (to excess)

alco(o)lizzato, -a [al·ko·lid·'dza:·to (al·ko·ɔ·lid·'dza:·to)] I. *agg* drunk II. *m, f* alcoholic

alco(o)ltest [al·kol·'tɛst (alko·ɔ:l·'tɛst)] <-> *m* Breathalyzer®

alcova [al·'kɔ:·va] *f* (*parte di una camera*) alcove

alcun, alcun' [al·'kun] *v.* **alcuno**

alcuno, -a [al·'ku:·no] I. *agg* 1. (*nessuno*) no; **non c'è alcun problema** there's no problem; **senza alcun riguardo** without any consideration 2. *pl* (*qualche*) some; **devo fare -e cose** I have to do a few things; **-i consigli utili** some useful advice; **abbiamo solo -e foto** we have only a few photos II. *pron indef* 1. (*nessuno*) (not) any; **non ne ho visto** ~ I haven't seen any of them; **senza che** ~ **mi udisse** without anyone hearing me 2. *pl* (*qualche*) some (of them); **-i ci danno la mano** some of them help us; **-e se le inventa** (*storie*) he makes some of them up

aldilà [al·di·'la] <-> *m* afterlife

alé [a'·le] *int inf* come on; ~ **Juve!** come on Juve!

aleatorio, -a [a·lea·'tɔ:·rio] <-i, -ie> *agg* (*dubbio: ipotesi, discorso*) dubious

aleggiare [a·led·'dʒa:·re] *vi* 1. (*profumo, aroma*) to float in the air 2. *fig* (*silenzio, paura*) to be in the air

aletta [a·'let·ta] *f* (*di pesce*) fin; (*di freccia*) feather; (*di tasca*) flap; ~ **parasole** AUTO visor; ~ (**della copertina**) (*risvolto*) (inside) flap

alfa ['al·fa] <-> *f* (*lettera*) alpha

alfabetico, -a [al·fa·'bɛ:·ti·ko] <-ci, -che> *agg* (*elenco, indice*) alphabetical; **in ordine** ~ in alphabetical order

alfabetizzare [al·fa·be·tid·'dza:·re] *vt* (*alunni, adulti*) to teach to read

alfabetizzazione [al·fa·be·tid·dzat·'tsio:·ne] *f* (*di alunni stranieri, adulti*) literacy

alfabeto [al·fa·'bɛ:·to] *m* alphabet

alfanumerico, -a [al·fa·nu·'mɛ:·ri·ko] <-ci, -che> *agg* COMPUT (*sigla, tastiera, display*) alphanumeric

alfiere [al·'fiɛ:·re] *m* 1. (*portabandiera*) standard-bearer 2. (*negli scacchi*) bishop

alfine [al·'fi:·ne] *avv liter* finally

alga ['al·ga] <-ghe> *f* alga; **alghe marine** seaweed

algebra ['al·dʒe·bra] *f* algebra

algebrico, -a [al·'dʒɛ:·bri·ko] <-ci, -che> *agg* (*calcolo, numero, metodo*) algebraic

Algeria [al·dʒe·'ri:·a] *f* Algeria

algerino, -a [al·dʒe·'ri:·no] I. *agg* Algerian II. *m, f* Algerian

algocoltura [al·go·kol·'tu:·ra] *f* cultivation of algae

aliante [a·'li·an·te] *m* glider

alibi ['a:·li·bi] <-> *m* alibi

alice [a·'li:·tʃe] *f* anchovy

alienare [a·lie·'na:·re] I. *vt a.* JUR (*vendere*) to alienate II. *vr* **-rsi qu** to alienate sb

alienato, -a [a·lie·'na:·to] I. *agg* 1. MED (*malato di mente*) insane 2. JUR (*venduto*) alienated II. *m, f* (*malato di mente*) insane person

alienazione [a·lie·nat·'tsio:·ne] *f* 1. PSYCH ~ **mentale** insanity 2. JUR, PHILOS alienation

alieno, -a [a·'liɛ:·no] *agg* **essere** ~ **da qc** (*privo di*) to be free from sth

alimentare¹ [a·li·men·'ta:·re] *agg* (*prodotto, additivo*) food; **generi -i** foodstuffs; **paste -i** pasta; **scienza** ~ nutrition

alimentare² I. *vt* 1. (*nutrire: persona, animale*) to feed 2. (*motore, computer, caldaia*) to power 3. *fig* (*mantenere vivo: interesse, sospetti*) to fuel II. *vr:* **-rsi** to eat

alimentari [a·li·men·'ta:·ri] <-> *m* (*negozio*) grocery store

alimentazione [a·li·men·tat·'tsio:·ne] *f* 1. (*con cibo*) diet; **scienza dell'** ~ nutrition 2. TEC (*fornitura*) ~ **elettrica** electricity supply; **auto ad** ~ **elettrica** electrically-powered vehicle; ~ **del carburante** fuel supply

alimento [a·li·'men·to] *m* 1. (*cibo*) food 2. *pl* JUR (*mezzi di sussistenza*) alimony

aliquota [a·'li:·kuo·ta] *f* 1. MATH (*quota*) aliquot 2. FIN rate

aliscafo [a·lis·'ka:·fo] *m* NAUT hydrofoil

alitare [a·li·'ta:·re] *vi* 1. (*respirare*) to breathe 2. *fig* (*soffiare: vento*) to blow

alito ['a:·li·to] *m a. fig* (*fiato*) breath; **aver l'**~ **cattivo** to have bad breath

all. *abbr di* **allegato, -i** attached

all', alla [all, 'al·la] *prep* = **a + l', la** *v.* **a**

allacciamento [al·lat·tʃa·'men·to] *m* 1. TEC (*elettrico, telefonico, del gas*) connection 2. FERR ~ **ferroviario** rail link

allacciare [al·la·'tʃa:·re] I. *vt* 1. (*scarpe*) to lace; (*cappotto, cintura*) to do up 2. TEC (*collegare*) to connect 3. *fig* (*stringere: amicizia*) to make II. *vr* (*cappotto, cintura*) to do up; (*scarpe*) to lace; **-rsi la cintura** (**di sicurezza**) to fasten one's seat belt

allagamento [al·la·ga·'men·to] *m* flooding

allagare [al·la·'ga:·re] *vt* to flood

allampanato, -a [al·lam·pa·'na:·to] *agg* (*alto e magro*) lanky

allargamento [al·lar·ga·'men·to] *m* 1. (*di strada, carreggiata, marciapiede*) widening 2. (*estensione*) enlargement

allargare [al·lar·'ga:·re] I. *vt* 1. (*rendere più largo*) to make wider; (*strada, stanza*) to widen; (*vestito*) to let out **2.**(*braccia, dita*) to spread **3.***fig* (*estendere*) to widen; **mi si allarga il cuore** I feel so happy **II.** *vr:* -rsi **1.**(*diventare più largo: strada, apertura*) to get wider **2.***fig* (*ampliarsi: gruppo, famiglia, gamma*) to expand **3.***fig* (*estendersi: protesta, crisi, ipotesi*) to spread

allarmare [al·lar·'ma:·re] **I.** *vt* **1.**(*dare l'allarme a*) to alert **2.***fig* (*mettere in agitazione*) to alarm **II.** *vr:* -rsi to become alarmed

allarme [al·'lar·me] *m* alarm; ~ **antifurto** burglar alarm; **dare l'~** to raise the alarm

allarmismo [al·lar·'miz·mo] *m* **1.**(*tendenza ad allarmare*) scaremongering **2.**(*stato di allarme*) alarm

allarmistico, -a [al·lar·'mis·ti·ko] <-ci, -che> *agg* (*tendenze, toni, messaggi*) alarmist

allattamento [al·lat·ta·'men·to] *m* (*di bambini, animali*) feeding

allattare [al·lat·'ta:·re] *vt* (*bambini, animali*) to feed

alle ['al·le] *prep* = a + le *v.* a

alleanza [al·le·'an·tsa] *f* alliance; **stringere un'~** to make an alliance

allearsi [al·le·'ar·si] *vr* ~ **a** [*o* **con**] **qu** to ally oneself with sb

alleato, -a [al·le·'a:·to] **I.** *agg* allied; HIST Allied **II.** *m, f* ally; **gli -i** HIST the Allies

allegare [al·le·'ga:·re] *vt* (*accludere: documenti*) to attach; ~ **qc a qc** to attach sth to sth

allegato [al·le·'ga:·to] *m* attachment; **in** ~ attached

allegato, -a *agg* attached; **qui** ~ attached herewith

alleggerire [al·led·dʒe·'ri:·re] <alleggerisco> **I.** *vt* **1.**(*rendere leggero: carico, peso*) to make lighter **2.***fig* (*rendere tollerabile: fatica, compito, dolore*) to lighten **3.***scherz* (*derubare*) ~ **qu di qc** to relieve sb of sth **II.** *vr:* -rsi (*diventare leggero*) to become lighter; -rsi **di qc** (*peso*) to relieve oneself of sth

allegoria [al·le·go·'ri:·a] <-ie> *f* allegory

allegorico, -a [al·le·'gɔ:·ri·ko] <-ci, -che> *agg* (*simbolo, significato*) allegorical; **figure -che** allegorical figures

allegria [al·le·'gri:·a] <-ie> *f* cheerfulness; **mettere ~ a qu** to cheer sb up

allegro, -a *agg* (*carattere, persona, colore*) cheerful; **c'è poco da stare -i** there's not much to be cheerful about; **essere un po'** ~ *inf* (*essere ubriaco*) to be merry

alleluia [al·le·'lu:·ia] <-> *m* hooray

allenamento [al·le·na·'men·to] *m* training; **esser fuori** ~ to be out of shape; **tenersi in** ~ to keep in shape

allenare [al·le·'na:·re] **I.** *vt* **1.**(*atleta, squadra, memoria*) to train **2.**(*cuore, muscoli*) to strengthen **II.** *vr* -rsi to train; -rsi (**per** [*o* **a**] **qc**) to train for sth

allenatore, -trice [al·le·na·'to:·re] *m, f* (*tecnico*) coach

allentare [al·len·'ta:·re] **I.** *vt* **1.**(*rendere meno stretto: presa, nodo*) to loosen **2.**(*diminuire:*

pressioni, sanzioni) to slacken **3.**(*loc*) ~ **un ceffone a qu** *inf* to whack sb; ~ **i cordoni della borsa** *fig* to loosen the purse strings **II.** *vr:* -rsi **1.**(*divenire lento: presa, nodo*) to come loose **2.**(*diminuire d'intensità: tensione*) to slacken

allergia [al·ler·'dʒi:·a] <-gie> *f* allergy

allergico, -a [al·'lɛr·dʒi·ko] <-ci, -che> *agg a. fig scherz* **essere** ~ (**a qc**) to be allergic (to sth)

allergologo, -a [al·ler·'gɔ:·lo·go] <-gi, -ghe> *m, f* MED allergist

allerta [al·'ler·ta] **I.** *avv* **stare** ~ to be alert **II.** *f* **essere in stato di** ~ to be in a state of alert

allestimento [al·les·ti·'men·to] *m* **1.**(*approntamento*) preparation **2.** FILM, THEAT production

allestire [al·les·'ti:·re] <allestisco> *vt* **1.**(*pranzo, cena, festa*) to hold **2.**(*vetrina*) to dress **3.** THEAT (*spettacolo*) to put on

allettamento [al·let·ta·'men·to] *m* enticement

allettare [al·let·'ta:·re] *vt* to entice

allevamento [al·le·va·'men·to] *m* **1.**(*di bestiame, cavalli*) rearing; (*di polli, pesci*) farming; (*di piante*) growing **2.**(*luogo*) farm **3.**(*di bambini*) raising

allevare [al·le·'va:·re] *vt* **1.**(*bestiame, cavalli*) to rear; (*polli, pesci*) to farm; (*piante*) to grow **2.**(*bambini*) to raise

allevatore, -trice [al·le·va·'to:·re] *m, f* (*di bestiame, cavalli, polli, pesci*) farmer; (*di piante*) grower

alleviare [al·le·'via:·re] *vt* (*pressione, peso*) to alleviate; (*dolore, fatica*) to relieve

allibire [al·li·'bi:·re] <allibisco> *vi* **essere** to be appalled

allibito, -a [al·li·'bi:·to] *agg* appalled

allibratore [al·li·bra·'to:·re] *m* bookmaker

allietare [al·lie·'ta:·re] *vt* (*ospiti*) to delight; (*giornata, vita*) to brighten

allievo, -a [al·'liɛ:·vo] *m, f* (*scolaro*) student; ~ **ufficiale** cadet

alligatore [al·li·ga·'to:·re] *m* alligator

allineamento [al·li·ne·a·'men·to] *m* **1.** *a.* COMPUT, POL alignment **2.**(*di stipendi, contratti*) adjustment **3.**(*di testi*) justification

allineare [al·li·ne·'a:·re] **I.** *vt* **1.**(*disporre in linea: oggetti, libri, atleti*) to line up **2.**(*adeguare: stipendi, ricavi, contratti*) to adjust **3.** COMPUT (*testi, punti*) to align **II.** *vr:* -rsi **1.**(*mettersi in linea*) to line up **2.**(*conformarsi*) to align oneself with

allineato, -a *agg* **1.** COMPUT (*testo*) justified; ~ **a sinistra/destra** left/right justified **2.** POL aligned; **i paesi non -i** the nonaligned countries

allo ['al·lo] *prep* = a + lo *v.* a

allocco [al·'lɔk·ko] <-cchi> *m* ZOO tawny owl

allocco, -a <-cchi, -cche> *m, f* (*sciocco*) idiot

allocuzione [al·lo·cut·'tsio:·ne] *f* (*discorso*) address

allodola [al·'lɔ:·do·la] *f* (sky)lark

allogeno, -a [al·'lɔ:·dʒe·no] **I.** *agg* (*cultura, gruppo*) ethnic minority **II.** *m, f* person from an ethnic minority

alloggiare [al·lod·'dʒa:·re] I. *vi* 1.(*dimorare: permanentemente*) to live; (*temporaneamente*) to stay 2. MIL to be quartered II. *vt* avere 1.(*dare ospitalità a*) to put up 2.(*contenere*) to contain 3. MIL to accommodate
alloggio [al·'lɔd·dʒo] <-ggi> *m* 1.*a.* MIL (*dimora*) accommodations; **vitto e ~** room and board 2.(*appartamento*) apartment
allontanamento [al·lon·ta·na·'men·to] *m* 1.(*distacco*) separation 2.(*espulsione: dalla scuola*) expulsion; (*dal posto di lavoro*) dismissal 3.*fig*(*estraniamento*) estrangement
allontanare [al·lon·ta·'na:·re] I. *vt* 1.(*collocare lontano*) to move away 2.(*dal posto di lavoro*) to dismiss; (*dalla scuola*) to expel 3.(*suscitare avversione*) to drive away 4.*fig* (*scongiurare: pericolo, sospetto*) to avert; (*ricordo*) to put out of one's mind II. *vr:* **-rsi** to move away; **~ dalla retta via** *fig* to stray
allora [al·'lo:·ra] I. *avv* then; **da ~ in poi** from then on; **fino ~** until then II. *cong* 1.(*in questo caso*) then 2.(*ebbene*) well; **Non ti piace? E ~?** You don't like it? so what?
alloro [al·'lɔ:·ro] *m* laurel; **dormire** [*o* **riposare**] **sugli -i** to rest on one's laurels
alluce ['al·lu·tʃe] *m* big toe
allucinante [al·lu·tʃi·'nan·te] *agg* (*incredibile: viaggio, storia, situazione*) terrible
allucinazione [al·lu·tʃi·nat·'tsio:·ne] *f* hallucination
alludere [al·'lu:·de·re] <alludo, allusi, alluso> *vi* **~ a qc** to refer to sth
alluminio [al·lu·'mi:·nio] <-i> *m* aluminum
allunaggio [al·lu·'nad·dʒo] <-ggi> *m* moon landing
allunare [al·lu·'na:·re] *vi* to land on the moon
allungamento [al·luŋ·ga·'men·to] *m* 1.(*di percorso, capelli*) extension; (*di tessuto*) stretching; **un ~ dei tempi** an extension of the time limit 2. LING lengthening
allungare [al·lun·'ga:·re] I. *vt* 1.(*accrescere di lunghezza: storia, libro, film*) to make longer; (*abito*) to lengthen; (*capelli*) to have extensions in; (*tavolo*) to extend; **~ il percorso** to go the long way round; **~ la strada** to take a detour; **~ il passo** to hurry up 2.(*accrescere di durata: vita, riunione*) to extend 3.(*diluire: vino*) to water down 4. LING (*vocale*) to lengthen 5.(*loc*) **~ un ceffone a qu** *inf* to whack sb; **allungare le mani su qc** *fig* (*per rubare*) to steal sth; **allungare le mani su qu** (*per toccare*) to touch sb; **~ le orecchie** *fig* to strain one's ears II. *vr:* **-rsi** 1.(*farsi più lungo: giornate*) to get longer 2.(*crescere*) to get taller 3.(*sdraiarsi*) to stretch out
allupato [al·lu·'pa:·to] *agg sl* horny
allusi [al·'lu:·zi] *1. pers sing pass rem di* **alludere**
allusione [al·lu·'zio:·ne] *f* allusion
allusivo, -a [al·lu·'zi:·vo] *agg* (*discorso, parole*) **fare discorsi -i** (**su**) to hint (at)
alluso [al·'lu:·zo] *pp di* **alludere**
alluvionale [al·lu·vio·'na:·le] *agg* alluvial;

deposito ~ alluvium; **pianura** ~ flood plain
alluvionato, -a [al·lu·vio·'na:·to] I. *agg* (*zona, città*) flooded II. *m, f* flood victim
alluvione [al·lu·'vio:·ne] *f a. fig* flood
almanacco [al·ma·'nak·ko] <-cchi> *m* almanac
almeno [al·'me:·no] I. *avv* at least II. *cong* if only
aloe ['a:·loe] <-> *f o m* aloe
alogeno [a·'lɔ:·dʒe·no] *m* CHEM halogen
alogeno, -a *agg* halogen; **lampada -a** halogen lamp
alone [a·'lo:·ne] *m* 1.*a.* FOTO (*di astri*) halo 2.*fig*(*aura*) air
alpe ['al·pe] *f* alp
alpeggio [al·'ped·dʒo] <-ggi> *m* mountain pasture
alpestre [al·'pɛs·tre] *agg* (*zona, paesaggio, pascolo*) alpine
Alpi ['al·pi] *fpl* Alps; **nelle ~** in the Alps
alpinismo [al·pi·'niz·mo] *m* climbing
alpinista [al·pi·'nis·ta] <-i , -e> *mf* climber
alpinistico, -a [al·pi·'nis·ti·ko] <-ci, -che> *agg* (*sci, scalate*) alpine
alpino [al·'pi:·no] *m member of the Italian Alpine troops*
alpino, -a *agg* (*paesaggio, fauna, flora*) alpine; **sci ~** alpine skiing; **soccorso ~** mountain rescue
alquanto [al·'kuan·to] I. *avv* (*piuttosto*) rather II. *agg* quite a few III. *pron indef* quite a few
alt¹ [alt] *int* stop
alt² <-> *m* halt; **dare l'~** to call a halt
altalena [al·ta·'le:·na] *f* 1.(*in bilico*) seesaw 2.(*con le funi*) swing 3.*fig* (*vicenda alterna*) roller coaster
altamente [al·ta·'men·te] *avv* highly
altare [al·'ta:·re] *m* altar; **~ maggiore** high altar
altarino [al·ta·'ri:·no] *m* small altar; **scoprire gli -i** *fig scherz* to reveal sb's guilty secrets
alterabile [al·te·'ra:·bi·le] *agg* 1.(*che può cambiare: cibo, colore, tessuto*) unstable 2.(*documento, password*) able to be changed 3.*fig* (*irritabile: persona*) irritable
alterare [al·te·'ra:·re] I. *vt* 1.(*modificare: clima, metabolismo, mente*) to change 2.(*far guastare: vino, prodotto*) to spoil 3.(*falsificare: documento, password, verità*) to falsify II. *vr:* **-rsi** 1.(*modificarsi: metabolismo, mente*) to change 2.(*guastarsi: cibo, vino, prodotto*) to be spoiled 3.*fig* (*turbarsi: persona*) to get angry
alterazione [al·te·rat·'tsio:·ne] *f* 1.(*modifica: di valori, materiali, ritmi*) alteration 2.(*falsificazione: di password, documento*) falsification 3.(*deterioramento: di frutta, prodotto*) deterioration 4. MED (*di cellule, mucose, funzioni vitali*) change 5. MUS change of pitch 6.*fig*(*turbamento*) irritation
alternanza [al·ter·'nan·tsa] *f* (*di fenomeni, stagioni*) alternation; (*di colture*) rotation; **~ scuola-lavoro** alternation of school and

work
furnace

alternare [al·ter·'na:·re] I. *vt* (*medicine, attività*) to alternate; (*colture*) to rotate II. *vr:* -**rsi** to alternate; -**rsi alla guida** to take turns driving

alternativa [al·ter·na·'ti:·va] *f* 1. (*possibilità di scegliere*) choice 2. (*scelta*) alternative

alternativo, -a [al·ter·na·'ti:·vo] *agg* (*medicina, musica, stampa,turismo*) alternative

alternato, -a [al·ter·'na:·to] *agg* (*colori, segni*) alternate; ~ **a** alternating with; **corrente -a** alternating current

alternatore [al·ter·na·'to:·re] *m* alternator

alterno, -a [al·'tɛr·no] *agg* (*turni, giorni, colori*) alternate; **a settimane -e** every other week; **targhe -e** alternating license plates, *system of allowing only vehicles with either odd or even license plate numbers to travel on a particular day*

altero, -a [al·'tɛ:·ro] *agg* proud

altezza [al·'tet·tsa] *f* 1. (*gener*) height 2. MUS pitch 3. (*livello*) **essere all'~** to be up to it 4. (*vicinanza*) proximity; **all'~ di** near 5. (*larghezza di tessuti*) width 6. (*titolo nobiliare*) **Sua Altezza** His/Her/Your Highness

altezzosità [al·tet·tso·si·'ta] <-> *f* hauteur

altezzoso, -a [al·tet·'tso:·so] *agg* haughty

alticcio, -a [al·'tit·tʃo] <-cci, -cce> *agg* (*ubriaco*) tipsy

altiforni *pl di* altoforno

altipiani *pl di* altopiano

altisonante [al·ti·so·'nan·te] *agg* 1. (*sonoro: voce*) ringing 2. (*nome, titolo*) aristocratic

altitudine [al·ti·'tu:·di·ne] *f* altitude

alto¹ ['al·to] *m* (*parte più elevata*) top; **guardare in ~** to look up; **mettere in ~** to put sth high up; **rivolto verso l'~** turned upwards; **mani in ~!** hands up!; **gli -i e i bassi** the highs and lows; **guardare qu dall'~ in basso** to look down on sb

alto² *avv* **mirare ~** to aim high

alto, -a <più alto *o* superiore, altissimo *o* supremo *o* sommo> *agg* 1. (*sviluppato in altezza: edificio, albero*) tall; (*montagna, muro*) high 2. (*statura*) tall; **quanto sei ~?** how tall are you? 3. (*elevato: prezzo, stipendio*) high 4. (*allegro: morale*) high 5. GEOG (*in luogo elevato*) upper; (*vicino alla sorgente*) **l'~ Isonzo** the upper reaches of the Isonzo; (*settentrionale*) northern 6. (*profondo: acqua, mare*) deep 7. (*tessuto*) wide 8. (*acuto: suono, voce*) high 9. *fig* (*eminente: carica, ufficiale*) high; **-a società** high society; **-a moda** high fashion; **avere un ~ concetto di sé** to have a high opinion of oneself 10. (*loc*) **-a stagione** high season; **-a finanza** high finance

Alto Adige ['al·to 'a:·di·dʒe] *m* Alto Adige; **Trentino ~** Trentino-Alto-Adige

altoatesino, -a [al·to·a·te·'zi:·no] I. *agg* from the Alto Adige II. *m, f* (*abitante*) person from the Alto Adige

altoforno [al·to·'for·no] <altiforni> *m* blast

altolocato, -a [al·to·lo·'ka:·to] *agg* (*amico, persona*) highly placed

altoparlante [al·to·par·'lan·te] *m* loudspeaker

altopiano [al·to·'pia:·no] <altipiani> *m* plateau

altrettanto [al·tret·'tan·to] *avv* equally

altrettanto, -a I. *agg* as much, as many II. *pron indef* as much, as many; **grazie ~!** thanks, and the same to you!

altri ['al·tri] <inv, solo al sing> *pron indef* 1. (*altra persona*) someone else 2. *liter* (*qualcuno*) others

altrimenti [al·tri·'men·ti] *avv* 1. (*in caso contrario*) otherwise 2. (*in modo diverso*) differently

altro ['al·tro] *m* something else; **che ~ vuoi?** what else do you want?; **ci vuol ben ~!** that won't do it at all!; **dell'~** more; **desidera ~?** would you like anything else?; **per ~** moreover; **più che ~** above all; **se non ~** at least; **senz'~** of course; **tra l'~** among other things; **tutt'~** quite the contrary; **l'un l'~** each other; **non fare ~ che studiare** she does nothing but study

altro, -a I. *agg* 1. (*distinto*) different; **in un ~ modo** differently; **sarà per un'~a volta** we'll do it another time 2. (*ulteriore*) another; **un ~ caffè, per favore!** another coffee please; **un'~a volta** again 3. (*passato*) last; **l'~a settimana** last week; **l'~a volta** last time; **l'~ giorno** the other day; **l'~ ieri** the day before yesterday 4. (*prossimo*) next; **domani l'~** the day after tomorrow; **quest'altr'anno** nex year II. *pron indef* another; **un giorno o l'~** one day or another; **da un momento all'~** from one moment to the next; **non avere ~ da fare** to have nothing else to do; **noi -i/voi -i** us/you

altroché [al·tro·'ke] *int* and how

altronde [al·'tron·de] *avv* **d'~** on the other hand

altrove [al·'tro:·ve] *avv* somewhere else

altrui [al·'tru:i] <inv> *agg* other people's

altruismo [al·tru·'iz·mo] *m* altruism

altruista [al·tru·'is·ta] <-i, -e> *mf* altruist

altura [al·'tu:·ra] *f* 1. (*luogo elevato*) high ground 2. (*alto mare*) deep sea

alunno, -a [a·'lun·no] *m, f* (*scolaro*) student

alveare [al·ve·'a:·re] *m* 1. (*arnia*) beehive 2. *fig* (*caseggiato*) rabbit warren

alveo ['al·veo] *m* riverbed

alzabandiera [al·tsa·ban·'diɛ:·ra] <-> *m* flag-raising ceremony

alzare [al·'tsa:·re] I. *vt* 1. (*gener*) to raise; (*peso*) to lift; (*bandiera, vela*) to hoist; **~ il bicchiere** to raise one's glass; **~ le carte** to cut the cards; **~ i tacchi** *fig* to take to one's heels; **~ gli occhi al cielo** to roll one's eyes; **~ le spalle** to shrug; **~ la cresta** *fig* to get too big for one's britches; **~ il gomito** *fig* to drink too much; **~ le mani su qu** *fig* to raise one's hand to sb; **non ~ un dito** *fig* to not lift a finger; **~ la voce** to raise one's voice 2. (*edificio, palizzata,* *muro*) to increase the height of **II.** *vr:* -**rsi** **1.**(*levarsi*) to get up; -**rsi in volo** to take off **2.**(*sorgere: sole, luna*) to rise **3.**(*aumentare: vento, mare*) to get up

alzata [al·'tsa:·ta] *f* (*sollevamento*) raising; ~ **di spalle** shrug; ~ **di scudi** outcry; **votare per ~ di mano** to vote by a show of hands

AM 1. *abbr di* **Aeronautica Militare** ≈ USAF **2.** *abbr di* **Modulazione d'Ampiezza** AM

amabile [a·'ma:·bi·le] *agg* **1.**(*persona*) likable **2.**(*vino*) sweet

amabilità [a·ma·bi·li·'ta] <-> *f* amiability

amaca [a·'ma:·ka] <-che> *f* hammock

amalgama [a·'mal·ga·ma] <-i> *m* (*lega*) amalgam

amalgamare [a·mal·ga·'ma:·re] **I.** *vt* **1.**(*unire in lega: metalli*) to amalgamate **2.**(*colori, ingredienti*) to mix **II.** *vr:* -**rsi** (*ingredienti*) to mix; (*musiche*) to combine

amante [a·'man·te] **I.** *agg* **essere ~ di qc** to be fond of sth **II.** *mf* lover; **è un ~ della buona tavola** he loves good food

amare [a·'ma:·re] **I.** *vt* to love; **non ~ la musica** to not like music **II.** *vr:* -**rsi** to love each other

amareggiare [a·ma·red·'dʒa:·re] **I.** *vt* to make sb bitter **II.** *vr:* -**rsi** to get upset

amarena [a·ma·'rɛ:·na] *f* sour black cherry

amaretto [a·ma·'ret·to] *m* **1.**(*biscotto*) amaretto (*almond-flavored cookie*) **2.**(*liquore*) amaretto (*almond-flavored liqueur*)

amarezza [a·ma·'ret·tsa] *f fig* (*dolore misto a rancore*) bitterness

amaro [a·'ma:·ro] *m* **1.**(*sapore*) bitter taste **2.**(*liquore*) aromatic liqueur usually drunk after a meal **3.** *fig* (*rancore*) bitterness

amaro, -a *agg* **1.**(*bibita, sapore, sconfitta, risata*) bitter; **cioccolato ~** dark chocolate; **rimanere con la bocca -a** *fig* to feel bitter **2.**(*senza zucchero: caffè, tè*) without sugar

amarone [a·ma·'ro:·ne] *m* Amarone (*a dry red wine obtained from withered grapes from the Valpolicella area*)

amatoriale [a·ma·to·'ria:·le] *agg* amateur; **teatro ~** amateur dramatics; **cinema ~** home movies; **sport ~** amateur sports

amazzone [a·'mad·dzo·ne] *f* amazon

ambasciata [am·baʃ·'ʃa:·ta] *f* **1.**(*luogo*) embassy **2.**(*messaggio*) message; **fare un'~** to pass on a message

ambasciatore, -trice [am·baʃ·ʃa·'to:·re] *m, f* **1.**(*diplomatico*) ambassador **2.**(*messaggero*) messenger; **ambasciator non porta pena** *prov* don't shoot the messenger

ambedue [am·be·'du:·e] **I.** <inv> *agg* both **II.** *pron* both

ambidestro, -a [am·bi·'dɛs·tro] *agg* (*guanto, tastiera, manovella*) that can be used with either hand

ambientale [am·bien·'ta:·le] *agg* environmental; **danni -i** environmental damage; **impatto ~** environmental impact; **tutela ~** environmental protection

ambientalismo [am·bien·ta·'liz·mo] *m* environmentalism

ambientalista [am·bien·ta·'lis·ta] <-i , -e> **I.** *mf* environmentalist **II.** *agg* (*associazione, politica, tematica*) environmental

ambientamento [am·bien·ta·'men·to] *m* (*adeguamento*) **periodo di ~** settling-in period

ambientare [am·bien·'ta:·re] **I.** *vt* LIT, FILM, THEAT to set **II.** *vr:* -**rsi** to settle in

ambientazione [am·bien·tat·'tsio:·ne] *f* FILM, THEAT setting

ambiente [am·'biɛn·te] *m* **1.**(*spazio*) place; **a temperatura ~** at room temperature **2.** BIOL environment; **tutela dell'~** protection of the environment **3.**(*stanza*) room **4.**(*politico, internazionale*) circle; **sentirsi nel proprio ~** to feel at home

ambiguità [am·bi·gui·'ta] <-> *f* **1.**(*di testo, parole, affermazioni*) ambiguity **2.** *pej* (*di comportamento*) duplicity

ambiguo, -a [am·'bi:·guo] <-i, -ie> *agg* **1.**(*testo, parole, affermazioni*) ambiguous **2.** *pej* (*comportamento*) dishonest

ambire [am·'bi:·re] <ambisco> **I.** *vt* to desire **II.** *vi* ~ (**a qc**) to aspire (to sth)

ambito ['am·bi·to] *m* field

ambivalente [am·bi·va·'lɛn·te] *agg* (*concetto, politica, parola*) with more than one possible meaning

ambivalenza [am·bi·va·'lɛn·tsa] *f* (*di atteggiamento, sentimento, termine*) ambivalence

ambizione [am·bit·'tsio:·ne] *f* (*aspirazione*) ambition

ambizioso, -a [am·bi·'tsio:·so] *agg* ambitious

ambo ['am·bo] *m* (*nel gioco*) double

ambo, -a <inv *o* -i, -e> *agg* both; ~ [*o* -i] **i lati** both sides

ambosessi [am·bo·'sɛs·si] <inv> *agg* of either sex

ambra ['am·bra] *f* amber; ~ **grigia** ambergris

ambrato, -a [am·'bra:·to] *agg* **1.**(*colore*) amber **2.**(*profumo*) musky

ambrosiano, -a [am·bro·'zia:·no] *agg* Milanese

ambulante [am·bu·'lan·te] **I.** *agg* (*venditore, commercio*) traveling **II.** *mf* street vendor

ambulanza [am·bu·'lan·tsa] *f* ambulance

ambulatorio [am·bu·la·'tɔ:·rio] <-i> *m* (*medico, dentistico*) surgery

amen ['a:·men] *m* **1.** REL amen **2.** *inf* (*pazienza*) never mind

amenità [a·me·ni·'ta] <-> *f* **1.**(*attrattiva: di luogo*) pleasantness **2.**(*facezia*) witticism

ameno, -a [a·'mɛ:·no] *agg* **1.**(*attraente: luogo, paesaggio, giardino*) pleasant **2.**(*piacevole: immagine*) enjoyable; **letteratura -a** light reading

America *f* America; ~ **Latina** Latin America; ~ **Centrale** Central America; ~ **del Nord/ Sud** North/South America

americanità [a·me·ri·ka·ni·'ta] <-> *f* Americanness

A

americano, -a [a·me·ri·'ka:·no] I. *agg* American II. *m, f* American

ametista [a·me·'tis·ta] *f* amethyst

amianto [a·'mian·to] *m* asbestos

amichetto, -a [a·mi·'ket·to] *m, f iron* (*innamorato*) boyfriend, girlfriend

amichevole [a·mi·'ke:·vo·le] *agg* 1. (*trattamento, parita*) friendly 2. (*accordo*) amicable

amicizia [a·mi·'tʃit·tsia] <-ie> *f* 1. (*affetto*) friendship; **fare ~ con qu** to make friends with sb 2. *pl fig* (*relazioni*) friends

amico, -a [a·'mi:·ko] <-ci, -che> I. *m, f* 1. (*conoscente*) friend; **~ intimo** [*o* **del cuore**] close friend; **~ di famiglia** family friend; **essere -ci per la pelle** to be great friends 2. (*amante*) lover II. *agg* (*persona, squadra, parole*) friendly

amido ['a:·mi·do] *m* starch

ammaccare [am·mak·'ka:·re] I. *vt* (*auto*) to dent II. *vr:* **-rsi** (*parti del corpo*) to bruise

ammaccatura [am·mak·ka·'tu:·ra] *f* 1. (*deformazione: di auto*) dent 2. (*contusione, di frutta*) bruise

ammaestramento [am·ma·es·tra·'men·to] *m* 1. (*insegnamento*) teaching 2. (*di animali*) training

ammaestrare [am·ma·es·'tra:·re] *vt* 1. (*istruire*) to teach 2. (*animali, soldati*) to train

ammainare [am·mai·'na:·re] *vt* (*vela, bandiera*) to lower

ammalarsi [am·ma·'la:r·si] *vr:* **-rsi** to get sick; **-rsi di ...** to fall sick with ...

ammalato, -a [am·ma·'la:·to] I. *agg* sick II. *m, f* sick

ammaliare [am·ma·'lia:·re] *vt* to bewitch

ammanettare [am·ma·net·'ta:·re] *vt* to handcuff

ammanicarsi [am·ma·ni·'kar·si] *vr* **~ (con qu)** to get in (with sb)

ammansire [am·man·'si:·re] *vt* (*animali*) to tame; (*persone*) to calm

ammantare [am·man·'ta:·re] I. *vt poet* 1. (*velare*) to shroud 2. (*coprire*) to cloak II. *vr:* **-rsi** *fig* **-rsi di qc** to wrap oneself in sth

ammassare [am·mas·'sa:·re] I. *vt* 1. (*oggetti*) to pile up 2. (*raccogliere: truppe*) to mass 3. (*accumulare: ricchezze, denaro*) to amass II. *vr:* **-rsi** 1. (*radunarsi*) to mass 2. (*accumularsi*) to pile up

ammasso [am·'mas·so] *m* (*mucchio*) heap

ammattire [am·mat·'ti:·re] <ammattisco> *vi essere* to go crazy

ammazzare [am·mat·'tsa:·re] I. *vt* 1. (*uccidere*) to kill 2. *fig* (*affaticare*) to exhaust 3. (*loc*) **~ la noia** to stave off boredom; **~ il tempo** to kill time II. *vr:* **-rsi** *a. fig* (*suicidarsi*) to kill oneself

ammenda [am·'mɛn·da] *f* 1. (*multa*) fine 2. *fig* (*riparazione*) **far ~ di qc** to make amends for sth

ammesso, -a [am·'mes·so] I. *agg* (*imprese, attività*) permitted; **~ che** +*conj* supposing

II. *m, f* (*candidato*) **gli -i agli esami** candidates who are allowed to take the exams

ammettere [am·'met·te·re] <irr> *vt* 1. (*supporre*) to suppose 2. (*riconoscere, accogliere*) to admit 3. (*permettere*) to accept 4. (*accettare*) **~ a qc** to be allowed to do sth

ammiccare [am·mik·'ka:·re] *vi* **~ a qu** to wink at sb

amministrare [am·mi·nis·'tra:·re] *vt* 1. ADM (*patrimonio, denaro pubblico*) to administer; (*azienda, condominio*) to run; **~ un sito Internet** to run a website; **~ la giustizia** to administer justice; **~ i sacramenti** to administer the sacraments 2. *fig* (*tempo*) to organize

amministrativo, -a [am·mi·nis·tra·'ti:·vo] *agg* (*personale, direttore, segreteria*) administrative

amministratore, -trice [am·mi·nis·tra·'to:·re] *m, f* (*di azienda, condominio, ospedale*) manager; **~ delegato** CEO

amministrazione [am·mi·nis·trat·'tsio:·ne] *f* 1. (*gestione*) administration; **~ della giustizia** the administration of justice; **cose di ordinaria ~** *fig* daily life 2. (*organi*) board; **~ comunale** local government; **~ pubblica** public administration 3. (*ufficio: di condominio, ospedale*) office

ammiraglia [am·mi·'raʎ·ʎa] <-glie> *f* MOT, NAUT flagship

ammiraglio [am·mi·'raʎ·ʎo] <-gli> *m* admiral

ammirare [am·mi·'ra:·re] *vt* to admire

ammiratore, -trice [am·mi·ra·'to:·re] *m, f* admirer

ammirazione [am·mi·rat·'tsio:·ne] *f* admiration

ammirevole [am·mi·'re:·vo·le] *agg* admirable

ammisi [am·'mi:·zi] *1. pers sing pass rem di* ammettere

ammissibile [am·mis·'si:·bi·le] *agg* (*spesa, investimento, carico*) allowable; **non è ~** (**fare**) **qc** sth is not allowed

ammissione [am·mis·'sio:·ne] *f* admission

ammobiliare [am·mo·bi·'lia:·re] *vt* (*appartamento, camera*) to furnish

ammobiliato, -a *agg* (*appartamento, camera*) furnished

ammodernamento [am·mo·der·na·'men·to] *m* (*di edificio, impianto, sistema*) modernization

ammodernare [am·mo·der·'na:·re] *vt* (*edificio, impianto, strada*) to modernize

ammodo [am·'mɔ:·do] <inv> I. *agg* nice II. *avv* well

ammogliare [am·moʎ·'ʎa:·re] I. *vt* to marry (off) II. *vr:* **-rsi** to get married

ammollare [a·mol·'la:·re] I. *vt* (*biancheria, biscotti*) to soak II. *vr:* **-rsi** (*pane, biscotti*) to get soaked

ammollo [am·'mɔl·lo] *m* (*di biancheria*) soaking; **lasciare in ~** to soak

ammoniaca [am·mo·'ni:·a·ka] <-che> *f* ammonia

ammonimento [am·mo·ni·'men·to] *m*

1.(*avvertimento*) warning **2.**(*rimprovero*) reprimand

ammonire [am·mo·'ni:·re] <ammonisco> *vt* **1.**(*mettere in guardia*) to warn **2.**SPORT (*calciatore*) to book

ammonizione [am·mo·nit·'tsio:·ne] *f* **1.**(*avvertimento*) warning **2.**SPORT (*di calciatore*) booking

ammontare[1] [am·mon·'ta:·re] *vi essere* ~ **a qc** to add up to sth

ammontare[2] *m* (*totale*) total amount

ammorbidente [am·mor·bi·'dɛn·te] *m* fabric softener

ammorbidire [am·mor·bi·'di:·re] <ammorbidisco> I. *vt avere a. fig* to soften II. *vr:* -**rsi** to soften

ammortamento [am·mor·ta·'men·to] *m* **1.**(*ammortizzazione*) amortization **2.**JUR, FIN (*estinzione*) redemption

ammortizzare [am·mor·tid·'dza:·re] *vt* **1.**(*investimento, spesa*) to amortize **2.**TEC (*attutire: colpo*) to cushion

ammortizzatore [am·mor·tid·dza·'to:·re] *m* AUTO shock absorber

ammucchiare [am·muk·'kia:·re] I. *vt* (*oggetti, libri*) to pile up II. *vr:* -**rsi** (*raccogliersi*) to crowd

ammucchiata [am·muk·'kia:·ta] *f* **1.**(*orgia*) group sex **2.** *fig* (*insieme confuso di persone o cose*) jumble **3.**SPORT (*nel rugby*) scrum

ammuffire [am·muf·'fi:·re] <ammuffisco> *vi essere* **1.**(*fare la muffa: frutta, pane, pareti*) to go moldy **2.** *fig* (*sciuparsi*) to molder (away)

ammutinamento [am·mu·ti·na·'men·to] *m* mutiny

ammutinarsi [am·mu·ti·'nar·si] *vr* to mutiny

ammutolire [am·mu·to·'li:·re] <ammutolisco> *vi essere* to be struck dumb

amnesia [am·ne·'zi:·a] <-ie> *f* amnesia

amniocentesi [am·nio·'tʃen·te·si] <-> *f* MED amniocentesis

amnioscopia [am·nio·sko·'pi:·a] <-ie> *f* MED amnioscopy

amniotico, -a [am·ni·'ɔ:·ti·ko] <-ci, -che> *agg* ANAT amniotic; **liquido** ~ amniotic fluid

amnistia [am·nis·'ti:·a] <-ie> *f* amnesty

amo ['a:·mo] *m* hook

amorale [a·mo·'ra:·le] *agg* (*discorso, lettura, insegnamento*) amoral

amore [a·'mo:·re] *m* **1.**(*sentimento*) love; ~ **del prossimo** love for one's neighbor; ~ **materno** motherly love; **amor patrio** love of one's country; **amor proprio** self esteem; ~ **per lo studio** love of study; **un** ~ **di casetta/di bambino** a delightful house/child; **far l'**~ [o **all'**~] **con qu** to make love with sb; **vivere d'**~ **e d'accordo** to get on like a house on fire; **per** ~ **di qu** for sb's sake; **per** ~ **o per forza** willy-nilly; **per amor di Dio!** for God's sake!; **l'**~ **è cieco** *prov* love is blind *prov* **2.**(*persona*) love

amoreggiare [a·mo·red·dʒa:·re] *vi* to flirt

amorevole [a·mo·'re:·vo·le] *agg* (*padre,*

madre, sguardo, cure) loving

amorfo, -a [a·'mɔr·fo] *agg* **1.**(*senza forma*) shapeless **2.**PHYS (*non cristallino: ghiaccio*) amorphous **3.**(*senza carattere: persona*) dull

amorino [a·mo·'ri:·no] *m* cupid

amoroso, -a [a·mo·'ro:·so] I. *agg* **1.**(*frase, dubbio*) amorous **2.vita** ~ love life; **relazione** ~ love affair II. *m, f* (*innamorato*) boyfriend, girlfriend

amovibile [a·mo·'vi:·bi·le] *agg* (*che si può spostare*) removable

amperaggio [am·pe·'rad·dʒo] <-ggi> *m* amperage

ampère [ã·'pɛ:r] <-> *m* amp

amperometro [am·pe·'rɔ:·me·tro] *m* ammeter

amperora [am·pe·'ro:·ra] <-> *f* ampere hour

ampiezza [am·'piet·tsa] *f* **1.**(*larghezza: di strada*) width; (*di locale*) size **2.**(*estensione: di fenomeno, epidemia*) scale **3.** *fig* (*abbondanza: di particolari*) wealth **4.**PHYS (*di onda, marea*) range

ampio, -a ['am·pio] <-i, -ie, amplissimo> *agg* **1.**(*spazioso: strada*) wide; (*locale*) large **2.**(*abbondante: abito*) loose **3.**(*esauriente: spiegazione*) full **4.**(*esteso: garanzia*) ample **5.**(*loc*) **una persona di -e vedute** a broad-minded person

amplesso [am·'plɛs·so] *m* **1.**(*coito*) intercourse **2.** *liter* (*abbraccio*) embrace

ampliamento [am·pli·a·'men·to] *m* **1.**(*di edificio*) extension; (*di strada*) widening **2.**COMPUT (*di memoria*) expansion

ampliare [am·pli·'a:·re] I. *vt* **1.**(*edificio*) to extend; (*strada*) to widen **2.**COMPUT (*memoria*) to expand **3.**(*conoscenze, attività sociale*) to broaden II. *vr:* -**rsi** (*prestazioni, attività*) to expand

amplificare [am·pli·fi·'ka:·re] *vt* **1.**(*fatti, notizie*) to broadcast **2.**TEC (*suono*) to amplify

amplificatore [am·pli·fi·ka·'to:·re] *m* TEC amplifier

amplificazione [am·pli·fi·kat·'tsio:·ne] *f* TEC (*di suono, segnale*) amplification

amplissimo [am·'plis·si·mo] *superlativo di* **ampio**

ampolla [am·'pol·la] *f* **1.**(*per olio, aceto*) cruet **2.**MED ampoule

ampolloso, -a [am·pol·'lo:·so] *agg* (*discorso*) pompous

amputare [am·pu·'ta:·re] *vt* **1.**MED (*arto*) to amputate **2.** *fig* (*eliminare una parte di: scritto*) to cut

amputazione [am·pu·tat·'tsio:·ne] *f* **1.**MED amputation **2.** *fig* (*di scritto*) cutting

amuleto [a·mu·'lɛ:·to/a·mu·'le:·to] *m* amulet

AN *f abbr di* **Alleanza Nazionale** National Alliance, *right-wing party*

anabbagliante [a·nab·baʎ·'ʎan·te] I. *agg* (*faro, luce*) dimmed II. *mpl* dimmed headlights *pl*

anacronismo [a·na·kro·'niz·mo] *m* anachronism

anacronistico, **-a** [a·na·kro·'nis·ti·ko] <-ci, -che> *agg* (*idea, affermazione*) anachronistic
anafora [a·'na·fo·ra] *f* LING anaphora
anagrafe [a·'naː·gra·fe] *f* **1.** (*registro*) register **2.** (*ufficio*) office of vital statistics
anagrafico, **-a** [a·na·'graː·fi·ko] <-ci, -che> *agg* (*elenco* ~) register; **dati -i** personal data
anagramma [a·na·'gram·ma] <-i> *m* anagram
analcolico [an·al·'kɔː·li·ko] <-ci> *m* non-alcoholic drink
analcolico, **-a** <-ci, -che> *agg* (*bevanda*) non-alcoholic
anale [a·'naː·le] *agg* (*orifizio, sesso*) anal
analfabeta [an·al·fa·'bɛː·ta] <-i , -e> **I.** *mf* illiterate person **II.** *agg* (*adulto, popolazione*) illiterate
analfabetismo [an·al·fa·be·'tiz·mo] *m* illiteracy
analgesico [an·al·'dʒɛː·zi·ko] <-ci> *m* analgesic
analgesico, **-a** <-ci, -che> *agg* (*efficacia, azione*) analgesic
analisi [a·'naː·li·zi] <-> *f* analysis; **fare l'~ della situazione** to analyze the situation; **~ di mercato** market analysis; **in ultima ~** in the final analysis
analista [a·na·'lis·ta] <-i , -e> *mf* PSYCH, CHEM analyst; **~ finanziario** financial analyst; **~ di sistemi** COMPUT systems analyst
analizzare [a·na·lid·'dzaː·re] *vt* (*dati, situazione, mercato*) to analyze
analizzatore [a·na·lid·dza·'toː·re] *m* (*strumento per analisi*) analyzer
anallergico, **-a** [an·al·'lɛr·dʒi·ko] *agg* (*che non genera allergie: crema, metallo, tessuto*) hypoallergenic
analogico, **-a** [a·na·'lɔː·dʒi·ko] <-ci, -che> *agg* **1.** (*metodo*) analogical **2.** (*orologio, telefono, videocamera*) analog
analogo, **-a** [a·'naː·lo·go] <-ghi, -ghe> *agg* (*simile: compito, circostanza, caso*) similar
ananas ['aː·na·nas/a·na·'nas] <-> *m* pineapple
anarchia [a·nar·'kiː·a] <-chie> *f* anarchy
anarchico, **-a** [a·'nar·ki·ko] <-ci, -che> **I.** *agg* (*idea, teoria, movimento, spirito*) anarchic **II.** *m, f* anarchist
anarchismo [a·nar·'kiz·mo] *m* anarchism
ANAS ['aː·nas] *f abbr di* **Azienda Nazionale Autonoma delle Strade** *National Highway Department*
anatema [a·na·'tɛː·ma] <-i> *m* **1.** (*maledizione*) curse **2.** (*scomunica*) excommunication
anatomia [a·na·to·'miː·a] <-ie> *f* **1.** (*scienza*) anatomy **2.** *fig* (*analisi minuziosa*) detailed analysis
anatomico, **-a** [a·na·'tɔː·mi·ko] <-ci, -che> *agg* (*relativo all'anatomia*) anatomical; **tavola -a** dissecting table; **sedile ~** orthopedic chair; **plantare ~** arch support
anatra ['aː·na·tra] *f* duck
anca ['aŋ·ka] <-che> *f* hip
anche ['aŋ·ke] *cong* **1.** (*pure*) too **2.** (*inoltre*)

as well **3.** (*perfino*) even; **~ se ...** +*conj* even if; **quand'~ ...** +*conj* even if
ancheggiare [aŋ·ked·'dʒaː·re] *vi* to wiggle one's hips
ancia ['an·tʃa] <-ce> *f* MUS reed
Ancona [aŋ·'koː·na] *f* Ancona, *city on the east coast of Italy*
anconetano, **-a** **I.** *agg* from Ancona **II.** *m, f* (*abitante*) person from Ancona
ancora[1] [aŋ·'koː·ra] *avv* **1.** (*tuttora*) still **2.** (*fino ad ora*) **non ~** not ... yet **3.** (*un'altra volta*) again **4.** (*in aggiunta*) (some) more; **~ più bella** even more beautiful
ancora[2] ['aŋ·koː·ra] *f* anchor; **essere all'~** to be at anchor; **gettare/levare** [*o* **salpare**] **l'~** to drop/raise anchor; **~ di salvezza** *fig* sheet anchor
ancoraggio [aŋ·ko·'rad·dʒo] <-ggi> *m* anchorage
ancorare [aŋ·ko·'raː·re] **I.** *vt a.* NAUT (*nave*) to anchor **II.** *vr:* **-rsi 1.** NAUT to drop anchor **2.** (*aggrapparsi: ipotesi, illusione, affetto*) **-rsi** (**a qc**) to cling (onto sth)
andai [an·'daːi] *1. pers sing pass rem di* **andare**[1]
andamento [an·da·'men·to] *m* **1.** (*di produzione, malattia*) progress; (*di mercato*) trend; **l'~ dei prezzi** price trends; **~ scolastico** academic progress **2.** MUS progression
andante [an·'dan·te] **I.** *agg* **1.** (*scadente: abito, prodotto*) cheap **2.** MUS andante **II.** *m* MUS andante
andare[1] [an·'daː·re] <vado, andai, andato> **I.** *vi essere* **1.** (*a piedi, con mezzo, recarsi*) to go; **~ a piedi** to walk; **~ avanti** to go forward; **~ a zonzo** to stroll around; **~ di fretta** to hurry; **~ via** to leave; **andiamo!** let's go!; **~ in treno** to go by train; **~ in macchina** to drive; **~ in aereo** to fly; **~ a cavallo** to ride; **~ a scuola in bicicletta** to go to school by bike; **~ a fare la spesa** to go shopping; **~ a mangiare** to go out to eat; **~ a prendere** to go and get; **~ a sciare** to go skiing; **~ a trovare** to visit **2.** (*recarsi*) to go; **~ a Roma** to go to Rome; **~ in Germania** to go to Germany **3.** (*strada*) to go; **questa strada va a Milano** this road goes to Milan **4.** (*venir messo*) to go; **dove vanno i piatti?** where do the plates go? **5.** *fig* (*svolgersi*) to go; **com'è andata?** how did it go?; **è andata bene** it went well **6.** (*vestiario*) to fit; **i pantaloni non mi vanno più** the pants don't fit me any more **7.** (*essere di moda*) to be in; **quest'anno vanno le gonne corte** short skirts are in this year **8.** (*funzionare*) to work; **la macchina non va?** won't the car start? **9.** (*piacere*) **ti va di andare a ballare?** do you want to go dancing?; **quel tipo non mi va proprio** I can't stand that guy **10.** (*procedere*) **come va? — bene grazie!** how are things? — good, thanks; **come vanno gli affari?** how's business? **11.** (*loc*) **~ a monte** to come to nothing; **~ a genio a qu** to be to sb's liking; **~ di mezzo** to get involved;

~ **pazzo per qc** to be crazy about sth; ~ **all'aria** to come to nothing; ~ **a male** to go bad; ~ **in fumo** to go up in smoke; **questa camicia va lavata** this shirt needs washing; **vai al diavolo!** *inf* go to hell! **II.** *vr* **andarsene** to go away; (*sparire*) to disappear; **andarsene all'altro mondo** to die; **me ne vado subito** I'm off

andare² *m* **a lungo** ~ in the long run; **con l'andar del tempo** with the passing of time

andata [an·'da:·ta] *f* **1.** (*percorso*) outward journey **2.** (*biglietto*) **biglietto di** (**sola**) ~ one-way ticket; **biglietto di** ~ **e ritorno** roundtrip ticket **3.** (*partenza*) journey **4.** SPORT leg

andatura [an·da·'tu:·ra] *f* **1.** (*modo di andare*) walk **2.** (*di auto*) speed **3.** SPORT pace **4.** NAUT tack

andazzo [an·'dat·tso] *m* **di questo** ~ the way things are going; **le cose hanno preso un brutto** ~ things have taken a turn for the worse

Ande ['an·de] *fpl* Andes

andirivieni [an·di·ri·'viɛː·ni] <-> *m* (*viavai*) coming and going

andito ['an·di·to] *m* corridor

Andorra [an·'dɔr·ra] *f* Andorra

androgino, -a [an·'drɔː·dʒi·no] *agg* (*donna, fattezze, mente*) androgynous

andrologia [an·dro·lo·'dʒi:·a] <-ie> *f* MED study of men's diseases

andrologo, -a [an·'drɔː·lo·go] <-gi, -ghe> *m, f* specialist in men's diseases

androne [an·'dro:·ne] *m* entrance hall

aneddoto [an·'nɛː·do·to] *m* anecdote

anelare [a·ne·'la:·re] *vi fig* ~ **a qc** to long for/to do sth

anelito [a·'nɛː·li·to] *m* (*brama*) ~ (**di qc**) longing (for sth)

anello [a·'nɛl·lo] *m* **1.** (*gioiello, forma*) ring; ~ **di fidanzamento** engagement ring; ~ **stradale** beltway **2.** SPORT (*pista*) circuit **3.** (*di catena*) link

anemia [a·ne·'mi:·a] <-ie> *f* anemia

anemico, -a [a·'nɛː·mi·ko] <-ci, -che> *agg* MED (*paziente, soggetto*) anemic

anemone [a·'nɛː·mo·ne] *m* anemone

anestesia [a·nes·te·'zi:·a] <-ie> *f* anesthetic; ~ **generale** general anesthetic; ~ **locale** local anesthetic

anestesista [a·nes·te·'zis·ta] <-i , -e> *mf* anesthesiologist

anestetico, -a <-ci, -che> *agg* (*pomata, soluzione, sostanza*) anesthetic

anestetizzare [a·nes·te·tid·'dza:·re] *vt* (*paziente, zona*) to anesthetize

aneto [a·'nɛː·to/a·'ne:·to] *m* dill

anfetamina [an·fe·ta·'mi:·na] *f* MED amphetamine

anfibi [an·'fi:·bi] *mpl* ZOO amphibia

anfibio [an·'fi:·bio] *m a.* MOT, AERO amphibian

anfiteatro [an·fi·te·'a:t·ro] *m* **1.** (*edificio*) amphitheater **2.** (*aula*) lecture hall

anfora ['an·fo·ra] *f* amphora

angariare [aŋ·ga·'ria:··re] *vt* to torment

angelico, -a [an·'dʒɛː·li·ko] <-ci, -che> *agg* angelic

angelo ['an·dʒe·lo] *m* angel; ~ **custode** *a. scherz* guardian angel

angheria [aŋ·ge·'ri:·a] <-ie> *f* tyranny

angina [an·'dʒi:·na] *f* MED angina

anglicano, -a [aŋ·gli·'ka:·no] **I.** *agg* Anglican **II.** *m, f* Anglican

angli(ci)smo [aŋ·'gli·zmo (aŋ·gli·'tʃiz·mo)] *m* LING anglicism

anglista [aŋ·'glis·ta] <-i , -e> *mf* scholar of English

anglistica [aŋ·'glis·ti·ka] <-che> *f* English

anglofono, -a [aŋ·'glɔː·fo·no] **I.** *agg* English-speaking **II.** *m, f* English speaker

anglosassone [aŋ·glo·'sas·so·ne] **I.** *agg* Anglo-Saxon **II.** *mf* Anglo Saxon

angolare [aŋ·go·'la:·re] *agg* (*velocità, distanza*) angular; **pietra** ~ ARCH cornerstone

angolazione [aŋ·go·lat·'tsio:·ne] *f a. fig* FILM, SPORT angle

angoliera *f* corner cupboard

angolo ['aŋ·go·lo] *m* **1.** (*in geometria*) angle **2.** *a.* SPORT (*di strada, stanza, fazzoletto, mobile*) corner; **calcio d'~** corner **3.** (*loc*) **starsene in un** ~ to stay by oneself; ~ **cottura** kitchen area

angoloso, -a [aŋ·go·'lo:·so] *agg* **1.** (*ossuto*) angular **2.** *fig* (*poco affabile*) prickly

angora ['aŋ·go·ra] *f* **d'~** angora

angoscia <-sce> *f* **1.** (*stato di ansia*) angst **2.** MED anxiety

angosciare [aŋ·goʃ·'ʃa:·re] **I.** *vt* ~ **qu** to upset sb **II.** *vr* to become upset; **-rsi** (**per qu/qc**) to get upset (about sb/sth)

angoscioso, -a [aŋ·goʃ·'ʃo:·so] *agg* **1.** (*che genera angoscia: attesa, silenzio*) agonizing; (*sogno*) upsetting **2.** (*di angoscia: grido*) agonized

anguilla [aŋ·'guil·la] *f* eel; **viscido come un'~** *fig* (as) slippery as an eel

anguillesco, -a [aŋ·guil·'les·ko] <-schi, -sche> *agg* (*ambiguità, politica, comportamento*) slimy

anguria [aŋ·'gu:·ria] <-ie> *f* sett watermelon

angustia [aŋ·'gus·tia] <-ie> *f* **1.** (*ristrettezza*) hardship **2.** (*angoscia*) distress

angustiare [aŋ·gus·'tia:·re] **I.** *vt* to bother **II.** *vr* **-rsi** (**per qc**) to worry (about sth)

angusto, -a [aŋ·'gus·to] *agg* **1.** (*stretto: sentiero, passaggio, locale*) narrow **2.** *fig* (*meschino: logica, pensiero*) narrow-minded

anice ['a:·ni·tʃe] *m* (*pianta*) anise; (*frutto*) aniseed

anima ['a:·ni·ma] *f* **1.** (*principio vitale, persona*) soul; **dedicarsi** ~ **e corpo a qc** to dedicate oneself to sth heart and soul; **essere un** ~ **in pena** to never be satisfied; **l'~ gemella di qu** sb's soulmate; **romper l'~ a qu** *inf* to pester sb **2.** (*nucleo centrale*) core **3.** (*elemento essenziale*) vital spirit

animale [a·ni·'ma:·le] **I.** *m* **1.** (*essere animato,* *bestia*) animal; ~ **domestico** pet **2.** *fig* (*persona violenta*) brute; (*persona stupida*) idiot **II.** *agg a. fig* animal

animalesco, -a [a·ni·ma·'les·ko] <-schi, -sche> *agg* (*istinto, fattezze, ritmo*) animal

animare [a·ni·'ma:·re] **I.** *vt* **1.** (*render più vivo: discussione, serata*) to liven up **2.** (*spingere*) ~ **qu** (**a fare qc**) to encourage sb (to do sth) **II.** *vr:* **-rsi 1.** (*vivacizzarsi: discussione, serata*) to become lively; (*luogo*) to come to life **2.** *fig* (*accalorarsi*) to become animated

animato, -a [a·ni·'ma:·to] *agg* **1.** (*vivace: discussione, serata, luogo*) animated **2.** (*vivente*) animate; **esseri -i** living things **3.** (*loc*) **disegni** [*o* **cartoni**] **-i** cartoons

animatore, -trice [a·ni·ma·'to:·re] *m, f* **1.** (*di villaggio turistico*) tour guide; (*di serata*) life and soul; ~ **socioculturale** coordinator of social and cultural activities (*in a particular area*) **2.** (*tecnico di cartoni animati*) animator

animazione [a·ni·mat·'tsio:·ne] *f* **1.** *a.* FILM animation; **film d'~** animated film **2.** (*folla*) bustle; **c'era molta ~ in giro** there were a lot of people about

animo ['a:·ni·mo] *m* **1.** (*spirito, anima, mente*) mind; **stato d'~** state of mind; **mettersi l'~ in pace** to set one's mind at rest; **leggere nell'~ di qu** to read sb's mind **2.** (*coraggio*) courage; **farsi ~** to pluck up one's courage; **perdersi d'~** to lose heart **3.** (*intendimento*) **di buon/mal ~** willingly/unwillingly; **aver in ~ di far qc** to be thinking of doing sth

animoso, -a [a·ni·'mo:·so] *agg* (*ostile: persona, azione*) hostile

anitra ['a:·ni·tra] *v.* **anatra**

ANLAIDS *f acro di* **Associazione Nazionale per la Lotta all'AIDS** *National Association for Combating AIDS*

ANMIC *f acro di* **Associazione Nazionale Mutilati e Invalidi Civili** *National Association for the Disabled*

annacquare [an·nak·'kua:·re] *vt* **1.** (*diluire: vino*) to water down **2.** *fig* (*mitigare: verità*) to soften

annacquato, -a [an·nak·'kua:·to] *agg* **1.** *a. fig* (*bevanda, vino, minestra*) watered down **2.** (*sguardo, occhi*) watery

annaffiare [an·naf·'fia:·re] *vt* **1.** (*orti, fiori, strade*) to water **2.** (*spruzzare: vivanda*) to sprinkle **3.** *fig* (*pasto*) to wash down with

annaffiatoio [an·naf·fia·'to:·io] <-oi> *m* watering can

annaffiatura [an·naf·fia·'tu:·ra] *f* watering

annali [an·'na:·li] *mpl* annals

annaspare [an·nas·'pa:·re] *vi* **1.** (*dibattersi*) to flounder **2.** *fig* (*nel parlare*) to stumble **3.** (*loc*) ~ **nel buio** *a. fig* to grope around in the dark

annata [an·'na:·ta] *f* **1.** (*durata di un anno*) year **2.** (*produzione*) vintage; **vini d'~** vintage wines **3.** (*di giornale*) year's worth (of copies)

annebbiamento [an·neb·bia·'men·to] *m* **1.** (*banco di nebbia*) fog patch **2.** *fig* (*offuscamento: di vista, mente, sensi*) clouding

annebbiare [an·neb·'bia:·re] **I.** *vt* **1.** (*velare di nebbia: cielo*) to cloud **2.** *fig* (*ottundere: vista*) to blur; (*mente, sensi*) to cloud **II.** *vr:* **-rsi 1.** (*riempirsi di nebbia: orizzonte*) to become foggy **2.** (*offuscarsi: vista*) to become blurred

annegare [an·ne·'ga:·re] **I.** *vt avere* to drown **II.** *vi* to drown **III.** *vr:* **-rsi** (*uccidersi*) to drown oneself

annerire [an·ne·'ri:·re] <annerisco> **I.** *vt avere* (*foglie, pentole*) to turn black; (*caselle*) to fill in **II.** *vi essere* to turn black

annessi¹ [an·'nɛs·si] *1. pers sing pass rem di* **annettere**

annessi² *mpl* **1.** ARCH (*di edificio*) annex **2.** (*cose*) **gli ~ e connessi** one thing and another

annessione [an·nes·'sio:·ne] *f* POL annexation

annesso, -a [an·'nɛs·so] *agg* **1.** (*edificio, documento*) attached **2.** POL (*Stato*) annexed

annettere [an·'nɛt·te·re] <annetto, annettei *o* annessi, annesso> *vt* **1.** POL (*Stato*) to annex **2.** *a. fig* (*allegare: documento*) to attach

annichilare, annichilire [an·ni·ki·'la:·re, an·ni·ki·'li:·re] **I.** *vt* **1.** (*annientare*) to annihilate **2.** (*prostrare: persona*) to destroy **II.** *vr:* **-rsi** to be destroyed

annidarsi [an·ni·'da:r·si] *vr* **1.** (*fare il nido*) to nest **2.** *fig* (*albergare*) to take root **3.** (*nascondersi*) to hide

annientamento [an·nien·ta·'men·to] *m* (*di nemico*) destruction

annientare [an·nien·'ta:·re] *vt* to destroy

anniversario [an·ni·ver·'sa:·rio] <-i> *m* (*ricorrenza*) anniversary; ~ **di matrimonio** wedding anniversary

anniversario, -a <-i, -ie> *agg* anniversary

anno ['an·no] *m* **1.** (*di calendario*) year; ~ **accademico** academic year; ~ **bisestile** leap year; ~ **civile** calendar year; ~ **commerciale** business year; ~ **corrente** this year; ~ **-luce** light year; ~ **nuovo** new year; ~ **scolastico** school year; **buon ~!** happy new year!; **capo d'~** *v.* **capodanno 2.** (*età*) year; **il bambino ha un ~** the baby's one; **ha tre -i** he [*o* she] is three; **compiere gli -i** to have one's birthday; **quanti -i hai?** how old are you?

annodare [an·no·'da:·re] *vt* **1.** (*stringere: corde, cravatta*) to tie **2.** *fig* (*relazioni*) to form

annoiare [an·no·'ia:·re] **I.** *vt* to bore **II.** *vr:* **-rsi** to get bored

annotare [an·no·'ta:·re] *vt* **1.** (*idee, dati, fatti*) to note; ~ **qc** to note sth (down) **2.** (*testo*) to annotate

annotazione [an·no·tat·'tsio:·ne] *f* **1.** (*registrazione: di idee, dati, fatti*) noting down **2.** (*postilla*) note

annottare [an·not·'ta:·re] *vi essere* (*impersonale*) **annotta** night is falling

annoverare [an·no·ve·'ra:·re] *vt* to number; ~ **tra ...** to number among ...

annuale [an·nu·'a:·le] *agg* annual

annualità [an·nua·li·'ta] <-> *f* (*somma*) annual installment

annuario [an·nu·'a:·rio] <-i> *m* yearbook

annuire [an·nu·'i:·re] <annuisco> *vi* to nod

annullamento [an·nul·la·'men·to] *m* 1.(*di risultato, prenotazione, ordine*) cancellation 2.(*di contratto, di matrimonio*) annulment

annullare [an·nul·'la:·re] I. *vt* 1.(*risultato, volo, prenotazione, francobollo*) to cancel 2.(*rendere nullo: contratto, matrimonio*) to annul; (*sentenza*) to quash 3.(*vanificare: sforzi, lavoro*) to undo 4.(*eliminare: effetti, conseguenze*) to eliminate 5.COMPUT undo; '**annulla e ripristina'** 'undo and redo' II. *vr:* -**rsi** 1.(*punti, forze*) to cancel each other out 2.(*annichilirsi*) to immerse oneself

annunciare [an·nun·'tʃa:·re] I. *vt* 1. *a.* RADIO, TV (*notizia, persona*) to announce 2.(*predire*) to foretell 3.(*far prevedere*) to be a sign of II. *vr:* -**rsi** to be on the horizon

annunciatore, -trice [an·nun·tʃa·'to:·re] *m, f* TV, RADIO announcer

Annunciazione [an·nun·tʃat·'tsio:·ne] *f* REL Annunciation

annuncio [an·'nun·tʃo] <-ci> *m* 1.(*comunicazione: di matrimonio, nascita, candidatura*) announcement 2.(*nel giornale*) advertisement; **mettere un ~ sul giornale** to place an advertisement in the paper; -**ci economici** classified ads; -**ci mortuari** death notices

annunziare [an·nun·'tsia:·re] *v.* **annunciare**

annuo, -a ['an·nuo] *agg* annual

annusare [an·nu·'sa:·re] *vt* 1. *a. fig* (*fiutare*) to sniff 2. **~ tabacco** to take snuff

annuvolarsi [an·nu·vo·'la:r·si] *vr* (*coprirsi di nuvole*) to cloud over

ano ['a:·no] *m* anus

anodizzato, -a [a·no·did·'dza:·to] *agg* (*alluminio*) anodized

anomalia [a·no·ma·'li:·a] <-ie> *f* 1. MED abnormality 2.(*irregolarità*) anomaly

anomalo, -a [a·'nɔ:·ma·lo] *agg a.* MED abnormal

anonimato [a·no·ni·'ma:·to] *m* anonymity; **conservare l'~** to remain anonymous

anonimo [a·'nɔ:·ni·mo] *m* unknown person

anonimo, -a *agg* 1.(*gener*) anonymous 2.(*insignificante: stile, cerimonia, colorazione*) colorless

anoressante [a·no·res·'san·te] I. *mf* appetite suppressant II. *agg* (*farmaco, prodotto*) appetite suppressing

anoressia [a·no·res·'si:·a] <-ie> *f* anorexia

anoressico, -a [a·no·'res·si·ko] <-ci, -che> I. *m, f* anorexic II. *agg* anorexic

anoressizzante [a·no·res·sit·'tsa:n·te] *m* appetite suppressant

anormale [a·nor·'ma:·le] I. *agg a.* MED abnormal II. *mf* MED person with learning disabilities

ANPA *f acro di* **Associazione Nazionale per la Protezione dell'Ambiente** *National Association for the Protection of the Environment*

ansa ['an·sa] *f a.* ANAT loop

ANSA ['an·sa] *f abbr di* **Agenzia Nazionale Stampa Associata**

ansia ['an·sia] <-ie> *f a.* PSYCH anxiety; **essere in ~ per qu** to worry about sb; **aspettare qc con ~** to be looking forward to sth

ansietà [an·sie·'ta] <-> *f* anxiety

ansimare [an·si·'ma:·re] *vi* to pant

ansioso, -a [an·'sio:·so] *agg* anxious; **~ di fare qc** anxious to do sth

anta ['an·ta] *f* 1.(*sportello: di armadio*) door 2.(*battente: di finestra, porta*) shutter

antagonismo [an·ta·go·'niz·mo] *m* rivalry

antagonista[1] [an·ta·go·'nis·ta] <-i , -e> *mf* (*rivale*) opponent

antagonista[2] <-i> *m* (*muscolo*) antagonist

antalgico [an·'tal·dʒi·ko] <-ci> *m* MED (*analgesico*) analgesic

antalgico, -a <-ci, -che> *agg* MED (*terapia, ginnastica*) for pain relief

antartico [ant·'ar·ti·ko] <-ci> *m* Antarctic

antartico, -a <-ci, -che> *agg* (*calotta, clima, spedizione*) Antarctic

Antartide [an·'tar·ti·de] *f* Antarctica

antecedente [an·te·tʃe·'dɛn·te] I. *agg* (*giorno, data*) preceding II. *mpl fig* history

antefatto [an·te·'fat·to] *m* background

anteguerra [an·te·'guɛr·ra] I. <inv> *agg* (*periodo, anni*) pre-war II. <-> *m* pre-war period

antenato, -a [an·te·'na:·to] *m, f* ancestor

antenna [an·'ten·na] *f* RADIO, TV, ZOO antenna; **~ parabolica** (satellite) dish

anteporre [an·te·'por·re] <irr> *vt* to put before; **~ qc a qc** to put sth before sth

anteprima [an·te·'pri:·ma] *f* preview

anteriore [an·te·'rio:·re] *agg* 1.(*davanti: routa, sedile*) front 2.(*precedente: data*) previous

anti- [an·ti] 1.(*indica anteriorità*) ante- 2.(*indica avversione*) anti-

antiabbaglianti [an·ti·ab·baʎ·'ʎan·ti] *mpl* AUTO (*anabbaglianti*) dimmed headlights *pl*

antiabortista [an·ti·a·bor·'tis·ta] <-i , -e> *mf* pro-lifer

antiacne [an·ti·'ak·ne] <inv> *agg* (*prodotto, crema, lozione*) anti-acne

antiaereo, -a [an·ti·a·'ɛ:·reo] *agg* (*difesa, rifugio*) anti-aircraft

antibatterico, -a [an·ti·bat·'tɛ:·ri·ko] <-ci, -che> *agg* (*terapia, prodotto, proprietà*) anti-bacterial

antibiotico [an·ti·bi·'ɔ:·ti·ko] <-ci> *m* antibiotic

antibiotico, -a <-ci, -che> *agg* (*terapia, crema, proprietà*) antibiotic

antibloccante [an·ti·blok·'kan·te] *agg* **sistema ~** antilock braking system

antiblocco [an·ti·'blɔk·ko] I. <-> *m* antilock braking system II. <inv> *agg* MOT (*sistema*) antilock

anticalcare [an·ti·kal·'ka:·re] *m* (*prodotto, sistema, trattamento*) anti-limescale

anticamera [an·ti·'ka:·me·ra] *f* hall; **fare ~** *fig* to cool one's heels; **non mi passa neppure per l'~ del cervello** *inf* in your dreams!

anticancro [an·ti·'kaŋ·kro] <inv> *agg* (*vaccino, farmaco*) cancer; (*cibo*) can-

cer-preventing; **terapia** ~ cancer treatment
anticarie [an·ti·'ka:·rie] <inv> *agg* (*dentifricio, colluttorio*) that fights decay
anticellulite [an·ti·tʃel·lu·'li:·te] <inv> *agg* (*dieta, massaggio, crema*) anti-cellulite
antichità [an·ti·ki·'ta] <-> *f* **1.** (*qualità*) (great) age **2.** (*età, oggetto*) antiquity
anticiclone [an·ti·tʃi·'klo:·ne] *m* anticyclone
anticipare [an·ti·tʃi·'pa:·re] *vt* **1.** (*fare prima: azione*) to bring forward **2.** (*dire prima: notizia*) to reveal in advance **3.** (*dare prima: somma*) to advance
anticipazione [an·ti·tʃi·pat·'tsio:·ne] *f* **1.** (*notizia in anteprima*) preview **2.** FIN advance
anticipo [an·'ti:·tʃi·po] *m* **1.** (*di tempo*) advance notice; **in** ~ early **2.** COM (*somma*) advance
antico [an·'ti:·ko] <-chi> *m* **1.** (*antichità*) **abbinare** ~ **e moderno** to combine (the) old and (the) new **2.** *pl* (*popoli dell'antichità*) ancients *pl*
antico, -a <-chi, -che> *agg* **1.** HIST (*epoca, popolo, arte*) ancient; **storia -a** ancient history **2.** (*non recente: mobile, oggetto, quadro*) antique **3.** (*tradizionale*) former
anticoncezionale [an·ti·kon·tʃet·tsio·'na:·le] I. *agg* (*pillola, metodo*) contraceptive II. *m* contraceptive
anticoncorrenziale [an·ti·kon·kor·ren·'tsia:·le] *agg* **1.** (*contro la concorrenza: intesa, programma*) anti-competitive **2.** (*sleale: comportamento*) dishonest
anticonformismo [an·ti·kon·for·'miz·mo] *m* nonconformism
anticonformista [an·ti·kon·for·'mis·ta] <-i , -e> I. *agg* (*idee, atteggiamento*) nonconformist II. *mf* nonconformist
anticongelante [an·ti·kon·dʒe·'lan·te] I. *agg* (*liquido, miscela*) antifreeze II. *m* antifreeze
anticorpo [an·ti·'kɔr·po] *m* antibody
anticostituzionale [an·ti·kos·ti·tut·tsio·'na:·le] *agg* (*riforma, legge, decreto*) unconstitutional
anticrimine [an·ti·'kri:·mi·ne] <inv> *agg* (*tecnica, piano*) crime-fighting; **squadra** ~ crime prevention unit
anticrittogamico, -a <-ci, -che> *agg* (*sostanza, protezione*) fungicidal
antidatare [an·ti·da·'ta:·re] *vt* (*lettera, certificato*) to predate
antideficit [an·ti·'dɛ:·fi·tʃit] <inv> *agg* (*misure, decreto*) anti-deficit
antidepressivo [an·ti·de·pres·'si:·vo] *m* antidepressant
antidepressivo, -a *agg* MED (*farmaco, massaggio, terapia*) antidepressant
antidolorifico [an·ti·do·lo·'ri:·fi·ko] <-ci> *m* MED painkiller
antidoping [an·ti·'dɔ·pin(g)] I. <-> *m* drug test II. <inv> *agg* (*commissione, campagna, normativa*) drug testing
antidoto [an·'ti:·do·to] *m a. fig* antidote
antidroga [an·ti·'drɔ:·ga] <inv> *agg* (*legge,*

operazione, prevenzione) anti-narcotics; **cane** ~ sniff dog; **squadra** ~ (anti-)narcotics unit
antiemorragico [an·ti·e·mor·'ra:·dʒi·ko] <-ci> *m* MED hemostatic
antiemorragico, -a <-ci, -che> *agg* (*proprietà, azione*) hemostatic
antifame [an·ti·'fa:·me] *agg* **farmaco** ~ appetite suppressant
antifascismo [an·ti·faʃ·'ʃiz·mo] *m* antifascism
antifecondativo [an·ti·fe·kon·da·'ti:·vo] *m* contraceptive
antifecondativo, -a *agg* (*farmaco, pillola, metodo*) contraceptive
antifemminismo [an·ti·fem·mi·'niz·mo] *m* anti-feminism
antifona [an·'ti:·fo·na] *f* **1.** *fig* (*allusione*) hint; **capire l'**~ *inf* to get the message **2.** *fig* (*discorso noioso*) lecture; **la solita** ~ *inf* the usual blah blah
antiforfora [an·ti·'for·fo·ra] <inv> *agg* **shampoo** ~ antidandruff shampoo
antifumo [an·ti·'fu:·mo] <inv> *agg* (*centro, legge, pillola*) antismoking; **campagna** ~ anti-smoking campaign
antifurto [an·ti·'fur·to] I. <inv> *agg* (*allarme, sistema*) anti-theft II. <-> *m* alarm
antigas [an·ti·'gas] <inv> *agg* (*allarme, filtro*) gas; **maschera** ~ gas mask
antigelo [an·ti·'dʒɛ:·lo] I. <inv> *agg* (*fluido, dispositivo, termostato*) antifreeze II. <-> *m* antifreeze
antiglobal [an·ti·'glou·bəl] <-> *mf* anti-globalization protestors
antigovernativo, -a [an·ti·go·ver·na·'ti:·vo] *agg* (*protesta, attività, politica*) anti-government; **giornale** ~ anti-government newspaper
antigraffio [an·ti·'graf·fio] <inv> *agg* (*vernice, trattamento*) scratch-resistant; **superficie** ~ scratch-resistant surface
anti(i)gienico, -a [an·ti·(i)·'dʒɛ:·ni·ko] <-ci, -che> *agg* (*alloggio, locali*) unhygienic
anti(i)nfiammatorio [an·ti·(i)n·fiam·ma·'tɔ:·rio] <-i> *m* MED anti-inflammatory
anti(i)nfiammatorio, -a <-i, -ie> *agg* (*farmaco, sostanza*) anti-inflammatory
Antille [an·'til·le] *fpl* **andare alle** ~ to go to the Antilles; **nelle** ~ in the Antilles
antilope [an·'ti:·lo·pe] *f* antelope
antimafia [an·ti·'ma:·fia] <inv> *agg* anti-Mafia; **squadra** ~ anti-Mafia squad; **commissione** ~ anti-Mafia commission; **legge** ~ anti-Mafia law
antimeridiano, -a [an·ti·me·ri·'dia:·no] *agg* (*seduta, colloquio*) morning; **nelle ore -e** in the morning
antimissile [an·ti·'mis·si·le] <inv> *agg* (*sistema, armi*) antimissile; **difesa** ~ antimissile defense; **scudo** ~ antimissile shield
antimuffa [an·ti·'muf·fa] <inv> *agg* (*pittura, additivo*) anti-mold
antincendio [an·tin·'tʃɛn·dio] I. <inv> *agg* (*allarme*) fire; (*impianto*) fire safety II. <-> *m* fire extinguisher

antinebbia [an·ti·'neb·bia] I. <inv> *agg* (*fari*) fog II. <-> *m* fog lights

antinflazionistico, **-a** [an·tin·fla·tsio·'nis·ti·ko] <-ci, -che> *agg* (*misura, politica*) anti-inflation; **provvedimento** ~ anti-inflation measure

antinfluenzale [an·tin·flu·en·'tsa:·le] I. *m* flu vaccine II. *agg* **vaccino** ~ flu vaccine

antinomia [an·ti·no·'mi:·a] <-ie> *f* antinomy

antinquinamento [an·tiŋ·kui·na·'men·to] <inv> *agg* (*azione, barriere, norma*) antipollution; **misure** ~ antipollution measures

antinquinante [an·tiŋ·kui·'na:n·te] *agg* ECO (*prodotto*) non-polluting; **motore** ~ low-emission engine

antinucleare [an·ti·nu·kle·'a:·re] *mf* antinuclear campaigner

antiorario, **-a** [an·ti·o·'ra:·rio] <-i, -ie> *agg* (*rotazione*) counterclockwise; **in senso** ~ counterclockwise

antiparassitario [an·ti·pa·ras·si·'ta:·rio] <-i, -ie> *m* insecticide

antiparassitario, **-a** *agg* (*prodotto, sostanza*) insecticidal

antipasto [an·ti·'pas·to] *m* antipasto (*cold food served at the start of an Italian meal*); ~ **misto** mixed antipasto

antipatia [an·ti·pa·'ti:·a] <-ie> *f* dislike; **provare** ~ **per qu** to dislike sb

antipatico, **-a** [an·ti·'pa:·ti·ko] <-ci, -che> I. *agg* **1.** (*persona*) not likable; **essere** ~ to be disliked; **stare** ~ **a qu** to be disliked by sb **2.** (*problema, malessere*) unpleasant II. *m, f* unpleasant person

antiplacca [an·ti·'plak·ka] <inv> *agg* (*colluttorio, dentifricio*) anti-plaque

antipodi [an·'ti:·po·di] *mpl* antipodes; **essere agli** ~ *fig* to be poles apart

antipolio [an·ti·'pɔ:·lio] <inv> *agg* anti-polio; **vaccino** ~ polio vaccine

antiproiettile [an·ti·pro·iet·'ti:·le] <inv> *agg* **giubbotto** ~ bulletproof vest; **cristallo** ~ bulletproof glass

antiquariato [an·ti·kua·'ria:·to] *m* antiques business; **pezzo d'**~ antique

antiquario, **-a** [an·ti·'kua:·rio] <-i, -ie> I. *agg* (*fiera, commercio*) antiques; **libreria** -a antiquarian bookshop II. *m, f* antiquarian

antiquato, **-a** [an·ti·'kua:·to] *agg* (*idea, termine*) obsolete; (*abbigliamento, equipaggiamento, software*) antiquated

antirabbico, **-a** [an·ti·'rab·bi·ko] <-ci, -che> *agg* (*vaccino*) rabies

antiracket [an·ti·'ra·ket] <inv> *agg* (*associazione, iniziativa, legge*) against organized crime

antirazzismo [an·ti·rat·'tsiz·mo] *m* anti-racism

antirazzista [an·ti·rat·'tsis·ta] I. *mf* anti-racist II. *agg* (*appello, commissione, movimento*) anti-racist

antireumatico, **-a** [an·ti·reu·'ma:·ti·ko] <-ci, -che> I. *m, f* anti-rheumatic drug II. *agg* MED

(*farmaco, terapia*) anti-rheumatic

antiriciclaggio [an·ti·ri·tʃi·'klad·dʒo] <inv> *agg* (*disciplina, normativa, norma*) anti-laundering

antiruggine [an·ti·'rud·dʒi·ne] I. <inv> *agg* (*vernice, fluido*) anti-rust II. <-> *m* anti-rust paint

antirughe [an·ti·'ru:·ge] I. <-> *m* anti-wrinkle cream II. <inv> *agg* (*iniezioni, trattamento, crema*) anti-wrinkle

antisala [an·ti·'sa:·la] *f* hall

antisatellite [an·ti·sa·'tɛl·lite] <inv> *agg* MIL (*armi*) anti-satellite

antiscippo [an·ti·'ʃip·po] <inv> *agg* (*borsa, valigia*) theft-resistant

antisdrucciolevole [an·ti·sdrut·tʃo·le·'vo:·le] *agg* (*rivestimento, superficie, scarpe*) nonslip; **pavimento** ~ nonslip floor

antisemita [an·ti·se·'mi:·ta] <-i , -e> I. *mf* anti-Semite II. *agg* (*persecuzione, razzismo, legge*) anti-Semitic

antisemitico, **-a** [an·ti·se·'mi:·ti·ko] <-ci, -che> *agg* (*propaganda, persecuzione, materiale*) anti-Semitic

antisemitismo [an·ti·se·mi·'tiz·mo] *m* anti-Semitism

antisequestro [an·ti·se·'kuɛs·tro] <inv> *agg* (*operazione, servizio di scorta, squadra*) anti-kidnapping

antisettico [an·ti·'sɛt·ti·ko] <-ci> *m* antiseptic

antisettico, **-a** <-ci, -che> *agg* (*soluzione, azione, liquido*) antiseptic

antisfondamento [an·ti·sfon·da·'men·to] <inv> *agg* shatterproof; **cristallo** ~ shatterproof glass

antisismico, **-a** [an·ti·'siz·mi·ko] <-ci, -che> *agg* (*costruzione, fondamenta*) earthquake-proof

antismog [an·ti·zmɔg] <inv> *agg* (*misura, piano*) anti-smog; **blocco** ~ *regulations designed to prevent smog from forming or getting worse*

antisolare [an·ti·so·'la:·re] *agg* (*vetro*) tinted; **crema** ~ sunblock

antistaminico [an·ti·sta·'mi:·ni·ko] <-ci> *m* antihistamine

antistaminico, **-a** <-ci, -che> *agg* (*collirio, pomata, terapia*) anithistamine

antistante [an·tis·'tan·te] *agg* ~ **qc** [*o* **a qc**] in front of sth

antistatico, **-a** [an·tis·'ta:·ti·ko] <-ci, -che> *agg* (*tessuto, scarpe, spazzola*) antistatic

antistrappo [an·ti·'strap·po] <inv> *agg* (*tessuto, materiale*) tear-resistant

antistress [an·ti·'stres] <inv> *agg* (*massaggio, dieta*) stress-reducing

antistupro [an·ti·'stu:·pro] <inv> *agg* **legge** ~ anti-rape law

antisudorifero [an·ti·su·do·'ri:·fe·ro] *m* (*proprietà*) sweat-reducing

antitarlo [an·ti·'tar·lo] <inv> *agg* (*trattamento, spray*) anti-woodworm

antitartaro [an·ti·'tar·ta·ro] <inv> *agg* (*denti-*

fricio, filo interdentale) anti-tartar

antitermico, -a [an·ti·'tɛr·mi·ko] <-ci, -che> *agg* (*rivestimento, scudo, vetro*) heatproof

antiterrorismo [an·ti·ter·ro·'riz·mo] I. <-> *m* anti-terrorism II. <inv> *agg* (*blitz, misure, reparto*) anti-terrorist

antitesi [an·'ti:·te·zi] *f* antithesis

antitetanico, -a [an·ti·te·'ta:·ni·ko] <-ci, -che> *agg* (*vaccino*) anti-tetanus

antitetico, -a [an·ti·'tɛ:·ti·ko] <-ci, -che> *agg* antithetical

antitraspirante [an·ti·tras·pi·'ran·te] *agg* (*deodorante*) antiperspirant

antitrust [æn·ti·'trʌst] I. <inv> *agg* (*legge, sentenza*) antitrust II. <-> *m* FIN competition authority

antitumorale [an·ti·tu·mo·'ra:·le] *agg* (*vaccino, terapia*) cancer

antiurto [an·ti·'ur·to] <inv> *agg* (*imbottitura, profilo*) shockproof

antivigilia [an·ti·vi·'dʒi:·lia] *f* **l'~ di Natale** the day before Christmas Eve

antivivisezione [an·ti·vi·vi·set·'tsio:·ne] <inv> *agg* (*campagna, iniziativa, lega*) anti-vivisection

antologia [an·to·lo·'dʒi:·a] <-gie> *f* (*raccolta: di scritti, testi*) anthology; (*di canzoni, brani musicali*) collection

antonomasia [an·to·no·ma·'zi:·a] *f* LING antonomasia; **per ~** par excellence

antracite[1] [an·tra·'tʃi:·te] <inv> *agg* charcoal

antracite[2] *f* (*carbon fossile*) anthracite

antro ['an·tro] *m* (*caverna*) cave

antropofago, -a [an·tro·'pɔ:·fa·go] <-gi, -ghe> *m, f* (*popolazione, pratica, rito*) cannibal

antropologia [an·tro·po·lo·'dʒi:·a] <-gie> *f* anthropology

antropologo, -a [an·tro·'pɔ:·lo·go] <-gi, -ghe> *m, f* anthropologist

anulare [a·nu·'la:·re] I. *agg* (*strada, circuito*) circular; **Grande Raccordo Anulare** beltway around Rome II. *m* (*dito*) ring finger

Anversa [an·'vɛr·sa] *f* Antwerp

anzi ['an·tsi] *avv* **1.** (*invece*) on the contrary **2.** (*o meglio*) or rather

anzianità [an·tsia·ni·'ta] <-> *f* **1.** (*condizione*) old age **2.** ADM length of service

anziano, -a [an·'tsia:·no] I. *agg* **1.** (*non giovane*) elderly **2.** ADM (*funzionario, ufficiale*) senior II. *m, f* senior (citizen); **gli -i** senior citizens

anziché, anzi che [an·tsi·'ke] *cong* **1.** (*invece di*) instead of **2.** (*piuttosto che*) rather than

anzidetto, -a [an·tsi·'det·to] *agg* aforementioned

anzitempo [an·tsi·'tɛm·po] *avv* prematurely

anzitutto [an·tsi·'tut·to] *avv* first of all

aorta [a·'ɔr·ta] *f* aorta

Aosta [a·'ɔs·ta] *f* Aosta, *city in northwest of Italy;* **Valle d'~** Valle d'Aosta

Aostano (*zona*) Aosta area; **nell'~** in the Aosta area

aostano, -a [a·os·'ta:·no] I. *agg* from Aosta

II. *m, f* (*abitante*) person from Aosta

apartheid [a·'part·hɛit] <-> *f* apartheid

apatia [a·pa·'ti:·a] <-ie> *f* apathy

apatico, -a [a·'pa:·ti·ko] <-ci, -che> *agg* (*persona*) apathetic

a.p.c. *abbr di* **a pronta cassa** collect on delivery

ape ['a:·pe] *f* bee; **~ domestica** honeybee; **~ maschio** drone; **~ operaia** worker bee; **~ regina** queen bee

aperitivo [a·pe·ri·'ti:·vo] *m* aperitif

i In many Italian cities, when people leave the office around 6:30 P.M. they make their way to a bar for an **aperitivo** (aperitif): *aperol®, bellini®, pink gin, campari®, campari® and orange, negroni,* or even just a tomato juice, accompanied by potato chips, peanuts, and olives. In recent years bars have competed to offer their customers ever more delicious and inventive aperitifs accompanied by snacks such as tartlets, mini pizzas, *bruschette* and *crostini* (toasted bread seasoned with oil and garlic or with various savory toppings), crudités and dips. In Padua, Treviso, and Venezia, on the other hand, the custom is to have a glass of wine known as an *ombra. Ombra* means "shadow" and it seems this custom derives its name from the fact that the wine was drunk in the shadow of the bell towers.

apersi [a·'pɛr·si] *1. pers sing pass rem di* **aprire**

aperto [a·'pɛr·to] *m* **all'~** outdoors; **cinema/teatro all'~** open-air cinema/theater

aperto, -a I. *pp di* **aprire** II. *agg* **1.** (*gener*) open; **essere ~ a qc** to be open to sth; **città -a** open city; **lettera -a** open letter; **all'aria -a** in the open air; **in -a campagna** in the country; **in mare ~** on the high seas **2.** (*gas*) on; (*rubinetto*) running **3.** (*loc*) **a braccia -e** with open arms; **rimanere a bocca -a** to be astounded

apertura [a·per·'tu:·ra] *f* **1.** (*gener*) opening; **articolo di ~** editorial; **discorso di ~** opening speech; **~ delle scuole** beginning of term **2.** *fig* openness; **~ mentale** open-mindedness **3.** (*ampiezza*) width; **~ alare** wingspan

API ['a:·pi] *f acro di* **Anonima Petroli Italiana** *Italian Gas Company*

apice ['a:·pi·tʃe] *m* **1.** (*culmine*) peak; **all'~ di qc** at the peak of sth **2.** ANAT, BOT apex **3.** ASTR zenith

apicoltore, -trice [a·pi·kol·'to:·re] *m, f* beekeeper

apicoltura [a·pi·kol·'tu:·ra] *f* beekeeping

apocalisse [a·po·ka·'lis·se] *f* **1.** REL Apocalypse **2.** (*disastro*) catastrophe

apocalittico, -a [a·po·ka·'lit·ti·ko] <-ci, -che> *agg* **1.** *a.* REL (*pessimista: previsione*) apocalyp-

tic **2.** (*spaventoso: catastrofe*) catastrophic
apogeo [a·po·'dʒɛː·o] *m* **1.** ASTR apogee **2.** *fig* (*culmine*) zenith
apolide [a·'pɔː·li·de] I. *agg* (*individuo*) stateless II. *mf* stateless person
apolitico, -a [a·po·'liː·ti·ko] <-ci, -che> *agg* (*associazione, magistrato*) non-political
apollo [a·'pɔl·lo] *m* Adonis
apologia [a·po·lo·'dʒiː·a] <-gie> *f* (*esaltazione*) glorification; ~ **di reato** glorification of a crime
apoplettico, -a [a·po·'plɛt·ti·ko] <-ci, -che> I. *agg* apoplectic; **colpo** ~ stroke II. *m, f* stroke patient
apostolico, -a [a·pos·'tɔː·li·ko] <-ci, -che> *agg* **1.** (*del Papa: benedizione, visita*) papal **2.** (*degli apostoli: predicazione*) apostolic
apostolo [a·'pɔs·to·lo] *m* apostle
apostrofare [a·pos·tro·'faː·re] *vt* **1.** (*rivolgersi duramente a*) to speak angrily to **2.** LING (*parola*) to write with an apostrophe
apostrofe [a·'pɔs·tro·fe] *f* (*figura retorica*) apostrophe
apostrofo [a·'pɔs·tro·fo] *m* (*segno*) apostrophe
apoteosi [a·po·te·'ɔː·zi] <-> *f* (*esaltazione*) apotheosis
app. *abbr di* **appendice** appendix
appagamento [ap·pa·ga·'men·to] *m* satisfaction
appagare [ap·pa·'gaː·re] I. *vt* to satisfy II. *vr* -**rsi di qc** to be satisfied with sth
appaio [ap·'pa·io] *1. pers sing pr di* **apparire**
appallottolare [ap·pal·lot·to·'laː·re] I. *vt* (*carta, biglietto, foglio*) to roll up II. *vr:* -**rsi** (*gatto, bambino*) to curl up
appaltare [ap·pal·'taː·re] *vt* (*dare in appalto: lavori, opere, servizi*) to contract out
appaltatore, -trice [ap·pal·ta·'toː·re] I. *agg* (*azienda, ente*) contracting II. *m, f* contractor
appalto [ap·'pal·to] *m* (*contratto*) contract; **dare in** ~ to contract out
appannaggio [ap·pan·'nad·dʒo] <-ggi> *m* **1.** POL (*somma*) annuity **2.** *fig* (*prerogativa*) prerogative
appannare [ap·pa·'naː·re] I. *vt* **1.** (*vetro, lente, finestra*) to steam up **2.** *fig* (*offuscare: mente, pensieri, riflessi*) to cloud II. *vr:* -**rsi** **1.** (*vetro, lente*) to steam up **2.** (*memoria, bellezza*) to fade
apparato [ap·pa·'raː·to] *m* **1.** ADM, ANAT apparatus; ~ **circolatorio** circulatory system; ~ **digerente** digestive system **2.** TEC (*impianto*) (piece of) equipment **3.** THEAT set; **l'**~ **scenico** the set **4.** MIL machinery; **l'**~ **bellico** the war machine **5.** (*sfoggio*) display
apparecchiare [ap·pa·rek·'kiaː·re] *vt* to set the table; **puoi** ~ **per favore** could you set the table, please?
apparecchiatura [ap·pa·rek·kia·'tuː·ra] *f* TEC (*strumento*) equipment
apparecchio [ap·pa·'rek·kio] <-cchi> *m* **1.** TEC (*strumento*) piece of equipment

2. (*aereo*) aircraft
apparente [ap·pa·'rɛn·te] *agg* apparent
apparenza [ap·pa·'rɛn·tsa] *f* **1.** (*aspetto*) appearance; **l'**~ **inganna** appearances can be deceptive **2.** *pl* (*forma*) appearances; **salvare le** -**e** to keep up appearances **3.** (*loc*) **in** ~ apparently
apparire [ap·pa·'riː·re] <appaio *o* apparisco, apparvi *o* apparii *o* apparsi, apparso> *vi essere* to appear
appariscente [ap·pa·riʃ·'ʃɛn·te] *agg* (*persona*) glamorous; (*abito*) showy
apparizione [ap·pa·rit·'tsio:·ne] *f* appearance
apparsi [ap·'par·si] *1. pers sing pass rem di* **apparire**
apparso [ap·'par·so] *pp di* **apparire**
appartamento [ap·par·ta·'men·to] *m* apartment
appartarsi [ap·par·'tar·si] *vr* to go off
appartenente [ap·par·te·'nɛn·te] I. *agg* belonging; ~ **a qc** belonging to sth II. *mf* member
appartenenza [ap·par·te·'nɛn·tsa] *f* membership; ~ **a qc** membership of sth
appartenere [ap·par·te·'neː·re] <irr> *vi essere o avere* **1.** (*essere di proprietà*) ~ **a qu** to belong to sb **2.** (*far parte*) ~ **a qc** to belong to sth
apparvi [ap·'par·vi] *1. pers sing pass rem di* **apparire**
appassimento [ap·pas·si·'men·to] *m* (*di pianta, foglia*) wilting
appassionare [ap·pas·sio·'naː·re] I. *vt* to grip II. *vr* -**rsi** (**a qc**) to become very interested in sth
appassionato, -a [ap·pas·sio·'naː·to] I. *agg* **1.** (*giocatore, musicista*) enthusiastic; **essere** ~ **di qc** to love sth **2.** (*parole, appello, sguardo*) passionate II. *m, f* enthusiast
appassire [ap·pas·'siː·re] <appassisco> *vi essere* (*fiore*) to wilt; (*pelle*) to age
appellare [ap·pel·'laː·re] I. *vt* JUR ~ **una sentenza** to appeal a sentence II. *vr:* -**rsi** **1.** -**rsi a qu/qc** to appeal to sb/sth **2.** JUR to appeal; -**rsi contro una sentenza** to appeal against a sentence
appellativo [ap·pel·la·'tiː·vo] *m* **1.** LING name **2.** (*soprannome*) nickname
appello [ap·'pɛl·lo] *m* **1.** (*chiamata*) roll-call; **fare l'**~ to call the roll **2.** *a.* JUR (*invocazione*) appeal; **fare** ~ **a qc** to appeal to sth; **corte d'**~ court of appeal; **ricorrere in** ~ to go to appeal **3.** UNIV (*sessione d'esami*) exam session
appena [ap·'peː·na] I. *avv* **1.** (*soltanto*) only just; **sono** ~ **le dieci** it's only just 10 **2.** (*da poco*) just; **sono** ~ **partite** they've just left **3.** (*a stento*) hardly; **ha parlato** ~ he [*o* she] hardly spoke II. *cong* as soon as
appendere [ap·'pɛn·de·re] <appendo, appesi, appeso> I. *vt* (*cappotto, giacca, quadro, lampada*) to hang (up); ~ **alla parete** to hang (up) on the wall; ~ **al soffitto** to hang from the ceiling; ~ **nell'armadio** to hang (up) in the cupboard II. *vr:* -**rsi** to hang
appendice [ap·pen·'diː·tʃe] *f* **1.** *a.* ANAT

A

(*aggiunta: di libro, enciclopedia*) appendix **2.**(*nei giornali*) supplement; **romanzo d'~** serial novel (*published in a newspaper*)

appendicite [ap·pen·di·'tʃi:·te] *f* appendicitis

Appennino [ap·pen·'ni:·no] *m* Appennine; **gli -i** the Appennines

appesantire [ap·pe·san·'ti:·re] <appesantisco> I. *vt* **1.**(*auto, barca, gambe*) to weigh down **2.**(*stomaco*) to overload **3.**(*pagine*) to overcrowd II. *vr:* **-rsi** *iron* (*ingrassare*) to put on weight

appesi [ap·'pe:·si] *1. pers sing pass rem di* **appendere**

appeso [ap·'pe:·so] *pp di* **appendere**

appestare [ap·pes·'ta:·re] *vt* **1.**MED (*contagiare*) to infect **2.**(*ammorbare: aria, locale*) to stink up

appestato, -a [ap·pes·'ta:·to] *m, f* person suffering from plague

appetibile [ap·pe·'ti:·bi·le] *agg* (*proposta, lavoro, prezzo*) attractive

appetito [ap·pe·'ti:·to] *m* (*fame*) appetite; **buon ~!** enjoy your meal!; **l'~ vien mangiando** *prov* eating makes you hungry, *said to encourage sb to eat*

appetitoso, -a [ap·pe·ti·'to:·so] *agg* (*pranzo, pietanza, insalata*) appetizing

appezzamento [ap·pet·tsa·'men·to] *m* plot; **~ di terreno** piece of land

appianare [ap·pia·'na:·re] *vt* **1.**(*terreno*) to level **2.** *fig* (*difficoltà*) to smooth out; (*lite, controversia*) to settle

appiattarsi [ap·pi·at·'tar·si] *vr* to flatten oneself

appiattire [ap·pi·at·'ti:·re] <appiattisco> I. *vt* (*superficie, terreno*) to flatten II. *vr:* **-rsi** **1.**(*divenire piatto*) to become flat **2.**(*farsi piatto*) to flatten oneself

appiccare [ap·pik·'ka:·re] *vt* **~ fuoco a qc** to set fire to sth

appiccicare [ap·pit·tʃi·'ka:·re] I. *vt* **1.**(*attaccare: etichetta, adesivo*) to stick; **~ qc su qc** to stick sth on(to) sth **2.** *fig* (*attribuire: nomignolo*) to give; **~ un nomignolo a qu** to give sb a nickname II. *vr:* **-rsi** to stick

appiccicaticcio, -a [ap·pit·tʃi·ka·'tit·tʃo] <-cci, -cce> *agg* **1.**(*attaccaticcio: mani*) sticky **2.** *fig* (*persona*) clingy

appiccicoso, -a [ap·pit·tʃi·'ko:·so] *agg* **1.**(*vischioso*) sticky **2.** *fig* (*persona*) clingy

appieno [ap·'piɛ:·no] *avv* fully

appigliarsi [ap·piʎ·'ʎar·si] *vr* **1.**(*aggrapparsi*) **~ a qu/qc** to grab hold of sb/sth **2.** *fig* **~ a qc** (*speranza, cavillo, pretesto*) to cling onto sth

appiglio [ap·'piʎ·ʎo] <-gli> *m* **1.**(*punto di appoggio*) handhold **2.** *fig* (*pretesto*) pretext

appiombo [ap·'piom·bo] *m* (*di giacca, cappotto*) line; (*di muro*) perpendicularity

appioppare [ap·piop·'pa:·re] *vt inf* **~ uno schiaffo a qu** to whack sb; **~ un nomignolo a qu** to pin a nickname on sb

appisolarsi [ap·pi·zo·'lar·si] *vr* to doze off

applaudire [ap·plau·'di:·re] <applaudo *o*

applaudisco> *vt, vi* **~** (**a**) **qu/qc** to applaud sb/sth

applauso [ap·'pla:u·zo] *m* **1.**(*battendo le mani*) applause **2.**(*approvazione*) approval

applicabile [ap·pli·'ka:·bi·le] *agg* **essere ~** (**a qc**) to be applicable (to sth)

applicare [ap·pli·'ka:·re] I. *vt* **1.**(*attaccare: cucendo*) to sew on; (*cerrotto, etichetta*) to stick on **2.**(*crema, legge, mente*) to apply **3.**(*far pagare: multa*) to impose II. *vr:* **-rsi** (*nello studio*) to apply oneself

applicativo, -a *agg* **programma ~** application

applicato, -a [ap·pli·'ka:·to] *agg* (*matematica, diritto*) applied

applicazione [ap·pli·kat·'tsio:·ne] *f* **1.** *a.* COMPUT application **2.**(*l'utilizzare: di multa*) imposition **3.**(*decorazione*) appliqué

applique [a·'plik] <-> *f* wall light

appoggiacapo [ap·pod·dʒa·'ka:·po] <-> *m* headrest

appoggiare [ap·pod·'dʒa:·re] I. *vt* **1.**(*posare*) to place; **~ qc su qc** to place sth on sth **2.**(*accostare*) to lean; **~ qc a qc** to lean sth against sth **3.** *fig* (*sostenere*) to support II. *vr:* **-rsi** **1.**(*sostenersi, reggersi*) **-rsi a qc** to lean against sth; **-rsi a qu** to lean on sb **2.** *fig* (*ricorrere*) **-rsi a qc** to rely on sth

appoggiatesta [ap·pod·dʒa·'tɛs·ta] <-> *m* headrest

appoggio [ap·'pɔd·dʒo] <-ggi> *m* support

appollaiarsi [ap·pol·la·'iar·si] *vr* **~ su qc** to perch on sth

appollaiato, -a [ap·pol·la·'ia:·to] *agg* (*uccello, persona, paese*) perched

apporre [ap·'por·re] <irr> *vt* **~ qc a qc** (*timbro, firma*) to append sth to sth

apportare [ap·por·'ta:·re] *vt* **1.**(*effettuare: modifica, variazione*) to carry out **2.**(*causare: danni*) to cause

apporto [ap·'pɔr·to] *m* (*contributo*) contribution

apposi [ap·'po:·zi] *1. pers sing pass rem di* **apporre**

appositamente [ap·po·zi·ta·'men·te] *avv* specially

apposito, -a [ap·'pɔ:·zi·to] *agg* appropriate

apposizione [ap·po·zit·'tsio:·ne] *f* **1.**LING apposition **2.**(*collocazione*) application

apposta [ap·'pɔs·ta] I. *avv* specially; **non l'ho fatto ~** I didn't do it on purpose II. <inv> *agg* special

appostamento [ap·pos·ta·'men·to] *m* **1.**(*agguato*) ambush **2.**MIL post **3.**(*a caccia*) blind

appostare [ap·pos·'ta:·re] I. *vt* **~ qu 1.**(*piazzare*) to station sb **2.**(*fare la posta a*) to lie in wait for sb II. *vr:* **-rsi** to lie in wait

apposto [ap·'pɔs·to] *pp di* **apporre**

apprendere [ap·'prɛn·de·re] <irr> *vt* to learn

apprendimento [ap·pren·di·'men·to] *m* learning; **capacità d'~** ability to learn

apprendista [ap·pren·'dis·ta] <-i, -e> *mf* apprentice

apprendistato [ap·pren·dis·'ta:·to] *m* apprenticeship

apprensione [ap·pren·'sio:·ne] *f* anxiety; **essere in** ~ to be worried

apprensivo, -a [ap·pren·'si:·vo] *agg* (*madre, genitori*) anxious

appresi [ap·'pre:·zi] *1. pers sing pass rem di* **apprendere**

appreso [ap·'pre:·zo] *pp di* **apprendere**

appresso [ap·'prɛs·so] I. *avv* 1. (*vicino*) portarsi ~ qc/qu to take sth/sb with oneself 2. *form* (*in seguito*) below; **come** ~ **indicato** as indicated below II. *prep* (*dietro*) behind; **andare** ~ **a qu** (*seguire*) to follow sb; (*corteggiare*) to chase after sb; **stare** ~ **a qu** to stay close to sb III. <inv> *agg* (*dopo*) after

apprestare [ap·pres·'ta:·re] I. *vt* (*servizio, assistenza*) to prepare II. *vr* **-rsi a fare qc** to get ready to do sth

appretto [ap·'prɛt·to] *m* starch; **dare l'~ a qc** to starch sth

apprezzabile [ap·pret·'tsa:·bi·le] *agg* 1. (*pregevole: sforzo, impegno*) admirable 2. (*notevole: somma*) significant

apprezzamento [ap·pret·tsa·'men·to] *m* 1. (*commento*) remark 2. FIN (*di investimento*) appreciation

apprezzare [ap·pret·'tsa:·re] *vt* to appreciate

approccio [ap·'prɔt·tʃo] <-cci> *m* 1. (*primo contatto*) encounter 2. (*metodo, corteggiamento*) approach

approdare [ap·pro·'da:·re] *vi essere o avere* 1. NAUT to land 2. (*arrivare*) to arrive 3. (*ottenere*) to arrive at; **non** ~ **a nulla** *fig* to come to nothing

approdo [ap·'prɔ:·do] *m* 1. (*manovra*) landing 2. (*luogo*) landing place

approfittare [ap·pro·fit·'ta:·re] I. *vi* 1. (*trarre vantaggio*) ~ **di qc** to take advantage of sth; ~ **dell'occasione** to take the opportunity 2. (*sfruttare*) ~ **di qu** to take advantage of sb II. *vr* **-rsi di qu/qc** to take advantage of sb/sth

approfondimento [ap·pro·fon·di·'men·to] *m* (*di materia, tecnica, studio*) study in greater depth

approfondire [ap·pro·fon·'di:·re] <approfondisco> I. *vt* 1. *fig* (*rendere* (*più*) *profondo: divario*) to deepen 2. *fig* (*studiare a fondo: materia, tecnica*) to go into in greater depth II. *vr:* **-rsi** *fig* (*divario*) to deepen

approntare [ap·pron·'ta:·re] *vt* (*bilancio, relazione, sito*) to prepare

appropriarsi [ap·pro·'pri·ar·si] *vr* ~ (**di**) **qc** to appropriate sth

appropriato, -a [ap·pro·'pria:·to] *agg* (*termine, titolo, scelta*) appropriate

appropriazione [ap·pro·pri·at·'tsio:·ne] *f* appropriation; ~ **indebita** embezzlement

approssimarsi [ap·pros·si·'mar·si] *vr* ~ (**a qc**) to approach (sth)

approssimativo, -a [ap·pros·si·ma·'ti:·vo] *agg* 1. (*non preciso: calcolo, cifra, dati, misura*) approximate 2. (*vago: lettura, risposta*) vague

approssimazione [ap·pros·si·mat·'tsio:·ne] *f* MATH approximation; **per** ~ approximately

approvare [ap·pro·'va:·re] *vt* to approve

approvazione [ap·pro·vat·'tsio:·ne] *f* approval

approvvigionamento [ap·prov·vi·dʒo·na·'men·to] *m* 1. (*rifornimento*) supply 2. *pl* (*provvista*) supplies *pl*

approvvigionare [ap·prov·vi·dʒon·'na:·re] *vt* a. MIL to supply

appuntamento [ap·pun·ta·'men·to] *m* 1. (*di piacere*) date; **darsi** (**un**) ~ to arrange a date; ~ **al buio** blind date 2. (*d'affari, dal medico*) appointment; **prendere un'~** to make an appointment

appuntare [ap·pun·'ta:·re] *vt* 1. (*matita*) to sharpen 2. (*decorazione, spilla*) to pin 3. (*prendere appunti*) to take notes of

appuntato [ap·pun·'ta:·to] *m* (*di carbinieri, guardia di finanza*) corporal

appuntire [ap·pun·'ti:·re] <appuntisco> *vt* (*matita*) to sharpen

appuntito, -a [ap·pun·'ti:·to] *agg* 1. (*matita*) sharp 2. (*naso, mento, lancia*) pointed

appunto[1] [ap·'pun·to] *avv* 1. just; **volevo per l'~ proporre ...** I was just going to suggest ... 2. (*nelle risposte*) exactly

appunto[2] *m* 1. (*nota*) note 2. (*rimprovero*) reproach

appurare [ap·pu·'ra:·re] *vt* (*controllare: verità, causa*) to ascertain; (*fatto*) to check

apribile [a·'pri:·bi·le] *agg* (*tavolo, divano*) that can be opened; **tettuccio** ~ sunroof

apribottiglie [a·pri·bot·'tiʎ·ʎe] <-> *m* bottle opener

aprii [a·'pri:·i] *1. pers sing pass rem di* **aprire**

aprile [a·'pri:·le] *m* April; **in** ~ [*o* **nel mese di**] ~ in April; **alla fine di** ~ at the end of April; **a fine** ~ at the end of April; **a metà** ~ in mid-April; **ai primi di** ~ in early April; ~ **ha 30 giorni** there are 30 days in April; **Firenze, (il) 15** ~ **2005** Florence, April 15, 2005; **oggi è il primo (di)** ~ today is the first of April; **l'undici/il venti/il ventun** ~ April eleventh/twentieth/twenty-first

aprire [a·'pri:·re] <apro, apersi *o* aprii, aperto> I. *vt* 1. (*gener*) to open; ~ **le braccia** to open one's arms; ~ **un conto** to open an account; ~ **il fuoco** to open fire 2. (*gas, acqua, rubinetto*) to turn on 3. (*creare un'apertura: varco, passaggio*) to clear 4. (*corteo*) to lead 5. (*loc*) **non** ~ **bocca** (*non parlare*) to not say a word; (*mantenere un segreto*) to keep mum; ~ **gli occhi** (*rendersi conto*) to open one's eyes (to sth); ~ **le orecchie** (*prestare attenzione*) to listen carefully; ~ **il cuore a qu** (*confidarsi*) to open one's heart to sb II. *vr:* **-rsi** 1. (*porta, mostra*) to open 2. (*confidarsi*) **-rsi con qu** to open up to sb

apriscatole [a·pris·'ka:·to·le] <-> *m* can opener

aquagym [a·kua·'dʒi:m] *f* aquarobics

A

aquila ['a:·kui·la] *f* eagle; ~ **selvaggia** *fig* (*sciopero*) wild eagle (*name given in the press to striking airline pilots*)

Aquilano (*zona*) Aquila area; **nell'**~ in the Aquila area

aquilano, -a [a·kui·'la:·no] **I.** *agg* from Aquila **II.** *m, f* (*abitante*) person from Aquila

aquilino, -a [a·kui·'li:·no] *agg* **naso** ~ aquiline nose

aquilone [a·kui·'lo:·ne] *m* kite

arabesco [a·ra·'bes·ko] <-schi> *m* (*decorazione*) arabesque

arabesco, -a <-schi, -sche> *agg* (*abito, scritta*) Arab

Arabia [a·'ra:·bia] *f* Arabia; ~ **Saudita** Saudi Arabia

arabo ['a:·ra·bo] *m* Arabic; **parlare** ~ *fig* to be incomprehensible

arabo, -a I. *agg* **1.** (*paese, cavallo*) Arab **2.** (*lingua*) Arabic **II.** *m, f* Arab

arachide [a·'ra:·ki·de] *f* peanut

aragosta [a·ra·'gos·ta] *f* lobster

araldica [a·'ral·di·ka] <-che> *f* heraldry

araldo [a·'ral·do] *m a.* HIST herald

aranceto [a·ran·'tʃe:·to] *m* orange grove

arancia [a·'ran·tʃa] <-ce> *f* orange

aranciata [a·ran·'tʃa:·ta] *f* orange soda

arancino [a·ran·'tʃi:·no] *m* CULIN *croquette made of rice*

arancio[1] [a·'ran·tʃo] <inv> *agg* orange

arancio[2] <-ci> *m* **1.** (*albero*) orange tree **2.** (*frutto*) orange **3.** (*colore*) orange

arancione [a·ran·'tʃo:·ne] <inv *o* -i> *agg* orange

arare [a·'ra:·re] *vt, vi* to plow

aratro [a·'ra:·tro] *m* plow

arazzo [a·'rat·tso] *m* tapestry

arbitraggio [ar·bi·'trad·dʒo] <-ggi> *m* **1.** JUR arbitration **2.** COM arbitrage **3.** SPORT (*nel calcio, nel pugilato*) refereeing; (*nel tennis*) umpiring

arbitrale [ar·bi·'tra:·le] *agg* **1.** COM (*camera, collegio, decisione*) arbitration **2.** SPORT **decisione** ~ (*nel calcio, nel pugilato*) referee's decision; (*nel tennis*) umpire's decision; **terna** ~ referee and linesmen (*in soccer*)

arbitrare [ar·bi·'tra:·re] *vt* **1.** (*controversia*) to arbitrate **2.** (*incontro: nel calcio, nel pugilato*) to referee; (*nel tennis*) to umpire

arbitrarietà [ar·bi·tra·rie·'ta] <-> *f* (*di giudizio, decisione*) arbitrariness

arbitrario, -a [ar·bi·'tra:·rio] <-i, -ie> *agg* (*giudizio, decisione, scelta*) arbitrary

arbitrio [ar·'bi:·trio] <-i> *m* (*facoltà di scelta*) will; **libero** ~ free will; **prendersi l'**~ **di fare qc** to take the liberty of doing sth

arbitro ['ar·bi·tro] *m* **1.** SPORT (*nel calcio, nel pugilato*) referee; (*nel tennis*) umpire **2.** JUR arbitrator

arbusto [ar·'bus·to] *m* shrub

arca ['ar·ka] <-che> *f* **1.** (*cassa di legno*) chest **2.** (*sepolcro*) sarcophagus **3.** (*nella Bibbia*) ark; **l'**~ **di Noè** Noah's ark

arcaico, -a [ar·'ka:·i·ko] <-ci, -che> *agg*

(*civiltà, rito, valori*) archaic

arcangelo [ar·'kan·dʒe·lo] *m* archangel

arcano [ar·'ka:·no] *m* mystery

arcano, -a *agg* (*magia, poteri*) occult

arcata [ar·'ka:·ta] *f* **1.** ANAT, ARCH arch **2.** MUS bow

archeologia [ar·keo·lo·'dʒi:·a] <-ie> *f* archeology

archeologico, -a [ar·keo·'lɔ:·dʒi·ko] <-ci, -che> *agg* (*museo, sito, scavo*) archeological

archeologo, -a [ar·ke·'ɔ:·lo·go] <-gi, -ghe> *m, f* archeologist

archetipico [ar·ke·'ti:·pi·ko] <-ci, -che> *agg* (*modello, forma*) archetypal

archetipo [ar·'kɛ:·ti·po] *m* archetype

archetto [ar·'ket·to] *m* MUS bow

architettare [ar·ki·tet·'ta:·re] *vt* (*piano*) to plot

architetto, -a [ar·ki·'tet·to] *m, f* architect

architettonico, -a [ar·ki·tet·'tɔ:·ni·ko] <-ci, -che> *agg* (*progetto, forme, restauro*) architectural

architettura [ar·ki·tet·'tu:·ra] *f* architecture

architrave [ar·ki·'tra:·ve] *m* architrave

archiviare [ar·ki·'via:·re] *vt* **1.** ADM (*documento, caso*) to file; ~ **una pratica** to put a file away **2.** *fig* (*non occuparsi più di*) to forget about

archivio [ar·'ki:·vio] <-i> *m a.* COMPUT archive

ARCI ['ar·tʃi] *m acro di* **Associazione Ricreativa Culturale Italiana** *Italian Association for Cultural Recreation*

arci- [ar·tʃi] (*in parole composte*) mega-

arciere [ar·'tʃɛ:·re] *m* archer

arcigno, -a [ar·'tʃiɲ·ɲo] *agg* (*persona*) severe; (*volto, espressione*) frowning

arcinoto, -a [ar·tʃi·'nɔ:·to] *agg inf* extremely well-known; **personaggio** ~ celeb

arcipelago [ar·tʃi·'pɛ:·la·go] <-ghi> *m* archipelago

arciricco, -a [ar·tʃi·'rik·ko] <-cchi, -cche> *agg inf* mega-rich

arcistufo, -a [ar·tʃi·'stu:·fo] *agg inf* **essere** ~ **di qc** to be sick to death of sth

arcivescovo [ar·tʃi·'ves·ko·vo] *m* archbishop

arco ['ar·ko] <-chi> *m* **1.** ARCHIT arch; ~ **a sesto acuto** pointed arch **2.** (*periodo*) period; ~ **di tempo** period of time **3.** MUS (*arma*) bow; **strumenti ad** ~ stringed instruments; **gli** -**chi** the strings **4.** arc

arcobaleno [ar·ko·ba·'le:·no] *m* rainbow

arcuare [ar·ku·'a:·re] *vt* (*sopracciglia, schiena*) to arch

ardente [ar·'dɛn·te] *agg* **1.** (*sole*) blazing; (*clima*) blazing hot **2.** (*passione, desiderio*) burning **3.** (*loc*) **camera** ~ funeral parlor

ardere ['ar·de·re] <ardo, arsi, arso> **I.** *vt avere* (*legna*) to burn **II.** *vi essere o avere* to burn

ardesia[1] [ar·'dɛ:·zia] <inv> *agg* slate gray

ardesia[2] <-ie> *f* slate

ardimento [ar·di·'men·to] *m* (*coraggio*) daring

ardire[1] [ar·'di:·re] <ardisco> *vi* ~ **fare qc** to dare (to) do sth

ardire² *m* (*impudenza*) impudence
ardito, -a *agg* 1.(*originale: paragone, idea*) bold 2.(*insolente: complimento*) impertinent
ardore [ar·'do:·re] *m* heat; **con ~** (*desiderare, discutere*) passionately
arduo, -a ['ar·duo] *agg* (*difficile: decisione, impresa, percorso*) difficult
area ['a:·rea] *f* 1.(*gener*) area; **~ di lavoro** COMPUT area; **~ ciclonica** low pressure area; **~ fabbricabile** building land; **~ linguistica** linguistic area; **~ di rigore** SPORT penalty area; **~ di servizio** rest area; **~ sismica** earthquake zone 2.*fig* POL (*raggruppamento*) grouping
arena¹ [a'·re:·na] *f* (*sabbia*) sand
arena² [a'·rɛ:·na] *f* (*stadio*) arena
arenarsi [a·re·'nar·si] *vr* 1.NAUT to run aground 2.*fig* (*bloccarsi*) to come to a standstill
areo- [a·reo] *v.* aero-
aretino, -a [a·re·'ti:·no] I. *agg* from Arezzo II. *m, f* (*abitante*) person from Arezzo; **L'Aretino** (*per antonomasia, narratore del Cinquecento*) Pietro Aretino
Arezzo *f* Arezzo, *town in southern Tuscany*
argentare [ar·dʒen·'ta:·re] *vt* (*metallo, posate*) to silver-plate
argenteo, -a [ar·'dʒɛn·teo] *agg* (*foglia, capelli, veste*) silver
argenteria [ar·dʒen·te·'ri:·a] <-ie> *f* silver; **~ da tavola** silverware
argentiere [ar·dʒen·'tiɛ:·re] *m* silversmith
Argentina [ar·dʒen·'ti:·na] *f* Argentina; **abitare in ~** to live in Argentina; **andare in ~** to go to Argentina
argentino, -a [ar·dʒen·'ti:·no] I. *agg* 1.(*suono, voce*) silvery 2.(*dell'Argentina*) Argentinian II. *m, f* (*abitante*) Argentinian
argento [ar·'dʒɛn·to] *m* silver; **~ vivo** mercury; **carta d'~** FERR *card giving discounts on rail travel for senior citizens;* **nozze d'~** silver wedding
argilla [ar·'dʒil·la] *f* clay
argilloso, -a [ar·dʒil·'lo:·so] *agg* (*terreno*) clay; (*roccia*) clay-rich
arginamento [ar·dʒi·na·'men·to] *m* 1.(*di fiume, acque*) embankment 2.*fig* (*di problema, conseguenze, spese*) limiting
arginare [ar·dʒi·'na:·re] *vt* 1.(*fiume, acque*) to embank 2.*fig* (*problema, conseguenze, spese*) to limit
argine ['ar·dʒi·ne] *m* 1.(*di fiume*) bank; **rompere gli ~i** to break the banks 2.*fig* check
argomentare [ar·go·men·'ta:·re] *vi* to argue
argomentazione [ar·go·men·tat·'tsio:·ne] *f* argument
argomento [ar·go·'men·to] *m* 1.(*tema*) subject 2.(*prova*) argument
arguire [ar·gu·'i:·re] <arguisco> *vt* **~ qc da qc** to deduce sth from sth
arguto, -a [ar·'gu:·to] *agg* 1.(*persona*) witty 2.(*osservazione, risposta, stratagemma*) clever 3.(*ingegno, sguardo*) keen
arguzia [ar·'gut·tsia] <-ie> *f* 1.(*vivacità d'in-*

gegno: di persona) intelligence 2.(*spirito*) wit 3.(*facezia*) witticism
aria ['a:·ria] <-ie> *f a.* MUS air; **~ di mare/montagna** sea/mountain air; **all'~ aperta** in the open air; **~ compressa** compressed air; **~ condizionata** air conditioning; **corrente d'~** draft; **non c'è un filo d'~** there isn't a breath of air; **prendere una boccata d'~** to get a breath of fresh air; **vuoto d'~** (*in aereo*) air pocket; **cambiare l'~** to have a change of scene; **prendere un colpo d'~** to get a chill; **vivere d'~** *fig* (*non mangiare*) to live on fresh air; **guardare in ~** to look up; **saltare in ~** (*esplodere*) to blow up; **sparare in ~** to fire into the air; **andare all'~** *fig* (*progetto, matrimonio*) to come to nothing; **avere la testa per ~** *fig* to have one's head in the clouds; **campato in ~** *fig* (*discorso, idea*) unsound; **mandare qc all'~** *fig* (*progetto, matrimonio*) to mess sth up; **c'è qc nell'~** *fig* there's sth in the air; **non tira ~ buona qui** *fig* I don't like the look of things; **avere un'~ stanca** (*espressione*) to look tired; **darsi delle -e** (*vantarsi*) to show off
aridità [a·ri·di·'ta] <-> *f* 1.(*siccità*) aridity 2.*fig* (*mancanza di sentimento*) lack of feeling
arido, -a ['a:·ri·do] *agg* 1.(*campagna, deserto*) arid 2.*fig* (*povero di sentimenti: persona*) unfeeling
arieggiare [a·ri·ed·'dʒa:·re] *vt* 1.(*cambiare l'aria a: materasso, stanza*) to air 2.(*imitare: forma, modello*) to have the air of
ariete [a·'riɛ:·te] *m* 1.ZOO ram 2.MIL battering ram 3.ASTR **Ariete** Aries; **sono** (**dell'** [*o* **un**]) **Ariete** I'm (an) Aries
aringa [a·'riŋ·ga] <-ghe> *f* herring
arioso, -a *agg* 1.(*spazioso: sala, piazza*) airy 2.MUS arioso
arista ['a:·ris·ta] *f* CULIN pork chine (*for roasting*)
aristocratico, -a [a·ris·to·'kra:·ti·ko] <-ci, -che> I. *agg* aristocratic II. *m, f* aristocrat
aristocrazia [a·ris·to·krat·'tsi:·a] <-ie> *f* 1.(*nobiltà*) *a.* POL aristocracy 2.*fig* (*comportamento raffinato*) refinement
aritmetica [a·rit·'mɛ:·ti·ka] <-che> *f* arithmetic
aritmetico, -a [a·rit·'mɛ:·ti·ko] <-ci, -che> *agg* (*problema, media, operatori*) arithmetic(al)
aritmia [a·rit·'mi:·a] <-ie> *f* MED arrhythmia
arlecchino¹ [ar·lek·'ki:·no] *m* harlequin
arlecchino² <inv> *agg* (*pigiama, tessuto, disegno*) diamond-patterned
arma ['ar·ma] <-i> *f* 1.(*strumento di difesa*) weapon; **-i a medio raggio** medium-range weapons; **~ automatica** automatic weapon; **~ azzurra** *the Italian air force;* **fatto d'-i** feat of arms; **deporre le -i** to lay down one's weapons; **~ a doppio taglio** *fig* double-edged sword; **essere alle prime -i** *fig* to be a beginner; **partire con -i e bagagli** *fig* to leave with bag and baggage 2.(*esercito*) army; **andare sotto le -i** to join the armed forces

armadillo [ar·ma·'dil·lo] *m* armadillo
armadio [ar·'ma:·dio] <-i> *m* wardrobe;
~ **blindato** armored closet; ~ **guardaroba**
closet; ~ **a muro** built-in closet
armaiolo [ar·ma·'iɔ:·lo] *m* 1.(*fabbricante*) ar-
morer 2.(*venditore*) arms dealer
armamento [ar·ma·'men·to] *m* 1. MIL weapons *pl* 2. NAUT (*attrezzatura*) fitting out 3. *pl*
(*armi*) arms; **corsa agli -i** arms race
armare [ar·'ma:·re] I. *vt* 1. MIL (*fornire di armi:
esercito*) to arm 2. ARCH (*rinforzare: parete,
trave*) to reinforce 3. NAUT (*nave, barca*) to fit
out II. *vr:* -**rsi -rsi di qc** *a. fig* to arm oneself
with sth
armata [ar·'ma:·ta] *f* army
armato, -a *agg* 1. MIL (*fornito di armi: esercito*)
armed; **carro** ~ tank; **a mano -a** armed 2. *fig* ~
di qc (*coraggio, pazienza, buona volontà*)
armed with sth 3. ARCH (*rinforzato*) reinforced;
cemento ~ reinforced concrete 4. NAUT (*nave,
barca*) fitted out
armatore, -trice [ar·ma·'to:·re] I. *agg* shipping; **società -trice** shipping company II. *m, f*
shipowner
armatura [ar·ma·'tu:·ra] *f* 1. HIST armor
2.(*struttura*) reinforcement
armeggiare [ar·med·'dʒa:·re] *vi* to mess
around; ~ **con qc** to mess around with sth;
~ **intorno a qc** to mess around sth
armeria [ar·me·'ri:·a] <-ie> *f* 1.(*magazzino*)
armory 2.(*negozio*) gun store 3.(*collezione*)
collection of weapons
armistizio [ar·mis·'tit·tsio] <-i> *m* armistice
armonia [ar·mo·'ni:·a] <-ie> *f* 1.(*concordia*)
harmony; **vivere in ~ con qu/qc** to live in
harmony with sb/sth 2. MUS harmony
armonica [ar·'mɔ:·ni·ka] <-che> *f* harmonica;
~ **a bocca** mouth organ
armonico, -a [ar·'mɔ:·ni·ko] <-ci, -che>
agg 1.(*convivenza, sviluppo*) harmonious
2.(*sapore*) balanced 3. MUS harmonic; **cassa -a**
sound box
armonioso, -a [ar·mo·'nio:·so] *agg* 1.(*proporzionato: corpo, forma*) well-proportioned
2.(*dotato di armonia: danza, movimento,
svolgimento*) graceful
armonium [ar·'mɔ:·ni·um] <-> *m* harmonium
armonizzare [ar·mo·nid·'dza:·re] I. *vt* (*far
accordare: norme, programmi, rapporti*) to
harmonize II. *vi* to go well together
armonizzazione [ar·mo·nid·dzat·'tsio:·ne] *f*
harmonization; ~ **fiscale** tax harmonization
arnese [ar·'ne:·se] *m* 1.(*attrezzo*) tool
2.(*oggetto*) thing
arnia ['ar·nia] <-ie> *f* beehive
aroma [a·'rɔ:·ma] <-i> *m* 1.(*sapore*) aroma
2. *pl* (*erbe*) herbs
aromaterapia [a·rɔ·ma·te·ra·'pi:·a] *f* aromatherapy
aromatico, -a [a·ro·'ma:·ti·ko] <-ci, -che> *agg*
(*sapore, vino*) aromatic; **erbe -che** herbs;
piante -che herbs; **oli -ci** flavored oils
aromatizzare [a·ro·ma·tid·'dza:·re] *vt*

(*bevanda, cibo, vino*) to flavor
arpa ['ar·pa] *f* harp
arpeggio [ar·'ped·dʒo] <-ggi> *m* MUS arpeggio
arpia [ar·'pi:·a] <-ie> *f fig* (*donna sgradevole*)
harpy
arpione [ar·'pio:·ne] *m* 1.(*gancio*) hook 2.(*da
pesca*) harpoon
arrabattarsi [ar·ra·bat·'tar·si] *vr* to struggle to
get by; ~ **a fare qc** to struggle to do sth
arrabbiare [ar·rab·'bia:·re] I. *vt* **far** ~ **qu** to
make sb angry II. *vr* -**rsi** (**con qu**) to get angry
(with sb)
arrabbiato, -a [ar·rab·'bia:·to] *agg* 1.(*irato*)
angry; **essere** ~ (**con qu**) to be angry with sb
2.(*accanito: musicista*) fanatical 3. CULIN **all'-a**
in a spicy sauce
arrabbiatura [ar·rab·bia·'tu:·ra] *f* fury; **prendersi un'**~ to get very angry
arraffare [ar·raf·'fa:·re] *vt* 1.(*afferrare:
oggetto*) to snatch 2.(*rubare: soldi*) to steal
arrampicarsi [ar·ram·pi·'kar·si] *vr* to climb;
~ **sugli specchi** *fig* to grasp at straws
arrampicata [ar·ram·pi·'ka:·ta] *f* (*scalata*)
climb
arrampicatore, -trice [ar·ram·pi·ka·'to:·re]
m, f a. fig climber; ~ **sociale** social climber
arrancare [ar·raŋ·'ka:·re] *vi* 1.(*camminare a
fatica*) to hobble 2. *fig* (*avanzare a fatica*) to
limp along
arrangiamento [ar·ran·dʒa·'men·to] *m* MUS
arrangement
arrangiare [ar·ran·'dʒa:·re] I. *vt* 1.(*aggiustare:
cosa, faccenda*) to settle 2. *inf* (*rimediare alla
meglio: pranzetto, cena*) to rustle up 3. MUS
(*pezzo, brano*) to arrange II. *vr:* -**rsi** (*indus-
triarsi*) to manage; **ci arrangiamo da soli,
grazie!** we can manage, thank you!
array [ə·'rei] <-> *m* COMPUT array
arrecare [ar·re·'ka:·re] *vt* (*causare: danno,
dolore*) to cause; ~ **disturbo** to bother
arredamento [ar·re·da·'men·to] *m* 1.(*mobili:
moderno, d'epoca*) furniture 2.(*attività*) fur-
nishing
arredare [ar·re·'da:·re] *vt* (*casa, ufficio*) to furnish
arredatore, -trice [ar·re·da·'to:·re] *m, f* interi-
or designer
arredo [ar·'rɛ:·do] *m* 1.(*arredamento*) furnish-
ing 2. *pl* (*mobili*) furniture
arrembaggio [ar·rem·'bad·dʒo] <-ggi> *m*
boarding; **buttarsi all'**~ **di qc** *fig* to scramble
for sth
arrendersi [ar·'rɛn·der·si] <irr> *vr* 1.(*darsi
vinto*) ~ (**a qu**) to surrender (to sb) 2. *fig*
(*desistere*) ~ (**a qc**) to give in (to sth); ~ **all'evidenza dei fatti** to accept the evidence
arrendevole [ar·ren·'de:·vo·le] *agg* (*carattere,
persona*) soft
arrestare [ar·res·'ta:·re] I. *vt* 1.(*catturare:
rapinatore, omicida*) to arrest 2.(*fermare*) to
stop II. *vr:* -**rsi** (*fermarsi*) to stop
arresto [ar·'rɛs·to] *m* 1.(*cattura*) arrest; **mandato d'**~ arrest warrant; **-i domiciliari** house

arrest 2.(*interruzione*) ~ **cardiaco** cardiac arrest **3.** TEC (*fermata*) **non aprire fino al completo** ~ **del motore** do not open until the engine has come to a complete stop **4.** *pl* MIL arrest

arretrare [ar·re·'tra:·re] **I.** *vi essere* to withdraw **II.** *vt avere* (*spostare indietro: giocatore, oggetto*) to move back

arretratezza [ar·ret·ra·'tet·tsa] *f* underdevelopment

arretrati [ar·re·'tra:·ti] *mpl* **1.**(*di stipendio*) back pay; (*di affitto*) arrears *pl* **2.** *fig* (*faccende in sospeso*) unfinished business

arretrato, -a [ar·re·'tra:·to] *agg* **1.**(*in ritardo: pagamento*) back; **del lavoro** ~ a backlog of work **2.**(*sottosviluppato: Paese*) underdeveloped **3.**(*antiquato: mentalità*) backward

arricchimento [ar·rik·ki·'men·to] *m* **1.**(*incremento dei beni*) (the fact of) becoming rich; **il suo improvviso** ~ his sudden wealth **2.** *a.* TEC (*linguistico, culturale, personale*) enrichment **3.**(*valorizzazione: di servizio, verde*) enhancement

arricchire [ar·rik·'ki:·re] <arricchisco> **I.** *vt avere* **1.** *a.* TEC (*rendere ricco*) to enrich **2.** *a. fig* (*valorizzare*) to enhance **II.** *vr:* **-rsi** to get rich; **-rsi alle spalle** [*o* **a spese**] **di qu** to get rich at sb else's expense

arricchito, -a [ar·rik·'ki:·to] *m*, *f pej* nouveau riche

arricciacapelli [ar·rit·tʃa·ka·'pel·li] <-> *m* curling tongs *pl*

arricciare [ar·rit·'tʃa:·re] *vt* **1.**(*capelli, labbra*) to curl **2.**(*manica, nastro, tessuto*) to roll up **3.** ~ **il naso** *a. fig* to turn up one's nose

arricciato, -a *agg* **1.**(*capelli*) curly **2.**(*manica, nastro, tessuto*) rolled up

arridere [ar·'ri:·de·re] <irr> *vi* (*vita, fortuna*) to smile on

arringa [ar·'rin·ga] <-ghe> *f* **1.** JUR address **2.**(*discorso*) speech

arringare [ar·rin·'ga:·re] *vt* (*folla, pubblico*) to address

arrischiare [ar·ris·'kia:·re] **I.** *vt* (*bilancio, giudizio, proposta*) to hazard **II.** *vr:* **-rsi -rsi a fare qc** to dare to do sth

arrischiato, -a [ar·ris·'kia:·to] *agg* **1.**(*pericoloso: sorpasso, manovra*) hazardous **2.**(*avventato: bilancio, giudizio, proposta*) rash

arrisi [ar·'ri:·zi] *1. pers sing pass rem di* **arridere**

arriso [ar·'ri:·zo] *pp di* **arridere**

arrivare [ar·ri·'va:·re] *vi essere* **1.**(*giungere*) to arrive; ~ **primo/secondo** SPORT to come first/ second **2.**(*raggiungere*) ~ **a ...** to reach; ~ **ad un accordo** to reach an agreement; ~ **a buon punto** to reach a good point **3.**(*affermarsi*) to succeed **4.**(*osare*) to dare **5. arrivarci** (*riuscire a toccare*) to reach; **io non ci arrivo** I can't reach (it); (*capire*) to get it; **non ci arriva** he [*o* she] doesn't get it

arrivato, -a [ar·ri·'va:·to] **I.** *agg* (*socialmente*) successful **II.** *m*, *f* (*socialmente*) person who has made it

arrivederci [ar·ri·ve·'der·tʃi] *int* (good)bye; ~ **(a) presto** see you soon

arrivederLa [ar·ri·ve·'der·la] *int* goodbye

arrivismo [ar·ri·'viz·mo] *m* social climbing

arrivista [ar·ri·'vis·ta] <-i , -e> *mf* social climber

arrivo [ar·'ri:·vo] *m* **1.**(*venuta*) arrival; **posta in** ~ incoming mail; **il treno è in** ~ **sul quarto binario** the train is arriving at platform four **2.** SPORT (*traguardo*) finishing line; **punto d'**~ culmination **3.** *pl* (*merce*) **i nuovi -i** the new stock **4.** *pl* (*in aeroporto*) arrivals

arrogante [ar·ro·'gan·te] *agg* arrogant

arroganza [ar·ro·'gan·tsa] *f* arrogance

arrogarsi [ar·ro·'gar·si] *vr* ~ **qc** (*merito*) to claim sth; (*diritto*) to assume sth

arrossare [ar·ros·'sa:·re] *vi essere* to blush

arrostire [ar·ros·'ti:·re] <arrostisco> **I.** *vt* (*al forno: carne, patate*) to roast; (*ai ferri: carne, verdura*) to grill; (*allo spiedo: pollo*) to spitroast; (*sulla graticola: castagne*) to roast **II.** *vi essere fig* (*al sole*) to roast

arrosto [ar·'rɔs·to] *m* roast

arrotare [ar·ro·'ta:·re] *vt* **1.**(*affilare: coltello, lama*) to sharpen **2.** *inf* (*investire*) to run over **3.** *fig* (*sfregare*) ~ **i denti** to grind one's teeth

arrotolare [ar·ro·to·'la:·re] *vt* (*filo, carta, nastro*) to roll up

arrotolatore [ar·ro·to·la·'to:·re] *m* AUTO (*per cinture di sicurezza*) roller

arrotondare [ar·ro·ton·'da:·re] *vt* **1.** MATH (*cifra, somma*) ~ **per eccesso** to round up; ~ **per difetto** to round down **2.**(*integrare: stipendio, pensione*) to supplement **3.**(*oggetto, forma*) to make round

arrovellarsi [ar·ro·vel·'lar·si] *vr* (*affannarsi*) ~ **il cervello** to rack one's brains

arroventare [ar·ro·ven·'ta:·re] **I.** *vt* (*ferro, pentola, lamiera*) to make red hot **II.** *vr:* **-rsi** **1.**(*ferro, pentola, lamiera*) to become red hot **2.**(*clima*) to become very hot; (*polemica*) to rage

arruffare [ar·ruf·'fa:·re] *vt* (*piume, penne, capelli*) to ruffle

arruffianarsi [ar·ruf·fia·'na:r·si] *vr* ~ (**qu**) *inf* to suck up (to sb)

arrugginire [ar·rud·dʒi·'ni:·re] <arruginisco> *vr:* **-rsi** **1.**(*ricoprirsi di ruggine: metallo*) to rust **2.** *fig* (*perdere elasticità: cervello*) to become rusty; (*muscoli*) to become stiff

arruolamento [ar·ruo·la·'men·to] *m* MIL, NAUT enlistment

arruolare [ar·ruo·'la:·re] **I.** *vt* MIL, NAUT to enlist **II.** *vr:* **-rsi** MIL, NAUT (*soldati*) to enlist

arsenale [ar·se·'na:·le] *m* **1.** NAUT dockyard **2.** MIL (*deposito*) arsenal

arsenico [ar·'sɛ·ni·ko] *m* arsenic

arsi ['ar·si] *1. pers sing pass rem di* **ardere**

arso, -a ['ar·so] **I.** *pp di* **ardere** **II.** *agg* **1.**(*bruciato: terreno, campo, erba*) burned **2.**(*secco: labbra, gola*) dry

arsura [ar·'su:·ra] *f* **1.**(*calore*) burning heat

2.(*aridità, siccità*) drought **3.**(*per sete, febbre*) raging thirst

art. *abbr di* **articolo** Art.

arte ['ar·te] *f* **1.**(*gener*) art; ~ **poetica** poetry; **-i grafiche** graphic arts; **-i meccaniche** mechanical arts; **le belle -i** the fine arts; **le -i figurative** the visual arts; **nome d'~** stage name; **opera d'~** work of art; **a regola d'~** perfectly; **storia dell'~** history of art **2.**(*mestiere*) craft; **non avere né ~ né parte** *fig* to be neither use nor ornament; **impara l'~ e mettila da parte** *prov* learn a trade for a rainy day **3.**(*artificio*) artifice; **ad ~** deliberately **4.**HIST (*corporazione*) guild

artefatto, -a [ar·te·'fat·to] *agg* **1.**(*non genuino: vino*) full of additives **2.**(*innaturale: posa, movenze*) artificial

artefice [ar·'te:·fi·tʃe] *mf* (*autore: di successo, sconfitta, trasformazione*) author

arteria [ar·'tε:·ria] <-ie> *f* **1.**ANAT artery **2.**(*strada*) arterial road

arteriosclerosi [ar·te·rio·skle·'rɔ:·zi] <-> *f* arteriosclerosis

arteriosclerotico, -a [ar·te·rio·skle·'rɔ:·ti·ko] <-ci, -che> I. *agg* **1.**MED (*paziente, lesione, patologia, placca*) arteriosclerotic **2.**inf(*rimbambito*) senile II. *m, f* person suffering from arteriosclerosis

arterioso, -a [ar·te·'rio:·so] *agg* (*pressione, sistema*) arterial

artico, -a ['ar·ti·ko] <-ci, -che> *agg* (*calotta, regione, spedizione*) Arctic

articolare¹ [ar·ti·ko·'la:·re] *agg* (*dolore, disturbo, protesi*) of the joints

articolare² *vt* **1.**(*pronunciare: parole, sillabe*) to articulate **2.**(*suddividere: corso, discorso, relazione*) to divide up

articolazione [ar·ti·co·lat·'tsio:·ne] *f* **1.**ANAT, TEC joint **2.**LING articulation **3.**(*suddivisione*) division

articolo [ar·'ti:·ko·lo] *m* **1.** *a.* JUR, LING (*di giornale*) article; ~ **di fondo** leading article; **l'~ determinativo/indeterminativo** the definite/indefinite article **2.**COM (*merce, di bilancio*) item

Artide ['ar·ti·de] *f* Arctic

artificiale [ar·ti·fi·'tʃa:·le] *agg* **1.**(*allattamento, lago, seta*) artificial **2.**(*sorriso*) forced

artificio [ar·ti·'fi:·tʃo] <-ci> *m* **1.**(*espediente*) device; ~ **scenico** dramatic device **2.**(*ricercatezza*) artificiality **3.**(*loc*) **fuochi d'~** fireworks

artificioso, -a [ar·ti·fi·'tʃo:·so] *agg* (*non spontaneo*) unnatural; (*sorriso*) forced

artigianale [ar·ti·dʒa·'na:·le] *agg* (*non industriale*) by hand; (*gioielleria, falegnameria, forno*) craftsman-made; (*gelato, prodotto*) handmade

artigianato [ar·ti·dʒa·'na:·to] *m* **1.**(*attività*) craftsmanship **2.**(*categoria*) craftspeople **3.**(*prodotti*) craft item; ~ **artistico** arts and crafts

artigiano, -a [ar·ti·'dʒa:·no] I. *agg* (*attività,*

2.(*aridità, siccità*) drought **3.**(*per sete, febbre*) raging thirst

impresa, prodotto) craft; (*lavorazione, produzione*) by hand; (*gioielleria, falegnameria, forno*) craftsman-made; (*gelato, prodotto*) handmade II. *m, f* craftsman *m*, craftswoman *f*

artigliere [ar·tiʎ·'ʎε:·re] *m* artilleryman

artiglieria [ar·tiʎ·ʎe·'ri:·a] <-ie> *f* artillery

artiglio [ar·'tiʎ·ʎo] <-gli> *m a. fig* (*di animale*) claw; **tirar fuori gli -gli** to show one's claws

artista [ar·'tis·ta] <-i, -e> *mf* **1.**(*attore, musicista, pittore, scultore*) artist; ~ **cinematografico** film actor; ~ **lirico** (*opera*) singer **2.**(*di circo*) artiste

artistico, -a [ar·'tis·ti·ko] <-ci, -che> *agg* **1.**artistic **2.**(*loc*) **direttore** ~ artistic director; **liceo** ~ *high school specializing in art;* **pattinaggio** ~ figure skating

arto ['ar·to] *m* limb

artrite [ar·'tri:·te] *f* arthritis

artritico, -a [ar·'tri:·ti·ko] <-ci, -che> *agg* arthritic

artrosi [ar·'trɔ:·zi] <-> *f* osteoarthritis

ARVA ['ar·va] *f acro di* **Apparecchio di Ricerca in VAlanga** *electronic device used for finding people caught by avalanches*

arzigogolare [ar·dzi·go·go·'la:·re] *vi* (*cavillare*) to quibble

arzillo, -a [ar·'dzil·lo] *agg* (*persona, bambino, vecchio*) lively

asce ['aʃ·ʃe] *pl di* **ascia**

ascella [aʃ·'ʃεl·la] *f* ANAT armpit

ascendente [aʃ·ʃen·'dεn·te] I. *agg* **1.**(*flusso, parabola, movimento*) upward **2.**MUS ascending **3.**LING (*intonazione*) rising II. *m* **1.**(*parente*) ancestor **2.***fig* (*influsso*) influence **3.**ASTR ascendant

ascendenza [aʃ·ʃen·'dεn·tsa] *f* (*parenti*) ancestry

ascendere [aʃ·'ʃen·de·re] <irr> *vi essere* (*salire*) to ascend; ~ **al trono** to ascend the throne; ~ **al soglio pontificio** to become Pope

ascensione [aʃ·ʃen·'sio:·ne] *f* **1.**(*scalata*) ascent **2.**(*al cielo*) ascension; **l'Ascensione** the Ascension

ascensore [aʃ·ʃen·'so:·re] *m* elevator

ascesa [aʃ·'ʃe:·sa] *f* ascent

ascesi¹ [aʃ·'ʃe:·zi] *1. pers sing pass rem di* **ascendere**

ascesi² [aʃ·'ʃε:·zi] <-> *f* asceticism

asceso [aʃ·'ʃe:·zo] *pp di* **ascendere**

ascesso [aʃ·'ʃεs·so] *m* abscess

asceta [aʃ·'ʃε:·ta] <-i , -e> *mf* ascetic

ascetico, -a [aʃ·'ʃε:·ti·ko] <-ci, -che> *agg* (*percorso, esperienza, vita*) ascetic

ascetismo [aʃ·ʃe·'tiz·mo] *m* asceticism

ascia ['aʃ·ʃa] <asce> *f* ax

ASCII *m acro di* **American Standard Code for Information Interchange codice standard** ~ standard ASCII code

asciugacapelli [aʃ·ʃu·ga·ka·'pel·li] <-> *m* hairdryer

asciugamano [aʃ·ʃu·ga·'ma:·no] *m* towel; ~ **di spugna** terry towel

asciugare [aʃ·ʃu·'ga:·re] I. *vt* to dry II. *vr:* **-rsi**

1.(*detergersi*) to dry oneself; **-rsi le mani/i capelli** to dry one's hands/hair 2.(*tergersi*) **-rsi la fronte** to wipe one's forehead 3.(*diventare asciutto*) to dry (out)

asciugatoio [aʃ·ʃu·ga·'to:·io] <-oi> *m* (*nell'industria tessile*) dryer

asciugatore [aʃ·ʃu·ga·'to:·re] *m* (*per le mani*) hand dryer

asciugatrice [aʃ·ʃu·ga·'tri:·tʃe] *f* (*per biancheria*) dryer

asciutto [aʃ·'ʃut·to] *m* dry; **rimanere** [*o* **restare**] **all'~** *fig* to be broke

asciutto, -a *agg* 1.dry; **restare a bocca -a** *fig* to be disappointed 2.(*prosciugato: pozzo*) dried-up 3.*fig* (*magro: persona, figura*) lean 4.(*brusco: commento, risposta*) curt

Ascolano (*zona*) the Ascoli area; **nell'~** in the Ascoli area

ascolano, -a [as·ko·'la:·no] I. *agg* from Ascoli; **olive all'-a** *stuffed green olives fried in breadcrumbs* II. *m, f* (*abitante*) person from Ascoli

Ascoli Piceno *f* Ascoli, *city in eastern central Italy*

ascoltare [as·kol·'ta:·re] I. *vt* 1.(*udire: radio, musica*) to listen to 2.(*dar retta a*) ~ **qu/qc** (*persona, consiglio*) to listen to sb/sth 3.(*esaudire: desiderio*) to grant II. *vi* to listen

ascoltatore, -trice [as·kol·ta·'to:·re] *m, f* listener

ascolto [as·'kol·to] *m* 1.(*l'ascoltare*) **apparecchiature per l'~ di brani musicali** equipment for listening to music 2.RADIO, TV **indice di ~** audience ratings 3.(*attenzione*) hearing; **dare ~ a qu** to listen to sb 4.(*origliare*) **stare in ~** to eavesdrop

ascrivere [as·'kri:·ve·re] <irr> *vt* (*attribuire*) to attribute

asessuato, -a [a·ses·su·'a:·to] *agg* BIOL asexual

asettico, -a [as·'sɛt·ti·ko] <-ci, -che> *agg* 1.MED aseptic 2.*fig* (*freddo, sterile: stile, arredamento*) clinical

asfaltare [as·fal·'ta:·re] *vt* (*strada*) to asphalt

asfalto [as·'fal·to] *m* asphalt

asfissia [as·fis·'si:·a] <-ie> *f* asphyxia

asfissiare [as·fis·'sia:·re] I. *vt avere* 1.MED to asphyxiate 2.*fig, inf* (*molestare*) to suffocate II. *vi essere* to suffocate

Asia ['a:·zia] *f* Asia; ~ **Minore** Asia Minor

asiatica [a·'zia:·ti·ka] <-che> *f* MED Asian flu

asiatico, -a [a·'zia:·ti·ko] <-ci, -che> I. *agg* (*civiltà, città, popolazione*) Asian II. *m, f* Asian

asilo [a·'zi:·lo] *m* 1.(*rifugio*) shelter 2.POL asylum; **diritto di ~** right of asylum; **richiesta di ~** (*politico*) request for (political) asylum 3.(*scuola materna*) nursery; **~ d'infanzia** nursery school; **~ nido** day nursery

asimmetria [a·sim·me·'tri:·a] *f* asymmetry

asimmetrico, -a [a·sim·'mɛ:·tri·ko] <-ci, -che> *agg* (*struttura, faro, vela*) asymmetric

asinino, -a [a·si·'ni:·no] *agg* **tosse -a** whooping cough

asino, -a ['a:·si·no] *m, f* (*animale, persona*) donkey; **a schiena d'~** (*strada*) saddle-backed; **qui casca l'~!** there's the rub!; **essere un ~** to be thick; **legare l'~ dove vuole il padrone** *prov* to tie up the donkey where the master wants, *to do what the boss says;* **meglio un ~ vivo che un dottore morto** *prov* better a live donkey than a dead doctor, *said as a warning not to study too much*

asintomatico, -a [a·sin·to·'ma:·ti·ko] <-ci, -che> *agg* (*malattia, persona*) asymptomatic

ASL *f abbr di* **Azienda Sanitaria Locale** *local health center*

asma ['az·ma] *f* asthma

asmatico, -a [az·'ma:·ti·ko] <-ci, -che> I. *agg* (*paziente, bronchite*) asthmatic II. *m, f* asthmatic

asociale [a·so·'tʃa:·le] *agg* (*comportamento, persona*) antisocial

asola ['a:·zo·la] *f* buttonhole

asparagicoltura [as·pa·ra·dʒi·kol·'tu:·ra] *f* asparagus growing

asparago [as·'pa:·ra·go] <-gi> *m* asparagus

asperità [as·pe·ri·'ta] <-> *f* 1.(*di terreno, strada, roccia*) roughness 2.(*difficoltà*) difficulty; **le ~ della vita** the trials of life

aspettare [as·pet·'ta:·re] I. *vt* 1.(*telefonata, ospite, accoglienza, dono*) to expect; ~ **un bambino** to be expecting a baby 2.(*treno, autobus*) to wait for; **farsi ~** to keep people waiting; **chi la fa l'aspetti** *prov* what goes around comes around II. *vi* (*attendere*) to wait III. *vr:* **-rsi** to expect

aspettativa [as·pet·ta·'ti:·va] *f* 1.(*speranza*) expectation 2.ADM leave

aspetto [as·'pɛt·to] *m* 1.(*apparenza*) appearance; **avere un bell'~** to be nice-looking 2.(*punto di vista*) aspect; **sotto questo ~** in this regard 3.(*attesa*) wait; **sala d'~** waiting room

aspirante [as·pi·'ran·te] I. *agg* (*forza, pompa*) suction II. *mf* candidate

aspirapolvere [as·pi·ra·'pol·ve·re] <-> *m* vacuum cleaner

aspirare [as·pi·'ra:·re] I. *vt* 1.(*respirare: aria*) to breathe (in) 2.TEC (*liquido, gas*) to suck up II. *vi* ~ (**a qc**) to aspire (to sth)

aspiratore [as·pi·ra·'to:·re] *m* 1.(*per gas*) extractor 2. *a.* MED (*per liquidi*) aspirator

aspirazione [as·pi·rat·'tsio:·ne] *f* 1.*fig* (*desiderio*) ambition 2.TEC extraction 3.MOT suction

aspirina® [as·pi·'ri:·na] *f* aspirin

asportabile [as·por·'ta:·bi·le] *agg* (*antenna, fodera*) removable

asportare [as·por·'ta:·re] *vt* to remove

asportazione [as·por·tat·'tsio:·ne] *f* removal

asprezza [as·'pret·tsa] *f* 1.(*di sapore*) sharpness 2.(*di terreno*) roughness 3.*a. fig* (*di inverno, clima, persona*) harshness 4.*fig* (*di battaglia, lotta, polemica*) bitterness

asprigno, -a [as·'priɲ·ɲo] *agg* (*gusto*) rather sharp

aspro, -a ['as·pro] <più aspro, asperrimo *o* asprissimo> *agg* **1.**(*acre: sapore*) sharp; (*odore*) pungent **2.**(*acuto: suono, voce*) shrill **3.**(*malagevole: terreno*) rough **4.**(*freddo: clima*) harsh **5.**(*spigoloso: carattere*) spiky **6.**(*severo: tono, rimprovero, risposta*) severe **7.**(*duro: battaglia, lotta, polemica*) bitter

Ass. *abbr di* **Assicurazione** Insurance

ass. *abbr di* **assegno** check

assaggiare [as·sad·'dʒa:·re] *vt* **1.**(*provare*) to try **2.**(*mangiare una piccola quantità di*) to taste; (*bere una piccola quantità di*) to sip

assaggio [as·'sad·dʒo] <-ggi> *m* **1.**(*degustazione*) tasting **2.**(*piccola quantità*) taste **3.**(*prova*) sample

assai [as·'sa:·i] I. *avv* **1.**(*molto*) very **2.**(*molto*) a lot; **m'importa ~ di lui!** *iron, inf* what do I care about him! II.<inv> *agg* (*parecchio*) a lot of

assale [as·'sa:·le] *m* axle

assalire [as·sa·'li:·re] <irr> *vt* **1.**to attack; **~ qu alle spalle** to attack sb from behind **2.** *fig* (*sopraffare*) to overcome

assaltare [as·sal·'ta:·re] *vt* (*banca*) to raid; (*convoglio, treno*) to attack; (*fortezza*) to storm

assalto [as·'sal·to] *m* **1.** MIL assault **2.**(*azione violenta*) attack; **prendere d'~ qc** (*biglietteria, treno, buffet*) to rush **3.** SPORT (*nella scherma*) bout

assaporare [as·sa·po·'ra:·re] *vt* to savor

assassinare [as·sas·si·'na:·re] *vt* (*uccidere*) to murder; POL to assassinate

assassinio [as·sas·'si:·nio] <-ii> *m* (*omicidio*) murder; POL assassination

assassino, -a [as·sas·'si:·no] I. *agg a. fig* murderous II. *m, f* (*omicida*) killer

assatanato, -a [as·sa·ta·'na:·to] *agg* **1.**(*indemoniato*) possessed **2.** *fig* (*sessualmente*) randy

asse ['as·se] I. *f* (*tavola di legno*) board; **l'~ del gabinetto** toilet seat; **~ di equilibrio** beam; **~ da stiro** ironing board II. *m* **1.** *a.* MATH axis **2.** TEC (*organo portante*) axle

assecondare [as·se·kon·'da:·re] *vt* **1.**(*favorire*) to encourage **2.**(*soddisfare*) **~ qc** to go along with sth; **~ qu in qc** to support sb in sth

assediare [as·se·'dia:·re] *vt* **1.** *a. fig* MIL to besiege **2.**(*bloccare*) to cut off

assedio [as·'sɛ:·dio] <-i> *m a. fig* MIL siege

assegnamento [as·seɲ·ɲa·'men·to] *m* reliance; **fare ~ su qc/qu** to rely on sth/sb

assegnare [as·seɲ·'ɲa:·re] *vt* **1.**(*dare*) **~ qc a qu** (*premio, borsa di studio*) to award sth to sb; (*compiti scolastici*) to give sth to sb; (*incarico*) to allocate sth to sb **2.**(*destinare*) to assign; **~ qu a qc** to assign sb to sth **3.**(*stabilire: scadenza*) to set

assegnazione [as·seɲ·ɲat·'tsio:·ne] *f* **1.**(*di premio, borsa di studio*) award; (*di prestito, alloggio*) allocation; (*di compiti scolastici*) setting **2.**(*di incarico*) assignment **3.**(*di persona*) posting

assegno [as·'seɲ·ɲo] *m* **1.** COM, FIN check; **~ in bianco** blank check; **~ postale** postal order; **~ sbarrato** crossed check; **~ scoperto** [*o* a vuoto] bad check **2.**(*sussidio*) welfare payment; **~ di maternità** maternity pay; **-i familiari** family welfare benefits

assemblaggio [as·sem·'blad·dʒo] <-ggi> *m* **1.**(*montaggio: di automobili, computer, componenti*) assembly **2.**(*di brani, sigle musicali*) compilation

assemblare [as·sem·'bla:·re] *vt* **1.**(*montare: automobili, computer, componenti*) to assemble **2.**(*brani, sigle musicali*) to compile

assemblatore, -trice [as·sem·bla·'to:·re] I. *m, f* assembly worker II. *agg* COMPUT (*programma ~*) assembler

assemblea [as·sem·'blɛ:·a] *f* **1.**(*riunione*) meeting; **~ plenaria** plenary meeting **2.**(*organo*) assembly

assembramento [as·sem·bra·'men·to] *m* gathering

assennato, -a [as·sen·'na:·to] *agg* wise

assenso [as·'sɛn·so] *m* **1.**(*approvazione*) approval **2.** DIR (*autorizzazione*) consent

assentarsi [as·sen·'tar·si] *vr* (*da un luogo*) to be absent (from a place)

assente [as·'sɛn·te] I. *agg* **1.**(*non presente: da scuola*) absent; (*per lavoro*) away **2.**(*inesistente*) non-existent **3.**(*distratto: aria, sguardo*) distracted II. *mf* absent person

assenteismo [as·sen·te·'iz·mo] *m* (*dal lavoro*) absenteeism

assenteista [as·sen·te·'is·ta] <-i , -e> *mf* absentee

assenteistico, -a [as·sen·te·'is·ti·ko] <-ci, -che> *agg* (*comportamento, fenomeno*) being frequently absent

assentire [as·sen·'ti:·re] *vi* to agree; **~ a qc** to agree to sth

assenza [as·'sɛn·tsa] *f* **1.**(*da luogo*) absence; **~ giustificata/ingiustificata** (*a scuola*) authorized/unauthorized absence **2.**(*mancanza*) lack; **l'~ di qc** the lack of sth

assenziente [as·sen·'tsiɛn·te] *agg* (*sguardo, risposta*) consenting; **essere ~** to be in agreement

assenzio [as·'sɛn·tsio] <-i> *m* **1.** BOT wormwood **2.**(*liquore*) absinthe

asserire [as·se·'ri:·re] <asserisco> *vt* to maintain

asservimento [as·ser·vi·'men·to] *m* enslavement; **~ a qc** (*potere, politica, padrone, interesse*) subservience to sth

asservire [as·ser·'vi:·re] <asservisco> I. *vt* **~ qc a qc** to subordinate sth to sth II. *vr: -rsi -rsi a qc* (*potere, politica, padrone, interesse*) to be subordinated to sth

asserzione [as·ser·'tsio:·ne] *f* (*dichiarazione*) assertion

assessorato [as·ses·so·'ra:·to] *m* (*ufficio*) department

assessore [as·ses·'so:·re] *m* councilor; **~ comunale** local councilor

assestamento [as·ses·ta·'men·to] *m* **1.** ARCH, GEOL (*di edificio, trave, terreno*) settlement **2.** (*sistemazione*) settling down

assestare [as·ses·'ta:·re] **I.** *vt* (*affibbiare*) ~ **un colpo** to deal a blow **II.** *vr:* **-rsi 1.** (*terreno, valore, dato*) to settle **2.** *fig* (*situazione*) to settle down

assestata [as·ses·'ta:·ta] *f* (*sistemata*) tidying up

assetare [as·se·'ta:·re] *vt* to deprive of water

assetato, -a [as·se·'ta:·to] **I.** *agg a. fig* thirsty; ~ **di qc** (*sapere, giustizia, vendetta*) thirsty for sth; ~ **di sangue** bloodthirsty **II.** *m, f* **gli -i** the thirsty

assettare [as·set·'ta:·re] **I.** *vt* (*stanza*) to tidy up **II.** *vr:* **-rsi** to tidy oneself up

assetto [as·'sɛt·to] *m* **1.** (*ordinamento*) organization **2.** (*equipaggiamento*) gear; ~ **di combattimento** action stations **3.** AERO, NAUT trim **4.** AUTO stability

assiale [as·'sia:·le] *agg* axial

assicurare [as·si·ku·'ra:·re] **I.** *vt* **1.** (*contro rischi: casa, auto, pacco*) to insure; ~ (**contro qc**) (*furto, rischio, incendio*) to insure (against sth) **2.** (*garantire, fissare*) to secure **3.** (*affermare*) ~ **qc a qu** to assure sb of sth; ~ **a qu che** to assure sb that **II.** *vr:* **-rsi 1.** (*fare un assicurazione*) to get insurance; **-rsi** (**contro qc**) (*furto, rischio, incendio*) to insure oneself (against sth) **2.** (*garantirsi*) to secure **3.** (*accertarsi*) to make sure

assicurato, -a [as·si·ku·'ra:·to] *m, f* policyholder

assicuratore, -trice [as·si·ku·ra·'to:·re] **I.** *agg* (*società, ente*) insurance **II.** *m, f* insurance agent

assicurazione [as·si·ku·rat·'tsio:·ne] *f* **1.** (*contratto*) insurance; ~ **casco/contro tutti i rischi** comprehensive insurance; ~ **contro la responsabilità civile** third party insurance; ~ **sulla vita** life insurance **2.** (*affermazione*) assurance

assideramento [as·si·de·ra·'men·to] *m* exposure

assiderare [as·si·de·'ra:·re] **I.** *vt* (*mani*) to freeze; (*pianta*) to frost **II.** *vi:* **-rsi** to suffer from exposure

assiduità [as·si·dui·'ta] <-> *f* **1.** (*abituale*) regularity; **con** ~ regularly **2.** (*perseveranza*) diligence

assiduo, -a [as·'si:·duo] *agg* **1.** (*regolare: cliente, lettore, visitatore*) regular **2.** (*costante: visita, attività, cura, interesse*) constant **3.** (*diligente: studente, lavoratore*) hardworking

assieme [as·'siɛ:·me] **I.** *avv* together **II.** *prep* ~ **a** (together) with **III.** <-> *m* **1.** (*complesso*) whole; **un quadro d'**~ an overall picture **2.** MUS, THEAT ensemble

assillare [as·sil·'la:·re] *vt* (*soggetto: problemi, preoccupazioni*) to nag at

assillo [as·'sil·lo] *m* (*problema*) worry

assimilabile [as·si·mi·'la:·bi·le] *agg* **1.** (*digeri-*

bile: alimento, medicinale) digestible **2.** (*paragonabile*) ~ **a qc** comparable to sth

assimilare [as·si·mi·'la:·re] *vt* **1.** BIOL (*assorbire: alimento, medicinale, sostanza*) to absorb **2.** *fig* (*far proprio*) to take in **3.** LING to assimilate

assimilazione [as·si·mi·lat·'tsio:·ne] *f a.* BIOL, LING (*di alimento, medicinale, sostanza*) assimilation

assioma [as·'sio:·ma] <-i> *m* axiom

assiomatico, -a [as·sio·'ma:·ti·ko] <-ci, -che> *agg* (*teoria, metodo*) axiomatic

assisano, -a [as·si·'za:·no] **I.** *agg* from Assisi **II.** *m, f* (*abitante*) person from Assisi

assise [as·'si:·ze] *fpl* **1.** JUR **Corte d'Assise** ≈ district court **2.** (*riunione plenaria*) meeting

Assisi *f* Assisi, *city in central Italy*

assistei [as·sis·'te:·i] *1. pers sing pass rem di* **assistere**

assistente [as·sis·'tɛn·te] **I.** *agg* assistant **II.** *mf* assistant; ~ **di bordo** flight attendant; ~ **alla regia** assistant director; ~ **sociale** social worker; ~ **universitario** ≈ instructor

assistenza [as·sis·'tɛn·tsa] *f* assistance; ~ **sanitaria** health care; ~ **sociale** welfare; ~ **tecnica** technical support; ~ **legale** legal aid

assistenziale [as·sis·ten·'tsia:·le] *agg* (*attività, ente, servizio*) welfare

assistenzialismo [as·sis·ten·tsia·'liz·mo] *m* welfarism

assistere [as·'sis·te·re] <assisto, assistei *o* assistetti, assistito> **I.** *vi* ~ **a qc** (*spettacolo, lezione*) to attend sth; (*incidente*) to witness sth **II.** *vt* **1.** (*curare*) ~ **qu** (*anziano, ferito, malato*) to care for **2.** (*aiutare*) to help **3.** (*cliente*) to assist

assistibile [as·sis·'ti:·bi·le] *agg* (*paziente, soggetto*) able to be cared for

asso ['as·so] *m* **1.** *a.* SPORT (*di carte da gioco*) ace; (*di dado*) one; **avere l'**~ **nella manica** *fig* to have an ace up one's sleeve; **un** ~ **del volante** an ace driver; **un** ~ **dello sport** a sporting champion **2.** (*loc*) **piantare** [*o* **lasciare**] **qu in** ~ to leave sb in the lurch

associare [as·so·'tʃa:·re] **I.** *vt* **1.** (*unire: idee, caratteristiche, prestazioni*) to associate **2.** (*a circolo, partito*) to enroll **3.** (*mettere insieme*) to bring together **II.** *vr:* **-rsi 1.** (*unirsi*) **-rsi con qu** to join sb **2.** **-rsi a qc** (*circolo, partito*) to join sth **3.** **-rsi a qc** (*protesta, brindisi*) to join in sth **4.** (*accompagnarsi*) to be associated with

associativo, -a [as·so·tʃa·'ti:·vo] *agg* (*quota*) membership

associazione [as·so·tʃat·'tsio:·ne] *f* association; ~ **di categoria** trade association; ~ **di idee** association of ideas; **per** ~ by association

assodare [as·so·'da:·re] *vt* to ascertain

assoggettabilità [as·sod·dʒet·ta·bi·li·'ta] <-> *f* liability, *for tax*

assoggettamento [as·sod·dʒet·ta·'men·to] *m* **1.** (*sottomissione: di Stato, popolazione*) subjection **2.** (*a tassa, controllo*) liability

assoggettare [as·sod·dʒet·'ta:·re] I. vt 1. (sottomettere: Stato, popolazione) to subjugate 2. (sottoporre) ~ a qc (a tassa, controllo) to subject to sth II. vr: -rsi -rsi a qc 1. (sottomettersi: nemico) to submit to sth 2. (sottoporsi: tassa, controllo) to comply with sth 3. (adattarsi) to adapt to sth

assolato, -a [as·so·'la:·to] agg (regione, isola, casa) sunny

assoldare [as·sol·'da:·re] vt 1. MIL (mercenari) to recruit 2. (killer, interprete, guida) to hire

assolsi [as·'sɔl·si] I. pers sing pass rem di assolvere

assolto [as·'sɔl·to] pp di assolvere

assolutamente [as·so·lu·ta·'men·te] avv 1. (senz'altro) definitely 2. (del tutto) absolutely

assolutismo [as·so·lu·'tiz·mo] m absolutism

assolutistico, -a [as·so·lu·'tis·ti·ko] <-ci, -che> agg (mire, potere, dominio) absolutist

assolutizzazione [as·so·lu·tid·dzat·'tsio:·ne] f making absolute

assoluto, -a [as·so·'lu:·to] agg 1. a. POL (generale: verità) absolute; in ~ absolutely 2. (totale: novità, silenzio) complete 3. SPORT (campione, record) undisputed 4. (urgente: bisogno) urgent

assoluzione [as·so·lut·'tsio:·ne] f 1. JUR (di imputato) acquittal 2. REL absolution

assolvere [as·'sɔl·ve·re] <assolvo, assolsi, assolto> vt 1. JUR (imputato) to acquit 2. a. REL (liberare) to absolve; ~ qu da qc to absolve sb of sth 3. (eseguire: compito, dovere) to carry out

assomigliare [as·so·miʎ·'ʎa:·re] I. vi ~ a qu/qc to resemble sb/sth II. vr: -rsi to look alike; -rsi come due gocce d'acqua to be like two peas (in a pod)

assonanza [as·so·'nan·tsa] f 1. LING assonance 2. fig (di colori, immagini) harmony

assonnato, -a [as·so·'na:·to] agg a. fig sleepy

assopirsi [as·so·'pir·si] <mi assopisco> vr (addormentarsi) to doze off

assorbente [as·sor·'bɛn·te] I. agg (carta, tessuto, sostanza) absorbent II. m ~ igienico sanitary towel; ~ interno tampon

assorbire [as·sor·'bi:·re] vt 1. (gener) to absorb 2. (incorporare: azienda, quota) to swallow up 3. (consumare: tempo) to take up

assordante [as·sor·'dan·te] agg (rumore, musica) deafening

assordare [as·sor·'da:·re] vt avere (render sordo) to deafen

assortimento [as·sor·ti·'men·to] m (di prodotti, articoli) range

assortire [as·sor·'ti:·re] <assortisco> vt 1. (combinare: colori) to mix 2. COM (rifornire) to supply

assortito, -a [as·sor·'ti:·to] agg 1. (misto: cioccolatini, pasticcini, colori) assorted 2. (che armonizza: coppia, gruppo) ben ~ well-matched

assorto, -a [as·'sɔr·to] agg ~ nei pensieri lost in thought

assottigliare [as·sot·tiʎ·'ʎa:·re] I. vt 1. (render sottile: caviglie, fianchi, gambe) to slim down 2. (ridurre: scorte, viveri, vantaggio) to reduce; (gruppo, numero, guadagno) to reduce the size of II. vr: -rsi 1. (diventar sottile: caviglie, fianchi, gambe) to become slimmer 2. (ridursi: scorte, viveri) to dwindle; (gruppo, numero, guadagno) to get smaller; (vantaggio) to narrow 3. (dimagrire) to slim down

assuefare [as·sue·'fa:·re] <irr> I. vt ~ qc a qc to accustom sth to sth II. vr -rsi a qc to get used to sth

assuefazione [as·sue·fat·'tsio:·ne] f addiction; l'~ a qc addiction to sth

assumere [as·'su:·me·re] <assumo, assunsi, assunto> I. vt 1. (responsabilità, impegno, personale, operaio) to take on 2. (colpa, merito, farmaco) to take 3. (fare proprio: atteggiamento) to put on 4. (ingerire: cibo) to eat 5. (procurarsi: informazioni) to obtain II. vr: -rsi 1. (prendersi: responsabilità, impegno) to take on 2. (attribuirsi: colpa, merito) to take

Assunta [as·'sun·ta] f 1. (Maria Vergine) the Virgin Mary 2. (festa) the feast of the Assumption

assunto¹ [as·'sun·to] m (tesi) argument

assunto² pp di assumere

assunzione [as·sun·'tsio:·ne] f 1. (di impiegato) employment 2. (di farmaco) taking 3. REL l'Assunzione (della Vergine) the Assumption (of the Virgin Mary)

assurdità [as·sur·di·'ta] <-> f 1. (caratteristica) absurdity 2. (cosa assurda) stupid thing

assurdo [as·'sur·do] m ridiculous thing

assurdo, -a agg (comportamento, idea, storia) ridiculous

asta ['as·ta] f 1. a. SPORT (bastone) pole; salto con l'~ pole vault; (di compasso, occhiali) arm; (di bandiera) flagpole; a mezz'~ (bandiera) at half mast 2. (lancia) lance 3. (nella scrittura) stroke 4. (vendita all'incanto) auction; mettere all'~ to auction (off)

astemio, -a [as·'tɛ:·mio] <-i, -ie> I. agg (persona) teetotal II. m, f teetotaler

astenersi [as·te·'ner·si] <irr> vr to abstain; ~ da qc (fumo, bere) to abstain from sth; ~ (dal voto) to abstain (from voting); ~ dal fare qc to refrain from doing sth

astensione [as·ten·'sio:·ne] f 1. (non votante) abstention 2. (sciopero) ~ dal lavoro withdrawal of labor

astenuto, -a [as·te·'nu:·to] I. pp di astenersi II. m, f (non votante) abstainer

asterisco [as·te·'ris·ko] <-schi> m TYP asterisk

asteroide [as·te·'rɔ:·i·de] m asteroid

Asti f Asti, town in northern Italy

astice ['as·ti·tʃe] m lobster

asticella [as·ti·'tʃɛl·la] f SPORT bar

Astigiano (zona) nell'~ in the Asti area

astigiano, -a [as·ti·'dʒa:·no] I. agg from Asti II. m, f (abitante) person from Asti astigmatico, -a [a·stig·'ma:·ti·ko] <-ci, -che> I. agg (paziente, lente) astigmatic II. m, f person with astigmatism

astinente [a·sti·'nɛn·te] agg (da droga, alcol, nicotina) abstinent

astinenza [a·sti·'nɛn·tsa] f (da droga, alcol, nicotina) abstinence

astio ['as·tio] <-i> m resentment

astioso, -a [as·'tio:·so] agg 1.(parola) hostile 2.(persona) resentful

astrarre [as·'trar·re] <irr> I. vt 1.(distogliere: sguardo, mente) to detach 2. PHILOS to abstract II. vi ~ da qc to disregard sth III. vr: -rsi to detach oneself

astratto [as·'trat·to] m abstract

astratto, -a I. pp di astrarre II. agg (concetto, rappresentazione) abstract

astringente [as·trin·'dʒɛn·te] I. agg (lozione) astringent II. m astringent

astro ['as·tro] m a. ASTR star

astrofisica [as·tro·'fi:·zi·ka] <-che> f astrophysics

astrologia [as·tro·lo·'dʒi:·a] <-gie> f astrology

astrologico, -a [as·tro·'lɔ:·dʒi·ko] <-ci, -che> agg (consulenza, previsione) astrological

astrologo, -a [as·'trɔ:·lo·go] <-gi, -ghe> m, f ASTR astrologer

astronauta [as·tro·'na:u·ta] <-i , -e> mf astronaut

astronautica [as·tro·'na:u·ti·ka] <-che> f astronautics

astronautico, -a [as·tro·'na:u·ti·ko] <-ci, -che> agg (attività, missione, ricerca) space

astronave [as·tro·'na:·ve] f spaceship

astronomia [as·tro·no·'mi:·a] <-ie> f astronomy

astronomico, -a [as·tro·'nɔ:·mi·ko] <-ci, -che> agg astronomical

astronomo, -a [as·'trɔ:·no·mo] m, f astronomer

astrusità [as·tru·zi·'ta] <-> f 1.(caratteristica) obscurity 2.(cosa assurda) to talk nonsense

astruso, -a [as·'tru:·zo] agg (calcolo, concetto, sistema) obscure

astuccio [as·'tut·tʃo] <-cci> m case

astuto, -a [as·'tu:·to] agg (persona, ragionamento, idea) smart

astuzia [as·'tut·tsia] <-ie> f 1.(furbizia) cunning 2.(trucco) trick

AT 1. abbr di Antico Testamento OT 2. abbr di Alta Tensione HT

ateismo [a·te·'iz·mo] m atheism

atelier [a·tə·'lje] <-> m (di pittore, fotografo, sarto) studio

Atene [a·'tɛ:·ne] f Athens

ateo, -a ['a:·te·o] I. agg (persona, pensiero) atheist II. m, f atheist

atesino, -a [a·te·'zi:·no] I. agg from Alto Adige II. m, f person from Alto Adige

ATI ['a:·ti] f abbr di Aereo Trasporti Italiani Italian Air Transport Company

atipico, -a [a·'ti:·pi·ko] <-ci, -che> agg (comportamento, sviluppo, caso) atypical

atlante [at·'lan·te] m atlas

atlantico, -a [at·'lan·ti·ko] <-ci, -che> agg (traversata, sommergibile, onda) Atlantic; l'Oceano Atlantico the Atlantic (Ocean)

atleta [at·'lɛ:·ta] <-i , -e> mf athlete

atletica [at·'lɛ:·ti·ka] f athletics; ~ leggera track and field

atletico, -a [at·'lɛ:·ti·ko] <-ci, -che> agg (corpo, persona, prestazioni) athletic

atmosfera [at·mos·'fɛ:·ra] f a. fig atmosphere

atmosferico, -a [at·mos·'fɛ:·ri·ko] <-ci, -che> agg (inquinamento, fenomeno, pressione) atmospheric; condizioni -che weather conditions

atomico, -a [a·'tɔ:·mi·ko] <-ci, -che> agg 1. CHEM PHYS atomic 2.(nucleare) bomba -ca atom bomb; centrale -ca nuclear power station

atomizzare [a·to·mid·'dza:·re] vt (nebulizzare) to spray

atomizzatore [a·to·mid·dza·'to:·re] m (nebulizzatore) atomizer

atomo ['a:·to·mo] m atom

atrio ['a:·trio] <-ii> m lobby

atroce [a·'tro:·tʃe] agg 1.(crudele: delitto, morte) appalling 2.(raccapricciante: scena, spettacolo) dreadful 3.(terribile: dolore, frastuono) awful 4.(angoscioso: dubbio) terrible

atrocità [a·tro·tʃi·'ta] <-> f 1.(caratteristica) awfulness 2.(cosa atroce) atrocity

atrofia [a·tro·'fi:·a] <-ie> f atrophy

atrofizzare [a·tro·fid·'dza:·re] I. vt (muscolo) to atrophy II. vr: -rsi (muscolo) atrophy

attaccabottoni [at·tak·ka·bot·'to:·ni] <-> mf inf gasbag

attaccabrighe [at·tak·ka·'bri:·ge] <-> mf inf quarrelsome person

attaccamento [at·tak·ka·'men·to] m attachment

attaccante [at·tak·'kan·te] I. agg (squadra) attacking II. mf SPORT forward

attaccapanni [at·tak·ka·'pan·ni] <-> m (a muro) hook; (a stelo) coatstand

attaccare [at·tak·'ka:·re] I. vt 1.(fissare) to attach 2.(con colla: etichetta, manifesto) to stick 3.(cucire) to sew 4.(appendere) to hang; ~ al chiodo fig (guanti da box, bicicletta) to hang up 5.(agganciare) to hook up 6.(alla corrente) to connect up 7. a. CHEM, SPORT (assalire, criticare) to attack 8. MED (malattia) ~ qc a qu to give sb sth 9.(iniziare) ~ discorso to start a conversation II. vi 1.(avere azione adesiva) to stick 2.(muovere all'assalto) to attack 3. fig (attecchire) to work; con me non attacca! inf that doesn't work with me! 4.(impersonale) to start; attacca a piovere it's starting to rain III. vr: -rsi 1. a. CULIN (restare aderente) to stick 2. MED to be catching 3.(aggrapparsi) -rsi a qu/qc to catch on to sb/sth; -rsi alla bottiglia to take to drink 4.(affezionarsi) -rsi a qu to become attached to sb

attaccaticcio [at·ta·ka·'tit·tʃo] <-cci> m

sapere di ~ to taste burned

attaccato, -a [at·tak·'ka:·to] *agg* (*legato*) attached; **essere ~ ai soldi/alla famiglia** to be fond of money/one's family

attaccatura [at·tak·ka·'tu:·ra] *f* (*di capelli*) hairline

attaccatutto [at·tak·ka·'tut·to] *m* (*colla*) superglue

attacchinaggio [at·tak·ki·'nad·dʒo] <-gi> *m* posting

attacchinare [at·tak·ki·'na:·re] *vi* to post bills

attacco [at·'tak·ko] <-cchi> *m* **1.** (*giunzione*) connection **2.** (*per sci*) binding **3.** *a. fig* MED, MIL, SPORT attack **4.** (*avvio, inizio*) beginning

attanagliare [at·ta·naʎ·'ʎa:·re] *vt a. fig* to grip

attardarsi [at·tar·'dar·si] *vr* to stay behind

attecchire [at·tek·'ki:·re] <attecchisco> *vi* **1.** BOT to take root **2.** *fig* (*moda*) to catch on

atteggiamento [at·ted·dʒa·'men·to] *m* attitude

atteggiare [at·ted·'dʒa:·re] I. *vt* ~ **qc** (*labbra, corpo, mani*) to fix sth; ~ **il volto a sofferenza** to put on a suffering face II. *vr:* **-rsi a qc** (*vittima, primadonna*) to pose as sth

attempato, -a [at·tem·'pa:·to] *agg* elderly

attendarsi [at·ten·'dar·si] *vr* to camp

attendere [at·'tɛn·de·re] <irr> I. *vt* to wait (for) II. *vi* ~ **a qc** to attend to sth

attendibile [at·ten·'di:·bi·le] *agg* (*giornale, fonte, notizia, testimone*) credible

attendista [at·ten·'dis·ta] *agg* wait-and-see

attenere [at·te·'ne:·re] <irr> I. *vi essere* ~ **a qc** to be relevant to sth II. *vr* **-rsi a qc** to stick to sth

attentare [at·ten·'ta:·re] *vi* ~ **alla vita di qu** to make an attempt on sb's life

attentato [at·ten·'ta:·to] *m* attack; **-i dinamitardi terroristici** terrorist bomb attacks; ~ **kamikaze** kamikaze attack

attentatore, -trice [at·ten·ta·'to:·re] *m, f* attacker

attenti [at·'tɛn·ti] I. *int* **1.** (*attenzione*) be careful; ~ **al cane!** beware of the dog! **2.** MIL attention! II. <-> *m* attention; **mettere qu sull'~** *fig* to call sb to order

attento, -a [at·'tɛn·to] I. *agg* **1.** (*concentrato: interlocutore, ascolto*) attentive **2.** (*diligente: scolaro*) diligent **3.** (*accurato: analisi*) careful II. *int* be careful!

attenuante [at·te·nu·'an·te] I. *agg* JUR **circostanze -i** extenuating circumstances II. *f* JUR extenuating circumstances

attenuare [at·te·nu·'a:·re] I. *vt* (*dolore*) to ease; (*rumore*) to deaden; (*colpo*) to soften II. *vr:* **-rsi** (*dolore*) to ease; (*maltempo*) to improve

attenuto [at·te·'nu:·to] *pp di* **attenere**

attenzione¹ [at·ten·'tsio:·ne] *f* **1.** *a.* COM (*concentrazione*) attention; **fare ~** to be careful; **alla cortese ~ di ...** for the attention of ... **2.** *pl* attentions *pl*

attenzione² *int* be careful!

atterraggio [at·ter·'rad·dʒo] <-ggi> *m* AERO,

SPORT landing; **campo d'~** landing strip; ~ **di fortuna** crash landing

atterrare [at·ter·'ra:·re] I. *vt* (*avversario*) to floor II. *vi* AERO, SPORT to land

atterrire [at·ter·'ri:·re] <atterrisco> I. *vt* to terrify; ~ **qu** to terrify sb II. *vr:* **-rsi** to become terrified

attesa [at·'te:·sa] *f* wait; **sala d'~** waiting room; **lista d'~** waiting list; **essere in ~ di qu/qc** to be waiting for sb/sth; **nell'~ della Sua risposta** awaiting your reply

attesi [at·'e:·si] *1. pers sing pass rem di* **attendere**

atteso, -a I. *pp di* **attendere** II. *agg* longawaited

attestare [at·tes·'ta:·re] *vt* **1.** (*testimoniare*) to state **2.** (*certificare*) to certify **3.** *fig* (*dimostrare*) to attest to

attestato [at·tes·'ta:·to] *m* (*certificato*) certificate; **rilasciare un ~** to issue a certificate

attestazione [at·tes·tat·'tsio:·ne] *f* **1.** (*testimonianza*) proof **2.** (*certificato*) declaration **3.** *fig* (*dimostrazione*) demonstration

attico ['at·ti·ko] <-ci> *m* (*appartamento*) penthouse

attiguo, -a [at·'ti:·guo] *agg* (*appartamento, stanza*) adjoining; ~ **a qc** next to sth

attillato, -a [at·til·'la:·to] *agg* (*abito*) tight

attimino [at·ti·'mi:·no] *m inf* (*breve istante*) second

attimo ['at·ti·mo] *m* moment; **in un ~** in a moment; **tra un ~** in a moment; **non ho un ~ di tempo** I don't have a spare minute

attinente [at·ti·'nɛn·te] *agg* ~ **a qc** relating to

attinenza [at·ti·'nɛn·tsa] *f* (*connessione*) connection

attingere [at·'tin·dʒe·re] <irr> *vt* **1.** (*acqua*) to draw **2.** *fig* (*informazioni, dati*) to obtain; FIN (*risorse finaziarie*) to draw on

attirare [at·ti·'ra:·re] I. *vt* **1.** *a. fig* (*tirare a sé*) to attract **2.** *fig* (*allettare*) to appeal to II. *vr:* **-rsi** to attract one another

attitudinale [at·ti·tu·di·'na:·le] *agg* aptitude; **test ~** aptitude test

attitudine [at·ti·'tu:·di·ne] *f* (*capacità*) aptitude; **l'~ a qc** a tendency toward sth; **l'~ per qc** aptitude for sth

attivare [at·ti·'va:·re] *vt* **1.** (*mettere in azione: motore di ricerca, leva*) to start **2.** *a.* CHEM, PHYS (*mettere in funzione: servizio, telefono, abbonamento*) to activate

attivazione [at·ti·vat·'tsio:·ne] *f* **1.** (*messa in azione: di meccanismo*) starting **2.** *a.* CHEM, PHYS (*di servizio, telefono*) activation

attivismo [at·ti·'viz·mo] *m* activism

attivista [at·ti·'vis·ta] <-i, -e> *mf* activist

attività [at·ti·vi·'ta] <-> *f* **1.** (*operosità*) activeness **2.** (*lavoro*) business; ~ **primaria** agriculture; ~ **secondaria** industry; ~ **terziaria** commerce **3.** occupazione; ~ **sportiva** sporting activity **4.** *pl* COM asset **5.** (*funzionamento, azione*) **essere in ~** to be in operation **6.** GEOL **in ~** active

attivo [at·'ti:·vo] *m* 1. COM assets *pl;* **essere in** ~ to be profitable 2. LING active 3. (*loc*) **avere al proprio** ~ to have to one's credit

attivo, -a *agg* 1. (*vita, mente, lavoratore, persona*) active 2. (*determinante*) **principio** ~ active ingredient; **prendere parte -a a qc** to take an active part in sth 3. (*in funzione*) TEC in operation 4. GEO, LING active 5. COM credit

attizzare [at·tit·'tsa:·re] *vt* 1. (*fiamma, fuoco*) to fan 2. *fig* (*odio*) to stir up

atto ['at·to] *m* 1. (*gesto*) act; (*azione*) action; **essere in** ~ to be underway; **mettere in** ~ **qc** to put sth into action; **all'**~ **di** at the moment of; **nell'**~ **di** in the act of 2. PHILOS, THEAT act; ~ **unico** one-act play 3. (*documento*) document; ~ **di accusa** indictment; ~ **di matrimonio** marriage certificate; ~ **di nascita** birth certificate; ~ **giuridico** instrument 4. *pl* (*documentazione*) proceedings; **passare agli -i** *fig* to be placed on record 5. REL ~ **di fede** act of faith 6. (*loc*) **dare** ~ **di qc** to give credit for sth; **fare** ~ **di presenza** to put in an appearance; **prendere** ~ **di qc** to take note of sth; **all'**~ **pratico** in practice

atto, -a *agg* 1. (*idoneo: persona*) ~ **a qc** able to do sth 2. (*adatto: mezzo*) ~ **a qc** suitable for sth

attonito, -a [at·'tɔ:·ni·to] *agg* 1. (*sconvolto*) dumbfounded 2. (*sorpreso*) amazed

attorcigliare [at·tor·tʃiʎ·'ʎa:·re] I. *vt* to twist II. *vr:* **-rsi** to become twisted

attore, attrice [at·'to:·re] *m, f* 1. (*in spettacoli*) actor; ~ **cinematografico** movie actor; ~ **comico** comic actor 2. *fig* (*protagonista*) central figure 3. JUR plaintiff

attorniare [at·tor·'nia:·re] I. *vt* (*circondare*) to surround II. *vr* **-rsi di qc** to surround oneself with sth; **-rsi di qu** to surround oneself with sb

attorno [at·'tor·no] I. *avv* around; **guardarsi** ~ to look around II. *prep* 1. ~ **a** around; **stare** ~ **a qu** to be around sb 2. (*circa*) about

attraente [at·tra·'ɛn·te] *agg* attractive

attrarre [at·'trar·re] <irr> *vt* 1. (*tirare a sé*) to attract 2. *fig* (*allettare: proposta, idea*) to appeal

attrattiva [at·trat·'ti:·va] *f* 1. (*fascino*) attraction 2. *pl* (*cose che attraggono*) attractions

attraversamento [at·tra·ver·sa·'men·to] *m* crossing; ~ **pedonale** pedestrian crossing

attraversare [at·tra·ver·'sa:·re] *vt* 1. (*passare attraverso*) to cross; ~ **la strada** to cross the road; ~ **il confine** to cross the border 2. *fig* (*trascorrere: periodo*) to go through

attraverso [at·tra·'ver·so] *prep* 1. (*da parte a parte*) across 2. (*mediante*) through

attrazione [at·trat·'tsio:·ne] *f* attraction; **provare** ~ **per qu** to be attracted to sb

attrezzare [at·tret·'tsa:·re] I. *vt* to fit out; ~ **qc** (**con qc**) to fit sth out with sth II. *vr:* **-rsi** to equip oneself

attrezzato, -a [at·tret·'tsa:·to] *agg* equipped; ~ **con qc** equipped with sth; **verde** ~ green spaces, *with facilities*

attrezzatura [at·tret·tsa·'tu:·ra] *f* 1. equipment; **-e sportive** sporting facilities 2. NAUT rigging

attrezzo [at·'tret·tso] *m* tool

attribuire [at·tri·bu·'i:·re] <attribuisco> I. *vt* 1. (*assegnare*) ~ **qc a qu** to award sth to sb 2. (*ascrivere*) to give; ~ **qc a qu/qc** to give sth to sb/sth II. *vr:* **-rsi** to claim

attributo [at·tri·'bu:·to] *m a.* LING attribute

attribuzione [at·tri·but·'tsio:·ne] *f* 1. (*assegnazione*) award 2. *pl* (*mansioni, funzioni*) duties

attrice *f v.* **attore**

attrito [at·'tri:·to] *m a. fig* PHYS (*contrasto*) friction

attuabile [at·tu·'a:·bi·le] *agg* feasible

attuale [at·tu·'a:·le] *agg* 1. (*odierno*) present 2. (*presente, tuttora valido*) current

attualità [at·tua·li·'ta] <-> *f* 1. (*modernità*) topicality; **tornare di** ~ to come to the fore again 2. (*avvenimento*) current affairs; **settimanale/programma di** ~ current affairs magazine/program

attuare [at·tu·'a:·re] I. *vt* to carry out II. *vr:* **-rsi** (*realizzarsi*) to be carried out

attuazione [at·tu·at·'tsio:·ne] *f* execution

attutire [at·tu·'ti:·re] <attutisco> *vt* (*dolore*) to ease; (*rumore*) to deaden; (*colpo*) to soften

audace [au·'da:·tʃe] *agg* 1. (*coraggioso*) daring 2. (*arrischiato: impresa, decisione*) bold 3. (*provocante: scollatura*) plunging

audacia [au·'da:·tʃa] <-cie> *f* 1. (*coraggio*) daring 2. (*atto arrischiato*) daring act 3. (*insolenza*) impudence

audience ['ɔ:·djens] <- *o* audiences> *f* audience, *for a TV show*

audio ['a:u·dio] <-> *m* sound

audiocassetta [au·dio·kas·'set·ta] *f* cassette

audiofrequenza [au·dio·fre·'kuɛn·tsa] *f* frequency

audioleso, -a [au·dio·'le:·zo] *agg* hearing-impaired

audiovisivo, -a [au·dio·vi·'zi:·vo] *agg* audiovisual

audiovisuale [au·dio·vi·zu·'a:·le] *agg* audiovisual

AUDITEL *m acro di* **AUD**Ience **TEL**evisiva AUDITEL, *system for monitoring the size of TV audiences;* **indice di ascolto** ~ ratings *pl*

auditivo, -a [au·di·'ti:·vo] *agg* hearing

auditorio [au·di·'tɔ:·rio] <-i> *m* auditorium

audizione [au·dit·'tsio:·ne] *f* 1. (*provino: di cantante, musicista*) audition 2. JUR (*di testimoni*) hearing

auge ['a:u·dʒe] *f fig* top; **essere in** ~ to be at the top

augurale [au·gu·'ra:·le] *agg* **cartolina** ~ greeting card

augurare [au·gu·'ra:·re] I. *vt* to wish; ~ **buon viaggio** to wish sb a good trip II. *vi* to wish III. *vr:* **-rsi** to hope

augurio [au·'gu:·rio] <-i> *m* 1. (*voto di felicità, benessere*) greeting; **fare** [*o* **porgere**] **gli -i a**

qu to give sb one's best wishes; **tanti -i di buon compleanno!** happy birthday! **2.** (*presagio*) omen; **essere di buon ~** to be a good omen

aula ['aːu·la] *f* **1.** (*di tribunale*) courtroom; (*di parlamento*) chamber **2.** (*di scuola*) classroom; (*di università*) lecture hall

aumentare [au·'men·'taː·re] **I.** *vt avere a. fig* to increase **II.** *vi essere* **1.** (*numero, prezzi, salari*) to rise **2.** (*quantità*) to increase; **~ di peso** to put on weight **3.** *inf* (*diventare più caro*) to go up

aumento [au·'men·to] *m* **1.** (*crescita, incremento*) increase; **~ di peso** weight gain; **~ salariale** raise; **~ di temperatura** rise in temperature; **essere in ~** to be going up **2.** (*rincaro*) increase in price

aureo, -a ['aːu·reo] *agg* **1.** (*d'oro*) gold **2.** (*colore, periodo*) golden

aureola [au·'rɛː·o·la] *f* REL halo

auricolare [au·ri·ko·'laː·re] **I.** *agg* MED ear; **padiglione ~** outer ear **II.** *m* earphone

aurora [au·'rɔː·ra] *f a. fig* dawn; **~ australe** Southern Lights; **~ boreale** Northern Lights; **~ polare** aurora

ausiliare [au·zi·'liaː·re] **I.** *agg* auxiliary **II.** *m* LING auxiliary **III.** *mf* auxiliary

ausiliario, -a [au·zi·'liaː·rio] <-i, -ie> **I.** *agg a.* MIL auxiliary **II.** *m, f* auxiliary

auspicare [au·spi·'kaː·re] *vt avere* to hope for

auspicio [aus·'piː·tʃo] <-ci> *m* **1.** (*pronostico*) omen; **essere di buon ~** to be a good omen **2.** (*desiderio*) hope

austerità [aus·te·ri·'ta] <-> *f a.* COM austerity; **misure di ~** austerity measures

austero, -a [aus·'tɛː·ro] *agg* **1.** (*rigido*) strict **2.** (*senza superfluità*) austere

australe [aus·'traː·le] *agg* southern

Australia [aus·'traː·lia] *f* Australia

australiano, -a [aus·tra·'lia··no] **I.** *agg* Australian **II.** *m, f* Australian

Austria ['aːus·tria] *f* Austria

austriaco, -a [aus·'triːa·ko] <-ci, -che> **I.** *agg* Austrian **II.** *m, f* Austrian

autarchia [au·tar·'kiː·a] <-chie> *f* autonomy

autarchico, -a [au·'tar·ki·ko] <-ci, -che> *agg* **1.** COM self-sufficient **2.** JUR autonomous

aut aut ['aːut 'aːut] <-> *m* ultimatum

autentica [au·'tɛn·ti·ka] <-che> *f* authentication

autenticare [au·ten·ti·'kaː·re] *vt* JUR, ADM to authenticate

autenticità [au·ten·ti·tʃi·'ta] <-> *f* **1.** (*di documento, firma, opera d'arte*) authenticity **2.** (*veridicità: di parole, risposte, intenzioni*) truthfulness

autentico, -a [au·'tɛn·ti·ko] <-ci, -che> *agg* **1.** (*firma, documento, mobile, opera d'arte*) genuine **2.** (*fatto, notizia*) true **3.** (*genuino, puro: sentimento*) sincere

autismo [au·'tiz·mo] *m* PSYCH autism

autista [au·'tis·ta] <-i, -e> **I.** *mf* **1.** (*conducente*) driver **2.** PSYCH person with autism

II. *agg* PSYCH autistic

autistico, -a [au·'tis·ti·ko] <-ci, -che> *agg* autistic

auto ['aːu·to] <-> *f* car; **~ civetta** unmarked car; **~ d'epoca** vintage car; **~ pubblica** taxi

autoabbronzante [au·to·ab·bron·'dzan·te] **I.** *agg* self-tanning **II.** *m* self-tanning cream

autoaccensione [au·to·at·tʃen·'sio:·ne] *f* MOT autoignition

autoaccessorio [au·to·at·tʃes·'sɔː·rio] *m* MOT car accessory

autoadesivo [au·to·ade·'ziː·vo] *m* sticker

autoadesivo, -a *agg* sticky

autoambulanza [au·to·am·bu·'lan·tsa] *f* ambulance

autoapprendimento [au·to·ap·pren·di·'men·to] *m* **1.** COMPUT **scanner con funzione di ~** scanner with a self-learning function; **programma con la funzione di ~** self-learning program **2.** (*senza insegnante*) self study

autobiografia [au·to·bi·o·gra·'fiː·a] *f* autobiography

autobiografico, -a [au·to·bi·o·'graː·fi·ko] <-ci, -che> *agg* autobiographical

autoblinda, autoblindata [au·to·'blin·da, au·to·blin·'daː·ta] *f* armored car

autoblindato, -a [au·to·blin·'daː·to] *agg* armored

autobloccante [au·to·blok·'kan·te] *agg* TEC self-locking

autobomba [au·to·'bom·ba] <-> *f* car bomb

autobotte [au·to·'bot·te] *f* (*per trasporto liquidi*) tanker

autobus ['aːu·to·bus] <-> *m* bus

autocaravan [au·to·'kaː·ra·van] <-> *m o f* camper

autocarro [au·to·'kar·ro] *m* truck

autocensura [au·to·tʃen·'suː·ra] *f* self-censorship

autocertificazione [au·to·tʃer·ti·fi·kat·'tsio:·ne] *f* self-certification

autocisterna [au·to·tʃis·'tɛr·na] *f* tanker

autocitarsi [au·to·tʃi·'tar·si] *vr* to quote oneself

autoclave [au·to·'klaː·ve] *f* autoclave

autocolonna [au·to·ko·'lon·na] *f* convoy

autocommiserarsi [au·to·kom·mi·ze·'rar·si] *vr* to feel sorry for oneself

autocompiacimento [au·to·kom·pia·tʃi·'men·to] *m* self-satisfaction

autoconcessionario [au·to·kon·tʃes·sio·'naː·rio] <-ri> *m* car dealership

autocontrollo [au·to·kon·'trɔl·lo] *m* self-control

autoconvocazione [au·to·kon·vo·kat·'tsio:·ne] *f* POL unofficial action, *by workers or a labor union*

autoconvoglio [au·to·kon·'vɔʎ·ʎo] *m* convoy

autocoscienza [au·to·koʃ·'ʃen·tsa] *f* PHILOS self-awareness; **gruppo di ~** encounter group

autocritica [au·to·'kriː·ti·ka] *f* self-criticism

autocritico, -a [au·to·'kriː·ti·ko] <-ci, -che> *agg* self-critical

autocross [au·to·'krɔs] <-> *m* autocross

autoctono, -a [au·'tɔk·to·no] *m*, *f* native

autodefinirsi [au·to·de·fi·'nir·si] <mi autodefinisco> *vr* to proclaim oneself; ~ **un genio** *iron* to proclaim oneself a genius

autodemolitore [au·to·de·mo·li·'to:·re] *m* wrecker

autodenuncia [au·to·de·'nun·tʃa] <-ce *o* -cie> *f* **1.** (*di errori*) admission **2.** JUR self-accusation

autodeterminazione [au·to·de·ter·mi·nat·'tsio:·ne] *f* self-determination

autodidatta [au·to·di·'dat·ta] <-i , -e> *mf* autodidact

autodidattico, -a [au·to·di·'dat·ti·ko] <-ci, -che> *agg* self-study

autodifesa [au·to·di·'fe:·sa] *f* self-defense

autodisciplina [au·to·diʃ·ʃi·'pli:·na] *f* self-discipline

autodistruggersi [au·to·dis·'trud·dʒer·si] <irr> *vr* to destroy oneself

autodistruzione [au·to·dis·trut·'tsio:·ne] *f a.* *fig* (*di missile*) self-destruction

autodromo [au·'tɔ:·dro·mo] *m* racetrack

autoescludersi [au·to·es·klu·'der·si] <irr> *vr* to exclude oneself

autoferrotranviario, -a [au·to·fer·ro·tran·'via:·rio] <-i, -ie> *agg* public transportation

autofficina [au·to·of·fi·'tʃi:·na] *f* garage

autofilotranviario, -a [au·to·fi·lo·tran·'via:·rio] <-i, -ie> *agg* road transportation

autofinanziamento [au·to·fi·nan·tsia·'men·to] *m* self financing

autofinanziarsi [au·to·fi·nan·'tsiar·si] *vr* to finance oneself

autoflagellazione [au·to·fla·dʒel·lat·'tsio:·ne] *f fig* (*autocritica*) self-criticism

autofocus [au·to·'fɔ·kus] I. <-> *m* FOTO autofocus II. <inv> *agg* **obiettivo** ~ lens with autofocus III. <-> *f* (*macchina fotografica*) camera with autofocus

autofurgone [au·to·fur·'go:·ne] *m* van

autogeno, -a [au·'tɔ:·dʒe·no] *agg* autogenic

autogestione [au·to·dʒes·'tio:·ne] *f* worker management

autogestire [au·to·dʒes·'ti:·re] <autogestisco> I. *vt* to run, *by workers themselves* II. *vr:* **-rsi** to run itself

autogestito, -a [au·to·dʒes·'ti:·re] *agg* worker-run

autogol [au·to·'gɔl] *m* own goal

autogovernarsi [au·to·go·ver·'nar·si] *vr* to govern itself

autogoverno [au·to·go·'vɛr·no] *m* (*di enti, gruppi, Stati*) self-government

autografo [au·'tɔ:·gra·fo] *m* (*firma*) autograph

autogrill® [au·to·'gril] <-> *m* service area, *on a freeway*

autogru [au·to·'gru] <-> *m o f* tow truck

autoguida [au·to·'gui:·da] *f* homing device

autoincensarsi [au·to·in·tʃen·'sar·si] *vr* to praise oneself

autoinvitarsi [au·to·in·vi·'tar·si] *vr* to invite oneself

autoironia [au·to·i·ro·'ni:·a] *f* self-mockery

autoironico, -a [au·to·i·'rɔ:·ni·ko] <-ci, -che> *agg* self-mocking

autolavaggio [au·to·la·'vad·dʒo] <-ggi> *m* carwash

autolesione [au·to·le·'zio:·ne] *f* PSYCH self harm

autolettiga [au·to·let·'ti:·ga] <-ghe> *f* ambulance

autolinea [au·to·'li:·nea] *f* bus route

automa [au·'tɔ:·ma] <-i> *m a. fig* automaton

automatico [au·to·'ma:·ti·ko] <-ci> *m* **1.** (*bottone*) snap **2.** (*fucile*) automatic

automatico, -a <-ci, -che> *agg* automatic; **pilota** ~ automatic pilot

automatismo [au·to·ma·'tiz·mo] *m* **1.** (*attrezzatura*) remote control device **2.** PSYCH automatism

automatizzare [au·to·ma·tid·'dza:·re] *vt* to automate

automazione [au·to·mat·'tsio:·ne] *f* automation

automezzo [au·to·'mɛd·dzo] *m* motor vehicle

automobile [au·to·'mɔ:·bi·le] *f* car; ~ **da corsa** racing car

automobilismo [au·to·mo·bi·'liz·mo] *m* **1.** (*delle auto*) motoring **2.** SPORT (*motor*) racing

automobilista [au·to·mo·bi·'lis·ta] <-i , -e> *mf* driver

automobilistico, -a [au·to·mo·bi·'lis·ti·ko] <-ci, -che> *agg* (*industria*) automotive; (*sport*) racing; (*incidente, traffico*) road; **patente -a** driver's license

automodellismo [au·to·mo·del·'liz·mo] *m* model making

automodellista [au·to·mo·del·'lis·ta] <-i , -e> *mf* model maker

automotrice [au·to·mo·'tri:·tʃe] *f* railcar

autonoleggiatore, -trice [au·to·no·led·dʒa·'to:·re] *m*, *f* owner [*o* manager] of a car rental company

autonoleggio [au·to·no·'led·dʒo] <-ggi> *m* car rental

autonomia [au·to·no·'mi:·a] <-ie> *f* **1.** (*indipendenza*) POL autonomy **2.** TEC range

autonomismo [au·to·no·'mis·mo] *m* autonomism

autonomo, -a [au·'tɔ:·no·mo] *agg* **1.** (*ente, regione*) autonomous **2.** (*persona, sindacato*) independent **3.** (*lavoro*) freelance

autoparco [au·to·'par·ko] <-chi> *m* parking lot

autopattuglia [au·to·pat·tuʎ·'ʎi:·a] *f* patrol car

autopilota [au·to·pi·'lɔ:·ta] *m* autopilot

autopista [au·to·'pis·ta] *f* **1.** (*per automobili*) track **2.** (*nei parchi di divertimento*) bumper car track **3.** (*giocattolo*) electric car track

autopompa [au·to·'pom·pa] *f* fire engine

autoporto [au·to·'pɔr·to] *m* (*parcheggio per camion*) truck park; ~ **doganale** truck park with customs facilities

autopsia [au·top·'si:·a] <-ie> *f* autopsy

autopulente [au·to·pu·'lɛn·te] *agg* TEC (*forno, filtro, vetro*) self-cleaning

autopullman [au·to·'pul·man] <-> *m* bus

autopunizione [au·to·pu·nit·'tsio:·ne] *f* PSYCH self-punishment

autoradio [au·to·'ra:·dio] <-> *f* 1.(*radio*) car radio 2.(*auto*) radio car

autoraduno [au·to·ra·'du:·no] *m* auto racing meeting

autore, -trice [au·'to:·re] *m, f* 1. *a.* LIT (*esecutore*) author 2.(*compositore*) composer 3.(*pittore*) painter; (*scultore*) sculptor

autoreggente [au·to·red·'dʒɛn·te] *agg* **calze -i** hold-up tights

autorete [au·to·'re:·te] *f* own goal

autoreverse [au·to·re·'vers] <-> *m* autoreverse

autorevole [au·to·'re:·vo·le] *agg* 1.(*potente: scienziato*) authoritative 2.(*competente: giudizio, parere*) definitive

autoriale [au·to·'ria:·le] *agg* (*stile, profilo, ricerca, attività*) authorial; **opera ~** authored work

autoricambio [au·to·ri·'kam·bio] <-bi> *m* car parts *pl;* **negozio di -i** car parts store

autoriflessivo, -a [au·to·rif·les·'si:·vo] *agg* PSYCH reflex

autorimessa [au·to·ri·'mes·sa] *f* garage

autorità [au·to·ri·'ta] <-> *f* 1. *a.* ADM, JUR authority 2. *pl* (*titolari di cariche*) authorities

autoritario, -a [au·to·ri·'ta:·rio] <-i, -ie> *agg* authoritarian

autoritratto [au·to·ri·'trat·to] *m* self-portrait

autorizzare [au·to·rid·'dza:·re] *vt* 1.(*permettere*) to authorize; **~ qu a fare qc** to authorize sb to do sth 2.(*giustificare*) justify

autorizzazione [au·to·rid·dzat·'tsio:·ne] *f* 1.(*permesso*) authorization 2.(*documento*) license

autosalone [au·to·sa·'lo:·ne] *m* car showroom

autoscontro [au·tos·'kon·tro] *m* bumper cars *pl*

autoscuola [au·to·'skuɔ:·la] <-> *f* driving school

autoservizio [au·to·ser·'vit·tsio] *m* (*trasporto pubblico*) bus service

autosilo [au·to·'si:·lo] *m* parking garage

autosnodato [au·toz·no·'da:·to] *m* articulated bus

autosoccorso [au·to·sok·'kor·so] *m* 1.(*veicolo*) tow truck 2.(*servizio*) towing and recovery service

autostazione [au·to·stat·'tsio:·ne] *f* 1.(*stazione di servizio*) service station 2.(*di autolinee*) bus station

autostima [au·to·'sti:·ma] *f* self-esteem

autostop [au·to·'stɔp] *m* hitchhiking; **fare (l')~** to hitchhike

autostoppista [au·to·stop·'pis·ta] <-i , -e> *mf* hitchhiker

autostrada [au·to·'stra:·da] *f* expressway; **~ a pedaggio** turnpike; **~ del Sole** *expressway linking Milan to the south of Italy*

autostradale [au·to·stra·'da:·le] *agg* (*di autostrade*) expressway; **casello ~** turnpike; **raccordo ~** access road; **svincolo ~** junction

autosufficiente [au·to·suf·fi·'tʃɛn·te] *agg* self-sufficient

autosuggestionarsi [au·to·sud·dʒes·tio·'nar·si] *vr* to get oneself into a state

autosuggestione [au·to·sud·dʒes·'tio:·ne] *f* autosuggestion

autotassazione [au·to·tas·sat·'tsio:·ne] *f* self-assessment

autotelaio [au·to·te·'la:·io] *m* chassis

autotelefono [au·to·te·'lɛ:·fo·no] *m* car phone

autotrasportatore, -trice [au·to·tras·por·ta·'to:·re] *m, f* 1.(*impresario*) hauler 2.(*camionista*) truck driver

autotrasporto [au·to·tras·'pɔr·to] *m* trucking

autotreno [au·to·'trɛ:·no] *m* tractor-trailer

autoveicolo [au·to·ve·'i:·ko·lo] *m* motor vehicle

autovelox® [au·to·'vɛ:·loks] <-> *m o f* speed trap

autovettura [au·to·vet·'tu:·ra] *f* car

autrice *f v.* **autore**

autunnale [au·tun·'na:·le] *agg* fall

autunno [au·'tun·no] *m* fall; **d'~** in fall

avallare [a·val·'la:·re] *vt* 1.(*progetto, cambiale*) to endorse 2. *fig* (*confermare: ipotesi*) to confirm

avallo [a·'val·lo] *m a. fig* (*di cambiale*) endorsement

avambraccio [a·vam·'brat·tʃo] <-cci> *m* forearm

avamposto [a·vam·'pos·to] *m* outpost

avances [a·'vãs] *fpl* **fare delle ~ a qu** to hit on sb

avancorpo [a·vaŋ·'kɔr·po] *m the projecting parts of a building*

avanguardia [a·vaŋ·'guar·dia] *f* 1. MIL vanguard 2.(*nell'arte, nella letteratura*) avant-garde; **essere all'~** *fig* to be on the cutting edge

avanguardismo [a·vaŋ·guar·'diz·mo] *m* avant-gardism

avanscoperta [a·van·sko·'pɛr·ta] *f* reconnaissance

avanti [a·'van·ti] **I.** *avv* 1.(*stato in luogo*) ahead 2.(*avvicinamento*) forward; **andare ~** to move forward; **farsi ~** to step forward; **venire ~** to come forward; **~ e indietro** backward and forward; **lasciar passare ~** to allow to go in front; **mettere le mani ~** *fig* to come clean 3.(*allontanamento*) ahead 4.(*tempo: successivamente*) **d'ora in ~** from now on; **l'orologio va ~** the watch is fast 5.(*loc*) **essere ~ negli studi** to be ahead in one's studies; **tirare ~** to manage; **tirare ~ la famiglia** to keep the family going **II.** *prep* 1.(*moto*) ahead 2.(*tempo*) before; **lo vidi ~ che partisse** I saw him before he left **III.** <inv> *agg* (*di tempo*) before; **il giorno ~** the day before **IV.** <-> *m* SPORT forward **V.** *int* 1.(*moto*) **~!** **entrate pure** come in!; **~! muovetevi** go on!

hurry up!; ~ **marsc!** MIL forward, march! **2.** (*esortazione*) come on; ~ **tutta!** NAUT full speed ahead!

avantieri, avant'ieri [a·van·'tiɛː·ri] *avv* the day before yesterday

avantreno [a·van·'trɛː·no] *m* front chassis

avanzamento [a·van·tsa·'men·to] *m* **1.** (*promozione*) promotion **2.** (*progresso*) progress; **stato di ~** (**dei lavori**) state of progress (of the work)

avanzare [a·van·'tsa·re] **I.** *vi essere* **1.** (*andare avanti*) to advance **2.** *fig* (*progredire: lavoro*) to progress **3.** (*essere promosso*) to be promoted **4.** (*sporgere in fuori*) to stick out **5.** (*rimanere come resto*) to be (left) over **6.** (*essere sovrabbondante*) to be left over **7.** *avere* MIL to advance **II.** *vt avere* **1.** (*spostare in avanti*) to move forward **2.** (*promuovere*) to promote **3.** (*presentare: proposta*) to put forward **4.** (*essere creditore*) ~ **qc** (**da qu**) to be owed sth (by sb)

avanzata [a·van·'tsa·ta] *f* MIL advance

avanzato, -a [a·van·'tsa·to] *agg* **1.** advanced **2.** (*residuo*) leftover

avanzo [a·'van·tso] *m* **1.** MATH (*resto*) remainder **2.** COM (*eccedenza*) surplus **3.** (*di cibo*) leftover; **mangiare gli -i** to eat leftovers **4.** (*di stoffa*) remnant

avaria [a·va·'riː·a] <-ie> *f* **1.** (*guasto*) breakdown **2.** NAUT damage

avariare [a·va·'ria·re] **I.** *vt* to spoil **II.** *vr:* **-rsi** to spoil

avariato, -a [a·va·'riaː·to] *agg* (*cibo, merce*) spoiled

avarizia [a·va·'rit·tsia] <-ie> *f* avarice

avaro, -a [a·'vaː·ro] **I.** *agg* **1.** (*persona*) cheap; ~ **di elogi** *fig* sparing with praise; ~ **di parole** *fig* of few words **2.** (*terreno*) poor **II.** *m, f* miser

avellinese [a·vel·li·'neː·se] **I.** *agg* from Avellino **II.** *mf* (*abitante*) person from Avellino

Avellinese area around Avellino

Avellino *f* Avellino

avem(m)aria [a·ve·m(m)a·'riː·a] <-ie> *f* Hail Mary; **sapere qc come l'~** to know sth by heart

avena [a·'veː·na] *f* oats *pl;* **fiocchi d'~** oat flakes

avere¹ [a·'veː·re] <ho, ebbi, avuto> *vt* **1.** (*possedere, tenere*) to have; **non ho soldi** I don't have any money; **ha gli occhi neri** she has dark eyes; **non ha i genitori** he doesn't have any parents; ~ **un bambino** to have a child; **ce l'aveva in mano** I had it in my hand; **ce l'hai tu la chiave?** do you have the key? **2.** (*portare*) to wear; **aveva il cappello?** was he wearing a hat? **3.** (*ricevere*) to receive; **l'ho avuto in dono** I was given it **4.** (*età*) to be; ~ **vent'anni** she's twenty **5.** (*provare*) to be; ~ **freddo** to be cold; ~ **sete** to be thirsty **6.** (*impegno*) **ho da fare** I have things to do; **abbiamo ospiti a cena** we are having people to dinner **7.** (*loc*) ~ **a che fare** [*o* **vedere**] **con**

qu to have sth to do with sb; **avercela con qu** to be angry with sb; ~ **un bambino** to have a baby; ~ **molto di qu** *fig* (*assomigliargli*) to take after sb

avere² *m* **1.** (*patrimonio*) property; **tutti i suoi -i** all his possession **2.** COM credit; **il dare e l'~** debit and credit

aviatore, -trice [a·via·'toː·re] *m, f* aviator

aviazione [a·viat·'tsioː·ne] *f* aviation; ~ **civile** civil aviation; ~ **militare** air force

avicoltura [a·vi·kol·'tuː·ra] *f* poultry farming

avidità [a·vi·di·'ta] <-> *f* avidity; **leggere con** ~ to read avidly; **mangiare con** ~ to eat hungrily; ~ **di sapere** thirst for knowledge

avido, -a ['aː·vi·do] *agg* greedy; ~ **di denaro** avaricious; ~ **di sapere** thirsty for knowledge

aviogetto [a·vio·'dʒet·to] *m* jet

aviorimessa [a·vio·ri·'mes·sa] *f* hangar

aviotrasporto [a·vio·tras·'pɔr·to] *m* air transport

avo, -a ['aː·vo] *m, f* ancestor

avocado [a·vo·'kaː·do] *m* avocado

avorio [a·'vɔː·rio] <-i> *m* **1.** (*sostanza, colore*) ivory **2.** GEOG **Costa d'Avorio** Ivory Coast

avuto [a·'vuː·to] *pp di* **avere¹**

avvalersi [av·va·'ler·si] <irr> *vr* ~ **di qc** to make use of sth

avvallamento [av·val·la·'men·to] *m* hollow

avvalorare [av·va·lo·'raː·re] *vt* to support

avvampare [av·vam·'paː·re] *vi essere* **1.** (*fiamma*) to blaze up **2.** (*arrossire per la vergogna*) to blush **3.** *fig* (*di rabbia*) to flare up

avvantaggiare [av·van·tad·'dʒaː·re] **I.** *vt* **1.** (*favorire*) to favor **2.** (*far progredire*) to benefit **II.** *vr:* **-rsi 1.** (*avvalersi con profitto*) to benefit; ~ **di qc** to benefit from sth **2.** (*guadagnar tempo*) to get ahead **3.** (*prevalere*) **-rsi su qu** to get ahead of sb

avvantaggiato, -a [av·van·tad·'dʒa·to] *agg* **partire -i** to have a head start

avvedersi [av·ve·'der·si] <irr> *vr* ~ **di qc** to notice sth

avvedutezza [av·ve·du·'tet·tsa] *f* shrewdness

avveduto, -a [av·ve·'duː·to] *agg* shrewd

avvelenamento [av·ve·le·na·'men·to] *m* poisoning

avvelenare [av·ve·le·'naː·re] **I.** *vt* to poison **II.** *vr:* **-rsi 1.** (*con veleno*) to take poison **2.** *fig* (*amareggiarsi*) to become bitter

avvenente [av·ve·'nɛn·te] *agg* attractive

avvenenza [av·ve·'nɛn·tsa] *f* attractiveness

avvenimento [av·ve·ni·'men·to] *m* event

avvenire¹ [av·ve·'niː·re] **I.** <-> *m* future **II.** <inv> *agg* future

avvenire² <irr> *vi essere* to become; **che è avvenuto di lui?** what became of him?

avventare [av·ven·'taː·re] **I.** *vt* (*scagliare addosso*) to hurl **II.** *vr* **-rsi** (**su qu/qc**) to hurl oneself on sth

avventatezza [av·ven·ta·'tet·tsa] *f* recklessness

avventato, -a [av·ven·'taː·to] *agg* **1.** (*giudizio, atto*) rash **2.** (*persona*) reckless

avventizio, **-a** [av·ven·'tit·tsio] <-i, -ie>
I. *agg* 1. (*provvisorio: personale*) ...: temporary
2. (*occasionale: lavoro*) occasional II. *m*, *f* occasional laborer

avvento [av·'vɛn·to] *m* 1. (*venuta*) coming
2. REL l' Avvento Advent

avventore, **-a** [av·ven·'to:·re] *m*, *f* regular

avventura [av·ven·'tu:·ra] *f* adventure

avventurarsi [av·ven·tu·'ra:r·si] *vr* a. fig
(*esporsi a rischi*) to venture; ~ **in qc** to venture into sth; ~ **a fare qc** to venture to do sth

avventuriero, **-a** [av·ven·tu·'riɛ:·ro] *m*, *f* adventurer

avventuroso, **-a** [av·ven·tu·'ro:·so] *agg*
1. (*storia, viaggio, persona*) adventurous 2. fig
(*rischioso: impresa*) risky

avvenuto [av·ve·'nu:·to] *pp di* **avvenire²**

avverare [av·ve·'ra:·re] I. *vt* to fulfill II. *vr:* **-rsi** to come true

avverbiale [av·ver·'bia:·le] *agg* adverbial

avverbio [av·'vɛr·bio] <-i> *m* adverb

avversare [av·ver·'sa:·re] *vt* to oppose

avversario, **-a** [av·ver·'sa:·rio] <-i, -ie> I. *agg* rival II. *m*, *f* opponent; MIL (*nemico*) adversary

avversione [av·ver·'sio:·ne] *f* aversion; **avere un'~ per qu/qc** to loathe sb/sth

avversità [av·ver·si·'ta] <-> *f* 1. (*ostilità*) loathing 2. *pl* (*disgrazia*) adversities

avverso, **-a** *agg* (*sorte, fortuna, condizioni atmosferiche*) adverse

avvertenza [av·ver·'tɛn·tsa] *f* 1. (*cautela*) good sense; **avere l'~ di fare qc** to take care to do sth 2. (*avviso*) warning 3. *pl* (*istruzioni per l'uso*) instructions

avvertimento [av·ver·ti·'men·to] *m* warning

avvertire [av·ver·'ti:·re] *vt* 1. (*avvisare*) ~ **qu** (**di qc**) to let sb know (about sth) 2. (*ammonire, minacciare*) to warn 3. (*percepire: freddo, stanchezza*) to feel

avvezzo, **-a** [av·'vet·tso] *agg* accustomed; **essere ~ a qc** to be accustomed to sth

avviamento [av·via·'men·to] *m* 1. (*formazione*) training; **l'~ a qc** training for sth 2. COM (*di negozio*) opening 3. TEC (*messa in moto*) starting; **motorino d'~** starter

avviare [av·vi·'a:·re] I. *vt* 1. fig (*indirizzare*) ~ **qu a qc** to direct sb toward sth 2. TEC (*mettere in moto*) to start 3. (*dare inizio a: attività*) to start up II. *vr:* **-rsi** 1. (*dirigersi, incamminarsi*) to set off 2. fig (*stare per*) **-rsi a fare qc** to be about to do sth

avvicendamento [av·vi·tʃen·da·'men·to] *m*
1. (*di personale*) turnover; ~ **alla presidenza** alternation of the presidency; ~ **ai comandi** alternation of leadership 2. (*di colture*) rotation

avvicendare [av·vi·tʃen·'da:·re] I. *vt* to alternate II. *vr:* **-rsi** to alternate

avvicinamento [av·vi·tʃi·na·'men·to] *m* MIL, AERO approach; **marcia di ~** approach march; **rotta di ~** approach route

avvicinare [av·vi·tʃi·'na:·re] I. *vt* 1. (*mettere vicino*) ~ **qc a qu/qc** to bring sth close to sb/sth 2. (*entrare in rapporti con qu*) ~ **qu** to ap-

proach sb II. *vr:* **-rsi** 1. (*farsi vicino*) **-rsi** (**a qu/qc**) to come closer (to ab/sth); **l'inverno si avvicina** winter is coming 2. (*essere simile*) to resemble

avvilente [av·vi·'lɛn·te] *agg* (*degradante*) degrading; (*scoraggiante*) disheartening

avvilire [av·vi·'li:·re] <avvilisco> I. *vt* (*scoraggiare*) to discourage II. *vr:* **-rsi** (*perdersi d'animo*) to become discouraged

avvilito, **-a** [av·vi·'li:·to] *agg* (*scoraggiato*) discouraged

avviluppare [av·vi·lup·'pa:·re] I. *vt* 1. (*avvolgere*) to wrap 2. (*aggrovigliare*) to entangle II. *vr:* **-rsi** 1. (*avvolgersi*) to wrap oneself up 2. (*aggrovigliarsi*) to become tangled

avvinazzato, **-a** [av·vi·nat·'tsa:·to] I. *agg* drunk II. *m*, *f* drunkard

avvincente [av·vin·'tʃɛn·te] *agg* (*racconto, spettacolo*) gripping

avvincere [av·'vin·tʃe·re] <irr> *vt* fig (*racconto, spettacolo*) to captivate

avvinghiare [av·viŋ·'gia:·re] I. *vt* to clutch II. *vr* **-rsi a qu/qc** to cling to sb/sth

avvio [av·'vi:·o] <-ii> *m* 1. (*inizio*) start; **dare** (**l'**)**~ a qc** to start sth 2. (*computer*) start

avvisaglia [av·vi·'zaʎ·ʎa] <-glie> *fpl* (*primi sintomi*) symptoms

avvisare [av·vi·'za:·re] *vt* 1. (*informare*) to inform 2. (*ammonire*) to warn

avvisatore [av·vi·za·'to:·re] *m* (*dispositivo*) alarm; ~ **acustico** horn; ~ **d'incendio** fire alarm

avviso [av·'vi:·zo] *m* 1. *a.* JUR (*informazione, notizia, cartello*) notice; **dare ~** to give notice; ~ **di sfratto** eviction order 2. (*sul giornale*) advertisement 3. (*consiglio, ammonimento*) warning; **metter qu sull'~** to put sb on their guard 4. (*parere, opinione*) opinion; **a mio ~** in my opinion

avvistare [av·vis·'ta:·re] *vt* to sight

avvitare [av·vi·'ta:·re] I. *vt* to screw II. *vr:* **-rsi** AERO to go into a spin

avvitatrice [av·vi·ta·'tri:·tʃe] *f* (electric) screwdriver

avviticchiare [av·vi·tik·'kia:·re] I. *vt* to twine II. *vr* **-rsi** (**a qc**) to twist (around sth)

avvizzire [av·vi·'tsi:·re] <avvizzisco> I. *vi essere* to wither II. *vt avere* to wither

avvocato, **-essa** [av·vo·'ka:·to] *m*, *f* 1. (*professionista*) lawyer; ~ **difensore** defense lawyer; ~ **dello Stato** prosecutor; ~ **penale** criminal lawyer; **parlare come un ~** fig, inf to be very persuasive 2. fig (*patrocinatore*) advocate; ~ **del diavolo** devil's advocate

avvolgere [av·'vɔl·dʒe·re] <irr> I. *vt* ~ **qu/qc** (*matassa, filo, cassetta*) to wind; ~ **qc attorno a qu/qc** to wind sth around sb/sth II. *vr:* **-rsi** to wind

avvolgibile [av·vol·'dʒi:·bi·le] I. *m* roller shutter II. *agg* (*persiana*) roller

avvolgitore, **-trice** *agg* (*dispositivo*) winding

avvolsi *1. pers sing pass rem di* **avvolgere**

avvolto *pp di* **avvolgere**

avvoltoio [av·vol·'to:·io] <-oi> *m a. fig* ZOO vulture

ayatollah [a·ja·tol·'la] <-> *m* ayatollah

azalea [ad·dza·'lε:·a] *f* azalea

azienda [ad·'dziεn·da] *f* firm

aziendale [ad·dzien·'da:·le] *agg* business; **economia** ~ UNIV business studies

aziendalizzare [ad·dzien·da·kid·'dza:·re] *vt* to privatize

azionabile [at·tsio·'na:·bi·le] *agg* **1.** (*macchina*) that can be operated **2.** JUR legally enforceable

azionamento [at·tsio·na·'men·to] *m* (*di macchina, pompa*) activation

azionare [at·tsio·'na:·re] *vt* (*leva, interruttore, tasto*) to activate

azionario, -a [at·tsio·'na:·rio] <-i, -ie> *agg* share; **mercato** ~ stock market

azionatore, -trice [at·tsio·na·'to:·re] I. *m, f* **1.** (*operatore*) operator **2.** (*dispositivo*) activation mechanism II. *agg* activation; **dispositivo** ~ activation mechanism

azione [at·'tsio:·ne] *f* **1.** (*l'agire, operato, effetto*) action; **passare all'**~ to go into action; **avere il coraggio delle proprie -i** to have the courage of one's convictions; **l'**~ **erosiva dell'acqua** the eroding action of water; **l'**~ **del vento sulle vele** the action of wind on sails; **l'**~ **delle piante utili alla salute** the action of plants that are beneficial to health **2.** TEC (*funzionamento*) working; **essere in** ~ to be working; **entrare in** ~ to start working **3.** ~ **dimostrativa** demonstration **4.** (*di romanzo, film*) story **5.** JUR action; **intraprendere un'**~ **legale contro qu** to start legal action against sb **6.** MIL operation **7.** FIN share **8.** FILM ~! action!

azionista [at·tsio·'nis·ta] <-i , -e> *mf* shareholder; **grande/piccolo** ~ major/minor shareholder

azoto [ad·'dzɔ:·to] *m* nitrogen

azzannare [at·tsan·'na:·re] *vt* to bite

azzardare [ad·dzar·'da:·re] I. *vt* (*arrischiare*) to take a risk II. *vr:* -**rsi** to dare; **non ti** ~ **a rispondermi così!** don't you dare speak to me like that!

azzardato, -a [ad·dzar·'da:·to] *agg* **1.** (*imprudente*) rash; **mossa -a** rash move; **fare un sorpasso** ~ to pass dangerously **2.** (*avventato: paragone, scelta*) daring **3.** (*rischioso*) risky; **investimento** ~ risky investment

azzardo [ad·'dzar·do] *m* **1.** (*rischio*) risk **2.** (*atto sconsiderato, temerario*) gamble; **giocatore d'**~ gambler

azzardoso, -a [ad·dzar·'do:·so] *agg* **1.** (*persona*) rash **2.** (*impresa, metodo*) risky

azzeccagarbugli [at·tsek·ka·gar·'buʎ·ʎi] <-> *m pej* quibbler

azzeccare [at·tsek·'ka:·re] *vt* **1.** (*colpire nel segno*) to hit **2.** *fig* (*indovinare*) to guess right

azzeccato, -a [at·tsek·'ka:·to] *agg* perfect; (*risposta*) correct

azzerare *vt* to reset (to zero)

azzoppare [at·tsop·'pa:·re] I. *vt* to lame II. *vr:* -**rsi** to become lame

Azzorre [ad·'dzɔr·re] *fpl* Azores

azzuffarsi [at·tsuf·'far·si] *vr* to fight

azzurro [ad·'dzur·ro] *m* **1.** (*colore*) blue **2.** SPORT **gli -i** the Italian national team

azzurro, -a *agg* blue; **principe** ~ Prince Charming

azzurrognolo, -a [ad·dzur·'roɲ·ɲo·lo] *agg* bluish

B

B, b [bi] <-> *f* B, b; ~ **come Bologna** B as in Boy

babbeo, -a [bab·'bε:·o] I. *agg* stupid II. *m, f* fool

babbo ['bab·bo] *m inf* dad; ~ **Natale** Santa Claus

babbuccia [bab·'but·tʃa] <-cce> *f* slipper

babbuino, -a [bab·bu·'i:·no] *m, f* **1.** ZOO baboon **2.** *fig* (*persona sciocca*) idiot

babele [ba·'bε:·le] *f* mess

Babele [ba·'bε:·le] *f* Babel

babordo [ba·'bor·do] *m* port side; **a** ~ to port

baby ['bei·bi] I. <·> *m* baby II. <inv> *agg* children's

baby-banda ['bε·bi·'ban·da] *f* teen gang

baby-doll ['bei·bi·dɔl] <-> *m* babydoll

baby-gang ['bε·bi·'gεng] <-> *f v.* **teen gang**

baby-pensionato, -a *m, f* early retiree

baby-sitter ['bei·bi·'si·tə] <-> *mf* babysitter

babysitteraggio [ba·bi·sit·te·'rad·dʒo] <-ggi> *m* babysitting; **servizio di** ~ daycare

bacato, -a [ba·'ka:·to] *agg* **1.** (*frutta*) rotten **2.** *fig, pej* (*corrotto*) crooked **3.** (*file, programma, computer*) COMPUT corrupt

bacca ['bak·ka] <-cche> *f* berry

baccalà [bak·ka·'la] <-> *m* CULIN dried cod

baccano [bak·'ka:·no] *m* racket; **fare un** ~ **infernale** to make a dreadful racket

bacchetta [bak·'ket·ta] *f* (*asticciola*) stick; (*di direttore d'orchestra*) baton; (*per tamburo*) drumstick; (*di mago, fata*) wand; ~ **magica** magic wand; **comandare qu a** ~ to rule sb with a rod of iron

bacheca [ba·'kε:·ka] <-che> *f* **1.** (*per affissione*) notice board **2.** (*di museo*) display case

bachelite [ba·ke·'li:·te] *f* bakelite®

baciamano [ba·tʃa·'ma:·no] <- o -i> *m* **fare il** ~ **a qu** to kiss sb's hand

baciare [ba·'tʃa:·re] I. *vt* to kiss II. *vr:* -**rsi** to kiss each other

bacillo [ba·'tʃil·lo] *m* germ

bacinella [ba·tʃi·'nεl·la] *f* bowl

bacino [ba·'tʃi:·no] *m* **1.** (*recipiente*) basin **2.** ANAT pelvis **3.** MIN (*giacimento*) bed **4.** GEOG basin; ~ **idrografico** catchment basin; ~ **idroe-**

lettrico hydroelectric basin **5.** NAUT dock; **~ di carenaggio** dry dock

bacio ['ba:·tʃo] <-ci> *m* kiss; **~ di Giuda** Judas kiss; **al ~** *fig, inf* fab

background ['bæk·graund] <-> *m* background

backup ['bæk·ʌp] <-> *m* COMPUT backup; **fare un ~ dei dati** to backup data

baco ['ba:·ko] <-chi> *m* ZOO, COMPUT (*verme*) worm; **~ da seta** silk worm

bacon ['bei·kən] <-> *m* bacon

bacucco, -a [ba·'kuk·ko] <-cchi, -cche> *agg inf* senile

bada ['ba:·da] *f* **tenere a ~ qu** to keep sb at bay; (*bambino*) to keep an eye on sb

badante [ba·'dan·te] *mf* (*per malati, anziani*) carer

badare [ba·'da:·re] *vi* **1.** (*accudire*) **~ a qu/qc** to look after sb/sth; **~ alla casa/ai bambini** to look after the house/the children **2.** (*stare attento*) to mind; **bada a come ti comporti** mind how you behave!; **bada a quello che fai!** mind what you're doing! **3.** (*dedicarsi*) to think of; **~ solo a divertirsi** to think only of enjoying oneself; **bada ai fatti tuoi!** mind your own business! **4.** (*dare importanza*) to mind; **non ~ a spese** to spare no expense

badessa [ba·'des·sa] *f* abbess

badge [bædʒ] <- *o* badges> *m* badge; **~ magnetico** swipe card

badia [ba·'di:·a] <-ie> *f* abbey

badile [ba·'di:·le] *m* shovel

baffo ['baf·fo] *m* (*di persona*) moustache; (*di animale*) whisker; **ridere sotto i -i** to snigger; **una cosa da leccarsi i -i** a mouthwatering thing; **me ne faccio un ~ di ...** *vulg* I don't give a damn about ...

baffuto, -a [baf·'fu:·to] *agg* (*..: uomo, donna*) with a moustache

bagagliaio [ba·gaʎ·'ʎa:·io] <-ai> *m* **1.** MOT (*di auto*) trunk **2.** FERR (*carrozza ferroviaria*) baggage car

bagaglio [ba·'gaʎ·ʎo] <-gli> *m* **1.** (*valigie*) luggage; **assicurazione (dei) -gli** luggage insurance; **deposito -gli** luggage room; **disfare i -gli** to unpack; **fare i -gli** to pack; **~ a mano** carryon luggage; **partire con armi e -gli** to pack up and leave **2.** *fig* (*formazione*) background; **~ culturale** cultural background

bagattella [ba·gat·'tɛl·la] *f* **1.** (*bazzecola*) trifle **2.** MUS bagatelle

baggianata [bad·dʒa·'na:·ta] *f* *pej, inf* nonsense; **non dire -e** don't talk nonsense

bagliore [baʎ·'ʎo:·re] *m* **1.** (*di lampo*) flash; (*di faro*) glare; (*di fuoco, tramonto, lampada*) glow **2.** *fig* (*manifestazione*) sign

bagnante [baɲ·'ɲan·te] *mf* swimmer

bagnare [baɲ·'ɲa:·re] I. *vt* **1.** (*con liquido*) to wet **2.** (*annaffiare: erba, fiori*) to water **3.** (*inumidire: fronte, labbra*) to moisten **4.** (*fiume*) to flow through; (*mare*) to wash; **Roma è bagnata dal Tevere** the Tiber flows through Rome II. *vr:* **-rsi 1.** (*fare il bagno*) to go for a

swim **2.** (*con pioggia, acqua*) to get soaked

bagnato [baɲ·'ɲa:·to] *m* wet surface

bagnato, -a *agg* **1.** (*con liquido*) wet; **~ fradicio** soaked **2.** (*umido*) damp

bagnino, -a [baɲ·'ɲi:·no] *m, f* lifeguard

bagno ['baɲ·ɲo] *m* **1.** (*stanza*) bathroom; **andare in ~** to go to the bathroom; **-i pubblici** public baths; **~ turco** Turkish bath **2.** (*immersione in acqua*) bathing; **costume da ~** (*da donna*) swimming costume; (*da uomo*) trunks *pl;* **fare il ~** (*nella vasca*) to have a bath; (*in piscina, nel mare*) to go swimming; **essere in un ~ di sudore** to be drenched in sweat **3.** (*lavaggio*) **mettere qc a ~** to leave sth to soak **4.** FOTO, CHEM bath **5.** *pl* (*stazione termale*) springs; (*stabilimento balneare*) lido; **fare la cura dei -i** to take the waters

bagnomaria [baɲ·ɲo·ma·'ri:·a] <-> *m* **a ~** in a bain-marie

bagnoschiuma [baɲ·ɲo·'ʃu:·ma] <-> *m* bubble bath

baia ['ba:·ia] <-aie> *f* GEOG bay

baionetta [ba·io·'net·ta] *f* bayonet

baita ['ba:·i·ta] *f* mountain hut

balaustra [ba·la·'us·tra] *f* balustrade

balbettare [bal·bet·'ta:·re] I. *vi* **1.** (*tartagliare*) to stammer **2.** (*bambino*) to gibber II. *vt* **1.** (*scusa*) to mumble **2.** (*lingua straniera*) to not be very fluent in; **balbetta un po' di inglese** he [*o* she]'s not very fluent in English

balbettio [bal·bet·'ti:·o] <-ii> *m* **1.** stammering **2.** (*bambini*) gibbering

balbuzie [bal·'but·tsi·e] <-> *f* stammer; **essere affetto da ~** to have a stammer

balbuziente [bal·but·'tsi·ɛn·te] I. *agg* stammering II. *mf* stammerer

Balcani [bal·'ka:·ni] *mpl* Balkans; **i ~** the Balkans; **nei ~** in the Balkans

balcanico, -a [bal·'ka:·ni·ko] <-ci, -che> *agg* (*popolazione, paese*) Balkan; **la penisola -a** the Balkan peninsula

balconata [bal·ko·'na:·ta] *f* balcony

balcone [bal·'ko:·ne] *m* balcony

baldacchino [bal·dak·'ki:·no] *m* canopy; **letto a ~** four-poster bed

baldanzoso, -a [bal·dan·'tso:·so] *agg* **1.** (*giovane, ragazza*) cocky **2.** (*passo, aria*) confident

baldoria [bal·'dɔ:·ria] <-ie> *f* fun; **fare ~** to have fun

balena [ba·'le:·na] *f* **1.** ZOO whale **2.** *fig, scherz* (*donna grassa*) lump of lard

balenare [ba·le·'na:·re] *vi* **essere 1.** METEO to lighten **2.** (*apparire improvvisamente*) to flash; **mi è balenata un'idea** I've just had an idea

baleno [ba·'le:·no] *m* **1.** (*lampo*) flash of lightning **2.** (*attimo*) **in un ~** *fig* in a flash

balera [ba·'lɛ:·ra] *f* dance hall

balia¹ ['ba:·lia] <-ie> *f* (*donna*) wet nurse; **~ asciutta** child minder

balia² [ba·'li:·a] *f* (*mercè*) mercy; **essere in ~ di qu/qc** to be at the mercy of sb/sth

balla ['bal·la] *f* **1.** *inf* (*frottola*) lie; **non raccontare -e!** don't tell lies! **2.** COM (*di cotone*)

bale
ballabile [bal·'la:·bi·le] I. *agg* (*musica*) good for dancing II. *m* dance music
ballare [bal·'la:·re] I. *vt* (*tango, valzer*) to dance II. *vi* 1. MUS (*danzare*) to dance; ~ **dalla** [*o* **per la**] **gioia** to dance for joy 2. NAUT (*barca, nave*) to toss 3. (*abiti*) ~ **addosso a qu** (*abito, cappotto*) to be too big for sb
ballata [bal·'la:·ta] *f* ballad
ballerina [bal·le·'ri:·na] *f* 1. (*scarpa*) ballet shoe 2. ZOO wagtail
ballerino, -a [bal·le·'ri:·no] I. *m, f* dancer; **prima -a** prima ballerina II. *agg* (*mutevole*) changeable; **terre -e** earthquake zones
balletto [bal·'let·to] *m* ballet
ballo ['bal·lo] *m* 1. (*il ballare*) dancing; **corpo di ~** corps de ballet; **festa da ~** ball; **scuola di ~** dancing school 2. (*movimenti, giro di danza*) dance; **mi permette questo ~?** may I have this dance? 3. (*festa*) ball 4. *fig* **essere in ~** to be involved; **tirare in ~ qu/qc** to bring sb/sth into play; **quando si è in ~, bisogna ballare** *prov* there's no turning back
ballottaggio [bal·lot·'tad·dʒo] <-ggi> *m* 1. POL second ballot 2. SPORT playoff
balneare [bal·ne·'a:·re] *agg* (*località, stabilimento*) seaside; **stagione ~** swimming season; **stazione ~** seaside resort
balneazione [bal·ne·at·'tsio:·ne] *f* swimming; '**divieto di ~**' 'no swimming'
balocco [ba·'lɔk·ko] <-cchi> *m* (*per bambini*) toy
balordo, -a [ba·'lor·do] I. *agg* stupid II. *m, f* fool
balsamico, -a [bal·'sa:·mi·ko] <-ci, -che> *agg* 1. MED (*unguento*) balsamic 2. (*salubre: aria*) balmy 3. (*loc*) **aceto ~** balsamic vinegar
balsamo ['bal·sa·mo] *m* 1. (*per capelli*) conditioner 2. MED balm 3. *fig* (*per la mente*) relief
baltico, -a ['bal·ti·ko] <-ci, -che> *agg* (*paese, popolazione*) Baltic; **il (Mar) Baltico** the Baltic (Sea)
balza ['bal·tsa] *f* 1. (*di vestito*) flounce 2. GEOG crag
balzare [bal·'tsa:·re] *vi* essere 1. (*saltare di scatto*) to leap; ~ **giù da qc** to leap down from sth; ~ **giù da cavallo** to dismount; ~ **giù dal letto** to leap out of bed; **è riuscita a ~ giù dall'auto** she managed to leap out of the car; ~ **in piedi** to leap to one's feet; **le balzò il cuore in gola** her heart leapt 2. *fig* (*risaltare*) to stand out; ~ **agli occhi** to be obvious
balzo ['bal·tso] *m* 1. (*salto*) leap; **prendere** [*o* **cogliere**] **la palla al ~** *fig* to seize the opportunity 2. (*avanzamento*) step
bambagia [bam·'ba:·dʒa] <-gie> *f* (*cotone*) absorbent cotton; **allevare** [*o* **tenere**] **qu nella ~** *fig* to mollycoddle sb; **stare** [*o* **vivere**] **nella ~** *fig* to be mollycoddled
bambinaia [bam·bi·'na:·ia] <-aie> *f* nanny
bambinata [bam·bi·'na:·ta] *f* 1. (*cosa di scarsa importanza*) trifle 2. (*atto puerile*) childish thing

bambino, -a [bam·'bi:·no] *m, f* 1. (*bimbo: maschio*) little boy; (*femmina*) little girl; **aspettare un ~** *inf* to be pregnant 2. *fig scherz* (*adulto ingenuo*) child; **non fare il ~!** don't be such a child!
bamboccio [bam·'bɔt·tʃo] <-cci> *m inf* 1. (*pupazzo*) rag doll 2. *fig* (*semplicione*) fool
bambola ['bam·bo·la] *f* doll
bambolotto [bam·bo·'lɔt·to] *m* (*bambola*) doll
bambù [bam·'bu] <-> *m* bamboo
banale [ba·'na:·le] *agg* 1. (*insignificante: persona, tipo*) ordinary; (*osservazione, domanda*) banal 2. (*poco importante: equivoco, incidente, caduta*) mere
banalità [ba·na·li·'ta] <-> *f* banality
banalizzare [ba·na·lid·'dza:·re] *vt* to trivialize
banalizzazione [ba·na·lid·dzat·'tsio:·ne] *f* trivialization
banana [ba·'na:·na] *f* (*frutto*) banana
banano [ba·'na:·no] *m* banana tree
banca ['baŋ·ka] <-che> *f* COM, COMPUT, MED bank; **andare in** [*o* **alla**] **~** to go to the bank; **Banca centrale europea** EU European Central Bank; ~ **dati** data bank; ~ **del sangue** blood bank
bancarella [baŋ·ka·'rɛl·la] *f* stall
bancario, -a [baŋ·'ka:·rio] <-i, -ie> I. *agg* (*estratto, operazione, saldo*) bank; **coordinate -ie** bank details; **sistema ~** banking system II. *m, f* 1. (*impiegato*) bank employee 2. FIN (*titolo*) bank share
bancarotta [baŋ·ka·'rot·ta] *f* bankruptcy; **fare ~** to go bankrupt; ~ **fraudolenta** fraudulent bankruptcy
banchetto [baŋ·'ket·to] *m* 1. (*bancarella*) stall 2. (*pranzo*) banquet
banchiere, -a [baŋ·'kiɛ:·re] *m, f* FIN (*proprietario di banca*) banker
banchina [baŋ·'ki:·na] *f* 1. NAUT wharf; ~ **di carico/di scarico** loading/unloading wharf 2. FERR (*in stazione*) platform 3. (*per ciclisti*) cycle lane; (*per pedoni*) footpath; ~ **spartitraffico** median strip
banco ['baŋ·ko] <-chi> *m* 1. (*sedile*) bench; ~ **degli imputati** [*o* **accusati**] dock; ~ **della giuria** jury box 2. (*di scuola*) desk; **scaldare i -chi** *fig* to pay no attention at school 3. (*di bar*) bar; (*di negozio*) counter; **vendere qc sotto ~** *fig* to sell sth under the counter 4. (*al mercato*) stall 5. FIN (*banca, a. nei giochi d'azzardo*) bank; ~ **del lotto** lottery outlet 6. TEC bench; ~ **di prova** testing bench 7. GEOL, ZOO layer; ~ **di nebbia** fog bank; ~ **di corallo** coral reef; ~ **di ghiaccio** ice floe; ~ **di pesci** shoal of fish
bancogiro [baŋ·ko·'dʒi:·ro] *m* credit transfer
bancomat [baŋ·ko·'mat/'baŋ·ko·mat] <-> *m* 1. (*servizio*) automated banking 2. (*sportello*) automated teller machine/ ATM; **prelevare soldi al ~** to get money out of the ATM 3. (*tessera*) cash card
bancone [baŋ·'ko:·ne] *m* (*di bar*) bar; (*di banca*) counter; (*di biglietteria*) ticket counter

banconota [baŋ·ko·'nɔ:·ta] *f* bill

bancoposta [baŋ·ko·'pɔs·ta] <-> *m* post-office bank

banda ['ban·da] *f* 1. MUS band 2. (*di malviventi, sfruttatori, truffatori*) gang 3. (*striscia*) stripe 4. RADIO, COMPUT, PHYS band

banderuola [ban·de·'ru·ɔ:·la] *f* METEO weathervane

bandiera [ban·'diɛ:·ra] *f* flag; ~ **bianca** white flag; **cambiare** [*o* **mutare**] ~ *fig* to change sides

bandierina [ban·die·'ri:·na] *f* 1. (*piccola bandiera*) small flag 2. (*nel calcio*) corner flag; **tiro dalla** ~ (*calcio d'angolo*) corner kick

bandire [ban·'di:·re] <bandisco> *vt* 1. (*indire*) to announce 2. (*eliminare*) to ban

bandito [ban·'di:·to] *m* (*fuorilegge*) outlaw

banditore, -trice [ban·di·'to:·re] *m*, *f* (*alle aste*) auctioneer

bando ['ban·do] *m* 1. (*pubblico annuncio*) announcement; ~ **di concorso** (*di lavoro*) announcement of job vacancies; (*di premio*) announcement of competition 2. (*divieto*) ban; **mettere al** ~ *a fig* to ban; ~ **a ...** that's enough ...

bandolo ['ban·do·lo] *m* end of a piece of wool; **perdere il** ~ **della matassa** *fig* to lose the plot; **trovare il** ~ **della matassa** *fig* to find the solution

bang [baŋg] I. *int* bang II. <-> *m* ~ **sonico** sonic boom

banketing manager ['bæŋ·ke·tiŋ 'mæ·ni·dʒə] <-> *m* banquet manager

BANKITALIA *f acro di* **BANCA d'ITALIA** *the Italian State Bank*

banner ['ban·ner] <-> *m* COMPUT banner; **campagna** ~ banner campaign

baobab [bao·'bab] <-> *m* baobab

bar [bar] <-> *m* 1. (*con licenza per alcolici*) bar; (*senza licenza per alcolici*) coffee shop; **andiamo al** ~ **a prendere un caffè** let's go to the coffee shop and have a coffee 2. PHYS bar

bara ['ba:·ra] *f* (*feretro*) coffin; **avere un piede nella** ~ *fig* to have one foot in the grave

baracca [ba·'rak·ka] <-cche> *f* 1. (*catapecchia*) hut 2. (*nelle fiere*) booth 3. *fig, inf* piece of junk; **mandare avanti la** ~ *inf* to keep things going; **piantare** ~ **e burattini** *fig* to pack up everything

baraccato, -a [ba·rak·'ka:·to] I. *agg* (*famiglie, cittadini*) living in a shantytown II. *m, f* shantytown dweller

baraccone [ba·rak·'ko:·ne] *m* (*nelle fiere*) booth

baraccopoli [ba·rak·'ko:·po·li] <-> *f* shantytown

baraonda [ba·ra·'on·da] *f* 1. (*movimento*) hubub 2. (*caos*) din

barare [ba·'ra:·re] *vi* 1. (*al gioco*) to cheat 2. (*imbrogliare su qc*) to lie about sth

baratro ['ba:·rat·ro] *m* 1. (*precipizio*) chasm 2. *fig* (*abisso*) abyss; **essere sul** ~ **di qc** to be on the point of sth; **siamo sul** ~ **del falli-**

mento economico we're on the brink of economic collapse

barattare [ba·rat·'ta:·re] *vt* ~ **qc** (**con qc**) to trade sth (for sth)

baratto [ba·'rat·to] *m* trade; **fare un** ~ to trade

barattolo [ba·'rat·to·lo] *m* (*di latta*) can; (*di vetro*) jar

barba ['bar·ba] *f* 1. (*peli*) beard; **farsi la** ~ to shave 2. *fig* (*noia*) bore; **che** ~ **quel tipo!** *fig* what a bore that guy is!; **che** ~! *fig, inf* what a pain! 3. (*loc*) **farla in** ~ **a qu** *fig* to make sb look like an idiot; **in** ~ **a qu/qc** *fig* in spite of sb/sth

barbabietola [bar·ba·'biɛ:·to·la] *f* beet; ~ **da zucchero** sugar beet

barbaresco [bar·ba·'res·ko] <-schi> *m* Barbaresco, *a red wine from the Piedmont region*

barbarico, -a [bar·'ba:·ri·ko] <-ci, -che> *agg* (*invasione, regno, dominazione*) barbarian

barbarie [bar·'ba:·ri·e] <-> *f* act of barbarism

barbaro ['bar·ba·ro] *m* 1. HIST Barbarian 2. *fig* barbarian

barbaro, -a *agg* 1. HIST (*dei barbari: popolo, capo*) barbarous 2. *fig* (*spietato: assassinio, tortura*) barbaric 3. *fig* (*rozzo: modi, gusti*) uncouth

barbecue ['ba:·bik·ju:] <-> *m* barbecue

barbera [bar·'bɛ:·ra] *m* Barbera, *a red wine from the Piedmont region*

barbie® ['bar·bi] <- *o* barbies> *f* 1. (*tipo di bambola*) Barbie® 2. *fig* doll

barbiere [bar·'biɛ:·re] *m* barber; **andare dal** ~ to go to the barber's

barbiturico [bar·bi·'tu:·ri·ko] <-ci> *m* barbiturate

barbone [bar·'bo:·ne] *m* 1. (*lunga barba*) long beard 2. *pej* (*vagabondo*) tramp 3. ZOO poodle

barboso, -a [bar·'bo:·so] *agg fig* (*film, giornata, conferenza*) boring

barbuto, -a [bar·'bu:·to] *agg* (*signore, donna*) bearded

barca ['bar·ka] <-che> *f* 1. NAUT boat; ~ **a motore** motorboat; ~ **a remi** rowing boat; ~ **a vela** sailboat; **andare in** ~ (*non a piedi*) to go by boat; (*fare vela*) to go sailing; **la** ~ **fa acqua da tutte le parti** *fig, inf* we [*o* you] [*o* they] 've had it 2. *fig, inf* (*famiglia, lavoro*) **mandare avanti la** ~ to keep things afloat; **è stata lei a mandare avanti la** ~ **facendo delle traduzioni** she kept things afloat by doing translations; **siamo tutti nella** [*o* **sulla**] **stessa** ~ *fig* (*condizione*) we're all in the same boat 3. *fig, inf* (*mucchio*) **una** ~ **di** loads of; **avere una** ~ **di soldi** *fig, inf* to have loads of money

barcamenarsi [bar·ka·me·'nar·si] *vr* to manage

barcata [bar·'ka:·ta] *f fig, inf* (*mucchio*) **una** ~ **di** loads of; **una** ~ **di tempo** loads of time

barcollare [bar·kol·'la:·re] *vi* 1. (*vacillare*) to stagger 2. *fig* (*perdere autorità, stabilità*) to totter

barcone [bar·'ko:·ne] *m* barge

bardare [bar·'da:·re] I. *vt* (*cavallo*) to harness

II. *vr:* -**rsi** *scherz* to dress up

bardolino [bar·do·'li:·no] *m* Bardolino, *a red wine from the Verona region*

barella [ba·'rɛl·la] *f* stretcher; **in** ~ on a stretcher

barese [ba·'re:·se] **I.** *agg* from Bari **II.** *mf* (*abitante*) person from Bari

Barese *m* (*zona*) Bari area; **nel** ~ in the Bari area

Bari *f* Bari, *city in Southern Italy*

baricentro [ba·ri·'tʃɛn·tro] *m* center of gravity

barile [ba·'ri:·le] *m* barrel

barista [ba·'ris·ta] <-i *m*, -e *f*> *mf* **1.**(*cameriere*) barman *m*, barmaid *f* **2.**(*proprietario*) landlord *m*, landlady *f*

baritonale [ba·ri·to·'na:·le] *agg* (*voce, canto*) baritone

baritono [ba·'ri:·to·no] *m* MUS baritone

baritono, -a *agg* LING baritone

barlume [bar·'lu:·me] *m* glimmer; ~ **di speranza** glimmer of hope

barocco [ba·'rɔk·ko] *m* Baroque

barocco, -a <-cchi, -cche> *agg* **1.**(*del barocco*) baroque **2.***fig pej* (*fastoso: gusto, stile*) over-the-top

barolo [ba·'rɔ:·lo] *m* Barolo, *a red wine from the Piedmont region*

barometro [ba·'rɔ:·met·ro] *m* barometer

barone, -essa [ba·'ro:·ne, ba·ro·'nes·sa] *m*, *f* **1.**(*titolo*) baron *m*, baroness *f* **2.***fig* top dog; **i -i della finanza** the top dogs of finance

barra ['bar·ra] *f* **1.**(*asta*) rod; (*di metallo*) bar **2.** TEC, MOT, COMPUT bar; ~ **dei menu** menu bar; ~ **di navigazione** navigation bar; ~ **di stato** status bar; ~ **dei task** task bar; ~ **del titolo** title bar; ~ **di scorrimento** scroll bar; **codice a -e** bar code **3.** NAUT helm **4.**(*segno grafico*) slash; ~ **inversa** backslash

barricare [bar·ri·'ka:·re] **I.** *vt* to barricade **II.** *vr:* -**rsi** to barricade oneself; -**rsi in casa** to barricade oneself in one's house; -**rsi in un silenzio assoluto** to not utter a single word

barricata [bar·ri·'ka:·ta] *f* barricade; **andare sulle -e** *fig* to go on the front line

barriera [bar·'riɛ:·ra] *f* **1.**(*sbarramento*) barrier; ~ **architettonica** access-limiting architectural feature; ~ **doganale** trade barrier; **le -e sociali** the social barriers **2.** GEOG reef; ~ **corallina** coral reef **3.** SPORT (*nel calcio*) wall

baruffa [ba·'ruf·fa] *f* **1.**(*zuffa*) brawl **2.**(*litigio*) row; **far** ~ to have a row

barzelletta [bar·dzel·'let·ta] *f* joke; **raccontare -e** to tell jokes

basamento [ba·za·'men·to] *m* **1.** ARCH (*di edificio, monumento*) base **2.** MOT, TEC bed **3.**(*di mobile*) bottom

basare [ba·'za:·re] **I.** *vt fig* (*fondare*) ~ **qc su qc** to base sth on sth **II.** *vr:* -**rsi** *fig* to base oneself; -**rsi su qc** (*argomento, valutazione*) to be based on sth; **mi baso su ...** I base my arguments on ...

basco ['bas·ko] <-schi> *m* (*cappello*) beret

basco, -a <-schi, -sche> **I.** *agg* (*lingua, paese*)

Basque **II.** *m*, *f* (*abitante*) Basque

base ['ba:·ze] *f* **1.**(*parte inferiore*) base **2.**(*principio, fondamento*) basis; **gettare** [*o* **porre**] **le -i di qc** to lay the basis for sth; **in** ~ **a** according to; **privo di -i** unsound **3.** CULIN basic ingredient(s); **minestra a** ~ **di carote** carrot soup; **piatto a** ~ **di carne** meat-based dish **4.** MIL, MATH, CHEM, SPORT base; ~ **aerea** air base; ~ **navale** naval base **5.** ASTR station; ~ **spaziale** space station **6.** POL rank-and-file

basetta [ba·'zet·ta] *f* sideburn

basilare [ba·zi·'la:·re] *agg* (*principio, elemento, regola*) basic

basilica [ba·'zi:·li·ka] <-che> *f* basilica

Basilicata [ba·zi·li·'ka:·ta] *f* Basilicata, *a region in Southern Italy*

basilico [ba·'zi:·li·ko] *m* basil

bassezza [bas·'set·tsa] *f* **1.***fig* (*viltà*) vileness; ~ **d'animo** meanness of spirit **2.**(*azione vile*) vile action

bassifondi *pl di* **bassofondo**

bassipiani *pl di* **bassopiano**

basso ['bas·so] *m* **1.**(*parte inferiore*) bottom; **in** ~ at the bottom; **più in** ~ further down; **clicca in** ~ **alla pagina** click at the bottom of the page; **cadere in** ~ *fig* to come down in the world **2.** MUS bass; **chiave di** ~ bass key

basso, -a <più basso *o* inferiore, bassissimo *o* infimo> **I.** *agg* **1.**(*di statura*) short **2.**(*edificio, muro, tacco*) low; **scarpe con i tacchi -i** low-heeled shoes **3.**(*inferiore: ripiano, parte, livello*) lower **4.**(*abbassato*) down, to keep one's eyes down **5.**(*d'intensità: pressione, temperatura*) low **6.**(*non profondo: acqua*) shallow **7.**(*prezzi*) cheap **8.**(*debole: voce*) soft; **parlare a voce -a** to speak quietly **9.** MUS (*nota*) bass **10.** HIST late; **il** ~ **Medioevo** the late Middle Ages **11.**(*ricorrenza, stagione*) early; **-a stagione** low season; **quest'anno la Pasqua è -a** Easter is early this year **12.** SOC (*ceti, classi*) lower **13.***fig* (*vile*) base **14.** GEO lower; **Bassa Italia** Southern Italy; **i Paesi Bassi** the Netherlands **II.** *avv* **1.**(*in basso*) low **2.**(*a bassa voce*) quietly

bassofondo [bas·so·'fon·do] <bassifondi> *m* **1.** *pl* SOC (*quartieri*) slums **2.** NAUT shallows *pl*

bassopiano [bas·so·'pia:·no] <-i *o* bassipiani> *m* lowland

bassorilievo [bas·so·ri·'liɛ:·vo] *m* bas-relief

bassotto [bas·'sɔt·to] *m* ZOO dachshund

basta ['bas·ta] *int* that's enough; **punto e** ~ period; *v.a.* **bastare**

bastardo, -a [bas·'tar·do] **I.** *agg* **1.**(*illeggittimo*) illegitimate **2.** ZOO (*animale*) crossbred; **cane** ~ mongrel **3.***fig* (*maledetto: domande*) damn **4.***fig* (*cattivo: professore, politico*) dreadful **II.** *m*, *f* **1.** *pej, inf* (*persona*) bastard **2.** ZOO (*animale*) crossbred; (*cane*) mongrel

bastare [bas·'ta:·re] *vi essere* **1.**(*essere sufficiente*) to be enough; ~ **a se stesso** to be self-sufficient; **basta poco per essere felici** it doesn't take much to be happy; **come se non bastasse** as if that wasn't enough; **basta che**

B

... +*conj* you [*o* we] [*o* they] [*o* he] [*o* she] just have to ...; **basta con** [*o* **di**] ... that's enough of ...; **basta con queste menzogne** that's enough of these lies; **basta così** that's enough; **punto e basta!** period! **2.** (*durare*) to last

bastian contrario [bas·'ti·aŋ kon·'tra:·rio] <- -i> *m inf* awkward so-and-so; **fare il ~** to be an awkward so-and-so

bastimento [bas·ti·'men·to] *m* **1.** (*nave*) ship **2.** (*carico*) load

bastonare [bas·to·'na:·re] **I.** *vt* to beat; **avere l'aria da cane bastonato** *fig* to look sorry for oneself **II.** *vr:* **-rsi** to beat each other up

bastonata [bas·to·'na:·ta] *f* blow (with a stick); **prendere qu a -e** *inf* to beat sb

bastoncino [bas·ton·'tʃi:·no] *m* **1.** (*piccolo bastone*) small stick **2.** SPORT (*da sci*) ski stick **3.** CULIN **~ di pesce** fish finger

bastone [bas·'to:·ne] *m* **1.** (*di legno*) stick; **~ da montagna** staff; **~ da passeggio** walking stick; **mettere il ~ tra le ruote a qu** *fig* to cause sb problems **2.** SPORT (*nel golf*) club **3.** *pl* (*di carte da gioco*) *suit in Italian playing cards* **4.** *fig* (*sostegno*) support; **essere il ~ della vecchiaia di qu** *fig* to be a support in sb's old age

batch processing [bætʃ 'prou·se·siŋ] <-> *m* COMPUT batch processing

batosta [ba·'tɔs·ta] *f fig* (*sconfitta*) slap in the face

battaglia [ba·'taʎ·ʎa] <-glie> *f* **1.** *a. fig* MIL battle; **campo di ~** *a. fig* battle field; **~ campale** open warfare; **dare ~ a qu/qc** to declare war on sb/sth **2.** (*campagna*) fight; **una ~ per** [*o* **contro**] **qc** a campaign for sth; **~ elettorale** electoral campaign

battagliero, -a [bat·taʎ·'ʎɛ:·ro] *agg* (*spirito, temperamento, tono*) aggressive

battaglione [bat·taʎ·'ʎo:·ne] *m* battalion

battello [bat·'tɛl·lo] *m* boat; **~ a vapore** steamboat; **~ pneumatico** (*gommone*) dinghy

battente [bat·'tɛn·te] *m* (*di porta*) wing; (*di finestra*) shutter; **chiudere i -i** *fig* to close up shop

battere ['bat·te·re] **I.** *vt* **1.** (*dar colpi*) to beat; **~ le ali** to beat one's wings; **~ i denti** (*per il freddo*) to chatter; **battevo i denti** my teeth were chattering; **~ le mani** to clap (one's hands); **~ le ore** to strike the hour; **~ i piedi** *fig* to stamp one's feet; **non so dove ~ il capo** [*o* **la testa**] *fig* I don't know what to do; **non ~ ciglio** to not bat an eyelid; **in un batter d'occhio** in a flash **2.** (*grano*) to thresh; (*carne*) to pound **3.** MUS, SPORT (*tempo, primato*) to beat **4.** SPORT (*tirare: rigore, calcio d'angolo*) to kick; **~ una punizione** to take a penalty **5.** FIN (*moneta*) to mint **6.** (*metallo, ferro*) to beat; **~ il ferro finché è caldo** *prov* to strike while the iron is hot *prov* **7.** (*dattilografare*) to type; **~ una lettera a macchina** to type a letter **8.** *inf* (*prostituirsi*) **~ il marciapiede** to be on the game **II.** *vi* **1.** (*pioggia, sole, cuore*) to beat; (*orologio*) to tick **2.** (*bussare*) to knock; **~ alla porta** to knock on the door **3.** MOT, TEC to knock **4.** (*insistere*) to go on about sth; **~ sempre sullo stesso tasto** *fig* to always go on about the same thing **III.** *vr:* **-rsi** **1.** *a. fig* MIL to fight; **-rsi per qc** to fight for sth **2.** *fig* to beat one's breast; **battersela** *inf* to beat it

batteria [bat·te·'ri:·a] <-ie> *f* **1.** MOT, EL (*di orologio, telefonino, motore*) battery **2.** (*insieme di cose: di pentole*) set **3.** MUS drums *pl* **4.** SPORT heat

battericida¹ [bat·te·ri·'tʃi:·da] <-i, -e> *agg* (*prodotto, azione*) bactericidal

battericida² <-i> *m* bactericide

batterio [bat·'tɛ:·rio] <-i> *m* bacterium

batteriologico, -a [bat·te·rio·'lɔ:·dʒi·ko] <-ci, -che> *agg* (*esame, armi, guerra*) biological

batterista [bat·te·'ris·ta] <-i *m*, -e *f*> *mf* MUS drummer

battesimo [bat·'te:·zi·mo] *m* **1.** REL baptism; **nome di ~** christian name; **tenere a ~ qu** to be godfather [*o* godmother] to sb **2.** (*cerimonia, rito*) christening; **il ~ dell'aria** first flight

battezzare [bat·ted·'dza:·re] **I.** *vt* **1.** REL to baptize **2.** (*denominare*) to christen **II.** *vr:* **-rsi** REL to be baptized

battibaleno [bat·ti·ba·'le:·no] *avv* **in un ~** in a flash

battibecco [bat·ti·'bek·ko] <-chi> *m* squabble

batticarne [bat·ti·'kar·ne] <-> *m* meat hammer

batticuore [bat·ti·'kuɔ:·re] *m* palpitations *pl*

battimani [bat·ti·'ma:·ni] *mpl* applause

battipanni [bat·ti·'pan·ni] <-> *m* (*per tappeti*) carpet beater

battiscopa [bat·tis·'ko:·pa] <-> *m* baseboard

battista [bat·'tis·ta] <-i *m*, -e *f*> **I.** *mf* Baptist; **San Giovanni Battista** Saint John the Baptist **II.** *agg* Baptist; **chiesa ~** Baptist Church

battistero [bat·tis·'tɛ:·ro] *m* baptistry

battistrada [bat·tis·'tra:·da] <-> *m* **1.** MOT thread **2.** SPORT pacemaker

battitappeto [bat·ti·tap·'pe:·to] <- *o* -i> *m* vacuum cleaner

battito ['bat·ti·to] *m* (*del cuore*) beat; (*dell'orologio*) tick; (*della pioggia*) patter

battitore, -trice [bat·ti·'to:·re] *m, f* SPORT (*nel baseball*) batter

battona [bat·'to:·na] *f dial, vulg* whore

battuta [bat·'tu:·ta] *f* **1.** (*percossa*) beating **2.** *scherz* (*frase spiritosa*) quip; **~ di spirito** witty remark; **avere la ~ pronta** to never be lost for words **3.** MUS bar; **~ d'arresto** (*insuccesso*) bar rest; **alle prime -e** *a. fig* at the beginning **4.** (*di macchina da scrivere, stampante*) stroke **5.** THEAT (*frase*) cue **6.** SPORT (*nel baseball*) strike **7.** (*caccia*) beat **8.** (*di polizia*) search operation

battuto, -a *agg* **1.** (*rame, ferro*) wrought; **di ferro ~** of wrought iron **2.** (*strada*) used **3.** (*sconfitto*) beaten

bau bau ['ba:·u 'ba:·u] *int* woof woof

baule [ba·'u:·le] *m* **1.** (*da viaggio*) trunk **2.** MOT (*di auto*) boot

bava ['baː·va] *f* 1.(*saliva: di persona*) dribble; (*di animale*) slobber; **avere la ~ alla bocca** *fig* to be foaming at the mouth 2.(*del baco da seta*) silk filament 3.(*alito*) breath; **~ di vento** breath of wind

bavaglino [ba·va·ʎ·'ʎiː·no] *m* bib

bavaglio [ba·'vaʎ·ʎo] <-gli> *m* gag; **mettere il ~ a qu** *fig* to gag sb

bavagliolo [ba·va·ʎ·'ʎɔː·lo] *m* bib

bavarese [ba·va·'reː·se] *f* CULIN bavarois

bavero ['baː·ve·ro] *m* collar; **afferrare qu per il ~** to grab sb by the collar

bazar [bad·'dzar] <-> *m* 1.(*mercato orientale*) bazaar 2.COM (*negozio, sito*) emporium

bazzecola [bad·'dzɛː·ko·la] *f* trifle

bazzicare [bat·tsi·'kaː·re] I. *vi* to hang out; **~ con qc/qu** to hang out with sb/sth; **bazzicano con l'informatica** they know a bit about computers; **in questo locale bazzicano molti artisti** lots of artists hang out in this bar II. *vt* (*ambiente, luogo, bar*) to hang out in

BCE *f abbr di* **Banca Centrale Europea** ECB

be' [bɛ] *int* **e ~ sì** well, yes; **va ~, non esageriamo** okay, let's not exaggerate

bè [bɛ] *int* (*della pecora*) baa

beach volley [biːtʃ 'vɔ·li] <-> *m* beach volleyball

beatitudine [be·a·ti·'tuː·di·ne] *f* 1.REL beatitude 2.(*felicità*) happiness

beato, -a [be·'aː·to] I. *agg* 1.(*felice*) happy 2.(*fortunato*) lucky; **~ te!** *inf* lucky you!; **~ tra le donne** *scherz* lucky so-and-so 3.REL blessed; **il Beatissimo Padre** God II. *m, f* REL soul in Paradise

bebè [be·'bɛ] <-> *m* baby

beccare [bek·'kaː·re] I. *vt* 1.ZOO (*colpire con il becco*) to peck 2.*inf* (*buscarsi: raffreddore*) to catch; **beccati questa!** *inf* take that! 3.*fig, inf* (*sorprendere*) to nab; **~ qu sul fatto** to catch sb in the act II. *vr:* **-rsi** 1.ZOO to peck (at) each other 2.*inf* (*bisticciarsi*) to snipe at each other

beccheggiare [bek·ked·'dʒaː·re] *vi* NAUT, AERO to pitch

becchime [bek·'kiː·me] *m* birdseed

becchino [bek·'kiː·no] *m* gravedigger

becco ['bek·ko] <-cchi> *m* 1.ZOO beak 2.*fig, inf* (*bocca umana*) mouth; **chiudi il ~!** *inf* shut up!; **mettere il ~ dappertutto** *inf* (*immischiarsi*) to stick one's nose in everywhere 3.ZOO (*caprone*) billy goat 4.CHEM burner; **~ di Bunsen** Bunsen burner 5.*inf* (*marito cornuto*) cuckold 6.(*loc*) **non avere il ~ d'un quattrino** *inf* to be broke

bee [bɛ] *v.* **bè**

beeper ['biː·pə] <- *o* beepers> *m* pager

befana [be·'faː·na] *f* 1.(*Epifania*) Italian national holiday on January 6th 2.(*vecchia che porta doni*) a witch who brings sweets to good children and coal to bad children on January 6th 3.*fig, inf* (*donna vecchia e brutta*) old hag

beffa ['bɛf·fa] *f* hoax; **farsi -e di qu** to make a

fool of sb; **restare col danno e con le -e** to have salt rubbed in the wound

beffardo, -a [bef·'far·do] *agg* (*sguardo, risata*) mocking

beffare [bef·'faː·re] I. *vt* (*raggirare*) to laugh at II. *vr* **-rsi di qu/qc** to laugh at sb/sth; **-rsi della legge** to laugh at the law

beffeggiare [bef·fed·'dʒaː·re] *vt* to laugh at

bega ['bɛː·ga] <-ghe> *f inf* 1.(*noia*) problem 2.(*litigio*) quarrel

begli ['bɛʎ·ʎi] *v.* **bello, -a**

begonia [be·'gɔː·nia] <-ie> *f* begonia

beh [bɛ] *int inf* well; **e ~ non importa** oh well, it doesn't matter

bei ['bɛː·i] *v.* **bello, -a**

beige [bɛʒ] I. <inv> *agg* (*maglione, pantaloni*) beige II. <-> *m* beige

bel [bɛl] *v.* **bello, -a**

belare [be·'laː·re] *vi a. fig* ZOO to bleat

belato [be·'laː·to] *m* ZOO (*di pecora, capra*) bleating

belga ['bɛl·ga] <-gi *m*, -ghe *f*> I. *agg* 1.(*popolo, persona, città*) Belgian 2.(*insalata*) endive II. *mf* Belgian

Belgio ['bɛl·dʒo] *m* il ~ Belgium

Belgrado [bel·'graː·do] *f* Belgrade

bell' [bɛll] *v.* **bello, -a**

bella ['bɛl·la] *f* 1.(*donna bella*) beauty; **la ~ addormentata nel bosco** Sleeping Beauty 2.(*innamorata*) girlfriend 3.(*copia*) fair copy; **ricopiare in ~** to copy out again 4.(*finale*) final

belladonna [bel·la·'dɔn·na] *f* deadly nightshade

bellezza [bel·'let·tsa] *f* 1.(*qualità, persona*) beauty; **istituto di ~** beauty parlor; **prodotti di ~** beauty products; **per ~** to look good; **le -e di Siena** the sights of Siena; **le -e della natura** the beauties of nature; **concorso di ~** beauty competition 2.(*loc*) **che ~!** wonderful!; **per finire in ~** *fig* to round (sth) off nicely; **la ~ di tremila euro** *inf* the princely sum of three thousand euros

bellicismo [bel·li·'tʃiz·mo] *m* warmongering

bellico, -a <-ci, -che> *agg* (*materiale, residuato, produzione*) war; **industria -a** war industry

bellicoso, -a [bel·li·'koː·so] *agg* 1.(*guerrafondaio: popolo, paese*) warmongering 2.(*battagliero: carattere, persona*) belligerent

belligerante [bel·li·dʒe·'ran·te] I. *agg* (*gruppo, paese*) belligerent II. *mf* belligerent

bellimbusto [bel·lim·'bus·to] *m inf* dandy

bello ['bɛl·lo] *m* 1.(*bellezza*) beauty; **che c'è di ~ alla televisione?** *inf* what's good on TV?; **che fai di ~?** what are you up to?; **ora viene il ~** *inf* now for the best bit; **il ~ è che ...** iron, *inf* best of all ...; **questo è il ~** *inf* the great thing is; **sul più ~** *inf* at that very moment 2.METEO good weather; **oggi fa ~** it's fine today; **il tempo s'è rimesso al ~** the weather has turned nice again

bello, -a I. *agg* 1.(*carino: auto, casa, donna,*

bambino) beautiful; (*uomo*) handsome; **il bel mondo** high society; **le -e arti** fine arts **2.**(*piacevole: camminata, viaggio*) lovely **3.**(*buono: idea, libro, film, voto*) good; **che -a idea!** what a good idea!; **prende sempre bei voti** he [*o she*] always gets good grades **4.**(*sereno: tempo*) fine **5.**(*nobile: gesto*) kind **6.**(*considerevole: somma*) large; **una -a somma** *inf* a lot of money **7.**(*rafforzativo*) **ha un bel dire** *inf* despite what he or she says; **un bel giorno te lo dirò** *inf* I'll tell you some day; **nel bel mezzo** *inf* bang in the middle; **un bel pasticcio!** a real mess!; **mi sono preso una -a paura** *inf* I was really scared; **sei un bel cretino** *inf* you're a real idiot; **non valere un bel nulla** *inf* to be worthless **8.** *iron* (*brutto*) fine; **questa è -a!** *inf* that's nice! **9.**(*loc*) **fare la -a vita** to lead an easy life; **l'ha fatta/detta -a!** *inf* that's done it!; **ne hai fatte delle -e** *inf* you've made a mess of that; **bell'e fatto** *inf* done and dusted; **bell'e buono** *inf* real; **alla bell'e meglio** *inf* somehow or other; **un bel niente** absolutely nothing; **bel ~ inf** slowly; **tante -e cose!** (*nelle lettere*) best wishes! **II.** *m, f* boyfriend *m*, girlfriend *f*

bellunese [bel·lu·'ne:·se] **I.** *agg* from Belluno **II.** *mf* (*abitante*) person from Belluno

Bellunese *m* (*zona*) Belluno area; **nel ~** in the Belluno area

Belluno *f* Belluno, *city in the Veneto*

bel paese® [bɛl pa·'e:·ze] <-> *m* (*formaggio*) bel paese®, *an Italian cheese, also available as a spread*

belva ['bel·va] *f* **1.**(*animale*) wild beast **2.** *fig* (*persona*) animal

belvedere [bel·ve·'de:·re] <-> *m* (*luogo*) lookout

benaccetto, -a [be·nat·'tʃɛt·to] *agg poet* welcome

benamato, -a [be·na·'ma:·to] *agg poet* beloved

benché [beŋ·'ke] *cong* although

benda ['bɛn·da] *f* **1.** MED bandage **2.**(*per occhi*) blindfold

bendare [ben·'da:·re] *vt* **1.** MED (*ferita, testa, arto*) to bandage **2.**(*occhi*) to blindfold; **avere gli occhi bendati** *fig* to be blinkered

bendisposto, -a [ben·dis·'pos·to] *agg* well-disposed

bene¹ ['bɛ:·ne] <meglio, benissimo *o* ottimamente> *avv* **1.**(*in modo giusto, soddisfacente, in salute*) well; **comportarsi ~** to behave well; **prenderla ~** to take sth well; **è andata ~** it went well; **star ~** (*di salute*) to be well; **non mi sento ~ oggi** I don't feel well today **2.**(*a proprio agio*) **trovarsi ~ con qu/qc** to get on well with sb/sth; **ti trovi ~ in Italia?** do you like being in Italy?; **con loro non mi trovo ~** I don't get on with them; **non mi trovo ~ con il nuovo computer** I'm having problems with the new compuer **3.**(*elegantemente*) **essere vestito ~** to be well-dressed; **gente per ~** respectable people; **quel cappello ti sta ~** that

hat suits you; **sta proprio ~ con quegli occhiali** he [*o she*] looks great with those glasses **4.**(*addirittura*) at least; **ben tremila euro m'è costato!** *inf* it cost me over three thousand euros! **5.**(*loc*) **di ~ in meglio** *a. iron* better and better; **~ o male** (*comunque sia*) whatever happens; **ben ~** *inf* (*accuratamente*) well; (*a fondo*) thoroughly; **lo credo ~** *inf* I can well believe it; **ben gli sta!, gli sta ~!** *inf* serves him right!; **ben detto!** *inf* well put!; **va ~!** *inf* okay!; **tutto è ~ quel che finisce ~** *prov* all's well that ends well *prov*

bene² *int* good; **~, basta così** good, that's enough; **~! bravo! bis!** well done! bravo! encore!

bene³ *m* **1.**(*ciò che è buono*) good **2.**(*amore, affetto*) affection; **voler ~ a qu** to love sb **3.**(*opera buona*) good deed; **opere di ~** charitable works **4.**(*benificio*) good; **per il tuo ~** for your own good; **lo dico per il tuo ~** I'm telling you for your own good; **fare qc a fin di ~** to do sth for a good reason **5.**(*benessere*) welfare; **far ~** (*alla salute*) to be good (for one's health); **ti auguro ogni ~** I wish you all the best **6.** COM, JUR goods *pl*; **-i culturali** cultural heritage; **-i di consumo** consumer goods; **-i immobili** real estate; **-i mobili** personal property **7.** *pl* (*averi*) goods *pl*

benedettino, -a **I.** *agg* (*abbazia, monastero*) Benedictine **II.** *m, f* REL Benedictine

benedetto, -a [be·ne·'det·to] *agg* **1.** REL (*santo: acqua*) holy; (*ostia*) consecrated; (*persona*) blessed; **Dio sia ~** praise the Lord **2.** *fig* (*maledetto*) damned

benedire [be·ne·'di:·re] <benedico, benedissi *o* benedii, benedetto> *vt* (*chiesa, campana, fedeli*) to bless; **mandare qu a farsi ~** *inf* to tell sb to go to hell

benedizione [be·ne·dit·'tsio:·ne] *f* **1.** REL (*atto*) blessing **2.** REL (*funzione*) benediction **3.** *fig* (*fonte di bene, di gioia*) boon

beneducato, ben educato, -a [be·ne·du·'ka:·to] *agg* polite

benefattore, -trice [be·ne·fat·'to:·re] *m, f* benefactor *m*, benefactress *f*

beneficenza [be·ne·fi·'tʃɛn·tsa] *f* charity; **fiera di ~** charity event

beneficiare [be·ne·fi·'tʃa:·re] *vi* **~ di qc** to benefit from sth

beneficiario, -a [be·ne·fi·'tʃa:·rio] <-i, -ie> *m, f* **1.** JUR (*di eredità, di lascito*) beneficiary **2.** COM (*di assegno, bonifico*) recipient

beneficio [be·ne·'fi:·tʃo] <-ci> *m a.* JUR (*giovamento*) benefit; **a ~ di qc/qu** for the benefit of sb/sth; **trarre ~ da qc** to benefit from sth

benefico, -a [be·'nɛ:·fi·ko] <-ci, -che> *agg* **1.**(*clima, cura, effetto*) beneficial **2.**(*persona, ente, iniziativa*) charitable

benefit ['be·ni·fit] <- *o* benefits> *m* benefit

beneplacito [be·ne·'pla:·tʃi·to] *m* (*approvazione*) consent

benessere [be·'nɛs·se·re] *m* **1.**(*di salute*) well-being **2.** COM (*economico, sociale*) affluence; **società del** ~ affluent society

benestante [ben·es·'tan·te] I. *agg* (*famiglia, ceto, classe*) well-off II. *mf* well-off person; **i -i** the well-off

benestare [be·nes·'ta:·re] <-> *m* ADM consent

benevolenza [be·ne·vo·'lɛn·tsa] *f* benevolence

benevolo, -a [be·'nɛ:·vo·lo] *agg* **essere ~ (con** [*o* **verso**] **qu**) to be kind (to sb)

benfatto, ben fatto, -a [ben·'fat·to] *agg* **1.**(*figura, corpo*) shapely **2.**(*lavoro, cosa*) good

beniamino, -a [be·nia·'mi:·no] *m, f* favorite

benigno, -a [be·'nip·po] *agg* **1.**(*benevolo: sguardo*) kind **2.** *fig* (*favorevole: sorte*) benevolent **3.** MED (*tumore*) benign **4.** METEO (*clima*) mild

beninformato, ben informato, -a [ben·in·for·'ma:·to] I. *agg* (*pubblico, persona*) well-informed II. *m, f* person in the know

benintenzionato, -a [ben·in·ten·tsio·'na:·to] *agg* well-meaning; **essere ~ nei confronti di qu** to be well-meaning towards sb

beninteso [ben·in·'te:·so] *avv* of course; **~, sei invitato anche tu** of course you're also invited

benissimo [be·'nis·si·mo] *superlativo di* **bene[1]**

benpensante, ben pensante [ben·pen·'san·te] I. *mf* conformist II. *agg* conformist

benservito [ben·ser·'vi:·to] *m* reference; **dare il ~ a qu** to sack sb; *iron* to send sb packing

bensì [ben·'si] *cong* but

bentornato, ben tornato [ben·tor·'na:·to] *m* welcome back; **dare il ~ a qu** to welcome sb back

benvenuto, ben venuto [ben·ve·'nu:·to] *m* welcome; **dare il ~ a qu** to welcome sb

benvenuto, ben venuto, -a I. *agg* welcome II. *int* welcome III. *m, f* **essere il ~ in un luogo** to be welcome in a place

benvisto, ben visto, -a [ben·'vis·to] *agg* well thought of

benvolere, ben volere[1] [ben·vo·'le:·re] <benvoluto> *vt* to like; **farsi ~ da qu** to win sb's affection; **prendere a ~ qu** to take a liking to sb

benvolere, ben volere[2] *m* affection

benvoluto, -a [ben·vo·'lu:·to] *agg* well-liked

benzina [ben·'dzi:·na] *f* gas; **~ normale** normal grade gasoline; **~ senza piombo/verde** unleaded gasoline; **~ super** premium gasoline; **serbatoio della ~** gas tank; **fare ~** to get gas

benzinaio, -a [ben·dzi·'na:·io] <-ai, -aie> *m, f* gas pump attendant

bere[1] ['be:·re] <bevo, bevvi *o* bevetti, bevuto> I. *vt* **1.**(*acqua, vino, caffè*) to drink; **~ dalla bottiglia** to drink from the bottle; **~ alla salute di qu** to drink to sb's health **2.**(*consumare*) to be heavy on; **la mia macchina beve benzina/olio** my car is heavy on petrol/gas **3.**(*credere*) to swallow; **darla a ~ a qu** *fig, inf* to get sb to swallow sth II. *vi* to drink; **~ come una spugna** to drink like a fish;

~ per dimenticare to drink to forget

bere[2] *m* (*vizio*) drink; **darsi al ~** to turn to drink

bergamasco [ber·ga·'mas·ko] *m* (*dialetto*) the dialect of Bergamo

Bergamasco *m* (*zona*) Bergamo area; **nel ~ in** the Bergamo area

bergamasco, -a <-chi, -che> I. *agg* from Bergamo II. *m, f* (*abitante*) person from Bergamo

Bergamo *f* Bergamo, *city in Lombardy*

bergamotto [ber·ga·'mɔt·to] *m* bergamot

berlina [ber·'li:·na] *f* **1.** AUTO sedan **2.** HIST (*antica pena*) pillory **3.**(*loc*) **mettere alla** [*o* **in**] **~** *fig* to ridicule sb

Berlino [ber·'li:·no] *f* Berlin

bermuda [ber·'mu:·da] *mpl* Bermuda shorts *pl*

Berna ['bɛr·na] I. *f* (*città*) Bern(e) II. *m* (*cantone*) Bern(e)

bernoccolo [ber·'nɔk·ko·lo] *m* **1.**(*in testa*) bump **2.** *fig* (*inclinazione*) bent; **avere il ~ di qc** to have a talent for sth

berretto [ber·'ret·to] *m* cap

bersagliare [ber·saʎ·'ʎa:·re] *vt* **1.** *fig* (*colpire, perseguitare*) to bombard; **~ qu di domande** to bomard sb with questions **2.** MIL (*nemico*) to fire on

bersagliere [ber·saʎ·'ʎɛ:·re] *m* MIL bersagliere, *member of the artillery corps of the Italian army*

bersaglio [ber·'saʎ·ʎo] <-gli> *m a. fig* MIL, SPORT target; **tiro al ~** target practice

besciamella [beʃ·ʃa·'mɛl·la] *f* bechamel sauce

bestemmia [bes·'tem·mia] <-ie> *f* swearword; REL blasphemy

bestemmiare [bes·tem·'mia:·re] I. *vi* to swear; REL to blaspheme; **~ contro la squadra avversaria** to swear at the opposing team; **~ come uno scaricatore di porto** to swear like a trooper II. *vt* to swear; REL to blaspheme

bestia ['bes·tia] <-ie> *f* (*animale*) beast; **una ~ rara** *fig* a rare breed; **brutta ~** *fig* horrible thing; **andare in ~** to fly into a rage; **lavorare come una ~** *inf* to work like a mule; **sudare come una ~** *inf* to sweat like a pig

bestiale [bes·'tia:·le] *agg* **1.** *fig* (*crudele: delitto*) brutal **2.** *fig, inf* (*intenso: caldo, fame*) terrible; **fa un caldo bestiale** it's terribly hot **3.** *fig, inf* (*incredibile*) incredible

bestialità [bes·tia·li·'ta] <-> *f* **1.** *fig* (*sproposito*) nonsense; **ha detto una ~** *inf* he talked nonsense **2.**(*brutalità*) brutality

bestiame [bes·'tia:·me] *m* livestock; (*mucche*) cattle *pl*

beta ['bɛ:·ta] I. <-> *f* (*lettera greca*) beta II. <inv> *agg* (*raggi, particelle, elettroni*) beta

betabloccante [be·ta·blok·'kan·te] I. *agg* MED betablocker II. *m* MED betablocker

Betlemme [be·'tlɛm·me] *f* Bethlehem

bettola ['bet·to·la] *f pej, inf* dive

betulla [be·'tul·la] *f* birch

bevanda [be·'van·da] *f* (*gassata, alcolica, rinfrescante*) drink

bevetti [be·'vɛt·ti] *1. pers sing pass rem di*

bere[1]

bevitore, -trice [be·vi·'to:·re] *m, f* drinker; **gran ~** heavy drinker

bevo ['be:·vo] *1. pers sing pr di* **bere**[1]

bevuta [be·'vu:·ta] *f* drink

bevuto [be·'vu:·to] *pp di* **bere**[1]

bevvi ['bev·vi] *1. pers sing pass rem di* **bere**[1]

BI *abbr di* **Banca d'Italia** Bank of Italy, *Italian State Bank*

biadesivo [bi·a·de·'zi:·vo] *m* double-sided adhesive tape

biadesivo, -a *agg* **nastro ~** double-sided adhesive tape

biancheria [bian·ke·'ri:·a] <-ie> *f* linen; **~ intima** underwear; **~ da letto** night clothes *pl;* **~ da tavola** table linen

bianchetto [bian·'ket·to] *m* (*per muri*) whitewash; (*per correggere*) whiteout

bianco ['bian·ko] <-chi> *m* 1.(*colore*) white; **foglio in ~** blank sheet of paper; **vestirsi di ~** to dress in white; **sposarsi in ~** to have a white wedding; **in ~ e nero** in black and white; **film in ~ e nero** black and white film; **mettere nero su ~** to write down; **dare il ~ a qc** to whitewash sth 2.(*parte bianca*) white; **~ dell'uovo** egg-white 3.COM **assegno in ~** blank check 4.CULIN **mangiare in ~** to eat bland food 5.(*loc*) **di punto in ~** suddenly; **notte in ~** sleepless night

bianco, -a <-chi, -che> I. *agg* 1.(*colore, chiaro: pane, vino, pelle, capelli*) white; **carni -che** white meat 2.(*non scritto: foglio*) blank 3.(*pallido: carnagione, viso*) pale; **essere ~ come un cencio lavato** to be as white as a sheet 4.(*pulito: lenzuola, camicia*) clean 5.(*invernale*) **settimana -a** winter sports holiday 6.(*di bambino*) **voce -a** child's voice II. *m, f* white person

biancoscudato, -a [bian·kos·ku·'da:·to] *agg* POL member of the Christian Democrat political party

biancospino [bian·kos·'pi:·no] *m* hawthorn

biascicare [biaʃ·ʃi·'ka:·re] *vt fig* (*lingua, parola*) to mumble; **biascica un po'd'inglese** he or she knows a couple of words of English

biasimare [bia·zi·'ma:·re] *vt* to criticize

biasimo ['bia:·zi·mo] *m* criticism

biat(h)lon [bi·a·'tlon] <-> *m* SPORT biathlon

bibagno [bi·'baɲ·ɲo] <inv> *agg* with two bathrooms; **vendesi appartamenti ~** apartments with two bathrooms for sale

Bibbia ['bib·bia] <-ie> *f* Bible

biberon [bi·be·'rɔn] <-> *m* baby's bottle

bibita ['bi:·bi·ta] *f* (*analcolica, gassata*) soft drink

biblico, -a ['bi:·bli·ko] <-ci, -che> *agg* 1.REL (*personaggio, episodio, testo*) biblical 2.*fig* (*imponente*) huge; **un'impresa -a** a huge task

bibliografia [bi·bli·o·gra·'fi:·a] <-ie> *f* bibliography

bibliografico, -a [bi·bli·o·'gra:·fi·ko] <-ci, -che> *agg* (*archivio, ricerca*) bibliographical

bibliografo, -a [bi·'bliɔ:·gra·fo] *m, f* bibliographer

biblioteca [bi·bli·o·'tɛ:·ka] <-che> *f* 1.(*edificio, stanza*) library 2.(*raccolta*) collection 3.(*mobile*) bookshelf 4.COMPUT **~ di programmi** program library

bibliotecario, -a [bi·bli·o·te·'ka:·rio] <-i, -ie> *m, f* librarian

bicamerale [bi·ka·me·'ra:·le] *agg* POL (*sistema*) bicameral

bicameralismo [bi·ka·me·ra·'li:z·mo] *m* bicameral system

bicamere, bicamera [bi·'ka:·me·re, bi·'ka:·me·ra] <inv> *agg* two-roomed

bicarbonato [bi·kar·bo·'na:·to] *m* bicarbonate; **~ di sodio** bicarbonate of soda

bicchierata [bik·kie·'ra:·ta] *f* drink

bicchiere [bik·'kiɛ:·re] *m* glass; **~ da vino/acqua** wine/water glass; **un ~ di vino/d'acqua** a glass of wine/water; **fondo di ~** fake diamond; **alzare il ~ (a)** to raise one's glass (to)

bicchierino [bik·kie·'ri:·no] *m* 1.(*bicchiere piccolo*) small glass 2.(*quantità di liquido*) tot

bichini [bi·'ki:·ni] <-> *m* bikini

bici ['bi:·tʃi] <-> *f inf* bike; **in ~** by bike; **andare in ~** to ride a bike

bicicletta [bi·tʃi·'klet·ta] *f* bicycle; **~ da corsa** bicycle race; **andare in ~** to ride a bicycle

bicipite [bi·'tʃi:·pi·te] I. *m* bicep(s) *sg o pl* II. *agg* (*in araldica*) two-headed; **aquila ~** two-headed

bicolore [bi·ko·'lo:·re] *agg* 1.(*a due colori: tessuto*) two-tone 2.*fig* POL (*governo*) two-party

bicromatico, -a [bi·kro·'ma:·ti·ko] <-ci, -che> *agg* (*a due colori: tela, tavola*) two-tone; **stampa -a** two-tone print; **emulsione -a** two-tone emulsion

bidè [bi·'dɛ] <-> *m* bidet

bidello, -a [bi·'dɛl·lo] *m, f* (*di una scuola*) janitor

bidimensionale [bi·di·men·sio·'na:·le] *agg* (*immagine, disegno*) two-dimensional

bidirezionale [bi·di·ret·tsio·'na:·le] *agg* (*antenna*) bidirectional; **segnale ~** COMPUT bidirectional signal

bidonare [bi·do·'na:·re] *vt inf* 1.(*fregare*) to rip off 2.(*piantare qc in asso*) to stand sb up

bidonata [bi·do·'na:·ta] *f inf* 1.(*fregatura*) ripoff 2.(*cosa scadente*) letdown; **questo film è una ~** this film is a letdown

bidone [bi·'do:·ne] *m* 1.(*recipiente*) drum; **il ~ della spazzatura** garbage can 2.*inf* (*imbroglio*) swindle 3.*inf* (*appuntamento mancato*) missed date; **mi ha fatto il ~** *inf* he stood me up 4.*pej, inf* (*apparecchio, veicolo*) no-hoper

bidonvia [bi·don·'vi:·a] <-ie> *f* cable car

bidonville [bi·dɔ̃·'vil] <-> *f* shantytown

bieco, -a ['biɛ:·ko] <-chi, -che> *agg* 1.(*sguardo*) menacing 2.(*proposito*) sinister

biella ['biɛl·la] *f* connecting rod

Bielorussia [bie·lo·'rus·sia] *f* Belarus

bielorusso, -a [bie·lo·'rus·so] I. *agg* (*cultura, cittadinanza*) Belarussian II. *m, f* (*abitante*)

Belarussian **III.** *m* (*lingua*) Belarussian

biennale [bien·'na:·le] **I.** *agg* **1.** (*che dura due anni*) two-year **2.** (*ogni due anni*) biannual **II.** *f* biennial

---

i The **Venice Biennale** is an international festival of modern art. Since 1895 it has taken place every two years in the **Giardini** public park in Venice. The Biennale Committee also organizes the international Film Festival. Held annually in September it is the second biggest film festival in Europe after Cannes.

---

biennio [bi·'ɛn·nio] <-i> *m* **1.** (*periodo*) two-year period **2.** (*corso universitario*) two-year foundation course **3.** (*nella scuola*) *the first two years of secondary school*

bierre [bi·'ɛr·re] **I.** <-> *m* (*brigatista*) *member of the Red Brigades terrorist group* **II.** *fpl* (*organizzazione*) Red Brigades **III.** <inv> *agg* Red Brigades

bietola ['biɛ:·to·la] *f* beet

bifamiliare [bi·fa·mi·'lia:·re] *agg* (*casa*) for two families; **villetta ~** small house for two families

bifase [bi·'fa:·ze] *agg* (*motore*) two-phase

bifocale [bi·fo·'ka:·le] *agg* (*lente, occhiali*) bifocal

bifolco, -a [bi·'fol·ko] <-chi, -che> *m, f pej* (*persona rozza, ignorante*) lout

biforcarsi [bi·for·'ka:r·si] *vr:* **-rsi** *a. fig* (*strade, fiumi, arterie*) to divide

biforcazione [bi·for·kat·'tsio:·ne] *f a. fig* (*strade, fiumi, arterie*) fork

biforcuto, -a [bi·for·'ku:·to] *agg* (*lingua, ramo, piede*) forked; **avere una lingua -a** *fig pej* to be a nasty piece of work

big [big] <-> *m* major player

bigamia [bi·ga·'mi:·a] <-ie> *f* bigamy

bigamo, -a ['bi:·ga·mo] **I.** *agg* (*moglie, marito, coppia*) bigamous **II.** *m, f* bigamist

bigemino, -a [bi·'dʒɛ:·mi·no] *agg* (*gravidanza, parto*) bigeminal

bighellonare [bi·gel·lo·'na:·re] *vi* to loaf around

bighellone, -a [bi·gel·'lo:·ne] *m, f inf* layabout

bigiotteria [bi·dʒot·te·'ri:·a] <-ie> *f* **1.** (*articoli*) costume jewelry **2.** (*negozio*) shop selling costume jewelry

bigiù [bi·'dʒu] <-> *m* gem

bigliettaio, -a [biʎ·ʎet·'ta:·io] <-ai, -aie> *m, f* (*su tram, treno, autobus*) ticket collector; (*di cinema*) box office clerk

biglietteria [biʎ·ʎet·te·'ri:·a] <-ie> *f* (*di ferrovie, autobus*) ticket office; (*di cinema, teatro*) box office

biglietto [biʎ·'ʎet·to] *m* **1.** (*cartoncino*) card; **~ d'auguri** greeting card; **~ da visita** business card **2.** (*di treno, autobus, teatro, lotteria*) ticket; **~ di andata e ritorno** roundtrip ticket; **fare il ~** to buy a ticket; **~ della lotteria** lottery ticket **3.** FIN bill; **~ di banca** bill **4.** (*fog-*

lietto) note; **lasciare un ~** to leave a note

Bignami® [big·'na:·mi] <-> *m paperback study guide*

bignè [biɲ·'pɛ] <-> *m* cream puff

bigodino [bi·go·'di:·no] *m* roller

bigotto, -a [bi·'gɔt·to] **I.** *agg* **1.** REL overly pious **2.** (*ipocrita*) hypocritical **II.** *m, f* bigot

bijou [bi·'ʒu] *v.* **bigiù**

bikini [bi·'ki:·ni] *v.* **bichini**

bilabiale [bi·la·'bia:·le] *agg* LING bilabial

bilama [bi·'la:·ma] <inv> *agg* double-bladed; **rasoio ~** double-bladed razor

bilancia [bi·'lan·tʃa] <-ce> *f* **1.** scales *pl;* **~ automatica/romana** automatic/lever scales; **porre qc sul piatto della ~** *fig* to weigh sth up; **essere l'ago della ~** *fig* to be the deciding factor **2.** ASTR **Bilancia** Libra; **sono (della** [*o* **una]) Bilancia** I'm Libra **3.** COM balance; **~ commerciale** balance of trade; **~ dei pagamenti** balance of payments

bilanciare [bi·lan·'tʃa:·re] **I.** *vt* **1.** *a fig* (*carico*) to distribute **2.** (*dieta, gomme, spese*) to balance; **saper ~ le entrate con le spese** to be able to balance income and expenditure **3.** *fig* (*valutare: argomenti*) to weigh up **II.** *vr:* **-rsi** **1.** (*equilibrarsi*) to be balanced **2.** (*equivalersi*) to balance each other out

bilanciere [bi·lan·'tʃɛ:·re] *m* **1.** (*di orologio*) balance **2.** NAUT outrigger **3.** TEC (*asta*) rod **4.** SPORT bar

bilancio [bi·'lan·tʃo] <-ci> *m* **1.** COM (*budget*) balance; **~ consolidato** consolidated balance; **~ consuntivo** final balance; **~ preventivo/pubblico** budget; **deficit di ~** budget deficit **2.** *fig* (*valutazione*) assessment; **fare il ~ della propria vita** *fig* to take stock of one's own life

bilaterale [bi·la·te·'ra:·le] *agg* (*accordo, incontro*) bilateral

bilateralismo [bi·la·te·ra·'liz·mo] *m* bilateralism

bile ['bi:·le] *f* **1.** ANAT bile **2.** *fig* (*collera*) anger; **essere verde dalla ~** *fig* to be absolutely livid

bilia ['bi:·li·a] <-ie> *f* **1.** (*gioco*) marble; **giocare a -ie** to play marbles **2.** (*palla da biliardo*) billiard ball; (*buca*) pocket

biliardo [bi·'liar·do] *m* **1.** (*gioco*) pool, billiards **2.** (*tavolo*) pool table

biliare [bi·'lia:·re] *agg* (*malattia*) bile

bilico ['bi:·li·ko] <-chi> *m* **in ~** in the balance; **tenere in ~** to balance; **tenere in ~ qu** to keep sb in suspense; **essere in ~ tra la vita e la morte** to fight for one's life

bilingue [bi·'liŋ·gue] **I.** *agg* (*educazione, dizionario, persona*) bilingual **II.** *mf* bilingual person

bilinguismo [bi·liŋ·'guiz·mo] *m* bilingualism

bilione [bi·'lio:·ne] *m* (*mille milioni*) billion; (*un milione di milioni*) trillion

bilocale [bi·lo·'ka:·le] **I.** *m* two-roomed apartment **II.** *agg* (*appartamento, mansarda*) two-roomed

bimbo, -a ['bim·bo] *m, f* child

bimensile [bi·men·'si:·le] *agg* (*ogni due set-*

timane) semimonthly

bimestrale [bi·mes·'traː·le] *agg* 1.(*che dura due bimestri*) two-month 2.(*ogni due bimestri*) bimonthly

bimestre [bi·'mɛs·tre] *m a.* COM (*periodo*) two month period

binario [bi·'naː·ri·o] <-i> *m* FERR platform; ~ **morto** dead-end track; **il treno per Pisa parte dal ~ 16** the train for Pisa leaves from platform 16

binocolo [bi·'nɔː·ko·lo] *m* binoculars *pl*

binomio [bi·'nɔː·mi·o] <-i> *m* 1.MATH binomial 2.*fig* (*coppia*) combination

bioagricoltore [bi·o·a·gri·kol·'toː·re] *m* organic farmer

bioagricoltura [bi·o·a·gri·kol·'tuː·ra] *f* organic farming

bioalimento [bi·o·a·li·'men·to] *m* biofood

biocarburante [bi·o·kar·bu·'ran·te] *m* biofuel

biochimica [bi·o·'kiː·mi·ka] <-che> *f* biochemistry

biochimico, -a [bi·o·'kiː·mi·ko] <-ci, -che> I. *agg* (*laboratorio, operatore*) biochemical II. *m, f* biochemist

biochip [ba·io·'tʃip] <- *o* biochips> *m* COMPUT biochip

biocida[1] [bi·o·'tʃiː·da] <-i> *m* biocide

biocida[2] <-i, -e> *agg* (*prodotto, medicinale, sostanza*) biocidal

biocompatibile [bi·o·kom·pa·'tiː·bi·le] *agg* (*prodotto, edificio, rivestimento*) biocompatible

biodegradabile [bi·o·de·gra·'daː·bi·le] *agg* (*detersivo, shampoo, rifiuti*) biodegradable

biodegradabilità [bi·o·de·gra·'daː·bi·li·'ta] <-> *f* (*di detergente, prodotto, rifiuti*) biodegradability

biodegradare [bi·o·de·gra·'daː·re] *vt* ECO (*rifiuti, cellulosa, petrolio*) to biodegrade

biodiesel ['bi·o·diː·zel] <-> *m* biodiesel

biodinamico, -a [bi·o·di·'naː·mi·ko] <-ci, -che> *agg* 1.BIOL biodynamical 2.AGR (*cibo, prodotto, produttore*) biodynamic

bioenergetica [bi·o·e·ner·'dʒɛː·ti·ka] <-che> *f* BIOL bioenergetics

bioenergetico, -a [bi·o·e·ner·'dʒɛː·ti·ko] <-ci, -che> *agg* BIOL (*terapia, esercizio*) bioenergetic

bioenergia [bi·o·e·ner·'dʒiː·a] *f* bioenergy

bioetica [bi·o·'ɛː·ti·ka] <-che> *f* bioethics

biofabbrica [bi·o·'fab·bri·ka] <-che> *f* biofactory

biofarmaceutica [bi·o·far·ma·'tʃɛːu·ti·ka] <-che> *f* biopharmaceutics

biofeedback [bi·o·fid·'bɛk] <-> *m* MED biofeedback

biofisica [bi·o·'fiː·zi·ka] <-che> *f* biophysics

biofisico, -a [bi·o·'fiː·zi·ko] <-ci, -che> I. *agg* (*fenomeno, scienze, profilo*) biophysical II. *m, f* biophysicist

biogas [bi·o·'gas] <-> *m* biogas

biogenesi [bi·o·'dʒɛː·ne·zi] *f* biogenesis

biogenetica [bi·o·dʒe·'nɛː·ti·ka] <-che> *f* biogenetics

biogenetico, -a [bi·o·dʒe·'nɛː·ti·ko] *agg* biogenetic

biografia [bi·o·gra·'fiː·a] *f* biography

biografico, -a [bi·o·'graː·fi·ko] <-ci, -che> *agg* (*film, romanzo, episodio*) biographical

biografo, -a [bi·'ɔː·gra·fo] *m, f* biographer

bioindicatore, -trice [bi·o·in·di·ka·'toː·re] *m, f* bioindicator; ~ **ambientale** environmental bioindicator

bioingegnere [bi·o·in·dʒeɲ·'pɛː·re] *m* bioengineer

bioingegneria [bi·o·in·dʒeɲ·ɲe·'riː·a] *m* bioengineering

bioinsetticida[1] [bi·o·in·set·ti·'tʃi·da] <-i, -e> *agg* (*prodotto, polvere*) bioinsecticide

bioinsetticida[2] <-i> *m* bioinsecticide

biologia [bi·o·lo·'dʒiː·a] <-ie> *f* biology

biologico, -a [bi·o·'lɔː·dʒi·ko] *agg* 1.(*cibo, coltura, produzione*) organic 2.(*ciclo, scienza, arma, bomba*) biological

biologo, -a [bi·'ɔː·lo·go] <-gi, -ghe> *m, f* biologist

biomanipolazione [bi·o·ma·ni·po·lat·'tsioː·ne] *f* biomanipulation

biomassa [bi·o·'mas·sa] *f* biomass

biomateriale [bi·o·ma·te·'riaː·le] *m* biomaterial

biomeccanica [bi·o·mek·'kaː·ni·ka] *f* biomechanics

biondo ['bion·do] *m* (*colore*) blond color

biondo, -a I. *agg* 1.(*donna*) blonde; (*uomo*) blond 2.(*capelli*) blond; ~ **cenere** ash blond; ~ **come l'oro** golden blond II. *m, f* (*donna*) blonde; (*uomo*) fair-haired

bionica ['biɔː·ni·ka] <-che> *f* bionics

bioparco [bi·o·'par·ko] <-chi> *m* ECO zoo, *a zoo in which the animals live in more humane conditions*

biopatia [bi·o·pa·'tiː·a] <-ie> *f* biopathy

biopsia [bi·o·'psiː·a] <-ie> *f* biopsy

bioreattore [bi·o·re·at·'toː·re] *m* bioreactor

bioritmo [bi·o·'rit·mo] *m* biorhythm

biosfera [bi·os·'fɛː·ra] *f* biosphere

biosistema [bi·o·sis·'tɛː·ma] <-i> *m* BIOL biosystem

biosociologia [bi·o·so·tʃo·lo·'dʒiː·a] <-gie> *f* biosociology

biossido [bi·'ɔs·si·do] *m* dioxide

biostatistica [bi·o·sta·'tis·ti·ka] <-che> *f* biostatistics

biotecnica [bi·o·'tɛk·ni·ka] <-che> *f* biotechnics

biotecnologia [bi·o·tɛk·no·lo·'dʒiː·a] *f* biotechnology

bioterapia [bi·o·te·ra·'piː·a] *f* MED biotherapy

biotopo [bi·'ɔː·to·po] *m* biotope

bipartisan [bi·'par·ti·zan] <inv> *agg* POL bipartisan

bipartitico, -a [bi·par·'tiː·ti·ko] *agg* two-party; **governo ~** two-party government

bipede ['biː·pe·de] I. *m* ZOO biped II. *agg* two-footed

biplano [bi·'pla:·no] *m* biplane
bipolare [bi·po·'la:·re] *agg* bipolar
bipolarismo [bi·po·la·'riz·mo] *m* POL bipolarism
bipolarità [bi·po·la·ri·'ta] <-> *f* PHYS bipolarism
bipolarizzazione [bi·po·la·rid·dzat·'tsio:·ne] *f* POL bipolarization
biposto [bi·'pos·to] <inv> *agg* two-seater; **automobile/aereo** ~ two-seater car/plane
birba ['bir·ba] *f scherz, inf* rascal
birbante [bir·'ban·te] *mf* **1.** *scherz, inf* (*monello*) rascal **2.** *pej* (*mascalzone*) rogue
birbone, -a [bir·'bo:·ne] *m, f scherz, inf* terror
bireattore [bi·re·at·'to:·re] *m* twin-engined aircraft
birichino, -a [bi·ri·'ki:·no] *inf* **I.** *agg* (*sguardo, aria*) mischievous **II.** *m, f* rascal
birillo [bi·'ril·lo] *m* pin
biro® ['bi:·ro] <-> *f* ballpoint pen
birra ['bir·ra] *f* beer; **lievito di** ~ brewer's yeast; ~ **alla spina** draft beer; **a tutta** ~ *inf* flat out
birraio [bir·'ra:·io] <-ai> *m* (*fabbricante*) brewer; (*venditore*) pub manager
birreria [bir·re·'ri:·a] <-ie> *f* **1.** (*locale*) pub **2.** (*fabbrica*) brewery
bis [bis] **I.** *int* encore! **II.** <-> *m* encore; **chiedere il** ~ to call for an encore; **concedere il** ~ to give an encore; **fare il** ~ **di qc** to give an encore of sth; (*nel mangiare*) to have a second helping **III.** <inv> *agg* (*supplementare*) additional; **treno** ~ additional train
bisavolo, -a [bi·'za:·vo·lo] *m, f* great-grandfather *m,* great-grandmother *f;* **i miei -i vengono dall'Italia** my ancestors were from Italy
bisbetico, -a [biz·'bɛ:·ti·ko] <-ci, -che> **I.** *agg* (*vecchio, donna*) cantankerous **II.** *m, f pej* cantankerous person
bisbigliare [biz·biʎ·'ʎa:·re] **I.** *vt* (*orazione, parole*) to whisper; ~ **qc nell'orecchio a qu** to whisper sth in sb's ear **II.** *vi* to whisper
bisbiglio[1] [biz·'biʎ·ʎo] <-gli> *m* (*sussurro*) whisper
bisbiglio[2] [biz·biʎ·'ʎi:·o] <-glii> *m* (*chiaccherio*) murmuring
bisca ['bis·ka] <-sche> *f pej* gambling den; ~ **clandestina** illegal gambling den
biscia ['biʃ·ʃa] <-sce> *f* grass snake
biscione [biʃ·'ʃo:·ne] *m* **1.** (*stemma di Milano*) coat of arms, featuring a large snake, of the city of Milan; **la TV del** ~ television companies based in Milan which form part of the Mediaset group; **il** ~ **dell'Inter** the snake emblem of Inter football club **2.** (*dolce emiliano*) almond-flavored cake in the form of a snake, a delicacy of Emilia-Romagna
biscottato, -a [bis·kot·'ta:·to] *agg* (*pane, torta*) crisp
biscottiera [bis·kot·'tiɛ:·ra] *f* cookie can
biscottificio [bis·kot·ti·'fi:·tʃo] <-ci> *m* cookie factory
biscotto [bis·'kɔt·to] *m* CULIN cookie
bisessuale [bi·ses·su·'a:·le] *agg* bisexual

bisestile [bi·zes·'ti:·le] *agg* **anno** ~ leap year
bisettimanale [bi·set·ti·ma·'na:·le] **I.** *agg* (*due volte alla settimana*) twice weekly **II.** *m* (*giornale*) biweekly newspaper
bisex [bi·'seks] **I.** <inv> *agg* **1.** (*persona*) bisexual **2.** (*capo di vestiario*) unisex **II.** <-> *mf* bisexual
bisillabico, -a [bi·sil·'la:·bi·ko] <-ci, -che> *agg* LING bisyllabic; **sostantivo** ~ bisyllabic noun
bisillabo [bi·'sil·la·bo] *m* LING bisyllable
bisillabo, -a *agg* bisyllabic
bislacco, -a [bi·'zlak·ko] <-cchi, -cche> *agg inf* (*idea*) weird
bislungo, -a [bi·'zluŋ·go] <-ghi, -ghe> *agg* (*figura, oggetto*) oblong
bisnipote [biz·ni·'po:·te] *mf* **1.** (*di nonno*) great-grandson *m,* great-granddaughter *f* **2.** (*di zio*) great-nephew *m,* great-niece *f*
bisnonno, -a [biz·'nɔn·no] *m, f* great-grandfather *m,* great-grandmother, f
bisognare [bi·zoɲ·'ɲa:·re] <bisogna, bisognano> *vi* essere (*essere necessario*) to be necessary; **bisogna che ... +*conj*, bisogna ... to** have to; **bisogna che tu lo faccia** you must[o have to] do it; **non bisogna crederci** you [o we] mustn't believe it; **bisogna farlo subito!** you [o we] [o he] [o she] must do it right away!
bisognino [bi·zoɲ·'ɲi:·no] *m inf* **fare un** ~ to go to the bathroom
bisogno [bi·'zoɲ·ɲo] *m* **1.** (*necessità*) need; **avere** ~ **di qc/qu** to need sb/sth; **in caso di** ~ if necessary; **secondo il** ~ as necessary; **al** ~ when necessary; **non c'è < TILDE> che ... +*conj*** there's no need for ...; **non c'è** ~ **che tu venga** there's no need for you to come; **non c'è** ~ **di ...** there's no need to ...; **non c'è** ~ **di alzare la voce** there's no need to raise your voice; **sentire il** ~ **di fare qc** to feel the need to do sth **2.** (*mancanza di mezzi*) want; **vivere nel** ~ to live in poverty **3.** *pl inf* (*corporali*) **fare i propri -i** to go to the toilet
bisognoso, -a [bi·zoɲ·'ɲo:·so] **I.** *agg* needy; ~ **di aiuto/cura** in need of help/care **II.** *m, f* needy person
bisonte [bi·'zon·te] *m* (*europeo*) bison; (*americano*) buffalo
bistecca [bis·'tek·ka] <-cche> *f* steak; ~ **alla fiorentina** T-bone steak
bistecchiera [bis·tek·'kiɛ:·ra] *f* grill
bisticciare [bis·tit·'tʃa:·re] *inf* **I.** *vi* to squabble **II.** *vr:* **-rsi** to squabble
bisticcio [bis·'tit·tʃo] <-cci> *m inf* squabble
bistrattare [bis·trat·'ta:·re] *vt* to mistreat
bistrò, bistrot [bis·'trɔ, bis·'tro] <-> *m* bistro
bisturi ['bis·tu·ri] <-> *m* scalpel
bisunto, -a [bi·'zun·to] *agg inf* greasy; **unto e** ~ *inf* completely filthy
bitume [bi·'tu:·me] *m* bitumen
biturbo [bi·'tur·bo] *m* twin-turbo
bivalente [bi·va·'lɛn·te] *agg* **1.** CHEM bivalent **2.** *fig* with two possibilities
bivio ['bi:·vio] <-i> *m* **1.** (*biforcazione*) fork **2.** *fig* (*svolta*) crossroads; **essere** (**giunto**) **a**

un ~ to be at a crossroads

bizantino, -a [bid·dzan·'ti:·no] *agg* **1.** HIST (*chiesa, icona*) Byzantine **2.** *fig pej* (*pedante: ragionamento*) pedantic

bizza ['bid·dza] *f* (*collera*) tantrum; **fare le -e** to have a temper tantrum

bizzarro, -a [bid·'dzar·ro] *agg* **1.** (*persona, idea*) weird **2.** (*cavallo*) high spirited

bizzeffe [bid·'dzɛf·fe] *avv* **a ~** galore; **avere denaro a ~** to have money galore

bla bla [bla 'bla] <-> *m* babble

blando, -a ['blan·do] *agg* **1.** (*leggero: medicinale*) mild **2.** (*parole*) soothing

blasfemo, -a [blas·'fɛ:·mo] **I.** *agg* (*affermazione, imprecazione*) blasphemous **II.** *m, f* blasphemer

blaterare [bla·te·'ra:·re] *vi inf* to babble on about

blindato, -a [blin·'da:·to] *agg* armored; **camera ~** strong room; **carro ~** tank; **auto -a** armored car; **vetro ~** bulletproof glass

blitz [blits] <-> *m* **1.** (*guerra*) blitz **2.** (*operazione a sorpresa*) raid

bloccabile [blok·'ka:·bi·le] *agg* (*forcella, ruota, sospensione*) blockable

bloccaggio [blok·'kad·dʒo] <-ggi> *m* **1.** TEC locking **2.** SPORT (*nel rugby*) two-man tackle

bloccare [blok·'ka:·re] **I.** *vt* **1.** (*fissare: porta, finestra*) to block **2.** TEC (*motore*) to block; (*sterzo*) to lock **3.** (*paziente, criminale, traffico*) to stop **4.** (*con posto di blocco*) to block off **5.** (*interrompere: comunicazioni, strada, paese*) to cut off **6.** (*intralciare: città, binari*) to immobilize **7.** (*prezzi, salari, licenziamenti*) to freeze **8.** FIN **~ un assegno** to stop a check; **~ un conto** to freeze an account **9.** SPORT (*avversario, pallone*) to stop **10.** (*inibire*) to inhibit **II.** *vr:* **-rsi 1.** (*fermarsi: computer*) to freeze; (*tastiera, freni*) to jam; (*motore*) to stall **2.** *fig* (*inibirsi*) to freeze

bloccaruota, bloccaruote [blok·ka·'ruɔ:·ta, blok·ka·'ruɔ:·te] <-> **I.** *m* wheel clamp **II.** <inv> *agg* clamping; **ceppo ~** wheel clamp

bloccasterzo [blok·kas·'tɛr·tso] *m* steering lock

blocco ['blɔk·ko] <-cchi> *m* **1.** (*pezzo*) block **2.** (*notevole quantità: di libri*) load; **vendere/ comprare in ~** (*tessuto*) to sell/buy in bulk **3.** TEC lock; **~ dello sterzo** steering lock; **~ motore** engine block **4.** (*per appunti*) notepad **5.** NAUT, MIL blockade; **~ navale** naval blockade; **~ stradale** roadblock; **posto di ~** (*alla frontiera*) checkpoint; (*per strada*) roadblock **6.** JUR, FIN (*sospensione: a. di lavoro, attività*) freeze; **~ dei fitti** rent freeze; **~ delle riforme** reform freeze; **~ dei salari** salary freeze **7.** (*arresto: di congegno*) jamming **8.** MED **~ renale** kidney failure; **~ cardiaco** cardiac arrest **9.** PSYCH (*di personalità, coscienza*) block; (*di memoria*) mental block

bloc-notes [blɔk·'nɔt] <-> *m* notepad

blu [blu] **I.** <inv> *agg* blue; **avere il sangue ~** to have blue blood **II.** <-> *m* (*colore*) blue;

~ di Prussia Prussian blue

blue-jeans ['blu: 'dʒi:nz] *mpl* jeans

bluffare [bluf·'fa:·re] *vt* to bluff

blusa ['blu:·za] *f* (*camicetta*) blouse

BNL *f abbr di* **Banca Nazionale del Lavoro** *an Italian bank*

boa¹ ['bɔ:·a] <-> *m* **1.** ZOO boa constrictor **2.** (*sciarpa*) feather boa

boa² *f* NAUT buoy

boato [bo·'a:·to] *m* rumbling

bob [bɔb] <-> *m* (*sport*) bobsled

bobbista [bob·'bis·ta] <-i *m*, -e *f*> *mf* (*sport*) bobsled rider

bobina [bo·'bi:·na] *f* **1.** (*rotolo: di filo*) reel **2.** ELEC coil

bocca ['bok·ka] <-cche> *f* **1.** ANAT mouth; **~ di leone** BOT snapdragon; **a ~ piena** with one's mouth full; **mettere ~ in qc** *fig* to interfere in sth; **restare a ~ aperta** *a fig* to be speechless; **tenere la ~ chiusa** *a fig* to keep one's mouth shut; **restare a ~ asciutta** *fig* to be left empty-handed; **essere di ~ buona** *fig* to be easily satisfied; **essere la ~ della verità** *fig* to be a truthful person; **essere sulla ~ di tutti** *fig* to be on everybody's lips; **in ~ al lupo!** *inf* good luck! **2.** *fig* (*apertura*) opening; (*di cannone*) mouth; (*di forno*) stokehole **3.** GEOG (*di fiume*) mouth; (*di mare: stretto*) strait

boccaccia [bok·'kat·tʃa] <-cce> *f* **1.** (*smorfia*) grimace; **fare le -cce** to make a face **2.** *fig pej* (*persona maldicente*) foul-mouthed person

boccale [bok·'ka:·le] *m* **1.** (*recipiente*) jug; (*per bere*) mug **2.** (*quantità*) jugful

boccata [bok·'ka:·ta] *f* (*d'aria, acqua*) mouthful; (*di sigaretta*) puff; **andare a prendere una ~ d'aria** *fig* to go and get some air

boccetta [bot·'tʃet·ta] *f* **1.** (*per inchiostro, medicinali*) small bottle **2.** *pl* (*al biliardo*) billiards

boccheggiante [bok·ked·'dʒan·te] *agg* **1.** (*per il caldo, la fatica*) gasping **2.** *fig* (*moribondo*) dying

boccheggiare [bok·ked·'dʒa:·re] *vi* to gasp

bocchino [bok·'ki:·no] *m* **1.** (*per sigaretta*) cigarette holder **2.** MUS mouthpiece

boccia ['bɔt·tʃa] <-cce> *f* **1.** (*per gioco*) bowl; **gioco delle -cce** bowls; **giocare alle -cce** to play bowls **2.** (*recipiente*) jug; (*per vino*) carafe

bocciare [bot·'tʃa:·re] *vt* **1.** (*agli esami*) to fail **2.** (*proposta, idea*) to reject **3.** (*alle bocce*) to hit

bocciatura [bot·tʃa·'tu:·ra] *f* **1.** (*agli esami*) failure **2.** (*di proposta, idea*) rejection

boccio ['bɔt·tʃo] <-cci> *m* BOT bud; **in ~** bud

bocciodromo [bot·'tʃɔ:·dro·mo] *m* (lawn) bowling ground

bocciofila [bot·tʃo·'fi:·la] *f* lawn bowler

bocciolo [bot·'tʃɔ:·lo] *m* bud

boccolo ['bok·ko·lo] *m* curl

bocconcino [bok·kon·'tʃi:·no] *m* **1.** (*piccolo pezzo*) bite-sized piece **2.** (*polpettina*) morsel **3.** (*piatto prelibato*) delicacy **4.** (*piccola moz-*

zarella) small mozzarella cheese

boccone [bok·'ko:·ne] *m* 1.(*piccolo pezzo*) mouthful 2.(*pasto*) light meal; **mangiare un** ~ to have a bite to eat; **col** ~ **in gola** *fig, inf* with one's mouth full 3.(*loc*) **un** ~ **amaro** bitter pill

bocconi [bok·'ko:·ni] *avv* face down; **stare** ~ to lie face down

body ['bɔ·di] <-> *m* (*intimo*) body; (*per ginnastica*) leotard

bofonchiare [bo·foŋ·'kia:·re] *vi inf* to mutter

boia ['bɔ:·ia] I.<-> *m* (*carnefice*) executioner II. *int vulg* ~ **d'un mondo!** damn it! III.<inv> *agg* (*terribile*) dreadful; **che tempo** ~! *inf* what awful weather!; **ho una sete** ~ I'm terribly thirsty

boiata [bo·'ia:·ta] *f* (*malriuscito: spettacolo, libro*) garbage

boicottaggio [boi·kot·'tad·dʒo] <-ggi> *m* boycott

boicottare [boi·kot·'ta:·re] *vt* 1. COM to boycott 2.(*ostacolare*) to sabotage

boiler ['bɔi·lə/'bɔi·ler] <-> *m* water heater

bolgia ['bɔl·dʒa] <-ge> *f fig* (*baraonda*) bedlam; **è una** ~ it's bedlam

bolide ['bɔ:·li·de] *m* 1. ASTR meteor 2. AUTO racing car

bolla ['bol·la] *f* 1.bubble; **finire in una** ~ **di sapone** *fig* to come to nothing 2. MED blister 3. REL bull; ~ **papale** papal bull 4. COM (*documento*) bill; ~ **di accompagnamento** waybill; ~ **di consegna** delivery note

bollare [bol·'la:·re] *vt* 1. ADM to stamp 2. *fig* (*marchiare*) to brand

bollato, -a [bol·'la:·to] *agg* 1. ADM stamped; **carta -a** stamped paper 2. *fig* (*marchiato*) branded

bollente [bol·'lɛn·te] *agg* 1.(*acqua, caffè*) boiling 2. *fig* (*temperamento, carattere*) fiery

bolletta [bol·'let·ta] *f* (*fattura*) bill; **essere in** ~ *inf* to be broke

bollettino [bol·let·'ti:·no] *m* 1.(*pubblicazione*) bulletin; ~ **medico** medical bulletin; ~ **meteorologico** weather report; **Bollettino Ufficiale** gazette 2.(*documento*) form; ~ **di versamento** paying-in slip

bollilatte [bol·li·'lat·te] <-> *m* milk pan

bollino [bol·'li:·no] *m* (*tagliando*) coupon; ~ **blu** AUTO ≈ Reduced Pollution Certificate

bollire [bol·'li:·re] I. *vi* PHYS, CULIN to boil; ~ **di rabbia** *fig* to seethe with rage; **cosa bolle in pentola** *fig* what's going on? II. *vt* to boil

bollito [bol·'li:·to] *m* (*pietanza*) boiled meat

bollito, -a *agg* boiled

bollitore [bol·li·'to:·re] *m* 1.(*per acqua*) kettle 2. TEC boiler

bollo ['bol·lo] *m* 1.(*marchio, strumento*) stamp; **carta da** ~ stamped paper; **marca da** ~ revenue stamp; ~ (**di circolazione**) road tax 2. *inf* (*francobollo*) postage stamp

bollore [bol·'lo:·re] *m* 1. CULIN, PHYS boiling; **dare un** ~ **a qc** to bring sth to a boil 2. *fig* (*caldo intenso*) boiling heat 3. *fig* (*agitazione*)

intensity

Bologna *f* Bologna, *a city in Emilia-Romagna*

bolognese [bo·loɲ·'ɲe:·se] I. *agg* from Bologna; **spaghetti alla** ~ spaghetti bolognese II. *m* (*abitante*) person from Bologna III. *m* (*dialetto*) Bolognese dialect

Bolognese *m* (*zona*) Bologna area

bolscevico, -a [bol·ʃe·'vi:·ko] <-chi, -che> I. *agg* POL Bolshevik II. *m, f* POL Bolshevik

bolzanino, -a [bol·tsa·'ni:·no] I. *agg* - II. *m, f* (*abitante*) person from Bolzano

Bolzano [bol·'tsa:·no] *f* Bolzano, *a city in the Trentino region*

bomba ['bom·ba] *f* MIL bomb; ~ **a idrogeno/ orologeria** hydrogen/time bomb; ~ **a mano** hand grenade; ~ **atomica** atomic bomb; ~ **vulcanica** [*o* **lavica**] volcanic bomb; **una notizia** ~ *fig* a bombshell; **fare scoppiare la** ~ *fig* to let the fox into the chicken coop; **a prova di** ~ watertight

bombardamento [bom·bar·da·'men·to] *m* 1. MIL, PHYS (*con bombe aeree*) air raid; (*con artiglieria pesante*) bombardment; ~ **a tappeto** carpet bombing; (*con artiglieria*) heavy fire 2. *fig* (*di domande*) storm

bombardare [bom·bar·'da:·re] *vt a. fig* MIL, PHYS (*città*) to bombard; ~ **qu di domande** to bombard sb with questions

bombardiere [bom·bar·'diɛ:·re] *m* 1.(*pilota*) bombardier 2.(*aereo*) bomber

bomber ['bɔm·bə/'bɔm·ber] <- *o* bombers> *m* 1. SPORT (*cannoniere*) striker 2.(*giubbotto*) bomber jacket

bombetta [bom·bet·'ta] *f* (*cappello*) bowler

bombing ['bɔm·bing] <-> *m* (*con bombolette spray*) fare ~ to bomb

bombola ['bom·bo·la] *f* (*contenitore*) cylinder; **-e da sub** oxygen cylinders; ~ **del gas** gas cylinder; ~ **ad ossigeno** oxygen cylinder

bomboletta [bom·bo·'let·ta] *f* aerosol

bombolone [bom·bo·'lo:·ne] *m* cream puff

bomboniera [bom·bo·'niɛ:·ra] *f* box of candy, *given as a present to guests at weddings and baptisms*

bonaccia [bo·'nat·tʃa] <-cce> *f* NAUT (*calma di mare e di vento*) dead calm

bonaccione, -a [bo·nat·'tʃo:·ne] *inf* I. *agg* good-natured II. *m, f* good-natured person

bonario, -a [bo·'na:·ri·o] <-i, -ie> *agg* good-natured

bonifica [bo·'ni:·fi·ka] <-che> *f* 1.(*operazione: di palude*) drainage; (*di terreno*) land reclamation 2. MIL clearing

bonificare [bo·ni·fi·'ka:·re] *vt* 1.(*palude*) to drain; (*terreno*) to reclaim 2. MIL to clear 3. FIN to credit

bonifico [bo·'ni:·fi·ko] <-ci> *m* FIN credit transfer

bontà [bon·'ta] <-> *f* 1.(*di persona*) goodness; **abbia la** ~ **di dirmelo** be so kind as to tell me 2.(*di prodotto*) high quality; **che** ~ **questa torta!** this cake is fabulous!

bonus ['bɔ:·nus] <-> *m* bonus

bonus-malus ['bɔ·nus·'ma·lus] <-> *m* no claims bonus

bora ['bɔːra] *f* bora

borbottare [bor·bot·'taːre] *vi, vt inf* **1.** (*parlare in modo indistinto*) to mutter **2.** (*brontolare*) to grumble

borchia ['bɔr·kia] <-chie> *f* stud

bordare [bor·'daːre] *vt* (*tovaglia, vestito*) to hem

bordello [bor·'dɛl·lo] *m* **1.** (*postribolo*) brothel **2.** *fig* (*disordine*) mess **3.** *fig* (*fracasso*) din

bordo ['bor·do] *m* **1.** (*di vestito*) hem; (*guarnizione*) border **2.** (*di tavolo, sedia*) edge; (*di strada*) side; **sul ~ della strada** at the roadside **3.** NAUT (*fiancata della nave*) ship's side; **virare di ~** (*in prua*) to tack; (*in poppa*) to jibe **4.** (*nave, aero, auto*) **salire a ~** to get on board; **prendere qu a ~** to take sb on board; **a ~** on board; **a ~ della macchina** in the car

bordura [bor·'duːra] *f* **1.** (*di aiuola, abito*) border **2.** CULIN garnish

boreale [bo·re·'aːle] *agg* northern; **aurora ~** northern lights

borgata [bor·'gaːta] *f* **1.** (*piccolo centro*) village **2.** (*rione*) working-class suburb

borghese [bor·'geːse] **I.** *agg* **1.** SOC (*della borghesia: famiglia*) middle-class **2.** *fig pej* (*conservatore: mentalità*) bourgeois **3.** ADM (*civile*) civilian; **abito ~** civilian clothes; **poliziotto in ~** plain-clothes policeman **II.** *mf* middle-class person; **piccolo ~** lower middle-class person; *pej* petty bourgeois **III.** *m* civilian

borghesia [bor·ge·'ziːa] <-ie> *f* bourgeoisie; **alta ~** upper middle class; **media ~** middle class; **piccola ~** lower middle class

borgo ['bor·go] <-ghi> *m* (*centro abitato*) village

borgomastro [bor·go·'mas·tro] *m* burgomaster

boria ['bɔːria] <-ie> *f* arrogance

borotalco® [bo·ro·'tal·ko] *m* talcum powder

borraccia [bor·'rat·tʃa] <-cce> *f* (*recipiente*) water bottle

borsa ['bor·sa] *f* **1.** (*sacco*) bag; (*da donna*) handbag; **~ da viaggio** travelling bag; **~ dell'acqua calda** hot water bottle; **~ del ghiaccio** ice bag; **~ della spesa** shopping bag; **o la ~ o la vita!** your money or your life! **2.** FIN Stock Market; **giocare in ~** to play the Stock Market **3.** *fig* (*denaro*) purse; **~ di studio** grant **4.** ANAT bursa; **avere le -e sotto gli occhi** to have bags under one's eyes

borsaiolo, -a [bor·sa·'iɔː·lo] *m, f* pickpocket

borsanera [bor·sa·'neːra] <borsenere> *f* black market

borseggiatore, -trice [bor·sed·dʒa·'toː·re] *m, f* pickpocket

borseggio [bor·'sed·dʒo] <-ggi> *m* pickpocketing

borsellino [bor·sel·'liː·no] *m* purse

borsello [bor·'sɛl·lo] *m* (*da uomo*) handbag

borsenere *pl di* **borsanera**

borsetta [bor·'set·ta] *f* (*da donna*) handbag

borsista [bor·'sis·ta] <-i *m*, -e *f*> *mf* (*chi ha una borsa di studio*) grant holder

boscaglia [bos·'kaʎ·ʎa] <-glie> *f* undergrowth

boscaiolo, -a [bos·ka·'iɔː·lo] *m, f* **1.** (*spaccalegna*) lumberjack **2.** (*guardaboschi*) forester

bosco ['bɔs·ko] <-schi> *m* wood; **~ da taglio** timber wood

boscosità [bos·ko·si·'ta] <-> *f* woodland density

boscoso, -a [bos·'koː·so] *agg* (*montagne, terreno*) wooded

Bosforo ['bɔs·fo·ro] *m* Bosphorous

Bosnia *f* Bosnia

bosniaco, -a [bos·'niaː·ko] <-ci, -che> **I.** *agg* Bosnian **II.** *m, f* (*abitante*) Bosnian

bossolo ['bɔs·so·lo] *m* MIL shell

bostik® ['bɔs·tik] <-> *m* bostik®

BOT, bot <-> *m acro di* **Buono Ordinario del Tesoro** Treasury bill

botanica [bo·'taː·ni·ka] <-che> *f* botany

botanico, -a [bo·'taː·ni·ko] <-ci, -che> **I.** *agg* botanical; **orto** [*o* **giardino**] **~** botanical garden **II.** *m, f* botanist

botola ['bɔː·to·la] *f* (*trabocchetto*) trap door

botta ['bɔt·ta] *f* **1.** (*percossa, colpo*) blow; **un sacco di -e** a thorough beating; **fare a -e** to come to blows; **è stata una bella ~ per lei** *fig* it was a bad blow for her **2.** (*rumore*) bang **3.** *fig* (*battuta pungente*) sarcastic remark; **fare a ~ e risposta** to give as good as one gets

botte ['bot·te] *f* **1.** (*di vino*) cask; **essere in una ~ di ferro** *fig* to be as safe as houses; **nella botte piccola sta** [*o* **c'è**] **il vino buono** *prov* (*persona*) good things come in small packages *prov;* **non si può avere la ~ piena e la moglie ubriaca** *prov* you can't have your cake and eat it too **2.** *a. fig, inf* barrel; **volta a ~** barrel vault

bottega [bot·'teː·ga] <-ghe> *f* **1.** (*negozio*) shop **2.** (*officina: di fabbro, falegname*) workshop **3.** POL **le Botteghe Oscure** headquarters of the Italian left wing political party the Democratici di Sinistra

bottegaio, -a [bot·te·'gaː·io] <-ai, -aie> *m, f* shopkeeper

botteghino [bot·te·'giː·no] *m* THEAT, FILM box office; (*di stadio*) ticket office

bottiglia [bot·'tiʎ·ʎa] <-glie> *f* bottle

bottiglione [bot·tiʎ·'ʎoː·ne] *m* large bottle

bottino [bot·'tiː·no] *m* MIL booty; (*di furto*) loot

botto ['bɔt·to] *m* **1.** (*colpo*) bang; (*di sparo*) crack; **di ~** all of a sudden; **in un ~** all at once **2.** (*fuochi d'artificio*) fire cracker

bottone [bot·'toː·ne] *m* **1.** (*per indumenti*) button; **~ automatico** snapper **2.** BOT **~ d'oro** buttercup **3.** TEC (*interruttore*) switch; **stanza dei -i** *fig* control room **4.** (*loc*) **attaccare ~** (**con qu**) *fig, inf* to strike up a conversation (with sb); **attaccare un ~** (**a qu**) *fig, inf* to buttonhole sb

botulismo [bo·tu·'liz·mo] *m* MED botulism

bouquet [bu·'kɛ] <-> *m* bouquet
boutique [bu·'tik] <-> *f* boutique
bovini [bo·'vi:·ni] *mpl* cattle
bovino [bo·'vi:·no] *agg* 1.(*carne, razza*) bovine 2.(*allevamento*) cattle; **occhi -i** protuberant eyes
bowling ['bou·liŋ] <-> *m* 1.(*gioco*) tenpin bowling 2.(*luogo*) bowling alley
box [bɔks] <-> *m* 1.(*recinto: per bambini*) playpen 2.(*comparto: per animali*) stall 3.(*garage*) garage 4.(*di corse automobilistiche*) pit; **sosta ai ~** pit stop
boxare [bok·'sa:·re] *vi* to box
boxe [bɔks] <-> *f* boxing; **incontro di ~** boxing match
boxer ['bɔk·sə/'bɔk·ser] <-> *m* 1.zoo (*cane*) boxer 2. *pl* (*mutande a calzoncino*) boxer shorts *pl*
boxeur [bɔk·'sœːr] <-> *m* SPORT boxer
boyfriend ['bɔi·frend] <- *o* boyfriends> *m* boyfriend
boy-scout ['bɔi·skaut] *m* scout
bozza ['bɔt·tsa] *f* 1.TYP proof; **correzione di -e** proofreading; **-e di stampa** proofs 2.(*di contratto, progetto*) draft
bozzetto [bot·'tset·to] *m* 1.(*disegno*) sketch 2.(*modello*) scale model
bozzolo ['bɔt·tso·lo] *m* zoo cocoon; **uscire dal ~** zoo to emerge from the cocoon; *fig* to come out of one's shell
BR *fpl abbr di* **Brigate Rosse** Red Brigades
braccare [brak·'ka:·re] *vt* 1.(*selvaggina*) to hunt 2.(*malviventi*) to hunt down
braccetto [brat·'tʃet·to] *m* **a ~** arm in arm; **prendere qu a ~** to take sb's arm
braccia ['brat·tʃa] *f pl di* **braccio¹**
bracciale [brat·'tʃa:·le] *m* 1.(*ornamento*) bracelet 2.(*fascia*) armband 3.(*per nuotare*) water wing
braccialetto [brat·tʃa·'let·to] *m* (*ornamento*) bracelet; **~ elettronico** electronic tag
bracciante [brat·'tʃan·te] *mf* (*lavoratore*) **~ agricolo** farm hand
braccio¹ ['brat·tʃo] <braccia> *m* 1.ANAT arm; **accogliere qu a braccia aperte** to welcome sb with open arms; **agitare le braccia** (*in cerca di aiuto*) to wave one's arms; (*in segno di saluto*) to wave; **portare un bambino in ~** to carry a child (in one's arms); **prendere qu per un ~** to grab sb by the arm; **offrire il ~ a qu** to offer one's arm to sb; **~ di ferro** arm-wrestling; *fig* I arm-wrestled my brother and won; **un ~ di ferro tra sindacati e governo** a tug of war between the unions and the government; **incrociare le braccia** *fig* to down tools; **stare a braccia conserte** to have one's arms crossed; **far cadere le braccia a qc** *fig* to make sb weep; **essere il ~ destro di qu** *fig* to be sb's right-hand man; **gettare le braccia al collo di qu** *fig* to thrown one's arms around sb's neck 2. *pl fig* (*manodopera*) manpower 3.NAUT (*misura di profondità*) fathom
braccio² <-cci> *m* GEOG **~ di fiume** arm of the river; **~ di mare** strait; **~ di terra** stretch of land
bracciolo [brat·'tʃɔ:·lo] *m* arm
brace ['bra:·tʃe] *f* embers *pl;* **una bistecca alla ~** a grilled steak
braciere [bra·'tʃɛː·re] *m* brazier
braciola [bra·'tʃɔ:·la] *f* chop; **~ di maiale** pork chop
brainstorming ['brein·'stɔ:·miŋ] <-> *m* brainstorming
brain trust ['brein 'trʌst] <-> *m* brain trust
brama ['bra:·ma] *f poet* longing; **~ di sapere** thirst for knowledge
bramare [bra·'ma:·re] *vt poet* to long for
bramosia [bra·mo·'si:·a] <-ie> *f* longing
bramoso, -a [bra·'mo:·so] *agg* longing; **essere ~ di qc** to be longing for sth
branca ['braŋ·ka] <-che> *f* (*ramo: di industria, scienza*) branch
branchiato, -a [braŋ·'kia:·to] *agg* (*pesce, creatura*) gilled
branchie ['braŋ·kie] *fpl* (*di pesce*) gills
branco ['braŋ·ko] <-chi> *m* 1.zoo (*di lupi, cani*) pack; (*di uccelli, pecore*) flock; (*di pesci, delfini, foche*) school 2. *fig pej* (*di persone*) gang
brancolare [braŋ·ko·'la:·re] *vi a fig* to grope; **~ nel buio** *fig* to grope in the dark
branda ['bran·da] *f* camp bed
brandello [bran·'dɛl·lo] *m* scrap; **fare a -i** to tear into shreds
brandina [bran·'di:·na] *f* camp bed
brandire [bran·'di:·re] <brandisco> *vt* (*spada, pugnale, coltello*) to brandish
brano ['bra:·no] *m* 1.MUS piece 2.(*di libro*) passage
branzino [bran·'tsi:·no] *m* sea bass
brasato [bra·'za:·to] *m* braised beef
Brasile [bra·'zi:·le] *m* **il ~** Brazil
brasiliano, -a [bra·zi·'lia:·no] I. *agg* Brazilian II. *m, f* Brazilian
bravata [bra·'va:·ta] *f* (*azione rischiosa*) act of bravado
bravo, -a ['bra:·vo] I. *agg* 1.(*abile: artigiano, dottore*) capable; **essere ~ in qc** [*o* a fare qc] to be good at sth [*o* at doing sth] 2.(*per bene: ragazza*) nice 3.(*buono: marito, padre, bambino*) good; **fare il ~** to be good; **su, da ~, vieni qua** *inf* good boy 4.(*loc*) **si è fatto i suoi bravi calcoli** he made his own plans; **la sua brava pizza ogni tanto se la mangia** every now and again he'll eat a pizza; **si fanno le loro brave litigate** they will have their differences II. *int* bravo; **-i bis!** bravo encore!
bravura [bra·'vu:·ra] *f* 1.(*abilità*) skill 2.MUS bravura; **con ~** con bravura
break ['breik/'brɛk] <-> *m* 1.(*pausa, intervallo*) break; **un ~ per il caffè** a coffee break 2.(*interruzione pubblicitaria*) advertising break 3.SPORT (*nel tennis*) break 4.MUS (*breve improvvisazione jazz*) improv
breccia ['bret·tʃa] <-cce> *f* 1.(*ghiaia*) gravel 2. *a. fig* MIL (*apertura*) breach 3.(*loc*) **essere sulla ~** to be at the top; **far ~** *fig* to be a hit

Brennero ['brɛn·ne·ro] *m* Brenner; **Passo del ~** Brenner Pass

bresaola [bre·'za:·o·la] *f sliced dried beef*

bretella [bre·'tɛl·la] *f* 1. *pl* (*per pantaloni, gonne*) braces 2. *fig* (*raccordo*) access road

brev. *abbr di* **brevetto** license

breve ['brɛ:·ve] *agg* short; **-i parole** a few words; **essere ~** *fig* to be brief; **a farla ~** in short; **a ~ termine** short-term; **a ~** shortly; **in ~** in short; **fra ~** shortly

brevettare [bre·vet·'ta:·re] *vt* (*prodotto, sistema, scoperta*) to patent

brevetto [bre·'vet·to] *m* 1. (*su invenzione, prodotto*) patent 2. (*patente*) license; **~** [*o* da] **sub** diving license; **~ da pilota** pilot's license

breviario [bre·'via:·ri·o] <-i> *m* REL (*libro*) breviary

brevità [bre·vi·'ta] <-> *f* (*di testo, periodo*) brevity

brezza ['bred·dza] *f* breeze

bricco ['brik·ko] <-cchi> *m* jug, coffeepot

briccone, -a [brik·'ko:·ne] *m*, *f inf* rascal

briciola ['bri:·tʃo·la] *f* 1. (*di pane*) crumb 2. *fig* (*quantità minima*) tiniest bit; **andare in -e** *fig* to be smashed to smithereens; **ridurre in -e** *fig* to smash to smithereens

briciolo ['bri:·tʃo·lo] *m fig* (*quantità minima*) tiniest bit; **avere un ~ di cervello** *fig* to have an ounce of common sense

bricolage [bri·ko·'laʒ] <-> *m* do-it-yourself

bridge [bridʒ] <-> *m* bridge; **il circolo del ~** the bridge club

briefing ['bri:·fiŋ] <-> *m* (*di piloti, skipper, turisti*) briefing; **fare ~** to hold a briefing

briga ['bri:·ga] <-ghe> *f* 1. (*problema*) trouble; **prendersi la ~ di fare qc** to take the trouble to do sth 2. (*lite*) quarrel; **attaccar ~ con qu** to start a quarrel with sb

brigadiere [bri·ga·'diɛ:·re] *m* (*di Carabinieri, Guardia di Finanza*) sergeant

brigante, -essa [bri·'gan·te, bri·gan·'tes·sa] *m*, *f* 1. (*bandito*) bandit 2. *scherz, inf* (*briccone*) rascal

brigare [bri·'ga:·re] *vi inf* **~ per avere qc** to pull some strings to get sth

brigata [bri·'ga:·ta] *f* 1. *inf* (*gruppo*) group 2. MIL brigade; **~ aerea** air brigade; **le Brigate Rosse** the Red Brigades

brigatista [bri·ga·'dis·ta] <-i *m*, -e *f*> *mf* **~ nero** member of the Black Brigades; **~ rosso** member of the Red Brigades

briglia ['briʎ·ʎa] <-glie> *f* 1. (*per cavalli*) bridle; **a ~ sciolta** *fig* quickly 2. (*di torrente*) dyke

brillantante [bril·lan·'tan·te] *m* (*per lavastoviglie*) dishwasher rinse agent, *especially designed to make dishes shine*

brillante [bril·'lan·te] **I.** *agg* 1. *a fig* (*che spicca: persona, ingegno, idea*) brilliant; **avere la ~ idea di fare qc** *a. iron* to have the brilliant idea of doing sth 2. (*mondano: vita*) full 3. (*che brilla: occhi, vetro, pavimento*) shining

4. (*vivace: colore*) bright **II.** *m* (*gioiello*) diamond

brillantina [bril·lan·'ti:·na] *f* brilliantine

brillare [bril·'la:·re] **I.** *vi* 1. (*stella, sole, occhi*) to shine 2. *fig* (*spiccare*) to stand out; **~ per qc** to be outstanding in sth; **dirigenti che brillano per intelligenza** managers who are outstandingly intelligent; **i giornalisti brillavano per la loro assenza** the journalists were conspicuous by their absence 3. (*esplodere: mina*) to explode **II.** *vt* 1. (*bomba, mina*) to explode 2. (*riso*) to husk

brillo, -a ['bril·lo] *agg* tipsy

brina ['bri:·na] *f* frost

brindare [brin·'da:·re] *vi* **~ a qu/qc** to toast sb/sth; **brindiamo alla tua promozione** let's drink to your promotion

brindisi ['brin·di·zi] <-> *m* toast; **fare un ~** (**a qu**) to toast (to sb)

Brindisi *f* Brindisi, *a city in the Puglia region*

Brindisino *m* (*zona*) Brindisi area

brindisino, -a [brin·di·'zi:·no] **I.** *agg* from Brindisi **II.** *m*, *f* (*abitante*) person from Brindisi

brio ['bri:·o] *m* 1. (*allegria*) verve 2. (*vivacità espressiva*) zest

brioche [bri·'ɔʃ] <-> *f* (*cornetto*) brioche

brioso, -a [bri·'o:·so] *agg* 1. (*allegro: persona*) bubbly 2. (*racconto, commedia*) joyful

briscola ['bris·ko·la] *f* 1. (*gioco*) briscola, *a type of card game* 2. (*carta*) trump card; **conta quanto il due di briscola** he counts for nothing

bristol ['bris·tol] <-> *m* colored card

brivido ['bri:·vi·do] *m* 1. (*tremore: per freddo, febbre*) shiver; **mi vengono i -i** it gives me the shivers 2. (*emozione*) thrill; **il ~ della velocità** the thrill of speed; **racconto del ~** suspense story; **sentire un ~ di piacere** to feel a thrill of pleasure

brizzolato, -a [brit·tso·'la:·to] *agg* 1. (*persona*) gray-haired 2. (*barba, capelli*) graying

brocca ['brɔk·ka] <-cche> *f* jug

broccato [brok·'ka:·to] *m* brocade

broccoli ['brɔk·ko·li] *mpl* CULIN broccoli

broche [brɔʃ] <-> *f* brooch

broda ['brɔ:·da] *f fig, pej* 1. (*minestra*) thin soup 2. (*acqua sporca*) dishwater

brodetto [bro·'det·to] *m* **~ di pesce** fish soup

brodo ['brɔ:·do] *m* broth; **~ ristretto** consommé; **~ di verdura** vegetable broth; **tortellini in ~** tortellini in a broth; **lasciar cuocere** [*o* **bollire**] **qu nel proprio ~** *fig* to let sb stew; **andare in ~ di giuggiole per qc** *fig* to go into raptures about sth; **tutto fa ~** *fig* every bit helps

broglio ['brɔʎ·ʎo] <-gli> *m* (*frode*) **~ elettorale** election rigging

broker ['brou·kə/'brɔ·ker] <-> *mf* FIN (*mediatore*) broker; **~ finanziario** financial broker; **~ di assicurazioni** insurance broker

bronchite [broŋ·'ki:·te] *f* bronchitis

broncio ['bron·tʃo] <-ci> *m inf* sulky face; **fare** [*o* **tenere**] **il ~** to sulk

bronco ['broŋ·ko] <-chi> *m* bronchial tube

brontolare [bron·to·'la:·re] *vi* 1.(*persona*) to grumble; (*borbottare*) to mutter 2.(*stomaco*) to rumble

brontolio [bron·to·'li:o] <-ii> *m* 1.(*di persona*) grumbling; (*borbottio*) muttering 2.(*di tuono, motore, di stomaco*) rumbling

brontolone, -a [bron·to·'lo:·ne] I. *agg* grumbling II. *m, f* grumbler

bronx [brɔŋks] *m fig* (*quartiere malfamato*) hood

bronzo ['bron·dzo] *m* bronze; **età del ~** Bronze Age; **faccia di ~** *fig* nerve; **che faccia di ~!** what nerve!; **ha avuto la faccia di ~ di dirmi che ...** he had the nerve to tell me that ...

brossura [bros·'su:·ra] *f* **in ~** paperback

browser ['brau·zə] <- *o* browsers> *m* COMPUT browser

brrr [br] *int* brrr

brucare [bru·'ka:·re] *vt* to nibble

bruciapelo [bru·tʃa·'pe:·lo] *avv* **a ~** (*all'improvviso*) out of the blue

bruciare [bru·'tʃa:·re] I. *vt avere* 1.(*carta, legna, pentola*) to burn; (*casa*) to burn down 2.(*con ferro da stiro*) to scorch 3.(*sole, vento, freddo*) to burn; (*gelo*) to blacken II. *vi essere* 1.(*fuoco, carta, rami*) to burn 2.(*casa, bosco*) to be on fire 3.(*sole, sabbia*) to be burning 4.(*cibi*) to be hot 5.*fig* (*ardere*) to be burning; **~ dal desiderio di fare qc** to be burning with desire to do sth; **~ di febbre** to be burning with fever III. *vr:* **-rsi** 1.(*scottarsi*) to burn oneself 2.(*arrosto, risotto, sugo*) to be burnt

bruciato [bru·'tʃa:·to] *m* 1.CULIN **il sugo sa di bruciato** the sauce tastes burnt 2.(*odore*) burning

bruciato, -a *agg* 1.(*dal fuoco, ustionato, troppo cotto*) burnt 2.(*dal sole: capelli, pelle*) sunburnt 3.(*inaridito: campo*) scorched 4.(*precocemente finito*) wasted; **gioventù -a** wasted youth

bruciatore [bru·tʃa·'to:·re] *m* burner

bruciatura [bru·tʃa·'tu:·ra] *f* (*scottatura*) burn

bruciore [bru·'tʃo:·re] *m* 1.MED burning; **~ di stomaco** stomach acid 2.*fig* (*ardore*) sting

bruco ['bru:·ko] <-chi> *m* grub

brufolo ['bru:·fo·lo] *m* spot

brughiera [bru·'giɛ:·ra] *f* heath

brûlé [bry·'le] <inv> *agg* **vino ~** mulled wine

brulicare [bru·li·'ka:·re] *vi* to be swarming; **il centro brulicava di gente** it was swarming with people downtown

brullo, -a ['brul·lo] *agg* (*campagna, paesaggio*) barren

bruma ['bru:·ma] *f* mist

Brunico [bru·'ni:·ko] *f* Bruneck

bruno ['bru:·no] *m* (*colore*) brown

bruno, -a I. *agg* (*capelli, occhi*) brown; (*carnagione*) dark; (*persona*) dark-haired II. *m, f* (*persona*) dark-haired person

brusco, -a ['brus·ko] <-schi, -sche> *agg* 1.(*maniere, modi, tono*) brusque 2.(*frenata, movimento*) abrupt

bruscolo ['brus·ko·lo] *m* speck

brusio [bru·'zi:·o] <-ii> *m* (*di voci*) buzzing

brutale [bru·'ta:·le] *agg* 1.(*crudele: gesto*) brutal 2.(*spietato: domanda*) blunt

brutalità [bru·ta·li·'ta] <-> *f* 1.(*ferocia*) brutality 2.(*spietatezza*) bluntness

bruto, -a ['bru:·to] I. *agg* (*animalesco*) brute; **forza -a** brute strength II. *m, f* brute

brutta ['brut·ta] *f inf* (*brutta copia*) rough copy

bruttezza [brut·'tet·tsa] *f* (*di città, edificio, film, persona*) ugliness

brutto ['brut·to] I. *m* 1. ugliness; **il ~ è che ...** the problem is that ...; **ha di ~ che ...** (*persona, cosa*) his [*o* her] [*o* its] problem is that ...; **Laura ha di ~ che non si sa vestire** Laura's problem is that she dresses badly 2.(*tempo*) bad weather; **il tempo si mette al ~** the weather is taking a turn for the worse II. *avv* **di ~** badly; **qui nevica di ~** it's snowing heavily here

brutto, -a I. *agg* 1.(*non bello: persona, quadro, spettacolo,*) ugly; **essere ~ come il peccato** to be as ugly as sin 2.(*abitudine, momento*) bad; **attraversare un ~ momento** to have a bad time 3.(*nuvoloso: tempo, giornata*) horrible; **fa ~ tempo** the weather is horrible 4.(*pesante: scherzo, tiro*) nasty; **un ~ tiro** a mean trick 5.(*forte: raffreddore*) heavy; (*tosse*) bad; **un ~ male** cancer 6.(*loc*) **-a copia** rough copy; **fare una -a figura** *fig* to create a bad impression; **fare una -a fine** *fig* to come to a bad end; **se l'è vista -a** he [*o* she] has had a bad time of it; **passarne delle -e** to go through a bad patch; **~ ignorante!** *pej, inf* pig! II. *m, f* ugly person

Bruxelles [bru·'ksɛl·le] *f* Brussels

BSE *f abbr di* Bovine Spongiform Encephalopathy BSE

bua ['bu:·a] *f* (*linguaggio infantile*) pain; **farsi la ~** *inf* to hurt oneself; **hai la ~ al pancino?** *inf* does your tummy ache?

buca ['bu:·ka] <-che> *f* 1.(*fossa*) pit 2.SPORT (*nel golf*) hole 3.(*nel biliardo*) pocket 4.(*loc*) **~ delle lettere** letterbox; **~ del suggeritore** prompter's box

bucaneve [bu·ka·'ne:·ve] <-> *m* snowdrop

bucare [bu·'ka:·re] I. *vt* 1.(*forare: biglietto, lamiera, legno*) **bucare qc** to make a hole in sth; **~ (una gomma)** to get a puncture 2.(*pungere: pelle, naso, orecchie*) to pierce II. *vr:* **-rsi** 1.(*pungersi*) to prick oneself 2.(*pneumatico*) to puncture 3.*sl* (*drogati*) to mainline

Bucarest [bu·ka·'rɛst/'bu:·ka·rest] *f* Bucharest

bucatini [bu·ka·'ti:·ni] *mpl* bucatini, *large spaghetti*

bucato [bu·'ka:·to] *m* washing; **fare il ~** to do the washing; **fresco di ~** freshly washed

bucato, -a *agg* with holes; (*metallo, pelle*) pierced; **avere le mani -e** *fig* to be a spendthrift

buccia ['but·tʃa] <-cce> *f* (*di frutta, verdura, salume*) skin; (*di agrumi, patate*) peel

buco ['buːko] <-chi> *m* 1.(*foro, debito, piercing*) hole 2.(*apertura*) opening; ~ **della chiave** keyhole 3.(*bugigattolo*) pokey space 4.(*intervallo*) gap 5. *sl* (*di eroina*) fix 6.(*loc*) **tappare un** ~ *a fig* to fill in a gap

Budapest ['buːda·pest/bu·da·'pɛst] *f* Budapest

buddismo [bud·'diz·mo] *m* Buddhism

buddista [bud·'dis·ta] <-i *m*, -e *f*> I. *agg* Buddhist II. *mf* Buddhist

budello [bu·'dɛl·lo] *m* 1.ANAT bowel 2.(*materiale*) gut 3.(*locale lungo e stretto*) oblong

budget ['bʌ·dʒit/'ba·dʒət] <-> *m* budget

budino [bu·'diː·no] *m* pudding

bue ['buː·e] <buoi> *m* 1.ZOO ox; **lavorare come un** ~ to work like a slave; ~ **muschiato** musk ox 2.*fig, inf* (*uomo ignorante*) ignoramus

bufala ['buː·fa·la] *f* 1.(*femmina del bufalo*) cow buffalo 2.(*errore*) howler; **fare una** ~ to make a howler 3.(*nel giornalismo: notizia falsa*) invented story

bufalo ['buː·fa·lo] *m* buffalo; **mangiare come un** ~ to tuck in

bufera [bu·'fɛː·ra] *f* 1.(*tempesta*) storm; ~ **di neve** snowstorm 2.(*agitazione*) upset

buffet [by·'fɛ] <-> *m* 1.(*mobile*) sideboard 2.(*pranzo*) buffet; ~ **freddo** cold buffet

buffetto [buf·'fet·to] *m* tap

buffo ['buf·fo] *m* 1.THEAT comedian 2.(*cosa*) funny thing

buffo, -a *agg* 1.(*cosa, persona*) funny 2.THEAT comic; **opera -a** comic opera

buffonata [buf·fo·'na:·ta] *f* (*cosa poca seria*) joke; **fare -e** to play a prank

buffone [buf·'foː·ne] *m*, *f* 1. *inf* (*pagliaccio*) clown; **fare il** ~ to play the clown 2.HIST (*di corte*) jester

bug [bʌg] <- *o* bugs> *m* COMPUT bug

bugia [bu·'dʒiː·a] <-gie> *f* (*menzogna*) lie; **dire le -gie** to tell lies; **le -gie hanno le gambe corte** *prov* truth will out *prov*

bugiardo, -a [bu·'dʒar·do] I. *agg* (*persona*) lying II. *m*, *f* liar

bugigattolo [bu·dʒi·'gat·to·lo] (*locale piccolo*) cubbyhole

buio ['buː·io] *m* dark; **al** ~ in the dark; ~ **pesto** pitch dark; **farsi** ~ to become dark; **prima del** ~ before dark; **brancolare** [*o* **brancicare**] **nel** ~ *fig* to grope in the dark; **fare un salto nel** ~ *fig* to take a leap into the unknown

buio, -a <bui, buie> *agg* 1.(*non illuminato: notte, finestra, stanza*) dark 2.(*periodo*) bad

bulbo ['bul·bo] *m* 1. BOT bulb 2.(*di lampadina, di termometro*) light bulb 3.ANAT ~ **oculare** [*o* **dell'occhio**] eyeball

Bulgaria [bul·ga·'riː·a] *f* Bulgaria

bulgaro ['bul·ga·ro] *m* (*lingua*) Bulgarian

bulgaro, -a I. *agg* Bulgarian II. *m*, *f* Bulgarian

bullo ['bul·lo] *m* 1.(*gradasso*) **fare il** ~ to act tough 2.(*teppista*) boor

bumerang ['buː·me·raŋg] *v.* **boomerang**

bungalow ['bʌŋ·gə·lou/'bun·ga·lov] <-> *m* chalet

bungee-jumping ['ban·dʒi·'dʒam·ping] <-> *m* SPORT bungee jumping; **fare il** ~ to go bungee jumping

buoi ['buɔː·i] *pl di* **bue**

buon, buon' [buɔn] *v.* **buono, -a**

buonafede, buona fede [buo·na·'feː·de] *f* **in** ~ in good faith

buonanima, buon'anima [buo·'na:·niː·ma] *f* late lamented; **la** ~ **del nonno** grandpa, God rest his soul

buonanotte, buona notte [buo·na·'nɔt·te] I. *int* good night; **... e** ~ **!** *inf* ... and that's that! II. <-> *f* **dare** [*o* **augurare**] **la** ~ **a qu** to say good night to sb

buonasera, buona sera [buo·na·'seː·ra] I. *int* good evening II. <-> *f* **dare** [*o* **augurare**] **la** ~ **a qu** to wish sb good evening

buoncostume, buon costume [buoŋ·kos·'tuː·me] <-> *m* public decency; **squadra del** ~ vice squad

buondì [buon·'di] *int* hello

buongiorno, buon giorno [buon·'dʒor·no] I. *int* good morning II.<-> *m* **dare** [*o* **augurare**] **il** ~ **a qu** to wish sb good morning

buongoverno, buon governo [buoŋ·go·'vɛr·no] <-> *m* good government

buongrado [buon·'gra:·do] *avv* **di** ~ willingly

buongustaio, -a [buoŋ·gus·'ta:·io] <-ai, -aie> *m*, *f* CULIN gourmet

buongusto, buon gusto [buoŋ·'gus·to] *m* 1.(*raffinatezza*) good taste; **con** ~ tastefully 2.(*tatto*) tact

buono ['buɔː·no] *m* 1.COM (*documento*) voucher; **un** ~ **per l'acquisto di libri** book token; ~ **del Tesoro** Treasury bill 2. *sing* (*ciò che è buono*) good thing; **sapere di** ~ to smell nice; **c'è di** ~ **che ...** at least

buono, -a <più buono *o* migliore, buonissimo *o* ottimo> I. *agg* 1.(*albergo, libro, voto*) good 2.(*gentile: persona, animo*) kind; **un'anima -a** a kind soul; **è -a gente** they're nice people; **essere** ~ **con qu** to be nice to sb; **essere** ~ **come il pane** to have a heart of gold 3.(*calmo: bambino, cane*) good 4.(*abile: medico, avvocato, artigiano*) good; **un buon medico** a good doctor; **un buon falegname** a good carpenter; **essere in -e mani** to be in good hands 5.(*utilizzabile: attrezzatura, auto*) good; **una -a macchina fotografica** a good camera 6.(*propizio: momento*) right; **il momento** ~ **per cambiare auto** the right time to buy a new car 7.(*vantaggioso: affare*) **fare un buon affare** to get a bargain 8.(*giusto: ragione*) valid 9.(*gradevole: odore*) nice; **c'è un buon odore qui** there's a nice smell 10.(*delizioso: pranzo, vino*) delicious 11.(*valido: biglietto*) valid; (*bancanote*) genuine; **questa moneta è ancora -a** this coin is still accepted; **a buon mercato** cheap(ly) 12.(*temperato: clima*) temperate 13.(*sano, robusto*) healthy 14.(*socialmente elevato*) high; **l'ingresso nella -a società** entry into high society **15.** (*adatto: maniere*) good; **con le -e** nicely **16.** (*loc*) **alla -a** simple; **ti ho aspettato un'ora -a** I waited a good hour for you **17.** (*espressioni esclamative*) **buon anno!** Happy New Year!; **buon appetito!** enjoy your meal!; **buon divertimento!** have a good time!; **buon giorno!** good morning!; **buon riposo!** sleep well!; **buon viaggio!** have a good journey!; **-a fortuna!** good luck!; **-a notte!** good night!; **-a sera!** good evening!; **Dio ~!** good God! **II.** *m, f* (*persona*) good person; **un ~ a nulla** a good-for-nothing; **essere un poco di ~** to be a nasty piece of work; **fare il ~** to be good

buonomini *pl di* **buonuomo**

buonora, buon'ora [buo·'no:·ra] <-> *f* **di ~** early; **alla ~!** about time!

buonsenso, buon senso [buoŋ·'sɛn·so] <-> *m* common sense

buontempone, -a [buoŋ·tem·'po:·ne] *m, f inf* cheerful person

buonumore, buon umore [buoŋ·u·'mo:·re] <-> *m* good mood; **essere di ~** to be in a good mood

buonuomo, buon uomo [buo·'nuɔ:·mo] <buon(u)omini> *m* (*uomo buono*) a good guy

buonuscita, buona uscita [buoŋ·uʃ·'ʃi:·ta, 'buɔ:·na uʃ·'ʃi:·ta] *f* **1.** (*per un appartamento*) *money paid when sb gives up a rented property* **2.** (*per un impiego*) golden handshake

burattinaio, -a [bu·rat·ti·'na:·io] <-ai> *m, f* puppet master

burattino [bu·rat·'ti:·no] *m* **1.** THEAT puppet; (*con fili*) marionette; **teatro dei -i** puppet theater **2.** *fig* (*persona manovrata da altri*) puppet; **piantare baracca e -i** *fig* to pack up and leave

burbero, -a ['bur·be·ro] *agg* (*aria, sguardo, tono*) surly

burla ['bur·la] *f* prank; **mettere in ~ qc** to make fun of sth; **per ~** for a joke

burlarsi [bur·'la:r·si] *vr* **-rsi di qu/qc** to make fun of sb/sth

burlone, -a [bur·'lo:·ne] **I.** *m, f inf* joker **II.** *agg inf* jokey

burocrate [bu·'rɔ:·kra·te] *mf* **1.** ADM bureaucrat **2.** *fig pej* (*persona pedante*) pedant

burocratese [bu·ro·kra·'te:·se] *m* bureaucratese

burocratico, -a [bu·ro·'kra:·ti·ko] <-ci, -che> *agg* bureaucratic

burocrazia [bu·ro·krat·'tsi:·a] <-ie> *f* **1.** ADM bureaucracy **2.** *pej* (*pedanteria, lungaggine*) pedantry

burrasca [bur·'ras·ka] <-sche> *f* **1.** (*tempesta*) storm; **il mare è in ~** the sea is stormy **2.** (*litigio*) **aria di ~** trouble brewing

burrascoso, -a [bur·ras·'ko:·so] *agg* stormy

burrata [bur·'ra:·ta] *f a full-fat soft cheese*

burro ['bur·ro] *m* butter; **al ~** in butter; **pane e ~** bread and butter

burrone [bur·'ro:·ne] *m* ravine

bus [bʌs] <-> *m* **1.** (*autobus*) bus **2.** COMPUT transfer speed of data

buscare [bus·'ka:·re] *vt, vr:* **-rsi** *inf* to catch; **-rsi l'influenza** to catch flu; **buscarne** [*o* **buscarle**] to catch it

business ['biz·nis] <-> *m* **1. fare ~** to do business **2.** (*azienda*) business

bussare [bus·'sa:·re] *vi* to knock; **~ alla porta** to knock on the door

busse ['bus·se] *fpl inf* blows; **prendere le ~** to get a thrashing

bussola ['bus·so·la] *f* NAUT compass; **perdere la ~** *fig* to lose one's bearings; (= *confondersi*)

bussolotto ['bus·so·'lɔt·to] *m* dice shaker

busta ['bus·ta] *f* **1.** (*per lettera*) envelope; **~ paga** pay packet **2.** (*custodia: per occhiali*) case **3.** (*borsa: per generi alimentari*) bag

bustarella [bus·ta·'rɛl·la] *f* bribe

busto ['bus·to] *m* **1.** ANAT, ART (*tronco*) bust **2.** MED (*a. da donna*) corset

buttafuori [but·ta·'fuɔ:·ri] <-> *m* bouncer

buttare [but·'ta:·re] **I.** *vt* **1.** (*gettare*) to throw; **buttare qc a qu** to throw sth at sb **2.** (*loc*) **~ all'aria** (*cassetto*) to turn inside out; (*piano, progetto*) to give up on; **~ giù un edificio** to knock down a building; **~ giù due righe** to jot down a couple of lines; **~ giù un boccone** to have a quick bite; **~ giù una bottiglia di cognac** to down a bottle of brandy; **~ (via)** (*nella spazzatura*) to throw away; (*sprecare*) to waste; **~ la pasta** to put the pasta on **II.** *vr:* **-rsi** to throw oneself; **-rsi dalla finestra** to throw oneself out of the window; **-rsi nelle braccia di qu** to throw oneself into sb's arms; **-rsi in mare** to dive into the sea; **-rsi nel fuoco per qu** *fig* to walk through fire for sb; **-rsi giù** *fig* to get depressed

bypass ['bai·'pa:s] <-* o* bypasses> *m a.* MED bypass

bypassare [bai·pas·'sa:·re] *vt* to bypass

byte [bait] <-> *m* COMPUT byte

C

C, c [tʃi] <-> *f* C; **~ come Catania** C for Charlie

c. *abbr di* **circa** c.

c.a. *abbr di* **corrente anno** current year

cabala ['ka:·ba·la] *f* **1.** (*nel misticismo ebraico*) Kabbalah **2.** *fig* (*tecnica*) *method of predicting the future using letters, symbols, or dreams*

cabaret [ka·ba·'rɛ] <-> *m* cabaret

cabina [ka·'bi:·na] *f* **1.** (*vano*) booth; **~ elettrica** substation; **~ di proiezione** projection booth; **~ di registrazione** recording booth; **~ telefonica** telephone booth **2.** (*di automezzo*) cab; **~ della funicolare** cable car;

~ di guida driver's cab **3.** (*di nave, velivolo*) cabin; **~ di pilotaggio** cockpit; **~ passeggeri** AERO passenger compartment **4.** (*al mare*) beach hut

cabinato [ka·bi·'naː·to] *m* NAUT (*barca*) cabin cruiser

cabotaggio [ka·bo·'tad·dʒo] <-ggi> *m* NAUT (*navigazione costiera*) coastal navigation

cabriolet [ka·bri·o·'lɛ] <-> *m* (*automobile scoperta*) convertible

cacao [ka·'kaːo] <-> *m* **1.** (*pianta*) cacao **2.** (*sostanza*) cocoa

cacare [ka·'kaː·re] **I.** *vi, vt* vulg to shit *vulg;* **ma va a ~!** just fuck off! **II.** *vr* vulg **cacarsi sotto** *fig* to shit oneself *vulg*

cacarella [ka·ka·'rɛl·la] *f* **1.** *vulg* shits *pl vulg* **2.** *fig* (*paura*) **avere la ~** to be shitting oneself *vulg*

cacata [ka·'kaː·ta] *f vulg* **1.** (*atto*) shit *vulg* **2.** *fig* (*cosa brutta*) piece of shit *vulg*

cacca ['kak·ka] <-cche> *f* inf poo inf; **fare la ~** to go poo

cacchio ['kak·kio] <-cchi> *m* vulg dick *vulg;* **che ~ vuoi?** what the hell do you want?; **non vale un ~** it's not worth a damn

caccia¹ ['kat·tʃa] <-cce> *f* **1.** (*arte venatoria*) hunting; **~ alla lepre** open field coursing; **~ grossa** big game hunting; **cane da ~** hunting dog; **andare a ~** to go hunting **2.** (*inseguimento*) hunt; **aereo da ~** fighter (plane); **dare la ~ a qu** to hunt sb **3.** (*ricerca*) search; **a ~ di guai** looking for trouble

caccia² <-> *m* **1.** AERO fighter (plane) **2.** NAUT destroyer

cacciabombardiere [kat·tʃa·bom·bar·'diɛ·re] *m* fighter-bomber

cacciagione [kat·tʃa·'dʒoː·ne] *f* game

cacciare [kat·'tʃaː·re] **I.** *vt* **1.** SPORT (*animali*) to hunt **2.** *fig* (*mettere*) to put; **dove ho cacciato l'orologio?** *inf* where have I put my watch? **3.** (*mandar via*) to throw out **4.** (*tirare fuori*) to get out; **~ i soldi** *inf* to fork out money *inf;* **~ fuori la lingua** to stick out one's tongue **5.** *inf* (*emettere*) to let out; **~ un urlo** to let out a yell **II.** *vr:* **-rsi 1.** *inf* (*nascondersi*) to hide (oneself); **dove si è cacciato?** *inf* where's he gotten to? *inf* **2.** (*introdursi*) to get; **-rsi nei pasticci** *fig* to get into trouble

cacciatora [kat·tʃa·'toː·ra] *f* **1.** (*giacca*) hunting jacket **2.** CULIN **alla ~** chasseur

cacciatore, -trice *m, f* hunter; **~ di frodo** poacher; **~ di teste** headhunter *a. fig*

cacciavite [kat·tʃa·'viː·te] <-> *m* screwdriver

caccola ['kak·ko·la] *m* **1.** *inf* (*di naso*) booger *inf* **2.** (*di occhi*) eye-gum **3.** (*cacca: di animale*) dropping

cache [kæʃ] **I.** <inv> *agg* COMPUT cache; **memoria ~** cache memory **II.** <-> *f* COMPUT cache

cachemire [kaʃ·'miːr] <-> *m* cashmere

cachet [ka·'ʃɛ] <-> *m* **1.** MED (*compressa*) tablet **2.** THEAT, FILM (*compenso*) fee

cachi ['kaː·ki] **I.** <inv> *agg* (*colore*) khaki **II.** <-> *m* **1.** (*colore cachi*) khaki **2.** (*albero, frutto*) persimmon

cacio ['kaː·tʃo] <-ci> *m* cheese; **una forma di ~** a cheese; **come il ~ sui maccheroni** *fig* at just the right time

caciocavallo [ka·tʃo·ka·'val·lo] <caci(o)cavalli> *m mer: pear-shaped cheese from Southern Italy*

caciotta [ka·'tʃot·ta] *f small flat cheese from Central Italy*

cacofonia [ka·ko·fo·'niː·a] <-ie> *f* cacophony

cactus ['kak·tus] <-> *m* cactus

CAD COMPUT *abbr di* **Computer Aided Design** CAD

cadavere [ka·'daː·ve·re] *m* corpse

cadaverico, -a [ka·da·'vɛ·ri·ko] <-ci, -che> *agg* **1.** (*del cadavere*) cadaveric; **rigidità -a** rigor or mortis **2.** *fig* (*simile ai cadaveri*) deathly

caddi ['kad·di] *1. pers sing pass rem di* **cadere¹**

cadente [ka·'dɛn·te] *agg* **1.** (*edificio*) crumbling **2.** *fig* (*persona*) decrepit **3.** (*astro*) **stella ~** shooting star

cadenza [ka·'dɛn·tsa] *f* **1.** LING (*intonazione*) intonation **2.** MUS cadenza

cadenzare [ka·den·'tsaː·re] *vt* **1.** (*ritmare*) to mark the rhythm of; **~ il passo** to walk at a fixed pace **2.** LIT (*modulare*) to modulate; **~ la voce** to modulate one's voice

cadere¹ [ka·'deː·re] <cado, caddi, caduto> *vi essere* **1.** (*cascare: persona*) to fall; (*aereo*) to crash; **~ lungo e disteso** to fall flat on one's face; **~ morto** to drop dead; **~ in piedi** *a fig* to land on one's feet; **~ dalle nuvole** *fig* to be shocked; **far ~ qc dall'alto** *fig* to flaunt sth **2.** (*staccarsi: capelli*) to fall out; (*foglie, frutta*) to fall **3.** (*abito*) to hang; **quest'abito cade bene** *fig* this suit hangs well **4.** (*trovarsi in difficoltà*) **~ ammalato** to fall sick; **~ in disgrazia** to fall out of favor; **~ in miseria** to fall on hard times; **~ nell'oblio** to be completely forgotten **5.** *fig* (*morire: in battaglia*) to fall *fig* **6.** (*crollare: edificio*) to fall down **7.** POL (*governo*) to fall; **far ~ un governo** to bring down a government **8.** (*venir giù: pioggia*) to fall **9.** (*finire: vento*) to drop **10.** (*capitare*) **~ a proposito** to come at the right time **11.** (*loc*) **~ nel ridicolo** to make a fool of oneself; **~ nel volgare** to descend into vulgarity; **~ dalla padella nella brace** *fig* to jump out of the frying pan into the fire

cadere² *m* **al ~ del sole** at sunset

cadetto [ka·'det·to] *m* **1.** (*figlio non primogenito*) younger son **2.** MIL cadet **3.** SPORT junior

cadetto, -a *agg* **1.** (*di figlio non primogenito*) younger **2.** SPORT junior

cadmio ['kad·mio] *m* cadmium

caduco, -a [ka·'duː·ko] <-chi, -che> *agg* **1.** BOT (*foglie, bosco*) deciduous **2.** *fig* (*effimero: pensiero*) fleeting; (*valore*) transitory; **mal ~** *inf* epilepsy

caduta [ka·'duː·ta] *f* (*il cadere*) fall; '**~ massi**' 'falling rocks'; **~ della temperatura** drop in temperature

caduto [ka·'du:·to] *m* MIL fallen soldier; **i -i** the fallen

caduto, -a *pp di* **cadere**[1]

caffè [kaf·'fɛ] <-> *m* **1.** CULIN coffee; ~ **espresso** espresso; ~ **corretto** liqueur coffee; ~ **macchiato** coffee with a dash of milk; ~ **in chicchi** coffee beans *pl;* ~ **in polvere** coffee powder; **macchinetta del** ~ coffee machine **2.** (*locale*) café; ~ **concerto** *café with live music* **3.** BOT coffee bush

> **i** The first coffee house in Europe opened in Venice in 1647. Since that time the drinking of coffee (**caffè**) has spread throughout Italy. Italians enjoy drinking several different varieties of coffee: **espresso** (small, strong black coffee), **cappuccino** (coffee with frothy milk), **caffellatte** (coffee with a lot of milk), **caffè macchiato** (espresso with a drop of hot milk), **latte macchiato** (hot milk with a drop of coffee), **caffè corretto** (black coffee with alcohol in it), and so on.

caffeina [kaf·fe·'i:·na] *f* caffeine; **caffè senza** ~ decaffeinated coffee

caffel(l)atte [kaf·fe·'lat·te (kaffel'latte)] <-> *m* white coffee

caffetteria [kaf·fet·te·'ri:·a] <-ie> *f* (*bar: di museo*) coffee bar

caffettiera [kaf·fet·'tiɛ:·ra] *f* **1.** (*macchina*) coffee-maker **2.** (*bricco*) coffeepot

cafone, -a [ka·'fo:·ne] **I.** *agg* boorish **II.** *m, f* boor

cagare [ka·'ga:·re] *v.* cacare

cagionare [ka·dʒo·'na:·re] *vt* to cause

cagionevole [ka·dʒo·'ne:·vo·le] *agg* delicate; **essere di salute** ~ to have delicate health

cagliare [kaʎ·'ʎa:·re] *vi, vr:* **-rsi** (*latte*) to curdle

Cagliari *f* Cagliari, *capital of Sardinia*

Cagliaritano Cagliari area; **nel** ~ in the Cagliari area

cagliaritano, -a [caʎ·ʎa·ri·'ta:·no] **I.** *agg* from Cagliari **II.** *m, f* (*abitante*) person from Cagliari

cagna ['kaɲ·ɲa] *f* **1.** ZOO bitch **2.** *pej, inf* (*sgualdrina*) slut *inf*

cagnara [kaɲ·'ɲa:·ra] *f pej, inf* racket *inf*

cagnesco, -a [kaɲ·'ɲes·ko] <-schi, -sche> *agg* hostile; **guardare qu in** ~ *fig* to look daggers at sb

CAI ['ka:·i] *m acro di* **Club Alpino Italiano** *Italian mountaineering organization*

Cairo ['ka:·i·ro] *m* **Il** ~ Cairo

cal *abbr di* (**piccola**) **caloria** cal.

cala ['ka:·la] *f* (*insenatura*) inlet

calabrese [ka·la·'bre:·se] **I.** *agg* Calabrian **II.** *mf* (*abitante*) Calabrian **III.** *sing* (*dialetto*) Calabrian

Calabria [ka·'la:·bri·a] *f* Calabria; **abitare in** ~ to live in Calabria; **andare in** ~ to go to Calabria

calabrone [ka·la·'bro:·ne] *m* ZOO hornet

calamaio [ka·la·'ma:·io] <-ai> *m* inkpot

calamaro [ka·la·'ma:·ro] *m* ZOO squid

calamita [ka·la·'mi:·ta] *f* magnet

calamità [ka·la·mi·'ta] <-> *f* disaster

calamitare [ka·la·mi·'ta:·re] *vt* **1.** (*ferro, acciaio*) to magnetize **2.** *fig* (*attirare*) to attract

calante [ka·'lan·te] *agg* **1.** (*luna*) waning; (*marea*) outgoing **2.** (*moneta, peso*) falling

calare [ka·'la:·re] **I.** *vt avere* **1.** (*abbassare: reti*) to cast; (*sipario*) to bring down **2.** (*buttare: pasta*) to add **3.** (*diminuire: maglie*) to decrease **4.** (*nei giochi a carte*) to lay down **II.** *vi essere* **1.** (*scendere: sipario, notte, nebbia*) to fall **2.** (*invadere*) to descend **3.** (*diminuire: vento*) to drop; (*acqua*) to subside; (*vista*) to get worse; (*prezzo*) to come down; ~ **di peso** to lose weight; ~ **di tono** *fig* to decline **III.** *vr:* **-rsi** to lower oneself

calca ['kal·ka] <-che> *f* crowd

calcagno [kal·'kaɲ·ɲo] *m* heel; **avere qu alle -a** *fig* to have sb at one's heels

calcare[1] [kal·'ka:·re] *vt* **1.** (*con i piedi*) to tread; ~ **le scene** to tread the boards **2.** (*con la voce: parole*) to emphasize **3.** (*disegno*) to trace **4.** (*premere*) to press down; ~ **la mano** *fig* (*esagerare*) to overdo it

calcare[2] *m* MIN limestone

calcareo, -a [kal·'ka:·reo] <-ei, -ee> *agg* calcareous

calce[1] ['kal·tʃe] *f* lime; **bianco di** ~ ART whitewash

calce[2] <-> *m* **in** ~ ADM at the bottom; **in** ~ **alla pagina** at the foot of the page

calcestruzzo [kal·tʃes·'trut·tso] *m* concrete

calcetto [kal·'tʃet·to] *m* **1.** SPORT five-a-side soccer **2.** (*gioco da tavolo*) foosball

calciare [kal·'tʃa:·re] **I.** *vi* (*tirar calci: persona, animale*) to kick **II.** *vt* to kick

calciatore, -trice [kal·tʃa·'to:·re] *m, f* soccer player

calcificare [kal·tʃi·fi·'ka:·re] *vt, vr:* **-rsi** BIOL to calcify

calcificazione [kal·tʃi·fi·ka·'tsio:·ne] *f* calcification

calcina [kal·'tʃi:·na] *f* lime mortar

calcinaccio [kal·tʃi·'nat·tʃo] <-cci> *m* **1.** (*pezzo di intonaco*) piece of plaster **2.** (*rovine*) rubble

calcio ['kal·tʃo] <-ci> *m* **1.** (*pedata, zampata*) kick; **prendere qu a -ci** to give sb a kicking; **tirare -ci** (*persona, animale*) to kick **2.** SPORT soccer; ~ **d'angolo** corner (kick); ~ **d'inizio** kick-off; ~ **di punizione** free kick; ~ **di rigore** penalty (kick); ~ **di rinvio** goal kick; **giocare a** ~ to play soccer **3.** (*impugnatura: di pistola, fucile*) butt **4.** CHEM calcium

> **i** **Calcio** (soccer) is the most popular sport in Italy. The teams in **Serie A** (the top league) have competed for the **scudetto** (trophy) since 1898. Italians are well-known

for being soccer-crazy. Soccer is simply a part of life all over the Peninsula, with its own rigid customs and rituals, whether one plays the game or is simply a spectator or supporter. The greatest Italian players are known throughout the world. What foreigners are often not aware of is the Sunday afternoon rituals of the *mondo del calcio*, the soccer world. Those with an *abbonamento* (season ticket) go to the stadium almost every Sunday to support their favorite team. If one is out and about, one must at least carry a radio in order to follow the half-time and final results. On Sunday evening, soccer mania rules on all possible TV channels, but the same goes for Monday, Tuesday, Wednesday, and sometimes Thursday evenings too. Every single game will be dissected and every detail examined and analyzed.

calciobalilla [kal·tʃo·ba·'lil·la] <-> *m* soccer
calciomercato [kal·tʃo·mer·'ka:·to] <-> *m* transfer market
calcioscommesse [kal·tʃos·kom·'mes·se] <-> *m illegal betting on the results of soccer games*
calcistico, -a <-ci, -che> *agg* (*tifo, risultati, società, stagione*) soccer
calco ['kal·ko] <-chi> *m* 1. (*copia: di scultura*) cast 2. TYP plate
calcolabile [kal·ko·'la:·bi·le] *agg* (*costo, danno, distanza*) calculable
calcolare [kal·ko·'la:·re] *vt* 1. MATH (*dimensioni, differenza, durata, valore*) to calculate 2. *fig* (*valutare*) to assess 3. (*tenere conto*) to take into account
calcolatore [kal·ko·la·'to:·re] *m* ~ **elettronico** COMPUT computer
calcolatore, -trice I. *agg* 1. MATH **regolo** ~ slide rule; **macchina -trice** calculator 2. *fig* (*persona, mente*) calculating II. *m, f fig* (*persona*) calculating person
calcolatrice [kal·ko·la·'tri:·tʃe] *f* TEC calculator; ~ **tascabile** pocket calculator
calcolo ['kal·ko·lo] *m* 1. MATH calculation; **fare i -i** to do the calculations; ~ **delle probabilità** probability theory; **agire per** ~ *fig* to act out of self-interest; ~ **dei costi** costing 2. MED calculus; ~ **renale** kidney stone
caldaia [kal·'da:·ia] <-aie> *f* (*per riscaldamento*) boiler
caldamente [kal·da·'men·to] *avv* highly
caldarrosta [kal·dar·'rɔs·ta] *f* roast chestnut
caldeggiare [kal·ded·'dʒa:·re] *vt* (*candidatura, progetto*) to back
calderone [kal·de·'ro:·ne] *m* cauldron; **mettere tutto nello stesso** ~ *fig* to lump everything together
caldo ['kal·do] *m* warmth; (~ *intenso*) heat;

fa ~ it's hot; **ho** [*o* **sento**] ~ I'm hot; **mettere** [*o* **tenere**] **le vivande in** ~ to keep the food warm; **a** ~ *fig* in the heat of the moment; **non mi fa né** ~ **né freddo** *fig* I don't care either way
caldo, -a *agg* 1. (*clima, giornata, fronte*) warm; (*molto* ~) hot 2. (*acqua, cibo*) hot; **pane** ~ (*appena sfornato*) warm bread 3. (*che tiene caldo: cappotto, sciarpa*) warm 4. (*colore, voce*) warm 5. (*di conflitto: zona, città, anni*) turbulent 6. (*passionale*) passionate; **essere una testa -a** *fig* to be a hothead; **avere il sangue** ~ *fig* to be hot-blooded
caleidoscopio [ka·lei·dos·'kɔ:·pio] <-i> *m* OPT kaleidoscope
calendario [ka·len·'da:·rio] <-i> *m* calendar
calende [ka·'lɛn·de] *fpl* **rimandare qc alle** ~ **greche** to postpone sth indefinitely
calesse [ka·'lɛs·se] *m* gig
calibro ['ka:·li·bro] *m* 1. (*di armi*) caliber; **di grosso** ~ (*arma*) large-caliber; *fig* (*importante*) prominent 2. (*strumento*) calipers *pl*
calice ['ka:·li·tʃe] *m* 1. (*bicchiere*) goblet 2. REL chalice
califfo [ka·'lif·fo] *m* caliph
caligine [ka·'li:·dʒi·ne] *f* 1. (*nebbia*) fog 2. (*fumo denso*) smog
calle ['kal·le] *f* (*a Venezia*) narrow street
callifugo [kal·'li:·fu·go] <-ghi> *m* corn plaster
calligrafia [kal·li·gra·'fi:·a] *f* 1. (*bella scrittura*) calligraphy 2. (*scrittura*) handwriting
callista [kal·'lis·ta] <-i, -e> *mf* podiatrist
callo ['kal·lo] *m* corn; ~ **osseo** callus; **fare il** ~ **a qc** *fig* to get used to sth; **pestare i -i a qu** *fig, inf* to tread on sb's toes
calma ['kal·ma] *f* 1. (*quiete*) quietness 2. (*tranquillità*) quiet; **periodo di** ~ peaceful period 3. (*autocontrollo*) calm; ~ **e sangue freddo!** keep calm! 4. (*flemma*) calmness; **prendersela con** ~ to take it easy 5. METEO calm(ness); ~ **di vento** lack of wind; ~ **di mare** calmness of the sea
calmante [kal·'man·te] I. *agg* 1. (*rilassante, che calma i nervi*) calming 2. (*che calma il dolore*) soothing II. *m* 1. (*del sistema nervoso*) sedative 2. (*contro il dolore*) painkiller
calmare [kal·'ma:·re] I. *vt* 1. (*persona*) to calm (down) 2. (*ira, rabbia*) to reduce; (*pianto*) to stop 3. (*dolore*) to alleviate II. *vr:* -**rsi** 1. (*persona*) to calm down 2. (*dolore*) to ease 3. (*vento*) to drop
calmata [kal·'ma:·ta] *f inf* **darsi una** ~ to calm down
calmierare [kal·mie·'ra:·re] *vt* ~ **qc** (*affitti, costi, prezzi*) to control
calmiere [kal·'miɛ:·re] *m* ceiling price
calmo, -a ['kal·mo] *agg* 1. (*posto, giornata*) quiet 2. (*persona, mare*) calm
calo ['ka:·lo] *m* 1. (*di mercato, prezzo, produzione*) fall 2. (*di peso, vista*) loss; (*di qualità*) reduction 3. (*di temperatura, pressione*) drop; ~ **di potenza** loss of power
calore [ka·'lo:·re] *m* 1. (*energia, calura*) heat

2. (*affetto*) warmth; ~ **familiare** familial warmth **3.** (*di animali*) **essere/andare in** ~ to be in/go into heat

caloria [ka·lo·'ri:·a] <-ie> *f* calorie; **grande** ~ large calorie

calorico, -a [ka·'lɔ:·ri·ko] <-ci, -che> *agg* caloric; **apporto** ~ caloric intake

caloroso, -a [ka·lo·'ro:·so] *agg* **1.** (*persona*) not feeling the cold **2.** *fig* (*cordiale: accoglienza, applauso*) warm

calotta [ka·'lɔt·ta] *f* **1.** GEOG ice cap; ~ **artica/ antartica** Arctic/Antarctic ice cap **2.** ANAT ~ **cranica** skullcap **3.** (*semisfera*) cap; (*di paracadute*) canopy; ~ **dello spinterogeno** AUTO distributor cap

calpestare [kal·pes·'ta:·re] *vt* **1.** (*con i piedi*) to tread on; '(**è**) **vietato** ~ **l'erba**' 'keep off the grass' **2.** *fig* (*sentimenti*) to trample on

Caltanissetta *f* Caltanissetta, *province in the south of Sicily*

calumet [ka·ly·'mɛ] <-> *m* peace pipe; **fumare il** ~ **della pace** *fig* to smoke the peace pipe

calunnia [ka·'lun·nia] <-ie> *f* **1.** (*accusa infondata*) slander **2.** (*bugia*) lie

calunniare [ka·lun·'nia:·re] *vt* to slander

calunniatore, -trice [ka·lun·nia·'to:·re] *m, f* slanderer

calvario [kal·'va:·rio] <-i> *m* **1.** REL Calvary **2.** *fig* ordeal

calvinismo [kal·vi·'niz·mo] *m* Calvinism

calvizie [kal·'vit·tsie] <-> *f* baldness

calvo, -a ['kal·vo] **I.** *agg* (*senza capelli*) bald **II.** *m, f* bald person

calza ['kal·tsa] *f* **1.** (*calzettone*) sock; **ferri da** ~ knitting needles; **fare la** ~ to knit **2.** (*da donna*) stocking; ~ **elastica** support stocking

calzamaglia [kal·tsa·'maʎ·ʎa] *f* leotard

calzare [kal·'tsa:·re] **I.** *vt avere* (*scarpe, guanti*) to wear **II.** *vi* **1.** *avere* (*scarpe, guanti*) to fit **2.** *essere fig* (*essere appropriato: esempio*) to be apt

calzascarpe [kal·tsas·'kar·pe] <-> *m* shoehorn

calzatura [kal·tsa·'tu:·ra] *f* footwear

calzaturificio [cal·tsa·tu·ri·'fi:·tʃo] <-ci> *m* shoe factory

calzetta [kal·'tset·ta] *f* ankle sock; **mezza** ~ (*persona mediocre*) lightweight

calzettone [kal·tset·'to:·ne] *m* knee-high sock

calzino [kal·'tsi:·no] *m* ankle sock

calzolaio, -a [kal·tso·'la:·io] <-ai, -aie> *m, f* **1.** (*che fa le scarpe*) shoemaker **2.** (*che aggiusta le scarpe*) shoe repairer

calzoleria [kal·tso·le·'ri:·a] <-ie> *f* **1.** (*negozio*) shoemaker's shop **2.** (*bottega del calzolaio*) shoe repair shop

calzoncini [kal·tson·'tʃi:·ni] *mpl* shorts *pl;* ~ **da bagno** trunks

calzone [kal·'tso:·ne] *m* **1.** (*indumento*) pants; **portare i** -**i** *fig, inf* (*comandare*) to wear the pants *fig* **2.** (*parte*) pants leg **3.** CULIN (*pizza*) calzone

camaleonte [ka·ma·le·'on·te] *m* chameleon

cambiale [kam·'bia:·le] *f* bill of exchange; ~ **a vista** demand note

cambiamento [kam·bia·'men·to] *m* change; ~ **d'aria** change of air; ~ **di stagione** change of season

cambiare [kam·'bia:·re] **I.** *vt avere* **1.** (*gener*) to change; ~ **casa** to move; ~ **idea** to change one's mind; ~ **marcia** to change gears; ~ **treno/aereo** to change trains/planes; ~ **euro in dollari** to change euros into dollars; **mi cambia cento euro?** can you give me change for a hundred euro bill? **2.** (*scambiare*) to exchange; ~ **qc con qc** to exchange sth for sth **II.** *vi essere* (*trasformarsi*) to change **III.** *vr:* -**rsi** (*d'indumento*) to change

cambiavalute [kam·bia·va·'lu:·te] <-> *mf* foreign exchange dealer

cambio ['kam·bio] <-i> *m* **1.** (*sostituzione: di pneumatico*) changing **2.** (*modifica, acquisto, indumenti*) change; ~ **di casa** house move **3.** MOT (*dispositivo*) gears *pl;* ~ **a cloche** stick shift; ~ **automatico** automatic transmission; ~ **manuale** manual transmission **4.** (*turno*) relief; **dare il** ~ **a qu** to take over from sb **5.** (*di merce*) exchange; **in** ~ **di qc** in exchange for sth **6.** FIN exchange rate; **agente di** ~ stockbroker

cambusa [kam·'bu:·za] *f* storeroom

camcorder ['kæm·'kɔ:·də] <-> *m* TEC camcorder

camelia [ka·'mɛ:·lia] <-ie> *f* camellia

camera ['ka:·me·ra] *f* **1.** (*locale d'abitazione*) room; ~ **da letto** bedroom; ~ **da pranzo** dining room; ~ **degli ospiti** guest room; ~ **matrimoniale** double room; ~ **singola** single room; ~ **ad un letto/a due letti** single/twin-bedded room; **prenotare/disdire una** ~ to book/to cancel a room **2.** (*mobilia*) bedroom suite **3.** POL, ADM chamber; **Camera di Commercio** Chamber of Commerce **4.** (*locale chiuso*) ~ **blindata** strongroom; ~ **iperbarica** decompression chamber; ~ **mortuaria** mortuary; ~ **oscura** camera obscura; ~ **a gas** gas chamber **5.** MOT (*di pneumatico*) ~ **d'aria** inner tube **6.** MUS **musica da** ~ chamber music

cameraman ['kæ·mə·rə·mən/'ka·me·ra·mɛn] *m* cameraman

camerata[1] [ka·me·'ra:·ta] *f* (*di collegio*) dormitory; (*di caserma*) barrack room

camerata² *mf* **1.** MIL, HIST comrade **2.** (*di collegio, università*) friend

cameratismo [ka·me·ra·'tiz·mo] *m* camaraderie

cameriera [ka·me·'riɛ:·ra] *f* **1.** (*di casa privata*) maid **2.** (*di locale*) waitress **3.** (*di albergo*) (chamber)maid

cameriere [ka·me·'riɛ:·re] *m* **1.** (*di casa privata*) servant **2.** (*di locale*) waiter; **~,** (**mi porti il conto,**) **per favore!** waiter, (check,) please! **3.** (*di albergo*) busboy

camerino [ka·me·'ri:·no] *m* THEAT dressing room

camice ['ka:·mi·tʃe] *m* **1.** MED (*di medico, chimico*) white coat; **-i bianchi** doctors **2.** REL alb

camicetta [ka·mi·'tʃet·ta] *f* blouse

camicia [ka·'mi:·tʃa] <-cie> *f* **1.** (*da uomo*) shirt; (*da donna*) blouse; **~ da notte** (*da uomo*) nightshirt; (*da donna*) nightdress; **~ di forza** straightjacket; **in maniche di ~** in one's shirt sleeves; **essere nato con la ~** *fig* to be born lucky; **giocarsi la ~** *fig* to bet one's life; **perdere anche la ~** *fig* to lose one's shirt; **sudare sette -cie** *fig* to sweat blood; **si toglierebbe la ~ di dosso** *fig* he [*o* she] would give the shirt off his [*o* her] back; **-cie nere** HIST blackshirts; **~ verde** POL green shirt, *Northern League militant* **2.** MOT, TEC (*rivestimento: di caldaia, motore*) jacket

caminetto [ka·mi·'net·to] *m* fireplace

camino [ka·'mi:·no] *m* **1.** (*focolare*) fireplace **2.** (*canna fumaria*) chimney

camion ['ka:·mion] <-> *m* truck

camionabile, camionale [ka·mio·'na:·bi·le, ka·mio·'na:·le] **I.** *agg* (*strada*) open to heavy traffic **II.** *f* road open to heavy traffic

camioncino [ka·mion·'tʃi:·no] *m* van

camionista [ka·mio·'nis·ta] <-i , -e> *mf* truck driver

camma ['kam·ma] *f* MOT cam; **albero a -e** camshaft

cammello¹ [kam·'mɛl·lo] *m* **1.** ZOO camel **2.** (*tessuto*) camelhair

cammello² <inv> *agg* (*colore*) camel

camminare [kam·mi·'na:·re] *vi* **1.** (*andare a piedi*) to walk; **~ a quattro zampe** to go on all fours; **cammina!** (*affrettati*) come on!; (*vattene*) go away!; **~ sulle uova** *fig, inf* to walk on eggshells; **~ sul filo del rasoio** to be on a razor's edge **2.** TEC (*funzionare*) to work

camminata [kam·mi·'na:·ta] *f* **1.** (*passeggiata*) walk **2.** (*modo di camminare*) gait

cammino [kam·'mi:·no] *m* **1.** (*viaggio*) walk; **mettersi in ~** to set off; **ci sono tre ore di ~** it's a three-hour walk **2.** (*strada*) way; **cammin facendo** *a. fig* on the way

camomilla [ka·mo·'mil·la] *f* **1.** (*pianta*) chamomile **2.** (*infuso*) chamomile tea

camorra [ka·'mɔr·ra] *f* (*associazione a delinquere*) Neapolitan mafia

camorrista [ka·mor·'ris·ta] <-i , -e> *mf* (*chi fa parte della camorra*) member of the Neapoli-

tan mafia

camoscio [ka·'mɔʃ·ʃo] <-sci> *m* **1.** ZOO chamois **2.** (*pelle*) suede

campagna [kam·'paɲ·ɲa] *f* **1.** AGR, GEOG country; **abitare in ~** to live in the country **2.** MIL, POL, COM campaign; **~ elettorale** election campaign; **~ promozionale** COM promotion; **~ pubblicitaria** advertising campaign

campagnola [kam·'paɲ·'ɲɔ:·la] *f* AUTO (*fuoristrada*) off-road vehicle

campagnolo, -a [kam·'paɲ·'ɲɔ:·lo] **I.** *agg* (*origini, usanza, specialità*) peasant **II.** *m, f* peasant

campale [kam·'pa:·le] *agg* field; **scontro** [*o* **battaglia**] **~** pitched battle; **giornata ~** *fig* hard day

campana [kam·'pa:·na] *f* bell; **~ per la raccolta del vetro** bottle bank; **~ pneumatica** diving bell; **a ~** bell-shaped; **pantaloni a ~** bell bottoms; **sordo come una ~** ~ deaf as a post; **sentire tutte e due le -e** *fig* to hear both sides; **vivere/tenere sotto una ~ di vetro** *fig* to be mollycoddled/to mollycoddle

campanaccio [kam·pa·'nat·tʃo] <-cci> *m* cowbell

campanella [kam·pa·'nɛl·la] *f* **1.** (*a scuola*) bell **2.** BOT campanula

campanello [kam·pa·'nɛl·lo] *m* (*della porta*) bell; **~ d'allarme** *fig* alarm bell

Campania [kam·'pa:·nia] *f* Campania; **abitare in ~** to live in Campania; **andare in ~** to go to Campania

campanile [kam·pa·'ni:·le] *m* **1.** ARCH bell tower **2.** *fig* (*paese nativo*) hometown

campanilismo [kam·pa·ni·'liz·mo] *m* parochialism

campano, -a [kam·'pa:·no] **I.** *agg* from Campania **II.** *m, f* (*abitante*) person from Campania

campanula [kam·'pa:·nu·la] *f* campanula

campare [kam·'pa:·re] *vi* essere *inf* to live; **~ alla giornata** to live from day to day; **~ di qc** to live on sth; **~ di aria** *fig* to live on nothing; **tirare a ~** to get by; **campa, cavallo** (**che l'erba cresce**) *prov* you'll have to wait a long time

campato, -a [kam·'pa:·to] *agg* **~ in aria** unrealistic

campeggiare [kam·ped·'dʒa:·re] *vi* **1.** (*far campeggio*) to camp **2.** (*spiccare*) to stand out

campeggiatore, -trice [kam·ped·dʒa·'to:·re] *m, f* camper

campeggio [kam·'ped·dʒo] <-ggi> *m* **1.** (*terreno*) campground **2.** (*turismo*) camping; **fare ~** to go camping

camper ['kæm·pə/'kam·per] *m* camper

campestre [kam·'pɛs·tre] *agg* country; **corsa ~** cross-country race

camping ['kæm·piŋ/'kam·piŋ] *m v.* **campeggio**

campionario [kam·pio·'na:·rio] <-i> *m* set of samples

campionario, -a <-i, -ie> *agg* **fiera -a** trade fair

campionato [kam·pio·'na:·to] *m* champion-

ship; ~ **mondiale di calcio** World Cup
campioncino [kam·pion·'tʃiː·no] *m* **1.** (*di prodotto*) sample **2.** *inf* (*persona*) budding champion
campione¹ [kam·'pioː·ne] <inv> *agg* **1.** SPORT championship-winning **2.** (*per indagini*) sample **3.** PHYS standard
campione² *m* **1.** (*di merce, materiale, test, sondaggio*) sample; ~ **senza valore** sample only **2.** PHYS standard
campione, -essa *m, f* **1.** SPORT champion **2.** *fig* (*chi eccelle in un'attività*) ace; **essere un ~ in qc** to be an expert at sth; **essere ~ di qc** to be the epitome of sth
campisanti *pl di* **camposanto**
campo ['kam·po] *m* **1.** (*gener*) field; ~ **giochi** play area; ~ **sportivo** sports field; ~ **da gioco** playing field; ~ **da golf** golf course; ~ **da tennis** tennis court; ~ **di calcio** soccer field; **abbandonare il** ~ *a. fig* to leave the field; **scendere in** ~ to join the fray; **scendere in** ~ **contro qu** *a. fig* to join the fray against sb; ~ **di forze** force field; ~ **visivo** field of vision; ~ **facoltativo** optional field; ~ **obbligatorio** required field **2.** (*area*) area; **avere ~ libero** *fig* to have a free hand; ~ **d'aviazione** airfield; ~ **di concentramento** concentration camp; ~ **profughi** refugee camp **3.** (*nell'arte: sfondo*) background **4.** TV, FILM shot **5.** *fig* (*ambito*) domain; ~ **d'azione** field of activity; **esula dal ~ delle mie competenze** it's outside my area of responsibility
Campobassano *m* Campobasso area; **nel ~ in** the Campobasso area
campobassano, -a [kam·po·bas·'saː·no] **I.** *agg* from Campobasso **II.** *m, f* (*abitante*) person from Campobasso
Campobasso *f* Campobasso, *city in Central Italy*
camposanto [kam·po·'san·to] <campisanti> *m* cemetery
camuffare [ka·muf·'faː·re] **I.** *vt* **1.** (*travestire*) to disguise; ~ **qu da qc** to disguise sb as sth **2.** *fig* (*nascondere*) to hide **II.** *vr:* **-rsi** to disguise oneself; **-rsi da qc** to disguise oneself as sth
Canada ['kaː·na·da] *m* **il ~** Canada; **abitare in ~** to live in Canada; **andare in ~** to go to Canada
canadese¹ [ka·na·'deː·se] **I.** *agg* Canadian **II.** *mf* Canadian
canadese² [ka·na·'deː·se] *f* (*tenda*) ridge tent
canaglia [ka·'naʎ·ʎa] <-glie> *f* **1.** *pej* (*persona malvagia*) scoundrel **2.** *scherz* (*birbante*) rascal
canale [ka·'naː·le] *m* **1.** (*artificiale*) canal; **il Canal Grande** the Grand Canal **2.** GEOG (*tratto di mare*) channel **3.** ANAT canal **4.** (*tubo, condotto*) pipe **5.** TV, RADIO, TEL, COMPUT, COM channel; ~ **di musica** music channel; ~ **telematico** data communications channel
canalizzare [ka·na·lid·'dzaː·re] *vt a. fig* to channel

canalizzazione [ka·na·lid·dzat·'tsioː·ne] *f a. fig* (*di attività*) channelling
canapa ['kaː·na·pa] *f* hemp
canapè [ka·na·'pɛ] <-> *m* CULIN canapé
Canarie [ka·'naː·rie] *fpl* **le ~** the Canaries; **abitare alle ~** to live in the Canaries; **andare alle ~** to go to the Canaries
canarino¹ [ka·na·'riː·no] *m* ZOO canary
canarino² <inv> *agg* (*colore*) canary yellow
canasta [ka·'nas·ta] *f* (*gioco di carte*) canasta
cancan [kaŋ·'kan] <-> *m* cancan
cancellare [kan·tʃel·'laː·re] *vt* **1.** (*con la gomma*) to erase; (*con la penna*) to cross out; (*sulla lavagna*) to wipe off; COMPUT to delete **2.** *fig* (*appuntamento, prenotazione, volo*) to cancel **3.** *fig* (*ricordo*) to erase
cancellatura [kan·tʃel·la·'tuː·ra] *f* crossing-out
cancellazione [kan·tʃel·lat·'tsioː·ne] *f* (*di prenotazione, volo, debito*) cancellation
cancelleria [kan·tʃel·le·'riː·a] <-ie> *f* **1.** POL (*ufficio del cancelliere*) chancellery **2.** JUR (*di tribunale*) clerk of the court's office **3.** (*materiale per scrivere*) stationery
cancelletto [kan·tʃel·'let·to] *m* TEL, COMPUT pound sign
cancelliere [kan·tʃel·'liɛ·re] *m* **1.** POL (*primo ministro*) chancellor **2.** JUR (*impiegato di tribunale*) clerk
cancello [kan·'tʃɛl·lo] *m* gate
cancerogeno [kan·tʃe·'rɔː·dʒe·no] *m* carcinogen
cancerogeno, -a *agg* (*agente, sostanza*) carcinogenic
cancrena [kaŋ·'krɛː·na] *f* gangrene; **andare in ~** to become gangrenous
cancro ['kaŋ·kro] *m* **1.** MED cancer **2.** ASTR **Cancro** Cancer; **sono (del [o un]) Cancro** I'm (a) Cancer **3.** *fig, pej* (*male incurabile*) cancer
candeggiante [kan·ded·'dʒan·te] **I.** *agg* bleaching **II.** *m* bleach
candeggiare [kan·ded·'dʒaː·re] *vt* (*bucato, biancheria*) to bleach
candeggina® [kan·ded·'dʒiː·na] *f* bleach
candeggio [kan·'ded·dʒo] <-ggi> *m* bleaching
candela [kan·'deː·la] *f* **1.** (*di cera*) candle; **a lume di ~** by candlelight; **tenere** [*o* **reggere**] **la ~** *a qu* to be a fifth wheel; **il gioco non vale la ~** *fig* the game's not worth the candle **2.** MOT spark plug **3.** EL candela; **una lampadina da 60 -e** a 60-watt bulb
candelabro [kan·de·'laː·bro] *m* candelabra
candeliere [kan·de·'liɛ·re] *m* candlestick
candelotto [kan·de·'lɔt·to] *m* ~ **di dinamite** stick of dynamite; ~ **fumogeno** smoke bomb; ~ **lacrimogeno** tear gas canister
candidare [kan·di·'daː·re] **I.** *vt* **1.** (*presentare come candidato*) to put forward as a candidate **2.** (*proporre come candidato*) to nominate **II.** *vr:* **-rsi** to run as a candidate
candidato, -a [kan·di·'daː·to] *m, f* candidate
candidatura [kan·di·da·'tuː·ra] *f* **1.** (*per lavoro, borsa di studio*) application; **pres-**

entare la propria ~ to put in an application
2. POL, ADM candidacy; **presentare la propria** ~ to put oneself forward as a candidate
candid camera ['kæn·did 'kæ·mə·rə] <-> *f*
candid camera
candido, -a ['kan·di·do] *agg* **1.** (*pulito: biancheria, bucato*) snow-white **2.** (*splendente:
neve, denti*) pure white **3.** (*colore*) pure **4.** *fig*
(*ingenuo*) naive; (*sincero*) candid
canditi [kan·'di:·ti] *mpl* candied fruit
candito, -a *agg* candied; **zucchero** ~ rock candy
candore [kan·'do:·re] *m* **1.** (*biancore*) whiteness **2.** *fig* (*ingenuità*) naivety; (*innocenza*) innocence
cane ['ka:·ne] *m* **1.** ZOO dog; ~ **da caccia** hunting dog; ~ **da guardia** guard dog; **figlio
d'un** ~ *inf* son of a bitch *vulg;* **vita da -i** dog's
life; **lavoro da -i** botched job; **mondo** ~! *inf*
damn it! *inf;* **solo come un** ~ all alone; **tempo
da -i** awful weather; **menare il can per l'aia**
to beat around the bush; **come un** ~ **bastonato** like a whipped dog; **fa un freddo** ~ *inf* it's
freezing cold *inf;* **non c'era un** ~ *fig, inf* there
wasn't a living soul; **essere come** ~ **e gatto** to
fight like cats and dogs; **can che abbaia non
morde** *prov* his [*o* her] bark is worse than his
[*o* her] bite **2.** (*di arma da fuoco*) hammer
canestro [ka·'nɛs·tro] *m* basket; **fare** ~ (*nella
pallacanestro*) to shoot a basket
canfora ['kan·fo·ra] *f* camphor
canguro [kaŋ·'gu:·ro] *m* kangaroo
canile [ka·'ni:·le] *m* **1.** (*cuccia*) kennel
2. (*luogo*) pound
canino [ka·'ni:·no] *m* canine
canino, -a *agg* **1.** (*di cani*) canine; **mostra -a**
dog show **2.** MED **tosse -a** whooping cough
3. ANAT **dente** ~ canine **4.** BOT **rosa -a** dog rose
canna ['kan·na] *f* **1.** BOT reed; ~ **da zucchero**
sugar cane; **essere povero in** ~ *fig* to be as
poor as a church mouse **2.** (*bastone*) stick;
~ **da pesca** fishing rod **3.** (*di organo*) pipe
4. (*di fucile*) barrel **5.** (*di bicicletta*) crossbar
6. *sl* (*di marijuana, hascisc*) joint; **farsi una** ~
to roll oneself a joint **7.** (*parte del camino*)
~ **fumaria** flue
cannare [kan·'na:·re] **I.** *vt sl* to flunk *inf* **II.** *vi sl*
(*fallire*) to get it wrong
cannella [kan·'nɛl·la] *f* **1.** CULIN cinnamon
2. (*tubo*) spout; (*di botte*) spigot
cannello [kan·'nɛl·lo] *m* **1.** TEC blowtorch **2.** (*di
pipa*) stem
cannelloni [kan·nel·'lo:·ni] *mpl* cannelloni
cannibale [kan·'ni:·ba·le] *mf* cannibal
cannocchiale [kan·nok·'kia:·le] *m* telescope
cannonata [kan·no·'na:·ta] *f* **1.** MIL cannon
shot **2.** *fig, inf* (*cosa eccezionale*) knockout
cannone [kan·'no:·ne] *m* **1.** MIL gun; ~ **sparan-
eve** snow cannon **2.** *fig, inf* (*asso*) ace *inf*
cannoniere [kan·no·'niɛ:·re] *m* **1.** (*bombardiere*) gunner **2.** (*nel calcio*) scorer
cannuccia [kan·'nut·tʃa] <-cce> *f* (*per bibite*)
straw

canoa [ka·'nɔ:·a] *f* canoe
canone [ka·'no:·ne] *m* **1.** (*norma*) canon
2. (*schema di riferimento*) ideal **3.** (*pagamento*) rent; ~ **d'affitto** rent; ~ **di abbonamento** RADIO, TV license fee **4.** MUS canon
5. REL canon
canonica [ka·'nɔ:·ni·ka] <-che> *f* presbytery
canonico [ka·'nɔ:·ni·ko] <-ci> *m* REL canon
canonico, -a <-ci, -che> *agg* **1.** (*regolare*)
standard **2.** REL canonical
canonizzare [ka·no·nid·'dza:·re] *vt* **1.** (*indicare come norma*) to standardize **2.** REL to canonize
canoro, -a [ka·'nɔ:·ro] *agg* **1.** (*per cantanti:
concorso, qualità*) singing; (*serata*) of song
2. (*di cantante: qualità*) vocal; **uccelli -i** song-
birds
canotta [ka·'not·ta] *f* (*maglietta*) undershirt
canottaggio [ka·not·'tad·dʒo] <-ggi> *m* rowing
canottiera [ka·not·'tiɛ:·ra] *f* undershirt
canottiere [ka·not·'tiɛ:·re] *m* rower
canotto [ka·'nɔt·to] *m* **1.** (*piccola barca*) dinghy; ~ **di salvataggio** lifeboat **2.** (*di gomma*)
(rubber) dinghy
canovaccio [ka·no·'vat·tʃo] <-cci> *m* **1.** (*da
cucina*) dishcloth **2.** (*tessuto*) canvas **3.** THEAT
(*trama*) plot
cantante [kan·'tan·te] *mf* singer; ~ **lirico** opera singer
cantare [kan·'ta:·re] **I.** *vi* **1.** MUS to sing; ~ **da
tenore** to sing tenor; **canta che ti passa** *prov*
don't worry and it'll be all right **2.** ZOO (*gallo*)
to crow; (*uccello*) to sing; (*grillo*) to chirp
3. *fig* (*fare la spia*) to squeal **II.** *vt* **1.** (*canzone*)
to sing **2.** (*persone, fatti*) to sing of; ~ **le lodi
di qu** to sing sb's praises; **cantar vittoria** to
claim victory; **cantarne quattro a qu** *inf* to
give sb a piece of one's mind
cantastorie [kan·tas·'tɔ:·rie] <-> *mf* ballad
singer
cantata [kan·'ta:·ta] *f* **1.** MUS cantata **2.** *inf*
(*canto*) sing-along
cantautore, -trice [kan·tau·'to:·re] *m, f* singer-songwriter
canterellare [kan·te·rel·'la:·re] *vt, vi* to hum
canticchiare [kan·tik·'kia:·re] *vt, vi* to hum
cantico [kan·ti·ko] <-ci> *m* canticle; **il** ~ **dei
-ci** the Song of Songs
cantiere [kan·'tiɛ:·re] *m* site; ~ **edile** construction site; ~ **navale** shipyard; **mettere qc in** ~
fig to get started on sth
cantilena [kan·ti·'lɛ:·na] *f* **1.** (*ninnananna*)
lullaby **2.** (*cadenza*) singsong **3.** *fig* (*discorso
noioso*) boring speech; **sempre la stessa** ~ always the same old story **4.** MUS psalmody
cantina [kan·'ti:·na] *f* **1.** ARCH (*di edificio*) cellar; (*per il vino*) (wine) cellar **2.** (*produzione e
vendita di vino*) vineyard; ~ **sociale** wine-
growers' cooperative
canto ['kanto] *m* **1.** MUS (*il cantare*) singing
2. (*canzone*) song; ~ **popolare** folksong **3.** ZOO
(*di gallo*) crowing; (*di uccelli*) singing; (*di*

cicala, grillo) chirping; **al ~ del gallo** at cock-crow **4.** *poet* canto **5.** (*parte*) part; **d'altro ~** on the other hand; **dal ~ mio/loro** for my/ their part **6.** (*angolo*) corner

cantonale [kan·to·'na:·le] *agg* (*in Svizzera*) cantonal

cantonata [kan·to·'na:·ta] *f* (*errore*) blunder; **prendere una ~** to make a blunder

cantone [kan·'to:·ne] *m* **1.** (*angolo*) corner; **il gioco dei quattro -i** the game of puss in the corner **2.** (*in Svizzera*) canton

cantoniera [kan·to·'niɛ:·ra] *agg* **casa ~** road-man's house

cantore [kan·'to:·re] *m* **1.** REL chorister **2.** LIT bard

cantuccio [kan·'tut·tʃo] <-cci> *m inf* (*angolo*) corner; **stare in un ~** to stand apart

canuto, -a [ka·'nu:·to] *agg* **1.** (*capelli*) white **2.** (*persona*) white-haired

canzonare [kan·tso·'na:·re] *vt* to tease

canzone [kan·'tso:·ne] *f* **1.** MUS song; **~ popolare** folksong **2.** LIT canzone

canzonetta [kan·tso·'net·ta] *f* MUS pop song

canzoniere [kan·tso·'niɛ:·re] *m* **1.** LIT (*raccolta di poesie*) poetry collection **2.** MUS (*raccolta di canzoni*) songbook

caos ['ka:·os] <-> *m* **1.** PHILOS (*disordine*) chaos **2.** (*rumore*) noise

caotico, -a [ka·'ɔ:·ti·ko] <-ci, -che> *agg* chaotic

cap. *abbr di* **capitolo** ch.

CAP [kap] *m acro di* **Codice di Avviamento Postale** zip code

capace [ka·'pa:·tʃe] *agg* **1.** (*in grado di*) capable; **essere ~ di fare qc** to be capable of do-ing sth; **~ d'intendere e di volere** JUR of sound mind **2.** (*abile*) able **3.** (*spazioso: ambiente*) spacious; (*borsa, valigia*) capacious

capacità [ka·pa·tʃi·'ta] <-> *f* **1.** (*di contenere*) capacity **2.** (*abilità*) ability **3.** JUR capacity; **~ giuridica** [*o* **di agire**] legal capacity

capacitarsi [ka·pa·tʃi·'tar·si] *vr* (*rendersi conto*) **non riuscire a ~ di qc** to be unable to understand sth

capanna [ka·'pan·na] *f* hut

capannello [ka·pan·'nɛl·lo] *m* (*di persone*) knot

capanno [ka·'pan·no] *m* (*in spiaggia: cabina*) hut

capannone [ka·pan·'no:·ne] *m* (*deposito*) shed; (*fabbrica*) warehouse

caparbietà [ka·par·bie·'ta] <-> *f* stubbornness

caparbio, -a [ka·'par·bio] <-i, -ie> *agg* stubborn

caparra [ka·'par·ra] *f* (*cauzione*) deposit

capatina [ka·pa·'ti:·na] *f* quick visit; **fare una ~** to make a quick visit

capeggiare [ka·ped·'dʒa:·re] *vt* to lead

capellini [ka·pel·'li:·ni] *mpl* angel hair pasta

capello [ka·'pel·lo] *m* hair; **-i d'angelo** angel hair pasta; **portare i -i lunghi/corti** to have long/short hair; **averne fin sopra i -i** to have had it up to here; **tirato per i -i** *fig* far-fetched;

non torcere neppure un ~ a qu not to touch [*o* harm] a hair on sb's head; **cose da far rizzare i -i** *fig* it'd make your hair stand on end; **mettersi le mani nei -i** *fig* to tear one's hair out; **mi fai venire i -i bianchi** *fig* you're giving me gray hair; **prendersi per i -i** *fig* to quarrel; **spaccare un ~ in quattro** *fig* to split hairs

capellone, -a [ka·pel·'lo:·ne] I. *m*, *f inf* (*hippy*) hippie II. *agg* hippie

capelluto, -a [ka·pel·'lu:·to] *agg* **cuoio ~** scalp

capezzale [ka·pet·'tsa:·le] *m* **1.** (*capo del letto*) bolster **2.** *fig* (*letto di un malato*) bedside

capezzolo [ka·'pet·tso·lo] *m* nipple

capi- [ka·pi] (*in compounds*) *v.a.* **capo-**

capiarea *pl di* **capoarea**

capibanda *pl di* **capobanda**

capicronisti *pl di* **capocronista**

capicuochi *pl di* **capocuoco**

capidivisione *pl di* **capodivisione**

capiente [ka·'piɛn·te] *agg* (*recipiente, valigia*) capacious; (*sala*) spacious

capienza [ka·'piɛn·tsa] *f* (*di sala, recipiente*) capacity

capifabbrica *pl di* **capofabbrica**

capifamiglia *pl di* **capofamiglia**

capigliatura [ka·piʎ·ʎa·'tu:·ra] *f* hair; **~ folta** thick hair

capigruppo *pl di* **capogruppo**

capilinea *pl di* **capolinea**

capilista *pl di* **capolista**[1]

capillare [ka·pil·'la:·re] I. *agg* **1.** ANAT **vasi -i** capillary **2.** (*minuzioso: indagine*) detailed **3.** (*diffuso: organizzazione*) widespread II. *m* capillary

capimafia *pl di* **capomafia**

capimastri *pl di* **capomastro**

capinera [ka·pi·'ne:·ra] *f* blackcap

capire [ka·'pi:·re] <capisco> I. *vt avere* to understand; **far ~ qc a qu** to make sth clear to sb; **~ fischi per fiaschi** to get the short end of the stick *inf* II. *vi essere* to understand; **farsi ~** to make oneself understood; **~ al volo** to be quick on the uptake; **si capisce** of course; **si capisce che ti telefono** of course I'll call you III. *vr:* **-rsi** to understand each other

capiredattori *pl di* **caporedattore**

capireparto *pl di* **caporeparto**

capirosso [ka·pi·'ros·so] *m* goldfinch

capisala *pl di* **caposala**

capisaldi *pl di* **caposaldo**

capiservizio *pl di* **caposervizio**

capisettore *pl di* **caposettore**

capisezione *pl di* **caposezione**

capisquadra *pl di* **caposquadra**

capistazione *pl di* **capostazione**

capitale [ka·pi·'ta:·le] I. *agg* **1.** (*principale: importanza, punto*) fundamental; **errore ~** major **2.** JUR capital; **sentenza ~** death sentence; **condannare alla pena ~** to condemn to death **3.** REL deadly; **i peccati -i** the deadly sins II. *f* (*città*) capital; **Capitale Europea della Cultura** European Capital of Culture

III. *m* (*patrimonio*) capital; ~ **a rischio** risk capital; ~ **sociale** (capital) stock; ~ **proprio** owner's equity; **fare ~ di qc** *a. fig* to capitalize on sth

capitalismo [ka·pi·ta·'liz·mo] *m* capitalism

capitalista [ka·pi·ta·'lis·ta] <-i , -e> **I.** *mf* capitalist **II.** *agg* capitalist

capitanare [ka·pi·ta·'na:·re] *vt* to lead; ~ **una squadra di calcio** SPORT to captain

capitaneria [ka·pi·ta·ne·'ri:·a] <-ie> *f* ~ (**di porto**) port authority

capitano [ka·pi·'ta:·no] *m* captain

capitare [ka·pi·'ta:·re] *vi essere* **1.** (*giungere*) to come; **capiti proprio a proposito!** you've come at just the right time!; ~ **bene/male** to have good luck/bad luck; ~ **nelle mani di qu** to fall into sb's hands **2.** (*succedere*) to happen; **capita a tutti** it happens to everyone; **sono cose che capitano anche nelle migliori famiglie** these things happen even to the best families; **dove capita** anywhere

capitavola *pl di* **capotavola**

capitello [ka·pi·'tɛl·lo] *m* capital

capitolare [ka·pi·to·'la:·re] *vi* **1.** MIL to capitulate **2.** *fig* to give in

capitolazione [ka·pi·to·lat·'tsio:·ne] *f* **1.** MIL capitulation **2.** *fig* surrender

capitolo [ka·'pi:·to·lo] *m* **1.** (*di libro*) REL chapter **2.** (*loc*) **avere voce in** ~ to have a say in the matter; **comincia un nuovo ~ della mia vita** a new chapter in my life is starting

capitombolo [ka·pi·'tom·bo·lo] *m* **1.** (*caduta*) tumble **2.** *fig* (*crollo*) collapse

capitone [ka·pi·'to:·ne] *m* eel

capitreno *pl di* **capotreno**

capi ufficio *pl di* **capo ufficio**

capo ['ka:·po] **I.** *m* **1.** ANAT head; **chinare il ~** *fig* to bow one's head; **lavata di ~** *fig, inf* telling-off *inf;* **rompersi il ~** *fig* to rack one's brains; **non avere né ~ né coda** to make no sense; **capitare fra ~ e collo** *fig* to come out of the blue **2.** (*persona: di azienda, istituto, organizzazione*) head; (*di associazione a delinquere*) boss; (*di tribù*) chief; ~ **del governo** leader of the government; ~ **dello Stato** head of state; **comandante in** ~ commander-in-chief; **essere a ~ di qu/qc** to head sb/sth; **fare ~ a qu/qc** to be the responsibility of sb/sth **3.** GEOG cape **4.** (*singolo oggetto*) item **5.** (*capitolo*) chapter; **per sommi -i** briefly **6.** (*estremità*) end; **in ~ al letto** at the head of the bed; **andare in ~ al mondo** to go to the ends of the earth **7.** (*principio*) **cominciare da ~** to start again; **andare a ~** to start a new paragraph; **punto e a ~** period, new paragraph **8.** (*fine, conclusione*) **in ~ ad un mese** in a month; **venire a ~ di qc** to get to the end of sth **II.** <inv> *agg* chief; **ispettore ~** chief inspector; **redattore ~** editor-in-chief

capoarea [ka·po·a·'re:·a] *mf* area manager

capobanda [ka·po·'ban·da] <capibanda> *m* **1.** MUS bandmaster **2.** *pej* (*caporione*) gang leader

capocchia [ka·'pɔk·kia] <-cchie> *f* (*di spillo, fiammifero, chiodo*) head

capoccia¹ [ka·'pɔt·tʃa] <-> *m* **1.** (*di famiglia*) head **2.** *scherz* (*di azienda*) boss **3.** (*caporione*) gang leader

capoccia² <-cce> *f dial, fam* (*testa*) nut *inf*

capocomico, -a [ka·po·'kɔ:·mi·ko] <-ci, -che> *m, f* manager of a theater company

capocronista [ka·po·kro·'nis·ta] *mf* news editor

capocuoco, -a [ka·po·'kuɔ:·ko] <-chi, -che> *m, f* head chef

capodanno, capo d'anno [ka·po·'dan·no] *m* New Year

capodivisione [ka·po·di·vi·'zio:·ne] *mf* **1.** MIL division commander **2.** ADM (*di azienda*) head of department

capofabbrica [ka·po·'fab·bri·ka] *mf* works manager

capofamiglia [ka·po·fa·'miʎ·ʎa] *mf* head of the family

capofitto [ka·po·'fit·to] *avv* **a ~** headlong; **buttarsi a ~ in qc** *fig* to throw oneself into sth

capogiro [ka·po·'dʒi:·ro] *m* dizziness; **prezzi da ~** *fig* exorbitant prices

capogruppo [ka·po·'grup·po] *mf* group leader; POL leader

capolavoro [ka·po·la·'vo:·ro] *m* masterpiece

capolinea [ka·po·'li:·nea] <capilinea> *m* terminus

capolino [ka·po·'li:·no] *m* **far ~** to peep out

capolista¹ [ka·po·'lis·ta] *mf* POL (*candidato*) top candidate

capolista² *f* top team

capolista³ <inv> *agg* **candidato ~** POL top candidate; **squadra ~** SPORT top team

capoluogo [ka·po·'luɔ:·go] <capoluoghi *o* capiluoghi> *m* ADM (*di regione, provincia*) capital

capomacchinista [ka·po·mak·ki·'nis·ta] *mf* chief engineer

capomafia [ka·po·'ma:·fia] <capimafia> *m* mafia boss

capomastro [ka·po·'mas·tro] <-i *o* capimastri> *m* (*capocantiere*) master builder; (*imprenditore*) contractor

capoofficina [ka·po·of·fi·'tʃi:·na] *mf* shop foreman *m,* shop forewoman *f*

caporale [ka·po·'ra:·le] *m* private first class

caporalmaggiore, caporal maggiore [ka·po·ral·mad·'dʒo:·re] *m* corporal

caporedattore, -trice [ka·po·re·dat·'to:·re] *m, f* editor-in-chief

caporeparto [ka·po·re·'par·to] *mf* foreman *m,* forewoman *f*

caporione, -a [ka·po·'rio:·ne] *m, f* leader

caposala [ka·po·'sa:·la] *mf* (*in ospedale*) head nurse

caposaldo [ka·po·'sal·do] <capisaldi> *m* **1.** *fig* (*punto fondamentale*) cornerstone **2.** MIL stronghold **3.** (*topografia*) datum point

caposervizio [ka·po·ser·'vit·tsio] *mf* **1.** (*di giornale*) senior editor **2.** ADM department head

caposettore [ka·po·set·'to:·re] *m* ADM divisional head

caposezione [ka·po·set·'tsio:·ne] *mf* ADM section head

caposquadra¹ [ka·pos·'kua:·dra] *mf* **1.** (*di operai, tecnici, vigili*) foreman *m*, forewoman *f* **2.** SPORT (team) captain

caposquadra² <capisquadra> *m* MIL squad leader

capostazione [ka·pos·ta·'tsio:·ne] *mf* station master

capostipite [ka·pos·'ti:·pi·te] *mf* founder

capotavola <capitavola> *m* head of the table; **sedersi a** ~ to sit at head of the table

capote [ka·'pɔt] <-> *f* top

capotreno [ka·po·'trɛ:·no] *mf* conductor

cap(o)ufficio, capo ufficio [ka·p(o)·uf·'fi:·tʃo] *mf* office manager

capoverso [ka·po·'vɛr·so] *m* paragraph

capovolgere [ka·po·'vɔl·dʒe·re] <irr> I. *vt* **1.** (*rovesciare: barca*) to capsize; (*rovesciare: auto*) to overturn; (*immagine, oggetto*) to turn upside down **2.** *fig* (*situazione, risultato*) to reverse II. *vr:* **-rsi 1.** (*barca*) to capsize; (*macchina*) to overturn **2.** *fig* (*cambiare radicalmente*) to be reversed

capovolgimento [ka·po·vol·dʒi·'men·to] *m* **1.** (*ribaltamento: di barca*) capsizing; (*di macchina*) overturning; (*di oggetti, immagini*) turning upside down **2.** *fig* (*rovesciamento*) reversal

cappa¹ ['kap·pa] *f* **1.** (*indumento*) cloak; **una ~ di piombo** *fig* a dead weight **2.** (*di camino, cucina*) hood

cappa² <-> *m o f* (*lettera*) *v.* **k**

cappella [kap·'pɛl·la] *f* **1.** REL chapel **2.** MUS choir **3.** (*di fungo*) cap

cappellano [kap·pel·'la:·no] *m* chaplain

cappelliera [kap·pel·'liɛ:·ra] *f* hatbox

cappello [kap·'pɛl·lo] *m* **1.** (*copricapo*) hat; **avere il ~ in testa** to have one's hat on one's head; **tanto di ~!** congratulations! **2.** (*introduzione: di scritto, discorso*) preamble

capperi ['kap·pe·ri] *int inf* wow!

cappero ['kap·pe·ro] *m* CULIN, BOT caper

cappio ['kap·pio] <-i> *m* noose; **il ~ al collo** *fig* a millstone around one's neck

cappone [kap·'po:·ne] *m* capon

cappotto [kap·'pɔt·to] *m* (*mantello*) coat

cappuccino [kap·put·'tʃi:·no] *m* **1.** CULIN cappuccino **2.** REL Capuchin **3.** ZOO capuchin (monkey)

cappuccio [kap·'put·tʃo] <-cci> I. *m* **1.** (*copricapo*) hood **2.** (*di penna, biro,tubo*) cap; (*di fiala, rossetto*) top **3.** *inf* CULIN cappuccino II. *agg* **cavolo ~** spring cabbage

capra ['ka:·pra] *f* ZOO goat; **arrampicarsi come una ~** to climb like a mountain goat; **salvare ~ e cavoli** *fig* to have the best of both worlds

caprese [ka·'pre:·se] I. *agg* from Capri II. *mf* (*abitante*) person from Capri III. *f* CULIN mozzarella, tomato and basil salad

capretto [ka·'pret·to] *m* kid; **guanti di** ~ kid gloves

Capri *f* Capri; **abitare a** ~ to live in Capri; **andare a** ~ to go to Capri

capriccio [ka·'prit·tʃo] <-cci> *m* **1.** (*voglia*) whim; **fare i -cci** to have a temper tantrum **2.** MUS caprice

capriccioso, -a [ka·prit·'tʃo:·so] *agg* **1.** (*bambino*) naughty; (*ragazza*) capricious **2.** (*tempo*) changeable

Capricorno [ka·pri·'kɔr·no] *m* ASTR Capricorn; **sono** (**del** [*o* **un**]) **Capricorno** I'm (a) Capricorn

caprifoglio [ka·pri·'fɔʎ·ʎo] *m* honeysuckle

caprino [ka·'pri:·no] *m* CULIN (*formaggio*) goat's cheese

capriola [ka·pri·'ɔ:·la] *f* **1.** (*salto*) somersault; **fare le -e** to do somersaults **2.** ZOO roe deer

capriolo [ka·pri·'ɔ:·lo] *m* ZOO roe deer

capro ['ka:·pro] *m* (he-)goat; **~ espiatorio** *fig* scapegoat

caprone [ka·'pro:·ne] *m* **1.** ZOO (he-)goat **2.** *fig pej* lout *pej*

capsula ['kapsula] *f* capsule

captare [kap·'ta:·re] *vt* **1.** TEL, RADIO to pick up **2.** *fig* (*cogliere: pensiero*) to read; (*intuire: desiderio*) to guess

capufficio [ka·puf·'fi:·tʃo] *v.* **cap(o)ufficio**

capzioso, -a [kap·'tsio:·so] *agg* (*ragionamento, scusa*) specious

CAR *m acro di* **Centro Addestramento Reclute** boot camp

carabina [ka·ra·'bi:·na] *f* rifle

carabiniere [ka·ra·bi·'niɛ:·re] *m* carabiniere, *member of Italian military police force*

> **i** The **Carabinieri** make up the fourth branch of the Italian armed forces along with the army – **Esercito** – navy – **Marina** – and air force – **Aviazione**. Working alongside the national police – **Polizia di Stato** – they perform both military and civil duties, such as the maintenance of public order.

caraffa [ka·'raf·fa] *f* carafe

caramba [ka·'ram·ba] <-> *m sl* carabiniere, *member of Italian military police force*

carambola [ka·'ram·bo·la] *f* **1.** (*nel biliardo: gioco, tiro*) carom **2.** (*collisione*) pileup

caramella [ka·ra·'mɛl·la] *f* **1.** CULIN piece of candy **2.** *fig, inf* (*monocolo*) monocle

caramello [ka·ra·'mɛl·lo] *m* caramel

carato [ka·'ra:·to] *m* **1.** (*di oro*) karat **2.** (*di pietre preziose*) carat

carattere [ka·'rat·te·re] *m* **1.** (*indole*) character; **mancare di** ~ to lack character **2.** (*natura*) character **3.** TYP (*segno*) character; **~ corsivo** italic; **~ grassetto** bold; **-i a stampatello** capital letters **4.** (*di scrittura*) character **5.** COMPUT character; **mappa dei -i** character map; **stringa di -i** character string **6.** BIOL characteristic

caratteriale [ka·rat·te·'ria:·le] **I.** *agg* disturbed **II.** *mf* disturbed child

caratterino [ka·rat·te·'ri:·no] *m iron* difficult character

caratteristica [ka·rat·te·'ris·ti·ka] <-che> *f* characteristic

caratteristico, -a [ka·rat·te·'ris·ti·ko] <-ci, -che> *agg* **1.** (*particolare*) characteristic **2.** (*tipico*) typical **3.** (*pittoresco*) picturesque

caratterizzare [ka·rat·te·rid·'dza:·re] *vt* to characterize

caratterizzato, -a [ka·rat·te·rid·'dza:·to] *agg* characterized; **essere ~ da qc** to be characterized by sth

caratterizzazione [ka·rat·te·rid·dzat·'tsio:·ne] *f* characterization

caratura [ka·ra·'tu:·ra] *f* **1.** (*di oro*) weighing in karats **2.** (*di diamanti*) weighing in carats **3.** (*valore*) caliber

caravan [kæ·rə·'væn] <-> *m* trailer

caravella [ka·ra·'vɛl·la] *f* (*nave*) caravel

carboidrato [kar·bo·i·'dra:·to] *m* carbohydrate

carbonaio, -a [kar·bo·'na:·io] <-ai, -aie> *m, f* **1.** (*lavoratore*) charcoal burner **2.** (*venditore*) coal merchant

carbonaro [kar·bo·'na:·ro] *m* **1.** HIST (*della Carboneria*) member of the Carbonari, *19th-century secret political organization* **2.** (*carbonaio: lavoratore*) charcoal burner; (*venditore*) coal merchant

carbonaro, -a *agg* **1.** HIST (*della Carboneria*) of the Carbonari, *19th-century secret political organization* **2.** CULIN **alla -a** carbonara, *made with eggs, bacon, and pecorino cheese*

carboncino [kar·bon·'tʃi:·no] *m* **1.** (*per disegnare*) charcoal **2.** (*disegno*) charcoal drawing

carbone [kar·'bo:·ne] *m* **1.** MIN coal; **nero come il ~** black as pitch; **essere** [*o* **stare**] **sui -i accesi** *fig* to be like a cat on a hot tin roof **2.** BOT (*malattia*) smut

carbonella [kar·bo·'nɛl·la] *f* slack

carbonico [kar·'bɔ:·ni·ko] <-ci> *m* Carboniferous period

carbonico, -a <-ci, -che> *agg* carbonic; **anidride -a** carbon dioxide

carbonifero [kar·bo·'ni:·fe·ro] *m* Carboniferous period

carbonifero, -a *agg* coal; **bacino ~** coalfield

carbonio [kar·'bɔ:·nio] *m* carbon; **ossido di ~** carbon monoxide

carbonizzare [kar·bo·nid·'dza:·re] **I.** *vt* to reduce to ashes **II.** *vr:* **-rsi** to be reduced to ashes; (*automobile*) to burn out

carbonizzazione [kar·bo·nid·dzat·'tsio:·ne] *f* carbonization

carburante [kar·bu·'ran·te] *m* fuel

carburare [kar·bu·'ra:·re] *vi* (*motore*) to fire; **oggi proprio non carburo** *sl* I'm not really firing on all cylinders today

carburatore [kar·bu·ra·'to:·re] *m* MOT carburetor

carcassa [kar·'kas·sa] *f* **1.** (*di animale*) carcass

2. TEC (*ossatura: di nave*) hulk **3.** *fig pej* (*macchina*) jalopy

carcerato, -a [kar·tʃe·'ra:·to] *m, f* prisoner

carcerazione [kar·tʃe·rat·'tsio:·ne] *f* imprisonment

carcere ['kar·tʃe·re] **1.** (*luogo*) prison **2.** (*pena*) imprisonment; **~ preventivo** remand

carcinoma [kar·tʃi·'nɔ:·ma] <-i> *m* carcinoma

carciofino [kar·tʃo·'fi:·no] *m* small artichoke

carciofo [kar·'tʃɔ:·fo] *m* BOT artichoke

card [ka:d] <-> *f* (*tessera, carta di credito*) card

cardanico, -a [kar·'da:·ni·ko] <-ci, -che> *agg* -; **albero ~** drive shaft; **giunto ~** universal joint

cardellino [kar·del·'li:·no] *m* ZOO goldfinch

cardiaco, -a [kar·'di:·a·ko] <-ci, -che> *agg* (*del cuore: attacco, battito*) heart; (*insufficienza*) cardiac

cardinale [kar·di·'na:·le] **I.** *agg* **1.** (*fondamentale*) cardinal; **numero ~** cardinal number **2.** GEOG cardinal; **punti -i** cardinal points **II.** *m* cardinal

cardine ['kar·di·ne] *m* **1.** (*di porta, finestra*) hinge **2.** *fig* (*fondamento, base*) cornerstone

cardiochirurgia [kar·dio·ki·rur·'dʒi·a] <-gie> *f* heart surgery

cardiochirurgico, -a [kar·dio·ki·'rur·dʒi·ko] <-ci, -che> *agg* (*intervento*) heart; (*reparto*) cardiology

cardiochirurgo, -a [kar·dio·ki·'rur·go] <-gi *o* -ghi, -ghe> *m, f* heart surgeon

cardiogramma [kar·dio·'gram·ma] <-i> *m* cardiogram

cardiologia [kar·dio·lo·'dʒi·a] <-gie> *f* cardiology

cardiologo, -a [kar·'diɔ:·lo·go] <-gi, -ghe> *m, f* cardiologist

cardiopatico, -a [kar·dio·'pa:·ti·ko] <-ci, -che> **I.** *agg* (*paziente*) heart **II.** *m, f* heart patient

cardiotelefono [kar·kio·te·'lɛ:·fo·no] *m* MED *cardiophone*

cardo ['kar·do] *m* **1.** BOT thistle **2.** CULIN cardoon

carena [ka·'rɛ:·na] *f* NAUT bottom

carente [ka·'rɛn·te] *agg* lacking; **essere ~ di qc** to be lacking in sth

carenza [ka·'rɛn·tsa] *f* lack; **la ~ di qc** the lack of sth; **per ~ di prove** JUR because of a lack of evidence

carestia [ka·res·'ti:·a] <-ie> *f* **1.** (*carenza di cibo*) famine **2.** (*scarsità*) scarcity; **~ di qc** scarcity of sth

carezza [ka·'ret·tsa] *f* caress; **fare una ~ a qu** to caress sb

carezzare [ka·ret·'tsa:·re] *vt* to stroke

cargo ['kar·go] <- *o* -ghi> *m* **1.** NAUT cargo ship **2.** AERO cargo plane

cariare [ka·'ria:·re] **I.** *vt* (*denti*) to rot **II.** *vr:* **-rsi** (*denti*) to rot

cariatide [ka·'ria:·ti·de] *f* ARCH caryatid; **starsene immobile come una ~** *fig* to stand there like a statue

caribico, -a [ka·'ri:·bi·ko] <-ci, -che> *agg* Caribbean

carica ['ka:·ri·ka] <-che> *f* **1.** ADM (*lavoro*) post; **in ~** in office **2.** (*di meccanismo*) winding **3.** EL, PHYS charge **4.** MIL (*attacco*) charge; **tornare alla ~** *fig* to try again **5.** SPORT tackle **6.** *fig* (*slancio*) drive; **dare la ~ a qu** *fig* to give sb a lift

caricabatteria [ka·ri·ka·bat·te·'ri:·a] <-> *m* (*per auto, notebook, telefono cellulare*) battery charger

caricare [ka·ri·'ka:·re] **I.** *vt* **1.** (*macchina, camion, nave, merce*) to load **2.** (*passeggeri*) to pick up **3.** (*batterie*) to charge **4.** (*fucile, pistola, macchina fotografica*) to load **5.** (*orologio*) to wind (up) **6.** MIL (*assaltare*) to charge **7.** SPORT to tackle **8.** COMPUT (*programma*) to load **9.** *fig* (*oberare*) to overload; **~ qu di qc** to overload sb with sth **10.** (*aumentare*) to increase; **~ il prezzo di qc** to put up the price of sth; **~ la dose** to increase the dose; *fig* (*esagerare*) to lay it on thick **II.** *vr:* **-rsi 1. -rsi di qc** (*di pacchi*) to load oneself with sth; (*di lavoro*) to overload oneself with sth **2.** *fig* (*gasarsi*) to psych oneself up

caricatore [ka·ri·ka·'to:·re] *m* **1.** (*di arma*) magazine; (*di macchina fotografica*) cartridge; (*di telefono cellulare*) charger **2.** (*operaio*) loader

caricatura [ka·ri·ka·'tu:·ra] *f* caricature

carico ['ka:·ri·ko] <-chi> *m* **1.** (*operazione*) loading **2.** (*merce*) load; NAUT cargo **3.** (*portata: di veicolo, ascensore*) load **4.** EL charge **5.** *fig* (*onere*) burden; **persone a ~** dependents; **avere la famiglia a ~** to have a dependent family; **a ~ di** payable by **6.** FIN **~ fiscale** [*o* **tributario**] tax burden

carico, -a <-chi, -che> *agg* **1.** *a. fig* (*pieno*) loaded; **~ di qc** loaded with sth **2.** (*persona*) laden; **~ di qc** (*pacchetti*) laden with sth; (*compiti, lavoro*) overloaded with sth **3.** (*pistola*) loaded; (*batteria*) charged; (*orologio, sveglia*) wound up

carie ['ka:·rie] <-> *f* decay

carillon [ka·ri·'jɔ] <-> *m* music box

carino, -a [ka·'ri:·no] *agg* **1.** (*grazioso*) nice **2.** (*gentile*) kind

carisma [ka·'riz·ma] <-i> *m* charisma

carismatico, -a [ka·ris·'ma:·ti·ko] <-ci, -che> *agg* (*personaggio, capo*) charismatic

carità [ka·ri·'ta] <-> *f* **1.** REL charity **2.** (*elemosina*) charity; **chiedere la ~** to ask for charity **3.** *inf* (*favore*) favor; **fammi la ~ di spegnere la radio** please turn off the radio; **per ~!** for heaven's sake!

carlona [kar·'lo:·na] *f* **alla ~** *inf* carelessly

carminio [kar·'mi:·nio] <-i> *m* carmine

carnagione [kar·na·'dʒo:·ne] *f* complexion

carnale [kar·'na:·le] *agg* **1.** (*sensuale: piaceri, peccato*) carnal; **violenza ~** rape **2.** (*fratello*) blood; (*cugino*) first

carne ['kar·ne] *f* **1.** (*cibo*) meat; **~ bianca** white meat; **~ rossa** red meat; **~ tritata** ground meat; **~ in scatola** canned meat; **mettere troppa ~ al fuoco** *fig* to have too many irons in the fire; **non essere né ~ né pesce** *fig* to be neither fish nor fowl **2.** (*muscoli*) flesh; **~ viva** living flesh; **bene in ~** plump; **in ~ ed ossa** in the flesh **3.** (*corpo*) flesh; **peccati della ~** sins of the flesh

carnefice [kar·'ne:·fi·tʃe] *m* **1.** (*boia*) executioner **2.** *fig* (*tormentatore*) torturer

carneficina [kar·ne·fi·'tʃi:·na] *f* **1.** (*strage*) massacre **2.** *fig* (*disastro*) disaster

carnet [kar·'nɛ] <-> *m* book; **~ di ballo** dance card; **~ degli assegni** checkbook

carnevale [kar·ne·'va:·le] *m* (*periodo festivo*) carnival; **veglione di ~** carnival masked ball; **a** [*o* **di**] **~ ogni scherzo vale** *prov* during carnival anything goes

i **Carnevale** (Carnival) is the period before the beginning of Lent when people celebrate with parties, processions, firework displays, and costumed balls. The high point of Carnival is **Martedì grasso** (Mardi Gras). The most famous Carnival processions in Italy are held in Venice and Viareggio.

carniere [kar·'niɛ:·re] *m* game bag

carnivori [kar·'ni:·vo·ri] *mpl* carnivores *pl*

carnivoro, -a [kar·'ni:·vo·ro] *agg* (*animale, pianta*) carnivorous

carnoso, -a [kar·'no:·so] *agg* **1.** (*labbra*) full **2.** (*foglie, petali*) fleshy

caro, -a ['ka:·ro] **I.** *agg* **1.** (*amato*) dear **2.** (*gentile*) kind; (*tanti*) **-i saluti** best wishes; **sono stati molto -i con me** they were very kind to me **3.** (*pregiato*) precious; **tenersi ~ qu/qc** to cherish sb/sth; **questo quadro mi è molto ~** this painting means a lot to me **4.** (*costoso: negozio, prodotto*) expensive; **pagare qc a ~ prezzo** *a fig* to pay a high price for sth **II.** *avv* a lot; **pagare ~ qc** to pay a lot for sth; **pagarla -a** *inf* to pay dearly **III.** *m, f* darling

carogna [ka·'roɲ·ɲa] *f* **1.** ZOO carcass **2.** *fig pej* (*persona vile*) swine

carognata [ka·roɲ·'ɲa:·ta] *f inf* dirty trick

carosello [ka·ro·'zɛl·lo] *m* (*torneo, giostra*) carousel

carota [ka·'rɔ:·ta] *f* BOT carrot; **pel di ~** *fig, inf* carrot top *inf*

carotene [ka·ro·'tɛ:·ne] *m* carotene

carotide [ka·'rɔ:·ti·de] *f* carotid

carovana [ka·ro·'va:·na] *f* **1.** (*convoglio*) caravan **2.** (*colonna*) convoy

carovaniere [ka·ro·va·'niɛ:·re] *m* caravaneer

carovita [ka·ro·'vi:·ta] <-> *m* high cost of living; **indennità di ~** cost of living allowance

carpa ['kar·pa] *f* ZOO carp

carpentiere [kar·pen·'tiɛ:·re] *m* carpenter

carpire [kar·'pi:·re] <carpisco> *vt* **~ qc a qu** (*segreto, denaro*) to get sth out of sb

carpo ['kar·po] *m* wrist joint

carponi [kar·'po:·ni] *avv* on all fours

carrabile [kar·'ra:·bi·le] *agg* suitable for vehicles; **passo** ~ driveway

carraio, -a [kar·'ra:·io] <-ai, -aie> *agg* **passo** ~ driveway

carré [ka·'re] <-> *m* **1.** (*di abito*) yoke **2.** CULIN loin; **pan** ~ sliced loaf

carreggiata [kar·red·'dʒa:·ta] *f* **1.** (*strada*) highway **2.** MOT (*di veicolo*) track **3.** *fig* (*retta via*) straight and narrow; **rimettere qu in** ~ *fig* to put sb back on the straight and narrow

carrellata [kar·rel·'la:·ta] *f* **1.** CINE tracking shot **2.** *fig* (*ricapitolazione*) roundup; **fare una** ~ **su qc** to take a quick look at sth

carrello [kar·'rɛl·lo] *m* **1.** (*per bagagli*) (baggage) cart; (*al supermercato*) (shopping) cart **2.** (*per cibi e bevande*) cart **3.** AERO landing gear **4.** TEC truck **5.** (*di macchina da scrivere*) carriage **6.** FILM dolly **7.** MIN bogie

carretta [kar·'ret·ta] *f* **1.** (*piccolo carro*) cart; **tirare la** ~ *fig* to plod along **2.** *pej* (*auto*) jalopy; ~ **del mare** tub

carriera [kar·'riɛ:·ra] *f* (*professione*) career; **far** ~ to get on in one's career

carrierista [kar·rie·'ris·ta] <-i , -e> *m* careerist

carriola [kar·ri·'ɔ:·la] *f* **1.** (*piccola carretta*) wheelbarrow **2.** (*quantità*) barrow load

carrista [kar·'ris·ta] <-i> *m* MIL tank crew member

carro ['kar·ro] *m* **1.** (*veicolo*) cart; ~ **armato** tank; ~ **attrezzi** tow truck; ~ **bestiame** stock car; ~ **ferroviario** rail car; ~ **funebre** hearse; ~ **merci** freight car; **il Gran/Piccolo Carro** ASTR the Big/Little Dipper; **mettere il** ~ **davanti** [*o* **innanzi**] **ai buoi** *fig* to put the cart before the horse **2.** (*contenuto*) cartload

carroccio [kar·'rɔ·tʃo] <-cci> *m* Northern League

carrozza [kar·'rɔt·tsa] *f* **1.** (*vettura*) carriage **2.** FERR car; ~ **ristorante** dining car; **signori, in** ~**!** all aboard!

carrozzella [kar·rot·'tsɛl·la] *f* **1.** (*per bambini*) baby carriage **2.** MED wheelchair

carrozzeria [kar·rot·tse·'ri:·a] <-ie> *f* **1.** MOT bodywork **2.** (*officina*) body shop

carrozziere [kar·rot·'tsiɛ:·re] *m* body shop worker

carrozzina [kar·rot·'tsi:·na] *f* (*per bambini*) baby carriage

carrozzone [kar·rot·'tso:·ne] *m* (*di circo*) wagon; **salire sul** ~ **di qc** to jump on the bandwagon of sth

carrucola [kar·'ru:·ko·la] *f* pulley

carta ['kar·ta] *f* **1.** (*materiale*) paper; ~ **assorbente** blotting paper; ~ **da lettere** writing paper; ~ **da pacchi** brown paper; ~ **da regalo** wrapping paper; ~ **igienica** toilet paper; ~ **oleata** waxed paper; ~ **millimetrata** graph paper; ~ **vetrata** sandpaper; ~ **velina** tissue paper; **dare** ~ **bianca a qu** *fig* to give sb carte blanche **2.** JUR, ADM paper; ~ **bancomat** ATM card; ~ **bollata** [*o* **da bollo**] stamped paper; ~ **costituzionale** constitution; ~ **d'identità**

identity card; **la** ~ **delle Nazioni Unite** the Charter of the United Nations; **avere le -e in regola** to have one's papers in order; *fig* to have what it takes; ~ **di credito** credit card; ~ **di credito telefonica** phone card; ~ **d'imbarco** boarding card; ~ **di soggiorno** JUR residence permit **3.** (*geografica*) map; ~ **stradale** street map **4.** CULIN menu; **mangiare alla** ~ to eat à la carte **5.** (*da gioco*) card; **cambiare le -e in tavola** *fig* to move the goalposts; **farsi fare le -e** to have one's fortune read in the cards; **giocare a -e** to play (at) cards; **giocare a -e scoperte** *fig* to lay one's cards on the table; **giocare l'ultima** ~ *fig* to play one's last card; **leggere le -e a qn** to read sb's fortune in the cards; **mettere le -e in tavola** *fig* to lay one's cards on the table; **chi è fortunato in amor non giochi a -e** *prov* lucky in love, unlucky at cards *prov*

cartacarbone [kar·ta·kar·'bo:·ne] <cartecarbone> *f* carbon paper

cartaceo, -a [kar·'ta:·tʃeo] *agg* FIN paper; **circolazione -a** paper currency; **moneta -a** paper money

cartamodello [kar·ta·mo·'dɛl·lo] *m* paper pattern

cartamoneta [kar·ta·mo·'ne:·ta] *f* paper money

cartapecora [kar·ta·'pɛ:·ko·ra] *f* parchment

cartapesta [kar·ta·'pes·ta] *f* papier mâché

cartastraccia [kar·tas·'trat·tʃa] <cartestracce> *f* waste paper

cartecarbone *pl di* **cartacarbone**

carteggio [kar·'ted·dʒo] <-ggi> *m* **1.** (*corrispondenza*) correspondence **2.** NAUT charting

cartella [kar·'tɛl·la] *f* **1.** (*scheda*) card; ~ **clinica** medical records *pl*; ~ **della tombola** tombola card **2.** TYP page **3.** FIN ~ **delle tasse** tax form; ~ **esattoriale** tax statement; ~ **pazza** wrong tax demand **4.** (*custodia: di plastica, di cartone*) folder **5.** (*borsa: per la scuola*) schoolbag

cartellino [kar·tel·'li:·no] *m* **1.** (*etichetta*) tag; ~ **dei prezzi** price tag **2.** (~ (*di presenza*)) time card; **timbrare il** ~ (*all'entrata*) to clock in; (*all'uscita*) to clock out; (*lavorare come dipendente*) to work as an employee **3.** SPORT (*nel calcio*) card; ~ **giallo/rosso** yellow/red card

cartello [kar·'tɛl·lo] *m* **1.** (*avviso*) notice; ~ (**stradale**) road sign **2.** (*insegna*) sign **3.** COM (*accordo*) cartel

cartellone [kar·tel·'lo:·ne] *m* **1.** (*per pubblicità*) poster **2.** (*della tombola*) board **3.** THEAT (*programma*) bill; **tenere il** ~ to run

carter ['kar·ter] <-> *m* **1.** (*di motocletta, bicicletta*) chain guard **2.** (*dell'olio*) oil reservoir

cartesiano, -a [kar·te·'sia:·no] *agg* MATH Cartesian; **coordinate -e** Cartesian coordinates

cartestracce *pl di* **cartastraccia**

cartevalori, carte-valori [kar·te·va·'lo:·ri] *fpl* paper money

cartiera [kar·'tiɛ:·ra] *f* paper mill

cartilagine [kar·ti·'la:·dʒi·ne] *f* cartilage
cartina [kar·'ti:·na] *f* **1.** GEO map **2.**(*per sigarette*) cigarette paper **3.**(*di aghi*) pack **4.** CHEM **~ al tornasole** litmus paper
cartoccio [kar·'tɔt·tʃo] <-cci> *m* **1.**(*involucro di carta*) paper cone **2.**(*contenuto*) paper coneful **3.** CULIN **al ~** in foil
cartografia [kar·to·gra·'fi:·a] *f* cartography
cartolaio, -a [kar·to·'la:·io] <-ai, -aie> *m, f* (*cartoleria*) stationery store
cartoleria [kar·to·le·'ri:·a] <-ie> *f* (*negozio*) stationery store
cartolibreria [kar·to·li·bre·'ri:·a] <-ie> *f* (*negozio*) book and stationery store
cartolina [kar·to·'li:·na] *f* postcard; **~ illustrata** picture postcard; **~ postale** stamped postcard; **~ precetto** [*o rosa inf*] draft card
cartomante [kar·to·'man·te] *mf* fortune-teller
cartoncino [kar·ton·'tʃi:·no] *m* **1.**(*cartone leggero*) cardboard **2.**(*biglietto*) card; **~ d'auguri** greeting card
cartone [kar·'to:·ne] *m* **1.**(*carta consistente*) cardboard **2.**(*disegno*) cartoon; **i -i animati** cartoons
cartongesso [kar·ton·'dʒɛs·so] *m* drywall; **parete di ~** drywall walls
cartonista [kar·to·'nis·ta] <-i , -e> *mf* CINE cartoonist
cartoon [ka:·'tu:·n] <-> *m* FILM cartoon
cartotecnica [kar·to·'tɛk·ni·ka] <-che> *f* **1.**(*tecnica*) paper-making **2.**(*produzione*) paper products *pl*
cartotecnico, -a [kar·to·'tɛk·ni·ko] <-ci, -che> *agg* (*industria, settore*) paper-making
cartuccia [kar·'tut·tʃa] <-cce> *f* (*di arma da fuoco, penna*) cartridge; **sparare l'ultima ~** *fig* to play one's last card; **essere una mezza ~** *fig* (*di statura*) to be a midget; (*valere poco*) to be a nobody
casa ['ka:·sa] *f* **1.**(*edificio*) house **2.**(*luogo in cui si vive*) home; **~ popolare** public housing unit; **a ~ mia** at my place; **andare a ~** to go home; **essere a ~** to be (at) home; **essere fuori (di) ~** to be out; **uscire di ~** to go out; **essere di ~** *fig* to be at home; **cercare/trovare ~** to look for/to find a house; **faccende** [*o lavori*] **di ~** housework; **spese per la ~** household expenditure; **mandare avanti la ~** *fig* to support one's family; **metter su ~** *fig* to set up home **3.** CULIN homemade; **fare gli onori di ~** to be the host; **passare di ~ in ~** to go from door to door **4.**(*istituto*) home; **~ di cura** nursing home; **~ di correzione** reformatory; **~ di pena** detention center; **~ di ricovero per anziani** (*old people's home*), **~ da gioco** casino; **~ dello studente** dormitory; **~ chiusa** [*o di tolleranza*] whorehouse **5.** COM (*ditta*) company; **~ editrice** publishing house **6.**(*casato*) house **7.** SPORT **giocare in/fuori ~** to play at home/away
casacca [ka·'zak·ka] <-cche> *f* coat
casaccio [ka·'zat·tʃo] *m* **a ~** *pej* at random
casalinghi [ka·sa·'liŋ·gi] *mpl* housewares *pl*

casalingo, -a [ka·sa·'liŋ·go] <-ghi, -ghe> **I.** *agg* **1.**(*vita*) home; (*persona*) homeloving **2.** CULIN homemade; **pane ~** homemade bread; **alla -a** made simply **3.** SPORT home **II.** *m, f* homeloving person
casato [ka·'sa:·to] *m* (*stirpe*) family
cascamorto [kas·ka·'mɔr·to] *m inf* lovesick Romeo; **fare il ~ con qu** *inf* to play the lovesick Romeo with sb
cascante [kas·'kan·te] *agg* (*floscio: guance, seno*) sagging; (*camicia*) loose-fitting
cascare [kas·'ka:·re] *vi essere inf* to fall; **~ dalla fame** to be fainting with hunger; **~ dal sonno** to be falling asleep on one's feet; **~ bene/male** *fig* to be lucky/unlucky; **far ~ qc dall'alto a qu** *fig* to rub sb's nose in sth *fig;* **cascarci** to fall for it; **caschi pure il mondo, io ci vado!** no matter what happens, I'm going!
cascata [kas·'ka:·ta] *f* GEOG waterfall
cascina [kaʃ·'ʃi:·na] *f* (*fattoria*) farm
cascinale [kaʃ·ʃi·'na:·le] *m* **1.**(*gruppo di case*) farmstead **2.**(*cascina*) farmhouse
casco[1] ['kas·ko] <-schi> *m* **1.**(*per bicicletta*) helmet; (*per motocicletta*) (crash) helmet; (*per equitazione*) (riding) hat; **-schi blu** MIL blue berets; **~ coloniale** pith helmet **2.**(*di parrucchiere*) (hair)dryer
casco[2] <inv> *agg* **assicurazione ~** comprehensive insurance
caseggiato [ka·sed·'dʒa:·to] *m* **1.**(*gruppo di case*) block of houses **2.**(*singolo edificio*) apartment building
caseificio [ka·zei·'fi:·tʃo] <-ci> *m* dairy
caseina [ka·ze·'i:·na] *f* casein
casella [ka·'sɛl·la] *f* **1.**(*scomparto: di mobile*) compartment; **~ postale** post office box **2.**(*riquadro: di foglio*) box; (*di scacchiera*) square **3.** COMPUT box; **~ di dialogo** dialog box
casellante [ka·sel·'lan·te] *mf* **1.** FERR railroad crossing keeper **2.** MOT (*di austostrada*) toll collector
casellario [ka·sel·'la:·rio] <-i> *m* **1.**(*per documenti*) filing cabinet; **~ postale** set of post office boxes **2.** JUR files *pl; ~* **giudiziale** court records *pl*
casello [ka·'sɛl·lo] *m* **1.** MOT (*di austostrada*) tollbooth **2.** FERR signal tower
casereccio, -a [ka·se·'ret·tʃo] <-cci, -cce> *agg* (*pane, pasta, salumi*) homemade
caserma [ka·'sɛr·ma/ka·'zɛr·ma] *f* barracks
casermone [ka·zɛr·'mo:·ne] *m* barracks
Caserta *f* Caserta, *town in Campania, southern Italy*
Casertano [ka·zer·'ta:·no] *m* (*zona*) Caserta area; **nel ~** in the Caserta area
casertano, -a I. *agg* from Caserta **II.** *m, f* (*abitante*) person from Caserta
cash [kæʃ] <-> *m* cash; **pagare in ~** to pay (in) cash
cash-and-carry ['kæʃ·ən(d)·'kæ·ri] <-> *m* COM cash-and-carry store
cash flow ['kæʃ flou] <-> *m* FIN, COM (*flusso di*

cassa) cash flow

cashmere [kæʃˈmiə] <-> *m v.* **cachemire**

casinista [ka·si·ˈnis·ta] <-i , -e> *mf inf* bungler

casino [ka·ˈsi:·no] *m* **1.** *inf* (*confusione*) mess **2.** *inf* (*chiasso*) racket *inf* **3.** *inf* (*pasticcio*) screw-up *inf* **4.** *inf* (*mucchio*) ton *inf* **5.** *vulg* (*bordello*) brothel **6.** (*di caccia*) lodge

casinò [ka·zi·ˈnɔ] <-> *m* casino

casistica [ka·ˈzis·ti·ka] <-che> *f* record of cases

caso [ˈka:·zo] *m* **1.** (*avvenimento fortuito*) chance; **per ~** by chance; **per puro ~** by sheer chance; **a ~** at random **2.** (*ipotesi*) case; **in** [*o* **nel**] **~ contrario** otherwise; **in qualunque ~** in any case; **in tal ~** in that case; **in ogni ~** in any case; **in nessun ~** in no case; **nel peggiore dei -i** if (the) worst comes to (the) worst; **nel ~ che** [*o* **in cui**] **...** +*conj* in case; **mettiamo** [*o* **poniamo**] **il ~ che ...** +*conj* let's suppose that ...; **si dà** (**il**) **~ che ...** +*conj* it so happens that ...; **i -i sono due** there are two possibilities; **non è il ~** +*conj* (*opportuno*) there's no need; **in ~ di morte/malattia** in case of death/illness **3.** (*fatto*) case; **~ limite** borderline case; **un ~ disperato** a desperate case; **il ~ Dreyfus** the Dreyfus Affair **4.** LING case

casolare [ka·so·ˈla:·re] *m* cottage

casomai, caso mai [ka·zo·ˈma:·i, ˈka:·zo ˈma:·i] *cong* (*eventualmente*) in case

caspita [ˈkas·pi·ta] *int inf* heavens!; **ma che ~ vuoi!** *inf* what the heck do you want! *inf*

cassa [ˈkas·sa] *f* **1.** (*recipiente*) crate; **~ da morto** coffin **2.** MUS **~ acustica** speaker **3.** (*di orologio*) case **4.** (*somma*) cash; **~ comune** kitty **5.** (*banca*) bank; **~ di risparmio** savings bank; **batter ~** *inf* to ask for money; **pagamento** (**a**) **pronta ~** cash payment **6.** (*di negozio*) cash desk; (*di supermercato*) checkout; **registratore di ~** cash register **7.** (*istituzione previdenziale*) fund; **~ integrazione** layoff fund; **~ malattia** health insurance program **8.** ANAT **~ toracica** ribcage

cassaforte [kas·sa·ˈfɔr·te] <casseforti> *f* safe

cassapanca [kas·sa·ˈpaŋ·ka] <-che *o* cassepanche> *f* chest

cassata [kas·ˈsa:·ta] *f* cassata

cassazione [kas·sat·ˈtsio:·ne] *f* **1.** ((*Corte di*) *Cassazione* ≈) Court of Appeals **2.** (*annullamento*) annulment by a higher court

casseforti *pl di* **cassaforte**

cassepanche *pl di* **cassapanca**

casseruola [kas·se·ˈruɔ:·la] *f* casserole

cassetta [kas·ˈset·ta] *f* **1.** (*piccola cassa*) box; **~ delle lettere** mailbox; **~ postale elettronica** COMPUT electronic mailbox; **~ di distribuzione** TEL junction box; **~ di sicurezza** safe-deposit box **2.** (*di registratore, video*) cassette **3.** CINE box-office receipts *pl;* **film di ~** box-office success **4.** (*di carrozza*) box

cassetto [kas·ˈset·to] *m* (*di mobile*) drawer

cassettone [kas·set·ˈto:·ne] *m* **1.** (*mobile*) chest of drawers **2.** ARCH coffer; **soffitto a -i** cof-

fered ceiling

cassiere, -a [kas·ˈsiɛ:·re] *m, f* (*di banca*) cashier; (*di supermercato*) checkout clerk

cassintegrato, -a [kas·sin·te·ˈgra:·to] **I.** *m, f* laid-off worker **II.** *agg* laid-off; **operaio** [*o* **lavoratore**] **~** laid-off worker

cassone [kas·ˈso:·ne] *m* **1.** (*grande cassa*) large box **2.** (*mobile*) chest

cassonetto [kas·so·ˈnet·to] *m* (*per rifiuti*) trashcan

cast [ka:st] <-> *m* cast

casta [ˈkas·ta] *f* **1.** (*ceto*) caste **2.** (*elite*) class

castagna [kas·ˈtaɲ·ɲa] *f* chestnut; **prendere qu in ~** *fig* to catch sb in the act

castagneto [kas·taɲ·ˈɲe:·to] *m* chestnut (wood)

castagno [kas·ˈtaɲ·ɲo] *m* chestnut

castano, -a [kas·ˈta:·no] *agg* (*capelli*) chestnut; (*occhi*) hazel

castellano [kas·tel·ˈla:·no] *m* lord of the manor

castello [kas·ˈtɛl·lo] *m* **1.** (*gener*) castle; **fare -i in aria** to build castles in the air **2.** (*impalcatura*) **letto a ~** bunk bed

castigare [kas·ti·ˈga:·re] *vt* (*punire*) to punish

castigato, -a [kas·ti·ˈga:·to] *agg* (*abiti*) sober; (*vita*) chaste

castigo [kas·ˈti:·go] <-ghi> *m* punishment; **essere in ~** *inf* to be being punished; **mettere qn in ~** *inf* to punish sb

castità [kas·ti·ˈta] <-> *f* chastity; **cintura di ~** chastity belt; **fare voto di ~** to take a vow of chastity

casto, -a [ˈkas·to] *agg* (*ragazza*) chaste; (*pensieri, parole*) sober

castorino [kas·to·ˈri:·no] *m* **1.** (*pelliccia*) nutria **2.** ZOO coypu

castoro [kas·ˈtɔ:·ro] *m* (*animale, pelliccia*) beaver

castrante [kas·ˈtran·te] *agg fig* (*che blocca*) inhibiting

castrare [kas·ˈtra:·re] *vt* (*animale, uomo*) to castrate

castrazione [kas·tra·ˈtsio:·ne] *f* castration

castronaggine [kas·tro·ˈnad·dʒi·ne] *f inf* nonsense

castroneria [kas·tro·ne·ˈri:·a] <-ie> *f inf* nonsense

casual [ˈkæ·ʒual] **I.** <inv> *agg* (*abiti, look*) casual; **abbigliamento ~** casual clothes *pl* **II.** *avv* casually; **vestirsi ~** to dress casually **III.** <-> *m* casual wear

casuale [ka·zu·ˈa:·le] *agg* (*dovuto al caso: incontro, episodio*) chance

casualità [ca·zua·li·ˈta] <-> *f* (*di eventi, incontri*) chance nature

casupola [ka·ˈsu:·po·la] *f* small house

cataclisma [ka·ta·ˈkliz·ma] <-i> *m a fig* cataclysm

catacomba [ka·ta·ˈkom·ba] *f* catacomb

catafalco [ka·ta·ˈfal·ko] <-chi> *m* **1.** (*impalcatura funebre*) catafalque **2.** (*struttura ingombrante*) monster catafascio [ka·ta·'faʃ·ʃo] *m* andare a ~ to go completely wrong; (*in rovina*) to go to rack and ruin; (*rapporto*) to go to the dogs; mandare a ~ to ruin completely

catalitico, -a [ka·ta·'liː·ti·ko] <-ci, -che> *agg* MOT catalytic; marmitta -a catalytic converter

catalizzare [ka·ta·lid·'dza:·re] *vt* 1. CHEM to catalyze 2. *fig* (*attirare*) to capture

catalizzato, -a [ka·ta·lid·'dza:·to] *agg* MOT (*dotato di catalizzatore: auto*) fitted with a catalytic converter

catalizzatore [ka·ta·lid·dza·'to:·re] *m* MOT catalytic converter

catalogare [ka·ta·lo·'ga:·re] *vt* 1. (*registrare: opere d'arte, pubblicazioni*) to catalog 2. (*elencare*) to list

catalogo [ka·'ta:·lo·go] <-ghi> *m* 1. (*di libri, oggetti*) catalog 2. *fig* (*elencazione*) list

catanese [ka·ta·'ne:·se] I. *agg* from Catania II. *mf* (*abitante*) person from Catania

Catanese (*zona*) Catania area; nel ~ in the Catania area

Catania *f* Catania, *port in eastern Sicily*

catanzarese [ka·tan·tsa·'re:·se] I. *agg* from Catanzaro II. *mf* (*abitante*) person from Catanzaro

Catanzarese (*zona*) Catanzaro area; nel ~ in the Catanzaro area

Catanzaro *f* Catanzaro, *city in Calabria, southern Italy*

catapecchia [ka·ta·'pek·kia] <-cchie> *f* hovel

catapulta [ka·ta·'pul·ta] *f* catapult

catapultare [ka·ta·pul·'ta:·re] *vt* 1. (*scagliare*) to catapult 2. *fig* (*far arrivare*) to throw

catarifrangente [ka·ta·ri·fran·'dʒɛn·te] *m* MOT reflector

catarro [ka·'tar·ro] *m* catarrh

catasta [ka·'tas·ta] *f* 1. (*di legna*) pile 2. *fig* (*mucchio*) stack

catasto [ka·'tas·to] *m* 1. (*registro*) land register 2. (*ufficio*) land office

catastrofe [ka·'tas·tro·fe] *f* 1. (*sciagura*) catastrophe; ~ ecologica ecological disaster 2. *fig* (*disastro*) disaster

catastrofico, -a [ka·tas·'trɔː·fi·ko] <-ci, -che> *agg* 1. (*disastroso: inondazione*) catastrophic 2. (*pessimista: previsioni*) pessimistic 3. (*sulle catastrofi: film*) disaster

catechismo [ka·te·'kiz·mo] *m* REL catechism; andare a ~ to go to catechism

catechizzare [ka·te·kid·'dza:·re] *vt* 1. REL to catechize 2. *fig* (*indottrinare*) to indoctrinate

categoria [ka·te·go·'riː·a] <-ie> *f* 1. (*classe*) category; ~ a rischio at-risk group; ~ di prezzo price bracket; ~ di reddito income bracket; ~ professionale professional group; associazione di ~ trade association 2. (*di albergo*) class 3. SPORT class

categorico, -a [ka·te·'gɔː·ri·ko] <-ci, -che> *agg* categorical; imperativo ~ categorical imperative

catena [ka·'te:·na] *f* 1. (*serie di anelli*) chain; la ~ dell'ancora the anchor chain; -e (da neve) snow chains 2. (*collana*) chain 3. (*gruppo di imprese*) chain; ~ di alberghi hotel chain; ~ di negozi chain of stores 4. (*serie*) chain; reazione a ~ *a. fig* FIS, BIOL chain reaction; una ~ di avvenimenti *fig* a chain of events

catenaccio [ka·te·'nat·tʃo] <-cci> *m* 1. (*spranga*) bolt 2. SPORT defensive game

cateratta [ka·te·'rat·ta] *f* MED, GEOG cataract

catering ['kei·tə·riŋ] <-> *m* 1. (*servizio*) catering 2. (*azienda*) catering company

caterpillar® [ka·ter·'pil·lar] <-> *m* (*veicolo*) Caterpillar®

caterva [ka·'tɛr·va] *f* (*mucchio*) pile

catetere [ka·te·'tɛː·re] *m* catheter

cateto [ka·'tɛː·to] *m* cathetus

catinella [ka·ti·'nɛl·la] *f* basin; piove a -e it's raining cats and dogs

catino [ka·'ti:·no] *m* 1. (*recipiente*) basin 2. (*quantità*) basinful

catodico, -a [ka·'tɔː·di·ko] <-ci, -che> *agg* (*tubo*) cathode-ray; (*raggi*) cathode

catodo ['ka:·to·do] *m* cathode

catorcio [ka·'tɔr·tʃo] <-ci> *m pej, inf* (*oggetto, veicolo*) wreck

catramare [ka·tra·'ma:·re] *vt* (*strada, marciapiede, tetto*) to tar

catrame [ka·'tra:·me] *m* tar

cattedra ['kat·te·dra] *f* 1. (*tavolo di scuola*) (teacher's) desk; stare in ~ *fig scherz* to pontificate 2. (*incarico*) chair 3. REL throne

cattedrale [kat·te·'dra:·le] cathedral

cattedratico, -a [kat·te·'dra:·ti·ko] <-ci, -che> I. *agg* (*corso, lezione*) university II. *m, f* professor

cattiveria [kat·ti·'vɛ:·ria] <-ie> *f* 1. (*qualità*) nastiness 2. (*azione*) nasty things 3. (*frase*) nasty thing

cattivo [kat·'ti:·vo] *m* (*non buono*) bad

cattivo, -a <più cattivo *o* peggiore, cattivissimo *o* pessimo> I. *agg* 1. (*gener*) bad; essere di ~ umore to be in a bad mood; essere in ~ stato to be in a bad state; fa ~ tempo the weather's bad; essere [*o* navigare] in -e acque *fig* to be in difficulty 2. (*irrequieto: bambino*) naughty II. *m, f* 1. (*malvagio: persona*) bad guy 2. (*irrequieto: bambino*) naughty child; fare il ~ to be naughty

cattolicesimo [kat·to·li·'tʃe:·zi·mo] *m* (Roman) Catholicism

cattolico, -a [kat·'tɔː·li·ko] <-ci, -che> I. *agg* (*chiesa, fede, persona*) (Roman) Catholic II. *m, f* (Roman) Catholic

cattura [kat·'tu:·ra] *f* (*di persona, animale*) capture; mandato [*o* ordine] di ~ arrest warrant

catturare [kat·tu·'ra:·re] *vt* (*persona, animale*) to capture

caucciù [kaut·'tʃu] <-> *m* India rubber

causa ['ka:u·za] *f* 1. (*origine*) cause; ~ ed effetto cause and effect; essere ~ di qc to be the cause of sth 2. JUR (*processo*) case; ~ civile civil case; ~ **penale** criminal case; **far ~ a qu** to take legal action against sb; **fare** [*o* **muovere**] ~ to take legal action 3. *fig* (*ideale*) cause; **perorare una** ~ to plead a cause 4. *fig* (*interessi*) cause; **fare ~ comune** to make common cause 5. (*motivo*) reason; **a** [*o* **per**] ~ **di qc** because of sth

causale [kau·'za:·le] I. *agg* causal II. *f* LING causal clause

causare [kau·'za:·re] *vt* (*danni, dolore, problemi*) to cause

caustico, -a ['ka:us·ti·ko] <-ci, -che> *agg a. fig* CHEM caustic

cautela [kau·'tɛ:·la] *f* 1. (*prudenza*) caution 2. (*precauzione*) precaution

cautelare¹ [kau·te·'la:·re] *agg* JUR precautionary

cautelare² I. *vt* (*proteggere: persona, interessi*) to protect II. *vr:* **-rsi -rsi contro qc** (*assicurarsi*) to protect oneself against sth; **-rsi da qc** (*proteggersi*) to protect oneself from sth

cauterizzazione [kau·te·rid·dza·'tsio:·ne] *f* (*di ferita, vaso sanguigno*) cauterization

cauto, -a ['ka:u·to] *agg* (*persona, parole, sorriso*) cautious

cauzionale [kau·tsio·'na:·le] *agg* **deposito ~** deposit

cauzione [kau·'tsio:·ne] *f* deposit

Cav. *abbr di* **Cavaliere** *Kt*

cava ['ka:·va] *f* (*di pietre*) quarry

cavalcare [ka·val·'ka:·re] I. *vt* (*cavallo, asino*) to ride II. *vi* to ride

cavalcata [ka·val·'ka:·ta] *f* (*di cavallo*) ride

cavalcavia [ka·val·ka·'vi:·a] <-> *m* (*ponte*) overpass

cavalcioni [ka·val·'tʃo:·ni] *avv* **a ~** astride

cavaliere [ka·va·'liɛ:·re] *m* 1. HIST knight 2. SPORT rider 3. (*accompagnatore*) escort 4. (*persona cortese*) gentleman 5. (*onorificenza*) Knight

cavalla [ka·'val·la] *f* mare

cavalleresco, -a [ka·val·le·'res·ko] <-schi, -sche> *agg* 1. LIT, HIST chivalric; **letteratura -a** chivalric literature; **poemi -schi** poems of chivalry 2. *fig* (*nobile: gesto*) chivalrous

cavalleria [ka·val·le·'ri:·a] <-ie> *f* 1. MIL cavalry 2. *fig* (*raffinata cortesia*) chivalry

cavallerizzo, -a [ka·val·le·'rit·tso] *m, f* 1. (*chi cavalca*) rider; **pantaloni alla -a** riding breeches *pl* 2. (*acrobata di circo*) circus rider

cavalletta [ka·val·'let·ta] *f* ZOO grasshopper

cavalletto [ka·val·'let·to] *m* 1. TEC (*per piani da lavoro, tavole*) trestle 2. (*da pittore*) easel 3. FOTO, FILM, MIL (*treppiede*) tripod

cavallina [ka·val·'li:·na] *f* 1. ZOO filly 2. SPORT (*attrezzo ginnico*) (vaulting) horse 3. (*gioco dei bambini*) leapfrog; **correre la ~** *fig* to sow one's wild oats

cavallo [ka·'val·lo] *m* 1. ZOO, SPORT horse; **~ a dondolo** rocking horse; **~ baio** bay (horse); **~ bianco** gray (horse); **~ sauro** chestnut (horse); **~ da corsa** racehorse; **~ da sella** saddle horse; **~ di battaglia** *fig* forte; (*di artista*)

signature piece; **coda di ~** ponytail; **ferro di ~** horseshoe; **andare a ~** to go riding; **montare** [*o* **salire**] **a ~** to mount; **scendere da ~** to dismount; **a ~ di** astride; **essere a ~** *a iron* to be home free; **a caval donato non si guarda in bocca** *prov* don't look a gift horse in the mouth 2. (*di scacchi*) knight 3. (*di calzoni, mutande*) crotch

cavallone [ka·val·'lo:·ne] *m* (*onda*) breaker

cavalluccio [ka·val·'lut·tʃo] <-cci> *m* **~ marino** seahorse; **portare a ~ (sulle spalle)** to carry piggyback

cavare [ka·'va:·re] *vt* 1. (*estrarre, tirare fuori*) to take out; (*dente*) to pull; (*marmo*) to quarry; (*liquidi*) to draw; **-rsi gli occhi** *fig* to ruin one's eyesight; **non ~ un ragno dal buco** *fig* to get nowhere 2. (*levarsi di dosso: vestiti*) to take off; **-rsi la fame** to satisfy one's hunger; **-rsi la sete** to quench one's thirst; **-rsi la voglia di far qc** to satisfy one's desire to do sth 3. **cavarsela** *inf* to get by; **come te la cavi?** *inf* how are you getting along?

cavatappi [ka·va·'tap·pi] <-> *m* corkscrew

cavaturaccioli [ka·va·tu·'rat·tʃo·li] <-> *m* corkscrew

caverna [ka·'vɛr·na] *f* 1. (*grotta*) cave 2. MED cavity

cavernicolo, -a [ka·ver·'ni:·ko·lo] I. *agg* (*animali, fauna*) cave II. *m, f* caveman *m*, cavewoman *f*

cavernoso, -a [ka·ver·'no:·so] *agg* 1. *fig* (*cupo: voce, risata*) deep 2. MED cavernous

cavia ['ka:·via] <-ie> *f a. fig* guinea pig

caviale [ka·'via:·le] *m* caviar

caviglia [ka·'viʎ·ʎa] <-glie> *f* (*di persona, animale*) ankle; (*malleolo*) ankle bone

cavigliera [ka·viʎ·'ʎɛː·ra] *f* ankle bandage

cavillo [ka·'vil·lo] *m* (*pretesto*) loophole

cavilloso, -a [ka·vil·'lo:·so] *agg* quibbling

cavità [ka·vi·'ta] <-> *f* 1. (*incavo*) hollow 2. (*grotta*) cave 3. MED cavity

cavo ['ka:·vo] *m* 1. (*cavità*) hollow; **nel ~ della mano** in the hollow of the hand 2. ANAT cavity; **~ orale** oral cavity 3. EL cable; **televisione via ~** cable televsion; **~ a fibbre ottiche** fiber-optic cable 4. (*corda*) cable

cavo, -a *agg* (*vuoto*) hollow

cavolata [ka·vo·'la:·ta] *f fig, inf* stupid thing

cavolfiore [ka·vol·'fio:·re] <-> *m* cauliflower

cavolo ['ka:·vo·lo] *m* cabbage; **~ cappuccio** spring cabbage; **~ di Bruxelles** Brussels sprout; **~ rapa** kohlrabi; **~ verzotto** savoy cabbage; **testa di ~** *fig, inf* moron *inf*; **non capire un ~** *inf* not to understand a thing; **non fare un ~** *inf* not to do a damn thing *inf*; **non me ne importa un ~** *inf* I don't give a damn *inf*; **col ~** *inf* no way *inf*; **sono -i tuoi** *inf* that's your problem; **entrarci come il ~ a merenda** to have nothing to do with it; **che ~ vuoi?** *inf* what the hell do you want? *inf*

cazzata [kat·'tsa:·ta] *f vulg* fucking stupid thing *vulg*; **non dire -e!** don't talk crap! *inf*

cazzo ['kat·tso] *m vulg* (*pene*) dick *vulg*; **testa**

di ~ *vulg* dickhead *vulg;* **non me ne importa un** ~ *vulg* I don't give a fuck *vulg;* **non capisce un** ~ *vulg* he doesn't understand a fucking thing *vulg*

cazzotto [kat·'tsɔt·to] *m inf* (*pugno*) punch; **fare a -i** (**con qu**) to have a fight (with sb)

cazzuola [kat·'tsu·ɔ:·la] *f* trowel

cazzuto, -a [kat·'tsu:·to] *agg vulg* **1.** (*scaltro, imbattibile*) badass *vulg* **2.** (*noioso, faticoso, sgradevole*) fucking *vulg*

CC *abbr di* **Carabinieri** Carabinieri, *Italian military police*

C.C. 1. *abbr di* **Codice Civile** civil code **2.** *abbr di* **Corte Costituzionale** Constitutional Court **3.** *abbr di* **Corte di Cassazione** ≈ Court of Appeals **4.** *abbr di* **Corte dei Conti** *court auditing public finances*

c/c *abbr di* **conto corrente** checking account

CCD *m abbr di* **Centro Cristiano Democratico** *Christian Democratic Center*

CCT, cct *m abbr di* **Certificato di Credito del Tesoro** ≈ Treasury bill

CD <-> *m abbr di* **Compact Disc** CD; **lettore** ~ CD player

CD-RAM *m abbr di* **Compact Disc Random Access Memory** COMPUT CD-RAM

CD-ROM, cd-rom *m abbr di* **Compact Disc Read Only Memory** COMPUT CD-ROM; **lettore** ~ CD-ROM drive

C.d.S. *abbr di* **Codice della Strada** ≈ rules of the road

CDU *m abbr di* **Classificazione Decimale Universale** UDC

ce [tʃe] *pron pers* (*davanti a lo, la, li, le, ne*) *v.* **ci** I., II., III.

cecchino [tʃek·'ki:·no] *m* sniper

cece ['tʃe:·tʃe] *m* chickpea

cecità [tʃe·tʃi·'ta] <-> *f* blindness

ceco ['tʃε:·ko] *m* (*lingua*) Czech

ceco, -a <-chi, -che> I. *agg* Czech II. *m, f* (*abitante*) Czech

Cecoslovacchia [tʃe·koz·lo·'vak·kia] *f* (**la**) ~ HIST Czechoslovakia

cecoslovacco, -a [tʃe·koz·lo·'vak·ko] <-chi, -che> I. *agg* HIST Czechoslovakian II. *m, f* HIST Czechoslovakian

cedere ['tʃε:·de·re] I. *vi* **1.** MIL to yield **2.** *fig* (*darsi per vinto*) to give in; ~ **a qc** to give in to sth **3.** (*pilastri, fondazioni*) to give way II. *vt* **1.** (*lasciare*) to give up; ~ **il passo a qu** to let sb go first; ~ **il passo a qc** *fig* to give way to sth; ~ **le armi** *a fig* to surrender; ~ **terreno** *fig* to give ground **2.** COM, JUR (*vendere*) to sell

cedevole [tʃe·'de:·vo·le] *agg* **1.** (*molle: terreno*) soft **2.** *fig* (*docile: carattere*) amenable

cedibile [tʃe·'di:·bi·le] *agg* (*diritto, biglietto*) transferable

cedimento [tʃe·di·'men·to] *m* **1.** (*di terreno, edificio, ponte*) subsidence **2.** *fig* MED (*momento di debolezza*) breakdown

cedola ['tʃε:·do·la] *f* **1.** (*tagliando*) voucher **2.** FIN (*di azioni*) coupon

cedro ['tʃε:·dro] *m* **1.** (*conifera*) cedar; (*albero da frutto*) citron (tree) **2.** (*frutto*) citron **3.** (*legno*) cedar(wood) **4.** (*candito*) candied citron

cefalea [tʃe·fa·'lε:·a] *f* headache

cefalo ['tʃε:·fa·lo] *m* mullet

ceffo ['tʃεf·fo] *m* **1.** *fig, pej* (*faccia*) mug *pej* **2.** (*persona*) troll

ceffone [tʃef·'fo:·ne] *m* slap

celare [tʃe·'la:·re] I. *vt poet* (*significato, tristezza, verità*) to conceal II. *vr:* **-rsi** to be concealed

celeberrimo, -a [tʃe·le·'bεr·ri·mo] *agg superlativo di* **celebre** very famous

celebrare [tʃe·le·'bra:·re] *vt* **1.** (*festeggiare: vittoria, festa*) to celebrate **2.** (*ufficiare: messa*) to celebrate; (*nozze*) to officiate at **3.** (*glorificare*) to celebrate

celebrazione [tʃe·le·brat·'tsio:·ne] *f* **1.** (*festeggiamento*) celebration **2.** (*svolgimento: di messa*) celebration; (*di matrimonio*) officiation; (*di processo*) hearing

celebre ['tʃε:·le·bre] <più celebre, celeberrimo> *agg* (*scrittore, fatto, prodotto*) famous

celebrità [tʃe·le·bri·'ta] <-> *f* **1.** (*fama*) fame **2.** (*persona*) celebrity

celere ['tʃε:·le·re] *agg* (*servizio, spedizione*) express

celeste [tʃe·'lεs·te] I. *agg* **1.** ASTR celestial; **corpi -i** celestial bodies **2.** REL (*divino*) heavenly **3.** (*occhi, cielo, tessuto*) light blue II. *m* (*colore*) light blue

celibato [tʃe·li·'ba:·to] *m* celibacy

celibe ['tʃε:·li·be] I. *agg* (*uomo*) single II. *m* bachelor

cella ['tʃεl·la] *f* **1.** (*gener*) cell **2.** (*vano*) ~ **frigorifera** cold store

cellofanare [se·lo·fa·'na:·re] *vt* TEC (*prodotti, CD, libri*) to wrap in cellophane®

cellophane® [se·lo·'fan] <-> *m* cellophane®

cellula ['tʃεl·lu·la] *f* BIOL, TEC, POL cell; **-e staminali** stem cells; ~ **fotoelettrica** photoelectric cell

cellulare [tʃel·lu·'la:·re] I. *agg* **1.** BIOL cell; **struttura** ~ cell structure **2.** (*telefono*) cellular **3.** (*carcere*) with one prisoner per cell; (*furgone*) police II. *m* **1.** (*telefono*) cellphone; ~ **GSM** GSM phone **2.** (*furgone*) police van

cellulite [tʃel·lu·'li:·te] *f* cellulite

celluloide [tʃel·lu·'lɔi·de] *f* celluloid; **mondo della** ~ world of movies; **divi della** ~ stars of the big screen

cellulosa [tʃel·lu·'lo:·sa] *f* cellulose

cembalo ['tʃem·ba·lo] *m* harpsichord

cementare [tʃe·men·'ta:·re] *vt a. fig* to cement

cemento [tʃe·'men·to] *m* **1.** (*nell'edilizia*) cement; ~ **armato** reinforced concrete **2.** (*per denti*) amalgam

cena ['tʃe:·na] *f* dinner; **l'ultima** ~ the Last Supper

cenacolo [tʃe·'na:·ko·lo] *m* **1.** (*nell'arte*) Last Supper **2.** *fig* (*di artisti e letterati*) coterie

cenare [tʃe·'na:·re] *vi* to have dinner

cencio ['tʃen·tʃo] <-ci> *m* (*straccio, abito*) rag;

bianco come un ~ *fig* white as a sheet
cenere¹ ['tʃe·ːne·re] *f* ash; (**mercoledì del**)**le -i** Ash Wednesday; **ridurre in ~** to reduce to ashes; **covare sotto la ~** *a fig* to smolder
cenere² <inv> *agg* ash
cenerentola [tʃe·ne·'rɛn·to·la] *f* Cinderella
cenno ['tʃen·no] *m* **1.** (*gesto*) signal; **~ di riscontro** reply; **salutare qu con un ~ della mano** to give sb a wave; **fare ~ di sì/no** (*con il capo*) to nod (in agreement)/to shake one's head (in disagreement) **2.** (*indizio*) sign **3.** (*informazione*) mention
cenone [tʃe·'no·ːne] *m* dinner; **~ di San Silvestro** New Year's Eve dinner
censimento [tʃen·si·'men·to] *m* (*di popolazione, fabbricati, documenti*) census
censire [tʃen·'si·ːre] <censisco> *vt* (*popolazione, animali, alberi, edifici*) to census
censura [tʃen·'su·ːra] *f* **1.** (*controllo*) censorship **2.** (*ufficio*) censor's office
censurare [tʃen·su·'ra·ːre] *vt* (*film, opera, libro*) to censor
centauro [tʃen·'ta:u·ro] *m* **1.** (*nella mitologia*) centaur **2.** ASTR Centaurus **3.** SPORT motorcyclist
centellinare [tʃen·tel·li·'na·ːre] *vt* **1.** (*bevanda, vino*) to sip **2.** (*dosare*) to ration
centenario [tʃen·te·'na·ːrio] <-i> *m* centennial
centenario, -a <-i, -ie> I. *agg* **1.** (*che ha cent'anni*) hundred-year-old **2.** (*che ricorre ogni cento anni*) centennial II. *m, f* centenarian
centennale¹ [tʃen·ten·'na·ːle] *agg* **1.** (*che ha cent'anni*) hundred-year-old **2.** (*che ricorre ogni cento anni*) centennial
centennale² [tʃen·ten·'na·ːle] *m* (*anniversario*) centennial
centesimale [tʃen·te·zi·'ma·ːle] *agg* (*cifra, sistema*) centesimal
centesimo [tʃen·'tɛ:·zi·mo] *m* **1.** (*frazione*) hundredth **2.** (*moneta*) cent **3.** *fig, inf* (*denaro*) **non avere un ~ in tasca** to not have a cent; **non valere un ~** to not be worth a dime
centesimo, -a I. *agg* hundredth II. *m, f* hundredth
centigrado, -a [tʃen·'ti:·gra·do] *agg* centigrade; **grado ~** degree centigrade
centigrammo [tʃen·ti·'gram·mo] *m* centigram
centilitro [tʃen·'ti:·lit·ro] *m* centiliter
centimetro [tʃen·'ti:·met·ro] *m* centimeter
centimilionesimo, -a [tʃen·ti·mil·io·'nɛː·zi·mo] *agg* hundred-millionth
centinaio [tʃen·ti·'na:·io] *m* hundred; **un ~ (di...)** about a hundred (...); **a -aia** by the hundred
centista [tʃen·'tis·ta] <-i, -e> *mf* hundred-meter runner
cento ['tʃɛn·to] I. *num* **1.** (*dieci decine*) **a** [*o* one] hundred **2.** (*moltissimi*) a hundred; **~ di questi giorni!** many happy returns! II. <-> *m* a [*o* one] hundred; **per ~** per cent; *v.a.* **cinque**
centometrista [tʃen·to·me·'tris·ta] <-i, -e> *mf* hundred-meter runner

centomila [tʃen·to·'mi:·la] I. *num* a [*o* one] hundred thousand II. <-> *m* a [*o* one] hundred thousand
centomillesimo, -a [tʃen·to·mil·'lɛː·zi·mo] *agg* hundred-thousandth
centone [tʃen·'to:·ne] *m scherz* (*banconota da cento*) hundred
centopiedi [tʃen·to·'piɛ:·di] <-> *m* centipede
centotredici [tʃen·to·'tre·di·tʃi] <-> *m* **1.** (*numero di telefono*) 113, emergency telephone number **2.** (*gruppo di pronto intervento*) emergency services *pl;* **chiamare il ~** to call the emergency services
centrale [tʃen·'tra·ːle] I. *agg* **1.** (*parte, appartamento, tema*) central; **riscaldamento ~** central heating; **Italia ~** central Italy **2.** ADM (*sede, ufficio*) head II. *f* head office; **~ elettrica** power plant; **~ telefonica** telephone exchange; **~ nucleare** [*o* atomica] nuclear power plant
centralinista [tʃen·tra·li·'nis·ta] <-i , -e> *mf* switchboard operator
centralino [tʃen·tra·'li:·no] *m* switchboard
centralismo [tʃen·tra·'liz·mo] *m* centralism
centralizzare [tʃen·tra·lid·'dza:·re] *vt* (*attività, servizi*) to centralize
centralizzazione [tʃen·tra·lid·dza·'tsio:·ne] *f* (*di attività, servizi*) centralization
centrare [tʃen·'tra:·re] *vt* **1.** (*bersaglio, canestro*) to hit in the center; (*canestro*) to score **2.** COMPUT, FOTO, SPORT to center **3.** *fig* (*argomento, tema*) to pinpoint **4.** TEC, MOT (*asse, ruote*) to balance
centrato, -a *agg* **1.** COMPUT, FOTO (*testo*) centered **2.** *fig* (*domanda, intervento*) pertinent
centrattacco [tʃen·trat·'tak·ko] <-cchi> *m* center-forward
centravanti [tʃen·tra·'van·ti] <-> *m* center-forward
centrifuga [tʃen·'tri:·fu·ga] <-ghe> *f* **1.** TEC centrifuge **2.** (*per frutta*) juicer **3.** (*per insalata*) salad spinner **4.** (*di lavatrice*) dryer
centrifugare [tʃen·tri·fu·'ga:·re] *vt* **1.** TEC (*soluzioni*) to centrifuge **2.** (*frutta*) to juice **3.** (*insalata*) to spin **4.** (*biancheria*) to dry
centrifugo, -a [tʃen·'tri:·fu·go] <-ghi, -ghe> *agg* () centrifugal; **forza -a** centrifugal force
centrino [tʃen·'tri:·no] *m* doily
centritavola *pl di* centrotavola
centro ['tʃɛn·tro] *m* **1.** MATH, POL, ANAT center **2.** (*punto di mezzo*) center **3.** (*di bersaglio*) bull's eye; **far ~** *a fig* to hit a bull's eye **4.** (*di città*) downtown; **andare in ~** to go downtown; **~ storico** old town **5.** (*insediamento*) **~ abitato** built-up area; **~ balneare** seaside resort **6.** (*servizio*) **~ commerciale** shopping center; **~ estetico** beauty parlor; **~ profughi** refugee hostel **7.** (*istituto di studi*) center; **~ meccanografico** [*o* elettronico] COMPUT data-processing center; **~ trapianti** transplant center **8.** *fig* (*punto fondamentale: di tema, questione*) core; **essere al ~ dell'attenzione** to be the center of attention **9.** (*baricentro*) **~ di gravità** center of gravity

Centroamerica [tʃen·tro·a·'mɛ:·ri·ka] *f* Central America
centrocampista [tʃen·tro·kam·'pis·ta] <-i, -e> *mf* midfielder
centrocampo [tʃen·tro·'kam·po] *m* midfield
centrodestra [tʃen·tro·'dɛs·tra] <-> *m* POL center-right
centrosinistra [tʃen·tro·si·'nis·tra] <-> *m* POL center-left
centrotavola [tʃen·tro·'ta:·vo·la] <centritavola> *m* centerpiece
centuplicare [tʃen·tu·pli·'ka:·re] *vt* 1. (*fatturato, prezzi*) to increase a hundredfold 2. *fig* (*accrescere di molto*) to increase greatly
centuplo, -a ['tʃɛn·tu·plo] I. *agg* hundredfold II. *m, f* a hundred times as much
ceppo ['tʃep·po] *m* 1. BOT (*di albero*) stump 2. (*da ardere*) log 3. (*stirpe*) stock 4. *pl* (*di prigioniero*) shackles
cera¹ ['tʃe:·ra] *f* 1. (*sostanza*) wax 2. (*per lucidare*) polish; ~ **da scarpe** shoe polish; ~ **per pavimenti** floor polish; ~ **per mobili** furniture polish; **dare la** ~ to give a polish 3. (*modello*) waxwork; **museo delle -e** waxwork museum
cera² ['tʃe:·ra/'tʃɛ:·ra] *f* (*aspetto: del viso*) **avere una bella/brutta** ~ to look well/sick
ceralacca [tʃe·ra·'lak·ka] <-cche> *f* sealing wax
ceramica [tʃe·'ra:·mi·ka] <-che> *f* 1. (*oggetto*) ceramic 2. (*arte*) ceramics 3. (*impasto*) ceramic
ceramista [tʃe·ra·'mis·ta] <-i , -e> *mf* ceramist
cerata [tʃe·'ra:·ta] *f* oilskins *pl*
cerato, -a [tʃe·'ra:·to] *agg* waxed; **tela -a** oilcloth
cerbiatto, -a [tʃer·'biat·to] *m, f* fawn
cerbottana [tʃer·bot·'ta:·na] *f* blowpipe
cerca ['tʃer·ka] <-che> *f* **in ~ di** looking for
cercamine [tʃer·ka·'mi:·ne] <-> *m* mine detector
cercapersone [tʃer·ka·per·'so:·ne] <-> *m* (*beeper*) pager
cercare [tʃer·'ka:·re] I. *vt* 1. (*tentare di trovare*) to look for; (*in un libro*) to look up; ~ **marito/moglie/** to look for a husband/wife; ~ **guai** to look for trouble; **'cercasi ...' '... wanted'** 2. (*tentare di ottenere: gloria, fama, potere*) to seek 3. (*desiderare: affetto, serenità, tranquillità*) to want II. *vi* (*sforzarsi*) to try; **cercherò di sbrigarmi** I'll try to be quick; **chi cerca trova** *prov* seek and ye shall find
cercatore, -trice I. *agg* **cannocchiale** ~ finder II. *m, f* searcher
cerchia ['tʃer·kia] <-chie> *f* (*di mura, montagne*) circle; ~ **di amici** *fig* circle of friends
cerchiare [tʃer·'kia:·re] *vt* 1. (*ruota*) to rim; (*botte*) to hoop 2. (*evidenziare*) to ring
cerchiato, -a [tʃer·'kia:·to] *agg* (*ruota*) rimmed; (*botte*) hooped; **con gli occhi -i** with bags under one's eyes
cerchietto [tʃer·'kiet·to] *m* 1. (*per capelli*)

hairband 2. (*anello*) band; (*braccialetto*) bracelet
cerchio ['tʃer·kio] <-chi> *m* 1. MATH circle 2. (*di botte*) hoop; **dare un colpo al ~ ed uno alla botte** *fig* to try to have it both ways 3. (*di ruota*) rim; **-chi in lega** alloy wheels 4. (*di persone*) circle; **disporsi in** ~ to form a circle 5. (*gioiello*) band 6. (*loc*) **avere un ~ alla testa** *fig* to have a headache
cerchione [tʃer·'kio:·ne] *m* rim
cereale [tʃe·re·'a:·le] *agg* (*piante, farine*) cereal
cereali [tʃe·re·'a:·li] *mpl* cereals
cerebrale [tʃe·re·'bra:·le] *agg* 1. ANAT (*malattia, materia*) brain 2. *fig* (*persona, artista, opera*) cerebral
cereo, -a ['tʃɛ:·reo] <-ei, -ee> *agg* 1. (*aspetto, volto*) wan 2. (*di cera*) wax
ceretta [tʃe·'ret·ta] *f* wax
cerimonia [tʃe·ri·'mɔ:·nia] <-ie> *f* 1. (*rito, festeggiamento*) ceremony; **abito da** ~ formal dress 2. *pl* (*complimenti*) ceremony
cerimoniale [tʃe·ri·mo·'nia:·le] *m* 1. (*regole*) etiquette 2. (*libro*) book of etiquette
cerino [tʃe·'ri:·no] *m* wax match
cerniera [tʃer·'niɛ:·ra] *f* 1. (*di borsa, abito*) zipper; ~ **lampo** zipper 2. (*cardine: di porta, finestra*) hinge
cernita [tʃer·'ni:·ta] *f* (*scelta*) selection
cero ['tʃe:·ro] *m* (*candela*) candle; ~ **pasquale** Pascal candle
cerone [tʃe·'ro:·ne] *m* (*cosmetico per attori*) greasepaint
cerotto [tʃe·'rɔt·to] *m* MED Band-Aid®
certamente [tʃer·ta·'men·te] *avv* certainly
certezza [tʃer·'tet·tsa] *f* certainty
certificare [tʃer·ti·fi·'ka:·re] *vt* (*qualità, conformità*) to certify; ~ **che** to certify that
certificato [tʃer·ti·fi·'ka:·to] *m* ADM (*attestato*) certificate; ~ **di garanzia** guarantee; ~ **di morte** death certificate; ~ **di nascita** birth certificate; ~ **di proprietà** proof of ownership; ~ **di residenza** proof of residence; ~ **medico** doctor's certificate
certo ['tʃɛr·to] *avv* certainly; ~ **che vengo!** of course I'll come!; **ma ~!** of course; ~ **che sì/no!** yes of course!/of course not!; **lei, ~, lo nega** she, of course, denies it
certo, -a I. *agg* 1. (*indubbio, sicuro*) definite 2. (*garantito, sicuro*) certain 3. (*convinto*) sure 4. (*vero*) **dare qc per** ~ to be sure that 5. (*qualche*) certain; **-i giorni** certain days 6. (*alquanto*) **avere una -a fame** to be rather hungry 7. (*non definito*) certain; **in un** ~ **senso** in a sense; **quel** ~ **non so che** that certain something 8. (*di tale genere*) such; **hai -e occhiaie oggi!** you've got such bags under your eyes today! 9. (*tale*) certain; **ha telefonato un** ~ **Davide** someone called Davide phoned II. *pron indef* (*alcuni*) some (people)
certosa [tʃer·'to:·za] *f* 1. REL, ARCH (*convento*) charterhouse 2. CULIN (*formaggio*) soft cheese from Lombardy
certosino [tʃer·to·'zi:·no] *m* 1. REL (*monaco*)

Carthusian (monk) **2.** CULIN (*formaggio*) *soft cheese from Lombardy* **3.** (*liquore*) chartreuse **4.** (*loc*) **pazienza da** [*o* **di un**] ~ patience of Job; **lavoro da** ~ painstaking work

certuno [tʃer·'tu:·no] *pron indef* certain person

cerume [tʃe·'ru:·me] *m* wax

cervelletto [tʃer·vel·'let·to] *m* cerebellum

cervello [tʃer·'vɛl·lo] *m* **1.** ANAT brain; **lavaggio del** ~ brainwashing; **avere il** ~ **di una gallina** *fig* to be a birdbrain *inf;* **farsi saltare le cervella** to blow one's brains out **2.** COMPUT brain; ~ **elettronico** electronic brain **3.** *fig* (*intelletto*) brains *pl;* **agire senza** ~ to act stupidly; **usare il** ~ to use one's head; **uscire di** ~ *fig* to go out of one's mind; **gli ha dato di volta il** ~ *fig* he's gone off his head; **lambiccarsi il** ~ *fig* to rack one's brains **4.** (*persona*) brains; **la fuga dei** ~ the brain drain

cervellone, -a [tʃer·vel·'lo:·ne] *m, f* brain

cervellotico, -a [tʃer·vel·'lɔ:·ti·ko] <-ci, -che> *agg* (*ragionamento*) tortuous; (*gioco*) complicated

cervicale [tʃer·vi·'ka:·le] *agg* (*arteria, muscoli, vertebre*) cervical

Cervino [tʃer·'vi:·no] *m* Matterhorn

cervo ['tʃɛr·vo] *m* deer; ~ **volante** ZOO stag beetle; (*giocattolo*) kite

cesareo [tʃe·'za:·reo] *agg* MED cesarean; **parto** ~ cesarean birth; **taglio** ~ cesarean section

cesellare [tʃe·zel·'la:·re] *vt* **1.** (*gioiello, metallo*) to chisel **2.** (*testo, scritto, stile*) to polish

cesello [tʃe·'zɛl·lo] *m* (*per incisioni*) chisel; **lavorare di** ~ *a fig* to polish

cespite ['tʃɛs·pi·te] *m* source of income

cespo ['tʃes·po] *m* tuft; ~ **d'insalata** head of lettuce

cespuglio [tʃes·'puʎ·ʎo] <-gli> *m* bush

cessare [tʃes·'sa:·re] **I.** *vi* to stop; *essere o avere;* ~ **di fare qc** to stop doing sth **II.** *vt avere* to stop

cessate il fuoco [tʃes·'sa:·te il 'fuɔ:·ko] <-> *m* ceasefire

cessazione [tʃes·sa·'tsio:·ne] *f* (*di attività, rapporto di lavoro*) suspension; ~ **delle ostilità** cessation of hostilities; ~ **di un contratto** expiration of a contract

cessione [tʃes·'sio:·ne] *f* (*di azienda*) sale; (*di diritto*) assignment

cesso ['tʃɛs·so] *m inf* john *inf*

cesta ['tʃes·ta] *f* **1.** (*recipiente*) basket **2.** (*contenuto*) basket(ful)

cestello [tʃes·'tɛl·lo] *m* **1.** (*piccola cesta*) little basket; (*per bottiglie*) crate **2.** (*di lavatrice*) drum; (*di lavastoviglie*) rack

cestinare [tʃes·ti·'na:·re] *vt* **1.** (*gettare*) to throw away **2.** *fig* (*rifiutare, non considerare*) to reject

cestino [tʃes·'ti:·no] *m* basket; ~ **da lavoro** work basket; ~ **da viaggio** lunchbox; ~ **della carta** wastebasket

cesto ['tʃes·to] *m* **1.** (*recipiente*) basket;

~ **regalo** gift basket **2.** (*contenuto*) basket(ful)

cesura [tʃe·'zu:·ra] *f* **1.** (*nella metrica*) caesura **2.** (*pausa, interruzione*) pause

cetaceo [tʃe·'ta:·tʃeo] *m* cetacean

ceto ['tʃɛ:·to] *m* (*classe*) class

cetra ['tʃe:·tra/'tʃɛ:·tra] *f* MUS zither

cetriolo [tʃe·tri·'ɔ:·lo] *m* cucumber

cf., cfr. *abbr di* **confronta** cf.

CFC *mpl abbr di* **clorofluorocarburo** CFC

CGIL *f abbr di* **Confederazione Generale Italiana del Lavoro** *left-wing Italian labor union assocation*

CH *abbr di* **Confoederatio Helvetica** CH

cha cha cha [tʃa tʃa 'tʃa] <-> *m* cha-cha

chalet [ʃa·'lɛ] <-> *m* chalet

champagne [ʃã·paɲ] **I.** <-> *m* CULIN champagne **II.** <inv> *agg* (*colore*) champagne

champignon [ʃã·pi·'ɲɔ̃] <- *o* champignons> *m* CULIN mushroom

chance [ʃã:s] <-> *f* chance

chantilly [ʃã·ti·'ji] <-> *f* CULIN (**crema**) ~ whipped cream

charme [ʃarm] <-> *m* charm

charter ['ʃa:·tə] **I.** <-> *m* AERO charter **II.** <inv> *agg* charter; **volo** ~ charter flight

chat-line [tʃæt·'lain] <-> *f* TEL chatline

chattare [tʃat·'ta:·re] *vi* COMPUT to chat

chatting ['tʃɛt·ting] <-> *m* COMPUT chat

chauffeur [ʃo·'fœ:r] <-> *m* chauffeur

che [ke] **I.** *pron* **1.** (*soggetto*) who; (*cosa, animale*) which **2.** (*complemento: persona*) who(m); (*cosa, animale*) which **3.** (*la qual cosa*) which **4.** (*temporale: in cui*) that **II.** *pron inter* what?; ~ (*cosa*)? what?; ~ **cosa vuoi da bere?** what do you want to drink?; ~ **ne dici?** what do you say?; ~ (*cosa*) **ne pensi?** what do you think?; **a** ~ (*cosa*) **stai pensando?** what are you thinking about?; **di** ~ (*cosa*) **ti lamenti?** what are you complaining about?; **non so** ~ (*cosa*) **dire** I don't know what to say **III.** *pron* what!; ~ **vedo!** what am I seeing!; ~, **sei già in piedi!** what, you're up already! **IV.** *pron indef* **ha un certo non so** ~ **di curioso** there's something rather curious about him [*o* her] [*o* it]; **il libro non è un gran** ~ the book isn't much good **V.** <inv> *agg* (*interrogativo*) what?; **a** ~ **pagina siamo arrivati?** what page are we on?; **con** ~ **diritto?** what right have you?; **in** ~ **mese andate in vacanza?** which month did you go on vacation?; ~ **uomo sei?** what sort of man are you? **VI.** <inv> *agg* (*esclamativo*) what!; ~ **bello!** how lovely!; ~ **stupido sono stato!** how stupid I've been! **VII.** *cong* **1.** (*dichiarativa*) that; **è ora** ~ **tu vada** it's time (that) you went; **spero** ~ **si fermi qualche giorno** I hope (that) you'll stay a few days **2.** (*causale*) that; **c'era un'afa** ~ **non si respirava** it was so close (that) you couldn't breathe; **era così triste** ~ **non voleva uscire dalla sua camera** she was so sad (that) she wouldn't come out of her room **3.** (*consecutiva*) that; **siediti in modo** ~ **ti veda** sit down so (that) I can see you **4.** (*temporale*) that; **prima ~ arrivi** before she arrives; **ogni volta ~ lo vedo** every time (that) I see him; **sono ore ~ lo aspetto** I've been waiting for him for hours **5.** (*concessiva*) **~ si comportino pure come vogliono** they can behave as they want; **sempre ~ si decida a farlo** provided that he decides to do it **6.** (*eccettuativa*) **nonostante ~ sia tardi** even though it's late **7.** (*in comparazioni*) than; **è andata meglio ~ non credessi** it went better than I thought **8.** (*limitativa*) **~ io sappia non è ancora arrivato** as far as I know, he's not arrived yet; **non fa altro ~ brontolare** she does nothing but complain **9.** (*nelle alternative*) **~ tu lo voglia o no, è lo stesso** it doesn't matter whether you want to or not; **sia ~ ..., sia ~ ...** whether ... or ...; **~ mi sia sbagliato?** or am I mistaken? **10.** (*imperativa*) **~ vada!** let him go!; **~ nessuno osi entrare!** no one should dare come in!

checca ['kek·ka] <-cche> *f pej, sl* queen *pej*
checché [kek·'ke] *pron, pron indef* whatever
check-in ['tʃek·'in] <-> *m* **1.** (*sportello*) check-in (desk) **2.** (*operazione*) check-in; **fare il ~** to check in
checkpoint ['tʃek·'pɔint] <-> *m* checkpoint
check-up ['tʃe·kʌp/tʃe·'kap] <-> *m* MED check-up
chef [ʃɛf] <-> *m* (*cuoco*) chef
chemioterapia [ke·mio·te·ra·'pi:·a] <-ie> *f* chemotherapy
chèque [ʃɛk] <-> *m* check
cherosene [ke·ro·'zɛ:·ne] *m* kerosene
cherubino [ke·ru·'bi:·no] *m* REL cherub
chetare [ke·'ta:·re] I. *vt* (*persona*) to calm; (*discussione*) to calm; (*fame*) to appease II. *vr:* -**rsi** (*persona*) to calm down; (*vento*) to drop; (*rumore*) to quiet down
chetichella [ke·ti·'kɛl·la] *f* **alla ~** on the quiet
cheto, -a ['ke:·to] *agg* quiet; **acqua -a** *fig* wolf in sheep's clothing; **acqua -a rompe i ponti** *prov* still waters run deep *prov*
chewing gum ['tʃu:·iŋ·ɡʌm] <-> *m* chewing gum
chi [ki] I. *pron* **1.** (*soggetto*) who; **si salvi ~ può** every man for himself **2.** (*oggetto*) who(m); **parlane a ~ vuoi** tell who you like; **il portale di ~ viaggia** the portal for travelers II. *pron indef* some; **~ dice una cosa, ~ un'altra** some say one thing; others say another III. *pron inter* **1.** (*soggetto*) who?; **~ c'è?** who is it? **2.** (*oggetto*) who(m)?; **~ hai incontrato al cinema?** who did you meet at the movie theater? **3.** (*complemento*) who(m)?; **a ~ hai dato le chiavi?** who did you give the keys to?; **con ~ esci?** who are you going out with?; **con ~ vieni alla festa?** who are you coming to the party with?; **di ~ hai paura?** who are you afraid of?; **di ~ è questo giornale?** whose is this newspaper?; **di ~ stavate parlando?** who were you talking about?; **su ~ vuoi far colpo stasera?** who are you out to impress tonight? IV. *pron* **1.** (*soggetto*) who

2. (*oggetto*) who(m); **~ si vede!** look who it is!
chiacchiera ['kiak·kie·ra] *f* **1.** *pl* (*conversazione*) chat; **fare quattro -e** *inf* to have a chat **2.** (*notizia infondata*) rumor; **tutte -e!** it's just gossip! **3.** *pl* CULIN *fried sweet pastry typically eaten at carnival time*
chiacchierare [kiak·kie·'ra:·re] *vi* **1.** (*parlare*) to chat **2.** *pej* (*spettegolare*) to gossip
chiacchierata [kia·kie·'ra:·ta] *f* chat
chiacchierio [kia·kie·'ri:·o] <-ii> *m* (*mormorio*) chatter
chiacchierone, -a [kia·kie·'ro:·ne] I. *agg* **1.** (*che chiacchiera molto*) chatty **2.** (*pettegolo*) gossipy II. *m, f* **1.** (*chi chiacchiera molto*) chatterbox **2.** (*pettegolo*) gossip
chiamare [kia·'ma:·re] I. *vt* **1.** (*rivolgersi a*) to call; **~ qu per nome** to call sb by name **2.** (*far venire: medico, polizia, taxi*) to call; **mandare a ~ qu** to send for sb **3.** (*telefonare a*) to call **4.** (*svegliare*) to call **5.** (*radunare*) **~ a raccolta** to gather together; **~ alle armi** (*al servizio di leva*) to call to arms **6.** (*mettere nome a*) to call; **lo hanno chiamato Davide** they called him Davide **7.** (*definire*) to call; **~ le cose col loro** (**vero**) **nome** to call a spade a spade **8.** JUR (*citare*) to call; **~ in giudizio** to summons; **~ in causa** *fig* to involve **9.** (*nominare: a carica*) to appoint II. *vr:* -**rsi** (*aver nome*) to be called; **come ti chiami?** what's your name?; **mi chiamo Davide** my name's Davide; **come si chiama questo fiore?** what's this flower called?
chiamata [kia·'ma:·ta] *f* **1.** (*telefonata*) call; **~ interurbana** long-distance call **2.** MIL **~ alle armi** draft
chianti ['kian·ti] <-> *m* Chianti, *red wine from Tuscany*
chiappa ['kiap·pa] *f vulg* buttock; **-e ass** *inf*
chiara ['kia:·ra] *f inf* (*egg*) white
chiarezza [kia·'ret·tsa] *f* **1.** (*comprensibilità*) clarity **2.** (*precisione*) clearness; **fare ~ su qc** to find out the truth about sth
chiarificare [kia·ri·fi·'ka:·re] *vt a. fig* to clarify
chiarimento [kia·ri·'men·to] *m* clarification
chiarire [kia'ri:re] <chia·ris·co> I. *vt* **1.** (*spiegare: concetto*) to clarify; (*dubbio*) to clear up **2.** (*risolvere: problema, faccenda*) to sort out II. *vr:* -**rsi** (*diventare chiaro*) to be cleared up
chiaro ['kia:·ro] I. *m* **1.** (*luminosità*) light; **quando fa ~** when it gets light; **al ~ di luna** by moonlight; **mettere in ~ una questione** *fig* to clear a matter up **2.** (*colore*) **vestirsi di ~** to wear light colors II. *avv* clearly; **parlar ~** to speak frankly; **vederci ~ in qc** to get to the bottom of sth; **~ e tondo** straight
chiaro, -a *agg* **1.** (*delicato: colore, legno, birra, occhi*) light; (*pelle, capelli*) fair; **blu/verde ~** light blue/green **2.** (*luminoso: giorno, luce*) bright; **~ come la luce del sole** *fig* clear as day **3.** (*limpido: cielo, acqua*) clear **4.** *fig* (*comprensibile: stile*) clear **5.** *fig* (*netto, deciso: rifiuto*) flat; **un no ~ e tondo** a definite no

chiarore [kia·'roː·re] *m* (*luce debole*) glimmer

chiaroscuro [kia·ros·'kuː·ro] *m* (*tecnica*) chiaroscuro

chiaroveggente [kia·ro·ved·'dʒɛn·te] **I.** *agg* clairvoyant **II.** *mf* clairvoyant

chiasso ['kias·so] *m* (*rumore*) din; **fare un ~ del diavolo** *inf* to make a hell of a racket *inf;* **la cosa ha fatto ~** *fig* the matter caused a stir

chiassoso, -a [kias·'soː·so] *agg* 1. (*persone, luoghi*) noisy 2. (*colore*) loud

chiatta ['kiat·ta] *f* (*per trasporto merci*) barge

chiavare [kia·'vaː·re] *vt vulg* to screw *vulg*

chiave¹ ['kiaː·ve] *f* 1. (*di armadio, casa, auto*) key; **chiudere a ~** to lock; **mettere sotto ~** to put under lock and key; **-i in mano** (*prodotto*) turnkey; **prezzo -i in mano** (*casa*) price with immediate occupation; (*auto*) sticker price 2. TEC (*attrezzo*) wrench; **~ inglese** monkey wrench 3. *fig* (*cardine*) key 4. *fig* (*tono*) viewpoint 5. COMPUT **~ di ricerca** search term 6. ARCH **~ di volta** keystone 7. MUS clef

chiave² <inv> *agg* -; **personaggio ~** key

chiavistello [kia·vis·'tɛl·lo] *m* (*spranga*) bolt

chiazza ['kiat·tsa] *f* 1. (*macchia: d'olio*) patch 2. (*su pelo*) patch; (*su pelle*) blotch

chiazzare [kiat·'tsaː·re] *vt* (*macchiare*) to stain

chic [ʃik] **I.** <inv> *agg* (*abito, casa, persona*) chic **II.** <-> *m* chic

chicchessia [kik·kes·'siː·a] <inv> *pron indef* anybody

chicchirichì [kik·ki·ri·'ki] <-> *m* (*verso del gallo*) cock-a-doodle-doo

chicco ['kik·ko] <-cchi> *m* 1. BOT (*di grano, riso*) grain; (*di caffè*) bean; **un ~ d'uva** a grape 2. (*di grandine*) hailtone

chiedere ['kiɛː·de·re] <chiedo, chiesi, chiesto> **I.** *vt* 1. (*per sapere*) to ask; **~ qc a qu** to ask sb for sth; **~ il prezzo di qc** to ask the price of sth; **~ notizie di qu** to ask after sb 2. (*per avere*) to ask for; **~ a qu di fare qc** to ask sb to do sth; **~ un favore a qu** to ask sb a favor; **~ la mano di una ragazza** to ask for a girl's hand **II.** *vi* to ask; **~ di qu** (*computarsi*) to ask about sb; (*al telefono*) to ask for sb

chierichetto [kie·ri·'ket·to] *m* altar boy

chiesa ['kiɛː·za] *f* church

chiesi ['kiɛː·si/'kiɛː·zi] *1. pers sing pass rem di* **chiedere**

chiesto ['kiɛs·to] *pp di* **chiedere**

Chieti *f* Chieti, *city and province in central Italy*

chietino, -a [kie·'tiː·no] **I.** *agg* from Chieti **II.** *m, f* (*abitante*) person from Chieti

chiffon [ʃi·'fɔ̃] <-> *m* chiffon

chiglia ['kiʎ·ʎa] <-glie> *f* keel

chignon [ʃi·'njɔ̃] <-> *m* chignon

chilo ['kiː·lo] *m abbr di* **chilogrammo** kilo

chilogrammo [ki·lo·'gram·mo] *m* kilogram

chilohertz [ki·lo·'ɛrts] *m* kilohertz

chilometraggio [ki·lo·me·'trad·dʒo] <-ggi> *m* =mileage

chilometrico, -a [ki·lo·'mɛː·tri·ko] <-ci, -che> *agg* 1. (*in chilometri*) kilometric; **percorso ~** distance in kilometers; **rimborso ~** =mileage allowance 2. *fig* (*interminabile*) endless

chilometro [ki·'lɔː·met·ro] *m* kilometer

chilowatt [ki·lo·'vat/'kiː·lo·vat] *m* kilowatt

chilowattora [ki·lo·vat·'toː·ra] <-> *m* kilowatt-hour

chimera [ki·'mɛː·ra] *f* 1. *fig* (*fantasticheria*) pipe-dream 2. (*in mitologia*) chimera

chimica ['kiː·mi·ka] <-che> *f* chemistry

chimico, -a ['kiː·mi·ko] <-ci, -che> **I.** *agg* (*analisi, processo, reazione*) chemical; **concime ~** chemical fertilizer **II.** *m, f* chemist

chimono [ki·'mɔː·no] <-> *m* kimono

china¹ ['kiː·na] <-> *f* (*inchiostro*) India ink

china² *f* (*pendio*) slope; **risalire la ~** *fig* to get back on one's feet

chinare [ki·'naː·re] **I.** *vt* (*testa, volto*) to bow; (*sguardo, occhi*) to lower; **~ il capo** *fig* (*sottomettersi*) to bow one's head **II.** *vr:* **-rsi** to bend down

chincaglieria [kiŋ·kaʎ·ʎe·'riː·a] <-ie> *f* 1. (*oggetti*) knick-knacks *pl* 2. (*negozio*) fancy goods store

chinino [ki·'niː·no] *m* quinine

chino, -a ['kiː·no] *agg* (*persona, schiena, testa*) bent

chinotto [ki·'nɔt·to] *m* 1. CULIN *sour orange soft drink* 2. BOT sour orange

chioccia ['kiɔt·tʃa] <-cce> *f* ZOO broody hen

chiocciola ['kiɔt·tʃo·la] *f* 1. ZOO snail 2. (*forma*) spiral; **scala a ~** spiral staircase 3. COMPUT at (sign)

chiodato, -a [kio·'daː·to] *agg* spiked

chiodo ['kiɔː·do] *m* 1. (*per legno, metallo*) nail; **~ da roccia** piton; **attaccare la bicicletta al ~** *fig* to give up cycling; **attaccare i guantoni al ~** *fig* to hang up one's gloves; **magro come un ~** *fig* (as) thin as a rake 2. *fig* (*idea fissa*) obsession 3. BOT **-i di garofano** cloves

chioma ['kiɔː·ma] *f* 1. (*capigliatura*) (head of) hair 2. BOT foliage

chiosco ['kiɔs·ko] <-schi> *m* (*padiglione*) kiosk

chiostro ['kiɔs·tro] *m* cloister

chip [tʃip] <-> *m* COMPUT chip

chiromante [ki·ro·'man·te] *mf* palm reader

chiromanzia [ki·ro·man·'tsiː·a] <-ie> *f* palm reading

chirurgia [ki·rur·'dʒiː·a] <-gie> *f* surgery; **~ plastica** plastic surgery

chirurgico, -a [ki·'rur·dʒi·ko] <-ci, -che> *agg* (*strumenti, operazione*) surgical; **intervento ~** surgical operation

chirurgo, -a [ki·'rur·go] <-gi *o* -ghi, -ghe> *m,* *f* surgeon

chissà [kis·'sa] *avv* who knows; **~ chi verrà** who knows who'll come; **~ quando/dove** who knows when/where; **~ mai** heaven knows

chitarra [ki·'tar·ra] *f* guitar; **suonare la ~** to play the guitar

chitarrista [ki·tar·'ris·ta] <-i , -e> *mf* guitarist

chiudere ['kiu:·de·re] <chiudo, chiusi, chiuso> I. *vt* **1.** (*finestra, libro, valigia, occhi*) to shut; (*ombrello*) to take down; (*mano*) to clench; **~ qc a chiave** to lock sth; **~ la bocca** *fig* to shut one's mouth; **~ un occhio** *fig* to turn a blind eye; **non ~ occhio tutta la notte** not to sleep a wink all night **2.** (*spegnere: acqua, gas*) to turn off **3.** (*delimitare: strada, passaggio*) to close **4.** (*bloccare: buco, falla*) to plug **5.** (*cessare l'attività di: fabbrica, negozio*) to close down **6.** (*terminare: lettera*) to end; (**comando**) **chiudi** COMPUT close (command) **7.** (*rinchiudere*) to shut; **~ qu sotto chiave** to lock sb up II. *vi* **1.** (*porta, finestra*) to close **2.** (*rubinetto*) to turn off **3.** (*scuola, locale*) to close **4.** COM (*cessare l'attività: fabbrica, negozio*) to close down; **~ in perdita** to show a loss III. *vr:* **-rsi** (*rinchiudersi*) to shut oneself; **-rsi in se stesso** to withdraw into oneself

chiunque [ki·'uŋ·kue] <inv, solo al sing> *pron* **1.** (*relativo*) whoever **2.** (*indefinito*) anybody

chiusa ['kiu:·sa] *f* **1.** (*di fiume, canale*) lock **2.** (*di lettera, discorso, poesia*) ending

chiusi ['kiu:·si] *1. pers sing pass rem di* **chiudere**

chiuso ['kiu:·so] *m* (*luogo riparato*) **al ~** indoors; **puzza di ~** musty smell

chiuso, -a I. *pp di* **chiudere** II. *agg* **1.** (*finestra, libro, ombrello, occhi*) closed; **tenere la bocca -a** *fig* to keep one's mouth shut; **avere il naso ~** to have a blocked nose; **~ a chiave** locked **2.** (*acqua, gas*) turned off **3.** (*strada, passaggio*) closed **4.** (*non più attivo: fabbrica, negozio*) closed down **5.** (*temporaneamente: scuola, museo*) closed **6.** (*concluso: capitolo*) closed **7.** (*riservato: persona*) reserved

chiusura [kiu·'su:·ra] *f* **1.** (*interruzione*) closing; **orario di ~** closing time **2.** (*cessazione: di attività*) closing down **3.** (*di strada*) closure **4.** (*abbottonatura*) fastener; **~ lampo** zipper **5.** (*serratura*) lock; **~ automatica** [*o* **a scatto**] latch; **~ centralizzata** central locking

ci [tʃi] I. *pron* **1.** (*oggetto: noi*) us **2.** (*complemento: a noi*) (to) us II. *pron* **1.** *pers pl* ourselves; **~ siamo divertiti** we enjoyed ourselves; **~ siamo lavate le mani** we washed our hands; **~ volevamo fermare per visitare il monastero** we wanted to stop to visit the monastery; **~ vediamo!** see you! III. *pron dem* **1.** (*a quella cosa*) it; **non ~ pensare più** don't think about it anymore; **non ~ credo** I don't believe it **2.** (*a quella persona*) him [*o* her] [*o* them]; **lo faccio perchè ~ tengo alla famiglia** I do it because I care about my family IV. *pron* **~ si diverte** it's fun V. *avv* **1.** (*qui*) here; **c'è** [*o* **ci**] **sono ...** there is [*o* there are] **... 2.** (*lì*) there **3.** (*per quel luogo*) that way

C.ia *abbr di* **compagnia** Co.

ciabatta [tʃa·'bat·ta] *f* **1.** (*pantofola*) mule **2.** (*tipo di pane*) ciabatta

ciac [tʃak] I. <-> *m* FILM clapperboard II. *int* **~**, **si gira!** action!

cialda ['tʃal·da] *f* (*wafer*) wafer

cialtrone, -a [tʃal·'tro:·ne] *m, f* **1.** (*persona incapace*) incompetent **2.** (*persona trasandata*) slob **3.** (*briccone*) scoundrel

ciambella [tʃam·'bɛl·la] *f* **1.** CULIN (*dolce*) doughnut; **non tutte le -e riescono col buco** *prov* you can't win them all **2.** (*salvagente*) lifebelt

ciancia ['tʃan·tʃa] <-ce> *f inf* (*pettegolezzo*) gossip

cianciare [tʃan·'tʃa:·re] *vi inf* to gossip

cianfrusaglia [tʃan·fru·'zaʎ·ʎa] <-glie> *f inf* knick-knack

cianidrico, -a [tʃa·'ni:·dri·ko] <-ci, -che> *agg* hydrocyanic; **acido ~** hydrocyanic acid

cianuro [tʃa·'nu:·ro] *m* cyanide

ciao ['tʃa:·o] *int* **1.** (*nell'incontrarsi*) hi! **2.** (*nel lasciarsi*) bye!

ciarla ['tʃar·la] *f* (*chiacchiere*) chatter

ciarlare [tʃar·'la:·re] *vi inf* (*chiacchierare*) to chatter

ciarlatano [tʃar·la·'ta:·no] *m* quack

ciarliero, -a [tʃar·'liɛ:·ro] *agg* chatty

ciarpame [tʃar·'pa:·me] *m* **1.** (*roba vecchia*) junk **2.** (*film, libro*) garbage

ciascuno, -a [tʃas·'ku:·no] <sing> I. *agg* each II. *pron indef* each (person); **a ~ il suo** to each his own

cibarsi [tʃi·'ba:r·si] *vr* to eat; **~ di qc** to live on sth

cibernetica [tʃi·ber·'nɛ:·ti·ka] <-che> *f* cybernetics

cibo ['tʃi:·bo] *m* food; **non toccare ~** to eat nothing

cicala [tʃi·'ka:·la] *f* ZOO cicada

cicatrice [tʃi·ka·'tri:·tʃe] *f* (*sulla pelle*) scar

cicatrizzare [tʃi·ka·trid·'dza:·re] I. *vi* to heal II. *vr:* **-rsi** to heal

cicca ['tʃik·ka] <-cche> *f* **1.** (*mozzicone di sigaretta*) butt **2.** (*sigaretta*) cigarette **3.** (*da masticare*) chewing gum **4.** (*loc*) **non valere una ~** *fig* to be worthless

cicchetto [tʃik·'ket·to] *m* **1.** (*di vino, liquore*) shot; **farsi un ~** to have a drink **2.** (*ramanzina*) telling-off *inf*

ciccia ['tʃit·tʃa] <-cce> *f inf* **1.** (*carne*) meat **2.** (*grasso*) flab *inf*

ciccione, -a [tʃit·'tʃo:·ne] *m, f inf* fatty *inf*

cicciotto, -a [tʃit·'tʃot·to] *agg* (*bambino*) chubby

cicerone [tʃi·tʃe·'ro:·ne] *m* (*guida*) guide

cicisbeo [tʃi·tʃiz·'bɛ:·o] *m* **1.** HIST gallant **2.** (*damerino*) ladies' man

ciclabile [tʃi·'kla:·bi·le] *agg* bicycle; **pista ~** bicycle lane

ciclamino[1] [tʃi·kla·'mi:·no] *m* cyclamen

ciclamino[2] <inv> *agg* (*colore*) cyclamen

ciclico, -a ['tʃi:·kli·ko] <-ci, -che> *agg* **1.** (*andamento, fenomeno, evento*) cyclical **2.** LIT (*romanzo*) cyclic

ciclismo [tʃi·'kliz·mo] *m* cycling

ciclista [tʃi·'klis·ta] <-i , -e> *mf* cyclist; **pista riservata ai -i** cycle lane

ciclistico, -a [tʃi·'klis·ti·ko] <-ci, -che> *agg*

C

(*evento, giro*) cycling; (*gara*) cycle; **lo sport** ~ the sport of cycling

ciclo ['tʃiː·klo] *m* **1.** (*gener*) cycle; ~ **biologico** life cycle; ~ **mestruale** menstrual cycle; ~ **di vita** life cycle **2.** (*serie*) series; ~ **di trasmissioni** series of programs

ciclomotore [tʃi·klo·mo·'toː·re] *m* moped

ciclone [tʃi·'kloː·ne] *m* METEO cyclone

ciclonico, -a [tʃi·'klɔː·ni·ko] <-ci, -che> *agg* **1.** METEO cyclonic **2.** *fig* (*esuberante*) high-spirited

ciclope [tʃi·'klɔː·pe] *m* Cyclops

ciclopico, -a [tʃi·'klɔː·pi·ko] <-ci, -che> *agg* (*gigantesco: opera, mangiata*) huge

ciclostilare [tʃi·klos·ti·'laː·re] *vt* (*volantino, documento*) to mimeograph

ciclostile [tʃi·klos·'tiː·le] *m* mimeograph

cicloturismo [tʃi·klo·tu·'riz·mo] *m* cycling vacations *pl*

cicloturista [tʃi·klo·tu·'ris·ta] <-i , -e> *mf* person on a cycling vacation

cicogna [tʃi·'koɲ·ɲa] *f* stork

cicoria [tʃi·'kɔː·ria] <-ie> *f* chicory

cicuta [tʃi·'kuː·ta] *f* hemlock

cieco, -a ['tʃɛː·ko] <-chi, -che> **I.** *agg* blind; **diventare** ~ to go blind; **essere** ~ **da un occhio** to be blind in one eye; **alla -a** *fig* blindly; **ubbidienza -a** *fig* blind obedience; **vicolo** ~ *fig* dead end **II.** *m, f* blind person

cielo ['tʃɛː·lo] **I.** *m* **1.** sky; **essere al settimo** ~ *fig* to be in seventh heaven; **toccare il** ~ **con un dito** *fig* to be walking on air; **non sta né in** ~ **né in terra** *fig* it's absolutely ludicrous; **sotto altri -i** *fig* in other climes; **per l'amore del** ~! for heaven's sake; ~ **a pecorelle, acqua a catinelle** *prov* mackerel sky, rain is nigh *prov* **2.** REL (*paradiso*) heaven **II.** *int inf* heavens!

cifra ['tʃiː·fra] *f* **1.** MATH figure; **un numero di tre -e** a three-figure number **2.** (*somma*) amount; **quel quadro costa una** ~ *fig inf* that painting costs a fortune *fig* **3.** *pl* (*monogramma*) initials **4.** (*scrittura segreta*) code

cifrare [tʃi·'fraː·re] *vt* (*messaggio, testo*) to encode

ciglio¹ ['tʃiʎ·ʎo] <-gli> *m* (*orlo*) edge

ciglio² *m* ANAT, ZOO eyelash; **senza batter** ~ *fig* without batting an eye(lid)

cigno ['tʃiɲ·ɲo] *m* swan

cigolare [tʃi·go·'laː·re] *vi* to squeak

cigolio [tʃi·go·'liː·o] <-ii> *m* squeaking

Cile ['tʃiː·le] *m* **il** ~ Chile

cilecca [tʃi·'lek·ka] *f* **far** ~ (*fucile*) to misfire; (*sessualmente*) not be able to get it up; *fig* to fail

cileno, -a [tʃi·'lɛː·no] **I.** *agg* Chilean **II.** *m, f* Chilean

cilicio [tʃi·'liː·tʃo] <-ci> *m* (*cintura*) hair shirt

ciliegia [tʃi·'liɛː·dʒa] <-ge *o* -gie> *f* cherry

ciliegio [tʃi·'liɛː·dʒo] <-gi> *m* **1.** (*albero*) cherry (tree) **2.** (*legno*) cherry

cilindrata [tʃi·lin·'draː·ta] *f* (cubic) capacity; **auto di grossa** ~ car with a powerful engine

cilindrico, -a [tʃi·'lin·dri·ko] <-ci, -che> *agg* (*rullo, vaso, costruzione*) cylindrical

cilindro [tʃi·'lin·dro] *m* **1.** MATH, MOT, TEC cylinder **2.** (*cappello*) top hat

cima ['tʃiː·ma] *f* **1.** (*vertice: di edificio, albero, gru*) top; (*di montagna*) peak; **-e di rapa** turnip tops; **da** ~ **a fondo** from top to bottom; **essere in** ~ **a qc** (*montagna*) to be on the top of sth; *fig* (*classifica, lista*) to be at the top of sth **2.** *iron, inf* (*campione*) genius

cimelio [tʃi·'mɛː·lio] <-i> *m* **1.** (*reliquia*) relic **2.** (*ricordo*) heirloom

cimentarsi [tʃi·men·'taː·r·si] *vr* **1.** (*impegnarsi*) ~ **in qc** to try one's hand at sth **2.** (*misurarsi*) ~ **con qu** to compete with sb

cimice ['tʃiː·mi·tʃe] *f* ZOO bug

ciminiera [tʃi·mi·'niɛː·ra] *f* smokestack

cimitero [tʃi·mi·'tɛː·ro] *m* cemetery; ~ **delle automobili** scrapyard

cimurro [tʃi·'mur·ro] *m* ZOO distemper

Cina ['tʃiː·na] *f* China; **la** ~ China; **abitare in** ~ to live in China; **andare in** ~ to go to China

cincilla [tʃin·'tʃil·la] <-> *m* chinchilla

cincin, cin cin [tʃin·'tʃin] *int inf* cheers!

cine ['tʃiː·ne] <-> *m inf* movies *pl*

cineamatore, -trice [tʃi·ne·a·ma·'toː·re] *m, f* amateur filmmaker

cineasta [tʃi·ne·'as·ta] <-i , -e> *mf* filmmaker

Cinecittà [tʃi·ne·tʃit·'ta] <-> *f* Cinecittà, *movie and TV studios in Rome*

ℹ️ **Cinecittà**, the Italian city of cinema, is a completely self-sufficient complex nine km outside Rome with streets, squares, parks, studios, and all the technical departments needed for making movies. It was built in 1937 and covers an area of 40 hectares. There are 22 studios, 280 dressing rooms and offices, 21 make-up rooms, and a 7,000 square meter swimming pool. Movies filmed wholly or partly at Cinecittà include "Quo vadis?" "Ben Hur", and "The Name of the Rose."

cineclub [tʃi·ne·'klub] *m* movie club

cineforum [tʃi·ne·'fɔː·rum] <-> *m* movie club

cinegiornale [tʃi·ne·dʒor·'naː·le] *m* newsreel

cinema ['tʃiː·ne·ma] <-> *m* **1.** (*locale*) movie theater **2.** (*arte*) movies *pl* **3.** (*produzione*) cinema

cinematica [tʃi·ne·'maː·ti·ka] *f* kinematics

cinematografia [tʃi·ne·ma·to·gra·'fiː·a] *f* **1.** (*arte*) cinematography **2.** (*produzione*) filmmaking

cinematografico, -a [tʃi·ne·ma·to·'graː·fi·ko] <-ci, -che> *agg* (*genere, produzione, sala*) movie

cinematografo [tʃi·ne·ma·'tɔː·gra·fo] *m* **1.** (*locale*) movie theater **2.** (*arte*) movies *pl*

cinepresa [tʃi·ne·'preː·sa] *f* movie camera

cinese [tʃi·'neː·ze] **I.** *agg* Chinese **II.** *mf* Chinese man *m*, Chinese woman *f* III. *m* (*lingua*) Chinese; **per me è** ~ *fig* it's all Greek to me

cinesiologia [tʃi·ne·zio·lo·'dʒi:·a] <-ie> *f* MED kinesiology

cinesiterapia [tʃi·ne·zi·te·ra·'pi:·a] *f* kinesitherapy

cineteca [tʃi·ne·'tɛ:·ka] <-che> *f* 1.(*raccolta*) movie collection 2.(*locale*) movie library

cinetica [tʃi·'nɛ:·ti·ka] <-che> *f* kinetics

cingere ['tʃin·dʒe·re] <cingo, cinsi, cinto> I. *vt* 1.(*circondare*) to surround; ~ **d'assedio** MIL to besiege 2.(*avvolgere*) to go around 3.(*con le braccia*) ~ **qc con un braccio** to put an arm around sth II. *vr:* **-rsi** *-rsi il collo con qc* to put sth around one's neck

cinghia ['tʃin·gia] <-ghie> *f* 1.(*cintura*) belt; **tirare** [*o* **stringere**] **la** ~ *fig* to tighten one's belt 2.(*di zaino*) strap; (*di sella*) girth 3. TEC belt; ~ **trapezoidale** fan belt

cinghiale [tʃin·'gia:·le] *m* 1.ZOO (wild) boar 2.(*pelle*) pigskin

cinguettare [tʃin·guet·'ta:·re] *vi* (*uccelli*) to chirp

cinguettio [tʃin·guet·'ti:·o] <-ii> *m* (*di uccelli*) chirping

cinico, -a ['tʃi:·niko] <-ci, -che> I. *agg* (*persona, osservazione*) cynical II. *m*, *f* (*persona*) cynic

cinismo [tʃi·'niz·mo] *m* cynicism

cinofilia [tʃi·no·fi·'li:·a] *f* dog lover

cinquanta [tʃin·'kuan·ta] I. *num* fifty II. <-> *m* fifty; **gli anni** ~ the Fifties; **essere sui** ~ to be about fifty (years old)

cinquantenario [tʃin·kuan·te·'na:·rio] <-i> *m* fiftieth anniversary

cinquantenne [tʃin·kuan·'tɛn·ne] I. *agg* fifty-year-old II. *mf* fifty-year-old

cinquantennio [tʃin·kuan·'tɛn·nio] <-i> *m* period of fifty years

cinquantesimo [tʃin·kuan·'tɛ:·zi·mo] *m* (*frazione*) fiftieth

cinquantesimo, -a I. *agg* fiftieth II. *m*, *f* fiftieth; *v.a.* **quinto**

cinquantina [tʃin·kuan·'ti:·na] *f* **una** ~ (**di ...**) about fifty ...; **essere sulla** ~ to be about fifty (years old)

cinque ['tʃin·kue] I. *num* five; **capitolo/pagina** ~ chapter/page five; **tre più due fa** ~ three plus two makes five; **siamo in** ~ there are five of us; **a** ~ **a** ~ in fives; **ho** ~ **anni** I'm five (years old); **di** ~ **anni** five-year-old; **ogni** ~ **anni** every five years; ~ **volte** five times II. <-> *m* 1.(*numero*) five; **abita al** (**numero**) ~ he lives at number five; **il** (**tram numero**) ~ the number five streetcar 2.(*nelle date*) fifth; **oggi è il** ~ **agosto** today is August fifth; **arriverò il** ~ I'm arriving on the fifth; **arriverò il** ~ **maggio** I'm arriving on May fifth; **Roma,** (**il**) ~ **dicembre 2000** Rome, December fifth, 2000 3.(*voto scolastico*) =D; **prendere un** ~ =to get a D 4.(*nei giochi a carte*) **il** ~ **di cuori** the five of hearts III.*fpl* five (o'clock); **alle** ~ at five (o'clock); **sono le** ~ (**del mat-**

tino/pomeriggio) it's five (in the morning/evening); **sono le** ~ **in punto** it's five (o'clock) exactly; **sono le quattro meno** ~ it's five to four; **sono le** ~ **e mezzo** it's half past five

cinquecentesco, -a [tʃin·kue·tʃen·'tes·ko] <-schi, -sche> *agg* 1.(*castello, mura*) sixteenth-century 2.(*nell'arte italiana*) of the Cinquecento

cinquecento [tʃin·kue·'tʃɛn·to] I. *num* five hundred II.<-> *m* il **Cinquecento** (*secolo*) the sixteenth century; (*nell'arte italiana*) the Cinquecento

cinquemila [tʃin·kue·'mi:·la] I. *num* five thousand II.<-> *m* five thousand

cinquina [tʃin·'kui:·na] *f* (*al lotto, alla tombola*) set of five winning numbers

cinsi ['tʃin·si] *1. pers sing pass rem di* cingere

cinta ['tʃin·ta] *f* 1.(*cerchia*) ~ **muraria** city walls *pl* 2.(*recinzione*) wall; **muro di** ~ boundary wall

cinto ['tʃin·to] *pp di* cingere

cintola ['tʃin·to·la] *f* 1. ANAT waist; **dalla** ~ **in su** from the waist up 2. *inf* (*cintura*) belt

cintura [tʃin·'tu:·ra] *f* belt; **allacciare le -e di sicurezza** to fasten seatbelts; ~ **verde** (*di una città*) green belt

cinturino [tʃin·tu·'ri:·no] *m* (*dell'orologio*) strap

ciò [tʃɔ] <solo sing> *pron dem* that, this; ~ **che ...** what ...; ~ **non di meno** nonetheless; **con tutto** ~ for all that

ciocca ['tʃɔk·ka] <-cche> *f* (*ciuffo*) lock

ciocco ['tʃɔk·ko] <-cchi> *m* (*pezzo di legno*) log

cioccolata [tʃok·ko·'la:·ta] *f* 1.(*liquida*) hot chocolate 2.(*solida*) chocolate; **una tavoletta di** ~ a bar of chocolate

cioccolatino [tʃok·ko·la·'ti:·no] *m* chocolate

cioccolato [tʃok·ko·'la:·to] *m* chocolate

cioè [tʃo·'ɛ] *avv* 1.(*vale a dire*) that is 2.(*o meglio*) or rather

ciondolare [tʃon·do·'la:·re] *vi* 1.(*dondolare*) to sway 2.(*pendere*) to dangle 3. *fig* (*aggirarsi oziosamente*) to loaf around

ciondolo ['tʃon·do·lo] *m* pendant

ciondoloni [tʃon·do·'lo:·ni] *avv* dangling; **con le gambe** ~ with one's legs dangling

ciononostante, ciò nonostante [tʃo·no·nos·'tan·te, tʃɔ no·nos·'tan·te] *avv* nevertheless

ciotola ['tʃɔ:·to·la] *f* 1.(*recipiente*) bowl 2.(*contenuto*) bowl(ful)

ciottolo ['tʃɔt·to·lo] *m* pebble

cip [tʃip] <-> *m* (*nel poker*) chip

cipolla [tʃi·'pol·la] *f* onion

cipollina [tʃi·pol·'li:·na] *f* 1.(*piccola cipolla*) small onion 2.(*erba cipollina*) (**erba**) ~ chives *pl*

cippo ['tʃip·po] *m* 1.(*funerario*) gravestone 2.(*di confine*) boundary stone

cipresso [tʃi·'prɛs·so] *m* (*albero, legno*) cypress

cipria ['tʃi:·pri·a] <-ie> *f* (face) powder

cipriota [tʃi·pri·'ɔ:·ta] <-i, -e> I. *agg* Cypriot

II. *mf* Cypriot

Cipro ['tʃi:·pro] *f* Cyprus

circa ['tʃir·ka] **I.** *avv* about **II.** *prep* (*a proposito*) about

circense [tʃir·'tʃen·se] *agg* (*arte, spettacolo, vita*) circus

circo ['tʃir·ko] <-chi> *m* circus

circolante [tʃir·ko·'lan·te] *agg* circulating

circolare¹ [tʃir·ko·'la:·re] *vi* essere o avere **1.** (*veicoli, traffico*) to be on the roads; ~! move along! **2.** (*sangue*) to circulate **3.** FIN (*capitale*) to be in circulation **4.** (*idee, notizie, voce, virus*) to go around

circolare² **I.** *agg* **1.** (*figura, stadio, tracciato*) circular **2.** FIN **assegno** ~ bank draft **II.** *f* **1.** ADM (*lettera*) circular **2.** (*linea di autobus*) circle line

circolatorio, -a [tʃir·ko·la·'tɔ:·rio] <-i, -ie> *agg* circulatory

circolazione [tʃir·ko·lat·'tsio:·ne] *f* **1.** BIOL circulation; **disturbi di** ~ circulation problems **2.** MOT traffic; **carta di** ~ registration **3.** (*di moneta, libro*) circulation; **mettere in** ~ (*moneta*) to put into circulation; *fig* (*notizie, voce*) to spread; **togliere dalla** ~ (*moneta*) to withdraw from circulation; (*libri, video*) to withdraw; (*persona*) to take off the streets

circolo ['tʃir·ko·lo] *m* **1.** MATH, GEOG circle **2.** (*associazione*) club **3.** ADM district **4.** (*loc*) ~ **vizioso** *fig* vicious circle

circoncidere [tʃir·kon·'tʃi:·de·re] <circoncido, circoncisi, circonciso> *vt* to circumcise

circoncisione [tʃir·kon·tʃi·'zio:·ne] *f* circumcision

circondare [tʃir·kon·'da:·re] **I.** *vt* **1.** (*accerchiare, contornare*) to surround **2.** *fig* (*colmare*) ~ **qu di qc** (*attenzioni, affetto*) to lavish sth on sb **II.** *vr:* **-rsi** **-rsi di qu/qc** to surround oneself with sb/sth

circondario [tʃir·kon·'da:·rio] <-i> *m* **1.** JUR, ADM district **2.** (*dintorni*) surrounding area

circonferenza [tʃir·kon·fe·'rɛn·tsa] *f* **1.** MATH circumference **2.** (*di tronco, torace*) measurement; ~ (**della**) **vita** waist measurement

circonflesso, -a [tʃir·kon·'flɛs·so] *agg* **accento** ~ circumflex accent

circonvallazione [tʃir·kon·val·la·'tsio:·ne] *f* beltway

circoscritto, -a [tʃir·kos·'krit·to] **I.** *pp di* **circoscrivere** **II.** *agg* **1.** MATH (*figura geometrica*) circumscribed **2.** (*delimitato: ambiente, luogo*) limited

circoscrivere [tʃir·kos·'kri:·ve·re] <irr> *vt* **1.** MATH to circumscribe **2.** *fig* (*delimitare*) to limit

circoscrizione [tʃir·kos·kri·'tsio:·ne] *f* ADM district; ~ **elettorale** constituency

circospetto, -a [tʃir·kos·'pɛt·to] *agg* circumspect

circospezione [tʃir·kos·pe·'tsio:·ne] *f* circumspection

circostante [tʃir·kos·'tan·te] *agg* (*area, territorio*) surrounding; (*persone*) nearby

circostanti [tʃir·kos·'tan·ti] *mpl* (*persone*) bystander

circostanza [tʃir·kos·'tan·tsa] *f* **1.** (*condizione*) circumstance; **-e attenuanti/aggravanti** JUR mitigating/aggravating circumstances **2.** (*occasione*) occasion; **aria di** ~ fitting air

circuire [tʃir·ku·'i:·re] <circuisco> *vt* (*ragazza, minore*) to take in

circuito [tʃir·'ku:i·to] *m* **1.** SPORT, EL circuit **2.** (~ *elettrico*) wiring; **corto** ~ short circuit

circumnavigare [tʃir·kum·na·vi·'ga:·re] *vt* to sail around

circumnavigazione [tʃir·kum·na·vi·ga·'tsio:·ne] *f* circumnavigation

cirillico, -a [tʃi·'ril·li·ko] <-ci, -che> *agg* (*carattere*) Cyrillic

cirrosi [tʃir·'rɔ:·zi] <-> *f* cirrhosis; ~ **epatica** cirrhosis of the liver

cisalpino, -a [tʃi·zal·'pi:·no] *agg* (*territorio, regione*) cisalpine

CISL [tʃizl] *f acro di* **Confederazione Italiana Sindacati Lavoratori** *center-right Italian labor union association*

CISNAL ['tʃiz·nal] *f acro di* **Confederazione Italiana Sindacati Nazionali dei Lavoratori** *right-wing Italian labor union association*

cispadano, -a [tʃis·pa·'da:·no] *agg* (*territorio, regione*) cispadane

cistercense [tʃis·ter·'tʃen·se] **I.** *agg* (*abbazia, monastero, monaco*) Cistercian **II.** *m* Cistercian

cisterna [tʃis·'tɛr·na] **I.** *f* (*serbatoio*) tank **II.** <inv> *agg* (*aereo, camion, nave*) tanker

cisti ['tʃis·ti] <-> *f* MED cyst

cistifellea [tʃis·ti·'fɛl·lea] *f* MED gall bladder

cistite [tʃis·'ti:·te] *f* MED cystitis

CIT [tʃit] *f acro di* **Compagnia Italiana Turismo** *Italian tourism company*

cit. *abbr di* **citato, -a** cited

citare [tʃi·'ta:·re] *vt* **1.** (*indicare*) to cite; ~ **ad esempio** to cite as an example **2.** (*testo, discorso*) to quote **3.** JUR ~ **qu in giudizio** to take sb to court

citazione [tʃi·ta·'tsio:·ne] *f* **1.** JUR summons **2.** LIT quotation **3.** (*menzione*) mention; **una** ~ **al merito** an honorable mention

citofonare [tʃi·to·fo·'na:·re] **I.** *vi* to call on the entrance phone **II.** *vt* to call on the entrance phone

citofono [tʃi·'tɔ:·fo·no] *m* entrance phone

citologia [tʃi·to·lo·'dʒi:·a] <-gie> *f* cytology

citologico, -a [tʃi·to·'lɔ:·dʒi·ko] <-ci, -che> *agg* (*esame, screening*) cytological

citrico, -a ['tʃi·tri·ko] <-ci, -che> *agg* citric; **acido** ~ citric acid

citrullo [tʃi·'trul·lo] *m, f* idiot

città [tʃit·'ta] <-> *f* city; ~ **nuova** new town; ~ **vecchia** old town; ~ **satellite** satellite town; ~ **degli studi** campus; ~ **dei ragazzi** boys' town; ~ **universitaria** university campus; **Città del Vaticano** Vatican City; **Città del Capo** Cape Town; **abitare in** ~ to live in town

cittadella [tʃit·ta·'dɛl·la] *f* **1.** MIL citadel **2.** *fig* (*roccaforte*) stronghold

cittadina [tʃit·ta·'di:·na] *f* small town

cittadinanza [tʃit·ta·di·'nan·tsa] *f* 1. JUR citizenship; **diritto di** ~ right of citizenship; ~ **onoraria** freedom of the city 2. (*insieme di cittadini*) town

cittadino, -a [tʃit·ta·'di:·no] I. *agg* (*infrastrutture, monumento, museo*) city II. *m*, *f* 1. JUR citizen 2. (*di città*) inhabitant; **primo** ~ mayor

citycar ['si·ti·car] *f* small car

ciucca ['tʃuk·ka] <-cche> *f inf* **s'è preso una bella** ~ he got plastered *inf*

ciucciare [tʃut·'tʃa:·re] *vt inf* to suck; ~ **il dito** to suck one's thumb

ciuccio ['tʃut·tʃo] <-cci> *m inf* (*tettarella*) pacifier

ciuco, -a ['tʃu:·ko] <-chi, -che> *m*, *f inf* 1. ZOO ass 2. *fig pej* (*stupido*) idiot 3. *fig* (*ubriaco*) drunk

ciuffo ['tʃuf·fo] *m* 1. (*di capelli*) lock 2. (*d'erba*) clump

civetta¹ [tʃi·'vet·ta] *f* 1. ZOO owl 2. *fig pej* (*donna frivola*) flirt; **fare la** ~ **con qu** to flirt with sb

civetta² <inv> *agg* **auto** ~ unmarked police car

civettare [tʃi·vet·'ta:·re] *vi* to flirt

civico, -a ['tʃi:·vi·ko] <-ci, -che> *agg* 1. (*di città: museo*) town; **numero** ~ house number 2. (*dovere, sentimento*) civic; **senso** ~ public spirit; **educazione -a** civics

civile [tʃi·'vi:·le] I. *agg* 1. (*del cittadino*) civil; **diritti -i** civil rights; **guerra** ~ civil war; **stato** ~ marital status 2. (*non militare: abiti*) civilian 3. (*non ecclesiastico*) civil; **matrimonio** ~ civil wedding 4. (*civilizzato: nazione, popolo*) civilized 5. (*educato: persona, maniere*) civil II. *m* (*non militare*) civilian; **essere vestito in** ~ to be in civilian clothes

civilizzare [tʃi·vi·lid·'dza:·re] I. *vt* (*popolo*) to civilize II. *vr:* -**rsi** (*popolo, persona*) to become civilized

civilizzazione [tʃi·vi·lid·dza·'tsio:·ne] *f* civilization

civilmente [tʃi·vil·'men·te] *avv* 1. (*educatamente*) civilly 2. ADM in a civil ceremony; **sposarsi** ~ to get married in a civil ceremony

civiltà [tʃi·vil·'ta] <-> *f* 1. (*cultura, progresso*) civilization 2. (*cortesia*) civility

civismo [tʃi·'viz·mo] *m* civic-mindedness

CL *abbr di* **Comunione e Liberazione** *lay Roman Catholic organization*

clacson ['klak·son] <-> *m* horn; **suonare il** ~ to sound one's horn

clamore [kla·'mo:·re] *m* 1. *fig* (*scalpore*) uproar; **suscitare** [*o* **destare**] ~ cause an uproar 2. (*chiasso*) din

clamoroso, -a [kla·mo·'ro:·so] *agg* (*successo, sconfitta*) resounding; (*notizia, novità*) sensational

clan [klan] <-> *m* clan

clandestinità [klan·des·ti·ni·'ta] <-> *f* (*illegalità*) secrecy

clandestino, -a [klan·des·'ti:·no] I. *agg* illegal; **passeggero** ~ stowaway II. *m*, *f* stowaway

clarinettista [kla·ri·net·'tis·ta] <-i , -e> *mf* clarinetist

clarinetto [kla·ri·'net·to] *m* clarinet

clarino [kla·'ri:·no] *m* clarinet

classe ['klas·se] *f* 1. (*servizio*) class; **viaggiare in prima** ~ to travel first class 2. (*corso scolastico*) class; (*aula*) class(room) 3. MIL ~ (**di leva**) class 4. *fig* (*ceto*) class; **lotta di** ~ class struggle; **la** ~ **dirigente** the ruling class 5. *fig* (*qualità*) class; **un uomo di** ~ a classy man; **avere** ~ to have class

classica ['klas·si·ka] <-che> *f* SPORT classic

classicismo [klas·si·'tʃiz·mo] *m* classicism

classico ['klas·si·ko] <-ci> *m* 1. (*autore*) classical author 2. (*romanzo*) classic

classico, -a <-ci, -che> *agg* classical; **danza -a** classical dance; **musica -a** classical music

classifica [klas·'si:·fi·ka] <-che> *f* 1. SPORT placings *pl;* **ultimo in** ~ in last place; **essere in testa alla** ~ to be in first place 2. (*graduatoria: di concorso*) list 3. (*di dischi*) charts *pl;* (*di libri*) list

classificare [klassifi'ka:re] I. *vt* 1. (*ordinare: materiale, libri*) to classify 2. (*valutare: scolaro, compito*) to grade 3. (*inquadrare*) to categorize II. *vr:* -**rsi** 1. (*arrivare*) to come; -**rsi bene** to be highly placed; -**rsi terzo** to come third 2. (*qualificarsi*) to qualify

classificatore [klas·si·fi·ka·'to:·re] *m* 1. (*raccoglitore*) loose-leaf file 2. (*mobile*) filing cabinet

classificazione [klas·si·fi·ka·'tsio:·ne] *f* 1. (*ordinazione per classi*) classification 2. (*valutazione*) categorization

classismo [klas·'siz·mo] *m* POL classism

classista [klas·'sis·ta] <-i , -e> I. *mf* classist II. *agg* classist; **lotta** ~ class struggle

clausola ['kla:u·zo·la] *f* (*di contratto, trattato*) clause

claustrofobia [klaus·tro·fo·'bi:·a] *f* claustrophobia

clausura [klau·'zu:·ra] *f* 1. REL enclosure; **una monaca di** ~ a nun belonging to a closed order 2. *fig* (*luogo appartato*) seclusion

clava ['kla:·va] *f* club

clavicembalo [kla·vi·'tʃem·ba·lo] *m* harpsichord

clavicola [kla·'vi:·ko·la] *f* collarbone

clear [kliə] <-> *m* COMPUT (*tasto*) clear key

clemente [kle·'mɛn·te] *agg* 1. (*clima, tempo*) mild 2. (*persona*) lenient

clemenza [kle·'mɛn·tsa] *f* 1. (*di clima*) mildness 2. (*di persona*) leniency

cleptomane [klep·'tɔ:·ma·ne] I. *agg* (*persona*) kleptomaniac II. *mf* kleptomaniac

cleptomania [klep·to·ma·'ni:·a] *f* kleptomania

clericale [kle·ri·'ka:·le] I. *agg* (*abito*) clerical; (*potere*) of the clergy II. *mf* clericalist

clericalismo [kle·ri·ka·'liz·mo] *m* clericalism

clero ['klɛ:·ro] *m* clergy; ~ **regolare/secolare** regular/secular clergy

clessidra [kles·'si:·dra] *f* (*a sabbia*) hourglass; (*ad acqua*) water clock

clic [klik] <-> *m* COMPUT click; ~ **del mouse** mouse click; **fare** (**doppio**) ~ **su qc** to (double-)click on sth

cliccare [klik·'ka:·re] I. *vt* (*icona, punto*) to click on II. *vi* ~ **su qc** to click on sth

cliché [kli·'ʃe] <-> *m fig* (*modello*) cliché

cliente [kli·'ɛn·te] *mf* (*di negozio, ristorante, bar*) customer; (*di albergo*) guest; (*di avvocato*) client; ~ **fisso** [*o* **abituale**] regular

clientela [klien·'tɛ:·la] *f* (*di negozio, ristorante, bar*) clientele; (*di albergo*) guests *pl;* (*di avvocato*) clients *pl*

clima ['kli:·ma] <-i> *m a. fig* climate

climatico, -a [kli·'ma:·ti·ko] <-ci, -che> *agg* (*cambiamento, zona*) climate; **stazione -a** health resort

climatizzare [kli·ma·tid·'dza:·re] *vt* (*ambiente, abitazione*) to air-condition

climatizzatore [kli·ma·tid·dza·'to:·re] *m* air conditioner

climatizzazione [kli·ma·tid·dza·'tsio:·ne] *f* air conditioning; **impianto di** ~ air conditioning system

climatologo, -a [kli·ma·'tɔ:·lo·go] <-gi, -ghe> *m, f* climatologist

clinica ['kli:·ni·ka] <-che> *f* clinic

clinico ['kli:·ni·ko] <-ci> *m* **1.** (*medico*) clinician **2.** (*docente*) professor of clinical medicine

clinico, -a <-ci, -che> *agg* clinical; **cartella -a** medical records *pl;* **avere l'occhio** ~ *fig* to have an expert eye

clip [klip] <-> *f* (*orecchino*) clip

CLIP [klɪp] *m* TEL caller ID

clipboard <-> *m* COMPUT clipboard

CLIR [klɪr] *m* TEL withhold number

clistere [klis·'tɛ:·re] *m* enema

clitoride [kli·'tɔ:·ri·de] *m o f* clitoris

cloaca [klo·'a:·ka] <-che> *f* **1.** (*canale, fogna*) sewer **2.** *fig* (*luogo corrotto*) cesspool **3.** *fig* (*persona*) pig

clonare [klo·na:·re] *vt* BIO, COMPUT to clone

clonazione [klo·na·'tsio:·ne] *f* BIO, COMPUT cloning

clone ['klɔ·ne] *m* BIO, COMPUT clone

cloridrico, -a [klo·'ri:d·ri·ko] <-ci, -che> *agg* hydrochloric; **acido** ~ hydrochloric acid

cloro ['klɔ:·ro] *m* chlorine

clorofilla [klo·ro·'fil·la] *f* chlorophyll

clorofilliano, -a [klo·ro·fil·'lia:·no] *agg* **sintesi -a** photosynthesis

cloroformio [klo·ro·'fɔr·mio] <-i> *m* chloroform

cloruro [klo·'ru:·ro] *m* chloride

clown [klaun] <-> *m* clown

club [klub] <-> *m* (*circolo*) club

cm *abbr di* **centimetro** cm.

c.m. *abbr di* **corrente mese** inst.

CNR *m abbr di* **Consiglio Nazionale delle Ricerche** *national research council*

c/o *abbr di* **care of** (*presso*) c/o

coabitare [ko·a·bi·'ta:·re] *vi* to live together

coabitazione [ko·a·bi·ta·'tsio:·ne] *f* cohabitation

coacervo [ko·a·'tʃɛr·vo] *m* (*di stili*) hodgepodge

coadiuvante [ko·ad·iu·'van·te] I. *agg* adjuvant II. *m* adjuvant

coagulante [ko·a·gu·'lan·te] I. *agg* (*fattore, prodotto, sostanza*) clotting II. *m* clotting agent

coagulare [ko·a·gu·'la:·re] I. *vt* **1.** MED (*sangue*) to clot **2.** (*latte*) to curdle II. *vi* **1.** MED (*sangue*) to clot **2.** (*latte*) to curdle III. *vr:* **-rsi** **1.** MED (*sangue*) to clot **2.** (*latte*) to curdle

coagulazione [ko·a·gu·la·'tsio:·ne] *f* **1.** MED (*di sangue*) clotting; **la** ~ **del sangue** blood clotting **2.** (*di latte*) curdling

coagulo [ko·'a:·gu·lo] *m* **1.** MED clot **2.** (*caglio*) curd

coalizione [koa·li·'tsio:·ne] *f* (*di partiti*) coalition

coalizzare [koa·lid·'dza:·re] I. *vt* (*unire: forze, sforzi*) to unite II. *vr:* **-rsi** (*unirsi: persone, partiti, Stati*) to form a coalition

coatto, -a [ko·'at·to] *agg* (*imposto*) compulsory

coautore, -trice [ko·au·'to:·re] *m, f* (*di libro, film, progetto*) coauthor

cobalto [ko·'bal·to] *m* **1.** CHEM cobalt **2.** (*colore*) cobalt blue

cobaltoterapia [ko·bal·to·te·ra·'pi:·a] *f* cobalt radiotherapy

cobas *m acro di* **Comitato di Base** *labor union organization functioning as an alternative to the main unions*

Coblenza [ko·'blɛn·tsa] *f* Koblenz

cobra ['kɔ:·bra] <-> *m* cobra

coca ['kɔ:·ka] <-che> *f* **1.** BOT coca **2.** *sl* (*cocaina*) coke **3.** *inf* (*bevanda*) Coke®

cocaina [ko·ka·'i:·na] *f* cocaine

cocainomane [ko·kai·'nɔ:·ma·ne] *mf* cocaine addict

coccarda [kok·'kar·da] *f* cockade

cocchiere, -a [kok·'kiɛ:·re] *m, f* coachman

cocchio ['kɔk·kio] <-cchi> *m* carriage

coccige [kot·'tʃi:·ge] *m* coccyx

coccinella [kot·tʃi·'nɛl·la] *f* ladybug

coccio ['kɔt·tʃo] <-cci> *m* **1.** (*terracotta*) earthenware **2.** (*frammento*) shard

cocciutaggine [kot·tʃu·'tad·dʒi·ne] *f* (*di persona*) pigheadedness

cocciuto, -a [kot·'tʃu:·to] I. *agg* (*persona*) pigheaded; (*speranza, pretesa*) stubborn II. *m, f* pigheaded person

cocco ['kɔk·ko] <-cchi> *m* **1.** BOT (*albero*) coconut palm; **noce di** ~ coconut **2.** BIOL coccus

cocco, -a <-cchi, -cche> *m, f scherz, inf* darling; **essere il** ~ **di mamma** to be mom's little darling; **povero** ~! *iron* poor dear!

coccodè [kok·ko·'dɛ] *int* (*di gallina*) cluck; **fare** ~ to cluck

coccodrillo [kok·ko·'dril·lo] *m* **1.** ZOO crocodile; **lacrime di** ~ *fig* crocodile tears *pl*

2. (*pelle*) crocodile skin

coccola [kok·'ko·la] *f* cuddle; **fare le -e a qu** to cuddle sb

coccolare [kok·ko·'la:·re] *vt inf* (*bambino, animale*) to cuddle

coccolone, -a [kok·ko·'lo:·ne] *m, f inf* liking being cuddled

coccoloni [kok·ko·'lo:·ni] *avv* squatting; **stare ~** to be squatting

cocente [ko·'tʃɛn·te] *agg* **1.** (*ardente: sole*) scorching **2.** *fig* (*delusione, sconfitta*) bitter

cocker ['kɔ·ka/'kɔ·ker] <-> *m* cocker spaniel

cocktail ['kɔk·teil/'kɔk·tel] <-> *m* **1.** CULIN cocktail; **~ di scampi** shrimp cocktail **2.** (*trattenimento*) cocktail party; **abito da ~** cocktail dress

cocomero [ko·'ko:·me·ro] *m* (*anguria*) watermelon

cocooning [kə·'ku:·niŋ] *sing* cocooning

cocuzzolo [ko·'kut·tso·lo] *m* (*di montagna*) summit

cod. *abbr di* **codice** code

coda ['ko:·da] *f* **1.** (*di animale*) tail; **~ di cavallo** (*acconciatura*) ponytail **2.** CULIN oxtail; **~ in umido** stewed oxtail; **~ di rospo** (*pesce*) angler fish **3.** ASTR (*di cometa*) tail **4.** (*di abito femminile*) train; (*di abito maschile*) tail **5.** (*di aereo*) tail; (*di treno*) rear; **vettura di ~** FERR rear car **6.** (*fila: di auto*) backup; (*di persone*) line; **fare la ~** to stand in line; **mettersi in ~** to get in line **7.** (*appendice*) **titoli di ~** FILM, TV credits **8.** (*loc*) **con la ~ dell'occhio** out of the corner of one's eye

codardo, -a [ko·'dar·do] **I.** *agg* (*persona, gesto*) cowardly **II.** *m, f* coward

codazzo [ko·'dat·tso] *m pej* pack *pej*

code [koud] <- *o* codes> *m* TEL, COMPUT password

codesto, -a [ko·'des·to] *pron dem, tosc, poet* this, that

codice ['kɔ:·di·tʃe] *m* **1.** (*gener*) code; **~ civile** civil code; **~ penale** penal code; **~ di procedura civile** code of civil procedure; **~ di procedura penale** code of criminal procedure; **~ della strada** ≈ rules of the road *pl*; **~ a barre** bar code; **~ ASCII** ASCII code; **~ di avviamento postale** zip code; **~ fiscale** tax code; **~ genetico** genetic code **2.** LIT (*manoscritto*) codex

codificare [ko·di·fi·'ka:·re] *vt* **1.** (*dati, messaggio segreto*) to encode **2.** JUR to codify

codificatore [ko·di·fi·ka·'to:·re] *m* COMPUT encoder

coeditore, -trice [ko·e·di·'to:·re] *m, f* copublisher

coedizione [ko·e·di·'tsio:·ne] *f* coedition

coefficiente [ko·ef·fi·'tʃɛn·te] *m* coefficient

coerente [ko·e·'rɛn·te] *agg fig* (*persona*) consistent; (*argomento, discorso, ragionamento*) coherent

coerenza [ko·e·'rɛn·tsa] *f* (*di persona*) consistency; (*di argomento, discorso, ragionamento*) coherence

coesione [ko·e·'zio:·ne] *f fig* (*di opera*) cohesion; (*di gruppo*) cohesiveness

coesistente [ko·e·zis·'tɛn·te] *agg* (*condizione, fenomeno*) coexistent

coesistere [ko·e·'zis·te·re] <irr> *vi essere* to coexist

coetaneo, -a [ko·e·'ta:·neo] **I.** *agg* (*della stessa età*) of the same age; **essere ~** (**di qu**) to be the same age (as sb) **II.** *m, f* (*della stessa età*) person of the same age

cofanetto [ko·fa·'net·to] *m* **1.** (*cassetta*) box; (*per gioielli*) jewel box **2.** (*per libri, CD, DVD*) boxed set

cofano ['kɔ:·fa·no] *m* MOT hood

cofirmatario, -a [ko·fir·ma·'ta:·rio] <-i, -ie> **I.** *agg* cosignatory **II.** *m, f* cosignatory

cofondatore, -trice [ko·fon·da·'to:·re] *m, f* cofounder

cogestione [ko·dʒes·'tio:·ne] *f* joint management

cogli ['koʎ·ʎi] *prep* = **con + gli** *v.* **con**

cogliere ['kɔʎ·ʎere] <colgo, colsi, colto> *vt* **1.** (*fiore, frutto*) to pick **2.** *fig* (*occasione*) to take; (*offerta*) to accept; **~ qc al volo** (*occasione, offerta*) to jump at sth **3.** (*sorprendere*) to catch; **~ qu in fallo** to catch sb out; **~ qu in flagrante** to catch sb redhanded **4.** *fig* (*significato, problema*) to understand **5.** (*colpire*) to strike; **~ nel segno** to hit the nail on the head

coglionata [koʎ·ʎo·'na:·ta] *f vulg* (*cosa fatta*) screw-up *vulg*; (*cosa detta*) bullshit *vulg*

coglione, -a [koʎ·ʎo:·ne] *m, f vulg* (*idiota*) dickhead *vulg*

coglioni [koʎ·ʎo:·ni] *mpl vulg* balls *vulg;* **rompere** [*o* **far girare**] **i ~ a qu** *vulg* to get on sb's nerves

cognac [kɔ·'ɲak/koɲ·'ɲak] <- *o* cognacs> *m* cognac

cognato, -a [koɲ·'ɲa:·to] *m, f* brother-in-law *m*, sister-in-law *f*

cognizione [koɲ·ɲi·'tsio:·ne] *f* **1.** (*nozione*) knowledge; **con ~ di causa** with full knowledge of the facts **2.** (*competenza*) cognizance

cognome [koɲ·'ɲo:·me] *m* surname; **nome e ~** first and last name; **~ da nubile** maiden name

coi ['ko:·i] *prep* = **con + i** *v.* **con**

coiffeur, coiffeuse [kwa·'fœr] <- *o* coiffeurs, coiffeuses> *m, f* hairdresser

coincidenza [ko·in·tʃi·'dɛn·tsa] *f* **1.** (*avvenimento*) coincidence **2.** (*di mezzi di trasporto*) connection **3.** (*corrispondenza*) correspondence

coincidere [ko·in·tʃi:·de·re] <irr> *vi* **1.** (*accadere insieme*) to coincide; **~ con qc** to coincide with sth **2.** (*corrispondere*) to concur; **~ con qc** to concur with sth **3.** MATH (*essere la stessa cosa*) to coincide

coinquilino, -a [ko·iɲ·kui·'li:·no] *m, f* (*di palazzo*) fellow tenant

cointestatario, -a [ko·in·tes·ta·'ta:·rio] <-i, -ie> **I.** *agg* JUR having a joint account **II.** *m, f* JUR joint account holder

coinvolgente [ko·in·vol·'dʒɛn·te] *agg* (*legame*) serious; (*libro, spettacolo*) engrossing

coinvolgere [ko·in·'vɔl·dʒe·re] <irr> *vt* ~ **qu in qc** to involve sb in sth

coinvolgimento [ko·in·'vɔl·dʒi·men·to] *m* involvement

coinvolto, -a [ko·in·'vɔl·to] I. *pp di* **coinvolgere** II. *agg* involved; **essere** ~ **in qc** to be involved in sth

coiote [ko·'iɔ:·te] <-> *m* coyote

coito ['kɔ:·i·to] *m* coitus

coke [kouk] <-> *m* coke

col [kol] *prep =* **con + il** *v.* **con**

colabrodo [ko·la·'brɔ:·do] <-> *m* colander; **essere un** ~ *fig* (*sistema, difesa*) to leak like a sieve

colapasta [ko·la·'pas·ta] <-> *m* colander

colare [ko·'la:·re] I. *vt avere* 1. (*liquido, brodo*) to strain; ~ **la pasta** to drain the pasta 2. (*metallo*) to cast II. *vi* 1. *essere o avere* (*gocciolare: liquido*) to run; (*cera*) to drip; **mi cola il naso** my nose is running 2. (*recipiente*) to leak 3. *essere* (*nave*) ~ **a picco** to sink to the bottom; *fig* to be in free fall

colata [ko·'la:·ta] *f* 1. GEOL flow; ~ **lavica** lava flow 2. (*di metallo, cemento*) casting

colazione [ko·la·'tsio:·ne] *f* 1. (*prima* ~) breakfast; **fare** ~ to have breakfast 2. (*seconda* ~) lunch; ~ **di lavoro** working lunch

cold boot [kold 'but] <-> *m* COMPUT cold boot

COLDIRETTI [kol·di·'rɛt·ti] *f abbr di* **Confederazione Nazionale Coltivatori Diretti** *Italian farmers' federation*

colei *f v.* **colui**

coleottero [ko·le·'ɔt·te·ro] *m* beetle

colera [ko·'lɛ:·ra] <-> *m* cholera

colerico, -a [ko·'lɛ:·ri·ko] <-ci, -che> *agg* (*epidemia, disturbo*) cholera

colesterina [ko·les·te·'ri:·na] *f* cholesterol

colesterolo [ko·les·te·'rɔ:·lo] *m* cholesterol

colf [kɔlf] <-> *f* home help

colgo ['kɔl·go] *1. pers sing pr di* **cogliere**

colibrì [ko·li·'bri] <-> *m* hummingbird

colica ['kɔ:·li·ka] <-che> *f* (*renale, intestinale, di fegato*) colic

colino [ko·'li:·no] *m* strainer

colite [ko·'li:·te] *f* MED colitis

colla¹ ['kɔl·la] *f* glue

colla² ['kɔl·la] *prep =* **con + la** *v.* **con**

collaborare [kol·la·bo·'ra:·re] *vi* 1. (*cooperare*) to work together; ~ **a un progetto** to be part of a project; ~ **con qu** to work together with sb 2. (*dare il proprio contributo a*) to contribute 3. (*confessare*) to cooperate 4. POL to collaborate

collaboratore, -trice [kol·la·bo·ra·'to:·re] *m, f* 1. (*aiutante*) coworker; **-trice domestica** home help 2. (*a giornale*) contributor; ~ **esterno** freelancer 3. (*pentito*) ~ **della giustizia** informer

collaborazione [kol·la·bo·ra·ra·'tsio:·ne] *f* 1. (*partecipazione*) collaboration; ~ **ad un**

progetto collaboration on a project 2. (*a giornale*) contribution

collage [ko·'la:ʒ] <-> *m* collage

collana [kol·'la:·na] *f* 1. (*di perle, oro, coralli*) necklace 2. (*di libri*) series

collant [kɔl·'lã] <-> *m* pantyhose

collare [kol·'la:re] *m* 1. (*per cani*) collar 2. REL (*di prete*) dog collar

collasso [kol·'las·so] *m* collapse; ~ **cardiaco** heart failure

collaterale [kol·la·te·'ra:·le] *agg* collateral; **effetti -i** side effects

collaudare [kol·lau·'da:·re] *vt* (*auto, motore, sistema*) to test

collaudatore, -trice [kol·lau·da·'to:·re] *m, f* (*di auto*) test driver; (*di aereo*) test pilot

collaudo [kol·'la:u·do] *m* (*di aereo, auto, impianto, edificio*) test; **volo di** ~ test flight

colle¹ ['kɔl·le] *m* 1. (*rilievo*) hill 2. (*passo*) pass

colle² ['kɔl·le] *prep =* **con + le** *v.* **con**

collega [kol·'lɛ:·ga] <-ghi , -ghe> *mf* colleague

collegamento [kol·le·ga·'men·to] *m* 1. (*connessione*) connection; ~ **ferroviario** rail link 2. COMPUT, TEL, RADIO, TV (*connessione*) link; ~ **Internet** Internet connection; ~ **radiofonico** radio link; ~ **telefonico** telephone link; **in** ~ **con Madrid, vi trasmettiamo** ... TV, RADIO live from Madrid we bring you ...; **icona di** ~ link 3. EL connection; ~ **in serie/parallelo** series/parallel connection 4. MIL liaison; **ufficiale di** ~ liaison officer

collegare [kol·le·'ga:·re] I. *vt* (*fili, cavi, computer*) to connect II. *vr:* **-rsi** to connect; **-rsi a qc** to connect to sth; **-rsi con qu/qc** to get a connection to sb/sth

collegato, -a [kol·le·'ga:·to] *agg* (*persona, telefono, computer*) connected; **essere** ~ **a qc** to be connected to sth; **questo computer è** ~ **a Internet** this computer has an Internet connection

collegiale [kol·le·'dʒa:·le] I. *agg* (*collettivo: organo, seduta*) collegiate; (*seduta*) joint II. *mf* 1. (*allievo*) boarder 2. *fig* (*giovane inesperto*) schoolboy *m*, schoolgirl *f*

collegio [kol·'lɛ:·dʒo] <-gi> *m* 1. (*istituto*) boarding school 2. (*professionale*) college 3. (*circoscrizione*) ~ **elettorale** constituency

collera ['kɔl·le·ra] *f* (*rabbia*) anger; **andare/ essere in** ~ to get/be angry; **essere in** ~ **con qu** to be angry with sb

collerico, -a [kol·'lɛ:·ri·ko] <-ci, -che> I. *agg* (*persona, carattere*) quick-tempered II. *m, f* quick-tempered person

colletta [kol·'lɛt·ta] *f* (*raccolta*) collection

collettività [kol·let·ti·vi·'ta] <-> *f* community

collettivo [kol·let·'ti:·vo] *m* collective

collettivo, -a [kol·let·'ti:·vo] *agg* collective

colletto [kol·'let·to] *m* 1. (*di camicia, abito*) collar; ~ **bianco** *fig* white-collar worker 2. ANAT (*di dente*) neck 3. BOT collar

collettore [kol·let·'to:·re] *m* 1. TEC manifold 2. EL collector

collezionare [kol·le·tsio·'na:·re] *vt* 1. (*franco-*

bolli, monete, oggetti) to collect **2.** (*delusioni, successi*) to notch up

collezione [kol·le·'tsio:·ne] *f* collection; **fare ~ di qc** to collect sth

collezionista [kol·le·tsio·'nis·ta] <-i , -e> *mf* collector

collier [kɔ·'lje] <-> *m* necklace

collimare [kol·li·'ma:·re] *vi* to agree

collina [kol·'li:·na] *f* hill

collirio [kol·'li:·rio] <-i> *m* eyedrops *pl*

collisione [kol·li·'zio:·ne] *f* collision; **entrare in ~** to collide

collo[1] ['kɔl·lo] *m* **1.** (*anat*) neck; **~ del piede** instep; **~ dell'utero** neck of the womb; **avere/portare al ~** to have/wear around one's neck; **allungare il ~** to crane one's neck; **con la testa sul ~** with a good head on one's shoulders; **tirare il ~ ad un pollo** to wring a chicken's neck; **essere nei debiti fino al ~** *fig* to be up to one's ears in debt; **prendere qu per il ~** *fig* to put the squeeze on sb *inf;* **rompersi l'osso del ~** to break one's neck; **rimetterci l'osso del ~** *fig* to lose everything **2.** (*di bottiglia, fiasco*) neck **3.** (*di abito*) neck; **a ~ alto** (*maglione*) high-necked **4.** TEC **albero a ~ d'oca** crankshaft **5.** COM (*pacco*) package

collo[2] ['kol·lo] = **con + lo**

collocamento [kol·lo·ka·'men·to] *m* **1.** (*in lavoro*) employment; **agenzia** [*o* **ufficio**] **di ~** employment agency **2.** (*disposizione*) placing

collocare [kol·lo·'ka:·re] I. *vt* to place II. *vr:* **-rsi** (*posizionarsi*) to be placed

collocazione [kol·lo·ka·'tsio:·ne] *f* **1.** (*sistemazione, lavoro, posizione politica*) position **2.** (*di libro*) classification **3.** LING collocation

colloquiale [kol·lo·'kui·a:·le] *agg* colloquial; **linguaggio ~** informal language; **tono ~** informal tone

colloquio [kol·'lɔ:·kui·o] <-qui> *m* **1.** (*conversazione*) talk **2.** (*incontro*) interview; **~ di lavoro** job interview **3.** (*esame*) oral exam

colloso, -a [kol·'lo:·so] *agg* (*particelle, liquidi*) sticky

collusione [kol·lu·'zio:·ne] *f* collusion

collut(t)orio [kol·lu·'tɔ:·rio (kol·lut·'tɔ:·rio)] <-i> *m* mouthwash

colmare [kol·'ma:·re] *vt* **1.** (*recipiente, lacuna*) to fill; **~ di qc** to fill with sth **2.** *fig* (*dare in abbondanza*) **~ qu di qc** to shower sb with sth

colmo ['kol·mo] *m* **1.** (*di cima, colle*) top **2.** *fig* (*apice*) height; **ma è il ~!** *inf* that beats everything! *inf*

colmo, -a *agg a. fig* full; **~ fino all'orlo** filled to the brim; **essere ~ di qc** (*dolore, bile, amarezze*) to be full of sth

colomba [ko·'lom·ba] *f* dove; **la ~ pasquale** (*dolce*) *caked shaped like a dove, eaten at Easter*

i A typical symbol of Easter in Italy is a cake in the shape of a dove – **colomba**. The Easter dove – **colomba pasquale** – has its roots in the distant past. Around the middle of the sixth century a raised ring-shaped loaf was offered to Alboin, the king of the Lombards, who was besieging the city of Pavia. The ingredients (eggs, flour, and yeast) were simple compared to those of today, which include butter, sugar, and candied fruit.

colombo [ko·'lom·bo] *m* pigeon; **tubano come due -i** *inf* (*innamorati*) they're like a pair of lovebirds

colon ['kɔ:·lon] <-> *m* ANAT colon

colonia [ko·'lɔ:·nia] <-ie> *f* **1.** POL, BIOL colony **2.** (*per le vacanze*) summer camp **3.** (*profumo*) cologne

Colonia [ko·'lɔ:·nia] *f* Cologne; **acqua di ~** cologne

coloniale [ko·lo·'nia:·le] I. *agg* colonial II. *mf* colonist

colonialismo [ko·lo·nia·'liz·mo] *m* colonialism

colonialista [ko·lo·nia·'lis·ta] <-i , -e> I. *mf* colonialist II. *agg* (*politica, teorie*) colonialist

colonico, -a [ko·'lɔ:·ni·ko] <-ci, -che> *agg* (*rurale*) farm; **casa -a** farmhouse

colonizzare [ko·lo·nid·'dza:·re] *vt* HIST, POL (*Paese, Stato*) to colonize

colonna [ko·'lon·na] *f* **1.** (*gener*) column **2.** (*di automobili: nel traffico*) backup; (*di veicoli militari*) convoy **3.** ANAT **~ vertebrale** spinal column **4.** *fig* (*sostegno*) mainstay **5.** CINE **~ sonora** soundtrack

colonnato [ko·lon·'na:·to] *m* (*portico*) colonnade

colonnello [ko·lon·'nɛl·lo] *m* colonel

colonnina [ko·lon·'ni:·na] *f* (*piccola colonna*) small column; **~ di mercurio** thermometer; **~ della benzina** gas pump; **~ di soccorso** emergency telephone

colonnista [ko·lon·'nis·ta] <-i , -e> *mf* (*columnist*) columnist

colono [ko·'lɔ:·no] *m* **1.** AGR farmer **2.** HIST colonist

colorante [ko·lo·'ran·te] I. *agg* (*sostanza, shampoo*) coloring II. *m* coloring; **-i alimentari** food coloring

colorare [ko·lo·'ra:·re] I. *vt* (*capelli, tessuti*) to color; (*disegno*) to color in II. *vr:* **-rsi di verde/rosso** to turn green/red

colorazione [ko·lo·ra·'tsio:·ne] *f* color

colore [ko·'lo:·re] *m* **1.** (*tinta*) color; **scatola di -i** paintbox; **uomo di ~** man of color; **-i a olio/tempera/dita** oil/tempera/finger paints *pl;* **dare una mano di ~ a qc** to give sth a coat of paint; **a -i** (*illustrazione, rivista*) color; **senza ~** colorless; **dirne di tutti i -i a qu** *fig* to lay into sb; **farne di tutti i -i** *fig* to get up to all sorts; **diventare di mille** [*o* **di tutti i**] **-i** *fig* (*vergognarsi*) to turn bright red **2.** (*folclore*) color; **il ~ locale** local color

colorificio [ko·lo·ri·'fi:·tʃo] <-ci> *m* paint fac-

tory
colorire [ko·lo·'ri:·re] <colorisco> *vt* **1.** (*colorare: disegno*) to color in **2.** *fig* (*racconto*) to embellish
colorito [ko·lo·'ri:·to] *m* (*della pelle*) complexion
colorito, -a *agg* **1.** (*viso, guance*) rosy **2.** *fig* (*linguaggio, parole, racconto*) colorful
coloro [ko·'lo:·ro] *pron dem pl di* **colui**
colossale [ko·los·'sa:·le] *agg a. fig* huge
colosso [ko·'lɔs·so] *m* **1.** (*statua*) colossus **2.** *fig* (*personalità*) giant; **un ~ dello schermo** a screen giant
colpa ['kol·pa] *f* fault; **dare la ~ a qu** to blame sb; **sentirsi in ~** to feel guilty; **per ~ di qu/qc** because of sb/sth; **non è ~ mia** it's not my fault
colpevole [kol·'pe:·vo·le] **I.** *agg* guilty; **~ di furto** guilty of theft **II.** *mf* culprit
colpevolizzare [kol·pe·vo·lid·'dza:·re] *vt ~ qu* (*far sentire colpevole*) to make sb feel guilty
colpire [kol·'pi:·re] <colpisco> *vt* **1.** (*avversario, bersaglio*) to hit; **~ qu con un pugno** to punch sb; **~ nel segno** *fig* to hit the nail on the head **2.** (*danneggiare: città, zona*) to strike **3.** *fig* (*impressionare*) to make an impression on
colpo ['kol·po] *m* **1.** (*botta*) blow; **~ basso** (*nel pugilato*) blow below the belt; *fig* low blow **2.** (*sparo, detonazione*) shot; **~ di grazia** *a. fig* coup de grâce; **al primo ~** *fig* at the first attempt; **andare a ~ sicuro** *fig* not to be able to go wrong; **sul ~** instantly **3.** (*rumore*) knock **4.** (*suono: di tosse*) fit; **dare un ~ di telefono a qu** *inf* to give sb a call **5.** *fig* (*movimento improvviso: d'ali*) flap; **a ~ d'occhio** at a glance; **~ di testa** *fig* impulse **6.** *fig* (*manifestazione improvvisa*) **~ di fortuna** stroke of luck; **un ~ di fulmine** *fig* love at first sight; **~ di vento** gust of wind; **~ di scena** CINE, THEAT coup de théâtre; *fig* unexpected turn of events; **di ~** suddenly **7.** (*malore*) stroke; **~ (apopletico)** stroke; **gli è venuto un ~** he's had a stroke; **~ d'aria** chill; **prendere un ~ di sole** to get sunstroke; **-i di sole** (*dal parrucchiere*) highlights **8.** *fig* (*spavento*) shock **9.** *fig* (*impressione*) impression; **la notizia ha fatto ~** *fig* the news caused a sensation **10.** *fig* (*azione sleale*) job; **fare un ~ in banca** to do a bank raid; **~ di Stato** coup (d'état)
colposo, -a [kol·'po:·so] *agg* JUR **omicidio ~** manslaughter
colsi ['kɔl·si] *1. pers sing pass rem di* **cogliere**
coltellata [kol·tel·'la:·ta] *f* (*colpo*) stab wound
coltello [kol·'tɛl·lo] *m* knife; **avere il ~ dalla parte del manico** *fig* to have the whip hand
coltivare [kol·ti·'va:·re] *vt* **1.** (*campo, terreno*) to cultivate **2.** (*patate, rape*) to grow **3.** *fig* (*amicizia, mente*) to cultivate; (*scienze, arti*) to go in for
coltivatore, -trice [kol·ti·va·'to:·re] *m, f* farmer; **~ diretto** small farmer

coltivazione [kol·ti·va·'tsio:·ne] *f* **1.** (*di campo*) cultivation **2.** (*di prodotto*) growing **3.** (*piantagione*) crop
colto ['kɔl·to] *pp di* **cogliere**
colto, -a ['kol·to] *agg* (*persona*) cultured; (*libro*) learned
coltre ['kol·tre] *f* (*strato*) blanket
coltura [kol·'tu:·ra] *f* **1.** AGR cultivation **2.** BIOL culture
colui, colei [ko·'lu:·i, ko·'lɛ:·i] <coloro> *pron dem ~ che ...* the one who ...
columnist ['kɔ·lə·nist] <-> *mf* columnist
coma ['kɔ:·ma] <-> *m* coma; **essere in ~** to be in a coma
comandamento [ko·man·da·'men·to] *m* commandment
comandante [ko·man·'dan·te] *m* **1.** MIL commander **2.** AERO, NAUT captain
comandare [ko·man·'da:·re] **I.** *vt* **1.** MIL (*reggimento, nave*) to command **2.** (*ordinare*) to order; **comandi!** yes, sir! **II.** *vi* to be in command; **~ a qu di fare qc** to order sb to do sth
comando [ko·'man·do] *m* **1.** (*ordine*) command **2.** (*comput*) command; **riga di ~** command line; **~ vocale** voice command **3.** TEC control; **leva di ~** control lever; **~ a distanza** remote control **4.** (*guida, potere*) charge **5.** MIL (*organo responsabile*) command; (*caserma*) headquarters **6.** SPORT (*prima posizione*) lead
comare [ko·'ma:·re] *f* (*donna pettegola*) gossip
Comasco [ko·'mas·ko] *m* Como area; **nel ~** in the Como area
comasco, -a <-schi, -sche> **I.** *agg* from Como **II.** *m, f* (*abitante*) person from Como
combaciare [kom·ba·'tʃa:·re] *vi* **1.** (*aderire: pezzi, tubi*) to fit together **2.** *fig* (*coincidere: idee*) to agree
combattente [kom·bat·'tɛn·te] **I.** *agg* (*esercito, popolazione*) combatant **II.** *mf* combatant
combattere [kom·'bat·te·re] **I.** *vi a. fig* to fight; **~ contro il nemico** to fight (against) the enemy; **~ contro qc** to fight (against) sth; **~ per qc** to fight for sth **II.** *vt* **1.** MIL (*nemico, guerra*) to fight **2.** *fig* (*malattia, ignoranza, delinquenza*) to combat
combattimento [kom·bat·ti·'men·to] *m* **1.** MIL combat **2.** SPORT match; **mettere fuori ~** to knock out; *fig* to see off
combattuto, -a [kom·bat·'tu:·to] *agg* **1.** (*confuso: persona*) undecided; (*decisione*) difficult; **essere ~ fra due possibilità** to be torn between two possibilities **2.** (*contrastato: partita*) hard-fought
combinare [kom·bi·'na:·re] **I.** *vt* **1.** (*unire: elementi, tecnologie, colori, sapori*) to combine **2.** (*organizzare: cena, gita, incontro, matrimonio*) to arrange **3.** (*concludere: affare*) to conclude **4.** *inf* (*fare*) to do; **~ un guaio** *inf* to mess up *inf*; **ne ha combinata un'altra delle sue** *inf* he's done it again *inf* **II.** *vr:* **-rsi 1.** CHEM to combine **2.** *inf* (*conciarsi*) to get oneself up;

ma come ti sei combinato oggi? *inf* what have you got on today?

combinazione [kom·bi·na·'tsio:·ne] *f* **1.** (*caso fortuito*) coincidence; **per** (**pura**) ~ by (sheer) chance **2.** (*di colori, idee, elementi*) combination **3.** (*numerica, di cassaforte*) combination

combriccola [kom·'brik·ko·la] *f* (*gruppo*) crowd

combustibile [kom·bus·'ti:·bi·le] **I.** *agg* (*materiale*) combustible **II.** *m* fuel

combustione [kom·bus·'tio:·ne] *f* CHEM combustion; **camera di** ~ combustion chamber; **motore a** ~ **interna** internal combustion engine

combutta [kom·'but·ta] *f pej* gang; **essere in** ~ **con qu** to be in league with sb

come ['ko:·me] **I.** *avv* **1.** (*nei paragoni*) as; **intelligenti** ~ **noi** as intelligent as us; **ridere** ~ **una matta** to split one's sides laughing; **un uomo buono** ~ **il pane** a man with a heart of gold **2.** (*interrogativo*) how?; ~ **stai?** how are you?; ~ **mai?** how come?; ~ **no?** of course!; ~ **hai detto?** what did you say? **3.** (*esclamativo*) how!; ~ **è cara!** how kind she is!; **ma** ~ **!** what! **4.** (*correlativo*) **ora** ~ **ora** right now; ~ **viene viene** *inf* any old how *inf* **5.** (*in qualità di*) as; **lavora** ~ **giornalista** he works as a reporter **II.** *cong* **1.** (*dichiarativo*) how; **guarda** ~ **li hai ridotti** look what you've done to them **2.** (*modale*) as; **si comporta** ~ **se non sapesse nulla** he acts as if he knew nothing **3.** (*temporale*) as soon as; ~ **mi ha visto, se n'è andata** as soon as she saw me, she left **4.** (*comparativo*) as … as; **non sei buono** ~ **pensavo** you're not as good as I thought **III.** <-> *m* how; **raccontami il** ~ **e il perché** tell me the whys and wherefores

COMECON ['kɔ:·me·kon] *m* COMECON

cometa [ko·'me:·ta] *f* comet

comfort ['kʌm·fət] <-> *m* comfort

comic ['kɔ·mik] <- *o* comics> *m* comic

comica ['kɔ:·mi·ka] <-che> *f* **1.** FILM silent comedy **2.** *fig* (*situazione farsesca*) farce

comicità [ko·mi·tʃi·'ta] <-> *f* (*di situazione*) funny side; (*di battuta*) comicality

comico ['kɔ:·mi·ko] <-ci> *m* **1.** (*attore*) comedian **2.** (*comicità*) funny side

comico, -a <-ci, -che> *agg* **1.** (*della commedia: attore*) comic **2.** (*buffo: scena, film*) funny

comignolo [ko·'miɲ·ɲo·lo] *m* chimney

cominciare [ko·min·'tʃa:·re] **I.** *vi* essere to start; **comincia a piovere** it's starting to rain; ~ **col dire** … to start by saying …; **a che ora cominciano le lezioni?** what time do lectures start?; **a** ~ **da oggi** starting from today; **ha cominciato a suonare la chitarra** she's started to play the guitar; **una parola che comincia per elle** a word that starts with 'l' **II.** *vt* avere (*lavoro, studi, discorso, libro*) to start

comitato [ko·mi·'ta:·to] *m* committee; **Comitato delle regioni** EU Committee of the Re-

gions; **Comitato economico e sociale** EU Economic and Social Committee

comitiva [ko·mi·'ti:·va] *f* group

comiziante [ko·mi·'tsian·te] *mf* speaker

comizio [ko·'mi·tsio] <-i> *m* rally

commedia [kom·'mɛ:·dia] <-ie> *f* comedy; ~ **musicale** musical; ~ **a soggetto** improvised comedy; ~ **dell'arte** commedia dell'arte; ~ **d'intreccio** situation comedy; **fare la** ~ *fig* to play-act

commediante [kom·me·'dian·te] *mf* **1.** THEAT comedian **2.** *fig pej* (*simulatore*) fake

commediografo, -a [kom·me·'diɔ:·gra·fo] *m, f* comedy writer

commemorare [kom·me·mo·'ra:·re] *vt* (*ricordare: evento, persona*) to commemorate

commemorativo, -a [kom·me·mo·ra·'ti:·vo] *agg* (*concerto, francobollo, targa, medaglia*) commemorative

commemorazione [kom·me·mo·ra·'tsio:·ne] *f* **1.** (*celebrazione*) commemoration **2.** (*cerimonia*) remembrance ceremony

commendatore [kom·men·da·'to:·re] *m* knight commander

commensale [kom·men·'sa:·le] *mf* fellow diner

commentare [kom·men·'ta:·re] *vt* **1.** (*passo, poesia*) to comment on **2.** (*evento*) to commentate on

commentatore, -trice [kom·men·ta·'to:·re] *m, f* RADIO, TV commentator

commento [kom·'men·to] *m* **1.** LIT, RADIO, TV commentary **2.** (*osservazione, giudizio*) comment **3.** FILM ~ **musicale** background music

commerciale [kom·mer·'tʃa:·le] *agg* commercial

commercialista [kom·mer·tʃa·'lis·ta] <-i, -e> *mf* **1.** (*consulente*) accountant **2.** (*esperto in diritto commerciale*) commercial lawyer

commercializzare [kom·mer·tʃa·lid·'dza:·re] *vt* **1.** COM (*vendere: prodotto*) to market **2.** *fig pej* (*rendere commerciale*) to commercialize

commerciante [kom·mer·'tʃan·te] *mf* **1.** (*negoziante*) storekeeper; ~ **all'ingrosso** wholesaler **2.** (*mercante*) dealer

commerciare [kom·mer·'tʃa:·re] *vi* to trade; ~ **in qc** to deal in sth

commercio [kom·'mɛr·tʃo] <-ci> *m* **1.** (*settore*) commerce; **essere nel** ~ to be in business **2.** (*attività*) trade; ~ **all'ingrosso** wholesale trade; ~ **al minuto** retail trade; ~ **elettronico** e-commerce **3.** (*distribuzione: prodotto, libro*) **essere in** ~ to be on sale

commessa [kom·'mes·sa] *f* **1.** (*di negozio*) sales clerk **2.** (*ordine*) order

commesso, -a [kom·'mes·so] **I.** *pp* di **commettere II.** *m, f* (*di negozio*) sales clerk; ~ **viaggiatore** traveling salesman

commestibile [kom·mes·'ti:·bi·le] *agg* edible

commettere [kom·'met·te·re] <irr> *vt* (*delitto, imprudenza*) to commit; (*errore*) to make

commiato [kom·'mia:·to] *m* (*congedo*) farewell; **prendere ~ da qu** to take one's leave of sb

commiserare [kom·mi·ze·'ra:·re] *vt* **1.** (*avere compassione per: persona, sorte*) to feel sorry for **2.** (*disprezzare*) to pity

commiserazione [kom·mi·ze·ra·'tsio:·ne] *f* sympathy

commisi [kom·'mi:·zi] *1. pers sing pass rem di* **commettere**

commissariato [kom·mis·sa·'ria:·to] *m* **~ di polizia** police station

commissario, -a [kom·mis·'sa:·rio] <-i, -ie> *m, f* **1.** ADM (*funzionario*) captain; **~ di pubblica sicurezza** police captain; **Commissario europeo** (*Unione europea*) European Commissioner **2.** (*membro di commissione*) commissioner; **~ d'esame** examiner **3.** SPORT steward; **~ tecnico** team manager

commissionare [kom·mis·sio·'na:·re] *vt* (*lavoro, ricerca, traduzione*) to commission

commissione [kom·mis·'sio:·ne] *f* **1.** COM (*ordine*) order; **prodotto su ~** made to order **2.** (*somma*) commission; **spese di ~** commission **3.** (*faccenda*) **fare una ~** to run an errand; **fare -i** to do the shopping **4.** (*comitato*) commission; **~ direttiva** executive committee; **~ esaminatrice** [*o* **d'esami**] board of examiners; **Commissione europea** EU European Commission; **~ d'inchiesta** committee of inquiry; **~ interna** shop committee

committente [kom·mit·'tɛn·te] *mf* customer

commossi *1. pers sing pass rem di* **commuovere**

commosso *pp di* **commuovere**

commovente [kom·mo·'vɛn·te] *agg* moving

commozione [kom·mo·'tsio:·ne] *f* **1.** (*turbamento*) emotion **2.** MED **~ cerebrale** MED concussion

commuovere [kom·'muɔ:·ve·re] <irr> **I.** *vt* (*momento, storia, cerimonia*) to move **II.** *vr:* **-rsi** to be moved

commutare [kom·mu·'ta:·re] *vt* **1.** (*scambiare: pena, sanzione*) to commute **2.** EL to switch

commutatore [kom·mu·ta·'to:·re] *m* EL, TEL switch

comò [ko·'mɔ] <-> *m* dresser

Como ['kɔ:·mo] *f* Como; **il lago di ~** Lake Como

comoda ['kɔ:·mo·da] *f* MED (*sedia*) commode

comodare [ko·mo·'da:·re] *vi* **essere** *inf* to suit; **fai come ti comoda** do as you like

comodino [ko·mo·'di:·no] *m* bedside table

comodità [ko·mo·di·'ta] <-> *f* **1.** (*agio*) ease **2.** (*comfort*) comfort

comodo ['kɔ:·mo·do] *m* **1.** (*agio*) comfort **2.** (*convenienza*) convenience; **con ~** at one's leisure; **fare** [*o* **tornare**] **~ a qu** to come in handy for sb; **fare il proprio ~** to do as one pleases

comodo, -a *agg* **1.** (*agiato: vita*) easy **2.** (*confortevole: divano, scarpe*) comfortable **3.** (*pratico: tavolo, indumento*) practical

4. (*conveniente: ora, momento*) convenient **5.** (*a proprio agio*) comfortable; **state -i!** don't get up!

compact disc [kəm·'pækt disk/'kɔm·pakt disk] <-> *m* (*disco*) compact disc

compaesano, -a [kom·pae·'za:·no] *m, f* person from the same town

compagnia [kom·paɲ·'ɲi:·a] <-ie> *f* **1.** (*lo stare insieme*) company; **essere di ~** to be good company; **fare** [*o* **tenere**] **~ a qu** to keep sb company **2.** (*gruppo*) group **3.** THEAT company **4.** REL society **5.** MIL company **6.** COM company; **~ aerea** airline; **~ di assicurazione** insurance company; **~ di navigazione** shipping company; **~ low-cost** budget airline

compagno, -a [kom·'paɲ·ɲo] *m, f* **1.** (*persona amica*) companion; (*di sport*) partner; **~ di classe** classmate; **~ di gioco** playmate; **~ di scuola** schoolfriend; **~ di stanza** roommate; **~ di sventura** companion in misfortune **2.** (*partner*) partner **3.** POL comrade

compaio [kom·'pa:·io] *1. pers sing pr di* **comparire**

comparare [kom·pa·'ra:·re] *vt* to compare

comparativo, -a *agg* **1.** (*studio, metodo*) comparative **2.** LING comparative; **grado ~** comparative degree

comparativo, -a *m, f* LING comparative

comparazione [kom·pa·ra·'tsio:·ne] *f* comparison

comparire [kom·pa·'ri:·re] <comparisco *o* compaio, comparvi *o* comparii, comparso> *vi* **essere** to appear

comparizione [kom·pa·ri·'tsio:·ne] *f* appearance; **mandato** [*o* **ordine**] **di ~** JUR summons

comparsa [kom·'par·sa] *f* **1.** THEAT walk-on; FILM extra; **fare la ~** to be a walk-on [*o* an extra] **2.** (*apparizione*) appearance

comparso [kom·'par·so] *pp di* **comparire**

compartecipe [kom·par·'te:·tʃi·pe] **I.** *agg* participating **II.** *mf* participant

compartimento [kom·par·ti·'men·to] *m* **1.** (*suddivisione*) compartment **2.** FERR compartment **3.** ADM (*circoscrizione*) district

comparvi [kom·'par·vi] *1. pers sing pass rem di* **comparire**

compassione [kom·pas·'sio:·ne] *f* **1.** (*pietà*) compassion; **avere ~ di** [*o* **per**] [*o* **verso**] **qu** to feel pity for sb; **far ~ a qu** to arouse sb's pity **2.** (*disprezzo*) pity

compasso [kom·'pas·so] *m* (*strumento*) compasses *pl*

compatibile [kom·pa·'ti:·bi·le] *agg* compatible; **essere ~ con qc** to be compatible with sth

compatibilità [kom·pa·ti·bi·li·'ta] <-> *f* compatibility

compatibilmente [kom·pa·ti·bil·'men·te] *avv* **~ con ...** depending on sth

compatimento [kom·pa·ti·'men·to] *m* **1.** (*compassione*) compassion **2.** (*disprezzo*) pity

compatire [kom·pa·'ti:·re] <compatisco> *vt* **1.** (*avere compassione di*) to feel sorry for **2.** (*disprezzare*) to pity

compatriota [kom·pa·tri·'ɔ:·ta] <-i , -e> *mf* compatriot

compattezza [kom·pat·'tet·tsa] *f* **1.** (*solidità*) solidity **2.** *fig* (*di gruppo*) unity

compatto, -a [kom·'pat·to] *agg* **1.** (*solido, denso: materiale*) solid **2.** (*piccolo: auto, videocamera*) compact **3.** (*unitario: gruppo*) close-knit

compendio [kom·'pɛn·dio] <-i> *m* compendium

compensare [kom·pen·'sa:·re] *vt* **1.** (*dare un compenso a*) to remunerate; ~ **qu per qc** to remunerate sb for sth **2.** (*ricompensare*) to make up for; ~ **qu di qc** to be compensation to sb for sth **3.** (*bilanciare: differenza*) to make up for

compensato *m* plywood

compensazione [kom·pen·sa·'tsio:·ne] *f* compensation

compenso [kom··'pɛn·so] *m* **1.** COM (*retribuzione*) remuneration **2.** COM (*risarcimento*) compensation **3.** (*loc*) **in** ~ on the other hand

compera ['kom·pe·ra] *f* purchase; **fare -e** to go shopping

competente [kom·pe·'tɛn·te] *agg* **1.** (*esperto: medico*) qualified **2.** ADM (*giudice*) with jurisdiction; (*ufficio*) appropriate

competenza [kom·pe·'tɛn·tsa] *f* **1.** (*preparazione*) competence **2.** ADM (*autorità*) jurisdiction **3.** ADM (*pertinenza*) responsibility; **non è di sua** ~ it's not his [*o* her] responsibility **4.** *pl* COM (*onorario*) fees

competere [kom·'pɛ:·te·re] <competo, competei> *manca il pp vi* **1.** (*gareggiare*) to compete; ~ **per qc** to compete for sth **2.** ADM **qc compete a qu** sth is sb's responsibility

competitività [kom·pe·ti·ti·vi·'ta] <-> *f* competitiveness

competitivo, -a [kom·pe·ti·'ti:·vo] *agg* competitive

competizione [kom·pe·ti·'tsio:·ne] *f* (*rivalità, gara*) competition

compiacente [kom·pia·'tʃɛn·te] *agg* (*accomodante*) amenable

compiacenza [kom·pia·'tʃɛn·tsa] *f* (*cortesia*) courtesy; **avere la** ~ **di fare qc** to have the courtesy to do sth

compiacere [kom·pia·'tʃe:·re] <irr> **I.** *vi* (*assecondare*) to please **II.** *vr:* **-rsi** to be pleased; **-rsi con qu per qc** to congratulate sb on sth

compiacimento [kom·pia·tʃi·'men·to] *m* satisfaction

compiangere [kom·'pian·dʒe·re] <irr> *vt* (*commiserare*) to feel sorry for

compianto [kom·'pian·to] *m* mourning

compianto, -a *agg* (*defunto*) late

compiere ['kom·pie·re] <compio, compii *o* compiei, compiuto> **I.** *vt* **1.** (*concludere:* *missione, studi*) to complete; ~ **gli anni** to have one's birthday; **ha compiuto 10 anni giovedì** he had his 10th birthday on Thursday **2.** (*fare*) to carry out **II.** *vr:* **-rsi** (*avverarsi*) to take place

compilare [kom·pi·'la:·re] *vt* **1.** (*riempire: modulo, questionario*) to fill out **2.** (*redigere: lista*) to draw up; (*vocabolario*) to compile

compilatore [kom·pi·la·'to:·re] *m* COMPUT compiler

compilazione [kom·pi·la·'tsio:·ne] *f* **1.** (*di modulo, questionario*) filling out **2.** (*di lista*) drawing up; (*di vocabolario*) compilation

compimento [kom·pi·'men·to] *m* (*fine*) end; **portare a** ~ **qc** to see sth through to the end

compire [kom·'pi:·re] *v.* **compiere**

compitare [kom·pi·'ta:·re] *vt* to spell out

compito ['kom·pi·to] *m* **1.** (*di scuola*) test; ~ **in classe** (**d'italiano**) class test (in Italian); **-i a casa** homework; **-i delle vacanze** vacation homework **2.** (*incarico*) duty

compito, -a [kom·'pi:·to] *agg* (*persona, aria*) polite

compiutamente [kom·piu·ta·'men·te] *avv* (*descrivere, esprimere, realizzare*) fully

compiuto, -a [kom·'piu·to] **I.** *pp di* **compiere** **II.** *agg* completed; **un fatto** ~ a fait accompli

compleanno [kom·ple·'an·no] *m* birthday; **tanti auguri di buon** ~! happy birthday!

complementare [kom·ple·men·'ta:·re] *agg* complementary

complemento [kom·ple·'men·to] *m* LING complement; ~ **di causa/tempo** adverbial phrase of reason/time; ~ **di specificazione** possessive phrase; ~ **di termine** indirect object

complessato, -a [kom·ples·'sa:·to] **I.** *agg* (*persona*) hung-up *inf* **II.** *m, f* person with hang-ups *inf*

complessità [kom·ples·si·'ta] <-> *f fig* complexity

complessivamente [kom·ples·si·va·'men·te] *avv* altogether

complessivo, -a [kom·ples·'si:·vo] *agg* (*quadro, valutazione*) overall; (*reddito*) total; **visione -a** overview

complesso [kom·'plɛs·so] *m* **1.** PSYCH complex; ~ **d'inferiorità** inferiority complex **2.** (*architettonico, industriale, ospedaliero, residenziale*) complex **3.** MUS (*gruppo*) group **4.** (*insieme*) whole; **in** [*o* **nel**] ~ altogether

complesso, -a *agg* **1.** (*di più elementi*) complex **2.** (*complicato: situazione, persona*) complicated

completamente [kom·ple·ta·'men·te] *avv* completely

completamento [kom·ple·ta·'men·to] *m* completion

completare [kom·ple·'ta:·re] *vt* to complete

completezza [kom·ple·'tet·tsa] *f* (*di opera, trattazione, computazione*) completeness

completo [kom·'plɛ:·to] *m* **1.** (*accessori*) set **2.** (*abito*) suit **3.** (*loc*) **al** ~ (*con tutti i partecipanti*) at full strength; (*teatro*) sold out;

(*albergo*) full
completo, -a *agg* 1.(*dettagliato, totale*) complete 2.(*pieno: cinema, teatro*) sold out; (*albergo*) full
complicare [kom·pli·'ka:·re] I. *vt* (*vita, situazione, scenario*) to complicate II. *vr:* **-rsi** (*situazione, trama*) to become complicated; **la malattia si è complicata** MED there have been complications
complicato, -a [kom·pli·'ka:·to] *agg* complicated
complicazione [kom·pli·ka·'tsio:·ne] *f* 1. MED complication 2.(*difficoltà*) problem
complice ['kɔm·pli·tʃe/'kom·pli·tʃe] *mf* JUR accomplice
complicità [kom·pli·tʃi·'ta] <-> *f* 1.(*l'essere complice*) complicity 2.(*intesa*) understanding
complimentarsi [kom·pli·men·'ta:r·si] *vr* ~ **con qu** (**per qc**) to compliment sb (on sth)
complimento [kom·pli·'men·to] *m* 1.(*lode*) compliment; **-i!** (*per azione, laurea, successo*) congratulations! 2. **-i** (*convenevoli*) ceremony; **non fare -i!** be my guest!; **no grazie, senza -i!** no, but thanks all the same!
complotto [kom·'plɔt·to] *m* plot; **un ~ contro qu** a plot against sb
componente [kom·po·'nɛn·te] *m* (*ingrediente, pezzo*) component
compongo 1. *pers sing pr di* **comporre**
componibile [kom·po·'ni:·bi·le] *agg* (*mobili*) modular; **cucina ~** fitted kitchen
componimento [kom·po·ni·'men·to] *m* 1.(*scolastico*) composition 2. LIT work 3. MUS composition
comporre [kom·'por·re] <irr> *vt* 1.(*formare*) to create; (*numero telefonico*) to dial 2. LIT, MUS to compose 3. TYP to typeset 4. DIR to settle
comportamento [kom·por·ta·'men·to] *m* behavior
comportare [kom·por·'ta·re] I. *vt* (*implicare*) to involve II. *vr:* **-rsi** to behave
composi 1. *pers sing pass rem di* **comporre**
compositore, -trice [kom·po·zi·'to:·re] *m, f* MUS composer
composizione [kom·po·zi·'tsio:·ne] *f* 1.(*struttura*) composition 2.(*sistemazione*) arrangement 3. MUS composition 4.(*a scuola*) composition 5. TYP typesetting
compostaggio [kɔm·pɔs·'tad·dʒo] <-ggi> *m* composting
compostezza [kom·pos·'tet·tsa] *f* composure
composto [kom·'pos·to] *m* (*mescolanza*) mixture
composto, -a [kom·'pɔs·to] I. *pp di* **comporre** II. *agg* 1.(*formato da più elementi*) composed 2.(*posizione*) **stare ~** to keep still
comprare [kom·'pra:·re] *vt* 1.(*acquistare*) to buy 2.(*corrompere: persona*) to bribe
compratore, -trice [kom·pra·'to:·re] *m, f* buyer
compravendita [kom·pra·'ven·di·ta] *f* COM buying and selling

comprendere [kom·'prɛn·de·re] <irr> I. *vt* 1.(*capire*) to understand 2.(*contenere*) to consist of II. *vr:* **-rsi** (*capirsi*) to understand each other
comprendonio [kom·pren·'dɔ:·nio] <-i> *m scherz, inf* wits *pl;* **essere duro di ~** to be slow on the uptake
comprensibile [kom·pren·'si:·bi·le] *agg* (*linguaggio, ragione, timore*) understandable
comprensione [kom·pren·'sio:·ne] *f* understanding
comprensivo, -a [kom·pren·'si:·vo] *agg* 1.(*indulgente: persona*) understanding 2. COM inclusive; **~ di qc** inclusive of sth; **prezzo ~ di I.V.A.** price inclusive of VAT
compresi [kom·'pre:·si] 1. *pers sing pass rem di* **comprendere**
compreso, -a [kom·'pre:·so] I. *pp di* **comprendere** II. *agg* 1.(*capito: persona*) understood 2.(*incluso*) included; **tutto ~** all inclusive; **I.V.A. -a** including VAT
compressa [kom·'prɛs·sa] *f* 1.(*pastiglia*) tablet 2.(*garza*) compress
compressi [kom·'prɛs·si] 1. *pers sing pass rem di* **comprimere**
compressione [kom·pres·'sio:·ne] *f* compression; **~ dati** COMPUT data compression
compresso, -a [kom·'prɛs·so] I. *pp di* **comprimere** II. *agg* 1.(*sottoposto a pressione: aria, gas*) compressed 2. COMPUT (*file*) zipped
compressore [kom·pres·'so:·re] I. *agg* compressing II. *m* compressor
comprimere [kom·'pri:·me·re] <comprimo, compressi, compresso> *vt* 1.(*sottoporre a pressione: aria, gas, fluido*) to compress 2. COMPUT (*file, dati, testo*) to zip
compromesso [kom·pro·'mɛs·so] *m* 1. *fig* (*accomodamento*) compromise; **arrivare** [*o* **scendere**] **ad un ~** to reach a compromise 2. JUR (*per l'acquisto di un immobile*) preliminary contract
compromesso, -a I. *pp di* **compromettere** II. *agg pej* (*persona, reputazione*) compromised
compromettente [kom·pro·met·'tɛn·te] *agg* (*dichiarazione, foto, lettera*) compromising
compromettere [kom·pro·'met·te·re] <irr> I. *vt* (*impresa, reputazione, salute*) to compromise II. *vr:* **-rsi** (*mettersi in cattiva luce*) to compromise oneself
comproprietà [kom·pro·prie·'ta] *f* joint ownership
comproprietario, -a [kom·pro·prie·'ta:·rio] *m, f* joint owner
comprovare [kom·pro·'va:·re] *vt* (*requisito, diritto, capacità*) to prove
compunto, -a [kom·'pun·to] *agg* (*persona, volto, espressione*) contrite
computare [kom·pu·'ta:·re] *vt* 1.(*contare*) to count 2. COM (*mettere in conto*) to charge
computazionale [kom·pu·ta·tsio·'na:·le] *agg* (*chimica, fisica, meccanica*) computational; **la linguistica ~** computational linguistics

computer [kəm·'pju:·tə/kom·'pju·ter] <-> *m* computer; ~ **portatile** laptop (computer); ~ **tascabile** pocket computer

computeristico, **-a** [kom·pju·te·'ris·ti·ko] <-ci, -che> *agg* (*scienza, sistema, terminologia*) computer

computerizzabile [kom·pju·te·rid·'dza:·bi·le] *agg* (*documenti, pratiche*) computerizable

computerizzare [kom·pu·te·rid·'dza:·re] *vt* (*dati, documenti, sistema, impianto*) to computerize

computerizzato, **-a** [kom·pju·te·rid·'dza:·to] *agg* (*sistema, impianto, macchinario*) computerized

computerizzazione [kom·pju·te·rid·dza·'tsio:·ne] *f* (*di sistema, impianto, macchinario*) computerization

computista [kom·pu·'tis·ta] <-i, -e> *mf* bookkeeper

computisteria [kom·pu·tis·te·'ri:·a] <-ie> *f* bookkeeping

comunale [ko·mu·'na:·le] *agg* **1.** ADM (*del comune: ufficio, servizio, consiglio, giunta*) town; (*biblioteca, teatro*) municipal; (*imposte*) local; **palazzo** ~ HIST town hall **2.** HIST (*dei comuni*) of the city states; **l'età** ~ the age of the city states

comune [ko·'mu:·ne] **I.** *agg* **1.** (*di tutti*) common; **bene** ~ common good; **il Mercato Comune** the Common Market **2.** (*di due o più persone: interessi*) common; (*amico*) mutual **3.** (*diffuso: opinione, uso*) common **4.** (*medio, normale*) ordinary; ~ **mortale** ordinary mortal **5.** (*ordinario: sale*) common **6.** (*non raffinato: gente*) ordinary **7.** LING (*generico*) common **II.** *m* **1.** ADM (*ente*) city council; (*sede*) city hall; **sposarsi in** ~ to get married at city hall **2.** HIST city state **3.** (*insieme*) **avere qc in** ~ to have sth in common **4.** (*ordinario*) **fuori dal** ~ out of the ordinary

i The **Comune** (municipality) is the smallest autonomous political unit. It keeps the registers of births, marriages, and deaths and has the power to raise taxes and to approve public works. The **Comune** is run by the **Giunta comunale** (governing group) whose members come from the **Consiglio comunale** (city council). Both groups report to the Mayor (**Sindaco**). The **Campidoglio** (Capitol), one of the Seven Hills of Rome, is the seat of the **Comune di Roma**, the Rome city council.

comunella [ko·mu·'nɛl·la] *f* (*accordo*) **fare** ~ to band together

comunicabile [ko·mu·ni·'ka:·bi·le] *agg* (*sapere, computazioni*) communicable

comunicante [ko·mu·ni·'kan·te] *agg* (*camere*) communicating; **vasi -i** communicating vessels

comunicare [ko·mu·ni·'ka:·re] **I.** *vt* (*notizia, data, dati, nomi, sentimenti*) to communicate; ~ **qc a qu** to inform sb of sth **II.** *vi* to communicate; ~ **con qc** to communicate with sth

comunicativa [ko·mu·ni·ka·'ti:·va] *f* communicativeness

comunicativo, **-a** [ko·mu·ni·ka·'ti:·vo] *agg* (*persona*) communicative

comunicato [ko·mu·ni·'ka:·to] *m* communiqué; ~ **stampa** press release

comunicazione [ko·mu·ni·ka·'tsio:·ne] *f* **1.** (*collegamento*) connection; **-i ferroviarie/marittime/stradali** rail/sea/road connections; **essere in** ~ to be connected; **mettersi in** ~ (**con qu**) to get in contact (with sb) **2.** (*informazione*) message **3.** (*trasmissione*) communication; ~ **telefonica/interurbana** telephone/long-distance call; **mezzi di** ~ means of communication

comunione [ko·mu·'nio:·ne] *f* **1.** REL communion; **prima** ~ first communion **2.** JUR community; ~ **dei beni** JUR community property **3.** *fig* (*di interessi*) community; (*di idee*) similarity

comunismo [ko·mu·'niz·mo] *m* communism

comunista [ko·mu·'nis·ta] <-i, -e> **I.** *mf* communist **II.** *agg* (*partito, ideologia*) communist

comunità [ko·mu·ni·'ta] <-> *f* **1.** (*collettività*) community **2.** (*di lavoro, terapeutica*) center **3.** (*organizzazione*) group; **Comunità Europea** European Community

comunitario, **-a** [ko·mu·ni·'ta:·rio] <-i, -ie> *agg* **1.** (*della comunità*) community **2.** (*della Comunità Europea*) Community

comunque [ko·'muŋ·kue] **I.** *avv* (*in ogni modo*) anyway **II.** *cong* **1.** (*in qualunque modo*) however; ~ **vada** whatever happens **2.** (*tuttavia*) nevertheless

con [kon] <col, collo, colla, coi, cogli, colle> *prep* **1.** (*compagnia, relazione*) with **2.** (*verso*) to; **essere gentile** ~ **qu** to be nice to sb **3.** (*unione*) with; **caffè col latte** coffee with milk; **un uomo coi capelli bianchi** a man with white hair **4.** (*mezzo, strumento*) with; **l'ho aperto** ~ **un coltello** I opened it with a knife; **viaggiare con treno/con la macchina** to travel by train/by car **5.** (*modo, maniera*) with; ~ **tutto il cuore** with all one's heart **6.** (*causa*) with; ~ **questo** with; ~ **questo caldo non si può uscire** you can't go out in this heat **7.** (*avversativo*) despite; ~ **tutti i suoi difetti, mi piace** despite all his faults, I like him; ~ **tutto che ...** despite all that ...

conca ['kon·ka] <-che> *f* **1.** (*recipiente*) bowl **2.** GEOG valley

concatenare [kon·ka·te·'na:·re] *vt* (*idee, computazioni*) to link

concatenazione [kon·ka·te·na·'tsio:·ne] *f* chain

concavo, **-a** ['kɔn·ka·vo] *agg* (*recipiente, lente, specchio*) concave

concedere [kon·'tʃɛː·de·re] <concedo, concessi *o* concedei *o* concedetti, concesso> **I.** *vt* (*grazia, prestito, proroga*) to grant **II.** *vr*:

-rsi (*permettersi: lusso, vacanza*) to allow oneself

concentramento [kon·tʃen·tra·'men·to] *m* (*ammassamento*) concentration; (*di truppe*) build-up; **campo di ~** concentration camp

concentrare [kon·tʃen·'tra:·re] I. *vt* 1. MIL (*truppe*) to mass 2. *fig* (*energie, risorse*) to concentrate; **~ qc su qc** to concentrate sth on sth II. *vr* **-rsi su qc** to concentrate on sth

concentrato [kon·tʃen·'tra:·to] *m* 1. CULIN concentrate; **~ di pomodoro** tomato purée 2. *fig* (*cumulo: di musica, tecnologia, comfort*) collection

concentrato, -a *agg* 1. (*assorto: persona*) absorbed 2. (*condensato: liquido*) concentrated

concentrazione [kon·tʃen·tra·'tsio:·ne] *f* (*raccoglimento*) concentration

concentrico, -a [kon·'tʃɛn·tri·ko] <-ci, -che> *agg* (*cerchio*) concentric

concepibile [kon·tʃe·'pi:·bi·le] *agg* conceivable; **non è ~ che ... +**conj* it is inconceivable that ...

concepimento [kon·tʃe·pi·'men·to] *m* 1. BIOL (*di bambino*) conception 2. *fig* (*ideazione*) conception

concepire [kon·tʃe·'pi:·re] <concepisco> *vt* 1. BIOL (*bambino*) to conceive 2. *fig* (*comprendere*) to understand 3. (*ideare: strategia, struttura*) to conceive

concernente [kon·tʃer·'nɛn·te] *agg* **~ qc** concerning sth

concernere [kon·'tʃɛr·ne·re] *mancano pass rem e pp vt* to concern

concertista [kon·tʃer·'tis·ta] <-i, -e> *mf* concert performer

concerto [kon·'tʃɛr·to] *m* MUS concert

concessi [kon·'tʃɛs·si] *1. pers sing pass rem di* **concedere**

concessionaria [kon·tʃes·sio·'na:·ria] <-ie> *f* dealership

concessionario [kon·tʃes·sio·'na:·rio] <-i> *m* 1. (*rivenditore*) dealer 2. (*destinatario di una concessione*) agent

concessionario, -a <-i, -ie> *agg* 1. (*di vendita*) **agente** ~ agent 2. (*destinatario di una concessione*) **società/ditta -a** agency

concessione [kon·tʃes·'sio:·ne] *f* 1. (*di prestito, mutuo, pensione*) granting 2. COM (*licenza*) franchise 3. DIR (*appalto*) contract

concessiva [kon·tʃes·'si:·va] *f* LING concessive clause

concessivo, -a [kon·tʃes·'si:·vo] *agg* (*congiunzione, proposizione*) concessive

concesso [kon·'tʃɛs·so] *pp di* **concedere**

concetto [kon·'tʃet·to] *m* 1. (*nozione*) concept 2. (*opinione*) opinion; **farsi un ~ di qc** to form an opinion of sth

concettuale [kon·tʃet·tu·'a:·le] *agg* (*analisi, metafora*) conceptual; **mappa ~** conceptual map

concezione [kon·tʃe·'tsio:·ne] *f* 1. (*concetto, idea*) concept 2. (*ideazione: di piano, progetto*) conception

conchiglia [koɲ·'kiʎ·ʎa] <-glie> *f* 1. ZOO shell 2. *pl* CULIN *pasta shell*

concia ['kon·tʃa] <-ce> *f* 1. (*di pelli*) tanning 2. (*di tabacco*) curing 3. (*sostanza*) tan

conciare [kon·'tʃa:·re] I. *vt* 1. (*pelli*) to tan 2. (*tabacco*) to cure 3. *fig, inf* (*ridurre in cattivo stato*) to make a mess of; **~ qu per le feste** *inf* to beat sb up II. *vr:* **-rsi** *pej* 1. (*ridursi male*) to get in a mess 2. (*vestirsi male*) to dress badly

conciliante [kon·tʃi·'lian·te] *agg* (*persona, tono, saluto*) conciliatory

conciliare [kon·tʃi·'lia:·re] I. *vt* 1. ADM (*pagare: multa*) to pay on the spot 2. (*sonno*) to be conducive to 3. (*controversia*) to settle 4. *fig* (*attività, interessi, passioni*) to reconcile II. *vr:* **-rsi** (*armonizzare*) to become reconciled

conciliatore, -trice [kon·tʃi·lia·'to:·re] I. *agg* 1. (*commissione*) conciliation; **giudice ~** justice of the peace 2. *fig* (*figura, posizione*) conciliatory II. *m, f* 1. (*intermediario*) conciliator 2. JUR (*giudice di pace*) justice of the peace

conciliazione [kon·tʃi·lia·'tsio:·ne] *f* JUR (*di avversari*) conciliation

concilio [kon·'tʃi:·lio] <-i> *m* 1. REL council 2. *scherz* (*riunione*) conference

concimare [kon·tʃi·'ma:·re] *vt* (*con prodotti chimici*) to put fertilizer on; (*con prodotti naturali*) to put manure on

concime [kon·'tʃi:·me] *m* (*chimico*) fertilizer; (*naturale*) manure

concisione [kon·tʃi·'zio:·ne] *f* (*di discorso, scritto*) conciseness

conciso, -a [kon·'tʃi:·zo] *agg* (*discorso, testo*) concise

concitazione [kon·tʃi·ta·'tsio:·ne] *f* excitement

concittadino, -a [kon·tʃit·ta·'di:·no] *m, f* fellow citizen

conclave [koɲ·'kla:·ve] *m* REL conclave

concludente [koɲ·klu·'dɛn·te] *agg* conclusive

concludere [koɲ·'klu:·de·re] <concludo, conclusi, concluso> I. *vt* 1. (*condurre a termine: discorso, viaggio*) to end; (*lavoro*) to finish 2. (*affare, trattato, vertenza, patto, pace*) to conclude 3. (*dedurre*) to conclude II. *vr:* **-rsi** to end

conclusione [koɲ·klu·'zio:·ne] *f* 1. (*fine: di conflitto, partita, discorso, libro*) end 2. (*deduzione*) conclusion; **giungere alla ~ che ...** to come to the conclusion that ...; **in ~** in conclusion

conclusivo, -a [koɲ·klu·'zi:·vo] *agg* (*osservazione, frase*) concluding

concluso, -a [kon·'klu:·zo] I. *pp di* **concludere** II. *agg* 1. (*affare, pace*) concluded 2. (*lavoro*) finished

concomitante [koɲ·ko·mi·'tan·te] *agg* (*circostanza*) concomitant

concomitanza [koɲ·ko·mi·'tan·tsa] *f* combination; **in ~ con qc** in conjunction with sth

concordanza [koɲ·kor·'dan·tsa] *f* 1. LING agreement 2. (*di opinioni, idee, fatti*) concord-

ance
concordare [koŋ·kor·'da:·ɾe] I. *vt* 1. LING to
make agree 2. (*data, prezzo*) to agree on II. *vi*
~ **con qc** to agree with sth; ~ **con qu su qc** to
agree with sb on sth
concordato [koŋ·kor·'da:·to] *m* 1. JUR
(*accordo*) composition 2. REL concordat
concorde [koŋ·'kɔr·de] *agg* in agreement
concordia [koŋ·'kɔr·dia] <-ie> *f* 1. (*accordo*)
agreement 2. (*armonia*) harmony
concorrente [koŋ·kor·'rɛn·te] I. *agg* 1. COM
(*azienda*) competing 2. MATH (*rette*) concurrent II. *mf* 1. SPORT, COM competitor 2. (*di concorso*) candidate
concorrenza [koŋ·kor·'rɛn·tsa] *f* 1. (*competizione*) competition; **fare** ~ **a qu** to compete
with sb 2. COM competition; ~ **libera/sleale**
free/unfair competition 3. COM (*concorrenti*)
competition
concorrenziale [koŋ·kor·ren·'tsia:·le] *agg*
(*prezzo, prodotto*) competitive
concorrere [koŋ·'kor·re·re] <irr> *vi* 1. (*competere*) to compete; ~ **a una gara** to compete
in a race 2. (*contribuire*) ~ **a fare qc** to contribute to doing sth; ~ **alle spese** to contribute
to expenses
concorso [koŋ·'kor·so] *m* 1. (*gara*) contest;
~ **di bellezza** beauty contest; ~ **a premi** prize
competition; **fuori** ~ out of competition
2. SPORT competition; ~ **ippico** horse show
concretezza [koŋ·kre·'tet·tsa] *f* concreteness
concretizzare [koŋ·kre·tid·'dza:·re] I. *vt* (*realizzare: idea, proposta*) to put into action II. *vr:*
-rsi (*realizzarsi: piano, progetto*) to be put into
action
concreto [koŋ·'krɛ:·to] *m* **venire al** ~ to get to
the crux of the matter; **in** ~ in reality
concreto, -a *agg* 1. (*materiale: oggetto*)
concrete 2. (*reale: esempio, ipotesi*) solid
3. (*pratico: persona*) practical
concussione [koŋ·kus·'sio:·ne] *f* extortion
condanna [kon·'dan·na] *f* 1. JUR sentence
2. *fig* (*disapprovazione*) condemnation
condannare [kon·dan·'na:·re] *vt* 1. JUR to sentence; ~ **qu a qc** to sentence sb to sth 2. *fig*
(*disapprovare*) to condemn
condensa [kon·'dɛn·sa] *f* condensation
condensamento [kon·den·sa·'men·to] *m* (*di
umidità*) condensation
condensare [kon·den·'sa:·re] I. *vt* 1. PHYS
(*aria, gas*) to condense 2. *fig* (*riassumere*) to
summarize II. *vr:* **-rsi** 1. PHYS (*aria, gas*) to condense 2. *fig* (*concentrarsi*) to be concentrated
condensato, -a *agg* 1. (*latte*) condensed
2. PHYS condensed 3. (*libro, racconto*) summar-
ized
condensatore [kon·den·sa·'to:·re] *m* EL condenser
condensazione [kon·den·sa·'tsio:·ne] *f* condensation
condimento [kon·di·'men·to] *m* CULIN (*per
insalata*) dressing; (*per pasta*) sauce
condire [kon·'di:·re] <condisco> *vt* 1. CULIN

(*insalata*) to dress; (*pasta*) to put the sauce on
2. *fig* to spice up
condiscendente [kon·diʃ·ʃen·'dɛn·te] *agg*
(*cedevole*) indulgent
condiscendere [kon·diʃ·'ʃen·de·re] <irr> *vi*
(*cedere*) to agree; ~ **a qc** to agree to sth
condividere [kon·di·'vi:·de·re] <irr> *vt* (*opinioni, idee*) to share; (*scelta*) to agree with
condivisibile [kon·di·vi·'zi:·bi·le] *agg* (*opinione, idea, punto di vista*) able to be shared;
(*decisione*) able to be agreed with
condivisione [kon·di·vi·'zio:·ne] *f* 1. (*di idee,
speranze*) sharing; **la** ~ **di qc** sharing in sth
2. COMPUT (*di dati, stampante*) sharing; **la** ~ **di
qc** sharing of sth
condizionale [kon·di·tsio·'na:·le] I. *agg* 1. LING
(*tempo, proposizione*) conditional 2. JUR **sospensione** ~ **della pena** suspended sentence
II. *m* LING conditional (mood) III. *f* 1. LING conditional (clause) 2. JUR suspended sentence
condizionamento [kon·di·tsio·na·'men·to]
m 1. (*climatizzazione*) air conditioning
2. PSYCH conditioning
condizionare [kon·di·tsio·'na:·re] *vt* 1. (*climatizzare*) to air-condition 2. PSYCH to condition
3. (*subordinare*) ~ **qc a qc** to make sth conditional on sth
condizionatore [kon·di·tsio·na·'to:·re] *m*
(~ *d'aria*) air-conditioner
condizione [kon·di·'tsio:·ne] *f* 1. (*requisito*)
condition; **porre delle -i** to lay down conditions; **a** ~ **che ...** +*conj* on condition that ...
2. *pl* COM conditions *pl* 3. (*stato*) condition; **-i
finanziarie** financial position; **-i di salute**
state of health; **essere in** ~ **di fare qc** to be in
a position to do sth
condoglianze [kon·doʎ·'ʎan·tse] *fpl* condolences; **fare le** ~ **a qu** to offer one's condolences to sb; '**sentite** ~' 'with deepest sympathy'
condominio [kon·do·'mi:·nio] <-i> *m* (*casa*)
condominium
condomino, -a [kon·'dɔ:·mi·no] *m, f* condominium owner
condonare [kon·do·'na:·re] *vt* (*pena, debito*)
to remit
condono [kon·'do:·no] *m* remission; ~ **fiscale**
tax amnesty; ~ **edilizio** amnesty for infringing
building regulations
condor ['kɔn·dor] <-> *m* condor
condotta [kon·'dot·ta] *f* 1. (*comportamento*)
conduct; **voto di** ~ grade for conduct 2. SPORT
~ **di gioco** play 3. TEC (*tubazione*) pipe
condottiero [kon·dot·'tiɛ:·ro] *m* HIST, MIL
leader
condotto [kon·'dɔt·to] *m* 1. ANAT duct;
~ **uditivo** auditory canal; ~ **lacrimale** tear
duct 2. TEC (*tubazione*) pipe
condotto, -a I. *pp di* **condurre** II. *agg*
medico ~ local authority country doctor
conducente [kon·du·'tʃɛn·te] *mf* (*di veicolo*)
driver
condurre [kon·'dur·re] <conduco, condussi,

condotto> I. *vt* 1.(*veicolo, treno*) to drive; (*nave*) to steer; ~ **in porto** *fig* (*affare, vittoria*) to pull off 2.(*accompagnare*) to take 3.(*azienda*) to run 4.(*trattative*) to hold 5.(*vita*) to lead 6. SPORT ~ **la gara** to lead 7. *fig* (*portare*) ~ **a termine qc** to complete sth II. *vi* 1. SPORT to lead; ~ **per due a zero** to lead two to nothing 2.(*strada*) to lead

conduttivo, -a [kon·dut·'tiː·vo] *agg* (*materiale, metallo*) conductive

conduttore [kon·dut·'toː·re] *m* PHYS conductor

conduttore, -trice I. *agg* leading; **filo** ~ *fig* leitmotif II. *m, f* 1. FERR (*bigliettaio*) guard 2. MOT (*di auto da corsa*) driver 3. DIR (*di contratto*) lessee 4. TV, RADIO (*di trasmissione*) host

conduttura [kon·dut·'tuː·ra] *f* (*di scarico*) pipe; (*elettrica, idrica*) main

conduzione [kon·du·'tsioː·ne] *f* 1.(*gestione*) management; **ristorante a** ~ **familiare** family-run restaurant 2. PHYS conduction 3. TV, RADIO (*presentazione: di trasmissione*) hosting

confabulare [kon·fa·bu·'laː·re] *vi scherz* to talk

confarsi [kon·'far·si] *vr* 1.(*addirsi*) ~ **a qu** to be suitable for sb 2.(*giovare*) ~ **a qu** to be good for sb

CONFARTIGIANATO [kon·far·ti·dʒa·'naː·to] *f acro di* Confederazione Generale dell'Artigianato Italiano *Italian crafts confederation*

CONFCOMMERCIO [konf·kom·'mɛr·tʃo] *f acro di* Confederazione Generale del Commercio *Italian trade confederation*

confederale [kon·fe·de·'raː·le] *agg* (*ente, organizzazione, sindacato*) confederal

confederato, -a [kon·fe·de·'raː·to] I. *agg* 1.(*ente, organizzazione, sindacato*) confederate 2.(*della guerra di secessione*) Confederate II. *m, f* (*della guerra di secessione*) Confederate

confederazione [kon·fe·de·ra·'tsioː·ne] *f* (*di Stati, organizzazioni, enti*) confederation; **la Confederazione Elvetica** the Swiss Confederation

conferenza [kon·fe·'rɛn·tsa] *f* 1.(*discorso*) lecture; **tenere una** ~ **su qc** to give a lecture on sth; ~ **stampa** press conference 2.(*riunione*) conference; ~ **al vertice** summit conference

conferimento [kon·fe·ri·'men·to] *m* (*di medaglia, premio, titolo*) awarding; (*di incarico*) assignment

conferire [kon·fe·'riː·re] <conferisco> I. *vt* (*premio, titolo*) to award; (*incarico*) to assign II. *vi* (*colloquiare*) to confer

conferma [kon·'fer·ma] *f* confirmation; **trovare** [*o* **avere**] ~ to get confirmation

confermare [kon·fer·'maː·re] I. *vt* to confirm II. *vr:* **-rsi** 1.(*rafforzarsi: sospetto, dubbio*) to be confirmed 2.(*affermarsi: come artista, autore*) to establish oneself

CONFESERCENTI [kon·fe·zer·'tʃɛn·ti] *f acro di* Confederazione degli Esercenti Attività Commerciali e Turistiche *Italian confedera-* tion for people working in commerce and tourism

confessare [kon·fes·'saː·re] I. *vt* 1. REL (*peccato*) to confess 2. REL (*fedeli*) ~ **qn** to hear sb's confession 3.(*a persona amica*) to confess 4.(*delitto*) to confess to 5.(*ammettere: colpa, errori*) to admit II. *vr:* **-rsi** REL to go to confession

confessionale [kon·fes·sio·'naː·le] I. *m* confessional II. *agg* confessional; **segreto** ~ secrecy of the confessional

confessione [kon·fes·'sioː·ne] *f* REL, JUR confession

confessore [kon·fes·'soː·re] *m* REL confessor

confetto [kon·'fɛt·to] *m* CULIN sugared almond

confettura [kon·fet·'tuː·ra] *f* (*marmellata*) jam

confezionamento [kon·fe·tsio·na·'men·to] *m* packaging; **data di** ~ date of packaging

confezionare [kon·fe·tsio·'naː·re] *vt* 1.(*vestito*) to make 2.(*incartare: merci, regali*) to wrap 3.(*imballare: pacco*) to package

confezionatrice [kon·fe·tsio·na·'triː·tʃe] *f* (*macchina*) packaging machine

confezione [kon·fe·'tsioː·ne] *f* 1.(*pacco*) pack; ~ **regalo** gift pack; ~ **di cioccolatini** box of chocolates 2.(*vestiti*) clothes *pl*

conficcare [kon·fik·'kaː·re] I. *vt* 1.(*ficcare: chiodo, palo*) to drive in 2. *fig* (*nella mente*) to put in II. *vr:* **-rsi** 1.(*penetrare*) to lodge 2.(*nella mente*) **quel film mi si è conficcato in testa!** I can't get that movie out of my head!

confidare [kon·fi·'daː·re] I. *vt* to confide; ~ **qc a qu** to confide sth to sb II. *vi* (*aver fiducia*) to have confidence; ~ **in qu** to have confidence in sb III. *vr* **-rsi con qu** to confide in sb

confidente [kon·fi·'dɛn·te] *mf* 1.(*persona amica*) confidant *m*, confidante *f* 2.(*informatore: di polizia*) informer

confidenza [kon·fi·'dɛn·tsa] *f* 1.(*familiarità*) familiarity; **essere in** ~ **con qu** to be friends with sb; **prendere** ~ **con qc** to become confident with sth; **prendersi la** ~ **di fare qc** to take the liberty of doing sth 2.(*segreto*) confidence; **fare una** ~ **a qu** to share a confidence with sb

configurare [kon·fi·gu·'raː·re] I. *vt* COMPUT to configure II. *vr:* **-rsi -rsi come qc** to look like being sth

configurazione [kon·fi·gu·ra·'tsioː·ne] *f* 1. COMPUT configuration 2.(*aspetto, forma*) shape 3. GEOG (*di terreno*) contour

confinante [kon·fi·'nan·te] *agg* (*stanza, terreno*) adjacent; **paese** ~ neighboring country

confinare [kon·fi·'naː·re] I. *vi* to be adjacent; ~ **con qc** to be adjacent to sth II. *vt* 1. HIST to intern 2. *fig* (*relegare*) to confine

confinato, -a [kon·fi·'naː·to] *m, f* HIST internee

CONFINDUSTRIA [kon·fin·'dus·tria] *f acro di* Confederazione Generale dell'Industria Italiana *Italian employers' confederation*

confine [kon·'fiː·ne] *m* border; **ai** ~ **-i del mondo** *fig* to the ends of the earth

confino [kon·'fiː·no] *m* HIST internment

confisca [kon·'fis·ka] <-sche> *f* JUR (*di beni, terreni*) confiscation

confiscare [kon·fis·'ka:·re] *vt* JUR (*beni, terreni*) to confiscate

conflitto [kon·'flit·to] *m* conflict; ~ **a fuoco** firefight; ~ **mondiale** world war; ~ **d'interessi** conflict of interests; **essere in** ~ to be in conflict

confluenza [kon·flu·'ɛn·tsa] *f* confluence

confluire [kon·flu·'i:·re] <confluisco> *vi* **1.** GEOG (*fiumi*) to meet **2.** *fig* (*convergere: persone, contributi, idee*) to come together

confondere [kon·'fon·de·re] <irr> **I.** *vt* to confuse **II.** *vr:* -rsi **1.** (*mescolarsi*) to mingle; -rsi **tra la folla** to mingle with the crowd **2.** (*immagini, suoni, colori*) to merge **3.** (*sbagliarsi*) to get confused **4.** (*turbarsi*) to get flustered

conformare [kon·for·'ma:·re] **I.** *vt* (*adeguare*) ~ **qc a qc** to adapt sth to sth **II.** *vr* -rsi **a qc** to comply with sth

conforme [kon·'for·me] *agg* **essere ~ a qc** to conform to sth; **essere ~ alle norme** to comply with the regulations

conformismo [kon·for·'miz·mo] *m* conformism

conformista [kon·for·'mis·ta] <-i , -e> *mf* conformist

conformità [kon·for·mi·'ta] <-> *f* conformity; **in ~ a** [*o* **con**] in conformity with

confort [kɔ̃·'fɔr/kon·'fɔrt] <-> *m* comfort

confortante [kon·for·'tan·te] *agg* (*parole, pensiero*) comforting

confortare [kon·for·'ta:·re] **I.** *vt* **1.** (*consolare*) to comfort **2.** (*tesi, assunto*) to support **II.** *vr:* -rsi **1.** (*farsi animo*) to console oneself **2.** (*consolarsi*) to comfort each other

confortevole [kon·for·'te:·vo·le] *agg* **1.** (*comodo: ambiente, auto*) comfortable **2.** (*consolante: parole, pensiero*) comforting

conforto [kon·'fɔr·to] *m* **1.** (*consolazione*) comfort; **portare ~ a qu** to give comfort to sb **2.** (*sostegno*) support

confraternita [kon·fra·ter·ni·'ta] *f* brotherhood

confrontare [kon·fron·'ta:·re] *vt* (*offerte, prezzi, tariffe*) to compare

confronto [kon·'fron·to] *m* **1.** (*paragone*) comparison; **fare un ~** (**fra**) to make a comparison (between); **mettere a ~** to compare; **in ~ a** in comparison with; **reggere al ~ con qu/qc** to stand in comparison with sb/sth; **senza -i** incomparable; **non c'è ~!** there's no comparison! **2.** JUR (*contraddittorio*) confrontation **3.** (*loc*) **nei -i di** toward

confusi [kon·'fu:·zi] *1. pers sing pass rem di* **confondere**

confusionario, -a [kon·fu·zio·'na:·rio] <-i, -ie> **I.** *agg* (*pensieri, ricordi*) jumbled; (*persona*) muddle-headed **II.** *m, f* muddlehead

confusione [kon·fu·'zio:·ne] *f* **1.** (*disordine*) mess **2.** (*agitazione*) confusion **3.** (*imbarazzo*) embarrassment

confuso, -a [kon·'fu:·zo] **I.** *pp di* **confondere**

II. *agg* (*discorso, situazione, persona*) confused

confutare [kon·fu·'ta:·re] *vt* (*tesi, teoria*) to refute

congedare [kon·dʒe·'da:·re] **I.** *vt* **1.** *geh* (*accomiatare: ospiti*) to say goodbye to **2.** MIL to dismiss **II.** *vr:* -rsi (*accomiatarsi*) to say goodbye

congedo [kon·'dʒɛ:·do] *m* leave; **prendere ~ da** to take one's leave of; **essere in ~** to be on leave; **~ parentale** parental leave

congegno [kon·'dʒeɲ·ɲo] *m* (*apparecchio*) device

congelamento [kon·dʒe·la·'men·to] *m* **1.** (*raffreddamento, blocco*) freezing **2.** MED frostbite

congelare [kon·dʒe·'la:·re] **I.** *vt* (*alimenti, embrioni, credito, finanziamento*) to freeze **II.** *vr:* -rsi PHYS, MED to freeze

congelatore [kon·dʒe·la·'to:·re] *m* freezer

congeniale [kon·dʒe·'nia:·le] *agg* (*clima, luogo, lavoro*) congenial

congenito, -a [kon·'dʒɛ:·ni·to] *agg* (*malformazione, malattia*) congenital

congestionare [kon·dʒes·tio·'na:·re] *vt* to congest

congestione [kon·dʒes·'tio:·ne] *f* congestion

congettura [kon·dʒet·'tu:·ra] *f* (*ipotesi*) conjecture

congiungere [kon·'dʒun·dʒe·re] <irr> **I.** *vt* (*tubi, linee, punti, mani*) to join; ~ **in matrimonio** to join in matrimony **II.** *vr* **1.** (*strade, linee*) to join **2.** *fig* -rsi **in matrimonio** to be joined in matrimony

congiuntivite [kon·dʒun·ti·'vi:·te] *f* conjunctivitis

congiuntivo [kon·dʒun·'ti:·vo] *m* LING subjunctive

congiunto, -a [kon·'dʒun·to] **I.** *agg* (*comunicato, divorzio*) joint **II.** *m, f* relative

congiuntura [kon·dʒun·'tu:·ra] *f* COM situation

congiunturale [kon·dʒun·tu·'ra:·le] *agg* (*analisi, crisi*) economic

congiunzione [kon·dʒun·'tsio:·ne] *f* LING, ASTR conjunction

congiura [kon·'dʒu:·ra] *f* conspiracy

congiurare [kon·dʒu·'ra:·re] *vi* to conspire; ~ **contro qu/qc** to conspire against sb/sth

conglomerare [koŋ·glo·me·'ra:·re] *vt* COM (*imprese*) to conglomerate

conglomerato [koŋ·glo·me·'ra:·to] *m* conglomerate

congratularsi [koŋ·gra·tu·'lar·si] *vr* ~ **con qu per qc** to congratulate sb on sth

congratulazione [koŋ·gra·tu·la·'tsio:·ne] *f* congratulation; **fare le -i a qu per qc** to congratulate sb on sth; **-i!** congratulations! *pl*

congrega [koŋ·'grɛ:·ga] <-ghe> *f* **1.** *pej* (*combriccola*) bunch *pej* **2.** REL congregation

congregazione [koŋ·gre·ga·'tsio:·ne] *f* REL congregation

congressista [koŋ·gres·'sis·ta] <-i , -e> *mf*

conference attendee
congresso [koŋ·'grɛs·so] *m* conference
congruente [koŋ·gru·'ɛn·te] *agg* **1.**(*rispondente*) ~ **a** [*o* **con**] **qc** consistent with sth **2.** MATH congruent
congruenza [koŋ·gru·'ɛn·tsa] *f* **1.**(*corrispondenza*) consistency **2.** MATH congruence
congruo, -a ['kɔŋ·gruo] *agg* **1.**(*adeguato: assegno, compenso*) adequate **2.** MATH congruent
conguaglio [koŋ·'guaʎ·ʎo] <-gli> *m* **1.**(*pareggio*) balancing; ~ **salariale** salary adjustment; ~ **fiscale** *tax adjustment* **2.**(*somma*) balance
coniare [ko·'nia:·re] *vt* **1.** FIN (*moneta*) to mint **2.** *fig* (*parola*) to coin
conico, -a ['kɔ:·ni·ko] <-ci, -che> *agg* (*bicchiere, vaso, valvola*) conical
conifera [ko·'ni:·fe·ra] *f* BOT conifer
coniglio [ko·'niʎ·ʎo] <-gli> *m* **1.** ZOO rabbit **2.** *fig* (*persona paurosa*) chicken
coniugare [kon·iu·'ga:·re] **I.** *vt* **1.** LING (*verbo*) to conjugate **2.** *fig* (*unire*) to combine **II.** *vr:* **-rsi** (*combinarsi*) to combine
coniugazione [kon·iu·ga·'tsio:·ne] *f* LING conjugation
coniuge ['kɔn·iu·dʒe] *mf* spouse
connazionale [kon·na·tsio·'na:·le] **I.** *agg* (*persona, cittadino*) from the same country **II.** *mf* fellow countryman *m*, fellow countrywoman *f*
connection [kə·'nɛk·ʃən] <-> *f* (*relazione*) connection altolocate; ~ **tra** ... connection between ...
connessi [kon·'nɛs·si] *mpl* **con tutti gli annessi e i** ~ with all that goes with it
connessione [kon·nes·'sio:·ne] *f* connection; ~ **a banda larga** broadband connection
connesso, -a [kon·'nɛs·so] *agg* connected
connettere [kon·'nɛt·te·re] <connetto, con­nettei, connesso> **I.** *vt* to connect **II.** *vi* (*pensare*) to think straight; **non riesco a** ~ I can't think straight **III.** *vr:* **-rsi** (*collegarsi*) to connect
connettivo, -a *agg* MED **tessuto** ~ connective tissue
connivente [kon·ni·'vɛn·te] **I.** *agg* conniving **II.** *mf* conniving person
connotato [kon·no·'ta:·to] *m* **cambiare i -i a qu** *scherz, inf* to beat sb up
connotazione [kon·no·ta·'tsio:·ne] *f* connotation
connubio [kon·'nu:·bio] <-i> *m fig* (*unione*) marriage *fig*
cono ['kɔ:·no] *m* MATH cone; ~ **gelato** ice-cream cone; **a** ~ cone-shaped
conobbi [ko·'nob·bi] *1. pers sing pass rem di* **conoscere**
conoscente [ko·noʃ·'ʃɛn·te] *mf* acquaintance
conoscenza [ko·noʃ·'ʃɛn·tsa] *f* **1.**(*apprendimento*) knowledge; **avere** ~ **di qc** to have knowledge of sth; **essere a** ~ **di qc** to know sth; **per** ~ for information; **venire a** ~ **di qc** to find out about sth; **prendere** ~ **di qc** ADM to

take cognizance of sth **2.** MED consciousness; **perdere la** ~ to lose consciousness; **privo di** ~ unconscious **3.**(*persona*) acquaintance; **avere molte -e** to have many acquaintances; **fare la** ~ **di qu** to make sb's acquaintance; **"piacere di fare la sua** ~**"** "pleased to meet you"; **una vecchia** ~ an old acquaintance
conoscere [ko·'noʃ·ʃe·re] <conosco, con­obbi, conosciuto> **I.** *vt* **1.**(*persona, metodo, ristorante, lingua*) to know; ~ **qu di vista/ personalmente** to know sb by sight/personally; **ti faccio** ~ **mio fratello** I'll introduce you to my brother; **conosco i miei polli** *scherz* I know who I'm dealing with **2.**(*incontrare*) to meet **II.** *vr:* **-rsi 1.**(*incontrarsi*) to meet **2.**(*essere amici*) to know each other
conoscitore, -trice [ko·noʃ·ʃi·'to:·re] *m, f* (*di musica, vini*) connoisseur
conosciuto, -a [ko·noʃ·'ʃu:·to] **I.** *pp di* **conoscere II.** *agg* (*albergo, personaggio, libro*) well-known
conosco [ko·'nos·ko] *1. pers sing pr di* **conoscere**
conquista [koŋ·'kuis·ta] *f* **1.**(*ottenimento: di diritto, potere, libertà*) gaining **2.** MIL conquest **3.**(*progresso: scientifico*) achievement **4.** *fig* (~ *amorosa*) conquest
conquistare [koŋ·kuis·'ta:·re] *vt* **1.**(*ottenere: diritto, potere, libertà*) to gain **2.** MIL to conquer **3.** *fig* (*persona*) to win over; (*amicizia, amore, simpatia*) to win
conquistatore, -trice [koŋ·kuis·ta·'to:·re] *m, f* MIL conqueror **2.** *fig* (*seduttore*) ladykiller
consacrare [kon·sa·'kra:·re] **I.** *vt* **1.** REL (*sacerdote*) to ordain **2.**(*re, imperatore*) to anoint **3.**(*dedicare: vita*) to devote **II.** *vr:* **-rsi** to devote oneself
consacrazione [kon·sak·ra·'tsio:·ne] *f* **1.** REL (*destinazione al culto*) consecration **2.** REL (*durante la messa*) Consacration
consanguineo, -a [kon·saŋ·'gui:·neo] <-ei, -ee> **I.** *agg* (*donatore*) related by blood **II.** *m, f* blood relative
consapevole [kon·sa·'pe:·vo·le] *agg* (*persona*) aware; **essere** ~ **di qc** to be aware of sth
consapevolizzare [kon·sa·pe·vo·lid·'dza:·re] **I.** *vt* to make aware; ~ **qu circa** [*o* **rispetto a**] **qc** to make sb aware of sth **II.** *vr* **-rsi di qc** to become aware of sth
conscio, -a ['kɔnʃ·ʃo] <-sci, -sce> *agg* conscious; **essere** ~ **di qc** to be conscious of sth
consecutiva [kon·se·ku·'ti:·va] *f* LING consecutive clause
consecutivo, -a [kon·se·ku·'ti:·vo] *agg* **1.**(*seguente: giorno*) next **2.**(*che si sussegue: numeri, ore, risultati*) consecutive **3.**(*traduzione, interprete, congiunzione, proposizione*) consecutive
consegna [kon·'seɲ·ɲa] *f* **1.**(*di merci*) delivery; **pagamento alla** ~ cash on delivery **2.** ADM **passare le -e a qu** to hand over to sb **3.**(*custodia*) care; **ricevere in** ~ to be entrusted with

consegnare [kon·seɲ·'ɲa:·re] *vt* **1.** (*recapitare: posta, merce*) to deliver **2.** (*affidare*) to hand over

conseguente [kon·se·'gu ɛn·te] *agg* **1.** (*danno, disturbi*) consequent **2.** (*ragionamento, deduzione*) consistent

conseguenza [kon·se·'gu ɛn·tsa] *f* (*effetto*) consequence; **in ~ di qc** as a consequence of sth; **agire di ~** to act accordingly

conseguimento [kon·se·gui·'men·to] *m* obtaining

conseguire [kon·se·'gui:·re] **I.** *vt* (*patente, diploma, qualifica, diritto*) to obtain; (*obiettivo*) to achieve **II.** *vi* to follow; **ne consegue che ...** it follows that ...

consenso [kon·'sɛn·so] *m* consent; **il ~ a qc** consent to sth; **dare il ~ a qc** to give one's consent to sth; **tacito ~** tacit consent

consensuale [kon·sen·su·'a:·le] *agg* (*separazione, accordo*) by mutual consent

consentire [kon·sen·'ti:·re] *vt* to allow

consenziente [kon·sen·'tsi ɛn·te] *agg* consenting

conserva [kon·'sɛr·va] *f* (*di frutta*) preserve; **~ di pomodoro** canned tomato sauce; **carciofi in ~** canned artichokes; **tonno/carne in ~** canned tuna/meat

conservabile [kon·ser·'va:·bi·le] *agg* (*cibo, vernice*) able to be kept

conservante [kon·ser·'van·te] *m* preservative

conservare [kon·ser·'va:·re] **I.** *vt* **1.** CULIN (*frutta, carne, pesce*) to preserve **2.** (*custodire*) to keep **3.** *fig* (*mantenere*) to hold **II.** *vr:* **-rsi** **1.** CULIN (*frutta, carne, pesce*) to keep **2.** (*mantenersi: persona*) **-rsi in salute** to keep (oneself) healthy; **-rsi bene** to be well preserved

conservatore, -trice [kon·ser·va·'to:·re] **I.** *agg* (*partito, idee, teorie*) conservative **II.** *m, f* conservative

conservatorio [kon·ser·va·'tɔ:·rio] <-i> *m* MUS conservatory

conservazione [kon·ser·va·'tsio:·ne] *f* **1.** (*gener*) preservation; **istinto di ~** instinct for self-preservation **2.** (*di edificio, quadro*) conservation

considerare [kon·si·de·'ra:·re] *vt* **1.** (*tenere conto, ritenere*) to consider; **tutto considerato** all things considered; **considerata la sua età** considering his [*o* her] age **2.** (*esaminare*) to examine **3.** (*stimare*) **~ qu molto** to think highly of sb

considerazione [kon·si·de·ra·'tsio:·ne] *f* **1.** (*osservazione*) observation **2.** (*esame*) consideration; **prendere in ~** to take into consideration; **in ~ di qc** in consideration of sth **3.** (*stima*) esteem; **essere tenuto in gran ~** to be held in high esteem

considerevole [kon·si·de·'re:·vo·le] *agg* (*somma, numero, sforzo, interesse*) considerable

consigliabile [kon·si ʎ·'ʎa:·bi·le] *agg* advisable

consigliare [kon·si ʎ·'ʎa:·re] **I.** *vt* to recom-

mend; **~ a qu di fare qc** to advise sb to do sth **II.** *vr:* **-rsi** to get advice

consigliere, -a [kon·si ʎ·'ʎ ɛ:·re] *m, f* **1.** (*chi dà consigli*) adviser **2.** ADM councilor; **~ d'amministrazione** member of the board; **~ di Stato** member of the Council of State

consiglio [kon·'si ʎ·ʎo] <-gli> *m* **1.** (*suggerimento*) advice; **chiedere un ~ a qu** to ask sb for advice; **dare un ~ a qu** to give sb advice; **la notte porta ~** *prov* it's best to sleep on it **2.** ADM (*organo, riunione*) council; **il ~ d'amministrazione** [*o* direttivo] the board of directors; **Consiglio Europeo** EU Council of Europe; **~ di fabbrica** works committee; **Consiglio dei Ministri** Cabinet; **Consiglio di Stato** Council of State; **sala del ~** council chamber

> **i** The **Consiglio dei Ministri** is the Italian cabinet. It is chaired by the **Presidente del Consiglio** (Prime Minister) and its members are taken from among the government ministers.

consistente [kon·sis·'tɛn·te] *agg* **1.** (*materiale, tessuto, sabbia*) firm **2.** *fig* (*notevole: somma, richiesta, aumento*) substantial

consistenza [kon·sis·'tɛn·tsa] *f* **1.** (*di crema*) consistency; (*di materiale, tessuto*) texture **2.** *fig* (*fondatezza*) substance; **prendere ~** to gain substance

consistere [kon·'sis·te·re] <consisto, consistei *o* consistetti, consistito> *vi* essere **1.** (*basarsi su*) **~ in qc** to consist in sth **2.** (*essere composto di*) **~ di qc** to consist of sth

consociata [kon·so·'t ʃa:·ta] *f* associated company

consociato, -a **I.** *agg* (*azienda*) associated **II.** *m, f* associate

consocio, -a [kon·'sɔ:·t ʃo] *m, f* associate; **~ in affari** business associate

consolare [kon·so·'la:·re] **I.** *vt* (*bambino*) to console **II.** *vr* **-rsi di qc** to console oneself with sth

consolato [kon·so·'la:·to] *m* consulate

consolatore, -trice [kon·so·la·'to:·re] *agg* (*parole, mano*) consoling

consolazione [kon·so·la·'tsio:·ne] *f* consolation; **premio di ~** consolation prize

console ['kɔn·so·le] *m* consul

consolidamento [kon·so·li·da·'men·to] *m* **1.** (*di struttura, terreno*) consolidation **2.** *fig* (*rinsaldamento: di amicizia, rapporti*) strengthening

consolidare [kon·so·li·'da:·re] **I.** *vt* **1.** (*rendere solido*) to consolidate **2.** *fig* (*rinsaldare: amicizia, conoscenza, posizione*) to strengthen **II.** *vr:* **-rsi** **1.** (*diventare solido*) to consolidate **2.** (*amicizia, conoscenza*) to strengthen

consolidato [kon·so·li·'da:·to] *m* funded debt

consolidato, -a *agg* **1.** COM (*bilancio*) consolidated **2.** *fig* (*rinsaldato: tradizione*) well-established

consolle [kon·'sɔl·le] <-> *f* (*tastiera*) console

consommé [kɔ̃·sɔ·'me] <-> *m* consommé

consonante [kon·so·'nan·te] *f* consonant

consono, -a ['kɔn·so·no] *agg* ~ **a qc** in keeping with sth

consorte [kon·'sɔr·te] *mf* consort

consorzio [kon·'sɔrt·sio] <-i> *m* JUR consortium

constare [kons·'ta:·re] *vi essere* 1. (*essere costituito*) ~ **di qc** to consist of sth 2. (*risultare*) **a quanto mi consta** as far as I know

constatare [kons·ta·'ta:·re] *vt* to note

constatazione [kons·ta·ta·'tsio:·ne] *f* observation

consueto, -a *agg* usual

consuetudine [kon·sue·'tu:·di·ne] *f* 1. (*abitudine*) habit; **avere la** ~ **di fare qc** to be in the habit of doing sth 2. (*costume*) custom

consulente [kon·su·'lɛn·te] *mf* consultant; ~ **legale/tributario** legal/tax consultant

consulenza [kon·su·'lɛn·tsa] *f* (*legale, tecnica*) advice

consulta [kon·'sul·ta] *f* (*Corte Costituzionale*) Constitutional Court

consultare [kon·sul·'ta:·re] I. *vt* (*medico, avvocato, libro*) to consult II. *vr:* **-rsi** to get advice; **-rsi con qu** to consult sb

consultazione [kon·sul·ta·'tsio:·ne] *f* (*dare consigli, ricerca*) consultation; **opere di** ~ reference works

consultivo, -a [kon·sul·'ti:·vo] *agg* consultative

consultorio [kon·sul·'tɔ:·rio] <-i> *m* clinic; ~ **familiare** family planning clinic

consumare [kon·su·'ma:·re] I. *vt* 1. (*rovinare: scarpe, cinturino, gomme*) to wear out 2. (*mangiare: pasti, cibo*) to consume 3. (*matrimonio*) to consummate; (*delitto*) to commit II. *vr:* **-rsi** (*logorarsi: scarpe, gomme*) to wear out; **-rsi la vista** to ruin one's eyesight

consumato, -a [kon·su·'ma:·to] *agg* 1. (*consunto: vestiti, scarpe*) worn-out 2. (*matrimonio*) consummated

consumatore, -trice [kon·su·ma·'to:·re] *m, f* consumer

consumazione [kon·su·ma·'tsio:·ne] *f* (*bevanda*) beverage; (*spuntino*) snack

consumismo [kon·su·'miz·mo] *m* consumerism

consumistico, -a [kon·su·'mis·ti·ko] <-ci, -che> *agg* (*società, logica, abitudini*) consumer

consumo [kon·'su:·mo] *m* (*uso*) consumption; **civiltà dei -i** consumer society; **beni di** ~ consumer goods

consunto, -a [kon·'sun·to] *agg* 1. (*consumato: scarpe, indumenti*) worn-out 2. (*volto*) haggard

consuocero, -a [kon·'suɔ:·tʃe·ro] *m, f* son's *m* father-in-law [*o* daughter's], son's *f* mother-in-law [*o* daughter's]

conta ['kon·ta] *f* **fare la** ~ (*nei giochi*) to de-

contabile [kon·ta··bi·le] I. *agg* (*operazione, revisione*) accounting II. *mf* accountant

contabilità [kon·ta·bi·li·'ta] <-> *f* 1. (*operazioni contabili*) accounting; **tenere la** ~ to do the bookkeeping; **ufficio** ~ accounts department 2. (*ragioneria*) accountancy

contachilometri [kon·ta·ki·'lɔ:·met·ri] <-> *m* odometer

contacopie [kon·ta·'kɔ:·pie] <-> *m* TEC sheet counter

contadino, -a [kon·ta·'di:·no] I. *m, f* 1. AGR farmer; **~, scarpe grosse e cervello fino** *prov* he [*o* she] is not as stupid as he [*o* she] looks 2. *pej* (*persona dai modi grossolani*) boor II. *agg* (*cultura, usanza*) peasant; **casa -a** country cottage

contagiare [kon·ta·'dʒa:·re] *vt a. fig* to infect

contagio [kon·'ta:·dʒo] <-gi> *m* infection

contagioso, -a [kon·ta·'dʒo:·so] *agg a. fig* infectious

contagiri [kon·ta·'dʒi:·ri] <-> *m* AUTO tachometer

contagocce [kon·ta·'got·tʃe] <-> *m* dropper; **con il** ~ *scherz* little by little

container [kən·'tei·nə/kon·'tɛi·ner] <-> *m* container

contaminare [kon·ta·mi·'na:·re] *vt* (*acqua, aria, cibo, ferita*) to contaminate

contaminazione [kon·ta·mi·na·'tsio:·ne] *f* (*di acqua, aria, cibo, ferita*) contamination

contaminuti [kon·ta·mi·'nu:·ti] <-> *m* timer

contante [kon·'tan·te] I. *agg* **denaro** [*o* **moneta**] ~ cash II. *m* cash; **pagare in -i** to pay (in) cash

contare [kon·'ta:·re] I. *vt* 1. (*numerare, calcolare*) to count; ~ **i giorni/le ore/i minuti** *fig* to count the days/the hours/the minutes *fig*; **senza** ~ not counting 2. (*proporsi*) ~ **di fare qc** +*inf* to think of doing sth II. *vi* 1. (*numeri*) to count; ~ **fino a trenta** to count up to thirty 2. (*valere*) to count 3. (*fare assegnamento*) ~ **su qu/qc** to count on sb/sth

contascatti [kon·ta·'skat·ti] <-> *m* TEL unit counter

contasecondi [kon·ta·se·'kon·di] <-> *m* stopwatch

contato, -a [kon·'ta:·to] *agg* **avere i soldi -i** (*pochi*) to have very little money; (*giusti*) to have the right money; **ha le ore -e** his [*o* her] [*o* its] days are numbered; **avere i minuti -i** not to have a minute to spare

contatore [kon·ta·'to:·re] *m* (*di gas, acqua*) meter

contattare [kon·tat·'ta:·re] *vt* (*persona, azienda, ufficio*) to contact

contatto [kon·'tat·to] *m* contact; **mantenere i -i con qu** to keep in contact with sb; **prendere** ~ **con qu** to get in contact with sb; **essere in** ~ **con qu** to be in contact with sb; **venire a** ~ **con** to come into contact with; **lenti a** ~ contact lenses

conte, -essa ['kon·te, kon·'tes·sa] *m, f* count

m [*o* countess] *f*

conteggio [kon·'ted·dʒo] <-ggi> *m* count; ~ **alla rovescia** countdown

contegno [kon·'teɲ·ɲo] *m* 1.(*compostezza*) composure; **darsi un** ~ to compose oneself 2.(*comportamento*) behavior

contemplare [kon·tem·'pla:·re] *vt* 1.(*ammirare: quadro, paesaggio, tramonto*) to gaze at 2.(*prevedere*) to provide for

contemplativo, -a [kon·tem·pla·'ti:·vo] *agg* contemplative

contemplazione [kon·tem·pla·'tsio:·ne] *f* contemplation

contempo [kon·'tɛm·po] *m* **nel** ~ in the meantime

contemporaneamente [kon·tem·po·ra·nea·'men·te] *avv* simultaneously

contemporaneità [kon·tem·po·ra·nei·'ta] <-> *f* contemporaneousness

contemporaneo, -a [kon·tem·po·'ra:·neo] <-ei, -ee> I. *agg* 1.(*simultaneo*) simultaneous 2.HIST contemporary; **storia -a** contemporary history II. *m, f* contemporary

contendente [kon·ten·'dɛn·te] I. *agg* competing II. *mf* adversary

contendere [kon·'tɛn·de·re] <irr> I. *vt* to compete for; ~ **qc a qu** to compete with sb for sth II. *vr* **-rsi qc** to compete for sth

contenere [kon·te·'ne:·re] <irr> I. *vt* 1.(*accogliere: persone, cose*) to contain 2.*fig* (*trattenere: lacrime*) to hold back; (*sdegno*) to keep in check; (*entusiasmo*) to contain; ~ **la piena di un fiume** to hold back a river in flood II. *vr:* **-rsi** (*moderarsi*) to contain oneself

contenitore [kon·te·ni·'to:·re] *m* container

contentare [kon·ten·'ta:·re] I. *vt* to satisfy II. *vr* **-rsi di qc** to content oneself with sth; **chi si contenta gode** *prov* enough is as good as a feast/ *prov*

contentezza [kon·ten·'tet·tsa] *f* happiness

contentino [kon·ten·'ti:·no] *m inf* sop

contento, -a [kon·'tɛn·to] *agg* 1.(*soddisfatto*) pleased; **essere** ~ **di qc** to be pleased with sth; **fare** ~ **qu** to please sb 2.(*lieto*) happy; **essere** ~ **di qc** to be happy about sth; **sono** ~ **per te** I'm happy for you

contenuto [kon·te·'nu:·to] *m* 1.(*di pacco, valigia*) contents *pl* 2.(*di libro, film*) content

contenuto, -a I. *pp di* **contenere** II. *agg* (*misurato: gioia, allegria*) restrained

contesa [kon·'te:·sa] *f* fight

contesi [kon·'te:·si] *1. pers sing pass rem di* **contendere**

conteso [kon·'te:·so] *pp di* **contendere**

contessa *f v.* **countess**

contestabile [kon·tes·'ta:·bi·le] *agg* questionable

contestare [kon·tes·'ta:·re] *vt* 1.(*negare: tesi, teoria*) to contest 2.JUR ~ **un infrazione a qu** to charge sb with an offense 3.POL, SOC (*protestare*) to protest against

contestatore, -trice [kon·tes·ta·'to:·re] *m, f* POL, SOC protester

contestazione [kon·tes·ta·'tsio:·ne] *f* 1.POL, SOC protest 2.JUR (*di infrazione*) notification 3.(*contrasto*) contesting

contesto [kon·'tɛs·to] *m a. fig* context

contestuale [kon·tes·tu·'a:·le] *agg* DIR (*contemporaneo*) contemporary

contestualizzare [kon·tes·tua·lid·'dza:·re] *vt* (*avvenimento, parola*) to contextualize

contiguità [kon·ti·gui·'ta] <-> *f* (*vicinanza*) proximity

contiguo, -a [kon·'ti:·guo] *agg* (*vicino: ambiente, edificio, terreno*) adjoining

continentale [kon·ti·nen·'ta:·le] I. *agg* (*clima, massa*) continental II. *mf* mainlander

continente [kon·ti·'nɛn·te] *m* 1.(*terre emerse*) continent; ~ **antico/nuovo** Old/New World 2.(*terraferma*) mainland

contingente [kon·tin·'dʒɛn·te] *m* 1.MIL contingent 2.COM quota

contingenza [kon·tin·'dʒɛn·tsa] *f* 1.(*circostanza*) contingency 2.(**indennità di**) ~ cost-of-living allowance

continuare [kon·ti·nu·'a:·re] I. *vt* (*studi, lavori, indagini*) to continue II. *vi* (*durare*) to continue; ~ **a fare qc** to continue to do sth; ~ **a dormire** to keep on sleeping

continuativo, -a [kon·ti·nua·'ti:·vo] *agg* (*lavoro*) permanent; (*attività*) continuous; **orario** ~ all-day opening; **impiego a carattere** ~ permanent job; **6 mesi -i** six consecutive months

continuazione [kon·ti·nua·'tsio:·ne] *f* (*di progetto*) continuation; (*di film, opera*) sequel; **in** ~ continuously

continuità [kon·ti·nui·'ta] <-> *f* continuity

continuo, -a [kon·'ti:·nuo] *agg* (*rumore*) continuous; (*lamentele*) continual; **di** ~ nonstop

conto ['kon·to] *m* 1.MATH count 2.COM (*di bar, ristorante*) check; **a -i fatti** *fig* all things considered; **fare i -i senza l'oste** *fig* to forget the most important thing 3.FIN (*in banca*) account 4.(*stima*) **tenere da** ~ **qc** to take great care of sth; **tenere in gran** ~ **qu/qc** to hold sb/sth in high regard 5.(*valutazione*) **tenere** ~ **di qc** to take account of sth 6.(*affidamento*) **far** ~ **su qu/qc** to count on sb/sth 7.(*interesse*) **per** ~ **di qu** on behalf of sb; **per** ~ **mio/tuo/suo** on my/your/his [*o* her] own 8.(*loc*) **fare i -i con qu** to sort things out with sb; **rendere** ~ **a qu di qc** to be accountable to sb for sth; **dire qc sul** ~ **di qu** to say sth about sb; **rendersi** ~ **di qc** to realize sth; **alla fin(e) dei -i** all things considered

contorcere [kon·'tɔr·tʃe·re] <irr> I. *vt* to twist II. *vr:* **-rsi** to twist

contorno [kon·'tor·no] *m* 1.CULIN side order 2.(*di disegno, volto*) outline

contorsi *1. pers sing pass rem di* **contorcere**

contorsione [kon·tor·'sio:·ne] *f* contortion

contorsionista [kon·tor·sio·'nis·ta] <-i , -e> *mf* contortionist

contorto, -a [kon·'tɔr·to] I. *pp di* **contorcere** II. *agg* 1.(*storto: tronco, rami*) twisted 2.*fig* (*pensiero, mente*) tortuous

contrabbandare [kon·trab·ban·'da:·re] *vt* to smuggle

contrabbandiere, -a [kon·trab·ban·'diɛ:·re] *m, f* smuggler

contrabbando [kon·trab·'ban·do] *m* smuggling; **di** ~ contraband

contrabbasso [kon·trab·'bas·so] *m* double bass

contraccambiare [kon·trak·kam·'bia:·re] *vt* (*amore, simpatia*) to reciprocate

contraccambio [kon·trak·'kam·bio] *m* reciprocation; **in** ~ in return

contraccettivo [kon·trat·tʃet·'ti:·vo] *m* contraceptive

contraccettivo, -a *agg* (*metodo, pillola*) contraceptive

contraccolpo [kon·trak·'kol·po] *m* 1.(*urto*) recoil 2.*fig* (*ripercussione*) repercussion

contraddire [kon·trad·'di:·re] <irr> I. *vt* to contradict II. *vr:* -**rsi** to contradict oneself

contraddistinguere [kon·trad·dis·'tiŋ·gue·re] <irr> I. *vt* to mark out II. *vr* -**rsi per qc** to stand out because of sth

contraddittorio, -a <-i, -ie> *agg* contradictory

contraddizione [kon·trad·di·'tsio:·ne] *f* contradiction; **spirito di** ~ argumentativeness; **cadere in** ~ to contradict oneself

contraereo, -a *agg* (*armi, fuoco, postazione*) antiaircraft

contraffare [kon·traf·'fa:·re] <irr> *vt* (*falsificare: firma, documento*) to forge

contraffazione [kon·traf·fa·'tsio:·ne] *f* (*falsificazione: di firma, documento*) forgery

contraggo [kon·'trag·go] *1. pers sing pr di* **contrarre**

contralto [kon·'tral·to] I. *m* 1.(*voce*) contralto 2.(*persona*) contralto II. <inv> *agg* MUS contralto; **sassofono** ~ alto saxophone

contrappeso [kon·trap·'pe:·so] *m* 1. TEC counterweight 2.*fig* (*compensazione*) counterbalance

contrapporre [kon·trap·'por·re] <irr> I. *vt fig* (*opporre*) to counter II. *vr:* -**rsi** (*essere in contrasto*) to contrast

contrapposizione [kontrappozit'tsio:ne] *f* contrast

contrapposto, -a I. *pp di* **contrapporre** II. *agg* opposing

contrappunto [kontrap'punto] *m* MUS counterpoint

contrariamente [kon·tra·ria·'men·te] *avv* ~ **a … contrary to …**

contrariare [kon·tra·'ria:·re] *vt* 1.(*contraddire*) to contradict 2.(*infastidire*) to annoy

contrarietà [kon·tra·rie·'ta] <-> *f* (*impedimento*) misfortune

contrario [kon·'tra:·rio] <-i> *m* opposite; **al** ~ on the contrary; **in caso** ~ otherwise; **avere qualcosa in** ~ to have an objection; **non avere nulla in** ~ to have no objection

contrario, -a <-i, -ie> *agg* 1.(*avverso*) opposing; **essere** ~ **a …** to be against …

2.(*opposto*) opposite

contrarre [kon·'trar·re] <irr> I. *vt* 1.(*patto*) to enter into; ~ **matrimonio** to get married 2.(*malattia, debito, muscoli*) to contract II. *vr: -***rsi** to contract

contrassegnare [kon·tras·seɲ·'ɲa:·re] *vt* (*prodotto, periodo*) to mark

contrassegno [kon·tras·'seɲ·ɲo] *m* 1.(*distintivo*) mark 2.(*modalità di pagamento*) cash on delivery

contrastare [kon·tras·'ta:·re] I. *vt* (*impedire*) to hinder II. *vi* (*essere in disaccordo*) ~ **con qc** to contrast with sth

contrasto [kon·'tras·to] *m* 1.(*diverbio*) dispute 2.(*di colori*) contrast

contrattaccare [kon·trat·tak·'ka:·re] *vt* to mount a counterattack against

contrattacco [kon·tra·'tak·ko] <-cchi> *m* counterattack

contrattare [kon·trat·'ta:·re] I. *vt* (*acquisto, retribuzione, prezzo*) to negotiate II. *vi* to negotiate

contrattazione [kon·trat·ta·'tsio:·ne] *f* negotiation

contrattempo [kon·trat·'tɛm·po] *m* (*impedimento*) hitch

contratto¹ [kon·'trat·to] *m* contract; ~ **d'affitto** lease; ~ (**collettivo**) **di lavoro** collective agreement; ~ **a termine** foward contract; ~ **a tempo determinato** fixed-term contract; ~ **a tempo indeterminato** permanent contract

contratto² *pp di* **contrarre**

contrattuale [kon·trat·tu·'a:·le] *agg* (*norme, condizioni, rapporti*) contractual

contravvenire [kon·trav·ve·'ni:·re] <irr> *vi* ~ **a qc** to contravene sth

contravventore, -trice [kon·trav·ven·'to:·re] *m, f* offender

contravvenzione [kon·trav·ven·'tsio:·ne] *f* 1.(*violazione*) contravention 2.(*multa*) fine

contrazione [kon·tra·'tsio:·ne] *f* 1.(*spasmo: di muscolo*) contraction 2.(*riduzione: di prezzi, mercato, vendite*) fall

contribuente [kon·tri·bu·'ɛn·te] *mf* taxpayer

contribuire [kon·tri·bu·'i:·re] <contribuisco> *vi* ~ **a qc** to contribute to sth

contributo [kon·tri·'bu:·to] *m* contribution; **dare un** ~ **a qc, -i previdenziali** welfare contributions *pl;* -**i sociali** social security contributions

contrito, -a [kon·'tri:·to] *agg* (*faccia, aria, espressione, voce*) contrite

contrizione [kon·tri·'tsio:·ne] *f* contrition

contro ['kon·tro] I. *prep* against; **sbattere** ~ **qc** to bump into sth; **sparare** ~ **qu** to shoot at sb; ~ **di me/te/lei** against me/you/her; ~ **natura** contrary to nature; ~ **assegno** cash on delivery; ~ **ricevuta/pagamento** on receipt/payment II. *avv* against; **votare/ essere** ~ to vote/to be against III. <-> *m* **i pro ed i** ~ the pros and cons

contro- [kon·tro] (*in parole composte*) counter-

controbattere [kon·tro·'bat·te·re] *vt fig* (*ribattere*) to rebut

controbilanciare [kon·tro·bi·lan·'tʃa:·re] I. *vt* 1. (*carico, pesi*) to counterbalance 2. *fig* (*compensare*) to make up for II. *vr:* **-rsi** (*pesi, pressioni*) to counterbalance each other

controcorrente [kon·tro·kor·'rɛn·te] *avv* against the current; **andare ~** to go against the current; *fig* to swim against the tide

controcultura [kon·tro·kul·'tu:·ra] *f* counter-culture

controdado [kon·tro·'da:·do] *m* locknut

controdomanda [kon·tro·do·'man·da] *f* counterquestion

controffensiva [kon·trof·fen·'si:·va] *f* 1. MIL counteroffensive 2. *fig* (*replica*) counterattack; **passare alla ~** to go on the counterattack

controfferta [kon·trof·'fɛr·ta] *f* COM counteroffer

controfigura [kon·tro·fi·'gu:·ra] *f* CINE double

controfinestra [kon·tro·fi·'nɛs·tra] *f* double-pane window

controfirma [kon·tro·'fir·ma] *f* countersignature

controfirmare [kon·tro·fir·'ma:·re] *vt* (*diagnosi, decreto, dichiarazione*) to countersign

controindicazione [kon·tro·in·di·ka·'tsio:·ne] *f* MED contraindication

controllabilità [kon·trol·la·bi·li·'ta] <-> *f* (*di teoria, sistema*) verifiability

controllare [kon·trol·'la:·re] I. *vt* 1. (*documenti, biglietti, risposta*) to check 2. (*attività*) to keep a watch on 3. (*mercato, avversario, gesti, emozioni*) to control II. *vr:* **-rsi** to control oneself; **non riuscire a -rsi** not to be able to control oneself; **-rsi nel mangiare** to watch what one eats

controllo [kon·'trɔl·lo] *m* 1. (*verifica*) check; **~ (dei) bagagli** baggage check; **~ dei biglietti** ticket inspection; **visita di ~** MED checkup; **~ di gestione** COM management control 2. *fig* (*di gesti, emozioni*) control; **perdere il ~** to lose control 3. TEC control

controllore [kon·trol·'lo:·re] *m* 1. FERR guard 2. AERO **-i di volo** [*o* **del traffico aereo**] air traffic controller

controluce [kon·tro·'lu:·tʃe] *avv* **fotografia in ~** backlit photograph; **guardare qc** [*o* **in**] **~** to look at sth against the light; **in ~** against the light

contromano [kon·tro·'ma:·no] *avv* on the wrong side of the road

contromarca [kon·tro·'mar·ka] <-che> *f* token

contromisura [kon·tro·mi·'zu:·ra] *f* countermeasure

controparte [kon·tro·'par·te] *f* opposing party

contropartita [kon·tro·par·'ti:·ta] *f* compensation

contropelo [kon·tro·'pe:·lo] I. *avv* against the nap; **prendere qu ~** *fig* to rub sb the wrong way II. *m* **fare** (**il pelo ed**) **il ~ a qu** *fig* to tear into sb

contropiede [kon·tro·'piɛ:·de] *m* **prendere** [*o* **cogliere**] **qu in ~** *fig* to wrong-foot sb

controproducente [kon·tro·pro·du·'tʃɛn·te] *agg* (*affermazioni*) counterproductive

controproposta [kon·tro·pro·'pos·ta] *f* counterproposal

controprova [kon·tro·'prɔ:·va] *f* counter-evidence

contrordine [kon·'tror·di·ne] *m* counter-order

controriforma [kon·tro·ri·'for·ma] *f* HIST Counter-Reformation

controrivoluzione [kon·tro·ri·vo·lu·'tsio:·ne] *f* counter-revolution

controsenso [kon·tro·'sɛn·so] *m* contradiction in terms

controsoffitto [kon·tro·sof·'fit·to] *m* false ceiling

controspionaggio [kon·tro·spio·'nad·dʒo] <-ggi> *m* counterespionage

controsterzare [kon·tro·ster·'tsa:·re] *vi* to countersteer

controtendenza [kon·tro·ten·'dɛn·tsa] *f* opposing trend; **in ~** against the trend

controvalore [kon·tro·va·'lo:·re] *m* equivalent

controvento [kon·tro·'vɛn·to] *avv* against the wind; **navigare ~** to sail into the wind

controversia [kon·tro·'vɛr·sia] <-ie> *f* controversy

controverso, -a [kon·tro·'vɛr·so] *agg* (*storia, situazione, tema*) controversial

controvoglia [kon·tro·'vɔʎ·ʎa] *avv* reluctantly

contumacia [kon·tu·'ma:·tʃa] <-cie> *f* JUR default

contundente [kon·tun·'dɛn·te] *agg* (*arma*) blunt

contusione [kon·tu·'zio:·ne] *f* bruise

contuso, -a [kon·'tu:·zo] *agg* (*persona, arto, occhio*) bruised

convalescente [kon·va·leʃ·'ʃɛn·te] I. *agg* (*paziente, malato*) convalescent II. *mf* convalescent

convalescenza [kon·va·leʃ·'ʃɛn·tsa] *f* convalescence; **essere in ~** (*paziente, malato*) to be convalescing

convalida [kon·'va:·li·da] *f* 1. (*di biglietto*) stamping 2. DIR (*riprova*) confirmation

convalidare [kon·va·li·'da:·re] *vt* 1. (*biglietto*) to stamp 2. JUR (*atto, provvedimento*) to confirm

convegno [kon·'veɲ·ɲo] *m* (*incontro: di medici, giuristi*) conference

convenevoli [kon·ve·'ne:·vo·li] *mpl* pleasantries *pl*

conveniente [kon·ve·'niɛn·te] *agg* 1. (*vantaggioso: prezzo*) low; (*economico: prodotto*) inexpensive 2. (*adatto: atteggiamento*) suitable

convenienza [kon·ve·'niɛn·tsa] *f* 1. (*cortesia*) **visita di ~** courtesy visit 2. (*economicità: di prodotto*) inexpensiveness; (*di prezzo*) lowness; **matrimonio di ~** marriage of convenience

convenire [kon·ve·'ni:·re] <irr> I. *vi* essere *o* avere 1. (*tornare utile*) to be worthwhile; **ci**

conviene tentare it's worth our while trying **2.** (*impersonale: essere opportuno*) it is advisable **3.** (*concordare*) ~ **su qc** to agree on sth; ~ **con qu** to agree with sb **4.** (*riunirsi*) to gather **II.** *vt avere* ~ **un prezzo** to agree on a price

convento [kon·'vɛn·to] *m* convent; **contentarsi di quello che passa il** ~ *fig scherz* to take potluck

convenuto, -a I. *pp di* **convenire II.** *agg* (*somma, cifra, luogo*) agreed; **come** ~ as agreed **III.** *m, f* **1.** JUR defendant **2.** *pl* (*a riunione*) people present *pl*

convenzionale [kon·ven·tsio·'na:·le] *agg* **1.** (*comune: metodo, medicina*) conventional **2.** *pej* (*banale: storia*) conventional **3.** (*stabilito: penale*) agreed

convenzione [kon·ven·'tsio:·ne] *f* **1.** (*accordo*) agreement **2.** *pl* (*regole tradizionali*) conventions *pl*

convergente [kon·ver·'dʒɛn·te] *agg* **1.** (*strade, linee*) converging **2.** *fig* (*coincidente: opinioni, indizi*) convergent **3.** PHYS (*lenti*) convergent

convergenza [kon·ver·'dʒɛn·tsa] *f* **1.** *a fig* (*di propositi, idee*) convergence **2.** AUTO (*di ruote*) toe-in

convergere [kon·'vɛr·dʒe·re] <convergo, conversi, converso> **I.** *vi essere* to converge **II.** *vt avere* **1.** PHYS to converge **2.** *fig* (*indirizzare*) **far** ~ **qc su qc** to concentrate sth on sth

conversare [kon·ver·'sa:·re] *vi* to talk; ~ **con qu** to talk with sb

conversazione [kon·ver·sa·'tsio:·ne] *f* conversation

conversi [kon·'vɛr·si] *1. pers sing pass rem di* **convergere**

conversione [kon·ver·'sio:·ne] *f* conversion; ~ **monetaria** currency conversion

converso, -a [kon·'vɛr·so] *pp di* **convergere**

convertire [kon·ver·'ti:·re] **I.** *vt* **1.** (*trasformare*) ~ **qc in qc** to convert sth into sth **2.** REL, POL ~ **qu a qc** to convert sb to sth **3.** COMPUT, TEL, FIN to convert **II.** *vr* **1.** (*trasformarsi*) **-rsi in qc** to be converted into sth **2.** REL, POL **-rsi a qc** to convert to sth

convertito, -a [kon·ver·'ti:·to] **I.** *agg* (*amico, fedele, popolo*) converted **II.** *m, f* convert

convertitore [kon·ver·ti·'to:·re] *m* converter; ~ **di frequenza** MOT frequency changer; ~ **di coppia** MOT torque converter

convesso, -a [kon·'vɛs·so] *agg* (*lente*) convex; (*angolo*) salient

convettore [kon·vet·'to:·re] *m* convector

convincere [kon·'vin·tʃe·re] <irr> **I.** *vt* ~ **qu** (**di qc**) to convince sb (of sth); **mi hanno convinto a venire** they convinced me to come **II.** *vr* **-rsi** (**di qc**) to be convinced (of sth)

convinto, -a [kon·'vin·to] *agg* (*assertore, sostenitore*) convinced; **essere** ~ **di qc** to be convinced of sth

convinzione [kon·vin·'tsio:·ne] *f* conviction

convitto [kon·'vit·to] *m* boarding school

convivenza [kon·vi·'vɛn·tsa] *f* **1.** (*di persone*) living together **2.** (*di popoli*) coexistence

convivere [kon·'vi:·ve·re] <irr> *vi essere o avere* **1.** (*persone*) to live together **2.** (*popoli, idee, dialetti*) to coexist

convocare [kon·vo·'ka:·re] *vt* **1.** POL, ADM (*indire: riunione*) to call; (*seduta*) to convene **2.** (*invitare: parti, contendenti, dipendenti*) to summon

convocazione [kon·vo·ka·'tsio:·ne] *f* **1.** POL, ADM (*di riunione*) calling; (*di seduta*) convening **2.** (*invito, in tribunale*) summons

convogliare [kon·voʎ·'ʎa:·re] *vt* (*traffico*) to direct; (*soccorsi, risorse*) to channel

convoglio [kon·'vɔʎ·ʎo] <-gli> *m* **1.** (*di navi, veicoli*) convoy **2.** FERR ~ **ferroviario** train

convulsione [kon·vul·'sio:·ne] *f* MED convulsion

convulso, -a *agg* **1.** MED convulsive; **tosse -a** whooping cough **2.** (*pianto, riso*) convulsive **3.** *fig* (*lavoro, attività*) feverish **4.** *fig* (*parole, discorso*) confused

cookie ['kʊ·kɪ] <-s> *m* COMPUT cookie

coop <-> *f acro di* **cooperativa** co-op

cooperare [ko·o·pe·'ra:·re] *vi* (*collaborare*) to cooperate; ~ **con qu/qc** to cooperate with sb/sth; ~ **a qc** to cooperate in sth

cooperativa [ko·o·pe·ra·'ti:·va] *f* cooperative

cooperazione [ko·o·pe·ra·'tsio:·ne] *f* cooperation

coordinamento [ko·or·di·na·'men·to] *m* (*di attività, servizi, progetti*) coordination

coordinare [ko·or·di·'na:·re] *vt* (*attività, servizi, progetti, movimenti*) to coordinate

coordinata [ko·or·di·'na:·ta] *f* coordinate; **-e cartesiane** Cartesian coordinates; **mandami le tue -e** send me your details; **-e bancarie** bank details

coordinato, -a *agg* **1.** (*armonioso: movimento*) coordinated **2.** LING (*proposizione*) coordinate

coordinatore, -trice [ko·or·di·na·'to:·re] *m, f* (*di attività, programma, progetto*) coordinator

coordinazione [ko·or·di·na·'tsio:·ne] *f* (*di movimenti, muscoli, progetto*) coordination

Copenaghen [ko·pe·'na:·gen] *f* Copenhagen

coperchio [ko·'pɛr·kio] <-chi> *m* (*di pentola, barattolo, contenitore, cofanetto, scatola*) lid; (*di flacone*) top

copersi [ko·'pɛr·si] *1. pers sing pass rem di* **coprire**

coperta [ko·'pɛr·ta] *f* **1.** (*panno*) blanket **2.** NAUT (*ponte*) deck

copertina [ko·per·'ti:·na] *f* (*di libro, quaderno, rivista*) cover; (*di disco*) sleeve

coperto [ko·'pɛr·to] *m* **1.** (*in tavola*) cover charge **2.** (*luogo riparato*) **stare al** ~ to be under cover

coperto, -a I. *pp di* **coprire II.** *agg* **1.** (*struttura*) covered; (*luogo*) indoor **2.** FIN (*assegno, rischio*) covered **3.** METEO (*cielo, tempo*) overcast **4.** (*cosparso*) **essere** ~ **di qc** to be covered with sth

copertone [ko·per·'to:·ne] *m* MOT tire

copertura [ko·per·'tu:·ra] *f* **1.**(*rivestimento*) cover **2.**fig (*di attività illegale*) cover **3.**FIN, TV coverage; ~ **assicurativa** insurance coverage **4.**MIL cover; **fuoco di** ~ covering fire

copia ['kɔ:·pia] <-ie> *f* **1.**(*trascrizione*) copy; **bella** ~ fair copy; **brutta** ~ rough copy; ~ **di sicurezza** COMPUT backup copy; ~ **conforme** ADM certified copy **2.**(*riproduzione: di chiavi*) duplicate

copiare [ko·'pia:·re] *vt* to copy

copilota [ko·pi·'lɔ:·ta] <-i , -e> *mf* AERO copilot

copione [ko·'pio:·ne] *m* THEAT, FILM script

coppa ['kɔp·pa/'kop·pa] *f* **1.**(*recipiente*) cup; ~ **da gelato** ice-cream bowl; ~ **da spumante** sparkling wine glass **2.**(*contenuto*) cup(ful); ~ **di gelato** bowl of ice cream; ~ **di spumante** glass of sparkling wine **3.**SPORT (*trofeo*) cup **4.**(*di reggiseno*) cup **5.**MOT ~ **dell'olio** oil pan **6.**pl (*di carte da gioco*) cups *pl, suit of deck of Neapolitan cards*

coppetta [kop·'pet·ta] *f* **1.**(*contenitore: per gelato*) small bowl **2.**(*contenuto*) small bowl(ful)

coppia ['kɔp·pia] <-ie> *f* **1.**A.SPORT pair; **a -ie, in** ~ in pairs; **gara a -ie** pairs competition **2.**(*due persone*) couple

copricapo [ko·pri·'ka:·po] *m* hat

copricostume [ko·pri·kos·'tu:·me] <-> *m* beach robe

copridivano [kɔ·pri·di·'va:·no] *m* sofa cover

coprifuoco [ko·pri·'fuɔ:·ko] *m* curfew

coprii [ko·'pri:·i] *1.pers sing pass rem di* **coprire**

copriletto [ko·pri·'lɛt·to] <-> *m* bedspread

coprimaterasso [ko·pri·ma·te·'ras·so] <-> *m* mattress cover

copripiumone [ko·pri·piu·'mo:·ne] <-> *m* comforter cover

copriradiatore [ko·pri·ra·dia·'to:·re] <-> *m* MOT (*per auto, moto*) radiator cover

coprire [ko·'pri:·re] <copro, coprii *o* copersi, coperto> I. *vt* **1.**(*gener*) to cover **2.**(*riempire*) ~ **qu di baci** to shower sb with kisses; ~ **qu di insulti** to hurl abuse at sb **3.**fig (*carica*) to hold II. *vr:* **-rsi 1.**FIN to cover oneself **2.**(*cielo*) to become overcast **3.**(*colmarsi*) **-rsi di qc** to cover oneself with sth **4.**(*con vestiti*) to wrap up; **-rsi bene** to wrap up well

coprocessore [ko·pro·tʃes·'so:·re] *m* COMPUT coprocessor

coproduzione [ko·pro·du·'tsio:·ne] *f* FILM coproduction

copy ['kɔ:·pi] <-> *mf* (*copywriter*) copywriter

copyright ['kɔ·pi·rait] <-> *m* copyright

coque [kɔk] <-> *f* **uovo alla** ~ soft-boiled egg

coraggio [ko·'rad·dʒo] *m* **1.**(*forza d'animo*) courage; **avere il** ~ **di fare qc** to have the courage to do sth; **fare** ~ **a qu** to cheer sb up **2.**(*sfacciataggine*) nerve

coraggioso, -a [ko·rad·'dʒo:·so] *agg* (*eroe, persona, decisione, scelta*) brave

corale [ko·'ra:·le] I. *agg* MUS choral; **canto** ~ choral singing; **musica** ~ choral music II. *m* MUS chorale

corallino, -a [ko·ral·'li:·no] *agg* GEOG coral; **barriera -a** coral reef

corallo [ko·'ral·lo] *m* coral

corano [ko·'ra:·no] *m* Koran

corazza [ka·'rat·tsa] *f* **1.**MIL armor **2.**ZOO shell

corazzare [ko·rat·'tsa:·re] I. *vt* **1.**MIL to armor **2.**fig (*difendere*) to protect II. *vr:* **-rsi 1.**MIL to put on armor **2.**(*difendersi*) to protect oneself

corazzato, -a [ko·rat·'tsa:·to] *agg* **1.**MIL armored **2.**(*rinforzato: vetro*) toughened **3.**(*protetto: persona*) hardened

corda ['kɔr·da] *f* **1.**(*fune*) rope; **dare** ~ **a qu** fig to encourage; **essere giù di** ~ fig to be feeling down; **tagliare la** ~ fig to slip off; **tenere qu sulla** ~ fig to keep sb on tenterhooks; **tirar troppo la** ~ fig to push it inf **2.**(*per pacchi*) string **3.**SPORT rope **4.**MUS string; **strumenti a** ~ string(ed) instruments; **essere teso come le -e di un violino** fig to be on edge **5.**(*di arco*) string **6.**ANAT **-e vocali** vocal cords

cordata [kor·'da:·ta] *f* **1.**SPORT (*nell'alpinismo*) roped party **2.**COM (*alleanza*) consortium

cordiale [kor·'dia:·le] *agg* (*accoglienza*) warm; (*atmosfera*) friendly; **"-i saluti"** (*nelle lettere*) "kind regards"

cordialità [kor·dia·li·'ta] <-> *f* **1.**(*affabilità*) friendliness; **accogliere qu con** ~ to give sb a warm welcome **2.** *pl* (*saluti*) best wishes *pl*

cordialmente [kor·dial·'men·te] *avv* **1.**(*accogliere, salutare*) warmly; **'~'** (*nelle lettere*) "best wishes" *pl* **2.**(*antipatico, odioso*) intensely

cordless [kɔ:d·les] I.<inv> *agg* TEL cordless II.<-> *m* cordless phone

cordoglio [kor·'dɔʎ·ʎo] <-gli> *m* grief

cordone [kor·'do:·ne] *m* **1.**(*di tenda*) rope; (*di cappello, saio*) cord **2.**ANAT ~ **ombelicale** umbilical cord **3.**EL cord **4.**(*sbarramento*) cordon; ~ **sanitario** cordon sanitaire

coreografia [ko·reo·gra·'fi:·a] *f* choreography

coreografico, -a [ko·reo·'gra:·fi·ko] <-ci, -che> *agg* **1.**THEAT choreographic **2.**fig (*cerimonia, manifestazione*) spectacular

coreografo, -a [ko·re·'ɔ:·gra·fo] *m, f* choreographer

coriaceo, -a [ko·'ria:·tʃeo] *agg* **1.**(*duro*) leathery **2.**fig (*insensibile*) hard

coriandolo [ko·'rian·do·lo] *m* **1.**BOT cilantro **2.** *pl* (*di carnevale*) confetti

coricare [ko·ri·'ka:·re] I. *vt* (*distendere, mettere a letto*) to lay down II. *vr:* **-rsi** to go to bed

corista [ko·'ris·ta] <-i , -e> *mf* choir member

cornacchia [kor·'nak·kia] <-cchie> *f* crow

cornamusa [kor·na·'mu:·za] *f* MUS bagpipes *pl*

cornea ['kɔr·nea] *f* MED cornea

corner ['kɔr·ner] <-> *m* SPORT corner

cornetta [kor·'net·ta] *f inf* (*di telefono*) receiver; **mettere giù la** ~ to put the receiver down

cornetto [kor·'net·to] *m* **1.**(*amuleto*) horn-shaped amulet **2.**CULIN croissant

cornice [kor·'ni:·tʃe] *f* **1.**(*di quadro, specchio*) frame **2.**(*ambientazione*) setting

corniciaio [kor·ni·'tʃa:·io] <-ai> *m* frame-maker

cornicione [kor·ni·'tʃo:·ne] *m* ARCHIT cornice

cornificare [kor·ni·fi·'ka:·re] *vt scherz* (*moglie, marito*) to cheat on

corno[1] ['kɔr·no] <-e, -a> *m* 1. ZOO (*di toro*) horn; (*di cervo, dell'alce*) antler; **prendere il toro per le -a** *fig* to take the bull by the horns *fig*; **rompere** [*o* **spezzare**] **le -a qu** *inf* to beat sb up *inf* 2. *pl fig, inf* (*tradimento*) **fare le -a alla moglie/al marito** to cheat on one's wife/one's husband 3. *inf* (*niente*) **non me ne importa un ~** I don't give a damn *inf* 4. *inf* (*scongiuro*) **fare le -a** to cross one's fingers

corno[2] *m* 1. (*sostanza*) horn 2. (*da scarpe*) shoehorn 3. MUS horn

cornuto, -a [kor·'nu:·to] I. *agg* 1. ZOO (*animale*) horned 2. *fig, inf* (*persona*) cheated on II. *m, f* 1. *fig, inf* (*persona tradita*) man [*o* woman] who has been cheated on 2. *vulg* (*insulto*) bastard *vulg*

corografia [ko·ro·gra·'fi:·a] *f* topography

corolla [ko·'rɔl·la] *f* corolla

corona [ko·'ro:·na] *f* 1. (*di metallo prezioso*) crown 2. *fig* (*potere*) crown 3. (*oggetto*) wreath; **~ funebre** funeral wreath; **~ di alloro** laurel wreath; **~ di spine** crown of thorns; **~ del rosario** rosary 4. ASTR corona; **~ solare** solar corona

coronamento [ko·ro·na·'men·to] *m* (*di sogni*) fulfillment; (*di carriera*) crowning achievement

coronare [ko·ro·'na:·re] *vt* 1. *fig* (*sogno*) to fulfill; (*carriera*) to be the crowning achievement of 2. (*cingere*) to ring

coronaria [ko·ro·'na:·ria] <-ie> *f* ANAT coronary artery

corpetto [kor·'pet·to] *m* (*di abito*) bodice

corpo ['kɔr·po] *m* 1. (*materia*) substance; **-i celesti** heavenly bodies 2. (*oggetto*) object; **~ del reato** JUR corpus delicti 3. (*umano e animale*) body; **guardia del ~** bodyguard; **avere qc in ~** to be consumed with sth; **avere il diavolo in ~** not to be able to stay still; **anima e ~** body and soul; **combattere ~ a ~** to grapple 4. (*cadavere*) body 5. (*forma*) substance; **dare ~ a qc** to give substance to sth; **prendere ~** to take shape 6. (*insieme di persone*) body; **~ insegnante** ADM teachers *pl*; **~ di ballo** corps de ballet 7. MUS (*cassa*) body 8. (*loc*) **andare di ~** *inf* to have a bowel movement

corporale [kor·po·'ra:·le] *agg* (*bisogni*) bodily; (*punizione*) corporal

corporation [kɔ:·pə·'rei·ʃən] <-> *f* corporation

corporatura [kor·po·ra·'tu:·ra] *f* physique

corporazione [kor·po·ra·'tsio:·ne] *f* 1. COM, ADM association 2. HIST guild

corporeo, -a [kor·'pɔ:·reo] <-ei, -ee> *agg* (*del corpo umano: peso, grasso*) body

corposo, -a [kor·'po:·so] *agg* 1. (*voluminoso*) fat 2. (*vino*) full-bodied

corpulento, -a [kor·pu·'lɛn·to] *agg* stout

corpulenza [kor·pu·'lɛn·tsa] *f* stoutness

corpuscolo [kor·'pus·ko·lo] *m* PHYS corpuscle

Corpus Domini ['kɔr·pus 'dɔ:·mi·ni] <-> *m* Corpus Christi

corredare [kor·re·'da:·re] *vt* to equip; **~ qc di qc** to equip sth with sth

corredo [kor·'rɛ:·do] *m* 1. (*di sposa*) trousseau 2. (*di laboratorio*) equipment

correggere [kor·'rɛd·dʒe·re] <irr> I. *vt* (*compiti, difetto, errore*) to correct II. *vr* **-rsi di qc** to break oneself of sth

correlazione [kor·re·la·'tsio:·ne] *f* 1. (*rapporto*) correlation 2. LING sequence of tenses

corrente [kor·'rɛn·te] I. *agg* 1. (*acqua*) running 2. (*mese, anno*) current 3. FIN **conto ~** checking account II. *m* **essere al ~ di qc** to know about sth; **mettere al ~ di qc** to inform about sth; **mettersi al ~ di qc** to find out about sth; **tenere qu al ~ (di** [*o* **su**] **qc)** to keep sb informed (about sth) III. *f* 1. (*di fiume, mare*) current 2. (*~ d'aria*) draft 3. EL current; **~ alternata** alternating current; **~ continua** direct current; **presa di ~** socket 4. *fig* (*moda, tendenza*) trend; **seguire la ~** *fig* to follow the trend; **andare contro ~** *fig* to swim against the tide

correntemente [kor·ren·te·'men·te] *avv* 1. (*bene*) fluently 2. (*comunemente*) commonly

correre ['kor·re·re] <corro, corsi, corso> I. *vi essere o avere* 1. (*persona*) to run; **~ dietro a qu** *fig* to chase after sb; **lasciar ~** *fig* to let it go; **~ a gambe levate** to run as fast as one's legs can carry one; **~ ai ripari** *fig* to take remedial action 2. (*in auto, moto*) to drive fast 3. SPORT (*gareggiare*) to race 4. *fig* (*strade*) to run 5. (*tempo*) to fly II. *vt avere* 1. SPORT (*distanza*) to run; (*gara*) to race in 2. (*rischio*) to run

corresponsabile [kor·res·pon·'sa:·bi·le] *agg* jointly responsible

corressi [kor·'rɛs·si] *1. pers sing pass rem di* correggere

correttezza [kor·ret·'tet·tsa] *f* (*rettitudine*) correctness

correttivo, -a *agg* corrective

corretto, -a [kor·'rɛt·to] I. *pp di* correggere II. *agg* 1. (*affermazione, risposta, persona, comportamento*) correct 2. (*compito, bozza*) corrected 3. (*caffè*) laced; **un caffè ~ alla grappa** a coffee laced with grappa

correttore, -trice [kor·ret·'to:·re] *m, f* **~ di bozze** proofreader

correzione [kor·re·'tsio:·ne] *f* (*di difetto, compiti*) correction; **~ di bozze** proofreading

corrida [kor·'ri:·da] *f* bullfight

corridoio [kor·ri·'do:·io] <-oi> *m* 1. (*di edificio, treno*) corridor; **voci di ~** backstairs gossip 2. (*di aereo*) aisle 3. POL **~ aereo** air corridor 4. SPORT (*nel tennis*) alley

corridore, -trice [kor·ri·'do:·re] *m, f* (*automobilista*) race car driver; (*ciclista*) racing cyclist; (*podista*) runner

C

corriera [kor·'riɛ:·ra] *f* bus

corriere [kor·'riɛ:·re] *m* **1.** (*spedizioniere*) courrier **2.** (*titolo di giornale*) Courier

corrimano [kor·ri·'ma:·no] *m* (*di scala, barca*) handrail

corrispettivo [kor·ris·pet·'ti:·vo] *m* compensation

corrispettivo, -a *agg* (*corrispondente*) corresponding

corrispondente [kor·ris·pon·'dɛn·te] **I.** *agg* corresponding; ~ **a qc** corresponding to sth **II.** *mf* (*di giornale*) correspondent; ~ **di guerra** war correspondent; ~ **dall'estero** foreign correspondent

corrispondenza [kor·ris·pon·'dɛn·tsa] *f* **1.** (*lettere*) correspondence; ~ **commerciale** business correspondence; ~ **epistolare** personal correspondence; **essere in** ~ **con qu** to be in correspondence with sb **2.** (*coincidenza*) connection

corrispondere [kor·ris·'pon·de·re] <irr> **I.** *vi* **1.** (*equivalere*) ~ **a qc** to correspond to sth **2.** (*soddisfare: requisiti, aspettative*) ~ **a qc** to meet sth **3.** (*per lettera*) to correspond **II.** *vt* **1.** (*pagare: somma, ammontare*) to pay **2.** (*sentimenti*) to reciprocate

corrodere [kor·'ro:·de·re] <irr> **I.** *vt* (*metalli*) to corrode; (*rocce*) to erode **II.** *vr:* **-rsi** (*metalli*) to corrode; (*rocce*) to erode

corrompere [kor·'rom·pe·re] <irr> **I.** *vt* **1.** *fig* (*con denaro*) to bribe **2.** (*moralmente*) to corrupt **3.** (*acqua, aria*) to contaminate **4.** COMPUT (*file*) to corrupt **II.** *vr:* **-rsi 1.** (*depravarsi*) to be corrupted **2.** COMPUT (*file*) to become corrupted

corrosi *1. pers sing pass rem di* **corrodere**

corrosione [kor·ro·'zio:·ne] *f* (*di metallo*) corrosion; (*di rocce*) erosion

corrosivo, -a *agg* corrosive

corroso *pp di* **corrodere**

corrotto *pp di* **corrompere**

corrucciarsi [kor·rut·'tʃa:r·si] *vr* to get upset

corrugare [kor·ru·'ga:·re] **I.** *vt* (*fronte*) to wrinkle; ~ **le sopracciglia** to frown **II.** *vr:* **-rsi** to wrinkle

corruppi [kor·'rup·pi] *1. pers sing pass rem di* **corrompere**

corruttore, -trice [kor·rut·'to:·re] **I.** *agg* (*azione, funzione*) corrupting **II.** *m, f* **1.** (*di giudici*) briber **2.** (*seduttore: di giovani*) corrupter

corruzione [kor·ru·'tsio:·ne] *f* **1.** (*con denaro*) bribery **2.** (*seduzione*) corruption

corsa ['kor·sa] *f* **1.** (*il correre*) running; **di** ~ in a hurry; **fare una** ~ (*gara*) to have a race; **ho fatto una** ~ **e sono sudato** I've been running and I'm all sweaty; **fare una** ~ **da qualche parte** to dash somewhere **2.** SPORT (*gara*) race; **automobile da** ~ racecar; **cavallo da** ~ racehorse **3.** (*di mezzo pubblico*) trip; **l'ultima** ~ **è alle 23:00** the last bus is at 11 o'clock **4.** (*movimento*) motion

corsaro, -a [kor·'sa:·ro] **I.** *m, f* (*pirata*) corsair **II.** *agg* (*nave, azione*) pirate

corsetto [kor·'set·to] *m* corset

corsi ['kor·si] *1. pers sing pass rem di* **correre**

corsia [kor·'si:·a] <-ie> *f* **1.** MED (*di ospedale*) ward **2.** (*di strada*) lane; ~ **di emergenza** shoulder; ~ **di sorpasso** passing lane **3.** SPORT lane

Corsica ['kɔr·si·ka] *f* Corsica; **abitare in** ~ to live in Corsica; **andare in** ~ to go to Corsica

corsivo [kor·'si:·vo] *m* italics *pl*

corsivo, -a *agg* (*scrittura, testo*) italic

corso¹ ['kor·so] *m* **1.** (*andamento*) course; **nel** ~ **dei secoli** in the course of the centuries; **seguire** [*o* **fare**] **il suo** ~ to take its course; **in** ~ **di stampa** at the printers; ~ **d'acqua** waterway **2.** (*insegnamento*) course; ~ **di sci** skiing course **3.** (*studente*) **fuori** ~ to have failed to finish one's course by the deadline **4.** FIN circulation; **aver** ~ to be legal tender; **moneta fuori** ~ money that is no longer in circulation **5.** (*strada*) main street **6.** ASTR course

corso² *pp di* **correre**

corso, -a ['kɔr·so] **I.** *agg* (*della Corsica*) Corsican **II.** *m, f* (*abitante della Corsica*) Corsican

corte ['kor·te] *f* **1.** (*reggia*) court **2.** ARCH (*cortile*) courtyard **3.** JUR court; ~ **d'appello** appeals court; **Corte di Cassazione** ≈ Court of Appeals; **Corte dei Conti** *court auditing public finances;* **Corte Costituzionale** Constitutional Court; ~ **di giustizia dell'Unione europea** European Court of Justice **4.** (*corteggiamento*) courtship; **fare la** ~ **a qu** to court sb

corteccia [kor·'tet·tʃa] <-cce> *f* **1.** (*di albero*) bark **2.** MED cortex; ~ **cerebrale** cerebral cortex

corteggiare [kor·ted·'dʒa:·re] *vt* (*persona*) to court

corteggiatore, -trice [kor·ted·dʒa·'to:·re] *m, f* suitor

corteo [kor·'tɛ:·o] *m* **1.** (*di matrimonio, funerale*) procession **2.** (*manifestazione*) march

cortese [kor·'te:·ze] *agg* (*garbato: parola, gesto*) polite; (*gentile: persona*) kind

cortesia [kor·te·'zi:·a] <-ie> *f* **1.** (*gentilezza*) politeness; **per** ~ please **2.** (*favore*) favor; **fammi la** ~ **di uscire** would you mind leaving?

cortigiano, -a [kor·ti·'dʒa:·no] *m, f* HIST courtier

cortile [kor·'ti:·le] *m* (*di edificio*) courtyard; (*di casa colonica*) farmyard

cortina [kor·'ti:·na] *f* **1.** (*tenda*) curtain **2.** *fig* (*strato*) ~ **di nebbia** blanket of fog; ~ **di fumo** pall of smoke; *fig* smokescreen

cortisone [kor·ti·'zo:·ne] *m* cortisone

corto, -a ['kor·to] **I.** *agg* short; **settimana -a** five-day week; **essere a** ~ **di soldi** to be short of money; **per farla -a** in short **II.** *avv* **tagliar** ~ to get straight to the point

cortocircuito [kor·to·tʃir·'ku:·ito] *m* short circuit

cortometraggio [kor·to·me·'trad·dʒo] <-ggi> *m* short

corvé [kor·'ve] <-> f 1. MIL **essere di ~** to be on fatigues 2. fig (lavoro ingrato e gravoso) chore

corvino, -a [kor·'viː·no] agg (capelli) jet-black

corvo ['kɔr·vo] m crow; **nero come un ~** as black as a crow

cosa ['kɔː·sa] f 1. (entità) thing; **arrivare a -e fatte** to arrive when it's all over; **credersi chissà che ~** to think one is somebody; **è ~ fatta** it's a done deal; **non è una gran ~** it's nothing special; **è la stessa ~** it's all the same thing; **è tutt'altra ~** it's quite another matter; **ho le mie -e** inf (mestruazioni) I've got my period; **una ~ tira l'altra, da ~ nasce ~** one thing leads to another; **dimmi una ~** tell me something; **sai una ~? ...** do you know something? ...; **per prima ~** first of all; **sopra ogni ~** more than anything; **fra le altre -e** among other things; **tante (belle) -e!** (auguri) all the best!; **qualche ~** something; **qualsiasi ~ succeda** whatever happens 2. (nelle interrogative) (che) **~?** what?; **a che ~ serve?** what's it for?; **a (che) ~ pensi?** what are you thinking about?; **~ vuoi, sono bambini!** what do you expect? they're children! 3. (situazione) thing; **le -e si mettono male** things are turning out badly; **raccontami come sono andate le -e** tell me how things went

cosca ['kɔs·ka] <-sche> f clan

coscia ['kɔʃ·ʃa] <-sce> f 1. ANAT thigh 2. CULIN (di pollo, maiale) leg

cosciente [koʃ·'ʃɛn·te] agg 1. (consapevole) aware 2. MED (lucido: paziente) conscious

coscienza [koʃ·'ʃɛn·tsa] f 1. (consapevolezza) awareness 2. MED (lucidità) consciousness; **perdere/riacquistare la ~** to lose/to regain consciousness 3. (valori morali) conscience; **avere la ~ pulita/sporca** to have a clear/guilty conscience; **avere qc sulla ~** to have sth on one's conscience; **caso di ~** matter of conscience; **esame di ~** soul-searching; **mettersi una mano sulla ~** to put one's hand on one's heart 4. (senso del dovere) conscientiousness; **agire con ~** to act conscientiously 5. (onestà) honesty

coscienzioso, -a [koʃ·ʃen·'tsio·so] agg (persona, opera, lavoro) conscientious

coscrizione [kos·kri·'tsio:·ne] f conscription

coseno [ko·'se:·no] m MATH cosine

Cosentino [ko·sen·'tiː·no] m (zona) Cosenza area; **nel ~** in the Cosenza area

cosentino, -a I. agg from Cosenza II. m, f (abitante) person from Cosenza

Cosenza f Cosenza

così [ko·'si] I. avv 1. (in questo modo) like this; **come va? — ~ ~** how's it going? — so-so; **non devi fare ~** you shouldn't do it like that; **per ~ dire** so to speak; **e ~ via** and so on; **è proprio ~** it's exactly like that 2. (tanto) so 3. (correlativo di come) **~ ... come** both ... and II. <inv> agg (siffatto) like that III. cong 1. (perciò) so 2. (nel modo) **~ ... come** as ... as; **~ sia** amen

cosicché [ko·sik·'ke] cong so

cosiddetto, -a [ko·sid·'det·to] agg so-called

cosmesi [koz·'mɛː·zi] <-> f cosmetics

cosmetico [kos·'mɛː·ti·ko] <-ci> m cosmetic

cosmetico, -a <-ci, -che> agg (prodotto, cura, azienda) cosmetic

cosmico, -a ['kɔz·mi·ko] <-ci, -che> agg 1. ASTR cosmic 2. fig (di tutti) universal

cosmo ['kɔz·mo] m cosmos

cosmologia [koz·mo·lo·'dʒi:·a] <-gie> f cosmology

cosmonauta [koz·mo·'na:u·ta] <-i , -e> mf astronaut

cosmonautico, -a [koz·mo·'na:u·ti·ko] <-ci, -che> agg (scienza, progetto, programma) astronautical

cosmonave [koz·mo·'na:·ve] f spaceship

cosmopolita [koz·mo·po·'li:·ta] <-i , -e> I. mf cosmopolitan II. agg (persona, città) cosmopolitan

coso ['kɔː·so] m inf thingy inf

cospargere [kos·'par·dʒe·re] <irr> vt to sprinkle; **~ qc di qc** to sprinkle sth with sth

cospetto [kos·'pɛt·to] m **al ~ di qu** in the presence of sb

cospicuo, -a [kos·'pi:·kuo] agg (somma, risorsa) considerable

cospirare [kos·pi·'ra:·re] vi to conspire; **~ contro qu/qc** to conspire against sb/sth

cospiratore, -trice [kos·pi·ra·'to:·re] m, f conspirator

cospirazione [kos·pi·ra·'tsio:·ne] f conspiracy

cossi ['kɔs·si] 1. pers sing pass rem di cuocere

Cost. abbr di **Costituzione** Constitution

costa ['kɔs·ta] f 1. GEOG coast 2. BOT (nervatura) rib 3. (di libro) spine 4. (di coltello) back 5. (di tessuto) ribbing; **velluto a -e** corduroy

costante [kos·'tan·te] I. agg 1. (continuo: moto, suono, vento) constant 2. (stabile: tempo) unchanging 3. (persona) persevering 4. (sentimenti, desideri) constant II. f 1. (caratteristica) constant feature 2. MATH, FIS constant

costanza [kos·'tan·tsa] f 1. (di persona) perseverance 2. TEC, SCIENT constancy

Costanza [kos·'tan·tsa] f Constance; **Lago di ~** Lake Constance

costare [kos·'ta:·re] vi, vt essere 1. (avere il prezzo di) to cost; **~ caro** to be expensive; **~ poco** to be inexpensive; **quanto costa?** how much is it?; **costi quel che costi** no matter what 2. (essere caro) to be expensive 3. (richiedere) to cost; **~ fatica a qu** to be hard for sb

costata [kos·'ta:·ta] f (bistecca) chop

costato [kos·'ta:·to] m side

costeggiare [kos·ted·'dʒa:·re] vt 1. NAUT to sail along 2. (strada, sentiero) to run along the side of

costei v. costui

costellazione [kos·tel·la·'tsio:·ne] f 1. ASTR constellation 2. (segno zodiacale) sign

costernazione [kos·ter·na·'tsio:·ne] *f* dismay
costì [kos·'ti] *avv* LIT (*lì*) there; (*qui*) here
costiera [kos·'tiɛ:·ra] *f* coast
costiero, **-a** [kos·'tiɛ:·ro] *agg* (*strada, zona*) coastal
costipare [kos·ti·'pa:·re] *vt* **1.** (*terreno*) to pack **2.** MED to cause constipation in
costituente [kos·ti·tu·'ɛn·te] I. *agg* (*elemento, fattore*) constituent; **assemblea ~** constituent assembly II. *f* POL (*assemblea*) constituent assembly III. *m* **1.** POL (*persona*) constituent assembly member **2.** CHEM constituent
costituire [kos·ti·tu·'i:·re] <costituisco> I. *vt* **1.** (*fondare: società*) to set up **2.** (*rappresentare*) to constitute **3.** (*formare*) to make up; **essere costituito da** to consist of II. *vr*: **-rsi** **1.** JUR (*consegnarsi alla giustizia*) to turn oneself in; **-rsi parte civile** to sue for damages; **-rsi in giudizio** to appear before the court **2.** (*formarsi*) to be formed
costituito, **-a** [kos·ti·tu·'i:·to] *agg* **1.** (*formato*) composed **2.** (*stabilito per legge: autorità, ordine*) constituted
costituzionale [kos·ti·tu·tsio·'na:·le] *agg* POL, JUR, MED constitutional; **governo/monarchia ~** constitutional government/monarchy; **Corte Costituzionale** Constitutional Court
costituzione [kos·ti·tu·'tsio:·ne] *f* **1.** JUR, MED constitution **2.** (*di società*) setting-up; (*di società, giuria*) formation
costo ['kɔs·to] *m a. fig* cost; **-i di nolo** freight costs; **a prezzo di ~** at cost (price); **sotto ~** for less than cost price; **il ~ della vita** the cost of living; **a qualunque** [*o* **ogni**] **~**, **a tutti i -i** at all costs
costola ['kɔs·to·la] *f* ANAT, BOT rib; **stare alle -e di qu** to be hot on sb's heels
costoletta [kos·to·'let·ta] *f* CULIN (*di vitello, maiale*) cutlet
costoro [kos·'to:·ro] *v.* **costui**
costoso, **-a** [kos·'to:·so] *agg* (*caro*) expensive
costringere [kos·'trin·dʒe·re] <irr> *vt* to force; **~ qu a fare qc** to force sb to do sth; **la febbre lo costringe a letto** he's laid up with a fever
costrizione [kos·tri·'tsio:·ne] *f* constraint
costruire [kos·tru·'i:·re] <costruisco> *vt* **1.** ARCH (*edificare: casa, muro*) to build **2.** TEC (*assemblare: motore, macchinario*) to construct **3.** *fig* (*società, vita*) to build
costruttore, **-trice** [kos·trut·'to:·re] *m, f* (*imprenditore edile*) builder
costruzione [kos·tru·'tsio:·ne] *f* **1.** (*edificio*) building **2.** (*fabbricazione, assemblaggio*) construction; **essere in ~** to be under construction **3.** *fig* (*di società, vita*) building **4.** LING construction
costui, costei [kos·'tu:·i, kos·'tɛ:·i] <costoro> *pron dem* he *m*, she *f*
costume [kos·'tu:·me] *m* **1.** THEAT costume **2.** (*foggia di vestire*) dress; **~ da bagno** (*da donna*) bathing suit; (*da uomo*) trunks *pl* **3.** (*usanze*) custom **4.** (*abitudine*) habit

5. (*condotta morale*) morality; **una donna di facili -i** a woman of easy virtue; **squadra del buon ~** vice squad
cotechino [ko·te·'ki:·no] *m* pork and bacon sausage, boiled and served with lentils
cotenna [ko·'ten·na] *f* bacon rind
cotogna [ko·'toɲ·ɲa] *f* quince
cotogno [ko·'toɲ·ɲo] *m* quince (tree)
cotoletta [ko·to·'let·ta] *f* CULIN (*di maiale*) chop; (*di vitello*) cutlet
cotonare [ko·to·'na:·re] I. *vt* (*capelli*) to tease II. *vr*: **-rsi -rsi i capelli** to tease one's hair
cotone [ko·'to:·ne] *m* cotton; **~** (**idrofilo**) cotton
cotonificio [ko·to·ni·'fi:·tʃo] <-ci> *m* cotton mill
cotta ['kɔt·ta] *f inf* (*passione*) crush; **avere una ~ per qu** to have a crush on sb; **prendersi una ~ per qu** to get a crush on sb
cottage ['kɔ·tidʒ] <-> *m* cottage
cottimo ['kɔt·ti·mo] *m* piecework; **lavorare a ~** to do piecework
cotto ['kɔt·to] *m* brickwork
cotto, **-a** I. *pp di* **cuocere** II. *agg* **1.** CULIN (*pronto*) done **2.** (*bollito*) boiled; (*preparato: al forno*) roast; (*in padella*) fried; (*in umido*) stewed; **ben ~** well done; **farne di -e e di crude** *fig* to get up to all kinds of tricks **3.** *inf* (*innamorato*) **essere ~ di qu** to be smitten with sb **4.** *inf* (*sfinito*) done in *inf*
cotton fioc® ['kɔ·tn fi·'ɔk] <-> *m* Q-tip®
cottura [kot·'tu:·ra] *f* CULIN cooking; (*bollitura: in acqua*) boiling; (*in padella*) frying; (*in umido*) stewing; (*in forno*) baking; **raggiungere il punto di ~** to be done
coupé [ku·'pe] <-> *f* (*mot*) coupe
coupon [ku·'pɔ̃] <-> *m* coupon
cova ['ko:·va] *f* brooding
covare [ko·'va:·re] I. *vt* **1.** ZOO (*uova*) to sit on **2.** *fig* (*malattia*) to go down with **3.** *fig* (*odio, sospetto*) to nurture II. *vi* **1.** ZOO to sit on its eggs **2.** *fig* (*stare celato*) to smolder; **il fuoco cova sotto la cenere** it's not what it seems; **qui gatta ci cova** there's something fishy going on here
covata [ko·'va:·ta] *f* clutch
cover story ['kʌ·və 'stɔ:·ri] <- *o* cover stories> *f* cover story
covo ['ko:·vo] *m* **1.** ZOO (*tana*) lair **2.** *fig* (*nascondiglio*) den; **~ di ladri** den of thieves
covone [ko·'vo:·ne] *m* sheaf
coyote [ko·'jo·te] *v.* **coyote**
cozza ['kɔt·tsa] *f* mussel
cozzare [kot·'tsa:·re] *vi* **1.** (*sbattere*) **~ contro qu/qc** to bang into sb/sth **2.** *fig* (*mettersi in contrasto*) **~ con qc** to clash with sth; **~ contro qc** to come up against sth
CP *mpl abbr di* **Cattolici Popolari** *Catholic student group*
C.P. *abbr di* **Casella Postale** P.O. box
CPU *f abbr di* **Central Processing Unit** COMPUT CPU
crac [krak] <-> *m* **1.** (*rumore*) crack **2.** *fig* COM

(*fallimento*) crash

cracker ['kræ·kə/'krɛ·ker] <-> *m* **1.**(*galletta*) cracker **2.** COMPUT (*pirata*) cracker

Cracovia *f* Kracow

cracoviano, -a [kra·ko·'via:·no] I. *agg* Kracovian II. *m*, *f* (*abitante*) Kracovian

crampo ['kram·po] *m* cramp

cranico, -a ['kra:·ni·ko] <-ci, -che> *agg* (*frattura, nevralgia*) cranial; **scatola -a** cranium; **trauma** ~ head injury

cranio ['kra:·nio] <-i> *m* skull

crash [kræʃ] <-> *m* **1.**(*rumore*) crash **2.** COMPUT crash; **avere un** ~ to crash **3.** *fig* COM (*fallimento*) crash

crash test [kræʃ test] <- *o* crash tests> *m* crash test

cratere [kra·'tɛ:·re] *m* GEOL (*di vulcano*) crater; ~ **lunare** lunar crater

crauti ['kra:u·ti] *mpl* CULIN sauerkraut

cravatta [kra·'vat·ta] *f* tie

crawl [krɔ:l] <-> *m* crawl; **nuotare a** ~ to swim the crawl

creanza [kre·'an·tsa] *f* (*buone maniere*) manners *pl*

creare [kre·'a:·re] *vt* **1.**(*gener*) to create **2.**(*nella moda*) to design **3.** COM (*società*) to set up **4.**(*nominare*) to appoint

creatività [kre·a·ti·vi·'ta] <-> *f* creativity

creativo, -a [kre·a·'ti:·vo] I. *agg* creative II. *m*, *f* (*in pubblicità*) copywriter

creatore, -trice [kre·a·'to:·re] I. *agg* creative II. *m*, *f* **1.**(*autore, ideatore*) creator **2.**(*di moda, di profumi*) designer **3.** REL (*Dio*) **il Creatore** the Creator

creatura [kre·a·'tu:·ra] *f* **1.**(*essere umano*) creature **2.**(*bambino*) baby **3.** *fig* (*cosa creata: programma, progetto*) creation

creazione [kre·a·'tsio:·ne] *f* **1.**(*il creare*) creation **2.**(*fondazione, realizzazione*) setting-up **3.**(*nella moda*) design

crebbi ['kreb·bi] *1. pers sing pass rem di* **crescere**

credei [kre·'de:·i] *1. pers sing pass rem di* **credere**[1]

credente [kre·'dɛn·te] I. *agg* believing II. *mf* REL believer

credenza [kre·'dɛn·tsa] *f* **1.**(*mobile*) hutch **2.**(*tradizione*) belief; **-e popolari** popular belief

credenziale [kre·den·'tsia:·le] I. *agg* **lettere -i** letters of credence II. *pl* credentials *pl*

credere[1] ['kre:·de·re] <credo, credetti *o* credei, creduto> I. *vt* **1.**(*ritenere vero*) to believe; **io non ci credo** I don't believe it; **lo credo bene!** *inf* I should think so! **2.**(*ritenere*) to think; **lo credo capace di tutto** I think he's capable of anything; **credo che ...** +*conj* I think (that) ... **3.**(*ritenere opportuno*) to think; **fa come credi** do as you like II. *vi* to believe; ~ **in qu/qc** to believe in sb/sth; ~ **a qu** to believe sb; **non potevo** ~ **ai miei occhi** I couldn't believe my eyes III. *vr:* **-rsi** to think oneself; **-rsi furbo/intelligente** to think one

is smart/intelligent; **ma chi ti credi di essere?** who do you think you are?

credere[2] *m* (*opinione*) opinion

credibilità [kre·di·bi·li·'ta] <-> *f* credibility

creditizio, -a [kre·di·'ti·tsio] <-i, -ie> *agg* (*politica, mediazione*) credit; **stretta -a** credit squeeze

credito ['kre:·di·to] *m* **1.** COM, FIN credit; **comprare/vendere a** ~ to buy/sell on credit; **essere in** ~ to be in credit; **fare** ~ **a qu** to give sb credit; ~ **d'imposta** tax credit **2.**(*voto, valutazione*) credit; ~ **formativo** extra credit; ~ **scolastico** school credit **3.** *fig* (*attendibilità*) credit; **godere di molto** ~ to be held in high esteem

creditore, -trice [kre·di·'to:·re] I. *agg* (*azienda, ente*) creditor II. *m*, *f* creditor

credo ['krɛ:·do] *m* **1.** REL creed **2.**(*convinzione*) credo

credulone, -a [kre·du·'lo:·ne] *inf* I. *agg* (*persona, gente*) gullible II. *m*, *f* gullible person

crema ['krɛ:·ma] I. *f* **1.**(*panna*) cream; **gelato alla** ~ vanilla ice cream; **la** ~ **della società** *fig* the cream of society **2.** CULIN (*passato*) purée; ~ **di pomodoro** tomato purée; (*per dolci*) cream; ~ **pasticcera** pastry cream **3.**(*cosmetico*) cream; ~ **antietà** antiaging cream; ~ **per le mani** handcream; ~ **da giorno/notte** day/night cream; ~ **da barba** shaving cream; ~ **solare** suntan lotion **4.**(*per scarpe*) polish; ~ **da scarpe** shoe polish II. <inv> *agg* (**color**) ~ cream(-colored)

cremare [kre·'ma:·re] *vt* (*defunto*) to cremate

crematorio [kre·ma·'tɔ:·rio] <-i> *m* crematorium

cremazione [kre·ma·'tsio:·ne] *f* cremation

crème [krɛm] <-> *f* *fig* cream; **la** ~ **della società** the cream of society

Cremlino [krem·'li:·no] *m* Kremlin

Cremona [kre·'mo:·na] *f* Cremona, *city in northern Italy*

cremonese [kre·mo·'ne:·se] I. *agg* Cremonese II. *mf* (*abitante*) Cremonese

Cremonese (*zona*) Cremona area; **nel** ~ in the Cremona area

cren [krɛn] <-> *m* CULIN horseradish sauce

crepa ['krɛ:·pa] *f* crack

crepaccio [kre·'pat·tʃo] <-cci> *m* (*di ghiacciaio*) crevasse

crepacuore [kre·pa·'kuɔ:·re] *m* (*dolore*) heartbreak; **morire di** ~ to die of a broken heart

crepapelle [kre·pa·'pɛl·le] *avv* **ridere a** ~ *inf* to split one's sides laughing

crepare [kre·'pa:·re] I. *vi* **essere** *fig, inf* (*morire*) to kick the bucket *inf*; ~ **dal caldo/dalla sete/fame** to be dying from the heat/of thirst/of hunger; ~ **di paura** to be scared to death; ~ **dalle risa** to kill oneself laughing; ~ **di rabbia** to be consumed with anger; **in bocca al lupo! — crepi (il lupo)!** *inf* good luck! — thanks! II. *vr:* **-rsi** (*muro, terra, pelle*) to crack

crêpe [krɛp] <-> *f* CULIN pancake

crepitare [kre·pi·'ta:·re] *vi* (*fuoco*) to crackle; (*pioggia*) to patter

crepitio [kre·pi·'ti:·o] <-ii> *m* (*di fuoco*) crackling; (*di pioggia*) pattering

crepuscolare [kre·pus·ko·'la:·re] *agg* (*cielo*) twilight; **luce** ~ twilight

crepuscolo [kre·'pus·ko·lo] *m a. fig* twilight

crescendo [kreʃ·'ʃɛn·do] *m a. fig* crescendo

crescente [kreʃ·'ʃɛn·tɛ] *agg* 1. (*luna*) waxing; (*marea*) rising 2. (*attenzione, partecipazione, malcontento*) growing

crescenza [kreʃ·'ʃɛn·tsa] *f* CULIN *soft cheese from Lombardy*

crescere ['kreʃ·ʃe·re] <cresco, crebbi, cresciuto> **I.** *vi essere* 1. (*svilupparsi: persona, pianta*) to grow; **farsi** ~ **i capelli** to grow one's hair; **come sei cresciuto!** how you've grown! 2. (*spuntare: denti*) to come through 3. (*aumentare*) to increase; ~ **di peso/volume** to increase in weight/volume 4. (*diventare adulto*) to grow up **II.** *vt avere* (*allevare: figli*) to raise

crescione [kreʃ·'ʃo:·ne] *m* watercress

crescita ['kreʃ·ʃi·ta] *f* 1. (*sviluppo*) growth 2. (*aumento*) increase; ~ **zero** COM zero growth

cresciuto [kreʃ·'ʃu:·to] *pp di* **crescere**

cresco ['kres·ko] *1. pers sing pr di* **crescere**

cresima ['krɛ:·zi·ma] *f* REL confirmation

cresimare [kre·zi·'ma:·re] **I.** *vt* REL to confirm **II.** *vr:* **-rsi** REL to be confirmed

crespella [kres·'pɛl·la] *f* CULIN *stuffed pancake*

crespo ['kres·po] *m* crêpe

crespo, -a *agg* (*capelli*) frizzy

cresta ['kres·ta] *f* ZOO, GEOG crest; **alzare la** ~ *fig* to get cocky; **essere sulla** ~ **dell'onda** *fig* to be on the crest of a wave

creta ['kre:·ta] *f* 1. GEOL clay 2. (*oggetto, statuetta*) clay object

cretinata [kre·ti·'na:·va] *f inf* 1. (*sciocchezza*) stupid thing 2. (*cosa di poca importanza*) trifle

cretino, -a [kre·'ti:·no] **I.** *agg inf* (*domanda, risposta*) stupid **II.** *m, f inf* (*stupido*) fool

CRI *f abbr di* **Croce Rossa Italiana** Italian Red Cross

cric [krik] <-> *m mot* jack

cricca ['krik·ka] <-cche> *f* clique

cricco ['krik·ko] <-cchi> *m v.* **cric**

criceto [kri·'tʃɛ:·to] *m* ZOO hamster

cricket ['kri·kit] <-> *m* cricket

criminale [kri·mi·'na:·le] **I.** *agg* criminal **II.** *mf* criminal

criminalità [kri·mi·na·li·'ta] <-> *f* 1. (*delinquenza*) crime; ~ **organizzata** organized crime 2. (*caratteristica*) criminality

crimine ['kri:·mi·ne] *m* crime; **-i di guerra** war crimes

criminologia [kri·mi·no·lo·'dʒi:·a] <-gie> *f* criminology

criminologo, -a [kri·mi·'nɔ:·lo·go] <-gi, -ghe> *m, f* criminologist

crine ['kri:·ne] *m* 1. (*di cavallo*) horsehair

2. BOT fiber; ~ **vegetale** vegetable fiber

criniera [kri·'niɛ:·ra] *f* (*di cavallo*) mane

cripta ['krip·ta] *f* (*di chiesa*) crypt

criptare [krip·'ta:·re] *vt* COMPUT (*messaggio, file, email*) to encrypt; ~ **un programma televisivo** to encrypt a TV program

criptato, -a [krip·'ta:·to] *agg* COMPUT encrypted; **programma televisivo** ~ encrypted TV program

crisantemo [kri·zan·'tɛ:·mo] *m* BOT chrysanthemum

crisi ['kri:·zi] <-> *f* 1. (*periodo difficile*) crisis; ~ **congiunturale** economic crisis; ~ **coniugale** marital crisis; ~ **economica** economic crisis; ~ **di governo** government crisis; **essere in** ~ (*persona*) to be going through a crisis; (*coppia*) to be in crisis 2. MED (*attacco*) attack; ~ **epilettica** epileptic fit; ~ **di nervi** attack of nerves; ~ **di pianto** fit of tears

crisma ['kriz·ma] <-i> *m* REL (*olio consacrato*) chrism; **con tutti i -i** *fig* in strict accordance with the rules

cristallino [kris·tal·'li:·no] *m* ANAT crystalline lens

cristallino, -a *agg* 1. *fig* (*voce, acqua*) crystal clear 2. MIN crystalline

cristallizzare [kris·tal·lid·'dza:·re] **I.** *vt* 1. CHEM (*minerale, sale*) to crystallize 2. *fig* (*fissare*) to preserve permanently **II.** *vr:* **-rsi** 1. CHEM (*minerale, sale*) to crystallize 2. *fig* (*situazione*) to remain unchanged

cristallizzazione [kris·tal·lid·dza·'tsio:·ne] *f* 1. CHEM (*di minerale, sale*) crystallization 2. *fig* (*di situazione*) maintaining

cristallo [kris·'tal·lo] *m* 1. MIN crystal 2. (*vetro*) glass 3. (*lastra di vetro*) window

cristianesimo [kris·tia·'ne:·zi·mo] *m* REL Christianity

cristianità [kris·tia·ni·'ta] <-> *f* 1. (*qualità*) Christianity 2. (*tutti i cristiani*) Christendom

cristianizzare [kris·tia·nid·'dza:·re] *vt* (*popolo*) to convert to Christianity; (*festa*) to Christianize

cristiano, -a [kris·'tia:·no] **I.** *agg* REL (*fede, religione, chiesa*) Christian **II.** *m, f* 1. REL Christian 2. *fig, inf* (*essere umano*) human being; **da** ~ *inf* in a civilized manner; **essere un buon** ~ *inf* to be a decent human being

cristo ['kris·to] *m* 1. REL **Cristo** Christ; **avanti/dopo Cristo** before Christ/Anno Domini 2. *inf* (*poveraccio*) **un povero** ~ a poor thing

criterio [kri·'tɛ:·rio] <-i> *m* 1. (*norma*) criterion 2. (*senno*) (common) sense; **fare qc con** ~ to show common sense in doing sth

critica ['kri:·ti·ka] <-che> *f* 1. (*giudizio negativo*) criticism; **rivolgere -che a qu** to criticize sb 2. (*valutazione*) criticism; ~ **storica/letteraria** historical/literary criticism 3. (*recensione*) review 4. (*critici*) critics *pl*

criticare [kri·ti·'ka:·re] *vt* 1. (*disapprovare: azioni, persona*) to criticize 2. LIT, FILM, THEAT, MUS (*valutare*) to review

critico, -a ['kriː·ti·ko] <-ci, -che> I. *agg* critical II. *m, f* LIT, FILM, THEAT, MUS critic; ~ **letterario/musicale** literary/music critic

criticone [kri·ti·'koː·ne] *m* fault-finder

croato, -a [kro·'aː·to] I. *agg* Croat(ian) II. *m, f* (*abitante*) Croat(ian) III. *m* (*lingua*) Croat(ian)

Croazia *f* Croatia; **abitare in** ~ to live in Croatia; **andare in** ~ to go to Croatia

croccante [krok·'kan·te] I. *agg* (*biscotto, pane*) crunchy II. *m* CULIN brittle

crocchetta [krok·'ket·ta] *f* CULIN croquette

crocchia ['krɔk·kia] <-cchie> *f* (*di capelli*) bun

crocchio ['krɔk·kio] <-cchi> *m* (*gruppo*) cluster

croce ['kroː·tʃe] *f* 1. REL (*di Gesù*) cross; **farsi il segno della** ~ to cross oneself 2. (*oggetto, onorificenza, segno*) cross; **in** ~ (*braccia*) crossed; **fare una** ~ **sopra qc** *fig* to forget about sth 3. (*organizzazione*) **Croce Rossa/Verde** Red/Green Cross 4. (*pena*) **ciascuno ha la sua** ~ *fig* we each have our cross to bear 5. (*di moneta*) tails; **testa o** ~? heads or tails?

crocerossina [kro·tʃe·ros·'siː·na] *f* Red Cross nurse

crocevia [kro·tʃe·'viː·a] <-> *m* crossroads

crociata [kro·'tʃaː·ta] *f* crusade

crociato [kro·'tʃaː·to] *m* crusader

crociato, -a *agg* 1. (*incrociato*) **parole -e** crossword (puzzle) 2. (*con la croce*) marked with a cross; **scudo** ~ shield with a cross on it

crocicchio [kro·'tʃik·kio] <-cchi> *m* crossroads

crociera [kro·'tʃɛː·ra] *f* 1. NAUT cruise 2. AERO **velocità di** ~ cruising speed

crocifiggere [kro·tʃi·'fid·dʒe·re] <crocifiggo, crocifissi, crocifisso> *vt a. fig* to crucify

crocifissione [kro·tʃi·fis·'sioː·ne] *f* crucifixion

crocifisso[1] [kro·tʃi·'fis·so] *m* REL (*immagine di Gesù*) crucifix

crocifisso[2] *pp di* **crocifiggere**

croco ['krɔː·ko] <-chi> *m* BOT crocus

crogiolarsi [kro·dʒo·'laːr·si] *vr* (*bearsi: al sole*) to bask; (*nel dolore*) to wallow

crogiolo [kro·'dʒɔː·lo] *m* 1. (*per fusioni*) crucible 2. *fig* (*di etnie, culture*) melting pot

crollare [krol·'laː·re] *vi essere* 1. (*costruzione*) to collapse 2. (*persona*) to break down; (*Stato*) to fall 3. (*prezzi, azioni*) to fall; (*borsa*) to crash

crollo ['krɔl·lo] *m* 1. (*di casa, ponte*) collapse 2. COM (*di prezzi, azioni*) fall; (*di borsa*) crash; ~ **delle nascite** fall in the birthrate 3. *fig* (*di persona*) breakdown; (*di Stato*) fall

croma ['krɔː·ma] *f* MUS eighth note

cromare [kro·'maː·re] *vt* (*metallo, plastica*) to chrome

cromatico, -a [kro·'maː·ti·ko] <-ci, -che> *agg* (*dei colori*) of colors

cromatura [kro·ma·'tuː·ra] *f* (*di metallo, plastica*) chroming

cromo ['krɔː·mo] *m* CHEM chromium

cromosoma [kro·mo·'sɔː·ma] <-i> *m* MED chromosome

cromosomico, -a [kro·mo·'sɔː·mi·ko] <-ci, -che> *agg* MED (*corredo, patrimonio, danno*) chromosome

cronaca ['krɔː·na·ka] <-che> *f* 1. (*reportage*) commentary 2. (*notizie*) news; ~ **bianca** general news; ~ **nera** crime news; ~ **politica** political column; ~ **rosa** [*o* **mondana**] gossip column; **fatti di** ~ news items; **per la** ~ *fig* for the record 3. (*resoconto*) account

cronico, -a ['krɔː·ni·ko] <-ci, -che> I. *agg* (*malattia, dolore, malato*) chronic II. *m, f* chronic invalid

cronista [kro·'nis·ta] <-i , -e> *mf* columnist

cronologia [kro·no·lo·'dʒiː·a] <-gie> *f* chronology

cronologico, -a [kro·no·'lɔː·dʒi·ko] <-ci, -che> *agg* (*ordine, tavole*) chronological

cronometraggio [kro·no·me·'trad·dʒo] <-ggi> *m* (*di gara*) timing

cronometrare [kro·no·me·'traː·re] *vt* (*gara, corsa*) to time

cronometro [kro·'nɔː·met·ro] *m* 1. (*orologio*) chronometer 2. SPORT stopwatch

cross [krɔs] <-> *m* 1. (*motociclismo*) motocross 2. (*nel calcio*) cross

crossare [kros·'saː·re] *vi* SPORT (*nel calcio*) to cross

crossista [kros·'sis·ta] <-i , -e> *mf* (*motociclista*) motocross rider

crosta ['krɔs·ta] *f* 1. (*di pane*) crust; (*di formaggio*) rind 2. MED scab; ~ **lattea** cradle cap 3. GEOG crust; ~ **terrestre** Earth's crust

crostacei [kros·'taː·tʃei] *mpl* shellfish

crostino [kros·'tiː·no] *m* CULIN canapé

crucciare [krut·'tʃaː·re] I. *vt* (*preoccupazioni, pensieri*) to trouble II. *vr:* **-rsi** to worry

cruccio ['krut·tʃo] <-cci> *m* (*problema*) worry

crucco, -a ['kruk·ko] <-cchi, -cche> *m, f pej, inf* Kraut *pej*

cruciale [kru·'tʃaː·le] *agg* (*decisivo: momento, partita*) crucial

cruciverba [kru·tʃi·'vɛr·ba] <-> *m* crossword

crudele [kru·'deː·le] *agg* cruel

crudeltà [kru·del·'ta] <-> *f* 1. (*di persona, animo, tortura*) cruelty 2. (*azione*) act of cruelty

crudo, -a ['kruː·do] *agg* 1. (*non cotto: carne, verdura*) raw 2. (*poco cotto*) undercooked 3. *fig* (*verità*) stark

cruento, -a [kru·'ɛn·to] *agg* (*battaglia, film, immagine*) bloody

crumiro, -a [kru·'miː·ro] *m, f* scab

cruna ['kruː·na] *f* (*di ago*) eye

crusca ['krus·ka] <-sche> *f* bran; **l'Accademia della Crusca** national academy that monitors the Italian language

cruscotto [krus·'kɔt·to] *m* AUTO dashboard

c.s. *abbr di* **come sopra** as above

cubatura [ku·ba·'tuː·ra] *f* cubic capacity

cubettatrice [ku·bet·ta·'triː·tʃe] *f* (*per alimenti, mangimi*) dicer

cubetto [ku·'bet·to] *m* (*di ghiaccio, di lievito*)

cube

cubico, -a ['ku:·bi·ko] <-ci, -che> *agg* cubic; **centimetri -ci** cubic centimeters; **radice -a** cube root

cubismo [ku·'biz·mo] *m* ART cubism

cubista [ku·'bis·ta] <-i , -e> I. *mf* ART cubist II. *agg* ART (*quadro, pittore*) cubist

cubito ['ku:·bi·to] *m* ANAT ulna

cubo ['ku:·bo] I. *m* cube II. *agg* cubic; **metro ~** cubic meter

cuccagna [kuk·'kaɲ·ɲa] *f* plenty; **il paese della ~** the land of plenty; **l'albero della ~** the greasy pole

cuccare [kuk·'ka:·re] I. *vt inf* 1.(*prendere*) to catch 2.*fig* (*rimorchiare*) to pick up II. *vr:* **-rsi** *inf* 1.(*prendersi*) to catch 2.(*sorbirsi*) to put up with

cuccetta [kut·'tʃet·ta] *f* NAUT (*di nave*) berth; FERR (*di treno*) couchette

cucchiaiata [kuk·kia·'ia:·ta] *f* spoonful

cucchiaino [kuk·kia·'i:·no] *m* 1.(*posata*) teaspoon; **essere da raccattare con il ~** *inf* to be pooped *inf* 2.(*quantità*) teaspoonful

cucchiaio [kuk·'kia:·io] <-ai> *m* 1.(*posata*) spoon 2.(*quantità*) spoonful

cuccia ['kut·tʃa] <-cce> *f* (*di cane*) dog basket; **a ~!** down!

cucciolata [kut·tʃo·'la:·ta] *f* litter

cucciolo, -a ['kut·tʃo·lo] *m, f* (*di cane*) puppy; (*di gatto*) kitten; (*di balena, elefante*) calf

cucco ['kuk·ko] <-cchi> *m* (*cuculo*) cuckoo; **vecchio come il ~** *inf* from out of the ark *inf*

cucina [ku·'tʃi:·na] *f* 1.(*luogo, mobili*) kitchen; **~ componibile** [*o* **all'americana**] fitted kitchen 2.(*arte, modo*) cooking; **libro di ~** cookbook 3.(*apparecchio*) stove; **~ a gas** gas stove; **~ elettrica** electric stove

cucinare [ku·tʃi·'na:·re] I. *vt* (*carne, pesce*) to cook II. *vi* to cook

cucinino [ku·tʃi·'ni:·no] *m* kitchenette

cucire [ku·'tʃi:·re] *vt* 1.(*orlo, abito*) to sew; **macchina da ~** sewing machine 2.(*ferita*) to sew up

cucito [ku·'tʃi:·to] *m* (*tecnica*) sewing

cucito, -a *agg* sewn; **~ a mano** hand-stitched; **avere le labbra -e** *fig* to know when to keep one's mouth shut

cucitrice [ku·tʃi·'tri:·tʃe] *f* (*spillatrice*) stapler

cucitura [ku·tʃi·'tu:·ra] *f* (*di tessuto*) seam

cucù [ku·'ku] I. <-> *m* 1. ZOO cuckoo 2. **orologio a ~** cuckoo clock II. *int* peekaboo!

cuculo [ku·'ku:·lo] *m* ZOO cuckoo

cuffia ['kuf·fia] <-ie> *f* 1.(*di lana*) hat; (*per neonati*) bonnet 2.(*impermeabile*) cap; **~ (da bagno**) (*per piscina*) swimming cap; **~ (da doccia**) shower cap 3.TEL, RADIO headphones *pl*

cugino, -a [ku·'dʒi:·no] *m, f* cousin

cui ['ku:·i] *pron* 1.(*con preposizioni*) **a ~** (*persona*) to whom; (*cosa*) to which; **con ~** (*persona*) with whom; (*cosa*) with which; **di ~** (*persona*) of whom; (*cosa*) of which; **in ~** in which; **per ~** (*persona*) for whom; (*cosa*) for

which 2.(*a cui*) to whom; (*cosa*) to which 3.(*di cui*) whose

culat(t)one [ku·la(t)·'to:·ne] *m vulg* faggot *pej*

culinaria [ku·li·'na:·ria] <-ie> *f* (*arte*) cooking

culinario, -a [ku·li·'na:·rio] <-i, -ie> *agg* (*doti, capacità, tradizioni*) culinary; **arte -a** cooking

culla ['kul·la] *f* cradle

cullare [kul·'la:·re] I. *vt* 1.(*bambino*) to rock 2.*fig* (*speranza*) to cherish II. *vr:* **-rsi** 1.(*dondolarsi*) to be rocked 2.*fig* (*abbandonarsi*) to indulge

culminante [kul·mi·'nan·te] *agg* (*fase, punto, momento*) culminating

culminare [kul·mi·'na:·re] *vi essere* 1.*fig* (*arrivare all'apice*) **~ in qc** to culminate in sth 2.ASTR to reach its highest point

culmine ['kul·mi·ne] *m* 1.*fig* (*apice: di carriera*) peak; (*apice: di stupidità, potenza*) height 2.(*di monte*) top

culo ['ku:·lo] *m vulg* ass *vulg*; **avere ~** to be lucky; **prendere qu per il ~** to take sb for a ride *inf*; **farsi il ~** [*o* **un ~ così**] to work one's ass off *vulg*; **va a fare in ~!** fuck off! *vulg*

culto ['kul·to] *m* 1.REL (*di reliquie, anime, morti*) cult 2.(*religione*) religion; **libertà di ~** religious freedom 3.*fig* (*venerazione*) cult; **avere il ~ della propria persona** to be vain about one's appearance

cultura [kul·'tu:·ra] *f* 1.(*conoscenze*) culture; **un uomo di ~** an educated man; **farsi una ~** to get an education 2.AGR crop

culturale [kul·tu·'ra:·le] *agg* cultural

culturismo [kul·tu·'riz·mo] *m* bodybuilding

culturista [kul·tu·'ris·ta] <-i , -e> *mf* bodybuilder

cumino [ku·'mi:·no] *m* cumin

cumulare [ku·mu·'la:·re] *vt* (*contributi, ore lavorative, sconti*) to accumulate

cumulativo, -a [ku·mu·la·'ti:·vo] *agg* (*biglietto, sconto, prezzo*) inclusive

cumulo ['ku:·mu·lo] *m* 1.(*mucchio: di macerie, terra, pietre*) heap 2.METEO cumulus

cuneense [ku·ne·'ɛn·se] I. *agg* from Cuneo II. *mf* (*abitante*) person from Cuneo

Cuneense *m* (*zona*) Cuneo area; **nel ~** in the Cuneo area

cuneiforme [ku·nei·'for·me] I. *agg* cuneiform; **caratteri -i** cuneiform characters *pl* II. *m* (*scrittura*) cuneiform

cuneo ['ku:·neo] *m* wedge

Cuneo *f* Cuneo

cunetta [ku·'net·ta] *f* 1.(*canaletto*) gutter 2.(*dosso*) dip

cunicolo [ku·'ni:·ko·lo] *m* tunnel

cuocere ['kuɔ:·tʃe·re] <cuocio, cossi, cotto> I. *vt avere* 1.to cook; (*bollire*) to boil; (*in padella*) to fry; (*in umido*) to stew; (*in forno*) to bake; **~ alla griglia** to broil; **~ sulla brace** to grill 2.(*ceramiche, mattoni, calcina*) to fire II. *vi essere* CULIN to cook; **il riso sta cuocendo** the rice is cooking

cuoco, -a ['kuɔ:·ko] <-chi, -che> *m, f* 1.(*chi cucina*) cook 2.(*di ristorante*) chef

cuoio ['kuɔː·io] *m* **1.**(*pelle conciata*) leather **2.** ANAT (*pelle dell'uomo*) ~ **capelluto** scalp **3.** *fig, inf* (*pelle dell'uomo*) skin; **tirare** [*o* **las-ciarci**] **le -a** *fig* to kick the bucket *inf*

cuore ['kuɔː·re] *m* **1.** ANAT heart **2.** *fig* (*sede dei sentimenti*) heart; **affari di** ~ affairs of the heart; **gente di** ~ kind-hearted people *pl;* **amica del** ~ bosom friend; **avere buon** ~ to have a big heart; **stare a** ~ to be important; **prendersi a** ~ **qc** to take sth to heart; **ridere di** ~ *fig* to laugh heartily; **spezzare il** ~ **a qu** *fig* to break sb's heart; **senza** ~ heartless; **con tutto il** ~ with all one's heart; **a** (**forma**) **di** ~ heart-shaped; **mi si stringe il** ~ *fig* my heart aches; **due -i e una capanna** love in a cottage; ~ **contento il ciel l'aiuta** *prov* God helps those who help themselves *prov* **3.** (*di carte da gioco*) hearts *pl* **4.** *fig* (*punto centrale*) heart; ~ **del carciofo** artichoke heart; **nel** ~ **della notte** in the dead of night

cupo, -a ['kuː·po] *agg* **1.**(*colore*) dark **2.**(*notte, foresta*) pitch-black **3.**(*voce*) deep **4.** *fig* (*volto, sguardo*) sullen

cupola ['kuː·po·la] *f* dome

cura ['kuː·ra] *f* **1.**(*interessamento*) care; **pren-dersi** ~ **di qu** to take care of sb; **avere** ~ **della propria salute** to take care of one's health **2.**(*accuratezza*) care; **a** ~ **di ...** (*libro*) edited by ... **3.** MED (*terapia*) treatment; **casa di** ~ nursing home; **luogo di** ~ **termale** thermal spa; **essere in** ~ **da qu** to be a patient of sb

curare [ku·raː·re] **I.** *vt* **1.**(*malato, malattia*) to treat **2.**(*occuparsi di: aziani, malati, affari, interessi*) to take care of **3.**(*testo*) to edit **II.** *vr:* **-rsi 1.**(*prendersi cura*) to take care of oneself **2.** MED (*sottoporsi a una terapia*) to get treat-ment **3.**(*preoccuparsi*) **-rsi di qc** to care about sth

curato [ku·raː·to] *m* REL parish priest

curia ['kuː·ria] <-ie> *f* REL curia

curiosare [ku·rio·'saː·re] *vi* **1.**(*guardare*) to browse **2.**(*ficcare il naso*) to nose around; ~ **in qc** to stick one's nose into sth

curiosità [ku·rio·si·'ta] <-> *f* curiosity; **mos-trare** ~ **per qc** to be curious about sth

curioso, -a [ku·'rio:·so] **I.** *agg* **1.**(*interes-sato*) curious **2.**(*indiscreto*) nosy **3.**(*bizzarro: oggetto, fatto*) curious **II.** *m, f* onlooker

curriculum (**vitae**) [kur·'riː·ku·lum ('viː·te)] <-> *m* résumé

curry ['kʌ·ri] <-> *m* (*polvere*) curry powder

cursore *m* COMPUT cursor

cursorio, -a [kur·'sɔː·rio] <-i, -ie> *agg* (*veloce*) cursory

curva ['kur·va] *f* **1.**(*su diagramma*) curve **2.**(*stradale*) bend; **doppia** ~ double bend

curvare [kur·'vaː·re] **I.** *vi* **1.**(*auto*) to turn **2.**(*strada*) to bend **II.** *vt* **1.**(*sbarra, ramo*) to bend **2.**(*capo, fronte*) to bow; (*schiena*) to make bent **III.** *vr:* **-rsi** (*ramo*) to bend; (*per-sona*) to bend down

curvo, -a ['kur·vo] *agg* (*linea, legno*) curved; (*spalle, persona*) bent

cuscinetto¹ [kuʃ·ʃi·'net·to] *m* **1.** TEC bearing; ~ **a sfere** ball bearing **2.**(*per spilli*) pincushion **3.**(*per timbri*) pad

cuscinetto² <inv> *agg* **stato** ~ buffer state; **zona** ~ buffer zone

cuscino [kuʃ·'ʃiː·no] *m* **1.**(*guanciale*) pillow **2.**(*per poltrona, divano*) cushion

cuscus ['kus·kus] <-> *m* CULIN couscous

cuspide ['kus·pi·de] *f* ARCH spire

custode [kus·'tɔː·de] **I.** *mf* **1.**(*di museo*) at-tendant; (*di palazzo*) superintendent; (*di scuola*) janitor **2.** *fig* (*di valore, bene ideale*) guardian **II.** *agg* **angelo** ~ guardian angel

custodia [kus·'tɔː·dia] <-ie> *f* **1.**(*cura*) care; **dare qu/qc in** ~ **a qu** to entrust sb/sth to sb's care **2.** JUR ~ **cautelare** custody **3.**(*astuccio: di occhiali, violino*) case

custodire [kus·to·'diː·re] <custodisco> *vt* (*conservare: casa, bambini*) to take care of; (*segreto*) to keep

customizing ['kʌs·tə·ai·ziŋ] *m* COM customiz-ing

cutaneo, -a [ku·'taː·neo] *agg* skin; **eruzione** -a rash

cute ['kuː·te] *f* skin

CV 1. *abbr di* **Cavallo Vapore** h.p. **2.** *abbr di* **curriculum vitae** résumé

cybercafé [sai·ber·ka·'fe] <-> *m* Internet café

cybernauta [sai·ber·'nau·ta] <-i , -e> *mf v.* **internettista**

cybersesso *m* COMPUT cybersex

cyberspazio [tʃi·ber·'spa·zio] <-i> *m* COMPUT cyberspace

cyclette® [si·'klɛt] <- *o* cyclettes> *f* exercise bike; **fare** ~ to ride an exercise bike

D

D, d [di] <-> *f* D, d; ~ **come Domodossola** D as in dog

d' *prep* = **di** *used before a vowel; v.* **di**

D 1. *abbr di* **Diretto** Dir. **2.** *abbr di* **Deutsch-land** DE

da [da] <dal, dallo, dall', dalla, dai, dagli, dalle> *prep* **1.**(*stato in luogo*) at; (*moto da luogo*) from; (*moto a luogo: con persone*) to; (*attraverso*) through; (*distanza*) from; **abito** ~ **mio zio** I live with my uncle; **andare** ~ **Torino a Stoccarda** to go from Turin to Stutt-gart; **vado** ~ **un amico** I'm going to a friend's house; **vengo** ~ **casa** I've come from home; **verrò** ~ **Firenze** I'll be coming from Florence; **trattoria "~ Giovanni"** "Giovanni's"; ~ **dove** where from **2.**(*con verbi passivi*) by **3.**(*causa*) with; **tremare dal freddo** to shiver with cold **4.**(*tempo*) ~ **principio** from the beginning; ~ **domani** from tomorrow; ~ **oggi in poi** from today on; **dal lunedì al venerdì** from Monday

to Friday; (**fin**) ~ **bambino** since childhood; ~ **allora** since then; ~ **cinque anni** for five years; ~ **molto/poco** for a long/short time; ~ **quanto tempo** how long **5.** (*fine, scopo*) **auto** ~ **corsa** racecar; **cane** ~ **caccia** hunting dog **6.** (*modo*) like; **comportarsi** ~ **vero amico** to behave like a true friend; **mi ha risposto** ~ **maleducato** he answered me very rudely; **ho fatto tutto** ~ **me** I did it all by myself; ~ **solo** alone **7.** (*qualità*) with; **una ragazza dai capelli rossi** a redheaded girl **8.** (*valore*) between; **ci vorranno dai due ai tre giorni** it will take two to three days; **un gelato** ~ **due euro** an ice cream for two euros **9.** (*con inf*) **essere così stanchi** ~ **non poter stare in piedi** to be so tired you can't stand up; **qualcosa** ~ **bere** something to drink; **non c'è niente** ~ **fare** there's nothing to be done
dabbasso [dab·'bas·so] *avv* downstairs
dabbenaggine [dab·be·'nad·dʒi·ne] *f* simple-mindedness
dabbene [dab·'bɛː·ne] <inv> *agg* decent
daccapo [dak·'kaː·po] *avv* again; **ricominciare** ~ to start again
dado ['daː·do] *m* **1.** (*cubetto*) dice; **giocare ai** -**i** to shoot dice **2.** CULIN bouillon cube **3.** (*per bulloni*) nut
daffare [daf·'faː·re] <-> *m* work; **avere un gran** ~ to be very busy; **darsi un gran** ~ to put oneself out
dagli, dai ['daʎ·ʎi, 'daː·i] *prep* = **da** + **gli, i** *v.* **da**
daino ['daː·i·no] *m* **1.** (*animale*) (fallow) deer **2.** (*pelle*) buckskin
dal [dal] *prep* = **da** + **il** *v.* **da**
dalia ['daː·lia] <-ie> *f* dahlia
dall', dalla, dallo, dalle [dall, 'dal·la, 'dal·lo, 'dal·le] *prep* = **da** + **l', la, lo, le** *v.* **da**
daltonico, -a [dal·'tɔː·ni·ko] <-ci, -che> **I.** *agg* colorblind **II.** *m, f* colorblind person
dama ['daː·ma] *f* **1.** HIST lady in waiting **2.** (*gioco*) checkers; (*scacchiera*) checkerboard; **giocare a** ~ to play checkers
damasco [da·'mas·ko] <-schi> *m* damask
damigella [da·mi·'dʒɛl·la] *f* HIST young woman, *of high social standing;* ~ **d'onore** bridesmaid
damigiana [da·mi·'dʒaː·na] *f* demijohn
dammeno [dam·'meː·no] <inv> *agg* **essere** ~ **di qu** to be outdone by sb; **è molto intelligente, ma sua sorella non è** ~ he's very intelligent, but so's his sister
DAMS [dams] *m acro di* **Discipline delle Arti, della Musica e dello Spettacolo** *degree in performing arts*
danaro [da·'naː·ro] *v.* **denaro**
danaroso, -a [da·na·'roː·so] *agg* wealthy
dancing ['daːn·siŋ/'dɛn·sin(g)] <-> *m* dance hall
danese [da·'neː·se] **I.** *agg* Danish **II.** *mf* (*persona*) Dane **III.** *m* (*cane*) Great Dane
Danimarca [da·ni·'mar·ka] *f* Denmark; **abitare in** ~ to live in Denmark; **andare in** ~ to

go to Denmark
dannare [dan·'naː·re] **I.** *vt* **far** ~ **qu** to drive sb crazy; -**rsi l'anima per qc** to move heaven and earth for sth **II.** *vr:* -**rsi** to fret
dannato, -a [dan·'naː·to] **I.** *agg inf* damn **II.** *m, f* **i** -**i** the damned
dannazione [dan·nat·'tsioː·ne] **I.** *f* **1.** (*dell'anima*) damnation **2.** *fig* (*tormento*) torment **II.** *int* ~! damn!
danneggiare [dan·ned·'dʒaː·re] *vt* **1.** (*oggetto*) to damage **2.** (*nuocere a*) to harm
danno ['dan·no] *m* damage; **far** -**i** to cause damage; **arrecare** ~ **a qc** to harm sth; **pagare i** -**i** to pay damages; **a** ~ [*o* **ai** -**i**] **di qu** to the detriment of sb; **rimanere** [*o* **restare**] **col** ~ **e con le beffe** to suffer twice over
dannoso, -a [dan·'noː·so] *agg* **essere** ~ (**per** [*o* **a**] **qu/qc**) harmful
dantesco, -a [dan·'tes·ko] <-schi, -sche> *agg* (*inferno, personaggio, stile, linguaggio*) Dantesque
Danubio [da·'nuː·bio] *m* Danube
danza ['dan·tsa] *f* dance; ~ **classica** classical ballet; ~ **popolare** folk dancing
danzare [dan·'tsaː·re] *vi, vt* to dance
danzatore, -trice [dan·tsa·'toː·re] *m, f* dancer
Danzica ['dan·tsi·ka] *f* Danzig
dappertutto [dap·per·'tut·to] *avv* everywhere
dappoco [dap·'pɔː·ko] <inv> *agg* **1.** (*inetto: medico, tipo*) useless **2.** (*di poca importanza: ferita, problema*) trivial
dapprima [dap·'priː·ma] *avv* at first
dare[1] ['daː·re] <do, diedi *o* detti, dato> **I.** *vt* **1.** (*gener*) ~ **qc a qu** to give sb sth; ~ **una notizia a qn** to give sb some news; ~ **un consiglio a qn** to give sb some advice; ~ **peso a qc** to give weight to sth; ~ **a qu il permesso di fare qc** to give sb permission to do sth; (~ *fuoco a qc*) to set sth on fire; (~ *uno sguardo a qc*) to look at sb; **darsi delle arie** to show off; ~ **una multa a qu** to fine sb; **non darsi pace** to not be able to stop thinking about sth **2.** (*produrre: frutti*) to produce **3.** (*causare*) ~ **preoccupazioni a qu** to worry sb; ~ **un dispiacere a qu** to upset sb **4.** (*fare: lezione*) to give; ~ **un esame** to take an exam; ~ **una conferenza** to give a lecture; ~ **una festa** to have a party **5.** (*dire*) to call; ~ **del Lei/tu a qu** to call sb Lei/tu; ~ **dell'imbecille a qu** to call sb an idiot **6.** (*augurare*) ~ **il buongiorno/la buonanotte a qu** to say hello/goodnight to sb **7.** (*pagare*) to pay **II.** *vi* **1.** (*guardare*) ~ **su qc** to overlook sth; **la finestra dà sul cortile** the window overlooks the courtyard **2.** (*prorompere*) ~ **in escandescenze** to go mad **3.** (*battere*) ~ **in qc** to hit sth **4.** (*fare effetto*) ~ **nell'occhio** to stick out; ~ **alla testa** to go to one's head **5.** (*tendere a*) ~ **sul rosso** to tend toward red **III.** *vr:* -**rsi 1.** (*dedicarsi*) to devote oneself to; **darsi alla pittura** to take up painting **2.** (*reciproco*) **si sono dati una mano l'un l'altro** they held hands; **ci siamo dati solo un bacio** we only kissed **3.** (*loc*) **si**

dà il caso che ... +*conj* it so happens that ...; **può darsi che ...** +*conj* perhaps ...; **darsela a gambe** to run away; **-rsi per vinto** to give in

dare² <-> *m* debits *pl;* **il ~ e l'avere** debits and credits

dark [daːk/dark] **I.** <inv> *agg* Goth **II.** <-> *mf* Goth

darsena ['dar·se·na] *f* dock

DAT ['dat] *m acro di* **Digital Audio Tape** DAT

data ['daː·ta] *f* date; **~ di nascita** date of birth; **~ di scadenza** expiration date; **rimandare qc a ~ da destinarsi** to postpone sth indefinitely; **un amico di lunga/vecchia ~** an old friend

datare [da·'taː·re] **I.** *vt avere* to date **II.** *vi essere* to date; **la nostra amicizia data dal 1998** our friendship dates back to 1998; **a ~ da oggi** *adm* dating from today

datario [da·'taː·rio] *m* **1.** (*timbro*) date stamp **2.** (*di orologio*) date window

dativo [da·'tiː·vo] *m* dative

dato ['daː·to] *m* datum; **-i anagrafici** personal data; **~ di fatto** fact; **banca -i** COMPUT data bank; **trasmissione (di) -i** COMPUT data transmission; **elaborazione elettronica dei -i** electronic data processing

dato, -a **I.** *pp di* **dare¹** **II.** *agg* **1.** (*determinato*) certain **2.** (*considerato*) given; **~ che ...** since; **-e le circostanze** under the circumstances

datore, -trice [da·'toː·re] *m, f* **~ di lavoro** employer

dattero ['dat·te·ro] *m* **1.** (*frutto*) date **2.** (*pianta*) date palm

dattilografare [dat·ti·lo·gra·'faː·re] *vt* to type

dattilografia [dat·ti·lo·gra·'fiː·a] *f* typing

dattilografo, -a [dat·ti·'lɔː·gra·fo] *m, f* typist

dattilogramma [dat·ti·lo·'gram·ma] <-i> *m* fingerprint

dattiloscritto, -a *agg* typewritten

dattorno [dat·'tor·no] **I.** *avv* around **II.** *prep* **~ a** around **III.** <inv> *agg* neighboring

davanti [da·'van·ti] **I.** *avv* (*di fronte*) opposite; (*nella parte anteriore*) in front **II.** *prep* **~ a** **1.** (*di fronte a*) in front of **2.** (*dirimpetto*) opposite **III.** <inv> *agg* front **IV.** *m* front

davanzale [da·van·'tsaː·le] *m* windowsill

davanzo, d'avanzo [da·'van·tso] *avv* more than enough

davvero [dav·'veː·ro] *avv* really; **per ~** really and truly

dazio ['dat·tsio] <-i> *m* duty

d.C. *abbr di* **dopo Cristo** A.D.

DC *f abbr di* **Democrazia Cristiana** HIST *former Italian centrist party*

dea ['dɛː·a] *f* goddess

deambulazione [de·am·bu·lat·'tsioː·ne] *f* walking

deamplificare [de·map·li·fi·'kaː·re] *vt* TEC to decrease, *in size*

deamplificazione [de·amp·li·fi·kat·'tsioː·ne] *f* TEC decrease, *in size*

débâcle [de·'ba·kl] <-> *f* debacle

debbo ['dɛb·bo] *1. pers sing pr di* **dovere¹**

debellare [de·bel·'laː·re] *vt form* (*malattia,*

corruzione) to overcome

debilitante [de·bi·li·'tan·te] *agg* (*malattia, clima, attività*) debilitating

debilitare [de·bi·li·'taː·re] *vt* to debilitate

debilitazione [de·bi·li·tat·'tsioː·ne] *f* weakness

debitamente [de·bi·ta·'men·te] *avv* duly

debito ['deː·bi·to] *m a.* FIN debt; **avere un ~ con qu** to be in debt to sb; **annullare un ~** to write off a debt; **~ pubblico** public debt; **sentirsi in ~ verso qu** to be in sb's debt

debito, -a *agg* **1.** (*doveroso*) due **2.** (*opportuno*) proper; **a tempo ~** at the right time

debitore, -trice [de·bi·'toː·re] *m, f* **1.** FIN debtor **2.** *fig* **ti sono ~** I'm in your debt

debitorio, -a [de·bi·'tɔː·rio] <-ri, -rie> *agg* JUR debt

debitrice *f v.* debitore

debole ['deː·bo·le] **I.** *agg* weak **II.** *m* **avere un ~ per qc/qu** to have a weakness for sth/sb; **avere il ~ del gioco** to have a weakness for gambling

debolezza [de·bo·'let·tsa] *f* weakness

debugging [diː·'bʌ·giŋ] <-> *m* COMPUT debugging

debuttante [de·but·'tan·te] **I.** *agg* THEAT young **II.** *mf* THEAT *actor/singer who is just starting out*

debuttare [de·but·'taː·re] *vi* to make one's debut

debutto [de·'but·to] *m* debut

decade ['dɛː·ka·de] *f* (*dieci giorni*) ten days

decadente [de·ka·'dɛn·te] *agg* decadent

decadentismo [de·ca·den·'tiz·mo] *m* LIT Decadence

decadentista [de·ka·den·'tis·ta] <-i *m*, -e *f*> *mf* LIT Decadent

decadentistico, -a [de·ka·den·'tis·ti·ko] <-ci, -che> *agg* LIT Decadent

decadenza [de·ca·'dɛn·tsa] *f* **1.** (*declino*) decadence **2.** JUR **~ dei termini** expiration of deadline

decadere [de·ka·'deː·re] <irr> *vi essere* (*declinare*) to fall into decline

decadimento [de·ka·di·'men·to] *m* decline

decaduto, -a [de·ka·'duː·to] *agg* **1.** (*impoverito*) impoverished; **nobiltà -a** decayed nobility; **antiche civiltà -e** ancient civilizations that fell into decline **2.** JUR expired

decaedro [de·ka·'ɛːd·ro] *m* MATH decahedron

decaffeinare [de·kaf·fei·'naː·to] *m* decaffeinated coffee

decaffeinato, -a *agg* decaffeinated

decagono [de·'ka··go·no] *m* MATH decagon

decagrammo [de·ka·'gram·mo] *m* decagram

decalcificare [de·kal·tʃi·fi·'kaː·re] *vt* CHEM, MED to decalcify

decalcomania [de·kal·ko·ma·'niː·a] <-ie> *f* decal

decalitro [de·'kaː·lit·ro] *m* decaliter

decalogo [de·'ka·lo·go] <-ghi> *m* **1.** (*di Mosè*) Decalogue **2.** (*norme*) rulebook

decano [de·'ka·no] *m* **1.** (*per anzianità*) doy-

D

en **2.**(*titolo*) dean

decantare¹ [de·kan·'ta:·re] *vt* (*lodare*) to sing the praises of

decantare² [de·kan·'ta:·re] **I.** *vt* **1.** CHEM to leave to settle **2.**(*vino*) to decant **II.** *vi* **1.** CHEM to settle **2.**(*vino*) to decant

decapitare [de·ka·pi·'ta:·re] *vt* to decapitate

decapitazione [de·ka·pi·tat·'tsio:·ne] *f* decapitation

decappottabile [de·kap·po·'ta:·bi·le] **I.** *agg* **auto** ~ convertible **II.** *f* convertible

decasillabo [de·ka·'sil·la·bo] *m* decasyllable

decathlon ['dɛ:·kat·lon] <-> *m* decathlon

decedere [de·'tʃɛ:·de·re] <decedo, decessi *o* decedetti, deceduto> *vi essere* lit to die

deceduto, -a [de·tʃe·'du:·to] *form* **I.** *agg* deceased **II.** *m, f* deceased

decelerare [de·tʃe·le·'ra:·re] *vt* to slow down

decelerazione [de·tʃe·le·rat·'tsio:·ne] *f* slowing down

decennale [de·tʃen·'na:·le] **I.** *agg* **1.**(*che dura 10 anni*) ten-year **2.**(*ogni 10 anni*) ten-yearly **II.** *m* **1.**(*anniversario*) tenth anniversary **2.**(*cerimonia*) tenth anniversary celebration

decenne [de·'tʃɛn·ne] *agg* ten-year-old

decennio [de·'tʃɛn·nio] <-i> *m* decade

decente [de·'tʃɛn·te] *agg* decent

decentralizzare [de·tʃen·tra·lid·'dza:·re] *vt* to decentralize

decentralizzazione [de·tʃen·tra·lid·dzat·'tsio:·ne] *f* decentralization; ~ **amministrativa** devolution; ~ **produttiva** outsourcing

decentramento [de·tʃen·tra·'men·to] *m* decentralization

decentrare [de·tʃen·'tra:·re] *vt* to decentralize

decentrato, -a [de·tʃen·'tra:·to] *agg* decentralized; **servizi/uffici -i** decentralized services/offices

decenza [de·'tʃɛn·tsa] *f* **1.**(*pudore, dignità*) decency **2.**(*convenienza*) suitability

decesse [de·'tʃɛs·si] *3. pers sing pass rem di* **decedere**

decesso [de·'tʃɛs·so] *m form* death

decibel [de·tʃi·'bɛl/'dɛ:·tʃi·bel] <-> *m* PHYS decibel; **scala in** ~ decibel scale; ~ **acustico** acoustic decibel

decidere [de·'tʃi:·de·re] <decido, decisi, deciso> **I.** *vt* (*stabilire*) to decide; (*scegliere*) to choose; ~ **di fare qc** to decide to do sth **II.** *vi* to decide; ~ **di qc** to decide about sth **III.** *vr:* **-rsi** to make up one's mind; **-rsi a fare qc** to make up one's mind to do sth

decifrabile [de·tʃi·'fra:·bi·le] *agg* (*codice, documento, scrittura*) decipherable

decifrare [de·tʃi·'fra:·re] *vt* (*scrittura*) to decipher; (*codice*) to work out; (*enigma*) to find the key to

decigrammo [de·tʃi·'gram·mo] *m* decigram

decilitro [de·'tʃi:·lit·ro] *m* deciliter

decima ['dɛ:·tʃi·ma] *f* MATH, MUS tenth; **7 alla** ~ 7 to the tenth

decimale [de·tʃi·'ma:·le] *agg* decimal

decimare [de·tʃi·'ma:·re] *vt* to decimate

decimazione [de·tʃi·mat·'tsio:·ne] *f* decimation

decimetro [de·'tʃi:·met·ro] *m* decimeter

decimilionesimo [de·tʃi·mi·lio·'nɛ:·zi·mo] *m* (*in frazioni*) ten millionth

decimilionesimo, -a **I.** *agg* ten millionth **II.** *m, f* ten millionth

decimillesimo [de·tʃi·mil·'lɛ:·zi·mo] *m* ten thousandth; **un** ~ **di secondo** a millisecond

decimillesimo, -a **I.** *agg* ten thousandth **II.** *m, f* ten thousandth

decimilligrammo [de·tʃi·mil·li·'gram·mo] *m* decimilligram

decimillimetro [de·tʃi·mil·'li:·met·ro] *m* decimillimeter

decimo ['dɛ:·tʃi·mo] *m* (*in frazione*) tenth

decimo, -a **I.** *agg* tenth **II.** *m, f* tenth; *v.a.* **quinto**

decina [de·'tʃi:·na] *f* MATH ten or so *pl;* **una** ~ (**di** ...) ten or so ...; **a -e** by the dozen

decisamente [de·tʃi·za·'men·te] *avv* **1.**(*veramente*) really **2.**(*con risolutezza*) decidedly

decisi [de·'tʃi:·zi] *1. pers sing pass rem di* **decidere**

decisionale [de·tʃi·zio·'na:·le] *agg* decision-making

decisione [de·tʃi·'zio:·ne] *f* **1.**(*risolutezza*) decisiveness **2.**(*deliberazione*) *a.* JUR decision; **prendere una** ~ to make a decision

decisivo, -a [de·tʃi·'zi:·vo] *agg* decisive

deciso, -a [de·'tʃi:·zo] **I.** *pp di* **decidere II.** *agg* **1.**(*convinto*) decided **2.**(*risoluto*) determined **3.**(*colore*) strong

decisorio, -a [de·tʃi·'zo:·rio] <-i, -ie> *agg* JUR decisive; **giuramento** ~ decisive judgement; **parere** ~ deciding opinion

declamare [de·kla·'ma:·re] **I.** *vt* to declaim **II.** *vi* to recite

declamazione [de·kla·mat·'tsio:·ne] *f* (*discorso*) declamation

declassamento [de·klas·sa·'men·to] *m* relegation

declassare [de·klas·'sa:·re] *vt* to downgrade

declinante [de·kli·'nan·te] *agg* **1.**(*strada, terreno*) sloping **2.**(*civiltà, impero*) declining

declinare [de·kli·'na:·re] **I.** *vt a.* LING to decline **II.** *vi* **1.**(*essere in pendenza*) to slope downwards **2.**(*diminuire: febbre*) to drop; (*tendenza*) to decline **3.**(*sole*) to set; (*giorno*) to draw to an end

declinazione [de·kli·nat·'tsio:·ne] *f* LING declination

declino [de·'kli:·no] *m* **1.**(*decadenza*) decline **2.** *lit* (*di bellezza, gioventù*) waning

declivio [de·'kli:·vio] <-i> *m* lit slope; **in** ~ sloping

decoder [di·'kou·də/de·co·der] *m* decoder

decodificabile [de·ko·di·fi·'ka:·bi·le] *agg* decodable

decodificare [de·ko·di·fi·'ka:·re] *vt* to decode

decodificatore [de·ko·di·fi·ka·'to:·re] *m* (*apparecchio*) decoder

decodificazione [de·ko·di·fi·kat·'tsio:·ne] *f*

decoding

decollare [de·kol·'la:·re] *vi* to take off

décolleté [de·kɔl·'te] I.<inv> *agg* (*abito*) low-cut; (*scarpe* ~) pumps II.<-> *m* 1.(*scarpa*) pumps 2.(*di abito*) low neckline 3.(*di donna*) cleavage

decolorante [de·ko·lo·'ran·te] I. *agg* (*crema, gel*) bleaching II. *m* bleach

decolorare [de·ko·lo·'ra:·re] *vt* (*peli, capelli*) to bleach

decompongo *1. pers sing pr di* **decomporre**

decomporre [de·kom·'por·re] <irr> I. *vt* 1. MAT to break down 2. CHEM to decompose II. *vr:* -**rsi** CHEM to decompose

decomposizione [de·kom·po·zit·'tsio:·ne] *f* 1.(*scomposizione*) breaking down 2.(*di cadavere*) decomposition

decomposto, -a [de·kom·'pɔs·to] I. *pp di* **decomporre** II. *agg* (*corpo*) decomposed

decompressione [de·kom·pres·'sio:·ne] *f* decompression

deconcentrato, -a [de·kon·tʃen·'tra:·to] *agg* distracted

decongelamento [de·kon·dʒe·la·'men·to] *m* 1.(*di alimenti*) defrosting 2. FIN ~ **di un credito** unfreezing

decongelare [de·kon·dʒe·'la:·re] *vt* 1.(*alimento*) to defrost 2.(*credito*) to unfreeze

decongestionamento [de·kon·dʒes·tio·na·'men·to] *m* decongestion

decongestionante [de·kon·dʒes·tio·'nan·te] I. *agg* decongestant II. *m* decongestant

decongestionare [de·kon·dʒes·tio·'na:·re] *vt* to decongest

decontaminare [de·kon·ta·mi·'na:·re] *vt* to decontaminate

decontaminazione [de·kon·ta·mi·nat·'tsio:·ne] *f* decontamination

decontrarre [de·kon·'trar·re] <irr> *vt* to relax

decontrazione [de·kon·trat·'tsio:·ne] *f* relaxation

decorare [de·ko·'ra:·re] *vt* to decorate

decorativo, -a [de·ko·ra·'ti:·vo] *agg* decorative; **arte -a** decorative art

decorato, -a [de·ko·'ra:·to] *agg* decorated

decoratore, -trice [de·ko·ra·'to:·re] *m, f* (*d'interno*) decorator; (*in teatro*) set designer

decorazione [de·ko·rat·'tsio:·ne] *f* decoration

decoro [de·'kɔ:·ro] *m* 1.(*dignità*) decorum 2.(*onore, prestigio*) honor

decoroso, -a [de·ko·'ro:·so] *agg* 1.(*dignitoso: atteggiamento, discorso*) dignified; (*stipendio*) decent 2.(*di prestigio*) desirable

decorrenza [de·kor·'rɛn·tsa] *f* con ~ da with effect from

decorrere [de·'kor·re·re] <irr> *vi essere* (*avere effetto*) to have effect; **a ~ da domani** from tomorrow

decorso [de·'kor·so] *m* 1.(*del tempo*) passage 2.(*di malattia*) course

decotto [de·'kɔt·to] *m* (*impacco*) decoction

decrebbi *1. pers sing pass rem di* **decrescere**

decremento [de·kre·'men·to] *m* decrease

decrepito, -a [de·'krɛ:·pi·to] *agg* 1.(*rafforzativo*) decrepit 2.(*idee, mentalità*) obsolete

decrescente [de·kreʃ·'ʃɛn·te] *agg* decreasing; **serie ~ di numeri** a falling sequence of numbers; **la fase ~ della luna** the waning of the moon; **costi -i** COM falling costs

decrescere [de·'kreʃ·ʃe·re] <irr> *vi essere* to fall

decretare [de·kre·'ta:·re] *vt* (*stabilire*) to order

decreto [de·'krɛ:·to] *m* decree; ~ **di citazione** summons; ~ **legge** decree passed by the Italian government without the consent of parliament; ~ **legislativo** decree passed by the Italian government with the consent of parliament; ~ **ministeriale** ministerial decree

decretone [de·kre·'to:·ne] *m* decree containing several provisions, especially financial ones

decriminalizzare [de·kri·mi·na·lid·'dza:·re] *vt* to decriminalize

decriminalizzazione [de·kri·mi·na·lid·dzat·'tsio:·ne] *f* decriminalization

decriptare [de·krit·'ta:·re] *vt* to decrypt

decubito [de·'ku:·bi·to] *m* MED **piaghe da ~** bedsores

decuplicare [de·kup·li·'ka:·re] *vt* to increase tenfold

decuplo ['dɛ:·kup·lo] *m* factor of ten

decuplo, -a *agg* tenfold

decurtare [de·kur·'ta:·re] *vt* to reduce

dedica ['dɛ:·di·ka] <-che> *f* dedication

dedicare [de·di·'ka:·re] I. *vt* to dedicate II. *vr:* -**rsi** to dedicate oneself

dedito, -a ['dɛ:·di·to] *agg* dedicated; ~ **ai vizi** addicted to vice

dedizione [de·dit·'tsio:·ne] *f* dedication; ~ **al dovere** devotion to duty

dedotto [de·'dot·to] *pp di* **dedurre**

deducibile [de·du·'tʃi:·bi·le] *agg* 1.(*concetto*) deducible 2. COM (*spese*) deductible

dedurre [de·'dur·re] <deduco, dedussi, dedotto> *vt* 1.(*concetto*) ~ **da qc** to deduce from sth 2. COM (*spese*) to deduct; ~ **le spese dalle tasse** to deduct expenses from taxes

deduzione [de·dut·'tsio:·ne] *f* deduction

deejay [di:·'dʒei] <-> *mf* deejay

de facto [de 'fak·to] *avv* JUR de facto; **riconoscimento ~ di uno Stato** de facto recognition of a state

defalcare [de·fal·'ka:·re] *vt* to deduct; ~ **le spese dalle tasse** to deduct expenses from taxes

defecare [de·fe·'ka:·re] *vi form* to defecate

defecazione [de·fe·kat·'tsio:·ne] *f form* defecation

defedato, -a [de·fe·'da:·to] *agg* MED weakened; **individuo ~** person who is in a weakened state; **organismo ~** body that is in a weakened state

defenestrare [de·fe·nes·'tra:·re] *vt destituire: presidente, ministro* to remove from office

deferente [de·fe·'rɛn·te] *agg* 1.(*rispettoso: atteggiamento, saluto, discorso*) deferential

2. ANAT **canale** ~ vas deferens

deferire [de·fe·'ri:·re] *vt* **1.** JUR ~ **qu all'autorità giudiziaria** to prefer charges against sb **2.** *form* (*consegnare*) to send

defezione [de·fet·'tsio:·ne] *f* defection

deficiente [de·fi·'tʃɛn·te] **I.** *agg* (*scarso: risorse, scorte*) insufficient **II.** *mf* (*imbecille*) idiot

deficienza [de·fi·'tʃɛn·tsa] *f* **1.** (*scarsità*) shortage **2.** (*lacuna*) weakness

deficit ['dɛ:·fi·tʃit] <-> *m* FIN deficit

deficitario, -a [de·fi·tʃi·'ta:·rio] <-i, -ie> *agg* **1.** FIN (*bilancio, gestione*) in deficit **2.** (*carente*) deficient

defilare [de·fi·'la:·re] **I.** *vt* MIL to defilade; ~ **le truppe** to defilade troops **II.** *vr:* **-rsi** *fig* to sneak off

défilé [de·fi·'le] <-> *m* fashion show

definibile [de·fi·'ni:·bi·le] *agg* definable

definire [de·fi·'ni:·re] <definisco> *vt* **1.** (*stabilire*) to decide **2.** (*spiegare: concetto, parola*) to define **3.** (*risolvere: questione*) to settle

definitivo, -a [de·fi·ni·'ti:·vo] *agg* definitive; **in -a** (*in conclusione*) in the end; (*tutto sommato*) all things considered

definito, -a [de·fi·'ni:·to] *agg* **1.** (*determinato: risposta*) definite **2.** (*nitido: contorni, colore, immagine*) clear

definizione [de·fi·nit·'tsio:·ne] *f* **1.** (*determinazione*) establishment **2.** (*di parola*) definition; **per** ~ by definition **3.** (*soluzione: di questione, lite*) settlement

defiscalizzare [de·fis·ka·lid·'dza:·re] *vt* FIN to make exempt from tax

deflagrazione [de·fla·grat·'tsio:·ne] *f* **1.** GEOL deflagration **2.** (*esplosione*) explosion

deflazione [de·flat·'tsio:·ne] *f* ECON deflation

deflazionistico, -a [de·flat·tsio·'nis·ti·ko] <-ci, -che> *agg* deflationary

deflettere [de·'flɛt·te·re] <irr> *vi* to deviate

deflettore [de·flet·'to:·re] *m* AUTO quarter window

defluire [de·flu·'i:·re] <defluisco> *vi* essere **1.** (*liquidi, capitale*) to flow **2.** (*folla*) to stream

deflusso [de·'flus·so] *m* **1.** (*di marea*) ebb **2.** (*di folla*) flow **3.** (*di onde*) ebbing

defogliante [de·foʎ·'ʎan·te] **I.** *agg* defoliant **II.** *m* defoliant

deforestazione [de·fo·res·tat·'tsio:·ne] *f* deforestation

deformabile [de·for·'ma:·bi·le] *agg* deformable

deformante [de·for·'man·te] *agg* deforming; **specchio** ~ distorting mirror

deformare [de·for·'ma:·re] *vt* **1.** (*corpo, mani, piedi*) to deform; (*maglione*) to put out of shape; (*lamiera, plastica*) to warp **2.** (*verità, fatti*) to distort

deformato, -a [de·for·'ma:·to] *agg* **1.** (*dita, corpo*) deformed; (*oggetto*) misshapen; (*carrozzeria, pneumatico*) warped **2.** (*verità, fatto*) distorted

deformazione [de·for·mat·'tsio:·ne] *f* **1.** (*di oggetto, corpo*) deformation **2.** (*di fatti, verità*) distortion; ~ **professionale** *the tendency to see everything in the light of one's job*

deforme [de·'for·me] *agg* (*corpo, mani, testa*) deformed

deformità [de·for·mi·'ta] <-> *f* (*di corpo, mani*) deformity

defraudare [de·frau·'da:·re] *vt* ~ **qu di qc** to cheat sb (out) of sth

defunto, -a [de·'fun·to] *form* **I.** *agg* (*morto*) deceased **II.** *m, f* deceased

degenerare [de·dʒe·ne·'ra:·re] *vi* (*cellule, tessuto, situazione*) to degenerate; ~ **in qc** to degenerate into sth

degenerativo, -a [de·dʒe·ne·ra·'ti:·vo] *agg* (*processo, fenomeno*) degenerative

degenerato, -a [de·dʒe·ne·'ra:·to] **I.** *agg* **1.** MED, BIOL degenerate **2.** (*depravato*) unnatural **II.** *m, f* degenerate

degenerazione [de·dʒe·ne·rat·'tsio:·ne] *f* **1.** MED, BIOL degeneration **2.** (*di costumi*) degeneracy

degenere [de·'dʒɛ:·ne·re] *agg* unnatural

degente [de·'dʒɛn·te] **I.** *agg* inpatient **II.** *mf* inpatient

degenza [de·'dʒɛn·tsa] *f* stay in bed; ~ **ospedaliera** stay in the hospital

degli ['deʎ·ʎi] *prep* = **di** + **gli** *v.* di

deglutire [de·glu·'ti:·re] <deglutisco> *vt* to swallow

degnare [deɲ·'ɲa:·re] **I.** *vt* **non mi ha neanche degnato di una risposta** he didn't even deign to answer me; **non** ~ **qu di uno sguardo** to not deign to look at sb **II.** *vr:* **-rsi** **-rsi di fare qc** to deign to do sth

degno, -a ['deɲ·ɲo] *agg* **1.** (*meritevole*) ~ **di qc** worthy of sth; ~ **di nota** worthy of note **2.** (*adatto*) suitable; **una -a ricompensa** a suitable reward

degradabile [de·gra·'da:·bi·le] *agg* CHEM degradable

degradabilità [de·gra·da·bi·li·'ta] <-> *f* degradability

degradante [de·gra·'dan·te] *agg* (*lavoro, ruolo*) degrading

degradare [de·gra·'da:·re] **I.** *vt* **1.** (*ufficiale*) to demote **2.** (*avvilire*) to degrade **II.** *vr:* **-rsi** **1.** (*peggiorare*) to deteriorate **2.** (*umiliarsi*) to demean oneself

degradazione [de·gra·dat·'tsio:·ne] *f* **1.** MIL demotion **2.** (*avvilimento morale*) degradation

degrado [de·'gra:·do] *m* decay

degustare [de·gus·'ta:·re] *vt* to taste

degustazione [de·gus·tat·'tsio:·ne] *f* **1.** (*assaggio*) taste **2.** (*locale*) store or bar where you can try specialties

dei¹ ['dɛ:·i] *m pl di* dio

dei² ['de:·i] *prep* = **di** + **i** *v.* di

deidratare [de·id·ra·'ta:·re] *vt* to dehydrate

deidratazione [de·id·ra·tat·'tsio:·ne] *f* dehydration

deificare [de·i·fi·'ka:·re] *vt* **1.** (*divinizzare*) to deify **2.** (*esaltare: attore, cantante*) to adulate

deificazione [de·i·fi·kat·'tsio:·ne] *f* 1. REL deification 2. (*esaltazione*) adulation

deindicizzare [de·in·di·tʃid·'dza:·re] *vt* COM, COMPUT to deindex; ~ **i salari/l'economia** to deindex salaries/the economy

deindicizzazione [de·in·di·tʃid·dzat·'tsio:·ne] *f* COM, COMPUT deindexing

deindustrializzare [de·in·dus·tria·lid·'dza:·re] *vt* to deindustrialize

deindustrializzazione [de·in·dus·tria·lid·dzat·'tsio:·ne] *f* deindustrialization

déjà vu [de·'ʒa 'vy] I. <inv> *agg* hackneyed II. <-> *m* PSYCH déjà vu

del [del] *prep* = **di + il** *v.* **di**

delatore, -trice [de·la·'to:·re] *m, f* informer

delatorio, -a [de·la·'tɔ:·rio] <-i, -ie> *agg* denunciatory

delazione [de·lat·'tsio:·ne] *f* informing

delega ['dɛ:·le·ga] <-ghe> *f* proxy; **per** ~ by proxy

delegare [de·le·'ga:·re] *vt* 1. to delegate; ~ **qc a qu** to delegate sth to sb 2. JUR to nominate

delegato, -a [de·le·'ga:·to] I. *agg* nominated II. *m, f* delegate

delegazione [de·le·gat·'tsio:·ne] *f* delegation

delegittimare [de·le·dʒit·ti·'ma:·re] *vt* to delegitimize

deleterio, -a [de·le·'tɛ:·rio] <-i, -ie> *agg* harmful

delfino [del·'fi:·no] *m* dolphin; **nuoto a** ~ butterfly

delibera [de·'li:·be·ra] *f* decision

deliberante [de·li·be·'ran·te] *agg* decision-making; **tribunale** ~ decision-making court; **potere** ~ decision-making power

deliberare [de·li·be·'ra:·re] I. *vt* 1. (*decidere*) to rule 2. (*nelle aste*) to knock down II. *vi* ~ **su qc** to rule on sth

deliberatamente [de·li·be·ra·ta·'men·te] *avv* deliberately

deliberato [de·li·be·'ra:·to] *m* decision

deliberato, -a *agg* deliberate

deliberazione [de·li·be·rat·'tsio:·ne] *f* 1. (*decisione*) decision 2. (*intenzione*) **con** ~ deliberately

delicatezza [de·li·ka·'tet·tsa] *f* 1. (*finezza: di colore, lineamenti*) delicacy 2. (*di sentimenti*) thoughtfulness 3. (*tatto*) tact 4. (*cibo, bevanda*) delicacy

delicato, -a [de·li·'ka:·to] *agg* 1. (*fine, fragile*) delicate 2. (*argomento, problema*) tricky 3. (*cibo, bevanda*) subtle

delimitabile [de·li·mi·'ta:·bi·le] *agg* subject to limits

delimitare [de·li·mi·'ta:·re] *vt* 1. (*terreno, zona*) to mark 2. *fig* (*definire*) to define

delimitazione [de·li·mi·tat·'tsio:·ne] *f* 1. (*di confini*) marking 2. *fig* (*di competenze*) definition

delineamento [de·li·ne·a·'men·to] *m fig* (*descrizione essenziale*) outline; ~ **di un problema** outline of a problem

delineare [de·li·ne·'a:·re] I. *vt* (*descrivere*) to outline II. *vr:* **-rsi** to take shape; (*presentarsi*)

delinquente [de·liŋ·'kuɛn·te] *mf* 1. JUR criminal 2. *fig, scherz* crook

delinquenza [de·liŋ·'kuɛn·tsa] *f* crime; ~ **minorile** juvenile delinquency

delinquere [de·'liŋ·kue·re] *vi* to commit crimes; **associazione per** [*o* **a**] ~ criminal syndicate

delirante [de·li·'ran·te] *agg* (*irragionevole: affermazioni, idee*) crazy

delirare [de·li·'ra:·re] *vi* 1. MED to be delirious 2. *fig* (*dire assurdità*) to rave

delirio [de·'li:·rio] <-i> *m* 1. MED delirium 2. *fig* (*follia*) madness 3. (*entusiasmo*) frenzy; **andare in** ~ to go wild; **la folla in delirio** the wildly cheering crowd

delitto [de·'lit·to] *m* 1. (*reato*) crime; ~ **colposo** criminal negligence; **corpo del** ~ corpus delicti 2. (*omicidio*) murder

delittuoso, -a [de·lit·tu·'o:·so] *agg* criminal

delizia [de·'lit·tsia] <-ie> *f* (*cosa piacevole*) delight; **la** ~ **di qu** sb's delight

delizioso, -a [de·lit·'tsio:·so] *agg* 1. (*cibo, bevanda*) delicious 2. (*persona, cosa*) delightful

dell', della, delle, dello [dell, 'del·la, 'del·le, 'del·lo] *prep* = **di + l', la, le, lo** *v.* **di**

delta ['dɛl·ta] <-> I. *m o f* (*lettera greca*) delta II. *m* (*di fiume*) delta

deltaplanista [del·ta·pla·'nis·ta] <-i *m*, -e *f*> *mf* hang glider

deltaplano [del·ta·'pla:·no] *m* hang glider; **fare** ~ to go hang gliding

delucidare [de·lu·tʃi·'da:·re] *vt* (*chiarire*) to clarify

delucidazione [de·lu·tʃi·dat·'tsio:·ne] *f* clarification

deludente [de·lu·'dɛn·te] *agg* disappointing

deludere [de·'lu:·de·re] <deludo, delusi, deluso> *vt* to disappoint

delusione [de·lu·'zio:·ne] *f* disappointment

deluso, -a [de·'lu:·zo] I. *pp di* **deludere** II. *agg* disappointed

demagogia [de·ma·go·'dʒi:·a] <-gie> *f* demagogy

demagogico, -a [de·ma·'gɔ:·dʒi·ko] <-ci, -che> *agg* demagogic

demandare [de·man·'da:·re] *vt form* (*affidare*) to refer

demaniale [de·ma·'nia:·le] *agg* **bene** ~ state property

demanio [de·'ma:·nio] <-i> *m* state property

demarcare [de·mar·'ka:·re] *vt* (*confini, limiti*) to demarcate

demarcazione [de·mar·kat·'tsio:·ne] *f* demarcation; **linea di** ~ demarcation line

demente [de·'mɛn·te] I. *agg* 1. MED demented 2. (*idiota*) crazy II. *mf* 1. MED person with dementia 2. (*idiota*) crazy person

demenza [de·'mɛn·tsa] *f* 1. MED dementia 2. *fig* (*stupidità*) insanity

demenziale [de·men·'tsia:·le] *agg* 1. MED (*stato, comportamento*) demented

2. (*assurdo: discorso, atteggiamento*) crazy; (*comicità, umorismo*) off-the-wall

demenzialità [de·men·tsia·li·'ta] <-> *f* (*di umorismo, film*) wackiness

demerito [de·'mɛː·ri·to] *m* **andare a ~ di qu** to reflect badly on sb; **nota di ~** demerit

demilitarizzare [de·mi·li·ta·rid·'dza:·re] *vt* to demilitarize

demilitarizzazione [de·mi·li·ta·rid·dzat·'tsio:·ne] *f* demilitarization

demistificante [de·mis·ti·fi·'kan·te] *agg* demystifying

demistificare [de·mis·ti·fi·'ka:·re] *vt* to demystify

demistificazione [de·mis·ti·fi·kat·'tsio:·ne] *f* demystification

demitizzare [de·mi·tid·'dza:·re] *vt* to debunk

demmo ['dem·mo] *1. pers pl pass rem di* **dare**[1]

democraticità [de·mo·kra·ti·tʃi·'ta] *f* (*di regime, decisione*) democratic nature

democratico, -a [de·mo·'kra:·ti·ko] <-ci, -che> I. *agg* **1.** POL (*regime, elezioni, principio*) democratic **2.** (*alla mano*) approachable II. *m, f* democrat; **Democratici di Sinistra** Democrats of the Left, *Italian center-left party*

democratizzare [de·mo·kra·tid·'dza:·re] *vt* to democratize

democratizzazione [de·mo·kra·tid·dzat·'tsio:·ne] *f* democratization

democrazia [de·mo·krat·'tsi:·a] <-ie> *f* democracy; **Democrazia Cristiana** HIST Christian Democrat Party, *former Italian governing party*

demografia [de·mo·gra·'fi:·a] *f* demography

demografico, -a [de·mo·'gra:·fi·ko] <-ci, -che> *agg* demographic

demolire [de·mo·'li:·re] <demolisco> *vt* **1.** (*distruggere: edificio*) to demolish; (*auto, nave*) to break up **2.** *fig* (*teoria*) to tear to pieces; (*reputazione*) to destroy; (*opera*) to savage

demolizione [de·mo·lit·'tsio:·ne] *f* (*distruzione: di edificio, teoria*) demolition; (*di auto, nave*) breakup

demone ['dɛː·mo·ne] *m* demon

demoniaco, -a [de·mo·'ni:·a·ko] <-ci, -che> *agg* demonic

demonio [de·'mɔː·nio] <-i> *m* (*ragazzo vivace*) devil; **fare il ~** to behave like a little devil

demonizzare [de·mo·nid·'dza:·re] *vt* to demonize

demoralizzante [de·mo·ra·lid·'dzan·te] *agg* demoralizing

demoralizzare [de·mo·ra·lid·'dza:·re] I. *vt* to demoralize II. *vr:* **-rsi** to get demoralized

demoralizzato, -a [de·mo·ra·lid·'dza:·to] *agg* demoralized

demoralizzazione [de·mo·ra·lid·dzat·'tsio:·ne] *f* demoralization

demoscopia [de·mos·ko·'pi:·a] <-ie> *f* market research

demoscopico, -a [de·mos·'kɔ:·pi·ko] <-ci, -che> *agg* market research; **indagine -a** opinion poll

demotivare [de·mo·ti·'va:·re] *vt* to demotivate

demotivato, -a [de·mo·ti·'va:·to] *agg* demotivated; **sentirsi ~** to feel demotivated

denaro [de·'na:·ro] *m* **1.** (*soldi*) money; **~ contante** cash; **~ spicciolo** change; **avere il ~ contato** *fig* to have just enough money; **il ~ è una chiave che apre tutte le porte** *prov* money is a key that opens every door **2.** *pl* (*di carte da gioco*) diamonds

denaturare [de·na·tu·'ra:·re] *vt* (*alcol, cloruro di sodio*) to denature

denaturato, -a [de·na·tu·'ra:·to] *agg* denatured

denazionalizzare [de·nat·tsio·na·lid·'dza:·re] *vt* (*privatizzare*) to denationalize

denigrare [de·ni·'gra:·re] *vt* to denigrate

denigratore, -trice [de·ni·gra·'to:·re] *m, f* denigrator

denigratorio, -a [de·ni·gra·'tɔ:·rio] <-i, -ie> *agg* denigratory

denigrazione [de·ni·grat·'tsio:·ne] *f* denigration

denim ['de·nim] <-> *m* denim

denocciolare [de·not·tʃo·'la:·re] *vt* (*ciliegie, albicocche, olive*) to pit

denocciolato, -a [de·not·tʃo·'la:·to] *agg* pitted; **olive -e** pitted olives

denocciolatrice [de·not·tʃo·la·'tri:·tʃe] *f* pitter

denominare [de·no·mi·'na:·re] I. *vt* to name greco-romane II. *vr:* **-rsi** to be named

denominativo, -a [de·no·mi·na·'ti:·vo] *agg* denominative

denominatore [de·no·mi·na·'to:·re] *m* MATH denominator

denominazione [de·no·mi·nat·'tsio:·ne] *f* **1.** (*attribuzione di un nome*) naming **2.** (*nome*) **vino a ~ di origine controllata** AOC wine, *wine whose origin is guaranteed*

denotare [de·no·'ta:·re] *vt* to show

densità [den·si·'ta] <-> *f* **1.** (*gener*) density; **~ della popolazione** population density; **~ assoluta** absolute density; **~ relativa** relative density **2.** (*compattezza: di nebbia, sugo*) thickness

denso, -a ['dɛn·so] *agg* **1.** (*spesso: nebbia, fumo, salsa*) thick **2.** (*ricco*) **~ di** full of; **una settimana -a di avvenimenti** an eventful week

dentale [den·'ta:·le] I. *agg* dental II. *f* LING dental

dentario, -a [den·'ta:·rio] <-i, -ie> *agg* dental; **carie -a** dental caries

dentata [den·'ta:·ta] *f* bite

dentato, -a [den·'ta:·to] *agg* TEC toothed; **ruota -a** toothed wheel

dentatura [den·ta·'tu:·ra] *f* **1.** ANAT teeth *pl* **2.** TEC (*di ruota, meccanismo*) serration

dente ['dɛn·te] *m* **1.** ANAT, TEC tooth; **~ canino** canine; **~ incisivo** incisor; **~ molare** molar; **~ del giudizio** wisdom tooth; **~ di latte** baby tooth; **avere mal di -i** to have a toothache; **batteva i -i** his teeth were chattering; **avere il ~ avvelenato contro qu** to bear sb a grudge contro la critica *fam;* **mettere qc sotto i -i** *fig* to eat sth; = **mangiare qc, mostrare i -i a qu** *fig* to show one's teeth to sb; = **essere aggressivo con qu, restare a -i asciutti** *fig* to remain empty-handed a -i asciutti; **stringere i -i** *fig* to grit one's teeth mettiti in marcia **2.** CULIN **al ~** (*spaghetti, pasta, riso*) al dente, *still firm* **3.** BOT **~ di leone** dandelion

dentellato, -a [den·tel·'la:·to] *agg* (*lama, coltello, bordo*) serrated

dentice ['dɛn·ti·tʃe] *m* ZOO (common) dentex

dentiera [den·'tiɛ:·ra] *f* **1.** (*protesi*) dentures *pl* **2.** (*cremagliera*) rack

dentifricio [den·ti·'fri:·tʃo] <-ci> *m* toothpaste

dentifricio, -a <-ci, -cie> *agg* **pasta -a** toothpaste

dentista [den·'tis·ta] <-i *m*, -e *f*> *mf* dentist

dentistico, -a [den·'tis·ti·ko] <-ci, -che> *agg* (*studio, gabinetto*) dentist's

dentizione [den·tit·'tsio:·ne] *f* dentition

dentro ['den·tro] **I.** *avv* (*stato, moto*) inside; **essere ~** *fam* (*in carcere*) to be inside; **mettere ~** *fam* to lock up **II.** *prep* **~** (**a**) (*stato*) inside; (*moto*) in; **~ casa** in the house; **~ di me** in my heart of hearts

denuclearizzare [de·nu·kle·a·tid·'dza:·re] *vt* to denuclearize

denuclearizzato, -a [de·nu·kle·a·rid·'dza:·to] *agg* denuclearized

denuclearizzazione [de·nu·kle·a·rid·dzat·'tsio:·ne] *f* denuclearization

denudare [de·nu·'da:·re] **I.** *vt* **1.** (*parte del corpo*) to bare **2.** *fig* (*ambiente, testo*) to strip **II.** *vr:* **-rsi** to strip

denuncia [de·'nun·tʃa] <-ce *o* -cie, -ie> *f* **1.** JUR **sporgere ~** to report to the police **2.** (*accusa*) accusation **3.** ADM (*di nascita, decesso, matrimonio*) registration; **~ dei redditi** tax return

denunciare [de·nun·'tʃa:·re] *vt* **1.** JUR to report to the police **2.** ADM (*nascita, decesso, matrimonio*) to register **3.** (*smascherare: scandalo, malasanità*) to criticize **4.** *fig* (*dimostrare*) to demonstrate

denutrito, -a [de·nu·'tri:·to] *agg* undernourished

denutrizione [de·nu·trit·'tsio:·ne] *f* malnutrition

deodorante [de·o·do·'ran·te] **I.** *agg* deodorant **II.** *m* deodorant; **~ per ambienti** room deodorant

deodorare [de·o·do·'ra:·re] *vt* to deodorize

deodorazione [de·o·do·rat·'tsio:·ne] *f* deodorizing

deorbitare [de·or·bi·'ta:·re] *vt* ASTR to take out of orbit; **~ un satellite** to take a satellite out of orbit

deossiribonucleico [de·os·si·ri·bo·nu·'klɛ:·i·ko] *agg* **acido ~** deoxyribonucleic acid

depauperare [de·pau·pe·'ra:·re] *vt lit* to impoverish

depauperato, -a [de·pau·pe·'ra:·to] *agg lit* impoverished

depenalizzare [de·pe·na·lid·'dza:·re] *vt* JUR to decriminalize

depennamento [de·pen·na·'men·to] *m* crossing out

depennare [de·pen·'na:·re] *vt* to cross out

deperibile [de·pe·'ri:·bi·le] *agg* perishable

deperimento [de·pe·ri·'men·to] *m* **1.** MED wasting away **2.** (*deterioramento: di alimenti, medicinali*) deterioration

deperire [de·pe·'ri:·re] <deperisco> *vi essere* **1.** (*di salute*) to waste away **2.** (*deteriorarsi: frutta*) to deteriorate

deperito, -a [de·pe·'ri:·to] *agg* (*persona, organismo*) weak

depilante [de·pi·'la:n·te] *agg* (*crema, gel*) depilatory

depilare [de·pi·'la:·re] *vt* (*gambe*) to depilate; **~ le sopracciglia** to pluck one's eyebrows

depilatore [de·pi·la·'to:·re] *m* (*apparecchio*) depilator

depilatorio [de·pi·la·'tɔ:·rio] *m* depilatory

depilatorio, -a <-i, -ie> *agg* (*crema, rasoio*) depilatory

depilazione [de·pi·lat·'tsio:·ne] *f* depilation

depistaggio [de·pis·'tad·dʒo] <-ggi> *m* (*di indagine, inquirenti*) putting off the scent

depistare [de·pis·'ta:·re] *vt* (*indagine, inquirenti*) to put off the scent

dépliant [de·pli·'jã] <-> *m* leaflet

deplorabile [de·plo·'ra:·bi·le] *agg* **1.** (*triste: morte, disgrazia*) terrible **2.** (*riprovevole: fatto, condotta*) disgraceful

deplorare [de·plo·'ra:·re] *vt* **1.** (*biasimare: condotta, azione*) to deplore **2.** (*compiangere: disgrazia, morte*) to lament

deplorevole [de·plo·'re:·vo·le] *agg* (*riprovevole*) deplorable

depoliticizzare [de·po·li·ti·tʃid·'dza:·re] *vt* to depoliticize

deporre [de·'por·re] <irr> **I.** *vt* **1.** (*oggetto*) to put down; **~ le armi** *fig* to lay down one's arms **2.** (*uova*) to lay **3.** (*testimoniare*) **~ il vero** to tell the truth; **~ il falso** to give false evidence **4.** *fig* (*rinunciare a: idea, intenzione*) to give up; (*corona*) to renounce **II.** *vi* **1.** (*testimoniare*) to give evidence; **~ a favore di / contro qu** to give evidence for/against sb **2.** *fig* **~ a favore di qu** to work in sb's favor

deportare [de·por·'ta:·re] *vt* to deport

deportato, -a [de·por·'ta:·to] *m, f* deportee

deportazione [de·por·tat·'tsio:·ne] *f* deportation

deposi *1. pers sing pass rem di* **deporre**

depositare [de·po·zi·'ta:·re] **I.** *vt* **1.** (*gener*) to deposit **2.** (*collocare*) to put **3.** (*in custodia*) to leave **II.** *vr:* **-rsi** (*materiale sedimento*) to settle

depositario, -a [de·po·zi·'ta:·rio] <-i, -ie> *m, f* custodian

deposito [de·'pɔ:·zi·to] *m* **1.** (*di denaro*) deposit **2.** (*luogo*) warehouse; **~ bagagli** luggage room **3.** (*oggetti*) collection **4.** (*di liquidi*) deposit

deposizione [de·po·zit·'tsio:·ne] *f* **1.** (*in tribunale*) deposition **2.** (*da una carica*) removal **3.** REL Deposition

deposto *pp di* **deporre**

depotenziare [de·po·ten·'tsia:·re] *vt* to weaken

depravato, -a [de·pra·'va:·to] I. *agg* depraved II. *m, f* degenerate

depravazione [de·pra·vat·'tsio:·ne] *f* depravity

deprecabile [de·pre·'ka:·bi·le] *agg* deplorable

deprecare [de·pre·'ka:·re] *vt* to deplore

depredare [de·pre·'da:·re] *vt* **1.** (*saccheggiare*) to loot **2.** (*derubare*) to rob; ~ **qu di qc** to rob sb of sth

depressi [de·'prɛs·si] *1. pers sing pass rem di* **deprimere**

depressione [de·pres·'sio:·ne] *f* depression

depressivo, -a [de·pres·'si:·vo] *agg* (*stato, comportamento*) depressive

depresso, -a [de·'prɛs·so] I. *pp di* **deprimere** II. *agg* depressed III. *m, f* MED person with depression

deprezzamento [de·pret·tsa·'men·to] *m* depreciation

deprezzare [de·pret·'tsa:·re] I. *vt* to reduce the value of II. *vr:* -**rsi** to depreciate

deprimente [de·pri·'mɛn·te] *agg* depressing

deprimere [de·'pri:·me·re] <deprimo, depressi, depresso> I. *vt fig* (*avvilire*) to depress II. *vr:* -**rsi** (*avvilirsi*) to get depressed

depurare [de·pu·'ra:·re] *vt* to purify

depurativo [de·pu·ra·'ti:·vo] *m* depurative

depurativo, -a *agg* purifying

depuratore [de·pu·ra·'to:·re] *m* (*apparecchio: di aria, acqua*) purifier

depuratore, -trice *agg* purifying

depurazione [de·pu·rat·'tsio:·ne] *f* purification

deputato, -a [de·pu·'ta:·to] *m, f* POL deputy

dequalificare [de·kua·li·fi·'ka:·re] *vt* to deskill

deragliamento [de·raʎ·ʎa·'men·to] *m* (*di treno*) derailment

deragliare [de·raʎ·'ʎa:·re] *vi essere* (*treno, vagone*) to derail

derattizzante [drat·tid·'dzan·te] I. *agg* CHEM **prodotto** ~ rat poison II. *m* CHEM rat poison

derattizzazione [de·rat·tid·dzat·'tsio:·ne] *f* disinfestation

derby ['dɛr·bi] <-> *m* (*partita*) derby

deregolamentare [de·re·go·la·men·'ta:·re] *vt* ADM to deregulate

deregolamentazione [de·re·go·la·men·tat·'tsio:·ne] *f* ADM deregulation

derelitto, -a [de·re·'lit·to] I. *agg* (*edificio, città*) derelict II. *m, f* (*persona*) derelict

deresponsabilizzare [de·res·pon·sa·bi·lid·'dza:·re] *vt* to relieve of responsibilities

deretano [de·re·'ta:·no] *m* backside

deridere [de·'ri:·de·re] <irr> *vt* to mock; ~ **qu per qc** to mock sb about sth

derisione [de·ri·'zio:·ne] *f* derision

derisorio, -a [de·ri·'zɔ:·rio] <-i, -ie> *agg* **1.** (*atteggiamento: discorso, parole, gesto*) derisive **2.** (*somma, compenso*) derisory

deriva [de·'ri:·va] *f* **1.** (*spostamento*) drift; ~ **dei continenti** continental drift; **andare alla** ~ *a. fig* to drift **2.** NAUT (*imbarcazione*) dinghy **3.** NAUT (*chiglia*) centerboard **4.** AER (*stabilizzatore*) vertical stabilizer

derivare [de·ri·'va:·re] I. *vi essere* **1.** (*aver origine*) ~ **da** to derive from; (*fiumi*) to spring from **2.** *fig* (*essere causato*) ~ **da** to be caused by; **ciò deriva da ...** the reason for that is ... II. *vt avere* **1.** (*canale*) to divert **2.** *fig* (*dedurre*) to conclude

derivata [de·ri·'va:·ta] *f* derivative

derivato [de·ri·'va:·to] *m* derivative

derivazione [de·ri·vat·'tsio:·ne] *f* **1.** (*di acqua*) diversion **2.** TEL extension **3.** EL shunt; **in ~** shunt-wound **4.** LING, MATH derivation

dermatite [der·ma·'ti:·te] *f* dermatitis

dermatologia [der·ma·to·lo·'dʒi:·a] <-gie> *f* dermatology

dermatologo, -a [der·ma·'tɔ:·lo·go] <-gi, -ghe> *m, f* dermatologist

dermatoplastica [der·ma·to·'plas·ti·ka] <-che> *f* MED dermatoplasty

dermatosi [der·ma·'tɔ:·zi] <-> *f* dermatosis

deroga ['dɛ:·ro·ga] <-ghe> *f* **in ~ a** contrary to

derrata [der·'ra:·ta] *f* agricultural product; -**e alimentari** foodstuffs

derubare [de·ru·'ba:·re] *vt* to rob; ~ **qu di qc** to steal sth from sb

derubato, -a [de·ru·'ba:·to] *agg* robbed; ~ **di ogni dignità** robbed of all dignity

deruralizzare [de·ru·ra·lid·'dza:·re] *vt* ADM to depopulate the countryside

desacralizzare [de·za·kra·lid·'dza:·re] *vt* to deconsecrate

desacralizzazione [de·zak·ra·lid·dzat·'tsio:·ne] *f* deconsecration

desalinizzare [de·za·li·nid·'dza:·re] *vt* to desalinate

desalinizzazione [de·sa·li·nid·dzat·'tsio:·ne] *f* desalination

desaparecido, -a [de·sa·pa·re·'tʃi:·do] <- *o* desaparecidos *m,* desaparecidas *f*> *m, f* (*in America Latina*) disappeared person

desco ['des·ko] <-schi> *m poet* table

descrissi *1. pers sing pass rem di* **descrivere**

descrittivo, -a [des·krit·'ti:·vo] *agg* (*romanzo, quadro*) descriptive

descrittore, -trice [des·krit·'to:·re] *m, f* person who describes something

descrivere [des·'kri:·ve·re] <irr> *vt* to describe; ~ **un cerchio** to describe a circle

descrivibile [des·kri·'vi:·bi·le] *agg* describable

descrizione [des·krit·'tsio:·ne] *f* description

desensibilizzare [de·sen·si·bi·lid·'dza:·re] *vt* to desensitize

desensibilizzazione [de·zen·si·bi·lid·dzat·'tsio:·ne] *f* FOTO desensitization

desertico, -a [de·'zɛr·ti·ko] <-ci, -che> *agg* (*zona, paesaggio*) desert

desertificazione [de·zer·ti·fi·kat·'tsio:·ne] *f* desertification

deserto [de·'zɛr·to] *m* desert

deserto, -a *agg* (*strada, locale, casa*) deserted

déshabillé [de·za·bi·'je] <-> *m* in ~ not dressed

desiderabile [de·si·de·'ra:·bi·le] *agg* desirable

desiderare [de·si·de·'ra:·re] *vt* to want; (*sessualmente*) to desire; ~ un figlio to want a child; ~ fare qc to want to do sth; farsi ~ to play hard to get; lasciare a ~ to leave a lot to be desired; ti desiderano al telefono you're wanted on the phone

desiderio [de·si·'dɛ:·rio] <-i> *m* 1. (*aspirazione*) wish 2. (*forte, sessuale*) desire; ~ di qc desire for sth

desideroso, -a [de·si·de·'ro:·so] *agg* desirous; *form;* essere ~ di qc to long for sth

designabile [de·ziɲ·'ɲa:·bi·le] *agg* designatable

designare [de·siɲ·'ɲa:·re] *vt* 1. (*indicare*) to appoint 2. (*significare*) to designate

designato, -a [de·ziɲ·'ɲa:·to] *agg* designated

designazione [de·siɲ·ɲat·'tsio:·ne] *f* 1. (*per incarico*) appointment 2. (*denotazione*) designation

desinenza [de·zi·'nɛn·tsa] *f* ending

desistenza [de·zis·'tɛn·tsa] *f* 1. (*rinuncia*) non dà nessun segno di ~ he shows no signs of giving up 2. DIR *agreement to give up criminal activity in return for a reduction in sentence* 3. POL *agreement by a political party to withdraw its own candidates in order to benefit candidates from an allied party*

desistere [de·'sis·te·re] <desisto, desistei *o* desistetti, desistito> *vi* 1. (*rinunciare*) ~ (da qc) to give (sth) up; ~ da un progetto to withdraw from a project 2. DIR ~ dalla causa to withdraw from a case; ~ dalla querela to withdraw a legal suit

desolante [de·zo·'lan·te] *agg* depressing

desolare [de·zo·'la:·re] *vt* (*addolorare*) to upset

desolato, -a [de·zo·'la:·to] *agg* 1. (*squallido*) desolate 2. (*dispiaciuto*) essere ~ di ... to be sorry that ...

desolazione [de·zo·lat·'tsio:·ne] *f* 1. (*squallore*) desolation 2. (*dolore*) sorrow

despota ['dɛs·po·ta] <-i *m*, -e *f*> *mf* despot

dessert [de·'sɛːr] <-> *m* dessert

dessi ['des·si] *1. e 2. pers sing conj imp di* dare[1]

destabilizzante [des·ta·bi·lid·'dzan·te] *agg* destabilizing

destabilizzare [des·ta·bi·lid·'dza:·re] *vt* to destabilize

destabilizzatore [des·ta·bi·lid·dza·'to:·re] *m* destabilizing influence

destabilizzatore, -trice *agg* destabilizing

destabilizzazione [des·ta·bi·lid·dzat·'tsio:·ne] *f* destabilization

destare [des·'ta:·re] I. *vt* 1. *poet* (*svegliare*) to waken 2. (*suscitare: curiosità, stupore*) to cause; (*sospetto*) to arouse II. *vr:* -rsi *poet* to awaken

deste ['des·te] *2. pers pl pass rem, 2. pers pl conj imp di* dare[1]

desti ['des·ti] *2. pers sing pass rem di* dare[1]

destinare [des·ti·'na:·re] *vt* ~ qc a qu/qc to set sth aside for sb/sth; destinato al fallimento destined to fail; essere destinato a fare qc to be destined to do sth

destinatario, -a [des·ti·na·'ta:·rio] <-i, -ie> I. *agg* banca -a receiving bank; paese ~ receiving country II. *m, f* (*di lettera, iniziativa*) addressee; (*di iniziativa*) recipient

destinazione [des·ti·nat·'tsio:·ne] *f* 1. (*scopo, fine*) purpose 2. (*di viaggio, treno*) destination; giungere a ~ to arrive

destino [des·'ti:·no] *m* destiny

destituire [des·ti·tu·'i:·re] <destituisco> *vt* to remove; ~ qu da qc to remove sb from sth

destituito, -a [des·ti·tu·'i:·to] *agg* lacking

destituzione [des·ti·tut·'tsio:·ne] *f* destitution

desto, -a ['des·to] *agg* 1. *lit* (*sveglio*) awake 2. (*pronto*) lively

destra ['dɛs·tra] *f* 1. (*mano*) right hand 2. (*lato*) a. POL right; a ~ right; alla mia ~ on my right

destreggiarsi [des·tred·'dʒar·si] *vr* to cope; ~ con qu/qc to handle sb/sth; ~ in qc to cope with sth

destrezza [des·'tret·tsa] *f* skill; ~ di mano manual dexterity; gioco di ~ game of skill

destrismo [des·'triz·mo] *m* 1. POL right-wing leanings 2. MED right-handedness

destro ['dɛs·tro] *m* SPORT right

destro, -a *agg* 1. (*lato, parte*) right; il braccio ~ di qu sb's right-hand man 2. (*abile*) skillful

destrorso, -a [des·'trɔr·so] *agg* rightist

destrutturato, -a [des·trut·tu·'ra:·to] *agg* unstructured

desumere [de·'su:·me·re] <desumo, desunsi, desunto> *vt* ~ qc (da qc) to deduce sth (from sth)

desumibile [de·su·'mi:·bi·le] *agg* è ~ che ... presumably ...

desunsi [de·'sun·si] *1. pers sing pass rem di* desumere

desunto [de·'sun·to] *pp di* desumere

detassazione [de·tas·sat·'tsio:·ne] *f* exemption from tax

detective [di·'tek·tiv/de·'tɛk·tiv] <-> *m* (*investigatore privato*) private detective

deteinato, -a [de·tei·'na:·to] *agg* decaffeinated

detenere [de·te·'ne:·re] <irr> *vt* 1. (*possedere*) to hold 2. (*in prigione*) to detain

detentivo, -a [de·ten·'ti:·vo] *agg* pena -a prison sentence

detentore, -trice [de·ten·'to:·re] I. *agg* il ~ del primato the record holder II. *m, f* holder; ~ di un titolo SPORT title holder

detenuto, -a [de·te·'nu:·to] *m, f* detainee

detenzione [de·ten·'tsio:·ne] *f* 1. (*possesso:*

di bene) holding; (*possesso illecito: di armi, esplosivi*) possession; ~ **di stupefacenti** possession of narcotics **2.** (*pena*) detention; ~ **preventiva** remand

detergente [de·ter·'dʒɛn·te] **I.** *agg* cleansing; **latte** ~ cleansing milk **II.** *m* (*detersivo*) detergent; (*cosmetico*) cleanser

detergere [de·'tɛr·dʒe·re] <irr> *vt* (*pulire: pavimento, ferita*) to clean; (*viso, volto, pelle grassa*) to cleanse

deteriorabile [de·te·rio·'ra:·bi·le] *agg* perishable

deterioramento [de·te·rio·ra·'men·to] *m* deterioration

deteriorare [de·te·rio·'ra:·re] **I.** *vt* **1.** (*danneggiare: oggetti*) to damage; (*cibi*) to spoil **2.** (*peggiorare: situazione, rapporti*) to cause to deteriorate **II.** *vr:* **-rsi 1.** (*cibi*) to go bad; (*oggetti*) to get damaged **2.** (*situazione, rapporti, edifici*) to deteriorate

deteriorato, -a [de·te·rio·'ra:·to] *agg* worsening; **rapporti -i** worsening relations

deteriore [de·te·'rio:·re] *agg* (*scadente*) second-rate

determinabile [de·ter·mi·'na:·bi·le] *agg* that can be determined

determinabilità [de·ter·mi·na·bi·li·'ta] <-> *f* ability to be determined

determinante [de·ter·mi·'nan·te] *agg* (*decisivo*) deciding; **essere** ~ **per qc** to be decisive for sth

determinare [de·ter·mi·'na:·re] *vt* **1.** (*stabilire*) to establish **2.** (*causare*) to cause

determinato, -a [de·ter·mi·'na:·to] *agg* **1.** (*stabilito*) certain; **in -i casi** in certain cases **2.** (*risoluto*) determined

determinazione [de·ter·mi·nat·'tsio:·ne] *f* **1.** (*definizione*) fixing **2.** (*decisione*) decision **3.** (*fermezza*) determination

deterrenza [de·ter·'rɛn·tsa] *f* deterrence

detersi *1. pers sing pass rem di* **detergere**

detersivo [de·ter·'si:·vo] *m* (*per pavimenti*) floor cleaner; (*per panni*) laundry detergent; (*per stoviglie*) dishwashing liquid

detersivo, -a *agg* detergent

deterso *pp di* **detergere**

detestabile [de·tes·'ta:·bi·le] *agg* (*persona, atteggiamento*) odious; (*sapore, odore*) disgusting

detestare [de·tes·'ta:·re] *vt* to detest

detonante [de·to·'nan·te] **I.** *agg* explosive **II.** *m* explosive

detonare [de·to·'na:·re] *vi* to detonate

detonatore [de·to·na·'to:·re] *m* detonator

detonazione [de·to·nat·'tsio:·ne] *f* **1.** (*scoppio*) detonation **2.** (*in motori*) firing

detraggo *1. pers sing pr di* **detrarre**

detraibile [de·tra·'i:·bi·le] *agg* deductible; **spese -i** deductible expenses

detraibilità [de·trai·bi·li·'ta] <-> *f* deductibility

detrarre [de·'trar·re] <irr> *vt* to deduct; ~ **le spese dall'incasso** to deduct expenditure

from receipts

detrazione [de·trat·'tsio:·ne] *f* (*sottrazione*) deduction

detrimento [de·tri·'men·to] *m* detriment; **a ~ di qu/qc** to the detriment of sb/sth

detritico, -a [de·'tri:·ti·ko] <-ci, -che> *agg* alluvial; **depositi -i** alluvial deposits

detrito [de·'tri:·to] *m* **1.** (*frammento*) fragment **2.** GEOL deposit

detronizzare [de·tro·nid·'dza:·re] *vt* **1.** (*sovrano*) to dethrone **2.** *fig* (*campione, presidente*) to unseat

detta ['det·ta] *f* **a ~ di ...** according to ...; **a ~ sua** by his/her own account

dettagliante [det·taʎ·'ʎan·te] *mf* retailer

dettagliato, -a [det·taʎ·'ʎa:·to] *agg* (*resoconto, descrizione*) detailed

dettaglio [det·'taʎ·ʎo] <-gli> *sing* **1.** (*particolare*) detail; **nei -i** in detail; **entrare nei -i** to go into detail **2.** (*piccola quantità*) retail; **al ~** retail

dettare [det·'ta:·re] *vt* to dictate; ~ **legge** *fig* to rule the roost

dettato [det·'ta:·to] *m* (*testo*) dictation

dettatura [det·ta·'tu:·ra] *f* dictation; **scrivere sotto ~** to write at sb's dictation

detti ['dɛt·ti] *1. pers sing pass rem di* **dare**[1]

detto ['det·to] *m* (*motto*) saying; ~ **popolare** popular saying

detto, -a **I.** *pp di* **dire**[1] **II.** *agg* **1.** (*soprannominato*) nicknamed **2.** (*suddetto*) above-mentioned **3.** (*loc*) ~ **fatto** no sooner said than done; **come non** ~ forget it

deturpare [de·tur·'pa:·re] *vt* to disfigure

deturpatore, -trice [de·tur·pa·'to:·re] *agg* disfiguring

deumidificatore [de·u·mi·di·fi·ka·'to:·re] *m* dehumidifier

devastare [de·vas·'ta:·re] *vt* **1.** (*rovinare*) to ruin **2.** (*scolvogere*) to devastate

devastatore, -trice [de·vas·ta·'to:·re] **I.** *agg* destructive **II.** *m, f* destroyer

devastazione [de·vas·tat·'tsio:·ne] *f* devastation

deviante [de·'vian·te] *agg* deviant; **comportamento** ~ deviant behavior

deviare [de·vi·'a:·re] **I.** *vi* **1.** (*cambiare direzione*) to take a detour; (*strada*) to come off **2.** *fig* (*divagare*) to deviate **II.** *vt* to divert; ~ **il discorso** to change the subject

deviazione [de·viat·'tsio:·ne] *f* **1.** (*spostamento*) deflection **2.** (*del traffico*) detour; (*strada*) turnoff **3.** (*allontanamento dalla norma*) deviation; (*comportamento anomalo*) deviance

devitalizzare [de·vi·ta·lid·'dza:·re] *vt* MED to kill; ~ **un molare** to kill a molar

devitaminizzante [de·vi·ta·mi·nid·'dzan·te] *agg* vitamin-reducing

devo ['dɛ:·vo] *1. pers sing pr di* **dovere**[1]

devolvere [de·'vɔl·ve·re] <devolvo, devolvei *o* devolvetti, devoluto> *vt* **1.** (*bene, diritto*) to transfer **2.** (*somma*) to donate

devoto, -a [de·'vɔː·to] I. *agg* 1. REL devout; **un cattolico molto** ~ a very devout Catholic; **essere** ~ **alla Madonna** to be devoted to the Madonna 2. (*affezionato*) devoted II. *m, f* 1. REL devout person 2. (*seguace*) follower

devozione [de·vot·'tsioː·ne] *f* 1. (*religiosità*) devoutness 2. (*deferenza*) devotion; ~ **a qu** devotion to sb; **la** ~ **alla Madonna** devotion to the Madonna

di [di] <d', del, dello, dell', della, dei, degli, delle> *prep* 1. (*specificazione*) of; **una donna** ~ **trent'anni** a woman of thirty; **un litro** ~ **latte** a liter of milk; **la città** ~ **Torino** the city of Turin; **il mese** ~ **gennaio** the month of January; **il presidente della Repubblica** the president of the Republic; **un libro** ~ **Calvino** a book by Calvino 2. (*materia*) **un tavolo** ~ **legno** a wooden table; **un anello d'oro** a gold ring 3. (*possessivo*) **la casa dei miei genitori** my parents' house; **il libro di Paolo** Paolo's book 4. (*argomento*) about; **un libro** ~ **geografia** a book about geography; **parlare** ~ **qc/qu** to speak about sth/sb 5. (*causa*) **gridare** ~ **gioia** to shout for joy 6. (*modo, mezzo*) **venire** ~ **corsa** to come running; **mangiare** ~ **gusto** to eat heartily; **fermarsi** ~ **colpo** to stop dead 7. (*fine, scopo*) **una camicia** ~ **riserva** a spare shirt; **pezzi** ~ **ricambio** spare parts; **uscita** ~ **emergenza** emergency exit 8. (*origine*) from; **essere** ~ **Trieste** to be from Trieste 9. (*luogo*) **uscire** ~ **casa** to leave the house; **andiamo via** ~ **qui** let's leave; **passiamo** ~ **qui** let's go this way 10. (*tempo*) ~ **mattina/sera** in the morning/evening; **d'estate/d'inverno** in summer/in winter; ~ **giorno/notte** by day/night 11. (*paragone*) than; **sono più alto** ~ **te** I'm taller than you 12. (*partitivo*) some; **vorrei del pane** I'd like some bread; **alcuni** ~ **noi** some of us; **non c'è niente** ~ **meglio** there's nothing better 13. (*con infinito*) **mi sembra** ~ **capire** it seems to me; **tentare** ~ **fuggire** to try to escape 14. (*loc*) **invece** ~ **lui** instead of him; **dopo/prima** ~ **me** before/after me

dia ['diː·a] *1., 2. e 3. pers sing conj pr di* **dare**[1]

diabete [dia·'bɛː·te] *m* diabetes

diabetico, -a [dia·'bɛː·ti·ko] <-ci, -che> I. *agg* diabetic II. *m, f* diabetic

diabolico, -a [dia·'bɔː·li·ko] <-ci, -che> *agg* devilish

diacronia [dia·kro·'niː·a] <-ie> *f* diachrony

diacronico, -a [dia·'krɔː·ni·ko] <-ci, -che> *agg* diachronic

diadema [dia·'dɛː·ma] <-i> *m* (*corona*) diadem

diafano, -a [di·'a·fa·no] *agg* 1. (*trasparente*) diaphanous 2. (*delicato: mani, pelle*) transparent

diaframma [dia·'fram·ma] <-i> *m* 1. (*elemento divisorio*) screen 2. ANAT, FOTO, CONTRACCETTIVO diaphragm

diagnosi [di·'aɲ·ɲoː·zi] <-> *f* diagnosis; **fare una** ~ to make a diagnosis

diagnosticare [di·aɲ·ɲos·ti·'kaː·re] *vt* to diagnose

diagnostico, -a [di·aɲ·'ɲɔs·ti·ko] <-ci, -che> I. *agg* diagnostic II. *m, f* diagnostician

diagonale [di·a·go·'naː·le] I. *agg* diagonal II. *m* 1. (*stoffa*) twill 2. SPORT (*nel calcio*) cross; (*nel tennis*) crosscourt shot III. *f* diagonal

diagramma [di·a·'gram·ma] <-i> *m* diagram; ~ **di flusso** COMPUT flow chart

dialettale [di·a·let·'taː·le] *agg* dialectal

dialettica [di·a·'lɛt·ti·ka] <-che> *f* dialectic

dialettico, -a [di·a·'lɛt·ti·ko] <-ci, -che> *agg* dialectical; **abilità -a** dialectical ability

dialettismo [di·a·let·'tiz·mo] *m* dialect word

dialetto [di·a·'lɛt·to] *m* dialect; **parlare in** ~ to speak in dialect

dialisi [di·'aː·li·zi] <-> *f* dialysis

dialogare [di·a·lo·'gaː·re] *vi* to open a dialog

dialogo [di·'aː·lo·go] <-ghi> *m* dialog

diamante [di·a·'man·te] *m* (*gemma*) diamond; **nozze di** ~ diamond wedding

diametralmente [di·a·me·tral·'men·te] *avv* diametrically; ~ **opposto** diametrically opposed

diametro [di·'aː·met·ro] *m* diameter

diamine ['di·aː·mi·ne] *int fam* good grief; **che** ~ **stai dicendo?** what the heck are you saying?

diapason [di·'aː·pa·zon] <-> *m* 1. (*strumento*) tuning fork 2. (*registro*) diapason

diapositiva [di·a·po·zi·'tiː·va] *f* slide

diaproiettore [di·a·pro·iet·'toː·re] *m* slide projector

diaria [di·'aː·ria] <-ie> *f* daily allowance, *for expenses;* ~ **parlamentare** parliamentary expense allowance

diario [di·'aː·rio] <-i> *m* diary; ~ **di bordo** log; ~ (**scolastico**) planner *per i genitori;* **tenere un** ~ to keep a diary

diarrea [di·ar·'rɛː·a] *f* diarrhea

diaspora [di·'as·po·ra] *f* diaspora

diatriba [di·'aː·tri·ba] *f* 1. (*discussione*) debate 2. (*invettiva*) diatribe

diavola ['di·aː·vo·la] *f* **pollo alla** ~ split roast chicken

diavoleria [dia·vo·le·'riː·a] <-ie> *f* 1. (*azione perfida*) piece of deviltry 2. *fam* (*oggetto strano*) contraption

diavoletto, -a [dia·vo·'let·to] *m, f scherz* little devil

diavolo ['diaː·vo·lo] *m* devil; **fare l'avvocato del** ~ to play devil's advocate; **un povero** ~ *fam* a poor devil; **avere il** ~ **addosso** to have ants in one's pants; **avere un** ~ **per capello** to be in a (bad) mood; **mandare qu al** ~ to tell sb to get lost; **mandare tutto al** ~ to throw up everything; **saperne una più del** ~ to be very cunning; **che** ~ **vuoi adesso?** what the hell do you want now?; **come/dove/perché** ~**?** how/where/why the hell?; **abitare a casa del** ~ *scherz* to live at the ends of the earth; **il** ~ **fa le pentole, ma non i coperchi** *prov* the devil makes the pots but not the lids, *you can* *do bad things but you can't hide them*

dibattere [di·'bat·te·re] I. *vt* (*discutere*) to debate II. *vr:* **-rsi** to struggle; (*divincolarsi*) to thrash around

dibattito [di·'bat·ti·to] *m* debate; **un ~ su qc** a debate about sth

dibattuto, -a [di·bat·'tu:·to] *agg* (*decisione, soggetto*) much-discussed

diboscamento [di·bos·ka·'men·to] *m* deforestation

dicembre [di·'tʃɛm·bre] *m* December; *v.a.* **aprile**

diceria [di·tʃe·'ri:·a] <-ie> *f* piece of gossip

dichiarante [di·kia·'ran·te] *mf* ADM declarant

dichiarare [di·kia·'ra:·re] I. *vt* to declare; **~ guerra a qu** to declare war on sb; **~ aperta la seduta** to declare the session open; **~ colpevole qu** to declare sb guilty; **~ le proprie generalità** ADM to give one's details; **vi dichiaro marito e moglie** I pronounce you man and wife; **~ qu in arresto** to formally arrest sb II. *vr:* **-rsi** (*a innamorato*) to declare oneself; **-rsi innocente** to declare one's innocence; **-rsi favorevole** to come out in favor

dichiaratamente [di·kia·ra·ta·'men·te] *avv* avowedly

dichiarativo, -a [di·kia·ra·'ti:·vo] *agg* (*nota*) declarative

dichiarazione [di·kia·rat·'tsio:·ne] *f* declaration; **~ dei redditi** tax return; **~ d'amore** declaration of love

diciannove [di·tʃan·'nɔ:·ve] I. *num* nineteen II. <-> *m* 1. (*numero*) nineteen 2. (*nelle date*) nineteenth III. *fpl* (*ore*) nineteen hundred (hours); *v.a.* **cinque**

diciannovenne [di·tʃan·no·'vɛn·ne] I. *agg* nineteen-year-old II. *mf* nineteen year old

diciannovesimo [di·tʃan·no·'vɛ:·zi·mo] *m* (*in frazione*) nineteenth

diciannovesimo, -a I. *agg* nineteenth II. *m, f* nineteenth; *v.a.* **quinto**

diciassette [di·tʃas·'sɛt·te] I. *num* seventeen II. <-> *m* 1. (*numero*) seventeen 2. (*nelle date*) seventeenth III. *fpl* (*ore*) seventeen hundred (hours); *v.a.* **cinque**

diciassettenne [di·tʃas·set·'tɛn·ne] I. *agg* seventeen-year-old II. *mf* seventeen year old

diciassettesimo [di·tʃas·set·'tɛ:·zi·mo] *m* (*in frazione*) seventeenth

diciassettesimo, -a I. *agg* seventeenth II. *m, f* seventeenth; *v.a.* **quinto**

diciottenne [di·tʃot·'tɛn·ne] I. *agg* eighteen-year-old II. *mf* eighteen year old

diciottesimo, -a [di·tʃot·'tɛ:·zi·mo] I. *agg* eighteenth II. *m, f* eighteenth III. *m* (*in frazione*) eighteenth; *v.a.* **quinto**

diciotto [di·'tʃɔt·to] I. *num* eighteen II. <-> *m* 1. (*numero*) eighteen 2. (*nelle date*) eighteenth III. *fpl* (*ore*) eighteen hundred (hours); *v.a.* **cinque**

dicitura [di·tʃi·'tu:·ra] *f* (*scritta*) wording

dico ['di:·ko] *1. pers sing pr di* **dire**[1]

didascalia [di·das·ka·'li:·a] <-ie> *f* 1. (*di*

immagine) caption 2. DI FILM subtitle 3. THEAT supertitle

didascalico, -a [di·das·'ka:·li·ko] <-ci, -che> *agg* didactic

didatta [di·'dat·ta] <-i *m*, -e *f*> *mf* (*insegnante*) teacher

didattica [di·'dat·ti·ka] <-che> *f* teaching methodology

didattico, -a [di·'dat·ti·ko] <-ci, -che> *agg* teaching

didietro [di·'diɛt·ro] I. <inv> *agg* back II. <-> *m* 1. (*parte posteriore*) bottom 2. *scherz* (*sedere*) backside

dieci ['diɛ:·tʃi] I. *num* ten II. <-> *m* 1. (*numero*) ten; (*nelle date*) tenth 2. (*voto scolastico*) ten (out of ten) III. *fpl* (*ore*) ten o'clock; *v.a.* **cinque**

diecimila [die·tʃi·'mi:·la] I. *num* ten thousand II. <-> *m* ten thousand

diecina [die·'tʃi:·na] *f v.* **decina**

diedi ['diɛ:·di] *1. pers sing pass rem di* **dare**[1]

dieresi [di·'ɛ:·re·zi] <-> *f* (*segno diacritico*) dierisis

diesis [di·'ɛ:·zis] <-> *m* MUS sharp; **do ~** C sharp

dieta ['diɛ:·ta] *f* diet; **essere a ~** to be on a diet

dietetica [die·'tɛ:·ti·ka] <-che> *f* dietetics

dietetico, -a [die·'tɛ:·ti·ko] <-ci, -che> *agg* diet

dietista [die·'tis·ta] <-i *m*, -e *f*> *mf* dietician

dietologia [die·to·lo·'dʒi:·a] <-gie> *f* dietetics

dietologo, -a [die·'tɔ:·lo·go] <-gi, -ghe> *m, f* dietician

dietro ['diɛt·ro] I. *prep* 1. **~ (a)** (*stato, moto*) behind; **~ di me** behind me 2. (*appresso*) **portarsi ~ qu** to take sb with one 3. *fig* (*alle spalle*) **tutti gli ridono ~** behind sb's back 4. (*temporale*) after; **un guaio ~ l'altro** one problem after another; **~ consegna** on delivery; **~ ricevuta** on receipt; **~ ricetta medica** on prescription II. *avv* (*stato, moto*) behind III. *m* back

dietrofront, dietro-front ['diɛt·ro 'front] I. <-> *m a. fig* about-face; **fare ~** to turn around II. *int* about-face

difatti [di·'fat·ti] *cong* in fact

difendere [di·'fɛn·de·re] <difendo, difesi, difeso> I. *vt* 1. (*gener*) *a.* DIR to defend 2. (*prendere le parti di*) to take the part of II. *vr* 1. (*da pericolo*) **-rsi da qu/qc** to protect oneself from sb/sth 2. (*cavarsela*) to get by

difenditrice *f v.* **difensore**

difensiva [di·fen·'si:·va] *f* defensive; **stare sulla ~** *fig* to be on the defensive

difensivo, -a [di·fen·'si:·vo] *agg* defensive

difensore, difenditrice [di·fen·'so:·re, di·fen·di·'tri:·tʃe] *m, f* 1. (*protettore*) *a.* SPORT defender 2. (*avvocato*) defense lawyer

difesa [di·'fe:·sa] *f* (*protezione*) *a.* DIR, MIL, SPORT defense; **la ~ da** [*o* **contro**] **qu/qc** defense against sb/sth; **la ~ di qc** the defense of sth; **legittima ~** self-defense; **~ antiaerea** anti-aircraft defenses

difesi [di·'fe:·si] *1. pers sing pass rem di* **difen-**

dere

difeso [di·fe:·so] *pp di* **difendere**

difettare [di·fet·'ta:·re] *vi* (*mancare*) to lack; ~ **di qc** to lack sth; **gli difetta la pazienza** he lacks patience

difetto [di·'fɛt·to] *m* 1.(*mancanza*) lack; **far ~** to lack 2.(*imperfezione*) defect; ~ **di fabbricazione** manufacturing defect 3.(*di carattere*) fault

difettoso, -a [di·fet·'to:·so] *agg* faulty

diffamare [dif·fa·'ma:·re] *vt* (*dire male di*) to slander; (*per iscritto*) to libel

diffamatore, -trice [dif·fa·ma·'to:·re] *m, f* (*a parole*) slanderer; (*per iscritto*) libeller

diffamatorio, -a [dif·fa·ma·'tɔ:·rio] <-i, -ie> *agg* (*affermazioni*) slanderous; (*lettera, scritto*) libelous; **campagna -a** defamation campaign

diffamatrice *f v.* **diffamatore**

diffamazione [dif·fa·mat·'tsio:·ne] *f* defamation; JUR libel

differente [dif·fe·'rɛn·te] *agg* different

differentemente [dif·fe·ren·te·'men·te] *avv* differently

differenza [dif·fe·'rɛn·tsa] *f* difference; ~ **di opinioni** difference of opinion; **a ~ di** unlike; **per me non fa ~** it's all the same to me

differenziare [dif·fe·ren·'tsia:·re] I.*vt* to distinguish II.*vr* **-rsi da qu/qc** to be different from sb/sth

differenziazione [dif·fe·ren·tsiat·'tsio:·ne] *f* differentiation

differire [dif·fe·'ri:·re] <differisco> I.*vt avere* (*rinviare*) to postpone; ~ **qc di un mese** to delay sth by a month II.*vi essere o avere* to be different; ~ **da qu/qc** to be different from sb/sth

difficile [dif·'fi:·tʃi·le] I.*agg* 1.(*gener*) difficult; **essere di gusti -i** to be fussy 2.(*improbabile*) unlikely; **è ~ che venga ...** he's unlikely to come II.*m* (*momento, fase*) difficult part III.*mf* (*persona*) **fare il** [*o* **la**] ~ to be difficult

difficilmente [dif·fi·tʃil·'men·te] *avv* (*con fatica*) with difficulty 2.(*con poca probabilità*) it's unlikely that

difficoltà [dif·fi·kol·'ta] <-> *f* 1.(*complessità, problema*) difficulty; **con ~** with difficulty; **incontrare delle ~** to run into difficulty; **ad ogni/alla minima ~** at the slightest difficulty 2.(*obiezione*) **fare ~** to make objections

difficoltoso, -a [dif·fi·kol·'to:·so] *agg* difficult

diffida [dif·'fi:·da] *f* warning (not to)

diffidare [dif·fi·'da:·re] I.*vi* ~ **di qu** to not trust sb II.*vt* ~ **qu dal fare qc** to warn sb not to do sth

diffidente [dif·fi·'dɛn·te] *agg* distrustful

diffidenza [dif·fi·'dɛn·tsa] *f* distrust

diffondere [dif·'fon·de·re] <irr> I.*vt* to spread II.*vr:* **-rsi** 1.(*luce, profumo, notizia, moda*) to spread 2.(*dilungarsi*) **-rsi troppo su una questione** to spend too long on a question

difforme [dif·'for·me] *agg a. fig* different

diffrazione [dif·frat·'tsio:·ne] *f* PHYS diffraction

diffusi *1. pers sing pass rem di* **diffondere**

diffusione [dif·fu·'zio:·ne] *f* 1.(*di luce, calore*) a. PHYS diffusion 2.(*di notizia, moda*) spread 3.(*di giornale*) circulation

diffusività [dif·fu·zi·vi·'ta] <-> *f* PHYS diffusiveness

diffuso, -a [dif·'fu:·zo] I.*pp di* **diffondere** II.*agg* widespread

diffusore [dif·fu·'zo:·re] *m* (*apparecchio*) diffuser; ~ **sonoro** speaker

difilato, -a [di·fi·'la:·to] *avv* (*subito*) straight; (*di seguito*) running; **tre giorni ~** three days running

difronte [di·'fron·te] I.<inv> *agg* opposite II.*avv* in front of; **me lo sono trovato ~ all'improvviso** he suddenly appeared in front of me; ~ **alle difficoltà** in the face of difficulty; **abito ~ alla stazione** I live opposite the station

difterite [dif·te·'ri:·te] *f* diphtheria

diga ['di:·ga] <-ghe> *f* dam; ~ **di ritenuta** retaining dam; ~ **marittima** seawall

digerente [di·dʒe·'rɛn·te] *agg* digestive

digeribile [di·dʒe·'ri:·bi·le] *agg* digestible

digerire [di·dʒe·'ri:·re] <digerisco> *vt* 1.MED (*cibo*) to digest 2.(*accettare: sconfitta*) to accept 3.*fig* (*sopportare: modi, persona*) to stomach

digestione [di·dʒes·'tio:·ne] *f* digestion

digestivo [di·dʒes·'ti:·vo] *m* (*bevanda*) after-dinner liqueur

digestivo, -a *agg* digestive

digitale [di·dʒi·'ta:·le] *agg* 1.(*delle dita*) **impronta ~** fingerprint 2.COMPUT digital

digitalizzare *vt* COMPUT to digitize

digitalizzato, -a [di·dʒi·ta·lid·'dza:·to] *agg* TEC, INFORM digitized

digitare [di·dʒi·'ta:·re] *vt* to key in

digiunare [di·dʒu·'na:·re] *vi* to fast

digiuno [di·'dʒu:·no] *m* (*astensione da alimenti*) fast; **a ~** on an empty stomach

digiuno, -a *agg* (*senza cibo*) **essere ~** to have an empty stomach; **essere (a) ~ di qc** *fig* (*non conoscere*) to know nothing about sth

dignità [diɲ·ɲi·'ta] <-> *f* dignity

dignitoso, -a [diɲ·ɲi·'to:·so] *agg* 1.(*pieno di contegno*) dignified 2.(*decoroso*) decent

DIGOS ['di:·gos] *f acro di* **Divisione Investigazioni Generali e Operazioni Speciali** *police department that deals with security matters*

digradare [di·gra·'da:·re] *vi lit* (*diminuire*) to decrease

digressione [di·gres·'sio:·ne] *f* (*divagazione*) digression

digrignare [di·griɲ·'ɲa:·re] *vt* ~ **i denti** (*persona*) to grind one's teeth; (*animale*) to bare one's teeth

dilagare [di·la·'ga:·re] *vi essere* 1.(*fiume*) to flood 2.(*diffondersi*) to spread

dilaniare [di·la·'nia:·re] *vt* 1.(*leone, cane*) to tear to pieces 2.*fig* (*rimorso, gelosia*) to rack

dilapidare [di·la·pi·'da:·re] *vt* (*patrimonio*) to

squander

dilatabile [di·la·'ta:·bi·le] *agg* dilatable

dilatare [di·la·'ta:·re] I. *vt* to cause to expand II. *vr:* **-rsi** 1.(*ampliarsi: pupille*) to dilate 2.(*gas, liquido, spazio*) to expand; (*tempo*) to stretch (out) 3.(*stomaco*) to distend 4.*fig* (*fenomeno*) to spread

dilatazione [di·la·tat·'tsio:·ne] *f* 1.(*di pupille*) dilation 2.(*di gas, liquido, spazio*) expansion 3.(*di stomaco*) distension 4.*fig* (*di tempo*) stretching (out)

dilazionabile [di·lat·tsio·'na:·bi·le] *agg* **pagamento ~ in rate mensili** payment that can be made by monthly installments

dilazionare [di·lat·tsio·'na:·re] *vt* (*pagamento*) to delay

dilazione [di·lat·'tsio:·ne] *f* (*proroga*) delay; **senza ~** without delay

dileggio [di·'led·dʒo] <-ggi> *m* mockery

dileguare [di·le·'gua:·re] I. *vt avere* lit to disperse II. *vr:* **-rsi** to vanish

dilemma [di·'lɛm·ma] <-i> *m* 1.(*scelta*) dilemma 2.(*problema difficile*) puzzler

dilettante [di·let·'tan·te] I. *agg* 1.(*non professionista*) amateur; **fotografo ~** amateur photographer; **pittore ~** amateur painter 2. *pej* (*non competente*) amateurish II. *mf a. pej* (*non professionista*) amateur; **compagnia di -i** THEAT amateur theater company

dilettantismo [di·let·tan·'tiz·mo] *m* 1.SPORT amateurism 2. *pej* (*incapacità*) amateurishness

dilettare [di·let·'ta:·re] I. *vt lit* to delight II. *vr:* **-rsi** to enjoy; **-rsi di qc** to have sth as a hobby

dilettevole [di·let·'te:·vo·le] I. *agg* enjoyable II. *m* **unire l'utile al ~** to mix business and pleasure

diletto [di·'lɛt·to] *m* pleasure; **fare qc per ~** to do sth for pleasure

diligente [di·li·'dʒɛn·te] *agg* (*persona*) diligent; (*lavoro*) careful

diligenza [di·li·'dʒɛn·tsa] *f* 1.(*accuratezza*) a. DIR care 2. HIST (*carrozza*) diligence

diluente [di·lu·'ɛn·te] *m* diluent

diluire [di·lu·'i:·re] <diluisco> *vt* 1.(*sostanze*) to dilute; (*sciogliere*) to dissolve 2.*fig* (*concetto, pensiero*) to water down

dilungare [di·luŋ·'ga:·re] *vr* **-rsi in qc** to go into great detail about sth; **~ nelle spiegazioni/descrizioni** to explain/describe sth at length

diluviare [di·lu·'via:·re] *vi essere o avere* to pour

diluvio [di·'lu:·vio] <-i> *m* 1.METEO downpour; **~ universale** the Flood 2.*fig* (*di parole, insulti*) torrent

dimagramento [di·mag·ra·'men·to] *m* 1.MED weight loss 2.AGR exhaustion

dimagrante [di·ma·'gran·te] *agg* **cura ~** diet

dimagrare [di·ma·'gra:·re] *vt avere* AGR to exhaust

dimagrimento [di·mag·ri·'men·to] *m* weight loss

dimagrire [di·ma·'gri:·re] <dimagrisco> *vi*

essere to lose weight

dimenare [di·me·'na:·re] I. *vt* (*braccia*) to wave; (*coda*) to wag II. *vr:* **-rsi** to struggle mettergli le manette; (*nel letto*) to toss and turn dormire

dimensione [di·men·'sio:·ne] *f* dimension; **-i** (*misure*) measurements

dimenticanza [di·men·ti·'kan·tsa] *f* 1.(*omissione*) oversight; (*cosa dimenticata*) omission 2.(*mancanza di memoria*) forgetfulness

dimenticare [di·men·ti·'ka:·re] I. *vt* 1.(*gener*) to forget tempo 2.(*lasciare*) to leave II. *vr* **-rsi di** to forget

dimenticatoio [di·men·ti·ka·'to:·io] <-oi> *m scherz* **finire nel ~** to be forgotten

dimesso, -a [di·'mes·so] I. *pp di* **dimettere** II. *agg* 1.(*modesto: atteggiamento, tono*) modest 2. *pej* (*trascurato: abbigliamento, tenuta*) shabby

dimestichezza [di·mes·ti·'ket·tsa] *f a. fig* familiarity; **avere ~ con qc** to be familiar with sth

dimettere [di·'met·te·re] <irr> I. *vt* (*da ospedale*) to discharge II. *vr:* **-rsi** to resign

dimezzare [di·med·'dza:·re] *vt* 1.(*in due*) to halve 2.(*ridurre*) to slash

diminuendo [di·mi·nu·'ɛn·do] *m* MUS diminuendo

diminuire [di·mi·nu·'i:·re] <diminuisco> I. *vt avere* to reduce II. *vi essere* to decrease; **~ di qc** to decrease by sth; **sono diminuito di cinque chili** I've lost five kilos; **~ di prezzo** to go down in price

diminutivo [di·mi·nu·'ti:·vo] *m* LING diminutive

diminutivo, -a *agg* diminutive

diminuzione [di·mi·nut·'tsio:·ne] *f* reduction; **~ dei costi** cost-cutting; **~ delle esportazioni** reduction in exports; **~ del personale** reduction of staff; **~ di peso** weight loss; **~ di temperatura** fall in temperature; **~ del valore** fall in value

dimisi *1. pers sing pass rem di* **dimettere**

dimissioni [di·mis·'sio:·ni] *fpl* resignation; **dare le ~** to resign; **lettera di ~** notice

dimora [di·'mɔ:·ra] *f* residence; **senza fissa ~** homeless

dimostrante [di·mos·'tran·te] *mf* demonstrator

dimostrare [di·mos·'tra:·re] I. *vt* 1.(*mostrare*) to show; **non dimostra affatto i suoi sessant'anni** she doesn't look sixty 2.(*provare*) to prove II. *vi* (*in corteo*) to demonstrate III. *vr:* **-rsi** to turn out to be; **la notizia si è dimostrata falsa** the news turned out to be false

dimostrativo, -a [di·mos·tra·'ti:·vo] *agg* LING demonstrative

dimostrazione [di·mos·trat·'tsio:·ne] *f* demonstration

dinamica [di·'na:·mi·ka] <-che> *f* 1.FIS dynamics 2.(*di fatti, incidente*) dynamic

dinamicità [di·na·mi·tʃi·'ta] <-> *f* (*di persona,*

azienda) dynamism

dinamico, -a [di·'na:·mi·ko] <-ci, -che> *agg* (*persona, azienda*) dynamic

dinamismo [di·na·'miz·mo] *m* dynamism

dinamitardo, -a [di·na·mi·'tar·do] **I.** *agg* **attentato** ~ bomb attack **II.** *m, f* bomber

dinamite [di·na·'mi:·te] *f* dynamite

dinamo ['di:·na·mo] <-> *f* dynamo

dinamoelettrico, -a [di·na·mo·e·'lɛt·tri·ko] <-ci, -che> *agg* **macchina -a** dynamoelectric machine

dinanzi [di·'nan·tsi] **I.** *avv* (*guardare, stare, mettere*) ahead **II.** *prep* ~ **a** in front of **III.** <inv> *agg* **1.** (*anteriore*) in front **2.** (*precedente*) before

dinastia [di·nas·'ti:·a] <-ie> *f* dynasty

dinastico, -a [di·'nas·ti·ko] <-ci, -che> *agg* dynastic

dindin, din din [din·'din] **I.** <-> *m* ringing **II.** *int* ding-dong

dindon, din don [din·'dɔn] **I.** <-> *m* ringing **II.** *int* bong

diniego [di·'niɛ:·go] <-ghi> *m* (*rifiuto*) refusal

dinoccolato, -a [di·nok·ko·'la:·to] *agg* lanky

dinosauro [di·no·'sa:u·ro] *m* dinosaur

dintorni [din·'tor·ni] *mpl* surrounding area; **nei ~ di** close to

dintorno [din·'tor·no] **I.** *avv* around **II.** *prep* ~ **a** around

dio ['di:·o] <dei> *m* god; **cantare come un ~** to sing beautifully

Dio *m* God; **la pioggia viene giù che ~ la manda** it's pouring; **grazie a ~** thank God; **~ me ne guardi!** God forbid!; **~ ce la mandi buona!** let's hope for the best!; **~ sia lodato** thank God pericolo; **se ~ vuole** God willing; **~ non voglia!** God forbid!; **per l'amor di ~!** for God's sake!

diocesi [di·'ɔ:·tʃe·zi] <-> *f* dioceses

dionisiaco, -a [dio·ni·'zi:·a·ko] <-ci, -che> *agg* Dionysiac

diossina [di·os·'si:·na] *f* dioxin

diottria [di·ot·'tri:·a] <-ie> *f* OPT diopter

dipanare [di·pa·'na:·re] *vt* **1.** (*lana*) to wind (into a ball) **2.** *fig* to disentangle

dipartimento [di·par·ti·'men·to] *m* **1.** (*gener*) department **2.** (*ministero*) Department

dipartita [di·par·'ti:·ta] *f* (*morte*) passing

dipendente [di·pen·'dɛn·te] **I.** *agg* ~ **da qu** dependent on sb **II.** *mf* employee

dipendenza [di·pen·'dɛn·tsa] *f* **1.** (*subordinazione*) dependence; **in ~ di ciò** therefore; **alle -e di qu** in sb's employ **2.** MED addiction

dipendere [di·'pɛn·de·re] <dipendo, dipesi, dipeso> *vi* essere ~ **da qu/qc** to depend on sb/sth; **dipende** it depends

dipingere [di·'pin·dʒe·re] <dipingo, dipinsi, dipinto> *vt* **1.** (*gener*) to paint; ~ **su qc** to paint on sth; ~ **ad acquerello** to paint in watercolors; ~ **ad olio** to paint in oils **2.** *fig* (*descrivere*) to portray

dipinto, -a I. *pp di* **dipingere II.** *agg* painted; **non voler vedere qu neanche ~** to not have

the slightest desire to see sb

dipl. *abbr di* **diploma** dip.

diploma [di·'plɔ:·ma] <-i> *m* diploma

diplomare [dip·lo·'ma:·re] **I.** *vt* to graduate **II.** *vr:* **-rsi** to graduate

diplomatico [dip·lo·'ma:·ti·ko] <-ci> *m* POL diplomat

diplomatico, -a <-ci, -che> *agg* diplomatic

diplomato, -a [dip·lo·'ma:·to] **I.** *agg* qualified **II.** *m, f* graduate; ~ **in agraria** graduate in agriculture

diplomazia [dip·lo·mat·'tsi:·a] <-ie> *f a. fig* diplomacy; **entrare nella ~** to enter the diplomatic service

dipoi, di poi [di·'pɔ:·i] <inv> *agg* following

diporto [di·'pɔr·to] *m* SPORT **imbarcazione da ~** pleasure boat

diradare [di·ra·'da:·re] **I.** *vt* **1.** (*rendere meno fitto: piante*) to thin out; (*nebbia*) to disperse **2.** *fig* (*visite*) to spread out **II.** *vr:* **-rsi** (*piante, capelli*) to become thinner; (*nebbia, folla*) to disperse

diramare [di·ra·'ma:·re] **I.** *vt* (*diffondere: comunicato, ordine*) to circulate **II.** *vr:* **-rsi** **1.** (*strada*) to branch off **2.** (*notizia*) to spread

diramazione [di·ra·mat·'tsio:·ne] *f* **1.** (*ramificazione*) branch; ~ **di un fiume** branch of a river **2.** (*diffusione: di comunicato, ordine, notizia*) circulation

dire[1] ['di:·re] <dico, dissi, detto> *vt* **1.** (*affermare, recitare*) to say; **dice di essere ammalato** he says he's sick; **si dice che sia molto ricco** people say he's very rich; ~ **di sì/no** to say yes/no; ~ **messa** to say mass **2.** (*chiedere, raccontare*) to tell; ~ **bugie** to tell lies; ~ **la propria** to have one's say; **dirle grosse** *fam* to talk nonsense; **dir male di qu** to speak ill of sb; **avere da ~ su qu** to have sth to say about sb; **lasciar ~** to let sth go; **a ~ il vero** to tell the truth; **per meglio ~** or rather; **lo dicevo io!** I told you ...; **dico bene?** am I right?; **come si dice in inglese?** what's the English for ...; ~ **pane al pane e vino al vino** to call a spade a spade; **dico sul serio** I mean it; **un film che non dice nulla** *fig* a nothing kind of movie; **così dicendo, ...** and with this, ...; **diciamo, ... suppose, ...**; (**mi**) **dica** can I help you?; **è facile a dirsi** it's easy for you to say **3.** (*significare*) **come sarebbe a ~?** what does that mean?; **voler ~** to mean; **vale a ~** that is **4.** (*pensare*) **che ne dici del mio abito nuovo?** what do you think of my new dress?; **che ne dici di uscire a cena?** shall we go out for dinner? **5.** (*chiamare*) to call

dire[2] *m* **hai un bel ~** that's easy for you to say; **tra il ~ e il fare c'è di mezzo il mare** *prov* it's easier said than done

directory [di·'rek·t(ə)·ri] <- *o* directories> *f* COMPUT directory

diressi [di·'rɛs·si] *1. pers sing pass rem di* **dirigere**

diretta [di·'rɛt·ta] *f* TV **in -a** live

direttamente [di·ret·ta·'men·te] *avv* **1.** (*senza*

tappe) straight **2.** (*senza intermediari*) directly

direttissima [di·ret·'tis·si·ma] *f* **1.** JUR **processo per** ~ summary trial **2.** (*linea ferroviaria*) high-speed railway line

direttiva [di·ret·'ti:·va] *f* (*istruzione*) directive; ~ **comunitaria** European Union directive

direttivo [di·ret·'ti:·vo] *m* leadership

direttivo, -a *agg* (*organo, comitato*) executive

diretto [di·'rɛt·to] *m* **1.** (*treno*) local train **2.** SPORT (*nel pugilato*) jab

diretto, -a I. *pp di* **dirigere** II. *agg* **1.** (*senza deviazioni, soste*) direct **2.** (*rivolto*) ~ **a qu** directed at sb **3.** (*destinato*) **il treno** ~ **a Roma** the train for Rome **4.** LING **complemento** ~ direct object; **discorso** ~ direct speech

direttore, -trice [di·ret·'to:·re] *m, f* director; ~ **di produzione** CINE producer; ~ **d'orchestra** conductor; ~ **artistico** THEAT artistic director; ~ (**didattico**) principal; ~ **tecnico** SPORT coach; ~ **responsabile** editor; ~ **delle vendite** sales director

direttrice [di·ret·'tri:·tʃe] *f* **1.** *v.* **direttore 2.** (*mat*) directrix **3.** POL, MIL line

direzionale [di·ret·tsio·'na:·le] *agg* **1.** (*della direzione: attività, norme, responsabilità*) managerial; **centro** ~ business center **2.** (*di direzione*) directional; **microfono** ~ directional microphone

direzione [di·ret·'tsio:·ne] *f* **1.** (*di azienda, partito*) management; ~ **amministrativa** administration **2.** (*senso*) direction; **in** ~ **di** toward

dirigente [di·ri·'dʒɛn·te] I. *agg* managerial; **classe** ~ ruling class II. *mf* manager; ~ **sindacale** union leader

dirigenza [di·ri·'dʒɛn·tsa] *f* management

dirigere [di·'ri:·dʒe·re] <dirigo, diressi, diretto> I. *vt* **1.** (*essere a capo di: azienda*) to manage; (*lavori, scuola*) to run; MUS (*orchestra*) to conduct **2.** (*indirizzare*) to direct; ~ **qu/qc a** [*o* **verso**] **qu/qc** to direct sb/sth to sb/sth II. *vr:* **-rsi** to make one's way; **-rsi verso qu** to make one's way toward sb; **-rsi verso** [*o* **a**] **qc** to make one's way toward sth

dirigibile [di·ri·'dʒi:·bi·le] *m* airship

dirimere [di·'ri:·me·re] <dirimo, *obs* dirimei *o* dirimetti, *manca il pp*> *vt form* (*lite, controversia*) to settle

dirimpettaio, -a [di·rim·pet·'ta:·io] <-ai, -aie> *m, f fam* neighbor living opposite

dirimpetto [di·rim·'pɛt·to] I. *avv* opposite II. *prep* ~ **a te** opposite you III. <inv> *agg* **la casa** ~ the house opposite

diritto [di·'rit·to] I. *m* **1.** (*complesso di norme, scienza*) law; ~ **civile** civil law; ~ **penale** criminal law; ~ **privato** private law; ~ **pubblico** public law **2.** (*interesse*) right; **avere** ~ **a qc** to have a right to sth; ~ **di proprietà** property right; ~ **di sciopero** right to strike; ~ **di voto** right to vote; **-i d'autore** copyright; **-i dell'uomo** human rights; **rivendicare un** ~ to demand a right; **di** ~ by right; **a buon** ~

quite rightly **3.** *pl* (*tassa*) fees; **avanzare dei -i** to claim fees **4.** (*di maglia, stoffa*) right side **5.** SPORT forehand II. *avv* **1.** (*in linea retta*) straight (on) **2.** (*direttamente*) straight assenza; **tirar** ~ **per la propria strada** *fig* to go one's own way; **rigare** [*o* **filare**] ~ to go straight

diritto, -a *agg* straight

dirittura [di·rit·'tu:·ra] *f* SPORT ~ **d'arrivo** home stretch; **essere in** ~ **d'arrivo** *fig* to be in the home stretch

diroccato, -a [di·rok·'ka:·to] *agg* (*edificio*) tumbledown

dirottamento [di·rot·ta·'men·to] *m* (*di nave, aereo*) hijacking

dirottare [di·rot·'ta:·re] I. *vt* **1.** (*far deviare*) to reroute **2.** (*con la forza*) to hijack II. *vi* (*cambiare rotta*) to change course

dirottatore, -trice [di·rot·ta·'to:·re] *m, f* hijacker

dirotto, -a [di·'rot·to] *agg* **scoppiare in un pianto** ~ to burst into tears; **piovere a** ~ to pour down rain

disabile [di·'za:·bi·le] I. *agg* disabled II. *mf* disabled person; **posti riservati ai -i** places reserved for the disabled

disabilità [di·za·bi·li·'ta] <-> *f* (*handicap*) disability

disabilitare [di·za·bi·li·'ta:·re] *vt* (*programma, macchina, funzione*) to disable

disabilitato, -a [di·za·bi·li·'ta:·to] *agg* disabled

disabitato, -a [di·za·bi·'ta:·to] *agg* uninhabited

disabituare [di·za·bi·tu·'a:·re] I. *vt* ~ **qu a qc** to break sb of a habit II. *vr:* **-rsi a qc** to break oneself of a habit

disaccordo [di·zak·'kɔr·do] *m* **1.** MUS discord **2.** (*contrasto*) disagreement; **essere in** ~ **su qc** to disagree about sth

disadattamento [di·za·dat·ta·'men·to] *m* alienation

disadattato, -a [di·za·dat·'ta:·to] I. *agg* alienated II. *m, f* alienated person

disadatto, -a [di·za·'dat·to] *agg* unsuitable; **essere** ~ **a** [*o* **per**] **qc** to be unsuitable for sth

disadorno, -a [di·za·'dor·no] *agg* (*stile, abbigliamento, muri*) unadorned

disagevole [di·za·'dʒe:·vo·le] *agg* **1.** (*scomodo: sistemazione, viaggio*) uncomfortable **2.** (*difficile: situazione, compito*) awkward

disaggregare [di·zag·gre·'ga:·re] I. *vt* to break up II. *vr:* **-rsi** to break up

disaggregazione [di·zag·gre·gat·'tsio:·ne] *f* breakup

disagiato, -a [di·za·'dʒa:·to] *agg* **1.** (*scomodo: sistemazione, viaggio*) uncomfortable **2.** (*povero: ceto, famiglia*) needy; **condizione -a** need

disagio [di·'za:·dʒo] *m* **1.** (*mancanza di comodità*) discomfort **2.** (*imbarazzo*) unease; **sentirsi a** ~ to feel awkward; **mettere a** ~ **qu** to make sb feel awkward

disambientato, -a [di·zam·bien·'ta:·to] *agg*

disoriented

disamorarsi [di·za·mo·'ra:r·si] *vr* ~ **di qc** to lose interest in sth; ~ **del lavoro** to lose interest in one's job; ~ **di qu** to fall out of love with sb

disancorare [di·zan·ko·'ra:·re] **I.** *vt* to raise the anchor of **II.** *vr:* **-rsi** (*liberarsi*) to free oneself; **-rsi dai pregiudizi** to free oneself of one's prejudices

disappetenza [di·zap·pe·'tɛn·tsa] *f* lack of appetite

disapprovare [di·zap·pro·'va:·re] *vt* to disapprove of

disapprovazione [di·zap·pro·vat·'tsio:·ne] *f* disapproval

disappunto [di·zap·'pun·to] *m* disappointment

disarmare [di·zar·'ma:·re] *vt* **1.** (*bandito, nemico, avversario*) to disarm **2.** (*pistola, fucile*) to put the safety on

disarmato, -a [di·zar·'ma:·to] *agg* **1.** (*senza armi*) unarmed **2.** (*indifeso*) defenseless

disarmo [di·'zar·mo] *m* **1.** (*di nazione*) disarmament **2.** (*di persone*) disarming

disarmonia [di·zar·mo·'ni:·a] *f* disharmony

disarticolato, -a [di·zar·ti·ko·'la:·to] *agg fig* (*suono*) disjointed

disassortito, -a [di·zas·sor·'ti:·to] *agg* unmatched; **scarpe -e** odd shoes

disastrato, -a [di·zas·'tra:·to] **I.** *agg* (*zona, paese*) devastated **II.** *m, f* victim

disastro [di·'zas·tro] *m* **1.** (*gener*) disaster **2.** (*caos*) disaster area

disastroso, -a [di·zas·'tro:·so] *agg* disastrous

disattento, -a [di·zat·'tɛn·to] *agg* inattentive

disattenzione [di·zat·ten·'tsio:·ne] *f* **1.** (*mancanza di attenzione*) carelessness **2.** (*svista*) oversight

disattivare [di·zat·ti·'va:·re] *vt* **1.** (*bomba*) to defuse **2.** (*macchina, impianto*) to deactivate

disavanzo [di·za·'van·tso] *m* deficit; **-i pubblici** public deficit

disavveduto, -a [di·zav·ve·'du:·to] *agg* (*gesto, affermazioni*) thoughtless

disavventura [di·zav·ven·'tu:·ra] *f* misadventure

disavvertenza [di·zav·ver·'tɛn·tsa] *f* **1.** (*mancanza di attenzione*) carelessness **2.** (*svista*) oversight

disbrigo [diz·'bri:·go] <-ghi> *m* ~ **di faccende** dealing with jobs; ~ **di lavori di casa** dealing with chores

discapito [dis·'ka:·pi·to] *m* **a** ~ **di qu** to the detriment of sb

discarica [dis·'ka:·ri·ka] <-che> *f* (*per rifiuti: pubblica, abusiva*) dump

discarico [dis·'ka:·ri·ko] <-chi> *m* **a** ~ (**di qu**) in sb's defense; **testimone a** ~ defense witness

discendente [diʃ·ʃen·'dɛn·te] **I.** *agg* descending **II.** *mf* descendant

discendenza [diʃ·ʃen·'dɛn·tsa] *f* **1.** (*origine*) descent **2.** (*discendenti*) descendants *pl*

discendere [diʃ·'ʃen·de·re] <irr> **I.** *vi* essere

1. (*provenire*) ~ **da qu** to descend from sb; ~ **da qc** to come from sth **2.** (*scendere*) to descend; (*da macchina*) to get out; (*da cavallo, bicicletta, treno, aereo*) to get off **3.** *fig* (*abbassarsi: prezzi, temperatura*) to fall **II.** *vt avere* ~ **le scale** to go downstairs

discensionale [diʃ·ʃen·sio·'na:·le] *agg* PHYS downward

discepolo, -a [diʃ·'ʃe:·po·lo] *m, f* **1.** *poet* (*allievo*) pupil; (*seguace*) follower **2.** REL disciple

discernere [diʃ·'ʃɛr·ne·re] <discerno, discernei, manca il pp> *vt* **1.** (*distinguere*) to distinguish **2.** (*scorgere*) to make out

discernimento [diʃ·ʃer·ni·'men·to] *m* (*giudizio*) discernment

discesa [diʃ·'ʃe:·sa] *f* **1.** (*azione*) descent **2.** (*pendenza*) slope; **in** ~ downward sloping **3.** (*invasione*) invasion **4.** SPORT ~ **libera** downhill race

discesi *1. pers sing pass rem di* **discendere**

discesista [diʃ·ʃe·'sis·ta] <-i *m*, -e *f*> *mf* (*nello sci*) downhill racer

disceso *pp di* **discendere**

dischetto [dis·'ket·to] *m* COMPUT diskette; **drive per -i** floppy drive

dischiudere [dis·'kiu:·de·re] <irr> *vt* **1.** (*aprire*) to open **2.** (*rivelare: segreto*) to disclose

disciogliere [diʃ·'ʃɔʎ·ʎe·re] <irr> *vt* **1.** (*liquefare: neve*) to melt **2.** (*diluire*) to dissolve

disciplina [diʃ·ʃi·'pli:·na] *f* **1.** (*ordine*) discipline **2.** (*materia di studio*) subject

disciplinare[1] [diʃ·ʃi·pli·'na:·re] *agg* (*provvedimento, misura*) disciplinary; **sanzioni -i** disciplinary measures

disciplinare[2] *vt* (*regolare*) to regulate

disciplinato, -a [diʃ·ʃi·pli·'na:·to] *agg* (*alunno, traffico*) disciplined

disc-jockey ['disk 'dʒɔ·ki/'dis 'dʒo·ki] <-> *mf* disc jockey

disco[1] [dis·ko] <-schi> *m* **1.** (*piastra rotonda*) *a.* ANAT disk; ~ **volante** flying saucer; ~ **orario** parking disk; **zona** ~ restricted parking area, *where a parking disk must be displayed* **2.** SPORT discus **3.** MUS record; **cambiare** ~ *fig* change the subject **4.** COMPUT (~ *magnetico*) magnetic disk; ~ **fisso** COMPUT hard disk **5.** FERR signal; ~ **rosso** red light **6.** MOT ~ **del freno** brake disk; ~ **della frizione** clutch plate

disco[2] <-> *f* (*discomusic*) disco

discobolo [dis·'kɔ:·bo·lo] *m* discus thrower

disco dance ['dis·kou 'da:ns] <-> *f* MUS disco dancing

discografia [dis·ko·gra·'fi:·a] *f* **1.** (*tecnica*) recording **2.** (*elenco*) discography

discografico, -a [dis·ko·'gra:·fi·ko] <-ci, -che> **I.** *agg* (*casa, mercato, produttore*) record **II.** *m, f* record producer

discolo, -a ['dis·ko·lo] *m, f* rascal

discolpa [dis·'kol·pa] *f* (*giustificazione*) excuse; **a** ~ **di qu** in sb's defense

discolpare [dis·kol·'pa:·re] **I.** *vt* (*giustificare*) to excuse; (*da accusa*) to prove innocent **II.** *vr:* -**rsi** (*giustificarsi*) to justify oneself

disco-mix ['dis·kou·miks/'dis·co·miks] <·> *m* disco album

disconoscere [dis·ko·'noʃ·ʃe·re] <irr> *vt* (*figlio, scrittura*) to disown

discontinuità [dis·kon·ti·nui·'ta] *f* discontinuity; **con** ~ with interruptions

discontinuo, -a [dis·kon·'ti:·nuo] *agg* **1.**(*non continuo: linea*) broken **2.**(*non costante: sforzo, allievo, rendimento*) erratic

discordante [dis·kor·'dan·te] *agg* (*opinioni, suoni*) discordant; (*colori*) clashing

discordanza [dis·kor·'dan·tsa] *f* (*di opinioni*) difference; (*di suoni*) discord; (*di colori*) clash

discordare [dis·kor·'da:·re] *vi* to conflict

discorde [dis·'kɔr·de] *agg* (*opinioni, versioni*) conflicting

discordia [dis·'kɔr·dia] <-ie> *f* discord

discorrere [dis·'kor·re·re] <irr> *vi* ~ **di qc** to talk about sth

discorsivo, -a [dis·kor·'si:·vo] *agg* **1.**(*relativo al discorso*) discursive **2.**(*scorrevole: testo, linguaggio*) flowing

discorso [dis·'kor·so] **I.** *pp di* **discorrere II.** *m* **1.**(*discussione*) conversation; **cambiare** ~ to change the subject; **attaccar** ~ (**con qu**) to start a conversation (with sb); **il** ~ **cadde su di te** your name was mentioned; **questo è un altro** ~ that's another matter; **un** ~ **campato in aria** a load of nonsense **2.**(*esposizione orale*) speech; ~ **inaugurale** opening speech; **pronunciare un** ~ to give a speech **3.** LING ~ **diretto/indiretto** direct/indirect speech

discosto, -a [dis·'kɔs·to] *avv* away; ~ **da qc** away from sth

discoteca [dis·ko·'tɛ:·ka] <-che> *f* club; **andare in** ~ to go clubbing

discount ['dis·kaunt] <·> *m* discount store

discreditare [dis·kre·di·'ta:·re] *vt* to discredit

discredito [dis·'kre:·di·to] *m* discredit

discrepanza [dis·kre·'pan·tsa] *f* **1.**(*differenza: di opinioni, mentalità*) difference **2.**(*discordia*) discord

discretamente [dis·kre·ta·'men·te] *avv* **1.**(*con discrezione*) discreetly **2.**(*abbastanza*) quite **3.**(*abbastanza bene*) quite well

discreto, -a [dis·'kre:·to] *agg* **1.**(*moderato*) modest **2.**(*riservato*) discreet **3.**(*abbastanza buono*) fair **4.**(*non importuno: domanda*) modest; (*ospite*) undemanding

discrezione [dis·kret·'tsio:·ne] *f* **1.**(*tatto*) tact; **con** ~ tactfully **2.**(*moderazione*) moderation; **senza** ~ excessively **3.**(*volontà*) **a** ~ **di qu** at sb's discretion

discriminante [dis·kri·mi·'nan·te] **I.** *agg* (*trattamento, politica*) discriminatory; (*fattore*) determining **II.** *m* MATH discriminant **III.** *f* JUR extenuating circumstances *pl*

discriminare [dis·kri·mi·'na:·re] *vt* **1.**(*differenziare*) to distinguish **2.**(*penalizzare: donne, immigrati, ceti meno abbienti*) to discriminate

discriminazione [dis·kri·mi·nat·'tsio:·ne] *f* (*trattamento inuguale*) discrimination; ~ **razziale** racial discrimination

discussi [dis·'kus·si] *1. pers sing pass rem di* **discutere**

discussione [dis·kus·'sio:·ne] *f* **1.**(*dibattito*) discussion **hanno espresso il loro parere; essere in** ~ to be in doubt; **mettere qc in** ~ to doubt sth; **essere fuori** ~ to be out of the question **2.**(*litigio*) argument

discusso, -a [dis·'kus·so] **I.** *pp di* **discutere II.** *agg* (*decisione, scelta*) controversial

discutere [dis·'ku:·te·re] <discuto, discussi, discusso> **I.** *vt* **1.**(*dibattere*) to discuss **2.**(*contestare*) to doubt **II.** *vi* **1.**(*parlare*) ~ **di** [*o* **su**] **qc** to discuss sth **2.**(*litigare*) to argue

discutibile [dis·ku·'ti:·bi·le] *agg* (*soggetto a critiche: opinione, scelta*) dubious

disdegnare [diz·deɲ·'ɲa:·re] *vt* to scorn

disdegno [diz·'deɲ·ɲo] *m* scorn

disdegnoso, -a [diz·deɲ·'ɲo:·so] *agg poet* (*sprezzante*) scornful

disdetta [diz·'det·ta] *f* **1.**(*sfortuna*) bad luck **2.**(*di contratto*) cancellation; **dare la** ~ to cancel

disdettare [diz·det·'ta:·re] *vt* JUR (*contratto*) to cancel; (*appartamento*) to give up

disdicevole [diz·di·'tʃe:·vo·le] *agg* (*comportamento, affermazioni*) improper

disdire [diz·'di:·re] <irr> *vt* **1.**(*annullare: appuntamento, prenotazione*) to cancel **2.**(*sciogliere: contratto, società*) to dissolve

diseconomia [di·ze·ko·no·'mi:·a] <-ie> *f* (*squilibrio economico*) diseconomy

diseducativo, -a [di·ze·du·ka·'ti:·vo] *agg* (*atteggiamento, programma tv*) harmful

disegnare [di·seɲ·'ɲa:·re] *vt* **1.**(*immagine, piantina*) to draw **2.**(*progettare: veicolo, edificio*) to design **3.**(*descrivere*) to outline **4.** *lit* (*avere intenzione*) ~ **di fare qc** to intend to do sth

disegnatore, -trice [di·seɲ·ɲa·'to:·re] *m, f* designer

disegno [di·'seɲ·ɲo] *m* **1.**(*immagine*) drawing; ~ **animato** cartoon **2.**(*motivo*) pattern **3.** *fig* (*intenzione*) plan **4.** JUR ~ **di legge** bill

disequilibrio [di·ze·kui·li·'bri:·o] <-ri> *m* imbalance

diserbante [di·zer·'ban·te] *m* herbicide

diserbare [di·zer·'ba:·re] *vt* to weed

diseredare [di·ze·re·'da:·re] *vt* to disinherit

disertare [di·zer·'ta:·re] **I.** *vi* **1.** MIL to desert **2.** *fig* (*abbandonare*) ~ **da qc** to leave sth **II.** *vt* to leave

disertore [di·zer·'to:·re] *m a. fig* MIL deserter

diserzione [di·zer·'tsio:·ne] *f a. fig* MIL desertion

disfacimento [dis·fa·tʃi·'men·to] *m* **1.**(*decomposizione*) decay; (*di cadavere*) decomposition **2.** GEO degradation **3.** *fig* (*sfacelo: di società, famiglia*) breakdown

disfare [dis·'fa:·re] <irr> **I.** *vt* (*scomporre: nodo*) to undo; (*letto*) to strip; (*cucitura, orlo*) to unpick; (*bagagli, valigie*) to unpack **II.** *vr:*

-rsi 1.(*nodo*) to come undone; (*cucitura, orlo*) to come unstitched; (*cibo*) to disintegrate **2.** *fig* (*famiglia, società*) to fall apart **3.**(*liberarsi*) **-rsi di qc/qu** to get rid of sth/sb

disfatta [dis·'fat·ta] *f* (*di esercito, squadra, partito*) crushing defeat

disfattismo [dis·fat·'tiz·mo] *m* defeatism

disfattista [dis·fat·'tis·ta] <-i *m*, -e *f*> **I.** *agg* defeatist **II.** *mf* defeatist

disfatto *pp di* **disfare**

disfeci *1. pers sing pass rem di* **disfare**

disfunzione [dis·fun·'tsio:·ne] *f a.* MED dysfunction

disgelare [diz·dʒe·'la:·re] **I.** *vt avere* to thaw **II.** *vr:* **-rsi** to thaw

disgelo [diz·'dʒɛ:·lo] *m* METEO, POL thaw

disgiungere [dis·'dʒun·dʒe·re] <irr> *vt poet* to separate

disgrazia [diz·'grat·tsia] *f* **1.**(*sfortuna*) misfortune; **per mia/tua ~** unfortunately for me/you **2.**(*avvenimento*) **è successa una ~** something terrible has happened **3.**(*sfavore*) **cadere in ~** to fall out of favor

disgraziatamente [diz·grat·tsia·ta·'men·te] *avv* unfortunately

disgraziato, -a [diz·grat·'tsia:·to] **I.** *agg* **1.**(*persona*) unfortunate **2.**(*evento*) unlucky **II.** *m, f* **1.**(*persona sfortunata*) poor soul **2.**(*sciagurato*) jerk

disgregamento [diz·gre·ga·'men·to] *m* (*di partito, famiglia, società*) breakup

disgregare [diz·gre·'ga:·re] **I.** *vt* **1.**(*frantumare*) to shatter **2.** *fig* (*partito, famiglia, società*) to break up **II.** *vr:* **-rsi 1.**(*andare in pezzi*) to shatter **2.** *fig* (*partito, famiglia, società*) to break up

disgregatore, -trice [diz·gre·ga·'to:·re] **I.** *agg* (*elemento, fattore*) disruptive **II.** *m, f* disruptive element

disgregazione [diz·gre·gat·'tsio:·ne] *f* **1.**(*di rocce, materia, cellule*) disintegration; **~ meteorica** weathering **2.**(*di partito, famiglia, società*) breakup

disguido [diz·'gui:·do] *m* **1.**(*errore: burocratico, tecnico*) error; (*postale*) postal error **2.**(*svista*) mistake

disgustare [diz·gus·'ta:·re] **I.** *vt* **1.**(*nauseare*) **~ qu** to make sb feel sick **2.** *fig* (*infastidire*) to disgust **II.** *vr:* **-rsi -rsi di qc** to grow sick of sth

disgusto [diz·'gus·to] *m a. fig* disgust

disgustoso, -a [diz·gus·'to:·so] *agg* disgusting

disidratare [di·zi·dra·'ta:·re] *vt* (*alimenti, organismo*) to dehydrate; (*pelle*) to dry out

disidratato, -a [di·zi·dra·'ta:·to] *agg* (*alimenti, organismo*) dehydrated; (*pelle*) dry

disidratazione [di·zi·dra·tat·'tsio:·ne] *f* (*di alimenti, organismo*) dehydration; (*di pelle*) drying out

disilludere [di·zil·'lu:·de·re] <irr> **I.** *vt* to disillusion; **~ le speranze di qu** to disappoint sb's hopes **II.** *vr:* **-rsi** to lose one's illusions

disillusione [di·zil·lu·'zio:·ne] *f* disillusion

disimparare [di·zim·pa·'ra:·re] *vt* to forget

disimpegnare [di·zim·peɲ·'ɲa:·re] **I.** *vt* **1.**(*gioiello, oggetto, somma*) to redeem **2.** *fig* (*da impegno, promessa*) to release **II.** *vr:* **-rsi 1.**(*liberarsi*) to free oneself **2.** SPORT (*nel calcio*) to run with the ball

disimpegnato, -a [di·zim·peɲ·'ɲa:·to] *agg* POL uncommitted

disimpegno [di·zim·'peɲ·ɲo] *m* **1.**(*verso obbligo*) freedom **2.** POL lack of commitment **3.**(*locale*) access room **4.** SPORT (*nel calcio*) jink

disimpiego [di·zim·'piɛ:·go] <-ghi> *sing* (*non uso*) disuse

disincagliare [di·ziŋ·kaʎ·'ʎa:·re] **I.** *vt* **1.** NAUT (*barca, nave*) to refloat **2.** *fig* (*negoziati, trattativa*) to restart **II.** *vr:* **-rsi 1.** NAUT (*barca, nave*) to get afloat again **2.** *fig* (*negoziati, trattativa*) to restart

disincantato, -a [di·ziŋ·kan·'ta:·to] *agg* (*disilluso*) disenchanted

disincentivare [di·zin·tʃen·ti·'va:·re] *vt* to discourage

disincentivo [di·zin·tʃen·'ti:·vo] *m* disincentive

disincrostante [di·zin·kros·'tan·te] **I.** *agg* descaling **II.** *m* descaler

disindustrializzare [di·zin·dus·tria·lid·'dza:·re] *vt* to deindustrialize

disinfestare [di·zin·fes·'ta:·re] *vt* (*da insetti, topi, erbacce*) to disinfest

disinfestazione [di·zin·fes·tat·'tsio:·ne] *f* (*da insetti, topi, erbacce*) disinfestation

disinfettante [di·zin·fet·'tan·te] **I.** *agg* disinfectant **II.** *m* disinfectant

disinfettare [di·zin·fet·'ta:·re] **I.** *vt* to disinfect; **~ una ferita** to disinfect a wound **II.** *vr:* **-rsi** to disinfect

disinfezione [di·zin·fet·'tsio:·ne] *f* disinfection

disinformato, -a [di·zin·for·'ma:·to] *agg* ignorant; **~ su qc** ignorant of sth

disinformazione [di·zin·for·mat·'tsio:·ne] *f* misinformation

disingannare [di·ziŋ·gan·'na:·re] **I.** *vt* **1.**(*togliere dall'errore*) to undeceive **2.**(*disilludere*) to disillusion **II.** *vr:* **-rsi** to become disillusioned

disinibito, -a [di·zi·ni·'bi:·to] *agg* (*persona, atteggiamento*) uninhibited

disinnescare [di·zin·nes·'ka:·re] *vt* (*bomba, mina*) to defuse

disinnesco [di·zin·'nes·ko] <-schi> *m* (*di bomba, mina*) defusing

disinnestare [di·zin·nes·'ta:·re] *vt* AUTO **~ la marcia** to disengage

disinnesto [di·zin·'nɛs·to] *m* AUTO (*disinserimento*) declutching

disinquinamento [di·ziŋ·kui·na·'men·to] *m* cleanup

disinquinare [di·ziŋ·kui·'na:·re] *vt* to clean up

disinserire [di·zin·se·'ri:·re] <disinserisco> *vt* to disconnect

disinserito, -a [di·zin·se·'ri:·to] **I.** *agg* socially excluded **II.** *m, f* socially excluded person

disinstallare [di·zins·tal·'la:·re] *vt* COMPUT to uninstall

disintegrare [di·zin·te·'gra:·re] I. *vt* 1.(*ridurre in frammenti*) to blow to pieces 2. PHYS (*atomo*) to split II. *vr: -rsi* 1.(*ridursi in frammenti*) to disintegrate 2. PHYS to split

disintegrazione [di·zin·te·grat·'tsio:·ne] *f* 1.(*distruzione*) disintegration 2. PHYS decay

disinteressamento [di·zin·te·res·sa·'men·to] *m* lack of interest; **il ~ per qc** lack of interest in sth

disinteressare [di·zin·te·res·'sa:·re] I. *vt* ~ **qu a qc** to make sb uninterested in sth II. *vr* -**rsi di qu/qc** (*non interessarsi*) to be uninterested in sb/sth; (*smettere di interessarsi*) to lose interest in sb/sth

disinteressato, -a [di·zin·te·res·'sa:·to] *agg* 1.(*privo di interesse*) **essere ~ (a qc)** to be uninterested (in sth) 2.(*senza fini personali*) disinterested

disinteresse [di·zin·te·'rɛs·se] *m* 1.(*indifferenza*) lack of interest; **mostrare ~ per qc** to show a lack of interest in sth 2.(*generosità*) disinterest

disintossicante [di·zin·tos·si·'kan·te] I. *agg* detoxifying II. *m* detoxifier

disintossicare [di·zin·tos·si·'ka:·re] I. *vt* (*organismo, tossicodipendente*) to detox II. *vr: -rsi* to detox

disintossicazione [di·zin·tos·si·kat·'tsio:·ne] *f* (*di organismo, tossicodipendente*) detox

disinvolto, -a [di·zin·'vɔl·to] *agg* 1.(*non timido*) confident 2. *pej* (*sfacciato*) familiar

disinvoltura [di·zin·vol·'tu:·ra] *f* 1.(*naturalezza*) ease 2. *pej* (*sfacciataggine*) insolence 3.(*superficialità*) flippancy

dislivello [diz·li·'vɛl·lo] *m* 1.(*differenza di altezza*) difference in height 2. *fig* (*divario*) gap; **~ tra classi sociali** inequality between social classes

dislocamento [diz·lo·ka·'men·to] *m* 1. NAUT displacement 2. MIL (*di truppe*) stationing

dislocazione [diz·lo·kat·'tsio:·ne] *f* 1.(*collocazione*) distribution 2. MIL (*di truppe*) movement

dismisura [diz·mi·'zu:·ra] *f* **a ~** beyond measure

disneyano, -a [diz·ne·'ia:·no] *agg* Disney; **personaggi -i** Disney characters

disobbediente [di·zob·be·'diɛn·te] *agg v.* **disubbidiente**

disobbligarsi [di·zob·bli·'ga:r·si] *vr* ~ **con qu per qc** to repay sb for sth

disoccupato, -a [di·zok·ku·'pa:·to] I. *agg* 1.(*senza lavoro*) unemployed 2. *poet* (*ozioso: periodo, vita*) leisurely II. *m, f* unemployed person; **~ di lunga durata** long-term unemployed person

disoccupazione [di·zok·ku·pat·'tsio:·ne] *f* unemployment; **~ giovanile** youth unemployment

disomogeneità [di·zo·mo·dʒe·nei·'ta] <-> *f* lack of homogeneity

disomogeneo, -a [di·zo·mo·'dʒɛ:·neo] <-ei, -ee> *agg* (*distribuzione, situazione*) unequal; (*conoscenze, forze, informazioni*) disparate

disonestà [di·zo·nes·'ta] *f* dishonesty

disonesto, -a [di·zo·'nɛs·to] *agg* (*privo di onestà: persona, negoziante, politico*) dishonest

disonorare [di·zo·no·'ra:·re] I. *vt* to disgrace II. *vr: -rsi* to disgrace oneself

disonore [di·zo·'no:·re] *m* 1.(*perdita dell'onore*) dishonor 2.(*persona*) disgrace

disonorevole [di·zo·no·'re:·vo·le] *agg* dishonorable

disopra, di sopra [di·'so:p·ra] I. *avv* upstairs II. <inv> *agg* upstairs III. <-> *m* (*parte superiore*) top; **essere al ~ di ogni cosa** to believe oneself superior; **essere al ~ di ogni sospetto** to be above suspicion

disordinato, -a [di·zor·di·'na:·to] I. *agg* 1.(*stanza*) untidy 2.(*idea, racconto*) incoherent 3.(*vita, alimentazione*) disorderly II. *m, f* untidy person

disordine [di·'zor·di·ne] *m* 1.(*scompiglio*) mess; **in ~** in a mess 2.(*situazione confusa*) disorder 3.(*sregolatezza: nel mangiare, bere*) irregularity 4. *pl* (*tumulti*) trouble

disorganico, -a [di·zor·'ga:·ni·ko] <-ci, -che> *agg* disorganized

disorganizzato, -a [di·zor·ga·nid·'dza:·to] *agg* disorganized

disorganizzazione [di·zor·ga·nid·dzat·'tsio:·ne] *f* disorganization

disorientamento [di·zo·rien·ta·'men·to] *m* disorientation

disorientare [di·zo·rien·'ta:·re] I. *vt* 1.(*nella direzione*) to disorient 2. *fig* (*confondere*) to confuse II. *vr: -rsi* 1.(*nella direzione*) to become disoriented 2. *fig* (*confondersi*) to become confused

disorientato, -a [di·zo·rien·'ta:·to] *agg* (*confuso*) confused

disossare [di·zos·'sa:·re] *vt* (*pollo, coniglio*) to bone

disossidante [di·zos·si·'dan·te] I. *agg* deoxidizing II. *m* deoxidizer

disossidare [di·zos·si·'da:·re] *vt* to deoxidize

disossidazione [di·zos·si·dat·'tsio:·ne] *f* deoxidation

disotto, di sotto [di·'sot·to] I. *avv* downstairs II. <inv> *agg* (*piano, camere*) downstairs III. <-> *m* (*parte inferiore*) bottom; **al ~ del livello del mare** below sea level; **al ~ di qu** (*dipendente*) below sb; **al ~ di qc** (*inferiore a*) below sth

dispaccio [dis·'pat·tʃo] <-cci> *m* (*comunicazione*) dispatch; **~ telegrafico** telegram

disparato, -a [dis·pa·'ra:·to] *agg* varied

dispari ['dis·pa·ri] <inv> *agg* MATH odd

disparità [dis·pa·ri·'ta] *f* difference

disparte [dis·'par·te] *avv* **lasciare qc in ~** to set sth aside; **tenersi [o starsene] in ~** to stay by oneself

dispendio [dis·'pɛn·dio] <-i> *m* (*spesa*

eccessiva) expense; (*consumo eccessivo*) waste; ~ **di energie** expenditure of energy

dispendioso, -a [dis·pen·'dio:·so] *agg* (*acquisto, vita*) extravagant; (*sport*) expensive

dispensa [dis·'pɛn·sa] *f* 1. (*fascicolo*) part; ~ **universitaria** lecture notes 2. (*esonero*) dispensation 3. (*mobile*) sideboard 4. (*stanzino*) pantry

dispensare [dis·pen·'sa:·re] *vt* 1. *iron* (*distribuire*) to hand out 2. (*esonerare: da tassa, servizio militare*) ~ **qu da qc** to exempt sb from sth

disperare [dis·pe·'ra:·re] I. *vt* ~ **di fare qc** to despair of doing sth II. *vi* to despair; ~ **di qc** to despair of sth; **far** ~ **qu** to drive sb crazy III. *vr:* -**rsi** to despair; -**rsi per qc** to be in despair about sth

disperato, -a [dis·pe·'ra:·to] I. *agg* 1. (*persona*) in despair 2. (*situazione*) desperate; **caso** ~ hopeless case II. *m, f* **un (povero)** ~ *fam* a poor wretch; **lavorare come un** ~ *fam* to work like crazy

disperazione [dis·pe·rat·'tsio:·ne] *f* 1. (*sconforto*) despair 2. (*che fa disperare*) **essere una** ~ to drive sb to distraction

disperdere [dis·'pɛr·de·re] <irr> I. *vt* 1. (*far allontanare: folla*) to disperse 2. (*consumare: averi*) to squander II. *vr:* -**rsi** 1. (*allontanarsi*) to disperse 2. (*andare sprecato*) to be lost 3. *fig* (*distrarsi*) -**rsi in qc** to get distracted by sth

dispersione [dis·per·'sio:·ne] *f* 1. (*allontamento: di folla, esercito*) dispersal 2. *fig* (*spreco: di energia, forze*) waste 3. PHYS (*di elettricità, suono*) dispersion; ~ **di calore** heat loss

dispersività [dis·per·si·vi·'ta] <-> *f a.* PSYCH dispersiveness

dispersivo, -a [dis·per·'si:·vo] I. *agg* dispersive II. *m, f* dispersive person

disperso, -a [dis·'pɛr·so] I. *agg* 1. (*sparso*) scattered 2. (*perso*) lost; **dare qu per** ~ to report sb missing II. *m, f* missing person

dispetto [dis·'pet·to] *m* 1. (*azione*) piece of spite; **fare un** ~ **a qu** to spite sb; **a** ~ **di qu** in spite of sb's opposition 2. (*irritazione*) **provare** ~ **per qc** to find sth annoying

dispettoso, -a [dis·pet·'to:·so] *agg* 1. (*che fa dispetti*) spiteful 2. (*fastidioso: tempo, vento*) unpleasant

dispiacere[1] [dis·pia·'tʃe:·re] *m* (*afflizione*) sorrow; **dare un** ~ **a qu** to upset sb

dispiacere[2] <irr> *vi* **essere** 1. (*causare dispiacere*) to upset; **mi dispiace (che ...)** I'm sorry (that ...); **ti dispiace posare il libro sul tavolo?** would you mind putting the book on the table?; **se non ti dispiace ...** if you don't mind ... 2. (*non piacere*) **il film non mi è dispiaciuto** I really liked the movie; **non mi dispiacerebbe vederlo** I wouldn't mind seeing him/it

dispiaciuto, -a [dis·pia·'tʃu:·to] *agg* sorry; **essere** ~ **di dover fare qc** to be sorry to have to do sth

dispongo *1. pers sing pr di* **disporre**

disponibile [dis·po·'ni:·bi·le] *agg* 1. (*a disposizione*) available; **non c'è più un posto** ~ there are no more seats 2. (*libero da impegni*) free; **questo pomeriggio sono** ~ I'm free this afternoon 3. (*gentile*) helpful

disponibilità [dis·po·ni·bi·li·'ta] <-> *f* 1. (*gener*) availability 2. (*gentilezza*) helpfulness 3. (*denaro*) available funds

disporre [dis·'por·re] <irr> I. *vt* 1. (*sistemare*) to arrange 2. (*preparare*) to prepare 3. (*prescrivere: legge*) to lay down; (*giudice*) to order II. *vi* 1. (*avere a disposizione*) ~ **di qc** to have (available) 2. (*decidere*) to decide 3. (*possedere*) to have III. *vr:* -**rsi** 1. (*sistemarsi: in fila, in cerchio*) to arrange oneself 2. (*prepararsi*) -**rsi a fare qc** to get ready to do sth

dispositivo [dis·po·zi·'ti:·vo] *m* 1. (*congegno*) device; ~ **di sicurezza** safety device 2. JUR operative part

dispositivo, -a *agg* regulating; ADM, JUR regulatory

disposizione [dis·po·zit·'tsio:·ne] *f* 1. (*sistemazione*) arrangement; **la** ~ **degli invitati a tavola** the seating of the guests 2. (*inclinazione*) bent; **avere** ~ **a [o per] qc** to have a bent for sth 3. (*stato d'animo*) mood 4. (*prescrizione*) instruction 5. (*servizio*) **essere a** ~ **di qu** to be at sb's disposal; **mettere qc a** ~ **di qu** to put sth at sb's disposal; **tenersi a** ~ to make oneself available

disposto [dis·'pos·to] *m* provision

disposto, -a I. *pp di* **disporre** II. *agg* 1. (*sistemato*) arranged 2. (*pronto*) **essere** ~ **a fare qc** to be disposed to do sth 3. (*psicologicamente*) **ben/mal** ~ **verso qu** well/ill disposed toward sb

dispotico, -a [dis·'pɔ:·ti·ko] <-ci, -che> *agg* 1. POL despotic 2. *fig* tyrannical

dispotismo [dis·po·'tiz·mo] *m* 1. POL despotism 2. *fig* tyranny

dispregiativo, -a [dis·pre·dʒa·'ti:·vo] *agg* LING pejorative

disprezzabile [dis·pret·'tsa:·bi·le] *agg* contemptible

disprezzare [dis·pret·'tsa:·re] *vt* 1. (*non stimare*) to despise 2. (*disdegnare: offerta*) to scorn 3. (*non tener conto di: pericolo, ordini*) to disregard

disprezzo [dis·'prɛt·tso] *m* 1. (*mancanza di stima*) contempt 2. (*noncuranza: di pericolo, tradizioni*) disregard

disputa ['dis·pu·ta] *f* 1. (*discussione*) discussion 2. (*lite*) dispute 3. SPORT **la** ~ **del campionato** the championship game

disputare [dis·pu·'ta:·re] I. *vt* SPORT (*partita, gara*) to take part in II. *vr* -**rsi qc** (*primo posto, premio, vittoria*) to compete for sth

disquisire [dis·kui·'zi:·re] <disquisisco> *vi* ~ (**su qc**) to hold forth (about sth)

disquisizione [dis·kui·zit·'tsio:·ne] *f* detailed discussion

dissacrante [dis·sa·'kran·te] *agg* debunking

D

dissacratore, **-trice** [dis·sa·kra·'to:·re] I. *agg* debunking II. *m*, *f* debunker

dissalare [dis·sa·'la:·re] *vt* to desalinate

dissalazione [dis·sa·lat·'tsio:·ne] *f* desalination

dissanguamento [dis·saŋ·gua·'men·to] *m* MED loss of blood

dissanguare [dis·saŋ·'gua:·re] I. *vt* 1. MED to cause to lose blood 2. *fig* (*spremere*) to bleed dry II. *vr:* **-rsi** 1. MED to lose blood 2. *fig* (*rovinarsi*) to bankrupt oneself

dissanguatore, **-trice** [dis·saŋ·gua·'to:·re] I. *agg fig* bloodsucking II. *m*, *f fig* bloodsucker

dissapore [dis·sa·'po:·re] *m* disagreement

disseminare [dis·se·mi·'na:·re] *vt* 1. (*spargere: oggetti*) to scatter 2. *fig* (*diffondere*) to spread

disseminazione [dis·se·mi·nat·'tsio:·ne] *f* 1. BOT dispersal 2. (*diffusione: di idee, dottrine*) dissemination

dissennato, **-a** [dis·sen·'na:·to] *agg* foolish

dissenso [dis·'sɛn·so] *m* 1. (*contrasto: di idee, opinioni*) disagreement 2. (*disapprovazione*) disapproval 3. POL, REL dissent

dissenteria [dis·sen·te·'ri:·a] <-ie> *f* dysentery

dissentire [dis·sen·'ti:·re] *vi* ~ **da qu su qc** to disagree with sb about sth

dissenziente [dis·sen·'tsiɛn·te] I. *agg* dissenting II. *mf* dissenter

disseppellire [dis·sep·pel·'li:·re] <disseppellisco> *vt* 1. (*rovine*) to excavate 2. (*cadavere*) to exhume

dissertare [dis·ser·'ta:·re] *vi* ~ **su** [*o* **di**] **qc** (*parlare*) to speak about sth; (*scrivere*) to write about sth

dissertazione [dis·ser·tat·'tsio:·ne] *f* dissertation; ~ **di laurea** dissertation, *for a first degree*

disservizio [dis·ser·'vit·tsio] *m* (*cattivo funzionamento*) inefficiency

dissesto [dis·'sɛs·to] *m fig* (*economico*) difficulty; (*sociale*) disorder; **azienda in** ~ failing company; ~ **finanziario** financial difficulties

dissetante [dis·se·'tan·te] I. *agg* thirst-quenching II. *m* thirst-quenching drink

dissetare [dis·se·'ta:·re] I. *vt* to quench the thirst of II. *vr:* **-rsi** to quench one's thirst

dissi ['dis·si] *1. pers sing pass rem di* **dire**[1]

dissidente [dis·si·'dɛn·te] I. *agg* dissident II. *mf* dissident

dissidenza [dis·si·'dɛn·tsa] *f* dissidence

dissidio [dis·'si:·dio] <-i> *m* (*politico, religioso*) disagreement

dissimile [dis·'si:·mi·le] *agg* dissimilar

dissimulare [dis·si·mu·'la:·re] *vt* 1. (*sentimento, pensiero*) to hide 2. (*fingere*) to pretend

dissimulatore, **-trice** [dis·si·mu·la·'to:·re] *m*, *f* deceiver

dissimulazione [dis·si·mu·lat·'tsio:·ne] *f* deceit

dissipare [dis·si·'pa:·re] I. *vt* 1. (*nebbia, fumo, nubi*) to disperse 2. (*dubbi, sospetti*) to dispel

3. (*patrimonio*) to squander II. *vr:* **-rsi** 1. (*nebbia*) to clear 2. (*dubbi*) to disappear

dissipatezza [dis·si·pa·'tet·tsa] *f* (*corruzione: di vita, costumi*) dissipation

dissipato, **-a** [dis·si·'pa:·to] I. *agg* dissolute II. *m*, *f* degenerate

dissipatore, **-trice** [dis·si·pa·'to:·re] *m*, *f* wastrel

dissipazione [dis·si·pat·'tsio:·ne] *f* 1. (*sperpero*) waste 2. (*condotta sregolata*) dissipation 3. FIS (*di calore, energia*) dissipation

dissociare [dis·so·'tʃa:·re] I. *vt a.* CHEM to separate II. *vr:* **-rsi -rsi da qc** to dissociate oneself from sth

dissodamento [dis·so·da·'men·to] *m* tilling

dissodare [dis·so·'da:·re] *vt* (*terra*) to till

dissolsi [dis·'sɔl·si] *1. pers sing pass rem di* **dissolvere**

dissolto [dis·'sɔl·to] *pp di* **dissolvere**

dissolubile [dis·so·'lu:·bi·le] *agg* (*matrimonio, legame*) that can be dissolved

dissolutezza [dis·so·lu·'tet·tsa] *f* (*corruzione*) dissoluteness

dissoluto, **-a** [dis·so·'lu:·to] I. *agg* (*vita, persona*) dissolute II. *m*, *f* dissolute person

dissoluzione [dis·so·lut·'tsio:·ne] *f* 1. (*disfacimento: di famiglia, istituzioni, società*) collapse 2. (*corruzione*) dissolution

dissolvenza [dis·sol·'vɛn·tsa] *f* FILM ~ **in apertura** fade-in; ~ **in chiusura** fade-out; ~ **incrociata** cross fading

dissolvere [dis·'sɔl·ve·re] <dissolvo, dissolsi, dissolto> I. *vt* 1. (*compressa, legame*) to dissolve 2. (*nebbia*) to dispel II. *vr:* **-rsi** (*sciogliersi*) to dissolve

dissonante [dis·so·'nan·te] *agg* 1. MUS dissonant 2. (*opinioni*) discordant

dissonanza [dis·so·'nan·tsa] *f* 1. MUS dissonance 2. (*di opinioni*) clash

dissotterrare [dis·sot·ter·'ra:·re] *vt* 1. (*rovine*) to excavate 2. (*cadavere*) to exhume

dissuadere [dis·sua·'de:·re] <dissuado, dissuasi, dissuaso> *vt* to dissuade; ~ **qu da qc/ dal fare qc** to dissuade sb from doing sth

dissuasione [dis·sua·'zio:·ne] *f* dissuasion

dissuaso [dis·su·'a:·zo] *pp di* **dissuadere**

distaccare [dis·tak·'ka:·re] I. *vt* 1. (*separare*) to separate 2. (*trasferire*) to transfer 3. SPORT (*gruppo, concorrenti*) to outstrip II. *vr:* **-rsi** 1. (*allontanarsi*) to detach oneself 2. (*distinguersi*) to stand out

distaccato, **-a** [dis·tak·'ka:·to] *agg* (*freddo: atteggiamento, tono, espressione*) detached

distacco [dis·'tak·ko] <-chi> *m* 1. (*rimozione: di parti, componenti*) removal 2. *fig* (*allontanamento*) separation 3. (*freddezza*) detachment 4. SPORT **ha vinto con un** ~ **di dieci secondi** he won by ten seconds; **avere un** ~ **di cinque metri/dieci secondi su qu** to have a five-meter/a ten-second lead over sb; **ridurre il** ~ to close the gap

distante [dis·'tan·te] I. *agg* 1. (*lontano*) faraway 2. (*opinioni*) different 3. *fig* (*freddo*) distant **II.** *avv* far away

distanza [dis·'tan·tsa] *f* **1.** (*spazio*) distance; ~ **di sicurezza** braking distance; **comando a ~** remote control; **tenere le -e** *fig* to keep one's distance; **prendere le -e da qu/qc** to distance oneself from sb/sth **2.** (*tempo*) time; **a ~ di dieci anni** after ten years **3.** *fig* (*differenza*) gulf

distanziare [dis·tan·'tsia:·re] *vt* **1.** (*disporre a distanza*) to move away from **2.** SPORT to outstrip

distare [dis·'ta:·re] <disto, *mancano pass rem e pp*> *vi* ~ (**da qc**) to be far away (from sth)

distendere [dis·'ten·de·re] <irr> **I.** *vt* **1.** (*coperta, vele*) to spread; (*braccia, mani, gambe*) to stretch **2.** (*sdraiare*) to lay down **3.** (*nervi, muscoli*) to relax **4.** (*vernice, colore*) ~ **qc su qc** to apply sth to sth **II.** *vr:* **-rsi 1.** (*rilassarsi*) to relax **2.** (*sdraiarsi*) to stretch out

distensione [dis·ten·'sio:·ne] *f* **1.** (*di muscoli, corda*) stretching **2.** (*rilassamento*) relaxation **3.** (*di rapporti*) improvement

distensivo, -a [dis·ten·'si:·vo] *agg* **1.** (*rilassante*) relaxing **2.** (*pacificatore: fase, misura*) conciliatory; **politica -a** policy of conciliation

distesa [dis·'te:·sa] *f* **1.** (*estensione*) expanse **2.** (*quantità*) collection

distesi *1. pers sing pass rem di* **distendere**

disteso, -a [dis·'te:·so] **I.** *pp di* **distendere** **II.** *agg* **1.** (*sdraiato, allungato*) stretched out **2.** (*rapporti*) improved **3.** (*rilassato*) relaxed

distillare [dis·til·'la:·re] **I.** *vt avere* **1.** CHEM to distill **2.** (*mandar fuori*) to secrete **II.** *vi essere* to drip

distillato [dis·til·'la:·to] *m* distillate

distillato, -a *agg* distilled

distillatore [dis·til·la·'to:·re] *m* distiller

distillatore, -trice *m, f* distiller

distillazione [dis·til·lat·'tsio:·ne] *f* distillation

distilleria [dis·til·le·'ri:·a] <-ie> *f* distillery

distinguere [dis·'tiŋ·gue·re] <distinguo, distinsi, distinto> **I.** *vt* **1.** (*differenziare*) to tell **2.** (*vedere, sentire*) to make out **3.** (*rendere riconoscibile: bagagli*) to identify; (*person*) to distinguish **II.** *vr* **-rsi da qu** (**per qc**) to be distinguished from sb (by sth)

distintivo [dis·tin·'ti:·vo] *m* badge

distintivo, -a *agg* (*carattere, tratto*) distinctive

distinto, -a [dis·'tin·to] **I.** *pp di* **distinguere** **II.** *agg* **1.** (*differente*) distinct **2.** (*chiaro*) clear **3.** (*elegante: uomo, portamento, modi*) distinguished **4.** *form* (*nelle lettere*) **-i saluti** yours truly

distinzione [dis·tin·'tsio:·ne] *f* distinction; **senza ~** without distinction

distogliere [dis·'tɔʎ·ʎe·re] <irr> *vt* to remove; (*attenzione*) to distract; ~ **lo sguardo** to look away; ~ **qu da qc** to dissuade sb from sth

distorcere [dis·'tɔr·tʃe·re] <irr> **I.** *vt* **1.** (*torcere, contorcere*) to twist **2.** TEC, PHYS to distort **II.** *vr:* **-rsi** to twist; **-rsi il polso** to sprain one's wrist

distorsione [dis·tor·'sio:·ne] *f* **1.** (*gener*) distortion **2.** MED sprain

distrarre [dis·'trar·re] <irr> **I.** *vt* **1.** (*deconcentrare*) to distract **2.** (*divertire*) to entertain **3.** (*somma*) to subtract **II.** *vr:* **-rsi 1.** (*deconcentrarsi*) to get distracted **2.** (*divertirsi*) to enjoy oneself

distratto, -a [dis·'trat·to] **I.** *agg* **1.** (*deconcentrato*) **ero ~** I wasn't paying attention **2.** (*sbadato*) absent-minded **II.** *m, f* absent-minded person

distrazione [dis·trat·'tsio:·ne] *f* **1.** (*disattenzione*) inattention **2.** (*divertimento*) amusement

distretto [dis·'tret·to] *m* (*circoscrizione*) district; ~ **di polizia** precinct

distribuire [dis·tri·bu·'i:·re] <distribuisco> *vt* **1.** (*assegnare: compiti, premi, ruoli*) to give out **2.** (*ripartire: peso*) to distribute **3.** (*diffondere: posta, giornali, pubblicità*) to deliver; (*acqua, elettricità*) to supply

distributore [dis·tri·bu·'to:·re] *m* TEC pump; ~ **di benzina** gas pump; ~ **di sigarette** cigarette machine; ~ **automatico** (*bancomat*) ATM

distribuzione [dis·tri·but·'tsio:·ne] *f* **1.** (*assegnazione: di compiti, regali, ruoli, prodotti*) distribution **2.** (*consegna: di posta, giornali, acqua*) delivery **3.** AUTO (*in un motore*) distributor

districare [dis·tri·'ka:·re] **I.** *vt* **1.** (*groviglio, capelli, fili*) to untangle **2.** (*questione*) to sort out **II.** *vr:* **-rsi 1.** (*da rovi*) to free oneself **2.** (*trarsi d'impaccio*) to extricate oneself

distruggere [dis·'trud·dʒe·re] <irr> *vt a. fig* to destroy

distruttivo, -a [dis·trut·'ti:·vo] *agg* destructive

distrutto [dis·'trut·to] *pp di* **distruggere**

distruttore [dis·trut·'to:·re] *m* ~ **di documenti** shredder

distruttore, -trice **I.** *agg* destructive **II.** *m, f* destroyer

distruzione [dis·trut·'tsio:·ne] *f a. fig* destruction

disturbare [dis·tur·'ba:·re] **I.** *vt* to disturb **II.** *vr:* **-rsi** to put oneself out; **non si disturbi** please don't get up; **grazie, ma non doveva -rsi** thank you, but you shouldn't have

disturbo [dis·'tur·bo] *m* **1.** (*fastidio*) trouble; **togliere il ~** to leave **2.** MED problem; ~ **di stomaco** upset stomach **3.** MALFUNZIONAMENTO interference

disubbidiente [di·zub·bi·'diɛn·te] *agg* disobedient

disubbidienza [di·zub·bi·'diɛn·tsa] *f* disobedience

disubbidire [di·zub·bi·'di:·re] <disubbidisco> *vi* ~ **a qu** to disobey sb; ~ **a un ordine** to disobey an order

disuguaglianza [di·zu·guaʎ·'ʎan·tsa] *f* **1.** *a.* MATH inequality; **-e sociali** social differences **2.** (*irregolarità*) unevenness

disuguale [di·zu·'gua·le] *agg* **1.** (*diverso*) unequal **2.** (*irregolare: rendimento, umore*) un-

D

certain; (*terreno*) uneven

disumano, -a [di·zu·'ma:·no] *agg* inhuman

disunione [di·zu·'nio:·ne] *f* (*discordia*) disharmony

disunire [di·zu·'ni:·re] <disunisco> *vt* 1. (*separare*) to separate 2. *fig* (*famiglia, amici, partito*) to divide

disuso [di·'zu:·zo] *m* **cadere in ~** (*usanza, espressione*) to fall into disuse

disutile [di·'zu:·ti·le] *m* (*danno*) damage

ditale [di·'ta:·le] *m* thimble

ditata [di·'ta:·ta] *f* 1. (*colpo*) poke 2. (*impronta*) fingerprint

dito ['di:·to] <nel loro insieme: -a *f*, considerati separatamente: -i *m*> *m* 1. (*della mano, guanto*) finger; (*del piede*) toe; **sapere qc sulla punta delle -a** *fig* to have sth at one's fingertips; **si contano sulle -a** they can be counted on the fingers of one hand; **leccarsi le -a** *fig* to enjoy sth a lot, *food;* **mettere il ~ sulla piaga** *fig* to put one's finger on a sore point; **mordersi le -a** *fig* to regret sth; **non muovere un ~ in favore di qu** to not lift a finger to help sb; **mostrare a ~ qu** *fig* to point the finger at sb; **toccare il cielo con un ~** to be in seventh heaven; **legarsi qc al ~** *fig* to not forget a wrong 2. (*misura, quantità*) inch; (*di bevande*) drop

ditta ['dit·ta] *f* firm

dittatore [dit·ta·'to:·re] *m* dictator

dittatoriale [dit·ta·to·'ria:·le] *agg* dictatorial

dittatura [dit·ta·'tu:·ra] *f* dictatorship

dittongo [dit·'tɔŋ·go] <-ghi> *m* LING diphthong

diuresi [diu·'rɛ:·zi] <-> *f* MED diuresis

diuretico [diu·'rɛ:·ti·ko] <-ci> *m* diuretic

diuretico, -a <-ci, -che> *agg* diuretic

diurno, -a [di·'ur·no] *agg* daily; **albergo ~** public restroom in a station where passengers can shower, shave etc.; **servizio ~ e notturno** 24-hour service

diva ['di:·va] *f* star

divagare [di·va·'ga:·re] I. *vi* to digress; **~ da qc** (*argomento, tema*) to stray from sth II. *vr:* **-rsi** to enjoy oneself

divagazione [di·va·gat·'tsio:·ne] *f* (*digressione*) digression

divampare [di·vam·'pa:·re] *vi essere* 1. (*incendio, fuoco*) to flare up 2. *fig* (*rivolta, guerra*) to break out; **~ d'ira** (*persone*) to fly into a rage

divano [di·'va:·no] *m* sofa; **~ letto** sofa bed

divaricare [di·va·ri·'ka:·re] *vt* 1. (*braccia, gambe*) to open wide 2. (*allargare*) to widen

divario [di·'va:·rio] *m* gap; **~ nord-sud** north-south divide

divenire [di·ve·'ni:·re] <irr> *vi essere* to become; **~ qc** to become sth amico

diventare [di·ven·'ta:·re] *vi essere* to become; **~ qc** to become sth; **~ vecchio** to grow old; **il bambino è diventato uomo** the child became a man; **mi fai ~ nervoso** you're getting on my nerves

diverbio [di·'vɛr·bio] <-i> *m* quarrel

divergente [di·ver·'dʒɛn·te] *agg* 1. (*in direzione diversa: strade, linee*) diverging 2. (*discordante: opinioni, mentalità*) divergent 3. OPT **lente ~** diverging lens

divergenza [di·ver·'dʒɛn·tsa] *f* 1. (*di due strade, linee*) divergence 2. (*di opinioni, giudizi, mentalità*) difference

divergere [di·'vɛr·dʒe·re] <divergo, mancano pass rem e pp> *vi* 1. (*andare in direzioni diverse: strade, binari*) to diverge 2. (*opinioni*) to differ

diversamente [di·ver·sa·'men·te] *avv* 1. (*in maniera diversa*) differently 2. (*altrimenti*) otherwise

diversificare [di·ver·si·fi·'ka:·re] I. *vt* 1. (*variare: attività, interessi, letture*) to vary 2. COM (*produzione*) to diversify II. *vr:* **-rsi** 1. (*differenziarsi*) to differ 2. COM to diversify

diversificazione [di·ver·si·fi·kat·'tsio:·ne] *f* 1. (*cambiamento*) change 2. COM diversification

diversione [di·ver·'sio:·ne] *f* MIL diversion

diversità [di·ver·si·'ta] <-> *f* 1. (*differenza*) difference 2. (*varietà*) diversity

diversivo [di·ver·'si:·vo] *m* (*distrazione*) distraction

diversivo, -a *agg* **manovra -a** diversion

diverso, -a [di·'vɛr·so] I. *agg* 1. (*differente*) different; **~ da qc/qu** different from sth/sb 2. *pl* (*vari*) various II. *pron pl* several

divertente [di·ver·'tɛn·te] *agg* (*buffo*) entertaining; (*piacevole*) enjoyable ~

divertimento [di·ver·ti·'men·to] *m* 1. (*piacere*) pleasure; **buon ~!** have a good time! 2. (*cosa che diverte*) pastime 3. MUS divertimento

divertire [di·ver·'ti:·re] I. *vt* to entertain II. *vr:* **-rsi** (*svagarsi*) to enjoy oneself; (*ridere*) to laugh; **-rsi un mondo** to have a great time; **-rsi a fare qc** to enjoy doing sth; **-rsi alle spalle di qu** to laugh at sb behind their back

divertito, -a [di·ver·'ti:·to] *agg* amused

dividendo [di·vi·'dɛn·do] *m* FIN, MATH dividend

dividere [di·'vi:·de·re] <divido, divisi, diviso> I. *vt* 1. (*gener*) to divide; **~ in quattro** to divide into four; **~ 9 per 3** to divide 9 by 3 2. (*separare*) to separate 3. (*distribuire, condividere*) to share II. *vr:* **-rsi** (*in gruppi, categorie*) to divide; (*tra attività*) to divide one's time; **-rsi tra casa e ufficio** to divide one's time between home and work

divieto [di·'viɛ:·to] *m* prohibition; **il ~ di fumare in locali pubblici** the ban on smoking in public places; **'~ di parcheggio'** 'No parking'; **'~ di sosta'** 'No waiting'; **'~ di transito'** 'No entry'

divincolamento [di·viŋ·ko·la·'men·to] *m* struggling free

divincolarsi [di·viŋ·ko·'lar·si] *vr* to struggle free

divinità [di·vi·ni·'ta] <-> *f* divinity

divino, -a *agg* 1. (*di Dio, di divinità*) divine

2. (*eccellente*) heavenly

divisa [di·'vi:·za] *f* 1. (*uniforme*) uniform; **essere in** ~ to be in uniform **2.** FIN currency; ~ **estera** foreign currency

divisi [di·'vi:·zi] *1. pers sing pass rem di* **dividere**

divisibile [di·vi·'zi:·bi·le] *agg* divisible

divisibilità [di·vi·zi·bi·li·'ta] <-> *f* divisibility

divisione [di·vi·'zio:·ne] *f* 1. (*gener*) division; ~ **in sillabe** syllable division; ~ **dei beni** JUR division of assets **2.** (*separazione*) separation; ~ **dei poteri** separation of powers **3.** SPORT league

diviso, -a [di·'vi:·zo] **I.** *pp di* **dividere II.** *agg* **1.** (*separato: coniugi*) separated **2.** (*distinto: zone, locali, unità*) separate

divisore [di·vi·'zo:·re] *m* **1.** MATH divisor; ~ **comune** common denominator **2.** TEC divider

divisorio [di·vi·'zɔ:·rio] *m* partition

divisorio, -a <-i, -ie> *agg* (*elemento, muro, siepe*) dividing; **parete -a** dividing wall

divo, -a ['di:·vo] *m, f* star

divorare [di·vo·'ra:·re] *vt* (*preda, piatto, libro*) to devour; ~ **la strada** to eat up the miles

divoratore, -trice [di·vo·ra·'to:·re] *m, f* ~ **di dolciumi** lover of desserts; ~ **di gialli** great reader of thrillers

divorziare [di·vor·'tsia:·re] *vi* JUR to get divorced; ~ **da qu** to divorce sb

divorzio [di·'vɔr·tsio] <-i> *m a. fig* JUR divorce; **chiedere il** ~ to seek a divorce

divulgare [di·vul·'ga:·re] **I.** *vt* (*notizie, informazioni*) to divulge; (*idee*) to popularize **II.** *vr:* -**rsi** to spread

divulgativo, -a [di·vul·ga·'ti:·vo] *agg* (*articolo, testo, seminario*) popularizing

divulgazione [di·vul·gat·'tsio:·ne] *f* (*di idee*) popularization; (*di notizie*) disclosure

dizionario [dit·tsio·'na:·rio] <-i> *m* dictionary; ~ **monolingue/bilingue** monolingual/bilingual dictionary; ~ **tecnico** technical dictionary; **consultare il** ~ to look in a dictionary

dizione [dit·'tsio:·ne] *f* (*locuzione*) expression

dl *abbr di* **decilitro** dl

D.L. *abbr di* **Decreto legge** *decree passed by the Italian government without the consent of parliament*

dm *abbr di* **decimetro** dm

D.M. *abbr di* **Decreto Ministeriale** *ministerial decree*

DNA *m abbr di* **Deoxyribonucleic acid** (*acido deossiribonucleico*) DNA

do[1] [dɔ] <-> *m* MUS C; ~ **maggiore/minore** C major/minor; **chiave di** ~ key of C

do[2] *1. pers sing pr di* **dare**[1]

dobbiamo [dob·'bia:·mo] *1. pers pl pr di* **dovere**[1]

DOC [dɔk] *acro di* **Denominazione di Origine Controllata** AOC, *mark guaranteeing the origin of a wine*

doccia ['dot·tʃa] <-cce> *f* **1.** (*nel bagno*) shower; **fare la** ~ to take a shower; **una** ~

fredda *fig* a slap in the face **2.** (*grondaia*) gutter **3.** MED douche

docciacrema [dot·tʃa·'krɛ:·ma] *m* shower gel

docente [do·'tʃɛn·te] **I.** *agg* teaching; **personale** ~ teaching staff **II.** *mf* teacher; ~ **universitario** professor

docenza [do·'tʃɛn·tsa] *f* (*incarico*) teaching position; (*insegnamento*) teaching

docile ['dɔ:·tʃi·le] *agg* **1.** (*persona, carattere, animale*) docile **2.** (*strumento*) manageable; (*materiale*) easy to work

docilità [do·tʃi·li·'ta] <-> *f* **1.** (*di persona, animale*) docility **2.** (*di strumenti*) manageability

documentare [do·ku·men·'ta:·re] **I.** *vt* to document **II.** *vr* -**rsi** (**su qc**) to find out (about sth)

documentario [do·ku·men·'ta:·rio] <-i> *m* documentary

documentazione [do·ku·men·tat·'tsio:·ne] *f* documentation

documento [do·ku·'men·to] *m* **1.** (*personale*) ~ (**di identità**) ID **2.** ADM document; ~ **contabile** COM accounting record **3.** (*testimonianza storica*) evidence

dodecafonia [do·de·ka·fo·'ni:·a] *f* twelve-tone system

dodecagono [do·de·'ka:·go·no] *m* dodecagon

dodicenne [do·di·'tʃɛn·ne] **I.** *agg* twelve-year-old **II.** *mf* twelve year old

dodicennio [do·di·'tʃɛn·nio] <-i> *m* period of twelve years

dodicesimo [do·di·'tʃɛ:·zi·mo] *m* (*in frazione*) twelfth

dodicesimo, -a **I.** *agg* twelfth **II.** *m, f* twelfth; *v. a.* **quinto**

dodici ['do:·di·tʃi] **I.** *num* twelve **II.** <-> *m* **1.** (*numero*) twelve; **essere in** ~ to be twelve **2.** (*nelle date*) twelfth **III.** *fpl* (*ore*) twelve o'clock; *v. a.* **cinque**

doga ['do:·ga] <-ghe> *f* stave

dogana [do·'ga:·na] *f* **1.** (*ufficio*) customs *pl;* **operazioni di** ~ customs operations; **passare la** ~ to go through customs **2.** (*impiegati*) customs officers

doganale [do·ga·'na:·le] *agg* customs

doganiere [do·ga·'niɛ:·re] *mf* customs officer

doge ['dɔ:·dʒe] *m* doge

doglia ['dɔʎ·ʎa] <-glie> *f* **1.** *poet* sorrow **2.** *pl* (*del parto*) labor; **avere le -glie** to have labor pains

dogma ['dɔg·ma] <-i> *m* dogma

dogmatica [dog·'ma:·ti·ka] *f* dogmatics

dogmatico [dog·'ma:·ti·ko] <-ci> *m* dogmatic person

dogmatico, -a <-ci, -che> *agg* dogmatic

dogmatismo [dog·ma·'tiz·mo] *m* dogmatism

dogmatizzare [dog·ma·tid·'dza:·re] *vi* to dogmatize

dolby® ['dɔl·bi] <-> *m* Dolby®

dolce ['dol·tʃe] **I.** *agg* sweet; ~ **come il miele** as sweet as honey; **acqua** ~ freshwater **II.** *m* **1.** (*dessert*) dessert **2.** (*torta*) cake

dolceamaro, -a [dol·tʃe·a·'ma:·ro] *agg* sweet

and sour

dolcetto [dol·'tʃet·to] *m* **1.** (*piccolo dolce*) small cake **2.** (*vino*) dolcetto, *red wine from Piedmont*

dolcezza [dol·'tʃet·tsa] *f* sweetness; **le -e della vita** the sweet things in life

dolciario, -a [dol·'tʃa:·rio] <-i, -ie> *agg* **industria -a** cakemaking industry

dolciastro, -a [dol·'tʃas·tro] *agg* **1.** (*sapore*) sickly sweet **2.** *fig* (*persona, maniera*) ingratiating

dolcificante [dol·tʃi·fi·'kan·te] **I.** *agg* sweetening **II.** *m* sweetener

dolcificare [dol·tʃi·fi·'ka:·re] *vt* **1.** (*rendere dolce*) to sweeten **2.** (*acqua*) to soften

dolciume [dol·'tʃu:·me] *m* **1.** (*sapore troppo dolce*) sickly sweetness **2.** *pl* (*prodotti*) sweet things

dolente [do·'lɛn·te] *agg* **1.** (*dolorante: testa, braccio*) painful **2.** *form* (*dispiaciuto*) sorry; **sono ~ per quanto è successo** I am sorry about what happened

dolere [do·'le:·re] <dolgo, dolsi, doluto> **I.** *vi essere o avere* **1.** *lit* (*far male*) to ache; **mi duole la testa** I have a headache **2.** *form* (*dare dispiacere*) to be (very) sorry; **mi duole di non potervi aiutare** I'm very sorry I can't help you **II.** *vr:* **-rsi** *lit* (*lamentarsi*) to complain; **-rsi con qu di qc** to complain to sb about sth; **-rsi di qc** to complain about sth

dollaro ['dɔl·la·ro] *m* dollar

dolo ['dɔ:·lo] *m* JUR malice

dolomite [do·lo·'mi:·te] *f* dolomite; **le Dolomiti** GEOG the Dolomite Alps

dolorante [do·lo·'ran·te] *agg* aching

dolore [do·'lo:·re] *m* **1.** MED pain; **~ di testa** headache; **~ alla schiena** backache **2.** (*afflizione*) grief; **con mio grande ~** to my sorrow

dolorifico, -a [do·lo·'ri:·fi·ko] <-ci, -che> *agg* (*stimolo*) painful

doloroso, -a [do·lo·'ro:·so] *agg* **1.** MED (*ferita, intervento*) painful **2.** (*triste: avvenimento, perdita*) sad

dolosità [do·lo·si·'ta] <-> *f* JUR malice

doloso, -a [do·'lo:·so] *agg* JUR malicious

dolsi ['dɔl·si] *1. pers sing pass rem di* **dolere**

doluto [do·'lu:·to] *pp di* **dolere**

domabile [do·'ma:·bi·le] *agg* **1.** (*animale*) tamable **2.** *fig* (*rivolta, incendio*) able to be controlled

domanda [do·'man·da] *f* **1.** (*interrogazione, quesito*) question; **fare una ~** to ask a question; **punto di ~** question mark **2.** (*richiesta: di rimborso, iscrizione*) request; **~ di lavoro** application; **~ di matrimonio** proposal **3.** COM demand

domandare [do·man·'da:·re] **I.** *vt* **1.** (*per sapere*) to ask; **~ qc a qu** to ask sb sth; **~ un consiglio a qu** to ask sb for advice; **~ notizie di qu** to ask sb for news; **~ il prezzo di qc** to ask the price of sth **2.** (*per ottenere*) to ask for; **~ un favore a qu** to ask sb for a favor; **~ la parola** to ask for permission to speak; **~ scusa** to

say sorry **II.** *vr:* **-rsi** to wonder

domani [do·'ma:·ni] **I.** *avv* tomorrow; **~ mattina** tomorrow morning; **~ pomeriggio** tomorrow afternoon; **a ~!** see you tomorrow! **II.** *m* (*futuro*) **il ~** the future

domare [do·'ma:·re] *vt* **1.** (*animali*) to tame **2.** *fig* (*passione*) to master; (*popolo, rivolta*) to subdue; **~ un incendio** to bring a fire under control

domatore, -trice [do·ma·'to:·re] *m, f* **1.** (*di cavalli*) horsebreaker **2.** (*di belve*) tamer

domattina [do·mat·'ti:·na] *avv* tomorrow morning

domenica [do·'me:·ni·ka] <-che> *f* Sunday; **la** [*o* **di**] **~** on Sundays; **l'ho visto ~** I saw him on Sunday; **~ scorsa/prossima** last/next Sunday; **tutta la ~** all day Sunday; **ogni ~,** **tutte le -che** every Sunday; **una ~ sì, una ~ no** on alternate Sundays; **una ~** one Sunday; **~ mattina/pomeriggio/sera** Sunday morning/afternoon/evening; **di ~ mattina/ pomeriggio/sera** on Sunday morning/afternoon/evening; **oggi è ~** it's Sunday today

domenicale [do·me·ni·'ka:·le] *agg* Sunday

domestico, -a [do·'mɛs·ti·ko] <-ci, -che> **I.** *agg* domestic; **pianta -ca** houseplant; **lavori -ci** housework; **per uso ~** for home use **II.** *m, f* servant

domiciliare [do·mi·tʃi·'lia:·re] *agg* house; **arresti -i** house arrest; **perquisizione ~** house search

domicilio [do·mi·'tʃi:·lio] <-i> *m* **1.** (*abitazione*) home; **consegna a ~** home delivery; **lavoro a ~** home working; **violazione di ~** breaking and entering **2.** ADM residence; **~ fiscale** residence for tax purposes

dominante [do·mi·'nan·te] *agg* dominant

dominare [do·mi·'na:·re] **I.** *vi* **1.** (*avere il controllo*) **~ (su qc/qu)** to control (sth/sb) **2.** *fig* (*primeggiare*) **~ su qu** to excel sb **II.** *vt* (*mercato, situazione*) to dominate; (*lingua*) to master **III.** *vr:* **-rsi** to control oneself

dominatore, -trice [do·mi·na·'to:·re] *m, f* ruler

dominazione [do·mi·nat·'tsio:·ne] *f* domination

dominio [do·'mi:·nio] <-i> *m* **1.** (*padronanza*) control; **avere il ~ di qc** to have control of sth **2.** (*controllo*) **~ di sé** self control **3.** JUR (*proprietà*) property; **essere di ~ pubblico** *fig* to be common knowledge **4.** (*territorio*) colony **5.** (*in Internet*) domain

domino ['dɔ:·mi·no] <-> *m* **1.** (*costume*) domino, *hooded cloak worn at Carnival* **2.** (*persona mascherata*) person dressed in a domino **3.** (*gioco*) dominoes

donare [do·'na:·re] **I.** *vt* **1.** (*regalo, sangue*) to give **2.** (*organi*) to donate **II.** *vi* (*star bene: abito, taglio di capelli*) **~ a qu** to suit sb **III.** *vr:* **-rsi** *lit* to dedicate oneself

donatore, -trice [do·na·'to:·re] *m, f* (*di sangue, organo*) donor

donazione [do·nat·'tsio:·ne] *f* donation; JUR

gift
dondolare [don·do·'la:·re] I. *vt* (*piedi, gambe*) to swing; (*culla, sedia, bambino*) to rock; (*corda*) to dangle; (*testa*) to nod II. *vr:* **-rsi** 1. (*muoversi oscillando: su una sedia*) to rock; (*sull'altalena*) to swing 2. *fig* (*oziare*) to laze around
dondolio [don·do·'li:·o] <-ii> *m* rocking
dondolo ['don·do·lo] *m* **cavallo a** ~ rocking horse; **sedia a** ~ rocking chair
dondoloni [don·do·'lo:·ni] *avv* **camminare** ~ *fig* to stroll around
dongiovanni [don·dʒo·'van·ni] <-> *m* Don Juan
donna ['dɔn·na] *f* 1. (*gener*) woman; ~ **di casa** housewife; ~ **di strada** prostitute; **bicicletta da** ~ woman's bicycle 2. (*nelle carte*) queen 3. (*domestica*) ~ (**di servizio**) cleaner
donnaiolo [don·na·'iɔ:·lo] *m* womanizer
donnina [don·'ni:·na] *f* young woman; **non è più una bambina, è già una** ~ she's not a girl anymore, she's a young woman; ~ **allegra** slut
donnola ['dɔn·no·la] *f* weasel
dono ['do:·no] *m* (*regalo*) gift; **in** ~ as a gift; ~ **di natura** natural gift
donzella [don·'dzɛl·la] *f poet* maiden
dopaggio [do·'pad·dʒo] <-ggi> *m* doping
dopante [do·'pan·te] *agg* performance-enhancing; **sostanza** ~ performance-enhancing drug
dopato, -a [do·'pa:·to] *agg* **atleta** ~ athlete who has taken performance-enhancing drugs
doping ['dou·piŋ/'dɔ·pin(g)] <-> *m* doping
dopo ['do:·po] I. *avv* 1. (*tempo*) afterwards; **poco** ~ shortly afterwards; **due anni** ~ two years later; **a** ~ see you later 2. (*luogo*) next II. *prep* 1. (*tempo*) after; ~ **pranzo/cena** after lunch/supper 2. (*luogo*) past III. *cong* after IV. <inv> *agg* next; **il giorno** ~ the next day
dopobarba [do·po·'bar·ba] <-> *m* aftershave
dopocena [do·po·'tʃe:·na] <-> *m* (*serata*) evening; (*trattenimento*) evening party
dopodiché, dopo di che [do·po·di·'ke, 'do:·po di 'ke] *avv* after which
dopodomani [do·po·do·'ma:·ni] *avv* the day after tomorrow
dopofestival [do·po·'fes·ti·val] <-> *m TV show broadcast in the evenings after the Sanremo Festival*
dopoguerra [do·po·'guɛr·ra] <-> *m* postwar period
dopolavoro [do·po·la·'vo:·ro] <-> *m recreational club for employees*
dopopranzo [do·po·'pran·dzo] I. <-> *m* afternoon II. *avv* this afternoon
doposci [do·poʃ·'ʃi] *mpl* (*scarponi*) après-ski boots
dopotutto, dopo tutto [do·po·'tut·to, 'do:·po 'tut·to] *avv* after all
dopovoto [do·po·'vo:·to] <-> *m* post-election period
doppiaggio [dop·'piad·dʒo] <-ggi> *m* FILM dubbing

doppiare [dop·'pia:·re] *vt* 1. NAUT to round 2. SPORT to lap 3. FILM to dub
doppiatore, -trice [dop·pia·'to:·re] *m, f* dubbing artist
doppietta [dop·'piet·ta] *f* 1. (*fucile*) double-barreled shotgun 2. SPORT (*nel pugilato*) one-two; (*nel calcio*) double 3. MOT **fare la** ~ to double-clutch
doppiezza [dop·'piet·tsa] *f* (*falsità*) duplicity
doppifondi *pl di* doppiofondo
doppio ['dop·pio] I. *m* 1. (*di quantità, numero, misura*) double 2. SPORT doubles; ~ **femminile/maschile** women's/men's doubles; ~ **misto** mixed doubles II. *avv* **vederci** ~ to see double
doppio, -a <-i, -ie> *agg* 1. (*gener*) double; **un caffè** ~ a double espresso; **filo** ~ two-ply; **chiudere a -a mandata** to double-lock; **in -a copia** in duplicate; **fare il** ~ **gioco** to play a double game 2. (*falso: atteggiamento, discorso, individuo*) deceitful
doppiofondo [dop·pio·'fon·do] <doppifondi> *m* (*di valigia, cassetto*) false bottom
doppione [dop·'pio:·ne] *m* duplicate
doppiopetto [dop·pio·'pɛt·to] <-> *m* double-breasted jacket
doppiovetro [dop·pio·'ve:·tro] <doppivetri> *m fam* (*vetrocamera*) double glazing
doppista [dop·'pis·ta] <-i *m*, -e *f*> *mf* SPORT doubles player
dorare [do·'ra:·re] *vt* 1. (*con oro*) to gild 2. CULIN (*rosolare*) to brown 3. *fig* (*rendere accettabile*) ~ **la pillola** to sugarcoat the pill
dorato, -a [do·'ra:·to] *agg* 1. (*rivestito d'oro*) gilt 2. (*color dell'oro*) golden 3. CULIN browned
doratura [do·ra·'tu:·ra] *f* 1. (*rivestimento*) gilding 2. (*ornamento*) gilt
dorico, -a ['dɔ:·ri·ko] <-ci, -che> *agg* ARTE Doric
dormicchiare [dor·mik·'kia:·re] *vi* to doze
dormiglione, -a [dor·miʎ·'ʎo:·ne] *m, f* sleepyhead
dormire [dor·'mi:·re] I. *vi* 1. (*essere addormentato*) to sleep; ~ **come un ghiro** to sleep like a log; **dormirci sopra** to sleep on it; ~ **in piedi** to be dead tired 2. *fig* **qui dorme in pace ...** (*su tombe*) here lies ...; ~ **sugli allori** to rest on one's laurels II. *vt* ~ **sonni tranquilli** to sleep soundly; ~ **il sonno del giusto** to sleep the sleep of the just
dormita [dor·'mi:·ta] *f* sleep
dormitina [dor·mi·'ti:·na] *f* nap
dormitorio [dor·mi·'tɔ:·rio] <-i> *m* 1. (*stanza*) dormitory; ~ (**pubblico**) shelter, *for homeless people* 2. (*città, quartiere*) commuter town
dormiveglia [dor·mi·'veʎ·ʎa] <-> *m* **essere nel** ~ to be half asleep
dorsale [dor·'sa:·le] I. *agg* MED back; **spina** ~ spine II. *m* 1. (*di letto*) headboard 2. (*di poltrona*) back III. *f* ridge, range
dorsista [dor·'sis·ta] <-i *m*, -e *f*> *mf* SPORT backstroke swimmer
dorso ['dɔr·so] *m* 1. (*gener*) back; **a** ~ **nudo**

barebacked; ~ **della mano** back of the hand **2.**SPORT backstroke

dosacaffè [do·sa·kaf·'fe] <-> *m* coffee measure

dosaggio [do·'zad·dʒo] <-ggi> *m* dosage

dosare [do·'za:·re] *vt* **1.**(*misurare*) to measure out **2.**fig (*parole*) to measure; (*forze*) to husband

dosaspaghetti [do·sas·pa·'get·ti] <-> *m* spaghetti measure

dosatura [do·za·'tu:·ra] *f* dosage

dosazucchero [do·sa·'tsuk·ke·ro] <-> *m* sugar pourer

dose ['dɔ:·ze] *f* **1.**(*quantità*) amount; **una buona ~ di** a lot of **2.**MED dose **3.**fig, scherz ration *fam;* **rincarare la ~** to compound the felony

dossier [do·'sje] <-> *m* dossier

dosso ['dɔs·so] *m* **1.**(*dorso*) **levarsi qc di ~** to get rid of sth **2.**(~ *stradale*) speed bump

dotare [do·'ta:·re] *vt* **1.**(*dare la dote a*) to give a dowry to **2.**(*corredare*) ~ **qc di qc** to provide sth with sth

dotato, -a [do·'ta:·to] *agg* **1.**(*di talento: attore, musicista, allievo*) gifted **2.**(*provvisto*) ~ **di qc** equipped with sth

dotazione [do·tat·'tsio:·ne] *f* **1.**(*rendita*) endowment **2.**(*mezzi e materiali*) equipment

dote ['dɔ:·te] *f* **1.**(*della sposa*) dowry; **cacciatore di ~** fortune hunter; **portare in ~** to bring as one's dowry **2.**fig (*pregio*) quality

Dott. *abbr di* **Dottore** Dr., *title given to medical doctors and to all university graduates*

dotto, -a ['dɔt·to] **I.** *agg* learned **II.** *m, f* scholar

dottorato [dot·to·'ra:·to] *m* doctorate; **fare il ~ di ricerca** to do a PhD

dottore, -essa [dot·'to:·re, dot·to·'res·sa] *m, f* **1.**(*laureato*) ~ **in legge/medicina** graduate in law/medicine **2.**fam (*medico*) doctor

dottrina [dot·'tri:·na] *f* **1.**(*gener*) doctrine **2.**(*cultura*) learning **3.**JUR law

Dott.ssa *abbr di* **Dottoressa** Dr., *title given to medical doctors and to all university graduates*

double-face [dub·le·'fa:s] *agg* (*giacca, impermeabile*) reversible

dove ['do:·ve] **I.** *avv* where; **da ~, ~ vai?** where are you going?; **la via ~ abito** the street where I live **II.** *m* where; **per ogni ~** everywhere

dovere¹ [do·'ve:·re] <devo *o* debbo, dovei *o* dovetti, dovuto> **I.** *vi* **1.**(*obbligo, necessità*) to have to; **devo essere a casa per le otto** I have to be home by eight; **sono dovuto andare** I had to go; **ho dovuto dirglielo** I had to tell him; **devo andare in bagno** I have to go to the bathroom; **devi dirlo alla polizia** you must tell the police; **fare qc come si deve** to do sth properly; **una persona come si deve** a respectable person; **grazie, ma non dovevi disturbarti** thanks, but you shouldn't have bothered **2.**(*probabilità*) **devono essere già le otto** it must be eight o'clock by now; **deve essere successo qc** something must

have happened; **strano, dovrebbe essere già qui** strange, he should be here by now **II.** *vt* (*essere debitore*) to owe; **essere dovuto a** to be due to

dovere² *m* duty; **farsi un ~ di qc** to undertake to do sth; **sentirsi in ~ di fare qc** to feel obliged to do sth; **fare le cose a ~** to do things properly

dovunque [do·'vuŋ·kue] *cong* **1.**(*in qualunque luogo*) wherever; ~ **tu sia** wherever you are; ~ **tu vada** wherever you go **2.**(*dappertutto*) everywhere

dovuto [do·'vu:·to] *m* due; **mi aspetto solo il ~** I only want what is due to me; **ho aspettato più del ~** I waited longer than I should have

dovuto, -a *agg* **1.**(*necessario*) due **2.**(*causato*) ~ **a** due to

download ['daʊn·ləʊd] *m* COMPUT downloading

dozzina [dod·'dzi:·na] *f* **una ~ (di ...)** a dozen (...); **a -e** by the dozen

dozzinale [dod·dzi·'na:·le] *agg pej* second-rate; **prodotti -i** shoddy goods

D.P. *abbr di* **Decreto Presidenziale** *presidential decree*

Dr. *abbr di* **Dottore, Dottoressa** Dr., *title given to medical doctors and to all university graduates*

dracma ['drak·ma] *f* drachma

draga ['dra:·ga] <-ghe> *f* (*macchina*) dredger

dragaggio [dra·'gad·dʒo] <-ggi> *m* dredging

dragamine [dra·ga·'mi:·ne] <-> *m* minesweeper

dragare [dra·'ga:·re] *vt* **1.**(*porto, fiume*) to dredge **2.**(*da mine*) to sweep

dragata [dra·'ga:·ta] *f* dredging

drago ['dra:·go] <-ghi> *m* dragon

dragone [dra·'go:·ne] *m* (*mostro*) dragon

dramma ['dram·ma] <-i> *m* **1.**THEAT drama **2.**(*vicenda dolorosa*) tragedy; **fare un ~ di qc** to make a drama out of sth

drammatica [dram·'ma:·ti·ka] <-che> *f* THEAT theater

drammaticità [dram·ma·ti·tʃi·'ta] <-> *f* drama

drammatico, -a [dram·'ma:·ti·ko] <-ci, -che> *agg* **1.**THEAT dramatic; **attore ~** theater actor **2.**(*doloroso*) terrible; **una situazione -a** a terrible situation

drammatizzare [dram·ma·tid·'dza:·re] *vt* **1.**(*esagerare*) to (over)dramatize **2.**(*opera*) to make into a play

drammaturgia [dram·ma·tur·'dʒi:·a] <-gie> *f* drama

drammaturgico, -a [dram·ma·'tur·dʒi·ko] <-ci, -che> *agg* dramatic

drammaturgo, -a [dram·ma·'tur·go] <-ghi, -ghe> *m, f* playwright

drappello [drap·'pɛl·lo] *m* MIL platoon; (*gruppo*) group

drappo ['drap·po] *m* (*tessuto*) cloth

drastico, -a ['dras·ti·ko] <-ci, -che> *agg* (*misure, decisione, soluzione*) drastic

drenaggio [dre·'nad·dʒo] <-ggi> *m* **1.** (*sistema*) drainage **2.** *a.* MED draining

drenare [dre·'na:·re] *vt* to drain

dribblare [drib·'bla:·re] *vi* to dribble

drindrin, drin drin [drin·'drin] I. <-> *m* ringing II. *int* ding-dong

drink [driŋk/drink] <-> *m* (alcoholic) drink

dritto, -a ['drit·to] *m, f fam* smart cookie

drive-in ['drai·vin] I. <inv> *agg* drive-in; **cinema** ~ drive-in movie theater; **ristorante** ~ drive-in restaurant II. <-> *m* drive-in

drizzare [drit·'tsa:·re] I. *vt* **1.** (*raddrizzare*) to straighten; ~ **le orecchie** *fig* to listen carefully **2.** (*innalzare*) to erect II. *vr:* **-rsi** to stand up

droga ['drɔ:·ga] <-ghe> *f* **1.** (*gener*) drug; **-ghe leggere/pesanti** soft/hard drugs **2.** (*in cucina*) spice

drogare [dro·'ga:·re] I. *vt* (*dare una droga a*) to drug; SPORT to dope II. *vr:* **-rsi** (*prendere droga*) to take drugs

drogato, -a [dro·'ga:·to] *m, f* drug addict

drogheria [dro·ge·'ri:·a] <-ie> *f* grocery store

droghiere, -a [dro·'giε:·re] *m, f* grocer

dromedario [dro·me·'da:·rio] <-i> *m* dromedary

DS *m abbr di* **Democratici di Sinistra** *Italian center-left party*

duale [du·'a:·le] *m* dual

dualismo [dua·'liz·mo] *m* dualism

dubbio ['dub·bio] *m* doubt; **essere in ~ su qc** to be doubtful about sth; **senza ~** without (a) doubt; **in caso di ~** if in doubt; **avere dei -i su qu** to have doubts about sb; **mi sorge un ~** I'm doubtful

dubbio, -a <-i, -ie> *agg* **1.** (*incerto: esito*) uncertain **2.** (*equivoco: reputazione*) dubious

dubbiosità [dub·bio·si·'ta] <-> *f* doubtfulness

dubbioso, -a [dub·'bio:·so] *agg* **1.** (*pieno di dubbi: espressione, sguardo*) doubtful **2.** (*motivo di dubbio*) dubious

dubitare [du·bi·'ta:·re] *vi* **1.** (*non credere*) to doubt; ~ **di qu/qc** to be doubtful about sb/sth **2.** (*essere incerto*) ~ **di qc** to doubt sth; **dubito assai che tu venga** I doubt very much you'll come

dubitativo, -a [du·bi·ta·'ti:·vo] *agg* (*tono*) doubtful

Dublino [du·'bli:·no] *f* Dublin

duca ['du:·ka] <-chi> *m* duke

ducale [du·'ka:·le] *agg* ducal

ducato [du·'ka:·to] *m* **1.** POL duchy **2.** (*moneta d'oro*) ducat

duce ['du:·tʃe] <-ci> *m* commander; **il Duce** (*Mussolini*) the Duce

duchessa [du·'kes·sa] *f* duchess

duchessina [du·kes·'si:·na] *f* duke's daughter

duchino [du·'ki:·no] *m* duke's son

due ['du:·e] I. *num* two; (*pochi*) a few; **non poter dividersi in** ~ *fig* to not be able to be in two places at once; **fare ~ passi** *fig* to have a walk; **scambiare ~ chiacchiere** to have a chat; **a ~ a ~** two by two; **su ~ piedi** *fig* on the spot II. <-> *m* **1.** (*numero*) two; **lavorare/**

mangiare per ~ *fig* to work/eat enough for two **2.** (*nelle date*) second **3.** (*voto scolastico*) *a flunk* **4.** SPORT (*nel canottaggio*) ~ **con/senza** coxed/uncoxed pair III. *fpl* (*ore*) two o'clock; *v.a.* **cinque**

duecentesco, -a [du·e·tʃen·'tes·ko] <-schi, -sche> *agg* thirteenth-century

duecento [du·e·'tʃεn·to] I. *num* two hundred II. <-> *m* two hundred; **il Duecento** the thirteenth century

duellare [du·el·'la:·re] *vi* to duel; ~ **con qu** to fight a duel with sb

duello [du·'εl·lo] *m* duel; **battersi a** ~ to fight a duel; **sfidare a** ~ to challenge to a duel

duemila [due·'mi:·la] I. *num* two thousand II. <-> *m* two thousand; **il** ~ the year 2000

duepezzi, due pezzi [du·e·'pεt·tsi, 'du:·e 'pεt·tsi] <-> *m* (*giacca e gonna*) suit; (*costume da bagno*) bikini

duetto [du·'et·to] *m* **1.** MUS duet **2.** *scherz* racket, *made by two people arguing*

duna ['du:·na] *f* dune

dunque ['duŋ·kue] I. *cong* **1.** (*perciò*) so **2.** (*allora*) well **3.** (*rafforzativo*) well then II. *m* **essere al** ~ to arrive at the moment of truth; **veniamo al** ~ let's get to the point

duo ['du:·o] <-> *m* duo

duodeno [du·o·'dε:·no] *m* duodenum

duomo ['du·ɔ:·mo] *m* cathedral

duplicare [du·pli·'ka:·re] *vt* to duplicate

duplicato [dup·li·'ka:·to] *m* (*di documento*) duplicate, copy

duplicazione [dup·li·kat·tsio:·ne] *f* duplication

duplice ['du:p·li·tʃe] *agg* **1.** (*in due parti*) double **2.** (*doppio*) **in ~ copia** in duplicate

duplicità [dup·li·tʃi·'ta] <-> *f* duplicity

durante [du·'ran·te] *prep* during; ~ **la guerra** during the war; **vita natural** ~ for life

durare [du·'ra:·re] *vi essere o avere* **1.** (*continuare*) to last; **così non può** ~ things can't go on like this **2.** (*mantenersi*) to keep **3.** *prov* **chi la dura la vince** slow and steady wins the race *prov*

durata [du·'ra:·ta] *f* duration; ~ **d'ascolto** (*di cassette*) playing time; **di lunga** ~ long-lasting

duraturo, -a [du·ra·'tu:·ro] *agg* lasting

durevole [du·'re:·vo·le] *agg* durable

durezza [du·'ret·tsa] *f* **1.** (*qualità*) hardness **2.** *fig* (*severità*) harshness

duro ['du:·ro] *m* hard part

duro, -a I. *agg* **1.** (*gener*) hard; **grano** ~ strong flour; **è un osso** ~ he's a tough cookie; **è** ~ **farlo ragionare** it's hard to make him see sense; **tempi -i** hard times; ~ **di comprendonio** slow; ~ **d'orecchi** hard of hearing **2.** (*ostinato*) stubborn; **più** ~ **di un mulo** stubborn as a mule **3.** (*freddo*) harsh II. *m, f* tough cookie; **fare il** ~ to act tough III. *avv* **tener** ~ to stand firm; **lavorare** ~ to work hard

durone [du·'ro:·ne] *m* hard skin

duttile ['dut·ti·le] *agg* **1.** (*materiale, metallo*) malleable **2.** *fig* (*carattere*) flexible

duttilità [dut·ti·li·'ta] <-> *f* **1.** (*di materiale, metallo*) malleability **2.** (*di carattere*) flexibility

DVD [di·vud·'di] <-> *m abbr di* **Digital Video Disc** DVD; **lettore** ~ DVD player

E

E, e [e] <-> *f* E, e; ~ **come Empoli** E for Echo; **vitamina** ~ vitamin E

e [e] *cong* **1.** (*correlativa*) and; **tutti** ~ **tre** all three of them; **e ... e ...** both ... and ... **2.** (*ma, invece*) but **3.** (*ebbene*) well

E *abbr di* est E

è [ɛ] *3. pers sing pr di* **essere**[1]

EAD *abbr di* **elaborazione automatica dei dati** ADP, *automatic data processing*

ebanite [e·ba·'ni:·te] *f* ebonite

ebano ['ɛ·ba·no] *m* **1.** BOT (*albero*) ebony (tree) **2.** (*legno*) ebony

ebbe ['ɛb·be] *3. pers sing pass rem di* **avere**[1]

ebbene [eb·'bɛ:·ne] *cong* **1.** (*dunque*) so **2.** (*interrogativo*) well

ebbi ['ɛb·bi] *1. pers sing pass rem di* **avere**[1]

ebbrezza [eb·'bret·tsa] *f* **1.** (*ubriachezza*) drunkenness; **guidare in stato di** ~ drunk driving **2.** *fig* (*euforia*) thrill; **l'**~ **della velocità** the thrill of speed

ebbro, -a ['ɛb·bro] *agg* **1.** *fig* (*euforico*) elated **2.** *lit* (*ubriaco*) drunk

ebete ['ɛ·be·te] **I.** *agg* idiotic **II.** *mf* idiot

ebetismo [e·be·'tiz·mo] *m* idiocy

ebollizione [e·bol·lit·'tsio:·ne] *f* boiling; **punto di** ~ boiling point

ebraico, -a [e·'bra:·i·ko] <-ci, -che> *agg* (*religione, festa, comunità*) Jewish

ebraismo [e·bra·'iz·mo] *m* REL Judaism

ebreo, -a [e·'brɛː·o] <-ei, -ee> **I.** *agg* (*popolazione, tradizione*) Jewish **II.** *m*, *f* Jew *m*, Jewess *f*

EC *abbr di* **EuroCity** FERR *European intercity train*

ecatombe [e·ka·'tom·be] *f* **1.** REL (*sacrificio*) hecatomb **2.** *fig* (*strage*) massacre

ecc. *abbr di* **eccetera** etc.

eccedente [et·tʃe·'dɛn·te] **I.** *agg* (*quantità, materiale*) surplus; (*bagaglio*) excess **II.** *m* excess

eccedenza [et·tʃe·'dɛn·tsa] *f* surplus; ~ **di qc** surplus of sth; **bagaglio in** ~ excess baggage

eccedere [et·'tʃɛː·de·re] **I.** *vt* (*superare: limiti, numero, peso*) to exceed **II.** *vi* to go too far; ~ **nel bere/nel mangiare** to drink/eat too much

eccellente [ettʃel'lɛnte] *agg* (*cibo, ristorante, risultato*) excellent

eccellenza [et·tʃel·'lɛn·tsa] *f* **1.** (*qualità*) excellence; **per** ~ par excellence **2.** (*titolo*) Excel-

lency

eccellere [et·'tʃɛl·le·re] <eccello, eccelsi, eccelso> *vi essere o avere* to excel; ~ **in qc** to excel at sth

eccelso, -a [et·'tʃɛl·so] *agg* **1.** *fig* (*mente, qualità*) excellent **2.** (*altissimo: vetta*) lofty

eccentricità [et·tʃen·tri·tʃi·'ta] <-> *f* **1.** *fig* (*stranezza*) eccentricity **2.** MAT, ASTR eccentricity

eccentrico, -a [et·'tʃɛn·tri·ko] <-ci, -che> *agg* **1.** *fig* (*stravagante: personaggio, abbigliamento*) eccentric **2.** MAT, ASTR eccentric

eccepire [et·tʃi·'pi:·re] <eccepisco> *vt* (*obiettare*) to object

eccessivo, -a [et·tʃes·'si:·vo] *agg* (*esagerato: prezzo, temperatura*) excessive; (*caldo, freddo*) extreme

eccesso [et·'tʃɛs·so] *m* **1.** (*superamento*) excess; ~ **di velocità** speeding; **per** ~ **di zelo** due to over-zealousness; **bagaglio in** ~ excess baggage **2.** (*sfrenatezza*) excess **3.** *pl* (*comportamento smodato*) extremes; **dare in -i** to burst into a rage

eccetera [et·'tʃɛː·te·ra] *avv* etcetera

eccetto [et·'tʃɛt·to] **I.** *prep* except for **II.** *cong* ~ **che ...** (*tranne*) except ...; (*a meno che*) unless ...

eccettuare [et·tʃet·tu·'a:·re] *vt* to exclude; **eccettuati i presenti** present company excepted

eccezionale [et·tʃet·tsio·'na:·le] *agg* exceptional; **in via** ~ as an exception

eccezione [et·tʃet·'tsio:·ne] *f* **1.** (*deroga*) exception; **fare** ~ to be an exception; **fare un** ~ to make an exception; **senza -i** without exception; **d'**~ celebrity; **ad** ~ **di** apart from; **l'**~ **conferma la regola** *prov* the exception proves the rule **2.** JUR plea

eccì [et·'tʃi] *int* kerchoo

eccidio [et·'tʃi:·dio] <-i> *m* (*strage*) massacre

eccitabile [et·tʃi·'ta:·bi·le] *agg* (*carattere, persona*) excitable

eccitabilità [et·tʃi·ta·bi·li·'ta] <-> *f* (*di carattere, persona*) excitability

eccitamento [et·tʃi·ta·'men·to] *m* **1.** (*nervoso*) excitement **2.** (*sessuale*) arousal

eccitante [et·tʃi·'tan·te] **I.** *agg* **1.** (*sostanza*) stimulating **2.** (*elettrizzante: atmosfera*) exciting **3.** (*sessualmente*) sexy **II.** *m* stimulant

eccitare [et·tʃi·'ta:·re] **I.** *vt* **1.** (*rendere nervoso*) to excite **2.** *fig* (*stimolare: curiosità, fantasia*) to stimulate **3.** (*sessualmente*) to arouse **II.** *vr:* **-rsi 1.** (*innervosirsi*) to get worked up **2.** (*sessualmente*) to become aroused

eccitazione [et·tʃi·tat·'tsio:·ne] *f* **1.** (*agitazione*) excitement **2.** (*sessuale*) arousal **3.** TEC, PHYS excitation

ecclesiastico [ek·kle·'zias·ti·ko] <-ci> *m* clergyman

ecclesiastico, -a <-ci, -che> *agg* (*abito, privilegio, istituzione*) ecclesiastical

ecco ['ɛk·ko] **I.** *avv* here; **eccomi** here I am; ~ **il libro** here's the book; ~ **perché ...** that's why ...; ~ **fatto** that's that; ~ **tutto** that's all **II.** *int* there

eccome [ek·'ko:·me] *avv* of course

ECG *abbr di* **elettrocardiogramma** ECG

echeggiare [e·ked·'dʒa:·re] *vi avere o essere* to echo

echi *pl di* **eco**

eclatante [e·kla·'tan·te] *agg* (*strepitoso: esempio, notizia*) sensational; **un successo** ~ a resounding success

eclettico, -a [e·'klɛt·ti·ko] <-ci, -che> *agg* (*persona, studioso*) versatile

eclettismo [e·klet·'tiz·mo] *m* versatility

eclissare [e·klis·'sa:·re] **I.** *vt* **1.** ASTR to eclipse **2.** *fig* (*far sfigurare*) to outshine **II.** *vr:* **-rsi 1.** ASTR to be eclipsed **2.** *fig* (*sparire*) to disappear

eclisse [e·'klis·se] *f* ASTR eclipse; ~ **di luna** lunar eclipse; ~ **di sole** solar eclipse

eco ['ɛ·ko] <echi *m*> *f o m* **1.** (*di suono, parole*) echo **2.** *fig* (*di notizia*) impact

ecocardiografia [e·ko·kar·dio·gra·'fi:·a] <-ie> *f* MED echocardiography

ecocardiografo [e·ko·kar·'diɔ:·gra·fo] *m* MED echocardiographer

ecocatastrofe [e·ko·ka·'tas·tro·fe] *f* ECO environmental disaster

ecocertificazione [e·ko·tʃer·ti·fi·ka·'tsio:·ne] *f* environmental certification

ecocompatibile [e·ko·kom·pa·'ti:·bi·le] *agg* (*turismo, agricoltura, prodotto*) environmentally-friendly

ecocontributo [ɛ·ko·kon·tri·'bu:·to] *m* ECO eco-tax

ecodiesel [ɛ·ko·'di:·zel] <-> *m o f* AUTO biodiesel

ecografia [e·ko·gra·'fi:·a] <-ie> *f* MED ultrasound scan

ecografico, -a [e·ko·'gra:·fi·ko] <-ci, -che> *agg* MED (*esame*) ultrasound

ecografo [e·'kɔ:·gra·fo] *m* ultrasonographer

ecogramma [e·ko·'gram·ma] <-i> *m* ultrasound photo

ecologia [e·ko·lo·'dʒi:·a] <-gie> *f* ecology

ecologico, -a [e·ko·'lɔ·dʒi·ko] <-ci, -che> *agg* **1.** (*sistema*) ecological **2.** (*prodotto*) eco-friendly

ecologista [e·ko·lo·'dʒis·ta] <-i *m*, -e *f*> *mf* ecologist

ecologo, -a [e·'kɔ:·lo·go] <-gi, -ghe> *m, f* ecologist

e-commerce [i·'kɔ·mers] <-> *m* COM e-commerce

economato [e·ko·no·'ma:·to] *m* (*di collegio, università*) bursar's office

economia [e·ko·no·'mi:·a] <-ie> *f* **1.** (*scienza*) economics **2.** (*sistema*) economy; ~ **di mercato** market economy; ~ **politica** political economy **3.** (*risparmio*) saving; **fare** ~ [*o* -ie] to economize; **in** ~ cheaply **4.** *pl* (*risparmi*) savings

economico, -a [e·ko·'nɔ:·mi·ko] <-ci, -che> *agg* **1.** (*dell'economia: crisi, criterio, settore*)

economic **2.** (*poco costoso: albergo, vacanze, volo*) cheap; **classe -a** economy class

economista [e·ko·no·'mis·ta] <-i *m*, -e *f*> *mf* economist

economizzare [e·ko·no·mid·'dza:·re] **I.** *vt* to save **II.** *vi* to economize

economizzatore [e·ko·no·mid·dza·'to:·re] *m* TEC economizer

economo, -a [e·'kɔ:·no·mo] *m, f* (*amministratore: di collegio, università*) bursar

ecopacifismo [e·ko·pa·tʃi·'fiz·mo] <*sing*> *m* ecopacifism

ecopacifista [e·ko·pa·tʃi·'fis·ta] <-i *m*, -e *f*> *mf* ecopacifist

ecoreato [ɛ·ko·re·'a:·to] *m* ECO environmental crime

ecoscandaglio [e·ko·skan·'daʎ·ʎo] <-gli> *m* NAUT echo sounder

ecosfera [e·ko·'sfɛ:·ra] *f* ECO, GEOG biosphere

ecosistema [e·ko·sis·'tɛ:·ma] *m* ecosystem

ecotassa [ɛ·ko·'tas·sa] *f* ECO eco-tax

ecoturismo [ɛ·ko·tu·'riz·mo] *m* ECO ecotourism

ecru [e·'kry] <inv> *agg* **1.** (*greggio: tessuto*) raw **2.** (*naturale: colore*) fawn

ecumenico, -a [e·ku·'mɛ:·ni·ko] <-ci, -che> *agg* REL ecumenical

eczema [ek·'dzɛ:·ma] <-i> *m* eczema

ed. *abbr di* **edizione** ed.

ed *cong* = **e** *davanti a vocale*

edelweiss ['e:·dəl·vais] <-> *f* edelweiss

edema [e·'dɛ:·ma] <-i> *m* edema

eden ['ɛ:·den] <-> *m* **1.** REL Eden **2.** *fig* paradise

edera ['e:·de·ra] *f* ivy

edicola [e·'di:·ko·la] *f* **1.** (*del giornalaio*) newsstand **2.** ARCH (*piccola cappella*) edicule, *column with a niche containing a statue*

edicolante [e·di·ko·'lan·te] *mf* newsdealer

edificabile [e·di·fi·'ka:·bi·le] *agg* (*area, terreno*) suitable for building

edificante [e·di·fi·'kan·te] *agg* (*esempio, storia*) uplifting

edificare [e·di·fi·'ka:·re] *vt* **1.** ARCH (*palazzo, ponte*) to build **2.** *fig* (*stato, società*) to build

edificio [e·di·'fi:·tʃo] <-ci> *m* **1.** ARCH building **2.** *fig* (*struttura*) structure

edile [e·'di:·le] **I.** *agg* (*cantiere, imprenditore, industria*) building **II.** *m* (*operaio*) construction worker

edilizia [e·di·'lit·tsia] <-ie> *f* **1.** (*costruzioni*) building **2.** (*settore*) construction industry

edilizio, -a [e·di·'lit·tsio] <-i, -ie> *agg* (*condono, regolamento, speculazione*) building

editing ['e·di·tiŋ] <-> *m* **1.** (*in editoria*) editing **2.** COMPUT editing

edito, -a ['ɛ:·di·to] *agg* (*pubblicato*) published

editor <-> *m* COMPUT editor

editore, -trice [e·di·'to:·re] **I.** *agg* **casa -trice** publishing house **II.** *m, f* publisher

editoria [e·di·to·'ri:·a] <-ie> *f* **1.** (*settore*) publishing industry **2.** (*attività*) publishing; ~ **elettronica** electronic publishing

editoriale [e·di·to·'ria:·le] **I.** *agg* (*dell'editoria:*

attività) editorial; **direttore** ~ publishing manager **II.** *m* (*articolo di fondo*) editorial

editorialista [e·di·to·ria·'lis·ta] <-i *m*, -e *f*> *mf* editorialist

editrice *f v.* **editore**

edizione [e·dit·'tsio:·ne] *f* 1.(*pubblicazione*) publication; ~ **economica** paperback; ~ **originale** original edition 2.(*libro*) edition; ~ **antica** old edition 3.(*tiratura*) print run; ~ **straordinaria** (*di giornale*) special edition 4.TV, RADIO program 5.(*di manifestazione*) edition; **la quinta** ~ **del concorso** the fifth year of the competition

edonismo [e·do·'niz·mo] *m* hedonism

edonista [e·do·'nis·ta] <-i *m*, -e *f*> *mf* hedonist

edonistico, -a [e·do·'nis·ti·ko] <-ci, -che> *agg* (*atteggiamento, piacere*) hedonistic

EDP *f abbr di* **Electronic Data Processing** EDP

educanda [e·du·'kan·da] *f* (*collegiale*) convent girl

educare [e·du·'ka:·re] *vt* 1.(*giovani*) to bring up; ~ **qu a fare qc** to bring sb up to do sth; ~ **i giovani al rispetto per gli altri** to teach young people to respect others 2.(*cane, gatto*) to train 3.*fig* (*affinare: mente, voce*) to train 4.(*allenare: corpo*) to train

educativo, -a [e·du·ka·'ti:·vo] *agg* (*metodo, progetto, problematica*) educational

educato, -a [e·du·'ka:·to] *agg* polite

educatore, -trice [e·du·ka·'to:·re] *m, f* (*professore*) teacher; (*studioso, teorico*) educationalist

educazione [e·du·kat·'tsio:·ne] *f* 1.(*di giovani*) education; ~ **fisica** physical education; ~ **stradale** road safety 2.(*buone maniere*) good manners *pl;* **gente senza** ~ ill-mannered people

EED *abbr di* **elaborazione elettronica dei dati** EDP, *electronic data processing*

EEG *abbr di* **elettroencefalogramma** MED EEG, *electroencephalogram*

effem(m)inato, -a *agg* effeminate

efferatezza [ef·fe·ra·'tet·tsa] *f* (*di delitto*) brutality

efferato, -a [ef·fe·'ra:·to] *agg* (*delitto*) brutal

efferente [ef·fe·'ren·te] *agg* (*condotto, via*) efferent

effervescente [ef·fer·veʃ·'ʃɛn·te] *agg* 1.(*frizzante: acqua, bibita*) fizzy; (*pasticca*) effervescent 2.*fig* (*carattere, persona*) bubbly; (*atmosfera*) exciting

effervescenza [ef·fer·veʃ·'ʃɛn·tsa] *f* 1.(*di pasticca*) effervescence; (*di acqua, vino*) bubbliness 2.*fig* (*vivacità*) effervescence

effettivamente [ef·fet·ti·va·'men·te] *avv* 1.(*in effetti*) indeed 2.(*realmente*) actually

effettivo [ef·fet·'ti:·vo] *m* 1.ADM, COM (*personale*) staff 2.SPORT (*di squadra*) member 3.MIL (*forze*) strength; **gli -i dell'esercito** the army's numbers

effettivo, -a *agg* 1.(*reale: costo, migliora-*

mento, valore) real; (*danno*) actual 2.(*socio, professore*) permanent; **personale** ~ permanent staff 3.MIL regular; **ufficiale** ~ regular officer

effetto [ef·'fɛt·to] *m* 1.(*risultato*) effect; ~ **ottico** optical illusion; ~ **serra** ECO greenhouse effect; **causa ed** ~ cause and effect; **avere** ~ to take effect; **ottenere l'**~ **voluto** to achieve the desired result 2.*fig* (*impressione*) impression; **fare** ~ to cause an impression 3.(*loc*) **in** -i indeed; -i **collaterali** side-effects; -i **personali** personal belongings

effettuare [ef·fet·tu·'a:·re] *vt* (*controllo*) to carry out; (*pagamento, vendita*) to make; ~ **una fermata** to stop

efficace [ef·fi·'ka:·tʃe] *agg* 1.(*metodo, medicina, risposta*) effective 2.(*descrizione, racconto*) vivid

efficacia [ef·fi·'ka:·tʃa] <-cie> *f* 1.(*di metodo, medicina*) effectiveness 2.(*di descrizione, racconto*) vividness

efficiente [ef·fi·'tʃɛn·te] *agg* efficient

efficientismo [ef·fi·tʃen·'tiz·mo] *m* over-efficiency

efficienza [ef·fi·'tʃɛn·tsa] *f* efficiency

effigie [ef·'fi:·dʒe] <- *o* -gi> *f poet* (*ritratto*) portrait; (*scultura*) effigy

effimero, -a [ef·'fi:·me·ro] *agg* (*fugace: moda, momento, gloria*) fleeting

efflusso [ef·'flus·so] *m* (*di gas, liquido*) outflow

effluvio [ef·'flu:·vio] <-i> *m* 1.*lit* (*profumo*) scent 2.*iron* (*puzza*) stink

effusione [ef·fu·'zio:·ne] *fpl fig* (*affettuosità*) effusions

egemone [e·'dʒɛː·mo·ne] *agg* (*potenza, mira*) hegemonic

egemonia [e·dʒe·mo·'ni:·a] <-ie> *f* hegemony

egemonico, -a [e·dʒe·'mɔː·ni·ko] <-ci, -che> *agg* (*mira, piano*) hegemonic

egemonizzare [e·dʒe·mo·nid·'dza:·re] *vt* (*politica, cultura*) to dominate

Egeo [e·'dʒɛː·o] *m* l'~ the Aegean; **il Mar** ~ the Aegean Sea

Egitto [e·'dʒit·to] *m* l'~ Egypt

egittologia [e·dʒit·to·lo·'dʒi:·a] <-ie> *f* Egyptology

egittologo, -a [e·dʒit·'tɔː·lo·go] <-gi, -ghe> *m, f* Egyptologist

egiziano, -a [e·dʒit·'tsia:·no] **I.** *agg* Egyptian **II.** *m, f* Egyptian

egizio, -a [e·'dʒit·tsio] <-i, -ie> **I.** *agg* (*dinastia, museo, piramide*) (ancient) Egyptian **II.** *m, f* (ancient) Egyptian

egli ['eʎ·ʎi] *pron 3. pers sing m* he

ego ['ɛː·go] <-> *m, agg* ego

egocentrico, -a [e·go·'tʃɛn·tri·ko] <-ci, -che> **I.** *agg* (*carattere, persona*) self-centered **II.** *m, f* self-centered person

egocentrismo [e·go·tʃen·'triz·mo] *m* egocentricity

egoismo [e·go·'iz·mo] *m* selfishness

egoista [e·go·'is·ta] <-i *m*, -e *f*> **I.** *mf* selfish person II. *agg* selfish

egoistico, -a [e·go·'is·ti·ko] <-ci, -che> *agg* (*bisogno, ragioni, motivazioni, scelta*) selfish

Egr. *abbr di* **egregio** Dear

egregio, -a [e·'grɛː·dʒo] <-gi, -gie> *agg* 1.(*eccellente: lavoro, qualità*) excellent 2.(*nelle lettere*) Dear

eguaglianza [e·guaʎ·'ʎan·tsa] *f v.* **uguaglianza**

egualitario, -a [e·gua·li·'taː·rio] <-i, -ie> *agg* (*dottrina, spirito, società*) egalitarian

egualitarismo [e·gua·li·ta·'riz·mo] *m* egalitarianism

eh [ɛ/e] *int fam* 1.(*richiamo*) hey 2.(*compatimento*) well; ~, **cosa ci vuoi fare?** well, what do you want to do about it? 3.(*sorpresa*) wow 4.(*domanda*) **niente male, ~?** not bad, is it?

ehi ['eː·i] *int fam* (*richiamo*) hey

ehm [m] *int fam* (*con esitazione*) er

E.I. *abbr di* **Esercito Italiano** *Italian army*

eiaculare [e·ia·ku·'laː·re] *vi* to ejaculate

eiaculazione [e·ia·ku·lat·'tsioː·ne] *f* ejaculation

eidomatica® [ei·do·'maː·ti·ka] <-che> *f* COMPUT computer imaging

eiettabile [e·iet·'taː·bi·le] *agg* **sedile** ~ ejector seat

elaborare [e·la·bo·'raː·re] *vt* 1.(*tesi, piano*) to devise; (*sistema*) to create 2.COMPUT (*dati*) to process 3.(*digerire*) to digest

elaborato [e·la·bo·'raː·to] *m* 1.(*a scuola, concorso: scritto, trattazione*) essay 2.COMPUT (*tabulato*) printout

elaborato, -a *agg* 1.(*ricercato: stile*) ornate; (*piatto, ricetta*) elaborate 2.(*potente: motore*) modified

elaboratore [e·la·bo·ra·'toː·re] *m* COMPUT ~ (**elettronico**) processor

elaborazione [e·la·bo·rat·'tsioː·ne] *f* 1.COMPUT (*di dati*) processing 2.(*di progetto, piano, teoria, modello*) creation

elargire [e·lar·'dʒiː·re] <elargisco> *vt* (*distribuire: fondi, soldi, sussidi*) to give out; (*regali, favori*) to lavish

elargizione [e·lar·dʒit·'tsioː·ne] *f* (*assegnazione*) donation

elasticità [e·las·ti·tʃi·'ta] <-> *f* 1.(*di molle, gomma*) elasticity 2.(*agilità: di persona*) agility 3.*fig* (*apertura*) flexibility; ~ **mentale** mental agility

elasticizzato, -a [e·las·ti·tʃid·'dzaː·to] *agg* (*tessuto, indumento*) elasticized

elastico [e·'las·ti·ko] <-ci> *m* 1.(*tessuto*) elastic 2.(*per fissare*) rubber band

elastico, -a <-ci, -che> *agg* 1.(*tessuto*) elastic; (*pelle*) supple 2.(*agile: persona, passo, mente*) nimble 3.(*flessibile: orario*) flexible 4.(*morale*) flexible

Elba *f* (*isola toscana*) Elba; **l'**~ Elba

elbano, -a [el·'baː·no] *m, f* (*abitante dell'isola d'Elba*) person from Elba

eldorado [el·do·'raː·do] *m* El Dorado

elefante [e·le·'fan·te] *m* elephant

elegante [e·le·'gan·te] *agg* elegant

eleganza [e·le·'gan·tsa] *f* elegance

eleggere [e·'lɛd·dʒe·re] <irr> *vt* to elect

elegia [e·le·'dʒiː·a] <-gie> *f* elegy

elegiaco, -a [e·le·'dʒiː·a·ko] <-ci, -che> *agg* (*atmosfera, melodia*) elegiac

elementare [e·le·men·'taː·re] I. *agg* 1.(*semplice: concetto*) basic 2.(*di base: regola*) basic 3.(*scuola*) elementary; **scuola** ~ elementary school II.*fpl* (*scuole*) elementary school

elemento [e·le·'men·to] *m* 1.(*sostanza*) element 2. CHEM element 3.(*parte: di macchina, cucina, frase*) part 4.*fig* (*ambiente*) element 5.(*dato*) fact 6.*fig, pej* (*individuo*) individual 7. *pl* (*nozione*) rudiments

elemosina [e·le·'mɔː·zi·na] *f* charity; **chiedere l'**~ to beg; **fare l'**~ to give charity

elemosinare [e·le·mo·zi·'naː·re] I. *vt a fig* to beg for II. *vi* to beg

elencare [e·leŋ·'kaː·re] *vt* 1.(*registrare: nomi, articoli*) to list 2.(*enumerare: pregi, difetti*) to count

elencazione [e·leŋ·kat·'tsioː·ne] *f* 1.(*registrazione: di nomi, articoli*) listing 2.(*enumerazione: di pregi, difetti*) counting

elenco [e·'lɛŋ·ko] <-chi> *m* list; ~ **telefonico** phone book

elessi *1. pers sing pass rem di* **eleggere**

elettivo, -a [e·let·'tiː·vo] *agg* 1.(*carica, monarchia*) elected 2.(*scelto: domicilio, patria*) chosen

eletto, -a [e·'lɛt·to] I. *pp di* **eleggere** II. *agg* 1.POL (*nominato*) elected 2.REL chosen; **il popolo** ~ the chosen people 3.*fig* select III. *m, f* (*a parlamento, camera, consiglio*) elected member

elettorale [e·let·to·'raː·le] *agg* electoral

elettorato [e·let·to·'raː·to] *m* (*elettori*) electorate

elettore, -trice [e·let·'toː·re] *m, f* voter

elettrauto [e·let·'tra·u·to] <-> *m* 1.(*persona*) car electrician 2.(*officina*) electrical repair shop, *for cars*

elettrice *f v.* **elettore**

elettricista [e·let·tri·'tʃis·ta] <-i *m*, -e *f*> *mf* electrician

elettricità [e·let·tri·tʃi·'ta] <-> *f* PHYS electricity

elettrico, -a [e·'lɛt·tri·ko] <-ci, -che> I. *agg* 1.PHYS (*carica*) electric; **centrale -a** power station; **energia -a** electric power 2.(*auto, scaldabagno, bollitore, pianola*) electric II. *m, f* electricity worker

elettrificare [e·let·tri·fi·'kaː·re] *vt* 1.(*luogo*) to supply with electricity 2.(*ferrovia*) to electrify

elettrificazione [e·let·tri·fi·kat·'tsioː·ne] *f* (*di ferrovia*) electrification

elettrizzante [e·let·trid·'dzan·te] *agg* (*atmosfera, esperienza, novità*) electrifying

elettrizzare [e·let·trid·'dzaː·re] I. *vt* 1.PHYS (*corpo*) to electrify 2.*fig* (*entusiasmare*) to electrify II. *vr*: **-rsi** 1.PHYS (*corpo*) to be electrified 2.*fig* (*entusiasmarsi*) to become electric

elettro- [e·let·tro] (*in parole composte*) electro-

elettrocalamita [e·let·tro·ka·la·'mi:·ta] *f* electromagnet

elettrocardiogramma [e·let·tro·kar·dio·'gram·ma] *m* electrocardiogram

elettrochimica [e·let·tro·'ki:·mi·ka] <-che> *f* electrochemistry

elettrochimico, -a [e·let·tro·'ki:·mi·ko] <-ci, -che> I. *agg* (*settore, impianto*) electrochemical II. *m, f* electrochemist

elettrochoc [e·let·troʃ·'ʃɔk] *m* electroshock

elettrodo [e·'lɛt·tro·do] *m* electrode

elettrodomestico [e·let·tro·do·'mɛs·ti·ko] *m* electrical appliance; **negozio di -ci** electrical appliance store

elettroencefalogramma [e·let·tro·en·tʃe·fa·lo·'gram·ma] *m* electroencephalogram

elettrofisica [e·let·tro·'fi:·zi·ka] <-che> *f* electrophysics

elettrolisi [e·let·'trɔ:·li·zi] <-> *f* electrolysis

elettrolitico, -a [e·let·tro·'li:·ti·ko] <-ci, -che> *agg* (*cella, conduzione*) electrolytic; **zincatura -a** electro-galvanizing

elettromagnetico, -a [e·let·tro·maɲ·'nɛ:·ti·co] <-ci, -che> *agg* (*campo, onda, inquinamento*) electromagnetic

elettromeccanica [e·let·tro·mek·'ka:·ni·ka] <-che> *f* electromechanics

elettromeccanico, -a [e·let·tro·mek·'ka:·ni·ko] <-ci, -che> I. *agg* (*pompa, componente, ricambio*) electromechanical II. *m, f* electrical mechanic

elettromotrice [e·let·tro·mo·'tri:·tʃe] *f* (*di treno*) electric locomotive

elettrone [e·let·'tro:·ne] *m* electron

elettronica [e·let·'trɔ:·ni·ka] <-che> *f* electronics

elettronico, -a [e·let·'trɔ:·ni·ko] <-ci, -che> *agg* 1. PHYS electronic 2. COMPUT (*giornale, rivista*) online; (*cartolina*) electronic; **posta -a** email; **commercio ~** e-commerce

elettroscopio [e·let·tros·'kɔ:·pio] <-i> *m* electroscope

elettroshock [e·let·tro·'ʃɔk] <-> *m* electroshock

elettrosmog [e·lɛt·tro·'zmɔg] <-> *m* ECO elettrosmog

elettrostatica [e·let·tro·'sta:·ti·ka] <-che> *f* PHYS electrostatics

elettrotecnica [e·let·tro·'tɛk·ni·ka] <-che> *f* electrical engineering

elettrotecnico, -a [e·let·tro·'tɛk·ni·ko] <-ci, -che> I. *agg* (*apparecchiatura, disciplina, azienda*) electrotechnical II. *m, f* electrical engineer

elevare [e·le·'va:·re] I. *vt* 1. (*edificio*) to erect; **~ un edificio di un piano** to add a floor to a building 2. *fig* (*migliorare*) to raise 3. (*aumentare*) to increase 4. ADM **~ una multa** to impose a fine 5. MAT **~ un numero al quadrato** to square a number II. *vr:* **-rsi** to rise

elevato, -a [e·le·va:·to] *agg* 1. (*alto: montagna, prezzo*) high 2. (*nobile: sentimenti*) no-

ble

elevatore [e·le·va·'to:·re] *m* TEC elevator

elevatore, -trice *agg* TEC elevatory; **carrello ~** forklift

elezione [e·let·'tsio:·ne] *f* 1. POL election 2. DIR (*scelta*) choice

eliambulanza [e·li·am·bu·'lan·tsa] *f* AERO medevac

elica ['ɛ:·li·ka] <-che> *f* (*di nave, aereo*) propellor

elicoidale [e·li·koi·'da:·le] *agg* (*a elica: corpo, scala*) spiral

elicottero [e·li·'kɔt·te·ro] *m* helicopter

elidere [e·'li:·de·re] <elido, elisi, eliso> *vt* LING (*vocale*) to elide

eliminare [e·li·mi·'na:·re] *vt* 1. (*togliere: macchia, ostacolo, errore*) to remove 2. *fig* (*scartare: dubbio, ipotesi*) to eliminate 3. (*estromettere: avversario, squadra*) to knock out 4. *inf* (*uccidere*) to rub out 5. (*espellere: tossine*) to eliminate

eliminatoria [e·li·mi·na·'tɔ:·ria] <-ie> *f* (*gara*) preliminary round

eliminazione [e·li·mi·nat·'tsio:·ne] *f* 1. SPORT (*esclusione: di avversario, squadra*) elimination 2. (*rimozione: di errore, ostacolo*) removal 3. *inf* (*uccisione*) killing 4. (*di tossine*) elimination

elio ['ɛ:·lio] *m* helium

eliocentrico, -a [e·lio·'tʃɛn·tri·ko] <-ci, -che> *agg* (*sistema*) heliocentric

eliografia [e·lio·gra·'fi:·a] *f* heliograph

eliporto [e·li·'pɔr·to] *m* heliport

elisi [e·'li:·zi] *1. pers sing pass rem di* **elidere**

elisione [e·li·'zio:·ne] *f* LING (*di vocale*) elision

elisir [e·li·'zir] <-> *m* elixir

eliso [e·'li:·zo] *pp di* **elidere**

elitario, -a [e·li·'ta:·rio] <-i, -ie> *agg* elite

élite [e·'lit] <-> *f* elite; **d'~** (*scuola, albergo*) elite

ella ['el·la] *pron 3. pers sing f* she

ellenico, -a [el·'lɛ:·ni·ko] <-ci, -che> *agg* (*bandiera, popolo*) Greek

ellenismo [el·le·'niz·mo] *m* HIST, LIT Hellenism

ellisse [el·'lis·se] *f* MAT ellipsis

ellittico, -a [el·'lit·ti·ko] <-ci, -che> *agg* (*ovale: tubo, cono*) elliptic

elmetto [el·'met·to] *m* (*per soldati, minatori, ciclisti*) helmet

elmo ['el·mo] *m* (*nelle antiche armature*) helmet

elogiare [e·lo·'dʒa:·re] *vt* (*persona, opera*) to praise

elogio [e·'lɔ:·dʒo] <-gi> *m* 1. (*orazione*) eulogy; **~ funebre** funeral oration 2. (*lode*) praise

eloquente [e·lo·'kuɛn·te] *agg* 1. (*oratore, discorso*) eloquent 2. (*sguardo, silenzio*) meaningful

eloquenza [e·lo·'kuɛn·tsa] *f a fig* eloquence

eludere [e·'lu:·de·re] <eludo, elusi, eluso> *vt* **~ qc** (*confronto*) to avoid sth; (*controllo*) to evade sth

elusivo, -a [e·lu·'zi:·vo] *agg* (*evasivo: discorso, parole*) evasive

eluso [e·'lu·zo] *pp di* **eludere**

elvetico, -a [el·'vɛ:·ti·ko] <-ci, -che> *agg* (*autorità, confederazione, cittadini*) Swiss

emaciato, -a [e·ma·'tʃa:·to] *agg* (*volto, guance, corpi*) emaciated

E-mail [i·'meil] <-> *f* e-mail

emanare [e·ma·'na:·re] *vt avere* **1.** (*luce, calore, profumo*) to give out; (*gas*) to give off **2.** JUR (*leggi*) to issue **3.** *fig* (*simpatia*) to exude

emanazione [e·ma·nat·'tsio:·ne] *f* **1.** (*di luce, calore, gas*) emission **2.** JUR (*di leggi*) enactment

emancipare [e·man·tʃi·'pa:·re] **I.** *vt* **1.** (*popolazione, cultura, paese*) to liberate **2.** (*donna, minore*) to emancipate **II.** *vr:* **-rsi 1.** (*popolazione, paese*) to be liberated **2.** (*donna*) to be emancipated

emancipato, -a [e·man·tʃi·'pa:·to] *agg* **1.** (*popolazione, paese*) free **2.** (*donna*) emancipated

emancipazione [e·man·tʃi·pat·'tsio:·ne] *f* (*di popolazione, paese*) liberation; ~ **della donna** women's liberation

emarginare [e·mar·dʒi·'na:·re] *vt fig* (*escludere: minoranza*) to marginalize

emarginati [e·mar·dʒi·'na:·ti] *mpl* outcasts *pl*

emarginato, -a [e·mar·dʒi·'na:·to] **I.** *agg* (*escluso: quartiere, gruppo, bambino*) outcast **II.** *m, f* (*persona*) outcast

ematico, -a [e·'ma:·ti·ko] <-ci, -che> *agg* MED blood; **controllo/prelievo** ~ blood test/sample

ematoma [e·ma·'tɔ:·ma] <-i> *m* (*livido*) bruise; MED hematoma

embargo [em·'bar·go] <-ghi> *m* embargo

emblema [em·'blɛ:·ma] <-i> *m* (*simbolo*) emblem

emblematico, -a [em·ble·'ma:·ti·ko] <-ci, -che> *agg* **1.** (*simbolico: personaggio, figura*) emblematic **2.** (*rappresentativo: caso, esperienza*) typical

embolia [em·bo·'li:·a] <-ie> *f* MED embolism

embrionale [em·bri·o·'na:·le] *agg* BIOL (*sviluppo*) embryonic; **cellula** ~ embryo cell

embrione [em·bri·'o:·ne] *m* **1.** BIOL embryo **2.** *fig* **essere in** ~ (*progetto, idea*) to be embryonic

emendamento [e·men·da·'men·to] *m* **1.** (*correzione*) correction **2.** JUR (*di legge*) amendment

emendare [e·men·'da:·re] *vt* **1.** (*correggere*) to correct **2.** JUR (*legge*) to amend

emergente [e·mer·'dʒɛn·te] *agg* (*cantante, autore*) up-and-coming; (*mercato*) emerging; **paesi -i** emerging countries

emergenza [e·mer·'dʒɛn·tsa] *f* (*situazione critica*) emergency; **stato di** ~ state of emergency; **freno di** ~ (*di treno*) emergency brake

emergere [e·'mɛr·dʒe·re] <emergo, emersi, emerso> *vi essere* **1.** (*venire a galla*) to emerge **2.** (*risultare*) to come out **3.** *fig* (*eccel-*

lere) to stand out

emerito, -a [e·'mɛ:·ri·to] *agg* **1.** (*professore*) emeritus **2.** (*insigne: studioso, statista*) eminent **3.** *fig, a. scherz* absolute; **sei un** ~ **stupido** you're an absolute fool

emersi [e·'mɛr·si] *1. pers sing pass rem di* **emergere**

emersione [e·mer·'sio:·ne] *f* **1.** (*di sommergibile, subaqcueo*) surfacing **2.** (*regolarizzazione: di lavoratore*) regularization

emerso [e·'mɛr·so] *pp di* **emergere**

emetico [e·'mɛ:·ti·ko] <-ci> *m* emetic

emetico, -a <-ci, -che> *agg* emetic

emettere [e·'met·te·re] <irr> *vt* **1.** (*mandare fuori: luce, radiazione, calore*) to emit; (*grido, sibilo, suono*) to let out **2.** FIN (*azioni, titoli, assegno*) to issue **3.** JUR (*sentenza*) to pass; (*mandato*) to issue

emiciclo [e·mi·'tʃi:·klo] *m* semicircle

emicrania [e·mi·'kra:·nia] <-ie> *f* MED migraine

emigrante [e·mi·'gran·te] *m* emigrant

emigrare [e·mi·'gra:·re] *vi essere o avere* **1.** (*espatriare*) to emigrate **2.** ZOO (*migrare*) to migrate

emigrato, -a [e·mi·'gra:·to] **I.** *agg* (*persona*) emigrant **II.** *m, f* emigrant

emigrazione [e·mi·grat·'tsio:·ne] *f* **1.** (*espatrio*) emigration **2.** FIN (*di capitali*) flight

Emilia *f* (*regione*) l'~ **Romagna** Emilia-Romagna

emiliano [e·mi·'lia:·no] <sing> *m* (*dialetto*) dialect spoken in the Emilia region

emiliano, -a **I.** *agg* from Emilia **II.** *m, f* (*abitante*) person from Emilia

Emilia-Romagna [e·'mi:·lia ro·'maɲ·ɲa] *f* Emilia-Romagna

eminente [e·mi·'nɛn·te] *agg fig* (*importante*) eminent

eminentemente [e·mi·nen·te·'men·te] *avv* (*soprattutto*) fundamentally

eminenza [e·mi·'nɛn·tsa] *f* **1.** REL (*titolo*) Eminence **2.** (*persona*) **eminent person** ~ **grigia,** éminence grise

emirato [e·mi·'ra:·to] *m* emirate

emiro [e·'mi:·ro] *m* emir

emisferico, -a [e·mis·'fɛ:·ri·ko] <-ci, -che> *agg* hemispherical

emisfero [e·mis·'fɛ:·ro] *m* **1.** GEOG hemisphere; ~ **australe/boreale** southern/northern hemisphere **2.** ANAT ~ **cerebrale** cerebral hemisphere **3.** MAT hemisphere

emisi *1. pers sing pass rem di* **emettere**

emissario [e·mis·'sa:·rio] <-i> *m* **1.** GEOG (*di fiume*) outlet **2.** (*rappresentante*) emissary

emissione [e·mis·'sio:·ne] *f* **1.** (*fuoriuscita: di gas, radiazioni, suoni*) emission **2.** FIN (*di azioni, titoli, francobolli*) issue

emittente [e·mit·'tɛn·te] **I.** *agg* **1.** RADIO (*antenna, stazione radio*) broadcasting **2.** FIN (*società*) issuing **II.** *f* TV, RADIO broadcast

emittenza [e·mit·'ten·tsa] *f* TV, RADIO broadcasting

emodialisi [e·mo·dia·'li:·zi] <-> *f* MED hemodialysis

emofilia [e·mo·fi·'li:·a] <-ie> *f* MED hemophilia

emofiliaco [e·mo·fi·'li:·a·ko] <-ci> *m* hemophiliac

emoglobina [e·mo·glo·'bi:·na] *f* hemoglobin

emolliente [e·mol·'li εn·te] I. *agg* (*cosmetico, crema, sapone*) emollient II. *m* MED (*per la tosse, crema*) emollient

emorragia [e·mor·ra·'dʒi:·a] <-gie> *f* MED hemorrhage

emorroidi [e·mor·'rɔ:·i·di] *fpl* hemorrhoids

emostatico [e·mos·'ta:·ti·ko] <-ci> *m* hemostatic

emostatico, -a <-ci, -che> *agg* (*cotone, laccio, matita*) hemostatic

emoteca [e·mo·'tε:·ka] *f* blood bank

emotività [e·mo·ti·vi·'ta] <-> *f* emotionality

emotivo, -a [e·mo·'ti:·vo] I. *agg* (*coinvolgimento, reazione, persona*) emotional II. *m, f* emotional person

emozionale [e·mot·tsio·'na:·le] *agg* (*equilibrio, disagio, sviluppo*) emotional

emozionante [e·mot·tsio·'nan·te] *agg* (*storia, vita*) inspiring

emozionare [e·mot·tsio·'na:·re] I. *vt* (*film, storia, paesaggio*) to thrill II. *vr:* -**rsi** ~ **per qc** to get excited by sth

emozione [e·mot·'tsio:·ne] *f* 1. (*agitazione*) emotion 2. (*impressione*) emotion; **provare una forte** ~ to feel strong emotions

empatia [em·pa·'ti:·a] <-ie> *f* PSYCH empathy

empietà [em·pie·'ta] <-> *f* (*spietatezza*) ruthlessness

empii [em·'pi:·i] *1. pers sing pass rem di* **empire**

empio, -a ['em·pio] <-i, -ie> *agg* (*spietato: guerra, persona*) cruel

empirico, -a [em·'pi:·ri·ko] <-ci, -che> *agg* (*rimedio, metodo*) empirical

emporio [em·'pɔ:·rio] <-i> *m* (*negozio*) general store

emù [e·'mu] <-> *m* ZOO emu

emulare [e·mu·'la:·re] *vt* 1. (*imitare: personaggio, gesta*) to emulate 2. COMPUT to emulate

emulazione [e·mu·lat·'tsio:·ne] *f* 1. (*imitazione*) emulation 2. COMPUT emulation

emulsionare [e·mul·sio·'na:·re] *vt* (*acqua e olio*) to emulsify

emulsionatore [e·mul·sio·na·'to:·re] *m* TECH (*apparecchio*) emulsifier

emulsione [e·mul·'sio:·ne] *f* (*di acqua e olio*) emulsion

Enalotto [e·na·'lɔt·to] *m* state lottery

encefalo [en·'tʃε:·fa·lo] *m* encephalon

encefalopatia [en·tʃe·fa·lo·pa·'ti:·a] <-ie> *f* MED encephalopathy

enciclica [en·'tʃik·li·ka] <-che> *f* encyclical

enciclopedia [en·tʃik·lo·pe·'di:·a] <-ie> *f* encyclopedia

enciclopedico, -a [en·tʃik·lo·'pε:·di·ko] <-ci, -che> *agg* (*dizionario, opera, sapere*) encyclopedic

encomio [eŋ·'kɔ:·mio] <-i> *m* (*lode*) tribute; **degno di** ~ praiseworthy

endemico, -a [en·'dε:·mi·ko] <-ci, -che> *agg* (*specie, malattia*) endemic

endocardio [en·do·'kar·dio] <-i> *m* ANAT endocardium

endocrino, -a [en·'dɔ:·kri·no] *agg* ANAT (*ghiandola*) endocrine

endogeno, -a [en·'dɔ:·dʒe·no] *agg* (*interno*) endogenous

endoscopio [en·dos·'kɔ:·pio] <-i> *m* endoscope

endovenosa [en·do·ve·'no:·sa] *f* MED (*iniezione*) intravenous injection

endovenoso, -a [en·do·ve·'no:·so] *agg* MED (*iniezione, infusione*) intravenous

ENEL ['ε:·nel] *m abbr di* **Ente Nazionale per l'Energia Elettrica** *state electricity company*

energetico, -a [e·ner·'dʒε:·ti·ko] <-ci, -che> *agg* 1. (*consumi, settore, titolo, risparmio*) energy; **fonti** -**che** electricity sources 2. (*cibo*) high-energy

energia [e·ner·'dʒi:·a] <-gie> *f* 1. PHYS energy; ~ **atomica** [*o* **nucleare**] nuclear power; ~ **elettrica** electric power; ~ **rinnovabile** renewable energy; ~ **solare** solar power 2. (*vigore*) energy; **con** ~ energetically; **senza** ~ apathetically

energico, -a [e·'nεr·dʒi·ko] <-ci, -che> *agg* (*persona, protesta*) energetic; (*passo*) determined

energizzare [e·ner·dʒid·'dza:·re] *vt* ~ **qc** to energize sth

energumeno, -a [e·ner·'gu:·me·no] *m, f* wild man *m*, wild woman *f*

enfant prodige [ã·'fã prɔ·'di:ʒ] <-> *m* golden boy

enfant terrible [ã·'fã te·'ri·bl] <-> *m* enfant terrible

enfasi ['εn·fa·zi] <-> *f* 1. (*foga*) emphasis; **con** ~ (*parlare*) enthusiastically 2. (*rilievo*) stress

enfatico, -a [en·'fa:·ti·ko] <-ci, -che> *agg* emphatic

enfatizzare [en·fa·tid·'dza:·re] *vt* 1. (*parole*) to emphasize 2. (*esagerare: racconto, notizia*) to dramatize

enfatizzazione [en·fa·tid·dzat·'tsio:·ne] *f* (*esagerazione*) dramatization

ENI ['ε:·ni] *m abbr di* **Ente Nazionale Idrocarburi** *state hydrocarbon agency*

enigma [e·'nig·ma] <-i> *m* 1. (*indovinello*) riddle 2. (*mistero*) mystery

enigmatico, -a [e·nig·'ma:·ti·ko] <-ci, -che> *agg* (*persona, comportamento, sorriso*) enigmatic

enigmistico, -a [e·nig·'mis·ti·ko] <-ci, -che> *agg* **gioco** ~ puzzle; **giornale** ~ puzzle magazine

Enna *f* Enna

ennese [en·'ne:·se] I. *agg* from Enna II. *mf* (*abitante*) person from Enna

Ennese <*sing*> *m* (*zona*) Enna region; **nell'** ~ in the Enna region

ennesimo, -a [en·'nɛː·zi·mo] *agg* 1. *fam* umpteenth; **per l'-a volta** for the umpteenth time 2. MAT nth

enologia [e·no·lo·'dʒiː·a] <-gie> *f* enology

enologo, -a [e·'nɔː·lo·go] <-gi, -ghe> *m, f* enologist

enorme [e·'nor·me] *agg* 1. (*oggetto, edificio*) enormous 2. (*fortuna, gioia*) great

enormità [e·nor·mi·'ta] <-> *f* 1. (*grandezza: di scoperta, aspettative, richiesta*) enormity 2. (*eccesso*) **costa un'~!** *fam* it costs a fortune! 3. (*stupidaggine*) nonsense; **dire un'~** to talk nonsense

enoteca [e·no·'tɛː·ka] *f* 1. (*raccolta*) (wine) cellar 2. (*locale*) wine bar

enoturismo [e·no·tu·'riz·mo] *m* wine tourism

en passant [ã pa·'sã] *avv* in passing

en plein [ã plɛ̃] <-> *m* 1. (*alla roulette*) en plein 2. *fig* **fare un ~** to make a clean sweep

ensemble [ã·'sã·bl] <-> *m* MUS (*complesso*) ensemble

ente ['ɛn·te] *m* 1. (*istituzione*) body 2. PHILOS (*cosa*) being

entità [en·ti·'ta] <-> *f* 1. (*importanza*) extent 2. PHILOS entity

entomologia [en·to·mo·lo·'dʒiː·a] <-gie> *f* entomology

entomologo, -a [en·to·'mɔː·lo·go] <-gi, -ghi> *m, f* entomologist

entraîneuse [ã·trɛ·'nø:z] <-> *f* hostess

entrambi, -e [en·'tram·bi] *agg, pron* (*tutti e due*) both; **-e le parti** DIR both parties

entrante [en·'tran·te] *agg* (*anno, mese*) coming

entrare [en·'traː·re] *vi essere* 1. (*in un luogo*) to enter, to go in; **~ in acqua** to get into the water; **~ in casa** to go indoors; **~ dalla porta/finestra** to go in through the door/window; **entrate pure!** please come in; **fare ~ qu** to bring sb in 2. *fig* (*in un gruppo*) to join; **~ nell'esercito** to join the army; **~ in convento** (*frate*) to enter a monastery; (*suora*) to enter a convent 3. (*vestito*) to fit; **la gonna non mi entra più** the skirt doesn't fit me anymore 4. (*trovare posto*) to fit; **qui non c'entra più nessuno** *fam* there's no room for anyone else 5. (*avere a che vedere*) to be relevant; **la politica non c'entra** *fig, fam* politics has nothing to do with it 6. *fig* (*iniziare*) **~ in contatto con qu** to get in touch with sb; **~ in carica** to take office; **~ in guerra** to go to war

entrata [en·'traː·ta] *f* 1. (*ingresso*) entrance 2. (*l'entrare*) entry; **~ in carica** appointment; **~ in vigore** (*di legge*) coming into force 3. *pl* COM (*guadagno*) income

entrecôte [ã·trə·'koːt] <-> *f* entrecôte

entro ['en·tro] *prep* within; **~ e non oltre il 30 ottobre** ADM no later than October 30; **si sposano ~ l'anno** they're getting married this year

entroterra [en·tro·'tɛr·ra] <-> *m* inland region; **nell'~** inland

entusiasmare [en·tuz·iaz·'maː·re] I. *vt* to ex-

cite II. *vr:* **-rsi -rsi per qc** to become excited about sth

entusiasmo [en·tu·'ziaz·mo] *m* enthusiasm

entusiasta [en·tu·'zias·ta] <-i *m*, -e *f*> I. *agg* (*persona, discorso, applauso*) enthusiastic; **essere ~ di qc** to be enthusiastic about sth II. *mf* enthusiast

entusiastico, -a [en·tu·'zias·ti·ko] <-ci, -che> *agg* (*applauso, partecipazione, parole*) enthusiastic

enucleare [e·nu·kl·'aː·re] *vt* (*chiarire: concetto, principio*) to explain

enumerare [e·nu·me·'raː·re] *vt* (*qualità, difficoltà*) to list

enumerazione [e·nu·me·rat·'tsio:·ne] *f* (*di qualità, difficoltà*) list

enunciare [e·nun·'tʃaː·re] *vt* (*principio, teoria*) to state

enunciato [e·nun·'tʃaː·to] *m* statement

enunciazione [e·nun·tʃat·'tsio:·ne] *f* (*di principio, teoria*) statement

enzima [en·'dziː·ma] <-i> *m* enzyme

eolico, -a [e·'ɔː·li·ko] <-ci, -che> *agg* (*del vento*) wind; **energia -a** wind power; **motore ~** wind generator

epatico, -a [e·'paː·ti·ko] <-ci, -che> *agg* (*del fegato*) liver; **cirrosi -a** cirrhosis

epatite [e·pa·'tiː·te] *f* hepatitis

epica ['ɛː·pi·ka] <-che> *f* epic

epicentro [e·pi·'tʃɛn·tro] *m a fig* epicenter

epico, -a ['ɛː·pi·ko] <-ci, -che> *agg* (*saga, avventure, film*) epic; **poema ~** epic poem

epicureo, -a [e·pi·ku·'rɛ·o] I. *agg* Epicurean II. *m, f* PHILOS Epicurean

epidemia [e·pi·de·'miː·a] <-ie> *f a fig* epidemic

epidemico, -a [e·pi·'dɛː·mi·ko] <-ci, -che> *agg* MED (*malattia, focolaio, infezione*) epidemic

epidermico, -a [e·pi·'dɛr·mi·ko] <-ci, -che> *agg* 1. ANAT (*cellule, tumore*) epidermal 2. (*superficiale: simpatia, sensazione*) superficial

epidermide [e·pi·'dɛr·mi·de] *f* ANAT epidermis

epifania [e·pi·fa·'niː·a] <-ie> *f* epiphany

> **i** **Epifania,** Epiphany, the Feast of the Three Kings at the end of the Christmas period, is a statutory holiday in Italy. According to tradition, on the night of January 6 the **Befana**, an old woman from fairy tales, comes down the chimney, bringing gifts for good children and pieces of coal for bad ones.

epigrafe [e·'pi·gra·fe] *f* epigraph

epilazione [e·pi·lat·'tsio:·ne] *f* depilation

epilessia [e·pi·les·'siː·a] <-ie> *f* epilepsy

epilettico, -a [e·pi·'lɛt·ti·ko] <-ci, -che> I. *agg* (*paziente, crisi*) epileptic II. *m, f* epileptic

epilogo [e·'piː·lo·go] <-ghi> *m* 1. LIT (*di romanzo*) epilogue 2. *fig* (*di storia, avvenimento*) end

episcopale [e·pis·ko·'pa:·le] *agg* episcopal

episcopato [e·pis·ko·'pa:·to] *m* **1.**(*ufficio di vescovo*) bishopric **2.**(*vescovi*) bishops *pl*

episodico, -a [e·pi·'zɔ:·di·ko] <-ci, -che> *agg* **1.**(*film, romanzo*) episodic **2.** *fig* (*fenomeno*) occasional

episodio [e·pi·'zɔ:·dio] <-i> *m* **1.**(*avvenimento*) episode **2.**(*di sceneggiato televisivo*) episode; (*di romanzo*) instalment

epistolare [e·pis·to·'la:·re] *agg* epistolary; **romanzo** ~ epistolary novel; **scambio** ~ correspondence

epitaffio [e·pi·'taf·fio] <-i> *m* epitaph

epiteto [e·'pi:·te·to] *m* **1.** LING (*denominazione*) epithet **2.** *pej* (*insulto*) insult

epoca ['ɛ:·po·ka] <-che> *f* **1.**(*periodo storico*) epoch; **auto d'**~ vintage car **2.**(*tempo*) time; **a quell'**~ at that time

epopea [e·po·'pɛ:·a] *f* **1.** LIT epic poem **2.** *fig* (*impresa*) epic achievement

epos ['ɛ:·pos] <-> *m* LIT epic poetry

eppure [ep·'pu:·re] *cong* (and) yet

epurare [e·pu·'ra:·re] *vt* POL (*mandar via*) to purge

epurazione [e·pu·rat·'tsio:·ne] *f* POL (*allontanamento*) purge

equanime [e·'kua:·ni·me] *agg* (*giudizio*) unbiased; (*giudice*) impartial

equanimità [e·kua·ni·mi·'ta] <-> *f* impartiality

equatore [e·kua·'to:·re] *m* equator

equatoriale [e·kua·to·'ria:·le] *agg* (*foresta, clima*) equatorial

equazione [e·kuat·'tsio:·ne] *f* equation

equestre [e·'kuɛs·tre] *agg* (*sport*) equestrian; **circo** ~ horse show

equiangolo, -a [e·kui·'aŋ·go·lo] *agg* equiangular

equidistante [e·kui·dis·'tan·te] *agg* (*punto*) equidistant

equidistanza [e·kui·dis·'tan·tsa] *f* equidistance

equilatero, -a [e·kui·'la:·te·ro] *agg* equilateral

equilibrare [e·kui·li·'bra:·re] I. *vt* **1.**(*tenere in equilibrio: piatti della bilancia, pesi*) to balance **2.** MOT (*ruote*) to balance II. *vr:* **-rsi** (*pesi, forze*) to balance (each other)

equilibrato, -a [e·kui·li·'bra:·to] *agg fig* (*persona, giudizio*) balanced

equilibratura [e·kui·li·bra·'tu:·ra] *f* MOT ~ **delle ruote** wheel balancing

equilibrio [e·kui·'li:·bri·o] <-i> *m* **1.**(*stabilità*) balance; **perdere/mantenere l'**~ to lose/keep one's balance; **stare in** ~ to be balanced **2.**(*di situazione, mercato*) balance **3.**(*interiore: di persona*) equilibrium

equilibrismo [e·kui·li·'briz·mo] *m* **1.**(*arte*) tightrope walking **2.** *fig* balancing act

equilibrista [e·kui·li·'bris·ta] <-i *m*, -e *f*> *mf* tightrope walker

equilizzatore [e·kui·lid·dza·'to:·re] *m* MUS equalizer

equini [e·'kui:·ni] *mpl* horses *pl*

equino, -a *agg* horse; **allevamento** ~ horse breeding

equinozio [e·kui·'nɔt·tsio] <-i> *m* ASTR equinox; ~ **di primavera/d'autunno** spring/autumnal equinox

equipaggiamento [e·kui·pad·dʒa·'men·to] *m* (*da sci, escursionismo, pesca*) equipment

equipaggiare [e·kui·pad·'dʒa:·re] I. *vt* (*esercito, nave*) to equip II. *vr:* **-rsi** to equip oneself

equipaggio [e·kui·'pad·dʒo] <-ggi> *m* (*di nave, aereo*) equipment

equiparare [e·kui·pa·'ra:·re] *vt* **1.**(*uguagliare*) to equalize **2.**(*comparare*) to compare

équipe [e·'kip] <-> *f* team; **lavoro d'**~ teamwork

equipollente [e·kui·pol·'lɛn·te] *agg* (*laurea, servizio*) equivalent

equità [e·kui·'ta] <-> *f* (*giustizia*) fairness; ~ **sociale** social justice

equitazione [e·kui·tat·'tsio:·ne] *f* horseback riding

equivalente [e·kui·va·'lɛn·te] I. *agg* equivalent II. *m* equivalent

equivalenza [e·kui·va·'lɛn·tsa] *f a fig* equivalence

equivalere [e·kui·va·'le:·re] <irr> I. *vi essere o avere* to be equivalent; ~ **a qc** to be equivalent to sth II. *vr:* **-rsi** to be equivalent (to each other)

equivocare [e·kui·vo·'ka:·re] *vi* to misunderstand; ~ **su qc** to misunderstand sth

equivoco [e·'kui:·vo·ko] <-ci> *m* (*malinteso*) misunderstanding

equivoco, -a <-ci, -che> *agg* **1.**(*ambivalente: frase, risposta*) ambiguous **2.** *fig* (*losco: persona, luogo*) dubious

equo, -a ['ɛ:·kuo] *agg* **1.**(*imparziale: persona, giudice*) impartial **2.** COM (*giusto: pagamento, condizioni, distribuzione*) fair

era[1] ['ɛ:·ra] *f* age; **l'**~ **atomica** the nuclear age; **l'**~ **cristiana/maomettana** the Christian/Islamic era; **le -e geologiche** the geological eras

era[2] *3. pers sing imp di essere*[1]

erariale [e·ra·'ria:·le] *agg* tax

erario [e·'ra:·rio] <-i> *m* treasury

erba ['ɛr·ba] *f* **1.** BOT grass; **un filo d'**~ a blade of grass; **fare d'ogni** ~ **un fascio** *fig* to lump everyone/everything together **2.** CULIN herb; **-e aromatiche** mixed herbs; ~ **cipollina** chives **3.** *sl* (*marijuana*) grass

erbaceo, -a [er·'ba:·tʃe·o] <-ei, -ee> *agg* (*colture, piante*) herbaceous

erbicida[1] [er·bi·'tʃi:·da] <-i *m*, -e *f*> *agg* herbicidal

erbicida[2] <-i> *m* weedkiller

erbivendolo, -a [er·bi·'ven·do·lo] *m, f* fruit and vegetable seller

erbivoro, -a [er'bi:voro] I. *agg* (*animale*) herbivorous II. *m, f* **1.**(*animale*) herbivore **2.** *scherz* (*vegetariano*) herbivore

erborista [er·bo·'ris·ta] <-i *m*, -e *f*> *mf* **1.**(*negozio*) herbalist shop **2.**(*esperto*) herbalist

erboristeria *f* **1.**(*negozio*) herbalist shop

2. (*disciplina*) herbal medicine

erboso, -a [er·'bo:·so] *agg* (*d'erba*) grassy; **tappeto** [*o* **manto**] ~ lawn

Ercolano [er·ko·'la:·no] *f* Herculaneum

erede [e·'rɛ:·de] *mf* heir

eredità [e·re·di·'ta] <-> *f* inheritance; **lasciare qc in** ~ to bequeath sth; **ricevere qc in** ~ to inherit sth

ereditare [e·re·di·'ta:·re] *vt* to inherit; ~ **qc da qu** to inherit sth from sb

ereditarietà [e·re·di·ta·rie·'ta] <-> *f* (*di malattia, titolo*) heritability

ereditario, -a [e·re·di·'ta:·rio] <-i, -ie> *agg* **1.** (*principe*) hereditary **2.** JUR (*bene, debiti, diritti*) inherited; **asse** ~ estate **3.** BIOL (*malattia, caratteri*) hereditary

ereditiera [e·re·di·'tiɛ:·ra] *f* heiress

eremita [e·re·'mi:·ta] <-i> *m* hermit

eremitaggio [e·re·mi·'tad·dʒo] <-ggi> *m* hermitage

eremo ['ɛ:·re·mo] *m* hermitage

eresia [e·re·'zi:·a] <-ie> *f* **1.** REL heresy **2.** (*assurdità*) nonsense

eressi [e·'rɛs·si] *1. pers sing pass rem di* **erigere**

eretico, -a [e·'rɛ:·ti·ko] <-ci, -che> **I.** *agg* REL heretical **II.** *m, f* **1.** REL heretic **2.** *fam* (*ateo*) atheist

eretto, -a [e·'rɛt·to] **I.** *pp di* **erigere II.** *agg* (*andatura, capo*) erect

erezione [e·ret·'tsio:·ne] *f* **1.** ARCH (*di edificio, monumento*) raising **2.** BIOL erection

ergastolano, -a [er·gas·to·'la:·no] *m, f prisoner serving a life sentence*

ergastolo [er·'gas·to·lo] *m* (*pena*) life sentence

ergersi ['ɛr·dʒer·si] <ergo, ersi, erto> *vr:* -**rsi** (*innalzarsi*) to rise; ~ **a qc** *fig* (*difensore, paladino*) to set oneself up as sth

ergo ['ɛr·go] *cong scherz* ergo

ergonomia [er·go·no·'mi:·a] <-ie> *f* ergonomics

ergonomico, -a [er·go·'nɔ:·mi·ko] <-ci, -che> *agg* (*sedile, impugnatura*) ergonomic

ergonomo, -a *m, f* ergonomist

eri ['ɛ:·ri] *2. pers sing imp di* **essere**[1]

erica ['ɛ:·ri·ka] <-che> *f* BOT heather

erigere [e·'ri:·dʒe·re] <erigo, eressi, eretto> **I.** *vt* **1.** ARCH (*edificio, città, monumento*) to build **2.** *fig* (*barriera, ostacolo*) to erect **II.** *vr:* -**rsi** to rise; -**rsi a qc** *fig* (*difensore, paladino*) to set oneself up as sth

eritema [e·ri·'tɛ:·ma] <-i> *m* erythema; ~ **solare** sunburn

ermafrodito [er·ma·fro·'di:·to] *m* hermaphrodite

ermellino [er·mel·'li:·no] *m* **1.** ZOO (*animale*) ermine **2.** (*pelliccia*) ermine

ermeneutica [er·me·'neu·ti·ka] <-che> *f* hermeneutics

ermetico, -a [er·'mɛ:·ti·ko] <-ci, -che> *agg* **1.** (*stagno*) hermetic **2.** LIT (*poesie, letteratura*) obscure **3.** *fig* (*persona, frase*) enigmatic

ernia ['ɛr·nia] <-ie> *f* MED hernia; ~ **al** [*o* **del**] **disco** slipped disc; ~ **inguinale** hernia of the groin

erniario, -a [er·'nia:·rio] <-i, -ie> *agg* (*strozzamento, sacco*) hernial; **cinto** ~ truss

ero ['ɛ:·ro] *1. pers sing imp di* **essere**[1]

erodere [e·'ro:·de·re] <irr> *vt a. fig* to erode

eroe, eroina [e·'rɔ:·e, e·ro·'i:·na] *m, f* hero

erogare [e·ro·'ga:·re] *vt* **1.** (*gas, luce, acqua*) to supply **2.** (*denaro*) to distribute

erogatore [e·ro·ga·'to:·re] *m* (*per subacqueo*) supply

erogatore, -trice *agg* (*ente, azienda*) distributor; **società -trice del gas** gas supply company

erogazione [e·ro·ga·'tsio:·ne] *f* **1.** (*di gas, luce, acqua*) supply **2.** (*di denaro*) distribution

eroico, -a [e·'rɔ:·i·ko] <-ci, -che> *agg* (*atto, impresa, avventura*) heroic

eroina[1] [e·ro·'i:·na] *f* heroine

eroina[2] [e·ro·'i:·na] *f* (*droga*) heroin

eroinomane [e·roi·'nɔ:·ma·ne] **I.** *mf* heroin addict **II.** *agg* (*persona*) addicted to heroin

eroismo [e·ro·'iz·mo] *m* (*qualità*) heroism

erompere [e·'rom·pe·re] <irr> *vi* (*gas*) to burst out; ~ **in qc** to break out into sth

eros ['ɛ:·ros] <-> *m* PSYCH (*erotismo*) eros

erosi *1. pers sing pass rem di* **erodere**

erosione [e·ro·'zio:·ne] *f a. fig* erosion

erosivo, -a [e·ro·'zi:·vo] *agg* (*azione, fenomeno*) erosive

eroso *pp di* **erodere**

erotico, -a [e·'rɔ:·ti·ko] <-ci, -che> *agg* erotic

erotismo [e·ro·'tiz·mo] *m* eroticism

erpice ['er·pi·tʃe] *m* AGR harrow

errante [er·'ran·te] *agg* (*cavaliere, ebreo*) wandering

errare [er·'ra:·re] *vi* **1.** (*sbagliare*) to make a mistake; **se non erro** if I'm not mistaken **2.** (*vagare*) to wander

errata corrige [er·'ra:·ta 'kɔr·ri·dʒe] <-> *m* TYP errata *pl*

errato, -a [er·'ra:·to] *agg* (*sbagliato: risposta, binario, indirizzo*) wrong

erroneità [er·ro·nei·'ta] <-> *f* (*di metodo, sentenza*) incorrectness

erroneo, -a [er·'rɔ:·ne·o] *agg* (*sbagliato: giudizio, scelta, definizione*) wrong

errore [er·'ro:·re] *m* error; ~ **di battitura** typo; ~ **di calcolo** miscalculation; ~ **d'ortografia** spelling mistake; **per** ~ by mistake

ersi ['er·si] *1. pers sing pass rem di* **ergere**

erta ['er·ta] *f* **stare all'**~ to be alert

erto ['er·to] *pp di* **ergere**

erudire [e·ru·'di:·re] <erudisco> *vt* **1.** (*educare: studenti*) to educate **2.** (*illuminare*) to enlighten

erudito, -a [e·ru·'di:·to] **I.** *agg* (*persona, commento*) scholarly **II.** *m, f* scholar

erudizione [e·ru·dit·'tsio:·ne] *f* (*cultura*) erudition

eruttare [e·rut·'ta:·re] *vt* to eject

eruttivo, -a [e·rut·'ti:·vo] *agg* GEOL eruptive; **rocce -e** eruptive rock

eruzione [e·rut·'tsio:·ne] *f* **1.** GEOL (*di vulcano*) eruption **2.** MED ~ **cutanea** rash

es. *abbr di* **esempio** e.g.

esacerbare [e·za·tʃer·'ba:·re] *vt poet* (*aggravare*) to exacerbate

esaedro [e·za·'ɛː·dro] *m* hexahedron

esagerare [e·za·dʒe·'ra:·re] **I.** *vt* to exaggerate **II.** *vi* to exaggerate; ~ **con qc** to go too far with sth; ~ **in qc** to overdo sth

esagerato, **-a** [e·za·dʒe·'ra:·to] **I.** *agg* (*richiesta, tassa, spesa*) excessive **II.** *m, f person who exaggerates*

esagerazione [e·za·dʒe·rat·'tsio:·ne] *f* **1.** (*forzatura*) exaggeration **2.** excessive amount

esagitato, **-a** [e·za·dʒi·'ta:·to] *agg* (*persona, reazione*) frantic

esagonale [e·za·go·'na:·le] *agg* (*forma*) hexagonal

esagono [e·'za:·go·no] *m* hexagon

esalare [e·za·'la:·re] **I.** *vt avere* (*respiro*) to exhale; (*profumo*) to give off **II.** *vi essere* to be given off

esalazione [e·za·lat·'tsio:·ne] *f* emission

esaltare [e·zal·'ta:·re] **I.** *vt* **1.** (*infervorare: folla*) to stir up **2.** (*evidenziare: pregio, difetto*) to bring out **II.** *vr:* **-rsi** (*entusiasmarsi*) to get excited

esaltato, **-a** [e·zal·'ta:·to] **I.** *agg* (*discorso, persona*) excited **II.** *m, f* (*fanatico*) hothead

esame [e·'za:·me] *m* **1.** (*nell'insegnamento*) exam; ~ **orale** oral exam; ~ **scritto** written exam; ~ **di guida** driving test; ~ **di laurea** finals; **-i di maturità** school exit exam; **dare un** ~ to take an exam; **passare un** ~ to pass an exam **2.** MED examination; ~ **del sangue** blood test

esametro [e·'za:·met·ro] *m* hexameter

esaminando, **-a** [e·za·mi·'nan·do] *m, f* candidate

esaminare [e·za·mi·'na:·re] *vt* **1.** (*studenti*) to test **2.** (*analizzare: situazione, cause*) to study **3.** MED to examine **4.** JUR (*testimone*) to question

esaminatore, **-trice** [e·za·mi·na·'to:·re] **I.** *agg* **commissione -trice** board of examiners **II.** *m, f* examiner

esangue [e·'zaŋ·gue] *agg* **1.** (*pallido: volto*) pallid **2.** MED (*dissanguato: corpo*) bloodless

esanime [e·'za:·ni·me] *agg* lifeless

esasperante [e·zas·pe·'ran·te] *agg* (*attesa, lentezza, timidezza*) infuriating

esasperare [e·zas·pe·'ra:·re] **I.** *vt* **1.** (*stressare: persona*) to exasperate **2.** (*aggravare: pena, sofferenza*) to aggravate **II.** *vr:* **-rsi** (*arrabbiarsi*) to become exasperated

esasperazione [e·zas·pe·rat·'tsio:·ne] *f* (*irritazione*) exasperation; **portare qu all'**~ to drive sb crazy

esattezza [e·zat·'tet·tsa] *f* **1.** (*di calcolo, metodo, risposta*) accuracy **2.** (*precisione: di descrizione*) precision

esatto [e·'zat·to] **I.** *pp di* **esigere II.** *agg* **1.** (*corretto: calcolo, risposta*) correct

2. (*preciso: descrizione*) precise

esattore, **-trice** [e·zat·'to:·re] *m, f* (*di crediti*) collector

esattoria [e·zat·to·'ri:·a] <-ie> *f* (tax) collector's office

esattrice *f v.* **esattore**

esaudire [e·zau·'di:·re] <esaudisco> *vt* (*desiderio, richiesta*) to fulfill

esauriente [e·zau·ri·'ɛn·te] *agg* (*spiegazione, chiarimento*) thorough

esaurimento [e·zau·ri·'men·to] *m* **1.** MED exhaustion; ~ **nervoso** nervous exhaustion **2.** (*consumo*) depletion; **fino ad** ~ **della merce** while stocks last

esaurire [e·zau·'ri:·re] <esaurisco> **I.** *vt* (*finire: merce*) to sell off **II.** *vr:* **-rsi 1.** (*finire: sorgente, miniera*) to be used up **2.** MED (*indebolirsi*) to become exhausted

esaurito, **-a** [e·zau·'ri:·to] *agg* **1.** (*libri, merce*) out of stock; (*biglietti, posti*) sold out; **far registrare il tutto** ~ to sell out **2.** (*miniera*) worked out; (*sorgente*) dry **3.** MED (*indebolito*) exhausted

esaustivo, **-a** [e·zau·'sti:·vo] *agg* (*completo: articolo, guida*) exhaustive

esausto, **-a** [e·'za:us·to] *agg* (*sfinito*) exhausted

esautorare [e·zau·to·'ra:·re] *vt* (*governo, Parlamento, potere*) to deprive of authority

esca ['es·ka] <esche> *f* (*per pescare*) bait

escandescenza [es·kan·deʃ·'ʃɛn·tsa] *f* **dare in -e** to fly into a rage

escavatore, **-trice** [es·ka·va·'to:·re] *m, f* (*macchina*) digger

escavazione [es·ka·vat·'tsio:·ne] *f* **1.** (*di pozzo*) excavation **2.** (*di marmo*) mining

eschimese [es·ki·'me:·se] **I.** *agg* (*lingua, popolazione*) Eskimo **II.** *mf* Eskimo

eschimo ['es·ki·mo] *m v.* **eskimo**

esclamare [es·kla·'ma:·re] *vt* to exclaim

esclamativo, **-a** [es·kla·ma·'ti:·vo] *agg* (*frase, pronome*) exclamatory; **punto** ~ exclamation mark

esclamazione [es·kla·mat·'tsio:·ne] *f* exclamation

escludere [es·'klu:·de·re] <escludo, esclusi, escluso> *vt* **1.** (*eliminare: da gara, concorso*) to eliminate; (*da lista*) to exclude **2.** (*dubitare*) to rule out **3.** (*eccettuare*) to exclude

esclusione [es·klu·'zio:·ne] *f* exclusion; **a** ~ **di** apart from; **andare per** ~ to work by process of elimination

esclusiva [es·klu·'zi:·va] *f* (*diritti*) exclusive right; **dare l'**~ **a qu** (*di intervista*) to grant sb an exclusive (interview); (*di prodotto*) to grant sb exclusive rights; **in** ~ (*intervista*) exclusive; (*prodotto*) exclusively

esclusivamente [es·klu·zi·va·'men·te] *avv* exclusively

esclusivista [es·klu·zi·'vis·ta] <-i *m*, -e *f*> *mf* COM exclusive distributor

esclusività [es·klu·zi·vi·'ta] <-> *f* **1.** (*per pochi*) exclusivity **2.** COM (*diritti*) exclusiveness

esclusivo, -a [es·klu·'zi:·vo] *agg* exclusive

escluso, -a [es·'klu:·zo] I. *pp di* **escludere** II. *agg* 1. (*eccetto*) excluded; **-i i presenti** present company excluded; **fino al 24 maggio ~** up to and excluding May 24 2. (*impossibile*) impossible; **non è ~ che ...** +*conj* it's not impossible that ... III. *m, f* unsuccessful candidate

esco ['ɛs·ko] *1. pers sing pr di* **uscire**

escogitare [es·ko·dʒi·'ta:·re] *vt* (*piano, metodo, sistema*) to come up with

escoriazione [es·ko·ri·at·'tsio:·ne] *f* graze

escrementi [es·kre·'men·ti] *mpl* (*feci*) excrement

escrescenza [es·kreʃ·'ʃɛn·tsa] *f* MED (*rigonfiamento*) outgrowth

escrezione [es·kret·'tsio:·ne] *f* MED (*espulsione*) excretion

escursione [es·kur·'sio:·ne] *f* 1. (*gita: in auto, battello*) trip; (*a piedi*) walk; **fare un'~ a** to go on a trip to 2. METEO (*differenza*) range; **~ termica** temperature range

escursionista [es·kur·sio·'nis·ta] <-i *m*, -e *f*> *mf* (*in auto, battello*) excursionist; (*a piedi*) walker

esecrabile [e·ze·'kra:·bi·le] *agg form* (*atto, comportamento*) disgraceful

esecrare [e·ze·'kra:·re] *vt* (*atto, comportamento*) to abhor

esecutivo [e·ze·ku·'ti:·vo] *m* (*comitato*) executive

esecutivo, -a *agg* 1. JUR (*potere*) executive 2. (*progetto, fase*) executive

esecutore, -trice [e·ze·ku·'to:·re] *m, f* JUR (*di delitto*) perpetrator; **~ testamentario** executor of a will 2. MUS performer

esecuzione [e·ze·ku·'tsio:·ne] *f* 1. realizzazione: di lavoro, performance 2. JUR (*di testamento*) execution 3. (*uccisione*) killing 4. MUS interpretazione, performance, un'ottima ~ del pianista cileno

eseguire [e·ze·'gui:·re] *vt* 1. (*fare: operazione, manovra*) to perform; (**comando**) **esegui** COMPUT run (command) 2. (*realizzare: lavoro*) to perform 3. (*effettuare: pagamento*) to make 4. (*mettere in atto: ordine*) to carry out 5. JUR (*sentenza*) to implement 6. MUS (*brano*) to perform

esempio [e·'zɛm·pio] <-i> *m* example; **dare il buon/cattivo ~** to give a good/bad example; **fare un ~** to give an example; **seguire l'~ di qu** to follow sb's example; **per ~** for example; **che ti serva d'~!** let that be a lesson for you!

esemplare [e·zem·'pla:·re] I. *agg* (*comportamento, punizione, persona*) exemplary II. *m* 1. (*copia*) copy 2. (*campione*) specimen 3. (*esempio*) model

esemplificare [e·zem·pli·fi·'ka:·re] *vt* (*processo, metodo*) to exemplify

esentare [e·zen·'ta:·re] *vt* **~ qu da qc** (*tasse, servizio militare*) to exempt sb from sth

esentasse [e·zen·'tas·se] <inv> *agg* (*credito, incentivo, utile*) tax-exempt

esente [e·'zɛn·te] *agg* exempt; **essere ~ da qc** (*da tasse*) to be exempt from sth; (*da difetti, colpe*) to be free of sth

esequie [e·'zɛ:·kui·e] *f form* funeral *sing*

esercente [e·zer·'tʃɛn·te] *mf* (*operatore*) storekeeper

esercitare [e·zer·tʃi·'ta:·re] I. *vt* 1. (*professione*) to practice 2. (*corpo, memoria*) to train 3. (*potere, diritto*) to exercise II. *vr* **-rsi** (**in qc**) to practice (sth)

esercitazione [e·zer·tʃi·ta·'tsio:·ne] *f* 1. (*allenamento*) training 2. (*lezione*) exercise

esercito [e·'zɛr·tʃi·to] *m* army

esercizio [e·zer·'tʃi·tsio] <-i> *m* 1. (*esercitazione*) exercise 2. (*pratica*) practice; **essere fuori ~** to be out of practice 3. (*sport*) practice; **fare ~** to train 4. (*albergo, bar*) business 5. COM (*gestione*) (fiscal) year

esibire [e·zi·'bi:·re] <esibisco> I. *vt* 1. (*passaporto, documento*) to show 2. (*bravura*) to demonstrate 3. (*nudità*) to display II. *vr:* **-rsi** 1. (*attore, musicista*) to perform; **~ in pubblico** to perform in public 2. (*mettersi in mostra*) to show off

esibizione [e·zi·bi·'tsio:·ne] *f* 1. THEAT performance 2. SPORT (*di squadre, atleti*) exhibition 3. (*di documenti*) presentation 4. (*sfoggio*) display 5. (*mostra*) exhibition

esibizionismo [e·zi·bi·tsio·'niz·mo] *m* 1. (*protagonismo*) exhibitionism 2. (*sessuale*) indecent exposure

esibizionista [e·zi·bi·tsio·'nis·ta] <-i *m*, -e *f*> *mf* 1. (*megalomane*) exhibitionist 2. (*sessuale*) exhibitionist, flasher *inf*

esigei [e·zi·'dʒe:·i] *1. pers sing pass rem di* **esigere**

esigente [e·zi·'dʒɛn·te] *agg* (*persona, cliente, pubblico*) demanding

esigenza [e·zi·'dʒɛn·tsa] *f* (*bisogno*) requirement

esigere [e·'zi:·dʒe·re] <esigo, esigei *o* esigetti, esatto> *vt* 1. (*richiedere*) to demand 2. (*riscuotere: somma*) to collect 3. *fig* (*necessitare: concentrazione, attenzione*) to require

esiguo, -a [e·'zi:·guo] *agg* (*piccolo*) meager

esilarante [e·zi·la·'ran·te] *agg* (*comicità, racconto, attore*) hilarious; **gas ~** laughing gas

esile ['ɛ:·zi·le] *agg* 1. (*persona, gambe, arbusto*) slender 2. (*tenue: speranza*) slender

esiliare [e·zi·'lia:·re] *vt* (*criminale, detenuto politico*) to exile

esiliato, -a [e·zi·'lia:·to] I. *agg* (*criminale, detenuto politico*) exiled II. *m, f* exile

esilio [e·'zi:·lio] <-i> *m* POL exile

esimere [e·'zi:·me·re] <esimo, *mancano pass rem e pp*> *vt* **~ qu da qc** to exempt sb of sth

esimio, -a [e·'zi:·mio] <-i, -ie> *agg* (*insigne*) eminent; (*nelle lettere*) dear

esistei [e·zis·'te:·i] *1. pers sing pass rem di* **esistere**

esistente [e·zis·'tɛn·te] *agg* (*persona, pro-*

dotto) existing

esistenza [e·zis·'tɛn·tsa] *f* **1.** (*vita*) life **2.** (*presenza*) existence

esistenziale [e·zis·ten·'tsia:·le] *agg* (*problemi, angoscia, disagio*) existential

esistere [e·'zis·te·re] <esisto, esistei *o* esistetti, esistito> *vi essere* **1.** (*essere*) to exist **2.** (*esserci*) to exist; **esistono diversi tipi di carta** there are various types of paper

esitare [e·zi·'ta:·re] *vi* to hesitate; ~ **a fare qc** to be hesitant about doing sth

esitazione [e·zi·ta·'tsio:·ne] *f* hesitation

esito ['ɛ:·zi·to] *m* (*risultato*) outcome

eskimo ['ɛs·ki·mo] <-> *m* parka

esodo ['ɛ:·zo·do] *m* REL, LIT exodus

esofago [e·'zɔ:·fa·go] <-gi> *m* esophagus

esogeno, -a [e·'zɔ:·dʒe·no] *agg* MED (*agente*) exogenous

esonerare [e·zo·ne·'ra:·re] *vt* to exonerate; ~ **qu da qc** to exonerate sb of sth

esonero [e·'zɔ:·ne·ro] *m* exemption; ~ **da qc** exemption from sth

esorbitante [e·zor·bi·'tan·te] *agg* (*prezzo, cifre*) exorbitant

esorcismo [e·zor·'tʃiz·mo] *m* exorcism

esorcista [e·zor·'tʃis·ta] <-i *m*, -e *f*> *mf* exorcist

esorcizzare [e·zor·tʃid·'dza:·re] *vt* **1.** REL to exorcize **2.** (*scacciare*) to drive away

esordiente [e·zor·'diɛn·te] **I.** *agg* (*cantante, attore, squadra, atleta*) budding **II.** *mf* beginner

esordio [e·'zɔr·dio] <-i> *m* **1.** (*inizio*) beginning **2.** THEAT, SPORT debut

esordire [e·zor·'di:·re] <esordisco> *vi* **1.** (*iniziare*) to start off **2.** SPORT, THEAT to make one's debut

esortare [e·zor·'ta:·re] *vt* to exhort; ~ **qu a fare qc** to urge sb to do sth

esortazione [e·zor·ta·'tsio:·ne] *f* exhortation

esoso, -a [e·'zɔ:·zo] *agg* (*eccessivo: prezzo, richiesta*) exorbitant

esoterico, -a [e·zo·'tɛ:·ri·ko] <-ci, -che> *agg* (*dottrina, disciplina, pratica*) esoteric

esotico, -a [e·'zɔ:·ti·ko] <-ci, -che> *agg* (*luogo, frutto*) exotic

espandere [es·'pan·de·re] <espando, espansi *o* espandetti, espanso> **I.** *vt* (*attività, rete, confini, orizzonti*) to expand **II.** *vr:* **-rsi 1.** (*ingrandirsi: macchia*) to spread **2.** (*aumentare: volume*) to expand **3.** *fig* (*diffondersi: notizia*) to spread **4.** COM (*azienda*) to grow

espandibile [es·pan·'di:·bi·le] *agg* **1.** COMPUT (*aumentabile: memoria*) expandable **2.** PHYS (*volume*) expansible

espansione [es·pan·'sio:·ne] *f* **1.** (*aumento di volume*) expansion **2.** COMPUT (*ingrandimento*) expansion **3.** (*diffusione*) spread

espansivo, -a [es·pan·'si:·vo] *agg* (*affettuoso*) affectionate

espanso, -a [es·'pan·so] **I.** *pp di* **espandere** **II.** *agg* (*polistirolo, resina, argilla*) expanded

espatriare [es·pa·tri·'a:·re] *vi essere* to emigrate

espatrio [es·'pa:·trio] <-i> *m* (*emigrazione*) authorization to travel abroad

espediente [es·pe·'diɛn·te] *m* (*accorgimento*) dodge

espellere [es·'pɛl·le·re] <espello, espulsi, espulso> *vt* **1.** (*allievo*) to expel; (*giocatore*) to send off; (*immigrato*) to deport **2.** MED (*tossine*) to expel

esperanto [es·pe·'ran·to] *m* LING Esperanto

esperienza [es·pe·'riɛn·tsa] *f* **1.** (*gener*) experience; **per** ~ from experience; **senza** ~ inexperienced **2.** SCIENT (*esperimento*) experiment

esperimento [es·pe·ri·'men·to] *m* experiment

esperto, -a [es·'pɛr·to] **I.** *agg* **1.** (*pratico*) experienced **2.** (*conoscitore*) expert **3.** (*abile: mani*) capable **II.** *m, f* expert

espiare [es·pi·'a:·re] *vt* **1.** JUR (*pena*) to serve **2.** REL (*peccato*) to atone for

espiatorio, -a [es·pia·'tɔ:·rio] <-i, -ie> *agg* **capro** ~ *fig* scapegoat

espiazione [es·pia·'tsio:·ne] *f* **1.** JUR (*di pena*) serving **2.** REL (*di peccato*) expiation

espirare [es·pi·'ra:·re] *vt* to breathe out

esplicare [es·pli·'ka:·re] *vt* (*esercitare: attività, funzione*) to perform

esplicito, -a [es·'pli:·tʃi·to] *agg* (*chiaro: parole, ordine*) explicit

esplodere [es·'plɔ:·de·re] <esplodo, esplosi, esploso> **I.** *vi essere o avere* **1.** (*bomba, dinamite*) to explode **2.** *fig* (*applauso, scandalo*) to break out; (*temporale*) to break **II.** *vt avere* (*colpo*) to fire

esplorare [es·plo·'ra:·re] *vt* **1.** (*scoprire: terra, giungla, mare*) to explore **2.** *fig* (*indagare: possibilità, scenario*) to investigate **3.** MED (*organo*) to explore

esploratore, -trice *m, f* explorer

esplorazione [es·plo·ra·'tsio:·ne] *f* **1.** (*di terra, giungla, mare*) exploration **2.** MED (*di organo*) exploration

esplosi [es·'plɔ:·zi] *1. pers sing pass rem di* **esplodere**

esplosione [es·plo·'zio:·ne] *f* **1.** (*di mina, bomba*) explosion **2.** *fig* (*di rabbia*) outburst

esplosivo [es·plo·'zi:·vo] *m* explosive

esplosivo, -a *agg* **1.** (*sostanza, miscela*) explosive **2.** *fig* (*intervista, scandalo*) dramatic

esploso [es·'plɔ:·zo] *pp di* **esplodere**

esponente [es·po·'nɛn·te] **I.** *mf* (*rappresentante: di partito, governo*) representative **II.** *m* MAT exponent

esponenziale [es·po·nen·'tsia:·le] MAT **I.** *agg* **1.** MAT (*curva, funzione*) exponential **2.** *fig* (*sviluppo, crescita*) dramatic **II.** *f* MAT exponential

esporre [es·'por·re] <irr> **I.** *vt* **1.** (*esibire: opera d'arte, merce*) to exhibit **2.** (*pelle*) to expose **3.** (*a rischio*) to expose **4.** (*spiegare*) to set out **II.** *vr:* **-rsi 1.** (*al sole*) to expose oneself **2.** (*a rischio*) to expose oneself **3.** (*compromettersi*) to leave oneself open

esportare [es·por·'ta:·re] *vt* **1.** COM (*prodotto*) to export **2.** COMPUT to export

esportatore, -trice [es·por·ta·'to:·re] **I.** *m, f* exporter **II.** *agg* (*azienda, paese*) exporting

esportazione [es·por·ta·'tsio:·ne] *f* export

esposi *1. pers sing pass rem di* **esporre**

esposimetro [es·po·'zi:·met·ro] *m* FOTO light meter

esposizione [es·po·zi·'tsio:·ne] *f* **1.** (*di opere d'arte*) exhibition; (*di prodotti*) display; **in ~** on display **2.** (*a luce, sole, vento*) exposure **3.** FOTO (*di pellicola*) exposure **4.** (*di edifici, terreni*) orientation **5.** (*narrazione: di fatto, brano*) presentation

esposto, -a [es·'pos·to] **I.** *pp di* **esporre** **II.** *agg* **1.** (*opera d'arte*) on display **2.** (*edificio, terreno*) **essere ~ a nord/sud** to face north/south

espressamente [es·pres·sa·'men·te] *avv* expressly

espressi [es·'prɛs·si] *1. pers sing pass rem di* **esprimere**

espressione [es·pres·'sio:·ne] *f* **1.** (*aspetto: di occhi, volto*) expression **2.** (*manifestazione*) expression **3.** LING (*termine, frase*) expression

espressionismo [es·pres·sio·'niz·mo] *m* ART, LIT, MUS expressionism

espressionista [es·pres·sio·'nis·ta] <-i *m*, -e *f*> **I.** *agg* (*pittore, tecnica, opera*) expressionist **II.** *mf* expressionist

espressionistico, -a [es·pres·sio·'nis·ti·ko] <-ci, -che> *agg* (*tecnica, opera*) expressionist

espressivo, -a [es·pres·'si:·vo] *agg* expressive

espresso [es·'prɛs·so] *m* **1.** (*caffè*) espresso **2.** FERR express (train) **3.** (*lettera*) express

espresso, -a **I.** *pp di* **esprimere** **II.** *agg* **1.** (*consenso*) express **2.** (*lettera, treno*) express **3. caffè ~** espresso

esprimere [es·'pri:·me·re] <esprimo, espressi, espresso> **I.** *vt* (*approvazione, giudizio, pensiero*) to express **II.** *vr:* **-rsi** (*parlare, manifestarsi*) to express oneself

espropriare [es·pro·'pria:·re] *vt* (*terreno*) to expropriate

esproprio [es·'prɔ:·pio] <-i> *m* (*di terreno*) expropriation

espugnare [es·puɲ·'ɲa:·re] *vt* MIL (*fortezza, città*) to take

espulsi [es·'pul·si] *1. pers sing pass rem di* **espellere**

espulsione [es·pul·'sio:·ne] *f* **1.** (*di allievo, socio*) expulsion; (*di giocatore*) sending off; (*di immigrato*) deportation **2.** MED (*di tossine, feci*) expulsion

espulso [es·'pul·so] *pp di* **espellere**

esquimese [es·kui·'me:·se] *mf v.* **eschimese**

essa ['es·sa] *pron 3. pers sing f* **1.** (*soggetto: persona*) she; (*animale, cosa*) it **2.** (*complemento: persona*) her; (*animale, cosa*) it

essai [e·'sɛ] <-> *m* **cinema d'~** arthouse cinema

esse ['es·se] *pron 3. pers pl f* **1.** (*soggetto*) they **2.** (*complemento*) them

essenza [es·'sɛn·tsa] *f* **1.** (*di discorso, problema*) essence **2.** CHEM essence; **~ di rose** rose oil

essenziale [es·sen·'tsia:·le] **I.** *agg* **1.** (*fondamentale: elemento, fattore*) essential **2.** (*scarno: stile, arredamento*) minimalist **3.** CHEM essential; **oli -i** essential oils **II.** *m* **l'~** the basics

essenzialmente [es·sen·tsial·'men·te] *avv* (*fondamentalmente*) essentially

essere¹ ['ɛs·se·re] <sono, fui, stato> *vi essere* **1.** (*gener*) to be; **c'è** there is; **ci sono** there are; **c'è odore di ...** there's a smell of ...; **c'era una volta ...** once upon a time there was ...; **c'eri anche tu?** were you there too?; **ci siamo!** (*siamo arrivati*) we're here!; *fig* (*è arrivato il momento*) the time has come; **~ di qu** to belong to sb; **è Natale** it's Christmas; **sono loro** it's them; **sono ore che t'aspetto** I've been waiting for you for hours; **chi è?** (*alla porta*) who is it?; **che ora è?, che ore sono?** what's the time?; **come sarebbe a dire?** what do you mean? **2.** (*trovarsi*) to be **3.** *fam* (*costare*) to cost; **quant'è?** *fam* (*al bar*) how much is it? **4.** (*provenire*) to be; **sono di Padova** I'm from Padua

essere² *m* **1.** (*esistenza*) existence **2.** (*creatura*) being; **gli -i viventi** living beings **3.** *fam* (*persona*) person

essi ['es·si] *pron 3. pers pl m* **1.** (*soggetto*) they **2.** (*complemento*) them

essiccare [es·sik·'ka:·re] **I.** *vt* **1.** (*palude*) to drain **2.** (*foglie, frutta, carne*) to dry **II.** *vr:* **-rsi** (*frutta, carne, legno*) to dry up

esso ['es·so] *pron 3. pers sing m* **1.** (*soggetto: persona*) he; (*animale, cosa*) it **2.** (*complemento: persona*) him; (*animale, cosa*) it

est [ɛst] <-> *m* east; **ad ~** east; **ad ~ di** (to the) east of; **verso ~** eastward

estasi ['ɛs·ta·zi] <-> *f* ecstasy; **andare in ~** to go into raptures

estasiare [es·ta·'zia:·re] **I.** *vt* to thrill **II.** *vr:* **-rsi** to go into raptures

estate [es·'ta:·te] *f* summer; **in** [*o* d'] **~** in summer

estatico, -a [es·'ta:·ti·ko] <-ci, -che> *agg* (*rapito: sguardo, epressione*) ecstatic

estendere [es·'tɛn·de·re] <irr> **I.** *vt* **1.** (*allungare: braccia, gambe*) to stretch **2.** *fig* (*ampliare: attività, struttura*) to expand **3.** (*comunicare*) to extend; **~ un invito a qu** to extend an invitation to sb **II.** *vr:* **-rsi** (*pianura, mare*) to extend

estensione [es·ten·'sio:·ne] *f* **1.** (*superficie*) extent **2.** (*di servizio, garanzia*) extension **3.** (*di arto*) stretching

estensivo, -a [es·ten·'si:·vo] *agg* (*allevamento, coltura*) extensive

estenuante [es·te·nu·'an·te] *agg* (*attesa, lavoro, negoziati*) lengthy

estenuare [es·te·nu·'a:·re] **I.** *vt* (*attesa, fatica*) to exhaust **II.** *vr:* **-rsi** to become exhausted

esteriore [es·te·'rio:·re] *agg* (*aspetto, qualità,*

doti) external

esternare [es·ter·'naː·re] *vt* (*manifestare: sentimento, disagio*) to display

esterno [es·'tɛr·no] *m* 1. (*di contenitore*) outside 2. (*di edificio*) exterior 3. THEAT outdoor scene

esterno, -a I. *agg* 1. (*fuori: lato*) outer; **per uso ~** (*farmaco*) for external use 2. (*fuori casa: parete, porta, pavimentazione*) outdoor; (*da fuori: nemico, pericolo*) external II. *m, f* (*di collegio*) day student

estero ['ɛs·te·ro] *m* **all'~** abroad; **andare all'~** to go abroad

estero, -a *agg* (*paese, politica, valuta*) foreign; **ministero degli affari -i** ministry of foreign affairs; **commercio ~** foreign trade

esterrefatto, -a [es·ter·re·'fat·to] *agg* (*sbalordito*) astonished

estesi *1. pers sing pass rem di* **estendere**

esteso, -a [es·'teː·so] I. *pp di* **estendere** II. *agg* 1. (*terreno, superficie*) extensive 2. (*testo*) full; **per ~** in full

esteta [es·'tɛː·ta] <-i *m*, -e *f*> *mf* aesthete

estetica [es·'tɛː·ti·ka] <-che> *f* 1. (*scienza*) aesthetics 2. (*bellezza*) beauty

estetico, -a [es·'tɛː·ti·ko] <-ci, -che> *agg* 1. (*aspetto, gusto*) aesthetic 2. (*medicina, chirurgia, trattamento, centro*) cosmetic

estetista [es·te·'tis·ta] <-i *m*, -e *f*> *mf* aesthetician

estinguere [es·'tiŋ·gue·re] <estinguo, estinsi, estinto> I. *vt* 1. (*incendio*) to put out 2. (*debito*) to settle II. *vr:* -**rsi** 1. (*incendio*) to go out 2. (*debito, diritto*) to expire; (*rapporto di lavoro*) to be terminated 3. (*specie*) to become extinct

estinto, -a [es·'tin·to] I. *agg* 1. (*vulcano*) extinct; (*incendio*) extinguished 2. (*diritto*) expired; (*debito*) settled; (*rapporto di lavoro*) terminated II. *m, f* (*defunto*) deceased

estintore [es·tin·'toː·re] *m* (fire) extinguisher

estinzione [es·tin·'tsioː·ne] *f* 1. BIOL (*di specie*) extinction 2. (*di incendio*) extinction 3. (*di debito*) settlement; (*di rapporto*) termination

estirpare [es·tir·'paː·re] *vt* 1. (*sradicare: erbacce*) to uproot 2. MED (*dente*) to pull out; (*tumore*) to remove 3. *fig* (*debellare: odio, corruzione*) to eradicate

estivo, -a [es·'tiː·vo] *agg* (*giornata, caldo, vacanze, abito*) summer

estone ['ɛs·to·ne] I. *agg* (*cittadino, città*) Estonian II. *mf* Estonian

Estonia [es·'tɔː·nia] *f* Estonia

estorcere [es·'tɔr·tʃe·re] <estorco, estorsi, estorto> *vt* **~ qc a qu** (*denaro*) to extort sth from sb; (*confessione*) to wring sth from sb

estorsione [es·tor·'sioː·ne] *f* extortion

estradizione [es·tra·dit·'tsioː·ne] *f* (*di imputato, criminale*) extradition

estraneità [es·tra·nei·'ta] <-> *f* (*non partecipazione*) non-involvement

estraneo, -a [es·'traː·neo] <-ei, -ee> I. *agg* 1. (*non conosciuto*) unknown 2. (*esterno*) external 3. (*non coinvolto*) uninvolved II. *m, f* 1. (*sconosciuto*) stranger 2. ADM unauthorized person; **'vietato l'ingresso agli -i'** 'authorized individuals only'

estraniare [es·tra·'niaː·re] I. *vt* (*allontanare*) to alienate; **~ qu da qc** to alienate sb from sth II. *vr* -**rsi da qc** (*mondo, realtà, famiglia*) to become alienated from sth

estrapolazione [es·tra·po·lat·'tsioː·ne] *f* MAT extrapolation

estrarre [es·'trar·re] <irr> *vt* 1. (*tirare fuori*) to pull out; **~ qc a sorte** to draw sth out of a hat 2. (*dente, carbone*) to extract 3. MAT (*radice*) to extract

estratto [es·'trat·to] *m* 1. CULIN (*di carne, pomodori*) extract 2. COM statement; **~ conto** bank statement 3. ADM certificate; **~ di nascita** birth certificate

estrazione [es·trat·'tsioː·ne] *f* 1. (*gener*) extraction 2. (*sorteggio*) draw 3. *fig* (*origine*) origins *pl*

estremismo [es·tre·'miz·mo] *m* extremism

estremista [es·tre·'mis·ta] <-i *m*, -e *f*> *mf* extremist

estremistico, -a [es·tre·'mis·ti·ko] <-ci, -che> *agg* (*organizzazione, dottrina*) extremist

estremità [es·tre·mi·'ta] <-> *f* 1. (*parte: di bastone, tavolo*) end 2. *pl* (*mani e piedi*) extremities *pl*

estremo [es·'trɛː·mo] *m* 1. (*punto estremo*) extreme 2. *pl, fig* extremes *pl* 3. *pl* ADM particulars *pl*

estremo, -a *agg* extreme; **l'Estremo Oriente** GEOG the Far East; **a mali -i, -i rimedi** *prov* desperate times call for desperate measures; **l'-a destra/sinistra** the extreme right/left

estrinsecare [es·trin·se·'kaː·re] I. *vt* (*dubbio, pensiero*) to express II. *vr:* -**rsi** to express oneself

estro ['ɛs·tro] *m* (*ispirazione*) inspiration; **~ creativo** creativity

estrogeno [es·'trɔː·dʒe·no] *m* estrogen

estroso, -a [es·'troː·so] *agg* 1. (*originale: abiti, stile, libro*) creative 2. (*capriccioso: persona, carattere*) whimsical

estroverso, -a [es·tro·'vɛr·so] I. *agg* (*persona, carattere*) extrovert II. *m, f* extrovert

estuario [es·tu·'aːr·io] <-i> *m* estuary

esuberante [e·zu·be·'ran·te] *agg* 1. (*sovrabbondante: raccolto, scorte*) overabundant 2. (*vivace: persona, carattere*) exuberant

esuberanza [e·zu·be·'ran·tsa] *f* 1. (*sovrabbondanza: di capitale, scorte*) overabundance 2. (*vivacità: di persona, temperamento*) exuberance

esule ['ɛː·zu·le] *mf* exile

esultare [e·zul·'taː·re] *vi* to rejoice; **~ per qc** to rejoice over sth

età [e·'ta] <-> *f* 1. (*anni*) age; **maggiore ~** majority 2. (*periodo*) age; **l'~ del bronzo/ferro** the bronze/iron age

etc. *abbr di* **eccetera** etc.

etere ['ɛː·te·re] *m* ether
eternit® [e·ter·'nit/'ɛː·ter·nit] <-> *m* asbestos cement
eternità [e·ter·ni·'ta] <-> *f a fig* eternity
eterno [e·'tɛr·no] *m* eternity; **in** ~ forever
eterno, -a *agg* **1.** (*illimitato*) eternal **2.** (*interminabile: attesa*) interminable **3.** *inf* (*perenne: ragazzina, giovanotto*) eternal
etero ['ɛ·te·ro] <inv> *agg v.* **eterosessuale**
eterogeneo, -a [e·te·ro·'dʒɛː·neo] *agg* (*gruppo, pubblico, risorse*) heterogeneous
eterosessuale [e·te·ro·ses·su·'aː·le] **I.** *agg* heterosexual **II.** *mf* heterosexual
etica ['ɛː·ti·ka] <-che> *f* (*scienza, morale*) ethics; ~ **professionale** professional ethics
etichetta [e·ti·'ket·ta] *f* **1.** COM (*su prodotto*) label; ~ **del prezzo** price tag **2.** (*cerimoniale*) etiquette
etico, -a ['ɛː·ti·ko] <-ci, -che> *agg* (*morale: codice, questione, problema*) ethical
etilato, -a [e·ti·'laː·to] *agg* **benzina -a** ethylbenzine
etilico, -a [e·'tiː·li·ko] <-ci, -che> *agg* **alcool** ~ ethyl alcohol
etilismo [e·ti·'liz·mo] *m* (*alcolismo*) alcoholism
etilometro [e·ti·'lɔː·me·tro] *m* drunkometer
etilotest [e·ti·lo·'tɛst] <-> *m* Breathalyzer; **sottoporsi all'**~ to take a Breathalyzer test
etimologia [e·ti·mo·lo·'dʒiː·a] <-gie> *f* (*etimo: di vocabolo*) etymology
etimologico, -a [e·ti·mo·'lɔː·dʒi·ko] <-ci, -che> *agg* (*dizionario, radice*) etymological
Etna ['ɛt·na] *m* Etna
etnico, -a ['ɛt·ni·ko] <-ci, -che> *agg* ethnic
etnocidio [et·no·'tʃiː·dio] <-di> *m* ethnocide
etnologia [et·no·lo·'dʒiː·a] <-gie> *f* ethnology
etnologo, -a [et·'nɔː·lo·go] <-gi, -ghe> *m, f* ethnologist
etologia [e·to·lo·'dʒiː·a] <-gie> *f* ethology
etologo, -a [e·'tɔː·lo·go] <-gi, -ghe> *m, f* ethologist
ETR 500 *m abbr di* **Elettrotreno** FERR *Italian high-speed train*
etrusco, -a [e·'trus·ko] <-schi, -sche> **I.** *agg* (*tomba, vaso*) Etruscan **II.** *m, f* Etruscan
ettaedro [et·ta·'ɛː·dro] *m* heptahedron
ettaro ['ɛt·ta·ro] *m* hectare
etto ['ɛt·to] *m* one hundred grams
ettolitro [et·'tɔː·lit·ro] *m* hectoliter
eucalipto [eu·ka·'lip·to] *m* eucalyptus
eucarestia, eucaristia [eu·ka·res·'tiː·a, eu·ka·ris·'tiː·a] <-ie> *f* REL Eucharist
eufemismo [eu·fe·'miz·mo] *m* euphemism
eufemistico, -a [eu·fe·'mis·ti·ko] <-ci, -che> *agg* (*espressione, valore*) euphemistic
euforia [eu·fo·'riː·a] <-ie> *f* euphoria
euforico, -a [eu·'fɔː·ri·ko] <-ci, -che> *agg* euphoric
eunuco [eu·'nuː·ko] <-chi> *m* eunuch
eureka [eu·'rɛː·ka] *int* eureka
euro <-> *m* euro
eurobbligazioni [eu·rob·bli·ga·'tsioː·ni] *fpl*

FIN Eurobond
eurobond ['juə·rou·bɔnd/eu·ro·'bɔnd] <-> *m* FIN (*eurobbligazione*) Eurobond
euroccidentale [eu·rot·tʃi·den·'taː·le] *agg* (*poesia, cinematografia*) western European
eurocent <-> *m* (*moneta*) eurocent
eurocheque [eu·ro·'ʃɛk] <-> *m* Eurocheck
eurocity [eu·ro·'si·ti] <-> *m* FERR *European intercity train*
eurocomunismo [eu·ro·ko·mu·'niz·mo] *m* Eurocommunism
eurocomunista [eu·ro·ko·mu·'nis·ta] <-i *m*, -e *f*> **I.** *agg* (*politica, strategia*) Eurocommunist **II.** *mf* Eurocommunist
eurocrate [eu·'rɔː·kra·te] *mf* POL Eurocrat
eurodeputato, -a [eu·ro·de·pu·'taː·to] *m, f* POL MEP, *Member of the European Parliament*
eurodestra [ɛu·ro·'dɛs·tra] *f* POL European right
eurodivisa [eu·ro·di·'viː·za] *f* FIN European currency
eurodollaro [eu·ro·'dɔl·la·ro] *m* Eurodollar
eurofilo, -a [eu·'rɔ·fi·lo] *m, f* Europhile
Eurolandia [ɛu·ro·'lan·dia] *f iron* (*Europa unita*) Euroland
euromercato [eu·ro·mer·'kaː·to] *m* FIN Euro zone
euromissile [eu·ro·'mis·si·le] *m* Euromissile
euromoneta [eu·ro·mo·'neː·ta] *f* FIN (*eurodivisa*) European currency
euronight [eu·ro·'nait] <-> *m* FERR *European intercity night train*
Europa [eu·'rɔː·pa] *f* Europe
europarlamentare [eu·ro·par·la·men·'taː·re] *mf* MEP, *Member of the European Parliament*
europarlamento [eu·ro·par·la·'men·to] *m* (*Parlamento*) European Parliament
europeismo [eu·ro·pe·'iz·mo] *m* Europeanism
europeista [eu·ro·pe·'is·ta] <-i *m*, -e *f*> **I.** *mf* pro-European **II.** *agg* pro-European
europeistico, -a [eu·ro·pe·'is·ti·ko] <-ci, -che> *agg* pro-European
europeizzare [eu·ro·peid·'dzaː·re] *vt* to Europeanize
europeizzazione [eu·ro·peid·dza·'tsioː·ne] *f* Europeanization
europeo, -a [eu·ro·'pɛː·o] <-ei, -ee> **I.** *agg* European; **il mercato comune** ~ the European Common Market **II.** *m, f* European
Europol [ɛu·ro·'pɔl] *m acro di* **European Police** Europol
europoliziotto, -a [ɛu·ro·po·li·'tsiɔt·to] *m, f* (*agente dell'Europol*) Europol agent
euroseggio [eu·ro·'sɛd·dʒo] <-ggi> *m seat in the European Parliament*
eurosinistra [ɛu·ro·si·'nis·tra] *f* POL European left
eurosocialismo [eu·ro·so·tʃa·'liz·mo] *m* European socialism
Eurostar [ɛu·ro·'staːr] <-> *m* FERR Eurostar
eurotassa [eu·ro·'tas·sa] *f tax to ensure compliance with European budgetary require-*

ments
euroterrorismo [eu·ro·ter·ro·'riz·mo] *m* Euroterrorism
euroterrorista [eu·ro·ter·ro·'ris·ta] <-i *m*, -e *f*> *mf* Euroterrorist
eurovaluta [eu·ro·va·'lu:·ta] *f* European currency
eurovisione [eu·ro·vi·'zio:·ne] *f* Eurovision; **collegamento in** ~ Eurovision link
eutanasia [eu·ta·na·'zi:·a] <-ie> *f* euthanasia
E.V. *abbr di* **Vostra Eccellenza** Your Excellency
evacuare [e·va·ku·'a:·re] I. *vt* 1.(*città, territorio*) to evacuate 2.(*feci*) to evacuate II. *vi* 1.(*luogo*) to evacuate; ~ **da una città** to evacuate from a city 2.(*defecare*) to defecate
evacuazione [e·va·ku·a·'tsio:·ne] *f* 1.(*di territorio, piazza*) evacuation 2.(*di feci*) evacuation
evadere [e·'va:·de·re] <evado, evasi, evaso> I. *vi essere* (*scappare*) to escape; ~ **dalla prigione** to escape from prison II. *vt avere* 1. ADM (*pratica, corrispondenza*) to deal with 2. JUR ~ **le tasse** to evade taxes
evanescente [e·va·neʃ·'ʃɛn·te] *agg* (*immagine, suono*) fading
evangelico, -a [e·van·'dʒɛː·li·ko] <-ci, -che> *agg* evangelical; (*chiesa, dottrina*) Protestant
evangelizzare [e·van·dʒe·lid·'dza:·re] *vt* (*convertire*) to evangelize
Evangelo [e·van·'dʒɛː·lo] *m v.* **Vangelo**
evaporare [e·va·po·'ra:·re] *vi essere o avere* to evaporate
evaporazione [e·va·po·ra·'tsio:·ne] *f* evaporation
evasi [e·'va:·zi] *1. pers sing pass rem di* **evadere**
evasione [e·va·'zio:·ne] *f* 1.(*fuga: da carcere*) escape 2. *fig* (*distrazione*) escape; **romanzo d'** ~ escapist novel 3. ADM (*di posta, pratiche*) dispatch 4.(*mancato pagamento*) avoidance; ~ **fiscale** tax evasion
evasivo, -a [e·va·'zi:·vo] *agg* (*vago: risposta*) evasive
evaso, -a [e·'va:·zo] I. *pp di* **evadere** II. *m, f* escapee
evasore [e·va·'zo:·re] *m* ~ (**fiscale**) tax evader
evenienza [e·ve·'niɛn·tsa] *f* eventuality; **all'**~ if required; **nell'**~ **che** ... +*conj* in the event that ...
evento [e·'vɛn·to] *m* (*fatto*) event; **lieto** ~ happy event
eventuale [e·ven·tu·'a:·le] I. *agg* (*possibile*) possible II. *fpl* **varie ed** -**i** any other business
eventualità [e·ven·tu·a·li·'ta] <-> *f* 1.(*circostanza*) eventuality; **nell'**~ **che** ... +*conj* in the event that ...; **per ogni** ~ for all eventualities 2.(*possibilità*) possibility
eventualmente [e·ven·tual·'men·te] *avv* (*in caso*) if necessary
eversivo, -a [e·ver·'si:·vo] *agg* (*sovversivo: attività, movimento*) subversive
evidente [e·vi·'dɛn·te] *agg* 1.(*visibile*) clear

2.(*indubitabile*) evident
evidenza [e·vi·'dɛn·tsa] *f* 1.(*indiscutibilità*) clarity 2.(*risalto*) **mettere in** ~ **qc** to highlight sth; **mettersi in** ~ to draw attention to oneself
evidenziare *vt* 1.(*sottolineare*) to stress 2.(*con evidenziatore*) to highlight
evidenziatore *m* (*pennarello*) highlighter
evirare [e·vi·'ra:·re] *vt* MED to castrate
evirazione [e·vi·ra·'tsio:·ne] *f* MED castration
evitare [e·vi·'ta:·re] *vt* (*scansare: pericolo, ostacolo*) to avoid; ~ **di fare qc** to avoid doing sth
evo ['ɛː·vo] *m* (*periodo*) era; **medio** ~ Middle Ages
evocare [e·vo·'ka:·re] *vt* 1.(*spiriti*) to evoke 2.(*richiamare: ricordo, avventura, fatto*) to recall
evolutivo, -a [e·vo·lu·'ti:·vo] *agg* (*processo, fase, psicologia*) developmental
evoluto, -a [e·vo·'lu:·to] I. *pp di* **evolvere** II. *agg* 1.(*civiltà, nazione, persona, specie*) developed 2.(*sistema, tecnologia*) advanced
evoluzione [e·vo·lut·'tsio:·ne] *f* 1.(*sviluppo: di tecnologia, situazione, malattia*) development 2. BIOL (*trasformazione: di specie*) evoluzion 3. *gener al pl* AERO (*picchiata*) evolutions *pl* 4. SPORT (*acrobazia*) evolutions *pl*
evoluzionismo [e·vo·lut·tsio·'niz·mo] *m* (*teoria*) evolutionism
evolvere [e·'vɔl·ve·re] <evolvo, evolvei *o* evolvetti, evoluto> I. *vt* to evolve II. *vr:* -**rsi** to evolve
evviva [ev·'vi:·va] *int fam* hurrah!; ~ **gli sposi!** three cheers for the bride and groom!
ex [ɛks] I. *prep* (*moglie, presidente*) ex-; (*paese*) former II. <-> *mf* (*amante, moglie*) ex
executive [ig·'ze·kju·tiv] I. <-> *mf* executive II. <-> *m* (*aereo*) private jet
expo [ɛks·'po] <-> *f* (*international*) exhibition
extra ['ɛks·tra] I. <inv> *agg* 1.(*speciale: qualità*) top-quality 2. COM (*spese*) additional II. <-> *m* (*spese*) additional expenses *pl* III. *prep* (*fuori*) extra
extracee [ɛks·tra·'tʃɛː·e] <-> *agg* (*cittadino, paese, imprenditore*) non-EU; **commercio** ~ trade with non-EU countries; **mercato** ~ non-EU market
extracomunitario, -a [ɛks·tra·ko·mu·ni·'ta:·rio] <-i, -ie> I. *agg* non-EU II. *m, f* non-EU citizen
extraconiugale [ɛks·tra·kon·iu·'ga:·le] *agg* (*amore, relazione*) extramarital
extracontrattuale [ɛks·tra·kon·trat·tu·'a:·le] *agg* 1.(*fuori dal contratto*) extra-contractual 2.(*non da rapporto contrattuale*) non-contractual
extracurricolare [ɛks·tra·kur·ri·ko·'la:·re] *agg* (*corso, esame*) extracurricular
extraeuropeo, -a [ɛks·tra·eu·ro·'pɛː·o] <-ei, -ee> *agg* (*paese, cittadino*) non-European
extragalattico, -a [ɛks·tra·ga·'lat·ti·ko] <-ci, -che> *agg* (*astronomia, nebulosa*) extragalactic

extragiudiziale [eks·tra·dʒu·dit·'tsia:·le] *agg* JUR extrajudicial

extramurale [eks·tra·mu·'ra:·le] *agg* (*università, corso, professione*) extramural

extranazionale [eks·tra·na·tsio·'na:·le] *agg* (*provenienza, territorio*) foreign

extraorario, -a [eks·tra·o·'ra:·rio] <-i, -ie> *agg* (*prestazione, servizio*) out-of-hours

extraparlamentare [eks·tra·par·la·men·'ta:·re] I. *agg* (*opposizione, politica*) extra-parliamentary II. *mf* member of an extra-parliamentary group

extraprocessuale [eks·tra·pro·tʃes·su·'a:·le] *agg* JUR 1. (*fuori dal processo*) out of court 2. (*extragiudiziale: spese*) extrajudicial

extraprofitto [eks·tra·pro·'fit·to] *m* FIN (*eccedenza di profitto*) excess profit

extrarapido, -a [eks·tra·'ra:·pi·do] *agg* 1. FOTO **lastra fotografica -a** high-speed film 2. TEC **acciaio ~** high-speed steel

extrascolastico, -a [eks·tra·sko·'las·ti·ko] <-ci, -che> *agg* (*attività, formazione*) after-school

extrasensoriale [eks·tra·sen·so·'ria:·le] *agg* (*percezione, potere, esperienza*) extrasensory

extrasistole [eks·tra·'sis·to·le] *f* MED extrasystole

extrasottile [eks·tra·sot·'ti:·le] *agg* (*apparecchio, materiale*) ultra-thin

extrastrong ['eks·trə·'strɔŋ] I. <-> *f* (*tipo di carta*) high-strength paper II. <inv> *agg* (*carta*) high-strength

extraterrestre [eks·tra·ter·'rɛs·tre] I. *agg* (*forme di vita*) extraterrestrial II. *mf* extraterrestrial

extraterritoriale [eks·tra·ter·ri·to·'ria:·le] *agg* (*zona, organismo*) extraterritorial

extraterritorialità [eks·tra·ter·ri·to·ri·a·li·'ta] <-> *f* (*privilegio*) extraterritoriality

extraurbano, -a [eks·tra·ur·'ba:·no] *agg* (*trasporti, tariffe, biglietti*) out-of-town

extravergine [eks·tra·'ver·dʒi·ne] <inv> *agg* extra-virgin; **olio di oliva ~** extra-virgin olive oil

ex voto [ɛks 'vɔ:·to] <-> *m* (*oggetto, quadro*) ex voto

F

F, f ['ɛf·fe] <-> *f* F, f; **~ come Firenze** F for Fox

fa¹ [fa] <-> *m* MUS fa; **~ maggiore/minore** F major/minor

fa² I. 3. pers sing pr di **fare¹** II. *avv* (*nel passato*) ago; **tre anni ~** three years ago

fabbisogno [fab·bi·'zoɲ·ɲo] *m* requirements *pl;* **~ di energia** energy requirements *pl*

fabbrica ['fab·bri·ka] <-che> *f* factory; **comprare a prezzo di ~** to buy at factory prices

fabbricabile [fab·bri·'ka:·bi·le] *agg* (*edificabile: area, terreno*) building

fabbricante [fab·bri·'kan·te] *mf* (*produttore: di scarpe, di orologi*) maker

fabbricare [fab·bri·'ka:·re] *vt* 1. (*costruire: muro, palazzo*) to build 2. (*produrre: mobili, scarpe*) to make

fabbricato [fab·bri·'ka:·to] *m* (*edificio*) building

fabbricazione [fab·bri·ka·'tsio:·ne] *f* (*produzione*) manufacture; **~ in serie** mass production; **difetto di ~** manufacturing defect

fabbro ['fab·bro] *m* smith

faccenda [fat·'tʃɛn·da] *f* 1. (*cosa da fare*) thing 2. *pl* (*lavori domestici*) housework 3. (*questione*) business

facchino [fak·'ki:·no] *m* 1. (*di stazione, albergo*) porter 2. *fig, pej* roughneck *pej;* **sgobbare come un ~** to work like a dog

faccia ['fat·tʃa] <-cce> *f* 1. (*volto, espressione*) face; **~ tosta** [*o* **di bronzo**] *fig* nerve; (*persona*) person with a lot of nerve; **~ a ~** face to face; **non guardare in ~ nessuno** not to look anyone in the face; **dire le cose in ~ a qu** to tell sb to their face; **alla ~!** *fam* good God!; **perdere la ~** to lose face; **salvare la ~** to save face 2. (*aspetto*) look 3. (*lato: di medaglia, cubo, poliedro*) face; (*di luna*) side

facciale [fat·'tʃa:·le] *agg* (*lifting*) face; (*chirurgia, nervo*) facial

facciata [fat·'tʃa:·ta] *f* 1. ARCH (*di edificio*) façade 2. (*di pagina*) side 3. *fig* (*aspetto esteriore*) appearances *pl*

faccina [fat·tʃi:·na] *f* COMPUT emoticon

faccio ['fat·tʃo] 1. pers sing pr di **fare¹**

faceto, -a [fa·'tʃɛ:·to] *agg* witty; **parlare tra il serio e il ~** to be half joking

facezia [fa·'tʃɛt·tsia] <-ie> *f* witticism

fachiro [fa·'ki:·ro] *m* fakir

facile ['fa:·tʃi·le] *agg* 1. (*lavoro, esercizio, testo, guadagno*) easy 2. (*incline*) **essere ~ al pianto/al riso** to cry/laugh easily 3. (*probabile*) likely; **è ~ che nevichi** it's probably going to snow 4. (*poco serio*) easy; **donna di -i costumi** woman of easy virtue

facilità [fa·tʃi·li·'ta] <-> *f* 1. (*d'uso, di manutenzione*) easiness 2. (*predisposizione*) aptitude; **avere ~ a fare qc** to have an aptitude for doing sth; **con ~** (*senza sforzo*) with ease

facilitare [fa·tʃi·li·'ta:·re] *vt* 1. (*lavoro, compito*) to make easier 2. COM (*pagamento*) to make easy

facilitazione [fa·tʃi·li·tat·'tsio:·ne] *f* (*agevolazione*) facility; **-i di pagamento** easy terms *pl*

facilone, -a [fa·tʃi·'lo:·ne] *m, f* (*superficiale*) cavalier person

faciloneria [fa·tʃi·lo·ne·'ri:·a] <-ie> *f* (*superficialità*) cavalier attitude

facoltà [fa·kol·'ta] <-> *f* 1. (*capacità*) faculty; **~ di intendere e di volere** JUR sound mind 2. (*potere*) power 3. (*possibilità: di scegliere, andarsene*) right 4. (*universitaria*) faculty

facoltativo, -a [fa·kol·ta·'ti:·vo] *agg* (*non*

obbligatorio) optional; **fermata** -a flag stop

facoltoso, -a [fa·kol·'to:·so] *agg* (*persona, famiglia*) well-off

façon [fa·'sɔ̃] <-> *f* **lavorazione a** ~ mass production

facsimile [fak·'si:·mi·le] <-> *m* (*riproduzione*) facsimile

factor ['fæk·tə] <-> *m* FIN factoring company

factoring ['fæk·tə·riŋ/'fak·to·rin(g)] *m* FIN factoring

factotum [fak·'tɔ:·tum] <-> *mf* factotum

faenza [fa·'ɛn·tsa] *f* faience

faggio ['fad·dʒo] <-ggi> *m* beech

fagiano [fa·'dʒa:·no] *m* pheasant

fagiolino [fa·dʒo·'li:·no] *m* green bean

fagiolo [fa·'dʒɔ:·lo] *m* bean; **andare a** ~ **a qu** *inf* to be to sb's liking; **capitare a** ~ *inf* to come at the right time

fagocitare [fa·go·tʃi·'ta:·re] *vt* 1. BIOL to phagocytize 2. *fig* (*assorbire*) to swallow up

fagocito [fa·go·'tʃi:·to] *m* BIOL phagocyte

fagotto [fa·'gɔt·to] *m* 1. MUS bassoon 2. (*involto*) bundle; **far** ~ *fig* to pack one's bags

faida ['fa:·i·da] *f* (*vendetta*) feud

faidaté, fai da te ['fa:i·da·'te] <-> *m* (*bricolage*) do-it-yourself

faina [fa·'i:·na] *f* ZOO stone marten

falange [fa·'lan·dʒe] *f* MIL, ANAT phalanx

falangetta [fa·lan·'dʒɛt·ta] *f* ANAT (*di dito*) terminal phalanx

falangina [fa·lan·'dʒi:·na] *f* ANAT (*di dito*) middle phalanx

falcata [fal·'ka:·ta] *f* (*di podista*) stride

falce ['fal·tʃe] *f* scythe

falciare [fal·'tʃa:·re] *vt* 1. (*tagliare: erba*) to mow; (*grano*) to reap 2. *fig* (*uccidere: vittime, vite*) to take 3. SPORT (*atterrare*) to bring down

falco ['fal·ko] <-chi> *m* hawk

falconiere [fal·ko·'niɛ:·re] *m* falconer

falda ['fal·da] *f* 1. GEOL stratum; ~ **acquifera** aquifer; ~ **freatica** water table 2. (*di monte*) lower slope 3. (*di cappello*) brim

falegname [fa·leɲ·'ɲa:·me] *m* carpenter

falegnameria [fa·leɲ·ɲa·me·'ri:·a] <-ie> *f* carpentry

falena [fa·'lɛ:·na] *f* moth

falesia [fa·'lɛ:·zia] <-ie> *f* GEOL cliff

falla ['fal·la] *f* 1. NAUT leak; **tamponare una** ~ to plug a leak 2. *fig* (*difetto*) failing 3. MIL (*rottura nello schieramento*) breach

fallace [fal·'la:·tʃe] *agg lit* 1. (*ingannevole: discorso*) deceptive 2. (*illusorio: promessa*) false; (*speranza*) vain

fallacia [fal·'la:·tʃa] <-cie> *f lit* (*falsità: prova*) falseness

fallico, -a ['fal·li·ko] <-ci, -che> *agg* phallic; **fase** -a phallic stage

fallimentare [fal·li·men·'ta:·re] *agg* 1. JUR (*procedimento, asta*) bankruptcy 2. *fig* (*gestione, politica*) disastrous

fallimento [fal·li·'men·to] *m* 1. JUR (*bancarotta*) bankruptcy; **dichiarare** ~ to declare bankruptcy 2. *fig* (*risultato, persona*) failure

fallire [fal·'li:·re] <fallisco> I. *vi essere* 1. (*azienda*) to go bankrupt 2. *fig* (*non riuscire*) ~ **in qc** to fail in sth II. *vt avere fig* (*mancare*) ~ **il colpo** [*o* **il bersaglio**] to miss

fallito, -a [fal·'li:·to] I. *agg* 1. JUR (*azienda*) bankrupt 2. *fig* (*tentativo, impresa, attore*) failed II. *m, f* 1. (*bancarottiere*) bankrupt 2. *fig* (*chi non si è affermato*) failure

fallo ['fal·lo] *m* 1. (*errore*) fault; **cogliere qu in** ~ to catch sb out 2. SPORT foul 3. ANAT (*pene*) phallus

falloso, -a [fal·'lo:·so] *agg* SPORT (*gioco, intervento*) illegal

fall-out [fɔ:l·'aut] <-> *m* fallout

falò [fa·'lɔ] <-> *m* bonfire

falsare [fal·'sa:·re] *vt* 1. (*distorcere: fatti, dati*) to falsify 2. (*alterare: voce*) to distort

falsariga [fal·sa·'ri:·ga] <-ghe> *f* 1. (*foglio*) lined page 2. *fig* (*esempio, modello*) model; **sulla** ~ **di qu** following sb's example

falsario [fal·'sa:·rio] <-i> *m* (*di quadri*) forger; (*di monete*) counterfeiter

falsetto [fal·'set·to] *m* MUS falsetto

falsificabile [fal·si·fi·'ka:·bi·le] *agg* (*firma, documento*) forgeable

falsificare [fal·si·fi·'ka:·re] *vt* 1. (*firma, banconota, quadro*) to forge 2. (*notizia*) to distort

falsificazione [fal·si·fi·kat·'tsio:·ne] *f* (*di firma, quadro*) forgery; (*di banconota*) counterfeiting

falsità [fal·si·'ta] <-> *f* 1. (*non autenticità, ipocrisia*) falseness 2. *pl* (*bugia*) lie

falso¹ ['fal·so] *m* 1. (*cosa non vera*) falsehood; **giurare il** ~ to commit perjury 2. JUR (*reato*) forgery; ~ **in bilancio** false accounting

falso² ['fal·so] I. *agg* 1. (*non vero: notizia, indizio*) false 2. (*errato: idea, sospetto*) mistaken 3. (*non sincero: sorriso, lacrime*) fake 4. (*falsificato: denaro*) counterfeit; (*quadro, gioielli*) fake 5. (*loc*) ~ **allarme** false alarm; **fare un passo** ~ to slip up; **-a partenza** false start; **-a testimonianza** perjured evidence; **sotto** ~ **nome** under a false name II. *m* (*ipocrita*) hypocrite

fama ['fa:·ma] *f* 1. (*reputazione*) reputation 2. (*celebrità*) fame

fame ['fa:·me] *f* 1. hunger; **avere poca** ~ to be not very hungry; **mi viene** ~ I feel hungry; **avere una** ~ **da lupi** *inf* to be starving; **morire di** ~ to starve to death; *fig* to be starving; **prendere uno stipendio da** ~ to get starvation wages; **essere un morto di** ~ *pej* to be a down-and-out 2. *fig* (*avidità: di denaro, potere*) hunger; (*desiderio: di giustizia, affetto*) desire

famelico, -a [fa·'mɛ:·li·ko] <-ci, -che> *agg* 1. (*affamato: animale*) ravenous 2. *fig* (*avido: sguardo, espressione*) eager

famigerato, -a [fa·mi·dʒe·'ra:·to] *agg* notorious

famiglia [fa·'miʎ·ʎa] <-glie> *f* 1. (*nucleo*) family; ~ **allargata** extended family; **essere uno di** ~ to be one of the family; **essere di**

buona ~ to come from a good family; **stato di** ~ *certificate giving details of the members of one's family;* **metter su** ~ to start a family; **sentirsi in** ~ to feel at home; **essere tutto casa e** ~ to be devoted to one's family; **la Sacra Famiglia** the Holy Family **2.** (*specie*) BIOL, BOT, MIN family

familiare [fa·mi·'lia:·re] I. *agg* **1.** (*vita, nucleo*) family **2.** (*consueto: viso, linguaggio*) familiar **3.** (*affabile: modi, tono*) familiar; (*semplice: pensione, trattamento*) friendly **4.** LING informal; **linguaggio** ~ informal language **II.** *mf* (*parente*) family member **III.** *f* AUTO station wagon

familiarità [fa·mi·lia·ri·'ta] <-> *f* (*confidenza, pratica*) familiarity

familiarizzare [fa·mi·lia·rid·'dza·re] *vi* ~ **con qu/qc** (*persone, ambiente*) to get to know sb/sth

familiarizzarsi [fa·mi·lia·rid·'dzar·si] *vr* (*impratichirsi*) to familiarize oneself

famoso, -a [fa·'mo:·so] *agg* famous

fan [fæn/fan] <-> *mf* fan

fanale [fa·'na:·le] *m* (*di automobile, bicicletta*) light; ~ **antinebbia** fog light

fanalino [fa·na·'li:·no] *m* light; ~ **di coda** AUTO tail light; *fig* (*ultimo in classifica*) tail-end Charlie *inf*

fanatico, -a [fa·'na:·ti·ko] <-ci, -che> **I.** *agg* **1.** *pej* (*intollerante*) fanatical **2.** (*appassionato*) **essere** ~ **di** [*o* **per**] **qc** to be mad about sth **II.** *m, f* fanatic

fanatismo [fa·na·'tiz·mo] *m* fanaticism

fanciullezza [fan·tʃul·'let·tsa] *f lit* childhood

fanciullo, -a [fan·'tʃul·lo] *m, f lit* child

fanculo [fan·'ku:·lo] *int vulg* (*vaffanculo*) fuck off!; **mandare qu a** ~ to tell sb to fuck off; **andare a** ~ to fuck off

fandonia [fan·'dɔ:·nia] <-ie> *f* lie

fanfara [fan·'fa:·ra] *f* **1.** (*banda*) brass band **2.** (*musica*) fanfare

fanfarone, -a [fan·fa·'ro:·ne] *m, f* boaster

fanghiglia [faŋ·'giʎ·ʎa] <-glie> *f* mud

fango ['faŋ·go] <-ghi> *m* **1.** (*melma*) mud **2.** *fig* (*infamia*) mire; **gettare** ~ **addosso a qu** to sling mud at sb **3.** *pl* MED (*termali*) mud baths *pl*

fannullone, -a [fan·nul·'lo:·ne] *m, f* layabout

fantapolitico, -a [fan·ta·po·'ti:·ti·ko] <-ci, -che> *agg* political-fantasy

fantascientifico, -a [fan·ta·ʃen·'ti:·fi·ko] <-ci, -che> *agg* science-fiction

fantascienza [fan·taʃ·'ʃɛn·tsa] *f* science fiction

fantasia [fan·ta·'zi:·a] <-ie> *f* **1.** (*immaginazione*) imagination **2.** (*capriccio*) whim **3.** (*tessuto*) pattern **4.** MUS fantasia

fantasioso, -a [fan·ta·'zio:·so] *agg* imaginative

fantasista [fan·ta·'zis·ta] <-i , -e> *mf* **1.** (*artista*) variety artist **2.** (*calciatore*) genius

fantasma¹ [fan·'taz·ma] <-i> *m* **1.** (*apparizione*) ghost **2.** PSYCH (*desiderio inconscio*) fantasy **3.** *pl* (*ossessione, incubo*) specters *pl*

fantasma² <inv> *agg* (*apparente: governo*)

shadow; (*abbandonato: nave, città*) ghost; **scrittore** ~ ghost writer

fantasmagoria [fan·taz·ma·go·'ri:·a] <-ie> *f* phantasmagoria

fantasmagorico, -a [fan·tas·ma·'gɔ:·ri·ko] <-ci, -che> *agg* phantasmagorical

fantasticare [fan·tas·ti·'ka:·re] **I.** *vt* to fantasize about **II.** *vi* to fantasize; ~ **su qc** to fantasize about sth

fantasticheria [fan·tas·ti·ke·'ri:·a] <-ie> *f* daydream; **perdersi in -e** to daydream

fantastico, -a [fan·'tas·ti·ko] <-ci, -che> *agg* **1.** (*irreale*) imaginary **2.** (*straordinario*) fantastic; ~ **!** fantastic!

fante ['fan·te] *m* **1.** MIL infantryman **2.** (*nelle carte*) jack

fanteria [fan·te·'ri:·a] <-ie> *f* infantry

fantino [fan·'ti:·no] *m* jockey

fantoccio [fan·'tɔt·tʃo] <-cci> *m a. fig* puppet

fantomatico, -a [fan·to·'ma:·ti·ko] <-ci, -che> *agg* (*misterioso*) mysterious

farabutto, -a [fa·ra·'but·to] *m, f* crook

faraglione [fa·raʎ·'ʎo:·ne] *m* stack

faraona [fa·ra·'o:·na] *f* ZOO guinea fowl

faraone [fa·ra·'o:·ne] *m* HIST pharaoh

farcire [far·'tʃi:·re] <farcisco> *vt* **1.** CULIN to stuff **2.** *fig* (*di errori, citazioni*) to pepper

farcitura [far·tʃi·'tu:·ra] *f* (*ripieno*) stuffing

fard [far(d)] <-> *m* (*cosmetico, belletto*) blusher

fardello [far·'dɛl·lo] *m* **1.** (*fagotto*) bundle **2.** *fig* (*di preoccupazioni*) burden

fare¹ ['fa:·re] <faccio, feci, fatto> **I.** *vt* **1.** (*compiere azioni*) to do; ~ **il bagno** to take a bath; ~ **colazione** to have lunch; ~ **un sonnellino** to have a nap; ~ **un favore a qu** to do sb a favor; ~ **del bene** to do good **2.** (*creare: quadro*) to paint; (*poesia*) to write **3.** (*ideare: progetto, programma*) to make **4.** (*suscitare*) **mi fa pena** I feel sorry for him; ~ **rabbia a qu** to annoy sb **5.** (*esercitare: mestiere*) to do; (*professione*) to follow; ~ **il medico/l'insegnante** to be a doctor/teacher; **che lavoro fai?** what do you do? **6.** (*ammontare*) to be; **tre più due fa cinque** three plus two is five; **quanto fa?** how much is it?; **fa 6 euro?** it's 6 euros? **7.** SPORT (*praticare*) ~ **sport** to do sport; ~ **vela** to sail; **il lago non è il luogo ideale per** ~ **vela** the lake isn't ideal for sailing; ~ **una partita a tennis** to have a game of tennis **8.** CULIN (*preparare: minestra, frittata*) to make **9.** (*comportamento*) ~ **lo scemo** to play the fool; ~ **il furbo** to try to be smart; **non** ~ **la sciocca!** don't play dumb!; ~ **buon viso a cattivo gioco** to make the best of it **10.** (*loc*) ~ **sapere qc a qu** to inform sb of sth; ~ **vedere** to show; ~ **a meno di qc** to do without sth; ~ **tardi** to be late; **farcela** to succeed; **farla finita con qu/qc** to have done with sb/sth; **strada facendo** on the way; **chi la fa l'aspetti** *prov* what goes around comes around *prov*; **far da sé** to do it oneself; **si è fatto da sé** *fig* he's a self-made man; **chi fa da**

sé fa per tre *prov* if you want something done well, do it yourself *prov* **II.** *vi* **1.** (*agire*) to act; **darsi da** ~ to get a move on *inf* **2.** (*essere adatto*) to do; **questo lavoro non fa per me** this job isn't for me **3.** (*loc*) **fa bello** it's nice; **fa caldo/freddo** it's hot/colld; ~ **in tempo** to be in time; **faccia pure!** go ahead!; **non mi fa né caldo né freddo** I don't care either way; ~ **a botte** to come to blows **III.** *vr:* **-rsi** (*loc*) **-rsi avanti** to step forward; **-rsi da parte** to move aside; **-rsi notare** to get oneself noticed; **-rsi pregare** to play hard to get; **farsela addosso** *inf* to wet oneself; **-rsi in quattro** to put oneself out; **-rsi strada** to make one's way; **si è fatto tardi** it's late; **farsene una ragione** to resign oneself; **-rsi** *inf* (*drogarsi*) to do drugs

fare² *m* **1.** (*lavoro*) doing; **tra il dire e il ~ c'è di mezzo il mare** *prov* there's many a slip 'twixt cup and lip *prov* **2.** (*atteggiamento: gentile, distaccato*) manner **3.** (*inizio*) **sul far del giorno** at daybreak

faretto [fa·'ret·to] *m* (*lampada*) spotlight

farfalla [far·'fal·la] *f* **1.** zoo, sport butterfly **2.** (*cravatta*) bow tie **3.** *pl* culin (*tipo di pasta*) bows *pl*

farfallone [far·fal·'lo:·ne] *m fig* philanderer

farfugliare [far·fuʎ·'ʎa:·re] *vi* to mutter

farina [fa·'ri:·na] *f* flour; ~ **gialla** (*di mais*) corn flour; ~ **di pesce** fish meal; **non è ~ del tuo sacco** *fig* that isn't your own idea

farinacei [fa·ri·'na:·tʃei] *mpl* starchy foods

farinaceo, -a *agg* farinaceous

faringe [fa·'rin·dʒe] *f* anat pharynx

faringite [fa·rin·'dʒi:·te] *f* pharyngitis

farinoso, -a [fa·ri·'no:·so] *agg* (*patata*) floury; (*neve*) powdery

fariseo, -a [fa·ri·'zɛ:·o] *m, f* Pharisee; *fig* pharisee

farmaceutico, -a [far·ma·'tʃɛu·ti·ko] <-ci, -che> *agg* (*industria, prodotto*) pharmaceutical

farmacia [far·ma·'tʃi:·a] <-cie> *f* (*scienza, negozio*) pharmacy; ~ **di turno** duty farmacy; **da vendersi solo in** ~ available only on prescription

farmacista [far·ma·'tʃis·ta] *mf* pharmacist

farmaco ['far·ma·ko] <-ci *o* -chi> *m* drug; ~ **generico** generic drug

farmacodipendente [far·ma·ko·di·pen·'dɛn·te] **I.** *mf* drug addict **II.** *agg* drug-addicted

farmacodipendenza [far·ma·ko·di·pen·'dɛn·tsa] *f* drug addiction

farmacologia [far·ma·ko·lo·'dʒi:·a] <-gie> *f* pharmacology

farmacologo, -a [far·ma·'kɔ:·lo·go] <-gi, -ghe> *m, f* pharmacologist

farmacopea [far·ma·ko·'pɛ:·a] *f* (*elenco ufficiale*) pharmacopoeia

Farnesina [far·ne·'zi:·na] <*sing*> *f* (*Ministero degli Affari Esteri italiano*) **la** ~ = the State Department

farneticare [far·ne·ti·'ka:·re] *vi* **1.** (*delirare*) to rave **2.** (*dire assurdità*) to talk nonsense

faro ['fa:·ro] *m* **1.** (*torre*) lighthouse **2.** (*di veicolo*) headlight; **-i antinebbia** fog lights *pl;* **-i anabbaglianti** low beams *pl*

farsa ['far·sa] *f a. fig* farce

farsesco, -a [far·'ses·ko] <-schi, -sche> *agg* farcical

fasc. *abbr di* **fascicolo** vol.

fascetta [faʃ·'ʃet·ta] *f* **1.** (*per libro*) wrapper **2.** tec strap

fascia ['faʃ·ʃa] <-sce> *f* **1.** (*striscia di tessuto*) sash; ~ **tricolore** tricolor sash **2.** med (*benda*) bandage; ~ **elastica** elastic bandage; **bambino in -sce** baby in diapers **3.** (*di territorio*) strip **4.** sport ~ **laterale** wing **5.** *fig* (*settore, gruppo*) group

fasciare [faʃ·'ʃa:·re] *vt* **1.** (*ferita*) to bandage **2.** (*neonato*) to put a diaper on **3.** (*aderire: abito*) to cling to

fasciatoio [faʃ·ʃa·'to:·io] <-oi> *m* changing table

fasciatura [faʃ·ʃa·'tu:·ra] *f* bandage

fascicolo [faʃ·'ʃi:·ko·lo] *m* **1.** (*di enciclopedia*) volume; (*di rivista*) issue **2.** (*dossier personale*) file **3.** jur (*di processo*) case file

fascina [faʃ·'ʃi:·na] *f* faggot

fascino ['faʃ·ʃi·no] *m* charm

fascio ['faʃ·ʃo] <-sci> *m* **1.** (*di erba, fieno*) sheaf; (*di banconote*) wad; **far d'ogni erba un** ~ (*loc*) to make generalizations **2.** anat (*nervoso, muscolare*) bundle **3.** pol, hist (*partito fascista*) Fascist Party **4.** (*emblema*) fasces

fascismo [faʃ·'ʃiz·mo] *m* fascism

fascista [faʃ·'ʃis·ta] <-i, -e> *m f* **I.** *agg* fascist **II.** *mf* fascist

fase ['fa:·ze] *f* **1.** (*di processo, malattia, lavoro*) stage; (*di motore*) stroke; ~ **di sviluppo** development stage; **essere fuori** ~ *fig* to feel out of sorts **2.** *pl* (*lunare, di Mercurio*) phase

fastello [fas·'tɛl·lo] *m* (*di legna, canne*) bundle

fasti ['fas·ti] *mpl* (*fatti memorabili*) glories *pl*

fastidio [fas·'ti:·dio] <-i> *m* **1.** (*molestia*) trouble; **dare** ~ **a qu** to annoy sb; **Le dà** ~ **il fumo?** is the smoke bothering you? **2.** (*insofferenza*) irritation **3.** (*seccatura, problema*) problem

fastidioso, -a [fas·ti·'dio:·so] *agg* **1.** (*irritante: persona, rumore*) annoying **2.** (*sgradevole: lavoro, questione*) difficult

fasto ['fas·to] *m* pomp

fastoso, -a [fas·'to:·so] *agg* sumptuous

fasullo, -a [fa·'zul·lo] *agg* **1.** (*moneta*) counterfeit; (*oro*) fake **2.** *fig* (*persona*) bogus

fata ['fa:·ta] *f* **1.** (*di fiaba*) fairy; **avere mani di** ~ *fig* to have nimble fingers **2.** ~ **morgana** (*miraggio*) Fata Morgana

fatale [fa·'ta:·le] *agg* **1.** (*fatidico: evento, incontro*) fateful **2.** (*letale: malattia, incidente*) fatal **3.** (*seducente: sguardo, donna*) irresistible; **donna** ~ femme fatale

fatalismo [fa·ta·'liz·mo] *m* fatalism

fatalista [fa·ta·'lis·ta] <-i, -e> *m f mf* fatalist

fatalità [fa·ta·li·'ta] <-> *f* **1.** (*inevitabilità*) inevitability **2.** (*sorte*) fate; **una tragica** ~ a tragic fate

fatica [fa·'ti:·ka] <-che> *f* 1.(*sforzo*) effort 2.(*affaticamento*) exhaustion 3.(*pena, difficoltà*) difficulty; **a** ~ with difficulty; **fare** ~ **a fare qc** to have a hard time doing sth 4.(*lavori pesanti*) labor

faticare [fa·ti·'ka:·re] *vi* 1.(*affaticarsi*) to work hard; ~ **dalla mattina alla sera** to work from morning till night 2.(*incontrare difficoltà*) to have trouble

faticoso, -a [fa·ti·'ko:·so] *agg* 1.(*stancante: lavoro, viaggio*) exhausting 2.(*difficile: respirazione*) labored

fatiscente [fa·tiʃ·'ʃɛn·te] *agg* 1.(*edificio*) dilapidated 2.*fig* (*organizzazione, sistema*) collapsing

fato ['fa:·to] *m* fate

Fatt. *abbr di* **fattura** inv.

fattezze [fat·'tet·tse] *fpl* features

fattibile [fat·'ti:·bi·le] *agg* feasible

fattispecie [fat·tis·'pɛ:·tʃe] <-> *f* **nella** ~ in this case

fattivo, -a [fat·'ti:·vo] *agg* (*efficace: intervento*) effective

fatto ['fat·to] *m* 1.(*azione*) fact; **cogliere qu sul** ~ to catch sb in the act; **dato di** ~ fact; **i -i parlano chiaro** the facts speak for themselves; **il** ~ **è che ...** the fact is that ...; ~ **sta che ...** the fact is that ...; **mettere qu davanti al** ~ **compiuto** to present sb with a fait accompli 2.JUR (*reato*) deed 3.(*avvenimento*) event; ~ **di cronaca** news item 4.(*loc*) **badare ai** [*o* **farsi i**] **-i propri** to mind one's own business; **sapere il** ~ **proprio** to know what one is doing; **impicciarsi dei -i altrui** to stick one's nose into other people's business

fatto, -a I. *pp di* **fare**[1] II. *agg* 1.(*fabbricato*) made; ~ **a macchina** machine-made; ~ **a mano** handmade; ~ **di legno/di plastica** made of wood/plastic; **pasta -a in casa** home-made pasta; **ben** ~! well done!; **a conti -i** all things considered; **detto** ~ no sooner said than done 2.(*maturo: uomo, donna*) grown; (*inoltrato*) **a giorno** ~ in broad daylight; **a notte -a** after dark 3.(*conformato*) **ben/mal** ~ with a good/poor body 4.(*adatto*) **essere** [*o* **non essere**] ~ **per qu/qc** to be made/not to be made for sb/sth 5.*inf* (*sfinito*) done in *inf* 6.*inf* (*drogato*) stoned

fattore[1] [fat·'to:·re] *m* factor

fattore[2] [fat·'to:·re/fat·to·'res·sa] *m* farm manager

fattoria [fat·to·'ri:·a] <-ie> *f* farm

fattorino [fat·to·'ri:·no] *m* (*per consegne*) delivery man

fattrice [fat·'tri:·tʃe] *f* zoo brood mare

fattura [fat·'tu:·ra] *f* 1.(*documento*) invoice; **rilasciare una** ~ to send out an invoice; ~ **pro forma** pro forma invoice 2.(*foggia: di abito*) tailoring; (*di mobile*) craftsmanship 3.*inf* (*maleficio*) spell

fatturare [fat·tu·'ra:·re] *vt* 1.(*merce, prestazione*) to invoice for 2.(*volume d'affari*) to

have a turnover of

fatturato [fat·tu·'ra:·to] *m* turnover

fatturatrice [fat·tu·ra·'tri:·tʃe] *f* invoicing machine

fatturazione [fat·tu·rat·'tsio:·ne] *f* invoicing

fatuo, -a ['fa:·tuo] *agg* 1.fatuous; **fuoco** ~ will-o'-the-wisp 2.*fig* (*illusione*) illusion

fauci ['fa:u·tʃi] *fpl* jaws *pl*

fauna ['fa:u·na] *f* fauna

fausto, -a ['fa:us·to] *agg* (*evento, ricorrenza*) auspicious

fautore, -trice [fau·'to:·re] *m, f* (*sostenitore*) supporter

fava ['fa:·va] *f* (*legume*) fava bean; **prendere due piccioni con una** ~ *prov* to kill two birds with one stone *prov*

favella [fa·'vɛl·la] *f* 1.(*parola*) speech; **perdere l'uso della** ~ to lose the power of speech 2. *lit* (*linguaggio*) language

favilla [fa·'vil·la] *f* (*scintilla*) spark; **far -e** *fig* to shine; **sprizzare -e dagli occhi** *fig* to have sparkling eyes

favola ['fa:·vo·la] *f* 1.(*fiaba*) fable; **le -e di Esopo** Aesop's fables; **la morale della** ~ the moral of the story; **vivere nel mondo delle -e** to live in a dream world 2.(*fandonia*) fairy tale 3.(*oggetto di chiacchiere*) **diventare la** ~ **del paese** to become the talk of the town 4.(*persona o cosa stupenda*) dream

favoloso, -a [fa·vo·'lo:·so] *agg* 1.(*fiabesco*) fabulous 2.(*straordinario: serata, spettacolo*) amazing

favore [fa·'vo:·re] *m* 1.(*benevolenza, cortesia*) favor; **per** ~ please; **fare un** ~ **a qu** to do sb a favor 2.(*aiuto*) **a** ~ **di qu** in aid of sb; **col** ~ **delle tenebre** under cover of darkness; **testimoniare a** ~ **di qu** to give evidence for sb; **trattamento di** ~ preferential treatment

favoreggiamento [fa·vo:·re·dschia·'men·to] *m* JUR aiding and abetting

favorevole [fa·vo·'re:·vo·le] *agg* 1.(*benevolo: voto, giudizio*) in one's favor; **essere** ~ **a qu/qc** to be in favor of sb/sth 2.(*propizio: situazione, vento*) favorable

favorire [fa·vo·'ri:·re] <favorisco> *vt* 1.(*avvantaggiare*) to favor 2.(*sostenere: iniziativa, commercio*) to encourage 3.(*in espressioni di cortesia*) **favorisca il biglietto** may I see your ticket, please?; **vuole** ~? (*offrendo da mangiare*) would you like some?

favorita [fa·vo·'ri:·ta] *f* (*amante*) mistress; (*negli harem*) favorite wife

favoritismo [fa·vo·ri·'tiz·mo] *m* favoritism

favorito, -a [fa·vo·'ri:·to] I. *agg* favorite II. *m, f* favorite

fax [faks] <-> *m* fax; **via** [*o* **per**] ~ by fax

faxare [fa·'ksa:·re] *vt* to fax

fazione [fat·'tsio:·ne] *f* faction

fazioso, -a [fat·'tsio:·so] I. *agg* partisan II. *m, f* partisan

fazzoletto [fat·tso·'let·to] *m* 1.(*per il naso*) handkerchief; ~ **di carta** paper handkerchief 2.(*foulard*) headscarf

F

febbraio [feb·'bra:·io] *m* February; *v.a.* **aprile**
febbre ['fɛb·bre] *f a fig* fever; **avere la ~** to have a temperature; **~ dell'oro** gold fever
febbricitante [feb·bri·tʃi·'tan·te] *agg* feverish
febbrifugo [feb·'bri:·fu·go] <-ghi> *m* febrifuge
febbrifugo, -a <-ghi, -ghe> *agg* febrifugal
febbrile [feb·'bri:·le] *agg* **1.** MED (*stato*) feverish **2.** *fig* (*inquieto: attesa*) anxious; (*convulso: attività*) feverish
fecale [fe·'ka:·le] *agg* fecal
feccia ['fɛt·tʃa] <-cce> *f a. fig, pej* dregs *pl*
feci[1] ['fɛ:·tʃi] *fpl* feces *pl*
feci[2] ['fe:·tʃi] *1. pers sing pass rem di* **fare**[1]
fecola ['fɛ:·ko·la] *f* starch
fecondare [fe·kon·'da:·re] *vt* to fertilize
fecondazione [fe·kon·dat·'tsio:·ne] *f* fertilization; **~ artificiale** artificial insemination; **~ in vitro** in vitro fertilization
fecondità [fe·kon·di·'ta] <-> *f a. fig* fertility
fecondo, -a [fe·'kon·do] *agg* **1.** (*persona, terreno*) fertile **2.** *fig* (*creativo: mente*) fertile; (*scrittore*) prolific
fede ['fe:·de] *f* **1.** *a.* REL faith **2.** (*anello*) wedding ring **3.** (*loc*) **far ~** to be proof; **in ~** ADM in witness whereof; **in buona ~** in good faith; **in mala ~** in bad faith
fedele [fe·'de:·le] **I.** *agg* faithful **II.** *mf* **1.** (*credente*) believer **2.** (*seguace*) follower
fedelissimo, -a [fe·de·'lis·si·mo] *m, f* acolyte
fedeltà [fe·del·'ta] <-> *f* **1.** (*gener*) faithfulness **2.** MUS **alta ~** high fidelity
federa ['fɛ:·de·ra] *f* pillowcase
federale [fe·de·'ra:·le] *agg* federal
federalismo [fe·de·ra·'liz·mo] *m* federalism
federato, -a [fe·de·'ra:·to] *agg* (*Stato*) federated
federazione [fe·de·rat·'tsio:·ne] *f* federation
FEDERCALCIO [fe·der·'kal·tʃo] *f abbr di* **Federazione Italiana Gioco Calcio** *Italian soccer association*
FEDERMECCANICA [fe·der·mek·'ka:·ni·ka] *f abbr di* **Federazione Sindacale dell'Industria Metalmeccanica Italiana** *Italian engineering industry federation*
fedina [fe·'di:·na] *f* **~ penale** criminal record
feedback ['fiːd·bæk/'fid·bɛk] *m a. fig* feedback
feeling ['fiː·liŋ/'fi·lin(g)] *m* connection; **non c'è ~ all'interno del gruppo** they have no team spirit
fegato ['fe:·ga·to] *m* ANAT liver; **avere ~** *fig* to have guts *inf;* **rodersi il ~** *fig* to sulk
felce ['fel·tʃe] *f* fern
felice [fe·'li:·tʃe] *agg* happy
felicità [fe·li·tsi·'ta] <-> *f* happiness
felicitarsi [fe·li·tʃi·'tar·si] *vr* **1.** (*rallegrarsi*) **~ di qc** to rejoice at sth **2.** (*complimentarsi*) **~ con qu per qc** to congratulate sb on sth
felicitazione [fe·li·tʃi·tat·'tsio:·ne] *f* **vivissime -i!** warmest congratulations!
felino [fe·'li:·no] *m* feline
felino, -a [fe·'li:·no] *agg* (*razza, sguardo*) feline
felliniano, -a [fel·li·'nia:·no] *agg* Fellinian

felpa ['fel·pa] *f* (*indumento*) sweatshirt
felpato, -a [fel·'pa:·to] *agg* (*indumento*) brushed-cotton; **con passo ~** *fig* stealthily
feltro ['fel·tro] *m* (*tessuto*) felt
feluca [fe·'lu:·ka] <-che> *f* **1.** NAUT felucca **2.** (*cappello*) cocked hat
femmina ['fem·mi·na] *f* **1.** (*bambina, ragazza*) girl **2.** ZOO, TEC female
femminile [fem·mi·'ni:·le] **I.** *agg* **1.** (*abbigliamento, squadra*) women's; (*scuola*) girls' **2.** (*astuzia, grazia*) feminine **3.** LING feminine; **genere ~** feminine gender **II.** *m* LING feminine
femminilità [fem·mi·ni·li·'ta] *f* femininity
femminilizzare [fem·mi·ni·lid·'dza:·re] *vt* to feminize
femminismo [fem·mi·'niz·mo] *m* feminism
femminista [fem·mi·'nis·ta] <-i, -e> *m f mf* feminist
femminuccia [fem·mi·'nut·tʃa] <-cce> *f* **1.** (*bambina*) baby girl **2.** *fig, pej* (*uomo debole*) sissy *pej*
femore ['fɛ:·mo·re] *m* thighbone
fendere ['fɛn·de·re] <fendo, fendei *o* fendetti, fenduto> *vt* **1.** (*spaccare: roccia, testa*) to split **2.** (*solcare: aria, onde*) to slice through; **~ la folla** (*farsi largo*) to push one's way through the crowd
fendinebbia [fen·di·'neb·bia] <-> *m* fog light
fenditura [fen·di·'tu:·ra] *f* (*fessura*) crack
fenice [fe·'ni:·tʃe] *f* phoenix
fenicottero [fe·ni·'kɔt·te·ro] *m* flamingo
fenolo [fe·'nɔ:·lo] *m* CHEM phenol
fenomenale [fe·no·me·'na:·le] *agg* (*straordinario: memoria, successo*) phenomenal
fenomeno [fe·'nɔ:·me·no] *m* phenomenon
feretro ['fɛ:·re·tro] *m* coffin
feriale [fe·'ria:·le] *agg* weekday; **giorni -i** workdays
ferie ['fɛ:·rie] *fpl* vacation; **andare in ~** to go on vacation; **essere in ~** to be on vacation; **prendere le ~** to take one's vacation
ferimento [fe·ri·'men·to] *m* wounding
ferire [fe·'ri:·re] <ferisco> *vt* **1.** to injure; **~ qu con qc** to wound sb with sth; **senza colpo ~** without striking a blow **2.** *fig* (*offendere*) to hurt
ferita [fe·'ri:·ta] *f* injury; **riaprire una ~** *fig* to open an old wound
ferito, -a [fe·'ri:·to] **I.** *agg* injured **II.** *m, f* casualty
feritoia [fe·ri·'to:·ia] <-oie> *f* **1.** MIL embrasure **2.** (*in ambienti*) opening
ferma ['fer·ma] *f* MIL service
fermacarte [fer·ma·'kar·te] <-> *m* paperweight
fermacravatta [fer·ma·kra·'vat·ta] <-e> *m* tie tack
fermaglio [fer·'maʎ·ʎo] <-gli> *m* **1.** (*borchia, fibbia*) clasp **2.** (*fermacapelli*) barrette
fermaporte [fer·ma·'por·te] <-> *m* doorstop
fermare [fer·'ma:·re] **I.** *vt* **1.** (*bloccare: motore*) to switch off; (*emorragia*) to stop **2.** (*trattenere: palla*) to trap **3.** (*per strada: per-*

sona, auto) to stop **4.** (*interrompere: lavoro, discorso*) to stop **5.** JUR (*arrestare*) to arrest **6.** (*fissare: bottone, persiana*) to sew on **7.** *fig* (*sguardo*) to fix **II.** *vr:* **-rsi** to stop; **senza -rsi** without stopping

fermata [fer·'ma:·ta] *f* (*di treno, metropolitana, autobus*) stop; ~ **facoltativa** [*o* **a richiesta**] flag stop; ~ **obbligatoria** compulsory stop

fermentare [fer·men·'ta:·re] **I.** *vi a. fig* to ferment **II.** *vt* to ferment

fermentazione [fer·men·tat·'tsio:·ne] *f* fermentation

fermento [fer·'men·to] *m* **1.** (*enzima*) enzyme; **-i lattici** lactobacilli *pl* **2.** (*lievito*) yeast **3.** *fig* (*agitazione*) ferment

fermezza [fer·'met·tsa] *f* firmness

fermo ['fer·mo] *m* **1.** (*chiusura: di porta, persiana*) catch **2.** JUR custody

fermo, -a *agg* **1.** (*immobile: persona*) still; (*veicolo*) stationary; **stai ~!** keep still! **2.** (*non funzionante: orologio, macchina*) stopped **3.** (*stagnante: acqua*) stagnant **4.** *fig* (*risoluto*) **avere il polso ~** [*o* **la mano -a**] to take a firm hand **5.** (*costante*) firm; ~ **restando che ...** it being understood that ...

fermoposta [fer·mo·'pɔs·ta] **I.** <inv> *agg* (*lettera, pacco*) general-delivery **II.** *avv* (*spedire, ricevere*) general delivery **III.** <-> *m* general delivery

feroce [fe·'ro:·tʃe] *agg* **1.** (*bestia*) ferocious **2.** (*crudele: tiranno, battaglia, vendetta*) fierce **3.** *fig* (*occhiata*) fierce

ferocia [fe·'rɔ:·tʃa] <-cie> *f* **1.** (*crudeltà: di persona, animale*) ferocity **2.** (*atti di crudeltà*) **-ie** barbarities

ferodo [fe·'rɔ:·do] *m* TEC ~ **per freni** brake lining

Ferr. *abbr di* **ferrovia** railroad

ferraglia [fer·'raʎ·ʎa] <-glie> *f* scrap iron

ferragosto [fer·ra·'gos·to] *m* **1.** (*festa*) Feast of the Assumption **2.** (*periodo*) *August 15 national holiday*

> ⓘ August 15 is a statutory holiday in Italy. This is the day on which Jesus' mother Mary was taken up into heaven and it is popularly known as **Ferragosto** (the height of August). Around the 15th, most Italians go on vacation, leaving the major Italian cities almost empty of people or populated almost exclusively by tourists.

ferramenta [fer·ra·'men·ta] *fpl* hardware; **negozio di** ~ hardware store

Ferrara *f* Ferrara

ferrare [fer·'ra:·re] *vt* (*cavallo*) to shoe

ferrarese [fer·ra·'re:·se] **I.** *agg* from Ferrara **II.** *mf* (*abitante*) person from Ferrara

Ferrarese <*sing*> *m* (*zona*) Ferrara area; **nel** ~ in the Ferrara area

ferrarista [fer·ra·'ris·ta] <-i, -e> *mf* **1.** (*pilota*)

Ferrari driver **2.** (*sostenitore*) Ferrari fan

ferrato, -a [fer·'ra:·to] *agg* **1.** (*cavallo*) shod; (*scarpa*) hobnailed **2.** *fig* (*esperto*) **essere ~ in qc** to be hot on sth *inf*

ferreo, -a ['fɛr·reo] <-ei, -ee> *agg fig* **1.** (*volontà, disciplina, regola*) iron; **salute -a** iron constitution **2.** (*memoria*) tenacious

ferro ['fɛr·ro] *m* **1.** MIN, CHEM iron; ~ **battuto** wrought iron; **di** ~ (*robusto: stomaco*) strong; (*salute*) iron; (*inattaccabile: alibi*) cast-iron **2.** (*oggetto*) ~ **da stiro** iron; ~ **da calza** knitting needle; ~ **di cavallo** horseshoe **3.** *pl* (*strumenti di lavoro*) tools; **i -i del mestiere** the tools of the trade **4.** CULIN (*alla griglia*) **ai -i** grilled **5.** (*loc*) **battere il ~ finché è caldo** *fig* to strike while the iron's hot; **toccare ~** *fig* to touch wood; **sentirsi in una botte di ~** *fig* to be safe as houses; **ai -i corti** *fig* at daggers drawn

ferroso, -a [fer·'ro:·so] *agg* ferrous

FERROTRANVIERI [fer·ro·tran·'viɛ:·ri] *mpl abbr di* **Federazione Nazionale Lavoratori Autoferrotranvieri e Internavigatori** *transportation workers' union*

ferrovecchio [fer·ro·'vɛk·kio] *m* <ferrivecchi> (*rigattiere*) junk dealer

ferrovia [fer·ro·'vi:·a] *f* **1.** (*strada ferrata, amministrazione*) railroad; ~ **a scartamento ridotto** narrow-gauge railroad; **Ferrovie dello Stato** *Italian state-owned railroad company* **2.** (*sistema di trasporto*) rail; **per** ~ by rail

ferroviario, -a [fer·ro·'via:·rio] *agg* railroad; **linea -a** railroad line

ferroviere, -a [fer·ro·'viɛ:·re] *m, f* railroad worker

fertile ['fɛr·ti·le] *agg* **1.** (*terreno, zona*) fertile **2.** *fig* (*creativo: fantasia*) fertile; (*scrittore*) prolific

fertilizzante [fer·ti·lid·'dzan·te] *m* fertilizer

fertilizzare [fer·ti·lid·'dza:·re] *vt* to fertilize

fervente [fer·'vɛn·te] *agg* **1.** (*sentimento: odio, amore*) burning **2.** (*zelante: persona*) devout

fervere ['fɛr·ve·re] <fervo, fervei *o* fervetti, manca il pp> *vi* (*preparativi*) to be in full swing

fervido, -a ['fɛr·vi·do] *agg fig* **1.** (*intenso: attività*) frantic **2.** (*caloroso: augurio*) warm **3.** (*creativo: fantasia*) vivid

fervore [fer·'vo:·re] *m* **1.** (*passione*) fervor; **fare qc con** ~ to do sth with fervor **2.** *fig* (*momento culminante*) heat

fesseria [fes·se·'ri:·a] <-ie> *f fam* **1.** (*idiozia*) stupid thing **2.** (*inezia*) trifle

fesso, -a ['fes·so] **I.** *pp di* fendere **II.** *agg fam* (*tonto*) dumb *inf;* **fare ~ qu** to take sb for a ride

fessura [fes·'su:·ra] *f* **1.** (*spaccatura: in terreno, muro*) crack **2.** (*spiraglio: di porta, finestra*) chink

festa ['fɛs·ta] *f* **1.** (*ricorrenza civile*) holiday; (*religiosa*) feast day; ~ **del Santo Patrono** patron saint's day; ~ **della mamma** [*o* **del papà**] Mother's [*o* Father's] Day; **l'otto marzo è la ~**

della donna March 8 is International Women's Day; **~ nazionale** national holiday; **Buone Feste!** Happy holidays! **2.** (*cerimonia, ricevimento*) party; **una ~ di compleanno** a birthday party; **invitare qu a una ~** to invite sb to a party **3.** (*dimostrazione gioiosa*) **far ~ a qu** to give sb a warm welcome; **fare la ~ a qu** *fig* (*uccidere*) to do sb in *inf* **4.** (*vacanza*) vacation

festeggiamenti [fes·ted·dʒa·'men·ti] *mpl* celebrations

festeggiare [fes·ted·'dʒa:·re] *vt* **1.** (*anniversario*) to celebrate **2.** (*persona*) to hold a celebration for

festino [fes·'ti:·no] *m* party

festival [fes·ti·'val/'fɛs·ti·val] *m* festival

i The first time a music festival was held in the Ligurian port of San Remo was in 1951. Over the course of more than half a century the **Festival of Sanremo**, which takes place at the end of February, has become essential viewing, followed by up to twenty million television viewers every year. Many of the best-known Italian songs and singers of the past sixty years became known through San Remo, from Domenico Modugno's worldwide hit "Nel blu dipinto di blu" (Volare) to the hits of Eros Ramazzotti.

festività [fes·ti·vi·'ta] <-> *f* (*giorno di festa*) holiday

festivo, -a [fes·'ti:·vo] *agg* holiday; **giorno ~** holiday; **orario ~** timetable for Sundays and public holidays; **riposo ~** Sunday rest

festone [fes·'to:·ne] *m* festoon

festoso, -a [fes·'to:·so] *agg* (*accoglienza*) warm; (*atmosfera*) festive

feticcio [fe·'tit·tʃo] <-cci> *m* fetish

feticismo [fe·ti·'tʃiz·mo] *m* fetishism

feticista [fe·ti·'tʃis·ta] <-i *m*, -e *f*> I. *mf* fetishist II. *agg* fetishistic

fetido, -a ['fɛ:·ti·do] *agg* fetid

feto ['fɛ:·to] *m* fetus

fetore [fe·'to:·re] *m* stench

fetta ['fet·ta] *f* **1.** (*di pane, torta, prosciutto, formaggio*) slice; **tagliare a -e** to slice; **-e biscottate** crackers *pl* **2.** (*striscia: di cielo, terra*) strip

fettina [fet·'ti:·na] *f* **1.** (*piccola fetta*) small slice **2.** (*carne*) minute steak

fettuccia [fet·tut·'tʃa] <-ce> *f* tape

fettuccine [fet·tut·'tʃi:·ne] *fpl* (*pasta*) fettuccine

feudale [feu·'da:·le] *agg* **1.** (*del feudo*) feudal **2.** (*dispotico: regime*) despotic **3.** (*antiquato: mentalità*) medieval

feudatario [feu·da·'ta:·rio] <-i> *m* HIST feudal lord

feudo ['fɛ:u·do] *m* **1.** HIST fief **2.** (*proprietà terriera*) estate

FF.AA. *fpl abbr di* **Forze Armate** *Armed Forces*

FI *f abbr di* **Forza Italia** *Italian center-right political party*

fiaba ['fia:·ba] *f* fairy tale

fiabesco, -a [fia·'bes·ko] <-schi, -sche> *agg* fairy-tale

fiacca ['fiak·ka] *f* **1.** (*stanchezza*) weariness **2.** (*svogliatezza*) listlessness; **battere la ~** to slack off

fiaccare [fiak·'ka:·re] *vt* (*spossare*) to weary

fiacco, -a ['fiak·ko] <-cchi, -cche> *agg* **1.** (*persona*) listless **2.** *fig* (*discorso, serata*) dull

fiaccola ['fiak·ko·la] *f* torch; **la ~ olimpica** SPORT the Olympic torch

fiaccolata [fiak·ko·'la:·ta] *f* torchlight procession

fiala ['fia:·la] *f* (*di medicinale*) vial; (*di profumo*) bottle

fiamma ['fiam·ma] *f* **1.** (*lingua di fuoco*) flame; **~ ossidrica** oxyhydrogen flame; **cuocere alla ~** to flambé; **andare in -e** to go up in flames; **fare fuoco e -e** *fig* (*strepitare*) to go all out **2.** *fig* (*sentimento intenso*) flames *pl*; (*persona amata*) **una mia vecchia ~** an old flame of mine **3.** (*rosso vivo: cielo, tramonto*) red; **diventare di ~** (*arrossire*) to go bright red

fiammante [fiam·'man·te] *agg* (*colore*) bright red; **nuovo ~** brand-new

fiammata [fiam·'ma:·ta] *f* **1.** (*fiamma*) blaze **2.** *fig* burst

fiammifero [fiam·'mi:·fe·ro] *m* match; **~ da cucina** kitchen match; **~ svedese** safety match

fiammingo, -a [fiam·'miŋ·go] <-ghi, -ghe> I. *agg* Flemish II. *m*, *f* Fleming III. *m* (*lingua*) Flemish

fiancata [fiaŋ·'ka:·ta] *f* (*di vettura, edificio*) side; (*di nave*) broadside

fiancheggiare [fiaŋ·ked·'dʒa:·re] *vt* **1.** (*stare a lato: alberi*) to line; (*persone*) to flank **2.** MIL (*proteggere*) to protect the flank of **3.** *fig* (*sostenere*) to back

fianco ['fiaŋ·ko] <-chi> *m* **1.** ANAT hip **2.** (*lato*) side; **~ a ~** *a. fig* side by side; **di ~** from the side; **di ~ a** next to; **stare al ~ di qu** *fig* (*essergli solidale*) to stand by sb

Fiandra ['fian·dra] *f* Flanders

fiasco ['fias·ko] <-schi> *m* **1.** (*recipiente*) bottle **2.** *fig* (*insuccesso: esame, spettacolo*) fiasco; **fare ~** to flop; (*a un esame*) to fail

FIAT *f acro di* **Fabbrica Italiana Automobili Torino** FIAT

fiatare [fia·'ta:·re] *vi fig* (*parlare*) to say a word; **senza ~** without saying a word

fiato ['fia:·to] *m* **1.** (*alito*) breath; **avere il ~ grosso** to pant; **trattenere il ~** to hold one's breath **2.** (*energia*) stamina **3.** MUS (*strumenti*) wind instruments *pl* **4.** *fig* (*loc*) **rimanere senza ~** to be speechless; **~ sprecato** a waste of breath; **col ~ sospeso** with bated breath tensione; **in un** [*o* **d'un**] **~** in one gulp; **prendere ~** to stop to catch one's breath; **a perdi~**

(*urlare*) at the top of one's voice; (*correre*) as fast as one's legs can carry one

fibbia ['fib·bia] <-ie> *f* buckle

fibra ['fi:b·ra] *f* 1. (*gener*) fiber 2. *pl* fiber; **-e alimentari** dietary fiber 3. *fig* (*costituzione fisica*) constitution

fibroso, -a [fi·'bro:·so] *agg* fibrous

fica ['fi:·ka] <-che> *f vulg* (*vulva*) cunt *vulg*

ficcanaso [fik·ka·'na:·so] <-i *o* - *m*, - *f*> *mf fam* nosy parker *inf*

ficcare [fik·'ka:·re] I. *vt* 1. (*conficcare*) to knock 2. *inf* (*mettere*) to put; ~ **il naso in qc** *fig* to stick one's nose into sth II. *vr:* **-rsi** *inf* 1. (*infilarsi*) **-rsi a letto** to get into bed; **-rsi le mani in tasca** to stick one's hands in one's pockets; **-rsi le dita nel naso** to pick one's nose 2. *fig* (*cacciarsi*) to get to; **-rsi nei guai** to get into trouble; **-rsi qc in testa** to get sth into one's head

fichidindia *pl di* **ficodindia**

fico ['fi:·ko] <-chi> *m* 1. (*albero*) fig (tree) 2. (*frutto*) fig; **non me n'importa un** ~ *inf* I don't give a damn; **non valere un** ~ **secco** *inf* no to be worth a damn

fico, -a <-chi, -che> I. *agg inf* cool *inf* II. *m*, *f inf* cool person *inf*; **che** ~! he' so cool!

ficodindia [fi·ko·'din·dia] <fichidindia> *m* (*pianta, frutto*) prickly pear

fidanzamento [fi·dan·tsa·'men·to] *m* engagement

fidanzarsi [fi·dan·'tsar·si] *vr* to get engaged

fidanzato, -a [fi·dan·'tsa:·to] *m*, *f* fiancé *m*, fiancée *f*

fidarsi [fi·'da:r·si] *vr* **-rsi di qu/qc** to trust sb/sth; **non -rsi a uscire da soli** not to dare go out alone; **-rsi è bene, non -rsi è meglio** *prov* better safe than sorry *prov*

fidato, -a [fi·'da:·to] *agg* trusted

fido ['fi:·do] *m* FIN credit; ~ **bancario** bank credit

fido, -a *agg lit* faithful

fiducia [fi·'du:·tʃa] <-cie> *f* trust; **avere** ~ **in qu/qc** to have faith in sb/sth; **di** ~ (*persona*) reliable; (*medico*) good; (*delicato: incarico*) responsible; **ispirare** ~ to inspire confidence

fiduciaria [fi·du·tʃa·'ri:·a] <-ie> *f* COM trust company

fiduciario, -a [fi·du·'tʃa:·rio] <-i, -ie> I. *agg* fiduciary II. *m*, *f* fiduciary

fiducioso, -a [fi·du·'tʃo:·so] *agg* confident; **essere** ~ **in qc** to be confident of sth

fiele ['fiɛ:·le] *m a. fig* bile

fienile [fie·'ni:·le] *m* hayloft

fieno ['fiɛ:·no] *m* hay; **febbre** [*o* **raffreddore**] **da** ~ hay fever

fiera ['fiɛ:·ra] *f* 1. (*mostra*) fair; ~ **del libro** book fair; ~ **campionaria** trade fair; ~ **di beneficenza** charity bazaar 2. (*sagra*) festival 3. *lit* (*belva*) wild beast

fierezza [fie·'ret·tsa] *f* pride

fiero, -a ['fiɛ:·ro] *agg* 1. (*orgoglioso*) proud; **essere** ~ **di qu/qc** to be proud of sb/sth 2. (*austero: portamento, sguardo*) haughty

fievole ['fie:·vo·le] *agg* (*voce, suono*) faint

fifa ['fi:·fa] *f fam* fear; **avere una** ~ **blu** to be scared stiff *inf*

fifo ['fi:·fo] <-> *m* COM FIFO

fifone, -a [fi·'fo:·ne] *m*, *f fam* wuss *inf*

fig. *abbr di* **figura** fig.

figata [fi·'ga:·ta] *f sl* beaut *inf*; **che** ~! what a beaut!

figg. *abbr di* **figure** figs

figlia ['fiʎ·ʎa] <-glie> *f* daughter

figliare [fiʎ·'ʎa:·re] *vt* to give birth to

figliastro, -a [fiʎ·'ʎas·tro] *m*, *f* stepchild

figliata [fiʎ·'ʎa:·ta] *f* litter

figlio ['fiʎ·ʎo] <-gli> *m* 1. son; ~ **unico** only child, ~ **naturale**, love child; ~ **di nessuno** foundling; ~ **di mammà** *fam* mama's boy *inf*; ~ **di papà** *fam* spoiled rich young man; ~ **di puttana** *vulg* son of a bitch *vulg* 2. *pl* (*prole*) children *pl*; **essere senza -gli** to be childless

figlioccio, -a [fiʎ·'ʎɔt·tʃo] <-cci, -cce> *m*, *f* (*di battesimo, di cresima*) godchild

figo ['fi:·go] <-ghi> *m sett v.* **fico 2**

figo, -a <-ghi, -ghe> *agg sett v.* **fico, -a**

figura [fi·'gu:·ra] *f* 1. (*gener*) figure 2. (*apparenza*) appearance 3. (*loc*) **fare** (**una**) **bella/ brutta** ~ to make a good/bad impression; **che** ~! *iron* how embarrassing!

figurare [fi·gu·'ra:·re] I. *vi* to appear II. *vr:* **-rsi** (*immaginarsi*) to imagine; **figurati!** of course not!; **ma si figuri!** not at all!

figurativo, -a [fi·gu·ra·'ti:·vo] *agg* (*stile: di pittura, di artista*) figurative; **arti -e** figurative arts

figurato, -a [fi·gu·'ra:·to] *agg* (*linguaggio, uso, significato*) figurative; **in senso** ~ in a figurative sense

figurina [fi·gu·'ri:·na] *f* 1. (*statuina*) figurine 2. (*su cartoncino*) picture card

figurino [fi·gu·'ri:·no] *m* (*disegno*) fashion sketch

figuro [fi·'gu:·ro] *m* (*tipo losco*) character

fila ['fi:·la] *f* 1. (*allineamento, coda*) line; **camminare in** ~ **indiana** to walk in single file; **far la** ~ to stand in line 2. *fig* (*serie continua*) series; **di** ~ in a row

filamento [fi·la·'men·to] *m* filament

filanca® [fi·'laŋ·ka] *f stretch material*

filanda [fi·'lan·da] *f* spinning mill

filantropia [fi·lan·tro·'pi:·a] *f* philanthropy

filantropo, -a [fi·'lan·tro·po] *m*, *f* philanthropist

filare¹ [fi·'la:·re] *m* (*di piante*) row

filare² I. *vt avere* 1. (*fibre tessili*) t spin 2. NAUT (*lasciar scorrere: fune, catena*) to pay out 3. *fig, inf* ~ [*o* **-rsi**] qu (*interessarsi a*) to show interest in sb II. *vi essere o avere* 1. (*ragno, baco da seta*) to spin 2. (*formaggio*) to go stringy 3. *fig* (*discorso, ragionamento*) to hang together 4. *fam* (*andare veloce*) to zoom along *inf*; (*andarsene*) to make oneself scarce; **-rsela all'inglese** to take French leave 5. *scherz* (*amoreggiare*) to go out 6. (*loc*) ~ **liscio** to go smoothly

filarmonica [fi·lar·'mɔ:·ni·ka] <-che> *f* philharmonic

filarmonico, -a [fi·lar·'mɔ:·ni·ko] <-ci, -che> I. *agg* philharmonic II. *m*, *f* philharmonic member

filastrocca [fi·las·'trɔk·ka] <-cche> *f* 1. (*per bambini*) nursery rhyme 2. *fig* (*tiritera*) litany

filato [fi·'la:·to] *m* yarn

filatura [fi·la·'tu:·ra] *f* 1. (*lavorazione*) spinning 2. (*opificio*) spinning mill

file [fail] <-> *m* COMPUT file; ~ **attuale** current file; ~ **immagine** image file; ~ **di testo** text file

filettare [fi·let·'ta:·re] *vt* TEC (*vite*) to thread

filettatura [fi·let·ta·'tu:·ra] *f* TEC (*di vite*) thread

filetto [fi·'let·to] *m* CULIN fillet

filiale [fi·'lia:·le] *f* branch

filibustiere [fi·li·bus·'tiɛ:·re] *m* *fig* (*mascalzone*) scoundrel

filiforme [fi·li·'for·me] *agg* threadlike

filigrana [fi·li·'gra:·na] *f* 1. (*in oreficeria*) filigree 2. (*sulla carta*) watermark

filisteo, -a [fi·lis·'tɛ:·o] I. *agg* 1. HIST Philistine 2. *fig* (*gretto*) conformist II. *m*, *f* 1. HIST Philistine 2. *fig* (*conformista*) conformist

film [film] <-> *m* 1. (*pellicola*) film 2. (*opera cinematografica*) movie; ~ **d'animazione** animated movie; ~ **giallo** thriller; **girare un** ~ to shoot a movie

filmare [fil·'ma:·re] *vt* (*riprendere*) to film

filmato [fil·'ma:·to] *m* short

filmina [fil·'mi:·na] *f* FILM filmstrip

filo ['fi:·lo] *m* 1. (*per cucire*) thread; ~ **di Scozia** lisle; **un** ~ **di perle** a string of pearls 2. (*di erba*) blade; (*di paglia*) piece 3. (*di ferro, rame*) wire; ~ **spinato** barbed wire 4. (*cavo: luce, telefono*) wire 5. *fig* (*di speranza*) glimmer; **con un** ~ **di voce** in a whisper 6. <fila> **tenere** [o **reggere**] **le -a** to pull the strings 7. (*loc*) ~ **conduttore** thread; **essere legato a** ~ **doppio con qu** to be hand in glove with sb; **dar del** ~ **da torcere a qu** to make things difficult for sb; **essere appeso a un** ~ to be hanging by a thread; **fare il** ~ **a qu** to be after sb; **perdere il** ~ to lose the thread; **per** ~ **e per segno** word for word

filoamericano, -a [fi·lo·a·me·ri·'ka:·no] *agg* pro-American

filoarabo, -a [fi·lo·'a:·ra·bo] *agg* pro-Arab

filobus ['fi:·lo·bus] *m* trolley bus

filocinese [fi·lo·tʃi·'ne:·se] *agg* pro-Chinese

filocomunista [fi·lo·ko·mu·'nis·ta] <-i *m*, -e *f*> *agg* procommunist

filodendro [fi·lo·'dɛn·dro] *m* philodendron

filodiffusione [fi·lo·dif·fu·'zio:·ne] *f* cable radio

filodrammatico, -a [fi·lo·dram·'ma:·ti·ko] <-ci, -che> I. *agg* amateur-dramatic II. *m*, *f* amateur actor *m* o *f*, amateur actress *f*

filofascista [fi·lo·faʃ·'ʃis·ta] <-i *m*, -e *f*> *agg* profascist

filogenesi [fi·lo·'dʒɛ:·ne·zi] *f* BIOL phylogenesis

filoisraeliano, -a [fi·lo·iz·ra·e·'lia:·no] *agg* pro-Israeli

filologia [fi·lo·lo·'dʒi:·a] <-gie> *f* philology; ~ **classica** classical philology

filologico, -a [fi·lo·'lɔ:·dʒi·ko] <-ci, -che> *agg* philological

filologo, -a [fi·'lɔ:·lo·go] <-gi, -ghe> *m*, *f* philologist

filonazista [fi·lo·na·'tsis·ta] <-i *m*, -e *f*> *agg* pronazi

filoncino [fi·lon·'tʃi:·no] *m* (*di pane*) baguette

filone [fi·'lo:·ne] *m* 1. (*di giacimento*) vein 2. *fig* (*di cultura*) tradition

filonucleare [fi·lo·nuk·le·'a:·re] *agg* pronuclear

filooccidentale [fi·lo·ot·tʃi·den·'ta:·le] *agg* pro-Western; **politica** ~ pro-Western policy

filorientale [fi·lo·rien·'ta:·le] *agg* pro-Eastern; **politica** ~ pro-Eastern policy

filosofale [fi·lo·zo·'fa:·le] *agg* **pietra** ~ philosopher's stone

filosofare [fi·lo·so·'fa:·re] *vi* *iron* to philosophize

filosofeggiare [fi·lo·so·fed·'dʒa:·re] *vi* *iron* to philosophize

filosofia [fi·lo·zo·'fi:·a] <-ie> *f* 1. (*dottrina, orientamento, concezione*) philosophy 2. *fig* (*serenità*) **con** ~ philosophically

filosofico, -a [fi·lo·'zɔ:·fi·ko] <-ci, -che> *agg* philosophical

filosofo, -a [fi·'lɔ:·zo·fo] *m*, *f* philosopher

filovia [fi·lo·'vi:·a] *f* trolley bus line

filtrare [fil·'tra:·re] I. *vt* avere a. *fig* to filter II. *vi* essere a. *fig* to filter

filtro[1] ['fil·tro] *m* filter; ~ **dell'aria** air filter; ~ **dell'olio** oil filter

filtro[2] ['fil·tro] *m* (*pozione magica*) philtre

filza ['fil·tsa] *f* a. *fig* string

fimosi [fi·'mɔ:·zi] <-> *f* MED phimosis

fin [fin] *prep* v. **fine, fino**

finale [fi·'na:·le] I. *agg* final II. *m* (*conclusione: di commedia*) ending; (*di gara*) end; (*di sinfonia*) finale III. *f* SPORT (*di calcio, tennis, pugilato*) final; **entrare in** ~ to reach the final

finalissima [fi·na·'lis·si·ma] *f* championship final

finalista [fi·na·'lis·ta] <-i *m*, -e *f*> *mf* finalist

finalità [fi·na·li·'ta] <-> *f* (*scopo*) aim

finalizzare [fi·na·lid·'dza:·re] *vt* (*indirizzare*) ~ **qc a qc** to aim sth at sth

finalmente [fi·nal·'men·te] *avv* finally

finanza [fi·'nan·tsa] *f* 1. (*gener*) finance 2. *pl* (*mezzi economici*) finance; **ministero delle Finanze** Department of the Treasury 3. MIL **Guardia di Finanza** branch of the military dealing with tax evasion and customs crimes such as smuggling

finanziamento *m* financing

finanziare [fi·nan·'tsia:·re] *vt* to finance

finanziaria [fi·nan·'tsia:·ria] <-ie> *f* 1. (*società*) investment company 2. (*legge*) finance act

finanziario, -a [fi·nan·'tsia:·rio] <-i, -ie> *agg* (*economico*) financial

finanziatore, -trice [fi·nan·tsia·'to:·re] *m*, *f* backer

finanziere [fi·nan·'tsiɛ:·re] *m* **1.** (*banchiere*) financier **2.** (*di Guardia di Finanza*) *member of the military dealing with tax evasion and customs crimes such as smuggling*

finché [fiŋ·'ke] *cong* **1.** (*fino a quando*) until **2.** (*per tutto il tempo che*) as long as

fine¹ ['fi:·ne] *agg* **1.** (*sottile: capello, tessuto*) fine **2.** *fig* (*acuto: vista, udito*) sharp **3.** (*astuto: espediente*) shrewd **4.** (*intelligente: ironia, mente*) subtle **5.** *fig* (*raffinato: persona, ambiente, palato*) refined **6.** (*delicato: lineamenti*) fine **7.** *fig* (*preciso: ricamo, meccanica*) delicate

fine² ['fi:·ne] **I.** *f* (*conclusione, morte*) end; **alla ~** in the end; **alla fin ~** at the end of the day; **senza ~** endless; **a ~ mese** at the end of the month; **che ~ ha fatto?** what's become of him?; **fare una brutta ~** to come to a bad end **II.** *m* **1.** (*scopo*) aim; **secondo ~** ulterior motive; **a fin di bene** with the best of intentions; **il ~ giustifica i mezzi** the end justifies the means **2.** (*esito*) end; **lieto ~** happy ending; **andare a buon ~** to be successful; **salvo buon ~** COM subject to collection

finesettimana ['fi:·ne set·ti·'ma:·na] <-> *m o f* weekend

finestra [fi·'nɛs·tra] *f* (*di edificio, busta*) COMPUT window; **affacciarsi alla ~** to appear at the window; **buttare i soldi dalla ~** *fig* to throw money down the drain *fig;* **uscire dalla porta e rientrare dalla ~** *fig* to be impossible to get rid of

finestrino [fi·nes·'tri:·no] *m* (*di automobile, treno, autobus*) window

finezza [fi·'net·tsa] *f* **1.** (*acume: di udito, intelletto*) sharpness **2.** (*raffinatezza: di gusto, modi*) refinement **3.** (*precisione*) delicacy **4.** (*premura*) subtleness; **conoscere le -e di qc** (*essere esperto*) to know the subtleties of sth

fingere ['fin·dʒe·re] <fingo, finsi, finto> **I.** *vt* (*gioia, dolore*) to feign *form* **II.** *vi* to pretend; **~ di fare qc** to pretend to do sth **III.** *vr* **-rsi malato/pazzo** to pretend to be sick/crazy

finimenti [fi·ni·'men·ti] *mpl* (*bardatura*) harness

finimondo [fi·ni·'mon·do] *m inf* (*confusione*) pandemonium

finire [fi·'ni:·re] <finisco> **I.** *vt avere* **1.** (*portare a compimento: libro, lavoro*) to finish; **~ di fare qc** to finish doing sth; **~ di mangiare** to finish eating **2.** (*smettere*) to stop; **finiscila!** stop it!; **finiamola!** let's be done with it! **3.** (*esaurire: scorte, soldi*) to get through **II.** *vi essere* **1.** (*concludersi*) to finish; **ho finito** I've finished **2.** (*esaurirsi*) **è finita la benzina** to run out **3.** (*terminare*) to end **4.** (*cacciarsi: persona, cosa*) to get to **5.** (*capitare*) to end up **6.** (*loc*) **com'è andata a ~?** what happened in the end?; **~ bene/male** to have a happy/unhappy ending; **~ in carcere** to end up in pris-

on; **~ sui giornali** to end up in the papers; **finirai con l'ammalarti** you'll end up making yourself sick

finito, -a [fi·'ni:·to] *agg* **1.** (*concluso*) finished; **farla -a con qu** to finish with sb; **farla -a con qc** to stop sth **2.** *fam* (*rovinato*) finished **3.** COM (*prodotto*) finished

finlandese [fin·lan·'de:·se] **I.** *agg* Finnish **II.** *mf* (*abitante*) Finn **III.** *m* (*lingua*) Finnish

Finlandia [fin·'lan·dia] *f* Finland; **abitare in ~** to live in Finland; **andare in ~** to go to Finland

fino ['fi:·no] <*davanti a consonante:* fin> *prep* **1.** (*tempo*) **~ a** until; **~ a domani** up until tomorrow; **~ a quando** until when; **~ a tardi** until late; **~ alle tre** until three o'clock; **andare ~ in fondo a qc** *fig* to get to the bottom of sth **2.** (*spazio, quantità*) as far as; **~ a qui** up to here; **~ a casa** all the way home; **~ in cima** right to the top; **~ all'ultimo centesimo** down to one's last penny **3.** (*loc*) **averne ~ sopra ai capelli** to have had it up to here; **~ a un certo punto** up to a point; **fin da piccolo** since childhood; **fin troppo** more than enough

fino, -a *agg* **1.** (*minuto: sale*) fine **2.** (*puro: oro, argento*) pure **3.** (*astuto: cervello*) sharp

finocchio [fi·'nɔk·kio] <-cchi> *m* **1.** BOT fennel **2.** *vulg* faggot *vulg*

finora [fi·'no:·ra] *avv* so far

finsi ['fin·si] *1. pers sing pass rem di* **fingere**

finta ['fin·ta] *f* **1.** (*simulazione*) pretense; **fare ~** to pretend; **fare ~ di niente** to pretend not to notice; **fare ~ di non sentire** to pretend not to hear **2.** SPORT feint

fintantoché [fin·tan·to·'ke] *cong v.* **finché**

finto, -a ['fin·to] **I.** *pp di* **fingere II.** *agg* **1.** (*nome, persona, denti*) false; (*gioiello, quadro*) fake; (*fiori*) artificial **2.** (*lacrime, cortesia*) feigned; (*attacco, battaglia*) pretend

finzione [fin·'tsio:·ne] *f* **1.** (*simulazione*) pretense **2.** (*doppiezza*) duplicity **3.** THEAT (*scenica, teatrale*) illusion

fioccare [fiok·'ka:·re] *vi essere* **1.** (*neve*) to fall **2.** *fig* (*applausi, proteste, multe*) to come thick and fast

fiocco ['fiɔk·ko] <-cchi> *m* **1.** (*di nastro*) bow; **coi -cchi** *fig* (*eccellente*) first-rate **2.** (*batuffolo: lana, cotone*) flock **3.** (*di neve, cereale*) flake; **-cchi d'avena** oat flakes

fiocina ['fiɔ:·tʃi·na] *f* harpoon

fioco, -a ['fiɔ:·ko] <-chi, -che> *agg* (*voce, luce*) faint

fionda ['fion·da] *f* slingshot

fiondarsi [fion·'dar·si] *vr inf* (*precipitarsi*) to dash

fioraio, -a [fio·'ra:·io] <-ai, -aie> *m*, *f* florist

fiordaliso [fior·da·'li:·zo] *m* **1.** BOT cornflower **2.** HIST (*giglio*) fleur-de-lys

fiordilatte [fior·di·'lat·te] <-> *m* **1.** (*mozzarella*) cow's milk mozzarella **2.** (*gelato*) plain ice cream

fiordo ['fiɔr·do] *m* fjord

fiore ['fio:·re] *m* **1.** BOT flower; (*di albero*) blossom; **un mazzo di -i** a bunch of flowers; **a -i** (*tessuto, tappezzeria*) flowery; **i -i di Bach** Bach flower remedies **2.** **il** (**fior**) ~ *fig* (*il meglio*) the cream; **un fior di mascalzone** *iron* a real bad apple *inf* **3.** (*apice*) **nel ~ degli anni** in one's prime **4.** *pl* (*di carte da gioco*) clubs *pl* **5.** (*loc*) **avere i nervi a fior di pelle** to be on edge; **a fior d'acqua** on the surface of the water; **a fior di labbra** in a whisper; **il ~ all'occhiello di qc** the pride of sth

fiorentino [fio·ren·'ti:·no] <*sing*> *m* (*dialetto*) Florentine

Fiorentino <*sing*> *m* (*zona*) Florence area; **nel ~** in the Florence area

fiorentino, -a **I.** *agg* Florentine; **bistecca alla -a** T-bone steak **II.** *m, f* (*abitante*) person from Florence

fioretto[1] [fio·'ret·to] *m* SPORT foil

fioretto[2] [fio·'ret·to] *m* **1.** (*motto*) **i -i di San Francesco** the Little Flowers of St Francis **2.** (*rinuncia*) small sacrifice; **fare un ~** to make a small sacrifice

fioriera [fior·'iɛ:·ra] *f* (*cassetta*) planter

fiorino [fio·'ri:·no] *m* HIST (*moneta*) florin

fiorire [fio·'ri:·re] <*fiorisco*> *vi essere* **1.** (*germogliare*) to flower **2.** *fig* (*prosperare*) to flourish; **se sono rose fioriranno** *prov* time will tell *prov*

fiorista [fio·'ris·ta] <-i *m*, -e *f*> *mf* florist

fiorito, -a [fio·'ri:·to] *agg* **1.** (*pianta*) in flower; (*prato, giardino*) in bloom **2.** *fig* (*stile*) flowery

fioritura [fio·ri·'tu:·ra] *f* **1.** (*di pianta*) flowering **2.** (*di iniziative, arte*) flourishing

Firenze [fi·'rɛn·tse] *f* Florence

firma ['fir·ma] *f* **1.** (*autografo*) signature; **~** [*o* **elettronica**] **digitale** digital signature; **autenticare una ~** to verify a signature; **mettere la ~ su qc** to put one's signature to sth; **ci metterei subito la ~!** *iron* I wouldn't say no to that!; **raccogliere -e** to collect signatures; **portare la ~ di qu** *fig* to bear sb's signature; **una grande ~** (*di giornalismo, moda*) a big name **2.** (*marchio, griffe*) label

firmamento [fir·ma·'men·to] *m a. fig* firmament

firmare [fir·'ma:·re] *vt* to sign

firmatario, -a [fir·ma·'ta:·rio] <-i, -ie> **I.** *agg* (*paese, ministro*) signatory **II.** *m, f* signatory

fisarmonica [fi·zar·'mɔ:·ni·ka] <-che> *f* accordion

fiscale [fis·'ka:·le] *agg* **1.** (*sistema, politica*) tax; **codice ~** tax code; **scontrino ~** cash-register receipt; **medico ~** *doctor who checks up on employees on sick leave* **2.** *fig* (*intransigente*) rigid; (*pignolo*) nitpicking

fiscalismo [fis·ka·'liz·mo] *m* **1.** (*sistema fiscale*) oppressive tax system **2.** *fig* (*intransigenza*) rigidity; (*pignoleria*) nitpicking

fiscalista [fis·ka·'lis·ta] <-i *m*, -e *f*> *mf* **1.** (*esperto*) tax adviser **2.** *fig* (*intransigente*) rigid person; (*pignolo*) nitpicker

fiscalizzare [fis·ka·lid·'dza:·re] *vt* to exempt from taxes

fiscalizzazione [fis·ka·lid·dzat·'tsio:·ne] *f* tax exemption

fischiare [fis·'kia:·re] **I.** *vi* (*persona, merlo, vento, treno, sirena*) to whistle; **mi fischiano le orecchie** *fig* my ears are burning **II.** *vt* **1.** (*zufolare*) to whistle **2.** (*per disapprovare*) to boo **3.** SPORT (*rigore, fallo*) to blow the whistle for

fischietto [fis·'kiet·to] *m* whistle

fischio ['fis·kio] <-schi> *m* (*di persona, merlo, vento, sirena, treno*) whistle; **prendere -schi per fiaschi** *fig* (*fraintendere*) to get hold of the wrong end of the stick

fisco ['fis·ko] *m* (*amministrazione*) =IRS

fisica ['fi:·zi·ka] <-che> *f* (*scienza*) physics; **~ nucleare** nuclear physics

fisico ['fi:·zi·ko] <-ci> *m* (*corporatura*) physique

fisico, -a <-ci, -che> **I.** *agg* physical; **educazione -a** physical education **II.** *m, f* physicist

fisima ['fi:·zi·ma] *f* (*mania*) fixation

fisiocinesiterapia [fi·sio·tʃi·ne·zi·te·ra·'pi:·a] <-ie> *f* physical therapy

fisiologia [fi·zio·lo·'dʒi:·a] *f* physiology

fisiologico, -a [fi·zio·'lɔ:·dʒi·ko] *agg* <-ci, -che> physiological

fisiologo, -a [fiz·'io·lo·go] <-gi, -ghe> *m, f* physiologist

fisionomia [fi·zio·no·'mi:·a] <-ie> *f* **1.** (*di persona*) physiognomy **2.** (*di città, paesaggio*) physical appearance

fisioterapia [fi·zio·te·ra·'pi:·a] *f* physical therapy

fisioterapista [fi·zio·te·ra·'pis·ta] <-i *m*, -e *f*> *mf* physical therapist

fissaggio [fis·'sad·dʒo] <-ggi> *m* FOTO fixing; **bagno di ~** fixing bath

fissamaiuscole [fis·sa·ma·'ius·ko·le] <-> *m* (*di computer, macchina da scrivere*) shift lock

fissare [fis·'sa:·re] **I.** *vt* **1.** (*chiodo*) to hammer in; (*imposta*) to fasten; (*foglio*) to pin **2.** (*capelli*) to keep in place; (*colore*) to make fast; (*pellicola*) to fix **3.** *fig* (*sguardo, attenzione*) to focus **4.** (*guardare intensamente*) to stare at **5.** (*imprimere*) to fix; **~ qc nella mente** (*imprimere*) to fix sth firmly in one's mind **6.** (*stabilire: data, prezzo*) to fix; (*appuntamento*) to arrange; (*domicilio*) to establish **7.** *fig* (*prenotare: camera, tavolo*) to reserve **II.** *vr:* **-rsi 1.** (*stabilirsi in un luogo*) to settle **2.** (*ostinarsi*) **-rsi di fare qc** to get it into one's head to do sth

fissativo [fis·sa·'ti:·vo] *m* CHEM fixative; FOTO fixer

fissato, -a [fis·'sa:·to] *m, f* (*maniaco*) obsessive

fissatore [fis·sa·'to:·re] *m* **1.** CHEM fixative; FOTO fixer **2.** (*per capelli*) setting lotion

fissazione [fis·sat·'tsio:·ne] *f* **1.** (*di data, di aliquota*) fixing **2.** (*ossessione*) fixation

fissile ['fis·si·le] *agg* PHYS fissile

fissionare [fis·sio·'na:·re] *vt* PHYS to fission

fissione [fis·'sio:·ne] *f* PHYS fission

fissità [fis·si·'ta] <-> *f* steadiness

fisso, -a *agg* **1.** (*gener*) fixed; **prezzo ~** fixed price; **avere un chiodo ~** *fig* to have an obsession **2.** (*invariabile: regola*) hard-and-fast; (*impiego*) permanent

fistola ['fis·to·la] *f* MED fistula

fitness ['fit·nis] <-> *f* SPORT fitness; **fare ~** to work out

fitocosmesi [fi·to·kos·'mɛː·zi] <-> *f* plant-based cosmetics *pl*

fitoterapia [fi·to·te·ra·'piː·a] *f* MED herbal medicine

fitta ['fit·ta] *f* (*dolore*) sharp pain; **sentire una ~ al cuore** *fig* (*angoscia*) to feel an ache in one's heart

fittavolo, -a [fit·'taː·vo·lo] *m, f* tenant

fittile ['fit·ti·le] *agg* fictile

fittizio, -a [fit·'tit·tsio] <-i, -ie> *agg* **1.** (*falso: nome*) fictitious; (*contratto*) bogus **2.** (*illusorio: immagine*) illusory

fitto I. *agg* **1.** (*folto: bosco*) dense; (*pelo*) thick **2.** (*compatto: pettine, rete*) fine **3.** (*denso: pioggia*) heavy; (*buio*) pitch; (*nebbia*) dense **4.** *fig* (*mistero*) impenetrable II. *avv* **piove** [*o* **nevica*] fitto** (*intensamente*) it's raining [*o* snowing] hard III. *m* **nel ~ del bosco** in the depths of the forest

fiumana [fiu·'maː·na] *f* **1.** (*piena*) torrent **2.** *fig* (*massa: di gente*) stream; (*di parole*) torrent

fiume[1] ['fiuː·me] *m* **1.** (*corso d'acqua*) river **2.** *fig* (*grande quantità: di lacrime*) flood; (*di parole*) torrent; **a -i** by the bucketful

fiume[2] <inv> *agg* long-drawn-out; **un romanzo ~** a roman-fleuve

fiutare [fiu·'taː·re] *vt* **1.** (*annusare*) to sniff **2.** (*aspirare: tabacco, cocaina*) to snort **3.** *fig* (*intuire: inganno, affare*) to smell

fiuto ['fiuː·to] *m* **1.** (*odorato*) sense of smell **2.** *fig* (*intuito*) nose

fix [fiks] <-> *f* (*dose di eroina*) fix

fixing ['fik·siŋ/'fik·sin(g)] *m* FIN fixing

flaccido, -a ['flat·tʃi·do] *agg* (*pelle*) saggy; (*seno, corpo*) flabby

flacone [fla·'koː·ne] *m* bottle

flagellare [fla·dʒel·'laː·re] *vt* **1.** (*fustigare*) to flog **2.** (*grandine, tempesta*) to beat against **3.** *fig* (*censurare*) to censure

flagello [flad·'dʒɛl·lo] *m* **1.** (*frusta*) whip **2.** *fig* (*calamità*) scourge

flagrante [fla·'gran·te] *agg* (*evidente*) flagrant; **cogliere qu in ~** to catch sb red-handed

flanella [fla·'nɛl·la] *f* flannel

flash [flæʃ/flɛʃ] I. <inv> *agg* (*breve*) **notizia ~** newsflash; **telegiornale ~** news summary II. <-> *m* **1.** FOTO flash **2.** (*notizia*) newsflash

flatulenza [fla·tu·'lɛn·tsa] *f* MED flatulence

flautista [flau·'tis·ta] <-i *m*, -e *f*> *mf* flutist

flauto ['flaːu·to] *m* flute; **~ dolce** recorder; **~ traverso** transverse flute

flebile ['flɛː·bi·le] *agg* (*voce, suono*) faint

flebite [fle·'biː·te] *f* MED phlebitis

flebo ['flɛː·bo] <-> *f fam* (*fleboclisi*) drip

fleboclisi [fle·bo·'kliː·zi] <-> *f* drip

flemma ['flɛm·ma] *f* calm

flemmatico, -a [flem·'maː·ti·ko] <-ci, -che> *agg* calm

flessibile [fles·'siː·bi·le] *agg* **1.** (*materiale*) flexible; **orario di lavoro ~** flextime **2.** *fig* (*carattere*) adaptable

flessione [fles·'sioː·ne] *f* **1.** (*nella ginnastica*) bend **2.** (*curvatura: di arco, sbarra*) bending **3.** LING inflection **4.** COM (*calo*) drop

flesso ['flɛs·so] *pp di* **flettere**

flessometro [fles·'sɔː·met·ro] *m* tape measure

flessore [fles·'soː·re] *m* (*muscolo*) flexor

flessuoso, -a [fles·su·'oː·so] *agg* (*corpo*) lithe

flettere ['flɛt·te·re] <fletto, fletei *o* flessi, flesso> I. *vt* **1.** (*membra*) to bend **2.** LING to inflect II. *vr*: **-rsi** (*curvarsi*) to bend; **-rsi sulle ginocchia** to squat

flicorno [fli·'kor·no] *m* MUS flugelhorn

flipper ['flip·per] <-> *m* pinball machine; **giocare a ~** to play pinball

flirt [fləːt] <-> *m* fling

flirtare [flir·'taː·re] *vi* to flirt

F.lli *abbr di* **fratelli** Bros

FLM *f abbr di* **Federazione Lavoratori Metalmeccanici** *Italian Engineering Workers Federation*

flora ['flɔː·ra] *f* flora

floreale [flo·re·'aː·le] *agg* **1.** (*decorazione*) floral **2.** (*stile*) Art Nouveau

floricoltore, -trice [flo·ri·kol·'toː·re] *m, f* flower-grower

floricoltura [flo·ri·kol·'tuː·ra] *f* flower-growing

floridezza [flo·ri·'det·tsa] *f* **1.** (*di vegetazione*) healthiness **2.** (*di commercio, nazione*) prosperousness

florido, -a ['flɔː·ri·do] *agg* **1.** (*aspetto*) healthy **2.** (*commercio*) flourishing

floscio, -a ['flɔʃ·ʃo] <-sci, -sce> *agg* **1.** (*flaccido: muscoli*) flabby **2.** (*non rigido: tessuto, cappello*) soft

flotta ['flɔt·ta] *f* fleet

fluente [flu·'ɛn·te] *agg* **1.** (*chioma, barba*) flowing **2.** (*lingua*) fluent

fluido ['fluː·ido] *m* **1.** PHYS fluid **2.** (*di medium, guaritore*) mystical power

fluido, -a *agg a. fig* fluid

fluire [flu·'iː·re] <fluisco> *vi essere a. fig* to flow

fluorescente [fluo·reʃ·'ʃɛn·te] *agg* fluorescent; **lampada ~** fluorescent light

fluorite [fluo·'riː·te] *f* MIN fluorite

fluoro [flu·'ɔː·ro] *m* CHEM fluorine

fluoruro [fluo·'ruː·ro] *m* fluoride

flusso ['flus·so] *m* **1.** (*gener*) flow; **~ mestruale** menstrual flow; **~ e riflusso** ebb and flow **2.** PHYS (*elettrico, magnetico*) flux; **~ luminoso** luminous flux

flûte [flyt] <-> *m* flute

fluttuare [flut·tu·'aː·re] *vi* **1.** (*ondeggiare: in acqua, nell'aria*) to float **2.** *fig* (*oscillare: stato d'animo, opinione*) to waver **3.** ECON, FIN (*valuta, titolo*) to fluctuate

fluttuazione [flut·tu·at·'tsioː·ne] *f* ECON, FIN

(*cambio, valuta*) fluctuation

fluviale [flu·'via:·le] *agg* **1.**(*bacino, naviga-zione, vegetazione*) river **2.**(*pesci*) freshwater

fly and drive ['flai ən 'draiv] <-> *m* (*biglietto, tour*) fly-drive

f.m. *abbr di* **fine mese** end of month

FMI *m abbr di* **Fondo Monetario Interna-zionale** IMF

fobia [fo·'bi:·a] <-ie> *f* PSYCH phobia

foca ['fɔ:·ka] <-che> *f* seal

focaccia [fo·'kat·tʃa] <-cce> *f* **1.**(*salata*) foc-caccia **2.**(*dolce*) bun **3.**(*loc*) **rendere pan per ~** to get one's own back

---

ℹ️ **Focaccia** is a flat bread rather like a pizza but thicker. It is made with dough similar to that used for making bread, but with the addition of salt and extra virgin olive oil. Both **focaccia** and the smaller *focaccine* are good eaten warm on their own; they can also be cut in half and filled with cold cuts or cheese. They are eaten as a mid-morning or afternoon snack, or for a quick lunch or supper. The Ligurian version is made with cheese.

---

focale [fo·'ka:·le] **I.** *agg* focal; **distanza ~** focal length; **punto ~** *fig* (*essenziale*) focal point **II.** *f* focal length

focalizzare [fo·ka·lid·'dza:·re] *vt* **1.**(*obiettivo*) to focus; (*immagine*) to get into focus **2.***fig* (*inquadrare: situazione*) to get into perspec-tive **3.***fig* (*concentrare: attenzione*) to focus

foce ['fo:·tʃe] *f* mouth

fochista [fo·'kis·ta] <-i *m*, -e *f*> *mf* stoker

focolaio [fo·ko·'la:·io] <-ai> *m* **1.**MED focus **2.***fig* (*di rivolta*) breeding ground

focolare [fo·ko·'la:·re] *m* (*camino*) hearth; **il ~ domestico** *fig* hearth and home

focoso, -a [fo·'ko:·so] *agg* (*temperamento*) fiery

fodera ['fɔ:·de·ra] *f* **1.**(*di cuscino*) cover **2.**(*di abito*) lining **3.**(*di libro*) jacket

foderare [fo·de·'ra:·re] *vt* **1.**(*abiti, cassetti*) to line **2.**(*libri*) to cover

fodero ['fɔ:·de·ro] *m* scabbard

foga ['fo:·ga] *f* (*impeto*) ardor; **nella ~ del discorso** in the heat of the discussion

foggia ['fɔd·dʒa] <-gge> *f* (*forma*) form; (*di abito*) style; **a ~ di** in the shape of

Foggia *f* Foggia

Foggiano [fod·'dʒa:·no] <*sing*> *m* (*zona*) Foggia area; **nel ~** in the Foggia area

foggiano, -a I. *agg* from Foggia **II.** *m, f* (*abi-tante*) person from Foggia

foglia ['fɔʎ·ʎa] <-glie> *f* leaf; **mangiare la ~** *fig* to smell a rat; **tremare come una ~** to shake like a leaf

fogliame [foʎ·'ʎa:·me] *m* (*di pianta*) foliage

foglio ['fɔʎ·ʎo] <-gli> *m* **1.**(*di carta*) sheet; **~ a righe/a quadretti** sheet of lined/squared

paper; **~ protocollo** foolscap; **~ illustrativo** instructions *pl* **2.**(*documento, modulo*) form; **~ rosa** AUTO learner's permit; **~ complement-are** AUTO registration **3.**(*banconota*) bill **4.**(*lamina*) sheet

fogna ['foɲ·ɲa] *f* **1.**(*discarica*) sewer **2.***fig, pej* (*ambiente sporco*) pigsty

fognatura [foɲ·ɲa·'tu:·ra] *f* sewers *pl*

föhn [fø:n] <-> *m* (*vento caldo*) föhn, warm Alpine wind

folata [fo·'la:·ta] *f* (*di vento*) gust

folclore [folk·'lo:·re] *m* folklore

folcloristico, -a [fol·klo·'ris·ti·ko] <-ci, -che> *agg* folk

folgorante [fol·go·'ran·te] *agg* **1.**(*luce*) daz-zling **2.***fig* (*ardente: amore, passione*) in-tense **3.**(*brillante: idea*) brilliant **4.**(*intenso: sguardo*) withering

folgorare [fol·go·'ra:·re] *vt* **1.**(*fulmine*) to strike **2.**(*scarica elettrica*) to electrocute; **~ qu con lo sguardo** *fig* to give sb a withering look

folgorazione [fol·go·rat·'tsio:·ne] *f* **1.**(*scarica elettrica*) electrocution **2.***fig* (*della mente*) brainstorm

folgore ['fol·go·re] *f liter* thunderbolt

folk [fouk/fɔlk] **I.**<inv> *agg* (*musica, canzone*) folk **II.**<-> *m* (*genere musicale*) folk (music)

folla ['fol·la/'fɔl·la] *f* crowd

folle ['fɔl·le] **I.** *agg* **1.**(*persona, idea, spesa*) crazy **2.**MOT neutral; **in ~** in neutral **II.** *mf* madman *m*, madwoman *f*

folleggiare [fol·led·'dʒa:·re] *vi* (*spassarsela*) to paint the town red

folletto [fol·'let·to] *m* (*nelle fiabe*) elf

follia [fol·'li:·a] <-ie> *f* madness; **alla ~** madly; **fare -ie per qu** to be crazy about sb

follicolo [fol·'li:·ko·lo] *m* ANAT follicle

folto ['fol·to] *m* **1.**(*di bosco*) depths *pl* **2.***fig* (*di mischia*) thick

folto, -a *agg* (*bosco, schiera*) dense; (*chioma*) thick

fomentare [fo·men·'ta:·re] *vt* (*istigare: odio, passioni, rivolta*) to stir up

fomentatore, -trice [fo·men·ta·'to:·re] *m, f* agitator

fonda ['fon·da] *f* NAUT anchorage; **essere alla ~** to be at anchor

fondaco ['fon·da·ko] <-chi> *m* HIST (*magaz-zino*) warehouse

fondale [fon·'da:·le] *m* **1.**(*di mare*) bottom **2.**THEAT backdrop

fondamentale [fon·da·men·'ta:·le] *agg* funda-mental

fondamento¹ [fon·da·'men·to] <le fonda-menta> *m* ARCH foundation; **gettare le -a** to lay the foundations

fondamento² *m fig* (*principio base*) founda-tion; **notizie prive di ~** (*non vere*) news that has no foundation

fondare [fon·'da:·re] **I.** *vt* **1.**(*città*) to found **2.**(*società, ordine religioso*) to establish **3.**(*teoria, accusa*) to base **II.** *vr* **-rsi su qc** (*bas-arsi: ipotesi, sospetto*) to be based on sth

fondatezza [fon·da·'tet·tsa] *f* soundness

fondatore, -trice [fon·da·'to:·re] *m, f* (*di città, società, ordine religioso*) founder

fondazione [fon·dat·'tsio:·ne] *f* foundation; (*la ~ Cini si occupa della salvaguardia di beni culturali*)

fondello [fon·'dɛl·lo] *m* 1. (*di bossolo*) bottom 2. (*di calzoni*) seat; **prendere qu per i -i** *fig* to pull sb's leg

fondente [fon·'dɛn·te] *agg* **cioccolato ~** dark chocolate

fondere ['fon·de·re] <fondo, fusi, fuso> I. *vt* 1. (*metallo, ghiaccio*) to melt 2. (*statua, campana*) to cast; **~** (**il motore**) AUTO to burn out the bearings 3. *fig* (*unire: aziende, partiti, gruppi*) to merge II. *vi* to melt III. *vr:* **-rsi** 1. (*sciogliersi: neve, cera*) to melt 2. *fig* (*unirsi: aziende, partiti, gruppi*) to merge; (*le due aziende si sono fuse*)

fonderia [fon·de·'ri:·a] <-ie> *f* foundry

fondiario, -a [fon·'dia:·rio] <-i, -ie> *agg* (*proprietà*) landed; (*rendita*) from land

fondista [fon·'dis·ta] <-i *m*, -e *f*> *mf* 1. SPORT long-distance runner 2. (*di giornale*) editorial writer

fondivalle *pl di* **fondovalle**

fondo ['fon·do] *m* 1. (*base: di pentola, valigia, pozzo,*) bottom; **avere uno stomaco senza ~** *fig* to have a bottomless stomach 2. (*fondale: di mare, lago, fiume*) bottom; **incagliarsi sul ~** to run aground; **andare a ~** to go to the bottom 3. (*bordo inferiore: di pagina, calzoni*) bottom 4. (*estremità: di strada*) end; (*di campo*) bottom; (*di scena*) back; **in ~ alla stanza** at the back of the room; **andare in ~ a qc** *fig* to get to the bottom of sth; **da cima a ~** from top to bottom 5. (*parte più interna: di cassetto*) back; **in ~ al cuore** *fig* deep in one's heart; **in ~** *fig* after all 6. SPORT **gara di ~** (*corsa*) distance race; **sci di ~** cross-country skiing 7. (*strato*) tinta foundation; **~ stradale** roadbed 8. (*deposito: di vino, aceto*) lees *pl;* **-i di caffè** grounds *pl;* **-i di magazzino** *fig* old stock 9. (*terreno*) estate 10. **articolo di ~** editorial 11. ECON (*denaro*) fund; **-i d'investimento** investment funds *pl;* **-i neri** slush fund; **~ pensioni** pension fund; **~ di cassa** float; **~ pubblico** public fund; **a ~ perduto** without security

fondo, -a *agg* (*profondo*) deep; **piatto ~** soup plate; **a notte -a** at dead of night

fondocampo [fon·do·'kam·po] <-> *m* SPORT back court

fondoschiena [fon·do·'skiɛ:·na] <-> *m inf* (*deretano*) backside

fondovalle [fon·do·'val·le] <fondivalle> *m* valley floor

fonduta [fon·'du:·ta] *f* CULIN fondue

fonema [fo·'nɛ:·ma] <-i> *m* LING phoneme

fonetica [fo·'nɛ:·ti·ka] <-che> *f* phonetics

fonetico, -a [fo·'nɛ:·ti·ko] <-ci, -che> *agg* (*scrittura, alfabeto*) phonetic

fonico ['fɔ:·ni·ko] <-ci> *m* FILM (*tecnico*) sound engineer

fonico, -a <-ci, -che> *agg* (*segnale, frequenza*) phonic

fonocassetta [fo·no·kas·'set·ta] *f* music cassette

fonografo [fo·'nɔ:·gra·fo] *m* MUS phonograph

fonogramma [fo·no·'gram·ma] <-i> *m* LING, PHYS phonogram

fonokit [fo·no·'kit] <-> *m voice recognition system*

fonologia [fo·no·lo·'dʒi:·a] <-gie> *f* LING phonology

fonometro [fo·'nɔ:·met·ro] *m* PHYS phonometer

fonomontaggio [fo·no·mon·'tad·dʒo] <-ggi> *m* edited recording

fonoriproduttore [fo·no·ri·pro·dut·'to:·re] *m* sound reproduction device

fonoriproduzione [fo·no·ri·pro·dut·'tsio:·ne] *f* sound reproduction

font [fɔnt] <-> *m o f* font

fontana [fon·'ta:·na] *f* fountain

fontanella [fon·ta·'nɛl·la] *f* 1. (*piccola fontana*) drinking fountain 2. ANAT fontanelle

fonte ['fon·te] I. *f* 1. (*sorgente*) spring 2. *fig* (*di guadagno, guai, informazioni*) source; **-i energetiche** energy sources *pl;* **-i scritte** written sources *pl* II. *m* **~ battesimale** font

footing ['fu·tiŋ] <-> *m* SPORT jogging; **fare ~** to go jogging

foraggiare [fo·rad·'dʒa:·re] *vt* 1. (*cavalli*) to provide fodder for 2. *fig, iron* (*mantenere*) to bankroll

foraggio [fo·'rad·dʒo] <-ggi> *m* fodder

forare [fo·'ra:·re] I. *vt* 1. (*parete, lamiera*) to make a hole in 2. (*biglietti*) to punch 3. (*pneumatico*) to burst II. *vi* (*pneumatico*) to burst

foratura [fo·ra·'tu:·ra] *f* 1. (*di legno, lamiera*) piercing 2. (*di pneumatico*) bursting

forbici ['fɔr·bi·tʃi] *fpl* scissors *pl;* **un paio di ~** a pair of scissors

forbito [for·'bi:·to] *agg fig* (*raffinato: linguaggio, stile*) elegant

forca ['for·ka] <-che> *f* 1. AGR pitchfork 2. (*patibolo*) gallows

forcella [for·'tʃɛl·la] *f* (*di carrucola, di bicicletta, di ramo*) fork

forchetta [for·'ket·ta] *f* fork; **essere una buona ~** *fig* to like one's food; **parlare in punta di ~** *fig* to speak affectedly

forchettata [for·ket·'ta:·ta] *f* forkful; **una ~ di spaghetti** a forkful of spaghetti; **ne assaggio una ~** I'll just have a little

forcina [for·'tʃi:·na] *f* hairpin

forcipe ['fɔr·tʃi·pe] *m* MED forceps *pl*

forcone [for·'ko:·ne] *m* pitchfork

forense [fo·'rɛn·se] *agg* forensic

foresta [fo·'rɛs·ta] *f* forest; **~ vergine** virgin forest

forestale [fo·res·'ta:·le] *agg* forest; **guardia ~** forest ranger; **Corpo ~ dello Stato =** Forest Service

foresteria [fo·res·te·'ri:·a] <-ie> *f* (*di collegio,*

convento) guest room; **uso** ~ for guest use

forestiero, -a [fo·res·'tiɛ:·ro] I. *agg* foreign II. *m, f* foreigner

forfait [fɔr·'fɛ] <-> *m* **1.** ECON (*prezzo fisso*) fixed price; **a** ~ for a fixed price; **lavoro a** ~ piecework **2.** SPORT (*ritiro*) default; **vincere per** ~ to win by default; **dichiarare** ~ *fig* to give in

forfettario, -a [for·fe·'ta:·rio] <-i, -ie> *agg* ECON fixed-price

forfora ['for·fo·ra] *f* dandruff

forgia ['fɔr·dʒa] <-ge> *f* (*fucina*) forge

forgiare [for·'dʒa:·re] *vt* **1.** (*metallo*) to forge **2.** *fig* (*plasmare: carattere*) to mold

Forlì *f* Forlì

forlivese [for·li·'ve:·se] I. *agg* from Forlì II. *mf* (*abitante*) person from Forlì

forma ['for·ma] *f* **1.** (*aspetto*) form; **prendere** ~ to take shape; **a** ~ **di ...** in the shape of ... **2.** *pl* (*fattezze*) figure **3.** (*condizione psicofisica*) form; **essere in** ~ to be in shape; **essere giù di** ~ to be feeling down; **peso** ~ ideal weight **4.** (*per calzature*) last; (*per dolci*) mold; **una** ~ **di formaggio** a whole cheese **5.** *fig* (*di governo, di ente*) form **6.** (*modalità*) **in** ~ **privata** privately **7.** (*convenzione*) convention

formaggiera [for·mad·'dʒɛ:·ra] *f* cheese bowl

formaggino [for·mad·'dʒi:·no] *m* processed cheese triangle

formaggio [for·'mad·dʒo] <-ggi> *m* cheese; ~ **fresco** fresh cheese; ~ **stagionato** mature cheese; ~ **pecorino** pecorino; ~ **molle** soft cheese

formaldeide [for·mal·'dɛ:·ide] *f* formaldehyde

formale [for·'ma:·le] *agg* formal

formalina [for·ma·'li:·na] *f* formalin

formalismo [for·ma·'liz·mo] *m* formalism

formalista [for·ma·'lis·ta] <-i *m*, -e *f*> *mf* formalist

formalità [for·ma·li·'ta] <-> *f* formality; **per** ~ as a formality

formalizzare [for·ma·lid·'dza:·re] I. *vt* (*rendere formale*) to formalize II. *vr* **-rsi per qc** (*risentirsi*) to take offense at sth

formare [for·'ma:·re] I. *vt* **1.** (*modellare: statua*) to make **2.** (*corteo, cerchio, famiglia, partito*) to form **3.** (*addestrare: ufficiali, tecnici, atleti*) to train **4.** *fig* (*carattere*) to mold **5.** TEL (*numero*) to dial II. *vr:* **-rsi 1.** (*prodursi*) to form **2.** (*svilupparsi*) to develop

format ['fɔ:·mæt] <-> *m* TV format

formato [for·'ma:·to] *m* format; ~ **tascabile** pocket size; **in** ~ **ridotto** small-sized; **fotografia** ~ **tessera** passport-size photo

formato, -a *agg* **1.** (*sviluppato*) fully developed **2.** (*costituito*) formed

formattare [for·mat·'ta:·re] *vt* COMPUT to format; ~ **un dischetto** to format a disk

formattato, -a *agg* COMPUT formatted

formattazione [for·mat·tat·'tsio:·ne] *f* COMPUT formatting

formazione [for·mat·'tsio:·ne] *f* **1.** (*gener*) for-

mation **2.** (*sviluppo*) development **3.** (*addestramento*) training; **contratto di** ~ (*professionale*) (vocational) training contract

formella [for·'mɛl·la] *f* ARCH (*motivo ornamentale*) tile

formica ~ **rossa** red ant; **avere un cervello di** ~ to be a bird-brain

formicaio [for·mi·'ka:·io] <-ai> *m* **1.** (*nido di formiche*) anthill **2.** *fig* (*luogo*) **essere un** ~ to be swarming with people

formichiere [for·mi·'kiɛ:·re] *m* anteater

formico, -a ['fɔr·mi·ko] <-ci, -che> *agg* CHEM formic; **acido** ~ formic acid

formicolare [for·mi·ko·'la:·re] *vi* **1.** *avere* (*brulicare*) ~ **di ...** to swarm with ... **2.** *essere* (*essere intorpidito*) **mi formicola il braccio** I've got pins and needles in my arm

formicolio [for·mi·ko·'li:·o] <-ii> *m* **1.** (*brulichio di gente*) swarming **2.** (*intorpidimento*) pins and needles

formidabile [for·mi·'da:·bi·le] *agg* **1.** (*fortissimo*) powerful **2.** (*eccezionale*) amazing

formoso, -a [for·'mo:·so] *agg* (*donna, fianchi, petto*) shapely

formula ['fɔr·mu·la] *f* **1.** (*di giuramento, liturgica*) form **2.** (*frase: di commiato, augurio*) formula **3.** MATH, CHEM formula; ~ **magica** magic spell **4.** (*metodo*) formula **5.** SPORT **Formula 1** Formula 1

formulare [for·mu·'la:·re] *vt* to formulate

formulario [for·mu·'la:·rio] <-i> *m* (*modulo*) form

formulazione [for·mu·lat·'tsio:·ne] *f* **1.** (*di domanda, ipotesi*) formulation **2.** (*testo: di legge*) phrasing

fornace [for·'na:·tʃe] *f* **1.** TEC kiln **2.** *fig* (*luogo caldo*) oven

fornaio, -a [for·'na:·io] <-ai, -aie> *m, f* **1.** (*operaio*) baker **2.** (*negozio*) bakery

fornello [for·'nɛl·lo] *m* (*cucina*) stova; (*fuoco*) burner; ~ **a gas** gas stove; ~ **elettrico** electric stove

fornicare [for·ni·'ka:·re] *vi poet* to fornicate *form*

fornire [for·'ni:·re] <fornisco> I. *vt* **1.** (*provvedere*) to supply; ~ **qu di qc** to supply sb with sth; ~ **qc a qu** to supply sth to sb **2.** (*informazioni, prova*) to provide II. *vr* **-rsi di qc** to provide o.s. with sth

fornito, -a [for·'ni:·to] *agg* provided; **un negozio ben** ~ a well-stocked store

fornitore, -trice [for·ni·'to:·re] *m, f* supplier; ~ **ufficiale** SPORT official supplier

fornitura [for·ni·'tu:·ra] *f* supply; **-e per ufficio** office supplies

forno ['for·no] *m* **1.** (*per cuocere*) oven; **pasta al** ~ baked pasta; **patate al** ~ baked potatoes; ~ **a microonde** microwave oven **2.** TEC furnace **3.** (*panetteria*) bakery

foro¹ ['fo:·ro] *m* (*buco*) hole

foro² ['fɔ:·ro] *m* **1.** HIST forum **2.** JUR (*tribunale*) court

forra ['for·ra] *f* ravine

forse ['for·se] I. *avv* perhaps II. *m* **essere in ~** to be doubtful

forsennato, -a [for·sen·'na:·to] *m, f* madman *m*, madwoman *f*

forte¹ ['fɔr·te] *avv* 1.(*a voce alta*) loud 2.(*velocemente*) fast

forte² I. *agg* 1.(*robusto*) strong 2.(*determinato: persona, carattere*) strong 3.(*elevato: somma*) large 4.(*acuto: dolore*) intense 5.(*intenso: colore*) bright; (*sapore, odore*) strong 6.(*abile*) good; **essere ~ in qc** to be good at sth 7. *inf* (*simpatico*) great 8.(*loc*) **dare man ~ a qu** to come to sb's aid; **farsi ~ di qc** to make use of sth II. *m* 1.(*persona*) **i -i** the strong 2.(*specialità*) forte; **la matematica non è il suo ~** math is not his forte 3. MIL fort

fortezza [for·'tet·tsa] *f* MIL fortress

fortificare [for·ti·fi·'ka:·re] *vt* 1.MIL (*mura, città*) to fortify 2.(*corpo*) to strengthen

fortificazione [for·ti·fi·kat·'tsio:·ne] *f* (*luogo fortificato*) fortification

fortilizio [for·ti·'lit·tsio] <-i> *m* fortalice

fortino [for·'ti:·no] *m* fort

fortuito, -a [for·'tu:i·to] *agg* (*coincidenza, incontro, incidente*) chance; **per un caso ~** by chance

fortuna [for·'tu:·na] *f* 1.(*destino*) fortune 2.(*buona sorte*) luck; **un colpo di ~** a stroke of luck; **avere ~ in qc** to be lucky in sth; **per ~** luckily 3.(*patrimonio*) fortune; **fare ~** to make one's fortune 4.(*loc*) **atterraggio di ~** emergency landing; **timone di ~** jury rudder

fortunato, -a [for·tu·'na:·to] *agg* lucky

fortunoso, -a [for·tu·'no:·so] *agg* (*fortuito: coincidenza*) chance

foruncolo [fo·'ruŋ·ko·lo] *m* boil

forviare [for·vi·'a:·re] *vt, vi v.* **fuorivare**

forwardare *vt* COMPUT (*mail*) to forward

forza ['fɔr·tsa] *f* 1.(*fisica, morale*) strength; **con ~** hard; **con tutte le -e** with all one's might; **farsi ~** to draw on one's reserves of courage 2.(*violenza*) force; **~ bruta** brute force; **~ maggiore** force majeure; **con la ~** by force; **per ~** (*controvoglia*) against one's will; (*naturalmente*) of course 3.(*efficacia*) force; **in ~ di** as provided by 4. *pl* MIL forces; **-e** (*armate*) (armed) forces; **arrivare in ~** *a. fig* to arrive in force 5.PHYS, NAUT force 6.(*loc*) **a ~ di ...** by dint of ...; **a ~ di gridare** through shouting

forzare [for·'tsa:·re] I. *vt* 1.(*porta*) to break down; (*serratura*) to force; (*blocco stradale*) to break through 2.(*accelerare*) **~ il passo** to speed up; *fig* to force the pace 3.(*costringere*) to force II. *vi* (*porta, cassetto*) to stick

forzato, -a [for·'tsa:·to] I. *agg* 1.(*sorriso, assenza, rinuncia*) forced 2.JUR (*esproprio*) compulsory; **lavori -i** forced labor II. *m, f* convict

forziere [for·'tsiɛ:·re] *m* strongbox

forzista [fort·'tsis·ta] <-i *m*, -e *f*> *mf* supporter of the Forza Italia party

forzuto, -a [for·'tsu:·to] *agg* brawny

foschia [fos·'ki:·a] <-schie> *f* mist

fosco, -a ['fos·ko] <-schi, -sche> *agg* 1.(*cupo: cielo*) overcast 2.(*incerto: previsione, futuro*) gloomy 3. *fig* (*minaccioso: sguardo*) menacing

fosfato [fos·'fa:·to] *m* phosphate

fosforescente [fos·fo·reʃ·'ʃɛn·te] *agg* phosphorescent

fosforescenza [fos·fo·reʃ·'ʃɛn·tsa] *f* phosphorescence

fosforo ['fɔs·fo·ro] *m* CHEM phosphorus

fossa ['fɔs·sa] *f* 1.(*buca*) hole 2.(*tomba*) grave; **~ comune** mass grave; **scavarsi la ~ con le proprie mani** *fig* to dig one's own grave *fig* 3.GEOL graben

fossato [fos·'sa:·to] *m* ditch

fosse ['fos·se] *3. per sing conj imp di* **essere¹**

fossetta [fos·'set·ta] *f* (*su guance*) dimple

fossi ['fos·si] *1.e 2.pers sing conj imp di* **essere¹**

fossile ['fɔs·si·le] I. *agg* (*di epoca remota: reperto, foresta*) fossil II. *m* fossil

fosso ['fɔs·so] *m* (*fossa*) ditch; **saltare il ~** *fig* to take the plunge

foste ['fos·te] *2.pers pl conj imp di* **essere¹**

fosti ['fos·ti] *2.pers sing pass rem di* **essere¹**

foto ['fɔ:·to] <-> *f* photo

foto- [fo·to] (*in parole composte*) photo-

fotocellula [fo·to·'tʃɛl·lu·la] *f* photoelectric cell

fotochimica [fo·to·'ki:·mi·ka] <*sing*> *f* photochemistry

fotocolor [fo·to·'ko·lor] <-> *f* FOTO color photography

fotocomposizione [fo·to·kom·po·zit·'tsio:·ne] *f* TYP photocomposition

fotocopia [fo·to·'kɔ:·pia] *f* photocopy

fotocopiare [fo·to·ko·'pia:·re] *vt* to photocopy

fotocopiatore [fo·to·ko·'pia:·re] *m* photocopier

fotocopiatrice [fo·to·ko·pia·'tri:·tʃe] *f* photocopier

fotocronaca [fo·to·'krɔ:·na·ka] <-che> *f* photojournalism

fotocronista [fo·to·kro·'nis·ta] <-i *m*, -e *f*> *mf* photojournalist

fotoelettrico, -a [fo·to·e·'lɛt·tri·ko] <-ci, -che> *agg* TEC (*barriera, cellula*) photoelectric; **effetto ~** photoelectric effect

fotofit [fo·to·'fit] <-> *m* (*identikit*) composite

fotogenico, -a [fo·to·'dʒɛ:·ni·ko] <-ci, -che> *agg* photogenic

fotogiornale [fo·to·dʒor·'na:·le] *m* illustrated magazine

fotografare [fo·to·gra·'fa:·re] *vt* FOTO to photograph

fotografia [fo·to·gra·'fi:·a] *f* 1.(*tecnica*) photography 2.(*immagine*) photograph; **~ a colori** color photograph; **~ in bianco e nero** black-and-white photograph; **~ formato tessera** passport-size photograph; **~ aerea** aerial photograph

fotografico, -a [fo·to·'gra:·fi·ko] <-ci, -che> *agg* FOTO photographic; **macchina -a** camera; **studio ~** photographer's studio

fotografo, -a [fo·'tɔ:·gra·fo] *m, f* photographer

fotogramma [fo·to·'gram·ma] <-i> *m* FOTO, FILM frame

fotokit [fo·to·'kit] <-> *m v.* **fotofit**

fotomeccanico, -a [fo·to·mek·'ka:·ni·ko] <-ci, -che> *agg* (*laboratorio, procedimento*) photomechanical

fotometria [fo·to·me·'tri:·a] <-ie> *f* (*scienza*) photometry

fotomodella [fo·to·mo·'dɛl·la] *f* model

fotomontaggio [fo·to·mon·'tad·dʒo] <-ggi> *m* photomontage

fotoreportage [fo·to·rə·por·'taʒ] <-> *m* photoreportage

fotoreporter [fo·to·re·'pɔr·ter] <-> *mf* news photographer

fotoriproduzione [fo·to·ri·pro·dut·'tsio:·ne] *f* FOTO photographic reproduction

fotoromanzo [fo·to·ro·'man·dzo] *m* photo story

fotosafari [fo·to·sa·'fa:·ri] <-> *m* photo safari

fotosensibile [fo·to·sen·'si:·bi·le] *agg* photosensitive

fotoservizio [fo·to·ser·'vi:·tsio] <-zi> *m* photoreportage

fotosintesi [fo·to·'sin·te·zi] <-> *f* BOT photosynthesis

fotosub [fo·to·'sub] <-> *mf* underwater photographer

fototeca [fɔ·to·'tɛ:·ka] <-che> *f* picture library

fototessera [fo·to·'tɛs·se·ra] *f* FOTO passport photo

fottere ['fot·te·re] I. *vt* 1. *vulg* to fuck; **va a farti ~!** *vulg* fuck off! 2. *fam* (*imbrogliare*) to screw *vulg* 3. *fam* (*rubare*) to steal II. *vr* **fottersene di qu/qc** *vulg* not to give a fuck about sb/sth

foulard [fu·'lar] <-> *m* (*fazzoletto*) scarf

fra [fra] *prep v.* **tra**

frac [frak] <-> *m* tails *pl*

fracassare [fra·kas·'sa:·re] I. *vt* (*frantumare*) to smash II. *vr:* **-rsi** (*frantumarsi*) to smash

fracasso [fra·'kas·so] *m* (*chiasso*) din

fradicio, -a <-ci, -ce> *agg* (*bagnato*) soaked; **~ di sudore** soaked in sweat; **bagnato ~** soaking wet

fragile ['fra:·dʒi·le] *agg* 1. (*vetro, oggetto*) fragile; (*capelli*) brittle; **'~'** (*su pacchi*) 'fragile' 2. (*salute, costituzione*) delicate

fragilità [fra·dʒi·li·'ta] <-> *f* 1. (*di vetro*) fragility; (*di capelli*) brittleness 2. (*gracilità: di persona, costituzione*) delicacy 3. (*insicurezza psicologica*) fragility

fragola ['fra:·go·la] *f* strawberry

fragore [fra·'go:·re] *m* (*di tuono*) rumble; (*di cascata, torrente*) roar; (*di motore*) noise

fragoroso, -a [fra·go·'ro:·so] *agg* (*tonfo, risata*) loud; (*applauso, esplosione*) deafening

fragrante [fra·'gran·te] *agg* (*aroma, profumo*) fragrant

fragranza [fra·'gran·tsa] *f* (*di pane, pulito*) fragrance

fraintendere [fra·in·'tɛn·de·re] <irr> *vt* to misunderstand; **ti prego di non fraintendermi** please don't misunderstand me

frammentare [fram·men·'ta:·re] *vt* 1. (*frantumare*) to break up 2. *fig* (*mercato*) to fragment; (*racconto*) to dissect; (*unità*) to shatter

frammentario, -a [fram·men·'ta:·rio] <-i, -ie> *agg fig* (*informazioni, racconto*) fragmentary

frammento [fram·'men·to] *m* 1. (*pezzo: di affresco, muro*) fragment 2. LIT (*di discorso, romanzo*) passage

frammettere [fram·'met·te·re] <irr> I. *vt* (*mettere in mezzo*) to interpose II. *vr:* **-rsi** 1. (*mettersi in mezzo*) to be interposed 2. *fig* (*immischiarsi*) to intervene

frammisi 1. *pers sing pass rem di* **frammettere**

frana ['fra:·na] *f* 1. (*di terreno*) landslide 2. *scherz, fam* (*persona*) disaster

franare [fra·'na:·re] *vi* essere a. *fig* to collapse

francamente [fraŋ·ka·'men·te] *avv* frankly

francescano [fran·tʃes·'ka:·no] *m* Franciscan

francescano, -a *agg* (*monastero, spirito*) Franciscan

francese [fran·'tʃe:·se] I. *agg* French II. *mf* Frenchman *m*, Frenchwoman *f*

francesismo [fran·tʃe·'ziz·mo] *m* LING Gallicism

francesista [fran·tʃe·'sis·ta] <-i *m*, -e *f*> *mf* French specialist

franchezza [fraŋ·'ket·tsa] *f* (*schiettezza*) frankness; **con ~** (*apertamente*) frankly

franchigia [fraŋ·'ki:·dʒa] <-gie> *f* 1. (*esenzione*) exemption; **~ fiscale** tax exemption 2. (*nelle assicurazioni*) franchise; **~** (*assicurativa*) insurance franchise

franchising [fræn·'tʃai·ziŋ/fran·'tʃai·sin(g)] *m* franchising

Francia ['fran·tʃa] *f* France; **abitare in ~** to live in France; **andare in ~** to go to France

franco ['fraŋ·ko] <-chi> *m* (*moneta*) franc

franco, -a <-chi, -che> I. *agg* 1. (*sincero*) frank 2. COM free; **porto ~** free port 3. (*mil*) **~ tiratore** (*cecchino*) sniper; *fig* (*al parlamento*) rebel 4. (*loc*) **farla -a** *fig* to get away with it; **lingua -a** lingua franca II. *avv* 1. (*apertamente*) frankly 2. COM **~ domicilio** carriage free; **~ fabbrica** ex works; **~ magazzino** ex warehouse

francobollo [fraŋ·ko·'bol·lo] *m* stamp

francofilo, -a [fraŋ·'kɔ:·fi·lo] *agg* Francophile

Francoforte [fraŋ·ko·'fɔr·te] *f* Frankfurt

frangente [fran·'dʒɛn·te] *m* 1. (*onda*) breaker 2. *fig* (*momento grave*) situation

frangere ['fran·dʒe·re] <frango, fransi, franto> I. *vt* (*olive*) to press II. *vr:* **-rsi** (*onde*) to break

frangetta [fran·'dʒet·ta] *f* bangs *pl*

frangia ['fran·dʒa] <-ge> *f* 1. (*di stoffa, tenda, sciarpa*) fringe 2. (*di capelli*) bangs *pl* 3. POL fringe

frangiflutti [fran·dʒi·'flut·ti] <-> *m* (*molo*) breakwater

frangitura [fran·dʒi·'tu:·ra] *f* pressing

frangivento [fran·dʒi·'vɛn·to] <-> *m* windbreak

fransi ['fran·si] *1. pers sing pass rem di* **frangere**

franto ['fran·to] *pp di* **frangere**

frantoio [fran·'to:·io] <-oi> *m* **1.** (*macina: per olive*) olive press **2.** (*oleificio*) crusher

frantumare [fran·tu·'ma:·re] **I.** *vt* (*spezzare: bicchiere, vaso*) to smash **II.** *vr:* **-rsi 1.** (*spezzarsi: bicchiere, vaso*) to smash **2.** *fig* (*speranza*) to be dashed; (*diritti*) to be lost

frantumi [fran·'tu:·mi] *mpl* pieces; **andare in ~** to smash to pieces; *fig* (*speranza*) to be dashed

frappé [frap·'pɛ] <-> *m* milk shake

frapporre [frap·'por·re] <irr> **I.** *vt* **1.** (*oggetti*) to interpose **2.** *fig* (*ostacoli*) to put in the way; **~ indugi** to delay **II.** *vr:* **-rsi 1.** (*barriera, oggetto*) to come; (*persona*) to stand **2.** *fig* (*ostacoli*) to be put in the way

frasario [fra·'za:·rio] <-i> *m* **1.** (*gergo*) language **2.** (*libro*) phrasebook

frasca ['fras·ka] <-sche> *f* (*fronda*) branch; **saltare di palo in ~** *fig* to jump from one subject to another

frascati [fras·'ka:·ti] <-> *m* Frascati

frase ['fra:·ze] *f* **1.** LING sentence **2.** (*espressione*) expression; **~ fatta** cliché **3.** MUS phrase

fraseggio [fra·'zed·dʒo] <-ggi> *m* MUS phrasing

fraseologia [fra·zeo·lo·'dʒi:·a] <-gie> *f* phraseology

frassino ['fras·si·no] *m* **1.** (*albero*) ash (tree) **2.** (*legno*) ash

frastagliato, -a [fras·ta·ʎ·'ʎa:·to] *agg* (*contorni, foglio, tessuto*) indented; (*terreno*) rugged; (*costa*) jagged

frastornato, -a [fras·tor·'na:·to] *agg* dazed

frastuono [fras·'tuɔ:·no] *m* (*di motore, musica, cascata*) noise

frate ['fra:·te] *m* REL monk; **farsi ~** to become a monk

fratellanza [fra·tel·'lan·tsa] *f* **1.** (*tra fratelli*) brotherliness **2.** (*solidarietà*) brotherhood

fratellastro [fra·tel·'las·tro] *m* stepbrother

fratello [fra·'tɛl·lo] *m* brother

fraternità [fra·ter·ni·'ta] <-> *f fig* (*amicizia*) fraternity

fraternizzare [fra·ter·nid·'dza:·re] *vi* to make friends

fraterno, -a [fra·'tɛr·no] *agg* **1.** (*di, tra fratelli: amore, relazione*) brotherly **2.** (*di amico: amicizia*) fraternal

fratricida [fra·tri·'tʃi:·da] <-i *m*, -e *f*> *mf* (*di fratello*) fratricide; **guerra ~** civil war

frattaglie [frat·'ta·ʎ·ʎe] *fpl* (*di pollo*) giblets; (*di agnello*) offal

frattale [frat·'ta:·le] *m* MAT fractal

frattanto [frat·'tan·to] *avv* meanwhile

frattempo [frat·'tɛm·po] *m* **nel ~** in the meantime

frattura [frat·'tu:·ra] *f* **1.** (*di ossa*) fracture **2.** *fig* (*contrasto*) split

fraudolento, -a [frau·do·'lɛn·to] *agg* (*azione, operazione, comportamento*) fraudulent

frazionare [frat·tsio·'na:·re] *vt* (*dividere*) to divide up

frazionario, -a [frat·tsio·'na:·rio] <-i, -ie> *agg* (*equazione, sistema*) fractional

frazione [frat·'tsio:·ne] *f* **1.** (*gener*) fraction **2.** (*borgata*) hamlet

freatico, -a [fre·'a:·ti·ko] <-ci, -che> *agg* (*falda, livello*) water; **acqua -a** groundwater

freccia ['fret·tʃa] <-cce> *f* arrow

frecciata [fret·'tʃa:·ta] *f* (*frase*) cutting remark

freddare [fred·'da:·re] *vt* **1.** (*cibi*) to cool **2.** (*entusiasmo*) to dampen **3.** (*uccidere*) to kill

freddezza [fred·'det·tsa] *f* **1.** (*indifferenza*) coldness **2.** (*sangue freddo*) cold-bloodedness

freddo ['fred·do] *m* cold; **a ~** in cold water; *fig* (*decidere*) in cold blood; **avere ~** to be cold; **fa ~** it's cold; **fa un ~ cane** *fam* it's freezing cold; **far venir ~ a qn** *fig* to give sb the creeps; **non mi fa né caldo né ~** it leaves me cold

freddo, -a *agg* **1.** (*acqua, vento, mani*) cold; **a sangue ~** (*uccidere*) in cold blood; **animali a sangue ~** cold-blooded animals; **guerra -a** cold war; **piatto ~** cold meal **2.** *fig* (*distaccato*) cool; **essere ~ con qu** to be cool with sb

freddoloso, -a [fred·do·'lo:·so] *agg* sensitive to the cold

freddura [fred·'du:·ra] *f* (*battuta*) quip

free lance ['fri:·læns] **I.** <inv> *agg* (*giornalista, collaboratore*) freelance **II.** <-> *mf* freelance(r)

freestyle ['fri:·stail] <-> *m* SPORT (*nello sci*) freestyle

freezer ['fri:·zə/'fri·zer] *m* freezer

fregare [fre·'ga:·re] **I.** *vt* **1.** (*strofinare: pavimento*) to wipe **2.** *fam* (*imbrogliare*) to rip off **3.** *fam* (*rubare*) to swipe **II.** *vr:* **-rsi** *fam* **fregarsene di qu/qc** not to give a damn about sb/sth

fregata [fre·'ga:·ta] *f* NAUT frigate

fregatura [fre·ga·'tu:·ra] *f fam* rip-off; **dare una ~ a qu** to rip sb off; **prendere una ~** to get ripped off

fregio ['fre:·dʒo] <-gi> *m* frieze

fregola ['fre:·go·la] *f* **1.** ZOO (*di animale*) heat **2.** *fig* (*smania*) passion

fremere ['frɛ:·me·re] <fremo, fremei *o* fremetti, fremuto> *vi* **~ per qc** to quiver with sth

fremito ['frɛ:·mi·to] *m* (*di paura*) shudder; (*di rabbia*) wave

frenare [fre·'na:·re] **I.** *vi* (*veicolo*) to brake **II.** *vt* **1.** (*veicolo*) to slow down **2.** (*trattenere: lacrime, riso*) to hold back **3.** (*contenere: immigrazione, inflazione*) to curb **III.** *vr:* **-rsi** (*dominarsi*) to control oneself

frenata [fre·'na:·ta] *f* braking

frenesia [fre·ne·'zi:·a] <-ie> *f* (*agitazione*) frenzy

frenetico, -a [fre·'nɛ:·ti·ko] <-ci, -che> *agg* (*attività, ritmo*) frenetic

frenico, -a ['frɛ:·ni·ko] <-ci, -che> *agg* ANAT (*nervo, arteria*) phrenic

frenista [fre·'nis·ta] <-i *m*, -e *f*> *mf* brake specialist

freno ['fre:·no] *m* **1.** TEC brake; ~ **a mano** emergency brake **2.** *fig (inibizione)* restraint; **mettere un ~ a qc** to restrain; **tenere a ~ qc** to keep in check; **senza -i** unrestrainedly

frequentare [fre·kuen·'ta:·re] *vt* **1.** *(persone)* to see; *(ambiente)* to go to; ~ **cattive compagnie** to be in with a bad crowd **2.** *(scuola, università)* to be in; *(corso)* to be on

frequentato, -a [fre·kuen·'ta:·to] *agg (locale, strada, porto)* busy

frequente [fre·'kuɛn·te] *agg (malattia, problema)* common; *(visita)* frequent; **di** ~ frequently

frequenza [fre·'kuɛn·tsa] *f* **1.** *(di incidenti, fatti)* frequency **2.** *(di scuola, università)* attendance; **obbligo di** ~ compulsory attendance **3.** *(di cuore, polso)* rate **4.** PHYS frequency **5.** COMPUT rate; ~ **di refresh** refresh rate

fresatrice [fre·za·'tri:·tʃe] *f* TEC mill

freschezza [fres·'ket·tsa] *f* freshness

fresco ['fres·ko] *m* **1.** *(temperatura)* coolness; **fa** ~ it's cool; **al** ~ outdoors; **conservare al** ~ store in a cool place; **mettere al** ~ *fig, fam* to put sb in the slammer *inf* **2.** *(tessuto)* light wool

fresco, -a <-schi, -sche> *agg* **1.** *(gradevole: aria, acqua)* fresh; *(clima)* cool **2.** *(appena fatto: latte, pane, caffè)* fresh **3.** *(appena colto: fiori, frutta)* fresh **4.** *(giovane: pelle)* young **5.** *(spontaneo: sorriso)* bright **6.** *(recente)* recent; **un dottore** ~ **di studi** a new graduate **7.** *(riposato)* refreshed **8.** *(loc)* **stare** ~ *fig, fam* to be in for it *inf*

frescura [fres·'ku:·ra] *f* coolness

fretta ['fret·ta] *f* hurry; **aver** ~ to be in a hurry; **far** ~ **a qu** to hurry sb; **non c'è** ~ there's no hurry; **in** ~ in a hurry; **in** ~ **e furia** in a terrible hurry

frettoloso, -a [fret·to·'lo:·so] *agg* **1.** *(rapido: passo)* hurried **2.** *(sommario: lavoro)* rushed

friabile [fri·'a:·bi·le] *agg (biscotti, pasta frolla)* crumbly; *(terreno, roccia)* friable

fricassea [fri·kas·'sɛ:·a] *f* CULIN fricassee

fricchettone [frik·ket·'to:·ne] *m sl* hippie

friggere ['frid·dʒe·re] <friggo, frissi, fritto> **I.** *vt* to fry; **andare a farsi** ~ *inf* to get lost; **mandare qu a farsi** ~ *inf* to tell sb to get lost **II.** *vi* **1.** *(crepitare)* to sizzle **2.** *fig (fremere)* to tremble

friggitoria [frid·dʒi·to·'ri:·a] <-ie> *f* store selling fried food

frigidità [fri·dʒi·di·'ta] <-> *f* MED frigidity

frigido, -a ['fri:·dʒi·do] *agg* MED frigid

frignare [friɲ·'ɲa:·re] *vi* to whine

frigo ['fri:·go] <-> *m fam* fridge

frigobar [fri·go·'bar] <-> *m* minibar

frigorifero [fri·go·'ri:·fe·ro] *m* refrigerator

frigorifero, -a *agg (impianto)* refrigeration; **cella -a** cold store

fringuello [friŋ·'guɛl·lo] *m* chaffinch

frinire [fri·'ni:·re] <frinisco> *vi (cicala)* to chirp

frissi ['fris·si] *1. pers sing pass rem di* **friggere**

frittata [frit·'ta:·ta] *f* omelette

frittella [frit·'tɛl·la] *f* CULIN fritter

fritto ['frit·to] *m* ~ **misto** mixed fried fish

fritto, -a I. *pp di* **friggere II.** *agg* **1.** CULIN fried **2.** *fig, inf (spacciato)* done for

frittura [frit·'tu:·ra] *f* fried food; ~ **di pesce** fried fish

friulano [fri·u·'la:·no] <*sing*> *m (lingua)* Friulian

friulano, -a I. *agg* Friulian **II.** *m, f (abitante)* Friulian

Friuli [fri·'u:·li] *m* Friuli

frivolezza [fri·vo·'let·tsa] *f* **1.** *(superficialità)* frivolousness **2.** *(discorso frivolo)* triviality

frivolo, -a ['fri:·vo·lo] *agg (argomento, discorso, giornale)* frivolous

frizionare [frit·tsio·'na:·re] *vt (corpo, pelle, cuoio capelluto)* to massage

frizione [frit·'tsio:·ne] *f* **1.** MOT clutch; **innestare la** ~ to engage the clutch; **disinnestare la** ~ to disengage the clutch **2.** *fig (dissenso)* friction **3.** *(massaggio)* massage

frizzante [frid·'dzan·te] *agg* **1.** *(bibita)* fizzy; *(vino)* sparkling **2.** *(aria)* crisp

frocio ['frɔ·tʃo] <-i> *m vulg (omosessuale)* faggot

frodare [fro·'da:·re] *vt* **1.** *(derubare)* to defraud; ~ **il fisco** to evade tax **2.** *(ingannare)* to cheat

frode ['frɔ:·de] *f* fraud; ~ **fiscale** tax fraud

frodo ['frɔ:·do] *m* **cacciare di** ~ to poach

frogia ['frɔ:·dʒa] <-gie *o* -ge> *f (di cavallo)* nostril

frollare [frol·'la:·re] **I.** *vt* avere *(carne, selvaggina)* to hang **II.** *vi* essere to become high

frollatura [frol·la·'tu:·ra] *f (di carne, selvaggina)* hanging

frollo, -a ['frɔl·lo] *agg* CULIN **pasta -a** pie crust

fronda ['fron·da] *f pl (fogliame)* foliage

frondoso, -a [fron·'do:·so] *agg (albero)* leafy

frontale [fron·'ta:·le] *agg* **1.** ANAT, LING frontal **2.** *(anteriore: pagina, vista)* front **3.** *(scontro)* head-on **4.** *fig (attacco)* frontal

frontaliero, -a [fron·ta·'liɛ:·ro] *m, f* cross-border worker

frontalino [fron·ta·'li:·no] *m (di autoradio)* front panel

fronte ['fron·te] **I.** *f* ANAT forehead; **a** ~ **alta/ bassa** *fig* with one's head held high/bowed; **di** ~ opposite **II.** *m* **1.** MIL, POL front **2.** *(loc)* **far** ~ **a qc** *(difficoltà)* to face; *(impegni)* to keep; *(spese)* to meet

fronteggiare [fron·ted·'dʒa:·re] *vt* to face

frontespizio [fron·tes·'pit·tsio] <-i> *m (di libro)* title page

frontiera [fron·'tiɛ:·ra] *f* **1.** *(confine: tra Stati)* border; **passare la** ~ to cross the border **2.** *(di tecnologia, comunicazioni)* frontier

frontone [fron·'to:·ne] *m* ARCH pediment

fronzolo ['fron·dzo·lo] *m a. fig* frill

Frosinone *f* Frosinone, *province in central Italy*

frotta ['frɔt·ta] *f (di persone)* crowd; *(di pesci)*

shoal; (*di animali*) herd; **a -e** in droves

frottola ['frɔt·to·la] *f* lie

frugale [fru·'ga:·le] *agg* (*cibo, pasto*) frugal

frugalità [fru·ga·li·'ta] <-> *f* (*di cibo, pasto*) frugality

frugare [fru·'ga:·re] I. *vi* to search II. *vt* to search

fruire [fru·'i:·re] <fruisco> *vi* ~ **di qc** to enjoy sth

frullare [frul·'la:·re] I. *vt avere* (*con frullatore: frutta, verdura*) to blend; (*con frullino: uova*) to whisk II. *vi essere o avere fig* to go on

frullato [frul·'la:·to] *m* shake

frullatore [frul·la·'to:·re] *m* blender; **~ a immersione** hand-held mixer

frullino [frul·'li:·no] *m* whisk

frumento [fru·'men·to] *m* wheat

fruscio [fruʃ·'ʃi:o] <-scii> *m* 1. (*di carta, seta, vento*) rustle 2. (*di telefono, registratore*) hiss

frusinate [fru·zi·'na:·te] I. *agg* from Frosinone II. *mf* (*abitante*) person from Frosinone

frusta ['frus·ta] *f* 1. (*sferza*) whip 2. (*da cucina*) whisk

frustare [frus·'ta:·re] *vt* (*con la frusta*) to whip

frustata [frus·'ta:·ta] *f* lash

frustino [frus·'ti:·no] *m* riding crop

frustrante [frus·'tran·te] *agg* frustrating

frustrare [frus·'tra:·re] *vt* (*persona, tentativi, speranze*) to frustrate

frustrazione [frus·trat·'tsio:·ne] *f* frustration

frutta ['frut·ta] <*sing*> *f* fruit; **~ candita** candied fruit; **~ secca** dried fruit; **essere alla ~** *fig, fam* to be at the end of one's tether

fruttare [frut·'ta:·re] *vt* to bring in

frutteto [frut·'te:·to] *m* orchard

frutticoltura [frut·ti·kol·'tu:·ra] *f* fruit growing

fruttiera [frut·'tiɛ:·ra] *f* fruit bowl

fruttifero, -a [frut·'ti:·fe·ro] *agg* 1. BOT (*albero*) fruit-bearing 2. FIN (*capitale, deposito*) interest-bearing

fruttivendolo, -a [frut·ti·'ven·do·lo] *m, f* 1. (*venditore*) produce dealer 2. (*negozio*) produce store

frutto ['frut·to] *m* 1. BOT fruit; **-i di bosco** berries; **mettere a ~ l'esperienza** to put one's experience to good use 2. *fig* (*risultato*) fruit 3. ZOO **-i di mare** seafood

fruttosio [frut·'tɔ:·zio] <-i> *m* fructose

fruttuoso, -a [frut·tu·'o:·so] *agg* (*attività, collaborazione, periodo*) fruitful

FS *fpl abbr di* **Ferrovie dello Stato** *Italian state railroad*

f.to *abbr di* **firmato** signed

fu [fu] I. 3. *pers sing pass rem di* **essere**[1] II. <inv> *agg* late; **il ~ Gino Martignon** the late Gino Martignon; **Martignon Davide ~ Gino** Davide Martignon, son of the late Gino

fucilare [fu·tʃi·'la:·re] *vt* to shoot

fucilata [fu·tʃi·'la:·ta] *f* shot

fucilazione [fu·tʃi·lat·'tsio:·ne] *f* shooting

fucile [fu·'tʃi:·le] *m* gun; **~ da caccia** shotgun; **~ mitragliatore** submachine gun

fuciliere [fu·tʃi·'liɛ:·re] *m* rifleman

fucina [fu·'tʃi:·na] *f* 1. (*di fabbro*) forge 2. *fig* (*di idee*) crucible

fuco ['fu:·ko] <-chi> *m* ZOO drone

fuga ['fu:·ga] <-ghe> *f* 1. (*atto del fuggire*) escape; **darsi alla ~** to flee; **mettere in ~** to put to flight 2. (*fuoriuscita: di gas, liquidi*) leak; **~ di notizie** leak; **~ di cervelli** brain drain; **~ di capitali** flight of capital 3. MUS fugue

fugace [fu·'ga:·tʃe] *agg* (*bellezza, incontro, momento*) fleeting

fugacità [fu·ga·tʃi·'ta] <-> *f* (*di bellezza, sensazione*) fleetingness

fuggiasco, -a [fud·'dʒas·ko] <-schi, -sche> I. *agg* runaway II. *m, f* fugitive

fuggifuggi [fud·dʒi·'fud·dʒi] <-> *m* stampede

fuggire [fud·'dʒi:·re] I. *vi essere* 1. (*scappare*) to escape; **~ via** to get away 2. (*passare*) fly; **il tempo fugge** time flies II. *vt avere* to avoid

fuggitivo, -a [fud·dʒi·'ti:·vo] I. *agg* (*persona*) runaway II. *m, f* fugitive

fui 1. *pers sing pass rem di* **essere**[1]

fulcro ['ful·kro] *m* 1. TEC fulcrum 2. *fig* (*di commercio*) hub; (*di conflitto*) nub

fulgido, -a ['ful·dʒi·do] *agg* 1. (*splendente: stelle*) bright 2. (*esempio*) shining; (*periodo*) brilliant

fulgore [ful·'go:·re] *m* 1. (*di astri*) brightness 2. (*di bellezza*) radiance

fuliggine [fu·'lid·dʒi·ne] *f* soot

fuligginoso, -a [fu·lid·dʒi·'no:·so] *agg* sooty

full immersion [ful i·'mə:·ʃən] <-> *f* full immersion; **fare un corso ~** to do a full-immersion course

full-time [ful·'taim] I. <inv> *agg* full-time II. *avv* full time III. <-> *m* full-time work

fulminante [ful·mi·'nan·te] *agg* 1. (*sguardo*) withering 2. (*malattia*) fulminating

fulminare [ful·mi·'na:·re] I. *vt* 1. (*folgorare*) to strike with lightning 2. (*uccidere: malattia, scarica elettrica, arma da fuoco*) to strike down 3. *fig* **~ qn con lo sguardo** to look daggers at sb II. *vi* to be lightning III. *vr:* **-rsi** (*lampadina*) to go

fulmine ['ful·mi·ne] *m* lightning; **un ~ a ciel sereno** a bolt from the blue; **un colpo di ~** *fig* love at first sight; **come un ~** like greased lightning

fulmineo, -a [ful·'mi:·neo] <-ei, -ee> *agg* 1. (*veloce: carriera*) rapid; (*riflessi*) lightning 2. (*improvviso: decisione, cambiamento*) sudden

fulvo, -a ['ful·vo] *agg* (*capelli, criniera*) tawny

fumaiolo [fu·ma·'iɔ:·lo] *m* (*di nave*) funnel

fumare [fu·'ma:·re] I. *vi* 1. (*persona*) to smoke 2. (*minestra, asfalto*) to steam II. *vt* (*sigarette, sigaro, pipa*) to smoke

fumata [fu·'ma:·ta] *f* 1. (*segnale*) smoke; **~ nera/bianca** black/white smoke 2. (*di tabacco*) smoke

fumatore, -trice [fu·ma·'to:·re] *m, f* smoker

fumetto [fu·'met·to] *m* 1. (*nuvoletta*) bubble 2. (*giornalino*) comic book; **a -i** cartoon

fummo ['fum·mo] 1. *pers pl pass rem di*

essere[1]

fumo ['fu:·mo] *m* **1.** (*prodotto di combustione*) smoke; **andare in ~** *fig* to fall through; **mandare in ~ qc** *fam* to scupper sth; **vendere ~** to be a phony; **molto ~ e poco arrosto** *fig* all show **2.** (*vapore*) steam **3.** (*di tabacco*) smoking

fumogeno, -a [fu·'mɔ:·dʒe·no] *agg* (*granata, razzo*) smoke; **cortina -a** smokescreen

fumoso, -a [fu·'mo:·so] *agg* **1.** (*pieno di fumo: ambiente*) smoky **2.** *fig* (*oscuro: storia, parole, proposta*) vague

funambolo, -a [fu·'nam·bo·lo] *m, f* tightrope walker

fune ['fu:·ne] *f* **1.** (*corda*) rope; **tiro alla ~** tug-of-war **2.** (*cavo d'acciaio*) cable

funebre ['fu:·ne·bre] *agg* **1.** (*cerimonia, rito*) funeral; **veglia ~** wake; **impresa di pompe -i** funeral home **2.** *fig* (*lugubre: aspetto, aria*) gloomy

funerale [fu·ne·'ra:·le] *m* funeral; **faccia da ~** *fig* long face

funerario, -a [fu·ne·'ra:·rio] <-i, -ie> *agg* (*arte, monumento*) funerary; (*rito*) funeral

funereo, -a [fu·'nɛ:·reo] <-ei, -ee> *agg fig* (*lugubre: atmosfera, aspetto*) funereal

funestare [fu·nes·'ta:·re] *vt* to ravage

funesto, -a [fu·'nɛs·to] *agg* (*triste: giorno, notizia*) sad

fungere ['fun·dʒe·re] <fungo, funsi, funto> *vi* **~ da** (*fare le veci: persona*) to act as; (*servire da: oggetto*) to function as

fungo ['fuŋ·go] <-ghi> *m* mushroom; **~ porcino** cep; **~ prataiolo** field mushroom; **~ velenoso** toadstool; **spuntare come -ghi** *fig* to spring up

funicolare [fu·ni·ko·'la:·re] *f* funicular

funivia [fu·ni·'vi:·a] <-ie> *f* cablecar

funsi ['fun·si] *1. pers sing pass rem di* **fungere**

funto ['fun·to] *pp di* **fungere**

funzionale [fun·tsio·'na:·le] *agg* functional

funzionalizzare [fun·tsio·na·lid·'dza:·re] *vt* (*rendere funzionale*) to make functional

funzionamento [fun·tsio·na·'men·to] *m* (*di macchina, sistema, organo*) functioning

funzionante [fun·tsio·'nan·te] *agg* (*meccanismo, sistema, relazione*) functioning

funzionare [fun·tsio·'na:·re] *vi* (*meccanismo, sistema, relazione*) to work; **come funziona?** how does it work?; **far ~ qc** to make sth work

funzionario, -a [fun·tsio·'na:·rio] <-i, -ie> *m, f* (*impiegato*) official

funzione [fun·'tsio:·ne] *f* **1.** (*gener*) function; **entrare in ~** to start operating **2.** (*ufficio*) post; **nell'esercizio delle proprie -i** while carrying out one's duties **3.** (*cerimonia, rito*) service; **~ funebre** funeral service; **~ religiosa** religious service

fuoco ['fuɔ:·ko] <-chi> *m* **1.** *gener* fire; **-chi d'artificio** fireworks; **dar ~ a qc** to set fire to sth; **prendere ~** to catch fire; **andare a ~** to go up in flames; **scherzare col ~** *fig* to play with fire; **mettere la mano sul ~ per qc** *fig* to

stake one's life on sth; **al ~!** fire! **2.** (*fornello*) burner **3.** FOTO, PHYS focus **4.** MIL fire; **fare ~** to fire; **aprire/cessare il ~** to open/cease fire

fuorché [fuor·'ke] **I.** *cong* except for **II.** *prep* except for

fuori [fu·'ɔ:·ri] **I.** *avv* **1.** (*all'esterno*) outside; **sporgersi in ~** to lean out; **~!** get out!; **~ i soldi!** hand over the money! **2.** (*di casa*) out **3.** (*da città*) away **4.** (*loc*) **essere ~ strada** *fig* to be way out; **far ~** *inf* (*uccidere*) to rub out; **ha fatto ~ il patrimonio di famiglia** he squandered his inheritance; **buttar ~** (*persona*) to throw out; **tagliar ~ qu** to exclude sb **II.** *prep* out of; **~ da** out (of); **~ di** out of; **~ di sé** beside oneself; **~ di testa** off one's head; **~ concorso** out of competition; **~ luogo** out of place; **~ mano** out of the way; **~ orario** out of hours; **~ pericolo** out of danger; **~ tempo** not in time; **~ tiro** out of range; **~ uso** not in use **III.** *m* **dal di ~** from the outside

FUORI ['fuɔ:·ri] *m abbr di* **Fronte Unitario Omosessuale Rivoluzionario Italiano** *Italian gay rights group*

fuoribordo [fuo·ri·'bor·do] <-> *m* NAUT (*motore*) outboard motor

fuoribusta [fuo·ri·'bus·ta] **I.** <-> *m* off-the-books payment **II.** <inv> *agg* off-the-books

fuoricampo [fuo·ri·'kam·po] **I.** <inv> *agg* FILM **voce ~** off-screen voice **II.** <-> *m* **1.** FILM (*suono, voce*) off-screen **2.** SPORT (*nel baseball*) home run

fuoriclasse [fuo·ri·'klas·se] <-> *mf* superstar

fuori combattimento [fuo·ri·kom·bat·ti·'men·to] **I.** <inv> *agg* out of action; **mettere qu ~** to knock sb out **II.** <-> *m* knockout

fuoricorso [fuo·ri·'kor·so] **I.** <inv> *agg* **studente ~** *student who has not completed his or her course within the prescribed time* **II.** <-> *mf* *student who has not completed his or her course within the prescribed time*

fuorigioco [fuo·ri·'dʒɔ:·ko] <-> *m* offside

fuorilegge [fuo·ri·'led·dʒe] <-> *mf* outlaw

fuorimano [fuo·ri·'ma:·no] **I.** *avv* off the beaten track; **abitare ~** (*o* **vivere**) to live off the beaten track **II.** <inv> *agg* (*strada*) out-of-the-way:

fuori misura, fuorimisura [fu·'ɔ:·ri mi·'zu:·ra] <inv> *agg* (*giacca, armadio*) non-standard-size

fuorimoda [fuo·ri·'mo:·da] <inv> *agg* (*acconciatura, abito*) unfashionable

fuoripasto [fuo·ri·'pas·to] *avv* between meals; **non mangio mai ~** I don't eat between meals

fuoripista [fuo·ri·'pis·ta] <-> *m* SPORT (*nello sci*) off-piste skiing; **fare un ~** to ski off piste

fuoriporta [fuo·ri·'pɔr·ta] **I.** *avv* outdoors **II.** <inv> *agg* outdoor; **ristorante ~** open-air restaurant

fuoriprogramma [fuo·ri·pro·'gram·ma] <-> *m* unscheduled program; **trasmettere un ~** to broadcast an unscheduled program

fuoriquota [fuo·ri·'kuɔ:·ta] <-> *mf* SPORT extra player

fuorisede [fuo·ri·'sɛ:·de] I.<inv> *agg* from out of town II. <-> *mf* out-of-towner

fuoriserie [fuo·ri·'sɛ:·rie] I.<inv> *agg* (*auto, modello*) custom-built II. <-> *f* custom-built model

fuoristrada [fuo·ri·'stra:·da] I. <-> *m* AUTO off-road vehicle II.<inv> *agg* (*moto, auto*) off-road

fuoriuscire [fuo·ri·uʃ·'ʃi:·re] <irr> *vi* ~ **da** to leak from

fuor(i)uscita [fuo·r(i)·uʃ·'ʃi:·ta] *f* (*di liquido, gas*) leak

fuor(i)uscito, a [fuo·r(i)·uʃ·'ʃi:·to] *m* exile

fuorviante [fuor·'vian·te] *agg* (*affermazione, ipotesi, proposta*) misleading

fuorviare [fuor·vi·'a:·re] *vt* (*sviare*) to mislead

furbacchione, -a [fur·bak·'kio:·ne] *m, f fam* cunning devil

furberia [fur·be·'ri:·a] <-ie> *f* 1. (*qualità*) cunning 2. (*atto*) trick

furbizia [fur·'bit·tsia] <-ie> *f* 1. (*qualità*) cunning 2. (*atto*) trick

furbo, -a ['fur·bo] I. *agg* smart II. *m, f* cunning person

furente [fu·'rɛn·te] *agg* furious

furetto [fu·'ret·to] *m* ZOO ferret

furfante [fur·'fan·te] *m* rascal

furgone [fur·'go:·ne] *m* van

furia ['fu:·ria] <-ie> *f* 1. (*collera*) rage; **andare su tutte le -ie** to fly into a rage 2. (*persona*) fury 3. (*di vento, mare*) fury 4. (*fretta*) hurry; **in fretta e** ~ in a real hurry 5. (*loc*) **a ~ di fare qu** by doing sth

furibondo, -a [fu·ri·'bon·do] *agg* (*persona, lotte*) furious

furiere [fu·'riɛ:·re] *m* MIL quartermaster

furioso, -a [fu·'rio:·so] *agg* (*persona, lotta, tempesta*) furious

furono ['fu:·ro·no] *3. pers pl pass rem di* **essere**[1]

furore [fu·'ro:·re] *m* (*rabbia, veemenza*) fury; **far ~** *fig* to be a great success

furoreggiare [fu·ro·red·'dʒa:·re] *vi* to be very popular

furtivo, -a [fur·'ti:·vo] *agg* (*sguardo*) furtive

furto ['fur·to] *m* (*azione*) theft

fusa ['fu:·sa] *fpl* **far le ~** to purr

fuscello [fuʃ·'ʃɛl·lo] *m* (*ramoscello*) twig

fuseaux [fy·'zo] <-> *mpl* leggings *pl*

fusi ['fu:·zi] *1. pers sing pass rem di* **fondere**

fusibile [fu·'zi:·bi·le] *m* ELEC fuse

fusilli [fu·'sil·li/fu·'zil·li] *m* fusilli

fusione [fu·'zio:·ne] *f* 1. (*di metalli, cera*) melting; **punto di ~** melting point; **~ nucleare** nuclear fusion 2. (*di colori, suoni*) blending 3. COM (*di aziende*) merger

fuso ['fu:·zo] I. *pp di* **fondere** II. *m* 1. (*in filatura*) spindle 2. GEO **~ orario** time zone

fusoliera [fu·zo·'liɛ:·ra] *f* AERO fuselage

fustagno [fus·'tan·ɲo] *m* moleskin

fustella [fus·'tɛl·la] *f* (*di medicinali*) price tag

fustigare [fus·ti·'ga:·re] *vt* 1. (*percuotere*) to flog 2. *fig* (*criticare*) to criticize

fustigazione [fus·ti·gat·'tsio:·ne] *f* (*flagellazione*) flogging

fustino [fus·'ti:·no] *m* (*di detersivo*) box

fusto ['fus·to] *m* 1. BOT (*di pianta*) stem 2. (*recipiente: di benzina*) drum 3. *fig* (*tronco umano*) trunk 4. *inf* (*giovane aitante*) hunk

futile ['fu:·ti·le] *agg* futile

futilità [fu·ti·li·'ta] <-> *f* futility

futuribile [fu·tu·'ri:·bi·le] *agg* feasible

futurismo [fu·tu·'riz·mo] *m* ARTE futurism

futurista [fu·tu·'ris·ta] <-i *m*, -e *f*> I. *agg* futurist II. *mf* futurist

futuro [fu·'tu:·ro] *m* future; **~ anteriore** future perfect

futuro, -a *agg* future

futurologia [fu·tu·ro·lo·'dʒi:·a] <-ie> *f* futurology

G

G, g [dʒi] <-> *f* g; ~ **come Genova** G for George

g *abbr di* **grammo** g

gabardina, gabardine [ga·bar·'di:·na, ga·bar·'din] <-> *f* (*tessuto*) gabardine

gabbana [gab·'ba:·na] *f fig* **voltar ~** to change sides

gabbia ['gab·bia] <-ie> *f* 1. ZOO (*per animali*) cage; (*per uccelli*) bird cage 2. MED (~ **toracica**) rib cage 3. (*di tribunale*) dock 4. *fig, fam* (*prigione*) jail; **mettere qu in ~** to send sb to jail 5. *fig, fam* ~ **di matti** (*manicomio*) madhouse

gabbiano [gab·'bia:·no] *m* (sea)gull

gabinetto [ga·bi·'net·to] *m* 1. (*toilette*) restroom; **andare al ~** to go to the restroom 2. (*studio*) study; ~ **medico** surgery 3. (*laboratorio*) laboratory; ~ **di fisica** physics laboratory 4. POL (*ministri*) cabinet

gadget ['ga·dʒit] <-> *m* 1. (*accessorio*) gadget 2. (*omaggio*) free gift

gaffe [gaf] <-> *f* blunder; **fare una ~** to put one's foot in it

gag [gæg/gag] *f* joke

gagà [ga·'ga] <-> *m pej* fop

gagliardetto [gaʎ·ʎar·'det·to] *m* pennant

gagliardo, -a [gaʎ·'ʎar·do] *agg* (*robusto*) strong; (*vivace*) lively

gaio, -a ['ga:·io] <-ai, -aie> *agg* (*allegro: persona, carattere*) cheerful

gala ['ga:·la] *f* (*sfarzo*) **abito di ~** formal dress; **in gran ~** in one's glad rags; **mettersi in gran ~** to put one's glad rags on

galà [ga·'la] *m* (*ricevimento*) gala; **serata di ~** gala performance

galante [ga·'lan·te] *agg* (*persona, gesto*) gallant

galanteria [ga·lan·te·'ri:·a] <-ie> *f* gallantry

galantina [ga·lan·'ti:·na] *f* CULIN galantine

galantuomo [ga·lan·'tuɔ:·mo] <galantu-
omini> *m* gentleman

galassia [ga·'las·sia] <-ie> *f* ASTRON galaxy

galateo [ga·la·'tɛ:·o] *m* etiquette

galattico, -a [ga·'lat·ti·ko] <-ci, -che> *agg*
1. ASTRON (*distanza, nucleo, ammassi*) galactic
2. *fig* (*eccezionale*) incredible

galeone [ga·le·'o:·ne] *m* (*nave*) galleon

galeotto [ga·le·'ɔt·to] *m* (*carcerato*) convict

galera [ga·'lɛ:·ra] *f* **1.** HIST (*nave*) galley **2.** (*prigione*) prison; **avanzo di ~** (*delinquente*)
crook

galla ['gal·la] *f* (*loc*) **a ~** on the surface; **stare
a ~** to float; **tenersi a ~** *fig* to keep one's head
above water; **venire a ~** *fig* to come out

galleggiamento [gal·led·dʒa·'men·to] *m* PHYS
flotation; (**linea di**) **~** water line

galleggiante [gal·led·'dʒan·te] **I.** *agg* (*ancora,
materiale, piattaforma*) free-floating **II.** *m*
1. (*per la pesca*) float **2.** (*del serbatoio della
benzina*) carburetor float; (*dello sciacquone
del WC*) ball cock **3.** (*boa*) buoy

galleggiare [gal·led·'dʒa:·re] *vi* to float

galleria [gal·le·'ri:·a] <-ie> *f* **1.** MOT, AERO, MIN
(*tunnel*) tunnel; **~ del vento** wind tunnel
2. ARCHIT arcade **3.** (*per esposizioni*) gallery
4. (*di cinema, teatro*) circle

gallerista [gal·le·'ris·ta] <-i *m*, -e *f*> *mf* (*proprietario*) art gallery owner; (*direttore*) art gallery manager *m*, art gallery manageress *f*

galletta [gal·'let·ta] *f* (*biscotto secco*) dry biscuit

galletto [gal·'let·to] *m* **1.** ZOO cockerel **2.** *fig,
fam* cock of the roost; **fare il ~** to play Casanova

gallicismo [gal·li·'tʃiz·mo] *m* LING French
word/expression

gallico, -a ['gal·li·ko] <-ci, -che> *agg* HIST
(*guerre, invasioni*) Gallic

gallina [gal·'li:·na] *f* hen; **avere il cervello di
una ~** *fam* to be bird-brained; **andare a letto
con le -e** to go to bed early; **~ vecchia fa
buon brodo** *prov, scherz* there's life in the old
bird yet

gallinacei [gal·li·'na:·tʃei] *mpl* gallinaceans

gallio ['gal·lio] *m* CHEM gallium

gallismo [gal·'liz·mo] *m fig* cock of the roost
attitude

gallo¹ ['gal·lo] *m* **1.** ZOO cock; **al canto del ~** at
daybreak **2.** *fig, fam* **fare il ~** to play Casanova

gallo² <inv> *agg* SPORT (*nel pugilato*) bantam;
peso ~ bantamweight

gallone [gal·'lo:·ne] *m* **1.** MIL stripe **2.** (*misura*)
gallon

galoppante [ga·lop·'pan·te] *agg* (*veloce:
epidemia, inflazione*) galloping

galoppare [ga·lop·'pa:·re] *vi* **1.** (*cavallo*) to
gallop **2.** *fig* (*persona*) to race around

galoppata [ga·lop·'pa:·ta] *f* gallop

galoppino [ga·lop·'pi:·no] *m* errand boy;
~ elettorale canvasser

galoppo [ga·'lɔp·po] *m* gallop; **andare al ~** to
gallop

galvanico, -a [gal·'va:·ni·ko] <-ci, -che> *agg*
(*procedimento, corrente, coppia*) galvanic

galvanizzare [gal·va·nid·'dza:·re] *vt a.* TEC to
galvanize

galvanizzazione [gal·va·nid·dzat·'tsio:·ne] *f*
TEC galvanization

gamba ['gam·ba] *f* (*di persona, animale,
mobile,*) leg; **andare a -e all'aria** to fall flat on
one's back; *fig* (*fallire*) to fall through; **camminare a quattro -e** to crawl; **darsela a -e
levate** to run away; **essere in ~** *fig* to be on
the ball; **prendere qc sotto ~** *fig* to take sth
too lightly; **sedere a -e incrociate** to sit
cross-legged; (*di tavolo, sedia*)

gambale [gam·'ba:·le] *m* (*di stivale*) leg

gamberetto [gam·be·'ret·to] *m* shrimp

gambero ['gam·be·ro] *m* prawn; **diventare
rosso come un ~** to turn as red as a tomato

gambo ['gam·bo] *m* (*di fiore*) stem; (*di frutta,
fungo*) stalk

gamma¹ ['gam·ma] *f* **1.** (*serie: di colori, prodotti*) range **2.** RADIO **~** (**di lunghezza**) **d'onda**
waveband

gamma² <inv> *agg* PHYS (*raggi*) gamma

ganascia [ga·'naʃ·ʃa] <-sce> *f* **1.** ANAT jaw
2. MOT (*di freno*) brake shoes *pl*

gancio ['gan·tʃo] <-ci> *m* hook; **~** (**di traino**)
AUTO tow hook

ganga ['gaŋ·ga] *f fam* gang

ganghero ['gaŋ·ge·ro] *m* (*di porte, finestre*)
hinge; **uscire dai -i** to fly off the handle;
essere fuori dai -i to be absolutely livid

ganglio ['gaŋ·glio] <-gli> *m* ANAT (*linfatico,
nervoso*) ganglion

gangrena [gaŋ·'grɛ:·na] *f v.* cancrena

ganimede [ga·ni·'mɛ:·de] *m* cock of the roost

ganzo, -a ['gan·dzo] **I.** *agg fam* drop dead gorgeous **II.** *m, f fam* (*in gamba*) smart person;
(*figo*) stunner

gara ['ga:·ra] *f* **1.** (*competizione*) competition;
(*di velocità*) race; **~ di solidarietà** charity
match; **fare una ~** to compete; **fare a ~ con
qu** to compete with sb; **essere fuori ~** to be
out of the running **2.** (*concorso*) competition;
~ d'appalto tender for bids

garagista [ga·ra·'dʒis·ta] <-i *m*, -e *f*> *mf*
(*meccanico*) auto mechanic; (*proprietario*)
garage owner; (*direttore*) garage manager *m*,
garage manageress *f*

garante [ga·'ran·te] **I.** *agg* **farsi ~ di qc** to
vouch for sth **II.** *mf* (*ente, persona*) guarantor

garantire [ga·ran·'ti:·re] <garantisco> **I.** *vt*
1. (*assicurare*) to ensure **2.** *a.* COM, JUR to guarantee; **~ qc a qu** to guarantee sb sth **II.** *vr:* **-rsi
-rsi contro qc** to insure oneself against sth

garantito, -a [ga·ran·'ti:·to] *agg* (*prodotto*)
guaranteed; **l'automobile è -a per un anno**
the car is under warranty for one year; **quei
soldi, ~, non li rivedi più!** *fam* you'll never
see that money again, that's for sure!

garanzia [ga·ran·'tsi:·a] <-ie> *f* **1.** *a.* COM guarantee; **in ~** under warranty; **~ di serietà** guarantee of reliability **2.** (*impegno: su finanzia-*

mento) security **3.** JUR **avviso di ~** *written warning given to a suspect that he/she is under investigation*

garbare [gar·'baː·re] *vi essere fam* to like; **il suo comportamento non mi garba** I don't like his [o her] behavior

garbatamente [gar·ba·ta·'men·te] *f* (*gentilmente*) kindly; (*educatamente*) politely

garbato, -a [gar·'baː·to] *agg* (*gentile*) kind; (*educato*) polite

garbo ['gar·bo] *m* (*educazione*) politeness; **con ~** politely

garbuglio [gar·'buʎ·ʎo] <-gli> *m* (*di cavi, fili*) tangle

garçonne [gar·'sɔn] <-> *f* **capelli alla ~** butch haircut

garçonnière [gar·sɔ·'njɛːr] <-> *f* love nest

Garda ['gar·da] *f* **il Lago di ~** Lake Garda

Gardena [gar·'deː·na] *f* **la Val ~** Val Gardena; **andare in Val ~** to go to Val Gardena; **abitare in Val ~** to live in Val Gardena

gardenia [gar·'dɛː·nia] <-ie> *f* gardenia

gardesano, -a [gar·de·'zaː·no] *agg* (*del Lago di Garda*) of Lake Garda

gareggiare [ga·red·'dʒaː·re] *vi* (*fare a gara*) to compete; **~ in qc con qc** to compete in sth with sth

garganella [gar·ga·'nɛl·la] *f* **bere a ~** to drink from the bottle

gargarismo [gar·ga·'riz·mo] *m* (*azione, colluttorio*) gargle; **fare i -i** to gargle

garofano [ga·'rɔː·fa·no] *m* carnation

garrese [gar·'reː·se] *m* withers *pl*

garrire [gar·'riː·re] <garrisco> *vi* (*uccelli*) to chirp

garrito [gar·'riː·to] *m* (*di uccelli*) chirping

garrotta [gar·'rɔt·ta] *f* garrote

garrulo, -a ['gar·ru·lo] *agg* (*uccelli*) chirping

garza ['gar·dza] *f* **1.** (*tessuto*) gauze **2.** MED (*per fasciare*) gauze bandage

garzone, -a [gar·'dzoː·ne] *m, f* (*di macellaio, panettiere*) boy

gas [gas] <-> *m* gas; **a tutto ~** (*veloce*) at full speed; **~ di scarico** exhaust gas; **~ asfissiante** asphyxiating gas; **~ esilarante** laughing gas; **~ lacrimogeno** tear gas; **~ nobile** inert gas; **~ serra** greenhouse gas; **bolletta del ~** gas bill

gasare [ga·'zaː·re] *v.* gassare

gasarsi [ga·'sar·si] *vr fig, fam* (*esaltarsi*) to get excited; (*montarsi*) to get big-headed

gasato, -a [ga·'saː·to] **I.** *agg* (*gassato: acqua, bibita*) fizzy **II.** *m, f fig, fam* (*esaltato*) excited person; (*montato*) big head

gasdotto [gaz·'dot·to] *m* gas pipeline

gasolio [ga·'zɔː·lio] *m* diesel

gasometro [ga·'zɔː·me·tro] *m* gasometer

gassare [gas·'saː·re] *vt* to make fizzy

gassato, -a [gas·'saː·to] *agg* (*bevanda*) fizzy

gassometro [gas·'sɔː·me·tro] *v.* gasometro

gassosa [gas·'soː·sa] *f* gassosa, *a clear fizzy drink*

gassoso, -a [gas·'soː·so] *agg* (*emissione, inquinante*) gaseous

gastrico, -a ['gas·tri·ko] <-ci, -che> *agg* (*dello stomaco: succo, ulcera, disturbo*) gastric; **lavanda -a** stomach pumping

gastrite [gas·'triː·te] *f* MED gastritis

gastroenterite [gas·tro·en·te·'riː·te] *f* MED gastroenteritis

gastrointestinale [gas·tro·in·tes·ti·'naː·le] *agg* MED (*disturbo, malattia*) gastrointestinal

gastronomia [gas·tro·no·'miː·a] <-ie> *f* (*arte culinaria*) cuisine

gastronomico, -a [gas·tro·'nɔː·mi·ko] <-ci, -che> *agg* (*prodotto, turismo, cultura*) gastronomic

gastronomo, -a [gas·'trɔː·no·mo] *m, f* (*intenditore*) gourmet

gastropatia [gas·tro·pa·'tiː·a] <-ie> *f* MED gastropathy

gastroscopia [gas·tros·ko·'piː·a] <-ie> *f* MED gastroscopy

gastroscopio [gas·tros·'kɔː·pio] <-i> *m* MED gastroscope

gatta ['gat·ta] *f* (female) cat; **una ~ da pelare** (*problema*) a thorny problem; **qui ~ ci cova!** there's something fishy going on!; **la ~ frettolosa fa i gattini ciechi** *prov* more haste, less speed *prov*

gattabuia [gat·ta·'buː·ia] <-ie> *f fam* nick

gattinara [gat·ti·'naː·ra] <-> *m* Gattinara, *a red wine from the Piedmont region*

gatto ['gat·to] *m* (*animale*) cat; (*maschio*) tomcat; **~ selvatico** wild cat; **~ delle nevi** snowcat; **il ~ con gli stivali** Puss in Boots; **c'erano quattro -i** *fig* there weren't many people; **quando il ~ non c'è i topi ballano** *prov* when the cat's away the mice will play *prov*

gattoni [gat·'toː·ni] *avv* on all fours; **andare a ~** to crawl

gattopardo [gat·to·'par·do] *m* ZOO leopard; **~ africano** serval; **~ americano** ocelot

gavetta [ga·'vet·ta] *f* **1.** (*portavivande*) mess kit **2.** (*apprendistato*) **fare la ~** to start at the bottom; **venire dalla ~** to come up through the ranks

gavettone [ga·vet·'toː·ne] *m* (*scherzo*) water-filled bag

gay ['gei] **I.** <-> *mf* gay person **II.** <inv> *agg* gay; **locale ~** gay bar; **matrimonio ~** gay marriage

gazza ['gad·dza] *f* ZOO magpie; **~ ladra** magpie

gazzarra [gad·'dzar·ra] *f fam* din

gazzella [gad·'dzɛl·la] *f* **1.** ZOO gazelle; **occhi da ~** doe eyes **2.** *sl* (*dei carabinieri*) police car

gazzetta [gad·'dzet·ta] *f* (*nome di giornale*) gazette; **la Gazzetta Ufficiale** the Official Gazette, *newspaper published by the government containing all new laws*

gazzettino [gad·dzet·'tiː·no] *m* **1.** (*nome di giornale*) gazette **2.** (*notiziario*) section

gazzosa [gad·'dzoː·sa] *v.* gassosa

Gazz. Uff. *abbr di* **Gazzetta Ufficiale** Official Gazette *newspaper published by the government containing all new laws*

G

GB *abbr di* **gigabyte** GB

gelare [dʒe·'la:·re] I. *vi* 1. *essere* (*acqua, lago*) to freeze 2. *essere o avere* (*impersonale*) METEO to freeze II. *vt avere* 1. (*dita, mani*) to freeze 2. *fig* (*sangue*) to run cold; **mi gelava il sangue nelle vene** my blood ran cold III. *vr:* **-rsi** to freeze

gelata [dʒe·'la:·ta] *f* frost

gelataio, -a [dʒe·la·'ta:·io] <-ai, -aie> *m, f* (*chi vende gelati*) ice-cream seller; (*chi fa gelati*) ice-cream maker

gelateria [dʒe·la·te·'ri:·a] <-ie> *f* ice-cream parlor

gelatiera [dʒe·la·'tiɛ:·ra] *f* ice-cream maker

gelatina [dʒe·la·'ti:·na] *f* CULIN, CHEM gelatine; **~ di frutta** fruit jelly

gelato [dʒe·'la:·to] *m* ice-cream

ℹ️ Many regions claim to be the home of **gelato** (ice cream), but in fact it seems to have spread from Sicily, after being introduced there by the Arabs. Indeed ice cream is believed to have originated from the ancient sorbet – from the Arabic word "sherbet" – which was invented by them to combat the searing heat of their desert home and taken by them to Sicily, where local ingredients were added. Sicilian ice cream is still renowned today, both for the exotic flavors ranging from mulberry to prickly pear and for the way in which it is served, in cones or cups but also sandwiched in the middle of a brioche. Throughout Italy, ice cream is served not in scoops but with a spatula, with the result that the size of the portions varies and depends on the whim of the person who is serving.

---

gelato, -a *agg* (*mani, piedi*) frozen; **cono ~** ice-cream cone

gelido, -a ['dʒɛ:·li·do] *agg* 1. (*acqua, aria, stanza*) freezing 2. *fig* (*persona, sguardo, accoglienza*) cold

gelo ['dʒɛ:·lo] *m* 1. METEO cold weather 2. *fig* (*ostilità*) chill

gelone [dʒe·'lo:·ne] *m* chilblain

gelosia [dʒe·lo·'si:·a] <-ie> *f* 1. (*stato d'animo*) jealousy; **fare una scenata di ~** to throw a jealous fit 2. (*cura attenta*) great care; **custodire qc con ~** to look after sth very carefully 3. (*di finestra*) shutter

geloso, -a [dʒe·'lo:·so] *agg* (*marito, moglie*) jealous; **~ di qu** jealous of sb

gelso ['dʒɛl·so] *m* BOT mulberry tree

gelsomino [dʒel·so·'mi:·no] *m* BOT jasmine

gemellaggio [dʒe·mel·'lad·dʒo] <-ggi> *m* (*di città, scuole*) twinning

gemellare¹ [dʒe·mel·'la:·re] *agg* twin; **parto ~** twin birth

gemellare² *vt* (*città, scuole*) to twin

gemelli [dʒe·'mɛl·li] *mpl* 1. ASTR **Gemelli** Gemini; **sono** (**dei**) **Gemelli** I'm Gemini 2. (*bottoni*) cufflinks

gemello, -a [dʒe·'mɛl·lo] I. *agg* (*fratello, letto*) twin II. *m, f* twin

gemere ['dʒɛ:·me·re] *vi* (*lamentarsi*) to groan; **~ di** to groan with

gemito ['dʒɛ:·mi·to] *m* (*lamento: di ferito, ammalato*) groan

gemma ['dʒɛm·ma] *f* 1. BOT bud 2. *a. fig* gem

gemmazione [dʒem·mat·'tsio:·ne] *f* BOT budding

gemmologia [dʒem·mo·lo·'dʒi:·a] <-gie> *f* gemology

gendarme [dʒen·'dar·me] *m* MIL (*guardia*) policeman

gendarmeria [dʒen·dar·me·'ri:·a] <-ie> *f* (*polizia*) police force

gene ['dʒɛ:·ne] *m* BIO gene

genealogia [dʒe·ne·a·lo·'dʒi:·a] <-gie> *f* genealogy

genealogico, -a [dʒe·ne·a·'lɔ:·dʒi·ko] <-ci, -che> *agg* (*ricerca, tavola*) genealogical; **albero ~** family tree

generale [dʒe·ne·'ra:·le] I. *agg* 1. (*fatti, principi, norma*) general 2. (*comune a tutti: sciopero, lutto*) national; (*sorpesa*) widespread; (*opinione*) public; **in ~** in general 3. (*direttore, ispettore, segretario*) general II. *m* MIL general; **~ di brigata** brigadier; **~ di corpo d'armata** lieutenant general

generalessa [dʒe·ne·ra·'les·sa] *f fig pej* (*di carattere*) battle-ax

generalità [dʒe·ne·ra·li·'ta] <-> *f* 1. *pl* ADM (*nome, cognome*) personal details 2. (*maggioranza*) majority 3. (*di discorso, concetto*) generality

generalizzare [dʒe·ne·ra·lid·'dza:·re] I. *vt* 1. (*diffondere*) to spread 2. (*uniformare*) to generalize II. *vi* (*uniformare*) to generalize

generalizzazione [dʒe·ne·ra·lid·dzat·'tsio:·ne] *f* generalization

generalmente [dʒe·ne·ral·'men·te] *avv* generally

generare [dʒe·ne·'ra:·re] *vt* 1. (*figlio*) to give birth to 2. *a. fig* (*produrre, causare*) to generate

generatore [dʒe·ne·ra·'to:·re] *m* (*gruppo elettrogeno*) generator

generatrice [dʒe·ne·ra·'tri:·tʃe] *f* MATH generatrix

generazionale [dʒe·ne·rat·tsio·'na:·le] *agg* (*differenza, conflitto*) generational

generazione [dʒe·ne·rat·'tsio:·ne] *f* generation; **tramandare di ~ in ~** to pass on from generation to generation

genere ['dʒɛ:·ne·re] *m* 1. LING gender 2. LIT (*letterario, rosa, poliziesco*) genre 3. BOT, ZOO genus 4. (*insieme di persone*) **il ~ umano** mankind 5. (*tipo*) type 6. *pl* COM goods; **-i alimentari** foodstuffs; **-i di consumo** consumer goods; **-i di prima necessità** staple commodities 7. (*loc*) **in ~** in general

genericità [dʒe·ne·ri·tʃi·'ta] <-> f (*indeterminatezza*) vagueness

generico [dʒe·'nɛː·ri·ko] m general; **restare nel ~** to be non-specific

generico, -a <-ci, -che> agg **1.**(*discorso, significato*) generic **2.** MED **medico ~** general practicioner; **medicinali -ci** generic drugs

genero ['dʒɛː·ne·ro] m son-in-law

generosità [dʒe·ne·ro·si·'ta] <-> f generosity

generoso, -a [dʒe·ne·'roː·so] agg generous

genesi ['dʒɛː·ne·zi] <-> I. f (*origine*) genesis; (*di opera d'arte*) birth II. f o m REL **Genesi** Genesis

genetica [dʒe·'nɛː·ti·ka] <-che> f genetics

genetico, -a [dʒe·'nɛː·ti·ko] <-ci, -che> agg (*evoluzione, patrimonio, malattia*) genetic; **ingegneria -a** genetic engineering

genetista [dʒe·ne·'tis·ta] <-i m, -e f> mf geneticist

gengiva [dʒen·'dʒiː·va] f gum

gengivite [dʒen·dʒi·'viː·te] f (*med*) gingivitis

genia [dʒe·'niː·a] <-ie> f **1.**(*stirpe*) line **2.**(*banda*) gang

geniale [dʒe·'niaː·le] agg (*persona, idea, trovata, invenzione*) brilliant

genialità [dʒen·ia·li·'ta] <-> f (*di persona, idea, trovata, invenzione*) brilliance

genio ['dʒɛː·nio] <-i> m **1.**(*talento, persona*) genius; **un uomo di ~** a genius; **Leonardo da Vinci era un ~** Leonardo da Vinci was a genius; **lampo di ~** brainwave **2.**(*folletto*) genie **3.** ADM (*organismo*) **~ civile** civil engineers pl; **il ~ militare** the corps of engineers **4.**(*loc*) **non mi va a ~** I don't like it [o him] [o her]

genitale [dʒe·ni·'taː·le] agg (*apparato, organo, malattia*) genital

genitali [dʒe·ni·'taː·li] mpl genitals

genitivo [dʒe·ni·'tiː·vo] m LING genitive

genitivo, -a agg LING (*forma, desinenza*) genitive; **caso ~** genitive case

genitore [dʒe·ni·'toː·re] m **1.**(*padre, madre*) parent **2.** pl (*padre e madre*) parents

genitrice [dʒe·ni·'triː·tʃe] f poet mother

gennaio [dʒen·'naː·io] m January; v.a. **aprile**

genocidio [dʒe·no·'tʃiː·dio] <-i> m genocide

genotipo [dʒe·no·'tiː·po/dʒe·'nɔː·ti·po] m genotype

Genova ['dʒɛː·no·va] f Genoa, *the capital of the Liguria region*

genovese [dʒe·no·'veː·se] I. agg Genoese; **pesto alla ~** pesto, *a sauce for pasta consisting of basil, olive oil and pine nuts* II. mf (*abitante*) Genoese III. <*sing*> m (*dialetto*) Genoese dialect

Genovese <*sing*> m (*zona*) Genoa area; **nel ~** in the Genoa area

gentaglia [dʒen·'taʎ·ʎa] <-glie> f pej riffraff

gente ['dʒɛn·te] f <*sing*> (*persone*) people pl; **~ di campagna** country folk; **~ di teatro** people from the theater world; **la ~ dice ...** word has it that ...; **abbiamo ~ a cena** fam we've got guests for dinner

gentildonna [dʒen·til·'dɔn·na] f (*nobildonna*) lady

gentile [dʒen·'tiː·le] agg **1.**(*persona*) kind; (*maniere*) courteous **2.**(*sentimenti, animo*) gentle; **il gentil sesso** the fair sex **3.**(*nelle lettere*) **~ signora** dear madam

gentilezza [dʒen·ti·'let·tsa] f **1.**(*di persona*) kindness; (*di modi*) courtesy **2.**(*piacere*) favor; **per ~** please; **fammi la ~ di ...** +*inf* please just ...; **fare una ~ a qu** to do sb a favor

gentiluomo [dʒen·ti·'luɔ·mo] <gentiluomini> m (*nobile*) gentleman; **comportarsi da ~** to behave like a gentleman

genuflessione [dʒe·nu·fles·'sioː·ne] f genuflection; **fare una ~** to genuflect

genuflettersi [dʒe·nu·'flɛt·ter·si] <irr> vr to genuflect

genuinità [dʒe·nui·ni·'ta] <-> f **1.**(*di prodotto*) naturalness **2.**(*di affermazione, notizia, fonte*) authenticity

genuino, -a [dʒe·nu·'iː·no] agg natural

genziana [dʒen·'tsia·na] f BOT gentian

geocentrico, -a [dʒe·o·'tʃɛn·tri·ko] <-ci, -che> agg (*sistema, teoria*) geocentric

geocentrismo [dʒe·o·tʃen·'triz·mo] m geocentricism

geochimica [dʒe·o·'kiː·mi·ka] <-che> f geochemistry

geodesia [dʒe·o·de·'ziː·a] <-ie> f geodesy

geodinamica [dʒe·o·di·'naː·mi·ka] <-che> f geodynamics

geofisica [dʒe·o·'fiː·zi·ka] <-che> f geophysics

geofisico, -a [dʒe·o·'fiː·zi·ko] <-ci, -che> I. agg (*osservatorio, metodo*) geophysical II. m, f (*studioso*) gephysicist

geografia [dʒe·o·gra·'fiː·a] f geography

geografico, -a [dʒe·o·'graː·fi·ko] <-ci, -che> agg geographical; **atlante ~** atlas; **carta -a** map

geografo, -a [dʒe·'ɔː·gra·fo] m, f geographer

geolinguistica [dʒe·o·liŋ·'guis·ti·ka] <-che> f geolinguistics

geologia [dʒe·o·lo·'dʒiː·a] <-gie> f geology

geologico, -a [dʒe·o·'lɔː·dʒi·ko] <-ci, -che> agg (*materiale, fenomeno, era*) geological

geologo, -a [dʒe·'ɔː·lo·go] <-gi, -ghe> m, f geologist

geomagnetismo [dʒe·o·maɲ·ɲe·'tiz·mo] m geomagnetism

geometra [dʒe·'ɔː·met·ra] <-i m, -e f> mf surveyor

geometria [dʒe·o·me·'triː·a] <-ie> f MATH geometry

geometrico, -a [dʒe·o·'mɛː·tri·ko] agg a. fig geometric(al)

geomorfologia [dʒe·o·mor·fo·lo·'dʒiː·a] f geomorphology

geopolitica [dʒe·o·po·'liː·ti·ka] <-che> f geopolitics

geopolitico, -a [dʒe·o·po·'liː·ti·ko] <-ci, -che> agg (*atlante, carta*) geopolitical

geotermica [dʒe·o·'tɛr·mi·ka] <-che> f geothermics

geotermico, -a [dʒe·o·'tɛr·mi·ko] <-ci, -che>

G

agg (*energia, gradiente*) geothermal

geotropico, -a [dʒe·o·'trɔ:·pi·ko] <-ci, -che> *agg* (*andamento, inclinazione*) geotropic

geotropismo [dʒe·o·tro·'piz·mo] *m* (*di radice*) geotropism

geranio [dʒe·'ra:·nio] <-i> *m* BOT geranium

gerarca [dʒe·'rar·ka] <-chi> *m* HIST party official

gerarchia [dʒe·rar·'ki:·a] <-chie> *f* hierarchy

gerarchico, -a [dʒe·'rar·ki·ko] <-ci, -che> *agg* hierarchical

gerbera [dʒer·'bɛ:·ra] *f* BOT gerbera

gerente [dʒe·'rɛn·te] *mf* (*di società, negozio*) manager *m*, manageress *f*

gergale [dʒer·'ga:·le] *agg* (*di slang*) slang; (*di linguaggio professionale*) jargon; **espressione** ~ slang expression

gergo ['dʒer·go] <-ghi> *m* (*linguaggio informale*) slang; (*linguaggio professionale*) jargon; ~ **giornalistico** newspaper jargon

geriatra [dʒe·'ria:·tra] <-i *m*, -e *f*> *mf* geriatrician

geriatria [dʒe·ria·'tri:·a] <-ie> *f* geriatrics

geriatrico, -a [dʒe·'ria:·tri·ko] <-ci, -che> *agg* (*malattia, ambulatorio*) geriatric; **clinica -a** geriatric clinic

gerla ['dʒer·la] *f* cone-shaped wicker basket carried on the back

Germania [dʒer·'ma:·nia] *f* Germany; **la** ~ Germany; **abitare in** ~ to live in Germany; **andare in** ~ to go to Germany

germanico, -a [dʒer·'ma:·ni·ko] <-ci, -che> *agg* HIST (*popolazioni, impero*) Germanic

germanista [dʒer·ma·'nis·ta] <-i *m*, -e *f*> *mf* Germanist

germanofilia [dʒer·ma·no·fi·'li:·a] *f* germanophile

germanofobia [dʒer·ma·no·fo·'bi:·a] *f* Germanophobia

germanofono, -a [dʒer·ma·'nɔ:·fo·no] *agg* (*popolazione, comunità, gruppo*) German-speaking

germe ['dʒer·me] *m* BIOL germ

germicida¹ [dʒer·mi·'tʃi:·da] <-i, -e> *agg* (*apparecchio, prodotto, sapone*) germicidal

germicida² <-i> *m* germicide

germinale [dʒer·mi·'na:·le] *agg* germinal

germinare [dʒer·mi·'na:·re] *vi essere o avere* BOT to germinate

germinazione [dʒer·mi·nat·'tsio:·ne] *f* BOT germination

germogliare [dʒer·moʎ·'ʎa:·re] *vi essere o avere* 1. (*seme*) to germinate 2. (*albero, ramo*) to bud

germoglio [dʒer·'moʎ·ʎo] <-gli> *m* 1. (*di seme*) shoot 2. (*di albero, ramo*) bud

geroglifico [dʒe·ro·'gli:·fi·ko] *m a. fig* LING hieroglyphic

geroglifico, -a <-ci, -che> *agg* LING (*scrittura, iscrizione*) hieroglyphic

gerontologia [dʒe·ron·to·lo·'dʒi:·a] <-gie> *f* gerontology

gerontologo, -a [dʒe·ron·'tɔ:·lo·go] <-gi,

-ghe> *m, f* gerontologist

gerundio [dʒe·'run·dio] <-i> *m* LING gerund

gerundivo, -a [dʒe·run·'di:·vo] *agg* LING gerundive

Gerusalemme [dʒe·ru·za·'lɛm·me] *f* Jerusalem; **abitare a** ~ to live in Jerusalem; **andare a** ~ to go to Jerusalem

gessato [dʒes·'sa:·to] *m* (*abito*) pinstripe suit

gessato, -a *agg* (*abito, pantaloni*) pin-stripe

gessetto [dʒes·'set·to] *m* piece of chalk

gesso ['dʒɛs·so] *m* 1. (*per lavagna*) chalk 2. MIN gypsum 3. MED, SCULTURA plaster cast

gesta ['dʒɛs·ta] *fpl* LIT feats

gestante [dʒes·'tan·te] *f* pregnant woman

gestazione [dʒes·tat·'tsio:·ne] *f* MED (*gravidanza*) pregnancy

gesticolare [dʒes·ti·ko·'la:·re] *vi* to gesticulate

gestionale [dʒes·tio·'na:·le] *agg* (*analisi, processi, software*) management

gestione [dʒes·'tio:·ne] *f* (*di albergo, azienda, negozio, fondi*) management; ~ **dei costi** cost management; ~ **del motore** AUTO running; ~ **fondi** FIN fund management; **società di** ~ FIN management trust; ~ **prestiti** FIN loan management

gestire [dʒes·'ti:·re] <gestisco> *vt* (*amministrare: albergo, azienda, negozio*) to run; (*fondi*) to manage; (*tempo*) to organize

gesto ['dʒɛs·to] *m* gesture

gestore, -trice [dʒes·'to:·re] *m, f* 1. (*di albergo, azienda, negozio*) manager *m*, manageress *f* 2. (*fornitore di servizio*) supplier; **il** ~ **della rete elettrica** the electricity network supplier

gestuale [dʒes·tu·'a:·le] *agg* **linguaggio** ~ sign language

Gesù [dʒe·'zu] *m* Jesus

gesuita [dʒe·zu·'i:·ta] <-i> *m* REL Jesuit

gesuitico, -a [dʒe·zu·'i:·ti·ko] <-ci, -che> *agg* REL Jesuitical

gettare [dʒet·'ta:·re] I. *vt* 1. (*lanciare*) to throw; ~ **via qc** to throw sth away; ~ **le braccia al collo a qu** to throw one's arms around sb's neck 2. NAUT (*ancora*) to drop; (*reti*) to cast 3. ARCH (*fondamenta*) to lay II. *vi* BOT to sprout III. *vr:* **-rsi** 1. (*buttarsi*) **-rsi a terra** to throw oneself down on the ground; **-rsi ai piedi di qu** to throw oneself at sb's feet; **-rsi contro qu** to attack sb; **-rsi dalla finestra** to throw oneself out of the window; **-rsi in acqua** to jump into the water 2. (*fiume*) to flow into

gettata [dʒet·'ta:·ta] *f* (*di cemento*) casting

gettito ['dʒɛt·ti·to] *m* (*introiti*) revenue

getto ['dʒɛt·to] *m* 1. BOT shoot 2. (*di liquido*) jet; **stampanti a** ~ **d'inchiostro** ink-jet printers 3. (*di metallo, calcestruzzo*) casting 4. *fig* **a** ~ **continuo** continuously; **di** ~ straight off

gettonato, -a [dʒet·to·'na:·to] *agg fam* (*cantante, canzone*) popular

gettone [dʒet·'to:·ne] *m* token; ~ **del telefono** [*o* **telefonico**] telephone token; **telefono a -i** telephone which operates with tokens

gettoniera [dʒet·to·'niɛ:·ra] *f* (*di telefono*) slot

ghepardo [ge·'par·do] *m* cheetah

gheriglio [ge·'riʎ·ʎo] <-gli> *m* (*di noce*) kernel

ghermire [ger·'mi:·re] *vt* (*afferrare: preda*) to seize

ghetta ['get·ta] *f* (*gambale*) gaiter

ghettizzare [get·tid·'dza:·re] *vt* (*minoranze*) to segregate

ghettizzazione [get·tid·dzat·'sio:·ne] *f* (*di minoranze*) segregation

ghiacciaia [giat·'tʃa:·ia] <-aie> *f* icebox

ghiacciaio [giat·'tʃa:·io] <-ai> *m* glacier

ghiacciare [giat·'tʃa:·re] **I.** *vt avere* (*gelare*) to freeze **II.** *vr:* **-rsi** to freeze

ghiacciato, -a [giat·'tʃa:·to] *agg* frozen

ghiaccio ['giat·tʃo] <-cci> *m* ice; ~ **secco** dry ice; **pattinaggio sul** ~ ice skating; **rompere il** ~ *a. fig* to break the ice; **rimanere di** ~ *fig* to be astounded; **essere un pezzo di** ~ *fig* to be as cold as ice

ghiacciolo [giat·'tʃɔ:·lo] *m* **1.** (*pezzo di ghiaccio*) icicle **2.** CULIN popsicle

ghiaia ['gia:·ia] <-aie> *f* gravel

ghiaione [gia·'io:·ne] *m* scree

ghiaioso, -a [gia·'io:·so] *agg* (*superficie, spiagge*) gravelly

ghianda ['gian·da] *f* BOT (*di quercia*) acorn

ghiandola ['gian·do·la] *f* ANAT gland

ghiandolare [gian·do·'la:·re] *agg* (*tessuto, febbre*) glandular

ghigliottina [giʎ·ʎot·'ti:·na] *f* guillotine

ghigliottinare [giʎ·ʎot·ti·'na:·re] *vt* (*decapitare*) to guillotine

ghignare [giɲ·'ɲa:·re] *vi* to snicker

ghignata [giɲ·'ɲa:·ta] *f* snicker

ghigno ['giɲ·ɲo] *m* sneer

ghingheri ['giɲ·ge·ri] *avv* **mattersi in** ~ *scherz, fam* to put on one's finery

ghiotto, -a ['giot·to] *agg* **1.** (*persona*) greedy; **è** ~ **di dolci** he's [*o* she's] a glutton for cakes **2.** (*cibo*) delicious

ghiottone, -a [giot·'to:·ne] *m, f* (*persona*) glutton

ghiottoneria [giot·to·ne·'ri:·a] <-ie> *f* **1.** (*golosità*) gluttony **2.** (*leccornia*) delicacy

ghiribizzo [gi·ri·'bid·dzo] *m fam* (*capriccio*) whim

ghirigoro [gi·ri·'gɔ:·ro] *m* scribble

ghirlanda [gir·'lan·da] *f* (*di fiori, foglie*) garland

ghiro ['gi:·ro] *m* ZOO dormouse; **dormire come un** ~ to sleep like a log

ghisa ['gi:·za] *f* cast iron

già [dʒa] *avv* **1.** (*fatto compiuto*) already; **sono** ~ **partiti** they've already left; **hai** ~ **fatto i compiti?** have you already done your homework? **2.** (*prima d'ora*) before; **l'ho** ~ **fatto** I've done it before; (*in frasi interrogative*) yet; **hai** ~ **fatto i compiti?** have you done your homework yet? **3.** (*ormai*) by now **4.** (*sin d'ora*) right; ~ **da ora** right now; ~ **da oggi**

from today **5.** (*sin da alllora*) ever since **6.** (*ex*) formerly **7.** (*rafforzativo*) quite; ~ **tanto** quite something **8.** (*loc*) ~ **che** while

giacca ['dʒak·ka] <-cche> *f* (*indumento*) jacket; ~ **a vento** windbreaker; ~ **ad un petto** single-breasted jacket; ~ **a doppio petto** double-breasted jacket

giacché [dʒak·'ke] *cong* (*poiché*) since

giacchetta [dʒak·'ket·ta] *f* jacket

giaccio ['dʒat·tʃo] *1. pers sing pr di* **giacere**

giacente [dʒa·'tʃɛn·te] *agg* **1.** (*posta normale*) unclaimed; (*posta elettronica*) unopened **2.** (*pratica*) pending

giacenza [dʒa·'tʃɛn·tsa] *f* (*deposito*) **in** ~ in abeyance; **posta in** ~ unclaimed mail; **capitale in** ~ uninvested capital; **-e di magazzino** (*resti*) unsold stock

giacere [dʒa·'tʃe:·re] <giaccio, giacqui, giaciuto> *vi essere* **1.** (*essere disteso*) to lie; ~ **bocconi** to lie on one's face; ~ **sul fianco** to lie on one's side; ~ **supino** to lie on one's back **2.** (*essere sepolto*) to be buried; **qui giace ...** (*sulle tombe*) here lies ... **3.** (*essere inattivo*) to lie idle

giaciglio [dʒa·'tʃiʎ·ʎo] <-gli> *m* (*letto*) pallet

giacimento [dʒa·tʃi·'men·to] *m* (*di petrolio, di gas*) deposit

giacinto [dʒa·'tʃin·to] *m* BOT hyacinth

giaciuto [dʒa·'tʃu:·to] *pp di* **giacere**

giacomo giacomo ['dʒa:·ko·mo 'dʒa:·ko·mo] **far** ~ ~ *fam* to tremble

giacqui ['dʒak·kui] *1. pers sing pass rem di* **giacere**

giada[1] ['dʒa:·da] *f* jade

giada[2] <inv> *agg* **verde** ~ jade green

giaggiolo [dʒad·'dʒɔ:·lo] *m* BOT iris

giaguaro [dʒa·'gua:·ro] *m* ZOO jaguar

giallastro, -a [dʒal·'las·tro] *agg* yellowish

giallino, -a [dʒal·'li:·no] *agg* light yellow

giallista [dʒal·'lis·ta] <-i *m*, -e *f*> *mf* crime writer

giallo, -a ['dʒal·lo] *m* **1.** (*colore*) yellow; **il** ~ **dell'uovo** the egg yolk; **passare col** ~ to go through a yellow light **2.** LIT detective story; CINE thriller

giallo, -a *agg* **1.** (*colore*) yellow; **farina -a** corn flour; **febbre -a** yellow fever; **Pagine -e**® Yellow Pages® **2.** (*romanzo*) detective story; (*film*) thriller

giallognolo, -a [dʒal·'loɲ·ɲo·lo] *agg* yellowish

giallorosa [dʒal·lo·'rɔ:·za] <inv> *agg* (*film, commedia*) romantic thriller

giammai [dʒam·'ma:·i] *avv poet* never

gianduia [dʒan·'du:·ia] <-> *m* CULIN nut chocolate

Giappone [dʒap·'po:·ne] *m* Japan; **il** ~ Japan; **abitare in** ~ to live in Japan; **andare in** ~ to go to Japan

giapponese [dʒap·po·'ne:·se] **I.** *agg* Japanese **II.** *mf* Japanese **III.** <sing> *m* (*lingua*) Japanese

giara ['dʒa:·ra] *f* (*recipiente*) earthenware jar

giardinaggio [dʒar·di·'nad·dʒo] <-ggi> *m*

G

gardening

giardinetta® [dʒar·di·'net·ta] *f* station wagon

giardiniera [dʒar·di·'niɛː·ra] *f* CULIN (*sottaceti*) pickled vegetables

giardiniere, -a [dʒar·di·'niɛː·re] *m, f* gardener

giardino [dʒar·'diː·no] *m* garden; **in** ~ in the garden; ~ **botanico** botanic garden; **da** ~ garden; **mobili da** ~ garden furniture; **-i pubblici** public gardens; ~ **zoologico** zoo

giarrettiera [dʒar·ret·'tiɛː·ra] *f* garter

giavellottista [dʒa·vel·lot·'tis·ta] <-i *m*, -e *f*> *mf* javelin thrower

giavellotto [dʒa·vel·'lɔt·to] *m* SPORT javelin

gibbone [dʒib·'boː·ne] *m* ZOO gibbon

gibbosità [dʒib·bo·si·'ta] <-> *f* (*di terreno, superficie*) unevenness

giberna [dʒi·'bɛr·na] *f* (*per cartucce, munizioni*) cartridge box

Gibilterra [dʒi·bil·'tɛr·ra] *f* Gibraltar; **la** ~ Gibraltar; **abitare a** ~ to live in Gibraltar; **andare a** ~ to go to Gibraltar

gigabyte [gi·ga·bait] <-> *m* COMPUT gigabyte

gigante [dʒi·'gan·te] I. *agg* (*confezione, scatola, formato*) giant-size II. *m* (*titano*) giant; **fare passi da** ~ *fig* to make great leaps forward

gigantesco, -a [dʒi·gan·'tes·ko] <-schi, -sche> *agg* gigantic

gigantismo [dʒi·gan·'tiz·mo] *m* MED gigantism

giglio ['dʒiʎ·ʎo] <-gli> *m* BOT lily

gilè [dʒi·'lɛ] <-> *m* vest

gillette® [dʒi·'let] *m* (*rasoio*) razor

gimcana [dʒim·'kaː·na] *v.* gincana

gincana [dʒiŋ·'kaː·na] *f* 1. (*gara*) obstacle race 2. (*percorso a zig zag*) **fare la** ~ to zigzag

ginecologia [dʒi·ne·ko·lo·'dʒiː·a] <-gie> *f* gynecology

ginecologico, -a [dʒi·ne·ko·'lɔː·dʒi·ko] <-ci, -che> *agg* (*malattia, reparto, visita*) gynecological

ginecologo, -a [dʒi·ne·'kɔː·lo·go] <-gi, -ghe> *m, f* gynecologist

ginepro [dʒi·'neː·pro] *m* BOT juniper

ginestra [dʒi·'nɛs·tra] *f* BOT broom

Ginevra [dʒi·'neːv·ra] *f* (*città*) Geneva; **abitare a** ~ to live in Geneva; **andare a** ~ to go to Geneva

gingillarsi [dʒin·dʒil·'lar·si] *vr* 1. (*giocherellare*) ~ **con qc** to fiddle with sth 2. (*perdere tempo*) to loaf around

gingillo [dʒin·'dʒil·lo] *m* 1. (*ninnolo*) trinket 2. (*gadget*) gadget 3. (*balocco*) plaything

ginnasiale [dʒin·na·'zia·le] I. *agg* (*classe, studi*) of the first and second years of a high school which specializes in Latin and Greek (*the Liceo Classico*) II. *mf* first and second-year students in the the Liceo Classico

ginnasio [dʒin·'naː·zio] <-i> *m the first and second years of a high school which specializes in Latin and Greek* (*the Liceo Classico*); **quarta** ~ *the first year of the Liceo Classico;* **quinta** ~ *the second year of the Liceo Classico*

ginnasta [dʒin·'nas·ta] <-i *m*, -e *f*> *mf* gymnast

ginnastica [dʒin·'nas·ti·ka] <-che> *f* 1. (*esercizio*) gymnastics; ~ **correttiva** [*o* **medica**] therapeutic gymnastics 2. *fig* (*materia scolastica*) physical education

ginnico, -a ['dʒin·ni·ko] <-ci, -che> *agg* (*attrezzo, attrezzature*) gymnastic; **percorso** ~ training

ginocchiera [dʒi·nok·'kiɛː·ra] *f* 1. (*per sport*) knee pad 2. (*fascia elastica*) knee bandage

ginocchio [dʒi·'nɔk·kio] <-cchi *m o* -cchia *f*> *m* knee; **stare in** ~ to kneel; **mettersi in** ~ to kneel down

ginocchioni [dʒi·nok·'kioː·ni] *avv* on one's knees; **andare** ~ to crawl

giocare [dʒo·'kaː·re] I. *vi* 1. *a.* SPORT (*divertirsi, trastullarsi*) to play; ~ **a carte** to play cards; ~ **a palla** to play ball; ~ **con qc** to play with sth; ~ **a rugby** to play rugby; **gioca nell'Inter** he plays for Inter; ~ **con la propria vita** to risk one's life 2. (*scommettere*) to bet; ~ **al lotto** to play the lottery; ~ **al totocalcio** to bet the pools 3. FIN to speculate; ~ **in borsa** to play the Stock Market II. *vt* 1. (*partita, carta*) to play 2. (*scommettere: somma*) to bet 3. *fig* (*ingannare*) to fool; ~ **un tiro mancino a qu** to play a dirty trick on sb III. *vr:* **-rsi** *fig* **-rsi l'anima** to risk one's neck; **-rsi anche la camicia** to lose the shirt off one's back

giocata [dʒo·'kaː·ta] *f* 1. (*puntata*) bet 2. (*partita*) game

giocatore, -trice [dʒo·ka·'toː·re] *m, f* 1. (*a carte, pallone, tennis*) player; ~ **d'azzardo** gambler 2. (*in borsa*) speculator

giocattolo [dʒo·'kat·to·lo] *m* toy

giocherellare [dʒo·ke·rel·'laː·re] *vi* to play

giocherellone, -a [dʒo·ke·rel·'loː·ne] *agg* playful

giochetto [dʒo·'ket·to] *m* 1. (*divertimento*) game 2. (*scherzo*) joke 3. (*lavoro facile*) piece of cake

gioco ['dʒɔː·ko] <-chi> *m* 1. (*divertimento*) game; ~ **d'azzardo** game of chance; ~ **di parole** pun; ~ **di società** parlor game; ~ **degli scacchi** chess; ~ **del lotto** lottery; ~ **da bambini** children's game; *fig* child's play; **i -chi olimpici** the Olympic Games; **campo da** ~ pitch; **fare il** ~ **di qu** *fig* to play sb's game; **fare il doppio** ~ *fig* to double-cross; **esserci in** ~ *fig* to be at stake; **mettere in** ~ **qc** *fig* to risk sth; **cambiar** ~ *fig* to change tack; **prendersi** ~ **di qu** *fig* to make fun of sb; **il** ~ **non vale la candela** *prov* the game is not worth the candle *prov;* **ogni bel** ~ **dura poco** *prov* don't take the joke too far 2. (*giocattolo*) toy 3. (*lavoro facile*) child's play

giocoliere, -a [dʒo·ko·'liɛː·re] *m, f* juggler

Gioconda [dʒo·'kon·da] *f* **La** ~ the Mona Lisa

giocoso, -a [dʒo·'koː·so] *agg* (*bambini, cuccioli*) playful

giogo ['dʒoː·go] <-ghi> *m* (*attrezzo*) yoke

gioia ['dʒɔː·ia] <-ie> *f* 1. (*emozione*) joy;

darsi alla pazza ~ to live things up **2.** (*gioiello*) jewel **3.** (*persona*) darling

gioielleria [dʒo·iel·le·'riː·a] <-ie> *f* **1.** (*negozio*) jeweler's shop **2.** (*arte*) jeweler's craft **3.** (*goielli*) jewelry

gioielliere, -a [dʒo·iel·'liɛː·re] *m, f* **1.** (*persona*) jeweler **2.** (*negozio*) jeweler's

gioiello [dʒo·'iel·lo] *m* **1.** (*monile*) jewel **2.** *fig* (*cosa, persona*) gem

gioioso, -a [dʒo·'io:so] *agg* (*persona, musica, momento*) joyful

gioire [dʒo·'iː·re] <gioisco> *vi* to delight; ~ **di** [*o* **per**] **qc** to delight in sth

giornalaio, -a [dʒor·na·'laː·io] <-ai, -aie> *m, f* newsdealer

giornale [dʒor·'naː·le] *m* **1.** (*quotidiano*) newspaper **2.** RADIO, TV news bulletin; ~ **radio** radio news **3.** (*registro*) journal; ~ **di bordo** ship's log

giornalese [dʒor·na·'leː·se] <-> *m iron, pej* newsspeak

giornaletto [dʒor·na·'let·to] *m fam* comic

giornaliero, -a [dʒor·na·'liɛː·ro] *agg* (*quotidiano: biglietto, servizio, volo*) daily

giornalino [dʒor·na·'liː·no] *m fam* comic

giornalismo [dʒor·na·'liz·mo] *m* journalism

giornalista [dʒor·na·'lis·ta] <-i *m*, -e *f*> *mf* journalist

giornalistico, -a [dʒor·na·'lis·ti·ko] <-ci, -che> *agg* (*stile, gergo, notizie*) journalistic

giornalmente [dʒor·nal·'men·te] *avv* on a daily basis

giornata [dʒor·'naː·ta] *f* **1.** (*giorno*) day; **uova di** ~ freshly-laid egg; **in** ~ by the end of the day; **andare a -e** to be up and down; **vivere alla** ~ to live from day to day **2.** (*lavoro*) day's work; (*paga*) day's pay

giorno [dʒor·no] *m* **1.** (*24 ore*) day; ~ **feriale** weekday; ~ **festivo** holiday; ~ **lavorativo** work day; ~ **libero** day off; **piatto del** ~ today's specialty; **al** ~ per day; **di** ~ **in** ~ from day to day; **da un** ~ **all'altro** suddenly; **un** ~ **o l'altro** one of these days; ~ **per** ~ day by day; **a -i alterni** on alternate days; **uno di questi -i** one of these days **2.** (*ore di luce*) daylight; **di** ~ by day; **in pieno** ~ in broad daylight; **sul far del** ~ at daybreak **3.** (*ricorrenza*) **il** ~ **dei morti** All Souls' Day **4.** (*loc*) **al** ~ **d'oggi** nowadays; **ai nostri -i** in our time; **buon** ~ *v.* **buongiorno**

> **i** On November 2, the **Giorno dei Morti** (All Souls Day), Italians visit cemeteries and think about their dead friends and relatives.

giostra ['dʒɔs·tra] *f* (*al luna park*) merry-go-round

giostrarsi [dʒos·'traːr·si] *vr* to hold one's own

giovamento [dʒo·va·'men·to] *m* benefit

giovane ['dʒo·va·ne] **I.** *agg* **1.** (*persona, animale*) young **2.** (*moda, letteratura*) youth; **festival internazionale del cinema** ~ international youth film festival **II.** *mf* (*ragazzo*) young man; (*ragazza*) young woman; **da** ~ as a young man [*o* woman]; **Plinio il** ~ Pliny the Younger

giovanetto, -a [dʒo·va·'net·to] *m, f* (*ragazzo*) lad; (*ragazza*) girl

giovanile [dʒo·va·'niː·le] *agg* **1.** (*amore, delusione*) youthful **2.** (*movimento, politica*) youth

giovanotto [dʒo·va·'nɔt·to] *m* young man

giovare [dʒo·'vaː·re] **I.** *vi avere o essere* **1.** (*essere utile*) to be useful; **non giova ...** +*inf* it's no use ...; **a che giova ...** ? what's the point of ...? **2.** (*fare bene*) to do good; **un bicchiere di vino ti gioverà** a glass of wine will do you good **II.** *vr* **-rsi di qu/qc** to take advantage of sb/sth

Giove ['dʒɔː·ve] *m* Jupiter; **per ~!** *fam* by Jove!

giovedì [dʒo·ve·'di] <-> *m* Thursday; ~ **grasso** last Thursday before Lent; ~ **santo** Thursday before Easter; *v.a.* **domenica**

giovenca [dʒo·'vɛŋ·ka] <-che> *f* heifer

gioventù [dʒo·ven·'tu] <-> *f* **1.** (*età*) youth; **errori di** ~ errors of youth; **in** ~ in one's youth **2.** (*giovani*) young people *pl*

gioviale [dʒo·'viaː·le] *agg* (*accoglienza*) hearty; (*persona, clima*) jovial

giovialità [dʒo·via·li·'ta] <-> *f* (*di persona*) joviality

giovinastro [dʒo·vi·'nas·tro] *m* young hoodlum

giovinetto [dʒo·vi·'net·to] *v.* **giovanetto**

giovinezza [dʒo·vi·'net·tsa] *f* youth; **la seconda** ~ the golden years

GIP ['dʒip] <-> *mf abbr di* **giudice per le indagini preliminari** *the magistrate appointed to supervise the initial police investigation into a case*

giradischi [dʒi·ra·'dis·ki] <-> *m* record player

giraffa [dʒi·'raf·fa] *f* **1.** ZOO giraffe **2.** FILM, TV, RADIO boom

giramento [dʒi·ra·'men·to] *m* ~ **di testa** *fam* dizzy spell; **questo lavoro è un** ~ **di scatole** *fam* this job is a pain

giramondo [dʒi·ra·'mon·do] <-> *mf* globetrotter

giranastri [dʒi·ra·'nas·tri] <-> *m* tape recorder

girandola [dʒi·'ran·do·la] *f* **1.** (*giocattolo*) pinwheel **2.** (*per fuochi d'artificio*) catherine wheel **3.** (*di avvenimenti*) whirl

girante [dʒi·'ran·te] *f* TEC (*di pompa*) impeller; (*di motore*) rotor

girante [dʒi·'ran·te] *mf* FIN endorser

girare [dʒi·'raː·re] **I.** *vt* **1.** (*chiave, testa, occhi*) to turn **2.** *fig* (*domanda, lettera*) to pass on **3.** (*film*) to shoot **4.** (*assegno*) to endorse **5.** (*città, isola*) to go around; ~ **il mondo** to travel around the world **6.** *fam* (*mescolare: sugo*) to stir **II.** *vi* **1.** (*ruotare*) to revolve; **mi girano le scatole** *fam* I'm fed up; **mi girano per la testa un sacco di idee** *fam* I'm bursting with lots of ideas; **mi gira la testa** I feel dizzy; **far ~ la testa a qu** (*fare innamorare*) to

G

turn sb's head; ~ **alla larga** to keep clear; **gira e rigira** which ever way you look at it; **se mi gira vengo** *fam* if I feel like it, I'll come 2.(*camminare*) to go around 3.(*voltare*) to turn 4.(*notizie, dicerie*) to circulate III. *vr:* **-rsi** (*voltarsi*) to turn; **-rsi nel letto** to turn over in bed; **-rsi dall'altra parte** to turn away

girarrosto [dʒi·rar·'rɔs·to] *m* spit

girasole [dʒi·ra·'so:·le] *m* BOT sunflower

girata [dʒi·'ra:·ta] *f* 1.(*passeggiata*) stroll 2.*fam* (*mescolata*) stir 3.FIN (*di assegno*) endorsement

giratario, -a [dʒi·ra·'ta:·rio] <-i, -ie> *m, f* FIN endorsee

girato, -a [dʒi·'ra:·to] *agg* 1.(*persona*) turned 2.FIN endorsed

giratubi [dʒi·ra·'tu:·bi] <-> *m* TEC pipe wrench

giravolta [dʒi·ra·'vɔl·ta] *f* (*piroetta*) pirouette

girellare [dʒi·rel·'la:·re] *vi* ~ **per** to wander around

girello [dʒi·'rɛl·lo] *m* 1.(*per bambini*) baby walker 2.CULIN bottom round

giretto [dʒi·'ret·to] *m fam* (*a piedi*) stroll; (*in macchina, bicicletta*) ride

girevole [dʒi·'re:·vo·le] *agg*(*porta, ponte, piastra*) revolving

girgentino, -a [dʒir·dʒen·'ti:·no] *agg v.* **agrigentino**

girino [dʒi·'ri:·no] *m* ZOO tadpole

girl [gə:l] <-> *f* chorus dancer

giro ['dʒi:·ro] *m* 1.(*circonferenza: di collo*) circumference 2.(*rotazione: di astro, motore*) revolution; **su di -i** (*motore*) revved-up; *fig* (*persona*) high-spirited; ~ **di valzer** waltz 3.(*passeggiata*) stroll; (*in macchina, bicicletta*) ride; (*percorso*) trip; ~ **turistico** sightseeing tour; **essere in ~ per lavoro/affari** to be out and about on work/business; **esserci in ~** to be around; **andare in ~** to go around; **lasciare in ~** (*abiti, libri*) to leave lying around; **mettere in ~** (*voci, dicerie*) to spread 4.SPORT (*di pista*) lap 5.SPORT (*gara*) tour; **il ~ di Francia** the Tour de France 6.(*periodo di tempo*) course; **nel ~ di un mese/anno** in a month's/year's time 7.(*cerchia*) circle; (*ambiente*) scene 8.COM ~ **d'affari** turnover 9.(*loc*) **prendere in ~ qu** to make fun of sb; **fare un ~ d'orizzonte** to make general inquiries; ~ **di parole** long-winded expression

i The **Giro d'Italia** took place for the first time in 1909. This cycle race comprises both climbs and flat stages and the route passes through many of the major Italian cities.

girocollo [dʒi·ro·'kɔl·lo] *m* 1.(*collana*) choker 2.(*maglione*) crewneck sweater

giroconto [dʒi·ro·'kon·to] *m* credit transfer

girone [dʒi·'ro:·ne] *m* 1.SPORT leg; ~ **d'andata** away leg; ~ **di ritorno** return leg 2.LIT circle

gironzolare [dʒi·ron·dzo·'la:·re] *vi fam* to wander about; ~ **intorno a qu/qc** to hang

around sb/sth

girotondo [dʒi·ro·'ton·do] *m* ring-around-the-rosey

girovagare [dʒi·ro·va·'ga:·re] *vi* to wander around

girovago, -a [dʒi·'rɔ:·va·go] <-ghi, -ghe> I. *agg* (*attori, suonatori*) traveling II. *m, f* wanderer

girovita [dʒi·ro·'vi:·ta] <-> *m* waist measurement; **prendere il ~** to measure sb's waist

gita ['dʒi:·ta] *f* trip; **andare in ~ a ...** to go on a trip to ...

gitano, -a [dʒi·'ta:·no] I. *agg* (*popolazioni, famiglie*) gypsy II. *m, f* gypsy

gitante [dʒi·'tan·te] *mf* tripper

gittata [dʒit·'ta:·ta] *f* (*di cannone, missile*) range; **missile a ~ intermedia** medium-range missile

giù [dʒu] *avv* (*in basso*) down; (*dabbasso*) downstairs; **ti aspetto ~** I'll wait for you downstairs; **andare su e ~** to go up and down; **mandare ~** *a fig* to swallow; **mettere ~** to put down; **essere ~** *fig* to be depressed; **essere ~ di morale** to be down in the dumps; **quella storia non mi va ~** I don't like that story; **la notizia l'ha buttato ~** the news depressed him; **i prezzi sono andati ~** prices have gone down; **su per ~** more or less; ~ **di lì** thereabouts; **in ~** down(wards); **scendi ~** get down; ~ **le mani!** get your hands off!

giubba ['dʒub·ba] *f* (*da militare*) tunic

giubbetto [dʒub·'bet·to] *m* jacket; ~ **salvagente** life jacket

giubbino [dʒub·'bi:·no] *m* (*di pelle, jeans*) jacket

giubbotto [dʒub·'bɔt·to] *m* (*di pelle*) jacket; ~ **antiproiettile** bulletproof vest; ~ **salvagente** life jacket

giubilare [dʒu·bi·'la:·re] *vi poet* ~ **per qc** to rejoice at sth

giubileo [dʒu·bi·'lɛ:·o] *m* REL Jubilee

giubilo ['dʒu:·bi·lo] *m poet* rejoicing

giuda ['dʒu:·da] <-> *m pej* (*traditore*) traitor

giudaico, -a [dʒu·'da:·i·ko] <-ci, -che> *agg* (*calendario, tradizione, rito*) Judaic

giudaismo [dʒu·da·'iz·mo] *m* Judaism

giudicare [dʒu·di·'ka:·re] *vt* 1.*a.* JUR (*persona*) to judge; **fu giudicato colpevole** he was found guilty; **non ~ dalle apparenze** don't judge by appearances 2.(*ritenere*) to consider; **giudicò opportuno tacere** he [*o* she] considered it advisable to keep quiet

giudicato [dʒu·di·'ka:·to] *m* JUR (*sentenza*) sentence; **passare in ~** to be the final verdict

giudicatore, -trice [dʒu·di·ka·'to:·re] *agg* (*commissione*) judging

giudice ['dʒu:·di·tʃe] *mf* 1.JUR judge; ~ **conciliatore** magistrate; ~ **costituzionale** Constitutional Court judge; **giudice per le indagini preliminari** *the magistrate appointed to supervise the initial police investigation into a case;* ~ **penale** criminal judge; ~ **popolare** juror 2.SPORT judge; ~ **di gara** (*tennis*) umpire;

(*calcio, rugby*) referee
giudiziale [dʒu·dit·'tsia:·le] *agg* (*separazione, conciliazione*) judicial
giudiziario, -a [dʒu·dit·'tsia:·rio] <-i, -ie> *agg* (*attività, atto*) judicial; **carcere** ~ prison; **uffi-ciale** ~ bailiff
giudizio [dʒu·'dit·tsio] <-i> *m* **1.** (*senno*) judg-ment **2.** opinion; **rimettersi al** ~ **di qu** to ac-cept sb's decision; **farsi un** ~ **su qu/qc** to form an opinion about sb/sth; **a mio/tuo/suo** ~ in my/your/his/her opinion **3.** JUR (*pro-cesso*) trial; **comparire in** ~ to appear before the court; **trascinare qu in** ~ to take sb to court; **rinviare qu a** ~ to commit sb for trial **4.** JUR (*sentenza*) verdict; ~ **di assoluzione** ac-quittal; ~ **di condanna** guilty verdict **5.** REL judgement; **il** ~ **universale** the Last Judge-ment
giudizioso, -a [dʒu·dit·'tsio:·so] *agg* (*per-sona,*) sensible; (*soluzione, scelta*) judicious
giuggiola ['dʒud·dʒo·la] *f* BOT jujube; **andare in brodo di -e per qu/qc** *fig* to be nuts about sb/sth
giugno ['dʒuɲ·ɲo] *m* June; *v.a.* **aprile**
giuliano, -a [dʒu·'lia:·no] **I.** *agg* **1.** (*del Venezia Giulia*) from Venezia Giulia **2.** (*di Giulio Cesare*) Julian; **calendario** ~ Julian calendar **II.** *m, f* (*abitante del Venezia Giulia*) person from Venezia Giulia
giulivo, -a [dʒu·'li:·vo] *agg* happy; **oca -a** silly goose
giullare [dʒul·'la:·re] *m* jester
giumenta [dʒu·'men·ta] *f* ZOO mare
giunco ['dʒuŋ·ko] <-chi> *m* BOT rush
giungere ['dʒun·dʒe·re] <giungo, giunsi, giunto> **I.** *vi essere* to reach; **mi giunge nuovo** it's news to me; ~ **all'orecchio di qu** to reach sb's ears **II.** *vt avere poet* to join
giungla ['dʒuŋ·gla] *f* jungle
giunsi ['dʒun·si] *1. pers sing pass rem di* **giun-gere**
giunta ['dʒun·ta] *f* **1.** ADM (*consiglieri*) council **2.** (*per indumenti*) extra piece **3.** (*loc*) **per** ~ what's more
giuntare [dʒun·'ta:·re] *vt* (*fare una giunta*) to join
giuntatrice [dʒun·ta·'tri:·tʃe] *f* FILM splicer
giunto ['dʒun·to] *m* MOT joint; ~ **cardanico** universal joint; ~ **rotante** rotating joint
giunto *pp di* **giungere**
giuntura [dʒun·'tu:·ra] *f a.* ANAT joint
giunzione [dʒun·'tsio:·ne] *f* connection
giuocare [dʒuo·'ka:·re] *v.* **giocare**
giuoco ['dʒuɔ:·ko] *v.* **gioco**
giuramento [dʒu·ra·'men·to] *m* oath; **pre-stare** ~ to swear an oath
giurare [dʒu·'ra:·re] **I.** *vt* to swear; ~ **il falso** to commit perjury **II.** *vi* ~ **su qc** to swear on sth
giurato, -a [dʒu·'ra:·to] **I.** *agg* (*nemico, perito*) sworn; **guardia** ~ security guard **II.** *m, f* JUR ju-ror
giureconsulto [dʒu·re·kon·'sul·to] *m* jurist
giurì [dʒu·'ri] <-> *m* jury

giuria [dʒu·'ri:·a] <-ie> *f* jury
giuridicità [dʒu·ri·di·tʃi·'ta] <-> *f* legality
giuridico, -a [dʒu·'ri:·di·ko] <-ci, -che> *agg* (*ordinamento, consulenza*) legal
giurisdizionale [dʒu·riz·dit·tsio·'na:·le] *agg* (*organo, sede*) jurisdictional
giurisdizione [dʒu·riz·dit·'tsio:·ne] *f a.* JUR ju-risdiction
giurisprudenza [dʒu·ris·pru·'dɛn·tsa] *f* (*scienza*) law
giurista [dʒu·'ris·ta] <-i *m*, -e *f*> *mf* jurist
giustapporre [dʒus·tap·'por·re] <irr> *vt* to juxtapose
giustapposizione [dʒus·tap·po·zit·'tsio:·ne] *f* juxtaposition
giustapposto *pp di* **giustapporre**
giustezza [dʒus·'tet·tsa] *f* **1.** (*esattezza*) accu-racy **2.** (*equità*) justness **3.** TYP justification
giustificare [dʒus·ti·fi·'ka:·re] **I.** *vt* to justify **II.** *vr:* **-rsi** (*scusarsi*) to justify oneself
giustificativo [dʒus·ti·fi·ka·'ti:·vo] *m* receipt
giustificativo, -a *agg* (*documento, pezza*) jus-tificatory; **pezza -a** receipt
giustificazione [dʒus·ti·fi·kat·'tsio:·ne] *f* **1.** (*spiegazione*) justification **2.** (*a scuola*) ab-sence note; **libretto delle -i** absences' book
giustizia [dʒus·'tit·tsia] <-ie> *f* **1.** (*equità*) jus-tice; **rendere** ~ **a qu** to do sb justice **2.** JUR (*autorità giudiziaria*) law; **ricorrere alla** ~ to take legal steps
giustiziare [dʒus·tit·'tsia:·re] *vt* (*condannato, prigioniero*) to execute
giustiziato, -a [dʒus·tit·'tsia:·to] *m, f* executed person
giustiziere [dʒus·tit·'tsiɛ:·re] *m* **1.** (*boia*) ex-ecutioner **2.** (*vendicatore*) avenger
giusto[1] ['dʒus·to] *m* right; **essere nel** ~ to be in the right; **chiedere il** ~ to ask for one's due
giusto[2] **I.** *avv* **1.** (*esattamente*) correctly **2.** (*proprio*) exactly; **arrivare** ~ **in tempo** to arrive just in time **3.** (*appena*) just **II.** *int* (*in ris-posta*) right
giusto, -a I. *agg* **1.** (*equo: persona, causa, pun-izione*) just **2.** (*vero: osservazione, inform-azioni*) true **3.** (*adeguato: salario, prezzo, momento*) right **4.** (*corretto: risposta, conto*) correct; **essere** ~ **di sale** to not be too salty **II.** *m, f* just person
glabro, -a ['gla:·bro] *agg* (*guance, viso*) hair-less
glaciale [gla·'tʃa:·le] *agg* **1.** (*gelato*) frozen **2.** *fig* (*accoglienza, persona, sguardo*) icy
glaciazione [gla·tʃat·'tsio:·ne] *f* glaciation
gladiatore [gla·dia·'to:·re] *m* gladiator
gladiolo [gla·'di:·o·lo] *m* BOT gladiolus
glande ['glan·de] *m* ANAT glans
glassa ['glas·sa] *f* (*per torte*) icing
glassare [glas·'sa:·re] *vt* (*torta*) to ice
glaucoma [glau·'kɔ:·ma] <-i> *m* MED glauco-ma
gli [ʎi] **I.** *art det m pl* (*davanti a s impura, gn, pn, ps, x, z*) the **II.** *pron pers 3. pers m sing* **1.** (*a lui, persona*) (to) him; (*a esso, animale*)

(to) it [o him]; ~ **ho detto che venivi** I told him you were coming **2.** (*unito a la, le, li, lo, ne: a lei, a lui, a loro ecc.*) non glielo dare don't give it to him [o her] [o it] [o them]; **dagliele subito** give them to him [o her] [o it] [o them] immediately; **diglielo tu** you tell him [o her] [o it] [o them] it; **faglielo tu** you do it to him [o her] [o it] [o them]; **prendiglieli tu dallo scaffale** take them down from the shelf for him [o her] [o it] [o them]; **gliene parlerò domani** I'll talk to him [o her] [o it] [o them] about it tomorrow; **gliene ho dato un pezzo** I gave him a piece [o her] [o it] [o them] of it **3.** (*unito a la, le, li, lo, ne: forma di cortesia: Lei*) to [o for] you; **gliele metto da parte** I'll put them on one side for you

glicemia [gli·tʃe·'mi:·a] <-ie> *f* MED glycemia

glicemico, -a [gli·'tʃɛ:·mi·ko] <-ci, -che> *agg* MED (*contenuto, tasso*) glycemic

gliceride [gli·'tʃɛ:·ri·de] *m* glyceride

glicerina [gli·tʃe·'ri:·na] *f* glycerine

glicine ['gli:·tʃi·ne] *m* BOT wisteria

gliela, gliele, glieli, glielo, gliene ['ʎe:·la, 'ʎe:·le, 'ʎe:·li, 'ʎe:·lo, 'ʎe:·ne] = **gli/le + la, le, li, lo, ne**

glissare [glis·'sa:·re] *vi* ~ **su qc** to skate over sth

globale [glo·'ba:·le] *agg* **1.** (*totale: costo*) total **2.** (*mondiale: economia, mercato*) global

globalità [glo·ba·li·'ta] <-> *f* entirety

globalizzare [glo·ba·lid·'dza:·re] *vt* (*mercato, linguaggio*) to globalize

globalizzazione [glo·ba·lid·dzat·'tsio:·ne] *f* (*di mercato, linguaggio*) globalization

globo ['glɔ:·bo] *m* **1.** (*sfera*) globe **2.** ASTR ~ **celeste** celestial globe; ~ **terrestre** Earth **3.** ANAT ~ **oculare** eyeball

globulare [glo·bu·'la:·re] *agg* **1.** ASTR globular; **ammasso** ~ globular cluster **2.** MED corpuscular

globulina [glo·bu·'li:·na] *f* MED globulin

globulo ['glɔ:·bu·lo] *m* **1.** (*sferetta*) capsule **2.** MED corpuscle

gloria¹ ['glɔ:·ria] <-ie> *f* glory; **farsi ~ di qc** to take pride in sth

gloria² <-> *m* (*preghiera*) Gloria

gloriarsi [glo·'riar·si] *vr* ~ **di qc** (*vantarsi*) to take pride in sth

glorificare [glo·ri·fi·'ka:·re] *vt* to glorify

glorioso, -a [glo·'rio:·so] *agg* glorious

glossa ['glɔs·sa] *f* (*nota*) gloss

glossare [glos·'sa:·re] *vt* to gloss

glossario [glos·'sa:·rio] <-i> *m* glossary

glottide ['glɔt·ti·de] *f* ANAT glottis

glottologia [glot·to·lo·'dʒi:·a] <-gie> *f* linguistics

glottologico, -a [glot·to·'lɔ:·dʒi·ko] <-ci, -che> *agg* (*analisi, studio*) linguistic

glottologo, -a [glot·'tɔ:·lo·go] <-gi, -ghe> *m, f* linguist

glucide [glu·'tʃi:·de] *m* glucide

glucosio [glu·'kɔ:·zio] <-i> *m* glucose

glutammato [glu·tam·'ma:·to] *m* glutamate

glutammico, -a [glu·'tam·mi·ko] <-ci, -che> *agg* glutamic; **acido** ~ glutamic acid

gluteo ['glu:·teo] *m* gluteus; **i -i** buttocks

glutine ['glu:·ti·ne] *m* gluten

gnao, gnau ['ɲa:·o, 'ɲa:·u] *int* meow, meow

gnaulare [ɲau·'la:·re] *vi* (*gatto*) to meow

gnocco ['ɲɔk·ko] <-cchi> *m* CULIN gnocco, *small potato dumpling eaten with pasta sauce;* **-cchi al pomodoro** gnocchi in tomato sauce

gnomo ['ɲɔ:·mo] *m* gnome

gnorri ['ɲɔr·ri] *m* **fare lo ~** *fam* to look blank

gnoseologia [ɲo·ze·o·lo·'dʒi:·a] <-gie> *f* gnoseology

gnosi ['ɲɔ:·zi] <-> *f* gnosis

gnosticismo [ɲos·ti·'tʃiz·mo] *m* gnosticism

gnostico, -a ['ɲɔs·ti·ko] <-ci, -che> **I.** *agg* gnostic **II.** *m, f* gnostic

gnu [ɲu] <-> *m* ZOO gnu

goal [goul/gɔl] <-> *m* goal; **fare** [o **segnare**] **un** ~ to score a goal

gobba ['gɔb·ba] *f* **1.** *a. fam* (*sulla schiena, di camello, dromedario*) hump; **avere la** ~ *fam* to be hunch-backed **2.** (*di naso*) bump

gobbo, -a ['gob·bo] **I.** *agg* **1.** (*che ha la gobba*) hunch-backed **2.** (*con le spalle curve*) round-shouldered; **diventare** ~ to become round-shouldered; **stare** ~ to be bent over **3.** *fig, scherz* **colpo** ~ stab in the back **II.** *m, f* hunch-back

goccia ['got·tʃa] <-cce> *f* drop; **somigliarsi come due -cce d'acqua** to be like two peas in a pod; **la ~ che fa traboccare il vaso** *fig* the straw that broke the camel's back; **fino all'ultima** ~ to the last drop; **a ~ a** ~ drop by drop; **a** ~ drop-shaped; **orecchini a** ~ drop-earrings

goccio ['got·tʃo] <-cci> *m fam* (*piccola quantità*) drop

gocciola ['got·tʃo·la] *f* drop

gocciolare [got·tʃo·'la:·re] **I.** *vt avere* (*acqua, sudore, sangue*) to drip **II.** *vi essere o avere* **1.** (*rubinetto, liquido*) to drip **2.** (*naso*) to run

gocciolio [got·tʃo·'li:·o] <-ii> *m* dripping

godere [go·'de:·re] <godo, godei *o* godetti, goduto> **I.** *vi* **1.** (*provare piacere*) to enjoy; ~ **nel fare qc** to enjoy doing sth **2.** (*sessualmente*) to come **3.** (*beneficiare*) ~ **di qc** to benefit from sth; ~ **della fiducia di qu** to enjoy sb's trust **II.** *vt* to enjoy; ~ **ottima salute** enjoy excellent health; **-rsi la vita/le vacanze** to enjoy life/ one's holidays; **godersela** *fam* to have a good time

godereccio, -a [go·de·'ret·tʃo] <-cci, -cce> *agg fam* pleasure-loving

godibile [go·'di:·bi·le] *agg* (*lettura, musica*) enjoyable

godimento [go·di·'men·to] *m* **1.** *a.* JUR (*diletto, uso*) enjoyment **2.** (*sessuale*) pleasure

goduroso, -a [ga·du·'riɔ:·so] *agg scherz* blissful

goffaggine [gof·'fad·dʒi·ne] *f* awkwardness

goffo, -a ['gɔf·fo] *agg* **1.** (*impacciato: persona*) awkward **2.** (*sgraziato: movimento*) clumsy

gogò [go·'gɔ] <-> *m* **a** ~ endless; **andare a** ~

(*macchina, attrezzo*) to go wild

gol [gɔl] *v.* **goal**

gola ['goːla] *f* 1. ANAT (*collo*) throat; **aver il mal di** ~ to have a sore throat; **prendere qu per la** ~ to tempt sb; **avere l'acqua alla** ~ *fig* to be up to one's neck in problems 2. (*vizio*) gluttony; **peccati di** ~ sins of gluttony; **sono ingrassata per i troppi peccati di** ~ I've put on weight because I can't resist food; **far** ~ **a qu** *fig* to tempt sb 3. GEOG gorge

golf [gɔlf] <-> *m* 1. SPORT golf; **giocare a** ~ to play golf 2. (*maglione*) sweater

golfista [gol·'fis·ta] <-i *m*, -e *f*> *mf* golfer

golfistico, -a [gol·'fis·ti·ko] <-ci, -che> *agg* (*turismo, percorso*) golfing

golfo ['gol·fo] *m* gulf; **guerra del Golfo** Gulf War

goliardia [go·liar·'diː·a] <-ie> *f* 1. (*spirito universitario*) student spirit 2. (*insieme dei goliardi*) student body

goliardico, -a [go·'liar·di·ko] <-ci, -che> *agg* (*spirito, canzone*) student

golosità [go·lo·si·'ta] <-> *f* 1. (*ghiottoneria*) gluttony 2. (*leccornia*) delicacy

goloso, -a [go·'loː·so] I. *agg* 1. (*ghiotto: persona*) greedy, I'm a glutton for pizza 2. (*appetitoso: cibo*) delicious II. *m, f* glutton

golpe ['gɔl·pe] <-> *m* (*colpo di Stato*) coup

golpista [gol·'pis·ta] <-i *m*, -e *f*> *mf* member of a coup

golpistico, -a [gol·'pis·ti·ko] <-ci, -che> *agg* (*macchinazione, intenzione*) of a coup; **tentativo** ~ coup attempt

gomena ['goː·me·na] *f* NAUT hawser

gomitata [go·mi·'taː·ta] *f* shove with the elbow; **fare a -e** to elbow; *fig* to fight tooth and nail

gomito ['goː·mi·to] *m* 1. ANAT elbow; **alzare il** ~ *fig* to drink a lot 2. (*di fiume, tubazioni*) bend

gomitolo [go·'mi·to·lo] *m* (*di lana*) ball

gomma ['gom·ma] *f* 1. (*materiale*) rubber; ~ **naturale** natural rubber; ~ **americana** [*o* **da masticare**] chewing gum 2. *fam* (*pneumatico: di auto, moto*) tire; **cambiare una** ~ to change a tire; **forare una** ~ to have a flat 3. (*per cancellare*) eraser; ~ **da matita** pencil eraser

gommapiuma® [gom·ma·'piuː·ma] *f* foam rubber

gommato, -a [gom·'maː·to] *agg* (*tela*) rubberized; (*carta*) gummed; **nastro** ~ adhesive tape

gommatura [gom·ma·'tuː·ra] *f* MOT set of tires

gommino [gom·'miː·no] *m* rubber washer

gommista [gom·'mis·ta] <-i *m*, -e *f*> *mf* tire specialist

gommone [gom·'moː·ne] *m* NAUT rubber dinghy

gommoso, -a [gom·'moː·so] *agg* (*simile a gomma: caramella, sostanza, torta*) rubbery

gonade ['gɔː·na·de] *f* gonad

gondoliere [gon·do·'liɛː·re] *m* gondolier

gonfalone [gon·fa·'loː·ne] *m* (*insegna*) banner

ner

gonfaloniere [gon·fa·lo·'niɛː·re] *m* (*portabandiera*) banner bearer

gonfiabile [gon·'fiaː·bi·le] *agg* (*materassino, pallone, piscina*) inflatable

gonfiare [gon·'fiaː·re] I. *vt* 1. (*pallone, materassino*) to inflate; (*gomma*) to pump up; (*vele*) to fill; (*guance*) to puff out 2. (*dilatare: stomaco*) to bloat 3. *fig* (*notizia*) to blow out of proportion II. *vr:* -**rsi** 1. (*diventare gonfio: mani, piedi, occhi*) to swell (up); (*occhi*) to puff up 2. (*dilatarsi*) to get bloated

gonfiato, -a [gon·'fiaː·to] *agg* (*pallone, materassino*) inflated; **un pallone** ~ *fig, pej* a big-head

gonfio, -a ['gon·fio] <-i, -ie> *agg* 1. (*mani, piedi*) swollen; (*occhi*) puffy 2. (*stomaco, pancia*) bloated 3. (*vela*) full; **andare a -ie vele** (*progetto*) to go really well

gonfiore [gon·'fioː·re] *m* swelling

gongolare [goŋ·go·'laː·re] *vi* ~ **per qc** to be very pleased about sth; ~ **di gioia per qc** to be overjoyed with sth

gonna ['gon·na/'gɔn·na] *f* skirt; ~ **a pieghe** pleated skirt; ~ **pantalone** culottes *pl*

gonnella [gon·'nɛl·la] *f* skirt; **attaccato alle -e della mamma** *fam* tied to his mother's apronstrings; **correre dietro alle -e** *fam* to chase skirts

gonorrea [go·nor·'rɛː·a] *f* gonorrhea

gonzo, -a ['gon·dzo] *m, f pej, fam* idiot

gorgheggiare [gor·ged·'dʒaː·re] *vi* 1. (*uccello*) to warble 2. (*cantante*) to trill

gorgheggio [gor·'ged·dʒo] <-ggi> *m* 1. (*di uccello*) warbling 2. (*di cantante*) trill

gorgo ['gor·go] <-ghi> *m* (*mulinello*) whirlpool

gorgogliare [gor·goʎ·'ʎaː·re] *vi* (*liquido*) to gurgle

gorgoglio[1] [gor·'goʎ·ʎo] <-gli> *m* (*di liquido*) gurgle

gorgoglio[2] [gor·goʎ·'ʎiː·o] <-glii> *m* (*di liquido*) gurgling

gorgonzola [gor·gon·'dzɔː·la] *m* gorgonzola, *a blue-veined cheese*

gorilla [go·'ril·la] <-> *m* 1. ZOO gorilla 2. *fig* bodyguard

Gorizia *f* Gorizia, *a town in the Friuli Venezia Giulia region*

Goriziano [go·ri·'tsiaː·no] <*sing*> *m* (*zona*) Gorizia area

goriziano, -a I. *agg* from Gorizia II. *m, f* (*abitante*) person from Gorizia

gotico *m* Gothic

gotico, -a ['gɔː·ti·ko] <-ci, -che> *agg* (*chiesa, cattedrale*) Gothic

goto ['gɔː·to] *m* HIST Goth

gotta ['got·ta] *f* MED gout

governante [go·ver·'nan·te] I. *mf* POL ruler II. *f* 1. (*bambinaia*) nanny 2. (*di casa, albergo*) housekeeper

governare [go·ver·'naː·re] I. *vt* 1. (*amministrare: Paese, Stato, comune, regione*) to gov-

G

ern **2.** (*guidare: famiglia, azienda*) to run **3.** (*regolare: organizzazione, rapporti*) to regulate **4.** (*nave, veicolo*) to handle **II.** *vr:* **-rsi** to govern oneself

governativo, -a [go·ver·na·'ti:·vo] *agg* (*del governo: associazione, decreto, provvedimento*) government

governatorato [go·ver·na·to·'ra:·to] *m* **1.** (*territorio*) protectorate **2.** (*periodo*) governorship

governatore, -trice [go·ver·na·'to:·re] *m, f* governor

governatrice *f v.* **governatore**

governissimo [go·ver·'nis·si·mo] *m* POL multi-party alliance

governo [go·'vɛr·no] *m* **1.** POL government; ~ **fantasma** shadow cabinet; ~ **fantoccio** puppet government; ~ **federale** federal government; ~ **monocolore** single party government; ~ **ponte** caretaker government; ~ **di coalizione** coalition government **2.** (*di azienda*) running **3.** (*di nave, veicolo*) handling

gozzo ['got·tso] *m* MED goiter; **stare sul** ~ *fig* to annoy

gozzovigliare [got·tso·viʎ·'ʎa:·re] *vi* to have a good time

GR *m abbr di* **Giornale Radio** (radio) news bulletin; **il** ~ **1** the news bulletin on Radio 1

gracchiare [grak·'kia:·re] *vi* **1.** (*corvo*) to caw; (*rana*) to croak **2.** (*disco, giradischi*) to crackle

gracchio ['grak·kio] <-cchi> *m* (*di corvo*) caw; (*di rana*) croak

gracidare [gra·tʃi·'da:·re] *vi* (*rana*) to croak

gracidio [gra·tʃi·'di:·o] <-ii> *m* (*di rana*) croak

gracile ['gra:·tʃi·le] *agg* **1.** (*esile*) slender **2.** (*debole*) frail

gracilità [gra·tʃi·li·'ta] <-> *f* **1.** (*esilità*) slenderness **2.** (*debolezza*) frailty

gradasso [gra·'das·so] *m pej* braggart; **fare il** ~ to bluster

gradatamente [gra·da·ta·'men·te] *avv* gradually

gradazione [gra·dat·'tsio:·ne] *f* **1.** (*di vino, liquore*) percent; ~ **alcolica** alcohol content **2.** (*di colori, luci*) shade

gradevole [gra·'de:·vo·le] *agg* (*piacevole: sensazione, temperatura, suono*) pleasant

gradevolezza [gra·de·vo·'let·tsa] *f* (*di immagine, suono*) pleasantness

gradimento [gra·di·'men·to] *m* **1.** (*soddisfacimento*) liking; **la temperatura non è di suo** ~ the temperature is not to his [*o* her] liking **2.** (*accettazione*) (customer) satisfaction; **sondaggio di** ~ customer satisfaction survey; **indice di** ~ TV, RADIO popularity rating

gradinata [gra·di·'na:·ta] *f* (*scalinata*) flight of stairs; (*di stadio*) terraces *pl;* (*tiers*)

gradino [gra·'di:·no] *m* step

gradire [gra·'di:·re] <gradisco> *vt* **1.** (*apprezzare*) to appreciate; **voglia** ~ **i più sentiti auguri** please accept my best wishes **2.** (*desiderare*) to like; **gradisci un caffè?**

would you like a coffee?

gradito, -a [gra·'di:·to] *agg* (*apprezzato: dono, sorpresa*) welcome; (*ricordo*) pleasant; **è** ~ **l'abito scuro** black-tie only

grado ['gra:·do] *m* **1.** MATH, PHYS, GEO degree **2.** (*in una graduatoria*) place; **interrogatorio di terzo** ~ the third degree; **ustioni di terzo** ~ third-degree burns **3.** (*di alcolici, vino*) percent; ~ **alcolico** alcohol content **4.** (*di parentela*) **una cugina di primo/secondo** ~ a first/second cousin **5.** (*stadio*) phase; **andare per -i** to proceed step by step; **a** ~ **a** ~ step by step; **al massimo** ~ to the highest degree **6.** (*rango*) MIL rank **7.** LING form; ~ **comparativo** comparative form; ~ **superlativo** superlative form **8.** (*loc*) **essere in** ~ **di fare qc** to be able to do sth; **di buon** ~ *poet* willingly

graduale [gra·du·'a:·le] *agg* (*aumento, processo*) gradual

gradualmente [gra·dual·'men·te] *avv* gradually

graduare [gra·du·'a:·re] *vt* **1.** TEC (*termometro, righello*) to graduate **2.** (*ordinare per gradi*) to grade; ~ **le priorità** to prioritize

graduato [gra·du·'a:·to] *m* MIL non-commissioned officer

graduato, -a *agg* (*lente, scala*) graduated; (*esercizio*) graded

graduatoria [gra·dua·'tɔ:·ria] <-ie> *f* (*classifica*) list

graduazione [gra·duat·'tsio:·ne] *f* (*di scala*) ranking

graffa ['graf·fa] *f* **1.** (*metallica*) bracket **2.** (*parentesi*) braces

graffetta [graf·'fet·ta] *f* (*per fogli*) paper clip

graffiante [graf·'fian·te] *agg fig* (*critica, ironia, satira*) biting

graffiare [graf·'fia:·re] **I.** *vt* to scratch **II.** *vr:* **-rsi** to scatch oneself

graffiata [graf·'fia:·ta] *f* (*atto*) scratch

graffio ['graf·fio] <-i> *m* scratch

graffitaro, -a [graf·fit·'t:a·ro] *m, f* graffiti artist

graffito [graf·'fi:·to] *m* graffito; **i -i** graffiti

grafia [gra·'fi:·a] <-ie> *f* **1.** (*modo di scrivere*) handwriting **2.** (*ortografia*) spelling

grafica ['gra:·fi·ka] <-che> *f* **1.** *a.* COMPUT (*arte*) graphics; ~ **computerizzata** computerized graphics **2.** (*opera*) graphic work

grafico ['gra:·fi·ko] <-ci> *m* (*diagramma*) graph

grafico, -a <-ci, -che> **I.** *agg* (*rappresentazione, punto*) graphic **II.** *m, f* (*tecnico*) graphic designer

grafite [gra·'fi:·te] *f* graphite

grafologia [gra·fo·lo·'dʒi:·a] <-gie> *f* graphology

grafologico, -a [gra·fo·'lɔ:·dʒi·ko] <-ci, -che> *agg* (*analisi, perizia, scienza*) handwriting

grafologo, -a [gra·'fɔ:·lo·go] <-gi, -ghe> *m, f* handwriting expert

gramaglie [gra·'maʎ·ʎe] *fpl* **in** ~ in mourning

gramigna [gra·'miɲ·ɲa] *f* BOT Bermuda grass;

crescere come la ~ *fig* to grow like weeds

graminacee [gra·mi·'na:·tʃee] *fpl* grasses

grammatica [gram·'ma:·ti·ka] <-che> *f* grammar

grammaticale [gram·ma·ti·'ka:·le] *agg* (*analisi, regola*) grammatical; **errore** ~ grammatical error

grammo ['gram·mo] *m* (*unità di misura*) gram

grammofono [gram·'mɔ:·fo·no] *m* gramophone

gramo, -a ['gra:·mo] *agg* (*vita*) miserable

gran [gran] *v.* **grande** I.

grana[1] ['gra:·na] *f* 1. *sl* (*denaro*) dough 2. *fig, fam* (*guaio*) problem; **piantare una** ~ to cause problems; **un sacco di** -e a load of problems; **avere -e con la giustizia** to have trouble with the law 3. FOTO grain; **pellicola a** ~ **grossa** coarse-grained film

grana[2] <-> *m* CULIN grana, *a cheese similar to Parmesan*

granaglie [gra·'naʎ·ʎe] *fpl* corn

granaio [gra·'na:·io] <-ai> *m* 1. (*deposito*) barn; (*per il grano*) granary 2. *fig* (*regione*) granary

granata [gra·'na:·ta] *f* 1. (*bomba*) grenade 2. BOT (*melagrana*) pomegranate

granatiere [gra·na·'tiɛ:·re] *m* 1. MIL grenadier 2. *fig* (*persona alta e robusta*) giant

granato [gra·'na:·to] *m* (*pietra preziosa*) garnet

granato, -a *agg* garnet red; **mela -a** red apple; **rosso** ~ garnet red

Gran Bretagna ['gram bre·'taɲ·ɲa] *f* Great Britain; **la** ~ Great Britain; **abitare in** ~ to live in Great Britain; **andare in** ~ to go to Great Britain

grancassa [gran·'kas·sa] *f* (*tamburo*) bass drum

granchio ['graŋ·kio] <-chi> *m* 1. ZOO crab 2. *fig* (*sbaglio*) mistake; **prendere un** ~ to make a mistake

grand' [grand] *v.* **grande** I.

grandangolare [gran·daŋ·go·'la:·re] I. *m* FOTO wide-angle lens II. *agg* FOTO **obiettivo** ~ wide-angle lens

grande ['gran·de] <più grande *o* maggiore, grandissimo *o* massimo *o* sommo> I. *agg* 1. (*vasto*) big; (*largo*) wide 2. (*alto: persona*) tall; **come ti sei fatto** ~! you've really grown!; (*montagna*) high 3. (*di età*) big; (*adulto*) grown-up; **sono piu** ~ **di lui** I'm older than him 4. *fig* (*bravo*) brilliant 5. (*intenso*) great 6. (*rafforzativo*) **una gran bella donna** a really good-looking woman; **un gran bevitore/fumatore** a heavy drinker/smoker; **avere una gran fame** *fam* to be starving; (**una**) **gran cosa** *fam* a wonderful thing; **non è un gran che** it's not up to much II. *mf* 1. (*adulto*) grown-up 2. (*chi eccelle*) great person 3. HIST **Federico il Grande** Frederick the Great III. *m* (*grandezza*) greatness; **fare le cose in** ~ to do things on a grand scale

grandezza [gran·'det·tsa] *f* 1. PHYS, MATH quantity 2. (*dimensione*) size; **a** ~ **naturale** life-size 3. *fig* (*nobiltà*) greatness; ~ **d'animo** magnanimity 4. *fig* (*sfarzo*) grandeur; **mania di** ~ delusions of grandeur *pl*

grandinare [gran·di·'na:·re] *vi* essere *o* avere METEO to hail; **grandina** it's hailing

grandinata [gran·di·'na:·ta] *f* METEO hailstorm

grandine ['gran·di·ne] *f* METEO hail

grandiosità [gran·dio·si·'ta] <-> *f* (*imponenza*) grandeur

grandioso, -a [gran·'dio:·so] *agg* (*imponente*) grandiose; (*grosso*) huge

grandissimo [gran·'dis·si·mo] *superlativo di* **grande**

granduca, -duchessa [gran·'du:·ka] *m, f* grand duke *m*, grand duchess *f*

granducato [gran·du·'ka:·to] *m* (*territorio*) grand duchy

granduchessa *f v.* **granduca**

granello [gra·'nɛl·lo] *m a. fig* (*di sale, sabbia*) grain; (*di polvere*) speck; **un** ~ **di pepe** a peppercorn; **un** ~ **di buon senso** an ounce of common sense

granita [gra·'ni:·ta] *f a kind of crushed ice drink which can be of different flavors*

granitico, -a [gra·'ni:·ti·ko] <-ci, -che> *agg* 1. MIN (*rocce, formazioni*) granite 2. *fig* (*carattere, fede, volontà*) rock-like

granito [gra·'ni:·to] *m* MIN granite

gran maestro ['gram ma·'ɛs·tro] *m* (*di Massoneria*) Grand Master

grano ['gra:·no] *m* 1. BOT (*frumento*) wheat; ~ **saraceno** buckwheat 2. (*chicco*) grain; **un** ~ **di pepe** a peppercorn; **un** ~ **di caffè** a coffee bean 3. (*di rosario*) bead 4. *fig* (*quantità minima*) ounce; **un** ~ **di buon senso** an ounce of common sense; **un** ~ **di sale** *fig* a pinch of salt

gran(o)turco [gran(o)·'tur·ko] <-chi> *m* corn

granulare[1] [gra·nu·'la:·re] *agg* (*in grani: brodo, concime, insetticida*) granular

granulato [gra·nu·'la:·to] *m* (*materiale in granuli*) ~ **di gomma/marmo** rubber/marble granules *pl*

granulato, -a *agg* 1. (*ridotto in granuli*) granulated 2. (*ruvido*) raised

granulo ['gra:·nu·lo] *m* (*di polline*) granule; (*di polvere*) speck

granulosità [gra·nu·lo·si·'ta] <-> *f* (*di superficie*) granulosity; (*di pellicola*) graininess

granuloso, -a [gra·nu·'lo:·so] *agg* (*cellula, materiale. superficie*) granular

grappa ['grap·pa] *f* CULIN grappa, *a spirit distilled from wine residues*

grappino [grap·'pi:·no] *m fam* (*bicchierino*) tot of grappa

grappolo ['grap·po·lo] *m* bunch; **un** ~ **d'uva** a bunch of grapes; **fiori a** ~ clusters of flowers

grassaggio [gras·'sad·dʒo] <-ggi> *m* greasing

grassetto [gras·'set·to] *m* bold

grasso ['gras·so] *m* 1. *a.* CULIN (*adipe, di animale*) fat; ~ **animale/vegetale** animal/vegetable fat 2. (*sostanza untuosa*) grease; ~ **per**

lubrificare lubricating grease

grasso, -a *agg* **1.** (*persona*) fat **2.** (*pelle, capelli*) greasy **3.** (*carne, formaggio, brodo*) fatty; (*cucina, cibo*) rich **4.** (*fertile: terreno*) fertile; **piante -e** succulent plants **5.** *fig* (*ricco: guadagno*) rich **6.** (*di carnevale*) **martedì ~** Shrove Tuesday

grassoccio, -a [gras·'sɔt·tʃo] <-cci, -cce> *agg* (*bambino, ragazzina*) plump

grassone, -a [gras·'so:·ne] *m, f* fat person

grata ['gra:·ta] *f* grating

gratella [gra·'tɛl·la] *f* CULIN grill; **bistecca in ~** grilled steak

graticcio [gra·'tit·tʃo] <-cci> *m* **1.** (*stuoia*) mat **2.** (*per proteggere*) screen; (*per sostenere*) trellis

graticola [gra·'ti:·ko·la] *f* **1.** CULIN grill; **pesce in ~** grilled fish **2.** (*di confessionale*) grille

gratifica [gra·'ti:·fi·ka] <-che> *f* COM (*compenso*) bonus; **~ natalizia** Christmas bonus

gratificante [gra·ti·fi·'kan·te] *agg* (*esperienza, lavoro, stipendio*) rewarding

gratificare [gra·ti·fi·'ka:·re] *vt* (*dare soddisfazione a*) to reward; **uno sport che lo gratifica** a sport he finds rewarding

gratificazione [gra·ti·fi·kat·'tsio:·ne] *f* (*soddisfazione*) reward

gratin [gra·'tɛ̃] <-> *m* CULIN gratin; **al ~** au gratin

gratinare [gra·ti·'na:·re] *vt* to cook au gratin

gratis ['gra:·tis] *avv* free of charge

gratitudine [gra·ti·'tu:·di·ne] *f* gratitude

grato, -a ['gra:·to] *agg* (*riconoscente*) grateful; **essere ~ a qu per** [*o* **di**] **qc** to be grateful to sb for sth; **ti sono -a dell' aiuto** I'm grateful for your help

grattacapo [grat·ta·'ka:·po] *m fam* (*preoccupazione*) headache

grattacielo [grat·ta·'tʃɛ:·lo] *m* skyscraper

gratta e vinci ['grat·ta e 'vin·tʃi] <-> *m* scratchcard

grattare [grat·'ta:·re] **I.** *vt* **1.** (*pelle*) to scratch **2.** (*grattugiare: formaggio*) to grate **3.** (*raschiare*) to scrape **4.** *sl* (*rubare*) to nick **II.** *vi* **1.** (*produrre rumore metallico*) to screech **2.** *fam* to grind **III.** *vr:* **-rsi** to scratch oneself

grattata [grat·'ta:·ta] *f* **1.** *fam* MOT grinding of the gears **2.** CULIN (*di tartufo, formaggio*) shaving

grattugia [grat·'tu:·dʒa] <-gie> *f* grater

grattugiare [grat·tu·'dʒa:·re] *vt* (*pane, tartufo, formaggio*) to grate

gratuito, -a [gra·'tu:i·to/gra·tu·'i:·to] *agg* **1.** (*gratis*) free; **biglietto ~** free ticket **2.** *fig* (*arbitrario: offesa, critica*) gratuitous

gravare [gra·'va:·re] **I.** *vt* **1.** (*caricare*) **~ il peso di qc su qc** to rest the weight of sth on sth **2.** *fig* (*di tasse, costi*) **~ qu/qc di qc** to burden sb/sth with sth **II.** *vi* **~ su qu/qc** (*pesare*) to weigh on sb/sth; *fig* to lie on sb/sth

grave ['gra:·ve] *agg* **1.** (*importante: errore*)

grave 2. (*serio: situazione, caso, malattia, malato*) serious **3.** (*solenne: atteggiamento, tono*) solemn **4.** MUS (*suono, nota*) low **5.** LING (*accento*) grave

gravidanza [gra·vi·'dan·tsa] *f* pregnancy

gravido, -a ['gra:·vi·do] *agg* pregnant

gravimetria [gra·vi·me·'tri:·a] <-ie> *f* gravimetry

gravità [gra·vi·'ta] <-> *f* **1.** PHYS **forza di ~** force of gravity **2.** *fig* (*di situazione, malattia*) seriousness

gravitare [gra·vi·'ta:·re] *vi* **1.** ASTR to gravitate; **~ intorno a qc** to gravitate around sth **2.** *fig* **~ intorno a qc** to be found around sth; **~ verso qc** to gravitate towards sth

gravitazionale [gra·vi·tat·tsio·'na:·le] *agg* (*attrazione, energia, forza*) gravitational

gravitazione [gra·vi·tat·'tsio:·ne] *f* gravitation; **la legge di ~** the law of gravitation

gravoso, -a [gra·'vo:·so] *agg a. fig* (*compito, lavoro, onere*) heavy

grazia ['grat·tsia] <-ie> *f* **1.** (*armonia, delicatezza*) grace **2.** (*gentilezza*) graciousness; **con ~** graciously **3.** (*benevolenza*) favor; **essere nelle -ie di qu** to be in sb's good books **4.** (*nella mitologia*) Grace; **le tre -ie** the three Graces **5.** REL grace; **per ~ di Dio** *fam* thank God; **nell'anno di ~ ...** in the year of grace ...; **troppa ~ Sant'Antonio!** *fam* when it rains it pours!; **colpo di ~** *fam* last straw **6.** JUR pardon; **concedere la ~ a qu** to pardon sb

graziare [grat·'tsia:·re] *vt* JUR (*condannato*) to pardon

graziato, -a [grat·'tsia:·to] **I.** *agg* **1.** JUR pardoned person **2.** REL blessed **II.** *m, f* **1.** JUR pardoned person **2.** REL blessed person

grazie ['grat·tsie] *int* thank you; **tante ~!** thank you very much!; **~ mille!, mille ~!** thank you very much indeed!; **sì/no, ~** yes/no thanks; **~ a** thanks to; **~ a Dio/al cielo** thank God/heavens; **~ per l'ospitalità** thank you for your hospitality

graziosità [grat·tsio·si·'ta] <-> *f* (*di lineamenti, modi, movimenti*) gracefulness

grazioso, -a [grat·'tsio:·so] *agg* **1.** (*bello*) beautiful **2.** (*piacevole*) charming

greca ['grɛ:·ka] <-che> *f* (*motivo ornamentale*) fret

Grecia ['grɛ:·tʃa] *f* Greece; **la ~** Greece; **abitare in ~** to live in Greece; **andare in ~** to go to Greece

grecismo [gre·'tʃiz·mo] *m* Greek word/expression

greco ['grɛ:·ko] <*sing*> *m* LING Greek; **~ antico/moderno** ancient/modern Greek

greco, -a <-ci, -che> **I.** *agg* (*della Grecia: civiltà, tragedia*) Greek; **~-ortodosso** Greek Orthodox; **~-romano** Greco-Roman **II.** *m, f* Greek

gregario [gre·'ga:·rio] <-i> *m* **1.** (*di partito, organizzazione*) supporter **2.** (*ciclista*) support rider

gregario, -a <-i, -ie> *agg* **1.** (*mentalità, spirito*) herd **2.** ZOO (*animale, tendenza*) gregarious

gregge ['gred·dʒe] <*pl*: -i *f*> *m* **1.** ZOO (*di pecore*) flock **2.** *fig* (*di persone*) herd; **uscire dal ~** *fig* to stand out from the crowd

greggio ['gred·dʒo] *m* (*petrolio*) crude oil

greggio, -a <-ggi, -gge> *agg* (*materiali, prodotti*) raw; (*petrolio*) crude; (*diamante*) uncut; (*tessuto*) unbleached; **allo stato ~** untreated

grembiale, grembiule [grem·'bia:·le, grem·'biu:·le] *m* **1.** (*per cucina*) apron **2.** (*camice*) coveralls; (*per bambini*) smock

grembo ['grɛm·bo/'grem·bo] *m* **1.** (*ventre materno*) womb **2.** (*incavo*) lap; **in grembo** on one's lap

gremire [gre·'mi:·re] <gremisco> I. *vt* to pack II. *vr* -rsi di to be packed with

greppia ['grep·pia] <-ie> *f* (*mangiatoia*) manger

greto ['gre:·to] *m* (*di fiume*) exposed part of the river bed

grettezza [gret·'tet·tsa] *f* (*meschinità*) meanness

gretto, -a ['gret·to] *agg fig* (*meschino*) mean; **animo ~** mean spirit

greve ['grɛ:·ve] *agg* oppressive

grezzo ['gred·dzo] *agg* **1.** (*materiali, prodotti*) raw; (*petrolio*) crude; (*diamante*) uncut; (*tessuto*) unbleached; **allo stato ~** untreated **2.** (*grossolano*) rough

gridare [gri·'da:·re] I. *vi* (*urlare*) to shout; (*strillare*) to scream; **~ a squarcia gola** to shout at the top of one's lungs II. *vt* (*dire ad alta voce*) to shout; **~ aiuto** to cry for help

grido[1] ['gri:·do] <*pl*: -a *f*> *m* **1.** (*urlo*) shout; (*strillo*) scream **2.** *fig* (*moda*) fashion; **di ~** fashionable; **essere l'ultimo ~** to be the latest thing

grido[2] <*pl*: -i *m*> *m* (*di animali*) call

griffe [grif] <-> *f* (*marchio*) designer label; (*stilista*) designer

grifone [gri·'fo:·ne] *m* (*uccello*) griffon

grigiastro, -a [gri·'dʒas·tro] *agg* grayish

grigio ['gri:·dʒo] <-gi> *m* gray

grigio, -a <-gi, -gie> *agg* **1.** (*colore*) gray; **~ cenere** ash gray; **~ perla** pearl gray **2.** *fig* (*scialbo*) drab

grigiore [gri·'dʒo:·re] *m* **1.** (*di paesaggio*) grayness **2.** *fig* (*di situazione*) dreariness

grigioverde [gri·dʒo·'ver·de] I. *agg* gray-green II. *m* gray-green; MIL the uniform of the Italian army

griglia ['griʎ·ʎa] <-glie> *f* **1.** CULIN grill; **pollo/bistecca alla ~** grilled chicken/steak **2.** MOT (*grata*) grille; **~ del radiatore** radiator grille

grill [gril] <-> *m* **1.** (*griglia*) grill **2.** *fam* (*ristorante*) highway restaurant

grilletto [gril·'let·to] *m* (*di pistola, fucile*) trigger; **premere il ~** to pull the trigger

grillo ['gril·lo] *m* **1.** ZOO cricket **2.** *fig* (*capriccio*) whim; **avere -i per la testa** *fam* to have some strange ideas

grinfia ['grin·fia] <-ie> *f fam* **cadere** [*o* **finire**]

nelle -ie di qu *fig, fam* to fall into sb's clutches

grinta ['grin·ta] *f fig* (*di persona: energia*) determination; (*di motore*) acceleration

grinza ['grin·tsa] *f* **1.** (*di vestito*) crease; (*di calze, pelle*) wrinkle **2.** *fig* **non fare una ~** (*ragionamento, discorso, logica*) to be faultless; (*vestito*) to fit like a glove; **il mio maglione non fa una ~** my sweater fits me like a glove

grinzoso, -a [grin·'tso:·so] *agg* (*vestito*) creased; (*pelle, volto*) wrinkled

grippare [grip·'pa:·re] I. *vi* MOT to jam II. *vr:* -rsi MOT (*motore, moto*) to jam

grisou [gri·'zu] <-> *m* firedamp

grissino [gris·'si:·no] *m* CULIN breadstick; **è magro come un ~** *fig* he's as thin as a lathe

groenlandese [gro·en·lan·'de:·se] I. *agg* Greenland II. *mf* Greenlander

Groenlandia [gro·en·'lan·dia] *f* Greenland; **la ~** Greenland; **abitare in ~** to live in Greenland; **andare in ~** to go to Greenland

grondaia [gron·'da:·ia] <-aie> *f* gutter

grondare [gron·'da:·re] I. *vi* to pour; **~ di sudore** to drip with sweat II. *vt* to pour

groppa ['grɔp·pa] *f* (*dorso*) back; **salire in ~ a un cavallo** to mount a horse

groppo ['grɔp·po] *m fig* (*nodo*) **un ~ alla gola** a lump in one's throat

groppone [grop·'po:·ne] *m scherz, fam* back; **restare sul ~ a qu** to be left with; **ti restano sul groppone** you'll be left with them; **un po'di anni ce li ho sul ~** I'm getting on a bit

grossa ['grɔs·sa] *f fig fam* **dormire della ~** to sleep like a log

Grossetano [gros·se·'ta:·no] <*sing*> *m* (*zona*) Grosseto area

grossetano, -a I. *agg* from Grosseto II. *m, f* (*abitante*) person from Grosseto

Grosseto *f* Grosseto, *a town in Tuscany*

grossista [gros·'sis·ta] <-i *m*, -e *f*> *mf* wholesaler

grosso ['grɔs·so] *m* (*maggior parte*) majority; **sbagliarsi di ~** *fam* to be very wrong

grosso, -a *agg* **1.** (*grande: sasso, pesce, recipiente*) big **2.** (*spesso: muro, filo*) thick; **sale ~** coarse salt **3.** (*robusto: persona, mani*) big; **avere le spalle -e** *fig* to have wide shoulders **4.** *fig* (*autorevole: persona*) important; **un pezzo ~** a big shot; **un ~ industriale** an important industrialist **5.** (*notevole: somma, guadagno*) large; (*affare, successo, occasione*) big **6.** (*grave: errore*) serious; **questa sì che è -a!** *fam* that's a good one!; **spararle -e** *fam* to talk big; **farla -a** *fam* to land oneself in it **7.** (*tonante: voce*) loud; **fare la voce -a** to raise one's voice **8.** (*agitato*) **mare ~** rough sea **9.** (*affannato*) **fiato ~** out of breath

grossolano, -a [gros·so·'la:·no] *agg* **1.** (*rozzo: persona, modi*) coarse **2.** (*grande: errore*) huge

grossomodo [gros·so·'mɔ:·do] *avv* more or less

grotta ['grɔt·ta] *f* cave

G

grottesco [grot·'tes·ko] *m* **cadere nel** ~ to become ridiculous

grottesco, -a <-schi, -sche> *agg* (*ridicolo*) ridiculous

groviera [gro·'viε:·ra] <-> *m o f* CULIN gruyère cheese

groviglio [gro·'viʎ·ʎo] <-gli> *m* 1. (*di fili, cavi, tubi*) tangle 2. (*di emozioni, bugie, idee*) muddle

gru [gru] <-> *f* ZOO, TEC crane

gruccia ['grut·tʃa] <-cce> *f* 1. (*stampella*) crutch; **camminare con le -cce** to walk with crutches 2. (*per abiti*) hanger

grufolare [gru·fo·'la:·re] *vi* (*maiale*) to root

grugnire [gruɲ·'ɲi:·re] <grugnisco> *vi* (*maiale*) to grunt

grugnito [gruɲ·'ɲi:·to] *m* (*di maiale*) grunt

grugno ['gruɲ·ɲo] *m* 1. ZOO (*muso*) snout 2. *pej* (*faccia*) face; **spaccare il ~ a qu** to smash sb's face in

grumo ['gru:·mo] *m* (*di sangue*) clot; (*di farina*) lump

gruppo ['grup·po] *m* 1. *a.* POL, MUS (*di persone*) group; **lavoro di ~** teamwork 2. SPORT pack 3. BIO group; **~ sanguigno** blood type 4. COM (*di aziende*) group; **~ finanziario** financial group 5. MOT **~ elettrogeno** generating set

gruppuscolo [grup·'pus·ko·lo] *m* POL small political group

gruviera [gru·'viε:·ra] *v.* **groviera**

gruzzolo ['grut·tso·lo] *m fam* tidy sum of money

GSM *m abbr di* **Global System for Mobile communication** GSM

G.U. *v.* **Gazzetta Ufficiale** Official Gazette, *newspaper published by the government containing all new laws*

guadagnare [gua·daɲ·'ɲa:·re] I. *vt* 1. (*denaro*) to earn; **tanto di guadagnato** *fig* so much the better 2. *a. fig* to gain; **~ tempo** to gain time; **~ terreno** to gain ground 3. (*raggiungere: cima, vetta*) to reach II. *vi* 1. (*ricevere uno stipendio*) to earn; **~ per vivere** to have to work for a living 2. (*risaltare*) to look better

guadagno [gua·'daɲ·ɲo] *m* (*profitto*) profit; **~ lordo/netto** gross/net profit

guadare [gua·'da:·re] *vt* (*fiume, torrente*) to wade

guado ['gua:·do] *m* (*passaggio*) ford

guai ['gua:·i] *int* woe betide; **~ a te se ci riprovi!** woe betide you if you try that again!

guaina [gua·'i:·na] *f* sheath

guaio ['gua:·io] <-ai> *m* 1. (*disgrazia*) trouble; **ficcarsi nei -ai** *fam* to get into trouble; **passare un ~** to go through a rough patch 2. (*fastidio*) nuisance; **che ~!** what a nuisance!

guaire [gua·'i:·re] *vi* (*cane*) to whine

guaito [gua·'i:·to] *m* (*di cane*) whine

guancia ['guan·tʃa] <-ce> *f* ANAT cheek

guanciale [guan·'tʃa:·le] *m* (*cuscino*) pillow; **dormire fra due -i** *fig* to sleep easy

guanto ['guan·to] *m* glove; **trattare qu coi -i** to handle sb with kid gloves

guantone [guan·'to:·ne] *m* (*da pugilato*) boxing glove

guardaboschi [guar·da·'bos·ki] <-> *m* forester

guardacaccia [guar·da·'kat·tʃa] <-> *m* gamekeeper

guardacoste [guar·da·'kɔs·te] <-> *m* coastguard

guardalinee [guar·da·'li:·nee] <-> *m* SPORT (*nel calcio*) assistant referee

guardare [guar·'da:·re] I. *vt* 1. (*vedere*) to look at; **guarda!** look!; **~ la televisione** to watch television; **~ un film** to watch a film; **~ qu/qc con la coda dell'occhio** to look at sb/sth out of the corner of one's eye; **~ qu dall'alto in basso** to look sb up and down; **~ qu di sbieco** to look askance at sb; **stare a ~** to stand and stare 2. (*cercare: parola*) to look up 3. (*vigilare su: bambino, condannato*) to look after; **Dio ce ne guardi!** *fam* God forbid! II. *vi* 1. (*badare*) **~ a qc** to mind sth; **non ~ a spese** he [*o* she] doesn't bother about the expense 2. (*fare in modo*) **~ di fare qc** to try to do sth 3. (*edificio, finestra*) **~ su qc** to look onto sth; **le finestre guardano a sud** the windows face South III. *vr:* **-rsi** 1. (*osservarsi*) to look at oneself; (*reciproco*) to look at each other; **non si guardano più in faccia** they cut each other dead 2. (*stare in guardia*) **-rsi da qc** to be wary of sth

guardaroba [guar·da·'rɔ:·ba] <-> *m* 1. (*armadio, indumenti*) wardrobe 2. (*stanza*) coatroom

guardarobiere, -a [guar·da·ro·'biε:·re] *m, f* (*in teatro*) coatroom attendant

guardata [guar·'da:·ta] *f* look; **dare una ~ a qc** to have a look at sth

guardia ['guar·dia] <-ie> *f* 1. (*attività*) guard duty; **cane da ~** guard dog; **essere di ~** (*soldato*) to be on guard duty; (*medico*) to be on call; **fare la ~** to keep watch; **corpo di ~** guard; **~ medica** first-aid station; **medico di ~** doctor on call 2. (*sentinella*) guard; **cambio della ~** *a. fig* changing of the guard 3. (*persona*) guard; **~ forestale** forest ranger; **~ giurata** security guard; **~ del corpo** bodyguard; **giocare a -ie e ladri** to play cops and robbers 4. (*corpo armato*) guard; **~ di finanza** Customs, *a military body which investigates financial crimes* 5. SPORT guard; **in ~!** on guard!; **mettere qu in ~** to put sb on their guard; **mettersi/stare in ~** to put sb/be on one's guard 6. (*limite*) **livello di ~** safety limit; (*di fiume*) **high-water mark**; **segnale di ~** (*di fiume*) high-water mark

---

i | The **Guardia di Finanza** is a special corps run by the Finance ministry and is part of the country's armed forces. Its duties include the prevention, investigation, and reporting of tax evasion and financial crimes, oversight of compliance with finance laws, and maritime surveillance in matters of financial policing.

guardiano, -a [guar·'dia:·no] *m, f* **1.** (*di edificio*) caretaker **2.** (*di zoo*) keeper

guardina [guar·'di:·na] *f* cell; **in ~** in the cells

guardingo, -a [guar·'diŋ·go] <-ghi, -ghe> *agg* wary

guardone [guar·'do:·ne] *m* peeping Tom

guarigione [gua·ri·'dʒo:·ne] *f* recovery

guarire [gua·'ri:·re] <guarisco> **I.** *vt avere* **1.** (*ferita*) to heal; (*malattia*) to cure **2.** (*persona, animale*) to cure; **~ qu da qc** *a. fig* to cure sb of sth **II.** *vi essere* **1.** (*ferita*) to heal; (*malattia*) to disappear **2.** (*persona, animale*) to recover; **~ da qc** to recover from sth; *fig* (*da vizio, noia*) to be cured of sth

guaritore, -trice [gua·ri·'to:·re] *m, f* healer

guarnigione [guar·ni·'dʒo:·ne] *f* (*distaccamento*) garrison

guarnire [guar·'ni:·re] <guarnisco> *vt* **1.** (*indumento, tovaglia*) to trim **2.** CULIN (*piatto, pietanza*) to garnish

guarnizione [guar·nit·'tsio:·ne] *f* **1.** TEC washer **2.** MOT gasket; (*dei freni*) lining **3.** (*di indumento, tenda*) trimming **4.** CULIN garnish

guastafeste [guas·ta·'fɛs·te] <-> *mf* spoilsport

guastare [guas·'ta:·re] **I.** *vt* **1.** (*rovinare: meccanismi, strada*) to damage **2.** (*corrompere: persona*) to change for the worse **3.** (*turbare: equilibrio, serata, vacanza*) to spoil **4.** (*disturbare*) to do harm **II.** *vr:* **-rsi 1.** (*tempo*) to change for the worse **2.** (*computer, meccanismo*) to go wrong **3.** (*cibi*) to go off **4.** (*rapporti*) to break down

guasto ['guas·to] *m* TEC, MOT breakdown; **~ al motore** engine failure

guasto, -a *agg* **1.** (*rotto*) broken; **il motore è ~** the engine has failed; **l'ascensore è ~** the elevator is out of order **2.** (*frutta, uova*) rotten **3.** (*dente*) decayed

guazzabuglio [guat·tsa·'buʎ·ʎo] <-gli> *m* (*confusione*) muddle

guercio, -a ['guɛr·tʃo] <-ci, -ce> *agg* (*occhio*) cross-eyed

guerra ['guɛr·ra] *f* **1.** *a. fig* MIL, POL, COM (*conflitto*) war; **~ civile** civil war; **~ fredda** Cold War; **~ atomica** atomic war; **-e stellari** star wars; **la prima/seconda ~ mondiale** the First/Second World War; **entrare in ~** to go to war; **essere in ~ con qu** to be at war with sb; **~ d'interessi** clash of interests; **la ~ contro la droga/criminalità** the war on drugs/crime **2.** (*tecnica*) warfare; **~ aerea** air warfare; **~ batteriologica** germ warfare; **~ chimica** chemical warfare; **~ lampo** blitzkrieg; **~ psicologica** psychological warfare

guerriero, -a [guer·'riɛ:·ro] *m, f* warrior

guerriglia [guer·'riʎ·ʎa] <-glie> *f* guerilla (warfare)

guerrigliero, -a [guer·riʎ·'ʎɛ:·ro] *m, f* guerrilla

gufare [gu·'fa:·re] *vt sl* **~ qu/qc** (*portare sfortuna*) to put a jinx on sb/sth

gufata [gu·'fa:·ta] *f sl* (*iettatura*) jinx

gufo ['gu:·fo] *m* ZOO owl; **~ reale** eagle-owl; **~ comune** long-eared owl

guglia ['guʎ·ʎa] <-glie> *f* **1.** ARCH spire **2.** GEOG needle

gugliata [guʎ·'ʎa:·ta] *f* (*di filo*) piece of thread

guida ['gui:·da] *f* **1.** MOT driving; **scuola ~** driving school; **patente di ~** driver's license; **posto di ~** driving seat **2.** (*libro*) guide; **~ telefonica** telephone directory; **~ turistica** guidebook; (*persona*) guide **3.** (*persona*) guide; **fare da ~ a qu** (*la strada*) to show sb the way; (*un posto*) to show sb the sights; **~ turistica** (*persona*) guide **4.** TEC (*traccia*) runner

guidare [gui·'da:·re] *vt* **1.** (*veicolo*) to drive; **non sa ~** he [*o* she] can't drive **2.** **~ qu** (*far da guida a*) to show sb around **3.** (*indirizzare*) to guide **4.** SPORT (*classifica*) to head **5.** (*capeggiare: gruppo, rivolta*) to lead

guidatore, -trice [gui·da·'to:·re] *m, f* driver

guinness® <-> *m* the Guinness Book of Records®

guinzaglio [guin·'tsaʎ·ʎo] <-gli> *m* leash

guizzare [guit·'tsa:·re] *vi essere* **1.** *a. fig* (*pesce, serpente, persona*) to dart; (*fiamme*) to flicker **2.** (*lampi*) to flash

guizzo ['guit·tso] *m a. fig* (*di pesce, serpente, persona*) dart; (*di fiamme*) flicker

guscio ['guʃ·ʃo] <-sci> *m* **1.** *a. fig* ZOO shell; **chiudersi nel ~** to retreat into one's shell; **uscire dal ~** to come out of one's shell **2.** BOT (*di piselli*) pod; (*di noce*) nutshell

gustare [gus·'ta:·re] **I.** *vt* **1.** CULIN (*provare*) to taste **2.** (*assaporare*) to enjoy **II.** *vr:* **-rsi** to enjoy

gustativo, -a [gus·ta·'ti:·vo] *agg* (*impatto, analisi, sensazione*) taste; **papille -e** taste buds

gusto ['gus·to] *m* **1.** (*sapore*) flavor; **al ~ di lampone** raspberry-flavored **2.** (*senso*) taste **3.** (*piacere*) pleasure; **mangiare/ridere di ~** to eat/laugh heartily; **prenderci ~** to get a taste for sth **4.** (*eleganza*) taste; **avere buon ~** to have good taste; **vestire con ~** to dress tastefully; **uno scherzo di pessimo ~** a joke in the worst possible taste **5.** (*preferenza*) taste; **è questione di -i** it's a question of tastes; **non è di mio ~** it's not to my taste; **i -i son -i** *prov* there's no accounting for taste *prov*

gustoso, -a [gus·'to:·so] *agg* **1.** CULIN (*ricette, piatti*) tasty **2.** *fig* (*che diverte: scherzo, racconto*) amusing

gutturale [gut·tu·'ra:·le] *agg* (*suono, consonante*) guttural

G

H

H, h ['akka] <-> *f* H, h; ~ **come hotel** H for hotel; **bomba H** H-bomb
h 1. *abbr di* **ora** h, *hour* 2. *abbr di* **etto** *100 g.*
ha *abbr di* **ettaro** hectare
ha [a] *3. pers sing pr di* **avere**[1]
habitat ['aːˑbiˑtat] <-> *m* 1. BIOL habitat 2. *fig* (*ambiente adatto*) setting
habitué [aˑbiˑ'tɥe] <-> *mf* regular
hacker ['hæˑkə, 'haˑker] <-> *mf* COMPUT hacker
hackeraggio [aˑkeˑ'radˑdʒo] *m* (*pirateria informatica*) hacking
hai ['aːˑi] *2. pers sing pr di* **avere**[1]
hall [hɔːl] <-> *f* (*di albergo*) lobby
hamburger [amˑ'burˑger] <-> *m* hamburger
hamburg(h)eria [amˑburˑgeˑ'riːˑa] <-ie> *f* burger bar
handheld <-> *m* COMPUT handheld
handicap ['hænˑdiˑkæp, 'ɛnˑdiˑkap] <-> *m* 1. MED disability 2. SPORT handicap
handicappare [anˑdiˑkapˑ'paːˑre] *vt* to handicap
handicappato, -a [anˑdiˑkapˑ'paːˑto] I. *agg* MED disabled II. *m, f* MED disabled person
hangar [ãˑ'gaːr] <-> *m* hangar
hanno ['anˑno] *3. pers pl pr di* **avere**[1]
happening ['hæˑpəˑniŋ, 'ɛpˑpeˑnin(g)] <-> *m* event
happy end [hæˑpi 'end, ɛpˑpi 'ɛnd] <-> *m* happy ending
happy hour ['ɛpˑpi 'auˑar] <-> *f* happy hour
hard discount [ard disˑ'kaunt] <-> *m* discount store
hard disk [haːd disk] <-> *m* COMPUT hard disk
hard top [haːd tɔp, ard top] <-> *m* hardtop
hardware ['haːdˑwɛˑə, 'ardˑwer] <-> *m* COMPUT hardware
hardwarista [ardˑweˑ'risˑta] <-i *m*, -e *f*> *mf* COMPUT hardware engineer
harem [aˑ'rem, 'aˑrem] <-> *m* harem
harmonium [arˑmoˑ'njom, arˑ'moˑniˑum] <-> *m* harmonium
hascisc [aʃˑ'ʃiʃ] <-> *m* hashish
HDTV *abbr di* **high definition television** HDTV
head hunter [hed 'hʌnˑtə, ɛd 'anˑter] <-> *m* headhunter
heavy metal ['heˑvi 'meˑt(a)l] I. <-> *m* MUS (*rock duro*) heavy metal II. *agg* MUS heavy metal; **gruppo** ~ heavy metal group
help [help, ɛlp] <-> *m* COMPUT help
Helsinki ['hɛlˑsiŋˑki] *f* Helsinki
henna ['ɛnˑna] *f* 1. (*tintura*) henna 2. BOT henna
herpes ['ɛrˑpes] <-> *m* herpes
hertz [(h)ɛrts] <-> *m* hertz
hg *abbr di* **ettogrammo** *100 g.*
hi-fi ['haiˑfai, 'aiˑfai] *m abbr di* **high-fidelity** hi-fi
hippy ['hiˑpi, 'ipˑpi] I. <-> *mf* hippie II. *agg* hip-

pie
hit [hit, it] <-> *m* hit
hit-parade ['(h)it pəˑ'reid] <-> *f* MUS charts *pl*; **entrare nella** ~ to hit the charts
hl *abbr di* **ettolitro** hectoliter
ho [ɔ] *1. pers sing pr di* **avere**[1]
hobby ['hɔˑbi, 'ɔbˑbi] <-> *m* hobby
hockey ['hɔˑki, 'ɔˑkei] <-> *m* hockey; ~ **su prato** field hockey; ~ **sul ghiaccio** ice hockey
holding ['houlˑdiŋ, 'ɔlˑdin(g)] <-> *f* holding company
Hong Kong [xoŋˑ'kɔŋ] *f* Hong Kong
horror ['ɔrˑror] <-> *m* 1. (*genere*) horror 2. (*film*) horror movie
hostaria [osˑtaˑ'riːˑa] <-ie> *f* tavern
hostess ['ɔsˑtes] <-> *f* 1. (*assistente di volo*) flight attendant 2. (*accompagantrice*) hostess
hot dog ['(h)ɔt dɔg] <-> *m* 1. (*panino*) hot dog 2. SPORT hot dog
hotel [oˑ'tɛl] <-> *m* hotel
hot line ['hɔt 'lain] <- *o* hot lines> *f* hotline
HTML *abbr di* **Hypertext Markup Language** COMPUT HTML; **codice** ~ HTML code
humour ['hjuːˑmə, 'juˑmor] <-> *m* humor; **avere senso dello** ~ to have a sense of humor
humus ['umˑus] <-> *m* 1. BOT humus 2. *fig* soil
Hz *abbr di* **hertz** Hz

I

I, i [i] <-> *f* I; ~ **come Imola** I for item; ~ **lunga** j
i *art m pl* (*dav a consonante, che non sia a s+consonante, gn, ps, x, y, z*) the
I *abbr di* **Italia**
IA *abbr di* **Intelligenza Artificiale** AI
IAL ['iˑal] *m acro di* **Istituto Addestramento Lavoratori** Vocational Training Institute
iato [iˑ'aːˑto] *m a. fig* LING hiatus
ib., ibid. *abbr di* **ibidem**
iberico, -a [iˑ'bɛˑriˑko] <-ci, -che> *agg* (*territorio*) Iberian; **penisola -a** Iberian peninsula
ibidem ['iˑbiˑdem] *avv* (*in bibliografia*) ibidem
ibernazione [iˑberˑnatˑ'tsioːˑne] *f* ZOO, MED hibernation
ibisco [iˑ'bisˑko] <-schi> *m* (*pianta*) hibiscus
ibrido[1] ['iːˑbriˑdo] *agg a. fig* ZOO, BOT hybrid; **animale** ~ hybrid animal
ibrido[2] *m a. fig* ZOO, BOT hybrid
IC *abbr di* **InterCity** FERR Intercity
ICE ['iˑtʃiˑ'e] *m abbr di* **InterCity Express** Intercity Express
ICI ['iˑtʃi] *f acro di* **Imposta Comunale sugli Immobili** property tax
icona [iˑ'kɔːˑna] *f a. fig* COMPUT, REL icon
iconografia [iˑkoˑnoˑgraˑ'fiːˑa] *f* ART iconography
iconografico [iˑkoˑnoˑ'graˑfiˑko] <-ci, -che>

agg (*studio, ricerca*) iconographical

ics [iks] <-> *f v.* **X, x**

ictus ['ik·tus] *m* MED ictus

id. *abbr di* **idem**

Iddio [id·'di:·o] *m* God; **Santo ~**! Good God!; **Signore ~**! Good Lord!

idea [i·'dɛ:·a] <-ee> *f* 1. (*pensiero*) thought; **associazione di -ee** association of ideas; **neanche per ~**! not on your life! 2. (*nozione*) idea; **non avere la minima** [*o* **la più pallida**] **~ di qc** to not have the slightest idea about sth 3. (*opinione*) idea; **cambiare ~** to change one's mind; **essere dell'~ che ... +**cong to think that ...; **essere dell'~ di ... +**inf to be thinking of ...; **essere di -ee liberali/conservatrici** to have liberal/conservative tendencies; **farsi un'~ di qc/qu** to form an opinion about sth/sb; **~ fissa** fixation 4. (*intenzione, progetto*) idea; **avere una mezza ~ di ... inf** to have half a mind to ... 5. (*trovata*) idea; **che ~**! what an idea!; **m'è venuta** [*o* **ho**] **un'~**! I've had an idea! 6. *inf* (*piccola quantità*) touch

ideale [i·de·'a:·le] I. *agg* (*perfetto*) ideal II. *m* 1. (*modello*) ideal 2. (*cosa migliore*) ideal thing 3. (*valore, idea*) ideal

idealista [i·de·a·'lis·ta] <-i *m*, -e *f*> *mf* (*sognatore*) idealist

idealizzare [i·de·a·lid·'dza:·re] *vt* to idealize

idealizzazione [i·de·a·lid·dzat·'tsio:·ne] *f* idealization

idealmente [i·de·al·'men·te] *avv* ideally

ideare [i·de·'a:·re] *vt* (*inventare*) to think up

ideatore, -trice [i·de·a·'to:·re] *m, f* (*inventore*) inventor

ideazione [i·de·at·'tsio:·ne] *f* (*invenzione*) invention

idem ['i:·dem] <-> I. *pron* (*in bibliografia*) idem II. *avv inf* likewise; **~ come sopra** just the same

identico, -a [i·'dɛn·ti·ko] <-ci, -che> *agg* (*uguale*) identical; **~ a qc** identical to sth; **essere ~ a qu** to be just like sb; **lo stesso ~** the very same

identificabile [i·den·ti·fi·'ka:·bi·le] *agg* (*impronta, persona*) identifiable

identificare [i·den·ti·fi·'ka:·re] I. *vt* to identify II. *vr*: **-rsi -rsi con qu** to identify with sb

identificazione [i·den·ti·fi·kat·'tsio:·ne] *f* identification; **processo di ~** identification

identità [i·den·ti·'ta] <-> *f* 1. (*di persona*) identity; **carta d'~** identity card; **crisi d'~** identity crisis 2. (*uguaglianza*) identical nature

ideogramma [i·de·o·'gram·ma] <-i> *m* ideogram

ideologia [i·de·o·lo·'dʒi:·a] <-gie> *f* ideology

ideologico, -a [i·de·o·'lɔ:·dʒi·ko] <-ci, -che> *agg* ideological

ideologo, -a [i·de·'ɔ:·lo·go] <-gi, -ghe> *m, f* ideologue

idilliaco, -a [i·dil·'li:·a·ko] <-ci, -che> *agg* (*romantico*) idyllic

idillico, -a [i·'dil·li·ko] <-ci, -che> *agg v.* **idil-** liaco

idillio [i·'dil·lio] <-i> *m* 1. *fig* (*vita felice*) idyll 2. *fig* (*amore*) romance 3. *fig* (*armonia*) idyll

idioma [i·'diɔ:·ma] <-i> *m* (*lingua*) idiom

idiomatico, -a [i·dio·'ma:·ti·ko] <-ci, -che> *agg* idiomatic; **frase/locuzione -a** idiomatic phrase/expression

idiota [i·'diɔ:·ta] <-i *m*, -e *f*> I. *agg* (*stupido*) idiotic II. *mf* (*persona*) idiot

idiozia [i·diot·'tsi:·a] <-ie> *f* 1. (*stupidità*) idiocy 2. (*cosa stupida*) idiotic thing

idolatrare [i·do·la·'tra:·re] *vt* 1. REL to worship 2. *fig* (*amare, ammirare*) to idolize

idolatria [i·do·la·'tri:·a] <-ie> *f* 1. REL idolatry 2. *fig* (*amore, ammirazione*) passion; **~ di** [*o* **per**] **qc/qu** love of [*o* for] sb/sth

idolo ['i:·do·lo] *m a. fig* REL idol

idoneità [i·do·nei·'ta] <-> *f* (*a lavoro, funzione*) suitability; **~ a qc** fitness for [*o* to] sth; **esami di ~** qualifying exam

idoneo, -a [i·'dɔ:·neo] <-ei, -ee> *agg* 1. (*persona*) fit; **essere ~ a qc** to be fit for sth; **~ al servizio militare** fit for military service 2. (*cosa*) suitable

idrante [i·'dran·te] *m* (*per incendi*) fire hydrant

idratante [i·dra·'tan·te] *agg* (*crema, lozione*) moisturizing

idratare [i·dra·'ta:·re] *vt* (*pelle, viso*) to moisturize

idrato [i·'dra:·to] *m* CHEM hydrate

idraulica [i·'dra:u·li·ka] <-che> *f* (*scienza*) hydraulics

idraulico, -a [i·'dra:u·li·ko] <-ci, -che> I. *agg* (*freno, pompa*) hydraulic; **energia -a** hydraulic energy; **impianto ~** plumbing II. *m, f* (*artigiano*) plumber

idrico, -a ['i:·dri·ko] <-ci, -che> *agg* (*bacino, fornitura*) water

idrocarburo [i·dro·kar·'bu:·ro] *m* CHEM hydrocarbon

idroelettrico, -a [i·dro·e·'lɛt·tri·ko] <-ci, -che> *agg* (*centrale, bacino*) hydroelectric

idrogeno [i·'drɔ:·dʒe·no] *m* CHEM hydrogen

idrografia [i·dro·gra·'fi:·a] *f* GEOG hydrography

idrolisi [i·'drɔ:·li·zi] <-> *f* CHEM hydrolisis

idromassaggio [i·dro·mas·'sad·dʒo] <-ggi> *m* 1. (*massaggio*) hydromassage 2. (*impianto*) jacuzzi; **vasca** (**da** [*o* con]) **~** jacuzzi

idrorepellente [i·dro·re·pel·'lɛn·te] *agg* (*materiale, sostanza*) waterproof

idroscalo [i·dro·'ska:·lo] *m* AERO, MAR hydroport

idrossido [i·'drɔs·si·do] *m* CHEM hydroxide

idrovolante [i·dro·vo·'lan·te] *m* AERO seaplane

iella ['i·ɛl·la] *f inf* (*sfortuna*) bad luck; **avere ~** to be jinxed; **che ~**! what bad luck!; **portare ~** to bring bad luck

iellato, -a [iel·'la:·to] *agg inf* jinxed; **essere ~** to be jinxed

iena ['iɛ:·na] *f* 1. (*animale*) hyena 2. *fig* (*persona*) nasty piece of work

ieri ['iɛ:·ri] I. *avv* yesterday; **~ l'altro** the day be-

H
I

fore yesterday; ~ **mattina/pomeriggio/ sera** yesterday morning/afternoon/evening; ~ **notte** last night; ~ **a mezzogiorno** midday yesterday; **nato** ~ *fig* born yesterday II. <-> *m* (*giorno precedente*) yesterday

igiene [iˑ'dʒɛːˑne] *f* (*pulizia*) cleanliness; ~ **dentale** dental hygiene; ~ **intima** personal hygiene; ~ **orale** oral hygiene; ~ **personale** personal hygiene; **ufficio d'**~ public health office; ~ **mentale** mental health

igienico, -a [iˑ'dʒɛːˑniˑko] <-ci, -che> *agg* 1.(*della salute*) healthy 2.(*della pulizia*) hygienic; **assorbente** ~ sanitary napkin; **carta -a** toilet paper; **impianto ~ -sanitario** sanitary fittings *pl*

igienista [iˑdʒeˑ'nisˑta] <-i *m*, -e *f*> *mf* 1.(*studioso*) hygienist 2.(*salutista*) health freak

ignaro, -a [iɲ'naːˑro] *agg* **essere** ~ **di qc** to be unaware of sth

ignifugo, -a [iɲ'ɲiːˑfuˑgo] <-ghi, -ghe> *agg* (*materiale, tessuto*) fireproof

ignobile [iɲ'nɔːˑbiˑle] *agg* despicable

ignominia [iɲˑɲoˑ'miːˑnia] <-ie> *f* 1.(*disonore*) disgrace 2.(*cosa, azione*) disgraceful deed

ignorante [iɲˑɲoˑ'ranˑte] I. *agg* 1.(*incolto*) ignorant 2.(*senza nozioni*) ignorant; **essere** ~ **in qc** to be ignorant about sth 3.(*incompetente*) incompetent 4. *inf* (*maleducato*) rude II. *mf* 1.(*incolto*) ignoramus 2.(*maleducato*) hood

ignoranza [iɲˑɲoˑ'ranˑtsa] *f* 1.(*mancanza d'istruzione*) ignorance 2.(*mancanza di nozioni*) ignorance 3. *inf*(*maleducazione*) rudeness

ignorare [iɲˑɲoˑ'raːˑre] I. *vt* 1.(*non sapere*) to not know 2.(*non considerare*) to ignore II. *vr:* **-rsi** to ignore each other

ignorato, -a [iɲˑɲoˑ'raːˑto] *agg* (*trascurato*) ignored

ignoto¹ [iɲ'ɲɔːˑto] <*sing*> *m* l'~ the unknown

ignoto² I. *agg* (*sconosciuto*) unknown; **cause -e** unknown causes; **di autore** ~ anonymous II. *m* (*persona*) unknown person; **sporgere denuncia contro -i** to make a complaint against unknown persons

il [il] *art m sing* (*dav a consonante, che non sia a s+consonante, gn, ps, x, y, z*) the; ~ **ragazzo** the boy; ~ **Lussemburgo** Luxembourg; **preferisco** ~ **caffé** I prefer coffee; **ha** ~ **naso grande** he [*o* she] has a big nose; **Mario vive con** ~ **fratello** Mario lives with his brother

ilarità [iˑlaˑriˑ'ta] <-> *f* (*risata*) laughter; **suscitare l'**~ **generale** to make everybody laugh

ill. *abbr di* **illustrazione**

illecito¹ [ilˑ'lɛːˑtʃiˑto] *agg* (*comportamento, guadagno*) unlawful; **relazione -a** illicit affair

illecito² *m* JUR offense; ~ **amministrativo** misdemeanor; ~ **civile/penale** civil/criminal offense

illegale [ilˑleˑ'gaːˑle] *agg* (*attività, operazione*) illegal

illegalità [ilˑleˑgaˑliˑ'ta] *f* (*atto*) illegal act;

(*condizione*) illegality

illeggibile [ilˑledˑ'dʒiːˑbiˑle] *agg* (*firma, scrittura*) illegible

illegittimità [ilˑleˑdʒitˑtiˑmiˑ'ta] *f a. fig* JUR illegitimacy

illegittimo, -a [ilˑleˑ'dʒitˑtiˑmo] *agg a. fig* JUR illegitimate

illeso, -a [ilˑ'leːˑzo] *agg* 1.(*persona*) unharmed 2.(*cosa*) intact

illiberale [ilˑliˑbeˑ'raːˑle] *agg* (*legge, provvedimento*) illiberal

illimitato, -a [ilˑliˑmiˑ'taːˑto] *agg* 1.(*spazio, tempo, risorsa*) unlimited 2.(*fiducia*) infinite

Ill.mo *abbr di* **illustrissimo** (*nelle lettere*) Mr.

illogico, -a [ilˑ'lɔːˑdʒiˑko] <-ci, -che> *agg* (*ragionamento, discorso*) illogical

illudere [ilˑ'luːˑdeˑre] <illudo, illusi, illuso> I. *vt* ~ **qu** (**con qc**) to deceive sb (with sth) II. *vr:* **-rsi** to deceive oneself; **-rsi su qc** to be mistaken about sth; **-rsi di ...** *inf* to kid oneself that ...; **-rsi che ...** +*cong* to mistakenly believe that ...

illuminante [ilˑluˑmiˑ'nanˑte] *agg* illuminating

illuminare [ilˑluˑmiˑ'naːˑre] I. *vt* 1.(*luce, lampada*) to light up; ~ **qc a giorno** to floodlight sth 2. *fig* (*occhi, sguardo, viso*) to light up 3. *fig* (*mente, persona*) to enlighten 4. *fig* (*informare*) to update; ~ **qu su qc** to update sb about sth II. *vr:* **-rsi** 1.(*ambiente, luogo*) to light up 2. *fig* (*persona*) to light up; **-rsi di contentezza/gioia** to light up with happiness/joy

illuminato, -a [ilˑluˑmiˑ'naːˑto] *agg* 1.(*ambiente, luogo*) lit (up) 2. *a. fig* HIST, POL enlightened

illuminazione [ilˑluˑmiˑnatˑ'tsioːˑne] *f* 1.(*di ambiente, luogo*) lighting 2. *fig, inf* (*intuizione, idea*) bright idea

illuminismo [ilˑluˑmiˑ'nizˑmo] *m* HIST, PHILOS Enlightenment

illuminista [ilˑluˑmiˑ'nisˑta] <-i *m*, -e *f*> HIST, PHILOS I. *agg* (*filosofo, opera*) Enlightenment II. *mf* (*pensatore*) follower of the Enlightenment

illusi [ilˑ'luːˑzi] *1. pers sing pass rem di* **illudere**

illusione [ilˑluˑ'zioːˑne] *f* illusion; **farsi/non farsi -i** to deceive/not deceive oneself; **vivere nell'**~ **che ...** +*cong* to deludingly hope that ...

illusionismo [ilˑluˑzioˑ'nizˑmo] *m* (*arte*) conjuring

illusionista [ilˑluˑzioˑ'nisˑta] <-i *m*, -e *f*> *mf* (*artista*) conjurer

illuso, -a [ilˑ'luːˑzo] I. *pp di* **illudere** II. *m*, *f* (*sognatore*) dreamer

illusorio, -a [ilˑluˑ'zɔːˑrio] <-i, -ie> *agg* 1.(*parole, promesse*) deceptive 2.(*benessere, felicità*) illusory

illustrare [ilˑlusˑ'traːˑre] *vt* to illustrate

illustrativo, -a [ilˑlusˑtraˑ'tiːˑvo] *agg* (*materiale, foglio*) illustrative; **nota -a** explanatory note

illustrato, -a [il·lus·'tra:·to] *agg* (*libro, rivista*) illustrated; **cartolina -a** picture postcard

illustratore, -trice [il·lus·tra·'to:·re] *m*, *f* (*persona*) illustrator

illustrazione [il·lus·trat·'tsio:·ne] *f* illustration

illustre [il·'lus·tre] *agg* (*celebre*) famous; **un ~ sconosciuto** *scherz* a nobody

illustrissimo, -a [il·lus·'tris·si·mo] *agg a. scherz* (*titolo*) most illustrious; (*nelle lettere*) Mr.

imballaggio [im·bal·'lad·dʒo] <-ggi> *m* 1. (*operazione*) packing 2. (*contenitore*) pack

imballare [im·bal·'la:·re] *vt* (*merce, mobile*) to pack

imbandito [im·ban·'di:·toe] *agg* (*tavola*) lavishly laid

imbarazzante [im·ba·rat·'tsan·te] *agg* (*domanda, situazione*) embarrassing

imbarazzato, -a [im·ba·rat·'tsa:·to] *agg* embarrassed

imbarazzo [im·ba·'rat·tso] *m* (*disagio*) embarrassment; **essere** [*o* **trovarsi**] [*o* **sentirsi**] **in ~** to be embarrassed; **mettere qu in ~** to embarrass sb; **avere l'~ della scelta** to be spoiled for choice

imbarcadero [im·bar·ka·'dɛ:·ro] *m* (*pontile*) pier

imbarcare [im·bar·'ka:·re] **I.** *vt* 1. (*merce*) to load 2. (*passeggeri*) to embark; **~ acqua** MAR to ship water **II.** *vr:* **-rsi** 1. (*passeggero*) to embark; **-rsi su qc** to board sth; (*equipaggio*) to sign on 2. **-rsi in qc** *fig* (*in avventura, impresa*) to embark on sth

imbarcazione [im·bar·kat·'tsio:·ne] *f* boat; **~ a motore** motorboat; **~ a vela** sailing boat; **~ da diporto** pleasure boat

imbarco [im·'bar·ko] <-chi> *m* 1. (*di merci, passeggeri*) boarding; **carta d'~** boarding card 2. (*luogo*) departure point; (*in aeroporto*) boarding gate

imbastire [im·bas·'ti:·re] <imbastisco> *vt* (*abito*) to tack

imbattersi [im·'bat·ter·si] *vr* 1. **~ in qu** to run into sb 2. **~ in qc** *fig* (*difficoltà*) to run up against sth

imbattibile [im·bat·'ti:·bi·le] *agg* unbeatable

imbattuto, -a [im·bat·'tu:·to] *agg* (*campione, record*) unbeaten

imbecille [im·be·'tʃil·le] *mf pej, inf* idiot

imbecillità [im·be·tʃil·li·'ta] <-> *f* 1. (*caratteristica*) idiocy 2. (*comportamento, discorso*) idiotic thing

imbevuto [im·be·'vu:·to] *agg* **~ di qc** (*liquido*) soaked in sth

imbiancatura [im·biaŋ·ka·'tu:·ra] *f* (*di parete*) painting; (*di muro*) whitewashing

imbianchino [im·biaŋ·'ki:·no] *m* (*operaio*) decorator

imboccare [im·bok·'ka:·re] *vt* 1. (*persona*) to feed 2. (*strada, uscita*) to take

imboccatura [im·bok·ka·'tu:·ra] *f* 1. (*di bottiglia, tubo,*) mouth; (*di galleria, porto*) entrance 2. (*di strumento*) mouthpiece

imbocco [im·'bok·ko] <-cchi> *m* (*di autostrada, tunnel*) entrance

imboscata [im·bos·'ka:·ta] *f* (*di guerriglieri*) ambush

imbottigliamento [im·bot·tiʎ·ʎa·'men·to] *m* 1. (*di liquido*) bottling 2. *fig* (*di veicoli*) build-up

imbottigliato, -a [im·bot·tiʎ·'ʎa:·to] *agg* 1. (*vino*) bottled 2. *fig* (*veicolo*) trapped

imbottito, -a [im·bot·'ti:·to] *agg* 1. (*divano*) upholstered 2. (*abito, materasso*) padded 3. (*panino*) filled 4. (*persona*) stuffed full of

imbottitura [im·bot·ti·'tu:·ra] *f* 1. (*lavoro su divano*) upholstery work; (*su abito*) padding 2. (*materiale per divano*) upholstery; (*per abito*) padding

imbranato, -a [im·bra·'na:·to] *inf* **I.** *agg* awkward **II.** *m, f* hopeless case

imbrattare [im·brat·'ta:·re] **I.** *vt* (*sporcare*) to dirty; **~ qc** (**di qc**) to dirty sth (with sth); **gli hai imbrattato la camicia di sugo!** you've got sauce on his shirt! **II.** *vr:* **-rsi** (*sporcarsi*) to get dirty; **-rsi di qc** to get sth on oneself; **-rsi la camicia di sugo** to get sauce on one's shirt

imbrigliare [im·briʎ·'ʎa:·re] *vt* 1. (*cavallo, mulo*) to harness 2. *fig* (*persona, fantasia*) to bridle

imbrogliare [im·broʎ·'ʎa:·re] *vt* (*truffare*) to swindle

imbroglio [im·'brɔʎ·ʎo] *m* (*truffa*) swindle

imbroglione, -a [im·broʎ·'ʎo:·ne] *m, f* (*truffatore*) swindler

imbrunire¹ [im·bru·'ni:·re] <imbrunisco> *vi essere* (*farsi sera*) to get dark

imbrunire² <*sing*> *m* (*tramonto*) dusk; **all'~** at dusk

imbucare [im·bu·'ka:·re] *vt* 1. (*lettera*) to mail 2. (*nascondere*) to hide

imburrato, -a [im·bur·'ra:·to] *agg* (*pane*) buttered; (*teglia*) greased

imbuto [im·'bu:·to] *m* (*utensile*) funnel; **a ~** funnel-shaped

IME ['i:·me] *m acro di* **Istituto Monetario Europeo** European Monetary Institute

imene [i·'mɛ:·ne] *m* ANAT hymen

imitare [i·mi·'ta:·re] *vt* 1. (*modello, stile*) to imitate 2. (*suono, voce, gesto*) to mimic; (*come caricatura*) to impersonate 3. (*firma, scrittura*) to forge

imitatore, -trice [i·mi·ta·'to:·re] *m, f* (*attore*) mimic

imitazione [i·mi·tat·'tsio:·ne] *f* 1. (*di modello, stile*) imitation 2. (*di suono, voce, gesto*) mimicry; (*come caricatura*) impersonation 3. (*oggetto, prodotto*) forgery

immacolato, -a [im·ma·ko·'la:·to] *agg* (*coscienza, vita*) clean; **l'Immacolata** REL the Immaculate Conception

immagazzinaggio [im·ma·gad·dzi·'nad·dʒo] *m v.* **immagazzinamento**

immagazzinamento [im·ma·gad·dzi·na·'men·to] *m* (*di merce*) storing

immagazzinare [im·ma·gad·dzi·'na:·re] *vt*

1.(*merce, grano*) to store **2.**_fig_ (*esperienze, nozioni*) to harbor **3.**COMPUT (*dati*) to store
immaginabile [im·ma·dʒi·'na:·bi·le] *agg* (*pensabile*) conceivable; **tutte le cure possibili e -i** all possible cures
immaginare [im·ma·dʒi·'na:·re] *vt* **1.**(*raffigurarsi*) to imagine **2.** *inf* (*enfatico*) to imagine; **puoi ~ come mi sono sentito** you can just imagine how I felt; **è la cosa più bella che si possa ~** it's the most beautiful thing you can imagine; **s'immagini!** (*come risposta*) not at all!; **Grazie! — S'immagini!** Thanks! — Don't mention it! **3.**(*ideare*) to think up **4.**(*credere, supporre*) to suppose
immaginario¹ [im·ma·dʒi·'na:·rio] <-i, -ie> *agg* (*mondo, paura*) imaginary; (*personaggio*) fictitious; **malato ~** hypochondriac
immaginario² *m* PSYCH imagination; **~ collettivo** collective imagination
immaginazione [im·ma·dʒi·nat·'tsio:·ne] *f* **1.**(*facoltà*) imagination **2.**(*cosa immaginata*) figment of one's imagination
immagine [im·'ma:·dʒi·ne] *f* **1.**(*percepita*) image **2.**(*mentale*) memory **3.**(*disegno, foto*) image; **~ sacra** holy image **4.**(*incarnazione, simbolo*) symbol; **essere l'~ della salute** to be the picture of health; **essere l'~ di qu** to be the image of sb **5.**(*di azienda, prodotto*) image; **curare la propria ~** to look after one's own image
immancabile [im·maŋ·'ka:·bi·le] *agg* **1.**(*solito*) inevitable **2.**(*inevitabile*) certain
immane [im·'ma:·ne] *agg* (*fatica, lavoro*) huge
immanente [im·ma·'nɛn·te] *agg* PHILOS (*causa, principio*) immanent
immangiabile [im·man·'dʒa:·bi·le] *agg* (*cibo*) inedible
immateriale [im·ma·te·'ria:·le] *agg* (*forma, bellezza*) immaterial; **beni -i** JUR intangible assets
immatricolare [im·ma·tri·ko·'la:·re] *vt* (*veicolo*) to register
immatricolazione [im·ma·tri·ko·lat·'tsio:·ne] *f* (*di veicolo*) registration
immaturità [im·ma·tu·ri·'ta] <-> *f* (*di persona*) immaturity
immaturo, -a [im·ma·'tu:·ro] *agg* (*persona*) immature; **essere ~ per qc** to be too young for sth
immedesimarsi [im·me·de·zi·'ma:r·si] *vr* **~ in qu** to identify with sb; **~ nella situazione di qu** to put oneself in sb's shoes
immediatamente [im·me·dia·ta·'men·te] *avv* immediately
immediatezza [im·me·dia·'tet·tsa] *f* **1.**(*di atto, decisione*) immediacy **2.**_fig_ (*di poesia, stile*) spontaneity
immediato¹ [im·me·'dia:·to] *agg* **1.**(*contatto, soccorso, reazione*) immediate; **pagamento ~** immediate payment **2.**_fig_ (*stile*) spontaneous
immediato² *sing* **nell'~** immediately; **per l'~** at the moment
immemorabile [im·me·mo·'ra:·bi·le] *agg* da

tempo ~ from time immemorial
immemore [im·'mɛ:·mo·re] *agg* **~ di qc** forgetful of sth
immensità [im·men·si·'ta] <-> *f* **1.**(*di spazio*) immensity **2.**(*grande quantità*) load
immenso, -a [im·'mɛn·so] *agg* **1.**(*spazio*) vast **2.**(*ricchezza*) immense; (*folla*) huge **3.**_fig_ (*amore, dolore*) immense
immergere [im·'mɛr·dʒe·re] <immergo, immersi, immerso> I. *vt* **~ qc in qc** (*liquido*) to dip sth in sth II. *vr:* **-rsi 1.**(*in liquido, vasca*) to plunge **2.**(*in profondità*) to dive **3.**_fig_ (*in pensieri, attività*) to immerse oneself
immersi [im·'mɛr·si] *1. pers sing pass rem di* **immergere**
immersione [im·mer·'sio:·ne] *f* **1.**(*atto, sport*) submersion; **corso di ~** diving course; **~ subacquea** scuba diving **2.**_fig_ immersion; **~ totale** total immersion
immerso [im·'mɛr·so] *pp di* **immergere**
immesso [im·'mes·so] *pp di* **immettere**
immettere [im·'met·te·re] <immetto, immisi, immesso> *vt* **1.**(*liquido, gas*) to introduce **2.**COMPUT (*dati*) to enter **3.**(*prodotto, denaro*) **~ qc sul mercato** to introduce sth into the market **4.**(*strada, corridoio*) to lead
immigrato, -a [im·mi·'gra:·to] *m, f* immigrant
immigrazione [im·mi·grat·'tsio:·ne] *f* (*fenomeno, atto*) immigration
imminente [im·mi·'nɛn·te] *agg* (*pericolo, evento*) imminent
imminenza [im·mi·'nɛn·tsa] *f* (*di pericolo, evento*) imminence; **nell'~ di qc** with sth on the doorstep
immisi [im·'mi:·zi] *1. pers sing pass rem di* **immettere**
immissione [im·mis·'sio:·ne] *f* **1.**(*di acqua, gas*) introduction **2.**COMPUT (*di dati*) entering **3.**ADM (*di personale*) intake; **~ in ruolo** (*di insegnanti, precari*) intake of permanent staff
immobile [im·'mɔ:·bi·le] I. *agg* **1.**(*persona, cosa*) motionless **2.bene ~** JUR real estate II. *m* **1.**(*edificio*) property **2.** *pl* JUR (*beni*) real estate
immobiliare [im·mo·bi·'lia:·re] I. *agg* (*mercato, patrimonio*) property; **agenzia/società ~** realtor; **proprietà ~** real estate II. *f* (*agenzia, società*) realtor
immobiliarista [im·mo·bi·lia·'ris·ta] <-i *m*, -e *f*> *mf* (*professionista*) realtor
immobilismo [im·mo·bi·'liz·mo] *m* POL, ECON inactivity
immobilità [im·mo·bi·li·'ta] <-> *f* **1.**(*di persona, cosa*) immobility **2.**_fig_ (*di situazione*) inactivity
immobilizzare [im·mo·bi·lid·'dza:·re] *vt* **1.** *a.* _fig_ MED to immobilize **2.**FIN (*capitale*) to lock up
immobilizzato, -a [im·mo·bi·lid·'dza:·to] *agg* **1.** *a.* _fig_ MED immobilized **2.**FIN (*capitale*) locked up
immodificabile [im·mo·di·fi·'ka:·bi·le] *agg* (*dato, elemento*) unchangeable

immondizia [im·mon·'dit·tsia] <-ie> *f* (*rifiuti*) garbage

immondo, -a [im·'mon·do] *agg* 1. *lit* (*animale*) dirty 2. *fig* (*colpa, individuo*) foul

immorale [im·mo·'ra:·le] *agg* immoral

immoralità [im·mo·ra·li·'ta] <-> *f* 1. (*di persona, dottrina*) immorality 2. (*atto*) immoral act

immortalare [im·mor·ta·'la:·re] *vt a. scherz* to immortalize

immortale [im·mor·'ta:·le] *agg* 1. (*anima*) immortal 2. (*sentimento*) undying; (*artista, fama, opera*) immortal

immortalità [im·mor·ta·li·'ta] <-> *f* immortality

immotivato, -a [im·mo·ti·'va:·to] *agg* (*senza motivo*) unjustified

immune [im·'mu:·ne] *agg* 1. MED immune; **essere ~ a** [*o* **da**] **qc** to be immune to sth 2. (*privo*) **essere ~ da qc** to have no sth

immunità [im·mu·ni·'ta] <-> *f* MED, JUR immunity; **~ parlamentare** parliamentary immunity

immunitario, -a [im·mu·ni·'ta:·rio] <-i, -ie> *agg* MED immune; **sistema ~** immune system

immunizzazione [im·mu·nid·dza·'tʃio:·ne] *f* MED immunization

immunodeficienza [im·mu·no·de·fi·'tʃɛn·tsa] *f* MED immunodeficiency; **sindrome da ~ acquisita** acquired immunodeficiency syndrome, *AIDS*

immunologia [im·mu·no·lo·'dʒi:·a] *f* MED immunology

immunologico, -a [im·mu·no·'lɔ:·dʒi·ko] <-ci, -che> *agg* MED immunological

immutabile [im·mu·'ta:·bi·le] *agg* (*legge, decisione*) unchangeable; (*amore*) unchanging

immutabilità [im·mu·ta·bi·li·'ta] <-> *f* (*di legge, decisione*) immutability

immutato, -a [im·mu·'ta:·to] *agg* unchanged

impacciato, -a [im·pat·'tʃa:·to] *agg a. fig* awkward

impaccio [im·'pat·tʃo] <-cci> *m* 1. (*oggetto, persona*) hindrance; **essere d'~ (a qu)** to be in the way (of sb) 2. (*situazione*) awkward situation; **trarre qu d'~** to get sb out of an awkward situation; **trarsi d'~** to get oneself out of an awkward situation

impacco [im·'pak·ko] <-cchi> *m* (*con panno, garza*) compress

impadronirsi [im·pa·dro·'nir·si] <m'impadronisco> *vr* **~ di qc** (*denaro, potere*) to take possession of sth; *fig* (*materia, mestiere*) to become proficient in sth

impagabile [im·pa·'ga:·bi·le] *agg* 1. (*favore, servizio*) incomparable 2. (*persona*) invaluable

impaginare [im·pa·dʒi·'na:·re] *vt* TYP to make up

impaginazione [im·pa·dʒi·nat·'tsio:·ne] *f* TYP making-up

impalcatura [im·pal·ka·'tu:·ra] *f* 1. (*nel cantiere*) scaffolding 2. (*portante*) framework

impallidire [im·pal·li·'di:·re] <impallidisco> *vi essere* 1. (*in volto*) to grow pale 2. *fig* (*per*

importanza) to fade

impalpabile [im·pal·'pa:·bi·le] *agg* (*tessuto, polvere*) fine

impanato, -a [im·pa·'na:·to] *agg* CULIN in breadcrumbs

imparare [im·pa·'ra:·re] *vt* 1. (*con studio*) to learn; **~ a fare qc** to learn to do sth; **~ qc a memoria** to learn sth by heart 2. (*con esperienza*) to learn; **~ la lezione** *fig* to learn one's lesson; **~ qc a proprie spese** *fig* to learn sth at one's own expense; **così impari!** that'll teach you!; **sbagliando s'impara** *prov* you learn from your mistakes

impareggiabile [im·pa·red·'dʒa:·bi·le] *agg* 1. (*bellezza, eleganza*) incomparable 2. (*amico, artista*) unique

imparentato, -a [im·pa·ren·'ta:·to] *agg* (*famiglia, persona*) related; **essere ~ con qu** to be related to sb

impari ['im·pa·ri] <inv> *agg* (*forze, lotta*) unequal

impartire [im·par·'ti:·re] <impartisco> *vt* **~ qc a qu** (*ordine, lezione*) to give sb sth [*o* to give sth to sb]

imparziale [im·par·'tsia:·le] *agg* (*arbitro, giudice*) unbiased; (*valutazione, giudizio*) impartial

imparzialità [im·par·tsia·li·'ta] <-> *f* impartiality

impassibile [im·pas·'si:·bi·le] *agg* impassive

impastare [im·pas·'ta:·re] *vt* (*pane*) to knead; (*farina, colori, cemento*) to mix

impasto [im·ˠpas·to] *m* (*amalgama*) mixture; (*di pasta di pane*) dough

impatto [im·'pat·to] *m* 1. (*di veicolo*) collision 2. *fig* **~ con qc** (*con realtà*) impact of sth; **~ su qc/qu** (*su ambiente, persona*) impact on sth/sb; **~ ambientale** impact on the environment

impaurito, -a [im·pau·'ri:·to] *agg* (*spaventato*) frightened

impavido, -a [im·'pa:·vi·do] *agg* (*sguardo, comportamento*) fearless

impaziente [im·pat·'tsiɛn·te] *agg* 1. (*per nervosismo*) impatient 2. **essere ~ di fare qc** (*per l'attesa*) to be anxious to do sth

impazienza [im·pat·'tsiɛn·tsa] *f* 1. (*nervosismo*) impatience 2. (*per l'attesa*) anxiety

impazzata [im·pat·'tsa:·ta] *f* **all'~** wildly

impazzire [im·pat·'tsi:·re] <impazzisco> *vi essere* (*ammattire*) to go crazy; **cosa dici, sei impazzito?** what are you saying, have you gone crazy?; **mi sembra di ~** I think I'm going crazy; **c'è da ~** it's enough to drive you crazy!; **~ dal mal di schiena** to have a horrible backache; **fare ~ qu** to drive sb crazy; **da ~** *inf* incredible; **ho un mal di testa da ~** I've got an incredible headache; **~ di qc** *fig* (*gioia, gelosia*) to be mad with sth; **~ per qc/qu** *fig* to be crazy about sth/sb

impeccabile [im·pek·'ka:·bi·le] *agg* impeccable

impedimento [im·pe·di·'men·to] *m* (*ostacolo*) problem; **essere d'~ a qc/qu** to be in

the way of sb/sth
impedire [im·pe·'diː·re] <impedisco> *vt*
1.(*vietare*) to prevent; ~ **a qu di fare qc** to
prevent sb from doing sth **2.**(*evitare*) to stop
3.(*vista, passaggio*) to block; (*movimenti*) to
restrict
impegnare [im·peɲ·'ɲaː·re] **I.** *vt* **1.**(*gioiello,
oggetto*) to pawn **2.** ~ **qu a fare qc** (*contratto,
onore*) to oblige sb to do sth **3.**(*lavoro, studio*)
to keep busy **II.** *vr:* **-rsi 1. -rsi** (**con qu**) **a fare
qc** to agree to do sth (with sb) **2. -rsi in qc**
(*studio, lavoro*) to work hard at sth; (*lotta*) to
commit oneself to sth
impegnativo, **-a** [im·peɲ·ɲa·'tiː·vo] *agg*
1.(*lavoro, compito*) demanding **2.**(*cena,
abito*) formal **3.**(*firma, promessa*) binding
impegnato, **-a** [im·peɲ·'ɲaː·to] *agg* **1.**(*occupato*) busy; **essere** ~ (*fidanzato*) to be going
steady **2.**(*militante*) politically committed
impegno [im·'peɲ·ɲo] *m* **1.**(*obbligo*) undertaking; **senza** ~ no strings attached **2.**(*incombenza*) commitment; **avere un** ~ to have a pri-
or commitment; **liberarsi da un** ~ to get out
of a commitment **3.**(*dedizione*) enthusiasm
4.(*militanza*) political commitment
impellente [im·pel·'lɛn·te] *agg* (*bisogno,
motivo*) urgent
impenetrabile [im·pe·ne·'traː·bi·le] *agg*
1.(*foresta, buoi, nebbia*) impenetrable **2.** *fig*
(*sguardo, occhi*) inscrutable; (*persona*) mysterious
impenitente [im·pe·ni·'tɛn·te] *agg* (*fumatore,
donnaiolo*) diehard
impennarsi [im·pen·'nar·si] *vr* **1.**(*cavallo,
moto*) to rear up **2.** AERO, MAR to zoom up
impennata [im·pen·'naː·ta] *f* **1.**(*di cavallo,
moto*) rearing up; (*di aereo*) zoom **2.**(*di
prezzo, valore*) upsurge
impensabile [im·pen·'saː·bi·le] *agg* (*inimmaginabile, assurdo*) inconceivable; **essere** ~
... +*inf* to be out of the question ...; **essere** ~
che ... +*cong* to be inconceivable that ...
impensierire [im·pen·sie·'riː·re] <impensier-
isco> *vt* ~ **qu** to worry sb
imperante [im·pe·'ran·te] *agg fig* (*moda, malcostume*) prevailing
imperativo[1] [im·pe·ra·'tiː·vo] *agg* **1.**(*tono, esigenza*) authoritative **2. modo** ~ LING imperative
imperativo[2] *m* LING, PHILOS imperative
imperatore, **-trice** [im·pe·ra·'toː·re] *m*, *f* emperor *m*, empress *f*
impercettibile [im·per·tʃet·'tiː·bi·le] *agg*
1.(*movimento, suono*) imperceptible
2.(*molto piccolo*) very slight
imperdonabile [im·per·do·'naː·bi·le] *agg*
(*errore, mancanza*) unforgivable
imperfetto[1] [im·per·'fɛt·to] *agg* **1.**(*funzionamento, meccanismo*) faulty **2. tempo** ~ LING
imperfect
imperfetto[2] *m* LING imperfect
imperfezione [im·per·fet·'tsio·ne] *f* **1.**(*caratteristica*) imperfection **2.**(*difetto*) flaw;

~ **fisica** physical imperfection
Imperia [im·pe·'riː·a] *f* Imperia, *a city in the
Liguria region*
imperiale [im·pe·'ria·le] *agg*(*dell'imperatore*)
imperial
imperialismo [im·pe·ria·'liz·mo] *m* (*espansionismo*) imperialism
imperialista [im·pe·ria·'lis·ta] <-i *m*, -e *f*>
I. *agg* (*politica, governo*) imperialist **II.** *mf*
(*fautore*) imperialist
imperioso, **-a** [im·pe·'rio·so] *agg* (*tono,
sguardo*) imperious
impermeabile [im·per·me·'a·bi·le] **I.** *agg*
1.(*tessuto, terreno*) waterproof; (*orologio*)
water-resistant **2.** *fig* (*persona*) impervious
II. *m* (*soprabito*) raincoat
impermeabilità [im·per·me·a·bi·li·'ta] <-> *f*
(*di tessuto, materiale*) impermeability
impermeabilizzante [im·per·me·a·bi·lid·
'dzan·te] **I.** *agg* (*sostanza, materiale*) water-
proofing **II.** *m* (*prodotto*) waterproofer
imperniato, **-a** [im·per·'nia·to] *agg* (*film, discorso, racconto*) ~ **su qc** based on sth
impero[1] [im·'pɛː·ro] *m a. fig* empire; ~ **coloniale** colonial Empire
imperscrutabile [im·per·skru·'taː·bi·le] *agg*
(*disegno, ragione*) inscrutable
impersonale [im·per·so·'na·le] *agg* **1.**(*non
mirato*) general **2.**(*stile, tono*) impersonal
3. LING (*verbo, forma*) impersonal
impersonare [im·per·so·'na·re] *vt* **1.**(*concetto, caratteristica*) to personify **2.**(*personaggio*) to play
imperterrito, **-a** [im·per·'tɛr·ri·to] *agg*(*impassibile*) calm; **continuare** ~ **a fare qc** to calmly
carry on doing sth; **rimanere** ~ [*o* **restare**] to
be unperturbed
impertinente [im·per·ti·'nɛn·te] **I.** *agg* (*persona, domanda*) impertinent **II.** *mf* (*persona*)
impertinent person
imperturbabile [im·per·tur·'baː·bi·le] *agg*
1.(*persona, carattere*) impassive **2.**(*calma,
serenità*) undisturbed
impervio, **-a** [im·'per·vio] (*sentiero, strada,
terreno*) impassable
impeto ['im·pe·to] *m* **1.**(*di onda, vento*) force;
(*di nemico, attacco*) onslaught; (*di discorso,
ragionamento*) heat; **con** ~ forcefully **2.** *fig* (*di
passione, collera*) outburst; **agire/reagire**
d'~ to act/react on impulse
impetuoso, **-a** [im·pe·'tuoː·zo] **1.**(*vento, corrente*) violent **2.**(*uomo, carattere*) impetuous
impiantare [im·pian·'taː·re] *vt* **1.**(*palo,
antenna*) to erect **2.** MED (*dente, protesi*) to
implant; (*pace-maker*) to implant **3.**(*attività,
azienda*) to set up
impianto [im·'pian·to] *m* **1.**(*allestimento*) installation **2.**(*attrezzature*) plant; ~ **di risalita**
lifts; ~ **di riscaldamento** heating; ~ **sportivo**
sports facility; ~ **stereo** stereo **3.** MED implant
impiccagione [im·pik·ka·'dʒoː·ne] *f* (*pena*)
hanging
impiccato, **-a** [im·pik·'kaː·to] **I.** *agg* hanged

II. *m, f* **1.**(*persona*) hanged person **2.**(*gioco*) hangman

impiccio [im·'pit·tʃo] <-cci> *m* (*ostacolo*) hindrance; **essere d'~** to be in the way

impiegare [im·pie·'ga:·re] *vt* **1.**(*strumento, oggetto*) to use; (*capacità, energie*) to employ **2.**(*tempo*) to take **3.**(*denaro*) to spend **4.**(*esperto, specialista*) to employ

impiegatizio, -a [im·pie·ga·'tit·tsio] <-i, -ie> *agg* (*lavoro, settore*) white-collar

impiegato, -a [im·pie·'ga:·to] *m, f* (*dipendente*) employee; **~ statale** civil servant

impiego [im·'piɛ:·go] <-ghi> *m* **1.**(*di strumento, attrezzo*) use; (*di manodopera*) employment; (*di forze, energie*) expending; (*di tempo, denaro*) spending **2.**(*lavoro*) job; **~ fisso** permanent job; **~ a tempo determinato/indeterminato** temporary/permanent job; **~ a tempo parziale/pieno** part-time/full-time job; **~ pubblico** public sector post

impietoso, -a [im·pie·'to:·so] *agg* merciless

implacabile [im·pla·'ka:·bi·le] *agg* (*odio, vendetta*) implacable; (*giudice, insegnante*) cruel

implementare [im·ple·men·'ta:·re] *vt* TEC, COMPUT (*programma, sistema*) to implement

implicare [im·pli·'ka:·re] *vt* **1.**(*come conseguenza*) to mean **2.**(*coinvolgere*) **~ qu in qc** to involve sb in sth

implicato, -a [im·pli·'ka:·to] *agg* **essere/rimanere ~ in qc** to be involved in sth

implicazione [im·pli·kat·'tsio:·ne] *f* **1.**(*conseguenza*) implication **2.**(*di persona*) involvement

implicito, -a [im·'pli:·tʃi·to] *agg* **1.**(*sottinteso*) implicit **2.frase** [*o* **proposizione**] **-a** LING implicit clause **3.funzione -a** MATH implicit function

implorare [im·plo·'ra:·re] *vt* **1.**(*aiuto, perdono*) to beg for **2. ~ qn per qc/di fare qc** to beg sb for sth/to do sth

imponente [im·po·'nɛn·te] *agg* impressive

imponenza [im·po·'nɛn·tsa] *f* **1.**(*di edificio, statura, aspetto*) impressiveness **2.**(*di persona*) stateliness

impongo [im·'po·ŋo] *1.pers sing pr di* **imporre**

imponibile [im·po·'ni:·bi·le] ADM, FIN I. *agg* (*reddito, patrimonio*) taxable II. *m* taxable income

impopolare [im·po·po·'la:·re] *agg* unpopular

imporre [im·'por·re] <impongo, imposi, imposto> I. *vt* **1.***fig* (*obbligo, ordine, legge*) to impose; (*condizione*) to set; (*tassa, tributo*) to levy **2. ~ qc a qu** to impose sth on sb; **~ a qu di fare qc** to make sb do sth **3.**(*sacrifici, impegno*) to demand II. *vr:* **-rsi 1.**(*persona*) to assert oneself; **-rsi all'attenzione di qu** to attract sb's attention **2.**(*moda, prodotto*) to become popular **3.-rsi su qu** to dominate sb **4.**(*essere necessario*) to be required **5.-rsi qc** to impose sth on oneself; **-rsi di fare qc** to make oneself do sth

importante [im·por·'tan·te] I. *agg* **1.**(*ril-*

evante) important **2.**(*persona*) high-ranking **3.**(*pranzo, vestito*) important **4.**(*naso, cappello*) large II.<*sing*> *m* **l'~** the important thing

importanza [im·por·'tan·tsa] *f* **1.**(*rilevanza*) importance; **avere ~** to matter; **di una certa ~** of some importance; **non dare ~ a qc/qu** not to bother about sth/sb **2.**(*di persona*) importance; **darsi ~** to put on airs

importare [im·por·'ta:·re] I. *vt avere* ECON to import II. *vi essere* (*interessare*) to matter; **non importa** (*a. come risposta*) it doesn't matter; **non gli importa niente di lei** he doesn't care about her at all; **non me ne importa niente** I don't care about it

importatore, -trice [im·por·ta·'to:·re] I. *agg* (*paese*) importing II. *m, f* importer

importazione [im·por·tat·'tsio:·ne] *f* **1.**(*di merce*) import; **merce d'~** import goods **2.** *pl* **le -i** (*merci*) imports

importo [im·'pɔr·to] *m* (*di fattura*) amount; (*somma*) sum

imposi [im·'po:·zi] *1.pers sing pass rem di* **imporre**

imposizione [im·po·zit·'tsio:·ne] *f* **1.**(*di divieto, obbligo*) enforcement **2.**(*con la forza*) imposition **3.**FIN (*di tassa, tributo*) levy

impossessarsi [im·pos·ses·'sar·si] *vr* **~ di qc** to get hold of sth

impossibile [im·pos·'si:·bi·le] I. *agg* **1.**(*irrealizzabile*) impossible; **è ~ continuare così** it can't go on like this; **~ a dirsi** impossible to say; **~ a farsi** impossible to do; **sembra** [*o* **pare**] **~** it seems incredible **2.**(*persona, situazione, traffico*) impossible; (*cibo, bevanda*) disgusting; (*freddo, caldo*) unbelievable; **c'era un caldo ~** it was unbelievably hot II.<*sing*> *m* **l'~** the impossible; **fare** [*o* **tentare**] **l'~** to do [*o* try] everything possible

impossibilità [im·pos·si·bi·li·'ta] <-> *f* impossibility; **essere** [*o* **trovarsi**] **nell'~ di fare qc** to be unable to do sth

impossibilitato, -a [im·pos·si·bi·li·'ta:·to] *agg* (*persona*) unable; **essere ~ a fare qc** to be unable to do sth

imposta [im·'pɔs·ta] *f* **1.**(*di finestra, porta*) shutter **2.**FIN (*tassa*) tax; **~ diretta/indiretta** direct/indirect tax; **esente da ~** tax free; **~ patrimoniale** property tax; **~ sul reddito delle persone fisiche** income tax; **soggetto a ~** taxable; **ufficio delle -e** Internal Revenue Service; **~ sul valore aggiunto** value-added tax

impostare [im·pos·'ta:·re] *vt* **1.**(*edificio, mura*) to build **2.***fig* (*lavoro*) to set up; (*progetto, problema, questione*) to set out; (*opera, dipinto, romanzo*) to plan out **3.**MATH to formulate **4.**TYP (*pagina, giornale*) to lay out **5.**MUS (*voce*) to pitch **6.**(*lettera, cartolina*) to mail

impostato, -a [im·po·'sta:·to] *agg* **1.** *a. fig* (*gioco, questione*) formulated **2.**(*atleta, cantante*) technically prepared **3.**MUS (*voce*) pitched

impostazione [im·pos·tat·'tsio:·ne] *f* **1.**(*di edificio*) building **2.***fig* (*di lavoro*) setting up; (*di opera, dipinto, romanzo*) planning out; (*di problema, questione, progetto*) setting out **3.**MATH (*di operazione, problema*) formulation **4.**TYP (*di pagina, giornale*) layout **5.**MUS (*di voce*) pitch **6.***fig*(*preparazione*) training

imposto, -a [im·'pos·to] I.*pp di* **imporre** II. *agg* **prezzo** ~ fixed retail price

impostore, -a [im·pos·'to:·re] *m, f* (*ciarlatano*) charlatan

impotente [im·po·'tɛn·te] *agg* **1.**(*persona*) powerless; (*governo, legge*) impotent **2.***fig* (*dolore, rabbia*) impotent **3.**MED impotent

impotenza [im·po·'tɛn·tsa] *f* **1.**(*di persona*) powerlessness; (*di governo, legge*) impotence **2.**MED impotence

impoverimento [im·po·ve·ri·'men·to] *m* impoverishment

impoverire [im·po·ve·'ri:·re] <impoverisco> I. *vt avere* **1.**(*persona, territorio*) to impoverish **2.**AGR (*terreno*) to impoverish II. *vi* (*persona*) to become poor(er) III. *vr:* **-rsi 1.**(*persona*) to become poor(er) **2.**AGR (*terreno*) to become impoverished

impraticabile [im·pra·ti·'ka:·bi·le] *agg* **1.**(*strada, sentiero*) impassable; (*campo da gioco*) unplayable **2.**(*ipotesi, piano*) infeasible

impraticabilità [im·pra·ti·ka·bi·li·'ta] <-> *f* **1.**(*di strada, sentiero*) impassable nature; (*di campo da gioco*) unplayable condition **2.**(*di ipotesi, piano*) infeasibility

imprecare [im·pre·'ka:·re] *vi* to curse; ~ **contro qc/qu** to curse sb/sth

imprecazione [im·pre·kat·'tsio:·ne] *f* (*parola, frase*) curse; **lanciare un'**~ to curse

imprecisato, -a [im·pre·tʃi·'za:·to] *agg* unspecified

imprecisione [im·pret·tʃi·'zio:·ne] *f* **1.**(*approssimazione*) imprecision **2.**(*errore*) inaccuracy

impreciso, -a [im·pre·'tʃi:·zo] *agg* **1.**(*lavoro, calcolo*) imprecise; (*strumento*) inaccurate **2.**(*persona*) careless

impregnato, -a [im·preɲ·'ɲa:·to] *agg* ~ **di qc** (*liquido*) soaked in sth; *fig* thick with sth

imprendibile [im·pren·'di:·bi·le] *agg* **1.**(*palla, giocatore, corridore*) uncatchable **2.**(*ladro, assassino*) elusive

imprenditore, -trice [im·pren·di·'to:·re] *m, f* entrepreneur

imprenditoriale [im·pren·di·to·'ria:·le] *agg* entrepreneurial

impreparato, -a [im·pre·pa·'ra:·to] *agg* **1.**(*a scuola*) **essere** ~ **in qc** to not have studied sth properly **2.**(*non competente*) badly trained **3.**(*non pronto*) unprepared; **essere** ~ **a qc** to be unprepared for sth

impreparazione [im·pre·pa·ra·'zio:·ne] *f* **1.**(*di studente*) lack of preparation **2.**(*di professionista*) lack of training **3.**(*mancanza di prontezza*) lack of preparation; ~ **a qc** unreadi-

ness for sth

impresa [im·'pre:·za] *f* **1.**(*azione*) enterprise; **essere un'**~ *inf* to be hard work **2.**(*ditta*) company; ~ **edile** construction company; ~ **familiare** family firm; ~ **pubblica** public company **3.** *pl* (*di eroe*) feats

impresario, -a [im·pre·'za:·rio] <-i, -ie> *m, f* **1.**(*di ditta*) director; ~ **edile** building contractor **2.**(*di teatro*) producer

imprescindibile [im·preʃ·ʃin·'di:·bi·le] *agg* (*bisogno, dovere*) unavoidable

impressi [im·'prɛs·si] *I. pers sing pass rem di* **imprimere**

impressionante [im·pres·sio·'nan·te] *agg* **1.**(*incidente, delitto, scena*) shocking **2.**(*eccezionale*) incredible; **faceva un caldo** ~ it was incredibly hot

impressionare [im·pres·sio·'na:·re] I. *vt* **1.**(*turbare*) to upset **2.**(*fare buona impressione*) to impress II. *vr:* **-rsi** (*turbarsi*) to get upset

impressione [im·pres·'sio:·ne] *f* **1.**(*sensazione*) sensation **2.**(*idea, opinione*) impression; **fare buona/cattiva** ~ (**a qu**) to make a good/bad impression (on sb); **prima** ~ first impression; **avere l'**~ **di ...** +*inf* to have the impression that ...; **avere l'**~ **che ...** +*ind, cong* to have the impression that ... **3.**(*turbamento*) **che** ~! it was dreadful!; **fare** ~ (**a qu**) to upset (sb)

impressionismo [im·pres·sio·'niz·mo] *m* ART, LIT, MUS Impressionism

impressionista [im·pres·sio·'nis·ta] <-i *m*, -e *f*> ART I. *agg* (*opera, pittore*) Impressionist II. *mf* (*artista*) Impressionist

impresso [im·'prɛs·so] *pp di* **imprimere**

imprevedibile [im·pre·ve·'di:·bi·le] *agg* **1.**(*circostanza, motivo*) unforeseeable **2.**(*persona, carattere*) unpredictable

imprevisto [im·pre·'vis·to] *agg* (*ritardo, spesa*) unforeseen

imprevisto² *m* (*contrattempo*) unforeseen event; **salvo -i** unless something happens

impreziosire [im·pret·tsio·'si:·re] <imprezio-sisco> *vt a. fig* to embellish

imprigionare [im·pri·dʒo·'na:·re] *vt* **1.**(*ladro, malvivente*) to imprison; (*animale*) to cage **2.***fig*(*bloccare*) to trap

imprimere [im·'pri:·me·re] <imprimo, impressi, impresso> I. *vt* **1.**a. *fig* (*segno*) to stamp; (*orma*) to leave **2.***fig* (*concetto, ricordo*) to fix **3.**PHYS (*movimento, velocità*) to give II. *vr:* **-rsi 1.**a. *fig*(*segno*) to be stamped; (*orma*) to be left **2.***fig* (*concetto, ricordo*) to fix oneself

improbabile [im·pro·'ba:·bi·le] *agg* **1.**(*quasi escluso*) unlikely **2.**(*inverosimile*) improbable

improduttivo, -a [im·pro·dut·'ti:·vo] *agg* **1.**(*terreno*) infertile **2.***fig* (*investimento, sforzo*) unprofitable **3.**(*persona*) unproductive

impronta [im·'pron·ta] *f* **1.**(*segno*) mark; (*di mano, piede, zampa*) print; **-e digitali** fingerprints; ~ **del piede** footprint; **lasciare le -e** to leave prints **2.** *fig* mark; **lasciare un'~ indelebile** to leave an indelible mark **3.** MED cast

improntare [im·pron·'ta:·re] *vt* ~ **qc a qc** (*sentimento, principio*) to endow sth with sth; ~ **qc su qc** (*argomento*) to base sth around sth

improprio, -a [im·'prɔ:·prio] <-i, -ie> *agg* **1.** (*inesatto*) improper; **uso** ~ improper use; (*termine, parola*) incorrect **2.** (*inadatto*) unsuitable

improrogabile [im·pro·ro·'ga:·bi·le] *agg* (*impegno, termine*) binding; (*decision*) that cannot be delayed

improvvisamente [im·prov·vi·za·'men·te] *avv* suddenly

improvvisare [im·prov·vi·'za:·re] *vt* **1.** (*discorso, canzone*) to improvise **2.** (*pranzo, festa*) to throw together; (*risposta, scusa*) to think up

improvvisata [im·prov·vi·'za:·ta] *f inf* (*visita*) surprise visit; **fare un'~ a qu** to pay sb a surprise visit

improvvisato, -a [im·prov·vi·'za:·to] *agg* **1.** (*canzone, cena*) improvised; (*visita*) surprise; **discorso** ~ improvised speech **2.** *pej* (*raffazzonato: lavoro*) makeshift

improvvisazione [im·prov·vi·zat·'tsio:·ne] *f a. fig* MUS, LIT, THEAT improvisation

improvviso¹ [im·prov·'vi:·zo] *agg* sudden; (*cambiamento del tempo*) unexpected

improvviso² *m* **all'~** suddenly

imprudente [im·pru·'dɛn·te] **I.** *agg* (*persona*) rash; (*guidatore*) careless **II.** *mf* rash person

imprudenza [im·pru·'dɛn·tsa] *f* **1.** (*caratteristica*) rashness; (*di guidatore*) carelessness **2.** (*azione*) rash action; **commettere un'~** to do sth rash

impugnabile [im·puɲ·'ɲa:·bi·le] *agg* JUR (*sentenza*) subject to appeal; (*testamento*) contestable

impugnare [im·puɲ·'ɲa:·re] *vt* **1.** (*fucile, racchetta*) to grip **2.** JUR (*sentenza, testamento*) to contest

impugnatura [im·puɲ·ɲa·'tu:·ra] *f* (*manico*) handle

impugnazione [im·puɲ·ɲat·'tsio:·ne] *f* JUR (*di sentenza, testamento*) contestation

impulsività [im·pul·si·vi·'ta] <-> *f* (*di gesto, risposta*) impulsiveness

impulsivo, -a [im·pul·'si:·vo] **I.** *agg* **1.** (*persona, carattere*) impulsive **2.** (*atto, gesto*) instinctive **II.** *m, f* (*persona*) impulsive person

impulso [im·'pul·so] *m* **1.** MEC, EL impulse; ~ **di corrente** electrical impulse; ~ **telefonico** (*scatto*) unit **2.** *fig* (*stimolo*) impetus; **dare ~ a qc** to boost sth **3.** *fig* (*istinto*) impulse; **d'~** impulsively

impunemente [im·pu·ne·'men·te] *avv* with impunity

impunità [im·pu·ni·'ta] <-> *f* (*di persona*) impunity

impunito, -a [im·pu·'ni:·to] *agg* unpunished

impurità [im·pu·ri·'ta] *f* **1.** (*stato: di aria,* *acqua*) impurity **2.** *pl* (*particelle*) impurities **3.** REL impurity

impuro, -a [im·'pu:·ro] *agg a. fig* REL impure

imputabile [im·pu·'ta:·bi·le] *agg* **1. essere ~ a qc/qu** (*attribuibile*) to be due to sth/sb **2.** JUR (*accusabile*) chargeable

imputabilità [im·pu·ta·bi·li·'ta] <-> *f* JUR liability

imputare [im·pu·'ta:·re] *vt* **1.** ~ **qc a qc/qu** (*attribuire*) to attribute sth to sth/sb **2.** JUR ~ **qu di qc** (*accusare*) to charge sb with sth

imputato, -a [im·pu·'ta:·to] *m, f* JUR defendant; **banco degli -i** dock

imputazione [im·pu·tat·'tsio:·ne] *f* JUR charge

in¹ [in] <nel, nello, nell', nella, nei, negli, nelle> *prep* **1.** (*stato in luogo*) in; **essere ~ casa** to be at home; **abitare ~ campagna/città/montagna** to live in the countryside/city/mountains; **abitare ~ via Garibaldi** to live in via Garibaldi; **vivere ~ Francia** to live in France; **lavorare ~ Sicilia** to work in Sicily; **lavorare ~ fabbrica** to work in a factory; **giocare ~ strada** to play in the street; **dormire ~ albergo** to sleep in a hotel; **dormire ~ un letto comodo** to sleep in a comfortable bed; **tenere un oggetto ~ mano/nella borsa** to keep sth in one's hand/bag; **avere un bambino ~ braccio** to have a child in one's arms; **avere un conto ~ banca** to have a bank account **2.** (*moto a luogo*) to; **andare ~ campagna/città/montagna** to go to the countryside/into the city/to the mountains; **entrare ~ casa** to go into the house; **andare ~ cucina** to go into the kitchen; **scendere ~ piazza** to take to the streets; **andare ~ Spagna** to go to Spain; **trasferirsi negli Stati Uniti** to move to the United States; **versare il vino nel bicchiere** to pour the wine into the glass **3.** (*moto per luogo*) in; **passeggiare nel parco** to walk in the park; **viaggiare ~ Australia** to travel around Australia **4.** (*tempo determinato*) in; **nel 2007** in 2007; ~ **primavera/estate/autunno/inverno** in Spring/Summer/Fall/Winter; ~ **gennaio** in January; **nel pomeriggio** in the afternoon; ~ **gioventù** in one's youth; ~ **tempo di guerra/pace** in times of war/peace **5.** (*durata: entro*) within [*o* in]; **finirò il lavoro ~ due mesi** I'll finish the work within two months; ~ **tre giorni/settimane/mesi/anni** within three days/weeks/months/years; ~ **un attimo** in a moment; **ho terminato tutto ~ poco tempo** I finished everything quickly; ~ **giornata** before the end of the day **6.** (*modo*) in; **parlare ~ fretta** to talk quickly; **ascoltare ~ silenzio** to listen silently; **mettersi ~ cerchio/fila** to get into a circle/line; **stare ~ piedi/~ ginocchio** to be standing/kneeling; **essere ~ vacanza** to be on vacation; **andare ~ vacanza** to go on vacation; **vivere ~ miseria/nel benessere** to live in poverty/prosperously; **vivere ~ pace** to live in peace; **essere ~ servizio/congedo/pensione** to be on duty/on leave/retired; **colorare ~ rosso** to

color red; **trasmettere ~ diretta** to transmit live; **mettersi ~ abito da sera** to wear evening dress; **uscire ~ pigiama** to go out in one's pyjamas; **parlare ~ tedesco** to speak German; **donna ~ carriera** career woman; **casa ~ vendita** house for sale; **carne ~ umido** stewed meat; **riso ~ bianco** boiled rice **7.**(*mezzo*) by; **viaggiare ~ aereo/macchina/treno** to travel by plane/car/train; **pagare ~ contanti** to pay cash **8.**(*materia*) in; **pilastro ~ cemento armato** pillar in reinforced concrete; **mobile ~ legno** wooden piece of furniture **9.**(*fine, scopo*) to; **correre ~ aiuto** to run to help; **dare ~ omaggio** to give away free; **festa ~ onore di qu** party in sb's honor; **ricevere ~ premio** to receive as a prize; **dare ~ prestito** to lend; **un patrimonio ~ libri** a lot of valuable books **10.**(*quantità, distribuzione*) in; **essere ~ pochi** to be only a few; **giocare ~ sei** to play amongs six people; **spettacolo ~ tre atti** show in three acts; **tagliare ~ due** to cut into two; **~ tutto sono dieci euro** that's ten euros in total **11.**(*area di competenza*) in; **dottore ~ legge** doctor of law; **essere bravo ~ matematica** to be good in math; **laurearsi ~ medicina** to get a degree in medicine; **commerciare ~ gioielli** to trade in jewels **12.**(*trasformazione*) into; **cambiare gli euro ~ dollari** to change euros into dollars; **tradurre dal francese ~ italiano** to translate from French into Italian; **l'acqua si trasforma ~ vapore** the water is transformed into steam
in² [in] I. *avv* **essere ~** to be front page news; **fare ~** to be very popular II. <inv> *agg* (*locale, personaggio*) in
INA ['iːna] *m acro di* Istituto Nazionale delle Assicurazioni National Insurance Service
inabile [i·'naː·bi·le] *agg* **essere ~ a qc** to be unfit for sth; **~ al lavoro** unfit for work; **~ al servizio militare** unfit for military service
inabilità [in·a·bi·li·'ta] <-> *f* unfitness; (*per infortunio*) disability
inabitabile [in·a·bi·'taː·bi·le] *agg* uninhabitable
inaccessibile [in·at·tʃes·'siː·bi·le] *agg* **1.**(*luogo*) inaccessible **2.** *fig* (*persona*) unapproachable **3.** *fig* (*prezzo*) unaffordable
inaccettabile [in·at·tʃet·'taː·bi·le] *agg* unacceptable
inadatto, -a [in·a·'dat·to] *agg* **~ (a qc)** (*abito, strumento*) unsuited (for sth); (*persona*) unfit (for sth)
inadeguatezza [in·a·de·gua·'tet·tsa] *f* **1.**(*di cosa*) inadequacy; (*di comportamento*) unsuitability **2.**(*di persona*) unfitness
inadeguato, -a [in·a·de·'guaː·to] *agg* **1.**(*mezzo, compenso, capacità*) inadequate **2.**(*persona*) unfit
inadempiente [in·a·dem·'piɛn·te] *agg* JUR defaulting
inadempienza [in·a·dem·'piɛn·tsa] *f* JUR default

inadempimento [in·a·dem·pi·'men·to] *m v.* **inadempienza**
inafferrabile [in·af·fer·'raː·bi·le] *agg* **1.**(*ladro, evaso, preda*) elusive **2.**(*suono, parole*) inaudible **3.** *fig* (*concetto, significato*) incomprehensible
inagibile [in·a·'dʒiː·bi·le] *agg* (*edificio*) unfit for use; (*strada*) impassable
INAIL ['in·ail] *m acro di* Istituto Nazionale per l'Assicurazione contro gli Infortuni sul Lavoro National Institute for Insurance against Occupational Injuries
inalazione [in·a·lat·'tsioː·ne] *f a. fig* MED inhalation
inalienabile [in·a·lie·'naː·bi·le] *agg a. fig* JUR inalienable
inalterato, -a [in·al·te·'raː·to] *agg* **1.**(*materiale*) fresh **2.** *fig* (*programma*) unchanged; (*sentimento, interesse*) constant
inammissibile [in·am·mis·'siː·bi·le] *agg* (*opinione*) inadmissible; (*errore, comportamento*) unjustifiable
inanimato, -a [in·a·ni·'maː·to] *agg* **1.**(*cosa*) inanimate **2.**(*corpo*) lifeless
inappellabile [in·ap·pel·'laː·bi·le] *agg* **1.** JUR (*sentenza, giudizio*) not subject to appeal **2.**(*decisione, parere*) final
inapplicabile [in·ap·pli·'kaː·bi·le] *agg* (*norma, legge*) inapplicable; (*metodo, sistema*) unappliable
inappropriato, -a [in·ap·pro·'priaː·to] *agg* inappropriate
inarrestabile [in·ar·res·'taː·bi·le] *agg* **1.**(*aumento, crescita*) unstoppable **2.**(*pianto, discorso*) never ending
inarrivabile [in·ar·ri·'vaː·bi·le] *agg* (*qualità*) unattainable; (*persona*) incomparable
inaspettato, -a [in·as·pet·'taː·to] *agg* (*evento, notizia, ospite*) unexpected
inasprimento [in·as·pri·'men·to] *m* (*di conflitto, rapporti*) worsening; (*di pena*) increase; (*di carattere*) souring
inasprire [in·as·'priː·re] <inasprisco> I. *vt* **1.**(*conflitto, rapporti*) to worsen **2.**(*pena*) to increase **3.**(*carattere*) to embitter II. *vr:* **-rsi 1.**(*vino*) to turn bitter **2.**(*conflitto, rapporti*) to worsen **3.**(*persona, carattere*) to become embittered
inattaccabile [in·at·tak·'kaː·bi·le] *agg* **1.**(*città, fortezza*) impregnable **2.**(*metallo*) proofed **3.** *fig* (*persona, reputazione*) unassailable; (*fede, principio*) solid
inattendibile [in·at·ten·'diː·bi·le] *agg* unreliable
inatteso, -a [in·at·'teː·so] *agg* (*notizia, ospite*) unexpected
inattività [in·at·ti·vi·'ta] <-> *f* **1.**(*di persona, di impianto*) inactivity **2.**(*di vulcano*) dormancy
inattivo, -a [in·at·'tiː·vo] *agg* **1.**(*persona, impianto*) inactive; **capitale ~** unemployed capital **2.**(*vulcano*) dormant
inaudito, -a [in·au·'diː·to] *agg* **1.**(*fatto, fer-*

ocia) unheard-of **2.**(*esclamativo*) outrageous

inaugurale [in·au·gu·'ra:·le] *agg* (*cerimonia, discorso*) inaugural

inaugurare [in·au·gu·'ra:·re] *vt* **1.**(*ospedale, stadio*) to inaugurate; (*negozio, mostra*) to open; (*anno accademico*) to begin **2.** *inf* (*vestito, automobile*) to christen **3.** *fig* (*era*) to usher in; (*metodo*) to introduce

inaugurazione [in·au·gu·rat·'tsio:·ne] *f* (*di ospedale, stadio*) inauguration; (*di negozio, mostra*) opening; (*di anno accademico*) start; **discorso di** ~ opening speech

inavvertitamente [in·av·ver·ti·ta·'men·te] *avv* (*involontariamente*) inadvertently

inca ['in·ka] I. *agg* (*degli Inca*) Inca II. <-> *mf* Inca; **gli Inca** the Incas

incalcolabile [in·kal·ko·'la:·bi·le] *agg* **1.**(*distanza*) incalculable **2.**(*danno, vantaggio*) inestimable

incallito, -a [in·cal·'li:·to] *agg* (*fumatore, bevitore*) inveterate

incalzante [in·kal·'tsan·te] *agg* (*domande, richieste*) urgent; (*ritmo*) insistent

incalzare [in·kal·'tsa:·re] I. *vt* **1.**(*nemico, avversario*) to pursue **2.** to pressure II. *vi fig* (*tempo*) to press; (*pericolo*) to be imminent

incamerare [in·ca·me·'ra:·re] *vt* JUR (*beni*) to expropriate

incamminarsi [in·kam·mi·'nar·si] *vr:* **-rsi** *a. fig* to set off; **-rsi verso qc** to set off toward sth

incanalare [in·ka·na·'la:·re] I. *vt* **1.**(*acqua*) to canalize **2.**(*folla, traffico*) to channel II. *vr* **1.**(*acqua*) to canalize **2.**(*folla, traffico*) to flow

incancellabile [in·kan·tʃel·'la:·bi·le] *agg fig* (*ricordo, immagine*) indelible

incandescente [in·kan·deʃ·'ʃɛn·te] *agg* **1.**(*metallo*) incandescent **2.** *fig* (*atmosfera*) heated

incandescenza [in·kan·de·'ʃɛn·tsa] *f* PHYS incandescence; **lampada a** ~ incandescent lamp

incantare [in·kan·'ta:·re] I. *vt* **1.** *fig* (*affascinare*) to enchant **2.** *fig* (*abbindolare*) to get around **3.**(*serpente*) to charm II. *vr:* **-rsi** **1.**(*restare assorto*) to fall under a spell **2.**(*restare affascinato*) to be spellbound **3.**(*meccanismo*) to get stuck

incantato, -a [in·kan·'ta:·to] *agg* **1.**(*castello, giardino*) enchanted **2.**(*paesaggio, aspetto*) enchanting **3.**(*persona: assorto*) in a daze; (*affascinato*) enchanted

incantatore, -trice [in·kan·ta·'to:·re] *m, f* (*mago*) sorcerer *m*, sorceress *f*; ~ **di serpenti** snake charmer

incantesimo [in·kan·'te:·zi·mo] *m* (*magia*) spell; **fare un** ~ to make a spell; **rompere l'**~ to break the spell

incantevole [in·kan·'te:·vo·le] *agg* (*persona, luogo*) enchanting

incanto [in·'kan·to] *m* **1.**(*magia*) spell; **come per** ~ as if by magic **2.** *fig* (*fascino*) enchantment; **d'**~ (*a meraviglia*) wonderfully; (*all'improvviso*) suddenly; **questo giardino è un** ~ this garden is a wonder **3.**(*asta*) auction; **met-**

tere qc all'~ to put sth up for auction

incapace [in·ka·'pa:·tʃe] I. *agg* **1.** ~ **di fare qc** incapable of doing sth; ~ **di intendere e di volere** JUR not in full possession of one's faculties **2.**(*nella professione*) incompetent II. *mf* (*nella professione*) incompetent

incapacità [in·ka·pa·tʃi·'ta] <-> *f* **1.** ~ **di fare qc** inability to do sth; ~ **d'intendere e di volere** JUR incapacity **2.**(*nella professione*) incompetency

incappare [in·kap·'pa:·re] *vi* essere ~ **in qu** to run into sb; ~ **in qc** to fall into sth

incappucciato, -a [in·kap·put·'tʃa:·to] (*persona, testa*) hooded

incarcerare [in·kar·tʃe·'ra:·re] *vt* (*persona*) to imprison

incaricare [in·ka·ri·'ka:·re] I. *vt* ~ **qu di qc** to entrust sb with sth; ~ **qu di fare qc** to give sb the job of doing sth II. *vr* **-rsi di fare qc** to see about doing sth

incaricato, -a [in·ka·ri·'ka:·to] I. *agg* ~ **di qc** responsible for sth II. *m, f* (*addetto*) employee

incarico [in·'ka:·ri·ko] <-chi> *m* **1.**(*compito*) task; **avere l'**~ **di fare qc** to have the job of doing sth; **per** [*o* **su**] ~ **di qu** on behalf of sb **2.**(*funzione*) position; (*di insegnante*) temporary teaching position

incarnare [in·kar·'na:·re] *vt* **1.**(*ideale, concetto*) to embody **2.**(*personaggio*) to play

incarnato, -a [in·kar·'na:·to] *agg a. fig* REL incarnate

incarnazione [in·kar·nat·'tsio:·ne] *f a. fig* REL incarnation

incartare [in·kar·'ta:·re] *vt* (*merce, regalo*) to wrap (up)

incasinato, -a [in·ka·zi·'na:·to] *agg inf* **1.**(*cosa*) topsy turvy **2.**(*persona: disordinato*) disorganized; **oggi sono incasinata** today I have a lot to do

incassare [in·kas·'sa:·re] *vt* **1.**(*mobile, elettrodomestico*) to set **2.**(*contante*) to take; (*assegno*) to cash **3.** *fig* (*critica, offesa*) to take; ~ **il colpo** to suffer the blow **4.** SPORT (*pugilato: colpi*) to take; (*calcio: reti, gol*) to let in

incasso [in·'kas·so] *m* **1.**(*di contante*) collection; (*di assegno*) cashing; **all'**~ for collection **2.**(*somma*) takings *pl*

incastonato, -a [in·kas·to·'na:·to] *agg* (*gemma, pietra*) mounted

incastrare [in·kas·'tra:·re] I. *vt* **1.**(*pezzi, elementi*) to fit together; ~ **qc in qc** to fit sth in sth **2.** *fig* (*persona*) to trap; *scherz, inf* to catch out II. *vr:* **-rsi** **1.**(*combinarsi*) to fit **2.**(*bloccarsi*) to get stuck

incastro [in·'kas·tro] *m* **1.**(*operazione*) fitting **2.**(*punto*) joint; **a** ~ jointed

incauto, -a [in·'ka:u·to] *agg* unwise

incavo [in·'ka:·vo] *m* (*di pietra, stampo*) groove; (*di parete*) hollow

incazzarsi [in·kat·'tsar·si] *vr vulg* (*arrabbiarsi*) to get pissed off

incazzato, -a [in·kat·'tsa:·to] *agg vulg* (*arrabbiato*) pissed off; **sono** ~ **nero** I'm really pissed

incazzatura [iŋ·kat·tsa·'tuː·ra] *f vulg* (*arrabbiatura*) **prendersi un'~** to get pissed off

incedere [in·'tʃɛː·de·re] <*sing*> (*andatura*) gait

incendiare [in·tʃen·'diaː·re] I. *vt* 1. (*bosco, casa*) to set fire to 2. *fig* (*animi, cuori*) to inflame II. *vr:* **-rsi** (*prendere fuoco*) to catch fire

incendiario, -a [in·tʃen·'diaː·rio] <-i, -ie> I. *agg* (*materiale, sostanza*) incendiary II. *m, f* (*persona*) arsonist

incendio [in·'tʃɛn·dio] <-i> *m* (*fuoco*) fire; **~ doloso** arson

incenerimento [in·tʃe·ne·ri·'men·to] *m* (*di rifiuti*) incineration

inceneritore [in·tʃe·ne·ri·'toː·re] *m* (*impianto*) incinerator

incenso [in·'tʃɛn·so] *m* (*resina*) incense

incensurato, -a [in·tʃen·su·'raː·to] JUR I. *agg* **essere ~** to have a clean record II. *m, f* first-time offender

incentivante [in·tʃen·ti·'van·te] *agg* (*premio, compenso*) motivating

incentivare [in·tʃen·ti·'vaː·re] *vt* 1. ECON to boost 2. (*persona*) to motivate

incentivazione [in·tʃen·ti·vat·'tsioː·ne] *f* ECON boosting

incentivo [in·tʃen·'tiː·vo] *m* 1. (*a studio, lavoro*) incentive 2. ECON boost; **-i alle assunzioni** employment incentives; **-i fiscali** tax incentives

incentrato, -a [in·tʃen·'traː·to] **~ su qc/qu** (*basato*) based on sth/sb

inceppare [in·tʃep·'paː·re] I. *vt* 1. *fig* (*andamento, sviluppo*) to hamper 2. (*meccanismo*) to jam II. *vr:* **-rsi** (*meccanismo*) to jam

incertezza [in·tʃer·'tet·tsa] *f* 1. (*di notizia, fonte*) doubtful nature 2. (*di condizione, sviluppi*) uncertainty 3. (*titubanza*) uncertainty

incerto¹ [in·'tʃɛr·to] *agg* 1. (*notizia, attribuzione*) doubtful 2. (*esito, sviluppi, data*) uncertain 3. (*persona*) uncertain 4. (*luce*) feeble; (*suono*) indistinct; (*confine*) unclear 5. (*passo, scrittura*) hesitant 6. (*tempo*) variable

incerto² I. <*sing*> *m* **l'~** the unknown II. *m* **gli -i** the risks

incessante [in·tʃes·'san·te] *agg* 1. (*pioggia, pianto*) incessant 2. (*impegno, pensiero*) constant

incesto [in·'tʃɛs·to] *m* incest

incetta [int·'ʃet·ta] *f* **fare ~ di qc** (*merce, prodotto*) to stockpile sth

inchiesta [iŋ·'kiɛs·ta] *f* 1. (*ricerca*) investigation; (*giornalistica*) report; **~ di mercato** market survey 2. ADM, JUR inquiry; **commissione d'~** commission of inquiry

inchinarsi [iŋ·ki·'naːr·si] *vr* (*per riverenza*) to bow; **~ davanti a qc/qu** to bow down before sb/sth

inchino [iŋ·'kiː·no] *m* (*atto*) bow; **fare un ~** to bow

inchiodare [iŋ·kio·'daː·re] *vt* 1. (*con chiodi*) to nail 2. *fig* (*persona*) to keep; (*con la forza*)

to hold 3. *fig* (*veicolo, ruote*) to stall

inchiodata [iŋ·kio·'daː·ta] *f inf* (*frenata*) **fare un'~** to brake hard

inchiodato, -a [iŋ·kio·'daː·to] *agg* (*persona*) glued; **prezzi -i** prices kept low

inchiostro [iŋ·'kiɔs·tro] *m* 1. (*per scrivere*) ink; **~ di china** Indian ink; **~ simpatico** invisible ink; **nero come l'~** as black as ink; **versare fiumi d'~ su qc** *fig* to write volumes about sth 2. (*di seppia*) cuttlefish ink

inciampare [in·tʃam·'paː·re] *vi* essere *o* avere (*col piede*) to trip; **~ in qc** to trip over sth

incidentale [in·tʃi·den·'taː·le] *agg* 1. (*casuale*) accidental 2. (*secondario*) incidental

incidente [in·tʃi·'dɛn·te] *m* 1. (*disgrazia*) accident; **~ sul lavoro** occupational accident; **~ stradale** traffic accident 2. *fig* (*fatto spiacevole*) incident; **~ diplomatico** diplomatic incident; **~ di percorso** hitch

incidenza [in·tʃi·'dɛn·tsa] *f* 1. *fig* (*peso: di spese*) effect 2. *fig* (*frequenza: di malattia*) frequency

incidere [in·'tʃiː·de·re] <incido, incisi, inciso> I. *vi* avere **~ su qc** (*pesare*) to have an effect on sth II. *vt* 1. (*tagliare*) to carve; (*cute*) to cut into 2. (*scolpire*) to engrave; **~ il legno** to carve wood; **~ la pietra/il rame** to engrave stone/copper 3. (*disco, canzone*) to record

incinta [in·'tʃin·ta] *agg* pregnant; **è ~ di cinque mesi** she's five months pregnant

incipiente [in·tʃi·'piɛn·te] *agg* (*malattia*) incipient

incirca [in·'tʃir·ka] *avv* **all'~** about

incisi [in·'tʃiː·zi] *1. pers sing pass rem di* **incidere**

incisione [in·tʃi·'zioː·ne] *f* 1. (*taglio*) carving; MED (*di ascesso*) lancing; (*della cute*) incision 2. (*tecnica, quadro*) engraving 3. (*di disco, canzone*) recording; **sala d'~** recording studio

incisività [in·tʃi·zi·vi·'ta] <-> *f* (*di discorso, stile*) incisiveness

incisivo¹ [in·tʃi·'ziː·vo] *agg fig* (*discorso, stile*) incisive

incisivo² *m* ANAT incisor

inciso¹ [in·'tʃiː·zo] *pp di* **incidere**

inciso² *m* LING parenthesis; **per ~** in passing

incisore [in·tʃi·'zoː·re] *m* (*artigiano*) engraver

incitamento [in·tʃi·ta·'men·to] *m* 1. (*esortazione*) incitement 2. (*stimolo*) incentive

incitare [in·tʃi·'taː·re] *vt* to urge

inciucio [in·'tʃuː·tʃo] <-ci> *m pej* POL deal

incivile [in·tʃi·'viː·le] I. *agg* 1. (*popolo, legge*) uncivilized 2. (*comportamento, persona*) rude II. *mf* (*persona*) peasant

inciviltà [in·tʃi·vil·'ta] *f* 1. (*di popolo, legge*) barbarity 2. (*di persona, comportamento*) rudeness 3. (*azione*) barbarism

inclassificabile [iŋ·klas·si·fi·'kaː·bi·le] *agg* 1. (*minerale, pianta*) unclassifiable 2. *fig* (*atto, gesto*) disgraceful

inclinabile [iŋ·kli·'naː·bi·le] *agg* (*sedile, piano*) reclining

inclinare [iŋ·kli·'na:·re] **I.** *vt* (*corpo, oggetto, test*) to tilt; (*schienale*) to tilt back **II.** *vi* (*schienale*) to tilt

inclinato, -a [in·kli·'na:·to] *agg* (*corpo, oggetto*) tilted; (*retta, superficie*) sloping; **piano** ~ inclined plane

inclinazione [iŋ·kli·nat·'tsio:·ne] *f* **1.** (*di corpo, piano, superficie*) slope **2.** *fig* (*predisposizione*) inclination

incline [iŋ·'kli:·ne] *agg* **essere** ~ **a qc** to be inclined to sth

includere [iŋ·'klu:·de·re] <includo, inclusi, incluso> *vt* **1.** (*comprendere*) to include **2.** (*in busta, lettera*) to enclose

inclusione [iŋ·klu·'zio:·ne] *f* inclusion

inclusivo, -a [iŋ·klu·'zi:·vo] *agg* (*prezzo*) ~ **di qc** including sth

incluso, -a [iŋ·'klu:·zo] **I.** *pp di* **includere II.** *agg* (*servizio, spese*) included; *inf;* **saremo in sette, -i noi** there will be seven including us

incoerente [iŋ·ko·e·'rɛn·te] *agg* **1.** (*persona, comportamento*) inconsistent **2.** (*discorso, testo*) incoherent

incoerenza [iŋ·ko·e·'rɛn·tsa] *f* **1.** (*caratteristica*) inconsistency **2.** (*cosa incoerente*) incoherency

incognita [iŋ·'kɔɲ·ɲi·ta] *f a. fig* MATH unknown quantity

incognito [iŋ·'kɔɲ·ɲi·to] *m* **in** ~ incognito

incollare [iŋ·kol·'la:·re] **I.** *vt* to stick; **incolla** COMPUT paste **II.** *vr* **1.** (*francobollo*) to stick **2. -rsi a qc/qu** *fig* to stick to sth/sb like glue

incolmabile [iŋ·kol·'ma:·bi·le] *agg* **1.** (*lacuna, vuoto*) unbridgeable; (*dolore*) overwhelming **2.** SPORT (*distacco*) irretrievable

incolore [iŋ·ko·'lo:·re] *agg* **1.** (*liquido, sostanza*) colorless **2.** *fig* dull

incolpare [iŋ·kol·'pa:·re] *vt* **1.** (*persona*) to blame; ~ **qu di qc** to accuse sb of sth **2.** (*destino, circostanze*) to blame

incolto, -a [iŋ·'kol·to] *agg* **1.** (*terreno*) uncultivated **2.** *fig* (*barba, capelli*) unkempt **3.** *fig* (*persona*) uneducated

incolumità [iŋ·ko·lu·mi·'ta] <-> *f* (*di persona*) safety

incombente [iŋ·kom·'bɛn·te] *agg* (*pericolo, rischio*) imminent

incombenza [iŋ·kom·'bɛn·tsa] *f* (*incarico*) task

incombere [iŋ·'kom·be·re] <incombo, incombei *o* incombetti, *manca il pp*> *vi* (*pericolo, rischio*) to threaten

incominciare [iŋ·ko·min·'tʃa:·re] **I.** *vt* (*dare inizio*) to start [*o* to begin]; ~ **a fare qc** to start [*o* begin] to do sth; **incomincia a piovere** it's starting [*o* beginning] to rain **II.** *vi* essere (*avere inizio*) to start [*o* begin]

incommensurabile [iŋ·kom·men·su·'ra:·bi·le] *agg* (*spazio, distanza*) immeasurable; (*bene, valore*) incalculable; (*sentimento*) boundless

incomodo, -a *agg* **terzo** ~ (*persona inoppor-*

tuna) gooseberry

incomparabile [iŋ·kom·pa·'ra:·bi·le] *agg* (*eccezionale*) incomparable

incompatibile [iŋ·kom·pa·'ti:·bi·le] *agg* (*inconciliabile*) incompatible

incompatibilità [iŋ·kom·pa·ti·bi·li·'ta] <-> *f* (*inconciliabilità*) incompatibility; ~ **di carattere** mutual incompatibility

incompetente [iŋ·kom·pe·'tɛn·te] **I.** *agg* incompetent; **essere** ~ **in qc** to know nothing about sth **II.** *mf* **1.** (*in una materia*) ignoramus **2.** (*nella professione*) incompetent

incompetenza [iŋ·kom·pe·'tɛn·tsa] *f* **1.** (*in una materia*) lack of knowledge **2.** (*nella professione*) incompetence

incompiuto, -a [iŋ·kom·'piu:·to] *agg* (*progetto, opera*) unfinished

incompleto, -a [iŋ·kom·'plɛ:·to] *agg* (*informazione, raccolta*) incomplete

incomprensibile [iŋ·kom·pren·'si:·bi·le] *agg* (*discorso, scrittura, comportamento*) incomprehensible; (*persona*) hard to understand

incomprensione [iŋ·kom·pren·'sio:·ne] *f* **1.** (*caratteristica*) incomprehension **2.** (*malinteso*) misunderstanding

incompreso, -a [iŋ·kom·'pre:·so] **I.** *agg* misunderstood **II.** *m, f* (*persona*) misunderstood person; **sono un** ~! nobody understands me!

incomunicabilità [iŋ·ko·mu·ni·ka:·bi·li·'ta] <-> *f* (*tra persone*) lack of communication

inconcepibile [iŋ·kon·tʃe·'pi:·bi·le] *agg* (*assurdo, incredibile*) inconceivable

inconciliabile [iŋ·kon·tʃi·'lia:·bi·le] *agg* (*punto di vista, tesi*) irreconcilable

inconcludente [iŋ·koɲ·klu·'dɛn·te] *agg* **1.** (*sforzo, discorso*) inconclusive **2.** (*persona*) ineffectual

incondizionato, -a [iŋ·kon·dit·tsio·'na:·to] *agg* unconditional; **resa -a** unconditional surrender

inconfondibile [iŋ·kon·fon·'di:·bi·le] *agg* (*voce, stile*) unmistakable

inconfutabile [iŋ·kon·fu·'ta:·bi·le] *agg* (*prova, teoria*) irrefutable

incongruenza [iŋ·koɲ·gru·'ɛn·tsa] *f* **1.** (*caratteristica*) contradictory nature **2.** (*contraddizione*) inconsistency

incongruo, -a [iŋ·'kɔɲ·gruo] *agg* (*compenso, retribuzione*) inadequate

inconsapevole [iŋ·kon·sa·'pe:·vo·le] *agg* **1.** (*persona*) unaware **2.** (*gesto*) unconscious

inconscio¹ [iŋ·'kɔn·ʃo] <-sci, -sce> *agg* (*atto, desiderio*) unconscious

inconscio² <*sing*> *m* PSYCH l'~ the unconscious; l'~ **collettivo** the collective unconscious

inconsistente [iŋ·kon·sis·'tɛn·te] *agg* **1.** (*tessuto, materiale*) flimsy **2.** *fig* (*accusa, prova*) unfounded; (*discorso, tesi*) groundless **3.** *fig* (*persona*) shallow

inconsistenza [iŋ·kon·sis·'tɛn·tsa] *f* **1.** (*di tessuto, materiale*) flimsiness **2.** *fig* (*di accusa, prova*) lack of foundation; (*di discorso, tesi*) groundlessness

inconsueto, -a [iŋ·kon·su·'ɛː·to] *agg* (*insolito*) unusual

incontaminato, -a [iŋ·kon·ta·mi·'na:·to] *agg* (*luogo*) uncontaminated

incontenibile [in·kon·te·'ni:·bi·le] *agg* (*impeto, avanzata*) unstoppable; (*riso, pianto*) uncontrollable

incontestabile [iŋ·kon·tes·'ta:·bi·le] *agg* indisputable

incontinenza [iŋ·kon·ti·'nɛn·tsa] *f* MED incontinence

incontrare [iŋ·kon·'tra:·re] I. *vt* 1. (*per appuntamento*) to meet; (*per caso*) to bump into 2. (*difficoltà, problema*) to come up against; (*favore*) to win over 3. SPORT (*avversario, squadra*) to meet II. *vr:* -**rsi** 1. (*per appuntamento*) to meet each other; (*per caso*) to bump into each other; -**rsi con qu** to meet with sb 2. SPORT to meet each other 3. (*strade, fiumi*) to meet up

incontrastato, -a [iŋ·kon·tras·'ta:·to] *agg* (*successo, dominio*) undisputed

incontro¹ [iŋ·'kon·tro] *m* 1. (*casuale*) encounter; **fare un brutto ~** to have a nasty encounter; (*per appuntamento*) meeting; **~ di lavoro** work meeting; **~ al vertice** summit; (*convegno*) conference 2. SPORT match

incontro² *prep* 1. **~ a qu/qc** (*in direzione di*) toward sb/sth; **andare ~ a qc/qu** to go toward sth/sb; **venire ~ a qc/qu** to come toward sth/sb 2. **andare ~ a qc** *fig* (*pericoli, difficoltà*) to come up against sth; **andare/ venire ~ a qu** *fig* (*aiutarlo*) to meet sb halfway

incontrollabile [iŋ·kon·trol·'la:·bi·le] *agg* 1. (*desiderio, impulso*) uncontrollable 2. (*notizia, dato*) unverifiable

incontrollato, -a [iŋ·kon·trol·'la:·to] *agg* 1. (*gesto, reazione*) uncontrolled 2. (*notizia, fonte*) unverified

incontrovertibile [iŋ·kon·tro·ver·'ti:·bi·le] *agg* (*diritto, prova*) incontrovertible

inconveniente [iŋ·kon·ve·'niɛn·te] *m* 1. (*ostacolo*) difficulty 2. (*svantaggio*) drawback

incoraggiamento [iŋ·ko·rad·dʒa·'men·to] *m* (*incitamento, esortazione*) encouragement; **parole di ~** words of encouragement; **premio di ~** consolation prize

incoraggiante [in·ko·rad·'dʒan·te] *agg* (*parole, notizie, risultato*) encouraging

incoraggiare [iŋ·ko·rad·'dʒa:·re] *vt* to encourage

incorniciare [iŋ·kor·ni·'tʃa:·re] *vt* (*foto, quadro*) to frame; **da ~** (*memorabile: vittoria, trionfo*) memorable

incoronazione [iŋ·ko·ro·nat·'tsio:·ne] *f* (*di re, vincitore*) coronation

incorporare [iŋ·kor·po·'ra:·re] *vt* 1. (*elementi, sostanze*) to mix (in) 2. *fig* (*provincia, azienda*) to incorporate

incorrere [iŋ·'kor·re·re] <incorro, incorsi, incorso> *vi* **essere ~ in qc** (*errore, sanzione*) to incur sth; **~ in un pericolo** to run into danger

ger

incorruttibile [iŋ·kor·rut·'ti:·bi·le] *agg* (*persona*) incorruptible

incorsi [iŋ·'kor·si] *l. pers sing pass rem di* **incorrere**

incorso [iŋ·'kor·so] *pp di* **incorrere**

incosciente [iŋ·koʃ·'ʃɛn·te] I. *agg* 1. (*svenuto*) unconscious 2. (*irresponsabile*) irresponsible II. *mf* (*irresponsabile*) irresponsible person; **agire da ~** to behave irresponsibly

incoscienza [iŋ·ko·'ʃɛn·tsa] *f* 1. (*stato*) unconsciousness 2. (*irresponsabilità*) irresponsibility

incostante [iŋ·kos·'tan·te] *agg* 1. (*persona, carattere*) fickle; **essere ~ in qc** to be inconsistent in sth 2. (*impegno, rendimento*) inconsistent

incostituzionale [iŋ·kos·ti·tut·tsio·'na:·le] *agg* JUR (*provvedimento, norma*) unconstitutional

incredibile [iŋ·kre·'di:·bi·le] *agg* incredible

incredulità [iŋ·kre·du·li·'ta] <-> *f* incredulity

incredulo, -a [iŋ·'krɛ:·du·lo] *agg* (*persona, sguardo*) incredulous

incrementare [iŋ·kre·men·'ta:·re] *vt* to increase

incremento [iŋ·kre·'men·to] *m* (*di produzione, consumo*) increase; **~ della popolazione** population growth

increscioso, -a [iŋ·kreʃ·'ʃo:·so] *agg* (*episodio, incidente*) regrettable

incriminato, -a [in·kri·mi·'na:·to] *agg* JUR (*persona, arma*) indicted

incriminazione [iŋ·kri·mi·nat·'tsio:·ne] *f* JUR indictment

incrinare [iŋ·kri·'na:·re] I. *vt* 1. (*bicchiere, piatto*) to crack 2. *fig* (*rapporto, amicizia*) to spoil II. *vr:* -**rsi** 1. (*bicchiere, piatto, voce*) to crack 2. *fig* (*rapporto, amicizia*) to worsen

incrociare [iŋ·kro·'tʃa:·re] I. *vt* 1. (*assi, bastoni, gambe*) to cross; **~ le braccia** *fig* to strike; **~ le dita** *fig* to cross one's fingers 2. (*strada*) to cut across 3. (*persona, veicolo*) to meet 4. BIOL to cross II. *vr:* -**rsi** 1. (*strade*) to cross 2. (*persone, veicoli*) to meet 3. BIOL to cross

incrocio [iŋ·'kro:·tʃo] <-ci> *m* 1. (*di assi, travi*) crossing 2. (*di strade*) junction 3. BIOL cross

incrollabile [iŋ·krol·'la:·bi·le] *agg* 1. (*edificio, muro*) indestructible 2. *fig* (*fede, volontà*) unwavering

incubatrice [iŋ·ku·ba·'tri:·tʃe] *f* (*per neonati*) incubator

incubazione [iŋ·ku·bat·'tsio:·ne] *f* (*di malattia*) incubation

incubo ['iŋ·ku·bo] *m a. fig* nightmare

incudine [iŋ·'ku:·di·ne] *f* (*attrezzo*) anvil; **tra l'~ e il martello** *fig* between the devil and the deep blue sea

incurabile [iŋ·ku·'ra:·bi·le] *agg* (*malattia, malato*) incurable; **male ~** (*cancro*) cancer

incurante [iŋ·ku·'ran·te] *agg* **~ di qc** (*pericolo, critiche*) indifferent to sth

incuria [iŋ·'ku:·ria] *f* (*negligenza*) neglect

incuriosire [iŋ·ku·rio·'si:·re] <incuriosisco>

I. *vt* to intrigue II. *vr:* **-rsi** to become curious; **-rsi di qc** to become curious about sth

incursione [iŋ·kur·'sio:·ne] *f* **1.** (*di soldati, polizia, ladri*) raid **2.** *inf* (*di ospiti*) invasion; (*in cucina, dispensa*) foray

incustodito, -a [iŋ·kus·to·'di:·to] *agg* (*macchina, bagaglio*) unattended; (*parcheggio, passaggio a livello*) unmanned

indaco ['in·da·ko] **I.** *m* (*colore*) indigo **II.** <inv> *agg* indigo

indaffarato, -a [in·daf·fa·'ra:·to] *agg* busy; **essere ~ in qc** to be busy with sth

indagare [in·da·'ga:·re] *vi* to investigate; **~ su qc** JUR to investigate sth

indagato, -a [in·da·'ga:·to] **I.** *agg* (*persona*) investigated **II.** *m*, *f* person under investigation; **registro degli -i** *list of people under investigation by the police*

indagine [in·'da:·dʒi·ne] *f* **1.** (*ricerca*) research; **~ di mercato** market research **2.** JUR investigation; **giudice per le -i preliminari** [*o* **GIP**] *the magistrate appointed to supervise the initial police investigation into a case*

indebitamento [in·de·bi·ta·'men·to] *m* indebtedness

indebito, -a [in·'de:·bi·to] *agg* (*illecito*) illegal

indebolimento [in·de·bo·li·'men·to] *m* (*di persona*) weakening; (*di udito, vista*) failing

indebolire [in·de·bo·'li:·re] <indebolisco> **I.** *vt avere* **1.** (*persona*) to weaken; (*vista, udito*) to worsen **2.** *fig* (*autorità, capacità*) to weaken **II.** *vr:* **-rsi** (*persona, autorità, capacità*) to grow weak; (*vista, udito*) to worsen

indecente [in·de·'tʃɛn·te] *agg* **1.** (*scollatura, proposta*) indecent **2.** (*indecoroso*) dreadful

indecenza [in·de·'tʃɛn·tsa] *f* **1.** (*caratteristica*) indecency **2.** (*cosa vergognosa*) disgrace; **è un'~!** it's a disgrace!

indecifrabile [in·de·tʃi·'fra:·bi·le] *agg* **1.** (*scrittura, messaggio*) indecipherable **2.** *fig* (*persona, sguardo*) unreadable

indecisione [in·de·tʃi·'zio:·ne] *f* indecision

indeciso, -a [in·de·'tʃi:·zo] **I.** *agg* (*persona, carattere*) undecided **II.** *m*, *f* wobbler

indecoroso, -a [in·de·ko·'ro:·so] *agg* (*comportamento, condizioni*) unseemly

indefinibile [in·de·fi·'ni:·bi·le] *agg* (*colore, odore, sapore*) nondescript; (*sentimento, sensazione*) indefinable

indefinito, -a [in·de·fi·'ni:·to] *agg* **1.** (*quantità*) indefinite; (*sensazione, idea*) vague **2.** (*questione*) unresolved **3.** LING (*modo, pronome*) indefinite

indegno, -a [in·'deɲ·ɲo] *agg* (*persona, comportamento*) shameful; **essere ~ di qc/qu** to be unworthy of sth/sb

indelebile [in·de·'lɛ:·bi·le] *agg a. fig* indelible

indelicato, -a [in·de·li·'ka:·to] *agg* (*persona, comportamento, domanda*) tactless

indenne [in·'dɛn·ne] *agg* **1.** (*da incidente*) unharmed **2.** (*da malattia*) uncontaminated

indennità [in·den·ni·'ta] <-> *f* **1.** (*compenso*) allowance; **~ parlamentare** parliamentary salary; **~ di trasferta** travel expenses *pl* **2.** (*sussidio*) benefit

indennizzare [in·den·nid·'dza:·re] *vt* JUR to compensate; **~ qu di qc** to compensate sb for sth

indennizzo [in·den·'nid·dzo] *m* JUR compensation

inderogabile [in·de·ro·'ga:·bi·le] *agg* (*principio*) binding; (*impegno*) unavoidable

indescrivibile [in·des·kri·'vi:·bi·le] *agg* indescribable

indesiderato, -a [in·de·si·de·'ra:·to] *agg* **1.** (*persona, ospite*) unwanted **2.** (*effetto, conseguenza*) undesired

indeterminatezza [in·de·ter·mi·na·'tet·tsa] *f* vagueness

indeterminato, -a [in·de·ter·mi·'na:·to] *agg* (*quantità, luogo, tempo*) undetermined; **contratto a tempo ~** permanent employment contract

indetto [in·'det·to] *pp di* **indire**

indi ['in·di] *avv lit* (*dopo*) then

India ['in·dia] *f* l'**~** India; **abitare in ~** to live in India; **andare in ~** to go to India

indiano, -a [in·'dia:·no] **I.** *agg* **1.** (*dell'India*) Indian; **Oceano Indiano** Indian Ocean **2.** (*d'America*) Native American; **in fila -a** single file **II.** *m*, *f* **1.** (*dell'India*) Indian **2.** (*d'America*) Native American

indiavolato, -a [in·dia·vo·'la:·to] *agg* (*bambino*) unruly; (*ritmo, chiasso*) frenzied

indicare [in·di·'ka:·re] *vt* **1.** (*con parole*) to show; (*con gesto*) to point out **2.** (*strumento, segnale*) to indicate; (*orologio*) to say; (*etichetta, istruzioni*) to explain **3.** (*consigliare*) to recommend **4.** (*rivelare*) to indicate; (*vocabolo*) to indicate

indicativo¹ [in·di·ka·'ti:·vo] *agg* **1.** (*rivelatore*) indicative **2.** (*cifra, prezzo*) approximate **3. modo ~** LING indicative

indicativo² *m* LING indicative

indicato, -a [in·di·'ka:·to] *agg* (*adatto*) suitable

indicatore¹ [in·di·ka·'to:·re] *agg* (*cartello, tabella*) explanatory

indicatore² *m* **1.** (*dispositivo*) gauge; **~ di direzione** indicator; **~ di velocità** speedometer **2.** ECON indicator

indicazione [in·di·kat·'tsio:·ne] *f* **1.** (*informazione*) information **2.** (*suggerimento*) recommendation **3.** *pl* (*istruzioni*) instructions

indice ['in·di·tʃe] *m* **1.** (*dito*) index finger **2.** (*di libro*) index; **~ analitico** index **3.** (*di strumento*) needle **4.** (*rapporto*) index; **~ d'ascolto** ratings *pl;* **~ di gradimento** popularity rating; **~ di natalità** birth rate; **~ del costo della vita** cost of living index **5.** *fig* (*indizio*) indication

indicibile [in·di·'tʃi:·bi·le] *agg* unspeakable

indicizzare [in·di·tʃid·'dza:·re] *vt* ECON to index

indicizzato, -a [in·di·tʃid·'dza:·to] *agg* ECON indexed

indicizzazione [in·di·tʃid·dzat·'tsio:·ne] *f* ECON indexing

indico [in·'di:·ko] *1. pers sing pr di* **indire**

indietro [in·'diɛ:·tro] *avv* 1. (*luogo*) back; **rimanere** ~ to be left behind; **tornare** ~ to turn back; **voltarsi** ~ to turn around; **all'**~ backwards 2. (*tempo*) **essere** ~ **col lavoro** to be behind with one's work 3. (*orologio*) **essere** ~ to be slow; **il mio orologio va** ~ **di cinque minuti** my watch is five minutes slow 4. (*paese, agricoltura*) backward

indifeso, -a [in·di·'fe:·so] *agg* 1. (*luogo, postazione*) undefended 2. (*persona*) defenseless

indifferente [in·dif·fe·'rɛn·te] I. *agg* 1. (*persona*) indifferent; **lasciare qu** ~ to leave sb cold 2. (*non importante*) qc/qu è ~ a qu to not care less about sth/sb; **quel ragazzo mi è** ~ I couldn't care less about that boy 3. (*scelta, questione*) **essere** ~ to be all the same; **non** ~ (*notevole: somma*) considerable II. *m* (*persona*) indifferent person; **fare l'**~ to pretend not to care

indifferenza [in·dif·fe·'rɛn·tsa] *f* indifference

indigeno, -a [in·'di:·dʒe·no] I. *agg* (*popolazione*) indigenous; (*prodotto*) local II. *m, f* (*persona*) native

indigenza [in·di·'dʒɛn·tsa] *f* (*povertà*) poverty

indigestione [in·di·dʒes·'tio:·ne] *f* 1. (*di cibo*) indigestion; **fare un'**~ **di dolci** to eat too much cake 2. *fig* (*di libri, film*) **ho fatto un'**~ **di latino** I've had more than enough of Latin

indignarsi [in·diɲ·'ɲa:r·si] *vr* to get indignant; **-rsi per qc** to get indignant about sth

indignato, -a [in·diɲ·'ɲa:·to] *agg* (*persona, reazione*) indignant; ~ (**contro qu**) (**per qc**) indignant (with sb) (about sth)

indignazione [in·diɲ·ɲat·'tsio:·ne] *f* indignation; **suscitare** ~ to cause indignation

indimenticabile [in·di·men·ti·'ka:·bi·le] *agg* (*fatto, persona*) unforgettable

indipendente [in·di·pen·'dɛn·te] *agg* 1. (*persona, gruppo, nazione*) independent; **essere** ~ **da qu/qc** to independent of sb/sth 2. (*fatto, evento*) unrelated; **essere** ~ **da qu/qc** to have nothing to do with sb/sth

indipendenza [in·di·pen·'dɛn·tsa] *f* (*di persona, gruppo, nazione*) independence

indire [in·'di:·re] <indico, indissi, indetto> *vt* (*concorso*) to announce; (*elezioni*) to call

indiretto, -a [in·di·'rɛt·to] *agg* 1. (*causa, conseguenza*) indirect; **per vie -e** indirectly 2. LING **complementi -i** indirect; **discorso** ~ indirect speech

indirizzare [in·di·rit·'tsa:·re] *vt* 1. (*persona*) to send; ~ **i passi** [*o* **il cammino**] **verso un luogo** to set off toward a place; ~ **qu da qu** to send sb to sb; ~ **qu a qc** *fig* to direct sb toward sth 2. (*posta*) to address

indirizzario [in·di·rit·'tsa:·rio] *m* mailing list

indirizzo [in·di·'rit·tso] *m* 1. (*di persona*) address; ~ **di posta elettronica** e-mail address 2. *fig* (*orientamento*) **a indirizzo umanistico** humanistically oriented

indisciplinato, -a [in·di·ʃi·pli·'na:·to] *agg* (*persona, comportamento*) undisciplined

indiscreto, -a [in·dis·'kre:·to] *agg* 1. (*persona*) intrusive; **se non sono** ~ (*formula di cortesia*) if you don't mind me asking 2. (*domanda*) indiscreet; (*sguardo*) prying

indiscrezione [in·dis·kret·'tsio:·ne] *f* 1. (*atto indelicato*) impertinence 2. (*notizia segreta*) gossip

indiscriminato, -a [in·dis·kri·mi·'na:·to] *agg* (*uso, aumento*) indiscriminate

indiscusso, -a [in·dis·'kus·so] *agg* (*fama, competenza*) undisputed

indiscutibile [in·dis·ku·'ti:·bi·le] *agg* unquestionable

indispensabile [in·dis·pen·'sa:·bi·le] I. *agg* 1. (*necessario*) essential; (*firma, consenso*) indispensable 2. (*persona*) indispensable II. *sing* **l'**~ the necessities *pl;* **lo stretto** ~ the bare necessities *pl*

indisponibile [in·dis·po·'ni:·bi·le] *agg* 1. (*cosa*) unavailable 2. (*persona, non pronto*) unwilling; (*non libero*) unavailable; ~ **a** [*o* **per**] **qc** (*non pronto*) to not be open to sth; (*non libero*) to be unavailable for sth 3. JUR (*bene, diritto*) inalienable

indissi [in·'dis·si] *1. pers sing pass rem di* **indire**

indissolubile [in·dis·so·'lu:·bi·le] *agg* (*legame, patto*) indissoluble

indistinto, -a [in·dis·'tin·to] *agg* 1. (*figura, suono*) indistinct 2. (*insieme, massa*) amorphous

indistruttibile [in·dis·trut·'ti:·bi·le] *agg* 1. (*materiale, macchina*) indestructible 2. (*fede, principio*) unwavering

indisturbato, -a [in·dis·tur·'ba:·to] *agg* undisturbed

indivia [in·'di:·via] <-ie> *f* endive

individuale [in·di·vi·du·'a:·le] *agg* individual

individualismo [in·di·vi·dua·'liz·mo] *m* (*egoismo*) individualism

individualista [in·di·vi·dua·'lis·ta] <-i *m*, -e *f*> *mf* (*egoista*) individualist

individualità [in·di·vi·dua·li·'ta] <-> *f* individuality

individuare [in·di·vi·du·'a:·re] *vt* 1. (*colpevole*) to identify; (*obiettivo*) to locate; ~ **qu tra la folla** to pick sb out of the crowd 2. (*causa, guasto*) to identify

individuazione [in·di·vi·duat·'tsio:·ne] *f* 1. (*di colpevole*) identification; (*di obiettivo*) location 2. (*di causa, guasto*) identification

individuo [in·di·'vi:·duo] *m a. pej* individual

indivisibile [in·di·vi·'zi:·bi·le] *agg* (*entità, numero*) indivisible

indiziato, -a [in·dit·'tsia:·to] I. *agg* suspected II. *m, f* suspect

indizio [in·'dit·tsio] <-i> *m* 1. (*sintomo*) sign 2. JUR evidence

Indocina [in·do·'tʃi:·na] *f* **l'**~ Indochina; **vivere in** ~ to live in Indochina; **andare in** ~ to go to Indochina

indoeuropeo, -a <-ei, -ee> *agg* (*lingua, popolazione*) Indo-European

indole ['inˑdoˑle] *f* (*temperamento*) temperament

indolente [inˑdoˑ'lɛnˑte] *agg* (*persona, carattere*) indolent

indolenza [inˑdoˑ'lɛnˑtsa] *f* (*di persona, carattere*) indolence

indolore [inˑdoˑ'loːˑre] *agg a. fig* painless

indomabile [inˑdoˑ'maːˑbiˑle] *agg* **1.** (*cavallo*) unbreakable **2.** *fig* (*incendio*) uncontrollable; (*carattere, volontà*) indomitable

indomani [inˑdoˑ'maːˑni] *m* l'~ the next day

indomito, -a [inˑ'doˑmiˑto] *agg fig, lit* (*cuore, spirito*) indomitable

Indonesia [inˑdoˑ'neːˑzia] *f* l'~ Indonesia; **abitare in** ~ to live in Indonesia; **andare in** ~ to go to Indonesia

indonesiano¹ [inˑdoˑneˑ'ziaːˑno] <*sing*> *sing* (*lingua*) Indonesian

indonesiano² **I.** *agg* (*dell'Indonesia*) Indonesian **II.** *m* (*abitante*) Indonesian

indossare [inˑdosˑ'saːˑre] *vt* **1.** (*portare*) to wear **2.** (*mettersi*) to put on

indossatore, -trice [inˑdosˑsaˑ'toːˑre] *m, f* (*uomo*) male model; (*donna*) model

indosso [inˑ'dɔsˑso] *avv* **avere/mettersi** ~ **qc** to have/put sth on

indotto¹ [inˑ'dɔtˑto] **I.** *pp di* **indurre** **II.** *agg* **1.** (*fatto, fenomeno*) caused **2.** PHYS (*carica, corrente*) induced

indotto² <*sing*> *m* ECON supplier industry; ~ **automobilistico** automotive supplier industry

indovinare [inˑdoˑviˑ'naːˑre] *vt* **1.** (*intuire*) to guess; (*risultato, gusti*) to predict; (*soluzione, risposta*) to get right; **tirare a** ~ to have a guess **2.** (*scegliere bene*) to choose well; **non indovinarne una** to get nothing right

indovinato, -a [inˑdoˑviˑ'naːˑto] *agg* (*regalo, scelta*) successful

indovinello [inˑdoˑviˑ'nɛlˑlo] *m* (*quesito*) puzzle

indovino, -a [inˑdoˑ'viːˑno] *m, f* (*mago*) fortuneteller

indù [inˑ'du] **I.** <*inv*> *agg* (*dell'India, dell'induismo*) Hindu **II.** <-> *mf* (*abitante*) Hindu

indubbio, -a [inˑ'dubˑbio] <-i, -ie> *agg* undeniable

indubitabile [inˑduˑbiˑ'taːˑbiˑle] *agg* unquestionable

induco [inˑ'duːˑko] *1. pers sing pr di* **indurre**

indugiare [inˑduˑ'dʒaːˑre] *vi* (*tardare*) to delay; ~ **a fare qc** to hesitate to do sth

indugio [inˑ'duːˑdʒo] <-gi> *m* (*ritardo*) delay; **senza** ~ without delay

induismo [inˑduˑ'izˑmo] *m* REL Hinduism

induista [inˑduˑ'isˑta] <-i *m*, -e *f*> *mf* (*seguace*) Hindu

indulgente [inˑdulˑ'dʒɛnˑte] *agg* **1.** (*persona, sguardo, sorriso*) indulgent **2.** (*giudizio, critica*) lenient

indulgenza [inˑdulˑ'dʒɛnˑtsa] *f* (*comprensione*) leniency

indumento [inˑduˑ'menˑto] *m* (*abito*) garment; **-i intimi** underwear

indurimento [inˑduˑriˑ'menˑto] *m a. fig* MED hardening

indurre [inˑ'durˑre] <induco, indussi, indotto> *vt* **1.** *fig* (*spingere*) to persuade; ~ **qu a fare qc** to persuade sb do sth; ~ **qu in errore** to mislead sb; ~ **qu in tentazione** to tempt sb **2.** (*medicinale*) to cause

indussi [inˑ'dusˑsi] *1. pers sing pass rem di* **indurre**

industria [inˑ'dusˑtriˑa] <-ie> *f* **1.** (*attività*) industry; ~ **leggera** light industry; ~ **pesante** heavy industry **2.** (*fabbrica*) factory

industriale [inˑdusˑ'triaːˑle] **I.** *agg* industrial; **zona** ~ industrial area **II.** *mf* (*imprenditore*) industrialist

industrializzato [inˑdusˑtriaˑlidˑ'dzaːˑto] *agg* (*paese, regione*) industrialized

industrializzazione [inˑdusˑtriaˑlidˑdzatˑ'tsioːˑne] *f* (*di paese, settore*) industrialization

induttivo, -a *agg* (*procedimento, ragionamento*) inductive

induzione [inˑdutˑ'tsioːˑne] *f* **1.** (*supposizione*) deduction **2.** PHYS, JUR induction

inebriante [inˑeˑbriˑ'anˑte] *agg* (*profumo, bevanda*) intoxicating

ineccepibile [inˑetˑtʃeˑ'piːˑbiˑle] *agg* **1.** (*ragionamento*) unassailable **2.** (*persona, comportamento*) exemplary

inedia [iˑ'neːˑdia] *f* **1.** (*digiuno*) starvation **2.** *fig* (*noia*) boredom

inedito¹ [iˑ'nɛːˑdiˑto] *agg* (*scritto, autore*) unpublished

inedito² *m* (*testo*) unpublished work

inefficace [inˑefˑfiˑ'kaːˑtʃe] *agg* ineffective

inefficacia [inˑefˑfiˑ'kaːˑtʃa] *f* ineffectiveness

inefficiente [inˑefˑfiˑ'tʃɛnˑte] *agg* inefficient

inefficienza [inˑefˑfiˑ'tʃɛnˑtsa] *f* inefficiency

ineguagliabile [inˑeˑguaʎˑ'ʎaːˑbiˑle] *agg* (*artista, atleta*) incomparable; (*record, talento*) unbeatable

ineguale [inˑeˑ'guaːˑle] *agg* **1.** (*altezza, forza, valore*) unequal **2.** (*terreno, stile*) uneven

ineleggibilità [inˑeˑledˑdʒiˑbiˑliˑ'ta] <-> *f* ineligibility

ineluttabile [inˑeˑlutˑ'taːˑbiˑle] *agg* (*destino, sorte*) inevitable

ineluttabilità [inˑeˑlutˑtaˑbiˑliˑ'ta] <-> *f* (*di destino, evento*) inevitability

inequivocabile [inˑeˑkuiˑvoˑ'kaːˑbiˑle] *agg* (*atteggiamento, risposta*) unequivocal

inerente [inˑeˑ'rɛnˑte] *agg* ~ **a qc** regarding sth

inerme [iˑ'nɛrˑme] *agg* **1.** (*senza armi*) unarmed **2.** *fig* (*senza difese*) defenseless

inerte [iˑ'nɛrˑte] *agg* **1.** (*persona*) motionless **2.** (*corpo, arto*) lifeless **3.** CHEM, PHYS inert

inerzia [iˑ'nɛrˑtsia] <-ie> *f a. fig* PHYS inertia; **fare qc per** ~ *fig* to do sth by force of habit

inesattezza [inˑeˑzatˑ'tetˑtsa] *f* **1.** (*caratteristica*) inaccuracy **2.** (*errore*) mistake

inesatto, -a [inˑeˑ'zatˑto] *agg* (*calcolo, ris-*

posta) inaccurate

inesauribile [in·e·zau·'ri:·bi·le] *agg* **1.** (*fonte, risorsa*) inexhaustible **2.** *fig* (*fantasia, argomento*) endless

inesistente [in·e·zis·'tɛn·te] *agg* inexistent

inesistenza [in·e·zis·'tɛn·tsa] *f* inexistence

inesorabile [in·e·zo·'ra:·bi·le] *agg* **1.** (*giudice*) harsh; (*vendetta*) relentless **2.** (*destino, malattia*) relentless

inesperienza [in·es·pe·'riɛn·tsa] *f* inexperience

inesperto, -a [in·es·'pɛr·to] *agg* inexperienced; **essere ~ di qc** to have no experience of sth

inesplorato, -a [in·es·plo·'ra:·to] *agg* **1.** (*luogo*) unexplored **2.** *fig* untouched

inespugnabile [in·es·puɲ·'ɲa:·bi·le] *agg* (*città, fortezza*) impregnable

inestimabile [in·es·ti·'ma:·bi·le] *agg* (*bene, valore*) inestimable

inestricabile [in·es·tri·'ka:·bi·le] *agg a. fig* inextricable

inettitudine [in·et·ti·'tu:·di·ne] *f* (*incapacità*) incompetency

inetto, -a [i·'nɛt·to] I. *agg* (*persona*) incompetent II. *m, f* incompetent

inevitabile¹ [in·e·vi·'ta:·bi·le] *agg* **1.** (*errore, danno*) unavoidable **2.** (*risultato, conseguenza*) inevitable

inevitabile² *<sing> m* l'~ the inevitable

in extremis [in eks·'trɛ:·mis] *avv* at the last moment

inezia [i·'nɛt·tsia] *<-ie> f* (*piccolezza*) trifle; **costare/pagare un'~** to cost/pay next to nothing

infallibile [in·fal·'li:·bi·le] *agg* **1.** (*persona*) infallible **2.** (*mira*) unerring; (*metodo, sistema*) foolproof

infamante [in·fa·'man·te] *agg* (*accusa*) defamatory

infame [in·'fa:·me] I. *agg* **1.** (*persona*) heinous **2.** (*tradimento, accusa*) vile **3.** *inf* (*tempo, viaggio*) foul; (*fatica*) dreadful II. *mf* (*persona*) wicked person

infamia [in·'fa:·mia] *<-ie> f* **1.** (*condizione*) infamy; **senza ~ e senza lode** nothing special **2.** (*cosa vergognosa*) disgraceful deed

infanticidio [in·fan·ti·'tʃi:·dio] *<-i> m* JUR infanticide

infantile [in·fan·'ti:·le] *agg* **1.** (*di bambino*) childrens'; **asilo ~** nursery school **2.** *fig* (*persona, atteggiamento*) childish

infanzia [in·'fan·tsia] *<-ie> f* **1.** (*periodo*) childhood; **prima ~** infancy **2.** (*bambini*) children

infarto [in·'far·to] *m* MED heart attack; **da ~** *fig, inf* (*velocità, partita*) frightening

infastidire [in·fas·ti·'di:·re] <infastidisco> I. *vt* to bother II. *vr* **-rsi per qc** to get annoyed with sth

infaticabile [in·fa·ti·'ka:·bi·le] *agg* (*persona*) untiring

infatti [in·'fat·ti] *cong* in fact; (*come risposta*) indeed

infatuazione [in·fa·tua·'tsio:·ne] *f* infatuation; **avere un'~ per qu/qc** to be infatuated with sb/sth

infausto, -a [in·'faus·to] *agg* (*luogo, giorno*) unhappy; (*presagio*) unfavorable

infedele [in·fe·'de:·le] *agg* (*amico*) disloyal; (*amante*) unfaithful

infedeltà [in·fe·del·'ta] *f* (*caratteristica*) disloyalty; (*di un coniuge*) infidelity

infelice [in·fe·'li:·tʃe] I. *agg* **1.** (*persona, infanzia, vita*) unhappy; **amore ~** unhappy love story **2.** (*scelta, frase*) unfortunate **3.** (*clima, posto*) poor II. *mf* (*persona*) wretch

infelicità [in·fe·li·tʃi·'ta] *<-> f* (*di persona*) unhappiness

inferiore [in·fe·'rio:·re] *comp di* **basso** lower I. *agg* **1.** (*per posizione*) lower **2.** (*per dimensioni, quantità*) smaller; **~ a qc** below sth **3.** *fig* (*per qualità*) inferior; **~ a qu/qc** inferior to sb/sth **4.** *fig* (*per grado*) lower II. *mf* inferior

inferiorità [in·fe·rio·ri·'ta] *<-> f* inferiority

inferire [in·fe·'ri:·re] <inferisco, infersi, inferto> *vt* (*danni*) to inflict; **~ un colpo** to strike

infermeria [in·fer·me·'ri:·a] *<-ie> f* (*ambulatorio*) sick bay

infermiere, -a [in·fer·'miɛ:·re] *m, f* male nurse *m*, nurse *f*

infermieristico, -a [in·fer·mie·'ris·ti·ko] *<-ci, -che> agg* nursing

infermità [in·fer·mi·'ta] *<-> f* (*malattia*) illness; **~ mentale** mental illness

infermo, -a [in·'fer·mo] I. *agg* (*malato*) ill II. *m, f* sick person

infernale [in·fer·'na:·le] *agg* **1.** (*piano, macchinazione*) infernal; **macchina ~** *fig* infernal device **2.** (*rumore, caldo, giornata*) hellish; (*danza, ritmo*) frenetic **3.** (*creatura, fuoco*) infernal

inferno [in·'fɛr·no] *m a. fig* REL hell; **mandare qu all'~** *fig* to tell sb to go to hell; **d'~** hellish; **questa casa è un ~** this house is bedlam; **durante la rissa si è scatenato l'~** during the fight all hell broke loose

inferriata [in·fer·'ria:·ta] *f* (*di finestra*) grating

infersi [in·'fɛr·si] *1. pers sing pass rem di* **inferire**

inferto [in·'fɛr·to] *pp di* **inferire**

infettare [in·fet·'ta:·re] I. *vt* **1.** (*ferita*) to infect **2.** (*acqua, aria*) to pollute **3.** (*persona, territorio*) to infect II. *vr*: **-rsi 1.** (*ferita*) to become infected **2.** (*persona*) to infect oneself

infettivo, -a [in·fet·'ti:·vo] *agg* (*malattia*) infectious

infetto, -a [in·'fɛt·to] *agg* **1.** (*ferita, persona*) infected **2.** (*acqua, aria*) polluted

infezione [in·fet·'tsio:·ne] *f* MED infection; **fare ~** to become infected

infiammabile [in·fiam·'ma:·bi·le] *agg* (*liquido, gas*) inflammable

infiammabilità [in·fiam·ma·bi·li·'ta] *<-> f* (*di sostanza*) inflammability

infiammato, -a [in·fiam·'ma:·to] *agg* MED inflamed

infiammatorio, -a [in·fiam·ma·'tɔ:·rio] <-i, -ie> *agg* MED inflammatory

infiammazione [in·fiam·mat·'tsio:·ne] *f* MED inflammation

inficiare [in·fit·'ʃa:·re] *vt* **1.** ADM, JUR to nullify **2.** (*ragionamento, tesi*) to invalidate

infido, -a [in·'fi:·do] *agg* **1.** (*persona, comportamento*) unreliable **2.** (*mare, sentiero*) treacherous

infierire [in·fie·'ri:·re] <infierisco> *vi* (*accanirsi*) ~ **su** to turn on; *fig* to rage at

infilare [in·fi·'la:·re] **I.** *vt* **1.** (*ago, perle*) to thread **2.** ~ **qc in qc** to put sth in sth **3.** (*indumento*) to put on **II.** *vr:* **-rsi 1.** (*indumento*) to put on **2.** **-rsi in qc** to get into sth; **-rsi sotto le coperte** to get under the covers; **-rsi tra qu** to mingle with sb

infiltrarsi [in·fil·'trar·si] *vr* **1.** (*umidità, fumo*) to seep **2.** *fig* (*spia*) to infiltrate

infiltrato, -a [in·fil·'tra:·to] *m, f* (*spia*) infiltrator

infiltrazione [in·fil·trat·'tsio:·ne] *f* **1.** (*di acqua, gas*) leak **2.** *fig* (*di spia*) infiltration

infimo, -a ['in·fi·mo] *agg superl di* **basso** (*grado, qualità, valore*) lowest

infine [in·'fi:·ne] *avv* **1.** (*alla fine*) finally **2.** (*insomma*) in short

infinità [in·fi·ni·'ta] <-> *f* **un'~ di qc** (*enorme quantità*) a mass of sth

infinitamente [in·fi·ni·ta·'men·te] *avv* (*immensamente*) infinitely; **vi ringrazio ~** thank you very much indeed

infinitesimale [in·fi·ni·te·zi·'ma:·le] *agg* **1.** (*piccolissimo*) tiniest **2.** MATH infinitesimal

infinito¹ [in·fi·'ni:·to] *agg* **1.** (*spazio, tempo*) infinite; (*quantità*) countless; **grazie -e** many thanks **2.** LING infinitive

infinito² *m* **1.** (*spazio, tempo illimitato*) infinity; **all'~** endlessly **2.** MATH infinity **3.** LING infinitive

infisso [in·'fis·so] *m* (*di porta, finestra*) frame

inflazione [in·flat·'tsio:·ne] *f* **1.** ECON inflation; ~ **galoppante** runaway inflation **2.** *fig* (*eccessiva diffusione*) proliferation

inflessibile [in·fles·'si:·bi·le] *agg* (*persona, carattere*) inflexible

inflessione [in·fles·'sio:·ne] *f* (*cadenza*) inflection

infliggere [in·'flid·dʒe·re] <infliggo, inflissi, inflitto> *vt* **1.** (*condanna, punizione*) to impose **2.** (*sconfitta*) to inflict

inflissi [in·'flis·si] *1. pers sing pass rem di* **infliggere**

inflitto [in·'flit·to] *pp di* **infliggere**

influente [in·flu·'ɛn·te] *agg* (*persona*) influential

influenza [in·flu·'ɛn·tsa] *f* **1.** (*influsso, prestigio*) influence **2.** MED flu

influenzale [in·flu·en·'tsa:·le] *agg* MED flu

influenzare [in·flu·en·'tsa:·re] *vt* to influence; **lasciarsi** [*o* **farsi**] ~ **da qu/qc** to be influenced by sb/sth

influenzato, -a [in·flu·en·za:·to] *agg* (*ammalato*) with the flu; **essere** ~ to have the flu

influire [in·flu·'i:·re] <influisco> *vi* ~ **su qu/ qc** to influence sb/sth

influsso [in·'flus·so] *m* (*di persona, cosa, pianeta*) influence

infondatezza [in·fon·da·'tet·tsa] *f* (*di accusa, teoria*) groundlessness

infondato, -a [in·fon·'da:·to] *agg* (*accusa, notizia*) unfounded; (*dubbio, sospetto*) groundless

infondere [in·'fon·de·re] <infondo, infusi, infuso> *vt* (*coraggio, fiducia*) to give

informale [in·for·'ma:·le] *agg* (*invito, colloquio*) informal

informare [in·for·'ma:·re] **I.** *vt* (*con notizie*) to tell; ~ **qu** (**di** [*o* **su**] **qc**) to tell sb (about sth) **II.** *vr* to keep oneself up-to-date; **-rsi su** [*o* **di**] **qc** to inquire about sth

informatica [in·for·'ma:·ti·ka] <-che> *f* (*disciplina*) computer science

informatico, -a [in·for·'ma:·ti·ko] <-ci, -che> **I.** *agg* (*sistema, linguaggio*) computer **II.** *m, f* (*studioso*) computer scientist; (*tecnico*) computer technician

informativa [in·for·ma·'ti:·va] *f* ADM office memorandum

informativo, -a [in·for·ma·'ti:·vo] *agg* (*articolo, foglio*) informative; **prospetto** ~ prospectus; **a titolo** ~ for information only

informatizzazione [in·for·ma·tid·dzat·'tsio:· ne] *f* computerization

informato, -a [in·for·'ma:·to] *agg* informed; ~ **su qc** knowledgeable about sth; **tenere qu** ~ (**su qc**) to keep sb informed (about sth); **tenersi** ~ to keep oneself well-informed

informatore, -trice [in·for·ma·'to:·re] *m, f* (*di polizia*) informant; ~ **medico** [*o* **scientifico**] pharmaceutical representative

informazione [in·for·mat·'tsio:·ne] *f* **1.** (*scambio*) information **2.** (*notizia*) information; **ufficio/sportello -i** information office/desk **3.** COMPUT **scienza dell'~** information science **4.** BIOL ~ **genetica** genetic code

informe [in·'for·me] *agg* **1.** (*massa, materia*) shapeless **2.** (*idea, progetto*) undeveloped

infornare [in·for·'na:·re] *vt* (*pane, torta*) to put in the oven

infortunato, -a [in·for·tu·'na:·to] **I.** *agg* (*lavoratore, atleta*) injured **II.** *m, f* injured person

infortunio [in·for·'tu:·nio] <-i> *m* (*incidente*) accident; ~ **sul lavoro** occupational accident

infortunistica [in·for·tu·'nis·ti·ka] *f* (*disciplina*) study of occupational accidents

infradito [in·fra·'di:·to] **I.** <inv> *agg* (*sandali*) thong **II.** <-> *m o f* thong

infrangere [in·'fran·dʒe·re] <infrango, infransi, infranto> **I.** *vt* **1.** (*vetro, vaso*) to smash **2.** *fig* (*resistenza, sogno*) to destroy **3.** *fig* (*divieto, legge*) to break **II.** *vr:* **-rsi 1.** (*vaso*) to smash; (*onde*) to break **2.** *fig* (*sogno*) to be destroyed

infrangibile [in·fran·'dʒi:·bi·le] *agg* (*vetro, bic-*

chiere) unbreakable

infransi *1. pers sing pass rem di* **infrangere**

infranto, -a [inˈfranˑto] I. *pp di* **infrangere** II. *agg* **1.** (*vaso*) smashed **2.** *fig* (*sogno*) unfulfilled; **cuore** ~ broken heart

infrarosso, -a [inˑfraˈrosˑso] *agg* PHYS (*raggi, radiazioni*) infrared

infrasettimanale [inˑfraˑsetˑtiˑmaˑˈnaːˑle] *agg* (*chiusura, festività*) midweek

infrastruttura [inˑfraˑstrutˈtuːˑra] *f* infrastructure

infrazione [inˑfratˈtsioːˑne] *f* (*di norma, regolamento*) violation; ~ **al codice stradale** traffic violation

infrequente [inˑfreˈkuɛnˑte] *agg* (*caso, fenomeno*) infrequent

infruttuoso, -a [inˑfrutˑtuˈoːˑso] *agg* **1.** (*terreno, stagione*) poor **2.** *fig* (*capitale, investimento*) unprofitable **3.** *fig* (*tentativo, ricerca*) unfruitful

infuori [inˈfuɔːˑri] I. *avv* **all'**~ outwards II. *prep* **all'**~ **di** (*tranne*) except

infuriare [inˑfuˈriaːˑre] I. *vi* (*vento, tempesta*) to rage II. *vr:* **-rsi** (*persona*) to fly into a rage

infusi [inˈfuːˑzi] *1. pers sing pass rem di* **infondere**

infusione [inˑfuˈzioːˑne] *f* **1.** (*macerazione*) infusion; **lasciare in** ~ to let soak **2.** (*bevanda*) infusion

infuso[1] [inˈfuːˑzo] *pp di* **infondere**

infuso[2] *m* (*bevanda*) infusion

ing. *abbr di* **ingegnere**

ingaggiare [iŋˑgadˈdʒaːˑre] *vt* **1.** (*operaio, attore*) to hire; (*soldato*) to recruit **2.** SPORT (*giocatore*) to sign **3.** MAR to sign on

ingaggio [iŋˈgadˑdʒo] <-ggi> *m* **1.** (*di operaio, attore*) hiring; (*di soldato*) recruitment **2.** SPORT (*di giocatore*) signing **3.** (*somma*) fee

ingannare [iŋˑganˈnaːˑre] I. *vt* **1.** (*indurre in errore*) to deceive; **l'apparenza inganna** *prov* don't judge a book by its cover *prov* **2.** (*cliente, amico*) to deceive; (*marito, moglie*) to cheat on **3.** *fig* (*speranza, fiducia*) to betray **4.** *fig* (*attesa, noia*) to while away; ~ **il tempo** to pass the time II. *vr:* **-rsi** (*sbagliarsi*) to be mistaken

ingannevole [iŋˑganˈneːˑvoˑle] *agg* (*parole, apparenza*) deceptive; **consiglio** ~ misleading advice

inganno [iŋˈganˑno] *m* **1.** (*imbroglio*) fraud **2.** (*errore*) **cadere in** ~ to be mistaken; **trarre qu in** ~ to mislead sb

ingegnere [inˑdʒeɲˈɲɛːˑre] *m* engineer

ingegneria [inˑdʒeɲˑɲeˈriːˑa] <-ie> *f* (*disciplina*) engineering; ~ **civile** civil engineering; ~ **genetica** BIOL genetic engineering

ingegno [inˈdʒeɲˑɲo] *m* (*intelligenza*) intelligence

ingegnoso, -a [inˑdʒeɲˈɲoːˑso] *agg* (*persona, macchina, risposta*) ingenious

ingente [inˈdʒenˑte] *agg* (*danno, somma*) huge

ingenuità [inˑdʒeˑnuiˈta] <-> *f* **1.** (*innocenza*) innocence **2.** (*sprovedutezza*) ingenuousness **3.** (*atto*) ingenuous thing

ingenuo, -a [inˈdʒɛːˑnuo] I. *agg* **1.** (*innocente*) innocent **2.** (*sprovveduto*) ingenuous **3.** (*sorriso, domanda*) ingenuous II. *m, f* (*persona*) ingenuous person; **fare l'**~ to play the innocent

ingerenza [inˑdʒeˈrɛnˑtsa] *f* interference

ingerire [inˑdʒeˈriːˑre] <ingerisco> *vt* (*cibo, medicina*) to swallow

ingessato, -a [inˑdʒesˈsaːˑto] *agg* (*braccio, gamba*) in a cast

ingestione [inˑdʒesˈtioːˑne] *f* (*di cibo, farmaco*) swallowing

Inghilterra [iŋˑgilˈtɛrˑra] *f* **l'**~ England; **abitare in** ~ to live in England; **andare in** ~ to go to England

inghiottire [iŋˑgiotˈtiːˑre] <inghiottisco *o* inghiotto> *vt a. fig* to swallow

inghippo [iŋˈgipˑpo] *m* catch

inginocchiarsi [inˑdʒiˑnokˈkiarˑsi] *vr* (*piegarsi*) to kneel down

ingiù [inˈdʒu] *avv* **all'**~ downward

ingiuntivo, -a [inˑdʒunˈtiːˑvo] *agg* JUR **decreto** ~ injunction

ingiunzione [inˑdʒunˈtsioːˑne] *f* JUR injunction; ~ **di pagamento** order to pay

ingiuria [inˈdʒuːˑria] *f* **1.** (*offesa*) affront **2.** (*insulto*) insult

ingiustificabile [inˑdʒusˑtiˑfiˈkaːˑbiˑle] *agg* inexcusable

ingiustificato, -a [inˑdʒusˑtiˑfiˈkaːˑto] *agg* **1.** (*assenza*) unexplained **2.** (*dubbio, sospetto*) unwarranted

ingiustizia [inˑdʒusˈtitˑtsia] *f* injustice

ingiusto, -a [inˈdʒusˑto] *agg* **1.** (*persona*) unfair **2.** (*condanna, critica, tassa*) unjust

inglese[1] [iŋˈgleːˑse] <sing> *m* (*lingua*) English

inglese[2] I. *agg* English II. *mf* (*abitante*) Englishman *m*, Englishwoman *f*

inglobare [iŋˑgloˈbaːˑre] *vt* to absorb

ingoiare [iŋˑgoˈiaːˑre] *vt* **1.** (*cibo, medicina*) to gulp down **2.** *fig* (*amarezze, umiliazioni*) to swallow; ~ **il rospo** to bite the bullet

ingombrante [iŋˑgomˈbranˑte] *agg* **1.** (*mobile*) cumbersome **2.** *fig* (*personaggio, ospite*) difficult

ingombro[1] [iŋˈgomˑbro] *agg* ~ **di qc** cluttered with sth

ingombro[2] *m* **1.** (*impaccio*) encumbrance; **essere d'**~ to be in the way **2.** (*spazio occupato*) size

ingordigia [iŋˑgorˈdiːˑdʒa] <-gie> *f a. fig* greed; ~ **di qc** greed for sth

ingordo, -a [iŋˈgorˑdo] *agg* greedy; ~ **di qc** greedy for sth

ingorgo [iŋˈgorˑgo] <-ghi> *m* **1.** (*di tubatura*) blockage **2.** (*di traffico*) traffic jam

ingranaggio [iŋˑgraˈnadˑdʒo] <-ggi> *m* **1.** (*di motore*) gear; (*di orologio*) cog **2.** *fig* mechanism

ingrandimento [in·gran·di·'men·to] *m* **1.**(*di edificio*) extension; (*di attività, azienda*) expansion **2.**FOTO, OPT enlargement; **lente d'~** magnifying glass

ingrandire [in·gran·'di:·re] <ingrandisco> **I.** *vt avere* **1.**(*edificio*) to extend; (*attività, azienda*) to expand **2.**FOTO, OPT to enlarge **3.** *fig* (*problemi, difficoltà*) to exaggerate **II.** *vr:* **-rsi** (*città*) to increase; (*attività, azienda*) to expand

ingrassare [in·gras·'sa:·re] **I.** *vt avere* **1.**(*animale*) to fatten **2.**(*persona*) to make fat **3.**(*ingranaggio, motore*) to grease **II.** *vi essere* (*diventare grasso*) to put on weight **III.** *vr:* **-rsi** (*diventare grasso*) to put on weight

ingratitudine [in·gra·ti·'tu:·di·ne] *f* (*caratteristica*) ingratitude

ingrato, -a [in·'gra:·to] **I.** *agg* **1.**(*persona*) ungrateful **2.**(*compito, lavoro*) thankless **II.** *m, f* (*persona*) ingrate

ingrediente [in·gre·'diɛn·te] *m a. fig* ingredient

ingresso [in·'grɛs·so] *m* **1.**(*atto*) entry **2.**(*facoltà di entrare*) admission; **~ libero** free admission; **~ a pagamento** admission by ticket only **3.**(*porta, cancello*) entrance; (*atrio*) hallway

ingrossamento [in·gros·sa·'men·to] *m* swelling

ingrossare [in·ros·'sa:·re] **I.** *vt avere* **1.**(*fiume*) to swell **2.**(*aspetto*) to make look bigger **3.**(*quantità, volume*) to increase **II.** *vi essere* **1.**(*fiume*) to swell **2.**(*aspetto*) to put on weight **3.**(*quantità, volume*) to increase **III.** *vr:* **-rsi 1.**(*fiume*) to swell; (*mare*) to get rough **2.**(*numero, quantità*) to increase **3.**(*muscoli*) to develop **4.**(*in peso*) to put on weight

ingrosso [in·'grɔs·so] *avv* **all'~** COM wholesale

inguaribile [in·gua·'ri:·bi·le] *agg* **1.**(*malattia*) incurable **2.** *fig* (*vizio, bevitore, giocatore*) hardened; *scherz* (*romantico, sognatore*) incurable

inguine ['in·gui·ne] *m* ANAT groin

inibire [i·ni·'bi:·re] <inibisco> PSYCH **I.** *vt* to inhibit **II.** *vr:* **-rsi 1.**(*frenarsi*) to be inhibited **2.**(*intimidirsi*) to become inhibited

inibito, -a [i·ni·'bi:·to] *agg* (*intimidito*) inhibited

inibitore, -trice [i·ni·bi·'to:·re] **I.** *agg* BIOL, CHEM, PSYCH inhibitory; **freni -i** inhibitory reflexes **II.** *m, f* BIOL, CHEM inhibitor

inibizione [i·ni·bit·'tsio:·ne] *f* PSYCH inhibition

iniettare [in·iet·'ta:·re] **I.** *vt* (*vaccino, farmaco*) to inject **II.** *vr:* **-rsi 1.**(*sostanza*) to inject oneself **2.**(*loc*) **-rsi di sangue** (*occhi*) to become bloodshot

iniezione [in·iet·'tsio:·ne] *f* MED, TEC injection; **motore a ~** fuel injection engine

inimicizia [i·ni·mi·'tʃit·tsia] <-ie> *f* enmity

inimitabile [i·ni·mi·'ta:·bi·le] *agg* (*esecuzione, stile*) inimitable

inimmaginabile [i·nim·ma·dʒi·'na:·bi·le] *agg* unimaginable

ininterrotto, -a [in·in·ter·'rot·to] *agg* (*serie, flusso*) uninterrupted

iniquità [i·ni·kui·'ta] <-> *f* **1.**(*caratteristica*) iniquity **2.**(*atto*) wicked act

iniquo, -a [i·'ni·kuo] *agg* (*legge, governo*) iniquitous

iniziale [i·nit·'tsia:·le] **I.** *agg* **1.**(*momento, fase*) initial; **stipendio ~** starting salary **2.**(*lettera, sillaba*) initial **II.** *f* (*lettera*) initial; **le -i** (*di nome*) the initials; **firmare con le -e** to initial

iniziare [i·nit·'tsia:·re] **I.** *vt avere* **1.**(*attività, studio*) to start [*o* begin]; **~ a fare qc** to start [*o* begin] to do sth **2.** **~ qu a qc** (*rito*) to initiate sb into sth; (*attività*) to introduce sb to sth **II.** *vi* (*avere inizio*) to begin [*o* start]

iniziativa [i·nit·tsia·'ti:·va] *f* **1.**(*decisione*) initiative; **di propria ~** on one's own iniative **2.**(*attitudine*) enterprise; **essere ricco** [*o* **pieno**] **di ~** to be enterprising; **spirito di ~** enterprising spirit **3.**(*opera, attività*) initiative; **~ privata** ECON private enterprise

iniziatore, -trice [i·nit·tsia·'to:·re] *m, f* (*di movimento, ideologia*) initiator

iniziazione [i·nit·tsiat·'tsio:·ne] *f* (*cerimonia*) initiation

inizio [i·'nit·tsio] <-i> *m* **1.**(*atto, momento*) start [*o* beginning]; **avere ~** to start [*o* begin]; **dare ~ a qc** to start [*o* begin] sth; **all'~** at the start [*o* beginning] **2.**(*prima parte*) start [*o* beginning]; **gli -i** the beginning [*o* start]

innalzamento [in·nal·tsa·'men·to] *m* **1.**(*di livello, temperatura*) rise **2.** *fig* (*di tenore di vita*) increase

innalzare [in·nal·'tsa:·re] **I.** *vt* **1.**(*calice, bandiera*) to raise **2.**(*antenna, palo*) to erect **3.**(*livello, temperatura*) to raise **II.** *vr:* **-rsi** to rise

innamoramento [in·na·mo·ra·'men·to] *m* passion

innamorare [in·na·mo·'ra:·re] **I.** *vt* **far ~ qu** to make sb fall in love **II.** *vr:* **-rsi** (*reciproco*) to fall in love with each other; **-rsi di qu/qc** to fall in love with sb/sth

innamorato, -a [in·na·mo·'ra:·to] **I.** *agg* in love; **essere ~ di qu** to be in love with sb; **essere ~ cotto** [*o* **pazzo**] (**di qu**) to be madly in love (with sb); **essere ~ di qc** to be mad about sth **II.** *m, f* (*fidanzato*) boyfriend *m*, girlfriend *f*

innanzi [in·'nan·tsi] *lit* **I.** *avv* **1.**(*avanti*) forward; **farsi ~** to step forward **2.**(*prima*) previously **3.**(*poi, in seguito*) later; **d'ora ~** from now on **II.** *prep* **~ a qu/qc** (*davanti a*) in front of sb/sth **III.** <inv> *agg* (*precedente*) previous

innanzitutto [in·nan·tsi·'tut·to] *avv* above all

innato, -a [in·'na:·to] *agg* **1.**(*istinto, difetto*) inborn; (*talento*) natural **2.**(*gentilezza, eleganza*) innate

innaturale [in·na·tu·'ra:·le] *agg* (*gesto, recitazione*) unnatural

innegabile [in·ne·'ga:·bi·le] *agg* (*principio, verità*) undeniable; **essere ~** to be true

I

inneggiare [in·ned·'dʒa:·re] *vi* ~ **a qc** to extol sth

innervosire [in·ner·vo·'si:·re] <innervosisco> **I.** *vt* to get on sb's nerves **II.** *vr:* **-rsi** to get annoyed

innescare [in·nes·'ka:·re] *vt* **1.** (*amo*) to bait **2.** (*bomba, mina*) to prime **3.** *fig* (*reazione, rivolta*) to set off

innesco [in·'nes·ko] <-schi> *m* (*di bomba*) primer

innestare [in·nes·'ta:·re] *vt* **1.** AGR, MED to graft **2.** TEC (*spina*) to insert; (*marcia*) to go into

innesto [in·'nɛs·to] *m* **1.** AGR, MED graft **2.** TEC (*attacco*) joint; EL (*presa*) socket

innevamento [in·ne·va·'men·to] *m* snowfall; ~ **artificiale** artificial snow

innevato, -a [in·ne·'va:·to] *agg* (*montagna, cima*) covered in snow

inno ['in·no] *m a. fig* hymn; ~ **nazionale** national anthem

innocente [in·no·'tʃɛn·te] **I.** *agg* **1.** (*non colpevole*) not guilty; (*ingenuo*) innocent **2.** (*domanda, scherzo*) innocent **II.** *mf* **1.** (*non colpevole*) innocent person **2.** (*bambino*) innocent

innocenza [in·no·'tʃɛn·tsa] *f* innocence

innocuo, -a [in·'nɔ:·kuo] *agg* **1.** (*sostanza, farmaco*) innocuous **2.** (*persona, animale, scherzo*) harmless; *pej* innocuous

innovare [in·no·'va:·re] *vt* (*modernizzare*) to update

innovativo, -a [in·no·va·'ti:·vo] *agg* (*idea, proposta, persona*) innovative

innovatore, -trice [in·no·va·'to:·re] **I.** *agg* innovative **II.** *m, f* (*persona*) innovator

innovazione [in·no·vat·'tsio:·ne] *f* **1.** (*cambiamento*) change **2.** (*elemento nuovo*) innovation

innumerevole [in·nu·me·'re:·vo·le] *agg* countless

inodore, -a [i·no·'do:·re] *agg* (*sostanza, gas*) odorless

inoffensivo, -a [in·of·fen·'si:·vo] *agg* **1.** (*parole, frasi*) inoffensive **2.** (*persona, animale*) harmless

inoltrare [in·ol·'tra:·re] **I.** *vt* **1.** ADM (*domanda, pratica*) to submit **2.** (*posta*) to forward **II.** *vr:* **-rsi** **-rsi in qc** (*in luogo*) to go into sth

inoltrato, -a [in·ol·'tra:·to] *agg* (*nel tempo*) late; **a notte/a sera** **-a** late at night/in the evening

inoltre [i·'nol·tre] *avv* furthermore

inoltro [i·'nol·tro] *m* ADM (*di domanda, pratica*) submission

inondare [in·on·'da:·re] *vt* **1.** (*acque*) to flood; (*lacrime, luce*) to bathe **2.** *fig* (*folla*) to flood into; (*merce*) to flood

inondazione [in·on·dat·'tsio:·ne] *f* **1.** (*di acque*) flooding **2.** *fig* (*di turisti, film*) flood

inopportunità [in·op·por·tu·ni·'ta] <-> *f* (*di atto, comportamento*) untimeliness

inopportuno, -a [in·op·por·'tu:·no] *agg* untimely

inoppugnabile [in·op·puɲ·'ɲa:·bi·le] *agg*

1. (*verità, teoria*) incontrovertible **2.** JUR (*sentenza*) not open to appeal

inorganico, -a [in·or·'ga:·ni·ko] <-ci, -che> *agg* CHEM (*elemento, sostanza*) inorganic

inospitale [in·os·pi·'ta:·le] *agg* **1.** (*persona, paese*) unfriendly **2.** (*casa, regione*) inhospitable

inosservanza [in·os·ser·'van·tsa] *f* (*di norma, regolamento*) non-observance

inosservato, -a [in·os·ser·'va:·to] *agg* (*non notato*) unobserved; **passare** ~ to escape notice

inossidabile [in·os·si·'da:·bi·le] *agg* **1.** (*metallo*) rustproof; **acciaio** ~ stainless steel **2.** *fig* (*persona, rapporto*) indestructible

INPS [imps] *m acro di* **Istituto Nazionale Previdenza Sociale** *Italian social security system*

input ['in·put] <-> *m* **1.** COMPUT input **2.** (*impulso*) start

inquadramento [iɲ·kua·dra·'men·to] *m* ADM, MIL (*di lavoratore, soldato*) placement

inquadrare [iɲ·kua·'dra:·re] **I.** *vt* **1.** FOTO to frame **2.** *fig* (*opera*) to place; (*problema, situazione*) to identify **3.** ADM, MIL (*lavoratore, soldato*) to place **II.** *vr:* **-rsi** (*collocarsi*) to be part of

inquadratura [iɲ·kua·dra·'tu:·ra] *f* FOTO, FILM, TV shot

inquietante [iɲ·kui·e·'tan·te] *agg* **1.** (*silenzio, atmosfera*) worrying **2.** (*film, libro, sogno*) disturbing

inquieto, -a [iɲ·'kui·ɛ:·to] *agg* **1.** (*agitato*) restless **2.** (*preoccupato*) worried

inquietudine [iɲ·kui·e·'tu:·di·ne] *f* (*stato d'animo*) worry

inquilino, -a [iɲ·kui·'li:·no] *m, f* (*affittuario*) tenant; (*abitante*) resident

inquinamento [iɲ·kui·na·'men·to] *m* **1.** ECO pollution; ~ **acustico** noise pollution; ~ **ambientale** environmental pollution; ~ **atmosferico** air pollution **2.** JUR ~ **delle prove** tampering with the evidence

inquinante [iɲ·kui·'nan·te] *agg* (*agente, sostanza*) polluting

inquinare [iɲ·kui·'na:·re] *vt* **1.** ECO to pollute **2.** JUR ~ **le prove** to tamper with the evidence

inquinato, -a [iɲ·kui·'na:·to] *agg* (*ambiente*) polluted

inquirente [iɲ·kui·'rɛn·te] *agg* (*magistrato, giudice*) examining

inquirenti [iɲ·kui·'rɛn·te] *mpl* **gli -i** the investigating authorities

inquisito, -a [iɲ·kui·'zi:·to] **I.** *agg* JUR under investigation **II.** *m, f* person under investigation

inquisitore, -trice [iɲ·kui·zi·'to:·re] *agg* (*occhio, sguardo*) inquiring

inquisizione [iɲ·kui·zit·'tsio:·ne] *f* HIST Inquisition

insaccati [in·sak·'ka:·ti] *mpl* (*salumi*) sausages

insalata [in·sa·'la:·ta] *f* salad; **in** ~ in a salad; ~ **di mare** seafood salad; ~ **russa** Russian salad

insalatiera [in·sa·la·'tiɛː·ra] *f* salad bowl

insalubre [in·sa·'luː·bre] *agg* (*aria, clima*) unhealthy

insanabile [in·sa·'naː·bi·le] *agg* 1. *fig* (*danno, errore*) irreperable 2. *fig* (*contrasto*) permanent; (*odio, rancore*) undying

insanguinato, -a [in·saŋ·gui·'naː·to] *agg* (*corpo, mani*) covered in blood

insano, -a [in·'saː·no] *agg* (*gesto, sentimento*) mad

insaporire [in·sa·po·'riː·re] <insaporisco> *vt* CULIN to flavor

insaputa [in·sa·'puː·ta] *f* **all'~ di qu** without sb's knowledge

insaziabile [in·sat·'tsia·bi·le] *agg a. fig* (*persona, fame, appetito*) insatiable

inscindibile *agg* (*legame, cosa*) inseparable

insediamento [in·se·dia·'men·to] *m* 1. (*in carica*) swearing in 2. GEOG settlement

insediare [in·se·'diaː·re] I. *vt* 1. (*in carica*) to swear in 2. (*in luogo*) to settle II. *vr:* **-rsi** 1. (*in carica*) to take up office 2. (*in luogo*) to settle

insegna [in·'seɲ·ɲa] *f* 1. (*di negozio, locale*) sign; ~ **stradale** road sign 2. (*di città, partito*) banner 3. (*di carica, ordine*) insignia *pl;* **all'~ di** *fig* characterized by

insegnamento [in·seɲ·ɲa·'men·to] *m* 1. (*attività, professione*) teaching 2. (*precetto*) lesson; **trarre ~ da qc** to learn from sth

insegnante [in·seɲ·'ɲan·te] I. *agg* (*corpo, personale*) teaching II. *mf* (*professore*) teacher; ~ **di sostegno** support teacher

insegnare [in·seɲ·'ɲaː·re] I. *vt* 1. (*materia, attività*) to teach; ~ **qc a qu** to teach sb sth [*o* to teach sth to sb]; ~ **a qu a fare qc** to teach sb how to do sth 2. (*comportamento, valori*) to teach 3. (*storia, esperienza*) to show II. *vi* (*come professione*) to teach

inseguimento [in·se·gui·'men·to] *m* 1. (*atto*) pursuit 2. (*corsa*) chase

inseguire [in·se·'guiː·re] *vt a. fig* (*persona, animale, successo*) to chase after

inseguitore, -trice [in·se·gui·'toː·re] *m, f* (*persona*) pursuer

inseminazione [in·se·mi·nat·'tsioː·ne] *f* BIOL insemination; ~ **artificiale** artificial insemination

insenatura [in·se·na·'tuː·ra] *f* inlet

insensatezza [in·sen·sa·'tet·tsa] *f* 1. (*caratteristica*) foolishness 2. (*atto*) foolish thing

insensato, -a [in·sen·'saː·to] *agg* 1. (*persona*) foolish 2. (*idea, gesto, discorso*) senseless.

insensibile [in·sen·'siː·bi·le] *agg* 1. (*arto*) numb; **essere ~ a qc** (*al freddo, dolore*) to not be susceptible to sth 2. *fig* **essere ~ a qc** (*a fascino, lusinghe, musica*) to be indifferent to sth 3. (*crescita, calo*) minute

insensibilità [in·sen·si·bi·li·'ta] <-> *f* 1. (*fisica*) numbness 2. *fig* (*affettiva*) indifference

inseparabile [in·se·pa·'raː·bi·le] *agg* inseparable

inserimento [in·se·ri·'men·to] *m* 1. (*di mon-*

eta, chiave, spina) insertion; (*di marcia*) setting 2. (*di foglio, nominativo*) inclusion; (*di dati*) entry 3. *fig* (*di persona*) integration

inserire [in·se·'riː·re] <inserisco> I. *vt* 1. (*moneta, chiave, spina*) to insert; (*marcia*) to go into 2. (*foglio, nominativo*) to put; (*dati*) to enter 3. *fig* (*persona*) to integrate 4. (*sul giornale: annuncio*) to place 5. (*audio, corrente*) to switch on II. *vr:* **-rsi** 1. (*meccanismo, congegno*) to fit 2. (*riforma, progetto, opera*) to be part of 3. *fig* (*persona: in ambiente*) to fit in 4. (*entrare: in una discussione*) to enter

inserto [in·'sɛr·to] *m* 1. (*di giornale, rivista*) supplement 2. (*di film*) clip; ~ **pubblicitario** commercial 3. (*di abito, accessorio*) inlay

inservibile [in·ser·'viː·bi·le] *agg* useless

inserviente [in·ser·'viɛn·te] *mf* (*in ospedale, istituto*) attendant

inserzione [in·ser·'tsioː·ne] *f* (*annuncio*) advert

inserzionista [in·ser·tsio·'nis·ta] <-i *m*, -e *f*> *mf* advertiser

insetticida¹ [in·set·ti·'tʃiː·da] <-i *m*, -e *f*> *agg* (*prodotto, sostanza*) insecticidal

insetticida² <-i> *m* insecticide

insetto [in·'sɛt·to] *m* (*animale*) insect

insicurezza [in·si·ku·'ret·tsa] *f* (*di situazione, persona*) insecurity

insicuro, -a [in·si·'kuː·ro] I. *agg* 1. (*persona, carattere*) insecure 2. (*voce, andatura*) faltering 3. (*luogo, strada, scala*) unsafe; (*lavoro*) precarious 4. (*notizia*) unconfirmed II. *m, f* (*persona*) insecure person

insidia [in·'siː·dia] <-ie> *f* 1. (*agguato*) ambush; (*di corteggiatore*) machination 2. (*pericolo*) hidden danger

insidiare [in·si·'diaː·re] *vt* 1. (*nemico*) to ambush 2. (*onore, reputazione*) to sully

insidioso, -a [in·si·'dioː·so] *agg* (*percorso, arma*) dangerous

insieme [in·'siɛː·me] I. *avv* 1. (*in compagnia, associazione*) together; (*di comune accordo*) as a body; **tutti** [*o* **tutti quanti**] ~ all together; **si sono messi ~** they started dating each other 2. (*unitamente*) together; **tutto** [*o* **tutto quanto**] ~ everything at once; **mettere ~** to put together 3. (*contemporaneamente*) at the same time II. *prep* ~ **a** (*compagnia*) with; (*contemporaneità*) at the same time as III. *m* 1. (*complesso*) whole; **nell'~** on the whole; **visione d'~** overall view 2. MATH set

insigne [in·'siɲ·ɲe] *agg* 1. (*persona*) eminent 2. (*monumento, opera*) outstanding

insignificante [in·siɲ·ɲi·fi·'kan·te] *agg* 1. (*banale*) insignificant; (*parole, gesti*) meaningless 2. (*particolare, differenza*) trifling

insindacabile [in·sin·da·'kaː·bi·le] *agg* (*giudizio, decisione*) final

insinuare [in·si·nu·'aː·re] I. *vt* 1. (*dubbio, sospetto*) to instil 2. (*sottintendere*) to insinuate; **cosa vorresti ~?** what are you insinuating? II. *vr:* **-rsi** 1. (*infilarsi*) to slip 2. *a. fig* (*in un gruppo*) to insinuate oneself 3. *fig* (*dubbio,* *sospetto*) to creep

insinuazione [in·si·nu·at·'tsio:·ne] *f* (*allusione*) insinuation

insipido, -a [in·'si:·pi·do] *agg* **1.**(*cibo*) tasteless **2.** *fig* (*persona, faccia*) insipid; (*film, storia*) dull

insistente [in·sis·'tɛn·te] *agg* **1.**(*persona, domande, richieste*) insistent **2.**(*pioggia*) persistent

insistenza [in·sis·'tɛn·tsa] *f* **1.**(*ostinazione*) insistence; **con** ~ insistently **2.** *pl* (*richieste*) insistent requests

insistere [in·'sis·te·re] <insisto, insistei *o* insistetti, insistito> *vi* **1.** ~ **su qc** (*argomento*) to insist on sth; **non insisto!** I won't insist! **2.** ~ **in qc** to persist in sth; ~ **nel** [*o* a] **fare qc** to persist in doing sth

insito, -a ['in·si·to] *agg* ~ **in qc/qu** inherent to sth/sb

insoddisfacente [in·sod·dis·fat·'ʃɛn·te] *agg* (*risultato, prestazione*) unsatisfactory

insoddisfatto, -a [in·sod·dis·'fat·to] *agg* **1.**(*persona*) dissatisfied; **essere/rimanere** ~ **di qc** to be unhappy about sth **2.**(*bisogno, desiderio*) not met

insoddisfazione [in·sod·dis·fat·'tsio:·ne] *f* dissatisfaction

insofferente [in·sof·fe·'rɛn·te] *agg* (*persona, carattere*) impatient; **essere** ~ **a qc** to not be able to stand sth

insofferenza [in·sof·fe·'rɛn·tsa] *f* (*di persona, carattere*) impatience; ~ **a qc** lack of tolerance of sth

insolazione [in·so·lat·'tsio:·ne] *f* MED sunstroke

insolente [in·so·'lɛn·te] *agg* (*persona, modo, tono*) insolent

insolenza [in·so·'lɛn·tsa] *f* **1.**(*caratteristica*) insolence; **con** ~ insolently **2.**(*parola, frase*) insolent remark

insolito, -a [in·'sɔ:·li·to] I. *agg* unusual II. *m, f* **qualcosa d'**~ something unusual

insolubile [in·so·'lu:·bi·le] *agg* **1.** *fig* (*caso, problema*) unsolvable **2.** CHEM insoluble

insoluto, -a [in·so·'lu:·to] *agg* **1.**(*caso, problema*) unsolved **2.**(*debito*) outstanding

insolvente [in·sol·'ven·te] *agg* JUR insolvent

insolvenza [in·sol·'ven·tsa] *f* JUR insolvency

insomma [in·'som·ma] I. *avv* **1.**(*in conclusione*) in short **2.**(*così così*) so, so II. *int* right; **ma** ~ ! well really!

insonne [in·'sɔn·ne] *agg* (*persona*) awake; (*notte*) sleepless

insonnia [in·'sɔn·nia] <-ie> *f* **1.**(*disturbo*) insomnia **2.**(*stato*) sleeplessness

insonorizzazione [in·so·no·rid·dzat·'tsio:·ne] *f* TEC soundproofing

insopportabile [in·sop·por·'ta:·bi·le] *agg* **1.**(*dolore, caldo, persona*) unbearable **2.**(*affronto, prepotenza*) intolerable

insopprimibile [in·sop·pri·'mi:·bi·le] *agg* insuppressible

insorgenza [in·sor·'dʒɛn·tsa] *f* (*di malattia,*

sintomo) onset

insorgere [in·'sor·dʒe·re] <insorgo, insorsi, insorto> *vi essere* **1.** ~ **contro qu/qc** to rebel against sb/sth **2.**(*malattia, difficoltà*) to arise

insormontabile [in·sor·mon·'ta:·bi·le] *agg* (*ostacolo, difficoltà*) insurmountable

insorsi *1. pers sing pass rem di* **insorgere**

insorto, -a [in·'sor·to] I. *pp di* **insorgere** II. *agg* **1.**(*popolazione*) rebellious **2.**(*difficoltà*) manifested III. *m, f* rebel

insospettabile [in·sos·pet·'ta:·bi·le] *agg* **1.**(*persona*) above suspicion **2.**(*qualità*) unsuspected

insospettire [in·sos·pet·'ti:·re] <insospettisco> I. *vt avere* ~ **qu** to make sb suspicious II. *vr:* -**rsi** to become suspicious

insostenibile [in·sos·te·'ni:·bi·le] *agg* **1.**(*spesa, sforzo*) unsustainable; (*situazione*) intolerable **2.**(*argomento, tesi*) untenable

insostituibile [in·sos·ti·tu·'i:·bi·le] *agg* irreplaceable

insperato, -a [in·spe·'ra:·to] *agg* unexpected

inspiegabile [in·spie·'ga:·bi·le] *agg* inexplicable

inspirazione [in·spi·rat·'tsio:·ne] *f* (*di aria*) inhaling

instabile [ins·'ta:·bi·le] *agg* **1.**(*carico, ponte, sedia, passo*) unsteady; **equilibrio** ~ *a. fig* unstable equilibrium **2.** *fig* (*tempo, clima*) changeable; (*prezzo*) variable; (*situazione, governo*) unstable; (*persona, carattere*) unstable

instabilità [in·sta·bi·li·'ta] <-> *f* **1.**(*di costruzione, scala*) instability **2.** *fig* (*di tempo, clima*) changeability; (*di prezzo*) variability; (*di situazione*) instability **3.** *fig* (*di persona*) instability

installare [in·stal·'la:·re] I. *vt* **1.**(*apparecchio, impianto*) to install **2.** COMPUT (*programma*) to install II. *vi:* -**rsi** -**rsi in qc** (*in luogo*) to settle in sth

installatore, -trice [in·stal·la·'to:·re] *m, f* (*tecnico*) installer

installazione [in·stal·lat·'tsio:·ne] *f* **1.**(*di apparecchio, impianto*) installation **2.**(*impianto: sportivo, portuale*) facilities *pl* **3.** COMPUT installation

instancabile [in·staŋ·'ka:·bi·le] *agg* tireless

instaurare [in·stau·'ra:·re] I. *vt* **1.**(*regime*) to institute **2.**(*metodo, tendenza*) to introduce **3.**(*amicizia, rapporto*) to establish II. *vr:* -**rsi** (*regime*) to be instituted; (*clima, atmosfera, rapporto*) to be established

instaurazione [in·stau·rat·'tsio:·ne] *f* (*di ordinamento, metodo*) institution

insù [in·'su] *avv* **all'**~ upwards; **naso all'**~ snub nose

insubordinazione [in·sub·or·di·na·'tsio:·ne] *f* *a. fig* MIL insubordination; **atto di** ~ act of insubordination

insuccesso [in·sut·'tʃɛs·so] *m* (*di impresa, progetto*) failure; **essere un** ~ to be a failure

insufficiente [in·suf·fi·'tʃɛn·te] I. *agg* **1.**(*per* *quantità, qualità*) insufficient **2.** (*a scuola: compito*) below standard **II.** *m* (*voto*) fail

insufficienza [in·suf·fi·'tʃɛn·tsa] *f* **1.** (*per quantità, qualità*) shortage; ~ **di prove** JUR lack of evidence **2.** (*incapacità*) inability **3.** (*a scuola*) fail **4.** MED insufficiency; ~ **cardiaca** cardiac insufficiency

insulare [in·su·'la:·re] *agg* island

insulina [in·su·'li:·na] *f* BIOL, MED insulin

insulso, -a [in·'sul·so] *agg* **1.** (*discorso, comportamento, film*) silly **2.** (*persona*) dull

insultare [in·sul·'ta:·re] *vt* (*offendere*) to insult

insulto [in·'sul·to] *m* insult; **coprire qu di -i** to hurl insults at sb; **essere un** ~ **a qc** to be an insult to sth

insuperabile [in·su·pe·'ra:·bi·le] *agg* **1.** (*montagna, distanza, difficoltà*) insuperable **2.** *fig* (*persona*) unequalled **3.** (*qualità, modello, prodotto*) unbeatable

insurrezione [in·sur·ret·'tsio:·ne] *f* insurrection

intaccare [in·tak·'ka:·re] *vt* **1.** (*acido, ruggine*) to corrode **2.** (*malattia*) to attack **3.** (*risparmi, patrimonio*) to eat into **4.** *fig* (*onore, amicizia*) to sully

intagliato, -a [in·taʎ·'ʎa:·to] *agg* carved

intaglio [in·'taʎ·ʎo] *m* **1.** (*lavorazione*) intaglio **2.** (*opera, figura*) intaglio

intangibile [in·tan·'dʒi:·bi·le] *agg* **1.** (*eredità, patrimonio*) untouchable **2.** *fig* (*diritto, norma*) inviolable

intanto [in·'tan·to] **I.** *avv* **1.** (*temporale*) in the meantime **2.** (*avversativo*) yet; **e** ~ **devo pagare io!** and yet I'll end up paying! **II.** *cong* ~ **che** ... +*ind* while ...

intarsiato, -a [in·tar·'sia:·to] *agg* (*mobile, pavimento*) inlaid

intarsio [in·'tar·sio] <-i> *m* **1.** (*tecnica*) intarsia **2.** (*opera*) intarsia

intasamento [in·ta·za·'men·to] *m* **1.** (*di tubo, canale*) blockage **2.** (*di strada*) traffic jam; ~ **del traffico** traffic jam

intasare [in·ta·'za:·re] **I.** *vt* **1.** (*tubo, canale*) to block **2.** (*strada, traffico*) to block **II.** *vr:* **-rsi** (*tubo, canale, naso*) to become blocked

intasato, -a [in·ta·'za:·to] *agg* blocked

intatto, -a [in·'tat·to] *agg* **1.** (*neve*) untouched **2.** (*serratura, edificio*) intact **3.** (*patrimonio, eredità*) untouched **4.** *fig* (*onore, reputazione*) unsullied

intavolare [in·ta·vo·'la:·re] *vt* (*argomento, discussione*) to broach

integrale [in·te·'gra:·le] **I.** *agg* **1.** (*intero*) complete; **edizione** ~ unabridged edition **2.** (*farina, pane*) wholewheat **3.** MATH integral **II.** *m* MATH integral

integralismo [in·te·gra·'liz·mo] *m* integralism

integralista [in·te·gra·'lis·ta] <-i *m*, -e *f*> **I.** *agg* (*movimento, posizione*) integralist **II.** *m* (*fautore*) integralist

integrante [in·te·'gran·te] *agg* (*elemento, parte*) integral; **essere parte** ~ **di qc** to be an integral part of sth

integrare [in·te·'gra:·re] **I.** *vt* **1.** (*completare*) to supplement **2.** (*persona*) ~ **qu in qc** to integrate sb into sth **II.** *vr:* **-rsi 1.** (*persona*) to fit in **2.** (*reciproco*) to complement one another

integrativo, -a [in·te·gra·'ti:·vo] *agg* (*contratto, norma, quota*) supplementary; (*anno, esame*) extra

integrato, -a [in·te·'gra:·to] *agg* **1.** (*persona*) integrated **2.** (*ciclo, processo*) built-in

integratore [in·te·gra·'to:·re] *m* vitamin supplement; ~ **alimentare** nutritional supplement

integrazione [in·te·grat·'tsio:·ne] *f* **1.** (*gener*) integration **2.** (*completamento: di stipendio, alimentazione*) supplement; **cassa** ~ *fund for workers who are temporarily laid-off*

integrità [in·te·gri·'ta] <-> *f a. fig* integrity; ~ **fisica e mentale** physical and mental well-being

integro, -a ['in·te·gro] <più integro, integerrimo> *agg* **1.** (*intatto*) intact; (*energie, facoltà*) unimpaired **2.** *fig* (*persona*) upright

intelaiatura [in·te·la·ia·'tu:·ra] *f* (*di finestra, costruzione*) framework

intelletto [in·tel·'lɛt·to] *m* intellect

intellettuale [in·tel·let·tu·'a:·le] **I.** *agg* **1.** (*doti, lavoro*) mental **2.** (*luogo, ambiente, persona*) intellectual **II.** *mf* (*persona*) intellectual; **fare l'~** *iron, pej* to act highbrow

intelligente [in·tel·li·'dʒen·te] *agg* **1.** (*pensante*) thinking **2.** (*acuto: persona, osservazione*) intelligent; **vacanze -i** planned vacation including excursions/visits

intelligenza [in·tel·li·'dʒen·tsa] *f* **1.** (*facoltà*) mind; ~ **artificiale** COMPUT artificial intelligence **2.** (*acutezza*) intelligence; **quoziente d'~** intelligence quotient

intellighenzia [in·tel·li·'gen·tsia] *f* (*di nazione, partito*) intelligentsia

intelligibile [in·tel·lid·'ʒi:·bi·le] *agg* (*comprensibile*) intelligible

intemperanza [in·tem·pe·'ran·tsa] *f* **1.** (*caratteristica*) lack of moderation **2.** (*atto*) excess

intemperie [in·tem·'pɛ:·rie] *fpl* inclement weather

intendente [in·ten·'dɛn·te] *m* ADM (*funzionario*) official; ~ **di finanza** internal revenue officer

intendenza [in·ten·'dɛn·tsa] *f* ADM office; ~ **di finanza** internal revenue office

intendere [in·'tɛn·de·re] <intendo, intesi, inteso> **I.** *vt* **1.** (*capire*) to understand; **dare a** ~ **qc a qu** to give sb to understand sth; **lasciare** [*o* **fare**] ~ **qc** to make sb understand; ~ **qc al volo** to immediately grasp sth; **s'intende** of course **2.** (*udire*) to hear **3.** (*accettare*) to listen to; **non** ~ **ragioni** to not listen to reason **4.** (*volere*) to wish; **non intendevo offenderti** I didn't mean to offend you **5.** (*voler dire*) to mean **II.** *vr:* **-rsi 1.** (*andare d'accordo*) to get along; **intendersela con qu** *inf* to have an affair with sb **2.** (*accordarsi, capirsi*) to understand each other; **-rsi su qc** to agree on sth; **tanto per intenderci** just to be clear **3.** (*essere esperto di*) **-rsi di qc** (*argomento, materia*) to know sth about sth; **non m'intendo di quadri/di politica** I don't know anything about paintings/politics

intenditore, -trice [in·ten·di·'to:·re] *m*, *f* (*esperto*) connoisseur; **a buon intenditor poche parole** *prov* a word to the wise *prov*

intensificare [in·ten·si·fi·'ka:·re] **I.** *vt* **1.** (*colore*) to intensify **2.** (*controlli, sforzi, produzione*) to increase **II.** *vr:* **-rsi** (*rumore, traffico*) to intensify; (*produzione*) to increase

intensificazione [in·ten·si·fi·kat·'tsio:·ne] *f* (*di traffico, sforzi*) increase

intensità [in·ten·si·'ta] <-> *f a. fig* PHYS intensity

intensivo, -a [in·ten·'si:·vo] *agg* (*corso, cura*) intensive; **terapia -a** MED intensive care

intenso, -a [in·'tɛn·so] *agg* **1.** (*suono, dolore, desiderio*) intense; (*nebbia, pioggia*) heavy; (*odore, sapore*) overpowering; (*colore*) deep; (*luce*) bright **2.** (*giornata, vita*) busy; (*lavoro, studio*) demanding; **traffico ~** heavy traffic

intentare [in·ten·'ta:·re] *vt* JUR (*causa, processo*) to initiate

intentato¹ [in·ten·'ta:·to] *agg* (*impresa, esperimento*) untried

intentato² <*sing*> *m* **non lasciare nulla d'~** to leave no stone unturned

intento¹ [in·'tɛn·to] *agg* (*concentrato*) intent; **essere ~ a qc** to be absorbed in sth; **essere ~ a fare qc** to be busy doing sth

intento² *m* (*scopo*) aim; **riuscire/fallire nell'~** to achieve/not achieve one's aim; **con l' [o nell']** ~ **di ...** +*inf* with the aim of ...

intenzionale [in·ten·tsio·'na:·le] *agg* (*offesa, errore*) intentional

intenzionato, -a [in·ten·tsio·'na:·to] *agg* **essere ~ a fare qc** to intend to do sth; **essere bene/male ~** to have good/bad intentions

intenzione [in·ten·'tsio:·ne] *f* (*proposito*) intention; **avere (l')~ di fare qc** to intend to do sth; **avere buone/cattive -i** to have good/bad intentions; **con/senza ~** intentionally/unintentionally

interagire [in·te·ra·'dʒi:·re] <interagisco> *vi* **~ con qc/qu** (*fenomeni, elementi, persone*) to interact with sth/sb

interattività [in·ter·at·ti·vi·'ta] <-> *f* (*di sistema, fenomeno*) interactivity

interattivo, -a [in·ter·at·'ti:·vo] *agg a. fig* COMPUT interactive

interazione [in·ter·at·'tsio:·ne] *f* interaction

interbancario, -a [in·ter·baŋ·'ka:·rio] <-i, -ie> *agg* (*accordo, rapporti*) interbank

intercalare¹ [in·ter·ka·'la:·re] *m* (*parola, frase*) pet phrase

intercalare² *vt* (*parola, frase*) to insert; **~ qc a qc** (*testo*) to insert sth into sth; *fig* to alternate sth with sth

intercambiabile [in·ter·kam·'bia:·bi·le] *agg* (*pezzi, elementi, ruoli*) interchangeable

intercapedine [in·ter·ka·'pɛ:·di·ne] *f* **1.** (*con-* *tro infiltrazioni*) cofferdam **2.** (*per isolamento*) gap

intercedere [in·ter·'tʃɛ:·de·re] *vi* avere ~ **presso qu** (**per qu/qc**) (*intervenire*) to intercede with sb (on behalf of sb/sth)

intercessione [in·ter·tʃes·'sio:·ne] *f* (*intervento*) intercession

intercettare [in·ter·tʃet·'ta:·re] *vt* (*aereo, lettera, telefonata*) to intercept

intercettazione [in·ter·tʃet·tat·'tsio:·ne] *f* **1.** (*di aereo*) interception **2.** (*di telefonata*) tapping; **~ telefonica** phone tapping

intercity [in·ter·'si·ti] <-> *m* FERR intercity train

intercomunale [in·ter·ko·mu·'na:·le] *agg* intermunicipal

intercomunicante [in·ter·ko·mu·ni·'kan·te] *agg* (*stanze, impianti*) intercommunicating

interconfederale [in·ter·kon·fe·de·'ra:·le] *agg* (*patto, accordo*) inter-union

interconnessione [in·ter·kon·nes·'sio:·ne] *f a. fig* TEC interconnection

intercontinentale [in·ter·kon·ti·nen·'ta:·le] *agg* (*telefonata, volo*) intercontinental

intercorrere [in·ter·'kor·re·re] <intercorro, intercorsi, intercorso> *vi essere* **1.** (*tempo*) to elapse **2.** *fig* (*rapporto, colloquio*) to exist

intercorso, -a [in·ter·'kor·so] **I.** *pp di* **intercorrere II.** *agg* (*colloquio, corrispondenza*) past

interculturale [in·ter·kul·tu·'ra:·le] *agg* intercultural

interdetto, -a **I.** *pp di* **interdire II.** *agg* **1.** (*sconcertato*) disconcerted **2.** JUR (*persona*) banned

interdipendenza [in·ter·di·pen·'dɛn·tsa] *f* (*tra fatti, fenomeni*) interdependence

interdire [in·ter·'di:·re] <interdico, interdissi, interdetto> *vt* JUR **~ qu (da qc)** to ban sb (from sth)

interdisciplinare [in·ter·diʃ·ʃi·pli·'na:·re] *agg* interdisciplinary

interdissi [in·ter·'dis·si] *1. pers sing pass rem di* **interdire**

interdizione [in·ter·dit·'tsio:·ne] *f* JUR disqualification; **~ dai pubblici uffici** ban from holding public office

interessamento [in·te·res·sa·'men·to] *m* (*intervento*) intervention

interessante [in·te·res·'san·te] *agg* interesting

interessare [in·te·res·'sa:·re] **I.** *vt* avere **1.** (*incuriosire*) to interest; **~ qu a qc** to interest sb in sth **2.** (*riguardare*) to affect **II.** *vi* *essere* (*importare*) **~ a qu** to matter to sb; **non gli interessa vincere** he's not interested in winning **III.** *vr:* **-rsi 1. -rsi a qc** (*incuriosirsi*) to be interested in sth **2. -rsi di qu/qc** (*occuparsi*) to take an interest in sb/sth; (*intervenire*) to intervene

interessato, -a [in·te·res·'sa:·to] **I.** *agg* **1.** (*incuriosito*) interested; **~ a qc** interested in sth **2.** (*calcolatore*) interested; (*amicizia, proposta*) selfish **3.** (*in causa*) concerned **II.** *m*, *f* (*persona in causa*) person concerned

interesse [in·te·'rɛs·se] *m* **1.** (*curiosità*) interest **2.** (*rilevanza*) interest; **di grande** ~ of great interest **3.** *pl* (*attività*) interests *pl;* **avere molti -i** to have a lot of interests **4.** FIN interest; **tasso d'**~ interest rate; ~ **attivo/passivo** interest received/charged; ~ **composto** compound interest **5.** (*vantaggio*) self-interest; **nell'**~ **di qu** in sb's interest

interezza [in·te·'ret·tsa] *f* (*totalità*) entirety

interfaccia [in·ter·'fat·tʃa] <-cce> *f* COMPUT interface; ~ **utente** user interface

interfacciare [in·ter·fat·'tʃa:·re] *vt* COMPUT to interface

interfacoltà [in·ter·fa·kol·'ta] <inv> *agg* (*regolamento, assemblea*) joint faculty

interferenza [in·ter·fe·'rɛn·tsa] *f* **1.** PHYS, TEL interference **2.** *fig* (*intromissione*) meddling

interferire [in·ter·fe·'ri:·re] <interferisco> *vi* **1.** *a. fig* PHYS (*elementi, fattori*) to interfere; ~ **in** [*o* con] **qc** to interfere with sth **2.** *fig* (*persona*) to interfere

interferone [in·ter·fe·'ro:·ne] *m* BIOL interferon

interfono [in·ter·'fɔ:·no] <-> *m* TEL intercom

intergalattico, -a [in·ter·ga·'lat·ti·ko] <-ci, -che> *agg* (*spazio*) intergalactic

intergenerazionale [in·ter·dʒe·ne·rat·tsio·'na:·le] *agg* intergenerational

interiezione [in·te·ri·et·'tsio:·ne] *f* LING interjection

interim ['in·te·rim] <-> *m* interim; **ad** ~ temporary

interinale [in·te·ri·'na:·le] *agg* temporary; **lavoro** ~ temporary job

interiora [in·te·'rio:·ra] *fpl* innards *pl*

interiore [in·te·'rio:·re] *agg* **1.** (*parte, lato*) internal **2.** (*spirituale*) inner; **mondo/vita** ~ interior world/life

interiorità [in·te·rio·ri·'ta] <-> *f fig* (*di persona*) inner life

interiorizzazione [in·te·rio·rid·dzat·'tsio:·ne] *f* (*di valore, norma*) interiorization

interista [in·te·'ris·ta] <-i *m*, -e *f*> SPORT I. *agg* (*dell'Inter*) Inter II. *mf* (*giocatore*) Inter player; (*tifoso*) Inter fan

interlinea [in·ter·'li:·nea] *f* (*spazio*) line spacing

interlocutore, -trice [in·ter·lo·ku·'to:·re] *m*, *f* **1.** (*conversatore*) speaker **2.** (*controparte*) counterpart

intermediario, -a [in·ter·me·'dia:·rio] <-i, -ie> I. *agg* (*funzione, attività*) intermediary II. *m, f* (*persona*) intermediary; **fare da** ~ to act as an intermediary

intermediazione [in·ter·me·diat·'tsio:·ne] *f* COM, FIN mediation

intermedio, -a [in·ter·'mɛ:·dio] *agg* **1.** (*periodo, punto, condizione*) intermediate **2.** *fig* (*soluzione*) compromise

intermezzo [in·ter·'mɛd·dzo] *m* **1.** (*intervallo*) interlude **2.** MUS intermezzo

interminabile [in·ter·mi·'na:·bi·le] *agg* (*troppo lungo*) interminable

interministeriale [in·ter·mi·nis·te·'ria:·le] *agg*

POL, ADM interdepartmental

intermittente [in·ter·mit·'tɛn·te] *agg* (*segnale, luce, pioggia*) intermittent

intermittenza [in·ter·mit·'tɛn·tsa] *f* **1.** (*di segnale, allarme*) intermittency **2.** EL (*dispositivo*) intermittence

internamento [in·ter·na·'men·to] *m* (*di malato*) confinement; (*di prigioniero*) internment

internazionale [in·ter·nat·tsio·'na:·le] *agg* international

internazionalismo [in·ter·nat·tsio·na·'liz·mo] *m* POL, ECON internationalism

internazionalità [in·ter·nat·tsio·na·li·'ta] <-> *f* (*di iniziativa, organismo*) internationality

internazionalizzare [in·ter·nat·tsio·na·lid·'dza:·re] *vt* (*aeroporto, provvedimento*) to internationalize

internazionalizzazione [in·ter·nat·tsio·na·lid·dzat·'tsio:·ne] *f* (*di istituzione, organizzazione*) internationalization

Internet [in·ter·'net] <-> *f* COMPUT Internet; **essere in** [*o* su] ~ to be on the Internet; **navigare in** [*o* su] ~ to go on the Internet; **sito** ~ website

interni [in·'tɛr·ni] *mpl* **1.** FILM interior shots **2.** ART interiors **3. gli Interni** POL, **ministero/ ministro degli Interni** Minister of the Interior

interno¹ [in·'tɛr·no] I. *agg* **1.** (*parte, lato*) inner **2.** (*regolamento, membro*) internal **3.** (*politica, affari*) national; (*volo*) domestic **4.** GEOG inland; **acque -e** inland waters **5.** *fig* (*interiore*) inner II. *m* (*allievo, candidato*) internal candidate

interno² <*sing*> *m* **1.** (*di struttura*) inside; (*di indumento*) lining; **all'**~ inside; **all'**~ **di qc** inside sth; **dall'**~ from the inside; **dall'**~ **di qc** from inside sth **2.** (*di territorio*) interior **3.** (*telefono*) extension; (*abitazione*) apartment number **4.** *fig* (*animo*) inner being **5.** (*di stato*) home; **notizie dall'**~ national news; **l'Interno** Minister of the Interior

intero¹ [in·'te:·ro] *agg* **1.** (*completo*) whole; **prezzo** ~ full price; **biglietto** ~ full fare ticket; **costume** ~ bathing suit; **latte** ~ full fat milk **2.** (*intatto*) whole

intero² *m* whole; **per** ~ in full

interpellanza [in·ter·pel·'lan·tsa] *f* POL question; ~ **parlamentare** parliamentary question

interpellare [in·ter·pel·'la:·re] *vt* **1.** (*persona, medico, avvocato*) to consult **2.** POL to question

interpellato, -a [in·ter·pel·'la:·to] I. *agg* (*persona*) questioned; (*medico, avvocato*) consulted II. *m, f* ADM person questioned

interpersonale [in·ter·per·so·'na:·le] *agg* (*rapporto, relazione*) interpersonal

interporre [in·ter·'por·re] <interpongo, interposi, interposto> I. *vt* (*ostacolo, difficoltà*) to put II. *vr:* **-rsi** **1.** (*ostacolo*) to be **2.** *fig* (*persona*) to intervene

interposi [in·ter·'po:·zi] *1. pers sing pass rem di* **interporre**

interposto, -a [in·ter·'pos·to] I. *pp di* **interporre** II. *agg* (*difficoltà, ostacolo*) intervening; **per -a persona** via a third party

interpretabile [in·ter·pre·'ta:·bi·le] *agg* (*testo*) interpretable

interpretare [in·ter·pre·'ta:·re] *vt a. fig* FILM, THEAT, MUS to interpret

interpretariato [in·ter·pre·ta·'ria:·to] *m* (*attività*) interpreting

interpretativo, -a [in·ter·pre·ta·'ti:·vo] *agg* 1.(*metodo, modello*) acting 2. JUR (*norma*) interpretative

interpretazione [in·ter·pre·tat·'tsio:·ne] *f a. fig* FILM, THEAT, MUS interpretation

interprete [in·'tɛr·pre·te] *mf* 1.(*di testo, opera*) interpreter 2.(*traduttore*) interpreter; **~ simultaneo** simultaneous interpreter 3.(*attore, musicista*) performer 4.(*portavoce*) spokesperson; **farsi ~ di qc** to act as spokesperson for sth

interprovinciale [in·ter·pro·vin·'tʃa:·le] *agg* interprovincial

interramento [in·ter·ra·'men·to] *m* 1.(*di tubo*) laying; (*di bulbo*) planting 2.(*di canale, palude*) filling in

interrato, -a [in·ter·'ra:·to] *agg* **piano ~** basement

interregionale [in·ter·re·dʒo·'na:·le] I. *agg* interregional II. *m* (*treno*) *stopping train which travels through different regions*

interrogare [in·ter·ro·'ga:·re] *vt* 1.(*testimone, sospetto*) to question 2.(*a scuola*) to test

interrogativo¹ [in·ter·ro·ga·'ti:·vo] *agg* 1.(*sguardo, espressione*) questioning 2. LING interrogative; **punto ~** question mark

interrogativo² *m* (*dubbio*) question

interrogato, -a [in·ter·ro·'ga:·to] I. *agg* (*testimone*) questioned; (*studente*) tested II. *m, f* (*testimone*) person questioned; (*studente*) student tested

interrogatorio [in·ter·ro·ga·'tɔ:·rio] <-i> *m* JUR questioning

interrogazione [in·ter·ro·gat·'tsio:·ne] *f* 1.(*a scuola*) test 2. POL **~ parlamentare** parliamentary question

interrompere [in·ter·'rom·pe·re] <interrompo, interruppi, interrotto> I. *vt* 1.(*lavoro, trattativa, persona*) to interrupt 2.(*strada, passaggio, linea, corrente*) to cut off II. *vr:* **-rsi** 1.(*in attività*) to break off; (*nel parlare*) to stop talking 2.(*trattativa*) to be interrupted 3.(*linea, corrente, strada*) to be cut off

interrotto [in·ter·'rot·to] *pp di* **interrompere**

interruppi [in·ter·'rup·pi] *1. pers sing pass rem di* **interrompere**

interruttore [in·ter·rut·'to:·re] *m* (*dispositivo*) switch

interruzione [in·ter·rut·'tsio:·ne] *f* 1.(*sospensione*) suspension; (*di linea, corrente*) interruption; (*di strada*) break; **senza ~** without stopping; **~ di gravidanza** termination of a pregnancy 2.(*pausa*) break; **~ pubblicitaria** advertising break 3.(*intervento*) interruption

interscambio [in·ters·'kam·bio] *m* exchange

intersettoriale [in·ter·set·to·'ria:·le] *agg* intersectorial

intersezione [in·ter·set·'tsio:·ne] *f* (*di linee, strade*) intersection; **punto di ~** junction

intersindacale [in·ter·sin·da·'ka:·le] *agg* inter-union

interurbana [in·ter·ur·'ba:·na] *f* (*telefonata*) long-distance call

interurbano, -a [in·ter·ur·'ba:·no] *agg* 1.(*linea ferroviaria, trasporto*) interurban 2.(*telefonata, tariffa*) long distance

intervallo [in·ter·'val·lo] *m* 1.(*di spazio*) interval 2.(*di tempo*) interval; **a -i** at intervals 3.(*pausa*) break; (*di spettacolo, conferenza*) interval; (*a scuola*) break 4. SCIENT, MUS interval

intervenire [in·ter·ve·'ni:·re] <intervengo, intervenni, intervenuto> *vi essere* 1.(*intromettersi*) to intervene 2. SPORT **~ su qu/qc** to get sb/sth 3.(*partecipare*) **~ a qc** to take part in sth 4.(*parlare*) to intervene 5. MED to operate

intervenni [in·ter·'ven·ni] *1. pers sing pass rem di* **intervenire**

interventismo [in·ter·ven·'tiz·mo] *m* HIST, POL interventionism

intervento [in·ter·'vɛn·to] *m* 1.(*intromissione*) intervention 2. SPORT tackle 3.(*partecipazione*) participation 4.(*discorso*) intervention 5. MED operation; **~ chirurgico** heart surgery

intervenuto, -a [in·ter·ve·'nu:·to] I. *pp di* **intervenire** II. *agg* (*persona, pubblico*) present III. *m, f* those present

intervista [in·ter·'vis·ta] *f* interview

intervistare [in·ter·vis·'ta:·re] *vt* to interview

intervistatore, -trice [in·ter·vis·ta·'to:·re] *m, f* interviewer

intesa [in·'te:·sa] *f* 1. *a. fig* POL agreement 2.(*affiatamento*) understanding

intesi [in·'te·zi] *1. pers sing pass rem di* **intendere**

inteso, -a [in·'te:·zo] I. *pp di* **intendere** II. *vt* **restare** [*o* **rimanere**] **~ che ...** to agree that ...; **(siamo) intesi?** agreed?

intessere [in·'tɛs·se·re] *vt* 1.(*cesto, stuoia*) to weave 2. *fig* **~ lodi a qu** to sing sb's praise

intestare [in·tes·'ta:·re] *vt* 1.(*lettera, pagina*) to head 2. JUR **~ qc a qu** (*bene, casa*) to register sth in sb's name; (*assegno*) to make out sth in sb's name

intestatario, -a [in·tes·ta·'ta:·rio] <-i, -ie> *m, f* 1.(*di lettera*) sender 2. JUR (*di bene*) owner, di conto, holder

intestato, -a [in·tes·'ta:·to] *agg* 1. JUR **~ a qu** (*bene, conto*) registered in sb's name 2.(*lettera, foglio*) headed; **carta -a** letterhead

intestazione [in·tes·tat·'tsio:·ne] *f* 1.(*di foglio*) heading; (*di libro, articolo*) title 2. JUR (*di bene*) registration; (*di conto*) holding

intestinale [in·tes·ti·'na:·le] *agg* ANAT intestinal

intestino¹ [in·tes·'ti:·no] *agg* (*guerra, lotta*) internal

intestino² *m* ANAT intestine; ~ **crasso/tenue** large/small intestine

intiepidire [in·tie·pi·'di:·re] <intiepidisco> **I.** *vt avere* **1.** CULIN (*riscaldare*) to warm up; (*far raffreddare*) to cool down **2.** *fig* (*sentimento*) to dampen **II.** *vi* **1.** CULIN (*riscaldarsi*) to warm up; (*raffreddarsi*) to cool down **2.** *fig* (*sentimento*) to cool

intimare [in·ti·'ma:·re] *vt* **1.** (*alt, silenzio*) to order; ~ **a qu di fare qc** to order sb to do sth **2.** (*pagamento*) to order; (*sfratto*) to serve

intimazione [in·ti·mat·'tsio:·ne] *f* **1.** (*ordine*) order; ~ **di fare qc** order to do sth **2.** (*di pagamento*) order; ~ **di sfratto** eviction order

intimidatorio, -a [in·ti·mi·da·'to:·rio] *agg* (*atto, parole*) intimidatory

intimidazione [in·ti·mi·dat·'tsio:·ne] *f* intimidation

intimidire [in·ti·mi·'di:·re] <intimidisco> *vt avere* **1.** (*imbarazzare*) to make shy **2.** (*minacciare*) to intimidate

intimità [in·ti·mi·'ta] <-> *f* **1.** (*ambito privato*) privacy; **nell'~** (*in casa, in famiglia*) in private; (*nella vita amorosa*) at intimate moments **2.** (*confidenza*) familiarity; **essere in ~ con qu** to be on close terms with sb

intimo¹ ['in·ti·mo] **I.** *agg* **1.** *fig* (*amico, amicizia*) close; **avere rapporti -i con qu** to have sex with sb; **ambiente ~** intimate atmosphere; **cenetta -a** romantic meal; **cerimonia -a** private ceremony **2.** *fig* (*convinzione, gioia*) inner; (*ragioni, significato*) innermost **3.** (*nascosto*) hidden; **parti -e** private parts; **biancheria -a** underwear; **igiene -a** personal hygiene **II.** *m* (*persona*) close friend

intimo² <*sing*> *m* **1.** (*interiorità*) heart **2.** (*biancheria*) underwear

intimorire [in·ti·mo·'ri:·re] <intimorisco> **I.** *vt* to frighten **II.** *vr:* **-rsi** to get frightened

intitolare [in·ti·to·'la:·re] **I.** *vt* **1.** (*libro, film*) to give a title to **2.** (*strada, edificio*) to name; ~ **qc a qu** to name sth after sb **II.** *vr:* **-rsi** (*libro, film*) to be called

intoccabile [in·tok·'ka:·bi·le] **I.** *agg* **1.** (*oggetto, patrimonio*) untouchable **2.** *fig* (*argomento*) indisputable **3.** *fig* (*persona*) unassailable **II.** *mf* **1.** (*persona*) person with powerful backing **2.** (*in India*) untouchable

intollerabile [in·tol·le·'ra:·bi·le] *agg* **1.** (*sopruso, offesa*) intolerable **2.** (*caldo, dolore*) unbearable

intollerante [in·tol·le·'ran·te] *agg* (*persona, carattere*) intolerant

intolleranza [in·tol·le·'ran·tsa] *f* intolerance

intonaco [in·'tɔ:·na·ko] <-ci *o* -chi> *m* (*per muro*) plaster

intonare [in·to·'na:·re] **I.** *vt* **1.** MUS (*strumento, voce*) to tune up; (*canzone, nota*) to intone **2.** (*colori, indumenti*) to match **II.** *vr:* **-rsi** (*colori, indumenti*) to match; **-rsi a qc** to go with sth

intonato, -a [in·to·'na·to] *agg* **1.** (*strumento, voce*) tuneful **2.** (*persona*) **essere ~** to be able

to sing in tune **3.** (*colori, indumenti*) matched

intonazione [in·to·nat·'tsio:·ne] *f* **1.** MUS tuning; (*della voce*) pitch **2.** LING intonation; (*inflessione*) inflection

intoppo [in·'tɔp·po] *m* (*ostacolo*) hitch

intorno [in·'tor·no] **I.** *avv* around; **guardarsi ~** to look around; **qui ~ non ci sono bar** there aren't any bars around here; **tutto ~** all around; **togliersi qu d'~** to get rid of sb **II.** *prep* **1.** ~ **a** around; (*spazio*) round **2.** (*tempo, quantità*) around about **3.** (*argomento*) on **III.** <inv> *agg* surrounding; **ho comprato la casa e il terreno ~** I've bought the house and the surrounding land

intossicazione [in·tos·si·kat·'tsio:·ne] *f* MED poisoning

intralciare [in·tral·'tʃa:·re] *vt* **1.** (*traffico*) to hold up; (*movimento*) to hamper **2.** *fig* (*attività, progetto*) to hinder

intralcio [in·'tral·tʃo] <-ci> *m* (*ostacolo*) hindrance

intramontabile [in·tra·mon·'ta:·bi·le] *agg* (*celebrità, fama*) timeless; (*attore, cantante*) immortal

intramuscolare [in·tra·mus·ko·'la:·re] MED **I.** *agg* (*iniezione*) intramuscular **II.** *f* intramuscular injection

Intranet [in·tra·'net] <-> *f* COMPUT Intranet

intransigente [in·tran·si·'dʒɛn·te] *agg* **1.** (*giudice, insegnante*) harsh **2.** (*politico, corrente*) intransigent **3.** (*atteggiamento*) intolerant

intransigenza [in·tran·si·'dʒɛn·tsa] *f* intransigence

intrappolare [in·trap·po·'la:·re] *vt* **1.** (*topo, ladro*) to trap **2.** *fig* (*raggirare*) to catch out

intrappolato, -a [in·trap·po·'la:·to] *agg* trapped

intraprendente [in·tra·pren·'dɛn·te] *agg* (*persona*) enterprising; (*in amore*) forward

intraprendenza [in·tra·pren·'dɛn·tsa] *f* enterprise

intraprendere [in·tra·'prɛn·de·re] <intraprendo, intrapresi, intrapreso> *vt* (*attività, viaggio*) to undertake; (*carriera, studi*) to start

intrapresi [in·tra·'pre:·zi] *1. pers sing pass rem di* **intraprendere**

intrapreso [in·tra·'pre:·zo] *pp di* **intraprendere**

intrattabile [in·trat·'ta:·bi·le] *agg* (*persona, carattere*) impossible

intrattenere [in·trat·te·'ne:·re] <intrattengo, intrattenni, intrattenuto> **I.** *vt* **1.** (*ospite, pubblico*) to entertain **2.** *fig* (*rapporti, corrispondenza*) to have **II.** *vr* **1.** **-rsi con qu** to stop with sb **2.** **-rsi su qc** to concentrate on sth

intrattenimento [in·trat·te·ni·'men·to] *m* entertainment

intrattenni [in·trat·'ten·ni] *1. pers sing pass rem di* **intrattenere**

intravedere [in·tra·ve·'de:·re] <intravedo, intravidi, intravisto> *vt* **1.** (*persona, cosa*) to glimpse **2.** *fig* (*soluzione, possibilità*) to see

intravidi [in·tra·'vi:·di] *1. pers sing pass rem di*

intravedere
intravisto [in·tra·'vis·to] *pp di* **intravedere**
intrecciare [in·tret·tʃa··re] I. *vt* **1.**(*capelli, paglia*) to pleat **2.**_fig_ (*rapporti*) to establish II. *vr:* **-rsi** (*fili, rami*) to become interwined; (*capelli*) to be pleated; (*strade*) to intersect
intreccio [in·'tret·tʃo] <-cci> *m* **1.**(*azione*) weaving **2.**(*di fili*) interlacing; (*di capelli*) pleating **3.**(*di tessuto*) weave **4.**_fig_ (*di fatti, fenomeni*) interweaving; (*di storia*) plot
intrepido, -a [in·'trɛː·pi·do] *agg* (*passo, sguardo*) intrepid; (*soldato, animo*) fearless
intricato, -a [in·tri·'ka·to] *agg* **1.**(*nodo, bosco*) tangled **2.**_fig_ (*vicenda, questione*) complicated
intrico [in·'tri·ko] <-chi> *m* **1.**(*di rami, fili*) tangle; (*di strade*) jumble **2.**_fig_ jumble
intrigante [in·tri·'gan·te] I. *agg* **1.**(*invadente*) meddlesome **2.**(*interessante*) intriguing II. *mf* (*persona invadente*) meddler
intrigo [in·'tri·go] <-ghi> *m* **1.**(*macchinazione*) plot **2.**(*situazione confusa*) difficult situation
intrinseco, -a [in·'trin·se·ko] <-ci, -che> *agg* (*proprio, interno*) intrinsic; **valore ~ di qc** intrinsic value of sth
intriso, -a *agg* **~ di qc** (*liquido*) soaked in [*o* with] sth; _fig_(*sentimento*) steeped in sth
introdurre [in·tro·'dur·re] <introduco, introdussi, introdotto> I. *vt* **1.**(*chiave, moneta, scheda*) to put **2.**(*prodotto, moda, uso*) to introduce; (*legge, riforma*) to bring in **3.**(*discorso, tema*) to start **4.**(*persona*) to show; **~ qu in qc** (*ambiente*) to introduce sb into sth; **~ qu a qc** (*disciplina*) to introduce sb to sth **5.** LING to introduce II. *vr* **-rsi in qc** (*luogo*) to enter sth; (*ambiente*) to join sth
introduttivo, -a [in·tro·dut·'ti:·vo] *agg* (*discorso, capitolo*) introductory
introduzione [in·tro·dut·'tsio:·ne] *f* **1.**(*gener*) introduction **2.**(*di moneta, scheda, disco*) insertion
introito [in·'trɔː·i·to] *m* (*incasso*) income
intromissione [in·tro·mis·'sio:·ne] *f* (*ingerenza*) interference
introspettivo, -a [in·tro·spet·'ti:·vo] *agg* (*esame, metodo, atteggiamento*) introspective
introspezione [in·tro·spet·'ʃio:·ne] *f* PSYCH introspection
introvabile [in·tro·'va:·bi·le] *agg* **1.**(*libro, francobollo*) untraceable **2.**(*persona*) nowhere to be found
introverso, -a [in·tro·'vɛr·so] I. *agg* (*persona, carattere*) introverted II. *m, f* introvert
intrusione [in·tru·'zio:·ne] *f* (*di persona*) intrusion
intruso, -a [in·'tru:·zo] *m, f* (*persona*) intruder
intuibile [in·tu·'i:·bi·le] *agg* (*conseguenza, motivo*) imaginable
intuire [in·tu·'i:·re] <intuisco> *vt* (*percepire*) to perceive
intuitivo, -a [in·tui·'ti:·vo] *agg* **1.**(*facoltà, conoscenza*) intuitive **2.**(*verità, giudizio*) ob-

vious **3.**(*persona*) intuitive
intuito [in·'tu:i·to] *m* (*attitudine*) intuition
intuizione [in·tuit·'tsio:·ne] *f* **1.**(*presentimento*) intuition **2.**(*trovata*) insight **3.**(*intuito*) intuition
inumano, -a [i·nu·'ma:·no] *agg* inhumane
inutile [i·'nu:·ti·le] *agg* **1.**(*oggetto, attrezzo*) useless; (*spesa, consiglio, discorso*) worthless; (*lavoro, sforzo*) pointless **2.**(*persona*) useless
inutilità [i·nu·ti·li·'ta] <-> *f* **1.**(*di oggetto*) uselessness **2.**(*di rimedio, sforzo*) pointlessness
inutilizzabile [i·nu·ti·lid·'dza:·bi·le] *agg* (*oggetto, attrezzo*) unusable
inutilizzato, -a [i·nu·ti·lid·'dsa:·to] *agg* (*attrezzo, impianto*) unused; (*energie, forze*) unspent
invadente [in·va·'dɛn·te] I. *agg* (*persona*) intrusive II. *mf* busybody
invadenza [in·va·'dɛn·tsa] *f* intrusiveness
invadere [in·'va:·de·re] <invado, invasi, invaso> *vt* **1.**(*territorio, paese*) to invade **2.**(*folla*) to invade; (*animali, piante*) to take over; (*acque*) to flood **3.**_fig_ (*malattia*) to infect; (*prodotto, moda*) to flood
invalicabile [in·va·li·'ka:·bi·le] *agg* (*passo, monte*) impassable; **limite ~** no access allowed
invalidare [in·va·li·'da:·re] *vt* JUR, ADM (*atto, documento*) to invalidate
invalidità [in·va·li·di·'ta] <-> *f* (*fisica*) disability; **~ permanente** permanent disability; **pensione di ~** disability benefit
invalido, -a [in·'va:·li·do] I. *agg* (*disabile*) disabled II. *m, f* disabled person; **~ di guerra** disabled veteran; **~ del lavoro** occupationally injured person
invano [in·'va:·no] *avv* in vain
invariabile [in·va·'ria:·bi·le] *agg* **1.**(*grandezza, tempo*) constant; (*comportamento*) invariable **2.** LING indeclinable
invariato, -a [in·va·'ria:·to] *agg* unchanged
invasi [in·'va:·zi] *1. pers sing pass rem di* **invadere**
invasione [in·va·'zio:·ne] *f* **1.**(*di truppe*) invasion **2.**(*di persone*) invasion; **~ di campo** SPORT field invasion **3.**(*di animali, piante*) invasion; (*di malattia*) spreading; (*di acque*) flooding **4.**_fig_ (*di prodotto*) flood
invaso [in·'va:·zo] *pp di* **invadere**
invasore, invaditrice [in·va·'zo:·re, in·va·di·'tri:·tʃe] I. *agg* (*esercito*) invading II. *m, f* invader
invecchiamento [in·vek·kia·'men·to] *m* **1.**(*di organismo*) aging; **~ della pelle** aging of the skin **2.**(*di vino*) maturing process
invecchiare [in·vek·'kia:·re] I. *vi essere* **1.**(*diventare vecchio*) to grow old **2.**(*vino, formaggio*) to mature **3.**_fig_ (*moda, opera*) to go out of date II. *vt avere* **1.**(*persona*) to age **2.**(*vino, formaggio*) to mature
invece [in·'ve:·tʃe] I. *avv* instead II. *prep* **~ di** instead of
inveire [in·ve·'i:·re] <inveisco> *vi* **~ contro**

qu/qc to rail against sb/sth

inventare [in·ven·'ta:·re] *vt* **1.**(*oggetto, fiaba*) to invent **2.**(*notizia, scuse*) to make up; (*bugia*) to tell; **inventarne di tutti i colori** to tell tall tales

inventario [in·ven·'ta:·rio] <-i> *m* **1.**COM stocktaking **2.**(*elenco*) inventory; **fare l'~** (**di qc**) to draw up an inventory (of sth)

inventiva [in·ven·'ti:·va] *f* (*fantasia*) invention

inventore, -trice [in·ven·'to:·re] *m, f* (*ideatore*) inventor

invenzione [in·ven·'tsio:·ne] *f* **1.**(*di oggetto, fiaba*) invention **2.**(*di notizia, bugia, scuse*) lie **3.**(*capacità, atto*) invention

invernale [in·ver·'na:·le] *agg* (*stagione, clima*) wintry; (*vacanze, sport, abbigliamento*) winter

inverno [in·'vɛr·no] *m* winter; **d'~** in winter

inverosimile [in·ve·ro·'si:·mi·le] **I.** *agg* **1.**(*improbabile*) unlikely **2.**(*enorme, straordinario*) incredible **II.**<*sing*> *m* improbability; **una storia che ha dell'~** an unlikely story; (**fino**) **all'~** incredibly

inversione [in·ver·'sio:·ne] *f* **1.**(*di direzione*) reverse; **fare ~** to make a U-turn; **~ a U** U-turn **2.**(*di ordine*) inversion **3.***fig* (*di parti, ruoli*) reversal; **~ di campo** SPORT changing of goals

inverso¹ [in·'vɛr·so] *agg* **1.**(*direzione, ordine*) reverse; (*ragionamento, situazione, caso*) opposite **2.**CHEM, PHYS reverse

inverso² <*sing*> *m* (*contrario*) opposite; **all'~** the wrong way around

invertebrato¹ [in·ver·te·'bra:·to] *agg* ZOO invertebrate

invertebrato² *m* ZOO invertebrate; **gli Invertebrati** the Invertebrates

invertire [in·ver·'ti:·re] *vt* **1.**(*direzione*) to reverse **2.**(*ordine, posizione*) to invert **3.**(*parti, ruoli*) to swap

invertito, -a [in·ver·'ti:·to] *m, f* homosexual

investigare [in·ves·ti·'ga:·re] **I.** *vt* (*cause, ragioni*) to investigate **II.** *vi* **~ su qc** to investigate sth

investigativo, -a [in·ves·ti·ga·'ti:·vo] *agg* (*attività, lavoro*) investigatory; (*ufficio, squadra*) detective

investigatore, -trice [in·ves·ti·ga·'to:·re] *m, f* investigator; **~ privato** private detective

investigazione [in·ves·ti·gat·'tsio:·ne] *f* investigation

investimento [in·ves·ti·'men·to] *m* **1.**ECON, FIN investment **2.***fig* (*di energie, risorse*) investment **3.**(*incidente*) traffic accident

investire [in·ves·'ti:·re] *vt* **1.**ECON, FIN to invest **2.***fig* (*energie, risorse*) to invest **3.**(*bufera, ondata, valanga*) to hit **4.**(*veicolo*) to crash into; (*pedone*) to run over **5.~ qu di qc** (*carica, titolo*) to give sb sth

investitore, -trice [in·ves·ti·'to:·re] *m, f* **1.**(*in incidente*) driver responsible **2.**ECON, FIN investor

investitura [in·ves·ti·'tu:·ra] *f* investiture

invettiva [in·vet·'ti:·va] *f* invective; **lanciare**

delle -e contro qu to hurl abuse at sb

inviare [in·vi·'a:·re] *vt* (*lettera, merce, persona*) to send; **le invio i miei migliori saluti** best wishes

inviato, -a [in·vi·'a:·to] *m, f* **1.**(*delegato*) envoy **2.**(*giornalista*) correspondent; **~ speciale** special correspondent; **dal nostro ~** from our correspondent

invidia [in·'vi:·dia] <-ie> *f* **1.**(*astio*) envy **2.**(*enfatico*) envy; **hai un giardino splendido, che ~!** you have a marvelous garden, I really envy you!; **ha una casa che è l'~ di tutti** his [*o* her] house is the envy of everybody

invidiabile [in·vi·'dia:·bi·le] *agg* enviable

invidiare [in·vi·'dia:·re] *vt* **1.**(*persona*) to envy; **~ qu per qc** to envy sb sth **2.**(*cosa*) to envy; **~ qc a qu** to envy sb's sth; **non avere nulla** [*o* **niente**] **da ~ a qu/qc/nessuno** to be the equal of sb/sth/anybody

invidioso, -a [in·vi·'dio:·so] **I.** *agg* envious **II.** *m, f* (*persona*) envious person

invincibile [in·vin·'tʃi:·bi·le] *agg* **1.**(*avversario, nemico*) invincible **2.***fig* (*ostacolo, difficoltà*) insurmountable **3.***fig* (*desiderio, sensazione*) irrepressible

invio [in·'vi:·o] <-ii> *m* **1.**(*di lettera, pacco, persona*) sending; (*di merce*) dispatch **2.**(*oggetto, merce*) consignment **3.**COMPUT (*tasto*) return

inviolabile [in·vio·'la:·bi·le] *agg* (*patto, segreto*) unbreakable; (*diritto, principio*) inviolable

inviolabilità [in·vio·la·bi·li·'ta] <-> *f* inviolability

invischiato, -a [in·vis·'kia:·to] *agg* (*persona*) caught up

invisibile [in·vi·'zi:·bi·le] *agg* **1.**(*non visibile*) invisible **2.**(*piccolissimo*) tiny

invisibilità [invizibili'ta] <-> *f* invisibility

invitante [in·vi·'tan·te] *agg* **1.**(*piatto, proposta*) inviting **2.**(*sguardo, sorriso*) alluring

invitare [in·vi·'ta:·re] *vt* **1.**(*a cena, festa*) to invite **2.**(*esortare*) to ask **3.***fig* (*invogliare*) to tempt

invitato, -a [in·vi·'ta:·to] *m, f* (*persona*) guest

invito [in·'vi:·to] *m* **1.**(*a cena, festa*) invitation; (*biglietto*) invitation; **~ a nozze** *fig* wedding invitation **2.**(*esortazione*) request **3.***fig* (*richiamo*) temptation

in vitro [in 'vi:t·ro] BIOL, MED **I.** *agg* in vitro **II.** *avv* in vitro

invivibile [in·vi·'vi:·bi·le] *agg* (*ambiente, clima*) unbearable

invocare [in·vo·'ka:·re] *vt* **1.**(*Dio, persona*) to call upon **2.**(*aiuto, grazia*) to ask for; (*pace, riforme*) to call for

invocazione [in·vo·kat·'tsio:·ne] *f* **1.**(*preghiera*) prayer **2.**(*richiesta*) request

invogliare [in·voʎ·'ʎa:·re] *vt* to entice

involontario, -a [in·vo·lon·'ta:·rio] *agg* (*errore, gesto, offesa*) involuntary

involtino [in·vol·'ti:·no] *m* CULIN roulade; **~ primavera** spring roll

involucro [in·'vɔ:·lu·kro] *m* (*confezione*) wrapping; (*per protezione*) casing

involuzione [in·vo·lut·'tsio:·ne] *f* (*di fenomeno, società*) decline

invulnerabile [in·vul·ne·'ra:·bi·le] *agg* (*eroe, fortezza*) unassailable

io ['i:·o] **I.** *pron 1. pers sing* I; **sono** ~ it's me; ~ **stesso/stessa** I personally; **neanch'**~ me neither; **neach'**~ **sono stato invitato** I haven't been invited either; **proprio** ~ I **II.** <-> *m* **1.** (*se stesso*) self **2.** l'**Io** PSYCH the ego

iodato, -a *agg* **sale** ~ iodized salt

iodio ['iɔ:·dio] *m* CHEM iodine

ione ['io:·ne] *m* CHEM ion

ionico, -a ['iɔ:·ni·ko] <-ci, -che> *agg* **1.** HIST, ARCH Ionic **2.** GEOG Ionian

Ionio ['io:·nio] *m* **il Mar(e)** ~/lo ~ the Ionian Sea

iosa ['iɔ:·za] *avv* **a** ~ galore

iperattività [i·pe·rat·ti·vi·'ta] <-> *f* (*di persona, bambino*) hyperactivity

iperattivo, -a [i·pe·rat·'ti:·vo] *agg* (*persona, bambino*) hyperactive

iperbole [i·'pɛr·bo·le] *f* MATH hyperbola; LING hyperbole

ipercalorico, -a [i·per·ka·'lɔ:·ri·ko] <-ci, -che> *agg* (*cibo, dieta*) high in calories

ipercritico, -a [i·per·'kri:·ti·ko] <-ci, -che> *agg* hypercritical

iperglicemia [i·per·gli·tʃe·'mi:·a] <-ie> *f* MED hyperglycemia

ipermercato [i·per·mer·'ka:·to] *m* superstore

ipersensibilità [i·per·sen·si·bi·li·'ta] <-> *f* *a. fig* MED hypersensitivity

ipertensione [i·per·ten·'sio:·ne] *f* MED hypertension

ipertesto [i·per·'tɛs·to] *m* COMPUT hypertext

ipertestuale [i·per·tes·tu·'a:·le] *agg* COMPUT hypertextual

ipnosi [ip·'nɔ:·zi] <-> *f* PSYCH hypnosis

ipnotico, -a [ip·'nɔ:·ti·ko] <-ci, -che> *agg* hypnotic

ipnotizzare [ip·no·tid·'dza:·re] *vt a. fig* to hypnotize

ipoallergenico, -a [i·po·al·ler·'dʒɛ:·ni·ko] <-ci, -che> *agg* (*cosmetico, alimento*) hypoallergenic

ipocalorico, -a [i·po·ka·'lɔ:·ri·ko] <-ci, -che> *agg* (*alimento, dieta*) low-calorie

ipocondria [i·po·kon·'dri:·a] <-ie> *f* PSYCH, MED hypochondria

ipocrisia [i·po·kri·'zi:·a] <-ie> *f* hypocrisy

ipocrita [i·'pɔ:·kri·ta] <-i *m*, -e *f*> **I.** *agg* hypocritical **II.** *mf* (*persona*) hypocrite

ipofisi [i·'pɔ:·fi·zi] <-> *f* ANAT pituitary gland

ipoglicemia [i·po·gli·tʃe·'mi:·a] *f* MED hypoglycemia

ipoteca [i·po·'tɛ:·ka] <-che> *f* JUR mortgage

ipotecare [i·po·te·'ka:·re] *vt* **1.** JUR (*casa, terreno*) to mortgage **2.** *fig* (*vittoria, promozione*) to believe sth is in the bag; ~ **il futuro** to count one's chickens before they hatch

ipotecario, -a [i·po·te·'ka:·rio] <-i, -ie> *agg*

(*mutuo, cambiale*) mortgage

ipotensione [i·po·ten·'sio:·ne] *f* MED hypotension

ipotesi [i·'pɔ:·te·zi] <-> *f* **1.** (*supposizione*) hypothesis; **per** ~ supposing **2.** (*teoria*) theory **3.** (*eventualità*) eventuality; **nell'**~ **che ...** +*cong* should ...; **nella migliore/peggiore delle** ~ at best/worst

ipotetico, -a [i·po·'tɛ:·ti·ko] <-ci, -che> *agg* **1.** (*caso, ragionamento, successo*) hypothetical **2.** LING **periodo** ~ conditional clause

ipotizzare [i·po·tid·'dza:·re] *vt* (*caso, situazione*) to imagine; ~ **che ...** +*cong* to suppose that ...; ~ **di ...** +*inf* to suppose that ...

ippica ['ip·pi·ka] <-che> *f* (*sport*) horse racing; **darsi all'**~ *scherz, inf* to get a new life

ippico, -a ['ip·pi·ko] <-ci, -che> *agg* (*gara, concorso*) horse

ippocampo [ip·po·'kam·po] *m* ZOO sea horse

ippocastano [ip·po·kas·'ta:·no] *m* (*albero*) horse chestnut tree

ippodromo [ip·'pɔ:·dro·mo] *m* (*impianto*) racetrack

ippopotamo [ip·po·'pɔ:·ta·mo] *m* (*animale*) hippopotamus

IPZS *m abbr di* **Istituto Poligrafico e Zecca dello Stato** State Printing Office and Mint

IR *abbr di* **InterRegionale** FERR Interregional (train)

ira ['i:·ra] *f* (*collera*) anger; **in** (**preda ad**) **uno scatto d'**~ in a fit of anger; **fare l'**~ **di Dio** *fig* to wreak havoc; **costare l'**~ **di Dio** *fig* to cost an arm and a leg

iracheno, -a [i·ra·'kɛ:·no] **I.** *agg* (*dell'Iraq*) Iraqi **II.** *m, f* (*abitante*) Iraqi

Iran [i·'ran] *m* **l'**~ Iran; **abitare in** ~ to live in Iran; **andare in** ~ to go to Iran

iraniano, -a [i·ra·'nia:·no] **I.** *agg* (*dell'Iran*) Iranian **II.** *m, f* (*abitante*) Iranian

Iraq, Irak [i·'rak] *m* **l'**~ Iraq; **abitare in** ~ to live in Iraq; **andare in** ~ to go to Iraq

irascibile [i·raʃ·'ʃi:·bi·le] *agg* (*persona, carattere*) irascible

IRI ['i:·ri] *m acro di* **Istituto per la Ricostruzione Industriale** Institute for Industrial Reconstruction

iride ['i:·ri·de] *f* **1.** (*arcobaleno*) rainbow **2.** ANAT iris

iridescente [i·ri·deʃ·'ʃɛn·te] *agg* (*riflesso, cristallo*) iridescent

IRL *abbr di* **IRLanda**

Irlanda [ir·'lan·da] *f* **l'**~ Ireland; **l'**~ **del Nord** Northern Ireland; **abitare in** ~ to live in Ireland; **andare in** ~ to go to Ireland

irlandese [ir·lan·'de:·se] **I.** *agg* (*dell'Irlanda*) Irish **II.** *mf* (*abitante*) Irishman *m*, Irishwoman *f*

ironia [i·ro·'ni:·a] <-ie> *f* irony; **fare dell'**~ (**su qc**) to be ironic (about sth); ~ **della sorte** irony of fate

ironico, -a [i·'rɔ:·ni·ko] <-ci, -che> *agg* ironic

ironizzare [i·ro·nid·'dza:·re] *vi* ~ **su qc/qu** to be ironic about sth/sb

IRPEF ['ir·pef] *f acro di* **Imposta sul Reddito delle PErsone Fisiche** Personal Income Tax

IRPEG ['ir·peg] *f acro di* **Imposta sul Reddito delle PErsone Giuridiche** Corporate Tax

Irpinia [ir·'pi:·nia] *f* **l'~** Irpinia, *part of the Campania region;* **abitare in ~** to live in Irpinia; **andare in ~** to go to Irpinia

irpino, -a [ir·'pi:·no] **I.** *agg* (*dell'Irpinia*) from Irpinia **II.** *m, f* (*abitante*) person from Irpinia

irradiare [ir·ra·'dia:·re] **I.** *vt avere* **1.** (*luce*) to light up; (*calore*) to give off **2.** *fig* (*felicità, gioia*) to radiate **3.** MED to irradiate **II.** *vi essere* (*propagarsi*) to radiate **III.** *vr:* **-rsi** (*calore, dolore*) to spread; (*strade*) to radiate

irradiazione [ir·ra·diat·'tsio:·ne] *f* **1.** (*di luce, calore*) radiation **2.** (*di dolore*) spread **3.** MED irradiation

irraggiamento [ir·rad·dʒa·'men·to] *m* radiation

irraggiungibile [ir·rad·dʒun·'dʒi:·bi·le] *agg* **1.** (*meta, luogo*) inaccessible **2.** *fig* (*traguardo, risultato*) unattainable

irragionevole [ir·ra·dʒo·'ne:·vo·le] *agg* **1.** (*persona, comportamento, opinione*) unreasonable **2.** (*paura, sospetto*) irrational; (*prezzo, punizione*) unreasonable

irrazionale [ir·rat·tsio·'na:·le] *agg* **1.** (*creatura, essere*) irrational **2.** (*persona, gesto, reazione*) irrational **3.** (*abitazione, metodo*) impractical

irrazionalità [ir·rat·tsio·na·li·'ta] <·> *f* **1.** (*di comportamento, gesto*) irrationality **2.** (*di abitazione, metodo*) impracticality

irreale [ir·re·'a:·le] *agg* (*atmosfera, immagine, luogo*) unreal

irrealizzabile [ir·re·a·lid·'dza:·bi·le] *agg* (*desiderio, sogno*) unattainable; (*impresa, progetto*) unworkable

irrealtà [ir·re·al·'ta] <·> *f* (*di ipotesi, racconto, sogno*) fantastic nature

irrecuperabile [ir·re·ku·pe·'ra:·bi·le] *agg* **1.** (*denaro, perdita*) lost **2.** (*distanza, ritardo*) irrecoverable **3.** (*macchinario, elettrodomestico*) dead **4.** (*malato, delinquente*) irredeemable

irrefrenabile [ir·re·fre·'na:·bi·le] *agg* (*impulso, slancio*) uncontrollable

irregolare [ir·re·go·'la:·re] *agg* **1.** (*procedura, documento*) irregular; **unione ~** unlawful union **2.** (*forma, dimensione*) irregular **3.** (*andamento, funzionamento*) erratic; (*persona*) inconsistent **4.** MED (*polso, respiro*) intermittent **5.** LING (*nome, verbo*) irregular

irregolarità [ir·re·go·la·ri·'ta] <·> *f* **1.** (*di procedura, documento*) irregularity **2.** (*di forma, dimensione*) irregularity **3.** (*di andamento, funzionamento*) erratic nature **4.** (*violazione*) unlawful act **5.** SPORT foul

irremovibile [ir·re·mo·'vi:·bi·le] *agg* **1.** (*carattere, opinione*) inflexible **2.** (*persona*) adamant

irreparabile [ir·re·pa·'ra:·bi·le] *agg* (*danno, errore, offesa*) irreparable

irreperibile [ir·re·pe·'ri:·bi·le] *agg* **1.** (*pro-*

dotto, documento) untraceable **2.** (*persona*) unable to be found; **rendersi ~** to make oneself scarce

irreprensibile [ir·re·pren·'si:·bi·le] *agg* **1.** (*persona*) irreproachable **2.** (*comportamento, vita*) faultless

irrequietezza [ir·re·kuie·'tet·tsa] *f* (*di persona, gesto*) restlessness

irrequieto, -a [ir·re·'kui·ɛ:·to] *agg* (*persona, animo, sguardo*) restless; (*bambino*) lively

irresistibile [ir·re·sis·'ti:·bi·le] *agg* irresistible

irrespirabile [ir·res·pi·'ra:·bi·le] *agg* **1.** (*aria, esalazione*) unbreathable **2.** *fig* (*atmosfera, clima*) stifling

irresponsabile [ir·res·pon·'sa:·bi·le] **I.** *agg* irresponsible **II.** *mf* (*persona*) irresponsible person

irresponsabilità [ir·res·pon·sa·bi·li·'ta] <·> *f* (*di persona, atto*) irresponsibility

irreversibile [ir·re·ver·'si:·bi·le] *agg a. fig* MED, CHEM irreversible

irrevocabile [ir·re·vo·'ka:·bi·le] *agg* (*decisione, scelta*) irrevocable

irriconoscibile [ir·ri·ko·noʃ·'ʃi:·bi·le] *agg* (*persona, voce*) unrecognizable

irriducibile [ir·ri·du·'tʃi:·bi·le] *agg* **1.** (*volontà, tenacia*) unshakeable **2.** (*fumatore, giocatore*) die-hard

irrigare [ir·ri·'ga:·re] *vt* **1.** (*terreno, campo*) to water **2.** (*fiume, canale*) to irrigate

irrigazione [ir·ri·gat·'tsio:·ne] *f a. fig* MED irrigation

irrigidimento [ir·ri·dʒi·di·'men·to] *m* **1.** (*di arto, corpo*) stiffening **2.** *fig* (*di pena*) increase; (*di clima*) fall

irrigidire [ir·ri·'di:·re] <irrigidisco> **I.** *vt* **1.** (*arto, corpo*) to stiffen **2.** *fig* (*pena*) to increase **II.** *vr:* **-rsi** **1.** (*arto, corpo*) to stiffen **2.** (*temperatura*) to drop **3.** *fig* (*ostinarsi*) **-rsi su** [*o* in] qc to cling doggedly to sth

irrilevante [ir·ri·le·'van·te] *agg* (*danno, problema*) insignificant

irrilevanza [ir·ri·le·'van·tsa] *f* (*di danno, problema*) insignificance

irrimediabile [ir·ri·me·'dia:·bi·le] *agg* (*danno*) irreparable; (*errore*) unrectifiable

irrinunciabile [ir·ri·nun·'cia:·bi·le] *agg* (*bene, diritto*) inalienable

irripetibile [ir·ri·pe·'ti:·bi·le] *agg* **1.** (*momento, esperienza*) one-time **2.** (*frase, insulto*) unrepeatable

irrisolto, -a [ir·ri·'sol·to] *agg* (*questione, problema*) unresolved

irrisorio, -a [ir·ri·'zɔ:·rio] <-i, -ie> *agg* (*prezzo, compenso*) derisory

irrispettoso, -a [ir·ris·pet·'to:·so] *agg* (*persona, comportamento*) disrespectful

irritabile [ir·ri·'ta:·bi·le] *agg a. fig* MED irritable

irritabilità [ir·ri·ta·bi·li·'ta] <·> *f a. fig* MED irritability

irritante [ir·ri·'tan·te] *agg* **1.** (*persona, comportamento*) irritating **2.** (*sostanza, liquido*) irritant

irritare [ir·ri·'ta:·re] I. *vt a. fig* MED to irritate II. *vr:* **-rsi** 1. (*persona*) to get irritated 2. MED (*pelle*) to become irritated

irritazione [ir·ri·tat·'tsio:·ne] *f a. fig* MED irritation

irriverente [ir·ri·ve·'rɛn·te] *agg* (*persona, gesto*) irreverent

irriverenza [ir·ri·ve·'rɛn·tsa] *f* (*di gesto, parole*) irreverence

irrobustire [ir·ro·bus·'ti:·re] <irrobustisco> I. *vt* (*corpo*) to make stronger II. *vr:* **-rsi** (*persona*) to become stronger

irrogare [ir·ro·'ga:·re] *vt* JUR (*sanzione, pena*) to impose

irrogazione [ir·ro·ga·'tsio:·ne] *f* JUR (*di sanzione, pena*) imposition

irrompere [ir·'rom·pe·re] <irrompo, irruppi, irrotto> *vi essere* ~ **in qc** to flood into sth

irrotto [ir·'rot·to] *pp di* **irrompere**

irruenza [ir·ru·'ɛn·tsa] *f* (*di persona, carattere*) impetuousness

irruppi [ir·'rup·pi] *1. pers sing pass rem di* **irrompere**

irruzione [ir·rut·'tsio:·ne] *f* 1. (*di polizia, ladri*) raid 2. (*entrata*) irruption; **fare** ~ **in qc** to burst into sth

irto, -a ['ir·to] *agg* 1. (*capelli, barba, baffi*) bristly 2. ~ **di qc** (*superficie*) bristling with sth 3. *fig* (*pieno*) full

Ischia ['is·kia] *f* Ischia, *island off the coast of the region of Campania;* **l'isola d'**~ the isle of Ischia; **abitare a** ~ to live on Ischia; **andare a** ~ to go to Ischia

iscrissi [is·'kris·si] *1. pers sing pass rem di* **iscrivere**

iscritto¹ [is·'krit·to] I. *pp di* **iscrivere** II. *agg* 1. (*a corso, partito, circolo, università*) enrolled; (*a gara*) entered 2. (*in registro*) listed; ~ **nel registro degli indagati** JUR named in the list of people under investigation by the police III. *m* 1. (*a corso*) pupil 2. (*a gara*) competitor 3. (*a partito, circolo*) member; (*all'università*) student

iscritto² *m* **per** ~ in writing

iscrivere [is·'kri:·ve·re] <iscrivo, iscrissi, iscritto> I. *vt* 1. ~ **qu** (**a qc**) (*a corso*) to enrol sb (in sth); (*a gara*) to enter sb (for sth) 2. (*in registro*) to enter II. *vr* **-rsi** (**a qc**) (*all'università, a corso*) to enroll in sth; (*a gara*) to enter oneself (for sth); (*a partito, circolo*) to join (sth)

iscrizione [is·krit·'tsio:·ne] *f* 1. (*a corso, all'università*) enrollment; (*a gara*) entry; (*a partito*) subscription; **quota d'**~ subscription fee 2. (*in registro*) registration 3. (*su pietra, metallo*) inscription

ISEF ['i:·zef] *m acro di* **Istituto Superiore di Educazione Fisica** Physical Education College

Isernia [i·'zer·nia] *f* Isernia, *city in the Molise region*

Islam [iz·'lam] <-> *m* (*religione*) Islam

islamico, -a [iz·'la:·mi·ko] <-ci, -che> *agg* (*dell'Islam*) Islamic

islamismo [iz·la·'miz·mo] *v.* **Islam**

islamista [iz·la·'mis·ta] <-i *m,* -e *f*> *mf* (*studioso*) Islamicist

Islanda [iz·'lan·da] *f* l'~ Iceland; **abitare in** ~ to live in Iceland; **andare in** ~ to go to Iceland

islandese¹ [iz·lan·'de:·se] <*sing*> *m* (*lingua*) Icelandic

islandese² I. *agg* (*dell'Islanda*) Icelandic II. *mf* (*abitante*) Icelander

isola ['i:·zo·la] *f* 1. GEOG island; ~ **deserta** desert island; **le Isole** Sicily and Sardinia 2. (*area staccata*) island; ~ **pedonale** pedestrian area 3. *fig* (*oasi*) little world

isolamento [i·zo·la·'men·to] *m* 1. (*solitudine*) solitude 2. (*di popolo, nazione*) isolation 3. (*di malato, detenuto*) isolation; **cella di** ~ solitary confinement 4. PHYS insulation; ~ **acustico** soundproofing; ~ **termico** thermal insulation

isolano, -a [i·zo·'la:·no] I. *agg* (*dell'isola*) island II. *m, f* (*abitante*) islander

isolante [i·zo·'lan·te] PHYS, TEC I. *agg* (*materiale, sostanza*) insulating; **nastro** ~ insulating tape II. *m* insulation

isolare [i·zo·'la:·re] I. *vt* 1. (*zona*) to screen; (*per sicurezza*) to isolate 2. (*malato, detenuto*) to isolate; (*da amici, contatti*) to cut off 3. PHYS, TEC (*filo, stanza*) to insulate II. *vr:* **-rsi** (*persona*) to isolate oneself; **-rsi da qu/qc** to cut oneself off from sb/sth

isolato¹ [i·zo·'la:·to] *agg* 1. (*luogo, caso, persona*) isolated 2. PHYS, TEC (*parete, stanza*) insulated

isolato² *m* (*edifici*) block

isolotto [i·zo·'lot·to] *m* islet

isontino, -a [i·zon·'ti:·no] *agg* (*dell'Isontino, dell'Isonzo*) from Isonzo

Isontino <*sing*> *m* (*zona*) Isonzo area; **nell'**~ in the Isonzo area

Isonzo [i·'zon·tʃo] *m* Isonzo river, *river in the Friuli-Venezia Giulia region*

isotermico, -a [i·zo·'ter·mi·ko] *agg* TEC (*contenitore, imballaggio*) isothermal

ispessimento [is·pes·si·'men·to] *m* thickening

ispettivo [is·pet·'ti:·vo] *agg* (*incarico, visita*) inspectional

ispettorato [is·pet·to·'ra:·to] *m* (*ente*) department; ~ **del lavoro** Department of Labor

ispettore, -trice [is·pet·'to:·re] *m, f* (*funzionario*) inspector; ~ **di polizia** police inspector

ispezionare [is·pet·'tsio·'na:·re] *vt* (*luogo, impianto*) to inspect

ispezione [is·pet·'tsio:·ne] *f* 1. (*di luogo, impianto*) inspection; **fare/compiere un'**~ to carry out an inspection 2. ADM audit

ispirare [is·pi·'ra:·re] I. *vt* 1. (*fiducia*) to inspire; (*compassione*) to arouse 2. *inf* (*piacere*) to like 3. (*artista*) to inspire 4. (*suggerire*) to prompt II. *vr* **-rsi a qc** (*a natura, bellezza, modello*) to be inspired by sth; (*a ideale, principio*) to be based on sth

ispirato, -a [is·pi·'ra:·to] *agg* inspired; **essere/sentirsi** ~ *inf* to be/feel in the mood

ispiratore, -trice [is·pi·ra·'to:·re] I. *agg* (*modello, principio*) inspirational II. *m*, *f* (*guida*) inspiration; (*musa*) muse

ispirazione [is·pi·rat·'tsio:·ne] *f* 1.(*potenza creativa*) inspiration 2.(*intuizione*) sudden idea 3.(*tendenza*) leaning

Israele [iz·ra·'ɛ:·le] *m* Israel; **lo Stato d'~** the State of Israel; **abitare in ~** to live in Israel; **andare in ~** to go to Israel

israeliano, -a [iz·ra·el·'ia:·no] I. *agg* (*di Israele*) Israeli II. *m*, *f* (*abitante*) Israeli

Istanbul [is·'tam·bul] *f* Istanbul

istantanea [is·tan·'ta:·nea] <-ee> *f* (*fotografia*) snap

istantaneo, -a [is·tan·'ta:·neo] <-ei, -ee> *agg* 1.(*immediato*) instantaneous 2.(*cibo*) instant

istante [is·'tan·te] *m* (*momento*) instant; **all'~** at once; **tra un ~** in a moment

istanza [is·'tan·tsa] *f* 1.JUR, ADM application; **presentare** [*o* **inoltrare**] **~** to apply; **in ultima ~** (*alla fine*) finally 2.(*esigenza*) need

ISTAT ['is·tat] *m acro di* Istituto (**Centrale**) di STATistica

isteria [is·te·'ri:·a] <-ie> *f* PSYCH, MED hysteria

isterico, -a [is·'tɛ:·ri·ko] <-ci, -che> I. *agg* hysterical II. *m*, *f* (*persona*) hysteric

istigazione [is·ti·gat·'tsio:·ne] *f* 1.(*incitamento*) instigation; **su** [*o* **per**] **~ di qu** at sb's instigation 2.JUR incitement; **~ a delinquere** incitement to crime

istintivo, -a [is·tin·'ti:·vo] *agg* instinctive

istinto [is·'tin·to] *m* instinct; **~ di conservazione** self-preservation instinct; **~ materno** maternal instinct; **seguire il proprio ~** to follow one's own instinct; **d'~** instinctively

istituire [is·ti·tu·'i:·re] <istituisco> *vt* (*tradizione, premio*) to found; (*commissione, cattedra*) to set up

istituto [is·ti·'tu:·to] *m* 1.(*ente*) institution; **~ di bellezza** beauty salon; **~ di credito** bank; **~ di cultura** cultural institute; **~ di pena** prison 2.(*scuola*) school; **~ professionale** teachers college; **~ tecnico** technical college 3.(*di università*) department 4.JUR institution; **~ del matrimonio** institution of marriage

istituzionale [is·ti·tut·tsio·'na:·le] *agg a. fig* POL institutional; **riforma ~** institutional reform

istituzione [is·ti·tut·'tsio:·ne] *f* 1.(*di servizio, governo, premio*) founding 2.(*ente*) institution; **-i pubbliche** public institutions; **è un'~!** *inf* (*persona*) he [*o* she] 's an institution!

istmo ['ist·mo] *m* GEOG isthmus

istogramma [is·to·'gram·ma] <-i> *m* (*in statistica*) histogram

istologia [is·to·lo·'dʒi:·a] *f* BIOL histology

istologico [is·to·'lo:·dʒi·ko] <-ci, -che> *agg* (*esame*) histological

istrice ['is·tri·tʃe] *m* (*animale*) porcupine

Istria ['is·tria] *f* l'~ Istria; **abitare in ~** to live in Istria; **andare in ~** to go to Istria

istriano [is·tri·'a:·no] I. *agg* (*dell'Istria*) Istrian

II. *m* (*abitante*) Istrian

istruire [is·tru·'i:·re] <istruisco> *vt* 1.(*educare*) to teach; **~ qu** (**in qc**) to teach sb (sth) 2.(*consigliare*) to instruct; **~ qu su qc** to instruct sb about sth 3.JUR (*causa, processo*) to prepare; **~ una pratica** to prepare the documentation

istruito [is·tru·'i:·to] *agg* (*colto*) educated

istruttivo, -a [is·trut·'ti:·vo] *agg* (*libro, film, viaggio*) informative

istruttore, -trice [is·trut·'to:·re] I. *agg* **giudice ~** JUR committing magistrate II. *m*, *f* (*insegnante*) instructor; **~ di guida** driving instructor; **~ di volo** flying instructor

istruzione [is·trut·'tsio:·ne] *f* 1.(*insegnamento*) education; **~ obbligatoria** compulsory education; **~ primaria** [*o* **elementare**] elementary education; **~ secondaria** secondary education; **~ professionale** vocational training; **~ pubblica/privata** public/private education 2.(*cultura*) education 3. *pl* (*direttive*) instructions *pl* 4. *pl* (*norme*) instructions *pl;* **manuale d'-i** instructions booklet; **-i per l'uso** instructions for use

Italia [i·'ta:·lia] *f* Italy; l'~ Italy; l'~ **centrale** Central Italy; l'~ **del Nord** [*o* **settentrionale**] Northern Italy; l'~ **del Sud** [*o* **meridionale**] Southern Italy; **abitare in ~** to live in Italy; **andare in ~** to go to Italy

italianistica [i·ta·lia·'nis·ti·ka] <-che> *f* (*disciplina*) Italian Studies *pl;* **dipartimento/istituto di ~** department of Italian Studies

italianità [i·ta·lia·ni·'ta] <-> *f* (*conformità, appartenenza*) Italianness

italiano¹ [i·ta·'lia:·no] <*sing*> *m* (*lingua*) Italian

italiano² I. *agg* (*dell'Italia*) Italian II. *m* (*abitante*) Italian

italico, -a [i·'ta:·li·ko] <-ci, -che> *agg* (*popolo, regno*) Italic; **carattere ~** TYP italic

ITALTEL [i·tal·'tel] *f acro di* società ITALiana TELecomunicazioni

iter ['i:·ter] <-> *m* ADM (*di pratica*) process; **~ burocratico** bureaucratic process

iterativo, -a [i·te·ra·'ti:·vo] *agg* 1.(*sviluppo, metodo*) repetitive 2.LING (*verbo, prefisso*) iterative

itinerante [i·ti·ne·'ran·te] *agg* (*spettacolo, mostra*) traveling

itinerario [i·ti·ne·'ra:·rio] <-i> *m* (*di viaggio, gita*) itinerary

ITIS ['i:·tis] *m acro di* Istituto Tecnico Industriale Statale

ittero ['it·te·ro] *m* MED jaundice

ittico, -a ['it·ti·ko] <-ci, -che> *agg* (*mercato, prodotto*) fish

Iugoslavia [iu·goz·'la:·via] *f* la ~ Yugoslavia; l'ex ~ the former Yugoslavia

iugoslavo, -a [iu·goz·'la:·vo] I. *agg* (*della Iugoslavia*) Yugoslav(ian) II. *m*, *f* (*abitante*) Yugoslav(ian)

iuta ['iu:·ta] *f* (*fibra*) jute

IVA ['i:·va] *f acro di* Imposta sul Valore

Aggiunto VAT; ~ **inclusa** VAT included; **partita** ~ VAT number

ivato, -a [i·'vaː·to] *agg* (*prezzo, prodotto*) VAT included

Ivrea [i·'vreː·a] *f* Ivrea, *city in the Piedmont region*

J

J, j [i l·'luŋ·ga] <-> *f* J, j; ~ **come jersey** J for Juliet

J *abbr di* **Joule** J; (*joule*)

jack [dʒæk] <-> *m* (*nelle carte da gioco*) Jack

jackpot ['dʒæk·pɔt] <-> *m* jackpot

jacquard [ʒa·'kar] <inv> *agg* (*disegno, tessuto*) jacquard

jazz [dʒæz, ʒɛts] <-> *m* jazz

jazzista [dʒad·'dzis·ta] <-i *m*, -e *f*> *mf* jazz musician

jeans [dʒiːnz] *mpl* jeans *pl*

jeanseria [dʒin·se·'riː·a] <-ie> *f* (*negozio*) jeans store

jeep® [dʒiːp] <-> *f* Jeep®

jersey ['dʒəː·zi, 'dʒer·zi] <-> *m* jersey

jet [dʒɛt] <-> *m* (*aeroplano*) jet

jetlag [dʒɛt·'læg, 'dʒɛt·lɛg] <-> *m* jetlag

jet-set [dʒɛt·'sɛt] <-> *m* jet set

jingle ['dʒɪŋ·gəl] <-> *m* (*per cellulari*) ringtone

job [dʒɔb] <- *o* jobs> *m* COMPUT job

jockey ['dʒɔ·ki] <-> *m* (*fantino*) jockey

jogging ['dʒɔ·giŋ] <-> *m* jogging; **fare** ~ to go jogging

joint ['dʒɔ·int] <- *o* joints> *m sl* (*spinello*) joint

joint venture ['dʒɔ·int 'vɛn·tʃə] <- *o* joint ventures> *f* COM, FIN joint venture

jolly ['dʒɔ·li] <-> *m* **1.** (*nelle carte*) joker **2.** *fig* wildcard

joule [dʒuːl, dʒaul] <-> *m* joule

joystick ['dʒɔi·stik] <- *o* joysticks> *m* COMPUT joystick

jr. *abbr di* **junior** jr.

judo ['dʒiː·do, 'dʒuː·dɔ] <-> *m* judo

judoista [dʒuː·dɔ·'is·ta] <-i *m*, -e *f*> *mf* judoist

jukebox ['dʒuː·k·bɔks] <-> *m* jukebox

jumbo [dʒʌm·bou, dʒum·bo] *m* <->, *m* AERO jumbo

junior¹ ['iun·jor] <inv> *agg* junior

junior² ['iun·jor, iu'n·jɔː·res] <juniores> *mf* SPORT junior

juventino, -a I. *agg* (*della Juventus*) **giocatore/tifoso** ~ Juventus player/fan **II.** *m*, *f* **1.** (*giocatore*) Juventus player **2.** (*tifoso*) Juventus fan

K

K, k ['kap·pa] <-> *m o f* K, k; ~ **come Kursaal** K for kilo

kalashnikov [ka·'laʃ·ni·kɔf] <-> *m* Kalashnikov

kamikaze [ka·mi·'ka·dze] <-> *m* kamikaze

karaoke [ka·ra·'ɔ·ke] <-> *m* karaoke

karatè [ka·ra·'tɛ, ka·'ra·te] <-> *m* karate

kart [kaːt] <-> *m* go-cart

kashmir ['ka·ʃmir, ka·'ʃmir] <-> *m* cashmere; **maglione di** ~ cashmere sweater

kayak [ka·'jak] <-> *m* kayak

kB *abbr di* **kilobyte** COMPUT KB

Kbyte [kei·'bait] *m abbr di* **kilobyte** kilobyte

kefir ['kɛ·fir, kɛ·'fir] <-> *m* kefir

képi [ke·'pi] <-> *m* kepi

kermesse [ker·'mɛs] <-> *f* **1.** (*festa*) kermis **2.** SPORT gala

kerosene [ke·ro·'zɛː·ne] *v.* **cherosene**

ketch [kɛtʃ] <-> *m* ketch

ketchup ['kɛ·tʃəp] <-> *m* ketchup

keyboard ['kiː·bɔːd] <- *o* keyboards> *f* COMPUT, MUS keyboard

kg *abbr di* **chilogrammo** kg

kibbu(t)z [kib·'buts] <-> *m* kibbutz

killer ['ki·lə, 'kil·ler] <-> *m* hitman

kilobyte ['ki·lə bait] <- *o* kilobytes> *m* COMPUT (*unità pari a 1024 byte*) KB

kiloton [ki·lo·'ton] <-> *m* kiloton

kit [kit] <- *o* kits> *m* kit; ~ **di montaggio** self-assembly kit

kitesurf [kait·'səf] <-> *m* SPORT kitesurfing

kitsch [kitʃ] **I.** <inv> *agg* (*arredamento, gusto*) kitsch **II.** <-> *m* kitsch

kiwi ['ki·wi] <-> *m* kiwi

kleenex® ['kliː·neks] <-> *m* kleenex®

km *abbr di* **chilometro** km

knockdown [nɔk·'daun, 'knok·'daun] **I.** <-> *m* SPORT knockdown **II.** <inv> *agg* knockdown

knockout [nɔk·'aut] **I.** <-> *m* knockout **II.** <inv> *agg* knockout

know-how [nou·'hau] <-> *m* know-how

K.O. [kap·pa·'ɔ] **I.** *m* K.O.; **vincere per** ~ to win by a knockout **II.** <inv> *agg fig* exhausted; **essere** ~ to be completely wiped out **III.** <inv> *avv a. fig* **mettere qu** ~ to knock sb out

koala [ko·'aː·la] <-> *m* koala

kolossal [ko·lɔs·'saː·l] <-> *m* FILM epic

krapfen ['krap·fən, 'kra·fen] <-> *m* donut

kW *abbr di* **chilowatt** KW

K-Way® ['ki 'wei] <-> *m o f* rain parka

kWh *abbr di* **chilowattora** kWh

L

L, l ['ɛl·le] <-> *f* L, l; ~ **come Livorno** L for Lima

l *abbr di* **litro** l.

l' I. *art det m e f sing davanti a vocale* the II. *pron pers* **1.** *3. pers m sing* (*persona*) him; (*cosa*) it **2.** *3. pers f sing* (*persona*) her; (*cosa*) it **3.** (*forma di cortesia*) **L'** you

L *abbr di* **lira** lira

la[1] [la] I. *art det f sing* the II. *pron pers* **1.** *3. pers f sing* (*persona*) her; (*cosa*) it **2.** (*forma di cortesia*) **La** you

la[2] <-> *m* MUS A; **dare il** ~ to give an A; *fig* to give the go-ahead

là [la] *avv* (*in quel posto*) there; **andare troppo in** ~ *fig* to go too far; **tirarsi in** ~ to budge up; **chi va** ~? MIL who goes there?; **di** ~ (*nella stanza accanto*) there; (*da quel luogo*) from there; (*attraverso quel luogo*) over there; **al di** ~ **del fiume** across the river; **per di** ~ that way; **via di** ~! get away from there!

labbro[1] ['lab·bro] <*pl*: -a *f*> *m* ANAT lip; **pendere dalle -a di qu** *fig* to hang on sb's every word; **rifarsi le -a** to have one's lips done; ~ **leporino** harelip

labbro[2] *m* (*di ferita*) edge

labiale [la·'bia·le] I. *agg* **1.** LING (*consonante*) labial **2.** (*lettura, metodo*) lip-reading II. *f* LING labial III. *m* (*linguaggio*) lip movements *pl;* **leggere il** ~ to lip-read

labile ['la·bi·le] *agg* (*persona, carattere*) unstable; (*memoria*) weak; (*concetto, confine*) shifting

labiolettura [la·bio·let·'tu:·ra] *f* lip-reading

labirinto [la·bi·'rin·to] *m* **1.** (*nella mitologia*) labyrinth **2.** (*di siepi*) maze **3.** (*di strade*) maze

laboratorio [la·bo·ra·'tɔ:·rio] <-i> *m* **1.** (*nella scuola: di chimica, fisica*) laboratory; ~ **linguistico** language lab **2.** MED laboratory; ~ **di analisi** analysis laboratory; **analisi di** ~ laboratory [*o* lab] tests **3.** (*officina*) workshop

laboriosità [la·bo·rio·si·'ta] <-> *f* **1.** (*operosità*) industriousness **2.** (*difficoltà: di procedure, operazioni*) laboriousness

laborioso, -a [la·bo·'rio:·so] *agg* **1.** (*operoso*) hard-working **2.** (*difficile: operazione, procedura*) laborious

lacca ['lak·ka] <-cche> *f* **1.** (*vernice*) lacquer **2.** (*per capelli*) hairspray

laccare [lak·'ka:·re] *vt* (*mobile, parquet*) to lacquer

laccio ['lat·tʃo] <-cci> *m* **1.** (*nastro*) (piece of) string **2.** (*per scarpe*) lace

lacerante [la·tʃe·'ran·te] *agg* **1.** (*penetrante: urlo*) piercing **2.** (*straziante: dolore, dubbio*) agonizing

lacerare [la·tʃe·'ra:·re] I. *vt* **1.** (*strappare: tessuto*) to tear **2.** (*assordare*) to deafen **3.** (*addolorare: cuore, anima*) to tear at **4.** *fig* (*distruggere: rapporto, famiglia*) to tear apart II. *vr:*

-**rsi 1.** (*strapparsi: tessuto*) to tear **2.** MED (*legamenti, muscoli, ferita*) to tear **3.** *fig* (*tormentarsi*) to torment oneself **4.** *fig* (*spezzarsi: gruppo, famiglia*) to split

lacerazione [la·tʃe·rat·'tsio:·ne] *f* **1.** MED laceration **2.** *fig* (*contrasto*) rift

lacero, -a ['la:·tʃe·ro] *agg* **1.** (*abito, persona, vela*) ragged **2.** MED **ferita -a** lacerated wound

laconicità [la·ko·ni·tʃi·'ta] <-> *f* **1.** (*concisione: di discorso, risposta*) brevity **2.** (*di persona*) curtness

laconico, -a [la·'kɔ:·ni·ko] <-ci, -che> *agg* **1.** (*conciso: risposta*) brief **2.** (*persona*) laconic

lacrima ['la:·kri·ma] *f* **1.** (*pianto*) tear; **avere le -e agli occhi** to have tears in one's eyes; **ridere fino alle -e** to laugh oneself to tears; **-e di coccodrillo** *fig* crocodile tears **2.** (*goccia: di burro, olio*) drop

lacrimare [la·kri·'ma:·re] *vi* (*persona*) to cry; (*occhi*) to water

lacrimazione [la·kri·mat·'tsio:·ne] *f* lacrimation

lacrimevole [la·kri·'me:·vo·le] *agg* (*patetico: storia, vicenda*) pitiful

lacrimogeno, -a [la·kri·'mɔ:·dʒe·no] *agg* **gas** ~ tear gas

lacuna [la·'ku:·na] *f* (*vuoto*) gap

lacunoso, -a [la·ku·'no:·so] *agg* (*conoscenze, informazioni*) incomplete

ladro, -a ['la:·dro] *m, f* thief

ladrocinio [la·dro·'tʃi:·nio] <-i> *m* theft

ladruncolo, -a [la·'druŋ·ko·lo] *m, f* (*ladro da poco*) petty crook

lager ['la:·gər] <-> *m* concentration camp

laggiù [lad·'dʒu] *avv* down there

lagna ['laɲ·ɲa] *f fam* **1.** (*lamento*) whining **2.** (*persona*) whiner **3.** (*canzone, discorso*) drag

lagnanza [laɲ·'ɲan·tsa] *f* complaint

lagnarsi [laɲ·'ɲar·si] *vr* (*lamentarsi*) ~ **per** [*o* **di**] **qc** to complain about sth

lago ['la:·go] <-ghi> *m* GEOG lake; ~ **artificiale** artificial lake; **Lago Maggiore/di Garda** Lake Maggiore/Garda

laguna [la·'gu:·na] *f* lagoon

lagunare [la·gu·'na:·re] *agg* lagoonal

L'Aia ['la:·ia] *f* The Hague

laicizzare [lai·tʃid·'dza:·re] *vt* (*istituzioni, scuola, Stato*) to secularize

laico, -a ['la:·i·ko] <-ci, -che> I. *agg* **1.** (*non ecclesiastico*) lay **2.** (*non confessionale: Stato*) secular II. *m, f* layperson

lama[1] ['la:·ma] *f* (*di coltello*) blade

lama[2] <-> *m* REL lama

lama[3] <-> *m* ZOO llama

lambiccarsi [lam·bik·'ka:r·si] *vr* ~ **il cervello** to rack one's brains

lambire [lam·'bi:·re] <lambisco> *vt* (*sfiorare*) to lap against

lambrusco [lam·'brus·ko] <-schi> *m* Lambrusco, *sparkling red wine*

lamella [la·'mɛl·la] *f* **1.** TEC (*di radiatore, collet-*

tore) strip; (*di persiana, veneziana*) slat **2.** BIO (*di fungo*) gill

lamentare [la·men·'ta:·re] **I.** *vt* to deplore **II.** *vr* **-rsi per** [*o* **di**] **qc** to complain about sth

lamentela [la·men·'tɛ:·la] *f* complaint

lamento [la·'men·to] *m* (*gemito*) groan

lamentoso, -a [la·men·'to:·so] *agg* (*voce, grido*) mournful

lametta [la·'met·ta] *f* (*per rasoio*) (razor)blade

lamiera [la·'miɛ:·ra] *f* plate; ~ **ondulata** corrugated iron

lamina ['la:·mi·na] *f* **1.** (*piastra*) (thin) plate; ~ **d'oro** gold foil **2.** (*di sci*) edge

laminare *vt* **1.** (*ridurre in lamine: vetro, legno*) to roll **2.** (*coprire*) to laminate

laminato [la·mi·'na:·to] *m* laminate

laminato, -a *agg* **1.** (*metallo*) rolled **2.** (*tessuto*) lamé

lampada ['lam·pa·da] *f* lamp; ~ **al neon** neon lamp

lampadario [lam·pa·'da:·rio] <-i> *m* chandelier

lampadato, -a [lam·pa·'da:·to] *agg with a sun-lamp tan*

lampadina [lam·pa·'di:·na] *f* lightbulb

lampante [lam·'pan·te] *agg* (*evidente*) clear

lampeggiare [lam·ped·'dʒa:·re] *vi* **1.** *avere* TEC (*spia, indicatore luminoso*) to flash; ~ **con gli abbaglianti** MOT to flash one's headlights **2.** *avere fig* to gleam **3.** *essere o avere* (*impersonale*) **sta lampeggiando** there is lightning

lampeggiatore [lam·ped·dʒa·'to:·re] *m* MOT turn signal

lampioncino [lam·pion·'tʃi:·no] *m* paper lantern

lampione [lam·'pio:·ne] *m* streetlamp

lampo[1] ['lam·po] *m* **1.** (*fulmine*) flash of lightning **2.** (*bagliore*) flash **3.** *fig* (*batter d'occhio*) flash; **in un** ~ in a flash **4.** (*intuizione*) flash; ~ **di genio** brainwave

lampo[2] <inv> *agg* **1.** **chiusura** [*o* **cerniera**] ~ zipper **2.** (*veloce*) lightning; **visita** ~ lightning visit

lampone [lam·'po:·ne] *m* **1.** (*pianta*) raspberry bush **2.** (*frutto*) raspberry

lana ['la:·na] *f* wool; ~ **d'acciaio** steel wool; ~ **di legno** wood curls; ~ **di vetro** glass wool

lancetta [lan·'tʃet·ta] *f* (*di orologio*) hand

lancia ['lan·tʃa] <-ce> *f* **1.** (*asta*) spear; **spezzare una** ~ **in favore di qu** *fig* to strike a blow for sb **2.** (*imbarcazione*) launch

lanciafiamme [lan·tʃa·'fiam·me] <-> *m* flamethrower

lanciamissili [lan·tʃa·'mis·si·li] **I.** <inv> *agg* rocket-launching **II.** <-> *m* rocket-launcher

lanciarazzi [lan·tʃa·'rad·dzi] <-> *f* (*pistola*) flare gun

lanciare [lan·'tʃa:·re] **I.** *vt* **1.** (*gettare: oggetti*) to throw; (*bombe*) to drop; ~ **un'occhiata a qu** to throw sb a look **2.** (*far andare a gran velocità: auto*) to drive at full speed; (*cavallo*) to ride at a gallop **3.** COMPUT (*programma, software*) to launch **4.** (*razzo, capsula spaziale*) to

launch **5.** COM (*prodotto*) to launch **6.** (*emettere: grido*) to let out **II.** *vr:* **-rsi 1.** (*buttarsi*) to throw oneself; **-rsi contro qu/qc** to throw oneself against sb/sth **2.** *fig* (*avventura*) **-rsi in qc** to throw oneself into sth

lanciasiluri [lan·tʃa·si·'lu:·ri] <-> *m* MAR torpedo tube

lancinante [lan·tʃi·'nan·te] *agg* (*dolore*) piercing

lancio ['lan·tʃo] <-ci> *m* **1.** (*di oggetto, palla, sasso*) throwing; (*di bombe*) dropping **2.** (*salto: con paracadute*) jump **3.** SPORT **lancio del giavellotto** javelin throwing; **lancio del peso** shot put **4.** (*di razzo, capsula spaziale*) launch **5.** COM (*di prodotto, campagna*) launch

landa ['lan·da] *f* (*pianura sterile*) heath

languidezza [laŋ·gui·'det·tsa] *f* **1.** (*spossatezza*) listlessness **2.** *fig* (*di sguardo*) languor

languido, -a ['laŋ·gui·do] *agg* **1.** (*fiacco*) listless **2.** *fig* (*svenevole: sguardo, occhi*) languid

languire [laŋ·'gui:·re] <languo *o* languisco, languii, languito> *vi* **1.** (*indebolirsi: per fame*) to grow weak **2.** (*lavoro, discorsi*) to languish

languore [laŋ·'guo:·re] *m* (*fiacchezza, struggimento*) languor

laniero, -a [la·'niɛ:·ro] *agg* (*industria, settore*) wool

lanificio [la·ni·'fi:·tʃo] <-ci> *m* woolen mill

lanolina [la·no·'li:·na] *f* lanolin

lanterna [lan·'tɛr·na] *f* (*lume*) lantern

lanternino [lan·ter·'ni:·no] *m* **cercare qc col** ~ to search high and low for sth

lanugine [la·nu·'dʒi:·ne] *f* (*di pulcino, pianta*) down

lapalissiano, -a [la·pa·lis·'sia:·no] *agg* (*ovvio*) self-evident; **verità -a** truism

lapidare [la·pi·'da:·re] *vt* **1.** (*uccidere a sassate*) to stone **2.** *fig* (*criticare*) to pan

lapidario, -a [la·pi·'da:·rio] *agg* <-i, -ie> *agg fig* (*frase, dichiarazione*) lapidary

lapidazione [la·pi·dat·'tsio:·ne] *f* (*uccisione a sassate*) stoning

lapide ['la:·pi·de] *f* **1.** (*su tomba*) gravestone **2.** (*su muro*) plaque

lapis ['la:·pis] <-> *m* (*matita*) pencil

lapislazzuli [la·piz·'lad·dzu·li] <-> *m* lapis lazuli

lapsus ['lap·sus] <-> *m* (*distrazione*) slip; ~ **calami** slip of the pen; ~ **freudiano** Freudian slip; ~ **linguae** slip of the tongue

L'Aquila *f* L'Aquila

lardellare [lar·del·'la:·re] *vt* CULIN to lard

lardo ['lar·do] *m* lard

largheggiare [lar·ged·'dʒa:·re] *vi* ~ **di** [*o* **in**] **qc** to be generous with sth

larghezza [lar·'get·tsa] *f* **1.** (*ampiezza*) breadth **2.** *fig* (*di idee, vedute*) liberality

largire [lar·'dʒi:·re] <largisco> *vt poet* to bestow

largo ['lar·go] <-ghi> *m* **1.** *sing* (*larghezza*) breadth; **farsi** ~ **tra la folla** to push one's way through the crowd; **girare al** ~ **da qu** to steer clear of sb; **fate ~!** make way! **2.** *sing* (*mare*) open sea; **prendere il ~** NAUT to put out to sea; *fig* (*andarsene*) to push off **3.** MUS largo **4.** (*piccola piazza*) small square; **~ Garibaldi** Garibaldi Square

largo, -a <-ghi, -ghe> *agg* **1.** (*ampio*) wide; **~ tre metri** three meters long; **essere ~ di fianchi** to have broad hips; **~ di spalle** broad-shouldered; **curva -a** open bend; **stare alla -a da qu** to give sb a wide berth; **su -a scala** far-reaching **2.** (*vestito*) loose

larice ['la·ri·tʃe] *m* BOT larch

laringe [la·'rin·dʒe] *f o m* ANAT larynx

laringite [la·rin·'dʒi·te] *f* MED laryngitis

laringotomia [la·rin·go·to·'mi:·a] <-ie> *f* MED laryngotomy

larva ['lar·va] *f* **1.** ZOO larva **2.** *fig* (*persona smagrita*) skeleton

larvale [lar·'va:·le] *agg* (*stadio, sviluppo, ciclo*) larval

larvato, -a [lar·'va:·to] *agg* (*nascosto*) hidden

lasagne [la·'zaɲ·ɲe] *fpl* lasagna *sing*

lasciapassare [laʃ·ʃa·pas·'sa:·re] <-> *m* pass

lasciare [laʃ·'ʃa:·re] **I.** *vt* **1.** (*gener*) to leave; **~ detto** to leave a message; **il discorso a mezzo** to stop in the middle of the speech; **~ le cose come stanno** to leave things as they are; **prendere o ~** take it or leave it **2.** (*mollare la presa*) to let; **lasciami andare** let me go **3.** (*consentire*) to allow; **~ andare** (*non curarsi di*) to neglect; **~ fare qu** to leave sb alone; **~ perdere** to give up; **~ correre** to let it pass; **~ a desiderare** to leave a lot to be desired; **~ stare qu** to let sb be; **lasciar stare** to forget (about) it; **lasciamo stare!** forget it! **4.** (*non chiudere*) to leave; **~ acceso** to leave on; **~ aperto** to leave open **II.** *vr:* **-rsi** (*coppia*) to split up; **-rsi andare** *fig* (*non avere freni*) to let oneself go; (*non curarsi*) to neglect oneself

lascito ['laʃ·ʃi·to] *m* (*eredità*) legacy

lascivia [laʃ·'ʃi:·via] <-ie> *f* lasciviousness

lascivo, -a [laʃ·'ʃi:·vo] *agg* lascivious

laser ['la:·zer] **I.** *sing* laser **II.** <inv> *agg* laser

laserista [la·ze·'ris·ta] <-i *m*, -e *f*> *mf* laser operative

La Spezia *f* La Spezia

lassativo [las·sa·'ti:·vo] *m* laxative

lassativo, -a *agg* (*medicinale*) laxative

lassismo [las·'siz·mo] *m* (*permissivismo*) laxity

lasso ['las·so] *m* **~ di tempo** interval

lassù [las·'su] *avv* (*in montagna*) up there; (*in cielo*) up above

lastra ['las·tra] *f* **1.** (*piastra: di metallo, di pietra*) slab; (*di vetro*) sheet **2.** (*radiografia*) X-ray

lastricato [las·tri·'ka:·to] *m* paving

lastrico ['las·tri·ko] <-chi *o* -ci> *m* **1.** (*di strada*) paving **2.** *fig* (*miseria*) **finire sul ~** to be on the rocks; **ridurre qu sul ~** to reduce sb to poverty

lastrone [las·'tro:·ne] *m* slab

latente [la·'tɛn·te] *agg* **1.** (*malattia, conflitto*) latent **2.** PHYS (*energia, calore*) latent

laterale [la·te·'ra:·le] **I.** *agg* **1.** (*ingresso, parete, bordo*) side **2.** SPORT (*nel calcio*) **linea ~** touchline; (*nel tennis*) sideline **II.** *m* SPORT (*nel calcio*) **~ sinistro/destro** left-/right-sided midfielder

laterizi [la·te·'rit·tsi] *mpl* brickwork

latice ['la·ti·tʃe] *m* latex

latifoglio, -a [la·ti·'fɔʎ·ʎo] <-gli, -glie> **I.** *agg* BOT (*pianta, cespuglio*) broad-leaved **II.** *m, f* BOT broad-leaved tree

latifondista [la·ti·fon·'dis·ta] <-i *m*, -e *f*> *mf* large landowner

latifondo [la·ti·'fon·do] *m* (large) estate

Latina [la·'ti:·na] *f* Latina

latine(n)se [la·ti·'nɛ(n)·se] **I.** *agg* (*di Latina*) from Latina **II.** *mf* (*abitante*) person from Latina

latinismo [la·ti·'niz·mo] *m* Latinism

latino [la·'ti:·no] <*sing*> *m* Latin

latino, -a I. *agg* Latin; **America -a** Latin America; **~-americano** Latin American **II.** *m, f* **1.** (*antico romano, neolatino*) Latin **2.** (*latino-americano*) Latino

latitante [la·ti·'tan·te] **I.** *agg* fugitive **II.** *mf* fugitive

latitanza [la·ti·'tan·tsa] *f* being in hiding

latitudine [la·ti·'tu:·di·ne] *f* latitude

lato ['la:·to] *m* **1.** (*parte*) side; **a ~ di qc** next to **2.** *fig* (*aspetto*) aspect; **d'altro ~** on the other hand; **da un ~ ..., dall'altro ...** on one hand ..., on the other ...

lato, -a *agg fig, poet* **in senso ~** broadly speaking

latore, -trice [la·'to:·re] *m, f* bearer

latrare [la·'tra:·re] *vi* to bark

latrato [la·'tra:·to] *m* bark

latrice *f v.* latore

latrina [la·'tri:·na] *f* public restroom; MIL latrine

latta ['lat·ta] *f* **1.** (*lamiera*) tin **2.** (*recipiente*) can

lattaio, -a [lat·'ta:·io] <-i, -ie> *m, f* milkman *m*, milkwoman *f*

lattante [lat·'tan·te] *mf* (*bebè*) baby

latte ['lat·te] <*sing*> *m* milk; **~ condensato** condensed; **~ detergente** (*per struccare*) cleansing lotion; **~ intero** whole milk; **~ materno** breast milk; **~ scremato** skimmed milk; **~ in polvere** powdered milk; **denti da ~** baby teeth; **fior di ~** (*mozzarella*) made from cow's milk, mozzarella; (*gelato*) plain ice cream; **bianco come il ~** as white as snow

latteo, -a ['lat·teo] <-ei, -ee> *agg* **1.** (*di latte: alimento, prodotto*) milk **2.** (*simile al latte*) milky; **via -a** ASTR Milky Way

latteria [lat·te·'ri:·a] <-ie> *f* (*negozio*) dairy

lattice ['lat·ti·tʃe] *v.* latice

latticello [lat·ti·'tʃɛl·lo] *m* buttermilk

latticini [lat·ti·'tʃi:·ni] *mpl* dairy products

lattico, -a ['lat·ti·ko] <-ci, -che> *agg* (*acido, fermento*) lactic

lattiera [lat·'tiɛ:·ra] *f* milk jug

lattiginoso, -a [lat·ti·dʒi·'no:·so] *agg* (*simile al*

latte) milky
lattina [lat·'ti:·na] *f* can
lattosio [lat·'tɔ:·zio] <-i> *m* lactose
lattuga [lat·'tu:·ga] <-ghe> *f* CULIN lettuce
laurea ['la:u·rea] *f* degree; ~ **breve** *bachelor's degree;* **esame di** ~ finals *pl;* **tesi di** ~ degree thesis; **conseguire la** ~ to graduate; **prendere la** ~ **in giurisprudenza** to do a law degree

i The **laurea** is awarded to students at the successful conclusion of their studies. A course of study lasts between four and six years. The final exam consisting of the discussion of a dissertation. Passing this exam entitles the person to use the title **Dottore/Dottoressa**. The **laurea breve** is awarded after a two- or three-year course of study.

laureando, -a [lau·re·'an·do] *m, f* final year student
laureare [lau·re·'a:·re] I. *vt* to award a degree to II. *vr:* **-rsi** to graduate; **-rsi in medicina** to graduate in medicine
laureato, -a [lau·re·'a:·to] I. *agg* (*studente*) graduate II. *m, f* graduate; ~ **in legge/lettere** law/arts graduate
lauto, -a ['la:u·to] *agg* (*compenso, retribuzione*) generous; (*pasto*) lavish
LAV *f abbr di* **Lega Anti Vivisezione** *Anti-Vivisection Law*
lava ['la:·va] *f* lava
lavabiancheria [la·va·biaŋ·ke·'ri:·a] <-> *f* washing machine
lavabile [la·'va:·bi·le] *agg* (*vernice*) cleanable; (*pannolino*) machine-washable
lavabo [la·'va:·bo] *m* (*lavandino*) sink
lavacristallo [la·va·kris·'tal·lo] <-> *m* MOT windshield washer
lavaggio [la·'vad·dʒo] <-ggi> *m* washing; ~ **a secco** dry-cleaning; ~ **del cervello** *fig* brainwashing
lavagna [la·'vaɲ·ɲa] *f* 1. GEOL slate 2. (*nelle scuole*) blackboard; ~ **luminosa** overhead projector
lavamano [la·va·'ma:·no] <-> *m* washstand
lavamoquette [la·va·mo·'kɛt] <-> *f* carpet cleaner
lavanda [la·'van·da] *f* 1. MED lavage; **fare una** ~ **gastrica a qu** to pump sb's stomach out 2. (*pianta, profumo*) lavender
lavandaia [la·van·'da:·ia] *f* washerwoman
lavanderia [la·van·de·'ri:·a] <-ie> *f* 1. (*negozio*) laundry 2. (*stanza*) laundry(room)
lavandino [la·van·'di:·no] *m* sink
lavapavimenti [la·va·pa·vi·'men·ti] <-> *f* floor cleaning machine
lavapiatti[1] [la·va·'piat·ti] <-> *f* dishwasher
lavapiatti[2] [la·va·'piat·ti] <-> *mf* dishwasher
lavare [la·'va:·re] I. *vt* (*biancheria, stoviglie*) to wash; (*pavimento, denti, vetri*) to clean; ~ **a secco** to dry-clean II. *vr:* **-rsi** to wash; **-rsi**

come i gatti to give oneself a sponge bath; **lavarsene le mani** (**di qc**) *fig* to wash one's hands (of sth)
lavasciuga, lavasciugatrice [la·vaʃ·'ʃu:·ga/la·vaʃ·ʃu:·ga·'tri:·tʃe] (*per biancheria*) washer dryer
lavasecco [la·va·'sek·ko] <-> *m o f* (*negozio*) dry cleaner's
lavastoviglie [la·vas·to·'viʎ·ʎe] <-> *f* dishwasher
lavata [la·'va:·ta] *f* wash; **dare una** ~ **di capo a qu** *fig* to give sb a dressing down
lavatergifari [la·va·tɛr·dʒi·'fa:·ri] <-> *m* MOT headlight washer
lavatergilunotto [la·va·tɛr·dʒi·lu·'nɔt·to] <-> *m* MOT rear windshield washer
lavativo [la·va·'ti:·vo] *m* shirker
lavatrice [la·va·'tri:·tʃe] *f* (*per biancheria*) washing machine
lavavetri [la·va·'ve:·tri] <-> *mf* 1. (*chi pulisce le finestre*) window cleaner 2. (*chi pulisce i parabrezza*) squeegee man *inf, pej* 3. (*attrezzo*) squeegee
lavello [la·'vɛl·lo] *m* sink
lavico, -a ['la:·vi·ko] <-ci, -che> *agg* (*pietra, colata*) lava
lavina [la·'vi:·na] *f* 1. (*di neve*) avalanche 2. (*di terra*) landslide
lavorante [la·vo·'ran·te] *mf* worker
lavorare [la·vo·'ra:·re] I. *vt* (*ferro, pasta, terreno*) to work II. *vi* 1. (*gener*) to work 2. (*negozio*) to do business; ~ **bene** to do good business III. *vr* **-rsi qu** *fam* to soften sb up
lavorativo, -a [la·vo·ra·'ti:·vo] *agg* (*attività, orario*) working; **giorno** ~ working day; **settimana -a** working week
lavoratore, -trice [la·vo·ra·'to:·re] I. *agg* working; **la classe -trice** the working class II. *m, f* worker; ~ **agricolo** agricultural worker; ~ **autonomo** self-employed worker; ~ **dipendente** employee; ~ **qualificato** skilled worker; ~ **specializzato** specialized worker
lavorazione [la·vo·rat·'tsio:·ne] *f* (*di materie prime*) processing; (*di film*) production; (*di pasta*) working; ~ **in serie** mass-production; **essere in** ~ to be in progress
lavorio [la·vo·'ri:·o] <-ii> *m* 1. (*attività*) intense activity 2. *fig* (*intrigo*) intrigue
lavoro [la·'vo:·ro] *m* 1. (*attività di produzione*) work; ~ **nero** *work in the black economy;* **-i domestici** housework; **-i forzati** forced labor; **-i in corso** (*su strade*) work in progress 2. (*rimunerato*) job; **senza** ~ unemployed; **andare al** ~ to go to work 3. (*opera*) work; ~ **teatrale** play
laziale [lat·'tsia:·le] I. *mf* 1. (*abitante*) person from the Lazio region 2. SPORT (*giocatore*) Lazio player; (*tifoso*) Lazio fan II. *agg* 1. (*abitante, dialetto*) Lazio 2. SPORT (*giocatore, tifoso*) Lazio
Lazio ['lat·tsio] <*sing*> I. *m* Lazio region II. *f* SPORT (*squadra di calcio*) Lazio (soccer team)
lazzaretto [lad·dza·'ret·to] *m* lazaretto

lazzarone [lad·dza·'ro:·ne] *m* **1.**(*canaglia*) rascal **2.**(*fannullone*) shirker

lazzo ['lad·dzo/'lat·tso] *m* **1.**(*nella Commedia dell'Arte*) comic scene **2.**(*battuta*) joke

le [le] **I.** *art det f pl* the; ~ **signore** the women **II.** *pron pers 3. pers f sing* **1.**(*complemento di termine*) (to) her; **non ~ hai detto nulla?** didn't you say anything to her? **2.**(*complemento di termine, forma di cortesia: Le*) (to) you; **Le dà fastidio se apro la finestra?** do you mind if I open the window? **III.** *pron pers 3. pers f pl* **1.**(*complemento oggetto*) them; **non ~ conosco** I don't know them **2.**(*in espressioni ellittiche, spesso non tradotto*) **guarda che ~ prendi!** you're heading for a smack!

leale [le·'a:·le] *agg* **1.**(*onesto, sincero: persona*) honest; (*comportamento*) fair **2.**(*fedele*) loyal

lealista [le·a·'lis·ta] <-i *m*, -e *f*> **I.** *mf* HIST loyalist **II.** *agg* (*comportamento, politica, truppe*) loyalist

lealtà [le·al·'ta] <-> *f* **1.**(*onestà, sincerità*) honesty; (*di comportamento*) fairness **2.**(*fedeltà*) loyalty

leasing ['li:·sin] <-> *m* FIN leasing; **prendere qc in ~** to lease sth; **società di ~** leasing firm; **~ immobiliare** real-estate leasing; **~ finanziario** financial leasing

lebbra ['leb·bra] *f* MED leprosy

lebbrosario [leb·bro·'sa:·rio] <-i> *m* leper colony

lebbroso, -a [leb·'bro:·so] **I.** *agg* leprous **II.** *m, f* leper

leccaculo [lek·ka·'ku:·lo] <-li *o* -> *m vulg* ass kisser

lecca lecca [lek·ka·'lek·ka] <-> *m* lollipop

leccapiedi [lek·ka·'piɛ:·di] <-> *mf pej* brown-noser

leccare [lek·'ka:·re] **I.** *vt* to lick; ~ **i piedi a qu** *fig* to suck up to sb **II.** *vr:* -**rsi** -**rsi le dita** [*o* i **baffi**] *fig* to lick one's lips; -**rsi le ferite** *fig* to lick one's wounds

leccata [lek·'ka:·ta] *f* lick

leccato, -a [lek·'ka:·to] *agg fig* primped

Lecce *f* Lecce

leccese [lek·'ke:·se] **I.** *agg* (*di Lecce*) from Lecce **II.** *mf* (*abitante*) person from Lecce

Leccese <*sing*> *m* Lecce area; **nel ~** in the Lecce area

lecchese [lek·'ke:·se] **I.** *agg* (*di Lecco*) from Lecco **II.** *mf* (*abitante*) person from Lecco

Lecchese <*sing*> *m* Lecco area; **nel ~** in the Lecco area

leccio ['let·tʃo] <-cci> *m* **1.**(*albero*) holm oak **2.**(*legno*) holm wood

Lecco *f* Lecco

leccornia [lek·kor·'ni:·a] <-ie> *f* delicacy

lecitina [le·tʃi·'ti:·na] *f* lecithin

lecito, -a ['le:·tʃi·to] *agg* (*azione, intercettazione*) lawful; (*copia*) legal; **non è ~ intercettare le telefonate** tapping phone calls is illegal

ledere ['lɛ:·de·re] <ledo, lesi, leso> *vt* **1.** MED

(*ferire*) to injury **2.** *fig* (*danneggiare*) to harm

lega ['le:·ga] <-ghe> *f* **1.**(*associazione*) league; **La Lega Nord** POL the Northern League **2.**(*di metalli*) alloy; ~ **in argento** silver alloy; **di bassa ~** (*oro*) with a low gold content; *fig* cheap

legaccio [le·'gat·tʃo] <-cci> *m* (piece of) string

legale [le·'ga:·le] **I.** *agg* **1.**(*secondo la legge*) legal; **studio ~** law firm; **spese legali** legal costs **2.**(*legittimo*) lawful **II.** *mf* lawyer

legalità [le·ga·li·'ta] <-> *f* legality

legalizzare [le·ga·lid·'dza:·re] *vt* (*autenticare, rendere legale*) to legalize

legalizzazione [le·ga·lid·dzat·'tsio:·ne] *f* legalization

Legambiente [le·gam·'biɛn·te] *f* ECO environmental league

legame [le·'ga:·me] *m* **1.**(*vincolo*) link **2.**(*rapporto*) relationship **3.**(*nesso logico*) link

legamento [le·ga·'men·to] *m* ANAT ligament

Lega Nord ['le:·ga nɔrd] *f* POL Northern League

legare [le·'ga:·re] **I.** *vt* **1.**(*collegare*) to bind; (*con spago, funi*) to tie up; **avere le mani legate** *fig* to have one's hands tied; **se l'è legata al dito** *fam* he didn't forget it **2.** *fig* (*unire*) to bind together **II.** *vi fig* (*andare d'accordo*) to get on **III.** *vr* **1.**(*attaccarsi*) to tie oneself **2.** CHEM to bind **3.**(*unirsi*) -**rsi a qu** to become involved with sb

legatoria [le·ga·to·'ri:·a] <-ie> *f* bookbindery

legatura [le·ga·'tu:·ra] *f* **1.** MED ligature **2.** MUS ligature **3.**(*rilegatura*) binding; ~ **in pelle** leather binding

legge ['led·dʒe] *f* JUR law; **per ~** by law; ~ **dell'onore** *fig* law of honor; **dottore in ~** law graduate

leggenda [led·'dʒɛn·da] *f* **1.** LIT legend **2.** *fig* (*invenzione*) myth; ~ **metropolitana** urban myth **3.**(*iscrizione*) legend

leggendario, -a <-i, -ie> *agg* (*evento, gesta, personaggio*) legendary

leggere ['lɛd·dʒe·re] <leggo, lessi, letto> **I.** *vt* (*libro, testo*) to read; ~ **il futuro** to read the future; ~ **la mano a qu** to read sb's palm; ~ **la musica** to read music; ~ **le labbra** to lip-read **II.** *vi* to read

leggerezza [led·dʒe·'ret·tsa] *f* **1.**(*di oggetto, tessuto, pasto*) lightness **2.**(*agilità*) nimbleness; **con ~** nimbly **3.** *fig* (*superficialità*) levity **4.** *fig* (*spensieratezza*) thoughtlessness

leggero, -a [led·'dʒɛ:·ro] *agg* **1.**(*gener*) light **2.**(*malessere, variazione*) mild **3.** *fig* (*superficiale*) frivolous; **prendere le cose alla -a** to take things lightly **4.**(*loc*) **atletica -a** track and field; **musica -a** light music

leggibile [led·'dʒi:·bi·le] *agg* **1.**(*scrittura*) legible **2.**(*libro*) readable

leggio [led·'dʒi:·o] <-ii> *m* **1.**(*per libri*) bookstand **2.** MUS music stand

leggiucchiare [led·dʒuk·'kia:·re] *vt* to browse

leghismo [le·'giz·mo] *m* POL *support for the Northern League*

leghista [le·'gis·ta] <-i *m*, -e *f*> I. *mf* POL supporter of the Northern League II. *agg* POL (*della Lega Nord*) Northern League; **deputato** ~ Northern League deputy

legiferare [le·dʒi·fe·'ra:·re] *vi* JUR to legislate

legionario [le·dʒo·'na:·rio] <-i> *m* 1. HIST legionary 2. (*della Legione straniera*) Legionnaire

legione [le·'dʒo:·ne] *f* MIL legion; **la Legione Straniera** the Foreign Legion

legislativo, -a [le·dʒiz·la·'ti:·vo] *agg* (*decreto, disposizione*) legislative; **potere** ~ legislative power

legislatore, -trice [le·dʒiz·la·'to:·re] *m*, *f* legislator

legislatura [le·dʒiz·la·'tu:·ra] *f* (*periodo*) legislature

legislazione [le·dʒiz·lat·'tsio:·ne] *f* 1. (*attività*) legislation 2. (*le leggi*) legislation

legittima [le·'dʒit·ti·ma] *f* JUR portion of a person's estate to which the spouse and offspring are legally entitled, regardless of the will

legittimare [le·dʒit·ti·'ma:·re] *vt a. fig* to legitimize

legittimazione [le·dʒit·ti·mat·'tsio:·ne] *f a. fig* legitimation

legittimità [le·dʒit·ti·mi·'ta] <-> *f a. fig* legitimacy

legittimo, -a [le·'dʒit·ti·mo] *agg a. fig* legitimate; **-a difesa** self-defense

legna ['leɲ·ɲa] <- *o* -e> *f* wood; **far** ~ to gather wood

legnaia [leɲ·'ɲa:·ia] <-aie> *f* woodshed

legname [leɲ·'ɲa:·me] *m* wood; ~ **da costruzione** timber

legnata [leɲ·'ɲa:·ta] *f* (*bastonata*) blow (with a stick); **prendere qu a -e** to give sb a thrashing

legno ['leɲ·ɲo] *m* wood

legnosità [leɲ·ɲo·si·'ta] <-> *f* (*di fusto, tronco*) woodiness

legnoso, -a [leɲ·'ɲo:·so] *agg* 1. BOT (*fusto, tronco*) woody 2. (*carne*) tough 3. (*rigido: movimento, arto*) stiff

legumi [le·'gu:·mi] *m pl* pulses

lei ['lɛ:·i] *pron pers* 1. 3. *pers f sing* (*soggetto*) she; **beata** ~! lucky her! 2. (*oggetto*) her 3. (*con preposizione*) her 4. 3. *pers m e f sing* (*forma di cortesia soggetto: Lei*) you 5. 3. *pers m e f sing* (*con preposizione: Lei*) you; **dare del Lei a qu** to address sb using the polite form

lembo ['lem·bo] *m* 1. (*di indumento, lenzuolo*) corner 2. (*pezzo, fascia*) piece

lemma ['lɛm·ma] <-i> *m* entry

lemmario [lem·'ma:·rio] <-i> *m* wordlist

lemme lemme ['lɛm·me 'lɛm·me] *avv fam* very slowly

lena ['le:·na] *f* (*vigore*) energy; **lavorare di buona** ~ to work with a will

leninismo [le·ni·'niz·mo] *m* Leninism

lenitivo [le·ni·'ti:·vo] *m* calmant

lenitivo, -a *agg* (*prodotto, trattamento*) soothing

lente ['lɛn·te] *f* lens; ~ **d'ingrandimento** magnifying lens; **-i a contatto** [*o* **corneali**] contact lenses

lentezza [len·'tet·tsa] *f* (*di persona, film*) slowness

lenticchia [len·'tik·kia] <-cchie> *f* BOT lentil

lentiggine [len·'tid·dʒi·ne] *f* freckle

lentigginoso, -a [len·tid·dʒi·'no:·so] *agg* (*volto, persona*) freckled

lento ['lɛn·to] *m* MUS slow dance

lento, -a *agg* 1. (*non veloce: passo, persona, traffico*) slow; **essere** ~ **di comprendonio** to be slow on the update 2. (*veleno, medicina*) slow-acting; **cuocere a fuoco** ~ to cook over low heat 3. *fig* (*monotono: film, racconto*) slow 4. (*allentato: vite*) loose

lenza ['lɛn·tsa] *f* (*per pescare*) line

lenzuolo [lɛn·'tsuɔ:·lo] <-i *m*, *o* -a *f*> *m* (*da letto*) sheet; ~ **con gli angoli** fitted sheet

leone [le·'o:·ne] *m* 1. ZOO lion; **fare la parte del** ~ *fig* to take the lion's share 2. ASTR **Leone** Leo; **sono del** [*o* **un**] **Leone** I'm Leo

leonessa [le·o·'nes·sa] *f* lioness

leopardo [le·o·'par·do] *m* leopard

leporino [le·po·'ri:·no] *agg* **labbro** ~ MED cleft lip

lepre ['lɛ:·pre] *f* hare; ~ **in salmì** jugged hare

lercio, -a ['lɛr·tʃo/ler·tʃo] <-ci, -ce> *agg* (*sporco: pavimento, abiti*) filthy

lerciume [ler·'tʃu:·me] *m* filth

lesbica ['lɛz·bi·ka] <-che> *f* lesbian

lesbico, -a ['lɛz·bi·ko] <-ci, -che> *agg* (*bacio, cinema, film*) lesbian

lesi ['le:·zi] *1. pers sing pass rem di* **ledere**

lesinare [le·zi·'na:·re] I. *vt* ~ **qc a qu** to grudge sth to sb; ~ **il centesimo** to count the pennies II. *vi* ~ **su qc** to skimp on sth

lesionare [le·zio·'na:·re] *vt* to damage

lesione [le·'zio:·ne] *f* (*ferita*) injury

lesivo, -a [le·'zi:·vo] *agg* (*che danneggia*) harmful

leso, -a ['le:·zo] I. *pp di* **ledere** II. *agg* JUR injured

lessare [les·'sa:·re] *vt* (*patate, carne, riso*) to boil

lessi ['lɛs·si] *1. pers sing pass rem di* **leggere**

lessicale [les·si·'ka:·le] *agg* (*analisi, competenza*) lexical

lessico ['lɛs·si·ko] <-ci> *m* 1. (*dizionario, glossario*) lexicon 2. LING vocabulary

lessicografia [les·si·ko·gra·'fi:·a] *f* lexicography

lessicografo, -a [les·si·'kɔ:·gra·fo] *m*, *f* lexicographer

lessicologia [les·si·ko·lo·'dʒi:·a] <-ie> *f* lexicography

lessicologo, -a [les·si·'kɔ:·lo·go] <-gi, -ghe> *m*, *f* lexicologist

lesso ['les·so] *m* (*carne lessata*) boiled meat

lesso, -a *agg* (*carne, patate, castagne*) boiled

lesto, -a ['lɛs·to] *agg* (*veloce*) nimble; **essere** ~ **di mano** to be light-fingered

letale [le·'ta:·le] *agg* (*colpo, arma, veleno*) lethal

letamaio [le·ta·'ma:·io] <-ai> *m* **1.**(*per letame*) dung-heap **2.** *fig* (*luogo sporco*) pigsty

letame [le·'ta:·me] *m* manure

letargia [le·tar·'dʒi:·a] <-gie> *f* MED lethargy

letargico, -a [le·'tar·dʒi·ko] <-ci, -che> *agg fig* (*ozioso: giornata, attesa*) lethargic

letargo [le·'tar·go] <-ghi> *m* **1.** MED lethargy **2.** ZOO hibernation

letizia [le·'tit·tsia] <-ie> *f* joy

letta ['lɛt·ta] *f* read; **dare una ~ a qc** to have a read of sth

lettera ['lɛt·te·ra/'let·te·ra] *f* **1.**(*di alfabeto*) letter; **alla ~** to the letter **2.**(*comunicazione scritta*) letter; **~ assicurata** special delivery letter; **~ circolare** circular; **~ di credito** credit note; **~ espresso** express letter; **~ raccomandata** registered letter; **per ~** by letter **3.** *pl* (*materie letterarie*) literature; **Lettere** Arts; **uomo di -e** man of letters

letterale [let·te·'ra:·le] *agg* literal

letteralmente [let·te·ral·'men·te] *avv a fig* literally

letterario, -a [let·te·'ra:·rio] <-i, -ie> *agg* (*critica, rivista, testo*) literary; **lingua -a** literary language; **materie -ie** arts subjects

letterato, -a [let·te·'ra:·to] *m, f* scholar

letteratura [let·te·ra·'tu:·ra] *f* literature

lettiga [let·'ti:·ga] <-ghe> *f* **1.**(*portantina*) litter **2.**(*barella*) stretcher

lettino [let·'ti:·no] *m* **1.**(*per bambini*) crib **2.**(*branda: dal dottore*) bed; (*per spiaggia*) sun lounger **3. ~ solare** tanning bed

letto ['lɛt·to] *m* **1.**(*mobile*) bed; **~ matrimoniale** [*o a due piazze*] double bed; **~ a castello** bunk beds; **andare a ~** to go to bed; **andare a ~ con qu** *fam* to go to bed with sb; **rifare il ~** to make the bed **2.** GEOL (*di fiume*) bed **3.** *fig* (*matrimonio*) **figlio di primo ~** child from the first marriage

letto <-a> I. *pp di* **leggere** II. *agg* **~ ed approvato** ADM read and approved

lettorato [let·to·'ra:·to] *m* (*carica*) assistantship

lettore [let·'to:·re] *m* TEC reader; **~ CD** [*o di compact disc*] CD player; **~ CD-ROM** CD-ROM drive; **~ DVD** DVD player; **~ ottico** optical character reader; **~ MP3** MP3 player; **~ per microfilm** microfilm reader

lettore, -trice *m, f* **1.**(*chi legge*) reader **2.**(*professione*) foreign language assistant

lettura [let·'tu:·ra] *f* **1.**(*atto del leggere*) reading **2.**(*scritto*) (piece of) writing; **-e per l'infanzia** children's writing

leucemia [leu·tʃe·'mi:·a] <-ie> *f* MED leukemia

leucocita [leu·ko·'tʃi:·ta] <-i> *m* leukocyte

leucorrea [leu·kor·'rɛ:·a] *f* MED leukorrhea

leva ['lɛ:·va] *f* **1.** TEC lever, gearshift **2.** *fig* (*stimolo*) lever; **fare ~ su qc** to play on sth **3.**(*arruolamento*) conscription; **essere di ~** to be liable for military service; **le nuove -e** *fig* the next generation

levante [le·'van·te] I. *agg* rising; **sole ~** rising

sun II. *m* **1.**(*est*) east **2.**(*vento*) east wind **3.**(*Paesi del Mediterraneo orientale*) **il Levante** the Levant

levapunti [le·va·'pun·ti] <-> *m o f* staple remover

levare [le·'va:·re] I. *vt* **1.**(*togliere*) to remove; **~ di mezzo qu** to get sb out of the way; **levati di mezzo** [*o dai piedi*]! get out of the way!; **~ le tende** to strike camp **2.**(*estrarre: dente, chiodo*) to pull out **3.**(*alzare*) to raise; **~ le braccia in alto** to raise one's arm; **~ gli occhi al cielo** to look heavenwards II. *vr*: **-rsi 1.**(*indumenti*) to take off **2.**(*dubbio, voglia, vizio*) to dispel; **-rsi qu/qc dalla testa** *fig* to put sb/sth out of one's mind **3.**(*togliersi*) **-rsi** (**dai piedi**) to get out of the way **4.**(*alzarsi*) to get up; **-rsi in volo** to fly up **5.**(*sollevarsi: vento*) to blow up

levata [le·'va:·ta] *f* **1. ~ del sole** sunrise **2.**(*prelievo: di posta*) collection **3.**(*sollevamento*) **~ di scudi** uproar

levataccia [le·va·'tat·tʃa] <-cce> *f* **fare una ~** to get up at an ungodly hour

levato, -a [le·'va:·to] *agg* (*sollevato: braccia*) raised; **a gambe -e** hotfoot

levatoio, -a [le·va·'to:·io] <-oi, -oie> *agg* **ponte ~** drawbridge

levatrice [le·va·'tri:·tʃe] *f* (*ostetrica*) midwife

levigare [le·vi·'ga:·re] *vt* (*lisciare: superficie, pelle*) to smooth down

levitazione [le·vi·tat·'tsio:·ne] *f* levitation

levriere, levriero [le·'vriɛ:·re, le·'vriɛ:·ro] *m* greyhound

lezione [let·'tsio:·ne] *f* **1.**(*a scuola, all'università*) lesson; **~ di ballo** dance lesson; **~ di storia** history lesson; **assistere alla ~** to attend class; **fare ~** to teach a class; **dare -i** to give classes; **prendere -i** to take classes **2.**(*in libro*) lesson **3.** *fig* (*ammaestramento*) lesson; **dare a qu una ~** to teach sb a lesson

leziosità [let·tsio·si·'ta] <-> *f* affectation

lezioso, -a [let·'tsio:·so] *agg* (*stile*) affected

li [li] *pron pers* **3.** *pers m pl* them

lì [li] *avv* (*stato*) there; **essere ~ ~ per fare qc** to be just about to do sth; **di ~ a pochi giorni** a few days later; **fin ~** up to there; **giù di ~** thereabouts; **per (di) ~** that way; **~ per ~** right then

liana [li·'a:·na] *f* creeper

libbra ['lib·bra] *f* (*unità di misura*) pound

libellula [li·'bɛl·lu·la] *f* dragonfly

liberale [li·be·'ra:·le] I. *agg* **1.**(*genitori, partito, politica*) liberal **2.**(*generoso*) generous II. *m a.* POL liberal

liberalismo [li·be·ra·'liz·mo] *m* liberalism

liberalità [li·be·ra·li·'ta] <-> *f* (*generosità*) generosity

liberalizzare [li·be·ra·lid·'dza:·re] *vt* (*abolire restrizioni*) to liberalize

liberalizzazione [li·be·ra·lid·dzat·'tsio:·ne] *f* liberalization

liberamente [li·be·ra·'men·te] *avv* (*parlare, muoversi, circolare*) freely

L

liberare [li·be·'ra:·re] I. *vt* 1.(*prigioniero, ostaggio*) to release 2.(*da invasione, assedio*) to liberate 3.(*sgombrare: tavolo, strada*) to clear 4.(*camera, casa*) to vacate II. *vr* 1.-**rsi da** [*o* di] **qc** to get rid of sth 2.(*posto, casa*) to become free

liberatorio, -a [li·be·ra·'tɔ:·rio] <-i, -ie> *agg* 1.(*risata, urlo*) liberating 2.FIN (*pagamento*) redemption

liberazione [li·be·rat·'tsio:·ne] *f* 1.(*di prigioniero, ostaggio*) release 2.(*di città, paese*) liberation; **Festa della Liberazione** Liberation Day 3.*fig* (*sollievo*) relief

> **i** April 25 is Liberation Day – **Anniversario della Liberazione**. This statutory holiday marks the liberation of Italy from Nazi and fascist rule in 1945.

liberismo [li·be·'riz·mo] *m* (*dottrina*) free trade

liberista [li·be·'ris·ta] <-i *m*, -e *f*> I. *mf* (*seguace del liberismo*) free trader II. *agg* (*del liberismo: dottrina, politica*) free trade

libero, -a ['li:·be·ro] *agg* 1.(*gener*) free; ~ **arbitrio** free will; **essere** ~ **di fare qc** +*inf* to be free to do sth; **mercato** ~ free market 2.(*indipendente*) independent; ~ **professionista** self-employed professional

libertà [li·ber·'ta] <-> *f* freedom; ~ **di parola** freedom of speech; ~ **vigilata** probation; **giorno di** ~ (*vacanza*) day off; **rimettere in** ~ (*prigioniero*) to release; **prendersi la** ~ **di fare qc** to take the liberty of doing sth

libertario, -a [li·ber·'ta:·rio] <-i, -ie> I. *agg* (*anarchico*) libertarian II. *m*, *f* (*anarchico*) libertarian

libertino, -a [li·ber·'ti:·no] I. *agg* (*dissoluto*) libertine II. *m*, *f* (*chi fa una vita dissoluta*) libertine

liberty ['li:·ber·ti] I. (*lampada, mobili, stile*) Art Nouveau II. <-> *m* Art Nouveau

libidine [li·'bi:·di·ne] *f* 1.(*sessuale*) lust 2.*fam* (*goduria*) luxury; **che** ~! what luxury!

libidinoso, -a [li·bi·di·'no:·so] *agg* 1.(*sessualmente*) lustful 2.*fam* (*goduroso*) luxurious

libido [li·'bi:·do] <-> *f* libido

libraio, -a [li·'bra:·io] <-ai, -aie> *m*, *f* (*chi vende libri*) bookseller

librario, -a [li·'bra:·rio] <-i, -ie> *agg* (*settore, industria*) book

librarsi [li·'brar·si] *vr* to glide

libreria [li·bre·'ri:·a] <-ie> *f* 1.(*negozio*) bookstore 2.(*mobile*) bookshelf

librettista [li·bret·'tis·ta] <-i *m*, -e *f*> *mf* librettist

libretto [li·'bret·to] *m* 1.(*opuscolo*) booklet 2.MUS libretto 3.(*documento, carnet*) book; ~ **di circolazione** vehicle registration book; ~ **universitario** university record book; ~ **di risparmio** savings book; ~ **degli assegni** checkbook

libro ['li:·bro] *m* book; ~ **di cucina** cookbook; ~ **di testo** textbook; ~ **illustrato** illustrated book; **Libro Verde** EU Green Paper

licantropo [li·'kan·tro·po] *m* werewolf

liceale [li·tfe·'a:·le] I. *agg* (*classe, studente, programma*) senior high school II. *mf* senior high school

licenza [li·'tʃen·tsa] *f* 1.(*autorizzazione*) license; ~ **di caccia** hunting license; ~ **di esercizio** trade license; ~ **di porto d'armi** firearms permit 2.COM (*concessione*) license; **su** ~ **americana** under American license 3.MIL (*congedo*) leave; ~ **premio** special leave 4.(*attestato*) certificate; ~ **elementare** *elementary school leaving certificate* 5.(*abuso*) license; ~ **poetica** poetic license

licenziabile [li·tʃen·'tsia:·bi·le] *agg* dismissible

licenziamento [li·tʃen·tsia·'men·to] *m* dismissal; ~ **per riduzione del personale** layoff; ~ **senza giusta causa** unfair dismissal

licenziare [li·tʃen·'tsia:·re] I. *vt* (*impiegato*) to dismiss; (*per riduzione del personale*) to lay off II. *vr:* -**rsi** (*da un impiego*) to resign

licenziosità [li·tʃen·tsio·si·'ta] <-> *f* (*di discorsi, costumi, immagini*) licentiousness

licenzioso, -a [li·tʃen·'tsio:·so] *agg* (*dissoluto*) licentious

liceo [li·'tʃɛ:·o] *m* senior high school; ~ **classico** senior high school specializing in classics; ~ **linguistico** senior high school specializing in languages

lichene [li·'kɛ:·ne] *m* lichen

licitare [li·tʃi·'ta:·re] *vi* (*all'asta, nel bridge*) to bid

licitazione [li·tʃi·tat·'tsio:·ne] *f* (*all'asta, nel bridge*) bid

lido ['li:·do] *m* (*spiaggia*) bathing beach; **il Lido** (**di Venezia**) the Venice Lido

lieto, -a ['liɛ:·to] *agg* cheerful; ~ **evento** (*nascita*) happy event; ~ **fine** happy ending; **sono** ~ **di conoscerLa** pleased to meet you

lieve ['liɛ:·ve] *agg* 1.(*poco pesante: peso*) light 2.(*leggero: rumore, scossa, passo*) slight 3.(*delicato: carezza, tocco*) delicate

lievitare [lie·vi·'ta:·re] *vi* essere to rise

lievitazione [lie·vi·tat·'tsio:·ne] *f* 1.(*di pasta*) rising 2.*fig* (*di prezzi, tassi d'interesse*) rise

lievito ['liɛ:·vi·to] *m* BIOL yeast; ~ **di birra** brewer's yeast; ~ **in polvere** baking powder

lift [lift] <-> *m* elevator attendant

lifting ['lif·ting] <-> *m* face-lift; ~ **facciale** face-lift

ligio, -a ['li:·dʒo] <-gi, -gie> *agg* (*rispettoso*) faithful; ~ **al dovere** dutiful

ligneo, -a ['liɲ·ɲeo] <-ei, -ee> *agg* (*mobile, statua*) wooden

lignite [liɲ·'ɲi:·te] *f* lignite

ligure[1] [li·'gu:·re] <*sing*> *m* (*dialetto*) Ligurian (dialect)

ligure[2] I. *mf* (*abitante*) person from Liguria II. *agg* (*costa, cucina, tradizioni*) Ligurian

Liguria [li·'gu:·ria] <*sing*> *f* Liguria

lilla, lillà ['lil·la, lil·'la] I. <inv> *agg* lilac II. <->

m (*colore, fiore*) lilac

lillipuziano, -a [lil·li·put·'tsia:·no] *agg* (*piccolo*) minute

lima ['li:·ma] *f* file

limaccioso, -a [li·mat·'tʃo:·so] *agg* (*acqua, lago*) muddy

limare [li·'ma:·re] I. *vt* 1. (*sbarra, superficie, unghia*) to file 2. *fig* (*scritto, stile*) to polish II. *vr* **-rsi le unghie** to file one's nails

limatura [li·ma·'tu:·ra] *f* filing

limbo ['lim·bo] *m a. fig* limbo

limetta [li·'met·ta] *f* nail file

limitare [li·mi·'ta:·re] I. *vt* 1. (*ridurre: costi, libertà*) to restrict 2. (*delimitare: zona*) to delimit II. *vr* **-rsi** (**in qc**) to cut down (on sth); **-rsi a qc** to restrict oneself to sth

limitativo, -a [li·mi·ta·'ti:·vo] *agg* restrictive

limitato, -a [li·mi·'ta:·to] *agg* 1. (*delimitato: traffico, durata*) restricted 2. (*determinato: potere*) limited 3. (*di piccola entità*) modest 4. (*scarso: prestazioni, risorse*) limited 5. (*stupido*) slow

limitazione [li·mi·tat·'tsio:·ne] *f* 1. (*limite: di orario, responsabilità*) limit 2. (*restrizione: di libertà*) restriction 3. (*riduzione: di assunzioni, circolazione stradale*) restriction

limite ['li:·mi·te] I. *m* 1. (*confine*) limit; **fuori ~** SPORT out of play 2. *fig* (*ultimo grado*) limit; **nei -i del possibile** as far as is possible 3. (*restrizione: di potere, periodo di tempo*) restriction; **-i di età** age restrictions; **~ di velocità** speed limit 4. (*loc*) **al ~** at worst II. <inv> *agg* **caso ~** extreme case

limitrofo, -a [li·'mi:·tro·fo] *agg* (*paese, zona*) bordering

limonata [li·mo·'na:·ta] *f* lemonade

limone [li·'mo:·ne] *m* 1. (*frutto*) lemon 2. (*pianta*) lemon tree

limpido, -a ['lim·pi·do] *agg* (*trasparente: cielo, aria, acqua*) clear

lince ['lin·tʃe] *f* ZOO lynx

linciaggio [lin·'tʃad·dʒo] <-ggi> *m* lynching; **~ morale** moral witch-hunt

linciare [lin·'tʃa:·re] *vt* to lynch

lindo, -a ['lin·do] *agg* (*pulito e ordinato*) neat

linea [li·'nea] *f* 1. (*segno, su strada*) line; **a grandi -e** in broad terms; **in ~ di massima** broadly speaking; **~ continua** solid line; **~ di mezzeria** center line 2. SPORT line; **~ di partenza** starting line 3. (*su termometro*) degree 4. TEL (*di telefono*) line; **restare in ~** to hold the line; **è caduta la ~** the call was cut off 5. EL (power) line 6. (*di aero, autobus*) service; **di ~** regular 7. (*di treno*) line 8. (*figura*) figure; **tenerci alla ~** to look after one's figure 9. (*di abito, veicolo, oggetto*) line 10. (*serie: di prodotti*) line 11. (*norma*) **in ~ con** in line with; **~ guida** guideline

lineamenti [li·nea·'men·ti] *mpl* (*fisionomia*) features *pl*

lineare [li·ne·'a:·re] *agg* 1. (*algebra, metro, misure, scala*) linear 2. *fig* (*coerente: ragionamento, rapporto*) straightforward

linearità [li·ne·a·ri·'ta] <-> *f* (*di comportamento*) straightforwardness; (*di discorso, ragionamento*) directness

lineetta [li·ne·'et·ta] *f* (*trattino*) hyphen

linfa ['lin·fa] *f* 1. ANAT lymph 2. BOT sap 3. *fig* **~ vitale** lifeblood

linfatico, -a [lin·'fa:·ti·ko] <-ci, -che> *agg* (*ghiandola, sistema*) lymphatic

linfatismo [lin·fa·'tiz·mo] *m* lymphatic disease

lingotto [liŋ·'gɔt·to] *m* (*blocco di metallo*) ingot

lingua ['liŋ·gua] *f* 1. ANAT tongue; **mala ~** gossip; **avere la ~ lunga** *fig* to have a loose tongue; **avere qc sulla punta della ~** *fig* to have sth on the tip of one's tongue; **mordersi la ~** *fig* to bite one's tongue 2. (*linguaggio*) language; **di ~ inglese** English-speaking; **~ parlata** spoken language; **studiare -e** to study languages 3. (*striscia*) tongue; **~ di terra** tongue of land

linguaccia [liŋ·'guat·tʃa] <-cce> *f* 1. (*boccaccia*) rude face; **fare le -cce a qu** to stick one's tongue out at sb 2. *fig* (*persona pettegola*) gossip

linguacciuto, -a [liŋ·guat·'tʃu:·to] I. *agg* (*pettegolo*) gossipy II. *m, f* (*persona pettegola*) gossip

linguaggio [liŋ·'guad·dʒo] <-ggi> *m* language; **~ simbolico** COMPUT symbolic language; **~ tecnico** technical language; **~ di programmazione** COMPUT programming language

linguetta [liŋ·'guet·ta] *f* 1. (*di buste*) flap 2. (*di scarpe*) tongue

linguista [liŋ·'guis·ta] <-i *m*, -e *f*> *mf* linguist

linguistica [liŋ·'guis·ti·ka] <-che> *f* linguistics *sing*; **~ computazionale** computational linguistics

linguistico, -a [liŋ·'guis·ti·ko] <-ci, -che> *agg* linguistic

lino ['li:·no] *m* 1. (*pianta*) flax 2. (*tessuto*) linen

linoleum [li·'nɔ:·le·um] <-> *m* linoleum

liofilizzare [lio·fi·lid·'dza:·re] *vt* (*alimenti*) to freeze dry; (*cellule*) to lyophilize

liofilizzato [lio·fi·lid·'dza:·to] *m* (*alimento*) freeze-dried product

liofilizzato, -a *agg* (*alimenti*) freeze-dried; (*cellule*) lyophilized

liofilizzazione [lio·fi·lid·dzat·'tsio:·ne] *f* (*di alimenti*) freeze-drying; (*di cellule*) lyophilization

lipoaspirazione [li·po·as·pi·rat·'tsio:·ne] *f* MED liposuction

lipoma [li·'po:·ma] <-i> *m* MED lipoma

liposolubile [li·po·so·'lu:·bi·le] *agg* (*vitamina, sostanza*) fat-soluble

liposuzione [li·po·sut·'tsio:·ne] *f v.* lipoaspirazione

LIPU *f acro di* **Lega Italiana per la Protezione degli Uccelli** *Italian bird protection association*

liquame [li·'kua:·me] *m* 1. (*di fogna*) sewage

2. (*per concimare*) slurry
liquefare [li·kue·'fa:·re] <irr> **I.** *vt* **1.** (*gas*) to liquefy **2.** (*metalli, neve*) to melt **II.** *vr:* **-rsi** **1.** (*gas*) to liquefy **2.** (*metalli, ghiaccio*) to melt
liquefazione [li·kue·fat·'tsio:·ne] *f* **1.** (*di gas*) liquefaction **2.** (*di metalli, ghiaccio*) melting
liquefeci *1. pers sing pass rem di* **liquefare**
liquidare [li·kui·'da:·re] *vt* **1.** (*calcolare: conto, somma, pensione*) to settle **2.** (*pagare: creditori*) to pay; (*debito*) to settle **3.** (*svendere: merce*) to sell off **4.** (*chiudere: azienda*) to liquidate **5.** *fig* (*criticare*) to write off **6.** (*uccidere: avversario*) to dispose of **7.** (*sbrigare: pratica*) to deal with **8.** (*mandar via: persona*) to get rid of
liquidatore, -trice [li·kui·da·'to:·re] *m, f* **1.** (*di assicurazioni*) loss adjuster **2.** (*di eredità*) executor **3.** (*di azienda*) liquidator
liquidazione [li·kui·dat·'tsio:·ne] *f* **1.** (*svendita*) clearance; ~ **di fine stagione** end of season sale **2.** (*somma liquidata per*) settlement **3.** (*di azienda*) liquidation **4.** (*di pensione, danni*) settlement
liquidità [li·kui·di·'ta] <-> *f* PHYS, FIN liquidity
liquido ['li:·kui·do] *m* **1.** PHYS liquid; ~ **amniotico** amniotic fluid; ~ **per freni** brake fluid; ~ **refrigerante** coolant **2.** FIN liquidity
liquido, -a *agg* **1.** PHYS liquid **2.** (*panna, vernice, metallo*) liquid **3.** FIN **denaro** ~ liquid cash
liquirizia [li·kui·'rit·tsia] <-ie> *f* licorice
liquore [li·'kuo:·re] *m* liquor; **negozio di -i** liquor store
liquoroso, -a [li·kuo·'ro:·so] *agg* (*vino*) fortified; (*crema, bevanda*) liqueur
lira ['li:·ra] *f* **1.** (*moneta*) lira; **non avere una** ~ not to have a cent **2.** MUS (*strumento*) lyre
lirica ['li:·ri·ka] <-che> *f* **1.** LIT (*componimento poetico*) lyric **2.** LIT (*arte poetica*) poetry **3.** MUS opera
liricità [li·ri·tʃi·'ta] <-> *f* (*poeticità*) lyricism
lirico, -a ['li:·ri·ko] <-ci, -che> *agg* MUS opera; **cantante -a** opera singer; **musica -a** opera music; **stagione -a** opera season
Lisbona [liz·'bo:·na] *f* Lisbon
lisca ['lis·ka] <-sche> *f* (*di pesce*) bone
lisciare [liʃ·'ʃa:·re] *vt* **1.** (*levigare: superficie*) to polish **2.** (*pelle*) to smooth **3.** (*capelli*) to straighten
liscio ['liʃ·ʃo] *m* (*ballo*) ballroom dance
liscio, -a <-sci, -sce> *agg* **1.** (*superficie, pelle*) smooth **2.** (*capelli*) straight **3.** *fig* (*bene*) smooth; **è andato tutto** ~ everything went smoothly; **passarla -a** to get away with it **4.** CULIN (*acqua*) still; (*caffè*) straight; (*bevanda alcolica*) neat
liso, -a ['li:·zo] *agg* (*cappotto, tessuto*) worn
lista ['lis·ta] *f* **1.** (*striscia*) strip **2.** (*elenco*) list; **la** ~ **dei vini** the winelist
listare [lis·'ta:·re] *vt* to edge
listello [lis·'tɛl·lo] *m* (*di legno*) batten
listino [lis·'ti:·no] *m* list; ~ **dei prezzi** price list; ~ **di Borsa** Stock list
litania [li·ta·'ni:·a] <-ie> *f a. fig* litany

lite ['li:·te] *f* **1.** (*litigio*) quarrel **2.** JUR dispute
litigante [li·ti·'gan·te] *mf* litigant; **fra i due -i il terzo gode** *prov* there's nothing to be gained by arguing
litigare [li·ti·'ga:·re] *vi* to quarrel
litigio [li·'ti:·dʒo] <-gi> *m* quarrel
litigiosità [li·ti·dʒo·si·'ta] <-> *f* quarrelsomeness
litigioso, -a [li·tid·'dʒo:·so] *agg* quarrelsome
litografare [li·to·gra·'fa:·re] *vt* to lithograph
litografia [li·to·gra·'fi:·a] *f* **1.** (*opera, arte*) lithography **2.** (*stabilimento*) lithographer's
litografico, -a [li·to·'gra:·fi·ko] <-ci, -che> *agg* lithographic
litografo [li·'tɔ:·gra·fo] *m* lithographer
litorale [li·to·'ra:·le] *m* (*costa*) coast
litoranea [li·to·'ra:·nea] *f* (*strada*) coastal road
litoraneo, -a [li·to·'ra:·neo] *agg* (*zona, fondale*) coastal
litote [li·'to:·te] *f* LING (*figura retorica*) litotes
litro ['li:·tro] *m* liter
Lituania [li·tu·'a:·nia] *f* Lithuania
lituano [li·tu·'a:·no] *m sing* (*lingua*) Lithuanian
lituano, -a [li·tu·'a:·no] **I.** *agg* Lithuanian **II.** *m, f* (*abitante*) Lithuanian
liturgia [li·tur·'dʒi:·a] <-gie> *f* REL liturgy
liturgico, -a [li·'tur·dʒi·ko] <-ci, -che> *agg* (*formula, musica*) liturgical; (*anno, calendario, ricorrenza*) ecclesiastical
liutista [liu·'tis·ta] <-i *m*, -e *f*> *mf* MUS lutenist
liuto [li·'u:·to] *m* MUS lute
livella [li·'vɛl·la] *f* spirit level
livellamento [li·vel·la·'men·to] *m* **1.** (*di terreno*) leveling **2.** (*di differenze, linguaggio, prezzi*) leveling out
livellare [li·vel·'la:·re] *vt* **1.** TEC (*terreno*) to level **2.** *fig* (*differenze, persone, prezzi*) to level out
livello [li·'vɛl·lo] *m* **1.** (*gen*) level; **sotto il** ~ **del mare** below sea level; ~ **dei prezzi** price level; ~ **di sussistenza** level of subsistence; **ad alto** ~ high-level **2.** (*grado*) standard
livido ['li:·vi·do] *m* bruise
livido, -a *agg* (*occhi*) black; (*cielo*) leaden
livornese [li·vor·'ne:·se] **I.** *mf* (*abitante*) person from Livorno **II.** *agg* from Livorno
Livornese <*sing*> *m* (*zona*) Livorno area; **nel** ~ in the Livorno area
Livorno [li·'vɔ:r·no] <*sing*> *f* Livorno
livrea [li·'vrɛ:·a] *f* livery
lizza ['lit·tsa] *f* **scendere in** ~ to enter the arena
lo [lo] **I.** *art m sing davanti a s impura, gn, pn, ps, x, z* the **II.** *pron* **1.** (*persona*) him **2.** (*cosa*) it
lobbismo [lɔb·'biz·mo] *m* lobbying
lobbista [lɔb·'bis·ta] <-i *m*, -e *f*> *mf* lobbyist
lobby ['lɔ·bi] <- *o* lobbies> *f* lobby
lobbying ['lɔ·bi·iŋ] <-> *m* lobbying
lobo ['lɔ:·bo] *m* ANAT lobe; ~ **dell'orecchio** earlobe; ~ **polmonare** lobe of the lung
locale [lo·'ka:·le] **I.** *agg* local; **anestesia** ~ local anesthesia **II.** *m* **1.** (*stanza*) room **2.** (*luogo*)

pubblico: caffe) café; (*ristorante*) restaurant; **una zona piena di -i** an area with lots of bars and restaurants; ~ **notturno** nightclub

localino [lo·ka·'li:·no] *m* (*luogo pubblico: caffe*) café; (*ristorante*) restaurant; **ci sono tanti -i** it's full of bars and restaurants con gli amici

località [lo·ka·li·'ta] <-> *f* locality; **una ~ di mare** a seaside resort

localizzabile [lo·ka·lid·'dza:·bi·le] *agg* locatable

localizzare [lo·ka·lid·'dza:·re] *vt* (*individuare: aereo, telefono*) to locate

localizzazione [lo·ka·lid·dzat·'tsio:·ne] *f* (*di aereo, telefono*) location

locanda [lo·'kan·da] *f* inn

locandiere, -a [lo·kan·'diɛ:·re] *m, f* innkeeper

locandina [lo·kan·'di:·na] *f* playbill

locare [lo·'ka:·re] *vt* JUR (*dare in affitto: fabbricati*) to rent out

locatario, -a [lo·ka·'ta:·rio] <-i, -ie> *m, f* (*di casa*) tenant

locativo [lo·ka·'ti:·vo] *m* LING locative

locatore, -trice [lo·ka·'to:·re] *m, f* (*di casa*) landlord *m*, landlady *f*

locazione [lo·kat·'tsio:·ne] *f* rental; **dare in ~** to rent out; **prendere in ~** to rent

locomotiva [lo·ko·mo·'ti:·va] *f* engine

locomotore [lo·ko·mo·'to:·re] *m* electric engine

locomotorio, -a [lo·ko·mo·'tɔ:·rio] <-i, -ie> *agg* MED locomotive

locomotrice [lo·ko·mo·'tri:·tʃe] *f* electric engine

locomozione [lo·ko·mot·'tsio:·ne] *f* 1. (*deambulazione*) movement 2. (*con veicolo*) transport; **mezzo di ~** means of transport

loculo ['lɔ:·ku·lo] *m* (*in cimitero*) niche

locusta [lo·'ku:s·ta] *f* ZOO locust

locuzione [lo·kut·'tsio:·ne] *f* phrase

lodare [lo·'da:·re] *vt* (*elogiare, celebrare*) to praise; **sia lodato il cielo!** thank heavens!

lode ['lɔ:·de] *f* 1. (*elogio*) praise 2. (*voto*) **prendere trenta e ~** to get full marks; **laurearsi con 110 e ~** to graduate magna cum laude

loden ['lo:·dən] <-> *m* (*panno, cappotto*) loden

lodevole [lo·'de:·vo·le] *agg* (*meritevole di lode*) praiseworthy

lodo ['lɔ:·do] *m* DIR arbitration award

logaritmico, -a [lo·ga·'rit·mi·ko] <-ci, -che> *agg* (*equazioni, funzioni*) logarithmic

logaritmo [lo·ga·'rit·mo] *m* logarithm

loggia ['lɔd·dʒa] <-gge> *f* 1. ARCH gallery 2. (*nella massoneria*) lodge

loggione [lɔd·'dʒo:·ne] *m* THEAT gallery

logica ['lɔ:·dʒi·ka] <-che> *f* logic; **a rigor di ~** logically speaking

logicità [lo·dʒi·tʃi·'ta] <-> *f* logicality

logico, -a ['lɔ:·dʒi·ko] <-ci, -che> *agg* logical

login [log·'in] <-> *f* COMPUT login; **fare il ~** to log in

logistica [lo·'dʒis·ti·ka] <-che> *f* logistics

logistico, -a [lo·'dʒis·ti·ko] <-ci, -che> *agg* (*attività, settore*) logistic

logo ['lo·go] <-> *m* logo; ~ **per cellulare** cell phone screensaver

logopedista [lo·go·pe·'dis·ta] <-i *m*, -e *f*> *mf* MED speech therapist

logoramento [lo·go·ra·'men·to] *m* 1. (*usura: di pavimento*) wear 2. (*deterioramento: di rapporto*) breakdown

logorante [lo·go·'ran·te] *agg* (*attività, giornata, passione*) exhausting

logorare [lo·go·'ra:·re] I. *vt* (*pavimento, vestiti, salute*) to wear out II. *vr:* **-rsi** 1. (*consumarsi: scarpe, ingranaggi*) to become worn out 2. *fig* (*per passione, rabbia*) to be consumed

logorio [lo·go·'ri:·o] <-ii> *m* 1. (*logoramento*) wear and tear 2. *fig* (*stress*) exhaustion

logoro, -a ['lo:·go·ro] *agg* (*vestito, gomiti, scarpe*) worn-out

logorrea [lo·gor·'rɛ:·a] *f* 1. MED logorrhea 2. *fig, scherz* long-windedness

logoterapeuta [lo·go·te·ra·'pɛu·ta] *mf* MED *v.* **logopedista**

logoterapia [lo·go·te·ra·'pi:·a] *f* MED speech therapy

logoterapista [lo·go·te·ra·'pis·ta] <-i *m*, -e *f*> *mf* MED *v.* **logopedista**

lombaggine [lom·'bad·dʒi·ne] *f* lumbago

Lombardia [lom·bar·'di:·a] *f* Lombardy

lombardo [lom·'bar·do] <*sing*> *m* (*dialetto*) Lombard (dialect)

lombardo, -a I. *agg* from Lombardy II. *m, f* (*abitante*) person from Lombardy

lombare [lom·'ba:·re] *agg* (*scoliosi, ernia, dolore*) lumbar

lombata [lom·'ba:·ta] *f* (*taglio di carne*) loin

lombrico [lom·'bri:·ko] <-chi> *m* earthworm

londinese [lon·din·'e:·se] I. *agg* (*di Londra*) from London II. *mf* (*abitante*) Londoner

Londra ['lon·dra] *f* London

longevità [lon·dʒe·vi·'ta] <-> *f* (*di persona, famiglia, razza*) longevity

longevo, -a [lon·'dʒɛ:·vo] *agg* (*persona, famiglia, razza*) long-lived

longilineo, -a [lon·dʒi·'li:·neo] <-ei, -ee> *agg* (*persona, fisico*) long-limbed

longitudinale [lon·dʒi·tu·di·'na:·le] *agg* (*taglio, sezione*) longitudinal

longitudine [lon·dʒi·'tu:·di·ne] *f* longitude

long play ['lɔŋ 'plei] <- *o* long plays> *m* MUS album

lontanamente [lon·ta·na·'men·te] *avv* distantly; **non ci penso neanche ~** I wouldn't dream of it

lontananza [lon·ta·'nan·tsa] *f* 1. (*distanza*) distance; **in ~** in the distance 2. (*assenza, mancanza*) absence

lontano, -a [lon·'ta:·no] I. *agg* 1. (*nello spazio*) far away; **quanto è ~ ...?** how far away is ...? 2. (*nel tempo*) distant 3. (*estraneo*) far 4. (*assente: sguardo*) distant 5. (*vago: somiglianza*) vague II. *avv* far; **andare ~** to go far; **vedere ~** *fig* to be far-sighted; **alla -a** in a roundabout way; **parenti alla -a** distant relatives; ~ **dagli occhi**, ~ **dal cuore** *prov* out of sight, out of mind

lontra ['lon·tra] *f* ZOO otter

look [luk] <- *o* looks> *m* (*immagine*) look; ~ **casual** casual look

loquace [lo·'kua:·tʃe] *agg* **1.** (*persona*) talkative **2.** *fig* (*silenzio*) eloquent

loquacità [lo·kua·tʃi·'ta] <-> *f* **1.** (*di persona*) talkativeness **2.** *fig* (*di silenzio*) eloquence

lordo, -a ['lor·do] *agg* (*peso, cifra, retribuzione*) gross

loro ['lɔ:·ro] **I.** *pron pers* **1.** *3. pers pl* (*soggetto*) they; ~ **due** the two of them; **beati ~!** lucky them! **2.** (*complemento oggetto*) them **3.** (*complemento di termine*) (to) them **4.** (*con preposizione*) them **5.** *3. pers pl* (*forma di cortesia soggetto: Loro*) you **6.** *3. pers pl* (*forma di cortesia complemento: Loro*) you **II.** <inv> *agg* their; **le ~ speranze** their hopes; **il ~ padre/zio** their father/uncle; **un ~ amico** one of their friends **III.** *pron* il [*o* la] [*o* i] [*o* le] ~ theirs **IV.** *m* **1.** (*averi*) their property **2.** (*famiglia*) their family **3.** (*gruppo, amici*) their friends **V.** *f* **1.** (*parte*) their side **2.** (*opinione*) their opinion

losanga [lo·'zaŋ·ga] <-ghe> *f* lozenge

losco, -a ['los·ko] <-schi, -sche> *agg fig* (*traffico, locale, tipo*) suspicious

loto ['lɔ:·to] *m* BOT lotus

lotta ['lɔt·ta] *f* **1.** (*combattimento*) combat; ~ **a corpo a corpo** hand to hand combat; **fare la ~** to wrestle **2.** SPORT wrestling; ~ **libera** professional wrestling **3.** *fig* (*contro fumo, malattia*) fight **4.** *fig* (*dissidio*) struggle; ~ **di classe** class struggle; ~ **per l'esistenza** struggle for existence

lottare [lot·'ta:·re] *vi* **1.** (*combattere*) to fight **2.** SPORT (*fare alla lotta*) to wrestle **3.** *fig* (*opporsi a: sonno, accuse*) to fight

lottatore, -trice [lot·ta·'to:·re] *m, f* SPORT wrestler

lotteria [lot·te·'ri:·a] <-ie> *f* lottery

lottizzabile [lot·tid·'dza:·bi·le] *agg* (*terreno, area*) edificable

lottizzare [lot·tid·'dza:·re] *vt* **1.** (*terreno, area*) to parcel out (for building) **2.** (*assunzioni*) to carve up

lottizzazione [lot·tid·dzat·'tsio:·ne] *f* **1.** (*di terreno*) parceling out (for building) **2.** (*di assunzioni, cariche*) distribution

lotto ['lɔt·to] *m* **1.** (*gioco*) bingo; **giocare al ~** to play bingo **2.** (*terreno*) plot **3.** (*partita: di merce*) batch **4.** (*negli appalti*) lot

---

i The **lotto** is one of the oldest games of chance and is still very popular. In Italy one bets on the numbers between 1 and 90, with the winning combinations being: **ambo** (two correct), **terno** (three correct), **quaterna** (four), and **cinquina** (five).

---

love story [lʌv 'stɔ:·ri] <- *o* love stories> *f* affair

lozione [lot·'tsio:·ne] *f* lotion

LP <-> *m* LP

lubrificante [lu·bri·fi·'kan·te] **I.** *agg* (*olio, prodotto*) lubricant **II.** *m* lubricant

lubrificare [lu·bri·fi·'ka:·re] *vt* (*motore, parti meccaniche*) to lubricate

lubrificazione [lu·bri·fi·kat·'tsio:·ne] *f* (*di motore, parti meccaniche*) lubrification

lucano [lu·'ka:·no] <sing> *m* (*dialetto della Basilicata*) dialect of the Basilicata region

lucano, -a **I.** *agg* (*della Basilicata*) from the Basilicata region **II.** *m, f* (*abitante della Basilicata*) person from the Basilicata region

Lucca *f* Lucca

lucchese [luk·'ke:·se] **I.** *mf* (*abitante*) person from Lucca **II.** *agg* from Lucca

Lucchese <sing> *m* (*zona*) Lucca area; **nel ~** in the Lucca area

lucchetto [luk·'ket·to] *m* padlock

luccicare [lut·tʃi·'ka:·re] *vi* (*stelle, gioielli, occhi*) to sparkle

luccichio [lut·tʃi·'ki:·o] <-chii> *m* (*di stelle, gioielli, occhi*) sparkle

luccio ['lut·tʃo] <-cci> *m* ZOO pike

lucciola ['lut·tʃo·la] *f* glow-worm; **prendere -e per lanterne** *fig* to get the short end of the stick

luce ['lu:·tʃe] *f* **1.** PHYS light; **dare alla ~** to give birth (to); **fare ~ su qc** to shed light on sth; **alla ~ dei fatti** in the light of the evidence; **mettere in ~ qc** to show sth up; **mettere qu in cattiva ~** to show sb in a bad light; **mettersi in ~** to come to the fore; **riportare qc alla ~** to bring sth to light **2.** (*sorgente luminosa*) light; ~ **intermittente** flashing light; **contro ~** against the light **3.** (*lampada*) light; **cinema a -i rosse** blue movie **4.** AUTO light; **-i di posizione** parking lights **5.** (*di ponte*) span; (*di negozio*) window **6.** (*sole*) **alle prime -i** at first light

lucente [lu·'tʃɛn·te] *agg* (*stella, lama, occhi*) bright

lucentezza [lu·tʃen·'tet·tsa] *f* (*di occhi*) brightness; (*di perle, oro*) shine; (*di seta*) sheen

lucerna [lu·'tʃɛr·na] *f* (*lampada*) oil lamp

lucernario [lu·tʃer·'na:·rio] <-i> *m* skylight

lucertola [lu·'tʃɛr·to·la] *f* ZOO lizard

lucidalabbra [lu·tʃi·da·'lab·bra] <-> *m* lip gloss

lucidare [lu·tʃi·'da:·re] *vt* (*scarpe, mobili*) to polish

lucidatrice [lu·tʃi·da·'tri:·tʃe] *f* floor polisher

lucidità [lu·tʃi·di·'ta] <-> *f* (*consapevolezza*) lucidity

lucido ['lu:·tʃi·do] *m* **1.** (*lucentezza*) shine **2.** (*per scarpe*) (shoe) polish **3.** (*disegno*) tracing; (*per lavagna luminosa*) slide

lucido, -a *agg* **1.** (*lucente: scarpe, pavimento*) shiny; **carta -a** glossy paper **2.** *fig* (*mente, analisi*) lucid

lucignolo [lu·'tʃiɲ·ɲo·lo] *m* (*stoppino*) wick

lucrare [lu·'kra:·re] *vt* (*somme*) to make

lucrativo, -a [lu·kra·'ti:·vo] *agg* lucrative

lucro ['lu:·kro] *m* profit; (**non**) **a scopo di ~** (not) for profit

ludico, -a ['lu:·di·ko] <-ci, -che> *agg* (*attività, materiali, modelli*) play

ludoteca [lu·do·'tɛ:·ka] <-che> *f* games library

luglio ['luʎ·ʎo] *m* July; *v.a.* **aprile**

lugubre ['lu:·gu·bre] *agg* (*aspetto, grida*) gloomy

lui ['lu:·i] *pron pers 3. pers m sing* **1.** (*soggetto*) he; **beato ~!** lucky him! **2.** (*oggetto*) him **3.** (*con preposizione*) him

lumaca [lu·'ma:·ka] <-che> *f* slug

lumbard [lum·'ba:rd] **I.** <inv> *agg dial* (*della Lega Nord*) Northern League **II.** <-> *mf dial* (*simpatizzante della Lega Nord*) Northern League supporter

lume ['lu:·me] *m* (*lampada*) lamp; **perdere il ~ della ragione** *fig* to lose one's mind

lumicino [lu·mi·'tʃi:·no] *m* small light

luminare [lu·mi·'na:·re] *m* luminary

lumino [lu·'mi:·no] *m* small lamp

luminosità [lu·mi·no·si·'ta] <-> *f* **1.** (*lucentezza*) brightness **2.** PHYS luminosity

luminoso, -a [lu·mi·'no:·so] *agg* **1.** (*che emette luce: astro, sorgente*) luminous **2.** (*limpido: cielo*) bright **3.** *fig* (*sorriso, occhi*) bright

luna ['lu:·na] *f* **1.** ASTR moon; **~ calante** waning moon; **~ crescente** waxing moon; **~ piena** full moon; **a mezza ~** half-moon; **~ di miele** honeymoon **2.** *fig* (*umore*) **avere la ~ di traverso** [*o* **storta**] to be in a bad mood

luna park ['lu:·na 'park] <-> *m* amusement park

lunare [lu·'na:·re] *agg* (*luce, paesaggio, calendario*) lunar

lunario [lu·'na:·rio] <-i> *m* (*almanacco*) almanac; **sbarcare il ~** to scrape a living

lunatico, -a [lu·'na:·ti·ko] <-ci, -che> *agg* (*strano*) moody

lunedì [lu·ne·'di] <-> *m* Monday; *v.a.* **domenica**

lunetta [lu·'net·ta] *f* ARCH fanlight

lungaggine [luŋ·'gad·dʒi·ne] *f* **-i della burocratiche** red tape

lungamente [luŋ·ga·'men·te] *avv* at length

lungarno [luŋ·'gar·no] *m* banks of the Arno

lunghezza [luŋ·'get·tsa] *f* length; **~ d'onda** wavelength

lungimirante [lun·dʒi·mi·'ran·te] *agg* (*persona, idea, scelta*) far-sighted

lungimiranza [lun·dʒi·mi·'ran·tsa] *f* (*di persona, idea, scelta*) long-sightedness

lungo ['luŋ·go] **I.** *m* length; **per il ~** lengthwise; **in ~ e in largo** far and near **II.** *prep* **1.** (*luogo*) along **2.** (*tempo*) during

lungo, -a <-ghi, -ghe> *agg* **1.** (*estenso*) long; **avere le mani -ghe** *fig* to be light fingered; **saperla -a** *fig* to know what's what **2.** (*che dura*) long; **alla -a** in the long run; **a ~ andare** long term **3.** (*alto*) tall **4.** (*lento*) slow **5.** (*caffè, brodo*) weak **6.** (*loc*) **di gran -a** by far

lungomare [luŋ·go·'ma:·re] *m* seafront

lungometraggio [luŋ·go·me·'trad·dʒo] <-ggi> *m* feature film

lunotto [lu·'nɔt·to] *m* MOT rear window; **~ termico** heated rear window

luogo ['luɔ:·go] <-ghi> *m* **1.** (*posto*) place; **in ogni ~** everywhere; **~ di nascita** birthplace; **le autorità del ~** the local authorities **2.** (*di delitto, avvenimento*) scene; **sul ~** on the scene **3.** (*locale*) place **4.** (*loc*) **in primo ~, ... in secondo ~** firstly, ... secondly; **fuori ~** out of place; **aver ~** to take place; **dar ~ a qc** give rise to sth

luogotenente [luo·go·te·'nɛn·te] *m* (*sostituto*) lieutenant

lupa ['lu:·pa] *f* ZOO she-wolf

lupetto [lu·'pet·to] *m* **1.** ZOO (*cucciolo di lupo*) wolf cub; (*cucciolo di cane lupo*) German shepherd pup **2.** (*negli scout*) cub scout **3.** (*maglione*) turtle neck

lupino [lu·'pi:·no] *m* BOT lupin

lupo ['lu:·po] *m* wolf; **~ mannaro** werewolf; **cane ~** German shepherd; **avere una fame da -i** to be really hungry; **tempo da -i** really bad weather; **~ di mare** (old) sea dog; **al ~!** wolf!; **il ~ perde il pelo ma non il vizio** *prov* a leopard cannot change his spots

luppolo ['lup·po·lo] *m* BOT hops *pl*

lurido, -a ['lu:·ri·do] *agg* (*sporco*) filthy

luridume [lu·ri·'du:·me] *m* (*sporcizia*) filth

lusinga [lu·'zin·ga] <-ghe> *f* temptation

lusingare [lu·zin·'ga:·re] *vt* **~ qu** to flatter sb

lusinghiero, -a [lu·zin·'giɛ:·ro] *agg* (*proposta, offerta, complimento*) flattering

lussemburghese [lus·sem·bur·'ge:·se] **I.** *agg* Luxembourgeois **II.** *mf* Luxemburger

Lussemburgo [lus·sem·'bur·go] *m* **il ~** Luxemburg

lusso ['lus·so] *m* luxury

lussuoso, -a [lus·su·'o:·so] *agg* (*villa, crociera, arredamento*) luxurious

lussureggiante [lus·su·red·'dʒan·te] *agg* (*giardino, piante*) luxuriant

lussuria [lus·'su:·ria] <-ie> *f* lust

lussurioso, -a [lus·su·'rio:·so] *agg* (*pensiero, atteggiamento, persona*) lustful

lustrare [lus·'tra:·re] *vt* (*mobili, scarpe*) to polish

lustrascarpe [lus·tras·'kar·pe] <-> *mf* bootblack

lustrata [lus·'tra:·ta] *f* polish; **dare una ~ a qc** to polish sth

lustrino [lus·'tri:·no] *m* (*paillette*) sequin

lustro ['lus·tro] *m* **1.** (*lucentezza*) shine **2.** *fig* (*splendore*) splendor **3.** (*periodo di cinque anni*) five-year period

lustro, -a *agg* **1.** (*scarpe*) polished **2.** (*occhi*) watery

luterano, -a [lu·te·'ra:·no] **I.** *agg* Lutheran **II.** *m, f* Lutheran

lutto ['lut·to] *m* **1.** (*dolore*) grief **2.** (*abiti*) mourning (clothes); **essere in ~** to be in mourning **3.** (*perdita*) bereavement; **chiuso**

L

per ~ closed due to a death in the family
luttuoso, -a [lut·tu·'o:·so] *agg* **1.**(*doloroso*) distressing **2.**(*funesto*) sorrowful

M

M, m ['ɛm·me] <-> *f* M, m; ~ **come Milano** M for Mike
m metro
ma [ma] I. *cong* **1.**(*contrapposizione*) but; **gli ho telefonato,** ~ **non l'ho trovato** I called him, but he wasn't there; **non ..., ma ...** not ..., but ...; **non solo ...,** ~ **anche ...** not only ..., but also ...; **non solo ci ha fatto compagnia,** ~ **ci ha anche aiutati** not only did he keep us company, but he also gave us a hand **2.**(*nuovo argomento*) but; ~ **torniamo al problema principale** but let's return to the main problem **3.**(*enfasi*) but; ~ **che bella notizia!** but what wonderful news!; ~ **insomma!** for heaven's sake!; ~ **no!** no!; ~ **si!** go on!; ~ **va** (**là**) yeah, yeah II.<-> *m* (*obiezione*) if and but
macabro, -a ['ma:·ka·bro] I. *agg* (*scena, scoperta*) macabre II. *m, f* (*cose macabre*) macabre
macaco [ma·'ka:·ko] <-chi> *m* **1.**(*scimmia*) macaque **2.** *fig, scherz* (*persona*) idiot
macché [mak·'ke] *int* (*assoluta negazione*) are you kidding?
maccheroni [mak·ke·'ro:·ni] *mpl* (*pasta*) macaroni
macchia ['mak·kia] <-cchie> *f* **1.**(*di sporco*) stain **2.**(*di colore diverso*) spot; **a** ~ **di leopardo** unevenly; **a** ~ **d'olio** rapidly **3.** *fig* (*colpa*) stain; **senza** ~ blameless
macchiare [mak·'kia:·re] I. *vt* **1.**(*sporcare*) to stain **2.**(*caffé, tè*) to add milk to; (*latte*) to add coffee to **3.** *fig* (*onore, nome*) to sully II. *vr:* **-rsi 1.**(*sporcarsi*) to get dirty **2.** *fig* (*rendersi colpevole*) **-rsi di qc** to be guilty of sth
macchiato, -a [mak·'kia:·to] *agg* **1.**(*sporco*) dirty **2.**(*maculato*) spotted **3.**(*caffè*) with a dash of milk; **latte** ~ a glass of hot milk with a single espresso
macchietta [mak·'kiet·ta] *f* **1.**(*persona*) wierdo **2.** THEAT, FILM oddball; (*caricatura*) charicature
macchina ['mak·ki·na] *f* **1.**(*apparecchio*) machine; ~ **da cucire** sewing machine; ~ **da presa** movie camera; ~ **da scrivere** typewriter; ~ **fotografica** camera; **a** ~ by machine; **fatto a** ~ machine-made; **battitura a** ~ typing; **battere** [*o* **scrivere**] **a** ~ to type **2.**(*auto*) car; **andare in** ~ to go by car **3.** *fig* (*persona, organizzazione*) machine
macchinare [mak·ki·'na:·re] *vt* (*scherzo, insidia*) to plot

macchinario [mak·ki·'na:·rio] <-i> *m* machinery
macchinazione [mak·ki·nat·'tsio:·ne] *f* (*intrigo*) intrigue
macchinetta [mak·ki·'net·ta] *f* **1.**(*del caffé*) espresso maker **2.**(*per i denti*) brace **3.**(*del parrucchiere*) clippers *pl*
macchinista [mak·ki·'nis·ta] <-i *m*, -e *f*> *mf* **1.**(*di locomotiva*) driver **2.**(*di nave*) engineer
macchinoso, -a [mak·ki·'no:·so] *agg* (*ragionamento, pensieri*) over elaborate
macedone¹ [mat·'ʃe·do·ne] <*sing*> *m* (*lingua*) Macedonian
macedone² [mat·'ʃe·do·ne] *mf* **1.**(*della Macedonia*) Macedonian **2.**(*abitante*) Macedonian
macedonia [mat·ʃe·'dɔ:·nia] <-ie> *f* ~ (**di frutta**) fruit salad
Macedonia *f* Macedonia; **la** ~ Macedonia; **abitare in** ~ to live in Macedonia; **andare in** ~ to go to Macedonia
macellaio, -a [ma·tʃel·'la:·io] <-i, -ie> *m, f* (*venditore*) butcher
macellare [ma·tʃel·'la:·re] *vt* (*animale*) to slaughter
macellazione [ma·tʃel·la·tsio:·ne] *f* slaughter
macelleria [ma·tʃel·le·'ri:·a] <-ie> *f* (*negozio*) butcher's
macello [ma·'tʃɛl·lo] *m* **1.**(*mattatoio*) slaughterhouse **2.** *inf* (*disastro*) disaster
macerare [ma·tʃe·'ra:·re] I. *vt* (*fibra*) to macerate; (*cibo*) to marinate II. *vr:* **-rsi** (*tormentarsi*) to torment oneself; **-rsi nel rimorso/nella gelosia** to be consumed with remorse/jealousy
Macerata [ma·tʃe·'ra:·ta] *f* Macerata, *a city in the Marches region*
maceratese [ma·tʃe·ra·'te:·ze] I. *agg* (*di Macerata*) from Macerata II. *mf* (*abitante*) person from Macerata
Maceratese *sing m* (*zona*) Macerata area; **nel** ~ in the Macerata area
macerazione [ma·tʃe·rat·'tsio:·ne] *f* maceration
macerie [ma·'tʃɛ:·rie] *fpl* (*rovine*) rubble
macero ['ma:·tʃe·ro] *m* **carta da** ~ paper for pulping
machiavellico, -a [ma·kia·'vɛl·li·ko] <-ci, -che> *agg* (*piano, stratagemma*) Machiavellian
macho ['ma·tʃo] I. <inv> *agg* (*atteggiamento, abbigliamento*) macho II.<-> *m* (*uomo*) macho man
macigno [ma·'tʃiɲ·ɲo] *m* (*masso*) rock; **duro come un** ~ as hard as rock; *fig* (*cocciuto*) as stubborn as a bull; **è pesante come un** ~ it weighs a ton; *fig* (*indigesto*) it's like a millstone; (*noioso*) it's as boring as hell
macina ['ma:·tʃi·na] *f* (*di mulino, frantoio*) millstone
macinacaffè [ma·tʃi·na·kaf·'fɛ] <-> *m* coffee grinder
macinapepe [ma·tʃi·na·'pe:·pe] <-> *m* pep-

per mill

macinare [ma·tʃi·'na:·re] *vt* **1.**(*grano, caffè, pepe, carne*) to grind; (*olive*) to crush **2.** *fig* (*chilometri*) to cover; (*denaro*) to get through

macinato, -a [ma·tʃi·'na:·to] *agg* (*caffé, pepe, carne*) ground

macinazione [ma·tʃi·nat·'tsio:·ne] *f* grinding

macinino [ma·tʃi·'ni:·no] *m* **1.**(*da caffè*) grinder; (*da pepe*) mill **2.** *scherz* (*auto*) clunker

maciste [ma·'tʃis·te] *m scherz* (*colosso*) colossus

maciullare [ma·tʃul·'la:·re] *vt* (*stritolare*) to crush

macrobiotica [ma·kro·bi·'ɔ:·ti·ka] <-che> *f* (*alimentazione*) macrobiotics

macrobiotico, -a [ma·kro·bi·'ɔ:·ti·ko] <-ci, -che> *agg* (*alimento, dieta*) macrobiotic

macroeconomia [ma·kro·e·ko·no·'mi:·a] *f* ECON macroeconomics

macroeconomico, -a [ma·kro·e·ko·'nɔ:·mi·ko] <-ci, -che> *agg* ECON macroeconomic

macroscopico, -a [ma·kros·'kɔ:·pi·ko] <-ci, -che> *agg fig* (*differenza*) huge; (*errore*) glaring

maculato, -a [ma·ku·'la:·to] *agg* (*tessuto, pelo*) spotted

madera [ma·'de:·ra] <-> *m* (*vino*) Madeira

Madonna [ma·'dɔn·na] *f* **1.** REL Madonna **2.**(*in esclamazioni*) good God!; **della** ~ *inf, vulg* incredible; **ho una fame/sete della** ~ I'm incredibly hungry/thirsty

madonnaro, -a [ma·don·'na:·ro] *m, f* (*artista*) sidewalk artist of religious subjects

madonnina [ma·don·'ni:·na] *f* **1.**(*immagine*) figure of the Madonna; **la Madonnina** the Madonnina, *golden statue of the Madonna on top of Milan Cathedral* **2.**(*ciondolo*) medal of the Madonna

madornale [ma·dor·'na:·le] *agg* (*errore, sproposito*) huge

madre¹ ['ma:·dre] *f* **1.**(*genitrice*) mother; ~ **natura** Mother Nature **2.**(*suora*) Mother **3.** *fig* (*origine, causa*) cause; **la ~ di tutte ...** the mother of all ... **4.**(*di aceto, vino*) mother

madre² ['ma:·dre] *agg* mother; **lavoratrice** ~ working mother; **lingua** ~ mother tongue; **ragazza** ~ single mother

madrelingua [ma·dre·'liŋ·gua] I.<madrelingue *o* madrilingue> *f* mother tongue; **è di** ~ **francese** his [*o* her] mother tongue is French II.<inv> *agg* mother tongue III.<-> *mf* (*persona*) native speaker

madrepatria [ma·dre·'pa:·tria] *f* (*patria d'origine*) homeland

madreperla [ma·dre·'pɛr·la] *f* mother-of-pearl

madrigale [ma·dri·'ga:·le] *m* (*mus, lit*) madrigal

madrina [ma·'dri:·na] *f* **1.**(*di battesimo, cresima*) godmother **2.**(*di manifestazione*) patroness; (*di nave*) christener

maestà [ma·es·'ta] <-> *f* **1.**(*di edificio, spettacolo naturale, atteggiamento*) majesty

2.(*titolo*) Majesty; (**Sua**) **Maestà** (His) Majesty *m*, (Her) Majesty *f*

maestosità [ma·es·to·si·'ta] <-> *f* (*di edificio, spettacolo naturale, atteggiamento*) majesty

maestoso, -a [ma·es·'to:·so] *agg* **1.**(*edificio, spettacolo naturale, atteggiamento*) majestic **2.** MUS maestoso

maestra [ma·'ɛs·tra] *f v.* maestro

maestrale [ma·es·'tra:·le] *m* (*vento*) northwest wind

maestranze [ma·es·'tran·tse] *fpl* (*dipendenti*) workers *pl*

maestria [ma·es·'tri:·a] <-ie> *f* (*abilità*) skill

maestro, -a [ma·'ɛs·tro/ma·'es·tro] I. *m, f* **1.**(*insegnante elementare*) elementary school teacher; ~ **d'asilo** nursery school teacher **2.**(*di danza*) teacher; (*di sci*) instructor **3.**(*musicista*) maestro; ~ **del coro** chorus master; ~ **d'orchestra** conductor **4.**(*esperto, artigiano*) master; ~ **d'arte** art school graduate; **da** ~ masterly **5.**(*di vita, stile*) master II. *agg* **1.**(*abile*) skilled **2.**(*principale*) main; **strada -a** main road; **muro** ~ main wall

mafia ['ma:·fia] *f* (*organizzazione*) Mafia

mafioso, -a [ma·'fio:·so] I. *agg* (*della mafia*) Mafia II. *m, f* (*affiliato*) member of the Mafia

magagna [ma·'gaɲ·ɲa] *f* (*malanno*) ailment

magari [ma·'ga:·ri] I. *int* (*desiderio*) you bet!; (*affermazione*) certainly! II. *cong* (*desiderio, rimpianto*) if only; ~ **fosse vero!** if only it was true! III. *avv* **1.**(*forse*) perhaps **2.**(*se possibile*) if possible; (*se necessario*) if necessary **3.**(*persino*) even

magazziniere, -a [ma·gad·dzi·'niɛ:·re] *m, f* (*custode, gestore*) warehouse keeper

magazzino [ma·gad·'dzi:·no] *m* **1.**(*deposito*) warehouse **2. grande** ~ department store

maggio ['mad·dʒo] *m* May; **il primo** ~ the first of May; *v.a.* **aprile**

maggiolino [mad·dʒo·'li:·no] *m* **1.**(*insetto*) June bug **2.**(*automobile*) Beetle

maggiorana [mad·dʒo·'ra:·na] *f* marjoram

maggioranza [mad·dʒo·'ran·tsa] *f* majority; ~ **assoluta** absolute majority

maggiorare [mad·dʒo·'ra:·re] *vt* (*prezzo*) to increase

maggiorazione [mad·dʒo·rat·'tsio:·ne] *f* (*di prezzo, salario*) increase

maggiordomo [mad·dʒor·'dɔ:·mo] <-i> *m* (*capo di servitù*) butler

maggiore¹ [mad·'dʒo:·re] I. *agg comp di* **grande 1.**(*comparativo: per dimensioni*) bigger [*o* biggest]; ~ **di** bigger than; **il/la** ~ the biggest **2.**(*per numero*) greater [*o* greatest]; **la maggior parte di** most of; (*per intensità*) greater; **avere** ~ **pazienza** to be more patient **3.**(*per importanza*) more [*o* most] important; **le opere -i** the major works; **a maggior ragione** even more so **4.**(*per età*) older [*o* oldest]; **essere** ~ **di qu** (**di un anno**) to be (a year) older than sb; **la** ~ **età** the age of majority **5.** MUS major II. *mf* (*il più anziano*) oldest

maggiore² *m* MIL major

maggiorenne [mad·dʒo·'rɛn·ne] I. *agg* of age II. *mf* adult

maggioritario, -a [mad·dʒo·ri·'ta:·rio] <-i, -ie> *agg* (*partito, gruppo*) majority; **sistema ~** POL first past the post system

maggiormente [mad·dʒor·'men·te] *avv* **1.** (*di più*) more **2.** (*più di tutto*) more than anything else

magi ['ma:·dʒi] *mpl* **i** (**tre**) (**re**) ~ the Magi

magia [ma·'dʒi:·a] <-gie> *f* **1.** (*arte*) magic; **~ bianca/nera** white/black magic **2.** (*incantesimo*) spell **3.** *fig* (*fascino*) magic

magico, -a ['ma:·dʒi·ko] <-ci, -che> *agg* **1.** (*di magia*) magic; **bacchetta -a** magic wand; **formula -a** magic words *pl;* **pozione -a** magic potion **2.** *fig* (*straordinario, suggestivo*) magical

magistero [ma·dʒis·'tɛ:·ro] *m* **1.** (*funzione educatrice*) teaching; **il ~ della Chiesa** the Church's teaching **2.** (*professione*) teaching; **facoltà di ~** faculty of Education

magistrale [ma·dʒis·'tra:·le] I. *agg* **1.** (*per maestri*) elementary school teaching; **istituto ~** *secondary school which trains elementary school teachers* **2.** (*eccellente*) masterly II. **le -i** *secondary school which trains elementary school teachers*

magistrato [ma·dʒis·'tra:·to] *m* (*giudice*) judge; **~ di Cassazione** Supreme Court judge; **~ di Corte d'Appello** Appeals Court judge; **~ inquirente** committing magistrate

magistratura [ma·dʒis·tra·'tu:·ra] *f* (*potere giudiziario*) judiciary

maglia ['maʎ·ʎa] <-glie> *f* **1.** (*golf*) sweater; (*indumento intimo*) vest **2.** SPORT shirt; **~ azzurra** Italian national teams' shirt; **~ rosa** *pink jersey worn by the winner of the Giro d'Italia bike race* **3.** (*punto*) stitch; **lavorare a ~** to knit **4.** (*tessuto*) jersey **5.** (*di catena, collana, bracciale*) link **6.** *pl a. fig* (*intreccio*) mesh

maglieria [maʎ·ʎe·'ri:·a] <-ie> *f* **1.** (*indumenti*) knitwear **2.** (*negozio*) knitwear shop

maglietta [maʎ·ʎet·ta] *f* (*indumento intimo*) vest; (*indumento estivo*) T-shirt

maglificio [maʎ·ʎi·'fi:·tʃo] <-ci> *m* (*fabbrica*) knitwear factory

maglione [maʎ·ʎo:·ne] *m* (*golf*) sweater

magnaccia [maɲ·'nat·tʃa] <-> *m vulg* (*sfruttatore*) pimp

magnanimità [maɲ·na·ni·mi·'ta] <-> *f* (*generosità, clemenza*) magnanimity

magnanimo, -a [maɲ·'na:·ni·mo] *agg* (*generoso, clemente*) magnanimous

magnate [maɲ·'na:·te] *m* (*capitalista*) magnate

magnesio [maɲ·'nɛ:·zio] *m* CHEM magnesium

magnete [maɲ·'nɛ:·te] *m* (*calamita*) magnet

magnetico, -a [maɲ·'nɛ:·ti·ko] <-ci, -che> *agg a. fig* PHYS magnetic; **campo ~** magnetic field; **polo ~** magnetic pole

magnetismo [maɲ·ne·'tiz·mo] *m a. fig* magnetism

magnificenza [maɲ·ni·fi·'tʃɛn·tsa] *f* (*sfarzo*) magnificence

magnifico, -a [maɲ·'ni:·fi·ko] <-ci, -che> *agg* (*gioiello, casa*) magnificent; (*interpretazione, esecuzione, spettacolo*) wonderful; (*idea, serata, giornata*) marvellous

magnolia [maɲ·'nɔ:·lia] <-ie> *f* (*pianta*) magnolia

mago, -a ['ma:·go] <-ghi, -ghe> *m, f* **1.** (*indovino*) fortune-teller **2.** (*nelle fiabe*) wizard; **il ~ Merlino** Merlin the wizard **3.** (*illusionista*) magician **4.** *fig* (*persona abile*) wizard

magra ['ma:·gra] *f* **1.** (*di fiume*) low water; **essere in ~** to be low **2.** *fig* hardship; **tempo** [*o* **periodo**] **di ~** hard times *pl*

magrezza [ma·'gret·tsa] *f* **1.** (*di corpo*) thinness **2.** *fig* (*di guadagno, risultato*) scantiness

magro, -a¹ ['ma:·gro] *agg* **1.** (*persona, animale, gambe, braccia*) thin; **~ come un chiodo** [*o* **uno stecco**] thin as a rail **2.** (*alimento*) low-fat; **di ~** without meat **3.** *fig* poor; **una -a soddisfazione** a scant consolation

magro, -a² *m, f* **1.** (*persona*) thin person; **falso ~** person who is not as thin as he seems [*o* she] **2.** *sing* (*parte magra*) lean part

mah [ma:] *int* **1.** (*dubbio, incertezza*) well **2.** (*rassegnazione, disapprovazione*) huh

mai ['ma:·i] *avv* **1.** (*in nessun tempo, in nessun caso*) never; **non mi saluta ~** he [*o* she] never says hello to me; **~ più** never again; **più che ~** more than ever **2.** (*risposta*) never; **lasceresti la tua città? — ~!** would you ever leave your hometown? — never!; **~ e poi ~** never in a million years **3.** (*in interrogative*) ever; **sei ~ stato a Venezia?** have you ever been to Venice?; (*enfatico*) ever; **come ~ sei ancora qui?** why ever are you still here?; **chi ~ sarà stato?** whoever can that have been?

maiala [ma·'ia:·la] *f vulg* slut

maiale [ma·'ia:·le] *m* **1.** (*animale*) pig **2.** (*carne*) pork **3.** *fig, inf* (*sporcaccione, persona dissoluta*) pig

maiolica [ma·'iɔ:·li·ka] <-che> *f* majolica

maionese [ma·io·'ne:·se] *f* (*salsa*) mayonnaise

Maiorca [ma·'iɔr·ka] *f* Majorca; **la Maiorca** Majorca; **abitare a ~** to live in Majorca; **andare a ~** to go to Majorca

mais ['ma:·is] <-> *m* (*cereale*) corn; (*chicchi*) sweetcorn

maitre ['me·tr] *m* (*in ristorante*) head waiter; (*in albergo*) maître d'hotel

maiuscola [ma·'ius·ko·la] *f* (*lettera*) capital (letter)

maiuscolo, -a¹ [ma·'ius·ko·lo] *agg* (*lettera, carattere*) capital

maiuscolo² *m* (*carattere*) capital letters *pl*

make-up ['mei·kap] <-> *m* makeup

mal [mal] *m v.* **male²**

mala ['ma:·la] *f inf v.* **malavita**

malaccio [ma·'lat·tʃo] *m* **non c'è ~** *inf* not bad at all

malafede [ma·la·'fe:·de] <malefedi> *f* (*slealtà*) bad faith; **in ~** in bad faith

malaffare [ma·laf·'fa:·re] *m* **di** ~ shady
malaga ['ma:·la·ga] <-> *m* **1.**(*vino*) Malaga
2.(*gelato*) rum-and-raisin icecream
malalingua [ma·la·'liŋ·gua] <malelingue> *f*
(*persona maldicente*) gossip
malamente [ma·la·'men·te] *avv* **1.**(*in modo
scorretto*) rudely **2.**(*in modo impreciso*) badly **3.**(*in modo violento*) badly
malandato, -a [ma·lan·'da:·to] *agg* **1.**(*indumento*) shabby; (*edificio, veicolo*) dilapidated
2.(*persona: malato, trasandato*) in a bad way
malandrino, -a [ma·lan·'dri:·no] **I.** *agg scherz,
inf* (*occhi, sorriso*) roguish **II.** *m, f scherz, inf*
(*ragazzo*) little devil
malanno [ma·'lan·no] *m* (*malattia*) ailment
malapena [ma·la·'pe:·na] *f* **a** ~ only just
malaria [ma·'la:·ria] <-ie> *f* malaria
malarico, -a [ma·'la:·ri·ko] <-ci, -che> *agg*
(*zona, palude*) malarial; **febbre -a** malarial fever
malasanità [ma·la·sa·ni·'ta] <-> *f* medical
malpractice
malaticcio, -ccia [ma·la·'tit·tʃo] <-cci, -cce>
agg sickly
malato, -a [ma·'la:·to] **I.** *agg* **1.**(*persona, animale*) ill; (*pianta*) diseased; **essere** ~ **di qc** to
suffer from sth; ~ **di mente** mentally ill
2.(*parte del corpo*) diseased **3.** *fig* (*ossessionato*) sick **II.** *m, f* (*persona malata*) ill person;
(*in ospedale*) patient; ~ **terminale** terminally
ill person [*o* patient]
malattia [ma·lat·'ti:·a] <-ie> *f* **1.**(*di persona,
animale*) illness; (*di pianta*) disease; **prendersi** [*o* **prendere**] **una** ~ to catch an illness;
essere/mettersi in ~ to be/go on sick leave
2. *fig* (*vizio*) vice
malaugurato, -a [ma·lau·gu·'ra:·to] *agg* (*ipotesi*) unlucky
malaugurio [ma·lau·'gu:·rio] <-i> *m* bad luck;
uccello del ~ *fig* albatross
malavita [ma·la·'vi:·ta] *f* **1.**(*delinquenza*)
crime; **darsi alla** ~ to turn to crime **2.**(*insieme
di persone*) underworld; ~ **organizzata** organized crime; **il gergo della** ~ underworld
slang
malavitoso [ma·la·vi·'to:·zo] **I.** *agg* (*attività,
clan*) underworld **II.** *m* member of the underworld
malavoglia [ma·la·'vɔʎ·ʎa] <malevoglie> *f*
di ~ unwillingly
malcapitato, -a [mal·ka·pi·'ta:·to] **I.** *agg* unlucky **II.** *m, f* unlucky person
malcelato, -a [mal·tʃe·'la:·to] *agg* (*sentimento, stato d'animo*) ill-concealed
malconcio, -a [mal·'kon·tʃo] <-ci, -ce> *agg*
(*persona, abito*) worse for wear; (*libro*) battered
malcontento [mal·kon·'tɛn·to] *m* discontent;
~ **generale** general discontent
malcostume [mal·kos·'tu:·me] *m* corruption;
~ **politico** political corruption
maldestro, -a [mal·'dɛs·tro] *agg* (*persona, tentativo, approccio*) clumsy

maldicenza [mal·di·'tʃɛn·tsa] *f* (*pettegolezzo*)
gossip
maldisposto, -a [mal·dis·'pos·to] *agg* hostile;
essere ~ **verso qu** to be hostile towards sb
male[1] ['ma:·le] <peggio, malissimo> *avv* **1.**(*in
modo insoddisfacente*) badly; **andare** ~ to go
badly; **comportarsi** ~ to behave badly; **guadagnare** ~ to not earn very much; **vestire** ~ to
dress badly **2.**(*in modo malevolo*) badly; **par-
lare/pensare** ~ **di qu** to talk/think badly of
sb; **rispondere** ~ **a qu** to answer sb rudely;
trattare ~ **qu** to treat sb badly **3.**(*in cattiva
salute*) ill; **sentirsi/stare** ~ to feel/be ill **4.**(*a
disagio*) uneasy; **rimanere/restare** ~ to feel
let down **5.**(*in modo imperfetto*) badly; **funzionare** ~ to not work properly; **riuscire** [*o*
venire] ~ to not turn out well; **la foto è
venuta** ~ the photo hasn't come out well;
quel vestito ti sta ~ you look awful in that
dress; **vedere/sentire** ~ to see/hear badly
6.(*loc*) **niente** ~ not bad; **non è** ~ it's not bad;
di ~ **in peggio** from bad to worse; **hai fatto** ~
a non farlo! you were wrong not to do it!
male[2] *m* **1.**(*in senso morale*) evil **2.**(*danno,
svantaggio*) bad thing; **andare a** ~ (*cibo*) to go
off; **che** ~ **c'è?** what's wrong with that?; **non
c'è** ~ not bad; **non c'è nulla di** ~ it's pretty
good; **poco** ~ never mind **3.**(*sofferenza*) pain;
fare (**del**) ~ **a qu** to hurt sb; **mi fa** ~ **vederlo
così** it upsets me to see him like that **4.**(*malattia*) illness; **un brutto** ~ cancer; **mal di denti**
toothache; **mal di gola** a sore throat; **mal
di pancia/stomaco** stomachache; **mal di
schiena** backache; **mal di testa** a headache;
mal d'aria [*o* **d'aereo**] air sickness; **mal
d'auto** car sickness; **mal di mare** seasickness
maledetto [ma·le·'det·to] **I.** *pp di* **maledire**
II. *agg* **1.**(*segnato da maledizione*) cursed
2.(*causa di sventura*) damned; **un viaggio** ~ a
jinxed trip **3.**(*detestabile*) damned; **ho di
nuovo perso quel** ~ **treno!** I've missed that
damned train again! **4.** *inf* (*fame, caldo*) incredible; **ho una sete -a** I'm incredibly thirsty;
(*paura, voglia*) real; **ho una voglia -a di partire** I really want to leave; **una fretta -a** an incredible hurry **III.** *m* damned person
maledire [ma·le·'di:·re] <irr> *vt* to curse
maledizione [ma·le·dit·'tsio:·ne] **I.** *f* **1.**(*condanna, disgrazia*) curse **2.**(*imprecazione*)
curse **II.** *int* damn
maleducato, -a [mal·e·du·'ka:·to] **I.** *agg* (*persona, gesto*) rude **II.** *m, f* rude person
maleducazione [ma·le·du·kat·'tsio:·ne] *f*
1.(*abitudine*) bad manners *pl* **2.**(*atto*) rudeness
malefatta [ma·le·'fat·ta] *f* wrongdoing
malefedi *pl di* **malafede** bad faith
malefico, -a [ma·'lɛ:·fi·ko] <-ci, -che> *agg*
1.(*persona*) evil; (*risposta*) nasty; (*azione,
influsso*) malevolent **2.**(*aria, clima*) bad
malelingue *pl di* **malalingua**
maleodorante [ma·le·o·do·'ran·te] *agg*
(*immondizia, luogo*) smelly

malese¹ [ma·'le:·ze] <*sing*> *m* (*lingua*) Malay
malese² I. *agg* (*della Malesia*) Malaysian II. *mf* (*abitante*) Malaysian
malessere [ma·ᵛlɛs·se·re] *m* 1.(*malore*) ailment 2.(*disagio*) uneasiness
malevoglie *pl di* **malavoglia**
malevolenza [ma·le·vo·'lɛn·tsa] *f* malevolence; **con** ~ malevolently
malevolo, -a [ma·'lɛ:·vo·lo] *agg* malevolent
malfamato, -a [mal·fa·'ma:·to] *agg* (*quartiere, bar*) rough
malfatto, -a [mal·'fat·to] *agg* 1.(*malriuscito*) badly done 2.(*persona*) misshapened; (*gambe, naso*) bent
malfattore, -trice [mal·fat·'to:·re] *m, f* criminal
malfermo, -a [mal·'fer·mo] *agg* 1.(*sedia, passo, voce*) unsteady 2.*fig* (*persona, salute*) frail; **essere di salute -a** to be frail
malformazione [mal·for·mat·'tsio:·ne] *f* MED malformation
malfunzionamento [mal·fun·tsio·na·'men·to] *m* malfunction
malga ['mal·ga] <-ghe> *f* (*baita*) shepherd's hut
malgoverno, mal governo [mal·go·'vɛr·no] *m* misrule
malgrado [mal·'gra:·do] I. *prep* in spite of; **mio/tuo/suo** ~ against my/your/his [*o* her] will II. *cong* + *conj* even though
malia [ma·'li:·a] <-ie> *f* (*fascino*) charm
malignare [ma·liɲ·'ɲa:·re] *vi* to malign; ~ **su qu/qc** to malign sth/sb
malignità [ma·liɲ·ɲi·'ta] <-> *f* 1.(*caratteristica*) malice 2.(*parola*) malicious remark; (*pensiero*) malicious thought
maligno, -a¹ [ma·'liɲ·ɲo] *agg* 1.(*spirito, persona*) evil 2.(*pensiero, voce*) malicious; **un sorrisetto** ~ a malicious smile 3.(*tumore*) malignant
maligno, -a² *m, f* (*persona*) malicious person; **il Maligno** the Devil
malinconia [ma·liɲ·ko·'ni:·a] <-ie> *f* 1.(*stato d'animo*) melancholy 2.(*pensiero*) melancholy thought
malinconico, -a [ma·liɲ·'kɔ:·ni·ko] <-ci, -che> *agg* 1.(*persona, carattere, sguardo*) melancholy 2.(*ricordo, musica*) sad
malincuore [ma·liɲ·'kuɔ:·re] *m* **a** ~ unwillingly
malinformato, -a [mal·in·for·'ma:·to] *agg* misinformed; **essere** ~ **su qc** to be misinformed about sth
malintenzionato, -a [mal·in·ten·tsio·'na:·to] I. *agg* up to something II. *m, f* suspicious character
malinteso [mal·in·'te:·so] *m* (*equivoco*) misunderstanding
malissimo [ma·'lis·si·mo] *avv superlativo di* **male¹**
malizia [ma·'lit·tsia] <-ie> *f* 1.(*cattiveria*) malice; **con/senza** ~ maliciously/without malice 2.(*allusività*) cunning 3.(*espediente*) trick

malizioso, -a [ma·lit·'tsio:·so] *agg* 1.(*allusivo*) cunning 2.(*birichino*) mischievous
malleabile [mal·le·'a:·bi·le] *agg* malleable
malleolo [mal·'lɛ:·o·lo] *m* ANAT malleolus
malloppo [mal·'lɔp·po] *m* 1.(*fagotto*) bundle 2.*inf* (*refurtiva*) loot 3.*fig* (*preoccupazione*) worry
malmenare [mal·me·'na:·re] *vt* (*picchiare*) to beat up
malnutrito, -a [mal·nu·'tri:·to] *agg* malnourished
malo, -a ['ma:·lo] *agg* **in** ~ **modo** badly; **cadere/scivolare in** ~ **modo** to fall/slip badly; **comportarsi in** ~ **modo** to behave awkwardly; **rispondere in** ~ **modo** to reply rudely
malocchio [ma·'lɔk·kio] *m* evil eye
malora [ma·'lo:·ra] *f* **andare in** ~ to go to the dogs; **essere in** ~ to be in serious trouble; **mandare in** ~ to ruin; **della** ~ *inf* from hell; (**va'**) **in** ~! [*o* **alla** ~!] *fam* go to hell!
malore [ma·'lo:·re] *m* sudden illness; **essere colto da** ~ to be suddenly taken ill
malridotto, -a [mal·ri·'dot·to] *agg* 1.(*abito, casa, libro*) in a sorry state 2.(*persona*) in a bad way
malriuscito, -a [mal·ri·uʃ·'ʃi:·to] *agg* (*tentativo, esperimento*) unsuccessful
malsano, -a [mal·'sa:·no] *agg* 1.(*clima, luogo, aspetto*) unhealthy 2.(*idea, pensiero*) unwholesome
malta ['mal·ta] *f* (*nelle costruzioni*) mortar
Malta ['mal·ta] *f* Malta; **abitare a** ~ to live in Malta; **andare a** ~ to go to Malta
maltagliati [mal·taʎ·'ʎa:·ti] *mpl* CULIN *irregular pasta squares for soup*
maltempo [mal·'tɛm·po] *m* bad weather
maltese¹ *m* <*sing*> (*lingua*) Maltese
maltese² [mal·'te·ze] I. *agg* (*di Malta*) Maltese; **cane** ~ Maltese II. *mf* (*abitante*) Maltese
malto ['mal·to] *m* malt
maltrattamento [mal·trat·ta·'men·to] *m* ill-treatment
maltrattare [mal·trat·'ta:·re] *vt* to mistreat
malumore [ma·lu·'mo:·re] *m* 1.(*cattivo umore*) bad mood; **di** ~ in a bad mood 2.(*rancore, scontento*) ill feeling
malva ['mal·va] I. *f* (*pianta*) mallow II. <-> *m* (*colore*) mauve III. <inv> *agg* mauve
malvagio, -a [mal·'va:·dʒo] <-gi, -gie> I. *agg* 1.(*persona, animo, atto, intenzione*) wicked 2.*inf* (*pessimo*) terrible; **non è un'idea -gia** it's not a bad idea II. *m, f* wicked person
malvagità [mal·va·dʒi·'ta] <-> *f* 1.(*inclinazione*) wickedness 2.(*atto*) wicked deed
malvasia [mal·va·'zi:·a] *m o f* (*vino*) Malvasia, *a type of Italian wine*
malvestito, -a [mal·ves·'ti:·to] *agg* 1.(*dimesso*) shabby 2.(*inelegante*) badly dressed
malvisto, -a [mal·'vis·to] *agg* disliked; **essere** ~ **da qu** to be disliked by sb
malvivente [mal·vi·'vɛn·te] *mf* (*delinquente*)

crook
malvolentieri [mal·vo·len·'tiɛː·ri] *avv* unwillingly
mamma[1] ['mam·ma] *f inf* (*madre*) mom
mamma[2] *int* heavens; ~ **mia!** good heavens!
mammario, -a [mam·'maː·rio] <-i, -ie> *agg* ANAT mammary
mammella [mam·'mɛl·la] *f* ANAT breast
mammifero [mam·'mi:·fe·ro] *m* mammal
mammo ['mam·mo] *m scherz* househusband
mammografia [mam·mo·gra·'fiː·a] *f* MED mammogram
mammola ['mam·mo·la] *f* (*fiore*) violet
mammone, -na [mam·'moː·ne] I. *agg* (*bambino, uomo*) attached to his [*o* her] mother II. *m, f inf* mama's boy *m*, mama's girl *f*
mammut [mam·'mut] <-> *m* (*animale estinto*) mammoth
manageriale [ma·na·dʒe·'riaː·le] *agg* (*attività, criterio*) managerial; **capacità -i** managerial abilities
manca ['man·ka] *f* **a destra** [*o* **a dritta**] **e a ~** all over the place
mancamento [maŋ·ka·'men·to] *m* (*svenimento*) fainting fit; **avere un ~** to faint
mancante [man·'kan·te] *agg* 1. (*assente*) missing 2. **~ di qc** (*privo*) lacking in sth
mancanza [maŋ·'kan·tsa] *f* 1. (*carenza*) lack; **~ di qc** lack of sth; **in ~ di** if there is [*o* are] no; **in ~ di meglio** if there's nothing better 2. (*assenza*) absence; **sentire la ~ di qu** to miss sb 3. (*errore*) mistake
mancare [maŋ·'ka:·re] I. *vi* 1. *essere* (*non esserci, non bastare*) to be lacking; (*acqua, corrente, luce*) to go off 2. *essere* (*essere assente*) to not be there; (*provocare nostalgia*) to miss; **ti sono mancato?** did you miss me?; **mi manca molto** I miss him [*o* her] a lot 3. *essere* (*distare*) to be; **c'è mancato poco che ...** +*conj* very nearly ... 4. *essere* (*forze*) **~ a qu** to fail sb; **mi manca il fiato** I'm out of breath; **mi sono mancate le forze** my strength failed 5. *essere* (*morire*) to die 6. *essere* (*svenire*) to faint; **sentirsi ~** to feel faint 7. *avere* (*essere privo*) **~ di qc** to be lacking in sth 8. *avere* (*venir meno*) **~ a qc** to not keep sth; **~ a una promessa** to not keep a promise; **~ di qc** to be lacking in sth; **~ di parola** to not keep one's word 9. *avere* (*sbagliare*) to make a mistake; **~ in qc** to get sth wrong; **ho mancato nel rispondergli così** I was wrong to answer him in that way II. *vt avere* 1. (*bersaglio, colpo, palla*) to miss 2. (*occasione, opportunità*) to miss 3. (*omettere*) **non ~ di ...** +*inf* to not fail to ...; **non mancherò!** I certainly will!
mancato, -a [maŋ·'ka:·to] *agg* 1. (*pagamento, funzionamento*) non-; **il ~ arrivo** the non-arrival; (*colpo, goal, obbiettivo*) missed; (*tentativo, accordo, film, libro*) unsuccessful; (*occasione*) wasted 2. (*attore, cantante, pittore*) manqué
manche [mãːʃ] <-> *f* 1. SPORT heat 2. (*nei gio-*

chi di carte) hand
mancia ['man·tʃa] <-ce> *f* (*per servizio*) tip
manciata [man·'tʃa:·ta] *f* 1. (*pugno*) handful 2. *fig* (*piccola quantità*) couple; **una ~ di secondi** a couple of seconds
mancino, -a [man·'tʃiː·no] I. *agg* left-handed; **essere ~** to be left-handed II. *m, f* (*persona*) left-handed person
manco ['maŋ·ko] *avv inf* (*nemmeno*) not even; **~ morto** over my dead body; **~ per idea** [*o* **per sogno**] [*o* **per scherzo**] not on your life; **~ a dirlo** needless to say
mandante [man·'dan·te] *mf* (*di delitto*) instigator
mandarancio [man·da·'ran·tʃo] <-ci> *m* clementine
mandare [man·'da:·re] *vt* 1. (*persona*) to send; (*a sede, ufficio*) to post; **~ a chiamare qu** to summons sb; **~ a dire qc a qu** to send word to sb; **~ qu a prendere qc/qu** to send sb to get sth/sb; **~ via qu** to send sb away 2. (*lettera, pacco, fiori*) to send; **~ qc per posta/col corriere** to send sth by mail/courier 3. (*luce, fumo, odore*) to give off; (*grido, verso*) to let out 4. (*loc*) **~ qc all'aria** [*o* **a monte**] [*o* **in fumo**] to ruin sth; **~ avanti qu** to send sb on; **~ avanti qc** (*famiglia, azienda*) to keep sth going; **~ avanti/indietro** (*cassetta, nastro*) to forward/rewind; **~ qu al diavolo** [*o* **a quel paese**] to tell sb to go to hell; **~ giù qc** (*cibo*) to swallow; (*offesa*) to get over; **~ in onda** to broadcast
mandarino [man·da·'riː·no] *m* (*frutto*) mandarin
mandata [man·'da:·ta] *f* (*di serratura*) turn; **chiudere a doppia ~** to double-lock
mandatario, -a [man·da·'ta:·rio] <-i, -ie> *m, f* (*incaricato*) representative
mandato [man·'da:·to] *m* 1. (*incarico*) job; **agire su ~ di qu** to act on sb's orders 2. JUR warrant; **~ di arresto/cattura** arrest warrant; **~ di comparizione** summons; **~ di perquisizione** search warrant
mandibola [man·'di:·bo·la] *f* ANAT jaw
mandolino [man·do·'liː·no] *m* (*strumento*) mandolin
mandorla ['man·dor·la] *f* (*frutto*) almond; **olio di -e** almond oil; **pasta di -e** almond paste; **occhi a ~** almond-shaped eyes
mandorlato [man·dor·'la:·to] *agg* (*cioccolato, torrone*) almond
mandorlo ['man·dor·lo] *m* almond tree
mandria ['mand·ria] <-ie> *f* 1. (*di buoi, cavalli*) herd 2. *fig, pej* (*di persone*) gang
mandriano [mand·ri·'a:·no] *m* herdsman
maneggevole [ma·ned·'dʒeː·vo·le] *agg* easy to handle
maneggiare [ma·ned·'dʒaː·re] *vt* 1. (*trattare*) to handle; **~ con cura** handle with care 2. (*usare*) to use 3. (*amministrare*) to manage
maneggio [ma·'ned·dʒo] <-ggi> *m* 1. (*pista*) ring; (*addestramento*) manège 2. (*intrigo*) intrigue 3. (*uso*) handling 4. (*amministrazione*)

M

managing

manesco, -a [ma·'nes·ko] <-schi, -sche> I. *agg* (*persona*) aggressive II. *m, f* agressive type

manetta [ma·'net·ta] *f* 1.(*manopola*) lever 2. *pl* (*per polsi*) handcuffs *pl;* **mettere le -e a qu** to handcuff sb

manganello [maŋ·ga·'nɛl·lo] *m* (*sfollagente*) billy club

manganese [maŋ·ga·'ne:·se] *m* CHEM manganese

mangia-e-bevi [man·dʒa·e·'be:·vi] <-> *m* (*gelato*) ice cream sundae

mangiare¹ [man·'dʒa:·re] I. *vt* 1.(*ingerire*) to eat; **dare da ~ qc a qu** to give sb sth to eat; **fare da ~** to get some food ready; **~ alla carta/a prezzo fisso** to eat à la carte/ from the set menu; **~ di magro** to not eat meat; **~ in bianco** to eat plain food; **~ la foglia** *fig* to catch on; **~ con gli occhi qu/qc** to devour sb/sth with one's eyes 2.(*rosicchiare, corrodere*) to eat away at 3.(*denaro*) to get through 4.(*nei giochi*) to take II. *vr:* **-rsi** to eat; **mi sono mangiato un panino** I ate a roll; **-rsi il fegato** *fig* to be consumed with rage; **-rsi le mani** *fig* to really regret; **-rsi la parola** *fig* to not keep one's word; **-rsi le parole** *fig* to mumble; **-rsi le unghie** to bite one's nails

mangiare² *m* (*cibo, pasto*) food

mangiasoldi [man·dʒa·'sɔl·di] <inv> *agg* **macchina ~** slot-machine

mangiata [man·'dʒa:·ta] *f* blowout; **farsi una bella ~ di qc** to stuff oneself on sth

mangiatoia [man·dʒa·'to:·ia] <-oie> *f* (*nella stalla*) manger

mangiatore, -trice [man·dʒa·'to:·re] *m, f* (*consumatore*) eater

mangime [man·'dʒi:·me] *m* (*per pesci, uccelli*) feed

mangione, -a [man·'dʒo:·ne] *m, f* big eater

mania [ma·'ni:·a] <-ie> *f* 1.(*ossessione*) mania; **avere la ~ dell'ordine** to be obsessively tidy; **~ di grandezza** delusions of grandeur *pl;* **~ di persecuzione** persecution complex 2.(*fanatismo*) craze

maniaco, -a [ma·'ni:·a·ko] <-ci, -che> *m, f* 1.(*squilibrato*) maniac; **~ sessuale** sex maniac 2.(*fanatico*) fanatic

manica ['ma:·ni·ka] <-che> *f* 1.(*di indumento*) sleeve; **a -che corte/lunghe** short/ long -sleeved; **a mezze -che** short-sleeved; **senza -che** sleeveless; **in -che di camicia** in one's shirt sleeves; **rimboccarsi** [*o* tirarsi su] **le -che** *a. fig* to roll one's sleeves up; **essere di ~ larga** *fig* to be indulgent 2. *pej* (*gruppo*) gang

Manica ['ma:·ni·ka] *f* **la Manica** the English Channel; **il canale della Manica** the English Channel

manicaretto [ma·ni·ka·'ret·to] *m* delicacy

manichino [ma·ni·'ki:·no] *m* dummy

manico ['ma:·ni·ko] <-chi *o* -ci> *m* (*impugnatura*) handle

manicomio [ma·ni·'kɔ:·mio] <-i> *m* 1. *inf* (*ospedale psichiatrico*) mental hospital 2. *inf* (*luogo caotico*) madhouse

manicure [ma·ni·'ku:·re, ma·ni·'ku:r] <-> *mf* 1.(*persona*) manicurist 2.(*trattamento*) manicure

maniera [ma·'niɛ:·ra] *f* 1.(*modo*) way; **alla ~ di qu** like sb; **in ~ che ... +***conj* so that ... 2.(*stile*) style; **alla ~ di qu** in the style of sb; **di ~** mannered 3. *pl* (*comportamento, modo di fare*) manners *pl;* **belle** [*o* **buone**]/**brutte** [*o* **cattive**] **-e** good/bad manners; **che -e sono queste?** what sort of way to behave is this?

manierismo [ma·nie·'riz·mo] *m* ART, LIT Mannerism

maniero [ma·'nie:·ro] *m* (*castello*) castle

manifattura [ma·ni·fat·'tu:·ra] *f* 1.(*lavorazione*) manufacture 2.(*azienda*) factory

manifatturiero, -a [ma·ni·fat·tu·'riɛ:·ro] *agg* (*industria, produzione, settore*) manufacturing

manifestante [ma·ni·fes·'tan·te] *mf* demonstrator

manifestare [ma·ni·fes·'ta:·re] I. *vt* 1.(*desiderio, opinione, sentimento*) to express 2.(*denotare*) to show II. *vi* (*protestare*) to demonstrate III. *vr:* **-rsi** (*rivelarsi*) to show oneself

manifestazione [ma·ni·fes·tat·'tsio:·ne] *f* 1.(*di affetto, gioia*) display 2.(*di malattia, fenomeno*) sign 3.(*di protesta, appoggio*) demonstration 4.(*artistica, musicale, sportiva*) event

manifestino [ma·ni·fes·'ti:·no] *m* (*volantino*) leaflet

manifesto, -a¹ [ma·ni·'fes·to] *agg* (*evidente*) obvious; **rendere ~ qc** to make sth obvious; **è ~ che ... +***ind* it's obvious that ...

manifesto² *m* 1.(*elettorale, pubblicitario*) poster 2.(*poster*) poster 3.(*programma*) manifesto; **il Manifesto del Partito Comunista** the manifesto of the Communist Party

maniglia [ma·'niʎ·ʎa] <-glie> *f* 1.(*di porta, finestra, cassetto*) handle; **-e di sostegno** strap 2. *fig, inf* (*raccomandazione*) backing; **avere una** [*o* qualche] **~** to have some backing

manipolare [ma·ni·po·'la:·re] *vt* 1.(*lavorare: cera, creta*) to work; (*mescolare: pasta*) to mix 2.(*alterare: vino, alimento*) to adulterate 3. *fig* (*notizia, risultato, idea, opinione*) to manipulate

manipolazione [ma·ni·po·lat·'tsio:·ne] *f* 1.(*lavorazione*) working; (*mescolazione*) mixing 2.(*alterazione*) adulteration 3. *fig* (*di notizia, risultato, idea, opinione*) manipulation

manipolo [ma·'ni:·po·lo] *m* (*di attivisti, fanatici*) gang

maniscalco [ma·nis·'kal·ko] <-chi> *m* (*artigiano*) blacksmith

manna ['man·na] *f* 1. REL manna 2. *fig* (*bene inatteso*) godsend; **aspettare la ~ dal cielo** to expect manna from heaven

mannaggia [man·'nad·dʒa] *int* damn; ~ **a te!** damn you!; ~, **sono in ritardo!** damn it, I'm late!

mannaia [man·'na:·ia] <-aie> *f* (*da taglialegna*) ax; (*da macellaio*) cleaver

mannaro [man·'na:·ro] *agg* **lupo** ~ *inf* werewolf

mano ['ma:·no] *f* 1.(*estremità*) hand; **a** ~ by hand; **bagaglio a** ~ hand luggage; **a portata di** ~ (*soldi, documenti*) close at hand; **alla** ~ (*persona*) easy-going; **alzare la** ~ to raise one's hand; **avere le -i bucate** to be a spendthrift; **ho le -i legate** my hands are tied; **avere** [*o* **tenere**] **qc in** ~ to hold sth; **avere qc per le -i** to have sth on the go; **battere le -i** to applaud; **dare** [*o* **stringere**] **la** ~ **a qu** to shake sb's hand; **dare una** ~ **a qu** to lend sb a hand; ~ **nella** ~ hand in hand; **presentarsi a -i vuote** to turn up empty handed; **di seconda** ~ second-hand; **starsene con le -i in** ~ to twiddle one's thumbs; **venire alle -i** to come to blows; **Mani Pulite** *Clean Hands investigation of the 1990s into bribes* 2.(*di vernice, smalto*) coat 3.(*nel gioco*) hand 4.(*nella guida*) side; **andare contro** ~ to go against traffic

manodopera [ma·no·'dɔ:·pe·ra] *f* labor

manomesso *pp di* **manomettere**

manomettere [ma·no·'met·te·re] <irr> *vt* 1.(*prove, documento, lettera*) to tamper with 2.(*serratura*) to force

manopola [ma·'nɔ:·po·la] *f* 1.(*guanto*) wash mitt 2.(*di radio, televisore*) knob 3.(*di manubrio, leva*) grip

manoscritto, -a¹ [ma·nos·'krit·to] *agg* (*testo, lettera*) handwritten

manovalanza [ma·no·va·'lan·tsa] *f* 1.(*manodopera*) labor 2.(*lavoratori*) workers *pl*

manovale [ma·no·'va:·le] *m* (*operaio*) worker

manovella [ma·no·'vɛl·la] *f* handle

manovra [ma·'nɔ:·v·ra] *f* 1.(*di macchinario, veicolo*) maneuver; ~ **di atterraggio/di decollo** landing/take-off; **fare** ~ to maneuver; **treno in** ~ train being shunted 2. MIL maneuver 3. *fig* (*intrigo*) scheme 4. POL measure

manovrare [ma·no·'vra:·re] **I.** *vt* 1.(*dispositivo, macchinario*) to maneuver 2. *fig* (*persona, situazione*) to manipulate 3. MIL to maneuver **II.** *vi* 1.(*fare manovra*) to maneuver 2. *fig* (*tramare*) to plot

manrovescio [ma·nro·'vɛʃ·ʃo] *m* (*schiaffo*) slap with the back of the hand

mansarda [man·'sar·da] *f* (*abitazione*) attic

mansione [man·'sio:·ne] *f* (*incarico*) duty

mansueto, -a [man·su·'ɛ:·to] *agg* (*animale*) docile; (*persona, aspetto, sguardo*) meek

mantella [man·'tɛl·la] *f* cape

mantello [man·'tɛl·lo] *m* 1.(*indumento*) cloak 2.(*pelo*) coat

mantenere [man·te·'ne:·re] <irr> **I.** *vt* 1.(*disciplina, calma, ordine*) to keep; ~ **una buona condotta** to behave well; ~ **i contatti con qu** to keep in contact with sb; ~ **il ritmo** to keep

up the pace 2.(*in vita, funzione*) to keep; ~ **giovane** to keep young; ~ **vivo l'interesse** to keep the interest going 3.(*impegno, promessa, segreto*) to keep 4.(*figli, famiglia*) to support; (*casa, auto*) to maintain **II.** *vr:* -**rsi** 1.(*conservarsi*) to keep; **si mantiene molto bene** he [*o* she] keeps himself [*o* herself] in good condition 2.(*sostentarsi*) to support oneself; **suo fratello si mantiene agli studi lavorando** his [*o* her] brother pays for school by working

mantenimento [man·te·ni·'men·to] *m* 1.(*di disciplina, impegno, promessa*) keeping 2.(*in vita*) keeping; ~ **in funzione** upkeep 3.(*di figli, famiglia*) maintenance

mantenni *1. pers sing pass rem di* **mantenere**

mantenuto **I.** *pp di* **mantenere** **II.** *m pej* kept man *m*, kept woman *f*

mantice ['man·ti·tʃe] *m* bellows *pl*

manto ['man·to] *m* 1.(*di cemento, bitume*) layer; ~ **stradale** road surface 2.(*di erba, neve, nubi*) coating

Mantova ['man·to·va] *f* Mantua, *a city in the Lombardy region*

mantovana [man·to·'va:·na] *f* 1.(*di tetto*) bargeboard 2.(*di tenda*) pelmet

mantovano¹ [man·to·'va:·no] <sing> *m* (*dialetto*) Mantuan dialect

mantovano, -a² **I.** *agg* (*di Mantova*) from Mantua **II.** *m, f* (*abitante*) person from Mantua

Mantovano <sing> *m* (*zona*) Mantua area; **nel** ~ in the Mantua area

manuale¹ [ma·nu·'a:·le] *agg* 1.(*lavoro, attività, comando*) manual 2.(*orologio*) hand-wound

manuale² *m* 1.(*di cucina, giardinaggio*) manual; ~ **di istruzioni** instruction booklet; **da** ~ textbook; **un goal da** ~ a textbook goal 2.(*scolastico*) textbook

manualità [ma·nua·li·'ta] *f* 1.(*caratteristica*) manual nature 2.(*abilità*) manual skills *pl*

manubrio [ma·'nu:·bri·o] <-i> *m* 1.(*di bicicletta, moto*) handlebars *pl* 2. SPORT dumbbell

manufatto [ma·nu·'fat·to] *m* (*artigianale, tessile*) handmade article

manutenzione [ma·nu·ten·'tsio:·ne] *f* (*di edificio, impianto, strada*) maintenance; ~ **ordinaria/straordinaria** ordinary/extraordinary maintenance; **spese di** ~ maintenance costs

manzo ['man·dzo] *m* 1.(*bovino*) steer 2.(*carne*) beef

maori [ma·'o:·ri] **I.** <inv> *agg* (*dei Maori*) Maori **II.** <-> *mf* Maori; **i Maori** the Maoris

mappa ['map·pa] *f* 1.(*di zona, città*) map; ~ **catastale** land registry map; ~ **del tesoro** treasure map 2.(*di fenomeno, situazione*) overview

mappamondo [map·pa·'mon·do] *m* (*globo*) globe

mappare [map·'pa:·re] *vt* to map out

mappatura [map·pa·'tu:·ra] *f* 1.(*di territorio*) mapping 2.(*di fenomeno, situazione*) map-

M

ping out

maquillage [ma·ki·'ja:ʒ] <-> *m* (*trucco*) make-up

marasma [ma·'raz·ma] <-i> *m fig* (*caos*) mess

maratona [ma·ra·'to:·na] *f a. fig* SPORT marathon

maratoneta [ma·ra·to·'ne:·ta] <-i *m*, -e *f*> *mf* marathon runner

marca ['mar·ka] <-che> *f* 1. (*marchio*) brand name 2. (*produttore, ditta*) brand; **di** ~ brand-name 3. (*contrassegno*) stamp; ~ **da bollo** revenue stamp

marcare [mar·'ka:·re] *vt* 1. (*articolo, indumento*) to mark; (*bestiame*) to brand 2. (*linea, contorno, accento*) to highlight 3. SPORT (*rete*) to score; (*avversario*) to mark

marcato, -a [mar·'ka:·to] *agg* 1. (*articolo, indumento, bestiame*) branded 2. (*lineamenti, tratti, accento*) pronounced

marcatore, -trice [mar·ka·'to:·re] *m*, *f* SPORT (*di gol*) scorer; (*di avversario*) marker

marcatura [mar·ka·'tu:·ra] *f* 1. (*di articolo, prodotto*) marking 2. SPORT (*di rete*) scoring; (*di avversario*) marking; ~ **a uomo/a zona** man-/zonal marking

Marche ['mar·ke] *fpl* **le** ~ the Marches; **abitare nelle** ~ to live in the Marches; **andare nelle** ~ to go to the Marches

marchese, -a [mar·'ke:·ze] *m*, *f* (*nobile*) marquis *m*, marquess *f*

marchetta [mar·'ket·ta] *f inf* (*prestazione sessuale*) **fare -e** to turn tricks

marchiare [mar·'kia:·re] *vt* 1. (*oggetto*) to mark; (*bestiame*) to brand 2. *fig* (*persona*) to brand

marchigiano, -a I. *agg* (*delle Marche*) from the Marches II. *m*, *f* (*abitante*) person from the Marches

marchingegno [mar·kinŋ·'geɲ·ɲo] *m* 1. (*attrezzo*) contraption 2. *fig* (*espediente*) way out

marchio ['mar·kio] <-chi> *m* 1. (*su oggetto, prodotto*) brand symbol; ~ **di fabbrica** trademark; ~ **di qualità** seal of quality; ~ **registrato** registered trademark 2. (*su animali*) brand

marcia ['mar·tʃa] <-ce> *f* 1. (*passo, camminata*) march; **mettersi in** ~ to get going; ~ **forzata** MIL forced march 2. SPORT walk 3. (*corteo*) march 4. MUS march 5. (*di veicolo*) gear; **andare a** ~ **indietro** [*o* **in retromarcia**] to reverse; **fare** ~ **indietro** *fig* to change one's mind; **avere una** ~ **in più** to be better than everybody else

marciapiede [mar·tʃa·'piɛ:·de] *m* 1. (*di strada*) sidewalk 2. (*do stazione ferroviaria*) platform

marciare [mar·'tʃa:·re] *vi* 1. *a. fig* to march 2. SPORT to walk 3. (*veicolo*) to go 4. (*motore, meccanismo*) to work

marcio, -a[1] ['mar·tʃo] <-ci, -ce> *agg* 1. (*cibo, legno, muro*) rotten 2. *fig* (*società, ambiente*) corrupt; **avere torto** ~ to be completely wrong

marcio[2] <*sing*> *m* 1. (*di cibo*) rotten part;

(*odore*) bad smell; (*sapore*) bad taste 2. *fig* (*corruzione*) rot; **c'è del** ~ something's not right

marcire [mar·'tʃi:·re] <marcisco> *vi essere* 1. (*cibo*) to go off 2. (*legno, carta*) to become moldy 3. *fig* (*nell'ozio, in prigione, casa*) to rot away

marciume [mar·'tʃu:·me] *m* 1. (*cose marce*) rotten part 2. *fig* (*corruzione*) rot

marco ['mar·ko] <-chi> *m* (*moneta*) mark

mare ['ma:·re] *m* 1. (*massa d'acqua*) sea; **in alto** ~ in [*o* on] the open sea; ~ **grosso** heavy sea; **andare al** ~ to go to the seaside 2. *fig* (*grande quantità*) load; **un** ~ **di qc** a load of sth

marea [ma·'rɛ:·a] <-ee> *f* 1. GEOG tide; **alta/bassa** ~ high/low tide 2. (*di fango*) river 3. *fig* (*grande quantità*) load; **una** ~ **di qc** a load of sth

mareggiata [ma·red·'dʒa:·ta] *f* sea storm

maremma [ma·'rem·ma] *f* (*pianura*) maremma; **la Maremma** (**toscana**) the (Tuscan) Maremma

maremmano, -a [ma·rem·'ma:·no] I. *agg* 1. (*della maremma*) maremma 2. (*cavallo, cane*) Maremma II. (*abitante*) person from the Maremma

maremoto [ma·re·'mɔ:·to] *m* GEOG tsunami

maresciallo [ma·reʃ·'ʃal·lo] *m* (*sottoufficiale*) warrant officer

maretta [ma·'ret·ta] *f* 1. (*in mare*) choppy sea 2. *fig* (*fra persone*) tension

margarina [mar·ga·'ri:·na] *f* margarine

margherita [mar·ge·'ri:·ta] *f* 1. (*fiore*) daisy 2. CULIN (**pizza**) ~ *pizza with tomato paste and mozzarella cheese* 3. POL **la Margherita** *Italian center-left political party*

marginale [mar·dʒi·'na:·le] *agg* (*secondario*) marginal

margine ['mar·dʒi·ne] *m* 1. (*di strada, fiume, bosco*) edge 2. (*di società, legalità*) fringe 3. (*di foglio*) margin; **a** ~ in the margin 4. (*di guadagno, tempo, azione, autonomia*) margin; ~ **di errore** margin of error; ~ **di sicurezza** safety margin

mariano, -a [ma·ri·'a:·no] *agg* REL Marian; **mese** ~ month of Mary

marina[1] [ma·'ri:·na] *f* 1. (*flotta*) navy; ~ **mercantile** merchant marine; ~ **militare** U.S. Navy 2. (*costa*) coast 3. (*quadro*) seascape

marina[2] [ma·'ri:·na] *m e f* (*porticciolo*) marina

marinaio [ma·ri·'na:·io] <-ai> *m* sailor

marinara [ma·ri·'na:·ra] *f* **alla** ~ CULIN with seafood; (*abbigliamento*) sailor; **vestire alla** ~ to dress like a sailor

marinare [ma·ri·'na:·re] *vt* 1. CULIN to marinate 2. (*loc*) ~ **la scuola** *fig, inf* to play hooky

marinaro, -a [ma·ri·'na:·ro] *agg* (*di mare*) seafaring; **repubbliche** -e maritime republics; **borgo** ~ coastal village

marinata [ma·ri·'na:·ta] *f* CULIN marinade

marino, -a [ma·'ri:·no] *agg* (*del mare*) marine; **blu** ~ navy blue; **cavalluccio** ~ sea horse;

stella -a starfish

marionetta [ma·rio·'net·ta] *f a. fig* puppet

marito [ma·'ri:·to] *m* husband; **tra moglie e ~ non mettere il dito** *prov* never interfere between husband and wife

marittimo, -a¹ [ma·'rit·ti·mo] I. *agg* (*città, stazione*) seaside; (*attività, trasporto*) maritime; (*clima*) coastal II. *m, f* (*persona*) maritime worker

marittimo² *m* (*marinaio*) seaman

marker ['ma:·kə] <- *o* markers> *m* **1.** (*evidenziatore*) highlighter (pen) **2.** BIOL, MED marker

marketing ['ma:·ki·tiŋ/'mar·ke·ting] <-> *m* marketing; **ricerca di ~** market research

marmaglia [mar·'maʎ·ʎa] <-glie> *f* (*gentaglia*) rabble

marmellata [mar·mel·'la:·ta] *f* jam; (*di arance*) marmalade

marmitta [mar·'mit·ta] *f* AUTO muffler; **~ catalitica** catalytic converter

marmo ['mar·mo] *m* marble

marmocchio, -a [mar·'mɔk·kio] <-cchi, -cchie> *m, f scherz, a. pej* brat

marmoreo, -a [mar·'mɔ:·reo] <-ei, -ee> *agg* (*di marmo*) marble

marmotta [mar·'mɔt·ta] *f* (*animale*) marmot; **dormire come una ~** to sleep like a log

marocchino, -a [ma·rok·'ki:·no] I. *agg* (*del Marocco*) Moroccan II. *m, f* **1.** (*abitante*) Moroccan **2.** *a. pej, inf* (*extracomunitario*) illegal immigrant

Marocco [ma·'rɔk·ko] *m* Morocco; **il ~** Morocco; **abitare in ~** to live in Morocco; **andare in ~** to go to Morocco

marrone¹ <inv *o* -i> *agg* brown

marrone² [mar·'ro:·ne] *m* **1.** (*castagna*) chestnut **2.** (*colore*) brown **3.** *pl, vulg* **i** -i balls

marsala [mar·'sa:·la] <-> *m* Marsala

marsigliese [mar·siʎ·'ʎie:·ze] I. *agg* (*di Marsiglia*) from Marseille II. *mf* (*abitante*) person from Marseille

Marsigliese [mar·siʎ·'ʎie:·ze] *f* **la ~** the Marseillaise

marsupio [mar·'su:·pio] <-i> *m* **1.** ZOO pouch **2.** (*per neonati*) baby sling **3.** (*borsello*) fanny pack **4.** (*tasca*) front pocket

Marte ['mar·te] <-> *m* (*pianeta*) Mars

martedì [mar·te·'di] <-> *m* Tuesday; **~ grasso** Shrove Tuesday; *v.a.* **domenica**

martellante [mar·tel·'lan·te] *agg* (*incalzante*) incessant; **un interrogatorio ~** a relentless questioning; **un mal di testa ~** a thumping headache; **una pubblicità ~** a never-ending advertising campaign

martellare [mar·tel·'la:·re] I. *vt* **1.** (*con martello*) to hammer **2.** (*con pugni*) to beat; **~ di pugni l'avversario** to beat up the opponent **3.** *fig* (*con domande, richieste*) to bombard; **~ qu di domande** to bombard sb with questions II. *vi* (*cuore, sangue, tempie*) to throb

martellata [mar·tel·'la:·ta] *f* (*colpo*) hammer blow; **darsi una ~ sulle dita** to hit one's fingers with a hammer

martelletto [mar·tel·'let·to] *m* **1.** MED reflex hammer **2.** (*di macchina da scrivere*) typebar; (*di orologio, pianoforte*) hammer

martello [mar·'tɛl·lo] *m* **1.** (*attrezzo*) hammer; **~ pneumatico** pneumatic drill **2.** SPORT hammer

martin pescatore [mar·'tin pes·ka·'to:·re] <-i> *m* kingfisher

martire ['mar·ti·re] *mf a. fig* martyr; **fare il ~** to play the martyr

martirio [mar·'ti:·rio] <-i> *m* **1.** (*per fede, ideale*) martyrdom **2.** *fig* hell

marxismo [mark·'siz·mo] *m* PHILOS, POL Marxism

marxista [mark·'sis·ta] <-i *m*, -e *f*> I. *agg* Marxist II. *mf* (*seguace*) Marxist

marzapane [mar·tsa·'pa:·ne] *m* marzipan

marzemino [mar·dse·'mi:·no] *m* (*vino*) Italian red wine from the Trento region

marziale [mar·'tsia:·le] *agg* **1.** (*della guerra*) martial; **arti -i** martial arts; **corte ~** court-martial; **legge ~** martial law **2.** *fig* (*aspetto, passo*) military

marziano, -a [mar·'tsia:·no] I. *agg* ASTR Martian II. *m, f* **1.** (*extraterrestre*) Martian **2.** *fig, inf* (*estraneo*) weirdo

marzo ['mar·tso] *m* March; *v.a.* **aprile**

mascalzone [mas·kal·'tso:·ne] *m* rogue

mascarpone [mas·kar·'po:·ne] *m* Italian soft cheese

mascella [maʃ·'ʃɛl·la] *f* ANAT jaw

maschera ['mas·ke·ra] *f* **1.** (*finto volto*) mask **2.** (*costume*) fancy dress; **essere/mettersi in ~** to be in/put on fancy dress **3.** (*persona*) masked person **4.** *fig* mask **5.** (*dispositivo*) mask; **~ antigas** gas mask; **~ a ossigeno** oxygen mask; **~ subacquea** diving mask; **~ di bellezza** face pack **6.** (*al cinema*) usher *m*, usherette *f* **7.** COMPUT screen

mascherare [mas·ke·'ra:·re] I. *vt* **1.** (*viso*) to mask; (*persona*) to dress up; **~ qu da qu/qc** to dress sb up as sb/sth **2.** *fig* (*sentimento*) to mask II. *vr* **-rsi da qu/qc** to dress up as sb/sth

mascherata [mas·ke·'ra:·ta] *f* (*sfilata, festa*) masquerade

mascherato, -a [mas·ke·'ra:·to] *agg* **1.** (*volto*) masked **2.** (*persona*) dressed-up **3.** (*ballo, corso*) fancy dress

mascherina [mas·ke·'ri:·na] *f* **1.** (*mezza maschera*) half mask **2.** (*per proteggersi*) mask **3.** (*per disegnare, verniciare*) mask

maschietto [mas·'kiet·to] *m* (*bambino*) little boy

maschile [mas·'ki:·le] I. *agg* **1.** (*sesso*) male; (*voce, aspetto*) masculine **2.** (*per uomini*) men's; (*per ragazzi*) boy's **3.** LING masculine II. *m* LING masculine

maschilismo [mas·ki·'liz·mo] *m* male chauvinism

maschilista [mas·ki·'lis·ta] <-i *m*, -e *f*> I. *agg* (*atteggiamento, mentalità*) male chauvinist II. *mf* male chauvinist

M

maschio¹ ['mas·kio] <-schi> agg 1. BIOL male 2. (voce, carattere) masculine

maschio² m 1. BIOL male; (ragazzo) boy; (uomo) man 2. TEC male

mascolino, -a [mas·ko·'li:·no] agg (donna, modi, tratti) masculine

mascotte [mas·'kɔt] <-> f mascot

maso ['ma:·zo] m family farm

masochismo [ma·zo·'kiz·mo] m masochism

masochista [ma·zo·'kis·ta] <-i m, -e f> I. agg (atteggiamento, carattere) masochistic II. mf (persona) masochist

massa ['mas·sa] f 1. (di terra, aria) mass; (di acqua) body 2. a. fig (di pietre, legna, errori) pile 3. (di gente) crowd; **di ~** (cultura) mass; **in ~** en masse 4. PHYS mass 5. EL earth; **collegare** [o **mettere**] **a ~** to earth

Massa ['mas·sa] f Massa, a city in Tuscany

massacrante [mas·sa·'kran·te] agg (corsa, fatica, viaggio) exhausting

massacrare [mas·sa·'kra:·re] vt 1. (trucidare) to massacre 2. (malmenare) to pulverize 3. fig (rovinare) to ruin; (grammatica, lingua) to murder; (film, opera teatrale) to massacre 4. (stancare) to murder

massacro [mas·'sa:·kro] m 1. (strage) massacre 2. fig (disastro) disaster

massaggiare [mas·sad·'dʒa:·re] vt (muscolo, arto) to massage

massaggiatore, -trice [mas·sad·dʒa·'to:·re] m, f masseur m, masseuse f

massaggio [mas·'sad·dʒo] <-ggi> m massage; **~ cardiaco** heart massage

massaia [mas·'sa:·ia] <-aie> f housewife

massello [mas·'sel·lo] m (legno massiccio) solid wood

masseria [mas·se·'ri:·a] <-ie> f (fattoria) farm

masserizie [mas·se·'rit·tsie] fpl (suppellettili) household furnishings

massiccio, -a¹ [mas·'sit·tʃo] <-cci, -cce> agg 1. (oro, legno) solid; (edificio) massive 2. (persona, corporatura) massive 3. fig (intervento) huge; (opera) massive

massiccio² <-cci> m GEOG massif

massificazione [mas·si·fi·kat·'tsio:·ne] f (di idee, cultura) homogenization

massima ['mas·si·ma] f 1. (principio) maxim; **di ~** general; **in linea di ~** on the whole 2. (motto) saying 3. (temperatura) maximum temperature 4. MED (pressione) highest level of blood pressure

massimale [mas·si·'ma:·le] m (di assicurazione) maximum liability

massimalista [mas·si·ma·'lis·ta] <-i m, -e f> I. agg POL (programma, corrente) maximalist II. mf POL (seguace) maximalist

massimizzare [mas·si·mid·'dza:·re] vt ECON (rendimento, profitto) to maximize

massimizzazione [mas·si·mid·dzat·'tsio:·ne] f ECON (di profitti, investimenti) maximization

massimo, -a¹ ['mas·si·mo] I. agg superl di **grande** 1. (il più grande) biggest 2. (altezza, temperatura, velocità, peso, tempo) maxi-

mum; **tempo ~** time limit; **campionato dei pesi -i** heavyweight championship 3. (risultato, vantaggio) best 4. (attenzione, importanza, stima) greatest II. avv (negli annunci) max

massimo² m 1. (il grado più alto) maximum; **al ~** (al grado più alto) on maximum 2. (tutt'al più) at the outside; **sfruttare qc al ~** to make full use of sth 3. (il meglio) best

massivo, -a [mas·'si:·vo] agg 1. (di massa, massiccio) mass 2. MED (asportazione, infezione) massive

mass media [mæs 'mi:·djə/mas 'mɛ·dia] mpl mass media

masso ['mas·so] m (sasso) rock; **caduta -i** falling rocks

massone [mas·'so:·ne] m (affiliato) freemason

massoneria [mas·so·ne·'ri:·a] <-ie> f (società segreta) freemasonry

massonico, -a [mas·'sɔ:·ni·ko] <-ci, -che> agg (loggia, rituale) masonic

mastectomia [mas·tek·to·'mi:·a] f MED mastectomy

mastello [mas·'tɛl·lo] m (per uva) vat; (per il bucato) tub

master ['ma:s·tə/'mas·ter] m 1. (corso) masters (degree); **~ in economia aziendale** masters (degree) in business administration 2. SPORT **i -s di golf** the Golf Masters

masterizzare [mas·te·rid·'dza:·re] vt COMPUT to burn

masterizzatore [mas·te·rid·dza·'to:·re] m COMPUT CD burner

masticare [mas·ti·'ka:·re] vt 1. (cibo) to chew 2. fig (conoscere poco) **~ qc** to know a little bit of sth

masticazione [mas·ti·kat·'tsio:·ne] f chewing

mastice ['mas·ti·tʃe] m (adesivo) mastic

mastino [mas·'ti:·no] m (cane) mastiff

mastite [mas·'ti:·te] f MED mastitis

mastodontico, -a [mas·to·'dɔn·ti·ko] <-ci, -che> agg (costruzione, diga) gigantic; inf (cappello, sciocchezza) huge

mastro ['mas·tro] I. agg **libro ~** ledger II. m (artigiano) **~ falegname** master carpenter

masturbarsi [mas·tur·'bar·si] vr to masturbate

masturbazione [mas·tur·bat·'tsio:·ne] f masturbation

matassa [ma·'tas·sa] f (di lana) skein; (di cotone) hank

matematica [ma·te·'ma:·ti·ka] <-che> f mathematics

matematicamente [ma·te·ma·ti·ka·'men·te] avv (assolutamente) one hundred percent

matematico, -a [ma·te·'ma:·ti·ko] <-ci, -che> I. agg 1. (calcolo, principio, regola) mathematical 2. (certezza, evidenza) absolute II. m, f (studioso) mathematician

Matera f Matera, a city in the Basilicata region

materassino [ma·te·ras·'si:·no] m 1. (da ginnastica) mat 2. (da spiaggia, tenda) inflatable mattress

materasso [ma·te·'ras·so] m (da letto) mattress; ~ **ad acqua** water bed; ~ **in lattice** latex mattress; ~ **a molle** spring mattress; ~ **ortopedico** orthopedic mattress

materia [ma·'tɛː·ria] <-ie> *f* **1.**(*sostanza*) material; ~ **grigia** BIOL, ANAT gray matter; *scherz* (*intelligenza*) little gray cells; **-ie plastiche** plastic materials; **-ie prime** raw materials **2.**(*argomento, disciplina*) subject; **in** ~ on the subject; **entrare in** ~ to discuss a subject; **non sapere nulla in** ~ to be ignorant about sth; **in** ~ **di** on the subject of

materiale¹ [ma·te·'ria:·le] *agg* **1.**(*aiuto, bisogno*) material; **beni -i** material goods; **lavoro** ~ manual labor **2.**(*tempo, possibilità*) necessary **3.**(*persona*) materialistic **4.**(*sostanza*) material

materiale² *m* **1.**(*sostanza*) material; ~ **da costruzione** building materials *pl;* ~ **plastico** plastic **2.**(*strumenti*) equipment; ~ **chirurgico** surgical equipment **3.**(*documenti*) material

materialismo [ma·te·ria·'liz·mo] *m* materialism

materialista [ma·te·ria·'lis·ta] <-i *m*, -e *f*> *mf* materialist

materialmente [ma·te·rial·'men·te] *avv* **1.**(*concretamente*) materially **2.**(*oggettivamente*) **essere** ~ **impossibile** to be absolutely impossible

maternità [ma·ter·ni·'ta] <-> *f* **1.**(*condizione*) motherhood; **essere alla prima/alla seconda** ~ to become a mother for the first/second time **2.**(*reparto*) maternity **3.**(*congedo*) maternity leave; **essere/ entrare** [*o* **mettersi**] **in** ~ to be/go on maternity leave **4.**ADM (*nome*) mother's name

materno, -a [ma·'tɛr·no] *agg* **1.**(*latte, istinto*) maternal; **scuola** ~ **a** nursery school **2.**(*parente, eredità*) mother's

matita [ma·'ti:·ta] *f* pencil

matriarcale [mat·riar·'ka:·le] *agg* (*società*) matriarchal

matriarcato [mat·riar·'ka:·to] *m* matriarchy

matrice [ma·'tri:·tʃe] *f* **1.**fig (*fonte*) origin **2.**(*originale*) matrix **3.**(*di assegno, biglietto*) counterfoil **4.**MATH matrix

matricola [ma·'tri:·ko·la] *f* **1.**(*registro*) register **2.**(*numero*) registration number **3.**(*studente*) freshman

matricolato, -a [mat·ri·ko·'la:·to] *agg scherz, pej* (*bugiardo, ladro*) out-and-out

matrigna [ma·'triɲ·ɲa] *f* stepmother

matrimoniale¹ [ma·tri·mo·'nia:·le] *agg* **1.**(*cerimonia*) wedding; (*vita*) married **2.**(*lenzuolo, letto, coperta*) double; **camera** ~ double room

matrimoniale² *f* (*camera*) double room

matrimonio [mat·ri·'mɔ:·nio] <-i> *m* **1.**(*unione*) marriage **2.**(*cerimonia*) wedding

matrioska, matriosca [ma·tri·'os·ka] <-ske, -sche> *f* Russian nesting doll

matrona [ma·'trɔ:·na] *f,fig* (*donna imponente*) matron

matta ['mat·ta] *f* (*jolly*) joker

mattanza [mat·'tan·tsa] *f* **1.**(*massacro*) series of killings **2.** *mer* (*di tonni*) tuna killing

mattatoio [mat·ta·'to:·io] <-oi> *m* slaughterhouse

mattatore [mat·ta·'to:·re] *m* star

matterello [mat·te·'rɛl·lo] *m* rolling pin

mattina [mat·'ti:·na] *f* morning; **di/la** ~ in the morning; **di prima** ~ early in the morning; **ieri/domani** ~ yesterday/tomorrow morning; **lunedì/martedì** ~ Monday/Tuesday morning; **questa** ~ this morning; **dalla** ~ **alla sera** from morning to night; **dalla sera alla** ~ (*improvvisamente*) all of a sudden

mattinata [mat·ti·'na:·ta] *f* **1.**(*mattina*) morning; **in** ~ in the morning **2.**(*spettacolo*) matinée

mattiniero, -a [mat·ti·'niɛː·ro] **I.** *agg* **essere** ~ to be an early bird **II.** *m, f* (*persona*) early bird

mattino [mat·'ti:·no] *m* morning; **al** ~ in the morning; **di buon** ~ early in the morning; **edizione/giornale del** ~ morning edition/ newspaper

matto, -a ['mat·to] **I.** *agg* **1.**(*malato*) mad; **andare** ~ **per qc** to be crazy about sth; **essere** ~ **da legare** *inf* to be as mad as a hatter; **sei** ~/**siamo -i?** are you/we insane? **2.**(*bizzarro*) crazy **3.***fig* (*voglia, paura*) incredible; **provare un gusto** ~ **a fare qc** to get a kick out of doing sth; **avere l'idea -a di fare qc** to have the crazy idea of doing sth; **avere una paura -a di qc/qu** to be incredibly scared of sth/sb; **avere una voglia -a di qc/di fare qc** to really want sth/to do sth **4.***fig* (*tempo*) crazy **5.***fig* (*oro, gioiello*) imitation **6.**(*negli scacchi*) **scacco** ~ checkmate **II.** *m, f* (*malato, bizzarro*) madman *m,* madwoman *f;* **da -i** really; **cose** [*o* **roba**] **da -i** unbelievable; **gabbia di -i** *inf* madhouse

mattone [mat·'to:·ne] **I.** *m* **1.**(*da costruzione*) brick **2.***fig* (*libro, film, persona*) bore **3.***fig* (*cibo*) lead weight **II.** *agg* (*colore*) brick red; **color** ~ brick red color

mattonella [mat·to·'nɛl·la] *f* (*piastrella*) tile

mattutino, -a *agg* morning

maturando, -a [ma·tu·'ran·do] *m, f* (*studente*) student taking high school final exams

maturare [ma·tu·'ra:·re] **I.** *vi* **essere 1.**(*frutto*) to ripen; (*vino, formaggio*) to mature **2.***fig* (*persona*) to grow up; **le esperienze lo hanno maturato** those experiences have made him grow up **3.**ECON (*interesse, dividendo*) to mature **II.** *vt avere* (*idea, proposito*) to develop; ~ **una decisione** to come to a decision

maturazione [ma·tu·rat·'tsio:·ne] *f* **1.**(*di frutto*) ripening; (*di vino, formaggio*) maturing **2.***fig*(*di persona*) maturing **3.***fig*(*di idea, proposito*) development; (*di decisione*) taking **4.**ECON (*di interesse, dividendo*) maturity

maturità [ma·tu·ri·'ta] <-> *f* **1.**(*età adulta*) maturity **2.**(*consapevolezza*) maturity **3.**(*diploma*) high school exit exam; **esame di** ~ *high school exit exam*

M

ⓘ Italian students take the **esame di maturità** (school-leaving exam) at the end of the **secondo ciclo d'istruzione** (second-stage education, equivalent to the U.S. high school). They can attend a range of different high schools including **liceo classico** (specializing in Greek, Latin, and the humanities), **liceo scientifico** (specializing in sciences), **liceo linguistico** (specializing in modern languages), **liceo artistico** (specializing in art), **istituto magistrale** (for teacher training), and **istituto tecnico e professionale** (specializing in commercial or vocational subjects).

maturo, -a [ma·'tu:·ro] **I.** *agg* **1.** (*frutto*) ripe; (*vino*) mature **2.** (*adulto*) mature **3.** *fig* (*consapevole*) mature **4.** (*studente*) *student who has passed the final high school exam* **II.** *m, f* (*studente*) *high school graduate*

mausoleo [mau·zo·'lɛ:·o] *m* (*sepolcro*) mausoleum

max [maks] *avv v.* **massimo** max

maxiemendamento [maks·ie·men·da·'men·to] *m* POL major amendment

maxiprocesso [mak·si·pro·'tʃɛs·so] *m* *trial against a large number of people*

maxischermo [mak·si·'sker·mo] *m* giant screen

maya ['ma:·ia] **I.** <-> *agg* (*dei Maya*) Maya **II.** <inv> *mf* (*persona*) Maya; **i Maya** the Maya

mazurka, mazurca [ma·'dsur·ka] <-ke, -che> *f* MUS mazurka

mazza ['mat·tsa] *f* **1.** (*bastone*) club **2.** (*martello*) sledgehammer **3.** SPORT ~ **da baseball** baseball bat; ~ **da golf** golf club **4.** (*loc*) **non capire/-rci una** ~ *vulg* to understand sweet nothing

mazzata [mat·'tsa:·ta] *f a. fig* heavy blow

mazzetta [mads·'set·ta] *f* **1.** (*di banconote*) wad **2.** *inf* (*tangente*) bribe

mazzetto [mads·'set·to] *m* **1.** (*di fiori, erbe*) bunch **2.** (*di carte da gioco*) pack; (*di carte, penne*) bundle

mazziniano [mat·tʃi·'nia:·no] *agg* (*di Giuseppe Mazzini*) Mazzinian

mazzo ['mat·tso] *m* **1.** (*di fiori, erbe, chiavi,*) bunch **2.** (*di funi, documenti, matite*) bundle **3.** (*di carte da gioco*) pack **4.** *vulg* (*loc*) **farsi il** ~ to work one's butt off

MB *abbr di* **megabyte** MB

MBA *m abbr di* **Master in Business Administration** MBA

MCD *abbr di* **Massimo Comune Divisore** HCF

mcm *abbr di* **minimo comune multiplo** lcm

me [me] *pron* **1.** *pers sing* **1.** (*complemento oggetto*) me; **cercate** ~ **o mio fratello?** are you looking for me or my brother? **2.** (*comple-*

mento di termine) me; **lo ha regalato a** ~ he [*o she*] gave it to me **3.** (*con preposizione*) me; **venite da** ~ come to my house; **parlavo fra** ~ **e** ~ I was talking to myself; **c'è posta per** ~ **?** is there any mail for me?; **per/secondo** ~ in my opinion; **se tu fossi in** ~, **lo faresti?** if you were me, would you do it? **4.** (*nelle comparazioni, esclamazioni*) I [*o me*]; **fa come** ~, **non dare retta a nessuno!** do as I do, pay no attention to anybody!; **è contento come** ~ he's as happy as me [*o I am*]; **lavorano quanto** ~ they work as hard as me [*o I do*]; **è più brava di** ~ she's better than me [*o I am*]; **povero** ~! poor me! **5.** (*davanti a lo, la, li, le, ne*) *v.* **mi**

meandro [me·'an·dro] *m* **1.** (*di strade*) maze **2.** *pl fig* ins-and-outs

MEC [mɛk] *m acro di* **Mercato Comune Europeo** ECM

Mecca ['mɛk·ka] <-cche> *f* **1. La Mecca** Mecca **2.** *fig* mecca

meccanica [mek·'ka:·ni·ka] <-che> *f* **1.** PHYS, TEC mechanics **2.** (*congegno, funzionamento*) mechanism **3.** (*modalità*) process; (*di avvenimento*) sequence of events

meccanico, -a [mek·'ka:·ni·ko] <-ci, -che> **I.** *agg a. fig* mechanical; **officina di riparazioni -che** garage **II.** *m, f* (*di automobili*) mechanic; (*tecnico*) technician

meccanismo [mek·ka·'niz·mo] *m* **1.** (*congegno*) mechanism **2.** (*funzionamento*) mechanics *pl* **3.** *pl, fig* mechanisms

meccanizzazione [mek·ka·nid·dzat·'tsio:·ne] *f* mechanization

mecenate [me·tʃe·'na:·te] *mf* patron

mecenatismo [me·tʃe·na·'tiz·mo] *m* patronage

mèche [mɛʃ] <-> *f* highlight

medaglia [me·'daʎ·ʎa] <-glie> *f* **1.** (*oggetto*) medal; **il rovescio della** ~ *fig* the other side of the coin **2.** (*onorificenza*) medal; (*persona*) medalist; ~ **d'oro/d'argento/di bronzo** gold/silver/bronze medal

medaglietta [me·daʎ·'ʎet·ta] *f* (*ciondolo*) small medal

medaglione [me·daʎ·'ʎo:·ne] *m* **1.** (*gioiello*) locket **2.** CULIN medallion

medesimo, -a [me·'de:·zi·mo] **I.** *agg* **1.** (*identico, uguale*) same; **fare sempre le -e cose** to always do the same things; **nel** ~ **tempo** at the same time; **le due case hanno il** ~ **valore** the two houses are worth the same **2.** (*rafforzativo*) very; **siamo responsabili noi -i** we ourselves are responsible **II.** *pron* (*persona*) same person [*o thing*]

media¹ ['mɛ:·dia] <-ie> *f* **1.** MATH mean; ~ **aritmetica** arithmetical mean **2.** (*misura di mezzo*) average; **al di sopra/sotto della** ~ above/below average; **in** [*o di*] ~ on average; ~ **oraria** average speed **3.** (*votazione*) average overall grade **4.** (*scuola*) **le -e** *first three years of junior high school* **5.** (*taglia*) medium size **6.** (*birra*) *measure equivalent to one third of a liter*

media² ['miː·dʒe] *mpl* media
mediano, -a [me·'diaː·no] I. *agg* (*di mezzo*) middle II. *m, f* SPORT (*nel calcio*) halfback; (*nel rugby*) back
mediante [me·'dian·te] *prep* by (means of); **pagare ~ assegno** to pay by check
mediare [me·'diaː·re] I. *vt* (*accordo, conflitto, disputa*) to mediate II. *vi* to mediate
mediateca [me·dia·'tɛː·ka] <-che> *f* multimedia library
mediatico, -a [me·'diaː·ti·ko] *agg* (*evento, fenomeno*) media
mediato, -a [me·'diaː·to] *agg* (*indiretto*) indirect
mediatore, -trice [me·dia·'toː·re] I. *m, f* 1. (*intermediario*) mediator; **fare da ~** to mediate 2. COM broker II. *agg* mediating
mediazione [me·di·at·'tsioː·ne] *f* 1. (*intervento*) mediation 2. COM brokerage
medicamento [me·di·ka·'men·to] *m* (*farmaco*) medication
medicalizzare [me·di·ca·lid·'dzaː·re] *vt* to medically supervise
medicare [me·di·'kaː·re] I. *vt* 1. (*persona*) to treat 2. (*ferita*) to dress II. *vr:* **-rsi** to treat oneself; **-rsi le ferite** to dress one's wounds
medicazione [me·di·kat·'tsioː·ne] *f* dressing
medicina [me·di·'tʃiː·na] *f* 1. (*scienza*) medicine; **~ del lavoro** occupational medicine; **~ legale** forensic medicine 2. (*farmaco*) medicine 3. *a. fig* (*rimedio*) cure
medicinale [me·di·tʃi·'naː·le] I. *agg* (*erba, preparato*) medicinal II. *m* medicine
medico, -a¹ ['mɛː·di·ko] <-ci, -che> *agg* 1. (*ambulatorio, visita*) doctor's 2. (*erba, preparato*) medicinal
medico² *m* 1. (*persona*) doctor; **andare dal ~** to go to the doctor's; **~ di base** [*o* **di famiglia**] [*o* **generico**] GP; **~ fiscale** *state doctor who checks adherence to sick leave regulations;* **~ di guardia** duty doctor; **~ legale** forensic scientist 2. *fig* cure
medievale [me·die·'vaː·le] *agg* medieval
medio ['mɛː·dio] <-i> *m* (*dito*) middle finger
medio, -a <-i, -ie> *agg* 1. (*valore, grandezza*) average; **ceto ~** middle class; **dito ~** middle finger; **scuola -a** *school for pupils of 11 to 14 years* 2. (*normale*) average 3. (*centrale*) middle; **Medio Oriente** Middle East
mediocre [me·'diɔː·kre] *agg* 1. (*per dimensioni, valore*) poor 2. (*per capacità, doti, qualità*) mediocre
mediocredito [me·dio·'kreː·di·to] *m* FIN medium-term credit
mediocrità [me·dio·kri·'ta] <-> *f* (*scarso valore*) mediocrity
medioevale [me·dio·e·'vaː·le] *agg v.* **medievale**
Medioevo [me·dio·'ɛː·vo] *m* Middle Ages *pl*
mediorientale [me·dio·rien·'taː·le] *agg* Middle Eastern
meditabondo, -a [me·di·ta·'bon·do] *agg* pensive

meditare [me·di·'taː·re] I. *vt* 1. (*esaminare*) to ponder 2. (*progettare*) to plan II. *vi* **~ su qc** to think about sth
meditato, -a [me·di·'taː·to] *agg* (*decisione, scelta*) considered
meditazione [me·di·tat·'tsioː·ne] *f* 1. (*riflessione*) consideration 2. (*ascetica*) meditation
Mediterraneo [me·di·ter·'raː·neo] *m* **il** (**Mare**) **Mediterraneo** the Mediterranean (Sea)
mediterraneo, -a <-ei, -ee> *agg* Mediterranean
medium ['mɛd·jum] <-> *mf* (*persona*) medium
medusa [me·'duː·za] *f* (*animale*) jellyfish
megabit [mɛ·ga·'bit] <-> *m* COMPUT megabit
megabyte, Megabyte ['me·gə·bait/'me·ga·'bait] <-> *m* COMPUT megabyte
megaconcerto [me·ga·kon·'tʃɛr·to] *m* megaconcert
megafono [me·'ga·fo·no] *m* megaphone
megagalattico, -a [mɛ·ga·ga·lat·'tiː·ko] <-ci, -che> *agg scherz, inf* (*persona*) mega important; (*oggetto, posto*) huge
megalomane [me·ga·'lɔː·ma·ne] *mf* megalomaniac
megalomania [me·ga·lo·ma·'niː·a] *f* megalomania
megalopoli [me·ga·'lɔː·po·li] <-> *f* megalopolis
meglio¹ ['mɛʎ·ʎo] I. *avv comp di* **bene** 1. (*comparativo*) better; **~ di** better than; **o ~** or even better; (**o**) **per ~ dire** (or) to be more precise 2. (*superlativo*) best; **il ~ possibile** in the best possible way II. *agg comp di* **buono** (*migliore*) better; **di ~** better; **qualcosa di ~** something better
meglio² <-> I. *m* (*cosa migliore*) best; **fare del proprio ~** to do one's best; **per il ~** for the best; **per il tuo/suo/vostro ~** for your/his/her own good II. *f* **alla ~** as best as possible; **avere la ~** (**su qu**) to get the better (of sb)
mela ['meː·la] *f* (*frutto*) apple; **~ cotogna** quince
melagrana [me·la·'graː·na] *f* (*frutto*) pomegranate
melanina [me·la·'niː·na] *f* BIOL melanin
melanzana [me·lan·'dzaː·na/me·lan·'tsaː·na] *f* (*ortaggio*) aubergine
melassa [me·'las·sa] *f* molasses
melatonina [me·la·to·'niː·na] *f* melatonin
melenso, -a [me·'lɛn·so] *agg* (*persona, discorso, romanzo*) dull; (*faccia, sorriso*) dopey
melissa [me·'lis·sa] *f* (*essenza*) lemon balm
mellifluo, -a [mel·'liː·fluo] *agg* (*persona*) unctuous; (*voce, frasi*) sugary
melma ['mel·ma] *f* 1. (*fango*) mud 2. *fig* squalor
melmoso, -a [mel·'moː·so] *agg* muddy
melo ['meː·lo] *m* (*albero*) apple tree
melodia [me·lo·'diː·a] <-ie> *f* 1. MUS melody 2. (*armonia*) melodiousness
melodico, -a [me·'lɔː·di·ko] <-ci, -che> *agg*

M

1. (*di melodia*) melodic **2.** (*genere*) sing-a-long
melodioso, -a [me·lo·'dio:·so] *agg* melodious
melodramma [me·lo·'dram·ma] <-i> *m* MUS melodrama; **da ~** *fig* over-the-top
melodrammatico, -a [me·lo·dram·'ma:·ti·ko] <-ci, -che> *agg a. fig* MUS melodramatic
melograno [me·lo·'gra:·no] *m* (*albero*) pomegranate tree
melone [me·'lo:·ne] *m* (*frutto*) melon
membrana [mem·'bra:·na] *f* ANAT, BIOL membrane
membro¹ ['mɛm·bro] *m* **1.** (*componente: persona*) member **2.** (*pene*) penis
membro² <-a *f*> *m* ANAT limb; **le -a** the limbs
memorabile [me·mo·'ra:·bi·le] *agg* (*impresa, azione*) memorable
memorandum [me·mo·'ran·dum] <-> *m* **1.** JUR memorandum **2.** (*taccuino*) notebook
memore ['mɛː·mo·re] *agg* **~ di qc** *lit* mindful of sth; (*riconoscente*) grateful for sth
memoria [me·'mɔː·ria] <-ie> *f* **1.** (*facoltà*) memory; **a ~** by heart; *pej* by rote **2.** (*ricordo*) memory; **la ~ di qu/qc** the memory of sb/sth; **in ~ di qu/qc** in memory of sb/sth **3.** *pl* (*opera*) memoirs *pl* **4.** COMPUT memory
memorial [mi·'mɔː·riəl] <- *o* memorials> *m* (*manifestazione*) memorial event
memoriale [me·mo·'ria:·le] *m* **1.** (*relazione*) memoirs *pl* **2.** (*difesa, richiesta*) petition
memorizzare [me·mo·rid·'dza:·re] *vt* **1.** (*imparare*) to memorize **2.** COMPUT to store
memorizzazione [me·mo·rid·dzat·'tsio:·ne] *f* **1.** (*apprendimento*) learning by heart **2.** COMPUT storage
menadito [me·na·'di:·to] *avv* **a ~** perfectly
ménage [me·'na:j] <-> *m* (*rapporto*) relationship; **~ à trois** [*o* a tre] ménage à trois
menagramo [me·na·'gra:·mo] *m* *inf* jinx
menare [me·'na:·re] **I.** *vt* **1.** *lit* (*condurre*) to lead; **~ il can per l'aia** *fig* to beat around the bush; **~ qu per il naso** to lead sb by the nose **2.** (*coda*) to wag; (*frusta*) to wield; **~ le mani** to fight **3.** (*colpo, schiaffo*) to give **4.** *inf* (*picchiare*) to beat up **II.** *vr*: **-rsi** (*picchiarsi*) to beat each other up
menata [me·'na:·ta] *f* **1.** *inf* (*lamentela*) whine **2.** *inf* (*cosa noiosa*) pain
mendicante [men·di·'kan·te] *mf* beggar
mendicare [men·di·'ka:·re] **I.** *vt* **~ qc** to beg for sth; **~ un favore da qc** to beg a favor from sb **II.** *vi* to beg
menefreghismo [me·ne·fre·'giz·mo] *m* couldn't-give-a-damn attitude
menefreghista [me·ne·fre·'gis·ta] <-i *m*, -e *f*> **I.** *agg* couldn't-give-a-damn **II.** *mf* person who couldn't give a damn
meninge [me·'nin·dʒe] *f* **1.** ANAT meninx **2.** *pl* *inf* (*cervello*) brains *pl*; **spremere/-rsi le -i** to rack one's brains
meningite [me·nin·'dʒi:·te] *f* MED meningitis
menisco [me·'nis·ko] <-schi> *m* ANAT meniscus
meno ['me:·no] **I.** *avv* *comp di* **poco 1.** (*nei*

comparativi) less [*o* not as]; **questa lana è ~ soffice dell'altra** this wool is less soft than the other one [*o* this wool is not as soft as the other one]; **oggi ha nevicato ~ di quanto ci sperava** it snowed less than we had hoped today; **Maria è ~ brava di Anna** Maria is not as good as Anna **2.** (*nei superlativi*) least; **questo è il giorno ~ bello della mia vita** this is the worst day of my life **3.** (*negazione*) **o ~** or not; **non ricordo se gliel'ho detto o ~** I don't remember if I told him or not **4.** MATH minus; (*nelle temperature*) below freezing; (*nei voti scolastici*) minus; (*nell'ora*) to; **sono le undici ~ un quarto** it's a quarter to eleven; **cinque chili ~ tre etti** four point seven kilos; **in** [*o* **di**] **~** less **5.** (*nelle correlazioni*) the less; **~ studi, ~ impari** the less you study, the less you learn **6.** (*loc*) **chi più chi ~** somehow or other; **fare a ~ di qu/qc** to do without sb/sth; **giorno più giorno ~** give or take a day; **~ male** (**che ...**) just as well (that ...); **più o ~** more or less; **tanto** [*o* **ancora**] **~** even less (reason why); **venir ~** (*coraggio, aiuto*) to be lacking **II.** <inv> *agg* **1.** (*nei comparativi*) less; **ha ~ rughe di me** she's got fewer wrinkles than me; **~ di così non potevo** it was the least I could do **2.** (*nelle correlazioni*) the less; **~ dolci mangi, più dimagrisci** the less sweets you eat, the thinner you'll get **III.** *prep* (*tranne*) except for; **a ~ che ...** +*cong* unless ... **IV.** <-> *m* **1.** **il ~** the least; **parlare del più e del ~** to talk about this and that **2.** MATH minus (sign)
menomare [me·no·'ma:·re] *vt* (*danneggiare*) to damage
menomato [me·no·'ma:·to] **I.** *agg* damaged **II.** *m* disabled person
menomazione [me·no·mat·'tsio:·ne] *f* disability
menopausa [me·no·'pa:u·za] *f* menopause
mensa ['mɛn·sa] *f* **1.** (*locale*) canteen **2.** (*tavola*) table
mensile [men·'si:·le] **I.** *agg* monthly **II.** *m* (*periodico*) monthly
mensilità [men·si·li·'ta] <-> *f* (*stipendio*) monthly salary
mensola ['mɛn·so·la] *f* shelf
menta ['men·ta] *f* **1.** (*pianta*) mint; **~ piperita** peppermint **2.** (*aroma*) mint; **alla ~** mint-flavored **3.** *inf* (*sciroppo*) peppermint cordial; (*caramella*) mint
mentale [men·'ta:·le] *agg* mental; **malattia ~** mental illness
mentalità [men·ta·li·'ta] <-> *f* mentality
mentalmente [men·tal·'men·te] *avv* mentally
mente ['men·te] *f* **1.** (*pensiero, testa*) mind; **un uomo tutto ~ e niente cuore** he's all head and no heart; **a ~ fresca** [*o* riposata] when one's mind is fresh; **a ~ lucida** with a clear head; **avere in ~ di fare qc** to have one's heart set on doing sth; **saltare in ~ a qu** to occur to sb; **mi è saltato** [*o* venuto] **in mente che ...** it occurred to me that ...; **cosa ti è sal-**

tato [*o* **venuto**] **in ~?** what got into you? **2.** (*intelligenza*) brain; (*attitudine*) mind **3.** (*attenzione*) attention; **avere la ~ altrove** to be thinking about sth else; **fare ~ locale** to concentrate **4.** (*memoria*) mind; **a ~** by heart; **venire in ~ a qu** to remember **5.** (*persona*) brain

mentecatto, -a [men·te·'kat·to] *agg pej* mad

mentina [men·'ti:·na] *f* mint

mentire [men·'ti:·re] *vi* (*dire il falso*) to lie

mento ['men·to] *m* chin; **doppio ~** double chin

mentolo [men·'tɔ:·lo] *m* CHEM menthol; **al ~** menthol flavored

mentre ['men·tre] **I.** *cong* **1.** (*nel tempo, nel momento in cui*) while; **non mi ascolti mai ~ parlo** you never listen to me when I'm talking **2.** (*invece*) whereas; **ti lamenti, ~ dovresti essere contento** you complain, whereas you should be satisfied **II.** *m* **in quel ~** at that moment

menu [me·'nu] <-> *m* **1.** (*lista*) menu; **~ degustazione** *set menu offering smaller portions of selected dishes;* **~ turistico** tourist menu **2.** COMPUT menu

menzionare [men·tsio·'na:·re] *vt* to mention

menzione [men·'tsio:·ne] *f* mention; **fare ~ di qc/qu** to mention sth/sb

menzogna [men·'tsoɲ·ɲa] *f* lie

Merano [me·'ra:·no] *f* Merano, *a city in the Trentino-Alto Adige region*

meraviglia [me·ra·'viʎ·ʎa] <-glie> *f* **1.** (*stupore*) amazement; **a ~** perfectly **2.** (*cosa, persona*) wonder; **che ~** how wonderful; **essere una ~** to be a complete joy

meravigliare [me·ra·viʎ·'ʎa:·re] **I.** *vt* (*stupire*) to amaze **II.** *vr:* **-rsi di qc/qu** to be amazed at sth/sb; **mi meraviglio di te!** I'm surprised at you!; **non -rsi di qc/qu** to not be surprised about sth/sb

meraviglioso, -a [me·ra·viʎ·'ʎo:·so] *agg* wonderful

mercante, -essa [mer·'kan·te, mer·kan·'tes·sa] *m, f* **1.** (*commerciante*) merchant; **~ di vini/d'olio** wine/oil merchant; **~ d'arte** art dealer **2.** *pej* dealer

mercanteggiare [mer·kan·ted·'dʒa:·re] **I.** *vi* **1.** (*commerciare*) **~ in qc** to deal in sth **2.** (*contrattare*) to haggle **II.** *vt fig, pej* (*voto, carica*) to flog

mercantile [mer·kan·'ti:·le] **I.** *agg* (*attività, spirito, traffico*) commercial; (*nave*) merchant **II.** *m* (*nave*) merchant ship

mercanzia [mer·kan·'tsi:·a] <-ie> *f* **1.** (*merce*) goods *pl* **2.** *a. pej, scherz, inf* stuff

mercatino [mer·ka·'ti:·no] *m* (*rionale*) local market; **~ delle pulci** flea market; **~ dell'usato** swap meet

mercato [mer·'ka:·to] *m* **1.** (*luogo*) market; **~ coperto** covered market; **~ all'ingrosso** wholesale market; **~ al minuto** retail market **2.** ECON market; **Mercato Comune Europeo** European Common Market; **~ nero** black market; **a buon ~** cheap; *fig* easily **3.** (*commercio*) market **4.** *pej* bargain; **fare ~ di qc** to bargain sth

merce ['mɛr·tʃe] *f* **1.** (*prodotto*) goods *pl;* **scalo -i** goods yard; **treno -i** goods train **2.** *fig* commodity

mercé [mert·'tʃe] <-> *f* **alla ~ di qc/qu** at the mercy of sth/sb

mercenario, -a [mer·tʃe·'na:·rio] <-i, -ie> **I.** *agg* **1.** (*soldato, truppe*) mercenary **2.** *pej* hack **II.** *m, f a. fig* mercenary

merceologia [mer·tʃe·o·lo·'dʒi:·a] <-ie> *f* (*disciplina*) commodity economics

merceria [mer·tʃe·'ri:·a] <-ie> *f* **1.** (*negozio*) haberdashery **2.** (*articoli*) haberdashery

mercificazione [mer·tʃi·fi·ka·'tʃio:·ne] *f* (*del corpo, della cultura*) commercialization

mercoledì [mer·ko·le·'di] <-> *m* Wednesday; **~ delle Ceneri** Ash Wednesday; *v.a.* **domenica**

mercurio [mer·'ku:·rio] *m* CHEM mercury

Mercurio [mer·'ku:·rio] *m* (*pianeta*) Mercury

merda ['mɛr·da] *f* **1.** *vulg* (*escremento*) shit **2.** *fig, inf, vulg* (*persona, cosa*) (piece of) shit; (*situazione*) shit; **essere nella ~** to be in the shit; **~!** shit! **3.** **di ~** *inf, vulg* shitty

merenda [me·'rɛn·da] *f* (*spuntino*) snack; **fare (la) ~** to have a snack

merendina [me·ren·'di:·na] *f* (*dolce preconfezionato*) snack

meridiana [me·ri·'dia:·na] *f* (*orologio*) sundial

meridiano, -a[1] [me·ri·'dia:·no] *agg* (*di mezzogiorno*) midday

meridiano[2] *m* GEOG meridian

meridionale [me·ri·dio·'na:·le] **I.** *agg* **1.** (*a sud, del sud*) southern; **l'Asia ~** Southern Asia **2.** (*del Sud d'Italia*) Southern Italian; **l'Italia ~** Southern Italy **II.** *mf* **1.** (*nativo, abitante*) southerner **2.** (*del Sud d'Italia*) Southern Italian

meridione [me·ri·'dio:·ne] *m* **1.** (*sud*) south **2.** (*territorio*) South; **il Meridione** (*d'Italia*) the South of Italy

meringa [me·'riŋ·ga] <-ghe> *f* CULIN meringue

merino [me·'ri·no] *agg* (*lana*) merino

meritare [me·ri·'ta:·re] **I.** *vt* **1.** (*premio, punizione*) to deserve **2.** *inf* (*prezzo*) to be worth **3.** *solo 3a pers.* (*valere la pena*) to be worth; **non merita!** it's not worth it! **II.** *vr:* **-rsi** to deserve

meritato [me·ri·'ta:·to] *agg* (*giusto*) well-deserved

meritevole [me·ri·'te:·vo·le] *agg* deserving; **~ di qc** worthy of sth

merito ['mɛ:·ri·to] *m* **1.** (*valore*) merit; **premiare/punire qu secondo il ~** to reward/punish sb according to merit; **a pari ~** (*in competizioni*) tied; **per ~ di qu** thanks to sb **2.** (*qualità*) merit **3.** (*di problema, questione*) heart; **entrare nel ~ di qc** to go to the heart of sth; **in ~ a** with reference to

meritocratico, -a [me·ri·to·'kra:·ti·co] *agg* (*sistema, criterio*) meritocratic

M

meritocrazia [me·ri·to·kra·'tʃiː·a] *f* meritocracy

merletto [mer·'let·to] *m* (*pizzo*) lace

merlo[1] ['mɛr·lo] *m* ARCH battlement

merlo, -a[2] *m, f* (*uccello*) blackbird

merluzzo [mer·'lut·tso] *m* (*pesce*) cod

mescere ['meʃ·ʃe·re] *vt lit* (*versare*) to pour

meschinità [mes·ki·ni·'ta] <-> *f* 1. (*grettezza*) pettiness 2. (*cosa gretta*) pettiness 3. (*miseria*) stinginess

meschino, -a [mes·'kiː·no] *agg* 1. (*gretto: persona*) petty 2. (*idea, sentimento*) petty 3. (*dono, ricompensa*) stingy; (*risultato*) poor

mescolanza [mes·ko·'lan·tsa] *f* 1. (*di sapori, stili*) mixture 2. (*di persone*) mix

mescolare [mes·ko·'laː·re] I. *vt* 1. (*rimestare*) to stir 2. (*mischiare: ingredienti*) to mix 3. (*scompigliare: oggetti*) to mix up; (*carte da gioco*) to shuffle; **~ le carte** *fig* to confuse the issue 4. *fig* (*elementi diversi*) to confuse II. *vr:* **-rsi** 1. (*mischiarsi: ingredienti*) to mix 2. (*scompigliarsi: oggetti*) to get mixed up 3. (*confondersi: persone*) to mingle; **-rsi alla folla** to mingle with the crowd; (*frequentare*) to go around with 4. *fig* (*trovarsi, unirsi*) to be mixed

mescolata [mes·ko·'laː·ta] *f* **dare una ~ a qc** (*cibi*) to stir sth; (*carte*) to shuffle

mese ['meː·se] *m* 1. (*di calendario, periodo*) month; **il ~ di settembre** the month of September; **da -i** for ages; **essere al primo/secondo/terzo ~** to be one/two/three month(s) pregnant 2. (*stipendio*) monthly salary; (*affitto, canone, rata*) monthly payment

mesetto [me·'set·to] *m* about a month

messa ['mes·sa] *f* (*il mettere*) **~ a fuoco** FOTO focusing; *fig* highlighting; **~ in moto** ignition; **~ in opera** installation; **~ in piega** set; **~ a punto** adjustment; **~ in scena** *v.* **messinscena**

messa, Messa *f* 1. REL mass; **andare a ~** to go to mass 2. MUS Mass

messaggero, -a [mes·sad·'dʒeː·ro] *m, f* (*inviato*) messenger

messaggiare [mes·sad·'dʒaː·re] I. *vi inf* to text II. *vt* **~ qc a qu** *inf* to text sb sth III. *vr:* **-rsi** *inf* to text each other

messaggino [mes·sad·'dʒiː·no] *m* TEL text

messaggio [mes·'sad·dʒo] <-ggi> *m a. fig* message; **~ pubblicitario** (*nei giornali*) advertisement; (*alla radio, in tv*) commercial; **il ~ di Natale del Papa** the Pope's Christmas message; **il ~ di un film/di un libro** a film's/book's message

messale [mes·'saː·le] *m* REL missal

messia [mes·'siː·a] <-> *m* REL **il Messia** the Messiah

messicano, -a [mes·si·'kaː·no] I. *agg* (*del Messico*) Mexican II. *m, f* (*abitante*) Mexican

Messico ['mɛs·si·ko] *m* **il ~** Mexico; **abitare in ~** to live in Mexico; **andare in ~** to go to Mexico

Messina [mes·'siː·na] *f* Messina, *a city in Sici-*

ly; **lo stretto di ~** the Strait of Messina

messinese [mes·si·'neː·se] I. *agg* (*di Messina*) from Messina II. *mf* (*abitante*) person from Messina

Messinese <*sing*> *m* (*zona*) Messina area; **nel ~** in the Messina area

messinscena, messa in scena [mes·sin·'ʃɛː·na] <messe in scena> *f* 1. THEAT production 2. *fig* act

messo[1] ['mes·so] *pp di* **mettere**

messo[2] *m* ADM messenger; **~ comunale** municipal messenger; **~ del tribunale** usher

mestiere [mes·'tiɛː·re] *m* 1. (*lavoro*) job; (*lavoro manuale*) trade; **essere del ~** to be an expert 2. (*pratica*) experience 3. *pej* money-spinner

mesto, -a ['mɛs·to] *agg* (*triste*) sad

mestolo ['mes·to·lo] *m* (*da cucina*) ladle

mestruale [mes·tru·'aː·le] *agg* (*ciclo, flusso*) menstrual

mestruazione [mes·trua·'tsio··ne] *f* (*ciclo*) menstruation; **avere le -i** to have one's period

meta ['mɛː·ta] *f* 1. (*destinazione*) destination 2. *fig* (*scopo*) purpose 3. SPORT try

metà [me·'ta] <-> *f* 1. (*parte*) half; **si è mangiato ~ torta** he ate half the cake 2. (*punto di mezzo*) middle; **a ~** in half; **a ~ libro** half-way through the book; **a ~ prezzo** half-price; **a ~ settimana** mid-week; **a ~ strada** half-way there 3. *fig, scherz* (*partner*) half; **la mia dolce ~** my better half

metabolico, -a [me·ta·'bɔː·li·ko] <-ci, -che> *agg* BIOL metabolic

metabolismo [me·ta·bo·'liz·mo] *m* BIOL metabolism

metadone [me·ta·'dɔː·ne] *m* CHEM, MED methadone

metafisica [me·ta·'fiː·zi·ka] *f* PHILOS metaphysics

metafisico, -a [me·ta·'fiː·zi·ko] <-ci, -che> *agg* PHILOS metaphysical

metafora [me·'taː·fo·ra] *f* LING metaphor

metaforico, -a [me·ta·'fɔː·ri·ko] <-ci, -che> *agg* LING metaphorical

metallaro, -a [me·tal·'laː·ro] *m, f* heavy metal fan

metallico, -a [me·'tal·li·ko] <-ci, -che> *agg* 1. (*di metallo*) metal 2. (*suono, voce, colore*) metallic

metallizzato, -a [me·tal·lid·'dzaː·to] *agg* (*colore*) metallic; (*auto*) metallized

metallo [me·'tal·lo] *m* metal; **di ~** metal

metallurgia [me·tal·lur·'dʒiː·a] <-gie> *f* (*tecnica*) metallurgy

metallurgico, -a [me·tal·'lur·dʒi·ko] <-ci, -che> I. *agg* (*impianto, stabilimento*) metal II. *m, f* (*operaio*) metal worker

metalmeccanico, -a [me·tal·mek·'kaː·ni·ko] I. *agg* (*industria, produzione*) engineering II. *m, f* (*operaio*) engineering worker

metamorfosi [me·ta·'mɔr·fo·zi] <-> *f a. fig* metamorphosis

metano [me·'taː·no] *m* CHEM methane; **a ~** me-

thane; **funzionare/andare a** ~ to be me-
thane-powered
metanodotto [me·ta·no·'dot·to] *m* methane
pipeline
metanolo [me·ta·'no:·lo] *m* CHEM methanol
metastasi [me·'tas·ta·zi] <-> *f* MED metastasis
meteo ['mɛ:·teo] I.<inv> *agg* (*bollettino,
previsioni*) weather II.<-> *m* (*bollettino*)
weather forecast
meteora [me·'tɛ:·o·ra] *f* ASTR meteor
meteorismo [me·te·o·'ri:z·mo] *m* MED meteor-
ism
meteorite [me·te·o·'ri:·te] *m o f* ASTR meteorite
meteorologia [me·te·o·ro·lo·'dʒi:·a] <-gie> *f*
meteorology
meteorologico, -a [me·te·o·ro·'lɔ:·dʒi·ko]
<-ci, -che> *agg* weather
meteorologo, -a [me·te·o·'rɔ:·lo·go] <-gi,
-ghe> *m, f* weather forecaster
meteosat ['mɛ:·te·o·sat] <-> *m* weather satellite
meticcio, -a [me·'tit·tʃo] <-cci, -cce> *m, f*
(*persona*) half-caste
meticolosità [me·ti·ko·lo·si·'ta] <-> *f* (*accuratezza*) meticulousness
meticoloso, -a [me·ti·ko·'lo:·so] *agg* meticulous
metodica [me·'tɔ:·di·ka] <-che> *f* (*metodo*)
method
metodico, -a [me·'tɔ:·di·ko] <-ci, -che> *agg*
methodical
metodista [me·to·'dis·ta] <-i *m,* -e *f*> I. *agg*
(*chiesa, religione*) Methodist II. *mf* (*seguace*)
Methodist
metodo ['mɛ:·to·do] *m* 1.(*sistema*) method
2.(*modo di agire*) way 3.(*ordine*) method;
fare qc con ~ to do sth methodically 4.(*manuale*) manual
metodologia [me·to·do·lo·'dʒi:·a] <-gie> *f*
(*metodo*) methodology
metodologico, -a [me·to·do·'lɔ:·dʒi·ko] <-ci,
-che> *agg*(*approccio, presupposto*) methodo-
logical
metratura [met·ra·'tu:·ra] *f* 1.(*lunghezza*)
length 2.(*superficie*) size 3.(*misurazione*)
measurement
metrica ['mɛ:·tri·ka] <-che> *f* LIT, LING metrics
metrico, -a ['mɛ:·tri·ko] *agg* 1.MATH metric
2.LIT, LING metrical
metro[1] ['mɛ:·tro] *m* 1.(*unità di misura*) meter;
~ **cubo** cubic meter, square meter 2.(*strumento*) rule; ~ **a nastro** tape measure 3. *fig*
(*criterio*) criteria *pl* 4.LIT, LING meter
metro[2] ['mɛ:·tro] *f inf* subway
metró [me·'trɔ] <-> *m* subway
metronomo [me·'trɔ:·no·mo] *m* MUS metronome
metropoli [me·'trɔ:·po·li] <-> *f* metropolis
metropolitana [me·tro·po·li·'ta:·na] *f* subway
metropolitano, -a *agg* (*di metropoli*) metropolitan
mettere ['met·te·re] <metto, misi, messo>
I. *vt* 1.(*collocare: in luogo*) to put; (*in pos-*

izione) to place; ~ **in ordine/disordine** to
tidy/untidy; ~ **ad asciugare** to put out to dry;
~ **a cuocere** to start cooking; **guarda dove
metti i piedi!** watch where you put your feet!
2.(*francobollo*) to stick; (*ingrediente*) to add;
(*liquido*) to pour; (*chiave, chiodo*) to put;
(*quadro, tende*) to hang 3.(*persona*) to put;
~ **qu in carcere/collegio** to send sb to pris-
on/boarding school; ~ **a letto** to put to bed; (*a
ufficio, direzione*) to appoint 4.(*indumento*)
to put on 5.(*telefono, ascensore*) to install
6.(*abbaglianti*) to switch on; (*marcia*) to go
into; ~ **la sveglia** to set the alarm 7.(*denaro,
annuncio, firma, visto*) to put 8.(*sentimento,
stato d'animo*) to make 9.(*energia, forza*) to
put; **mettercela tutta** to give one's all; **metterci un'ora/un giorno/un anno** to take an
hour/a day/ a year; **ci hanno messo due
anni per finire il lavoro** it took them two
years to finish the work 10.(*loc*) ~ **a confronto** to compare; ~ **a disposizione** to make
available; ~ **su qc** (*casa, attività*) to set up;
(*famiglia*) to start; **metti/mettiamo che ...**
+*cong* suppose (that) ... II. *vr:* -**rsi** 1.(*in posizione*) to put oneself; -**rsi in piedi** to stand
up; -**rsi a letto** to go to bed 2.(*in condizione*)
to make oneself; -**rsi comodi** to make oneself
comfortable; -**rsi nei guai** to get into trouble;
-**rsi a dieta** to go on a diet; -**rsi in aspettativa**
to take a leave of absence; -**rsi in malattia/
maternità** to go on sick/maternity leave
3.(*indossare*) to put on; -**rsi in qc** to wear sth
4.(*infilarsi*) to put 5.(*cominciare*) -**rsi a fare
qc** to start to do sth 6.(*unirsi*) -**rsi con qu** to
join up with sb 7.(*evolversi: situazione*) to
turn out; -**rsi bene/male** to turn out well/
badly
meublé [m ·'ble] <-> *m* bed and breakfast
mezza ['med·dza] <-> *f inf* (*ora*) twelve thirty
mezzadria [med·dza·'dri:·a] <-ie> *f* JUR share-
cropping
mezzadro [med·'dza:·dro] *m* JUR sharecropper
mezzaluna [med·dza·'lu:·na] <mezzelune> *f*
1.(*luna*) crescent 2.(*arnese*) chopping knife
mezzanino [med·dza·'ni:·no] *m* (*di edificio*)
mezzanine
mezzano, -a [med·'dza:·no] *agg* (*intermedio*)
middle; **statura -a** medium build
mezzanotte [med·dza·'nɔt·te] <mezzenotti>
f (*ora*) midnight; **a** ~ at midnight
mezz'aria [med·'dza:·ria] *f* **a** ~ in mid-air
mezzasega [med·dza·'se:·ga] <mezze-
seghe> *mf vulg* 1.(*basso*) dwarf 2.(*mediocre*) no-hoper
mezz'asta [med·'dzas·ta] *f* **a** ~ at half-mast
mezzelune *pl di* **mezzaluna**
mezzenotti *pl di* **mezzanotte**
mezzeria [med·dze·'ri:·a] <-ie> *f* (*di strada*)
center line
mezzibusti *pl di* **mezzobusto**
mezzisoprani *pl di* **mezzo soprano**
mezzo, -a[1] ['mɛd·dzo] *agg* 1.(*metà*) half;
~ **litro di acqua/di olio** half a liter of water/

M

oil; **-a giornata** half a day; **mezz'ora** half an hour; **-a pensione** half-board **2.** (*dopo numerale*) half; **tre litri e ~** three and a half liters; **sei mesi e ~** six and a half months; **otto anni e ~** eight and a half years **3.** (*nelle ore*) half; **le nove e mezza** [*o* **mezzo**] half-past nine **4.** (*intermedio*) middle; **a -a strada** halfway; **di mezza età** middle-aged; **-a stagione** spring and fall **5.** (*davanti a aggettivo*) half; **la porta è -a chiusa** the door is half-closed; **un teatro ~ vuoto** a half-empty theater; **essere ~ morto** *fig* to be half-dead **6.** *inf* (*quasi intero*) a bit of a; **avere una -a idea** to have a vague idea; **un ~ scandalo** a bit of a scandal; **non dire neanche ~ parola** to not even open one's mouth; **mi dai ~ minuto?** can I have just a minute?; **~ mondo** everybody and his uncle

mezzo² *m* **1.** (*metà*) half **2.** (*parte centrale*) middle; **in ~ a** in the middle of; **nel** (**bel**) **~ di** (right) in the middle of; **via di ~** middle way; **andarci di ~** to be involved; **esserci di ~** to be at stake; **levarsi** [*o* **togliersi**] **di ~** to get out of the way **3.** (*strumento*) means *inv;* **-i di comunicazione** (**di massa**) mass media *pl;* **~** (**di**) by; **per ~ di** by means of; **il fine giustifica i -i** *prov* the end justifies the means *prov* **4.** (*veicolo*) vehicle; **-i pubblici** public transport **5.** *pl* (*denaro*) means *pl;* **essere privo di -i** to have no money **6.** *pl* (*capacità*) capability **7.** PHYS, CHEM (*sostanza, fluido*) medium

mezzobusto, mezzo busto [med·dzo·'bus·to] <mezzibusti> *m* bust; **a ~** head and shoulders

mezzofondista [med·dzo·fon·'dis·ta] <-i *m*, -e *f*> *mf* SPORT middle-distance runner

mezzofondo [med·dzo·'fon·do] *m* SPORT middle-distance

mezzogiorno [med·dzo·'dʒor·no] *m* **1.** (*ora*) noon; **a ~** at noon **2.** (*sud*) south **3.** (*meridione*) South; **il Mezzogiorno** the South of Italy

mezz'ora, mezzora [med·'dzo:·ra] <mezze ore> *f* **1.** (*metà ora*) half an hour **2.** (*periodo troppo lungo*) for ages; (*periodo troppo breve*) two seconds

mezzosoprano, mezzo soprano [med·dzo·so·'pra:·no] <mezzosoprani *o* mezzisoprani> *m* MUS mezzo soprano

mi¹ [mi] I. *pron* *1. pers sing* **1.** (*me: complemento oggetto*) me; **non ~ toccare!** don't touch me!; **~ stai ascoltando?** are you listening to me? **2.** (*a me: complemento di termine*) (to) me; **datemi una mano!** give me a hand!; **~ ha regalato dei fiori** he gave me some flowers; (*davanti a lo, la, li, le, ne diventa me*) (to) me; **me lo presterai?** will you lend me it ? [*o* will you lend it to me?]; **puoi prestarmelo?** can you lend me it ? [*o* can you lend it to me?]; **me la porterai dopo** you can bring me it later [*o* you can bring it to me later]; **potresti portarmela dopo** you could bring me it later [*o* you could bring it to me later]; **me le hai già date** you've already given me them [*o* you've

already given them to me]; **vuoi darmele subito?** do you want to give me them right away ? [*o* do you want to give them to me right away ?]; **me ne hanno parlato** they talked to me about it II. *pron 1. pers sing* myself; **~ vesto** I get dressed; **mi sono lavata la faccia** I washed my face; **mi sono fatto male** I hurt myself

mi² <-> *m* MUS E

miagolare [mia·go·'la:·re] *vi* (*gatto*) to meow

miagolio [mia·go·'li:·o] <-ii> *m* (*di gatto*) meowing

miao ['mia:·o] *int* meow

MIB I. *m* *abbr di* **Milano Indice Borsa** FIN Milan Stock Exchange Index II. *agg* **indice ~** Milan Stock Exchange Index

MIBTEL I. *m* *abbr di* **Milano Indice Borsa Telematico** FIN Milan Stock Exchange Telematic Index II. *agg* **indice ~** Milan Stock Exchange Telematic Index

mica ['mi:·ka] *avv* **1.** *inf* (*affatto, per niente*) at all; **non sono ~ arrabbiato** I'm not at all angry **2.** *inf* (*non: senza altra negazione*) not; **~ sono matto!** I'm not mad!; **~ tanto** not that much; **~ male!** not bad! **3.** *inf* (*per caso*) by chance

miccia ['mit·tʃa] <-cce> *f* (*dispositivo*) fuse

micidiale [mi·tʃi·'dia:·le] *agg* **1.** (*mortale: arma, gas, veleno*) lethal **2.** (*dannoso: alimento, clima*) dangerous **3.** *inf* (*intollerabile, terribile*) terrible; **una battuta ~** a conversation stopper; **una risposta/una frase ~** a cutting reply/sentence **4.** *inf* (*potente: pugno, tiro*) murderous

micio, -a ['mi:·tʃo] <-ci, -ce> *m, f* *inf* (*gatto*) puss

micosi [mi·'kɔ:·zi] <-> *f* MED mycosis

microanalisi [mi·kro·a·'na:·li·zi] <-> *f* CHEM, SCIENT microanalysis

microbico, -a [mi·'kro:·bi·ko] *agg* BIOL microbial

microbiologia [mi·kro·bi·o·lo·'dʒi:·a] *f* microbiology

microbiologico, -a [mi·kro·bi·o·'lɔ:·dʒi·ko] <-ci, -che> *agg* BIOL microbiological

microbo ['mi:·kro·bo] *m* **1.** (*germe*) germ **2.** *fig, pej* (*persona mediocre, nullità*) ignoramus

microchirurgia [mi·kro·ki·rur·'dʒi:·a] *f* MED microsurgery

microcircuito [mi·kro·tʃir·'ku:·i·to] *m* IN ELETTRONICA microcircuit

microclima [mi·kro·'kli:·ma] *m* **1.** GEOG, METEO microclimate **2.** (*di ambiente chiuso*) hothouse atmosphere

microcosmo [mi·kro·'kɔz·mo] *m a. pej* microcosm

microcriminalità [mi·kro·kri·mi·na·li·'ta] <-> *f* petty crime

microdelinquenza [mi·kro·de·liŋ·'kuen·tsa] *f* *v.* **microcriminalità**

microeconomia [mi·kro·e·ko·no·'mi:·a] *f* ECON microeconomics

microelettronica [mi·kro·e·let·'trɔ:·ni·ka] *f* microelectronics

microfibra [mi·kro·'fi:·bra] *f* microfiber

microfiche [mi·kro·'fiʃ] <- *o* microfiches> *f* (*microscheda*) microfiche

microfilm [mi·kro·'film] <-> *m* (*pellicola*) microfilm

microfilmare [mi·kro·fil·'ma:·re] *vt* to microfilm

microflora [mi·kro·'flɔ:·ra] *f* BIOL, BOT, ECO (*batterica*) microflora

microfonare [mi·kro·fo·'na:·re] *vt* (*persona, luogo, strumento*) to fit with a microphone

microfono [mi·'krɔ:·fo·no] *m* 1.(*amplificatore*) microphone 2.*inf* (*cornetta del telefono*) receiver

microlettore [mi·kro·let·'to:·re] *m* TEC microreader

microonda [mi·kro·'on·da] *f* PHYS microwave; **forno a -e** microwave oven

microonde [mi·kro·'on·de] <-> *m inf* (*forno*) microwave oven

microprocessore [mi·kro·pro·tʃes·'so:·re] *m* COMPUT microprocessor

microregistratore [mi·kro·re·dʒis·tra·'to:·re] *m* (*tascabile*) microrecorder

microrganismo [mi·kro·or·ga·'niz·mo] *m* BIOL microorganism

microscopia [mi·kro·sko·'pi:·a] <-ie> *f* SCIENT microscope

microscopico, -a [mi·kros·'kɔ:·pi·ko] <-ci, -che> *agg a. scherz* SCIENT microscopic

microscopio [mi·kro·'skɔ:·pio] *m* microscope

microsecondo [mi·kro·se·'kon·do] *m* 1.PHYS microsecond 2.*inf* (*istante*) instant

microsonda [mi·kro·'son·da] *f* TEC microsound

microspia [mi·kros·'pi:·a] *f* bug

microstruttura [mi·kro·strut·'tu:·ra] *f a. fig* microstructure

MIDI ['mi·di] *abbr di* **Musical Instrument Digital Interface** I.<-> *m* COMPUT, MUS MIDI II. *agg* <inv> (*brano, canzone, file*) MIDI

midollo [mi·'dol·lo] <-a *f*> *m* 1.ANAT, CULIN marrow; ~ **osseo** bone marrow; ~ **spinale** spinal cord 2.*fig* (*profondo, intimo*) marrow; **fino alle -a** [*o* al ~] through and through

mie, miei ['mi:·e, 'mi:·i] *v.* **mio**

miele ['mie:·le] *m* (*alimento*) honey; **luna di ~** honeymoon

mietere ['mie:·te·re] *vt* 1.(*tagliare: avena, grano, orzo*) to harvest 2.*fig* (*uccidere*) to kill; ~ **vittime** to claim victims; *inf* (*conquistare*) to conquer all and sundry 3.*fig* (*conseguire: consensi, successi*) to gather

mietitore, -trice [mie·ti·'to:·re] *m, f* harvester

mietitrebbiatrice [mie·ti·treb·bia·'tri:·tʃe] *f* (*mietitrebbia*) combine harvester

mietitrice [mie·ti·'tri:·tʃe] *f* (*macchina*) harvester

mietitura [mie·ti·'tu:·ra] *f* 1.(*attività*) harvesting 2.(*periodo*) harvest

migliaio [miʎ·'ʎa:·io] <-aia *f*> *m* 1.(*mille, circa mille*) thousand; **un ~ di qc** about a thousand sth 2.(*grande numero*) thousand; **-aia di ...** thousands of ...; **a -aia** by the thousand

miglio¹ ['miʎ·ʎo] <-glia *f*> *m* 1.(*unità di misura*) mile 2.*fig* (*grande distanza*) mile; **essere lontano un ~** [*o* mille -glia] *fig* to be nowhere near; **si vede lontano un ~** (**che ...**) *fig* you can see from a mile away (that ...)

miglio² <-gli> *m* BOT millet

miglioramento [miʎ·ʎo·ra·'men·to] *m* 1.(*di situazione, salute, edificio*) improvement 2.(*di stipendio*) rise

migliorare [miʎ·ʎo·'ra:·re] I. *vt avere* (*rendere migliore*) to improve II. *vi essere* 1.(*diventare migliore*) to improve 2.(*stare meglio*) to get better III. *vr:* -rsi to improve oneself

migliorativo, -a [miʎ·ʎo·ra·'ti:·vo] *agg* (*intervento, provvedimento*) remedial

migliore [miʎ·'ʎo:·re] I. *agg comp di* **buono ~ di** (*comparativo*) better; **il ~** (*superlativo relativo*) the best; **nel ~ dei casi** at best; **nella ~ delle ipotesi** at best II. *mf* the best

miglioria [miʎ·ʎo·'ri:·a] <-ie> *f* (*di edificio, strada*) improvement

mignolo ['min·ɲo·lo] *m* 1.(*della mano*) little finger 2.(*del piede*) little toe

mignon [min·'ɲon] <inv> *agg* (*piccolo*) miniature; **pasticceria ~** petit fours *pl*

mignotta [min·'ɲot·ta] *f vulg* (*sgualdrina*) whore

migrare [mi·'gra:·re] *vi essere* (*uccelli*) to migrate

migratore, -trice [mi·gra·'to:·re] I. *agg* (*animale, popolo*) migrant II. *m, f* migrant

migrazione [mi·grat·'tsio:·ne] *f* (*di popolo, animale*) migration

mila ['mi:·la] *pl di* **mille**

milanese¹ [mi·la·'ne:·se] <sing> *m* (*dialetto*) Milanese dialect

milanese² I. *agg* (*di Milano*) Milanese; **cotoletta alla ~** fried cutlet Milan style; **risotto alla ~** risotto with saffron II. *mf* (*abitante*) Milanese

milanese³ *f* (*cotoletta*) wiener schnitzel

Milanese <sing> *m* (*zona*) Milan area; **nel ~** in the Milan area

milanista [mi·la·'nis·ta] <-i *m*, -e *f*> I. *agg* SPORT (*del Milan*) Milan II. *mf* SPORT (*giocatore*) Milan player; (*tifoso*) Milan fan

Milano [mi·'la:·no] *f* Milan

miliardario, -a [mil·iar·'da:·rio] <-i, -ie> I. *agg* billionaire II. *m, f* (*persona ricchissima*) billionaire

miliardesimo, -a¹ [mil·iar·'dɛ:·zi·mo] I. *agg* 1.(*numerale ordinale*) billionth 2.*inf* (*ennesimo*) umpteenth II. *m, f* umpteenth person [*o* thing]

miliardesimo² *m* (*frazione*) billionth

miliardo [mi·'liar·do] *m* 1.(*numero*) billion; (*di euro*) billion 2.*inf* (*quantità enorme*) million

miliare [mi·'lia:·re] *agg* **pietra ~** *a. fig* mile-

M

stone
milieu [mi·'liœ̃] <-> *m* (*ambiente, contesto*) milieu
milionario, -a [mi·lio·'na:·rio] <-i, -ie> I. *agg* millionaire II. *m, f* millionaire
milione [mi·'lio:·ne] *m* 1.(*numero, di soldi*) million; (*di euro*) million euros 2. *inf*(*quantità enorme*) million
milionesimo, -a¹ [mi·lio·'nɛ:·zi·mo] I. *agg* 1.(*numerale ordinale*) millionth 2. *inf* (*ennesimo*) millionth II. *m, f* millionth
milionesimo² *m* (*frazione*) millionth
militante [mi·li·'tan·te] I. *agg* (*impegnato*) militant II. *mf* (*attivista*) activist
militanza [mi·li·'tan·tsa] *f* 1.(*impegno, attivismo*) militancy 2.(*insieme di persone*) team
militare¹ [mi·li·'ta:·re] I. *agg* (*di soldati, esercito*) military; **servizio** ~ military service; **zona** ~ military zone II. *mf* (*soldato*) soldier; **fare il** ~ to do one's military service
militare² *vi* 1.(*fare il soldato*) to serve 2.(*impegnarsi*) to be involved
militaresco [mi·li·ta·'res·ko] *agg* military
militarismo [mi·li·ta·'riz·mo] *m* militarism
militarista [mi·li·ta·'ris·ta] <-i *m*, -e *f*> I. *agg* (*politica, propaganda, stato*) militaristic II. *mf* (*persona*) militarist
militarizzare [mi·li·ta·rid·'dza:·re] *vt* (*città, porto, territorio*) to militarize
militarizzazione [mi·li·ta·rid·dzat·'tsio:·ne] *f* (*di città, porto, territorio*) militarization
militassolto, -a [mi·li·tas·'sɔl·to] *agg* ADM (*in annunci economici*) exempt from military service
milite ['mi:·li·te] *m* 1.LIT (*soldato*) soldier; ~ **ignoto** unknown soldier 2.(*militare*) member
militesente [mi·li·te·'zɛn·te] *agg* ADM (*in annunci economici*) exempt from military service
milizia [mi·'lit·tsia] <-ie> *f* (*corpo armato*) militia
miliziano, -a [mi·lit·'tsia:·no] *m, f* (*civile armato*) militiaman
millantatore, -trice [mil·lan·ta·'to:·re] I. *agg* (*spaccone*) boastful II. *m, f* (*persona spaccona*) boaster
mille ['mil·le] <mila> I. *num* 1.(*numerale cardinale*) a [*o* one] thousand; ~ **euro** a [*o* one] thousand euros; **da** ~ **e una notte** out of this world 2.(*posposto: numerale ordinale*) one thousand 3. *inf* (*moltissimi*) thousands of; **ho** ~ **cose da fare** I've got thousands of things to do; ~ **auguri!** very best wishes!; ~ **grazie!** thank you so much!; ~ **scuse!** I'm so sorry! II. <-> *m* 1.(*numero*) a [*o* one] thousand; **il Mille** the year one thousand A.D.; **i Mille** *the Thousand* (*supporters of Garibaldi*) 2.(*nelle percentuali*) thousand; **per** ~ per thousand
millecento [mil·le·'tʃɛn·to] I. <*sing*> *m* il **Millecento** (*secolo*) the twelfth century II. <-> *f* (*automobile*) *type of Italian car with a 1100 cc engine*

millefoglie [mil·le·'fɔʎ·ʎe] <-> *m o f* CULIN millefeuille
millenario, -a¹ [mil·le·'na:·rio] <-i, -ie> *agg* 1.(*di mille anni*) millenial 2.(*ogni mille anni*) millenary
millenario² <-i> *m* (*ricorrenza*) millenium
millennio [mil·'lɛn·nio] <-i> *m* millenium
millepiedi [mil·le·'piɛ:·di] <-> *m* millipede
millesimale [mil·lɛ·zi·'ma:·le] *agg* 1.(*millesima parte*) thousandth 2.(*piccolissimo*) minute
millesimo, -a¹ [mil·'lɛ:·zi·mo] I. *agg* 1.(*numerale ordinale*) thousandth 2. *inf* (*ennesimo*) thousandth II. *m, f* thousandth
millesimo² *m* (*frazione*) thousandth
milleusi [mil·le·'u:·zi] <inv> *agg* multi-purpose
milligrammo [mil·li·'gram·mo] *m* milligram
millilitro [mil·'li·lit·ro] *m* milliliter
millimetrato, -a [mil·li·me·'tra:·to] *agg* **carta -a** graph paper
millimetro [mil·'li:·met·ro] *m* 1.(*unità di misura*) millimeter 2. *a. fig, inf* (*minimo*) inch; **al** ~ *fig* (*con precisione*) to the last millimeter
milza ['mil·tsa] *f* ANAT spleen
mimare [mi·'ma:·re] *vt* 1.(*scena*) to mime 2.(*persona*) to imitate
mimetico, -a [mi·'mɛ:·ti·ko] <-ci, -che> *agg* 1. *a. fig* MIL (*tuta, vettura, vernice*) camouflage 2. ZOO, BOT mimetic 3.(*arte, abilità, forza*) mimetic
mimetismo [mi·me·'tiz·mo] *m* 1.ZOO, BOT camouflage 2.*fig, pej* (*opportunismo*) opportunism
mimetizzare [mi·me·tid·'dza:·re] I. *vt* MIL (*carro armato, trincea*) to camouflage II. *vr:* -**rsi** (*soldato, animale, pianta*) to camouflage oneself
mimica ['mi:·mi·ka] <-che> *f* 1.(*gestualità*) gestures 2.(*arte*) mime
mimico, -a ['mi:·mi·ko] <-ci, -che> *agg* 1.(*gestuale*) mime; **linguaggio** ~ sign language 2.(*del mimo: arte, teatro*) mime
mimo, -a ['mi:·mo] *m, f* 1.(*attore*) mime artist 2.(*arte*) mime
mimosa [mi·'mo:·sa] *f* (*pianta*) mimosa
min. 1.minuto 2.minimo
mina ['mi:·na] *f* 1.MIL (*ordigno*) mine; ~ **antiuomo** anti-personnel mine; ~ **vagante** *fig* ticking bomb; *scherz* walking time bomb 2.(*carica esplosiva*) mine 3.(*di matita*) lead
minaccia [mi·'nat·tʃa] <-cce> *f* threat
minacciare [mi·nat·'tʃa:·re] *vt* to threaten; ~ **qu di qc** to threaten sb with sth; ~ **di fare qc** to threaten to do sth
minaccioso, -a [mi·nat·'tʃo:·so] *agg* threatening
minare [mi·'na:·re] *vt* 1.(*terreno, ponte, strada*) to mine 2. *fig* (*insidiare*) to undermine
minareto [mi·na·'re:·to] *m* minaret
minatore, -trice [mi·na·'to:·re] *m, f* (*in miniera*) miner
minatorio, -a [mi·na·'tɔ:·rio] <-i, -ie> *agg* (*frase, discorso*) threatening; **lettera -a** threat-

ening letter

minchia ['miŋ·kia] <-chie> *f mer, vulg* (*pene*) cock

minchione, **-a** [miŋ·'kioː·ne] *m*, *f vulg* (*sciocco*) prick

minerale[1] [mi·ne·'raː·le] I. *agg* (*elemento, sostanza, sale*) mineral; **acqua** ~ mineral water II. *m* mineral

minerale[2] *f* (*acqua, bottiglia*) mineral water

mineralogia [mi·ne·ra·lo·'dʒiː·a] <-gie> *f* mineralogy

minerario, **-a** [mi·ne·'raː·rio] <-i, -ie> *agg* (*delle miniere*) mining

minerva®[1] [mi·'nɛr·va] <-> *mpl* (*fiammiferi*) safety matches *pl*

minestra [mi·'nɛs·tra] *f* 1. (*zuppa*) soup; ~ **riscaldata** *fig* the same soup, just reheated 2. *fig* (*faccenda, storia*) story; **è sempre la solita** ~! it's the same old story!

minestrina [mi·nes·'triː·na] *f* broth

minestrone [mi·nes·'troː·ne] *m* 1. (*zuppa*) minestrone 2. *fig, inf* (*miscuglio*) jumble

mingherlino, **-a** [miŋ·ger·'liː·no] *agg* (*persona, corpo*) skinny

mini ['miː·ni] I. <inv> *agg* (*piccolo, corto, breve*) mini II. <-> *f* (*minigonna*) miniskirt

miniabito [mi·ni·'aː·bi·to] *m* mini-dress

minialloggio [mi·ni·al·'lɔd·dʒo] <-ggi> *m v.* miniappartamento

miniappartamento [mi·ni·ap·par·ta·'men·to] *m* small apartment

miniatura [mi·nia·'tuː·ra] *f* 1. (*tecnica*) miniature painting 2. (*dipinto*) miniature 3. (*modellino*) miniature model; **in** ~ in miniature

minibasket [mi·ni·'bas·ket] *m* SPORT mini-basketball

miniera [mi·'niɛː·ra] *f a. fig* mine; ~ **d'oro** *fig* gold mine

minigonna [mi·ni·'gon·na/mi·ni·'gɔn·na] (*indumento*) miniskirt

minima ['miː·ni·ma] *f* 1. (*temperatura*) minimum temperature 2. (*pressione*) minimum blood pressure level 3. MUS (*nota*) minim 4. (*pensione*) minimum pension

minimale [mi·ni·'maː·le] *agg* minimum

minimalismo [mi·ni·ma·'liz·mo] *m* ART, LIT, MUS, POL minimalism

minimalista [mi·ni·ma·'lis·ta] <-i *m*, -e *f*> I. *agg* ART, LIT, MUS, POL, FASHION minimalist II. *mf* (*seguace*) minimalist

minimamente *avv* (*per nulla, affatto*) at all

minimarket [mi·ni·'maː·kit] <-> *m* mini market

minimizzare [mi·ni·mid·'dza:·re] *vt* to minimalize

minimo, **-a**[1] ['miː·ni·mo] *agg superl di* piccolo 1. (*piccolissimo*) very small 2. (*il più piccolo*) least; **non avere la -a idea di qc** to not have the faintest idea about sth 3. (*tempo*) minimum 4. (*voto, temperatura, pressione*) lowest; **prezzo** ~ lowest price 5. (*importanza, particolare, problema*) slightest

minimo[2] *m* 1. (*la quantità/misura più piccola*)

minimum; **al** ~ (*volume, gas*) on low; **come** [*o* **al**] ~ (*almeno*) at the very least 2. (*la cosa più piccola*) least 3. (*di motore*) low gear

miniregistratore [mi·ni·re·dʒis·tra·'toː·re] *m* minirecorder

miniserie [mi·ni·'sɛː·rie] <-> *f* TV miniseries

ministeriale [mi·nis·te·'riaː·le] *agg* (*di un ministero*) ministerial; **decreto** ~ ministerial decree

ministero [mi·nis·'tɛː·ro] *m* 1. (*dicastero*) department; **Ministero dell'Ambiente** Environmental Protection Agency; **Ministero degli** (**Affari**) **Esteri** Department of State; **Ministero degli** (**Affari**) **Interni** [*o* **Ministro dell'Interno**] Department of the Interior; **Ministero dei Beni e delle Attività Culturali** Department of Arts and Culture; **Ministero della Difesa** Department of Defense; **Ministero dell'Economia e delle Finanze** Department of the Treasury; **Ministero della Giustizia** Department of Justice; **Ministero dell'Istruzione, dell'Università e della Ricerca** Department of Education; **Ministero per le Pari Opportunità** Equal Employment Opportunity Commission; **Ministero della Salute** Department of Health and Human Services 2. (*edificio*) department 3. (*periodo, governo*) administration 4. JUR **pubblico** ~ (*magistrato*) District Attorney

ministro [mi·'nis·tro] *m* (*del governo*) secretary; **primo** ~ Prime Minister

minoranza [mi·no·'ran·tsa] *f* 1. (*gener*) minority 2. POL (*opposizione*) Opposition

minorato, **-a** [mi·no·'raː·to] I. *agg* (*disabile*) disabled II. *m*, *f* disabled person

minorazione [mi·no·rat·'tsio:·ne] *f* (*menomazione*) handicap

minore [mi·'noː·re] I. *agg comp di* piccolo 1. (*comparativo*) ~ **di** less than; **il/la** ~ (*superlativo relativo*) the least 2. (*per dimensioni*) smaller 3. (*per quantità*) lower 4. (*per intensità, forza, gravità*) lesser 5. (*per importanza*) minor; **Asia Minore** Asia Minor; **Orsa** ~ Ursa Minor 6. (*di età*) younger 7. MATH less 8. MUS (*accordo, scala*) minor II. *mf* 1. (*più giovane*) youngest 2. (*minorenne*) minor

minorenne [mi·no·'rɛn·ne] I. *agg* underage II. *mf* minor

minorile [mi·no·'riː·le] *agg* juvenile; **delinquenza** ~ juvenile delinquency; **lavoro** ~ child labor

minoritario, **-a** [mi·no·ri·'taː·rio] <-i, -ie> *agg* (*gruppo, partito, voto*) minority

minuetto [mi·nu·'et·to] *m* MUS minuet

minuscola [mi·'nus·ko·la] *f* lower case letter

minuscolo, **-a** [mi·'nus·ko·lo] *agg* 1. (*lettera, carattere, iniziale*) lower case 2. (*piccolissimo*) miniscule

minuta [mi·'nuː·ta] *f* (*brutta copia*) draft

minuto, **-a**[1] [mi·'nuː·to] I. *agg* 1. (*piccolo*) minute 2. (*sabbia, neve, pioggia*) fine 3. (*corporatura, lineamenti*) delicate II. **al** ~ retail

minuto[2] *m* 1. (*unità di tempo*) minute;

M

~ **primo** minute; ~ **secondo** second; **al** ~ per minute; **spaccare il** ~ *fig* (*persona*) to always be on time; (*orologio*) to always be accurate **2.** (*momento*) moment; **a -i** any time now; **da un** ~ **all'altro** suddenly; **in** [*o* tra] **un** ~ immediately; **avere i -i contati** (*avere fretta*) to be in a rush; (*essere sul punto di morire*) to have little time left

minuzioso, -a [mi·nut·'tsio:·so] *agg* **1.** (*persona*) meticulous **2.** (*lavoro*) detailed

mio, -a ['mi:·o] <miei, mie> **I.** *agg* my; **la -a speranza** my hope; ~ **padre/zio** my father/uncle; **il** ~ **caro cugino** my dear cousin; **i miei fratelli** my brothers; **un** ~ **amico** a friend of mine; **a casa -a** (*stato*) at my house; (*moto*) to my house; **mamma -a!** good heavens!; **Dio** ~! [*o* ~ **Dio!**] my God!; **dei miei stivali** *pej* completely useless **II.** *pron* **1.** **il** ~, **la -a** mine **2.** **la -a** (*lettera*), **rispondo con questa -a alla tua ultima** I'm replying to your last letter; (*opinione*) my say; **dalla -a** (*parte*) on my side **3.** **il** ~ (*ciò che mi appartiene*) mine; (*patrimonio, denaro, proprietà*) my own (income/money/property); (*apporto personale*) my own contribution; **non c'è niente di** ~ **qui** there's nothing of mine here; **i miei** (*genitori*) my parents; (*parenti*) relatives; **le mie** (*scappatelle, sciocchezze*) some silly mistakes; **ne ho fatta una delle -e** I've done it again!; **sono stato sulle mie** I kept to myself

miope ['mi:·o·pe] **I.** *agg* MED (*occhio, persona, vista*) short-sighted **II.** *mf* MED short-sighted person

miopia [mio·'pi:·a] <-ie> *f fig* MED short-sightedness

mira ['mi:·ra] *f* **1.** (*di tiro*) aim; **prendere la** ~ to take aim; **prendere di** ~ **qu** *fig* to pick on sb **2.** *fig* (*scopo*) goal

miracolato, -a [mi·ra·ko·'la:·to] *agg* **1.** (*infermo, malato, cieco*) miraculously cured **2.** *fig* (*salvato, graziato*) miraculously saved

miracolo [mi·'ra:·ko·lo] *m* **1.** *a. fig* miracle; **conoscere** [*o* **sapere**] **vita, morte e -i di qu** to know everything about sb; **per** ~ miraculously; ~ **economico** economic miracle **2.** *fig* (*genio, mostro*) wonder

miracoloso, -a [mi·ra·ko·'lo:·so] *agg* miraculous

miraggio [mi·'rad·dʒo] <-ggi> *m* **1.** (*ottico*) mirage **2.** *fig* (*illusione*) illusion

mirare [mi·'ra:·re] *vi a. fig* to aim; ~ **a qc** (*parte del corpo*) to aim at sth; (*potere, denaro*) to aspire to sth; ~ **lontano** [*o* **in alto**] to aim high

mirato [mi·'ra:·to] *agg* (*intervento, provvedimento, cura*) with the aim of

miriade [mi·'ri:·a·de] *f* (*grande quantità*) host

mirino [mi·'ri:·no] *m* **1.** (*di arma*) sight; **essere** [*o* **trovarsi**] **nel** ~ **di qu** *a. fig* to have sb's eyes on one **2.** (*di apparecchio*) viewfinder

mirra ['mir·ra] *f* BOT myrrh

mirtillo [mir·'til·lo] *m* (*frutto*) blueberry

mirto ['mir·to] *m* (*pianta*) myrtle

misantropo, -a [mi·'zan·tro·po] **I.** *agg* (*atteg-*

giamento, comportamento) misanthropic **II.** *m, f* (*persona scontrosa*) misanthrope

miscela [miʃ·'ʃɛ:·la] *f* **1.** (*carburante*) mixture *of 98% gasoline and 2% oil* **2.** (*di caffè*) blend **3.** (*di elementi diversi*) mixture

miscelare [miʃ·ʃe·'la:·re] *vt* (*mescolare*) to mix

miscelatore [miʃ·ʃe·la·'to:·re] *m* **1.** (*apparecchio*) mixer **2.** (*rubinetto*) mixer tap **3.** (*per cocktail*) mixer

miscellanea [miʃ·ʃel·'la:·nea] *f* **1.** (*volume*) miscellany **2.** (*di opuscoli*) collection **3.** (*rubrica*) miscellaneous news

miscellaneo, -a [miʃ·ʃel·'la:·neo] <-ei, -ee> *agg* (*libro, testo, volume*) miscellaneous

mischia ['mis·kia] <-schie> *f* **1.** (*rissa*) brawl; **buttarsi** [*o* **gettarsi**] **nella** ~ to enter the fray **2.** SPORT (*nel rugby*) scrum

mischiare [mis·'kia:·re] **I.** *vt* **1.** *a. fig* to mix **2.** (*confondere*) to mix up; ~ **le carte** to shuffle the deck **II.** *vr* (*unirsi: persona*) to mix

misconosciuto, -a [mis·ko·noʃ·'ʃu:·to] *agg* (*sottovalutato*) underrated

miscredente [mis·kre·'dɛn·te] **I.** *agg* (*persona, comportamento*) non-religious **II.** *mf* (*ateo*) non-believer

miscuglio [mis·'kuʎ·ʎo] <-gli> *m* **1.** (*di elementi, sostanze*) mixture **2.** (*di persone, razze*) mix **3.** *fig* (*di idee, pensieri, sentimenti*) hotchpotch

miserabile [mi·ze·'ra:·bi·le] **I.** *agg* **1.** (*povero*) wretched **2.** *pej* (*spregevole*) despicable **3.** (*scarso: compenso, offerta, paga*) poor **II.** *mf* **1.** (*persona povera*) poor person **2.** (*persona spregevole*) wretch

miserere [mi·ze·'rɛ:·re] <-> *m* REL (*salmo*) Miserere

miserevole [mi·ze·'re:·vo·le] *agg* (*condizione, vita, stato*) wretched

miseria [mi·'zɛ:·ria] <-ie> *f* **1.** (*povertà*) poverty **2.** (*somma esigua*) next-to-nothing **3.** *fig* (*meschinità*) pettiness **4.** (*loc*) **la** ~! [*o* **per la miseria!**] [*o* **porca** ~!] *inf* damn it!

misericordia [mi·ze·ri·'kɔr·dia] <-ie> *f* (*pietà*) mercy; **avere** ~ **di qu** to have mercy on sb

misericordioso, -a [mi·ze·ri·kor·'dio:·so] *agg* (*caritatevole*) merciful

misero, -a ['mi:·ze·ro] **I.** *agg* **1.** (*povero*) poor **2.** (*infelice*) wretched **3.** (*scarso, inadeguato*) scant **4.** (*spregevole*) wretched **II.** *m, f* (*persona povera, infelice*) poor person

misfatto [mis·'fat·to] *m* crime

misi ['mi:·zi] *1. pers sing pass rem di* **mettere**

misogino, -a [mi·'zɔ:·dʒi·no] **I.** *agg* (*atteggiamento, comportamento*) misogynistic **II.** *m, f* (*persona*) mysoginist

miss [mis] <-> *f* (*in un concorso*) beauty queen; ~ **Universo** Miss Universe

missile ['mis·si·le] *m* AERO (*veicolo, arma*) missile

missilistico, -a [mis·si·'lis·ti·ko] <-ci, -che> *agg* missile; **base -a** missile base

missionario, -a [mis·sio·'na:·rio] <-i, -ie>
I. *agg a. fig* missionary II. *m*, *f* 1. (*religioso*)
missionary 2. *fig* (*propugnatore*) envoy
missione [mis·'sio:·ne] *f* 1. (*incarico*) mission 2. (*scientifica*) mission 3. ADM (*trasferta*)
indennità di ~ travel allowance 4. REL (*apos-
tolato*) mission 5. (*alto compito*) mission
missiva [mis·'si:·va] *f a. scherz* (*lettera*) missive
mister ['mis·tə] <-> *m* 1. (*in un concorso*) mister 2. SPORT (*allenatore*) manager
misterioso, -a [mis·te·'rio:·so] I. *agg*
1. (*inspiegabile*) mysterious 2. (*sospetto*) suspicious; (*enigmatico*) enigmatic 3. (*sconosciuto, segreto*) secret II. *m*, *f* 1. (*cosa inspiegabile*) mystery 2. (*persona sospetta, enig-
matica*) mystery man *m*, mystery woman *f*
mistero [mis·'tɛ:·ro] *m* 1. (*enigma*) mystery;
~! who knows! 2. (*segreto*) secret; (**non**) **fare**
~ **di qc** to (not) make a mystery of sth 3. REL
mystery
mistica ['mis·ti·ka] <-che> *f* 1. REL, LIT mysticism 2. (*di partito, ideologia*) mystique
misticismo [mis·ti·'tʃiz·mo] *m* 1. REL mysticism 2. (*adesione totale*) total faith
mistico, -a ['mis·ti·ko] <-ci, -che> I. *agg* REL
(*contemplazione, ascesi*) mystical II. *m*, *f*
mystic
mistificare [mis·ti·fi·'ka:·re] *vt* (*realtà, verità,
fatto*) to distort
mistificatore, -trice [mis·ti·fi·ka·'to:·re] *m*, *f*
(*impostore*) hoaxer
mistificazione [mis·ti·fi·kat·'tsio:·ne] *f* (*di
realtà, verità, fatto*) distortion
misto, -a[1] ['mis·to] *agg* 1. (*mescolato*) mixed;
antipasti -i mixed appetizers; **classe/scuola**
-a mixed class/school; **fritto** ~ *dish of different types of fried fish or meat*; **insalata -a**
mixed salad; **matrimonio** ~ mixed marriage
2. (*tessuto*) blended
misto[2] *m* 1. (*miscuglio*) mixture 2. (*tessuto*)
blend
mistura [mis·'tu:·ra] *f* 1. (*mescolanza*) mixture 2. (*intruglio*) concoction
misura [mi·'zu:·ra] *f* 1. (*grandezza*) measure
2. (*dimensioni*) size; **prendere le -e a qu** to
take sb's measurements; **su** ~ custom made
3. (*taglia*) size 4. (*misurazione*) measurement;
avere due pesi e due -e to see things in two
different ways 5. (*limite*) limit; **oltre** ~ excessive; **oltrepassare la** ~ to go too far 6. *fig*
(*moderazione, equilibrio*) moderation; **senso**
della ~ sense of proportion 7. *fig* (*proporzione*) measure; **a** ~ **di** for; **a** ~ **d'uomo** on a
human scale; **in ugual** ~ equally; **nella** ~ **in**
cui equal to 8. *fig* (*criterio, parametro*) measure 9. *pl* (*provvedimento*) measures *pl;* **-e di**
sicurezza security measures
misurare [mi·zu·'ra:·re] I. *vt* 1. (*calcolare*) to
measure; ~ **ad occhio** to measure roughly
2. (*indossare*) to try on 3. (*moderare*) to measure 4. (*stimare*) to weigh up II. *vi* to measure
III. *vr:* **-rsi** 1. *fig* (*cimentarsi*) to measure one-

self; **-rsi con qu** to measure oneself against sb
2. (*limitarsi*) to control
misurato, -a [mi·zu·'ra:·to] *agg* 1. (*pacato:
tono, discorso, gesto*) measured 2. (*moderato:
persona*) moderate
misurazione [mi·zu·rat·'tsio:·ne] *f* measuring
misurino [mi·zu·'ri:·no] *m* measure
mite ['mi:·te] *agg* 1. (*persona, sguardo, animale*) mild-mannered 2. (*clima*) mild 3. (*pena,
giudice*) lenient
mitezza [mi·'tet·tsa] *f* 1. (*di carattere, persona, animale*) mild-manneredness 2. (*di
clima*) mildness 3. (*di animale*) meekness
4. (*di giudizio, pena, provvedimento*) leniency
mitico, -a ['mi:·ti·ko] <-ci, -che> *agg* 1. (*del
mito*) mythical 2. (*memorabile*) legendary
3. *inf* (*eccezionale, straordinario*) brilliant
mitigare [mi·ti·'ga:·re] I. *vt* 1. (*dolore, fatica*)
to relieve 2. *fig* (*sentimento, stato d'animo*) to
dampen 3. (*condanna, pena, punizione*) to reduce II. *vr:* **-rsi** 1. (*freddo, dolore*) to lessen;
(*carattere, sentimento, stato d'animo*) 2. to
calm down
mitilo ['mi:·ti·lo] *m* (*cozza*) mussel
mitizzare [mi·tid·'dza:·re] *vt* (*idealizzare*) to
turn into a legend
mito ['mi:·to] *m* 1. (*gener*) myth; **il** ~
dell'uguaglianza sociale the myth of social
equality 2. *fig* (*sogno individuale*) dream
3. *fig, a. scherz, inf* star; **sei un** ~! you're a
star!
mitologia [mi·to·lo·'dʒi:·a] <-gie> *f* mythology
mitologico, -a [mi·to·'lɔ:·dʒi·ko] <-ci, -che>
agg (*di mito*) mythological
mitra[1] ['mi:·tra] <-> *m* (*arma*) submachine gun
mitra[2] *f* REL (*copricapo*) miter
mitraglia [mi·'traʎ·ʎa] <-glie> *f* 1. *inf* (*mitragliatrice*) machine gun 2. (*raffica di colpi*) machine gun fire
mitragliatore [mi·traʎ·ʎa·'to:·re] *m* (*fucile*)
light machine gun
mitragliatrice [mi·traʎ·ʎa·'tri:·tʃe] *f* (*arma*)
machine gun
mitt. *abbr di* **mittente** sender
mitteleuropeo, -a ['mit·tel·eu·ro·'pe·o] *agg*
(*città, cultura*) mitteleuropean
mittente [mit·'tɛn·te] *mf* (*di lettera, pacco*)
sender
mixaggio [mik·'sad·dʒo] *m* MUS, FILM, TV mixing
mixare [mik·'sa:·re] *vt* to mix
mixer ['mik·sə] <-> I. *m* 1. (*frullatore*) blender
2. FILM, TV (*strumento*) mixer II. *mf* TV (*tecnico*) mixer
mms ['em·me·em·me·es·se] *m* mms
mnemonico, -a [mne·'mɔ:·ni·ko] <-ci, -che>
agg 1. (*della memoria*) mnemonic 2. *a. pej*
(*meccanico*) by rote
mo' [mɔ] *m* **a** ~ **di** *inf* (*come*) as
mobbing ['mɔ·biɲ] <-> *m* workplace bullying
mobile ['mɔ:·bi·le] I. *agg* 1. (*non fisso*) movable 2. (*in movimento*) moving; **scala** ~ esca-

M

lator; **squadra** ~ police rapid response team **3.** (*instabile*) wobbly **II.** *m* (*di arredamento*) piece of furniture **III.** *f* (*squadra mobile*) police rapid response team

mobilia [mo·'bi:·lia] <-> *f* furniture

mobiliare [mo·bi·'lia:·re] *agg* ECON (*investimento, patrimonio*) stock; **mercato** ~ stock market

mobilificio [mo·bi·li·'fi:·tʃo] <-ci> *m* **1.** (*fabbrica*) furniture factory **2.** (*negozio*) furniture shop

mobilio [mo·'bi:·lio] <-i> *m v.* mobilia

mobilità [mo·bi·li·'ta] <-> *f* **1.** (*caratteristica*) mobility **2.** (*sociale, professionale*) mobility; ~ **del lavoro** ECON labor mobility **3.** JUR, ECON **lista di** ~ *workers who have been laid off and receive unemployment help until they find new jobs;* **mettere in** ~ to lay off

mobilitare [mo·bi·li·'ta:·re] **I.** *vt a. fig* to mobilize; ~ **tutte le proprie forze** to gather one's strength **II.** *vr:* **-rsi** (*impegnarsi*) to take action

mobilitazione [mo·bi·li·tat·'tsio:·ne] *f* mobilization

moca ['mo:·ka] <-che> *f* (*macchinetta*) mocha coffee maker

mocassino [mo·kas·'si:·no] *m* (*scarpa*) moccasin

moccio ['mot·tʃo] <-cci> *m inf* snot

moccioso, -a [mot·'tʃo:·so] *m, f pej* (*bambino, ragazzino*) snot-nosed kid

moccolo ['mɔk·ko·lo/'mok·ko·lo] *m* **1.** (*candela*) small candle; **reggere il** ~ *fig, scherz* to be the third wheel **2.** *inf* (*moccio*) booger

moda ['mɔ:·da] *f* **1.** (*tendenza*) fashion; **alla** ~ fashionable; **vestirsi alla** ~ to dress fashionably; **all'ultima** ~ in the latest fashion; **fuori** ~ out of fashion; **andare** [*o* **essere**] **di** ~ to be fashionable; **passare di** ~ to go out of fashion **2.** (*industria*) fashion; **sfilata di** ~ fashion show; **alta** ~ haute couture

modale [mo·'da:·le] *agg* modal

modalità [mo·da·li·'ta] <-> *f* **1.** (*forma, modo*) method; ~ **di pagamento** method of payment; ~ **d'uso** instructions for use **2.** (*procedura*) procedure

modella [mo·'dɛl·la] *f* model

modellare [mo·del·'la:·re] **I.** *vt* **1.** (*plasmare*) to model **2.** (*sagomare*) to shape **3.** (*far risaltare*) to cling **4.** *fig* (*conformare*) ~ **qc su qc** to model sth on sth **II.** *vr* **-rsi su qc** *a. fig* to model oneself on sth

modellino [mo·del·'li:·no] *m* model

modellismo [mo·del·'liz·mo] *m* (*hobby*) model making

modellistica [mo·del·'lis·ti·ka] <-che> *f* (*tecnica, studio*) model making

modello [mo·'dɛl·lo] *m* **1.** (*originale, tipo, prototipo*) model **2.** *fig* (*di coerenza, stile*) model; **essere un** ~ **di qc** to be a model of sth; **prendere qu a** ~ to take sb as a model **3.** (*plastico, modellino*) model **4.** (*forma, stampo*) mold **5.** (*capo d'abbigliamento*) model; (*del sarto*) pattern **6.** ADM (*modulo, stam-*

pato) form

modello [mo·'dɛl·lo] *m* model

Modena ['mo·de·na] *f a city in the Emilia-Romagna region*

modenese [mo·de·'ne:·se] **I.** *agg* (*di Modena*) from Modena **II.** *mf* (*abitante*) person from Modena

Modenese <*sing*> *m* (*zona*) Modena area; **nel** ~ in the Modena area

moderare [mo·de·'ra:·re] **I.** *vt* **1.** (*spese, velocità*) to curb; (*tono, collera*) to moderate; ~ **i termini** [*o* **le parole**] to weigh one's words **2.** (*dibattito*) to chair **II.** *vr:* **-rsi** to keep oneself in check; **-rsi in qc** to do sth moderately; **-rsi nel bere** to drink moderately

moderato, -a [mo·de·'ra:·to] **I.** *agg* **1.** (*prezzo, consumo*) moderate **2.** (*misurato: persona*) measured; **essere** ~ **in qc** to do sth moderately; **è** ~ **nel mangiare** he eats moderately **3.** POL moderate **4.** MUS moderato **II.** *m, f* POL moderate

moderatore, -trice *m, f* (*in dibattito*) chairperson

moderazione [mo·de·rat·'tsio:·ne] *f* **1.** (*misura*) moderation **2.** (*contenimento: di prezzi, spese*) modesty

modernismo [mo·der·'niz·mo] *m a. fig* ART, LIT, MUS, REL modernism

modernità [mo·der·ni·'ta] <-> *f* **1.** (*caratteristica, attualità*) modernity **2.** (*l'oggi*) present day

modernizzare [mo·der·nid·'dza:·re] **I.** *vt* (*rinnovare*) to modernize **II.** *vr:* **-rsi** to modernize oneself

moderno, -a *agg* **1.** (*attuale*) modern; **storia -a** early modern history **2.** (*aggiornato*) up-to-date

modestia [mo·'dɛs·tia] <-ie> *f* **1.** (*virtù*) modesty; **falsa** ~ false modesty; ~ **a parte** *scherz, inf* If I do say so myself **2.** (*moderazione*) moderation **3.** (*di arredamento, indumento, lavoro*) modesty

modesto, -a [mo·'dɛs·to] *agg* **1.** (*non presuntuoso*) modest **2.** (*non lussuoso*) modest **3.** (*origine, estrazione, condizione*) humble **4.** (*prezzo, paga, spesa*) moderate **5.** (*mediocre*) modest; **un libro** ~ a mediocre book

modico, -a ['mɔ:·di·ko] <-ci, -che> *agg* (*prezzo, spesa*) moderate

modifica [mo·'di:·fi·ka] <-che> *f* **1.** (*cambiamento*) alteration **2.** (*miglioramento*) improvement

modificare [mo·di·fi·'ka:·re] **I.** *vt* **1.** (*cambiare*) to alter; **modifica** COMPUT modify **2.** (*migliorare*) to improve **II.** *vr:* **-rsi** to change

modo ['mɔ:·do] *m* **1.** (*maniera*) way; **in** ~ ... *adj* in a ... way; ~ **di dire** expression; **di** [*o* **in**] ~ **che** ... +*conj* so that ...; **in** ~ **da** ... +*inf* so as to ... **2.** (*comportamento, atteggiamento*) manners *pl* **3.** (*mezzo, metodo*) means *inv* **4.** (*occasione, opportunità*) chance; **ad** [*o* **in**] **ogni** ~ anyway; **avere** ~ **di fare qc** to have the chance to do sth; **dare** ~ **a qu di fare qc** to

give sb the chance to do sth **5.** LING mood
6. MUS mode
modulare¹ [mo·du·'la:·re] *agg* modular
modulare² *vt* (*voce, suono*) to modulate
modulazione [mo·du·lat·'tsio:·ne] *f* **1.** (*di voce, suono*) modulation **2.** RADIO modulation;
~ **di frequenza** frequency modulation
modulo ['mɔ:·du·lo] *m* **1.** (*stampato*) form;
~ **d'iscrizione** enrollment form; ~ **di versamento** deposit slip **2.** (*parte, elemento*) unit
3. (*all'università*) module
mogano ['mɔ:·ga·no] *m* (*legno*) mahogany
mogio, -a ['mɔ:·dʒo] <-gi, -ge> *agg* (*abbattuto*) dejected
moglie ['moʎ·ʎe] <-gli> *f* wife; **mia/tua/sua** ~ my/your/his wife; **prendere** ~ to get married; ~ **e buoi dei paesi tuoi** *prov* best to stick to your own kind; **tra** ~ **e marito non mettere il dito** *prov* never intefere between husband and wife
moina [mo·'i:·na] *fpl* (*smancerie*) sweet-talking; **fare le -e a qu** to sweet-talk sb
molare [mo·'la:·re] **I.** *agg* **dente** ~ molar tooth **II.** *m* (*dente*) molar
Moldavia [mol·'da:·via] *f* Moldavia
moldavo [mol·'da:·vo] **I.** *agg* (*della Moldavia*) Moldovan **II.** *m* (*abitante*) Moldovan
mole ['mɔ:·le] *f* **1.** (*massa enorme*) sheer size **2.** (*edificio*) mausoleum **3.** *fig* (*quantità*) amount
molecola [mo·'lɛː·ko·la] *f* CHEM molecule
molecolare [mo·le·ko·'la:·re] *agg* CHEM molecular
molestare [mo·les·'ta:·re] *vt* **1.** (*infastidire*) to bother **2.** (*donna*) to sexually harass
molestia [mo·'lɛs·tia] <-ie> *f* **1.** (*fastidio*) bother **2.** ~ **sessuale** [*o* -**e sessuali**] sexual harassment
molesto, -a [mo·'lɛs·to] *agg* (*fastidioso*) bothersome
molisano, -a **I.** *agg* (*del Molise*) from Molise **II.** *m, f* (*abitante*) person from Molise
Molise [mo·'li:·ze] *m* Molise, *region in Central Italy*
molla ['mɔl·la] *f* **1.** (*meccanismo*) spring; **materasso a -e** spring mattress **2.** *fig* (*stimolo*) incentive **3.** *pl* (*pinza*) tongs; **prendere** [*o* **trattare**] **qu con le -e** *fig* to treat sb with kid gloves
mollare [mol·'la:·re] **I.** *vt* **1.** (*allentare*) to cast off; **molla!** let go!; ~ **la presa** to let go **2.** *inf* (*dare*) to give; ~ **un pugno a qu** to land a punch on sb **3.** *fig, inf* (*famiglia, lavoro, partner*) to leave **II.** *vi* **1.** *inf* (*cedere*) to give in **2.** *fig, inf* (*smettere*) to stop
molle ['mɔl·le] *agg* **1.** (*soffice*) soft **2.** *fig* (*debole: animo, carattere*) weak; (*non severo*) easy-going
molleggiato [mol·led·'dʒa:·to] *agg* **1.** (*materasso, divano, vettura*) sprung; **una vettura ben -a** a vehicle with good suspension **2.** (*andatura, passo*) bouncy
molletta [mol·'let·ta] *f* **1.** (*da bucato*) clothes-

pin **2.** (*per capelli*) hairpin
mollettone [mo·let·'to:·ne] *m* undercloth
mollica [mol·'li:·ka] <-che> *f* (*di pane*) soft part of a roll/loaf
molliccio, -a [mol·'lit·tʃo] <-cci, -cce> *agg* (*materia, terreno, carne*) soft
mollo ['mɔl·lo] *agg v.* **molle**
mollusco [mol·'lus·ko] <-schi> *m* (*mollusc*) cozze e vongole sono -schi
molo ['mɔ:·lo] *m* (*di porto*) jetty
molotov ['mɔ:·lo·tov] **I.**<inv> *agg* (*bomba, bottiglia*) Molotov **II.**<-> *f* Molotov cocktail
molteplice [mol·'te:·pli·tʃe] *agg* **1.** (*composito: forma, struttura*) composite **2.** *pl* (*numerosi*) many
molteplicità [mol·te·pli·tʃi·'ta] <-> *f* (*varietà*) range
moltiplicare [mol·ti·pli·'ka:·re] **I.** *vt* MATH to multiply; ~ **qc per qc** to multiply sth by sth **II.** *vr:* -**rsi** **1.** (*aumentare*) to increase **2.** (*riprodursi*) to multiply
moltiplicazione [mol·ti·pli·kat·'tsio:·ne] *f* **1.** MATH multiplication **2.** (*aumento*) increase
moltissimo [mol·'tis·si·mo] *superl di* **molto** the most
moltitudine [mol·ti·'tu:·di·ne] *f* **1.** (*di persone*) vast number; *a. pej* (*folla*) crowd; **distinguersi dalla** ~ to stand out from the crowd **2.** (*di insetti*) swarm; (*di oggetti, pensieri*) load
molto¹ ['mol·to] <più, moltissimo> **I.** *avv* **1.** (*intensità*) very much; **mi piace** ~ I like it [*o* him] [*o* her] a lot **2.** (*con aggettivi e avverbi*) very; ~ **prima** much earlier; ~ **al di sotto delle aspettative** much below expectations; **sono** ~ **felice del tuo successo** I'm very happy for your success **3.** (*tempo*) for a long time; **esci** ~ **la sera?** do you often go out in the evening? **4.** (*distanza*) much farther **5.** (*con comparativi*) much **II.** *pron* **1.** (*quantità, misura, numero*) a lot; **hai voglia di uscire?** — **io non ne ho -a** do you feel like going out? — I don't really feel like it **2.** (*tempo*) a long time; **ci vuole** ~? will it take a long time?; **è da** ~ **che mi aspetti?** have you been waiting for me long?; **fra non** ~ shortly **3.** (*distanza*) far **4.** (*denaro*) a lot; **costa** ~ it costs a lot; **non costa** ~ it doesn't cost much [*o* a lot] **5.** (*intelligenza, sforzo*) much **6.** (*cosa importante*) something **7.** *pl* (*persone*) many [*o* a lot of] people
molto, -a² <più, moltissimo> *agg* **1.** (*quantità, misura, numero*) a lot of **2.** (*intenso, grande*) very; **fa** ~ **caldo** it's very hot; **c'è** ~ **vento** it's very windy **3.** (*lungo*) **c'è ancora -a strada prima di arrivare?** is it much farther before we arrive?; **è passato** ~ **tempo da allora** it was a long time ago
momentaccio [mo·men·'tat·tʃo] <-cci> *m inf* (*situazione sfavorevole*) bad time
momentaneamente [mo·men·ta·nea·'men·te] *avv* at present
momentaneo, -a [mo·men·'ta:·neo] <-ei,

-ee> *agg* (*malore, interesse, gioia*) momentary

momentino [mo·men·'ti:·no] *m inf* (*attimo*) moment

momento [mo·'men·to] *m* **1.**(*attimo*) moment; **al** [*o* **per il**] **~** at the moment; **al ~ di fare qc** when it came to doing sth; **a -i** (*tra poco*) any time now; *inf* (*per poco*) almost; **dal ~ che ...** (*dato che*) given that ...; **da un ~ all'altro** from one moment to the next; **sul ~** there and then; **un ~!** just a moment! **2.**(*periodo*) period; **del ~** of the moment **3.**(*circostanza*) chance; (*istante opportuno*) right moment; **~ magico** magic moment; **~ no** bad period

monaca ['mɔ:·na·ka] <-che> *f* (*religiosa*) nun

monacale [mo·na·'ka:·le] *agg* **1.**(*abito, ordine*) monastic **2.***fig* (*rigore, vita*) monkish

monaco ['mɔ:·na·ko] <-ci> *m* (*religioso*) monk; **l'abito non fa il ~** *prov* don't judge a book by its cover *prov*

Monaco ['mɔ:·na·ko] *f* **1. ~** (**di Baviera**) Munich **2.**(**il Principato di**) **~** (the Principality of) Monaco

monarca [mo·'nar·ka] <-chi> *m* (*re*) monarch

monarchia [mo·nar·'ki:·a] <-chie> *f* monarchy

monarchico, -a [mo·'nar·ki·ko] <-ci, -che> **I.** *agg* (*regime, potere*) monarchic; (*partito*) monarchist **II.** *m, f* (*sostenitore*) monarchist

monastero [mo·nas·'tɛ:·ro] *m* (*edificio*) monastery

monastico, -a [mo·'nas·ti·ko] <-ci, -che> *agg* (*abito, ordine, vita*) monastic

moncherino [moŋ·ke·'ri:·no] *m* (*braccio*) stump

monco, -a ['moŋ·ko] <-chi, -che> *agg* **1.**(*braccio, gamba*) maimed, to have only one arm **2.**(*parola, frase*) incomplete

moncone [moŋ·'ko:·ne] *m a. fig* stump

mondanità [mon·da·ni·'ta] <-> *f* **1.**(*modo di vivere*) worldly pleasures *pl* **2.**(*insieme di persone*) haut monde

mondano, -a [mon·'da:·no] *agg* **1.**(*persona, vita*) worldly **2.**(*evento*) society

mondare [mon·'da:·re] *vt* (*frutto*) to peel; (*riso*) to rinse

mondiale [mon·'dia:·le] **I.** *agg* **1.**(*internazionale*) world; **di fama ~** world-famous **2.***fig, inf* (*eccezionale*) awesome **II.** *m* SPORT (*campionato*) world championship; **i -i** the World Cup

mondo ['mon·do] *m a. fig* world; **al ~** in the world; **il bel** [*o* **gran**] **~** the jet set; **uomo/ donna di ~** jet setter; **andare all'altro ~** to pass on; **mettere al ~ qu** to give birth to sb; **venire al ~** to be born; **un ~ a** lot; **un ~ di qc** a lot of sth; **ti voglio un ~ di bene** I love you very much; **un ~ di auguri** very best wishes

mondovisione [mon·do·vi·'zio:·ne] *f* **in ~** TV worldwide

monegasco, -sca [mo·ne·'gas·ko] <-schi, -sche> **I.** *agg* (*del Principato di Monaco*) from

monello, -a [mo·'nɛl·lo] *m, f* (*birichino*) rascal

moneta [mo·'ne:·ta] *f* **1.**(*di metallo*) coin **2.**(*valuta*) currency **3.**(*denaro*) money **4.**(*spiccioli*) change

monetario, -a [mo·ne·'ta:·rio] <-i, -ie> *agg* ECON, FIN monetary

monetina [mo·ne·'ti:·na] *f* **1.**(*spicciolo*) coin **2. lanciare la ~** to toss a coin

monetizzare [mo·ne·tid·'dza:·re] *vt* (*convertire in denaro*) to convert into cash

mongolfiera [moŋ·gol·'fiɛ:·ra] *f* hot-air balloon

Mongolia [moŋ·'go:·lia] *f* Mongolia

mongolo, -a ['mon·go·lo] **I.** *agg* (*della Mongolia*) Mongol **II.** *m, f* (*persona*) Mongol

monito ['mɔ:·ni·to] *m* (*rimprovero*) warning

monitoraggio [mo·ni·to·'ra:·dʒio] <-ggi> *m a. fig* monitoring

monitorare [mo·ni·to·'ra:·re] *vt* to monitor

monoblocco [mo·no·'blɔk·ko] <-cchi> *m* cylinder block

monocolore [mo·no·ko·'lo:·re] <inv> *agg* POL one-party

monocromatico, -a [mo·no·kro·'ma:·ti·ko] <-ci, -che> *agg* (*pittura, effetto*) monochrome

monofamiliare [mo·no·fa·mi·'lia:·re] *agg* (*casa, villetta*) for single family use

monofase [mo·no·'fa:·ze] <inv> *agg* PHYS, EL single-phase

monogamia [mo·no·ga·'mi:·a] <-ie> *f* monogamy

monogamo, -a [mo·'no·ga·mo] **I.** *agg* **1.**(*società, tribù, animale*) monogamous **2.***scherz* (*persona*) faithful **II.** *m, f a. scherz* (*persona*) monogamist

monografia [mo·no·gra·'fi:·a] *f* monograph

monografico, -a [mo·no·'gra:·fi·ko] <-ci, -che> *agg* (*opera, ricerca, saggio*) monographic; (*corso*) dedicated

monogramma [mo·no·'gram·ma] <-i> *m* monogram

monolingue [mo·no·'liŋ·gue] <inv> *agg* LING monolingual; **dizionario/vocabolario ~** monolingual dictionary

monolitico, -a [mo·no·'li:·ti·ko] <-ci, -che> *agg* **1.**(*colonna, statua*) monolithic **2.***fig* (*persona*) strong-minded; (*gruppo*) compact

monolito [mo·'nɔ:·li·to] *m* monolith

monolocale [mo·no·lo·'ka:·le] *m* studio apartment

monologo [mo·'nɔ:·lo·go] <-ghi> *m* monologue

monopattino [mo·no·'pat·ti·no] *m* scooter

monopoli® [mo·'nɔ:·po·li] <-> *m* (*gioco*) Monopoly®

monopolio [mo·no·'pɔ:·lio] <-i> *m a. fig* ECON monopoly; **~ di stato** state monopoly

monopolizzare [mo·no·po·lid·'dza:·re] *vt a. fig* to monopolize

monoposto [mo·no·'pos·to] **I.** <inv> *agg* (*cabina, seggiovia*) single-seater **II.** <-> *f* (*auto*) single-seater car

monoreddito [mo·no·'rɛd·di·to] <inv> *agg* **famiglia ~** single-income family

monoscì [mo·no·'ʃi] <-> *m* SPORT (*alpino*) monoski; (*sci d'acqua*) water ski

monosillabo [mo·no·'sil·la·bo] *m* (*parola*) monosyllable; **parlare/rispondere a -i** to talk/reply to oneself in monosyllables

monossido [mo·'nɔs·si·do] *m* CHEM **~ di carbonio** carbon monoxide

monoteismo [mo·no·te·'iz·mo] *m* REL monotheism

monoteista [mo·no·te·'is·ta] <-i *m*, -e *f*> *agg* (*religione, culto*) monotheist

monoteistico, -a [mo·no·te·'is·ti·ko] <-ci, -che> *agg* (*concezione, corrente*) monotheistic

monotematico [mo·no·te·'ma·ti·ko] *agg* monothematic

monotonia [mo·no·to·'ni·a] <-ie> *f* monotony

monotono, -a [mo·'nɔ·to·no] *agg* monotonous

monouso [mo·no·'u:·zo] <inv> *agg* disposable

monovolume [mo·no·vo·'lu:·me] <-> *f* (*automobile*) minivan

monsignore [mon·siɲ·'ɲo:·re] *m* (*titolo*) Monsignor

monsone [mon·'so:·ne] *m* monsoon

monta ['mon·ta] *f* 1.(*accoppiamento*) covering 2.(*in equitazione*) riding

montacarichi [mon·ta·'ka:·ri·ki] <-> *m* elevator

montaggio [mon·'tad·dʒo] <-ggi> *m* 1.(*assemblaggio*) assembly; **catena di ~** assembly line 2. FILM editing

montagna [mon·'taɲ·ɲa] *f* 1.(*monte*) mountain; **-e russe** roller coaster 2.(*regione*) mountains *pl;* **da ~** mountain; **di ~** mountain; **in ~** in [*o* to] the mountains 3. *fig*(*grande quantità*) mountain

montagnoso, -a [mon·taɲ·'ɲo:·so] *agg* (*regione, zona*) mountainous

montanaro, -a [mon·ta·'na:·ro] I. *agg* (*abitudine, canto*) mountain II. *m, f* 1.(*abitante*) mountain dweller 2. *pej* (*persona rozza*) peasant

montano, -a [mon·'ta:·no] *agg*(*clima, paesaggio*) mountain

montare [mon·'ta:·re] I. *vt avere* 1.(*scala, pendio*) to climb 2.(*cavallo*) to ride 3.(*fecondare*) to cover 4. CULIN to whisk; **~ a neve** to whisk until peaks form 5.(*mobile, pezzi*) to assemble; (*scaffale*) to put up 6. *fig*(*notizia, fatto*) to exaggerate 7. *fig* (*persona*) **~ qu** to make sb big-headed; **~ qu contro qu/qc** to set sb against sb/sth; **~ la testa a qu** *inf* to make sb big-headed 8.(*fotografia, diamante*) to mount 9. FILM, PELLICOLA to edit II. *vi essere* 1.(*salire*) to climb; (*in bicicletta*) to get on; (*in macchina*) to get in; **monta in macchina!** get in the car! 2. CULIN to rise 3. *a. fig* (*acque, tono, malcontento*) to rise 4.(*iniziare un turno*) to

clock in III. *vr:* **-rsi -rsi** (**la testa**) *inf*to become big-headed

montato, -a [mon·'ta:·to] *agg* 1.CULIN **panna -a** whipped cream 2. *inf*(*persona*) big-headed

montatore, -trice [mon·ta·'to:·re] *m, f* 1.(*operaio*) fitter 2. FILM editor

montatura [mon·ta·'tu:·ra] *f* 1.(*di occhiali*) frames *pl* 2.(*di gioielli*) setting 3. *fig*(*esagerazione*) invention

monte ['mon·te] *m* 1.(*montagna*) mountain; **il Monte Bianco** Mont Blanc; **a ~** uphill; *fig*at the source; **promettere mari e -i** to promise the world 2. *fig* (*di libri, pacchi, problemi*) mountain 3.(*istituto*) **~ di pietà** pawnshop 4. ANAT **~ di Venere** mons veneris 5.(*loc*) **andare a ~** *fig* to fall apart; **mandare a ~** *fig* to finish off

Montecitorio [mon·te·tʃi·'to:·rio] *m* 1.(*palazzo*) seat of the Italian parliament 2.(*Camera*) the lower house of the Italian parliament

montepremi [mon·te·'pre:·mi] *m* (*di lotteria, concorso*) jackpot

montessoriano [mon·tes·so·'ria:·no] *agg* (*in pedagogia*) Montessori

montgomery [moɲ·'o·me·ri] <-> *m* (*cappotto*) duffle coat

montone [mon·'to:·ne] *m* 1.(*animale*) ram; **carne di ~** mutton 2. *inf*(*cappotto*) sheepskin jacket/coat

montuoso, -a [mon·tu·'o:·so] *agg* (*regione, paesaggio*) mountainous; **catena -a** mountain range

monumentale [mo·nu·men·'ta:·le] *agg* 1.(*arte, pittura*) on [*o* of] a monument 2.(*imponente*) monumental

monumento [mo·nu·'men·to] *m* 1.(*commemorativo*) monument; **~ ai caduti** war memorial 2.(*artistico*) monument; **~ nazionale** national monument

moquette [mo·'kɛt] <-> *f* fitted carpet

mora ['mɔ:·ra] *f* 1.(*di rovo*) blackberry; (*di gelso*) mulberry 2. JUR (*ritardo*) delay; **essere in ~** to be in arrears; **interesse di ~** interest on arrears 3.(*somma*) surcharge on arrears

morale¹ [mo·'ra:·le] *agg* moral; **forza ~** moral strength; **schiaffo ~** slap in the face; **vincitore ~** moral winner

morale² I. *f* 1.(*norme*) morality 2.(*dottrina*) morals *pl* 3.(*di favola, racconto*) moral; **~ della favola** *scherz* moral of the story II. *m inf*(*umore*) morale; **essere giù/su di ~** to be in good/low spirits; **avere il ~ alle stelle** to be as happy as a clam; **avere il ~ sotto i tacchi** [*o* a terra] to be downhearted

moralismo [mo·ra·'liz·mo] *m* 1. *pej* (*intransigenza*) moralizing 2.(*dottrina*) moralism

moralista [mo·ra·'lis·ta] <-i *m*, -e *f*> I. *agg* moralistic II. *mf* 1. *pej*(*persona intransigente*) moralizer 2.(*pensatore*) moralist

moralità [mo·ra·li·'ta] <-> *f* (*rettitudine*) morality

moralizzare [mo·ra·lid·'dza:·re] *vt* (*costumi,*

vita pubblica) ~ **qc** to raise the moral standards of sth

moratoria [mo·ra·'tɔ:·ria] <-ie> *f* **1.**(*sospensione*) suspension **2.** JUR moratorium

morbidezza [mor·bi·'det·tsa] *f* softness

morbido, -a ['mɔr·bi·do] *agg* soft

morbillo [mor·'bil·lo] *m* MED measles

morbo ['mɔr·bo] *m* **1.**(*malattia*) disease; ~ **di Alzheimer** Alzheimer's disease; ~ **di Parkinson** Parkinson's disease; ~ **della mucca pazza** mad cow disease **2.** *fig* evil

morbosità [mor·bo·si·'ta] <-> *f* (*di atteggiamento, passione*) morbidness

morboso, -a [mor·'bo:·so] *agg fig* (*attaccamento, curiosità*) morbid; (*persona*) overly attached

mordace [mor·'da:·tʃe] *agg fig* (*battuta, scrittore*) scathing; **satira** ~ biting satire

mordente [mor·'dɛn·te] *m* **1.** *fig* (*grinta*) drive; (*incisività*) bite **2.**(*vernice*) mordant

mordere ['mɔr·de·re] <mordo, morsi, morso> **I.** *vt* **1.**(*mela, panino*) to bite into; (*cane, vipera*) to bite **2.** *inf*(*insetto*) to sting **II.** *vi fig* (*freddo*) to bite; (*sapore*) to be sharp **III.** *vr:* -**rsi** (*lingua, labbro, unghie*) to bite; -**rsi la lingua** [*o* **le labbra**] *fig* to bite one's tongue; -**rsi le mani** [*o* **le dita**] [*o* **le unghie**] *fig* to kick oneself

mordicchiare [mor·dik·'kia:·re] *vt* (*matita, pane*) to chew

morente [mo·'rɛn·te] **I.** *agg a. fig* dying **II.** *mf* (*persona*) dying person

morfema [mor·'fɛː·ma] <-i> *m* LING morpheme

morfina [mor·'fi:·na] *f* morphine

morfinomane [mor·fi·'nɔ:·ma·ne] *mf* morphine addict

morfologia [mor·fo·lo·'dʒi:·a] <-gie> *f* morphology

morfologico, -a [mor·fo·'lɔ:·dʒi·ko] *agg* (*analisi, livello*) morphological

moria [mo·'ri:·a] <-ie> *f* (*di animali*) high death rate

moribondo, -a [mo·ri·'bon·do] **I.** *agg* dying; **essere** ~ to be dying **II.** *m, f* dying person

morigerato, -a [mo·ri·dʒe·'ra:·to] *agg* (*sobrio, moderato*) moderate

morire [mo·'ri:·re] <muoio, morii, morto> *vi essere* **1.**(*persona, animale, pianta*) to die; ~ **di qc** to die from sth; **è morto di morte naturale/violenta** he died a natural/violent death **2.** *fig*(*soffrire*) ~ **di fame/di sete** to die of hunger/thirst; ~ **dall'invidia** to be green with envy; ~ **di freddo/di noia** to be frozen/bored stiff; ~ **dal ridere/dalle risate** to die laughing; ~ **dal sonno** to be dead tired; ~ **dalla voglia di fare qc** to be dying to do sth; **fa un caldo/un freddo da** ~ *inf* it's boiling hot/bitterly cold; **bello/brutto da** ~ drop-dead gorgeous/as ugly as sin; **mi piace da** ~ I love it; ~ **dietro a qu** to be madly in love with sb **3.** *fig* (*istituzione, tradizione*) to die **4.** *fig* (*conversazione, discorso*) to die off; (*progetto, questione*) to die **5.** *fig*(*fuoco, luce*) to die out;

(*passione, speranza*) to die off

mormone [mor·'mo:·ne] *m* (*seguace*) Mormon

mormorare [mor·mo·'ra:·re] *vi* **1.**(*bisbigliare*) to whisper **2.**(*lamentarsi*) to murmur **3.**(*sparlare*) ~ **su qu** to speak ill of sb **4.**(*acqua, vento*) to murmur; (*foglie*) to rustle

mormorio [mor·mo·'ri:·o] <-ii> *m* **1.**(*di persone*) murmur **2.**(*di acqua, vento*) murmuring; (*di foglie*) rustling

moro[1] ['mɔ:·ro] *m* BOT mulberry tree

moro, -a[2] **I.** *agg* (*persona*) dark-skinned; (*capelli*) dark-haired **II.** *m, f* (*persona*) dark-skinned [*o* dark-haired] person

Moro, -a *m, f* HIST **i Mori** the Moors

morosità [mo·ro·si·'ta] <-> *f* JUR arrears *pl*

moroso, -a[1] [mo·'ro:·zo/mo·'ro:·so] *agg* JUR in arrears

moroso, -a[2] *m, f sett* (*innamorato*) boyfriend *m*, girlfriend *f*

morsa ['mɔr·sa] *f* **1.**(*attrezzo*) vise **2.**(*stretta*) grip **3.** *fig* (*disagio*) grip

Morse ['mor·se] *agg* (*alfabeto, codice*) Morse

morsetto [mor·'set·to] *m* **1.**(*attrezzo*) clamp **2.** EL terminal

morsi ['mɔr·si] *1. pers sing pass rem di* **mordere**

morsicare [mor·si·'ka:·re] *vt* **1.**(*mela, pane*) to bite into **2.**(*cane*) to bite **3.** *inf*(*insetto*) to sting

morso[1] ['mɔr·so] *pp di* **mordere**

morso[2] *m* **1.**(*gener*) bite; (*di insetto*) sting **2.** *fig*(*fitta*) pang **3.**(*per cavallo*) bit

mortadella [mor·ta·'dɛl·la] *f* mortadella

mortaio [mor·'ta:·io] <-ai> *m* (*recipiente*) mortar

mortale [mor·'ta:·le] **I.** *agg* **1.**(*non eterno*) mortal **2.**(*umano, terreno*) human; **beni -i** worldly goods **3.**(*malattia, ferita, veleno*) deadly; **nemico** ~ deadly enemy; **odio** ~ mortal hatred; **salto** ~ somersault **4.**(*insopportabile*) terrible **II.** *m* (*essere umano*) mortal

mortalità [mor·ta·li·'ta] <-> *f* (*dato statistico*) mortality rate; ~ **infantile** infant mortality

mortalmente [mor·tal·'men·te] *avv* **1.**(*a morte*) mortally **2.** *fig* (*enormemente*) **offendere** ~ **qu** to mortally offend sb; **odiare** ~ **qu** to hate sb's guts; **annoiarsi** ~ to be bored to death

mortaretto [mor·ta·'ret·to] *m* (*petardo*) firecracker

morte ['mɔr·te] *f* **1.**(*decesso*) death; ~ **cerebrale** [*o* **clinica**] brain death; **essere fra la vita e la** ~ to be fighting for one's life; **in punto di** ~ on one's deathbed; **colpire/ferire qu a** ~ to mortally wound sb; **odiare qu a** ~ *inf* to really hate sb's guts **2.**(*pena*) death; **pena di** ~ death penalty **3.** *fig*(*fine*) end **4.** *inf* CULIN best way of cooking

mortificante [mor·ti·fi·'kan·te] *agg* mortifying

mortificare [mor·ti·fi·'ka:·re] **I.** *vt* (*persona*) to humiliate **II.** *vr:* -**rsi 1.**(*avvilirsi*) to feel humiliated **2.**(*punirsi*) to punish oneself

mortificato [mor·ti·fi·'ka:·to] *agg* (*dispiaciuto*) mortified

mortificazione [mor·ti·fi·kat·'tsio:·ne] *f* 1.(*umiliazione*) humiliation 2.(*di corpo, carne*) mortification

morto, -a ['mɔr·to] I. *pp di* **morire** II. *agg* 1.(*persona, animale, albero*) dead; ~ **e sepolto** dead and buried 2.*fig* (*sfinito*) dying; **essere** ~ **di fame/di sete/di freddo** to be dying of hunger/thirst/cold; **essere** ~ **di fatica** to be dead tired; **stanco** ~ dead tired; **essere** ~ **di paura** to be really scared 3.*fig* (*città, festa, stagione*) quiet III. *m, f* (*persona*) dead person; **i Morti** [*o* **il giorno dei -i**] All Soul's Day; **fare il** ~ to float; **un** ~ **di fame** *fig, pej* poor wretch

mortorio [mor·'tɔ:·rio] <-i> *m* **essere un** ~ *fig* (*noia*) to be deadly dull

mortuario, -a [mor·tu·'a:·rio] <-i,-ie> *agg* (*annuncio*) death; (*servizio*) funeral; **camera -a** mortuary

mosaico [mo·'za:·i·ko] <-ci> *m* 1.(*opera*) mosaic; **pavimento a** ~ mosaic floor 2.*fig* (*di idee, genti*) mixture

mosca ['mos·ka] <-sche> *f* (*insetto*) fly; ~ **bianca** rare breed; ~ **cieca** (*gioco*) blind man's bluff; **non farebbe male ad una** ~ he [*o* she] wouldn't hurt a fly; **non si sente volare una** ~ you couldn't hear a pin drop; **far saltare la** ~ **al naso a qu** *fig* to make sb lose their cool

Mosca ['mos·ka] *f* Moscow

moscatello [mos·ka·'tɛl·lo] *m* (*vino*) muscatel

moscato [mos·'ka:·to] *m* (*vino*) muscatel

moscato, -a *agg* **uva** ~ muscat grape; **noce -a** nutmeg

moscerino [moʃ·ʃe·'ri:·no] *m* (*insetto*) gnat

moschea [mos·'kɛ:·a] <-schee> *f* mosque

moschettiere [mos·ket·'tiɛ:·re] *m* (*guardia reale*) musketeer; **"I tre -i"** "The Three Musketeers"

moschettone [mos·ket·'to:·ne] *m* carabiner

moschicida [mos·ki·'tʃi:·da] <-i> *agg* (*carta, veleno*) fly

moscio, -a ['moʃ·ʃo] <-sci, -sce> *agg* 1.(*frutta, carne, pelle*) soft; (*fiore*) wilted 2.*fig* (*noioso*) flat 3.*fig* (*avvilito*) down 4.(*loc*) **avere** [*o* **parlare con**] **la erre -a** to not be able to roll one's "r"s

moscone [mos·'ko:·ne] *m* 1.(*insetto*) bluebottle 2.*fig* (*corteggiatore*) admirer 3.(*imbarcazione*) pedal boat

moscovita [mos·ko·'vi:·ta] <-i *m*, -e *f*> I. *agg* (*di Mosca*) from Moscow II. *mf* (*abitante*) Muscovite

mossa ['mɔs·sa] *f* 1.(*movimento*) movement; **fare la** ~ **di** to make as if to 2.(*strategica*) move 3.SPORT move; **fare la prima** ~ *a. fig* to make the first move 4.(*loc*) **darsi una** ~ *inf* to get a move on

mossi ['mɔs·si] *1. pers sing pass rem di* **muovere**

mosso, -a ['mɔs·so] I. *pp di* **muovere** II. *agg* 1.(*mare*) rough 2.(*fotografia*) blurred; (*capelli*) wavy 3.(*paesaggio*) varied 4.MUS mosso

mostarda [mos·'tar·da] *f* 1.(*salsa*) mustard 2.~ **di Cremona** *pickled fruit in a mustard-based sauce*

mosto ['mos·to] *m* (*d'uva*) must

mostra ['mos·tra] *f* 1.(*sfoggio*) show; **mettere in** ~ **qc** to show sth off; **mettersi in** ~ to draw attention to oneself 2.(*d'arte*) exhibition; (*di prodotti*) display; (*di animali*) show; ~ **mercato** market

mostrare [mos·'tra:·re] I. *vt* 1.(*far vedere*) to show; ~ **qc a qu** to show sb sth [*o* to show sth to sb]; (*gambe*) to show off 2.(*additare*) to point out 3.(*spiegare, dimostrare*) to explain 4.(*palesare*) to show 5.(*fingere*) to pretend II. *vr:* **-rsi** 1.(*farsi vedere*) to appear 2.(*dimostrarsi*) to appear

mostriciattolo [mos·tri·'tʃat·to·lo] *m* (*persona, animale*) runt

mostrina [mos·'tri:·na] *f* MIL stripe

mostro ['mos·tro] *m* 1.*a. fig, a. scherz* monster 2.(*persona eccezionale*) **un** ~ **di bontà** an incredibly good person; **un** ~ **di bravura** an incredibly skillful person; ~ **sacro** mythical figure

mostruosità [mos·truo·zi·'ta] <-> *f* 1.(*aspetto*) monstrosity 2.*fig* (*atto, malvagità*) dreadful deed 3.*fig* (*difformità*) anomaly

mostruoso, -a [mos·tru·'o:·zo] *agg* 1.(*orrendo*) monstrous 2.*fig* (*eccezionale*) incredible 3.*fig* (*malvagio*) monstrous

motivare [mo·ti·'va:·re] *vt* 1.(*spiegare*) to justify 2.(*causare*) to cause 3.(*stimolare*) to motivate

motivato [mo·ti·'va:·to] *agg* 1.(*giustificato*) justified 2.(*incentivato: persona*) motivated

motivazione [mo·ti·vat·'tsio:·ne] *f* 1.(*giustificazione*) justification 2.(*stimolo*) motivation

motivo [mo·'ti:·vo] *m* 1.(*ragione*) reason; **avere** ~ **di qc** to have reason to sth; **dare** ~ **di qc** to give rise to sth; **per quale** ~? why?; **per questo** ~ this is why; **dar** ~ **di** to give reason to 2.MUS (*tema, melodia*) motif; (*brano*) tune 3.(*tematica*) theme 4.(*floreale, geometrico*) motif

moto[1] ['mɔ:·to] *m* 1.PHYS motion 2.(*di apparecchio, macchina*) movement; **mettere in** ~ (*auto*) to start up; *fig* to set sth in motion; **mettersi in** ~ *fig* to get moving 3.(*ginnastica*) exercise 4.(*gesto*) movement; (*impulso*) gesture 5.MUS **con** ~ con moto

moto[2] <-> *f* (*motocicletta*) motorcycle

motocarro [mo·to·'kar·ro] *m* van

motocicletta [mo·to·tʃi·'klet·ta] *f* motorcycle

motociclismo [mo·to·tʃi·'kliz·mo] *m* motorcycling

motociclista [mo·to·tʃi·'klis·ta] <-i *m*, -e *f*> *mf* motorcyclist

motociclistico, -a [mo·to·tʃi·'klis·ti·ko] *agg* (*club, gara*) motorcycling

motociclo [mo·to·'tʃi:·klo] *m* motorcycle

M

motonave [mo·to·'na:·ve] *f* motor vessel

motopeschereccio [mo·to·pes·ke·'ret·tʃo] *m* trawler

motore, -trice[1] [mo·'to:·re] *agg* (*forza, albero*) driving; (*nervo*) motor

motore[2] *m* **1.** TEC engine; **a** ~ motor-powered; ~ **a benzina** gas engine; ~ **Diesel** diesel engine **2.** *fig* (*movente*) motivating force **3.** COMPUT ~ **di ricerca** search engine

motorino [mo·to·'ri:·no] *m* **1.** *inf* (*ciclomotore*) moped **2.** ~ **d'avviamento** AUTO starter

motorio, -a [mo·'tɔ:·rio] <-i, -ie> *agg* **1.** BIOL, ANAT motor **2.** (*sviluppo, disturbo*) motory; **attività -a** exercise

motoristico, -a [mo·to·'ris·ti·ko] <-ci, -che> *agg* (*sport, settore*) motor-sports

motorizzare [mo·to·rid·'dza:·re] **I.** *vt* **1.** (*esercito, truppe*) to motorize **2.** (*persona*) to give a car [*o* motorcycle] to **II.** *vr:* **-rsi** *inf* to get some wheels

motorizzato [mo·to·rid·'dza:·to] *agg* **1.** (*reparto, truppa*) motorized **2.** (*persona*) with own car/motorcycle; **sei ~ o ti serve un passaggio?** have you got wheels or do you need a ride? **3.** (*imbarcazione, veicolo*) motor

motorizzazione [mo·to·rid·dzat·'tsio:·ne] *f inf* ADM Department of Motor Vehicles

motoscafo [mo·tos·'ka:·fo] *m* motorboat

motosega [mo·to·'se:·ga] <-ghe> *f* power saw

motovedetta [mo·to·ve·'det·ta] *f* (*guardacoste*) patrol boat

motoveicolo [mo·to·ve·'i:·ko·lo] *m* motor vehicle

motrice [mo·'tri:·tʃe] *f* (*di tram, treno*) engine

motto [mɔt·to] *m* **1.** (*massima*) motto; ~ **popolare** popular saying **2.** (*battuta*) witticism; ~ **di spirito** witty remark

mou [mu] <inv> *agg* **caramella** ~ *soft milk-flavored candy*

mouse [maus] <-> *m* COMPUT mouse

mousse [mus] <-> *f* CULIN mousse

movente [mo·'vɛn·te] *m* (*di delitto*) motive

movenza [mo·'vɛn·tsa] *f* (*movimento*) movement

movimentare [mo·vi·men·'ta:·re] *vt* (*festa, serata, lezione*) to liven up

movimentato, -a [mo·vi·men·'ta:·to] *agg* (*festa, serata, lezione*) lively; (*strada*) busy; (*discussione*) animated

movimento [mo·vi·'men·to] *m* **1.** (*del corpo*) movement; **fare** ~ to exercise **2.** (*spostamento*) movement; **essere in** ~ to be moving; **mettersi in** ~ to begin to move; ~ **di cassa** cash flow; ~ **di denaro** movement of money; ~ **di impiegati/funzionari** labor mobility; ~ **di truppe** troop movement **3.** (*animazione*) bustle; (*traffico*) traffic **4.** *fig* (*corrente, tendenza*) movement **5.** MUS (*velocità*) tempo; (*parte*) movement

moviola [mo·'viɔ:·la] *f* TV slow motion replay; **alla** ~ on the replay

Mozambico, -a [mo·tsam·'bi:·ko] *m, f* Mozambique

mozartiano [mo·dzar·'tia·no] *agg* MUS Mozart

mozione [mot·'tsio:·ne] *f* motion; ~ **di fiducia/sfiducia** POL motion of confidence/no-confidence

mozzafiato [mott·tsa·'fia:·to] <inv> *agg* **1.** (*corsa*) fast; (*salita*) steep **2.** *fig* breathtaking

mozzare [mot·'tsa:·re] *vt* **1.** (*testa*) to cut off; (*coda*) to dock **2.** (*fiato, respiro*) ~ **il fiato a qu** (*salita*) to make sb pant; (*puzza*) to take sb's breath away; **da** ~ **il fiato** *fig* breathtakingly

mozzarella [mott·tsa·'rɛl·la] *f* mozzarella; ~ **di bufala** *mozzarella made from buffalo's milk*

> **i** **Mozzarella** is a famous fresh Italian cheese made from buffalo milk in the northwest of the Campania region. A large amount of imitation mozzarella made from cow's milk is produced; but anyone who has tasted the real **mozzarella di bufala campana** can tell the difference between them.

mozzicone [mot·tsi·'ko:·ne] *m* (*di sigaretta*) butt; (*di candela*) end; (*di matita*) stub

mozzo, -a[1] ['mot·tso] *agg* **1.** (*testa, dito*) cut off; **coda -a** docked tail **2.** *fig* (*parola, voce*) choked

mozzo[2] *m* **1.** MAR deck hand **2.** (*di ruota, elica*) hub

mucca ['muk·ka] <-cche> *f* cow; ~ **pazza** *inf* mad cow, mad cow disease

mucchio ['muk·kio] <-cchi> *m* **1.** (*di carte, pietre, stracci*) heap **2.** (*grande quantità*) a lot

muco ['mu:·ko] <-chi> *m* (*nasale, intestinale*) mucus

mucosa [mu·'ko:·za] *f* ANAT mucous membrane

muffa ['muf·fa] *f* mold; **fare la** ~ to go moldy; *fig* to gather dust

muggire [mud·'dʒi:·re] <muggisco> *vi* **1.** (*bovino*) to moo **2.** *fig* (*mare, tuono, vento*) to roar

muggito [mud·'dʒi:·to] *m* **1.** (*di bovino*) moo **2.** *fig* (*di mare, tuono, vento*) roar

mughetto [mu·'get·to] *m* **1.** (*fiore*) lily of the valley **2.** MED thrush

mugnaio, -a [muɲ·'ɲa:·io] <-i, -ie> *m, f* miller; **sogliola alla -a** CULIN sole meunière

mugolare [mu·go·'la:·re] **I.** *vi* **1.** (*cane*) to whimper **2.** (*persona*) to groan **3.** *fig* (*vento*) to groan **II.** *vt* (*borbottare: parole, scuse*) to mutter

mugolio [mu·go·'li:·o] <-ii> *m* **1.** (*di cane*) whining **2.** (*di dolore, piacere*) groaning **3.** *fig* (*di vento*) groaning

mugugnare [mu·guɲ·'ɲa:·re] *vi inf* (*brontolare*) to grumble

mulattiera [mu·lat·'tiɛ:·ra] *f* muletrack

mulatto, -a [mu·'lat·to] **I.** *agg* mulatto **II.** *m, f* mulatto

mulinello [mu·li·'nɛl·lo] *m* **1.** (*vortice: di*

acqua, vento) eddy **2.** (*di canna da pesca*) reel
mulino [mu·'li:·no] *m* mill; ~ **ad acqua** water mill; ~ **a vento** windmill; **tirare** [*o* **portare**] **l'acqua al proprio** ~ *fig* to add grist to one's own mill; **combattere contro i -i a vento** *fig* to tilt at windmills
mulo ['mu:·lo] *m* (*animale*) mule; **testardo** [*o* **ostinato**] **come un** ~ as stubborn as a mule
multa ['mul·ta] *f* (*ammenda*) fine
multare [mul·'ta:·re] *vt* to fine
multicanale [mul·ti·ka·'na:·le] <inv> *agg* TEC, TEL multichannel
multicentrico, -a [mul·ti·'tʃɛn·tri·ko] <-ci, -che> *agg* multicentric
multicolore [mul·ti·ko·'lo:·re] *agg* multicolored
multiculturale [mul·ti·kul·tu·'ra:·le] *agg* (*società, città*) multicultural
multidisciplinare [mul·ti·diʃ·ʃi·pli·'na:·re] *agg* (*insegnamento, ricerca*) multidisciplinary
multietnico, -a [mul·ti·'ɛt·ni·ko] <-ci, -che> *agg* (*società, cultura*) multiethnic
multiforme [mul·ti·'for·me] <inv> *agg* **1.** (*vita, interessi*) varied **2.** (*ingegno, intelligenza*) lively
multifunzionale [mul·ti·fun·tsio·'na:·le] *agg* (*apparecchio, macchina, sistema*) multifunctional
multifunzione [mul·ti·funt·'tsio:·ne] <inv> *agg* (*dispositivo, stampante, tasto*) multifunctional
multilaterale [mul·ti·la·te·'ra:·le] <inv> *agg* ECON, POL (*accordo, negoziato, scambio*) multilateral
multilingue [mul·ti·'liŋ·gue] <inv *o* -i> *agg* (*gruppo, paese, documento*) multilingual
multimedia [mul·ti·'mɛ:·dia] <inv> *agg* multimedia
multimediale [mul·ti·mɛ·'dia:·le] *agg* multimedia; **enciclopedia** ~ multimedia encyclopedia
multimiliardario, -a [mul·ti·mi·liar·'da:·rio] <-i, -ie> I. *agg* (*persona, vincita*) multibillionaire II. *m, f* multibillionaire
multimilionario, -a [mul·ti·mi·lio·'na:·rio] <-i, -ie> I. *agg* (*persona, vincita*) multimillionaire II. *m, f* multimillionaire
multinazionale [mul·ti·nat·tsio·'na:·le] I. *agg* (*azienda, società, impresa*) multinational II. *f* multinational
multipartitico, -a [mul·ti·par·'ti:·ti·ko] <-ci, -che> *agg* POL multiparty; **sistema** ~ multiparty system
multipiano [mul·ti·'pia:·no] <inv> *agg* (*edificio, parcheggio, struttura*) multi-floored
multiplo ['mul·ti·plo] *m* MATH multiple; **il minimo comune** ~ the least common multiple
multiplo, -a *agg* **1.** MATH multiple **2.** (*di più parti*) multiple; **gravidanza -a** multiple pregnancy; **presa di corrente -a** multiple outlet; **vettura** [*o* **auto**] **-a** minivan; (*furgone*) large van

multiproprietà [mul·ti·pro·prie·'ta] <-> *f* **1.** JUR (*comproprietà*) time-sharing **2.** (*immobile*) time-share
multirazziale [mul·ti·rat·'tsia:·le] *agg* (*società, politica*) multiracial
multisala [mul·ti·'sa:·la] I. <inv> *agg* (*cinema*) multiplex II. <- *m*, -e *f*> *m o f* (*cinema*) multiplex
multisettoriale [mul·ti·set·to·'ria:·le] *agg* (*attività, studio, progetto*) cross-sector
multistrato [mul·ti·'stra:·to] <inv> *agg* TEC multilayered; **pannello** ~ multilayered panel
multiuso [mul·ti·'u:·zo] <inv> *agg* (*attrezzo, strumento*) multi-purpose
mummia ['mum·mia] <-ie> *f* **1.** (*cadavere*) mummy **2.** *fig* (*persona vecchia*) living corpse; (*persona taciturna, asociale*) sphinx; (*persona antiquata*) old fogey
mundial [mun·'dial] <-> *m* SPORT (*di calcio*) World Cup; (*di altri sport*) world championship
mungere ['mun·dʒe·re] <mungo, munsi, munto> *vt a. fig* to milk
mungitura [mun·dʒi·'tu:·ra] *f* (*atto*) milking; (*quantità di latte*) milk yield
municipale [mu·ni·tʃi·'pa:·le] *agg* (*comunale*) municipal; **palazzo** ~ city hall
municipio [mu·ni·'tʃi:·pio] <-i> *m* **1.** (*amministrazione*) city council **2.** (*edificio*) city hall; **sposarsi in** ~ to get married at city hall
munire [mu·'ni:·re] <munisco> I. *vt* (*dotare*) to equip; ~ **qu/qc di qc** to equip sb/sth with sth II. *vr* -**rsi di qc** (*dotarsi*) to equip oneself with sth; *fig* to muster; -**rsi contro qc** (*premunirsi*) to arm oneself against sth
munito, -a [mu·'ni:·to] *agg* (*dotato*) equipped; ~ **di qc** equipped with sth
munizioni [mu·nit·'tsio:·ni] *fpl* (*bombe, cartucce, proiettili*) munitions *pl*
munsi ['mun·si] *1. pers sing pass rem di* **mungere**
munto ['mun·to] *pp di* **mungere**
muoio ['muɔ:·io] *1. pers sing pr di* **morire**
muovere ['muɔ:·ve·re] <muovo, mossi, mosso> I. *vt avere* **1.** (*parte del corpo*) to move; **non** ~ **un dito** to not lift a finger; ~ **i primi passi** to take one's first steps; *fig* to start out **2.** (*azionare*) to drive **3.** (*spostare*) to move; (*vento*) to blow **4.** (*nella dama, negli scacchi*) to move **5.** *fig* (*attacco*) to launch; (*inganno, tranello*) to set; ~ **guerra a** [*o* contro] **qu** to wage war on sb; ~ **una causa contro qu** to take sb to court **6.** *fig* (*accusa*) to level; (*obiezione*) to raise; (*osservazione*) to make **7.** *fig* (*a riso, pianto, compassione*) to move **8.** *fig* (*stimolare, spingere*) to motivate **9.** *fig* (*distogliere, dissuadere*) to budge II. *vi* **1.** (*dirigersi*) to move **2.** *fig* (*provenire*) to come from III. *vr:* -**rsi 1.** (*mettersi in movimento: persona*) to move; (*cosa, meccanismo*) to move; (*veicolo*) to move off; (*essere in moto*) to be moving **2.** (*dirigersi*) to move **3.** (*allontanarsi*) to move **4.** *fig* (*desistere*) to

budge **5.** (*sbrigarsi*) to get a move on **6.** *fig* (*decidersi*) to make up one's mind **7.** *fig* (*intervenire*) to move **8.** *fig* (*a compassione, pietà*) to be moved

muraglia [mu·'raʎ·ʎa] <-glie> *f* (*muro di difesa*) defensive wall; ~ **cinese** Great Wall of China

muraglione [mu·raʎ·'ʎo:·ne] *m* (*autostradale, ferroviario*) embankment

murale [mu·'ra:·le] *agg* (*pittura, disegno, scritta*) mural; (*carta, giornale, manifesto*) wall

murales [mu·'ra·les] *mpl* (*dipinti*) murals *pl*

murare [mu·'ra:·re] I. *vt* **1.** (*porta, finestra*) to wall up **2.** (*presa, gancio*) to fix on a wall; (*cassaforte, libreria*) to fix in [*o on*] a wall; (*gioielli, argenteria*) to put in a wall **3.** *a. scherz* (*persona*) to wall up II. *vr:* **-rsi** (*rinchiudersi*) to wall oneself up

murario, -a [mu·'ra:·rio] <-i, -ie> *agg* **1.** (*opera, arte*) masonry **2. cinta -a** wall

muratore [mu·ra·'to:·re] *m* (*operaio*) bricklayer

muratura [mu·ra·'tu:·ra] *f* **1.** (*lavoro*) walling; **in ~** (*di pietra*) built of stone; (*di mattoni*) built of brick **2.** (*muro*) wall

murena [mu·'rɛ:·na] *f* moray eel

muretto [mu·'ret·to] *m* (*muro basso*) small wall

muriatico, -a [mu·'ria:·ti·ko] <-ci, -che> *agg* CHEM **acido ~** muriatic acid

muro¹ ['mu:·ro] <-a *f*> *m a. fig* (*di città*) wall; **entro/fuori le mura** within/outside the walls; **chiudersi fra quattro -a** *fig* to shut oneself up in the house

muro² *m* **1.** (*di edificio*) wall; **~ divisorio** dividing wall; **~ maestro** main wall; **~ portante** bearing wall; **a ~** wall; **~ di Berlino** Berlin Wall; **~ del pianto** Western Wall; **essere scritto anche sui -i** *fig* to be common knowledge; **mettere qu con le spalle al ~** *fig* to put sb with their back to the wall; **parlare al ~** *fig* to talk to the wall; **sbattere la testa contro il ~** *fig* to bang one's head against a (brick) wall **2.** (*di nebbia, acqua*) wall **3.** *fig* (*di indifferenza, omertà, silenzio*) wall; **~ di gomma** wall of indifference

musa ['mu:·za] *f* **1.** (*dea*) Muse **2.** *fig* (*fonte d'ispirazione*) muse

muschiato, -a [mus·'kia:·to] *agg* (*odore*) musky

muschio ['mus·kio] <-schi> *m* **1.** (*pianta*) moss **2.** (*essenza*) musk

musco ['mus·ko] *m* BOT *v.* **muschio**

muscolare [mus·ko·'la:·re] *agg* (*fibra, forza, dolore*) muscular

muscolatura [mus·ko·la·'tu:·ra] *f* musculature

muscolo ['mus·ko·lo] *m* **1.** ANAT muscle **2.** *pl fig* (*forza fisica*) muscles; **essere tutto -i** to be all muscles; *pej* to be all brawn and no brain **3.** (*carne*) stew meat

muscoloso, -a [mus·ko·'lo:·so] *agg* (*uomo,*

braccia) muscular

museo [mu·'zɛ:·o] *m* museum; **da ~** rare; *fig, pej* oldfangled

museruola [mu·ze·'ruɔ:·la] *f* (*per cani*) muzzle; **mettere la ~ a qu** *fig* to muzzle sb

musica ['mu:·zi·ka] <-che> *f* **1.** (*arte, esecuzione, notazione*) music; **leggere la ~** to read music **2.** *fig* (*suono gradevole*) music **3.** *fig, iron* (*suono fastidioso*) din **4.** *fig, iron* (*litigio, scenata*) brawl **5.** *fig, inf* (*solfa, storia*) story; **è sempre la stessa ~!** it's always the same old story!; **è ora di cambiar ~!** it's time to change the record!

musicale [mu·zi·'ka:·le] *agg* musical; (**non**) **avere orecchio ~** to (not) have an ear for music

musicalità [mu·zi·ka·li·'ta] <-> *f* (*di melodia, verso, lingua*) musicality

musicare [mu·zi·'ka:·re] *vt* (*poesia, testo*) to set to music

musicassetta [mu·zi·kas·'set·ta] *f* music tape

music hall ['mju:·zik hɔːl] <-> *m* (*teatro di varietà*) vaudeville theater; (*spettacolo musicale*) vaudeville

musichetta [mu·zi·'ket·ta] *f* **1.** (*brano breve, leggero*) short piece of music **2.** *pej* (*di poco valore*) poor piece of music

musicista [mu·zi·'tʃis·ta] <-i *m*, -e *f*> *mf* **1.** (*compositore*) composer **2.** (*esecutore*) musician

musicologia [mu·zi·ko·lo·'dʒi:·a] *f* (*disciplina*) musicology

musicologo, -ga [mu·zi·'ko·lo·go] <-gi, -ghe> *m, f* (*studioso*) musicologist

musicoterapia [mu·zi·ko·te·ra·'pi:·a] *f* MED, PSYCH music therapy

muso ['mu:·zo] *m* **1.** (*di animale*) muzzle **2.** *pej, scherz* (*faccia*) face; **a ~ duro** *fig* resolutely; **rompere** [*o* **spaccare**] **il ~ a qu** *inf* to smash sb's face in **3.** (*broncio*) sulky expression; **avere** [*o* **fare**] [*o* **tenere**] **il ~ (lungo)** *inf* to sulk

musone, -a [mu·'zo:·ne] *m, f fig* (*scontroso*) sulky person

mussola ['mus·so·la] *f* muslin

mussoliniano [mus·so·li·'nia:·no] *agg* HIST, POL (*regime, totalitarismo*) of Mussolini

must [mast] <-> *m* (*in pubblicità*) must

musulmano, mussulmano, -a [mu·sul·'ma:·no] I. *agg* (*civiltà, cultura*) Muslim II. *m, f* (*persona*) Muslim

muta ['mu:·ta] *f* **1.** ZOO (*di uccelli*) molting; (*di rettili*) shedding **2.** SPORT (*tuta*) wetsuit **3.** (*di cani*) pack

mutamento [mu·ta·'men·to] *m* change

mutande [mu·'tan·de] *fpl* (*da uomo*) underpants; (*da donna*) panties; **in ~** *fig, inf* penniless

mutandine [mu·tan·'di:·ne] *fpl* (*da donna*) panties; (*da bambino*) pants

mutandoni [mu·tan·'do:·ni] *mpl* (*lunghi*) long johns

mutante [mu·'tan·te] *m a. fig* BIOL (*gene,*

individuo) mutant

mutare [mu·'ta:·re] I. *vt avere* (*idea, aspetto, città, abito*) to change; (*pelle, penne, squame*) to shed II. *vi essere* (*diventare diverso*) to change

mutazione [mu·tat·'tsio:·ne] *f* 1.(*di clima*) change 2.BIOL mutation

mutevole [mu·'te:·vo·le] *agg* 1.(*tempo, situazione*) changeable 2.(*umore, carattere*) moody

mutilare [mu·ti·'la:·re] *vt* 1.(*corpo, arto*) to amputate 2.*fig* (*opera*) to mutilate

mutilato, -a [mu·ti·'la:·to] I. *agg* (*persona*) maimed II. *m, f* (*invalido*) disabled person

mutilazione [mu·ti·lat·'tsio:·ne] *f* 1.(*di corpo, arto*) amputation 2.*fig* (*di opera, insieme organico*) mutilation

mutismo [mu·'tiz·mo] *m* 1.MED mutism 2.(*silenzio*) silence

muto[1] ['mu:·to] *m <sing>* (*cinema*) silent cinema

muto, -a[2] I. *agg* 1.MED dumb 2.(*silenzioso*) silent; (*ammutolito*) dumbstruck; **essere ~ come un pesce** *scherz* to be as silent as the grave 3.(*senza suono, senza voce*) silent; **cinema ~** silent cinema; **consonante -a** LING silent consonant; **fare scena -a** *fig* to not utter a word II. *m, f* (*persona*) dumb person

mutua ['mu:·tua] *f inf* (*ente*) Italian National Health Service; **essere/mettersi in ~** to be/go on certified sick leave

mutuabile [mu·'tua:·bi·le] *agg* (*farmaco, analisi*) available on the Italian National Health Service

mutualistico, -a [mu·tua·'lis·ti·ko] <-ci, -che> *agg* ADM (*ente, organizzazione*) Health Service

mutuare [mu·'tua:·re] *vt* 1.*fig* (*adottare, prendere*) to adopt 2.(*insegnamento, materia*) to provide

mutuato, -a [mu·tu·'a:·to] *m, f* (*assistito*) National Health Service patient

mutuo[1] ['mu:·tuo] *agg* (*reciproco*) mutual

mutuo[2] *m* JUR. ECON (*prestito*) loan; **~ ipotecario** mortgage

N

N, n ['ɛn·ne] <-> *f* N, n; **~ come Napoli** N for November

n *abbr di* **numero** no.

N *abbr di* **nord** N

nacchere ['nak·kere] *fpl* castanets *pl*

nacqui ['nak·kui] *I. pers sing pass rem di* **nascere**

nafta ['naf·ta] *f* 1.CHEM naphtha 2.(*olio combustibile*) oil

naftalina [naf·ta·'li:·na] *f* naphthalene; **met-**

tere qc sotto ~ *a. fig* to put sth into mothballs

naïf [na·'if] <inv> *agg* naive

nailon ['na:i·lon] *m v.* **nylon**

nanismo [na·'niz·mo] *m* dwarfism

nanna ['nan·na] *f* (*linguaggio infantile*) night-night; **andare a ~** to go to night-night; **fare la ~** to go to sleep

nano, -a ['na:·no] I. *agg* (*razza, pianta*) dwarf II. 1.(*di favole*) dwarf 2.(*persona bassa*) dwarf; *pej* midget

napoletana [na·po·le·'ta:·na] *f* (*caffettiera*) stovetop espresso maker

napoletano [na·po·le·'ta:·no] *m* (*dialetto*) Neapolitan

Napoletano *m* (*zona*) the Naples area; **nel ~** in the Naples area

napoletano, -a I. *m, f* (*abitante*) Neapolitan II. *agg* Neapolitan; **canzone -a** Neapolitan song; **pizza alla -a** pizza with tomato, mozzarella, oregano and anchovies

Napoli ['na:·po·li] *f* Naples

nappa ['nap·pa] *f* 1.(*ornamento*) tassel 2.(*pelle*) Nappa leather

narcisismo [nar·tʃi·'ziz·mo] *m* narcissism

narcisista [nar·tʃi·'zis·ta] <-i *m*, -e *f*> *mf* narcissist

narciso [nar·'tʃi:·zo] *m* 1.BOT daffodil 2.*fig* **è un narcisista** he's extremely vain

narciso, -a *agg* vain

narco ['nar·ko] <narcos> *m* drug dealer

narcosi [nar·'kɔ:·zi] <-> *f* narcosis

narcotest [nar·ko·'tɛst] <-> *m* MED drug test

narcotico [nar·'kɔ:·ti·ko] <-ci> *m* narcotic

narcotico, -a <-ci, -che> *agg* narcotic

narcotizzare [nar·ko·tid·'dza:·re] *vt* to narcotize

narcotrafficante [nar·ko·traf·fi·'kan·te] *mf* drug trafficker

narcotraffico [nar·ko·'traf·fi·ko] <-ci> *m* drug trafficking

narice [na·'ri:·tʃe] *f* nostril

narrare [nar·'ra:·re] I. *vt* (*storia, leggenda*) to tell; (*libro, film*) to narrate II. *vi* **~ di qu/qc** to tell of sb/sth

narrativa [nar·ra·'ti:·va] *f* LIT narrative

narrativo, -a [nar·ra·'ti:·vo] *agg* narrative

narratore, -trice [nar·ra·'to:·re] *m, f* narrator

narrazione [nar·ra·'tsio:·ne] *f* 1.(*di fatto, viaggio*) account 2.(*in libro, film*) narration

NAS *acro di* **Nucleo Antisofisticazioni Sanità** (**dei Carabinieri**) *health investigation department of the Carabinieri*

NASA ['na:·za] *f* NASA

nasale [na·'sa:·le] I. *agg* ANAT, LING nasal II. *f* LING nasal

nasata [na·'sa:·ta] *f* bang on the nose

nascente [naʃ·'ʃɛn·te] *agg* (*giorno*) breaking; (*astro, sole*) rising

nascere [naʃ·ʃe·re] <nasco, nacqui, nato> *vi essere* 1.(*persone, animali*) to be born; **non sono nato ieri** I wasn't born yesterday 2.(*pianta*) to come up; (*fiore*) to come out 3.(*fiumi*) to rise 4.(*sole*) to rise; (*giorno*) to break **5.** *fig* (*avere origine: tradizione, iniziativa*) to come from **6.** *fig* (*formarsi: associazione*) to be created **7.** *fig* (*amore*) to be born **8.** *fig* **far** ~ (*dubbio, sospetto*) to give rise to

nascita ['naʃ·ʃi·ta] *f* **1.** (*di bambino*) birth; **di** ~ by birth **2.** BOT appearance **3.** *fig* (*di sentimento*) beginning

nascituro, -a [naʃ·ʃi·'tu:·ro] I. *agg* unborn II. *m, f* unborn child

nascondere [nas·'kon·de·re] <nascondo, nascosi, nascosto> I. *vt* **1.** (*oggetto*) to hide **2.** (*sentimento, verità*) to conceal; ~ **qc a qu** to hide sth from sb II. *vr:* **-rsi** to hide

nascondiglio [nas·kon·'diʎ·ʎo] <-gli> *m* (*di persona, oggetto*) hiding place

nascondino [nas·kon·'di:·no] *m* **giocare a ~** to play hide-and-seek

nascosi [nas·'ko:·si] *1. pers sing pass rem di* **nascondere**

nascosto, -a [nas·'kos·to] I. *pp di* **nascondere** II. *agg* **1.** (*oggetto*) hidden; (*luogo*) secret; **rimanere** ~ to remain hidden **2.** *fig* **di** ~ (*sposarsi, vedersi*) in secret; (*uscire*) unseen; (*fumare, mangiare*) on the sly

nasello [na·'sɛl·lo] *m* hake

naso ['na:·so] *m* nose; ~ **all'insù** snub nose; **avere buon** ~ to have a good nose; **ficcare il** ~ **negli affari altrui** to stick one's nose into other people's business; **non vedere più in là del proprio** ~ to see no further than the end of one's nose

nastro ['nas·tro] *m* (*per capelli, abiti*) ribbon; ~ **adesivo** adhesive tape; ~ **biadesivo** double-sided tape; ~ **isolante** insulating tape; ~ **magnetico** magnetic tape; ~ **trasportatore** conveyor belt

natale [na·'ta:·le] *agg* native

Natale [na·'ta:·le] *m* Christmas

natalità [na·ta·li·'ta] <-> *f* birth rate

natalizio, -a [na·ta·'lit·tsio] <-i, -ie> *agg* (*atmosfera, festeggiamento, vacanze*) Christmas

natante [na·'tan·te] *m* craft

natica ['na:·ti·ka] <-che> *f* buttock

nativo, -a [na·'ti:·vo] I. *agg* **1.** (*paese*) home; (*lingua*) native; **essere** ~ **di Firenze/Parigi** to be from Florence/Paris **2.** MIN (*ferro*) native II. *m, f* native

N.A.T.O. ['na:·to] *f* NATO

nato, -a ['na:·to] I. *pp di* **nascere** II. *agg* born; **un attore** ~ *fig* a born actor

natura [na·'tu:·ra] *f* **1.** (*universo*) nature; ~ **morta** still life; **contro** ~ unnatural **2.** (*indole*) character

naturale [na·tu·'ra:·le] *agg* **1.** (*non artefatto*) natural; **a grandezza** ~ life-size; **scienze -i** natural sciences **2.** (*ovvio*) natural

naturalezza [na·tu·ra·'let·tsa] *f* naturalness; **con** ~ naturally

naturalismo [na·tu·ra·'liz·mo] *m* naturalism

naturalizzare [na·tu·ra·lid·'dza:·re] *vt* to naturalize

naturalmente [na·tu·ral·'men·te] *avv* **1.** (*sec-*ondo *natura*) naturally **2.** (*ovviamente*) of course

naturismo [na·tu·'riz·mo] *m* nudism

naufragare [nau·fra·'ga:·re] *vi* essere o avere *fig* (*progetto*) to fail

naufragio [nau·'fra:·dʒo] <-gi> *m* **1.** NAUT shipwreck **2.** *fig* (*progetto*) failure

naufrago, -a ['na:u·fra·go] <-ghi, -ghe> *m, f* shipwreck survivor

nausea ['na:u·ze·a] *f* **1.** MED nausea; **avere la** ~ to feel nauseous **2.** *fig* **mi dà la** ~ it makes me feel sick

nauseante [nau·ze·'an·te] *agg* nauseous

nauseare [nau·ze·'a:·re] *vt* to nauseate

nautica ['na:u·ti·ka] <-che> *f* (*attività*) sailing; **salone della** ~ boat show

nautico, -a ['na:u·ti·ko] <-ci, -che> *agg* (*di mare*) nautical; **sport -ci** water sports

navale [na·'va:·le] *agg* **1.** (*accademia*) naval **2.** (*cantiere, industria*) shipbuilding

navata [na·'va:·ta] *f* ~ **centrale** nave; ~ **laterale** aisle

nave ['na:·ve] *f* ship; ~ **a vapore** steamboat; ~ **a vela** sailing ship; ~ **da carico** cargo ship; ~ **da guerra** warship; ~ **cisterna** tanker; ~ **traghetto** ferry

navetta [na·'vet·ta] *f* **1.** (*di telaio*) shuttle **2.** (*treno, autobus*) shuttle; ~ **spaziale** space shuttle

navicella [na·vi·'tʃɛl·la] *f* (*di dirigibile*) gondola; (*di aerostato*) basket; ~ **spaziale** capsule

navigabile [na·vi·'ga:·bi·le] *agg* navigable

navigante [na·vi·'gan·te] *mf* seaman *m,* seawoman *f*

navigare [na·vi·'ga:·re] *vi* **1.** NAUT to sail; ~ **in cattive acque** *fig* to be in trouble **2.** COMPUT to surf the Internet; ~ **in Internet/in Rete** to surf the Internet/the Net

navigato, -a [na·vi·'ga:·to] *agg* **1.** (*percorso da navi*) navigated; **molto** ~ very busy **2.** *fig* (*persona*) experienced

navigatore, -trice [na·vi·ga·'to:·re] *m, f* (*marinaio*) sailor

navigatore [na·vi·ga·'to:·re] *m* TEC ~ (**satellitare**) GPS navigator

navigazione [na·vi·ga·'tsio:·ne] *f* NAUT, AERO navigation

naviglio [na·'viʎ·ʎo] <-gli> *m* vessel

nazionale [nat·tsio·'na:·le] I. *agg* (*di nazione*) national; (*mercato*) domestic II. *f* (national) team; **la** ~ **italiana** the Italian soccer team

nazionalismo [nat·tsio·na·'liz·mo] *m* nationalism

nazionalista [nat·tsio·na·'lis·ta] <-i *m,* -e *f*> *mf* nationalist

nazionalistico, -a [nat·tsio·na·'lis·ti·ko] <-ci, -che> *agg* nationalistic

nazionalità [nat·tsio·na·li·'ta] <-> *f* nationality

nazionalizzare [nat·tsio·na·lid·'dza:·re] *vt* to nationalize

nazionalizzazione [na·tsio·na·lid·dza·'tsio:·ne] *f* nationalization

nazionalsocialismo [na·tsio·nal·so·tʃa·'liz·mo] *m* National Socialism

nazionalsocialista [na·tsio·nal·so·tʃa·'lis·ta] <-i *m*, -e *f*> I. *agg* Nazi II. *mf* Nazi

nazione [na·'tsio:·ne] *f* nation; **le Nazioni Unite** the United Nations

naziskin ['na:·tsi·skin] <-> *mf* (neonazi) skinhead

nazismo [na·'tsiz·mo] *m* Nazism

nazista [na·'tsis·ta] I. *agg* Nazi II. *mf* Nazi

N.B., n.b. *abbr di* **nota bene** NB

N.d.A. *abbr di* **nota dell'autore** author's note

'ndrangheta [n·'draŋ·ge·ta] *f Calabrian Mafia*

ne [ne] I. *pron* 1. (*persona: di lui*) about him; (*di lei*) about her; (*di loro*) about them 2. (*di ciò*) about it; **~ parlano molto** they talk about it a lot; **non ~ vedo proprio la ragione** I can't see the point of it; **non ~ ho proprio idea** I haven't got a clue; **non me ~ importa** (**niente**) I don't care (at all) 3. (*da ciò*) from it 4. (*con valore partitivo: di questo*) of it; (*di questi*) of them; **me ~ daresti un po'?** could you give me some of it?; **~ ho già mangiati tantissimi** I've already eaten lots of them; **quanti anni hai?** — **~ ho 29** how old are you? — I'm 29; **hai dei giornali?** — **sì, ~ ho** do you have any newspapers? — yes, I do II. *avv* 1. (*da un luogo*) from there; (*da una situazione*) from it; **andarsene** to go away; **non te ~ andare** don't go away 2. (*rafforzativo*) **me ~ sto qui** I'm just sitting here; **vorrei solo rimanermene a casa** I'd just like to stay at home

né [ne] *cong* neither; **~ ... ~ ...** neither ... nor ...; **non è ~ nuovo ~ vecchio** it's neither old nor new; **~ più ~ meno** no more, no less

NE *abbr di* **nordest** NE

neanche [ne·'aŋ·ke] *avv v.* **nemmeno**

nebbia ['neb·bia] <-ie> *f* 1. METEO fog 2. *fig* (*nebulosità*) mist

nebbiolo [neb·'biɔ:·lo] *m* nebbiolo, *type of red wine from Piedmont*

nebbiosità [neb·bio·si:·'ta] <-> *f* 1. METEO fogginess; (*foschia*) mistiness 2. *fig* (*di idee, ricordo, progetto*) vagueness

nebbioso, -a [neb·'bio:·so] *agg* METEO foggy; (*coperto da foschia*) misty

nebulizzare [ne·bu·lid·'dza:·re] *vt* to atomize

nebulizzatore [ne·bu·lid·dza·'to:·re] *m* atomizer

nebulizzazione [ne·bu·lid·dza·'tsio:·ne] *f* atomization

nebulosità [ne·bu·lo·si:·'ta] <-> *f fig* (*di idee, ricordo, progetto*) vagueness

nebuloso, -a [ne·bu·'lo:·so] *agg fig* (*non chiaro: frase, immagine, ricordo*) vague

nécessaire [ne·sɛ·'ser] <-> *m* sponge bag; **~ per le unghie** manicure set

necessariamente [ne·tʃes·sa·ria·'men·te] *avv* necessarily

necessario [ne·tʃes·'sa:·rio] *m* **portati il ~ per cambiarti** bring what you need to get changed; **lo stretto ~** the bare essentials;

guadagna lo stretto ~ per vivere she earns just enough to live on

necessario, -a <-i, -ie> *agg* necessary

necessità [ne·tʃes·si·'ta] <-> *f* need; (*povertà*) poverty; **avere ~ di qc** to need sth; **in caso di ~** if need be; **per ~** out of necessity

necessitare [ne·tʃes·si·'ta:·re] I. *vt* to need; **questa questione necessita tutta la nostra attenzione** this issue demands our full attention II. *vi* 1. (*avere bisogno*) **~ di qc** to need sth 2. (*impersonale*) to require

necessitato, -a [ne·tʃes·si·'ta:·to] *agg* obliged

necrofilia [ne·kro·fi·'li:·a] <-ie> *f* necrophilia

necrofilo, -a [ne·'krɔ:·fi·lo] I. *agg* necrophiliac II. necrophiliac

necroforo [ne·'krɔ:·fo·ro] *m* gravedigger

necrologio [ne·kro·'lɔ:·dʒo] <-gi> *m* (*annuncio*) obituary

necropoli [ne·'krɔ:·po·li] <-> *f* necropolis

nefasto, -a [ne·'fas·to] *agg* fateful

negare [ne·ga:·re] *vt* 1. (*contestare*) to deny 2. (*rifiutare*) to deny

negatività [ne·ga·ti·vi·'ta] <-> *f* negativity

negativo [ne·ga·'ti:·vo] *m* FOTO negative

negativo, -a *agg* negative

negato, -a [ne·'ga:·to] *agg fig* (*non portato*) **essere ~ per qc** to be hopeless at sth

negazione [ne·gat·'tsio:·ne] *f* 1. (*rifiuto*) denial 2. (*contrario*) opposite 3. LING negation

negletto, -a [neg·'lɛt·to] *agg lit* neglected

negli ['neʎ·ʎi] *prep v.* **in + gli** *v.* in[1]

négligé [ne·gli·'ʒe] <-> *m* negligee

negligente [ne·gli·'dʒen·te] I. *agg* negligent II. *mf* negligent person

negligenza [ne·gli·'dʒen·tsa] *f* negligence

negoziabile [ne·go·'tsia·bi·le] *agg* COM (*accordo, compenso, prezzo*) negotiable

negoziante [ne·go·'tsian·te] *mf* storekeeper

negoziare [ne·go·'tsia:·re] *vt* 1. (*contratto, pace*) to negotiate 2. FIN (*titoli, cambiali*) to negotiate

negoziato [ne·go·'tsia:·to] *m* negotiation; **-i di pace** peace negotiations

negoziatore, -trice [ne·go·tsia·'to:·re] *m*, *f* negotiator

negoziazione [ne·go·tsia·'tsio:·ne] *f* 1. (*trattativa*) negotiation 2. FIN (*di titoli, cambiali*) negotiation

negozio [ne·'gɔ·tsio] <-i> *m* store

negro, -a ['ne:·gro] I. *agg* negro II. *m*, *f* negro

negromante [ne·gro·'man·te] *mf* necromancer

nel, nell', nella, nelle, nello, nei [nel, 'nel·la, 'nel·le, 'nel·lo, 'ne:·i] *prep v.* **in + il, l', la, le, lo, i** *v.* in[1]

nembo ['nem·bo] *m* METEO nimbus

nemico, -a [ne·'mi:·ko] <-ci, -che> I. *agg* 1. (*attacco, esercito*) enemy; **essere ~ di qu** to be sb's enemy; **farsi ~ qu** to make an enemy of sb 2. (*atteggiamento, parole*) hostile; **essere ~ di qu/qc** to be opposed to sb/sth II. *m*, *f* enemy; **~ mortale** sworn enemy

nemmeno [nem·'me:·no] *avv* 1. (*neppure*)

neither; ~ **io** me neither **2.**(*rafforzativo*) not even; ~ **una settimana dopo** not even a week later; ~ **uno** not even one; ~ **per idea** [*o* **per sogno**]! no chance!

nenia ['nɛːˑnia] <-ie> *f* **1.**(*canzone monotona*) dirge **2.**(*discorso noioso*) spiel

neo ['nɛːˑo] *m* **1.**ANAT mole **2.***fig* (*piccolo difetto*) flaw

neoassunto, -a [ne·o·asˑ'sunˑto] **I.** *agg* newly-appointed **II.** *m*, *f* recent appointment

neoclassicismo [ne·o·klasˑsiˑ'tʃizˑmo] *m* neo-classicism

neocomunista [ne·o·ko·muˑ'nisˑta] *mf* neo-communist

neodiplomato, -a [ne·o·di·plo·'maːˑto] *m*, *f* newly-qualified person

neofascismo [ne·o·faʃˑ'ʃizˑmo] *m* neo-fascism

neofascista [ne·o·faʃˑ'ʃisˑta] <-i *m*, -e *f*> **I.** *agg* neo-fascist **II.** *mf* neo-fascist

neolaureato, -a [ne·o·lau·re·'aːˑto] *m*, *f* recent graduate

neologismo [ne·o·lo·'dʒizˑmo] *m* neologism

neomarxista [ne·o·markˑ'sisˑta] <-i *m*, -e *f*> **I.** *mf* POL neo-Marxist **II.** *agg* neo-Marxist

neon ['nɛːˑon] <-> *m* neon

neonato, -a [ne·o·'naːˑto] **I.** *agg* **1.**(*bambino*) newborn **2.***fig, scherz* brand new **II.** *m*, *f* newborn infant

neonazismo [ne·o·naˑ'tsizˑmo] *m* neo-Nazism

neonazista [ne·o·naˑ'tsisˑta] <-i *m*, -e *f*> **I.** *agg* neo-Nazi **II.** *mf* neo-Nazi

neopatentato, -a [ne·o·pa·tenˑ'taːˑto] *m*, *f* newly-qualified driver

neoplatonico, -a [ne·o·pla·'tɔːˑni·ko] *agg* neo-Platonic

neopositivismo [ne·o·po·zi·ti·'vizˑmo] *m* neopositivism

neorealismo [ne·o·re·aˑ'lizˑmo] *m* neo-realism

neozelandese [ne·oˑˑdze·lanˑ'deːˑse] **I.** *agg* New Zealand **II.** *m* New Zealander

nepotismo [ne·po·'tizˑmo] *m* nepotism

neppure [nepˑ'puːˑre] *avv v.* **nemmeno**

nerastro, -a [ne·'rasˑtro] *agg* blackish

nerazzurri [ne·radˑ'dzurˑri] *mpl Inter Milan* soccer team

nerazzurro, -a *agg* **giocatore/tifoso** ~ Inter Milan player/fan

nerbo ['nɛrˑbo] *m* **1.**(*staffile*) whip **2.***fig* vigor; (*forza*) strength

nerboruto, -a [ner·bo·'ruːˑto] *agg scherz* brawny

neretto [ne·'retˑto] *m* TYP bold; **in** ~ in bold

nero ['nɛːˑro] *m* black; ~ **di seppia** cuttlefish ink; ~ **su bianco** in writing

nero, -a *agg a. fig* (*colore*) black; **cronaca -a** crime news; **vedere tutto** ~ to look on the down side of everything

nerofumo, nero fumo [ne·ro·'fuːˑmo] *m* lampblack

nervatura [ner·va·'tuːˑra] *f* **1.**BOT nervation **2.**(*elemento di sostegno*) rib

nervo ['nɛrˑvo] *m* **1.**ANAT nerve; **avere i -i a fior di pelle** *fig* to be on edge; **avere i -i a pezzi** *fig* to be a nervous wreck; **far venire i -i a qu** *fig* to get on sb's nerves **2.** BOT vein **3.** *inf* (*tendine*) tendon **4.***fig* spirit

nervosismo [ner·vo·'sizˑmo] *m* nervousness

nervosità [ner·vo·si·'ta] <-> *f* **1.**(*nervosismo*) nervousness **2.***fig* (*incisività*) incisiveness

nervoso [ner·'voːˑso] *m inf* irritability; **mi viene il** ~ I get annoyed; **far venire il** ~ **a qu** to annoy sb

nervoso, -a *agg* **1.**ANAT nervous **2.**(*irritabile*) on edge

nespola ['nɛsˑpo·la] *f* **1.**BOT medlar **2.***fig, inf* blow

nespole ['nɛsˑpo·le] *int* wow

nespolo ['nɛsˑpo·lo] *m* medlar tree

nesso ['nɛsˑso] *m* link

nessuno [nesˑ'suːˑno] *m* nobody

nessuno, -a I. *agg* no; (*con negazione*) any; **in nessun caso** under no circumstances; **in nessun luogo** nowhere; **non ho -a voglia di farlo/di andarci** I don't feel at all like doing it/going there **II.** *pron* **1.**(*non uno*) nobody; **non ho visto** ~ I didn't see anybody **2.**(*qualcuno*) anybody

netiquette <-> *m* COMPUT netiquette

nettare ['nɛtˑta·re] *m* nectar

nettezza [netˑ'tetˑtsa] *f* (*pulizia*) cleanliness; ~ **urbana** street cleaning and garbage collection

netto, -a ['netˑto] *agg* **1.**(*risposta, rifiuto*) straight; **tagliare qc di** ~ to cut sth (clean) off **2.**COM net; **stipendio** ~ net salary; **al** ~ net

netturbino [net·tur·'biːˑno] *m* garbage man

network ['netˑwəːk] <- *o* networks> *m* RADIO, TV network

neuro ['nɛuˑro] *f inf* MED (*clinica neurologica*) insane asylum

neurobiologia [neu·ro·bi·o·lo·'dʒiːˑa] *f* neurobiology

neurobiologico, -a [neu·ro·bi·o·'lɔːˑdʒi·ko] <-ci, -che> *agg* neurobiological

neurobiologo, -a [neu·ro·'biɔːˑlo·go] <-gi, -ghe> *m*, *f* neurobiologist

neurochimica [neu·ro·'kiːˑmi·ka] *f* neurochemistry

neurochirurgia [neu·ro·ki·rur·'dʒiːˑa] *f* neurosurgery

neurofarmacologia [neu·ro·far·ma·ko·lo·'dʒiːˑa] *f* MED neuropharmacology

neurofisiologia [neu·ro·fi·zio·lo·'dʒiːˑa] *f* MED neurophysiology

neurofisiologo, -a [neu·ro·fi·'ziɔːˑlo·go] <-gi, -ghe> *m*, *f* MED neurophysiologist

neurologia [neu·ro·lo·'dʒiːˑa] *f* neurology

neurologico, -a [neu·ro·'lɔːˑdʒi·ko] <-ci, -che> *agg* neurological

neurologo, -a [neu·'rɔːˑlo·go] <-gi, -ghe> *m*, *f* neurologist

neuropatologia [neu·ro·pa·to·lo·'dʒiːˑa] *f* neuropathology

neuropatologo, -a [neu·ro·pa·'tɔːˑlo·go]

<-gi, -ghe> *m*, *f* neuropathologist

neuropsicologia [neu·ro·psi·ko·lo·'dʒi:·a] *f* PSYCH, MED neuropsychology

neuroscienze [neu·roʃ·'ʃɛn·tse] *fpl* neuroscience

neurovegetativo, -a [neu·ro·ve·dʒe·ta·'ti:·vo] *agg* autonomic; **sistema** ~ autonomic system

neutrale [neu·'tra:·le] I. *agg* neutral II. *mf* neutral

neutralità [neu·tra·li·'ta] <-> *f* neutrality

neutralizzare [neu·tra·lid·'dza:·re] *vt* 1. CHEM to neutralize 2. (*rendere inoffensivo*) to neutralize 3. (*rendere inutile*) to cancel out

neutralizzazione [neu·tra·lid·dzat·'tsio:·ne] *f* a. *fig* neutralization

neutro ['nɛu·tro] *m* 1. EL neutral 2. LING neuter

neutro, -a *agg* 1. (*non definibile: atteggiamento, stile, tinta*) neutral 2. CHEM, EL, POL neutral 3. LING neuter

neutrone [neu·'tro:·ne] *m* PHYS neutron

nevaio [ne·'va:·io] <-ai> *m* snowfield

neve ['ne:·ve] *f* 1. METEO snow; ~ **fresca** fresh snow; **fiocco di** ~ snowflake; **palla di** ~ snowball; **bianco come la** ~ as white as snow 2. *sl* (*cocaina*) coke

nevicare [ne·vi·'ka:·re] *vi essere o avere* to snow

nevicata [ne·vi·'ka:·ta] *f* snowfall

nevischio [ne·'vis·kio] <-schi> *m* sleet

nevosità [ne·vo·si·'ta] <-> *f* snowfall

nevoso, -a [ne·'vo:·so] *agg* snowy

nevralgia [ne·vral·'dʒi:·a] <-gie> *f* neuralgia

nevralgico, -a [nev·'ral·dʒi·ko] <-ci, -che> *agg* neuralgic; **punto** ~ *fig* key point

nevrastenia [nev·ra·ste·'ni:·a] <-ie> *f* neurasthenia

nevrastenico [nev·ras·'tɛ:·ni·ko] *m* MED neurasthenic; *fig* nervous wreck

nevrastenico, -a <-ci, -che> *agg* MED neurasthenic; **essere** ~ *fig* to be a nervous wreck

nevrite [ne·'vri:·te] *f* neuritis

nevrosi [ne·'vrɔ:·zi] <-> *f* neurosis

nevrotico, -a [nev·'rɔ:·ti·ko] <-ci, -che> I. *agg* neurotic II. neurotic

nevrotizzare [nev·ro·tid·'dza:·re] *vt* ~ **qu** to drive sb mad

news [nju:z] *fpl* TV news *sing*

newsgroup <-> *m* COMPUT newsgroup

nicchia ['nik·kia] <-cchie> *f* ARCH niche; (*nella roccia*) recess

nichel ['ni:·kel] *m* nickel

nichelare [ni·ke·'la:·re] *vt* to nickel-plate

nichelatura [ni·ke·la·'tu:·ra] *f* nickel-plating

nichilismo [ni·ki·'liz·mo] *m* nihilism

nichilista [ni·ki·'lis·ta] <-i *m*, -e *f*> I. *agg* nihilistic II. *mf* nihilist

nicotina [ni·ko·'ti:·na] *f* nicotine; **senza** ~ nicotine-free

nidiata [ni·'dia:·ta] *f* 1. (*di uccelli*) nestful; (*di topi, conigli*) litter 2. *fig, scherz* brood

nidificare [ni·di·fi·'ka:·re] *vi* to nest

nido ['ni:·do] I. *m* 1. ZOO nest; **a** ~ **d'ape** *fig* honeycomb 2. *fig* (*casa*) **abbandonare il** ~ to leave the nest II. *agg* **asilo** ~ nursery

niente ['niɛn·te] I. *pron* 1. (*nessuna cosa*) nothing; **non fa** ~ it doesn't matter; ~ **di** ~ nothing at all; **per** ~ (*assolutamente non*) not at all; **di** ~ you're welcome 2. (*interrogativo*) anything; **ti serve** ~? do you need anything? 3. (*poca cosa*) nothing; **è una cosa da** ~ it was nothing II. *m* 1. (*nessuna cosa*) nothing; **un bel** ~ nothing at all 2. (*poca cosa*) anything III. *avv* **non è** ~ **male** it's not at all bad; ~ **affatto** not at all; **nient'altro** nothing else IV. *agg fam* no; ~ **paura!** never fear!

nientedimeno, nientemeno [nien·te·di·'me:·no, nien·te·'me:·no] I. *avv* no less II. *int* you don't say!

nietzschiano, -a [nit·'tʃa:·no] I. *agg* Nietzschean II. *m*, *f* Nietzschean

nightclub ['nait·klʌb/'nait·kleb] *m* nightclub

Nilo ['ni:·lo] *m* Nile

ninfa ['nin·fa] *f* (*in mitologia*) nymph

ninfea [nin·'fɛ:a] *f* water lily

ninfomane [nin·'fɔ:·ma·ne] I. *agg* nymphomaniac II. *f* nymphomaniac

ninfomania [nin·fo·ma·'ni:·a] *f* nymphomania

ninnananna [nin·na·'nan·na] <ninnenanne> *f* lullaby

ninnare [nin·'na:·re] *vt* to sing to sleep

ninnolo ['nin·no·lo] *m* 1. (*giocattolo*) (baby's) toy 2. (*soprammobile*) knick-knack

nipote [ni·'po:·te] *mf* 1. (*di zio*) nephew *m*, niece *f* 2. (*di nonno*) grandson *m*, granddaughter *f* 3. (*discendenti*) descendants *pl*

nippomania [nip·po·ma·'ni:·a] *f love of Japan and Japanese culture*

nipponico, -a [nip·'pɔ:·ni·ko] <-ci, -che> I. *agg* Japanese II. *m*, *f* Japanese

nirvana [nir·'va:·na] *m* nirvana

nisseno, -a [nis·'se:·no] I. *m*, *f* (*abitante*) *person from Caltanissetta* II. *agg from Caltanissetta*

nitidezza [ni·ti·'det·tsa] *f* 1. (*chiarezza*) clarity 2. (*di immagine, contorno*) clarity

nitido, -a ['ni:·ti·do] *agg* 1. (*chiaro*) clear 2. (*immagine, contorno*) clear

nitrato [ni·'tra:·to] *m* nitrate

nitrico, -a ['ni:·tri·ko] <-ci, -che> *agg* nitric

nitrire [ni·'tri:·re] <nitrisco> *vi* to neigh

nitrito [ni·'tri:·to] *m* 1. (*di cavallo*) whinny 2. CHEM nitrite

nitro ['ni:·tro] *m* niter

nitrocellulosa [ni·tro·tʃel·lu·'lo:·sa] *f* nitrocellulose

nitroglicerina [ni·tro·gli·tʃe·'ri:·na] *f* nitroglycerine

NN *abbr di* **nescio nomen** (*di padre ignoto*) *unknown father*

no [nɔ] I. *avv* not; **parti o** ~? are you leaving or not?; **lo farai,** ~? you'll do it, won't you?; **pare di** ~ it seems not; **come** ~! I'll bet!; **perché** ~? why not?; ~ **e poi** ~ absolutely not; **dire di** ~ to say no; **rispondere di** ~ to answer no; **non dico di** ~ (*per accettare*) I wouldn't say no; (*lo ammetto*) I don't deny it

N

II. <-> *m* **1.**(*risposta*) no **2.**(*voto*) no (vote)
NO *abbr di* **nordovest** NW
nobildonna [no·bil·'dɔn·na] *f* noblewoman
nobile ['nɔ:·bi·le] I. *agg* **1.**(*di origine*) noble **2.**(*generoso*) noble **3.** CHEM (*gas, metallo*) noble II. *mf* nobleman *m*, noblewoman *f; i* -i the nobility
nobiliare [no·bi·'lia:·re] *agg* noble
nobiltà [no·bil·'ta] <-> *f a. fig* nobility
nobiluomo [no·bi·'luɔ:·mo] <nobiluomini> *m* nobleman
nocca ['nɔk·ka] <-cche> *f* (*di mani*) knuckle
noccio ['nɔt·tʃo] *1. pers sing pr di* **nuocere**
nocciola[1] [not·'tʃɔ:·la] *f* hazelnut
nocciola[2] <inv> *agg* (*colore*) (light) brown; (*occhi*) hazel
nocciolato [not·tʃo·'la:·to] *m* chocolate with hazelnuts
nocciolina [not·tʃo·'li:·na] *f* peanut
nocciolo[1] ['nɔt·tʃo·lo] *m* **1.** BOT stone **2.** *fig* heart
nocciolo[2] [not·'tʃɔ:·lo] *m* BOT hazel
noce ['no:·tʃe] I. *m* (*albero, legno*) walnut II. *f* **1.** BOT walnut; **~ moscata** nutmeg **2.**(*di bue, vitello*) knuckle **3.**(*misura*) knob
nocepesca [no·tʃe·'pɛs·ka] <nocipesche> *f* nectarine
nocino [no·'tʃi:·no] *m* walnut liqueur
nociuto [no·'tʃu:·to] *pp di* **nuocere**
nocività [no·tʃi·vi·'ta] <-> *f* harmfulness
nocivo, -a [no·'tʃi:·vo] *agg* harmful
nocqui ['nɔk·kui] *1. pers sing pass rem di* **nuocere**
nodo ['nɔ:·do] *m* **1.**(*intreccio*) knot; **~ linfatico** ANAT lymph node; **avere un ~ alla gola** *fig* to have a lump in one's throat; **fare il ~ alla cravatta** to knot one's tie; **tutti i -i vengono al pettine** *prov* everything comes out in the end **2.**(*trama: di azione, dramma*) plot; (*problema*) sticking point; (*impedimento*) obstacle **3.**(*punto centrale: di problema, questione*) nub **4.** MOT, FERR **~ ferroviario** railway junction; **~ stradale** road junction
nodoso, -a [no·'do:·so] *agg* (*bastone, ramo, dita*) gnarled
nodulo ['nɔ:·du·lo] *m* BIOL, MED nodule
no frost [nou 'frɔst] I. <-> *m* frost-free system II. <inv> *agg* **congelatore ~** frost-free freezer
noi ['no:·i] *pron* **1.**(*soggetto*) we **2.**(*oggetto*) us
noia ['nɔ:·ia] <-oie> *f* **1.**(*tedio*) boredom **2.**(*seccatura*) nuisance; **dar ~ a qu** to annoy sb
noialtri [no·'ial·tri] *pron 1. pers pl* we
noioso, -a [no·'io:·so] *agg* **1.**(*tedioso: libro, persona*) boring **2.**(*che dà fastidio*) annoying
noleggiare [no·led·'dʒa:·re] *vt* **1.**(*dare a nolo*) to rent (out) **2.**(*prendere a nolo*) to rent; (*navi, aerei*) to charter
noleggiatore, -trice [no·led·dʒa·'to:·re] *m, f* **1.**(*che dà a nolo*) renter **2.**(*che prende a nolo*) renter; (*di navi, aerei*) charterer
noleggio [no·'led·dʒo] <-ggi> *m* **1.**(*affitto*) rental; (*di navi, aerei*) charter **2.**(*prezzo*) rental charge; (*di navi, aerei*) charter fee **3.**(*impresa*) rental company
nolente [no·'lɛn·te] *agg* **verrai, volente o ~** you'll come, whether you like it or not
nolo ['nɔ:·lo] *m* **1.**(*noleggio*) rental; **dare a ~ qc** to rent sth out; **prendere a ~ qc** to rent sth **2.**(*prezzo*) rental charge; (*per navi, aerei*) charter fee
nomade ['nɔ:·ma·de] I. *agg* nomadic II. *mf* nomad
nomadismo [no·ma·'diz·mo] *m* nomadism
nome ['no:·me] *m* **1.**(*nome e cognome*) name; (*opposto a cognome*) first name; **~ di battesimo** baptismal name; **farsi un ~** to make a name for oneself; **a ~ di qu** in sb's name; **di ~** (*chiamato*) called; **conoscere qu di ~** to know sb's name **2.**(*di cosa, luogo*) name; **~ depositato** registered trademark **3.** LING noun; **~ astratto** abstract noun; **~ collettivo** collective noun; **~ comune** common noun; **~ proprio** proper name
nomenclatura [no·men·kla·'tu:·ra] *f* nomenclature
nomignolo [no·'miɲ·ɲo·lo] *m* (*soprannome*) nickname
nomina ['nɔ:·mi·na] *f* appointment
nominale [no·mi·'na:·le] *agg* **1.** LING nominal **2.**(*teorico*) in name **3.** COM (*valore, capitale*) nominal
nominare [no·mi·'na:·re] *vt* **1.**(*citare*) to mention; **mai sentito ~!** I've never heard of him [*o* her] [*o* it]! **2.**(*eleggere*) to nominate; (*commissione, avvocato*) to appoint **3.**(*chiamare: via, pianta, astro*) to name
nominativo [no·mi·na·'ti:·vo] *m* **1.** LING nominative **2.** ADM name
nominativo, -a *agg* (*biglietto, abbonamento*) nominative
non [non] *avv* **1.**(*con verbi*) not **2.**(*con aggettivi, sostantivi, avverbi*) non-; **~ fumatori** non-smokers; **~ violenza** non-violence **3.**(*con un'altra negazione*) **~ appena** as soon as; **~ ... niente** not at all; **~ ... mai** never
nonagenario, -a [no·na·dʒe·'na:·rio] <-i, -ie> I. *agg* nonagenarian II. *m, f* nonagenarian
non aggressione [non ag·gres·'sio:·ne] *f* JUR non-aggression
non allineamento [non al·li·ne·a·'men·to] *m* JUR non-alignment
non allineato, -a *agg* non-aligned
non belligerante [non bel·li·dʒe·'ran·te] I. *agg* JUR non-belligerant II. *m* non-combatant
non belligeranza [non bel·li·dʒe·'ran·tsa] *f* JUR non-combatancy
nonchalance [nɔ̃·ʃa·'lãs] <-> *f* nonchalance
nonché [noɲ·'ke] *cong* **1.**(*e inoltre*) as well **2.**(*e tanto meno*) far less
nonconformismo [non·kon·for·'miz·mo] *m* nonconformism
nonconformista [noɲ·kon·for·'mis·ta] <-i *m*, -e *f*> I. *agg* nonconformist II. *mf* nonconformist

non credente [non kre·'dɛn·te] *mf* REL non-believer

noncurante [noŋ·ku·'ran·te] *agg* **essere ~ di qc** to pay no attention to sth

noncuranza [noŋ·ku·'ran·tsa] *f* **1.** (*nonchalance*) nonchalance **2.** (*inosservanza*) lack of attention

nondimeno [non·di·'meː·no] *cong* nonetheless

non docente [non do·'tʃɛn·te] *agg* non-teaching; **personale ~** non-teaching staff

nonetto [no·'net·to] *m* MUS nonet

non interferenza [non in·ter·fe·'rɛn·tsa] *f* non-interference

non intervento [non in·ter·'vɛn·to] *m* JUR, POL non-intervention

nonni ['nɔn·ni] *mpl* grandparents; (*antenati*) ancestors

nonnismo [non·'niz·mo] *m inf* MIL hazing

nonno, -a ['nɔn·no] *m, f* grandpa *m*, grandma *f*

nonnulla [non·'nul·la] <-> *m* **un ~** a trifle

nono ['nɔː·no] *m* (*frazione*) ninth

nono, -a I. *agg* ninth II. *m, f* ninth; *v.a.* **quinto**

nonostante [no·nos·'tan·te] I. *prep* despite II. *cong* although

non plus ultra [nɔn plus 'ul·tra] <-> *m* **il ~ di** the height of

non professionale [non pro·fes·sio·'naː·le] *agg* **1.** (*amatoriale*) non-professional **2.** *pej* (*senza serietà e competenza*) amateurish

non profit [non 'pro·fit] <inv> *agg* JUR not for profit

non so che [non sɔ k·'ke] <-> *m* **un** (**certo**) **~** a certain something

nonstop, non stop [nɔn stɔp] I. <inv> *agg* nonstop; **orario ~** 24 hours a day; **volo ~** nonstop flight II. <-> *f* TV continuous program

nontiscordardime, **non-ti-scordar-di-me** [non·tis·kor·dar·di·'me] <-> *m* forget-me-not

non udente [non u·'dɛn·te] I. *mf form* ADM (*sordo*) hearing-impaired person II. *agg* hearing-impaired

non vedente [non ve·'dɛn·te] I. *mf form* ADM (*cieco*) blind person II. *agg* blind

non violento, -a [non vio·'lɛn·to] I. *agg* non-violent II. *m, f* advocate of non-violence

norcino, -a [nor·'tʃiː·no] *m, f* person from Norcia

nord [nɔrd] *m* north; **l'Italia del ~** northern Italy; **a ~ di ...** to the north of ...; **verso ~** northwards; **il Mare del Nord** the North Sea; **il Polo Nord** the North Pole

nord- (*in parole composte*) north-

nordest [nɔr·'dɛst] *m* north-east; **di ~** north-easterly

nordico, -a ['nɔr·di·ko] <-ci, -che> I. *agg* Nordic II. *m, f* Nordic

nordismo [nor·'diz·mo] *m* POL *ideology of the Northern League, advocating autonomy for the northern regions of Italy*

nordista [nor·'dis·ta] <-i *m*, -e *f*> I. *agg* POL *relating to the Northern League* II. *mf* POL *supporter of the Northern League*

nordovest [nor·'dɔː·vest] *m* **1.** GEOG northwest; **di ~** northwesterly **2.** (*cappello*) southwester hat

norma ['nɔr·ma] *f* **1.** (*regola*) rule; **-e per l'uso** instructions; **a ~ di legge** in accordance with the law; **di ~** (*abitualmente*) as a rule **2.** (*uso*) custom **3.** (*in statistica*) norm

normale [nor·'maː·le] *agg* **1.** (*conforme alla norma*) normal **2.** (*regolare*) normal

normalità [nor·ma·li·'ta] <-> *f* normality

normalizzare [nor·ma·lid·'dzaː·re] I. *vt* **1.** (*rendere normale*) to normalize **2.** (*standardizzare*) to standardize II. *vr:* **-rsi** to normalize

normalmente [nor·mal·'men·te] *avv* **1.** (*secondo la norma*) normally **2.** (*abitualmente*) usually

normanno, -a [nor·'man·no] I. *agg* GEOG, HIST Norman II. *m, f* GEOG, HIST Norman

normativa [nor·ma·'tiː·va] rules *pl*

normativo, -a [nor·ma·'tiː·vo] *agg* prescriptive

normografo [nor·'mɔː·gra·fo] *m* lettering guide

norvegese [nor·ve·'dʒeː·se] I. *agg* Norwegian II. *mf* Norwegian

Norvegia [nor·'vɛː·dʒa] *f* Norway

nossignora [nos·siɲ·'ɲoː·ra] *int* no, Madam; *iron* no way

nossignore [nos·siɲ·'ɲoː·re] *int* no, Sir; *iron* no way

nostalgia [nos·tal·'dʒiː·a] <-gie> *f* (*rimpianto*) nostalgia; **sentire ~ del proprio paese** to be homesick for one's town; **avere ~ della famiglia** to miss one's family

nostalgico, -a [nos·'tal·dʒi·ko] <-ci, -che> I. *agg* (*discorso, atteggiamento, persona*) nostalgic II. *m, f* nostalgic

nostrano, -a [nos·'traː·no] *agg* (*formaggio, vino, frutta*) local

nostro, -a ['nɔs·tro] I. *agg* our; **la -a speranza** our hope; **~ padre/zio** our father/uncle; **un ~ amico** a friend of ours II. *pron* **il ~, la -a** ours

nostromo [nos·'trɔː·mo] *m* boatswain

nota ['nɔː·ta] *f* **1.** (*contrassegno*) feature **2.** (*appunto*) note; **prendere ~ di qc** to take note of sth; **degno di ~** noteworthy **3.** (*a scuola*) reprimand slip **4.** (*conto*) check; **~ spese** expense sheet **5.** (*comunicazione*) note **6.** MUS note; **trovare la giusta ~** to hit the right note

nota bene ['nɔː·ta 'bɛː·ne] <-> *m* NB

notabile [no·'taː·bi·le] *m* worthy

notaio [no·'taː·io] <-ai> *m* notary (public)

notare [no·'taː·re] *vt* **1.** (*rilevare*) to notice; **farsi ~** to attract attention **2.** (*prender nota*) to note **3.** (*considerare*) to note; **far ~ a qu qc** to point sth out to sb

notariato [no·ta·'ria·to] *m* notaries (public) *pl*

notarile [no·ta·'riː·le] *agg* notarial

notazione [no·ta·'tsioː·ne] *f* **1.** (*annotazione*) notation **2.** MUS notation **3.** *fig* (*osservazione*) remark

notebook ['nout·buk/not·'buk] *m* COMPUT notebook

notes ['nɔː·tes] <-> *m* notepad

notevole [no·'teː·vo·le] *agg* **1.** (*degno di nota*) notable **2.** (*grande*) significant

notifica [no·'tiː·fi·ka] <-che> *f* ADM notification

notificabile [no·ti·fi·'kaː·bi·le] *agg* ADM notifiable

notificare [no·ti·fi·'kaː·re] *vt* **1.** ADM to notify; JUR (*sentenza*) to serve **2.** (*dichiarare*) to declare

notificazione [no·ti·fi·ka·'tsioː·ne] *f* DIR notificatoin

notizia [no·'tiː·tsia] <-ie> *f* (*novità*) piece of news; **-ie** news *sing*

notiziario [no·ti·'tsiaː·rio] <-i> *m* TV, RADIO news program

noto, -a ['nɔː·to] *agg* well-known; **ben ~** notable; *pej* (*criminale, truffatore, dongiovanni*) notorious

notoriamente [no·to·ria·'men·te] *avv* notoriously

notorietà [no·to·rie·'ta] <-> *f* **1.** (*conoscenza*) **di ~ pubblica** common knowledge **2.** (*fama*) fame

notorio, -a [no·'tɔː·rio] <-i, -ie> *agg* **1.** (*conosciuto*) well-known **2.** ADM **atto ~** affidavit

nottambulismo [not·tam·bu·'liz·mo] *m* sleepwalking

nottambulo, -a [not·'tam·bu·lo] **I.** *agg* nighttime **II.** *m, f* night owl

nottata [not·'taː·ta] *f* night; **far ~** to stay up very late

notte ['nɔt·te] *f* night; **nel cuore della ~** in the middle of the night; **~ bianca** [*o* **in bianco**] sleepless night; **di ~** at night

nottetempo [not·te·'tɛm·po] *avv* at night

nottola ['nɔt·to·la] *f* ZOO (*pipistrello*) noctule bat

notturno [not·'tur·no] *m* **1.** (*in liturgia*) nocturn **2.** MUS (*in pittura*) nocturne **3.** FOTO, FILM night scene

notturno, -a *agg* (*orario, turno, ore, veduta*) nocturnal

novanta [no·'van·ta] **I.** *num* ninety **II.** <-> *m* ninety; **pezzo da ~** (*persona importante*) big shot; *v.a.* **cinquanta**

novantenne [no·van·'tɛn·ne] **I.** *agg* ninety-year-old **II.** *mf* ninety-year-old

novantennio [no·van·'tɛn·nio] <-i> *m* ninety years *pl*

novantesimo [no·van·'tɛː·zi·mo] *m* ninetieth

novantesimo, -a I. *agg* ninetieth **II.** *m, f* ninetieth; *v.a.* **quinto**

novantina [no·van·'tiː·na] *f* **una ~ (di ...)** about ninety (...); **essere sulla ~** to be about ninety

Novara *f* Novara

novarese [no·va·'reː·se] **I.** *mf* (*abitante*) person from Novara **II.** *agg* from Novara

Novarese *m* (*zona*) Novara region

nove ['nɔː·ve] **I.** *num* nine **II.** <-> *m* **1.** (*numero*) nine **2.** (*nelle date*) ninth **3.** (*voto*

scolastico) *9 out of 10* **III.** *fpl* nine (o'clock); *v.a.* **cinque**

novecento [no·ve·'tʃɛn·to] **I.** *num* nine-hundred **II.** <-> *m* nine-hundred; **il Novecento** the Twentieth Century

novella [no·'vɛl·la] *f* LIT short story

novellino, -a [no·vel·'liː·no] **I.** *agg* inexperienced **II.** *m, f* novice

novellistica [no·vel·'lis·ti·ka] *f* short story writing

novello, -a *agg* **1.** (*patate*) new; (*vino*) young **2.** (*nuovo*) **-i sposi** newlyweds

novembre [no·'vɛm·bre] *m* November; *v.a.* **aprile**

novembrino, -a [no·vem·'briː·no] *agg* November

novemila [no·ve·'miː·la] **I.** *num* nine-thousand **II.** <-> *m* nine-thousand

novena [no·'vɛː·na] *f* novena

novennale [no·ven·'naː·le] *agg* **1.** (*che dura nove anni*) nine-year **2.** (*ricorrente ogni nove anni*) nine-yearly

novennio [no·'vɛn·nio] <-i> *m* nine years *pl*

novità [no·vi·'ta] <-> *f* **1.** (*qualità*) novelty **2.** (*notizia*) news

noviziato [no·vi·'tsiaː·to] *m* **1.** REL (*stato, periodo, collegio*) novitiate **2.** (*tirocinio*) apprenticeship

novizio, -a [no·'vi·tsio] <-i, -ie> *m, f* **1.** REL novice **2.** *fig* (*inesperto*) novice

nozione [not·'tsioː·ne] *f* **1.** (*conoscenza*) knowledge; **perdere la ~ del tempo** to lose track of time **2.** (*concetto*) notion

nozionismo [no·tsio·'niz·mo] *m* superficiality

nozionistico, -a [no·tsio·'nis·ti·ko] <-ci, -che> *agg* superficial

nozze ['nɔt·tse] *fpl* wedding; **~ d'argento/di diamante/d'oro** silver/diamond/gold wedding; **andare a ~** *fig* to

NT *abbr di* **Nuovo Testamento** NT

NU *abbr di* **Nazioni Unite** UN

nuance [nɥ·ãːs] <-> *f* **1.** (*di colore*) shade **2.** *fig* nuance

nube ['nuː·be] *f* **1.** (*nuvola*) cloud **2.** SCIENT (*radioattiva, tossica, cosmica, ionica*) cloud

nubifragio [nu·bi·'fraː·dʒo] <-gi> *m* downpour

nubile ['nuː·bi·le] **I.** *agg* unmarried **II.** *f* unmarried woman

nuca ['nuː·ka] <-che> *f* nape

nucleare [nu·kle·'aː·re] *agg* nuclear; **armi -i** nuclear weapons

nuclearizzazione [nu·kle·a·rid·dza·'tsioː·ne] *f* acquisition of nuclear weapons

nucleico, -a [nu·'klɛː·i·ko] <-ci, -che> *agg* **acido ~** nucleic acid

nucleo ['nuː·kleo] *m* **1.** SCIENT nucleus **2.** *fig* (*gruppo*) unit

nudismo [nu·'diz·mo] *m* nudism

nudista [nu·'dis·ta] <-i *m*, -e *f*> *mf* nudist

nudità [nu·di·'ta] <-> *f* nudity

nudo ['nuː·do] *m* nude

nudo, -a *agg* **1.** (*persona*) naked; (*piedi,*

gambe) bare; (*terreno*) bare **2.** *fig* **verità -a e cruda** the naked truth; **a occhio ~** with the naked eye; **mettere a ~ qc** *fig* to reveal sth

nulla ['nul·la] I. <inv> *pron v.* **niente** II. *avv* **non contare ~** to count for nothing III. *m* nothing

nulladimeno [nul·la·di·'me:·no] *cong v.* **nondimeno**

nullaosta, nulla osta [nul·la·'ɔs·ta] <-> *m* authorization

nullatenente [nul·la·te·'nɛn·te] I. *agg* destitute II. *mf* destitute person

nullità [nul·li·'ta] <-> *f* **1.** DIR nullity **2.** (*persona*) nonentity

nullo, -a ['nul·lo] *agg* **1.** (*non valido*) null and void **2.** SPORT disallowed; **dichiarare ~ un gol** to disallow a goal

nume ['nu:·me] *m* deity

numerabile [nu·me·'ra:·bi·le] *agg* numerable

numerale [nu·me·'ra:·le] I. *agg* numeral II. *m* numeral

numerare [nu·me·'ra:·re] *vt* **1.** (*segnare con un numero*) to number **2.** (*quantificare*) to count

numeratore [nu·me·ra·'to:·re] *m* **1.** MAT numerator **2.** TEC counter

numerazione [nu·me·ra·'tsio:·ne] *f* (*sequenza*) numbering

numerico, -a [nu·'mɛ:·ri·ko] <-ci, -che> *agg* MAT, COMPUT numerical

numero ['nu:·me·ro] *m* **1.** *gener* number; **~ civico** street number; **~ di telefono** phone number; **~ di emergenza** emergency number; **~ di gara** competitor's number; **~ verde** TEL toll-free number; **chiamare un ~** TEL to ring a number; **sbagliare ~** TEL to dial a wrong number; **dare i -i** *inf* to go out of one's head **2.** (*quantità*) number; **far ~** *a. fig* to make up the numbers; **in gran ~** in large numbers; **~ chiuso** UNIV restricted *number of places* **3.** (*di giornale, rivista*) issue; **~ unico** special issue; **-i arretrati** back issues **4.** (*di spettacolo*) number **5.** (*di scarpe*) size; **che ~ (di scarpe) porti?** what's your shoe size? **6.** LING number

numeroso, -a [nu·me·'ro:·so] *agg* **1.** (*famiglia, pubblico*) large **2.** *pl* many; **-e possibilità** many chances

nunzio ['nun·tsio] <-i> *m* nuncio

nuocere ['nuɔ:·tʃe·re] <noccio *o* nuoccio, nocqui, nociuto> *vi* to be harmful; **~ a qu/qc** to harm sb/sth

nuora ['nuɔ:·ra] *f* daughter-in-law

nuorese [nuo·'re:·se] I. *mf* (*abitante*) person from Nuoro II. *agg* from Nuoro

Nuorese *m* (*zona*) the Nuorese area; **nel ~** in the Nuorese area

Nuoro *f* Nuoro

nuotare [nuo·'ta:·re] *vi* to swim; **~ a farfalla** to swim butterfly (stroke); **~ a rana** to swim breaststroke; **~ nell'abbondanza** *fig* to be drowning in abundance

nuotata [nuo·'ta:·ta] *f* swim; **fare una ~** to go for a swim

nuotatore, -trice [nuo·ta·'to:·re] *m, f* swimmer

nuoto [ɔ:·to] *m* swimming; **traversare a ~ un fiume** to swim across a river

nuova ['nuɔ:·va] *f* **nessuna ~, buona ~** *prov* no news is good news

Nuova Zelanda ['nuɔ:·va ddze·'lan·da] *f* New Zealand

nuovo ['nuɔ:·vo] *m* **1.** (*novità*) **che c'è di ~?** what's new? **2.** COM (*immobili*) new property; **i prezzi del ~ e dell'usato** (*auto*) new and used car prices

nuovo, -a <più nuovo, nuovissimo> *agg* new; **~ fiammante** [*o* di zecca] brand new; **questa è proprio -a!** that's quite something!; **di ~** (*ancora*) again

nutria ['nu:·tria] <-ie> *f* coypu

nutrice [nu·'tri:·tʃe] *f* (*balia*) wet nurse

nutriente [nu·tri·'ɛn·te] *agg* (*sostanzioso: piatto, merenda*) nutritious

nutrimento [nu·tri·'men·to] *m* nourishment

nutrire [nu·'tri:·re] I. *vt* **1.** (*alimentare*) to feed **2.** *fig* (*mente*) to nourish; (*fiducia*) to foster; (*odio*) to harbor II. *vr:* **-rsi** to feed; **-rsi di** to feed on

nutritivo, -a [nu·tri·'ti:·vo] *agg* **valore ~** nutritional value

nutrito, -a [nu·'tri:·to] *agg* **1. ben ~** well-nourished; **mal ~** malnourished **2.** (*ampio*) healthy

nutrizione [nu·tri·'tsio:·ne] *f* **1.** (*atto del nutrire*) nutrition **2.** (*cibo*) nourishment

nutrizionistica [nu·tri·tsio·'nis·ti·ka] *f* nutrition

nuvola ['nu:·vo·la] *f* cloud; **avere la testa tra le -e** *inf* to have one's head in the clouds; **cadere** [*o* cascare] **dalle -e** *inf* to come down to earth with a bang; **vivere nelle -e** *inf* to wander around in a daze

nuvolone [nu·vo·'lo:·ne] *m* raincloud

nuvolosità [nu·vo·lo·si·'ta] <-> *f* cloudiness

nuvoloso, -a [nu·vo·'lo:·so] *agg* cloudy

nuziale [nu·'tsia:·le] *agg* (*festa, rito*) wedding; **anello ~** wedding ring

nylon® ['nai·lən] <-> *m* nylon®

O

O, o [ɔ] <-> *f* O, o; **~ come Otranto** O for Oscar

o [o] I. <davanti a vocale spesso *od*> *cong* **1.** (*oppure*) or **2.** (*ossia, vale a dire*) or; **~ ... ~** either ... or II. *int* oh

O *abbr di* **ovest** W

oasi ['ɔ:·a·zi] <-> *f* oasis

obbediente [ob·be·'diɛn·te] *agg v.* **ubbidiente**

obbligare [ob·bli·'ga:·re] I. *vt* **1.** (*costringere*) to force; **~ qu a fare qc** to make sb do sth;

~ **qu a letto** (*malattia*) to confine sb to their bed **2.**JUR (*vincolare*) to compel **II.** *vr:* **-rsi 1.**JUR (*vincolarsi*) to be bound **2.**(*impegnarsi*) to force oneself

obbligato, -a [ob·bli·'ga:·to] *agg* **1.**(*costretto*) obliged **2.**(*vincolato*) bound **3.**(*per riconoscenza*) indebted **4.**(*inevitabile: percorso, tappa*) obligatory

obbligatorio, -a [ob·bli·ga·'tɔ:r·io] <-i, -ie> *agg* (*materia, vaccinazione, dotazione*) compulsory

obbligazione [ob·bli·gat·'tsio:·ne] *f* **1.** *a.* JUR (*obbligo*) obligation **2.**FIN bond; **-i dello Stato** government bonds; **-i convertibili europee** European convertible bonds

obbligo ['ɔb·bli·go] <-ghi> *m* obligation; ~ **scolastico** compulsory education; **scuola dell'**~ compulsory education; **d'** ~ obligatory; **essere in** [*o* **avere l'**]~ **di fare qc** to be obliged to do sth; **sentirsi in** ~ to feel indebted to sb

obbrobrio [ob·'brɔ:·brio] <-i> *m* **1.**(*azione vergognosa*) disgrace **2.**(*cosa brutta*) horror

obbrobrioso, -a [ob·bro·'brio:·so] *agg* **1.**(*vergognoso*) shameful **2.**(*brutto*) ugly

obelisco [o·be·'lis·ko] <-schi> *m* obelisk

oberato, -a [o·be·'ra:·to] *agg* **1.**(*di debiti*) overburdened **2.** *fig* (*sovraccarico*) overloaded

obesità [o·be·zi·'ta] <-> *f* obesity

obeso, -a [o·'bɛ:·zo] **I.** *agg* obese **II.** *m, f* obese person

obiettare [o·biet·'ta:·re] *vt* to object

obiettività [ob·iet·ti·vi·'ta] <-> *f* objectivity

obiettivo [ob·iet·'ti:·vo] *m* **1.**FOTO lens **2.**MIL (*bersaglio*) target **3.**(*scopo*) objective

obiettivo, -a *agg* (*imparziale: giudizio, arbitro*) objective

obiettore, -trice [ob·iet·'to:·re] *m, f* ~ (**di coscienza**) conscientious objector

obiezione [ob·iet·'tsio:·ne] *f* objection; ~ **di coscienza** conscientious objection

obitorio [o·bi·'tɔ:·rio] <-i> *m* mortuary

oblio [o·'bli:·o] <-ii> *m poet* oblivion

obliquo, -a [ob·'li:·kuo] *agg* **1.**(*sghembo: lato, parete*) oblique **2.**LING indirect

obliterare [ob·li·te·'ra:·re] *vt* (*biglietto*) to stamp

obliteratrice [ob·li·te·ra·'tri:·tʃe] *f* (*di biglietti*) ticket stamping machine

oblò [or·'blɔ] <-> *m* (*di nave*) porthole; (*di aereo*) window

oblungo, -a [o·'bluŋ·go] <-ghi, -ghe> *agg* (*sagoma, foglia, frutto*) oblong

oboe ['ɔ:·bo·e] *m* oboe

oboista [o·bo·'is·ta] <-i *m*, -e *f*> *mf* oboist

obsoleto, -a [ob·so·'lɛ:·to] *agg* (*parola, merce*) obsolete

OC *abbr di* **onde corte** SW

oca ['ɔ:·ka] <oche> *f* ZOO goose; **pelle d'**~ *fig* goose bumps *pl*

ocarina [o·ka·'ri:·na] *f* ocarina

occasionale [ok·ka·zio·'na:·le] *agg* **1.**(*saltuario: lavoro*) occasional **2.**(*per caso: incontro*) chance

occasione [ok·ka·'zio:·ne] *f* **1.**(*opportunità*) opportunity; **cogliere l'**~ to take the opportunity; **perdere un'**~ to miss an opportunity **2.**COM (*affare*) bargain; **auto d'**~ bargain car **3.**(*circostanza*) occasion; **adatto all'**~ suitable to the occasion; **in** ~ **di ...** on the occasion of ...; **per l'**~ for the occasion; **l'**~ **fa l'uomo ladro** *prov* opportunity makes the thief **4.**(*motivo*) cause

occhi *pl di* **occhio**

occhiaie [ok·'kia:·ie] <-aie> *fpl* bags *pl* under the eyes; **avere le** ~ to have bags under one's eyes

occhiali [ok·'kia:·li] *mpl* glasses *pl;* ~ **da sole** sunglasses

occhiata [ok·'kia:·ta] *f* glance; **dare un'**~ **a qc** to take a look at sth; **dare un'**~ **al giornale** to take a quick look at the newspaper; **dare un'**~ **ai bambini** to check on the children; **lanciare un'**~ **a qu** to glance at sb; **un'**~ **di disapprovazione** a disapproving look

occhiello [ok·'kiɛl·lo] *m* (*asola*) buttonhole

occhio ['ɔk·kio] <-chi> *m* **1.**ANAT eye; **uova all'**~ **di bue** fried egg, sunny side up; **a colpo d'**~ at a glance; **costare un** ~ **della testa** to cost an arm and a leg; **non credere ai propri -chi** not to believe one's eyes; **dare nell'**~ to attract attention; **non togliere gli occhi di dosso a qu** not to take one's eyes off sb; **non perdere d'**~ not to lose sight of; **vedere di buon** ~ **qu** to look kindly on sb; **a** ~ at a glance; **a** ~ **e croce** at an estimate; **valutare** (**qc**) **ad** ~ **e croce** to make a rough estimate (of sth); **avere** ~ to have a good eye; **a -chi chiusi** *fig* with one's eyes closed; **essere un pugno in un** ~ *fig* to be an eyesore; **in un batter d'**~ in a flash; ~! watch out!; ~ **per** ~, **dente per dente** an eye for an eye, a tooth for a tooth; ~ **non vede, cuore non duole** *prov* out of sight, out of mind **2.**(*foro*) eye; **l'**~ **del ciclone** *fig* the eye of the storm

occhiolino [ok·kio·'li:·no] *m* **fare l'**~ **a qu** to wink at sb

occidentale [ot·tʃi·den·'ta:·le] **I.** *agg* **1.**(*lato, confine*) western **2.**(*civiltà mondo*) Western **II.** *mf* Westerner

occidente [ot·tʃi·'dɛn·te] *m* **1.**(*ponente*) west; **a** ~ **di** to the west of **2.**(*civiltà*) West

occludere [ok·'klu:·de·re] <occludo, occlusi, occluso> *vt* (*arteria, passaggio, tubo*) to block

occlusione [ok·klu·'zio:·ne] *f* **1.**MED obstruction; ~ **intestinale** gastrointestinal obstruction **2.**LING occlusion

occlusivo, -a [ok·klu·'zi:·vo] *agg* LING occlusive

occluso, -a [ok·'klu:·zo] *pp di* **occludere**

occorrente [ok·kor·'rɛn·te] **I.** *agg* necessary **II.** *m* materials *pl;* **l'**~ **per scrivere** writing materials

occorrenza [ok·kor·'rɛn·tsa] *f* **1.**(*evenienza*) event; **all'**~ if necessary **2.**LING (*frequenza*) occurrence

occorrere [ok·'kor·re·re] <irr> *vi essere*
1. (*essere necessario*) to be needed; **occor-
rono medicinali** medicine is needed; **mi
occorre del latte** I need some milk 2. (*impersonale*) **occorre ...** +*inf* it's necessary to ...;
occorre che ... +*cong* it is necessary that ...;
**occorre che l'altoparlante sia di buona
qualità** the loudspeaker must be of good quality; **non occorre ...** +*inf* there's no need to
...; **non occorre che ...** +*cong* it is not necessary that ...

occultare [ok·kul·'ta:·re] *vt* 1. (*nascondere*) to
hide 2. *fig* to conceal 3. ASTR to occult

occulto, -a [ok·'kul·to] *agg* (*scienze, forze*) occult

occupante [ok·ku·'pan·te] I. *agg* (*esercito,
forze*) occupying II. *mf* (*di veicolo, edificio*)
occupant

occupare [ok·ku·'pa:·re] I. *vt* 1. (*casa, fabbrica, scuola*) to occupy 2. MIL (*città paese*) to
occupy 3. (*abitare: appartamento*) to occupy
4. (*riempire: spazio*) to take up 5. (*ricoprire:
carica*) to hold II. *vr:* **-rsi** 1. (*interessarsi*) **-rsi
di qc** to be involved in 2. (*prendersi cura*) **-rsi
di qu** to look after sb 3. (*impicciarsi*) **-rsi di qc**
to interfere with sth; **occupati dei fatti tuoi**
mind your own business

occupato, -a [ok·ku·'pa:·to] *agg* 1. (*posto*)
taken 2. (*telefono, linea*) busy; (*affaccendato*)
busy 3. (*impiegato*) employed

occupatore, -trice [ok·ku·pa·'to:·re] *m, f* occupier

occupazionale [ok·ku·pat·tsio·'na:·le] *agg*
(*livello, politica, terapia, malattia*) occupational

occupazione [ok·ku·pat·'tsio:·ne] *f* 1. (*di
casa, fabbrica, scuola*) occupation 2. MIL occupation 3. (*impiego*) job 4. (*attività*) pastime
5. (*lavoro*) employment; **piena ~** full employment

oceanico, -a [o·tʃe·'a:·ni·ko] <-ci, -che> *agg*
1. (*dell'oceano: onde, veliero, pesce*) oceanic
2. *fig* (*immenso: adunata, folla*) immense

oceano [o·'tʃɛː·a·no] *m* 1. GEOG ocean 2. *fig*
(*immensità*) huge quantity

oceanografia [o·tʃe·a·no·gra·'fiː·a] *f* oceanography

oceanografico, -a [o·tʃe·a·no·'gra:·fi·ko]
<-ci, -che> *agg* (*museo, ricerche, nave*)
oceanographic

oche *pl di* **oca**

ocra[1] ['ɔ:·k·ra] <inv> *agg* (*colore*) ocher

ocra[2] *f* (*minerale*) ocher

OCSE *f abbr di* **Organizzazione per la Collaborazione e lo Sviluppo Economico**
OECD

oculare [o·ku·'la:·re] *agg* (*nervo*) ocular;
bulbo ~ eyebulb; **testimone ~** eyewitness

oculista [o·ku·'lis·ta] <-i *m*, -e *f*> *mf* opthal-
mologist

od [od] *cong* = **o** *or*

ode ['ɔ:·de] *f* ode

odiare [o·'dia:·re] *vt* (*nemico, persona,
materia, cibo*) to hate

odierno, -a [o·'diɛr·no] *agg* 1. (*di oggi: riunione, seduta*) today's 2. (*attuale: società
monumento*) present-day

odio ['ɔ:·dio] <-i> *m* hatred; **avere in ~ qc/qu**
to hate sth/sb; **venire in ~ a qu** to become
hated by sb

odioso, -a [o·'dio:·so] *agg* 1. (*detestabile*) unpleasant 2. (*antipatico: persona*) dislikable

odissea [o·dis·'sɛː·a] *f fig* odyssey

odo ['ɔ:·do] *1. pers sing pr di* **udire**

odontalgia [o·don·tal·'dʒiː·a] <-gie> *f* toothache

odontoiatra [o·don·to·'ia:·tra] <-i *m*, -e *f*> *mf*
dentist

odontoiatria [o·don·to·ia·'tri:·a] <-ie> *f* dentistry

odontotecnico, -a [o·don·to·'tɛk·ni·ko] <-ci,
-che> I. *agg* (*apparecchiature, materiali, laboratorio*) dental II. *m, f* dental technician

odorare [o·do·'ra:·re] *vi ~* **di qc** to smell of sth

odorato [o·do·'ra:·to] *m* (*olfatto*) sense of
smell

odore [o·'do:·re] *m* 1. (*esalazione*) smell; **sentire ~ di qc** to smell sth 2. *fig* (*sentore*) scent
3. *pl* CULIN (*spezie*) herbs *pl*

offendere [of·'fɛn·de·re] <offendo, offesi,
offeso> I. *vt* 1. *fig* (*persona*) to offend 2. (*danneggiare*) to damage II. *vr:* **-rsi** 1. (*risentirsi*) to
take offense 2. (*insultarsi*) to insult each other

offensiva [of·fen·'si:·va] *f* 1. MIL offensive
2. POL campaign

offensivo, -a [of·fen·'si:·vo] *agg* 1. (*parole,
messaggio*) offensive 2. MIL (*arma, azione,
guerra*) offensive

offerente [of·fe·'rɛn·te] *mf* bidder; **aggiudicare qc al migliore ~** to sell sth to the highest
bidder

offersi [of·'fɛr·si] *1. pers sing pass rem di* **offrire**

offerta [of·'fɛr·ta] *f* 1. (*proposta*) offer; **~ di
lavoro** job offer 2. COM supply; **domanda e ~**
supply and demand 3. (*donazione*) donation;
(*obolo*) offering

offerto [of·'fɛr·to] *pp di* **offrire**

offesa [of·'fe:·sa] *f* 1. (*insulto*) insult
2. (*attacco*) offensive

offesi [of·'fe:·si] *1. pers sing pass rem di* **offendere**

offeso, -a [of·'fe:·so] I. *pp di* **offendere** II. *agg*
1. (*insultato*) insulted 2. (*ferita*) injured 3. JUR
injured; **la parte -a** the injured party III. *m, f*
offended person; **fare l'~** to take offense

officina [of·fi·'tʃi:·na] *f* 1. (*fabbrica*) workshop
2. (*per auto*) garage

officinale [of·fi·tʃi·'na:·le] *agg* **erba ~** medicinal herb

offline ['ɔ:f·lain] <inv> I. *agg* COMPUT offline
II. *avv* COMPUT offline

offrire [of·'fri:·re] <offro, offersi *o* offrii,
offerto> I. *vt* 1. (*gener*) to offer; **chi mi offre
una sigaretta?** has anyone got a cigarette?
2. (*fornire: pretesto, appiglio, scusa*) to pro-

O

vide **3.** (*regalare*) to give **4.** *fam* (*pagare*) to pay; **oggi offre lui** he's paying today **II.** *vr:* **-rsi** to offer oneself

offset ['ɔːf·set] <-> *m* (*stampa, stampante, macchina*) offset

offuscamento [of·fus·ka·'men·to] *m* **1.** (*di vista*) blurring **2.** *fig* (*di mente*) clouding

offuscare [of·fus·'kaː·re] *vt* **1.** (*oscurare: luce, vista*) to obscure **2.** *fig* (*mente*) to cloud

oftalmico, -a [of·'tal·mi·ko] <-ci, -che> *agg* (*lente, medico, malattia*) ophthalmic; **ospedale** ~ eye hospital

oggettistica [od·dʒet·'tis·ti·ka] <-che> *f* fancy goods *pl*

oggettività [od·dʒet·ti·vi·'ta] <-> *f* objectivity

oggettivo, -a [od·dʒet·'tiː·vo] *agg* **1.** (*reale, obiettivo*) objective **2.** LING object

oggetto [od·'dʒet·to] *m* **1.** (*cosa*) object; **-i preziosi** valuables **2.** (*scopo*) object; **avere per** ~ to have the aim of **3.** (*argomento*) subject; ~ **del discorso** subject of the speech **4.** JUR matter **5.** PHILOS object **6.** LING object; (*complemento* ~) direct object **7.** ADM (*nelle lettere*) re:; **con riferimento a quanto indicato in** ~ ... ADM with reference to the subject of this letter ...

oggi ['ɔd·dʒi] **I.** *avv* today; ~ **stesso** today **II.** *m* today; **il giornale di** ~ today's paper; **al giorno d'**~ nowadays; **dall'**~ **al domani** from one day to the next

oggigiorno [od·dʒi·'dʒor·no] *avv* nowadays

ogiva [o·'dʒiː·va] *f* **1.** ARCH ogive **2.** MIL (*di un missile*) cone; ~ **nucleare** nuclear warhead

OGM *acro di* **Organismi Geneticamente Modificati** GMO

ogni ['oɲ·ɲi] <inv, solo al sing> *agg* every; **uno** ~ **dieci** one in ten; ~ **tre giorni** every three days; ~ **tanto** now and then; ~ **momento** all the time; **ad** ~ **modo** at any rate; **con** ~ **mezzo** with every means available; **in** ~ **caso** in any case; **in** ~ **luogo** everywhere; **in** ~ **modo** in every way

Ognissanti [oɲ·ɲis·'san·ti] <-> *m* All Saints' Day

ognuno, -a [oɲ·'ɲuː·no] <sing> *pron indef* everyone; ~ **di noi/voi/loro** each of us/you/them

oh [ɔ/o] *int* oh

ohè [o·'e] *int fam* hey

ohi ['ɔː·i] *int* ouch

ohibò [oi·'bɔ] *int* ooh

ohimè [oi·'mɛ] *int* oh dear

ohm [oːm] <-> *m* ohm

oibà *int v.* **ohibà**

OL *abbr di* **onde lunghe** LW

olà [o·'la] *int* hey

Olanda [o·'lan·da] *f* Holland; **l'**~ Holland

olandese[1] [o·lan·'deː·se] <sing> *m* (*lingua*) Dutch

olandese[2] **I.** *agg* Dutch **II.** *mf* Dutchman *m*, Dutchwoman *f*

oleandro [o·le·'an·dro] *m* BOT oleander

oleario, -a [o·le·'aː·rio] <-i, -ie> *agg* (*dell'olio:*

industria, macina, macchine) oil

oleato, -a [o·le·'aː·to] *agg* **carta -a** greaseproof paper

oleificio [o·lei·'fiː·tʃo] <-ci> *m* oil mill

oleodotto [o·le·o·'dot·to] *m* oil pipeline

oleoso, -a [o·le·'oː·so] *agg* oily

olfatto [ol·'fat·to] *m* sense of smell

oliare [o·'liaː·re] *vt* **1.** (*motore, ingranaggi*) to oil **2.** CULIN to grease

oliera [o·'lieː·ra] *f* oil jug

oligarchia [o·li·gar·'kiː·a] <-chie> *f* oligarchy

olimpiade [o·lim·'piː·a·de] *f* Olympic Games *pl*

olimpico, -a [o·'lim·pi·ko] <-ci, -che> *agg* (*campione, sport*) Olympic

olimpionico, -a [o·lim·'piɔː·ni·ko] <-ci, -che> **I.** *agg* (*campione, piscina*) Olympic **II.** *m, f* Olympic athlete

olimpo [o·'lim·po] *m* Olympus

olio ['ɔː·lio] <-i> *m* oil; ~ **abbronzante** suntan lotion; ~ **combustibile** fuel oil; ~ **commestibile** cooking oil; ~ **essenziale** essential oil; ~ **di oliva** olive oil; ~ **di ricino** castor oil; ~ **di semi** corn oil; **quadro ad** ~ oil painting; **andare liscio come l'**~ to go like clockwork; **estendersi a macchia d'**~ to spread like wildfire; **sott'**~ CULIN in oil

oliva[1] [o·'liː·va] *f* olive

oliva[2] <inv> *agg* (*colore*) olive green

olivastro, -a [o·li·'vas·tro] *agg* (*colorito*) olive

oliveto [o·li·'veː·to] *m* olive grove

olivo [o·'liː·vo] *m* BOT olive tree

olmo ['ol·mo] *m* BOT elm

olocausto [o·lo·'kaːus·to] *m* HIST holocaust

OLP [ɔlp] *m abbr di* **Organizzazione per la Liberazione della Palestina** PLO

oltraggiare [ol·trad·'dʒaː·re] *vt* (*offendere*) to offend

oltraggio [ol·'trad·dʒo] <-ggi> *m* offense; ~ **a pubblico ufficiale** insulting a public official

oltraggioso, -a [ol·trad·'dʒoː·so] *agg* (*parole, scritte*) offensive

oltralpe, oltr'alpe [ol·'tral·pe] **I.** *avv* north of the Alps **II.** *m* north of the Alps

oltranza [ol·'tran·tsa] *f* **ad** ~ to the last

oltranzismo [ol·tran·'tsiz·mo] *m* extremism

oltranzista [ol·tran·'tsis·ta] <-i *m*, -e *f*> *mf* extremist

oltre ['ol·tre] **I.** *avv* **1.** (*di tempo*) longer **2.** (*di luogo*) further; **andare** ~ to go further; **andare troppo** ~ *fig* to go too far **II.** *prep* **1.** (*dall'altra parte di*) beyond **2.** (*pi di*) more than; **non** ~ **il 15 giugno** no later than June 15 **3.** (*in aggiunta, in più*) ~ **a** apart from **4.** (*eccetto*) ~ **a** apart from

oltrefrontiera [ol·tre·fron·'tieː·ra] **I.** <inv> *agg* foreign **II.** *avv* **1.** (*stato in luogo*) abroad **2.** (*moto a luogo*) abroad **III.** <sing> *m* **paesi d'**~ foreign countries

oltremanica [ol·tre·'maː·ni·ka] **I.** <sing> *m* GEOG **d'**~ British **II.** *avv* **1.** (*stato in luogo*) in Britain **2.** (*moto a luogo*) to Britain

oltremare [ol·tre·'maː·re] **I.** *avv* (*stato, moto*)

overseas II.<inv> *agg* **blu** ~ ultramarine III.<*sing*> *m* **d'**~ overseas

oltremisura, oltre misura [ol·tre·mi·'zu:·ra] *avv* excessively

oltremodo, oltre modo [ol·tre·'mɔ:·do] *avv* extremely

oltreoceano [ol·tre·'tʃɛ:·a·no] I. *avv* 1.(*stato*) in America 2.(*moto*) to America II.<*sing*> *m* **d'**~ American

oltrepassare [ol·tre·pas·'sa:·re] *vt* 1.(*superare*) to cross 2.*fig*(*limite, soglia*) to exceed

oltretomba [ol·tre·'tom·ba] <-> *m* afterworld

OM *abbr di* **onde medie** MW

omaggio¹ [o·'mad·dʒo] <-ggi> *m* 1.(*offerta*) gift; **in** ~ complimentary 2.*fig* (*segno di rispetto*) tribute; **rendere** ~ **a qu** to pay homage to sb 3. *pl* (*ossequi*) regards *pl;* **gradisca i miei -ggi** kindest regards

omaggio² <inv> *agg* complimentary

ombelicale [om·be·li·'ka:·le] *agg* umbilical; **cordone** ~ umbilical cord

ombelico [om·be·'li:·ko] <-chi> *m* navel

ombra ['om·bra] *f* 1.(*zona non illuminata*) shade; **all'**~ **di** in the shade of 2.*fig*(*oscurità*) darkness; **restare nell'**~ to stay in the background 3.(*sagoma*) shadow; **aver paura della propria** ~ to be afraid of one's own shadow; **senz'**~ **di dubbio** *fig* without a shadow of a doubt

ombrellino [om·brel·'li:·no] *m* (*parasole per signora*) parasol

ombrello [om·'brɛl·lo] *m* umbrella; ~ **atomico** [*o* **nucleare**] MIL nuclear umbrella

ombrellone [om·brel·'lo:·ne] *m* (*per spiaggia*) beach umbrella

ombretto [om·'bret·to] *m* eye shadow

ombroso, -a [om·'bro:·so] *agg* 1.(*ricco d'ombra: luogo*) shady 2.(*che dà ombra: albero, fronde*) shady 3.(*nervoso: animale*) skittish

omega [o·'mɛ:·ga] <-> *m* omega

omelette [ɔm·'lɛt] <-> *f* omelette

omelia [o·me·'li:·a] <-ie> *f* REL homily

omeopatia [o·me·o·pa·'ti:·a] <-ie> *f* homeopathy

omeopatico¹ [o·me·o·'pa:·ti·ko] <-ci, -che> *agg* (*cura, medicina*) homeopathic

omeopatico² [o·me·o·'pa:·ti·ko] <-ci> *m* (*medicinale*) homeopathic remedy

omero ['ɔ:·me·ro/'o:·me·ro] *m* ANAT humerus

omertà [o·mer·'ta] <-> *f* code of silence

omettere [o·'met·te·re] <irr> *vt* (*tralasciare*) to omit; ~ **di dire/fare qc** to fail to say/do sth

ometto [o·'met·to] *m* 1.(*omino*) small man 2.(*bambino*) little man

omicida [o·mi·'tʃi:·da] <-i *m*, -e *f*> I. *mf* murderer II. *agg* (*follia, mire, padre*) murderous

omicidio [o·mi·'tʃi:·dio] <-i> *m* homicide; ~ **colposo** negligent homicide; ~ **doloso** first-degree murder; ~ **premeditato** premeditated murder; ~ **volontario** voluntary manslaughter

omisi *1. pers sing pass rem di* **omettere**

omissione [o·mis·'sio:·ne] *f* 1.(*dimenticanza*) omission 2.(*mancata attuazione*) failure; ~ **di soccorso** failure to help

omofonia [o·mo·fo·'ni:·a] <-ie> *f* LING homophony

omofono [o·'mɔ:·fo·no] *m* LING homophone

omofono, -a *agg* LING homophonic

omogeneità [o·mo·dʒe·nei·'ta] <-> *f* 1.(*di gruppi, materiali*) homogeneity 2.(*di dati, procedure*) consistency

omogeneizzare [o·mo·dʒe·neid·'dza:·re] *vt* 1.(*dati, gruppo*) to make consistent 2.(*materiali, soluzione*) to homogenize

omogeneizzati [o·mo·dʒe·neid·'dza:·ti] *mpl* (*alimenti*) baby food

omogeneizzato, -a [o·mo·dʒe·neid·'dza:·to] *agg* (*pollo, pesce, latte*) homogenized

omogeneo, -a [o·mo·'dʒɛ:·ne·o] *agg* (*materiale, testo, gruppo*) homogeneous

omografia [o·mo·gra·'fi:·a] *f* LING homography

omografo [o·'mɔ:·gra·fo] *m* LING homograph

omografo, -a *agg* LING homographic

omologare [o·mo·lo·'ga:·re] *vt* 1.(*autoveicoli*) to homologate 2.(*riconoscere: risultato*) to recognize

omologazione [o·mo·lo·gat·'tsio:·ne] *f* 1.(*di autoveicoli*) homologation 2.(*riconoscimento: di risultato*) recognition

omonimia [o·mo·ni·'mi:·a] <-ie> *f a.* LING homonymy

omonimo [o·'mɔ:·ni·mo] *m* LING homonym

omonimo, -a I. *agg a.* LING homonymous II. *m, f* namesake

omosessuale [o·mo·ses·su·'a:·le] I. *agg* homosexual II. *mf* homosexual

omosessualità [o·mo·ses·su·a·li·'ta] *f* homosexuality

onanismo [o·na·'niz·mo] *m* 1. REL onanism 2.(*masturbazione*) masturbation

onanista [o·na·'nis·ta] <-i *m*, -e *f*> *mf* onanist

oncia ['on·tʃa] <-ce> *f* ounce

onda ['on·da] *f* 1.(*del mare*) wave; **essere sulla cresta dell'**~ *fig* to be riding on the crest of a wave 2. PHYS wave; **-e corte/lunghe/medie** short/long/medium waves; ~ **d'urto** shockwave; **andare in** ~ TV, RADIO to be broadcast; **mandare in** ~ TV, RADIO to broadcast 3.(*loc*) ~ **verde** ALLA RADIO travel bulletin; (*semafori*) synchronized traffic lights

ondata [on·'da:·ta] *f* 1.(*di mare*) wave 2.(*afflusso*) heatwave, cold snap 3.*fig* (*di scandali, disordini*) wave

ondeggiare [on·ded·'dʒa:·re] *vi* 1.(*aquilone*) to fly; (*barca*) to roll 2.(*capelli, spighe*) to ripple

ondoso, -a [on·'do:·so] *agg* (*mare*) wavy; **moto** ~ wave motion

ondulato, -a [on·du·'la:·to] *agg* (*capelli*) wavy; (*cartone, lamiera*) corrugated

ondulatorio, -a [on·du·la·'tɔ:·rio] <-i, -ie> *agg* PHYS undulatory

ondulazione [on·du·lat·'tsio:·ne] *f* 1.(*di terreno*) undulation 2.(*oscillazione*) oscillation

O

3. (*di capelli*) waviness

onere ['ɔ:·ne·re] *m* **1.** (*obbligo*) burden; ~ **fiscale** JUR tax burden **2.** (*responsabilità*) responsibility

oneroso, -a [o·ne·'ro:·so] *agg* (*gravoso*) burdensome

onestà [o·nes·'ta] <-> *f* honesty; **in tutta ~ in** all honesty

onestamente [o·nes·ta·'men·te] *avv* honestly

onesto, -a [o·'nɛs·to] I. *agg* **1.** (*retto: persona*) honest **2.** (*decoroso: prezzo*) fair II. *m, f* honest person

onice ['ɔ:·ni·tʃe] *m* onyx

onirico, -a [o·'ni:·ri·ko] <-ci, -che> *agg* (*letteratura, musica, visione*) oneiric

online ['ɔ:n·'lain] <inv> *agg* COMPUT online; **servizio ~** online service

onni- [onni] (*in parole composte*) omni-

onnicomprensivo, -a [on·ni·kom·pren·'si:·vo] *agg* all-inclusive

onnipotente [on·ni·po·'tɛn·te] *agg* omnipotent

onnipotenza [on·ni·po·'tɛn·tsa] *f* omnipotence

onnipresente [on·ni·pre·'zɛn·te] *agg* omnipresent

onnipresenza [on·ni·pre·'zɛn·tsa] *f* omnipresence

onnisciente [on·niʃ·'ʃɛn·te] *agg* omniscient

onniscienza [on·niʃ·'ʃɛn·tsa] *f* omniscience

onniveggente [on·ni·ved·'dʒɛn·te] *agg* all-seeing

onniveggenza [on·ni·ved·'dʒɛn·tsa] *f* all-embracing vision

onnivoro [on·'ni:·vo·ro] *m* omnivore

onnivoro, -a *agg* omnivorous

onomastico [o·no·'mas·ti·ko] *m* (*festa*) name day

onomatopea [o·no·ma·to·'pɛ:·a] <-ee> *f* LING onomatopoeia

onomatopeico, -a [o·no·ma·to·'pɛ:·i·ko] <-ci, -che> *agg* LING onomatopoeic

onoranze [o·no·'ran·tse] *fpl* honors *pl;* **agenzia di ~ funebri** funeral director's

onorare [o·no·'ra:·re] *vt* **1.** (*rendere onore a*) to honor **2.** REL (*venerare, adorare*) to honor **3.** (*rispettare: impegno*) to fulfill

onorario [o·no·'ra:·rio] *m* fee

onorario, -a <-i, -ie> *agg* (*console, cittadino, cittadinanza*) honorary

onorato, -a [o·no·'ra:·to] *agg* **1.** (*stimato*) honored **2.** (*onorevole*) honorable **3.** (*contento*) honored **4.** (*in frasi di cortesia*) honored; **molto ~ di fare la Sua conoscenza** it's an honor to meet you

onore [o·'no:·re] *m* **1.** (*reputazione*) honor; **parola d'~** word of honor; **uomo d'~** man of honor **2.** (*gloria*) glory; **farsi ~ in qc** to distinguish oneself in sth; **fare ~ a qc** to honor sth; (*cucina*) to do justice to sth **3.** (*favore*) honor **4.** (*omaggio*) tribute; **in ~ di** in honor of; **damigella d'~** bridesmaid **5.** (*privilegio*) honor; **ho l'~ di presentarLe ...** I have the honor

of introducing ... **6.** (*titolo*) Honor; **Vostro Onore** Your Honor

onorevole [o·no·'re:·vo·le] I. *agg* **1.** (*degno di onore: comportamento, sconfitta*) honorable **2.** (*parlamentare*) Honorable II. *mf Member of the Italian Parliament*

onorificenza [o·no·ri·fi·'tʃɛn·tsa] *f* (*decorazione*) distinction

onorifico, -a [o·no·'ri:·fi·ko] <-ci, -che> *agg* (*carica, titolo, qualifica*) honorary

onta ['on·ta] *f* (*disonore*) disgrace; **ad ~ di** in spite of

ontologia [on·to·lo·'dʒi:·a] <-gie> *f* ontology

ontologico, -a [on·to·'lɔ:·dʒi·ko] *agg* ontological

ONU ['ɔ:·nu] *f acro di* **Organizzazione delle Nazioni Unite** UN

opacità [o·pa·tʃi·'ta] <-> *f* **1.** (*di vetro*) opacity **2.** (*di metallo*) dullness

opacizzare [o·pa·tʃid·'dza:·re] *vt* **1.** (*vetro*) to make opaque **2.** (*metallo*) to tarnish **3.** (*pelle*) to smooth

opaco, -a [o·'pa:·ko] <-chi, -che> *agg* **1.** (*vetro, lente*) opaque **2.** (*metallo*) matte **3.** (*pelle*) smooth **4.** *fig* (*sguardo*) glazed

opalina [o·pa·'li:·na] *f* opaline

op. cit. *abbr di* **opera citata** op. cit.

opera ['ɔ:·pe·ra] *f* **1.** (*attività*) work; **mettersi all'~** to get to work; **è ~ sua** it's his/her work **2.** (*prodotto*) work; **-e pubbliche** works **3.** LIT, ARTE work; **~ d'arte** work of art **4.** MUS opera; **~ buffa** comic opera; **~ lirica** opera **5.** (*teatro*) play

operaio, -a [o·pe·'ra:·io] <-ai, -aie> I. *agg* (*sciopero, movimento, lotta*) workers'; **classe -a** working class II. *m, f* worker; **~ qualificato** skilled worker; **~ specializzato** specialist worker

operante [o·pe·'ran·te] *agg* **1.** (*valido*) operative **2.** (*attivo*) active

operare [o·pe·'ra:·re] I. *vt* **1.** (*fare: controllo*) to exercise; (*scelta, taglio*) to make **2.** MED (*paziente*) to operate on II. *vr:* **-rsi 1.** (*realizzarsi*) to be undertaken **2.** MED to be operated on

operativo, -a [o·pe·ra·'ti:·vo] *agg* (*attivo*) operative; **ricerca -a** operational research

operato [o·pe·'ra:·to] *m* actions *pl*

operato, -a *agg* **1.** MED *who has undergone surgery* **2.** (*stoffa*) textured

operatore, -trice [o·pe·ra·'to:·re] *m, f* **1.** (*specialista*) operator; **~ di borsa** stockbroker; **~ economico** businessperson; **~ sociale** social worker; **~ turistico** tour operator **2.** MED (*chirurgo*) surgeon **3.** COMPUT operator **4.** TV, FILM cameraman

operazione [o·pe·rat·'tsio:·ne] *f* MAT, MED, MIL, COM operation; **~ finanziaria** financial operation

operetta [o·pe·'ret·ta] *f* MUS light opera

operistico, -a [o·pe·'ris·ti·ko] <-ci, -che> *agg* (*musica, repertorio, registrazione*) opera

operosità [o·pe·ro·si·'ta] <-> *f* (*di persona,*

insetto) industriousness

operoso, -a [o·pe·'ro:·so] *agg* (*persona, insetto, mani*) industrious

opificio [o·pi·'fi:·tʃo] <-ci> *m* factory

opinabile [o·pi·'na:·bi·le] *agg* (*discutibile: scelta, gusto*) debatable

opinione [o·pi·'nio:·ne] *f* opinion; **questione di -i** matter of opinion; **~ pubblica** public opinion; **condividere l'~ di qu** to share sb's opinion

opinionista [o·pi·nio·'nis·ta] <-i *m*, -e *f*> *mf* columnist

op là [op·'la] *int* whoops

opossum [o·'pɔs·sum] <-> *m* opossum

oppiato [op·'pia:·to] *m* (*medicinale*) opiate

oppio ['ɔp·pio] <-i> *m* opium

opponente [op·po·'nɛn·te] *mf* DIR opposing party

opporre [op·'por·re] <irr> I. *vt* 1.(*argomenti, rifiuto*) to oppose 2.(*resistenza*) to offer II. *vr* **-rsi a qu/qc** to oppose sb/sth

opportunismo [op·por·tu·'niz·mo] *m* opportunism

opportunista [op·por·tu·'nis·ta] <-i *m*, -e *f*> *mf* opportunist

opportunità [op·por·tu·ni·'ta] <-> *f* 1.(*occasione*) opportunity 2.(*utilità*) advisability

opportuno, -a [op·por·'tu:·no] *agg* (*adatto*) advisable

opposi *1. pers sing pass rem di* **opporre**

oppositore, -trice [op·po·zi·'to:·re] *m*, *f* opponent

opposizione [op·po·zit·'tsio:·ne] *f* 1.(*resistenza*) opposition 2. POL opposition 3.(*contrapposizione*) opposition

opposto [op·'pos·to] *m* opposite

opposto, -a *agg* 1.(*situato di fronte*) opposite 2.(*contrario*) opposite

oppressi [op·'prɛs·si] *1. pers sing pass rem di* **opprimere**

oppressione [op·pres·'sio:·ne] *f* 1.(*sopraffazione*) oppression 2.(*sensazione*) constriction

oppressivo, -a [op·pres·'si:·vo] *agg a. fig* oppressive

oppresso, -a [op·'prɛs·so] I. *pp di* **opprimere** II. *agg* (*popolo*) oppressed III. *m*, *f* **gli -i** the oppressed

oppressore [op·pres·'so:·re] *m* oppressor

opprimente [op·pri·'mɛn·te] *agg* 1.(*caldo*) oppressive 2.(*persona*) overbearing

opprimere [op·'pri:·me·re] <opprimo, oppressi, oppresso> *vt* 1.(*vessare: tiranno, governo*) to oppress 2.(*affliggere: persona, angoscia*) to oppress

oppugnabilità [op·puɲ·ɲa·bi·li·'ta] <-> *f* (*di teoria, tesi*) refutability

oppugnare [op·puɲ·'ɲa:·re] *vt* (*teoria, tesi*) to refute

oppure [op·'pu:·re] *cong* 1.(*o*) or 2.(*altrimenti*) otherwise

optare [op·'ta:·re] *vi* (*scegliere*) to choose; **~ per qc** to choose sth

optimum ['ɔp·ti·mum] <-> *m* optimum

optional(s) ['ɔp·ʃə·nəl(s)/'ɔp·ʃo·nal(s)] *mpl* extras *pl*

optoelettronica [op·to·e·le·'trɔ:·ni·ka] <-che> *f* TEC optoelectronics *sing*

opulento, -a [o·pu·'lɛn·to] *agg* (*banchetto, pranzo*) opulent; (*stile*) luxuriant

opulenza [o·pu·'lɛn·tsa] *f* (*di banchetto, pranzo*) opulence; (*di stile*) luxuriance

opuscolo [o·'pus·ko·lo] *m* pamphlet

opzionale [op·tsio·'na:·le] *agg* optional

opzione [op·'tsio:·ne] *f* 1.(*scelta*) option 2. FIN option

ora¹ ['o:·ra] I. *avv* 1.(*adesso*) now; **d'~ in avanti** [*o* **in poi**] from now on; **fin d'~** straight away; **prima d'~** until now 2.(*poco fa*) (just) now; **or ~** just now 3.(*tra poco*) (right) now 4.(*in correlazioni*) **~ ... ~ ...** now ... now ...; **~ come ~** right now; **fin ~** *v.* **finora** II. *cong* 1.(*invece*) but 2.(*dunque, allora*) now

ora² *f* 1.(*unità*) hour; **a -e** by the hour; **correre a cento all'~** to do sixty miles an hour; **tra mezz'~** in half an hour; **per -e e -e** for hours 2.(*nelle indicazioni temporali*) time; **~ civile** standard time; **~ legale** daylight-saving time; **~ locale** local time; **che ~ è** — è l'una what's the time? — (it's) one o'clock; **che -e sono? — sono le quattro** what's the time? — (it's) four o'clock 3. *fig* (*momento*) time; **di buon'~** in good time; **è ~ di partire** it's time to leave; **era ora!** about time!; **far le -e piccole** to stay up late; **non veder l'~ di ... +** *inf* not to be able to wait to ...

oracolo [o·'ra:·ko·lo] *m* oracle

orafo, -a ['ɔ:·ra·fo] *m*, *f* goldsmith

orale [o·'ra:·le] I. *agg* 1.(*della bocca: chirurgia, igiene*) oral; **per via ~** orally 2.(*esame, poesia, tradizione*) oral; **prova ~** oral exam II. *m* oral

oramai [o·ra·'ma:·i] *avv v.* **ormai**

orango [o·'raŋ·go] <-ghi> orangutan

orario [o·'ra:·rio] <-i> *m* 1.(*di lavoro, ufficio, negozio*) hours *pl*; **~ continuato** all-day opening; **~ elastico** [*o* **flessibile**] flextime; **~ d'apertura dei negozi** opening hours; **~ di lavoro** working hours; **~ di sportello** business hours; **~ delle visite** visiting hours; **~ d'ufficio** office hours 2. AERO, FERR timetable; **in ~** on time 3.(*tabella: di lezioni*) timetable

orario, -a <-i, -ie> *agg* 1.(*di ora, delle ore*) time; **disco ~** parking disk; **fascia ~** time slot; **fuso ~** time zone 2.(*all'ora: retribuzione, paga*) hourly 3.(*dell'orologio*) **in senso ~** clockwise

orata [o·'ra:·ta] *f* gilthead bream

oratore, -trice [o·ra·'to:·re] *m*, *f* orator

oratorio [o·ra·'tɔ:·rio] *m* (*nelle parrocchie*) parish youth center

oratorio, -a <-i, -ie> *agg* (*arte, capacità dote*) oratory

orbene, or bene [or·'bɛ:·ne] *cong* so

orbettino [or·bet·'ti:·no] *m* slowworm

orbita ['ɔr·bi·ta] *f* 1. ASTR, PHYS (*traiettoria*) orbit 2. ANAT socket; **con gli occhi fuori delle -e**

O

fig in amazement

orbitale [or·bi·'ta:·le] *agg* ASTR orbital; **stazione** ~ space station; **velocità** ~ orbital velocity

orbitante [or·bi·'tan·te] *agg* ASTR orbiting

orbitare [or·bi·'ta:·re] *vi* **1.** ASTR to orbit; ~ **intorno alla terra** to orbit the earth **2.** *fig* to hang around; ~ **intorno a qu** to hang around sb

orbo, -a ['ɔr·bo] *agg* **1.** (*cieco*) blind **2.** (*che vede male*) **essere** ~ to have poor sight

orca ['ɔr·ka] <-che> *f* ZOO killer whale

orchestra [or·'kɛs·tra] *f* orchestra

orchestrale [or·kes·'tra:·le] **I.** *agg* (*musica, concerto, repertorio*) orchestral; **complesso** ~ orchestra **II.** *mf* orchestral musician

orchestrare [or·kes·'tra:·re] *vt a. fig* to orchestrate

orchestrazione [or·kes·trat·'tsio:·ne] *f a. fig* orchestration

orchestrina [or·kes·'tri:·na] *f* band

orchidea [or·ki·'dɛ:·a] *f* orchid

orco ['ɔr·ko] <-chi> *m* (*nelle fiabe*) ogre

ordigno [or·'diɲ·ɲo] *m* **1.** (*congegno*) device **2.** (*bomba*) bomb; ~ **esplosivo** explosive device

ordinale [or·di·'na:·le] **I.** *agg* ordinal **II.** *m* ordinal

ordinamento [or·di·na·'men·to] *m* (*regolamento: scolastico, legislativo*) system

ordinanza [or·di·'nan·tsa] *f* **1.** JUR (*provvedimento*) order **2.** MIL **uniforme d'**~ service uniform

ordinare [or·di·'na:·re] **I.** *vt* **1.** (*gener*) to order **2.** (*mettere in ordine: carte, idee, elementi*) to organize **3.** REL to ordain; ~ **qu sacerdote** to ordain sb as a priest **II.** *vr:* **-rsi** to arrange oneself

ordinario [or·di·'na:·rio] <-i> *m* **1.** (*normalità*) **fuori dell'**~ out of the ordinary **2.** (*professore di ruolo*) full professor

ordinario, -a <-i, -ie> *agg* **1.** (*normale*) ordinary; **tariffa -a** standard rate **2.** (*di ruolo: docente*) full **3.** (*grossolano*) vulgar

ordinata *f* MATH ordinate

ordinato, -a [or·di·'na:·to] *agg* (*persona, casa*) tidy

ordinazione [or·di·nat·'tsio:·ne] *f* **1.** COM order; **su** ~ to order **2.** (*al bar, ristorante*) order **3.** REL ordination

ordine ['or·di·ne] *m* **1.** (*sistemazione, struttura*) order; ~ **alfabetico** alphabetic order; **mettere** ~ to tidy up; **richiamare qu all'**~ to call sb to order; **in** ~ **sparso** a few at a time; **con** ~ in an orderly fashion **2.** (*comando*) order; ~ **del giorno** agenda; ~ **di comparizione** JUR summons; **parola d'**~ password; **fino a nuovo** ~ until further orders; **ai vostri -i** at your command; **agli -i!** yes, sir!; **per** ~ **di** by order of **3.** COMPUT (*comando*) command **4.** COM order; ~ **di consegna** delivery order; ~ **di pagamento** payment order **5.** (*categoria professionale*) profession, the medical/legal

profession **6.** (*cavalleresco, religioso*) order **7.** (*qualità*) quality; **di prim'**~ first-rate; **di terz'**~ third-rate; **d'infimo** ~ poor quality **8.** THEAT tier; **secondo** ~ **di palchi** second tier of boxes

ordire [or·'di:·re] <ordisco> *vt fig* (*congiura, complotto, trama*) to hatch

ordito [or·'di:·to] *m* (*di tessuto*) warp

orecchia [o·'rek·kia] <-cchie> *f* ANAT ear; **fare le -cchie alle pagine** to fold the corners of the pages; *v.a.* **orecchio**

orecchiabile [o·rek·'kia:·bi·le] *agg* (*musica, canzone*) catchy

orecchino [o·rek·'ki:·no] *m* (*gioiello*) earring

orecchio [o·'rek·kio] <-cchi *m*, -cchie *f*> *m* **1.** ANAT ear **2.** (*udito*) hearing **3.** (*per la musica*) ear; **avere molto** ~ to have a very good ear; **cantare a** ~ to sing by ear **4.** (*loc*) **entrare da un** ~ **e uscire dall'altro** to go in one ear and out the other; **essere duro d'-cchi** to be hard of hearing; **fare -cchie da mercante** to turn a deaf ear; **mettere una pulce nell'**~ **a qu** to arouse sb's suspicions; **tirare le -cchie a qu** to give sb a slap on the wrist; **da questo** ~ **non ci sento** I'm not listening; **aprir bene le -cchie** to prick up one's ears; **essere tutt'-cchi** to be all ears

orecchioni [o·rek·'kio:·ni] *mpl fam* mumps *sing*

orefice [o·'re:·fi·tʃe] *mf* **1.** (*artigiano*) goldsmith **2.** (*negoziante*) jeweler

oreficeria [o·re·fi·tʃe·'ri:·a] <-ie> *f* **1.** (*arte*) goldwork **2.** (*laboratorio*) goldsmith's workshop **3.** (*negozio*) goldsmith's

oretta [o·'ret·ta] *f* about an hour

orfano, -a ['or·fa·no] **I.** *agg* orphan; **essere** ~ **di madre** to have lost one's mother **II.** *m, f* orphan

orfanotrofio [or·fa·no·'trɔ:·fio] <-i> *m* orphanage

organetto [or·ga·'net·to] *m* (*organo meccanico mobile*) barrel organ

organicità [or·ga·ni·tʃi·'ta] <-> *f* (*ordine: di discorso, trattato, progetto*) coherence

organico [or·'ga:·ni·ko] <-ci> *m* **1.** ADM (*personale*) staff **2.** MIL (*personale*) members *pl*

organico, -a <-ci, -che> *agg* **1.** (*degli organismi*) organic **2.** (*degli organi*) organic **3.** *fig* (*strutturato*) comprehensive

organigramma [or·ga·ni·'gram·ma] <-i> *m* ADM organizational chart

organismo [or·ga·'niz·mo] *m* **1.** (*essere vivente*) organism **2.** (*corpo umano*) body **3.** *fig* (*ente*) body

organista [or·ga·'nis·ta] <-i *m*, -e *f*> *mf* organist

organizzare [or·ga·nid·'dza:·re] **I.** *vt* (*lavoro, conferenza, viaggio*) to organize **II.** *vr:* **-rsi** to organize oneself

organizzativo, -a [or·ga·nid·dza·'ti:·vo] *agg* **1.** (*capacità aspetto*) organizational **2.** (*comitato, segreteria*) organizing

organizzato, -a [or·ga·nid·'dza:·to] **I.** *agg*

(*ordinato*) organized; **viaggio** ~ package tour **II.** *m*, *f* (*sindacalmente*) union member

organizzatore, -trice [or·ga·nid·dza·'to:·re] **I.** *agg* (*comitato, segreteria*) organizing **II.** *m*, *f* organizer

organizzazione [or·ga·nid·dzat·'tsio:·ne] *f* (*ordine, attività associazione*) organization

organo ['ɔr·ga·no] *m* **1.** ANAT organ **2.** TEC component **3.** MUS organ **4.** (*ente*) body **5.** (*giornale*) organ

orgasmo [or·'gaz·mo] *m* orgasm

orgia ['ɔr·dʒa] <-ge *o* -gie> *f* orgy

orgiastico, -a [or·'dʒas·ti·ko] <-ci, -che> *agg* (*esaltazione, eccitazione, danza*) orgiastic

orgoglio [or·'goʎ·ʎo] <-gli> *m* **1.** (*superbia*) pride **2.** (*motivo di vanto*) pride

orgoglioso, -a [or·goʎ·'ʎo:·so] *agg* proud; **essere** ~ **di qu/qc** to be proud of sb/sth

orientabile [o·rien·'ta:·bi·le] *agg* (*antenna, lampada, lamella*) adjustable

orientale [o·rien·'ta:·le] **I.** *agg* **1.** (*a est: parte, frontiera, lato*) eastern **2.** (*civiltà, popolazioni*) oriental; **tappeto** ~ oriental rug **II.** *mf* Asian

orientalista [o·rien·ta·'lis·ta] <-i *m*, -e *f*> *mf* orientalist

orientalistica [o·rien·ta·'lis·ti·ka] <-che> *f* oriental studies *pl*

orientamento [o·rien·ta·'men·to] *m* **1.** (*consapevolezza della direzione*) orientation; **perdere l'~** to lose one's bearings **2.** (*indirizzo*) orientation **3.** (*scelta di un indirizzo*) guidance; ~ **professionale** guidance counseling

orientare [o·rien·'ta:·re] **I.** *vt* **1.** (*disporre*) to point; ~ **qc a sud/nord** to point sth towards the south/north; ~ **qc verso l'alto** to point sth upwards **2.** *fig* (*indirizzare*) to direct; ~ **qu verso** [*o* **a**] **qc** to direct sb towards sth **II.** *vr:* **-rsi 1.** (*orizzontarsi*) to find one's bearings **2.** (*indirizzarsi*) **-rsi verso qc** to opt for sth

orientativo, -a [o·rien·ta·'ti:·vo] *agg* **1.** (*indicativo: prezzo, stima*) indicative; **a titolo** ~ as a guideline **2.** (*per orientarsi: corso, tirocinio, test*) guidance

orientazione [o·rien·tat·'tsio:·ne] *f* orientation

oriente [o·'riɛn·te] *m* **1.** (*est*) east **2.** (*civiltà*) East; **l'Estremo** ~ the Far East; **il Medio** ~ the Middle East; **il Vicino** ~ the Near East

orifizio [o·ri·'fit·tsio] <-i> *m a.* ANAT orifice

origami [o·ri·'ga·mi] <-> *m* ARTE origami

origano [o·'ri:·ga·no] *m* **1.** (*pianta*) wild marjoram **2.** (*spezia*) oregano

originale [o·ri·dʒi·'na:·le] **I.** *agg* **1.** (*opera, peccato, idea*) original **2.** (*stravagante: persona*) eccentric **II.** *m* **1.** (*gener*) original; **copia conforme all'~** true copy of the original document **2.** (*lingua originale*) original language **III.** *mf* eccentric

originalità [o·ri·dʒi·na·li·'ta] <-> *f* **1.** (*autenticità*) authenticity **2.** (*novità*) originality **3.** (*stravaganza*) eccentricity

originare [o·ri·dʒi·'na:·re] *vt* (*causare*) to give rise to

originario, -a [o·ri·dʒi·'na:·rio] <-i, -ie> *agg* **1.** (*proveniente: persona, pianta*) native; **essere** ~ **di** to come from **2.** (*archetipo*) original

origine [o·'ri:·dʒi·ne] *f* **1.** (*gener*) origin; **dare** ~ **a qc** to give rise to sth; **in** ~ originally; **ha** ~ **da** it has it's origins in **2.** *pl* origins *pl*

origliare [o·riʎ·'ʎa:·re] *vi* to eavesdrop

orina [o·'ri:·na] *f* urine

orinale [o·ri·'na:·le] *m* (*vaso da notte*) chamber pot

orinare [o·ri·'na:·re] **I.** *vi* to urinate **II.** *vt* to urinate

oristanese [o·ris·ta·'ne:·se] **I.** *mf* (*abitante*) person from Oristano **II.** *agg* from Oristano

Oristanese <*sing*> *m* (*zona*) Oristano area; **nell'~** in the Oristano area

Oristano [o·ri·'sta:·no] *f* Oristano

orizzontale [o·rid·dzon·'ta:·le] **I.** *agg* horizontal; **in posizione** ~ in a horizontal position **II.** *f* (*nei cruciverba*) **le -i** the across clues

orizzontarsi [o·rid·dzon·'tar·si] *vr* **1.** (*orientarsi*) to find one's bearings **2.** *fig* (*raccapezzarsi*) to find one's way

orizzonte [o·rid·'dzon·te] *m* **1.** GEO horizon; **giro d'~** to survey the horizon **2.** *fig* (*prospettiva*) opportunity

orlare [or·'la:·re] *vt* **1.** (*fiancheggiare*) to flank **2.** (*nel cucito*) to hem

orlo [or·lo] *m* **1.** (*margine*) edge **2.** (*di tessuto*) hem **3.** *fig* brink; **essere sull'~ della pazzia** to be on the brink of madness

orma ['or·ma] *f* **1.** (*di persona*) footprint **2.** (*di animale*) track **3.** *fig* footstep; **seguire** [*o* **calcare**] **le -e di qu** to follow in sb's footsteps

ormai [or·'ma:·i] *avv* **1.** (*a questo punto*) now **2.** (*a quel punto*) by then **3.** (*già*) already

ormeggiare [or·med·'dʒa:·re] **I.** *vt* NAUT to moor **II.** *vi:* **-rsi** to moor

ormeggio [or·'med·dʒo] <-ggi> *m* **1.** NAUT (*manovra, luogo*) mooring **2.** *pl* NAUT (*cime*) moorings *pl*; **mollare gli -ggi** to slip one's moorings

ormonale [or·mo·'na:·le] *agg* (*cura, terapia, sistema*) hormonal

ormone [or·'mo:·ne] *m* hormone

ornamentale [or·na·men·'ta:·le] *agg* ornamental; **piante -i** ornamental plants

ornamento [or·na·'men·to] *m* (*decorazione*) ornament

ornare [or·'na:·re] **I.** *vt* (*abbellire: abito, tavola*) to decorate **II.** *vr:* **-rsi** to decorate oneself

ornato, -a *agg* (*decorato*) ornate

ornitologia [or·ni·to·lo·'dʒi:·a] <-gie> *f* ornithology

ornitologo, -a [or·ni·'tɔ:·lo·go] <-gi, -ghe> *m*, *f* ornithologist

oro ['ɔ:·ro] *m* **1.** (*metallo, colore*) gold; ~ **bianco/giallo/rosso** white/yellow/red gold; **d'~** gold; **anello/catena d'~** gold ring/chain; **il secolo d'~** the Golden Age; **valere tant'~ quanto pesa** to be worth one's weight

O

in gold; **non è tutto ~ quel che luccica** *prov* all that glitters is not gold **2.**(*denaro*) money; **nemmeno per tutto l'~ del mondo** not for all the tea in China; **nuotare nell'~** to be rolling in it **3.** *pl* (*oggetti d'~*) gold items *pl* **4.** *pl* (*di carte*) coins *pl, suit in Italian card deck*

orologeria [o·ro·lo·dʒe·'ri:·a] <-ie> *f* **1.**(*arte*) clockmaking **2.**(*industria*) clockmaking industry **3.**(*negozio*) watchmaker's (shop) **4.**(*dispositivo*) clockwork; **bomba a ~** time bomb

orologiaio, -a [o·ro·lod·'dʒa:·io] <-giai, -giaie> *m, f* **1.**(*fabbricante*) clockmaker; (*di orologi da polso*) watchmaker **2.**(*riparatore*) clock repairer; (*di orologi da polso*) watch repairer **3.**(*negozio*) clock seller's; (*di orologi da polso*) watch seller's

orologio [o·ro·'lɔ:·dʒo] <-gi> *m* clock; (*da polso*) watch; **~ al quarzo** quartz clock; (*da polso*) quartz watch; **~ da polso** wristwatch; **~ da tasca** pocket watch; **caricare l'~** to wind up the clock; (*da polso*) to wind up the watch; **essere come un ~** *fig* to be as regular as clockwork; **l'~ va avanti/indietro** the click is fast/slow

oroscopo [o·'rɔs·ko·po] *m* ASTR horoscope

orrendo, -a [or·'rɛn·do] *agg* horrible

orribile [or·'ri:·bi·le] *agg* **1.**(*atroce: delitto, morte, disgrazia*) awful **2.**(*fig (pessimo: gusto, film*) terrible

orrido ['ɔr·ri·do] *m* **l'~** the gorge

orrido, -a *agg* (*aspetto, creatura*) horrible

orripilante [or·ri·pi·'lan·te] *agg* (*aspetto, immagine*) terrifying

orrore [or·'ro:·re] *m* **1.**(*repulsione*) horror; **avere ~ di qc** to loathe sth **2.**(*terrore*) terror; **avere un sacro ~ di qc** to be terrified of sth; **film dell'~** horror movie **3.**(*cosa brutta*) fright **4.**(*cosa orribile*) horror; **gli -i della guerra** the horrors of war

orsa ['or·sa] *f* **1.** ZOO bear **2.** ASTR **l'Orsa maggiore** Ursa Major; *inf* the Big Dipper; **l'Orsa minore** Ursa Minor

orsacchiotto [or·sak·'kiɔt·to] *m* **1.**(*piccolo orso*) bear cub **2.**(*di peluche*) teddy bear

orso ['ors·o] *m* bear; **~ bianco** [*o* **polare**] polar bear; **~ bruno** brown bear; **~ grigio** grizzly bear

ortaggio [or·'tad·dʒo] <-ggi> *m* vegetable

ortensia [or·'tɛn·sia] <-ie> *f* hortensia

ortica [or·'ti:·ka] <-che> *f* stinging nettle

orticante [or·ti·'kan·te] *agg* stinging

orticaria [or·ti·'ka:·ria] <-ie> *f* hives *sing*

orticoltore, -trice [or·ti·kol·'to:·re] *m, f* horticulturist

orticoltura [or·ti·kol·'tu:·ra] *f* horticulture

orto ['ɔr·to] *m* (vegetable) garden; **~ botanico** botanical gardens

ortodontista [or·to·don·'tis·ta] <-i *m*, -e *f*> *mf* MED orthodontist

ortodossia [or·to·dos·'si:·a] <-ie> *f a. fig* orthodoxy

ortodosso, -a [or·to·'dɔs·so] **I.** *agg a. fig* orthodox **II.** *m, f* REL **gli -i** the Orthodox

ortofrutticolo, -a [or·to·frut·'ti:·ko·lo] *agg* (*mercato, prodotto*) fruit and vegetable

ortogonale [or·to·go·'na:·le] *agg* orthogonal

ortografia [or·to·gra·'fi:·a] *f* spelling

ortografico, -a [or·to·'gra:·fi·ko] <-ci, -che> *agg* (*errori, convenzione*) spelling

ortolano, -a [or·to·'la:·no] *m, f* (*venditore*) fresh produce vendor

ortomercato [or·to·mer·'ka:·to] *m* wholesale produce market

ortopedia [or·to·pe·'di:·a] <-ie> *f* orthopedics *sing*

ortopedico, -a [or·to·'pɛ:·di·ko] <-ci, -che> **I.** *agg* (*scarpe, busto*) orthopedic **II.** *m, f* (*medico*) orthopedic surgeon

orvieto [or·'vie:·to/or·'vie:·to] *m* Orvieto, *white wine from the Umbria region*

orzaiolo [or·dza·'iɔ:·lo] *m* MED sty

orzata [or·'dza:·ta] *f* CULIN (*bevanda*) drink *made using almond milk*

orzo ['ɔr·dzo] *m* barley; **~ perlato** pearl barley

osanna [o·'zan·na] **I.** *int* hosanna **II.** <-> *m* hosanna

osannare [o·zan·'na:·re] *vt* to praise

osare [o·'za:·re] *vt* to dare; **non oso chiedere** I don't dare ask

oscenità [oʃ·ʃe·ni·'ta] <-> *f* **1.**(*indecenza*) obscenity **2.**(*atto indecente*) indecent act **3.**(*parole indecenti*) obscenity **4.** *fam* (*cosa brutta*) monstrosity

osceno, -a [oʃ·'ʃɛ:·no] *agg* **1.**(*indecente: atto, gesto, film*) obscene **2.** *fam* (*bruttissimo*) disgusting

oscillare [oʃ·ʃil·'la:·re] *vi* **1.** PHYS (*pendolo*) to oscillate **2.**(*variare*) to fluctuate

oscillatore [oʃ·ʃil·la·'to:·re] *m* oscillator

oscillatorio, -a [oʃ·ʃil·la·'tɔ:·rio] <-i, -ie> *agg* PHYS oscillatory

oscillazione [oʃ·ʃil·lat·'tsio:·ne] *f* **1.** PHYS oscillation **2.**(*di prezzo, temperatura*) fluctuation

oscuramento [os·ku·ra·'men·to] *m* **1.**(*di cielo*) darkening **2.**(*in guerra*) blackout **3.**(*di sito Internet, rete televisiva*) blackout

oscurare [os·ku·'ra:·re] **I.** *vt* **1.**(*rendere oscuro: cielo*) to darken **2.**(*rete televisiva*) to block out **II.** *vr:* **-rsi 1.**(*diventare oscuro*) to darken **2.** *fig* (*vista*) to cloud over

oscurità [os·ku·ri·'ta] <-> *f* **1.**(*assenza di luce*) darkness **2.** *fig* (*di stile, linguaggio*) obscurity

oscuro [os·'ku:·ro] *m* darkness; **essere all'~ di qc** to be in the dark about sth

oscuro, -a *agg* **1.**(*buio: notte, zona*) dark; **camera -a** PHOT dark room **2.** *fig* (*pensiero, testo*) gloomy

ospedale [o·pe·'da:·le] *m* hospital; **~ da campo** field hospital; **fare sei mesi d'~** to spend six months in the hospital

ospedaliero, -a [os·pe·da·'liɛ:·ro] *agg* (*ente, struttura*) hospital; **cure -e** hospital treatment

ospedalizzare [os·pe·da·lid·'dza:·re] *vt* (*paziente*) to hospitalize

ospitale [os·pi·'ta:·le] *agg* (*persona, casa*) hospitable

ospitalità [os·pi·ta·li·'ta] <-> *f* **1.** (*caratteristica*) hospitality **2.** (*accoglienza*) hospitality; **dare ~ a qu** to offer hospitality to sb

ospitare [os·pi·'ta:·re] *vt* **1.** (*dare ospitalità a*) to accommodate **2.** SPORT to host **3.** (*accogliere: convegno*) to host **4.** (*contenere: persone, barche*) to hold **5.** (*custodire: quadro, statua*) to house

ospite ['ɔs·pi·te] I. *mf* **1.** (*persona che ospita*) host **2.** (*persona ospitata*) guest; **l'~ è come il pesce, dopo tre giorni puzza** *prov* guests, like fish, begin to smell after three days II. *agg* **1.** (*che ospita*) host **2.** (*ospitato*) guest

ospizio [os·'pit·tsio] <-i> *m* (*per anziani*) nursing home

ossatura [os·sa·'tu:·ra] *f* **1.** ANAT (*insieme delle ossa*) skeleton **2.** ANAT (*struttura ossea*) bone structure **3.** (*struttura portante: di edificio, economia*) framework

osseo, -a ['ɔs·se·o] <-ei, -ee> *agg* (*frattura, protesi, struttura*) bone; **callo ~** callus; **midollo ~** bone marrow

ossequio [os·'sɛ·kui·o] <-qui> *m* **1.** (*rispetto*) respect **2.** *pl* (*saluto*) regards *pl*; **gradisca i miei -qui** (*nelle lettere*) kindest regards

ossequioso, -a [os·se·'kui·o:·so] *agg* obsequious

osservante [os·ser·'van·te] I. *agg* **1.** REL practicing **2.** (*rispettoso*) respectful; **essere ~ di qc** to observe sth II. *mf* REL churchgoer

osservanza [os·ser·'van·tsa] *f a.* REL observance

osservare [os·ser·'va:·re] *vt* **1.** (*guardare attentamente*) to observe **2.** (*rispettare: norme, regole, silenzio*) to observe **3.** (*rilevare*) to notice

osservatore, -trice [os·ser·va·'to:·re] I. *agg* observant II. *m, f* observer

osservatorio [os·ser·va·'tɔ:·rio] <-i> *m* observatory; **~ astronomico** astronomical observatory; **~ meteorologico** weather station

osservazione [os·ser·vat·'tsio:·ne] *f* **1.** (*atto*) observation; **spirito di ~** power of observation; **essere tenuto in ~** to be kept under observation **2.** (*considerazione critica*) observation **3.** (*rimprovero*) reproach

ossessionante [os·ses·sio·'nan·te] *agg* **1.** desiderio, idea, ricordo all-consuming **2.** (*persona*) obsessive **3.** (*danza, musica*) haunting

ossessionare [os·ses·sio·'na:·re] *vt* **1.** (*tormentare: ricordo, idea*) to obsess **2.** (*infastidire: persona*) to pester

ossessione [os·ses·'sio:·ne] *f* obsession; **avere l'~ di qc** to be obsessed with sth

ossessivo, -a [os·ses·'si:·vo] *agg* **1.** PSYCH obsessive **2.** (*ritmo, musica*) haunting

ossesso, -a [os·'sɛs·so] *m, f* (*indemoniato*) possessed person

ossia [os·'si:·a] *cong* that is

ossibuchi *pl di* **ossobuco**

ossidabile [os·si·'da:·bi·le] *agg* (*metallo, vit-*

amina) oxidizable

ossidare [os·si·'da:·re] I. *vt* to oxidize II. *vr:* **-rsi** to oxidize

ossidazione [os·si·dat·'tsio:·ne] *f* oxidation

ossido ['ɔs·si·do] *m* oxide; **~ di azoto** nitric oxide

ossidrico, -a [os·'si:·dri·ko] <-ci, -che> *agg* (*fiamma*) oxyhydrogen; **cannello ~** blowtorch

ossigenare [os·si·dʒe·'na:·re] I. *vt* **1.** CHEM to oxygenate **2.** (*decolorare*) to bleach II. *vr:* **-rsi** **1.** (*capelli*) to bleach one's hair **2.** (*polmoni*) to get some fresh air

ossigenato, -a [os·si·dʒe·'na:·to] *agg* **1.** CHEM oxygenated; **acqua -a** peroxide **2.** (*capelli*) bleached; **bionda -a** peroxide blonde

ossigenazione [os·si·dʒe·nat·'tsio:·ne] *f* oxygenation

ossigeno [os·'si:·dʒe·no] *m* CHEM oxygen

ossimoro [os·si·'mɔ:·ro] *m* LIT oxymoron

osso¹ ['ɔs·so] <*pl:* **-a** *f*> *m* **1.** ANAT bone; **avere le -a rotte** to be exhausted; **ridursi pelle e -a** to become nothing but skin and bones; **farsi le -a** to cut one's teeth; **un ~ duro** *fig* (*difficoltà*) a hard nut to crack; (*persona*) a tough customer **2.** (*nocciolo*) stone; **sputa l'~!** *scherz, fam* spit it out!

osso² *m* (*osso animale lavorato*) bone

ossobuco [os·so·'bu:·ko] <ossibuchi> *m* CULIN osso buco

ossuto, -a [os·'su:·to] *agg* (*persona*) skinny; (*volto, mani, gambe*) bony

ostacolare [os·ta·ko·'la:·re] *vt* (*movimenti*) to obstruct; (*decisioni*) to block; (*ingresso, sviluppo, ricerca*) to hinder

ostacolo [os·'ta:·ko·lo] *m* **1.** (*impedimento*) obstacle **2.** *fig* (*intralcio*) hindrance; **essere d'~ a qc** to be a hindrance to sth **3.** SPORT **corsa a -i** obstacle race

ostaggio [os·'tad·dʒo] <-ggi> *m* hostage; **tenere qu in ~** to hold sb hostage

oste, -essa ['ɔs·te, os·'tes·sa] *m, f* innkeeper; **fare i conti senza l'~** *fig* to forget the most important thing

osteggiare [os·ted·'dʒa:·re] *vt* (*progetto, matrimonio*) to oppose

ostello [os·'tɛl·lo] *m* dwelling; **~ della giovent** youth hostel

ostensorio [os·ten·'sɔ:·rio] <-i> *m* REL ostensory

ostentare [os·ten·'ta:·re] *vt* **1.** (*fare sfoggio di: ricchezza*) to flaunt **2.** (*simulare: cinismo, indifferenza*) to affect

ostentato, -a [os·ten·'ta:·to] *agg* **1.** (*ricchezza, lusso*) ostentatious **2.** (*simulato: cinismo, indifferenza*) affected

ostentazione [os·ten·tat·'tsio:·ne] *f* **1.** (*di ricchezza, lusso*) ostentation **2.** (*di cinismo, indifferenza*) display

osteopatia [os·teo·pa·'ti:·a] *f* osteopathy

osteria [os·te·'ri:·a] <-ie> *f* tavern

ostessa *f v.* **oste**

ostetrica [os·'tɛ:·tri·ka] <-che> *f* obstetrician

ostetricia [os·te·'tri:·tʃa] <-cie> *f* obstetrics

O

sing

ostetrico, -a [os·'tɛ:·tri·ko] <-ci, -che> *agg* (*clinica*) obstetric

ostia ['ɔs·tia] <-ie> *f* 1. REL Host 2. (*per medicinali*) wafer

ostico, -a ['ɔs·ti·ko] <-ci, -che> *agg* (*materia, linguaggio, termine*) difficult

ostile [os·'ti:·le] *agg* (*atto, forze*) hostile; **essere ~ a qc** (*ambiente*) to be hostile to sth; (*persona*) to be opposed to sth; **acquisizione ~** COM hostile takeover

ostilità [os·ti·li·'ta] <-> *f* 1. (*avversione*) hostility 2. *pl* (*atto ostile*) hostilities *pl*

ostinarsi [os·ti·'nar·si] *vr* ~ **a fare qc** to insist on doing sth; ~ **a non fare qc** to refuse to do sth

ostinato, -a [os·ti·'na:·to] *agg* 1. (*persona*) obstinate 2. (*dolore*) persistent 3. (*ricerca*) relentless

ostinazione [os·ti·nat·'tsio:·ne] *f* (*di persona*) obstinacy

ostracismo [os·tra·'tʃiz·mo] *m* 1. (*esilio*) ostracism 2. (*preconcetto*) prejudice

ostrica ['ɔs·tri·ka] <-che> *f* oyster

ostruire [os·tru·'i:·re] <ostruisco> *vt* (*passaggio, strada*) to block

ostruzione [os·trut·'tsio:·ne] *f* 1. (*di passaggio*) obstruction 2. MED blockage

ostruzionismo [os·trut·tsio·'niz·mo] *m* stonewalling; **fare ~** to stonewall

ostruzionista [os·trut·tsio·'nis·ta] <-i *m*, -e *f*> *mf* stonewaller

otite [o·'ti:·te] *f* MED ear infection

otorinolaringoiatra [o·to·ri·no·la·riŋ·go·'ia:·tra] <-i *m*, -e *f*> *mf* ear, nose and throat specialist

ottaedro [ot·ta·'ɛ:·dro] *m* octahedron

ottagonale [ot·ta·go·'na:·le] *agg* octagonal

ottagono [ot·'ta:·go·no] *m* octagon

ottanta [ot·'tan·ta] I. *num* eighty II. <-> *m* eighty; *v.a.* **cinquanta**

ottantenne [ot·tan·'tɛn·ne] I. *agg* eighty-year-old II. *mf* eighty-year-old

ottantennio [ot·tan·'tɛn·nio] <-i> *m* eighty years *pl*

ottantesimo [ot·tan·'tɛ:·zi·mo] *m* (*frazione*) eightieth

ottantesimo, -a I. *agg* eightieth II. *m*, *f* eightieth; *v.a.* **quinto**

ottantina [ot·tan·'ti:·na] *f* **un'~ (di …)** about eighty (…); **essere sull'~** to be about eighty

ottativo [ot·ta·'ti:·vo] *m* LING optative

ottativo, -a *agg* LING optative

ottava [ot·'ta:·va] *f* MUS octave

ottavino [ot·ta·'vi:·no] *m* MUS piccolo

ottavo [ot·'ta:·vo] *m* 1. (*frazione*) eighth 2. (*formato*) octavo 3. SPORT **-i di finale** quarterfinals

ottavo, -a I. *agg* eighth II. *m*, *f* eighth; *v.a.* **quinto**

ottemperanza [ot·tem·pe·'ran·tsa] *f* ADM compliance; **in ~ alla legge** in accordance with the law

ottenebrare [ot·te·ne·'bra:·re] *vt poet* (*offuscare: mente*) to cloud

ottenere [ot·te·'ne:·re] <irr> *vt* 1. (*conseguire: risultato, totale, vittoria*) to obtain 2. (*ricevere: ricompensa, premio*) to gain 3. (*ricavare: prodotto*) to obtain

ottenibile [ot·te·'ni:·bi·le] *agg* obtainable

ottenimento [ot·te·ni·'men·to] *m* (*di diploma, finanziamento*) achievement; (*di premio*) winning

ottenni *1. pers sing pass rem di* ottenere

ottenuto *pp di* ottenere

ottetto [ot·'tet·to] *m* octet

ottica ['ɔt·ti·ka] <-che> *f* 1. PHYS optics *sing* 2. (*tecnica*) optics *sing* 3. (*lenti*) optical system 4. *fig* (*punto di vista*) point of view

ottico ['ɔt·ti·ko] <-ci> *m* (*negozio*) optician's

ottico, -a <-ci, -che> I. *agg* 1. (*dell'occhio: nervo*) optic 2. COMPUT (*cavo*) optical; **lettore ~** OCR II. *m*, *f* (*tecnico*) optician

ottimale [ot·ti·'ma:·le] *agg* optimal

ottimamente [ot·ti·ma·'men·te] *avv superlativo di* **bene**[1] very well

ottimare [ot·ti·'ma:·re] *v.* ottimizzare

ottimismo [ot·ti·'miz·mo] *m* optimism

ottimista [ot·ti·'mis·ta] <-i *m*, -e *f*> I. *agg* (*persona*) optimistic II. *mf* optimist

ottimistico, -a [ot·ti·'mis·ti·ko] <-ci, -che> *agg* (*previsione, dichiarazione, dati*) optimistic

ottimizzare [ot·ti·mid·'dza:·re] *vt* (*processo, sistema, produttività*) to optimize

ottimo ['ɔt·ti·mo] *m* (*ideale*) ideal

ottimo, -a *agg superlativo di* **buono, -a** excellent

otto ['ɔt·to] I. *num* eight II. <-> *m* 1. (*numero*) eight 2. (*nelle date*) eighth 3. (*voto scolastico*) 8 out of 10 4. SPORT (*nel pattinaggio*) figure eight; (*nel canottaggio*) (rowing) eight 5. (*a forma di otto*) ~ **volante** roller coaster III. *fpl* eight o'clock; *v.a.* **cinque**

ottobre [ot·'to:·bre] *m* October; *v.a.* **aprile**

ottocentesco, -a [ot·to·tʃen·'tes·ko] <-schi, -sche> *agg* nineteenth-century

ottocento [ot·to·'tʃen·to] I. *num* nineteenth century II. <-> *m* (*numero*) eight-hundred; **l'Ottocento** the nineteenth century

ottomana [ot·to·'ma:·na] *f* (*divano*) ottoman

ottomano, -a [ot·to·'ma:·no] I. *agg* 1. *poet* Turkish 2. (*turco*) Ottoman II. *m*, *f* 1. *poet* Turk 2. (*turco*) Ottoman

ottomila [ot·to·'mi:·la] I. *num* eight-thousand II. <-> *m* eight-thousand

ottone [ot·'to:·ne] *m* 1. (*lega*) brass 2. *pl* MUS brass section

ottuagenario, -a [ot·tu·a·dʒe·'na:·rio] <-i, -ie> I. *agg* octogenarian II. *m*, *f* octogenarian

otturare [ot·tu·'ra:·re] I. *vt* 1. MED (*dente*) to fill 2. TEC (*tubo*) to block II. *vr*: **-rsi** to become blocked

otturatore [ot·tu·ra·'to:·re] *m* FOTO shutter

otturazione [ot·tu·rat·'tsio:·ne] *f* 1. (*di scarico, tubo*) blockage 2. (*di dente*) filling

ottusi [ot·'tu:·zi] *1. pers sing pass rem di*

ottundere

ottusità [ot·tu·zi·'ta] <-> *f* (*mente, persona*) obtuseness

ottuso, -a [ot·'tu:·zo] I. *pp di* **ottundere** II. *agg a fig* obtuse

output ['aut·put] <-> *m* COMPUT output

outsider [aut·'sai·də/aut·'sai·der] *mf* outsider

ouverture [u·vɛr·'ty:r] <-> *f* MUS overture

ovaia [o·'va:·ia] <-aie> ovary

ovaio [o'va:io] <*pl*: -aia *f*> *m* ovary

ovale [o·'va:·le] I. *agg* oval II. *m* oval

ovarico, -a [o·'va:·ri·ko] <-ci, -che> *agg* ANAT ovarian

ovatta [o·'vat·ta] *f* cotton wool

overdose ['ou·və·dous/o·ver·'dɔ·z(e)] <overdosi> *f* overdose

ovest ['ɔ:·vest] *m* west; **ad** ~ to the west; **ad** ~ **di** west of; **verso** ~ westwards

ovile [o·'vi:·le] *m* sheepfold; **tornare all'**~ *fig* to return to the fold

ovino [o·'vi:·no] *m* sheep

ovino, -a *agg* ovine; **carne** ~ mutton

ovolo ['ɔ:·vo·lo] *m* BOT (~ *buono*) Caesar's mushroom

ovulazione [o·vu·lat·'tsio:·ne] *f* BIOL ovulation

ovulo ['ɔ:·vu·lo] *m* 1. BOT ovule 2. BIOL ovum

ovunque [o·'vuŋ·kue] *avv* 1. (*dovunque*) wherever 2. (*dappertutto*) everywhere

ovvero [ov·'ve:·ro] *cong* that is

ovviare [ov·vi·'a:·re] *vi* ~ **a qc** (*situazione*) to remedy sth; (*inconveniente*) to solve sth

ovvietà [ov·vie·'ta] <-> *f* 1. (*caratteristica*) obviousness 2. (*cosa banale*) clichè

ovvio, -a ['ɔv·vio] <-i, -ie> *agg* 1. (*normale*) normal 2. (*logico: fatto, soluzione, conclusione*) obvious 3. (*scontato: considerazione*) predictable

ozelot [od·dze·'lɔt] *m* ocelot

oziare [ot·'tsia:·re] *vi* to loaf around

ozio ['ɔt·tsio] <-i> *m* 1. (*abituale inoperosità*) idleness; **l'**~ **è il padre dei vizi** *prov* idle hands are the devil's tools 2. (*inattività temporanea*) inactivity 3. (*tempo libero*) leisure

oziosità [ot·tsio·si·'ta] <-> *f* (*pigrizia*) laziness

ozioso, -a [ot·'tsio:·so] *agg* 1. (*fannullone*) idle 2. (*inoperoso: giornata*) idle 3. (*futile*) pointless

ozono [od·'dzɔ:·no] *m* CHEM ozone; **buco nell'**~ ozone hole

ozonosfera [od·dzo·nos·'fɛ:·ra] *f* ozonosphere

P

P, p [pi] <-> *f* P, p; ~ **come Palermo** P for Papa

p. *abbr di* **pagina** p.

PA *abbr di* **Pubblica Amministrazione** Civil Service

pacatezza [pa·ka·'tet·tsa] *f* calmness

pacato, -a [pa·'ka:·to] *agg* calm

pacca ['pak·ka] <-cche> *f fam* (*manata*) slap

pacchetto [pak·'ket·to] *m* 1. (*piccolo pacco*) package 2. (*confezione*) pack; **un** ~ **di sigarette** a pack of cigarettes 3. (*azionario*) block 4. COMPUT package

pacchia ['pak·kia] <-cchie> *f fam* blast

pacchiano, -a [pak·'kia:·no] *agg* (*di cattivo gusto*) vulgar

pacco ['pak·ko] <-cchi> *m* 1. (*involto*) package; **le faccio un** ~ **regalo?** would you like it gift-wrapped?; ~ **bomba** mail bomb 2. *fam* (*fregatura*) rip-off; **mi ha tirato un** ~ he stood me up

paccottiglia [pak·kot·'tiʎ·ʎa] <-glie> *f* (*cose senza valore*) junk

pace ['pa:·tʃe] *f* peace; **fare** ~ **con qu** to make it up with sb; **mettersi il cuore in** ~ to resign oneself; **non trovar** ~ to find no peace; **lasciare qu in** ~ to leave sb alone; **starsene in** (*santa*) ~ to have some peace

pacemaker ['peis·mei·kə] <-> *m* MED pacemaker

pachiderma [pa·ki·'dɛr·ma] <-i> *m* (*elefante*) pachyderm

Pachistan [pa·kis·'tan] *m il* ~ Pakistan; **in** ~ in Pakistan

pachistano, -a [pa·kis·'ta:·no] I. *agg* Pakistani II. *m, f* Pakistani

paciere, -a [pa·'tʃɛ:·re] *m, f* peacemaker

pacificare [pa·tʃi·fi·'ka:·re] I. *vt* 1. (*nemici*) to reconcile 2. (*animi*) to pacify II. *vr:* **-rsi** (*trovar pace*) to become reconciled

pacifico, -a [pa·'tʃi:·fi·ko] <-ci, -che> *agg* 1. (*uomo, indole*) peace-loving 2. (*intervento, manifestazione*) peaceful 3. *fig* (*chiaro*) clear 4. GEOG **il** [*o* **l'Oceano**] **Pacifico** the Pacific (Ocean)

pacifismo [pa·tʃi·'fiz·mo] *m* pacifism

pacifista [pa·tʃi·'fis·ta] <-i *m*, -e *f*> I. *mf* pacifist II. *agg* pacifist

pacioccone, -a [pa·tʃok·'ko:·ne] *m, f fam* plump easygoing person

pack [pæk] <-> *m* pack ice

package ['pæ·kidʒ] <- *o* packages> *m* COMPUT package

packaging ['pæ·ki·dʒiŋ] <-> *m* COM packaging

padano, -a [pa·'da:·no] *agg* Po; **pianura -a** Po Valley

padella [pa·'dɛl·la] *f* 1. (*pentola*) frying pan; ~ **antiaderente** nonstick frying pan; **cadere dalla** ~ **nella brace** *fig* to jump out of the frying pan into the fire 2. (*per malati*) bedpan

padiglione [pa·diʎ·'ʎo:·ne] *m* 1. (*di fiera, edificio*) pavilion 2. ~ **auricolare** auricle

Padova ['pa:·do·va] *f* Padua, *city in northeast Italy*

Padovano <*sing*> *m* the Padua area; **nel** ~ in the Padua

padovano, -a [pa·do·'va:·no] I. *agg* Paduan II. *m, f* (*abitante*) Paduan

padre ['pa:·dre] *m* 1. *a. fig* (*genitore*) father;

~ **adottivo** adoptive father; ~ **putativo** putative father; **di** ~ **in figlio** from father to son; **per via di** ~ on one's father's side; **tale il** ~ **tale il figlio** *prov* like father, like son *prov* 2. REL (*Dio*) Father 3. REL (*titolo*) Father; **il santo Padre** (*Papa*) the Holy Father 4. *pl* (*antenati*) forefathers

Padrenostro [pad·re·'nɔs·tro] <-> *m* Our Father

padrino [pa·'dri:·no] *m* (*di battesimo, nella mafia*) godfather; (*di cresima*) sponsor

padronale [pa·dro·'na:·le] *agg* 1.(*del padrone*) owner's 2.(*imprenditoriale*) employers'

padronanza [pa·dro·'nan·tsa] *f* 1.(*di materia, argomento*) command 2.(*di emozioni*) control

padronato [pa·dro·'na:·to] *m* (*imprenditori*) employers *pl*

padroncino, -a [pa·dron·'tʃi:·no] *m, f* taxi driver who owns his or her own cab

padrone, -a [pa·'dro:·ne] *m, f* 1.(*proprietario*) owner; ~ **di casa** landlord 2.(*datore di lavoro*) employer 3.(*dominatore*) master; **essere** ~ **di fare qc** (*libero*) to be free to do sth 4.(*conoscitore*) expert

padroneggiare [pa·dro·ned·'dʒa:·re] I. *vt* 1.(*emozioni*) to control 2.(*materia, argomento*) to master II. *vr:* **-rsi** (*dominarsi*) to control oneself

paesaggio [pae·'zad·dʒo] <-ggi> *m* 1. GEOG landscape; ~ **alpino** Alpine landscape 2.(*panorama*) view 3.(*pittura*) landscape (painting); FOTO landscape (photograph)

paesaggista [pae·zad·'dʒis·ta] <-i *m*, -e *f*> *mf* landscape painter

paesano, -a [pae·'za:·no] I. *agg* country; **alla -a** in a rustic style II. *m, f* (*abitante*) villager

paese [pa·'e:·ze] *m* 1.(*nazione, Stato*) country; ~ **emergente** developing country; ~ **industrializzato** industrialized nation; ~ **in via di sviluppo** developing country 2.(*l'Italia*) Italy; **i Paesi Bassi** the Netherlands *pl;* ~ **che vai, usanze che trovi** *prov* when in Rome, do as the Romans do *prov* 3.(*villaggio*) village 4.(*territorio*) land; **mandare qu a quel** ~ *fig, fam* to tell sb to go to hell

paffuto, -a [paf·'fu:·to] *agg* chubby

pag. *abbr di* **pagina** p.

paga ['pa:·ga] <-ghe> *f* 1.(*stipendio*) pay; **giorno di** ~ payday; **busta** ~ pay envelope 2. *fig* (*ricompensa*) reward

pagabile [pa·'ga:·bi·le] *agg* payable; ~ **a rate** payable in installments; ~ **a vista** payable on demand; ~ **alla consegna** payable on delivery; ~ **alla scadenza** payable on maturity

pagaia [pa·'ga:·ia] <-aie> *f* paddle

pagamento [pa·ga·'men·to] *m* payment; ~ **anticipato** advance payment; ~ **alla consegna** payment on delivery; ~ **a mezzo assegno** payment by check; ~ **a pronta cassa** cash payment; ~ **a rate** payment in installments; ~ **contro assegno** cash on delivery;

mancato ~ non-payment

paganesimo [pa·ga·'ne:·zi·mo] *m* paganism

pagano, -a [pa·'ga:·no] I. *agg* pagan II. *m, f* pagan

pagante [pa·'gan·te] I. *agg* paying II. *mf* payer

pagare [pa·'ga:·re] *vt* 1.(*persona*) to pay; (*acquisto, servizio*) to pay for; ~ **caro qc** to pay a lot for sth; *fig* (*errori*) to pay dearly for sth; **farla** ~ **a qu** *fam* to make sb pay for sth 2.(*offrire*) to buy; ~ **da bere a qu** to buy sb a drink 3. *fig* (*ricompensare*) to repay; ~ **qu con qc** to pay sb back for sth

pagella [pa·'dʒɛl·la] *f* (*a scuola*) report card

paggio ['pad·dʒo] <-ggi> *m* page

pagherò [pa·ge·'rɔ] <-> *m* IOU

pagina ['pa:·dʒi·na] *f* page; **prima** ~ (*di giornale*) front page; **terza** ~ (*pagina culturale*) culture page; **Pagine gialle** Yellow Pages®; **voltar** ~ to turn the page; (*cambiare vita*) to turn over a new leaf; (*cambiare discorso*) to move on; **mettere in** ~ TYP to print; ~ **web** Web page

paginatura [pa·dʒi·na·'tu:·ra] *f* (*numerazione delle pagine*) pagination

paglia ['paʎ·ʎa] <-glie> *f* 1.(*materiale*) straw; **fuoco di** ~ *fig* flash in the pan 2.(*oggetto*) straw object; (*cappello*) straw hat

pagliaccetto [paʎ·ʎat·'tʃet·to] *m* 1.(*da bambino*) rompers *pl* 2.(*da donna*) teddy

pagliacciata [paʎ·ʎat·'tʃa:·ta] *f fam* farce

pagliaccio [paʎ·'ʎat·tʃo] <-cci> *m* 1.(*di circo*) clown 2. *fig* (*buffone*) fool

pagliaio [paʎ·'ʎa:·io] <-ai> *m* haystack; **cercare un ago nel** ~ *fig* to look for a needle in a haystack

pagliericcio [paʎ·ʎe·'rit·tʃo] <-cci> *m* straw mattress

paglierino, -a [paʎ·ʎe·'ri:·no] *agg* straw-colored

paglietta [paʎ·'ʎet·ta] *f* 1.(*cappello*) boater 2.(*d'acciaio*) steel wool

pagliuzza [paʎ·'ʎut·tsa] *f* 1.(*di paglia*) straw 2.(*d'oro, d'argento*) speck

pagnotta [paɲ·'nɔt·ta] *f* (*pane*) round loaf

pago, -a ['pa:·go] <-ghi, -ghe> *agg* (*soddisfatto*) satisfied

pagoda [pa·'gɔ:·da] *f* (*monumento*) pagoda

paguro [pa·'gu:·ro] *m* hermit crab

paia *pl di* **paio²**

paillard [pa·'ja:·r] <-> *f* grilled sirloin

paillette [pa·'jɛt] <-> *f* sequin

paio¹ ['pa:·io] *1. pers sing pr di* **parere¹**

paio² <*pl*: **paia** *f*> *m* (*coppia*) pair; **un** ~ **di** (*alcuni*) a couple of; **un** ~ **di calzoni** a pair of pants; **un** ~ **di forbici** a pair of scissors; **un** ~ **di occhiali** a pair of glasses

paiolo [pa·'jɔ:·lo] *m* (*pentola*) pot

Pakistan [pa·kis·'tan] *m v.* **Pachistan**

pakistano, -a [pa·kis·'ta:·no] I. *agg v.* **Pakistani** II. *m, f v.* **Pakistani**

pala ['pa:·la] *f* 1.(*attrezzo*) shovel 2. REL ~ **d'altare** altar piece 3.(*di elica, turbina*) blade

paladino [pa·la·'di:·no] *m* (*cavaliere*) paladin

paladino, **-a** *m*, *f* (*difensore*) champion
palafitta [pa·la·'fit·ta] *f* HIST pile-dwelling
palaghiaccio [pa·la·'gia:t·tʃo] <-> *m* SPORT ice rink
palanca [pa·'laŋ·ka] <-che> *f* 1. (*trave*) plank 2. *pl*, *fam* (*soldi*) dough
palandrana [pa·lan·'dra:·na] *f* *scherz*, *fam* tent
palasport [pa·la·'spɔrt] <-> *m* SPORT sports arena
palata [pa·'la:·ta] *f* 1. (*quantità*) shovelful; **aver soldi a -e** *fam* to have lots of money 2. (*colpo di pala*) blow with a shovel
palatale [pa·la·'ta:·le] I. *agg* ANAT, LING palatal II. *f* LING palatal
palatino, **-a** [pa·la·'ti:·no] *agg* Palatine
palato [pa·'la:·to] *m* *a*. *fig* palate
palazzina [pa·lat·'tsi:·na] *f* *small apartment building*
palazzo [pa·'lat·tso] *m* 1. (*edificio signorile*) palace; **~ reale** royal palace 2. (*condominio*) apartment building 3. (*sede amministrativa*) **il ~ di giustizia** the law courts *pl*; **il Palazzo** (*governo*) the government; **Palazzo Chigi** *prime minister's office*; **Palazzo Madama** (*sede del Senato*) Senate

> **i** There are a number of **Palazzi** in Rome whose names have become synonymous with the political institutions with which they are connected. **Palazzo Chigi** in Piazza Colonna was built in the 16th century and in 1919 was purchased by the state to be the seat of the Foreign Ministry. Since 1961 it has been the office of the Prime Minister and the place where the cabinet meets. **Palazzo Madama** was built by the Medici family in the 16th century and has been the seat of the Senate since 1871. **Palazzo di Montecitorio** has been the home of the **Camera dei deputati** (the lower house) since 1870. The **Palazzo del Viminale**, named after one of the Seven Hills of Rome, is the home of the Interior Ministry. The **Palazzo del Quirinale**, named after one of the famous Seven Hills of Rome, is the official residence of the **Presidente della Repubblica**.

palco ['pal·ko] <-chi> *m* 1. THEAT box 2. (*piano sopraelevato*) platform
palcoscenico [pal·koʃ·'ʃɛ:·ni·ko] <-ci> *m* stage
paleocristiano, **-a** [pa·le·o·kris·'tia:·no] *agg* early Christian
paleontologia [pa·le·on·to·lo·'dʒi:·a] <-gie> *f* paleontology
Palermitano <*sing*> *m* Palermo area; **nel ~** in the Palermo area
palermitano, **-a** I. *agg* from Palermo II. *m*, *f*

(*abitante*) person from Palermo
Palermo *f* Palermo, *capital of Sicily*
palesare [pa·le·'za:·re] I. *vt* to reveal II. *vr*: **-rsi** to reveal oneself
palese [pa·'le:·ze] *agg* (*chiaro*) clear
palestra [pa·'lɛs·tra] *f* 1. (*locale*) gym; (*attività*) working out; **fare ~** to work out 2. *fig* **~ di vita** training ground for life
paletot [pal·'to] <-> *m* overcoat
paletta [pa·'let·ta] *f* 1. (*piccola pala*) spade; (*per brace, carbone*) shovel 2. (*di carabinieri, vigili, capostazione*) signal bat 3. (*per dolci*) cake slice
paletto [pa·'let·to] *m* 1. (*chiavistello*) bolt 2. (*nel terreno*) stake; (*per tenda*) peg
palio [pa·'lio] <-i> *m* 1. (*drappo*) banner, = *drappo ricamato dato in premio al vincitore di una gara* 2. (*gara*) competition; **il Palio di Siena** the Palio 3. *fig* **essere in ~** to be at stake; **mettere in ~** to offer as a prize

> **i** The **Palio** is a horse race that is run in a number of Italian cities. The best known is the **Palio di Siena**. This race dates back to the 13th century and is run twice a year, on July 2 and August 16 in the Piazza del Campo in Siena. Ten of the city's seventeen **contrade** (districts) take part; the winner is the first horse to pass the winning post, whether it still has a rider or not. Before the race there is a procession with members of the various districts dressed in historical costumes.

palissandro [pa·lis·'san·dro] *m* rosewood
palizzata [pa·lit·'tsa:·ta] *f* (*steccato*) palisade
palla ['pal·la] *f* 1. (*gener*) ball; **~ di neve** snowball; **~ da tennis** tennis ball; **giocare a ~** to play ball; **prendere la ~ al balzo** *fig* to seize one's chance; **essere una ~ al piede per qu** to be a millstone around sb's neck 2. (*proiettile*) bullet 3. *pl*, *vulg* (*testicoli*) balls; **che -e!** what a drag!; **averne le -e piene di qc** *vulg* to have had enough of sth; **far girare le -e a qu** *vulg* to piss sb off; **non mi rompere le -e!** *vulg* don't be such a pain in the ass!
pallabase [pal·la·'ba:·ze] *f* baseball
pallacanestro [pal·la·ka·'nɛs·tro] *f* basketball
pallamano [pal·la·'ma:·no] *f* handball
pallanuoto [pal·la·'nuɔ:·to] *f* water polo
pallavolo [pal·la·'vo:·lo] *f* volleyball
palleggiamento [pal·led·dʒa·'men·to] *m* 1. SPORT practice with the ball 2. *fig* (*di colpe, responsabilità*) shifting
palleggiare [pal·led·'dʒa:·re] *vi* (*nella pallacanestro*) to dribble; (*nel calcio*) to practice with the ball
palleggio [pal·'led·dʒo] <-ggi> *m* (*nel calcio*) practice with the ball; (*nel basket*) dribbling
palliativo [pal·lia·'ti:·vo] *m* 1. MED palliative 2. *fig* (*rimedio inefficace*) stopgap

pallido, -a ['pal·li·do] *agg* **1.** (*viso, colore*) pale **2.** (*luce, immagine*) faint; **non avere la più -a idea di qc** *fig* to not have the faintest idea about sth

pallina [pal·'li:·na] *f* small ball; **~ da ping-pong** ping-pong ball

pallino [pal·'li:·no] *m* **1.** (*del biliardo*) cue ball; (*delle bocce*) jack **2.** *pl* (*di fucile*) pellet **3.** (*su stoffa*) dot **4.** *fig, fam* (*fissazione*) craze; **avere il ~ della pulizia** to be fanatical about cleanliness

pallonata [pal·lo·'na:·ta] *f* blow with a ball

palloncino [pal·lon·'tʃi:·no] *m* **1.** (*gonfiabile*) balloon **2.** *fam* (*alcoltest*) **fare la prova del ~** to blow into the Breathalyzer®

pallone [pal·'lo:·ne] *m* **1.** (*grossa palla*) ball; **avere** [*o* **sentirsi**] **la testa come un ~** *fam* to feel dazed **2.** *fam* to be full of oneself **3.** (*calcio*) **giocare a ~** to play soccer **4.** (*aerostato*) balloon

pallonetto [pal·lo·'net·to] *m* lob

pallore [pal·'lo:·re] *m* pallor

pallottola [pal·'lɔt·to·la] *f* **1.** (*proiettile*) bullet **2.** (*di carta, legno, vetro*) ball

pallottoliere [pal·lo·to·'liɛ:·re] *m* abacus

palma ['pal·ma] *f* **1.** (*albero*) palm (tree); **~ da cocco** coconut palm **2.** (*ramo*) palm branch; **la domenica delle Palme** Palm Sunday **3.** (*della mano*) palm **4.** *fig* to have great admiration for sb

palmare [pal·'ma:·re] *m* (*computer*) palmtop

palmato, -a [pal·'ma:·to] *agg* **1.** ZOO webbed **2.** BOT palmate

palmo ['pal·mo] *m* **1.** (*spanna*) span; **restare con un ~ di naso** to be disappointed **2.** (*di mano*) palm

palo ['pa:·lo] *m* **1.** (*di legno*) stake; (*del telegrafo*) pole; (*della luce*) post; **fare il** [*o* **da**] **~ sl** to act as lookout; **star dritto come un ~** to be as straight as a ramrod; **saltare di ~ in frasca** *fig* to jump from one thing to another **2.** SPORT (*calcio*) (goal)post

palombaro [pa·lom·'ba:·ro] *m* diver

palombo [pa·'lom·bo] *m* (*squalo*) dogfish

palpare [pal·'pa:·re] *vt* (*tastare*) to feel; MED to palpate

palpebra ['pal·pe·bra] *f* eyelid

palpitante [pal·pi·'tan·te] *agg* (*cuore*) beating; **una notizia di ~ attualità** a highly topical piece of news

palpitare [pal·pi·'ta:·re] *vi* **1.** (*cuore*) to beat **2.** *fig* (*di paura, emozione*) to tremble

palpitazione [pal·pi·tat·'tsio:·ne] *f a. fig* palpitation; **avere le -i** *fam* to have palpitations

palpito ['pal·pi·to] *m* **1.** (*del cuore*) beat **2.** *fig* (*agitazione*) pang; **~ d'amore** pang of love

paltò [pal·'tɔ] <-> *m* overcoat

paludarsi [pa·lu·'dar·si] *vr pej* (*conciarsi*) to dress up

palude [pa·'lu:·de] *f* marsh

paludoso, -a [pa·lu·'do:·so] *agg* marshy

palustre [pa·'lus·tre] *agg* marsht

pampa ['pam·pa] <pampas> *f* pampas

pamphlet [pã·'flɛ] <-> *m* pamphlet

pampino ['pam·pi·no] *m* vine leaf

panacea [pa·na·'tʃɛ:·a] <-ee> *f* panacea

panama ['pa:·na·ma] <-> *m* (*cappello*) panama (hat)

panare [pa·'na:·re] *vt* to coat in breadcrumbs

panca ['paŋ·ka] <-che> *f* (*sedile*) bench

pancarré [paŋ·kar·'re] <-> *m* sliced bread

pancetta [pan·'tʃet·ta] *f* **1.** CULIN bacon **2.** *fam* (*ventre*) belly

panchetto [paŋ·'ket·to] *m* (*sgabello*) stool

panchina [paŋ·'ki:·na] *f* bench; **rimanere in ~** *fig* to stay on the bench

pancia ['pan·tʃa] <-ce> *f a. fig, fam* (*ventre*) belly; **avere** (**il**) **mal di ~** to have a stomachache; **metter su ~** *fam* to get a potbelly; **starsene a ~ all'aria** *fam* not to do jack

panciera [pan·'tʃɛ:·ra] *f* (*maglia*) corset

pancione [pan·'tʃo:·ne] *m fam* **1.** (*grossa pancia*) big belly **2.** (*persona*) person with a big belly

panciotto [pan·'tʃɔt·to] *m* vest

panciuto, -a [pan·'tʃu:·to] *agg* **1.** (*persona*) potbellied **2.** (*vaso*) rounded

pancreas ['paŋ·kre·as] <-> *m* pancreas

panda ['pan·da] <-> *m* panda

pandemia [pan·de·'mi:·a] *f* pandemic

pandemonio [pan·de·'mɔ:·nio] <-i> *m* (*confusione*) pandemonium

pandoro [pan·'dɔ:·ro] *m cone-shaped sponge cake, originally from Verona, eaten at Christmas*

pane ['pa:·ne] *m* **1.** (*alimento*) bread; **~ bianco** white bread; **~ integrale** wholewheat bread; **~ nero** whole-wheat bread; **Pan di Spagna** sponge cake; **dire ~ al ~ e vino al vino** *fig* to call a spade a spade; **trovare ~ per i propri denti** *fig* to meet one's match; **rendere pan per focaccia** *fam* to give tit for tat; **essere buono come il ~** to have a heart of gold **2.** (*pagnotta*) loaf **3.** (*blocchetto: di burro*) pat; (*di cera*) bar

---

i Most Italian bread – *pane* – is made with white flour – *ciabatte* (flat loaves), *filoni* (long, large loaves), *panini al latte*, and *all'acqua* (rolls made with milk or water) – but there are more than 250 types of bread officially classified by the baking industry. Every region has its own kinds of bread, which vary according to the type of flour used and the length of time for which the bread needs to be kept. One special regional bread is the Piedmontese *biova*, an oblong crusty loaf that is hollow inside, made from soft-grain flour, water, yeast, and salt. Another specialty is *grissini rubatà*, bread sticks that are left to rise for a long time, then rolled out by hand and cooked until they reach their characteristic lightness and fragrance. Tuscan bread on the other hand is usually oval in shape with a thin crisp crust and open texture; it is made without salt. In Sardinia, where bread was baked once a week or even once a month, you can find *pane carasau*, which is flat, round, and crisp.

panegirico [pa·ne·'dʒi:·ri·ko] <-ci> *m* **1.** LIT panegyric **2.** (*lode esagerata*) hype
panetteria [pa·net·te·'ri:·a] <-ie> *f* bakery
panettiere, -a [pa·net·'tiɛ:·re] *m, f* baker
panettone [pa·net·'to:·ne] *m dome-shaped sweet loaf containing sultanas and candied fruit eaten at Christmas, originally from Milan*

i Originally from Milan, industrial production has led to **panettone** becoming the Christmas cake for the whole of Italy. The ingredients are flour, yeast, butter, sugar, eggs, raisins, and candied fruit.

panfilo ['pan·fi·lo] *m* yacht
panforte [pan·'fɔr·te] *m round, flat cake containing candied fruit and nuts, spices and honey, originally from Siena*
pangrattato, pan grattato [paŋ·grat·'ta:·to] *m* breadcrumbs *pl*
panico ['pa:·ni·ko] *m* panic; **farsi prendere dal ~** to panic
paniere [pa·'niɛ:·re] *m* basket; **un ~ di frutta** a basket of fruit; **il ~ valutario** the basket of currencies
panificazione [pa·ni·fi·kat·'tsio:·ne] *f* bread-making
panificio [pa·ni·'fi:·tʃo] <-ci> *m* bakery
panino [pa·'ni:·no] *m* roll; **un ~ al prosciutto** a ham roll
panna ['pan·na] *f* **1.** CULIN cream; **~ montata** whipped cream **2.** MOT (*guasto*) breakdown
panne [pan] <-> *f* MOT breakdown; **essere** [*o* **rimanere**] **in ~** to have broken down
pannello [pan·'nɛl·lo] *m* panel; **~ isolante** insulating board; **~ solare** solar panel
panno ['pan·no] *m* **1.** (*tessuto, pezzo di stoffa*) cloth **2.** *pl* (*vestiti*) clothes; **lavare i -i** to do the laundry; **stendere i -i** to hang out the laundry; **mettersi nei -i di qu** to put oneself in sb's shoes; **non stare più nei propri -i** *fam* to be beside oneself
pannocchia [pan·'nɔk·kia] <-cchie> *f* **1.** (*infiorescenza*) cob **2.** (*spiga*) ear
pannolino [pan·no·'li:·no] *m* **1.** (*per neonato*) diaper **2.** (*da donna*) sanitary napkin
panorama [pa·no·'ra:·ma] <-i> *m* **1.** (*veduta*) panorama **2.** *fig* (*contesto*) context
panoramica [pa·no·'ra:·mi·ka] <-che> *f* **1.** (*veduta*) panorama **2.** FOTO panorama; FILM pan shot **3.** *fig* (*rassegna*) survey **4.** (*strada*) scenic route
panoramico, -a [pa·no·'ra:·mi·ko] <-ci, -che>

agg **1.** (*strada, percorso*) scenic; **veduta -a** panoramic **2.** *fig* (*rassegna*) general **3.** (*obiettivo*) wide-angle; (*schermo*) wide
panpepato [pam·pe·'pa:·to] *m cake containing honey, almonds, candied fruit, orange peel and spices*
pansé [pan·'se] <-> *f v.* **pensée**
pantacollant [pan·ta·kol·'lan] *mpl* leggings *pl*
pantaloncini [pan·ta·lon·'tʃi:·ni] *mpl* (*corti*) shorts
pantalone [pan·ta·'lo:·ne] <inv> *agg* **gonna ~** culottes *pl*
pantaloni [pan·ta·'lo:·ni] *mpl* pants; **un paio di ~** a pair of pants; **~ alla pescatora** pedal pushers
pantano [pan·'ta:·no] *m* (*fango*) mud
pantera [pan·'tɛ:·ra] *f* **1.** ZOO panther **2.** *sl* (*auto della polizia*) police car
pantofola [pan·'tɔ:·fo·la] *f* slipper
pantofolaio, -a [pan·to·fo·'la:·io] <-ai, -aie> *m, f* (*pigro*) slob
pantomima [pan·to·'mi:·ma] *f* **1.** THEAT pantomime **2.** *fig* (*finzione*) play-acting
panzana [pan·'tsa:·na] *f fam* tall tale
panzanella [pan·tsa·'nɛl·la] *f slice of stale bread with olive oil, salt, vinegar, tomato, and basil*
panzarotto, panzerotto [pan·tsa·'rɔt·to, pan·tse·'rɔt·to] *m large piece of ravioli filled with cheese or cooked meat and fried*
paonazzo, -a [pao·'nat·tso] *agg* (*viso*) purple
papa ['pa:·pa] <-i> *m* pope; **ad ogni morte di ~** *fig* once in a blue moon; **morto un ~ se ne fa un altro** *prov* no one is indispensable
papà [pa·'pa] <-> *m fam* dad; **figlio di ~** *pej* spoiled boy
papaia [pa·'pa:·ia] <-aie> *f* papaya
papale [pa·'pa:·le] *agg* papal
papalina [pa·pa·'li:·na] *f* skullcap
paparazzo [pa·pa·'rat·tso] *m* paparazzo
papato [pa·'pa:·to] *m* papacy
papavero [pa·'pa:·ve·ro] *m* BOT poppy
papera ['pa:·pe·ra] *f* **1.** ZOO gosling **2.** *fig* (*errore*) gaffe; **fare una ~** to make a gaffe **3.** *pej, fam* (*donna sciocca*) airhead
papilla [pa·'pil·la] *f* ANAT **-e gustative** taste buds
papillon [pa·pi·'jɔ̃] <-> *m* bow tie
papiro [pa·'pi:·ro] *m* **1.** (*gener*) papyrus **2.** *scherz* (*scritto prolisso*) screed
papismo [pa·'piz·mo] *m* (*teoria*) papalism
pappa ['pap·pa] *f* **1.** (*per bambini*) babyfood **2.** *pej* (*minestra troppo cotta*) mush **3.** *sostanza* **~ reale** royal jelly **4.** (*nel linguaggio infantile: mangiare*) din-din; **trovare la ~ pronta** *fig, fam* to have it handed to one on a plate
pappagallo [pap·pa·'gal·lo] *m* **1.** (*uccello*) parrot **2.** *fig* (*uomo*) wolf **3.** (*per urinare*) urine bottle **4.** *fam* (*pinza*) pipe wrench
pappagorgia [pap·pa·'gɔr·dʒa] <-ge> *f* double chin
pappardella [pap·par·'dɛl·la] <-> *f* **1.** *pl* CULIN

wide pasta strips **2.** *fig* (*tiritera*) blather
pappare [pap·'pa:·re] *vt fam* **1.** (*divorare*) to scarf **2.** *fig* (*accaparrarsi*) to pocket
pappina [pap·'pi:·na] *f fam* (*per bambini*) babyfood
paprica ['pa:·pri·ka] <-che> *f* paprika
pap-test [pap·'test] *m* Pap smear
par. *abbr di* **paragrafo** par.
para ['pa:·ra] *f* crepe
parabancario [pa·ra·baŋ·'ka:·rio] *m* para-banking
parabile [pa·'ra:·bi·le] *agg* SPORT able to be saved
parabola [pa·'ra:·bo·la] *f* **1.** DEL VANGELO parable **2.** MATH parabola **3.** (*antenna*) satellite dish **4.** *fig* (*evoluzione: di moda, movimento*) trajectory
parabolico, -a [pa·ra·'bɔ:·li·ko] <-ci, -che> *agg* parabolic; **antenna -a** parabolic antenna
parabrezza [pa·ra·'bred·dza] <-> *m* windshield
paracadutare [pa·ra·ka·du·'ta:·re] *vt* to parachute
paracadute [pa·ra·ka·'du:·te] <-> *m* parachute
paracadutismo [pa·ra·ka·du·'tiz·mo] *m* parachuting
paracadutista [pa·ra·ka·du·'tis·ta] <-i *m*, -e *f*> I. *mf* **1.** parachutist **2.** MIL paratrooper II. *agg* parachute
paracarro [pa·ra·'kar·ro] *m* curbstone
paradenti [pa·ra·'dɛn·ti] <-> *m* SPORT mouthpiece
paradigma [pa·ra·'dig·ma] <-i> *m* paradigm
paradigmatico, -a [pa·ra·dig·'ma:·ti·ko] <-ci, -che> *agg* (*esemplare*) paradigmatic
paradisiaco, -a [pa·ra·di·'zi:·a·ko] <-ci, -che> *agg a. fig* heavenly
paradiso [pa·ra·'di:·zo] *m a. fig* paradise; **~ terrestre** earthly paradise
paradontale [pa·ra·don·'ta:·le] *agg* paradontal
paradossale [pa·ra·dos·'sa:·le] *agg* paradoxical
paradosso [pa·ra·'dɔs·so] *m* **1.** (*argomentazione*) paradox **2.** (*assurdità*) nonsense
parafango [pa·ra·'faŋ·go] <-ghi> *m* (*di macchina*) mudguard; (*di motocicletta*) fender
parafarmaceutico, -a [pa·ra·far·ma·'tʃɛu·ti·ko] <-ci, -che> *agg* over-the-counter
parafarmaco [pa·ra·'far·ma·ko] <-ci> *m* MED over-the-counter medication
paraffina [pa·raf·'fi:·na] *f* paraffin
parafrasare [pa·ra·fra·'za:·re] *vt* to paraphrase
parafrasi [pa·'ra:·fra·zi] <-> *f* paraphrase
parafulmine [pa·ra·'ful·mi·ne] *m* lightning conductor
parafumo [pa·ra·'fu:·mo] *m* smoke screen
parafuoco [pa·ra·'fuɔ:·ko] <-> *m* firescreen
paraggi [pa·'rad·dʒi] *mpl* **nei ~** in the vicinity
paragonabile [pa·ra·go·'na:·bi·le] *agg* comparable; **essere ~ a qc** to be comparable to sth
paragonare [pa·ra·go·'na:·re] I. *vt* (*confrontare*) to compare II. *vr:* **-rsi** to compare oneself

paragone [pa·ra·'go:·ne] *m* **1.** (*confronto*) comparison; **a ~ di** in comparison with; **essere senza ~** [*o* **non avere -i**] to be incomparable **2.** (*esempio*) analogy
paragrafare [pa·ra·gra·'fa:·re] *vt* to paragraph
paragrafo [pa·'ra:·gra·fo] *m* paragraph
paralisi [pa·'ra:·li·zi] <-> *f a. fig* paralysis
paralitico, -a [pa·ra·'li:·ti·ko] <-ci, -che> I. *agg* **1.** (*persona*) paralyzed **2.** (*di paralisi*) paralytic II. *m, f* paralytic
paralizzare [pa·ra·lid·'dza:·re] *vt a. fig* to paralyze
parallela [pa·ral·'lɛ:·la] *f* **1.** MATH parallel (line); **una ~ di via Roma** () a street running parallel to via Roma **2.** *pl* SPORT parallel bars
parallelepipedo [pa·ral·le·le·'pi:·pe·do] *m* MATH parallelepiped
parallelo [pa·ral·'lɛ:·lo] *m* parallel; **collegamento in ~** parallel connection
parallelo, -a *agg* **1.** (*retta, linea*) parallel **2.** (*simile*) similar
parallelogramma [pa·ral·le·lo·'gram·ma] <-i> *m* parallelogram
paraluce [pa·ra·'lu:·tʃe] <-> *m* lens cover
paralume [pa·ra·'lu:·me] *m* lampshade
paramedico [pa·ra·'mɛ:·di·ko] <-ci> *m* paramedic
paramedico, -a <-ci, -che> *agg* paramedical; **personale ~** paramedics *pl*
paramento [pa·ra·'men·to] *m* **1.** *pl* REL vestments *pl* **2.** ARCH face
parametrizzare [pa·ra·me·trid·'dza:·re] *vt* to parameterize
parametrizzazione [pa·ra·met·rid·dzat·'tsio:·ne] *f* parameterization
parametro [pa·'ra:·met·ro] *m* parameter
paramilitare [pa·ra·mi·li·'ta:·re] *agg* paramilitary
paramosche [pa·ra·'mos·ke] <-> *m* fly screen
paranco [pa·'raŋ·ko] <-chi> *m* hoist
paranoia [pa·ra·'nɔ:·ia] <-oie> *f* paranoia; **andare in ~** to get paranoid
paranoico, -a [pa·ra·'nɔ:·i·ko] <-ci, -che> I. *agg* paranoid II. *m, f* paranoid
paranormale [pa·ra·nor·'ma:·le] *agg* paranormal
paraocchi [pa·ra·'ɔk·ki] <-> *m* blinders *pl;* **avere i ~** *fig* to be blind
paraorecchie [pa·rao·'rek·kie] <-> *m* **1.** SPORT rugby helmet **2.** (*contro il freddo*) ear muffs *pl*
parapendio [pa·ra·pen·'di:·o] <-> *m* **1.** (*paracadute*) paraglider **2.** (*attività*) paragliding
parapetto [pa·ra·'pɛt·to] *m* **1.** (*di balcone, ponte*) parapet **2.** NAUT rail **3.** MIL breastwork
parapiglia [pa·ra·'piʎ·ʎa] <-> *m fam* commotion
parapioggia [pa·ra·'piɔd·dʒa] <-> *m* umbrella
paraplegia [pa·ra·ple·'dʒi:·a] <-gie> *f* paraplegia
paraplegico, -a [pa·ra·'plɛ:·dʒi·ko] <-ci, -che> I. *agg* paraplegic II. *m, f* paraplegic
parapolitico, -a [pa·ra·po·'li:·ti·ko] <-ci, -che>

agg parapolitical

parapsicologia [pa·ra·psi·ko·lo·'dʒi:·a] *f* parapsychology

parapsicologico, -a [pa·ra·psi·ko·'lɔ:·dʒi·ko] <-ci, -che> *agg* parapsychological

parare [pa·'ra:·re] I. *vt* 1.(*colpo*) to parry; SPORT (*tiro*) to save 2.(*ornare*) to adorn 3.(*schermare*) ~ qc da qc to protect sth from sth II. *vi* (*finire*) **dove vuoi andare a ~?** what are you driving at? III. *vr* 1.(*ripararsi*) -rsi da qc to shelter from sth 2.(*presentarsi*) -rsi davanti a qu to appear in front of sb

parasailing ['pæ·rə·'sai·liŋ] <-> *m* SPORT parasailing

parascientifico, -a [pa·ra·ʃen·'ti:·fi·ko] <-ci, -che> *agg* parascientific

parascintille [pa·ra·ʃin·'til·le] <-> *m* EL spark screen

parascolastico, -a [pa·ras·ko·'las·ti·ko] <-ci, -che> *agg* extracurricular

parasole [pa·ra·'so:·le] I.<-> *m* 1.(*ombrello*) parasol 2.FOTO lens cover II.<inv> *agg* sun

paraspalle [pa·ra·'spal·le] <-> *m* SPORT shoulder pad

paraspruzzi [pa·ras·'prut·tsi] <-> *m* MOT mudguard

parassita [pa·ras·'si:·ta] <-i *m*, -e *f*> I. *mf a.* *fig* parasite II. *agg a.* *fig* parasitic

parassitario, -a [pa·ras·si·'ta:·rio] <-i, -ie> *agg a.* *fig* parasitic

parastatale [pa·ras·ta·'ta:·le] I. *agg* state-controlled II. *mf* employee of a state-controlled organization

parastato [pa·ra·'sta:·to] *m* 1.(*enti*) state-controlled organizations *pl* 2.(*dipendenti*) employees of state-controlled organizations

parastinchi [pa·ra·'stiŋ·ki] <-> *m* SPORT shinguards

parata [pa·'ra:·ta] *f* 1.SPORT (*calcio*) save; (*scherma*) parry 2.MIL parade; **abito da ~** formal dress

parati [pa·'ra:·ti] *mpl* **carta da ~** wallpaper

paratia [pa·ra·'ti:·a] <-ie> *f* NAUT bulkhead

parauniversitario, -a [pa·ra·u·ni·ver·si·'ta:·rio] <-i, -ie> *agg* extramural

paraurti [pa·ra·'ur·ti] <-> *m* 1.MOT bumper 2.FERR buffer

paravalanghe [pa·ra·va·'laŋ·ge] <-> *m* avalanche shelter

paravento [pa·ra·'vɛn·to] <-> *m* 1.(*mobile*) screen 2.*fig* **fare da ~ a qu** to be a cover for sth

parca ['par·ka] <-che> *f* (*in mitologia*) Fate

parcella [par·'tʃɛl·la] *f* 1.(*di terreno*) parcel 2.(*di professionista*) fee

parcellare [par·tʃel·'la:·re] *agg* (*terreno*) parceled out

parcellazione [par·tʃel·lat·'tsio:·ne] *f* (*di terreno*) parceling out

parcellizzazione [par·tʃel·lid·dzat·'tsio:·ne] *f* (*di terreno, lavoro*) parceling out

parcheggiare [par·ked·'dʒa:·re] I. *vt a.* *fig* to park II. *vi* (*fare manovra*) to park

parcheggio [par·'ked·dʒo] <-ggi> *m* 1.(*area*) parking lot; **~ a pagamento** pay parking lot; **~ custodito** parking lot with an attendant 2.(*sosta, manovra*) parking; **area di ~** parking area; **divieto di ~** no parking 3.*fig* (*sistemazione*) parking place

parchimetro [par·'ki:·me·tro] *m* parking meter

parco ['par·ko] <-chi> *m* 1.(*spazio verde*) park; **~ nazionale** national park 2.(*area attrezzata*) ~ **giochi** playground; **~ dei divertimenti** amusement park 3.(*materiali*) ~ **macchine** carpool

parco, -a <-chi, -che> *agg* (*nel mangiare, bere*) moderate; (*nello spendere*) careful

parcometro [par·'kɔ·me·tro] *m* *v.* **parchimetro**

par condicio [par kon·'di·tʃo] <-> *f* DIR, POL equal opportunity

pardon [par·'dɔ̃] *int* (*per chiedere scusa, correggersi*) sorry

parecchio [pa·'rek·kio] *avv* 1.(*molto*) quite 2.(*a lungo*) quite a while; **mi sono fermato ~** I stayed quite a while

parecchio, -a <-cchi, -cchie> I. *agg* (*con sostantivo singolare*) quite a lot of; (*con sostantivo plurale*) several; **-cchie volte** several times; ~ **tempo** quite a long time; **c'è ~ vento** it's quite windy; **c'è ancora -a strada** there's still quite a way to go II. *pron indef* (*singolare*) quite a lot; (*plurale*) several; **-cchi di noi** several of us III. *avv* (*molto tempo*) long

pareggiare [pa·red·'dʒa:·re] I. *vt* 1.(*terreno*) to level 2.(*bilancio*) to balance; **~ i conti** to balance the books; *fig* to get even 3.(*uguagliare*) ~ **qu** (**in qc**) to equal sb (in sth) II. *vi* ~ (**con qu**) to tie (with sb)

pareggio [pa·'red·dʒo] <-ggi> *m* 1.COM balance 2.SPORT tie; **finire con un ~** to end in a tie

parentado [pa·ren·'ta:·do] *m* *scherz* (*insieme dei parenti*) relatives *pl*

parentale [pa·ren·'ta:·le] *agg* 1.(*vincolo, autorità*) parental 2.(*malattia*) hereditary

parente [pa·'rɛn·te] *mf* (*congiunto*) relative; **i miei -i** my relatives

parentela [pa·ren·'tɛ:·la] *f* 1.(*insieme dei parenti*) relatives *pl* 2.(*legame*) relationship; **grado di ~** degree of kinship 3.*fig* (*affinità*) kinship

parentesi [pa·'rɛn·te·zi] <-> *f* 1.(*segno grafico*) parenthesis; **~ tonda** parenthesis; **~ quadra** square bracket; **~ graffa** brace; **fra ~** *fig* incidentally 2.(*digressione*) digression 3.*fig* (*periodo*) interlude

parentetico, -a [pa·ren·'tɛ:·ti·ko] <-ci, -che> *agg* parenthetic(al)

parere[1] [pa·'re:·re] <paio, parvi, parso> *vi essere* 1.(*apparire*) to seem; **mi pare di averlo visto** I think I saw him; **non mi par vero** I can't believe it; **pare di sì/no** it seems so/not; **pare impossibile** it seems impossible; **pare che non sia vero** it seems it's not true; **a**

quanto pare apparently **2.** (*avere l'impressione*) **ti pare di aver ragione?** do you think you're right?; **che te ne pare?** what do you think?; **non ti pare?** don't you think?; **ma Le pare!** not at all!; **fai come ti pare** do as you like

parere² *m* **1.** (*opinione*) opinion; **a mio ~ in** my opinion; **essere del ~ che ...** to be of the opinion that ... **2.** (*di esperto*) advice

parete [pa·'re:·te] *f* wall; **tra le -i domestiche** *fig* at home

pargolo ['par·go·lo] *m poet* (*bambino*) child

pari ['pa:·ri] I.<inv> *agg* **1.** (*uguale*) equal; **essere ~ a qc** to be equal to sth; **di ~ passo** at the same pace **2.** (*superficie, piano, strada*) level **3.** MATH (*numero*) even **4.** SPORT (*nei giochi*) tied **5.** ANAT paired **6.** (*loc*) **alla ~** (*lavorare*) as an au pair; **ragazza alla ~** au pair (girl) II.<inv> *avv* evenly; **~ ~** (*alla lettera*) word for word III. <-> *mf* equal; **trattare qu da ~ a ~** to treat sb as an equal; **non aver ~** to be unequaled; **senza ~** without equal IV.<-> *m* **1.** (*parità*) tie; **al ~ di** just like; **mettersi in ~** (*con programma*) to catch up **2.** (*numero pari*) even number; **fare a ~ e dispari** to play odds and evens

parietale [pa·rie·'ta:·le] I. *agg* **1.** (*graffito, pittura*) wall **2.** ANAT parietal II. *m* parietal

parificare [pa·ri·fi·'ka:·re] *vt* (*rendere uguale*) to make equal

parificato, -a [pa·ri·fi·'ka:·to] *agg* (*scuola*) officially recognized

Parigi [pa·'ri:·dʒi] *f* Paris

pariglia [pa·'riʎ·ʎa] <-glie> *f* **1.** (*gener*) pair **2.** (*trattamento*) **rendere la ~** to give tit for tat

parigrado [pa·ri·'gra:·do] <-> *mf* equal

parità [pa·ri·'ta] <-> *f* **1.** (*uguaglianza*) equality; **~ di diritti** equal rights; **a ~ di condizioni** all things being equal; **a ~ di voti** with equal votes **2.** SPORT (*punteggio*) tie; **finire in ~** to end in a tie **3.** COM parity; **~ salariale** equal pay

paritario, -a [pa·ri·'ta:·rio] <-i, -ie> *agg* equal

paritetico, -a [pa·ri·'tɛ:·ti·ko] <-ci, -che> *agg* joint

parka ['par·ka] <-> *m* (*giacca*) parka

parlamentare [par·la·men·'ta:·re] I. *agg* parliamentary II. *mf* POL Congressman *m*, Congresswoman *f*

parlamentarismo [par·la·men·ta·'riz·mo] *m* parliamentarianism

parlamento [par·la·'men·to] *m* (*organo*) parliament, sede; **sedere in ~** to have a seat in parliament; **Parlamento europeo** European Parliament

parlante [par·'lan·te] I. *agg* **1.** (*che parla*) talking **2.** *fig* (*evidente: prova, fatti*) clear II. *mf* speaker

parlantina [par·lan·'ti:·na] *f fam* patter; **avere una bella** [*o buona*] **~** to have the gift of gab

parlare¹ [par·'la:·re] I. *vi* **1.** (*esprimersi*) to speak; **~ a caso** to ramble on; **~ a vanvera** to talk nonsense; **~ con le mani** [*o a gesti*] to use one's hands to communicate; **~ tra i denti** to mumble; **~ tra sé e sé** to talk to oneself; **~ come un libro stampato** to talk like a book; **~ male di qn** to speak ill of sb; **far ~ di sé** to get oneself talked about; **per non ~ di** not to mention **2.** (*conversare*) to talk; **~ a qu** to talk to sb; **~ con qu** to talk to sb; **~ di qu/qc** to talk about sb/sth; **non parliamone più** let's say no more about it; **~ al vento** [*o al muro*] *fig* to talk to the wall **3.** *fig* (*trattare*) **~ di qu/qc** to be about sb/sth II. *vt* to speak; **~ tedesco/francese/inglese** to speak German/French/English III. *vr:* **-rsi** to speak (to each other)

parlare² *m* **1.** (*discorso*) way of speaking **2.** (*parlata*) dialect

parlata [par·'la:·ta] *f* dialect

parlato, -a [par·'la:·to] *agg* (*linguaggio, uso*) spoken

parlatorio [par·la·'tɔ:·rio] <-i> *m* (*in convento*) parlor; (*in carcere*) visiting room

parlottare [par·lot·'ta:·re] *vi* (*bisbigliare*) to mutter

parlottio [par·lot·'ti:·o] <-ii> *m* muttering

Parma ['par·ma] *f* Parma, *city in northern Italy*

parmense [par·'mɛn·se] I. *agg* from Parma II. *mf* (*abitante*) person from Parma

Parmense <*sing*> *m* Parma area; **nel ~** in the Parma area

parmigiana [par·mi·'dʒa:·na] *f* dish consisting of layers of sliced fried vegetables, tomato sauce, and Parmesan cheese; **~ di melanzane** eggplant Parmesan

parmigiano [par·mi·'dʒa:·no] *m* (*formaggio*) Parmesan (cheese)

parmigiano, -a I. *agg* from Parma II. *m, f* (*abitante*) person from Parma

parodia [pa·ro·'di:·a] <-ie> *f* (*di film, canzone*) parody

parodiare [pa·ro·'dia:·re] *vt* to parody

parodista [pa·ro·'dis·ta] <-i *m*, -e *f*> *mf* parodist

parola [pa·'rɔ:·la] *f* **1.** (*vocabolo, discorso*) word; **~ d'ordine** password; **~ chiave** keyword; **-e** (**in**)**crociate** crossword; **mangiarsi le -e** to mumble; ~ **per** ~ word for word; **nel vero senso della** ~ in the true sense of the word; **rivolgere la** ~ **a qu** to speak to sb; **avere l'ultima** ~ to have the last word; **una** ~ **tira l'altra** one thing leads to another; **cavare le -e di bocca a qu** to drag it out of sb; **senza giri di -e** without beating around the bush; **solo a -e** in word only 2. *pl* (*consiglio*) advice 3. *pl* (*chiacchiere*) talk 4. (*facoltà*) speech; **restare senza -e** to be speechless 5. (*diritto di parlare*) **chiedere la** ~ to ask to speak; **dare la** ~ **a qu** to call on sb to speak; **prendere la** ~ to take the floor 6. (*promessa*) word; ~ **d'onore** word of honor; **essere di** ~ [*o* **mantenere la** ~] to keep one's word; **credere a qu sulla** ~ to take sb's word for it; **prendere qu in** ~ to take sb at their word 7. (*loc*) **avere la** ~ **facile** to be a fluent speaker; **è una** ~! it's easier said than done!

parolaccia [pa·ro·'lat·tʃa] <-cce> *f* (*termine volgare*) swearword

paroliere, -a [pa·ro·'liɛ:·re] *m, f* lyricist

parolina [pa·ro·'li:·na] *f* 1. (*affettuosa*) sweet nothing 2. (*rimprovero*) word

parossismo [pa·ros·'siz·mo] *m* paroxysm

parotite [pa·ro·'ti:·te] *f* mumps

parquet [par·'kɛ] <-> *m* parquet

parricida [par·ri·'tʃi:·da] <-i *m*, -e *f*> *mf* parricide

parricidio [par·ri·'tʃi:·dio] <-i> *m* parricide

parrocchia [par·'rɔk·kia] <-ie> *f* 1. (*circoscrizione, insieme dei fedeli*) parish 2. (*chiesa*) parish church

parrocchiano, -a [par·rok·'kia:·no] *m, f* parishioner

parroco ['par·ro·ko] <-ci> *m* parish priest

parrucca [par·'ruk·ka] <-cche> *f* (*capelli posticci*) wig

parrucchiere, -a [par·ruk·'kiɛ:·re] *m, f* hairdresser

parrucchino [par·ruk·'ki:·no] *m* (*mezza parrucca*) hairpiece

parsimonia [par·si·'mɔ:·nia] *f* thrift

parsimonioso, -a [par·si·mo·'nio:·so] *agg* (*persona, abitudine*) thrifty

parso ['par·so] *pp di* **parere**[1]

partaccia [par·'tat·tʃa] <-cce> *f fam* (*rimprovero*) telling-off; **fare una** ~ **a qu** to tell sb off

parte[1] ['par·te] *f* 1. (*gener*) part; ~ **del discorso** part of speech; **-i intime** private parts; **a** ~ (*separato*) separate; (*separatamente*) separately; (*senza contare*) apart from; **in** ~ in part; **far** ~ **di qc** to belong to sth; **prendere** ~ **a qc** to take part in sth; **la maggior** ~ **di** the majority of 2. (*quota*) share; **l'occhio vuole la sua** ~ *fig* appearance is important too 3. (*luogo*) **da ogni** ~ everywhere; **da queste -i** around here; **da un'altra** ~ somewhere else; **da qualche** ~ somewhere 4. (*lato*) side; (*direzione*) **da** ~ **di** from; **da una** ~ ... **dall'altra** on the one hand ... on the other (hand); **mettere da** ~ (*metter via*) to put

aside; (*tralasciare*) to leave aside; **non sapere da che** ~ **voltarsi** *fig* not to know which way to turn; **fatti da** ~! *fam* to move aside; **da un anno a questa** ~ for about a year now 5. (*fazione*) faction; **di** ~ (*fazioso*) partisan; **prendere le -i di qu** to take sb's side; **essere** [*o* **stare**] **dalla** ~ **del torto** to be in the wrong 6. JUR party; **essere** ~ **in causa** *fig* to be an interested party; **costituirsi** ~ **civile** to file suit 7. THEAT, MUS part

parte[2] *avv* **gli scolari furono** ~ **promossi e** ~ **bocciati** some students passed, while some failed

partecipante [par·te·tʃi·'pan·te] I. *mf* participant II. *agg* participating

partecipare [par·te·tʃi·'pa:·re] I. *vi* ~ **a qc** to participate in sth; FIN to share in sth; ~ **al dolore/alla gioia di qu** to share sb's pain/joy II. *vt* (*rendere noto*) to announce

partecipazione [par·te·tʃi·'pat·'tsio:·ne] *f* 1. (*presenza*) participation 2. (*coinvolgimento*) involvement 3. (*di matrimonio, nascita*) announcement card 4. FIN (*in società*) interest; ~ **agli utili** profit-sharing

partecipe [par·'te:·tʃi·pe] *agg* (*interessato*) interested; **essere** ~ **di qc** to share sth

parteggiare [par·ted·'dʒa:·re] *vi* ~ **per qu/qc** to support sb/sth

partenariato [par·te·na·'ria:·to] *m* partnership

partenza [par·'tɛn·tsa] *f* 1. (*atto, momento*) departure; **-e** (*in stazione, aeroporto*) departures; **punto di** ~ *fig* (*inizio*) starting point; **in** ~ leaving 2. (*di veicolo*) starting 3. SPORT start 4. COMPUT boot; ~ **a caldo** COMPUT warm boot; ~ **a freddo** COMPUT cold boot

parterre [par·'tɛːr] <-> *m* THEAT parterre

particella [par·ti·'tʃɛl·la] *f* LING, PHYS particle

participio [par·ti·'tʃi:·pio] <-i> *m* LING participle

particola [par·'ti:·ko·la] *f* REL host

particolare [par·ti·ko·'la:·re] I. *m* detail; **entrare** [*o* **scendere**] **nei -i** to go into detail; **fin nei minimi -i** in minute detail II. *agg* 1. (*caratteristico: di individuo, problema*) particular 2. (*diverso dagli altri: caso, situazione*) special 3. (*fuori dal comune: carattere*) unusual

particolareggiato, -a [par·ti·ko·la·red·'dʒa:·to] *agg* detailed

particolarità [par·ti·kla·ri·'ta] <-> *f* 1. (*caratteristica*) peculiarity 2. (*dettaglio*) detail

particolarizzare [par·ti·ko·la·rid·'dza:·re] *vt* to describe in detail

partigiano, -a [par·ti·'dʒa:·no] I. *m, f* 1. HIST partisan 2. (*sostenitore*) supporter II. *agg* partisan

partire [par·'ti:·re] *vi essere* 1. (*andare via*) to leave; ~ **per Napoli** to leave for Naples; ~ **per le vacanze** to go away on vacation; ~ **in quarta** *fig, fam* to jump right in; ~ **è un po' morire** *prov* parting is such sweet sorrow 2. (*colpo*) to go off 3. (*macchina*) to start; SPORT to start 4. *fig* (*avere inizio*) to start; **a** ~

da starting from **5.**(*provenire*) **~ da qc** to come from sth **6.** *fam* (*rompersi*) to break; (*staccarsi*) to come off

partita [par·'ti:·ta] *f* **1.**(*incontro sportivo, gioco*) game; **fare una ~ a carte/scacchi** to have a game of cards/chess; **dare ~ vinta a qu** to admit defeat at the hands of sb **2.** COM entry; **~ semplice/doppia** single-entry/double-entry bookkeeping; **~ IVA** VAT number **3.**(*di caccia*) party **4.** MUS partita

partitico, -a [par·'ti:·ti·ko] <-ci, -che> *agg* party

partitino [par·ti·'ti:·no] *m* POL minor party

partitismo [par·ti·'tiz·mo] *m* party politics

partitivo, -a [par·ti·'ti:·vo] *agg* partitive

partito [par·'ti:·to] *m* **1.** POL party **2.**(*decisione*) **non sapere che ~ prendere** not to know what to do; **prendere ~ per qu** to side with sb; **per ~ preso** because of preconceived ideas **3.**(*condizione*) **essere** [*o* trovarsi] **a mal ~** to be in dire straits **4.**(*persona da sposare*) catch; **essere un buon ~** to be a good catch

partitocrazia [par·ti·to·krat·'tsi:·a] *f* POL *control of state institutions by political parties*

partitura [par·ti·'tu:·ra] *f* MUS score

partizione [par·tit·'tsio:·ne] *f* **1.**(*suddivisione*) subdivision **2.** COMPUT partition

partner ['pa:t·nə/'part·ner] *mf* partner

partnership ['pa:t·nə·ʃip/part·ner·'ʃip] *f* partnership

parto ['par·to] *m* **1.**(*di bambino*) birth **2.** *fig* (*prodotto della fantasia*) product

partoriente [par·to·'riɛn·te] *f* woman in labor

partorire [par·to·'ri:·re] <partorisco> *vt* **1.** MED to give birth to **2.** *fig* (*produrre: romanzo, invenzione*) to produce

part-time [pa:t·'taim/part·'taim] **I.**<inv> *agg* (*lavoro, segretaria*) part-time **II.** *avv* (*lavorare*) part-time **III.**<-> *m* part-time job

party ['pa:·ti/'par·ti] <-> *m* party

parure [pa·'ry:r] <-> *f* **1.**(*da letto*) set of sheets and pillow cases **2.**(*di gioielli*) jewelry

parvenu [par·və·'ny] <-> *mf* upstart

parvenza [par·'vɛn·tsa] *f* semblance

parvi ['par·vi] *1. pers sing pass rem di* **parere**[1]

parziale [par·'tsia:·le] *agg* partial

parzialità [par·tsia·li·'ta] <-> *f* (*atteggiamento*) partiality

pascià [paʃ·'ʃa] <-> *m* pasha; **vivere come un ~** to live in the lap of luxury

pasciuto, -a [paʃ·'ʃu:·to] *agg* (**ben**) **~** plump

pascolare [pas·ko·'la:·re] **I.** *vi* to graze **II.** *vt* to graze

pascolo ['pas·ko·lo] *m* pasture

Pasqua ['pas·kua] *f* (*nel cristianesimo*) Easter; (*nell'ebraismo*) Passover; **essere contento come una pasqua** to be as happy as a lark

pasquale [pas·'kua:·le] *agg* Easter

pasquetta [pas·'kuet·ta] *f* (*lunedì di Pasqua*) Easter Monday

i The official name for Easter Monday in Italy is **Lunedì dell'Angelo** (Angel Monday); however it is popularly known as **Pasquetta**. Many Italians make trips to the countryside on this day.

pass [pa:s] <-> *m* pass

passabile [pas·'sa:·bi·le] *agg* passable

passaggio [pas·'sad·dʒo] <-ggi> *m* **1.**(*transito*) passing by; **essere di ~** to be passing through **2.**(*luogo*) passage; **~ pedonale** crosswalk; **~ a livello** grade crossing **3.**(*di veicoli, persone*) traffic **4.**(*su veicolo*) ride; **dare un ~ a qu** to give sb a ride **5.** *fig* (*cambiamento di stato*) change; **~ di proprietà** change of ownership **6.** LIT, MUS (*brano*) passage **7.** SPORT pass

passamaneria [pas·sa·ma·ne·'ri:·a] <-ie> *f* **1.**(*guarnizioni*) trimmings *pl* **2.**(*negozio*) trimmings store

passamontagna [pas·sa·mon·'taɲ·ɲa] <-> *m* balaclava

passante [pas·'san·te] **I.** *mf* passerby **II.** *m* **1.**(*per cintura*) loop **2.**(*collegamento*) **~ ferroviario** rail link

passaparola [pas·sa·pa·'rɔ:·la] <-> *m* **1.** MIL order passed by word of mouth **2.**(*gioco*) telephone; **giocare a ~** to play telephone **3.**(*sistema di diffusione*) word of mouth

passaporto [pas·sa·'pɔr·to] *m* passport

passare [pas·'sa:·re] **I.** *vi* essere **1.**(*transitare*) to pass; **~ per qc** to pass through sth; **di qui non si passa** you can't go this way; **~ per la mente** to go through one's mind; **~ inosservato** *fig* to go unnoticed; **~ sopra a qc** *fig* to overlook sth **2.**(*strada, canale*) to run **3.**(*andare*) to call in; **~ a prendere qu** to call for sb; **~ a trovare qu** to go and see sb; **passo da te più tardi** I'll drop by your place later **4.**(*attraversare un'apertura*) to get in; (*penetrare*) to come in **5.**(*trasferirsi*) to go **6.**(*da una persona all'altra*) to pass; **~ alla storia** to go down in history **7.**(*trascorrere*) to go by **8.**(*cambiare stato*) **~ da qc a qc** to change from sth to sth **9.**(*cambiare argomento*) to move on **10.**(*sparire*) to pass; **~ di moda** to go out of fashion; **~ di mente** to go out of sb's head **11.**(*essere accettabile*) to do; **per questa volta passi!** I'll let it go this time! **12.**(*a livello superiore*) to change; **~ di grado** to be promoted; **~ di ruolo** to be made permanent **13.**(*agli esami*) to pass; (*legge*) to be passed **14.**(*essere considerato*) **~ per qc** to be considered sth **15.** SPORT to pass **II.** *vt* avere **1.**(*attraversare: confine*) to cross **2.**(*oltrepassare: semaforo, strada*) to go past **3.**(*trafiggere*) to go through **4.** *fig* (*superare*) to pass; **~ il segno** [*o* la misura] to go too far; **ha passato la sessantina** he's over sixty **5.**(*trascorrere*) to spend; **passarsela bene/male** *fam* to get on well/badly **6.**(*dare*) to pass **7.** TEL **~ qu a qu** to put sb through to sb; **mi**

può passare la signora Magnetti, per favore? can you put Mrs. Magnetti on, please; **le passo il servizio assistenza** I'll transfer you to customer service 8.(*notizia*) to tell; **~ la voce** to spread the word 9.(*patire*) to undergo; **passarne di tutti i colori** to go through it 10.(*perdonare*) to forgive 11.(*legge*) to pass 12.(*superare: esame, controllo*) to pass 13.(*patate, verdura*) to purée 14.(*spugna, mano di vernice*) to apply 15.(*loc*) **passarla liscia** *fam* to get away with it; **~ qc sotto silenzio** to say nothing about sth

passata [pas·'sa:·ta] *f* 1.(*lettura veloce*) glance 2.(*pulita*) clean; (*stirata*) iron 3.(*di vernice*) coat 4.(*in padella*) fry 5.DI VERDURE **~ di pomodoro** tomato sauce

passatempo [pas·sa·'tɛm·po] *m* pastime; **per ~** as a hobby

passato [pas·'sa:·to] *m* 1.(*tempo*) past; **in ~** in the past 2.LING **~ prossimo** (present) perfect; **~ remoto** past historic 3.CULIN (*di verdura*) purée

passato, -a *agg* 1.(*trascorso: tempi, fatti, usanze*) past; **è acqua -a** *fig* it's water under the bridge 2.(*scorso*) last; **l'anno ~** last year 3.CULIN puréed 4.(*frutta*) overripe

passatoia [pas·sa·'to:·ia] <-oie> *f* (*tappeto*) carpet

passatutto [pas·sa·'tut·to] <-> *m* vegetable mill

passaverdura, passaverdure [pas·sa·ver·'du:·ra, pas·sa·ver·'du:·re] <-> *m* vegetable mill

passeggero, -a [pas·sed·'dʒe:·ro] I. *agg* passing II. *m, f* passenger; **~ clandestino** stowaway

passeggiare [pas·sed·'dʒa:·re] *vi* 1.(*andare a spasso*) to walk 2.(*andare su e giù*) to pace up and down

passeggiata [pas·sed·'dʒa:·ta] *f* 1.(*a piedi*) walk; (*in macchina*) drive; (*in bicicletta*) ride 2.(*strada*) walk 3.(*loc*) **essere una ~** to be a piece of cake

passeggiatrice [pas·sed·dʒa·'tri:·tʃe] *f* (*eufemismo*) streetwalker

passeggino [pas·sed·'dʒi:·no] *m* stroller; **~ trekking** jogging stroller

passeggio [pas·'sed·dʒo] <-ggi> *m* (*camminata*) **andare a ~** to go for a walk; **portare a ~** to take for a walk

passe-partout [pas·par·'tu] <-> *m* 1.(*chiave*) master key 2.(*cornice*) passepartout

passera ['pas·se·ra] *f* 1.ZOO (*uccello*) hen sparrow; **~ di mare** plaice 2.*vulg* pussy

passerella [pas·se·'rɛl·la] *f* 1.(*ponte*) footbridge 2.NAUT, AERO gangway 3.THEAT forestage 4.(*per indossatrici*) catwalk

passero, -a ['pas·se·ro] *m, f* sparrow

passerotto [pas·se·'rɔt·to] *m* 1.ZOO young sparrow 2.*fam* (*appellativo*) sweetie

passibile [pas·'si:·bi·le] *agg* **~ di** liable to; **prezzo ~ d'aumento** prices subject to increase

passino [pas·'si:·no] *m fam* (*colino*) sieve

passionale [pas·sio·'na:·le] *agg* passionate; **delitto ~** crime of passion

passionalità [pas·sio·na·li·'ta] <-> *f* passionateness

passione [pas·'sio:·ne] *f* 1.(*gener*) passion 2.REL Passion

passività [pas·si·vi·'ta] <-> *f* 1.(*inerzia*) passivity 2.COM liabilities *pl*

passivo [pas·'si:·vo] *m* 1.LING passive 2.COM liabilities *pl;* **chiudere in ~** to end up in the red

passivo, -a *agg* 1.(*gener*) passive 2.COM debit

passo ['pas·so] *m* 1.(*gener*) step; **fare due** [*o* **quattro**] **-i** *fig* to go for a little walk; **fare il ~ più lungo della gamba** *fig* to bite off more than one can chew; **muovere i primi -i** *fig* to take one's first steps; **tornare sui propri -i** to retrace one's steps; (*cambiare idea*) to change one's mind; *fig* one step at a time; **essere a pochi -i** to be a stone's throw away 2.(*andatura*) pace; **a ~ d'uomo** at walking pace; **camminare di buon ~** to proceed at a brisk pace; **~ ~** step by step; **e via di questo ~** *fam* and so on; **di questo ~** *fig* like this; **essere al ~ con i tempi** to be up to date 3.(*impronta*) footprint 4.TEC thread 5.MOT wheelbase 6.FILM gauge 7.(*brano*) MUS passage 8.(*passaggio*) **~ carrabile** [*o* **carraio**] driveway 9.(*valico*) pass 10.(*stretto di mare*) strait 11.*fig* (*loc*) **fare un ~ falso** to slip up; **fare il primo ~** to make the first move

password ['pa:s·wə:d/'pas·word] *f* COMPUT password

pasta ['pas·ta] *f* 1.(*pastasciutta*) pasta 2.(*impasto*) dough; **~ frolla** shortcrust pastry; **~ sfoglia** puff pastry 3.(*dolce*) cake 4.*fig* (*indole*) **essere della stessa ~** to be cast in the same mold 5.(*preparazione: d'acciughe, olive*) paste

> **i** In ancient times fresh noodles were made from flour, water, and salt. It was in the Middle Ages, during the Arab rule of Sicily, that people first began to dry and store noodle dough, a process which suddenly allowed **pasta** to spread first throughout Italy and then all over the world. The dozens of types of pasta known today include not only **spaghetti** and **maccheroni**, but also **penne, tubetti, lumaconi, conchiglie, bucatini, fusilli, capelli d'angelo, rigatoni, linguine, ziti,** and **vermicelli.**

pastafrolla [pas·ta·'frɔl·la] *f v.* pasta

pastasciutta [pas·taʃ·'ʃut·ta] *f* pasta

pasteggiare [pas·ted·'dʒa:·re] *vi* **~ a champagne** to have champagne with one's meal

pastella [pas·'tɛl·la] *f* (*per fritture*) batter

pastello[1] [pas·'tɛl·lo] *m* pastel

pastello[2] <inv> *agg* pastel; **tinta ~** pastel color

P

pasticca [pas·'tik·ka] <-cche> *f* (*pastiglia*) pastille

pasticceria [pas·tit·tʃe·'ri:·a] <-ie> *f* 1. (*negozio*) cake shop 2. (*pasticcini*) cakes *pl* 3. (*arte*) patisserie

pasticciare [pas·tit·'tʃa:·re] *vt* 1. (*fare male*) to mess up 2. (*imbrattare*) to make a mess on

pasticciato, -a [pas·tit·'tʃa:·to] *agg* 1. (*malfatto*) messed up 2. (*imbrattato*) messy 3. CULIN *with a meat and cheese sauce*

pasticciere, -a [pas·tit·'tʃɛ·re] *m, f* pastry cook

pasticcino [pas·tit·'tʃi:·no] *m* cake

pasticcio [pas·'tit·tʃo] <-cci> *m* 1. CULIN pie 2. *fig, fam* (*faccenda imbrogliata, cosa malfatta*) mess; **mettersi nei -cci** *fam* to get into trouble 3. MUS pastiche

pasticcione, -a [pas·tit·'tʃo:·ne] I. *m, f fam* messy person II. *agg fam* messy

pastificio [pas·ti·'fi:·tʃo] <-ci> *m* pasta factory

pastiglia [pas·'tiʎ·ʎa] <-glie> *f* 1. (*pasticca*) pastille 2. MOT (*dei freni*) pad

pastina [pas·'ti:·na] *f* 1. (*per brodo*) small pasta shapes *pl* 2. (*pasticcino*) cake

pasto ['pas·to] *m* meal; **vino da ~** table wine; **saltare il ~** to skip a meal; **fare due -i al giorno** to have two meals a day

pastone [pas·'to:·ne] *m* 1. (*per polli*) feed; (*per maiali*) swill 2. (*cibo troppo cotto*) mush

pastorale [pas·to·'ra:·le] I. *agg* pastoral II. *f* 1. (*lettera*) pastoral letter 2. (*missione*) pastoral mission 3. MUS pastorale III. *m* (*bastone*) crook

pastore, -a [pas·'to:·re] *m, f* 1. (*di greggi*) shepherd *m,* shepherdess *f* 2. (*cane*) **~ tedesco** German shepherd 3. REL (*ministro*) pastor

pastorizia [pas·to·'rit·tsia] <-ie> *f* sheep farming

pastorizzare [pas·to·rid·'dza:·re] *vt* (*latte*) to pasteurize

pastoso, -a [pas·'to:·so] *agg* 1. (*morbido*) doughy 2. *fig* (*colore, voce, vino*) mellow

pastrano [pas·'tra:·no] *m* greatcoat

pastrocchio [pas·'trɔk·kio] <-cchi> *m fam* mess

pastura [pas·'tu:·ra] *f* 1. (*per bestiame*) pasture 2. (*esca*) bait

patacca [pa·'tak·ka] <-cche> *f* 1. (*cosa senza valore*) piece of junk 2. *scherz* (*distintivo*) gong 3. *fig, fam* (*macchia*) mark

patata [pa·'ta:·ta] *f* potato; **~ americana** [*o* dolce] sweet potato; **-e fritte** (French) fries; **-e lesse** boiled potatoes; **sacco di -e** *fam* clumsy person

patatina [pa·ta·'ti:·na] *f* (*in sacchetto*) chip

patatrac [pa·ta·'trak] I. <-> *m* (*disastro*) disaster II. *int* crash

patella [pa·'tɛl·la] *f* (*mollusco*) limpet

patema [pa·'tɛ:·ma] <-i> *m* worry; **~ d'animo** anxiety

patentato, -a [pa·ten·'ta:·to] *agg* 1. (*munito di patente*) licensed 2. *scherz, fam* (*ladro, imbro-*

glione) out-and-out

patente [pa·'tɛn·te] *f* license; **~ (di guida)** (driver's) license; **~ a punti** *driver's license with a demerit points system*

patentino [pa·ten·'ti:·no] *m* (*per motorini*) moped license

paternale [pa·ter·'na:·le] *f* reprimand

paternalismo [pa·ter·na·'liz·mo] *m* 1. POL paternalism 2. (*condiscendenza*) patronizing attitude

paternalistico, -a [pa·ter·na·'lis·ti·ko] <-ci, -che> *agg* 1. POL paternalistic 2. (*condiscendente: tono, atteggiamento*) patronizing

paternità [pa·ter·ni·'ta] <-> *f* 1. (*condizione di padre*) fatherhood 2. ADM paternity 3. (*di opera*) authorship

paterno, -a [pa·'tɛr·no] *agg* 1. (*istinto, affetto*) paternal 2. (*da padre: consiglio*) fatherly

patetico, -a [pa·'tɛ:·ti·ko] <-ci, -che> *agg* pathetic

pathos ['pa:·tos] *m* pathos

patibolo [pa·'ti:·bo·lo] *m* (*per esecuzioni*) gallows

patimento [pa·ti·'men·to] *m* (*sofferenza*) suffering

patina ['pa:·ti·na] *f* 1. (*su metallo*) patina 2. (*vernice*) varnish 3. MED **~ linguale** fur on the tongue

patire [pa·'ti:·re] <patisco> I. *vt* (*offesa, torto*) to suffer; (*fame, sete, freddo, caldo*) to suffer from II. *vi* to suffer

patito, -a [pa·'ti:·to] I. *agg* (*deperito*) sickly II. *m, f* (*appassionato*) fan

patogeno, -a [pa·'tɔ:·dʒe·no] *agg* pathogenic

patologia [pa·to·lo·'dʒi:·a] <-gie> *f* (*malattia*) pathology

patologico, -a [pa·to·'lɔ:·dʒi·ko] <-ci, -che> *agg a. fig, scherz* pathological

patologo, -a [pa·'tɔ:·lo·go] <-gi, -ghe> *m, f* pathologist

patos *m v.* **pathos**

patria ['pa:·tria] <-ie> *f* 1. (*nazione*) home country; (*città, paese*) birthplace; **~ d'elezione** adoptive country; **la madre ~** the mother country 2. (*luogo d'origine*) home

patriarca [pa·tri·'ar·ka] <-chi> *m* patriarch

patriarcale [pa·tri·ar·'ka:·le] *agg* patriarchal

patriarcato [pa·tri·ar·'ka:·to] *m* 1. (*in famiglia*) patriarchy 2. REL patriarchate

patrigno [pa·'triɲ·ɲo] *m* stepfather

patrimoniale [pa·tri·mo·'nia:·le] I. *agg* property II. *f* (*imposta*) property tax

patrimonio [pa·tri·'mɔ:·nio] <-i> *m* 1. JUR estate; (*beni materiali*) possessions *pl;* **un ~** (*grossa somma*) a fortune 2. BIOL **~ genetico** gene pool 3. *fig* (*ricchezza*) heritage; **~ culturale** cultural heritage

patriota [pa·tri·'ɔ:·ta] <-i *m,* -e *f*> *mf* patriot

patriottico, -a [pa·tri·'ɔt·ti·ko] <-ci, -che> *agg* patriotic

patriottismo [pa·tri·ot·'tiz·mo] *m* patriotism

patrizio, -a [pa·'trit·tsio] <-i, -ie> I. *agg* patrician II. *m, f* patrician

patrocinare [pa·tro·tʃi·'na:·re] *vt* **1.** JUR to defend **2.** (*iniziativa*) to support

patrocinio [pa·tro·'tʃi:·nio] <-i> *m* **1.** (*patronato*) patronage; **sotto il ~ di** under the patronage of **2.** JUR defense

patronato [pa·tro·'na:·to] *m* **1.** (*ente*) charity **2.** (*sostegno*) patronage

patrono, -a [pa·'trɔ:·no] *m, f* **1.** (*protettore*) patron; REL patron saint **2.** (*socio di patronato*) charity official

patta ['pat·ta] *f* **1.** (*di tasca*) flap; (*di pantaloni*) fly **2.** (*pareggio*) tie

patteggiare [pat·ted·'dʒa:·re] **I.** *vt* (*resa, pena*) to negotiate **II.** *vi* **~ con qu** to negotiate with sb

pattinaggio [pat·ti·'nad·dʒo] <-ggi> *m* skating; **~ a rotelle** roller skating; **~ su ghiaccio** ice skating

pattinare [pat·ti·'na:·re] *vi* **1.** (*su ghiaccio, a rotelle*) to skate **2.** MOT (*slittare*) to skid

pattino¹ ['pat·ti·no] *m* **1.** skate; **-i da ghiaccio** ice skates; **-i a rotelle** roller skates; **-i in linea** Rollerblades® *pl* **2.** (*di slitta*) runner; (*di aereo*) skid **3.** TEC sliding block

pattino² [pat·'ti:·no] *m* (*barca*) twin-hulled rowboat

patto ['pat·to] *m* **1.** (*accordo*) pact; **venire** [*o* **scendere**] **a -i con qu** to come to terms with sb; **stare ai -i** to keep to an agreement; **Patto Atlantico** Atlantic Charter; **~ di non aggressione** nonaggression pact **2.** (*condizione*) condition; **a ~ che ... +**conj on condition that ...; **a nessun ~** on no condition

pattuglia [pat·'tuʎ·ʎa] <-glie> *f* patrol; **~ stradale** traffic patrol; **~ di ricognizione** reconnaissance patrol; **essere di ~** to be on patrol

pattugliare [pat·tuʎ·'ʎa:·re] **I.** *vi* to patrol **II.** *vt* to patrol

pattuire [pat·tu·'i:·re] <pattuisco> *vt* to agree on

pattuito [pat·tu·'i:·to] *m* agreement

pattuito, -a *agg* agreed

pattumiera [pat·tu·'miɛ:·ra] *f* garbage can

paura [pa·'u:·ra] *f* fear; **aver ~ di qu/qc** to be afraid of sb/sth; **avere una ~ da morire** to be scared to death; **niente ~!** don't worry!; **aver ~ che ...** to be afraid that ...; **far ~ a qu** [*o* **mettere ~ a qu**] to scare sb; **brutto da far ~** (as) ugly as sin

pauroso, -a [pau·'ro:·so] *agg* **1.** (*scena, incidente*) frightening **2.** (*persona, carattere*) fearful **3.** *fig* (*straordinario*) incredible

pausa ['pa·u·za] *f* pause; (*interruzione*) break; **~ caffè** coffee break

pavese I. *agg* from Pavia **II.** *mf* (*abitante*) person from Pavia

Pavese <sing> *m* Pavia area; **nel ~** in the Pavia area

Pavia *f* Pavia, *city in Lombardy*

pavimentare [pa·vi·men·'ta:·re] *vt* (*stanza*) to floor; (*strada*) to pave

pavimentazione [pa·vi·men·tat·'tsio:·ne] *f* paving

pavimento [pa·vi·'men·to] *m* (*di stanza*) floor

pavone¹ [pa·'vo:·ne] *m* ZOO peacock; **fare il ~** (*vantarsi*) to show off

pavone² <inv> *agg* **azzurro/verde ~** peacock

pavoneggiarsi [pa·vo·ned·'dʒar·si] *vr* to show off

pazientare [pat·tsien·'ta:·re] *vi* to be patient

paziente [pat·'tsiɛn·te] **I.** *agg* **1.** (*persona*) patient **2.** (*lavoro, ricerca*) painstaking **II.** *mf* (*malato*) patient

pazienza [pat·'tsiɛn·tsa] *f* patience; **~!** *fam* never mind!; **perdo** [*o* **mi scappa**] **la ~** I'm losing my patience

pazzesco, -a [pat·'tses·ko] <-schi, -sche> *agg* **1.** (*di, da pazzo: comportamento, discorso*) crazy **2.** *fam* (*straordinario*) incredible

pazzia [pat·'tsi:·a] <-ie> *f* **1.** MED madness **2.** (*azione stravagante*) something crazy **3.** *fig* (*assurdità*) crazy behavior

pazzo, -a ['pat·tso] **I.** *agg* **1.** MED mad **2.** (*insensato*) crazy; **essere ~ da legare** *fig* to be a raving lunatic; **essere innamorato ~ di qu** to be madly in love with sb; **andare ~ per qc** to be crazy about sth; **darsi alla ~ gioia** to live it up **II.** *m, f* **1.** MED madman *m*, madwoman *f* **2.** (*persona insensata*) crazy person

p.c. *abbr di* per conoscenza cc.

PC <-> *m abbr di* **personal computer** PC

PCI *m* HIST *abbr di* **Partito Comunista Italiano** *former Italian Communist Party*

PDCI *m abbr di* **Partito dei Comunisti Italiani** *Italian Communist Party*

PDS *m abbr di* **Partito Democratico della Sinistra** *left-wing Italian party*

pecca ['pɛk·ka] <-cche> *f* (*difetto*) flaw

peccaminoso, -a [pek·ka·mi·'no:·so] *agg* (*pensiero, vita*) sinful; (*lettura*) immoral

peccare [pek·'ka:·re] *vi* **1.** REL to sin; **~ di superbia** to commit the sin of pride **2.** (*commettere errori*) to err; **~ di leggerezza** to be guilty of thoughtlessness; **~ di presunzione** to be presumptuous

peccato [pek·'ka:·to] *m* **1.** REL sin; **~ capitale** deadly sin; **~ mortale** mortal sin; **~ originale** original sin **2.** (*errore*) error **3.** *fig* (*per esprimere rammarico*) (**che**) **~!** (what a) shame!; **è un ~ che ... +**conj it's a shame that ...

peccatore, -trice [pek·ka·'to:·re] **I.** *agg* sinning **II.** *m, f* sinner

pece ['pe:·tʃe] *f* pitch; **nero come la ~** (as) black as pitch

pechinese [pe·ki·'ne:·se] **I.** *agg* from Beijing **II.** *mf* **1.** (*abitante*) person from Beijing **2.** (*cane*) Pekinese

Pechino [pe·'ki:·no] *f* Beijing

pecora ['pɛ:·ko·ra] *f* sheep; **~ nera** *fig* black sheep

pecorella [pe·ko·'rɛl·la] *f* **1.** ZOO lamb **2.** (*nuvola*) **cielo a -e** mackerel sky

pecorino [pe·ko·'ri:·no] *m* pecorino

peculiare [pe·ku·'lia:·re] *agg* peculiar

peculiarità [pe·ku·lia·ri·'ta] <-> *f* peculiarity

pecuniario, -a [pe·ku·'nia:·rio] <-i, -ie> *agg*

pecuniary

pedaggio [pe·'dad·dʒo] <-ggi> *m* toll; ~ **autostradale** highway toll; **a** ~ toll

> **i** In Italy travel on superhighways is paid for by a system of **pedaggio** (tolls), which ensures that the user pays for the use that he or she makes of the superhighway infrastructure. The network of tolled superhighways totals about 5,500 km and is run by 24 concessionaire companies. Tolls are normally paid in cash at the tollgate. However payment can also be made using the *Viacard®* system, a magnetic card that can be used either at automatic barriers or handed to the tollgate operator; or with *Telepass®*, a telematic system that works by means of a small machine placed on the windshield allowing the driver to pass through the appropriate lanes without stopping.

pedagogia [pe·da·go·'dʒi:·a] <-gie> *f* pedagogy

pedagogico, -a [pe·da·'gɔ:·dʒi·ko] <-ci, -che> *agg* pedagogic(al)

pedalare [pe·da·'la:·re] *vi* 1. (*in bicicletta*) to pedal 2. *fam* (*camminare in fretta*) to hurry up

pedalata [pe·da·'la:·ta] *f* push on a pedal

pedale [pe·'da:·le] *m* pedal; ~ **del freno** brake pedal; ~ **dell'acceleratore** gas pedal

pedaliera [pe·da·'liɛ:·ra] *f* 1. (*di bicicletta*) pedal and gear mechanism; DI MACCHINA, PIANOFORTE pedals *pl* 2. (*di organo*) pedal board

pedalò® [pe·da·'lɔ] <-> *m* pedal boat

pedalone [pe·da·'lo:·ne] *m v.* **pedalò®**

pedana [pe·'da:·na] *f* 1. (*di scrivania*) footrest 2. (*per salti*) springboard; (*per lancio del disco*) throwing circle

pedante [pe·'dan·te] I. *agg* pedantic II. *m* pedant

pedanteria [pe·dan·te·'ri:·a] <-ie> *f* pedantry

pedata [pe·'da:·ta] *f* 1. (*calcio*) kick; **prendere qu a -e** to kick sb 2. (*impronta*) footprint 3. (*di gradino*) tread

pederasta [pe·de·'ras·ta] <-i> *m pej* pederast

pediatra [pe·'dia:·tra] <-i *m*, -e *f*> *mf* pediatrician

pediatria [pe·dia·'tri:·a] <-ie> *f* pediatrics

pediatrico, -a [pe·'dia:·tri·ko] <-ci, -che> *agg* pediatric

pedicure [pe·di·'ku:·re] <-> I. *m* (*trattamento*) pedicure II. *mf* podiatrist

pediluvio [pe·di·'lu:·vio] <-i> *m* footbath; **farsi un** ~ to have a footbath

pedina [pe·'di:·na] *f* 1. (*nella dama*) checker; (*negli scacchi*) pawn 2. *fig* (*persona*) pawn

pedinare [pe·di·'na:·re] *vt* to tail

pedonale [pe·do·'na:·le] *agg* ·; **isola** [*o* **zona**] ~ pedestrian mall; **strisce -i** crosswalk

pedonalizzazione [pe·do·na·lid·dzat·'tsio:ne] *f* pedestrianization

pedone [pe·'do:·ne] *m* 1. (*persona*) pedestrian; **zona riservata ai -i** pedestrian zone 2. (*negli scacchi*) pawn

pedopornografia [pɛ·do·por·no·gra·'fia] <-ie> *f* child pornography

peeling ['pi·liŋ] <-> *m* MED exfoliation

peggio ['pɛd·dʒo] *comparativo di* **male¹** I. *avv* 1. (*comparativo*) worse; **andare di male in** ~ to go from bad to worse; **cambiare in** ~ to change for the worse 2. (*superlativo*) worst II. <*inv*> *agg* worse; (*tanto*) ~ **per lui!** that's his loss! III. <-> *m* worst IV. <-> *f* **avere la** ~ to come off worst; **alla meno** ~ (*come si può*) as best one can; **alla** ~ (*nella peggiore ipotesi*) if (the) worst comes to (the) worst

peggioramento [ped·dʒo·ra·'men·to] *m* worsening

peggiorare [ped·dʒo·'ra:·re] I. *vt avere* to make worse II. *vi essere* to get worse

peggiorativo [ped·dʒo·ra·'ti:·vo] *m* pejorative

peggiorativo, -a *agg* LING pejorative

peggiore [ped·'dʒo:·re] *comparativo di* **cattivo, -a** I. *agg* 1. (*comparativo*) worse 2. (*superlativo*) worst; **nel** ~ **dei casi** if (the) worst comes to (the) worst II. *mf* worst

pegno ['peɲ·ɲo] *m* 1. JUR security 2. *fig* (*testimonianza: d'amore, di amicizia*) pledge

pelandrone, -a [pe·lan·'dro:·ne] *m, f fam* slacker

pelapatate [pe·la·pa·'ta:·te] <-> *m* potato peeler

pelare [pe·'la:·re] I. *vt* 1. (*patate, castagne*) to peel 2. (*pollo*) to pluck; (*selvaggina*) to skin 3. (*tagliare a zero*) to scalp 4. (*lasciare senza soldi*) to rip off II. *vr:* **-rsi** 1. (*perdere i capelli*) to lose one's hair 2. (*spellarsi*) to peel

pelata [pe·'la:·ta] *f* 1. (*testa calva*) bald head 2. *fig* (*taglio di capelli*) scalping 3. (*in negozio, ristorante*) rip-off; **ti hanno dato una bella** ~**!** they've really ripped you off

pelati [pe·'la:·ti] *mpl* CULIN skinned tomatoes

pelato [pe·'la:·to] *m* (*calvo*) bald man

pelato, -a *agg* 1. (*testa, persona*) bald 2. CULIN skinned

pelatura [pe·la·'tu:·ra] *f* skinning

pellaccia [pel·'lat·tʃa] <-cce> *f fam* 1. (*persona astuta*) rogue 2. (*persona resistente*) tough cookie

pellame [pel·'la:·me] *m* (*pelli conciate*) hides *pl*

pelle ['pɛl·le] *f* 1. (*cute*) skin; **avere la** ~ **dura** *fig* to be tough; **avere la** ~ **d'oca** *fig* to have goose bumps; **essere** ~ **ed ossa** to be (all) skin and bone(s); **non stare più nella** ~ *fig* to be beside oneself 2. (*pellame*) leather; **oggetti di** [*o* **in**] ~ leather goods *pl* 3. *fig, fam* (*vita*) **amici per la** ~ close friends; **lasciarci** [*o* **rimetterci**] **la** ~ to lose one's life; **salvare la** ~ to save one's skin 4. (*buccia*) peel

pellegrinaggio [pel·le·gri·'nad·dʒo] <-ggi> *m* pilgrimage

pellegrino, -a [pel·le·'gri:·no] *m, f* (*in luoghi*

santi) pilgrim
pellerossa [pel·le·'ros·sa] <pellirosse> *mf* Red Indian *pey*
pelletteria [pel·let·te·'ri:·a] <-ie> *f* 1.(*industria*) leather industry 2.(*articoli*) leather goods *pl* 3.(*negozio*) leather goods store
pellicano [pel·li·'ka:·no] *m* pelican
pelliccia [pel·'lit·tʃa] <-cce> *f* 1.(*di animale*) fur 2.(*in abbigliamento*) fur (coat); ~ **ecologica** fake fur
pellicola [pel·'li:·ko·la] *f* 1.FOTO film 2.(*film*) movie 3.(*strato sottile*) layer
pellirossa [pel·li·'ros·sa] *mf v.* pellerossa
pellirossa *pl di* pellerossa, pellirossa
pelo ['pɛ:·lo] *m* 1.(*di uomo, animale, pianta*) hair; **per un ~** *fig, fam* by the skin of one's teeth; **non avere -i sulla lingua** *fig* to say what one thinks; **cercare il ~ nell'uovo** *fig* to split hairs 2.(*pelame*) coat 3.(*su indumenti*) fur; **il lupo perde il ~, ma non il vizio** *prov* a leopard can't change its spots 4.*fig* (*superficie*) surface; **a ~ d'acqua** on the surface
peloso, -a [pe·'lo:·so] *agg* hairy
peltro ['pel·tro] *m* pewter
peluche [pə·'luʃ] <-> *m* (*pupazzo*) **di** plush
peluria [pe·'lu:·ria] <-ie> *f* down
pena ['pe:·na] *f* 1.JUR penalty; (*punizione*) punishment; ~ **capitale** capital punishment; ~ **di morte** death penalty; ~ **pecuniaria** fine 2.(*sofferenza*) sorrow; **-e d'amore** heartache; **soffrire le -e dell'inferno** to suffer the torments of hell 3.(*angoscia*) **essere** [*o* **stare**] **in ~ per qu** to be worried for sb 4.(*pietà*) pity; **mi fa veramente ~** I feel really sorry for him 5.(*fatica, stento*) difficulty; **a mala ~** barely; **valere la ~** to be worth it
penale [pe·'na:·le] I. *agg* criminal; **azione ~** criminal action; **causa ~** criminal trial; **il codice ~** the penal code II. *f* (*somma*) penalty
penalista [pe·na·'lis·ta] <-i *m*, -e *f*> *mf* criminal lawyer
penalità [pe·na·li·'ta] <-> *f* penalty
penalizzare [pe·na·lid·'dza:·re] *vtt* to penalize
penalizzazione [pe·na·lid·dzat·'tsio:·ne] *f* SPORT penalty
penare [pe·'na:·re] *vi* 1.(*soffrire*) to suffer 2.(*faticare*) to struggle
pen computer [pɛn kom·'piu·ter] <-> *m* COMPUT pen computer
pendaglio [pen·'daʎ·ʎo] <-gli> *m* (*monile*) pendant
pendant [pã·'dã] <-> *m* companion; **fare ~** (**con qc**) to match (sth)
pendente [pen·'dɛn·te] I. *agg* 1.(*che pende*) hanging; (*inclinato*) leaning; **la torre ~** the leaning tower 2.JUR **carichi -i** charges pending 3.(*fattura*) outstanding; **crediti -i** outstanding credits II. *m* (*ciondolo*) pendant
pendenza [pen·'dɛn·tsa] *f* 1.(*inclinazione*) slope 2.MATH gradient 3.JUR pending suit 4.COM (*conto*) outstanding account
pendere ['pɛn·de·re] *vi* 1.(*essere appeso*) ~ **da qc** to hang from sth; ~ **dalle labbra di**

qu *fig* to hang on sb's every word 2.(*essere inclinato*) to slant 3.*fig* (*incombere*) ~ **su qu** to hang over sb 4.(*causa, questione*) to be pending 5.*fig* (*propendere*) ~ **verso qc** to tend toward sth; ~ **dalla parte di qu** to lean toward taking sb's part
pendici [pen·'di:·tʃi] *fpl* slopes *pl*
pendio [pen·'di:·o] <-ii> *m* slope
pendola ['pɛn·do·la] *f* pendulum clock
pendolare I. *agg* 1.(*moto*) pendular 2.(*lavoratore, studente*) commuting II. *mf* commuter
pendolarismo [pen·do·la·'riz·mo] *m* (*fenomeno*) commuting
pendolino® [pen·do·'li:·no] *m* FERR *tilting train*
pendolo ['pɛn·do·lo] *m* 1.PHYS pendulum 2.(*orologio*) pendulum clock 3.(*filo a piombo*) plumb line
pene ['pɛ:·ne] *m* penis
penetrante [pe·ne·'tran·te] *agg* 1.(*odore*) pungent; (*freddo, gelo*) penetrating 2.(*parole, osservazione*) incisive; (*sguardo*) searching
penetrare [pe·ne·'tra:·re] I. *vi* essere (*in un materiale*) ~ **in qc** to penetrate sth; (*in un luogo*) to get into sth II. *vt* avere 1.(*significato, concetto*) to understand 2.(*sessualmente*) to penetrate
penetrazione [pe·ne·trat·'tsio:·ne] *f* penetration; **quota di ~** COM market share
penicillina [pe·ni·tʃil·'li:·na] *f* penicillin
peninsulare [pen·in·su·'la:·re] *agg* peninsular
penisola [pe·'ni:·zo·la] *f* peninsula
penitenza [pe·ni·'tɛn·tsa] *f* 1.(*gener*) penance 2.(*nei giochi*) forfeit
penitenziario [pe·ni·ten·'tsia:·rio] <-i> *m* penitentiary
penna ['pen·na] *f* 1.ZOO feather; **lasciarci** [*o* **rimetterci**] **le -e** *fig* to get one's fingers burned 2.(*per scrivere*) pen; ~ **biro** [*o* **a sfera**] ballpoint; ~ **luminosa** COMPUT light pen; ~ **ottica** COMPUT optical pen; ~ **stilografica** fountain pen 3. *pl* (*pasta*) penne *pl*
pennacchio [pen·'nak·kio] <-cchi> *m a. fig* plume
pennarello [pen·na·'rɛl·lo] *m* felt-tip (pen)
pennellare [pen·nel·'la:·re] *vi* 1.(*col pennello*) to paint 2.*fig* (*descrivere*) to paint a picture of
pennellata [pen·nel·'la:·ta] *f* (*di pennello*) brush stroke
pennello [pen·'nɛl·lo] *m* brush; ~ **da barba** shaving brush; **andare** [*o* **stare**] **a ~** (*vestito*) to fit perfectly
pennino [pen·'ni:·no] *m* (*di stilografica*) nib
pennone [pen·'no:·ne] *m* 1.NAUT yard 2.(*di bandiera*) flagstaff
pennuto [pen·'nu:·to] *m* bird
penombra [pe·'nom·bra] *f* (*luce scarsa*) half-light
penoso, -a [pe·'no:·so] *agg* 1.(*triste*) distressing 2.(*sgradevole*) unpleasant 3.(*negativo*) pathetic
pensare [pen·'sa:·re] I. *vt* 1.(*gener*) to think;

P

cosa stai pensando? what are you thinking?; penso che ... +*conj* I think that ...; la penso anch'io così I think so too 2.(*escogitare*) to think of; una ne fa e cento ne pensa *fam* he's always up to something 3.(*avere intenzione*) ~ di fare qc to think of doing sth II. *vi* 1.(*riflettere*) to think; ~ a qc to think of sth; dar da ~ to give food for thought; pensarci su to think about it 2.(*volgere il pensiero*) ~ a qu/qc to think about sb/sth 3.~ a qc/fare qc (*occuparsi di*) to think about sth/doing sth; (*provvedere a*) to take care of sth/doing sth; pensa ai fatti tuoi! mind your own business! 4.(*giudicare*) ~ bene/male di qu to think well/badly of sb

pensata [pen·'sa:·ta] *f* idea

pensatore, -trice [pen·sa·'to:·re] *m, f* thinker; libero ~ free thinker

pensée [pã·'se] <-> *f* BOT pansy

pensierino [pen·sie·'ri:·no] *m* 1.(*pensiero*) farci un ~ to think about it 2.*fam* (*regalino*) little something 3.(*composizione scolastica*) composition

pensiero [pen·'siɛ:·ro] *m* 1.(*gener*) thought; essere sopra ~ to be lost in thought 2.(*opinione*) thoughts *pl* 3.(*preoccupazione*) worry; stare in ~ per qu/qc to be worried about sb/sth; dar -i a qu to worry sb; togliersi il ~ to get it over and done with 4.*fam* (*regalo*) present

pensieroso, -a [pen·sie·'ro:·so] *agg* thoughtful

pensile ['pɛn·si·le] *agg* (*mobile*) wall; (*giardino*) hanging

pensilina [pen·si·'li:·na] *f* (*di fermata di autobus*) bus shelter; (*di stadio*) overhanging roof

pensionabile [pen·sio·'na:·bi·le] *agg* pensionable

pensionamento [pen·sio·na·'men·to] *m* retirement; ~ anticipato early retirement

pensionante [pen·sio·'nan·te] *mf* (*ospite di pensione*) guest

pensionare [pen·sio·'na:·re] *vt* to pension off

pensionato [pen·sio·'na:·to] *m* (*per studenti*) hostel

pensionato, -a I. *agg* retired II. *m, f* (*persona*) pensioner

pensione [pen·'sio:·ne] *f* 1.(*vitto e alloggio*) board; ~ completa American plan; mezza ~ modified American plan; essere [*o* stare] a ~ da [*o* presso] qu to board with sb 2.(*albergo*) guesthouse 3.(*retribuzione*) pension; ~ integrativa personal pension 4.(*condizione*) retirement; essere in ~ to be retired; andare in ~ to retire

pensionistico, -a [pen·sio·'nis·ti·ko] <-ci, -che> *agg* pension

pensoso, -a [pen·'so:·so] *agg* thoughtful

pentagonale [pen·ta·go·'na:·le] *agg* pentagonal

pentagono [pen·'ta:·go·no] *m* pentagon; il Pentagono the Pentagon

pentagramma [pen·ta·'gram·ma] <-i> *m* staff

pentathlon, pentatlon ['pɛn·ta·tlon] <-> *m* pentathlon

Pentecoste [pen·te·'kɔs·te] *f* Pentecost

pentimento [pen·ti·'men·to] *m* (*rimorso*) remorse

pentirsi [pen·'tir·si] *vr* ~ di qc/di aver fatto qc (*provare rimorso*) to feel remorse for sth/having done sth; (*rimpiangere*) to regret sth/having done sth

pentola ['pen·to·la] *f* pot; ~ a pressione pressure cooker; bollire in ~ *fig, fam* to be going on

pentolino [pen·to·'li:·no] *m* small saucepan

penultimo, -a [pe·'nul·ti·mo] I. *agg* penultimate II. *m, f* penultimate

penuria [pe·'nu:·ria] <-ie> *f* shortage

penzolare [pen·dzo·'la:·re] *vi* to dangle

penzoloni [pen·dzo·'lo:·ni] *avv* (a) ~ dangling

peonia [pe·'ɔ:·nia] <-ie> *f* peony

pepare [pe·'pa:·re] *vt* to pepper

pepato, -a [pe·'pa:·to] *agg* 1.(*con pepe*) peppered 2.(*piccante*) peppery 3.*fig* (*risposta*) caustic

pepe[1] ['pe:·pe] *m* pepper; ~ bianco/nero white/black pepper; ~ in grani peppercorns *pl;* tutto ~ *fig* high-spirited

peperonata [pe·pe·ro·'na:·ta] *f sliced peppers fried in oil with onions, garlic, and tomatoes*

peperoncino [pe·pe·ron·'tʃi:·no] *m* (*piccante*) chili (pepper)

peperone [pe·pe·'ro:·ne] *m* (bell) pepper; diventare rosso come un ~ to get as red as a beet

pepita [pe·'pi:·ta] *f* nugget

peppermint ['pe·pə·mint] <-> *m* peppermint

per [per] *prep* 1.(*moto per luogo*) through; (*moto a luogo*) for; (*stato in luogo*) on; passare ~ Firenze to pass through Florence; partire ~ Londra to leave for London; ~ terra on the ground 2.(*tempo: durata, momento esatto*) for; (*scadenza*) by; ~ il momento for the moment; ~ ora for now; ~ tempo in time; ~ poco nearly; ~ questa volta this time; ho preso appuntamento ~ domani I've made an appointment for tomorrow; sarò di ritorno ~ le otto I'll be back by eight 3.(*scopo, fine*) for; un libro ~ bambini a book for children; ~ iscritto in writing; ~ esempio for example 4.(*mezzo, modo*) by; spedire ~ posta to send by mail 5.(*causa*) because of; ~ caso by chance; ~ ciò [*o* questo] for this reason; ~ il fatto che ... because of the fact that ...; ~ quale motivo? for what reason? 6.(*destinazione, vantaggio*) for; c'è una lettera ~ te there's a letter for you; farebbe qualsiasi cosa ~ i figli he'd do anything for his children 7.(*prezzo*) for; l'ho venduto ~ 100 euro I sold it for a 100 euros 8.(*estensione*) for; correre ~ 30 chilometri to run (for) 30 kilometers 9.(*distributivo*) for; uno ~ volta one at a time; in fila ~ tre in threes 10. MATH by; tre ~ tre three times three; dividere ~ sette to divide by seven; moltiplicare ~ sette to multiply by seven; **il tre ~ cento** three percent **11.** (*come*) as; **prendere ~ moglie** to take as one's wife; **l'ho preso ~ un altro** I took him for someone else **12.** (*in esclamazioni*) for; **~ l'amor del cielo** [*o di Dio*]**!** for heaven's sake!; **~ carità!** *fam* for goodness sake! **13.** (*con infinito: finale*) (in order) to; **sono venuto ~ aiutarti** I've come to help you; (*consecutiva*) to; **sei troppo piccolo ~ capire** you're too little to understand; (*causale*) for; **sono stato punito ~ non aver obbedito** I was punished for disobedience **14.** (*loc*) **stare ~ ... +*inf*** to be about to ...

pera ['pe:·ra] *f* **1.** (*frutto*) pear **2.** *sl* (*di eroina*) fix; **farsi una ~** to give oneself a fix **3.** (*loc*) **a ~** (*sconclusionato*) illogical

peraltro [pe·'ral·tro] *avv* moreover

perbacco [per·'bak·ko] *int fam* goodness!

perbene [per·'bɛ:·ne] **I.** <inv> *agg* (*famiglia, persona*) respectable **II.** *avv* (*comportarsi, sedersi*) properly

perbenismo [per·be·'niz·mo] *m pej* supposed respectability

percento [per·'tʃɛn·to] <-> *m* percent

percentuale [per·tʃen·tu·'a:·le] **I.** *agg* percentage **II.** *f* **1.** MATH percentage **2.** (*provvigione*) commission

percepire [per·tʃe·'pi:·re] <percepisco> *vt* **1.** (*ricevere: compenso, stipendio, somma*) to receive **2.** (*sentire: diffidenza, ostilità*) to perceive

percezione [per·tʃet·'tsio:·ne] *f* (*facoltà*) perception

perché [per·'ke] **I.** *avv* why **II.** *cong* **1.** (*causale*) because **2.** +*conj* (*finale*) so that **3.** +*conj* (*consecutivo*) **era troppo lontano ~ potessimo vederlo** it was too far off for us to be able to see it **III.** <-> *m* **1.** (*motivo*) reason **2.** (*interrogativo*) question

perciò [per·'tʃɔ] *cong* so

percorrere [per·'kor·re·re] <irr> *vt* **1.** (*distanza*) to cover; (*strada*) to drive along **2.** (*territorio*) to travel through

percorso [per·'kor·so] *m* **1.** (*tragitto*) route **2.** (*tempo di percorrenza*) journey **3.** SPORT (*nell'equitazione*) round **4.** COMPUT path

percorso, -a I. *pp di* **percorrere II.** *agg* covered

percossa [per·'kɔs·sa] *f* blow

percuotere [per·'kuɔ:·te·re] <percuoto, percossi, percosso> *vt* (*colpire*) to strike

percussione [per·kus·'sio:·ne] *f* percussion; **strumenti a ~** percussion instruments

percussore [per·kus·'so:·re] *m* (*di arma*) hammer

perdei [per·'de:·i] *1. pers sing pass rem di* **perdere**

perdente [per·'dɛn·te] **I.** *agg* losing **II.** *mf* loser

perdere ['pɛr·de·re] <perdo, persi *o* perdei *o* perdetti, perso *o* perduto> **I.** *vt* **1.** (*gener*) to lose; **~ la vita** to lose one's life; **~ (il) colore** (*tessuto*) to fade; **~ le staffe** *fig, fam* to lose one's temper; **~ la testa** *fig* to lose one's head;

~ ogni speranza to lose all hope **2.** (*treno, film, evento, occasione*) to miss; **non ti sei perso niente** you haven't missed anything **3.** (*sprecare*) to waste **4.** (*acqua, gas*) to leak; (*sangue*) to lose **5.** (*loc*) **lasciar ~ qu/qc** to forget sb/sth; **lasciamo ~** let's forget it; **~ qu di vista** to let sb out of your sight; **fare qc a tempo perso** *fam* to do sth in one's spare time **II.** *vi* (*diminuire*) **~ di qc** (*interesse, valore*) to lose sth **III.** *vr:* **-rsi 1.** (*smarrirsi*) to get lost; **-rsi d'animo** to get discouraged; **-rsi in chiacchiere** to waste time chatting; **-rsi in un bicchiere d'acqua** *fig* to be easily discouraged **2.** (*svanire*) to disappear **3.** (*rovinarsi*) to be ruined; **-rsi dietro a qu** to fall head over heels for sb

perdiana [per·'dia:·na] *int* goodness!

perdifiato [per·di·'fia:·to] *avv* **a ~** (*gridare*) at the top of one's voice; (*correre*) at breakneck speed

perdigiorno [per·di·'dʒor·no] <-> *mf* slacker

perdinci [per·'din·tʃi] *int fam* goodness!

perdindirindina [per·din·di·rin·'di:·na] *int scherz* goodness!

perdio, per Dio [per·'di:·o] *int fam* God!

perdita ['pɛr·di·ta] *f* **1.** (*gener*) loss; **a ~ d'occhio** *fig* as far as the eye can see **2.** COM **essere in ~** to be running at a loss **3.** (*di acqua, gas*) leak

perditempo [per·di·'tɛm·po] <-> *mf fam* (*persona*) time-waster

perdizione [per·dit·'tsio:·ne] *f* (*rovina morale*) perdition

perdonare [per·do·'na:·re] **I.** *vt* **1.** (*per colpa, errore*) to forgive; **non ~ qc a qu** not to forgive sb sth **2.** (*per disturbo*) to excuse **II.** *vi* **non ~** (*essere inesorabile*) not to forgive; **una malattia che non perdona** an incurable disease **III.** *vr:* **-rsi** to forgive oneself

perdono [per·'do:·no] *m* **1.** REL forgiveness **2.** (*scusa*) pardon; **chiedere ~ a qu** to apologize to sb **3.** JUR **~ giudiziale** pardon

perdurare [per·du·'ra:·re] *vi* **1.** (*permanere: maltempo*) to continue **2.** (*persistere*) **~ in qc** (*proposito, intenzione*) to persist in sth

perdutamente [per·du·ta·'men·te] *avv* desperately

perduto, -a [per·'du:·to] *agg* lost; **andare ~** to get lost

peregrinare [pe·re·gri·'na:·re] *vi* (*vagare*) to wander

peregrinazione [pe·re·gri·nat·'tsio:·ne] *f* (*vagabondaggio*) wandering

perenne [pe·'rɛn·ne] *agg* **1.** (*neve*) perpetual; (*gloria*) everlasting **2.** BOT perennial **3.** *fig* (*continuo: disturbo*) continual

perentorio, -a [pe·ren·'tɔ:·rio] <-i, -ie> *agg* **1.** (*improrogabile: termine*) final **2.** (*tono, risposta*) peremptory

perequazione [pe·re·kuat·'tsio:·ne] *f* ADM equalization

perestroika [pe·res·'trɔi·ka] <*sing*> *f* POL perestroika

peretta [pe·'ret·ta] *f* 1.(*interruttore*) switch 2.(*clistere*) enema

perfettamente [per·fet·ta·'men·te] *avv* perfectly

perfetto, -a [per·'fɛt·to] *agg* 1.(*privo di difetti, irreprensibile*) perfect; **un ~ idiota** an utter fool 2.(*completo*) complete

perfezionamento [per·fet·tsio·na·'men·to] *m* improvement; **corso di ~** proficiency course

perfezionare [per·fet·tsio·'na:·re] I.*vt* 1.(*opera*) to improve; (*metodo, macchina*) to perfect 2.(*contratto*) to draw up II.*vr:* **-rsi** 1.(*tecnica, scienza*) to improve 2.(*materia*) **-rsi in inglese** to perfect one's English

perfezione [per·fet·'tsio:·ne] *f* perfection; **alla ~** perfectly

perfezionismo [per·fet·tsio·'niz·mo] *m* perfectionism

perfezionista [per·fet·tsio·'nis·ta] <-i *m*, -e *f*> *mf* perfectionist

perfidia [per·'fi:·dia] <-ie> *f* 1.(*caratteristica*) treachery 2.(*azione*) treacherous act

perfido, -a ['pɛr·fi·do] *agg* treacherous

perfino [per·'fi:·no] *avv* even

perforante [per·fo·'ran·te] *agg* perforating; **appendicite ~** perforating appendicitis

perforare [per·fo·'ra:·re] *vt* (*carta, scheda, banda*) to punch; (*organo, tessuto*) to pierce

perforato, -a [per·fo·'ra:·to] *agg* (*carta, scheda, nastro*) punched; (*tessuto*) pierced

perforazione [per·fo·rat·'tsio:·ne] *f* 1.(*gener*) perforation 2.(*di terreno, roccia*) drilling

performance [pə·'fɔ:·məns/per·'fɔr·məns] <-> *f* performance

performante [per·for·'man·te] *agg* high-performance

pergamena [per·ga·'mɛ:·na] *f* parchment

pergola ['pɛr·go·la] *f* (*tettoia*) pergola

pergolato [per·go·'la:·to] *m* pergola

pericolante [pe·ri·ko·'lan·te] *agg* (*edificio, ponte*) unsafe

pericolo [pe·'ri:·ko·lo] *m* danger; **~ di morte** danger; **essere in ~** to be in danger; **essere fuori ~** to be out of danger; **a proprio rischio e ~** at one's own risk; **correre un ~** to run a risk; **essere un ~ pubblico** to be a public menace; **c'è ~ che ...** +*conj* there's a danger that ...

pericolosità [pe·ri·ko·lo·si·'ta] <-> *f* danger

pericoloso, -a [pe·ri·ko·'lo:·so] *agg* dangerous

periferia [pe·ri·fe·'ri:·a] <-ie> *f* 1.(*di città*) suburbs *pl;* **quartiere di ~** suburb; **abitare in ~** to live in the suburbs 2.ANAT periphery

periferica [pe·ri·'fɛ:·ri·ka] <-che> *f* COMPUT peripheral

periferico, -a [pe·ri·'fɛ:·ri·ko] <-ci, -che> *agg* 1.(*questione, critica*) peripheral 2.(*quartiere, scuola*) suburban

perifrasi [pe·'ri:·fra·zi] <-> *f* periphrasis

perimetrale [pe·ri·me·'tra:·le] *agg* perimeter

perimetro [pe·'ri:·me·tro] *m* perimeter

periodico [pe·'riɔ:·di·ko] <-ci> *m* (*rivista*) periodical

periodico, -a <-ci, -che> *agg* 1.(*ricorrente: fatto, crisi, ricerca*) periodic 2.MATH recurring

periodo [pe·'ri:·o·do] *m* 1.(*intervallo di tempo*) period; **attraversare un brutto ~** to go through a bad patch; **~ di aspettativa** leave; **~ di prova** trial period; **~ elettorale** election time 2.*fig* to be patchy

peripezie [pe·ri·pet·'tsi:·e] *fpl* ups and downs *pl*

perire [pe·'ri:·re] <perisco> *vi essere poet* to perish

periscopio [pe·ris·'kɔ:·pio] <-i> *m* periscope

perito, -a [pe·'ri:·to] I.*m, f* 1.(*esperto*) expert 2.(*titolo di studio*) **~ agrario/chimico** qualified agronomist/chemist II.*agg* (*morto*) perished

peritonite [pe·ri·to·'ni:·te] *f* peritonitis

perizia [pe·'rit·tsia] <-ie> *f* 1.(*abilità*) skill 2.(*esame: calligrafica, balistica, psichiatrica*) report

perizoma [pe·rid·'dzɔ:·ma] <-i> *m* thong

perla[1] ['pɛr·la] *f* 1.(*gioiello*) pearl; **~ coltivata** cultivated pearl 2.*fig* (*persona eccellente*) gem

perla[2] <inv> *agg* **grigio ~** pearl gray

perlaceo, -a [per·'la:·tʃeo] <-ei, -ee> *agg* pearly

perlato, -a [per·'la:·to] *agg* 1.(*diadema*) decorated with pearls 2.(*orzo, cotone*) pearl

perlina [per·'li:·na] *f* (*per collane*) bead

perlomeno, per lo meno [per·lo·'me:·no] *avv* at least

perlopiù, per lo più [per·lo·'piu] *avv* for the most part

perlustrare [per·lus·'tra:·re] *vt* to patrol

perlustrazione [per·lus·trat·'tsio:·ne] *f* patrol

permaloso, -a [per·ma·'lo:·so] I.*agg* touchy II.*m, f* touchy person

permanente [per·ma·'nɛn·te] I.*agg* permanent II.*f* (*di capelli*) perm

permanentemente [per·ma·nen·te·'men·te] *avv* permanently

permanenza [per·ma·'nɛn·tsa] *f* 1.(*soggiorno*) stay; **buona ~!** enjoy your stay! 2.(*di situazione, condizioni*) permanence

permanere [per·ma·'ne:·re] <permango, permasi, permaso> *vi essere* (*durare*) to remain

permeabile [per·me·'a:·bi·le] *agg* permeable

permeabilità [per·me·a·bi·li·'ta] <-> *f* permeability

permeare [per·me·'a:·re] *vt a. fig* to permeate

permesso [per·'mes·so] I.*m* 1.(*autorizzazione*) permission; **~ di lavoro** work permit; **~ di soggiorno** residence permit; **~ di caccia** hunting license; **~ di pesca** fishing license; **chiedere il ~ di fare qc** to ask permission to so sth; **con ~** (*entrando*) may I? 2.MIL leave; **essere in ~** to be on leave II.*agg* (*è*) **permesso?** (*entrando*) may I?; (*passando*) can I get past?

permettere [per·'met·te·re] <irr> I.*vt* 1.(*dare il permesso per*) to allow; **~ a qu di fare qc** to allow sb to do sth 2.(*dare la possibilità*) to permit **3.**(*concedersi*) to afford **II.** *vr:* **-rsi** to take the liberty; **come si permette!** how dare you!

permissivo, -a [per·mis·'si:·vo] *agg* (*genitori, educazione*) permissive

permuta ['pɛr·mu·ta] *f* (*contratto*) exchange

permutare [per·mu·'ta:·re] *vt* (*barattare: merci, valori*) to exchange

pernice [per·'ni:·tʃe] *f* partridge; **occhio di ~** *fam* (*callo*) corn

perno ['pɛr·no] *m* **1.** TEC pivot **2.** *fig* (*di famiglia, organizzazione*) linchpin

pernottamento [per·not·ta·'men·to] *m* overnight stay

pernottare [per·not·'ta:·re] *vi* to stay the night

pero ['pe:·ro] *m* pear tree

però [pe·'rɔ] *cong* **1.**(*avversativo*) but **2.**(*concessivo*) nevertheless

perorare [pe·ro·'ra:·re] *vt* (*difendere: causa*) to plead

perpendicolare [per·pen·di·ko·'la:·re] **I.** *agg* (*retta, strada*) perpendicular **II.** *f* (*retta*) perpendicular (line)

perpendicolo [per·pen·'di:·ko·lo] *m* **a ~** perpendicularly

perpetua [per·'pɛ:·tua] *f* (*domestica*) priest's housekeeper

perpetuare [per·pe·tu·'a:·re] **I.** *vt* (*nome, ricordo*) to immortalize; (*stirpe, opera*) to perpetuate **II.** *vr:* **-rsi** to be immortalized

perpetuo, -a [per·'pɛ:·tuo] *agg* **1.**(*eterno: ricordo, felicità*) everlasting **2.**(*continuo: indecisione, lamentele*) perpetual

perplessità [per·ples·si·'ta] <-> *f* (*incertezza*) perplexity

perplesso, -a [per·'plɛs·so] *agg* (*indeciso*) undecided; (*disorientato*) perplexed

perquisire [per·kui·'zi:·re] <perquisisco> *vt* (*stanza, persona*) to search

perquisizione [per·kui·zit·'tsio:·ne] *f* search; **mandato di ~** search warrant

persecutore, -trice [per·se·ku·'to:·re] **I.** *m, f* persecutor **II.** *agg* (*movimento*) persecuting

persecuzione [per·se·kut·'tsio:·ne] *f* **1.**(*repressione*) persecution; **mania di ~** persecution complex **2.** *fig* (*assillo*) nuisance ~!

perseguibile [per·se·'gui:·bi·le] *agg* **1.**(*fine, obiettivo*) pursuable **2.** JUR (*reato*) prosecutable

perseguire [per·se·'gui:·re] *vt* **1.**(*scopo*) to pursue **2.**(*criminale, reato*) to prosecute

perseguitare [per·se·gui·'ta:·re] *vt* **1.**(*sottoporre a persecuzione*) to persecute **2.** *fig* (*ossessionare*) to hound

perseguitato, -a [per·se·gui·'ta:·to] **I.** *agg* persecuted **II.** *m, f* victim of persecution; **i -i politici** victims of political persecution

perseveranza [per·se·ve·'ran·tsa] *f* perseverance

perseverare [per·se·ve·'ra:·re] *vi* **~ in qc** to persevere in sth

persi ['pɛr·si] *1. pers sing pass rem di* **perdere**

Persia ['pɛr·sia] *f* **la ~** Persia; **abitare in ~** to live in Persia; **andare in ~** to go to Persia

persiana [per·'sia:·na] *f* (*imposta*) shutter;

~ avvolgibile roller shutter

persiano [per·'sia:·no] *m* **1.**(*lingua*) Persian **2.**(*gatto*) Persian **3.**(*pelliccia*) Persian lamb

persiano, -a **I.** *agg* Persian **II.** *m, f* (*abitante*) Persian

persico, -a ['pɛr·si·ko] <-ci, -che> *agg* **1.** GEOG Persian; **il golfo ~** the Persian Gulf **2.** ZOO **pesce ~** perch

persino [per·'si:·no] *avv v.* **perfino**

persistente [per·sis·'tɛn·te] *agg* (*pioggia, odore*) persistent

persistenza [per·sis·'tɛn·tsa] *f* persistence

persistere [per·'sis·te·re] <persisto, persistetti *o* persistei, persistito> *vi* **~ in qc** to persist in sth; **~ nel** [*o* a] **fare qc** to persist in doing sth

perso ['pɛr·so] *pp di* **perdere**

persona [per·'so:·na] *f* person; (*al plurale*) people; **~ fisica/giuridica** natural/legal person; **~ di fiducia** trustworthy person; **in prima ~** personally; **di ~** (*conoscere*) personally; (*andare*) in person; **in ~** (*personalmente*) in person; (*personificato*) personified

personaggio [per·so·'nad·dʒo] <-ggi> *m* **1.**(*persona importante*) figure **2.**(*di romanzo, film*) character **3.** *fig* (*tipo*) individual

personal computer ['pə:s·nəl kəm·'pju:·tə] <-> *m* INFORM personal computer

personale [per·so·'na:·le] **I.** *agg* personal **II.** *m* **1.**(*impiegati*) personnel; **~ di servizio** domestic staff; **~ di volo** flight crew; **~ qualificato** skilled workers *pl;* **~ insegnante** faculty; **reparto** (**del**) **~** personnel (department) **2.**(*aspetto fisico*) figure

personalità [per·so·na·li·'ta] <-> *f* **1.**(*gener*) personality **2.** DIR **~ giuridica** legal status

personalizzare [per·so·na·lid·'dza:·re] *vt* (*ambiente, arredamento*) to personalize; (*prodotto*) to customize

personalizzato, -a [per·so·na·lid·'dza:·to] *agg* (*ambiente*) personalized; (*prodotto*) customized

personalizzazione [per·so·na·lid·dzat·'tsio:·ne] *f* (*di ambiente*) personalization; (*di prodotto*) customization

personalmente [per·so·nal·'men·te] *avv* personally

personificare [per·so·ni·fi·'ka:·re] *vt* **1.**(*rappresentare*) to represent **2.**(*essere simbolo di*) to personify

personificazione [per·so·ni·fi·kat·'tsio:·ne] *f* personification

perspicace [per·spi·'ka:·tʃe] *agg* (*persona, ingegno, politica, provvedimento*) shrewd

perspicacia [per·spi·'ka:·tʃa] <-cie> *f* shrewdness

persuadere [per·sua·'de:·re] <persuado, persuasi, persuaso> **I.** *vt* **1.**(*convincere*) to persuade; **~ qu di qc** to persuade sb of sth; **~ qu di fare qc** to persuade sb to do sth **2.**(*suscitare consenso*) to convince **II.** *vr:* **-rsi 1.**(*convincersi*) to convince oneself **2.**(*capacitarsi*) **-rsi di qc** to understand sth

persuasi [per·su·'a:·zi] *1. pers sing pass rem di* **persuadere**

persuasione [per·sua·'zio:·ne] *f* 1.(*opera di convincimento*) persuasion 2.(*opinione*) conviction

persuasivo, -a [per·sua·'zi:·vo] *agg* persuasive

persuaso [per·su·'a:·zo] *pp di* **persuadere**

pertanto [per·'tan·to] *cong* (*perciò*) therefore

pertica ['pɛr·ti·ka] <-che> *f* pole

pertinente [per·ti·'nɛn·te] *agg* (*domanda, osservazione*) pertinent

pertinenza [per·ti·'nɛn·tsa] *f* 1.(*attinenza*) pertinence 2.(*competenza*) **essere di ~ di qu** to be down to sb

pertosse [per·'tos·se] *f* whooping cough

perturbare [per·tur·'ba:·re] I. *vt* to disturb II. *vr:* **-rsi** METEO to get worse

perturbazione [per·tur·bat·'tsio:·ne] *f* 1. METEO ~ (**atmosferica**) atmospheric disturbance 2. SCONVOLGIMENTO upheaval

Perù [pe·'ru] *m* **il ~** Peru; **abitare in ~** to live in Peru; **andare in ~** to go to Peru

Perugia *f* Perugia, *city in central Italy*

Perugino <*sing*> *m* Perugia area

perugino, -a [pe·ru·'dʒi:·no] I. *m, f* (*abitante*) Perugian II. *agg* Perugian

peruviano, -a [pe·ru·'via:·no] I. *agg* Peruvian II. *m, f* Peruvian

pervadere [per·'va:·de·re] <pervado, pervasi, pervaso> *vt fig, poet* (*occupare*) to pervade

pervenire [per·ve·'ni:·re] <irr> *vi* **essere ~ a qc** to reach sth; **far ~** to send

perversione [per·ver·'sio:·ne] *f* perversion

perversità [per·ver·si·'ta] <-> *f* perversity

perverso, -a [per·'vɛr·so] *agg* (*persona, sentimento*) perverse

pervertire [per·ver·'ti:·re] I. *vt* (*animo, persona*) to pervert II. *vr:* **-rsi** to become perverted

pervertito, -a [per·ver·'ti:·to] I. *agg* perverted II. *m, f* pervert

p. es. *abbr di* **per esempio** e.g.

pesa ['pe:·sa] *f* 1.(*operazione*) weighing 2.(*luogo*) weigh-house; (*apparecchio*) weighing machine

pesalettere [pe·sa·'lɛt·te·re/pe·sa·'let·te·re] <-> *m* letter scales

pesante [pe·'san·te] *agg* 1.(*valigia, pacco, cibo, passo*) heavy; (*maglia, giacca*) thick; **artiglieria ~** heavy artillery; **industria ~** heavy industry **~**; **avere il sonno ~** to be a heavy sleeper; **sentirsi la testa ~** to have a headache 2. *fig* (*atmosfera*) oppressive; (*discorso*) boring 3.(*situazione, danno*) serious 4.(*lavoro*) physically demanding 5.(*stile*) ponderous 6.(*moneta*) hard 7.(*gioco*) physical

pesantezza [pe·san·'tet·tsa] *f* (*di oggetto*) weight; (*di movimento, stile*) heaviness; **~ di stomaco** bloated feeling

pesare [pe·'sa:·re] I. *vt* 1.(*persona, merce*) to weigh 2. *fig* (*valutare*) to weigh up; **~ le parole** to weigh one's words II. *vi* 1.(*avere un peso*) to weigh; (*essere pesante*) to be heavy

2.(*essere sgradevole*) **~ a qu** to be difficult for sb; **~ sulla coscienza** to weigh on one's conscience; **~ sullo stomaco** to lie heavily on one's stomach 3.(*influire*) **~ su qc** to influence sth; **far ~ qc a qu** to remind sb of sth 4. *fig* (*incombere*) **~ su qu/qc** to hang over sb/sth III. *vr:* **-rsi** to weigh oneself

pesarese [pe·sa·'re:·se] I. *mf* (*abitante*) person from Pesaro II. *agg* from Pesaro

Pesarese <*sing*> *m* Pesaro area

Pesaro *f* Pesaro, *city on the east coast of central Italy*

pesca[1] ['pɛs·ka] <-sche> *f* (*frutto*) peach; **~ noce** nectarine

pesca[2] ['pes·ka] <-sche> *f* 1.(*attività*) fishing; (*pescato*) catch; **~ subacquea** underwater fishing; **canna da ~** fishing rod 2.(*lotteria*) lucky dip

pescaggio [pes·'kad·dʒo] <-ggi> *m* draft

Pescara *f* Pescara, *city on the east coast of central Italy*

pescare [pes·'ka:·re] I. *vt* 1.(*pesci*) to catch 2. *fig* (*trovare*) to get 3. *fig* (*carta*) to pick 4. *fig* (*sorprendere*) to catch; **~ qu con le mani nel sacco** *fam* to catch sb red-handed sacco II. *vi* (*imbarcazione*) to draw

pescarese [pes·ka·'re:·se] I. *mf* (*abitante*) person from Pescara II. *agg* from Pescara

Pescarese <*sing*> *m* Pescara area

pescatore, -trice [pes·ka·'to:·re] I. *m, f* (*persona*) fisherman *m*, fisherwoman *f* II. *agg* ZOO **martin ~** kingfisher; **rana -trice** angler fish

pesce ['peʃ·ʃe] *m* 1. ZOO, GASTRON fish; **~ d'acqua dolce** freshwater fish; **~ di mare** saltwater fish; **~ d'aprile** *fam* April fool; **non sapere che -i prendere** [*o* **pigliare**] *fig, fam* not to know which way to turn; **chi dorme non piglia -i** *prov* the early bird catches the worm 2. TYP omission 3. ASTR **Pesci** Pisces; **sono dei Pesci** I'm (a) Pisces

i The **Pesce d'aprile** (April fish) is the Italian equivalent of April Fool. Its name comes from the paper fish that is attached to the back of the person one wants to trick. These days, all kinds of tricks are played on April Fool's Day.

pescecane [peʃ·ʃe·'ka:·ne] <pescicani *o* pescecani> *m* 1. ZOO shark 2.(*persona senza scrupoli*) profiteer

peschereccio [pes·ke·'ret·tʃo] <-cci> *m* (*imbarcazione*) fishing boat

peschereccio, -a <-cci, -cce> *agg* fishing

pescheria [pes·ke·'ri:·a] <-ie> *f* (*negozio*) fish shop

peschiera [pes·'kiɛ:·ra] *f* (*vivaio*) fish farm

pescicani *pl di* **pescecane**

pesciera [peʃ·'ʃɛ:·ra] *f* (*pentola*) fish kettle; (*vassoio*) fish plate

pescivendolo, -a [peʃ·ʃi·'ve:n·do·lo] *m, f* (*venditore*) fish merchant; (*negozio*) fish shop

pesco ['pɛs·ko] <-schi> *m* peach tree
pescosità [pes·ko·si·'ta] <-> *f* abundance of fish
pescoso, -a [pes·'ko:·so] *agg* full of fish
pesista [pe·'sis·ta] <-i *m*, -e *f*> *mf* (*in sollevamento pesi*) weightlifter; (*nel lancio del peso*) shot putter
peso ['pe:·so] *m* **1.** (*gener*) weight; (*cosa pesante*) heavy object; ~ **lordo/netto** gross/net weight; **eccedenza di** ~ (*di bagaglio*) excess weight; **dar** ~ **a qu/qc** *fig* to pay attention to sb/sth **2.** SPORT (*in atletica*) shot; **lancio del** ~ shot put; (*nel pugilato*); ~ **massimo/medio** heavyweight/middleweight; **sollevamento** -i weightlifting **3.** *fig* (*incombenza, angoscia*) burden vita; **togliersi un** ~ (**dalla coscienza**) to clear one's conscience
pessimismo [pes·si·'miz·mo] *m* (*tendenza*) pessimism
pessimista [pes·si·'mis·ta] <-i *m*, -e *f*> **I.** *mf* pessimist **II.** *agg* pessimistic
pessimistico, -a [pes·si·'mis·ti·ko] <-ci, -che> *agg* pessimistic
pessimo, -a ['pɛs·si·mo] *agg superlativo di* cattivo, -a very bad; **di** ~ **gusto** in very bad taste
pestare [pes·'ta:·re] *vt* **1.** (*calpestare*) to tread on; ~ **i piedi** to stamp one's foot **2.** (*pepe, sale*) to grind **3.** *fig* (*picchiare*) to beat
peste ['pɛs·te] *f* **1.** (*malattia*) plague **2.** (*bambino vivace*) pest **3.** *fig* (*rovina*) curse; **dire** ~ **e corna di qu** *fam* to tear sb to pieces
pestello [pes·'tɛl·lo] *m* (*di mortaio*) pestle
pestifero, -a [pes·'ti:·fe·ro] *agg fig* (*cattivo*) pestilential; (*nauseabondo*) noxious
pestilenza [pes·ti·'lɛn·tsa] *f* **1.** (*odore, esalazione*) stench; (*dannoso: vizio, veleno*) curse; (*bambino*) pest **2.** MED pestilence
pesto [pes·to] *m* pesto
pesto, -a *agg* **1.** (*ossa, membra*) aching **2.** (*occhi*) black con un occhio ~ **3.** *fig* **è buio** ~ it's pitch-black
pestone [pes·'to:·ne] *m fam* (*pedata*) stamp
petalo ['pɛː·ta·lo] *m* petal
petardo [pe·'tar·do] *m* **1.** (*bombetta di carta*) firecracker **2.** FERR torpedo
petizione [pe·tit·'tsio:·ne] *f* JUR petition
peto ['pe:·to] *m* fart
petro(l)chimica [pe·tro(l)·'ki:·mi·ka] <-che> *f* petrochemical industry
petro(l)chimico, -a [pe·tro(l)·'ki:·mi·ko] <-ci, -che> *agg* petrochemical
petro(l)dollari [pe·tro(l)·'dɔl·la·ri] *mpl* petrodollar
petroliera [pe·tro·'liɛː·ra] *f* (*oil*) tanker
petroliere [pe·tro·'liɛː·re] *m* oilman
petrolifero, -a [pe·tro·'li:·fe·ro] *agg* oil; **industria** -a oil industry
petrolio [pe·'trɔː·lio] *m* oil; (*cherosene*) kerosene; ~ **grezzo** crude oil
pettegolare [pet·te·go·'la:·re] *vi* to gossip
pettegolezzo [pet·te·go·'led·dzo] *m* gossip
pettegolo, -a [pe·'te:·go·lo] **I.** *agg* (*persona*)

gossipy **II.** *m, f* gossip
pettinare [pet·ti·'na:·re] **I.** *vt* to comb; (*acconciare*); ~ **qu** to do sb's hair **II.** *vr:* -**rsi** (*ravviarsi i capelli*) to comb one's hair; (*acconciarsi*) to do one's hair
pettinata [pet·ti·'na:·ta] *f* **darsi una** ~ to give one's hair a comb
pettinato, -a *agg* **1.** (*persona*) with one's hair combed **2.** (*filato*) combed; (*cotone*) brushed
pettinatrice [pet·ti·na·'tri:·tʃe] *f* (*donna*) hairdresser
pettinatura [pet·ti·na·'tu:·ra] *f* (*di capelli*) hairstyle
pettine ['pɛt·ti·ne] *m* comb
petting ['pɛ·tiŋ] <-> *m* petting
pettirosso [pet·ti·'ros·so] <-i> *m* robin
petto ['pɛt·to] *m* **1.** ANAT chest; (*di donna*) bust; (*organi*) breasts *pl*; GASTR breast; **do di** ~ high C; **prendere qc di** ~ to tackle sth head on **2.** (*di abito*) front; **a doppio** ~ double-breasted **3.** *fig* (*cuore*) **tenersi qc in** ~ to keep sth bottled up
pettorina [pet·to·'ri:·na] *f* (*di grembiule*) bib
petulante [pe·tu·'lan·te] *agg* (*impertinente*) impertinent
petunia [pe·'tu:·nia] <-ie> *f* petunia
pezza ['pɛt·tsa] *f* **1.** (*pezzo di tessuto*) cloth; (*rotolo di tessuto*) bolt; **trattare qu come una** ~ **da piedi** *fam* to treat sb like dirt **2.** (*toppa, macchia*) patch
pezzato, -a *agg* (*animale, manto*) piebald
pezzente [pet·'tsɛn·te] *mf pej* (*straccione*) beggar
pezzo ['pet·tso] *m* **1.** (*gener*) piece; **un** ~ **di dolce/pane** a piece of candy/bread; **un uomo tutto d'un** ~ a man of great integrity; **andare in mille** -i to smash into a thousand pieces; **cadere a** [*o* **in**] -i *fig* to fall to pieces; **fare a** -i **qc** to smash sth to pieces; **fare a** -i **qc/qu** (*denigrare*) to tear sb/sth to pieces; **un** ~ **da museo** *iron* a museum piece; **un due** -i (*costume da bagno*) a two-piece; **essere un** ~ **di legno** *fig* to be made of stone; **costano tre euro al** ~ they cost three euros each; **un servizio da tavola di 48** -i a 48-piece dinner service **2.** (*di meccanismo, macchina*) part; ~ **di ricambio** spare part autorizzati **3.** LIT (*brano*) passage licenziato **4.** (*di strada*) stretch **5.** *fig* (*tempo*) **un** ~ a while; **è un** ~ **che non ci vediamo** we haven't seen each other for a while **6.** (*loc*) **un** ~ **grosso** a big shot; **un bel** ~ **di ragazza** a babe
pH [pi·'ak·ka] <-> *m* pH
phone banking [fon 'bɛn·king] <-> *m* FIN telephone banking
piaccio ['piat·tʃo] *1. pers sing pr di* piacere[1]
piacente [pia·'tʃɛn·te] *agg* attractive
Piacentino <*sing*> *m* Piacenza area
piacentino, -a [pia·tʃen·'ti:·no] **I.** *m, f* (*abitante*) person from Piacenza **II.** *agg* from Piacenza
Piacenza *f* Piacenza, *town in northern Italy*
piacere[1] [pia·'tʃeː·re] <piaccio, piacqui, pia-

ciuto> *vi essere* **mi piace nuotare** I like swimming; **mi piace molto la pasta** I like pasta a lot; **quello rosso mi piace di più di quello verde** I like the red one more than the green one; **il libro che mi piace di più** the book I like best; **mi piacerebbe rivederti** I'd like to see you again; **mi piacerebbe che tu mi accompagnassi** I'd like you to come with me; **che ti piaccia o no** whether you like it or not

piacere[2] *m* 1. (*gener*) pleasure; **provare ~ a fare qc** to take pleasure in doing sth; **viaggio di ~** pleasure trip; **~!** it's a pleasure!; **è un ~ conoscerla** pleased to meet you; **con (molto) ~!** with (great) pleasure! 2. (*favore*) favor; **fare un ~ a qu** to do sb a favor; **fammi il (santo) ~ di ...** +*inf fam* please ...; **ma mi faccia il ~!** for goodness sake ~!; **per ~** please 3. (*volontà*) **a ~** as much as one likes

piacevolezza [pia·tʃe·vo·'let·tsa] *f* (*amabilità*) pleasantness

piacimento [pia·tʃi·'men·to] *m* **a ~** as much as one likes

piaciuto [pia·'tʃuː·to] *pp di* **piacere**[1]

piacqui ['piak·kui] *1. pers sing pass rem di* **piacere**[1]

piadina [pia·'diː·na] *f flat unleavened bread from the Emilia Romagna region*

piaga ['piaː·ga] <-ghe> *f* 1. MED sore 2. *fig* (*danno*) scourge 3. *fig* (*ricordo doloroso*) wound; **mettere il dito nella** [*o* **nella**] **sulla ~** to touch (on) a sore point 4. *fam* (*persona noiosa*) pain

piagare [pia·'gaː·re] *vt* (*ferire*) to damage

piagnisteo [piaɲ·nis·'tɛː·o] *m* whining

piagnone, -a [piaɲ·'ɲoː·ne] *m, f fam* (*bambino*) whiner

piagnucolare [piaɲ·ɲu·ko·'laː·re] *vi* to whine

piagnucolio [piaɲ·ɲu·ko·'liː·o] <-ii> *m* whining

piagnucolone, -a [piaɲ·ɲu·ko·'loː·ne] *m, f fam* whiner

pialla ['pial·la] *f* plane

piallare [pial·'laː·re] *vt* to plane

piana ['piaː·na] *f* (*pianura*) plain

pianeggiante [pia·ned·'dʒan·te] *agg* (*strada, terreno*) flat

pianerottolo [pia·ne·'rɔt·to·lo] *m* landing

pianeta [pia·'neː·ta] <-i> *m* ASTR planet

piangente [pian·'dʒɛn·te] *agg* (*persona*) crying; **salice ~** weeping willow

piangere ['pian·dʒe·re] <piango, piansi, pianto> I. *vi* to cry; **~ di gioia/dolore/rabbia** to cry with joy/in pain/with rage; **~ sul latte versato** *fig, fam* to cry over spilled milk; **mi piange il cuore** it breaks my heart II. *vt* 1. (*lacrime*) to cry 2. (*lamentare*) to mourn

pianificare [pia·ni·fi·'kaː·re] *vt* to plan

pianificato, -a [pia·ni·fi·'kaː·to] *agg* planned

pianificazione [pia·ni·fi·kat·'tsio··ne] *f* planning; **~ familiare** family planning

pianista [pia·'nis·ta] <-i *m*, -e *f*> *mf* (*musicista*) pianist

pianistico, -a [pia·'nis·ti·ko] <-ci, -che> *agg* pianistic

piano[1] ['piaː·no] *m* 1. (*livello*) level; MAT plane; **mettere sullo stesso ~** *fig* to put on the same level; **sul ~ politico/economico** politically/economically 2. (*superficie*) surface; **~ di cottura** stovetop 3. (*di edificio*) floor; **abitare al primo ~** to live on the second floor 4. (*progetto*) plan; **~ regolatore** ADM city-planning project 5. FOTO, FILM **primo ~** (*viso*) close-up; **in primo/secondo ~** in the foreground/the background si vedono i soldati; **di primo ~** *fig* prominent; **passare in secondo ~** *fig* to become less important 6. MUS piano

piano[2] *avv* 1. (*senza fretta*) slowly; **andarci ~** to take it easy; **pian(o) ~** little by little; **chi va ~, va sano e va lontano** *prov* slow and steady wins the race 2. (*a bassa voce*) quietly

piano, -a *agg* (*superificie, strada, terreno*) flat

piano-bar [pia·no·'bar] <-> *m* piano bar

pianoforte [pia·no·'fɔr·te] *m* piano; **~ a coda** grand piano

pianola [pia·'nɔː·la] *f* player piano

pianoro [pia·'nɔː·ro] *m* plateau

pianoterra [pia·no·'tɛr·ra] <-> *m fam* first floor

piansi ['pian·si] *1. pers sing pass rem di* **piangere**

pianta ['pian·ta] *f* 1. BOT plant 2. (*del piede*) sole 3. (*di edificio, città*) layout 4. (*ruolo*) **in ~ stabile** (*essere assunto*) on a permanent basis; *fig* permanently 5. (*loc*) **inventare qc di sana ~** to make sth up completely

piantagione [pian·ta·'dʒoː·ne] *f* (*di caffè, tabacco, cotone*) plantation

piantagrane [pian·ta·'graː·ne] <-> *mf fam* troublemaker

piantare [pian·'taː·re] I. *vt* 1. (*fiori, alberi, terreno*) to plant 2. (*conficcare*) to hammer 3. *fig* (*lasciare*) to leave; **piantala!** *fam* stop it!; **~ in asso qu** to leave sb in the lurch II. *vr:* **-rsi** 1. (*conficcarsi*) **-rsi una spina nel piede** to get a thorn in one's foot 2. (*fermarsi*) **-rsi in casa di qc** to settle into sb's house

pianterreno [pian·ter·'reː·no] *m* first floor

pianto ['pian·to] *m* (*lacrime*) crying

pianto, -a *pp di* **piangere**

piantonare [pian·to·'naː·re] *vt* to guard

piantone [pian·'toː·ne] *m* 1. MIL guard; **essere di ~** to be on guard 2. AUTO **~ di guida** [*o* **di sterzo**] steering column

pianura [pia·'nuː·ra] *f* plain; **la ~ Padana** the Po Valley

piastra ['pias·tra] *f* 1. (*lastra*) plate; **~ di cottura** hotplate 2. HIST (*moneta*) piaster

piastrella [pias·'trel·la] *f* (*mattonella*) tile

piastrellare [pias·trel·'laː·re] *vt* (*bagno, pavimento*) to tile

piastrellista [pias·trel·'lis·ta] <-i *m*, -e *f*> *mf* tiler

piastrina [pias·'triː·na] *f* 1. BIOL platelet 2. MIL **~ di riconoscimento** dog tag 3. (*medaglietta*) tag

piattaforma [piat·ta·'for·ma] <piatteforme> *f*

1. (*gener*) platform; ~ **petrolifera** oil platform Collettivo Nazionale di Lavoro **2.** (*per tuffi*) board

piattello [piat·'tɛl·lo] *m* (*bersaglio*) skeet; **tiro al** ~ skeet shooting

piattino [piat·'ti:·no] *m* (*di tazzina*) saucer

piatto ['piat·to] *m* **1.** (*recipiente*) plate; ~ **fondo/piano** soup/dinner plate **2.** GASTR (*vivanda*) dish; **un** ~ **di minestra/di spaghetti** a plate of soup/spaghetti; (*portata*) course; **primo** ~ first course; ~ **del giorno** today's special **3.** (*di bilancia*) pan **4.** *pl* MUS cymbals

piatto, -a *agg* **1.** (*piano*) flat; MAT (*angolo*) straight **2.** (*monotono*) dull

piattola ['piat·to·la] *f* **1.** ZOO crab **2.** *fam* (*persona noiosa*) pain

piazza ['piat·tsa] *f* **1.** (*di città*) squadre; **scendere in** ~ (*manifestare*) to take to the streets; **fare** ~ **pulita** (*sbarazzarsi*) to make a clean sweep **2.** (*luogo di operazioni*) market; **rovinare la** ~ **a qu** to ruin sb's reputation **3.** (*posto*) **letto ad una** ~ single bed; **letto a due -e** double bed **4.** *fig* (*gente*) crowd; **mettere in** ~ *fig* to make public

piazzale [piat·'tsa:·le] *m* **1.** (*piazza*) square **2.** (*di stazione*) forecourt; (*di aeroporto*) apron

piazzamento [piat·tsa·'men·to] *m* (*in classifica, graduatoria*) placing

piazzare [piat·'tsa:·re] I. *vt* **1.** (*gener*) to place **2.** COM to sell II. *vr:* **-rsi 1.** SPORT to be placed **2.** *fam* (*mettersi*) to plant oneself

piazzata [piat·'tsa:·ta] *f fam* (*scenata*) scene

piazzato, -a [piat·'tsa:·to] *agg* **1.** (*nell'ippica*) placed **2.** (*robusto*) **ben** ~ well-built **3.** *fig* (*con solida posizione*) established

piazzista [piat·'tsis·ta] <-i *m*, -e *f*> *mf* traveling salesman *m*, traveling saleswoman *f*

piazzola [piat·'tsɔ:·la] *f* **1.** (*su una strada*) pulloff; ~ **di sosta** pull-off; ~ **di emergenza** emergency pull-off **2.** (*in campeggio*) spot

picca ['pik·ka] <-cche> *f* **1.** (*puntiglio*) pique **2.** *pl* (*di carte da gioco*) spades; **rispondere -cche** *fam* to refuse point-blank

piccante [pik·'kan·te] *agg* **1.** (*piatto, salsa*) spicy; (*formaggio*) strong **2.** (*storiella*) racy; (*particolare*) juicy

piccarsi [pik·'kar·si] *vr* (*vantarsi*) ~ **di fare qc** to pride oneself on doing sth

picchettaggio [pik·ket·'tad·dʒo] <-ggi> *m* picketing

picchettare [pik·ket·'ta:·re] *vt* **1.** (*fabbrica*) to picket **2.** (*area*) to stake out

picchetto [pik·'ket·to] *m* **1.** (*paletto*) peg **2.** MIL (*gruppo di scioperanti*) picket

picchiare [pik·'kia:·re] I. *vt* **1.** (*dare colpi su*) to beat **2.** (*percuotere*) to beat up II. *vi* **1.** (*dare colpi*) to beat **2.** (*sole*) to beat down **3.** AUTO ~ **in testa** to knock III. *vr:* **-rsi** to fight

picchiata [pik·'kia:·ta] *f* AERO **scendere in** ~ to nosedive

picchiatello, -a [pik·kia·'tɛl·lo] I. *agg fam* crazy II. *m, f fam* crazy person

picchiato, -a [pik·'kia:·to] *agg fam* (*strambo*) crazy

picchiatore, -trice [pik·kia·'to:·re] *m, f* goon *inf*

picchiettare [pik·kiet·'ta:·re] I. *vi* (*con le dita*) to tap; (*pioggia*) to patter II. *vt* to spatter

picchio ['pik·kio] <-cchi> *m* **1.** ZOO woodpecker **2.** (*colpo*) tap

piccineria [pit·tʃi·ne·'ri:·a] <-ie> *f* (*meschinità*) pettiness

piccino, -a [pit·'tʃi:·no] I. *agg* **1.** (*piccolo*) little **2.** *fig* (*meschino*) petty II. *m, f* little one

picciolo [pit·'tʃɔ:·lo] *m* (*di mela*) stalk

piccionaia [pit·tʃo·'na:·ia] <-aie> *f* **1.** (*riparo per piccioni*) pigeon loft **2.** (*soffitta*) loft **3.** THEAT (*loggione*) gallery

piccioncino, -a [pit·tʃon·'tʃi:·no] *m, f fam* lovebird

piccione [pit·'tʃo:·ne] *m* pigeon; ~ **viaggiatore** carrier pigeon; **tiro al** ~ pigeon shooting; **prendere due -i con una fava** *fig* to kill two birds with one stone

picco ['pik·ko] <-cchi> *m* peak; **a** ~ (*perpendicolare*) vertically; **colare a** ~ to sink

piccolezza [pik·ko·'let·tsa] *f* **1.** (*dimensione*) smallness simile **2.** (*inezia*) trifle **3.** (*meschinità*) pettiness

piccolo, -a ['pik·ko·lo] <più piccolo *o* minore, piccolissimo *o* minimo> I. *agg* **1.** (*non grande*) small ~; ~ **imprenditore** small businessman **2.** (*breve*) short **3.** (*di età*) young **4.** (*di poco conto*) little **5.** *fig* (*meschino*) petty II. *m, f* **1.** (*gener*) little one; **da** ~ as a child **2.** (*loc*) **nel mio/tuo/suo** ~ in my/your/his [*o* her] [*o* its fondi] own small way; **in** ~ on a smaller scale

piccone [pik·'ko:·ne] *m* pickax

piccozza [pik·'kɔt·tsa] *f* ice ax

pick-up ['pik·ʌp] <-> *m* (*furgone*) pick-up

picnic [pik·'nik] <-> *m* picnic

pidocchio [pi·'dɔk·ko] <-cchi> *m* **1.** (*di persona, pianta*) louse **2.** (*persona avara*) stingy person

pidocchioso, -a [pi·dok·'ki·io:·so] *agg pej* **1.** (*con i pidocchi*) lice-infested **2.** (*avaro*) stingy

piè [piɛ] *m* **a** ~ **di pagina** at the foot of the page

pied-à-terre [pie·ta·'tɛːr] <-> *m* pied-à-terre

pied-de-poule [piet·'pul] <-> *m* hound's-tooth cloth

piede ['piɛ:·de] *m* **1.** ANAT (*unità di misura*) foot; **stare in -i** to stand viaggio; **essere a -i** to be on foot; **non stare in -i** (*ragionamento, teoria*) not to stand up; **andare a -i** to go on foot; **levarsi** [*o* **togliersi**] **dai -i** *fam* to go away; **prender** ~ to gain ground; **tenere in -i** (*azienda, famiglia*) to keep going famiglia; **mettere i -i in testa a qu** (*trattar male*) to walk all over sb; **mettere in -i qc** (*allestire*) to set sth up; **puntare i -i** (*intestardirsi*) to dig one's heels in; **fatto coi -i** *fam* (*malfatto*) badly done; **a -i nudi** barefoot; **da capo a -i** from head to toe; **su due -i** (*immediatamente*) im-

P

mediately **2.** (*di mobile*) leg; (*di lampada*) base; ~ **del tavolo** table leg **3.** (*estremità inferiore*) **ai -i della montagna** at the foot of the mountain; **ai -i del letto** at the foot of the bed

piedestallo [pie·des·'tal·lo] *m v.* **piedistallo**

piedino [pi·'di:·no] *m* **fare ~ a qu** to play footsie with sb

piedipiatti [pie·di·'piat·ti] <-> *m sl* (*poliziotto*) cop

piedistallo [pie·dis·'tal·lo] *m* (*di statua, colonna*) pedestal

piega ['piɛ:·ga] <-ghe> *f* fold; **gonna a -ghe** pleated skirt; **messa in ~** set; **non fare una ~** (*rimanere impassibile*) not to bat an eye; **prendere una brutta ~** *fig* to take a turn for the worse

piegaciglia [pie·ga·'tʃiʎ·ʎa] <-> *m* eyelash curler

piegamento [pie·ga·'men·to] *m* SPORT push-up

piegare [pie·'ga:·re] **I.** *vt* **1.** (*sbarra, fil di ferro, braccia, gambe, testa, corpo*) to bend; (*foglio, vestiti*) to fold **2.** (*dominare*) to subdue **II.** *vi* (*voltare*) to turn **III.** *vr:* **-rsi 1.** (*incurvarsi*) to bend schiena **2.** (*arrendersi*) to submit

pieghevole [pie·'ge:·vo·le] *agg* **1.** (*metallo, ramo*) pliant **2.** (*sedia, tavolo*) folding

Piemonte [pie·'mon·te] *m* Piedmont

piemontese¹ <*sing*> *m* (*dialetto*) Piedmontese

piemontese² **I.** *mf* (*abitante*) Piedmontese **II.** *agg* Piedmontese

piena ['piɛ:·na] *f* **1.** (*di corso d'acqua*) flood; **in ~** in spate **2.** (*calca*) crowd

pieno ['piɛ:·no] *m* **1.** (*culmine*) **nel ~ dell'estate** at the height of summer; **nel ~ dell'inverno** in the depths of winter; **nel ~ della notte** at the dead of night; **in ~** (*completamente*) completely **2.** (*carico*) **fare il ~ (di benzina)** to fill up (with gas)

pieno, -a *agg* **1.** (*gener*) full; **~ di** full of; **essere ~ di sé** to be full of oneself; **~ zeppo** completely full; **a stomaco ~** on a full stomach; **luna -a** full moon; **in ~ giorno** in broad daylight; **in ~ inverno** in the depths of winter **2.** (*oro*) solid **3.** (*giornata, periodo*) busy

pienone [pie·'no:·ne] *m* (*folla*) crowd

piercing ['pi:r·sing] <-> *m* piercing

pietà [pie·'ta] <-> *f* **1.** (*compassione*) pity; **avere ~ di qu** to feel pity for sb; **muovere qu a ~** to move sb to pity **2.** REL piety; (*in arte*) Pietà

pietanza [pie·'tan·tsa] *f* dish

pietismo [pie·'tiz·mo] *m* (*pietà ostentata*) pietism

pietoso, -a [pie·'to:·so] *agg* **1.** (*che prova pietà*) compassionate **2.** (*che ispira pietà*) pitiful **3.** *fam* (*pessimo*) pathetic

pietra ['piɛ:·tra] *f* stone; **~ preziosa** precious stone; **~ dura** semiprecious stone; **età della ~** Stone Age; **porre la prima ~** *fig* to lay the foundations sistema sanitario; **mettere una ~ sopra qc** *fig* to say no more about sth

pietrificare [pie·tri·fi·'ka:·re] **I.** *vt* to petrify **II.** *vr:* **-rsi** to become petrified

pietrina [pie·'tri:·na] *f* (*di accendino*) flint

pietrisco [pie·'tris·ko] <-schi> *m* aggregate

piffero ['pif·fe·ro] *m* (*strumento*) pipe

pigiama [pi·'dʒa:·ma] <-i> *m* pajamas

pigia pigia ['pi:·dʒa 'pi:·dʒa] <-> *m* crowd

pigiare [pi·'dʒa:·re] *vt* (*premere*) to press; (*dare spintoni a*) to push; (*uva*) to tread

pigiatura [pi·dʒa·'tu:·ra] *f* (*dell'uva*) treading

pigione [pi·'dʒo:·ne] *f* (*affitto*) rent

pigliare [piʎ·'ʎa:·re] *vt fam* to take; **pigliarle** (*essere picchiato*) to get a hiding

pigmentazione [pig·men·tat·'tsio:·ne] *f* (*di fibre tessili*) pigmentation

pigmento [pig·'men·to] *m* (*per vernici*) pigment

pigna ['piɲ·ɲa] *f* (*di pino*) pine cone

pignoleria [piɲ·ɲo·le·'ri:·a] <-ie> *f* (*caratteristica*) fussiness

pignolo, -a **I.** *agg* fussy **II.** *m, f* fussbudget

pignone [piɲ·'ɲo:·ne] *m* ARCHIT gable

pignoramento [piɲ·ɲo·ra·'men·to] *m* distraint

pignorare [piɲ·ɲo·'ra:·re] *vt* JUR to distrain

pigolare [pi·go·'la:·re] *vi* (*pulcino, uccello*) to chirp

pigolio [pi·go·'li:·o] <-ii> *m* chirping

pigrizia [pi·'grit·tsia] <-ie> *f* laziness

pigro, -a ['pi:·gro] **I.** *agg* (*indolente*) lazy **II.** *m, f* lazybones *inf*

PIL [pil] *abbr di* **Prodotto Interno Lordo** GDP

pila ['pi:·la] *f* **1.** (*batteria*) battery **2.** (*cumulo*) pile **3.** *fam* (*lampadina tascabile*) flashlight

pilastro [pi·'las·tro] *m* **1.** ARCH pillar **2.** *fig* (*sostegno*) mainstay

pile [pail] *m* fleece

pillola ['pil·lo·la] *f* **1.** (*pastiglia*) pill; (*anticoncezionale*); **prendere la ~** to be on the pill; **la ~ del giorno dopo** the morning-after pill **2.** *fig* (*difficoltà*) **indorare la ~** to sweeten the pill

pilone [pi·'lo:·ne] *m* **1.** ARCH pier **2.** (*nel rugby*) prop

pilota¹ [pi·'lɔ:·ta] <-i> *m* TEC **~ automatico** automatic pilot

pilota² <-i *m*, -e *f*> *mf* AERO, NAUT pilot; MOT driver

pilota³ <inv> *agg* pilot

pilotaggio [pi·lo·'tad·dʒo] <-ggi> *m* AERO, NAUT piloting

pilotare [pi·lo·'ta:·re] *vt* **1.** (*automobile*) to drive **2.** (*nave, aereo*) to pilot

piluccare [pi·luk·'ka:·re] *vt* to pick at

pimento [pi·'men·to] *m* (*spezia*) allspice

pimpante [pim·'pan·te] *agg* (*allegro*) perky

pin [pin] <-> *m acro di* **personal identification number** PIN

pina ['pi:·na] *f v.* **pigna**

pinacoteca [pi·na·ko·'tɛ:·ka] <-che> *f* art gallery capitolina

Pinco ['piŋ·ko] *m* **~ Pallino** *fam* so-and-so

pineta [pi·'ne:·ta] *f* pinewood

ping-pong® [piŋg'pɔŋg] <-> *m* table tennis

pingue ['piŋ·gue] *agg* **1.** (*corpo, persona, braccia*) fat **2.** (*terra, pianura*) fertile **3.** (*guadagno, patrimonio*) large

pinguedine [piŋ·'guɛ:·di·ne] *f* (*grassezza*) fatness

pinguino [piŋ·'gui:·no] *m* **1.** (*uccello*) penguin **2.** (*gelato*) *chocolate-covered ice cream on a stick*

pinna ['pin·na] *f* **1.** (*di pesce, imbarcazione*) fin **2.** (*calzatura*) flipper

pinnacolo [pin·'na:·ko·lo] *m* pinnacle

pino ['pi:·no] *m* (*albero, legno*) pine

pinolo [pi·'nɔ:·lo] *m* pine kernel

pin-up (**girl**) ['pin·ʌp 'gə:l] <-> *f* pinup ~

pinza ['pin·tsa] *f* **1.** TEC pliers *pl*; MED forceps *pl* **2.** *fam* pincer

pinzare [pin·'tsa:·re] *vt* (*con la pinzatrice*) to staple

pinzetta [pin·'tset·ta] *f* (*per sopracciglia, francobolli*) tweezers *pl*

pinzimonio [pin·tsi·'mɔ:·nio] <-i> *m* tosc: *olive oil, salt and pepper dip for crudités*

pio, -a ['pi:·o] <pii, pie> *agg* **1.** (*devoto*) pious **2.** (*caritatevole*) charitable

pioggerella [piod·dʒe·'rɛl·la] *f* drizzle

pioggia ['piɔd·dʒa] <-gge> *f* **1.** METEO rain; ~ **acida** acid rain; ~ **fine/fitta/scrosciante** light/heavy/pouring rain; **la stagione delle -gge** the rainy season **2.** (*grande quantità*) torrent

piolo ['piɔ:·lo] *m* **1.** (*legnetto*) peg **2.** (*di scala*) rung; **scala a -i** ladder

piombare [piom·'ba:·re] **I.** *vi essere* **1.** (*cadere dall'alto*) to fall **2.** (*sprofondare*) ~ **nella disperazione/depressione** to be plunged into despair/depression **3.** (*disgrazie, aggressore*) ~ **addosso a qu** to descend on sb **4.** (*arrivare all'improvviso*) to turn up **II.** *vt avere* (*pacco, carro*) to seal with lead

piombatura [piom·ba·'tu:·ra] *f* **1.** (*di dente*) filling **2.** (*rivestimento di piombo*) sealing with lead

piombino [piom·'bi:·no] *m* **1.** (*proiettile*) lead pellet **2.** (*di lenza, rete*) sinker **3.** (*di pacco*) lead seal **4.** (*di filo a piombo*) plumb; (*scandaglio*) lead

piombo ['piom·bo] *m* **1.** CHEM lead; **pesare come il** ~ to weigh a ton; **andare coi piedi di** ~ *fig* to tread carefully; **senza** ~ (*benzina*) unleaded **2.** (*di lenza, rete*) sinker; **filo a** ~ plumb line; **cadere a** ~ to hang straight **3.** (*sigillo*) lead seal **4.** (*proiettili*) bullets

pioniere [pio·'niɛ:·re] *m* pioneer

pio pio ['pi:·o 'pi:·o] **I.** <-> *m* cheep-cheep **II.** *int* cheep-cheep

piovano, -a [pio·'va:·no] *agg* **acqua** ~ rainwater

piovere ['piɔ:·ve·re] <piove, piovve, piovuto> *vi essere o avere* **1.** METEO to rain; ~ **a catinelle** [o **dirotto**] [o **scrocio**] to pour (down); **su questo non ci piove** *fig, fam* there's no doubt about it; **piove sul bagnato** (*in senso posi-*

tivo) some people have all the luck **sul bagnato!**; (*in senso negativo*) it never rains but it pours **2.** *cadere come pioggia* to rain down; ~ **dal cielo** *fig* to fall into one's lap **3.** (*arrivare in grande quantità*) to come thick and fast ~ **gli insulti**; ~ **addosso a qu** (*disgrazia*) to assail sb

piovigginare [pio·vid·dʒi·'na:·re] *vi essere o avere* to drizzle

piovigginoso, -a [pio·vid·dʒi·'no:·so] *agg* (*giorno, tempo*) drizzly

piovoso, -a [pio·'vo:·so] *agg* (*inverno, giornata, tempo*) rainy

piovra ['piɔ:·vra] *f* **1.** ZOO octopus **2.** *mafia* **la** ~ the Mafia

piovve ['piɔv·ve] *3. pers sing pass rem di* **piovere**

pipa ['pi:·pa] *f* (*per fumare*) pipe; **fumare la** ~ to smoke a pipe

pipeline ['paip·lain] <-> *m* pipeline

pipetta [pi·'pet·ta] *f* (*tubo di vetro*) pipette

pipì [pi·'pi] <-> *f fam* pee; **fare** (**la**) ~ to have a pee

pipistrello [pi·pis·'trɛl·lo] *m* ZOO bat

piqué [pi·'ke] <-> *m* piqué

piramidale [pi·ra·mi·'da:·le] *agg* **1.** (*forma, organizzazione*) pyramidal **2.** (*madornale*) huge

piramide [pi·'ra:·mi·de] *f* pyramid

piranha [pi·'re·ɲa] <-> *m* piranha

pirata <inv> *agg* (*illegale*) pirate; **copia** ~ pirate copy; **emittente** ~ pirate station

pirata [pi·'ra:·ta] <-i> *m* **1.** (*uomo di mare*) pirate; ~ **della strada** hit-and-run driver; ~ **dell'aria** hijacker **2.** (*persona senza scrupoli*) shark **3.** INFORM ~ **informatico** hacker

piratare [pi·ra·'ta:·re] *vt* (*software, canale televisivo*) to pirate

piratato, -a [pi·ra·'ta:·to] *agg* (*sofware, canale televisivo*) pirated

pirateria [pi·ra·te·'ri:·a] <-ie> *f* **1.** (*in mare*) piracy; (*su un aereo*) hijacking **2.** (*attività abusiva*) pirating; ~ **informatica** hacking **3.** (*ruberia*) stealing

Pirenei [pi·re·'nɛ:·i] *mpl* **i** ~ the Pyrenees

pirico, -a ['pi:·ri·ko] <-ci, -che> *agg* **polvere -a** gunpowder

pirite [pi·'ri:·te] *f* pyrite

piritico, -a [pi·'ri:·ti·ko] <-ci, -che> *agg* pyritic

piroetta [pi·ro·'et·ta] *f* pirouette

piroettare [pi·ro·et·'ta:·re] *vi* to pirouette

pirofila [pi·'rɔ:·fi·la] *f* (*tegame*) Pyrex® dish

piroga [pi·'rɔ:·ga] <-ghe> *f* dugout (canoe)

piromane [pi·'rɔ:·ma·ne] *mf* pyromaniac

piromania [pi·ro·ma·'ni:·a] *f* pyromania

piroscafo [pi·'rɔs·ka·fo] *m* steamship

pirotecnico [pi·ro·'tɛk·ni·ko] <-ci> *m* MIL munitions factory

pirotecnico, -a <-ci, -che> **I.** *agg* (*arte*) pyrotechnical; (*spettacolo*) fireworks **II.** *m, f* fireworks maker

Pisa *f* Pisa, *city in northwest Italy*

Pisano <sing> *m* Pisa area

pisano, -a [pi·'sa:·no] I. *m, f* (*abitante*) Pisan II. *agg* Pisan

piscia ['piʃ·ʃa] <-sce> *f vulg* piss

pisciare [piʃ·'ʃa:·re] *vi vulg* to piss; **pisciarsi addosso** [*o* **sotto**] *fig* to piss oneself

pisciata [piʃ·'ʃa:·ta] *f vulg* piss; **fare una ~** to take a piss

piscicoltore, -trice [piʃ·ʃi·kol·'to:·re] *m, f* fish farmer

piscicoltura [piʃ·ʃi·kol·'tu:·ra] *f* fish farming

piscina [piʃ·'ʃi:·na] *f* (swimming) pool; **~ olimpionica** Olympic pool; **~ coperta** indoor pool; **~ scoperta** open-air pool

piscio ['piʃ·ʃo] <-sci> *m vulg* piss

pisello¹ [pi·'sɛl·lo] *m* 1. BOT, GASTR pea 2. *fam* (*pene*) dick

pisello² <inv> *agg* verde **~** pea-green

pisolino [pi·zo·'li:·no] *m fam* nap; **fare** [*o* **schiacciare**] **un ~** to take a nap

pisside ['pis·si·de] *f* REL pyx

pissi pissi ['pis·si 'pis·si] <-> *m* whispering

pista ['pis·ta] *f* 1. (*gener*) track 2. (*spazio libero*) **~ da ballo** dance floor; **~ da bowling** bowling alley; **~ di pattinaggio** skating rink; **~ del circo** ring 3. (*nello sci*) run 4. AERO **~ di atterraggio** landing strip; **~ di rullaggio** taxiway 5. (*via*) **~ ciclabile** bike lane

pistacchio¹ [pis·'tak·kio] <-cchi> *m* (*albero, frutto*) pistachio

pistacchio² <inv> *agg* pistachio

pistillo [pis·'til·lo] *m* pistil

Pistoia *f* Pistoia, *city in northern Italy*

pistoiese [pis·toi·'e:·se] I. *mf* (*abitante*) person from Pistoia II. *agg* from Pistoia

Pistoiese <*sing*> *m* Pistoia area

pistola [pis·'tɔ:·la] *f* 1. (*arma*) pistol; **~ ad acqua** water pistol 2. (*strumento*) **~ a spruzzo** spray gun

pistolero [pis·to·'lɛ:·ro] *m* gunfighter

pistone [pis·'to:·ne] *m* 1. (*di motore*) piston 2. (*di strumenti a fiato*) valve

pitagorico, -a <-ci, -che> *agg* tavola **-a** multiplication table

pitocco, -a [pi·'tɔk·ko] <-cchi, -cche> I. *m, f* skinflint II. *agg* (*avaro*) stingy

pitone [pi·'to:·ne] *m* (*serpente, pelle*) python

pittografia [pit·to·gra·'fi:·a] *f* pictography

pittografico, -a [pit·to·'gra:·fi·ko] <-ci, -che> *agg* pictographic

pittogramma [pit·to·'gram·ma] <-i> *m* pictogram

pittore, -trice [pit·'to:·re] *m, f* painter

pittoresco, -a [pit·to·'res·ko] <-schi, -sche> *agg* (*suggestivo*) picturesque; (*stravagante*) colorful

pittorico, -a [pit·'tɔ:·ri·ko] <-ci, -che> *agg* 1. (*tecnica, scuola*) painting 2. *fig* (*vivacità, descrizione*) colorful

pittura [pit·'tu:·ra] *f* 1. (*arte, dipinto*) painting 2. *fam* (*vernice*) paint

pitturare [pit·tu·'ra:·re] *vt* (*verniciare*) to paint

più [piu] *comparativo di* **molto, -a** I. *avv* 1. (*comparativo*) more; (*superlativo*) most;

~ intelligente/bello more intelligent/beautiful; **~ piccolo/grande** smaller/bigger; **il ~ interessante** the most interesting; **il ~ vecchio di tutti** the oldest of them all; **il ~ vecchio dei due** the older of the two; **di ~ more**; **mi piace di ~ il rosso** I like the red one better; **la canzone che mi piace di ~** the song I like best; **tanto ~ che** especially since; **~ ... che mai** more ... than ever; **~ ... che ... more ...** than ...; **sono ~ sorpreso che arrabbiato** I'm more surprised than angry; **chi ~ chi meno** some more than others; **tra non ~ di un mese** in less than a month; **e chi ~ ne ha ~ ne metta** the more the merrier 2. (*oltre*) **non ... ~** not ... anymore; **non ci pensare ~** don't think about it anymore; **mai ~** never again; **non ne posso ~** I can't take any more; **per di ~** what's more; **a ~ non posso** *fam* (*correre*) as fast as possible 3. (*nelle temperature*) MAT plus; **~ tre** plus three; **tre ~ tre fa sei** three plus three is six; **in ~** more; **~ o meno** more or less 4. (*nei voti scolastici*) plus II. *prep* plus III. <inv> *agg* 1. (*comparativo*) more; (*superlativo*) most; **ho ~ amici di te** I've got more friends than you; **quello con ~ possibilità di vincere** the one with the best chance of winning; **ci vuole ~ tempo** more time is needed; **~ persone vengono e meglio è** the more people that come the better; **al ~ presto** as soon as possible; **al ~ tardi** at the latest 2. (*parecchi*) several; **te l'ho ripetuto ~ volte** I've told you several times IV. <-> *m* 1. (*massimo*) most; (**tutt'**)**al ~** at most; **per lo ~** usually; **parlare del ~ e del meno** to talk about this and that 2. (*parte maggiore*) most; **il ~ è fatto** most of it is done; **il ~ delle volte** most of the time 3. *pl* (*la maggioranza*) majority 4. MAT plus sign

piuma¹ ['piu·ma] *f* 1. (*penna*) feather 2. (*ornamento*) plume

piuma² <inv> *agg* peso **~** SPORT featherweight

piumaggio [piu·'mad·dʒo] <-ggi> *m* plumage

piumato, -a [piu·'ma:·to] *agg* feathered

piumino [piu·'mi:·no] *m* 1. (*degli uccelli*) down 2. (*per la cipria*) powder puff 3. (*coperta*) comforter 4. (*giacca*) padded jacket 5. (*per spolverare*) feather duster 6. (*proiettile*) dart

piumone® [piu·'mo:·ne] *m* comforter

piuttosto [piut·'tɔs·to] *avv* (*anzi, alquanto*) rather; **~ che ... +***inf* rather than ...; (*anziché*); **~ che** rather than

piva ['pi:·va] *f* bagpipes *pl*

pivello, -a [pi·'vel·lo] *m, f fam* tenderfoot

pixel ['pik·səl] <-> *m* pixel

pizza ['pit·tsa] *f* 1. GASTR pizza; **~ al taglio** pizza by the slice 2. *fig* (*persona o cosa noiosa*) bore; **che ~!** what a bore! 3. (*pellicola*) reel

---

i Although its ultimate origins are disputed, the pizza that is loved all over the world comes from Naples. There are more than fifty types of pizza (**Margherita, Calzone, Capricciosa, Quattro Stagioni**, etc.) **Margherita**, the best-known pizza, was invented in the late nineteenth century in honor of the then Queen of Italy, Margherita. This pizza unites the three colors of the Italian flag: green basil, white mozzarella, and red tomato sauce.

pizzaiolo, -a [pit·tsa·'iɔ:·lo] *m, f* **1.** (*chi fa le pizze*) pizza chef; **alla -a** *cooked with tomato, parsley and garlic* **2.** (*gestore di pizzeria*) pizzeria owner

pizzeria [pit·tse·'ri:·a] <-ie> *f* pizzeria

pizzicare [pit·tsi·'ka:·re] I. *vt* **1.** (*con le dita*) to pinch; (*solleticare*) to tickle **2.** (*pungere*) to sting **3.** (*stuzzicare*) to tease **4.** *fam* (*cogliere*) to catch **5.** MUS to pluck II. *vi* **1.** (*prudere*) to tingle **2.** (*essere piccante*) to be hot

pizzicato [pit·tsi·'ka:·to] *m* (*tecnica*) pizzicato

pizzico ['pit·tsi·ko] <-chi> *m* **1.** (*gener*) pinch **2.** (*puntura d'insetto*) bite

pizzicotto [pit·tsi·'kɔt·to] *m* (*con le dita*) pinch

pizzo ['pit·tso] *m* **1.** (*merletto*) lace **2.** (*barba*) goatee **3.** (*tangente*) protection money; **pagare il ~** to pay protection money

placare [pla·'ka:·re] I. *vt* **1.** (*collera*) to appease; (*persona*) to calm down **2.** (*fame*) to satisfy; (*sete*) to quench II. *vr:* **-rsi** (*persona*) to calm down; (*dolore*) to ease; (*tempesta*) to die down

placca ['plak·ka] <-cche> *f* **1.** (*lamina*) EL plate **2.** (*targhetta, sulla pelle*) plaque; **~ batterica** [*o* **dentaria**] dental plaque

placcare [plak·'ka:·re] *vt* **1.** (*rivestire*) **~ qc d'oro/argento** to gold-/silver-plate sth **2.** (*nel rugby*) to tackle

placchetta [plak·'ket·ta] *f* (*di occhiali*) nose pad

placebo [pla·'tʃɛ:·bo] <-> I. *m* placebo II. *agg* **effetto ~** placebo effect

placenta [pla·'tʃɛn·ta] *f* placenta

placido, -a ['pla:·tʃi·do] *agg* (*persona, carattere*) placid; (*serata*) calm

plafond [pla·'fɔ̃] <-> *m* FIN, COM ceiling

plafoniera [pla·fo·'niɛ:·ra] *f* ceiling light

plagiare [pla·'dʒa:·re] *vt* **1.** (*opera*) to plagiarize **2.** (*persona*) to subject to duress

plagio ['pla:·dʒo] <-gi> *m* **1.** (*di opera*) plagiarism **2.** (*di persona*) duress

plaid [plɛd] <-> *m* lap robe

planare [pla·'na:·re] *vi* (*aereo*) to glide; (*imbarcazione*) to skim

planata [pla·'na:·ta] *f* glide

plancia ['plan·tʃa] <-ce> *f* **1.** AUTO dashboard **2.** NAUT (*ponte*) bridge; (*passerella*) gangway

planetario [pla·ne·'ta:·rio] <-i> *m* (*macchina*) orrery; (*edificio*) planetarium

planetario, -a <-i, -ie> *agg* (*dei pianeti*) planetary; (*della Terra*) worldwide

planetologia [pla·ne·to·lo·'dʒi:·a] *f* ASTR planetology

planetologo, -a [pla·ne·'tɔ:·lo·go] <-ghi, -ghe> *m, f* ASTR planetologist

planimetria [pla·ni·me·'tri:·a] <-ie> *f* **1.** MAT planimetry **2.** (*pianta*) plan sito web

planisfero [pla·nis·'fɛ:·ro] *m* planisphere; **~ celeste** celestial planisphere

plantare [plan·'ta:·re] *m* (*protesi*) arch support

plasma ['plaz·ma] <-i> *m* (*del sangue*) plasma

plasmabile [plaz·'ma:·bi·le] *agg* (*materia*) moldable; (*carattere*) malleable

plasmare [plaz·'ma:·re] *vt* (*materiale, carattere, gusti*) to mold

plastica ['plas·ti·ka] <-che> *f* **1.** (*materiale*) plastic **2.** MED plastic surgery **3.** (*in arte*) plastic art

plasticità [plas·ti·tʃi·'ta] <-> *f* (*di materiale, raffigurazione*) plasticity ~

plastico ['plas·ti·ko] <-ci> *m* **1.** (*rappresentazione topografica*) scale model **2.** (*esplosivo*) plastic explosive

plastico, -a <-ci, -che> *agg* plastic; (*materiale, consistenza*); **arti -che** plastic arts; **modello ~** scale model; **chirurgia -a** plastic surgery

plastificare [plas·ti·fi·'ka:·re] *vt* **1.** (*rendere plastico*) to plasticize **2.** (*rivestire di plastica*) to coat with plastic

plastilina® [plas·ti·'li:·na] *f* Play-Doh®

platano ['pla:·ta·no] *m* plane (tree)

platea [pla·'tɛ:·a] *f* (*parte del teatro*) orchestra; (*spettatori*) audience

plateale [pla·te·'a:·le] *agg* (*evidente*) theatrical

platinato [pla·ti·'na:·to] *agg* (*capelli*) platinum-blond

platino ['pla:·ti·no] *m* platinum

platonico, -a <-ci, -che> *agg* (*pensiero, opera*) Platonic; (*amore, amicizia*) platonic

plausibile [plau·'zi:·bi·le] *agg* (*spiegazione, argomento*) plausible

plausibilità [plau·zi·bi·li·'ta] <-> *f* plausibility

plauso ['pla:u·zo] *m* (*approvazione*) approval

playback ['plei·bæk] <-> *m* miming

playboy ['plei·bɔi] <- *o* playboys> *m* playboy

plebaglia [ple·'baʎ·ʎa] <-glie> *f* pej rabble

plebe ['plɛ:·be] *f* HIST plebs *pl*

plebeo, -a [ple·'bɛ:·o] *agg* HIST plebeian

plebiscito [ple·biʃ·'ʃi:·to] *m* **1.** POL plebiscite ~ **2.** *fig* **un ~ di consensi** unanimous agreement

Pleiadi ['plɛ:·ia·di] *fpl* Pleiades *pl*

plenario, -a [ple·'na:·rio] <-i, -ie> *agg* **1.** (*riunione*) plenary **2.** (*totale*) complete; **indulgenza -a** REL plenary indulgence

plenilunio [ple·ni·'lu:·nio] <-i> *m* full moon

plenum ['plɛ:·num] <-> *m* plenum

pleonasmo [ple·o·'naz·mo] *m* pleonasm

pleonastico, -a [ple·o·'nas·ti·ko] <-ci, -che> *agg* **1.** LING pleonastic **2.** *fig* (*superfluo*) unnecessary

pleura ['plɛ:u·ra] *f* pleura

pleurite [pleu·'ri:·te] *f* pleurisy

PLI *m abbr di* **Partito Liberale Italiano** HIST *Italian Liberal Party*

plico ['pliːko] <-chi> *m* package; (*insieme di documenti*) sheaf of papers

plissé [pli·'se] I.<inv> *agg* (*gonna, tessuto*) pleated II. <-> *m* pleated fabric

plissettato [plis·set·'ta:·to] *agg* pleated

plot [plɔt] <-> *m* (*di film*) plot

plotone [plo·'to:·ne] *m* 1. MIL platoon; ~ **d'ese-cuzione** firing squad 2. (*nel ciclismo*) pack

plotter ['plɔ·tə] <- *o* plotters> *m* INFORM plotter

plug-in [plʌg·'ɪn] <-> *m* INFORM plug-in

plumbeo, -a ['plum·beo] <-ei, -ee> *agg* (*cielo, colore*) leaden

plurale [plu·'ra:·le] I. *agg* plural II. *m* plural; **al** ~ in the plural

pluralismo [plu·ra·'liz·mo] *m* pluralism

pluralista [plu·ra·'lis·ta] <-i *m*, -e *f*> *mf* pluralist

pluralistico, -a [plu·ra·lis·ti·ko] <-ci, -che> *agg* (*sistema, informazione*) pluralist

pluri- [plu·ri] (*in parole composte*) multi-

pluricellulare [plu·ri·tʃel·lu·'la:·re] *agg* (*organismo*) multicellular

pluridimensionale [plu·ri·di·men·sio·'na:·le] *agg* multidimensional

pluridirezionale [plu·ri·di·ret·tsio·'na:·le] *agg* multidirectional

pluridisciplinare [plu·ri·diʃ·ʃi·pli·'na:·re] *agg* multidisciplinary

pluriennale [plu·rien·'na:·le] *agg* lasting many years

plurietnico, -a [plu·ri·'ɛt·ni·ko] <-ci, -che> *agg* multiethnic

plurigemellare [plu·ri·dʒe·mel·'la:·re] *agg* MED **parto** ~ multiple birth

plurigemino, -a [plu·ri·'dʒe:·mi·no] *agg* MED *v.* **plurigemellare**

plurilingue [plu·ri·'liŋ·gue] <inv> *agg* multilingual

plurilinguismo [plu·ri·liŋ·'guiz·mo] *m* (*di zona, comunità*) multilingualism

plurimandatario, -a [plu·ri·man·da·'ta:·rio] I. *m, f* COM *representative working for several companies* II. *agg* working for several companies

plurimiliardario, -a [plu·ri·mi·liar·'da:·rio] I. *agg* multimillionaire II. *m, f* multimillionaire

plurimilionario, -a [plu·ri·mi·lio·'na:·rio] I. *agg* multimillionaire II. *m, f* multimillionaire

plurimillenario, -a [plu·ri·mil·le·'na:·rio] *agg* thousands of years old

plurimo, -a ['plu:·ri·mo] *agg* multiple

plurinominale [plu·ri·no·mi·'na:·le] *agg* multimember

pluriomicida [plu·rio·mi·'tʃi:·da] *mf* multiple murderer

pluripartitico, -a [plu·ri·par·'ti:·ti·ko] <-ci, -che> *agg* multiparty

plurisecolare [plu·ri·se·ko·'la:·re] *agg* centuries-old

plurisettimanale [plu·ri·set·ti·ma·'na:·le] *agg* lasting several weeks

plurisettoriale [plu·ri·set·to·'ria:·le] *agg* COM multisector

plurisillabo, -a [plu·ri·'sil·la·bo] *agg* polysyllabic

plurivalente [plu·ri·va·'lɛn·te] *agg* plurivalent

plusvalore [pluz·va·'lo:·re] *m* surplus value

plutocrate [plu·'tɔ:·kra·te] *mf* plutocrat

plutocratico, -a [plu·to·'kra:·ti·ko] <-ci, -che> *agg* plutocratic

plutocrazia [plu·to·krat·'tsi:·a] <-ie> *f* plutocracy

plutonio [plu·'tɔ:·nio] *m* CHIM plutonium

pluviale [plu·'via:·le] *agg* **foresta** ~ rainforest

pluviometro [plu·'viɔ:·met·ro] *m* rain gauge

PM *m abbr di* **Pubblico Ministero** District Attorney

pneumatico [pneu·'ma:·ti·ko] <-ci> *m* tire

pneumatico, -a <-ci, -che> *agg* 1. TEC pneumatic; **martello** ~ jackhammer 2. (*gonfiabile*) inflatable; **materassino** ~ air mattress piscine

po' [pɔ] *avv fam* **un** ~ a little; **un bel** ~ quite a while; **un** ~ **di ...** a little ...; **guarda un** ~! good heavens! simile!

pochezza [pok·'ket·tsa] *f* 1. (*scarsezza*) scarcity 2. (*inadeguatezza*) inadequacy ~

pochino [po·'ki:·no] *m fam* **un** ~ a little; **un** ~ **di ...** a little ...

poco¹ ['pɔ:·ko] <meno, pochissimo> *avv* 1. (*con verbo: in piccola misura*) not very much; **il film mi è piaciuto** ~ I didn't like the movie very much; (*con verbo: per breve tempo*) a little while; **ho dormito** ~ I slept for a little while; **pesa** ~ **più di ...** it weighs slightly more than ...; **(a)** ~ **(a)** ~ little by little 2. (*con aggettivo, avverbio*) not very; **è** ~ **gentile** she's not very nice; ~ **dopo/prima** shortly after/before; ~ **fa** a short time ago; **stare** ~ **bene** to not be very well; ~ **male** (*pazienza*) it doesn't matter

poco² <-chi> *m* little; **un** ~ a little; **un** ~ **di ...** a little ...; **accontentarsi del** ~ **che si ha** to be content with the little one has; **un** ~ **di buono** *fam* a bad egg; *v.a.* **po'**

poco, -a <-chi, -che> I. *agg* 1. (*una piccola quantità di*) not very much; (*in piccolo numero*) not very many; **è -a cosa** it's nothing 2. (*con valore ellittico*) **mangia** ~ he doesn't eat much; **ho** ~ **da fare** I don't have much to do; **ci vuol** ~ **a capirlo** it's not hard to understand; **fra** ~ soon; **per** ~ **non** (*quasi*) nearly; **un errore da** ~ a trivial mistake; **un oggetto da** ~ a worthless object; **siamo arrivati da** ~ we've just arrived; ~ **importa** it doesn't matter risultato; **meglio** ~ **che niente** *prov* take what you can get II. *pron* 1. (*piccola quantità*) little 2. *pl* (*non numerosi*) few -chi; **essere in -chi** to be few in number

podere [po·'de:·re] *m* (*fondo agricolo*) farm

poderoso, -a [po·de·'ro:·so] *agg* 1. (*muscoli, braccia*) powerful 2. (*esercito*) mighty 3. *fig* (*sforzo*) great; (*memoria*) good

podestà [po·des·'ta] <-> *m* HIST (*nel medioevo*) podestà; (*nel fascismo*) mayor

podio ['pɔ:·dio] <-i> *m* podium

podismo [po·'diz·mo] *m* running

podista [po·'dis·ta] <-i *m*, -e *f*> *mf* runner
podistico, -a [po·'dis·ti·ko] <-ci, -che> *agg* running
poema [po·'ε:·ma] <-i> *m* **1.** LIT poem; ~ **epico** epic poem **2.** *fig* (*scritto prolisso*) epic ~
poesia [poe·'zi:·a] <-ie> *f* **1.** (*genere, complesso di opere*) poetry **2.** (*componimento*) poem
poeta, -tessa [po·'ε:·ta, poe·'tes·sa] <-i, -esse> *m, f* poet
poetica [po·'ε:·ti·ka] <-che> *f* (*di artista, movimento*) poetics
poeticità [poe·ti·tʃi·'ta] <-> *f* poeticalness
poetico, -a [po·'ε:·ti·ko] <-ci, -che> *agg* poetic
poggiare [pod·'dʒa:·re] **I.** *vt* (*posare*) to place **II.** *vi* (~ *su qc*) ARCH to rest on sth; *teoria* to be based on sth
poggiatesta [pod·dʒa·'tes·ta] <-> *m* (*in auto*) headrest
poggio ['pɔd·dʒo] <-ggi> *m* hill
poggiolo [pod·'dʒɔ:·lo] *m* (*terrazzino*) balcony
pogrom [pa·'grɔm] <-> *m* pogrom
poi ['pɔ:·i] *avv* **1.** (*dopo, infine*) then; (*più tardi*) later; **prima o** ~ sooner or later; **d'ora in** ~ from now on **2.** (*inoltre*) besides **3.** (*enfatico*) really; **no e** ~ **no** absolutely not
poiché [poi·'ke] *cong* (*dato che*) since
pois [pwa] <-> *m* **a** ~ polka-dot
poker ['pou·kər/'po·ker] <-> *m* **1.** (*gioco*) poker; **giocare a** ~ to play poker **2.** (*combinazione di carte*) ~ **d'assi/di fanti** four aces/jacks
polacca [po·'lak·ka] <-cche> *f* (*danza*) polonaise
polacco, -a [po·'lak·ko] <-cchi, -cche> **I.** *agg* Polish **II.** *m, f* Pole
polare [po·'la:·re] *agg* (*del polo*) polar
polarità [po·la·ri·'ta] <-> *f* **1.** PHYS polarity **2.** *fig* (*opposizione*) diametrical opposition
polarizzare [po·la·rid·'dza:·re] *vt* **1.** PHYS to polarize **2.** (*attenzione, interesse*) to attract
polarizzazione [po·la·rid·dzat·'tsio:·ne] *f* PHYS polarization
polca ['pɔl·ka] <-che> *f v.* polka
polemica [po·'lε:·mi·ka] <-che> *f* (*contrasto di opinioni*) argument; (*attacco*) attack; **fare delle -che** to be argumentative
polemico, -a [po·'lε:·mi·ko] <-ci, -che> *agg* (*spirito, scritto*) controversial; (*tono, atteggiamento*) argumentative
polemizzare [po·le·mid·'dza:·re] *vi* (*cavillare*) ~ **su qc** to argue about sth
polenta [po·'lεn·ta] *f* polenta
polentone, -a [po·len·'to:·ne] *m, f* **1.** *fam* (*persona lenta*) slowpoke **2.** *pej* North Italian
polesine [po·'le:·zi·ne] *m* **il Polesine** Polesine
poli- [po·li] (*in parole composte*) poly-
poliambulatorio [po·li·am·bu·la·'tɔ:·rio] <-i> *m* MED clinic
poliammidico, -a [po·li·am·'mi:·di·ko] <-ci, -che> *agg* **fibre -che** polyamide
poliatomico, -a [po·lia·'tɔ:·mi·ko] <-ci, -che>

agg PHYS (*molecola*) polyatomic
policlinico [po·li·'kli:·ni·ko] <-ci> *m* general hospital
policoltura [po·li·kol·'tu:·ra] *f* AGR polyculture
policromo, -a [po·'li:·kro·mo] *agg* polychrome
poliedrico, -a [po·li·'εd·ri·ko] <-ci, -che> *agg* **1.** *fig* (*ingegno, mente*) versatile **2.** MAT polyhedral
poliedro [po·li·'εd·ro] *m* MAT polyhedron
poliestere¹ [po·liv'εs·te·re] *m* polyester
poliestere² <inv> *agg* polyester
polifase [po·li·'fa:·ze] <inv> *agg* multiphase
polifonico, -a [po·li·'fɔ:·ni·ko] <-ci, -che> *agg* MUS polyphonic
polifunzionale [po·li·fun·tsio·'na:·le] *agg* multipurpose
poligamia [po·li·ga·'mi:·a] <-ie> *f* polygamy
poligamo, -a [po·'li:·ga·mo] **I.** *agg* polygamous **II.** *m, f* polygamist
poliglotta [po·li·'glɔt·ta] <-i *m*, -e *f*> **I.** *mf* polyglot **II.** *agg* polyglot
poligonale [po·li·go·'na:·le] *agg* MAT polygonal
poligono [po·'li:·go·no] *m* **1.** MAT polygon **2.** MIL ~ **di tiro** firing range
polimero [po·'li:·me·ro] *m* polymer
polimero, -a *agg* CHEM polymeric
polinomio [po·li·'nɔ:·mio] <-i> *m* polynomial
polio ['pɔ:·lio] <-> *f* MED polio
poliomielite [po·lio·mie·'li:·te] *f* poliomyelitis
poliomielitico, -a [po·lio·mie·'li:·ti·ko] <-ci, -che> **I.** *m, f* MED person with polio **II.** *agg* MED poliomyelitic
polipo ['pɔ:·li·po] *m* MED polyp
polistirolo [po·lis·ti·'rɔ:·lo] *m* Styrofoam®
politeismo [po·li·te·'iz·mo] *m* polytheism
politeista [po·li·te·'is·ta] **I.** *mf* polytheist **II.** *agg* (*religione, culto*) polytheistic
politica [po·'li:·ti·ka] <-che> *f* **1.** (*scienza, ambito*) politics **2.** (*strategia*) policy; ~ **estera** foreign policy; ~ **interna** domestic policy; ~ **finanziaria** financial policy; ~ **salariale** pay policy; ~ **sociale** social policy; ~ **dei prezzi** pricing policy; ~ **del non intervento** policy of nonintervention
politicante [po·li·ti·'kan·te] *mf pej* politico
politichese [po·li·ti·'ke:·se] *m pej* POL political jargon
politicismo [po·li·ti·'tʃiz·mo] *m* politicization
politicizzare [po·li·ti·tʃid·'dza:·re] *vt* to politicize
politicizzazione [po·li·ti·tʃid·dzat·'tsio:·ne] *f* politicization
politico [po·'li:·ti·ko] <-ci> *m* (*uomo politico*) politician
politico, -a <-ci, -che> *agg* political; **economia -a** political economy; **elezioni -che** general election; **scienze -che** political science
politologia [po·li·to·lo·'dʒi:·a] <-gie> *f* political science
politologo, -a [po·li·'tɔ:·lo·go] <-gi, -ghe> *m, f* political scientist
polittico [po·'lit·ti·ko] <-ci> *m* (*dipinto*) polyptych

polivalente [po·li·va·'lɛn·te] *agg (multifunzione)* multipurpose

polizia [po·lit·'tsi:·a] <-ie> *f (corpo)* police; *(commissariato)* police station; **agente di ~** police officer; **~ sanitaria** public health officials *pl;* **~ stradale** highway patrol; **~ tributaria** IRS agents *pl;* **~ municipale** local police

i The duties of the **Polizia di stato** (state police) include the maintenance of public order, and the prevention and solving of crime. They come under the authority of the Interior Minister.

poliziesco, -a [po·lit·'tsies·ko] <-schi, -sche> *agg (romanzo, film)* detective

poliziotto [po·lit·'tsiɔt·to] <inv> *agg* **cane ~** police dog; **donna ~** policewoman

poliziotto, -a *m, f* **1.** *(agente)* policeman *m* **2.** policewoman *f*

polizza ['pɔ:·lit·tsa] *f* COM policy; **~ (di assicurazione)** insurance policy

polka ['pɔl·ka] *f* polka

pollaio [pol·'la:·io] <-ai> *m* **1.** *(per polli)* henhouse **2.** *fig, fam (luogo sporco)* pigsty

pollame [pol·'la:·me] *m* poultry

polleria [pol·le·'ri:·a] <-ie> *f* poultry store

pollice ['pɔl·li·tʃe] *m* **1.** ANAT *(della mano)* thumb; **avere il ~ verde** *fig* to have a green thumb **2.** *(unità di misura)* inch; **non cedere di un ~** *fig* not to give an inch

pollicoltura [pol·li·kol·'tu:·ra] *f* chicken farming

polline ['pɔl·li·ne] *m* pollen

pollo ['pol·lo] *m* **1.** *(animale)* chicken; **conoscere i propri -i** *fam* to know who one is dealing with; **far ridere i -i** to be ridiculous **2.** *fig (individuo ingenuo)* sucker

polluzione [pol·lut·'tsio:·ne] *f* pollution

polmonare [pol·mo·'na:·re] *agg* pulmonary

polmone [pol·'mo:·ne] *m* **1.** ANAT lung; **gridare a pieni -i** to shout at the top of one's voice; **respirare a pieni -i** to breathe deeply **2.** *fig (stimolo)* beating heart **3.** *fig (di città)* lungs *pl*

polmonite [pol·mo·'ni:·te] *f* pneumonia

polo[1] ['pɔ:·lo] *m* **1.** GEOG, PHYS pole; **il ~ nord** the North Pole; **il ~ sud** the South Pole; **da un ~ all'altro** *fig* from one end of the Earth to the other all'altro **2.** *fig* **essere ai -i opposti** to be poles apart **3.** POL *(coalizione)* coalition; **il Polo (per le libertà)** POL the House of Freedom Coalition **4.** SPORT polo

polo[2] <-> *f (maglia)* polo shirt

Polonia [po·'lɔ:·nia] *f* **la ~** Poland; **abitare in ~** to live in Poland; **andare in ~** to go to Poland

polpa ['pol·pa] *f (di frutto)* flesh; *(di carne)* lean meat

polpaccio [pol·'pat·tʃo] <-cci> *m (della gamba)* calf

polpastrello [pol·pas·'trɛl·lo] *m* pad

polpetta [pol·'pet·ta] *f* GASTR meatball in salsa; **far -e di qu** *[o* **ridurre qu in -e]** *scherz* to make mincemeat of sb

polpettone [pol·pet·'to:·ne] *m* **1.** GASTR meat loaf **2.** *(film, libro)* mishmash

polpo ['pol·po] *m* octopus

polsino [pol·'si:·no] *m (di camicia)* cuff

polso ['pol·so] *m* **1.** ANAT wrist **2.** *(carattere)* firmness; **un uomo di ~** a strong man **3.** MED pulse; **tastare il ~ a qu** to take sb's pulse; **sentire il ~ di qc** *fig* to take the pulse of sth delle elezioni

poltiglia [pol·'ti/·ʎa] <-glie> *f* **1.** *(miscuglio)* mush ~; **ridurre qu in ~** to make mincemeat of sb **2.** *(fango)* mud

poltrire [pol·'tri:·re] <poltrisco> *vi* **1.** *(riposarsi)* to laze **2.** *(vivere nell'ozio)* to laze around

poltrona [pol·'tro:·na] *f* **1.** *(mobile)* armchair **2.** THEAT orchestra seat **3.** *fig (carica)* position

poltrone, -a [pol·'tro:·ne] *m, f* lazybones

polvere ['pol·ve·re] *f* **1.** *(sui mobili, in strada)* dust; **togliere la ~** to do the dusting; **ridurre qu in ~** *fig* to pulverize sb **2.** *(sostanza sminuzzata)* powder; **~ di carbone/d'oro** coal/gold dust; **in ~** powdered; **caffè in ~** instant coffee **3.** MIL **~ da sparo** gunpowder

polveriera [pol·ve·'riɛ:·ra] *f* **1.** *(magazzino)* munitions store **2.** *fig (territorio)* powder keg

polverina [pol·ve·'ri:·na] *f* **1.** *(medicinale)* powder **2.** *sl (cocaina)* snow

polverizzare [pol·ve·rid·'dza:·re] **I.** *vt* **1.** *(ridurre in polvere)* to pulverize **2.** *(nebulizzare)* to atomize **3.** *(annientare)* to crush; *(record)* to smash **4.** GASTR to dust **II.** *vr:* **-rsi** *(disintegrarsi)* to disintegrate

polverizzazione [pol·ve·rid·dzat·'tsio:·ne] *f* **1.** *(di piante, terreno)* pulverization **2.** *(disgregazione)* splitting

polverone [pol·ve·'ro:·ne] *m (nuvola di polvere)* dust cloud

polveroso, -a [pol·ve·'ro:·so] *agg (pieno di polvere)* dusty

pomata [po·'ma:·ta] *f* ointment

pomello [po·'mɛl·lo] *m* **1.** *(zigomo)* cheekbone **2.** *(di porta, cassetto)* knob

pomeridiano, -a [po·me·ri·'dia:·no] *agg* afternoon

pomeriggio [po·me·'rid·dʒo] <-ggi> *m* afternoon; **di ~** in the afternoon; **domani/oggi ~** tomorrow/this afternoon; **nel primo/tardo ~** in the early/late afternoon; **venerdì ~** Friday afternoon

pomice ['po:·mi·tʃe] <-ci> *f* **pietra ~** pumice (stone)

pomiciare [po·mi·'tʃa:·re] *vi sl (baciarsi)* to smooch

pomo ['po:·mo] *m* **1.** ANAT **~ d'Adamo** Adam's apple **2.** *(di letto, bastone)* knob

pomodoro [po·mo·'dɔ:·ro] *m* tomato; **diventare rosso come un ~** to get as red as a beet

pompa ['pom·pa] *f* **1.** *(strumento)* pump **2.** *fam (di benzina)* pump **3.** *(sfarzo)* pomp; **impresa di -e funebri** funeral home; **in ~**

magna *scherz* in all one's finery
pompare [pom·'pa:·re] *vt* **1.**(*acqua, benzina*) to pump **2.**(*pneumatico*) to pump up **3.**(*notizia, fatto*) to exaggerate
Pompei [pom·'pɛ:·i] *f* Pompeii
pompelmo [pom·'pɛl·mo] *m* grapefruit
pompiere [pom·'piɛ:·re] *m* (*vigile del fuoco*) firefighter
pompon [p5·'p5] <-> *m* pompom
pomposità [pom·po·si·'ta] <-> *f* pomposity
pomposo, -a [pom·'po:·so] *agg* (*festa, cerimonia*) grand; (*abbigliamento*) magnificent; (*tono, atteggiamento*) pompous
ponderare [pon·de·'ra:·re] *vt* (*conseguenze, decisione*) to consider
ponderato, -a [pon·de·'ra:·to] *agg* **1.**(*discorso, decisione*) considered **2.**(*persona*) sensible
ponderoso, -a [pon·de·'ro:·so] *agg* (*carico*) heavy; (*trattato*) weighty
ponente [po·'nɛn·te] *m* **1.**(*ovest*) west **2.**(*vento*) west wind
pongo [po'poŋ·go] *1. pers sing pr di* **porre**
ponte ['pon·te] *m* **1.**(*su fiume, strada, protesi*) bridge; ~ **levatoio** drawbridge; ~ **sospeso** suspension bridge; **rompere** [*o* **tagliare**] **i -i** *fig* to sever all ties **2.**(*collegamento*) ~ **aereo** airlift; ~ **radio** radio link **3.**(*di nave*) deck; ~ **di comando** bridge **4.**(*impalcatura*) scaffold **5.**(*in ginnastica*) crab **6.**(*vacanza*) long weekend; **fare il** ~ to make a long weekend of it
pontefice [pon·'te:·fi·tʃe] <-ci> *m* **1.** REL pontiff **2.** HIST pontifex
ponticello [pon·ti·'tʃɛl·lo] *m* **1.**(*piccolo ponte*) small bridge **2.**(*di occhiali*) bridge
pontiere [pon·'tiɛ:·re] *m* MIL bridge builder
pontificale [pon·ti·fi·'ka:·le] **I.** *agg* pontifical **II.** *m* (*messa*) pontifical mass; (*libro*) pontifical
pontificare [pon·ti·fi·'ka:·re] *vi* to pontificate
pontificato [pon·ti·fi·'ka:·to] *m* (*papato*) pontificate
pontificio, -a [pon·ti·'fi:·tʃo] <-ci, -cie> *agg* **1.**(*del papa*) pontifical **2.** HIST **lo stato** ~ the Papal State
pontile [pon·'ti:·le] *m* pier
pony ['pou·ni] <-> *m* pony
pony express ['pou·ni iks·'pres] <-> *m* courier company
pool [pu:l] <-> *m* **1.**(*accordo*) agreement **2.**(*gruppo di persone*) group **3.**(*giudici*) team; ~ **antimafia** anti-Mafia team **4.** BIOL ~ **genetico** [*o* **genico**] gene pool **5.**(*gioco, inform*) pool
pop [pɔp] <inv> *agg* (*musica, cantante*) pop
pop art ['pɔp a:t] <-> *f* pop art
pop-corn ['pɔp·kɔ:n] <-> *m* popcorn
popeline [pɔ·pə·'lin/po·pe·'li·ne] <-> *m o f* poplin
pop jazz [pɔp 'dʒæz/pɔp 'dʒets] <-> *m* MUS pop jazz
pop music [pɔp 'mju:·zik] <-> *f* MUS pop music
popò [po·'pɔ] <-> **I.** *f fam* (*feci*) poop **II.** *m fam*

(*sedere*) bottom
popolamento [po·po·la·'men·to] *m* population
popolano, -a [po·po·'la:·no] **I.** *m, f* working-class person **II.** *agg* (*persona*) working-class
popolare[1] [po·po·'la:·re] *agg* **1.**(*gener*) popular **2.**(*delle classi inferiori*) working-class; **casa** ~ public housing unit; **musica** ~ popular music
popolare[2] I. *vt* to populate nella speranza di ~ quelle regioni territorio **II.** *vr:* **-rsi 1.**(*diventare popolato*) to become populated **2.**(*affollarsi*) to fill up
popolaresco, -a [po·po·la·'res·ko] <-schi, -sche> *agg* popular
popolarità [po·po·la·ri·'ta] <-> *f* (*fama*) popularity
popolazione [po·po·lat·'tsio:·ne] *f* **1.**(*abitanti di un luogo*) population; ~ **civile** civilian population; **densità di** ~ population density **2.**(*popolo*) people **3.**(*fauna*) wildlife **4.**(*gruppo etnico*) ethnic group
popolino [po·po·'li:·no] *m pej* masses *pl*
popolo ['pɔ:·po·lo] *m* **1.**(*gener*) people **2.**(*classi più basse*) common people
popoloso, -a [po·po·'lo:·so] *agg* (*quartiere, città*) populous
poppa ['pop·pa] *f* **1.** NAUT stern **2.** *fam* (*mammella*) boob
poppante [pop·'pan·te] *mf* **1.**(*lattante*) unweaned child **2.** *fig, fam* tenderfoot
poppare [pop·'pa:·re] *vt* (*latte*) to feed
poppata [pop·'pa:·ta] *f* feed
poppatoio [pop·pa·'to:·io] <-oi> *m* (*biberon*) bottle
pop star ['pɔp star] <-> *f* MUS pop star
populismo [po·pu·'liz·mo] *m* populism
populistico, -a [po·pu·'lis·ti·ko] <-ci, -che> *agg* populist
porcaio [por·'ka:·io] <-ai> *m* (*luogo sporco*) pigsty
porcata [por·'ka:·ta] *f* **1.**(*cosa disgustosa*) crap **2.** *fam* (*cosa brutta, malfatta*) piece of crap
porcellana [por·tʃel·'la:·na] *f* (*materiale*) porcelain; (*oggetto*) piece of porcelain
porcellino [por·tʃel·'li:·no] *m* **1.** ZOO ~ **d'India** guinea pig **2.**(*stufa*) stove **3.** *fig, fam* (*bambino sporco*) messy little thing
porcello, -a [por·'tʃɛl·lo] *m, f* **1.**(*maiale giovane*) piglet **2.** *fam* (*persona sporca, immorale*) pig
porcheria [por·ke·'ri:·a] <-ie> *f* **1.**(*sporcizia*) mess **2.**(*cibo disgustoso*) muck; (*cibo non sano*) garbage **3.** *fig* (*azione*) dirty trick; *fam* (*cosa brutta*) piece of junk
porchetta [por·'ket·ta] *f* GASTR roast suckling pig
porcile [por·'tʃi:·le] *m* pigsty
porcino [por·'tʃi:·no] *m* (*fungo*) porcino
porco, -a ['pɔr·ko] <-ci, -che> **I.** *m, f* **1.** ZOO (*persona viziosa*) pig; **piede** [*o* **piè**] **di** ~ TEC

jimmy; **mangiare come un** ~ to eat like a pig; **gettar le perle ai -ci** *fig* to cast pearls before swine -i **2.** (*carne*) pork **II.** *agg* **1.** *pej* (*indecente*) disgusting **2.** *vulg* (*in esclamazioni*) **-a miseria!** shit!

porcospino [por·kos·'pi:·no] *m* (*istrice*) porcupine; *fam* (*riccio*) hedgehog

Pordenone [por·de·'no:·ne] *f* Pordenone, *city in northeastern Italy*

pordenonese [por·de·no·'ne:·se] **I.** *mf* (*abitante*) person from Pordenone **II.** *agg* from Pordenone

Pordenonese <*sing*> *m* Pordenone area

porfido ['pɔr·fi·do] *m* porphyry

porgere ['pɔr·dʒe·re] <porgo, porsi, porto> *vt* (*dare*) to hand; ~ **la mano** to hold out one's hand; ~ **orecchio** to pay attention

poriferi [po·'ri:·fe·ri] *mpl* Porifera *pl*

porno ['por·no] **I.** <-> *m* porn **II.** <inv> *agg* porno; **film** ~ porno movie; **rivista** ~ porno magazine

pornoattore, -trice [por·no·at·'to:·re] *m, f* FILM porno actor

pornocassetta [por·no·kas·'set·ta] *f* porno video

pornodivo, -a [por·no·'di:·vo] *m, f* porno star

pornografia [por·no·gra·'fi:·a] *f* pornography

pornografico, -a [por·no·'gra:·fi·ko] <-ci, -che> *agg* pornographic

pornoshop [pɔr·no·'ʃɔp] <-> *m* porno shop

pornostar [por·no·'sta:] <-> *mf* porno star

pornovideo [por·no·'vi:·deo] <-> *m* porno video

poro ['pɔ:·ro] *m* pore; **sprizzare veleno da tutti i -i** *fig* to filled with resentment; **sprizzare gioia da tutti i -i** to be overjoyed

porosità [po·ro·si·'ta] <-> *f* (*di materiale*) porosity

poroso, -a [po·'ro:·so] *agg* porous

porpora ['por·po·ra] *f* (*colorante*) purple dye; (*colore*) purple

porporato [por·po·'ra:·to] *m* cardinal

porporina [por·po·'ri:·na] *f* purpurin

porporino, -a [por·po·'ri:·no] *agg* purple

porre ['por·re] <pongo, posi, posto> **I.** *vt* **1.** (*mettere*) to put **2.** *fig* (*supporre*) to suppose; **poni caso che ...** suppose that ... **3.** (*loc*) ~ **una domanda a qu** to ask sb a question; ~ **un problema a qu** to pose a problem for sb; ~ **fine** [*o* **termine**] **a qc** to put an end to sth **II.** *vr:* **-rsi 1.** (*mettersi*) **-rsi in marcia** to set off; **-rsi in salvo** to reach safety **2.** (*atteggiarsi*) to behave

porro ['pɔr·ro] *m* **1.** BOT leek **2.** *fam* (*verruca*) wart

porsi ['pɔr·si] *1. pers sing pass rem di* **porgere**

porta ['pɔr·ta] *f* **1.** (*di stanza, edificio, armadio*) door; ~ **di servizio** service entrance; **a -e chiuse** JUR in camera; **prendere la** ~ *fam* to leave; **sfondare una** ~ **aperta** *fig* to preach to the choir; **mettere qu alla** ~ to throw sb out; **chiudere la** ~ **in faccia a qu** *fig* to slam the door in sb's face; **aprire tutte le -e a** to open doors **2.** SPORT goal **3.** (*nello sci*) gate

portaaghi [por·ta·'a:·gi] <-> *m* needle box

portabagagli [por·ta·ba·'gaʎ·ʎi] <-> *m* **1.** (*sul tetto di automobile*) luggage rack; *fam* (*bagagliaio*) trunk; (*per biciclette*) bicycle rack **2.** (*facchino*) porter

portabandiera [por·ta·ban·diɛ:·ra] <-> *mf a. fig* (*esponente principale*) standard-bearer

portabastoni [por·ta·bas·'to:·ni] <-> *m* SPORT (*nel golf*) caddy

portabile [por·'ta:·bi·le] *agg* (*abito*) wearable

portabilità [por·ta·bi·li·'ta] <-> *f* **1.** (*di abbigliamento*) wearability **2.** TEC portability

portabiti [por·'ta:·bi·ti] **I.** <-> *m* (*gruccia*) coat hanger **II.** <inv> *agg* **gruccia** ~ coat hanger

portaborse [por·ta·'bor·se] <-> *mf pej* gofer

portabottiglie [por·ta·bo·'tiʎ·ʎe] <-> *m* (*scaffale*) bottle rack

portacarta [por·ta·'kar·ta] <-> *m* (*portarotolo*) toilet-paper holder

portacarte [por·ta·'kar·te] <-> *m* (*borsa*) briefcase

portacassette [por·ta·kas·'set·te] <-> *m* cassette holder

portacenere [por·ta·'tʃe:·ne·re] <-> *m* ashtray

portachiavi [por·ta·'kia:·vi] <-> *m* keyring

portacipria [por·ta·'tʃi:·pria] <-> *m* compact

portacravatte [por·ta·kra·'vat·te] <-> *m* tie rack

portadocumenti [po·ta·do·ku·'men·ti] <-> *m* (*custodia*) document holder

portadolci [por·ta·'dol·tʃi] <-> *m* (*piatto*) cake stand

portafinestra [por·ta·fi·'nɛs·tra] <portefinestre> *f* French door

portafiori [por·ta·'fio:·ri] **I.** <inv> *agg* flower **II.** <-> *m* vase

portafoglio [por·ta·'fɔʎ·ʎo] *m* **1.** (*per banconote*) wallet **2.** (*per documenti*) briefcase **3.** (*pol, fin*) portfolio; ~ **estero** foreign bills

portaformaggio [por·ta·for·'mad·dʒo] <-i *o* -> *m* cheese box

portafortuna [por·ta·for·'tu:·na] **I.** <inv> *agg* lucky ~ **II.** <-> *m* lucky charm

portafoto [por·ta·'fɔ:·to] <-> *m* frame

portafotografie [por·ta·fo·to·gra·'fi:·e] <-> *m* frame

portafrutta [por·ta·'frut·ta] <-> *m* fruit bowl

portaghiaccio [por·ta·'giat·tʃo] **I.** <-> *m* (*secchiello*) ice bucket **II.** <inv> *agg* ice

portagioie, portagioielli [por·ta·'dʒɔ:·ie, por·ta·dʒo·'iel·li] <-> *m* (*cofanetto*) jewelry box

portale [por·'ta:·le] *m* portal

portalettere [por·ta·'lɛt·te·re/por·ta·'let·te·re] *mf* mail carrier

portamatite [por·ta·ma·'ti:·te] <-> *m* (*astuccio*) pencil case

portamento [por·ta·'men·to] *m* (*modo di muoversi*) bearing

portamine [por·ta·'mi:·ne] <-> *m* mechanical pencil

portamissili [por·ta·'mis·si·li] <-> *agg* missile-carrying

portamonete [por·ta·mo·'ne:·te] <-> *m* change purse

portante [por·'tan·te] *agg* (*struttura, muro*) load-bearing; **piano** [*o* **superficie**] ~ lifting surface

portantina [por·tan·'ti:·na] *f* **1.** (*per ammalati*) stretcher **2.** HIST (*sedia portatile*) sedan chair

portantino, -a [por·tan·'ti:·no] *m, f* (*negli ospedali*) orderly

portanza [por·'tan·tsa] *f* PHYS lift

portaobiettivi [por·ta·o·biet·'ti:·vi] <-> *m* OPT lens holder

portaocchiali [por·ta·ok·'kia:·li] <-> *m* glasses case

portaoggetti [por·ta·od·'dʒɛt·ti] I.<inv> *agg* **vano** ~ MOT glove compartment II.<-> *m* holder

portaolio [por·ta·'ɔ:·lio] <-> *m* cruet

portaombrelli [por·ta·om·'brɛl·li] <-> *m* umbrella stand

portapacchi [por·ta·'pak·ki] <-> *m* **1.** (*di automobile*) luggage rack; (*di bicicletta*) carrier **2.** (*fattorino*) delivery man

portapenne [por·ta·'pen·ne] <-> *m* (*astuccio*) pencil case

portapiatti [por·ta·'piat·ti] I.<-> *m* **1.** (*scolapiatti*) plate rack **2.** (*vassoio*) tray II.<inv> *agg* **vassoio** ~ tray

portapillole [por·ta·'pil·lo·le] <-> *m* pillbox

portapipe [por·ta·'pi:·pe] <-> *m* pipe rack

portaposate [por·ta·po·'sa:·te] <-> *m* silverware tray

portare [por·'ta:·re] I. *vt* **1.** (*trasportare, trascinare*) to carry **2.** (*trasferire, accompagnare, prendere con sé*) to take; ~ **qc in tavola** to serve sth; ~ **su/giù** to take up/down; ~ **dentro/fuori** to take in/out; ~ **fuori qu** (*a cena, al cinema*) to take sb out; ~ **a spasso qu** to take sb for a walk; ~ **via** (*allontanare*) to take away; (*rubare*) to steal **3.** (*dare, causare*) to bring; ~ **qc in dote** to bring a dowry of sth; ~ **qc in regalo** to give sth as a present; ~ **bene** [*o* **fortuna**] **a qu** to bring sb good luck; ~ **male** [*o* **sfortuna**] **a qu** to bring sb bad luck **4.** (*indossare*) to wear **5.** (*condurre*) to lead; (*veicoli*) to go **6.** (*taglia*) to take; **porto la 44/il 39** I wear a size 44/39 **7.** (*indurre*) ~ **qu a qc/a fare qc** to lead sb to sth/to do sth **8.** (*proporre, presentare*) to provide; ~ **un esempio** to provide an example **9.** (*dimostrare*) ~ **bene/male gli anni** not to look/to look one's age **10.** (*provare*) ~ **rancore a qu** to bear sb a grudge; ~ **rispetto a qu** to show respect for sb; ~ **pazienza** to have patience **11.** (*reggere*) to support II. *vr:* **-rsi 1.** (*recarsi*) to go **2.** (*stare di salute*) to be

portareliquie [por·ta·re·'li:·kuie] <-> *m* reliquary

portaritratti [por·ta·ri·'trat·ti] <-> *m* frame

portariviste [por·ta·ri·'vis·te] <-> *m* magazine rack

portarossetto [por·ta·ros·'set·to] <-> *m* lip-

stick case

portarotoli [por·ta·'rɔ:·to·li] <-> *m* toilet paper holder

portasapone [por·ta·sa·'po:·ne] <-> *m* soap dish

portasci [por·taʃ·'ʃi] <-> *m* ski rack

portasciugamano [por·taʃ·ʃu·ga·'ma:·no] <-> *m* towel rail

portasigarette [por·ta·si·ga·'ret·te] <-> *m* cigarette case

portaspazzolini [por·ta·spat·tso·'li:·ni] <-> *m* (*in bagno*) toothbrush holder

portaspazzolino [por·ta·spat·tso·'li:·no] <-> *m* (*astuccio*) toothbrush case

portaspilli [por·tas·'pil·li] <-> *m* pincushion

portata [por·'ta:·ta] *f* **1.** (*di pranzo*) course **2.** (*capacità di carico*) capacity **3.** (*di arma*) range **4.** (*di fiume*) flow **5.** *fig* (*importanza*) importance **6.** (*livello*) **alla ~ di** (*libro*) within the grasp of; (*spesa*) within the means of; **a ~ di mano** to hand; *fig* within one's grasp ~ di mano

portatessera [por·ta·'tɛs·se·ra] <-> *m* card holder

portatile [por·'ta:·ti·le] I. *agg* (*televisione, computer, stufa, radio*) portable II. *m* (*computer*) laptop

portato, -a *agg* **1.** (*abito, giacca*) secondhand **2.** *fig* (*predisposto*) **essere ~ per qc** to have a gift for sth

portatore, -trice [por·ta·'to:·re] *m, f* **1.** (*trasportatore*) FIN bearer; **al ~** to the bearer **2.** (*di malattia, virus*) carrier aviaria; ~ **sano** healthy carrier malato

portatovagliolo [por·ta·to·vaʎ·'ʎɔ:·lo] *m* (*busta*) napkin holder; (*anello*) napkin ring

portatrice *f v.* portatore

portattrezzi [por·tat·'tret·tsi] <-> *m* (*cassetta*) toolbox

portauova [por·ta·'uɔ:·va] <-> *m* (*per uovo alla coque*) eggcup

portauovo [por·ta·'uɔ:·vo] <-> *m* (*di frigorifero*) egg compartment; (*per trasporto*) egg box

portautensili [por·ta·u·ten·'si:·li] <-> *m* TEC attachment holder

portavalori [por·ta·va·'lo:·ri] I.<inv> *agg* **furgone** ~ armored truck II.<-> *mf* (*persona*) security guard

portavasi [por·ta·'va:·zi] <-> *m* (*sostegno*) flower stand; (*di ceramica*) flowerpot holder

portavivande [por·ta·vi·'van·de] <-> *m* (*carrello*) food cart; (*cesta*) insulated food carrier

portavoce [por·ta·'vo:·tʃe] <-> *mf* spokesman *m*, spokeswoman *f*

porte-enfant ['pɔrt ã·'fã] <-> *m* Portacrib®

portefinestre *pl di* portafinestra

portello [por·'tɛl·lo] *m* **1.** (*sportello*) door **2.** NAUT, AERO hatch

portellone [por·tel·'lɔ:·ne] *m* (*di nave, aereo*) hatch; (*di automobile*) tailgate

portento [por·'tɛn·to] *m* **1.** (*medicina, strumento*) marvel **2.** (*persona*) **essere un ~ di**

memoria to have an amazing memory
portentoso, -a *agg* **1.**(*fatto, avvenimento*) extraordinary **2.**(*medicina, atleta*) marvelous
porticato [por·ti·'ka:·to] *m* colonnade
porticato, -a *agg* porticoed
portico ['pɔr·ti·ko] <-ci> *m* **1.** ARCH portico **2.**(*costruzione rurale*) lean-to
portiera [por·'tiɛ:·ra] *f* (*di veicolo*) door
portiere, -a [por·'tiɛ:·re] *m, f* **1.**(*di albergo*) porter; (*di ufficio*) superintendent **2.** SPORT goalkeeper
portinaio, -a [por·ti·'na:·io] <-i, -ie> *m, f* (*di condominio*) superintendent
portineria [por·ti·ne·'ri:·a] <-ie> *f* superintendent's apartment
porto¹ ['pɔr·to] *pp di* porgere
porto² *m* **1.** NAUT port; **essere un ~ di mare** *fig* to be like Grand Central Station **2.** *fig* (*punto d'arrivo*) **giungere in ~** to reach a successful conclusion; **condurre in ~ un affare** to bring a matter to a successful conclusion **3.**(*autorizzazione*) **~ d'armi** gun license **4.**(*spesa di trasporto*) carriage; **franco di ~** carriage free
porto³ <-> *m* (*vino*) port
Portogallo [por·to·'gal·lo] *m* **il ~** Portugal; **vivere in ~** to live in Portugal; **andare in ~** to go to Portugal
portoghese [por·to·'ge:·se] I. *agg* Portuguese II. *mf* **1.**(*abitante*) Portuguese **2.** *fig* (*chi entra senza pagare*) **fare il ~** to get in without paying
portone [por·'to:·ne] *m* (*di palazzo*) main door
portuale [por·tu·'a:·le] I. *agg* (*zona, attività*) port II. *m* longshoreman
porzione [por·'tsio:·ne] *f* (*di cibo*) portion; (*di eredità, responsabilità*) share
posa ['pɔ:·sa] *f* **1.**(*di materiale*) laying **2.** FOTO exposure **3.**(*atteggiamento*) pose; **mettersi in ~** to pose **4.**(*riposo*) **senza ~** without a break **5.** FILM **teatro di ~** photographic studio
posacenere [po·sa·'tʃe:·ne·re] <-> *m* ashtray
posare [po·'sa:·re] I. *vt* (*metter giù*) to put down II. *vi* **1.**(*poggiare*) to rest **2.**(*stare in posa*) to pose **3.** *fig* (*fondarsi*) to be based III. *vr:* **-rsi** (*uccello*) to alight; (*sguardo*) to light
posata [po·'sa:·ta] *f* (*per mangiare*) piece of silverware
posateria [po·sa·te·'ri:·a] <-ie> *f* silverware
posato, -a [po·'sa:·to] *agg* (*equilibrato*) level-headed
poscritto [pos·'krit·to] *m* postscript
posi ['po:·si] *1. pers sing pass rem di* porre
positiva [po·zi·'ti:·va] *f* print
positivismo [po·zi·ti·'vis·mo] *m* PHILOS positivism
positivo [po·zi·'ti:·vo] *m* **1.**(*certo*) positive **2.** FOTO print
positivo, -a *agg* positive
posizionare [po·zit·tsio·'na:·re] *vt* (*collocare*) to position
posizione [po·zit·'tsio:·ne] *f* position **~; luci**

di ~ MOT parking lights; **farsi una ~** to make a career for oneself; **prendere ~** to come out
posologia [po·zo·lo·'dʒi:·a] <-gie> *f* dosage
posporre [pos·'por·re] <irr> *vt* **1.**(*collocare dopo*) **~ qc** to put sth after **2.**(*rimandare*) to postpone
possedere [pos·se·'de:·re] <possiedo, possedetti *o* possedei, posseduto> *vt* (*beni*) to have; (*dote*) to possess
possedimento [pos·se·di·'men·to] *m* **1.**(*proprietà terriera*) property **2.**(*colonia*) possession
posseditrice *f v.* possessore
possente [pos·'sɛn·te] *agg* (*fisico, individuo*) owner
possessivo, -a [pos·ses·'si:·vo] *agg* possessive
possesso [pos·'sɛs·so] *m* **1.**(*di bene, facoltà*) possession; **entrare in ~ di qc** to come into possession of sth **2.**(*padronanza*) command; **essere nel pieno ~ delle proprie facoltà mentali** to be in full possession of one's faculties **3.** *pl* (*proprietà terriera*) property
possessore, posseditrice [pos·ses·'so:·re, pos·se·di·'tri:·tʃe] *m, f* owner
possibile [pos·'si:·bi·le] I. *agg* possible; **è ~ che ...** it is possible that ...; **con la maggior cura ~** with the greatest possible care; **il prima** [*o* **più presto**] **~** as soon as possible II. *m* possible; **nei limiti del ~** as far as possible
possibilità [pos·si·bi·li·'ta] <-> *f* **1.**(*attuabilità, capacità*) possibility **2.**(*opportunità*) opportunity **3.** *pl* (*mezzi*) means *pl* **~**
possibilmente [pos·si·bil·'men·te] *avv* (*se possibile*) possibly
possidente [pos·si·'dɛn·te] *mf* property owner
posso ['pɔs·so] *1. pers sing pr di* potere¹
posta ['pɔs·ta] *f* **1.**(*servizio*) postal service; (*ufficio postale*) post office; **spedire** [*o* **mandare**] **qc per ~** to mail sth; **fermo ~** general delivery; **~ aerea** airmail; **~ elettronica** INFORM electronic mail; **~ prioritaria** first class mail **2.**(*corrispondenza*) mail **3.**(*rubrica di giornale*) **~ del cuore** advice column; **piccola ~** letters to the editor **4.**(*nei giochi*) stake; **la ~ in gioco** *fig* the stakes *pl* alta
postacelere [pos·ta·'tʃe:·le·re] *m* (*corriere*) special delivery
postagiro [pos·ta·'dʒi:·ro] *m* postal transfer
postale [pos·'ta:·le] I. *agg* (*servizio, ufficio*) postal; (*pacco*) mail; **cartolina ~** stamped postcard; **casella ~** post office box II. *m* NAUT mail boat; FERR mail train; AERO mail plane
Postamat® [pos·ta·'mat] <-> *m* ATM
postarsi [pos·'tar·si] *vr* (*appostarsi*) to station oneself
postazione [pos·tat·'tsio:·ne] *f* **1.** MIL emplacement **2.**(*apparecchiature*) **~ di lavoro** workstation
postbellico, -a [post·'bɛl·li·ko] <-ci, -che> *agg* postwar
postcomunismo [post·ko·mu·'niz·mo] *m* POL

post-communism

postcomunista [post·ko·mu·'nis·ta] <-i *m*, -e *f*> I. *mf* post-communist II. *agg* post-communist

postdatare [post·da·'ta:·re] *vt* (*lettera, documento*) to postdate

posteggiare [pos·ted·'dʒa:·re] I. *vt* to park II. *vi* to park

posteggiatore, -trice [post·ed·dʒa·'to:·re] *m*, *f* (*custode*) parking lot attendant

posteggio [pos·'ted·dʒo] <-ggi> *m* (*luogo*) parking lot; ~ **a pagamento** pay parking lot; ~ **dei taxi** taxi stand; **divieto di** ~ no parking

postelegrafico, -a [pos·te·le·'gra:·fi·ko] <-ci, -che> I. *agg* mail-and-telegraph II. *m*, *f* mail and telegraph worker

poster ['pɔs·ter] <-> *m* poster

posteri ['pɔs·te·ri] *mpl* posterity

posteriore [pos·te·'rio:·re] I. *agg* 1. (*nello spazio*) back 2. (*nel tempo*) later 3. (*arto*) hind II. *m scherz, fam* (*sedere*) behind

posteriorità [pos·te·rio·ri·'ta] <-> *f* (*di evento*) posteriority

posterità [pos·te·ri·'ta] <-> *f* posterity

postfazione [post·fat·'tsio:·ne] *f* afterword

posticcio [pos·'tit·tʃo] <-ci> *m* (*toupet*) hairpiece

posticcio, -a <-cci, -cce> *agg* (*baffi, capelli*) false

posticino [pos·ti·'tʃi:·no] *m fam* spot

posticipare [pos·ti·tʃi·'pa:·re] *vt* (*data, appuntamento*) to postpone

postilla [pos·'til·la] *f* (*su lettera, libro*) marginal note; (*su contratto, atto*) rider

postillare [pos·til·'la:·re] *vt* (*libro, lettera*) to annotate

postindustriale [pos·tin·dus·'tria:·le] *agg* postindustrial

postino, -a [pos·'ti:·no] *m*, *f* (*portalettere*) mailman *m*, mailwoman *f*

post-it® ['pous·tit] <-> *m* Post-it®

postmoderno, -a [post·mo·'dɛr·no] *agg* ARCH postmodern

posto ['pɔs·to] *m* 1. (*gener*) place; **fuori** ~ out of place; (**ri**)**mettere a** ~ **qc** to put sth back (in its place); **mettere a** ~ (*riordinare*) to tidy up; **mettere la testa a** ~ *fig* to sort oneself out; **al** ~ **di qu** in sb's place; **essere a** ~ (*in ordine*) to be tidy; (*in regola*) in order; **una persona a** ~ *fig* an OK kind of guy; **del** ~ local; **sul** ~ there; ~ **di polizia** police station; ~ **di blocco ferroviario** signal tower ... 2. (*spazio libero*) space; **far** ~ **a qu** to make room for sb 3. (*sedia*) seat; ~ **a sedere** seat; ~ **in piedi** standing place; ~ **di guida** driver's seat; ~ **letto** bed 4. MIL post; ~ **di guardia** sentry post; ~ **di blocco** roadblock 5. (*impiego*) position ~

posto, -a I. *pp di* **porre** II. *agg* 1. (*collocato*) situated 2. (*dato*) ~ **che** ... +*conj* given that ...; ~ **ciò** given that

postoperatorio, -a [pos·to·pe·ra·'tɔ:·rio] *agg* postoperative

postproduzione [post·pro·dut·'tsio:·ne] *f*

FILM, TV postproduction

post scriptum [post 'skrip·tum] <-> *m* postscript

postulare [pos·tu·'la:·re] *vt* (*principio*) to postulate

postulato [pos·tu·'la:·to] *m* (*premessa*) postulate

postumo ['pɔs·tu·mo] *m* 1. (*di malattia*) aftereffect 2. *pl* (*conseguenze*) aftermath

postumo, -a *agg* (*scritto, figlio*) posthumous

post-universitario, -a [pos·tu·ni·ver·si·'ta:·rio] <-i, -ie> *agg* postuniversity

potabile [po·'ta:·bi·le] *agg* drinkable

potare [po·'ta:·re] *vt* (*pianta*) to prune

potassio [po·'tas·sio] *m* potassium

potei [po·'te:·i] *I. pers sing pass rem di* **potere**[1]

potente [po·'tɛn·te] *agg* powerful

Potentino <*sing*> *m* Potenza area

potentino, -a [po·ten·'ti:·no] I. *m*, *f* (*abitante*) person from Potenza II. *agg* from Potenza

potenza [po·'tɛn·tsa] *f* 1. (*gener*) power; ~ **elettrica** electrical power; **all'ennesima** ~ *fig* to the nth degree 2. (*forza fisica*) strength 3. (*nazione*) **le grandi -e** the great powers

Potenza *f* Potenza, *town in southern Italy*

potenziale [po·ten·'tsia:·le] I. *agg* (*possibile*) potential II. *m* potential

potenziamento [po·ten·tsia·'men·to] *m* (*rafforzamento*) strengthening

potenziare [po·ten·'tsia:·re] *vt* (*rafforzare*) to strengthen

potere[1] [po·'te:·re] <posso, potei, potuto> *vi* 1. (*gener*) to be able to; **posso fare un tentativo** I can have a try; **non potevo saperlo** I couldn't have known; **verrò se potrò** I'll see if I can; **non ne posso più** I can't take any more; **può darsi** [*o* **essere**] **che** ... +*conj* perhaps ... 2. (*avere il permesso di*) may; **permesso, si può?** excuse me, may I?

potere[2] *m* 1. (*gener*) power; **farò tutto quello che è in mio** ~ I'll do everything in my power; ~ **temporale** temporal power; **essere al** ~ to be in power; **pieni -i** full powers; ~ **legislativo/esecutivo/giudiziario** legislative/executive/judicial power; ~ **d'acquisto** purchasing power 2. MED ~ **nutritivo** nutritive value

potestà [po·tes·'ta] <-> *f* DIR power; **patria** ~ JUR parental authority

pot-pourri ['po pu·'ri] <-> *m* 1. CULIN stew 2. (*per profumare*) potpourri

poveraccio, -a [po·ve·'rat·tʃo] <-cci, -cce> *m*, *f* (*disgraziato*) poor soul

poverino, -a [po·ve·'ri:·no] I. *agg* poor II. *m*, *f fam* poor soul

povero, -a ['pɔ:·ve·ro] I. *agg* 1. (*senza mezzi*) poor; ~ **in canna** dirt poor; **un** ~ **diavolo** *fam* poor devil 2. (*stile, arredamento*) plain; (*terreno*) barren; (*fantasia*) limited; **in parole -e** in short 3. (*scarso: proteine, idee*) ~ **di** (*proteine, idee*) lacking in 4. (*defunto*) late; **il mio** ~ **marito** my late husband II. *m*, *f* poor person

povertà [po·ver·'ta] <-> *f* (*indigenza*) poverty

pozione [pot·'tsio:·ne] *f* potion

pozza ['pot·tsa] *f* pool

pozzanghera [pot·'tsaŋ·ge·ra] *f* puddle

pozzetto [pot·'tset·to] *m* 1.(*nelle fognature*) shaft 2. NAUT cockpit

pozzo ['pot·tso] *m* 1.(*d'acqua*) well; ~ **artesiano** artesian well; ~ **petrolifero** oil well 2.(~ *nero*) cesspool 3.*fig* (*grande quantità*) load; **un** ~ **di soldi** a load of money; **essere un** ~ **di scienza** to be a mine of information; **essere un** ~ **senza fondo** *fig* to be a bottomless pit

PPI *m abbr di* **Partito Popolare Italiano** *center-right Italian political party*

Praga ['pra:·ga] *f* Prague

pragmatico, -a [prag·'ma:·ti·ko] <-ci, -che> *agg* pragmatic

pragmatismo [prag·ma·'tiz·mo] *m* pragmatism

pragmatista [prag·ma·'tis·ta] <-i *m*, -e *f*> *mf* pragmatist

pralina [pra·'li:·na] *f* praline

prammatica [pram·'ma:·ti·ka] *f* **essere di** ~ to be usual

prammatico, -a [pram·'ma:·ti·ko] <-ci, -che> *agg v.* **pragmatico**

pranzare [pran·'dza:·re] *vi* to have lunch

pranzo ['pran·dzo] *m* lunch; ~ **di gala** gala dinner; **sala da** ~ dining room; **all'ora di** ~ at lunchtime; **dopo** ~ after lunch

prassi ['pras·si] <-> *f* 1.(*procedura corrente*) usual procedure 2.(*pratica*) practice

prataiolo [pra·ta·'iɔ:·lo] *m* (*fungo*) field mushroom

prataiolo, -a *agg* field

prateria [pra·te·'ri:·a] <-ie> *f* (*pianura*) prairie

pratica ['pra:·ti·ka] <-che> *f* 1.(*gener*) practice; **mettere in** ~ **qc** to put sth into practice; **in** ~ in practice 2.(*esperienza*) experience; **avere** ~ **di qc** to have experience of sth 3. ADM (*dossier*) file 4. *pl* (*procedura*) proceedings 5.(*tirocinio*) training

praticabile [pra·ti·'ka:·bi·le] *agg* 1.(*idea, progetto*) feasible 2.(*strada*) passable

praticabilità [pra·ti·ka·bi·li·'ta] <-> *f* 1.(*di idea, progetto*) feasibility 2.(*di strada*) passability

praticamente [pra·ti·ka·'men·te] *avv* practically

praticante [pra·ti·'kan·te] I. *agg* REL practicing II. *mf* (*tirocinante*) trainee

praticare [pra·ti·'ka:·re] *vt* 1.(*mettere in pratica: legge*) to bring into force 2.(*esercitare: professione*) to practice 3.(*effettuare: taglio*) to make; (*sconto*) to give 4.(*frequentare: persona*) to associate with; (*luogo*) to frequent

praticità [pra·ti·tʃi·'ta] <-> *f* practicality

pratico, -a ['pra:·ti·ko] <-ci, -che> *agg* 1.(*gener*) practical 2.(*esperto*) ~ **di qc** experienced in sth; **non sono** ~ **del posto** I'm not familiar with the place

prato ['pra:·to] *m* (*in campagna*) meadow; (*di*

giardino, parco) lawn

pratolina [pra·to·'li:·na] *f* daisy

pre- [pre] (*in parole composte*) pre-

prealpino, -a [pre·al·'pi:·no] *agg* of the Pre-Alps

preambolo [pre·'am·bo·lo] *m* 1.(*introduzione*) preamble 2. *pl, fam* (*cerimonie*) **senza tanti -i** *fam* without beating around the bush

preannunciare, preannunziare [pre·an·nun·'tʃa:·re, pre·an·nun·'tsia:·re] I. *vt* to give advanced warning of II. *vr:* **-rsi** to look

preavvisare [pre·av·vi·'za:·re] *vt* to inform in advance

preavviso [pre·av·'vi:·zo] *m* 1.(*avviso preventivo*) warning; ~ **di pagamento** payment notice 2. JUR (*comunicazione, periodo*) notice

prebarba [pre·'bar·ba] I. <-> *m* preshave II. <inv> *agg* preshave

prebellico, -a [pre·'bɛl·li·ko] <-ci, -che> *agg* prewar

precampionato¹ [pre·kam·pio·'na:·to] <inv> *agg* prechampionship

precampionato² *m* SPORT prechampionship games

precariato [pre·ka·'ria:·to] *m* temporary employment

precarietà [pre·ka·rie·'ta] <-> *f* precariousness

precario, -a [pre·'ka:·rio] <-i, -ie> I. *agg* 1.(*situazione, salute*) precarious 2.(*lavoro, lavoratore*) temporary; **personale** ~ temporary staff II. *m, f* (*lavoratore*) temporary worker

precauzionale [pre·kaut·tsio·'na:·le] *agg* (*misura*) precautionary

precauzione [pre·kaut·'tsio:·ne] *f* (*prudenza*) caution; (*misura*) precaution; **prendere le proprie -i** to take precautions

precedei 1. *pers sing pass rem di* **precedere**

precedente [pre·tʃe·'dɛn·te] I. *agg* (*nello spazio, nel tempo*) previous II. *m* 1.(*evento*) precedent; **senza -i** unprecedented 2. *pl* (*di persona*) history; **-i penali** criminal record

precedenza [pre·tʃe·'dɛn·tsa] *f* 1. MOT right of way; **dare la** ~ to give way; **strada con diritto di** ~ road with right of way 2.(*anteriorità*) **in** ~ previously 3.(*priorità*) priority

precedere [pre·'tʃɛ:·de·re] <precedo, precedetti *o* precedei, preceduto> *vt* to precede

precetto [pre·'tʃɛt·to] *m* 1.(*insegnamento*) rule; REL precept; **festa di** ~ day of obligation 2. JUR (*ordine*) order 3. MIL draft notice

precettore, -trice [pre·tʃet·'to:·re] *m, f* tutor

precipitare [pre·tʃi·pi·'ta:·re] I. *vt avere* 1.(*gettare*) to throw 2.*fig* (*affrettare*) to rush II. *vi essere* 1.(*cadere*) to fall 2.*fig* to plunge III. *vr:* **-rsi** 1.(*gettarsi*) to throw oneself 2.(*recarsi in fretta*) to rush

precipitato, -a *agg* (*decisione, giudizio*) hasty

precipitazione [pre·tʃi·pi·tat·'tsio:·ne] *f* 1. METEO rainfall 2.*fig* (*fretta*) hurry

precipitosamente [pre·tʃi·pi·to·sa·'men·te] *avv* (*in fretta*) hastily

precipitoso, -a [pre·tʃi·pi·'to:·so] *agg* (*per-*

sona, decisione) hasty; (*fuga*) headlong
precipizio [pre·tʃi·'pit·tsio] <-i> *m* **1.**(*abisso*) precipice; **correre a ~** *fig* to run headlong **2.** *fig* **essere sull'orlo del ~** to be on the brink
precipuo, -a [pre·'tʃi:·puo] *agg* (*principale*) main
precisamente [pre·tʃi·za·'men·te] *avv* exactly
precisare [pre·tʃi·'za:·re] *vt* (*definire*) to specify
precisazione [pre·tʃi·zat·'tsio:·ne] *f* (*chiarimento*) clarification
precisino, -a [pre·tʃi·'si:·no] I. *agg* (*pignolo*) precise II. *m, f iron* (*pignolo*) stickler
precisione [pre·tʃi·'zio:·ne] *f* (*esattezza*) precision; **strumento di ~** precision instrument; **esprimersi con ~** to express oneself clearly; **sapere qc con ~** to know sth exactly
preciso, -a [pre·'tʃi:·zo] *agg* **1.**(*esatto*) exact; (*chiaro*) clear; **sono le 10 -e** it's exactly ten o'clock **2.**(*scrupoloso*) precise **3.**(*uguale*) exactly the same
precludere [pre·'klu:·de·re] <precludo, preclusi, precluso> *vt* (*fuga*) to prevent; (*possibilità*) to preclude
preclusione [pre·klu·'zio:·ne] *f* (*esclusione*) bar; JUR ban
precluso [pre·'klu:·zo] *pp di* **precludere**
precoce [pre·'kɔ:·tʃe] *agg* **1.**(*bambino, ragazzo*) precocious **2.**(*inverno, frutto*) early; (*morte*) premature
precocemente [pre·ko·tʃe·'men·te] *avv* (*anzitempo*) prematurely
precocità [pre·ko·tʃi·'ta] <-> *f* (*di persona*) precociousness
preconcetto [pre·kon·'tʃɛt·to] *m* (*pregiudizio*) prejudice; **avere dei -i nei confronti di qu** to be prejudiced against sb
preconcetto, -a *agg* preconceived
preconfezionato, -a *agg* (*prodotto, alimento*) prepackaged; (*abito*) off-the-rack
preconizzare [pre·ko·nid·'dza:·re] *vt* (*pronosticare*) to predict
precorrere [pre·'kor·re·re] <irr> *vt* **~ i tempi** (*moda, evento*) to be ahead of its time
precorritore, -trice [pre·kor·ri·'to:·re] I. *m, f* precursor II. *agg* precursory
precorsi *1. pers sing pass rem di* **precorrere**
precorso *pp di* **precorrere**
precostituire [pre·kos·ti·tu·'i:·re] <precostituisco> *vt* to establish in advance
precotto, -a [pre·'kɔt·to] *agg* precooked
precursore, -corritrice [pre·kur·'so:·re] I. *agg* precursory II. *m, f* precursor
preda ['prɛ:·da] *f* prey; **uccello da ~** bird of prey; **essere in ~ a qc** to be prey to sth
predare [pre·'da:·re] *vt* to plunder
predatore, -trice [pre·da·'to:·re] I. *agg* (*esercito, popolazione*) plundering II. *m, f* **1.**(*mammifero, uccello*) predator **2.**(*predone: del mare, deserto*) plunderer
predecessore [pre·de·tʃes·'so:·re] *m* (*in una carica, attività*) predecessor; **-i** (*antenati*) forefathers

predellino [pre·del·'li:·no] *m* (*di treno, tram*) footboard
predestinare [pre·des·ti·'na:·re] *vt* to predestine
predestinazione [pre·des·ti·nat·'tsio:·ne] *f* REL predestination
predeterminare [pre·de·ter·mi·'na:·re] *vt* to predetermine
predeterminato, -a [pre·de·ter·mi·'na:·to] *agg* predetermined
predetto, -a [pre·'dɛt·to] I. *pp di* **predire** II. *agg* aforementioned
predica ['prɛ:·di·ka] <-che> *f* **1.** REL sermon **2.** *fam* (*rimprovero*) telling-off
predicare [pre·di·'ka:·re] I. *vt* (*pace, fratellanza*) to preach II. *vi* **1.**(*prete*) to preach **2.** *fig* **~ al vento** to waste one's breath
predicativo, -a [pre·di·ka·'ti:·vo] *agg* (*aggettivo, uso*) predicative
predicato [pre·di·'ka:·to] *m* LING predicate; **~ verbale** verbal predicate
predicatore, -trice [pre·di·ka·'to:·re] *m, f* **1.** REL preacher **2.** *pej* (*moralista*) sermonizer
predicatrice *f v.* **predicatore**
predico [pre·'di:·co] *1. pers sing pr di* **predire**
predicozzo [pre·di·'kɔt·tso] *m scherz, fam* talking-to
predilessi [pre·di·'lɛs·si] *1. pers sing pass rem di* **prediligere**
prediletto, -a [pre·di·'lɛt·to] I. *pp di* **prediligere** II. *agg* favorite III. *m, f* favorite
predilezione [pre·di·let·'tsio:·ne] *f* (*preferenza*) fondness
prediligere [pre·di·'li:·dʒe·re] <prediligo, predilessi, prediletto> *vt* (*preferire*) to favor
predire [pre·'di:·re] <irr> *vt* to predict
predisporre [pre·dis·'por·re] <irr> I. *vt* to prepare; **~ qu a qc** to prepare sb for sth II. *vr* **-rsi a qc** to prepare oneself for sth
predisposizione [pre·dis·po·zit·'tsio:·ne] *f* **1.**(*inclinazione*) aptitude; **avere ~ alla musica** to be musical **2.** MED predisposition **3.**(*preparazione*) preparation
predisposto, -a [pre·dis·'pos·to] I. *pp di* **predisporre** II. *agg* **1.**(*organizzato*) prepared **2.**(*impianto, sistema*) ready **3.**(*propenso*) inclined **4.** MED predisposed
predissi *1. pers sing pass rem di* **predire**
predizione [pre·dit·'tsio:·ne] *f* prediction
predominante [pre·do·mi·'nan·te] *agg* predominant
predominare [pre·do·mi·'na:·re] *vi* **1.**(*prevalere*) to be dominant **2.**(*dominare*) **~ su qc/ qn** to predominate over sb/sth
predominio [pre·do·'mi:·nio] <-i> *m* (*supremazia*) dominance
predone [pre·'do:·ne] *m* marauder
preesame [pre·e·'za:·me] *m* preliminary examination
preesistei *1. pers sing pass rem di* **preesistere**
preesistente [pre·e·zis·'tɛn·te] *agg* pre-existing

P

preesistenza [pre·e·zis·'tɛn·tsa] *f* pre-existence

preesistere [pre·e·'zis·te·re] <irr> *vi essere* to pre-exist

prefabbricare [pre·fab·bri·'ka:·re] *vt* **1.** (*edificio*) to prefabricate **2.** (*prove*) to manufacture

prefabbricato [pre·fab·bri·'ka:·to] *m* (*edificio*) prefabricated house

prefabbricato, -a *agg* (*edificio*) prefabricated; **casa -a** prefabricated house

prefazione [pre·fat·'tsio:·ne] *f* (*di scritto*) preface

preferenza [pre·fe·'rɛn·tsa] *f* preference; **voto di ~** preference vote; **dare** [*o* **accordare**] **la ~ a qc/qu** to prefer sb/sth; **di ~** by preference; **fare -e** to have favorites; **non ho -e** I've no preference

preferenziale [pre·fe·ren·'tsia:·le] *agg* preferential; **corsia ~** bus lane; **trattamento ~** preferential treatment

preferibile [pre·fe·'ri:·bi·le] *agg* preferable

preferibilmente [pre·fe·ri·bil·'men·te] *avv* preferably

preferire [pre·fe·'ri:·re] <preferisco> *vt* to prefer; **~ il nuoto allo sci** I prefer swimming to skiing

preferito, -a [pre·fe·'ri:·to] **I.** *agg* favorite **II.** *m, f* favorite

prefestivo, -a [pre·fes·'ti:·vo] *agg* before a holiday

prefetto [pre·'fɛt·to] *m* (*funzionario*) prefect

prefettura [pre·fet·'tu:·ra] *f* prefecture

prefiggere [pre·'fid·dʒe·re] <prefiggo, prefissi, prefisso> *vt* **-rsi uno scopo/un obiettivo** to set oneself a goal/an objective

prefinanziamento [pre·fi·nan·tsia·'men·to] *m* prefinancing

prefinanziare [pre·fi·nan·'tsia:·re] *vt* FIN to prefinance

prefissare [pre·fis·'sa:·re] *vt* to arrange in advance; **-rsi una meta** to set oneself a goal

prefissato, -a [pre·fis·'sa:·to] *agg* **1.** (*termine, scadenza*) prearranged **2.** (*parola*) prefixed

prefissi [pre·'fis·si] *1. pers sing pass rem di* **prefiggere**

prefisso¹ [pre·'fis·so] *pp di* **prefiggere**

prefisso² *m* **1.** LING prefix **2.** TEL (~ (*telefonico*)) area code

pregare [pre·'ga:·re] *vt* **1.** REL to pray to **2.** (*chiedere*) to beg; **ti prego di farmi un favore** please do me a favor; **farsi ~** to play hard to get **3.** (*in frasi di cortesia*) **si prega di non fumare** please do not smoke; **entri, La prego** please come in

pregevole [pre·'dʒe:·vo·le] *agg* **1.** (*oggetto, opera*) valuable **2.** (*persona*) valued

preghiera [pre·'giɛ:·ra] *f* **1.** REL prayer **2.** (*richiesta*) request

pregiarsi [pre·'dʒar·si] *vr poet* **~ di fare qc** to be pleased to do sth

pregiatissimo, -a [pre·'dʒa·'tis·si·mo] *agg form* (*nelle lettere*) Dear

pregiato, -a [pre·'dʒa:·to] *agg* (*vino, tessuto*) fine; (*quadro*) valuable; (*nelle lettere*) Dear

pregio ['prɛ:·dʒo] <-gi> *m* **1.** (*valore*) value **2.** (*qualità*) quality **3.** (*stima*) regard; **tenere in ~ qu** to esteem sb; **farsi ~ di ... +***inf* (*nelle lettere*) to be honored to ...

pregiudicare [pre·dʒu·di·'ka:·re] *vt* (*compromettere*) to prejudice

pregiudicato, -a [pre·dʒu·di·'ka:·to] *m, f* convicted criminal

pregiudiziale [pre·dʒu·dit·'tsia:·le] JUR **I.** *agg* preliminary **II.** *f* precondition

pregiudizio [pre·dʒu·'dit·tsio] <-zi> *m* **1.** (*preconcetto*) prejudice; **avere -i nei confronti di** [*o* **contro**] **qu/qc** to be prejudiced against sb/sth; **senza -i** without prejudice **2.** (*danno*) detriment; **recare ~ a qu** to harm sb

Preg.mo *abbr di* **pregiatissimo** Dear

pregnante [preɲ·'ɲan·te] *agg* (*discorso, frase*) pregnant

pregnanza [preɲ·'ɲan·tsa] *f* (*di discorso, frase*) significance

pregno, -a ['preɲ·ɲo] *agg* **1.** ZOO pregnant **2.** *fig* (*impregnato*) **~ di** full of

prego ['prɛ:·go] *int* **1.** (*come invito*) please; **~?** excuse me? **2.** (*come risposta*) you're welcome

pregustare [pre·gus·'ta:·re] *vt* to look forward to

preistoria [pre·is·'tɔ:·ria] *f* **1.** HIST prehistory **2.** *fig* (*primi passi*) early days *pl*

preistorico, -a [pre·is·'tɔ:·ri·ko] <-ci, -che> *agg scherz, a. fam* prehistoric

prelavaggio [pre·la·'vad·dʒo] <-ggi> *m* prewash

prelevamento [pre·le·va·'men·to] *m* **1.** (*operazione bancaria, somma*) withdrawal **2.** (*di persona, oggetto*) collection

prelevare [pre·le·'va:·re] *vt* **1.** (*in banca*) to withdraw **2.** (*sangue, campione*) to take **3.** (*andare a prendere: merce, persona*) to collect; (*arrestare*) to pick up

prelibato, -a [pre·li·'ba:·to] *agg* (*vino, cibo*) delicious

prelievo [pre·'liɛ:·vo] *m* **1.** (*di sangue, urina*) sample **2.** (*di denaro*) withdrawal

preliminare [pre·li·mi·'na:·re] *agg* (*introduttivo*) preliminary; **corso ~** introductory course

preliminari [pre·li·mi·'na:·ri] *mpl* (*di trattato*) preliminaries *pl*; (*di rapporto sessuale*) foreplay

preludere [pre·'lu:·de·re] <preludo, prelusi, preluso> *vi* **~ a qc** (*preannunciare*) to herald sth

preludio [pre·'lu:·dio] <-i> *m* **1.** (*di guerra, crisi, rivolta*) prelude **2.** (*di poema, discorso*) introduction

prelusi [pre·'lu:·zi] *1. pers sing pass rem di* **preludere**

preluso [pre·'lu:·zo] *pp di* **preludere**

pré-maman [pre ma·'mã] **I.** <-> *m* maternity dress **II.** <inv> *agg* maternity

premarcato, -a [pre·mar·'ka:·to] *agg* (*bollet-*

tino, modulo) preprinted

prematrimoniale [pre·ma·tri·mo·'nia:·le] *agg* (*accordo, contratto*) prenuptial

prematuro, -a [pre·ma·'tu:·ro] I. *agg a. fig* premature II. *m, f* (*neonato*) premature baby

premeditare [pre·me·di·'ta:·re] *vt* to plan

premeditato, -a [pre·me·di·'ta:·to] *agg* premeditated; **omicidio ~** premeditated murder

premeditazione [pre·me·di·tat·'tsio:·ne] *f* premeditation; **con/senza ~** with/without premeditation

premere ['prɛ:·me·re] I. *vt* 1.(*spingere su*) to press; **~ il freno/l'acceleratore** to put one's foot on the brake/the gas 2. *fig* (*incalzare*) to pursue II. *vi* 1.(*esercitare una pressione*) **~ su qc** to press on sth; **~ su qu** *fig* to put pressure on sb 2. *fig* (*gravare*) **~ su qu** to weigh on sb 3. *fig* (*stare a cuore*) to be important

premessa [pre·'mes·sa] *f* 1.(*di discorso*) introductory statement; (*di libro*) introduction 2.(*presupposto*) basis; (*di ragionamento*) premise

premettere [pre·'met·te·re] <irr> *vt* to start by saying; **premesso ciò, ...** that said, ...

premiare [pre·'mia:·re] *vt* (*vincitore*) to give a prize to; (*sforzo, sincerità*) to reward

premiazione [pre·mi·at·'tsio:·ne] *f* prize-giving; **~ degli Oscar** Oscars ceremony

premier ['prəm·jə/'prɛm·jer] <-> *m* (*primo ministro*) premier

première [prə·'mjɛr] <- *o* premières> *f* FILM, COMMEDIA premiere

preminente [pre·mi·'nɛn·te] *agg* (*posizione, personaggio*) prominent

premio¹ ['prɛ:·mio] <-i> *m* 1.(*gener*) prize; (*ricompensa*) reward; **Premio Nobel** Nobel Prize 2.(*indennità*) bonus; **~ di produzione** productivity bonus 3. IN CONTRATTO **~ di assicurazione** insurance premium

> **i** The **Gran Premio d'Italia** usually takes place in Monza on the second Sunday in September. This Italian high point of the Formula 1 year is identified with Team Ferrari, which has millions of supporters in Italy and around the world. Founded in Modena in 1939 by the industrialist Enzo Ferrari, the Ferrari "Casa del cavallino rampante" (House of the rearing stallion) is one of the most successful Formula 1 teams of all time.

premio² <inv> *agg* prize; **viaggio ~** prize trip

premisi *1. pers sing pass rem di* **premettere**

premonitore, -trice [pre·mo·ni·'to:·re] *agg* warning

premonizione [pre·mo·nit·'tsio:·ne] *f* premonition

premunire [pre·mu·'ni:·re] <premunisco> I. *vt* (*predisporre*) to protect II. *vr* **-rsi contro qc** to protect oneself against sth

premunizione [pre·mu·nit·'tsio:·ne] *f* MED premunition

premura [pre·'mu:·ra] *f* 1.(*fretta*) hurry 2.(*cura*) care 3. *pl* (*attenzioni*) kindness

premuroso, -a [pre·mu·'ro:·so] *agg* (*pieno d'attenzioni*) considerate

prenatale [pre·na·'ta:·le] *agg* prenatal

prenatalizio, -a [pre·na·ta·'lit·tsio] <-i, -ie> *agg* pre-Christmas

prendere ['prɛn·de·re] <prendo, presi, preso> I. *vt* 1.(*gener*) to take; **~ qn per mano** to take sb by the hand; **prendi la prima a destra dopo il semaforo** take the first right after the traffic lights; **~ la parola** to speak; **se esci, prenditi le chiavi** if you go out, take your keys; **per andare a lavorare, prendo l'autobus** I take the bus to work; **qualcuno mi ha preso la penna** someone's taken my pen; **-rsi un giorno di ferie** to take a day off; **-rsi una vacanza** to take a vacation 2.(*procurarsi, ricevere, derivare*) to get; **devo uscire a ~ il pane** I have to go out and get the bread; **~ in affitto** to rent 3.(*malattia*) to catch 4.(*al bar, al ristorante*) to have; **cosa prendi?** what would you like?; **prendo solo un caffè** I'll just have a coffee 5.(*catturare, sorprendere*) to catch; **~ qu alla sprovvista** to catch sb unawares 6.(*ritirare*) to pick up 7.(*misurare*) to measure; **~ le misure** (*di persona, oggetto*) to measure 8.(*far pagare*) to charge 9.(*assumere*) to take on; **-rsi cura di qu** to take care of sb 10.(*spazio*) to take up; **questa traduzione mi ha preso tutto il pomeriggio** this translation took me all afternoon 11.(*scambiare*) **~ qu per qu** to take sb for sb 12.(*loc*) **~ appunti** to take notes; **~ aria** (*persona*) to get some fresh air; **~ qu con le buone** *fam* to be nice to sb; **~ una decisione** to make a decision; **~ forma** to take shape; **~ fuoco** to catch fire; **~ in giro qn** to make fun of sb; **~ piede** to catch on; **~ posizione** to take sides; **~ il sole** to sunbathe; **~ sonno** to go to sleep; **~ qu sul serio** to take sb seriously; **~ tempo** to play for time; **~ qu in braccio** to take sb in one's arms; **prender(se)le** *fam* to get a licking; **prendersela** (*offendersi*) to get upset; **prendersela con qu** to get angry with sb; **prendersela comoda** [*o* con comodo] *fam* to take it easy II. *vi* 1.(*piante*) to take 2.(*fuoco*) to catch 3.(*colla, cemento*) to set 4.(*avviarsi*) to go; **~ per qc** to go across sth 5.(*cominciare*) **~ a fare qc** to start to do sth 6.(*venire in mente*) **ma cosa ti prende?** what got into you? III. *vr:* **-rsi** 1.(*azzuffarsi*) **-rsi a pugni/calci** to punch/kick each other 2.(*aggrapparsi*) **-rsi a qu/qc** to grab hold of sb/sth 3.(*assumersi*) to take on

prendisole [pren·di·'so:·le] <-> *m* sundress

prenotare [pre·no·'ta:·re] I. *vt* (*posto, tavolo, camera*) to reserve II. *vr* **-rsi per qc** to put one's name down for sth

prenotazione [pre·no·tat·'tsio:·ne] *f* reservation

preoccupante [pre·ok·ku·'pan·te] *agg* worrying

preoccupare [pre·ok·ku·'pa:·re] I. *vt* (*causare apprensione a*) to worry II. *vr* **-rsi** (**per qu/ qc**) to worry (about sb/sth); **-rsi di fare qc** to think to do sth

preoccupazione [pre·ok·ku·pat·'tsio:·ne] *f* worry

preolimpico, -a [pre·o·'lim·pi·ko] <-ci, -che> *agg* SPORT pre-Olympic

preordinato, -a [pre·or·di·'na:·to] *agg* preordained

prepagamento [pre·pa·ga·'men·to] *m* prepayment

prepagato, -a [pre·pa·'ga:·to] *agg* prepaid

preparare [pre·pa·'ra:·re] I. *vt* 1. (*letto, pranzo, lista*) to make; (*stanza*) to get ready; ~ **la tavola** to set the table; ~ **le valigie** to pack one's bags 2. (*piano, sorpresa, persona*) to prepare; ~ **il terreno** *fig* to prepare the ground II. *vr* 1. (*predisporsi*) **-rsi a qc** to prepare oneself for sth; **-rsi a fare qc** to get ready to do sth 2. (*vestirsi*) to get ready

preparativi [pre·pa·ra·'ti:·vi] *mpl* (*di viaggio, festa*) preparations

preparato [pre·pa·'ra:·to] *m* (*farmaco*) preparation

preparato, -a *agg* 1. (*letto, bagagli*) ready 2. (*per interrogazione*) prepared

preparazione [pre·pa·rat·'tsio:·ne] *f* 1. (*attività*) preparation; (*di atleta*) training; **la ~ agli esami** reviewing for the exams 2. (*conoscenze*) knowledge; ~ **generale** general knowledge

prepensionamento [pre·pen·sio·na·'men·to] *m* early retirement

preponderante [pre·pon·de·'ran·te] *agg* predominant

preponderanza [pre·pon·de·'ran·tsa] *f* predominance

preporre [pre·'por·re] <irr> *vt* 1. (*anteporre*) to place before; (*mettere a capo*); ~ **qu a qc** to put sb in charge of sth 2. *fig* (*privilegiare*) ~ **qc a qc** to put sth before sth

preposizione [pre·po·zit·'tsio:·ne] *f* preposition

preposto *pp di* **preporre**

prepotente [pre·po·'tɛn·te] I. *agg* 1. (*persona*) domineering 2. (*bisogno, impulso*) overwhelming II. *mf* bully

prepotenza [pre·po·'tɛn·tsa] *f* 1. (*caratteristica*) overbearingness 2. (*atto*) bullying

preprint ['pri:·print] <- *o* preprints> *m* preprint

prerogativa [pre·ro·ga·'ti:·va] *f* 1. (*caratteristica propria*) quality 2. (*privilegio*) prerogative

preromanticismo [pre·ro·man·ti·'tʃiz·mo] *m* pre-Romanticism

presa ['pre:·sa] *f* 1. (*atto del prendere*) grip 2. (*di città, postazione*) taking 3. (*di cemento, colla*) setting 4. (*del gas, dell'acqua*) point; ~ **d'aria** air intake; ~ (**di corrente**) outlet 5. (*per le pentole*) oven mitt 6. (*di sale, pepe, tabacco*) pinch 7. (*loc*) ~ **di posizione** *fig*

stance; ~ **di possesso** taking possession; ~ **in giro** *fam* joke; **essere alle -e con qc** to be struggling with sth

presagio [pre·'za:·dʒo] <-gi> *m* 1. (*segno premonitore*) omen 2. (*presentimento*) premonition

presagire [pre·za·'dʒi:·re] <presagisco> *vt* 1. (*annunciare*) to herald 2. (*presentire*) to have a premonition of 3. (*prevedere*) to foresee

presalario [pre·sa·'la:·rio] *m* grant

presbite ['prɛz·bi·te] I. *agg* far-sighted II. *mf* far-sighted person

presbiterio [prez·bi·'tɛ:·rio] <-i> *m* presbytery

prescegliere [preʃ·'ʃeʎ·ʎe·re] <irr> *vt* to select

presciistico, -a [pre·ʃi·'is·ti·ko] <-ci, -che> *agg* (*esercizio, ginnastica*) pre-ski

prescindere [preʃ·'ʃin·de·re] <irr> *vi* ~ **da qc** to leave sth aside; **a ~ da** regardless of

prescolare [pre·sko·'la:·re] *agg* **età ~** pre-school age

prescolastico, -a [pre·sko·'las·ti·ko] <-ci, -che> *agg* preschool

prescrivere [pres·'kri:·ve·re] <irr> *vt* to prescribe

prescrizione [pres·krit·'tsio:·ne] *f* 1. (*regola*) rule 2. JUR, MED prescription

preselezione [pre·se·let·'tsio:·ne] *f* 1. (*di atleta, candidato*) shortlisting 2. TEC preselector

presentare [pre·zen·'ta:·re] I. *vt* 1. (*mostrare: documento, passaporto*) to show; (*sottoporre: domanda, proposta*) to submit 2. (*far conoscere*) ~ **qu a qu** to introduce sb to sb 3. (*comportare*) to offer 4. (*prodotto*) to present 5. *form* (*saluti*) to give 6. (*programma televisivo*) to host II. *vr:* **-rsi** 1. (*andare*) to go 2. (*apparire*) to appear; **-rsi bene/male** to make a good/bad impression 3. (*farsi conoscere*) to introduce oneself 4. (*occasione*) to present itself; (*difficoltà*) to come up

presentatore, -trice [pre·zen·ta·'to:·re] *m, f* (*di spettacolo*) host

presentazione [pre·zen·tat·'tsio:·ne] *f* 1. (*di passaporto, biglietto*) production; (*di domanda, ricorso*) submission; (*di candidato*) nomination 2. (*di modello, merce*) presentation 3. (*di persona, scritto, discorso*) introduction; **fare le -i** to do the introductions; **lettera di ~** letter of introduction 4. (*di film*) trailer

presente [pre·'zɛn·te] I. *agg* 1. (*gener*) present; **aver ~ qu/qc** *fig* to know sb/sth; **far ~ qc a qu** *fig* to point sth out to sb; **tener ~ qu/ qc** *fig* to bear sb/sth in mind; **il tempo ~** the present time 2. (*questo*) this II. *mf* those present III. *m* 1. (*tempo*) present 2. LING present (tense); **al ~** in the present 3. *form* (*dono*) gift IV. *f* (*lettera*) **con la ~ Le comunichiamo ...** we hereby inform you ...

presentimento [pre·sen·ti·'men·to] *m* feeling

presentire [pre·sen·'ti:·re] *vt* to have a presentiment of

presenza [pre·'zɛn·tsa] *f* 1. (*in un luogo, esis-*

tenza) presence; **in ~ di** in the presence of; **fare atto di ~** to put in an appearance **2.** (*aspetto*) **di bella ~** neat-looking

presenziare [pre·zen·'tsia:·re] *vt, vi* **~** (**a**) **qc** to be present at sth

presepe, presepio [pre·'zε:·pe] <-i> *m* nativity scene

preservare [pre·ser·'va:·re] *vt* **~ qu/qc da qc** to protect sb/sth from sth

preservativo [pre·ser·va·'ti:·vo] *m* condom

presi ['pre:·si] *1. pers sing pass rem di* **prendere**

preside ['prε:·si·de] *mf* (*di scuola*) principal; (*di facoltà*) dean

presidente, -essa [pre·si·'dεn·te, pre·si·den·'tes·sa] *m, f* POL president; JUR presiding judge; **Presidente della Regione** regional president; **Presidente della Repubblica** President of the Republic; **Presidente del Consiglio** (**dei ministri**) Prime Minister

> ℹ️ The **Presidente del Consiglio**, the Italian Prime Minister, is the head of the government. He or she proposes ministerial candidates to the **Presidente della Repubblica** and is responsible for those appointed. He or she is appointed by the **Presidente della Repubblica** after a vote by party leaders, former heads of state, **Presidente della Camera**, and the **Presidente del Senato** (the speakers of the two chambers). The **Presidente della Repubblica** is the head of state. He or she must be an Italian citizen and at least 50 years old. He or she holds office for seven years.

presidenza [pre·si·'dεn·tsa] *f* **1.** (*carica di presidente*) presidency **2.** (*sede*) president's office **3.** (*personale*) president's staff

presidenziale [pre·si·den·'tsia:·le] *agg* presidential

presidenzialismo [pre·si·den·tsia·'liz·mo] *m* (*sistema*) presidentialism

presidiare [pre·si·'dia:·re] *vt* **1.** (*città, zona, ingresso*) to guard **2.** *fig* (*difendere*) to defend

presidio [pre·'si:·dio] <-i> *m* **1.** (*truppe*) garrison **2.** (*occupazione*) occupation **3.** MED **-i ospedalieri** hospital facilities; **-i medici e chirurgici** medical and surgical supplies

presiedere [pre·'siε:·de·re] <presiedo, presiedei *o* presiedetti, presieduto> I. *vt* (*riunione, assemblea*) to chair II. *vi* **~ a qc** (*essere a capo di*) to be in charge of sth

preso ['pre:·so] *pp di* **prendere**

press agent ['pres·ei·dʒənt/'pres·a·dʒənt] <*o* press agents> *mf* press agent

pressante [pres·'san·te] *agg* (*bisogno*) pressing

pressappoco, press'a poco [pres·sap·'pɔ:·ko] *avv* about

pressare [pres·'sa:·re] *vt* **1.** TEC to press **2.** *fig*

(*incalzare*) to pressure

pressi ['prεs·si] *mpl* **nei -i di** near

pressing ['prεs·sin] <-> *m* SPORT pressure

pressione [pres·'sio:·ne] *f* pressure; **~ atmosferica** atmospheric pressure; **pentola a ~** pressure cooker; **~ tributaria** tax burden; **far ~ su qu** to put pressure on sb; **essere sotto ~** to be under pressure; **~** (**sanguigna**) blood pressure; **avere la ~ alta/bassa** to have high/low blood pressure

presso ['prεs·so] I. *avv* nearby II. *prep* **1.** (*vicino a*) near **2.** (*azienda, negozio, ufficio*) at; (*a casa di*) with; (*nell'ambito di*) among **3.** (*nelle lettere*) care of

pressoché [pres·so·'ke] *avv* (*quasi*) nearly

pressofusione [pres·so·fu·'zio:·ne] *f* TEC die-casting

pressurizzare [pres·su·rid·'dza:·re] *vt* to pressurize

pressurizzazione [pres·su·rid·dzat·'tsio:·ne] *f* pressurization

prestabilire [pres·ta·bi·'li:·re] <prestabilisco> *vt* to settle in advance

prestabilito, -a [pres·ta·bi·'li:·to] *agg* (*prefissato*) prearranged; **una data -a** a prearranged date

prestampato [pres·tam·'pa:·to] *m* (*modulo*) form

prestampato, -a *agg* (*modulo*) preprinted

prestanome [pres·ta·'no:·me] <-> *mf* front man

prestante [pres·'tan·te] *agg* good-looking

prestanza [pres·'tan·tsa] *f* presence

prestare [pres·'ta:·re] I. *vt* **1.** (*dare in prestito*) to lend **2.** *fig* (*dare*) to give; **~ attenzione** (**a qc**) to pay attention (to sth); **~ fede a qc** to believe sth; **~ giuramento** to take an oath; **~ orecchio a qc** to listen to sth II. *vr:* **-rsi 1.** (*offrirsi*) to offer; (*acconsentire*) to agree **2.** (*essere adatto*) **-rsi a** [*o* **per**] **qc** to be appropriate for sth

prestatore, -trice [pres·ta·'to:·re] *m, f* **~ di lavoro** [*o* **d'opera**] employee

prestazione [pres·tat·'tsio:·ne] *f* **1.** (*di atleta, squadra*) performance; **-i** (*di macchina*) performance **2.** (*servizio*) service

prestigiatore, -trice [pres·ti·dʒa·'to:·re] *m, f* (*illusionista*) conjurer

prestigio [pres·'ti:·dʒo] <-gi> *m* **1.** (*fama*) prestige **2.** (*illusione*) **giochi di ~** conjuring tricks

prestigioso, -a [pres·ti·'dʒo:·so] *agg* prestigious

prestito ['prεs·ti·to] *m* **1.** (*somma*) loan **2.** (*atto*) **dare in** [*o* **a**] **~ qc** to lend sth; **prendere in** [*o* **a**] **~ qc** to borrow sth

presto ['prεs·to] I. *avv* **1.** (*fra breve*) soon; **a ~!** see you soon! **2.** (*in fretta*) quickly; **fare ~** to hurry up; **al più ~** as soon as possible; **è ~ detto/fatto** it's easily said/done **3.** (*prima del tempo, di buon'ora*) early II. *m* MUS presto

presumere [pre·'zu:·me·re/pre·'su:·me·re] <presumo, presunsi, presunto> *vt* **1.** (*sup-*

porre) to presume **2.** (*avere la pretesa di*) to think

presumibile [pre·su·'mi:·bi·le] *agg* likely

presunsi [pre·'zun·si] *1. pers sing pass rem di* **presumere**

presunto, -a [pre·'zun·to/pre·'sun·to] I. *pp di* **presumere** II. *agg* presumed

presuntuoso, -a [pre·zun·tu·'o:·so] *agg* presumptuous

presunzione [pre·zun·'tsio:·ne/pre·sun·'tsio:·ne] *f* **1.** (*arroganza*) presumptuousness **2.** (*congettura*) presumption

presupporre [pre·sup·'por·re] <irr> *vt* **1.** (*immaginare*) to suppose **2.** (*implicare*) to presuppose

presupposizione [pre·sup·po·zit·'tsio:·ne] *f* (*congettura*) supposition

presupposto [pre·sup·'pos·to] *m* condition

presupposto, -a I. *pp di* **presupporre** II. *agg* supposed

prêt-à-porter ['prɛt a por·'te] <-> *m* **1.** (*settore*) ready-to-wear sector **2.** (*abito*) ready-to-wear clothes

prete ['prɛ:·te] *m* priest; **scherzo da ~** *fam* dirty trick

pretendente [pre·ten·'dɛn·te] *mf* **1.** (*aspirante*) **~ al trono** pretender to the throne **2.** (*corteggiatore*) suitor

pretendere [pre·'tɛn·de·re] <irr> *vt* **1.** (*esigere*) to demand **2.** (*presumere*) to presume **3.** (*affermare*) to claim

pretenzioso, -a [pre·ten·'tsio:·so] *agg* pretentious

preterintenzionale [pre·te·rin·ten·tsio·'na:·le] *agg* involuntary; **omicidio ~** involuntary manslaughter

pretesa [pre·'te:·sa] *f* (*richiesta, presunzione*) claim; (*esigenza eccessiva*) demand; **avere la ~ di fare qc** to expect to do sth; **senza -e** (*persona, arredamento*) unpretentious

pretesi *1. pers sing pass rem di* **pretendere**

preteso *pp di* **pretendere**

pretesto [pre·'tɛs·to] *m* **1.** (*scusa*) excuse; **con il ~ di ...** with the excuse of ... **2.** (*occasione*) chance

pretestuosità [pre·tes·tuo·si·'ta] <-> *f* spuriousness

pretestuoso, -a [pre·tes·tu·'ɔ:·so] *agg* (*discorso, ragionamento*) spurious

pretore [pre·'to:·re] *m* **1.** JUR magistrate **2.** HIST praetor

pretura [pre·'tu:·ra] *f* **1.** JUR (*carica*) magistracy; (*sede*) county court **2.** HIST praetorship

prevalente [pre·va·'lɛn·te] *agg* (*caratteristica, colore*) predominant; (*opinione*) prevailing

prevalentemente [pre·va·len·te·'men·te] *avv* predominantly

prevalenza [pre·va·'lɛn·tsa] *f* **1.** (*maggioranza*) majority **2.** (*superiorità*) superiority

prevalere [pre·va·ˇle:·re] <irr> *vi* **essere** *o* **avere 1.** (*predominare*) to prevail **2.** (*vincere*) **~ su qu** to prevail over sb

prevaricare [pre·va·ri·'ka:·re] *vi* (*abusare*) to abuse one's power

prevaricazione [pre·va·ri·kat·'tsio:·ne] *f* (*uso della forza*) abuse of power

prevedere [pre·ve·'de:·re] <irr> *vt* **1.** (*anticipare*) to foresee; (*programmare*) to plan **2.** (*prescrivere*) to provide for

prevedibile [pre·ve·'di:·bi·le] *agg* foreseeable

prevendita [pre·'ven·di·ta] *f* advance sale

prevenire [pre·ve·'ni:·re] <irr> *vt* **1.** (*anticipare*) to anticipate **2.** (*impedire*) to prevent **3.** (*avvertire*) to warn

preventivo [pre·ven·'ti:·vo] *m* estimate

preventivo, -a *agg* preventive; **carcere ~** custody

prevenuto, -a [pre·ve·'nu:·to] I. *pp di* **prevenire** II. *agg* **essere ~ contro qu/qc** to be prejudiced against sb/sth

prevenzione [pre·ven·'tsio:·ne] *f* **1.** (*provvedimenti*) prevention; **~ degli infortuni sul lavoro** prevention of accidents in the workplace **2.** (*pregiudizio*) prejudice

previdente [pre·vi·'dɛn·te] *agg* prudent

previdenza [pre·vi·'dɛn·tsa] *f* **1.** (*assistenza*) welfare system; **~ sociale** welfare **2.** (*caratteristica*) foresight

previdenziale [pre·vi·den·'tsia:·le] *agg* (*contributo*) welfare

previdi *1. pers sing pass rem di* **prevedere**

previo, -a ['prɛ:·vio] <-i, -ie> *agg* ADM **~ pagamento** on payment

previsione [pre·vi·'zio:·ne] *f* (*pronostico*) METEO prediction; **le -i del tempo** the weather forecast

previsto *pp di* **prevedere**

preziosità [pret·tsio·si·'ta] <-> *f* **1.** (*valore*) value **2.** (*eleganza*) refinement

prezioso, -a [pret·'tsio:·so] I. *agg* **1.** (*oggetto*) valuable; (*pietra, metallo*) precious **2.** (*stile, modi*) refined II. *m, f fam* **fare il ~** to play hard to get

prezzemolo [pret·'tse:·mo·lo] *m* parsley; **essere come il ~** *fig* to turn up like a bad penny

prezzo ['prɛt·tso] *m* **1.** *a. fig* (*valore*) price **2.** (*cartellino*) price tag; **~ di favore** special price; **~ di listino** list price; **a ~ di grossi** [*o* **grandi**] **sacrifici** at the cost of great sacrifices; **a metà ~** half price; **a qualunque ~** *fig* at any price; **pagare qc a caro ~** *fig* to pay dearly for sth; **non avere ~** to be priceless; **tirare sul ~** to haggle over the price

PRI *m abbr di* **Partito Repubblicano Italiano** *former Italian political party*

prigione [pri·'dʒo:·ne] *f* **1.** (*carcere, ambiente opprimente*) prison **2.** *fig* (*stanza buia*) dungeon

prigionia [pri·dʒo·'ni:·a] <-ie> *f* imprisonment

prigioniero, -a [pri·dʒo·'niɛ:·ro] I. *agg* **1.** (*carcerato*) captive; **tenere/fare ~ qu** to keep/take sb prisoner **2.** *fig* **essere ~ di qc** to be a prisoner of sth II. *m, f* prisoner; **~ di guerra** prisoner of war

prima¹ ['pri:·ma] *avv* **1.** (*in precedenza, nello*

spazio) before; (*più presto*) earlier; **tre giorni** ~ three days earlier; **come** ~ as before; **quanto** ~ as soon as possible; **ne so quanto** ~ I'm none the wiser; ~ **di** before; ~ **che** +*conj*, ~ **di** +*inf*before; ~ **o poi** sooner or later **2.** (*per prima cosa*) first; ~ **di tutto** first of all; ~ **il dovere, poi il piacere** duty first, pleasure later

prima² *f* **1.** THEAT, FILM premiere; ~ **tv** TV premiere **2.** MOT (*classe*) first **3.** (*scuola: elementare*) first grade; (*media*) sixth grade; (*superiore*) tenth grade **4.** SPORT (*nella scherma*) prime

primario, -a [pri·'ma:·rio] <-i, -ie> **I.** *agg* primary; **scuola -a** elementary school; **era -a** Paleozoic Era **II.** *m, f* **1.** (*medico*) chief physician **2.** (*settore economico*) primary sector

primati [pri·'ma:·ti] *mpl* primates

primato [pri·'ma:·to] *m* **1.** SPORT record **2.** (*superiorità*) primacy

primavera [pri·ma·'vɛ:·ra] *f* **1.** (*stagione*) spring; **in** ~ in spring **2.** *scherz* (*anno*) year

primaverile [pri·ma·ve·'ri:·le] *agg* (*clima, abito*) spring

primeggiare [pri·med·'dʒa:·re] *vi* (*essere superiore*) to excel

primitivo, -a [pri·mi·'ti:·vo] **I.** *agg* **1.** (*originario*) original **2.** (*rudimentale*) rudimentary; (*rozzo*) uncouth **II.** *m, f* **1.** (*abitante preistorico*) primitive **2.** *pej* (*persona rozza*) uncouth person

primizia [pri·'mit·tsia] <-ie> *f* **1.** (*frutto*) early fruit; (*ortaggio*) early vegetable **2.** (*notizia*) scoop

primo ['pri:·mo] *m* **1.** (*primo giorno*) first; **il** ~ **dell'anno** New Year's Day; **il** ~ **maggio** the first of May **2.** *pl* **ai -i di maggio** at the beginning of May; **sui -i del Novecento** around the beginning of the twentieth century **3.** CULIN first course; **per** ~ **prenderò il risotto** I'll have the risotto for my first course

primo, -a **I.** *agg* **1.** (*gener*) first; **Alessandro** ~ Alexander the First; **arrivare** ~ to come first; **di prim'ordine** first-rate; **di -a qualità** top-quality; **il** ~ **cittadino** (*presidente della Repubblica*) the President of the Republic; (*sindaco*) the mayor **2.** (*iniziale*) initial; **nelle -e ore del mattino** in the early hours of the morning; **in un** ~ **tempo** [*o momento*] at first; **sulle -e** at first; **a -a vista** at first sight **3.** (*principale*) main; **in** ~ **luogo** in the first place; **di** ~ **piano** prominent **II.** *m, f* (*di successione*) first (person); **il** ~ **che capita** the first person to come along; **il** ~ **della classe** first in the class; **per** ~ first

primogenito, -a [pri·mo·'dʒɛ:·ni·to] **I.** *m, f* firstborn **II.** *agg* firstborn

primordi [pri·'mɔr·di] *mpl* beginnings

primordiale [pri·mor·'dia:·le] *agg* **1.** (*dei primordi*) early; (*originario*) original **2.** (*fondamentale*) **di** ~ **importanza** of fundamental importance; **istinto** ~ basic instinct **3.** *fig* (*antiquato*) primitive

primula ['pri:·mu·la] *f* primula

principale [prin·tʃi·'pa:·le] **I.** *agg* **1.** (*più importante*) main **2.** LING (*proposizione*) principal **II.** *mf* (*capo*) boss

principalmente [prin·tʃi·pal·'men·te] *avv* mainly

principato [prin·tʃi·'pa:·to] *m* **1.** (*stato*) principality **2.** (*governo*) reign

principe¹ ['prin·tʃi·pe] *m* prince; **il** ~ **azzurro** Prince Charming; **vivere come un** ~ to live like a king

principe² <inv> *agg* **edizione** ~ first edition

principesco, -a [prin·tʃi·'pes·ko] <-schi, -sche> *agg* princely

principessa [prin·tʃi·'pes·sa] *f* princess

principiante [prin·tʃi·'pian·te] *mf* beginner

principio [prin·'tʃi:·pio] <-i> *m* **1.** (*inizio*) beginning; **da** [*o* **in**] [*o* **al**] ~ at first; **(sin) dal** ~ (right) from the start **2.** (*origine*) origin **3.** *pl* (*concetto fondamentale*) principles **4.** (*concetto, norma etica*) principle; **una questione di** ~ a matter of principle; **per** ~ on principle; **in linea di** ~ in principle

priore [pri·'o:·re] *m* REL prior

priorità [pri·o·ri·'ta] <-> *f* priority

prioritario, -a [pri·o·ri·'ta:·rio] <-i, -ie> *agg* priority; **posta -a** first-class mail

privacy ['prai·va·si/'prai·va·si] <-> *f* privacy; **legge sulla** ~ privacy law

privare [pri·'va:·re] **I.** *vt* ~ **qu di qc** to deprive sb of sth **II.** *vr* **-rsi di qc** to go without sth

privatizzare [pri·va·tid·'dza:·re] *vt* to privatize

privatizzazione [pri·va·tid·dzat·'tsio:·ne] *f* FIN privatization

privato [pri·'va:·to] *m* **1.** (*sfera privata*) private life **2.** (*settore economico*) private sector

privato, -a **I.** *agg* private; **in** ~ in private **II.** *m, f* (*semplice cittadino*) private citizen

privazione [pri·vat·'tsio:·ne] *f* **1.** (*rinuncia*) privation **2.** (*azione*) loss

privilegiare [pri·vi·le·'dʒa:·re] *vt* **1.** (*favorire*) to favor **2.** (*preferire*) to prefer

privilegiato, -a [pri·vi·le·'dʒa:·to] **I.** *agg* **1.** (*trattamento*) preferential **2.** (*persona*) fortunate **3.** (*posizione, condizione*) favorable **II.** *m, f* privileged person

privilegio [pri·vi·'lɛ:·dʒo] <-gi> *m* **1.** (*onore*) privilege; **avere il** ~ **di ...** *form* to have the honor to ... **2.** (*vantaggio*) advantage

privo, -a ['pri:·vo] *agg* ~ **di** without; ~ **di sensi** unconscious

pro [prɔ] **I.** *prep* for **II.** <-> *m* (*utilità*) **a che** ~? what's the use?; **il** ~ **ed il contro** the pros and cons

probabile [pro·'ba:·bi·le] *agg* probable

probabilità [pro·ba·bi·li·'ta] <-> *f* (*caratteristica*) probability; (*possibilità*) chance; **avere una** ~ **su cento** to have a hundred to one chance; **con molta** [*o* **tutta**] [*o* **ogni**] ~ in all probability

probabilmente [pro·ba·bil·'men·te] *avv* probably

problema [pro·'blɛ:·ma] <-i> *m* (*gener*) prob-

P

lem; (*quesito*) question; **non c'è** ~ it's no problem

problematica [pro·ble·'ma:·ti·ka] <-che> *f* problems *pl*

problematicità [pro·ble·ma·ti·tʃi·'ta] <-> *f* problematic nature

problematico, -a [pro·ble·'ma:·ti·ko] <-ci, -che> *agg* (*situazione, questione*) problematic; (*persona*) difficult

proboscide [pro·'bɔʃ·ʃi·de] *f* (*di elefante*) trunk

procacciare [pro·kat·'tʃa:·re] *vt* (*procurare*) to get

procace [pro·'ka:·tʃe] *agg* (*provocante*) provocative

pro capite [pro·'ka:·pi·te] *avv* per capita

procedere [pro·'tʃɛ:·de·re] <procedo, procedei *o* procedetti, proceduto> *vi* 1. *essere* (*veicolo, persona*) to proceed 2. *avere* (*continuare*) to continue 3. *essere* (*affari, attività*) to go 4. *avere* (*dare inizio*) ~ **a qc** to proceed with sth 5. *avere* JUR ~ **contro qu** to start proceedings against sb

procedimento [pro·tʃe·di·'men·to] *m* 1. (*metodo*) process 2. JUR proceedings *pl*

procedura [pro·tʃe·'du:·ra] *f* procedure

procedurale [pro·tʃe·du·'ra:·le] *agg* JUR procedural

processare [pro·tʃes·'sa:·re] *vt* (*sottoporre a processo*) to try

processione [pro·tʃes·'sio:·ne] *f* REL procession

processo [pro·'tʃɛs·so] *m* 1. JUR lawsuit; ~ **civile** civil suit; ~ **penale** criminal trial 2. (*successione di fenomeni, metodo*) process

processore *m* COMPUT processor

processuale [pro·tʃes·su·'a:·le] *agg* (*atto*) trial; (*spese*) legal

procinto [pro·'tʃin·to] *m* **in ~ di ... +** *inf* on the point of ...

procione [pro·'tʃo:·ne] *m* raccoon

proclamare [pro·kla·'ma:·re] *vt* (*dichiarare ufficialmente*) to declare; ~ **lo sciopero generale** to declare a general strike

proclamazione [pro·kla·mat·'tsio:·ne] *f* (*dichiarazione ufficiale*) declaration

procrastinare [pro·kras·ti·'na:·re] *vt* form (*rimandare: pagamento*) to defer; (*decisione*) to postpone

procreare [pro·kre·'a:·re] *vt* to procreate

procreazione [pro·kre·at·'tsio:·ne] *f* procreation

procura [pro·'ku:·ra] *f* 1. JUR (*delega*) power of attorney; **matrimonio per ~** marriage by proxy 2. (*ufficio*) district attorney's office

procurare [pro·ku·'ra:·re] *vt* 1. (*fare avere*) to get; **procurarsi qc** to get oneself sth 2. (*causare*) to cause

procuratore, -trice [pro·ku·ra·'to:·re] *m, f* 1. (*magistrato*) prosecutor; **Procuratore Generale** Attorney General; ~ **della Repubblica** district attorney 2. (*laureato in legge*) ~ (**legale**) lawyer

prodezza [pro·'det·tsa] *f* 1. (*coraggio*) valor 2. (*impresa*) feat

prodigarsi [pro·di·'gar·si] *vr* ~ **per qu** to do one's best for sb

prodigio¹ [pro·'di:·dʒo] <-gi> *m* 1. (*gener*) marvel 2. (*persona*) prodigy

prodigio² <inv> *agg* marvelous; **bambino ~** child prodigy

prodigioso, -a [pro·di·'dʒo:·so] *agg* (*straordinario: fatto, evento*) marvelous; (*eccezionale: memoria, cultura*) prodigious

prodigo, -a ['prɔ:·di·go] <-ghi, -ghe> *agg* 1. *pej* (*dissipatore*) prodigal; **il figliol ~** the prodigal son 2. *fig* (*generoso*) ~ **di qc** generous with sth

prodotto¹ [pro·'dot·to] *pp di* **produrre**

prodotto² *m* 1. (*gener*) product; (*della terra*) produce; ~ **alimentare** foodstuff; **-i di bellezza** beauty products 2. (*risultato*) result; ~ **interno lordo** gross domestic product; ~ **nazionale lordo** gross national product

produco *1. pers sing pr di* **produrre**

produrre [pro·'dur·re] <produco, produssi, prodotto> I. *vt* 1. (*gener*) to produce 2. (*opera*) to write 3. (*causare*) to cause II. *vr:* **-rsi** 1. THEAT to appear 2. (*formarsi*) to develop

produttività [pro·dut·ti·vi·'ta] <-> *f* (*capacità produttiva*) productivity

produttivo, -a [pro·dut·'ti:·vo] *agg* 1. (*albero, investimento, atteggiamento*) productive; (*terreno*) fertile 2. (*metodo, ciclo*) production

produttore, -trice [pro·dut·'to:·re] I. *m, f* producer II. *agg* producing; **i paesi -i di cacao** the cocoa-producing countries

produzione [pro·dut·'tsio:·ne] *f* 1. (*gener*) production; (*di frutta, ortaggi*) yield; ~ **in serie** mass production; **costo di ~** manufacturing cost 2. (*letteraria, artistica*) work

profanare [pro·fa·'na:·re] *vt* (*chiesa, tomba, ricordo*) to profane

profanazione [pro·fa·nat·'tsio:·ne] *f* (*di chiesa, tomba, ricordo*) profanation

profano [pro·'fa:·no] *m* (*cosa non sacra*) profane

profano, -a I. *agg* profane II. *m, f* (*persona non competente*) **essere un ~** to be no expert

proferire [pro·fe·'ri:·re] <proferisco> *vt* 1. (*parola, frase*) to utter 2. (*giuramento*) to take; (*voto*) to make

professare [pro·fes·'sa:·re] I. *vt* 1. (*gratitudine, amore*) to declare 2. (*opinione*) to make known; (*religione*) to profess **per la politica** II. *vr:* **-rsi** (*dichiararsi*) to declare oneself; **si professa mio amico** he claims to be my friend

professionale [pro·fes·sio·'na:·le] *agg* (*gener*) professional; (*scuola, formazione*) vocational

professionalità [pro·fes·sio·na·li·'ta] <-> *f* (*competenza*) professionalism

professione [pro·fes·'sio:·ne] *f* profession; **libera ~** profession; ~ **di fede** profession of faith

professionismo [pro·fes·sio·'niz·mo] *m* SPORT

professionalism

professionista [pro·fes·sio·'nis·ta] <-i *m*, -e *f*> *mf* professional; **libero** ~ professional person

professionistico, **-a** [pro·fes·sio·'nis·ti·ko] <-ci, -che> *agg* SPORT professional

professore, **-essa** [pro·fes·'so::re, pro·fes·so·'res·sa] *m*, *f* (*di scuola*) teacher; (*di università*) professor; ~ **a contratto** professor without tenure; ~ **di ruolo** tenured professor

profeta, **-tessa** [pro·'fɛ::ta, pro·fe·'tes·sa] <-i, -esse> *m*, *f* prophet

profetico, **-a** [pro·'fɛ::ti·ko] <-ci, -che> *agg* prophetic

profetizzare [pro·fe·tid·'dza::re] I. *vt* to prophesy II. *vi* to prophesy

profezia [pro·fet·'tsi::a] <-ie> *f* prophecy

proficuo, **-a** [pro·'fi::kuo] *agg* (*attività*) profitable

profilare [pro·fi·'la::re] I. *vt* 1. TEC (*sbarra, trave*) to profile 2. (*orlare: tovaglia, vestito*) to edge II. *vr:* -**rsi** (*essere imminente*) to loom

profilassi [pro·fi·'las·si] <-> *f* prophylaxis

profilato [pro·fi·'la::to] *m* section bar

profilato, **-a** *agg* 1. (*sbarra, trave*) profiled 2. (*abito, gonna*) trimmed

profilattico [pro·fi·'lat·ti·ko] <-ci> *m* condom

profilattico, **-a** <-ci, -che> *agg* (*metodo*) prophylactic

profilo [pro·'fi::lo] *m* (*gener*) profile; (*di montagna, edificio*) outline; **di** ~ (*persona*) in profile; **sotto il** ~ ... from the point of view of

profiterole [prɔ·fi·'trɔl] <-> *m* profiterole

profittare [pro·fit·'ta::re] *vi v.* **approfittare**

profittatore, **-trice** [pro·fit·ta·'to::re] *m*, *f v.* **approfittatore**

profitto [pro·'fit·to] *m* 1. (*giovamento*) advantage; **trarre** ~ **da qc** to benefit from sth 2. (*negli studi, nel lavoro*) progress 3. (*utile*) profit

profondamente [pro·fon·'da·men·te] *avv* (*molto*) deeply; **dormire** ~ to sleep soundly

profondersi [pro·'fon·der·si] *vr* ~ **in qc** to be lavish with sth

profondità [pro·fon·di·'ta] <-> *f* depth

profondo [pro·'fon·do] *m* 1. (*del mare*) depth 2. (*del mare*) heart of hearts; **dal** ~ **del cuore** from the bottom of one's heart

profondo, **-a** *agg* 1. (*gener*) deep 2. (*pensiero, delusione, rispetto*) profound

proforma, **pro forma** [pro·'for·ma, prɔ 'for·ma] I. <inv> *agg* (*formale: esame, controllo*) perfunctory; (*fattura*) pro forma II. *avv* (*per formalità*) as a matter of form III. <-> *m* (*formalità*) formality

profugo, **-a** ['prɔ::fu·go] <-ghi, -ghe> I. *agg* refugee II. *m*, *f* refugee

profumare [pro·fu·'ma::re] I. *vt* **avere** ~ **qc** to make sth smell nice II. *vi* **essere** ~ (**di qc**) to have a nice smell (of sth) III. *vr:* -**rsi** to put on perfume

profumatamente [pro·fu·ma·ta·'men·te] *avv* handsomely; **pagare qc** ~ to pay handsomely

for sth

profumeria [pro·fu·me·'ri::a] <-ie> *f* perfumery

profumo [pro·'fu::mo] *m* 1. (*fragranza: di fiore*) scent; (*di caffè*) aroma 2. (*essenza*) perfume

profusi 1. *pers sing pass rem di* **profondere**

profusione [pro·fu·'zio::ne] *f* **a** ~ lavishly

profuso *pp di* **profondersi**

progenitore, **-trice** [pro·dʒe·ni·'to::re] *m*, *f* (*di famiglia, stirpe*) ancestor

progesterone [pro·dʒes·te·'ro::ne] *m* progesterone

progettare [pro·dʒet·'ta::re] *vt* 1. (*viaggio, spedizione*) to plan 2. (*ponte, edificio*) to design

progettazione [pro·dʒet·tat·'tsio::ne] *f* (*di ponte, edificio*) designing

progettista [pro·dʒet·'tis·ta] <-i *m*, -e *f*> *mf* designer

progettistica [pro·dʒet·'tis·ti·ka] <-che> *f* designing

progetto [pro·'dʒɛt·to] *m* plan; ~ **di legge** bill; **essere in** ~ to be being planned; **avere qc in** ~ to have sth planned

prognosi ['prɔɲ·ɲo·zi] <-> *f* prognosis; **in** ~ **riservata** on the critical list

programma [pro·'gram·ma] <-i> *m* 1. (*gener*) program; (*di lavoro*) schedule; **installare un** ~ **sul computer** to install a program on the computer; **fuori** ~ unscheduled 2. (*progetto*) plan; **avere in** ~ **qc** to have sth planned 3. (*di corso, esame*) syllabus

programmare [pro·gram·'ma::re] *vt* 1. (*viaggio, incontro, riforma*) to plan 2. (*piano economico*) to devise 3. (*lavastoviglie, videoregistratore*) to set 4. COMPUT to program

programmatico, **-a** [pro·gram·'ma::ti·ko] <-ci, -che> *agg* (*dichiarazione*) policy

programmatore, **-trice** [pro·gram·ma·'to::re] *m*, *f* 1. COMPUT programmer 2. COM planner

programmazione [pro·gram·mat·'tsio::ne] *f* 1. (*di piano economico*) devising; (*di produzione*) planning 2. (*di lavastoviglie, videoregistratore*) setting 3. COMPUT programming 4. (*a scuola*) syllabus

progredire [pro·gre·'di::re] <progredisco> *vi* essere o avere 1. (*avanzare*) to progress 2. (*far progressi*) to make progress

progredito, **-a** [pro·gre·'di::to] *agg* (*tecnica, paese*) advanced

progressione [pro·gres·'sio::ne] *f* 1. MATH, MUS progression 2. (*avanzamento*) progress; (*aumento*) increase; **essere in** ~ to be on the increase

progressismo [pro·gres·'siz·mo] *m* POL progressivism

progressista [pro·gres·'sis·ta] <-i *m*, -e *f*> I. *mf* progressive II. *agg* progressive

progressivo, **-a** [pro·gres·'si::vo] *agg* (*aumento, calo*) progressive; **imposta** -**a** progressive tax

progresso [pro·'grɛs·so] *m* progress; **far** -**i** to make progress

proibire [pro·i·'bi:·re] <proibisco> *vt* (*vietare*) to forbid; ~ **a qu di fare qc** to forbid sb to do sth

proibitivo, -a [pro·i·bi·'ti:·vo] *agg* 1. (*decreto, provvedimento*) prohibitory 2. (*prezzo*) prohibitive

proibizione [pro·i·bit·'tsio:·ne] *f* (*divieto*) prohibition

proibizionismo [pro·i·bit·tsio·'niz·mo] *m* HIST prohibition

proiettare [pro·iet·'ta:·re] I. *vt* 1. (*film, diapositive*) to project 2. (*gettar fuori*) to throw 3. *fig* ~ **qc su qc** to project sth onto sth II. *vr:* -**rsi** 1. (*gettarsi*) to be thrown 2. (*riflettersi*) to project

proiettile [pro·iet·'ti:·le] *m* (*di arma da fuoco*) bullet

proiettore [pro·iet·'to:·re] *m* 1. (*per film, diapositive*) projector 2. (*per illuminare*) floodlight; MOT headlight

proiezione [pro·iet·'tsio:·ne] *f* 1. (*gener*) projection 2. (*spettacolo*) showing; ~ **elettorale** electoral projection; ~ **demografica** demographic projection

project manager ['prɔ·dʒekt 'mæ·ni·dʒə] <o project managers> *mf* project manager

proletariato [pro·le·ta·'ria:·to] *m* proletariat

proletario, -a [pro·le·'ta:·rio] <-i, -ie> I. *agg* proletarian II. *m, f* (*contadino, operaio*) proletarian

proliferare [pro·li·fe·'ra:·re] *vi* 1. BIOL to proliferate 2. *fig* (*moltiplicarsi: case*) to spring up everywhere; (*moda*) to become increasingly popular

prolificare [pro·li·fi·'ka:·re] *vi* 1. BIOL to procreate; BOT to proliferate 2. *fig* (*espandersi: idea, moda*) to become increasingly popular

prolifico, -a [pro·'li:·fi·ko] <-ci, -che> *agg* prolific

prolissità [pro·lis·si·'ta] <-> *f* prolixity

prolisso, -a [pro·'lis·so] *agg* prolix

prologo ['prɔ:·lo·go] <-ghi> *m* prologue

prolunga [pro·'luŋ·ga] <-ghe> *f* 1. EL extension 2. (*di tavolo*) leaf

prolungamento [pro·luŋ·ga·'men·to] *m* extension

prolungare [pro·luŋ·'ga:·re] I. *vt* to extend II. *vr:* -**rsi** (*estendersi nello spazio*) to extend; (*estendersi nel tempo*) to continue

promemoria [pro·me·'mɔ:·ria] <-> *m* note

promessa [pro·'mes·sa] *f* 1. (*impegno*) promise; **fare una ~ (a qu)** to make (sb) a promise 2. (*persona*) **una ~ del teatro/della letteratura** a promising young actor/author

promesso, -a [pro·'mes·so] I. *pp di* **promettere** II. *m, f* (*fidanzato*) fiancé *m*, fiancée *f*

promettente [pro·met·'tɛn·te] *agg* (*inizio, giovane*) promising

promettere [pro·'met·te·re] <irr> *vt* to promise; ~ **di fare qc** to promise to do sth; ~ **bene/male** to be/not to be promising

prominente [pro·mi·'nɛn·te] *agg* (*zigomi,*

mascelle) prominent

promiscuità [pro·mis·kui·'ta] <-> *f* 1. (*di lingue, religioni*) multiplicity 2. (*sessuale*) promiscuity

promiscuo, -a *agg* 1. (*classe, scuola*) mixed; **matrimonio** ~ mixed marriage 2. (*sessualmente*) promiscuous

promisi 1. *pers sing pass rem di* **promettere**

promontorio [pro·mon·'tɔ:·rio] <-i> *m* GEOGR promontory

promossi 1. *pers sing pass rem di* **promuovere**

promosso, -a [pro·'mɔs·so] I. *pp di* **promuovere** II. *m, f student who passes an exam*

promotore, -trice [pro·mo·'to:·re] I. *m, f* (*di iniziativa, ideologia*) promoter II. *agg* organizing

promozionale [pro·mot·'tsio·'na:·le] *agg* (*attività, campagna*) promotional

promozione [pro·mot·'tsio:·ne] *f* 1. (*gener*) promotion 2. (*a scuola, a un esame*) pass

promulgare [pro·mul·'ga:·re] *vt* to promulgate

promuovere [pro·'muɔ:·ve·re] <irr> *vt* 1. (*gener*) to promote 2. (*a scuola, a un esame*) to pass

pronipote [pro·ni·'po:·te] *mf* 1. (*di nonni*) great-grandchild; (*di zii*) great-nephew *m*, great-niece *f* 2. *pl* (*discendenti*) descendants

pronome [pro·'no:·me] *m* pronoun

pronominale [pro·no·mi·'na:·le] *agg* pronominal

pronosticare [pro·nos·ti·'ka:·re] *vt* (*predire*) to predict

pronostico [pro·'nɔs·ti·ko] <-ci> *m* (*predizione*) prediction

prontezza [pron·'tet·tsa] *f* (*di parola, riflessi*) quickness

pronto ['pron·to] *int* TEL hello

pronto, -a *agg* 1. (*preparato*) ready; **essere ~ per qc** to be ready for sth 2. (*disposto*) **essere ~ a fare qc** to be ready to do sth; **essere ~ a tutto** to be ready to do anything 3. (*rapido*) prompt; ~ **soccorso** first aid; **auguri di -a guarigione** best wishes for a speedy recovery

pronuncia [pro·'nun·tʃa] <-ce> *f* 1. (*articolazione*) pronunciation; (*accento*) accent 2. JUR pronouncement

pronunciare [pro·nun·'tʃa:·re] I. *vt* (*parola, consonante*) to pronounce; (*giudizio, sentenza*) to pronounce; (*discorso*) to deliver II. *vr:* -**rsi** 1. (*esprimere giudizio*) to comment 2. JUR to pronounce

pronunciato, -a *agg* (*naso, mento*) 1. prominent 2. (*gusto, simpatia, preferenza*) strong

propaganda [pro·pa·'gan·da] *f* propaganda

propagandare [pro·pa·gan·'da:·re] *vt* (*idea, partito*) to hype

propagandistico, -a [pro·pa·gan·'dis·ti·ko] <-ci, -che> *agg* (*di propaganda*) propagandistic

propagare [pro·pa·'ga:·re] I. *vt* (*fede, dottrina*) to propagate; (*notizia, diceria*) to spread

II. *vr:* **-rsi 1.** (*luce, calore, onde*) to be propagated **2.** (*epidemia, notizia*) to spread

propagazione [pro·pa·gat·'tsio:·ne] *f* **1.** (*di luce, calore, onde*) BIOL propagation **2.** (*di notizie, scandalo*) spread

propaggine [pro·'pad·dʒi·ne] *f* (*ramo*) layer; (*di un monte*) foot

propano [pro·'pa:·no] *m* propane

propedeutico, -a [pro·pe·'dɛːu·ti·ko] <-ci, -che> *agg* (*corso, trattato*) introductory

propellente [pro·pel·'lɛn·te] *m* propellent

propendere [pro·'pɛn·de·re] <propendo, propendei *o* propesi, propenso> *vi* to be inclined; **~ per qu/qc** to tend toward sb/sth

propensione [pro·pen·'sio:·ne] *f* **1.** (*preferenza*) preference; **avere ~ a fare qc** to be inclined to do sth **2.** (*disposizione*) **avere ~ per qc** to have a bent for sth

propenso, -a [pro·'pɛn·so] **I.** *pp di* **propendere II.** *agg* **essere ~ a fare qc** to be inclined to do sth

propesi [pro·'pe:·si] *1. pers sing pass rem di* **propendere**

propinare [pro·pi·'na:·re] *vt pej, scherz* to inflict

propiziatorio, -a [pro·pit·tsia·'tɔː·rio] <-i, -ie> *agg* propitiatory

propizio, -a [pro·'pit·tsio] <-i, -ie> *agg* (*occasione, momento*) propitious

propongo *1. pers sing pr di* **proporre**

proponibile [pro·po·'niː·bi·le] *agg* proposable

proponimento [pro·po·ni·'men·to] *m* resolution

proporre [pro·'por·re] <irr> *vt* **1.** (*suggerire*) to propose **2.** (*scopo*) **-rsi qc** to set sth for oneself; **-rsi una meta** to set oneself a goal

proporzionale [pro·por·tsio·'na:·le] *agg* proportional; **sistema ~** proportional representation

proporzionato, -a [pro·por·tsio·'na:·to] *agg* proportionate

proporzione [pro·port·'tsio:·ne] *f* **1.** GENER proportion; **in ~ a** in proportion to **2.** *pl* (*grandezza*) proportions *pl;* **avere il senso delle -i** *fig* to have a sense of proportion

proposi *1. pers sing pass rem di* **proporre**

proposito [pro·'pɔː·zi·to] *m* **1.** (*intenzione*) intention; **di ~** (*apposta*) on purpose **2.** (*argomento*) **a ~ di** with regard to; **a ~!** by the way; **capitare a ~** to be just in time; **a questo ~** on this subject

proposizione [pro·po·zit·'tsio:·ne] *f* clause

proposta [pro·'pos·ta] *f* proposal; **~ di matrimonio** marriage proposal; **~ di legge** bill

proposto *pp di* **proporre**

propriamente [pro·pria·'men·te] *avv* **1.** (*veramente*) really **2.** (*in senso proprio*) strictly

proprietà [pro·prie·'ta] <-> *f* **1.** (*diritto*) ownership; (*bene, caratteristica*) property **2.** (*di linguaggio*) correctness

proprietario, -a [pro·prie·'ta:·rio] <-i, -ie> *m*, *f* owner

proprio¹ ['prɔː·prio] *avv* **1.** (*precisamente*) ex-

actly **2.** (*davvero*) really

proprio² <-i> *m* **lavorare in ~** to be self-employed

proprio, -a <-i, -ie> *agg* **1.** (*impersonale*) one's **2.** (*insieme a possessivo*) own **3.** (*tipico*) typical **4.** (*linguaggio*) correct; **vero e ~** real

propugnare [pro·puɲ·'ɲa:·re] *vt* (*sostenere*) to support

propulsione [pro·pul·'sio:·ne] *f* **1.** TEC propulsion **2.** *fig* (*spinta*) boost

propulsivo, -a [pro·pul·'si:·vo] *agg* propulsive

propulsore [pro·pul·'so:·re] *m* TEC propeller

proroga ['prɔː·ro·ga] <-ghe> *f* extension

prorogare [pro·ro·'ga:·re] *vt* to extend

prorompente [pro·rom·'pɛn·te] *agg* (*gioia*) overwhelming; (*entusiasmo*) boundless

prorompere [pro·'rom·pe·re] <irr> *vi* **~ in lacrime** to burst into tears; **~ in una risata** to burst out laughing

prosa ['prɔː·za] *f* (*forma letteraria*) prose; (*componimento*) prose work

prosaico, -a [pro·'za:i·ko] <-ci, -che> *agg* (*discorso, atteggiamento*) prosaic

prosciogliere [proʃ·'ʃɔʎ·ʎe·re] <irr> *vt* **1.** (*da obbligo, giuramento*) to release **2.** JUR to acquit

prosciugare [proʃ·ʃu·'ga:·re] **I.** *vt* (*terreno*) to drain; (*finanze*) to use up **II.** *vr:* **-rsi** (*terreno*) to be drained; (*finanze*) to get used up

prosciutto [proʃ·'ʃut·to] *m* ham

proscrissi *1. pers sing pass rem di* **proscrivere**

proscritto, -a [pros·'krit·to] **I.** *pp di* **proscrivere II.** *m, f* (*esule*) exile

proscrizione [pros·krit·'tsio:·ne] *f* **1.** (*esilio*) banishment **2.** (*divieto*) banning

prosecco [pro·'sek·ko] <-chi> *m* sparkling dry white wine

prosecuzione [pro·se·kut·'tsio:·ne] *f* continuation

proseguimento [pro·se·gui·'men·to] *m* (*continuazione*) continuation; **buon ~!** (*viaggio*) enjoy the rest of your trip!; (*serata*) enjoy the rest of the evening!

proseguire [pro·se·'gui:·re] **I.** *vt* to continue **II.** *vi* to carry on; **~ in qc** to continue with sth

prosperare [pros·pe·'ra:·re] *vi* to prosper

prosperità [pros·pe·ri·'ta] <-> *f* prosperity

prospero, -a ['prɔs·pe·ro] *agg* (*commercio*) flourishing; (*salute*) excellent; (*paese*) prosperous

prosperoso, -a [pros·pe·'ro:·so] *agg* **1.** (*commercio*) flourishing; (*regione*) prosperous **2.** (*donna, forme*) curvaceous

prospettare [pros·pet·'ta:·re] **I.** *vt* (*esporre*) to put forward **II.** *vr:* **-rsi** to look

prospettiva [pros·pet·'tiː·va] *f* **1.** (*tecnica*) perspective **2.** (*vista*) view **3.** (*punto di vista*) point of view **4.** (*possibilità*) prospect

prospetto [pros·'pɛt·to] *m* **1.** (*tabella*) table **2.** (*veduta*) view; **di ~** from the front **3.** (*facciata*) facade **4.** (*disegno*) elevation

prossimamente [pros·si·ma·'men·te] *avv* (*fra breve*) soon

P

prossimità [pros·si·mi·'ta] <-> *f* proximity; **in ~ di** near

prossimo ['prɔs·si·mo] *m* (*gli altri*) neighbor; **il tuo ~** your neighbor

prossimo, -a *agg* **1.**(*vicino*) near; **un parente ~** a close relative **2.**(*successivo*) next; **passato ~** LING present perfect; **trapassato ~** LING past perfect; **la -a volta** the next time; **ci vediamo venerdì ~** see you next Friday

prostata ['prɔs·ta·ta] *f* ANAT prostate

prosternarsi [pros·ter·'nar·si] *vr* to prostrate oneself

prostituirsi [pros·ti·tu·'i:r·si] <prostituisco> *vr* to prostitute oneself

prostituta [pros·ti·'tu:·ta] *f* prostitute

prostituzione [pros·ti·tut·'tsio:·ne] *f* prostitution

prostrare [pros·'tra:·re] **I.** *vt fig* (*fiaccare*) to wear out **II.** *vr:* **-rsi 1.**(*gettarsi a terra*) to prostrate oneself **2.** *fig*(*umiliarsi*) to kowtow

prostrazione [pros·trat·'tsio:·ne] *f* **1.**(*fisica*) exhaustion **2.**(*morale*) depression

protagonista [pro·ta·go·'nis·ta] <-i *m*, -e *f*> *mf* protagonist

proteggere [pro·'tɛd·dʒe·re] <proteggo, protessi, protetto> **I.** *vt* (*difendere*) to protect; (*soccorrere*) to defend **II.** *vr* to protect oneself

proteggi-slip [pro·'tɛd·dʒi·zlip] <-> *m* pantyliner

proteico, -a [pro·'tɛ:·i·ko] <-ci, -che> *agg* protein

proteina [pro·te·'i:·na] *f* protein

protendere [pro·'tɛn·de·re] <irr> **I.** *vt* (*mano, braccia*) to stretch out **II.** *vr:* **-rsi** (*sporgersi in avanti*) to lean forward

protesi[1] [pro·'te:·si] *1. pers sing pass rem di* **protendere**

protesi[2] ['prɔ:·te·zi] <-> *f* MED prosthesis

proteso *pp di* **protendere**

protessi [pro·'tɛs·si] *1. pers sing pass rem di* **proteggere**

protesta [pro·'tɛs·ta] *f* protest; **per ~** in protest

protestante [pro·tes·'tan·te] **I.** *agg* Protestant **II.** *mf* Protestant

protestantesimo [pro·tes·tan·'te:·zi·mo] *m* Protestantism

protestare [pro·tes·'ta:·re] **I.** *vt* (*cambiale, assegno*) to dishonor **II.** *vi ~* (**contro qc**) to protest (against sth)

protettivo, -a [pro·tet·'ti:·vo] *agg* protective

protetto, -a [pro·'tɛt·to] **I.** *pp di* **proteggere** **II.** *m, f* protégé *m*, protégée *f* **III.** *agg* protected

protettorato [pro·tet·to·'ra:·to] *m* **1.**(*tutela*) protection **2.**(*territorio*) protectorate

protettore, -trice [pro·tet·'to:·re] **I.** *m, f* **1.**(*difensore*) protector **2.**(*santo*) patron **3.**(*di prostitute*) pimp **II.** *agg* **santo ~** patron saint; **società -trice degli animali** animal protection society

protezione [pro·tet·'tsio:·ne] *f* protection; **la**

~ civile (*attività*) emergency management; (*ente*) ≈Federal Emergency Management Agency

protezionismo [pro·tet·tsio·'niz·mo] *m* (*politica economica*) protectionism

protezionista [pro·tet·tsio·'nis·ta] <-i *m*, -e *f*> I. *mf* protectionist II. *agg* protectionist

protezionistico, -a [pro·tet·tsio·'nis·ti·ko] <-ci, -che> *agg* protectionist

protocollare [pro·to·kol·'la:·re] *agg* (*cerimonia, ordine*) formal

protocollo [pro·to·'kɔl·lo] *m* **1.**(*registro*) register; **carta** (**formato**) **~** foolscap (paper); **mettere a ~** to record **2.**(*accordo, cerimoniale*) protocol

protone [pro·'to:·ne] *m* proton

prototipo [pro·'tɔ:·ti·po] *m* **1.**(*modello*) prototype **2.** *scherz* (*esempio perfetto*) epitome

protrarre [pro·'trar·re] <irr> **I.** *vt* (*prolungare*) to prolong; (*rimandare*) to postpone **II.** *vr:* **-rsi** to continue

protuberanza [pro·tu·be·'ran·tsa] *f* (*su una superficie, sul corpo*) protuberance

Prov. *abbr di* **provincia** Prov.

prova ['prɔ:·va] *f* **1.**(*esperimento*) test; **mettere qu alla ~** to put sb to the test; **a ~ di bomba** (*oggetto*) bombproof; (*rapporto, contratto*) indestructible; **periodo di ~** (*nel lavoro*) trial period **2.**(*esame*) examination; **~ orale/scritta** oral/written examination **3.**(*dimostrazione*) JUR proof; **dar ~ di qc** to show sth; **fino a ~ contraria** until proven otherwise **4.**(*theat, mus*) rehearsal; **~ generale** dress rehearsal **5.**(*tentativo*) try **6.** SPORT competition

provare [pro·'va:·re] **I.** *vt* **1.**(*gener*) to try; TEC, SCIENT to test; (*abito, scarpe*) to try on; **~ a fare qc** to try to do sth; **provarci** to try **2.**(*indebolire*) to weaken **3.**(*dolore, simpatia, pietà*) to feel **4.**(*dimostrare*) to prove **5.** MUS, THEAT, FILM to rehearse **II.** *vr:* **-rsi 1.**(*osare*) to dare; **-rsi a fare qc** to dare to do sth **2.**(*mettersi alla prova*) **-rsi in qc** to try sth

provato, -a [pro·'va:·to] *agg* **1.**(*dimostrato*) proven **2.**(*affaticato*) exhausted

provengo *1. pers sing pr di* **provenire**

provenienza [pro·ve·'niɛn·tsa] *f* **1.**(*luogo*) provenance **2.**(*origine*) origin

provenire [pro·ve·'ni:·re] <irr> *vi essere* **1.**(*arrivare*) **~ da** to come from **2.** *fig* (*trarre origine*) **~ da qc** to derive from sth

provenuto *pp di* **provenire**

proverbiale [pro·ver·'bia:·le] *agg* (*detto, espressione*) proverbial; (*leggendario*) legendary

proverbio [pro·'vɛr·bio] <-i> *m* proverb

provetta [pro·'vet·ta] *f* (*recipiente*) test tube; **figlio in ~** test tube baby

provider <- *o* providers> *m* COMPUT (*Internet*) provider

provincia [pro·'vin·tʃa] <-cie *o* -ce> *f* provinces; **di ~** *pej* provincial

i The **Provincia** is the political unit that comes between the **Comune** and the **Regione**. There are 110 **provinces** in Italy, each one containing several **comuni**. The **Provincia** has responsibility for public health care, highway maintenance and public buildings such as schools, as well as for agriculture and fisheries. Each **provincia** has a **capoluogo**, a capital, and is governed by a **Giunta provinciale** (provincial government) whose members are chosen from the **Consiglio provinciale** (provincial council).

provinciale [pro·vin·'tʃa:·le] *agg a. pej* provincial; **strada** ~ highway
provincialismo [pro·vin·tʃa·'liz·mo] *m pej* provincialism
provino [pro·'vi:·no] *m* 1. (*di fotografie*) contact print 2. (*campione*) specimen 3. (*di attore*) screen test
provocante [pro·vo·'kan·te] *agg* (*abbigliamento, sguardo*) provocative
provocare [pro·vo·'ka:·re] *vt* 1. (*causare*) to cause 2. (*sfidare*) to provoke 3. (*sessualmente*) to behave provocatively toward
provocatore, -trice [pro·vo·ka·'to:·re] I. *agg* (*atteggiamento,* *discorso*) provocative; **agente** ~ agent provocateur II. *m, f* troublemaker
provocatorio, -a [pro·vo·ka·'tɔ:·rio] <-i, -ie> *agg* (*tono, domanda, atteggiamento*) provocative
provocatrice *f v.* provocatore
provocazione [pro·vo·kat·'tsio:·ne] *f* (*sfida*) provocation
provvedere [prov·ve·'de:·re] <irr> I. *vi* ~ **a** **qc/a fare qc** to take care of sth/of doing sth II. *vt* (*fornire*) ~ **qu/qc di qc** to provide sb/sth with sth III. *vr* **-rsi di qc** to provide oneself with sth
provvedimento [prov·ve·di·'men·to] *m* 1. (*misura*) step; **prendere -i** to take steps 2. JUR measure
provveditorato [prov·ve·di·to·'ra:·to] *m* ~ **agli studi** local education department
provveditore, -trice [prov·ve·di·'to:·re] *m, f* ~ **agli studi** commissioner of education
provvidenza [prov·vi·'dɛn·tsa] *f* REL (*assistenza divina*) providence
provvidenziale [prov·vi·den·'tsia:·le] *agg* providential
provvidi 1. *pers sing pass rem di* provvedere
provvigione [prov·vi·'dʒo:·ne] *f* (*retribuzione*) commission
provvisorietà [prov·vi·zo·rie·'ta] <-> *f* temporary nature
provvisorio, -a [prov·vi·'zɔ:·rio] <-i, -ie> *agg* (*lavoro, soluzione*) temporary; (*governo*) provisional
provvista [prov·'vis·ta] *f* 1. (*rifornimento*) **fare** ~ **di qc** to stock up on sth 2. *pl* (*scorte*) supplies
provvisto, -a [prov·'vis·to] I. *pp di* provvedere II. *agg* **essere** ~ **di qc** to be provided with sth
prozio, -a [prot·'tsi:·o] *m, f* great uncle *m,* great aunt *f*
prua ['pru:·a] *f* (*di imbarcazione*) bow
prudente [pru·'dɛn·te] *agg* cautious
prudenza [pru·'dɛn·tsa] *f* caution; **guidare con** ~ to drive carefully; **la** ~ **non è mai troppa** *prov* you can't be too careful
prudere ['pru:·de·re] <*manca il pp*> *vi* to itch; **mi prude la schiena/il naso** my back/my nose is itchy
prugna ['pruɲ·ɲa] *f* plum
prugno ['pruɲ·ɲo] <-i> *m* plum (tree)
pruno ['pru:·no] *m* 1. BOT blackthorn 2. (*spina*) thorn
prurito [pru·'ri:·to] *m* (*sensazione*) itch
PS 1. *abbr di* **Pubblica Sicurezza** Police 2. *abbr di* postscriptum P.S.
PSDI *m* HIST *abbr di* **Partito Socialista Democratico Italiano** *former Italian social democratic party*
pseudonimo [pseu·'dɔ:·ni·mo] *m* pseudonym
PSI *m* HIST *abbr di* **Partito Socialista Italiano** *Italian Socialist Party*
psicanalisi [psi·ka·'na:·li·zi] *f* psychoanalysis
psicanalista [psi·ka·na·'lis·ta] <-i *m,* -e *f*> *mf* psychoanalyst
psicanalitico, -a [psi·ka·na·'lis·ti·ko] <-ci, -che> *agg* psychoanalytic(al)
psiche ['psi:·ke] *f* (*mente*) psyche
psichedelico, -a [psi·ke·'dɛ:·li·ko] <-ci, -che> *agg* (*luce, musica*) psychedelic
psichiatra [psi·'kia:·tra] <-i *m,* -e *f*> *mf* psychiatrist
psichiatria [psi·kia·'tri:·a] <-ie> *f* psychiatry
psichiatrico, -a [psi·'kia:·tri·ko] <-ci, -che> *agg* psychiatric
psichico, -a ['psi:·ki·ko] <-ci, -che> *agg* (*mentale*) mental
psicofarmaco [psi·ko·'far·ma·ko] *m* psychotropic drug
psicologia [psi·ko·lo·'dʒi:·a] <-gie> *f* psychology
psicologico, -a [psi·ko·'lɔ:·dʒi·ko] <-ci, -che> *agg* psychological
psicologo, -a [psi·'kɔ:·lo·go] <-gi, -ghe> *m, f* psychologist
psicopatico, -a [psi·ko·'pa:·ti·ko] <-ci, -che> I. *agg* psychopathic II. *m, f* psychopath
psicosi [psi·'kɔ:·zi] <-> *f* psychosis; ~ **collettiva** collective fear; ~ **degli esami** fear of exams
psicosociologia [psi·ko·so·tʃo·lo·'dʒi:·a] <*sing*> *f* psychosociology
psicosomatico, -a [psi·ko·so·'ma:·ti·ko] <-ci, -che> *agg* (*malattia, disturbo*) psychosomatic
psicoterapia [psi·ko·te·ra·'pi:·a] *f* psychotherapy
psicoterapico, -a [psi·ko·te·'ra:·pi·ko] <-ci,

P

-che> *agg* psychotherapeutic

psicoterapista [psi·ko·te·ra·'pis·ta] <-i *m*, -e *f*> *mf* psychotherapist

psicotico, -a [psi·'kɔ:·ti·ko] <-ci, -che> *agg* psychotic

psoriasi [pso·'ri:·a·zi] <-> *f* psoriasis

pss, pst [ps] *int* **1.** (*per imporre silenzio*) sh! **2.** (*per richiamare attenzione*) psst!

PT *abbr di* **Poste e Telecomunicazioni** ≈ Postal Service

puah [puah] *int* ugh!

pub [pʌb/pab] <- *o* pubs> *m* pub

pubblicare [pub·bli·'ka:·re] *vt* (*opera*) to publish

pubblicazione [pub·bli·kat·'tsio:·ne] *f* **1.** (*attività, opera*) publication **2.** *pl* -i (**matrimoniali**) (wedding) banns; **fare le** -i to publish the banns

pubblicista [pub·bli·'tʃis·ta] <-i *m*, -e *f*> *mf* **1.** (*giornalista*) freelance journalist **2.** JUR public law expert

pubblicistica [pub·bli·'tʃis·ti·ka] <-che> *f* **1.** (*attività*) current affairs reporting **2.** JUR public law

pubblicità [pub·bli·tʃi·'ta] <-> *f* **1.** (*gener*) publicity **2.** (*annuncio*) advertisement **3.** (*di documento*) availability to the public; (*di udienza*) openness to the public

pubblicitario, -a [pub·bli·tʃi·'ta:·rio] <-i, -ie> **I.** *agg* (*annuncio, campagna*) advertising **II.** *m, f* advertising executive

pubblicizzare [pub·bli·tʃid·'dza:·re] *vt* to publicize

pubblico ['pub·bli·ko] *m* (*gente*) public; (*spettatori, ascoltatori*) audience; **in ~** in public

pubblico, -a <-ci, -che> *agg* public; **la ~ amministrazione** the civil service; **i mezzi (di trasporto)** -ci public transportation; **l'opinione** -a public opinion; **-che relazioni** public relations; **rendere ~ qc** (*divulgare*) to make sth public

pube ['pu:·be] *m* pubis

pubertà [pu·ber·'ta] <-> *f* puberty

pubico, -a ['pu:·bi·co] *agg* pubic

public company ['pʌb·lik 'kʌm·pə·ni] <- *o* public companies> *f* FIN public company

pudico, -a [pu·'di:·ko] <-chi, -che> *agg* (*persona, sguardo*) modest

pudore [pu·'do:·re] *m* **1.** (*riserbo*) modesty **2.** (*contegno*) decency

puerile [pue·'ri:·le] *agg* **1.** (*dei fanciulli*) **età ~** childhood **2.** *pej* (*immaturo*) childish

puerilità [pue·ri·li·'ta] <-> *f* (*immaturità*) childishness

puerpera [pu·'ɛr·pe·ra] *f* woman who has recently given birth

pugilato [pu·dʒi·'la:·to] *m* SPORT boxing

pugile ['pu:·dʒi·le] *m* boxer

Puglia ['puʎ·ʎa] *f* Puglia

pugliese¹ [puʎ·'ʎe:·se] <*sing*> *m* (*dialetto*) Puglia dialect

pugliese² **I.** *mf* (*abitante*) person from Puglia **II.** *agg* from Puglia

pugnalare [puɲ·ɲa·'la:·re] *vt* to stab

pugnalata [puɲ·ɲa·'la:·ta] *f* (*ferita*) stab wound

pugnale [puɲ·'ɲa:·le] *m* dagger

pugno ['puɲ·ɲo] *m* **1.** (*mano chiusa*) fist; **avere qc in ~** *fig* to have sth within one's grasp; **essere (come) un ~ in un occhio** *fig* to be an eyesore **2.** (*colpo*) punch; **fare a -i** to fight; *fig* (*colori, accessori*) to clash; **prendere a -i qu** to punch sb **3.** (*quantità*) handful; **restare con un ~ di mosche** *fig* to be left with nothing

pulce ['pul·tʃe] *f* (*insetto*) flea; **mercato delle -i** flea market; **mettere una ~ nell'orecchio a qu** *fig* to arouse sb's suspicions

pulcinella [pul·tʃi·'nɛl·la] <-> *m* (*maschera*) Punch

pulcino [pul·'tʃi:·no] *m* (*di gallina*) chick

puledro, -a [pu·'le:·dro] *m, f* (*cavallo*) colt *m*, filly *f*

pulire [pu·'li:·re] <pulisco> **I.** *vt* to clean; **-rsi le orecchie** to clean out one's ears; **-rsi la bocca** to wipe one's mouth **II.** *vr* to clean oneself up

pulita [pu·'li:·ta] *f* **dare una ~ a qc** to clean sth; **darsi una ~** to wash up

pulito [pu·'li:·to] *m* (*pulizia*) cleanness

pulito, -a *agg* **1.** (*gener*) clean **2.** (*coscienza*) clear **3.** (*faccenda*) shady

pulitura [pu·li·'tu:·ra] *f* (*operazione di pulire*) cleaning; **~ a secco** dry-cleaning

pulizia [pu·lit·'tsi:·a] <-ie> *f* **1.** (*azione*) cleaning; **donna delle -ie** cleaning woman; **fare le -ie** to do the cleaning; **fare ~** *fig* to clear everything out; **~ etnica** ethnic cleansing **2.** (*condizione*) cleanliness

pullman ['pul·man] <-> *m* bus

pullover [pul·'lɔ:·ver] <-> *m* pullover

pullulare [pul·lu·'la:·re] *vi* **1.** (*essere numeroso*) to abound **2.** (*essere pieno*) **~ di** to be full of

pulmino [pul·'mi:·no] *m* minibus

pulpito ['pul·pi·to] *m* (*di chiesa*) pulpit; **montare** [*o* **salire**] **sul ~** *fig* to get on one's soapbox; **da che ~ viene la predica!** *fam* look who's talking!

pulsante [pul·'san·te] **I.** *m* button; **~ del campanello** bell-push **II.** *agg* (*throbbing*) **cuore ~** *fig* beating heart

pulsare [pul·'sa:·re] *vi* (*cuore*) to beat; *fig* (*attività*) to be vibrant

pulsazione [pul·sat·'tsio:·ne] *f* (*battito*) beat

pulviscolo [pul·'vis·ko·lo] *m* (*polvere*) dust

puma ['pu:·ma] <-> *m* puma

punch [pʌntʃ] <-> *m* (*bevanda*) punch

pungente [pun·'dʒɛn·te] *agg* **1.** (*freddo*) biting **2.** (*battuta*) cutting; (*critica*) stinging; (*desiderio*) burning; (*nostalgia*) bittersweet

pungere ['pun·dʒe·re] <pungo, punsi, punto> **I.** *vt* **1.** (*soggetto: spina, spillo*) to prick; (*insetto, ortica*) to sting **2.** (*offendere*) to offend **II.** *vr:* **-rsi** to prick oneself

pungiglione [pun·dʒiʎ·'ʎo:·ne] *m* (*di insetto*)

stinger
punibile [pu·'ni:·bi·le] *agg* punishable
punire [pu·'ni:·re] <punisco> *vt* (*bambino, criminale*) to punish
punitivo, -a [pu·ni·'ti:·vo] *agg* (*azione, misura*) punitive
punizione [pu·nit·'tsio:·ne] *f* 1.(*castigo*) punishment; **per** ~ as a punishment 2.(*nel calcio*) (**tiro di**) ~ free kick
punk [pʌŋk] <-> I. *mf* punk II. *agg* punk
punsi ['pun·si] *1. pers sing pass rem di* **pungere**
punta ['pun·ta] *f* 1.(*estremità: di coltello, bastone*) point; (*di naso, dita, lingua*) tip; **camminare in** ~ **di piedi** to walk on tiptoe; **ballare sulle -e** to dance on points; **fare la** ~ **ad una matita** to sharpen a pencil; **avere qc sulla** ~ **della lingua** to have sth on the tip of one's tongue; **prendere qu di** ~ *fig* to tackle sb head on; **naso a** ~ pointed nose; **avere le doppie -e** (*ai capelli*) to have split ends 2.(*cima, valore massimo*) peak; **ore di** ~ peak time 3.(*di trapano*) bit 4.CULIN ~ (**di petto**) brisket 5. NEL CALCIO forward
puntare [pun·'ta:·re] I. *vt* 1.(*appoggiare*) to brace; ~ **i piedi** *fig* to dig one's heels in 2.(*dirigere*) to point; ~ **il dito verso qu** to point the finger at sb 3.(*scommettere*) ~ **qc su qc** to bet sth on sth II. *vi* 1.(*dirigersi*) ~ **su qc** to head for sth 2.*fig* (*mirare*) ~ **a qc** to be after sth 3.(*contare*) ~ **su qu/qc** to count on sb/sth
puntaspilli [pun·tas·'pil·li] <-> *m* pincushion
puntata [pun·'ta:·ta] *f* 1.TV, RADIO episode; **a -e** (*romanzo, sceneggiato*) serialized 2.(*breve gita*) flying visit 3.(*scommessa, somma scommessa*) bet
puntatore [pun·ta·'to:·re] *m* COMPUT pointer
puntatore, -trice [pun·ta·'to:·re] *m, f* (*scommettitore*) bettor
punteggiatura [pun·ted·dʒa·'tu:·ra] *f* LING punctuation
punteggio [pun·'ted·dʒo] <-ggi> *m* (*di gara*) score; (*di esame*) grade
puntellare [pun·tel·'la:·re] *vt* (*muro*) to prop up
puntello [pun·'tɛl·lo] *m* (*trave*) prop
punteruolo [pun·te·'ruɔ:·lo] *m* (*per forare*) bradawl
puntiforme [pun·ti·'for·me] *agg* dot-like
puntiglio [pun·'tiʎ·ʎo] <-gli> *m* (*ostinazione*) stubbornness
puntiglioso, -a [pun·tiʎ·'ʎo:·so] *agg* (*persona*) punctilious; (*lavoro*) painstaking
puntina [pun·'ti:·na] *f* 1.(*di giradischi*) stylus 2.(*chiodino*) ~ (**da disegno**) thumb tack
puntino [pun·'ti:·no] *m* dot; **-i di sospensione** suspension points; **mettere i -i sulle i** *fig* to cross the t's and dot the i's; **a** ~ perfectly
punto¹ ['pun·to] *pp di* **pungere**
punto² *m* 1. GENER point; ~ **di fusione/ebollizione** melting/boiling point; **i -i cardinali** the cardinal points; **alle tre in** ~ at exactly three o'clock; ~ **di vista** point of view; **venire al** ~

to get to the point; **questo è il** ~ that's the point; **essere sul** ~ **di ...** to be on the point of ...; **in** ~ **di morte** on the point of death; **ad un certo** ~ at a certain point; **di** ~ **in bianco** suddenly; **cotto al** ~ **giusto** cooked perfectly; **messa a** ~ TEC adjustment 2. *nella punteggiatura* ~ (**fermo**) period; ~ **esclamativo** exclamation point; ~ **interrogativo** question mark; **-i di sospensione** suspension points; ~ **e virgola** semicolon; **due -i** colon; ~ **e basta!** *fam* period! 3.(*tondino*) spot; **-i neri** blackhead 4.(*luogo*) place; ~ (**di**) **vendita** sales outlet; ~ **di ritrovo** meeting place 5.(*nel cucito, ricamo*) stitch; ~ **croce** cross-stitch; **dare un** ~ **a qc** to sew sth up 6. MED ~ (**di sutura**) stitch 7.(*riassunto*) **fare il** ~ to sum up 8.(*sfumatura di colore*) shade
puntuale [pun·tu·'a:·le] *agg* 1.(*rispettoso di orario, scadenza*) punctual; **essere** [*o* **arrivare**] ~ to be punctual 2.(*esatto: critica, osservazione*) accurate
puntualità [pun·tua·li·'ta] <-> *f* 1.(*di persona, treno*) punctuality 2.(*di osservazione, critica*) accuracy
puntualizzare [pun·tua·lid·'dza:·re] *vt* to clarify
puntualizzazione [pun·tua·lid·dzat·'tsio:·ne] *f* clarification
puntura [pun·'tu:·ra] *f* 1.*fam* (*iniezione*) injection 2.(*di zanzara*) bite; (*di ago, spina*) prick 3.(*fitta*) sharp pain
punzecchiare [pun·tsek·'kia:·re] *vt* 1.(*pungere*) to prick 2.*fig* (*provocare*) to tease
punzone [pun·'tso:·ne] *m* (*asticciola*) stamp; (*punteruolo*) punch
può ['pu·ɔ] *3. pers sing pr di* **potere¹**
puoi ['puɔ:·i] *2. pers sing pr di* **potere¹**
pupa ['pu:·pa] *f fam* (*ragazza*) babe
pupazzo [pu·'pat·tso] *m* (*fantoccio*) puppet
pupilla [pu·'pil·la] *f* ANAT pupil
pupillo, -a [pu·'pil·lo] *m, f* 1.JUR ward 2.(*preferito*) favorite
pupo ['pu:·po] *m* 1.(*marionetta*) puppet 2.*fam* (*bambino*) little boy
pur *v.* **pur(e)**
puramente [pu·ra·'men·te] *avv* (*semplicemente*) simply
purché [pur·'ke] *cong* (*a condizione che*) provided (that)
purchessia [pur·kes·'si:·a] <inv> *agg* (*qualsiasi*) any
pure [pur ('pu:·re)] I. *cong* 1.(*anche se*) even if 2.(*tuttavia*) but II. *avv* 1.(*anche*) too 2.(*rafforzativo*) surely; **faccia** ~! please do! 3.(*con valore finale*) **pur di fare qc** +*inf* (in order) to do sth
purè [pu·'rɛ] <-> *m* purée; ~ (**di patate**) mashed potatoes *pl*
purezza [pu·'ret·tsa] *f* purity
purga ['pur·ga] <-ghe> *f* (*lassativo*) laxative
purgante [pur·'gan·te] I. *m* laxative II. *agg* (*lassativo*) laxative
purgare [pur·'ga:·re] I. *vt* 1. MED to give a laxa-

tive to **2.**(*purificare: aria, sangue*) to purify; (*stile, scritto*) to expurgate **3.** POL (*epurare*) to purge **II.** *vr:* **-rsi 1.** MED to take a laxative **2.** *fig* (*da colpe, peccati*) to purge oneself

purgativo, -a [pur·ga·'ti:·vo] *agg* (*lassativo*) laxative

purgatorio [pur·ga·'tɔ:·rio] <-i> *m* REL purgatory

purificare [pu·ri·fi·'ka:·re] **I.** *vt* to purify **II.** *vr:* **-rsi 1.** (*sostanza, organismo, animo*) to be purified **2.** (*persona*) to purify oneself

purificatore, -trice [pu·ri·fi·ka·'to:·re] *m, f* (*dal peccato*) purificatory; (*sauna, dieta*) detoxifying

purificazione [pu·ri·fi·kat·'tsio:·ne] *f* purification

purismo [pu·'riz·mo] *m* LING purism

purista [pu·'ris·ta] <-i *m*, -e *f*> *mf* purist

puritanesimo [pu·ri·ta·'ne:·zi·mo] *m* HIST Puritanism; (*moralismo*) puritanism

puritano, -a [pu·ri·'ta:·no] **I.** *agg* HIST Puritan; (*moralista*) puritanical **II.** *m, f* HIST Puritan; (*moralista*) puritan

puro, -a ['pu:·ro] *agg* **1.** (*gener*) pure; (*vino*) undiluted **2.** (*semplice: curiosità*) simple; (*verità*) absolute; **~ e semplice** pure and simple; **per ~ caso** by sheer chance

purosangue [pu·ro·'saŋ·gue] **I.** <inv> *agg* **1.** (*cavallo*) thoroughbred **2.** (*nobile, piemontese*) full-blooded **II.** <-> *mf* (*cavallo*) thoroughbred

purpureo, -a [pur·'pu:·reo] *agg* (*labbra, abito*) crimson

purtroppo [pur·'trɔp·po] *avv* unfortunately

purulento, -a [pu·ru·'lɛn·to] *agg* festering

pus [pus] *m* pus

pusillanime [pu·zil·'la:·ni·me] **I.** *agg* cowardly **II.** *mf* coward

pustola ['pus·to·la] *f* (*sulla pelle*) pustule

putativo, -a [pu·ta·'ti:·vo] *agg* (*figlio, padre*) putative

putiferio [pu·ti·'fɛ:·rio] <-i> *m* (*schiamazzo*) uproar; *fig* (*confusione*) confusion

putrefare [pu·tre·'fa:·re] <irr> **I.** *vi* essere to rot **II.** *vr:* **-rsi** to rot

putrefazione [pu·tre·fat·'tsio:·ne] *f* (*decomposizione*) putrefaction

putrefeci *1. pers sing pass rem di* **putrefare**

putrescente [pu·treʃ·'ʃɛn·te] *agg* (*corpo*) rotting

putrido, -a ['pu:·tri·do] *agg* (*carne*) rotten; (*acqua, odore*) foul

putsch [putʃ] <-> *m* POL, MIL putsch

puttana [put·'ta:·na] *f vulg* (*prostituta*) whore

puttanesco, -a [put·ta·'nes·ko] <-schi, -sche> *agg* **spaghetti alla -a** spaghetti with a tomato, anchovy, caper, and olive sauce

puttaniere [put·ta·'niɛ:·re] *m fam* (*dongiovanni*) Don Juan

putto ['put·to] *m* cherub

puzza ['put·tsa] *f dial* (*puzzo*) stink; **avere la ~ sotto il naso** *fig* to be a snob

puzzare [put·'tsa:·re] *vi* **1.** (*mandare puzzo*) to

stink; **~ di qc** to stink of sth; **gli puzza l'alito** he's got really bad breath **2.** *fig* (*essere sospetto*) to sound fishy

puzzle ['pʌ·zəl/'pat·sle] <-> *m* jigsaw (puzzle)

puzzo ['put·tso] *m* (*cattivo odore*) stink

puzzola ['put·tso·la] *f* polecat

puzzolente [put·tso·'lɛn·te] *agg* smell

puzzone, -a [put·'tso:·ne] *m, f dial, fam* (*persona puzzolente*) smelly person; *fig* (*mascalzone*) rat

P.za *abbr di* **Piazza** Sq.

Q

Q, q [ku] <-> *f* Q, q; **~ come quarto** Q for Queen

q *abbr di* **quintale** q, *quintal* (*metric unit of weight = 100 kg*)

QI *abbr di* **quoziente d'intelligenza** IQ

qua [kua] **I.** *avv* **1.** (*stato, moto*) here; **dammi ~** give it here; **siamo ~** we're here; **vieni ~** come here; **per di ~** this way; **andare di ~ e di là** to wander around; **questo ~ mi piace di più** I prefer this one; **~ i soldi!** *fam* give me the money!; **essere più di là che di ~** *fig* to be more dead than alive **2.** (*temporale*) **da quando in ~?** *fam* since when?; **da un anno in ~** since last year **II.** <-> *m* (*di oche, anatre*) quack **III.** *int* quack

quaderno [kua·'dɛr·no] *m* (*di scuola*) notebook; **~ a quadretti/a righe** notebook with squared/lined pages

quadrangolare [kua·draŋ·go·'la:·re] *agg* **1.** MAT quadrangular **2.** SPORT four-sided

quadrangolo [kua·'draŋ·go·lo] *m* quadrangle

quadrante [kua·'dran·te] *m* **1.** (*di orologio*) face **2.** (*di bussola, cerchio*) quadrant

quadrare [kua·'dra:·re] **I.** *vt* avere a. *fig* (*conti*) to balance; **~ il bilancio** to balance the books **II.** *vi* essere o avere **1.** (*corrispondere*) **~ con qc** to square with sth **2.** *fig, fam* (*convincere*) to add up; **c'è qualcosa che non quadra** there's something that doesn't add up **3.** (*conti, calcoli*) to tally

quadrato [kua·'dra:·to] *m* **1.** MAT (*quadrangolo*) square **2.** MAT (*potenza*) square; **7 al ~ 7** squared; **elevare un numero al ~** to square a number **3.** SPORT (*nel pugilato*) ring

quadrato, -a *agg* **1.** (*forma*) square **2.** *fig* (*equilibrato*) sensible **3.** MAT square; **radice -a** square root

quadratura [kua·dra·'tu:·ra] *f* MAT, ASTR squaring

quadrettato [kua·dret·'ta:·to] *agg* (*carta*) squared; (*tessuto*) checked

quadretto [kua·'dret·to] *m* **1.** (*piccolo quadrato*) (small) square; **a -i** (*foglio, quaderno*) squared **2.** (*di cioccolato*) square **3.** (*piccolo* *quadro*) (small) picture **4.** *fig* (*scena*) picture

quadriennale [kua·dri·en·'na:·le] I. *agg* **1.** (*che dura quattro anni*) four-year **2.** (*che ricorre ogni quattro anni*) four-yearly II. *f* quadrennial

quadriennio [kua·dri·'ɛn·nio] <-i> *m* four-year period

quadrifoglio [kua·dri·'fɔʎ·ʎo] <-gli> *m* BOT four-leaf clover

quadriglia [kua·'driʎ·ʎa] <-glie> *f* (*ballo*) quadrille

quadrilatero [kua·dri·'la:·te·ro] *m* **1.** MAT quadrilateral **2.** (*forma, zona*) area

quadrilatero, -a *agg* quadrilateral

quadrimestre [kua·dri·'mɛs·tre] *m* **1.** (*periodo*) four-month period **2.** (*di scuola*) quarter

quadrimotore [kua·dri·mo·'to:·re] *m* four-engined plane

quadripartito [kua·dri·par·'ti:·to] *m* POL four-party government

quadripartito, -a *agg* four-party; **governo ~** four-party government; **accordo ~** four-party agreement

quadrisillabo, -a [kua·dri·'sil·la·bo] I. *agg* (*vocabolo*) four-syllable II. *m*, *f* **1.** (*parola*) word with four syllables **2.** (*verso*) four-syllable line

quadrivio [kua·'dri:·vio] <-i> *m* (*incrocio*) crossroads

quadro ['kua:·dro] *m* **1.** (*dipinto*) painting **2.** (*quadrato*) square; **a -i** checked **3.** *fig* (*descrizione*) picture; **fare un ~ della situazione** to give an account of the situation **4.** *fig* (*scena*) sight **5.** *fig* (*tabella*) table **6.** *fig* (*ambito*) area **7.** THEAT scene; FILM frame **8.** TEC panel **9.** *pl* ADM cadres; **-i amministrativi** administration; **-i direttivi** (senior) management **10.** *pl* (*di carte da gioco*) diamonds

quadro, -a *agg* **1.** (*quadrato*) square **2.** MAT square; **metro/centimetro ~** square meter/centimeter

quadrupede [kua·'dru:·pe·de] I. *m* quadruped II. *agg* (*animali*) four-footed

quadruplicare [kua·dru·pli·'ka:·re] I. *vt avere* to quadruple II. *vr:* **-rsi** to quadruple

quadruplice [kua·'dru:·pli·tʃe] *agg* (*copia*) four

quadruplo ['kua:·drup·lo] *m* four times as much

quadruplo, -a *agg* (*salto*) quadruple; **camera -a** four-bedded room

quaggiù [kuad·'dʒu] *avv* down here; (*~ sulla terra*) down here on earth; **~ in Sicilia** down here in Sicily

quaglia ['kuaʎ·ʎa] <-glie> *f* quail

qual [kual] *v.* **quale**

qualche ['kual·ke] <inv, solo al sing> *agg* **1.** (*alcuni*) some; (*nelle frasi interrogative*) a few; **hai qualche minuto?** do you have a few minutes?; **~ ora/giorno/mese** a few hours/days/months; **~ volta** sometimes **2.** (*uno*) some; (*nelle frasi interrogative*) any; **in ~ modo** somehow **3.** (*un certo*) some; **~ cosa** *v.*

qualcosa

qualcheduno [kual·ke·'du:·no] *pron v.* **qualcuno**

qualcosa [kual·'kɔ:·sa] <inv> *pron* (*una cosa*) something; (*nelle frasi interrogative*) anything; **~ di bello** something nice; **~ come 50 euro** around 50 euros; **è già ~** that's something

qualcuno, -a [kual·'ku:·no] <solo al sing> *pron* **1.** (*alcuni*) some people; **~ di loro** some of them **2.** (*uno*) someone; (*nelle frasi interrogative*) anyone; **c'è ~?** is anyone there? **3.** (*persona importante*) somebody

quale ['kua:·le] <*davanti a consonante spesso* qual> I. *agg* **1.** (*interrogativo*) which; **qual è il tuo libro preferito?** which is your favorite book? **2.** (*indefinito*) some; **in certo qual modo** in some ways **3.** (*esclamativo*) what; **ma -i vacanze: sono pieno di lavoro!** what vacation: I have a ton of work to do! **4.** (*come*) **tale ~** just like; **è tale ~ te l'ho descritto** it's just as I described it to you II. *pron* **1.** (*interrogativo*) which (one) **2.** (*relativo: persona*) who; (*cosa*) that; **il bambino del ~ ti ho accennato** the child (who) I told you about; **la storia sulla ~ si basa il film** the story that the film is based on; **è tale e ~ sua madre** *fam* she's exactly like her mother; **una persona non tanto per la ~** *fam* someone who is not to be trusted **3.** (*come*) such as; **erbe, -i la menta e l'origano** herbs such as mint and oregano

qualifica [kua·'li:·fi·ka] <-che> *f* **1.** (*titolo*) qualification **2.** (*categoria professionale*) job title **3.** (*giudizio*) label

qualificare [kua·li·fi·'ka:·re] I. *vt* **1.** (*definire*) to define **2.** (*formare*) to qualify II. *vr:* **-rsi** **1.** (*definirsi*) to describe oneself **2.** SPORT to qualify

qualificativo, -a [kua·li·fi·ka·'ti:·vo] *agg* qualifying; **aggettivo ~** qualifying adjective

qualificato, -a [kua·li·fi·'ka:·to] *agg* **1.** (*operaio, tecnico*) skilled **2.** (*esperto*) qualified

qualificazione [kua·li·fi·ka·'tsio:·ne] *f* qualification

qualità [kua·li·'ta] <-> *f* **1.** (*gener*) quality; **prodotti di ~** quality products; **di ~** high quality; **di prima ~** top quality; **di ~ superiore** superior quality **2.** (*varietà*) type

qualitativo, -a [kua·li·ta·'ti:·vo] *agg* qualitative

qualora [kua·'lo:·ra] *cong* if

qualsiasi [kual·'si:·a·si] <inv, solo al sing> *agg* any; **vieni un giorno ~** come any day; **a ~ prezzo** at any cost

qualunque [kua·'luŋ·kue] <inv, solo al sing> *agg* **1.** (*ogni, uno qualsiasi*) any; **a ~ costo** at any cost; **in ~ modo** in any way; **è una persona ~** he's [*o* she's] an ordinary person **2.** +*conj* (*relativo*) whatever

qualunquismo [kua·luŋ·'kuiz·mo] *m* apathy toward politics

qualunquista [kua·luŋ·'kuis·ta] <-i *m*, -e *f*> *mf* person who is apathetic about politics

Q

quando ['kuan·do] I. *avv* 1. (*interrogativo*) when; **per ~?** when?; **per ~ è previsto il funerale?** when is the funeral expected to be?; **da ~?** since when?; **di ~?** when from?; **di ~ sono le foto?** when are the photos from?; **fino a ~?** how long?; **fino a ~ ti fermi?** how long are you staying? 2. (*correlativo*) **di ~ in ~** from time to time II. *cong* 1. (*temporale*) when; **da ~** since; **da ~ ci siamo lasciati sono passati sei anni** it's been six years since we split up; **quand'ecco che ...** when suddenly ... 2. (*tutte le volte che*) whenever 3. (*mentre*) while 4. (*esclamativo*) **~ si dice la fortuna!** talk about your good luck! III. *m* when
quantificare [kuan·ti·fi·'ka:·re] *vt* to quantify
quantificatore, -trice [kuan·ti·fi·ka·'to:·re] *m*, *f* quantifier
quantificazione [kuan·ti·fi·ka·'tsio:·ne] *f* measurement
quantistico, -a [kuan·'tis·ti·ko] <-ci, -che> *agg* PHYS quantum; **teoria/meccanica -a** quantum theory/mechanics
quantità [kuan·ti·'ta] <-> *f* 1. (*numero*) quantity 2. (*gran numero*) load; **in ~** in large quantities
quantitativo, -a [kuan·ti·ta·'ti:·vo] I. *agg* quantitative II. *m*, *f* quantity
quanto¹ ['kuan·to] *m* PHYS quantum; **teoria dei -i** quantum theory
quanto² *avv* 1. (*interrogativo*) how much; **~ costa?** how much is it?; **~ sei alto?** how tall are you?; (*tempo*) how long; **~ ci impieghi?** how long does it take you?; (*distanza*) how far; **~ è lontano?** how far is it? 2. (*esclamativo*) **~ sei grande!** you're so tall! 3. (*nella misura che*) as much as; **aggiungere olio ~ basta** add as much oil as is necessary 4. (*come*) as; **tanto ... ~ ... as ... as ...; tanto bello ~ intelligente** as handsome as he is clever; **in ~** because; **per ~** +*conj* as far as; **per ~ ne sappia io** as far as I know; **~ mai** (*estremamente*) extremely; **~ prima** as soon as possible
quanto, -a I. *agg* 1. (*interrogativo: singolare*) how much; (*plurale*) how many; **~ tempo ci vuole?** how long does it take?; **-i anni hai?** how old are you?; **-i ne abbiamo oggi?** what's the date today? 2. (*esclamativo*) **-e storie!** what a fuss!; **-a fretta!** you're in a hurry! 3. (*nella quantità che*) **compra -e cartoline vuoi** buy as many cards as you like; **tutti -i** everyone 4. (*quello che*) **da ~ ho capito** as I understand it II. *pron* 1. (*interrogativo: singolare*) how much; (*plurale*) how many; **~ ne metto?** how much should I put in?; **-i ne hai?** how many do you have? 2. (*relativo: singolare*) as much as; (*plurale*) as many as 3. *pl* (*coloro che*) those who 4. (*con partitivo*) **ho comprato ~ di meglio si possa trovare** I bought the best you can buy
quantunque [kuan·'tuŋ·kue] *cong* although
quaranta [kua·'ran·ta] I. *num* forty II. <-> *m* forty; *v.a.* **cinquanta**
quarantena [kua·ran·'tɛ:·na] *f* MED quarantine;

mettere in ~ MED to quarantine
quarantenne [kua·ran·'tɛn·ne] I. *agg* forty-year-old II. *mf* forty year old
quarantennio [kua·ran·'tɛn·nio] <-i> *m* forty years
quarantesimo [kua·ran·'tɛ:·zi·mo] *m* (*frazione*) fortieth
quarantesimo, -a I. *agg* fortieth II. *m*, *f* fortieth
quarantina [kua·ran·'ti:·na] *f* **una ~ (di ...)** around forty; **essere sulla ~** to be around forty
quarantotto [kua·ran·'tɔt·to] I. *num* forty-eight II. <-> *m* 1. (*numero*) forty-eight 2. *fig, fam* (*confusione*) **fare un ~** to hit the roof
quaresima [kua·'re:·zi·ma] *f* Lent
quarta ['kuar·ta] *f* 1. (*classe: nelle elementari*) fourth grade; (*nelle superiori*) twelfth grade 2. MOT (*marcia*) fourth (gear); **partire in ~** *fig* (*arrabbiarsi*) to fly off the handle; (*entusiasmarsi*) to jump in with both feet 3. MUS fourth
quartetto [kuar·'tet·to] *m* MUS quartet
quartiere [kuar·'tiɛ:·re] *m* 1. (*di città*) neighborhood 2. MIL quarters; **~ generale** headquarters *pl*
quartina [kuar·'ti:·na] *f* 1. LIT (*strofa*) quatrain 2. MUS quadruplet
quartino [kuar·'ti:·no] *m fam* (*di vino*) quarter liter
quarto ['kuar·to] *m* (*frazione, quantità*) quarter; **~ d'ora** quarter of an hour; **sono le tre e un ~** it's a quarter after three; **i -i di finale** the quarterfinals; **un ~ di vino** a quarter of a liter of wine
quarto, -a I. *agg* fourth II. *m*, *f* fourth; *v.a.* **quinto**
quarzo ['kuar·tso] *m* quartz
quasi ['kua:·zi] I. *avv* 1. (*circa*) around 2. (*pressoché*) almost 3. (*forse*) **penserei ~ ad un furto** it looks almost like a robbery; **~ ~ vengo anch'io** I've half a mind to come to 4. (*come se fosse*) **sembrare ~ qc** to be like sth; **sembra ~ una farsa** it's like a farce II. *cong* +*conj* as if
quassù [kuas·'su] *avv* up here; **~ al Nord** up here in the north; **~ in montagna** up here in the mountains
quaterna [kua·'tɛr·na] *f* (*nel lotto, nella tombola*) set of four winning numbers
quaternario [kua·ter·'na:·rio] *m* GEOL quaternary
quatto, -a ['kuat·to] *agg* (*zitto zitto*) **~ ~** as quiet as a mouse
quattordicenne [kuat·tor·di·'tʃɛn·ne] I. *agg* fourteen-year-old II. *mf* fourteen year old
quattordicesima [kuat·tor·di·'tʃe·zi·ma] *f* (*retribuzione*) bonus equivalent to one month's pay
quattordicesimo [kuat·tor·di·'tʃe·zi·mo] *m* (*frazione*) fourteenth
quattordicesimo, -a I. *agg* fourteenth II. *m*, *f* fourteenth; *v.a.* **quinto**
quattordici [kuat·'tor·di·tʃi] I. *num* fourteen

II. <-> *m* **1.** (*numero*) fourteen **2.** (*nelle date*) fourteenth III. *fpl* 2 pm; *v.a.* **cinque**

quattrino [kuat·'tri:·no] *m* (*soldi*) money; **non ha il becco di un** ~ he doesn't have a penny; **costa fior di -i** it costs a fortune; **avere un sacco di -i** *fam* to be loaded

quattrinoso, -a [kuat·tri·'no:·so] *agg fam* loaded; **una persona -a** a wealthy person

quattro ['kuat·tro] I. *num* four II. *agg fig* (*pochi*) **alla festa c'erano** ~ **gatti** there were only a few people at the party; **gridare ai** ~ **venti** to tell all and sundry; **dirne** ~ **a qu** to give sb a piece of one's mind; **fare** ~ **chiacchiere** to have a chat; **fare** ~ **passi** to go for a stroll; **fare** ~ **salti** to go dancing; **fare il diavolo a** ~ to move heaven and earth; **farsi in** ~ **per qu** to bend over backwards to help sb; **in** ~ **e quattr'otto** in no time III. <-> *m* **1.** (*numero*) four **2.** (*nelle date*) fourth **3.** (*voto scolastico*) = D, *below average grade* **4.** SPORT (*nel canottaggio*) four IV. *fpl* four o'clock; *v.a.* **cinque**

quattrocchi, quattr'occhi [kuat·'trɔk·ki] *avv* **a** ~ face to face; **parlare a quattr'occhi con qu** to speak to someone privately

quattrocentesco, -a [kuat·tro·tʃen·'tes·ko] <-schi, -sche> *agg* (*arte, mura, edifici*) fifeenth century

quattrocento [kuat·tro·'tʃɛn·to] I. *num* four hundred II. <-> *m* four hundred; **il Quattrocento** the fifteenth century

quattroesettanta [kuat·tro·e·set·'an·ta] <*sing*> *m* SPORT 470, *Olympic sailing dinghy*

quattromila [kuat·tro·'mi:·la] I. *num* four thousand II. <-> *m* four thousand

quello, -a ['kuel·lo] I. <quel, quell', quei, quegli> *agg* (*singolare*) that; (*plurale*) those; **-a casa** that house; **-e montagne** those mountains; **-a ragazza di cui ti parlavo** that girl I was telling you about; **-e cose che ti ho detto** those things I said to you II. *pron* **1.** (*persona, animale, cosa lontana: singolare*) that (one); (*plurale*) those (ones), I'd like that one, not this one **2.** (*colui*) the one; ~ **che** the one who **3.** (*ciò*) ~ **che** what; **digli** ~ **che pensi** tell him what you think; **parlami di** ~ **che vuoi** tell me what you want; **tutto** ~ **che ...** everything (that) ...; **per quel che ne so io** as far as I know **4.** (*uomo*) he; (*donna*) she; **una di -e** *pej* one of those; **arriva** ~ **dei gelati** the ice-cream man is coming **5.** (*persone*) they

quercia ['kuɛr·tʃa] <-ce> *f* oak; **forte come una** ~ *fig* strong as an oak

querela [kue·'rɛ:·la] *f* lawsuit; **sporgere** ~ **contro qu** to take sb to court

querelante [kue·re·'lan·te] *mf* plaintiff

querelare [kue·re·'la:·re] *vt* to sue

querelato, -a [kue·re·'la:·to] *m, f* defendant

quesito [kue·'zi:·to] *m* question

questionare [kues·tio·'na:·re] *vi* (*litigare*) ~ (**con qu su qc**) to argue (with sb about sth)

questionario [kues·tio·'na:·rio] <-i> *m* questionnaire

questione [kues·'tio:·ne] *f* **1.** POL, SOC, HIST (*problema*) question; **in** ~ in question **2.** (*controversia*) issue **3.** (*faccenda*) matter; ~ **d'onore** affair of honor; **è** ~ **di un minuto** it will only take a minute; **è** ~ **di vita o di morte** it's a matter of life and death

questo, -a ['kues·to] I. *agg* (*singolare*) this; (*plurale*) these; **-a casa** this house; **-i libri** these books; **in** ~ **momento** at this moment; **quest'oggi** today; **uno di -i giorni** one of these days II. *pron* **1.** (*persona, animale, cosa vicina: singolare*) this (one); (*plurale*) these (ones) **2.** (*ciò*) ~ **mai** never; ~ **no** not this; ~ **sì** this is OK; **senti -a!** listen to this!; **in** ~ **ti dò ragione** I take your point; **per** ~ **ti ho chiamato** this is why I called you; **su** ~ **non sono d'accordo** I don't agree on this point; **con** ~ with this; **-a proprio non ci voleva!** *fam* that's all we need!; **-a sì che è bella!** *fam* amazing!

questore [kues·'to:·re] *m* (*funzionario di polizia*) ≈ police commissioner

questura [kues·'tu:·ra] *f* **1.** (*organo*) police department **2.** (*sede*) police headquarters; **andare in** ~ to go to the police headquarters

qui [kui] *avv* **1.** (*stato, moto*) here; **siamo** ~ we're here; **vieni** ~ come here; ~ **dentro/fuori/sopra/sotto/vicino** in/out/over/under/near here; **da** ~ from here; **da** ~ **in avanti** from here (on); **di** ~ through here; **per di** ~ this way; **fin** ~ up to here **2.** (*temporale*) now; **fin** ~ until now

quiescenza [kuieʃ·'ʃɛn·tsa] *f* payment of a lump sum instead of a pension

quietanza [kuie·'tan·tsa] *f* receipt; **per** ~ received with thanks

quietare [kuie·'ta:·re] I. *vt* (*tranquillizzare*) to calm; ~ **le acque** *fig* to pour oil on troubled waters II. *vr:* **-rsi** to calm down

quiete ['kuiɛ:·te] *f* **1.** (*calma: di sera, notte, campagna*) peace **2.** (*pace dell'anima*) calm **3.** (*silenzio*) quiet

quieto, -a ['kuiɛ:·to] *agg* **1.** (*mare, persona*) calm **2.** (*aria*) still **3.** (*zona, notte*) peaceful

quindi ['kuin·di] I. *cong* (*perciò*) so II. *avv* (*poi*) then

quindicenne [kuin·di·'tʃɛn·ne] I. *agg* fifteen-year-old II. *mf* fifteen year old

quindicennio [kuin·di·'tʃɛn·nio] <-i> *m* fifteen-year period

quindicesimo [kuin·di·'tʃɛ:·zi·mo] *m* (*frazione*) fifteenth

quindicesimo, -a I. *agg* fifteenth II. *m, f* fifteenth; *v.a.* **quinto**

quindici ['kuin·di·tʃi] I. *num* fifteen; **fra** ~ **giorni** in two weeks II. <-> *m* **1.** (*numero*) fifteen **2.** (*nelle date*) fifteenth III. *fpl* 3 p.m.; *v.a.* **cinque**

quindicina [kuin·di·'tʃi:·na] *f* **1.** (*serie*) about fifteen; **una** ~ (**di ...**) about fifteen (...) **2.** (*periodo*) two weeks; **la prima** ~ **di luglio** the first two weeks in July

quindicinale [kuin·di·tʃi·'na:·le] I. *agg* **1.** (*che* *dura quindici giorni*) two-weekly **2.**(*che ricorre ogni quindici giorni*) semimonthly **II.** *m* (*giornale, pubblicazione*) bimonthly

quinquennale [kuin·kuen·'na:·le] *agg* **1.**(*che dura 5 anni*) five year **2.**(*che ricorre ogni 5 anni*) five-yearly

quinquennio [kuin·'kuen·nio] <-i> *m* five year period

quinta ['kuin·ta] *f* **1.** THEAT flat; **stare dietro le -e** to be backstage; *fig* to be behind the scenes **2.**(*classe: nelle elementari*) fifth grade; (*nelle superiori*) freshman year, *at college* **3.** MOT fifth (gear) **4.** MUS fifth; *v.a.* **quinto**

quintale [kuin·'ta:·le] *m* quintal, *metric unit of weight = 100 kg*

quintetto [kuin·'tet·to] *m* quintet

quinto ['kuin·to] *m* (*frazione*) fifth; **quattro -i** four fifths

quinto, -a I. *agg* fifth; **la -a volta** the fifth time; **la -a parte di** one fifth of **II.** *m, f* fifth; **arrivare ~** to come fifth

quintuplicare [kuin·tup·li·'ka:·re] **I.** *vt* to increase fivefold **II.** *vr:* **-rsi** (*aumentare*) to increase fivefold

quintuplo ['kuin·tu·plo] *m* five times as much

quintuplo, -a *agg* (*formazione*) five-part; **camera -a** five-bedded room

qui pro quo [kui prɔ kuɔ] <-> *m* misunderstanding

Quirinale [kui·ri·'na:·le] *m* POL *residence of the President of Italy*

quisquilia [kuis·'kui:·lia] <-ie> *f* trifle

quiz [kuidz] <-> *m* **1.**(*domanda*) question **2.** TV (*programma*) quiz

quorum ['kuɔ:·rum] *m* (*numero legale*) quorum

quota ['kuɔ:·ta] *f* **1.**(*percentuale*) share **2.**(*somma*) fee; **~ di partecipazione** enrollment fee; **~ d'ammortamento** FIN depreciation allowance **3.**(*altitudine*) height; **perdere ~** to lose height

quotare [kuo·'ta:·re] *vt* FIN (*società*) to list

quotato, -a [kuo·'ta:·to] *agg* **1.**(*apprezzato*) highly rated **2.** FIN (*azioni, titoli*) listed

quotazione [kuo·ta·'tsio:·ne] *f* **1.** FIN (*azioni, titoli*) listing **2.**(*di persona*) rating

quotidiano [kuo·ti·'dia:·no] *m* (*giornale*) daily newspaper

quotidiano, -a *agg* **1.**(*di tutti i giorni*) daily **2.**(*solito*) everyday

quoziente [kuo·'tsiɛn·te] *m* **1.** MAT, MED, PSYCH quotient; **~ di intelligenza** intelligence quotient; **~ di sviluppo** development quotient **2.**(*in statistica*) rate

R

R, r ['ɛr·re] <-> *f o m* (*lettera*) r; **~ come Roma** r for Roger

rabarbaro [ra·'bar·ba·ro] *m* **1.**(*pianta*) rhubarb **2.**(*liquore*) rhubarb liqueur

rabberciare [rab·ber·'tʃa:·re] *vt a. fig* to patch together

rabbi ['rab·bi] <-> *m* (*religione ebraica*) rabbi

rabbia ['rab·bia] <-ie> *f* **1.** MED (*idrofobia*) rabies **2.**(*collera, furore*) anger; **sfogare la propria ~ su qu** to take one's anger out on sb; **essere divorato dalla ~** to be consumed with anger **3.**(*stizza, disappunto*) irritation; **fare ~ a qu** to make sb cross; **che ~!** *fam* how annoying! **4.** *fig* (*impeto, furia*) fury; **con ~** furiously

rabbico, -a [rab·bi·ko] <-ci, -che> *agg* MED rabies

rabbino [rab·'bi:·no] *m* (*religione ebraica*) rabbi

rabbioso, -a [rab·'bio:·so] *agg* **1.** MED (*cane*) rabid **2.**(*pieno di rabbia: persona, sguardo*) angry **3.**(*furioso: gesto, scatto*) furious **4.**(*vento, mare*) raging

rabbonire [rab·bo·'ni:·re] <rabbonisco> **I.** *vt* (*calmare*) to calm down **II.** *vr:* **-rsi** (*placarsi*) to calm down

rabbrividire [rab·bri·vi·'di:·re] <rabbrividisco> *vi essere* to shiver

rabbuffare [rab·buf·'fa:·re] *vt* **1.**(*scompigliare: capelli*) to ruffle **2.** *fig* (*rimproverare*) to tell off

rabbuffo [rab·'buf·fo] *m* (*rimprovero*) telling-off

rabbuiarsi [rab·bu·'ia:·r·si] *vr* (*oscurarsi*) to darken

rabdomante [rab·do·'man·te] *mf* dowser

rabdomanzia [rab·do·man·'tsi:·a] <-ie> *f* dowsing

racc. *abbr di* **raccomandata** certified mail

raccapezzarsi [rak·ka·pet·'tsa:·r·si] *vr fam* (*riuscire ad orientarsi*) to get one's head around sth; **non mi ci raccapezzo** I can't get my head around it

raccapricciante [rak·ka·prit·'tʃa:n·te] <-i> *agg* (*scena, visione, spettacolo*) horrifying

raccapriccio [rak·ka·'prit·tʃo] <-ci> *m* horror

raccattapalle [rak·kat·ta·'pal·le] <-> (*nel tennis*) ball boy *m*, ball girl *f*

raccattare [rak·kat·'ta:·re] *vt* **1.**(*raccogliere da terra*) to pick up **2.** *fig* (*radunare*) to get together

racchetta [rak·'ket·ta] *f* SPORT racket; **~ da tennis** tennis racket; **~ da ping-pong** table tennis paddle; **~ da neve** snowshoe; **~ da sci** ski stick

racchettone [rak·ket·'tɔ:·ne] *m* (*per beach tennis*) beach tennis racket

racchio, -a ['rak·kio] <-cchi, -cchie> **I.** *agg fam* ugly **II.** *m, f fam* ugly mug

racchiudere [rak·'kiu:·de·re] <irr> *vt* **1.**(*con-*

tenere) to contain **2.** *fig* (*implicare*) to imply
raccoglibriciole [rak·koʎ·ʎi·'bri:·tʃo·le] <-> *m* (*per la tavola*) hand-held vacuum cleaner
raccogliere [rak·'kɔʎ·ʎe·re] <irr> I. *vt* **1.** (*da terra*) to pick up **2.** (*frutti, fiori*) to pick; (*grano*) to harvest **3.** (*mettere insieme: soldi*) to collect; (*idee, energie*) to gather **4.** (*collezionare: francobolli*) to collect II. *vr:* **-rsi 1.** (*radunarsi*) to gather **2.** *fig* (*concentrarsi*) to gather one's thoughts
raccoglimento [rak·koʎ·ʎi·'men·to] *m* concentration
raccoglitore [rak·koʎ·ʎi·'to:·re] *m* (*per documenti*) file
raccolgo *1. pers sing pr di* **raccogliere**
raccolsi *1. pers sing pass rem di* **raccogliere**
raccolta [rak·'kɔl·ta] *f* **1.** (*atto*) collecting; (*di frutta*) picking; (*di grano*) harvesting; ~ **dei rifiuti** garbage collection; ~ **differenziata** recycling collection; ~ **di fondi** fundraising **2.** (*le cose raccolte*) collection; (*di frutta, grano*) harvest **3.** (*collezione: di opere d'arte*) collection **4.** (*loc*) **chiamare a** ~ to gather together
raccolto [rak·'kɔl·to] *m* harvest; (*di frutta*) crop
raccolto, -a I. *pp di* **raccogliere** II. *agg* **1.** (*capelli: tenuti insieme*) gathered back; (*tirati su*) gathered up; (*documenti*) gathered together **2.** *fig* (*concentrato: persona*) absorbed **3.** *fig* (*composto: atteggiamento*) calm **4.** *fig* (*tranquillo: ambiente*) secluded
raccomandabile [rak·ko·man·'da:·bi·le] *agg* commendable; **un tizio poco** ~ a guy not to be trusted
raccomandare [rak·ko·man·'da:·re] I. *vt* **1.** (*affidare alle cure*) to entrust **2.** (*consigliare*) to advise; ~ **a qu di fare qc** to advise sb to do sth **3.** (*appoggiare: candidato*) to recommend II. *vr:* **-rsi a qc** (*clemenza, bontà*) to beg for sth; **mi raccomando!** don't forget!
raccomandata [rak·ko·man·'da:·ta] *f* (*lettera*) certified letter
raccomandato, -a [rak·ko·man·'da:·to] I. *agg* **1.** (*lettera, pacco*) certified **2.** (*favorito: candidato*) recommended II. *m, f* (*persona raccomandata*) well-connected person
raccomandazione [rak·ko·man·dat·'tsio:·ne] *f* **1.** (*consiglio*) advice **2.** (*segnalazione: per lavoro, concorso*) recommendation
raccontare [rak·kon·'ta:·re] *vt* (*riferire*) ~ **qc a qu** to tell sb sth; ~ **qc per filo e per segno** to go into every detail about sth; **raccontamela giusta!** be honest!
racconto [rak·'kon·to] **1.** (*narrazione*) account **2.** (*fatto raccontato*) story **3.** LIT story; (*novella*) short story
raccordare [rak·kor·'da:·re] *vt* (*collegare: strade, tubi*) to connect
raccordo [rak·'kɔr·do] (*strada*) junction; (*ferroviario*) siding; ~ **anulare** beltway
rachitico, -a [ra·'ki:·ti·ko] <-ci, -che> I. *agg* **1.** MED (*affetto da rachitismo*) suffering from rickets **2.** (*debole*) scrawny II. *m, f* MED person

suffering from rickets
rachitismo [ra·ki·'tiz·mo] *m* rickets
racimolare [ra·tʃi·mo·'la:·re] *vt fig* (*soldi*) to scrape together
radar ['ra:·dar] I. <-> *m* radar II. <inv> *agg* radar
radarlocalizzazione [ra·dar·lo·ka·lid·dzat·'tsio:·ne] *f* TEC radar detection
radarmeteorologia [ra·dar·me·te·o·ro·lo·'dʒi:·a] *f* TEC, METEO radar meteorology
radarnavigazione [ra·dar·na·vi·gat·'tsio:·ne] *f* AERO, NAUT radar navigation
radarriflettente [ra·dar·ri·flet·'tɛn·te] *agg* TEC radar reflective
radarsonda [ra·dar·'son·da] *f* TEC radarsonde
radartachimetro [ra·dar·ta·'ki:·me·tro] *m* TEC radar tachometer
raddensarsi [rad·den·'sa:r·si] *vr* (*salsa, nuovle*) to thicken
raddolcire [rad·dol·'tʃi:·re] <raddolcisco> I. *vt* **1.** to sweeten **2.** (*metalli, carattere*) to soften II. *vr:* **-rsi** *fig* (*carattere*) to soften
raddoppiamento [rad·dop·pia·'men·to] *m* doubling
raddoppiare [rad·dop·'pia:·re] I. *vt avere* to double II. *vi essere* to double
raddoppio [rad·'dop·pio] <-pi> *m* **1.** FERR doubling **2.** MUS doubling
raddrizzamento [rad·drit·tsa·'men·to] *m* **1.** (*correzione*) straightening **2.** (*di immagine, fotografia*) correction **3.** EL rectification
raddrizzare [rad·drit·'tsa:·re] I. *vt* **1.** (*lama, chiodo, quadro*) to straighten **2.** *fig* (*correggere*) to straighten out **3.** EL to rectify II. *vr:* **-rsi 1.** (*mettersi eretto*) to straighten oneself up **2.** (*rimettersi sulla buona strada*) to straighten oneself out
radente [ra·'dɛn·te] *agg* (*volo*) skimming; (*tiro*) grazing
radere ['ra:·de·re] <rado, rasi, raso> I. *vt* **1.** (*barba, baffi*) to shave **2.** (*distruggere*) ~ **al suolo** to raze to the ground **3.** (*sfiorare*) to graze II. *vr:* **-rsi** (*barba, baffi*) to shave
radiale [ra·'dia:·le] *agg* MAT, PHYS, ASTR radial; **pneumatico** ~ radial tire
radiante [ra·'dian·te] *agg* PHYS radiant; **terapia** ~ radiation therapy
radiare [ra·'dia:·re] *vt* ADM (*da scuola*) to expel; (*da albo professionale*) to strike off
radiatore [ra·dia·'to:·re] *m* radiator
radiazione [ra·diat·'tsio:·ne] *f* PHYS radiation
radica ['ra:·di·ka] <-che> *f* (*legno pregiato*) walnut; (*per pipe*) briar
radicale [ra·di·'ka:·le] *agg* **1.** *a. fig* radical **2.** (*partito*) Radical
radicalizzare [ra·di·ka·lid·'dza:·re] I. *vt avere* (*inasprire: lotta, protesta*) to radicalize II. *vr:* **-rsi** (*inasprirsi: conflitto*) to worsen
radicarsi [ra·di·'ka:r·si] *vr* (*idee, valori*) to take root
radicato, -a [ra·di·'ka:·to] *agg* (*idee, valori*) rooted
radice [ra·'di:·tʃe] *f a. fig* root; **mettere -i** *fig* to

R

put down roots

radi e getta ['ra:·di e 'dʒɛt·ta] I. <-> *m* disposable razor II. <inv> *agg* disposable

radio¹ ['ra:·dio] I. <-> *f* 1. (*collegamento, emittente*) radio; **trasmettere per** ~ to broadcast on the radio; ~ **ricevente** receiver; ~ **trasmittente** transmitter 2. (*apparecchio*) radio; **sentire** [*o* **ascoltare**] **la** ~ to listen to the radio II. <inv> *agg* radio; **contatto** ~ radio contact; **giornale** ~ radio news bulletin; **ponte** ~ radio link

radio² *m* CHEM radium

radioamatore, -trice [ra·dio·a·ma·'to:·re] *m*, *f* radio ham

radioamatoriale [ra·dio·a·ma·to·'ria:·le] *agg* ham radio operator

radioascoltatore, -trice [ra·dio·as·kol·ta·'to:·re] *m*, *f* radio listener

radioassistenza [ra·dio·as·sis·'tɛn·tsa] *f* radio assistance

radioattività [ra·dio·at·ti·vi·'ta] *f* radioactivity

radioattivo, -a [ra·dio·at·'ti:·vo] *agg* radioactive; **scorie -e** radioactive waste

radiocollegamento [ra·dio·kol·le·ga·'men·to] *m* radio link

radiocomandare [ra·dio·ko·man·'da:·re] *vt* to radio control

radiocomando [ra·dio·ko·'man·do] *m* radio control

radiocomunicazione [ra·dio·ko·mu·ni·kat·'tsio:·ne] *f* radio communication

radiocontaminazione [ra·dio·kon·ta·mi·nat·'tsio:·ne] *f* ECO radioactive contamination

radiocronaca [ra·dio·'krɔ:·na·ka] *f* radio commentary

radiocronista [ra·dio·kro·'nis·ta] *mf* radio commentator

radiodiffusione [ra·dio·dif·fu·'zio:·ne] *f* radio broadcasting

radiodisturbo [ra·dio·dis·'tur·bo] *m* static

radiodramma [ra·dio·'dram·ma] *m* radio play

radioelettrico, -a [ra·dio·e·'lɛt·tri·ko] <-ci, -che> *agg* radioelectric

radiofonia [ra·dio·fo·'ni:·a] <-ie> *f* radio broadcasting

radiofonico, -a [ra·dio·'fɔ:·ni·ko] <-ci, -che> *agg* radiophonic

radiografia [ra·dio·gra·'fi:·a] *f* 1. (*operazione, tecnica*) radiography 2. (*lastra*) X-ray 3. (*esame*) scrutiny

radiografico, -a [ra·dio·'gra:·fi·ko] <-ci, -che> *agg* radiographic

radiogramma [ra·dio·'gram·ma] <-i> *m* 1. (*telegramma*) radiogram 2. LASTRA X-ray

radiolina [ra·dio·'li:·na] *f* 1. (*piccola radio*) pocket radio 2. (*radio a transistor*) transistor radio

radiologia [ra·dio·lo·'dʒi:·a] <-gie> *f* MED radiology

radiologico, -a [ra·dio·'lɔ:·dʒi·ko] <-ci, -che> *agg* radiological

radiologo, -a [ra·'diɔ:·lo·go] <-gi, -ghe> *m*, *f* radiologist

radiomessaggio [ra·dio·mes·'sad·dʒo] <-ggi> *m* radio message

radiomicrofono [ra·dio·mi·'krɔ:·fo·no] *m* radio microphone

radiomobile [ra·dio·'mɔ:·bi·le] *f* (*automezzo*) radio car

radiooperatore, -trice [ra·dio·o·pe·ra·'to:·re] *m*, *f* radio operator

radioregistratore [ra·dio·re·dʒis·tra·'to:·re] *m* cassette radio

radioricevente [ra·dio·ri·tʃe·'vɛn·te] I. *agg* radio receiving II. *f* radio receiver

radioricevitore [ra·dio·ri·tʃe·vi·'to:·re] *m* radio receiver

radioripetitore [ra·dio·ri·pe·ti·'to:·re] *m* radio repeater

radioscanner ['rei·dio·'skæ·nə] <- *o* -s> *f* radio scanner

radioscopia [ra·dio·sko·'pi:·a] <-ie> *f* radioscopy

radiosità [ra·dio·si·'ta] <-> *f* radiance

radioso, -a [ra·'diɔ:·so] *agg a. fig* radiant

radiosveglia [ra·dioz·'veʎ·ʎa] *f* clock radio

radiotaxi, radiotassì [ra·dio·'tak·si, ra·dio·tas·'si] <-> *m* radio taxi

radiotecnica [ra·dio·'tɛk·ni·ka] <-che> *f* radio engineering

radiotecnico, -a [ra·dio·'tɛk·ni·ko] <-ci, -che> I. *agg* radio engineering II. *m*, *f* radio engineer

radiotelefono [ra·dio·te·'lɛ:·fo·no] *m* radio telephone

radiotelevisione [ra·dio·te·le·vi·'zio:·ne] *f* radio and television broadcasting company

radiotelevisivo, -a [ra·dio·te·le·vi·'zi:·vo] *agg* radio and television broadcasting

radioterapia [ra·dio·te·ra·'pi:·a] *f* radiotherapy

radiotrasmettere [ra·dio·traz·'met·te·re] <irr> *vt* to broadcast on the radio

radiotrasmettitore [ra·dio·traz·met·ti·'to:·re] *m* radio transmitter

radiotrasmisi *1. pers sing pass rem di* **radiotrasmettere**

radiotrasmissione [ra·dio·traz·mis·'sio:·ne] *f* 1. (*il trasmettere*) radio broadcasting 2. (*trasmissione*) radio broadcast

radiotrasmittente [ra·dio·traz·mit·'tɛn·te] I. *agg* broadcasting II. *f* radio broadcasting station

rado, -a ['ra:·do] *agg* 1. (*nebbia, tela, capelli*) thin 2. (*infrequente*) rare; **di** ~ rarely

radunare [ra·du·'na:·re] I. *vt* to gather together II. *vr:* **-rsi** to gather

radunata [ra·du·'na:·ta] *f* gathering

raduno [ra·'du:·no] *m* gathering

radura [ra·'du:·ra] *f* glade

rafano ['ra:·fa·no] *m* horseradish

raffa ['raf·fa] *f* **di riffa o di** ~ *fam* somehow

raffazzonato [raf·fat·tso·'na:·to] *vt* (*discorso, articolo*) thrown together

raffermo, -a [raf·'fer·mo] *agg* (*pane*) stale

raffica ['raf·fi·ka] <-che> *f* 1. METEO gust; ~ **di**

vento gust of wind **2.**(*di mitra*) burst **3.**(*di domande*) barrage **4.** *fig* spate; **scioperi a** ~ a spate of strikes

raffigurare [raf·fi·gu·'ra:·re] *vt* **1.**(*rappresentare*) to depict **2.**(*simboleggiare*) to represent

raffinare [raf·fi·'na:·re] **I.** *vt* to refine **II.** *vr:* -**rsi** to become refined

raffinatezza [raf·fi·na·'tet·tsa] *f* refinement

raffinato, -a [raf·fi·'na:·to] *agg* refined

raffinazione [raf·fi·nat·'tsio:·ne] *f* refining

raffineria [raf·fi·ne·'ri:·a] <-ie> *f* refinery

rafforzamento [raf·for·tsa·'men·to] *m* **1.**(*irrobustimento*) reinforcement **2.**(*di carattere*) strengthening

rafforzare [raf·for·'tsa:·re] **I.** *vt* **1.**(*rinforzare*) to reinforce **2.**(*carattere*) to strengthen **II.** *vr:* -**rsi** to get stronger

raffreddamento [raf·fred·da·'men·to] *m* cooling; ~ **ad acqua/aria** water/air cooling

raffreddarsi [raf·fred·'da:r·si] *vr* **1.**(*diventar freddo*) to get cold **2.** *fig* (*rapporti*) to cool **3.**(*prendere un raffredore*) to catch a cold

raffreddato, -a [raf·fred·'da:·to] *agg* **sono raffreddato** I've got a cold

raffreddore [raf·fred·'do:·re] *m* cold

raffronto [raf·'fron·to] *m* comparison

ragazza [ra·'gat·tsa] *f* **1.**(*giovane donna*) girl; ~ **copertina** cover girl; ~ **madre** single mother **2.** *fam* (*fidanzata*) girlfriend

ragazzata [ra·gat·'tsa:·ta] *f fam* childish prank

ragazzo [ra·'gat·tso] *m* **1.**(*giovane uomo*) boy **2.**(*inesperto*) lad **3.** *fam* (*fidanzato*) boyfriend **4.**(*garzone*) boy

raggelarsi [rad·dʒe·'la:r·si] *vr a. fig* to freeze

raggiante [rad·'dʒan·te] *agg* radiant

raggio ['rad·dʒo] <-ggi> *m* **1.**(*gener*) ray; -**ggi alfa** alpha rays; -**ggi X** X-rays; ~ **di speranza** ray of hope **2.** MATH radius **3.**(*zona*) radius; (*ambito*) range; ~ **d'azione** range of action **4.**(*di ruota*) spoke

raggirare [rad·dʒi·'ra:·re] *vt* to trick

raggiro [rad·'dʒi:·ro] *m* trick

raggiungere [rad·'dʒun·dʒe·re] <irr> *vt* **1.**(*meta, vetta*) to reach; (*persone*) to join **2.** *fig* (*obiettivo*) to achieve **3.**(*colpire: bersaglio, cuore*) to hit

raggiungimento [rad·dʒun·dʒi·'men·to] *m* achievement

raggiunsi *1. pers sing pass rem di* **raggiungere**

raggiunto *pp di* **raggiungere**

raggomitolare [rag·go·mi·to·'la:·re] **I.** *vt* (*lana*) to wind **II.** *vr:* -**rsi** (*rannicchiarsi*) to curl up

raggranellare [rag·gra·nel·'la:·re] *vt fam* to scrape together

raggrinzato, raggrinzito [rag·grin·'tsa:·to, rag·grin·'tsi:·to] *agg* **1.**(*pelle*) wrinkled **2.**(*stoffa*) creased

raggrumarsi [rag·gru·'ma:r·si] *vr* (*sangue*) to clot; (*latte*) to curdle

raggruppamento [rag·grup·pa·'men·to] *m* **1.**(*azione*) grouping **2.**(*gruppo*) group

raggruppare [rag·grup·'pa:·re] **I.** *vt* (*riunire*) to gather together **II.** *vr:* -**rsi** to gather

ragguagliare [rag·guaʎ·'ʎa:·re] *vt* (*informare*) to update

ragguaglio [rag·'guaʎ·ʎo] <-gli> *m* (*informazione*) update

ragguardevole [rag·guar·'de:·vo·le] *agg* **1.**(*importante: persona*) distinguished **2.**(*notevole: somma*) considerable

ragia ['ra:·dʒa] <-gie *o* -ge> *f* (*resina*) resin; **acqua** ~ turpentine

ragionamento [ra·dʒo·na·'men·to] *m* **1.**(*pensiero*) reasoning **2.**(*argomentazione*) argument

ragionare [ra·dʒo·'na:·re] *vi* **1.**(*riflettere*) to think **2.** *fam* (*discorrere*) ~ **di qc** to discuss sth

ragionato, -a [ra·dʒo·'na:·to] *agg* (*discorso, proposta*) logical; (*bibliografia, grammatica*) annotated

ragionatore, -trice [ra·dʒo·na·'to:·re] *m, f* thinker

ragione [ra·'dʒo:·ne] *f* **1.**(*facoltà*) reason; **perdere l'uso** [*o* **il lume**] **della** ~ to go out of one's mind; **farsi una** ~ **di qc** to come to terms with sth; **ridurre qu alla** ~ to bring sb back to his/her senses **2.**(*motivo*) reason; **non sentir** ~ to refuse to listen to reason; **per -i di famiglia** for family reasons; **per -i di forza maggiore** due to circumstances beyond one's control; **a maggior** ~ all the more reason why **3.**(*diritto*) right; **avere** ~ to be right; **dare** ~ **a qu** to admit that sb's right **4.** MATH (*misura*) ratio; **in** ~ **di** at the rate of **5.**(*loc*) **picchiare qu di santa** ~ *fam* to give sb a good hiding; **a ragion veduta** after due consideration

ragioneria [ra·dʒo·ne·'ri:·a] <-ie> *f* **1.**(*disciplina*) accountancy **2.**(*ufficio*) accounts department

ragionevole [ra·dʒo·'ne:·vo·le] *agg* **1.**(*di buon senso: persona*) sensible **2.**(*giusto: prezzo*) reasonable

ragioniere, -a [ra·dʒo·'niɛ:·re] *m, f* accountant

ragliare [raʎ·'ʎa:·re] *vi* **1.**(*asino*) to bray **2.** *pej* (*cantare male*) to caterwaul

raglio ['raʎ·ʎo] <-gli> *m* **1.**(*di asino*) bray **2.** *pej* (*canto*) caterwaul

ragnatela [raɲ·ɲa·'te:·la] *f* **1.**(*di ragno*) cobweb **2.** *fig* (*intreccio: di contatti, relazioni*) web

ragno ['raɲ·ɲo] *m* spider

ragù [ra·'gu] <-> *m* (*sugo*) bolognese sauce

Ragusa [ra·'gu:·sa] *f* Ragusa, *city in Sicily*

Ragusano <sing> *m* (*zona*) Ragusa area; **nel** ~ in the Ragusa area

ragusano, -a [ra·gu·'sa:·no] **I.** *m, f* (*abitante*) person from Ragusa **II.** *agg* from Ragusa

RAI ['ra:·i] *f acro di* **Radio Audizione Italiana** *Italian public television and radio broadcasting company*

raid [reid/raid] <-> *m* **1.** SPORT rally **2.** MIL raid

RAI-TV ['ra:i tiv·'vu] *f abbr di* **Radio Televisione Italiana** *Italian public television company*

R

rallegramenti [ral·le·gra·'men·ti] *mpl* congratulations

rallegrare [ral·le·'gra:·re] I. *vt* to cheer up II. *vr:* **-rsi** 1. (*diventar allegro*) to cheer up 2. (*provare allegrezza*) **-rsi a qc** to rejoice at sth 3. (*congratularsi*) **-rsi con qu per qc** to congratulate sb on sth

rallentamento [ral·len·ta·'men·to] *m* 1. (*di velocità, intensità*) slowdown 2. FILM slow motion

rallentare [ral·len·'ta:·re] I. *vt* 1. (*rendere più lento*) to slow down; ~ **il passo** to slow down 2. *fig* (*diventare meno intenso*) to slacken II. *vi* to slow down

rallentatore [ral·len·ta·'to:·re] *m* TV slow motion; **al ~** very slowly

RAM [ram] *m acro di* **Random Access Memory** (*memoria ad accesso casuale*) RAM

ramanzina [ra·man·'dzi:·na] *f fam* telling-off; **fare una ~ a qu** to give sb a telling-off

ramarro [ra·'mar·ro] *m* green lizard

ramato, -a *agg* 1. (*filo*) copper-coated; **zolfo ~** copper sulfate 2. (*capelli, barba*) copper-colored

ramazza [ra·'mat·tsa] *f* broom; **essere di ~** MIL to be on fatigue duty

rambo ['ram·bo] <-> *m fig* (*persona atletica*) action man

rame ['ra:·me] I. *m* 1. CHEM copper 2. (*incisione*) copperplate II. <inv> *agg* (*colore*) copper; **biondo ~** copper blond; **rosso ~** copper red

ramificarsi [ra·mi·fi·'ka:r·si] *vr:* **-rsi** (*distribuirsi*) to branch out

ramificazione [ra·mi·fi·kat·'tsio:·ne] *f* 1. BOT branching 2. (*diramazione*) branch

ramino [ra·'mi:·no] *m* rummy

rammaricarsi [ram·ma·ri·'ka:r·si] *vr:* **-rsi** (*rincrescersi*) **~ di** [*o* **per**] **qc** to regret sth

rammarico [ram·'ma:·ri·ko] <-chi> *m* (*rincrescimento*) regret

rammendare [ram·men·'da:·re] *vt* to darn

rammendatrice [ram·men·da·'tri:·tʃe] *f* darner

rammendo [ram·'mɛn·do] *m* 1. (*azione*) darning 2. (*risultato*) darn

rammentare [ram·men·'ta:·re] *vt* 1. (*ricordare*) to remember 2. (*far presente*) **~ qc a qu** to remind sb of sth 3. (*assomigliare*) **~ qu a qu** to remind sb of sb

rammollire [ram·mol·'li:·re] <rammollisco> I. *vt a. fig* to make soft II. *vr:* **-rsi** *a. fig* (*diventar molle*) to go soft

rammollito, -a [ram·mol·'li:·to] *m, f* runt

ramo ['ra:·mo] *m a. fig* branch

ramoscello [ra·moʃ·'ʃɛl·lo] *m* twig

rampa ['ram·pa] *f* 1. (*di scale*) flight 2. AERO **~ di lancio** launch pad 3. (*salita*) ramp

rampante [ram·'pan·te] *agg* 1. (*leone, grifo*) rampant 2. *fig* (*arrivista: persona*) ambitious

rampicante [ram·pi·'kan·te] I. *agg* BOT climbing II. *m* climber

rampichino [ram·pi·'ki:·no] <-> *m* BOT climbing plant

rampino [ram·'pi:·no] *m* 1. (*gancio*) hook 2. NAUT grapnel

rampollo [ram·'pol·lo] *m* 1. (*discendente*) descendant 2. *scherz* (*figlio*) son

rampone [ram·'po:·ne] *m* 1. (*fiocina*) harpoon 2. SPORT (*nell'alpinismo*) crampon

rana ['ra:·na] *f* frog

rancido ['ran·tʃi·do] *m* rancid taste [*o* smell]

rancido, -a *agg* (*olio, burro*) rancid

rancio ['ran·tʃo] <-ci> *m* MIL mess

rancore [raŋ·'ko:·re] *m* rancor

randagio, -a [ran·'da:·dʒo] <-gi, -ge *o* -gie> *agg* stray

randellare [ran·del·'la:·re] *vt* to cudgel

randellata [ran·del·'la:·ta] *f* blow with a cudgel

randello [ran·'dɛl·lo] *m* cudgel

random ['ræn·dəm] *agg* 1. SCIENT random 2. COMPUT **accesso ~** random access

rango ['raŋ·go] <-ghi> *m* 1. (*condizione sociale*) social standing 2. MIL rank

ranking ['ræŋ·kiŋ] <- *o* rankings> *m* ranking

rannicchiarsi [ran·nik·'kiar·si] *vr* (*raccogliersi*) to crouch down

rannuvolamento [ran·nu·vo·la·'men·to] *m* METEO clouding over

rannuvolarsi [ran·nu·vo·'lar·si] *vr* METEO to cloud over

ranocchio [ra·'nɔk·kio] <-cchi> *m* frog

rantolare [ran·to·'la:·re] *vi* 1. (*emettere rantoli*) to wheeze 2. (*in agonia*) to be breathing one's last breath

rantolio [ran·to·'li:·o] <-ii> *m* wheezing

rantolo ['ran·to·lo] *m* 1. (*respiro affannoso*) wheeze 2. (*in agonia*) death rattle

ranuncolo [ra·'nun·ko·lo] *m* buttercup

rapa ['ra:·pa] *f* turnip; **cavolo ~** kohlrabi; **cima di ~** turnip top; **testa di ~** *fig, scherz* dumbo

rapace [ra·'pa:·tʃe] I. *agg* 1. (*uccello*) predatory; **uccello ~** bird of prey 2. (*ladri, amministratori*) rapacious 3. (*sguardo*) greedy II. *m* bird of prey

rapare [ra·'pa:·re] *vt* (*capelli*) to shave

rapida ['ra:·pi·da] *f* rapids *pl*

rapidità [ra·pi·di·'ta] <-> *f* speed

rapido ['ra:·pi·do] *m* (*treno*) express

rapido, -a *agg* rapid

rapimento [ra·pi·'men·to] *m* 1. (*di persona*) kidnapping 2. REL rapture

rapina [ra·'pi:·na] *f* robbery; **~ in banca** bank robbery; **~ a mano armata** armed robbery

rapinare [ra·pi·'na:·re] *vt* 1. (*rubare: soldi, oggetti*) to steal 2. (*derubare: persone*) to rob

rapinatore, -trice [ra·pi·na·'to:·re] *m, f* robber

rapire [ra·'pi:·re] <rapisco> *vt* 1. (*persone*) to kidnap 2. *fig* (*estasiare*) to enchant

rapitore, -trice [ra·pi·'to:·re] *m, f* kidnapper

rappacificare [rap·pa·tʃi·fi·'ka:·re] I. *vt* to reconcile II. *vr:* **-rsi** to become reconciled

rappacificazione [rap·pa·tʃi·fi·kat·'tsio:·ne] *f* reconciliation

rappezzare [rap·pet·'tsa:·re] *vt a. fig* to patch

up

rappezzo [rap·'pɛt·tso] *m* **1.**(*riparazione*) patching up **2.**(*parte riparata*) patch **3.***fig* (*rimedio*) patch job

rapportare [rap·por·'ta:·re] **I.** *vt* **1.**(*confrontare*) ~ **qc a qc** to compare sth with sth **2.**(*riprodurre*) to reproduce **II.** *vr* (*mettersi in relazione*) -**rsi a qu** to relate to sb

rapporto [rap·'pɔr·to] *m* **1.**(*resoconto*) report **2.**(*legame*) relationship; **essere in buoni -i con qu** to be on good terms with sb; **in ~ a** with relation to **3.** MAT, TEC ratio; **avere un buon ~ qualità-prezzo** to be good value for money

rapprendersi [rap·'prɛn·der·si] <irr> *vr* (*sugo*) to thicken

rappresaglia [rap·pre·'saʎ·ʎa] <-glie> *f* reprisal

rappresentante [rap·pre·zen·'tan·te] *mf* **1.**(*chi fa le veci*) representative; ~ **di classe** class representative **2.** COM (*venditore*) sales representative

rappresentanza [rap·pre·zen·'tan·tsa] *f* **1.**(*delegazione*) delegation; **in ~ di qu** on behalf of sb **2.** COM agency

rappresentare [rap·pre·zen·'ta:·re] *vt* **1.**(*raffigurare*) to depict **2.**(*simboleggiare*) to represent **3.** THEAT (*pezzo teatrale*) to stage; (*ruolo*) to play **4.**(*agire per conto di*) to represent

rappresentativo, -a [rap·pre·zen·ta·'ti:·vo] *agg a. fig* representative

rappresentazione [rap·pre·zen·tat·'tsio:·ne] *f* **1.**(*gener*) depiction **2.** THEAT performance

rappresi *1. pers sing pass rem di* **rapprendere**

rappreso *pp di* **rapprendere**

rapsodia [rap·so·'di:·a] <-ie> *f* rhapsody

raptus ['rap·tus] <-> *m* **1.** MED, PSYCH raptus **2.***fig* (*ispirazione*) flash of inspiration

rarefarsi [ra·re·'fa:r·si] <irr> *vr* **1.**(*aria*) to become rarified **2.***fig* (*visite, incontri*) to become rarer

rarefazione [ra·re·fat·'tsio:·ne] *f* **1.** PHYS (*di aria*) rarefaction **2.***fig* (*di attività, visite, incontri*) decrease

rarefeci *1. pers sing pass rem di* **rarefare**

rarità [ra·ri·'ta] <-> *f* rarity

raro, -a ['ra:·ro] *agg* (*esemplare, animale*) rare; **una bestia -a** *fig* a rare breed

rasare [ra·'sa:·re] **I.** *vt* **1.**(*barba, capelli*) to shave **2.**(*siepe*) to trim; (*prato*) to mow **II.** *vr:* -**rsi** (*barba, capelli*) to shave

rasato, -a *agg* **1.**(*barba*) shaven off; (*persona*) clean-shaven **2.**(*tessuto*) smooth; **maglia -a** stockinette stitch

rasatura [ra·sa·'tu:·ra] *f* shave

raschiamento [ras·kia·'men·to] *m* MED curettage

raschiare [ras·'kia:·re] *vt* to scrape; ~ **il fondo** to be on one's last legs

raschiatura [ras·kia·'tu:·ra] *f* **1.**(*azione*) scraping **2.**(*effetto*) scrape

raschietto [ras·'kiet·to] *m* scraper

rasentare [ra·zen·'ta:·re] *vt* (*sfiorare*) to graze;

~ **qc** *fig* to border on sth; ~ **il ridicolo** to border on the ridiculous

rasente [ra·'zɛn·te] *prep* ~ (**a**) close to

rasi ['ra:·si] *1. pers sing pass rem di* **radere**

raso ['ra:·so] *m* satin

raso, -a **I.** *pp di* **radere** **II.** *agg* **1.**(*volto, testa*) shaven **2.**(*bicchiere*) full; (*cucchiaio*) level; ~ **terra** *v.* **rasoterra**

rasoio [ra·'so:·io] <-oi> *m* razor; **sul filo del ~** *fig* on the razor's edge

rasoterra [ra·so·'tɛr·ra] **I.** *avv* close to the ground **II.** <inv> *agg fig* indifferent

rassegna [ras·'seɲ·ɲa] *f* **1.** MIL inspection **2.**(*esame accurato*) review; **passare in ~ qc** *fig* to review sth **3.**(*elenco*) listing; ~ **degli spettacoli** theater listings *pl* **4.**(*mostra*) exhibition; ~ **cinematografica** film festival

rassegnare [ras·seɲ·'ɲa:·re] **I.** *vt* ~ **le dimissioni** to resign **II.** *vr:* -**rsi a qc** to resign oneself to sth

rassegnazione [ras·seɲ·ɲat·'tsio:·ne] *f* resignation

rasserenamento [ras·se·re·na·'men·to] *m* (*di cielo, tempo*) brightening up

rasserenare [ras·se·re·'na:·re] **I.** *vt* **1.**(*cielo*) to brighten up **2.***fig* (*persona*) to cheer up **II.** *vr:* -**rsi** **1.** METEO to brighten up **2.***fig* (*persona*) to cheer up; -**rsi in volto** to brighten

rassettare [ras·set·'ta:·re] **I.** *vt* **1.**(*stanza, casa*) to tidy **2.**(*riparare: abiti*) to mend **II.** *vr:* -**rsi** to tidy oneself up

rassicurare [ras·si·ku·'ra:·re] **I.** *vt* to reassure **II.** *vr:* -**rsi** to be reassured

rassicurazione [ras·si·ku·rat·'tsio:·ne] *f* reassurance

rassodamento [ras·so·da·'men·to] *m* firming up

rassodare [ras·so·'da:·re] **I.** *vt* (*muscoli*) to firm up **II.** *vr:* -**rsi** (*muscoli*) to become firm

rassomigliare [ras·so·miʎ·'ʎa:·re] **I.** *vi* ~ **a qc** to resemble sth **II.** *vr:* -**rsi** to look like each other

rastrellamento [ras·trel·la·'men·to] *m* **1.** AGR raking **2.** MIL combing

rastrellare [ras·trel·'la:·re] *vt* **1.** AGR to rake **2.** MIL to comb

rastrelliera [ras·trel·'liɛ:·ra] *f* **1.**(*per fieno*) hayrack **2.**(*per biciclette*) bicycle rack

rastrello [ras·'trɛl·lo] *m* rake

rata ['ra:·ta] *f* installment; **pagare/comprare a -e** to pay for/buy sth in installments

rateale [ra·te·'a:·le] *agg* (*acquisto*) in installments

rateizzare [ra·te·id·'dza:·re] *vt* to split into installments

rateo ['ra:·teo] *m* **1.**(*in contabilità*) accrual **2.**(*rateizzazione*) splitting into installments

ratifica [ra·'ti:·fi·ka] <-che> *f* ratification

ratificare [ra·ti·fi·'ka:·re] *vt* to ratify

rating ['rei·tiŋ] <-> *m* **1.** FIN credit rating **2.** TV, RADIO ratings *pl*

ratticida [rat·ti·'tʃi:·da] <-i *m*, -e *f*> **I.** *m* rat poison **II.** *agg* rat poison

R

ratto ['rat·to] *m* **1.** ZOO rat **2.** JUR abduction
rattoppare [rat·top·'pa:·re] *vt a. fig* to patch up
rattrappimento [rat·trap·pi·'men·to] *m* stiffening
rattrappire [rat·trap·'pi:·re] <rattrappisco> I. *vt* to make stiff II. *vr:* **-rsi** to become stiff
rattristare [rat·tris·'ta:·re] I. *vt* to sadden II. *vr:* **-rsi** to become sad
raucedine [rau·'tʃɛ:·di·ne] *f* hoarseness
rauco, -a ['ra:u·ko] <-chi, -che> *agg* hoarse
ravanello [ra·va·'nɛl·lo] *m* radish
ravegnano, -a [ra·veɲ·'ɲa:·no] I. *m, f* (*abitante*) person from Ravenna II. *agg* from Ravenna
Ravenna *f* Ravenna, *city in the Emilia-Romagna region*
ravennate [ra·ven·'na:·te] I. *mf* (*abitante*) person from Ravenna II. *agg* from Ravenna
Ravennate *m* (*zona*) Ravenna area; **nel** ~ in the Ravenna area
ravioli [ra·'vio:·li] *mpl* ravioli
ravvedersi [rav·ve·'der·si] <irr> *vr* to become a reformed character
ravvedimento [rav·ve·di·'men·to] *m* reform
ravveduto *pp di* **ravvedersi**
ravvicinamento [rav·vi·tʃi·na·'men·to] *m* **1.** (*tra partiti, paesi*) rapprochement **2.** *fig* (*tra coniugi*) reconciliation
ravvicinare [rav·vi·tʃi·'na:·re] I. *vt* **1.** (*avvicinare di più*) to move closer **2.** *fig* (*rappacificare*) to bring closer together II. *vr:* **-rsi** **1.** (*avvicinarsi*) to get to know one another better **2.** (*rappacificarsi*) to make it up
ravvicinato, -a [rav·vi·tʃi·'na:·to] *agg* close
ravvisare [rav·vi·'za:·re] *vt* to recognize
ravvivare [rav·vi·'va:·re] I. *vt* (*fiamma, sentimento*) to rekindle II. *vr:* **-rsi** (*interesse*) to revive
raziocinio [rat·tsio·'tʃi:·nio] <-i> *m* **1.** (*ragione*) reason **2.** (*buon senso*) common sense
razionale [rat·tsio·'na:·le] I. *agg* **1.** (*persona, metodo*) rational **2.** (*architettura*) functional; (*alimentazione*) balanced **3.** MATH rational II. *m* rational
razionalismo [rat·tsio·na·'liz·mo] *m* rationalism
razionalista [rat·tsio·na·'lis·ta] <-i *m*, -e *f*> *mf* rationalist
razionalità [rat·tsio·na·li·'ta] <-> *f* **1.** (*facoltà*) common sense **2.** (*funzionalità: di edificio*) functionality
razionalizzare [rat·tsio·na·lid·'dza:·re] *vt* to rationalize
razionalizzazione [rat·tsio·na·lid·dzat·'tsio:·ne] *f* rationalization
razionamento [rat·tsio·na·'men·to] *m* rationing
razionare [rat·tsio·'na:·re] *vt* to ration
razione [rat·'tsio:·ne] *f* **1.** (*quantità*) ration **2.** *fig* (*porzione*) share
razza¹ ['rat·tsa] *f* **1.** (*di uomini*) race **2.** (*di animali*) breed; **di** ~ **pura** thoroughbred **3.** (*di*

piante) type **4.** (*famiglia, stirpe*) family **5.** *pej, fam* kind; **che** ~ **di uomo sei!** you're a real piece of work!
razza² ['rad·dza] *f* ZOO skate
razzia [rat·'tsi:·a] <-ie> *f* raid
razziale [rat·'tsia:·le] *agg* racial; **conflitto** ~ racial conflict; **odio** ~ racial hatred
razziare [rat·'tsia:·re] *vt* to raid
razzismo [rat·'tsiz·mo] *m* racism
razzista [rat·'tsis·ta] <-i *m*, -e *f*> I. *mf* racist II. *agg* racist
razzo ['rad·dzo] *m* rocket
razzolare [rat·tso·'la:·re] *vi* to scratch around
RC *f abbr di* **Rifondazione Comunista** *Italian Communist party*
re¹ [re] <-> *m a. fig* king
re² [rɛ] <-> *m* MUS D
reagente [rea·'dʒɛn·te] *m* reagent
reagire [re·a·'dʒi:·re] <reagisco> *vi* to react
reale [re·'a:·le] I. *agg* **1.** (*di, da re*) royal; **aquila** ~ golden eagle **2.** (*vero: oggetto, fatto*) real **3.** (*effettivo: stipendio*) actual **4.** JUR, MAT real II. *m* reality
realismo [re·a·'liz·mo] *m* realism
realista [re·a·'lis·ta] <-i *m*, -e *f*> I. *mf* (*persona concreta*) realist II. *agg* realistic
realistico, -a [re·a·'lis·ti·ko] <-ci, -che> *agg* realistic
realizzabile [re·a·lid·'dza:·bi·le] *agg* feasible
realizzare [re·a·lid·'dza:·re] I. *vt* to realize II. *vr:* **-rsi** **1.** (*aspirazioni*) to come true **2.** (*come persona*) to find fulfillment
realizzazione [re·a·lid·dzat·'tsio:·ne] *f* realization
realizzo [re·a·'lid·dzo] *m* **1.** COM realization **2.** FIN proceeds *pl*
realmente [re·al·'men·te] *avv* really
realtà [re·al·'ta] <-> *f* reality; **in** ~ really; ~ **virtuale** TEL, COMPUT virtual reality
reame [re·'a:·me] *m* realm
Reatino <*sing*> *m* (*zona*) Rieti area; **nel** ~ in the Rieti area
reatino, -a [re·a·'ti:·no] I. *m, f* (*abitante*) person from Rieti II. *agg* from Rieti
reato [re·'a:·to] *m* crime; **corpo del** ~ material evidence; **il fatto non costituisce** ~ it was not a criminal offense; **-i contro l'ambiente** crimes against the environment
reattivo, -a *agg* **1.** (*persona*) with it; **è troppo stanco, non è più** ~ he's too tired, he's out of it **2.** CHEM, EL reactive
reattore [re·at·'to:·re] *m* **1.** AERO (*motore*) jet engine; (*aeroplano*) jet **2.** PHYS reactor
reazionario, -a [re·at·tsio·'na:·rio] <-i, -ie> I. *agg* reactionary II. *m, f* reactionary
reazione [re·at·'tsio:·ne] *f* **1.** (*gener*) reaction **2.** AERO **motore a** ~ jet engine; **aereo a** ~ jet
rebus ['rɛ:·bus] <-> *m* **1.** (*gioco*) rebus **2.** *fig* (*persona, cosa*) puzzle
recalcitrare [re·kal·tʃi·'tra:·re] *v.* **ricalcitrare**
recapitare [re·ka·pi·'ta:·re] *vt* to deliver
recapito [re·'ka:·pi·to] *m* (*indirizzo*) address
recare [re·'ka:·re] I. *vt* **1.** (*portare*) to bring

2. (*avere su di sé*) to bear **3.** (*causare*) to cause; ~ **disturbo a qu** to inconvenience sb; ~ **offesa a qu** to offend sb **II.** *vr:* -**rsi** to go

recedere [re·'tʃɛ·de·re] <recedo, recedetti *o* recedei, receduto> *vi a. fig* JUR (*tirarsi indietro*) to withdraw

recensione [re·tʃen·'sio:·ne] *f* review

recensore, -a [re·tʃen·'so:·re] *m, f* reviewer

recente [re·'tʃɛn·te] *agg* recent; **di** ~ recently

recentemente [re·tʃen·te·'men·te] *avv* recently

recentissime [re·tʃen·'tis·si·me] *fpl* latest news

recepire [re·tʃe·'pi:·re] <recepisco> *vt* (*capire*) to recognize

reception [ri·'sep·ʃən] <- *o* receptions> *f* (*di albergo*) reception desk

recessione [re·tʃes·'sio:·ne] *f* COM recession

recessivo, -a [re·tʃes·'si:·vo] *agg* **1.** BIOL (*carattere*) recessive **2.** COM (*economia*) recessionary

recesso [re·'tʃɛs·so] *m* **1.** *fig* (*della mente*) recess **2.** JUR (*da contratto*) withdrawal **3.** MED recess

recidere [re·'tʃi:·de·re] <recido, recisi, reciso> *vt* to cut off

recidivo, -a [re·tʃi·'di:·vo] **I.** *agg* (*incorreggibile: persona*) lapsing into old habits **II.** *m, f* **1.** JUR (*imputato*) habitual offender **2.** MED (*malattia*) recidivist **3.** (*persona incorreggibile*) sb who returns to his/her old habits

recingere [re·'tʃin·dʒe·re] <irr> *vt* (*città, giardino*) to enclose

recintare [re·tʃin·'ta:·re] *vt* (*giardino*) to fence off

recinto¹ [re·'tʃin·to] *pp di* **recingere**

recinto² *m* **1.** (*spazio circoscritto*) enclosure; (*per animali*) pen **2.** (*recinzione: di legno*) fence; (*di mattoni*) wall

recinzione [re·tʃin·'tsio:·ne] *f* (*di legno*) fence; (*di mattoni*) wall

recipiente [re·tʃi·'piɛn·te] *m* container

reciprocità [re·tʃi·pro·tʃi·'ta] <-> *f* reciprocity

reciproco, -a <-ci, -che> *agg* reciprocal

recisi [re·'tʃi:·zi] *1. pers sing pass rem di* **recidere**

reciso, -a [re·'tʃi:·zo] **I.** *pp di* **recidere II.** *agg* (*tagliato*) cut off

recita ['rɛ:·tʃi·ta] *f* (*teatrale*) performance; (*di poesie*) recital

recitare [re·tʃi·'ta:·re] **I.** *vt* **1.** (*poesia, lezioni, orazioni*) to recite **2.** THEAT, FILM to act; ~ **una parte** to play a part **II.** *vi* (*fingere*) to pretend

recitativo, -a *agg* recitative

recitazione [re·tʃi·tat·'tsio:·ne] *f* **1.** (*interpretazione*) delivery **2.** (*disciplina*) acting

reclamare [re·kla·'ma:·re] **I.** *vi* ~ **contro** [*o* per] qc to complain about sth **II.** *vt* (*diritto*) to demand

réclame [re·'klam] <-> *f* **1.** (*pubblicità*) advertising **2.** (*avviso pubblicitario*) advertisement

reclamizzare [re·kla·mid·'dza:·re] *vt* to advertise

reclamo [re·'kla:·mo] *m* complaint; **fare/**

sporgere ~ to complain; **ufficio -i** complaints department

reclinare [re·kli·'na:·re] *vt* **1.** (*capo*) to bow **2.** (*sedia*) to tilt

reclusione [re·klu·'zio:·ne] *f* JUR imprisonment

recluso, -a [re·'klu:·zo] **I.** *agg* secluded; JUR imprisoned **II.** *m, f* prisoner

recluta ['rɛ:·klu·ta] *f* recruit

reclutamento [re·klu·ta·'men·to] *m* recruitment

reclutare [re·klu·'ta:·re] *vt* to recruit

recondito, -a [re·'kɔn·di·to] *agg poet* **1.** (*luogo*) secluded **2.** *fig* (*nascosto: pensieri*) hidden

record ['rɛ:·kord] **I.** <-> *m* **1.** SPORT record; **battere un** ~ to beat a record; ~ **mondiale** world record; **a tempo di** ~ in record time **2.** COMPUT record **II.** <inv> *agg* record

recriminare [re·kri·mi·'na:·re] *vi* ~ **su qc** to complain about sth

recriminazione [re·kri·mi·nat·'tsio:·ne] *f* complaint

recrudescenza [re·kru·deʃ·'ʃɛn·tsa] *f* recurrence

recuperare [re·ku·pe·'ra:·re] *v.* **ricuperare**

redarguire [re·dar·gu·'i:·re] <redarguisco> *vt* to rebuke

redarre [re·'dar·re] <usato solo all'inf> *v.* **redigere**

redassi [re·'das·si] *1. pers sing pass rem di* **redigere**

redatto [re·'dat·to] *pp di* **redigere**

redattore, -trice [re·dat·'to:·re] *m, f* **1.** (*di giornale, casa editrice*) editor **2.** (*di atti, documenti*) author

redazionale [re·dat·tsio·'na:·le] *agg* editorial

redazione [re·dat·'tsio:·ne] *f* **1.** (*stesura*) writing; ~ **di un documento** drawing up of a document **2.** (*attività*) editing **3.** (*team*) editorial staff **4.** (*ufficio*) editorial office

redditività [red·di·ti·vi·'ta] <-> *f* profitability

redditizio, -a [red·di·'tit·tsio] <-i, -ie> *agg* profitable

reddito ['rɛd·di·to] *m* income; ~ **imponibile** taxable income; ~ **non imponibile** non-taxable income

redditometro [red·di·'tɔ:·me·tro] *m* system used by the state for assessing income

redensi [re·'dɛn·si] *1. pers sing pass rem di* **redimere**

redento, -a [re·'dɛn·to] **I.** *pp di* **redimere II.** *m, f* redeemed sinner **III.** *agg* redeemed

redentore, -trice [re·den·'to:·re] *m* redeemer; **il** ~ the Redeemer

redentore, -trice *agg* redeeming

redenzione [re·den·'tsio:·ne] *f* redemption

redigere [re·'di:·dʒe·re] <redigo, redassi, redatto> *vt* **1.** (*scrivere*) to draw up; ~ **un verbale** to draw up a record; ~ **un articolo** to write an article **2.** (*curare*) to edit

redimere [re·'di:·me·re] <redimo, redensi, redento> *vt poet* to redeem

redimibile [re·di·'mi:·bi·le] *agg* (*debito*) redeemable

redini ['rɛːdi·ni] *fpl* reins *pl*

redivivo, -a [re·di·'viːvo] *agg* returned to life

reduce ['rɛːdu·tʃe] I. *agg* **essere ~ da qc** (*guerra*) to be back from sth; *fig* (*influenza*) to have gone through sth II. *mf* veteran

refe ['reːfe] *m* thread

referendarista [re·fe·ren·da·'risːta] <-i *m*, -e *f*> *mf* POL supporter of the calling of a referendum

referendum [re·fe·'rɛnːdum] <-> *m* 1. JUR referendum 2. (*indagine*) survey

referenza [re·fe·'rɛnːtsa] *f* reference

referenziato, -a [re·fe·ren·'tsiaːto] *agg* with references

referto [re·'fɛrːto] *m* MED report

refettorio [re·fet·'tɔːrio] <-i> *m* cafeteria

reflazione [re·flat·'tsioːne] *f* FIN, COM reflation

refrattario, -a [re·frat·'taːrio] <-i, -ie> *agg* 1. (*materiale*) refractory 2. MED (*paziente*) unresponsive

refrigerante [re·fri·dʒe·'ranːte] I. *agg* refrigerating II. *m* 1. (*liquido*) coolant 2. (*apparecchio*) refrigerator

refrigerare [re·fri·dʒe·'raːre] *vt* to refrigerate

refrigeratore [re·fri·dʒe·ra·'toːre] *m* refrigerator

refrigerazione [re·fri·dʒe·rat·'tsioːne] *f* refrigeration

refrigerio [re·fri·'dʒɛːrio] <-i> *m* coolness; **~ dalla calura estiva** relief from the summer heat

refurtiva [re·fur·'tiːva] *f* loot

refuso [re·'fuːzo] *m* TYP typographical error

regalare [re·ga·'laːre] *vt* 1. (*gener*) to give 2. COM (*vendere a buon mercato*) to give away

regale [re·'gaːle] *agg* 1. (*del re*) royal 2. *fig* (*comportamento*) regal

regalità [re·ga·li·'ta] <-> *f* majesty

regalo [re·'gaːlo] *m* present; **fare un ~ a qu** to give sb a present

regata [re·'gaːta] *f* regatta

reggente [red·'dʒɛnːte] I. *mf* regent II. *f* LING main clause III. *agg* (*principe, sovrano*) reigning

reggenza [red·'dʒɛnːtsa] *f* regency

reggere ['redːdʒe·re] <reggo, ressi, retto> I. *vt* 1. (*tenere*) to hold; (*sostenere*) to support; (*tenere fermo*) to hold still 2. (*resistere a*) to deal with 3. (*governare*) to rule 4. LING to govern 5. (*sopportare: alcol, vino*) to take II. *vi* 1. (*resistere*) to deal with 2. (*durare: bel tempo*) to last; (*cibi*) to stay fresh III. *vr:* **-rsi** 1. (*sostenersi*) to stand up; **-rsi a galla** to keep afloat 2. *fig* (*controllarsi*) to contain oneself 3. (*attaccarsi*) to hold on

reggia ['redːdʒa] <-gge> *f a. fig* palace

reggiano, -a [red·'dʒiaːno] I. *m*, *f* (*abitante*) person from Reggio Emilia II. *agg* from Reggio Emilia

Reggiano *m* 1. (*zona*) Reggio Emilia area; **nel ~** in the Reggio Emilia area 2. (*formaggio*) Parmesan cheese

reggicalze [red·dʒi·'kalːtse] <-> *m* garter belt

reggimento [red·dʒi·'menːto] *m* 1. MIL regiment 2. *fig* (*moltitudine*) crowd

reggino, -a [red·'dʒiːno] I. *m*, *f* (*abitante*) person from Reggio Calabria II. *agg* from Reggio Calabria

Reggino *m* (*zona*) Reggio Calabria area; **nel ~** in the Reggio Calabria area

Reggio Calabria *f* Reggio Calabria, *city in Calabria*

Reggio Emilia *f* Reggio Emilia, *city in the Emilia-Romagna area*

reggipetto, reggiseno [red·dʒi·'pɛtːto, red·dʒi·'seːno] *m* bra; **~ a balconcino** underwire bra

reggitesta [red·dʒi·'tɛsːta] <-> *m* headrest

regia [re·'dʒiːa] <-gie> *f* 1. FILM, TV direction 2. *fig* (*di festa, viaggio*) organization

regime [re·'dʒiːme] *m* 1. POL regime 2. (*dieta*) diet; **tenersi a ~** to be on a diet 3. (*regola di vita*) regime 4. TEC, MOT speed

regina [re·'dʒiːna] *f* queen

reginetta [re·dʒi·'netːta] *f* **~ di bellezza** beauty queen

regio, -a ['rɛːdʒo] <-gi, -gie> *agg* royal

regionale [re·dʒo·'naːle] *agg* regional

regionalismo [re·dʒo·na·'lizːmo] *m* regionalism

regione [re·'dʒoːne] *f* region

regista [re·'dʒisːta] <-i *m*, -e *f*> *mf* director

registrare [re·dʒis·'traːre] *vt* 1. (*con registratore: musica*) to record 2. FIN (*entrate, uscite*) to enter 3. (*aumento, diminuzione*) to report

registratore [re·dʒis·tra·'toːre] *m* 1. (*magnetofono*) tape recorder 2. (*apparecchio*) recorder; **~ di cassa** till; **~ di volo** flight recorder

registratore, -trice *agg* (*barometro, apparecchio*) recording

registrazione [re·dʒis·trat·'tsioːne] *f* 1. (*di musica, spettacolo*) recording 2. ADM (*di atto, società*) registration 3. (*in contabilità*) entry

registro [re·'dʒisːtro] *m* 1. (*libro*) register 2. TEC regulator

regnante [reɲ·'ɲanːte] I. *agg* (*famiglia, monarca*) reigning II. *mf* (*sovrano*) ruler

regnare [reɲ·'ɲaːre] *vi* to reign

regno ['reɲːɲo] *m* 1. (*gener*) kingdom 2. (*autorità, durata*) reign

regola ['rɛːgo·la] *f* 1. (*norma*) rule; **di regola** as a rule 2. (*ordine*) order; **essere in ~** to be in order; **mettere in ~** (*immigrato*) to regularize illegal workers 3. (*misura*) measure 4. REL rule

regolabile [re·go·'laːbi·le] *agg* adjustable

regolamentare¹ [re·go·la·men·'taːre] *agg* regulation; **tempi regolamentari** SPORT regulation (time)

regolamentare² *vt* to regulate

regolamentazione [re·go·la·men·tat·'tsioːne] *f* regulations *pl*

regolamento [re·go·la·'menːto] *m* 1. (*norme*) regulations *pl* 2. (*sistemazione: di questione*) settling 3. COM (*di conto*) settlement; (*di debito*) repayment

regolare¹ [re·go·'la:·re] I. *vt* 1.(*ordinare*) to organize 2.*fig* (*sistemare*) to fix 3.COM (*conto*) to settle; (*debito*) to repay 4.TEC to adjust; (*orologio*) to set II. *vr:* -**rsi** 1.(*comportarsi*) to behave 2.(*controllarsi*) to control oneself

regolare² *agg* 1.LING, MAT regular 2.(*a norma*) standard 3.(*costante: velocità, andatura*) steady 4.(*superficie*) even

regolarità [re·go·la·ri·'ta] <-> *f* regularity

regolarizzare [re·go·la·rid·'dza:·re] *vt* 1.(*posizione, immigrato*) to regularize 2.COM (*conto*) to settle

regolarizzazione [re·go·la·rid·dzat·'tsio:·ne] *f* 1.(*di posizione, immigrato*) regularization 2.COM (*di conto*) settlement

regolata [re·go·'la:·ta] *f* TEC adjustment; **darsi una** ~ *fig, fam* to pull oneself together

regolatezza [re·go·la·'tet·tsa] *f* moderation

regolazione [re·go·lat·'tsio:·ne] *f* regulation

regolo ['rɛ:·go·lo] *m* (*righello*) ruler

regredire [re·gre·'di:·re] <regredisco, regredii, regredito *o* regresso> *vi essere* to go backwards

regressione [re·gres·'sio:·ne] *f* regression

regressivo, -a [re·gres·'si:·vo] *agg a. fig* backwards

regresso¹ [re·'grɛs·so] *pp di* **regredire**

regresso² *m* 1.MED regression 2. *a. fig* decline

reimpiego [re·im·'piɛ:·go] <-ghi> *m* re-employment

reincarnazione [re·iŋ·kar·nat·'tsio:·ne] *f* reincarnation

reinserimento [re·in·se·ri·'men·to] *m* reintegration

reinserire [re·in·se·'ri:·re] <reinserisco> I. *vt* (*persona, paziente*) to reinstate II. *vr:* -**rsi** (*in gruppo*) to reinstate oneself

reintegrare [re·in·te·'gra:·re] I. *vt* (*nella società*) to reintegrate; (*in una carica*) to reinstate II. *vr:* -**rsi** (*in gruppo, attività*) to reinstate oneself

reintegrazione [re·in·te·grat·'tsio:·ne] *f* reintegration

reinvestimento [re·in·ves·ti·'men·to] *m* reinvestment

reinvestire [re·in·ves·'ti:·re] *vt* to reinvest

relais [re·'lɛ] <-> *m* relay

relativa [re·la·'ti:·va] *f* relative clause

relativamente [re·la·ti·va·'men·te] *avv* relatively; ~ **a qc** with reference to sth

relativista [re·la·ti·'vis·ta] <-i *m*, -e *f*> *mf* relativist

relativistico, -a [re·la·ti·'vis·ti·ko] <-ci, -che> *agg* relativistic

relatività [re·la·ti·vi·'ta] <-> *f* relativity

relativizzare [re·la·ti·vid·'dza:·re] *vt* (*problema*) to view objectively

relativo, -a [re·la·'ti:·vo] *agg* 1.(*pertinente*) relevant 2.(*limitato*) relative 3.LING **pronome** ~ relative pronoun

relatore, -trice [re·la·'to:·re] *m, f* speaker

relax [re·'laks] <-> *m* relaxation

relazione [re·lat·'tsio:·ne] *f* 1.(*esposizione*) account 2.(*rapporto tra persone*) relationship

relè [re·'lɛ] *m v.* **relais**

relegare [re·le·'ga:·re] *vt* to relegate

religione [re·li·'dʒo:·ne] *f* religion

religioso, -a [re·li·'dʒo:·so] I. *agg a. fig* religious; **matrimonio** ~ church wedding II. *m, f* monk *m*, nun *f*

reliquia [re·'li:·ku·ia] <-quie> *f* relic

reliquiario [re·li·'ku·ia:·rio] <-i> *m* reliquary

relitto [re·'lit·to] *m a. fig* wreck

rem [rɛm] <-> *m acro di* **röntgen equivalent man** TEC rem

remainder [ri·'mein·də] <-> *m* 1.(*libro*) remainder 2.(*libreria*) remainder bookshop

remare [re·'ma:·re] *vi* to row

remata [re·'ma:·ta] *f* 1.(*il remare*) row 2.(*colpo di remo*) stroke of the oar

rematore, -trice [re·ma·'to:·re] *m, f* rower

reminiscenza [re·mi·niʃ·'ʃen·tsa] *f* reminiscence

remissione [re·mis·'sio:·ne] *f* 1.REL (*perdono*) remission 2.JUR withdrawal 3.(*sottomissione*) submissiveness

remissività [re·mis·si·vi·'ta] <-> *f* submissiveness

remissivo, -a [re·mis·'si:·vo] *agg* 1.(*docile*) submissive 2.JUR remitting

remo ['rɛ:·mo] *m* oar

remora ['rɛ:·mo·ra] *f poet* hesitation

remoto, -a [re·'mɔ:·to] *agg* 1.(*tempo, causa*) distant 2.(*paese, località*) remote 3.LING **passato** ~ past simple

remunerare [re·mu·ne·'ra:·re] *v.* **rimunerare**

rena ['rɛ:·na] *f* sand

renale [re·'na:·le] *agg* MED renal

rendere ['rɛn·de·re] <rendo, resi, reso> I. *vt* 1.(*soldi, merce, libro*) to return; ~ **giustizia a qu/qc** to do justice to sb/sth; **a buon** ~ it's my turn next time 2.(*tributare*) ~ **omaggio a qu** to pay homage to sb; ~ **lode a qu** to praise sb 3.(*esprimere: senso, messaggio, sensazione*) to convey; ~ **l'idea di qc** to give the idea of sth 4.(*far diventare: felice, indispensabile, importante*) to make 5.(*fruttare: investimento, attività*) to earn II. *vr:* -**rsi** 1.(*diventare*) to become 2.(*sembrare*) to seem 3.(*loc*) -**rsi conto di qc** to realize sth

rendez-vous [rã·de·'vu] <-> *m* (*appuntamento*) date

rendiconto [ren·di·'kon·to] *m* 1.COM (*di conto*) statement 2.(*racconto: di fatto, evento*) report

rendimento [ren·di·'men·to] *m* 1.(*di macchina, persona*) performance; **avere un buon** ~ (*persona*) to do well 2.(*reddito*) return

rendita ['rɛn·di·to] *f* income

rene ['rɛ:·ne] *m* kidney

reni ['rɛ:·ni] *fpl* back

renitente [re·ni·'tɛn·te] *agg* unwilling

renitenza [re·ni·'tɛn·tsa] *f* unwillingness

renna ['rɛn·na] *f* ZOO reindeer

reo, -a ['rɛ:·o] *m, f* criminal

reografia [re·o·gra·'fi:·a] *f* MED rheography

reogramma [re·o·'gram·ma] <-i> *m* MED rheogram

reostato [re·'ɔ:·sta·to] *m* rheostat

reparto [re·'par·to] *m* **1.**(*di azienda*) department **2.**(*di ospedale*) ward; ~ **psichiatrico** psychiatric ward

repellente [re·pel·'lɛn·te] *agg* (*cibo, vista*) repulsive

repentaglio [re·pen·'taʎ·ʎo] <-gli> *m* **mettere a** ~ to risk

repentino, -a [re·pen·'ti:·no] *agg* sudden

reperibile [re·pe·'ri:·bi·le] *agg* (*professore, medico*) contactable; (*prodotto, informazione*) available

reperimento [re·pe·ri·'men·to] *m* finding

reperire [re·pe·'ri:·re] <reperisco> *vt* to find

reperto [re·'pɛr·to] *m* **1.**(*archeologico*) find **2.**(*giudiziario*) exhibit **3.** MED report

repertorio [re·per·'tɔ:·'rio] <-i> *m* **1.** THEAT, MUS repertoire **2.**(*raccolta*) stock

replay [ri:·'plei] <- *o* replays> *m* TV, SPORT action replay

replica ['rɛ:·pli·ka] <-che> *f* **1.**(*risposta*) answer **2.** THEAT repeat performance **3.** TV, RADIO repeat

replicare [re·pli·'ka:·re] *vt* **1.**(*rispondere*) to say something in reply; (*obiettare*) to make an objection **2.**(*ripetere: impresa, iniziativa*) to repeat **3.**(*spettacolo*) to perform again; (*trasmissione*) to show again

reportage [rə·pɔr·'taʒ] <-> *m* report

repressi [re·'prɛs·si] *1. pers sing pass rem di* **reprimere**

repressione [re·pres·'sio:·ne] *f* repression

repressivo, -a [re·pres·'si:·vo] *agg* repressive

represso, -a [re·'prɛs·so] *agg* (*emozioni*) repressed

reprimere [re·'pri:·me·re] <reprimo, repressi, represso> **I.** *vt* to repress **II.** *vr:* **-rsi** to keep a grip on oneself

reprint ['ri·print] <-> *m* modern reprint

reprobo, -a ['rɛ:·pro·bo] *agg* reprobate

repubblica [re·'pub·bli·ka] <-che> *f* republic

repubblicano, -a [re·pub·bli·'ka:·no] **I.** *agg* republican **II.** *m, f* republican

repulsione [re·pul·'sio:·ne] *f a. fig* repulsion

reputare [re·pu·'ta:·re] **I.** *vt* to consider **II.** *vr:* **-rsi** to consider oneself

reputazione [re·pu·tat·'tsio:·ne] *f* reputation

requie ['rɛ:·kui·e] <*sing*> *f* peace

requiem ['rɛ:·kui·em] <-> *m o f* requiem

requisire [re·kui·'zi:·re] <requisisco> *vt* to requisition

requisito [re·kui·'zi:·to] *m* requirement

requisitoria [re·kui·zi·'tɔ:·ria] <-ie> *f* JUR prosecution's closing argument

requisizione [re·kui·zit·'tsio:·ne] *f* requisition

resa ['rɛ:·sa] *f* **1.** MIL surrender **2.**(*restituzione*) return **3.**(*rendimento*) performance **4.**(*loc*) ~ **dei conti** *a. fig* day of reckoning

rescindere [reʃ·'ʃin·de·re] <irr> *vt* to annul;

~ **un contratto** to cancel a contract

rescissione [reʃ·ʃis·'sio:·ne] *f* annulment

rescisso *pp di* **rescindere**

resettare [re·set·'ta:·re] *vi* COMPUT to reset

resi ['re:·si] *1. pers sing pass rem di* **rendere**

residence ['rɛ·zi·dəns] <-> *m* building offering fully-equipped and serviced apartments for medium- to long-term rents

residente [re·si·'dɛn·te] **I.** *agg* resident **II.** *mf* resident

residenza [re·si·'dɛn·tsa] *f* residence

residenziale [re·si·den·'tsia:·le] *agg* residential

residuo [re·'si:·duo] *m* **1.** GENER remainder **2.**(*di sostanza, trattamento chimico*) residue **3.** COM surplus

residuo, -a *agg* remaining

resina ['rɛ:·zi·na] *f* resin

resistei [re·sis·'te:·i] *1. pers sing pass rem di* **resistere**

resistente [re·sis·'tɛn·te] *agg* resistant; (*materiale, tessuto, legno*) durable; ~ **al calore** heat-resistant; ~ **all'acqua** waterproof

resistenza [re·sis·'tɛn·tsa] *f* **1.**(*gener*) resistance; ~ **aerodinamica** aerodynamic drag; **opporre** ~ to put up a fight **2.**(*energia*) stamina **3.** HIST **la Resistenza** the Resistance

resistere [re·'sis·te·re] <resisto, resistei *o* resistetti, resistito> *vi* **1.**(*opporsi*) ~ **a qu/qc** to resist sb/sth **2.**(*sopportare*) ~ **a qc** to put up with sth; **resisti!** hang on in there!

reso ['re:·so] *m* (*merce restituita*) returned goods *pl*

reso, -a **I.** *pp di* **rendere** **II.** *agg* returned

resoconto [re·so·'kon·to] *m* account

respingente [res·pin·'dʒɛn·te] *m* bumper

respingere [res·'pin·dʒe·re] <irr> *vt* **1.**(*nemico, aggressore*) to repel **2.**(*regalo*) to return **3.**(*proposta*) to reject; (*accusa*) to deny **4.**(*bocciare*) to fail **5.** SPORT to ward off

respirare [res·pi·'ra:·re] **I.** *vi* **1.** BIOL to breathe; ~ **con la bocca** to breathe through one's mouth; ~ **col naso** to breathe through one's nose; ~ **a pieni polmoni** to take deep breaths **2.** *fig* (*riposarsi*) to have a rest **II.** *vt* to breathe

respiratore [res·pi·ra·'to:·re] *m* **1.**(*per sub, pompieri*) breathing apparatus **2.** MED respirator

respiratorio, -a [res·pi·ra·'tɔ:·rio] <-i, -ie> *agg* breathing

respirazione [res·pi·rat·'tsio:·ne] *f* breathing; ~ **artificiale** artificial respiration

respiro [res·'pi:·ro] *m* **1.**(*il respirare*) breathing; **da togliere il** ~ breathtaking **2.**(*singolo atto*) breath **3.**(*sollievo*) respite

responsabile [res·pon·'sa:·bi·le] **I.** *agg* responsible; **essere** ~ **di qc** to be in charge of sth **II.** *mf* person in charge

responsabilità [res·pon·sa·bi·li·'ta] <-> *f* **1.**(*consapevolezza*) responsibility **2.** JUR liability

responsabilizzare [res·pon·sa·bi·lid·'dza:·re] **I.** *vt* ~ **qu** to make sb aware of his [*o* her] responsibilities **II.** *vr:* **-rsi** to become aware of one's responsibilities

responso [res·'pɔn·so] *m* **1.** (*di oracolo*) reply **2.** (*di giuria, commissione*) verdict

ressa ['rɛs·sa] *f* crowd

ressi ['rɛs·si] *1. pers sing pass rem di* **reggere**

restante [res·'tan·te] *agg* remaining

restare [res·'ta:·re] *vi essere* **1.** (*continuare a stare*) to remain; **~ in piedi/seduto** to remain standing/seated; **~ indietro** *a. fig* to get behind **2.** (*diventare*) to be; **~ deluso** to be disappointed **3.** (*trovarsi*) **~ d'accordo** to agree **4.** (*avanzare*) to be left; **non gli rimane altro che accettare** he has no choice but to accept **5.** (*essere situato*) to be

restaurare [res·tau·'ra:·re] *vt* to restore

restauratore, -trice [res·tau·ra·'to:·re] *m, f* restorer

restaurazione [res·tau·rat·'tsio:·ne] *f* restoration

restauro [res·'ta:u·ro] *m* restoration

restio, -a [res·'ti:·o] <-ii, -ie> *agg* **1.** (*riluttante*) reluctant **2.** (*mulo, cavallo*) restive

restituire [res·ti·tu·'i:·re] <restituisco> *vt* (*libro, vestito, CD*) to give back; (*soldi*) to refund

restituzione [res·ti·tut·'tsio:·ne] *f* (*di libro, di bene*) return; (*di soldi*) refund

resto ['rɛs·to] *m* **1.** (*di tempo, di oggetti, di persone*) rest **2.** (*in denaro*) change **3.** *pl* (*di monumenti*) remains *pl* **4.** *pl* (*di cibo*) leftovers *pl* **5.** (*loc*) **del ~** besides

restringere [res·'trin·dʒe·re] <irr> **I.** *vt* **1.** (*abito*) to take in **2.** *fig* (*campo d'azione*) to limit **II.** *vr:* **-rsi** **1.** (*diventar stretto: strada*) to narrow **2.** (*stoffa*) to shrink

restrinsi *1. pers sing pass rem di* **restringere**

restrittivo, -a [res·trit·'ti:·vo] *agg* restrictive

restrizione [res·trit·'tsio:·ne] *f* restriction

resurrezione [re·sur·ret·'tsio:·ne] *f v.* **risurrezione**

resuscitare [re·suʃ·ʃi·'ta:·re] *v.* **risuscitare**

retaggio [re·'tad·dʒo] <-ggi> *m* **1.** *poet* (*eredità*) heritage **2.** *fig* (*culturale*) legacy

retard [ri·'ta:d] <inv> *agg* MED retard

retata [re·'ta:·ta] *f* **1.** *fig* (*di persone*) roundup **2.** (*di pesci, uccelli*) catch

rete ['re:·te] *f* **1.** (*di filo*) net **2.** (*di letto*) base of the bed **3.** (*stradale, commerciale*) network; **~ di distribuzione** distribution network; **~ stradale** road network **4.** COMPUT network; **~ locale** local network; **essere in Rete** to be on the Internet; **accesso alla ~** Internet access **5.** TV channel

reticella [re·ti·'tʃɛl·la] *f* (*per capelli*) hairnet

reticente [re·ti·'tʃɛn·te] *agg* reticent

reticenza [re·ti·'tʃɛn·tsa] *f* reticence

reticolato [re·ti·ko·'la:·to] *m* **1.** (*di linee, strade*) grid **2.** (*metallico*) chainlink fence; **~ di filo spinato** barbed wire fence

reticolo [re·'ti:·ko·lo] *m* grid

retina ['rɛ:·ti·na] *f* **1.** ANAT retina **2.** (*per capelli*) hairnet

retino [re·'ti:·no] *m* (*piccola rete*) small net

retore ['rɛ:·to·re] *m poet* rhetorician

retorica [re·'tɔ:·ri·ka] <-che> *f* rhetoric

retorico, -a [re·'tɔ:·ri·ko] <-ci, -che> *agg* LIT rhetorical

retribuire [re·tri·bu·'i:·re] <retribuisco> *vt* to pay

retributivo, -a [re·tri·bu·'ti:·vo] *agg* pay

retribuzione [re·tri·but·'tsio:·ne] *f* pay

retro[1] ['rɛ:·tro] *avv* vedi **~** see over

retro[2] *m* back; **sul ~** on the back

retro[3] [re·'tro] <inv> *agg* (*abbigliamento, arredamento*) retro; (*mostra*) retrospective

retroattività [re·tro·at·ti·vi·'ta] *f* retroactivity

retroattivo, -a [re·tro·at·'ti:·vo] *agg* retroactive

retrobottega [re·tro·bot·'te:·ga] <-> *m* back of the store

retrocedere [re·tro·'tʃɛ:·de·re] <retrocedo, retrocessi, retrocesso> **I.** *vi essere* **1.** (*indietreggiare*) to move back **2.** SPORT to be relegated **II.** *vt avere* **1.** SPORT to relegate **2.** MIL to demote

retrocessione [re·tro·tʃes·'sio:·ne] *f* **1.** SPORT relegation **2.** MIL demotion

retrocesso [re·tro·'tʃɛs·so] *pp di* **retrocedere**

retrodatare [re·tro·da·'ta:·re] *vt* to backdate

retrodatazione [re·tro·da·tat·'tsio:·ne] *f* backdating

retrogrado, -a [re·'trɔ:·gra·do] **I.** *agg* **1.** (*persone, idee*) backward looking **2.** (*moto, movimento*) retrograde **II.** *m, f* backward looking person

retroguardia [re·tro·'guar·dia] *f* rearguard

retroilluminato, -a [re·tro·il·lu·mi·'na:·to] *agg* back lit

retroilluminazione [re·tro·il·lum·na·'tsio:·ne] *f* TEC back lighting

retromarcia [re·tro·'mar·tʃa] <-ce> *f* **1.** (*rapporto*) reverse gear **2.** (*movimento*) reverse; **fare ~** *fig* to change one's mind

retroscena[1] [re·troʃ·'ʃɛ:·na] <-> *m* **1.** THEAT backstage **2.** *pl, fig* behind-the-scenes goings-on

retrospettiva [re·troc·spet·'ti:·va] *f* retrospective

retrospettivo, -a [re·tro·spet·'ti:·vo] *agg* (*sguardo*) retrospective; **mostra -a** retrospective

retrospezione [re·tro·spet·'tsio:·ne] *f* retrospection

retrostante [re·tros·'tan·te] *agg* at the back

retroterra [re·tro·'tɛr·ra] <-> *m* **1.** (*territorio*) hinterland **2.** *fig* (*culturale*) background

retrovia [re·tro·'vi:·a] *f* area behind the battle line

retrovisivo, -a [re·tro·vi·'zi:·vo] *agg* rearview

retrovisore [re·tro·vi·'zo:·re] *m* rearview mirror

retta ['rɛt·ta] *f* **1.** (*di convitto, pensionato*) charge **2.** MATH straight line **3.** (*loc*) **dar ~ a qu** to pay attention to sb

rettale [ret·'ta:·le] *agg* MED rectal

rettangolare [ret·taŋ·go·'la:·re] *agg* rectangular

R

rettangolo [ret·'taŋ·go·lo] I. *agg* (*triangolo*) right-angled II. *m* **1.** MATH rectangle **2.** SPORT ~ **di gioco** pitch

rettifica [ret·ˠti:·fi·ka] <-che> *f* **1.**(*correzione*) correction **2.** TEC grinding

rettificare [ret·ti·fi·'ka:·re] *vt* **1.** *fig* (*correggere*) to correct **2.** TEC to grind

rettile ['rɛt·ti·le] *m a. fig, pej* reptile

rettilineo [ret·ti·'li:·neo] *m* stretch

rettilineo, -a *agg* straight

rettitudine [ret·ti·'tu:·di·ne] *f* rectitude

retto, -a I. *pp di* **reggere** II. *agg* **1.**(*gener*) straight; **angolo** ~ right angle **2.**(*onesto*) upright

rettore [ret·'to:·re] <-trice> *m, f* (*di università*) chancellor

reuma ['rɛ:u·ma] <-i> *m* rheumatism

reumatico, -a [reu·'ma:·ti·ko] <-ci, -che> *agg* rheumatic

reumatismo [reu·ma·'tiz·mo] *m* rheumatism

reumatologico, -a [reu·ma·to·'lɔ:·dʒi·ko] <-ci, -che> *agg* rheumatological

reverendo [re·ve·'rɛn·do] *m* priest

reverendo, -a *agg* Reverend

reverenziale [re·ve·ren·'tsia:·le] *agg* reverential

revers [rə·'vɛr] <-> *m* lapel

reversibile [re·ver·'si:·bi·le] *agg* **1.**(*moto, processo*) reversible **2.** JUR (*pensione*) reversionary

reversibilità [re·ver·si·bi·li·'ta] <-> *f* **1.**(*gener*) reversibility **2.** JUR (*di pensione*) reversion

revisionare [re·vi·zio·'na:·re] *vt* **1.**(*testo, documento*) to check **2.** TEC to overhaul **3.**(*conti*) to audit

revisione [re·vi·'zio:·ne] *f* **1.** checking **2.** TEC (*di parti meccaniche*) overhaul **3.** FIN (*dei conti*) audit

revisore, -a [re·vi·'zo:·re] *m, f* checker; ~ **dei conti** auditor; ~ **di bozze** proofreader

revoca ['rɛ:·vo·ka] <-che> *f* revocation

revocabile [re·vo·'ka:·bi·le] *agg* revocable

revocare [re·vo·'ka:·re] *vt* to revoke

revocazione [re·vo·kat·'tsio:·ne] *f* revocation

revolverata [re·vol·ve·'ra:·ta] *f* revolver shot

rhum [rum] *m v.* **rum**

RI *abbr di* **Repubblica Italiana** *Italian Republic*

ri- [ri] (*in parole composte*) re-; (*di nuovo*) re-

riabilitare [ri·a·bi·li·'ta:·re] I. *vt* to rehabilitate II. *vr:* **-rsi** to rehabilitate oneself

riabilitazione [ri·a·bi·li·tat·'tsio:·ne] *f* MED rehabilitation

riaccendere [ri·at·'tʃɛn·de·re] <irr> I. *vt* **1.**(*luce*) to switch on again **2.**(*fuoco, sigaretta*) to light again II. *vr:* **-rsi 1.**(*luce*) to come on again **2.**(*fuoco, sigaretta*) to catch fire again **3.** *fig* (*speranza, discussione*) to be rekindled; (*lotta*) to flare up again

riaccompagnare [ri·ak·kom·paɲ·'ɲa:·re] *vt* to take back

riacquistare [ri·ak·kuis·'ta:·re] *vt* **1.**(*bene, gioiello*) to buy back **2.** *fig* (*fiducia*) to regain

riacquisto [ri·ak·'kuis·to] *m* repurchase

riaffacciarsi [ri·af·fat·'tʃa:r·si] *vr:* **-rsi 1.**(*affacciarsi di nuovo*) to reappear **2.** *fig* (*rappresentarsi: ricordo*) to return

riaggiustare [ri·ad·dʒus·'ta:·re] *vt* **1.**(*sistemare: sito, trucco*) to readjust **2.** *fig* to fix

rialzamento [ri·al·tsa·'men·to] *m* **1.**(*di terreno*) elevation **2.**(*di prezzi*) rise

rialzare [ri·al·'tsa:·re] I. *vt avere* **1.**(*alzare di nuovo*) to pick up again **2.** *fig* (*testa*) to lift up again **3.**(*muro, edificio*) to raise **4.**(*prezzi*) to increase II. *vr:* **-rsi 1.**(*risollevarsi*) to get back up again **2.** *fig* (*riprendersi*) to get back on one's feet

rialzato, -a [ri·al·'tsa:·to] *agg* **piano** ~ mezzanine

rialzo [ri·'al·tso] *m* **1.**(*dei prezzi*) increase **2.**(*in borsa*) rise **3.**(*loc*) **giocare al** ~ (*in borsa*) to force up the price; *fig* to up the stakes

rialzista [ri·al·'tsis·ta] <-i *m*, -e *f*> *mf* bull

riammissione [ri·am·mis·'sio:·ne] *f* readmission

rianimare [ri·a·ni·'ma:·re] I. *vt* **1.**(*restituire fiducia*) to revive **2.** MED to resuscitate II. *vr:* **-rsi 1.**(*riprendere forza*) to come around **2.** *fig* (*riprendere coraggio*) to take heart **3.** *fig* (*luogo*) to come alive again

rianimazione [ri·a·ni·mat·'tsio:·ne] *f* MED resuscitation; **reparto (di)** ~ intensive care unit

riannessione [ri·an·nes·'sio:·ne] *f* (*di Stato, di territorio*) reannexation

riaperto *pp di* **riaprire**

riapertura [ri·a·per·'tu:·ra] *f* reopening

riaprire [ri·a·'pri:·re] <irr> I. *vt* to reopen II. *vr:* **-rsi** to reopen

riarmo [ri·'ar·mo] *m* (*di Stato*) rearmament; **corsa al** ~ arms race

riarso, -a [ri·'ar·so] *agg* **1.**(*terreno*) arid **2.**(*gola*) dry

riassetto [ri·as·'sɛt·to] *m* (*di amministrazione, servizio*) reorganization

riassorbimento [ri·as·sor·bi·'men·to] *m* **1.**(*nuovo assorbimento: di liquidi*) reabsorption **2.** *fig* (*nuova assunzione: di dipendenti*) new intake

riassorbire [ri·as·sor·'bi:·re] I. *vt* **1.**(*assorbire di nuovo: liquidi*) to reabsorb **2.** *fig* to take on II. *vr:* **-rsi** (*liquido, ematoma*) to be reabsorbed

riassumere [ri·as·'su:·me·re] <irr> *vt* **1.**(*operaio*) to re-employ **2.**(*carica, funzione*) to take on again **3.**(*riepilogare*) to recap

riassunto [ri·as·'sun·to] *m* summary

riassunto, -a I. *pp di* **riassumere** II. *agg* re-employed

riassunzione [ri·as·sun·'tsio:·ne] *f* **1.**(*di dipendenti*) re-employment **2.** JUR (*di processo*) resumption

riattare [ri·at·'ta:·re] *vt* (*appartamento, negozio, strada*) to renovate

riattivare [ri·at·ti·'va:·re] *vt* **1.**(*processo, rapporto, servizio*) to reactivate **2.** COMPUT to restart **3.** MED to stimulate

riattivazione [ri·at·ti·vat·'tsio:·ne] *f* **1.**(*di pro* *cesso, rapporto, servizio*) reactivation **2.** COM-PUT restart **3.** MED stimulation

riavere [ri·a·'ve:·re] <irr> **I.** *vt* **1.** (*libri, soldi*) to get back **2.** (*malattia*) to get again **II.** *vr:* **-rsi 1.** *fig* (*ricuperare la salute*) to recover **2.** (*riprendere i sensi*) to come around

riavvicinamento [ri·av·vi·tʃi·na·'men·to] *m* **1.** (*trasferimento*) move back **2.** *fig* (*di persone, governi*) rapprochement

riavvicinare [ri·av·vi·tʃi·'na:·re] **I.** *vt* **1.** (*oggetti*) ~ qc a qc to put sth closer to sth **2.** *fig* (*riconciliare: persone*) to bring closer together **II.** *vr:* **-rsi** (*riconciliarsi*) to come closer together

riavvio <-ii> *m* COMPUT restart

riavvolgere [ri·av·'vɔl·dʒe·re] <irr> *vt* to rewind

riavvolgimento [ri·av·vol·dʒi·'men·to] *m* FILM, MUS rewinding; ~ **rapido** fast rewind

ribadire [ri·ba·'di:·re] <ribadisco> *vt* (*affermazione, concetto*) to confirm

ribaldo [ri·'bal·do] *m* rogue

ribalta [ri·'bal·ta] *f* **1.** THEAT footlights *pl* **2.** (*sportello: di scrittoio*) flap **3.** (*loc*) **venire alla ~** to come into the limelight; **tornare alla ~** to make a comeback

ribaltabile [ri·bal·'ta:·bi·le] **I.** *agg* **1.** (*sedile*) reclining **2.** (*risultato, situazione*) reversible **II.** *m* **1.** (*parte di autocarro*) dump bed **2.** (*autocarro*) dump truck

ribaltamento [ri·bal·ta·'men·to] *m* overturning

ribaltare [ri·bal·'ta:·re] **I.** *vt* **1.** (*capovolgere*) to tip over **2.** *fig* (*governo, decisione*) to overturn; (*situazione, risultato*) to reverse **II.** *vr:* **-rsi 1.** (*auto, autocarro*) to overturn **2.** (*situazione, tendenza*) to reverse

ribassare [ri·bas·'sa:·re] **I.** *vt avere* (*prezzo*) to lower **II.** *vi essere* to come down

ribassista [ri·bas·'sis·ta] <-i *m*, -e *f*> *mf* bear

ribasso [ri·'bas·so] *m* **1.** (*di prezzi*) fall **2.** (*in borsa*) **essere in ~** to be down; **in ~** down; **giocare al ~** to force down the price **3.** *fig* (*di popolarità*) **essere in ~** to be on the wane

ribattere [ri·'bat·te·re] *vt* **1.** SPORT (*palla*) to return **2.** (*posizioni, affermazioni*) to refute **3.** (*replicare*) to reply

ribattezzare [ri·bat·ted·'dza:·re] *vt* **1.** REL to rebaptize **2.** *fig* (*dare un nuovo nome a*) to rename

ribattino [ri·bat·'ti:·no] *m* rivet

ribellarsi [ri·bel·'lar·si] *vr* ~ **a qu/qc** to rebel against sb/sth

ribelle [ri·'bɛl·le] **I.** *agg* **1.** (*insorto: popolazione, villaggio*) rebel **2.** (*indocile: animo*) rebellious **II.** *mf* rebel

ribellione [ri·bel·'lio:·ne] *f* rebellion

ribes ['ri:·bes] <-> *m* currant

ribollire [ri·bol·'li:·re] *vi* **1.** (*acqua, minestra*) to boil again **2.** *fig* (*dalla collera*) to boil

ribollita [ri·bol·'li:·ta] *f* vegetable soup which is cooked, left to stand and then reheated before serving

ribonucleico, **-a** [ri·bo·nu·'klɛ:·i·ko] <-ci, -che> *agg* ribonucleic; **acido ~** ribonucleic acid

ribrezzo [ri·'bred·dzo] *m* (*repulsione*) revulsion; **fare ~** to disgust

ributtante [ri·but·'tan·te] *agg* disgusting

ributtare [ri·but·'ta:·re] **I.** *vt* (*buttare di nuovo*) to throw again **II.** *vr:* **-rsi 1.** (*buttarsi di nuovo*) to throw oneself down **2.** *fig* (*dedicarsi*) to throw oneself back

ricacciare [ri·kat·'tʃa:·re] **I.** *vt* **1.** (*nemico, invasore*) to drive back **2.** (*mandar via*) to drive out **II.** *vr:* **-rsi 1.** (*tornare: nel bosco, nella mischia*) to return **2.** *fig* (*in gola*) to hold back

ricadere [ri·ka·'de:·re] <irr> *vi essere* **1.** (*cadere di nuovo: giornale, libro*) to fall down again **2.** (*prezzi*) to fall again **3.** *fig* ~ **in qc** to fall back into sth **4.** (*abiti*) to hang down **5.** (*palla*) to fall back down **6.** (*compito, responsabilità*) to fall on

ricaduta [ri·ka·'du:·ta] *f* **1.** MED relapse **2.** (*conseguenza*) fallout

ricalcare [ri·kal·'ka:·re] *vt* **1.** (*cappello*) to push down **2.** (*disegno*) to trace **3.** *fig* (*seguire un modello*) to copy; ~ **le orme di qu** *fig* to follow in sb's footsteps

ricalcitrante [ri·kal·tʃi·'tran·te] *agg* (*riluttante*) recalcitrant

ricalcitrare [ri·kal·tʃi·'tra:·re] *vi* **1.** (*cavallo, asino*) to kick **2.** *fig* (*opporsi*) to kick up a fuss

ricamare [ri·ka·'ma:·re] *vt a. fig* to embroider

ricamatrice [ri·ka·ma·'tri:·tʃe] *f* embroiderer

ricambiare [ri·kam·'bia:·re] **I.** *vt avere* **1.** (*favore, amore, invito*) to return; (*auguri*) to reciprocate **2.** (*cambiare di nuovo*) to change **II.** *vr* (*cambiarsi di nuovo*) to get changed again

ricambio [ri·'kam·bio] <-i> *m* **1.** (*rinnovamento: di personale*) turnover **2.** (*di scorta: calze, maglietta*) **di ~** spare **3.** TEC replacement; **pezzo di ~** spare part

ricamo [ri·'ka:·mo] *m* **1.** (*lavoro*) piece of embroidery **2.** (*operazione*) embroidery **3.** *fig* (*aggiunta arbitraria*) embellishment

ricandidarsi [ri·kan·di·'da:r·si] *vr* (*politico*) to run again

ricapitalizzazione [ri·ka·pi·ta·lid·dzat·'tsio:·ne] *f* FIN, COM recapitalization

ricapitolare [ri·ka·pi·to·'la:·re] *vt* to recap

ricarica [ri·'ka:·ri·ka] <-che> *f* **1.** (*di cellulare*) top up; (*operazione*) topping up **2.** (*di biro, stampante*) refill; (*operazione*) refilling

ricaricare [ri·ka·ri·'ka:·re] *vt* **1.** (*fucile*) to reload **2.** (*batteria*) to recharge **3.** (*orologio*) to wind up again **4.** (*bombole, accendini*) to refill

ricattare [ri·kat·'ta:·re] *vt* to blackmail

ricatto [ri·'kat·to] *m* blackmail

ricavare [ri·ka·'va:·re] *vt* **1.** (*estrarre: minerali*) to extract **2.** COM (*guadagnare*) to make **3.** (*ottenere: risultato, vantaggio*) to get **4.** (*dedurre: consequenza, conclusioni*) to draw **5.** (*insegnamento, lezione*) to learn

R

ricavato [ri·ka·'va:·to] *m* (*somma*) proceeds *pl*
ricavato, -a *agg* (*somma*) earned; (*vino*) obtained
ricavo [ri·'ka:·vo] *m* COM proceeds *pl*
ricchezza [rik·'ket·tsa] *f* 1. (*gener*) wealth 2. (*di luogo, colore*) richness 3. (*abbondanza: di doni, risorse*) abundance
riccio ['rit·tʃo] <-cci> *m* 1. ZOO hedgehog; **chiudersi come un ~** *fig* to clam up like an oyster 2. (*di castagna*) chestnut husk 3. (*di capelli*) curl
riccio, -a <-cci, -cce> *agg* 1. (*capelli*) curly 2. **insalata -a** curly leafed lettuce
ricciolo [rit·'tʃɔ:·lo] *m* curl
ricciuto, -a [rit·'tʃu:·to] *agg* (*testa*) curly
ricco, -a ['rik·ko] <-cchi, -cche> I. *agg* 1. (*paese, persona, vegetazione*) rich; **~ sfondato** filthy rich 2. (*abbondante: documentazione, gamma di prodotti*) vast; **~ di qc** (*risorse, informazioni*) full of sth 3. (*sfarzoso*) ostentatious II. *m, f* wealthy person
riccone, -a [rik·'ko:·ne] *m, f fam* moneybags
ricerca [ri·'tʃer·ka] <-che> *f* 1. (*di lavoro, di colpevole, di cause*) search; **andare alla ~ di qc/qu** to go looking for sth/sb; **motore di ~** COMPUT search engine 2. SCIENT research; **centro di -che** research center; **dottorato di ~** PhD 3. (*indagine*) investigation; **~ di mercato** market research 4. (*a scuola*) research
ricercare [ri·tʃer·'ka:·re] *vt* 1. (*indagare*) to investigate 2. *fig* (*parole*) to look for
ricercatezza [ri·tʃer·ka·'tet·tsa] *f* (*di stile, design, modi*) taste
ricercato, -a [ri·tʃer·'ka:·to] I. *agg* 1. (*apprezzato: persona, locale*) popular 2. (*affettato: persona, modi*) affected 3. (*raffinato: maniere, stile, design*) tasteful II. *m, f* wanted person
ricercatore, -trice [ri·tʃer·ka·'to:·re] *m, f* (*studioso*) researcher
ricetrasmittente [ri·tʃe·traz·mit·'tɛn·te] *f* transceiver
ricetta [ri·'tʃɛt·ta] *f* 1. (*di cucina*) recipe 2. (*del medico*) prescription 3. (*rimedio*) cure
ricettacolo [ri·tʃet·'ta:·ko·lo] *m* 1. (*luogo di raccolta*) gathering place 2. *pej* (*rifugio: di criminali*) hangout
ricettare [ri·tʃet·'ta:·re] *vt* to receive stolen goods
ricettario [ri·tʃet·'ta:·rio] <-i> *m* 1. MED prescription pad 2. (*di cucina*) recipe book
ricettatore, -trice [ri·tʃet·ta·'to:·re] *m, f* receiver of stolen goods
ricettazione [ri·tʃet·tat·'tsio:·ne] *f* receiving stolen goods
ricettività [ri·tʃet·ti·vi·'ta] <-> *f* 1. (*gener*) receptivity 2. (*di luogo, di albergo*) accommodation
ricettivo, -a [ri·tʃet·'ti:·vo] *agg* 1. (*gener*) receptive 2. (*luogo*) accommodating
ricevente [ri·tʃe·'vɛn·te] I. *agg* (*radio*) receiving II. *f* (*radio*) receiver III. *mf* recipient
ricevere [ri·'tʃe:·ve·re] I. *vi* (*medico, professore*) to receive patients II. *vt* 1. (*ospiti,*

regalo, lettera,) to receive 2. (*insulto, condanna*) to get 3. (*sacramento*) to be given 4. RADIO, TEL to pick up
ricevimento [ri·tʃe·vi·'men·to] *m* (*cerimonia, festa*) reception
ricevitoria [ri·tʃe·vi·to·'ri:·a] <-ie> *f* (*del totocalcio, del lotto*) outlet
ricevuta [ri·tʃe·'vu:·ta] *f* (*di versamento, pagamento*) receipt; **~ fiscale** receipt for tax purposes; **raccomandata con ~ di ritorno** certified letter with return receipt
ricezione [ri·tʃet·'tsio:·ne] *f* (*di onde*) reception
richiamare [ri·kia·'ma:·re] I. *vt* 1. (*chiamare di nuovo*) to call again; **~ qu all'ordine** to call sb to order 2. (*per far tornare*) to call back 3. MIL to recall 4. (*attrarre: turisti, folla*) to attract; **~ l'attenzione di qu su qc** to call sb's attention to sth 5. (*sgridare*) to reprimand 6. (*rievocare*) to recall; **~ alla memoria di qu** to remind sb 7. COMPUT (*programma*) to open; (*dati*) to get access to II. *vr* **-rsi a qc** (*riferirsi*) to refer to sth
richiamo [ri·'kia:·mo] *m* 1. (*invito al ritorno*) recall 2. (*invito: a dovere, obbedienza*) call 3. (*rimprovero*) reprimand 4. (*attrazione*) attraction 5. (*fascino: di luoghi, di persone*) charm 6. (*rimando: in libro*) cross-reference 7. MED (*vaccinazione*) booster 8. COMPUT link
richiedente [ri·kie·'dɛn·te] *mf* applicant
richiedere [ri·'kiɛː·de·re] <irr> *vt* 1. (*chiedere di nuovo*) to ask again 2. (*con fermezza: aiuto, sostegno, sussidio*) to request 3. ADM (*congedo, permesso di soggiorno*) to apply for 4. (*esigere: concentrazione, impegno*) to require 5. (*parere*) to ask for 6. (*libri, oggetti prestati*) to request the return of
richiesta [ri·'kiɛs·ta] *f* 1. (*domanda*) request 2. ADM (*di congedo, permesso di soggiorno*) application 3. (*di compenso*) charge 4. (*esigenza*) necessity; **a ~ (di)** on (sb's) request; **dietro ~ (di)** at the request (of)
richiesto, -a [ri·'kiɛs·to] I. *pp di* **richiedere** II. *agg* requested
riciclabile [ri·tʃi·'kla·bi·le] *agg* (*carta, metallo*) recyclable
riciclaggio [ri·tʃi·'klad·dʒo] <-ggi> *m* 1. (*di rifiuti, materiali*) recycling 2. (*di denaro sporco*) money laundering
riciclare [ri·tʃi·'kla:·re] *vt* 1. (*rifiuti, carta, metalli*) to recycle 2. (*denaro sporco*) to launder
riciclato, -a [ri·tʃi·'kla:·to] *agg* (*carta*) recycled
ricino ['ri:·tʃi·no] *m* castor-oil plant
riclassificazione [ri·klas·si·fi·kat·'tsio:·ne] *f* reclassification
ricognitore [ri·koɲ·ɲi·'to:·re] *m* reconnaissance aircraft
ricognizione [ri·koɲ·ɲit·'tsio:·ne] *f a. scherz* reconnaissance
ricollegare [ri·kol·le·'ga:·re] I. *vt* 1. (*collegare di nuovo: fili*) to reconnect 2. *fig* (*ragionamenti, concetti*) to connect II. *vr:* **-rsi**

1. (*riferirsi: a discorso*) **-rsi a qu/qc** to refer to sb/sth **2.** (*studio televisivo*) **-rsi con qu/qc** to go back to sb/sth

ricolmare [ri·kol·'ma:·re] *vt* ~ **qu/qc di qc** to cover sb/sth with sth

ricolmo, -a [ri·'kol·mo] *agg a. fig* (*pieno*) full

ricominciare [ri·ko·min·'tʃa:·re] **I.** *vt avere* to start again **II.** *vi essere* to start again; **si ricomincia!** *fam* we're off again!

ricomparsa [ri·kom·'par·sa] *f* (*di malattie, sintomi*) reappearance

ricompattare [ri·kom·pat·'ta:·re] *vt* (*gruppo*) to reunite

ricompensa [ri·kom·'pɛn·sa] *f* reward

ricompensare [ri·kom·pen·'sa:·re] *vt* (*premiare*) to reward

riconciliare [ri·kon·tʃi·'lia:·re] **I.** *vt* (*persone*) to reconcile **II.** *vr:* **-rsi** to be reconciled

riconciliazione [ri·kon·tʃi·liat·'tsio:·ne] *f* reconciliation

ricondotto *pp di* **ricondurre**

riconducibile [ri·kon·du·'tʃi:·bi·le] *agg* ~ **a** related to

ricondurre [ri·kon·'dur·re] <irr> *vt* **1.** (*riportare: persone*) to take back; ~ **qu alla ragione** to bring sb back to his [*o* her] senses **2.** (*far risalire a*) ~ **qc a qc** to trace sth to sth

riconferma [ri·kon·'fer·ma] *f* **1.** (*di incarico*) reappointment **2.** (*nuova conferma*) confirmation; (*dimostrazione, prova*) proof

riconfermare [ri·kon·fer·'ma:·re] **I.** *vt* **1.** (*notizia, informazione*) to reconfirm **2.** (*in un incarico*) to reappoint **II.** *vr:* **-rsi** (*campione*) to prove oneself again

ricongiungere [ri·kon·'dʒun·dʒe·re] <irr> **I.** *vt* (*famiglie*) to reunite **II.** *vr:* **-rsi a qu** to rejoin sb

riconobbi *1. pers sing pass rem di* **riconoscere**

riconoscente [ri·ko·noʃ·'ʃɛn·te] *agg* (*parole, tono*) grateful; **essere ~ a qu per qc** to be grateful to sb for sth

riconoscenza [ri·ko·noʃ·'ʃɛn·tsa] *f* gratitude

riconoscere [ri·ko·'noʃ·ʃe·re] <irr> **I.** *vt* **1.** (*persona, oggetto*) to recognize; ~ **qu dalla voce** to recognize sb by his [*o* her] voice **2.** (*distinguere: intenzioni, verità, qualità*) to distinguish **3.** (*ammettere: errori*) to admit **4.** (*stato di emergenza, calamità naturale*) to declare **5.** (*considerare: colpevole, conforme*) to find **6.** JUR, POL (*Stato, ente*) to recognize; (*figlio*) to acknowledge **II.** *vr:* **-rsi 1.** (*colpevole, capace, incapace*) to admit **2.** (*identificarsi: in idea, partito*) **-rsi in qc/qu** to identify with sth/sb

riconoscibile [ri·ko·noʃ·'ʃi:·bi·le] *agg* recognizable

riconoscimento [ri·ko·noʃ·ʃi·'men·to] *m* **1.** (*identificazione*) identification **2.** JUR, POL (*di figlio, persona giuridica*) acknowledgement; (*di Stato, titolo*) recognition **3.** (*compenso*) recognition **4.** (*di colpa, di errore*) admission

riconosciuto [ri·ko·noʃ·'ʃu:·to] **I.** *pp di* **rico-**

noscere II. *agg* (*festa, titolo*) recognized

riconquista [ri·kon·'kuis·ta] *f* (*di città, di territorio*) reconquest

riconquistare [ri·koɲ·kuis·'ta:·re] *vt* **1.** (*territorio, regione*) to reconquer **2.** *fig* (*fiducia, speranza*) to regain

riconsegna [ri·kon·'seɲ·ɲa] *f* reconsignment

riconsegnare [ri·kon·seɲ·'na:·re] *vt* **1.** (*consegnare di nuovo*) to redeliver **2.** (*restituire: libri, gioielli*) to return

riconsiderare [ri·kon·si·de·'ra:·re] *vt* (*questione, fatti, problema*) to reconsider

riconversione [ri·kon·ver·'sio:·ne] *f* (*di industria, organizzazione, società*) reorganization

ricopersi *1. pers sing pass rem di* **ricoprire**

ricoperto *pp di* **ricoprire**

ricopiare [ri·ko·'pia:·re] *vt* **1.** (*copiare di nuovo*) to copy out again **2.** (*trascrivere*) to copy; ~ **in bella** to make a fair copy of sth

ricoprire [ri·ko·'pri:·re] <irr> **I.** *vt* **1.** (*coprire di nuovo*) to re-cover **2.** (*mobili, poltrone*) to cover **3.** *fig* (*colmare*) ~ **qu/qc di qc** to shower sb/sth with sth **4.** ADM (*carica*) to hold **II.** *vr:* **-rsi** ~ **di qc** (*crema*) to cover oneself with sth; (*bolle, macchie*) to be covered in sth

ricordare [ri·kor·'da:·re] **I.** *vt* **1.** (*serbare memoria di*) ~ **qu/qc** to remember sb/sth **2.** (*richiamare alla memoria*) ~ **a qu qc/qu** to remind sb of sth/sb **3.** (*far presente*) ~ **qc a qu** to remind sb about sth **4.** (*assomigliare*) ~ **qu a qu** to remind sb of sb **5.** (*citare*) to mention **6.** (*commemorare*) to commemorate **II.** *vr:* **-rsi** (*serbare memoria di*) **-rsi di qu/qc** to remember sb/sth; **me ne ricorderò** *fam* (*minaccia*) I won't forget it

ricordino [ri·kor·'di:·no] *m* souvenir

ricordo [ri·'kɔr·do] *m* **1.** (*di persona, periodo*) memory; **serbare un buon ~ di qu/qc** to have happy memories of sb/sth **2.** (*souvenir*) souvenir; (*libro, quadro*) memento; **per ~** as a memento **3.** (*traccia, vestigia*) reminder

ricorrente [ri·kor·'rɛn·te] **I.** *agg* **1.** (*fatto, fenomeno*) recurring **2.** JUR **parte ~** plaintiff-side **II.** *mf* DIR plaintiff

ricorrenza [ri·kor·'rɛn·tsa] *f* **1.** (*festività*) holiday; (*anniversario*) anniversary **2.** (*ritorno: di sintomi, di fenomeno*) recurrence

ricorrere [ri·'kor·re·re] <irr> *vi essere* **1.** (*tornare indietro*) to rush back **2.** (*rivolgersi*) ~ **a qu** to turn to sb **3.** (*servirsi*) ~ **a qc** to use sth **4.** (*festa, anniversario*) to take place **5.** (*ripetersi: evento, fenomeno*) to recur **6.** (*comparire: parola*) to appear **7.** JUR ~ **alle vie legali** to take legal action

ricorso [ri·'kor·so] *m* **1.** JUR appeal **2.** (*loc*) **fare ~ a qu/qc** to turn to sb/sth

ricostituente [ri·kos·ti·tu·'ɛn·te] **I.** *agg* (*cura, terapia*) tonic **II.** *m* tonic

ricostituire [ri·kos·ti·tu·'i:·re] <ricostituisco> **I.** *vt* (*governo, gruppo*) to re-form **II.** *vr:* **-rsi** (*società, gruppo, comitato*) to re-form

ricostituzione [ri·kos·ti·tut·'tsio:·ne] *f* (*di partito, organizzazione*) re-formation

R

ricostruire [ri·kos·tru·'iː·re] <ricostruisco> *vt* **1.** (*edificio, industria, vita*) to rebuild **2.** (*fatti, eventi*) to reconstruct

ricostruttivo, -a [ri·kos·trut·'tiː·vo] *agg* **1.** MED (*intervento*) reconstructive; (*trattamento*) fortifying **2.** (*piano*) reconstruction

ricostruzione [ri·kos·trut·'tsioː·ne] *f* **1.** (*di paese, economia*) rebuilding **2.** (*di fatti, trama*) reconstruction

ricotta [ri·'kɔt·ta] *f soft cheese made from sheep's milk*

ricoverare [ri·ko·ve·'raː·re] I. *vt* (*in ospedale, in clinica*) to admit II. *vr:* -**rsi** (*in ospedale, in clinica*) to be admitted

ricoverato, -a [ri·ko·ve·'raː·to] *m, f* (*di ospedale*) patient

ricovero [ri·'koː·ve·ro] *m* **1.** (*in ospedale*) admission; ~ **d'urgenza** emergency admission **2.** (*istituto*) institution; (*per anziani*) old people's home **3.** *fig* (*rifugio*) refuge

ricreare [ri·kre·'aː·re] I. *vt* **1.** (*ristorare*) to restore **2.** (*divertire*) to amuse **3.** (*creare di nuovo*) to recreate II. *vr:* -**rsi 1.** (*divertirsi*) to enjoy oneself **2.** (*situazione, atmosfera*) to be recreated

ricreativo, -a [ri·kre·a·'tiː·vo] *agg* (*gioco, attività*) recreational; (*centro*) recreation

ricreazione [ri·kre·at·'tsioː·ne] *f* **1.** (*intervallo*) break **2.** (*svago*) entertainment

ricredersi [ri·'kreː·der·si] *vr* -**rsi su qc/qu** to change one's mind about sth/sb

ricucire [ri·ku·'tʃiː·re] *vt* **1.** (*strappo, buco*) to mend **2.** MED (*ferita*) to stitch **3.** *fig* (*dialogo, strappo, frattura*) to patch up

ricuperare [ri·ku·pe·'raː·re] *vt* **1.** (*documenti, portafoglio*) to get back; (*salute, vista, parola, forze*) to regain **2.** (*tempo*) to make up **3.** (*naufraghi*) to rescue; (*relitti*) to salvage **4.** (*carcerato, tossicodipendente*) to rehabilitate **5.** SPORT (*in una partita*) to add on **6.** (*materiali, dati*) to recover

ricupero [ri·'kuː·pe·ro] *m* **1.** (*riacquisto: di dati, valori, tempo*) recovery **2.** (*ricostruzione: di patrimonio, centro storico, rustici*) renovation **3.** (*di nave*) salvage; (*di naufraghi*) rescue **4.** (*di carcerato*) rehabilitation **5.** SPORT overtime

ricurvo, -a [ri·'kur·vo] *agg* bent

ridacchiare [ri·dak·'kiaː·re] *vi* to snicker

ridare [ri·'daː·re] <irr> *vt* **1.** (*dare di nuovo*) to give again; **dagli e ridagli** *fam* after a lot of effort **2.** (*rifare: esami*) to retake **3.** (*restituire*) to give back

ridarella [ri·da·'rɛl·la] *f fam* giggles *pl*

ridente [ri·'dɛn·te] *agg* (*località, centro*) charming

ridere ['riː·de·re] <rido, risi, riso> I. *vi* to laugh; ~ **fino alle lacrime** to laugh until one cries; **fare per** ~ *fam* to joke; **farsi** ~ **dietro** *fam* to make a fool of oneself; **far** ~ **i polli** *fam* to make everybody laugh; **ma non farmi** ~! *fam* don't make me laugh!; **ride bene chi ride ultimo** *prov* he who laughs last laughs

longest *prov* II. *vr:* -**rsi 1.** (*burlarsi*) -**rsi di qc** to laugh at sth **2.** (*infischiarsene*) to not care

ridetti *1. pers sing pass rem di* **ridare**

ridetto *pp di* **ridire**

ridico *1. pers sing pr di* **ridire**

ridicolizzare [ri·di·ko·lid·'dzaː·re] *vt* ~ **qu/qc** to ridicule sb/sth

ridicolo [ri·'diː·ko·lo] *m* **cadere nel** ~ to make oneself look ridiculous; **mettere qu/qc nel** ~ to make sb/sth look ridiculous

ridicolo, -a *agg* (*goffo: atteggiamento, pretesa*) ridiculous

ridiedi *1. pers sing pass rem di* **ridare**

ridimensionamento [ri·di·men·sio·na·'men·to] *m* downsizing

ridimensionare [ri·di·men·sio·'naː·re] I. *vt* **1.** (*industria*) to downsize **2.** (*fatti, importanza*) to put into perspective II. *vr:* -**rsi** (*ambizioni, pretese*) to become more realistic

ridire [ri·'diː·re] <irr> *vt* **1.** (*dire di nuovo*) to repeat **2.** (*criticare*) **avere qc da** ~ **su qc/qu** to object to sth/sb

ridissi *1. pers sing pass rem di* **ridire**

ridistribuzione [ri·dis·tri·but·'tsioː·ne] *f* redistribution

ridiventare [ri·di·ven·'taː·re] *vi essere* to become again

ridondante [ri·don·'dan·te] *agg* (*testo, informazioni*) bombastic

ridondanza [ri·don·'dan·tsa] *f* excess

ridosso [ri·'dɔs·so] *m* **a** ~ **di** behind

ridotto, -a I. *pp di* **ridurre** II. *agg* **1.** (*prezzi, biglietto*) discounted; **prezzo** ~ cut-price **2.** (*loc*) **a** ~ (*diventato*) nothing more than

ridurre [ri·'dur·re] <riduco, ridussi, ridotto> I. *vt* **1.** (*diminuire: impegni, tasse, velocità*) to reduce **2.** (*far diventare*) ~ **al silenzio** to silence; ~ **all'obbedienza** to bring to heel; ~ **alla disperazione** to drive to despair; ~ **in cenere** *a. fig* to reduce to ashes; ~ **in polvere** *a. fig* to crush; ~ **uno straccio** to leave like a wet rag **3.** (*costringere*) **essere ridotto a fare qc** to be reduced to doing sth **4.** MATH to reduce II. *vr:* -**rsi 1.** (*diventare*) to be reduced **2.** (*diminuire*) to decrease

riduzione [ri·dut·'tsioː·ne] *f* **1.** (*di prezzi, tasse*) reduction **2.** THEAT, FILM adaptation **3.** MATH reduction

riedizione [ri·e·dit·'tsioː·ne] *f* **1.** (*ristampa*) new edition **2.** THEAT revival; (*film*) re-release

rieducare [ri·e·du·'kaː·re] *vt* **1.** (*ragazzo*) to re-educate; (*detenuto*) to rehabilitate **2.** MED (*sordo, muto*) to re-teach; (*braccio, vista*) to rehabilitate

rieducazione [ri·e·du·kat·'tsioː·ne] *f* **1.** (*di ragazzo*) re-education; (*di detenuto, di condannato*) rehabilitation; **istituto di** ~ **minorile** rehabilitation center for juvenile offenders **2.** MED rehabilitation

rielaborare [ri·e·la·bo·'raː·re] *vt* **1.** (*progetto, testo*) to rework **2.** *fig* (*idee, convinzioni*) to rethink

rielaborazione [ri·e·la·bo·rat·'tsioː·ne] *f* (*di*

testo) reworking

rieleggere [ri·e·'lɛd·dʒe·re] <irr> *vt* to re-elect

rielezione [ri·e·let·'tsio:·ne] *f* re-election

riemergere [ri·e·'mɛr·dʒe·re] <irr> *vi essere a. fig* to re-emerge

riempimento [ri·em·pi·'men·to] *m* (*di contenitori*) filling

riempire [ri·em·'pi:·re] I. *vt* 1. (*bicchiere, sacco*) to fill 2. (*modulo*) to fill in 3. (*loc*) ~ qu di gioia to fill sb with joy II. *vr:* -rsi 1. (*mangiare troppo*) -rsi di qc *fam* to stuff oneself with sth; -rsi lo stomaco di qc to eat sth 2. (*diventare pieno: d'acqua, persone*) -rsi di qc to fill with sth; (*di brufoli, macchie*) to be covered in sth 3. (*loc*) -rsi la bocca di promesse [*o* belle parole] to spout promises [*o* fine words]

riempitivo [ri·em·pi·'ti:·vo] *m* 1. (*materiale*) filler 2. *fig* (*passatempo, occupazione*) time-filler

rientrante [ri·en·'tran·te] *agg* (*guance*) hollow; (*parete*) receding

rientranza [ri·en·'tran·tsa] *f* (*di superficie*) recess

rientrare [ri·en·'tra:·re] *vi essere* 1. (*entrare di nuovo*) to come [*o* go] back in 2. (*tornare*) to return; (*a casa*) to come [*o* go] home 3. (*piegarsi in dentro*) to recede 4. (*fare parte*) ~ in qc to be part of sth

rientro [ri·'en·tro] *m* (*da viaggio, vacanze*) return

riepilogare [ri·e·pi·lo·'ga:·re] *vt* to summarize

riepilogo [ri·e·'pi:·lo·go] <-ghi> *m* summary

riesco *1. pers sing pr di* riuscire

riessere [ri·'ɛs·se·re] <irr> *vi essere fam* (*essere di nuovo*) to be again; ci risiamo! *fig, fam* here we go again!

riesumare [ri·e·zu·'ma:·re] *vt* 1. (*cadavere*) to exhume 2. (*abito, articolo, manuale*) to bring out again

Rieti *f* Rieti, *city in the Lazio region*

Rietino [ri·e·'ti:·no] *m* (*zona*) Rieti area; nel ~ in the Rieti area

rietino, -a I. *agg* from Rieti II. *m, f* (*abitante*) person from Rieti

rievocare [ri·e·vo·'ka:·re] *vt* (*passato, episodio, racconto*) to remember

rievocazione [ri·e·vo·kat·'tsio:·ne] *f* (*di evento passato*) commemoration

rifacimento [ri·fa·tʃi·'men·to] *m* 1. (*di palazzo, di edificio*) reconstruction 2. (*di opera, di film*) remake

rifare [ri·'fa:·re] <irr> I. *vt* 1. (*esame*) to retake; (*compito*) to redo 2. (*stanza*) to clean; (*letto*) to make 3. (*imitare*) to imitate 4. (*compensare*) to compensate 5. (*compiere un'altra volta*) to do again; ~ la strada to retrace one's steps II. *vr:* -rsi 1. (*diventare nuovamente*) to become again 2. -rsi di qc (*prendersi la rivincita*) to get one's revenge for sth 3. (*loc*) ~ una vita to rebuild one's life; ~ gli occhi to be a sight for sore eyes; ~ la bocca [*o* il seno] to have one's mouth [*o* breasts] redone

riferimento [ri·fe·ri·'men·to] *m* (*richiamo*) reference; fare ~ a to refer to; punto di ~ *a. fig* reference point

riferire [ri·fe·'ri:·re] <riferisco> I. *vt* 1. (*riportare: fatto, episodio*) to report 2. (*mettere in relazione*) ~ qc a qc to relate sth to sth II. *vi* (*presentare una relazione*) ~ su qc to report on sth III. *vr:* -rsi -rsi a qc (*fare riferimento*) to refer to sth; (*alludere*) to allude to sth

riffa ['rif·fa] *f tosc* di ~ o di raffa *fam* however one looks at it

rifilare [ri·fi·'la:·re] *vt* 1. *fam* (*affibbiare*) ~ qc a qu to land sb with sth 2. *fam* (*vendere*) to palm off

rifinire [ri·fi·'ni:·re] *vt* (*perfezionare: opera, disegno, abito*) to add the finishing touches to

rifinitura [ri·fi·ni·'tu:·ra] *f* 1. (*perfezionamento*) finishing touch 2. (*guarnizione: di tessuto*) trimming

rifiutare [ri·fiu·'ta:·re] I. *vt* 1. (*non accettare: proposta, invito*) to turn down; (*consigli*) to reject 2. (*negare*) ~ qc a qu to refuse sb sth II. *vr:* -rsi -rsi di fare qc to refuse to do sth

rifiuto [ri·'fiu·to] *m* 1. (*negazione*) refusal 2. *pl* (*immondizie*) garbage; -i organici (compostabili) organic waste; -i nucleari [*o* radioattivi] nuclear [*o* radioactive] waste; -i tossici toxic waste 3. (*loc*) essere un ~ della società to be the dregs of society

riflessante [rif·les·'san·te] *m* (*shampoo*) highlight enhancer

riflessi [ri·'flɛs·si] *1. pers sing pass rem di* riflettere

riflessione [ri·fles·'sio:·ne] *f* 1. (*considerazione*) reflection; (*osservazione*) remark 2. PHYS reflection

riflessivo, -a [ri·fles·'si:·vo] *agg* 1. (*persona, mente, carattere*) thoughtful 2. LING verbo ~ reflexive verb; pronome ~ reflexive pronoun

riflesso [ri·'flɛs·so] *m* 1. (*di sole, luce*) reflection 2. (*conseguenza*) repercussion 3. MED reflex

riflesso, -a I. *pp di* riflettere II. *agg* (*raggio, luce, immagine*) reflected; brillare di luce -a *fig* to bask in reflected glory

riflessologia [ri·fles·so·lo·'dʒi:·a] *f* reflexology; ~ plantare reflexology

riflettere [ri·'flɛt·te·re] <irr> I. *vt* to reflect II. *vi* ~ su qc to think about sth III. *vr:* -rsi 1. (*specchiarsi*) to be reflected 2. *fig* (*influire*) -rsi su qc to influence sth

riflettore [ri·flet·'to:·re] *m* EL reflector; sotto i -i *a. fig* in the spotlight

rifluire [ri·flu·'i:·re] <rifluisco> *vi essere* 1. (*tornare a scorrere: sangue, traffico*) to flow again 2. (*fluire indietro: liquido*) to flow back 3. (*tornare ad affluire: pubblico*) to flow back 4. *fig* (*ripercuotersi*) to be reflected

riflusso [ri·'flus·so] *m a. fig* reflux; flusso e ~ ebb and flow

rifocillare [ri·fo·tʃil·'la:·re] I. *vt* (*persona, stomaco*) to feed II. *vr:* -rsi to eat

rifondazione [ri·fon·dat·'tsio:·ne] *f* (*di par-*

tito, movimento) refoundation; **Rifondazione Comunista** POL *Italian Communist party*

rifondere [ri·'fon·de·re] <irr> *vt* 1.(*statua, metallo*) to melt down again 2.*fig* (*danni*) to pay compensation for; (*spese*) to reimburse

riforestazione [ri·fo·res·tat·'tsio·ne] *f* ECO reforestation

riforma [ri·'for·ma] *f* 1.(*di ordinamento, di partito*) reform 2.REL reform; ~ **protestante** Protestant Reformation 3.MIL (*congedo*) medical discharge

riformabile [ri·for·'ma:·bi·le] *agg* (*sistema, paese*) open to reform

riformare [ri·for·'ma:·re] I.*vt* 1.(*formare di nuovo: squadra, gruppo*) to re-form 2.(*partito, ordinamento*) to reform 3.REL to reform 4.MIL to medically discharge II.*vr:* -**rsi** (*formarsi di nuovo*) to re-form

riformato [ri·for·'ma:·to] *m* MIL *soldier deemed unfit for active duty*

riformato, -a I.*agg* **Chiesa -a** Reformed Church II.*m, f* REL member of the Reformed Church

riformatore, -trice [ri·for·ma·'to:·re] I.*agg* 1.(*programma*) reformist 2.REL reformist II.*m, f* POL, REL reformer

riformatrice *f v.* **riformatore**

riformismo [ri·for·'miz·mo] *m* reformism

riformista [ri·for·'mis·ta] <-i *m*, -e *f*> I.*mf* reformist II.*agg* reformist

rifornimento [ri·for·ni·'men·to] *m* 1.(*di benzina*) refueling; **fare ~ di benzina** to fill up with gasoline 2.(*fornitura: di gas*) provision 3.*pl* (*viveri*) supplies *pl*

rifornire [ri·for·'ni:·re] <rifornisco> I.*vt* ~ **qu/ qc di qc** to supply sb/sth with sth II.*vr* -**rsi di qc** to stock up on sth

rifrazione [ri·frat·'tsio·ne] *f* refraction

rifriggere [ri·'frid·dʒe·re] <irr> *vt* 1.CULIN to fry again 2.*fig, fam* (*ripetere: idee, concetti*) to churn out again

rifuggire [ri·fud·'dʒi:·re] *vi essere* 1.(*fuggire di nuovo*) to flee again 2.(*evitare*) ~ **da qc** to avoid sth

rifugiarsi [ri·fu·'dʒar·si] *vr a. fig* to seek refuge

rifugiato, -a [ri·fu·'dʒa:·to] *m, f* refugee

rifugio [ri·'fu:·dʒo] <-gi> *m* 1.(*riparo*) shelter 2.(*luogo*) refuge; ~ **alpino** alpine refuge; ~ **antiatomico** fallout shelter 3.*fig* (*conforto*) refuge

rifui *1. pers sing pass rem di* **riessere**

rifulgere [ri·'ful·dʒe·re] <rifulgo, rifulsi, rifulso> *vi* ~ **di qc** (*luce, colori*) to glow with sth

riga ['ri:·ga] <-ghe> *f* 1.(*linea*) line; **carta/ quaderno a -ghe** lined paper/excercise book 2.(*striscia: su tessuto*) stripe 3.(*di scritto*) line; **leggere fra le -ghe** *fig* to read between the lines 4.(*di persone, cose*) line; **mettersi in ~** to get in line 5.(*di capelli*) parting 6.(*asticella*) ruler 7.COMPUT ~ **di comando** command line; ~ **di commento** comment line

rigagnolo [ri·'gaɲ·ɲo·lo] *m* brook

rigare [ri·'ga:·re] I.*vt* 1.(*auto, CD*) to scratch 2.*fig* (*volto, guance*) to bathe II.*vi* **rigar diritto** to behave oneself

rigatoni [ri·ga·'to:·ni] *mpl* rigatoni, *tube-shaped pasta*

rigattiere [ri·gat·'tiɛ:·re] *m* secondhand dealer

rigenerare [ri·dʒe·ne·'ra:·re] I.*vt* to regenerate II.*vr:* -**rsi** 1.BIOL to regenerate 2.*fig* (*rimettersi*) to feel reborn

rigettare [ri·dʒet·'ta:·re] I.*vt* 1.(*gettare di nuovo*) to throw again 2.(*respingere: domanda, richiesta, ricorso*) to reject 3.*fam* (*vomitare*) to throw up II.*vr:* -**rsi** *a. fig* (*gettarsi di nuovo*) to throw oneself back

rigetto [ri·'dʒet·to] *m a. fig* BIOL rejection

righello [ri·'gɛl·lo] *m* ruler

rigidezza [ri·dʒi·'det·tsa] *f* rigidity

rigidità [ri·dʒi·di·'ta] <-> *f* 1.(*severità: di carattere, di regolamento*) severity; (*di clima*) harshness 2.TEC (*di struttura*) rigidity 3.MED stiffness

rigido, -a ['ri:·dʒi·do] *agg* 1.(*colletto, dito*) stiff; (*cappello*) hard 2.(*clima, inverno*) harsh 3.*fig* (*severo: carattere, educazione*) strict; (*tono*) harsh

rigirare [ri·dʒi·'ra:·re] I.*vt* 1.(*girare più volte*) to turn 2.(*percorrere*) to go around 3.*fig* (*discorso*) to change; (*situazione*) to switch; ~ **la frittata** to turn the situation around; **saperla ~** *fam* to manipulate the situation; **gira e rigira** *fam* in the end II.*vi* to go around III.*vr:* -**rsi** (*girarsi di nuovo*) to turn around; (*nel letto*) to turn over

rigiro [ri·'dʒi:·ro] *m* (*imbroglio*) swindle

rigoglio [ri·'goʎ·ʎo] <-gli> *m* 1.BOT luxuriance 2.*fig* (*grande vigore: di giovinezza, di vita*) prime

rigoglioso, -a [ri·goʎ·'ʎo:·so] *agg* 1.BOT luxuriant 2.*fig* (*crescita, mente*) flourishing

rigonfiamento [ri·gon·fia·'men·to] *m* (*parte rigonfia*) swelling

rigonfiare [ri·gon·'fia:·re] I.*vt* (*pallone, ruota*) to blow up again II.*vr:* -**rsi** (*braccio, guancia, legno*) to swell up again

rigore [ri·'go:·re] *m* 1.(*severità: di condanna, provvedimento*) severity; **a rigor di logica** logically speaking 2.(*esattezza: di scienza, logica*) precision 3.(*di clima*) harshness 4.SPORT penalty

rigorosità [ri·go·ro·si·'ta] <-> *f* (*precisione: di controllo, ricerca*) precision

rigoroso, -a [ri·go·'ro:·so] *agg* 1.(*severo: atteggiamento, persona*) strict 2.(*esatto: ragionamento, logica*) rigorous 3.(*preciso: controllo*) precise

rigovernare [ri·go·ver·'na:·re] *vt* (*piatti*) to wash up; (*cucina*) to clean up

riguadagnare [ri·gua·daɲ·'ɲa·re] *vt* (*stima, favore*) to regain; (*tempo, soldi*) to make up

riguardante [ri·guar·'dan·te] *agg* (*concernente*) regarding

riguardare [ri·guar·'da:·re] I.*vt* 1.(*guardare di nuovo*) to look at again 2.(*rivedere*) to revise; (*ricontrollare*) to check **3.** (*concernere*) to concern; **per quanto riguarda ...** as far as ... is concerned **II.** *vr:* **-rsi 1.** (*stare in guardia*) **-rsi da qc** to steer clear of sth **2.** (*aver cura della salute*) to look after oneself

riguardata [ri·guar·'da:·ta] *f* **dare una ~ a qc** to have another look at sth

riguardo [ri·'guar·do] *m* **1.** (*cura: di oggetto*) care; **avere ~ per la propria salute** to take care of one's health; **non avere alcun ~** to not care about **2.** (*stima: di persona*) respect; **ospite di ~** special guest **3.** (*relazione*) **nei -i di** with reference to sth; **~ a** regarding

riguardoso, -a [ri·guar·'do:·so] *agg* (*rispettoso*) respectful

rigurgitare [ri·gur·dʒi·'ta:·re] **I.** *vi* essere o avere **~ di qc** *fig* (*persone, sapori, simboli*) to be brimming with sth **II.** *vt* avere (*neonato*) to regurgitate

rigurgito [ri·'gur·dʒi·to] *m* **1.** MED (*di neonato*) regurgitation **2.** *fig* (*ritorno: di razzismo, nazionalismo*) revival

rilanciare [ri·lan·'tʃa:·re] *vt* **1.** (*palla, sasso*) to throw again [*o* back] **2.** (*prodotto, film, moda*) to relaunch

rilancio [ri·'lan·tʃo] <-i> *m a. fig* COM relaunch

rilasciamento [ri·laʃ·ʃa·'men·to] *m* relaxation

rilasciare [ri·laʃ·'ʃa:·re] **I.** *vt* **1.** ADM (*certificato, permesso di soggiorno*) to issue **2.** (*prigioniero*) to release **II.** *vr:* **-rsi** (*lasciarsi di nuovo*) to split up again

rilascio [ri·'laʃ·ʃo] <-sci> *m* **1.** ADM (*di certificato, permesso di soggiorno*) issue **2.** (*di prigioniero*) release

rilassamento [ri·las·sa·'men·to] *m* **1.** (*di muscoli, nervi*) relaxation **2.** (*di costumi*) laxity

rilassare [ri·las·'sa:·re] **I.** *vt* (*muscoli, nervi*) to relax **II.** *vr:* **-rsi** (*distendersi*) to relax

rilassatezza [ri·las·sa·'tet·tsa] *f* (*tranquillità*) relaxation

rilegare [ri·le·'ga:·re] *vt* (*libro*) to bind

rilegatore, -trice [ri·le·ga·'to:·re] *m, f* bookbinder

rilegatura [ri·le·ga·'tu:·ra] *f* (*di libro*) binding

rileggere [ri·'lɛd·dʒe·re] <irr> *vt* **1.** (*leggere di nuovo: lettera, racconto*) to reread **2.** (*rivedere: relazione, traduzione*) to read over

rilento [ri·'lɛn·to] *avv* **a ~** slowly

rilessi *1. pers sing pass rem di* **rileggere**

riletta [ri·let·'ta] *f fam* read through

riletto *pp di* **rileggere**

rilevabile [ri·le·'va:·bi·le] *agg* identifiable

rilevamento [ri·le·va·'men·to] *m* **1.** (*di dati*) identification **2.** (*topografico*) survey **3.** (*di negozio, di attività*) takeover

rilevante [ri·le·'van·te] *agg* (*importante*) important

rilevare [ri·le·'va:·re] *vt* **1.** (*mettere in evidenza*) to highlight **2.** (*notare: errori, inesattezze*) to note **3.** (*raccogliere: dati*) to gather **4.** (*azienda, negozio*) to takeover **5.** (*fare un rilevamento topografico*) to map out

rilevazione [ri·le·vat·'tsio:·ne] *f* survey

rilievo [ri·'liɛ:·vo] *m* **1.** GEOG relief **2.** (*scultura*) **alto/basso ~** haut/bas relief **3.** *fig* (*importanza*) importance; **mettere in ~ qc** to highlight sth

riluttante [ri·lut·'tan·te] *agg* reluctant

riluttanza [ri·lut·'tan·tsa] *f* reluctance

rima ['ri:·ma] *f* rhyme; **rispondere per le -e** *fig* to say one's piece

rimandare [ri·man·'da:·re] *vt* **1.** (*mandare di nuovo*) to send back **2.** (*restituire*) to give back **3.** (*rinviare: incontro, esame*) to postpone **4.** (*alunno*) *to take an exam in September or October due to unsatisfactory grades during the school year* **5.** (*fare riferimento: in libro*) **~ a qc** to refer to sth

rimando [ri·'man·do] *m* (*riferimento, rinvio*) reference

rimaneggiare [ri·ma·ned·'dʒa:·re] *vt* **1.** (*articolo*) to rework **2.** (*edificio*) to restore

rimanente [ri·ma·'nɛn·te] **I.** *agg* remaining **II.** *mf* person remaining **III.** *m* (*ciò che rimane*) remainder

rimanenza [ri·ma·'nɛn·tsa] *f* **1.** (*di denaro*) remainder **2.** (*di magazzino*) **-e di magazzino** unsold stock

rimanere [ri·ma·'ne:·re] <rimango, rimasi, rimasto> *vi* essere **1.** (*restare*) to stay; **~ male/confuso** to be offended/confused; **~ a bocca aperta** to be amazed **2.** (*avanzare*) to be left **3.** (*loc*) **non gli rimane altro che accettare** he can only accept

rimangiare [ri·man·'dʒa:·re] *vt* **1.** (*mangiare di nuovo*) to eat again **2.** *fig* **-rsi qc** (*promessa, parola*) to go back on sth; (*cattiverie*) to take back sth

rimango [ri·'maŋ·go] *1. pers sing pr di* **rimanere**

rimarcare [ri·mar·'ka:·re] *vt* (*sottolineare*) to highlight

rimare [ri·'ma:·re] *vi* to rhyme

rimarginabile [ri·mar·dʒi·'na:·bi·le] *agg* **1.** (*ferita*) healable **2.** *fig* (*offesa*) easy to get over

rimarginarsi [ri·mar·dʒi·'na:r·si] *vr a. fig* to heal

rimasi [ri·'ma:·si] *1. pers sing pass rem di* **rimanere**

rimasterizzare [ri·mas·te·rid·'dza:·re] *vt* to remaster

rimasterizzazione [ri·mas·te·rid·dzat·'tsio:·ne] *f* remastering

rimasto [ri·'mas·to] *pp di* **rimanere**

rimasuglio [ri·ma·'suʎ·ʎo] <-gli> *m pej* vestige

rimbalzare [rim·bal·'tsa:·re] *vi* essere o avere **1.** (*palla*) to bounce **2.** *fig* (*notizia*) to spread

rimbalzo [rim·'bal·tso] *m* **di ~** indirectly

rimbambire [rim·bam·'bi:·re] <rimbambisco> **I.** *vi* essere (*rincretinire*) to become stupid; (*con l'età*) to become senile **II.** *vt* to make stupid **III.** *vr:* **-rsi** (*rincretinirsi*) to become stupid; (*con l'età*) to become senile

rimbambito, -a [rim·bam·'bi:·to] **I.** *agg* (*per-*

R

sona) stupid; (*vecchio*) senile **II.** *m, f* senile person

rimbeccare [rim·bek·'ka:·re] **I.** *vt* to scold **II.** *vr* (*contraddirsi*) to squabble

rimbecillire [rim·be·tʃil·'li:·re] <rimbecillisco> **I.** *vi essere* (*diventare imbecille*) to become stupid **II.** *vt avere* (*rendere imbecille*) to make stupid **III.** *vr:* **-rsi** (*diventare imbecille*) to become stupid

rimbecillito, -a [rim·be·tʃil·'li:·to] **I.** *agg* stupid **II.** *m, f* idiot

rimboccare [rim·bok·'ka:·re] *vt* **1.** (*lenzuola, coperta*) to tuck in **2.** (*loc*) **-rsi le maniche** *fig* to roll up one's sleeves

rimbombante [rim·bom·'ban·te] *agg* (*suono*) thundering

rimbombare [rim·bom·'ba:·re] *vi essere o avere* (*voce, rumore*) to thunder

rimbombo [rim·'bom·bo] *m* (*di suono*) rumble

rimborsabile [rim·bor·'sa:·bi·le] *agg* repayable

rimborsare [rim·bor·'sa:·re] *vt* **1.** (*denaro*) to repay **2.** (*persone*) to refund

rimborso [rim·'bor·so] *m* (*di spese*) refund

rimboscamento [rim·bos·ka·'men·to] *m v.* rimboschimento

rimboscare [rim·bos·'ka:·re] *vt* to reforest

rimboschimento [rim·bos·ki·'men·to] *m* reforestation

rimboschire [rim·bos·'ki:·re] <rimboschisco> **I.** *vt avere* (*terreno, bosco*) to reforest **II.** *vi essere* (*terreno, bosco*) to wood over

rimbrottare [rim·brot·'ta:·re] *vt* (*rimproverare*) to tell off

rimbrotto [rim·'brɔt·to] *m* telling-off

rimediare [ri·me·'dia:·re] **I.** *vi* ~ **a qc** (*errore, torto, carenza*) to make sth good **II.** *vt* **1.** (*procurarsi*) to get hold of **2.** *fig, fam* (*subire: sconfitta, ammonizione*) to suffer

rimedio [ri·'mɛː·dio] <-i> *m* **1.** (*provvedimento*) remedy; **mettere** [*o* **porre**] ~ **a qc** to remedy sth **2.** MED cure

rimescolamento [ri·mes·ko·la·'men·to] *m fig* (*turbamento*) turmoil

rimescolare [ri·mes·ko·'la:·re] **I.** *vt* **1.** (*carte*) to remix; ~ **le carte** *fig* to confuse the issue **2.** CULIN to stir again **3.** *fig* (*modificare*) to change **II.** *vr:* **-rsi** *..: fig* **mi si è rimescolato il sangue** I got upset

rimescolata [ri·mes·ko·'la:·ta] *f* CULIN stir

rimessa [ri·'mes·sa] *f* **1.** (*per veicoli*) garage; (*per attrezzi*) shed **2.** SPORT throw-in; (*del portiere*) goal kick **3.** (*il rimettere*) **la ~ in funzione** the return to service

rimesso, -a [ri·'mes·so] **I.** *pp di* **rimettere** **II.** *agg* **1.** (*ristabilito: paziente, malato*) recovered **2.** (*peccato, colpa*) forgiven

rimestare [ri·mes·'ta:·re] *vt* **1.** (*salsa, minestra*) to stir **2.** *fig* (*passato, vecchie questioni*) to bring up again

rimettere [ri·'met·te·re] <irr> **I.** *vt* **1.** (*mettere di nuovo a posto*) to put back **2.** (*indossare di*

nuovo: indumento) to put on again **3.** (*affidare: decisione*) to entrust **4.** (*pena, colpa*) to forgive **5.** SPORT to throw in **6.** *fam* (*vomitare*) to puke up **7.** (*loc*) **rimetterci** *fam* to lose; **rimetterci la salute** *fam* to ruin one's health **II.** *vr:* **-rsi** **1.** (*riprendersi*) to recover **2.** (*tempo*) to improve **3.** (*affidarsi*) **-rsi a qu/qc** to place one's trust in sb/sth **4.** (*ricominciare*) **-rsi a studiare** to begin to study again

riminese [ri·mi·'ne:·se] **I.** *mf* (*abitante*) person from Rimini **II.** *agg* from Rimini

Riminese <*sing*> *m* (*zona*) Rimini area; **nel** ~ in the Rimini area

Rimini *f* Rimini, *seaside resort in Emilia-Romagna*

rimisi *1. pers sing pass rem di* **rimettere**

rimmel® ['rim·mel] <-> *m* mascara

rimodernare [ri·mo·der·'na:·re] *vt* (*edificio, linea di prodotto*) to modernize

rimonta [ri·'mon·ta] *f* SPORT comeback

rimontare [ri·mon·'ta:·re] **I.** *vt avere* **1.** (*montare di nuovo: scaffale, motore*) to put back together again **2.** SPORT to catch up **II.** *vi essere* **1.** (*montare di nuovo*) to climb back on **2.** (*in macchina, treno*) to climb back in

rimorchiare [ri·mor·'kia:·re] *vt* **1.** (*veicolo*) to tow; (*nave*) to tug **2.** *fig, fam* (*abbordare: in discoteca*) to pull

rimorchio [ri·'mɔr·kio] <-chi> *m* trailer

rimordere [ri·'mɔr·de·re] <irr> *vt fig* to prick

rimorso [ri·'mɔr·so] *m* remorse

rimostranza [ri·mos·'tran·tsa] *f* complaint

rimozione [ri·mot·'tsio:·ne] *f* **1.** (*allontanamento*) removal **2.** (*da carica, impiego*) dismissal **3.** PSYCH repression

rimpaginazione [rim·pa·dʒi·nat·'tsio:·ne] *f* TYP re-paging

rimpallo [rim·'pal·lo] SPORT rebound

rimpastare [rim·pas·'ta:·re] *vt* **1.** (*pasta*) to reknead **2.** (*governo*) to reshuffle

rimpasto [rim·'pas·to] *m* (*di governo*) reshuffle

rimpatriare [rim·pa·'tria:·re] **I.** *vi essere* to return home **II.** *vt avere* to repatriate

rimpatriata [rim·pa·'tria:·ta] *f fam* get-together

rimpatrio [rim·'pa:·trio] <-ii> *m* repatriation

rimpetto [rim·'pɛt·to] *avv* **di** ~ **a** opposite

rimpiangere [rim·'pian·dʒe·re] <irr> *vt* ~ **qc** to regret sth; (*passato*) to miss

rimpianto [rim·'pian·to] *m* regret

rimpianto, -a *agg* (*persona*) much missed

rimpiattino [rim·piat·'ti:·no] *m* hide-and-seek

rimpiazzare [rim·piat·'tsa:·re] *vt* (*sostituire*) to replace

rimpicciolirsi [rim·pit·tʃo·'li:·r·si] <rimpicciolisco> *vr* to grow smaller

rimpinguare [rim·piŋ·'gua:·re] *vt* (*casse, erario, risorse*) to boost

rimpinzare [rim·pin·'tsa:·re] *fam* **I.** *vt* (*di cibo*) ~ **qu di qc** to stuff sb with sth **II.** *vr:* **-rsi** (*di cibo*) **-rsi di qc** to stuff oneself with sth

rimpolpare [rim·pol·'pa:·re] *vt* (*arricchire: articolo, finanze*) to fatten up

rimpossessarsi [rim·pos·ses·'sar·si] *vr* ~ **di qc** to get sth back

rimproverare [rim·pro·ve·'ra:·re] I. *vt* (*biasimare*) to tell off II. *vr:* **-rsi -rsi** (**di**) **qc** to reproach oneself for sth

rimprovero [rim·'prɔ:·ve·ro] *m* telling-off

rimuginare [ri·mu·dʒi·'na:·re] *vt* to ponder

rimunerare [ri·mu·ne·'ra:·re] *vt* 1. (*ricompensare*) to reward 2. (*dare profitto: azienda, mercato*) to pay a profit

rimunerativo, -a [ri·mu·ne·ra·'ti:·vo] *agg* profitable

rimunerazione [ri·mu·ne·rat·'tsio:·ne] *f* 1. (*ricompensa*) reward 2. (*paga*) pay

rimuovere [ri·'muɔ:·ve·re] <irr> *vt* 1. (*togliere*) to remove 2. ADM (*destituire*) to dismiss 3. PSYCH to repress

rinascere [ri·'naʃ·ʃe·re] <irr> *vi essere* 1. (*nascere di nuovo*) to be born again 2. BOT to spring up again 3. (*unghie, capelli*) to grow back 4. *fig* to become a new person

rinascimentale [ri·naʃ·ʃi·men·'ta:·le] *agg* Renaissance

rinascimento [ri·naʃ·ʃi·'men·to] *m* Renaissance

rinascita [ri·'naʃ·ʃi·ta] *f* (*di impresa, di museo, di città*) revival

rinato *pp di* **rinascere**

rincarare [riŋ·ka·'ra:·re] I. *vt avere* to put up (the price of); ~ **la dose** *fig* to stir things up even more II. *vi essere* (*prezzo, prodotto*) to go up

rincaro [riŋ·'ka:·ro] *m* (*di prezzi, tariffe*) increase; ~ **della vita** rise in the cost of living

rincasare [riŋ·ka·'sa:·re] *vi essere* to go [*o* come] home

rinchiudere [riŋ·'kiu:·de·re] <irr> I. *vt* (*prigioniero, gioielli*) to shut up II. *vr:* **-rsi** 1. (*chiudersi*) to shut oneself up 2. *fig* (*in se stesso*) to withdraw into one's shell

rincitrullire [rin·tʃi·trul·'li:·re] <rincitrullisco> *fam* I. *vt avere* (*rendere stupido*) to make stupid II. *vr:* **-rsi** (*diventare stupido*) to become stupid

rincoglionirsi [riŋ·koʎ·ʎo·'ni:r·si] <mi rincoglionisco> *vr vulg* to become totally thick

rincontrare [riŋ·kon·'tra:·re] *vt* ~ **qu** to bump into sb

rincorare [riŋ·ko·'ra:·re] *vt v.* **rincuorare**

rincorrere [riŋ·'kor·re·re] <irr> I. *vt a. fig* ~ **qc/qu** to chase after sth/sb II. *vr:* **-rsi** (*corrersi dietro*) to chase each other

rincorsa [riŋ·'kor·sa] *f* 1. (*breve corsa*) run-up; **prendere la** ~ to take a run-up 2. *fig* (*corsa al successo: di squadra, di impresa*) hunt for success

rincrescere [riŋ·'kreʃ·ʃe·re] <irr> *vi essere* (*impersonale*) **mi rincresce che ...** I regret that ...

rincrescimento [riŋ·kreʃ·ʃi·'men·to] *m* regret

rinculo [riŋ·'ku:·lo] *m* (*di armi da fuoco*) recoil

rincuorare [riŋ·kuo·'ra:·re] I. *vt* (*dare coraggio*) to give strength II. *vr:* **-rsi** (*riprendere coraggio*) to take heart

rinegoziare [ri·ne·got·'tsia:·re] *vt* (*accordo, finanziamento, debito*) to renegotiate

rinegoziazione [ri·ne·go·tsiat·'tsio:·ne] *f* renegotiation

rinfacciare [rin·fat·'tʃa:·re] *vt* ~ **qc a qu** to throw sth in sb's face

rinfocolare [rin·fo·ko·'la:·re] *vt fig* (*rancore, dibattito*) to rekindle

rinforzare [rin·for·'tsa:·re] I. *vt avere* 1. (*edificio, muro*) to reinforce 2. (*muscoli, potere*) to strengthen 3. MIL to reinforce II. *vr:* **-rsi** (*diventare più forte*) to become stronger

rinforzo [rin·'fɔr·tso] *m* 1. (*sostegno*) reinforcement 2. *fig* (*aiuto*) support 3. MIL reinforcement

rinfrancare [rin·fraŋ·'ka:·re] I. *vt* (*ridare coraggio*) to encourage II. *vr:* **-rsi** (*riacquistare fiducia*) to take heart

rinfrescante [rin·fres·'kan·te] *agg* (*doccia, bibita*) refreshing

rinfrescare [rin·fres·'ka:·re] I. *vt avere* 1. (*ambienti, gola*) to freshen; (*vino*) to cool 2. *fig* (*memoria*) to refresh II. *vi essere* (*diventare fresco: tempo, aria*) to grow cooler III. *vr:* **-rsi** 1. (*lavarsi*) to freshen oneself up 2. (*con bibita*) to have sth to drink

rinfrescata [rin·fres·'ka:·ta] *f* (*lavata*) freshen-up; **darsi una** ~ to freshen oneself up

rinfresco [rin·'fres·ko] <-schi> *m* reception

rinfusa [rin·'fu:·za] *f* **alla** ~ (*merci*) in bulk; **sistemato alla** ~ mixed up

ringalluzzire [riŋ·gal·lut·'tsi:·re] <ringalluzzisco> *fam* I. *vt* (*rendere baldanzoso*) to make cocky II. *vr:* **-rsi** (*diventare baldanzoso*) to become cocky

ringhiare [riŋ·'gia:·re] *vi* 1. (*cane*) to growl 2. *fig* (*persona*) to snarl

ringhiera [riŋ·'giɛː·ra] *f* railing

ringhio ['riŋ·gio] <-ghi> *m* (*di cane*) growl

ringhioso, -a [riŋ·'gio:·so] *agg* 1. (*cane*) growling 2. (*tono*) snarling

ringiovanimento [rin·dʒo·va·ni·'men·to] *m* (*di pelle, società*) rejuvenation

ringiovanire [rin·dʒo·va·'ni:·re] <ringiovanisco> *vi essere* to become [*o* seem] younger

ringraziamento [riŋ·grat·tsia·'men·to] *m* (*espressione di gratitudine*) thank you; **-i** thanks; **lettera** [*o* **biglietto**] **di** ~ thank you letter [*o* card]

ringraziare [riŋ·grat·'tsia:·re] *vt* ~ **qu** to thank sb

rinnegare [rin·ne·'ga:·re] *vt* 1. (*ideale, passato*) to renounce 2. (*figlio, genitore*) to disown

rinnegato, -a [rin·ne·'ga:·to] I. *agg* renegade II. *m, f* renegade

rinnovamento [rin·no·va·'men·to] *m* (*di società, partito, tecnologie*) renewal

rinnovare [rin·no·'va:·re] I. *vt* 1. (*rendere nuovo: sito, offerta, direttivo*) to change 2. (*contratto, abbonamento, alleanza*) to renew 3. (*domanda, istanza*) to repeat II. *vr:* **-rsi** (*diventare nuovo*) to change

R

rinnovo [rin·'nɔː·vo] *m* (*di contratto, tessera*) renewal

rinoceronte [ri·no·tʃe·'ron·te] *m* rhinoceros

rinomato, -a [ri·no·'maː·to] *agg* (*celebre*) famous

rinsaldare [rin·sal·'daː·re] I. *vt* (*legame, amicizia*) to strengthen II. *vr:* **-rsi** (*rapporto, impegno*) to get stronger

rinsavire [rin·sa·'viː·re] <rinsavisco> *vi essere* (*ravvedersi*) to come to one's senses

rinsecchire [rin·sek·'kiː·re] <rinsecchisco> *vi essere* 1. (*diventare magro*) to get thin 2. (*diventare secco*) to wither

rintanarsi [rin·ta·'nar·si] *vr a. fig* to hide oneself

rintoccare [rin·tok·'kaː·re] *vi essere o avere* (*orologio*) to strike; (*campana*) to ring

rintocco [rin·'tok·ko] <-cchi> *m* (*di orologio*) stroke; (*di campana*) toll

rintracciare [rin·trat·'tʃaː·re] *vt* (*trovare*) to find

rintronare [rin·tro·'naː·re] I. *vi essere o avere* (*risuonare*) to boom II. *vt avere fig* (*stordire*) to deafen

rinuncia [ri·'nun·tʃa] <-ie> *f* 1. (*il rinunciare: a gara*) ~ **a** withdrawal 2. JUR (*a eredità*) renunciation 3. (*privazione*) sacrifice

rinunciare [ri·nun·'tʃaː·re] *vi* 1. (*rifiutare*) ~ **a qc** (*carriera, progetto, eredità*) to give up sth; **ci rinuncio volentieri** *iron, fam* it's no skin off my nose 2. (*astenersi*) ~ **a fare qc** to decide not to do sth

rinunciatario, -a [ri·nun·tʃia·'taː·rio] <-i, -ie> I. *agg* (*atteggiamento*) defeatist II. *m, f* defeatist

rinvenimento [rin·ve·ni·'men·to] *m* 1. (*ritrovamento*) discovery 2. (*ripresa dei sensi*) coming around

rinvenire [rin·ve·'niː·re] <irr> I. *vt avere* (*scoprire: reperti, affreschi*) to discover II. *vi essere* (*ricuperare i sensi*) to come around

rinviare [rin·vi·'aː·re] *vt* 1. (*mandare indietro: lettera, merce*) to send back 2. SPORT to clear 3. (*rimandare a: opera, capitolo, nota*) ~ **a** to refer to 4. (*differire: riunione, partita*) to postpone

rinvigorire [rin·vi·go·'riː·re] <rinvigorisco> I. *vt avere a. fig* to reinvigorate II. *vr:* **-rsi** *a. fig* to be reinvigorated

rinvio [rin·'viː·o] *m* 1. (*restituzione*) return 2. SPORT clearance 3. (*differimento: di seduta, udienza*) postponement 4. (*rimando: a pagina, nota*) reference

riò [ri·'ɔ] *1. pers sing pr di* **riavere**

rionale [rio·'naː·le] *agg* neighborhood

rione [ri·'oː·ne] *m* (*quartiere*) neighborhood

riordinamento [ri·or·di·na·'men·to] *m* (*riorganizzazione*) reorganization

riordinare [ri·or·di·'naː·re] *vt* 1. (*casa, stanza*) to tidy 2. (*dare un nuovo ordinamento a*) to reorganize

riordino [ri·'or·di·no] *m* ADM reorganization

riorganizzare [ri·or·ga·nid·'dzaː·re] I. *vt* 1. (*organizzare di nuovo*) to reorganize 2. (*riordinare*) to tidy up II. *vr:* **-rsi** (*organizzarsi di nuovo*) to reorganize oneself

riorganizzazione [ri·or·ga·nid·dzat·'tsio·ne] *f* (*di servizio, impresa*) reorganization

riottoso, -a [ri·ot·'toː·so] *agg* (*indocile: carattere*) unruly

ripagare [ri·pa·'gaː·re] *vt* 1. (*pagare di nuovo*) ~ **qc** to pay for sth again; ~ **con la stessa moneta** *fig* to give as good as one gets 2. ~ **qu di qc** (*ricompensare*) to repay sb for sth 3. (*risarcire*) ~ **qc** to pay for sth

riparare [ri·pa·'raː·re] I. *vt* 1. (*accomodare: abiti, radio, muro*) to fix 2. (*proteggere: da sole, vento*) to protect 3. (*rimediare a: torto, ingiustizia*) to put right II. *vi fam* (*provvedere*) ~ **a qc** to put sth right III. *vr* 1. (*cercare riparo*) to shelter 2. *fig* (*proteggersi*) to protect oneself

riparato, -a [ri·pa·'raː·to] *agg* 1. (*luogo*) sheltered 2. (*tetto, vestito*) repaired

riparatore, -trice [ri·pa·ra·'toː·re] I. *agg* reparatory II. *m, f* repairer

riparazione [ri·pa·rat·'tsio·ne] *f* 1. (*di mobile, di auto*) repairing 2. (*di danno*) repair 3. *fig* (*di torto*) reparation

riparo [ri·'paː·ro] *m* 1. (*protezione*) shelter; **mettersi al** ~ to take shelter 2. (*rimedio*) **porre** [*o* **mettere**] ~ **a qc** to do sth about sth

ripartire [ri·par·'tiː·re] <ripartisco> I. *vt* 1. (*dividere*) to divide up 2. (*distribuire: compiti, mansioni*) to share out II. *vi essere* (*partire di nuovo*) to set off again; (*macchina*) to start again

ripartizione [ri·par·tit·'tsio·ne] *f* 1. (*divisione*) division 2. (*distribuzione: di compiti, mansioni*) sharing out

ripassare [ri·pas·'saː·re] I. *vi essere* (*ritornare*) to call in again II. *vt avere* 1. (*passare sopra*) to go over again 2. (*ripetere: lezione*) to revise

ripassata [ri·pas·'saː·ta] *f* 1. (*a lezione*) brush-up 2. *fam* (*sgridata*) telling-off

ripasso [ri·'pas·so] *m* revision

ripensamento [ri·pen·sa·'men·to] *m* (*cambiamento di idea*) rethink

ripensare [ri·pen·'saː·re] *vi* 1. (*riflettere*) ~ **a qc** to think about sth 2. (*cambiare parere*) to change one's mind 3. (*riandare con la memoria*) ~ **a qu/qc** to think back to sb/sth

ripercorrere [ri·per·'kor·re·re] <irr> *vt* 1. (*itinerario, tragitto*) to follow again 2. (*rianalizzare*) to review 3. *fig* (*esperienze vissute*) ~ **qc** to return to sth

ripercuotersi [ri·per·'kwɔː·ter·si] <irr> *vr:* **-rsi** *a. fig* to have an incidental effect

ripercussione [ri·per·kus·'sio·ne] *f fig* (*effetto*) incidental effect

ripescare [ri·pes·'kaː·re] *vt* 1. (*dall'acqua*) to fish out 2. *fig, fam* (*ritrovare*) to unearth

ripetente [ri·pe·'tɛn·te] I. *agg* repeat II. *mf* repeat student

ripetere [ri·'pɛː·te·re] I. *vt* 1. (*rifare: esperimento, esame*) to repeat 2. (*ripassare:*

lezione) to go over again **3.**(*ridire*) to repeat **II.** *vr:* **-rsi 1.**(*dire o fare le stesse cose*) to repeat oneself **2.**(*accadere di nuovo*) to happen again

ripetitivo, -a [ri·pe·ti·'ti:·vo] *agg* repetitive

ripetitore [ri·pe·ti·'to:·re] *m* RADIO, TV repeater

ripetizione [ri·pe·tit·'tsio:·ne] *f* **1.**(*di prova, registrazione*) repetition **2.**(*lezione privata*) private lesson

ripetuto, -a [ri·pe·'tu:·to] *agg* repeated

ripiano [ri·'pia:·no] *m* **1.**(*di mobile, scaffale*) shelf **2.**(*terreno pianeggiante*) terrace

ripicca [ri·'pik·ka] <-cche> *f* (*dispetto*) act of spite; **per ~** out of spite

ripido, -a ['ri:·pi·do] *agg* (*sentiero, versante, declivio*) steep

ripiegare [ri·pie·'ga:·re] **I.** *vt* **1.**(*foglio, tessuto*) to fold **2.**(*piegare di nuovo*) to fold again **II.** *vi* **1.** *fig* (*rinunciare*) **~ su qc** to make do with sth **2.** MIL to retreat **III.** *vr:* **-rsi** (*incurvarsi*) to bend

ripiego [ri·'piɛ:·go] <-ghi> *m* (*via d'uscita*) stopgap; **soluzione di ~** makeshift solution

ripieno [ri·'piɛ:·no] *m* CULIN (*di verdura*) filling; (*di carne*) stuffing

ripieno, -a *agg* CULIN stuffed

ripigliare [ri·piʎ·'ʎa:·re] *fam* **I.** *vt* (*ricuperare*) **~ fiato** to catch one's breath; **~ forza** to regain one's strength **II.** *vr:* **-rsi** to recover

ripopolamento [ri·po·po·la·'men·to] *m* (*di paese*) repopulation; (*con animali*) restocking

ripopolare [ri·po·po·'la:·re] **I.** *vt* (*con abitanti*) to repopulate; (*con animali*) to restock **II.** *vr:* **-rsi** (*tornare a popolarsi*) to be repopulated

riporre [ri·'por·re] <irr> *vt* **1.**(*mettere via: oggetti, abiti*) to put away **2.** *fig* (*affidare*) **~ fiducia/speranze in qu** to place one's trust/hopes in sb

riportare [ri·por·'ta:·re] **I.** *vt* **1.**(*portare di nuovo o indietro*) to take back **2.**(*riferire: notizie, dichiarazioni*) to report **3.**(*ricavare: impressione*) to get **4.** MATH to carry over **5.**(*ottenere: vittoria, utile*) to achieve **6.**(*subire: danni*) to suffer **7.** DIR (*condanna*) to receive **II.** *vr:* **-rsi** (*richiamarsi*) **-rsi a qc** to refer to sth

riporto [ri·'pɔr·to] *m* **1.** MATH amount carried over **2.**(*di capelli*) combover

riposante [ri·po·'san·te] *agg* (*effetto*) soothing; (*lettura, vacanza*) relaxing

riposare [ri·po·'sa:·re] **I.** *vi* **1.**(*dormire*) to sleep **2.**(*fermarsi*) to stop; **~ in pace** (*defunto*) to rest in peace **II.** *vt* **1.**(*mente, membra, vista*) to rest **2.**(*posare di nuovo*) to put back again **III.** *vr:* **-rsi 1.**(*dormire*) to sleep **2.**(*prendere ristoro*) to rest

riposato, -a [ri·po·'sa:·to] *agg* (*ritemprato: viso, aspetto*) rested

riposi *1. pers sing pass rem di* **riporre**

riposino [ri·po·'si:·no] *m fam* nap

riposizionare [ri·po·sit·tsio·'na:·re] *vt* to reposition

riposo [ri·'pɔ:·so] *m* **1.**(*sospensione dell'at-*

tività) rest; **casa di ~** old folk's home; **giornata di ~** day off **2.**(*sonno*) sleep; **buon ~!** sleep well! **3.** ADM (*pensione*) **a ~** retired

ripostiglio [ri·pos·'tiʎ·ʎo] <-gli> *m* closet

riposto, -a [ri·'pos·to] **I.** *pp di* **riporre II.** *agg* secret

riprendere [ri·'prɛn·de·re] <irr> **I.** *vt* **1.**(*prendere di nuovo*) to pick up again; **~ posto** to go back to one's seat; **~ quota/velocità** to regain height/speed; **~ le forze** *fig* to regain one's strength; **~ i sensi** to come around **2.**(*prendere indietro*) to get back **3.**(*ricominciare*) to start again **4.**(*rimproverare*) to tell off **5.** FILM to shoot **II.** *vi* (*ricominciare*) to start again **III.** *vr:* **-rsi** (*ricuperare vigore*) to recover

ripresa [ri·'pre:·sa] *f* **1.**(*inizio*) resumption **2.** COM (*economico, di paese*) recovery **3.**(*da malattia*) recovery **4.** FILM, TV filming **5.** MOT acceleration **6.** SPORT second half

ripresentare [ri·pre·zen·'ta:·re] **I.** *vt* (*presentare di nuovo: progetto, proposta*) to resubmit **II.** *vr:* **-rsi 1.**(*manifestarsi di nuovo: problema, dolore*) to return **2.**(*presentarsi di nuovo: persona*) to turn up again

ripresi *1. pers sing pass rem di* **riprendere**

ripreso *pp di* **riprendere**

ripristinare [ri·pris·ti·'na:·re] *vt poet* **1.**(*consuetudine*) to reinstate; (*ordine*) to restore **2.**(*edificio, facciata*) to restore

ripristino [ri·'pris·ti·no] *m* **1.**(*ricupero: di dati*) recovery **2.**(*di edificio*) restoration

riprodotto *pp di* **riprodurre**

riproducibile [ri·pro·du·'tʃi:·bi·le] *agg* (*immagine, modello, materiale*) reproducible

riproducibilità [ri·pro·du·tʃi·bi·li·'ta] <-> *f* (*di immagine, opera d'arte*) reproducibility

riprodurre [ri·pro·'dur·re] <irr> **I.** *vt* (*immagine, opera d'arte*) to reproduce; (*documento, libro*) to print **II.** *vr:* **-rsi 1.** BIOL to reproduce **2.**(*formarsi di nuovo: macchia*) to reappear **3.**(*ripetersi: situazione*) to recur

riproduttivo, -a [ri·pro·dut·'ti:·vo] *agg* BIOL, TEC reproductive

riproduttore [ri·pro·dut·'to:·re] **I.** *m* player **II.** *agg* BIOL reproductive

riproduzione [ri·pro·dut·'tsio:·ne] *f* reproduction

ripromettersi [ri·pro·'met·ter·si] <irr> *vr* **~ di fare qc** to promise oneself to do sth

riprova [ri·'prɔ:·va] *f* (*conferma*) confirmation

riprovare [ri·pro·'va:·re] **I.** *vt* **1.**(*vestito, cappello*) to try on again **2.** *fig* (*sentimento*) to feel again **II.** *vi* (*ritentare*) to try again

riprovazione [ri·pro·vat·'tsio:·ne] *f* (*biasimo*) disapproval

ripudiare [ri·pu·'dia:·re] *vt* **1.**(*persone, passato*) to disown **2.**(*fede, ideologia*) to reject

ripudio [ri·'pu:·dio] <-i> *m* (*rifiuto*) repudiation

ripugnante [ri·puɲ·'nan·te] *agg* repugnant

ripugnanza [ri·puɲ·'nan·tsa] *f* repugnance

ripugnare [ri·puɲ·'ɲa:·re] *vi* **~ a qu** to disgust sb

ripulire [ri·pu·'li:·re] <ripulisco> *vt* **1.**(*pulire di nuovo*) to clean again **2.** *fig, fam* (*svaligiare: appartamento*) to clean out

ripulsione [ri·pul·'sio:·ne] *f* (*rifiuto*) repugnance

riquadro [ri·'kua:·dro] *m* **1.**(*casella*) box **2.** ARCH, COMPUT panel

riqualificare [ri·kua·li·fi·'ka:·re] I. *vt* **1.**(*dipendenti*) to retrain **2.**(*valorizzare: area, paesaggio, edificio*) to upgrade II. *vr:* **-rsi** (*nel lavoro*) to retrain

riqualificazione [ri·kua·li·fi·kat·'tsio:·ne] *f* (*di lavoratore*) retraining

RIS *m acro di* **reparto investigazioni scientifiche** Crime Scene Investigation Team

risacca [ri·'sak·ka] <-cche> *f* backwash

risaia [ri·'sa:·ia] <-aie> *f* rice paddy

risalire [ri·sa·'li:·re] <irr> I. *vt avere* (*scale*) to go up again; (*albero, scale*) to climb back up II. *vi essere* **1.**(*salire di nuovo*) to go up again; (*su albero, scale*) to climb back up **2.**(*prezzi*) to go up again **3.**...: *fig* (*a causa, origine*) ~ **a qc** to trace sth **4.** *fig* (*essere avvenuto*) ~ **a** to date back to

risalita [ri·sa·'li:·ta] *f* climb back up; **impianti di** ~ ski lifts

risaltare [ri·sal·'ta:·re] *vi essere o avere* **1.** *fig* (*spiccare, eccellere*) to stand out **2.** *fig* (*risultare evidente da*) ~ **da** to be obvious from

risalto [ri·'sal·to] *m* (*spicco*) prominence; **mettere** [*o* **porre**] **in** ~ **qc** to highlight sth

risanabile [ri·sa·'na:·bi·le] *agg* (*azienda*) savable; *fig* (*strappo, ferita*) healable

risanamento [ri·sa·na·'men·to] *m* **1.**(*di terreno*) redevelopment **2.**(*di azienda, bilancio*) reorganization

risanare [ri·sa·'na:·re] *vt avere* **1.**(*azienda, economia, bilancio*) to reorganize **2.**(*zona paludosa*) to reclaim; (*terreno, quartiere*) to redevelop

risaputo, -a [ri·sa·'pu:·to] *agg* (*noto*) well-known

risarcimento [ri·sar·tʃi·'men·to] *m* compensation

risarcire [ri·sar·'tʃi:·re] <risarcisco> *vt* **1.**(*danno*) to pay for **2.**(*persone*) ~ **qu** to pay compensation to sb

risata [ri·'sa:·ta] *f* laugh

riscaldamento [ris·kal·da·'men·to] *m* **1.**(*impianto*) heating; ~ **a gas** gas heating; ~ **centrale** central heating **2.**(*azione*) warming; ~ **del pianeta** global warming **3.**(*di motore*) warm-up **4.** SPORT warm-up

riscaldare [ris·kal·'da:·re] I. *vt* **1.**(*minestra*) to warm up again **2.**(*stanza, casa*) to heat **3.**(*loc*) ~ **gli animi** to get people worked up II. *vr:* **-rsi** (*diventare caldo*) to get warm

riscattare [ris·kat·'ta:·re] I. *vt* **1.**(*gener*) to redeem; (~ *una polizza*) to surrender a policy **2.**(*prigioniero*) to ransom II. *vr:* **-rsi** *fig* (*redimersi*) to redeem oneself

riscatto [ris·'kat·to] *m* **1.**(*gener*) redemption **2.**(*per persona, prigioniero*) ransom

rischiarare [ris·kia·'ra:·re] I. *vt avere a. fig* to light up II. *vr:* **-rsi 1.**(*cielo*) to become clearer **2.** *fig* (*persona*) to brighten up

rischiare [ris·'kia:·re] I. *vt* to risk II. *vi* ~ **di fare qc** to risk doing sth

rischio ['ris·kio] <-schi> *m* risk; **correre un** ~ to run a risk; **mettere qc a** ~ to put sth at risk

rischioso, -a [ris·'kio:·so] *agg* risky

risciacquare [riʃ·ʃak·'kua:·re] *vt* (*stoviglie, bucato*) to rinse

risciacquo [riʃ·'ʃak·kuo] *m* (*di capelli, abiti, stoviglie*) rinsing

risciò [riʃ·'ʃɔ] <-> *m* rickshaw

riscontrabile [ris·kon·'tra:·bi·le] *agg* verifiable

riscontrare [ris·kon·'tra:·re] I. *vt* **1.**(*rilevare: diffetto, irregolarità*) to identify **2.**(*confrontare*) to compare **3.**(*avere: successo*) to enjoy II. *vi essere* (*corrispondere*) to match

riscontro [ris·'kon·tro] *m* **1.**(*confronto*) comparison **2.**(*risposta*) reply **3.** *fig* (*risposta*) feedback

riscoperta [ris·ko·'pɛr·ta] *f* rediscovery

riscossa [ris·'kɔs·sa] *f* counterattack; **alla** ~ on the counterattack

riscossione [ris·kos·'sio:·ne] *f* (*di contributo, vincita, affitto*) collection

riscuotere [ris·'kuɔ:·te·re] <irr> *vt* **1.**(*stipendio*) to draw; (*pagamento, assegno*) to cash **2.**(*successo*) to enjoy

risentimento [ri·sen·ti·'men·to] *m* (*sdegno*) resentment

risentire [ri·sen·'ti:·re] I. *vt* **1.**(*sentire di nuovo: rumore*) to hear again **2.**(*ascoltare di nuovo: disco*) to listen again to II. *vi* ~ **di qc** to be affected by sth III. *vr:* **-rsi 1.**(*sentirsi di nuovo*) to talk to each other again **2.**(*offendersi*) to be offended

risentito, -a [ri·sen·'ti:·to] *agg* (*offeso*) resentful

riserbo [ri·'sɛr·bo] *m* discretion

riserva [ri·'sɛr·va] *f* **1.**(*provvista: di cibo, munizioni*) stock **2.** SPORT, MIL reserve **3.**(*di caccia, pesca*) reserve **4.**(*dubbio*) reservation **5.** MOT **in** ~ low on gasoline

riservare [ri·ser·'va:·re] I. *vt* **1.**(*tavolo, posto*) to reserve **2.**(*tenere in serbo*) to save **3.**(*facoltà, diritto*) to reserve II. *vr* **-rsi di fare qc** to reserve the right to do sth

riservatezza [ri·ser·va·'tet·tsa] *f* discretion

riservato, -a [ri·ser·'va:·to] *agg* **1.**(*notizia, informazione*) confidential **2.**(*prenotato: posto, tavolo*) reserved **3.**(*timido: persona, carattere*) reserved

risi ['ri:·si] *1. pers sing pass rem di* **ridere**

risicare [ri·zi·'ka:·re] *vt fam v.* **rischiare chi non risica non rosica** *prov* faint hearts never won the day

risiedere [ri·siɛ:·de·re] *vi* **1.**(*abitare*) to be based **2.** *fig* (*consistere*) ~ **in qc** to lie in sth

risma ['riz·ma] *f* **1.**(*di carta*) ream **2.** *fig, pej* (*genere*) type

riso[1] ['ri:·so] *pp di* **ridere**

riso[2] <*pl:* **-a** *f*> *m* (*risata*) laughing

riso[3] *m* **1.** BOT rice **2.** CULIN rice

risolsi [ri·'sɔl·si] *1. pers sing pass rem di* **risolvere**

risolto [ri·'sɔl·to] *pp di* **risolvere**

risolutezza [ri·so·lu·'tet·tsa] *f* determination

risolutivo, -a [ri·so·lu·'ti:·vo] *agg* (*decisivo: intervento*) decisive

risoluto, -a [ri·so·'lu:·to] I. *pp di* **risolvere** II. *agg* (*deciso: tipo, carattere, piglio*) decisive

risoluzione [ri·so·lut·'tsio:·ne] *f* **1.** (*decisione*) decision **2.** (*di dubbio, quesito*) solution **3.** (*composizione: di conflitto, questione*) settlement **4.** JUR (*di contratto*) cancellation **5.** MATH (*soluzione*) solution

risolvere [ri·'sɔl·ve·re] <risolvo, risolsi, risolto *o* risoluto> I. *vt* **1.** (*equazione, problema, indovinello*) to solve; (*questione, controversia*) to resolve **2.** (*dubbio*) to settle **3.** JUR (*contratto*) to cancel II. *vr:* **-rsi 1.** (*decidersi*) **-rsi a fare qc** to decide to do sth **2.** *fig* (*andare a finire*) **-rsi in qc** to turn into sth **3.** (*problema, questione*) to resolve oneself

risonanza [ri·so·'nan·tsa] *f* **1.** *fig* (*di evento, avvenimento*) interest **2.** PHYS resonance

risonare [ri·so·'na:·re] *v.* **risuonare**

risorgere [ri·'sor·dʒe·re] <irr> *vi essere* **1.** (*gener*) to rise again **2.** *fig* (*rifiorire*) to become a different person

risorgimento [ri·sor·dʒi·'men·to] *m* Risorgimento

risorsa [ri·'sor·sa] *f* resource

risorsi *1. pers sing pass rem di* **risorgere**

risorto *pp di* **risorgere**

risotto [ri·'sɔt·to] *m* risotto; **~ ai funghi** mushroom risotto; **~ alla marinara** seafood risotto

risparmiare [ris·par·'mia:·re] I. *vt* **1.** (*gener*) to save **2.** (*salvare: persona, vita*) to spare **3.** (*loc*) **-rsi di fare qc** to not bother to do sth II. *vr:* **-rsi** (*avere riguardo di sé*) to look after oneself

risparmiatore, -trice [ris·par·mia·'to:·re] *m, f* saver

risparmio [ris·'par·mio] <-i> *m* saving

rispecchiare [ris·pek·'kia:·re] I. *vt a. fig* to reflect II. *vr:* **-rsi** *a. fig* to be reflected

rispedire [ris·pe·'di:·re] <rispedisco> *vt* **1.** (*spedire di nuovo*) to send again **2.** (*spedire indietro*) to send back

rispettabile [ris·pet·'ta:·bi·le] *agg* **1.** (*persone*) respectable **2.** (*notevole: somma*) considerable

rispettare [ris·pet·'ta:·re] *vt* **1.** (*persone, opinioni, diritti*) to respect **2.** (*ordini*) to obey **3.** (*feste*) to observe **4.** (*mantenere: parola*) to keep

rispettivamente [ris·pet·ti·va·'men·te] *avv* respectively

rispettivo, -a [ris·pet·'ti:·vo] *agg* respective

rispetto [ris·'pɛt·to] *m* **1.** (*stima*) respect **2.** (*di legge, regolamento*) observance **3.** **~ a qu/qc** (*riguardo*) with reference to sb/sth; (*in confronto*) compared to sb/sth

risplendere [ris·'plɛn·de·re] *vi essere o avere* (*sole, occhi*) to shine

rispolverare [ris·pol·ve·'ra:·re] *vt* **1.** (*spolverare di nuovo*) to dust again **2.** *fig* (*rinfrescare: conoscenze, lingua*) to brush up

rispondere [ris·'pon·de·re] <rispondo, risposi, risposto> *vi* **1.** (*dare una risposta*) to answer; **~ ad una domanda/lettera** to reply to a question/letter; **~ al telefono** to answer the phone **2.** (*replicare*) to answer back **3.** (*essere responsabile*) **~ di qc** to answer for sth **4.** (*soddisfare: desideri, requisiti, aspettative*) **~ a qc** to meet sth

risposta [ris·'pos·ta] *f* **1.** answer; **in ~ a** in answer to **2.** (*reazione*) **la ~ a qc** the reply to sth **3.** TEC response

rispostina [ris·pos·'ti:·na] *f* **1.** *dim di* **risposta** **2.** (*risposta pungente*) sarcastic reply

risposto [ris·'pos·to] *pp di* **rispondere**

rissa ['ris·sa] *f* brawl

rissoso, -a [ris·'so:·so] *agg* (*atteggiamento, carattere*) quarrelsome

ristabilire [ris·ta·bi·'li:·re] <ristabilisco> I. *vt* (*potere, ordine, autorità*) to re-establish II. *vr:* **-rsi** (*rimettersi*) to get better

ristagnare [ris·taɲ·'ɲa:·re] *vi a. fig* to stagnate

ristagno [ris·'taɲ·ɲo] *m a. fig* stagnation

ristampa [ris·'tam·pa] *f* **1.** (*azione*) reprinting **2.** (*opera*) reprint

ristampare [ris·tam·'pa:·re] *vt* (*libro*) to reprint

ristato *pp di* **riessere**

ristorante[1] [ris·to·'ran·te] *m* restaurant

ristorante[2] <inv> *agg* FERR **vagone ~** restaurant car

ristorare [ris·to·'ra:·re] I. *vt* (*rifocillare*) to give sth to eat [*o* drink] II. *vr:* **-rsi** (*rifocillarsi*) to have sth to eat [*o* drink]

ristoratore, -trice [ris·to·ra·'to:·re] *agg* (*gestore di ristorante*) restaurateur

ristoro [ris·'tɔ:·ro] *m* (*sollievo*) relief

ristrettezza [ris·tret·'tet·tsa] *f* **1.** (*di spazio*) narrowness **2.** (*di mezzi*) scarcity **3.** *fig* (*di mente, idee, vedute*) narrowmindedness

ristretto, -a [ris·'tret·to] I. *pp di* **restringere** II. *agg* **1.** (*limitato: numero, quantità*) small **2.** CULIN **brodo ~** consommé; **caffè ~** strong coffee **3.** *fig* (*meschino: mente*) narrow

ristrutturabile [ris·trut·tu·'ra:·bi·le] *agg* (*edificio*) renovatable

ristrutturare [ris·trut·tu·'ra:·re] *vt* **1.** (*edificio*) to renovate **2.** (*azienda*) to reorganize

ristrutturato, -a [ris·trut·tu·'ra:·to] *agg* (*edificio*) renovated

ristrutturazione [ris·trut·tu·rat·'tsio:·ne] *f* **1.** (*di edificio*) renovation **2.** (*di azienda*) reorganization

risucchiare [ri·suk·'kia:·re] *vt fig* (*assorbire*) to absorb

risucchio [ri·'suk·kio] <-cchi> *m* suction; (*di onda*) undertow

risultare [ri·sul·'ta:·re] *vi essere* **1.** (*derivare*) to be shown **2.** (*essere accertato*) to be clear **3.** (*rivelarsi*) to prove to be

risultato [ri·sul·'ta:·to] *m* result

R

risuonare [ri·suo·'na:·re] *vi essere o avere* **1.**(*gener*) to echo **2.**(*campane, campanello*) to ring again **3.**fig(*echeggiare*) to ring

risurrezione [ri·sur·ret·'tsio:·ne] *f* REL resurrection

risuscitare [ri·suʃ·ʃi·'ta:·re] **I.** *vt* **1.**(*morti*) to bring back to life **2.**fig(*tradizione, moda*) to revive **II.** *vi essere* **1.**REL to rise from the dead **2.**fig(*riprendersi*) to recover

risvegliare [riz·veʎ·'ʎa:·re] **I.** *vt* **1.**(*svegliare*) to wake up **2.**fig(*memoria, emozioni, gelosia*) to reawaken **II.** *vr:* **-rsi 1.**(*svegliarsi*) to wake up **2.**fig(*rinascere: speranza*) to revive

risveglio [ris·'veʎ·ʎo] <-gli> *m* **1.**(*dal sonno*) awakening **2.**fig(*rinascita: di speranze, paure, ostilità*) revival

risvolto [riz·'vɔl·to] *m* **1.**(*di pantaloni*) turn-up; (*di giacca*) lapel **2.**fig(*ripercussione*) implication

ritagliare [ri·taʎ·'ʎa:·re] *vt* (*articolo, fotografia*) to cut out

ritaglio [ri·'taʎ·ʎo] <-gli> *m* **1.**(*di giornale*) clipping **2.**(*di stoffa*) remnant **3.**(*loc*) **-i di tempo** spare time

ritardare [ri·tar·'da:·re] **I.** *vi* (*persona*) to be late; (*treno*) to be running late; (*orologio*) to be slow **II.** *vt* **1.**(*far tardare*) to delay **2.**(*differire*) to defer

ritardatario, -a [ri·tar·da·'ta:·rio] <-i, -ie> *m, f* latecomer

ritardato, -a [ri·tar·'da:·to] **I.** *agg* **1.**(*moto, scoppio, pagamento*) delayed; **reazione a scoppio ~** fig delayed reaction **2.**(*persona*) mentally challenged; (*scolaro*) with learning difficulties **II.** *m, f* (*mentale*) mentally challenged person

ritardo [ri·'tar·do] *m* **1.**(*non puntualità*) delay; **essere in ~** to be late **2.**(*indugio*) delay **3.** MED, PSYCH (*mentale*) retardation

ritegno [ri·'teɲ·ɲo] *m* restraint; **senza ~** without restraint

ritemprare [ri·tem·'pra:·re] **I.** *vt* fig (*forze, spirito*) to restore **II.** *vr:* **-rsi** (*persona*) to recover

ritenere [ri·te·'ne:·re] <irr> **I.** *vt* **1.**(*considerare*) to consider **2.**(*trattenere: somma, importo*) to deduct **II.** *vr:* **-rsi** (*considerarsi*) to consider oneself

ritenuta [ri·te·'nu:·ta] *f* (*detrazione*) deduction; **~ d'acconto** tax withholding at the source

ritirare [ri·ti·'ra:·re] **I.** *vt* **1.**(*tirare di nuovo*) to throw again **2.**(*tirare indietro*) to pull back **3.**(*truppe, squadra, moneta*) to withdraw **4.**(*farsi consegnare*) to pick up **5.**(*riscuotere: stipendio*) to get **6.**fig (*promessa*) to take back **7.**(*revocare: legge*) to abrogate **II.** *vr:* **-rsi 1.**(*appartarsi*) to withdraw **2.**(*abbandonare: gara*) **-rsi da qc** to withdraw from sth **3.**(*restringersi: maglione*) to shrink

ritirata [ri·ti·'ra:·ta] *f* MIL retreat; **~ strategica** *a.* fig strategic retreat

ritirato, -a [ri·ti·'ra:·to] *agg*(*appartato: vita*) se-cluded

ritiro [ri·'ti:·ro] *m* **1.**(*di truppe, squadra, merce*) withdrawal **2.**(*di pacco, merce*) collection **3.**(*di patente*) suspension

ritmico, -a ['rit·mi·ko] <-ci, -che> *agg* rhythmic

ritmo ['rit·mo] *m* rhythm

rito ['ri:·to] *m* **1.** REL rite; (*cerimonia*) ceremony **2.**(*usanza*) custom; **di ~** (*discorso, presentazioni*) customary

ritoccare [ri·tok·'ka:·re] *vt* **1.**(*toccare di nuovo*) to touch again **2.**(*correggere: disegno*) to retouch; (*trucco, labbra*) to touch up

ritocco [ri·'tok·ko] <-cchi> *m* (*rifinitura*) alteration; FOTO retouching

ritorcersi [ri·'tɔr·tʃer·si] <irr> *vr:* **-rsi** (*rivolgersi contro*) **~ contro** to backfire on

ritornare [ri·tor·'na:·re] *vi essere* **1.**(*venire di nuovo*) to go [o come] back; **~ a casa** to go [o come] home; **~ in sé** to return to normal **2.**(*ricomparire*) to return **3.**(*ridiventare*) to become again

ritornello [ri·tor·'nɛl·lo] *m* **1.**MUS refrain **2.**fig (*ripetizione*) story

ritorno [ri·'tor·no] *m* (*rientro*) return; **essere di ~** to be back; **biglietto di andata e ~** roundtrip ticket

ritorsi *1. pers sing pass rem di* **ritorcere**

ritorsione [ri·tor·'sio:·ne] *f* (*rivalsa*) retaliation

ritrarre [ri·'trar·re] <irr> *vt* **1.**(*tirare indietro*) to pull back **2.**(*dipingere*) to portray **3.**(*raccontare*) to depict

ritrattare [ri·trat·'ta:·re] *vt* **1.**(*trattare di nuovo: questione, argomento*) to deal with again **2.**(*ritirare: accusa*) to withdraw; **il testimone ha ritrattato** the witness retracted his statement

ritrattista [ri·trat·'tis·ta] <-i *m*, -e *f*> *mf* portrait painter

ritratto¹ [ri·'trat·to] *pp di* **ritrarre**

ritratto² *m* **1.**(*immagine*) portrait; **farsi fare il ~** to have one's portrait done **2.**fig (*descrizione*) picture **3.**(*somiglianza*) double; **essere il ~ della salute** to be the picture of health

ritrosia [ri·tro·'si:·a] <-ie> *f* (*timidezza*) shyness

ritroso, -a [ri·'tro:·so] *agg* **1.**(*riservato: carattere*) shy **2.**(*restio*) reluctant

ritrovare [ri·tro·'va:·re] **I.** *vt* **1.**(*persone, cose smarrite*) to find **2.**fig (*salute, pace*) to regain **3.**fig (*cammino, filo del discorso*) to find again **II.** *vr:* **-rsi 1.**(*incontrarsi di nuovo*) to meet up again **2.**(*senza accorgersi*) to end up **3.**fig (*in situazione*) to find oneself **4.**(*raccapezzarsi*) **-rsi con qc** to understand sth **5.** *fam* (*avere: sfortuna*) to have

ritrovo [ri·'trɔ:·vo] *m* **1.**(*luogo*) meeting place **2.**(*riunione*) gathering

rituale [ri·tu·'a:·le] **I.** *agg* **1.**(*di un rito*) ritual **2.**fig (*abituale: brindisi, discorso*) customary **II.** *m* ritual

riunificazione [ri·u·ni·fi·kat·'tsio:·ne] *f* reunification

riunione [ri·u·'nio:·ne] *f* (*raduno*) gathering

riunire [ri·u·'ni:·re] <riunisco> I. *vt* 1. (*elementi*) to unite 2. (*mettere insieme: pezzi, fogli*) to gather 3. (*riconciliare: coniugi*) to reconcile 4. (*convocare: squadra*) to gather together II. *vr:* **-rsi** 1. (*fare una riunione*) to meet 2. (*tornare insieme: squadra*) to reunite

riuscire [ri·uʃ·'ʃi:·re] <irr> *vi essere* 1. (*raggiungere*) ~ **a fare qc** to manage to do sth 2. (*avere esito: foto, film*) to come out 3. (*risultare*) to be; ~ **difficile a qu** to be difficult for sb 4. (*avere successo*) to succeed

riuscita [ri·uʃ·'ʃi:·ta] *f* (*di esperimento, progetto, persona*) success

riutilizzare [ri·u·ti·lid·'dza:·re] *vt* (*utilizzare di nuovo*) to reuse

riva ['ri:·va] *f* (*di mare*) shore; (*di fiume*) bank

rivale [ri·'va:·le] I. *agg* (*banda*) rival; (*squadra*) opposing II. *mf* rival

rivaleggiare [ri·va·led·'dʒa:·re] *vi* (*essere rivale*) to compete

rivalità [ri·va·li·'ta] <-> *f* rivalry

rivalsa [ri·'val·sa] *f* (*rivincita*) revenge

rivalutare [ri·va·lu·'ta:·re] *vt* 1. FIN to revalue; ~ **gli stipendi** to raise salaries 2. (*riconoscere il valore di*) to re-evaluate

rivalutazione [ri·va·lu·tat·'tsio:·ne] *f* (*monetaria, di terreni, beni*) revaluation; (*di opera d'arte*) re-evaluation

rivangare [ri·vaŋ·'ga:·re] *vt fig* (*passato, storia*) to dig up again

rivedere [ri·ve·'de:·re] <irr> I. *vt* 1. (*persona, luogo, film*) to see again 2. (*revisionare: testo*) to have another look at 3. (*rileggere*) to reread II. *vr:* **-rsi** (*vedersi di nuovo*) to see one another again

rivedibile [ri·ve·'di:·bi·le] *agg* MIL temporarily unfit for duty

rivelare [ri·ve·'la:·re] I. *vt* 1. (*notizia, segreto*) to disclose; (*intenzioni*) to reveal 2. (*manifestare*) to reveal II. *vr:* **-rsi** (*risultare*) to turn out to be

rivelazione [ri·ve·lat·'tsio:·ne] *f* 1. (*gener*) revelation 2. (*di notizie, segreti*) disclosure

rivendicare [ri·ven·di·'ka:·re] *vt* JUR 1. to claim 2. (*libertà, diritto*) to demand 3. (*assumersi la responsabilità di*) ~ **qc** to claim responsibility for sth

rivendicazione [ri·ven·di·kat·'tsio:·ne] *f* 1. (*di diritto*) claim 2. (*di attentato*) claiming of responsibility

rivendita [ri·'ven·di·ta] *f* 1. (*di auto, immobile*) resale 2. (*negozio*) shop

rivenditore, -trice [ri·ven·di·'to:·re] *m, f* (*venditore*) retailer

riverbero [ri·'vɛr·be·ro] *m* 1. (*riflesso: del sole*) reflection 2. MUS reverberation

riverente [ri·ve·'rɛn·te] *agg* (*atteggiamento, inchino*) reverent

riverenza [ri·ve·'rɛn·tsa] *f* (*rispetto*) reverence

riverire [ri·ve·'ri:·re] <riverisco> *vt* 1. (*rispettare*) to revere 2. (*salutare*) ~ **qu** to pay one's respects to sb

riversare [ri·ver·'sa:·re] *vt* 1. (*versare di nuovo*) to pour again 2. *fig* (*energia, capacità*) to pour

rivestimento [ri·ves·ti·'men·to] *m* (*operazione, materiale*) covering

rivestire [ri·ves·'ti:·re] I. *vt* 1. (*ricoprire: parete, divano*) to cover 2. *fig* (*carica*) to hold 3. *fig* (*avere*) ~ **una grande importanza** to be very important II. *vr:* **-rsi** (*vestirsi di nuovo*) to get dressed again

rividi *1. pers sing pass rem di* **rivedere**

riviera [ri·'viɛ:·ra] *f* coast; **la Riviera ligure** the Ligurian Riviera

rivincita [ri·'vin·tʃi·ta] *f* 1. (*seconda partita*) return match 2. *fig* (*rivalsa*) revenge; **prendersi la ~** to get one's revenge

rivissi *1. pers sing pass rem di* **rivivere**

rivissuto *pp di* **rivivere**

rivista [ri·'vis·ta] *f* (*periodico*) magazine

rivisto *pp di* **rivedere**

rivitalizzare [ri·vi·ta·lid·'dza:·re] *vt* (*tradizione, commercio, attività*) to revitalize

rivivere [ri·'vi:·ve·re] <irr> I. *vi essere* 1. (*rinascere: pianta*) to come back to life 2. *fig* (*riacquistare vigore: persona*) to be reborn 3. *fig* (*tornare in uso: tradizione*) to be revived 4. *fig* (*vivere in altra forma: persona, ricordo*) to live on; (*passato*) to come alive again II. *vt avere* to relive

rivolgere [ri·'vol·dʒe·re] <irr> I. *vt* to turn; ~ **l'attenzione a qu/qc** to turn one's attention to sb/sth; ~ **la parola a qu** to speak to sb II. *vr:* **-rsi -rsi a qu** (*per parlargli*) to turn to sb; (*per chiedere aiuto, informazioni*) to go and see sb

rivolgimento [ri·vol·dʒi·'men·to] *m* POL upheaval

rivolsi [ri·'vɔl·si] *1. pers sing pass rem di* **rivolgere**

rivolta [ri·'vɔl·ta] *f* (*insurrezione*) revolt

rivoltante [ri·vol·'tan·te] *agg* (*ripugnante*) revolting

rivoltare [ri·vol·'ta:·re] I. *vt* 1. (*sottosopra*) to turn over 2. (*ripetutamente*) to turn over again 3. (*provocare disgusto*) to disgust II. *vr:* **-rsi** 1. (*ribellarsi*) **-rsi contro qu/qc** to rebel against sb/sth 2. (*girarsi indietro*) to turn around 3. (*loc*) **mi si rivolta lo stomaco** it turns my stomach

rivoltella [ri·vol·'tɛl·la] *f* revolver

rivoltellata [ri·vol·tel·'la:·ta] *f* revolver shot

rivolto *pp di* **rivolgere**

rivoltoso, -a [ri·vol·'to:·so] I. *agg* rebellious II. *m, f* rebel

rivoluzionamento [ri·vo·lut·tsio·na·'men·to] *m* (*profondo cambiamento*) revolutionizing

rivoluzionare [ri·vo·lut·tsio·'na:·re] *vt* 1. (*società, mercato, moda*) to revolutionize 2. *fig* (*vita*) to change

rivoluzionario, -a [ri·vo·lut·tsio·'na:·rio] <-i, -ie> I. *agg* (*partito, idee, corrente*) revolutionary II. *m, f* revolutionary

R

rivoluzione [ri·vo·lut·'tsio:·ne] *f* **1.** POL, SOC revolution; **la Rivoluzione Francese** the French Revolution; ~ **industriale** Industrial Revolution **2.** *fig, fam* earthquake

rizzare [rit·'tsa:·re] **I.** *vt* **1.** (*bandiera*) to hoist; (*tenda*) to pitch **2.** (*loc*) ~ **le orecchie** to prick up one's ears; ~ **la cresta** to become arrogant **II.** *vr:* **-rsi** (*alzarsi in piedi*) to stand up

RNA *m abbr di* **ribonucleic acid** (*acido ribonucleico*) RNA

roba ['rɔ:·ba] *f* **1.** (*cose, abiti*) things *pl* **2.** (*materiale, stoffa*) material **3.** (*oggetti*) stuff; ~ **da mangiare** *fam* things to eat **4.** (*da vendere*) goods *pl*; ~ **usata** second hand goods **5.** *sl* (*droga*) dope

robotica [ro·'bɔ:·ti·ka] <-che> *f* robotics

robotizzare [ro·bo·tid·'dza:·re] *vt a. fig* (*meccanizzare*) to robotize

robustezza [ro·bus·'tet·tsa] *f* (*solidità*) sturdiness

robusto, -a [ro·'bus·to] *agg* **1.** (*persona, costituzione, braccia*) strong; (*grasso*) overweight **2.** (*valigia, scarpe*) sturdy

roccaforte [rok·ka·'fɔr·te] <roccheforti> *f* **1.** (*fortificazione*) fortress **2.** *fig* (*di partito, di turisti*) stronghold

roccia ['rɔt·tʃa] <-cce> *f a. fig* rock

roccioso, -a [rot·'tʃo:·so] *agg* (*terreno, panorama*) rocky; **giardino** ~ rock garden

rockettaro, -a [ro·ket·'ta:·ro] *m, f* **1.** (*compositore*) rocker **2.** (*appassionato*) rock fan

rococò [ro·ko·'kɔ] **I.** <-> *m* Rococo **II.** <inv> *agg* rococo

rodaggio [ro·'dad·dʒo] <-ggi> *m* **1.** TEC, MOT breaking in **2.** *fig* (*periodo per abituarsi a qc*) time to adjust

rodere ['ro:·de·re] <rodo, rosi, roso> *vt* **1.** (*rosicchiare*) to gnaw **2.** (*corrodere: roccia*) to erode **3.** *fig* (*gelosia, sconfitta*) ~ **qu** to get to sb

rodigino, -a [ro·di·'dʒi:·no] **I.** *agg* from Rovigo **II.** *m, f* (*abitante*) person from Rovigo

roditore [ro·di·'to:·re] *m* rodent

rododendro [ro·do·'dɛn·dro] *m* rhododendron

rogito ['rɔ:·dʒi·to] *m* deed

rogna ['roɲ·ɲa] *f* **1.** MED mange **2.** *fig, fam* (*problema*) hassle

rognoso, -a [roɲ·'ɲo:·so] *agg* **1.** MED mangy **2.** *fig* (*questione, problema*) annoying

rogo ['rɔ:·go/'ro:·go] <-ghi> *m* (*incendio*) fire

roller ['rou·lə] <- *o* rollers> *m* (*pattini*) Rollerblade *pl*

ROM [rɔm] *m acro di* **Read Only Memory** (*memoria a sola lettura*) ROM

Roma ['ro:·ma] *f* Rome, *capital city of Italy*

Romagna [ro·'maɲ·ɲa] *f* Romagna, *area in Northern Italy*

romagnolo [ro·maɲ·'ɲo:·lo] <sing> *m* (*dialetto*) Romagna dialect

romagnolo, -a **I.** *m, f* (*abitante*) person from Romagna **II.** *agg* from Romagna

romanesco, -a [ro·ma·'nes·ko] <-schi, -sche> *agg* Roman

Romania [ro·ma·'ni:·a] *f* Romania; **abitare in** ~ to live in Romania; **andare in** ~ to go to Romania

romanico [ro·'ma:·ni·ko] *m* ARCH Romanesque

romanico, -a <-ci, -che> *agg* ARCH Romanesque

romanista [ro·ma·'nis·ta] <-i *m*, -e *f*> *mf* **1.** (*tifoso della Roma*) fan of Roma football club **2.** (*studioso*) Romanist

romanità [ro·ma·ni·'ta] <-> *f* Roman spirit

romano, -a [ro·'ma:·no] **I.** *agg* Roman **II.** *m, f* (*abitante*) Roman

romanticismo [ro·man·ti·'tʃiz·mo] *m* **1.** (*movimento*) Romanticism **2.** (*di persona*) romanticism

romantico, -a [ro·'man·ti·ko] <-ci, -che> **I.** *agg* **1.** (*del romanticismo*) Romantic **2.** (*sentimentale*) romantic **II.** *m, f* **1.** (*scrittore, artista*) Romantic **2.** (*persona sentimentale*) romantic

romanza [ro·'man·dza] *f* MUS romance

romanzesco, -a [ro·man·'dzes·ko] <-schi, -sche> *agg* **1.** LIT fictional **2.** (*avventura, amore*) fantastic

romanziere, -a [ro·man·'dziɛ:·re] *m, f* LIT novelist

romanzo [ro·'man·dzo] *m a. fig* novel

romanzo, -a *agg* LIT Romance

rombare [rom·'ba:·re] *vi* (*veicolo, tuono*) to rumble

rombo ['rom·bo] *m* **1.** MATH rhombus **2.** (*rumore*) rumble **3.** ZOO turbot

romeno, -a [ru·'mɛ:·no] *agg, v.* **rumeno**

rompere ['rom·pe·re] <rompo, ruppi, rotto> **I.** *vt* **1.** (*vetro, vaso*) to smash; (*bastone*) to break; ~ **i timpani a qu** to deafen sb; ~ **la faccia a qu** to smash sb's face in; ~ **le scatole** [*o* **palle**] **a qu** *fam* to annoy sb **2.** *fig* (*silenzio, incanto*) to break **3.** (*interrompere: amicizia*) to break off; (*dieta*) to stop **4.** (*file, righe*) to break **II.** *vi* (*troncare*) ~ **con qu** to break up with sb **III.** *vr:* **-rsi 1.** (*spezzarsi: vaso, bicchiere*) to smash; **-rsi la testa** *fig* to rack one's brains; **-rsi un braccio/una gamba** to break one's arm/leg **2.** (*macchina, radio, lavatrice*) to break down

rompi ['rom·pi] *mf fam* pain

rompiballe [rom·pi·'bal·le] **I.** <-> *mf vulg* pain in the ass **II.** <inv> *agg vulg* pain-in-the-ass

rompicapo [rom·pi·'ka:·po] *m* brain teaser

rompicoglioni [rom·pi·koʎ·'ʎo:·ni] <-> *mf vulg v.* **rompiballe**

rompimento [rom·pi·'men·to] *m fig, fam* pain

rompipalle [rom·pi·'pal·le] <-> *mf vulg v.* **rompiballe**

rompiscatole [rom·pis·'ka:·to·le] <-> *mf fam* pain in the neck

ronda ['ron·da] *f* MIL patrol

rondine ['ron·di·ne] *f* swallow

rondò [ron·'dɔ] <-> *m* **1.** MUS rondo **2.** (*rotatoria*) traffic circle

ronfare [ron·'fa:·re] *vi* **1.** (*russare*) to snore

2.(*gatto*) to purr
ronfata [ron·'fa:·ta] *f* snooze
ronzare [ron·'dza:·re] *vi a. fig* to buzz
ronzio [ron·'dzi:·o] <-ii> *m* (*di insetti*) buzzing
rosa[1] ['rɔ:·za] *f* BOT rose; ~ **dei venti** wind
rose; **all'acqua di -e** *fig* superficial; **se son -e,**
fioriranno *fig* time will tell
rosa[2] **I.**<inv> *agg* (*colore*) pink; **foglio** ~
learner's permit; **romanzo** ~ romantic novel
II.<-> *m* pink
rosario [ro·'za:·rio] <-i> *m* rosary
rosato, -a *agg* **1.**(*vino*) rosé **2.**(*labbra*) pink
rosbif ['rɔs·bif] <-> *m* roast beef
roseo, -a ['rɔ:·zeo] *agg a. fig* rosy
rosetta [ro·'zet·ta] *f* **1.**(*in gioielleria*) rose
2. TEC washer **3.**(*panino*) *a large crusty white*
bread roll
rosi ['ro:·si] *1. pers sing pass rem di* **rodere**
rosicchiare [ro·sik·'kia:·re] *vt* (*osso, mela*) to
gnaw
rosmarino [roz·ma·'ri:·no] *m* rosemary
roso ['ro:·so] *pp di* **rodere**
rosolare [ro·zo·'la:·re] *vt* **1.**CULIN to brown
2.(*loc*) **rosolarsi al sole** to bask
rosolata [ro·zo·'la:·ta] *f* browning
rosolia [ro·zo·'li:·a] <-ie> *f* German measles
rosone [ro·'zo:·ne] *m* **1.**(*motivo ornamen-*
tale) rosette **2.**(*vetrata*) rose window
rospo ['rɔs·po] *m* toad; **ingoiare un** ~ *fig* to
bite the bullet
rossastro, -a [ros·'sas·tro] *agg* reddish
rossetto [ros·'set·to] *m* lipstick
rossiccio, -a [ros·'sit·tʃo] <-cci, -cce> *agg* reddish
rosso ['ros·so] *m* red
rosso, -a I. *agg* red; **vino** ~ red wine **II.** *m, f*
1.(*persona rossa di capelli*) redhead **2.**COM
essere in ~ to be in the red
rossore [ros·'so:·re] *m* (*del viso*) blush
rosticceria [ros·tit·tʃe·'ri:·a] <-ie> *f* rotisserie
rosticciere, -a [ros·tit·'tʃɛ:·re] *m, f* owner of a
rotisserie
rota ['rɔ:·ta] *f* **Tribunale della Sacra Rota** Tribunal of the Sacred (Roman) Rota
rotaia [ro·'ta:·ia] <-aie> *f* FERR rail
rotatoria [ro·ta·'tɔ:·ria] *f* traffic circle
rotatorio, -a [ro·ta·'tɔ:·rio] <-i, -ie> *agg* (*movi-*
mento) rotating
rotazione [ro·tat·'tsio:·ne] *f* rotation
rotella [ro·'tɛl·la] *f* (*piccola ruota*) small wheel;
gli manca una [*o* **qualche**] ~ *fam* he's got a
screw loose
rotocalco [ro·to·'kal·ko] *m* (*rivista*) illustrated
magazine
rotolamento [ro·to·la·'men·to] *m* (*di corpo*)
rolling
rotolare [ro·to·'la:·re] **I.** *vi essere* (*botte,*
masso, tronco) to roll **II.** *vr:* **-rsi** (*girarsi*) to roll
over
rotolo ['rɔ:·to·lo] *m* **1.**(*di carta, stoffa*) roll
2.(*loc*) **andare a -i** to go to the dogs
rotondità [ro·ton·di·'ta] <-> *f* (*di persone,*
arti) curve

rotondo, -a [ro·'ton·do] *agg* round
rotore [ro·'to:·re] *m* TEC rotor
rotta ['rot·ta] *f* **1.**(*percorso*) route; **cam-**
biare ~ *a. fig* to change direction **2.**(*loc*)
essere in ~ **con qu** to not be on good terms
with sb
rottamare [rot·ta·'ma:·re] *vt* (*auto*) to scrap
rottamazione [rot·ta·mat·'tsio:·ne] *f* (*di auto*)
scrapping
rottame [rot·'ta:·me] *m* **1.**(*residuo*) scrap
2.(*ammasso inservibile*) wreck **3.** *fig, fam*
(*persona*) wreck
rotto ['rot·to] *m fig, fam* **per il ~ della cuffia**
by the skin of one's teeth
rotto, -a I. *pp di* **rompere II.** *agg* **1.**(*vaso, bic-*
chiere) broken **2.**(*automobile*) broken down
3.(*scarpe*) worn out; (*pantaloni*) torn
4.(*ossa*) aching **5.** *fig* (*voce*) broken
rottura [rot·'tu:·ra] *f* **1.**(*di tubo*) breaking; (*di*
vetro) smashing **2.**(*di automobile*) breakdown
3.(*di tregua*) breaking; (*di trattative, fidanza-*
mento) breaking-off **4.**(*di fidanzamento,*
amicizia) split
rotula ['rɔ:·tu·la] *f* kneecap
roulotte [ru·'lɔt] <-> *f* trailer
rovente [ro·'vɛn·te] *agg* **1.**(*caldo, estate*) boiling hot **2.**(*ferro*) red-hot **3.** *fig* (*polemica,*
questione) prickly
rovere ['ro:·ve·re] *m o f* oak
rovesciamento [ro·veʃ·ʃa·'men·to] *m* **1.**(*di*
situazione) reversal **2.**(*di governo*) overturning
rovesciare [ro·veʃ·'ʃa:·re] **I.** *vt* **1.**(*inavvertita-*
mente: olio, latte) to spill **2.**(*far cadere: bottig-*
lia, sedia) to knock over **3.**(*ribaltare: barca*) to
overturn; ~ **il governo** to overturn the government; ~ **la situazione** to reverse the situation
4.(*voltare: indumento*) to turn inside out
II. *vr:* **-rsi 1.**(*capovolgersi*) to overturn
2.(*versarsi*) to spill
rovescio, -a <-sci, -sce> *agg* **a** ~ inside out
Rovigo *f* Rovigo, *city in the Veneto area*
rovigotto, -a [ro·vi·'gɔt·to] **I.** *m, f fam* (*abi-*
tante) person from Rovigo **II.** *agg fam* from
Rovigo
rovina [ro·'vi:·na] *f* **1.**(*disfacimento*) collapse
2. *pl* (*macerie*) ruins *pl* **3.** *fig* (*sfacelo*) ruin
rovinare [ro·vi·'na:·re] **I.** *vt a. fig* to ruin **II.** *vi*
1.(*cadere giù*) to collapse **2.**(*precipitare: cas-*
cata, acqua) to rush **III.** *vr:* **-rsi** (*danneggiarsi*)
to ruin oneself
rovinoso, -a [ro·vi·'no:·zo] *agg* disastrous
rovistare [ro·vis·'ta:·re] *vt* ~ **qc** to rummage in
sth
rozzezza [rod·'dzet·tsa] *f* coarseness
rozzo, -a ['rod·dzo] *agg* (*persone, parole*)
coarse
R.R. *abbr di* **ricevuta di ritorno** return receipt
Rrr *abbr di* **raccomandata con ricevuta di**
ritorno certified letter with return receipt
RSM *m abbr di* **Repubblica di San Marino** Republic of San Marino
ruba ['ru:·ba] *f* **andare a** ~ *fam* to sell like hot-

R

cakes
rubacuori [ru·ba·'kuɔ:·ri] I.<inv> *agg* womanizing II. <-> *mf* heartbreaker
rubare [ru·'ba:·re] *vt* 1.(*portafogli, gioielli*) to steal 2.*fig*(*segreto, cuore*) to steal; (*tempo*) to take up
rubicondo, -a [ru·bi·'kon·do] *agg* (*guance, viso*) ruddy
rubinetteria [ru·bi·net·te·'ri:·a] <-ie> *f* taps and fittings *pl*
rubinetto [ru·bi·'net·to] *m* tap
rubino[1] [ru·'bi:·no] *m* ruby
rubino[2] <inv> *agg* (*colore*) ruby
rublo ['ru:·blo] *m* ruble
rubrica [ru·'bri:·ka] <-che> *f* 1.(*degli indirizzi*) address book 2.RADIO, TV feature 3.(*di giornale*) column
rucola ['ru:·ko·la] *f* rocket
rude ['ru:·de] *agg* (*persona, modi*) coarse
rudere ['ru:·de·re] *m* 1.(*rovine*) ruins *pl* 2.*fig* (*persona malandata*) wreck
rudimentale [ru·di·men·'ta:·le] *agg* rudimentary
rudimento [ru·di·'men·to] *m* -i (*di matematica, fisica*) rudiments *pl*
ruffiano, -a [ruf·'fia:·no] *m, f fam* creep
ruga ['ru:·ga] <-ghe> *f* wrinkle
ruggine[1] ['rud·dʒi·ne] *f* 1.(*sostanza*) rust; **fare la** ~ *a. fig* to get rusty 2.*fig, fam*(*attrito*) bad blood
ruggine[2] <inv> *agg*(*colore*) rust
ruggire [rud·'dʒi:·re] <ruggisco> *vi* 1.(*leone*) to roar 2.(*mare*) to crash; (*tempesta*) to roar
ruggito [rud·'dʒi:·to] *m* 1.(*del leone*) roar 2.(*del mare*) crashing; (*roaring*)
rugiada [ru·'dʒa:·da] *f* dew
rugosità [ru·go·si·'ta] <-> *f* roughness
rugoso, -a [ru·'go:·so] *agg* 1.(*volto*) wrinkled 2.(*superficie*) rough
rullare [rul·'la:·re] *vi* (*tamburo*) to roll
rullino [rul·'li:·no] *m* roll of film
rullio [rul·'li:·o] <-ii> *m* (*di tamburo*) roll
rullo ['rul·lo] *m* 1.(*di tamburo*) roll 2.(*cilindro*) roller
rumeno [ru·'mɛ:·no] *m sing* (*lingua*) Romanian
rumeno, -a [ru·'mɛ:·no] I. *agg* Romanian II. *m, f*(*abitante*) Romanian
ruminanti [ru·mi·'nan·ti] *mpl* ruminants *pl*
ruminare [ru·mi·'na:·re] *vt a. fig* to ruminate
rumore [ru·'mo:·re] *m* 1.(*suono*) noise 2.*fig* (*scalpore*) fuss; **fare** ~ *fig* to cause a fuss
rumoreggiare [ru·mo·red·'dʒa:·re] *vi* 1.(*fare rumore*) to make a noise; (*di tamburo, tuono*) to rumble 2.*fig*(*persone*) to murmur
rumoroso, -a [ru·mo·'ro:·so] *agg* noisy
ruolo ['ruɔ:·lo] *m* 1.(*funzione*) role 2.THEAT part 3.ADM **insegnanti di** ~ tenured teachers
ruota ['ruɔ:·ta] *f* 1.TEC, MOT wheel 2.(*del lotto*) one of the Italian cities, e.g. Milan, Naples, where lottery numbers are drawn 3.(*di luna park*) ~ **panoramica** big wheel
rupe ['ru:·pe] *f* rock

rupestre [ru·'pɛs·tre] *agg*(*paesaggio*) rocky
ruppi ['rup·pi] *1. pers sing pass rem di* **rompere**
rurale [ru·'ra:·le] *agg*(*paesaggio, popolazione*) rural
ruscello [ruʃ·'ʃɛl·lo] *m* stream
ruspa ['rus·pa] *f* excavator
ruspante [rus·'pan·te] *agg* 1.(*pollo*) free-range 2.*fig*(*carattere*) down-to-earth
russare [rus·'sa:·re] *vi* to snore
Russia ['rus·sia] *f* Russia; **abitare in** ~ to live in Russia; **andare in** ~ to go to Russia
russo ['rus·so] *m sing*(*lingua*) Russian
russo, -a ['rus·so] I. *agg*(*della Russia*) Russian; **insalata -a** Russian salad; **montagne -e** big dipper II. *m, f*(*abitante*) Russian
rustico ['rus·ti·ko] <-ci> *m* (*edificio*) cottage
rustico, -a <-ci, -che> *agg* 1.(*campagnolo*) rustic 2.(*persona*) rough
ruttare [rut·'ta:·re] *vi* to burp
ruttino [rut·'ti:·no] *m* burp; **fare il** ~ to burp
rutto ['rut·to] *m* burp; **fare un** ~ to burp
ruvidezza [ru·vi·'det·tsa] *f a. fig* roughness
ruvido, -a ['ru:·vi·do] *agg a. fig* rough
ruzzolare [rut·tso·'la:·re] *vi* to tumble
ruzzolone [rut·tso·'lo:·ne] *m* tumble
ruzzoloni [rut·tso·'lo:·ni] *avv* with a tumble

S

S, s ['ɛs·se] <-> *f* (*lettera*) S; ~ **come Savona** S for Sugar
S *abbr di* **sud** S
sabato ['sa:·ba·to] *m* Saturday; ~ **Santo** Holy Saturday; *v.a.* **domenica**
sabba ['sab·ba] <-> *m* witches' Sabbath
sabbia ['sab·bia] <-ie> *f* sand; **costruire sulla** ~ *fig* to build on sand; (**di**) **color** ~ sand-colored
sabbiato, -a [sab·'bia:·to] *agg* TEC sandblasted
sabbiatura [sab·bia·'tu:·ra] *f* 1.MED sandbath 2.TEC sandblasting
sabotaggio [sa·bo·'tad·dʒo] <-ggi> *m* sabotage
sabotare [sa·bo·'ta:·re] *vt* to sabotage
sabotatore, -trice [sa·bo·ta·'to:·re] *m, f* saboteur
sacca ['sak·ka] <-cche> *f* 1.(*borsa*) bag 2.MED, ANAT sac
saccarina [sak·ka·'ri:·na] *f* saccharin
saccarosio [sak·ka·'rɔ:·sio] <-i> *m* saccharose
saccente [sat·'tʃɛn·te] I. *agg* 1.(*ragazzo, modo di fare*) know-it-all 2.(*vecchio, modo di fare*) opinionated II. *mf* know-it-all
saccheggiare [sak·ked·'dʒa:·re] *vt* 1.(*città, villaggio*) to sack 2.(*banca*) to rob; (*casa, negozio*) to ransack 3.(*frigorifero, negozio*) to raid

saccheggiatore, -trice [sak·ked·dʒa·'to:·re] I. *agg* plundering II. *m, f* plunderer

saccheggio [sak·'ked·dʒo] <-ggi> *m* HIST sack; (*al giorno d'oggi*) looting; (*di negozio*) plunder

sacchetto [sak·'ket·to] *m* bag

sacco ['sak·ko] <-cchi> *m* 1. (*recipiente*) bag; ~ **a pelo** sleeping bag; **pranzo al** ~ packed lunch; **farina del proprio** ~ one's own work; **cogliere** [*o* **pescare**] qu con le mani nel ~ *fig* to catch sb red-handed; **vuotare il** ~ *fig* to spill the beans 2. *fig, fam* un ~ di loads of 3. ANAT sac

saccopelista [sak·ko·pe·'lis·ta] <-i *m*, -e *f*> *mf* backpacker

sacerdote, -essa [sa·tʃer·'dɔ:·te, sa·tʃer·do·'tes·sa] *m, f* priest

sacerdozio [sa·tʃer·'dɔt·tsio] <-i> *m* REL priesthood

sacramentale [sa·kra·men·'ta:·le] *agg* (*rito, celebrazione, grazia*) sacramental

sacramentare [sa·kra·men·'ta:·re] *vt* 1. REL to administer the sacraments 2. *fig* (*giurare*) to swear 3. *fam* (*bestemmiare*) to blaspheme

sacramento [sa·kra·'men·to] *m* sacrament; (*l'Eucarestia*) host

sacrario [sa·'kra:·rio] <-i> *m* 1. (*di tempio*) sanctuary 2. (*dei caduti*) memorial monument [*o* chapel]

sacrato [sa·'kra:·to] *v.* sagrato

sacrestano [sa·kres·'ta:·no] *v.* sagrestano

sacrestia [sa·kres·'ti:·a] *f v.* sagrestia

sacrificale [sa·kri·fi·'ka:·le] *agg* (*altare, rito, vittima*) sacrificial

sacrificare [sa·kri·fi·'ka:·re] I. *vt* (*animali, persone*) to sacrifice II. *vr:* **-rsi** 1. (*offrirsi in sacrificio*) to sacrifice oneself 2. (*sopportare privazioni*) to make sacrifices

sacrificato, -a [sa·kri·fi·'ka:·to] *agg* 1. (*pieno di rinunce: vita, anni*) full of hardship 2. (*non valorizzato: mente, edificio*) wasted; **essere** ~ to be wasted 3. (*offerto in sacrificio: animale, vittima*) sacrificial

sacrificio [sa·kri·'fi:·tʃo] <-ci> *m* sacrifice

sacrifizio [sa·kri·'fit·tsio] <-i> *m* sacrifice

sacrilegio [sa·kri·'lɛ:·dʒo] <-gi> *m* sacrilege

sacrilego, -a [sa·'kri:·le·go] <-ghi, -ghe> *agg* 1. (*profanatorio: atto, furto, ladro*) sacrilegious 2. (*irriverente: furto, atto, parole*) audacious

sacro, -a *agg* sacred; **la -a famiglia** the Holy Family; **le -e scritture** the holy scriptures

sacrosanto, -a [sa·kro·'san·to] *agg* 1. REL holy 2. (*inviolabile: diritto, principio*) sacrosanct 3. *fam* (*opportuno*) justified; **parole -e!** you're absolutely right!

sadico, -a ['sa:·di·ko] <-ci, -che> I. *agg* sadistic II. *m, f* PSYCH sadist

sadismo [sa·'diz·mo] *m* sadism

saetta [sa·'et·ta] *f* 1. LIT (*freccia*) arrow 2. (*fulmine*) lightning; **come una** ~ like lightning; **è una** ~ to be like lightning

safari [sa·'fa:·ri] <-> *m* safari

saga ['sa:·ga] <-ghe> *f* 1. (*racconto, leg-*

genda) saga 2. *fig* (*di famiglia*) story

sagace [sa·'ga:·tʃe] *agg* (*persona, risposta, mente*) shrewd

saggezza [sad·'dʒet·tsa] *f* wisdom

saggiare [sad·'dʒa:·re] *vt* (*provare, verificare*) to test

saggina [sad·'dʒi:·na] *f* sorghum

saggio ['sad·dʒo] <-gi> *m* 1. (*prova: di forza, di volontà*) proof; **dare** ~ **di qc** to demonstrate sth; ~ **di ginnastica** gymnastics display; ~ **musicale** recital 2. (*scritto*) essay 3. FIN (*tasso*) rate

saggio, -a <-ggi, -gge> I. *agg* wise II. *m, f* (*persona saggia*) wise man *m*, wise woman *f*

saggista [sad·'dʒis·ta] <-i *m*, -e *f*> *mf* essayist

saggistica [sad·'dʒis·ti·ka] <-che> *f* essays *pl*

sagittario [sa·dʒit·'ta:·rio] *m* ASTR Sagittarius; **sono** (**del** [*o* **un**]) **Sagittario** I'm (a) Sagittarius

sagoma ['sa:·go·ma] *f* 1. (*profilo: di uomo, di animale, di vettura*) outline 2. (*nel tiro a segno*) target 3. (*modello: in legno, cartone, metallo*) template 4. *fig, fam* **è una** ~ he's a scream

sagomare [sa·go·'ma:·re] *vt* (*roccia, dune*) to sculpt; (*pezzo di legno, di metallo*) to shape

sagomato, -a [sa·go·'ma:·to] *agg* molded

sagra ['sa:·gra] *f* (*festa popolare*) festival

sagrato [sa·'gra:·to] *m* churchyard

sagrestano, -a [sa·gres·'ta:·no] *m, f* sexton

sagrestia [sa·gres·'ti:·a] <-ie> *f* sacristy

saio ['sa:·io] <sai> *m* REL habit

sala ['sa:·la] *f* room; (*grande*) hall; ~ **d'aspetto** waiting room; ~ **da ballo** ballroom; ~ **da pranzo** dining room

salace [sa·'la:·tʃe] *agg* 1. (*lascivo: parole, frasi*) salacious 2. (*pungente: commento, ironia*) cutting

salamandra [sa·la·'man·dra] *f* salamander

salame [sa·'la:·me] *m* 1. CULIN salami 2. *fig, fam* dope

salamelecco [sa·la·me·'lɛk·ko] <-cchi> *m* bowing and scraping; **senza -cchi** without ceremony

salamoia [sa·la·'mɔ:·ia] <-oie> *f* brine

salare [sa·'la:·re] *vt* (*minestra, pasta, carne*) to salt

salariato, -a [sa·la·'ria:·to] *m, f* wage-earner

salario [sa·'la:·rio] <-i> *m* (*di operaio*) wage; (*di dipendente*) salary; ~ **garantito** guaranteed wage; ~ **da fame** starvation wage

salassare [sa·las·'sa:·re] *vt fig* (*spremere denaro a*) to bleed dry

salasso [sa·'las·so] *m fig* (*esborso di denaro*) drain on resources

salatino [sa·la·'ti:·no] *m* cocktail snack

salato, -a [sa·'la:·to] *agg* 1. (*burro*) salted; (*pane*) made with salt; **torta -a** savory pie 2. (*acqua del mare*) salt 3. (*troppo salato: pasta, carne*) salty 4. *fig* (*prezzo*) high

salciccia [sal·'tʃit·tʃa] *f fam v.* salsiccia

saldare [sal·'da:·re] *vt* 1. TEC (*pezzi metallici*) to weld 2. (*conto*) to pay; (*debito*) to pay off

saldatore [sal·da·'to:·re] *m* TEC (*utensile*) soldering iron

saldatore, -trice *m, f* TEC (*operaio*) welder

saldatrice [sal·da·'tri:·tʃe] *f* EL welder

saldatura [sal·da·'tu:·ra] *f* TEC welding; **punto di ~** weld point

saldezza [sal·'det·tsa] *f* (*morale, di nervi*) strength

saldo ['sal·do] *m* **1.** (*svendita*) sale; **-i di fine stagione** end of season sales **2.** (*di conto, fattura*) settlement; **~ attivo** credit; **~ passivo** deficit

saldo, -a *agg fig* (*stabile: carattere, natura, convinzioni*) firm

sale ['sa:·le] *m* **1.** GASTR, CHEM salt; **~ da cucina** cooking salt; **~ iodato** iodized salt; **~ marino** sea salt; **un pizzico di ~** a pinch of salt; **-i da bagno** bath salts; **sotto ~** CULIN salted **2.** *fig* (*senno*) **avere poco ~ in zucca** *fam* to not have much sense

Salernitano <*sing*> *m* (*zona*) Salerno area; **nel ~** in the Salerno area

salernitano, -a [sa·ler·ni·'ta:·no] **I.** *agg* from Salerno **II.** *m, f* (*abitante*) person from Salerno

Salerno [sa·'lɛr·no] *f* Salerno, *city in southwestern Italy*

salgemma [sal·ˠdʒem·ma] *m* rock salt

salgo ['sal·go] *1. pers sing pr di* **salire**

salice ['sa:·li·tʃe] *m* willow; **~ piangente** weeping willow

saliente [sa·'liɛn·te] *agg fig* (*fondamentale: fatto, punto, elemento*) main

saliera [sa·'liɛ:·ra] *f* saltcellar

salii [sa·'li:·i] *1. pers sing pass rem di* **salire**

salina [sa·'li:·na] *f* **1.** (*impianto*) saltworks **2.** MIN salt pan

salinità [sa·li·ni·'ta] <-> *f* salinity

salino, -a [sa·'li:·no] *agg* (*contenente sale: liquido, integratore*) saline

salire [sa·'li:·re] <**salgo, salii, salito**> **I.** *vt avere* (*scale, gradini, montagna*) to climb **II.** *vi essere* **1.** (*gener*) to go up **2.** (*aereo, strada, sentiero*) to climb **3.** (*catena montuosa, fumo, urla*) to rise **4.** (*montare: sul treno*) to get on; (*sull'auto*) to get in **5.** (*aumentare: livello, numero, temperatura*) to rise **6.** (*diventare più caro: prezzo, affitto, frutta*) to go up (in price)

saliscendi [sa·liʃ·'ʃen·di] <-> *m* **1.** (*chiusura*) latch **2.** (*salite e discese*) series of ups and downs

salita [sa·'li:·ta] *f* **1.** (*azione*) climb **2.** (*strada*) hill; **in ~** uphill

saliva [sa·'li:·va] *f* saliva

salivare¹ [sa·li·'va:·re] *agg* salivary

salivare² *vi* to salivate

salivazione [sa·li·vat·'tsio:·ne] *f* salivation

salma ['sal·ma] *f* body

salmastro [sal·'mas·tro] *m* salty smell [*o* taste]

salmastro, -a *agg* (*odore, sapore*) salty; **acque -e** brackish water

salmì [sal·'mi] *m* salmi, *a kind of rich stew;* **lepre in ~** salmi of hare

salmistrato, -a [sal·mis·'tra:·to] *agg* corned

salmo ['sal·mo] *m* psalm

salmonato, -a [sal·mo·'na:·to] *agg* **1.** (*relativo al salmone*) salmon; **trota -a** salmon trout **2.** (*colore*) salmon (colored)

salmone [sal·'mo:·ne] *m* salmon

salmonella [sal·mo·'nɛl·la] *f* salmonella

salmonellosi [sal·mo·nel·'lɔ:·zi] <-> *f* salmonella poisoning

salone [sa·'lo:·ne] *m* **1.** (*ampia sala*) hall **2.** (*esposizione*) show; **~ dell'automobile** auto show

salopette [sa·lɔ·'pɛt] <- *o* salopettes> *f* overalls *pl*

salotto [sa·'lɔt·to] *m* **1.** (*stanza*) living room **2.** (*mobilio*) living room furniture **3.** (*letterario, aritstico*) salon

salpare [sal·'pa:·re] **I.** *vi essere* to set sail **II.** *vt avere* **~ l'ancora** to raise the anchor

salsa ['sal·sa] *f* sauce; **~ di pomodoro** tomato sauce

salsedine [sal·'sɛ:·di·ne] *f* **1.** (*del mare*) saltiness **2.** (*residuo*) (dried) salt

salsiccia [sal·'sit·tʃa] <-cce> *f* sausage

salsicciotto [sal·sit·'tʃɔt·to] *m* (*grossa salsiccia*) large sausage

salsiera [sal·'siɛ:·ra] *f* sauceboat

saltare [sal·'ta:·re] **I.** *vi essere o avere* **1.** (*da terra*) to jump; **~ dalla finestra** to jump out of the window; **~ dal ponte** to jump off the bridge; **~ dalla gioia** to jump for joy; **~ al collo di qu** (*abbracciare*) to throw one's arms around sb; (*aggredire*) to jump on sb; **~ fuori** (*essere trovato*) to turn up; (*esprimere*) to come out with; **~ agli occhi (a qu)** to jump out (at sb); **~ in mente** to think of; **ma cosa ti è saltato in mente?** what got into you?; **~ di palo in frasca** to jump from one subject to another **2.** (*esplodere*) **~ in aria** *fig* to blow up **II.** *vt avere* **1.** (*ostacolo*) to jump (over); **~ la corda** to jump rope **2.** CULIN to sauté **3.** *fig* (*omettere, non frequentare*) to skip; **~ il pasto** to skip a meal

saltellare [sal·tel·'la:·re] *vi* to skip

saltello [sal·'tɛl·lo] *m* hop

salterellare [sal·te·rel·'la:·re] *v. saltellare*

saltimbanco, -a [sal·tim·'baŋ·ko] <-chi, -che> *m, f* (*acrobata*) acrobat

saltimbocca [sal·tim·'bok·ka] <-> *m* rolled veal with ham and sage

salto ['sal·to] *m* **1.** *fig, fam, a* SPORT jump; **~ in alto** high jump; **~ in lungo** long jump; **~ con l'asta** pole vault; **~ mortale** somersault; **fare i -i mortali** *fig* to bust a gut; **fare quattro -i** *fam* to dance **2.** (*scappata*) **fare un ~ in centro** to pop into town; **fare un ~ da qu** to drop in on sb; **in un ~** **vado e torno** *fam* I'll take just a second **3.** (*rapido passaggio*) step up the ladder **4.** MUS leap

salubre [sa·'lu:·bre] *agg* (*ambiente, aria*) healthy

salume [sa·'lu:·me] *m* (type of) cured pork; **-i** cold cuts, *made of pork*

salumeria [sa·lu·me·'ri:·a] <-ie> *f* ≈ delicatessen

salumiere, -a [sa·lu·'miɛ:·re] *m, f* ≈ person who works in/owns a delicatessen

salumificio [sa·lu·mi·'fi:·tʃo] <-ci> *m* ≈ factory producing cured pork

salutare¹ [sa·lu·'ta:·re] *agg* (*alimento, vacanza, trattamento*) healthy

salutare² I. *vt* to greet; **salutami tua moglie** say hello to your wife for me; **andare a ~ qu** to go and see sb II. *vr* (*incontrandosi*) to greet one another; (*lasciandosi*) to say goodbye to one another

salute [sa·'lu:·te] *f* **1.** (*benessere fisico*) (good) health; (*benessere mentale*) mental health **2.** (*loc*) **bere alla ~ di qu** to drink to sb's health; **~!** (*nei brindisi*) cheers!; (*quando si starnutisce*) bless you!

saluto [sa·'lu:·to] *m* greeting; **portare a qu i -i di qu** to say hello to sb for sb; **rivolgere un ~ a qu** to greet sb; **togliere il ~ a qu** *fig* to (deliberately) ignore sb; **tanti cari -i** love from; **cordiali -i** with best wishes

salva ['sal·va] *f* (*sparo senza proiettile*) salvo; **cartuccia a -e** blank

salvabile [sal·'va:·bi·le] *agg* **salvare il ~ to** save what can be saved

salvacondotto [sal·va·kon·'dot·to] *m* (*permesso*) safe conduct

salvadanaro [sal·va·da·'na:·ro] *m* piggy bank

salvagente [sal·va·'dʒen·te] I. <inv> *agg* **giubbotto ~** life jacket II. <-> *m* **1.** (*per nuotare*) rubber ring **2.** (*isola pedonale*) safety island

salvaguardare [sal·va·guar·'da:·re] I. *vt* (*diritti, onore, salute*) to safeguard II. *vr* **-rsi da qc** to protect oneself from sth

salvare [sal·'va:·re] I. *vt* **1.** *a.* COMPUT (*gener*) to save; **~ la vita a qu** to save sb's life **2.** (*proteggere: onore, reputazione*) to preserve II. *vr:* **-rsi 1.** (*dalla morte*) to survive **2.** (*trovare scampo*) to find safety; **si salvi chi può!** it's every man for himself!

salvaschermo [sal·va·'sker·mo] <-> *m* screen saver

salvaslip [sal·va·'zlip] <-> *m* panty liner

salvataggio [sal·va·'tad·dʒo] <-ggi> *m a.* COMPUT rescue; **operazioni di ~** rescue operations

salvatore, -trice [sal·va·'to:·re] *m, f* savior; **il Salvatore** the Savior

salve ['sal·ve] I. *f v.* **salva** II. *int* hi

salvezza [sal·'vet·tsa] *f a.* REL salvation; **ancora di ~** *fig* safety net; **la ~ eterna** eternal salvation

salvia ['sal·via] <-ie> *f* sage

salvietta [sal·'viet·ta] *f* hand towel; **~ rinfrescante** wet wipe

salvo¹ ['sal·vo] *msing* **trarre qu in ~** to lead sb to safety; **mettere qc in ~** to keep sth safe

salvo² I. *prep* (*ad eccezione*) except (for) II. *cong* **~ che ...** +*conj* unless

salvo, -a *agg* safe; **avere -a la vita** to have one's life spared

sambuca [sam·'bu:·ka] <-che> *f* sambuca, *li-*

queur similar to anisette

sambuco [sam·'bu:·ko] <-chi> *m* elder

san [san] *v.* **santo** I.

sanabile [sa·'na:·bi·le] *agg* JUR reparable

sanare [sa·'na:·re] *vt* **1.** (*gener*) to heal **2.** (*bilancio*) to put right; **~ un debito** to pay (off) a debt **3.** JUR to settle

sanatoria [sa·na·'tɔ·ria] *f* JUR act of indemnity; **~ fiscale** tax amnesty

sanatorio [sa·na·'tɔ·rio] <-i> *m* sanatorium

San Bernardo <- - o - -i> *m* Saint Bernard

sancire [san·'tʃi:·re] <sancisco> *vt* **1.** (*patto, alleanza, accordo*) to ratify **2.** JUR to sanction

sandalo ['san·da·lo] *m* **1.** (*calzatura*) sandal **2.** BOT sandalwood

sangiovese [san·dʒo·'ve:·se] <-> *m* Sangiovese, *red wine from Tuscany and Romagna*

sangria [san·'gri:·a] <-> *f* sangria

sangue¹ ['saŋ·gue] *m* blood; **donatore di ~** blood donor; **legami** [*o* **vincoli**] **di ~** blood ties; **un** (**cavallo**) **puro ~** a thoroughbred; **~ freddo** *fig* sang-froid; **a ~ freddo** in cold blood; **una bistecca al ~** a rare steak; **avere la musica nel ~** to have music in one's blood; **fra loro non c'è buon ~** there's bad blood between them; **buon ~ non mente** *prov* blood will out

sangue² <inv> *agg* blood

sanguigno, -a [saŋ·'guiɲ·ɲo] *agg* MED blood; **pressione -a** blood pressure

sanguinaccio [saŋ·gui·'nat·tʃo] <-cci> *m* (*insaccato*) black pudding

sanguinare [saŋ·gui·'na:·re] *vi* to bleed

sanguinario, -a [saŋ·gui·'na:·rio] <-i, -ie> *agg* (*killer, guerriero*) bloodthirsty

sanguinoso, -a [saŋ·gui·'no:·so] *agg* (*conflitto, battaglia*) bloody

sanguisuga [saŋ·gui·'su:·ga] <-ghe> *f* **1.** ZOO leech **2.** *fig, pej* bloodsucker

sanità [sa·ni·'ta] <-> *f* **1.** (*salute: fisica, mentale*) health **2.** ADM public health

sanitario, -a [sa·ni·'ta:·rio] <-i, -ie> *agg* ADM health; **ufficiale ~** health inspector

sano, -a ['sa:·no] *agg* **1.** MED healthy; **~ come un pesce** in perfect health **2.** (*intero*) in one piece; **di -a pianta** *fig* completely

sanscrito ['san·skri·to] *m* Sanskrit

sant' [sant] *v.* **santo** I.

santarellina [san·ta·rel·'li:·na] *f* goody-goody

santerello [san·te·'rɛl·lo] *m* goody-goody

santificare [san·ti·fi·'ka:·re] *vt* **1.** (*rendere santo*) to sanctify **2.** (*dichiarare santo*) to canonize **3.** (*le feste*) to observe

santino [san·'ti:·no] *m* holy picture

santissimo [san·'tis·si·mo] *m* **il ~** the Blessed Sacrament

santissimo, -a *agg* **il ~ Padre** the Holy Father; **il ~ Sacramento** the Blessed Sacrament

santità [san·ti·'ta] <-> *f* holiness; **Sua ~** His Holiness

santo, -a ['san·to] I. *agg* **1.** (*gener*) holy; **acqua -a** holy water; **la settimana -a** Holy Week; **la terra -a** the Holy Land **2.** (*con nome* *proprio*) Saint **3.** (*loc*) **tutto il ~ giorno** *fam* all day long; **fammi il ~ piacere ...** *fam* for goodness' sake ...; **Sant'Iddio!** *fam* for God's sake! **II.** *m*, *f a.* REL saint; (**tutti**) **i Santi** All Saints; **pazienza di un ~** patience of a saint; **non ci sono -i che tengano** *fig* there's nothing for it; **deve avere qualche ~ dalla sua** *fig* he must have a guardian angel

santone, -a [san·'to:·ne] *m*, *f* **1.** REL holy man **2.** *fig* guru

santuario [san·tu·'a:·rio] <-i> *m* (*edificio sacro*) sanctuary

sanzionare [san·tsio·'na:·re] *vt* **1.** (*infliggere una sanzione*) to penalize **2.** (*confermare: accordo, intesa*) to ratify

sanzione [san·'tsio:·ne] *f* **1.** JUR, ADM sanction **2.** (*punizione*) penalty; **~ disciplinare** punishment; **-i penali** legal sanctions

sapere[1] [sa·'pe:·re] <so, seppi, saputo> **I.** *vt* **1.** (*gener*) to know; **sa il fatto suo** he [*o* she] knows his [*o* her] stuff; **saperla lunga** to know a thing or two; **lo so** I know; **non saprei** I don't know; **non si sa mai** you never know; **buono a sapersi** that's good to know; **averlo saputo!** I wish I'd known! **2.** (*essere in grado di fare qualcosa*) to know how to; **saper fare qc** to know how to do sth; **so nuotare** I can swim; **sa giocare bene a basket** he's [*o* she's] good at basketball **3.** (*apprendere*) to find out; **come hai fatto a saperlo?** how did you find out (about it)? **II.** *vi* **1.** (*aver sapore*) **~ di qc** to taste of sth; **non sa di niente** it has no flavor **2.** (*avere un odore*) **~ di qc** to smell of sth **3.** *fig* (*avere un'impressione*) **mi sa che oggi non viene** I don't think he'll [*o* she'll] come today; **mi sa che racconta un sacco di bugie** I think he's [*o* she's] telling a pack of lies

sapere[2] *m* **1.** (*conoscenze*) knowledge **2.** (*loc*) **il saper vivere** the art of living; **il saper fare** practical ability

sapiente [sa·'pjɛn·te] **I.** *agg* **1.** (*saggio*) learned **2.** (*abile: uso, gioco, mano*) masterly **II.** *mf* wise man *m*, wise woman *f*

sapientone, -a [sa·pjen·'to:·ne] *pej* **I.** *agg* know-it-all **II.** *m*, *f* know-it-all

sapienza [sa·'pjɛn·tsa] *f* wisdom

sapone [sa·'po:·ne] *m* soap; **~ da barba** shaving soap; **~ da bucato** laundry soap; **bolla di ~** *a fig* soap bubble

saponetta [sa·po·'net·ta] *f* bar of soap

sapore [sa·'po:·re] *m a. fig* flavor; **avere ~ di qc** to smack of sth; **senza ~** flavorless

saporito, -a [sa·po·'ri:·to] *agg* **1.** CULIN tasty **2.** *fig* (*gustoso: risata*) hearty

saputello, -a [sa·pu·'tɛl·lo] *pej* **I.** *agg* precocious **II.** *m*, *f* know-it-all

saputo, -a [sa·'pu:·to] **I.** *agg* (*noto*) well-known **II.** *m*, *f pej* know-it-all

sarà [sa·'ra] *3. pers sing futuro di* **essere**[1]

sarabanda [sa·ra·'ban·da] *f* **1.** (*danza*) sarabande **2.** *fig* (*confusione*) uproar

saraceno, -a [sa·ra·'tʃɛ:·no] **I.** *agg* Saracen; **grano ~** buckwheat **II.** *m*, *f* Saracen

saracinesca [sa·ra·tʃi·'nes·ka] <-sche> *f* (*di porte e finestre*) rolling shutter

sarcasmo [sar·'kaz·mo] *m* sarcasm

sarcastico, -a [sar·'kas·ti·ko] <-ci, -che> *agg* sarcastic

sarcofago [sar·'kɔ:·fa·go] <-gi *o* -ghi> *m* sarcophagus

sarda ['sar·da] *f* sardine

Sardegna [sar·'deɲ·ɲa] *f* Sardinia

sardella [sar·'dɛl·la] *f fam* sardine

sardina [sar·'di:·na] *f* sardine; **-e sott'olio** sardines in oil

sardo ['sar·do] <*sing*> *m* (*lingua*) Sardinian

sardo, -a **I.** *agg* Sardinian **II.** *m*, *f* Sardinian

sareste, saresti [sa·'res·te, sa·'res·ti] *2. pers pl, 2. pers sing condizionale di* **essere**[1]

sarto, -a ['sar·to] *m*, *f* tailor [*o* m], dressmaker [*o* f]

sartoria [sar·to·'ri:·a] <-ie> *f* **1.** (*per uomo*) tailor's; (*per donna*) dressmaker's **2.** (*settore*) tailoring

sassarese [sas·sa·'re:·se] **I.** *agg* from Sassari **II.** *mf* (*abitante*) person from Sassari

Sassarese *sing f* (*zona*) Sassari area; **nel ~** in the Sassari area

Sassari *f* Sassari, *city in NW Sardinia*

sassata [sas·'sa:·ta] *f* **tirare una ~ a qu** to throw a stone at sb

sasso ['sas·so] *m* (*pietra*) stone; (*masso*) rock; (*ciottolo*) pebble; **duro come un ~** *a. fig* (as) hard as a rock; **restare di ~** *fig* to be astounded

sassofonista [sas·so·fo·'nis·ta] <-i *m*, -e *f*> *mf* saxophonist

sassofono [sas·'sɔ:·fo·no] *m* saxophone

sassoso, -a [sas·'so:·so] *agg* (*strada, percorso*) stony

Satana ['sa:·ta·na] *m* Satan

satanico, -a [sa·'ta:·ni·ko] <-ci, -che> *agg* satanic; *fig* (*ghigno*) devilish

satellitare [sa·tel·li·'ta:·re] *agg* satellite

satellite [sa·'tɛl·li·te] **I.** *m* satellite; **~ meteorologico** weather satellite; **~ televisivo** TV satellite; **~ di comunicazione** communications satellite; **trasmissione via ~** satellite transmission **II.** *agg* satellite; **città ~** satellite town

satin [sa·'tɛ̃] <-> *m* satin

satinare [sa·ti·'na:·re] *vt* to satinize

satira ['sa:·ti·ra] *f* satire

satirico, -a [sa·'ti:·ri·ko] <-ci, -che> **I.** *agg* (*scrittore, pezzo*) satirical **II.** *m*, *f* satirist

satiro ['sa:·ti·ro] *m* satyr

satollarsi [sa·tol·'la:r·si] *vr* **-rsi di qc** to eat one's fill of sth

satollo, -a [sa·'tol·lo] *agg* full

saturare [sa·tu·'ra:·re] *vt* **1.** CHEM to saturate **2.** *fig* (*riempire troppo*) to over-fill

saturazione [sa·tu·rat·'tsio:·ne] *f* saturation; **~ del mercato** market saturation

saturo, -a ['sa:·tu·ro] *agg* CHEM saturated

saudita [sau·'di:·ta] <-i *m*, -e *f*> *agg* Saudi; **Arabia Saudita** Saudi Arabia

sauna ['sa:u·na] *f* sauna; **fare la ~** to have a

sauna
savana [sa·'va:·na] *f* savannah
savoiardo [sa·vo·'iar·do] *m* CULIN sponge finger
Savona [sa·'vɔ:·na] *f* Savona, *town in north-western Italy*
savonese [sa·vo·'ne:·se] **I.** *agg* from Savona **II.** *mf* (*abitante*) person from Savona
Savonese <*sing*> *m* (*zona*) Savona area; **nel ~** in the Savona area
saxofonista [sak·so·fo·'nis·ta] *mf v.* **sassofonista**
saxofono [sa·'ksɔ:·fo·no] *m v.* **sassofono**
saziare [sat·'tsia:·re] **I.** *vt a. fig* to satisfy **II.** *vr:* -**rsi 1.** (*riempirsi*) to eat one's fill; -**rsi di qc** to eat one's fill of sth **2.** *fig* to have one's fill
sazietà [sat·tsie·'ta] <-> *f* **1.** (*essere sazio*) fullness; **mangiare a ~** to eat one's fill **2.** *fig* satisfaction
sazio, -a ['sat·tsio] <-i, -ie> *agg* **1.** (*di cibo*) full (up) **2.** *fig, pej* sated; **non esser mai ~** *a. fig* to never be satisfied
sbaciucchiare [zba·tʃuk·'kia:·re] **I.** *vt* to kiss and cuddle **II.** *vr:* -**rsi** to kiss and cuddle
sbadataggine [zba·da·'tad·dʒi·ne] *f* carelessness
sbadato, -a [zba·'da:·to] *agg* careless
sbadigliare [zba·diʎ·'ʎa:·re] *vi* to yawn
sbadiglio [zba·'diʎ·ʎo] <-gli> *m* yawn
sbafare [zba·'fa:·re] *vt fam* **1.** (*mangiare a scrocco*) to scrounge **2.** (*mangiare avidamente*) to scoff
sbafo ['zba:·fo] *m pej, fam* **vivere/mangiare a ~** to scrounge a living/a meal
sbagliare [zbaʎ·'ʎa:·re] **I.** *vt* **1.** *a. fig* (*colpo, mira*) to miss **2.** (*scambiare*) to get wrong; **~ i calcoli** to make a mistake in the calculations; **~ indirizzo** to get the wrong address; **~ strada** to take the wrong road; **~ treno** to catch the wrong train **II.** *vi, vr:* -**rsi** to make a mistake; **~ a leggere/scrivere** to read/write sth wrong; **sbagliando s'impara** *prov* you live and learn
sbagliato, -a [zbaʎ·'ʎa:·to] *agg* wrong; **giudizio ~** erroneous judgment; **investimento ~** bad investment
sbaglio ['zbaʎ·ʎo] <-gli> *m* mistake; **per ~** by mistake
sbalestrato, -a [zba·les·'tra:·to] *agg* unsettled
sballare [zbal·'la:·re] *vt* (*merce, pacco*) to unpack
sballato, -a [zbal·'la:·to] *agg fam* wacko
sballo ['zbal·lo] **I.** *m sl* blast; **che ~** what a blast **II.** *agg sl* (*fantastico*) **da ~** fantastic
sballottamento [zbal·lot·ta·'men·to] *m* **1.** (*di oggetti, persone*) bouncing around **2.** *fig* back-and-forth
sballottare [zbal·lot·'ta:·re] *vt* to toss (around)
sbalordimento [zba·lor·di·'men·to] *m* (*incredulità*) amazement
sbalordire [zba·lor·'di:·re] <sbalordisco> *vt* (*stupire profondamente*) to amaze
sbalorditivo, -a [zba·lor·di·'ti:·vo] *agg* (*sor-*

prendente) incredible
sbalzare [zbal·'tsa:·re] *vt* avere (*da auto, cavallo*) to throw
sbalzo ['zbal·tso] *m* **1.** (*spostamento*) jolt **2.** *fig* (*oscillazione: di temperatura*) change **3.** (*lavorazione*) embossing
sbancare [zbaŋ·'ka:·re] *vt* (*banco*) to break the bank; *fig* (*persona*) to clean out
sbandamento [zban·da·'men·to] *m* **1.** MOT skid **2.** *fig* confusion; **avere un momento di ~** *fig* to lose it briefly
sbandare [zban·'da:·re] *vi* (*auto*) to skid
sbandato, -a [zban·'da:·to] **I.** *agg fig* (*gioventù*) wild **II.** *m, f* misfit
sbandierare [zban·die·'ra:·re] *vt* **1.** (*bandiera, vessilli*) to wave **2.** *fig* to flaunt; **e non andare a sbandierarlo a tutti!** and don't go telling everyone about it!
sbando ['zban·do] *m* **allo ~** floundering
sbaraccare [zba·rak·'ka:·re] *vt fam* **1.** (*togliere di mezzo*) to clear away **2.** (*smontare tutto*) to clear out
sbaragliare [zba·raʎ·'ʎa:·vre] *vt* **1.** MIL to rout **2.** SPORT, POL to defeat **3.** *fig* to beat
sbaraglio [zba·'raʎ·ʎo] <-gli> *m* **gettarsi** [*o* **buttarsi**] **allo ~** to plunge recklessly into sth; **mandare allo ~ qu** to put sb in danger
sbarazzarsi [zba·rat·'tsa:r·si] *vr* **~ di qu/qc** to get rid of sb/sth
sbarazzino, -a [zba·rat·'tsi:·no] **I.** *m, f* (*ragazzo*) scamp **II.** *agg* (*sorriso*) cheeky; (*pettinatura*) gamine; (*carattere*) impish
sbarbarsi [zbar·'ba:r·si] *vr:* -**rsi** to shave
sbarbatello [zbar·ba·'tɛl·lo] *m* beardless youth
sbarcare [zbar·'ka:·re] **I.** *vt* avere **1.** (*passeggeri*) to disembark; (*merce*) to unload **2.** (*loc*) **~ il lunario** to make ends meet **II.** *vi essere* NAUT to disembark; AERO to get off
sbarco ['zbar·ko] <-chi> *m* **1.** (*atto*) disembarkation; (*di merci*) unloading **2.** MIL landing
sbarra ['zbar·ra] *f* **1.** SPORT (*gener*) bar; **essere dietro le -e** *fig* to be behind bars **2.** (*barriera*) barrier **3.** TYP slash
sbarramento [zbar·ra·'men·to] *m* **1.** (*atto*) closing off **2.** (*barriera*) barrier
sbarrare [zbar·'ra:·re] *vt* **1.** (*chiudere*) to close off **2.** (*assegno*) to endorse **3.** (*occhi*) to widen
sbarrato, -a [zbar·'ra:·to] *agg* **1.** (*bloccato*) closed **2.** FIN **assegno ~** endorsed check **3.** (*occhi*) wide
sbarretta [zbar·'ret·ta] *f* (*segno grafico*) slash
sbatacchiare [zba·tak·'kia:·re] **I.** *vt* to bang **II.** *vi* to bang
sbattere ['zbat·te·re] **I.** *vt* **1.** (*panni, tappeti*) to beat **2.** (*ali*) to flap **3.** (*battere forte*) to slam; **~ qc sul tavolo** to slam sth down on the table **4.** (*urtare*) to bang; **non sapere dove ~ la testa** *fig* to not know which way to turn **5.** CULIN to whip **II.** *vi* **1.** (*porta*) to bang **2.** (*urtare*) **~ contro qc** to bang into sth **III.** *vr* **sbattersene** *vulg* to not give a damn
sbattitore [zbat·ti·'to:·re] *m* beater
sbattuto, -a [zbat·'tu:·to] *agg* **1.** CULIN beaten

S

2. (*viso*) worn out

sbavare [zba·'va:·re] *vi* **1.** (*dalla bocca*) to drool **2.** (*colore*) to run

sbavatura [zba·va·'tu:·ra] *f* **1.** (*di colore*) bleeding **2.** *fig* flaw

sbellicarsi [zbel·li·'kar·si] *vr* ~ **dalle risate** to kill oneself laughing

sberla ['zbɛr·la] *f fam* slap; **prendere a -e qu** to slap sb

sberleffo [zber·'lɛf·fo] *m* grimace

sbevazzare [zbe·vat·'tsa:·re] *vi fam* to booze

sbiadire [zbia·'di:·re] <sbiadisco> I. *vi essere* to fade II. *vr:* **-rsi** to fade

sbiadito, -a [zbia·'di:·to] *agg* **1.** (*colore, tessuto*) faded **2.** *fig* (*ricordo*) faint; (*stile*) colorless

sbiancare [zbiaɲ·'ka:·re] I. *vt avere* (*abiti*) to bleach II. *vr:* **-rsi** *fig* (*in volto*) to go pale

sbieco ['zbiɛ:·ko] *m* **guardare qu di** ~ to look askance at sb

sbieco, -a <-chi, -che> *agg* (*muro, linea, inquadratura*) sloping

sbigottimento [zbi·got·ti·'men·to] *m* (*sgomento*) dismay

sbigottire [zbi·got·'ti:·re] <sbigottisco> *vt avere* (*rendere sgomento*) to dismay

sbilanciamento [zbi·lan·tʃa·'men·to] *m* **1.** (*disequilibrio*) displacement **2.** (*propensione per: persona, proposta*) bias

sbilanciare [zbi·lan·'tʃa:·re] I. *vt a. fig* to throw off balance II. *vr:* **-rsi** (*esporsi troppo*) to compromise oneself

sbilancio [zbi·'lan·tʃo] *m* COM deficit

sbilenco, -a [zbi·'lɛŋ·ko/zbi·'leŋ·ko] <-chi, -che> *agg* (*cane, salto, edificio*) crooked

sbirciare [zbir·'tʃa:·re] *vt* (*guardare di nascosto*) to peep

sbirciata [zbir·'tʃa:·ta] *f* (*rapido sguardo*) peep

sbirro ['zbir·ro] *m pej* cop

sbizzarrirsi [zbid·dzar·'rir·si] <mi sbizzarrisco> *vr* to amuse oneself; ~ **a fare qc** to amuse oneself (by) doing sth

sbloccare [zblok·'ka:·re] I. *vt* **1.** (*cancello, catena*) to undo; (*cambio, ingranaggio*) to release **2.** *fig* (*situazione*) to unblock; (*partita*) to open up **3.** (*fondo, finanziamento, aiuti*) to free up II. *vr* **1.** (*computer*) to unfreeze; (*chiavistello*) to come free **2.** *fig* (*situazione, problema*) to be resolved; (*partita*) to open up; (*traffico*) to start moving again

sblocco ['zblɔk·ko] <-cchi> *m* **1.** TEL (*di cellulare*) unblocking **2.** (*di merci*) release **3.** *fig* (*di situazione, risultato*) resolution

sbobba ['zbɔb·ba] *f pej, fam* slop

sbobinare [zbo·bi·'na:·re] *vt* (*trascrivere*) to transcribe

sboccare [zbok·'ka:·re] *vi essere* **1.** (*fiume*) to flow; (*strada*) to come out **2.** *fig* (*discussione*) to end up

sboccato, -a [zbok·'ka:·to] *agg* foul-mouthed

sbocciare [zbot·'tʃa:·re] *vi essere* **1.** (*fiore*) to bloom **2.** *fig* (*persona, bellezza*) to blossom

sbocco ['zbok·ko] <-cchi> *m* **1.** (*di fiume*)

mouth; (*di strada*) end; **strada senza** ~ dead end **2.** *fig* (*soluzione*) resolution

sbollire [zbol·'li:·re] <sbollisco *o* sbollo> *vi essere o avere* **1.** CULIN to stop boiling **2.** *fig* (*placarsi: rabbia*) to cool

sbolognare [zbo·loɲ·'ɲa:·re] *vt fam* **1.** (*rifilare*) ~ **qc a qu** to palm sth off on sb **2.** *fig* (*levarsi di torno*) to get rid of

sboom [zbum] <-> *m* COM slump

sbornia ['zbɔr·nia] <-ie> *f fam* **prendersi una** ~ to get hammered

sborsare [zbor·'sa:·re] *vt* (*pagare*) to pay out

sbottare [zbot·'ta:·re] *vi essere fam* (*scoppiare*) to explode; ~ **a ridere** *fam* to burst out laughing; ~ **a piangere** *fam* to burst into tears

sbotto ['zbɔt·to] *m fam* (*sfogo*) outburst

sbottonare [zbot·to·'na:·re] I. *vt* (*camicia, giacca*) to undo II. *vr fig, fam* (*confidarsi*) to unburden oneself

sbracato, -a [zbra·'ka:·to] *agg fam* **1.** (*vestito male*) disheveled **2.** (*disordinato: vita*) slovenly **3.** (*sguaiato: allegria, risate*) unbridled

sbracciarsi [zbrat·'tʃar·si] *vr* **1.** (*agitare le braccia*) to wave (one's arms) **2.** *fig* (*darsi da fare*) to busy oneself

sbracciato, -a [zbrat·'tʃa:·to] *agg* **1.** (*senza maniche: abito, camicia*) sleeveless **2.** (*persona*) bare-armed

sbraitare [zbrai·'ta:·re] *vi fam* to yell

sbranare [zbra·'na:·re] I. *vt* **1.** (*fare a pezzi*) to tear to pieces **2.** *fig* (*distruggere: avversario*) to hammer; (*a parole*) to tear to pieces II. *vr:* **-rsi** *a. fig* to tear one another to pieces

sbriciolare [zbri·tʃo·'la:·re] I. *vt* (*pane, biscotti*) to crumble up II. *vr:* **-rsi** *a. fig* to crumble

sbrigare [zbri·'ga:·re] I. *vt* (*faccenda, questione*) to deal with II. *vr:* **-rsi** **1.** (*affrettarsi*) to hurry up **2.** *fam* to deal with sth oneself

sbrigativo, -a [zbri·ga·'ti:·vo] *agg* **1.** (*persona, modi*) brusque; (*risposta*) quick **2.** *pej* (*superficiale: soluzione, approccio*) hasty

sbrinare [zbri·'na:·re] *vt* (*frigorifero*) to defrost

sbrinatore [zbri·na·'to:·re] *m* defroster

sbrindellato, -a [zbrin·del·'la:·to] *agg* (*pantaloni, giacca*) tattered

sbrodolare [zbro·do·'la:·re] I. *vt* (*vestito, tovaglia*) to dirty II. *vr:* **-rsi** to dirty oneself

sbrodolone, -a [zbro·do·'lo:·ne] *m, f fam* messy eater

sbrogliare [zbroʎ·'ʎa:·re] *vt* **1.** (*matassa, filo*) to untangle **2.** *fig* (*questione, situazione*) to resolve **3.** (*loc*) ~ **la matassa** to solve the problem

sbronza ['zbron·tsa/'zbron·dza] *f fam* **prendersi una** ~ to get hammered

sbronzarsi [zbron·'tsar·si/zbron·'dzar·si] *vr fam* to get hammered

sbronzo, -a ['zbron·tso/'zbron·dzo] *agg fam* hammered

sbruffone, -a [zbruf·'fo:·ne] *m, f pej, fam* braggart

sbucare [zbu·'ka:·re] *vi essere* **1.** (*animale*) to pop out **2.** (*apparire improvvisamente*) to appear

sbucciapatate [zbut·tʃa·pa·'ta:·te] <-> *m* potato peeler

sbucciare [zbut·'tʃa:·re] *vt* **1.** (*patate, castagne*) to peel **2.** MED to skin

sbucciatura [zbut·tʃa·'tu:·ra] *f* **1.** (*lo sbucciare*) peeling **2.** *fam* (*graffio*) graze

sbudellare [zbu·del·'la:·re] **I.** *vt* (*pollo, pesce*) to clean **II.** *vr* **-rsi dalle risate** *fam* to laugh one's head off

sbuffare [zbuf·'fa:·re] *vi* **1.** (*persona*) to snort **2.** (*locomotiva*) to puff

sbuffo ['zbuf·fo] *m* **1.** (*lo sbuffare*) snort **2.** (*di vento*) gust **3.** (*di fumo, vapore*) puff **4.** (*di vestiti*) **maniche a ~** puffed sleeves

scabbia ['skab·bia] <-ie> *f* scabies *sing*

scabro, -a ['ska:·bro] *agg* (*superficie*) rough

scabrosità [ska·bro·si·'ta] <-> *f* **1.** (*di superficie*) roughness **2.** *fig* (*impudicizia*) indecency

scabroso, -a [ska·'bro:·so] *agg* **1.** (*strada*) uneven **2.** *fig* (*tema, argomento*) delicate **3.** *fig* (*impudico: fatto*) indecent

scacchiera [skak·'kiɛ:·ra] *f* chessboard

scacchiere [skak·'kiɛ:·re] *m* MIL, POL theater

scacchista [skak·'kis·ta] <-i *m*, -e *f*> *mf* chess player

scacciacani [skat·tʃa·'ka:·ni] **I.** <-> *m o f* blank gun **II.** <inv> *agg* **pistola ~** blank gun

scacciapensieri [skat·tʃa·pen·'siɛ:·ri] <-> *m* Jew's harp

scacciare [skat·'tʃa:·re] *vt* **1.** (*persone*) to throw out **2.** *fig* (*noia, malinconia*) to chase away

scacco ['skak·ko] <-cchi> *m* **1.** *pl* (*gioco*) chess *sing;* **giocare a -cchi** to play chess **2.** (*mossa*) checkmate **3.** *fig* (*sconfitta*) setback **4.** (*quadratino*) **a -cchi** checked

scaccomatto, scacco matto [skak·ko·'mat·to] *m* (*mossa vincente*) checkmate; **dare ~ a qu** *a. fig* to checkmate sb

scaddi ['skad·di] *1. pers sing pass rem di* **scadere**

scadente [ska·'dɛn·te] *agg* **1.** (*voto*) unsatisfactory **2.** (*merce*) shoddy; (*prodotto*) poor-quality

scadenza [ska·'dɛn·tsa] *f* **1.** (*di abbonamento, contratto*) expiry; (*di bando*) deadline **2.** FIN due date **3.** (*periodo*) timescale; **a breve/lunga ~** short-/long-term **4.** (*di alimento*) expiration date

scadenzare [ska·den·'tsa:·re] *vt* ADM to schedule

scadere [ska·'de:·re] <scado, scaddi, scaduto> *vi essere* **1.** COM, ADM to expire **2.** (*perdere valore*) to decline

scafandro [ska·'fan·dro] *m* protective suit; (*dei palombari*) diving suit; (*degli astronauti*) spacesuit

scaffale [skaf·'fa:·le] *m* (*per libri*) set of shelves

scafo ['ska:·fo] *m* hull

scagionare [ska·dʒo·'na:·re] **I.** *vt* (*discolpare*) to exonerate **II.** *vr:* **-rsi** (*discolparsi: da accusa*) to clear oneself

scaglia ['ska·ʎ·ʎa] <-glie> *f* **1.** (*di pesce*) scale **2.** (*di pietra, di vetro*) splinter; (*di cioccolato, di formaggio*) flake

scagliare [ska·ʎ·'ʎa:·re] **I.** *vt* (*lanciare*) to throw **II.** *vr:* **-rsi 1.** (*aggredire, avventarsi*) to hurl oneself **2.** (*inveire*) to hurl abuse

scaglionamento [ska·ʎ·ʎo·na·'men·to] *m* (*distribuzione*) staggering

scaglionare [ska·ʎ·ʎo·'na:·re] *vt* (*distribuire nel tempo*) to stagger

scaglione [ska·ʎ·'ʎo:·ne] *m* **1.** (*gruppo*) batch; **a -i** in groups **2.** FIN bracket; **~ d'imposta** tax bracket

scagnozzo, -a [skaɲ·'ɲɔt·tso] *m, f* hanger-on

scala ['ska:·la] *f* **1.** ARCH staircase; **~ a chiocciola** spiral staircase; **~ di servizio** back stairs; **~ mobile** escalator **2.** (*apparecchio*) ladder **3.** *a. fig* TEC, PHYS, MUS, GEOG scale; **~ Fahrenheit** Fahrenheit scale; **~ Richter** Richter scale; **~ Celsius/centigrada** Celsius/centigrade scale; **in ~ ridotta** to scale; **su larga ~** *fig* on a grand scale; **economia di ~** economy of scale; **~ in do maggiore** C major scale **4.** COM **~ mobile** escalator

scalare[1] [ska·'la:·re] *agg* **1.** (*disposto a scala*) ladderlike **2.** MATH scalar

scalare[2] *vt* **1.** (*montagna*) to climb; **~ un muro** to climb over **2.** COM (*scontare*) to take off **3.** (*capelli*) to layer **4.** MOT (*marcia*) to downshift

scalata [ska·'la:·ta] *f* (*di montagna*) ascent

scalatore, -trice [ska·la·'to:·re] *m, f* (*alpinismo, ciclismo*) climber

scalciare [skal·'tʃa:·re] *vi* (*tirar calci*) to kick

scalcinato, -a [skal·tʃi·'na:·to] *agg* **1.** (*muro, casa*) unplastered **2.** *fig* (*persona, aspetto*) shabby

scaldabanchi [skal·da·'baŋ·ki] <-> *mf pej* seat warmer

scaldaletto [skal·da·'lɛt·to] <-i> *m* bedwarmer

scaldare [skal·'da:·re] **I.** *vt* **1.** (*acqua*) to boil; (*minestra*) to heat (up); (*stanza, motore*) to warm (up) **2.** *fig* (*agitare: animi, testa*) to stir up **II.** *vr:* **-rsi 1.** *a.* SPORT (*diventare caldo*) to warm up **2.** *fig* (*accalorarsi, irritarsi*) to grow heated

scaldata [skal·'da:·ta] *f* **dare una ~ all'arrosto** to warm the roast through

scaldavivande [skal·da·vi·'van·de] <-> *m* dishwarmer

scaletta [ska·'let·ta] *f* **1.** (*piccola scala*) small staircase; (*a pioli*) small ladder **2.** THEAT, FILM treatment **3.** (*abbozzo*) summary

scalfire [skal·'fi:·re] <scalfisco> *vt fig* (*danneggiare, intaccare: immagine*) to tarnish; (*entusiasmo*) to diminish

scalinata [ska·li·'na:·ta] *f* flight of steps

scalino [ska·'li:·no] *m* step

scalmanato, -a [skal·ma·'na:·to] **I.** *agg* (*turbolento: tifoso*) fanatical **II.** *m, f* (*persona turbolenta*) lunatic

scalo ['ska:·lo] *m* **1.** NAUT slipway **2.** FERR yard;

S

~ merci freight yard **3.** AERO stopover; **volo senza ~** nonstop flight; **fare ~** to make a stopover

scalogna [ska·'loɲ·ɲa] *f fam* bad luck

scalognato, -a [ska·loɲ·'ɲa:·to] *fam* **I.** *agg* unlucky **II.** *m, f* unlucky person

scalogno [ska·'loɲ·ɲo] *m* shallot

scalone [ska·'lo:·ne] *m* (*di palazzo*) staircase

scaloppa, scaloppina [ska·'lɔp·pa, ska·lop·'pi:·na] *f* escalope

scalpellare [skal·pel·'la:·re] *vt* (*incidere: marmo, roccia*) to chisel

scalpellino [skal·pel·'li:·no] *m* stonemason

scalpello [skal·'pɛl·lo] *m* (*gener*) chisel; MED scalpel

scalpiccio [skal·pit·'tʃi:·o] <-ccii> *m* (*di piedi*) shuffling

scalpitare [skal·pi·'ta:·re] *vi* **1.** ZOO to paw the ground **2.** *fig, scherz* (*essere impazienti*) to be unable to wait; **sto scalpitando!** I can't wait!

scalpitio [skal·pi·'ti:·o] <-ii> *m* pawing

scalpo ['skal·po] *m* scalp; **fare lo ~ a qu** to scalp sb

scalpore [skal·'po:·re] *m* sensation; **destare** [*o* **fare**] **~** to cause a sensation

scaltrezza [skal·'tret·tsa] *f* (*astuzia*) cunning

scaltro, -a ['skal·tro] *agg* (*furbo*) cunning

scalzare [skal·'tsa:·re] *vt* **1.** (*albero*) to bare the roots of; (*radice*) to bare **2.** *fig* (*autorità, potere*) to undermine **3.** *fig* (*da posizione, classifica, potere*) to unseat

scalzo, -a ['skal·tso] *agg* barefoot; **a piedi -i** barefoot

scambiare [skam·'bia:·re] **I.** *vt* **1.** (*confondere*) **~ qu per qu** to mistake sb for sb; **~ qc per qc** *fig* to mistake sth for sth **2.** (*fare uno scambio*) to exchange; **~ qc con qc** to exchange sth for sth **3.** (*impressioni, opinioni*) to share; (*parole*) to exchange; **~ due chiacchiere** to have a chat **II.** *vr:* **-rsi 1.** (*sostituirsi*) to change over; **-rsi di posto** to change places **2.** (*dare l'un l'altro*) to exchange

scambio ['skam·bio] <-i> *m* **1.** (*di persona*) case of mistaken identity **2.** (*di doni, cortesie, idee*) exchange; **~ culturale** cultural exchange **3.** COM trade; **-i commerciali** trade; **libero ~** free trade **4.** FERR switches *pl*

scamiciato [ska·mi·'tʃa:·to] *m* jumper

scamiciato, -a *agg* in shirt sleeves

scamorza [ska·'mɔr·tsa] *f* **1.** CULIN *soft cheese in a pear shape* **2.** *fig, scherz* wimp

scamosciato, -a [ska·moʃ·'ʃa:·to] *agg* suede

scampagnata [skam·paɲ·'ɲa:·ta] *f fam* trip to the country

scampanata [skam·pa·'na:·ta] *f* peal (of bells)

scampanellare [skam·pa·nel·'la:·re] *vi* to ring loudly

scampanellata [skam·pa·nel·'la:·ta] *f* ring(ing)

scampare [skam·'pa:·re] **I.** *vi essere* (*sfuggire: a pericolo, morte, massacro*) to escape **II.** *vt avere* (*sfuggire a: morte, prigione*) to escape; **scamparla** *fam* to have a lucky escape

scampo ['skam·po] *m* **1.** (*salvezza*) safety; (*via d'uscita*); **senza ~** with no way out **2.** ZOO Norway lobster; **risotto agli -i** risotto with scampi

scampolo ['skam·po·lo] *m* (*di stoffa*) remnant

scanalare [ska·na·'la:·re] *vt* to make a groove in

scanalatura [ska·na·la·'tu:·ra] *f* **1.** (*incavo*) groove **2.** (*operazione*) grooving

scandagliare [skan·daʎ·'ʎa:·re] *vt* **1.** NAUT to sound **2.** *fig* (*analizzare in profondità*) to probe

scandaglio [skan·'daʎ·ʎo] <-gli> *m* **1.** NAUT (*strumento*) sounding line **2.** *fig* (*analisi profonda*) probing

scandalistico, -a [skan·da·'lis·ti·ko] <-ci, -che> *agg* scandalmongering; **giornale ~** tabloid

scandalizzare [skan·da·lid·'dza:·re] **I.** *vt* (*suscitare sdegno*) to scandalize **II.** *vr* (*provare sdegno*) **-rsi di qc** to be scandalized by sth

scandalo ['skan·da·lo] *m* scandal

scandaloso, -a [skan·da·'lo:·so] *agg* (*che suscita sdegno*) scandalous

Scandinavia [skan·di·'na:·via] *f* Scandinavia

scandinavo, -a [skan·di·'na:·vo] **I.** *agg* Scandinavian **II.** *m, f* Scandinavian

scandire [skan·'di:·re] <scandisco> *vt* **1.** (*dividere a intervalli*) to mark out **2.** *fig* (*parole, nome*) to pronounce

scannare [skan·'na:·re] **I.** *vt* **1.** (*animale, persona*) to slaughter **2.** *fig* (*opprimere*) to rip off **II.** *vr:* **-rsi** (*darsi battaglia: persone, popoli*) to slaughter one another

scannatoio [skan·na·'to:·io] <-oi> *m a. fig, pej* slaughterhouse

scanner ['skan·ner] <- *o* scanners> *m* scanner

scannerizzare [skan·ne·rid·'dza:·re] *vt* COMPUT to scan

scanning ['skan·niŋ] <-> *m* COMPUT scanning; **fare lo ~ di qc** to scan sth

scansafatiche [skan·sa·fa·'ti:·ke] <-> *mf fam* lazybones

scansare [skan·'sa:·re] **I.** *vt* **1.** (*schivare*) **~ qu/qc** to dodge sb/sth **2.** (*evitare*) **~ qu/qc** to avoid sb/sth **II.** *vr:* **-rsi** (*spostarsi*) to move

scansione [skan·'sio:·ne] *f* **1.** LIT scansion **2.** COMPUT, TV scanning

scanso ['skan·so] *m* **a ~ di qc** in order to avoid; **a ~ di equivoci** in order to avoid misunderstandings

scantinato [skan·ti·'na:·to] *m* basement

scanzonato, -a [skan·tso·'na:·to] *agg* easygoing

scapaccione [ska·pat·'tʃo:·ne] *m* smack

scapestrato, -a [ska·pes·'tra:·to] **I.** *agg* (*dissoluto*) good-for-nothing **II.** *m, f fam* good-for-nothing

scapigliato, -a [ska·piʎ·'ʎa:·to] *agg* **1.** (*arruffato*) disheveled **2.** *fig* dissolute

scapito ['ska:·pi·to] *m* **a ~ di** at the expense of

scapola ['ska:·po·la] *f* shoulder blade

scapolo ['ska:·po·lo] *m* bachelor

scapolo, -a *agg* unmarried

scapolone [ska·po·'lo:·ne] *m fam* confirmed bachelor

scappamento [skap·pa·'men·to] *m* MOT exhaust

scappare [skap·'pa:·re] *vi essere* **1.** (*darsi alla fuga*) to flee **2.** (*di prigione*) to escape **3.** (*andar via in fretta*) to run **4.** *fig* (*sfuggire*) to slip out; **gli è scappato di mente** he [*o* she] has forgotten it; **mi scappa la pazienza** I've run out of patience **5.** *fam* (*loc*) **mi scappa la pipì!** I'm bursting; **mi scappa da ridere** I can't help laughing

scappata [skap·'pa:·ta] *f* (*breve visita*) **ho fatto una ~ dalla nonna** I popped in to see grandma; **ho fatto una ~ in ufficio** I popped into the office; **abbiamo fatto una ~ a Asolo** we popped over to Asolo

scappatella [skap·pa·'tɛl·la] *f* adventure

scappatoia [skap·pa·'to:·ia] <-oie> *f* way out

scarabeo [ska·ra·'bɛ:·o] *m* **1.** (*insetto*) scarab beetle **2.** (*gioiello*) scarab **3.** (*gioco*) Scarabeo® Scrabble®

scarabocchiare [ska·ra·bok·'kia:·re] *vt* to scribble

scarabocchio [ska·ra·'bɔk·kio] <-cchi> *m* **1.** (*parola*) scribble **2.** (*disegno*) doodle

scarafaggio [ska·ra·'fad·dʒo] <-ggi> *m* cockroach

scaramanzia [ska·ra·man·'tsi:·a] <-ie> *f* **per ~** for luck

scaramuccia [ska·ra·'mut·tʃa] <-cce> *f* (*litigio*) squabble

scaraventare [ska·ra·ven·'ta:·re] **I.** *vt* (*gettare con impeto*) to hurl **II.** *vr*: **-rsi** (*gettarsi con impeto*) to hurl oneself

scarcassato, -a [skar·kas·'sa:·to] *agg fam* (*auto, aereo, computer*) rickety

scarcerare [skar·tʃe·'ra:·re] *vt* to release (from prison)

scarcerazione [skar·tʃe·rat·'tsio:·ne] *f* release

scardinare [skar·di·'na:·re] *vt* **1.** (*porta, finestra*) to take off its hinges **2.** (*demolire: sistema, modello, concetto*) to demolish

scarica ['ska:·ri·ka] <-che> *f* **1.** MIL **una ~ di mitra** a burst of machine-gun fire **2.** *fig* (*di grandine, pugni*) shower; (*bestemmie*) torrent **3.** EL discharge

scaricabarili [ska·ri·ka·ba·'ri:·li] <-> *m* **fare a ~** *fig, fam* to blame one another

scaricabile *agg* COMPUT downloadable

scaricamento [ska·ri·ka·'men·to] *m* **1.** (*di merci*) unloading **2.** (*di file, software*) download

scaricare [ska·ri·'ka:·re] **I.** *vt* **1.** (*macchina, merci, bagagli*) to unload **2.** (*arma*) to unload; (*sparare*) to discharge **3.** (*riversare su altri: responsabilità*) to offload **4.** COMPUT to download **5.** (*loc*) **~ la coscienza** to ease one's conscience; **~ la propria collera su qu** to take out one's anger on sb; **~ la colpa addosso a qu** to lay the blame on sb; **~ qu** to dump sb

II. *vr*: **-rsi 1.** (*peso*) to unburden oneself **2.** *fig* (*tensione nervosa*) to let off **3.** (*rilassarsi*) to unwind **4.** (*batteria, accumulatore*) to go flat; (*orologio*) to wind down

scaricatore, -trice *m*, *f* laborer; **~ di porto** longshoreman

scarico ['ska:·ri·ko] *m* **1.** (*di merci, nave, vagone*) unloading **2.** (*di rifiuti*) dumping; (*luogo*) garbage dump; **-chi industriali** industrial waste **3.** (*di acque*) draining **4.** MOT discharge; (*impianto*) exhaust

scarico, -a <-chi, -che> *agg* **1.** (*carro*) empty **2.** (*batteria*) dead; (*orologio*) wound down **3.** *fig* (*stanco*) run down

scarlattina [skar·lat·'ti:·na] *f* scarlet fever

scarlatto, -a *agg* scarlet

scarno, -a ['skar·no] *agg* **1.** (*viso, mani*) bony **2.** *fig* (*povero: programma, sito, arredamento*) meager

scarpa ['skar·pa] *f* (*calzatura*) shoe; **~ da ginnastica** sneakers; **~ di cuoio** leather shoes; **numero di -e** shoe size; **fare le -e a qu** *fig* to stab sb in the back

scarpata [skar·'pa:·ta] *f* escarpment

scarpiera [skar·'piɛ:·ra] *f* shoe rack

scarpinare [skar·pi·'na:·re] *vi fam* to trek

scarpinata [skar·pi·'na:·ta] *f fam* trek

scarpone [skar·'po:·ne] *m* (walking) boot; **~ da sci** ski boot; **~ da montagna** climbing boot

scarrozzare [ska·rot·'tsa:·re] *vt, vi* to drive around

scarseggiare [skar·sed·'dʒa:·re] *vi* to be lacking; **~ di** to lack

scarsezza [skar·'set·tsa] *f* (*insufficienza*) inadequacy

scarsità [skar·si·'ta] <-> *f* (*mancanza*) scarcity

scarso, -a ['skar·so] *agg* **1.** (*insufficiente: risultato, voto, interesse*) poor; **essere ~ in inglese** to not be very good at English **2.** (*chilo, metro, anno*) just under; **è lungo un metro ~** it's just under a meter long

scartabellare [skar·ta·bel·'la:·re] *vt* (*leggere disordinatamente*) to skim through

scartamento [skar·ta·'men·to] *m* FERR gauge

scartare [skar·'ta:·re] *vt* **1.** (*pacco, regalo*) to unwrap **2.** *fig* (*escludere: ipotesi, proposta, idea*) to reject **3.** (*nelle carte*) to discard **4.** SPORT to dodge

scarto ['skar·to] *m* **1.** (*eliminazione*) dumping **2.** (*di produzione, fabbrica, magazzino*) **materiali di ~** waste materials; **-i di magazzino** seconds; *fig;* **essere uno ~ della società** to be an outcast **3.** (*nelle carte*) discard **4.** (*differenza*) gap

scartoffia [skar·'tɔf·fia] <-ie> *f pej, fam* pile of paper

scassare [skas·'sa:·re] **I.** *vt* **1.** *fam* (*rompere*) to wreck **2.** *fam* (*loc*) **non ~!** stop bugging me! **II.** *vr*: **-rsi** *fam* (*rompersi*) to be wrecked

scassinare [skas·si·'na:·re] *vt* to force

scassinatore, -trice [skas·si·na·'to:·re] *m, f* burglar

S

scasso ['skas·so] *m* breaking and entering; **furto con** ~ burglary

scatenante [ska·te·'nan·te] *agg* (*causa, motivo, fattore*) triggering

scatenare [ska·te·'na:·re] I. *vt* (*provocare: guerra, reazione, ira*) to trigger II. *vr:* **-rsi** 1. (*prorompere: battaglia, discussione*) to break out; (*tempesta, temporale*) to break 2. (*sfogarsi: bambini*) to let off steam

scatola ['ska:·to·la] *f* 1. (*di biscotti, delle scarpe*) tin; (*di carne, piselli*) can; **cibo in** ~ canned food 2. *fam* (*loc*) **rompere** [*o* **far girare**] **le -e a qc** to get on sb's nerves; **levarsi dalle -e** to get out 3. (*elemento, dispositivo*) ~ **cranica** cranium; AERO; ~ **nera** black box; MOT; ~ **dello sterzo** steering box

scatolame [ska·to·'la:·me] *m* CULIN canned goods

scatoletta [ska·to·'lɛt·ta] *f* box

scattante [skat·'tan·te] *agg* (*auto, motore*) speedy

scattare [skat·'ta:·re] I. *vi essere o avere* 1. (*congegno*) to be tripped; (*allarme*) to go off 2. (*avere inizio: operazione*) to begin; (*diritto, legge*) to come into effect 3. (*muoversi repentinamente: persona*) to leap; ~ **in piedi** to jump to one's feet; ~ **sull'attenti** to leap to attention 4. MOT to go 5. *fig* (*per l'ira*) to fly off the handle 6. SPORT (*al via*) to spring forward; (*durante la corsa*) to put a spurt on II. *vt avere* (*foto*) to take

scattista [skat·'tis·ta] <-i *m*, -e *f*> *mf* SPORT sprinter

scatto ['skat·to] *m* 1. (*dispositivo*) release; **serratura a** ~ spring lock 2. (*moto brusco*) jump 3. SPORT spurt 4. MOT acceleration 5. *fig* (*d'ira*) outburst; **avere uno** ~ **di rabbia** to fly off the handle 6. *fig* (*aumento*) increment; ~ **di anzianità** long-service increment 7. TEL unit

scaturire [ska·tu·'ri:·re] <scaturisco> *vi essere* 1. (*liquidi*) to gush 2. *fig* (*derivare*) to derive

scavalcare [ska·val·'ka:·re] *vt* 1. (*ostacolo*) to climb over 2. *fig* (*saltare*) ~ **qu** to bypass sb 3. *fig* (*superare: in una competizione*) to pass; (*nella professione*) to be promoted over

scavare [ska·'va:·re] *vt* 1. (*fosso, galleria, pozzo*) to dig 2. (*legno, pietra*) to hollow out 3. (*città, tesoro*) to excavate 4. *fig* (*indagare*) in investigate

scavatore, -trice [ska·va·'to:·re] *m, f* digger

scavezzacollo [ska·vet·tsa·'kɔl·lo] <-> *m, f* hothead

scavo ['ska:·vo] *m* excavation

scazzato, -a [skat·'tsa:·to] *agg vulg* pissed (off)

scegliere ['ʃeʎ·ʎe·re] <scelgo, scelsi, scelto> *vt* to choose

sceicco [ʃe·'ik·ko] <-cchi> *m* sheik

scelgo ['ʃel·go] *1. pers sing pr di* **scegliere**

scelleratezza [ʃel·le·ra·'tet·tsa] *f* 1. (*inclinazione al male*) wickedness 2. (*azione*) wicked act

scellerato, -a [ʃel·le·'ra:·to] I. *agg* (*patto,*

gesto, progetto) wicked II. *m, f* villain

scelsi ['ʃel·si] *1. pers sing pass rem di* **scegliere**

scelta ['ʃel·ta] *f* choice; **fare una buona/cattiva** ~ to make a good/bad choice; **a** ~ of one's choice; **a** ~ **dello studente** of the student's choice; **merce di prima/seconda** ~ top quality products; **merce di seconda** ~ second-class products

scelto, -a ['ʃel·to] I. *pp di* **scegliere** II. *agg* 1. (*vestito, prodotto, facoltà*) selected 2. (*di buona qualità: vino, frutta, merce*) top quality 3. (*addestrato: tiratore, guardia*) **tiratore** ~ marksman; **guardia -a** elite guard

scemare [ʃe·'ma:·re] *vi essere* (*entusiasmo, interesse, desiderio*) to decline

scemata [ʃe·'ma:·ta] *f fam* (*sciocchezza*) stupid thing

scemenza [ʃe·'mɛn·tsa] *f* (*sciocchezza*) stupid thing

scemo, -a ['ʃe:·mo] I. *agg* stupid II. *m, f* idiot; ~ **del villaggio** village idiot

scempio ['ʃem·pio] *m* 1. (*massacro*) massacre 2. *fig* (*rovina: di ambiente, patrimonio artistico*) destruction

scena ['ʃɛ:·na] *f* 1. (*palcoscenico*) stage; **calcare le -e** to tread the boards; **entrare in** ~ to come on stage; *fig* to come on the scene; **essere di** ~ to be on; *fig* to take the stage; **mettere in** ~ to stage 2. *a. fig* scene; **colpo di** ~ coup de théâtre; *fig* dramatic turn of events; **la** ~ **del delitto** the scene of the crime; **fare -e** to make a scene; **scomparire dalla** ~ **politica** to disappear from the scene 3. (*loc*) **fare** ~ **muta** to not open one's mouth

scenario [ʃe·'na:·rio] <-i> *m* 1. THEAT setting; FILM location 2. (*paesaggio*) backdrop 3. POL background

scenata [ʃe·'na:·ta] *f* scene; **fare una** ~ **a qu** to make a scene

scendere ['ʃen·de·re] <scendo, scesi, sceso> *vi essere* 1. (*andare giù*) to go down; ~ **a valle** to go back down the mountain/hill; ~ **a patti con qu** *fig* to come to an agreement with sb 2. (*smontare: da macchina*) to get out of; (*da bus, treno*) to get off; (*da cavallo*) to dismount 3. (*essere in pendenza*) to descend 4. (*calare*) to drop; (*notte*) to fall; (*sole*) to set 5. (*di grado*) to decline 6. (*loc*) ~ **in piazza** to take to the streets; ~ **in campo** *a. fig* to take the field

scendiletto [ʃen·di·'lɛt·to] <-> *m* bedside rug

sceneggiare [ʃe·ned·'dʒa:·re] *vt* THEAT, FILM, TV to dramatize

sceneggiato [ʃe·ned·'dʒa:·to] *m* TV (television) drama

sceneggiato, -a *agg* (*soggetto*) dramatized

sceneggiatore, -trice [ʃe·ned·dʒa·'to:·re] *m, f* screenwriter

sceneggiatura [ʃe·ned·dʒa·'tu:·ra] *f* TV, RADIO, FILM screenplay

scenetta [ʃe·'net·ta] *f* sketch

scenico, -a ['ʃɛ:·ni·ko] <-ci, -che> *agg* (*spazio,*

effetto) stage; **realizzazione -a** staging

scenografia [ʃe·no·gra·'fiː·a] *f* **1.** (*tecnica*) set design **2.** (*elementi scenici*) scenery

scenografico, -a [ʃe·no·'graː·fi·ko] <-ci, -che> *agg* **1.** THEAT stage **2.** *fig* (*spettacolare*) spectacular

scenografo, -a [ʃe·'nɔː·gra·fo] *m*, *f* set designer

sceriffo [ʃe·'rifˑfo] *m* sheriff

scervellarsi [stʃer·vel·'larˑsi] *vr* ~ **su** [*o* **intorno a**] qc to rack one's brains over sth

scervellato, -a [stʃer·vel·'laː·to] **I.** *agg* (*privo di senno*) idiotic **II.** *m*, *f* idiot

scesi ['ʃeː·si] *1. pers sing pass rem di* **scendere**

sceso ['ʃeː·so] *pp di* **scendere**

scespiriano, -a [ʃes·pi·'riaː·no] *agg* (*dramma, personaggio, classico*) Shakespearean

scetticismo [ʃet·ti·'tʃiz·mo] *m* skepticism

scettico, -a ['ʃetˑti·ko] <-ci, -che> **I.** *agg* (*diffidente*) skeptical **II.** *m*, *f* (*persona scettica*) skeptic

scettro ['ʃetˑtro] *m* **1.** (*del re*) scepter **2.** *fig* (*potere, primato*) crown

scheda ['skɛː·da] *f* ADM card; ~ **elettorale** ballot paper; ~ **grafica** COMPUT graphics card; ~ **madre** COMPUT motherboard; ~ **magnetica** swipe card; ~ **perforata** punch card

schedare [ske·'daː·re] *vt* **1.** (*registrare*) to catalog **2.** ADM to put on record

schedario [ske·'daː·rio] <-i> *m* **1.** (*raccolta*) file **2.** (*mobile*) filing cabinet; (*dispositivo*) box file

schedato, -a [ske·'daː·to] *m*, *f* person with a police record

schedina [ske·'diː·na] *f* (*di Lotto*) ticket; (*di Totocalcio*) coupon

scheggia ['skedˑdʒa] <-gge> *f* (*di legno*) splinter

scheggiare [sked·'dʒaː·re] **I.** *vt* (*rovinare*) to shatter **II.** *vr:* **-rsi** (*rovinarsi*) to shatter

scheletrico, -a [ske·'lɛː·tri·ko] <-ci, -che> *agg* a. *fig* ANAT skeletal

scheletro ['skɛː·le·tro] *m* **1.** ANAT skeleton **2.** (*di nave, mobile*) frame **3.** (*di romanzo, racconto*) outline

schema ['skɛː·ma] <-i> *m* **1.** (*modello*) diagram **2.** JUR draft; ~ **di legge** bill **3.** *fig* (*mentale, della società*) pattern **4.** SPORT game plan

schematicità [ske·ma·ti·tʃi·'ta] <-> *f* over simplification

schematico, -a [ske·'maː·ti·ko] <-ci, -che> *agg* (*quadro, esempio, raffigurazione*) schematic

schematizzare [ske·ma·tid·'dzaː·re] *vt* to schematize

schematizzazione [ske·ma·tid·dzat·'tsio·ne] *f* schematization

scherma ['sker·ma] *f* fencing; **tirare di** ~ to fence

schermaglia [sker·'maʎˑʎa] <-glie> *f* (*disputa*) skirmish

schermare [sker·'maː·re] *vt* (*proteggere medi-*

ante schermo) to screen

schermata [sker·'maː·ta] *f* (*videata*) screen

schermo ['sker·mo] *m* a. *fig* screen; **diva dello** ~ screen goddess; **grande** ~ big screen; **piccolo** ~ small screen; ~ **a cristalli liquidi** liquid crystal screen; ~ **a colori** color screen

schernire [sker·'niː·re] <schernisco> *vt* (*deridere*) to mock

scherno ['sker·no] *m* (*derisione*) scorn; **farsi** ~ **di qu/qc** to sneer at sb/sth

scherzare [sker·'tsaː·re] *vi* to joke; ~ **col fuoco** to play with fire; **c'è poco da** ~ it's no laughing matter

scherzo ['sker·tso] *m* **1.** (*azione, parola scherzosa*) joke; ~ **da prete** *fam* stupid trick; **stare allo** ~ to take a joke; **per** ~ for fun; **neppure per** ~ not even in fun; **-i a parte!** seriously! **2.** (*sorpresa sgradevole*) trick **3.** *fig* (*impresa facile*) child's play

scherzoso, -a [sker·'tsoː·so] *agg* (*tono, brano*) jokey; (*persona*) fun

schiaccianoci [skiat·tʃa·'noː·tʃi] <-> *m* nutcracker

schiacciante [skiat·'tʃan·te] *agg* (*vittoria, prova*) overwhelming

schiacciapatate [skiat·tʃa·pa·'taː·te] <-> *m* potato masher

schiacciare [skiat·'tʃaː·re] *vt* **1.** (*patate*) to mash; (*dito*) to squash; (*noci, mandorle*) to crack **2.** SPORT to smash **3.** (*premere: pedale, pulsante*) to push **4.** *fig* (*annientare*) to thrash **5.** (*travolgere*) to crush **6.** (*loc*) ~ **un pisolino** [*o* **sonnellino**] *fam* to take a nap

schiacciata [skiat·'tʃaː·ta] *f* **1.** SPORT smash **2.** CULIN *type of flat, usually salty bread*

schiacciato, -a [skiat·'tʃaː·to] *agg* **1.** (*naso*) flat **2.** SPORT (*tiro* ~) smash

schiaffare [skiaf·'faː·re] *vt* **1.** *fam* (*gettare*) to chuck **2.** (*loc*) **l'hanno schiaffato dentro** they locked him up

schiaffeggiare [skiaf·fed·'dʒaː·re] *vt* to slap

schiaffo ['skiaf·fo] *m* slap; **prendere qu a -i** to slap sb around

schiamazzare [skia·mat·'tsaː·re] *vi* **1.** ZOO (*galline*) to squawk; (*oche*) to cackle **2.** (*persone*) to make a racket

schiamazzo [skia·'mat·tso] *m* **1.** ZOO (*di galline*) squawking; (*di oche*) cackling **2.** (*di persone*) racket

schiantare [skian·'taː·re] **I.** *vt avere* **1.** (*distruggere*) to smash **2.** *fig* (*sconfiggere*) to thrash **II.** *vr:* **-rsi** (*rompersi violentemente*) to crash

schianto ['skian·to] *m* (*boato*) crash; **di** ~ suddenly

schiappa ['skiap·pa] *f pej, fam* **essere una** ~ to be hopeless

schiarimento [skia·ri·'men·to] *m* lightening

schiarire [skia·'riː·re] <schiarisco> **I.** *vt avere* (*rendere più chiaro*) to lighten; **-rsi la voce** to clear one's throat **II.** *vr:* **-rsi** **1.** (*cielo, tempo*) to brighten **2.** (*capelli, tessuto*) to become lighter

schiarita [skia·'riː·ta] *f* **1.** METEO bright spell

S

2. *fig* (*miglioramento*) improvement

schiattare [skiat·'ta:·re] *vi essere fig, fam* (*crepare*) to die

schiavismo [skia·'viz·mo] *m* slavery

schiavitù [skia·vi·'tu] <-> *f a. fig* slavery; **ridurre in** ~ to enslave

schiavo, -a ['skia·vo] I. *agg* enslaved; **essere** ~ **della droga** to be hooked on drugs II. *m, f* slave

schiena ['skiɛ·na] *f* back; **colpire alla** ~ **qu** to attack sb from behind

schienale [skie·'na:·le] *m* (*di sedile, di divano*) back

schiera ['skiɛ·ra] *f* **1.** (*moltitudine*) crowd; **a -e** in large numbers **2.** MIL force **3.** (*loc*) **casa a** ~ row house

schieramento [skie·ra·'men·to] *m* **1.** MIL, SPORT formation **2.** POL alliance

schierare [skie·'ra:·re] I. *vt* (*esercito, soldati*) to draw up; (*squadra, giocatori*) to select II. *vr:* **-rsi 1.** MIL to line up **2.** *fig* (*prendere posizione*) to align oneself; **-rsi dalla parte di/contro qu** to side with/against sb; **-rsi dalla parte di/contro qc** to take a stand against sth

schiettezza [skiet·'tet·tsa] *f* frankness

schietto, -a ['skiɛt·to/'skiet·to] *agg* (*carattere, tono, risposta*) frank

schifare [ski·'fa:·re] *vt* to disgust

schifezza [ski·'fet·tsa] *f* junk; **è una** ~ it's a piece of junk

schifiltoso, -a [ski·fil·'to:·so] *agg* fussy

schifo ['ski:·fo] *m* disgust; **i funghi mi fanno** ~ I can't stand mushrooms; **la minestra è uno** ~ the soup is disgusting; **che** ~! yuck!

schifoso, -a [ski·'fo:·so] *agg* disgusting

schioccare [ski·ok·'ka:·re] *vt* (*frusta*) to crack; (*lingua, dita*) to click

schiocco ['ski·ɔk·ko] <-cchi> *m* click; **bacio con lo** ~ smacking kiss

schioppettata [skiop·pet·'ta:·ta] *f* gunshot

schioppo ['skiɔp·po] *m* bang

schiribizzo [ski·ri·'bid·dzo] *v.* **sghiribizzo**

schiudere ['skiu:·de·re] <irr> I. *vt* to open II. *vr:* **-rsi 1.** (*fiori*) to open; (*uova*) to crack open **2.** *fig* (*futuro, orizzonte, scenario*) to open up

schiuma ['skiu:·ma] *f* foam; ~ **da barba** shaving foam; **fare molta/poca** ~ to make a lot of/not much foam

schiumoso, -a [skiu·'mo:·so] *agg* (*sapone*) foaming; (*latte*) frothy

schiusi ['skiu:·si] *1. pers sing pass rem di* **schiudere**

schiuso ['skiu:·so] *pp di* **schiudere**

schivare [ski·'va:·re] *vt* (*evitare*) to avoid; ~ **un colpo** to dodge a blow

schivo, -a ['ski:·vo] *agg* **1.** (*contrario*) **essere** ~ **di qc** to be wary of sth **2.** (*timido*) reserved

schizofrenia [skid·dzo·fre·'ni:·a] <-ie> *f* schizophrenia

schizofrenico, -a [skid·dzo·'frɛ:·ni·ko] <-ci, -che> I. *agg* **1.** MED schizophrenic **2.** *fig* (*folle*)

crazy II. *m, f* schizophrenic

schizzare [skit·'tsa:·re] I. *vt avere* **1.** (*liquidi*) to splash **2.** (*sporcare*) to spatter **3.** (*disegnare*) to sketch II. *vi essere* **1.** (*liquidi*) to spurt **2.** *fig* (*guizzare*) to shoot III. *vr:* **-rsi** to spatter oneself

schizzato, -a [skit·'tsa:·to] *agg* **1.** (*sporcato*) spattered **2.** *fig* (*persona*) crazy

schizzinoso, -a [skit·tsi·'no:·so] *agg* fussy

schizzo ['skit·tso] *m* **1.** (*di fango, inchiostro*) splash **2.** (*abbozzo*) sketch

sci [ʃi] <-> *m* **1.** (*attrezzo*) ski **2.** (*attività*) skiing

sciabola ['ʃa·bo·la] *f* saber

sciacallaggio [ʃa·kal·'la:d·dʒo] <-ggi> *m* **1.** (*furto*) looting **2.** *fig* (*azione cinica*) cynical maneuver

sciacallo [ʃa·'kal·lo] *m* **1.** ZOO jackal **2.** *fig* (*in guerra*) looter **3.** *fig* (*approfittatore*) profiteer

sciacchetrà [ʃak·ke·'tra] *m* sciacchetrà, *sweet white wine from Liguria*

sciacquare [ʃak·'kua:·re] *vt* (*piatti, bicchieri*) to rinse; (*panni*) to rinse (out); **-rsi la bocca** to rinse one's mouth (out); **-rsi le mani** to wash one's hands

sciacquata [ʃak·'kua:·ta] *f* rinse

sciacquo ['ʃak·kuo] *m* **fare gli -i** to rinse one's mouth (out)

sciacquone [ʃak·'kuo:·ne] *m* flush; **tirare lo** ~ to flush

sciagura [ʃa·'gu:·ra] *f* **1.** (*disgrazia*) disaster; ~ **ecologica** environmental disaster **2.** *fig* (*sfortuna*) misfortune

sciagurato, -a [ʃa·gu·'ra:·to] I. *agg* **1.** (*persone*) unlucky **2.** (*malvagio*) wicked **3.** (*dissennato*) insane II. *m, f* (*disgraziato*) wretch

scialacquare [ʃa·lak·'kua:·re] *vt* (*patrimonio*) to squander

scialacquatore, -trice [ʃa·lak·kua·'to:·re] I. *m, f* spendthrift II. *agg* spendthrift

scialbo, -a ['ʃal·bo] *agg* (*privo di carattere*) dull

scialle ['ʃal·le] *m* shawl

scialo ['ʃa:·lo] *m* (*divertimento*) blast

scialuppa [ʃa·'lup·pa] *f* sloop; ~ **di salvataggio** lifeboat

sciamano [ʃa·'ma:·no] *m* shaman

sciamare [ʃa·'ma:·re] *vi essere o avere a. fig* to swarm

sciame ['ʃa:·me] *m* **1.** (*di api*) swarm **2.** *fig* (*di persone*) crowd

sciampo ['ʃam·po] *m fam* shampoo

sciangai [ʃaŋ·'ga:i] <-> *m* pickup sticks

sciarada [ʃa·'ra:·da] *f* word game in which two words are joined together to form a third

sciare [ʃi·'a:·re] *vi* SPORT to ski

sciarpa ['ʃar·pa] *f* scarf

sciata [ʃi·'a:·ta] *f fam* **fare una** ~ to go skiing

sciatica ['ʃa:·ti·ka] <-che> *f* sciatica

sciatico, -a ['ʃa:·ti·ko] <-ci, -che> *agg* **nervo** ~ sciatic nerve

sciatore, -trice [ʃia·'to:·re] *m, f* skier

sciatto, -a ['ʃat·to] *agg* (*persona*) unkempt;

(*abito*) shabby; (*stile*) sloppy

scibile [ˈʃiːbiˌle] *m* knowledge

sciccoso, -a [ʃikˈkoːso] *agg fam* (*elegante: persona, abito*) chic

scientifica [ʃenˈtiːfiˌka] <-che> *f* (*polizia*) forensics

scientificità [ʃenˌtifiˌtʃiˈta] <-> *f* scientific nature

scientifico, -a <-ci, -che> *agg* 1.(*studio, analisi, articolo*) scientific 2.(*liceo*) high school specializing in science subjects

scienza [ˈʃɛnˌtsa] *f* science; ~ **dell'alimentazione** nutrition; ~ **dell'educazione** science of education; **-e economiche** economics; **-e naturali** natural science

scienziato, -a [ʃɛnˈtsiaːto] *m, f* scientist

sciistico, -a [ʃiˈisˌtiˌko] <-ci, -che> *agg* ski

scimmia [ˈʃimˌmia] <-ie> *f* monkey; (*più grande*) ape; **brutto come una** ~ ugly as sin

scimpanzé [ʃimˌpanˈtse] <-> *m* chimpanzee

scimunito, -a [ʃiˌmuˈniːto] I. *agg* stupid II. *m, f* idiot

scindere [ˈʃinˌdeˌre] <scindo, scissi, scisso> I. *vt* to split II. *vr:* **-rsi** (*dividersi: partito, società, gruppo*) to split

scintilla [ʃinˈtilˌla] *f* (*di fuoco*) spark; **fare -e** *fig* (*brillare*) to perform brilliantly

scintillare [ʃinˌtilˈlaːre] *vi* 1.PHYS to give off sparks 2.(*luccicare*) to sparkle; (*risplendere di luce*) to glitter

scintillio [ʃinˌtilˈliːo] <-ii> *m* (*di spade, luci, vetrine*) glitter

sciò [ʃɔ] *int* shoo

scioccante [ʃokˈkanˌte] *agg* (*verità, immagine, rivelazione*) shocking

scioccare [ʃokˈkaːre] *vt fam* to shock

scioccato, -a [ʃokˈkaːto] *agg* shocked

sciocchezza [ʃokˈketˌtsa] *f* 1.(*scemenza*) stupid thing; **è stata una** ~ it was a stupid thing to do 2.*fig* (*cosa da nulla*) **è una** ~ it's nothing

sciocco, -a [ˈʃɔkˌko] <-cchi, -cche> I. *agg* silly II. *m, f* idiot

sciogliere [ˈʃɔʎˌʎeˌre] <sciolgo, sciolsi, sciolto> I. *vt* 1.(*slegare: capelli*) to loosen; (*nodo*) to undo 2.(*liberare: cane*) to let off the leash 3.CHEM to dissolve 4.(*porre fine a: contratto*) to cancel; (*società*) to wind up 5.(*seduta, manifestazione, riunione*) to bring to an end; (*parlamento*) to dissolve 6.(*risolvere: dubbio, problema*) to resolve 7.(*muscoli, gambe*) to loosen up II. *vr:* **-rsi** 1.(*neve*) to melt 2.(*superare l'imbarazzo*) to relax

scioglilingua [ʃoʎˌʎiˈlinˌgua] <-> *m* tongue twister

scioglimento [ʃoʎˌʎiˈmenˌto] *m* 1.(*di nodo*) untying 2.POL (*di parlamento*) dissolution 3.JUR (*di matrimonio*) annulment; (*di contratto*) cancellation 4.REL (*di voto*) fulfilment 5.(*di nevi, ghiaccio*) melting

sciolgo [ˈʃɔlˌgo] *1. pers sing pr di* **sciogliere**

sciolina [ʃioˈliːna] *f* wax

sciolsi [ˈʃɔlˌsi] *1. pers sing pass rem di* **sciog-**liere

scioltezza [ʃolˈtetˌtsa] *f* 1.(*di movimenti*) suppleness 2.(*disinvoltura*) fluency

sciolto, -a [ˈʃɔlˌto] I. *pp di* **sciogliere** II. *agg* 1.(*slegato*) loose 2.(*ritmo, movimento*) supple; **avere la lingua -a** to have the gift of the gab

scioperare [ʃoˌpeˈraːre] *vi* to strike

sciopero [ˈʃɔːpeˌro] *m* strike; ~ **bianco** slowdown; ~ **della fame** hunger strike; **domani c'è lo** ~ **degli autobus** there's a bus strike tomorrow; **fare** ~ to (go on) strike

sciorinare [ʃoˌriˈnaːre] *vt a. fig* (*mettere in mostra*) to display; (*dati, fatti*) to rattle off

sciovia [ʃioˈviːa] *f* ski tow

scippare [ʃipˈpaːre] *vt* ~ **qu** to rob sb in the street

scippatore, -trice [ʃipˌpaˈtoːre] *m, f* street robber

scippo [ˈʃipˌpo] *m* street robbery

scirocco [ʃiˈrɔkˌko] <-cchi> *m* sirocco

sciroppo [ʃiˈrɔpˌpo] *f* MED syrup; ~ **per la tosse** cough syrup

scisma [ˈʃizˌma] <-i> *m* 1.REL schism 2.POL split

scismatico, -a [ʃizˈmaːˌtiˌko] <-ci, -che> I. *agg* (*corrente, atto, principio*) schismatic II. *m, f* schismatic

scissi [ˈʃisˌsi] *1. pers sing pass rem di* **scindere**

scissione [ʃisˈsioːne] *f* (*di partito*) split; (*di società*) division

scisso [ˈʃisˌso] *pp di* **scindere**

sciupare [ʃuˈpaːre] I. *vt* 1.(*rovinare: abito, mobile*) to ruin 2.*fig* (*rovinare: sorpresa*) to spoil 3.(*sprecare: tempo, fatica*) to waste II. *vr:* **-rsi** 1.(*indumenti*) to be ruined 2.(*persone*) to become run down

scivolare [ʃiˌvoˈlaːre] *vi essere* 1.(*perdere l'equilibrio*) to slip; ~ **di mano a qu** to slip out of sb's hand 2.(*scorrere*) to slide

scivolo [ˈʃiːvoˌlo] *m* slide

scivolone [ʃiˌvoˈloːne] *m fig* (*grave errore*) blunder

scivoloso, -a [ʃiˌvoˈloːso] *agg* (*terreno*) slippery

sclerosi [skleˈrɔːzi] <-> *f* MED sclerosis; ~ **multipla** multiple sclerosis

scocca [ˈskɔkˌka] <-cche> *f* (*di auto*) body

scoccare [skokˈkaːre] I. *vt avere* 1.(*freccia*) to shoot 2.(*ore*) to strike 3.*fig* ~ **un bacio a qu** to give sb a smacker II. *vi essere* (*ore*) to strike

scocciare [skotˈtʃaːre] *fam* I. *vt* (*stufare*) to annoy II. *vr:* **-rsi** (*stufarsi*) to grow tired of sth

scocciatore, -trice [skotˌtʃaˈtoːre] *m, f fam* pain (in the neck)

scocciatura [skotˌtʃaˈtuːra] *f fam* pain; **che ~!** what a pain!

scodella [skoˈdɛlˌla] *f* bowl

scodinzolare [skoˌdinˌtsoˈlaːre] *vi* ZOO to wag its tail

scogliera [skoʎˈʎɛːra] *f* (*scogli*) rocks *pl;* (*a strapiombo*) cliffs *pl;* ~ **corallina** coral reef

scoglio [ˈskɔʎˌʎo] <-gli> *m* 1.GEOG rock 2.*fig*

obstacle

scoglioso, -a [skoʌ·'ʎoː·so] *agg* rocky

scoiattolo [sko·'iat·to·lo] *m* squirrel

scolapasta [sko·la·'pas·ta] <-> *m* colander

scolapiatti [sko·la·'piat·ti] <-> *m* drainboard

scolare¹ [sko·'laː·re] *agg* età ~ school age

scolare² *vt avere* to drain; **scolarsi una bottiglia di vino** to drink a whole bottle of wine

scolaresca [sko·la·'res·ka] <-sche> *f* schoolchildren *pl*

scolaretto, -a [sko·la·'ret·to] *m, f* schoolboy *m*, schoolgirl *f*

scolaro, -a [sko·'laː·ro] *m, f* student

scolastico, -a [sko·'las·ti·ko] <-ci, -che> *agg* **1.** (*anno, tasse, programma*) school **2.** *fig, pej* superficial; **inglese** ~ basic English

scoliosi [sko·'liɔː·zi] <-> *f* scoliosis

scollato, -a [skol·'laː·to] *agg* (*abito*) low-cut; **scarpa -a** pump

scollatura [skol·la·'tuː·ra] *f* **1.** (*di abito*) neckline **2.** (*parte scoperta*) cleavage

scolorina® [sko·lo·'riː·na] *f* ink remover

scolorirsi [sko·lo·'riːr·si] <scolorisco> *vr:* -rsi (*colore, abito, legno*) to fade

scolpire [skol·'piː·re] <scolpisco> I. *vt* **1.** (*marmo, statua*) to sculpt; (*legno*) to carve **2.** (*incidere*) to engrave II. *vr* (*imprimersi*) to become engraved

scombinare [skom·bi·'naː·re] *vt* to upset

scombussolare [skom·bus·so·'laː·re] *vt* to unsettle

scommessa [skom·'mes·sa] *f* bet; **fare una** ~ to (make a) bet

scommettere [skom·'met·te·re] <irr> *vt* **1.** ~ qc to bet sth **2.** (*affermare con certezza*) to bet

scomodare [sko·mo·'daː·re] I. *vt* **1.** *fig* (*chiamare in causa*) to drag in **2.** (*rivolgersi a*) to invoke II. *vr:* -rsi (*disturbarsi*) to bother (oneself)

scomodità [sko·mo·di·'ta] *f* inconvenience

scomodo, -a *agg* uncomfortable

scomparire [skom·pa·'riː·re] <irr> *vi essere* **1.** (*sparire*) to disappear **2.** (*morire*) to die **3.** *fig* (*fare poca figura*) to fade into the background

scomparsa [skom·'par·sa] *f* **1.** (*sparizione*) disappearance **2.** (*morte*) death

scomparso, -a [skom·'par·so] *agg* **1.** (*popolo, continente*) vanished **2.** (*irreperibile: documento*) lost; (*persona*) missing

scompartimento [skom·par·ti·'men·to] *m* **1.** FERR compartment; ~ **fumatori/non fumatori** smoking/non-smoking compartment **2.** (*di armadio, di stiva*) section

scomparto [skom·'par·to] *m* (*di borsa, di cassetto, di portadocumenti*) section

scompenso [skom·'pɛn·so] *m* MED decompensation

scompigliare [skom·piʌ·'ʎaː·re] *vt* (*capelli*) to mess up

scompiglio [skom·'piʌ·ʎo] <-gli> *m* confusion

scompisciarsi [skom·piʃ·'ʃar·si] *vr* ~ **dalle risate** *vulg* to pee one's pants laughing

scomponibile [skom·po·'niː·bi·le] *agg*

(*mobile, modello*) modular

scomporre [skom·'por·re] <irr> I. *vt* **1.** (*disgregare: elementi*) to break up **2.** MATH to factor II. *vr:* -rsi (*mostrare turbamento*) to lose one's composure

scomposto, -a [skom·'pos·to] I. *pp di* **scomporre** II. *agg* (*sguaiato: atteggiamento, gesto*) unseemly

scomunica [sko·'muː·ni·ka] <-che> *f* REL excommunication

scomunicare [sko·mu·ni·'kaː·re] *vt* REL to excommunicate

sconcertante [skon·tʃer·'tan·te] *agg* (*verità, episodio*) disconcerting

sconcertare [skon·tʃer·'taː·re] *vt* (*turbare*) to disconcert

sconcerto [skon·'tʃɛr·to] *m* (*turbamento*) bewilderment

sconcio, -a <-ci, -ce> *agg* (*parola, foto, battuta*) dirty

sconclusionato, -a [skon·klu·zio·'naː·to] *agg* (*discorso, frase*) inconclusive

scondito, -a [skon·'diː·to] *agg* without dressing

sconfessare [skon·fes·'saː·re] *vt* **1.** (*rinnegare*) to repudiate **2.** (*disapprovare*) to denounce

sconfiggere [skon·'fid·dʒe·re] <sconfiggo, sconfissi, sconfitto> *vt* **1.** *a.* MIL to defeat **2.** *fig* (*eliminare*) to overcome

sconfinare [skon·fi·'naː·re] *vi fig* (*oltrepassare i limiti*) to spill over

sconfissi [skon·'fis·si] *1. pers sing pass rem di* **sconfiggere**

sconfitta [skon·'fit·ta] *f* defeat; ~ **elettorale** electoral defeat; **infliggere una** ~ **a qu** to defeat sb; **subire una** ~ to be defeated

sconfitto [skon·'fit·to] *pp di* **sconfiggere**

sconfortante [skon·for·'tan·te] *agg* (*dato, notizia*) discouraging

sconfortare [skon·for·'taː·re] I. *vt* (*togliere coraggio*) to discourage II. *vr:* -rsi (*perdere coraggio*) to become discouraged

sconforto [skon·'fɔr·to] *m* (*abbattimento*) dejection

scongelamento [skon·dʒe·la·'men·to] *m* defrosting

scongelare [skon·dʒe·'laː·re] *vt* to defrost

scongiurare [skon·dʒu·'raː·re] *vt* **1.** (*pregare*) to beg **2.** (*pericolo, disastro, tragedia*) to avert

scongiuro [skon·'dʒuː·ro] *m* (*atto rituale*) charm

sconnesso, -a [skon·'nɛs·so] *agg* (*discorso*) disconnected

sconosciuto, -a [sko·noʃ·'ʃuː·to] I. *agg* unknown II. *m, f* stranger

sconsacrare [skon·sa·'kraː·re] *vt* (*chiesa*) to deconsecrate

sconsigliabile [skon·siʌ·'ʎaː·bi·le] *agg* inadvisable

sconsigliare [skon·siʌ·'ʎaː·re] *vt* ~ qc a qu to advise sb against sth; ~ **a qu di ...** + *inf* to advise sb not to ...

sconsolato, -a [skon·so·'la:·to] *agg* (*espressione, faccia, atteggiamento*) disconsolate

scontare [skon·'ta:·re] *vt* **1.** COM to take off; **~ una cambiale** to discount a bill of exchange **2.** JUR to serve; **~ il debito con la giustizia** to serve one's time **3.** *fig* (*pagare le conseguenze di*) to pay for

scontato, -a [skon·'ta:·to] *agg* (*previsto: successo, risultato, risposta*) expected

scontentezza [skon·ten·'tet·tsa] *f* dissatisfaction

scontento [skon·'tɛn·to] *m* (*insoddisfazione*) discontent

scontento, -a *agg* discontented

sconto ['skon·to] *m* COM discount

scontrarsi [skon·'tra:r·si] *vr:* **-rsi** **1.** (*treno, auto*) to crash **2.** MIL to clash **3.** *fig* (*divergere*) to differ

scontrino [skon·'tri:·no] *m* receipt; **~ fiscale** cash register receipt

scontro ['skon·tro] *m* **1.** MOT, FERR, AERO crash **2.** MIL, SPORT clash **3.** *fig* (*diverbio*) confrontation

scontrosità [skon·tro·si·'ta] <-> *f* surliness

scontroso, -a [skon·'tro:·so] *agg* (*atteggiamento, carattere*) surly

sconveniente [skon·ve·'niɛn·te] *agg* (*contegno, parole, risposta*) improper

sconvolgente [skon·vol·'dʒɛn·te] *agg* (*notizia, evento*) devastating

sconvolgere [skon·'vɔl·dʒe·re] <irr> *vt* **1.** (*turbare profondamente*) to devastate **2.** (*piano, progetto*) to upset

sconvolgimento [skon·vol·dʒi·'men·to] *m* (*interiore*) **la notizia mi provocò un grande ~** I was devastated by the news

sconvolsi *1. pers sing pass rem di* **sconvolgere**

sconvolto *pp di* **sconvolgere**

scoop [sku(:)p] <- *o* scoops> *m* scoop; **~ pubblicitario** marketing scoop

scooter ['sku:·tə/'sku·ter] <-> *m* scooter

scopa ['sko:·pa] *f* broom

scopare [sko·'pa:·re] *vt* **1.** (*pavimento*) to sweep **2.** *vulg* to screw

scopata [sko·'pa:·ta] *f* **1.** (*spazzata*) **dare una ~ a qc** to give sth a sweep **2.** *vulg* screw; **farsi una ~** to screw

scoperchiare [sko·per·'kia:·re] *vt* **1.** (*pentola*) to uncover; **~ una casa** to take the roof off a house **2.** *fig* (*mettere a nudo*) to reveal

scoperta [sko·'pɛr·ta] *f* discovery

scoperto [sko·'pɛr·to] *m* **1.** (*luogo aperto*) **dormire allo ~** to sleep in the open **2.** COM, FIN overdraft

scoperto, -a *agg* **1.** (*terrazzo*) roofless **2.** (*braccia, capo*) bare; **essere troppo ~** to be wearing too few clothes **3.** COM, FIN overdrawn **4.** *fig* (*sincero*) **a viso ~** openly

scopiazzare [sko·piat·'tsa:·re] *vt* to copy

scopo ['skɔ:·po] *m* (*fine*) aim; **a che ~?** why?

scoppiare [skop·'pia:·re] *vi essere* **1.** (*guerra, rissa, epidemia*) to break out; (*estate, inverno*)

to arrive **2.** (*bomba, moda*) to explode **3.** (*gomma*) to burst **4.** *fig* (*per aver mangiato troppo*) to burst; **~ a piangere** to burst into tears; **~ a ridere** to burst out laughing; **~ dal caldo** to be boiling (hot) **5.** SPORT to collapse

scoppio ['skɔp·pio] <-i> *m* **1.** (*di bomba, mina*) explosion; **a ~ ritardato** *fig* delayed action **2.** (*rumore*) bang **3.** *fig* burst; **uno ~ di risa** a burst of laughter **4.** MOT **motore a ~** internal combustion engine

scoprire [sko·'pri:·re] <scopro, scoprii *o* scopersi, scoperto> **I.** *vt* **1.** (*gener*) to discover; **~ l'acqua calda** *fam* to reinvent the wheel **2.** (*pentola, statua, gambe*) to uncover **3.** *fig* (*palesare*) to reveal **II.** *vr:* **-rsi** **1.** (*spogliarsi*) to take some clothes off; **si è scoperta troppo** she was wearing too few clothes **2.** *fig* (*rivelarsi*) to give oneself away

scopritore, -trice [sko·pri·'to:·re] *m, f* discoverer

scoraggiante [sko·rad·'dʒan·te] *agg* discouraging

scoraggiare [sko·rad·'dʒa:·re] **I.** *vt* (*togliere il coraggio*) to discourage **II.** *vr:* **-rsi** (*perdere il coraggio*) to lose heart

scorbutico, -a [skor·'bu:·ti·ko] <-ci, -che> *agg fig* surly

scorciatoia [skor·tʃa·'to:·ia] <-oie> *f a. fig* shortcut

scordare [skor·'da:·re] **I.** *vt* **1.** (*dimenticare*) to forget **2.** MUS to put out of tune **II.** *vr:* **-rsi** **1.** (*dimenticarsi*) to forget **2.** (*lasciare*) to leave; **mi sono scordato gli appunti a casa** I left my notes at home **3.** MUS to go out of tune

scoreggia [sko·'red·dʒa] <-gge> *f vulg* fart

scoreggiare [sko·red·'dʒa:·re] *vi vulg* to fart

scorfano ['skɔr·fa·no] *m* ZOO scorpion fish

scorfano, -a *m, f fam* (*persona brutta*) dog

scorgere ['skɔr·dʒe·re] <scorgo, scorsi, scorto> *vt* **1.** (*riconoscere: persona*) to see **2.** *fig* (*riconoscere: pericolo, inganno, minaccia*) to recognize

scorpacciata [skor·pat·'tʃa:·ta] *f fam* feast; **fare una ~ di qc** to feast on sth

scorpione [skor·'pio:·ne] *m* **1.** ZOO scorpion **2.** ASTR **sono (dello** [*o* uno]**) Scorpione** I'm (a) Scorpio

scorrazzare [skor·rat·'tsa:·re] *vi* **1.** (*bambino*) to run around **2.** *fig* (*girovagare*) to roam

scorrere ['skor·re·re] <irr> **I.** *vi essere* **1.** (*fiume, lacrime, discorso*) to flow **2.** (*tempo*) to pass **3.** (*traffico*) to move **II.** *vt avere* **1.** (*libro, testo, righe, parole*) to scan **2.** COMPUT to scroll (through)

scorreria [skor·re·'ri:·a] <-ie> *f* (*incursione*) incursion

scorrettezza [skor·ret·'tet·tsa] *f* **1.** (*errore*) mistake **2.** (*azione*) act of rudeness; (*condizione*) rudeness

scorretto, -a [skor·'rɛt·to] *agg* **1.** (*sbagliato: nome, uso*) incorrect **2.** (*disonesto: gesto, azione, comportamento*) improper; (*nello sport*); **gioco ~** foul play; **è molto ~ in**

S

campo he's a dirty player

scorrevole [skor·'re:·vo·le] *agg* **1.** (*traffico, discorso*) flowing **2.** (*su rotaie*) **porta** ~ sliding door

scorribanda [skor·ri·'ban·da] *f* **1.** (*breve scorreria*) raid **2.** (*breve gita*) trip

scorsi ['skɔr·si] *1. pers sing pass rem di* **scorgere, scorrere**

scorso, -a ['skor·so] **I.** *pp di* **scorrere II.** *agg* (*passato*) last; **l'anno** ~ last year

scorta ['skɔr·ta] *f* **1.** (*accompagnamento*) bodyguard **2.** MIL escort **3.** (*provvista*) supply; **fare** ~ **di qc** to stock up on sth; **ruota di** ~ spare tire

scortare [skor·'ta:·re] *vt* (*accompagnare*) to escort

scortese [skor·'te:·ze] *agg* rude

scortesia [skor·te·'zi:·a] *f* **1.** (*essere scortese*) rudeness **2.** (*gesto*) ...: act of rudeness

scorticare [skor·ti·'ka:·re] *vt* to skin

scorto ['skɔr·to] *pp di* **scorgere**

scorza ['skɔr·dza/'skɔr·tsa] *f* **1.** (*di albero*) bark **2.** (*di frutto*) peel **3.** *fig* (*esteriorità*) exterior; **avere la** ~ **dura** to have thick skin

scosceso, -a [skoʃ·'ʃe:·so] *agg* (*pendio, promontorio*) steep

scossa ['skɔs·sa] *f* **1.** EL shock; **prendere una** ~ to get an electric shock **2.** (*sbalzo*) ~ **di terremoto** tremor **3.** *fig* (*grande dolore*) blow

scossi ['skɔs·si] *1. pers sing pass rem di* **scuotere, scuocere**

scosso, -a ['skɔs·so] **I.** *pp di* **scuotere II.** *agg* (*sconvolto*) shaken

scossone [skos·'so:·ne] *m* shake

scostante [skos·'tan·te] *agg* (*non coerente: atteggiamento, carattere*) inconsistent

scostare [skos·'ta:·re] **I.** *vt* (*spostare: vaso, cesto*) to move **II.** *vr:* -**rsi** (*farsi da parte*) to move

scostumato, -a [skos·tu·'ma:·to] *agg* (*vita, donna*) immoral

scotch [skɔtʃ] <-> *m* (*whisky*) Scotch

scotch® <-> *m* (*nastro autoadesivo*) Scotch tape®

scottante [skot·'tan·te] *agg fig* (*grave*) sensitive; (*urgente*) pressing

scottare [skot·'ta:·re] **I.** *vt* **1.** (*fiamma, sole*) to burn; (*liquido*) to scald **2.** CULIN (*carne*) to sear; (*verdure*) to cook quickly **3.** *fig* (*ferire*) to wound **II.** *vi* **1.** (*minestra, acqua*) to be very hot **2.** *fig* (*destare interesse*) **è una questione/un tema che scotta** it's a burning question/issue **III.** *vr:* -**rsi 1.** MED to burn oneself **2.** *fig* (*rimanere deluso*) to be burned

scottatura [skot·ta·'tu:·ra] *f* **1.** MED burn **2.** (*di sole*) sunburn

scotto ['skɔt·to] *pp di* **scuocere**

scout [skaut] **I.** <-> *mf* scout **II.** <inv> *agg* scout

scovare [sko·'va:·re] *vt* **1.** (*lepre, volpe*) to flush **2.** *fig* (*scoprire*) to discover

Scozia ['skɔt·tsia] *f* Scotland

scozzese [skot·'tse:·se] **I.** *agg* Scottish;

gonna ~ kilt **II.** *mf* Scot

screditare [ske·di·'ta:·re] **I.** *vt* (*privare di stima*) to discredit **II.** *vr:* -**rsi** (*perdere credito*) to be discredited

scremare [skre·'ma:·re] *vt* **1.** (*latte*) to skim **2.** *fig* (*selezionare: concorrenti*) to cream off

screpolare [skre·po·'la:·re] **I.** *vt* (*mani, labbra*) to chap **II.** *vr:* -**rsi** (*mani, labbra*) to chap

screzio ['skrɛt·tsio] <-i> *m* disagreement

scribacchiare [skri·bak·'kia:·re] *vt pej* (*scrivere malamente*) to scribble

scribacchino [skri·bak·'ki:·no] *m* **1.** *pej* (*scrittore*) scribbler **2.** *pej* (*impiegato*) pencil pusher

scricchiolare [skrik·kio·'la:·re] *vi* to squeak

scricchiolio [skrik·kio·'li:·o] <-ii> *m* (*di ramo, ossa*) creaking

scricciolo ['skrit·tʃo·lo] *m fig, fam* doll

scrigno ['skriɲ·ɲo] *m* (*per gioielli*) casket

scrissi ['skris·si] *1. pers sing pass rem di* **scrivere**

scriteriato, -a [skri·te·'ria:·to] *agg* (*privo di senno*) crazy

scritta ['skrit·ta] *f* writing

scritto ['skrit·to] *m* **1.** (*cosa scritta*) written word; **per** ~ in writing **2.** (*opera*) work

scritto, -a **I.** *pp di* **scrivere II.** *agg a. fig* written; **ce l'hai** ~ **in fronte** it's written all over your face

scrittoio [skrit·'to:·io] <-oi> *m* (writing) desk

scrittore, -trice [skrit·'to:·re] *m, f* writer

scrittura [skrit·'tu:·ra] *f* **1.** (*attività*) writing; COMPUT; **programma di** ~ word processing program **2.** REL scripture **3.** JUR document **4.** THEAT, FILM, MUS engagement

scritturare [skrit·tu·'ra:·re] *vt* (*attore*) to engage

scrivania [skri·va·'ni:·a] <-ie> *f* **1.** (*tavolo per scrivere*) desk **2.** COMPUT desktop

scrivere ['skri:·ve·re] <scrivo, scrissi, scritto> *vt* to write; ~ **a mano** to write by hand; ~ **alla lavagna** to write on the board; **come si scrive?** how do you spell?

scroccare [skrok·'ka:·re] *vt fam* to scrounge

scrocco ['skrɔk·ko] *m fam* **a** ~ to scrounge; **mangiare a** ~ to scrounge a meal; **vivere a** ~ to sponge

scroccone, -a [skrok·'ko:·ne] *m, f fam* scrounger

scrofa ['skrɔ:·fa] *f* sow

scrollare [skrol·'la:·re] **I.** *vt* (*tovaglia, ramo*) to shake; ~ **le spalle** to shrug one's shoulders **II.** *vr:* -**rsi** *fig* (*scuotersi dall'abbattimento*) to give oneself a shake

scrollata [skrol·'la:·ta] *f* (*scuotimento*) shake; **dare una** ~ **a qu/qc** to give sb/sth a shake

scrosciare [skroʃ·'ʃa:·re] *vi* **1.** (*fiume*) to thunder; (*pioggia, acqua*) to pour (down) **2.** *fig* **scrosciavano gli applausi** there was thunderous applause; **scrosciano le risate** there are gales of laughter

scrostare [skros·'ta:·re] **I.** *vt* (*muro*) to strip; (*intonaco*) to scrape off **II.** *vr:* -**rsi** (*muro*) to peel; (*intonaco*) to flake off; **la ferita si sta scrostando** the scab is coming off

scroto ['skrɔːto] *m* scrotum

scrupolo ['skru:·po·lo] *m* **1.** (*timore*) scruple; **senza -i** unscrupulous **2.** (*diligenza*) care

scrupolosità [skru·po·lo·si·'ta] <-> *f* scrupulousness

scrupoloso, -a [skru·po·'lo:·so] *agg* scrupulous

scrutare [skru·'ta:·re] *vt* (*osservare intensamente*) to scrutinize

scrutatore, -trice [skru·ta·'to:·re] I. *m, f* scrutinizer II. *agg* (*sguardo, occhio*) searching

scrutinare [skru·ti·'na:·re] *vt* **1.** JUR to count **2.** (*nell'insegnamento*) to assign grades to students, *at the end of a term*

scrutinio [skru·'ti:·nio] <-i> *m* **1.** JUR counting, *of votes* **2.** (*a scuola*) assignment of grades, *at the end of a term*

scucire [sku·'tʃi:·re] I. *vt* **1.** (*orlo*) to unpick **2.** *fam* (*soldi*) to cough up II. *vr:* **-rsi** (*orlo, tasca*) to come unstitched

scuderia [sku·de·'ri:·a] <-ie> *f* **1.** ZOO stable **2.** SPORT (*automobilismo*) team

scudetto [sku·'det·to] *m* SPORT championship; **vincere lo ~** to win the championship

scudo ['sku:·do] *m* **1.** (*gener*) shield; **fare da ~ a qu** to shield sb; **lo ~ crociato** *symbol of the Christian Democrat party* **2.** (*moneta*) scudo; **~ europeo** ECU

scugnizzo [skuɲ·'ɲit·tso] *m* (*napoletano*) *Neapolitan street urchin*

sculacciare [sku·lat·'tʃa:·re] *vt* to spank

sculacciata [sku·lat·'tʃa:·ta] *f* spanking

sculaccione [sku·lat·'tʃo:·ne] *m* spank

sculettare [sku·let·'ta:·re] *vi* to wiggle one's hips

scultore, -trice [skul·'to:·re] *m, f* sculptor

scultoreo, -a [skul·'tɔ:·reo] *agg* **1. l'arte -a** the art of scuplture **2.** (*bellezza, fisico*) sculptural

scultura [skul·'tu:·ra] *f* sculpture

scuocere ['skwɔ:·tʃe·re] <scuocio, scossi, scotto> *vi* (*cuocere troppo*) to overcook

scuola ['skwɔ:·la] *f* school; **~ elementare** elementary school; **~ media** middle school; **~ superiore** high school; **~ materna** (*dai 3 ai 5 anni*) nursery school; (*da 5 a 6 anni*) kindergarten; **~ guida** driving school; **~ serale** night school; *fig;* **fare ~** to show the way

scuolabus ['skwɔ:·la·bus/skuo·la·'bus] *m* school bus

scuotere ['skwɔ:·te·re] <scuoto, scossi, scosso> I. *vt a. fig* to shake; **~ le spalle ...:** to shrug; **....:** **~ la testa** to shake one's head II. *vr:* **-rsi 1.** *fig* (*dal torpore*) to shake oneself **2.** (*turbarsi*) to be shaken

scurire [sku·'ri:·re] <scurisco> I. *vt avere* (*colore, metallo*) to make darker II. *vr:* **-rsi** (*colore, capelli, pelle, metallo*) to become darker

scuro, -a *agg* **1.** (*gener*) dark **2.** *fig* (*fosco*) **si fece ~ in volto** his [*o* her] face darkened

scurrile [sku·'ri:·le] *agg* (*volgare: linguaggio, espressione*) scurrilous

scusa ['sku:·za] *f* **1.** (*lo scusarsi*) apology;

chiedere [*o* **domandare**] **~** to apologize **2.** (*pretesto*) excuse; **avere sempre una ~ pronta** to always have an excuse

scusare [sku·'za:·re] I. *vt* to excuse; (*perdonare*) to forgive; **scusi, che ore sono?** excuse me, do you have the time?; **mi scusi!** I beg your pardon II. *vr:* **-rsi con qu di/per qc** to apologize to sb for sth

sdebitarsi [zde·bi·'tar·si] *vr fig* **~ con qu di qc** to repay sb for sth

sdegnare [zdeɲ·'ɲa:·re] I. *vt* **1.** (*rifiutare*) to despise **2.** (*provocare sdegno*) to disgust II. *vr:* **-rsi** (*indignarsi*) to become angry

sdegno ['zdeɲ·ɲo] *m* (*indignazione*) indignation

sdegnoso, -a [zdeɲ·'ɲo:·so] *agg* (*che mostra sdegno: rifiuto, sguardo*) scornful

sdentato, -a [zden·'ta:·to] *agg* toothless

sdoganare [zdo·ga·'na:·re] *vt* **1.** (*merce*) to clear through customs **2.** *fig* (*liberare*) to legitimize

sdolcinato, -a [zdol·tʃi·'na:·to] *agg* sugary; **parole -e** sweet nothings

sdoppiamento [zdop·pia·'men·to] *m* **1.** (*divisione*) splitting **2.** MED **~ della personalità** split personality

sdraiare [zdra·'ia:·re] I. *vt* (*mettere a terra*) to lay II. *vr:* **-rsi** (*stendersi*) to lie down

sdraio <-> *f* beach chair; **sedia a ~** deck chair

sdrammatizzare [zdram·ma·tid·'dza:·re] *vt* (*racconto, notizia*) to play down

sdrucciolevole [zdrut·tʃo·'le:·vo·le] *agg* (*terreno, strada*) slippery

se¹ [se] I. *cong* **1.** (*condizionale*) if; **~ mai** if ever; **~ non altro** at least; **~ non che** but; **~ ben ricordo** if I remember rightly; **~ me l'avesse detto, avrei accettato** if he [*o* she] had told me, I would have said yes **2.** (*dubitativa, interrogativa, indiretta*) if; **come ~** as if; **come ~ non lo sapessi!** as if I didn't know! **3.** (*esclamativa, desiderativa*) if only; **~ solo l'avessi saputo!** if only I'd known! II. *m* if

se² *pron* (*davanti a lo, la, li, le, ne*) *v.* si¹

SE *abbr di* **sudest**

sé [se] *pron refl. 3. pers* (*impersonale*) oneself; (*persona*) himself *m*, herself *f*; (*plurale*) themselves; (*cosa*) itself; **essere fuori di ~** to be beside oneself; **è completamente fuori di ~ dal dolore** he [*o* she] is beside himself [*o* herself] with grief; **uscire di ~** to go crazy; **fra ~ (e ~)** to oneself; **stava pensando fra ~ e ~** he [*o* she] was thinking to himself [*o* herself]; **parlano solo di ~** they only talk about themselves; **la cosa di per ~ ha poca importanza** in itself, it's not very important; **~ stesso, ~ medesimo** oneself; **dentro di ~** inside; **un caso a ~** a special case; **va da ~ che ...** it goes without saying that ...; **è un uomo che si è fatto da ~** he's a self-made man; **chi fa da ~ fa per tre** *prov* if you want something done, do it yourself

sebbene [seb·'bɛ:·ne] *cong* although

sec *abbr di* **secondo** sec

seccante [sek·'kan·te] *agg* (*fastidioso*) annoying

seccare [sek·'ka:·re] I. *vt avere* 1. (*terreno, aria*) to dry (out); (*fiori*) to wither 2. *fig, fam* (*infastidire*) to annoy II. *vr:* -**rsi** 1. (*diventare secco: frutta, pianta*) to wither; (*pelle*) to dry out 2. (*diventare asciutto*) to dry up 3. *fam* (*stancarsi*) -**rsi di fare qc** to grow tired of doing sth

seccato, -a [sek·'ka:·to] *agg* 1. (*pianta, fiore*) dried 2. *fam* (*irritato: tono, aria, fare*) annoyed

seccatore, -trice [sek·ka·'to:·re] *m, f fam* nuisance

seccatura [sek·ka·'tu:·ra] *f fam* nuisance

secchiello [sek·'kiɛl·lo] *m* (*piccolo secchio*) bucket; ~ **per il ghiaccio** ice bucket

secchio ['sek·kio] <-cchi> *m* bucket; ~ **della spazzatura** trash can

secchione, -a [sek·'kio:·ne] *m, f pej, fam* grind

secco ['sek·ko] *m* **portare in** ~ **una barca** to beach a boat; **lavatura a** ~ dry cleaning; **murare a** ~ to dry wall; **rimanere a** ~ **di carburante** *fig* to run out of gas

secco, -a <-cchi, -cche> *agg* 1. (*terreno, clima, pelle*) dry; (*palude, fiume*) dried-up 2. (*frutta, funghi, rami*) dried 3. (*vino, liquore*) dry 4. (*persona, gambe*) skinny 5. *fig* (*privo di garbo: tono, modo*) brusque; (*risposta*) curt 6. *fig* (*netto: sconfitta*) decisive 7. (*loc*) **fare** ~ **qu** *fam* to do sb in; *fam* (*morire*); **c'è rimasto** ~ he bought it

secentesco, -a [se·tʃen·'tes·ko] <-schi, -sche> *agg* seventeenth-century

secernere [se·'tʃɛr·ne·re] <secerno, secernei *o* secernetti, secreto> *vt* MED to secrete

secessione [se·tʃes·'sio:·ne] *f* (*seprazione di territorio*) secession

secessionismo [se·tʃes·sio·'niz·mo] *m* secessionism

secolare [se·ko·'la:·re] *agg* 1. (*che ha uno, più secoli*) age-old 2. (*laico, mondano*) secular

secolo ['sɛ:·ko·lo] *m* 1. (*periodo*) century; **lo scandalo del** ~ the scandal of the century 2. *fam* age; **è un** ~ **che non ti vedo** I haven't seen you for ages

seconda [se·'kon·da] *f* 1. (*classe: nelle elementari*) second grade; (*nelle medie*) seventh grade; (*nelle superiori*) tenth grade 2. MOT second gear 3. (*loc*) **a** ~ **di** according to; **a** ~ **dei casi** according to circumstances

secondariamente [se·kon·da·ria·'men·te] *avv* secondly

secondario, -a [se·kon·'da:·rio] <-i, -ie> *agg* (*di minore importanza*) secondary; **proposizione -a** secondary proposition; **scuola -a** secondary school

secondino [se·kon·'di:·no] *m* prison guard

secondo[1] [se·'kon·do] *prep* 1. (*conformemente a*) according to; ~ **l'uso** according to current practice; ~ **me/te** in my/your opinion 2. (*nel modo prescritto*) in accordance with 3. (*in base a*) depending on 4. (*nella direzione di*) along

secondo[2] *m* 1. CULIN main course 2. (*unità di misura del tempo*) second

secondo, -a I. *agg* second; **abiti di -a mano** hand-me-downs; ~ **fine** ulterior motive; **di** ~ **piano** *fig* of lesser importance II. *m, f* second

secondogenito, -a [se·kon·do·'dʒɛ:·ni·to] I. *agg* second II. *m, f* second-born

secreto[2] *pp di* **secernere**

secrezione [se·kret·'tsio:·ne] *f* secretion

sedano ['sɛ:·da·no] *m* celery

sedare [se·'da:·re] *vt* 1. (*tumulto*) to calm; (*rivolta*) to put down 2. (*dolore*) to soothe

sedativo [se·da·'ti:·vo] *m* sedative

sedativo, -a *agg* sedative

sede ['sɛ:·de] *f* 1. (*di governo*) seat; (*di partito, società*) headquarters; (*di università*) administration 2. (*di manifestazione, di evento*) site 3. (*loc*) **in** ~ **di** during; **in separata** ~ *a. fig* on another occasion; **Santa Sede** Holy See

sedentario, -a [se·den·'ta:·rio] <-i, -ie> *agg* sedentary

sedere[1] [se·'de:·re] <siedo, sedetti *o* sedei, seduto> I. *vi essere* to be sitting; **è seduto sulla panca** he is sitting on the bench; **mettersi a** ~ to sit down; ~ **a tavola** to sit (down) at the table II. *vr:* -**rsi** to sit (down); -**rsi a tavola** to sit (down) at the table

sedere[2] *m* ANAT bottom; **mi stai prendendo per il** ~? *fam* are you pulling my leg?

sedia ['sɛ:·dia] <-ie> *f* chair; ~ **a sdraio** lounger; ~ **elettrica** electric chair

sedicenne [se·di·'tʃɛn·ne] I. *agg* sixteen-year-old II. *mf* sixteen year old

sedicente [se·di·'tʃɛn·te] *agg pej* self-styled

sedicesimo [se·di·'tʃɛ:·zi·mo] *m* (*frazione*) sixteenth

sedicesimo, -a I. *agg* sixteenth II. *m, f* sixteenth; *v.a.* **quinto**

sedici ['sɛ:·di·tʃi] I. *num* sixteen II. <-> *m* (*numero*) sixteen; (*nelle date*) sixteenth III. *fpl* 4 pm; *v.a.* **cinque**

sedile [se·'di:·le] *m* seat; (*di più posti*); **il** ~ **posteriore** the back seat

sedimentazione [se·di·men·tat·'tsio:·ne] *f a.* GEOL sedimentation

sedimento [se·di·'men·to] *m a.* GEOL sediment

sedizione [se·dit·'tsio:·ne] *f* (*ribellione*) sedition

sedizioso, -a [se·dit·'tsio:·so] *agg* (*moto, adunata*) seditious

sedotto [se·'dot·to] *pp di* **sedurre**

seducente [se·du·'tʃɛn·te] *agg* (*donna, posa*) seductive

sedurre [se·'dur·re] <seduco, sedussi, sedotto> *vt* 1. (*donna, uomo*) to seduce 2. *fig* (*attrarre*) to appeal to

seduta [se·'du:·ta] *f* (*riunione*) meeting; ~ **stante** during the meeting; *fig* immediately

seduttore, -trice [se·dut·'to:·re] *m, f* seducer

seduzione [se·dut·'tsio:·ne] *f* (*capacità di affascinare*) charm

sega ['se:·ga] <-ghe> *f* 1. (*utensile*) saw; ~ **circolare** circular saw 2. *vulg* **farsi una** ~ to jerk off

segala, segale ['se:·ga·la, 'se:·ga·le] *f* rye

segare [se·'ga:·re] *vt* **1.**(*tronco*) to saw **2.** *sl* (*bocciare*) to flunk

segatura [se·ga·'tu:·ra] *f* **1.**(*di albero*) sawing **2.**(*residuo*) sawdust

seggio ['sɛd·dʒo] <-ggi> *m* PARL seat; ~ **elettorale** (*luogo*) polling station

seggiola ['sɛd·dʒo·la] *f* chair

seggiolino [sed·dʒo·'li:·no] *m* (*per bambini*) child's seat

seggiolone [sed·dʒo·'lo:·ne] *m* high chair

seghettato, -a [se·get·'ta:·to] *agg* serrated; **coltello** ~ serrated knife

segmento [seg·'men·to] *m* segment

segnalare [seɲ·ɲa·'la:·re] I. *vt* **1.**(*annunciare*) to signal **2.** *fig* (*richiamare l'attenzione su*) ~ **qc a qu** to tell sb about sth II. *vr* (*distinguersi*) -**rsi per qc** to be distinguished by sth

segnalazione [seɲ·ɲa·lat·'tsio:·ne] *f* **1.**(*segnale*) signal **2.**(*azione*) signalling **3.** *fig* (*di artista, di libro*) recommendation

segnale [seɲ·'ɲa:·le] *m* (*segno convenuto*) signal; ~ **stradale** road sign; ~ **d'allarme** alarm

segnaletica [seɲ·ɲa·'lɛ:·ti·ka] <-che> *f* signs *pl;* ~ **stradale** road signs *pl*

segnalibro [seɲ·ɲa·'li:·bro] *m* bookmark

segnaposto [seɲ·ɲa·'pos·to] *m* place card

segnare [seɲ·'ɲa:·re] I. *vt* **1.**(*gener*) to mark **2.**(*prendere nota di*) to jot down **3.** SPORT (*gol, punto*) to score **4.**(*indicare: orologio, termometro*) to show II. *vr:* -**rsi** (*fare il segno della croce*) to cross oneself

segno ['seɲ·ɲo] *m* **1.**(*indizio, accenno, gesto, atto*) sign; **non dar** ~ **di voler fare qc** to give no sign of wanting to do sth; ~ **della croce** sign of the cross; -**i dello zodiaco** signs of the zodiac; **fare** ~ **di sì** to nod; **fare** ~ **di no** to shake one's head; **fare** ~ **con la mano** to make a sign with one's hand; **fare** ~ **con la testa** to make a sign with one's head; **in** ~ **di** as a sign of **2.**(*traccia, espressione grafica, limite*) mark; **lasciare il** ~ *a. fig* to leave a mark; -**i di interpunzione** punctuation marks; **passare il** ~ to overstep the mark **3.**(*bersaglio*) **tiro a** ~ target shooting; **andare a** ~ to score; *fig* to strike home; **colpire nel** ~ to hit the target; *fig* to hit the nail on the head

segregare [se·gre·'ga:·re] I. *vt* (*rinchiudere*) to segregate II. *vr:* -**rsi** (*isolarsi*) to shut oneself up

segretario, -a [se·gre·'ta:·rio] <-i, -ie> *m, f* secretary; **Segretario di Stato** Secretary of State

segreteria [se·gre·te·'ri:·a] <-ie> *f* **1.**(*ufficio*) office **2.**(*loc*) ~ **telefonica** answering machine

segretezza [se·gre·'tet·tsa] *f* (*di informazione*) confidentiality

segreto [se·'gre:·to] *m* (*ciò che viene tenuto nascosto*) secret; **sai mantenere un ~?** can you keep a secret?; ~ **bancario** banking secrecy; ~ **confessionale** secrecy of the confession-

al; ~ **di stato** state secret; **fare qc in** ~ to do sth in secret

segreto, -a *agg* secret

seguace [se·'gua:·tʃe] *mf* (*di dottrina, maestro*) follower

seguente [se·'guɛn·te] *agg* (*successivo*) next

seguire [se·'gui:·re] I. *vt* *avere* **1.**(*gener*) ~ **qu/qc** to follow sb/sth; ~ **la moda** to follow fashion; ~ **il consiglio di qu** to follow sb's advice **2.**(*corso di studi*) to take **3.**(*con lo sguardo*) to watch; (*con l'attenzione*) to follow II. *vi essere* **1.**(*venir dopo, derivare*) to follow; **ne segue che ...** it follows that ... **2.**(*continuare*) to continue

seguito [se·'gui·to] *m* **1.**(*scorta*) retinue **2.**(*discepoli*) followers *pl* **3.**(*continuazione*) sequel; **dare** ~ **a qc** to follow sth up **4.** *fig* (*conseguenza*) repercussions *pl* **5.**(*loc*) **in** ~ **a** as a result of; **in** ~ later on; **di** ~ below

sei¹ ['sɛ:·i] I. *num* six II. <-> *m* **1.**(*numero*) six **2.**(*nelle date*) sixth **3.**(*voto scolastico*) =C, average grade III. *fpl* 6 o'clock

sei² **2. pers sing pr di essere¹**

seicentesco, -a [sei·tʃen·'tes·ko] <-schi, -sche> *agg v.* **secentesco**

seicento [sei·'tʃɛn·to] I. *num* six hundred II. <-> *m* **il Seicento** the seventeenth century

seimila [sei·'mi:·la] I. *num* six thousand II. <-> *m* six thousand

selciato [sel·'tʃa:·to] *m* (stone) paving

selettività [se·let·ti·vi·'ta] <-> *f* (*di scuola, procedura*) selectivity

selettivo, -a [se·let·'ti:·vo] *agg* **1.**(*criteri, metodo*) selective **2.**(*persona*) choosy

selezionare [se·let·tsio·'na:·re] *vt* (*scegliere, individuare*) to choose

selezione [se·let·'tsio:·ne] *f* **1.**(*scelta*) selection **2.** BIOL ~ **naturale** natural selection

self-service ['self·'sə:·vis] <-> *m* (*ristorante*) self-service restaurant

sella ['sɛl·la] *f* saddle

sellaio [sel·'la:·io] <-ai> *m* saddler

sellino [sel·'li:·no] *m* saddle

selvaggina [sel·vad·'dʒi:·na] *f* game

selvaggio, -a [sel·'vad·dʒo] <-ggi, -gge> I. *agg* (*luogo*) wild II. *m, f* savage

selvatico, -a [sel·'va:·ti·ko] <-ci, -che> *agg* **1.**(*gener*) wild; **gatto** ~ feral cat **2.** *fig* (*persona*) unsociable

semaforo [se·'ma:·fo·ro] *m* traffic lights *pl;* ~ **verde** *fig* green light

semantica [se·'man·ti·ka] <-che> *f* LING semantics

semantico, -a [se·'man·ti·ko] <-ci, -che> *agg* LING semantic

sembrare [sem·'bra:·re] *vi essere* **1.**(*parere*) to seem; **sembra che ...** +*conj* it seems (that) ...; **sembra contento** he seems happy; **sembra non ricordarsi dell'accaduto** he [*o* she] seems not to remember what happened **2.**(*ritenere*) **ti sembra di aver ragione?** do you think you're right?; **come ti sembra?** what do you think (of it)? **3.**(*avere l'aspetto*) to look like

S

seme ['se:·me] *m* 1.(*gener*) seed 2.(*delle carte*) suit

semente [se·'mɛn·te] *f* seed

semestrale [se·mes·'tra:·le] *agg* (*corso*) six-month; (*rivista*) biannual

semestre [se·'mɛs·tre] *m* semester

semi- [se·mi] (*in parole composte*) semi-

semianalfabeta [se·mi·an·al·fa·'bɛ:·ta] <-i *m*, -e *f*> I. *agg* semi-literate II. *mf* semi-literate

semiaperto, -a [se·mi·a·'pɛr·to] *agg* (*porta, occhi*) half open

semicerchio [se·mi·'tʃer·kio] *m* semicircle

semicircolare [se·mi·tʃir·ko·'la:·re] *agg* semi-circular

semifinale [se·mi·fi·'na:·le] *f* (*gara*) semifinal

semifreddo [se·mi·'fred·do] *m* (*dolce*) cold dessert made with ice cream

seminare [se·mi·'na:·re] *vt* 1.(*campo, grano, odio, discordia*) to sow 2.SPORT to leave behind 3.(*inseguitore*) to shake off

seminario [se·mi·'na:·rio] <-i> *m* 1.REL seminary 2.(*corso*) seminar 3.(*convegno*) conference

seminato, -a *agg fig* ~ **di** scattered with

seminfermità [se·min·fer·mi·'ta] *f* partial infirmity; ~ **mentale** partial insanity

seminudo, -a [se·mi·'nu:·do] *agg* half-naked

semiologia [se·mio·lo·'dʒi:·a] <-gie> *f* semiology

semioscurità [se·mio·sku·ri·'ta] <-> *f* semi-darkness

semirigido, -a *agg* TEC semi-rigid; **lenti a contatto -e** semi-rigid contact lenses

semirimorchio [se·mi·ri·'mɔr·kio] *m* TEC semitrailer

semisfera [se·mis·'fɛ:·ra] *f* hemisphere

semisferico, -a [se·mis·'fɛ:·ri·ko] <-ci, -che> *agg* hemispherical

semitono [se·mi·'tɔ:·no] *m* semitone

semitrasparente [se·mi·tras·pa·'rɛn·te] *agg* semi-transparent

semivuoto, -a [se·mi·'vuɔ:·to] *agg* half empty; **un bicchiere** ~ a half-empty glass

semmai [sem·'ma:·i] *cong* if anything

semola ['se:·mo·la] *f* (*farina*) flour; ~ **di grano duro** durum wheat flour

semolino [se·mo·'li:·no] *m* 1.(*farina*) semolina 2.(*minestra*) semolina soup

semplice ['sem·pli·tʃe] *agg* 1.(*gener*) simple 2.(*schietto: persona*) straightforward; (*ingenuo*) ingenuous

semplicemente [sem·pli·tʃe·'men·te] *avv* simply

sempliciotto, -a [sem·pli·'tʃɔt·to] *fam* I. *agg* simple-minded II. *m, f* simpleton

semplicità [sem·pli·tʃi·'ta] <-> *f* 1. *a. fig* simplicity 2. *pej* (*ingenuità*) simple-mindedness

semplificare [sem·pli·fi·'ka:·re] I. *vt a.* MATH to simplify II. *vr:* -**rsi** (*diventare più semplice*) to become simpler

semplificazione [sem·pli·fi·kat·'tsio:·ne] *f* simplification

sempre ['sɛm·pre] *avv* 1.(*gener*) always; **da** ~ always; **è** ~ **la mia musica preferita** it's always been my favorite music; **una volta per** ~ once and for all 2.(*ancora, tuttavia, nondimeno*) still 3. ~ **che** +*conj* as long as

sempreverde [sem·pre·'ver·de] I. *agg* ever-green II. *m o f* evergreen

sempronio, -a [sem·'prɔ:·nio] <-i, -ie> *m, f fam* **Tizio, Caio e Sempronio** Tom, Dick, and Harry

senape[1] ['sɛ:·na·pe] *f* mustard

senape[2] <inv> *agg* mustard-colored

senato [se·'na:·to] *m* (*ramo del parlamento*) Senate

senatore, -trice [se·na·'to:·re] *m, f* senator

senese[1] <*sing*> *m* (*dialetto*) Sienese

senese[2] [se·'ne:·se] I. *agg* Sienese II. *mf* (*abitante*) person from Siena

Senese <*sing*> *m* Siena area; **nel** ~ in the Siena area

senile [se·'ni:·le] *agg* old; **l'età** ~ old age

senilità [se·ni·li·'ta] <-> *f* old age

senior[1] ['sɛ:n·ior] <inv> *agg* 1.(*più vecchio*) **il signor Giorgi** ~ Mr. Giorgi Senior 2. SPORT senior

senior[2] <seniores> *mf* COM senior employee

senno ['sen·no] *m* judg(e)ment; **uscire di** [*o* **perdere il**] ~ to lose one's mind

sennò [sen·'nɔ] *avv fam* otherwise

seno ['se:·no] *m* 1.(*mammella*) breast; (*petto*) breasts *pl* 2. MATH sine

senonché [se·noɲ·'ke] *v.* sennonché

sensato, -a [sen·'sa:·to] *agg* sensible

sensazionale [sen·sat·tsio·'na:·le] *agg* (*notizia, avvenimento*) sensational

sensazione [sen·sat·'tsio:·ne] *f* 1.(*tattile, visiva*) sensation 2.(*impressione*) feeling; **ho la sensazione che ...** I have the feeling that ... 3.(*loc*) **fare** ~ to cause a sensation

sensibile [sen·'si:·bi·le] *agg* 1.(*gener*) sensitive; **essere** ~ **a qc** to be sensitive to sth 2.(*notevole*) noticeable

sensibilità [sen·si·bi·li·'ta] <-> *f* 1.(*capacità di percepire*) feeling 2.(*emotiva*) sensitivity

sensibilizzare [sen·si·bi·lid·'dza:·re] *vt fig* ~ **qu a qc** to make sb aware of sth

sensitivo, -a [sen·si·'ti:·vo] I. *agg* 1.(*facoltà*) clairvoyant 2.(*sensibile, emotivo*) sensitive II. *m, f* medium

senso ['sɛn·so] *m* 1.(*gener*) sense; **buon** ~ good sense; ~ **comune** common sense; ~ **della misura** sense of proportion; **avere** ~ **pratico** to be practical; **fare** ~ **a qu** to disgust sb 2. *pl* (*coscienza*) **riprendere i** -**i** to regain consciousness; **perdere i** -**i** to lose consciousness 3.(*sensazione*) feeling 4.(*significato*) meaning; **a** ~ logically 5.(*direzione*) direction; **'~ vietato'** 'no entry'; **strada a** ~ **unico** one way street; **in** ~ **opposto** from the opposite direction; **in** ~ **orario/antiorario** clockwise/counterclockwise

sensore [sen·'so:·re] *m* TEC (*dispositivo*) sensor

sensoriale [sen·so·'ria:·le] *agg* sensory

sensuale [sen·su·'a:·le] *agg* (*sguardo, voce*) sensual

sensualità [sen·su·a·li·'ta] <-> *f* sensuality

sentenza [sen·'tɛn·tsa] *f* 1. JUR sentence; ~ **di assoluzione** acquittal; ~ **di condanna** conviction 2. (*massima*) maxim; **sputar -e** to moralize

sentenziare [sen·ten·'tsia:·re] *vt* 1. JUR ~ **che** ... to rule that ... 2. *fig* (*giudicare con saccenteria*) to pontificate

sentiero [sen·'tiɛ:·ro] *m* path

sentimentale [sen·ti·men·'ta:·le] *agg* sentimental

sentimentalismo [sen·ti·men·ta·'liz·mo] *m pej* sentimentality

sentimento [sen·ti·'men·to] *m* 1. (*il sentire*) feeling 2. *pl* (*modo di pensare*) sentiments *pl*

sentinella [sen·ti·'nɛl·la] *f* guard; **fare la ~** *a. fig* to keep watch

sentire [sen·'ti:·re] I. *vt* 1. (*con le orecchie*) to hear; (*ascoltare*) to listen to; **farsi ~** to make one's voice heard; **stare a ~** (**qu**) to listen (to sb) 2. (*con il naso*) to smell 3. (*col gusto*) to taste 4. (*col tatto*) to feel 5. (*provare, accorgersi*) to feel; ~ **stanchezza** to feel tired; ~ **fame** to feel hungry; ~ **sonno** to feel sleepy; **sentire caldo/freddo** to feel hot/cold 6. (*venire a sapere*) to hear; **ho sentito che** ... I heard that ... II. *vr:* **-rsi** to feel; **mi sento bene** I feel well; **mi sento male** I feel ill; **-rsi svenire** to feel faint; **non me la sento** *fam* I don't feel like it; **non me la sento di venire con voi** I don't feel like coming with you

sentito, -a [sen·'ti:·to] *agg* 1. (*sincero*) sincere 2. (*loc*) **per ~ dire** by hearsay

sentore [sen·'to:·re] *m* **avere ~ di qc** to get wind of sth

senza ['sɛn·tsa] I. *prep* without; ~ **di me/te/lui** without me/you/him; ~ **casa** homeless; ~ **dubbio** without doubt; ~ **paragone** unequalled; **senz'altro** certainly; **fare ~ qc/qu** to do without sth/sb; **rimanere ~ qc** to have run out of sth II. *cong* without +*inf;* ~ **dire niente** without saying anything; ~ **che** +*conj* without; ~ **che io glielo chiedessi** without my asking him

senzatetto [sen·tsa·'tet·to] <-> *mf* homeless person

separare [se·pa·'ra:·re] I. *vt* 1. (*disgiungere*) to separate 2. (*tenere distinto*) to distinguish II. *vr:* **-rsi** (*lasciarsi: coniugi*) to separate; (*amici, soci*) to part company

separatamente [se·pa·ra·ta·'men·te] *avv* separately

separato, -a [se·pa·'ra:·to] *agg* 1. (*distinto*) separate 2. (*da coniuge*) separated; **marito ~** estranged husband; **moglie -a** estranged wife

separazione [se·pa·rat·'tsio:·ne] *f* separation

séparé [se·pa·'re] *m* (*in ristorante*) private dining room

sepolcrale [se·pol·'kra:·le] *agg* 1. (*monumento ~*) tomb 2. *fig* (*silenzio, voce*) sepulchral

sepolcro [se·'pol·kro] *m* tomb

sepolto, -a [se·'pol·to] I. *pp di* **seppellire** II. *agg* buried

sepoltura [se·pol·'tu:·ra] *f* (*cerimonia*) burial

seppellire [sep·pel·'li:·re] <seppellisco, seppellii, seppellito *o* sepolto> *vt* to bury

seppi ['sɛp·pi] *1. pers sing pass rem di* **sapere**[1]

seppia ['sep·pia] <-ie> *f* cuttlefish

seppure, se pure [sep·'pu:·re] *cong* +*conj* 1. (*anche se*) even if 2. (*se anche*) though

sequela [se·'kuɛ:·la] *f* series

sequenza [se·'kuɛn·tsa] *f* 1. (*serie*) sequence 2. FILM sequel

sequestrare [se·kues·'tra:·re] *vt* 1. JUR to seize 2. (*illegalmente*) to kidnap

sequestratore, -trice [se·kues·tra·'to:·re] *m, f* kidnapper

sequestro [se·'kuɛs·tro] *m* 1. JUR seizure; **mettere sotto ~** to seize 2. (*illegale*) kidnap; ~ **di persona** false imprisonment; **tenere sotto ~** to falsely imprison

sera ['se:·ra] *f* evening; **buona ~!** good evening; **di ~** in the evening; **domani/ieri ~** tomorrow/yesterday evening; **la ~ prima** the previous evening; **si fa ~** it's getting dark

serafico, -a [se·'ra:·fi·ko] <-ci, -che> *agg fig, fam* (*tranquillo*) serene

serale [se·'ra:·le] *agg* evening; **scuola ~** night school

serata [se·'ra:·ta] *f* evening

serbare [ser·'ba:·re] *vt* (*segreto*) to keep; ~ **rancore a qu** to bear a grudge against sb; ~ **odio a qu** to hate sb

serbatoio [ser·ba·'to:·io] <-oi> *m* tank

Serbia ['sɛr·bia] *f* Serbia

serbo ['sɛr·bo] *m* **in ~** in store

serbo, -a I. *agg* Serbian II. *m, f* (*abitante*) Serb

serbocroato [ser·bo·kro·'a:·to] *m* (*lingua*) Serbo-Croatian

serbocroato, -a *agg* Serbo-Croatian

serenata [se·re·'na:·ta] *f* serenade

serenità [se·re·ni·'ta] <-> *f* serenity

sereno, -a *agg* 1. METEO clear 2. (*persona*) calm; (*vita*) quiet

sergente [ser·'dʒɛn·te] *m* sergeant

serial ['sɛ·ri·al] <-> *m* serial

seriamente [se·ria·'men·te] *avv* seriously

serie ['sɛː·rie] <-> *f* 1. (*gener*) series; **modello di ~** standard model; **produzione in ~** mass production 2. SPORT league; ~ **A** *the top league of Italian soccer*

serietà [se·rie·'ta] <-> *f* seriousness

serio ['sɛː·rio] *m* **sul ~** seriously; **fare sul ~** *fam* to be serious; **prendere qc/qu sul ~** to take sth/sb seriously

serio, -a <-i, -ie> *agg* 1. (*uomo, condotta*) responsible 2. (*sguardo, voce, questione*) serious

sermone [ser·'mo:·ne] *m* 1. REL sermon 2. *fig, pej* (*ramanzina*) lecture

serpe ['sɛr·pe] *f* snake

serpeggiante [ser·ped·'dʒan·te] *agg* (*fiume, strada*) winding

serpeggiare [ser·ped·'dʒa:·re] *vi* 1. (*strada,*

fiume) to wind **2.** *fig* (*insinuarsi*) to spread

serpente [ser·'pɛn·te] *m* **1.** BOT snake **2.** *fig, pej* viper; **~ a sonagli** rattlesnake

serpentina [ser·pen·'ti:·na] *f* **1.** (*linea*) **strada a ~** winding road; **~ refrigerante** cooling coil **2.** (*traiettoria*) winding route

serra ['sɛr·ra] *f* BOT, AGR greenhouse; **effetto ~** greenhouse effect

serramanico [ser·ra·'ma:·ni·ko] *m* **coltello a ~** switchblade

serramento [ser·ra·'men·to] <-i *m o* -a *f*> *mf* fitting for a window or door

serranda [ser·'ran·da] *f* shutter

serrare [ser·'ra:·re] *vt* to close

serrata [ser·'ra:·ta] *f* lockout

serrato, -a [ser·'ra:·to] *agg* (*discorso*) incisive; (*interrogatorio*) penetrating; **a ritmo ~** quickly

serratura [ser·ra·'tu:·ra] *f* lock

serva ['sɛr·va] *f* (*donna di servizio*) maid

server ['sə:·və/'ser·ver] <- *o* servers> *m* COMPUT server

servile [ser·'vi:·le] *agg* **1.** (*condizione, mestiere*) menial **2.** *fig, pej* (*animo, modi*) servile

servire [ser·'vi:·re] I. *vt avere* (*gener*) to serve; (*come domestico*) to work; **~ qu** (*re, dio*) to serve sb; **~ la patria** to serve one's country II. *vi essere o avere* **1.** (*essere utile*) to be useful; **non ~ a niente** to be useless; (*aver bisogno*) to need; **mi serve una sedia** *fam* I need a chair **2.** MIL, SPORT to serve III. *vr:* **-rsi** **1.** (*usare*) **-rsi di qc** to use sth **2.** (*a tavola*) to help oneself; **servitevi pure** help yourselves **3.** (*essere cliente*) to shop

servitù [ser·vi·'tu] <-> *f* **1.** (*schiavitù*) slavery **2.** (*personale di servizio*) domestic staff

servizievole [ser·vit·'tsie:·vo·le] *agg* obliging

servizio [ser·'vit·tsio] <-i> *m* **1.** (*gener*) service; **il settore dei -i** the service sector; **~ assistenza clienti** customer services; **~ militare** military service; **essere in ~** to be in service; **~ pubblico** public service; **donna di ~** maid; **stazione di ~** gas station; **fuori ~** *fig* out of order **2.** (*giornalismo*) RADIO, TV report; **~ speciale** special report **3. ~ da tavola** dinner service **4.** *pl* bathroom

servo ['sɛr·vo] *m* (*schiavo*) serf

servoassistenza [ser·vo·as·sis·'tɛn·tsa] *f* MOT servo assistance

servofreno [ser·vo·'fre:·no/ser·vo·'frɛ:·no] *m* servo brake

servosterzo [ser·vos·'tɛr·tso] *m* power steering

sesamo ['sɛ:·za·mo] *m* sesame; **apriti ~!** open sesame!

sessanta [ses·'san·ta] I. *num* sixty II. <-> *m* sixty; *v.a.* **cinquanta**

sessantenne [ses·san·'tɛn·ne] I. *agg* sixty-year-old II. *mf* sixty year old

sessantennio [ses·san·'tɛn·nio] <-i> *m* sixty year period

sessantesimo [ses·san·'tɛ:·zi·mo] *m* (*frazione*) sixtieth

sessantesimo, -a I. *agg* sixtieth II. *m, f* sixti-

eth; *v.a.* **quinto**

sessantina [ses·san·'ti:·na] *f* **una ~ (di ...)** around sixty; **essere sulla ~** to be around sixty

sessantottino, -a [ses·san·tot·'ti:·no] I. *m, f* person who took part in the events of 1968 II. *agg* connected with the events of 1968

sessione [ses·'sio:·ne] *f* session

sessismo [ses·'siz·mo] *m* sexism

sessista [ses·'sis·ta] <-i *m*, -e *f*> I. *agg* sexist II. *mf* sexist

sesso ['sɛs·so] *m* sex; **~ sicuro** safe sex

sessoturista [sɛs·so·tu·'ris·ta] <-i *m*, -e *f*> *mf* sex tourist

sessuale [ses·su·'a:·le] *agg* sexual

sessualità [ses·sua·li·'ta] <-> *f* sexuality

sessuologia [ses·suo·lo·'dʒi:·a] <-gie> *f* sexology

sessuologo, -a [ses·su·'ɔ:·lo·go] <-gi, -ghe> *m, f* sexologist

sestetto [ses·'tet·to] *m* sextet

sesto ['sɛs·to] *m* **1.** ARCH curve; **arco a tutto ~** rounded arch; **arco a ~ acuto** pointed arch **2.** (*frazione*) sixth **3.** (*loc*) **rimettere in ~** to put back in order

sesto, -a ['sɛs·to] I. *agg* sixth II. *m, f* sixth; *v.a.* **quinto**

set [sɛt] <-> *m* set; **essere sul ~** to be on the set

seta ['se:·ta] *f* silk

setacciare [se·tat·'tʃa:·re] *vt* **1.** (*farina*) to sieve **2.** *fig* (*esaminare con cura*) to comb

setaccio [se·'tat·tʃo] <-cci> *m* sieve; **passare al ~** *fig* to comb

sete ['se:·te] *f* thirst; **avere ~** to be thirsty; **mi viene ~** I get thirsty; **~ di vendetta** thirst for revenge

setificio [se·ti·'fi:·tʃo] <-ci> *m* silk factory

setola ['se:·to·la] *f* bristle

setta ['sɛt·ta] *f* sect

settanta [set·'tan·ta] I. *num* seventy II. <-> *m* seventy; *v.a.* **cinquanta**

settantenne [set·tan·'tɛn·ne] I. *agg* seventy-year-old II. *mf* seventy year old

settantennio [set·tan·'tɛn·nio] <-i> *m* seventy year period

settantesimo [set·tan·'tɛ:·zi·mo] *m* seventieth

settantesimo, -a I. *agg* seventieth II. *m, f* seventieth; *v.a.* **quinto**

settantina [set·tan·'ti:·na] *f* **una ~ (di ...)** around seventy; **essere sulla ~** to be around seventy

settario, -a [set·'ta:·rio] <-i, -ie> I. *agg* (*movimento, omicidio*) sectarian II. *m, f* sectarian

sette ['sɛt·te] I. *num* seven II. <-> *m* **1.** (*numero*) seven **2.** (*nelle date*) seventh **3.** (*voto scolastico*) =B, above average grade III. *fpl* seven o'clock; *v.a.* **cinque**

settecentesco, -a [set·te·tʃen·'tes·ko] <-schi, -sche> *agg* eighteenth-century

settecento [set·te·'tʃɛn·to] I. *num* seven hundred II. <-> *m* seven hundred; **il Settecento** the eighteenth century

settembre [set·'tɛm·bre] *m* September; *v.a.* **aprile**

settemila [set·te·'mi:·la] I. *num* seven thousand II. <-> *m* seven thousand

settentrionale [set·ten·trio·'na:·le] I. *agg* northern II. *mf* 1. (*del Nord*) northerner 2. (*dell'Italia del Nord*) northern Italian

settentrione [set·ten·'trio:·ne] *m* 1. (*il nord*) north 2. (*d'Italia*) north of Italy

settimana [set·ti·'ma:·na] *f* week; **~ bianca** ski vacation; **~ santa** Holy Week; **fine ~** weekend

settimanale [set·ti·ma·'na:·le] I. *agg* weekly II. *m* weekly

settimino, -a [set·ti·'mi:·no] *m*, *f* baby born two months premature

settimo ['sɛt·ti·mo] *m* seventh

settimo, -a I. *agg* seventh II. *m*, *f* seventh; *v.a.* **quinto**

setto ['sɛt·to] *m* septum; **~ nasale** nasal septum

settore [set·'to:·re] *m* 1. GENER sector 2. *a. fig* (*zona*) area

settoriale [set·to·'ria:·le] *agg* 1. COM sector-based 2. *fig* (*circoscritto*) limited

settuplo ['sɛt·tup·lo] *m* **il ~** seven times as much

settuplo, -a *agg* sevenfold

severità [se·ve·ri·'ta] <-> *f* 1. (*di docente, genitore*) strictness 2. (*di metodo, studio*) rigor

severo, -a [se·'vɛ:·ro] *agg* (*genitore, docente*) strict

sevizia [se·'vit·tsia] <-ie> *f pl* torture

seviziare [se·vit·'tsia:·re] *vt* 1. (*usare sevizie*) to beat up 2. (*violentare*) to rape

sexy ['sek·si] <inv> *agg* sexy

sezionamento [set·tsio·na·'men·to] *m* (*di cadavere*) dissection

sezionare [set·tsio·'na:·re] *vt* 1. (*dividere*) to divide up 2. (*cadavere*) to dissect

sezione [set·'tsio:·ne] *f* 1. (*gener*) section 2. JUR division

sfaccendato, -a [sfat·tʃen·'da:·to] *m*, *f fam* lazybones

sfaccettatura [sfat·tʃet·ta·'tu:·ra] *f* (*aspetto*) facet

sfacchinare [sfak·ki·'na:·re] *vi* to slog

sfacchinata [sfak·ki·'na:·ta] *f* 1. (*lavoro intenso*) grind 2. (*sforzo intenso*) slog

sfacciataggine [sfat·tʃa·'ta:·dʒi·ne] *f* nerve

sfacciato, -a [sfat·'tʃa:·to] I. *agg* (*tono, gesto*) nervy II. *m*, *f* **è uno ~** he has no shame

sfacelo [sfa·'tʃɛ:·lo] *m* (*rovina*) ruin

sfaldarsi [sfal·'da:r·si] *vr* (*disfarsi*) to break up

sfamare [sfa·'ma:·re] I. *vt* to feed II. *vr:* -**rsi** to satisfy one's hunger

sfarzo ['sfar·tso] *m* opulence

sfarzosità [sfar·tso·si·'ta] <-> *f* opulence

sfarzoso, -a [sfar·'tso:·so] *agg* opulent

sfasamento [sfa·za·'men·to] *m* 1. EL phase displacement 2. *fig, fam* (*confusione*) disorientation

sfasare [sfa·'za:·re] *vt* 1. EL to adjust the phase of 2. *fig, fam* to disorient

sfasciacarrozze [sfaʃ·ʃa·kar·'rɔt·tse] <-> *m* wrecking yard

sfasciare [sfaʃ·'ʃa:·re] I. *vt* 1. (*ferita*) to unbandage 2. *a. fig* (*distruggere*) to wreck II. *vr:* -**rsi** (*rompersi*) to smash to pieces

sfascio ['sfaʃ·ʃo] *m fig* (*rovina*) ruin; **essere allo ~** to be on the verge of collapse

sfatare [sfa·'ta:·re] *vt* (*leggenda, mito*) to explode

sfaticato, -a [sfa·ti·'ka:·to] *m*, *f pej, fam* lazybones

sfatto, -a ['sfat·to] *agg* 1. (*letto*) unmade 2. *fig* (*persona*) flabby

sfavillare [sfa·vil·'la:·re] *vi* 1. (*luccicare*) to sparkle 2. *fig* (*esprimere gioia*) to glow

sfavillio [sfa·vil·'li:·o] <-ii> *m* sparkling

sfavore [sfa·'vo:·re] *m* **a ~ di** to the disadvantage of

sfavorevole [sfa·vo·'re:·vo·le] *agg* unfavorable

sfavorire [sfa·vo·'ri:·re] <sfavorisco> *vt* (*gener*) to work against; (*candidato*) to treat unfavorably

sfegatato, -a [sfe·ga·'ta:·to] I. *agg* fanatical II. *m*, *f fam* fanatic

sfera ['sfɛ:·ra] *f* 1. MATH sphere; **penna a ~** ballpoint (pen) 2. *fig* (*ambito*) area

sferico, -a ['sfɛ:·ri·ko] <-ci, -che> *agg* spherical

sferrare [sfer·'ra:·re] *vt* (*colpo, attacco*) to launch

sferruzzare [sfer·rut·'tsa:·re] *vi* to knit (away)

sferzare [sfer·'tsa:·re] *vt* 1. (*colpire con violenza*) to lash 2. *fig* (*criticare*) to lash out at

sferzata [sfer·'tsa:·ta] *f* 1. (*critica*) tongue-lashing 2. *fig* (*di energia, ottimismo*) wave

sfiancare [sfiaŋ·'ka:·re] I. *vt fig* (*spossare*) to exhaust II. *vr:* -**rsi** *fig* (*spossarsi*) to exhaust oneself

sfiatare [sfia·'ta:·re] I. *vi* to vent II. *vr:* -**rsi** *fam* (*perdere il fiato*) to shout oneself hoarse

sfiatatoio [sfia·ta·'to:·io] <-oi> *m* (*dispositivo*) vent

sfiato ['sfia:·to] *m* (*sfiatatoio*) vent

sfibrare [sfi·'bra:·re] *vt* (*svigorire*) to exhaust

sfida ['sfi:·da] *f* 1. (*invito a battersi*) challenge; **lanciare una ~ a qu** to challenge sb 2. *fig* (*provocazione*) defiance

sfidante [sfi·'dan·te] I. *agg* challenging II. *mf* challenger

sfidare [sfi·'da:·re] *vt* 1. (*gener*) to challenge; **~ qu a poker** to challenge sb to a game of poker; **~ qu a fare qc** to challenge sb to do sth 2. (*pericolo, morte*) to defy; **sfido io!** *fam* of course!

sfiducia [sfi·'du:·tʃa] *f* mistrust; **voto di ~** vote of no confidence

sfigato, -a [sfi·'ga:·to] *vulg* I. *agg* 1. (*sfortunato*) unlucky 2. (*squallido*) bleak II. *m*, *f* (*sfortunato*) unlucky person

sfigurare [sfi·gu·'ra:·re] I. *vt fig* (*deturpare*) to disfigure II. *vi* (*fare brutta figura*) to make a bad impression

S

sfilacciarsi [sfi·lat·'tʃa·r·si] *vr* to fray

sfilare [sfi·'la:·re] I. *vt avere* (*anello, indumenti*) to take off II. *vr:* **-rsi** 1. (*calze, maglia*) to run 2. (*collana*) to come unstrung

sfilata [sfi·'la:·ta] *f* (*di persone*) procession; **~ di moda** fashion show

sfilettare [sfi·let·'ta:·re] *vt* to fillet

sfilza ['sfil·tsa] *f* (*lunga serie*) series

sfinge ['sfin·dʒe] *f* sphinx

sfinimento [sfi·ni·'men·to] *m* (*stanchezza*) exhaustion

sfinire [sfi·'ni:·re] <sfinisco> I. *vt* to exhaust II. *vr:* **-rsi** to exhaust oneself

sfiorare [sfio·'ra:·re] *vt* 1. (*toccare*) to brush 2. *fig* (*tema*) to touch on 3. (*successo, vittoria*) to come close to

sfiorire [sfio·'ri:·re] <sfiorisco> *vi essere* 1. BOT to wither 2. *fig* (*bellezza*) to fade

sfitto, -a ['sfit·to] *agg* vacant

sfizio ['sfit·tsio] <-i> *m dial* whim; **per ~** on a whim; **togliersi lo ~ di fare qc** to satisfy a whim

sfizioso, -a [sfit·'tsio:·so] *agg* (*cibo*) tasty

sfocato, -a [sfo·'ka:·to] *agg* (*foto*) out of focus

sfociare [sfo·'tʃa:·re] *vi essere* 1. (*fiume*) **~ in** to flow into 2. *fig* (*andare a finire*) **~ in qc** to develop into sth

sfocio ['sfo:·tʃo] <-ci> *m fig* (*soluzione*) way out

sfoderabile [sfo·de·'ra:·bi·le] *agg* **un divano ~** a sofa with removable covers

sfoderare [sfo·de·'ra:·re] *vt* 1. (*spada*) to draw 2. *fig* (*argomenti*) to bring out; (*coraggio*) to reveal

sfoderato, -a [sfo·de·'ra:·to] *agg* unlined

sfogare [sfo·'ga:·re] I. *vt avere* (*rabbia, odio*) to work off II. *vr:* **-rsi** (*manifestare ansia*) to unburden oneself; **-rsi su** [*o* **contro**] **qu** to take it out on sb

sfoggiare [sfod·'dʒa:·re] *vt* (*abiti, oggetti di lusso*) to show off

sfoggio ['sfɔd·dʒo] <-ggi> *m* **fare ~ di qc** to show sth off

sfoglia ['sfɔʎ·ʎa] *f* CULIN pasta dough; **pasta ~** puff pastry

sfogliare [sfoʎ·'ʎa:·re] *vt* (*libro, rivista*) to flick through

sfogliata [sfoʎ·'ʎa:·ta] *f* (*lettura sommaria*) glance; **dare una ~ al giornale** to glance through the newspaper

sfogliatella [sfoʎ·ʎa·'tɛl·la] *f* type of cake consisting of puff pastry filled with candied fruit and cream cheese

sfogo ['sfo:·go] <-ghi> *m* 1. (*gener*) outlet 2. *fam* MED rash 3. *fig* (*manifestazione di sentimenti*) outburst; **dare ~ ai propri sentimenti** to give vent to one's feelings

sfollagente [sfol·la·'dʒen·te] <-> *m* nightstick

sfollamento [sfol·la·'men·to] *m* (*di paese, scuola*) evacuation

sfollare [sfol·'la:·re] *vt avere* (*sgombrare: persone*) to displace; (*luogo*) to empty

sfoltire [sfol·'ti:·re] <sfoltisco> I. *vt* 1. (*bosco,*

capelli) to thin (out) 2. (*testo*) to prune II. *vr:* **-rsi** (*diventare meno folto*) to thin (out)

sfondamento [sfon·da·'men·to] *m* 1. (*rottura*) knocking down 2. SPORT bringing down

sfondare [sfon·'da:·re] I. *vt* 1. (*porta, cassa*) to break down; **~ una porta aperta** *fig* to push at an open door 2. MIL to break through II. *vi* (*avere successo*) to make a name for oneself

sfondato, -a *agg* (*botte, parete*) broken; (*scarpe*) worn-out; (*maglione*) out-of-shape; **essere ricco ~** *fam* to be rolling in it

sfondo ['sfon·do] *m* background; **sullo ~** in the background

sformare [sfor·'ma:·re] I. *vt* (*scarpe, giacca*) to put out of shape II. *vr:* **-rsi** (*scarpe, giacca*) to go out of shape

sformato [sfor·'ma:·to] *m savory dish made of vegetables and eggs*

sfornare [sfor·'na:·re] *vt* 1. CULIN to take out of the oven 2. *fig* (*far uscire in abbondanza*) to churn out

sfornito, -a [sfor·'ni:·to] *agg* (*cucina*) badly equipped; (*supermercato*) badly stocked

sfortuna [sfor·'tu:·na] *f* bad luck

sfortunato, -a [sfor·tu·'na:·to] *agg* unlucky; **essere ~ al gioco** to be unlucky at cards

sforzare [sfor·'tsa:·re] I. *vt* 1. (*gener*) to force 2. (*vista*) to strain II. *vr:* **-rsi** (*impegnarsi*) to make an effort

sforzo ['sfɔr·tso] *m* 1. (*impiego di forze*) effort; **senza ~ non si ottiene nulla** you won't get anywhere if you don't try; **fare uno ~** to make an effort; **non fare -i!** *fam* don't tire yourself out! 2. TEC stress

sfottere ['sfot·te·re] *vt fam* to tease

sfracellare [sfra·tʃel·'la:·re] I. *vt* (*rompere*) to smash (up) II. *vr:* **-rsi** (*rompersi*) to smash (up)

sfrattare [sfrat·'ta:·re] *vt* **~ qu** to evict sb

sfratto ['sfrat·to] *m* eviction

sfrecciare [sfret·'tʃa:·re] *vi essere* to shoot past

sfregamento [sfre·ga·'men·to] *m* (*movimento*) rubbing

sfregare [sfre·'ga:·re] *vt* 1. (*occhi*) to rub 2. (*auto*) to scrape

sfregiare [sfre·'dʒa:·re] *vt* (*rivale, quadro, viso*) to slash

sfregio ['sfre:·dʒo] <-gi> *m* 1. (*di persona*) scar 2. (*di cosa*) scrape

sfrenato, -a [sfre·'na:·to] *agg* (*ritmo*) frenetic; (*passione*) unbridled

sfrondare [sfron·'da:·re] *vt* to prune

sfrontatezza [sfron·ta·'tet·tsa] *f* impudence

sfrontato, -a [sfron·'ta:·to] *agg* impudent

sfruttamento [sfrut·ta·'men·to] *m* exploitation

sfruttare [sfrut·'ta:·re] *vt* 1. AGR, MIN to work 2. (*spazio*) to make the most of 3. *fig* (*situazione, circostanze, persona*) to take advantage of 4. (*dipendenti*) to exploit

sfruttatore, -trice [sfrut·ta·'to:·re] *m, f* exploiter

sfuggire [sfud·'dʒi:·re] *vi essere* **~ a** (*inseguitori*) to escape; (*discussione*) to avoid; **~ alla**

morte to escape death; **mi è sfuggita la penna di mano** the pen slipped out of my hand; **mi sfugge il titolo del film** I can't remember the name of the movie; **mi è sfuggito che ...** I forgot (that) ...; **mi sono sfuggiti molti errori** I missed a lot of mistakes; **mi è sfuggito di bocca che ...** I let it slip that ...

sfuggita [sfud·'dʒiː·ta] *f* **di ~** in passing

sfumare [sfu·'maː·re] I. *vt avere* 1. (*colori*) to shade 2. *fig* (*polemica*) to soften II. *vi essere* 1. (*dissolversi: nebbia, fumo*) to disappear 2. *fig* (*svanire: sogno*) to vanish 3. (*colore*) to shade into

sfumato, -a *agg* soft

sfumatura [sfu·ma·'tuː·ra] *f* 1. (*gradazione*) tone 2. *fig* (*di testo*) shade of meaning 3. *fig* (*accenno*) hint

sfuriata [sfu·'riaː·ta] *f fam* outburst

sfuso, -a ['sfuː·zo] *agg* 1. (*burro*) melted 2. COM loose

sg. *abbr di* **seguente** ff

sgabello [zga·'bɛl·lo] *m* stool

sgabuzzino [zga·bud·'dziː·no] *m* storage room

sgambato, -a [zgam·'baː·to] *agg* high-cut

sgambettare [zgam·bet·'taː·re] I. *vi* to kick one's legs II. *vt* **~ qu** to trip sb up

sgambetto [zgam·'bet·to] *m a. fig* **fare lo ~ a qu** to trip sb up

sganasciarsi [zga·naʃ·'ʃar·si] *vr fam* **~ dalle risa** to laugh one's head off

sganciare [zgan·'tʃaː·re] I. *vt* 1. (*veicolo*) to uncouple 2. (*bomba, siluro*) to launch 3. *fig, fam* (*denaro*) to fork out II. *vr:* **-rsi** 1. (*staccarsi: rimorchio*) to come uncoupled; (*oggetto legato, appeso*) to come undone 2. *fig, fam* (*da persona, impegno*) to get away

sgarbato, -a [zgar·'baː·to] *agg* (*tono, modi*) ill-mannered

sgarbo ['zgar·bo] *m* **fare uno ~ a qu** to be rude to sb

sgargiante [zgar·'dʒan·te] *agg* (*colore*) garish

sgarrare [zgar·'raː·re] *vi* to step out of line

sga(s)sare [zga(s)·'saː·re] I. *vt* (*bevande*) to make flat II. *vr:* **-rsi** *fam* (*abbattersi*) to become deflated

sgattaiolare [zgat·ta·io·'laː·re] *vi essere* (*fuggire via*) to sneak off

sgelare [zdʒe·'laː·re] I. *vt avere* (*scongelare*) to defrost II. *vr:* **-rsi** 1. (*scongelarsi*) to defrost 2. *fig* (*distendersi: atmosfera*) to thaw

sghembo, -a ['zgem·bo] *agg* (*storto*) crooked

sghignazzare [zgiɲ·ɲat·'tsaː·re] *vi fam* to laugh scornfully

sghimbescio, -a [zgim·'bɛʃ·ʃo] <-sci, -sce> *agg* **a** [*o* **di**] **~** crookedly

sghiribizzo [zgi·ri·'bid·dzo] *m fam* whim

sgobbare [zgob·'baː·re] *vi fam* (*lavorare duramente*) to slave (away); **~ sui libri** to study hard

sgobbata [zgob·'baː·ta] *f fam* slog

sgobbone, -a [zgob·'boː·ne] *m, f fam* workaholic

sgocciolare [zgot·tʃo·'laː·re] I. *vi essere o avere* (*liquidi*) to drip II. *vt avere* 1. (*liquidi*) to drip 2. (*recipienti*) to drain

sgocciolo ['zgot·tʃo·lo] *m fig* **essere agli -i** to be almost over

sgolarsi [zgo·'lar·si] *vr* to shout oneself hoarse

sgomb(e)rare [zgom·'braː·re (zgom·be·'raː·re)] *vt* 1. (*tavolo, stanza, strada*) to clear; **puoi ~ il tavolo dai tuoi libri?** can you clear your books off the table? 2. (*appartamento*) to vacate

sgombro ['zgom·bro] *m* ZOO mackerel

sgombro, -a *agg* (*casa, appartamento*) vacant

sgomentare [zgo·men·'taː·re] *vt* to dismay

sgomento [zgo·'men·to] *m* dismay

sgomento, -a *agg* dismayed

sgominare [zgo·mi·'naː·re] *vt* (*sconfiggere*) to defeat

sgommare [zgom·'maː·re] *vi* to make one's tires screech

sgommata [zgom·'maː·ta] *f* screech of tires

sgonfiare [zgon·'fiaː·re] I. *vt* 1. (*pneumatico, pallone*) to let the air out of 2. MED to bring down the swelling of II. *vr:* **-rsi** 1. (*ruota, pallone*) to go flat 2. MED to go down 3. *fig* (*ridimensionarsi*) to become deflated

sgonfio, -a ['zgon·fio] <-i, -ie> *agg* 1. (*pallone, ruota*) flat 2. MED no longer swollen

sgorbio ['zgɔr·bio] <-i> *m* 1. (*scrittura*) scrawl; (*disegni*) scribble 2. *fig, pej* (*persona brutta*) dog

sgorgare [zgor·'gaː·re] *vi essere* to gush

sgozzamento [zgot·tsa·'men·to] *m* slaughter

sgozzare [zgot·'tsaː·re] *vt* to slaughter

sgradevole [zgra·'deː·vo·le] *agg* unpleasant

sgradito, -a [zgra·'diː·to] *agg* unwelcome

sgraffignare [zgraf·fiɲ·'ɲaː·re] *vt fam* to swipe

sgrammaticato, -a [zgram·ma·ti·'kaː·to] *agg* ungrammatical

sgranare [zgra·'naː·re] *vt* (*piselli, fave*) to shuck; **~ gli occhi** to open one's eyes wide

sgranchire [zgraŋ·'kiː·re] <sgranchisco> *vt* to stretch; **-rsi le gambe** to stretch one's legs

sgranocchiare [zgra·nok·'kiaː·re] *vt fam* to munch

sgrassare [zgras·'saː·re] *vt* (*brodo*) to remove the fat from

sgravare [zgra·'vaː·re] I. *vt fig* (*liberare*) to relieve II. *vr:* **-rsi** (*liberarsi*) to free oneself

sgravio ['zgra·vio] <-i> *m* (*alleggerimento: di imposte*) relief; **~ fiscale** tax relief

sgraziato, -a [zgrat·'tsiaː·to] *agg* (*andatura, persona*) ungainly

sgretolamento [zgre·to·la·'men·to] *m a. fig* (*disfacimento*) crumbling

sgretolarsi [zgre·to·'lar·si] *vr a. fig* (*disgregarsi*) to crumble

sgridare [zgri·'daː·re] *vt* **~ qu** to tell sb off

sgridata [zgri·'daː·ta] *f* telling off

sguaiato, -a [zgua·'iaː·to] *agg* (*risata, gesto*) vulgar

sguainare [zguai·'naː·re] *vt* (*spada, sciabola*) to draw

sgualcire [zgual·'tʃi:·re] <sgualcisco> *vt* (*sciupare: abito*) to crush

sgualdrina [zgual·'dri:·na] *f* whore

sguardo ['zguar·do] *m* look; **alzare/abbassare lo** ~ to look up/down; **dare uno** ~ **a qc** to look at sth; **non degnare qu/qc di uno** ~ to not deign to look at sb/sth

sguarnito, -a [zguar·'ni:·to] *agg* (*negozio*) badly stocked; (*assortimento*) scanty

sguattero, -a ['zguat·te·ro] *m, f* scullery boy *m,* scullery maid *f;* **trattare qu come uno** ~ to treat sb like a servant

sguazzare [zguat·'tsa:·re] *vi* **1.** (*nell'acqua*) to splash around **2.** *fig* ~ **nell'oro** to be rolling in it

sguinzagliare [zguin·tsaʎ·'ʎa:·re] *vt* **1.** (*cani*) to let off the leash **2.** *fig* (*mandare alla ricerca*) ~ **un detective dietro qu** to hire a private detective to follow sb

sgusciare [zguʃ·'ʃa:·re] **I.** *vt avere* (*uova, fagioli, fave*) to shell **II.** *vi essere fig* (*svignarsela*) ~ **via** to slip away

shampoo [ʃæm·'pu:/'ʃam·po] <-> *m* shampoo

share ['ʃɛ·ə] <-> *m* TV audience ratings

shareware <-> *m* COMPUT shareware

shoccare [ʃok·'ka:·re] *v.* scioccare

shoccato, -a [ʃok·'ka:·to] *agg v.* scioccato

shock [ʃɔk] <-> *m* shock

shockato, -a *agg v.* scioccato

shopper ['ʃɔ·pə] <-> *m* shopping bag

short [ʃɔːt] <-> *m* short (film)

shorts [ʃɔːts] *mpl* shorts

si¹ [si] *pron 3. pers m e f sing e pl* **1.** (*riflessivo, complemento oggetto: impersonale*) oneself; (*maschile*) himself; (*femminile*) herself; (*neutro*) itself; (*plurale*) themselves; **si è tagliato** he cut himself; **si è scottata** she burned herself; **si alzano sempre tardi** they always get up late; ~ **veste con eleganza** he [*o* she] dresses well **2.** (*riflessivo, complemento di termine*) **si è rotta un piede** she broke her foot; **si è tagliato un dito** he cut his finger; **si è messo il cappotto** he put on his coat **3.** (*intensivo*) **si è comprata un vestito nuovo** she bought herself a new dress; **si è mangiato mezza torta da solo** he ate half a cake all on his own; **guardarsi un film** to watch a movie **4.** (*reciproco*) each other; **vogliono conoscersi meglio** they want to get to know each other better; ~ **sono separati** they split up **5.** (*impersonale*) **in Australia si parla inglese** they speak English in Australia; **cercasi segretaria** secretary wanted; ~ **apre alle ... opening time ...**; **non** ~ **sa mai** you never know; ~ **sa!** we know! **6.** (*passivante*) **non accettano assegni** checks not accepted

si² <-> *m* MUS B; (*nel solfeggio*) ti

sì [si] **I.** *avv* yes; **certo che** ~ of course; **rispondere di** ~ to say yes; **credo di** ~ I think so; **e** ~ **che** to think that; **un giorno** ~ **ed uno no** on alternate days; ~ **e no** yes and no **II.** <-> *m* yes

sia¹ ['si:·a] *cong* ~ **... o** whether ... or; ~ **... che** both ... and; ~ **che gli piaccia,** ~ **che**

non gli piaccia whether he likes it or not

sia² *1., 2. e 3. pers sing conj pr di* **essere¹**

SIAE *f abbr di* **Società Italiana Autori ed Editori** *Italian Association of Authors and Publishers*

siamese [sia·'me:·se] **I.** *agg* Siamese; **gatto** ~ Siamese cat; **fratelli -i** conjoined twins **II.** *mf* **1.** (*abitante*) Siamese **2.** ZOO Siamese cat

siamo ['si:·a·mo] *1. pers pl pr di* **essere¹**

Siberia [si·'bɛ:·ria] *f* Siberia

sibilante [si·bi·'lan·te] **I.** *agg* (*pronuncia*) sibilant; (*respiro*) wheezing **II.** *f* LING sibilant

sibilare [si·bi·'la:·re] *vi* (*emettere sibili*) to whistle

sibilla [si·'bil·la] *f* **1.** (*nella mitologia*) sibyl **2.** *fig* clairvoyant

sibilo ['si:·bi·lo] *m* whistling

sicché [sik·'ke] *cong* **1.** (*così che, perciò*) so **2.** (*ebbene*) well

siccità [sit·tʃi·'ta] <-> *f* drought

siccome [sik·'ko:·me] *cong* since

Sicilia [si·'tʃi:·lia] *f* Sicily

siciliano [si·tʃi·'lia:·no] <*sing*> *m* (*dialetto*) Sicilian

siciliano, -a I. *agg* Sicilian; **scuola -a** LIT Sicilian school; **cassata -a** *Sicilian cake consisting of ricotta and candied fruit* **II.** *m, f* (*abitante*) Sicilian

sicura [si·'ku:·ra] *f* **1.** (*di arma*) safety **2.** (*dispositivo*) safety lock

sicurezza [si·ku·'ret·tsa] *f* safety; (*certezza*) certainty; ~ **stradale** road safety; **cintura di** ~ seat belt; **uscita di** ~ emergency exit

sicuro [si·'ku:·ro] **I.** *m* **1.** **essere al** ~ to be safe; **sentirsi al** ~ to feel safe; **mettersi al** ~ *fig* to take cover **2. dare qc per** ~ to be sure about sth; **andare sul** ~ to play (it) safe **II.** *avv* certainly; **di** ~ certainly

sicuro, -a *agg* **1.** (*luogo, posto*) safe **2.** (*che sa con certezza*) sure **3.** (*abile*) **essere** ~ **in matematica** to be good at math; **mi sento** ~ **per l'esame** I'm confident about the exam; **essere** ~ **di sé** to be self-confident **4.** (*che dà certezza di avvenire*) certain

siderurgia [si·de·rur·'dʒi:·a] <-gie> *f* iron and steel industry

siderurgico [si·de·'rur·dʒi·ko] <-ci> *m* steelworker

siderurgico, -a <-ci, -che> *agg* iron and steel

sidro ['si:·dro] *m* cider

Siena *f* Siena, *city in Tuscany*

siepe ['siɛ:·pe] *f* BOT hedge

siero ['siɛ:·ro] *m* **1.** (*del latte*) whey **2.** MED serum

sieronegativo, -a [sie·ro·ne·ga·'ti:·vo] **I.** *agg* MED (*AIDS*) HIV negative **II.** *m, f* person who is HIV negative

sieropositivo, -a [sie·ro·po·si·'ti:·vo] **I.** *agg* MED (*AIDS*) HIV positive **II.** *m, f* person who is HIV positive

siesta ['siɛs·ta] *f* siesta

siete ['siɛ:·te] *2. pers pl pr di* **essere¹**

sifilide [si·'fi:·li·de] *f* syphilis

Sig. *abbr di* **signore** Mr.

sigaretta [si·ga·'ret·ta] *f* cigarette; ~ **con filtro** filter tip; ~ **senza filtro** unfiltered cigarette; **farsi una ~** to roll a cigarette

sigaro ['si:·ga·ro] *m* cigar

Sigg. *abbr di* **signori** Messrs.

sigillare [si·dʒil·'la:·re] *vt* (*chiudere con sigillo*) to seal

sigillatura [si·dʒil·la·'tu:·ra] *f* 1. (*chiusura*) seal 2. TEC sealing; ~ **delle cavità** cavity sealing

sigla ['si:·gla] *f* 1. (*abbreviazione*) acronym 2. MUS, TV, RADIO signature tune

siglare [si·'gla:·re] *vt* to initial

Sig.na *abbr di* **signorina** Miss

significante [siɲ·ɲi·fi·'kan·te] *agg* (*importante*) meaningful

significare [siɲ·ɲi·fi·'ka:·re] *vt* to mean

significativo, -a [siɲ·ɲi·fi·ka·'ti:·vo] *agg* (*sguardo, silenzio*) meaningful

significato [siɲ·ɲi·fi·'ka:·to] *m* 1. (*concetto*) meaning 2. (*importanza*) significance

signora [siɲ·'ɲo:·ra] *f* 1. (*gener*) lady; **fare la ~** to act the lady; **signori e -e** ladies 2. (*appellativo*) Mrs.; **la ~ Trevisan** Mrs. Trevisan 3. (*moglie*) wife 4. (*padrona di casa*) owner

signore [siɲ·'ɲo:·re] *m* 1. (*gener*) gentleman; **il signor dottore/avvocato** the doctor/lawyer; **il signor Martignon** Mr. Martignon; **i -i Berla** the Berlas; **egregio signor Colombo** Dear Mr. Colombo; **-i e signore** ladies and gentlemen 2. (*padrone di casa*) owner

signorile [siɲ·ɲo·'ri:·le] *agg* (*gesto, atteggiamento*) refined; (*da signore*) gentlemanly; (*da signora*) ladylike

signorilità [siɲ·ɲo·ri·li·'ta] <-> *f* refinement

signorina [siɲ·ɲo·'ri:·na] *f* 1. (*donna nubile, appellativo*) Miss; **la ~ Marchi** Mrs. Marchi 2. (*donna giovane*) young lady

signorino [siɲ·ɲo·'ri:·no] *m* 1. (*figlio del padrone di casa*) son of the house *liter* 2. *iron* (*ragazzo viziato*) **il ~** his lordship

signornò [siɲ·ɲor·'nɔ] *avv* no sir

signorsì [siɲ·ɲor·'si] *avv* yes sir

Sig.ra *abbr di* **signora** Mrs.

silenzio [si·'lɛn·tsio] <-i> *m* silence; **fare ~** to be quiet; **passare qc sotto ~** to hush sth up; ~ **stampa** press silence

silenzioso, -a [si·len·'tsio:·so] *agg* quiet

silhouette [si·'lwɛt] <-> *f* silhouette

silicio [si·'li:·tʃo] *m* silicon

siliconato, -a [si·li·ko·'na:·to] *agg* (*labbra*) surgically-enhanced; **seno ~** boob job

silicone [si·li·'ko:·ne] *m* silicone

sillaba ['sil·la·ba] *f* syllable; **parola di tre -e** three-syllable word

sillabare [sil·la·'ba:·re] *vt* (*dividire in sillabe*) to divide into syllables

sillabico, -a [sil·'la:·bi·ko] <-ci, -che> *agg* syllabic

silo- [si·lo] *v.* **xilo-**

siluramento [si·lu·ra·'men·to] *m* 1. (*di nave,*

idea, progetto) torpedoing 2. (*di persona*) ousting

silurare [si·lu·'ra:·re] *vt* to torpedo

siluro [si·'lu:·ro] *m* torpedo

silvestre [sil·'vɛs·tre] *agg* (*pino, profumo*) woodland

simbiosi [sim·bi·'ɔ:·zi] <-> *f* symbiosis

simboleggiare [sim·bo·led·'dʒa:·re] *vt* to symbolize

simbolico, -a [sim·'bɔ:·li·ko] <-ci, -che> *agg* (*significato, gesto, dono*) symbolic

simbolismo [sim·bo·'liz·mo] *m* 1. (*arte*) Symbolism 2. (*complesso di simboli*) symbolism

simbolo ['sim·bo·lo] *m* symbol

simbologia [som·bo·lo·'dʒi:·a] <-ie> *f* (*insieme di simboli*) symbolism

similare [si·mi·'la:·re] *agg* (*simile*) similar

simile ['si:·mi·le] I. *agg* 1. (*analogo*) similar; **essere ~ a qu/qc** to be similar to sb/sth 2. (*tale*) such; **non ho mai visto una confusione ~** I've never seen such a mess II. *mf* (*il prossimo*) neighbor

similpelle [si·mil·'pɛl·le] *f* imitation leather

simmetria [sim·me·'tri:·a] <-ie> *f* (*di oggetto, corpo*) symmetry

simmetrico, -a [sim·'mɛ:·tri·ko] <-ci, -che> *agg* symmetrical

simpatia [sim·pa·'ti:·a] <-ie> *f* 1. (*di carattere*) pleasant nature 2. (*inclinazione*) liking; **avere ~ per qu/qc** to like sb/sth; **prendere qu in ~** to take a liking to sb

simpatico, -a [sim·'pa:·ti·ko] <-ci, -che> I. *agg* nice II. *m, f* nice person

simpaticone, -a [sim·pa·ti·'ko:·ne] *m, f fam* really nice person

simpatizzante [sim·pa·tid·'dzan·te] *mf* sympathizer

simpatizzare [sim·pa·tid·'dza:·re] *vi* (*di ideologia*) ~ **per qc** to support sth

simposio [sim·'pɔ:·zio] <-i> *m* (*convegno*) symposium

simulare [si·mu·'la:·re] *vt* 1. (*fingere*) to fake 2. TEC to simulate

simulazione [si·mu·lat·'tsio:·ne] *f* 1. (*finzione*) faking; **è stata tutta una ~** it was all a pretence 2. TEC simulation

simultaneità [si·mul·ta·nei·'ta] <-> *f* simultaneity

simultaneo, -a [si·mul·'ta:·neo] *agg* simultaneous; **traduzione -a** simultaneous translation

sinagoga [si·na·'gɔ:·ga] <-ghe> *f* synagogue

sinceramente [sin·tʃe·ra·'me:n·te] *avv* honestly; ~ **non so cosa pensare** honestly I don't know what to think

sincerarsi [sin·tʃe·'rar·si] *vr* to make sure

sincerità [sin·tʃe·ri·'ta] <-> *f* honesty; **con tutta ~** in all honesty

sincero, -a [sin·'tʃɛ:·ro] *agg* 1. (*persona*) honest 2. *fig* (*gesto, parole*) sincere

sincope ['siɲ·ko·pe] *f* fainting fit

sincronia [siɲ·kro·'ni:·a] <-ie> *f* (*simultaneità*) synchrony

sincronizzare [siɲ·kro·nid·'dza:·re] *vt* to syn-

chronize
sincronizzatore [siŋ·kro·nid·dza·'to:·re] *m* synchronizer
sindacale [sin·da·'ka:·le] *agg* (*del sindacato*) (trade) union
sindacalista [sin·da·ka·'lis·ta] <-i *m*, -e *f*> *mf* trade unionist
sindacare [sin·da·'ka:·re] *vt* 1. ADM to inspect 2. *fig* (*criticare*) to criticize
sindacato [sin·da·'ka:·to] *m* (*di lavoratori*) (trade) union
sindaco ['sin·da·ko] <-ci> *m* ADM mayor
sindone ['sin·do·ne] *f* shroud
sindrome ['sin·dro·me] *f* syndrome; ~ **di Down** Down syndrome; ~ **da immunodeficienza acquisita** acquired immune deficiency syndrome; ~ **da iperattività** hyperactivity syndrome
sinergia [si·ner·'dʒ:·a] *f* COM synergy
sinfonia [sin·fo·'ni:·a] <-ie> *f* MUS symphony
sinfonico, -a [sin·'fɔ:·ni·ko] <-ci, -che> *agg* symphonic
singhiozzare [siŋ·giot·'tsa:·re] *vi* 1. (*piangere*) to sob 2. (*avere il singhiozzo*) to hiccup
singhiozzo [siŋ·'giot·tso] *m* 1. MED hiccups *pl* 2. (*pianto*) sob 3. (*loc*) **a** ~ in fits and starts
single ['siŋ·gl] <-> *mf* single person
singolare [siŋ·go·'la:·re] I. *agg* 1. (*particolare*) strange 2. (*insolito*) remarkable II. *m* LING singular
singolarità [siŋ·la·ri·'ta] <-> *f* (*unicità*) uniqueness
singolo ['siŋ·go·lo] *m* SPORT (*tennis*) singles *pl;* (*canottaggio*) single sculls
singolo, -a I. *agg* single II. *m*, *f* individual
singulto [siŋ·'gul·to] *v.* **singhiozzo**
sinistra [si·'nis·tra] *f* 1. (*gener*) left; **partito di** ~ party of the left; **a** ~ on the left; **girare** [*o* **voltare**] **a** ~ to turn left; **tenere la** ~ to keep left; **alla mia** ~ on my left 2. (*mano*) left hand
sinistrato, -a [si·nis·'tra:·to] I. *agg* damaged II. *m*, *f* victim
sinistro [si·'nis·tro] *m* 1. (*infortunio*) accident 2. SPORT (*piede*) left foot; (*mano, pugno*) left
sinistro, -a *agg* 1. (*che è a sinistra*) left 2. *fig* (*infausto*) sinister
sino ['si:·no] *prep* ~ **a** until
sinologia [si·no·lo·'dʒi:·a] <-gie> *f* sinology
sinologo, -a [si·'nɔ:·lo·go] <-gi *o* -ghi, -ghe> *m*, *f* sinologist
sinonimia [si·no·ni·'mi:·a] <-ie> *f* LING synonymy
sinonimo [si·'nɔ:·ni·mo] *m* synonym
sinora [si·'no:·ra] *v.* **finora**
sintagma [sin·'tag·ma] <-i> *m* LING construction
sintassi [sin·'tas·si] <-> *f* LING syntax
sintattico, -a [sin·'tat·ti·ko] <-ci, -che> *agg* LING syntactic
sintesi ['sin·te·zi] <-> *f* 1. PHILOS, BIOL, CHEM, MED synthesis 2. (*riassunto*) summary; **in** ~ in short
sinteticamente [sin·te·ti·ka·'men·te] *avv* (*in*

sintesi) briefly
sinteticità [sin·te·ti·tʃi·'ta] <-> *f* (*l'essere sintetico*) succinctness
sintetico, -a [sin·'tɛ:·ti·ko] <-ci, -che> *agg* 1. (*schematico*) concise 2. (*tessuto*) synthetic
sintetizzare [sin·te·tid·'dza:·re] *vt* 1. (*riassumere*) to summarize 2. CHEM to synthesize
sintetizzatore [sin·te·tid·dza·'to:·re] *m* MUS synthesizer
sintomatico, -a [sin·to·'ma:·ti·ko] <-ci, -che> *agg* 1. (*significativo*) significant 2. MED symptomatic
sintomo ['sin·to·mo] *m* symptom
sintonia [sin·to·'ni:·a] <-ie> *f* *fig* (*perfetto accordo*) harmony; **essere in** ~ **con** to be in harmony with
sintonizzare [sin·to·nid·'dza:·re] *vt* RADIO to tune
sintonizzatore [sin·to·nid·dza·'to:·re] *m* tuner
sinuoso, -a [si·nu·'o:·so] *agg* winding
sinusite [si·nu·'zi:·te] *f* sinusitis
sionismo [sio·'niz·mo] *m* Zionism
sionista [sio·'nis·ta] <-i *m*, -e *f*> *mf* Zionist
sipario [si·'pa:·rio] <-i> *m* curtain
Siracusa [si·ra·'ku:·za] *f* Syracuse, *city in southeastern Sicily*
Siracusano <*sing*> *m* (*zona*) Syracuse area; **nel** ~ in the Syracuse area
siracusano, -a [si·ra·ku·'sa:·no] I. *agg* from Syracuse II. *m*, *f* (*abitante*) person from Syracuse
sirena [si·'rɛ:·na] *f* mermaid
Siria ['si:·ria] *f* Syria
siriano, -a [si·'ria:·no] I. *agg* Syrian II. *m*, *f* Syrian
siringa [si·'riŋ·ga] <-ghe> *f* 1. MED syringe; ~ **monouso** single-use syringe 2. CULIN piping bag
siringare [si·riŋ·'ga:·re] *vt* MED to syringe
sisal ['si:·zal] <-> *f* (*fibra tessile*) sisal
sisma ['siz·ma] <-i> *m* earthquake
SISMI ['siz·mi] *m acro di* **Servizio per l'Informazione e la Sicurezza Militare** *Italian military security service*
sismico, -a ['siz·mi·ko] <-ci, -che> *agg* seismic; **zona -a** earthquake zone
sismografo [siz·'mɔ:·gra·fo] *m* seismograph
sismologia [siz·mo·lo·'dʒi:·a] <-gie> *f* seismology
sismologo, -a [siz·'mɔ:·lo·go] <-gi, -ghe> *m*, *f* seismologist
sissignore [sis·siŋ·'po:·re] *int iron* yes sir!
sistema [sis·'tɛ:·ma] <-i> *m* 1. (*gener*) system; ~ **antibloccaggio** AUTO antilock braking system; ~ **antisbandamento** AUTO anti-skid system; ~ **immunitario** immune system; ~ **di irrigazione** irrigation system; ~ **di navigazione satellitare** satellite navigation system; ~ **nervoso** nervous system; ~ **operativo** operating system; ~ **solare** solar system 2. *fig* (*ordine*) way; ~ **di vita** way of life
sistemare [sis·te·'ma:·re] I. *vt* 1. (*mettere a*

posto) to tidy (up) **2.** (*faccenda*) to sort out **3.** (*procurare un lavoro*) to fix up **4.** (*procurare un alloggio a*) to put; **abbiamo sistemato i tuoi amici nella stanza degli ospiti** we've put your friends in the guest room **5.** *fam* (*punire*) to chew out **II.** *vr:* **-rsi 1.** (*trovare lavoro*) to find a job **2.** (*trovare alloggio*) to find a place to stay; **per una notte mi sono sistemato sul divano letto** for one night I slept on the sofa bed **3.** (*sposarsi*) to settle down

sistematicamente [sis·te·ma·ti·ka·'men·te] *avv* **1.** (*secondo un piano organico*) systematically **2.** (*regolarmente*) regularly

sistematicità [sis·te·ma·ti·tʃi·'ta] <-> *f* **con grande** ~ very systematically

sistematico, -a [sis·te·'ma:·ti·ko] <-ci, -che> *agg* (*metodo, ordine*) systematic

sistemazione [sis·te·mat·'tsio:·ne] *f* **1.** (*risoluzione*) settling **2.** (*impiego*) job **3.** (*alloggio*) accomodations

sistemista [sis·te·'mis·ta] <-i *m*, -e *f*> *mf* COMPUT systems engineer

sito ['si·to] *m* **1.** *poet* place **2.** COMPUT site; ~ **Internet** Internet site; ~ **Web** web site

situare [si·tu·'a:·re] *vt* to locate

situato, -a [si·tu·'a:·to] *agg* situated

situazione [si·tu·at·'tsio:·ne] *f* situation

skateboard ['skeit·bɔːd/'skeit·bɔrd] <-> *m* **1.** (*tavola*) skateboard **2.** (*sport*) skateboarding

skating ['skei·tiŋ/'skei·tiŋg] <-> *m* SPORT (*su ghiaccio*) ice-skating; (*a rotelle*) roller skating

skibob ['ski:·bɔb] <-> *m* skibob

skipass [ski·'pas] <-> *m* ski pass

ski roll ['ski: roul] <-> *m* **1.** (*attrezzo*) roller ski **2.** (*sport*) roller skiing

ski stopper ['ski: 'stɔ·pə] <-> *m* ski stopper

skysurfing [skai·'sə·fiŋ] <*sing*> *m* SPORT skysurfing

slacciare [zlat·'tʃa:·re] **I.** *vt* (*giacca, bottoni, scarpe*) to undo **II.** *vr:* **-rsi** (*giacca, bottoni, scarpe*) to come undone

slalom ['zla:·lom] <-> *m* SPORT slalom; ~ **gigante** giant slalom

slalomista [zla·lo·'mis·ta] <-i *m*, -e *f*> *mf* slalom racer

slanciarsi [zlan·'tʃar·si] *vr* ~ **contro** [*o* **su**] **qu** to hurl oneself at sb

slanciato, -a [zlan·'tʃa:·to] *agg* (*ragazza, fisico*) slim

slancio ['zlan·tʃo] <-ci> *m* **1.** (*balzo*) leap **2.** *fig* (*impeto*) gusto; **in uno ~ di entusiasmo** in a burst of enthusiasm

slargo ['zlar·go] <-ghi> *m* widening

slavato, -a [zla·'va:·to] *agg* (*sbiadito*) faded

slavina [zla·'vi:·na] *f* snowslide

slavismo [zla·'viz·mo] *m* **1.** LING Slavic word **2.** POL Pan-Slavism

slavistica [zla·'vis·ti·ka] <-che> *f* Slavic studies

slavo, -a ['zla:·vo] **I.** *agg* Slavic **II.** *m*, *f* Slav

slavofilia [zla·vo·fi·'li:·a] *f* pro-Slavism

slavofobia [zla·vo·fo·'bi:·a] *f* anti-Slavism

slavofono, -a [zla·'vɔː·fo·no] **I.** *m*, *f* Slavic

speaker **II.** *agg* Slavic-speaking

sleale [zle·'a:·le] *agg* (*persona, avversario*) cheating; **una persona** ~ a cheat

slealtà [zle·al·'ta] <-> *f* cheating

slegare [zle·'ga:·re] *vt* (*cane*) to untie

slegato, -a [zle·'ga:·to] *agg* (*senza connessione: concetti, frasi*) disconnected

slip [zlip] <-> *m* (*da uomo*) briefs *pl*; (*da donna*) panties *pl*

slitta ['zlit·ta] *f* sledge

slittamento [zlit·ta·'men·to] *m* **1.** (*di ruote*) skidding **2.** (*rinvio*) postponement

slittare [zlit·'ta:·re] *vi* essere *o* avere **1.** (*ruote*) to skid **2.** COM, FIN to slide **3.** (*essere rinviato*) to be postponed

slittino [zlit·'ti:·no] *m* toboggan

s.l.m. *abbr di* **sul livello del mare** asl, *above sea level*

slogan ['zlɔː·gan] <-> *m* slogan

slogare [zlo·'ga:·re] *vt* (*spalla*) to dislocate; (*polso, caviglia*) to sprain

slogatura [zlo·ga·'tu:·ra] *f* (*di spalla*) dislocation; (*di polso, caviglia*) sprain

sloggiare [zlod·'dʒa:·re] *vi* **1.** (*abbandonare un alloggio*) to move out **2.** *fam* (*andarsene*) to clear out

slot [slɔt/zlɔt] <-> *m* AERO landing slot; COMPUT slot

slot-machine ['slɔt mə·'ʃiːn/'zlɔt ma·'ʃin] <-> *f* slot machine

Slovacchia [zlo·vak·'kia] *f* Slovakia

slovacco, -a [zlo·'vak·ko] <-cchi, -cche> **I.** *agg* Slovak **II.** *m*, *f* Slovak

Slovenia [zlo·'vɛː·nia] *f* Slovenia

sloveno, -a [zlo·'vɛː·no] **I.** *agg* Slovenian **II.** *m*, *f* Slovenian

slurp [zlurp] *int* *fam* (*rumore di chi mangia o beve*) slurping noise, *written in comic strips*

smacchiare [zmak·'kia:·re] *vt* to remove stains from

smacchiatore, -trice [zmak·kia·'to:·re] *m*, *f* stain remover

smacco ['zmak·ko] <-cchi> *m* (*sconfitta*) humiliating defeat

smack [zmak] *int* *fam* smack, *the sound of a loud kiss*

smagliante [zmaʎ·'ʎan·te] *agg* **1.** *fig* (*sorriso, bellezza*) radiant **2.** (*loc*) **in forma** ~ in great shape

smagliare [zmaʎ·'ʎa:·re] *vr:* **-rsi 1.** (*calze, maglia*) to run **2.** (*pelle*) to get stretch marks

smagliatura [zmaʎ·ʎa·'tu:·ra] *f* **1.** (*di calze*) run **2.** MED stretch mark

smagnetizzare [zmaɲ·ɲe·tid·'dza:·re] *vt* to demagnetize

smagrirsi [zma·'grir·si] <smagrisco> *vr:* **-rsi** (*dimagrire*) to lose weight

smaliziato, -a [zma·lit·'tsia:·to] *agg* (*non più ingenuo*) knowing

smaltare [zmal·'ta:·re] *vt* **1.** (*vaso*) to glaze; (*padella*) to enamel **2.** (*unghie*) to put nail polish on

smaltimento [zmal·ti·'men·to] *m* disposal; **lo**

S

~ dei rifiuti waste disposal

smaltire [zmal·'ti:·re] <smaltisco> *vt* **1.**(*digerire: cibo*) to digest **2.**(*far passare: sbornia, rabbia*) to get over **3.**(*eliminare: acque*) to drain away; (*rifiuti*) to dispose of

smalto ['zmal·to] *m* **1.**(*per decorare, dei denti*) enamel **2.**(*per unghie*) nail polish

smammare [zmam·'ma:·re] *vi fam* to clear out

smanceria [zman·tʃe·'ri:·a] <-ie> *f pej* (*moina*) affectation

smanettare [zma·net·'ta:·re] *vi sl* MOT to go flat out; **~ al computer** to mess around on the computer

smania ['zma:·nia] *f* **1.**(*agitazione*) agitation; **perché hai tutta questa ~?** why are you so agitated? **2.**fig (*intenso desidero*) **~ di qc** thirst for sth

smaniare [zma·'nia:·re] *vi* **1.**(*agitarsi*) to be agitated **2.**fig (*desiderare fortemente*) **~ di fare qc** to long to do sth

smanicato, -a [zma·ni·'ka:·to] *agg* sleeveless

smanioso, -a [zma·'nio:·so] *agg* (*desideroso*) **essere ~ di qc** to be eager for sth; **essere ~ di fare qc** to be eager to do sth

smantellamento [zman·tel·la·'men·to] *m* **1.**(*chiusura: di fabbrica*) shutting down **2.**fig (*di sistema politico*) dismantling

smantellare [zman·tel·'la:·re] *vt* **1.**(*mura*) to demolish; (*fabbrica*) to shut down **2.**(*tesi,accusa*) to take apart

smarrimento [zmar·ri·'men·to] *m* **1.**(*di oggetto*) loss **2.**fig (*mancanza di lucidità*) confusion

smarrire [zmar·'ri:·re] <smarrisco> I. *vt* **1.**(*perdere: oggetti*) to lose **2. ~ la strada** to lose one's way II. *vr:* **-rsi** (*perdersi*) to get lost

smascheramento [zmas·ke·ra·'men·to] *m* revelation

smascherare [zmas·ke·'ra:·re] I. *vt fig* (*mettere a nudo*) to reveal II. *vr:* **-rsi** *fig* (*rivelare la propria natura*) to give oneself away

smaterializzare [zma·te·ria·lid·'dza:·re] I. *vt* **~ qu/qc** to make sb/sth disappear II. *vr:* **-rsi** to disappear

SME *m abbr di* **Sistema Monetario Europeo** EMS

smembramento [zmem·bra·'men·to] *m* (*divisione*) dismantling

smembrare [zmem·'bra:·re] *vt* (*dividere in parti*) to dismantle

smemoratezza [zme·mo·ra·'tet·tsa] *f* forgetfulness

smemorato, -a [zme·mo·'ra:·to] I. *agg* forgetful II. *m, f* forgetful person; **è un inguaribile ~** he's hopelessly forgetful

smentire [zmen·'ti:·re] <smentisco> I. *vt* **1.**(*notizia, fatti*) to deny **2.**JUR to retract **3.**(*buon nome*) to lose; (*fama*) to disprove II. *vr:* **-rsi** (*contraddirsi*) to contradict oneself; **non si smentisce mai** he's [*o* she's] always consistent

smentita [zmen·'ti:·ta] *f* denial

smeraldo¹ [zme·'ral·do] *m* emerald

smeraldo² <inv> *agg* **verde ~** emerald green

smerciare [zmer·'tʃa:·re] *vt* (*vendere*) to sell off

smercio ['zmɛr·tʃo] <-ci> *m* (*vendita*) sale; **avere un ottimo ~** to sell very well

smerdare [zmer·'da:·re] I. *vt vulg* (*svergognare*) **~ qu** to show sb up II. *vr:* **-rsi** *vulg* (*svergognarsi*) to make a fool of oneself

smerigliato, -a [zme·riʎ·'ʎa:·to] *agg* **1.carta -a** emery paper **2.vetro ~** frosted glass

smettere ['zmet·te·re] <irr> I. *vt* (*interrompere: lavoro*) to stop; (*studi*) to give up; (*discussione*) to end; **smettila!** *fam* stop it! II. *vi* (*cessare*) to stop; **~ di fare qc** to stop doing sth; **ha smesso di piovere** it's stopped raining

smidollato, -a [zmi·dol·'la:·to] I. *agg fig, pej* spineless II. *m, f* wimp

smilitarizzare [zmi·li·ta·rid·'dza:·re] *vt* to demilitarize

smilzo, -a ['zmil·tso] *agg* (*persona*) skinny

sminuire [zmi·nu·'i:·re] <sminuisco> *vt* (*svalutare*) to belittle

sminuzzare [zmi·nut·'tsa:·re] *vt* (*ridurre in pezzettini: carne*) to grind; (*pomodori*) to chop up

smisi ['zmi·zi] *1. pers sing pass rem di* **smettere**

smistare [zmis·'ta:·re] *vt* **1.**(*corrispondenza, merci*) to sort **2.**FERR to shunt

smisurato, -a [zmi·zu·'ra:·to] *agg* (*spazio*) enormous; (*amore*) excessive

smitizzare [zmi·tid·'dza:·re] *vt* to demystify

smobilitare [zmo·bi·li·'ta:·re] *vt* **1.**(*truppe*) to demobilize **2.**fig (*riportare alla normalità*) to pack up

smobilitazione [zmo·bi·li·tat·'tsio:·ne] *f* (*di truppe*) demobilization

smodato, -a [zmo·'da:·to] *agg* (*desiderio, consumo*) excessive

smoderato, -a [zmo·de·'ra:·to] *agg* (*eccessivo*) excessive; **essere ~ nel mangiare/bere** to eat/drink to excess

smog [zmɔg] <-> *m* smog; **cappa di ~** blanket of smog; **allarme ~** smog alarm

smoking ['zmɔ:·kiŋ] <-> *m* tuxedo

smontabile [zmon·'ta:·bi·le] *agg* able to be taken apart

smontare [zmon·'ta:·re] I. *vt avere* **1.**(*scomporre: scaffare, motore*) to take apart **2.**fig (*scoraggiare*) to dishearten II. *vi essere o avere* **1.**(*scendere: da treno*) to get off; (*da cavallo*) to dismount **2.**(*di turno, lavoro*) to finish III. *vr:* **-rsi** (*scoraggiarsi*) to lose heart

smorfia ['zmɔr·fia] <-ie> *f* **1.**(*contrazione del viso*) grimace; **fare le -ie** to make faces **2.**fig (*atteggiamento lezioso*) **fare -e** to simper; **lascia perdere le tue -e** stop simpering

smorfioso, -a [zmor·'fio:·so] I. *agg* (*bambino*) simpering II. *m, f* spoiled brat

smorto, -a ['zmɔr·to] *agg fig* (*pallido*) pale

smorzare [zmor·'tsa:·re] *vt* **1.**(*spegnere: fuoco, candela*) to put out; (*luce*) to dim **2.**fig (*attutire: sete*) to quench; (*desiderio,* *passione*) to dampen **3.** *fig* (*attenuare: polemica, suoni*) to tone down

smossi *1. pers sing pass rem di* **smuovere**

smosso *pp di* **smuovere**

smottamento [zmot·ta·'men·to] *m* (*frana*) landslide

SMS ['ɛs·se·ɛm·me·'ɛs·se] <-> *m abbr di* **Short Message System** TEL (*messaggio*) text; **~ con immagini** text with pictures

smunto, -a ['zmun·to] *agg* (*pallido*) pale

smuovere ['zmuɔː·ve·re] <irr> I. *vt* **1.** (*spostare*) to shift **2.** *fig* (*dissuadere: da idea, decisione*) to dissuade II. *vr:* **-rsi 1.** (*spostarsi*) to shift **2.** *fig* (*cambiare idea*) **~ da qc** to change one's mind about sth

smussare [zmus·'saː·re] I. *vt* **1.** (*spigolo, stipite*) to smooth off; (*coltello*) to blunt **2.** *fig* (*carattere, asperità*) to soften II. *vr:* **-rsi** (*coltello*) to get blunt

snaturato, -a [zna·tu·'raː·to] I. *agg* (*madre, padre*) heartless II. *m, f* heartless person

snellezza [znel·'let·tsa] *f* (*di persona*) slimness

snellire [znel·'liː·re] <snellisco> I. *vt* **1.** (*rendere snello*) **~ qu** to make sb look slim **2.** *fig* (*procedura, servizio*) to slim down II. *vr:* **-rsi** (*diventare snello*) to slim down

snello, -a ['znɛl·lo] *agg* **1.** (*persona, figura*) slim **2.** *fig* (*stile*) easy; (*procedura*) slimmed-down

snervante [zner·'van·te] *agg* (*attesa*) nerve-wracking; (*polemica*) exhausting

snervare [zner·'vaː·re] I. *vt* (*logorare*) to wear out II. *vr:* **-rsi** (*perdere la pazienza*) to lose patience

snidare [zni·'daː·re] *vt* to flush (out)

sniffare [znif·'faː·re] *vt sl* (*cocaina*) to snort

sniffata [znif·'faː·ta] *f* sniff; **fare una ~ di cocaina** to sniff cocaine; **fare una ~ a un profumo** to sniff a perfume

snob [znɔb] I. <inv> *agg* snobbish II. <-> *mf* snob

snobbare [znob·'baː·re] *vt* (*mostrare disinteresse*) to snub

snobismo [zno·'biz·mo] *m* snobbery

snocciolare [znot·tʃo·'laː·re] *vt* **1.** (*ciliege, albicocche*) to pit **2.** *fig* (*orazioni, lezione*) to reel off

snodabile [zno·'daː·bi·le] *agg* TEC (*antenna, supporto*) adjustable

snodare [zno·'daː·re] I. *vt* **1.** (*fune, corda*) to untie **2.** (*gambe*) to loosen II. *vr:* **-rsi** (*fiume, strada*) to wind

snodo ['znɔː·do] *m* TEC joint; **fuso a ~** steering knuckle

snowbo(a)rdista [snou·bor·'dis·ta] <-i *m*, -e *f*> *mf* snowboarder

so [sɔ] *1. pers sing pr di* **sapere**[1]

SO *abbr di* **sudovest** SW

soave[1] [so·'aː·ve] *agg* (*profumo, gusto*) delicate

soave[2] <-> *m* Soave, *dry white wine produced in northern Italy*

sobbalzare [sob·bal·'tsaː·re] *vi* **1.** (*veicoli*) to jolt **2.** (*persone*) to jump

sobbalzo [sob·'bal·tso] *m* start

sobbarcarsi [sob·bar·'kaːr·si] *vr* **~ qc** to take on sth

sobborgo [sob·'bor·go] <-ghi> *m* suburb

sobillare [so·bil·'laː·re] *vt* (*istigare*) to stir up

sobillatore, -trice [so·bi·la·'toː·re] *m, f* troublemaker

sobrietà [so·brie·'ta] <-> *f* (*di stile*) simplicity

sobrio, -a ['sɔː·brio] <-i, -ie> *agg* **1.** (*stile, vita, abitudini*) simple **2.** (*non ubriaco*) sober

soc. *abbr di* **società** Soc.

socchiudere [sok·'kiuː·de·re] <irr> *vt* **1.** (*porta, finestra*) to leave ajar **2.** (*occhi*) to half-close

soccombere [sok·'kom·be·re] <soccombo, soccombei *o* soccombetti, soccombuto> *vi* essere (*restare vinto: persona*) to give up; (*società*) to go under

soccorrere [sok·'kor·re·re] <irr> *vt* **~ qu** to help sb

soccorritore, -trice [sok·kor·ri·'toː·re] *m, f* rescuer

soccorso [sok·'kor·so] *m* (*aiuto*) help; **-i** aid; **il pronto ~** the emergency room; **~ stradale** emergency road service; **cassetta di pronto ~** first aid kit; **colonnina di ~** emergency phone; **correre in ~ di qu** to rush to sb's aid; **omissione di ~** JUR failure to offer assistance

socialdemocratico, -a [so·tʃal·de·mo·'kraː·ti·ko] <-ci, -che> I. *agg* social democratic II. *m, f* social democrat

socialdemocrazia [so·tʃal·de·mo·krat·'tsiː·a] *f* social democracy

sociale [so·'tʃaː·le] *agg* **1.** (*gener*) social **2.** COM **capitale ~** authorized capital

socialismo [so·tʃa·'liz·mo] *m* socialism

socialista [so·tʃa·'lis·ta] <-i *m*, -e *f*> I. *mf* socialist II. *agg* socialist

socialità [so·tʃa·li·'ta] <-> *f* (*convivenza sociale*) sociality

socializzare [so·tʃa·lid·'dzaː·re] *vi* (*avere rapporti sociali*) to form relationships

società [so·tʃe·'ta] <-> *f* **1.** (*gener*) society; **~ dei consumi** consumer society; **~ industriale** industrial society; **alta ~** high society **2.** COM company; **~ per azioni** corporation; **~ a responsabilità limitata, ~ in accomandita semplice** limited partnership; **~ affiliata** affiliate; **~ finanziaria** finance company; **~ distributrice di film** movie distributor; **~ (di fornitura) di lavoro temporaneo** employment agency; **in ~** in partnership **3.** (*associazione*) club; **~ sportiva** sports club **4. giochi di ~** parlor games

socievole [so·'tʃeː·vo·le] *agg* sociable

socio, -a ['sɔː·tʃo] <-ci, -cie> *m, f* **1.** (*membro*) member **2.** COM partner **3.** *pej* (*compare*) pal

socioculturale [so·tʃo·kul·tu·'raː·le] *agg* sociocultural

socioeconomico, -a [so·tʃo·e·ko·'nɔː·mi·ko]

<-ci, -che> *agg* socioeconomic

sociologia [so·tʃo·lo·'dʒi:·a] <-gie> *f* sociology

sociologo, -a [so·'tʃɔ:·lo·go] <-gi, -ghe> *m, f* sociologist

sociosanitario, -a [so·tʃo·sa·ni·'ta:·rio] *agg* healthcare; **struttura -a** healthcare structure

soda ['sɔ:·da] *f* **1.** CHEM soda; **bicarbonato di** ~ bicarbonate of soda **2.** (*acqua*) (club) soda; **un whisky con** ~ a whiskey and soda

sodalizio [so·da·'lit·tsio] <-i> *m* (*vincolo*) fellowship

soddisfaccio [sod·dis·'fat·tʃo] *1. pers sing pr di* **soddisfare**

soddisfacente [sod·dis·fa·'tʃɛn·te] *agg* (*esito, risultato*) satisfactory

soddisfare [sod·dis·'fa:·re] <irr> *vt* to satisfy

soddisfatto, -a [sod·dis·'fat·to] *agg* (*contento*) satisfied

soddisfazione [sod·dis·fat·'tsio:·ne] *f* **1.** (*contentezza*) satisfaction; **le piccole -i della vita quotidiana** the small satisfactions of daily life; **con mia grande** ~ to my great satisfaction; **non c'è** ~ there's no satisfaction **2.** (*adempimento: di aspirazioni, richieste*) fulfillment

soddisfeci *1. pers sing pass rem di* **soddisfare**

sodio ['sɔ:·dio] *m* sodium

sodo ['sɔ:·do] **I.** *avv* **1.** (*con forza*) hard **2.** (*alacremente*) **lavorare/studiare** ~ to work/study hard **3.** (*profondamente*) **dormire** ~ to sleep soundly **II.** *m fam* **venire al** ~ to come to the point

sodo, -a *agg* **1.** (*carne, muscoli*) firm **2.** (*legname*) hard; **uova -e** hard-boiled eggs; **prenderle -e** *fam* to get a beating

sodomia [so·do·'mi:·a] <-ie> *f* sodomy

sofà [so·'fa] <-> *m* sofa

sofferente [sof·fe·'rɛn·te] *agg* **1. persona** ~ sufferer; **i malati più -i** the patients who are suffering the most **2.** pain-stricken; **cos'è quell'espressione** ~? what's that pained look for?

sofferenza [sof·fe·'rɛn·tsa] *f* suffering

soffermare [sof·fer·'ma:·re] **I.** *vt* ~ **lo sguardo su qc** to rest one's gaze on sth **II.** *vr:* **-rsi** *fig* **-rsi su qc** to dwell on sth

soffersi [sof·'fɛr·si] *1. pers sing pass rem di* **soffrire**

sofferto, -a [sof·'fɛr·to] **I.** *pp di* **soffrire II.** *agg* (*vittoria, risultato*) hard-fought

soffiare [sof·'fia:·re] **I.** *vi* to blow **II.** *vt* **1.** (*aria, fumo, vetro*) to blow; **-rsi il naso** to blow one's nose **2.** *fig, fam* (*portar via*) to steal, to swipe; **mi ha soffiato la ragazza!** he stole my girlfriend! **3.** *fam* (*spifferare: segreto*) to whisper

soffiata [sof·'fia:·ta] *f fam* (*rivelazione*) tip-off

soffice ['sɔf·fi·tʃe] *agg* soft

soffietto [sof·'fiet·to] *m* TEC bellows *pl;* **porta a** ~ folding door

soffio ['sof·fio] <-i> *m* **1.** (*gener*) puff; **in un** ~ in a sec; **c'è mancato un** ~ *fig* it was a close thing **2.** (*rumore*) MED **un** ~ **al cuore** a heart murmur

soffitta [sof·'fit·ta] *f* attic

soffitto [sof·'fit·to] *m* ceiling

soffocamento [sof·fo·ka·'men·to] *m* suffocation

soffocante [sof·fo·'kan·te] *agg* **1.** (*aria*) suffocating **2.** *fig* (*persona, atmosfera*) oppressive

soffocare [sof·fo·'ka:·re] **I.** *vt avere* to suffocate; ~ **qu con un cuscino** to suffocate sb with a pillow **II.** *vi essere* to suffocate; **un caldo che soffoca** suffocating heat; **mi sento** ~ I'm suffocating

soffriggere [sof·'frid·dʒe·re] <irr> *vt* to fry lightly

soffrire [sof·'fri:·re] <soffro, soffrii *o* soffersi, sofferto> **I.** *vt* **1.** (*patire*) to suffer; ~ **il caldo/freddo** to suffer from the heat/cold; ~ **la fame** to suffer from hunger **2.** (*sopportare*) to bear **II.** *vi* **1.** MED ~ **di qc** to suffer from sth; ~ **di mal di testa** he [*o* she] suffers from headaches **2.** (*patire*) to suffer

soffritto¹ [sof·'frit·to] *pp di* **soffriggere**

soffritto² *m a mixture of chopped herbs and onions fried in oil*

soffuso, -a [sof·'fu:·zo] *agg* (*luce*) diffuse

sofisticare [so·fis·ti·'ka:·re] *vi* (*sottilizzare*) to quibble

sofisticato, -a [so·fis·ti·'ka:·to] *agg* **1.** (*persona, impianto*) sophisticated **2.** (*linguaggio*) elevated

soft [sɔft] <inv> *agg* **1.** (*atmosfera*) relaxed **2.** (*luce, musica*) soft

software ['sɔft·wɛə] <-> *m* COMPUT software; ~ **didattico** educational software

soggettività [sod·dʒet·ti·vi·'ta] <-> *f* subjectivity

soggettivo, -a [sod·dʒet·'ti:·vo] *agg* subjective

soggetto [sod·'dʒɛt·to] *m* **1.** (*tema*) theme **2.** LING, MUS, PHILOS subject **3.** MED (*paziente*) patient **4.** *fam* (*persona, tipo*) character

soggetto, -a *agg* **1.** (*esposto*) **essere** ~ **a qc** to be subject to sth; ~ **a imposta** taxable **2.** MED **essere** ~ **a qc** to be prone to sth

soggezione [sod·dʒet·'tsio:·ne] *f* (*riguardo timoroso*) **ho molta** ~ **dei tuoi genitori** I find your parents very intimidating

sogghignare [sog·giɲ·'ɲa:·re] *vi* to snicker

sogghigno [sog·'giɲ·ɲo] *m* snicker; **-i** snickering

soggiacere [sod·dʒa·'tʃe:·re] <irr> *vi essere o avere* ~ **a qc** to be subject to sth

soggiogare [sod·dʒo·'ga:·re] *vt a. fig* (*sottomettere*) to subjugate

soggiornare [sod·dʒor·'na:·re] *vi* (*trattenersi*) to stay

soggiorno [sod·'dʒor·no] *m* **1.** (*permanenza*) stay; **località di** ~ resort; **permesso di** ~ residence permit **2.** (*stanza*) living room

soggiungere [sod·'dʒun·dʒe·re] <irr> *vt* to add

soglia ['sɔʎ·ʎa] <-glie> *f* threshold; ~ **della porta** doorstep; ~ **del dolore** pain threshold; **è alla soglia dei 40** he's [*o* she's] pushing 40;

la primavera è alle -e spring is nearly here

soglio *1. pers sing pr di* **solere**

sogliola ['sɔʎ·ʎo·la] *f* sole

sognante [soɲ·'ɲan·te] *agg* (*sguardo*) dreamy

sognare [soɲ·'ɲaː·re] *vt* **1.** (*vedere in sogno*) to dream; **ho sognato che ...** I dreamed (that) ...; **ho sognato il nonno** I dreamed about (my) granddad **2.** *fig* (*desiderare*) to dream of; **sogno una casa al mare** I dream of (having) a house on the coast **3.** *fig* (*illudersi*) **te la puoi ~!** in your dreams!; **te lo sogni che venga!** *fam* in your dreams he's [*o* she's] coming! **4.** *fig* (*immaginare*) **non mi sarei mai sognata di finire in questa città** I never dreamed I'd end up living here

sognatore, **-trice** [soɲ·ɲa·'toː·re] *m, f* dreamer

sogno ['soɲ·ɲo] *m a. fig* dream; **fare un ~** to dream; **nemmeno** [*o* **neppure**] [*o* **neanche**] **per ~** *fam* you've got to be kidding

soia ['sɔː·ia] <soie> *f* soy

sol [sɔl] <-> *m* MUS G; (*nel solfeggio*) so

solaio [so·'laː·io] <-ai> *m* attic

solare [so·'laː·re] *agg* **1.** (*gener*) solar; **eclissi ~** solar eclipse; **sistema ~** solar system; **energia ~** solar energy; **orologio ~** solar clock; **crema** [*o* **olio**] **~** suntan lotion **2.** *fig* (*raggiante*) sunny; **un'indole ~** a sunny nature **3.** *fig* (*evidente*) (crystal) clear

solarium [so·'laː·ri·um] <-> *m* solarium

solcare [sol·'kaː·re] *vt* **1.** AGR to plow **2.** *fig* (*fendere l'acqua*) **solcare le onde** [*o* **il mare**] to plow the waves [*o* the ocean]

solco ['sol·ko] <-chi> *m* **1.** AGR furrow **2.** (*incavatura*) track **3.** (*ruga*) wrinkle **4.** *fig* (*impronta*) mark

soldatino [sol·da·'tiː·no] *m* (*giocattolo*) toy soldier

soldato, **-essa** [sol·'daː·to] *m, f* soldier; **andare** (**a fare il**) **~** to join the army; **fare il ~** to serve in the army

soldo ['sɔl·do] *m* **1.** *pl* money; **fare -i a palate** to make a fortune **2.** *fig* (*quantità minima di denaro*) penny; **mio padre non aveva un ~** my father was penniless; **non valere un ~** (**bucato**) to not be worth a dime; **da pochi** [*o* **quattro**] **-i** *fig, fam* worthless

sole ['soː·le] *m* sun; **c'è il ~** it's sunny; **colpo di ~** sunstroke; **occhiali da ~** sunglasses; **prendere il ~** to sunbathe; **sdraiarsi al ~** to lie in the sun; **stare al ~** to stay in the sun; **chiaro come il ~** as clear as day

soleggiato, **-a** [so·led·'dʒaː·to] *agg* sunny

solei [so·'leː·i] *1. pers sing pass rem di* **solere**

solenne [so·'lɛn·ne] *agg* **1.** (*gener*) solemn; **la messa ~** High Mass **2.** *fam* **una lezione ~** a good lesson; **uno schiaffo ~** an almighty slap

solennità [so·len·ni·'ta] <-> *f* **1.** (*serietà*) solemnity **2.** (*ricorrenza*) (religious) holiday

solerte [so·'lɛr·te] *agg* diligent

soletta [so·'let·ta] *f* insole

solfa ['sɔl·fa] *f fam* old story; **è sempre la solita ~!** it's always the same old story!; **che**

~! what a pain!

solfato [sol·'faː·to] *m* sulfate

solfeggio [sol·'fed·dʒo] <-i> *m* MUS sol-fa

solforico, **-a** [sol·'fɔː·ri·ko] <-ci, -che> *agg* sulfuric; **acido ~** sulfuric acid

solfuro [sol·'fuː·ro] *m* sulfur

solidale [so·li·'daː·le] *agg* supportive

solidarietà [so·li·da·rie·'ta] <-> *f* support

solidarizzare [so·li·da·rid·'dzaː·re] *vi* **~ con qu/qc** to express one's support for sb/sth

solidificarsi [so·li·di·fi·'kaːr·si] *vr* to solidify

solidità [so·li·di·'ta] <-> *f* **1.** (*di costruzione*) solidity **2.** FIN strength **3.** (*di argomento, ragionamento*) soundness

solido ['sɔː·li·do] *m* MATH, PHYS solid

solido, **-a** *agg* **1.** MATH, PHYS solid **2.** (*argomento, base, costruzione*) strong **3.** COM sound

soliloquio [so·li·'lɔː·kuio] <-qui> *m* monologue

solista [so·'lis·ta] <-i *m*, -e *f*> *mf* soloist

solitario [so·li·'taː·rio] <-i> *m* solitaire; **fare un ~** to play solitaire

solitario, **-a** <-i, -ie> *agg* **1.** (*luogo, via*) lonely **2.** (*persona, animale*) solitary; **un tipo ~** a loner; **verme ~** tapeworm

solito ['sɔː·li·to] *m* (*nelle ordinazioni*) **il ~** the [*o* my] usual; **è più in ritardo del ~** he's [*o* she's] even later than usual; **di ~** usually; **come al ~** as usual

solito, **-a I.** *pp di* **solere II.** *agg* usual; **essere ~ fare qc** to usually do sth; **siamo alle -e** *fam* here we go again

solitudine [so·li·'tuː·di·ne] *f* loneliness

sollazzo [sol·'lat·tso] *m* (*piacere*) pleasure

sollecitare [sol·le·tʃi·'taː·re] *vt* **1.** (*cose*) to request urgently **2.** (*persone*) to urge **3.** (*stimolare: fantasia*) to stimulate **4.** TEC to stress

sollecitazione [sol·le·tʃi·tat·'tsio·ne] *f* **1.** (*il sollecitare*) (urgent) request **2.** (*stimolo*) encouragement **3.** PHYS, TEC stress

sollecito [sol·'leː·tʃi·to] *m* ADM **una lettera di ~ al pagamento** a payment reminder

sollecito, **-a** *agg* **1.** (*risposta*) speedy **2.** (*persona*) helpful

sollecitudine [sol·le·tʃi·'tuː·di·ne] *f* (*rapidità*) speed

solleone [sol·le·'o·ne] *m* **1.** (*gran caldo*) summer heat **2.** (*periodo*) dog days *pl*, period between the middle of July and the beginning of August

solleticare [sol·le·ti·'kaː·re] *vt* **1.** (*fare il solletico a*) to tickle **2.** *fig* (*appetito*) to whet; (*fantasia*) to stimulate

solletico [sol·'leː·ti·ko] <-chi> *m* (*sensazione*) tickling sensation; **fare il ~ a qu** to tickle sb; **soffrire il ~** to be ticklish

sollevamento [sol·le·va·'men·to] *m* **1.** (*il sollevare*) lifting; **impianto di ~** lifting gear **2.** SPORT **~ pesi** weightlifting

sollevare [sol·le·va·'re] *vt* **1.** (*peso*) to lift **2.** (*testa, occhi, questione*) to raise **3.** *fig* to cheer up; **~ qu dall'abbattimento** to cheer sb up **4.** *fig* (*far sorgere: protesta, polemica*) to stir up **II.** *vr:* **-rsi 1.** (*alzarsi: da tavola*) to get up; **si sollevò dal letto** he [*o* she] got out of bed **2.** *fig* (*ribellarsi*) to rise up **3.** *fig* (*riprendersi*) to recover

sollevato, -a [sol·le·'va:·to] *agg fig* relieved

sollevazione [sol·le·vat·'tsio:·ne] *f* rebellion

sollievo [sol·'liɛ:·vo] *m* relief

solo ['so:·lo] **I.** *avv* (*solamente*) only; **non ~ ..., ma anche ...** not only ..., but also ... **II.** *cong* (*ma*) but; **~ che** +*conj* only

solo, -a I. *agg* **1.** (*senza compagnia*) alone; **uno che s'è fatto da ~** a self-made man; **parlare da ~** to talk to oneself; **vivere (da) ~** to live alone; **meglio -i che male accompagnati** *prov: it's better to be alone than in bad company;* **sentirsi -i** to feel lonely **2.** (*unico*) he [*o* she] has only taken part in one meeting, he [*o* she] has only one child **II.** *m, f* the only one

solstizio [sols·'tit·tsio] <-i> *m* solstice

soltanto [sol·'tan·to] *avv* (*solo*) only; **non ~ ..., ma ...** not only ..., but ...

solubile [so·'lu:·bi·le] *agg* soluble; **caffè ~** instant coffee

solubilità [so·lu·bi·li·'ta] <-> *f* CHEM (*di sostanza*) solubility

soluzione [so·lut·'tsio:·ne] *f* solution; **ho pagato i miei debiti in un'unica ~** I paid all my debts at once

solvente [sol·'vɛn·te] **I.** *agg* solvent **II.** *m* CHEM solvent

solvenza [sol·'vɛn·tsa] *f* COM solvency

soma ['sɔ:·ma] *f* (*carico*) **bestia** [*o* **animale**] **da ~** pack animal

somaro, -a [so·'ma:·ro] *m, f* **1.** ZOO donkey **2.** *pej, fam* idiot

somatico, -a [so·'ma:·ti·ko] <-ci, -che> *agg* somatic

somigliante [so·miʎ·'ʎan·te] *agg* similar

somiglianza [so·miʎ·'ʎan·tsa] *f* resemblance

somigliare [so·miʎ·'ʎa:·re] **I.** *vi* (*essere simile*) to look like; **~ a qu** to look like sb; **tua sorella ti somiglia tantissimo** your sister looks a lot like you **II.** *vr:* **-rsi** (*essere simile: fisicamente*) to look alike; (*di carattere*) to be alike

somma ['som·ma] *f* sum; **fare la ~** to add up; **tirare le -e** *fig* to sum up; **una ~ di denaro** a sum of money

sommare [som·'ma:·re] *vt* **1.** MATH to add up **2.** (*aggiungere*) to add; **tutto sommato** all things considered

sommario [som·'ma:·rio] <-i> *m* (*riassunto*) summary

sommario, -a <-i, -ie> *agg* **1.** (*superficiale: lavoro*) perfunctory **2.** JUR (*procedimento, processo*) summary **3.** (*breve: racconto, esposizione*) brief

sommergere [som·'mɛr·dʒe·re] <irr> *vt* **1.** (*terre, villaggi*) to submerge **2.** *fig* (*di regali*) to overwhelm **3.** (*far affondare*) to sink

sommergibile [som·mer·'dʒi:·bi·le] *m* submarine

sommersi [som·'mɛr·si] *1. pers sing pass rem di* **sommergere**

sommerso, -a [som·'mɛr·so] **I.** *pp di* **sommergere II.** *agg* **economia -a** black economy

sommesso, -a [som·'mes·so] *agg* (*tono, voce, pianto*) subdued

somministrare [som·mi·nis·'tra:·re] *vt* (*medicine, sacramenti*) to administer

somministrazione [som·mi·nis·trat·'tsio:·ne] *f* (*di medicine, sacramenti*) administration

sommità [som·mi·'ta] <-> *f* (*cima*) summit

sommo, -a I. *superlativo di* **alto, -a II.** *superlativo di* **grande III.** *agg* **1.** (*superiore: capo, sacerdote*) chief **2.** (*eccellente: poeta*) outstanding **3.** *fig* (*massimo: rispetto*) greatest

sommossa [som·'mɔs·sa] *f* (*sollevazione*) uprising

sommozzatore [som·mot·tsa·'to:·re] *m* diver

sonaglio [so·'naʎ·ʎo] <-gli> *m* bell, *spherical metal type with a small ball inside*

sonare *v.* **suonare**

sonata *v.* **suonata**

sonatore *v.* **suonatore**

sonda ['son·da] *f* probe; **~ spaziale** space probe

sondaggio [son·'dad·dʒo] <-ggi> *m* **1.** (*indagine*) survey; **~ d'opinione** opinion poll **2.** (*con sonda*) sounding

sondare [son·'da:·re] *vt* **1.** (*con sonda*) to survey **2.** *fig* (*intenzioni*) to discover; **~ il terreno** to test the water

sondriese [son·'drie:·se] **I.** *agg* from Sondrio **II.** *mf* (*abitante*) person from Sondrio

Sondrio *f* Sondrio, *town in northern Italy*

soneria *v.* **suoneria**

sonetto [so·'net·to] *m* sonnet

sonnambulismo [son·nam·bu·'liz·mo] *m* sleepwalking

sonnambulo, -a [son·'nam·bu·lo] *m, f* sleepwalker

sonnecchiare [son·nek·'kia:·re] *vi fam* to doze

sonnellino [son·nel·'li:·no] *m* nap; **fare** [*o* **farsi**] **un ~** to take a nap

sonnifero [son·'ni:·fe·ro] *m* sleeping pill

sonno ['son·no] *m* sleep; **avere ~** to be sleepy; **prendere ~** to fall asleep; **cascare dal ~** to be asleep on one's feet; **morire di ~** to be half asleep

sonnolento, -a [son·no·'lɛn·to] *agg* sleepy

sonnolenza [son·no·'lɛn·tsa] *f* sleepiness

sono ['so:·no] *1. pers sing pr di* **essere**[1]

sonorità [so·no·ri·'ta] <-> *f* sonority

sonorizzare [so·no·rid·'dza:·re] *vt* to add a soundtrack to

sonorizzazione [so·no·rid·dzat·'tsio:·ne] *f* addition of a soundtrack

sonoro [so·'nɔ:·ro] *m* soundtrack; **~ surround** surround sound

sonoro, -a *agg* **1.** PHYS sound; **onde -e** soundwaves **2.** (*voce*) sonorous **3.** *fig* (*clamoroso: sconfitta*) resounding **4.** LING voiced **5.** FILM **colonna -a** soundtrack; **cinema ~** the talkies *pl*

sontuosità [son·tuo·si·'ta] <-> *f* sumptuousness

sontuoso, -a [son·tu·'o:·so] *agg* sumptuous
sopire [so·'pi:·re] <sopisco> *vt* (*calmare: animi*) to soothe
sopore [so·'po:·re] *m* drowsiness
soporifero, -a [so·po·'ri:·fe·ro] *agg* tedious
soppalco [sop·'pal·ko] <-chi> *m* platform
sopperire [sop·pe·'ri:·re] <sopperisco> *vi* ~ **a qc** to provide for sth; ~ **alle spese** to pay for expenses
soppesare [sop·pe·'sa:·re] *vt* **1.** *fig* (*valutare*) to weigh up **2.** (*oggetto*) ~ **qc** to feel the weight of sth
soppiantare [sop·pian·'ta:·re] *vt* **1.** (*subentrare a*) to supplant **2.** (*sostituire*) to replace
soppiatto [sop·'piat·to] *agg* **di** ~ furtively; **è entrata in cucina di** ~ she stole into the kitchen
sopportare [sop·por·'ta:·re] *vt* **1.** (*peso, sofferenza, spese*) to bear; **non sopporta il dolore fisico** he [*o* she] cannot bear physical pain; ~ **una perdita** to sustain a loss **2.** (*persona, caldo, freddo*) to stand
sopportazione [sop·por·tat·'tsio:·ne] *f* (*pazienza*) patience
soppressi [sop·'prɛs·si] *1. pers sing pass rem di* **sopprimere**
soppressione [sop·pres·'sio:·ne] *f* (*eliminazione: di organizzazione*) suppression; (*di servizio*) withdrawal
sopprimere [sop·'pri:·me·re] <irr> *vt* **1.** (*legge*) to abolish **2.** (*persona*) to eliminate
sopra ['so:·pra] **I.** *prep* **1.** (*gener*) over; **hanno costruito un ponte** ~ **il fiume** they've built a bridge over the river; **i vicini che abitano** ~ **di noi** our upstairs neighbors **2.** (*con contatto: stato*) on; **ha appoggiato il braccio sopra la mia spalla** he [*o* she] leaned his [*o* her] arm on my shoulder. **3.** (*in cima a*) on top of; **ho messo i miei documenti sopra i tuoi libri.** I put my documents on top of your books **4.** (*senza contatto: stato*) above **5.** (*oltre, più di*) above; ~ **ogni cosa** above all else **6.** (*addosso*) **queste responsabilità ricadranno** ~ **i tuoi figli** these responsibilities will fall on your children **II.** *avv* (*gener*) up; (*in cima*) on top; **vive al piano di sopra** he [*o* she] lives upstairs; **berci** ~ to have a drink, *in order to forget about sth;* **dormirci** ~ to sleep on it; **passarci** ~ to pass over it; **al di** ~ **di** above; **vedi** ~ see above; **di cui** ~ ADM as above **III.** <inv> *agg* above; **la figura** ~ the above figure; **Anna vive al piano** ~ Anna lives upstairs **IV.** <-> *m* (*parte superiore*) top
sopra- [so·pra] (*in parole composte*) **soprannome** nickname; **superstrada sopraelevata** elevated expressway; **sopracciglia** eyebrows
soprabito [so·'pra:·bi·to] *m* light coat
sopracciglio [so·prat·'tʃiʎ·ʎo] <*pl:* -glia *f*> *m* eyebrow
sopraddetto, -a [so·prad·'det·to] *agg* above-mentioned
sopraelencato, -a [so·pra·e·len·'ka:·to] *agg* listed above

sopr(a)elevare [so·pr(a)·e·le·'va:·re] *vt* **1.** (*strada*) to raise **2.** (*edificio*) to increase the height of
sopr(a)elevata [so·pr(a)·e·le·'va:·ta] *f* **1.** (*strada*) elevated highway **2.** (*ferrovia*) elevated railroad
sopr(a)elevato, -a [so·pr(a)·e·le·'va:·to] *agg* (*strada, ferrovia*) elevated
sopraffare [so·praf·'fa:·re] <irr> *vt* to overcome
sopraffazione [so·praf·fat·'tsio:·ne] *f* tyranny
sopraffeci *1. pers sing pass rem di* **sopraffare**
sopraffino, -a [so·praf·'fi:·no] *agg* **1.** (*pranzo*) excellent **2.** *fig* (*astuzia*) masterly
sopraffò [so·praf·'fɔ] *1. pers sing pr di* **sopraffare**
sopraggiungere [so·prad·'dʒun·dʒe·re] <irr> *vi essere* **1.** (*arrivare*) to arrive (unexpectedly) **2.** (*accadere*) to happen
sopraindicato, -a [so·pra·in·di·'ka:·to] *agg* above-mentioned
sopra(l)luogo [so·pra(l)·'luɔ:·go] <-ghi> *m* on-the-spot investigation
soprammobile [so·pram·'mɔ:·bi·le] *m* ornament
soprannaturale [so·pran·na·tu·'ra:·le] **I.** *agg* (*fatto, fenomeno*) supernatural **II.** *m* supernatural
soprannome [so·pran·'no:·me] *m* nickname
soprannominare [so·pran·no·mi·'na:·re] *vt* ~ **qu** to give sb a nickname
soprannominato, -a [so·pran·no·mi·'na:·to] *agg* nicknamed
soprannumero [so·pran·'nu:·me·ro] *m* **le ragazze sono in** ~ **rispetto ai ragazzi** there are more girls than boys
soprano [so·'pra:·no] *m* soprano; **mezzo** ~ mezzo (soprano)
soprappensiero, sopra pensiero [so·prap·pen·'siɛ:·ro] *avv* lost in thought
soprappiù [sop·rap·'piu] <-> *m* **1.** (*ciò che è in più*) **è un** ~ it is surplus to requirements **2.** (*aggiunta*) **in** [*o* per] ~ too many; **i ragazzi erano in** ~ there were too many boys
soprapprezzo [sop·rap·'prɛt·tso] *m* surcharge
soprassalto [sop·ras·'sal·to] *m* start; **di** ~ with a start; **mi sono svegliata di** ~ I woke up with a start
soprassedere [sop·ras·se·'de:·re] <irr> *vi* ~ **a qc** to let sth go
soprattassa [sop·rat·'tas·sa] *f* surtax
soprattutto [sop·rat·'tut·to] *avv* especially
sopra(v)valutare [sop·ra(v)·va·lu·'ta:·re] *vt* to overestimate
sopravvenire [sop·rav·ve·'ni:·re] <irr> *vi essere* (*accadere*) to arise
sopravvento [sop·rav·'vɛn·to] *m* **prendere il** ~ *fig* to prevail
sopravvissi *1. pers sing pass rem di* **sopravvivere**
sopravvissuto, -a [sop·rav·vis·'su:·to] **I.** *pp di* **sopravvivere II.** *agg* surviving **III.** *m, f* survivor

S

sopravvivenza [sop·rav·vi·'vɛn·tsa] *f* survival; **istinto di ~** survival instinct

sopravvivere [sop·rav·'vi:·ve·re] <irr> *vi* essere **1.** (*a persone, a disgrazia*) ~ **a qu** to outlive sb; ~ **a qc** to survive sth **2.** *fig* (*ricordo*) to live on

soprintendente [sop·rin·ten·'dɛn·te] *mf* superintendent

soprintendenza [sop·rin·ten·'dɛn·tsa] *f* supervision; **Soprintendenza per i beni archeologici** *government department responsible for the archeological heritage*

soprintendere [sop·rin·'tɛn·de·re] <irr> *vi* ~ **a qc** to supervise sth

sopruso [so·'pru:·zo] *m* abuse; **subire -i** to suffer abuse

soqquadro [sok·'kua:d·ro] *m* **mettere a ~** to turn upside down

sorbetto [sor·'bet·to] *m* sorbet

sorbire [sor·'bi:·re] <sorbisco> *vt fig* (*sopportare*) to put up with

sorcio ['sor·tʃo] <-ci> *m fam* mouse

sordido, -a ['sɔr·di·do/'sor·di·do] *agg pej* **1.** (*sporco*) squalid **2.** *fig* (*ignobile*) sordid

sordina [sor·'di:·na] *f* MUS mute; **in ~** *fig* on the quiet

sordità [sor·di·'ta] <-> *f* **1.** MED deafness **2.** *fig* (*disinteresse*) indifference

sordo, -a ['sor·do] **I.** *agg* **1.** *a. fig* deaf; **essere ~ da un orecchio** to be deaf in one ear; **~ come una campana** (as) deaf as a post **2.** LING voiceless **II.** *m, f* deaf person; **fare il ~** to play deaf; **parlare** [*o* **cantare**] **ai -i** *fig* to waste one's breath

sordomuto, -a [sor·do·'mu:·to] **I.** *agg* deaf-and-dumb **II.** *m, f* deaf mute

sorella [so·'rɛl·la] *f* sister

sorellastra [so·rel·'las·tra] *f* (*con un genitore in comune*) half sister, stepsister

sorgente [sor·'dʒɛn·te] *f* source

sorgere ['sor·dʒe·re] <sorgo, sorsi, sorto> *vi* essere **1.** (*gener*) to rise **2.** *fig* (*manifestarsi*) to arise; **mi sorge un dubbio** I'm starting to wonder

sorgivo, -a [sor·'dʒi:·vo] *agg* source

soriano [so·'ria:·no] *m* tabby (cat)

soriano, -a *agg* tabby

sormontare [sor·mon·'ta:·re] *vt* **1.** (*difficoltà, ostacolo*) to overcome **2.** (*acqua*) to overflow

sornione, -a [sor·'nio:·ne] *agg* (*sguardo, atteggiamento*) sly

sorpassare [sor·pas·'sa:·re] *vt* **1.** (*veicolo*) to pass **2.** (*in altezza: persona*) to be taller than; (*liquido*) to be higher than; **mi sorpassa di dieci cm** he [*o* she] is ten cm taller than me **3.** *fig* (*sopravanzare*) to be better than

sorpassato, -a [sor·pas·'sa:·to] *agg* (*antiquato*) outdated

sorpasso [sor·'pas·so] *m* **fare** [*o* **effettuare**] **un ~** to pass; **divieto di ~** no passing; **corsia di ~** passing lane

sorprendente [sor·pren·'dɛn·te] *agg* (*avvenimento, fatto*) surprising

sorprendere [sor·'prɛn·de·re] <irr> **I.** *vt* **1.** (*stupire*) to surprise; **la sua reazione mi ha sorpreso** his reaction surprised me; **mi ha sorpreso molto sapere che ...** I was very surprised to learn that ... **2.** (*raggiungere*) ~ **qu** to take sb by surprise **3.** *fig* (*cogliere*) ~ **qu** to catch sb in the act **II.** *vr* (*meravigliarsi*) **-rsi di qc** to be surprised about sth; **non mi soprendo più di nulla** nothing surprises me any more

sorpresa [sor·'pre:·sa] *f* surprise; **cogliere qu di ~** to take sb by surprise; **con mia grande ~** to my great surprise; **fare una ~ a qu** to give sb a surprise

sorreggere [sor·'rɛd·dʒe·re] <irr> *vt* to support

Sorrento [sor·'rɛn·to] *f* Sorrento, *town in southwestern Italy*

sorressi *1. pers sing pass rem di* **sorreggere**

sorretto *pp di* **sorreggere**

sorridente [sor·ri·'dɛn·te] *agg* smiling; **è sempre ~** he [*o* she] is always in a good mood

sorridere [sor·'ri:·de·re] <irr> *vi* **1.** (*ridere*) to smile; ~ **a qu** to smile at sb **2.** *fig* (*riuscire gradito*) ~ **a qu** to appeal to sb **3.** *fig* (*apparire favorevole*) to smile on; **la vita mi sorride** life is good

sorriso [sor·'ri:·so] *m* smile

sorsata [sor·'sa:·ta] *f* sip

sorseggiare [sor·sed·'dʒa:·re] *vt* to sip

sorsi ['sor·si] *1. pers sing pass rem di* **sorgere**

sorso ['sor·so] *m* sip

sorta ['sɔr·ta] *f* sort; **d'ogni ~** of every sort

sorte ['sɔr·te] *f* (*destino*) fate; **tirare** [*o* **estrarre**] **a ~** to draw lots

sorteggiare [sor·ted·'dʒa:·re] *vt* to draw

sorteggio [sor·'ted·dʒo] <-ggi> *m* draw; **per ~** by lot

sortilegio [sor·ti·'lɛ:·dʒo] <-gi> *m* (*incantesimo*) spell

sortire [sor·'ti:·re] <sortisco> *vt* (*effetto, risultato*) to produce

sorto ['sor·to] *pp di* **sorgere**

sorvegliante [sor·veʎ·'ʎan·te] *mf* supervisor

sorveglianza [sor·veʎ·'ʎan·tsa] *f* surveillance; **gli hanno affidato la ~ del castello** he is in charge of security at the castle

sorvegliare [sor·veʎ·'ʎa:·re] *vt* (*tenere sotto controllo: traffico*) to monitor; (*alunni*) to keep an eye on; (*operai*) to supervise

sorvolare [sor·vo·'la:·re] **I.** *vt* **1.** AERO to fly over **2.** *fig* (*passar sopra*) to pass over **II.** *vi* ~ **su qc** *fig* to pass over sth

S.O.S. ['ɛs·se·o·'ɛs·se] <-> *m* SOS; **lanciare un ~** *a. fig* to send out an SOS

sosia ['sɔ:·zia] <-> *mf* double

sospendere [sos·'pɛn·de·re] <irr> *vt* **1.** (*appendere*) to hang **2.** (*gener*) to suspend; ~ **qu da una carica** to suspend sb from office

sospensione [sos·pen·'sio:·ne] *f* **1.** (*gener*) suspension **2.** LING **puntini di ~** ellipsis points

sospesi [sos·'pe:·si] *1. pers sing pass rem di* **sospendere**

sospeso, -a [sos·'pe:·so] I. *pp di* **sospendere** II. *agg* **1.** (*sollevato verso l'alto*) raised; (*che pende dall'alto*) hanging; **ponte** ~ suspension bridge **2.** (*interrotto*) suspended; **col fiato** ~ with bated breath **3.** *fig* (*incerto, indeciso: pratica*) **in** ~ pending; **tenere qu in** ~ to keep sb in suspense **4.** *fig* (*ansioso*) **stare con il cuore** ~ to have one's heart in one's mouth

sospettare [sos·pet·'ta:·re] I. *vt* **1.** (*ritenere responsabile*) ~ **qu di** (**fare**) **qc** to suspect sb of (doing) sth **2.** (*immaginare*) to suspect II. *vi* (*diffidare*) ~ **di qu** to be suspicious of sb

sospetto [sos·'pɛt·to] *m* (*dubbio*) suspicion; **destare** ~ to arouse suspicion

sospetto, -a *agg* (*comportamento*) suspicious

sospettoso, -a [sos·pet·'to:·so] *agg* suspicious

sospirare [sos·pi·'ra:·re] I. *vi* to sigh II. *vt* to long for

sospiro [sos·'pi:·ro] *m* sigh; **fare** [*o* **tirare**] **un** ~ to sigh; **Ponte dei Sospiri** Bridge of Sighs, *famous bridge in Venice over which prisoners were led to prison*

sosta ['sɔs·ta] *f* **1.** (*fermata*) stop; ~ **limitata** restricted parking; **'divieto di ~'** 'No Parking'; **parcheggiare in** ~ **vietata** to park in a no parking area **2.** (*riposo*) break; **lavorare senza** ~ to work nonstop

sostantivo [sos·tan·'ti:·vo] *m* LING noun

sostanza [sos·'tan·tsa] *f* **1.** (*gener*) substance; ~ **nociva** harmful substance **2.** *pl* (*patrimonio*) wealth **3.** (*parte essenziale*) essence; **in** ~ in essence

sostanziale [sos·tan·'tsia:·le] *agg* (*fondamentale*) main

sostanzioso, -a [sos·tan·'tsio:·so] *agg* substantial

sostare [sos·'ta:·re] *vi* **1.** (*fermarsi*) to stop **2.** (*fare una pausa*) to take a break

sostegno [sos·'teɲ·ɲo] *m* support; **un pilastro di** ~ a supporting pillar; **mi è sempre stato di** ~ he has always supported me

sostenere [sos·te·'ne:·re] <irr> I. *vt* **1.** (*reggere*) to hold up **2.** (*spese*) to bear **3.** *fig* (*persona, legge, famiglia*) to support; (*tesi, idea*) to hold; **sostiene la tesi che ...** he maintains that ... **4.** (*esame*) to take **5.** (*affermare*) to maintain; **sostiene di essere figlio di un attore famoso** he maintains that he is the son of a famous actor II. *vr:* **-rsi 1.** (*tenersi ritto*) to support oneself **2.** *fig* (*mantenersi vigoroso*) to keep in good shape

sostenibile [sos·te·'ni:·bi·le] *agg* (*teoria*) plausible; **sviluppo** ~ sustainable development

sostenitore, -trice [sos·te·ni·'to:·re] I. *agg* supporting II. *m, f* supporter

sostentamento [sos·ten·ta·'men·to] *m* support; **mezzi di** ~ means of support

sostentare [sos·ten·'ta:·re] I. *vt* (*mantenere*) to support II. *vr:* **-rsi** (*mantenersi*) to support oneself

sostenuto, -a [sos·te·'nu:·to] *agg* (*tono*) distant; (*atteggiamento*) reserved; **fare il** ~ **con qu** to be standoffish with sb

sostituire [sos·ti·tu·'i:·re] <sostituisco> I. *vt* **1.** (*cambiare*) to replace **2.** (*prendere il posto di*) to stand in for II. *vr* (*prendere il posto di*) **-rsi a qu** to replace sb; **-rsi a qc** to replace sth

sostitutivo, -a [sos·ti·tu·'ti:·vo] *agg* replacement

sostituto, -a [sos·ti·'tu:·to] *m, f* replacement; ~ **procuratore** JUR ≈ assistant district attorney

sostituzione [sos·ti·tut·'tsio:·ne] *f* **1.** SPORT substitution **2.** (*di pezzo*) replacement; **in** ~ **di** (*collega*) in place of

sostrato [sos·'tra:·to] *m* substratum

sottaceti [sot·ta·'tʃe:·ti] *mpl* pickles

sottaceto, sott'aceto [sot·ta·'tʃe:·to] I. *agg* <inv> pickled; **cetriolini** ~ gherkins II. *avv* **mettere** ~ to pickle

sottana [sot·'ta:·na] *f* (*sottogonna*) petticoat; **stare attaccato alla** ~ **della mamma** *fig* to be tied to the mother's apron strings

sottecchi [sot·'tek·ki] *avv* **di** ~ secretly

sotterfugio [sot·ter·'fu:·dʒo] <-gi> *m* (*inganno*) subterfuge; **di** ~ secretly

sotterranea [sot·ter·'ra:·nea] *f* subway

sotterraneo [sot·ter·'ra:·neo] *m* cellar

sotterraneo, -a *agg* underground; **ferrovia -a** subway

sotterrare [sot·ter·'ra:·re] *vt* to bury

sottigliezza [sot·tiʎ·'ʎet·tsa] *f* **1.** *fig* (*acutezza*) subtlety **2.** *fig* (*cavillo*) detail

sottile [sot·'ti:·le] I. *agg* **1.** (*filo, strato, aria*) thin **2.** (*figura, gambe*) slim **3.** *fig* (*mente*) shrewd **4.** (*acuto: vista, odorato*) sharp **5.** (*sofistico: argomentazione, discorso*) subtle II. *m* **non andare per il** ~ to not get sidetracked

sottiletta [sot·ti·'let·ta] *f* processed cheese slice

sottilizzare [sot·ti·lid·'dza:·re] *vi* to split hairs

sottintendere [sot·tin·'tɛn·de·re] <irr> *vt* **1.** (*lasciare intendere*) to imply; **è sottinteso** it goes without saying **2.** (*non esprimere*) to mean

sottinteso [sot·tin·'te:·so] *m* insinuation

sottinteso, -a *agg* understood

sotto ['sot·to] I. *prep* **1.** (*gener*) under(neath); ~ **il tavolo** under the table; ~ **le coperte** under(neath) the covers; **essere nato** ~ **il segno del Cancro** to be born under the sign of Cancer; ~ **l'effetto dell'alcool** under the influence (of alcohol); **abita** ~ **di me** he [*o* she] lives downstairs from me; ~ **questo aspetto** from this point of view; ~ **la pioggia** in the rain **2.** (*più in basso di*) below; ~ **lo zero** below zero **3.** *fig* (*subordinazione, vigilanza*) under; ~ **il dominio austriaco** under Austrian rule; **ha tre collaboratori** ~ **di sé** he [*o* she] has three people under him [*o* her]; **mi ha preso** ~ **la sua ala protettrice** he [*o* she] took me under his [*o* her] wing **4.** (*condizione*) ~ **giuramento** under oath; **essere** ~ **esami** to be taking exams; **caffè** ~ **vuoto** vacuum packed coffee; **sott'aceto** pickled; **sott'olio** in oil II. *avv* **1.** (*stato*) down; **il piano di** ~ downstairs; **le stanze di** ~ the rooms downstairs; **qui c'è** ~ **qualcosa** *fig* there's more to this than meets the eye 2. (*moto*) forward; **farsi ~** *fig* to go for something; **fatti ~!** go for it!; **mettere ~** to run over; **mettersi ~** *fig, fam* to get going 3. (*addosso*) underneath 4. (*più giù, oltre*) below; **vedi ~** see below; **~ ~** *fig* deep down III. <inv> *agg* (*sottostante*) below IV. <-> *m* underneath

sotto- [sot·to] (*in parole composte*) **sottotono** under one's breath; **sottopassaggio** underpass

sottobanco [sot·to·'baŋ·ko] *avv* under the counter

sottobicchiere [sot·to·bik·'kiɛː·re] *m* coaster

sottobosco [sot·to·'bɔs·ko] <-schi> *m* 1. BOT undergrowth 2. *fig, pej* lowlife

sottobottiglia [sot·to·bot·'tiʎ·ʎa] <-glie *o* -> *m* coaster

sottobraccio [sot·to·'brat·tʃo] *avv* **prendere qu ~** to take sb by the arm; **passeggiare ~ con qu** to walk arm in arm with sb

sottocchio [sot·'tɔk·kio] *avv* in front of one; **tenere ~ la situazione** to keep an eye on things

sottochiave [sot·to·'kiaː·ve] *avv* under lock and key

sottocoperta[1] [sot·to·ko·'pɛr·ta] *f* below deck
sottocoperta[2] *avv* below (deck)

sottocosto [sot·to·'kɔs·to] I. *avv* below cost (price) II. <inv> *agg* below cost

sottocultura [sot·to·kul·'tuː·ra] *f* subculture

sottocutaneo, -a [sot·to·ku·'taː·neo] *agg* subcutaneous

sottoelencato, -a [sot·to·e·len·'kaː·to] *agg* listed below

sottoesporre [sot·to·es·'por·re] <irr> *vt* to underexpose

sottofondo [sot·to·'fon·do] *m* 1. MUS, FILM, TV background 2. (*strato sottostante*) lower layer 3. *fig* (*connotazione*) undertone

sottogamba [sot·to·'gam·ba] *avv* **prendere qc ~** to not take sth seriously

sottogonna [sot·to·'gon·na] *f* underskirt

sottogruppo [sot·to·'grup·po] *m* subgroup

sottolineare [sot·to·li·ne·'aː·re] *vt* 1. (*con matita, evidenziatore*) to underline 2. *fig* (*evidenziare: fatto, aspetto, forma*) to emphasize

sott'olio, sottolio [sot·'tɔː·lio] I. *avv* **mettere ~** to preserve in oil II. <inv> *agg* in oil

sottomano [sot·to·'maː·no] *avv* (*a portata di mano*) to hand

sottomarino [sot·to·ma·'riː·no] *m* submarine

sottomarino, -a *agg* underwater

sottomesso, -a [sot·to·'mes·so] *agg* 1. (*atteggiamento, persona*) submissive 2. (*popolo*) subjugated

sottomettere [sot·to·'met·te·re] <irr> I. *vt* (*popolo*) to subjugate II. *vr:* **-rsi** (*assoggettarsi*) to submit

sottomissione [sot·to·mis·'sioː·ne] *f* submission

sottomultiplo [sot·to·'mul·ti·plo] *m* MATH submultiple

sottopassaggio [sot·to·pas·'sad·dʒo] <-ggi> *m* underpass

sottopentola [sot·to·'pen·to·la] <-> *m* trivet

sottopiatto [sot·to·'piat·to] *m* plate, *that is placed under another plate*

sottoporre [sot·to·'por·re] <irr> I. *vt* 1. (*costringere*) **~ qu a qc** to subject sb to sth 2. *fig* (*presentare*) **~ qc a qu** to submit sth to sb 3. **~ qu ad un'operazione** to operate on sb II. *vr:* **-rsi** 1. (*sottomettersi*) to submit 2. (*affrontare*) to undergo

sottoprodotto [sot·to·pro·'dot·to] *m* byproduct

sottoprogramma [sot·to·pro·'gram·ma] *m* COMPUT subroutine

sottoscala [sot·tos·'kaː·la] <-> *m* closet under the stairs

sottoscritto, -a [sot·tos·'krit·to] I. *agg* signed II. *m, f* ADM **il** [*o* **la**] **~** the undersigned

sottoscrivere [sot·tos·'kriː·ve·re] <irr> *vt* 1. (*contratto, petizione, abbonamento*) to sign 2. *fig* (*condividere*) **~ qc** to agree with sth

sottoscrizione [sot·tos·krit·'tsioː·ne] *f* 1. ADM signing 2. (*raccolta di adesioni*) subscription

sottosegretario, -a [sot·to·se·gre·'taː·rio] *m, f* assistant secretary

sottosistema [sot·to·sis·'tɛː·ma] *m* COMPUT subsystem

sottosopra [sot·to·'soː·pra] *avv* in a mess

sottospecie [sot·tos·'pɛː·tʃe] *f* 1. BOT, ZOO subspecies 2. *fig, pej* **quella ~ di amico che ti ritrovi** that creep of a friend of yours; **quella ~ di discoteca** that dive of a club

sottostare [sot·tos·'taː·re] <irr> *vi* **essere** (*essere soggetto*) to submit

sottosterzante [sot·tos·ter·'tsan·te] *agg* understeering

sottostetti 1. *pers sing pass rem di* **sottostare**

sottosuolo [sot·to·'suɔː·lo] *m* AGR subsoil

sottosviluppato, -a [sot·toz·vi·lup·'paː·to] *agg* **paese ~** developing country

sottosviluppo [sot·toz·vi·'lup·po] *m* underdevelopment

sottotenente [sot·to·te·'nɛn·te] *m* sub-lieutenant

sottoterra [sot·to·'tɛr·ra] *avv* below ground

sottotetto [sot·to·'tet·to] *m* attic

sottotitolare [sot·to·ti·to·'laː·re] *vt* to subtitle

sottotitolato, -a [sot·to·ti·to·'laː·to] *agg* subtitled; **film ~ per non udenti** movie subtitled for the deaf

sottotitolo [sot·to·'tiː·to·lo] *m* subtitle

sottovalutare [sot·to·va·lu·'taː·re] *vt* (*situazione, difficoltà*) to undervalue

sottovaso [sot·to·'vaː·zo] *m* flowerpot holder

sottovento [sot·to·'vɛn·to] *avv* to sail leeward

sottoveste [sot·to·'vɛs·te] *f* petticoat

sottovoce [sot·to·'voː·tʃe] *avv* quietly

sottovuoto [sot·to·'vuɔː·to] <inv> *agg* vacuum-packed

sottrarre [sot·'trar·re] <irr> I. *vt* 1. MATH to subtract 2. (*rubare: denaro, documento*) to steal 3. **~ qc alla vista** to put sth out of sight II. *vr* (*sfuggire*) **-rsi a qu/qc** to avoid sb/sth; **-rsi al pericolo** to escape danger

sottrazione [sot·trat·'tsio:·ne] *f* **1.** MATH subtraction **2.** (*di denaro, documento*) theft

sottufficiale [sot·tuf·fi·'tʃa:·le] *m* noncommissioned officer

souvenir [suv·'ni:r] <-> *m* souvenir

sovente [so·'vɛn·te] *avv poet* frequently

soviet [so·'viet] <-> *m* soviet

sovietico, -a [so·'viɛ:·ti·ko] <-ci, -che> **I.** *agg* Soviet; **l'Unione Sovietica** the Soviet Union **II.** *m, f* (*cittadino sovietico*) Soviet citizen

sovra- [sov·ra] *v.a.* **sopra-**

sovrabbondante [sov·rab·bon·'dan·te] *agg* overabundant

sovrabbondanza [sov·rab·bon·'dan·tsa] *f* overabundance

sovrabbondare [sov·rab·bon·'da:·re] *vi* ~ **di qc** to abound with sth

sovraccaricare [sov·rak·ka·ri·'ka:·re] *vt* **1.** ~ **qc (di qc)** to overload sth (with sth) **2.** ~ **qu di qc** *fig* to overload sb with sth

sovraccarico [sov·rak·'ka:·ri·ko] <-chi> *m* **1.** (*carico eccessivo*) excess load **2.** *fig* ~ **di lavoro** excess work

sovraccarico, -a <-chi, -che> *agg* overloaded

sovradimensionato, -a [sov·ra·di·men·sio·'na:·to] *agg* outsize(d); **un ufficio** ~ an overstaffed office

sovraesporre [sov·ra·es·'por·re] <irr> *vt* FOTO to overexpose

sovraffollato, -a [sov·raf·fol·'la:·to] *agg* overcrowded

sovranità [sov·ra·ni·'ta] <-> *f* sovereignty

sovrano, -a [so·'vra:·no] **I.** *m, f* sovereign **II.** *agg* sovereign

sovrappongo *1. pers sing pr di* **sovrapporre**

sovrappopolato, -a [sov·rap·po·po·'la:·to] *agg* overpopulated

sovrapporre [sov·rap·'por·re] <irr> **I.** *vt* (*porre l'uno sopra l'altro*) to place on top of; **ho sovrapposto due tessuti l'uno all'altro** I placed two fabrics on top of each other **II.** *vr:* **-rsi** (*porsi l'uno sopra l'altro*) to be superimposed

sovrapposizione [sov·rap·po·zit·'tsio:·ne] *f* (*di due cose*) superimposition

sovrapprezzo [sov·rap·'prɛt·tso] *m* extra charge

sovrapproduzione [sov·rap·pro·dut·'tsio:·ne] *f* COM overproduction

sovrastare [sov·ras·'ta:·re] *vt avere* **1.** (*dominare*) to dominate **2.** *fig* (*essere imminente*) to threaten

sovrasterzante [sov·ras·ter·'tsan·te] *agg* oversteering

sovresporre [sov·res·'por·re] *v.* **sovraesporre**

sovrumano, -a [sov·ru·'ma:·no] *agg* superhuman

sovvenzionare [sov·ven·tsio·'na:·re] *vt* (*finanziare*) to subsidize

sovvenzione [sov·ven·'tsio:·ne] *f* (*finanziamento*) subsidy

sovversivo, -a [sov·ver·'si:·vo] **I.** *agg* (*spirito, corrente*) subversive **II.** *m, f* subversive

sovvertimento [sov·ver·ti·'men·to] *m* (*della società*) subversion

sovvertire [sov·ver·'ti:·re] *vt* (*ordinamenti, leggi*) to subvert

sozzo, -a ['sot·tso] *agg fam* filthy

S.p.A. *abbr di* **Società per Azioni** Corp.

spaccalegna [spak·ka·'leɲ·ɲa] <-> *mf* lumberjack

spaccapietre [spak·ka·'piɛ:·tre] <-> *mf* stonecutter

spaccare [spak·'ka:·re] **I.** *vt* **1.** (*rompere*) to break; ~ **la legna** to chop wood **2.** *fam* to smash sb's face in; **un orologio che spacca il minuto** a clock that keeps perfect time; **o la va o la spacca** *fam* it's sink or swim **II.** *vr:* **-rsi** (*rompersi*) to break; **-rsi in due** to break in half

spaccata [spak·'ka:·ta] *f* SPORT **fare la** ~ to do the splits

spaccato [spak·'ka:·to] *m fig* (*descrizione*) cross-section

spacciare [spat·'tʃa:·re] **I.** *vt* **1.** (*valuta falsa*) to deal in; (*droga*) to push **2.** (*far passare per*) ~ **per** to pass off as **3.** *fam* (*dichiarare inguaribile*) to give up on; **essere spacciato** to be done for **II.** *vr* (*far credere di essere qc*) **-rsi per qu** to pass oneself off as sb

spacciatore, -trice [spat·tʃa·'to:·re] *m, f* (*di droga*) pusher; **rete di -i** drug ring

spaccio ['spat·tʃo] <-cci> *m* (*negozio*) shop

spacco ['spak·ko] <-cchi> *m* **1.** (*nella pietra*) split **2.** (*di indumento*) slit

spacconata [spak·ko·'na:·ta] *f fam* boast; **fare una** ~ to show off

spaccone, -a [spak·'ko:·ne] *m, f fam* show-off

spada ['spa:·da] *f* **1.** (*gener*) sword; **pesce** ~ swordfish; **difendere qu a** ~ **tratta** to leap to sb's defense **2.** SPORT saber **3.** *pl* (*di carte da gioco*) one of the suits in Neapolitan cards

spadroneggiare [spa·dro·ned·'dʒa:·re] *vi pej* to lord it

spaesato, -a [spae·'za:·to] *agg* (*disorientato*) lost

spaghettata [spa·get·'ta:·ta] *f fam* pasta meal; **facciamo una bella** ~ let's have some pasta

spaghetteria [spa·get·te·'ri:·a] *f* pasta restaurant

spaghetti [spa·'get·ti] *mpl* CULIN spaghetti; ~ **aglio e olio** spaghetti with oil and garlic; ~ **alla chitarra** *handmade square-cut spaghetti*

spaghettini [spa·get·'ti:·ni] *mpl* angel-hair pasta

Spagna ['spaɲ·ɲa] *f* Spain

spagnola [spaɲ·'ɲɔ:·la] *f* Spanish flu

spagnoletta [spaɲ·ɲo·'let·ta] *f* peanut

spagnolo, -a [spaɲ·'ɲɔ:·lo] **I.** *agg* Spanish **II.** *m, f* Spaniard

spago ['spa:·go] <-ghi> *m* **1.** (*per legare*) string **2.** *fam* (*paura*) **prendersi un bello** ~ to get spooked **3.** (*loc*) **dare** ~ **a qu** to let sb have his [*o* her] way

spaiato, -a [spa·'ia:·to] *agg* (*calzino*) unpaired

S

spalancare [spa·laŋ·'ka:·re] I. *vt* **1.** (*porta, finestra*) to fling open **2.** *fig* (*occhi, bocca, braccia*) to open wide; (*gambe*) to spread II. *vr:* **-rsi** (*aprirsi*) to open wide

spalare [spa·'la:·re] *vt* to shovel

spalla ['spal·la] *f* **1.** ANAT shoulder; **alzare le -e** [*o* **stringersi nelle -e**] *a. fig* to shrug; **avere le -e larghe** to have broad shoulders; *fig* to have a broad back; **avere la famiglia sulle -e** *fig* to have a family to support; **avere 80 anni sulle -e** *fig* to be 80; **vivere alle -e di qu** to live off sb **2.** (*schiena*) back; **voltare le -e a qu** *a. fig* to turn one's back on sb; **ridere alle -e di qu** to laugh behind sb's back; **con le -e al muro** *fig* with one's back to the wall **3.** ARCH pier **4.** THEAT straight man

spallata [spal·'la:·ta] *f* (*urto*) push with one's shoulders

spalleggiare [spal·led·'dʒa:·re] I. *vt* **1.** (*sostenere*) to support **2.** MIL to carry on one's shoulders II. *vr:* **-rsi** (*difendersi*) to support one another

spalletta [spal·'let·ta] *f* **1.** (*di ponte*) parapet **2.** (*di fiume*) embankment

spalliera [spal·'liɛ:·ra] *f* **1.** (*di sedia, poltrona*) back **2.** (*di letto*) bedhead

spallina [spal·'li:·na] *f* **1.** (*di indumento*) shoulder strap **2.** (*imbottita*) shoulder pad **3.** MIL epaulet

spallucce [spal·'lut·tʃe] *fpl* **fare ~ fam** to shrug one's shoulders

spalmare [spal·'ma:·re] *vt* to spread

spalti ['spal·ti] *mpl* (*di stadio*) bleachers

spanciarsi [span·'tʃa:r·si] *vr* **~ dalle risate** *fam* to split one's sides

spanciata [span·'tʃa:·ta] *f* (*colpo*) belly flop; **prendere una ~** to do a belly flop

spandere [span·de·re] <spando, spandei *o* spansi *o* spandetti, spanto> I. *vt* **1.** (*liquidi*) to spill **2.** *fig* (*lacrime*) to shed **3.** (*distendere*) to spread **4.** *fam* (*sperperare*) to squander; **spendere e ~** to spend money like water II. *vr:* **-rsi** (*diffondersi*) to spread

spanna ['span·na] *f fig* **essere alto una ~** *scherz* to be very short; **a -e direi 20% della popolazione** I would say roughly 20% of the population

spansi ['span·si] *1. pers sing pass rem di* **spandere**

spanto ['span·to] *pp di* **spandere**

spaparacchiarsi [spa·pa·rak·'kiar·si] *vr dial, fam* to sprawl (out)

spaparanzato, -a [spa·pa·ran·'tsa:·to] *agg dial, fam* sprawled

spappolare [spap·po·'la:·re] I. *vt* (*ridurre in poltiglia*) to crush II. *vr:* **-rsi** to get crushed

sparagnino, -a [spa·raŋ·'ɲi:·no] I. *agg fam* stingy II. *m, f fam* tightwad

sparare [spa·'ra:·re] I. *vt* **1.** (*colpo*) to fire **2.** *fig* (~ *fandonie*) to tell (fairy) tales; **spararle** (**grosse**) *fam* to talk a load of bull II. *vi* MIL (*soldati*) to shoot; (*fucile, pistola*) to fire III. *vr:* **-rsi** to shoot oneself; **-rsi un colpo alla testa**

to blow one's head off

sparato, -a *agg* (*a gran velocità*) at full speed; **partire tutto ~** to be off like a shot

sparatoria [spa·ra·'tɔ:·ria] <-ie> *f* gunfight

sparecchiare [spa·rek·'kia:·re] *vt* **~** (**la tavola**) to clear (the table); **per favore sparecchia** could you clear the table?

spareggio [spa·'red·dʒo] <-ggi> *m* SPORT tiebreaker

spargere ['spar·dʒe·re] <spargo, sparsi, sparso> I. *vt* **1.** (*semi, fiori*) to scatter **2.** (*luce, calore, notizia*) to spread **3.** (*liquidi*) to spill; (*lacrime, sangue*) to shed II. *vr:* **-rsi 1.** (*persone, animali*) to scatter **2.** (*notizie, dicerie*) to spread

spargimento [spar·dʒi·'men·to] *m* (*di lacrime, sangue*) shedding; **-i di sangue** bloodshed

sparire [spa·'ri:·re] <sparisco> *vi* essere to disappear; **dove sei sparito?** where did you disappear to?

sparizione [spa·rit·'tsio:·ne] *f* (*scomparsa*) disappearance

sparlare [spar·'la:·re] *vi* **1.** *pej* **~ di qu** to badmouth sb **2.** (*farneticare*) to talk nonsense

sparo ['spa:·ro] *m* (*colpo*) shot

sparpagliare [spar·paʎ·'ʎa:·re] I. *vt* (*spargere*) to spread II. *vr:* **-rsi** (*spargersi*) to scatter

sparsi ['spar·si] *1. pers sing pass rem di* **spargere**

sparso, -a ['spar·so] I. *pp di* **spargere** II. *agg* (*non ordinato*) scattered; **in ordine ~** in open order

spartano, -a [spar·'ta:·no] *agg a. fig* (*modesto*) spartan

spartiacque [spar·ti·'ak·kue] <-> *m* **1.** *a. fig* (*linea di separazione*) watershed; **~ continentale** continental divide **2.** (*elemento discriminante*) divide

spartineve [spar·ti·'ne:·ve] <-> *m* snow plow

spartire [spar·'ti:·re] <spartisco> *vt* (*dividere*) to share out; **non avere niente da ~ con qu** *fig* to have nothing in common with sb

spartito [spar·'ti:·to] *m* (*partitura*) music

spartitraffico [spar·ti·'traf·fi·ko] I. <-> *m* median (strip) II. <inv> *agg* **banchina ~** median (strip)

spartizione [spar·tit·'tsio:·ne] *f* **1.** (*distribuzione*) sharing out **2.** (*di cariche*) division

sparuto, -a [spa·'ru:·to] *agg* **1.** (*viso, aspetto*) gaunt **2.** *fig* (*piccolo*) tiny

sparviere, sparviero [spar·'viɛ:·re, spar·'viɛ:·ro] *m* sparrow hawk

spasimante [spa·zi·'man·te] *mf scherz* admirer

spasimare [spa·zi·'ma:·re] *vi* **1.** (*patire*) to suffer **2.** *fig* (*desiderare*) **~ di fare qc** to long to do sth; **~ per qu** to be smitten by sb

spasimo ['spa:·zi·mo] *m* sharp pain; **-i della fame** hunger pangs; **-i d'amore** heartache

spasmo ['spaz·mo] *m* MED spasm

spasmodico, -a [spaz·'mɔ:·di·ko] <-ci, -che> *agg* **1.** MED spasmodic **2.** *fig* (*attesa, ricerca*) feverish

spassarsi [spas·'sa:r·si] *vr fam* (*divertirsi*) to enjoy oneself; **spassarsela con qu** to have a fling with sb

spassionato, -a [spas·sio·'na:·to] *agg* (*imparziale: consiglio, parere*) impartial

spasso ['spas·so] *m* **1.** (*divertimento*) fun; **è un vero ~** it's a lot of fun **2.** (*persona*) scream; **è un vero ~** he's [*o* she's] a scream **3.** (*passeggiata*) **andare a ~** to go for a walk; **mandare a ~** *fig* to fire

spassoso, -a [spas·'so:·so] *agg* entertaining

spastico, -a ['spas·ti·ko] <-ci, -che> **I.** *agg* spastic **II.** *m, f* **1.** MED person with cerebral palsy **2.** *scherz* klutz

spatola ['spa:·to·la] *f* **1.** (*arnese*) trowel **2.** MED spatula **3.** ZOO paddlefish

spauracchio [spau·'rak·kio] <-cchi> *m a. fig, fam* bugaboo

spaurire [spau·'ri:·re] <spaurisco> **I.** *vt* (*metter paura a*) to frighten **II.** *vr:* **-rsi** (*aver paura*) to be frightened

spavalderia [spa·val·de·'ri:·a] <-ie> *f* cockiness

spavaldo, -a [spa·'val·do] *agg* (*persona, aria*) cocky

spaventapasseri [spa·ven·ta·'pas·se·ri] <-> *m* **1.** (*fantoccio*) scarecrow **2.** *scherz* (*persona brutta*) freak

spaventare [spa·ven·'ta:·re] **I.** *vt* (*mettere paura a*) to frighten **II.** *vr:* **-rsi** to be frightened

spavento [spa·'vɛn·to] *m* (*paura*) fright; **fare uno ~ a qu** to frighten sb

spaventoso, -a [spa·ven·'to:·so] *agg* **1.** (*terribile*) terrible **2.** *fig* (*straordinario*) incredible; **ho una fame -a** I'm starving

spaziale [spat·'tsia:·le] *agg* **1.** (*dello spazio*) spatial **2.** (*cosmico*) space; **navicella ~** spacecraft **3.** *fam* (*straordinario*) amazing

spaziare [spat·'tsia:·re] **I.** *vi* **1.** (*vista*) to sweep; (*uccelli*) to fly freely **2.** *fig* (*pensieri*) to range widely **II.** *vt* TYP to space (out)

spazientirsi [spat·tsien·'tir·si] <mi spazientisco> *vr* to lose patience

spazio ['spat·tsio] <-i> *m* space; (*posto*) room; **fare ~ a qu/qc** to make room for sb/sth; **~ pubblicità** advertising space

spazioso, -a [spa·'tsio:·so] *agg* (*capiente*) spacious

spazzacamino [spat·tsa·ka·'mi:·no] *m* chimney sweep

spazzaneve [spat·tsa·'ne:·ve] <-> *m* snow plow

spazzare [spat·'tsa:·re] *vt* **1.** (*strada, stanza*) to sweep **2.** *fam* (*cibo*) to polish off

spazzatura [spat·tsa·'tu:·ra] *f a. fig* trash

spazzino [spat·'tsi:·no] *m* garbage collector

spazzola ['spat·tso·la] *f* **1.** (*arnese*) brush, hairbursh; **avere i capelli a ~** to have a flattop **2.** MOT wiper blade

spazzolare [spat·tso·'la:·re] *vt* to brush

spazzolata [spat·tso·'la:·ta] *f* brush; **darsi una ~ ai capelli** to brush one's hair

spazzolino [spat·tso·'li:·no] *m* (small) brush; **~ da denti** (**elettrico**) (electric) toothbrush; **~ per unghie** nail brush

spazzolone [spat·tso·'lo:·ne] *m* broom

speaker ['spi:·kə/'spi:·ker] <-> *m* TV, RADIO speaker

specchiarsi [spek·'kiar·si] *vr* **1.** (*guardarsi allo specchio*) to look at oneself in a mirror **2.** (*riflettersi*) to be reflected

specchiera [spek·'kiɛ:·ra] *f* wall mirror

specchietto [spek·'kiet·to] *m* **1.** (*piccolo specchio*) (small) mirror **2.** AUTO **~ retrovisore** rear-view mirror **3.** (*prospetto riassuntivo*) table

specchio ['spɛk·kio] <-cchi> *m* **1.** *gener* mirror; **guardarsi allo ~** to look in the mirror **2.** *fig* reflection

special ['spɛ:·tʃal] <-> *m* special

speciale [spe·'tʃa:·le] *agg* special; **inviato ~** special correspondent; **questo formaggio è davvero ~** this cheese is really excellent

specialista [spe·tʃa·'lis·ta] <-i *m*, -e *f*> *mf* **1.** MED specialist **2.** (*persona specializzata*) expert

specialità [spe·tʃa·li·'ta] <-> *f* specialty

specializzare [spe·tʃa·lid·'dza:·re] **I.** *vt* to specialize **II.** *vr* **-rsi in qc** to specialize in sth

specializzato, -a [spe·tʃa·lid·'dza:·to] *agg* (*operaio, medico*) specialized

specializzazione [spe·tʃa·lid·dzat·'tsio:·ne] *f* (*competenza specialistica*) specialization

specialmente [spe·tʃal·'men·te] *avv* especially

specie ['spɛ:·tʃe] **I.** <-> *f* **1.** BIOL species **2.** (*sorta, tipo*) kind; **una ~ di** a kind of; **d'ogni ~** of all kinds **II.** *avv* especially

specifica [spe·'tʃi:·fi·ka] <-che> *f* specification

specificare [spe·tʃi·fi·'ka:·re] *vt* to state

specificazione [spe·tʃi·fi·kat·'tsio:·ne] *f* specification; **complemento di ~** possessive case

specifico, -a [spe·'tʃi:·fi·ko] <-ci, -che> *agg* **1.** (*particolare*) particular **2.** PHYS, MED specific

speck [spɛk] <-> *m smoked ham from the South Tyrol region*

speculare[1] [spe·ku·'la:·re] *vi* **1.** FIN, COM to speculate **2.** *fig* (*sfruttare*) **~ su qc** to take advantage of sth

speculare[2] *agg* (*di specchio*) **immagine ~** mirror image

speculativo, -a [spe·ku·la·'ti:·vo] *agg* speculative

speculatore, -trice [spe·ku·la·'to:·re] *m, f* ECON speculator

speculazione [spe·ku·lat·'tsio:·ne] *f* speculation

spedire [spe·'di:·re] <spedisco> *vt* (*inviare*) to send

spedito, -a [spe·'di:·to] *agg* (*rapido*) fast; **camminare a passo ~** to walk quickly

spedizione [spe·dit·'tsio:·ne] *f* **1.** (*di pacco, merce*) dispatch; **spese di ~** postage and handling **2.** (*operazione*) mailing **3.** MIL, SCIENT expedition

spedizioniere [spe·dit·tsio·'niɛ:·re] *m* shipper

spegnere ['spɛɲ·ɲe·re/'speɲ·ɲe·re] <spengo, spensi, spento> I. *vt* **1.** (*fuoco, fiamma, sigaretta*) to put out **2.** (*luce, radio, motore, apparecchio*) to turn off **3.** *fig* (*entusiasmo*) to extinguish **4.** (*sete*) to quench II. *vr:* **-rsi 1.** (*fuoco, sigaretta*) to go out **2.** (*motore, apparecchio*) to go off **3.** *fig* (*entusiasmo*) to fizzle out **4.** *fig* (*morire*) to pass away

spelacchiato, -a [spe·lak·'kia:·to] *agg* **1.** (*pelliccia, animale*) mangy **2.** (*persona*) bald

spelare [spe·'la:·re] *vt, vr:* **-rsi** *v.* **spelacchiare**

speleologia [spe·le·o·lo·'dʒi:·a] <-gie> *f* **1.** (*studio*) speleology **2.** (*pratica*) spelunking

speleologo, -a [spe·le·'ɔ:·lo·go] <-gi, -ghe> *m, f* **1.** (*studioso*) speleologist **2.** (*hobbista*) spelunker

spellare [spel·'la:·re] I. *vt* **1.** **~ un animale** to skin **2.** *fam* **~qu** to rip sb off II. *vr:* **-rsi 1.** (*serpenti*) to shed one's skin **2.** MED to skin; **-rsi le ginocchia** to skin one's knees

spelonca [spe·'loŋ·ka] <-che> *f* **1.** (*grotta*) cave **2.** *fig, pej* (*casa*) hovel

spendaccione, -a [spen·dat·'tʃo:·ne] *m, f pej* spendthrift

spendere ['spɛn·de·re] <spendo, spesi, speso> *vt* **1.** (*soldi, tempo*) to spend; **~ molto in vestiti** he [*o* she] spends a lot on clothes; **~ e spandere** *fam* to spend money like water **2.** *fig* (*impiegare: energie, forze*) to expend

spendibilità [spen·di·bi·li·'ta] *f* marketability

spengere ['spɛn·dʒe·re/'spen·dʒe·re] *v.* **spegnere**

spengo ['spɛŋ·go/'speŋ·go] *1. pers sing pr di* **spegnere**

spennare [spen·'na:·re] *vt* **1.** (*animale*) to pluck; **~ una gallina** to pluck a hen **2.** *fig, fam* to fleece; **~ qu al gioco** to fleece sb at cards

spennellare [spen·nel·'la:·re] *vt* to paint

spennellata [spen·nel·'la:·ta] *f* coat of paint

spensi ['spɛn·si/'spen·si] *1. pers sing pass rem di* **spegnere**

spensieratezza [spen·sie·ra·'tetʋtsa] *f* lightheartedness

spensierato, -a [spen·sie·'ra:·to] *agg* (*ragazzo*) lighthearted

spento, -a ['spɛn·to/'spen·to] I. *pp di* **spegnere** II. *agg* **1.** (*fuoco*) **il fuoco è spento** the fire is out **2.** (*sigaretta*) extinguished **3.** *fig* (*colore, espressione*) dull

speranza [spe·'ran·tsa] *f* hope; **un filo** [*o* **un barlume**] **di ~** a glimmer [*o* ray] of hope; **avere riposto tutte le -e in qu** to place all one's hope in sb; **senza ~** hopeless

speranzoso, -a [spe·ran·'tso:·so] *agg* hopeful

sperare [spe·'ra:·re] I. *vt* to hope; **~ di fare qc** +*inf* to hope to do sth; **~ in qc** to hope for sth; **~ che** +*conj* to hope that; **spero di sì** I hope so; **spero di no** I hope not; **speriamo (bene)!** let's hope so II. *vi* **~ in qu/qc** to have great hopes of sb/sth

sperduto, -a [sper·'du:·to] *agg* **1.** (*paese, luogo*) remote **2.** (*persona*) lost

spergiurare [sper·dʒu·'ra:·re] *vi* (*giurare in modo solenne*) to swear; **giurare e ~** *fam* to swear to God

spericolato, -a [spe·ri·ko·'la:·to] *agg* reckless

sperimentale [spe·ri·men·'ta:·le] *agg* (*progetto, ricerca*) experimental; **centro ~** research center

sperimentare [spe·ri·men·'ta:·re] *vt* **1.** TEC to try out **2.** (*conoscere per esperienza*) to experience

sperimentazione [spe·ri·men·tat·'tsio:·ne] *f* TEC testing

sperma ['spɛr·ma] <-i> *m* semen

spermatozoo [sper·ma·tod·'dzɔ:·o] <-oi> *m* sperm

spermicida¹ [sper·mi·'tʃi:·da] <-i *m*, -e *f*> *agg* spermicidal

spermicida² <-i> *m* spermicide

speronare [spe·ro·'na:·re] *vt* (*nave, auto*) to ram

sperone [spe·'ro:·ne] *m* (*della scarpa*) spur

sperperare [sper·pe·'ra:·re] *vt* (*denaro, beni*) to squander

sperpero ['spɛr·pe·ro] *m* (*spreco*) waste

spesa ['spe:·sa] *f* **1.** (*somma*) expense; **non badare a -e** to spare no expense; **imparare qc a proprie -e** *fig* to learn sth to one's cost; **a -e di qu** *a. fig* at sb's expense **2.** (*compera*) shopping; **fare la ~** to do the shopping; **borsa della ~** shopping bag **3.** *pl* COM expenses; **-e d'esercizio** [*o* **di gestione**] operating expenses

spesare [spe·'sa:·re] *vt* **~ qu** to pay sb's expenses

spesi ['spe:·si] *1. pers sing pass rem di* **spendere**

speso ['spe:·so] *pp di* **spendere**

spesso ['spes·so] *avv* often

spesso, -a *agg* **1.** (*libro, muro*) thick **2.** (*aria*) heavy **3.** (*frequente*) **-e volte** often

spessore [spes·'so:·re] *m* thickness

Spett. *abbr di* **spettabile ~ Ditta ...** Dear Sirs; **(alla) ~ Ditta ...** Messrs. ...

spettabile [spet·'ta:·bi·le] *agg* (*nelle lettere*) Dear; **~ Signor Rossi, ...** Dear Mr. Rossi, ...

spettacolare [spet·ta·ko·'la:·re] *agg* (*straordinario*) fantastic

spettacolo [spet·'ta:·ko·lo] *m* **1.** THEAT performance **2.** FILM (*rappresentazione*) showing **3.** (*vista*) spectacle

spettanza [spet·'tan·tsa] *f* (*competenza*) province

spettare [spet·'ta:·re] *vi essere* (*appartenere per diritto*) to be due; **non spetta a me giudicare** it's not up to me to judge

spettatore, -trice [spet·ta·'to:·re] *m, f* **1.** THEAT, FILM spectator **2.** (*chi è presente*) onlooker; **sono stato ~ di un terribile incidente** I witnessed a terrible accident

spettegolare [spet·te·go·'la:·re] *vi pej* to gossip

spettinare [spet·ti·'na:·re] I. *vt* to muss *inf* II. *vr:* **-rsi** to get one's hair mussed (up)

spettrale [spet·'tra:·le] *agg* **1.** PHYS **analisi** ~ spectral analysis **2.** *fig* (*figura, aspetto*) spectral

spettro ['spɛt·tro] *m* **1.** *a. fig* (*fantasma*) ghost **2.** PHYS, ASTR spectrum

spezie ['spɛt·tsie] *fpl* spices

spezzare [spet·'tsa:·re] I. *vt* **1.** (*rompere*) to break **2.** *fig* (*dividere: viaggio, periodo*) ~ **qc in qc** to break sth into sth II. *vr:* **-rsi** (*rompersi*) to break

spezzatino [spet·tsa·'ti:·no] *m* stew

spezzato [spet·'tsa:·to] *m* (*abito maschile*) coordinated jacket and pants

spezzato, -a *agg* (*braccio, gamba*) broken; **cuore** ~ broken heart

spezzettare [spet·tset·'ta:·re] *vt* (*ridurre in pezzi*) ~ **qc** to break sth into pieces; ~ **il discorso** to speak in a disconnected way

Spezzino <*sing*> *m* La Spezia area

spezzino, -a [spet·'tsi:·no] I. *agg* from La Spezia II. *m, f* (*abitante*) person from La Spezia

spezzone [spet·'tso:·ne] *m* **1.** FILM clip **2.** MIL fragmentation bomb

spia ['spi:·a] <-ie> *f* **1.** (*persona*) spy; **fare la** ~ *fam* to tell tales **2.** TEC light **3.** (*fessura di porta*) spyhole

spiaccicare [spiat·tʃi·'ka:·re] *fam* I. *vt* (*schiacciare*) to squash II. *vr:* **-rsi** to splat

spiacente [spia·'tʃɛn·te] *agg* **sono** ~ I'm sorry

spiacere [spia·'tʃe:·re] <*irr*> *vi* **essere mi spiace non poterti aiutare** I'm sorry I can't help you; **mi spiace dover rifiutare** I'm sorry to have to refuse; **spiace vedere tanto disinteresse** it's sad to see such a lack of interest

spiacevole [spia·'tʃe:·vo·le] *agg* unpleasant

spiaggia ['spiad·dʒa] <-gge> *f* beach; **andare in** ~ to go to the beach

spianamento [spia·na·'men·to] *m* (*di terreno*) leveling (off)

spianare [spia·'na:·re] *vt* **1.** (*terreno, strada*) to level (off); ~ **la pasta** to roll out the dough **2.** *fig* (*eliminare difficoltà*) to smooth out; ~ **la via per qc** to smooth the way for sth **3.** (*demolire*) to flatten

spianata [spia·'na:·ta] *f* area of level ground

spiano ['spia:·no] *m* **a tutto** ~ flat out

spiantato, -a [spian·'ta:·to] *pej* I. *agg* (*senza soldi: persona*) penniless II. *m, f* dropout

spiare [spi·'a:·re] *vt* **1.** (*seguire di nascosto*) **spiare qu/qc** to spy on sb/sth **2.** (*fatti, segreti*) to find out

spiata [spi·'a:·ta] *f* tip-off

spiattellare [spiat·tel·'la:·re] *vt fam* (*riferire apertamente*) to blurt out

spiazzo ['spiat·tso] *m* clearing; ~ **erboso** patch of grass

spiccare [spik·'ka:·re] I. *vt* **1.** JUR (*mandato di cattura*) to issue **2.** (*salto, balzo*) ~ **un salto** [*o* **balzo**] to leap; ~ **il volo** to take flight; *fig* to spread one's wings II. *vi* (*distinguersi*) to stand out

spiccato, -a [spik·'ka:·to] *agg* (*accento, senso dell'umorismo*) strong; (*udito*) sharp

spicchio ['spik·kio] <-cchi> *m* (*di agrumi,*

aglio) segment

spicciare [spit·'tʃa:·re] I. *vt* (*faccenda*) to attend to II. *vr:* **-rsi** *fam* (*sbrigarsi*) to hurry; **spicciati!** hurry up!

spicciativo, -a [spit·tʃa·'ti:·vo] *agg* **1.** (*persona*) curt **2.** (*rimedio, metodo*) speedy

spiccicare [spit·tʃi·'ka:·re] *vt* **non** ~ **parola** to not say a word

spiccio, -a ['spit·tʃo] <-cci, -cce> *agg* (*sbrigativo*) brisk; **andare per le -cce** to cut to the chase

spicciolato, -a [spit·tʃo·'la:·to] *agg* **alla -a** in dribs and drabs

spiccioli ['spit·tʃo·li] *mpl* (small) [*o* (loose)] change

spicciolo, -a ['spit·tʃo·lo] *agg* **moneta -a** [*o* **soldi -i**] change

spicco ['spik·ko] <-cchi> *m* **fare** ~ to be prominent

spider ['spai·der] <-> *m o f* convertible

spiedino [spie·'di:·no] *m* **1.** (*arnese*) skewer **2.** (*piatto*) shish kebab

spiedo ['spiɛ:·do] *m* CULIN spit; **arrosto allo** ~ spit roast

spiegamento [spie·ga·'men·to] *m* deployment; ~ **di forze** deployment of forces

spiegare [spie·'ga:·re] I. *vt* **1.** (*far capire*) to explain **2.** (*tovaglia, cartina*) to unfold **3.** (*ali, vele*) to spread **4.** MIL (*truppe*) to deploy II. *vr:* **-rsi** (*chiarirsi*) to explain (oneself); (*con un'altra persona*) to sort things out; **cerca di spiegarti** try to explain; **mi spiego?, mi sono spiegato?** do you understand?

spiegazione [spie·gat·'tsio:·ne] *f* explanation; **avere una** ~ **con qu** to sort things out with sb

spiegazzare [spie·gat·'tsa:·re] *vt* (*foglio*) to crumple

spietato, -a [spie·'ta:·to] *agg* ruthless

spifferare [spif·fe·'ra:·re] *vt fam* to blab

spiffero ['spif·fe·ro] *m fam* draft

spiga ['spi:·ga] <-ghe> *f* (*di grano*) ear

spigato, -a [spi·'ga:·to] *agg* (*tessuto*) herringbone

spigliatezza [spiʎ·ʎa·'tet·tsa] *f* (*disinvoltura*) self-assurance

spigliato, -a [spiʎ·'ʎa:·to] *agg* self-assured

spigola ['spi:·go·la] *f* sea bass

spigolo ['spi:·go·lo] *m* **1.** (*angolo*) sharp edge **2.** *pl, fig* (*asprezza*) rough edges

spigoloso, -a [spi·go·'lo:·so] *agg* **1.** (*pieno di spigoli*) full of sharp edges **2.** *fig* (*difficile: carattere*) prickly

spilla ['spil·la] *f* (*gioiello*) brooch; (*da cravatta*) pin

spillare [spil·'la:·re] *vt avere* **1.** (*botte*) to tap **2.** *fig* ~ **soldi a qu** to tap sb for money

spillo ['spil·lo] *m* **1.** *gener* pin; **tacchi a** ~ stilettos **2.** (*per botti*) (wine) thief; (*foro*) tap hole

spillone [spil·'lo:·ne] *m* large pin

spilorceria [spi·lor·tʃe·'ri:·a] <-ie> *f* stinginess

spilorcio, -a [spi·'lor·tʃo] <-ci, -ce> I. *agg* stingy II. *m, f* tightwad

spilungone, -a [spi·luŋ·'go:·ne] *m, f fam*

S

beanpole

spina ['spi:·na] *f* **1.** BOT thorn **2.** ZOO (*di istrice*) spine; (*di pesce*) bone **3.** ANAT ~ **dorsale** spine **4.** EL plug; ~ **multipla** adapter **5.** TEC (*di botte*) tap; **birra alla** ~ draft beer **6.** (*loc*) **stare** [*o* essere] **sulle -e** to be on tenterhooks; **staccare la** ~ to wind down

spinacio [spi·'na:·tʃo] <-ci> *m* BOT spinach; **-ci** CULIN spinach

spinale [spi·'na:·le] *agg* spinal; **midollo** ~ spinal cord

spinato, -a [spi·'na:·to] *agg* **filo** ~ barbed wire

spinello [spi·'nɛl·lo] *m sl* joint

spingere ['spin·dʒe·re] <spingo, spinsi, spinto> I. *vt* **1.** (*spostare*) to push **2.** (*premere*) to press **3.** *fig* (*indurre*) ~ **qu a qc** to drive sb to sth **4.** (*fare ressa*) to push and shove II. *vr:* **-rsi 1.** (*inoltrarsi*) to go on **2.** *fig* (*osare*) **non pensavo che potesse spingersi fino a tal punto** I didn't think he [*o* she] would go that far

spinoso, -a [spi·'no:·so] *agg a. fig* prickly

spinotto [spi·'nɔt·to] *m* EL plug

spinsi ['spin·si] *1. pers sing pass rem di* **spingere**

spinta ['spin·ta] *f* **1.** (*urto, stimolo*) push **2.** PHYS thrust

spintarella [spin·ta·'rɛl·la] *f fig, fam* (*raccomandazione*) leg-up; **dare una** ~ **a qu** to give sb a leg-up

spinterogeno [spin·te·'rɔ:·dʒe·no] *m* TEC distributor

spinto, -a ['spin·to] I. *pp di* **spingere** II. *agg* (*scabroso: discorso, barzelletta*) risqué; (*film, scena*) steamy

spintone [spin·'to:·ne] *m* shove

spionaggio [spio·'nad·dʒo] <-ggi> *m* spying; ~ **telefonico** phone tapping

spioncino [spion·'tʃi:·no] *m* spyhole

spione, -a [spi·'o:·ne] *m, f pej* tattle-tale

spiovente [spio·'vɛn·te] I. *agg* **1.** (*rami*) drooping; (*tetto*) pitched **2.** SPORT (*tiro*) dipping II. *m* **1.** (*del tetto*) slope **2.** SPORT dipping shot

spiovere ['spiɔ:·ve·re] <irr> *vi essere o avere* to stop raining

spira ['spi:·ra] *f* coil

spiraglio [spi·'raʎ·ʎo] <-gli> *m* **1.** (*di porta, finestra*) chink **2.** (*di luce*) ray **3.** *fig* (*barlume*) glimmer

spirale [spi·'ra:·le] *f* **1.** (*gener*) spiral; ~ **negativa** downward spiral **2.** (*di fumo*) ring **3.** (*metallica*) spring

spirare [spi·'ra:·re] *vi avere* **1.** (*vento*) to blow **2.** *essere* (*morire*) to pass away

spiritato, -a [spi·ri·'ta:·to] *agg* (*faccia, occhi*) wild

spiritico, -a [spi·'ri:·ti·ko] <-ci, -che> *agg* (*seduta -a*) seance

spiritista [spi·ri·'tis·ta] <-i *m*, -e *f*> *mf* spiritualist

spirito ['spi:·ri·to] *m* **1.** REL **lo Spirito Santo** the Holy Spirit **2.** (*senso dell'umorismo*) wit; **una battuta di** ~ a witticism; **fare dello** ~ to make jokes **3.** (*fantasma*) ghost; **nel castello ci sono gli -i** the castle is haunted **4.** (*qualità*) ~ **di carità/giustizia** spirit of charity/justice; **ha un grande** ~ **di osservazione** he [*o* she] is very observant **5.** (*sostanza alcolica*) alcohol

spiritoso, -a [spi·ri·'to:·so] I. *agg* (*persona, carattere*) funny II. *m, f* clown; **smettila di fare lo** ~ stop clowning around

spirituale [spi·ri·tu·'a:·le] *agg* spiritual

spiritualità [spi·ri·tua·li·'ta] <-> *f* REL spirituality

splendere ['splɛn·de·re] *vi* to shine

splendido, -a ['splɛn·di·do] I. *agg* wonderful II. *int* great!

splendore [splen·'do:·re] *m* **1.** (*di sole, stelle*) brightness **2.** (*di persona*) **in tutto il suo** ~ in all his [*o* her] glory **3.** (*di festa*) splendor

spodestare [spo·des·'ta:·re] *vt* to remove from power

spoglia ['spɔʎ·ʎa] <-glie> *fpl* (*resti mortali*) remains *pl*

spogliare [spoʎ·'ʎa:·re] I. *vt* **1.** (*svestire*) to undress **2.** *fig* (*derubare*) to strip II. *vr:* **-rsi 1.** (*svestirsi*) to undress **2.** *fig* (*privarsi*) **-rsi di qc** (*beni,*) to strip oneself of sth

spogliarellista [spoʎ·ʎa·rel·'lis·ta] <-i *m*, -e *f*> *mf* stripper

spogliarello [spoʎ·ʎa·'rɛl·lo] *m* striptease; **fare lo** ~ to strip

spogliatoio [spoʎ·ʎa·'to:·io] <-oi> *m* (*di palestra, stadio*) locker room

spoglio ['spɔʎ·ʎo] *m* (*esame*) reading; **fare lo** ~ **della corrispondenza** to read through the correspondence; ~ **dei voti** count of the votes

spoglio, -a <-gli, -glie> *agg* **1.** (*albero, terreno*) bare **2.** *fig* ~ **di qc** (*pregiudizi*) free from sth

spoiler ['spɔi·lə] <-> *m* spoiler

spola ['spɔ:·la] *f* spool; **fare la** ~ *fig* to commute

spoletta [spo·'let·ta] *f* **1.** (*rocchetto*) cotton reel **2.** (*di bomba*) fuse

spolpare [spol·'pa:·re] *vt* **1.** (*osso*) to bone **2.** *fig* (*privare degli averi*) to fleece

spolverare [spol·ve·'ra:·re] I. *vt* **1.** (*gener*) to dust **2.** *fig, fam* (*mangiare tutto*) to polish off II. *vi* to dust

spolverata [spol·ve·'ra:·ta] *f* **1.** (*pulizia*) **dare una** ~ **a qc** to dust sth **2.** CULIN dusting

spolverino [spol·ve·'ri:·no] *m* duster

spompare [spom·'pa:·re] I. *vt fig, fam* (*affaticare*) to wear out II. *vr:* **-rsi** to wear oneself out

spompato, -a [spom·'pa:·to] *agg* exhausted

sponda ['spon·da] *f* **1.** (*di fiume*) bank **2.** (*di letto*) edge

sponsor ['spɔn·sor] <-> *m* sponsor

sponsorizzare [spon·so·rid·'dza:·re] *vt* to sponsor

sponsorizzazione [spon·so·rid·dzat·'tsio:·ne] *f* sponsorship

spontaneità [spon·ta·nei·'ta] <-> *f* spontaneity

spontaneo, -a [spon·'ta:·neo] *agg* **1.** (*per-*

sona, adesione, offerta) spontaneous **2.** (*vegetazione*) wild

spopolamento [spo·po·la·'men·to] *m* depopulation; ~ **delle campagne** flight from the countryside

spopolare [spo·po·'la:·re] **I.** *vt* to depopulate **II.** *vi fam* (*avere grande successo*) to be all the rage **III.** *vr:* **-rsi** to empty

spora ['spɔ:·ra] *f* BOT spore

sporadicità [spo·ra·di·tʃi·'ta] <-> *f* sporadic nature

sporadico, -a [spo·'ra:·di·ko] <-ci, -che> *agg* sporadic

sporcaccione, -a [spor·kat·'tʃo:·ne] *pej* dirty beast

sporcare [spor·'ka:·re] **I.** *vt* **1.** (*vestito, tovaglia*) to dirty **2.** *fig* (*nome, reputazione*) to sully **II.** *vr:* **-rsi** **1.** (*insudiciarsi*) to get dirty **2.** *fig* (*compromettersi*) to sully oneself

sporcizia [spor·'kit·tsia] <-ie> *f* **1.** (*mancanza di pulizia*) dirt **2.** *fig* (*volgarità*) obscenity; **dire -e** to use foul language

sporco ['spor·ko] *m* dirt

sporco, -a <-chi, -che> *agg* dirty; **avere la coscienza -a** to have something on one's conscience; **avere la fedina penale -a** to have a criminal record

sporgenza [spor·'dʒɛn·tsa] *f* (*su parete*) bulge

sporgere ['spor·dʒe·re] <irr> **I.** *vt avere* **1.** (*da finestra*) ~ **qc da qc** to stick sth out of sth **2.** JUR ~ **querela contro qu** to take sb to court **II.** *vi essere* to stick out **III.** *vr:* **-rsi** (*in fuori, avanti*) to lean out; **è pericoloso -rsi dal finestrino!** it is dangerous to lean out of the window!

sport [sport] <-> *m* sport; ~ **a squadre** team sport; ~ **estremi** extreme sports; **fare dello ~** to play sports; **per ~** *fig* for fun

sporta ['spɔr·ta] *f* **uno sacco e una** ~ a load; **ne ha prese uno sacco e una** ~ he got a good thrashing

sportello [spor·'tɛl·lo] *m* **1.** (*gener*) door **2.** (*di ufficio, banca*) window; ~ **automatico** ATM

sportivo, -a [spor·'ti:·vo] **I.** *agg* **1.** (*giornale, gara, auto*) sports; (*evento*) sporting; **campo ~** sports field **2.** (*persona*) sporty **3.** (*abbigliamento*) casual **4.** (*leale*) sporting **II.** *m, f* **1.** (*atleta*) sportsman *m*, sportswoman *f* **2.** (*persona leale*) sport

sposa ['spɔ:·za] *f* bride; (*moglie*) wife; **promessa** ~ fiancée; **abito** [*o* vestito] **da** ~ wedding dress; **andare** ~ **a qu** to marry sb

sposalizio [spo·za·'lit·tsio] <-i> *m* wedding

sposare [spo·'za:·re] **I.** *vt* **1.** (*gener*) to marry **2.** (*dare in moglie o marito*) to marry (off) **3.** *fig* (*causa, lavoro*) to be wedded to **II.** *vr* **-rsi con qu** to marry sb; **-rsi in chiesa/in comune** to get married in church/in city hall

sposo ['spɔ:·zo] *m* (bride)groom; (*marito*) husband; **-i** newlyweds

spossare [spos·'sa:·re] *vt* to exhaust

spossatezza [spos·sa·'tet·tsa] *f* exhaustion

spostamento [spos·ta·'men·to] *m* move-

ment; (~ *d'aria*) blast

spostare [spos·'ta:·re] **I.** *vt* **1.** (*mobile*) to move **2.** (*data*) to change **II.** *vr:* **-rsi** to move

spostato, -a [spos·'ta:·to] **I.** *agg* oddball **II.** *m, f* oddball

spot [spɔt] <-> *m* **1.** TV, RADIO ~ **pubblicitario** commercial **2.** (*riflettore*) spotlight

spranga ['spraŋ·ga] <-ghe> *f* (*sbarra*) (metal) bar

sprangare [spraŋ·'ga:·re] *vt* (*sbarrare*) to bolt

spray ['spra·i] **I.** <-> *m* spray **II.** <inv> *agg* **bomboletta** ~ spray can; **lacca** ~ hair spray

sprazzo ['sprat·tso] *m* **1.** (*gener*) flash **2.** (*spruzzo*) splash

sprecare [spre·'ka:·re] **I.** *vt* (*tempo, denaro*) to waste **II.** *vr:* **-rsi** **1.** *iron* to exert oneself **2.** (*perdersi*) **-rsi in qc** to waste one's energy on sth

sprecato [spre·'ka:·to] *agg* wasted; **fatica -a** a waste of energy; **è tempo** ~ it's a waste of time; **essere** ~ **per qc** to be wasted on sth

spreco ['sprɛ:·ko] <-chi> *m* waste

sprecone, -a [spre·'ko:·ne] *fam* **I.** *agg* wasteful **II.** *m, f* spendthrift

spregevole [spre·'dʒe:·vo·le] *agg* **1.** (*persona, cosa*) contemptible **2.** (*gesto*) despicable

spregiativo [spre·dʒa·'ti:·vo] *m* LING pejorative

spregiativo, -a *agg* (*suffisso, tono*) pejorative

spregio ['sprɛ:·dʒo] <-gi> *m* (*disprezzo*) contempt

spregiudicatezza [spre·dʒu·di·ka·'tet·tsa] *f* unscrupulousness

spregiudicato, -a [spre·dʒu·di·'ka:·to] *agg* unscrupulous

spremere ['sprɛ:·me·re] **I.** *vt* **1.** (*limone, arancia*) to squeeze **2.** *fig* (*far parlare*) to pump **II.** *vr:* **-rsi -rsi le meningi** to rack one's brains

spremiaglio [spre·mi·'aʎ·ʎo] <-> *m* garlic press

spremiagrumi [spre·mia·'gru:·mi] <-> *m* juicer

spremilimoni [spre·mi·li·'mo:·ni] <-> *m* lemon squeezer

spremitura [spre·mi·'tu:·ra] *f* (*delle olive*) pressing

spremuta [spre·'mu:·ta] *f* freshly-squeezed fruit juice; ~ **di pompelmo** fresh grapefruit juice

sprezzante [spret·'tsan·te] *agg* (*atteggiamento, sguardo, frase*) contemptuous

sprezzo ['sprɛt·tso] *m* **1.** (*disprezzo*) contempt **2.** (*noncuranza*) carelessness

sprigionare [spri·dʒo·'na:·re] **I.** *vt* (*emettere*) to give off **II.** *vr:* **-rsi** (*uscire: calore, fumo*) to come out of

sprint [sprint] <-> *m* **1.** SPORT sprint; ~ **finale** *a. fig* final sprint **2.** *fig* (*slancio*) oomph

sprizzare [sprit·'tsa:·re] **I.** *vt avere fig* (*manifestare*) ~ **qc** to be bubbling with sth; ~ **gioia da tutti i pori** to be bubbling with joy; ~ **salute da tutti i pori** to be bursting with health **II.** *vi essere* (*sangue, liquido*) to spurt

sprizzo ['sprit·tso] *m* **1.** (*getto*) spurt **2.** *fig* (*slancio*) burst

sprofondare [spro·fon·'da:·re] I. *vi essere* **1.** (*pavimento, casa*) to collapse **2.** (*affondare*) to sink **3.** *fig* sentirsi ~ dalla vergogna to die of embarrassment II. *vr:* -rsi **1.** (*lasciarsi andare*) to collapse **2.** *fig* (*immergersi*) to bury oneself

sproloquio [spro·'lɔ:·kui·o] <-qui> *m* rambling speech

spronare [spro·'na:·re] *vt* **1.** (*cavallo*) to spur **2.** *fig* (*stimolare*) ~ qu a fare qc to spur sb (on) to do sth

sprone ['spro:·ne] *m* spur; a spron battuto *fig* hell-for-leather

sproporzionato, -a [spro·por·tsio·'na:·to] *agg* **1.** (*braccia, persona*) out of proportion **2.** (*prezzo, reazione*) disproportionate

spropositato, -a [spro·po·zi·'ta:·to] *agg* (*eccessivo: cifra*) enormous; (*richiesta*) ridiculous

sproposito [spro·'pɔ:·zi·to] *m* (*errore*) mistake

sprovvedutezza [sprov·ve·du·'tet·tsa] *f* (*ingenuità*) gullibility; (*mancanza di preparazione*) ignorance

sprovveduto, -a [sprov·ve·'du:·to] I. *agg* (*ingenuo*) gullible; (*impreparato*) inexperienced II. (*incapace*) babe in arms

sprovvisto, -a [sprov·'vis·to] *agg* essere ~ di qc (*negozio*) to be out of sth; ~ passaporto/biglietto without passport/ticket; alla -a by surprise; prendere qu alla -a to take sb by surprise

spruzzare [sprut·'tsa:·re] *vt* to spray

spruzzata [sprut·'tsa:·ta] *f* **1.** CULIN sprinkling **2.** (*pioggia leggera*) shower **3.** (*di fango, acqua*) splash

spruzzatore [sprut·tsa·'to:·re] *m* spray

spruzzo ['sprut·tso] *m* **1.** (*d'acqua, fango*) splash **2.** TEC verniciatura a ~ spray-painting

spudoratezza [spu·do·ra·'tet·tsa] *f* impudence

spudorato, -a [spu·do·'ra:·to] *agg* (*sfrontato*) impudent

spugna ['spuɲ·ɲa] *f* **1.** (*per pulire*) sponge; gettare la ~ *fig* SPORT to throw in the towel; bere come una ~ to drink like a fish **2.** (*tessuto*) terry cloth

spugnoso, -a [spuɲ·'ɲo:·so] *agg* spongy

spulciare [spul·'tʃa:·re] I. *vt* **1.** (*cane, gatto*) to de-flea **2.** *fig* (*esaminare: documento, testo*) to sift through II. *vr:* -rsi to get rid of fleas

spuma ['spu:·ma] *f* **1.** (*schiuma*) foam **2.** (*bibita*) soda pop

spumante [spu·'man·te] *m* sparkling wine

spumeggiante [spu·med·'dʒan·te] *agg* **1.** (*vino*) frothy **2.** *fig* (*brillante*) sparkling

spumeggiare [spu·med·'dʒa:·re] *vi* (*mare*) to foam; (*vino*) to froth

spumoso, -a [spu·'mo:·so] *agg* **1.** (*birra, vino*) frothy **2.** (*mousse*) foamy

spuntare [spun·'ta:·re] I. *vt avere* **1.** (*penna, lapis*) to break the point of **2.** (*capelli, baffi*) to

trim **3.** *fig* (*superare*) spuntarla *fam* to win through **4.** (*depennare: lista*) to cross out II. *vi essere* **1.** (*venir fuori*) to poke up **2.** (*fiori*) to come out **3.** (*sole*) to rise; (*giorno*) to break **4.** (*apparire*) to appear; da dove spunti? where did you spring from? III. *vr:* -rsi (*penna, lapis*) to become blunt

spuntino [spun·'ti:·no] *m* snack

spuntone [spun·'to:·ne] *m* (*sporgenza di roccia*) ledge

spurgare [spur·'ga:·re] *vt* (*fogna*) to clean out; (*canale*) to dredge

spurgo ['spur·go] <-ghi> *m* **1.** (*operazione*) dredging **2.** (*materiale*) discharge

sputacchiare [spu·tak·'kia:·re] *vi* to spit

sputare [spu·'ta:·re] I. *vt* to spit (out); ~ sangue *fig* to sweat blood; ~ sentenze *fig* to hold forth; ~ veleno *fig* to say spiteful things; sputa l'osso! *fig, fam* spit it out! II. *vi* to spit; ~ su qc *fig, fam* to despise sth

sputo ['spu:·to] *m* spit

sputtanare [sput·ta·'na:·re] *vulg* I. *vt* ~ qu to dish the dirt on sb II. *vr:* -rsi to lose face

squadra ['skua:·dra] *f* **1.** (*complesso di persone*) troop **2.** SPORT team **3.** ADM, MIL squad; ~ mobile rapid response team **4.** (*da disegno*) set square

squadrare [skua·'dra:·re] *vt* **1.** (*foglio da disegno*) to square off **2.** *fig* (*osservare*) ~ qu to look sb up and down

squadrone [skua·'dro:·ne] *m* SPORT squadron

squagliarsi [skuaʎ·'ʎa:r·si] *vr* (*ghiaccio, gelato*) to melt; squagliarsela *fig, fam* to clear out

squalifica [skua·'li:·fi·ka] <-che> *f* SPORT disqualification

squalificare [skua·li·fi·'ka:·re] I. *vt* to disqualify II. *vr:* -rsi (*discreditarsi*) to discredit oneself

squallido, -a ['skual·li·do] *agg* (*luogo*) squalid; (*vita*) dreary

squallore [skual·'lo:·re] *m* **1.** (*di luogo*) dreariness **2.** (*miseria*) wretchedness

squalo ['skua:·lo] *m* shark

squama ['skua:·ma] *f* ZOO scale

squamare [skua·'ma:·re] I. *vt* (*pesce*) to scale II. *vr:* -rsi (*perdere la pelle*) to peel

squarciagola [skuar·tʃa·'go:·la] *avv* (*a tutta voce*) a ~ at the top of one's voice

squarciare [skuar·'tʃa:·re] I. *vt* (*aprire con violenza*) to rip open II. *vr:* -rsi (*aprirsi*) to be torn apart

squarcio ['skuar·tʃo] <-ci> *m* (*nel vestito*) rip; (*nel corpo*) gash

squartare [skuar·'ta:·re] *vt* **1.** (*vitello*) to quarter **2.** (*massacrare*) to butcher

squartatore, -trice [skuar·ta·'to:·re] *m, f* (*assassino*) ripper

squattrinato, -a [skuat·tri·'na:·to] *fam* I. *agg* penniless II. *m, f* penniless person; sei il solito ~! you're always stone broke!

squilibrato, -a [skui·li·'bra:·to] I. *agg* unbalanced II. *m, f* MED loony

squilibrio [skui·'li:·bri·o] <-i> *m* **1.** MED derangement; ~ **mentale/psichico** mental/ psychological derangement **2.** COM imbalance

squillante [skuil·'lan·te] *agg* **1.** (*acuto: voce*) shrill **2.** (*colore*) harsh

squillare [skuil·'laː·re] *vi essere o avere* **1.** (*trombe*) to sound **2.** (*telefono, campanello*) to ring

squillo[1] ['skuil·lo] *m* **1.** (*di tromba*) sounding **2.** (*di telefono, campanello*) ringing

squillo[2] <inv> *agg* **ragazza** ~ call girl

squinternato, -a [skuin·ter·'naː·to] *m, f* oddball

squisitamente [skui·zi·ta·'men·te] *avv* (*prettamente*) purely

squisitezza [skui·zi·'tet·tsa] *f* **1.** (*di cibo*) deliciousness **2.** (*di modi*) refinement

squisito, -a [skui·'ziː·to] *agg* **1.** (*cibo*) delicious **2.** (*modi*) delightful

squittire [skuit·'tiː·re] <squittisco> *vi* (*pappagallo, topo*) to squeak

sradicare [zra·di·'kaː·re] *vt* **1.** (*pianta*) to uproot **2.** *fig* (*vizio, male*) to root out

sragionare [zra·dʒo·'naː·re] *vi* (*parlando*) to talk nonsense

sregolatezza [zre·go·la·'tet·tsa] *f* **1.** (*di vita, costumi*) wildness **2.** (*comportamento, atto*) excess; **-e excesses**

sregolato, -a [zre·go·'laː·to] *agg* **1.** (*senza regola: nel mangiare*) disorderly **2.** (*dissoluto: vita*) wild

S.r.l. *abbr di* **Società a responsabilità limitata** Ltd.

srotolare [zro·to·'laː·re] *vt* to unroll

S.S. *abbr di* **Strada Statale** highway

stabbio ['stab·bio] <-i> *m* (*recinto*) fold

stabile ['staː·bi·le] **I.** *agg* **1.** (*scala, impiego*) steady **2.** (*governo, moneta, prezzi*) stable; **beni -i** real estate **3.** METEO (*tempo*) settled **4.** THEAT (*compagnia*) resident **II.** *m* **1.** ARCH building **2.** THEAT resident theater company

stabilimento [sta·bi·li·'men·to] *m* **1.** (*edificio*) building; ~ **termale** spa **2.** (*fabbrica*) factory

stabilire [sta·bi·'liː·re] <stabilisco> **I.** *vt* **1.** (*dimora, sede*) to set up **2.** (*decidere*) to establish **II.** *vr:* **-rsi** (*prendere dimora*) to set up home

stabilità [sta·bi·li·'ta] <-> *f* (*di edificio, impiego, prezzi*) stability

stabilito, -a [sta·bi·'liː·to] *agg* set; ~ **dalla legge** laid down by law; **entro il termine** ~ by the due date

stabilizzare [sta·bi·lid·'dzaː·re] **I.** *vt* to stabilize **II.** *vr:* **-rsi 1.** (*diventare stabile*) to stabilize **2.** METEO (*tempo*) to become settled

stabilizzatore [sta·bi·lid·dza·'toː·re] *m* MOT stabilizer

stabilizzatore, -trice *agg* stabilizing

stabilizzazione [sta·bi·lid·dzat·'tsio·ne] *f* stabilization; **la ~ dei cambi** the stabilization of exchange rates

staccare [stak·'kaː·re] **I.** *vt* **1.** (*francobollo, etichetta*) to remove **2.** (*quadro*) to take down; (*bottone*) to take off **3.** FERR (*vagone*) to detach

4. (*assegno, ricevuta*) to write **5.** SPORT to outdistance **6.** (*parole, sillabe*) to articulate **II.** *vi fam* (*finire di lavorare*) to knock off **III.** *vr:* **-rsi 1.** (*gener*) **-rsi da qc** to come off sth **2.** *fig* (*allontanarsi*) to detach oneself

staccato [stak·'kaː·to] *m* MUS staccato

staccato, -a *agg* detached

staccionata [stat·tʃo·'naː·ta] *f* fence

stacco ['stak·ko] <-cchi> *m* **1.** (*intervallo*) pause **2.** SPORT takeoff **3.** *fig* (*contrasto*) contrast

stadio ['staː·dio] <-i> *m* **1.** SPORT stadium **2.** (*fase*) stage

staffa ['staf·fa] *f* **1.** (*di sella*) stirrup; **perdere le -e** *fig* to lose it; **tenere il piede in due -e** *fig* to run with the hare and hunt with the hounds **2.** ANAT stirrup bone

staffetta [staf·'fet·ta] *f* SPORT relay (race)

stage [staːʒ] <-> *m* internship

stagionale [sta·dʒo·'naː·le] **I.** *agg* (*fenomeno, malattia*) seasonal **II.** *mf* seasonal worker

stagionare [sta·dʒo·'naː·re] **I.** *vt* (*vino, formaggio*) to age **II.** *vi* (*vino, formaggio*) to age

stagionato, -a [sta·dʒo·'naː·to] *agg* **1.** CULIN (*formaggio, prosciutto*) mature **2.** *fig, scherz* (*persona*) elderly

stagione [sta·'dʒoː·ne] *f* **1.** (*gener*) season; **alta/bassa** ~ high/low season; ~ **degli amori** ZOO mating season **2.** (*periodo adatto*) time of year

stagliarsi [staʎ·'ʎar·si] *vr* to stand out

stagnante [staɲ·'ɲan·te] *agg* **1.** (*acqua*) stagnant; (*aria*) stale **2.** COM (*economia*) sluggish

stagnare [staɲ·'ɲaː·re] *vi* to stagnate

stagnazione [staɲ·ɲat·'tsioː·ne] *f* COM stagnation

stagno ['staɲ·ɲo] *m* **1.** CHEM tin **2.** (*d'acqua*) pond

stagno, -a *agg* (*contenitore*) watertight; **compartimenti -i** watertight compartments

stagnola [staɲ·'ɲɔː·la] *f* foil

stalagmite [sta·lag·'miː·te] *f* stalagmite

stalattite [sta·lat·'tiː·te] *f* stalactite

stalinismo [sta·li·'niz·mo] *m* Stalinism

stalinista [sta·li·'nis·ta] <-i *m*, -e *f*> *mf* Stalinist

stalla ['stal·la] *f* **1.** (*per animali*) stable **2.** *fig* (*luogo sporco*) pigsty

stalliere [stal·'liɛː·re] *m* stable hand

stallone [stal·'loː·ne] *m* stallion

stamane, stamani [sta·'maː·ne, sta·'maː·ni] *avv* this morning

stamattina [sta·mat·'tiː·na] *avv* this morning

stambecco [stam·'bek·ko] <-cchi> *m* ibex

stamberga [stam·'bɛr·ga] <-ghe> *f* hovel

stampa[1] ['stam·pa] *f* **1.** TYP printing; **errore di** ~ misprint; **mandare in** ~ to print **2.** (*giornalismo*) press; **libertà di** ~ freedom of the press **3.** (*riproduzione*) print

stampa[2] <inv> *agg* press; **comunicato** ~ press release; **conferenza** ~ press conference

stampante [stam·'pan·te] *f* COMPUT printer; ~ **ad aghi** dot matrix printer; ~ **a getto d'in-**

chiostro inkjet printer; ~ **laser** laser printer

stampare [stam·'pa:·re] I. *vt* **1.**(*gener*) to print **2.**(*monete*) to mint **3.** TEC to press II. *vr:* -**rsi** (*imprimersi*) to be imprinted; **stamparsi nella mente di qu** to stick in sb's mind

stampatello [stam·pa·'tɛl·lo] *m* capital letters *pl;* **scrivere in** ~ to write in capital letters

stampato [stam·'pa:·to] *m* **1.**(*opuscolo*) leaflet **2.**(*modulo*) form

stampato, -a *agg* printed

stampatore, -trice [stam·pa·'to:·re] *m, f* printer

stampella [stam·'pɛl·la] *f* **1.**(*gruccia*) crutch **2.**(*per abiti*) hanger

stampo ['stam·po] *m* mold; **sono tutti dello stesso** ~ *fig* they are all cast from the same mold

stanare [sta·'na:·re] *vt a. fig* to flush (out)

stancare [staŋ·'ka:·re] I. *vt* **1.**(*gener*) ~ **qu** to tire sb out **2.**(*cose, discorso*) to weary II. *vr:* -**rsi 1.**(*affaticarsi*) to get tired **2.**(*stufarsi*) -**rsi di qc** to grow tired of sth; -**rsi di qu** to grow tired of sb

stanchezza [staŋ·'ket·tsa] *f* tiredness

stanco, -a ['staŋ·ko] <-chi, -che> *agg* tired; ~ **morto** *fam* dead tired; **essere ~ di vivere** to be tired of life

standard ['stæn·dəd/'stan·dard] I. <-> *m* standard; ~ **di vita** standard of living II. <inv> *agg* standard

standardizzare [stan·dar·did·'dza:·re] *vt* to standardize

standardizzazione [stan·dar·did·dzat·'tsio:·ne] *f* standardization

standista [stan·'dis·ta] <-i *m*, -e *f*> *mf* (*impiegato*) stand assistant, *at a trade show or exhibition*

stanga ['staŋ·ga] <-ghe> *f* **1.**(*asta*) plank **2.**(*di carro*) shaft **3.** *fig, fam* (*persona alta*) beanpole

stangare [staŋ·'ga:·re] *vt* **1.** *fig, fam* (*bocciare*) to flunk **2.** *fig, fam* (*tassare: contribuenti*) to fleece

stangata [staŋ·'ga:·ta] *f fig* (*duro colpo*) setback

stanghetta [staŋ·'get·ta] *f* (*degli occhiali*) arm

stanotte [sta·'nɔt·te] *avv* tonight

stante ['stan·te] *agg* **a sé** ~ separate; **seduta** ~ at once

stantio, -a [stan·'ti:·o] <-ii, -ie> *agg* **1.**(*pane*) stale **2.** *fig* (*superato*) out-of-date

stantuffo [stan·'tuf·fo] *m* TEC piston

stanza ['stan·tsa] *f* room; ~ **da letto** bedroom; ~ **da pranzo** dining room

stanziamento [stan·tsia·'men·to] *m* (*di denaro*) allocation

stanziare [stan·'tsia:·re] I. *vt* (*denaro*) to allocate II. *vr:* -**rsi** (*stabilirsi*) to settle

stanzino [stan·'tsi:·no] *m* utility room

stappare [stap·'pa:·re] *vt* (*bottiglia*) to uncork

star [sta:] <-> *f* star

stare ['sta:·re] <sto, stetti, stato> *vi essere* **1.**(*restare*) to stay; ~ **fermo** to stay still; ~ **seduto** to sit; **stai pure seduto** don't get up; ~ **in piedi** to stand **2.**(*trovarsi*) to be; **Luca è quel ragazzo che sta accanto al pianoforte** Luca is that boy (standing) next to the piano **3.**(*abitare*) to live; ~ **dai genitori** he [*o* she] lives with his [*o* her] parents; **Gianna sta a Roma** Gianna's lives in Rome **4.**(*di salute*) to be; **come stai?** how are you?; **sto bene/male/così così** I'm fine/not well/OK **5.**(*toccare*) ~ **a qu fare qc** to be up to sb to do sth; **sta a te decidere** it's up to you to decide **6.** MATH ~ **a qc** to be to sth; **3 sta a 9 come 6 sta a 18** 3 is to 9 as 6 is to 18 **7.**(*attenersi*) ~ **a qc** to stick to sth **8.**(*colore, indumento*) to suit; **questi pantaloni ti stanno bene/male** these pants suit you/don't suit you **9.**(*resistere*) to take; ~ **allo scherzo** to take a joke **10.**(*entrarci*) to fit; **non ci sta** it doesn't fit in here **11.**(*con gerundio*) **sto leggendo** I'm reading; **stavo guardando la TV** I was watching TV **12.**(*con infinito*) **stiamo a vedere cosa succede** let's wait and see what happens; ~ **a sentire** to wait and find out; ~ **per fare qc** to be about to do sth **13.**(*loc*) ~ **a cuore a qu** to be close to sb's heart; ~ **a dieta** to be on a diet; **lasciar ~ qc** to let sth drop; **ti sta bene!** *fam* that'll teach you!; **starci** *fig, fam* (*essere d'accordo*) to agree; **va bene, ci sto** OK, I agree; **le cose stanno così** this is how things stand; **sta tranquillo** don't worry

starnazzare [star·nat·'tsa:·re] *vi* **1.** ZOO to honk **2.** *fig, scherz* (*fare rumore*) to make a racket

starnutare, starnutire [star·nu·'ta:·re, star·nu·'ti:·re] <starnutisco> *vi* to sneeze

starnuto [star·'nu:·to] *m* sneeze; **fare uno** ~ to sneeze

starter ['star·ter] <-> *m* **1.** MOT starter (motor) **2.** SPORT starter

stasera [sta·'se:·ra] *avv* this evening

stasi ['sta:·zi] <-> *f* FIN stasis

statale [sta·'ta:·le] I. *agg* state; **impiegato** ~ civil servant II. *mf* civil servant III. *f* **1.**(*strada*) highway **2.** *pl* public schools

statalizzare [sta·ta·lid·'dza:·re] *vt* to bring under state control

statalizzazione [sta·ta·lid·dzat·'tsio:·ne] *f* bringing under state control

statica ['sta:·ti·ka] <-che> *f* statics

staticità [sta·ti·tʃi·'ta] <-> *f* static nature

statico, -a ['sta:·ti·ko] <-ci, -che> *agg* static

statista [sta·'tis·ta] <-i *m*, -e *f*> *mf* statesman *m*, stateswoman *f*

statistica [sta·'tis·ti·ka] <-che> *f* statistics; -**che degli infortuni** accident statistics

statistico, -a [sta·'tis·ti·ko] <-ci, -che> I. *agg* statistical II. *m, f* statistician

stato[1] ['sta:·to] *pp di* **essere**[1], **stare**

stato[2] *m* **1.**(*nazione*) state; **affare di** ~ *fig* affair of state; **esami di** ~ public exams; **capo dello** ~ head of state; **gli Stati Uniti d'America** the United States of America; **gli**

Stati del Benelux the Benelux states **2.** (*condizione*) state; ~ **d'animo** state of mind; ~ **d'emergenza** state of emergency; **essere in ~ d'assedio** to be under siege **3.** ADM (*ceto*) status; ~ **civile** [*o* **di famiglia**] civil status; ~ **coniugale** [*o* **maritale**] marital status; ~ **giuridico** legal status; ~ **patrimoniale** statement of assets and liabilities; **essere in ~ d'accusa** JUR to have been charged with an offense; **essere in ~ d'arresto** JUR to be under arrest **4.** MIL ~ **maggiore** general staff **5.** LING **verbo di ~** stative verb; **complemento di ~ in luogo** complement of place

statua ['sta:·tua] *f* statue; **immobile come una ~** stock-still

statuario, -a [sta·tu·'a:·rio] <-i, -ie> *agg* **1.** (*arte, opera*) sculptural **2.** *fig* (*bellezza, fisico*) statuesque

statunitense [sta·tu·ni·'tɛn·se] **I.** *agg* American **II.** *mf* American

statura [sta·'tu:·ra] *f* **1.** (*altezza*) height **2.** *fig* (*morale*) stature

status ['sta:·tus] <-> *m* status

statuto [sta·'tu:·to] *m* **1.** JUR, COM statute; **regione a ~ speciale** *Italian region that has a degree of political autonomy;* ~ **societario** articles *pl* of association **2.** POL, HIST constitution

stavolta [sta·'vɔl·ta] *avv fam* this time

stazionamento [stat·tsio·na·'men·to] *m* parking; **freno di ~** emergency brake

stazionare [stat·tsio·'na:·re] *vi* MOT (*sostare*) to park

stazionario, -a [stat·tsio·'na:·rio] <-i, -ie> *agg* (*invariato*) stable

stazione [stat·'tsio:·ne] *f* **1.** FERR station **2.** MOT ~ **di servizio** gas station **3.** RADIO (radio) station **4.** (*di polizia*) police station

stazza ['stat·tsa] *f* **1.** (*di nave*) tonnage **2.** *fig* (*mole*) large frame

st. civ. *abbr di* **stato civile** civil status

stecca ['stek·ka] <-cche> *f* **1.** (*di ombrello, ventaglio*) rib **2.** MED splint **3.** (*di sigarette*) carton **4.** MUS wrong note

steccare [stek·'ka:·re] **I.** *vt* **1.** MED to splint **2.** (*giardino*) to fence **II.** *vi* MUS to hit a wrong note

steccato [stek·'ka:·to] *m* fence

stecchetto [stek·'ket·to] *m* **tenere qu a ~** (*di cibo*) to keep sb on short rations; (*di soldi*) to keep sb short of money

stecchino [stek·'ki:·no] *m* (*stuzzicadenti*) toothpick

stecchire [stek·'ki:·re] <stecchisco> *vt sl* to bump off

stecchito, -a [stek·'ki:·to] *agg* **1.** (*rami, pianta*) dead **2.** (*loc*) **morto ~** stone dead; **lasciare qualcuno ~** to leave sb dumbstruck

stecco ['stek·ko] <-cchi> *m* **1.** (*ramoscello*) twig; **essere (magro come) uno ~** to be stick thin **2.** (*pezzetto di legno*) stick

stele ['stɛ:·le] <- *o rar* -i> *f* stele; ~ **funeraria** memorial slab

stella ['stel·la] *f* **1.** *fig* ASTR star; ~ **cadente** falling star; **essere nato sotto una buona/cattiva ~** to be born under a lucky/an unlucky star; **vedere le -e** *fig* to daydream; **i prezzi sono saliti alle -e** prices have gone sky high; **dalle -e alle stalle** *fig* to go from riches to rags **2.** FILM star; ~ **del cinema** movie star **3.** BOT ~ **alpina** edelweiss; ~ **di Natale** poinsettia **4.** ZOO ~ **di mare** starfish

stellare [stel·'la:·re] *agg* **luce ~** starlight

stellato, -a [stel·'la:·to] *agg* (*cielo, notte*) starry

stelletta [stel·'let·ta] *f pl* MIL stars

stellina [stel·'li:·na] *f* **1.** (*piccola stella*) little star **2.** *pl* CULIN *star-shaped pasta for putting in soup*

stelo ['stɛ:·lo] *m* **1.** (*di fiore*) stem **2.** (*asta di sostegno*) **lampada a ~** floor lamp

stemma ['stɛm·ma] <-i> *m* coat of arms

stemperare [stem·pe·'ra:·re] *vt* **1.** (*sostanza*) to mix **2.** *fig* (*tensione*) to defuse

stempiarsi [stem·'piar·si] *vr* to have a receding hairline

stendardo [sten·'dar·do] *m* banner

stendere ['stɛn·de·re] <irr> **I.** *vt* **1.** (*braccia, gambe, mano*) to stretch (out) **2.** (*biancheria*) to spread (out); (*tappeto, tovaglia*) to spread **3.** (*pasta*) to roll (out) **4.** (*colori*) to spread **5.** (*persona*) to lay; (*con pugno, pallottola*) to knock down **6.** ADM (*verbale*) to write (up) **II.** *vr*: **-rsi 1.** (*allungarsi*) to stretch out **2.** *fig* (*estendersi*) to extend

stendibiancheria [sten·di·bian·ke·'ri:·a] <-> *m* clotheshorse

stenditoio [sten·di·'to:·io] <-oi> *m* (*locale*) drying room; (*stendibiancheria*) clotheshorse

stenodattilografia [ste·no·dat·ti·lo·gra·'fi:·a] *f* shorthand typing

stenodattilografo, -a [ste·no·dat·ti·'lɔ:·gra·fo] *m, f* shorthand typist

stenografare [ste·no·gra·'fa:·re] *vt* to take down in shorthand

stenografia [ste·no·gra·'fi:·a] *f* shorthand

stenografico, -a [ste·no·'gra:·fi·ko] <-ci, -che> *agg* (*segni, resoconto*) stenographic

stenografo, -a [ste·'nɔ:·gra·fo] *m, f* stenographer

stentare [sten·'ta:·re] *vi* (*faticare*) to have difficulty; ~ **a leggere/scrivere/parlare** to have difficulty reading/writing/speaking

stentato, -a [sten·'ta:·to] *agg* **1.** (*lavoro*) labored **2.** (*vita*) hard

stento ['stɛn·to] *m* **1.** (*fatica*) difficulty; **a ~** with difficulty **2.** *pl* (*disagio*) hardships

steppa ['step·pa] *f* GEOG steppes *pl*

stepposo, -a [step·'po:·so] *agg* (*clima, paesaggio*) steppe

sterco ['stɛr·ko] <-chi> *m* dung

stereo ['stɛ:·reo] **I.** <-> *m fam* (*impianto*) stereo **II.** <inv> *agg* stereo

stereofonia [ste·re·o·fo·'ni:·a] <-ie> *f* stereo

stereofonico, -a [ste·re·o·'fɔ:·ni·ko] <-ci, -che> *agg* stereo

stereotipato, **-a** [ste·reo·ti·'pa:·to] *agg fig* (*convenzionale*) clichéd

sterile ['stɛː·ri·le] *agg* **1.** MED infertile **2.** BOT, AGR barren **3.** (*infecondo: discorso, atteggiamento*) sterile

sterilità [ste·ri·li·'ta] <-> *f* **1.** MED infertility **2.** BOT, AGR barrenness

sterilizzare [ste·ri·lid·'dza:·re] *vt* (*uomo, animale*) to sterilize

sterilizzazione [ste·ri·lid·dzat·'tsio:·ne] *f* sterilization

sterlina [ster·'li:·na] *f* pound (sterling)

sterminare [ster·mi·'na:·re] *vt* to exterminate

sterminato, **-a** [ster·mi·'na:·to] *agg* (*pianura*) endless

sterminio [ster·'mi:·nio] <-i> *m* (*distruzione*) extermination; **campo di** ~ death camp

sterno ['stɛr·no] *m* sternum

sterpaglia [ster·'paʎ·ʎa] *f* scrub

sterpo ['stɛr·po/'ster·po] *m* (*ramo*) dry branch; (*cespuglio*) thorny shrub

sterrare [ster·'ra:·re] *vt* (*canale*) to excavate

sterzare [ster·'tsa:·re] *vt* MOT to turn

sterzata [ster·'tsa:·ta] *f* turn of the wheel

sterzo ['stɛr·tso] *m* (*dispositivo*) steering; (*volante*) steering wheel

stesi *1. pers sing pass rem di* **stendere**

steso *pp di* **stendere**

stessi ['stes·si] *1. e 2. pers sing conj imp di* **stare**

stesso ['stes·so] **I.** *avv* **lo** ~ just the same **II.** *m* the same; **fa** [*o* **è**] **lo** ~ it makes no difference

stesso, **-a I.** *agg* **1.** (*medesimo*) **lo** ~ [*o* **la -a**] [*o* **le -e**] [*o* **gli -i**] the same **2.** (*rafforzativo*) **io** ~ myself; **tu** ~ yourself; **voi** ~ yourselves; **lo farò io** ~ I'll do it myself; **il presidente** ~ the president himself; **ci vado oggi** ~ I'll go today; **in quel momento** ~ at that very moment **II.** *pron* **lo** ~ [*o* **la -a**] the same (one); **le -e** [*o* **gli -i**] the same (ones)

steste ['stes·te] *2. pers pl pass rem di* **stare**

stesti ['stes·ti] *2. pers sing pass rem di* **stare**

stesura [ste·'su:·ra] *f* **1.** ADM (*di contratto, documento*) drawing up **2.** LIT writing

stetoscopio [ste·tos·'kɔ:·pio] <-i> *m* stethoscope

stetti ['stet·ti] *1. pers sing pass rem di* **stare**

stia *1., 2. e 3. pers sing conj pr di* **stare**

stick [stick] <-> *m* stick; **rossetto in** ~ stick lipstick

stigmate ['stig·ma·te] *fpl* REL stigmata

stigmatizzare [stig·ma·tid·'dza:·re] *vt fig* (*criticare*) to condemn

stilare [sti·'la:·re] *vt* (*documento*) to draw up; (*lettera*) to write

stile ['sti:·le] *m* style; ~ **libero** freestyle; ~ **di vita** lifestyle; **avere dello** ~ to have style; **in grande** ~ in style; **con** ~ stylishly

stilista [sti·'lis·ta] <-i *m*, -e *f*> *mf* (*designer*) stylist

stilistica [sti·'lis·ti·ka] <-che> *f* stylistics

stilistico, **-a** [sti·'lis·ti·ko] <-ci, -che> *agg* stylistic

stilizzare [sti·lid·'dza:·re] *vt* (*tracciare*) to outline

stillare [stil·'la:·re] **I.** *vi essere* to drip **II.** *vt avere* to ooze

stilografica [sti·lo·'gra:·fi·ka] <-che> *f* fountain pen

stilografico, **-a** [sti·lo·'gra:·fi·ko] <-ci, -che> *agg* **inchiostro** ~ fountain-pen ink

stima ['sti:·ma] *f* **1.** (*apprezzamento*) esteem; **avere** ~ **di qu** to esteem sb **2.** COM (*valutazione*) valuation; **fare la** ~ **di qc** to estimate sth

stimabile [sti·'ma:·bi·le] *agg* **1.** (*persona*) respected **2.** COM estimated

stimare [sti·'ma:·re] *vt* **1.** COM to value **2.** (*persona*) to esteem

stimmate ['stim·ma·te] *v.* **stigmate**

stimolante [sti·mo·'lan·te] **I.** *agg* (*conversazione, persona*) stimulating **II.** *m* (*sostanza, farmaco*) stimulant

stimolare [sti·mo·'la:·re] *vt* **1.** (*sensi*) to awaken; (*appetito*) to sharpen **2.** (*incitare*) to encourage

stimolazione [sti·mo·lat·'tsio:·ne] *f* stimulation

stimolo ['sti:·mo·lo] *m* **1.** (*incentivo*) stimulus **2.** (*fisiologico: della fame*) impulse

stinco ['stiŋ·ko] <-chi> *m* shin

stipare [sti·'pa:·re] **I.** *vt* (*ammassare*) to cram **II.** *vr:* **-rsi** (*accalcarsi*) to cram

stipendiare [sti·pen·'dia:·re] *vt* ~ **qu** to pay sb

stipendiato, **-a** [sti·pen·'dia:·to] *agg* (*finanziato*) receiving financial support

stipendio [sti·'pɛn·dio] <-i> *m* salary; ~ **netto/lordo** net/gross salary; **aumento di** ~ raise

stipite ['sti:·pi·te] *m* (*di porta, finestra*) jamb

stipula ['sti:·pu·la] *f* (*di contratto*) drawing up

stipulare [sti·pu·'la:·re] *vt* (*contratto, accordo*) to draw up

stipulazione [sti·pu·lat·'tsio:·ne] *f* (*di contratto*) drawing up

stiracchiarsi [sti·rak·'kia:r·si] *vr fam* to stretch

stiramento [sti·ra·'men·to] *m* MED strain

stirare [sti·'ra:·re] **I.** *vt* (*con il ferro*) to iron **II.** *vr:* **-rsi** *fam* to stretch

stiro ['sti:·ro] *m* **asse** [*o* **tavolo**] **da** ~ ironing board; **ferro da** ~ iron

stirpe ['stir·pe] *f* **1.** (*origine*) race **2.** (*discendenza*) line

stitichezza [sti·ti·'ket·tsa] *f* constipation

stitico, **-a** ['sti:·ti·ko] <-ci, -che> **I.** *agg* constipated **II.** *m, f* person with constipation

stiva ['sti:·va] *f* hold

stivale [sti·'va:·le] *m* boot

stivaletto [sti·va·'let·to] *m* ankle boot

stivare [sti·'va:·re] *vt* (*caricare*) to stow

stizza ['stit·tsa] *f* (*rabbia*) anger

stizzire [stit·'tsi:·re] <stizzisco> **I.** *vt* (*fare arrabbiare*) to annoy **II.** *vr:* **-rsi** (*arrabbiarsi*) to get angry

stizzoso, **-a** [stit·'tso:·so] *agg* (*persona*) irritable; (*parole*) petulant

sto [stɔ] *l. pers sing pr di* **stare**

stoccafisso [stok·ka·'fis·so] *m* dried cod

stoccaggio [stok·'kad·dʒo] <-ggi> *m* storage

stoccata [stok·'ka:·ta] *f* **1.** SPORT (*scherma*) thrust; (*calcio*) shot **2.** *fig* (*allusione*) dig

stock [stɔk] <-> *m* stock

stoffa ['stɔf·fa] *f* **1.** (*tessuto*) cloth **2.** *fig, fam* stuff; **avere della ~** *fam* to have what it takes

stoicismo [stoi·'tʃiz·mo] *m* PHILOS stoicism

stoico, -a ['stɔː·i·ko] <-ci, -che> *m, f* PHILOS stoic

stola ['stɔː·la] *f* stole

stoltezza [stol·'tet·tsa] *f* (*stupidità*) stupidity

stolto, -a ['stol·to] **I.** *agg* stupid **II.** *m, f* idiot

stomacare [sto·ma·'ka:·re] *vt* **~ qu** *a. fig* to make sb sick

stomachevole [sto·ma·'ke:·vo·le] *agg* disgusting

stomaco ['stɔː·ma·ko] <-chi *o* -ci> *m* stomach; **avere qc sullo ~** to not have digested sth; **dare di ~** to be sick; **rivoltare lo ~ a qu** to turn sb's stomach; **riempirsi lo ~** *fam* to eat one's fill

stonare [sto·'na:·re] **I.** *vt* MUS (*cantare*) to sing out of tune; (*suonare*) to play out of tune **II.** *vi fig* **~ con qc** to be out of tune with sth; (*colori*) to clash with sth

stonato, -a [sto·'na:·to] *agg* MUS (*strumento*) out of tune; **è stonato** (*persona*) he sings out of tune

stonatura [sto·na·'tu:·ra] *f* MUS wrong note

stop [stɔp] <-> *m* **1.** (*segnale stradale*) stop sign **2.** MOT (*fanalino*) brake light

stoppare [stop·'pa:·re] *vt* **1.** (*arrestare*) to put a stop to **2.** SPORT to block

stoppino [stop·'pi:·no] *m* (*di candela*) wick

stopposo, -a [stop·'po:·so] *agg* (*capelli*) matted

storcere ['stɔr·tʃe·re] <irr> *vt* **1.** (*chiave, chiodo*) to bend **2.** (*piede, gamba, braccio*) to twist; **~ la bocca** *fig* to curl one's lip; *fig* (**~ il naso**) to wrinkle one's nose **3.** *fig* (*senso, significato*) to distort

stordimento [stor·di·'men·to] *m* (*confusione*) befuddlement; **regnava un senso di ~ generale** everyone was in a daze

stordire [stor·'di:·re] <stordisco> **I.** *vt* (*provocare confusione*) to daze facevano male le orecchie **II.** *vr:* **-rsi** (*ubriacarsi*) to get drunk, *in order to forget one's sorrows*

stordito, -a [stor·'di:·to] *agg* **1.** (*tramortito*) dazed **2.** *fig* (*sventato*) scatterbrained

storia ['stɔː·ria] <-ie> *f* history; **~ naturale** natural history; **~ antica/medievale/moderna** ancient/medieval/modern history; **passare alla ~** to go down in history; **è sempre la solita ~** *fam* it's the same old same old; **sono tutte -ie!** *fam* it's a load of nonsense!; **quante -ie!** *fam* what a fuss!; **non fare tante -ie!** *fam* don't make such a fuss; **non fare -ie!** *fam* stop complaining!

storicizzare [sto·ri·tʃid·'dza:·re] *vt* to historicize

storico, -a ['stɔː·ri·ko] <-ci, -che> **I.** *agg* **1.** HIST historical; **centro ~** old town **2.** (*memorabile*) historic **II.** *m, f* historian

storiella [sto·'riɛl·la] *f* **1.** *fam* (*aneddoto*) story **2.** (*bugia*) fib

storiografia [sto·rio·gra·'fi:·a] *f* historiography

storiografo, -a [sto·'riɔː·gra·fo] *m, f* historiographer

storione [sto·'rio:·ne] *m* ZOO sturgeon

stormire [stor·'mi:·re] <stormisco> *vi* (*foglie*) to rustle

stormo ['stor·mo] *m* ZOO flock

stornare [stor·'na:·re] *vt* COM to cancel

storno ['stor·no] *m* **1.** ZOO starling **2.** COM cancellation

storpiare [stor·'pia:·re] *vt* **1.** (*persona*) to maim **2.** (*parola*) to mispronounce

storpiatura [stor·pia·'tu:·ra] *f fig* (*di discorso*) mangling

storpio, -a ['stɔr·pio] <-i, -ie> **I.** *agg* disabled **II.** *m, f* disabled person

storsi *l. pers sing pass rem di* **storcere**

storta ['stɔr·ta] *f fam* (*distorsione*) sprain; **prendere una ~** to sprain one's foot

storto, -a ['stɔr·to] **I.** *pp di* **storcere II.** *agg* **1.** (*gambe, righe*) crooked **2.** *fig* (*sfavorevole*) bad; **oggi mi va tutto ~!** everything's going wrong for me today!; **avere la luna -a** to be in a bad mood

stortura [stor·'tu:·ra] *f fig* (*cosa distorta*) distortion

stoviglie [sto·'viʎ·ʎe] *fpl* dishes; **lavare le ~** to wash the dishes

strabene [stra·'bɛː·ne] *avv* extremely well

strabico, -a ['stra:·bi·ko] <-ci, -che> **I.** *agg* cross-eyed; **essere ~** to be cross-eyed **II.** *m, f* cross-eyed person

strabiliante [stra·bi·'lian·te] *agg* (*straordinario*) astonishing

strabiliare [stra·bi·'lia:·re] *vt* (*sbalordire*) to astonish

strabiliato, -a [stra·bi·'lia:·to] *agg* (*sbalordito*) astonished; **rimanere ~** to be astonished

strabismo [stra·'biz·mo] *m* squint

stracarico, -a [stra·'ka:·ri·ko] <-ci, -che> *agg fam* packed

stracchino [strak·'ki:·no] *m* soft white cheese made in Lombardy

stracciare [strat·'tʃa:·re] **I.** *vt* **1.** (*lettera*) to tear up; (*vestito*) to tear **2.** *fam* SPORT (*avversario*) to crush **II.** *vr:* **-rsi** (*lacerarsi*) to tear

stracciatella [strat·tʃa·'tɛl·la] *f* (*gelato*) vanilla ice cream with chocolate chips

straccio ['strat·tʃo] <-cci> *m* **1.** (*cencio*) cloth; **~ per i pavimenti** floor cloth; **sentirsi uno ~** *fig* to be exhausted **2.** *pl, pej, fam* rags; **non avere uno ~ di vestito** *fam* to not have a thing to wear

straccio, -a <-cci, -cce> *agg* tatty; **carta -a** waste paper

straccione, -a [strat·'tʃo:·ne] *m, f* (*persona*) beggar

stracontento, -a [stra·kon·'tɛn·to] *agg* extremely happy

stracotto [stra·'kɔt·to] *m* beef stew

stracotto, -a *agg* overcooked

strada ['stra:·da] *f* 1. (*via*) road; (*in città*) street; ~ **ferrata** railroad; ~ **a senso unico** one-way street; ~ **senza uscita** dead end; **codice della** ~ traffic code; **donna di** ~ *pej* streetwalker; **vittima della** ~ accident victim; **andare per la propria** ~ to go one's own way; **farsi** ~ to get on in life; **mettere** [*o* **buttare**] **qu in mezzo alla** [*o* **sulla**] ~ *fig* to throw someone onto the street; **essere su una cattiva** ~ *fig* to be on the wrong track; **tagliare la** ~ **a qu** to cut sb up; ~ **facendo** *fig* on the way; **non c'è molta** ~ it's not far; **il paese è a molti chilometri di** ~ it's a long way 2. *fig* (*cammino*) journey

stradale [stra·'da:·le] I. *agg* street; **carta** ~ street map; **incidente** ~ accident; **lavori -i** roadwork II. *f* traffic police

stradario [stra·'da:·rio] <-i> *m* street map

stradino [stra·'di:·no] *m* street cleaner

stradone [stra·'do:·ne] *m* wide road

strafaccio [stra·'fat·tʃo] 1. *pers sing pr di* **strafare**

strafalcione [stra·fal·'tʃo:·ne] *m* (*errore*) blooper

strafare [stra·'fa:·re] <irr> *vt* (*esagerare*) to overdo it [*o* things]

strafatto, -a [stra·'fat·to] *agg sl* (*drogato*) stoned

strafeci 1. *pers sing pass rem di* **strafare**

strafò [stra·'fɔ] 1. *pers sing pr di* **strafare**

straforo [stra·'fo:·ro] *m* **di** ~ (*di nascosto*) secretly; (*di sfuggita*) briefly

strafottei [stra·fot·'te:·i] 1. *pers sing pass rem di* **strafottere**

strafottente [stra·fot·'tɛn·te] *agg* (*sfrontato*) arrogant

strafottenza [stra·fot·'tɛn·tsa] *f* (*sfrontatezza*) arrogance

strage ['stra:·dʒe] *f* 1. (*uccisione*) massacre 2. *fig, fam* ton

stragrande [stra·'gran·de] *agg fam* vast; **la** ~ **maggioranza** the vast majority

stralciare [stral·'tʃa:·re] *vt* (*eliminare*) to remove

stralcio ['stral·tʃo] <-ci> *m* 1. (*eliminazione*) removal 2. (*brano scelto*) extract

stralunare [stra·lu·'na:·re] *vt* ~ **gli occhi** to roll one's eyes

stralunato, -a [stra·lu·'na:·to] *agg* 1. (*occhi*) staring 2. (*persona*) dazed

stramaledetto, -a [stra·ma·le·'dɛt·to] *agg* goddamn

stramaledire [stra·ma·le·'di:·re] <irr> *vt* to curse

stramazzare [stra·mat·'tsa:·re] *vi essere* (*cadere*) to collapse

strambo, -a ['stram·bo] *agg* (*strano: persona*) weird

strampalato, -a [stram·pa·'la:·to] *agg* (*stravagante: persona, discorso*) strange

stranezza [stra·'net·tsa] *f* strangeness

strangolamento [straŋ·go·la·'men·to] *m* strangulation

strangolare [straŋ·go·'la:·re] *vt* to strangle

straniero, -a [stra·'niɛ:·ro] I. *agg* foreign; **lingua -a** foreign language II. *m, f* foreigner

stranito, -a [stra·'ni:·to] *agg* (*confuso: sguardo*) dazed

strano, -a ['stra:·no] *agg* strange

straordinario [stra·or·di·'na:·rio] <-ri> *m* overtime; **fare gli -i** to do [*o* work] overtime

straordinario, -a <-ri, -rie> *agg* extraordinary; **treno** ~ special train; **lavoro** ~ overtime

strapagare [stra·pa·'ga:·re] *vt* to pay too much for

straparlare [stra·par·'la:·re] *vi* to talk nonsense

strapazzare [stra·pat·'tsa:·re] I. *vt* 1. (*persone*) to tire out 2. (*cose*) to mistreat II. *vr:* **-rsi** (*affaticarsi*) to tire oneself out

strapazzato, -a [stra·pat·'tsa:·to] *agg* **uova -e** scrambled eggs

strapazzo [stra·'pat·tso] *m* strain; **da** ~ *pej* (*cosa*) trashy; (*autore*) third-rate

strapieno, -a [stra·'piɛ:·no] *agg fam* packed

strapiombo [stra·'piom·bo] *m* drop; **a** ~ with a sheer drop; **una strada a** ~ **sul mare** a road with a sheer drop to the sea

strapotere [stra·po·'te:·re] *m* excessive power

strappalacrime [strap·pa·'la:·kri·me] <inv> *agg* **film/libro** ~ tearjerker

strappare [strap·'pa:·re] I. *vt* 1. (*ramo, fiore*) to break off; (*pagina*) to tear out; (*carta*) to tear up 2. *fig* (*cuore*) to break; (*promessa, confessione*) to extract II. *vr:* **-rsi** (*lacerarsi*) to break

strappo ['strap·po] *m* 1. MED (*lacerazione*) strain 2. *fig* (*eccezione*) exception; **fare uno** ~ **alla regola** to make an exception 3. *fam* (*passaggio*) ride; **dare uno** ~ **a qu** to give sb a ride

straricco, -a [stra·'rik·ko] <-cchi, -cche> *agg fam* loaded

straripare [stra·ri·'pa:·re] *vi essere o avere* to overflow

strascicare [straʃ·ʃi·'ka:·re] I. *vt* 1. (*gambe, piedi*) to drag; ~ **una malattia** *fig* to be unable to shake off an illness 2. (*vestito, coperta*) to trail along the ground II. *vi* (*vestito, cintura*) to drag along the ground III. *vr:* **-rsi** (*prolungarsi*) to drag on

strascico ['straʃ·ʃi·ko] <-chi> *m* 1. (*di abito*) train 2. *fig* (*seguito*) installment

strass [stras] <-> *m* paste

stratagemma [stra·ta·'dʒɛm·ma] <-i> *m* stratagem

strategia [stra·te·'dʒi:·a] <-gie> *f* strategy

strategico, -a [stra·'tɛ:·dʒi·ko] <-ci, -che> *agg* (*mossa*) strategic

stratificare [stra·ti·fi·'ka:·re] I. *vt a. fig* to stratify II. *vr:* **-rsi** *a. fig* to become stratified

stratificazione [stra·ti·fi·kat·'tsio:·ne] *f a. fig* stratification

stratiforme [stra·ti·'for·me] *agg* (*terreno*) stratiform

strato ['stra:·to] *m* 1.(*gener*) stratum; **a -i** in layers 2. METEO (*nuvole*) stratus

stratosfera [stra·tos·'fɛː·ra] *f* stratosphere

stratosferico, -a [stra·tos·'fɛː·ri·ko] <-ci, -che> *agg* 1. METEO stratospheric 2. *fig* (*straordinario*) amazing

strattone [strat·'toː·ne] *m* push

stravaccarsi [stra·vak·'kar·si] *vr fam* to sprawl

stravaccato, -a [stra·vak·'kaː·to] *agg* sprawled

stravagante [stra·va·'gan·te] I. *agg* (*carattere, vestito, aspetto*) odd II. *mf* eccentric

stravaganza [stra·va·'gan·tsa] *f* oddness

stravecchio, -a [stra·'vɛk·kio] <-cchi, -cchie> *agg* very old; (*vino*) vintage; (*grana*) mature

stravedere [stra·ve·'deː·re] <irr> *vi* ~ **per qu** to dote on sb

stravincere [stra·'vin·tʃe·re] <irr> *vt* to win easily

stravisto *pp di* **stravedere**

stravolgere [stra·'vɔl·dʒe·re] <irr> *vt* 1. *fig* (*persona: brutta esperienza*) to upset; (*lavoro*) to exhaust 2.(*fatti*) to distort 3.(*volto*) to contort

stravolto, -a [stra·'vɔl·to] *agg* (*sconvolto: espressione, viso*) distraught

straziante [strat·'tsian·te] *agg*(*grida*) piercing; (*immagine*) horrifying; (*dolore*) excruciating

straziare [strat·'tsiaː·re] *vt* 1.(*maltrattare*) to torture 2. *fig* (*affliggere*) ~ **qu** to break sb's heart

strazio ['strat·tsio] <-i> *m* (*grande pena*) torment; **che ~!** *fam* what a disaster!

strega ['streː·ga] <-ghe> *f* witch; **caccia alle -ghe** witch-hunt

stregare [stre·'gaː·re] *vt a. fig* to bewitch

stregone [stre·'goː·ne] *m* 1.(*mago*) wizard 2.(*presso i popoli primitivi*) witch doctor

stregoneria [stre·go·ne·'riː·a] <-ie> *f* witchcraft

stregua ['streː·gua] *f* **alla ~ di** in the same way as

stremare [stre·'maː·re] *vt* to wear out

stremo ['strɛː·mo] *m* exhaustion; **essere allo ~ delle** (**proprie**) **forze** to be on one's last legs

strenuo, -a ['strɛː·nuo] *agg* 1.(*difesa*) strong 2.(*lavoratore*) tireless

strepitare [stre·pi·'taː·re] *vi* (*produrre rumori*) to make a racket

strepitio [stre·pi·'tiː·o] <-ii> *m* (*rumore*) clamor

strepitoso, -a [stre·pi·'toː·so] *agg* 1. **applausi -i** thunderous applause 2. *fig* (*successo*) resounding

stress [stres] <-> *m* stress; **essere sotto ~** to be stressed

stressante [stres·'san·te] *agg* (*giornata, lavoro*) stressful

stressare [stres·'saː·re] *vt* to put under stress

stressato, -a [stres·'saː·to] *agg* stressed (out)

stretch [stretʃ] <inv> *agg* stretch; **pantaloni ~** stretch pants

stretching ['stre·tʃiŋ] <-> *m* SPORT stretching

stretta ['stret·ta] *f* 1.(*pressione*) **dare una ~ a**

qc (*vite, rubinetto*) to tighten sth; **~ di mano** handshake; **dare una ~ di mano a qu** to shake hands with sb 2. *fig* (*turbamento*) **sentire una ~ al cuore** to feel one's heart jump 3.(*situazione difficile*) **mettere qu alle -e** to force sb into a corner

stretto ['stret·to] *m* GEO strait

stretto, -a I. *pp di* **stringere** II. *agg* 1.(*tavolo, strada*) narrow 2.(*vestito*) tight 3.(*parente, amico*) close 4.(*osservanza, disciplina*) strict

strettoia [stret·'toː·ia] <-oie> *f* 1.(*di strada*) narrowing 2. *fig* (*situazione grave*) tight spot

striato, -a [stri·'aː·to] *agg* striped

stridente [stri·'dɛn·te] *agg* 1.(*contrasto*) glaring 2.(*colori*) garish

stridere ['striː·de·re] <strido, stridei *o* stridetti, *rar* striduto> *vi* 1.(*animali*) to screech 2.(*freni*) to squeal; (*porta*) to squeak 3. *fig* (*essere in contrasto*) ~ **con qc** to jar with sth; **quei colori stridono fra loro** those colors clash

stridore [stri·'doː·re] *m* (*di freni*) squealing; (*di denti*) grinding

strigliare [striʎ·'ʎaː·re] *vt* 1.(*cavallo*) to curry 2. *fam* (*sgridare*) to lecture

strigliata [striʎ·'ʎaː·ta] *f* 1.(*a cavallo*) currying 2. *fig* (*sgridata*) talking-to

strillare [stril·'laː·re] I. *vi* (*gridare*) to shout II. *vt fam* (*sgridare urlando*) to shout at

strillo ['stril·lo] *m* yell

striminzito, -a [stri·min·'tsiː·to] *agg* 1.(*vestito*) skimpy 2.(*persona*) skinny

strimpellare [strim·pel·'laː·re] *vt fam* to plunk

stringa ['striŋ·ga] <-ghe> *f* 1.(*delle scarpe*) lace 2. COMPUT string

stringare [striŋ·'gaː·re] *vt fig* (*accorciare*) to condense

stringato, -a [striŋ·'gaː·to] *agg fig* (*discorso, risposta*) condensed

stringere ['strin·dʒe·re] <stringo, strinsi, stretto> I. *vt* 1.(*serrare*) to squeeze (together); ~ **la mano a qu** to shake sb's hand; ~ **qu fra le braccia** to hug sb 2.(*vite*) to tighten 3.(*denti, pugni*) to clench 4.(*vestito*) to take in 5. *fig* (*riassumere*) to condense; **stringi, stringi** when it comes down to it 6.(*loc*) ~ **alleanza** to make an alliance; ~ **amicizia** to make friends II. *vr:* **-rsi** 1.(*avvicinarsi*) **-rsi attorno a qu** to gather around sb 2.(*loc*) **-rsi nelle spalle** to shrug

striscia ['striʃ·ʃa] <-sce> *f* 1.(*di stoffa, carta*) strip; **a -sce** striped 2. *pl* **-sce** (**pedonali**) crosswalk

strisciante [striʃ·'ʃan·te] *agg* 1. ZOO crawling 2. *fig, pej* (*viscido*) **un essere ~** a creep 3.(*inflazione*) creeping

strisciare [striʃ·'ʃaː·re] I. *vi* 1. ZOO to crawl 2.(*rasentare*) to scrape; ~ **contro un muro** to scrape along a wall II. *vt* 1.(*piedi*) to drag 2.(*sfregare: auto, paraurti*) to scrape 3.(*passare rasente: proiettile*) to graze III. *vr:* **-rsi** (*sfregarsi*) **-rsi contro qc** to rub (up) against sth

S

striscio ['striʃ·ʃo] <-sci> *m* **1.** MED Pap smear **2.** (*loc*) **colpire qc di ~** to hit sth a glancing blow

striscione [striʃ·'ʃo:·ne] *m* advertising banner

stritolare [stri·to·'la:·re] *vt* to crush

strizza[1] ['strit·tsa] *f fam* (*paura*) fright; **prendersi una ~** to get spooked

strizzacervelli [strit·tsa·tʃer·'vɛl·li] <-> *mf scherz* (*psicanalista*) shrink

strizzare [strit·'tsa:·re] *vt* **1.** (*panni*) to wring **2.** (*loc*) **~ l'occhio a qu** to wink at sb

strofa ['strɔ:·fa] <-> *f* verse

strofinaccio [stro·fi·'nat·tʃo] <-cci> *m* floor cloth

strofinare [stro·fi·'na:·re] **I.** *vt* (*argenteria*) to polish; (*pavimento*) to wipe **II.** *vr:* **-rsi** (*strusciarsi*) to rub oneself; **-rsi gli occhi/le mani** to rub one's eyes/hands

strombazzare [strom·bat·'tsa:·re] **I.** *vt* to trumpet **II.** *vi* to sound one's horn repeatedly

stroncare [stroŋ·'ka:·re] *vt* **1.** (*ramo*) to break off **2.** *fig* (*interrompere*) to break up **3.** *fig* (*criticando*) to tear to pieces **4.** (*loc*) **~ la vita a qu** to cut sb's life short

stronzata [stron·'tsa:·ta] *f* (*stupidaggine*) stupid thing to do [*o* say]; **combinare una bella ~** to screw it up

stronzo ['stron·tso] *m* (*escremento*) turd

stronzo, -a *m, f vulg* asshole

stropicciare [stro·pit·'tʃa:·re] *vt* (*vestito*) to crumple

strozzare [strot·'tsa:·re] **I.** *vt* **1.** (*uccidere*) to strangle **2.** (*tubo, condotto*) to narrow **II.** *vr:* **-rsi** (*strangolarsi*) to strangle oneself

strozzatura [strot·tsa·'tu:·ra] *f* **1.** (*di tubo*) narrowing **2.** (*di valle, strada*) bottleneck

strozzino, -a [strot·'tsi:·no] *m, f* (*usuraio*) loan shark

struccante [struk·'kan·te] *m* makeup remover

struccare [struk·'ka:·re] **I.** *vt* to remove makeup from **II.** *vr:* **-rsi** to remove one's makeup

strudel ['stru·del] <-> *m* CULIN strudel

struggere ['strud·dʒe·re] <struggo, strussi, strutto> **I.** *vt fig* (*consumare lentamente*) to consume **II.** *vr* (*consumarsi*) **-rsi d'amore per qu** to be dying of love for sb

struggimento [strud·dʒi·'men·to] *m* (*patimento*) yearning

strumentale [stru·men·'ta:·le] *agg* **1.** MUS instrumental **2.** *fig* (*uso, polemica*) **fare un uso ~ di qc** to use sth for one's own ends

strumentalizzare [stru·men·ta·lid·'dza:·re] *vt* to exploit

strumentazione [stru·men·tat·'tsio:·ne] *f* instrumentation

strumento [stru·'men·to] *m* **1.** (*gener*) tool; **-i di precisione** precision tools **2.** MUS instrument; **-i a corda** stringed instruments; **-i a fiato** wind instruments; **-i a percussione** percussion instruments

strussi ['strus·si] *1. pers sing pass rem di* **struggere**

strutto[1] ['strut·to] *pp di* **struggere**

strutto[2] *m* lard

struttura [strut·'tu:·ra] *f* structure; **~ portante** loadbearing structure; **~ sociale** social structure

strutturale [strut·tu·'ra:·le] *agg* structural

strutturare [strut·tu·'ra:·re] *vt* to structure

struzzo ['strut·tso] *m* ostrich

stuccare [stuk·'ka:·re] *vt* **1.** (*preparare: parete*) to plaster; (*turare: buco*) to fill **2.** (*decorare*) to stucco

stucchevole [stuk·'ke:·vo·le] *agg* **1.** (*cibo*) sickly **2.** *fig* (*noioso: discorso*) tiresome

stucco ['stuk·ko] <-cchi> *m* **1.** (*malta*) plaster **2.** (*ornamento*) stucco **3.** (*loc*) **rimanere di ~** to be struck dumb

studente, -essa [stu·'dɛn·te, stu·den·'tes·sa] *m, f* student

studentesco, -a [stu·den·'tes·ko] <-schi, -sche> *agg* student

studentessa *f v.* **studente**

studiare [stu·'dia:·re] **I.** *vt* **1.** (*per imparare qc*) to study; **~ al liceo/all'università** to be a high school/university student **2.** (*esaminare, indagare*) to examine **3.** (*parole, mosse*) to weigh **II.** *vr:* **-rsi** (*osservarsi*) to weigh each other up

studio ['stu:·dio] <-i> *m* **1.** (*gener*) study; **borsa di ~** grant; **provveditorato agli -i** education department **2.** <*gener al pl*> (*all'università*) studies *pl* **3.** (*di professionista*) office; **~ legale** law firm **4.** FILM, TV, RADIO studio

studioso, -a [stu·'dio:·so] **I.** *agg* (*persona*) studious **II.** *m, f* scholar

stufa ['stu:·fa] *f* stove

stufare [stu·'fa:·re] **I.** *vt* **1.** CULIN to stew **2.** *fig, fam* (*stancare*) to weary; **mi hai stufato con le tue continue lamentele** I'm fed up with your incessant complaining **II.** *vr* **-rsi di qu/qc** *fam* to get fed up with sb/sth

stufato [stu·'fa:·to] *m* stew

stufo, -a ['stu:·fo] *agg fam* **essere ~ di qu/qc** to be fed up with sb/sth

stuoia ['stuɔ:·ia] <-oie> *f* mat

stuolo ['stuɔ:·lo] *m* crowd

stupefacente [stu·pe·fa·'tʃɛn·te] **I.** *agg* **1.** (*sorprendente*) astonishing **2.** MED **sostanze -i** drugs; **abuso di sostanze -i** drug abuse **II.** *m* narcotic

stupefare [stu·pe·'fa:·re] <irr> *vt* (*sorprendere*) to amaze

stupendo, -a [stu·'pɛn·do] *agg* (*bellissimo*) wonderful

stupidaggine [stu·pi·'dad·dʒi·ne] *f* stupidity

stupidità [stu·pi·di·'ta] <-> *f* stupidity

stupido, -a ['stu:·pi·do] **I.** *agg* stupid **II.** *m, f* idiot

stupire [stu·'pi:·re] <stupisco> **I.** *vt* *avere* (*meravigliare*) to amaze **II.** *vr:* **-rsi** (*meravigliarsi*) to be amazed

stupore [stu·'po:·re] *m* amazement

stupratore [stu·pra·'to:·re] *m* rapist

stupro ['stu:·pro] *m* rape

sturare [stu·'ra:·re] *vt* (*lavandino*) to unblock

stuzzicadenti [stut·tsi·ka·'dɛn·ti] <·> *m* toothpick

stuzzicare [stut·tsi·'ka:·re] *vt* **1.** (*molestare*) to tease **2.** (*stimolare: appetito*) to whet

su [su] <sul, sullo, sull', sulla, sui, sugli, sulle> I. *prep* **1.** (*con contatto*) on; **sul lago/ mare** by the lake/ocean; **Parigi è sulla Senna** Paris is on the Seine **2.** (*senza contatto*) over; **commettere errori ~ errori** *fig* to make one mistake after another; **giurare ~ qc/qu** *fig* to swear on sth/sb **3.** (*mezzi di trasporto*) on; **erano seduti sull'autobus** they were sitting on the bus; **salire sul treno** to get on the train **4.** (*complemento d'argomento*) **hanno discusso sul futuro dell'azienda** they discussed the future of the business **5.** (*complemento di modo*) **~ richiesta** on request; **~ misura** custom-made; **~ ordinazione** to order; **sull'esempio di** in the same way as **6.** (*circa*) around; **un uomo sulla sessantina** a man of around 60; **sono partiti sul far del mattino** they left around dawn; **sul momento ho reagito male** at the time I reacted badly **7.** (*di, fra*) out of; **sette volte ~ dieci** seven times out of ten; **un candidato ~ quattro** one candidate in four II. *avv* up; **andare ~ e giù** to walk up and down; **non andare né ~ né giù** *a. fig* to not go down; **~ per giù** around; **pensarci ~** *fam* to think about it; **metter ~ casa** to settle down; **dai 100 euro in ~** from 100 euros upwards; **~ le mani!** hands up!; **~ con la vita!** cheer up! III. *int* come on; **~ ragazzi, muoviamoci!** come on guys, let's go; **~ ~** never mind

suadente [sua·'dɛn·te] *agg* (*voce*) soft; (*parole*) persuasive

sub [sub] <·> *mf* scuba diver

sub- [sub] (*in parole composte*) sub-

subacqueo, -a [sub·'ak·kue·o] I. *agg* underwater II. *m, f* scuba diver

subaffittare [sub·af·fit·'ta:·re] *vt* to sublet

subaffitto [sub·af·'fit·to] *m* **una stanza in ~ a** sublet room

subalpino, -a [sub·al·'pi:·no] *agg* subalpine

subalterno, -a [sub·al·'tɛr·no] I. *agg* subordinate II. *m, f* (*dipendente*) subordinate

subappalto [sub·ap·'pal·to] *m* subcontract

subbuglio [sub·'buʎ·ʎo] <-gli> *m* (*agitazione*) **essere in ~** to be in an uproar; **mettere qc/qu in ~** to throw sth/sb into confusion

subconscio [sub·'kon·ʃo] *m* subconscious

subdolo, -a ['sub·do·lo] *agg* (*maligno*) underhand

subentrare [su·ben·'tra:·re] *vi essere* **1.** (*succedere*) to happen **2.** (*sostituire*) **~ a qu** to succeed sb

subire [su·'bi:·re] <subisco> *vt* **1.** (*ingiuria, danni, conseguenze*) to suffer **2.** (*sottoporsi a*) **~ un'operazione** to have an operation

subissare [su·bis·'sa:·re] *vt* **~ qu di qc** *fig* to bombard sb with sth

subito ['su:·bi·to] *avv* **1.** (*immediatamente*) at once **2.** (*in un attimo*) instantly

sublime [sub·'li:·me] *agg* (*eccellente*) wonderful

subodorare [sub·o·do·'ra:·re] *vt* (*intuire*) to smell

subordinare [sub·or·di·'na:·re] *vt* **~ qc a qc** to put sth before sth else; **ha subordinato i propri interessi a quelli della ditta** he [*o* she] put the interests of the business before his [*o* her] own

subordinata [sub·or·di·'na:·ta] *f* LING subordinate clause

subordinato, -a [sub·or·di·'na:·to] I. *agg* **1.** (*secondario*) subordinate; **~ a** subordinate to **2.** LING **proposizione -a** subordinate clause II. *m, f* subordinate

subordinazione [sub·or·di·nat·'tsio:·ne] *f* subordination

subtropicale [sub·tro·pi·'ka:·le] *agg* subtropical

suburbano, -a [sub·ur·'ba:·no] *agg* suburban

succedere [sut·'tʃɛː·de·re] <succedo, successi *o* succedetti, successo> I. *vi essere* **1.** (*prendere il posto di*) **~ a qu** to succeed sb **2.** (*venir dopo*) **~ a qc** to follow sth **3.** (*avvenire*) to happen; **cosa ti succede?** what's the matter?; **sono cose che succedono** these things happen II. *vr:* **-rsi** (*susseguirsi*) to follow one another

successi [sut·'tʃɛs·si] *1. pers sing pass rem di* **succedere**

successione [sut·tʃes·'sio:·ne] *f* succession; **~ al trono** succession to the throne

successivo, -a [sut·tʃes·'si:·vo] *agg* next

successo¹ [stu·'tʃɛs·so] *pp di* **succedere**

successo² *m* success; **un film di ~** a hit movie

successore, succeditrice [sut·tʃes·'so:·re, sut·tʃe·di·'tri:·tʃe] *m, f* successor

succhiare [suk·'kia:·re] *vt* (*latte, dito*) to suck; **-rsi il dito** to suck one's thumb

succhiotto [suk·'kiɔt·to] *m* **1.** (*per bambini*) pacifier **2.** *fam* (*traccia di bacio*) hickey

succinto, -a [sut·'tʃin·to] *agg* **1.** (*vestito*) skimpy **2.** (*resoconto*) scanty

succo ['suk·ko] <-cchi> *m* **1.** (*di frutta*) juice **2.** ANAT **-cchi gastrici** gastric juices **3.** *fig* (*contenuto*) gist

succoso, -a [suk·'ko:·so] *agg* **1.** (*frutta*) juicy **2.** *fig* (*ricco di contenuto*) meaty

succube ['suk·ku·be] *agg* **essere ~ di qu** to be under sb's thumb

succulento, -a [suk·ku·'lɛn·to] *agg* (*cibo*) delicious

succursale [suk·kur·'sa:·le] *f* (*filiale*) branch

sud [sud] <·> *m* south; **Mare del Sud** Southern Ocean; **Polo Sud** South Pole; **a ~ di** south of; **Napoli si trova a ~ di Roma** Naples is south of Rome

Sudafrica [su·'da:·fri·ka] *m* South Africa

sudare [su·'da:·re] I. *vi* to sweat II. *vt fig* **~ sangue** to sweat blood

sudata [su·'da:·ta] *f* **1.** (*il sudare*) **che ~!** I'm sweating like a pig! *inf* **2.** (*fatica*) slog

sudaticcio, -a [su·da·'tit·tʃo] <-cci, -cce> *agg* sweaty

sudato, -a [su·'da:·to] *agg* **1.** (*bagnato di sudore*) sweaty; ~ **fradicio** dripping with sweat **2.** *fig* (*guadagnato: successo, risultato*) hard-earned

suddetto, -a [sud·'det·to] *agg* above-mentioned

suddito, -a ['sud·di·to] *m, f* subject

suddividere [sud·di·'vi:·de·re] <irr> *vt* to subdivide

suddivisione [sud·di·vi·'zio:·ne] *f* subdivision

sudest [su·'dɛst] *m* southeast

sudicio, -a <-ci, -ce *o* -cie> *agg* **1.** (*mani, vestito, luogo*) filthy **2.** *fig, pej* (*affare, faccenda*) dirty; **è un affare** ~ it's a dirty business

sudoccidentale [su·dot·tʃi·den·'ta:·le] *agg* southwest; **l'Europa** ~ southwest Europe

sudorazione [su·do·rat·'tsio:·ne] *f* sweating

sudore [su·'do:·re] *m* sweat; **essere in un bagno di** ~ to be bathed in sweat; **guadagnarsi il pane col** ~ **della fronte** to earn one's living from the sweat of one's brow

sudorientale [sud·or·ien·'ta:·le] *agg* southeast

sudovest [su·'dɔ:·vest] *m* southwest

sufficiente [suf·fi·'tʃɛn·te] *agg* **1.** (*che basta*) sufficient **2.** *fig, pej* (*borioso: atteggiamento*) superior

sufficientemente [suf·fi·tʃen·te·'men·te] *avv* sufficiently

sufficienza [suf·fi·'tʃɛn·tsa] *f* **1.** (*l'essere sufficiente*) **c'è n'è a** ~ there's enough of it; **averne a** ~ **di qc** to have had enough of sth **2.** (*voto scolastico*) pass; **prendere la** ~ to pass **3.** *fig, pej* (*boria*) superiority

suffisso [suf·'fis·so] *m* LING suffix

suffragio [suf·'fra:·dʒo] <-gi> *m* **1.** JUR suffrage **2.** REL **una messa in** ~ **dei defunti** a mass in memory of the dead

suggellare [sud·dʒel·'la:·re] *vt fig* (*confermare: vittoria*) to seal

suggerimento [sud·dʒe·ri·'men·to] *m* (*consiglio*) suggestion

suggerire [sud·dʒe·'ri:·re] <suggerisco> *vt* **1.** (*a scuola*) ~ **la risposta a qn** to tell sb the answer **2.** THEAT to prompt **3.** (*consigliare*) to suggest; ~ **a qu di fare qc** to suggest that sb does sth

suggeritore, -trice [sud·dʒe·ri·'to:·re] *m, f* (*theat*) prompter

suggestionare [sud·dʒes·tio·'na:·re] *vt* (*affascinare*) to affect

suggestione [sud·dʒes·'tio:·ne] *f* **1.** PSYCH (power of) suggestion **2.** *fig* (*impressione: di paesaggio*) beauty; (*di racconto*) fascination

suggestivo, -a [sud·dʒes·'ti:·vo] *agg fig* (*paesaggio, spettacolo*) beautiful

sughero ['su:·ge·ro] *m* (*oggetto, materiale*) cork; **tappo di** ~ cork

sugli ['suʎ·ʎi] *prep* = **su + gli** *v.* **su**

sugo ['su:·go] <-ghi> *m* (*salsa*) sauce; ~ **di pomodoro** tomato sauce

sui ['su:·i] *prep* = **su + i** *v.* **su**

suicida [sui·'tʃi:·da] <-i *m*, -e *f*> I. *mf* suicide II. *agg* (*mania, impulso*) suicidal

suicidarsi [sui·tʃi·'dar·si] *vr* to commit suicide

suicidio [sui·'tʃi:·dio] <-i> *m* suicide

suino [su·'i:·no] *m* pig; **carne di** ~ pork

suino, -a *agg* **carne -a** pork

sul [sul] *prep* = **su + il** *v.* **su**

sull', sulla, sulle, sullo [sul, 'sul·la, 'sul·le, 'sul·lo] *prep* = **su + l', la, le, lo** *v.* **su**

sultanina [sul·ta·'ni:·na] *f* sultanas *pl*

sultano, -a [sul·'ta:·no] *m, f* sultan *m*, sultana *f*

sunto ['sun·to] *m* summary

suo, -a <suoi, sue> I. *agg* **1.** (*di lui*) his; (*di lei*) her; **la -a voce** his [*o* her] voice; ~ **padre/zio** his [*o* her] father/uncle; **un** ~ **amico** a friend of his [*o* hers]; **sono parole sue** those are his [*o* her] words; **ne ha fatta una delle sue** he's [*o* she's] been up to his [*o* her] usual tricks; **essere dalla -a** to be on his [*o* her] side; **dire la -a** to say one's piece; **sta sulle sue** he keeps to himself **2.** (*forma di cortesia: Suo*) your; **in seguito al Suo scritto del …** in reply to your letter of … II. *pron* **1.** **il** ~ [*o* **la -a**] (*di lui*) his; (*di lei*) hers; **i suoi** his [*o* her] parents **2.** (*forma di cortesia: Suo*) yours

suocero, -a ['suɔ:·tʃe·ro] *m, f* father-in-law *m*, mother-in-law *f*; **-i** in-laws

suoi ['suɔ:·i] *v.* **suo**

suola ['suɔ:·la] *f* sole

suolo ['suɔ:·lo] *m* (*terra*) ground

suonare [suo·'na:·re] I. *vt avere* **1.** MUS to play **2.** (*orologio*) to strike; (*campana, campanello*) to ring; ~ **il clacson** to sound the horn **3.** *fam* (*picchiare*) **suonarle a qu** to give sb a good beating II. *vi essere o avere* **1.** (*campana, telefono*) to ring; (*sveglia*) to go off; **sta suonando il campanello** the doorbell is ringing **2.** MUS to play **3.** (*parole, frasi*) to sound

suonata *f* **1.** MUS sonata **2.** *fam* (*imbroglio*) con; **si è preso una bella** ~! boy was he taken for a ride! **3.** *fam* (*bastonatura*) walloping

suonato, -a *agg fam* **essere** ~ to be crazy

suonatore, -trice [so·na·'to:·re] *m, f* player; **e buonanotte -i!** that's all, folks!

suoneria [so·ne·'ri:·a] <-ie> *f* ringtone

suono ['suɔ:·no] *m* sound

suora ['suɔ:·ra] *f* nun

super ['su:·per] <inv> *agg* fantastic; **benzina** ~ super unleaded gasoline

superaffollato, -a [su·per·af·fol·'la:·to] *agg* jam-packed

superalcolico [su·per·al·'kɔ:·li·ko] <-ci> *m* high-alcohol drink

superalcolico, -a <-ci, -che> *agg* high-alcohol; **bevanda -a** high-alcohol drink

superamento [su·pe·ra·'men·to] *m* (*di difficoltà*) overcoming

superare [su·pe·'ra:·re] *vt* **1.** (*per qualità*) to surpass; (*per dimensioni, quantità*) to be bigger than; (*di numero*) to be greater than; ~ **qu in qc** to be better than sb at sth; **nessuno lo supera in fatto di arroganza** no one is more arrogant than he is; **mi ha superato**

nell'esame di matematica he beat me in the math exam **2.** MOT (*sorpassare*) to pass **3.** *fig* (*età*) to be over; (*velocità*) to exceed; (*prova*) to overcome; (*esame*) to pass; (*malattia*) to get over; (*difficoltà, ostacolo, crisi*) to get through
superato, -a [su·pe·'ra:·to] *agg* outdated
superbia [su·'pɛr·bia] <-ie> *f* pride
superbo, -a [su·'pɛr·bo] *agg* **1.** *pej* proud **2.** *fig* (*grandioso*) superb
superbollo [su·per·'bol·lo] *m* tax on diesel cars
Superenalotto [su·pe·re·na·'lɔt·to] <-> *m* national lottery
superficiale [su·per·fi·'tʃa:·le] I. *agg* shallow II. *mf* shallow person
superficialità [su·per·fi·tʃa·li·'ta] <-> *f* shallowness
superficie [su·per·'fi:·tʃe] <-ci> *f* surface; **in ~** on the surface
superfluo [su·'pɛr·flu·o] *m* unnecessary things *pl*
superfluo, -a *agg* (*parole, spese*) unnecessary
super-io [su·pe·'ri:·o] <-> *m* PSYCH superego
superiore [su·pe·'rio:·re] I. *comparativo di alto, -a* II. *agg* **1.** (*di posizione*) upper; **al piano ~** upstairs **2.** (*maggiore, in una gerarchia*) higher; **~ alla media** above average; **scuola media ~** high school **3.** (*migliore*) better III. *m* (*capo*) boss
superiorità [su·pe·rio·ri·'ta] <-> *f* superiority
superlativo [su·per·la·'ti:·vo] *m* LING superlative
superlativo, -a *agg* **1.** (*massimo*) extraordinary **2.** *fig* (*grandioso*) superb **3.** LING **grado ~** superlative
superlavoro [su·per·la·'vo:·ro] *m* overwork
superleggero [su·per·led·'dʒɛ:·ro] *m* SPORT super lightweight
superleggero, -a *agg* **1.** (*vestito, oggetto*) extra light **2.** SPORT **categoria ~a** super lightweight
supermercato [su·per·mer·'ka:·to] *m* supermarket
superpotenza [su·per·po·'tɛn·tsa] *f* superpower
supersonico, -a [su·per·'sɔ:·ni·ko] <-ci, -che> *agg* supersonic
superstar ['sju:·pə·sta:] <-> *mf* superstar
superstite [su·'pɛr·sti·te] I. *agg* **persona ~** survivor II. *m, f* survivor
superstizione [su·per·stit·'tsio:·ne] *f* (*credenza*) superstition
superstizioso, -a [su·per·stit·'tsio:·so] I. *agg* (*credenza, persona*) superstitious II. *m, f* superstitious person; **è un grande ~** he's [*o* she's] very superstitious
superstrada [su·per·'stra:·da] *f* highway
supertassa [su·per·'tas·sa] *f* surtax
supertestimone [su·per·tes·ti·'mɔ:·ne] *mf* key witness
superuomo [su·pe·'ruɔ:·mo] <-uomini> *m* superman
supervisione [su·per·vi·'zio:·ne] *f* (*controllo*) supervision

supino, -a [su·'pi:·no] *agg* supine
suppellettile [sup·pel·'lɛt·ti·le] *f* **1.** (*arredamento*) ornament; **-i di casa** furnishings **2.** (*in archeologia*) object
suppergiù [sup·per·'dʒu] *avv fam* roughly
suppl. *abbr di* **supplemento** supplement
supplementare [sup·ple·men·'ta:·re] *agg* (*aggiuntivo*) extra; **tempi -i** SPORT overtime
supplemento [sup·ple·'men·to] *m* **1.** (*a giornale, libro, vocabolario*) supplement **2.** FERR surcharge; **~ rapido** surcharge payable on fast trains
supplente [sup·'plɛn·te] *mf* (*a scuola*) substitute teacher
supplenza [sup·'plɛn·tsa] *f* (*a scuola*) **fare ~** to do substitute teaching
supplica ['sup·pli·ka] <-che> *f* (*invocazione*) plea
supplicante [sup·pli·'kan·te] *agg* (*tono*) pleading
supplicare [sup·pli·'ka:·re] *vt* **~ qu di fare qc** to plead with sb to do sth
supplichevole [sup·pli·'ke:·vo·le] *agg* (*tono*) pleading
supplire [sup·'pli:·re] <supplisco> *vi* **~ (con qc) a qc** to make up for sth (with sth)
supplizio [sup·'plit·tsio] <-i> *m fig* (*tortura*) torture
supporre [sup·'por·re] <irr> *vt* to suppose
supporto [sup·'pɔr·to] *m* **1.** (*gener*) support **2.** (*di strumento, dipinto*) stand
supposi *1. pers sing pass rem di* **supporre**
supposizione [sup·po·zit·'tsio:·ne] *f* supposition
supposta [sup·'pos·ta] suppository
supposto *pp di* **supporre**
supremazia [sup·re·mat·'tsi:·a] <-ie> *f* (*di un paese*) supremacy
supremo, -a [su·'prɛ:·mo] *agg superlativo di alto, -a* supreme; **una ragazza di una bellezza -a** an incredibly beautiful girl
surf [sə:f/sərf] <-> *m* surfing
surfing ['sə:·fiŋ/'sər·fing] <-> *m* surfing; **tavola da ~** surfboard; **praticare il ~** to surf
surfista [sur·'fis·ta] <-i *m*, -e *f*> *mf* surfer
surgelare [sur·dʒe·'la:·re] *vt* to freeze
surgelato [sur·dʒe·'la:·to] *m* frozen food; **banco dei -i** frozen food counter
surgelato, -a *agg* frozen; **pesce ~** frozen fish
surplus [syr·'ply] <-> *m* surplus
surreale [sur·re·'a:·le] *agg* surreal
surrealismo [sur·re·a·'liz·mo] *m* surrealism
surrealista [sur·re·a·'lis·ta] <-i *m*, -e *f*> *mf* surrealist
surriscaldare [sur·ris·kal·'da:·re] I. *vt* to overheat II. *vr*: **-rsi** to overheat
surrogato [sur·ro·'ga:·to] *m* copy
suscettibile [suʃ·ʃet·'ti:·bi·le] *agg* **1.** (*capace*) **questo progetto è ~ di miglioramenti** this project could be improved **2.** (*sensibile*) touchy
suscettibilità [suʃ·ʃet·ti·bi·li·'ta] <-> *f* touchiness

suscitare [suʃ·ʃi·'ta:·re] *vt* (*reazione, odio, entusiasmo*) to arouse; ~ **la pietà di qu** to arouse sb's pity

susina [su·'si:·na/su·'zi:·na] *f* plum

susino [su·'si:·no/su·'zi:·no] *m* plum tree

suspense [səs·'pens] *m o f* suspense

susseguire [sus·se·'gui:·re] <irr> I. *vt* ~ **qu/ qc** to follow sb/sth II. *vr:* -**rsi** to follow one another

sussidiario [sus·si·'dia:·rio] <-i> *m* textbook used in elementary school

sussidio [sus·'si:·dio] <-i> *m* (*in denaro*) subsidy; ~ **di disoccupazione** unemployment insurance

sussistei [sus·sis·'te:·i] *1. pers sing pass rem di* sussistere

sussistenza [su·sis·'tɛn·tsa] *f* subsistence

sussistere [sus·'sis·te·re] <sussisto, sussistei *o* sussistetti, sussistito> *vi essere* to exist

sussultare [sus·sul·'ta:·re] *vi* 1.(*persona*) to jump 2.(*cosa*) to shake

sussulto [sus·'sul·to] *m* jump

sussurrare [sus·sur·'ra:·re] *vt* to whisper

sussurrato, -a [sus·sur·'ra:·to] *agg* whispered; **parole -e** whispers

sussurro [sus·'sur·ro] *m* whisper

sutura [su·'tu:·ra] *f* MED suture

suvvia [suv·'vi:·a] *int fam* come on

svagare [zva·'ga:·re] I. *vt* (*distrarre*) to distract II. *vr:* -**rsi** (*distrarsi*) to get distracted

svago ['zva:·go] *m* (*distrazione*) distraction

svaligiare [zva·li·'dʒa:·re] *vt* 1.(*banca*) to rob 2. *fig* (*negozio*) to ransack

svalutare [zva·lu·'ta:·re] I. *vt* 1.COM (*valuta*) to devalue 2. *fig* (*proposta*) to belittle II. *vr:* -**rsi** 1.COM (*valuta*) to be devalued 2.(*bene, immobile*) to depreciate

svalutazione [zva·lu·tat·'tsio:·ne] *f* (*di valuta*) devaluation; (*di bene*) depreciation

svampito, -a [zvam·'pi:·to] *agg fam* birdbrained

svanire [zva·'ni:·re] <svanisco> *vi essere* to disappear

svantaggiato, -a [zvan·tad·'dʒa:·to] *agg* disadvantaged; **essere ~ rispetto a qu** to be at a disadvantage compared to sb

svantaggio [zvan·'tad·dʒo] <-ggi> *m* 1.(*condizione*) disadvantage; **essere in ~ rispetto a qu** to be at a disadvantage compared to sb 2.SPORT **essere in ~** to be behind

svantaggioso, -a [zvan·tad·'dʒo:·so] *agg* (*condizione, situazione*) unfavorable

svastica ['zvas·ti·ka] <-che> *f* swastica

svecchiamento [zvek·kia·'men·to] *m* modernization

svedese [zve·'de:·se] I. *agg* Swedish II. *mf* Swede III. *m* (*fiammifero*) safety match

sveglia¹ ['zveʎ·ʎa] *f* 1.(*lo svegliare*) **dare la ~ a qu** to wake sb up 2.(*orologio*) alarm clock

sveglia² *int fam* wake up; ~, **che è tardi!** wake up, it's late!

svegliare [zveʎ·'ʎa:·re] I. *vt* 1.(*dal sonno*) to wake (up) 2. *fig*(*animare: persone*) to liven up

3. *fig* (*suscitare: emozioni*) to awaken II. *vr:* -**rsi** *a. fig* to wake up

sveglio, -a ['zveʎ·ʎo] <-gli, -glie> *agg* 1.(*non addormentato*) awake 2. *fig* (*perspicace*) smart

svelare [zve·'la:·re] *vt* (*segreto, verità*) to reveal

sveltina [zvel·'ti:·na] *f vulg* quickie

sveltire [zvel·'ti:·re] <sveltisco> I. *vt* to speed up II. *vr:* -**rsi** to speed up

svelto ['zvɛl·to] *avv* quickly

svelto, -a *agg* 1.(*rapido*) quick 2. *fig* (*vivace*) smart

svenare [zve·'na:·re] I. *vt* ~ **qu** *fig* to bleed sb dry II. *vr:* -**rsi** *fig* to wear oneself out

svendita ['zven·di·ta] *f* sale

svenimento [zve·ni·'men·to] *m* fainting fit

svenire [zve·'ni:·re] <irr> *vi essere* to faint

sventare [zven·'ta:·re] *vt* (*evitare*) to foil

sventatezza [zven·ta·'tet·tsa] *f* (*imprudenza*) thoughtlessness

sventato, -a [zven·'ta:·to] I. *agg* (*gesto, comportamento*) thoughtless II. *m, f pej, fam* scatterbrain

sventola ['zvɛn·to·la] *f* 1. *fam* (*schiaffone*) slap 2.(*loc*) **orecchie a ~** dumbo ears

sventolare [zven·to·'la:·re] I. *vt* (*bandiera*) to wave II. *vi* (*bandiera*) to wave

sventrare [zven·'tra:·re] *vt* 1.(*pollo*) to draw; (*pesce*) to gut 2.(*uccidere*) ~ **qu** to slay sb 3.(*distruggere: edificio*) to flatten

sventura [zven·'tu:·ra] *f* misfortune; **compagno di ~** companion in misfortune

sventurato, -a [zven·tu·'ra:·to] I. *agg* unlucky II. *m, f* unlucky person

svenuto *pp di* svenire

sverginare [zver·dʒi·'na:·re] *vt* to take the virginity of

svergognare [zver·goɲ·'ɲa:·re] *vt* to shame

svergognato, -a [zver·goɲ·'ɲa:·to] I. *agg* (*atteggiamento*) shameless II. *m, f* shameless person

svernare [zver·'na:·re] *vi* to spend the winter

svestire [zves·'ti:·re] I. *vt* (*spogliare*) to undress II. *vr:* -**rsi** (*spogliarsi*) to get undressed

svettare [zvet·'ta:·re] *vi* to stand out

Svezia ['zvɛt·tsia] *f* Sweden

svezzamento [zvet·tsa·'men·to] *m* (*di neonato*) weaning

svezzare [zvet·'tsa:·re] *vt* (*neonato*) to wean

sviare [zvi·'a:·re] *vt* 1. *fig* (*traviare*) to lead astray 2.(*colpo, tiro*) to deflect; ~ **il discorso** to change the subject

svicolare [zvi·ko·'la:·re] *vi essere o avere* to slip away

svignarsela [zviɲ·'ɲar·se·la] *vi essere fam* to slip away

svilire [zvi·'li:·re] <svilisco> *vt fig* (*spregiare*) to debase

sviluppare [zvi·lup·'pa:·re] I. *vt* to develop II. *vr:* -**rsi** to develop

sviluppo [zvi·'lup·po] *m* development; **paese in via di ~** developing country; ~ **sostenibile**

sustainable development

svincolare [zviŋ·ko·'la:·re] I. *vt* (*liberare*) to free II. *vr:* **-rsi** (*liberarsi*) to free oneself

svincolo ['zviŋ·ko·lo] *m* MOT junction; (*entrata*) on-ramp; (*uscita*) exit

sviolinata [zvio·li·'na:·ta] *f fam* **fare una ~ a qu** to sweet-talk sb

sviscerare [zviʃ·ʃe·'ra:·re] *vt* (*argomento, questione*) to analyze in depth

svista ['zvis·ta] *f* slip

svitare [zvi·'ta:·re] *vt* to unscrew

Svizzera ['zvit·tse·ra] *f* (**la**) ~ Switzerland

svogliatezza [zvoʎ·ʎa·'tet·tsa] *f* apathy

svogliato, -a [zvoʎ·'ʎa:·to] *agg* apathetic

svolazzare [zvo·lat·'tsa:·re] *vi* 1. (*uccelli, insetti*) to flutter 2. *fig* (*vagare*) to flit 3. (*al vento*) to flap

svolgere ['zvɔl·dʒe·re] <irr> I. *vt* 1. (*gomitolo*) to unwind 2. (*idea, tema*) to set out; (*programma, piano*) to carry out 3. (*lavoro*) to do; **svolge la professione dell'avvocato** he's [*o* she's] a lawyer II. *vr:* **-rsi** 1. (*accadere*) to happen 2. THEAT, LIT to be set

svolgimento [zvol·dʒi·'men·to] *m* 1. (*di tema, tesi*) **lo ~ della tesi è articolato in otto capitoli** the thesis is in eight chapters 2. *fig* (*sviluppo, esecuzione*) **lo ~ del lavoro/progetto avverrà nei tempi previsti** the work/project will be carried out according to schedule

svolsi *1. pers sing pass rem di* **svolgere**

svolta ['zvɔl·ta] *f* 1. (*azione*) turn; **divieto di ~ a destra/sinistra** no right/left turn 2. (*curva*) bend 3. *fig* (*cambiamento*) turning point

svoltare [zvol·'ta:·re] *vi* (*girare*) to turn; **~ a destra/a sinistra** turn right/left

svolto *pp di* **svolgere**

svuotare [zvuo·'ta:·re] *vt* 1. (*vuotare*) to empty 2. *fig* (*privare di*) ~ **qc di senso** [*o* **significato**] to deprive sth of meaning

Swaziland ['swa:·zi·land] *m* Swaziland

Sydney ['sid·nei] *f* Sydney

T

T, t [ti] <-> *f* T, t; ~ **come Torino** T for Tommy

tabaccaio, -a [ta·bak·'ka:·io] <-ccai, -ccaie> *m, f* tobacconist

tabaccheria [ta·bak·ke·'ri:·a] <-ie> *f* tobacconist's, *sells stamps, bus tickets, and sometimes gift items as well as cigarettes and tobacco*

tabacchiera [ta·bak·'kiɛ:·ra] *f* snuffbox

tabacco[1] [ta·'bak·ko] <-cchi> *m* tobacco; ~ **da fiuto** [*o* **da naso**] snuff

tabacco[2] <inv> *agg* tobacco

tabagismo [ta·ba·'dʒiz·mo] *m* nicotine addiction

tabella [ta·'bɛl·la] *f* 1. (*tavola*) table 2. (*pros-*

petto) list; ~ **di marcia** *fig* schedule; ~ **dei prezzi** price list

tabellone [ta·bel·'lo:·ne] *m* 1. (*di orari, punteggi*) board 2. (*per affiggere*) bulletin board 3. (*nella pallacanestro*) backboard

tabernacolo [ta·ber·'na:·ko·lo] *m* tabernacle

tabù [ta·'bu] I. <inv> *agg* taboo II. <-> *m* (*proibizione*) taboo

tabulato [ta·bu·'la·to] *m* printout

tabulatore [ta·bu·la·'to:·re] *m* tab

TAC *f o m acro di* **Tomografia Assiale Computerizzata** 1. (*apparecchiatura*) CAT [*o* CT] scanner 2. (*esame*) CAT [*o* CT] scan

tacca ['tak·ka] <-cche> *f* 1. (*incisione*) notch 2. (*di display*) block 3. (*di lama*) nick

taccagno, -a [tak·'kaɲ·ɲo] I. *agg* cheap II. *m, f* cheapskate

tacchetto [tak·'ket·to] *m* SPORT stud

tacchino, -a [tak·'ki:·no] *m, f* turkey; **petto di ~** turkey breast

tacciare [tat·'tʃa:·re] *vt* ~ **qu di qc** to accuse sb of sth

taccio ['tat·tʃo] *1. pers sing pr di* **tacere**

tacco ['tak·ko] <-cchi> *m* (*di scarpa*) heel; ~ **alto/basso** high/low heel; **-cchi alti** (*scarpe*) high heels; **alzare** *fig* **i -cchi** to go away

taccuino [tak·ku·'i:·no] *m* (*per appunti*) notebook

tacere [ta·'tʃe:·re] <taccio, tacqui, taciuto> I. *vt* (*non rivelare*) to say nothing about; ~ **la verità** to hide the truth II. *vi* 1. (*stare in silenzio*) to be quiet; (*non opporsi*) to keep quiet; **mettere a ~ qc** to hush sth up; **chi tace acconsente** *prov* silence is [*o* equals] consent 2. (*non esprimersi, non riferire*) to keep silent; ~ **su qc** to remain silent about sth

tachicardia [ta·ki·kar·'di:·a] <-ie> *f* tachycardia

tachimetro [ta·'ki:·met·ro] *m* speedometer

tacito, -a ['ta:·tʃi·to] *agg* 1. (*sottinteso: accordo*) tacit 2. *a. lit* (*silenzioso*) silent

taciturno, -a [ta·tʃi·'tur·no] *agg* (*introverso*) taciturn; (*silenzioso*) quiet

taciuto [ta·'tʃu:·to] *pp di* **tacere**

tacqui ['tak·kui] *1. pers sing pass rem di* **tacere**

tafano [ta·'fa:·no] *m* horsefly

tafferuglio [taf·fe·'ruʎ·ʎo] <-gli> *m* scuffle

taffettà [taf·fet·'ta] <-> *m* taffeta

taglia ['taʎ·ʎa] <-glie> *f* 1. (*di abito*) size; ~ **unica** one size 2. (*ricompensa*) bounty

tagliaboschi [taʎ·ʎa·'bɔs·ki] <-> *m* lumberjack

tagliacarte [taʎ·ʎa·'kar·te] <-> *m* paperknife

tagliacuce [taʎ·ʎa·'ku·tʃe] <-> *f* linking machine

tagliafuoco [taʎ·ʎa·'fuɔ:·ko] I. <inv> *agg* fire; **porta ~** fire door II. <-> *m* 1. (*muro*) firewall 2. (*nei boschi*) firebreak

taglialegna [taʎ·ʎa·'leɲ·ɲa] <-> *m* lumberjack

tagliando [taʎ·'ʎan·do] *m* (*cedola*) receipt; **fare il ~** AUTO to have the car serviced

tagliapietre [taʎ·ʎa·'piɛːt·re] <-> *mf* stone-cutter

tagliare [taʎ·'ʎaː·re] **I.** *vt* **1.** (*gener*) to cut; (*albero*) to cut down; **-rsi un dito** to cut one's finger **2.** (*in parti*) to cut up; **~ in due** to cut in half; **~ in quattro** to cut into four; **~ le carte** to cut the cards **3.** (*staccare con un taglio*) to cut off; **tagliarsi i capelli**/**le unghie** to cut one's hair/nails **4.** (*vino*) to blend **5. ~ i tempi** to shorten the time allowed **6.** (*attraversare*) to cut across; **~ il traguardo** SPORT to cross the finishing line **7.** (*loc*) **~ la corda** *fig* to get away; **~ i ponti con qu** *fig* to break off relations with sb; **~ la testa al toro** *fig* to settle sth once and for all **II.** *vi* **1.** (*percorrere la via più breve*) cut through **2. tagliar corto** to cut to the chase

tagliasfoglia [taʎ·ʎa·'sfɔʎ·ʎa] <-> *m* pastry cutter

tagliasigari [taʎ·ʎa·'siː·ga·ri] <-> *m* cigar cutter

tagliatelle [taʎ·ʎa·'tɛl·le] *fpl* tagliatelle

tagliato, -a [taʎ·'ʎaː·to] *agg* **1.** (*abbreviato: film*) abridged **2.** *fig* (*portato*) **essere ~ per qc** to be cut out for sth; **essere ~ per le lingue** to have a gift for languages

tagliaunghie [taʎ·ʎa·'uŋ·gie] <-> *m* nail clippers

tagliauova [taʎ·ʎa·'uɔː·va] <-> *m* egg slicer

taglieggiare [taʎ·ʎed·'dʒaː·re] *vt* (*estorcere denaro a*) to extort money from

tagliente [taʎ·'ʎɛn·te] **I.** *agg* sharp **II.** *m* edge

tagliere [taʎ·'ʎɛː·re] *m* (*per cucinare*) cutting board

taglierina [taʎ·ʎe·'riː·na] *f* cutter

taglierini [taʎ·ʎe·'riː·ni] *mpl* thin pasta, *for soup*

taglio ['taʎ·ʎo] <-gli> *m* **1.** (*operazione*) cutting; (*di vini*) blending; **dacci un ~!** *fig* cut it out! **2.** (*fenditura, linea*) cut; **~ cesareo** cesarean (section) **3.** *fig* (*di spese, film, scena*) cut **4.** (*pezzo: di stoffa, carne*) piece **5.** (*di capelli*) hairstyle **6.** (*impostazione: di discorso*) slant **7.** (*di lama*) edge; **arma a doppio ~** *fig* double-edged weapon **8.** (*di lastra, tavola*) short edge; **colpire la palla di ~** to put a spin on the ball **9.** FIN (*di banconote*) denomination

tagliola [taʎ·'ʎɔː·la] *f* (*per animali*) trap

tagliuzzare [taʎ·ʎut·'tsaː·re] *vt* to cut into small pieces

tailleur [ta·'jœːr] <-> *m* suit; **~ pantalone** pantsuit

takeaway ['teik·ə·wei] <-> *m* **1.** (*negozio*) takeout **2.** (*servizio*) **la pizzeria ha il ~** the pizzeria does takeout

tal [tal] *v.* tale

talaltro, -a [ta·'lal·tro] *pron* others

talare [ta·'laː·re] *agg* **veste ~** cassock

talco ['tal·ko] <-chi> *m* (*polvere*) talcum powder

tale ['taː·le] <*davanti a consonante spesso* tal>

I. *agg* **1.** (*di questa specie*) such (a) **2.** (*così grande*) so much; **a tal punto** so much **3.** (*questo*) that; **la tal persona** that person; **in tal caso** in that case **4.** (*indefinito*) **un ~ signor Veneruso** a certain Mr. Veneruso; **il giorno ~, all'ora ~** on such and such a day, at such and such a time **5. ~ (e) quale** exactly the same; **è ~ (e) quale suo padre** he's just like his father; **sono -i (e) quali!** they're identical! **II.** *pron* **1.** (*persona già menzionata*) that; **quel ~** that person **2.** (*indefinito*) **un/una ~** someone; **dei -i** some people

talento [ta·'lɛn·to] *m* (*inclinazione*) talent; **un giovane di ~** a talented young man; **avere (del) ~** to be talented

talismano [ta·liz·'maː·no] *m* (*oggetto*) talisman

tallonare [tal·lo·'naː·re] *vt* to be (hot) on the heels of; **~ il pallone** to heel the ball

talloncino [tal·lon·'tʃiː·no] *m* (*tagliando: di biglietto, versamento*) stub; (*di medicinale*) tear-off tag

tallone [tal·'loː·ne] *m* (*calcagno*) heel; **~ d'Achille** *fig* Achilles heel

talmente [tal·'men·te] *avv* so

talora [ta·'loː·ra] *avv* sometimes

talpa ['tal·pa] *f* mole

talvolta [tal·'vɔl·ta] *avv* sometimes

tamarindo [ta·ma·'rin·do] *m* **1.** BOT tamarind **2.** (*bibita*) tamarind juice

tamburellare [tam·bu·rel·'laː·re] *vi* to drum; **~ con le dita** to drum one's fingers

tamburello [tam·bu·'rɛl·lo] *m* **1.** MUS tambourine **2.** (*gioco*) tamburello, *racket game played in northern Italy*

tamburino [tam·bu·'riː·no] *m* **1.** MUS (*strumento*) tabor **2.** MUS (*suonatore*) drummer **3.** *sl* (*sui giornali*) entertainment guide

tamburo [tam·'buː·ro] *m* **1.** MUS (*strumento*) drum **2.** MUS (*suonatore*) drummer **3.** ARCH tambour **4.** AUTO **~ del freno** brake drum

Tamigi [ta·'miː·dʒi] *m* **il ~** the Thames

tamponamento [tam·po·na·'men·to] *m* **1.** (*di veicoli*) collision; **~ a catena** pile-up **2.** (*di ferita*) packing

tamponare [tam·po·'naː·re] *vt* **1.** (*veicolo*) to go into the back of **2.** (*ferita*) to pack

tampone [tam·'poː·ne] *m* **1.** (*per timbri*) ink pad **2.** (*per medicare*) pad **3.** (*assorbente interno*) tampon

tamtam, tam-tam [tam·'tam] <-> *m* (*tamburo, suono*) tom-tom

tana ['taː·na] *f* **1.** (*di animali*) den **2.** (*di criminali*) hideout **3.** *fig, pej* (*stamberga*) hovel

tandem ['tan·dem] <-> *m* **1.** (*bicicletta*) tandem **2.** (*di atleti*) duo; **lavorare in ~** *fig* to work as a pair

tanfo ['tan·fo] *m* stink

tangente [tan·'dʒɛn·te] **I.** *agg* tangential **II.** *f* **1.** (*retta*) tangent **2.** (*bustarella*) bribe; (*pizzo*) protection money

tangentopoli [tan·dʒen·'tɔː·po·li] <-> *f* Tangentopoli

i **Tangentopoli** (city of bribes) was the name given by journalists to the corruption scandal of the early 1990s which involved numerous politicians, government ministers, high-profile industrialists and businessmen. Judicial investigations uncovered an extensive network of bribery, paid for from both private and public funds. The scandal emerged in Milan, and the city was therefore known as **Tangentopoli**.

tangenziale [tan·dʒen·'tsia:·le] I. *agg* MATH tangential II. *f* (*strada*) bypass
tanghero ['taŋ·ge·ro] *m* bumpkin
tangibile [tan·'dʒi:·bi·le] *agg* (*manifesto: miglioramento, prova*) tangible
tango ['taŋ·go] <-ghi> *m* tango
tanica ['ta:·ni·ka] <-che> *f* (*recipiente*) jerrycan
tannino [tan·'ni:·no] *m* tannin
tantino [tan·'ti:·no] *avv* un ~ a little
tanto ['tan·to] I. *avv* 1. (*molto: con aggettivo*) very; (*con verbo*) so much; **ti ringrazio ~** thank you so much; **~ meno** still less; **~ meglio** so much the better 2. (*così*) so; **~ ... che ... +***indicativo*, **~ ... da ... +***inf* so ... that 3. (*altrettanto*) **~ ... quanto ...** as much ... as 4. (*soltanto*) **una volta ~** once in a while; **~ per cambiare** just for a change; **~ per fare qualcosa** just to pass the time; **dicevo così, ~ per scherzare** I said it just as a joke II. *cong* after all; **~ è lo stesso** but it doesn't matter
tanto, -a I. *agg* 1. (*così molto, così grande*) so much; **~ ... che ... +***indicativo* so much ... that; **~ ... da ... +***inf* enough ... to 2. *pl* (*in numero così grande*) so many; **-i ... che ... +***indicativo*, **-i ... da ... +***inf* so many ... that 3. (*molto grande*) **ho -a fame** I'm so hungry; **non ho ~ tempo** I don't have much time 4. *pl* (*molto numerosi*) **c'erano -e persone** there were such a lot of people; **non ho trovato -i errori** I didn't find (very) many mistakes; **-i saluti** best wishes; **-e grazie** many thanks; **-e volte** so many times 5. (*altrettanto*) **~ ... quanto ...** as much ... as ...; **-i ... quanti ...** the same number of ... as ... 6. *pl* (*distributivo*) **ogni -e/-i** every so many; **ogni -e settimane** every so many weeks 7. (*ellittico*) so much; **spende ~ in abbigliamento** she spends a fortune on clothes; **ti ci vuole ancora ~?** will you be long?; **oggi non ho ~ da fare** I don't have much to do today; **da ~** for ages; **di ~ in ~** once in a while; **ogni ~** every so often; **a dir ~** if that II. *pron* 1. (*molto*) a lot; **quel ~ che basta** as much as is needed 2. *pl* (*molti*) (so) many 3. (*quantità indeterminata*) some; **~ vale che tu rimanga** you may as well stay; **non più che ~** not much; **guardare con ~ d'occhi** to gaze wide-eyed 4. *pl* (*numero indeterminato*) some 5. *pl*

(*molte persone*) **-i** many people
tapino, -a [ta·'pi:·no] I. *agg* miserable II. *m, f* wretch
tapiro [ta·'pi:·ro] *m* tapir
tapis roulant [ta·'pi ru·'lã] <-> *m* moving sidewalk
tappa ['tap·pa] *f* 1. (*sosta*) stop 2. (*percorso, momento decisivo*) *a.* SPORT stage; **bruciare le -e** *fig* to get somewhere fast
tappabuchi [tap·pa·'bu:·ki] <-> *m* stopgap
tappare [tap·'pa:·re] *vt* (*buco*) to stop up; (*bottiglia*) to cork; **~ la bocca a qu** *fig* to shut sb up; **~ un buco** *fig* to fill a hole; **-rsi il naso** to hold one's nose; **-rsi le orecchie** *fig* to turn a deaf ear
tapparella [tap·pa·'rɛl·la] *f* rolling shutter
tappetino [tap·pe·'ti:·no] *m* COMPUT mouse pad
tappeto [tap·'pe:·to] *m* 1. (*per pavimenti*) carpet; **~ persiano** Persian carpet; **a ~** *fig* blanket 2. (*per tavoli*) cloth; **~ verde** *fig* gaming table 3. SPORT (*nel pugilato*) canvas; **mandare qu al ~** to knock sb down
tappezzare [tap·pet·'tsa:·re] *vt* 1. (*con carta da parati*) to paper; **~ i muri di qc** to cover the walls with sth 2. (*poltrona, divano*) to cover
tappezzeria [tap·pet·tse·'ri:·a] <-ie> *f* 1. (*per pareti*) wallpaper; **fare ~** *fig* to be a wallflower 2. *a.* AUTO (*per poltrone, tecnica*) upholstery
tappezziere, -a [tap·pet·'tsiɛ:·re] *m, f* upholsterer
tappo ['tap·po] *m* 1. (*turacciolo*) stopper; (*di sughero*) cork; **~ a corona** bottle top; **~ a vite** screw top 2. *scherz* (*persona piccola*) shorty
TAR [tar] *m abbr di* **Tribunale Amministrativo Regionale** *regional administrative court;* **fare ricorso al ~** to appeal to the TAR
tara ['ta:·ra] *f* 1. (*peso*) tare 2. (*malattia*) defect; **~ ereditaria** hereditary defect 3. *fam* (*difetto*) flaw
tarantella [ta·ran·'tɛl·la] *f* tarantella
Tarantino <*sing*> *m* Taranto area; **nel ~** in the Taranto area
tarantino, -a [ta·ran·'ti:·no] I. *agg* from Taranto II. *m, f* (*abitante*) person from Taranto
Taranto [ta·'ran·to] *f* Taranto, *city in the southeast of Italy*
tarantola [ta·'ran·to·la] *f* (*ragno*) tarantula
tarare [ta·'ra:·re] *vt* 1. (*recipiente*) to tare 2. (*strumento*) to calibrate
tarato, -a [ta·'ra:·to] *agg* 1. (*mentalmente*) crazy 2. (*strumento*) calibrated
taratura [ta·ra·'tu:·ra] *f* (*di strumento*) calibration
tarchiato, -a [tar·'kia:·to] *agg* stocky
tardare [tar·'da:·re] I. *vi* 1. (*arrivare tardi*) to be late 2. (*indugiare*) **~ a rispondere** to delay replying; **~ a venire** to delay coming 3. (*in consegna, pagamento*) to delay II. *vt* to delay
tardi ['tar·di] *avv* late; **far ~** to be late; **più ~** later; **a più ~!** see you later!; **sul ~** quite late; **al più ~** at the latest; **ieri sera ho fatto ~** I stayed out late last night; **chi ~ arriva male**

alloggia *prov* first come first served *prov*

tardivo, -a [tar·'di:·vo] *agg* **1.**(*pianta, primavera*) late **2.**(*scusa, rimedio*) belated **3.**(*persona*) slow

tardo, -a ['tar·do] *agg* **1.**(*rinascimento, serata*) late **2.** *a. pej* (*lento: reazione, persona*) slow

tardona [tar·'do:·na] *f scherz* all that glitters is not gold

targa ['tar·ga] <-ghe> *f* (*su porta, tomba*) plate; (*di veicolo*) license plate

targato, -a [tar·'ga:·to] *agg* with the license plate; **la vettura -a AT 405 FR** the car with the license plate AT 405 FR

target ['ta:·git/'tar·get] <-> *m* COM (*consumatori*) target market; (*vendite*) sales target

targhetta [tar·'get·ta] *f* plate

tariffa [ta·'rif·fa] *f* rate; **~ ordinaria** regular rate; **~ ridotta** reduced rate; **~ telefonica** phone rates *pl*

tariffario [ta·rif·'fa:·rio] <-i> *m* price list; (*di professionista*) scale of fees

tarlare [tar·'la:·re] I. *vt* (*legno*) to make holes in, *woodworm;* (*tessuto*) to make holes in, *moths* II. *vi:* **-rsi** (*legno*) to have woodworm; (*tessuto*) to be moth-eaten

tarlo ['tar·lo] *m* **1.** ZOO woodworm **2.** *fig* **essere roso dal ~ del dubbio** to be racked with doubt

tarma ['tar·ma] *f* moth

taroccare [ta·rok·'ka:·re] *vi sl* (*falsificare*) to fake

tarpare [tar·'pa:·re] *vt* **~ le ali a qu/qc** to clip the wings of sb/sth

tartagliare [tar·taʎ·'ʎa:·re] I. *vt* to stammer II. *vi* to stammer

tartaro ['tar·ta·ro] *m* tartar

tartaro, -a I. *agg* tartar; **salsa -a** tartar sauce II. *m, f* Tartar

tartaruga [tar·ta·'ru:·ga] <-ghe> *f* **1.** ZOO turtle; **camminare a passo di ~** to walk at a snail's pace **2.**(*materiale*) tortoiseshell

tartassare [tar·tas·'sa:·re] *vt* (*strapazzare*) to maltreat; **~ uno strumento musicale** to murder a musical instrument; **~ qu a un esame** to give sb a grilling

tartina [tar·'ti:·na] *f* canapé

tartufo [tar·'tu:·fo] *m* truffle

i Every fall in the misty Langhe region, men and dogs set out in search of the **tartufo bianco** (white truffle) of Alba, one of the most highly prized delicacies of Italian cuisine. It is an ingredient in Piedmontese fondue, and is eaten with tagliatelle, polenta and many other dishes, accompanied for preference with one of the great red wines of the area, *barolo, dolcetto*, or even *barbera*. The **tartufo** is a fungus that lives underground whose fruit, in the form of a tuber, consists of a fleshy mass and whose color, perfume, and flavor depend on the tree with which it lives symbiotically, principally poplar, lime, oak, and willow.

tasca ['tas·ka] <-sche> *f* **1.**(*nei vestiti*) pocket; **conoscere qc come le proprie -sche** to know sth like the back of one's hand; **fare i conti in ~ a qu** to try to work out how much sb is worth; **starsene con le mani in ~** *fig* to be idle; **ne ho piene le -sche** *fam* I've had it up to here; **non me ne viene nulla in ~** I'm not going to get anything out of it **2.**(*di borsa, valigia*) pocket

tascabile [task·'ka:·bi·le] I. *agg* (*libro, edizione*) pocket; **computer ~** palmtop II. *m* (*libro*) paperback

tascapane [task·ka·'pa:·ne] <-> *m* haversack

taschino [task·'ki:·no] *m* (*di giacca, camicia*) breast pocket; (*di gilet, pantaloni*) small pocket

tassa ['tas·sa] *f* **1.**(*su un servizio*) tax; **~ di circolazione** road tax; **~ sul consumo** indirect tax; **~ di soggiorno** tourist tax; **-e scolastiche** school fees; **esente da -e** tax exempt; **soggetto a -e** taxable **2.** *pl, fam* (*imposte*) taxes

tassabile [tas·'sa:·bi·le] *agg* taxable

tassametro [tas·'sa:·met·ro] *m* (*di taxi*) taximeter; **~ di parcheggio** parking meter

tassare [tas·'sa:·re] *vt* (*reddito, servizio*) to tax

tassativamente [tas·sa·ti·va·'men·te] *avv* without fail; **è ~ vietato fumare** smoking is strictly prohibited

tassativo, -a [tas·sa·'ti:·vo] *agg* absolute

tassazione [tas·sat·'tsio:·ne] *f* (*imposizione di una tassa*) taxation

tassello [tas·'sɛl·lo] *m* **1.**(*pezzetto di legno*) plug **2.** *fig* (*elemento*) piece

tassì [tas·'si] <-> *m* taxi

tassista [tas·'sis·ta] <-i *m*, -e *f*> *mf* taxi driver

tasso ['tas·so] *m* **1.**(*gener*) rate; **~ di mortalità/natalità** death/birth rate; **~ d'interesse/di sconto** interest/discount rate; **~ d'inflazione** rate of inflation; **-i di conversione** conversion rates **2.** ZOO badger **3.** ARBUSTO, LEGNO yew

tastare [tas·'ta:·re] *vt* to feel; **~ il polso a qu** to take sb's pulse; *fig* to sound sb out; **~ il terreno** *fig* to get the lay of the land

tastiera [tas·'tiɛ:·ra] *f* **1.**(*di computer, pianoforte*) keyboard; **telefono a ~** touch-tone phone **2.**(*di chitarra*) fingerboard **3.**(*strumento*) keyboards *pl*

tastierino *m* **~ numerico** (*di computer*) numeric keypad

tasto ['tas·to] *m* **1.**(*di computer, pianoforte*) key; **tasti di scelta rapida** hot keys **2.**(*di telefono, software*) button **3.** MUS (*di chitarra*) fret **4.**(*prelievo*) sample

tastoni [tas·'to:·ni] *avv* feeling one's way; **procedere a ~** *fig* to feel one's way forward

TAT *m abbr di* **Tariffa A Tempo** *rate for phone calls based on their duration*

tattica ['tat·ti·ka] <-che> *f* tactics *pl*
tattico, -a ['tat·ti·ko] <-ci, -che> *agg* tactical
tattile [tat·'ti:·le] *agg* tactile
tatto ['tat·to] *m* **1.** (*senso*) touch **2.** *fig* tact; **mancanza di ~** tactlessness
tatuaggio [ta·tu·'ad·dʒo] <-ggi> *m* tattoo
tatuare [t·tu·'a:·re] *vt* to tattoo
taurino, -a [tau·'ri:·no] *agg* bull-like; **forza -a** bull-like strength
taverna [ta·'vɛr·na] *f* tavern
tavola ['ta:·vo·la] *f* **1.** (*mobile*) table; **~ allungabile** extendable table; **~ calda** diner, *serving hot food;* **~ fredda** diner, *serving cold food;* **mettersi a ~** to sit down to eat; **mettere le carte in ~** *fig* to put one's cards on the table; **portare in ~** to put on the table; **il pranzo è in ~** lunch is on the table **2.** (*asse*) board; (*lastra*) plate; (*piastra*) slab; **~ da surf** surfboard **3.** (*pittura*) painting, *on wood;* (*illustrazione*) plate **4.** (*tabella*) table; **~ periodica** periodic table
tavolata [ta·vo·'la:·ta] *f* (*commensali*) group at table
tavoletta [ta·vo·'let·ta] *f* **1.** (*assicella*) board **2.** (*pezzo rettangolare*) bar; **~ di cioccolata** bar of chocolate **3.** *fam* (*a tutta velocità*) **andare a ~** to go flat out
tavoliere [ta·vo·'liɛ:·re] *m* (*da gioco*) gaming table; (*del biliardo*) pool table
tavolino [ta·vo·'li:·no] *m* (*piccolo tavolo*) (small) table; **lavoro di ~** *fig* desk work; **a ~** *fig* in theory
tavolo ['ta:·vo·lo] *m* table; **~ da disegno** drawing board; **~ da stiro** ironing board; **~ delle trattative** negotiating table
tavolozza [ta·vo·'lɔt·tsa] *f* palette
taxi ['tak·si] <-> *m* taxi
tazza ['tat·tsa] *f* cup; **una ~ da caffè** a coffee cup; **una ~ di caffè** a cup of coffee
tazzina [tat·'tsi·na] *f* (*per caffè*) espresso cup
tbc, TBC *m abbr di* **tubercolosi** MED TB
te [te] *pron* *2. pers sing* **1.** (*complemento oggetto*) you; **ho visto solo ~** I only saw you; **hanno cercato ~ e non me** they were looking for you, not me **2.** (*complemento di termine*) you; **lo ha regalato a ~** he gave it to you; **~ l'avevo detto** I had told you; **ricordatelo** remember that **3.** (*con preposizione*) you; **vengo con ~** I'll come with you; **c'è posta per ~?** is there any post for you? **4.** (*con funzione di soggetto e nelle comparazioni, esclamazioni*) you; **lo dici ~!** you're a fine one to talk!; **povero ~!** (you) poor thing!; **ne so quanto ~** I know as much about it as you do **5.** (*davanti a lo, la, li, le, ne*) *v.* **ti**
tè [tɛ] <-> *m* tea; **bustina di ~** tea bag; **biscotti da ~** tea biscuit
teatino, -a [te·a·'ti:·no] **I.** *agg* **1.** (*di Chieti*) from Chieti **2.** (*dell'ordine dei monaci*) Theatine; **padre ~** Theatine father **II.** *m, f* (*abitante*) person from Chieti
teatrale [te·a·'tra:·le] *agg* **1.** (*di, da teatro*) theater **2.** *fig* theatrical

teatralità [te·a·tra·li·'ta] <-> *f* (*esagerazione*) theatricality
teatro [te·'a:·tro] *m a. fig* theater; **~ all'aperto** open-air theater; **~ di posa** movie studio; **~ di prosa** theater; **~ lirico** opera

> **i** The **Teatro alla Scala**, Milan was built on the site of the ancient church of Santa Maria della Scala and opened in 1778 with a production of Antonio Salieri's "L'Europa riconosciuta". It was badly damaged by bombing in 1943, but restored and reopened in 1946 with a concert conducted by Arturo Toscanini. It closed for restoration and modernization at the end of 2001 and reopened to the public in December 2004 with the same opera by Salieri that had inaugurated the theater 226 years earlier. The Scala is known as an opera house all over the world, but it is also the home of a world-class ballet company.

teatro-tenda [te·'a:·tro 'tɛn·da] *m* marquee, *used for performances*
teca ['tɛ:·ka] <-che> *f* (*vetrina*) display case
tecnica ['tɛk·ni·ka] <-che> *f* (*norme*) technology; (*sistema*) technique; **~ delle comunicazioni** communication technology
tecnico ['tɛk·ni·ko] <-ci> *m* technician
tecnico, -a <-ci, -che> *agg* technical; **linguaggio ~** technical language; **termine ~** technical term; (*assistente*) **tecnico sanitario** medical technician, *with a degree*
tecnocratico, -a [tek·no·'kra:·ti·ko] <-ci, -che> *agg* technocratic
tecnocrazia [tek·no·kra·'tsi:·a] <-ie> *f* technocracy
tecnofibra [tek·no·'fi:·bra] *f* hi-tech fiber
tecnohouse [tek·nɔ·'haus] *f* MUS techno house
tecnologia [tek·no·lo·'dʒi:·a] <-gie> *f* technology; **alta ~** high technology; **-gie dolci** soft technologies
tecnologico, -a [tek·no·'lɔ:·dʒi·ko] *agg* technological
tedesco [te·'des·ko] <sing> *m* (*lingua*) German
tedesco, -a <-schi, -sche> **I.** *agg* German; **la Repubblica Federale Tedesca** the Federal Republic of Germany **II.** *m, f* German
tediare [te·'dia:·re] *vt* **1.** (*annoiare*) to bore **2.** (*seccare*) to annoy
tedio ['tɛ:·dio] <-i> *m* **1.** (*noia*) boredom **2.** (*fastidio*) annoyance
tedioso, -a [te·'dio:·so] *agg* **1.** (*noioso*) boring **2.** (*fastidioso*) annoying
tegame [te·'ga:·me] *m* skillet
teglia ['teʎ·ʎa] <-glie> *f* (*per arrostire*) roasting pan; (*per dolci*) cake pan
tegola ['tɛ:·go·la] *f* (roof) tile; **~ in testa** *fig* shock

T

teiera [te·'iɛ:·ra] *f* teapot
teina [te·'i:·na] *f* theine
tela ['tɛ:·la] *f* **1.** (*tessuto*) cloth; ~ **di canapa** hemp cloth; ~ **cerata** waxed cloth; ~ **di cotone** cotton cloth; ~ **di lino** linen cloth; ~ **di ragno** cobweb **2.** (*dipinto*) canvas
telaio [te·'la:·io] <-ai> *m* **1.** (*per tessitura*) loom **2.** (*di finestra*) frame; (*di auto*) chassis; (*di letto*) base
tele ['tɛ:·le] <-> **I.** *f fam* (*televisione*) TV **II.** *m* (*teleobiettivo*) telephoto lens
teleabbonato, -a [te·le·ab·bo·'na:·to] *m, f* television license holder
telebanking [te·le·'bɛn·king] <-> *m* home banking
telecamera [te·le·'ka:·me·ra] *f* television camera
Telecom [te·le·kom] *f* ~ **Italia** *Italian national phone company*
telecomandare [te·le·ko·man·'da:·re] *vt* to operate by remote control
telecomando [te·le·ko·'man·do] *m* remote control
telecomunicare [te·le·ko·mu·ni·'ka:·re] *vt* to communicate over distance
telecomunicazione [te·le·ko·mu·ni·kat·'tsio:·ne] *f* telecommunication
teleconferenza [te·le·kon·fe·'rɛn·tsa] *f* teleconference
telecontrollare [te·le·kon·trol·'la:·re] *vt* to operate by remote control
telecontrollo [te·le·kon·'trɔl·lo] *m* remote control
telecronaca [te·le·'krɔ:·na·ka] *f* television report
telecronista [te·le·kro·'nis·ta] *mf* television reporter
telediffusione [te·le·dif·fu·'zio:·ne] *f* broadcasting
teleelaborazione [te·le·e·la·bo·rat·'tsio:·ne] *f* teleprocessing
telefax ['tɛ:·le·faks] <-> *m* fax
teleferica [te·le·'fɛ:·ri·ka] <-che> *f* cableway
telefilm [te·le·'film] *m* TV film
telefonare [te·le·fo·'na:·re] **I.** *vt* to call **II.** *vi* (*fare una o più chiamate*) to call; ~ **a qu** to call sb; **mi fai telefonare?** can you ask him [*o* her] [*o* them] to call me?; **posso telefonare?** can I make a phone call?
telefonata [te·le·fo·'na:·ta] *f* phone call; ~ **interurbana** long distance phone call; ~ **urbana** local phone call; **fare una ~ a qu** to call sb; **posso fare una telefonata?** can I make a phone call?; **scusi posso fare una telefonata urbana?** excuse me, could I make a local phone call?
telefonia [te·le·fo·'ni:·a] *f* ~ **fissa** landline telephony; ~ **mobile** mobile telephony
telefonico, -a [te·le·'fɔ:·ni·ko] <-ci, -che> *agg* phone; **scheda -a** phone card; **cabina** ~ phone booth; **elenco** ~ phone book
telefonino [te·le·fo·'ni:·no] *m* cellphone
telefono [te·'lɛ:·fo·no] *m* phone; ~ **amico** *hot-*

line for people with psychological problems; ~ **azzurro** *hotline for reporting child abuse;* ~ **cellulare** cellphone; ~ **a scheda magnetica** card-operated phone; **bolletta del** ~ phone bill; ~ **senza filo** cordless phone; **dare un colpo di** ~ **a qu** *fam* to call sb
telefoto [te·le·'fɔ:·to] *f* **1.** (*sistema*) telephotography **2.** (*fotografia*) telephotograph
telegiornale [te·le·dʒor·'na:·le] *m* (television) news
telegrafare [te·le·gra·'fa:·re] *vt, vi* to telegraph
teleguida [te·le·'gui:·da] *f* radio control
teleguidare [te·le·gui·'da:·re] *vt* to operate by radio control
telelavorare [te·le·la·vo·'ra:·re] *vi* COMPUT to telecommute
telematica [te·le·'ma:·ti·ka] <-che> *f* telematics
telematico, -a [te·le·'ma:·ti·ko] <-ci, -che> *agg* telematic; **giornale** ~ COMPUT e-newspaper
telemedicina [te·le·me·di·'tʃi:·na] *f* e-medicine
telenovela [te·le·no·'vɛ·la] *f Latin American soap opera*
teleobiettivo [te·le·o·biet·'ti:·vo] *m* telephoto lens
telepass® [te·le·'pas] *m electronic transponder for use on toll roads*
telepatia [te·le·pa·'ti:·a] <-ie> *f* telepathy
telepilotare [te·le·pi·lo·'ta:·re] *vt* to operate by radio control
telepromozione [te·le·pro·mot·'tsio:·ne] *f* TV television advertising
telequiz [te·le·'kui·ts] *m* game show
teleriscaldamento [te·le·ris·kal·da·'men·to] *m* district heating
teleromanzo [te·le·ro·'man·dzo] *m* miniseries
teleschermo [te·les·'ker·mo/te·les·'kɛr·mo] *m* television screen
telescopico, -a [te·les·'kɔ:·pi·ko] <-ci, -che> *agg* telescopic
telescopio [te·les·'kɔ:·pio] <-i> *m* telescope
teleselezione [te·le·se·let·'tsio:·ne] *f* direct dialing
telespettatore, -trice [te·les·pet·ta·'to:·re] *m, f* viewer
teletex [te·le·'tɛks] <-> *m* teletex
teletext [te·le·'tɛkst] <-> *m* teletext®
teletrasmettere [te·le·traz·'met·te·re] <irr> *vt* to televise
teleutente [te·leu·'tɛn·te] *mf* television subscriber
televendita [te·le·'ven·di·ta] *f* teleshopping
televideo [te·le·'vi:·deo] <-> *m system of teletext used in Italy*
televisione [te·le·vi·'zio:·ne] *f* **1.** (*sistema*) television; ~ **via cavo** cable television **2.** *fam* (*televisore*) television; ~ **a colori** color television

i Italian **television** consists of three public channels (RAIUNO, RAIDUE, RAITRE) and numerous private channels, most of them local or regional. The three most important private channels (Canale5, Italia1, Rete4) broadcast nationwide and belong to Mediaset, which is controlled by Silvio Berlusconi. RAI, as a state-owned company, is run by the *Communications Minister.*

tellurico, -a [tel·'lu:·ri·ko] <-ci, -che> *agg* telluric

telo ['te:·lo] *m* piece of cloth; ~ **da bagno** beach towel; ~ **da salvataggio** safety blanket

telone [te·'lo:·ne] *m* 1. (*copertura*) tarpaulin 2. (*sipario*) safety curtain

tema ['tɛ:·ma] <-i> *m* 1. (*argomento*) subject; **andare fuori** ~ to wander off the subject 2. (*componimento scolastico*) essay 3. LING theme

tematica [te·'ma:·ti·ka] <-che> *f* themes *pl*

tematico, -a [te·'ma:·ti·ko] <-ci, -che> *agg* thematic

temerarietà [te·me·ra·rie·'ta] <-> *f* recklessness

temerario, -a [te·me·'ra:·rio] <-i, -ie> I. *agg* reckless II. *m, f* (*persona sconsiderata*) reckless person

temere [te·'me:·re] I. *vt* 1. (*avere paura di*) to be afraid of 2. (*non sopportare*) **questa pianta teme il freddo** this plant can't stand the cold II. *vi* 1. (*essere preoccupato*) ~ **per qu/qc** to worry about sb/sth; **non ~!** don't worry! 2. (*diffidare di*) ~ **di qu/qc** to distrust sb/sth

temibile [te·'mi:·bi·le] *agg* fearsome

tempario [tem·'pa·rio] *m manual showing the times different jobs should take*

temperalapis, temperamatite [tem·pe·ra·'la:·pis, tem·pe·ra·ma·'ti:·te] <-> *m* pencil sharpener

temperamento [tem·pe·ra·'men·to] *m* (*indole*) temperament

temperante [tem·pe·'ran·te] *agg* moderate

temperare [tem·pe·'ra:·re] *vt* 1. (*gener*) to temper 2. (*matita*) to sharpen

temperato, -a [tem·pe·'ra:·to] *agg* 1. (*gener*) moderate 2. (*clima*) temperate

temperatura [tem·pe·ra·'tu:·ra] *f* temperature; ~ **in aumento** rising temperature; ~ **in diminuzione** falling temperature; ~ **ambiente** room temperature; ~ **di ebollizione** boiling point; **sbalzo di** ~ sudden fall/rise in temperature

temperino [tem·pe·'ri:·no] *m* 1. (*per matite*) sharpener 2. (*coltello*) penknife

tempesta [tem·'pɛs·ta] *f* (*bufera*) storm; **c'è aria di** ~ *fig* there's a storm brewing

tempestare [tem·pes·'ta:·re] I. *vt* ~ **qu di qc** to bombard sb with sth II. *vi* (*impersonale*) **tempestava** a storm was raging

tempestato, -a [tem·pes·'ta:·to] *agg* ~ **di qc** (*diamanti*) smothered in sth

tempestina [tem·pes·'ti:·na] *f* CULIN *small cylindrical pasta for soup*

tempestività [tem·pes·ti·vi·'ta] <-> *f* timeliness

tempestivo, -a [tem·pes·'ti:·vo] *agg* timely

tempestoso, -a [tem·pes·'to:·so] *agg* 1. (*cielo, mare*) stormy 2. (*pensieri*) agitated 3. (*vita*) eventful

tempia ['tɛm·pia] <-ie> *f* ANAT temple

tempio ['tɛm·pio] <-i *o* templi> *m* temple

tempismo [tem·'piz·mo] *m* (good) timing

templi ['tɛm·pli] *pl di* **tempio**

tempo ['tɛm·po] *m* 1. (*gener*) time; ~ **libero** free time; ~ **reale** real time; **ammazzare il** ~ to kill time; **dar** ~ **al** ~ to let things run their course; **ai miei -i** in my day; **a** ~ **pieno** full time; **in** (*o per*) ~ in time; **in un primo** ~ at first; **un** ~ once; ~ **fa** a while ago; **con i -i che corrono** these days; **quanto** ~? how long?; **il** ~ **è denaro** (*o moneta*) *prov* time is money; **chi ha** ~ **non aspetti** ~ *prov* there's no time like the present 2. METEO weather; **previsioni del** ~ weather forecast; ~ **da cani** (*o da lupi*) terrible weather; **fare il buono e il cattivo** ~ *fig* to be the boss 3. LING tense 4. MUS time; **andare a** ~ to keep time; **andare fuori** ~ to be out of time; **a** ~ **di valzer** waltz time 5. (*di motore*) stroke 6. DI PARTITA half; **-i supplementari** extra time 7. (*di spettacolo*) part

temporale [tem·po·'ra:·le] I. *agg* 1. *a.* ANAT temporal 2. REL, POL worldly; **il potere** ~ earthly power 3. LING time II. *m* METEO storm

temporalesco, -a [tem·po·ra·'les·ko] <-schi, -sche> *agg* stormy

temporaneo, -a [tem·po·'ra:·neo] *agg* (*provvisorio*) temporary

temporeggiare [tem·po·red·'dʒa:·re] *vi* (*prendere tempo*) to play for time

tempra ['tɛm·pra] *f* 1. (*di vetro, metallo*) temper 2. (*di persona*) constitution

temprare [tem·'pra:·re] *vt* 1. (*vetro, metallo*) to temper; **acciaio temprato** tempered steel 2. (*persona, carattere*) to strengthen

tenace [te·'na:·tʃe] *agg* 1. (*resistente: filo, colore*) tough; (*duro: legno*) hard 2. (*persona*) tenacious; (*odio, avversione*) strong

tenacia [te·'na:·tʃa] <-cie> *f* tenacity

tenaglia [te·'naʎ·ʎa] *f* 1. TEC **un paio di -e** a pair of pliers 2. *fam* (*chele: di granchio, aragosta*) pincers

tenda ['tɛn·da] *f* 1. (*per finestre*) curtain 2. (*per negozi, balconi*) awning 3. (*da campeggio*) tent; **levare le -e** *fig* to hit the road 4. MED ~ **a ossigeno** oxygen tent

tendenza [ten·'dɛn·tsa] *f* 1. (*propensione*) tendency; **avere** ~ **a fare qc** to tend to do sth 2. (*orientamento*) trend

tendenziosità [ten·den·tsio·si·'ta] <-> *f* tendentiousness

tendenzioso, -a [ten·den·'tsio:·so] *agg* tendentious

tendere ['tɛn·de·re] <tendo, tesi, teso> I. *vt* 1. (*fune*) to tighten; (*lenzuolo*) to spread out; (*muscoli*) to stretch; ~ **un tranello** to set a trap 2. (*mano*) to hold out; (*braccio*) to stretch out; ~ **l'orecchio** *fig* to prick up one's ears **II.** *vi* **1.** (*aspirare*) ~ **a qc** to aim toward sth **2.** (*propendere*) ~ **a qc** to tend toward sth; **un giallo che tende all'arancione** an orangy yellow

tendina [ten·'di:·na] *f* (*per finestre*) curtain

tendine ['tɛn·di·ne] *m* tendon

tendinite [ten·di·'ni:·te] *f* tendonitis

tendone [ten·'do:·ne] *m* (*copertura*) (big) tent; (*di circo*) big top

tendopoli [ten·'dɔ:·po·li] <-> *f* tented camp, *for disaster victims*

tenebre ['tɛ:·ne·bre] *f* **1.** *pl* (*buio*) darkness **2.** (*ignoranza*) ignorance

tenebroso, -a [te·ne·'bro:·so] *agg* **1.** (*buio: notte, stanza*) dark **2.** (*schivo: persona*) mysterious

tenente [te·'nɛn·te] *m* lieutenant

tenere [te·'ne:·re] <tengo, tenni, tenuto> **I.** *vt* **1.** (*in mano, in braccio*) to hold; (*non lasciar sfuggire*) to hold onto; **ecco il resto: tenga!** here's your change **2.** (*mantenere*) to keep; ~ **la finestra aperta** to keep the window open; ~ **il posto a qu** to keep sb's seat; ~ **la lingua a freno** to hold one's tongue; ~ **a mente qc** to bear sth in mind; ~ **le distanze** *fig* to keep one's distance; ~ **una promessa** to keep a promise; **-rsi buono qu** to keep sb sweet; ~ **qc da conto** to take care of sth; ~ **la destra/sinistra** to keep to the right/left **3.** (*contenere*) to hold **4.** (*discorso, conferenza*) to give; (*riunione*) to hold; **la riunione si terrà domani mattina** the meeting will take place tomorrow morning **5.** *fig* (*occupare*) to take up; (*dominare*) to hold; ~ **banco** *fig* to hold the stage **6.** (*loc*) ~ **conto di qc** to bear sth in mind; ~ **compagnia a qu** to keep sb company; ~ **d'occhio qu** to keep an eye on sb; **l'auto tiene bene la strada** the car handles the road well **II.** *vi* **1.** (*reggere: scaffale*) to hold up; (*colla*) to stick; ~ **duro** *fam* (*resistere*) to hang on **2.** (*dare importanza*) ~ **a qc** to care about sth; **tengo a ... +** *inf* I would like to ... **3.** (*parteggiare*) ~ **per qu** to be on sb's side; ~ **per una squadra** to support a team **III.** *vr:* **-rsi 1.** (*reggersi*) to hold on **2.** (*mantenersi*) to keep; **tenersi a distanza da qc** to keep one's distance from sth; **tenersi aggiornato** to keep up to date; ~ **pronto** to be ready; **-rsi in piedi** to stand up **3.** (*trattenersi*) to keep oneself; **-rsi dal ridere** to keep oneself from laughing **4.** (*attenersi*) **-rsi a qc** to stick to sth

tenerezza [te·ne·'ret·tsa] *f* tenderness; **un bambino che fa** ~ a sweet baby

tenero ['tɛ:·ne·ro] *m* **1.** (*parte tenera*) tender part **2.** (*sentimento*) feelings *pl;* **tra quei due c'è del** ~ those two have feelings for each other

tenero, -a *agg* **1.** (*morbido: carne*) tender; (*legno, pietra*) soft **2.** (*affettuoso: sguardo, parole*) tender; (*non severo: madre, padre*) soft; **che** ~! how sweet! **3.** (*giovane*) **in -a età** at a tender age

tengo ['tɛŋ·go] *1. pers sing pr di* tenere

tenia ['tɛ:·nia] <-ie> *f* (*verme*) tapeworm

tenni ['ten·ni] *1. pers sing pass rem di* tenere

tennis ['tɛn·nis] <-> *m* tennis; ~ **da tavolo** table tennis

tennista [ten·'nis·ta] <-i *m*, -e *f*> *mf* tennis player

tennistico, -a [ten·'nis·ti·ko] <-ci, -che> *agg* tennis

tenore [te·'no:·re] **I.** *agg* tenor; **sax** ~ tenor sax **II.** *m* **1.** MUS tenor **2.** (*tasso, contenuto*) content **3.** (*modo*) way **4.** (*tono*) tone; ~ **di vita** standard of living

tensione [ten·'sio:·ne] *f* tension; **alta/bassa** ~ high/low tension; **in casa mia c'è un po' di** ~ things are a bit tense at home

tentabile [ten·'ta:·bi·le] *agg* worth trying; **tentare il** ~ to do what one can

tentacolo [ten·'ta:·ko·lo] *m a. fig* tentacle

tentare [ten·'ta:·re] *vt* **1.** (*provare*) to try; ~ **di fare qc** to try to do sth **2.** (*allettare*) to tempt

tentativo [ten·ta·'ti:·vo] *m* (*prova*) attempt

tentatore, -trice [ten·ta·'to:·re] **I.** *agg* tempting **II.** *m, f* tempter *m,* temptress *f*

tentazione [ten·tat·'tsio:·ne] *f* temptation; **indurre qu in** ~ to lead sb into temptation

tentennamento [ten·ten·na·'men·to] *m* (*indecisione*) hesitation

tentennare [ten·ten·'na:·re] **I.** *vt* (*testa*) to shake **II.** *vi* **1.** (*dente, tavolo*) to wobble **2.** (*esitare*) to waver

tentone, tentoni [ten·'to:·ne, ten·'to:·ni] *avv* **1.** (*alla cieca*) (a) ~ feeling one's way; **camminare** (a) ~ to feel one's way **2.** (*a caso*) (a) ~ haphazardly

tenue ['tɛ:·nue] *agg* **1.** (*colore*) soft **2.** (*speranza, luce*) faint; (*voce*) feeble

tenuta [te·'nu:·ta] *f* **1.** (*azione*) handling; ~ **di strada** road handling **2.** TEC sealing; **a** ~ **d'acqua** watertight; **a** ~ **stagna** hermetic **3.** (*podere agricolo*) estate **4.** (*abito: da lavoro*) clothes *pl;* (*uniforme*) uniform **5.** (*resistenza: di atleta*) stamina

tenuto, -a [te·'nu:·to] **I.** *pp di* tenere **II.** *agg* (*obbligato*) **essere** ~ **a fare qc** to be obliged to do sth

teologia [te·o·lo·'dʒi:·a] <-gie> *f* theology

teologico, -a [te·o·'lɔ:·dʒi·ko] <-ci, -che> *agg* theological

teologo, -a [te·'ɔ:·lo·go] <-ghi, -ghe> *m, f* theologian

teorema [te·o·'rɛ:·ma] <-i> *m* theorem

teoretico, -a [te·o·'rɛ:·ti·ko] <-ci, -che> *agg* theoretical

teoria [te·o·'ri:·a] <-ie> *f* theory; **in** ~ in theory

teorico, -a [te·'ɔ:·ri·ko] <-ci, -che> **I.** *agg* theoretical **II.** *m, f* theorist

teorizzare [te·o·rid·'dza:·re] *vi* to theorize

tepore [te·'po:·re] *m* warmth

teppa ['tep·pa] *f* BOT moss

teppaglia [tep·'paʎ·ʎa] <-glie> *f pej* rabble

teppismo [tep·'piz·mo] *m* (*comportamento*)

hooliganism
teppista [tep·'pis·ta] <-i *m*, -e *f*> *mf* hooligan
Teramano <*sing*> *m* Teramo area; **nel** ~ in the Teramo area
teramano, -a [te·ra·'ma:·no] **I.** *agg* from Teramo **II.** *m*, *f* (*abitante*) person from Teramo
Teramo *f* Teramo, *town in southeastern Italy*
terapeuta [te·ra·'pɛːu·ta] <-i *m*, -e *f*> *mf* (*medico*) therapist
terapeutico, -a [te·ra·'pɛːu·ti·ko] <-ci, -che> *agg* therapeutic
terapia [te·ra·'piː·a] <-ie> *f* **1.** (*cura*) treatment; ~ **intensiva** intensive care; ~ **del dolore** pain control; ~ **d'urto** massive-dose treatment **2.** *fam* (*psicoterapia*) therapy
terapista [te·ra·'pis·ta] <-i *m*, -e *f*> *mf* therapist
tergere ['tɛr·dʒe·re] <tergo, tersi, terso> *vt lit* (*pulire*) to wipe
tergicristallo [ter·dʒi·kris·'tal·lo] *m* MOT windshield wiper
tergilavalunotto [ter·dʒi·la·va·lu·'nɔt·to] *m* MOT rear windshield washer/wiper
tergilunotto [ter·dʒi·lu·'nɔt·to] *m* MOT rear windshield wiper
tergiversare [ter·dʒi·ver·'sa:·re] *vi* (*temporeggiare*) to prevaricate
tergo ['tɛr·go] <-ghi> *m* (*di foglio, moneta*) back; **a** ~ behind; **vedi a** ~ please turn over
termale [ter·'ma:·le] *agg* thermal; **stazione** ~ spa resort
terme ['tɛr·me] *fpl a.* HIST (thermal) baths
termico, -a ['tɛr·mi·ko] <-ci, -che> *agg* thermal; **energia -a** thermal energy; **variazioni -che** temperature variations
terminal ['tə:·mi·nəl/'tɛr·mi·nal] <-> *m* terminal
terminale [ter·mi·'na:·le] **I.** *agg* **1.** (*finale*) final **2.** (*malato*) terminal **II.** *m a.* COMPUT terminal
terminare [ter·mi·'na:·re] **I.** *vt avere* (*concludere*) to finish **II.** *vi essere* (*concludersi*) to end
terminazione [ter·mi·nat·'tsio:·ne] *f* ending
termine ['tɛr·mi·ne] *m* **1.** (*scadenza*) deadline; **a** ~ (*contratto, mandato*) fixed-term; **a breve** ~ short-term **2.** (*fine*) end; **aver** ~ to end; **portare a** ~ to finish; **volgere al** ~ to come to an end **3.** (*vocabolo, elemento*) term; ~ **tecnico** technical term; **ridurre ai minimi -i** to reduce to the lowest terms
terminologia [ter·mi·no·lo·'dʒi:·a] <-gie> *f* terminology
termite ['tɛr·mi·te] *f* termite
termoaderente [ter·mo·a·de·'rɛn·te] *agg* heat-shrinking
termoadesivo, -a [ter·mo·a·de·'zi:·vo] *agg* thermoadhesive
termodistruttore [ter·mo·dis·trut·'to:·re] *m* incinerator
termoelettrico, -a [ter·mo·e·'lɛt·tri·ko] *agg* thermoelectric; **centrale -a** thermoelectric power station
termoforo [ter·'mɔ:·fo·ro] *m* heating pad

termoisolante [ter·moi·zo·'lan·te] **I.** *agg* heatproof **II.** *m* insulator
termometro [ter·'mɔ:·me·tro] *m* thermometer
termonucleare [ter·mo·nu·kle·'a:·re] *agg* thermonuclear
termoreattore [ter·mo·re·at·'to:·re] *m* (*per laboratorio di analisi*) incubating shaker
termos ['tɛr·mos] <-> *m v.* **thermos**
termosifone [ter·mo·si·'fo:·ne] *m* **1.** (*radiatore*) radiator **2.** (*impianto*) central heating
termostato [ter·'mɔ:s·ta·to] *m* thermostat
termoventilazione [ter·mo·ven·ti·lat·'tsio:·ne] *f* warm-air heating
terna ['tɛr·na] *f* (*tre elementi*) set of three
Ternano <*sing*> *m* Terni area; **nel** ~ in the Terni area
ternano, -a [ter·'na:·no] **I.** *agg* from Terni **II.** *m*, *f* (*abitante*) person from Terni
ternario, -a [ter·'na:·rio] <-i, -ie> *agg* **1.** (*di tre elementi*) triple **2.** (*verso*) three-syllable **3.** CHEM ternary
Terni ['tɛr·ni] *f* Terni, *town in Umbria*
terno ['tɛr·no] *m* set of three winning numbers; **fare** ~ to get three winning numbers; ~ **al lotto** *fig* lucky break
terra ['tɛr·ra] *f* **1.** (*pianeta*) earth **2.** (*suolo*) ground; **-e emerse** land surface; **finire per** ~ to fall to the ground; **raso** ~ close to the ground; **avere una gomma a** ~ to have a flat *fam;* **essere a** ~ *fig* (*essere giù di morale*) to be at rock bottom; **sentirsi mancare la** ~ **sotto i piedi** to feel completely lost **3.** (*per vasi*) soil **4.** (*paese, campagna*) land **5.** (*terreno*) piece of land; ~ **di nessuno** no man's land **6.** EL ground; **mettere a** ~ to ground
terra-aria ['tɛr·ra 'a:·ria] <inv> *agg* earth-to-air
terracotta [ter·ra·'kɔt·ta] <terrecotte> *f* **1.** (*materiale*) terracotta **2.** (*manufatto*) earthenware
terraferma [ter·ra·'fer·ma] <-> *f* dry land
terraglia [ter·'raʎ·ʎa] <-glie> *f* pottery
terrapieno [ter·ra·'piɛː·no] *m* embankment
terrazza [ter·'rat·tsa] *f* (*di edificio*) terrace
terrazzino [ter·rat·'tsi:·no] *m* balcony
terrazzo [ter·'rat·tso] *m* terrace
terrecotte *pl di* **terracotta**
terremotato, -a [ter·re·mo·'ta:·to] **I.** *agg* (*zona*) affected by an earthquake **II.** *m*, *f* earthquake victim
terremoto [ter·re·'mɔ:·to] *m* **1.** (*movimento tellurico*) earthquake **2.** *fig, scherz* (*persona*) terror
terreno [ter·'re:·no] *m* **1.** *superficie di terra* land; ~ **fabbricabile** building land; **tastare il** ~ *fig* to get the lay of the land; **trovare il** ~ **adatto** *fig* to find fertile ground **2.** (*suolo*) ground; **guadagnare/perdere** ~ *fig* to gain/lose ground; **sentirsi mancare il** ~ **sotto i piedi** to feel completely lost **3.** SPORT ~ (**di gioco**) (sports) field **4.** MIL field
terreno, -a *agg* **1.** (*vita, beni*) earthly **2.** (*al livello del suolo*) **piano** ~ first floor
terreo, -a ['tɛr·reo] *agg* earthy

terrestre [ter·'rɛs·tre] I. *agg* 1. (*superficie, temperatura*) earth's 2. (*battaglia, animale*) land II. *mf* earthling

terribile [ter·'ri:·bi·le] *agg* 1. (*spaventoso: mostro, disastro*) terrible 2. (*molto intenso: freddo, fame*) awful

terriccio [ter·'rit·tʃo] <-cci> *m* compost

terriero, -a [ter·'riɛ:·ro] *agg* (*proprietà*) landed; **proprietario** ~ landowner

terrificante [ter·ri·fi·'kan·te] *agg* terrifying

terrificare [ter·ri·fi·'ka:·re] *vt* to terrify

terrina [ter·'ri:·na] *f* CULIN (*di lepre, anatra*) terrine

territoriale [ter·ri·to·'ria:·le] *agg* territorial; **acque -i** territorial waters; **confini -i** territorial limits

territorio [ter·ri·'tɔ:·rio] <-i> *m* (*regione*) region; ~ **nazionale** national territory

terrò [ter·'rɔ] *1. pers sing futuro di* **tenere**

terrone, -a [ter·'ro:·ne] *m*, *f pej*: derogatory term for someone from the South of Italy

terrore [ter·'ro:·re] *m* (*paura*) terror; **incutere** ~ **a qu** to terrify sb

terrorismo [ter·ro·'riz·mo] *m* terrorism

terrorista [ter·ro·'ris·ta] <-i *m*, -e *f*> *mf* terrorist

terroristico, -a [ter·ro·'ris·ti·ko] <-ci, -che> *agg* terrorist

terrorizzare [ter·ro·rid·'dza:·re] *vt* to terrorize

terroso, -a [ter·'ro:·so] *agg* 1. (*materiale*) earthy 2. (*mani, scarpe*) muddy

tersi ['tɛr·si] *1. pers sing pass rem di* **tergere**

terso, -a ['tɛr·so] I. *pp di* **tergere** II. *agg* (*cielo*) clear

terza ['tɛr·tsa] *f* 1. (*classe: elementare*) third grade; (*media*) eighth grade; (*superiore*) eleventh grade 2. MOT third gear 3. MUS third 4. MATH power of three

terzetto [ter·'tset·to] *m a.* MUS trio

terziario [ter·'tsia:·rio] *m* 1. GEOL tertiary 2. COM service sector

terziario, -a <-i, -ie> I. *agg* tertiary II. *m*, *f* tertiary

terzina [ter·'tsi:·na] *f* 1. (*strofe*) tercet 2. MUS triplet

terzino [ter·'tsi:·no] *m* fullback, *in soccer*

terzo ['tɛr·tso] *m* 1. (*frazione*) third 2. *pl* (*altri*) other people; **per conto -i** on behalf of a third party

terzo, -a I. *agg* third; **-a età** third age; **-a pagina** (*di giornale*) arts page; **di terz'ordine** third-rate II. *m*, *f* (*terza persona*) third; *v.a.* **quinto**

terzultimo, -a [ter·'tsul·ti·mo] I. *agg* third from last II. *m*, *f* third from last

tesa ['te:·sa] *f* (*di cappello*) brim

teschio ['tɛs·kio] <-schi> *m* skull

tesi¹ ['tɛ:·zi] <-> *f* 1. (*proposizione*) theory; **sostenere/confutare una** ~ to support/refute a theory 2. (*di laurea*) thesis; (*di dottorato*) doctoral thesis

tesi² ['te:·si] *1. pers sing pass rem di* **tendere**

tesina [te·'zi:·na] *f* short thesis

teso, -a ['te:·so] I. *pp di* **tendere** II. *agg*

1. (*corda, muscoli*) tight 2. (*nervoso*) tense

tesoriere, -a [te·zo·'riɛ:·re] *m*, *f* 1. (*di azienda*) treasurer 2. (*nella pubblica amministrazione*) treasury secretary

tesoro [te·'zɔ:·ro] *m* 1. (*cose preziose*) treasure; **fare ~ di qc** *fig* to take sth to heart 2. (*erario pubblico*) Treasury

tessera ['tɛs·se·ra] *f* 1. (*documento*) membership card; ~ **magnetica** swipe card; ~ **sanitaria** *card entitling its bearer to health care* 2. (*di mosaico*) tile 3. (*del domino*) domino

tesserare [tes·se·'ra:·re] *vt* 1. (*iscrivere*) ~ **qu** to make sb a member 2. (*razionare*) to ration

tesserato, -a [tes·se·'ra:·to] *m*, *f* (paid-up) member

tessere ['tɛs·se·re] *vt* 1. (*con telaio*) to weave; (*intrecciare*) to braid 2. (*inganno*) to plot

tesserino [tes·se·'ri:·no] *m* card; ~ **magnetico** swipe card; ~ **sanitario** *card entitling its bearer to health care*; ~ **universitario** student ID card

tessile ['tɛs·si·le] I. *agg* textile II. *mf* textile worker III. *m* 1. (*settore*) textile sector 2. *pl* (*prodotti*) textiles

tessitore, -trice [tes·si·'to:·re] *m*, *f* weaver

tessitura [tes·si·'tu:·ra] *f* weaving

tessuto [tes·'su:·to] *m* 1. (*stoffa*) material 2. *fig* ~ **sociale** social fabric 3. BIOL, ANAT tissue 4. *pl* textiles

test [tɛst] <-> *m* test; ~ **di gravidanza** pregnancy test

testa ['tɛs·ta] *f* 1. DI PERSONA head; **mal di** ~ headache; **andar fuori di** ~ *fam* to go crazy; **avere la** ~ **tra le nuvole** to have one's head in the clouds; **dare alla** ~ to go to sb's head; **fare a** ~ **e croce** to toss a coin; **fare di** ~ **propria** to do as one pleases; **mettersi in** ~ **qc** to get sth into one's head; **perdere la** ~ **per qu/qc** to lose one's head over sb/sth; **scommettere la** ~ to bet one's life; **non sapere dove sbattere la** ~ to be at one's wits' end 2. (*persona*) ~ **calda** hothead; ~ **dura** stubborn person; ~ **di cavolo** [*o* **di rapa**] *fam* idiot; **colpo di** ~ impulse; **a** ~ each 3. (*parte superiore*) top; **in** ~ **al treno** at the front of the train 4. (*di spillo, martello, vite*) head; ~ **d'aglio** head of garlic 5. (*di fila*) front; **essere in** ~ (*in classifica, gara*) to be [*o* come] first; **essere alla** ~ **di qc** (*azienda, partito*) to head sth up; **tener** ~ **a qu** to stand up to sb

testacoda [tes·ta·'ko:·da] <-> *m* spin; **fare** (**un**) ~ to spin around

testamentario, -a [tes·ta·men·'ta:·rio] <-i, -ie> *agg* testamentary

testamento [tes·ta·'men·to] *m* 1. (*atto*) will 2. (*Bibbia*) **l'Antico** ~ the Old Testament; **il Nuovo** ~ the New Testament

testardaggine [tes·tar·'dad·dʒi·ne] *f* stubbornness

testardo, -a [tes·'tar·do] I. *agg* stubborn II. *m*, *f* stubborn person

testare [tes·'ta:·re] *vi* to test

testata [tes·'ta:·ta] *f* 1. (*colpo*) **prendere/**

dare una ~ to bump one's head **2.** (*di letto*) headboard **3.** (*di motore*) (cylinder) head **4.** (*di giornale*) masthead **5.** (*di missile*) warhead

teste ['tɛs·te] *mf* witness

testicolare [tes·ti·ko·'la:·re] *agg* testicular

testicolo [tes·'ti:·ko·lo] *m* testicle

testiera [tes·'tiɛ:·ra] *f* **1.** (*per cavalli*) headstall **2.** (*di letto*) headboard; (*di poltrona*) headrest

testimone [tes·ti·'mɔ:·ne] *mf* **1.** (*persona*) witness; **~ a carico** prosecution witness; **~ a discarico** defense witness; **~ di nozze** witness, *at a wedding*; **~ oculare** eyewitness; **Testimone di Geova** REL Jehovah's Witness **2.** SPORT baton

testimonianza [tes·ti·mo·'nian·tsa] *f* **1.** JUR testimony **2.** (*prova*) proof; **rendere ~ di qc** to testify to sth

testimoniare [tes·ti·mo·'nia:·re] **I.** *vt* **1.** JUR to testify (that); **~ il falso** to commit perjury **2.** (*dimostrare*) to bear witness to **II.** *vi* **1.** (*deporre*) to testify **2.** (*far fede*) **~ di qc** to vouch for sth

testimonio [tes·ti·'mɔ:·nio] <-i> *m v.* **testimone**

testina [tes·'ti:·na] *f* CULIN, TEC head; **~ di registrazione** tape head

testo ['tɛs·to] *m* text; **libri di ~** textbooks

testone [tes·'to:·ne] *m* **1.** TESTA GROSSA big head **2.** *fig, fam* (*persona testarda*) stubborn person

testuale [tes·tu·'a:·le] *agg* **1.** (*del testo: analisi, critica*) textual **2.** (*esatto*) exact; **disse queste -i parole** these were his [*o* her] exact words

testuggine [tes·'tud·dʒi·ne] *f* turtle

tetano ['tɛ:·ta·no] *m* tetanus

tetro, -a ['tɛ:t·ro] *agg* (*buio*) dark; (*lugubre*) gloomy

tetta ['tet·ta] *f fam* tit

tettarella [tet·ta·'rɛl·la] *f* **1.** (*di biberon*) teat **2.** (*succhiotto*) pacifier

tetto ['tet·to] *m* **1.** (*di edificio, vettura*) roof; **~ scorrevole** sunroof **2.** (*casa*) home; **rimanere senza ~** to be homeless **3.** (*limite massimo*) ceiling

tettoia [tet·'to:·ia] <-oie> *f* (*copertura*) canopy

tettonica [tet·'tɔ:·ni·ka] <-che> *f* GEOL tectonics

tettonico, -a [tet·'tɔ:·ni·ko] <-ci, -che> *agg* GEOL tectonic

Tevere ['te:·ve·re] *m* Tiber

TG <-> *m abbr di* **Telegiornale** TV news; **il ~ della sera** the evening news

the [tɛ] *m v.* **tè**

thermos ['tɛr·mos] <-> *m* Thermos®

thrilling ['θri·liŋ/'tril·lin(g)] **I.** <inv> *agg* (*film*) horror **II.** <-> *m* thriller

ti [ti] **I.** *pron* **2.** *pers sing* **1.** (*oggetto: te*) you; **chi ~ ha invitato?** who invited you? **2.** (*complemento: a te*) (to) you; **~ farò un bel regalo** I'll give you a lovely present **II.** *pron* **2.** *pers sing* yourself

tiara ['tia:·ra] *f* (*del Papa*) crown

tibia ['ti:·bia] <-ie> *f* tibia

tic [tik] <-> *m* (*movimento*) tic

ticchettare [tik·ket·'ta:·re] *vi* (*orologio*) to tick; (*con le dita*) to drum; (*pioggia*) to patter

ticchettio [tik·ket·'ti:·o] <-ii> *m* (*di orologio*) ticking; (*di tacchi*) clicking; (*della pioggia*) patter

ticchio ['tik·kio] <-cchi> *m* (*capriccio*) whim

Ticino [ti·'tʃi:·no] *m* Ticino

ticket ['ti·kit/'ti·ket] <-> *m* **1.** (*buono pasto*) meal ticket **2.** (*di scommesse*) betting slip **3.** (*su medicine, esami*) charge for medicine and medical examinations

tiene, tieni ['tiɛ:·ne, 'tiɛ:·ni] *3. e 2. pers sing pr di* **tenere**

tiepido, -a ['tiɛ:·pi·do] *agg* **1.** (*poco caldo*) tepid **2.** (*poco entusiastico*) lukewarm

tifare [ti·'fa:·re] *vi fam* **~ per qu** to support sb

tifo ['ti:·fo] *m* **1.** MED typhus **2.** (*per squadra, atleta*) **fare il ~ per qu** to support sb

tifone [ti·'fo:·ne] *m* typhoon

tifoso, -a [ti·'fo:·so] **I.** *agg* **1.** MED typhous **2.** SPORT **essere ~ del Milan** to be a fan of Milan **II.** *m, f* **1.** MED typhus patient **2.** SPORT fan; **~ di calcio** soccer fan

ti(g)gì [ti(d)·'dʒi] <-> *m* (*telegiornale*) TV news; **il ~ delle otto** the eight o'clock news

tight [tait] <-> *m* morning suit

tiglio ['tiʎ·ʎo] <-gli> *m* (*albero*) linden (tree)

tiglioso, -a [tiʎ·'ʎo:·so] *agg* fibrous

tigna ['tiɲ·ɲa] *f* **1.** MED ringworm **2.** (*fastidio*) nuisance

tignola [tiɲ·'nɔ:·la] *f* moth

tignosa [tiɲ·'ɲo:·sa] *f* amanita, *type of mushroom*

tignoso, -a [tiɲ·'ɲo:·so] *agg* **1.** MED suffering from ringworm **2.** *fam* (*fastidioso*) troublesome

tigrato, -a [ti·'gra:·to] *agg* striped

tigratura [ti·gra·'tu:·ra] *f* tiger stripes

tigre ['ti:·gre] *f* tiger

tilde ['til·de] <-> *m o f* tilde

tilt [tilt] <-> *m* **andare in ~** (*macchina, orologio*) to go on the blink; (*traffico*) to go crazy; (*persona*) to lose it

TIM *f abbr di* **Telecom Italia Mobile** *Italian cellphone operator*

timballo [tim·'bal·lo] *m* CULIN timbale; **~ di riso** rice timbale

timbrare [tim·'bra:·re] *vt* to stamp; **~ il cartellino** (*all'entrata*) to clock in; (*all'uscita*) to clock out

timbro ['tim·bro] *m* **1.** (*marchio, strumento*) stamp **2.** (*di suono*) timbre

time out ['taim aut] <-> *m* SPORT time out

timer ['tai·mə/'tai·mer] <-> *m* timer

timidezza [ti·mi·'det·tsa] *f* shyness

timido, -a ['ti:·mi·do] *agg* (*persona, carattere*) shy; (*gesto, tentativo*) timid

timo ['ti:·mo] *m* thyme

timone [ti·'mo:·ne] *m* **1.** NAUT, AERO rudder **2.** (*di carro*) shaft

timoniere, -a [ti·mo·'niɛ:·re] *m, f* helmsman

timorato, -a [ti·mo·'ra:·to] *agg* conscientious; **~ di Dio** God-fearing

timore [ti·'mo:·re] *m* **1.** (*paura*) fear **2.** (*preoccupazione*) concern **3.** (*rispetto*) awe; ~ **di Dio** fear of God

timoroso, -a [ti·mo·'ro:·so] *agg* (*pauroso*) fearful

timpano ['tim·pa·no] *m* **1.** ANAT eardrum; **spaccare i -i** *fam* to be ear-splitting **2.** MUS kettledrum **3.** ARCH tympanum

tinello [ti·'nɛl·lo] *m* (*stanza*) small dining room

tingere ['tin·dʒe·re] <tingo, tinsi, tinto> I. *vt* (*capelli, stoffa*) to dye II. *vr:* **-rsi 1.** (*colorarsi*) **il cielo al tramonto si tinge di rosso** the sky turns red at sunset **2.** *fig* (*sentimenti*) **-rsi di qc** to be tinged with sth

tino ['ti:·no] *m* (*per il vino*) vat

tinozza [ti·'nɔt·tsa] *f* (*per il bucato*) tub; (*da bagno*) bathtub

tinsi ['tin·si] *1. pers sing pass rem di* **tingere**

tinta ['tin·ta] *f* **1.** (*sfumatura*) color; **in ~ unita** plain-colored **2.** (*per muri*) paint; **dare una mano di ~ a qc** to give sth a coat of paint **3.** (*per capelli*) dye; **farsi la ~** to dye one's hair **4.** (*loc*) **vedere tutto a -e fosche** *fig* to take a gloomy view of things

tintarella [tin·ta·'rɛl·la] *f* (*abbronzatura*) suntan; **prendere la ~** to get a suntan

tinteggiare [tin·ted·'dʒa:·re] *vt* (*casa, parete*) to paint

tinteggiatura [tin·ted·dʒa·'tu:·ra] *f* (*di casa, pareti*) painting

tintinnare [tin·tin·'na:·re] *vi* to tinkle

tintinnio [tin·tin·'ni:·o] <-ii> *m* tinkling

tinto ['tin·to] *pp di* **tingere**

tintoria [tin·to·'ri:·a] <-ie> *f* **1.** (*fabbrica*) dyeworks **2.** (*lavanderia*) dry cleaner's

tintura [tin·'tu:·ra] *f* **1.** (*azione*) dyeing **2.** (*colorante*) dye **3.** MED tincture; ~ **di iodio** tincture of iodine

tipico, -a ['ti:·pi·ko] <-ci, -che> *agg* (*di persona, cosa*) characteristic; (*di regione*) traditional

tipizzare [ti·pid·'dza:·re] *vt* typologize

tipo ['ti:·po] *m* **1.** (*genere*) type; (**del** [*o* **sul**]) **tipo** (**di**) like; **merce di tutti i -i** all kinds of goods **2.** (*individuo*) person; **un ~ ti vuole parlare** there's someone who wants to speak to you

tipografia [ti·po·gra·'fi:·a] *f* **1.** (*procedimento*) typography **2.** (*stabilimento*) print shop

tipografico, -a [ti·po·'gra:·fi·ko] <-ci, -che> *agg* typographic

tipografo, -a [ti·'pɔ:·gra·fo] *m, f* typographer

tipologia [ti·po·lo·'dʒi:·a] <-gie> *f* typology

TIR [tir] <-> *m* tractor-trailer

tiramisù [ti·ra·mi·'su] <-> *m* tiramisu, *dessert made of sponge cake, coffee, cream cheese and eggs*

tiranneggiare [ti·ran·ned·'dʒa:·re] I. *vt* to tyrannize II. *vi* to act in a tyrannical way

tirannia [ti·ran·'ni:·a] <-ie> *f a.* POL tyranny

tirannico, -a [ti·'ran·ni·ko] <-ci, -che> *agg* tyrannical

tirannide [ti·'ran·ni·de] *f* tyranny

tiranno, -a [ti·'ran·no] *m, f* tyrant

tirare [ti·'ra:·re] I. *vt* **1.** (*carro*) to pull; (*cassetto*) to open; (*tenda*) to draw; ~ **qu per i capelli** to pull sb's hair; ~ **su qc** to pick sth up; ~ **su le maniche** to roll up one's sleeves; ~ **su i figli** *fam* to bring up one's children; **-rsi su** *fig* to cheer up; **-rsi indietro** *fig* to back out; **una parola tira l'altra** one thing you say leads to another **2.** (*fune*) to stretch; ~ **qc per le lunghe** to let sth run on **3.** *fam* (*dente*) to take out **4.** (*linea*) to trace **5.** (*lanciare*) to throw; ~ (**in porta**) to score **6.** (*sparare: colpo*) to fire **7.** (*nel ciclismo*) ~ (**il gruppo**) to be the pacemaker **8.** (*dare*) to give; ~ **un sberla a qu** to give sb a slap; ~ **calci** to kick; ~ **pugni** to punch **9.** (*stampare*) to print **10.** (*loc*) ~ **il fiato** *fig* to breathe a sigh of relief; ~ **a lucido** to polish; ~ **le somme** *fig* to take stock; ~ **a sorte** to draw out of a hat II. *vi* **1.** *gener* to pull **2.** (*vento*) to blow; **con l'aria che tira** *fig* the way things are (today) **3.** (*abito*) to be tight **4.** (*camino*) to draw **5.** (*sparare*) to shoot **6.** (*loc*) ~ **sul prezzo** to bargain; ~ **avanti** *fig, fam* to get by; ~ **diritto** to keep right on going

i The expression **tirare a campare** (to get by) expresses a certain philosophy of life that involves avoiding getting worked up or worrying about things, especially in difficult situations. The art of getting through difficulties without getting too caught up in them is found also in the political and administrative arenas.

tirata [ti·'ra:·ta] *f* **1.** (*azione*) pull; **dare una ~ d'orecchi a qu** to give sb a telling off **2.** (*di pipa, sigaretta*) drag **3.** (*viaggio*) nonstop journey; **abbiamo fatto una ~ da Milano a Napoli** we drove nonstop from Milan to Naples; **600 chilometri in una ~** 600 kilometers in one go; **in una ~** in one go **4.** (*invettiva*) tirade

tirato, -a [ti·'ra:·to] *agg* **1.** (*corda, filo*) taut **2.** (*volto*) drawn **3.** *fig* (*avaro*) cheap **4.** *fig* (*sorriso*) forced

tiratore, -trice [ti·ra·'to:·re] *m, f* **1.** (*lanciatore*) thrower **2.** (*con armi da fuoco*) shot; ~ **scelto** marksman

tiratura [ti·ra·'tu:·ra] *f* (*numero di copie*) circulation

tirchieria [tir·kie·'ri:·a] <-ie> *f fam* cheapness

tirchio, -a ['tir·kio] <-chi, -chie> *fam* I. *agg* cheap II. *m, f* skinflint

tiremmolla [ti·rem·'mɔl·la] *m* shilly-shallying; **fare a ~** to shilly-shally

tiretto [ti·'ret·to] *m* (*cassetto*) drawer

tiritera [ti·ri·'tɛ:·ra] *f pej, fam* (*discorso noioso*) drivel

tiro ['ti:·ro] *m* **1.** (*azione di tirare*) pull; ~ **alla fune** tug-of-war **2.** (*azione di sparare*) shooting; (*sparo*) shot; ~ **al piattello** skeet shooting; **~ con l'arco** archery **3.** (*azione di lanciare*) throwing; (*lancio*) throw; **essere a un ~ di schioppo** *fig* to be close by **4.** (*attacco di cavalli*) team **5.** (*azione cattiva*) **fare** [*o giocare*] **un brutto ~ a qu** to play a dirty trick on sb

tirocinante [ti·ro·tʃi·'nan·te] **I.** *agg* trainee **II.** *mf* trainee

tirocinio [ti·ro·'tʃi:·nio] <-i> *m* (*formazione professionale*) training; (*stage*) internship

tiroide [ti·'rɔ:·i·de] *f* thyroid

tirolese [ti·ro·'le:·se] **I.** *agg* Tyrolean **II.** *mf* Tyrolean

Tirolo [ti·'rɔ:·lo] *m* Tyrol

tisana [ti·'za:·na] *f* tisane

tisi ['ti:·zi] <-> *f* tuberculosis

tisico, -a ['ti:·zi·ko] <-ci, -che> **I.** *agg* MED tubercular **II.** *m, f* tuberculosis patient

titanico, -a [ti·'ta:·ni·ko] <-ci, -che> *agg* (*gigantesco*) gigantic

titanio [ti·'ta:·nio] *m* CHEM titanium

titano [ti·'ta:·no] *m* (*nella mitologia*) titan

titolare [ti·to·'la:·re] **I.** *agg* **1.** (*professore*) tenured **2.** REL titular **II.** *m* **1.** (*di cattedra*) professor **2.** (*di azienda*) owner **3.** (*di conto corrente*) account holder

titolo ['ti:·to·lo] *m* **1.** (*di libro, quadro*) title; (*di articolo*) headline; **-i di prima pagina** front page headlines; **-i di testa** opening credits; **-i di coda** closing credits **2.** (*qualifica*) qualification; **~ di studio** academic qualification **3.** SPORT title **4.** (*diritto*) right; **a ~ di prestito** as a loan; **a ~ gratuito** free; **a ~ personale** in a private capacity **5.** FIN security; **~ azionario** stock; **~ di Stato** government security; **portafoglio -i** investment portfolio **6.** (*epiteto offensivo*) name

i In formal situations, a man should be addressed as 'signor' plus the surname; for a woman use 'signora', or 'signorina' if she is very young; both of these can be used without the surname. Italians regard professional titles as very important and these are often used instead of 'signor' or 'signora.' It is therefore usual to refer to a lawyer, for example, as 'l'avvocato Rossi.' The titles dottore / dottoressa are widely used as titles for anyone who has a university degree. Other common titles are professore / professoressa for teachers, ragioniere / ragioniera, architetto and ingegnere.

titubante [ti·tu·'ban·te] *agg* hesitant

titubanza [ti·tu·'ban·tsa] *f* hesitation

titubare [ti·tu·'ba:·re] *vi* to hesitate

tizio, -a ['tit·tsio] <-zi, -zie> *m, f* guy *m*, woman *f*; **un ~ qualunque** an ordinary guy; **Tizio, Caio e Sempronio** Tom, Dick, and Harry

tizzone [tit·'tso:·ne] *m* (*di carbone*) live coal; (*di legno*) brand *lit*

to' [tɔ] *int* **1.** (*con meraviglia*) **~, guarda un po' chi si vede!** look who's here! **2.** *fam* (*dando qualcosa*) here you are; **~! eccoti i soldi!** here you are, here's your money!

toast [toust/tɔst] <-> *m* toasted sandwich

toccante [tok·'kan·te] *agg* touching

toccare [tok·'ka:·re] **I.** *vt avere* **1.** (*gener*) to touch; **~ con mano** *fig* to see for oneself; **non ~ cibo** *fig* to not touch a thing; **~** (**il fondo**) (*in acqua*) to touch the bottom **2.** *a. fig* (*tasto*) to touch; **~ un tasto dolente** to touch a sore point **3.** (*giungere*) to reach; **~ terra** to reach land; **~ la sessantina** to turn sixty **4.** (*argomento*) to touch on **5.** (*commuovere*) to touch **6.** (*riguardare*) to concern; **la cosa mi tocca da vicino** this is something that concerns me closely **II.** *vi essere* **1.** (*accadere*) **~ a qu** to happen to sb **2.** (*essere obbligato*) **guarda un po' cosa mi tocca fare!** see what I have to do!; **mi è toccato andarmene** I had to leave **3.** (*spettare*) **tocca a te dirglielo** it's your job to tell him; **ti tocca una parte dei soldi** part of the money's for you; **a chi tocca tocca** that's life **4.** (*nei giochi*) it's my/your turn

toccasana [tok·ka·'sa:·na] <-> *m a. fig* panacea

toccata [tok·'ka:·ta] *f* **1.** (*azione*) touch **2.** MUS toccata

toccato, -a [tok·'ka:·to] *agg* **1.** (*nella scherma*) touché **2.** *fam* (*matto*) **è un po'~** he's a bit loopy

tocco ['tok·ko] <-cchi> *m* **1.** (*gener*) touch **2.** (*di campane, orologio*) stroke **3.** (*pezzo: di pane, formaggio*) chunk

tocco, -a ['tok·ko] <-cchi, -cche> *agg fam* (*matto*) loopy

toeletta [toe·'lɛt·ta] *f* **1.** (*operazione*) toilette **2.** (*abbigliamento*) dress

toga ['tɔ:·ga] <-ghe> *f* **1.** HIST toga **2.** JUR gown

togato, -a [to·'ga:·to] *agg* **1.** HIST toga-wearing **2.** JUR gowned

togliere ['tɔʎ·ʎe·re] <tolgo, tolsi, tolto> **I.** *vt* **1.** (*rimuovere*) to take away; (*dente*) to take out; (*vestito, cappello*) to take off; **~ di mezzo qu** to get sb out of the way; **-rsi la vita** to kill oneself; **ciò non toglie che ...** +*conj* that doesn't alter the fact that ... **2.** *fig* (*privare di: diritto*) to withdraw; **~ il saluto a qn** to ignore sb; **~ la parola a qn** to interrupt sb **3.** *fig* (*divieto*) to remove **4.** *fig* (*liberare*) **~ qu dai guai** to rescue sb; **~ qu dall'imbarazzo** to save sb from embarrassment **II.** *vr*: **-rsi** to remove oneself; **-rsi dai piedi** *fam* to get out

tolgo ['tɔl·go] *1. pers sing pr di* **togliere**

tollerabile [tol·le·'ra:·bi·le] *agg* tolerable

tollerabilità [tol·le·ra·bi·li·'ta] <-> *f* tolerability

tollerante [tol·le·'ran·te] *agg* tolerant

tolleranza [tol·le·'ran·tsa] *f* **1.** *a.* MED tolerance; **~ zero** zero tolerance; **casa di ~** brothel **2.** (*ritardo*) margin

tollerare [tol·le·'ra:·re] *vt* **1.** (*sopportare, ammettere*) to tolerate **2.** (*reggere a: freddo,* *alcolici*) to take

tolsi ['tɔl·si] *1. pers sing pass rem di* **togliere**

tolto[1] ['tɔl·to] *pp di* **togliere**

tolto[2] *agg* (*eccettuato*) except for

tomaia [to·'ma:·ia] <-aie> *f* upper

tomba ['tom·ba] *f* tomb; **c'era un silenzio di ~** it was deathly quiet; **essere** (**muto come**) **una ~** *fig* to be the soul of discretion; **avere un piede nella ~** *fig* to have one foot in the grave

tombarolo [tom·ba·'rɔː·lo] *m sl* grave robber

tombino [tom·'biː·no] *m* manhole cover

tombola ['tom·bo·la] *f* bingo

tombolo ['tom·bo·lo] *m* 1. (*lavorazione*) bobbin lacemaking 2. (*cuscino*) bobbin lace cushion

tomo ['tɔː·mo] *m* 1. (*volume*) volume 2. *fig, fam* (*persona bizzarra*) oddball

tomografia [to·mo·gra·'fiː·a] *f* tomography; **~ assiale computerizzata** Computerized Axial Tomography

tomografo [to·'mɔ·gra·fo] *m* CT scanner

tonaca ['tɔː·na·ka] <-che> *f* (*di frate, monaca*) habit; (*di prete*) cassock

tonale [to·'naː·le] *agg* tonal

tonalità [to·na·li·'ta] <-> *f* 1. MUS tonality 2. (*di colore*) shade

tonare [to·'naː·re] *v.* **tuonare**

tondeggiante [ton·ded·'dʒa·nte] *agg* rounded

tondino [ton·'diː·no] *m* (*profilato*) reinforcing rod

tondo ['ton·do] *m* (*cerchio*) circle; **girare in ~** to go around in circles

tondo, -a *agg* round; **numero ~** round number; **chiaro e ~** straight out

toner [tɔː·ner] <-> *m* toner

tonfete ['ton·fe·te] *int* (*per terra*) thud; (*nell'acqua*) plop

tonfo ['ton·fo] *m* 1. (*rumore*) thud; (*nell'acqua*) plop 2. (*caduta*) tumble; **fare un ~** to tumble

tonico ['tɔː·ni·ko] <-ci> *m* (*ricostituente*) tonic; (*per la pelle*) toner

tonico, -a <-ci, -che> *agg* 1. (*muscolo, fisico*) toned 2. *a.* LING tonic; **acqua -a** tonic water

tonificare [to·ni·fi·'kaː·re] *vt* 1. (*muscolo, pelle*) to tone 2. (*rinvigorire*) to invigorate

tonnato, -a [ton·'naː·to] *agg* **vitello ~** *veal with tuna sauce;* **salsa -a** tuna sauce

tonnellaggio [ton·nel·'lad·dʒo] <-ggi> *m* tonnage

tonnellata [ton·nel·'laː·ta] *f* ton

tonno ['ton·no] *m* tuna; **~ sott'olio** tuna in oil

tono ['tɔː·no] *m* 1. *a.* MUS, PHYS tone; **rispondere a ~** to respond in kind; **darsi un ~** *fig* to behave properly 2. (*di colore*) shade

tonsilla [ton·'sil·la] *f* ANAT tonsil

tonsillectomia [ton·sil·lek·to·'miː·a] <-ie> *f* tonsillectomy

tonsillite [ton·sil·'liː·te] *f* tonsillitis

tonsura [ton·'suː·ra] *f* tonsure

tonto, -a ['ton·to] *agg* dumb; **fare il finto ~** to play dumb

top [tɔp] <-> *m* top

topaia [to·'paː·ia] <-aie> *f fig* dump

topazio [to·'pat·tsio] <-i> *m* topaz

topicida <-i> *m* rat poison

topless ['tɔp·lis] <-> *m* **delle ragazze in ~** topless girls

top model [tɔp 'mɔ·dl] <-> *f* supermodel

topo ['tɔː·po] *m* rat; **~ di biblioteca** *fig* bookworm; **fare la fine del ~** *fig* to be caught like a rat in a trap

topografia [to·po·gra·'fiː·a] *f* topography

topografico, -a [to·po·'gra:·fi·ko] <-ci, -che> *agg* topographical

topolino [to·po·'liː·no] *m* (*piccolo topo*) mouse; **Topolino** Mickey Mouse

toponimo [to·'pɔː·ni·mo] *m* place name

toppa ['tɔp·pa] *f* 1. (*serratura*) keyhole 2. (*rappezzo*) patch

torace [to·'raː·tʃe] *m* chest

toracico, -a [to·'ra:·tʃi·ko] <-ci, -che> *agg* chest

torba ['tor·ba] *f* peat

torbido, -a ['tor·bi·do] *agg* 1. (*acqua, vino*) cloudy 2. (*pensieri, intenzioni*) dark

torcere ['tor·tʃe·re] <torco, torsi, torto> I. *vt* 1. (*filo, corda*) to twist; (*sbarra*) to bend; **~ il collo a qu** to wring sb's neck 2. (*biancheria*) to wring 3. (*storcere*) **~ la bocca** [*o* il naso] *fig* to wrinkle one's nose, *in disgust* II. *vr:* **-rsi** 1. (*sbarra*) to bend 2. (*contorcersi*) **-rsi dalle risa** to double up laughing

torchiare [tor·'kia:·re] *vt* 1. (*spremere*) to press 2. *fig* (*a un esame*) to grill

torchio ['tor·kio] <-chi> *m* press; **mettere qu sotto** (**il**) **~** *fig* to give sb the third degree

torcia ['tor·tʃa] <-ce> *f* (*fiaccola*) torch; **~ elettrica** flashlight

torcicollo [tor·tʃi·'kɔl·lo] *m* stiff neck; **avere il ~** to have a stiff neck

tordo ['tor·do] *m* thrush

torero [to·'rɛ:·ro] *m* bullfighter

torinese[1] [to·ri·'ne:·se] I. *agg* from Turin II. *mf* (*abitante*) person from Turin

torinese[2] <sing> *m* (*dialetto*) Turin dialect

Torinese <sing> *m* Turin area; **nel ~** in the Turin area

Torino [to·'riː·no] *f* Turin, *capital of Piedmont*

tormalina [tor·ma·'liː·na] *f* tourmaline

tormenta [tor·'men·ta] *f* blizzard

tormentare [tor·men·'ta:·re] I. *vt* (*dolore, rimorso*) to torment; (*assillare*) to pester II. *vr:* **-rsi** to worry

tormento [tor·'men·to] *m* 1. *fig* (*sofferenza*) torment 2. (*dolore*) agony

tormentone [tor·men·'to:·ne] <-i> *m* 1. THEAT (*battuta*) gag 2. (*argomento*) running story; **quella canzone è stata il ~ dell'estate** that song was the soundtrack of the summer

tormentoso, -a [tor·men·'to:·so] *agg* (*dubbio, pensiero*) nagging

tornaconto [tor·na·'kon·to] *m* (*guadagno*) benefit

tornado [tor·'na:·do] <-> *m* tornado

tornante [tor·'nan·te] *m* hairpin curve

tornare [tor·'na:·re] *vi* essere 1.(*venire di nuovo*) to come back; (*andare di nuovo*) to go back; ~ **in mente a qu** to come back to sb; ~ **a fare qc** to be able to do sth again; ~ **in sé** *fig* to be back to one's old self; ~ **sull'argomento** to come back to a subject; ~ **su una decisione** to change one's mind 2.(*ridiventare*) to become again; ~ **utile** to become useful again; ~ **di moda** to become fashionable again 3.(*essere esatto, giusto*) **il conto torna** the calculation is correct; **c'è qualcosa che non mi torna** there's something not quite right here

tornasole [tor·na·'so:·le] <-> *m* sunflower

torneo [tor·'nɛ:·o] *m* tournament

tornio ['tor·nio] <-i> *m* lathe

tornire [tor·'ni:·re] <tornisco> *vt* 1.TEC to turn, *on a lathe* 2.(*frase, testo*) to polish

tornitore, -trice [tor·ni·'to:·re] *m, f* turner

torno ['tor·no] *m* **levarsi di** ~ to go away; **levarsi qu di** ~ to get rid of sb

toro ['tɔ:·ro] *m* 1.ZOO bull; **prendere il** ~ **per le corna** *fig* to take the bull by the horns 2.ASTR Toro Taurus; **sono (del [o un]) Toro** I'm (a) Taurus

torpedine [tor·'pɛ:·di·ne] *f* 1.ZOO electric ray 2.MIL torpedo

torpedone [tor·pe·'do:·ne] *m* tourist bus

torpido, -a ['tɔr·pi·do] *agg* 1.(*gamba, piede*) numb 2.(*ingegno, volontà*) sluggish

torpore [tor·'po:·re] *m* drowsiness

torre ['tɔr·re] *f* 1.tower; ~ **di controllo** control tower 2.(*negli scacchi*) castle

torrefare [tor·re·'fa:·re] <irr> *vt* to roast, *coffee*

torrefazione [tor·re·fat·'tsio:·ne] *f* 1.(*azione: di caffè*) roasting 2.(*locale*) coffee store

torreggiare [tor·red·'dʒa:·re] *vi* to tower

torrente [tor·'rɛn·te] *m* 1.(*corso d'acqua*) torrent 2.*fig* (*di lava, lacrime*) flood; **a -i** in torrents

torrenziale [tor·ren·'tsia:·le] *agg* torrential; **pioggia** ~ torrential rain

torrido, -a ['tɔr·ri·do] *agg* scorching hot

torrione [tor·'rio:·ne] *m* fortified tower, *in a castle or city walls*

torrone [tor·'ro:·ne] *m type of nougat*

torsi ['tɔr·si] *1.pers sing pass rem di* torcere

torsione [tor·'sio:·ne] *f* 1.(*gener*) twisting 2.(*in ginnastica*) twist

torso ['tor·so] *m* 1.(*gener*) torso; **a** ~ **nudo** bare-chested 2.BOT (*di frutto*) core

torsolo ['tor·so·lo] *m* (*di mela*) core

torta ['tɔr·ta] *f* (*dolce*) cake; (*salata*) savory pie

tortellini [tor·tel·'li:·ni] *mpl* tortellini, *small round pasta filled with meat or vegetables*

tortelloni [tor·tel·'lo:·ni] *mpl* tortelloni, *large round pasta filled with cheese and spinach*

tortiera [tor·'tiɛ:·ra] *f* cake pan

torto¹ ['tɔr·to] *pp di* torcere

torto² *m* 1.(*ingiustizia*) wrong; **fare un** ~ **a qu** to do sb wrong; **questa domanda fa** ~ **alla mia intelligenza** this question is an insult to my intelligence 2.(*mancanza di ragione*) **avere** ~ to be wrong; **non avere tutti i -i** to not be completely wrong; **dar** ~ **a qu** to say that sb is wrong; **a** ~ wrongly; **essere dalla parte del** ~ to be in the wrong

tortora ['tor·to·ra] I.*f* turtle dove II.*agg* **grigio** ~ dove gray

tortuoso, -a [tor·tu·'o:·so] *agg* 1.(*strada, percorso*) winding 2.(*ragionamento*) tortuous

tortura [tor·'tu:·ra] *f* 1.(*corporale*) torture 2.*fig* (*sofferenza*) torment

torturare [tor·tu·'ra:·re] I.*vt* 1.(*corporalmente*) to torture 2.(*tormentare*) to torment; **-rsi il cervello** to rack one's brains II.*vr:* **-rsi** to torment oneself

torvo, -a ['tor·vo] *agg* grim

tosacani [to·za·'ka:·ni] <-> *mf* 1.dog groomer 2.*scherz* (*barbiere non bravo*) lousy barber

tosaerba [to·za·'ɛr·ba] <-> *m o f* lawnmower

tosare [to·'za:·re] *vt* 1.(*pecore*) to shear 2.*scherz* (*capelli*) to crop 3.(*siepi*) to clip

tosatore, -trice [to·za·'to:·re] *m, f* (sheep) shearer

tosatura [to·sa·'tu:·ra] *f* 1.(*operazione*) clipping 2.*scherz* (*di capelli*) crop 3.(*lana*) shearing

Toscana [tos·'ka:·na] *f* Tuscany

toscano, -a [tos·'ka:·no] I.*agg* Tuscan II.*m, f* (*abitante*) Tuscan

tosse ['tos·se] *f* cough; ~ **canina** [o **asinina**] whooping cough

tossicchiare [tos·sik·'kia:·re] *vi* (*per schiarirsi la voce*) to clear one's throat; (*per attirare l'attenzione*) to cough a few times

tossicità [tos·si·tʃi·'ta] <-> *f* toxicity

tossico ['tɔs·si·ko] <-ci> *m* (*veleno*) poison

tossico, -a <-ci, -che> I.*agg* toxic II.*m, f sl* junkie

tossicodipendente [tos·si·ko·di·pen·'dɛn·te] *mf* drug addict

tossicodipendenza [tos·si·ko·di·pen·'dɛn·tsa] *f* drug addiction

tossicologia [tos·si·ko·lo·'dʒi:·a] <-gie> *f* toxicology

tossicologo, -a [tos·si·'kɔ:·lo·go] <-gi, -ghe> *m, f* toxicologist

tossicomane [tos·si·'kɔ:·ma·ne] I.*agg* drug addicted II.*mf* drug addict

tossicomania [tos·si·ko·ma·'ni:·a] *f* drug addiction

tossina [tos·'si:·na] *f* toxin

tossire [tos·'si:·re] <tossisco> *vi* to cough

tostacaffè [tos·ta·kaf·'fɛ] <-> *m* coffee roaster

tostapane [tos·ta·'pa:·ne] <-> *m* toaster

tostare [tos·'ta:·re] *vt* (*caffè, mandorle*) to roast; (*pane*) to toast

tostatura [tos·ta·'tu:·ra] *f* (*di caffè, mandorle*) roasting; (*di pane*) toasting

tosto, -a ['tɔs·to] *agg* 1.(*duro*) tough; **faccia -a** nerve 2.*sl* (*bello*) cool

tot [tɔt] *fam* I.<inv> *agg* so much/many II.<-> *m* so much

totale [to·'ta:·le] I.*agg* total II.*m* total

totalità [to·ta·li·'ta] <-> *f* entirety; **la** ~ **di** all;

la ~ **degli studenti** all the students

totalitario, -a [to·ta·li·'ta:·rio] <-i, -ie> *agg* (*regime, Stato*) totalitarian

totalitarismo [to·ta·li·ta·'riz·mo] *m* totalitarianism

totalizzare [to·ta·lid·'dza:·re] *vt* (*ottenere*) to score

totalizzatore [to·ta·lid·dza·'to:·re] *m* (*gioco*) totalizator

totano ['tɔ:·ta·no] *m* squid

totem ['tɔ:·tɛm] *m* totem

totip [to·'tip] *m acro di* **totalizzatore ippico,** *weekly game of betting on horse races*

totocalcio [to·to·'kal·tʃo] *m acro di* **totalizzatore calcistico,** *weekly game of betting on soccer results*

toupet [tu·'pɛ] <-> *m* (*di capelli*) toupee

tour de force ['tur də 'fɔrs] <-> *m* tour de force

tournée [tur·'ne] <-> *f* tour; **essere in** ~ to be on tour

tovaglia [to·'vaʎ·ʎa] <-glie> *f* (*per tavolo*) tablecloth

tovagliolo [to·vaʎ·'ʎɔ:·lo] *m* napkin; ~ **di carta** paper napkin

tozzo ['tɔt·tso] *m* (*di pane*) crust; **per un** ~ **di pane** *fig* (*vendere*) for a song; (*lavorare*) for a pittance

tozzo, -a *agg* (*persona, fisico*) stocky; (*edificio*) squat

Tr. *abbr di* **tratta** draft, = *titolo di credito*

tra [tra] *prep* **1.** (*fra due persone, cose*) between; (*fra più persone, cose*) among; **siediti** ~ **di noi** sit between us; **che rimanga** ~ (**di**) **noi** let's keep this between ourselves; **un colore** ~ **il blu e il verde** a color between blue and green; **arriveremo** ~ **le sette e le otto** we'll be there between seven and eight; **la pace** ~ **i popoli** peace among nations; **sono amici** ~ **loro** they are friends; **sono incerto** ~ **il pesce e la carne** I can't decide whether to have fish or meat; ~ **sé e sé** to oneself **2.** (*attraverso*) through **3.** (*partitivo*) of; ~ **l'altro** among other things **4.** (*causale*) what with; ~ **vitto e alloggio ho speso quasi tutto** with food and lodging, I've spent almost all my money **5.** (*di tempo*) in; ~ **un'ora** in an hour; ~ **poco** soon

traballare [tra·bal·'la:·re] *vi* **1.** (*tavolo, dente*) to wobble **2.** *fig* (*speranza, convinzione*) to waver

trabiccolo [tra·'bik·ko·lo] *m scherz* (*auto scassata*) jalopy

traboccare [tra·bok·'ka:·re] *vi* **1.** *essere* (*liquido*) to overflow **2.** *avere* (*recipiente*) to overflow

trabocchetto [tra·bok·'ket·to] *m* **1.** (*congegno*) trap door **2.** *fig* (*trappola*) trap; **domanda a** ~ trick question; **tendere un** ~ **a qu** to set a trap for sb

tracagnotto, -a [tra·kaɲ·'ɲɔt·to] *agg* stocky

tracannare [tra·kan·'na:·re] *vt* to gulp down

traccia ['trat·tʃa] <-cce> *f* **1.** (*gener*) trace;

essere sulle -cce di qu to be on sb's trail; **non lasciar** ~ **di sé** to vanish without a trace; **far perdere le proprie -cce** to cover one's tracks **2.** (*impronta*) track **3.** (*scia: di nave*) wake; (*di aereo*) contrail **4.** (*di libro, testo*) outline

tracciante [trat·'tʃan·te] *agg* **proiettile** ~ tracer bullet

tracciare [trat·'tʃa:·re] *vt* **1.** (*linea, quadrato*) to draw **2.** (*strade, ferrovie*) to mark out **3.** *fig* (*discorso, lettera*) to draft

tracciato [trat·'tʃa:·to] *m* **1.** (*di strada, ferrovia, percorso*) route; ~ **di gara** course **2.** (*grafico*) trace **3.** COMPUT ~ **dell'archivio** trace archive

tracciatore [trat·tʃa·'to:·re] *m* COMPUT (*di grafici*) plotter

trachea [tra·'kɛ:·a] <-chee> *f* trachea

tracheotomia [tra·ke·o·to·'mi:·a] <-ie> *f* tracheotomy

tracolla [tra·'kɔl·la] *f* shoulder strap; **borsa a** ~ shoulder bag

tracollo [tra·'kɔl·lo] *m* (*nervoso, finanziario*) collapse

tracotante [tra·ko·'tan·te] *agg* arrogant

tracotanza [tra·ko·'tan·tsa] *f* arrogance

tradimento [tra·di·'men·to] *m* **1.** (*gener*) betrayal; **alto** ~ high treason; **attacco a** ~ surprise attack **2.** (*di coniuge*) infidelity

tradire [tra·'di:·re] <tradisco> I. *vt* **1.** (*gener*) to betray **2.** (*coniuge*) to cheat on **3.** (*promessa, patto*) to break **4.** (*ingannare*) **se la memoria non mi tradisce** if my memory doesn't deceive me II. *vr:* **-rsi** to give oneself away

traditore, -trice [tra·di·'to:·re] I. *m, f* traitor II. *agg* treacherous

tradizionale [tra·dit·tsio·'na:·le] *agg* **1.** (*festa, usanza*) traditional **2.** (*abituale*) usual

tradizione [tra·dit·'tsio:·ne] *f* **1.** (*di un popolo*) tradition **2.** (*consuetudine*) custom

tradotta [tra·'dot·ta] *f* troop train

tradotto [tra·'dot·to] *pp di* **tradurre**

traducibile [tra·du·'tʃi:·bi·le] *agg* **1.** (*parola, frase*) translatable **2.** (*sentimento*) **difficilmente** ~ **in parole** hard to put into words

tradurre [tra·'dur·re] <traduco, tradussi, tradotto> *vt* **1.** (*testo*) to translate; ~ **dall'italiano in inglese** to translate from Italian into English **2.** *fig* (*sentimento*) to put into words; ~ **in parole povere** to explain in simple terms **3.** (*detenuti*) to transfer

traduttivo, -a [tra·dut·'ti:·vo] *agg* (*processo, metodo*) translation

traduttologia [tra·dut·to·lo·'dʒi:·a] *f* translation studies

traduttore, -trice [tra·dut·'to:·re] *m, f* translator; ~ **elettronico** electronic translator

traduzione [tra·dut·'tsio:·ne] *f* **1.** (*di scritto, discorso*) translation; ~ **consecutiva** consecutive translation; ~ **simultanea** simultaneous translation **2.** (*di detenuti*) transfer

traente [tra·'ɛn·te] *m* drawer, *of a check*

trafelato, -a [tra·fe·'la:·to] *agg* breathless

trafficante [traf·fi·'kan·te] *mf pej* trafficker

trafficare [traf·fi·'ka:·re] I. *vi* 1. *pej*(*smerciare*) ~ **in** [*o* **con**] qc to traffic in sth 2. (*darsi da fare*) to fiddle II. *vt pej* to traffic in

traffico ['traf·fi·ko] <-ci> *m* 1. COM trafficking; ~ **di stupefacenti** drug trafficking 2. (*movimento*) traffic; ~ **aereo** air traffic; ~ **stradale** road traffic

trafficone, -a [traf·fi·'ko:·ne] *m*, *f* wheeler-dealer

trafiggere [tra·'fid·dʒe·re] <trafiggo, trafissi, trafitto> *vt* to pierce

trafila [tra·'fi:·la] *f* (*serie di difficoltà*) procedure

trafiletto [tra·fi·'let·to] *m* short article, *in a newspaper*

trafissi [tra·'fis·si] *1. pers sing pass rem di* **trafiggere**

trafitto [tra·'fit·to] *pp di* **trafiggere**

traforare [tra·fo·'ra:·re] *vt* 1. (*trapassare*) to pierce 2. (*stoffa, cuoio, metallo*) to cut patterns in

traforo [tra·'fo:·ro] *m* 1. (*galleria*) tunnel 2. (*su stoffa, cuoio, legno*) openwork; **seghetta** [*o* **sega**] **da** ~ fret saw

trafugamento [tra·fu·ga·'men·to] *m* (*di opere d'arte*) (secret) theft; (*di cadaveri*) theft

trafugare [tra·fu·'ga:·re] *vt* to steal secretly

tragedia [tra·'dʒɛ:·dia] <-ie> *f* 1. (*gener*) tragedy 2. *fig* (*dramma*) fuss

traggo ['trag·go] *1. pers sing pr di* **trarre**

traghettare [tra·get·'ta:·re] *vt* 1. (*cose, persone*) to ferry 2. (*fiume*) to cross on a ferry

traghettatore [tra·get·ta·'to:·re] *m* ferryman

traghetto [tra·'get·to] *m* (*imbarcazione*) ferry

tragicità [tra·dʒi·tʃi·'ta] <-> *f* tragedy

tragico ['tra:·dʒi·ko] *m* (*tragicità*) tragedy

tragico, -a <-ci, -che> *agg* tragic

tragicomico, -a [tra·dʒi·'kɔ:·mi·ko] <-ci, -che> *agg* tragicomic

tragicommedia [tra·dʒi·kom·'mɛ:·dia] *f* tragicomedy

tragitto [tra·'dʒit·to] *m* (*percorso*) journey

traguardo [tra·'guar·do] *m* 1. (*in gara*) finishing line; **tagliare il** ~ to cross the finishing line 2. *fig* (*obiettivo*) goal 3. (*di arma*) sight

traiettoria [tra·iet·'tɔ:·ria] <-ie> *f* trajectory

trainare [trai·'na:·re] *vt* to pull

training ['trei·niŋ] <-> *m* training; ~ **autogeno** autogenous training

traino ['trai·no] *m* 1. (*azione: di automobile*) towing 2. (*veicolo trainato*) trailer

trait d'union ['trɛ dy·'njɔ̃] <-> *m* TYP hyphen

tralasciare [tra·laʃ·'ʃa:·re] *vt* (*omettere*) to leave out

tralcio ['tral·tʃo] <-ci> *m* (*ramo*) shoot

traliccio [tra·'lit·tʃo] <-cci> *m* 1. (*per cavi di alta tensione*) pylon 2. (*per piante*) trellis

tralice [tra·'li:·tʃe] *avv* **in** ~ sideways

tralucere [tra·'lu:·tʃe·re] <traluco *mancano i tempi composti*> *vi* to shine

tram [tram] <-> *m* streetcar

trama ['tra:·ma] *f* 1. (*di tessuto*) weft 2. *a. pej* plot

tramandare [tra·man·'da:·re] *vt* to hand down

tramare [tra·'ma:·re] *vt fig* to plot

trambusto [tram·'bus·to] *m* racket

tramezzino [tra·med·'dzi:·no] *m* (*panino*) sandwich

tramezzo [tra·'mɛd·dzo] *m* partition

tramite¹ ['tra:·mi·te] *m* (*mezzo*) means; **per il** ~ **di** by means of

tramite² *prep* by

tramontana [tra·mon·'ta:·na] *f* north wind; **a** ~ from the north; **perdere la** ~ *fig, scherz* to lose one's bearings

tramontare [tra·mon·'ta:·re] *vi essere* 1. ASTR to set 2. (*civiltà*) to decline

tramonto [tra·'mon·to] *m* 1. ASTR (*del sole*) sunset; (*di astri*) setting 2. (*di civiltà*) decline

tramortire [tra·mor·'ti:·re] <tramortisco> *vt avere* to knock out

trampolino [tram·po·'li:·no] *m* (*per tuffi*) springboard; (*per sci*) ski jump

trampolo ['tram·po·lo] *m* stilt

tramutare [tra·mu·'ta:·re] I. *vt lit* (*cambiare*) ~ **qc in qc** to change sth into sth II. *vr:* **-rsi -rsi in qc** to change into sth

tramvai [tram·'va:·i] <-> *m v.* **tram**

trancia ['tran·tʃa] <-ce> *f* 1. (*tranciatrice*) shearing machine 2. (*fetta*) slice; **salmone in -ce** salmon steaks

tranciare [tran·'tʃa:·re] *vt* (*tagliare*) to cut off; TEC to shear

tranello [tra·'nɛl·lo] *m* 1. (*inganno*) trap; **tendere un** ~ **a qu** to set a trap for sb 2. (*difficoltà*) pitfall; **domanda a** ~ trick question

trangugiare [tran·gu·'dʒa:·re] *vt* to gulp down

tranne ['tran·ne] *prep* except

tranquillante [traŋ·kuil·'lan·te] *m* tranquilizer

tranquillità [traŋ·kuil·li·'ta] <-> *f* tranquility

tranquillizzare [traŋ·kuil·lid·'dza:·re] *vt* to reassure

tranquillo, -a [traŋ·'kuil·lo] *agg* 1. (*calmo: notte, luogo, sonno*) peaceful 2. (*persona*) calm; **sta ~!** don't worry!

transalpino, -a [tran·sal·'pi:·no] *agg* (*d'oltrealpe*) transalpine; (*francese*) French

transatlantico [tran·sat·'lan·ti·ko] <-ci> *m* transatlantic liner

transatlantico, -a <-ci, -che> *agg* transatlantic

transatto [tran·'sat·to] *pp di* **transigere**

transazione [tran·sat·'tsio:·ne] *f* 1. JUR settlement 2. COM deal

transcontinentale [trans·kon·ti·nen·'ta:·le] *agg* transcontinental

transenna [tran·'sɛn·na] *f* (*barriera*) barrier

transennare [tran·zen·'na:·re] *vt* to cordon off

transessuale [tran·ses·su·'a:·le] I. *agg* transsexual II. *mf* transsexual

transetto [tran·'sɛt·to] *m* transept

transgenico [trans·'dʒɛ:·ni·ko] <-ci, -che> *agg* genetically modified; **alimento** ~ GM food

transiberiano, -a [tran·si·be·'ria:·no] *agg* trans-Siberian

transigere [tran·'si:·dʒe·re] <transigo, transigei *o* transigetti, transatto> I. *vt* JUR to settle

II. *vi* ~ (**con qc**) to compromise (with sth)

transistor [tran·'sis·tor, (tran·sis·'to:·re)] <-> *m* (*dispositivo*) transistor; (*radio*) transistor (radio)

transitabile [tran·si·'ta:·bi·le] *agg* passable

transitare [tran·si·'ta:·re] *vt essere* to pass

transitivo, -a [tran·si·'ti:·vo] *agg* transitive

transito ['tran·si·to] *m* (*passaggio*) transit; '**divieto di** ~' 'no entry'; **stazione di** ~ transit station; **treno in** ~ train that is not stopping

transitorio, -a [tran·si·'tɔ:·rio] <-i, -ie> *agg* (*non duraturo*) transitory; (*provvisorio*) temporary

transizione [tran·sit·'tsio:·ne] *f* (*passaggio*) transition

transoceanico, -a [tran·so·tʃe·'a:·ni·ko] <-ci, -che> *agg* transoceanic

tran tran, trantran [tran 'tran] <-> *m* routine; **il solito** ~ **quotidiano** the same old daily routine

tranvai [tran·'va:·i] <-> *m v.* **tram**

tranvia [tran·'vi:·a] *f* streetcar line

tranviario, -a [tran·'via:·rio] *agg* streetcar

tranviere, -a [tran·'viɛ:·re] *m, f* streetcar driver

trapanare [tra·pa·'na:·re] *vt* **1.** TEC to drill **2.** MED to trephine

trapanazione [tra·pa·nat·'tsio:·ne] *f* **1.** TEC drilling **2.** MED trephination

trapanese [tra·pa·'ne:·se] **I.** *agg* from Trapani **II.** *mf* (*abitante*) person from Trapani

Trapanese <*sing*> *m* Trapani area; **nel** ~ in the Trapani area

Trapani *f* Trapani, *town in western Sicily*

trapano ['tra:·pa·no] *m* **1.** TEC drill **2.** MED trephine

trapassare [tra·pas·'sa:·re] **I.** *vt* (*passare da parte a parte*) to go through **II.** *vi essere lit* (*morire*) to pass away

trapassato [tra·pas·'sa:·to] *m* LING ~ **prossimo** past perfect; ~ **remoto** past pluperfect

trapasso [tra·'pas·so] *m lit* (*morte*) passing

trapelare [tra·pe·'la:·re] *vi essere* **1.** (*luce*) to filter in **2.** (*verità, fatto*) to leak out

trapezio [tra·'pɛt·tsio] <-i> *m* **1.** MAT trapezium **2.** (*di circo*) trapeze

trapezista [tra·pet·'tsis·ta] <-i *m*, -e *f*> *mf* trapeze artist

trapiantare [tra·pian·'ta:·re] **I.** *vt* to transplant **II.** *vr:* -**rsi** to move

trapianto [tra·'pian·to] *m* **1.** AGR, BOT transplantation **2.** MED transplant; ~ **renale/cardiaco** kidney/heart transplant

trapiantologico, -a [tra·pian·to·'lɔ:·dʒi·ko] *agg* transplant

trappola ['trap·po·la] *f* **1.** trap; ~ **per topi** mouse trap; **cadere in** ~ *fig* to fall into a trap; **tendere una** ~ **a qu** *fig* to set a trap for sb **2.** *fam* (*arnese malfunzionante*) wreck

trapunta [tra·'pun·ta] *f* quilt

trarre ['trar·re] <**traggo, trassi, tratto**> **I.** *vt* **1.** (*ricavare: guadagno, beneficio*) to obtain **2.** (*portare*) to bring; ~ **in inganno** to deceive;

~ **in salvo** to rescue **3.** (*derivare*) to derive; ~ **origine da** to derive from; ~ **le conseguenze** to draw the consequences; ~ **le conclusioni** to draw conclusions **II.** *vr:* -**rsi** -**rsi d'impaccio** (*togliersi*) to extricate oneself; -**rsi in salvo** (*salvarsi*) to reach safety

trasalire [tra·sa·'li:·re] <**trasalisco**> *vi essere o avere* to jump

trasandato, -a [tra·zan·'da:·to] *agg* (*sciatto*) scruffy

trasbordare [traz·bor·'da:·re] **I.** *vt* **1.** (*merci, persone*) to transfer **2.** NAUT to transship **II.** *vi* to transfer; NAUT to change ship

trasbordo [traz·'bor·do] *m* **1.** (*di merci, persone*) transfer **2.** NAUT transshipment

trascendentale [traʃ·ʃe·den·'ta:·le] *agg* **1.** PHILOS transcendental **2.** *fig* (*complicato*) difficult; **non è una cosa** ~ it's not difficult

trascendente [traʃ·ʃen·'dɛn·te] *agg* transcendental

trascendenza [traʃ·ʃen·'dɛn·tsa] *f* transcendence

trascendere [traʃ·'ʃen·de·re] <irr> *vi* (*eccedere*) to go beyond

trascinare [traʃ·ʃi·'na:·re] **I.** *vt* **1.** (*tirare*) to drag **2.** *fig* (*oratore, entusiasmo*) to enthuse **II.** *vr:* -**rsi** **1.** (*persona*) to drag oneself **2.** (*faccenda, questione*) to drag on

trascorrere [tras·'kor·re·re] <irr> **I.** *vt avere* (*vacanze, giornata*) to spend **II.** *vi essere* (*tempo*) to pass

trascorso [tras·'kor·so] **I.** *pp di* **trascorrere II.** *m* past; **un tipo dai -i dubbi** someone with a dubious past

trascrivere [tras·'kri:·ve·re] <irr> *vt* **1.** (*copiare*) to copy down; (*su registro*) to set down **2.** LING, MUS to transcribe

trascrizione [tras·krit·'tsio:·ne] *f* **1.** (*copiatura*) copying down; (*su registro*) setting down **2.** LING, MUS transcription; ~ **fonetica** phonetic transcription

trascurabile [tras·ku·'ra:·bi·le] *agg* negligible

trascurare [tras·ku·'ra:·re] **I.** *vt* **1.** (*non curare*) to neglect **2.** (*non tener conto di*) to ignore **3.** (*omettere*) ~ **di fare qc** to omit to do sth **II.** *vr:* -**rsi** to neglect oneself

trascuratezza [tras·ku·ra·'tet·tsa] *f* carelessness

trasecolare [tra·se·ko·'la:·re] *vi essere o avere* to be dumbfounded

trasferibile [tras·fe·'ri:·bi·le] *agg* transferable

trasferimento [tras·fe·ri·'men·to] *m* **1.** (*gener*) transfer **2.** (*di cosa*) transport

trasferire [tras·fe·'ri:·re] <**trasferisco**> **I.** *vt* **1.** (*gener*) to transfer **2.** (*cosa*) to transport **II.** *vr:* -**rsi** to move

trasferta [tras·'fɛr·ta] *f* **1.** DI IMPIEGATO temporary transfer **2.** SPORT away game; **giocare in** ~ to play away (from home)

trasfigurare [tras·fi·gu·'ra:·re] *vt* **1.** (*viso, persona*) to transfigure **2.** (*fatto*) to transform

trasformabile [tras·for·'ma:·bi·le] *agg* convertible

trasformare [tras·for·'ma:·re] I. *vt* 1.(*cambiare*) to transform 2. SPORT (*rigore, meta*) to convert II. *vr:* -**rsi** to change

trasformatore [tras·for·ma·'to:·re] *m* transformer

trasformazione [tras·for·mat·'tsio:·ne] *f* 1.(*gener*) transformation 2.(*nel rugby*) conversion

trasfusione [tras·fu·'zio:·ne] *f* transfusion

trasgredire [traz·gre·'di:·re] <trasgredisco> I. *vt* (*legge*) to break; (*ordini*) to disobey II. *vi* ~ **a qc** (*legge*) to break sth; (*ordini*) to disobey sth

trasgreditrice *f v.* **trasgressore**

trasgressione [traz·gres·'sio:·ne] *f* 1.(*violazione*) infringement 2.(*anticonformismo*) transgression

trasgressore, -greditrice [traz·gres·'so:·re, traz·gre·di·'tri:·tʃe] *m, f* transgressor

traslato [traz·'la:·to] *m* metaphor

traslato, -a *agg* (*senso*) figurative

traslazione [traz·lat·'tsio:·ne] *f* 1. JUR transfer 2. PHYS, GEOL translation

traslocare [traz·lo·'ka:·re] I. *vt* to move II. *vi* to move

trasloco [traz·'lɔ:·ko] <-chi> *m* move

traslucido, -a [traz·'lu:·tʃi·do] *agg* translucent

trasmesso *pp di* **trasmettere**

trasmettere [traz·'met·te·re] <irr> I. *vt* 1.(*diritto, malattia, notizia*) to pass on; (*eredità*) to hand down 2.(*ordine*) to give; (*lettera, dati*) to send 3. RADIO, TV to broadcast II. *vi* to broadcast III. *vr:* -**rsi** 1.(*eredità*) to be handed down 2.(*malattia, virus*) to be spread

trasmettitore [traz·met·ti·'to:·re] *m* transmitter

trasmisi *1. pers sing pass rem di* **trasmettere**

trasmissibile [traz·mis·'si:·bi·le] *agg* 1.(*eredità*) inheritable 2.(*malattia*) transmissible

trasmissione [traz·mis·'sio:·ne] *f* 1.(*gener*) transmission; ~ **dati** COMPUT data transmission 2.(*di beni, tradizione*) handing down 3. RADIO, TV (*programma*) broadcast

trasmittente [traz·mit·'tɛn·te] *f* 1.(*stazione*) station 2.(*apparecchio*) transmitter

trasognato, -a [tra·son·'ɲa:·to] *agg* dreamy

traspaio [tras·'pa:·io] *1. pers sing pr di* **trasparire**

trasparente [tras·pa·'rɛn·te] *agg* transparent

trasparenza [tras·pa·'rɛn·tsa] *f* transparency

trasparire [tras·pa·'ri:·re] <traspaio *o* trasparisco, trasparii *o* trasparsi, trasparso *o* trasparito> *vi essere* 1.(*intravedersi*) to be visible 2.(*rivelarsi*) to show; **lasciar** ~ to reveal

traspirare [tras·pi·'ra:·re] *vi essere* 1.(*sudore*) to perspire 2.(*liquido*) to transpire

traspirazione [tras·pi·rat·'tsio:·ne] *f* perspiration

trasporre [tras·'por·re] <irr> *vt a.* MUS to transpose

trasportabile [tras·por·'ta:·bi·le] *agg* transportable

trasportare [tras·por·'ta:·re] *vt* 1.(*merce, passeggeri*) to transport 2. *fig* **lasciarsi** ~ (*da impulso*) to let oneself be carried away

trasportatore [tras·por·ta·'to:·re] *m* 1.(*azienda, operaio*) hauler 2. TEC conveyor; ~ **a nastro** conveyor belt

trasporto [tras·'pɔr·to] *m* 1.(*di merce, passeggeri*) transportation; **mezzi di** ~ means of transportation; **-i pubblici** public transportation 2. *fig* (*impeto*) passion

trasposi *1. pers sing pass rem di* **trasporre**

trasposizione [tras·po·zit·'tsio:·ne] *f* transposition

trasposto *pp di* **trasporre**

trassi ['tras·si] *1. pers sing pass rem di* **trarre**

trastullare [tras·tul·'la:·re] I. *vt* (*divertire*) to amuse II. *vr:* -**rsi** 1.(*divertirsi*) to enjoy oneself 2.(*perdere tempo*) to waste time

trastullo [tras·'tul·lo] *m* (*divertimento*) pastime

trasudare [tra·su·'da:·re] I. *vi essere* (*fuoriuscire*) to ooze out II. *vt avere* (*mandar fuori*) ~ **qc** to ooze with sth

trasversale [traz·ver·'sa:·le] I. *agg* cross; MAT transverse; **via** ~ side street II. *f* side street

tratta ['trat·ta] *f* 1. COM (*cambiale*) draft 2.(*di persone*) trade

trattabile [trat·'ta:·bi·le] *agg* 1.(*prezzo*) negotiable; **due mila euro -i** offers in the neighborhood of 2000 euros 2. *fig* (*persona*) reasonable

trattamento [trat·ta·'men·to] *m* 1.(*gener*) treatment 2.(*retribuzione*) payment; ~ **di fine rapporto** JUR severance pay 3. COMPUT processing; ~ **automatico delle informazioni** automatic information processing

trattare [trat·'ta:·re] I. *vt* 1.(*gener*) to treat 2.(*argomento, pratica*) to deal with 3.(*affare, compravendita*) to negotiate 4. COM (*articoli*) to sell II. *vi* 1.(*avere per argomento*) ~ **di qc** to be about sth 2.(*avere a che fare*) ~ **con qu** to deal with sb 3.(*impersonale*) **dimmi pure di cosa si tratta** tell me what's the matter; **deve** -**rsi di un errore** there must be some mistake III. *vr* to treat oneself

trattativa [trat·ta·'ti:·va] *f* negotiation; **essere in** -**e** to be in negotiation

trattato [trat·'ta:·to] *m* 1.(*opera*) treatise 2. POL (*accordo*) treaty; **Trattato di Maastricht** Maastricht Treaty

trattato, -a [trat·'ta:·to] *agg* (*materiale*) treated; (*alimento*) processed; **frutta non trattata** fruit that has not been treated with pesticides

tratteggiare [trat·ted·'dʒa:·re] *vt* 1.(*disegnare*) ~ **una linea** to draw a dotted line 2. *fig* (*descrivere*) to sketch

tratteggio [trat·'ted·dʒo] <-ggi> *m* hatching

trattenere [trat·te·'ne:·re] <irr> I. *vt* 1.(*far rimanere: in ospedale*) to keep; (*in questura*) to detain; **non ti voglio** ~ I don't want to keep you; **siamo stati trattenuti in ufficio** we were delayed at the office; ~ **qu in caserma** to confine sb to barracks 2.(*non dare*) to with-

T

hold **3.**(*detrarre: somma*) to deduct **4.**(*riso, pianto*) to keep back; (~ *il fiato*) to hold one's breath **5.**(*impedire*) ~ **qu** (**dal fare qc**) to prevent sb (from doing sth) **II.** *vr:* -**rsi 1.**(*astenersi*) to help oneself **2.**(*fermarsi*) to stay

trattenimento [trat·te·ni·'men·to] *m* (*ricevimento*) party

trattenuta [trat·te·'nu:·ta] *f* (*sullo stipendio*) deduction

trattino [trat·'ti:·no] *m* (*in parole composte*) hyphen; (*tra parole*) dash

tratto ['trat·to] **I.** *pp di* **trarre II.** *m* **1.**(*di penna, pennello*) stroke **2.**(*di strada, cielo*) stretch **3.**(*di tempo*) period; **ti sento a -i** your voice keeps disappearing; **tutto ad un ~** suddenly **4.** *pl* (*lineamenti*) features; (*caratteristiche*) characteristics

trattore [trat·'to:·re] *m* tractor

trattoria [trat·to·'ri:·a] <-ie> *f* trattoria, *small restaurant serving simple food*

trauma ['tra:u·ma] <-i> *m* trauma

traumatico, -a [trau·'ma:·ti·ko] <-ci, -che> *agg* traumatic

traumatizzare [trau·ma·tid·'dza:·re] *vt* to traumatize

travaglio [tra·'vaʎ·ʎo] <-gli> *m* **1.**(*sofferenza*) anguish **2.**(*del parto*) labor pains *pl*

travasare [tra·va·'za:·re] *vt* (*vino*) to decant

travaso [tra·'va:·zo] *m* **1.**(*di vino*) decanting **2.** MED extravasation

travatura [tra·va·'tu:·ra] *f* beams *pl*

trave ['tra:·ve] *f* beam

traveggole [tra·'veg·go·le] *fpl* **avere le ~** *fam* to be seeing things

traversa [tra·'vɛr·sa] *f* **1.** TEC, ARCH crossbeam **2.**(*via*) side road **3.**(*di binario*) railroad tie **4.**(*nel calcio*) crossbar

traversare [tra·ver·'sa:·re] *vt* to cross

traversata [tra·ver·'sa:·ta] *f* crossing

traversie [tra·ver·'si:·e] *f pl, fig* (*disavventure*) mishaps

traversina [tra·ver·'si:·na] *f* (*di binario*) railroad tie

traverso [tra·'vɛr·so] *m* width; **di ~** (*obliquamente*) sideways; **la bevanda gli è andata di ~** his drink went down the wrong pipe; **guardare di ~ qu** to give sb a dirty look; **prendere qc di ~** to take sth the wrong way

traverso, -a *agg* cross; **per vie -e** *fig* in a roundabout way

travertino [tra·ver·'ti:·no] *m* travertine

travestimento [tra·ves·ti·'men·to] *m* **1.**(*azione*) dressing up **2.**(*costume*) costume

travestire [tra·ves·'ti:·re] **I.** *vt* ~ **qu da qc** to dress sb up as sth **II.** *vr* -**rsi da** to dress up as

travestito [tra·ves·'ti:·to] *m* transvestite

traviare [tra·vi·'a:·re] **I.** *vt* to lead astray **II.** *vr:* -**rsi** to be led astray

travisare [tra·vi·'za:·re] *vt* (*distorcere*) to distort

travolgente [tra·vol·'dʒen·te] *agg* (*coinvolgente: entusiasmo*) overwhelming

travolgere [tra·'vɔl·dʒe·re] <irr> *vt* **1.**(*trasci-*

nare via) to sweep away; (*con veicolo*) to run over **2.** *fig* (*sentimento*) to overwhelm

trazione [trat·'tsio:·ne] *f* **1.**(*gener*) traction **2.** AUTO drive; ~ **anteriore** front-wheel drive; ~ **posteriore** rear-wheel drive; ~ **integrale** four-wheel drive

tre [tre] **I.** *num* three; **chi fa da sé, fa per ~** *prov* if you want something done, you have to do it yourself **II.** <-> *m* **1.**(*numero*) three **2.**(*nelle date*) third **3.**(*voto scolastico*) =F, *very low grade* **III.** *fpl* (*ore*) three o'clock; *v.a.* **cinque**

trebbia ['treb·bia] <-ie> *f* **1.**(*trebbiatrice*) threshing machine **2.**(*trebbiatura*) threshing

trebbiare [treb·'bia:·re] *vt* to thresh

trebbiatrice [treb·bia·'tri·tʃe] *f* threshing machine

treccia ['tret·tʃa] <-cce> *f* braid

trecentesco, -a [tre·tʃen·'tes·ko] <-schi, -sche> *agg* fourteenth-century

trecentista [tre·tʃen·'tis·ta] <-i *m*, -e *f*> *mf* **1.**(*artista*) fourteenth-century artist/writer **2.**(*studioso*) *scholar who specializes in the fourteenth century*

trecento [tre·'tʃɛn·to] **I.** *num* three hundred **II.** *m* three hundred; **il Trecento** the fourteenth century

tredicenne [tre·di·'tʃɛn·ne] **I.** *agg* thirteen-year-old **II.** *mf* thirteen year old

tredicesima [tre·di·'tʃɛ:·zi·ma] *f* (*retribuzione*) thirteenth month, *extra money paid to employees as a Christmas bonus*

tredicesimo [tre·di·'tʃɛ:·zi·mo] *m* (*frazione*) thirteenth

tredicesimo, -a **I.** *agg* thirteenth **II.** *m, f* thirteenth; *v.a.* **quinto**

tredici ['tre:·di·tʃi] **I.** *num* thirteen **II.** <-> *m* **1.**(*numero*) thirteen; **fare** (**un**) ~ **al totocalcio** to hit the jackpot, *on the soccer pools, by guessing 13 results correctly* **2.**(*nelle date*) thirteenth **III.** *fpl* (*ore*) 1 pm; *v.a.* **cinque**

tregua ['tre:·gua] *f* **1.**(*gener*) truce **2.**(*sosta*) rest; **senza ~** nonstop

trekking ['trɛ·kiŋ] <-> *m* trekking; **fare ~** to go trekking

tremare [tre·'ma:·re] *vi* **1.**(*fiamma, terra*) to shake **2.**(*persona, voce*) to tremble; ~ **di freddo/per la rabbia** to tremble with cold/rage; ~ **per qu** *fig* to fear for sb

tremarella [tre·ma·'rɛl·la] *f* **1.**(*tremito*) trembling **2.** *fam* (*paura*) shivers *pl;* **avere la ~** to have the shivers

tremendo, -a [tre·'mɛn·do] *agg* (*spaventoso*) terrible; **faceva un freddo ~** it was terribly cold

trementina [tre·men·'ti:·na] *f* turpentine

tremila [tre·'mi:·la] **I.** *num* three thousand **II.** <-> *m* three thousand

tremito ['trɛ:·mi·to] *m* trembling

tremolare [tre·mo·'la:·re] *vi* (*gelatina*) to shake; (*foglie*) to tremble; (*suono*) to waver; (*luce, fiamma*) to flicker

tremolio [tre·mo·'li:·o] <-ii> *m* (*di mani,*

gambe, voce) shaking; (*di luce*) flickering
tremore [tre·'mo:·re] *m* MED tremor
tremulo, -a ['trɛ:·mu·lo] *agg* (*voce*) tremulous; (*luce*) flickering
trenette [tre·'net·te] *fpl long flat pasta*
treno ['trɛ:·no] *m* train; ~ **ad alta velocità** high-speed train; ~ **interregionale** long-distance train; ~ **locale** local train; ~ **rapido** express train; ~ **diretto** through train; ~ **merci** goods train; **prendere il** ~ to catch the train; **perdere il** ~ to miss the train; **il** ~ **per Venezia** the train to Venice

> **i** There are various types of **trains** in Italy. Local train services are provided either by *Locali*, which stop at almost every station, *Interregionali*, which link places in different regions, often tourist centers – these may run only on weekends or at certain times of the year – or *Diretti*, which travel both within and between regions and are generally faster than *Locali*. Express trains can be either *Intercity*, linking almost all Italian cities, or *Eurostar*, which serve only the most important cities. Travel on both these types of trains is subject to payment of a supplemental fare.

trenta ['tren·ta] I. *num* thirty II. <-> *m* 1. (*numero*) thirty 2. (*nelle date*) thirtieth; *v.a.* **cinquanta**
trentennale [tren·ten·'na:·le] I. *agg* 1. (*che dura 30 anni*) thirty-year 2. (*che ricorre ogni 30 anni*) happening every thirty years II. *m* (*ricorrenza*) thirtieth anniversary
trentenne [tren·'tɛn·ne] I. *agg* thirty-year-old II. *mf* thirty year old
trentennio [tren·'tɛn·nio] <-i> *m* thirty year period
trentesimo [tren·'tɛ:·zi·mo] *m* thirtieth
trentesimo, -a I. *agg* thirtieth II. *m, f* thirtieth; *v.a.* **quinto**
trentina [tren·'ti:·na] *f* **una** ~ (**di ...**) about thirty; **essere sulla** ~ to be about thirty
Trentino <*sing*> *m* 1. (*territorio intorno a Trento*) Trento area 2. (*regione*) Trentino; ~-**Alto Adige** Trentino-Alto Adige, *region in the north of Italy*
trentino, -a I. *agg* 1. (*di Trento*) from Trento 2. (*del Trentino*) from Trentino II. *m, f* 1. (*di Trento*) person from Trento 2. (*del Trentino*) person from Trentino
Trento ['trɛn·to] *f* Trento, *capital of Trentino-Alto Adige region*
trepidante [tre·pi·'dan·te] *agg* anxious
trepidare [tre·pi·'da:·re] *vi* ~ **per qu** to be anxious about sb
trepidazione [tre·pi·dat·'tsio:·ne] *f* anxiety
treppiede, treppiedi [trep·'piɛ:·de, trep·'piɛ:·di] <-> *m* (*cavalletto*) trivet; (*per cinepresa, macchina fotografica*) tripod
trequarti [tre·'kuar·ti] <-> *m* (*cappotto*)

three-quarter length coat; (*giacca*) three-quarter length jacket
tresca ['tres·ka] <-sche> *f* 1. (*intrigo*) plot 2. (*relazione*) affair
trespolo ['tres·po·lo] *m* 1. (*gener*) stand 2. *fig, scherz* (*catorcio*) piece of junk
tressette [tres·'sɛt·te] <-> *m Italian card game played with a deck of forty cards*
Trevigiano <*sing*> *m* Treviso area; **nel** ~ in the Treviso area
trevigiano, -a [tre·vi·'dʒia:·no] I. *agg* from Treviso II. *m, f* (*abitante*) person from Treviso
Treviso *f* Treviso, *town in north-eastern Italy*
triade ['tri:·a·de] *f* (*tre persone*) trio; MUS triad
triangolare [tri·aŋ·go·'la:·re] *agg* triangular
triangolo [tri·'aŋ·go·lo] *m* 1. (*poligono, forma*) triangle; ~ (**d'emergenza**) AUTO warning triangle; ~ **industriale** industrial triangle, *area between Milan, Turin and Genoa* 2. (*rapporto a tre*) love triangle
tribolare [tri·bo·'la:·re] *vi* (*patire*) to suffer
tribolato, -a [tri·bo·'la:·to] *agg* full of troubles
tribolazione [tri·bo·lat·'tsio:·ne] *f* (*patimento*) suffering
tribordo [tri·'bor·do] *m lit* starboard
tribù [tri·'bu] <-> *f a. scherz* tribe
tribuna [tri·'bu:·na] *f* 1. (*podio*) platform 2. (*negli stadi*) stand 3. (*trasmissione*) ~ **politica/elettorale** paid political/election broadcast
tribunale [tri·bu·'na:·le] *m* court; ~ **arbitrale** tribunal; ~ **internazionale** International Court of Justice; ~ **supremo** Supreme Court; **presentarsi in** ~ to appear in court
tribuno [tri·'bu:·no] *m* tribune
tributare [tri·bu·'ta:·re] *vt* to bestow
tributario, -a [tri·bu·'ta:·rio] <-i, -ie> *agg* 1. (*delle tasse*) tax; **riforma -a** tax reform 2. **fiume** ~ tributary
tributo [tri·'bu:·to] *m* 1. FIN tax 2. *fig* (*prezzo*) price
tricheco [tri·'kɛ:·ko] <-chi> *m* walrus
triciclo [tri·'tʃi:·k·lo] *m* (*per bambini*) tricycle
tricipite [tri·'tʃi:·pi·te] *agg* triceps
tricolore [tri·ko·'lo:·re] I. *agg* three-color II. *m* tricolor, *especially the Italian flag*
tricorno [tri·'kor·no] *m* three-cornered hat
tridente [tri·'dɛn·te] *m* trident
tridimensionale [tri·di·men·sio·'na:·le] *agg* three-dimensional
trielina [trie·'li:·na] *f* trichloroethylene
triennale [tri·en·'na:·le] I. *agg* 1. (*che dura tre anni*) three-year 2. (*che ricorre ogni tre anni*) triennial II. *f* (*manifestazione*) Triennale
triennio [tri·'ɛn·nio] <-i> *m* three-year period
Trieste [tri·'ɛs·te] *f* Trieste, *capital of Friuli region*
Triestino <*sing*> *m* Trieste area; **nel** ~ in the Trieste area
triestino [tri·es·'ti:·no] <*sing*> *m* (*dialetto*) Triestine dialect
triestino, -a I. *agg* from Trieste II. *m, f* (*abitante*) person from Trieste

T

trifase [tri·'fa:·ze] *agg* three-phase

trifoglio [tri·'fɔʎ·ʎo] *m* clover

trifolato, -a [tri·fo·'la:·to] *agg* cut up and cooked in oil, garlic and parsley

trifora ['tri:·fo·ra] *f* (*finestra*) window divided into three parts

trigemino [tri·'dʒɛ:·mi·no] *m* ANAT trigeminal

trigemino, -a *agg* **parto** ~ giving birth to triplets

triglia ['triʎ·ʎa] <-glie> *f* mullet

trigonometria [tri·go·no·me·'tri:·a] <-ie> *f* trigonometry

trilaterale [tri·la·te·'ra:·le] *agg* trilateral

trilingue [tri·'liŋ·gue] <-> *agg* trilingual

trilione [tri·'lio:·ne] *m* (*mille miliardi*) trillion

trillare [tril·'la:·re] *vi* (*campanello*) to ring; **allodola** to trill

trillo ['tril·lo] *m* (*di usignolo*) trill; (*di campanello*) ring

trilobato, -a [tri·lo·'ba:·to] *agg* **1.** (*foglia*) trilobate **2.** (*arco*) trefoil

trilocale [tri·lo·'ka:·le] **I.** *m* three-roomed apartment; **affittasi** ~ three-roomed apartment to rent **II.** *agg* three-roomed

trilogia [tri·lo·'dʒi:·a] <-gie> *f* trilogy

trimestrale [tri·mes·'tra:·le] *agg* **1.** (*che dura tre mesi*) three-month **2.** (*ogni tre mesi*) three-monthly

trimestre [tri·'mɛs·tre] *m* three-month period; UNIV term

trimotore [tri·mo·'to:·re] **I.** *agg* three-engined **II.** *m* three-engined airplane

trina ['tri:·na] *f* (*pizzo*) lave

trincare [triŋ·'ka:·re] *vt fam* **1.** (*vino, birra*) to knock back **2.** (*bere molto*) to booze

trincea [trin·'tʃɛ:·a] <-cee> *f* MIL trench

trincerare [trin·tʃe·'ra:·re] **I.** *vt* to dig trenches in **II.** *vr:* **-rsi 1.** MIL to dig oneself in **2.** *fig* (*nascondersi*) to hide; **-rsi nel silenzio** to take refuge in silence

trincetto [trin·'tʃet·to] *m* cobbler's knife

trinciapolli [trin·tʃa·'pol·li] <-> *m* poultry shears *pl*

trinciare [trin·'tʃa:·re] *vt* **1.** (*tagliare: lamiera*) to cut up **2.** CULIN to carve

trinciato [trin·'tʃa:·to] *m* (*tabacco*) loose-cut tobacco

trinciato, -a *agg* (*tagliato*) cut (up)

trinciatura [trin·tʃa·'tu:·ra] *f* **1.** (*operazione*) cutting up **2.** (*frammenti*) offcuts *pl*

trinità [tri·ni·'ta] <-> *f* REL trinity

trio ['tri:·o] <-ii> *m* **1.** MUS trio **2.** (*tre persone*) threesome

trionfale [tri·on·'fa:·le] *agg* triumphal

trionfante [tri·on·'fan·te] *agg* triumphant

trionfare [tri·on·'fa:·re] *vi* **1.** (*vincere*) to win **2.** (*prevalere*) to triumph

trionfatore [tri·on·fa·'to:·re] *m* victor

trionfo [tri·'on·fo] *m* **1.** (*vittoria*) victory **2.** (*successo*) triumph

tripartire [tri·par·'ti:·re] <tripartisco> *vt* to divide into three parts

tripartitico, -a [tri·par·'ti:·ti·ko] <-ci, -che>

agg tripartite

tripartito [tri·par·'ti:·to] *m* (*governo*) three-party government

tripartito, -a *agg* **governo** ~ three-party government

triplicare [tri·pli·'ka:·re] *vt* to triple

triplice ['tri:·pli·tʃe] *agg* triple

triplo ['tri:·plo] *m* **il** ~ (**di**) three times as much (as)

triplo, -a *agg* triple

trippa ['trip·pa] *f* **1.** CULIN tripe **2.** *scherz, fam* (*pancia*) paunch

tripudio [tri·'pu:·dio] <-i> *m* rejoicing

trisavolo, -a [tri·'za:·vo·lo] *m*, *f* great-great-grandfather *m*, great-great-grandmother *f*

triste ['tris·te] *agg* sad

tristezza [tris·'tet·tsa] *f* sadness

tritacarne [tri·ta·'kar·ne] <-> *m* grinder

tritaprezzemolo [tri·ta·pret·'tse:·mo·lo] <-> *m* parsley mill

tritare [tri·'ta:·re] *vt* (*carne*) to grind; (*verdura, cipolla, prezzemolo*) to chop finely

tritarifiuti [tri·ta·ri·'fiu:·ti] <-> *m* garbage disposal unit

tritatura [tri·ta·'tu:·ra] *f* (*di carne*) grinding; (*di verdure*) chopping

tritatutto [tri·ta·'tut·to] <-> *m* (*elettrico*) grinder

trito, -a ['tri:·to] *agg* **1.** CULIN (*carne*) ground; (*cipolla*) chopped **2.** (*argomento*) ~ (**e ritrito**) tired

trittico ['trit·ti·ko] <-ci> *m* **1.** ARTE triptych **2.** LIT trilogy

triturare [tri·tu·'ra:·re] *vt* to grind

triumvirato, triunvirato [tri·un·vi··'ra:·to] *m* triumvirate

triumviro, triunviro [tri·'un·vi·ro] *m* triumvir

trivella [tri·'vɛl·la] *f* (*sonda*) drill

trivellare [tri·vel·'la:·re] *vt* (*terreno, roccia*) to drill

trivellazione [tri·vel·lat·'tsio:·ne] *f* to drill; **torre di** ~ derrick

triviale [tri·'via:·le] *agg* vulgar

trivialità [tri·via·li·'ta] <-> *f* vulgarity

trofeo [tro·'fɛ:·o] *m* trophy

troglodita [tro·glo·'di:·ta] <-i *m*, -e *f*> *mf* **1.** (*uomo preistorico*) caveman **2.** *fig* (*persona rozza*) barbarian

troia ['trɔ:·ia] <-ie> *f* **1.** ZOO sow **2.** *fig, vulg* whore

tromba ['trom·ba] *f* **1.** MUS trumpet **2.** (*di auto*) horn **3.** METEO ~ **marina** waterspout; ~ **d'aria** whirlwind **4.** (*passaggio*) ~ **delle scale** stairwell **5.** ANAT ~ **di Eustachio** eustachian tube; ~ **di Fallopio** fallopian tube

trombare [trom·'ba:·re] *vt* **1.** *scherz* (*bocciare*) to fail **2.** *vulg* to screw

trombettiere [trom·bet·'tiɛ:·re] *m* MIL bugler

trombettista [trom·bet·'tis·ta] <-i *m*, -e *f*> *mf* trumpeter

trombone [trom·'bo:·ne] *m* **1.** MUS trombone **2.** *fig, pej* windbag

trombosi [trom·'bo:·zi] <-> *f* thrombosis

troncamento [troŋ·ka·'men·to] *m* **1.** (*interruzione*) cutting off **2.** LING apocope

troncare [tron·'ka:·re] *vt* **1.** (*tagliare*) to cut off **2.** *fig* (*interrompere*) to break off **3.** LING to apocopate **4.** (*stancare*) ~ **le gambe** to do sb in

tronco ['troŋ·ko] <-chi> *m* **1.** BOT, ANAT trunk **2.** (*tratto: di strada, ferrovia*) stretch **3.** MATH ~ **di cono/piramide** truncated cone/pyramid

tronco, -a <-chi, -che> *agg* **1.** (*tagliato*) cut off **2.** LING apocopated **3.** *loc* **essere licenziato in** ~ to be fired on the spot

troneggiare [tro·ned·'dʒa:·re] *vi* to dominate

tronfio, -a ['tron·fio] <-i, -ie> *agg* **1.** (*borioso: persona*) conceited **2.** (*parole*) pompous

trono ['trɔ:·no] *m* throne; **successione al** ~ succession to the throne

tropicale [tro·pi·'ka:·le] *agg* tropical

tropico ['trɔ:·pi·ko] <-ci> *m* tropic; **i -i** the tropics; **Tropico del Cancro** Tropic of Cancer; **Tropico del Capricorno** Tropic of Capricorn

troppo ['trɔp·po] **I.** *m* too much; **il ~ stroppia** *prov* enough is as good as a feast **II.** *avv* too much; **ho mangiato** ~ I've eaten too much; **non** ~ (*poco*) not much; **di** ~ too much; **essere/sentirsi di** ~ (*inopportuno*) to be/feel in the way

troppo, -a I. *agg* (*in quantità eccessiva*) too much; (*in numero eccessivo*) too many; **troppo lavoro** too much work; **troppe cose** too many things **II.** *pron* (*in quantità eccessiva*) too much; (*in numero eccessivo*) too many; **questo è** ~ *fig* this is too much!; **-i** (*troppe persone*) too many people

trota ['trɔ:·ta] *f* trout

trottare [trot·'ta:·re] *vi* **1.** (*gener*) to trot **2.** (*darsi da fare*) to rush around

trotterellare [trot·te·rel·'la:·re] *vi* **1.** (*cavalli*) to trot **2.** (*camminare in fretta*) to trot along

trotto ['trɔt·to] *m* trot

trottola ['trɔt·to·la] *f* spinning top

troupe [trup] <-> *f* (*di artisti*) company; ~ **televisiva** television crew

trovare [tro·'va:·re] **I.** *vt* **1.** (*gener*) to find; **andare a** ~ **qu** to visit sb; **ti trovo bene** you look well; ~ **da ridire** to find sth to criticize **2.** (*pensare*) to think; ~ **qu simpatico** to like sb **II.** *vr:* **-rsi 1.** (*essere*) to be; **-rsi bene con qu** to get on well with sb; **-rsi d'accordo** to agree **2.** (*incontrarsi*) to meet

trovarobe [tro·va·'rɔ:·be] <-> *mf* properties manager

trovata [tro·'va:·ta] *f* brainstorm; ~ **pubblicitaria** publicity stunt

trovatello, -a [tro·va·'tɛl·lo] *m, f* foundling

truccare [truk·'ka:·re] **I.** *vt* **1.** (*con cosmetici*) to make up **2.** (*falsificare: risultati, elezioni*) to rig; (*partita*) to fix **3.** (*motore*) to soup up **II.** *vr:* **-rsi** (*con cosmetici*) to put on makeup

trucco ['truk·ko] <-cchi> *m* **1.** (*cosmesi*) makeup **2.** (*espediente*) trick

truce ['tru:·tʃe] *agg* grim

trucidare [tru·tʃi·'da:·re] *vt* to slaughter

truciolo ['tru:·tʃo·lo] *m* (*di legno*) shaving; (*di polistirolo, plastica*) chip

truffa ['truf·fa] *f* **1.** (*imbroglio*) swindle **2.** DIR fraud

truffare [truf·'fa:·re] *vt* (*imbrogliare*) to swindle

truffatore, -trice [truf·fa·'to:·re] *m, f* swindler

truppa ['trup·pa] *f* **1.** MIL troop; ~ **d'occupazione** occupation forces **2.** *fig* (*gruppo numeroso*) band

trust [trʌst] <-> *m* trust; ~ **dei cervelli** brain trust

T-shirt, tee-shirt ['ti:·ʃə:t] <-> *f* T-shirt

tu [tu] *pron* **2.** *pers sing* you; **dare del** ~ **a qu** ≈ to be on a first name basis with sb; **parlare a** ~ **per** ~ to speak to sb privately; **trovarsi a** ~ **per** ~ to come face to face with sb

---

i There are two ways of addressing someone in Italian: **tu**, which is informal, and the formal *Lei*. *Lei* is usually used when speaking to people one doesn't know or with whom one is not on familiar terms. Generally young people call each other 'tu' even if they do not know each other; similarly an older person such as a shopkeeper may address a young person as **tu**. It is also usual for work colleagues to call one another **tu**.

---

tuba ['tu:·ba] *f* **1.** MUS tuba **2.** (*cappello*) top hat **3.** ANAT tube; ~ **uditiva** auditory canal; ~ **uterina** fallopian tube

tubare [tu·'ba:·re] *vi* **1.** (*colomba*) to coo **2.** (*innamorati*) to bill and coo

tubatura [tu·ba·'tu:·ra] *f* pipes *pl*

tubercolosi [tu·ber·ko·'lo:·zi] <-> *f* tuberculosis

tubercoloso, -a [tu·ber·ko·'lo:·so] **I.** *agg* tubercular **II.** *m, f* tuberculosis patient

tubetto [tu·'bet·to] *m* tube

tubo ['tu:·bo] *m* **1.** (*gener*) tube; ~ **flessibile** flexible tubing; ~ **di scappamento** exhaust pipe; ~ **digerente** digestive tract **2.** *fam* (*niente*) **un** ~ nothing; **non ho capito un** ~ I didn't understand a thing

tuffare [tuf·'fa:·re] **I.** *vt* (*immergere*) to plunge **II.** *vr:* **-rsi 1.** (*in acqua*) to dive; (*nel vuoto*) to throw oneself **2.** *fig* (*dedicarsi*) **-rsi in qc** to throw oneself into sth

tuffo ['tuf·fo] *m* **1.** (*gener*) dive **2.** (*sport*) diving **3.** *fig* (*emozione*) **ho provato un** ~ **al cuore** my heart skipped a beat

tufo ['tu:·fo] *m* tuff

tugurio [tu·'gu:·rio] <-i> *m* hovel

tulipano [tu·li·'pa:·no] *m* tulip

tulle ['tul·le] *m* tulle

tumefazione [tu·me·fat·'tsio:·ne] *f* swelling

tumido, -a ['tu:·mi·do] *agg* (*labbra*) swollen

tumorale [tu·mo·'ra:·le] *agg* tumoral

tumore [tu·'mo:·re] *m* (*cancro*) tumor

tumulare [tu·mu·'la:·re] *vt* to bury

tumulazione [tu·mu·lat·'tsio:·ne] *f* burial

tumulo ['tu:·mu·lo] *m* (*tomba*) tomb

tumulto [tu·'mul·to] *m* **1.**(*rumore*) tumult **2.**(*rivolta*) riot **3.** *fig*(*agitazione*) turmoil

tumultuare [tu·mul·tu·'a:·re] *vi* to riot

tumultuoso, -a [tu·mul·tu·'o:·so] *agg* **1.**(*folla*) unruly **2.**(*acque, fiume*) turbulent **3.** *fig*(*periodo*) tumultuous

tunica ['tu:·ni·ka] <-che> *f* tunic

tunnel ['tun·nel] <-> *m* tunnel

tuo, -a <tuoi, tue> I. *agg* your; **la -a voce/ mano** your voice/hand; **~ padre/zio** your father/uncle; **un ~ amico** a friend of yours II. *pron* **il ~, la -a** yours; **i tuoi** (*genitori*) your parents; **ti tieni sempre sulle -e** you always keep to yourself

tuonare [tuo·'na:·re] I. *vi avere* (*inveire*) to rage II. *vi essere o avere* (*impersonale*) to thunder

tuono ['tuɔ:·no] *m* thunder

tuorlo ['tuɔr·lo] *m* yolk

tu(p)pè [tu·'pɛ (tup·'pɛ)] <-> *m v.* **toupee**

tuppertù, tu per tu [tu·per·'tu] *avv* **essere a ~ con qu** to be face to face with sb

turacciolo [tu·'rat·tʃo·lo] *m* (*di sughero*) cork; (*di plastica*) stopper

turare [tu·'ra:·re] I. *vt* **1.**(*bottiglia*) to cork **2.**(*buco, falla*) to stop (up); **-rsi il naso** to hold one's nose; **-rsi le orecchie/gli occhi** to block up one's ears; **-rsi gli occhi** to cover one's eyes II. *vr:* **-rsi** to get blocked

turba ['tur·ba] *f* **1.**(*di persone*) crowd; *pej* mob **2.** MED disorder

turbamento [tur·ba·'men·to] *m* (*ansia*) agitation

turbante [tur·'ban·te] *m* turban

turbare [tur·'ba:·re] I. *vt* **1.**(*cerimonia, svolgimento*) to disrupt **2.**(*pace, rapporto*) to disturb **3.**(*persona*) to upset II. *vr:* **-rsi** (*agitarsi*) to get upset

turbina [tur·'bi:·na] *f* turbine

turbinare [tur·bi·'na:·re] *vi* (*foglie*) to whirl

turbine ['tur·bi·ne] *m* **1.**(*movimento d'aria*) whirlwind; **un ~ di sabbia** a sandstorm **2.**(*di pensieri*) whirl

turbo ['tur·bo] I. <-> *m* turbo II. <inv> *agg* turbo; **motore ~** turbo engine

turbocompressore [tur·bo·kom·pres·'so:·re] *m* turbocharger

turbodiesel [tur·bo·'di:·zəl] I. <-> *m* turbo diesel II. <inv> *agg* turbo diesel; **una macchina ~** a turbo diesel car

turbogas [tur·bo·'gas] <-> *m* turbogas

turbogetto [tur·bo·'dʒɛt·to] *m* **1.**(*motore*) jet engine **2.**(*aereo*) jet

turbolento, -a [tur·bo·'lɛn·to] *agg* **1.**(*persona*) unruly **2.**(*periodo*) turbulent

turbolenza [tur·bo·'lɛn·tsa] *f* **1.**(*gener*) turbulence **2.**(*di persona*) unruliness

turbomotore [tur·bo·mo·'to:·re] *m* turbine

turbonave [tur·bo·'na:·ve] *f* turbine ship

turboreattore [tur·bo·re·at·'to:·re] *m v.* **turbogetto**

turchese [tur·'ke:·se] I. *f* (*pietra*) turquoise II. *m* (*colore*) turquoise

Turchia [tur·'ki:·a] *f* **la ~** Turkey; **abitare in ~** to live in Turkey; **andare in ~** to go to Turkey

turchino, -a [tur·'ki:·no] *agg* deep blue

turco ['tur·ko] <*sing*> *m* Turkish; **parlare ~** *fig* to speak double talk

turco, -a <-chi, -che> I. *agg* Turkish; **sedere alla -a** to sit cross-legged II. *m, f* Turk; **fumare come un ~** to smoke like a chimney

turgido, -a ['tur·dʒi·do] *agg* swollen

turismo [tu·'riz·mo] *m* tourism; **~ di massa** mass tourism

turista [tu·'ris·ta] <-i *m*, -e *f*> *mf* tourist

turistico, -a [tu·'ris·ti·ko] <-ci, -che> *agg* tourist

turlupinare [tur·lu·pi·'na:·re] *vt* to cheat

turnista [tur·'nis·ta] <-i *m*, -e *f*> *mf* shift worker

turno ['tur·no] *m* **1.**(*di lavoro*) shift; **essere di ~** to be on duty; **~ di notte** night shift; **medico di ~** duty doctor; **farmacia di ~** late-night drugstore **2.**(*volta*) turn; **aspettare il proprio ~** to wait one's turn; **fare a ~** to take turns; **a ~, abbiamo guidato a ~** we took turns driving **3.** SPORT round

turpe ['tur·pe] *agg* (*infame*) vile

turpiloquio [tur·pi·'lɔ·ku·io] <-qui> *m* obscene language

tuta ['tu:·ta] *f* jumpsuit; **~ (da ginnastica)** sweatsuit; **~ da lavoro** coveralls; **~ mimetica** camouflage gear; **~ spaziale** spacesuit; **-e blu** *fig* blue-collar workers

tutela [tu·'tɛ:·la] *f* **1.**(*difesa*) protection; **~ del consumatore** consumer protection; **~ dell'ambiente** protection of the environment **2.** JUR (*di minore*) guardianship

tutelare¹ [tu·te·'la:·re] *agg* **1.**(*misura*) protection **2.** JUR tutelary; **giudice ~** *juvenile court judge*

tutelare² I. *vt* to protect; **~ i propri interessi** to look after one's own interests II. *vr:* **-rsi** to protect oneself

tutor ['tju:·tə] <-> *m* (*negli studi*) tutor; (*al lavoro*) mentor

tutore, -trice [tu·'to:·re] *m, f* **1.**(*protettore, difensore*) protector **2.** JUR guardian

tutrice *f v.* **tutore**

tuttavia [tut·ta·'vi:·a] *cong* but

tutto ['tut·to] *m* the (whole) shebang; **preferisco pagare il ~ ora** I'd rather pay the whole deal now; **rischiare [*o* tentare] (il) ~ per (il) ~** to go for broke

tutto, -a I. *agg* **1.**(*intero*) whole; **~ il denaro** all the money; **~ il giorno** the whole day (long); **-a la notte** all night; **-a velocità** at top speed **2.**(*la totalità di*) all; **-e le donne** all women; **-a la mia famiglia** all my family; **-e le sere** every evening; **-i e due** both **3.**(*qualsiasi*) **in -i i modi** whatever happens; **in -i i casi** in any case; **a -i i costi** at all costs; **-e le volte che** every time; **-e le volte che la invito trova una scusa** every time I invite her she makes some excuse **4.** (*rafforzativo*) **è -a una finzione** it's all made-up; **era ~ contento** he was all happy **II.** *pron* **1.** (*ogni cosa*) everything; **prima di ~** first of all; **in ~** altogether **2.** (*la totalità*) everyone; **-i risero** everyone laughed **III.** *avv* quite; **è ~ il contrario di suo fratello** he's the complete opposite of his brother; **c'è un giardino tutt'intorno alla casa** there's a garden all around the house; **del ~** completely; **tutt'al più** at (the) most; **tutt'altro** on the contrary

tuttofare [tut·to·'faː·re] **I.** <inv> *agg* **donna ~** maid; **una segretaria ~** a girl Friday **II.** <-> *mf* (*domestico*) handyman *m*, maid *f*

tuttora [tut·'toː·ra] *avv* still

tutù [tu·'tu] <-> *m* tutu

tv [tiv·'vu] <-> *f* *abbr di* **televisione** TV; **~ spazzatura** trash TV

tweed [twiːd] <-> *m* tweed; **giacca di ~** tweed jacket

twin-set ['twin·'sɛt] <-> *m* twin set

U

U, u [u] *f* U, u; **~ come Udine** U for Uncle; **profilo a U** U-shaped iron profile; **inversione a U** U-turn

ubbidiente [ub·bi·'diɛn·te] *agg* obedient

ubbidienza [ub·bi·'diɛn·tsa] *f* obedience

ubbidire [ub·bi·'diː·re] *ubbidisco vi* to obey; **~ a qu/qc** to obey sb/sth

ubicazione [u·bi·kat·'tsio·ne] *f* (*posizione*) location

ubiquità [u·bi·kui·'ta] *f* ubiquity

ubriacare [u·bri·a·'kaː·re] **I.** *vt* **1.** (*inebriare*) **~ qu** to get sb drunk **2.** *fig* (*stordire*) to intoxicate **II.** *vr:* **-rsi** to get drunk

ubriacatura [u·bri·a·ka·'tuː·ra] *f* **1.** (*sbornia*) drinking binge **2.** *fig* (*inebriamento*) intoxication

ubriachezza [u·bri·a·'ket·tsa] *f* (*ebbrezza*) drunkenness; **in stato di ~** under the influence of alcohol

ubriaco, -a [u·bri·'aː·ko] *-chi, -che* **I.** *agg* **1.** (*ebbro*) drunk; **~ fradicio** *fam* plastered **2.** *fig* (*stordito: per sonno*) groggy **II.** *m*, *f* drunk

ubriacone, -a [u·bri·a·'koː·ne] *m*, *f* drunk

uccelliera [ut·tʃel·'liɛ·ra] *f* (*gabbia*) aviary

uccello [ut·'tʃɛl·lo] *m* **1.** ZOO bird; **essere uccel di bosco** *fig* to be nowhere to be found; **fare l'~ del malaugurio** *fig* to be a prophet of doom **2.** *vulg* (*pene*) dick

uccidere [ut·'tʃiː·de·re] *uccido, uccisi, ucciso* **I.** *vt a. fig* to kill **II.** *vr:* **-rsi** **1.** (*suicidarsi*) to kill oneself **2.** (*vicendevolmente*) to kill each other **3.** (*perdere la vita*) to be killed

uccisi [ut·'tʃiː·zi] *1. pers sing pass rem di* **ucci-**

dere

uccisione [ut·tʃi·'zioː·ne] *f* killing

ucciso [ut·'tʃiː·zo] *pp di* **uccidere**

uccisore [ut·tʃi·'zoː·re] *m* killer

udibile [u·'diː·bi·le] *agg* audible

udienza [u·'diɛn·tsa] *f* **1.** (*colloquio*) audience; **chiedere** (**un'**)**~** to seek an audience; **concedere un'~** to grant an audience **2.** JUR hearing

Udine *f* Udine, *city in northeastern Italy*

udinese [u·di·'neː·se] **I.** *agg* from Udine **II.** *mf* (*abitante*) person from Udine

Udinese *sing m* Udine area; **nell'~** in the Udine area

udire [u·'diː·re] *odo, udii, udito vt* **1.** (*sentire*) to hear **2.** (*ascoltare*) to listen to

udito [u·'diː·to] *m* hearing; **esame dell'~** hearing examination

UDEUR *m* *Democratic Union for Europe, Italian centrist political party; abbr di* **Unione Democratici per l'Europa**

UE *f* EU; *abbr di* **Unione Europea**

UEM *f* *Econimic and Monetary Union*, EMU; *abbr di* **Unione economica e monetaria europea**

ufficiale [uf·fi·'tʃaː·le] **I.** *agg* official **II.** *m* **1.** ADM official; **~ di stato civile** registrar; **~ giudiziario** bailiff; **pubblico ~** public official **2.** MIL officer

ufficializzare [uf·fi·tʃa·lid·'dzaː·re] *vt* (*unione, situazione*) **~ qc** to make sth official

ufficio [uf·'fiː·tʃo] *-ci m* **1.** (*gen*) office; **~ postale** post office; **~** (**di**) **collocamento** employment office; **difensore d'~** public defender; **provvedimento d'~** official measure; **trasferire qu d'~** to give sb a compulsory transfer **2.** (*reparto*) department; **~ contabilità** accounts department; **~ informazioni** information office; **~ personale** personnel department; **~ vendite** sales department; **~ viaggi** travel agency

ufficioso, -a [uf·fi·'tʃoː·so] *agg* (*notizia, risultato, classifica*) unofficial

U.F.O. ['uː·fo] *m* UFO

ufo ['uː·fo] *avv* **a ~** without paying; **mangiare a ~** to scrounge a meal

ugello [u·'dʒɛl·lo] *m* nozzle

uggia ['ud·dʒa] *ugge f* (*noia*) dreariness

uggioso, -a [ud·'dʒoː·so] *agg* (*giornata, inverno, autunno*) dreary

ugola ['uː·go·la] *f* **1.** ANAT uvula **2.** *fig* (*gola*) throat

uguaglianza [u·gua·ʎ·'ʎan·tsa] *f* **1.** (*coincidenza*) similarity **2.** MATH, JUR equality

uguagliare [u·gua·ʎ·'ʎaː·re] **I.** *vt* **1.** (*gener*) to equal; **~ qu in qc** to equal sb in sth **2.** (*rendere uniforme: terreno*) to level **II.** *vr:* **-rsi** (*livellarsi*) to even out

uguale[1] [u·'guaː·le] **I.** *agg* **1.** (*identico*) identical; **per me è ~** it's all the same to me **2.** (*che rimane uguale*) the same; **essere sempre ~ a se stesso** to be consistent **3.** MATH equal **4.** (*uniforme: tono*) even **II.** *mf* equal

uguale[2] *avv fam* the same

U

ugualmente [u·gual·'men·te] *avv* all the same
uh [u] *int* **1.** (*dolore*) ow! **2.** (*meraviglia*) wow!
uhi ['uː·i] *int* (*dolore*) ow!
UIL [uil] *f Italian labor union; abbr di* **Unione Italiana del Lavoro**
ulcera ['ul·tʃe·ra] *f* (*piaga*) ulcer; ~ (**gastrica**) (stomach) ulcer
ulcerazione [ul·tʃe·rat·'tsio:·ne] *f* ulceration
uliva [u·'liː·va] *f v.* **oliva¹**
ulivista [u·li·'vis·ta] *-i, -e* **I.** *agg* (*partito, politica*) Olive Tree **II.** *mf* POL Olive Tree
ulivo [u·'liː·vo] *m v.* **olivo**
Ulivo [u·'liː·vo] *m* POL *Olive Tree, center-left Italian political party*
ulteriore [ul·te·'rio:·re] *agg* further
ultima ['ul·ti·ma] *f fam* (*novità*) latest; **vuoi sapere l'~?** do you want to know the latest?; **ti racconto l'~?** have I told you the latest?
ultimare [ul·ti·'maː·re] *vt* (*finire: lavoro, opera, cottura*) to complete
ultimatum [ul·ti·'maː·tum] *m* ultimatum
ultimazione [ul·ti·mat·'tsio:·ne] *f* (*di lavoro, opera*) completion
ultimissima [ul·ti·'mis·si·ma] *f* **1.** (*giornale*) latest edition **2.** *pl* (*notizie*) latest news
ultimo, -a ['ul·ti·mo] **I.** *agg* **1.** (*gener*) last; **all'~ momento** at the last moment; **lo studio è la sua -a preoccupazione, dire l'-a parola** to have the last word **2.** (*recente*) latest **3.** (*estremo*) utmost **II.** *m, f* last; **l'~ del mese** the last day of the month; **all'~** in the end; **da ~** finally; **fino all'~** to the last; **in ~** finally; **per ~** lastly; **gli -i saranno i primi** the last shall be first
ultrà [ult·'ra] *mf* **1.** POL extremist **2.** SPORT hardcore fans
ultracentenario, -a [ult·ra·tʃen·te·'naː·rio] *agg* more than a hundred years old
ultracompatto, -a [ult·ra·kom·'pat·to] *agg* (*auto, radio, cinepresa*) super-compact
ultracorto, -a [ult·ra·'kor·to] *agg* ultrashort; **onde -e** ultrashort waves
ultraleggero [ult·ra·led·'dʒɛ:·ro] *m* (*deltaplano a motore*) ultralight
ultramoderno, -a [ult·ra·mo·'dɛr·no] *agg* (*arredamento, design*) ultramodern
ultramondano, -a [ult·ra·mon·'daː·no] *agg* (*Dei*) otherwordly; **vita -a** afterlife
ultraortodosso, -a [ult·ra·or·to·'dɔs·so] **I.** *agg* (*partito, fazione, quartiere*) ultra-orthodox **II.** *m, f* ultra-orthodox Jew
ultrapiatto, -a [ult·ra·'piat·to] *agg* (*cellulare, microfono, tastiera*) ultrathin; **schermo ~** flat screen
ultrapotente [ult·ra·po·'tɛn·te] *agg* (*palmare, motore, videocamera*) high-powered
ultrarapido, -a [ult·ra·'raː·pi·do] *agg* high-speed
ultrasensibile [ult·ra·sen·'siː·bi·le] *agg* (*microfono, sensore*) ultrasensitive
ultrasinistra [ult·ra·si·'nis·tra] *f* POL far Left
ultrasottile [ult·ra·sot·'tiː·le] *agg* ultrathin
ultrasuono [ult·ra·'suɔ:·no] *m* ultrasound

ultraterreno, -a [ult·ra·ter·'re:·no] *agg* (*visioni*) of another world; **vita -a** afterlife
ultravioletto, -a [ult·ra·vio·'let·to] *agg* (*raggi*) ultraviolet
ululare [u·lu·'laː·re] *vi* (*lupo, vento*) to howl
ululato, ululo [u·lu·'laː·to, 'uː·lu·lo] *m* (*di lupo, vento*) howling
umanamente [u·ma·na·'men·te] *avv* **1.** (*dell'uomo*) humanly; **è ~ impossibile** it's not humanly possible **2.** *fig* (*con umanità*) humanely
umanesimo [u·ma·'neː·zi·mo] *m* (*movimento culturale*) humanism
umanista [u·ma·'nis·ta] *-i, -e mf* (*dell'umanesimo*) humanist
umanistico, -a [u·ma·'nis·ti·ko] *agg -ci, -che* **1.** (*dell'umanesimo*) humanistic **2.** (*materie, facoltà*) arts
umanità [u·ma·ni·'ta] *f* **1.** (*natura umana, genere umano*) humanity **2.** (*sentimento*) humaneness
umanitario, -a [u·ma·ni·'taː·rio] *-i, -ie agg* (*attività, associazione*) humanitarian; **aiuti -i** humanitarian aid
umano [u·'maː·no] *m* human
umano, -a *agg* **1.** (*dell'uomo*) human **2.** *fig* (*buono*) kind
umanoide [u·ma·'no·i·de] *agg* humanoid
Umbria ['um·bria] *f* Umbria
umbro ['um·bro] *sing m* (*dialetto*) Umbrian dialect
umbro, -a **I.** *agg* Umbrian **II.** *m, f* Umbrian
UME *f European Monetary Union*, EMU; *abbr di* **Unione Monetaria Europea**
umidificare [u·mi·di·fi·'kaː·re] *vt* (*aria, ambiente*) to humidify
umidificatore [u·mi·di·fi·ka·'to:·re] *m* humidifier
umidità [u·mi·di·'ta] *f* **1.** (*nell'aria*) humidity **2.** (*bagnato*) damp
umido ['uː·mi·do] *m* **1.** (*umidità*) damp **2.** CULIN **coniglio in ~** rabbit stew
umido, -a *agg* **1.** (*clima*) humid **2.** (*bagnato: biancheria*) damp
umile ['uː·mi·le] *agg* humble
umiliare [u·mi·'lia:·re] **I.** *vt* (*offendere*) to humiliate **II.** *vr:* **-rsi** (*abbassarsi*) to humiliate oneself
umiliazione [u·mi·liat·'tsio:·ne] *f* (*offesa*) humiliation
umiltà [u·mil·'ta] *f* (*modestia*) humility
umore [u·'mo:·re] *m* **1.** BIOL, BOT (*liquido*) humor **2.** (*indole*) temperament **3.** (*disposizione d'animo*) mood; **essere di buon ~** to be in a good mood; **essere di ~ nero** to be in a black mood
umorismo [u·mo·'riz·mo] *m* humor; **non avere il senso dell'~** to have no sense of humor
un' [un] *art f davanti a vocale* a, an; *v.* **un, una**
un, una [un, 'uː·na] *art m, f* a, an
una¹ ['uː·na] *art v.* **un, uno**
una² *f* **1.** (*temporale*) one (o'clock); **è l'~** it's

one (o'clock) **2.** (*storia*) **te ne racconto ~** I'll tell you a good one; **non me ne va bene ~** nothing ever goes right for me; **me n'è capitata ~** something happened to me

unanime [u·'na:·ni·me] *agg* **1.** (*assemblea*) whole **2.** (*decisione*) unanimous

unanimità [u·na·ni·mi·'ta] *f* unanimity; **all'~** unanimously

una tantum ['u:·na 'tan·tum] I. <inv> *agg* (*sussidio, contributo, retribuzione*) one-time II. <-> *f* one-time payment

uncinato, -a [un·tʃi·'na:·to] *agg* (*con uncini: aculeo, artigli*) hooked; **croce -a** swastika

uncinetto [un·tʃi·'net·to] *m* crochet

uncino [un·'tʃi:·no] *m* (*gancio*) hook

underground ['ʌn·də·'graund/an·der·'graund] I. <inv> *agg* (*musica, happening*) underground II. <-> *m* underground

undicenne [un·di·'tʃɛn·ne] I. *agg* (*ragazzi*) eleven-year-old II. *mf* eleven year old

undicesimo [un·di·'tʃɛ:·zi·mo] *m* (*frazione*) eleventh

undicesimo, -a I. *agg* eleventh II. *m, f* eleventh; *v.a.* **quinto**

undici ['un·di·tʃi] I. *num* eleven II. <-> *m* **1.** (*numero*) eleven **2.** (*nelle date*) eleventh **3.** SPORT eleven III. *fpl* eleven (o'clock); **le ~** (**di mattina/sera**) 11 (a.m./p.m.); *v.a.* **cinque**

UNESCO [u·'nɛs·ko] *m* UNESCO

ungere ['un·dʒe·re] *ungo, unsi, unto* I. *vt* **1.** (*ingranaggio, motore, teglia*) to grease; (*con creme, pomate: corpo*) to oil **2.** (*sporcare*) to get grease on **3.** REL to anoint **4.** *fig, fam* **~ qu** (*corrompere*) to bribe II. *vr:* **-rsi 1.** (*mettersi dell'unto*) to oil oneself **2.** (*sporcarsi d'unto*) to get grease on oneself

ungherese [un·ge·'re:·se] I. *agg* Hungarian II. *mf* Hungarian

Ungheria [un·ge·'ri:·a] *f* Hungary

unghia ['un·gia] <-ghie> *f* **1.** ANAT nail; **mangiarsi le -ghie** to bite one's nails **2.** ZOO (*di uccello, gatto*) claw; **tirar fuori le -ghie** *fig* to show one's claws **3.** *fig* (*minima grandezza*) speck

unghiata [un·'gia:·ta] *f* scratch

unguento [un·'guɛn·to] *m* (*pomata*) ointment

unica ['u:·ni·ka] *f* **l'unica** the only thing

unicamerale [u·ni·ka·me·'ra:·le] *agg* (*parlamento, iter*) unicameral

unicameralismo [u·ni·ka·me·ra·'liz·mo] *m* POL unicameral system

UNICEF ['u:·ni·tʃef] *m* UNICEF

unicellulare [u·ni·tʃel·lu·'la:·re] *agg* (*organismo*) single-cell

unicità [u·ni·tʃi·'ta] <-> *f* uniqueness

unico, -a ['u:·ni·ko] <-ci, -che> I. *agg* **1.** (*il solo esistente, ineguagliabile*) unique; **essere ~ nel suo genere** to be one of a kind **2.** (*che avviene una volta sola*) only; **figlio ~** only child; **numero ~** (*di giornale, rivista*) single issue II. *m, f* only one

unidimensionale [u·ni·di·men·sio·'na:·le] *agg* one-dimensional

unidirezionale [u·ni·di·ret·tsio·'na:·le] *agg* EL, TEL (*antenna*) unidirectional; **corrente** (**elettrica**) **~** unidirectional current

unifamiliare [u·ni·fa·mi·'lia:·re] *agg* (*casa, villetta*) single-family

unificare [u·ni·fi·'ka:·re] *vt* **1.** (*ridurre a unità*) to unify **2.** (*standardizzare*) to standardize

unificatore, -trice [u·ni·fi·ka·'to:·re] I. *agg* (*attività, forza, impulso, principio*) unifying II. *m, f* unifier

unificazione [u·ni·fi·kat·'tsio:·ne] *f* **1.** (*atto dell'unificare*) unification **2.** (*standardizzazione*) standardization

uniformare [u·ni·for·'ma:·re] I. *vt* **1.** (*unificare*) to homogenize **2.** (*adeguare*) **~ qc a qc** to make sth conform to sth II. *vr* **-rsi a qc** to conform to sth

uniforme [u·ni·'for·me] I. *agg* **1.** (*uguale: superficie*) even; (*colore*) uniform **2.** *fig* (*monotono: voce*) monotonous II. *f* uniform

uniformità [u·ni·for·mi·'ta] <-> *f* **1.** (*di colore, idee, opinioni*) uniformity **2.** (*di superficie*) evenness

unigenito [u·ni·'dʒɛ:·ni·to] <inv> *agg* (*Cristo*) only-begotten

unilaterale [u·ni·la·te·'ra:·le] *agg* **1.** JUR, POL (*accordo, tregua*) unilateral **2.** *fig, pej* (*visione, idea*) one-sided

uninominale [u·ni·no·mi·'na:·le] *agg* (*collegio*) single-member; (*votazione*) single-candidate; **sistema ~** single-candidate system

unione [u·'nio:·ne] *f* **1.** (*gener*) union; **Unione delle Repubbliche Socialiste Sovietiche** Union of Soviet Socialist Republics; **Unione europea** European Union; **Unione monetaria** monetary union; **Unione economica e monetaria europea** economic and monetary union **2.** *fig* (*concordia*) unity; **l'~ fa la forza** *prov* united we stand, divided we fall

unipolare [u·ni·po·'la:·re] *agg* EL (*cavo*) unipolar

unire [u·'ni:·re] <unisco> I. *vt* **1.** (*collegare: fili, cavi, tessuti*) to join **2.** (*aggiungere*) to add **3.** (*allegare*) to enclose **4.** (*persone*) to unite; **~ in matrimonio** to join in matrimony II. *vr:* **-rsi 1.** (*legarsi*) to be united; **-rsi in matrimonio** to be joined in matrimony **2.** (*associarsi*) to join together **3.** (*accompagnarsi*) **-rsi a qu** to join sb

unisex ['u:·ni·seks/u·ni·'sɛks] <inv> *agg* (*abiti*) unisex

unisono [u·'ni:·so·no] I. *agg* MUS unison II. *m* **all'~** *a. fig* MUS in unison

unità [u·ni·'ta] <-> *f* **1.** (*gener*) unit; **~ di misura del peso** unit of weight; **~ monetaria** unit of currency; **~ centrale** COMPUT central processing unit **2.** (*unione, concordia*) unity

unitario, -a [u·ni·'ta:·rio] <-i, -ie> *agg* **1.** (*congiunto: sforzo*) united; (*sindacato*) amalgamated **2.** (*per singolo pezzo*) **costo/prezzo ~** cost/price per unit

unito, -a [u·'ni:·to] *agg* **1.** (*congiunto*) united; **Stati Uniti d'America** United States of Ameri-

U

ca; **Nazioni Unite** United Nations **2.** (*affi-atato*) close; **una famiglia molto -a** a very close family **3.** (*uniforme*) plain; **in tinta -a** self-colored

universale [u·ni·ver·'sa:·le] **I.** *agg* **1.** (*gener*) universal; **diluvio** ~ Great Flood; **storia** ~ world history **2.** (*totale*) sole; **erede** ~ sole heir **3.** (*generale*) general; **concetto** ~ general concept; **suffragio** ~ universal suffrage **II.** *m* (*generale*) universal

universalità [u·ni·ver·sa·li·'ta] <-> *f* **1.** (*accolto da tutti*) universality **2.** (*totalità*) totality

università [u·ni·ver·si·'ta] <-> *f* university; ~ **della terza età** Institute for Learning in Retirement

---

i Italian universities (**università**), are divided into a number of different faculties (**facoltà**). The course of study ends with the award of the **laurea**. The first European university was the **scuola salernitana**, the medical school founded in Salerno in the 11th century. The universities of Bologna, Padua and, Naples are almost equally ancient.

---

universitario, -a [u·ni·ver·si·'ta:·rio] <-i, -ie> *agg* (*corso, istituto, studente*) university

universo [u·ni·'ver·so] *m* **1.** ASTR universe **2.** *fig* (*mondo*) world

univocità [u·ni·vo·tʃi·'ta] <-> *f* (*di affermazione, significato*) unambiguity

univoco, -a [u·'ni:·vo·ko] <-ci, -che> *agg* (*affermazione, discorso*) unambiguous

uno ['u:·no] **I.** *num* one **II.**<-> *m* **1.** (*numero*) one **2.** (*voto scolastico*) fail; *v.a.* **cinque**

uno, una I. *art m davanti a s impura, gn, pn, ps, x, z; f davanti a consonante* a, an **II.** *pron* **1.** (*cosa*) one; ~ **e mezzo** one and a half; **non** ~ not one; ~ **solo** just one **2.** (*persona*) someone; **a** ~ **a** ~ one by one; ~ **per volta** one at a time; **si aiutano l'un l'altro** they help each other **3.** (*impersonale*) you; **se** ~ **ci crede** if you believe in it

unsi ['un·si] *1. pers sing pass rem di* **ungere**

unto ['un·to] *m* grease

unto, -a I. *pp di* **ungere II.** *agg* (*capelli, mani, pelle*) greasy

untuoso, -a [un·tu·'o:·so] *agg* **1.** (*grasso: crema*) greasy **2.** *fig, pej* (*complimento, personaggio*) unctuous

unzione [un·'tsio:·ne] *f* REL unction; **estrema** ~ extreme unction

unzippare [ʌn·dzip·'pa:·re] *vt* COMPUT to unzip

uomo ['uɔ:·mo] <uomini> *m* **1.** (*essere umano*) person **2.** (*di sesso maschile*) man; ~ **d'affari** businessman; ~ **di mondo** man of the world; ~ **d'onore** man of honor; **l'~ della strada** the man on the street; **abito da** ~ man's suit

uovo ['uɔ:·vo] <*pl*: -a *f*> *m* egg; **bianco d'~** egg white; **rosso d'~** egg yolk; **pasta all'~** egg pasta; ~ **à la coque** (soft-)boiled egg; ~ **all'occhio di bue** eggs sunny-side up; ~ **al tegame** fried egg; ~ **sodo** (hard-)boiled egg; **-a affogate** poached eggs; **-a strapazzate** scrambled eggs; **essere pieno come un** ~ to be full up; **meglio un** ~ **oggi che una gallina domani** *prov* a bird in the hand is worth two in the bush

uploadare [ʌp·lou·'da:·re] *vt* COMPUT to upload

uragano [u·ra·'ga:·no] *m* (*ciclone*) hurricane

Urali [u·'ra:·li] *mpl* Urals; **negli** ~ in the Urals

uranio [u·'ra:·nio] *m* uranium

urbanesimo [ur·ba·'ne:·zi·mo] *m* urbanization

urbanista [ur·ba·'nis·ta] <-i *m*, -e *f*> *mf* city planner

urbanistica [ur·ba·'nis·ti·ka] <-che> *f* city planning

urbanistico, -a [ur·ba·'nis·ti·ko] <-ci, -che> *agg* (*piano, progetto*) city; (*regolamento*) planning

urbanizzare [ur·ba·nid·'dza:·re] *vt* (*aree rurali, costa*) to urbanize

urbanizzazione [ur·ba·nid·dzat·'tsio:·ne] *f* (*di aree rurali, costa*) urbanization

urbano, -a [ur·'ba:·no] *agg* **1.** (*della città*) urban; **nettezza -a** department of sanitation; **linea -a** city bus route; **rete -a** city transportation network; **vigile** ~ municipal police officer **2.** *fig* (*cortese*) urbane

urgente [ur·'dʒɛn·te] *agg* (*caso, affare, messaggio*) urgent; (*lettera, pacco*) express

urgenza [ur·'dʒɛn·tsa] *f* **1.** (*fretta*) urgency; **non c'è** ~ there's no hurry **2.** (*emergenza*) emergency; **ricoverare qu d'~** to rush sb to the hospital; **in caso d'~** in case of emergency

urgere ['ur·dʒe·re] <urgo *mancano il pass rem, il pp ed i tempi composti*> *vi* to be urgently needed

urico, -a ['u:·ri·ko] <-ci, -che> *agg* uric; **acido** ~ uric acid

urina [u·'ri:·na] *f v.* **orina**

urinare [u·ri·'na:·re] *v.* **orinare**

urlare [ur·'la:·re] **I.** *vi* **1.** (*persona, scimmia*) to scream **2.** (*parlare forte*) to shout **3.** (*vento*) to howl **II.** *vt* **1.** (*dire a voce alta*) to shout **2.** (*cantare a voce alta*) to belt out

urlo¹ ['ur·lo] <*pl*: -a *f*> *m* (*di dolore, spavento*) scream; (*di piacere*) moan

urlo² *m* **1.** (*di animale*) cry **2.** *fig* (*di vento, sirene*) howl

urna ['ur·na] *f* **1.** (*per le votazioni*) ~ (**elettorale**) ballot box; **responso delle -e** election results *pl;* **andare alle -e** to go to the polls **2.** (*recipiente*) ~ **cineraria** funeral urn

urologia [u·ro·lo·'dʒi:·a] <-gie> *f* urology

urologo, -a [u·'rɔ:·lo·go] <-gi, -ghe> *m, f* urologist

urrà [ur·'ra] **I.** *int* hooray!; **hip hip hip** ~! hip hip hooray! **II.** *m* hooray

URSS [urs] *f* USSR; *abbr di* **Unione delle**

Repubbliche Socialiste Sovietiche

urtare [ur·'ta:·re] I. *vt* 1.(*andare contro a*) to knock against; (*con veicoli*) to hit 2. *fig* (*irritare*) to annoy; ~ **i nervi di qu** to get on sb's nerves II. *vi* (*sbattere contro*) ~ **contro qc** to knock against sth; (*con veicolo*) to hit sth III. *vr:* -**rsi** 1.(*scontrarsi*) to collide 2. *fig* (*irritarsi*) to get annoyed

urto ['ur·to] *m* 1.(*colpo, spinta*) shove; **resistente agli -i** shockproof 2.(*scontro, collisione*) collision 3.(*loc*) **forza d'**~ strike force; **terapia d'**~ massive-dose therapy

u.s. ult.; *abbr di* ultimo scorso

U.S.A. ['u:·za] *mpl* USA; **negli** ~ in the USA

usa e getta ['u·za e 'dʒet·ta] <inv> *agg* disposable; **lenti a contatto** ~ disposable contact lenses; **rasoio** ~ disposable razor; **siringhe** ~ disposable syringes

usanza [u·'zan·tsa] *f* (*consuetudine*) custom

usare [u·'za:·re] I. *vt avere* 1.(*adoperare, impiegare*) to use; ~ **attenzione** to be careful 2.(*vestiti*) to wear 3. *avere* (*avere l'abitudine*) ~ **fare qc** to be in the habit of doing sth II. *vi* 1. *avere* (*essere di moda*) to be fashionable 2. *essere* (*impersonale*) to be the custom

usato [u·'za:·to] *m* (*non più nuovo*) second-hand goods; **mercato dell'**~ secondhand market; **negozio dell'**~ secondhand store

usato, -a *agg* (*non nuovo: oggetti, abiti*) secondhand; **auto -e** secondhand cars

uscente [uʃ·'ʃɛn·te] *agg* ADM (*presidente*) outgoing

usciere, -a [uʃ·'ʃɛ:·re] *m, f* usher

uscii [uʃ·'ʃi:·i] *I. pers sing pass rem di* uscire

uscio ['uʃ·ʃo] <usci> *m* door

uscire [uʃ·'ʃi:·re] <esco, uscii, uscito> *vi essere* 1.(*gener*) to come out; (*andare fuori, per svago*) to go out; (*da veicolo, carcere, ospedale*) to get out 2. *fig* (*esclamare, sbottare*) ~ **a dire qc** to come out with sth; **uscirsene con una battuta** to come out with a witty remark 3. *fig* (*da situazione*) to emerge; ~ **un da partito** to leave a party; ~ **indenne da un incidente** to escape unhurt from an accident 4. COMPUT to quit; (**comando**) **esci** escape 5.(*loc*) **mi è uscito di mente** it slipped my mind; ~ **di strada** to go off the road; ~ **dagli occhi a qn** *fig* to be coming out someone's ears; ~ **dai gangheri** *fig* to lose one's temper; ~ **di bocca a qn** to come out of sb's mouth

uscita [uʃ·'ʃi:·ta] *f* 1.(*movimento*) leaving 2.(*apertura, di autostrada*) exit; **strada senza** ~ dead end; ~ **di sicurezza** emergency exit; **senza via d'**~ *fig* with no way out 3.(*in aeroporto*) gate 4.(*di pubblicazioni*) publication; (*di film*) release 5.(*battuta*) remark 6. FIN (*spesa, passivo*) item of expenditure 7. MIL **essere in libera** ~ to be off duty 8. COMPUT output

uscito [uʃ·'ʃi:·to] *pp di* uscire

usignolo [u·ziɲ·'ɲɔ:·lo] *m* nightingale

uso ['u:·zo] *m* 1.(*gener*) use; **istruzioni per**

l'~ instructions for use; **fuori** ~ out of order; **ad** ~ **di qu** for the use of sb; **per** ~ **esterno** MED for external use; **con** ~ **di cucina** with use of the kitchen 2.(*usanza*) custom; -**i e costumi** customs and traditions

USSL *f local health department; abbr di* Unità Socio-Sanitaria Locale

ustionare [us·tio·'na:·re] I. *vt* to burn II. *vr:* -**rsi** to burn oneself

ustione [us·'tio:·ne] *f* burn

usuale [u·zu·'a:·le] *agg* (*solito*) habitual

usufruire [u·zu·fru·'i:·re] <usufruisco> *vi* (*giovarsi di*) ~ **di qc** to benefit from sth

usufrutto [u·zu·'frut·to] *m* usufruct

usufruttuario, -a [u·zu·frut·tu·'a:·rio] <-i, -ie> *m, f* usufructuary

usura [u·'zu:·ra] *f* 1.(*strozzinaggio*) usury 2. TEC wear

usuraio, -a [u·zu·'ra:·io] <-ai, -aie> *m, f* (*strozzino*) usurer

usurpare [u·zur·'pa:·re] *vt* to usurp

usurpatore, -trice [u·zur·pa·'to:·re] *m, f* usurper

usurpazione [u·zur·pat·'tsio:·ne] *f* (*di trono, potere*) usurpation

utensile [u·ten·'si:·le] I. *agg* **macchina** ~ machine tool II. *m* tool; -**i da cucina** kitchen utensils

utensileria [u·ten·si·le·'ri:·a] <-ie> *f* 1.(*complesso di utensili*) tools *pl* 2.(*reparto di officina*) tool room

utente [u·'tɛn·te] *mf* (*di vocabolario*) user; ~ **del telefono** telephone subscriber; ~ **della TV** viewer; ~ **della strada** road user; ~ **finale** end user

utenza [u·'tɛn·tsa] *f* 1.(*uso di un servizio*) use; (*di gas*) consumption; (*di telefono*) subscribing; (*di radio*) listening; (*di TV*) viewing 2.(*utenti*) users *pl*

uterino, -a [u·te·'ri:·no] *agg* (*fibroma, malformazione*) uterine

utero ['u:·te·ro] *m* uterus

utile ['u:·ti·le] I. *agg* 1.(*che è di aiuto*) useful; **rendersi** ~ to make oneself useful 2.(*vantaggioso*) handy 3. TEC (*utilizzabile*) **carico** ~ payload 4.(*in formule di cortesia*) **se posso essere** ~ **in qc ...** if I can be of help in sth ... II. *m* 1.(*ciò che serve*) usefulness; **unire l'**~ **al dilettevole** to mix business with pleasure 2.(*vantaggio*) benefit 3. FIN profit; ~ **lordo/netto** gross/net profit; **partecipazione agli -i dell'azienda** profit-sharing

utilità [u·ti·li·'ta] <-> *f* 1.(*funzionalità*) usefulness 2.(*vantaggio*) benefit

utilitaria [u·ti·li·'ta:·ria] *f* compact

utilitarismo [u·ti·li·ta·'riz·mo] *m* utilitarianism

utilitaristico, -a [u·ti·li·ta·'ris·ti·ko] <-ci, -che> *agg pej* (*fine, scopo, motivazione*) utilitarian

utilizzabile [u·ti·lid·'dza:·bi·le] *agg* (*oggetto, programma, memoria*) usable

utilizzare [u·ti·lid·'dza:·re] *vt* (*strumenti, servizi, tempo*) to use

U

utilizzazione [u·ti·lid·dzat·'tsio:·ne] *f* (*strumenti, servizi*) use
utilizzo [u·ti·'lid·dzo] *m* use
utopia [u·to·'pi:·a] <-ie> *f* utopia
utopico, -a [u·'tɔ:·pi·ko] <-ci, -che> *agg* (*progetti, idee*) utopian
uva ['u:·va] *f* grapes *pl;* ~ **bianca/nera** white/black grapes *pl;* ~ **passa** raisins *pl;* ~ **spina** gooseberry; ~ **da tavola** dessert grapes *pl*
uvetta [u·'vet·ta] *f* raisins *pl*

V

V, v [vu] <-> *f* V; ~ **come Venezia** V for Victor; ~ **doppia** double U; **scollo** [*o* **scollatura**] **a** ~ V-neck
V *abbr di* **volt**
va [va] *3. pers sing pr di* **andare**[1]
vacante [va·'kan·te] *agg* (*posto, sede*) vacant
vacanza [va·'kan·tsa] *f* 1.(*ferie*) vacation; **essere in** ~ to be on vacation; **andare in** ~ to go on vacation; **fare** ~ to take a vacation; **le -e** (*scolastiche*) the vacation; **-e estive** summer vacation; **-e natalizie** Christmas vacation; **-e pasquali** Easter vacation 2.(*di carica, posto, sede*) vacancy

ℹ️ During the long, hot Italian summer the schools close for almost three months of **vacanze estive** (summer vacation). Italian students are on vacation from mid June to mid September. In August many factories and offices also close, leaving the major cities practically deserted. Early August sees the *esodo* (exodus) from the major cities while at the end of August comes the *controesodo* (return). This leads to long lines of traffic on the superhighways and especially at the toll-gates.

vacanziere, -a [va·kan·'tsiɛ:·re] *m, f a. scherz* (*turista*) vacationer
vacca ['vak·ka] <-cche> *f* 1.(*mucca*) cow 2.*fig, pej, vulg* (*sgualdrina*) slut 3.(*loc*) **in tempo di -e grasse/magre** *fig* in prosperous/lean times
vaccinare [vat·tʃi·'na:·re] I.*vt* 1.(*immunizzare*) to vaccinate 2.(*loc*) **essere vaccinato contro qc** *fig* to be immune to sth II.*vr* **-rsi contro qc** to get vaccinated against sth
vaccinazione [vat·tʃi·nat·'tsio:·ne] *f* vaccination; **fare** [*o* **farsi**] **la** ~ to get a vaccination; ~ **obbligatoria** compulsory vaccination; ~ **di richiamo** booster vaccination
vaccino [vat·'tʃi:·no] *m* vaccine
vacillare [va·tʃil·'la:·re] *vi* 1.(*barcollare: per-*

sona) to stagger 2.(*oscillare: cosa*) to wobble; (*fiamma*) to flicker 3.*fig* (*governo, impero*) to totter 4.*fig* (*persona, sentimento*) to waver
vacuo, -a ['va:·kuo] *agg* 1.*fig* (*persona*) vacuous 2.(*discorso, promessa, speranza*) empty
vademecum [va·de·'mɛ:·kum] <-> *m* handbook
vado ['va:·do] *1. pers sing pr di* **andare**[1]
va e vieni ['va e 'viɛ:·ni] <-> *m* (*movimento*) coming and going
vaffanculo [vaf·fan·'ku:·lo] *int vulg* fuck off!; (*per esprimere stizza*) fuck!
vagabondaggio [va·ga·bon·'dad·dʒo] <-ggi> *m* 1.(*vita di vagabondo*) vagrancy; **darsi al** ~ to become a vagrant 2.(*il girovagare*) wanderings *pl*
vagabondare [va·ga·bon·'da:·re] *vi* 1.(*fare il vagabondo*) to live as a vagrant 2.(*girovagare*) to wander
vagabondo, -a [va·ga·'bon·do] I.*agg* 1.(*senza fissa dimora*) homeless 2.*a. fig* (*in continuo movimento*) wandering II.*m, f* 1.(*persona senza fissa dimora*) vagrant, bum *inf* 2.*fig, pej* (*fannullone*) loafer 3.*fig, scherz* (*viaggiatore*) wanderer
vagamente [va·ga·'men·te] *avv* vaguely
vagare [va·'ga:·re] *vi* 1.(*spostarsi senza meta*) to wander (around) 2.*fig* (*con mente, fantasia*) to wander
vagheggiare [va·ged·'dʒa:·re] *vt* (*successo, vittoria*) to long for
vaghezza [va·'get·tsa] *f* 1.(*di dichiarazione, promessa, ricordo*) vagueness 2.(*di tratto, contorno*) haziness
vagina [va·'dʒi:·na] *f* vagina
vaginale [va·dʒi·'na:·le] *agg* vaginal
vagire [va·'dʒi:·re] <vagisco> *vi* to cry
vagito [va·'dʒi:·to] *m* 1.(*pianto*) cry; **emettere** [*o* **mandare**] **un** ~ to let out a cry 2.*fig* (*di civiltà, arte*) the dawn
vaglia ['vaʎ·ʎa] <-> *m* money order; ~ **bancario** bank draft; ~ **cambiario** promissory note; ~ **postale** money order
vagliare [vaʎ·'ʎa:·re] *vt* (*esaminare: proposta, problema*) to examine
vaglio ['vaʎ·ʎo] <-gli> *m fig* (*esame: di proposta, tesi*) examination; **passare** [*o* **sottoporre**] **qc al** ~ to examine sth
vago, -a <-ghi, -ghe> *agg* (*somiglianza, ricordo*) vague
vagone [va·'go:·ne] *m* car; ~ **letto** sleeping car; ~ **ristorante** dining car
vai ['va:·i] *2. pers sing pr di* **andare**[1]
vaiolo [va·'iɔ:·lo] *m* MED smallpox
valanga [va·'laŋ·ga] <-ghe> *f* 1.(*di neve, ghiaccio*) avalanche 2.*fig* (*quantità enorme*) flood 3.SPORT **la** ~ **azzurra** the Italian ski team
valchiria [val·'ki:·ria] <-ie> *f* 1.(*figura mitologica*) Valkyrie 2.*scherz* (*biondona*) *tall, blonde woman*
Val d'Aosta [val·da·'ɔs·ta] *f* (**la**) ~ Val d'Aosta
valdese [val·'de:·se] I.*mf* REL Waldensian II.*agg* REL Waldensian

valdostano, -a [val·dos·'ta:·no] I. *agg* (*della Val d'Aosta*) from the Val d'Aosta II. *m, f* (*abitante*) person from the Val d'Aosta

valente [va·'lɛn·te] *agg* (*eccellente: professionista, artigiano*) skillful

valenza [va·'lɛn·tsa] *f* 1. CHEM valency 2. (*valore, significato*) importance 3. LING valency

valere [va·'le:·re] <valgo, valsi, valso> I. *vi essere* 1. (*avere potere, influenza*) **non ~ nulla** to count for nothing; **~ molto** to be worth a lot 2. (*essere capace*) to be good; **~ poco** not to be very good; **~ per tre** [*o* **dieci**] *inf* to be worth ten; **farsi ~** to show what one's worth 3. (*avere efficacia: legge*) to be valid; (*norma*) to apply 4. (*essere valido*) to be valid; **non vale!** *inf* that doesn't count! 5. (*costare*) to be worth; **~ un tesoro** [*o* **un occhio della testa**] to be priceless; **non ~ un fico** (**secco**) [*o* **una lira**] [*o* **una cicca**] *fam* not to be worth a fig 6. (*essere uguale a*) to be the same as; **uno vale l'altro** they're both the same; **tanto vale** [*o* **varrebbe**] +*inf* it's all the same; **tanto vale che ...** I [*o* you] [*o* he] etc. might as well ...; (**non**) **~ la pena** (not) to be worth the effort; **vale a dire** (*cioé, ovvero*) that is; **hai detto che arrivi tardi, vale a dire?** you said you'll be arriving late, but how late exactly? 7. (*loc*) **il gioco non vale la candela** *prov* it's more trouble than it's worth; **a Carnevale ogni scherzo vale** *prov: at Carnival time, anything goes* II. *vt avere* 1. (*rendere*) to earn 2. *fig* (*procurare*) to earn III. *vr* (*servirsi*) **-rsi di qc** to make use of sth

valeriana [va·le·'ria:·na] *f* 1. BOT (*pianta*) valerian 2. (*sostanza*) valerian

valevole [va·'le:·vo·le] *agg* (*biglietto*) valid; **partita ~** SPORT deciding game

valgo ['val·go] *1. pers sing pr di* **valere**

valicabile [va·li·'ka:·bi·le] *agg* (*passo, confine, ostacolo*) passable

valicare [va·li·'ka:·re] *vt* (*confine, frontiera, catena montuosa*) to cross

valico ['va:·li·ko] <-chi> *m* 1. (*passo*) pass; **~ di frontiera** border crossing 2. (*attraversamento*) crossing

validare [va·li·'da:·re] *vt* **~ qc** to validate sth

validità [va·li·di·'ta] <-> *f* (*di biglietto, documento, sentenza, argomento*) validity

valido, -a ['va:·li·do] *agg* 1. (*forte: uomo*) fit 2. (*di ottima qualità: prodotto*) good 3. (*efficace: aiuto, contributo*) effective; (*argomento, ragione, motivo*) valid 4. JUR (*matrimonio, votazione, documento*) valid 5. (*apprezzato: opera, scrittore, avvocato*) well-regarded 6. SPORT (*regolare: partenza*) valid; (*utile: incontro*) useful

valigeria [va·li·dʒe·'ri:·a] <-ie> *f* 1. (*assortimento*) leather goods *pl* 2. (*negozio*) leather goods store 3. (*fabbrica*) leather goods factory

valigia [va·'li:·dʒa] <-gie *o* -ge> *f* suitcase; **fare** [*o* **preparare**] **la ~** to pack (one's suitcase); **disfare la ~** to unpack (one's suitcase); **~ ventiquattr'ore** overnight bag; **fare le -gie**

fig to pack one's bags

vallata [val·'la:·ta] *f* valley

valle ['val·le] *f* valley; **a ~** (*di monte*) downhill; (*di fiume*) downstream

Valle d'Aosta [val·le·da·'ɔs·ta] *f v.* **Val d'Aosta**

Vallese [val·'le:·se] *m* Valais

valletta [val·'let·ta] *f female assistant to TV presenter*

valligiano, -a [val·li·'dʒa:·no] I. *m, f* (*abitante*) valley-dweller II. *agg* (*della valle*) valley

vallo ['val·lo] *m* 1. HIST (*fortificazione romana*) wall 2. MIL (*linea di difesa*) (defensive) wall

valore [va·'lo:·re] *m* 1. (*prezzo*) value; **aumentare di ~** to gain value; **diminuire di ~** to lose value; **~ aggiunto** added value; **imposta sul ~ aggiunto** value-added tax 2. (*ideale*) value; **-i umani** human values; **scala di -i** value scale 3. (*importanza, pregio*) value 4. (*validità*) validity; **avere ~ legale** to be legally valid 5. (*capacità*) worth 6. (*coraggio*) bravery 7. FIN (*moneta, titolo, obbligazione*) security; **borsa -i** stock exchange; **-i mobiliari** stocks and shares 8. *pl* (*gioielli, oggetti preziosi*) valuables *pl* 9. (*significato: di vocabolo, locuzione*) meaning

valorizzare [va·lo·rid·'dza:·re] *vt* 1. (*dare valore: terreno, immobile*) to value 2. (*mettere in risalto: idea, persona, risorsa*) to value 3. (*abiti, trucco*) to flatter

valorizzazione [va·lo·rid·dzat·'tsio:·ne] *f* 1. (*aumento: di valore, pregio*) increase 2. (*riconoscimento: di qualità, merito*) appreciation

valoroso, -a [va·lo·'ro:·so] *agg* 1. (*coraggioso: soldato, atleta*) brave; (*azione, impresa, gesta*) valiant 2. *a. iron* (*bravo: artista, scienziato*) outstanding

valpolicella [val·po·li·'tʃɛl·la] <-> *m* Valpolicella

valsi ['val·si] *1. pers sing pass rem di* **valere**

valso ['val·so] *pp di* **valere**

valuta [va·'lu:·ta] *f* 1. ECON (*moneta*) currency; **~ estera** foreign currency; **~ nazionale** national currency 2. FIN (*decorrenza degli interessi*) accrual date

valutare [va·lu·'ta:·re] *vt* 1. COM (*stimare*) to value; **la casa è valutata 350.000 euro** the house has been valued at 350,000 euros 2. (*calcolare*) to estimate 3. *fig* (*apprezzare: capacità, qualità, azione*) to value 4. (*esaminare: conseguenze*) to evaluate 5. (*a scuola, nei concorsi*) to mark

valutario, -a [va·lu·'ta:·rio] <-i, -ie> *agg* FIN currency

valutazione [va·lu·tat·'tsio:·ne] *f* 1. COM (*stima: di bene, danno*) valuation 2. (*apprezzamento: di capacità, azione*) appreciation 3. (*a scuola, nei concorsi: giudizio*) assessment 4. (*verifica: di prestazione, obiettivo*) assessment

valva ['val·va] *f* BOT, ZOO valve

valvola ['val·vo·la] *f* 1. EL, TEC, MED valve;

V

~ cardiaca heart valve; **~ a farfalla** butterfly valve **2.** *fig* escape valve; **~ di sicurezza** safety valve; *fig* escape valve

valzer ['val·tser] <-> *m* (*danza, musica*) waltz; **fare un giro di ~** *fig* to flirt

vamp [vamp] <-> *f* vamp

vampa ['vam·pa] *f* **1.** (*di fuoco*) flame; (*di calore*) blast **2.** *fig* (*sensazione di calore*) flush

vampata [vam·'pa:·ta] *f* **1.** (*di fuoco, calore*) blast **2.** (*sensazione di calore*) flush **3.** *fig* (*manifestazione improvvisa*) wave

vampiro [vam·'pi:·ro] *m* **1.** (*spettro*) vampire **2.** *fig, pej* bloodsucker

vanaglorioso, -a [va·na·glo·'rio:·so] *agg* boastful

vandalico, -a [van·'da:·li·ko] <-ci, -che> *agg* **1.** HIST (*dei Vandali*) Vandal **2.** *fig* (*teppistico: atto, gesto*) vandalistic

vandalismo [van·da·'liz·mo] *m* vandalism

vandalo ['van·da·lo] *m* **1.** HIST Vandal **2.** *fig* (*teppista*) vandal

vaneggiamento [va·ned·dʒa·'men·to] *m* ravings *pl*

vaneggiare [va·ned·'dʒa:·re] *vi* **1.** (*delirare*) to be delirious **2.** (*dire o pensare cose assurde*) to babble

vanesio, -a [va·'nɛ:·zio] <-i, -ie> I. *agg* **1.** (*frivolo, vanitoso: persona*) vain **2.** (*sciocco: sguardo, sorriso*) foolish II. *m, f* (*persona frivola*) **fare il ~** to behave vainly

vanga ['vaŋ·ga] <-ghe> *f* spade

vangare [vaŋ·'ga:·re] *vt* (*campo, orto, terreno*) to dig (over)

Vangelo [van·'dʒe:·lo] *m* **1.** REL Gospel **2.** (*durante la Messa*) Gospel reading **3.** (*libro*) New Testament; **giurare sul ~** to swear on the Bible **4.** *fig* (*fondamento ideologico*) gospel **5.** *fig, inf* (*verità sacrosanta*) gospel truth

vanificare [va·ni·fi·'ka:·re] *vt* (*tentativo, progetto*) to frustrate; (*speranze, desideri*) to thwart

vaniglia [va·'niʎ·ʎa] <-glie> *f* (*pianta, essenza*) vanilla; **gelato alla ~** vanilla ice-cream

vanigliato, -a [va·niʎ·'ʎa:·to] *agg* vanilla(-flavored); **zucchero ~** vanilla sugar

vanillina [va·nil·'li:·na] *f* CHEM vanillin

vaniloquio [va·ni·'lɔ·kui·o] <-qui> *m* raving

vanità [va·ni·'ta] <-> *f* **1.** (*fatuità: di persona*) vanity; **lusingare la ~ di qu** to flatter sb's ego **2.** (*inutilità: di sforzo, speranza*) futility **3.** (*caducità: di successo, bellezza*) worthlessness

vanitoso, -a [va·ni·'to:·so] I. *agg* **1.** (*frivolo: persona*) vain **2.** (*comportamento, atteggiamento, discorso*) conceited II. *m, f* (*persona*) vain person; **fare il ~** to be vain

vanno ['van·no] *3. pers pl pr di* **andare**[1]

vano ['va:·no] *m* **1.** (*cavità: di finestra*) opening; (*di scala*) (stair)well; (*di ascensore*) shaft **2.** (*stanza*) room **3.** (*scomparto*) compartment

vano, -a *agg* **1.** (*inconsistente: speranza, illusione*) vain **2.** (*caduco: bellezza, ricchezze*)

transient **3.** (*inefficace: tentativo, sforzo*) pointless; **rendere ~ qc** to frustrate sth **4.** (*frivolo, sciocco*) vain

vantaggio [van·'tad·dʒo] <-ggi> *m* **1.** (*privilegio*) advantage; **a ~ di qu/qc** to sb's/sth's advantage **2.** (*giovamento, convenienza*) benefit **3.** (*distacco*) A SPORT lead

vantaggioso, -a [van·tad·'dʒo:·so] *agg* (*condizione, offerta, accordo*) favorable; (*posizione*) advantageous

vantare [van·'ta:·re] I. *vt* **1.** (*lodare*) to praise; **~ i propri meriti** to sing one's own praises **2.** (*affermare di possedere*) to boast; **~ diritti su qc** to lay claim to sth II. *vr* **-rsi di qc** to boast about sth; **non (faccio) per vantarmi** I don't want to brag

vanto ['van·to] *m* **1.** (*il vantare, vantarsi*) boasting; **essere motivo di ~** to be something to boast about; **farsi ~ di qc** to boast about sth **2.** (*motivo di orgoglio*) pride **3.** (*merito*) merit

vanvera ['van·ve·ra] *avv* (*a caso*) **a ~** haphazardly; **parlare a ~** to talk nonsense

vapore [va·'po:·re] *m* **1.** PHYS vapor **2.** (*di acqua*) **~** (**acqueo**) steam; **bagno di ~** steam bath; **cuocere al ~** to steam; **a ~** (*locomotiva, macchina, turbina*) steam-powered **3.** *pl* (*nebbia, fumo, esalazione*) vapors *pl* **4.** NAUT (*piroscafo*) steamship

vaporetto [va·po·'ret·to] *m* steamboat

vaporizzare [va·po·rid·'dza:·re] I. *vt* **1.** (*far evaporare: liquido*) to vaporize **2.** (*nebulizzare: insetticida, profumo*) to spray **3.** (*nella cosmesi*) **~ il viso/la pelle** to apply steam treatment to one's face/skin II. *vi* essere to evaporate

vaporizzatore [va·po·rid·dza·'to:·re] *m* **1.** (*di profumo*) atomizer **2.** (*per aerosol*) vaporizer

vaporosità [va·po·ro·si·'ta] <-> *f fig* (*leggerezza: di tessuto, capelli*) gauziness

vaporoso, -a [va·po·'ro:·so] *agg* (*leggero: tessuto, capelli*) gauzy

varare [va·'ra:·re] *vt* **1.** NAUT to launch **2.** JUR (*promulgare: legge, decreto*) to issue **3.** *fig* (*avviare: iniziativa, progetto, opera*) to present **4.** SPORT (*formazione*) to build

varcare [var·'ka:·re] *vt* **1.** (*oltrepassare: fiume, confine, soglia*) to cross **2.** *fig* (*superare: limite*) to overstep; (*età*) to pass

varco ['var·ko] <-chi> *m* opening; **aprirsi un ~ tra la folla** to make one's way through the crowd; **aspettare qu al ~** to lie in wait for sb

varec(c)hina [va·re·'ki:·na (va·rek·'ki:·na)] *f* bleach

Varese *f* Varese

varesino [va·re·'si:·no] <*sing*> *m* (*dialetto*) dialect spoken in Varese

varesino, -a I. *agg* (*di Varese*) from Varese II. *m, f* (*abitante*) person from Varese

Varesotto [va·re·'zot·to] <*sing*> *m* (*zona*) Varese area; **nel ~** in the Varese area

variabile [va·'ria:·bi·le] I. *agg* **1.** METEO (*tempo*) changeable **2.** (*quantità, valore, prezzo*) variable **3.** (*umore*) changeable **4.** LING **le parti -i**

del discorso variable parts of speech **5.**MAT (*funzione, grandezza*) variable **II.** *f* variable; **~ indipendente** (*econ*) independent variable
variabilità [va·ria·bi·li·'ta] <-> *f* **1.**(*di tempo meteorologico*) changeability **2.**(*di umore*) volatility **3.** BIOL variability
variante [va·'rian·te] *f* **1.**(*alternativa*) variant **2.**(*modifica*) change **3.** LING (*forma diversa*) variant **4.**(*strada alternativa*) bypass
variare [va·'ria:·re] **I.** *vt* (*modifica*) **1.**(*modificare: data, programma*) to change **2.**(*diversificare: alimentazione*) to vary **3.** MUS to vary on **II.** *vi essere* (*subire cambiamenti*) to vary
variato, -a [va·'ria:·to] *agg* varied
variazione [va·riat·'tsio:·ne] *f* **1.**(*modificazione: di dato, programma, umore*) change; (*di clima, temperatura*) fluctuation **2.**(*di colori, toni*) variety **3.** MUS variation; **~ sul tema** *a fig* variation on a theme
varice [va·'ri:·tʃe] *f* MED varicose vein
varicella [va·ri·'tʃɛl·la] *f* chickenpox
varicoso, -a [va·ri·'ko:·so] *agg* varicose; **vena -a** varicose vein
variegato, -a [va·rie·'ga:·to] *agg* **1.**(*variopinto*) variegated **2.** *fig* (*multiforme: situazione, problema*) complex
varietà [va·rie·'ta] <-> **I.** *f* **1.**(*gener*) variety **2.**(*diversità: di prodotti*) diversity; (*di opinioni, gusti, idee*) range **II.** *m* **1.** THEAT vaudeville **2.**(*luogo*) music hall **3.** TV (*programma d'intrattenimento*) variety show
vario, -a [va·'rio] <-i, -ie> **I.** *agg* **1.**(*variato: alimentazione, paesaggio*) varied **2.**(*mutevole: tempo, umore*) changeable **3.**(*diverso*) various; **autori -i** various artists **4.** *pl* (*numerosi*) several; **-e ed eventuali** (*su ordine del giorno*) any other business **II.** *pron* (*molte persone*) several people
variopinto, -a [va·rio·'pin·to] *agg* multicolored
varo ['va:·ro] *m* **1.**(*di nave, progetto, iniziativa*) launch **2.** JUR (*di legge*) passing
varrò [var·'rɔ] *1. pers sing futuro di* **valere**
Varsavia [var·'sa:·via] *f* Warsaw
vasca ['vas·ka] <-sche> *f* **1.**(*recipiente*) basin; **~ da bagno** bathtub **2.**(*bacino di fontana*) basin **3.** SPORT (*piscina*) pool; **fare una ~** (*nuotare*) to swim a lap; *fig, scherz* (*passeggiare*) to go for a stroll
vascello [vaʃ·'ʃɛl·lo] *m* HIST, MAR vessel; **ufficiali di ~** naval officers
vascolare [vas·ko·'la:·re] *agg* ANAT vascular
vasectomia [va·zek·to·'mi:·a] <-ie> *f* MED vasectomy
vaselina® [va·ze·'li:·na] *f* vaseline®
vasellame [va·zel·'la:·me] *m* (*di ceramica, porcellana*) crockery; (*di vetro*) glassware; (*d'argento*) silverware
vasellina [va·zel·'li:·na] *f v.* **vaselina**
vasino [va·'zi:·no] *m inf* (*per bambini*) potty
vaso ['va:·zo] *m* **1.**(*recipiente*) vase; **~ da fiori** flower vase; (*per piante*) flower pot **2.**(*per alimenti*) jar; **~ da conserva** jam jar **3.**(*di gabinetto*) bowl; **~ da notte** chamber

pot **4.** ANAT, PHYS vessel; **-i comunicanti** communicating vessels
vasocostrittore, -trice [va·zo·kos·trit·'to:·re] *agg* MED vasoconstrictive
vasodilatatore, -trice [va·zo·di·la·ta·'to:·re] *agg* MED vasodilatory
vassoio [vas·'so:·io] <-oi> *m* tray; **su un ~ d'argento** *fig* on a silver platter
vastità [vas·ti·'ta] <-> *f* **1.**(*ampiezza: di spazio, superficie*) immensity **2.** *fig* (*di pensiero, tema*) depth
vasto, -a ['vas·to] *agg* **1.**(*esteso: territorio*) vast **2.** *fig* (*profondo: cultura, esperienza, argomento*) deep **3.**(*loc*) **di -a portata** (*fenomeno, conseguenze, rivolgimento*) far-reaching; **di -e proporzioni** (*incendio, rivolta, riforma*) widespread; **su -a scala** (*commercio, produzione, esperimento, attacco*) large-scale
vaticano, -a [va·ti·'ka:·no] *agg* Vatican
Vaticano *m* Vatican; **il Vaticano** the Vatican; **lo Stato del Vaticano** the Vatican State; **la Città del Vaticano** Vatican City

> **i** Città del Vaticano (Vatican City) is the smallest independent state in the world, covering an area of just 0.44 square km. It lies inside downtown Rome and consists of **Piazza San Pietro** (St. Peter's Square), St. Peter's Basilica (**Basilica di San Pietro**) and the **Palazzi Vaticani**, the Vatican Palaces, which include the Pope's official residence.

vattelapesca [vat·te·la·'pes·ka] *int inf* who knows
ve [ve] *pron* (*before lo, la, li, le, ne*) *v.* **vi**
vecchiaia [vek·'kia:·ia] <-aie> *f* (*età*) old age
vecchietto, -a [vek·'kiet·to] *m, f* little old man *m*, little old woman *f*
vecchio ['vɛk·kio] *m* <-> **1.**(*sapore, odore*) **sapere di ~** (*cibo*) to taste stale; (*di abito*) to smell musty **2.**(*cosa datata*) old; **il ~ e il nuovo** the old and the new

vecchio, -a <-cchi, -cchie> **I.** *agg* **1.**(*gener*) old; **da ~** in one's old age; **essere più ~ di qu** to be older than sb; **essere meno ~ di qu** not to be as old as sb **2.**(*superato*) outdated; (*mentalità, moda, sistema*) old-fashioned; **~ stile** old-style; **~ stampo** of the old school **3.**(*stagionato, invecchiato: alimenti*) mature; (*legna*) seasoned **4.**(*personaggio*) **Plinio/Catone il Vecchio** Pliny/Cato the Elder **5.**(*loc*) **essere più ~ di Matusalemme** to be as old as the hills; **essere ~ come il cucco** to be as old as the hills; **una -cchia conoscenza** an old acquaintance; **una -cchia conoscenza della polizia** *scherz* an ex-con; **essere ~ del mestiere** to be an old hand; **-cchia volpe** *fig* sly old fox; **-cchia guardia** old guard; **gallina -cchia fa buon brodo** *prov* there's no substitute for experience **II.** *m, f* **1.**(*persona anziana*) old person **2.**(*genitore, antenato*) **il mio ~** my old man; **i miei -cchi** *inf* my folks; **i**

-**cchi** the old folks **3.** (*persona esperta*) old hand; **Grande Vecchio** *fig* grand old man **4.** *scherz* (*capo*) boss

vece ['veːtʃe] *f* (*funzione, ufficio, mansione*) **fare le -i di qu** to act for sb; **in ~ di qu** instead of sb

vedente [ve·'dɛn·te] *mf* sighted person

vedere[1] [ve·'deː·re] <vedo, vidi, visto *o* veduto> I. *vt* **1.** (*gener*) to see; **~ con i propri occhi** to see with one's own eyes; (**guarda**) **chi si vede!** *inf* look who it is!; **non farsi ~** not to appear; **non essersi vivo** not to arrive; **farsi ~ dal medico** to see the doctor; **vedo!** I see!; **si vede che** it's clear that; **vediamo** (**un po'**) let's see; **~ di ...** +*inf* (*badare*) to take care to ...; **vederne delle belle** [*o* **di cotte e di crude**] [*o* **di tutti i colori**] to see a few things; **vedi** (*nell'editoria*) see **2.** (*visitare: museo, mostra*) to visit **3.** (*esaminare: giornale, legge, questione*) to look at **4.** (*loc*) **avere a che ~ con qc/qu** (*essere in rapporto con*) to have something to do with sth/sb; **chi s'è visto s'è visto** and that's that; **non ~ l'ora di ...** +*inf fig* (*desiderare*) not to be able to wait until ...; **non ~ l'ora che ...** +*conj* not to be able to wait until ...; **stiamo** [*o* **staremo**] **a ~!** let's wait and see!; **~ le stelle** *fig* to see stars; **vedrò** [*o* **vedremo**] well **II.** *vi avere* (*possedere la vista*) **vederci** to see **III.** *vr:* -**rsi 1.** (*vedere se stessi*) to see oneself **2.** (*incontrarsi, frequentarsi*) to see (one another); **con Maria mi vedo spesso** I see a lot of Maria; **ci vediamo domani** see you tomorrow **3.** (*riconoscersi*) to see oneself **4.** (*trovarsi in una situazione*) to be

vedere[2] *m* **1.** (*atto*) **al ~ ...** on seeing ... **2.** (*apparenza*) **essere un bel ~** to be a real sight **3.** (*opinione*) view

vedetta [ve·'det·ta] *f* **1.** MIL (*postazione*) lookout tower **2.** MIL (*sentinella*) sentry; **essere di ~** to be on sentry duty **3.** MAR (*guardacoste*) patrol boat

vedette [və·'dɛt] <-> *f a. fig* leading lady

vedovanza [ve·do·'van·tsa] *f* widowhood

vedovo, -a ['veː·do·vo] I. *m, f* (*uomo*) widower; (*donna*) widow II. *agg* **rimanere ~** to be widowed

veduta [ve·'duː·ta] *f* **1.** (*panorama, immagine*) view; **~ aerea** aerial view **2.** *pl fig* (*mentalità, idee*) views *pl* **3.** ARCH **~ prospettica** prospect

veemente [ve·e·'mɛn·te] *agg* **1.** (*impetuoso, violento: attacco*) fierce; (*onda*) wild **2.** *fig* (*discorso, parole*) vehement; (*reazione, passione*) intense

veemenza [ve·e·'mɛn·tsa] *f* **1.** (*impetuosità: di mare, fuoco, vento*) ferocity **2.** *fig* (*di persona, discorso*) vehemence; (*di reazione, passione*) intensity

vegan ['vɛ·gan] <-> *mf* vegan

vegetale [ve·dʒe·'taː·le] I. *agg* **1.** (*delle piante*) plant; **vita ~** plant life **2.** (*ricavato da piante*) vegetable; **olio ~** vegetable oil II. *m* **1.** (*pianta*) vegetable **2.** *fig* (*persona malata*) **ridursi a**

un ~ to be a vegetable

vegetaliano, -a [ve·dʒe·ta·'lia:·no] I. *agg* (*dieta*) vegan II. *m, f* vegan

vegetare [ve·dʒe·'taː·re] *vi* **1.** (*crescere: pianta*) to grow **2.** (*persona*) to vegetate

vegetariano, -a [ve·dʒe·ta·'ria:·no] I. *agg* vegetarian II. *m, f* (*persona*) vegetarian

vegetativo, -a [ve·dʒe·ta·'tiː·vo] *agg* vegetative

vegetazione [ve·dʒe·tat·'tsio:·ne] *f* vegetation

vegeto, -a ['vɛː·dʒe·to] *agg* **1.** (*sano: persona*) healthy; **vivo e ~** alive and well **2.** (*rigoglioso: pianta*) flourishing

veggente [ved·'dʒɛn·te] *mf* fortune-teller

veglia ['veʎ·ʎa] <-glie> *f* **1.** (*essere sveglio*) waking; **tra la ~ e il sonno** between sleep and waking **2.** (*periodo*) wakeful night; **fare la ~ a qu** to sit by sb's bedside; **fare la ~ a un morto** to keep vigil for a dead person; **~ funebre** wake **3.** (*pubblica*) vigil; **~ pasquale** Easter Vigil

vegliare [veʎ·'ʎaː·re] I. *vt* (*assistere: malato, morto*) to keep vigil for II. *vi* **1.** (*restare sveglio*) to keep vigil **2.** *fig* (*stare attenti*) to keep a watch

veglione [veʎ·'ʎoː·ne] *m* (*festa da ballo*) **~ di Capodanno** [*o* **di San Silvestro**] New Year's Eve ball; **~ di Carnevale** Carnival ball

> **i** Celebrating New Year's Eve with your family means either **il veglione** or *il cenone*. The **veglione** (literally staying up late) involves waiting for the arrival of the new year at midnight, passing the time with a New Year's Eve party or eating a large rich dinner (cenone) with friends or relatives. A typical dish for the Christmas period and New Year's Eve dinners is *cappone* (capon). Another is *zampone e lenticchie*, stuffed pig's trotter with lentils. The latter are considered important, because they will bring luck and money in the new year.

veicolare [ve·i·ko·'laː·re] I. *agg* (*traffico, circolazione*) vehicular II. *vt* **1.** (*trasmettere: malattie*) to carry **2.** *fig* (*comunicare: idee*) to communicate

veicolo [ve·'iː·ko·lo] *m* **1.** (*mezzo di trasporto*) vehicle **2.** *fig* (*di idee, atteggiamenti*) medium **3.** MED (*di malattie*) vector

vela ['veː·la] *f* **1.** NAUT (*tela*) sail; **barca a ~** sailboat; **andare a ~** to sail; **andare a gonfie -e** to have the wind in one's sails; *fig* to go really well; **a -e spiegate** *fig* splendidly **2.** SPORT sailing

velare [ve·'laː·re] I. *vt* **1.** (*con un velo: capo, viso*) to cover; (*quadro, statua*) to veil; (*luce, lampada*) to shade **2.** (*nuvole, nebbia*) to hide **3.** (*offuscare: occhi, sguardo, sorriso*) to cloud; (*voce*) to make husky; **le lacrime le velavano gli occhi** her eyes were clouded with tears **4.** *fig* (*attenuare: realtà, verità*) to obscure **5.** *fig* (*nascondere: difetto, proposito, sentimento*) to hide **II.** *vr:* **-rsi 1.** (*con velo*) to cover oneself; **-rsi il volto** to cover one's face; (*nell'Islam*) to wear the veil; **-rsi il capo** to cover one's head **2.** (*di rugiada*) to be covered **3.** (*offuscarsi: orizzonte, sole, luna*) to mist over; **il cielo si è velato di nubi** the sky clouded over **4.** *fig* (*occhi, sguardo, sorriso*) to mist over; (*voce*) to go husky

velato, -a [ve·'la··to] *agg* **1.** (*coperto da velo: capo, volto*) veiled **2.** (*cielo, sole*) hazy **3.** *fig* (*offuscato: sguardo*) misty; (*attenuato: voce*) husky **4.** *fig* (*celato: accenno, allusione, insinuazione*) veiled **5.** (*molto trasparente: calze*) gauzy

velatura [ve·la·'tu··ra] *f* NAUT sails *pl*

velcro® ['vel·kro] *m* velcro®

veleggiare [ve·led·'dʒa··re] *vi* **1.** (*navigare a vela*) to sail **2.** (*aliante*) to glide

veleno [ve·'le··no] *m* **1.** (*gener*) poison; (*di serpente*) venom **2.** *fig* (*odio, astio*) venom; **ingoiar** [*o* **mangiar**] [*o* **masticar**] **~** to swallow one's anger; **sputar ~** to spit bile **3.** *inf* (*bevanda, cibo disgustoso*) crap

velenoso, -a [ve·le·'no··so] *agg* poisonous

veletta [ve·'let·ta] *f* veil

velico, -a ['vɛ·li·ko] <-ci, -che> *agg* (*circolo, regata*) sailing

veliero [ve·'liɛ·ro] *m* sailing ship

velina [ve·'li·na] **I.** *f* **1.** (*carta*) tissue paper **2.** (*copia*) carbon copy **3.** TV *female assistant to TV presenter* **II.** *agg* **carta -a** tissue paper

velista [ve·'lis·ta] <-i *m*, -e *f*> *mf* sailor

velivolo [ve·'li:·vo·lo] *m* (*aeroplano*) airplane

velleità [vel·lei·'ta] <-> *f* (*ambizione*) unrealistic ambition

velleitario, -a [vel·lei·'ta:·rio] <-i, -ie> *agg* **1.** (*irrealizzabile: progetto, tentativo*) unrealistic **2.** (*che ha velleità: persona*) overambitious

vello ['vɛl·lo] *m* (*lana: di pecora, capra*) fleece; (*pelo: di volpe, leone*) pelt

vellutato, -a [vel·lu·'ta:·to] *agg* **1.** (*stoffa, pelle, petalo, buccia*) velvety **2.** (*suono, voce*) smooth; (*colore*) velvet **3.** CULIN **salsa -a** velouté sauce

velluto [vel·'lu:·to] *m a. fig* (*tessuto*) velvet; **~ a coste** corduroy

velo ['ve:·lo] *m* **1.** (*drappo*) veil; **~ da sposa** [*o* **nuziale**] bridal veil; **prendere il ~** REL to take the veil **2.** (*tessuto*) voile **3.** (*strato*) layer; **zucchero a ~** confectioners' sugar **4.** (*di nebbia, lacrime*) veil **5.** *fig* (*di mistero*) veil; (*di tristezza*) shadow; (*d'indifferenza*) cloak; **stendere un ~ pietoso su qc** to cover sth with a veil of silence **6.** ANAT, LING **~ palatino** soft palate

veloce [ve·'lo:·tʃe] **I.** *agg* **1.** (*veicolo, animale, pista*) fast **2.** (*segretaria, lavoratore*) quick **3.** (*lettura, riparazione, pasto*) quick **4.** (*tempo*) fast **5.** (*loc*) **~ come un lampo** as fast as lightning; **~ come il vento** like the wind **II.** *avv* quickly

velocista [ve·lo·'tʃis·ta] <-i *m*, -e *f*> *mf* SPORT sprinter

velocità [ve·lo·tʃi·'ta] <-> *f* speed; **~ di crociera** cruising speed; **limite di ~** speed limit; **~ media** average speed; **~ della luce** speed of light; **~ del suono** speed of sound

velocizzare [ve·lo·tʃid·'dza:·re] *vt* to speed up

velodromo [ve·'lɔ:·dro·mo] *m* SPORT velodrome

vena ['ve:·na] *f* **1.** ANAT vein; **tagliarsi le -e** to slit one's wrist **2.** GEOG, MIN vein **3.** *fig* (*poetica, musicale*) vein **4.** *fig* (*traccia: di malinconia, ironia*) trace **5.** *fig* (*disposizione, umore*) mood; **essere** [*o* **sentirsi**] **in ~ di fare qc** to be in the mood to do sth

venale [ve·'na:·le] *agg* **1.** *fig, pej* (*persona*) corrupt; (*amore*) mercenary **2.** (*di vendita*) selling

venato, -a [ve·'na:·to] *agg* **1.** (*marmo*) veined; (*legno*) grained **2.** *fig* (*pervaso: di malinconia, tristezza*) tinged

venatorio, -a [ve·na·'tɔ:·rio] <-i, -ie> *agg* (*della caccia*) hunting

venatura [ve·na·'tu·ra] *f* **1.** (*di marmo, foglio*) vein; (*di legno*) grain **2.** *fig* (*sfumatura: di tristezza, rimpianto*) trace

vendemmia [ven·'dem·mia] <-ie> *f* (grape) harvest

vendemmiare [ven·dem·'mia:·re] **I.** *vi* (*fare la vendemmia*) to harvest **II.** *vt a. fig* to gather

vendere ['ven·de·re] **I.** *vt* **1.** (*smerciare*) to sell; **vendesi** [*o* **vendonsi**] for sale; **da ~** *fig* (*moltissimo*) to spare **2.** (*tradire*) to sell out; **~ l'anima al diavolo** *fig* to sell one's soul to the devil **II.** *vr:* **-rsi** to sell oneself; **-rsi la camicia** (*ridursi sul lastrico*) to sell the shirt off one's back

vendetta [ven·'det·ta] *f* **1.** (*rivalsa*) revenge; **~ trasversale** *revenge targeted at a person's family* **2.** (*castigo*) vengeance; **gridare ~** *a. scherz* to demand justice

vendicare [ven·di·'ka:·re] **I.** *vt* to avenge **II.** *vr* **-rsi di qc** (*offesa, torto*) to avenge sth; **-rsi di qu** (*offensore*) to take revenge on sb

vendicativo, -a [ven·di·ka·'ti:·vo] *agg* (*pronto a vendicarsi*) vindictive

vendita ['ven·di·ta] *f* sale; **essere in ~** to be for sale; **~ all'asta** auction; **~ all'ingrosso** wholesale; **~ al minuto** retail sale; **~ di fine stagione** end of season sale; **~ porta a porta** door-to-door selling

venditore, -trice [ven·di·'to:·re] *m, f* **1.** COM salesperson; **~ ambulante** travelling salesperson; **~ di fumo** *fig* big mouth **2.** JUR seller

venduto, -a [ven·'du:·to] *agg* **1.** (*merce*) sold **2.** *fig, pej* (*corrotto: persona*) corrupt

venerabile [ve·ne·'ra:·bi·le] *agg* (*rispettabile*) venerable

venerando, -a [ve·ne·'ran·do] *agg* **-a età** *a. scherz* venerable

venerare [ve·ne·'ra:·re] *vt* **1.** REL (*adorare*) to venerate **2.** (*onorare: genitori, memoria*) to revere

venerazione [ve·ne·rat·'tsio:·ne] *f a.* REL ven-

V

eration

venerdì [ve·ner·'di] <-> *m* Friday; ~ **grasso** Carnival Friday; ~ **santo** Good Friday; **gli manca un** [*o* **qualche**] ~ *scherz* he's got a screw loose; *v.a.* **domenica**

Venere ['vɛː·ne·re] *f* **dea, pianeta** Venus

venere ['vɛː·ne·re] *f* (*donna*) beauty

venereo, -a [ve·'nɛː·reo] *agg* MED venereal; **malattia -a** venereal disease

Veneto *m* Veneto (region)

veneto ['vɛː·ne·to] <*sing*> *m* (*dialetto*) dialect spoken in the Veneto region

veneto, -a I. *agg* 1. (*del Veneto*) *from the Veneto region* 2. (*di Venezia*) Venetian II. *m, f* person from the Veneto region

Venezia [ve·'nɛt·tsia] *f* 1. (*città*) Venice 2. (*regione*) **la ~-Giulia** Venezia-Giulia

veneziana [ve·net·'tsia·na] *f* (*tenda*) Venetian blind

veneziano [ve·net·'tsia·no] <*sing*> *m* (*dialetto*) Venetian (dialect)

veneziano, -a I. *agg* (*di Venezia*) Venetian II. *m, f* (*abitante*) Venetian

Venezuela [ve·net·tsu·e··la] *m* il ~ Venezuela

venezuelano, -a [ve·net·tsu·e·'la·no] I. *agg* (*del Venezuela*) Venezuelan II. *m, f* (*abitante*) Venezuelan

vengo ['vɛŋ·go] *1. pers sing pr di* **venire**

veniale [ve·'nia·le] *agg* 1. REL (*non grave*) venial; **peccato** ~ venial sin 2. (*perdonabile: errore, mancanza, colpa*) forgivable

venire [ve·'niː·re] <vengo, venni, venuto> I. *vi essere* 1. (*gener*) to come; ~ **da qc/qu** to come from sth/sb; **far ~** (*chiamare*) to call out 2. (*uscire: liquido*) to come out 3. (*cadere: pioggia, neve*) to fall 4. (*alla mente*) to occur; **mi è venuta un'idea** I've had an idea 5. (*malattie*) **mi sta venendo l'influenza** I'm coming down with the flu 6. ~ **da ...** +*inf* (*sentire l'impulso di*) to feel like ... 7. (*ricordare*) to remember; **non mi viene!** I don't remember! 8. (*riuscire*) to turn out (well); **non mi viene mai la maionese** my mayonnaise never turns out well 9. (*risultare: numero*) to come to; (*nel lotto, nella tombola*) to come up 10. *inf* (*costare*) to come to; ~ **a costare** to come to a total of 11. *inf* (*spettare*) to come out; **ci vengono 100 euro a testa** it comes out at 100 euros each 12. (*nascere*) to arrive 13. (*crescere: pianta*) to come up 14. (*con participio passato*) to be 15. (*loc*) **a** ~ (*in futuro*) to come; **andare e** ~ to come and go; **come viene viene** (*alla meno peggio*) come what may; ~ **a conoscenza di qc** (*essere informato*) to come to know of sth; ~ **al dunque** [*o* **sodo**] to get to the point; ~ **alla luce** (*nascere: bambino*) to be born; (*essere scoperto: cosa*) to come to light; ~ **dentro** (*entrare*) to come in; ~ **fuori** (*uscire*) to come out; ~ **giù** (*scendere*) to come down; ~ **in mente a qu** (*essere ricordato*) to come to sb's mind; ~ **incontro a qu** *fig* (*aiutare*) to come to sb's help; ~ **meno** (*mancare*) to be lacking;

~ **prima di qc/qn** (*precedere, essere più importante*) to come before sth/sb; ~ **su** (*salire*) to come up; *fig* (*crescere*) to grow up; ~ **via** (*spostarsi: persona*) to come away; (*staccarsi: cosa*) to come off; (*scomparire: macchia*) to come out II. *vr* **venirsene** (*procedere*) to come; **venirsene** (**via**) *fam* (*allontanarsi*) to walk out

venoso, -a [ve·'noː·so] *agg* MED (*di vena*) venous

ventaglio [ven·'taʎ·ʎo] <-gli> *m* 1. (*oggetto*) fan; **a** ~ (*a raggiera*) in a fan shape 2. (*gamma*) range

ventata [ven·'taː·ta] *f* 1. (*di vento*) gust of wind 2. *fig* (*di entusiasmo*) surge; (*di novità, freschezza*) wave

ventennale [ven·ten·'naː·le] I. *agg* 1. (*che dura 20 anni*) twenty-year 2. (*che ricorre ogni 20 anni*) happening every twenty years II. *m* (*ventesimo anniversario*) twentieth anniversary

ventenne [ven·'tɛn·ne] I. *agg* twenty-year-old II. *mf* (*persona*) twenty-year-old

ventennio [ven·'tɛn·nio] <-i> *m* (*periodo di venti anni*) twenty years *pl;* **il Ventennio** the period of Fascist dictatorship in Italy

ventesimo [ven·'tɛː·zi·mo] *m* (*frazione*) twentieth

ventesimo, -a I. *agg* (*numerale ordinale*) twentieth; **il ~ secolo** the twentieth century II. *m, f* twentieth; *v.a.* **quinto**

venti ['ven·ti] I. *num* twenty II. <-> *m* 1. (*numero*) twenty 2. (*giorno*) twentieth 3. (*anno*) twenty; **gli anni Venti** the nineteen-twenties 4. (*numero civico*) number twenty 5. (*autobus, tram*) number twenty III. *fpl* (*ore*) eight (o'clock) in the evening IV. *mpl* (*minuti*) twenty; *v.a.* **cinquanta**

ventilare [ven·ti·'laː·re] *vt* 1. (*stanza, casa*) to air 2. (*fare vento*) to fan 3. *fig* (*prospettare: idea, ipotesi, progetto*) to air

ventilato, -a [ven·ti·'laː·to] *agg* 1. (*aerato: casa, stanza*) ventilated 2. (*esposto al vento*) windy

ventilatore [ven·ti·la·'toː·re] *m* fan

ventilazione [ven·ti·lat·'tsio··ne] *f* 1. (*aerazione*) ventilation 2. (*presenza di vento*) air

ventina [ven·'tiː·na] *f* 1. (*circa venti*) about twenty 2. (*età*) twentieth birthday; **essere sulla** ~ to be about twenty (years old)

ventiquattr'ore, ventiquattrore [ven·ti·kuat·'troː·re] *f* 1. (*valigetta*) overnight bag 2. SPORT (*gara*) twenty-four hour race 3. *pl* (*periodo*) twenty-four hours *pl;* ~ **su ventiquattro** twenty-four hours a day

ventitré [ven·ti·'tre] I. *num* twenty-three II. <-> *m* 1. (*numero*) twenty-three 2. (*giorno*) twenty-third 3. (*anno*) twenty-three 4. (*numero civico*) number twenty-three 5. (*autobus, tram*) number twenty-three III. *fpl* (*ore*) eleven (o'clock) in the evening; **portare il cappello sulle** ~ to wear one's hat to one side IV. *mpl* (*minuti*) twenty-three; *v.a.* **cinque**

vento ['vɛn·to] *m* (*spostamento d'aria*) wind; **giacca a ~** windbreaker; **mulino a ~** windmill; **correre come il ~** to run like the wind; **parlare al ~** *fig* to waste one's breath; **qual buon ~ (ti porta)**? *fig* to what do we owe the pleasure of your visit?; **spargere una notizia ai quattro -i** *fig* to tell a piece of news to anyone and everyone

ventola ['vɛn·to·la] *f* **1.** (*per il fuoco*) bellows *pl* **2.** (*di raffreddamento*) fan

ventosa [ven·'to:·sa] *f* **1.** (*adesiva*) suction cup; (*per sturare*) plunger **2.** ZOO (*di polipo, sanguisuga*) sucker

ventoso, -a [ven·'to:·so] *agg* windy

ventre ['vɛn·tre] *m* **1.** ANAT (*pancia*) stomach; **~ a terra** face down; **~ materno** *lit* womb **2.** *fig* (*cavità*) belly

ventricolo [ven·'tri:·ko·lo] *m* ANAT ventricle; **~ cardiaco** cardiac ventricle

ventriloquo, -a [ven·'tri:·lo·kuo] *m, f* ventriloquist

ventunenne [ven·tu·'nɛn·ne] **I.** *agg* twenty-one year old **II.** *mf* twenty-one year old

ventura [ven·'tu:·ra] *f* (*sorte*) chance; **andare alla ~** to trust to luck

venturo, -a [ven·'tu:·ro] *agg* (*prossimo*) next; **ci vediamo la settimana -a** see you next week; **prossimo ~** next

venuta [ve·'nu:·ta] *f* (*arrivo*) arrival

venuto, -a [ve·'nu:·to] **I.** *pp di* **venire II.** *m, f* person who has arrived; **nuovo ~** newcomer; **il primo ~** *fig* anybody who comes along; **non essere il primo ~** *fig* not to be just anybody

vera ['ve:·ra] *f* (*anello*) wedding band

verace [ve·'ra:·tʃe] *agg merid* (*genuino*) genuine

veramente [ve·ra·'men·te] *avv* **1.** (*gener*) really **2.** (*molto*) very **3.** (*a dire la verità*) actually

veranda [ve·'ran·da] *f* (*terrazzo*) veranda

verbale [ver·'ba:·le] **I.** *agg* **1.** (*accordo*) verbal **2.** (*in grammatica: del verbo*) verbal **3.** LING (*del linguaggio, della parola*) oral **II.** *m* ADM **1.** (*documento: di contravvenzione, processo*) record; **mettere qc a ~** to put sth on record **2.** (*di riunione*) minutes *pl*; **redigere** [*o* **stendere**] **un ~** to take the minutes

verbena [ver·'bɛ:·na] *f* (*pianta*) verbena

verbo ['vɛr·bo] *m* LING verb

vercellese I. *agg* (*di Vercelli*) from Vercelli **II.** *mf* (*abitante*) person from Vercelli

Vercellese <*sing*> *m* (*zona*) Vercelli area; **nel ~** in the Vercelli area

Vercelli *f* Vercelli

verdastro, -a [ver·'das·tro] *agg* (*colore*) greenish

verde ['ver·de] **I.** *agg* **1.** (*colore*) green **2.** (*frutta, verdura*) unripe **3.** (*territorio, area cittadina*) green; **zona ~** green zone **4.** (*ecologico: benzina, energia, veicolo*) green **5.** *fig* (*livido*) livid; **essere ~ per l'invidia** to be green with envy **6.** (*giovanile*) **anni -i** adolescence **7.** (*loc*) **carta ~** FIN international auto in-

surance card; **numero ~** toll free number **II.** *m* **1.** (*colore*) green **2.** (*parte*) green part; **essere** [*o* **ridursi**] **al ~** *fig, fam* to be broke **3.** (*vegetazione*) greenery **4.** (*di semaforo*) green **III.** *mf* POL green; **il partito dei -i** the Greens

verdeggiante [ver·ded·'dʒan·te] *agg* (*aiuola, campagna, valle*) verdant

verderame [ver·de·'ra:·me] <-> *m* CHEM copper acetate

verdetto [ver·'det·to] *m* **1.** JUR (*sentenza*) verdict; **~ di assoluzione** not guilty verdict; **~ di condanna** guilty verdict **2.** SPORT (*decisione: di arbitro, giuria*) ruling **3.** *fig* (*responso*) verdict

verdiano, -a [ver·'dia:·no] *agg* MUS (*di Giuseppe Verdi*) Verdian

verdicchio [ver·'dik·kio] <-cchi> *m* Verdicchio, *dry white wine from the Marche region*

verdognolo, -a [ver·'doɲ·ɲo·lo] *agg* **1.** (*verde sgradevole*) greenish **2.** (*livido: viso*) green

verdolino, -a [ver·do·'li:·no] *agg* light green

verdone, -a [ver·'do:·ne] **I.** *agg* (*verde scuro*) dark green **II.** *m* **1.** (*colore*) dark green **2.** *inf* (*dollaro in banconota*) greenback **3.** AUTO (*contrassegno*) green sticker indicating that a car complies with EU pollution limits

verdura [ver·'du:·ra] *f* vegetables *pl*

verduzzo [ver·'dut·tso] *m* Verduzzo, *dry white wine from the Friuli region*

verga ['ver·ga] <-ghe> *f* (*bacchetta*) rod; (*di pastore*) staff; (*di rabdomante*) divining rod

vergare [ver·'ga:·re] *vt* **1.** (*rigare: tessuto, foglio*) to rule **2.** (*scrivere a mano*) to write (by hand)

verginale [ver·dʒi·'na:·le] *agg* (*di vergine*) virginal

vergine ['ver·dʒi·ne] **I.** *f* **1.** (*donna illibata*) virgin **2.** *sing* REL **la Vergine** (*la Madonna*) the Virgin Mary **3.** *sing* ASTR **la Vergine** Virgo; **sono della** [*o* **una**] **Vergine** I'm Virgo **II.** *agg* **1.** (*illibato*) virgin **2.** (*naturale*) virgin; **foresta ~** virgin forest; **pura lana ~** pure virgin wool; **olio (extra)~ d'oliva** (extra) virgin oil; **terreno ~** virgin soil; **terra** [*o* **terreno**] **~** *fig* unexplored territory **3.** (*non inciso: nastro, cassetta, dischetto*) blank

verginità [ver·dʒi·ni·'ta] <-> *f* **1.** (*illibatezza*) virginity **2.** *fig* (*integrità morale*) reputation; **rifarsi una ~** *scherz* to rebuild one's reputation

vergogna [ver·'goɲ·ɲa] *f* **1.** (*gener*) shame; **provare ~ per qc** to be ashamed of sth; **essere la ~ della famiglia** to be the shame of the family; **che ~!** [*o* **~!**] what a disgrace! **2.** (*imbarazzo, disagio*) embarrassment; **avere ~ di qc** to be embarrassed about sth **3.** (*timidezza*) shyness; **avere ~ di fare qc** to be afraid to do sth

vergognarsi [ver·goɲ·'ɲar·si] *vr* **1.** (*essere mortificato*) to be ashamed; **~ di qc/qu** to be ashamed of sth/sb; **~ per qu** to be ashamed for sb; **~ come un ladro** to be deeply ashamed; **vergognati!** *fam* shame on you! **2.** (*imbarazzarsi*) to be embarrassed; **~ a fare**

qc to be embarrassed about doing sth **3.**(*essere timido*) to be shy

vergognoso, -a [ver·goɲ·'ɲoː·so] *agg* **1.**(*ignobile, disonorevole*) disgraceful **2.**(*imbarazzato: guardo, tono*) embarrassed **3.**(*timido*) shy

veridicità [ve·ri·di·tʃi·'ta] <-> *f* truthfulness

verifica [ve·'riː·fi·ka] <-che> *f* **1.**(*controllo: di passaporto, impianto*) check **2.** MAT (*di equazione, operazione, problema*) check **3.**(*di bilancio, conto*) audit; ~ **contabile** accounting audit **4.**(*a scuola*) test

verificabile [ve·ri·fi·'kaː·bi·le] *agg* (*dato, ipotesi*) verifiable

verificare [ve·ri·fi·'kaː·re] **I.** *vt* **1.**(*provare: qualità, funzionamento*) to test; (*documento, firma, affermazione*) to check; (*bilancio, conto*) to audit **2.**(*nella scienza: convalidare*) to confirm **II.** *vr:* **-rsi 1.**(*accadere: fatto*) to happen **2.**(*avverarsi: ipotesi, previsione*) to prove to be true

verismo [ve·'riz·mo] *m* realism

verità [ve·ri·'ta] <-> *f* truth; **in** [*o* **per la**] ~ (*veramente*) to tell the truth; **la ~ viene sempre a galla** *prov* the truth will out

veritiero, -a [ve·ri·'tiɛː·ro] *agg* **1.**(*persona*) truthful **2.**(*notizia, testimonianza, racconto*) accurate

verme ['vɛr·me] *m* **1.**(*animale*) worm; **fare i -i** (*cibo*) to go rotten; **essere nudo come un ~** to be bare naked; **~ solitario** tapeworm **2.** *fig* (*miserabile*) worm

vermicelli [ver·mi·'tʃɛl·li] *mpl* vermicelli *sing*

vermifugo [ver·'miː·fu·go] <-ghi> *m* vermifuge

vermifugo, -a <-ghi, -ghe> *agg* vermifuge

vermiglio, -a <-gli, -glie> **I.** *agg* vermillion **II.** *m, f* (*colore*) vermillion

vermouth, vermut ['vɛr·mut] <-> *m* vermouth

vernaccia [ver·'nat·tʃa] <-cce> *f* Vernaccia, dry white wine

vernice [ver·'niː·tʃe] *f* **1.**(*tinta*) paint; **'~ fresca!'** 'wet paint!' **2.**(*trasparente*) varnish **3.**(*pellame*) patent leather **4.** *fig* (*apparenza*) veneer

verniciare [ver·ni·'tʃaː·re] *vt* **1.**(*con tinta*) to paint **2.**(*con vernice trasparente*) to varnish

verniciata [ver·ni·'tʃaː·ta] *f* **1.**(*con tinta*) coat of paint **2.**(*con vernice trasparente*) coat of varnish

verniciatura [ver·ni·tʃa·'tuː·ra] *f* **1.**(*operazione*) painting **2.**(*strato*) (coat of) paint

vernissage [vɛr·ni·'saːʒ] <-> *m* (*di mostra*) opening

vero ['veː·ro] <-sing> *m* **1.**(*verità*) truth; **a dire il ~** to tell the truth **2.**(*realtà*) reality; **dal ~** (*dipingere*) from real life; **ritratto dal ~** life drawing

vero, -a *agg* **1.**(*affermazione, notizia, persona, amore*) true; (*pentimento*) genuine; **è ~ che ...** it's true that ...; **è incredibile, ma ~** it may seem incredible, but it's true **2.**(*autentico,*

reale: causa, significato, valore) real; ~ **e proprio** out and out **3.**(*genuino: prodotto, materiale*) genuine

Verona *f* Verona

veronese [ve·ro·'neː·se] <*sing*> *m* (*dialetto*) Veronese (dialect)

veronese I. *agg* (*di Verona*) from Verona **II.** *mf* (*abitante*) person from Verona

Veronese <*sing*> *m* (*zona*) Verona area; **nel ~** in the Verona area

verosimiglianza [ve·ro·si·miʎ·'ʎan·tsa] *f* (*di ipotesi, racconto*) plausibility

verosimile [ve·ro·'siː·mi·le] *agg* (*ipotesi, racconto*) plausible

verrò [ver·'rɔ] *1. pers sing futuro di* **venire**

verruca [ver·'ruː·ka] <-che> *f* MED wart; (*al piede*) verruca

versaccio [ver·'sat·tʃo] <-cci> *m pej* (*smorfia*) grimace; **fare i -cci a qu** to make faces at sb

versamento [ver·sa·'men·to] *m* **1.**(*deposito, pagamento*) deposit; **fare** [*o* **effettuare**] **un ~** to make a deposit **2.** MED (*di liquido*) effusion

versante [ver·'san·te] *m* GEOG side

versare [ver·'saː·re] **I.** *vt* **1.**(*liquido, farina, zucchero*) to pour; ~ **lacrime** (*piangere*) to cry; ~ **sangue** (*sanguinare*) to bleed **2.**(*spandere*) to spill; **piangere sul latte versato** *fig* to cry over spilt milk **3.**(*soldi*) to deposit **II.** *vi* (*essere, trovarsi*) to be; ~ **in fin di vita** to be dying **III.** *vr:* **-rsi 1.**(*spargersi, rovesciarsi addosso*) to spill **2.**(*fiume*) to flow

versatile [ver·'saː·ti·le] *agg* (*eclettico*) versatile

versato, -a [ver·'saː·to] *agg* **essere ~ in qc** (*competente*) to be knowledgeable about sth; (*capace*) to be skilled at sth

versetto [ver·'set·to] *m* **1.**(*verso*) line **2.** REL (*paragrafo*) verse

versione [ver·'sio·ne] *f* **1.**(*gener*) version **2.**(*traduzione*) translation

verso¹ ['vɛr·so] *prep* **1.**(*direzione*) toward **2.**(*vicino a, nei pressi di*) near **3.**(*nel tempo: circa*) around; (*prima di*) towards **4.**(*nei confronti di*) toward

verso² **I.** *m* **1.** LIT (*unità metrica*) line **2.** *pl* LIT (*composizione*) verse *sing* **3.**(*di animale*) call **4.**(*di persona: grido*) cry **5.**(*gesto, smorfia*) grimace; (*imitazione*) imitation; **fare il ~ a qu** to do a takeoff on sb **6.**(*direzione*) direction; **prendere qu per il suo ~** [*o* **per il ~ giusto**] to know how to handle sb; **tutto va per il ~ giusto** everything's going well **7.**(*di pelo, stoffa*) direction **8.** *fig* (*modo*) way; **per un ~** in one way **II.** *m* <-> (*di foglio*) back; (*di moneta, medaglia*) reverse

vertebra ['vɛr·te·bra] *f* ANAT vertebra

vertebrale [ver·te·'braː·le] *agg* ANAT, MED vertebral; **colonna ~** spine

vertebrato [ver·te·'braː·to] *m* vertebrate

vertebrato, -a *agg* vertebrate

vertenza [ver·'tɛn·tsa] *f* JUR, ADM (*controversia*) controversy; **~ sindacale** labor dispute

vertere ['vɛr·te·re] <*mancano il pp e le forme composte*> *vi* **~ su qc** (*discussione, ques-*

tione) to turn on sth
verticale [ver·ti·'ka:·le] I. *agg* vertical; **pianoforte** ~ upright piano II. *f* 1. (*retta*) vertical 2. SPORT (*esercizio*) handstand 3. (*nei cruciverba*) down
vertice ['vɛr·ti·tʃe] *m* 1. *fig* (*di successo, carriera*) peak 2. (*di impresa, organizzazione, partito*) leadership 3. (*incontro*) summit 4. MAT vertex
vertigine [ver·'ti:·dʒi·ne] *f* 1. (*capogiro*) dizziness 2. *fig* (*ebbrezza, turbamento*) intoxication
vertiginoso, -a [ver·ti·dʒi·'no:·so] *agg* 1. (*altezza*) dizzying 2. MED vertiginous 3. *fig* (*rapidissimo: ritmo, danza, velocità*) breakneck 4. *fig* (*enorme: cifra, prezzo, ricchezza*) breathtaking; **scollatura -a** plunging neckline
verve [vɛrv] <-> *f* verve
verza ['ver·dza] *f* Savoy cabbage
vescica [veʃ·'ʃi:·ka] <-che> *f* 1. ANAT bladder 2. MED (*bolla*) blister
vescovo ['ves·ko·vo] *m* REL bishop
vespa ['vɛs·pa] *f* (*insetto*) wasp; **avere un vitino di** ~ *fig* to have a wasp waist
Vespa® ['vɛs·pa] *f* (*scooter*) Vespa®
vespaio [ves·'pa:·io] <-ai> *m* (*nido*) wasp's nest; **suscitare un** ~ *fig* to stir up a hornet's nest
vespasiano [ves·pa·'zia:·no] *m* (*orinatoio*) urinal
vespro ['vɛs·pro] *m* 1. REL vespers *sing* 2. *poet* nightfall
vessare [ves·'sa:·re] *vt* (*con tributi*) to overburden; (*con richieste*) to harass
vessazione [ves·sa·'tsio:·ne] *f* oppression; **subire -i** to be oppressed
vessillo [ves·'sil·lo] *m* 1. (*bandiera, stendardo*) standard 2. *fig* (*emblema, simbolo*) emblem
vestaglia [ves·'taʎ·ʎa] <-glie> *f* dressing gown
vestaglietta [ves·taʎ·'ʎet·ta] *f* summer dress
vestale [ves·'ta:·le] *f fig* (*custode intransigente*) guardian
veste ['vɛs·te] *f* 1. (*abito*) garment; ~ **da camera** dressing gown 2. *pl* (*indumenti*) clothes *pl* 3. *fig* (*apparenza*) guise 4. TYP ~ **editoriale** [*o* **tipografica**] layout 5. (*titolo, funzione, qualità*) capacity 6. *fig* (*forma di espressione*) form
vestiario [ves·'tia:·rio] <-ri> *m* 1. (*indumenti personali*) clothes *pl;* **rinnovare il** ~ to renew one's wardrobe; **capo di** ~ item of clothing 2. (*assortimento*) clothes *pl*
vestire¹ [ves·'ti:·re] I. *vt* 1. (*abbigliare*) to dress 2. (*fornire di vestiti*) to clothe 3. (*indossare: abito, uniforme, taglia*) to wear; ~ **la divisa** to wear uniform; ~ **la toga** to be a magistrate; ~ **il saio** [*o* **la tonaca**] to take holy orders 4. (*cadere*) to fit II. *vi* (*abbigliarsi in un certo modo*) to dress; ~ **di bianco/nero** to dress in white/black III. *vr:* **-rsi** 1. (*abbigliarsi*) to get dressed 2. (*abbigliarsi in un certo modo*) to dress; **sapere** ~ to be well-dressed; **si veste da**

un grande sarto he buys his clothes from one of the best tailors 3. *fig* (*ricoprirsi*) ~ **di qc** to be attired in sth
vestire² *m* 1. (*abbigliamento*) clothing 2. (*modo di vestire*) fashion sense
vestito [ves·'ti:·to] *m* 1. (*da donna*) dress 2. (*da uomo*) suit
Vesuvio [ve·'zu:·vio] *m* Vesuvius
veterano [ve·te·'ra:·no] *m* MIL (*soldato*) veteran
veterano, -a I. *agg* (*anziano, esperto*) veteran II. *m, f fig* (*persona esperta*) veteran
veterinaria [ve·te·ri·'na:·ria] <-ie> *f* veterinary science
veterinario, -a [ve·te·ri·'na:·rio] <-i, -ie> I. *agg* (*ambulatorio, medico*) veterinary II. *m, f* (*medico*) vet
veto ['vɛ:·to] <-> *m* veto; **diritto di** ~ right of veto; **porre** [*o* **opporre**] **il** ~ **a qc** to veto sth
vetraio, -a [ve·'tra:·io] <-ai, -aie> *m, f* (*artigiano*) glazier; (*operaio*) glassmaker
vetrata [ve·'tra:·ta] *f* 1. (*porta*) glass door; (*finestra*) (large) window; (*soffitto*) glass ceiling 2. (*di chiesa, decorata*) stained glass window
vetrato, -a [ve·'tra:·to] *agg* 1. (*a vetri*) glass; **porta -a** glass door 2. (*con polvere di vetro*) **carta -a** sandpaper
vetrina [ve·'tri:·na] *f* 1. (*di negozio*) window; **mettersi in** ~ *fig* to put oneself on display 2. *fig* (*evento, luogo rappresentativo*) showcase 3. (*mobile*) display cabinet
vetrinista [ve·tri·'nis·ta] <-i *m*, -e *f*> *mf* (*professione*) window dresser
vetrino [ve·'tri:·no] *m* (*del microscopio*) slide
vetriolo [ve·tri·'ɔ:·lo] *m* (*solfato*) vitriol; **al** ~ *fig* vitriolic
vetro ['ve:·tro] *m* 1. (*materiale*) glass; ~ **infrangibile** shatterproof glass; ~ **soffiato** blown glass 2. (*oggetto*) piece of glassware 3. (*lastra*) pane 4. (*frammento*) piece of broken glass
vetroresina [ve·tro·'rɛ:·zi·na] *f* TEC fiberglass
vetta ['vet·ta] *f* 1. (*cima: di monte, campanile, albero*) peak; **in** ~ at the top 2. *fig* (*di classifica, graduatoria*) top 3. *fig* (*di successo, carriera*) peak
vettore [vet·'to:·re] *m* 1. PHYS, MAT vector 2. JUR (*trasportatore*) carrier
vettore, -trice *agg* 1. PHYS, MAT vector 2. (*razzo, missile*) carrier 3. BIOL, MED (*insetto, batterio*) carrier
vettovaglie [vet·to·'vaʎ·ʎe] *fpl* (*viveri*) victuals *pl*
vettura [vet·'tu:·ra] *f* 1. (*automobile*) car 2. FERR (*vagone*) car
vetturino [vet·tu·'ri:·no] *m* (*conducente*) driver
vezzeggiamento [vet·tsed·dʒa·'men·to] *m* pampering
vezzeggiare [vet·tsed·'dʒa:·re] *vt* (*coccolare*) to pet
vezzeggiativo [vet·tsed·dʒa·'ti:·vo] *m* 1. (*nome*) pet name 2. LING (*forma alterata*) di-

V

minutive

vezzeggiativo, -a *agg* **1.**(*affettuoso: espressione, parola*) affectionate **2.**LING (*alterato: aggettivo, sostantivo*) dimunitive

vezzo ['vet·tso] *m* **1.**(*abitudine*) habit; **avere il ~ di fare qc** to be in the habit of doing sth **2.** *pl* (*smancerie*) affectation

vezzoso, -a [vet·'tso:·so] **I.** *agg* **1.**(*lezioso*) affected **2.**(*grazioso*) charming **II.** *m, f* (*persona leziosa*) affected person; **fare il ~** to behave in an affected way

vi [vi] **I.** *pron* **1.**2. pers pl (*oggetto: voi*) you; **chi ~ ha invitati?** who invited you? **2.**(*complemento: a voi*) (to) you; **~ farò un bel regalo** I'll give you a lovely present **3.**(*forma di cortesia: Voi, a Voi*) (to) you **II.** *pron* 2. pers pl yourselves **III.** *pron* (*a ciò*) to it; (*in ciò*) in it; (*su ciò*) about it, I didn't pay much attention to it **IV.** *avv* **1.**(*qui*) here; (*lì*) there **2.**(*per di qua, per di là*) along it; (*attraverso*) through it **3. ~ sono** there are

via¹ ['vi:·a] <vie> *f* **1.**(*strada*) street; **abitare in ~ ...** to live on ... Street **2.**(*passaggio, varco*) path; **~ libera!** the path is clear! **3.**(*percorso*) route **4.**(*mezzo*) by; **~ aerea** by air; **~ fax** by fax **5.**(*tappa, stazione, scalo*) via **6.***fig* (*attività, carriera*) path **7.***fig* (*condotta morale*) path **8.***fig* (*modo*) way; **in ~ confidenziale** confidentially; **in ~ eccezionale** exceptionally; **~ di mezzo** compromise; **per vie traverse** by a roundabout route **9.***fig* (*modalità d'intervento*) method; **adire le** [*o* **ricorrere alle**] **-e legali** to resort to legal action **10.**ANAT (*canale*) channel **11.**MED (*modalità*) means *sing*; **~ orale** orally; **~ endovenosa** intravenously **12.**(*loc*) **essere in ~ di** *fig* to be on the road to; **per ~ di** (*a causa di*) because of; (*per mezzo di*) through

via² **I.** *avv* **1.**(*lontano*) away; **andare ~** to leave; **buttare** [*o* **gettare**] **~** to throw away; **essere** [*o* **stare**] **~** *inf*(*essere fuori casa*) to be out; (*essere fuori città*) to be away; **mandare ~ qu** to get rid of sb; **portare ~ qu** to take sb away **2.**(*andarsene*) to leave **3.**(*macchia*) to come out; (*bottone*) to come off **4.**(*con verbo di moto sottinteso: rapidità*) off **5.**(*eccetera*) **e così ~** [*o* **e ~ dicendo**] [*o* **e ~ di questo passo**] and so on **6. ~ ~** (*che ...*) (*gradualmente*) as (...) **II.** *int* **1.**(*per allontanare*) away **2.**(*esortazione*) come on **3.**(*incredulità, disapprovazione*) no way **4.**(*conclusione*) that's it **5.**SPORT go; **pronti, attenti, ~!** ready, steady, go! **III.** *m* (*segnale di partenza*) starting signal; **al ~** on the starting signal; **dare il ~** to start; *fig* (*dare inizio*) to start off

viabilità [vi·a·bi·li·'ta] <-> *f* **1.**(*transito*) passibility **2.**(*rete stradale*) road network

Viacard® [vi·a·'kard] <-> *f prepaid card for toll roads*

Via Crucis ['vi:·a 'kru:·tʃis] <inv *o* lat. viae crucis> *f* **1.**REL (*percorso di Gesù*) Via Crucis; (*esercizio devoto*) Way of the Cross; (*immagine*) Stations of the Cross **2.***fig* (*serie di sof-*

ferenze) ordeal

viado ['vi:a·do] <viados> *m transvestite or transsexual prostitute, typically from Brazil*

viadotto [via·'dot·to] *m* viaduct

viaggiare [vi·ad·'dʒa:·re] **I.** *vi* **1.**(*persona, treno, merce*) to travel **2.**(*come professione*) to be a traveling salesperson **3.***fig* (*fantasticare*) to travel **II.** *vt* (*percorrere*) to travel

viaggiatore, -trice [vi·ad·dʒa·'to:·re] **I.** *agg* traveling; **commesso ~** traveling salesperson **II.** *m, f* (*passeggero*) traveler

viaggio [vi·'ad·dʒo] <-ggi> *m* (*spostamento*) journey; (*breve*) trip; **buon ~!** have a good trip!; **da ~** traveling; **essere in ~** to be traveling; **mettersi in ~** to set off; **~ di nozze** honeymoon; **~ organizzato** vacation package

viagra® ['vi·ag·ra] <-> *m* MED Viagra®

viale [vi·'a:·le] *m* **1.**(*strada alberata*) avenue **2.**(*in un giardino*) path

viandante [vi·an·'dan·te] *mf poet* (*pellegrino*) wayfarer

viario, -a [vi·'a:·rio] <-i, -ie> *agg* (*stradale*) road; **rete -a** road network

viavai [vi·a·'va:·i] <-> *m* (*andirivieni*) coming and going

vibrafono [vi·'bra:·fo·no] *m* vibraphone

vibrante [vi·'bra·n·te] *agg* **1.**(*che vibra*) vibrating **2.**LING (*consonante*) trilled **3.**(*voce, tono*) vibrant **4.***fig* (*intenso: parole, discorso*) trembling **5.***fig* (*di rabbia, sdegno*) quivering

vibrare [vi·'bra:·re] **I.** *vt* **1.**(*scagliare: lancia, freccia*) to hurl **2.**(*colpo*) to strike; (*pugno*) to throw **3.**(*insulto, maledizione*) to hurl **4.**(*far risuonare*) to vibrate **II.** *vi* **1.**(*muoversi*) to vibrate **2.***fig* (*fremere*) to tremble **3.***fig* (*suono*) to vibrate

vibrato [vi·'bra:·to] *m* MUS vibrato

vibratore [vi·bra·'to:·re] *m* vibrator

vibrazione [vi·brat·'tsio:·ne] *f* **1.**(*oscillazione*) vibration **2.**(*tremolio: di luce*) flicker **3.**(*di voce, animo*) tremble **4.**MED (*massaggio*) vibration

vibromassaggiatore [vi·bro·mas·sad·dʒa·'to:·re] *m* massage vibrator

vicario [vi·'ka:·rio] <-i> **I.** *m* REL vicar; **~ apostolico** vicar apostolic; **~ parrocchiale** curate; **~ vescovile** vicar episcopal **II.** *agg* (*sostitutivo: funzione, ruolo*) replacement

vice ['vi:·tʃe] <-> *mf* deputy

vice- [vi·tʃe] (*in parole composte*) vice-; **il vicecomandante** the vice-commander; **il vicedirettore** the vice-director; **la vicepreside** the assistant principal

vicenda [vi·'tʃɛn·da] *f* **1.**(*evento, caso*) event **2.**(*storia, faccenda*) story **3.**(*loc*) **a ~** (*l'un l'altro*) each other; (*a turno*) in turns

vicendevole [vi·tʃen·'de:·vo·le] *agg* mutual

Vicentino [vi·tʃen·'ti:·no] <sing> *m* (*zona*) Vicenza area; **nel ~** in the Vicenza area

vicentino *sing* (*dialetto*) *dialect spoken in Vicenza*

vicentino, -a **I.** *agg* (*di Vicenza*) from Vicenza **II.** *m, f* (*abitante*) person from Vicenza

Vicenza [vi·'tʃɛn·tsa] *f* Vicenza

viceversa [vi·tʃe·'vɛr·sa] **I.** *avv* **1.** (*in modo inverso*) the other way around **2.** (*in direzione opposta*) return **II.** *cong* (*e invece*) on the contrary

vichingo, -a [vi·'kiŋ·go] <-ghi, -ghe> **I.** *agg* (*dei Vichinghi*) Viking **II.** *m, f* **1.** HIST Viking **2.** *scherz* (*persona nordica*) Scandinavian

vicinanza [vi·tʃi·'nan·tsa] *f* **1.** (*prossimità: nello spazio*) proximity; **in ~ di** near **2.** (*nel tempo*) nearness; **in ~ di** near **3.** *fig* (*affinità: di idee, opinioni*) affinity **4.** *pl* (*dintorni*) surrounding area; **nelle -e di qc** near sth

vicinato [vi·tʃi·'na:·to] *m* **1.** (*persone*) neighbors *pl* **2.** (*luoghi*) neighborhood **3.** (*condizione*) neighborliness

vicino [vi·'tʃi:·no] *avv* **1.** (*a poca distanza*) nearby; **~ a** near **2.** (*loc*) **andarci ~** *fig* to come close; **da ~** from close up; *fig* (*bene*) well

vicino, -a **I.** *agg* **1.** (*luogo*) nearby; (*strada, casa*) neighboring; (*confinante: nazione, stato*) neighboring; **~ a** close to **2.** (*tempo*) near; **essere ~ a qc** to be close to sth **3.** *fig* (*idealmente*) close **4.** (*stretto: parente*) close **5.** *fig* (*presente, partecipe: persona*) close **6.** (*affine: opinioni, idee*) close **7.** (*simile: colore*) close **II.** *m, f* (*di casa*) neighbor; (*di ombrellone, banco*) *person sitting next to sb;* **i nostri -i di tavola** our dining companions

vicissitudini [vi·tʃis·si·'tu:·di·ni] *fpl* ups and downs

vicolo ['vi:·ko·lo] *m* (*strada*) alleyway; **~ cieco** *a. fig* blind alley

videata [vi·de·'a:·ta] *f* COMPUT, TV (*schermata*) screen

video ['vi:·de·o] **I.** <-> *m* **1.** COMPUT, TV screen **2.** COMPUT, TV (*immagini*) video **3.** (*televisore*) TV **4.** (*videoclip*) video **II.** <inv> *agg* **1.** (*segnale, impianto*) video **2.** (*televisivo*) TV

video- [vi·de·o] (*in parole composte*) video-

videoamatore, -trice [vi·de·o·a·ma·'to:·re] *m, f* amateur film-maker

videocamera [vi·de·o·'ka:·me·ra] *f* video camera

videocassetta [vi·de·o·kas·'set·ta] *f* video (cassette)

videochiamare [vi·de·o·kia·'ma:·re] *vt* to video call

videochiamata [vi·de·o·kia·'ma:·ta] *f* video call

videocitofono [vi·de·o·tʃi·'tɔ:·fo·no] *m* video door phone

videoclip [vi·de·o·'klip] <-> *m* (music) video

videoconferenza [vi·de·o·kon·fe·'rɛn·tsa] *f* videoconference

videocontrollo [vi·de·o·kon·'trɔl·lo] *m* closed circuit TV monitoring

videocrazia [vi·de·o·cra·'tsi·a] *f* (*potere della tv*) tyranny of the TV; (*potere dell'immagine*) tyranny of the visual image

videodipendente [vi·de·o·di·pen·'dɛn·te] **I.** *agg* addicted to the TV **II.** *mf* TV addict

videodipendenza [vi·de·o·di·pen·'dɛn·tsa] *f* TV addiction

videofonino [vi·de·o·fo·'ni:·no] *m* video cellphone

videogame ['vi·diou geim/'vi·de·o 'geim] <-o videogames> *m* video game

videogioco [vi·de·o·'dʒɔ:·ko] *m* video game

videografia [vi·de·o·gra·'fi:·a] *f* list of published videos

videolento® [vi·de·o·'lɛn·to] *m* TEL *system for low-speed retransmission of TV images using phone network*

videoleso, -a [vi·de·o·'le:·zo] MED **I.** *agg* visually impaired **II.** *m, f* visually impaired person; **i -i** the visually impaired

videolettore [vi·de·o·let·'to:·re] *m* video player

videomessaggio [vi·de·o·mes·'sad·dʒo] *m* video message

videomusica [vi·de·o·'mu:·zi·ka] *f* video music

videonastro [vi·de·o·'nas·tro] *m* videotape

videopirateria [vi·de·o·pi·ra·te·'ri·a] *f* video piracy

videopolitica [vi·de·o·po·'li·ti·ka] *f* TV politics

videoproiettore [vi·de·o·pro·iet·'to:·re] *m* TEC video projector

videoproiezione [vi·de·o·pro·iet·'tsio:·ne] *f* TEC video projection

videoregistratore [vi·de·o·re·dʒis·tra·'to:·re] *m* video recorder

videoregistrazione [vi·de·o·re·dʒis·trat·'tsio:·ne] *f* video recording

videoripresa [vi·de·o·ri·'pre:·sa] *f* TV video filming

videoscrittura [vi·de·os·krit·'tu:·ra] *f* word processing

videosegnale [vi·de·o·sen·'ɲa:·le] *m* TV video signal

videotape ['vi·diou·teip/'vi·de·o·teip] <-o videotapes> *m* videotape

videoteca [vi·de·o·'tɛ:·ka] <-che> *f* **1.** (*negozio*) video store **2.** (*collezione*) video collection

Videotel® [vi·de·o·'tɛl] <-> *m* TEL *Italian Videotex*® *service*

videotelefonia [vi·de·o·te·le·fo·'ni:·a] *f* TEL videotelephony

videotelefonico, -a [vi·de·o·te·le·'fɔ:·ni·ko] *agg* videophone

videotelefono [vi·de·o·te·'lɛ:·fo·no] *m* videophone

videoterminale [vi·de·o·ter·mi·'na:·le] *m* COMPUT video display terminal

Videotex® [vi·de·o·'tɛks] <-> *m* TEL Videotex®

videotext [vi·de·o·'tekst] <-> *m* TEL videotext

vidi ['vi:·di] *1. pers sing pass rem di* **vedere**[1]

vidimare [vi·di·'ma:·re] *vt* ADM (*bilancio, documento*) to ratify

vidimazione [vi·di·mat·'tsio:·ne] *f* ADM (*di documento, certificato*) ratification

viene, vieni ['viɛ:·ne, 'viɛ:·ni] *3. e 2. pers sing pr di* **venire**

Vienna ['viɛn·na] *f* Vienna

V

viennese [vien·'ne:·ze] I. *agg* (*di Vienna*) Viennese II. *mf* (*abitante*) Viennese

vietare [vie·'ta:·re] *vt* (*proibire*) to prohibit; ~ qc a qu to forbid sth to sb; ~ a qu di fare qc to prevent sb from doing sth; '(è) **vietato entrare**' 'no entry'; '(è) **vietato fumare**' 'no smoking'; '(è) **vietato l'ingresso ai non addetti ai lavori**' 'authorized personnel only'; '(è) **vietato sporgersi dal finestrino**' 'do not lean out of the window'; '**film vietato ai minori**' 'must be over 18 to enter'; '**sosta vietata**' 'no parking'

Vietnam [viet·'nam] *m* il ~ Vietnam; nel [*o* in] ~ in Vietnam

vietnamita [viet·na·'mi:·ta] <-i *m*, -e *f*> I. *agg* (*del Vietnam*) Vietnamese II. *mf* (*abitante*) Vietnamese

vieto, -a ['viɛ:·to] *agg* (*usanza, idea, valore*) old-fashioned

vig. *abbr di* **vigente**

vigente [vi·'dʒɛn·te] *agg* JUR (*in vigore: disposizione, legge, regolamento*) applicable

vigere ['vi:·dʒe·re] <*usato solo nelle terze persone sing e pl*> *vi* (*disposizione, legge, regolamento*) to be applicable

vigilante [vi·dʒi·'lan·te] *mf* 1. (*guardia giurata*) security guard 2. *pl* (*cittadini organizzati*) vigilantes *pl*

vigilanza [vi·dʒi·'lan·tsa] *f* 1. (*sorveglianza*) supervision 2. (*di guardie giurate, polizia*) security

vigilare [vi·dʒi·'la:·re] I. *vt* (*sorvegliare*) to supervise II. *vi* (*badare*) to keep watch; ~ su qu/qc to supervise sb/sth

vigilato [vi·dʒi·'la:·to] *agg* JUR **libertà -a** probation

vigile ['vi:·dʒi·le] I. *agg* 1. (*attento: sguardo, occhio*) watchful 2. (*sveglio, pronto: mente*) alert II. *mf* ~ (*urbano*) (local) policeman/woman; ~ **del fuoco** firefighter

---

i The **vigili urbani** are a city police force under the command of the **Comune**. Their duties include making sure that laws on traffic, public facilities, and trade are observed.

---

vigilessa [vi·dʒi·'les·sa] *f scherz* (local) policewoman

vigilia [vi·'dʒi:·lia] <-ie> *f* 1. (*giorno prima*) **alla ~ di ...** the day before ...; **la ~ di Natale** Christmas Eve 2. (*periodo*) **alla ~ di ...** just before ...

vigliaccheria [viʎ·ʎak·ke·'ri:·a] <-ie> *f* 1. (*caratteristica*) cowardice 2. (*azione*) cowardly act

vigliacco, -a [viʎ·'ʎak·ko] <-cchi, -cche> I. *agg* 1. (*senza coraggio: persona, azione*) cowardly 2. (*prepotente*) **essere ~** to be a bully II. *m*, *f* 1. (*persona senza coraggio*) coward 2. (*persona prepotente*) bully

vigna ['viɲ·ɲa] *f* (*vigneto*) vineyard

vigneto [viɲ·'ɲe:·to] *m* vineyard

vignetta [viɲ·'ɲet·ta] *f* 1. (*satirica, umoristica*) cartoon 2. (*bollo autostradale*) Swiss highway toll sticker

vignettista [viɲ·ɲet·'tis·ta] <-i *m*, -e *f*> *mf* cartoonist

vigogna [vi·'goɲ·ɲa] *f* (*stoffa*) vicuña

vigore [vi·'go:·re] *m* 1. (*gener*) vigor 2. (*foga*) energy 3. JUR **in ~** in force; **entrare in ~** to come into force

vigoroso, -a [vi·go·'ro:·so] *agg* 1. (*forte: uomo, animale, corpo*) vigorous 2. *fig* (*intelligenza, stile, protesta*) lively 3. (*pianta*) thriving

vile ['vi:·le] I. *agg* 1. (*codardo: persona, azione*) cowardly 2. (*spregevole: denaro, interesse*) despicable II. *mf* (*persona codarda*) coward

vilipendio [vi·li·'pɛn·dio] <-i> *m* JUR (*di religione, costituzione*) defamation; (*di cadavere, tomba*) desecration

villa ['vil·la] *f* (*casa*) house; ~ **unifamiliare/bifamiliare** single/multi-family home

villaggio [vil·'lad·dʒo] <-ggi> *m* 1. (*paese*) village 2. (*complesso*) complex; ~ **globale** global village; ~ **olimpico** Olympic village; ~ **turistico** holiday resort; ~ **universitario** university campus

villanata [vil·la·'na:·ta] *f* (*maleducazione, villania*) rude piece of behavior

villania [vil·la·'ni:·a] <-ie> *f* 1. (*maleducazione*) rudeness 2. (*atto, detto da villano*) rudeness

villano, -a [vil·'la:·no] *pej* I. *agg* (*persona, comportamento*) rude II. *m*, *f* (*cafone*) rude person; **fare il ~** to behave rudely; **giochi** [*o* **scherzi**] **di mano, giochi** *prov* **da ~** physical horseplay is rude

villanzone, -a [vil·lan·'tso:·ne] *m*, *f* (*persona molto villana*) very rude person

villeggiante [vil·led·'dʒan·te] *mf* vacationer

villeggiare [vil·led·'dʒa:·re] *vi* to vacation

villeggiatura [vil·led·dʒa·'tu:·ra] *f* 1. (*vacanza*) vacation 2. (*luogo*) vacation destination

villetta [vil·'let·ta] *f* 1. (*in città*) (small) house; ~ **unifamiliare/bifamiliare** single/multi-family home; **-e a schiera** townhouse 2. (*in campagna, al mare*) cottage

villino [vil·'li:·no] *m* 1. (*in città*) (small) house 2. (*in campagna, al mare*) cottage

villoso, -a [vil·'lo:·so] *agg* (*peloso*) hairy

viltà [vil·'ta] <-> *f* 1. (*codardia*) cowardice 2. (*azione*) cowardly act

viluppo [vi·'lup·po] *m* 1. (*di capelli, cavi, fili, sterpi*) tangle 2. *fig* (*intrico, imbroglio*) maze

Viminale [vi·mi·'na:·le] *m* POL **il Viminale** Italian Ministry of the Interior

vimine ['vi:·mi·ne] *m* wicker; **di** [*o* **in**] **-i** (*cesto, sedia*) wicker

vinaccia [vi·'nat·tʃa] <-cce> I. *f* marc II. *agg* <-> (*colore*) claret

vinaio [vi·'na:·io] <-nai> *m* (*venditore*) wine merchant

vinavil® ['vi·na·vil] <-> *m* plastic glue

vincente [vin·'tʃen·te] *agg* (*biglietto, giocatore*) winning; **persona** ~ *fig* winner

vincere ['vin·tʃe·re] <vinco, vinsi, vinto> I. *vt* 1.(*superare: nemico, avversario*) to beat 2.(*guerra, concorso*) to win; ~ **una causa** JUR to win a case 3.(*ottenere: premio*) to win; (*posto, cattedra*) to obtain; ~ **un terno al lotto** *fig* to hit the jackpot 4. *fig* (*superare: difficoltà, timidezza*) to overcome 5.(*loc*) **chi la dura la vince** *prov* patience always pays II. *vi* (*prevalere*) to win III. *vr:* -**rsi** (*dominarsi*) to control oneself

vincita ['vin·tʃi·ta] *f* 1.(*vittoria*) victory 2.(*premio, somma*) winnings *pl*

vincitore, -trice [vin·tʃi·'to:·re] I. *agg* (*candidato, concorrente*) winning II. *m, f* (*di gara, concorso*) winner

vincolante [viŋ·ko·'lan·te] *agg* binding

vincolare [viŋ·ko·'la:·re] I. *vt* 1.(*impacciare, impedire*) to restrict 2. *fig* (*obbligare*) to bind 3. FIN (*conto, deposito, somma*) to tie up 4. ADM (*limitare*) to restrict II. *vr:* -**rsi** (*impegnarsi*) to bind oneself

vincolato, -a [viŋ·ko·'la:·to] *agg* 1.(*impacciato*) restricted 2. *fig* (*obbligato*) bound 3. FIN **conto** ~ term account

vincolo ['viŋ·ko·lo] *m* 1. JUR restraint 2. *fig* (*obbligo*) obligation 3. *fig* (*legame*) tie 4. FIN (*di conto, deposito*) fixed term 5. ADM (*limite*) restriction

vinello [vi·'nɛl·lo] *m* light wine

vinicolo, -a [vi·'ni:·ko·lo] *agg* wine-producing

vinificare [vi·ni·fi·'ka:·re] I. *vi* (*produrre vino*) to produce wine II. *vt* (*trasformare in vino*) ~ **qc** to make wine out of sth

vino ['vi:·no] I. *m* 1.(*di uva*) wine; **vin brûlé** mulled wine; ~ **d'annata** vintage wine; ~ **a denominazione d'origine controllata** [*o* **DOC**] DOC wine; ~ **della casa** house wine; ~ **nuovo** [*o* **novello**] young wine; ~ **passito** *wine made from raisins;* **reggere il** ~ to hold one's drink 2.(*di altro frutto*) wine II. *agg* <-> (*colore*) claret; **rosso** ~ claret

i A glass of wine (**vino**) is an essential part of the Italian mealtime. Italians are estimated to drink 70 liters per head every year. In the past, due to the competition from other countries and the lack of an official classification system, Italian wine was not drunk much abroad. These days, thanks to the recovery of old grape varieties and a revival of traditional manual harvesting methods, Italy has become a great producer and exporter both of white wines – such as vernaccia di San Gimignano, verduzzo, Sardinian vermentino, and red – *barolo, barbera, chianti, nero d'avola,* and *carignano del sulcis.* The law of 1992 introduced a degree of clarity into wine classification, with wines

being divided into the following categories: vino da tavola, where no indication of origin is given; IGT or Indicazione Geografica Tipica; DOC, Denominazione d'Origine Controllata; and DOCG, Denominazione d'Origine Controllata e Garantita.

vinsanto, vin santo [vin·'san·to] *m* Vinsanto, *white dessert wine*

vinsi ['vin·si] *1. pers sing pass rem di* **vincere**

vinto, -a ['vin·to] I. *pp di* **vincere** II. *agg* (*loc*) **averla -a** to get one's way; **darla -a a qu** to let sb have his [*o* her] way; **darsi per** ~ *a. fig* to give up III. *m, f* 1.(*sconfitto*) loser 2. *fig* (*fallito*) loser

viola[1] [vi·'ɔ:·la] *f* 1.(*fiore*) violet; ~ **del pensiero** pansy 2. MUS (*strumento, violista*) viola; ~ **da gamba** cello

viola[2] I. <inv> *agg* 1.(*colore*) purple 2. SPORT (*della Fiorentina*) of the Fiorentina soccer team II. <-> *m* 1.(*colore*) purple 2. SPORT **tifoso** ~ Fiorentina fan

violaceo, -a [vio·'la:·tʃeo] *agg* 1.(*viola*) purplish 2.(*livido: labbra, mani*) purple

violare [vio·'la:·re] *vt* 1.(*trasgredire: legge, patto, regolamento*) to break 2.(*invadere: confine*) to violate; (*domicilio*) to break into 3.(*profanare: chiesa, tomba*) to desecrate

violazione [vio·lat·'tsio:·ne] *f* 1.(*trasgressione: di legge, patto, regolamento*) violation 2.(*di confine*) violation; (*di domicilio*) burglary 3.(*profanazione: di chiesa, tomba*) desecration

violentare [vio·len·'ta:·re] *vt* 1.(*sessualmente*) to rape 2. *fig* (*coscienza, volontà, libertà*) to violate

violento, -a [vio·'lɛn·to] I. *agg* 1.(*persona, metodo, azione*) violent 2.(*temporale, terremoto*) violent; (*pioggia*) heavy; (*incendio*) fierce 3.(*passione, sentimento*) intense 4.(*sforzo*) huge; (*urto*) violent; (*febbre*) high 5.(*colore, suono*) harsh II. *m, f* (*persona*) brute

violenza [vio·'lɛn·tsa] *f* 1.(*aggressività, azione violenta*) violence; **ricorrere alla** ~ to resort to violence; ~ **sessuale** sexual violence 2.(*impeto: di temporale, terremoto*) violent; (*di incendio*) ferocity 3.(*intensità: di febbre, passione*) intensity

violetta [vio·'let·ta] *f* (*viola mammola*) violet

violetto [vio·'let·to] *m* (*colore*) violet

violetto, -a *agg* violet

violinista [vio·li·'nis·ta] <-i *m*, -e *f*> *mf* violinist

violino [vio·'li:·no] *m* (*strumento, violinista*) violin

violista [vio·'lis·ta] <-i *m*, -e *f*> *mf* violist

violoncellista [vio·lon·tʃel·'lis·ta] <-i *m*, -e *f*> *mf* cellist

violoncello [vio·lon·'tʃɛl·lo] *m* (*strumento, violoncellista*) cello

viottolo [vi·'ɔt·to·lo] *m* track

vip [vip] I. <-> *mf* celebrity II. <-> *agg* (*locale, sala*) exclusive

vipera ['vi:·pe·ra] *f* 1. (*serpente*) viper 2. *fig* (*persona*) snake

viraggio [vi·'rad·dʒo] <-ggi> *m* CHEM, FOTO toning

virago [vi·'ra:·go] <viragini> *f pej, scherz* dragon

virale [vi·'ra:·le] *agg* MED viral

virare [vi·'ra:·re] *vi* 1. NAUT, AERO to veer 2. CHEM, FOTO to tone

virata [vi·'ra:·ta] *f* 1. NAUT veer; ~ **in prua** going about; ~ **in poppa** jibe 2. AER turn 3. *fig* (*di tendenza, orientamento*) shift

virgola ['vir·go·la] *f* comma; **punto e** ~ semicolon; **non cambiare neanche una** ~ *fig* not to change a single word

virgolette [vir·go·'let·te] *fpl* quotation marks; **tra** ~ *a. fig* in quotes

virile [vi·'ri:·le] *agg* 1. (*maschile*) manly 2. (*da uomo adulto*) adult 3. (*sessualmente*) virile 4. *fig* (*coraggioso*) manly

virilità [vi·ri·li·'ta] <-> *f* 1. (*maturità di maschio*) manliness 2. (*sessuale*) virility 3. *fig* (*coraggio*) courage

virologia [vi·ro·lo·'dʒi:·a] <-gie> *f* BIOL, MED virology

virologo, -a [vi·'rɔ:·lo·go] <-gi, -ghe> *m, f* BIOL, MED virologist

virtù [vir·'tu] <-> *f* 1. (*pregio*) virtue 2. (*efficacia: di rimedio, terapia*) property; **in** ~ **di** by virtue of

virtuale [vir·tu·'a:·le] *agg* virtual; **realtà** ~ virtual reality

virtuosismo [vir·tuo·'siz·mo] *m* 1. (*abilità*) virtuosity 2. *pej* (*sfoggio*) over-elaboration

virtuoso, -a [vir·tu·'o:·so] I. *agg* 1. (*retto: persona, scelta*) virtuous 2. (*molto abile: artista, giocatore*) virtuoso II. *m, f* 1. (*persona virtuosa*) virtuous person 2. (*artista, giocatore*) genius; **essere un** ~ **di qc** to be brilliant at sth

virulento, -a [vi·ru·'lɛn·to] *agg* 1. BIOL, MED virulent 2. *fig* (*polemica, linguaggio*) heated; (*critica*) bitter

virulenza [vi·ru·'lɛn·tsa] *f* 1. BIOL, MED virulence 2. *fig* (*di polemica, linguaggio*) heatedness; (*critica*) bitterness

virus ['vi:·rus] <-> *m* 1. COMPUT, BIOL, MED virus 2. *fig* (*germe: di sentimento, passione, ideologia*) curse

visagista [vi·za·'dʒis·ta] <-i *m*, -e *f*> *mf* beautician

vis à vis [vi·za·'vi] *avv* face to face

viscerale [viʃ·ʃe·'ra:·le] *agg fig* (*profondo: amore, simpatia, stato d'animo*) deep; (*odio*) visceral

viscere ['viʃ·ʃe·re] *fpl* 1. ANAT innards *pl* 2. *fig* (*profondità: di terra, montagna*) bowels *pl*

vischio ['vis·kio] <-schi> *m* mistletoe

vischioso, -a [vis·'kio:·so] *agg* (*appiccicoso: liquido, sostanza*) viscous

viscidità [viʃ·ʃi·di·'ta] <-> *f* 1. (*scivolosità*) slipperiness 2. *fig, pej* (*ambiguità: di persona, modi*) unctuousness

viscido, -a ['viʃ·ʃi·do] *agg* 1. (*scivoloso: terreno, strada*) slippery 2. (*al tatto*) slimy 3. *fig* (*equivoco: persona, atteggiamento*) unctuous

visconte, -essa [vis·'kon·te, vis·kon·'tes·sa] *m, f* (*nobile*) viscount *m*, viscountess *f*

viscosa [vis·'ko:·sa] *f* (*fibra*) viscose

viscosità [vis·ko·si·'ta] <-> *f* PHYS viscosity

viscoso, -a [vis·'ko:·so] *agg* 1. PHYS (*fluido, liquido, olio*) viscous 2. (*appiccicoso*) slimy

visibile [vi·'zi:·bi·le] *agg* 1. (*con la vista*) visible 2. *fig* (*evidente*) clear

visibilio [vi·zi·'bi:·lio] <-i> *m* (*ammirazione estatica*) ecstasy; **andare** [*o* **essere**] **in** ~ **per qc/qu** to be in ecstasies over sth/sb

visibilità [vi·zi·bi·li·'ta] <-> *f a. fig* visibility

visiera [vi·'zie:·ra] *f* 1. (*di casco*) visor 2. (*di berretto*) peak

visionare [vi·zio·'na:·re] *vt* 1. (*per scegliere: merce, candidati*) to examine 2. (*vedere in anteprima: film, spettacolo*) to view

visionario, -a [vi·zio·'na:·rio] <-i, -ie> I. *agg* (*utopico: progetto, idee, persona*) visionary II. *m, f* (*utopista*) visionary

visione [vi·'zio:·ne] *f* 1. (*percezione visiva*) vision 2. (*esame*) examination; **prendere** ~ **di qc** to go through sth; **prendere in** ~ **qc** to examine sth 3. (*scena, panorama*) view 4. *fig* (*idea*) view; ~ **d'insieme** overview 5. (*di film, spettacolo, trasmissione*) viewing; **prima** ~ first showing 6. (*soprannaturale, allucinazione*) vision

visita ['vi:·zi·ta] *f* 1. (*presso persona*) visit; **andare in** ~ **da qu** to visit with sb; **essere in** ~ **da qu** to stay with sb; **fare (una)** ~ **a qu** to visit with sb 2. (*persona*) visitor; **biglietto da** ~ business card 3. (*in un luogo*) visit; ~ **guidata** guided tour 4. MED consultation; ~ **fiscale** visit by a doctor to check on a person on sick leave; ~ **di leva** military service medical examination 5. (*ispezione*) inspection visit

visitare [vi·zi·'ta:·re] *vt* 1. (*medico*) to examine; **farsi** ~ **da uno specialista** to go and see a specialist 2. (*luogo: città, museo*) to visit 3. (*andare a trovare: amici, parenti*) to visit with 4. (*ispezionare*) to inspect

visitatore, -trice [vi·zi·ta·'to:·re] *m, f* visitor

visivo, -a [vi·'zi:·vo] *agg* (*della vista*) visual; **campo** ~ field of vision; **memoria** -a visual memory; **arti** -e visual arts

viso ['vi:·zo] *m* 1. (*volto*) face 2. (*espressione*) expression; **a** ~ **aperto** *fig* openly; **far buon** ~ **a cattivo gioco** to put a brave face on things

visone [vi·'zo:·ne] *m* 1. (*animale, pelo*) mink 2. (*cappotto*) mink coat

visore [vi·'zo:·re] *m* FOTO, TEC viewer

vispo, -a ['vis·po] *agg* lively

vissi ['vis·si] *1. pers sing pass rem di* **vivere**[1]

vissuto, -a [vis·'su:·to] I. *pp di* **vivere**[1] II. *agg* 1. (*esperto: persona*) experienced 2. (*trascorso: esperienza, vita*) real III. *m, f* PSYCH (*passato, esperienza*) experiences *pl*

vista ['vis·ta] *f* 1.(*senso*) sight, eyesight 2.(*percezione, spettacolo*) view 3.(*visuale*) sight 4.(*scena, panorama*) view 5.(*loc*) **a** ~ on sight; **conoscere qu di** ~ to know sb by sight; **in** ~ (*visibile*) in view; *fig* (*imminente: novità*) coming up; *fig* (*importante: persona*) prominent; **in** ~ **di** (*di luogo*) in sight of; (*di avvenimento*) in the run-up to; **a** ~ **d'occhio** as far as the eye can see; *fig, scherz* (*molto rapidamente*) in a flash; **perdere di** ~ **qc/qu** to lose sight of sth/sb; **a prima** ~ at first sight; **punto di** ~ *fig* point of view

vistare [vis·'ta:·re] *vt* ADM 1.(*con timbro: certificato, documento*) to stamp 2.(*con visto: passaporto*) to apply a visa to

visto ['vis·to] *m* ADM 1.(*convalida: di documento, domanda*) ratification 2.(*su passaporto*) visa

visto, -a I. *pp di* **vedere**[1] II. *agg* 1.(*guardato*) seen; **mai** ~ unparalleled 2.(*considerato*) **essere ben/mal** ~ to be well/badly thought of; ~ **che ...** given that ...

vistoso, -a [vis·'to:·so] *agg* 1.(*appariscente*) showy 2.(*ingente: somma, ricompensa*) impressive

visuale [vi·zu·'a:·le] I. *agg* (*della vista*) visual II. *f* 1. view 2. *fig* (*punto di vista*) point of view

visualizzabile [vi·zu·a·lid·'dza:·bi·le] *agg* viewable

visualizzare [vi·zu·a·lid·'dza:·re] *vt* 1.(*rendere visibile*) to view 2.(*rappresentare*) to depict 3. COMPUT to display

visualizzatore [vi·zu·a·lid·dza·'to:·re] *m* COMPUT display

visualizzazione [vi·zu·a·lid·dzat·'tsio:·ne] *f* 1.(*il rendere visibile*) visualization 2. COMPUT display

vita[1] ['vi:·ta] *f* 1.(*gener*) life; **a** ~ for life; **dare la** ~ **a qu** to give birth to sb; **dare la** ~ **per qc/qu** to give one's life for sth/sb; **fare la bella** ~ to live it up; **rimanere in** ~ to stay alive; **essere in fin di** ~ to be at death's door; **perdere la** ~ to lose one's life; **togliersi la** ~ to take one's own life; **sto aspettando da una** ~ *inf* I've been waiting for ages 2.(*durata: di fenomeno, prodotto*) lifetime 3.(*sussistenza*) living; **guadagnarsi la** ~ to earn a living

vita[2] ['vi:·ta] *f* (*di persona, indumento*) waist

vitale [vi·'ta:·le] *agg* 1.(*gener*) vital; **spazio** ~ living space 2.(*capace di vivere: neonato, cucciolo*) viable 3. *fig* (*dinamico: persona, organismo*) dynamic

vitalità [vi·ta·li·'ta] <-> *f* 1.(*vivacità: di persona*) vitality 2.(*dinamismo: di istituzione, settore*) dynamism 3.(*capacità di vivere: di neonato*) viability

vitalizio [vi·ta·'lit·tsio] <-i> I. *m* life annuity II. *agg* life

vitamina [vi·ta·'mi:·na] *f* vitamin

vitaminico, -a [vi·ta·'mi:·ni·ko] <-ci, -che> *agg* vitamin; **carenza -a** vitamin deficiency

vitaminizzato [vi·ta·mi·nid·'dza·to] *agg* (*arricchito con vitamine*) vitamin-enriched

vite ['vi:·te] *f* 1. BOT (*pianta*) vine 2.(*elemento metallico*) screw; **a** ~ (*a spirale*) spiral; (*tappo*) screw top; **giro di** ~ *fig* turn of the screw

vitello [vi·'tɛl·lo] *m* 1.(*animale*) calf 2.(*carne*) veal; ~ **tonnato** CULIN veal with tuna sauce 3.(*pelle*) calfskin

vitellone [vi·tel·'lo:·ne] *m fig* (*giovane ozioso*) layabout

viterbese I. *agg* (*di Viterbo*) from Viterbo II. *mf* (*abitante*) person from Viterbo

Viterbese <*sing*> *m* (*zona*) Viterbo area; **nel** ~ in the Viterbo area

Viterbo *f* Viterbo

viticcio [vi·'tit·tʃo] <-cci> *m* BOT, ARTE tendril

viticolo, -a [vi·'ti:·ko·lo] *agg* wine-growing

viticoltore, viticultore, -trice [vi·ti·kol·'to:·re, vi·ti·kul·'to:·re] *m, f* wine-grower

viticoltura, viticultura [vi·ti·kol·'tu:·ra, vi·ti·kul·'tu:·ra] *f* (*coltivazione*) wine-growing

vitigno [vi·'tiɲ·ɲo] *m* variety of vine; ~ **lambrusco/nebbiolo** Lambrusco/Nebbiolo vine

vitivinicolo, -a [vi·ti·vi·'ni:·ko·lo] *agg* (*associazione, cooperativa, industria*) wine-growing and producing

vitreo, -a *agg* 1.(*di vetro*) glass 2.(*occhi, sguardo, superficie*) glassy 3. ANAT **corpo** ~ vitreous

vittima ['vit·ti·ma] *f* victim; **rimanere** ~ **di qc** to fall victim to sth; **fare la** ~ *inf* to play the victim

vittimismo [vit·ti·'miz·mo] *m* self-pity

vittimistico [vit·ti·'mis·ti·ko] *agg* self-pitying

vitto ['vit·to] *m* (*cibo*) food; ~ **e alloggio** board and lodging

vittoria [vit·'tɔ:·ria] <-ie> *f* (*militare, politica, elettorale*) victory; (*sportiva*) win

vittoriano [vit·to·'ria:·no] *agg* (*epoca, architettura, stile*) Victorian

vittorioso, -a [vit·to·'rio:·so] *agg* 1.(*vincitore*) victorious; SPORT winning 2.(*battaglia, gara*) victorious 3.(*trionfante: aspetto, sorriso*) triumphant

vituperare [vi·tu·pe·'ra:·re] *vt* (*insultare*) to vilify

viuzza [vi·'ut·tsa] *f* alley

viva ['vi:·va] *int* long live; ~ **gli sposi!** to the bride and groom!

vivacchiare [vi·vak·'kia:·re] *vi fam* to scrape a living

vivace [vi·'va:·tʃe] *agg* 1.(*esuberante: bambino, persona*) lively 2.(*acuto: intelligenza, mente*) lively; (*studente*) bright 3.(*concitato: discussione, protesta*) lively 4.(*intenso: fiamma, fuoco*) intense; (*colore*) bright 5. MUS (*esecuzione*) vivace

vivacità [vi·va·tʃi·'ta] <-> *f* 1.(*esuberanza: di bambino, ragazzo*) liveliness 2.(*acume: di intelligenza, mente*) liveliness; (*di studente*) brightness 3.(*fervore: di discussione*) liveliness 4.(*di fiamma, fuoco*) intensity 5.(*di colore*) brightness

vivacizzare [vi·va·tʃid·'dza:·re] *vt* 1.(*animare:*

festa, conversazione) to animate **2.** (*arredamento*) to brighten up

vivaio [vi·'va:·io] <-ai> *m* **1.** (*di piante*) (plant) nursery **2.** (*di pesci*) (fish) farm **3.** (*di personaggi*) breeding ground **4.** SPORT (*di atleti*) youth system

vivanda [vi·'van·da] *f* (*pietanza*) dish

viva voce ['vi:·va 'vo:·tʃe] <-> *m* TEL hands free set

vivente [vi·'vɛn·te] **I.** *agg* (*essere, organismo, specie*) living; (*persona*) alive **II.** *m* **i** -**i** the living *pl*

vivere[1] ['vi:·ve·re] <vivo, vissi, vissuto> **I.** *vi* essere **1.** (*gener*) to live; ~ **alla giornata** to live from day to day; ~ **di qc** *a. fig* to live on sth; ~ **per qc/qu** to live for sth/sb **2.** *fig* (*durare, sopravvivere*) to live on **II.** *vt avere* **1.** (*condurre: vita*) to lead **2.** (*passare*) to live through **3.** (*sentire: dolore, gioia, fede*) to live through **4.** (*parte, personaggio*) to live **5.** *fig* (*godere*) to enjoy

vivere[2] *msing* (*modo di vivere*) life; **per quieto** ~ for a quiet life

viveri ['vi:·ve·ri] *mpl* supplies *pl;* **tagliare i** ~ **a qu** *fig* to cut off sb's supplies; *scherz* to cut off sb's allowance

vivibile [vi·'vi:·bi·le] *agg* (*ambiente, città, clima*) pleasant

vivibilità [vi·vi·bi·li·'ta] <-> *f* liveability

vivificare [vi·vi·fi·'ka:·re] *vt* (*rinvigorire: campagna, terra*) to revive; (*corpo, mente*) to invigorate

viviparo, -a [vi·'vi:·pa·ro] **I.** *agg* ZOO live-bearing **II.** *m, f* ZOO livebearer

vivisezione [vi·vi·set·'tsio:·ne] *f* (*di animali*) vivisection

vivo ['vi:·vo] *m* **1.** *pl* (*persone viventi*) **i** -**i** the living *pl* **2.** (*parte vitale*) living flesh **3.** *fig* (*di argomento, questione, problema*) core; **colpire** [*o* **toccare**] **nel** ~ to get to the core **4.** MUS, RADIO, TV live **5.** (*disegno, ritratto*) **dal** ~ life

vivo, -a *agg* **1.** (*gener*) living; ~ **e vegeto** alive and kicking; **farsi** ~ to show one's face **2.** (*persistente: ricordo, dolore, immagine*) fresh; **è ancora** ~ **nel mio ricordo** he lives on in my memory **3.** (*espressione, intelligenza, conversazione*) lively **4.** (*intenso: sentimento, bisogno*) deep **5.** (*fuoco, fiamma*) high **6.** (*luce, colore*) bright **7.** (*nelle lettere*) **vivissimo** heartfelt

viziare [vit·'tsia:·re] *vt* (*diseducare: bambino, figlio*) to spoil

viziato, -a [vit·'tsia:·to] *agg* **1.** (*maleducato*) spoiled **2.** (*pesante: aria*) stale

vizio ['vit·tsio] <-i> *m* **1.** (*disposizione al male*) vice **2.** (*abitudine*) bad habit **3.** (*difetto*) fault **4.** JUR (*irregolarità*) error; ~ **di forma** procedural error

vizioso, -a [vit·'tsio:·so] **I.** *agg* **1.** (*depravato: persona, vita, comportamento*) dissolute **2.** (*imperfetto*) **circolo** ~ vicious circle **II.** *m, f* (*persona depravata*) dissolute person

vocabolario [vo·ka·bo·'la:·rio] <-i> *m* **1.** (*dizionario*) dictionary **2.** (*lessico*) vocabulary

vocabolo [vo·'ka:·bo·lo] *m* LING word

vocale [vo·'ka:·le] **I.** *agg* ANAT, MUS vocal **II.** *f* (*suono, lettera*) vowel

vocalico, -a [vo·'ka:·li·ko] <-ci, -che> *agg* LING vowel

vocativo [vo·ka·'ti:·vo] *m* LING vocative

vocativo, -a *agg* LING vocative

vocazione [vo·kat·'tsio:·ne] *f* **a.** *fig* vocation

voce ['vo:·tʃe] *f* **1.** *a. fig* voice; **a** ~ orally; **fare la** ~ **grossa** to make oneself heard; **a gran** ~ loudly; **sotto** ~ in a whisper; **avere** ~ **in capitolo** *fig* to have influence **2.** (*di strumento, mare*) sound **3.** (*notizia, diceria*) rumor; -**i di corridoio** idle rumors **4.** (*vocabolo*) word **5.** (*in dizionario, enciclopedia*) headword **6.** (*in grammatica*) form **7.** ADM (*capitolo*) item **8.** MUS voice; (*cantante*) singer

vociare[1] [vo·'tʃa:·re] *vi* (*gridare*) to shout

vociare[2] <-> *m* (*rumore*) noise

vociferare [vo·tʃi·fe·'ra:·re] *vt* (*dire, insinuare*) to rumor; **si vocifera che ...** rumor has it that ...

vocio [vo·'tʃi:·o] <- cii> *m* shouting

vodka ['vɔd·ka] <-> *f* vodka

voga ['vo:·ga] <-ghe> *f* **1.** (*popolarità*) fashion; **essere in** ~ to be in fashion **2.** SPORT (*attività*) rowing; (*remata*) stroke **3.** *fig* enthusiasm

vogare [vo·'ga:·re] *vi* to row

vogata [vo·'ga:·ta] *f* **1.** (*il vogare*) rowing **2.** (*remata*) stroke

vogatore [vo·ga·'to:·re] *m* (*attrezzo*) rowing machine

vogatore, -trice *m, f* (*rematore*) rower

voglia ['vɔʎ·ʎa] <-glie> *f* **1.** (*desiderio*) wish; **avere** ~ **di** (**fare**) **qc** to feel like (doing) sth; **morire dalla** ~ **di fare qc** to be dying to do sth; **togliersi la** ~ **di qc** to lose the urge for sth **2.** (*disposizione, volontà*) desire; **fare qc di mala** [*o* **contro**] ~ to do sth reluctantly **3.** *pej* (*capriccio*) whim **4.** *inf* (*in gravidanza*) craving **5.** *inf* (*macchia della pelle*) birthmark

voglio ['vɔʎ·ʎo] *1. pers sing pr di* **volere**[1]

voglioso, -a [voʎ·'ʎo:·so] *agg* **1.** (*capriccioso*) capricious **2.** (*lussurioso*) lewd **3.** (*desideroso: sguardo, espressione*) wishful

voi ['vo:·i] *pron* **1.** *2. pers pl* (*soggetto*) you **2.** (*oggetto, complemento di termine*) you, emphatic **3.** (*con preposizione*) you **4.** (*forma di cortesia*) **Voi** you

voialtri [vo·'ial·tri] *pron inf* you guys

volano [vo·'la:·no] *m* **1.** SPORT (*pallina*) shuttlecock **2.** (*gioco*) badminton

volant [vɔ·'lã] <-> *m* flounce

volante [vo·'lan·te] **I.** *agg* flying; **disco** ~ flying saucer; **foglio** ~ sheet of paper **II.** *f* (*in polizia: squadra*) flying squad; (*auto*) patrol car **III.** *m* MOT (*sterzo*) steering wheel; **stare** [*o* **essere**] [*o* **sedere**] **al** ~ *a. fig* to be behind the wheel; **un asso del** ~ an ace racing driver; **sport**

del ~ motor racing

volantinaggio [vo·lan·ti·'nad·dʒo] <-ggi> *m* leafleting; **fare** ~ to leaflet

volantino [vo·lan·'tiː·no] *m* (*pubblicitario, informativo*) leaflet

volare [vo·'laː·re] *vi essere o avere* 1.(*gener*) to fly; ~ **in cielo** [*o* **paradiso**] (*morire*) to go to heaven 2.(*piuma, foglia, polvere*) to fly around 3.(*precipitare*) to fall 4.(*correre*) to fly along 5.*fig* (*diffondersi: notizia, diceria, calunnia*) to travel fast 6.(*tempo*) to fly by

volata [vo·'laː·ta] *f* 1.*fam* (*corsa veloce*) rush; **fare una** ~ to rush; **di** ~ in a rush 2.SPORT (*scatto*) sprint 3.(*di uccelli*) flight

volatile [vo·'laː·ti·le] I. *agg* CHEM volatile II. *m* ZOO bird

volatilizzare [vo·la·ti·lid·'dzaː·re] I. *vi essere* CHEM to evaporate II. *vr:* **-rsi** 1.CHEM to evaporate 2.*fig, fam* (*sparire: persona, cosa*) to vanish

vol-au-vent [vɔ·lo·'vã] <-> *m* CULIN vol-au-vent

volente [vo·'lɛn·te] *agg* ~ **o nolente** willing or not

volenteroso, volonteroso, -a [vo·len·te·'roː·so, vo·lon·te·'roː·so] *agg* 1.(*atteggiamento, comportamento*) willing 2.(*persona*) keen

volentieri [vo·len·'tiɛː·ri] *avv* 1.(*di buon grado, con piacere*) willingly; **spesso e** ~ *inf* always 2.(*come risposta*) of course

volere[1] [vo·'leː·re] <voglio, volli, voluto> I. *vt* 1.(*intenzione, desiderio*) to want; **senza** ~ unintentionally; ~ **qu** (*per vederlo*) to want to see sb; (*per parlargli*) to want to speak to sb; (*in offerte e richieste*) would you like …?; **quanto vuole?** (*prezzo*) how much do you want? 2.(*decidere: potenza superiore*) to will 3.(*prescrivere: legge, regolamento*) to demand 4.(*richiedere*) to require; **volerci poco/molto** (*tempo, fatica, denaro*) to take a little/a lot 5.LING (*reggere*) to take 6.(*loc*) ~ **bene a qu** to love sb; ~ **dire** (*significare*) to mean; **voglio/volevo dire** … I mean/ meant … II. *vr* 1.**-rsi bene** (*reciprocamente*) to love each other 2.**-rsi bene** (*a se stessi*) to look after oneself

volere[2] *m* (*volontà, desiderio*) will

volgare [vol·'gaː·re] I. *agg* 1.*pej* (*comune, ordinario*) crude 2.*pej* (*triviale: gesto, parola, espressione*) trivial; (*grossolano: persona, bellezza, comportamento*) vulgar 3.(*non scientifico: nome, termine*) common 4.(*del volgo: lingua*) vulgar; **latino** ~ Vulgar Latin II. *m* (*lingua*) vernacular

volgarità [vol·ga·ri·'ta] <-> *f* 1.(*caratteristica: di persona*) vulgarity 2.(*espressione*) vulgar expression; (*gesto*) vulgar gesture; (*parola*) vulgar word

volgarizzare [vol·ga·rid·'dzaː·re] *vt* (*divulgare*) to popularize

volgarmente [vol·gar·'men·te] *avv* 1.(*in modo scurrile*) vulgarly 2.(*comunemente*) commonly

volgere[1] ['vɔl·dʒe·re] <volgo, volsi, volto>

I. *vt* 1.(*dirigere*) to turn; ~ **le spalle a qu** *a. fig* to turn one's back on sb 2.*fig* (*indirizzare: attenzione, pensiero, sentimento*) to turn 3.*fig* (*trasformare*) ~ **qc in qc** to turn sth into sth 4.(*tradurre*) to transform II. *vi* 1.(*dirigersi: verso luogo*) to turn 2.*fig* (*rivolgersi*) ~ **a qc** to turn towards sth 3.*fig* (*avvicinarsi*) to come; ~ **al termine** to be coming to an end 4.(*evolversi: tempo, situazione*) to turn 5.(*tendere: colore*) to shade towards III. *vr:* **-rsi** (*girarsi*) to turn; **-rsi indietro** to turn back

volgere[2] *m* passing

volgo ['vol·go] <-ghi> *m pej* (*plebe, massa*) masses *pl*

voliera [vo·'liɛː·ra] *f* aviary

volitivo [vo·li·'tiː·vo] *agg* (*determinato: persona, carattere*) keen

volli ['vɔl·li] *1. pers sing pass rem di* **volere**[1]

volo ['vo·lo] *m* 1.(*gener*) flight; **assistente di** ~ flight attendant; **al** ~ in mid-air 2.(*caduta*) fall 3.(*corsa*) dash 4.(*loc*) **al** ~ (*immediatamente*) at once

volontà [vo·lon·'ta] <-> *f* 1.(*facoltà di volere*) will; **forza di** ~ willpower 2.(*volere, desiderio*) desire; **a** ~ as much as one wishes; **ultime** ~ last will and testament 3.(*disposizione*) **buona** ~ goodwill; **cattiva** ~ ill will

volontariamente [vo·lon·ta·ria·'men·te] *avv* voluntarily

volontariato [vo·lon·ta·'ria·to] *m* 1.(*per assistenza, pratica*) voluntary work; **fare** ~ to work as a volunteer; **il** ~ the voluntary sector 2.(*servizio militare volontario*) voluntary service

volontario, -a [vo·lon·'taː·rio] <-i, -ie> I. *agg* 1.(*liberamente scelto*) voluntary 2.(*soldato, medico*) volunteer II. *m, f* volunteer

volpe ['vol·pe] *f* 1.(*animale*) fox 2.(*pelliccia*) fox-fur 3.*fig* (*persona astuta*) cunning person

volpino [vol·'piː·no] *m* (*cane*) Florentine spitz

volpino, -a *agg* (*da volpe*) foxlike

volpone, -na [vol·'poː·ne] *m, f fig* (*persona astuta*) crafty person

volsi ['vɔl·si] *1. pers sing pass rem di* **volgere**[1]

volt [vɔlt] <-> *m* EL volt

volta ['vɔl·ta] *f* 1.(*circostanza*) time; **la** ~ **che** … when …; **una** ~ (**che**) … once …; **una** ~ **tanto** every now and then; **una** ~ **per tutte** once and for all 2.(*con numerale*) time; **a -e** [*o* **certe -e**] [*o* **qualche** ~] sometimes; **di** ~ **in** ~ each time; **una** ~ once; **c'era una** ~ once upon a time 3.(*turno*) turn; **alla** [*o* **per**] ~ at a time; **tutto in una** ~ all at once 4.(*direzione*) **alla** ~ **di** towards 5.ARCH vault; **a** ~ vaulted 6.(*copertura*) ceiling; **la** ~ **celeste** [*o* **del cielo**] heaven 7.ANAT ~ **cranica** dome of the skull

voltafaccia [vol·ta·'fat·tʃa] <-> *m fig* U-turn

voltagabbana [vol·ta·gab·'baː·na] <-> *mf* **è un(a)** ~ turncoat

voltaggio [vol·'tad·dʒo] <-ggi> *m* voltage

voltare [vol·'taː·re] I. *vt* 1.(*rivolgere: occhi, viso, testa*) to turn; ~ **le spalle a qu** *a. fig* to turn one's back on sb **2.** (*girare: moneta, foglio, pagina*) to turn; **~ pagina** *fig* to move on **3.** (*oltrepassare: angolo*) to go around **II.** *vi* (*girare: persona, strada*) to turn **III.** *vr:* **-rsi** (*girarsi*) to turn; **non sapere da che parte -rsi** *fig* not to know where to turn; **-rsi contro qu** to turn against sb

voltastomaco [vol·tas·'tɔː·ma·ko] <-chi *o* -ci> *m* **ho il ~** to feel sick; **dare il ~** to turn sb's stomach; **far venire il ~** to be disgusting

volteggiare [vol·ted·'dʒaː·re] *vi* **1.** (*in aria: uccello, aereo*) to circle **2.** SPORT to vault; (*nella danza*) to twirl

volto ['vol·to] *m* **1.** (*viso, natura*) face **2.** *fig* (*aspetto*) aspect

volto, -a ['vɔl·to] **I.** *pp di* volgere[1] **II.** *agg* (*essere*) **~ a fare qc** (to be) intended to do sth

voltura [vol·'tuː·ra] *f* ADM (*di proprietà*) registration; (*di contratto*) transfer

volubile [vo·'luː·bi·le] *agg* (*instabile: individuo, carattere, umore*) volatile; (*tempo atmosferico*) changeable

volume [vo·'luː·me] *m* **1.** MAT (*misura, spazio*) volume **2.** (*ingombro*) volume; **auto a due -i** hatchback; **auto a tre -i** sedan **3.** COM (*di affari, produzione, vendite*) volume; **~ del traffico** traffic volume **4.** (*di suono*) volume; **a tutto ~** at full volume **5.** (*libro*) volume

voluminosità [vo·lu·mi·no·si·'ta] <-> *f* bulkiness

voluminoso, -a [vo·lu·mi·'noː·so] *agg* bulky

voluta [vo·'luː·ta] *f* **1.** (*spira, spirale*) whirl **2.** ARCH, ART scroll; (*di capitello*) volute

voluto, -a [vo·'luː·to] **I.** *pp di* volere[1] **II.** *agg* **1.** (*desiderato*) desired **2.** (*intenzionale*) intentional

voluttà [vo·lut·'ta] <-> *f* **1.** (*piacere sensuale*) pleasure **2.** (*godimento*) enjoyment

voluttuario, -a [vo·lut·tu·'aː·rio] <-i, -ie> *agg* (*articolo*) luxury; (*spese*) non-essential

voluttuoso, -a [vo·lut·tu·'oː·so] *agg* **1.** (*sensuale: bocca, danza, sguardo*) sensuous **2.** (*persona*) voluptuous; **una vita -a** a life of pleasure

vomere ['vɔː·me·re] *m* **1.** AGR plowshare **2.** ANAT vomer

vomitare [vo·mi·'taː·re] **I.** *vt* **1.** (*rimettere*) to throw up **2.** (*emettere*) to spew forth **3.** *fig* (*ingiurie, insulti, imprecazioni*) to hurl **II.** *vi* **1.** (*rimettere*) to throw up **2.** *fig* to make sb throw up

vomitevole [vo·mi·'teː·vo·le] *agg fig* (*disgustoso, sgradevole*) disgusting; (*brutto: film, spettacolo, libro*) nauseating

vomito ['vɔː·mi·to] *m* vomit; **far venire il ~ a qu** *a. fig* to make sb throw up

vongola ['voŋ·go·la] *f* clam

vorace [vo·'raː·tʃe] *agg* **1.** (*animale*) voracious **2.** (*ingordo: bambino, persona*) greedy **3.** *fig* (*avido*) voracious

voragine [vo·'raː·dʒi·ne] *f* **1.** (*baratro*) chasm **2.** (*gorgo d'acqua*) whirlpool

vorrò [vor·'rɔ] *1. pers sing futuro di* volere[1]

vortice ['vɔr·ti·tʃe] *m* **1.** (*di acqua*) whirlpool; (*di aria, sabbia*) whirlwind; (*di polvere*) dust devil **2.** (*movimento rotatorio*) whirl **3.** *fig* (*susseguirsi: di azioni, pensieri*) whirlwind

vorticoso, -a [vor·ti·'koː·so] *agg* **1.** (*con vortici: acque, fiume, vento*) swirling **2.** (*di ballo, danza*) swirling **3.** *fig* (*incalzante: ritmo*) whirlwind

vostro, -a **I.** *agg* **1.** your; **la -a speranza** your hope; **~ padre/zio** your father/uncle; **il ~ caro cugino** your dear cousin; **i -i fratelli** your brothers; **un ~ amico** one of your friends **2.** (*forma di cortesia*) your **II.** *pron* **1.** (*forma di cortesia*) yours **2.** (*forma di cortesia*) yours **3. alla -a!** (*salute*) cheers!; **la -a** (*lettera*) your letter; (*opinione*) your opinion; **dalla -a** (*parte*) on your side; **i -i** (*genitori, parenti*) your folks

votante [vo·'tan·te] **I.** *mf* voter **II.** *agg* voting

votare [vo·'taː·re] **I.** *vt* **1.** (*sottoporre a voto: legge, delibera, emendamento*) to vote on **2.** (*approvare: legge*) to pass **3.** (*sostenere con voto: candidato, partito*) to vote for **4.** (*consacrare, dedicare*) to devote **II.** *vi* (*partecipare al voto*) to vote; **~ per** [*o* **a favore di**] **qc/qu** to vote for sth/sb; **~ contro qc/qu** to vote against sth/sb **III.** *vr:* **-rsi 1.** REL (*offrirsi*) to devote oneself **2.** (*dedicarsi*) to dedicate oneself

votazione [vo·tat·'tsio·ne] *f* **1.** (*voto, risultato*) vote **2.** (*a scuola: punteggio*) grade

voto ['voː·to] *m* **1.** (*elettorale*) vote; **avere diritto di ~** to have the right to vote; **~ di fiducia** vote of confidence; **mettere ai -i qc** to put sth to the vote; **~ segreto** secret ballot **2.** (*a scuola: punteggio*) grade **3.** REL (*promessa*) vote; **prendere i -i** to take one's vows **4.** REL (*oggetto*) votive

voyeur [vwa·'jœːr] <-> *mf* voyeur

voyeurismo [vwa·jœ·'riz·mo] *m* voyeurism

v.r. *abbr di* **vedi retro** PTO

v.s. 1. *abbr di* **vedi sopra** see above **2.** *abbr di* **vedi sotto** see below

vs., Vs. *abbr di* **vostro** your

VT *abbr di* **Vecchio Testamento** OT, *Old Testament*

VU *abbr di* **Vigile Urbano ~ urbano** (local) policeman/woman

vu cumprà [vu·kum·'pra] <-> *mf pej, scherz: North African street vendor*

vulcanico, -a [vul·'kaː·ni·ko] <-ci, -che> *agg* **1.** GEOL volcanic **2.** *fig* (*persona, mente*) dynamic; (*fantasia*) vivid

vulcanizzare [vul·ka·nid·'dzaː·re] *vt* to vulcanize

vulcano [vul·'kaː·no] *m* **1.** GEOL volcano **2.** *fig* (*situazione tesa*) powder keg; **su un ~** *fig* on a powder keg **3.** *fig* (*persona, testa, mente*) dynamo

vulnerabile [vul·ne·'raː·bi·le] *agg* **1.** (*feribile*) vulnerable **2.** *fig* (*persona, carattere, idea*) vulnerable

vuoi, vuole ['vuɔ·i, 'vuɔ·le] *2. e 3. pers sing pr di* volere[1]

vuotare [vuo·'taː·re] **I.** *vt* **1.** (*armadio, cas-*

setto, valigia) to empty **2.**(*bacino idrico*) to drain **3.**(*bere tutto: bicchiere, bottiglia*) to drain; (*mangiare tutto: piatto*) to clear **4.**(*sgombrare: casa, magazzino*) to clear **5.**(*abbandonare: piazza, sala, teatro*) to clear **6.**(*loc*) ~ il sacco *fig* (*confessare*) to spill the beans; ~ **le tasche** [*o* **il portafoglio**] **a qu** (*far spendere tutto, derubare*) to clean sb out **II.** *vr:* **-rsi 1.**(*diventare vuoto*) to empty **2.**(*loc*) **-rsi le tasche** (*spendere tutto*) to empty one's pockets

vuoto ['vuɔːto] *m* **1.**(*spazio libero*) void; **avere paura del** ~ to be afraid of heights; ~ **d'aria** air pocket **2.**(*spazio senza oggetti*) empty space; (*senza persone*) gap **3.**(*cavità*) cavity **4.** PHYS (*di recipiente, ambiente*) vacuum; **conservato sotto** ~ vacuum-packed **5.**(*contenitore*) empty container; (*bottiglia*) empty bottle; ~ **a perdere** non-refundable container; ~ **a rendere** refundable container **6.** *fig* (*lacuna*) gap **7.**(*mancanza affettiva*) emptiness; **creare** [*o* **fare**] **il** ~ **intorno a sé** (*allontanare gli altri*) to drive everyone away **8.**(*loc*) **a** ~ (*senza effetto, inutilmente*) in vain; **assegno a** ~ bad check

vuoto, -a *agg* **1.**(*gener*) empty; **a stomaco** ~ on an empty stomach; **a mani -e** *a fig* empty-handed **2.**(*persona*) shallow

website <-> *m* COMPUT website
weekend ['wiːˌkɛnd/wiːˈkɛnd] <-> *m* weekend; ~ **di benessere** weekend health break
weekendista [wiˌkenˈdisˌta] <-i *m*, -e *f*> *mf* weekender
western ['wesˌtən/'wɛsˌtern] **I.**<inv> *agg* **un film** ~ a western **II.** <-> *m* western; ~ **all'italiana** spaghetti western
whisky ['wisˌki] <-> *m* whiskey
windsurf ['windˌsəːf] <-> *m* **1.**(*sport*) windsurfing **2.**(*tavola*) windsurfer
windsurfer ['windˌsəːfə] <- *o* windsurfers> *mf* SPORT windsurfer
windsurfing ['windˌsəːfiŋ] <-> *m* SPORT windsurfing
windsurfista [windˌserˈfisˌta] <-i *m*, -e *f*> *mf* SPORT windsurfer
woofer ['wuːfə] *m* (*altoparlante*) woofer
word processing [wəːd 'prouˌseˌsiŋ] <-> *m* COMPUT word processing
word processor [wəːd 'prouˌseˌsə] <-> *m* COMPUT word processor
workstation ['wəːkˈsteiˌʃən] <- *o* workstations> *f* COMPUT workstation
World Wide Web <-> *m* COMPUT World Wide Web
würstel ['vyrsˌtəl] <-> *m* frankfurter
WWF [vuˌvuˈɛfˌfe] *m abbr di* **Worldwide Fund for Nature** (*Fondo Mondiale per la Natura*) WWF
WWW [vuːvuˈvu] *m abbr di* **World Wide Web** WWW

W

W, w [vu 'dopˌpia] <-> *f* W, w; ~ **come Washington** W for William
W *abbr di* **watt** W
wafer ['vaːfer] <-> *m* wafer
wagon-lit [vaˌgɔ̃ˈli] <-> *m* sleeper
wagon-restaurant [vaˌgɔ̃ˌrɛsˌtɔˈrã] <-> *m* dining car
walkie-cup ['wɔːkiˌkʌp] <- *o* walkie-cups> *f* paper cup with lid
walkie-talkie ['wɔːkiˈtɔːki] <-> *m* walkie-talkie
walking ['wolˌking] <-> *m* SPORT power walking
walkman ['wɔːkˌmən] <- *o* walkmen> *m* Walkman®
WAP ['wap] *m acro di* **Wireless Application Protocol** WAP
war game ['wɔ geim] <- *o* war games> *m* war game
wash-and-wear ['wɔʃˌən(d)ˈwɛə] <inv> *agg* wash-and-wear
waterproof ['wɔːˌtəˌpruːf] <inv> *agg* waterproof
watt [vat] <-> *m* watt
wattora [vatˈtoːˌra] <-> *f* watt-hour
wc <-> *m* (*tazza del gabinetto*) toilet; (*stanza*) bathroom

X

X, x [iks] **I.**<-> *f* X, x; ~ **come xilofono** X for xylophone; **gambe a** ~ bandy legs; **l'asse delle** ~ MAT the X axis **II.** *agg* **il signor** ~ Mr. X; **l'ora/il giorno** ~ at a certain time/on a certain day; **raggi** ~ X-rays
xenofilia [kseˌnoˌfiˈliːˌa] <-ie> *f* (*esterofilia*) xenophilia, *a liking for foreign people, cultures, etc.*
xenofilo, -a [kseˈnɔːˌfiˌlo] **I.** *agg* (*esterofilo*) xenophilous **II.** *m*, *f* xenophile, *a person who likes foreign people, cultures, etc.*
xenofobia [kseˌnoˌfoˈbiːˌa] *f* xenophobia
xenofobo, -a [kseˈnɔːˌfoˌbo] **I.** *agg* xenophobic **II.** *m*, *f* xenophobe
xerocopia [kseˌroˈkɔːˌpia] *f* photocopy
xerografia [kseˌroˌgraˈfiːˌa] *f* photocopying
xerografico, -a [kseˌroˈgraːˌfiˌko] <-ci, -che> *agg* (*procedimento*) photocopying
xilofonista [ksiˌloˌfoˈnisˌta] <-i *m*, -e *f*> *mf* xylophonist
xilofono [ksiˈlɔːˌfoˌno] *m* xylophone
xilografia [ksiˌloˌgraˈfiːˌa] *f* **1.**(*arte*) wood engraving **2.**(*copia*) woodcut

Y

Y, y ['ip·si·lon] <-> *f* Y, y; ~ **come yacht** Y for Yoke
yacht [jɔt] <-> *m* (*a motore*) (motor) yacht; (*a vela*) (sailing) yacht
yachting ['jɔ·tiŋ] <-> *m* yachting
yak [jæk/jak] <-> *m* ZOO yak
yeti ['iɛ·ti] *m* yeti
yiddish I. <-> *m* (*lingua*) Yiddish II. <inv> *agg* (*lingua, letteratura*) Yiddish
yoga ['jo:·ga] I. <-> *m* yoga II. <inv> *agg* (*esercizio, insegnamento*) yoga
yogurt ['iɔ:·gurt] <-> *m v.* **iogurt**
yogurtiera [io·gur·'tie:·ra] *f* yogurt maker
yo-yo® ['jou·jou] <-> *m* 1. (*giocattolo*) yo-yo 2. *fig* **effetto** ~ yo-yo effect
ypsilon ['ip·si·lon] <-> *f o m v.* **ipsilon**
yucca ['iuk·ka] <-cche> *f* BOT yucca
yuppie ['jʌ·pi] I. <- *o* yuppies> *mf* yuppie II. <inv> *agg* **look** ~ yuppie look

Z

Z, z ['dzɛ:·ta] <-> *f* Z, z; ~ **come Zara** Z for Zebra; **dalla a alla** ~ from A to Z
zabaione [dza·ba·'io:·ne] *m* zabaglione, *sauce made of eggs, sugar and wine*
zaffata [tsaf·'fa:·ta] *f* stink
zafferano [dzaf·fe·'ra:·no] *m* 1. BOT saffron crocus 2. CULIN (*aroma*) saffron
zaffiro [dzaf·'fi:·ro] *m* (*pietra*) sapphire
Zagabria [dza·'ga:·bria] *f* Zagreb; **abitare a** ~ to live in Zagreb; **andare a** ~ to go to Zagreb
zaino ['dza:i·no] *m* backpack
zainetto ['dza:i·'net·to] *m* backpack
zampa ['tsam·pa] *f* 1. ZOO (*gamba*) leg; (*piede: di cane, gatto*) paw; (*di gallina, uccello*) foot; **-e di gallina** *fig* (*intorno agli occhi*) crow's feet; (*scrittura illeggibile*) scrawl 2. *fig, pej* (*di persona: mano*) paw; **giù le -e!** keep your paws off!; **a quattro -e** on all fours
zampata [tsam·'pa:·ta] *f* blow with a paw
zampettare [tsam·pet·'ta:·re] *vi fam* 1. (*animali*) to scamper 2. (*persone*) to toddle
zampetto [tsam·'pet·to] *m* CULIN (*di vitello*) calf's foot; (*di maiale*) pig's feet
zampillare [tsam·pil·'la:·re] *vi essere o avere* to gush
zampillo [tsam·'pil·lo] *m* jet
zampino [tsam·'pi:·no] *m fig, fam* paw; **mettere lo** ~ **in qc** to have a hand in sth
zampirone [dzam·pi·'ro:·ne] *m* mosquito coil
zampogna [tsam·'poɲ·ɲa] *f* (*mus*) Italian bagpipes *pl*
zampone [tsam·'po:·ne] *m* CULIN pig's feet

stuffed with minced meat and spices
zanna ['tsan·na] *f* ZOO (*di elefante, tricheco*) tusk; (*di lupo*) fang
zanzara [dzan·'dza:·ra] *f* ZOO mosquito
zanzariera [dzan·dza·'riɛ:·ra] *f* (*per letto*) mosquito net; (*per finestra*) mosquito screen
zappa ['tsap·pa] *f* hoe; **darsi la** ~ **sui piedi** *fig* to shoot oneself in the foot
zappare [tsap·'pa:·re] *vt* (*terreno, zolle*) to hoe
zappata [tsap·'pa:·ta] *f* 1. (*colpo*) blow with a hoe 2. (*azione*) **dare una** ~ **all'orto** to hoe the vegetable garden
zappatore, -trice *m, f* AGR hoer
zappatura [tsap·pa·'tu:·ra] *f* (*azione*) hoeing
zapping ['zæ·piŋ] <-> *m* channel surfing; **fare lo** ~ to channel-surf
zar [tsar] <-> *m* czar
zarina [tsa·'ri:·na] *f* czarina
zarista [tsa·'ris·ta] <-i *m*, -e *f*> I. *mf* czarist II. *agg* (*esercito, truppe*) czarist
zattera ['tsat·te·ra/'dzat·te·ra] *f* raft; ~ **di salvataggio** life raft; **ponte di -e** pontoon bridge
zavorra [dza·'vɔr·ra] *f* 1. NAUT, AERO ballast 2. *fig, pej* (*cosa*) junk; (*persona*) waste of space
zazzera ['tsat·tse·ra] *f scherz* (*capelli lunghi*) mop
zebra ['dzɛ:·bra] *f* 1. ZOO zebra 2. *pl, fam* crosswalk
zebrato, -a [dze·'bra:·to] *agg* (*tessuto, disegno*) black and white striped
zebù [dze·'bu] <-> *m* ZOO zebu
zecca ['tsek·ka] <-cche> *f* 1. (*officina*) mint; **nuovo di** ~ *fig* brand new 2. ZOO tick
zecchino [tsek·'ki:·no] *m* (*moneta*) gold coin; **oro** ~ pure gold
zelante [dze·'lan·te] *agg* (*persona*) diligent
zelo ['dzɛ:·lo] *m* zeal
zen [dzɛn] I. <-> *m* Zen II. <inv> *agg* (*pensiero, filosofia*) Zen
zenit ['dzɛ:·nit] <-> *m* zenith
zenzero ['dzen·dze·ro] *m* ginger
zeppa ['tsep·pa] *f* 1. (*cuneo*) wedge 2. (*di scarpa*) platform sole; **scarpe con le -e** platform shoes
zeppelin ['tsɛ·pə·li:n] <-> *m* zeppelin
zeppo, -a ['tsep·po] *agg fam* ~ **di** packed with; **essere pieno** ~ to be jam-packed
zerbino [dzer·'bi:·no] *m* doormat
zero ['dzɛ:·ro] I. <-> *m* 1. (*gener*) zero; ~ **virgola otto** zero point eight; **essere uno** ~ *fig* to be hopeless; **rasare a** ~ (*capelli*) to shave off all sb's hair; **sparare a** ~ **contro** [*o* su] qu *fig* to lay into sb; **3 gradi sotto** ~ 3 degrees below zero 2. (*voto scolastico*) F, *the lowest possible grade* II. *num* zero; **l'ora** ~ *fig* zero hour
zeta ['dzɛ:·ta] <-> *f v.* Z, z
zia ['tsi:·a] <zie> *f* aunt
zibaldone [dzi·bal·'do:·ne] *m* LIT author's notebook
zibellino [dzi·bel·'li:·no] *m* sable
zibibbo [dzi·'bib·bo] *m* BOT *type of sweet*

white grape

zigano, -a [tsi·'ga:·no] I. *m, f* Romany II. *agg* (*musica, danza*) Romany

zigomo ['dzi:·go·ma] *m* cheekbone

zigrinare [dzi·gri·'na:·re] *vt* 1. (*pelle*) to grain 2. (*moneta*) to mill

zigrinato, -a [dzi·gri·'na:·to] *agg* 1. (*ruvido: pelle*) grained 2. (*rigato*) ridged

zigrinatura [dzi·gri·na·'tu:·ra] *f* 1. (*di cuoio*) grain 2. (*di moneta, superficie*) milling

zigzag, zig-zag [dzig·'dzag] <-> *m* zigzag

zigzagare [dzig·dza·'ga:·re] *vi* to zigzag

zimbello [tsim·'bɛl·lo/dzim·'bɛl·lo] *m* 1. *fig* (*oggetto di scherno*) laughing stock 2. ZOO (*uccello*) decoy

zinco ['tsiŋ·ko/'dziŋ·ko] *m* zinc

zingaro, -a ['tsiŋ·ga·ro/'dziŋ·ga·ro] *m, f* Romany

zio ['tsi:·o] <zii> *m* 1. (*uomo*) uncle 2. *pl* (*zio e zia*) aunt and uncle

zip [dzip] <-> *m o f* (*cerniera*) zipper

zippare [dzip·'pa:·re] *vt* COMPUT (*file*) to zip

zippato, -a [dzip·'pa:·to] *agg* zipped; **file ~** zipped file

zircone [dzir·'ko:·ne] *m* zircon

zirlare [dzir·'la:·re/tsir·'la:·re] *vi* to whistle, *used about thrushes*

zirlo ['dzir·lo/'tsir·lo] *m* whistle

zit(t)ella [tsi·'tɛl·la/dzi·'tɛl·la (dzit·'tɛl·la)] *f* 1. (*donna nubile*) single woman 2. *pej* old maid

zit(t)ellone [tsi(t)·tel·'lo:·ne/dzi(t)·tel·'lo:·ne] *m scherz* bachelor

zittire [tsit·'ti:·re] <zittisco> I. *vt* to silence II. *vr:* **-rsi** to fall silent

zitto, -a ['tsit·to] I. *agg* quiet; **sta' ~!** *fam* be quiet!; **~ ~** *fam* quietly II. *int* be quiet!

zizzania [dzid·'dza:·nia] <-ie> *f* 1. *fig* (*discordia*) discord 2. BOT rye grass

zoccolo ['tsɔk·ko·lo] *m* 1. (*calzatura*) clog 2. ZOO (*di cavallo, mucca*) hoof 3. ARCH (*di edificio, colonna, monumento*) plinth 4. (*battiscopa*) baseboard 5. GEOL **~ continentale** continental shelf

zodiacale [dzo·dia·'ka:·le] *agg* (*costellazione, segno*) **segno ~** sign of the zodiac

zodiaco [dzo·'di:·a·ko] <-ci> *m* zodiac; **i segni dello ~** the signs of the zodiac

zolfanello [tsol·fa·'nɛl·lo] *m* (*fiammifero*) sulfur match

zolfo ['tsol·fo] *m* sulfur

zolla ['dzɔl·la/'tsɔl·la] *f* (*pezzo di terra*) clod

zolletta [dzol·'let·ta/tsol·'let·ta] *f* (*di zucchero*) cube; **zucchero in -e** cubed sugar

zombie ['zɔm·bi] <-> *m* zombie; **sembrare uno ~** *fig* to look like a zombie

zona ['dzɔ:·na] *f* 1. (*regione*) zone; **~ climatica** climate zone; **~ collinare** hilly area; **~ desertica** desert region; **~ di montagna** mountain region; **~ di libero scambio** free trade zone; **~ sismica** earthquake zone 2. ADM (*in una città*) area; **~ blu** *area where parking has to be paid for*; **~ disco** *area where you can*

park *as long as you display a parking sticker*; **~ industriale** industrial park; **~ pedonale** pedestrian mall; **~ residenziale** residential area; **~ verde** green area; **~ vietata** exclusion zone

zonizzare [dzo·nid·'dza:·re] *vt* (*in urbanistica*) to zone

zonzo ['dzon·dzo] *fam* **andare a ~** to wander around

zoo ['dzɔ:·o] <-> *m* zoo

zoologia [dzo·o·lo·'dʒi:·a] <-gie> *f* zoology

zoologico, -a [dzo·o·'lɔ:·dʒi·ko] <-ci, -che> *agg* (*scienze*) zoological; **giardino ~** zoo

zoologo, -a [dzo·'ɔ:·lo·go] <-gi, -ghe> *m, f* zoologist

zoom [zu:m] <-> *m* PHOT zoom

zoomare [dzu·'ma:·re] *v.* **zumare**

zoomata [dzu·'ma:·ta] *f v.* **zumata**

zootecnia [dzo·o·tek·'ni:·a] <-ie> *f* zootechnics

zootecnico, -a [dzo·o·'tɛk·ni·ko] <-ci, -che> I. *agg* (*settore, patromonio*) zootechnic II. *m, f* zootechnician

zoppicante [tsop·pi·'kan·te] *agg* (*persona, passo*) limping

zoppicare [tsop·pi·'ka:·re] *vi* 1. (*persona*) to limp 2. *fig, fam* (*periodo*) to lose its rhythm; (*ragionamento*) to be full of holes

zoppo, -a ['tsɔp·po] I. *m, f* lame person II. *agg* (*persona, gamba*) lame; **è ~ dalla gamba destra** his right leg is lame

zotico, -a ['dzɔ:·ti·ko] <-ci, -che> I. *agg* (*persona*) boorish II. *m, f* boor

zuavo, -a [dzu·'a:·vo] *m, f* (*loc*) **pantaloni alla ~** plus fours

zucca ['tsuk·ka] <-cche> *f* 1. BOT pumpkin 2. *scherz, fam* head

zuccherare [tsuk·ke·'ra:·re] *vt* to sweeten

zuccherato, -a [tsuk·ke·'ra:·to] *agg* (*caffè, tè*) sweet

zuccheriera [tsuk·ke·'riɛ:·ra] *f* sugar bowl

zuccherificio [tsuk·ke·ri·'fi:·tʃo] <-ci> *m* sugar factory

zuccherino [tsuk·ke·'ri:·no] *m* 1. (*pezzetto di zucchero*) sugar cube 2. *fig* sweetener

zuccherino, -a *agg* 1. (*che contiene zucchero*) sweet 2. (*dolce*) sugary

zucchero ['tsuk·ke·ro] *m* sugar; **~ filato** cotton candy; **~ vanigliato** vanilla sugar; **~ di canna** cane sugar; **~ in polvere** caster sugar; **~ in zollette** cubed sugar; **barbabietola da ~** sugar beet; **dolce come lo ~** *a. fig* sweet as sugar

zuccheroso, -a [tsuk·ke·'ro:·so] *agg* 1. (*frutta*) sweet 2. *fig* (*parole*) sugary

zucchina [tsuk·'ki:·na] *f* zucchini

zuccone, -a *m, f fig, fam* 1. (*tonto*) blockhead 2. (*testardo*) stubborn person

zuccotto [tsuk·'kɔt·to] *m* CULIN cold dessert made from sponge cake, cream, chocolate and candied fruit

zuffa ['tsuf·fa] *f* brawl

zufolo ['tsu:·fo·lo] *m* MUS tin whistle

zumare [dzu·'ma:·re] I. *vi* FILM, TV to zoom; **~ su un particolare** to zoom in on a detail

Y

Z

II. *vt* FILM, TV to zoom in on; COMPUT to zoom in on

zumata [dzu·'ma:·ta] *f* FILM, TV zoom

zuppa ['tsup·pa] *f* CULIN soup; **~ di pesce** fish soup; **~ di verdura** vegetable soup; **~ inglese** *cold dessert made from sponge soaked in liquor with cream and chocolate;* **se non è ~ è pan bagnato** *prov* there's nothing to choose between them

zuppetta [tsup·'pe·ta] *f* (*loc*) **fare** (**la**) **~** to dunk, *cookies in milk or bread in wine*

zuppiera [tsup·'piɛ:·ra] *f* soup tureen

zuppo, -a ['tsup·po] *agg fam* (*bagnato*) soaked

Zurigo [dzu·'ri:·go] *m* Zurich; **andare a ~** to go to Zurich; **abitare a ~** to live in Zurich

zuzzerellone, -a [dzud·dze·rel·'lo:·ne] *m, f fam* clown

SVIZZERA
SWITZERLAND

LIECHTENSTEIN

AUSTRIA

UNGHERIA
HUNGARY

Lago di Ginevra
Lake Geneva

Rodano
Rhône

Reno
Rhine

Adige

Bolzano-Bozen

Trentino-Alto Adige/
Trentino-
South Tyrol

Friuli-
Venezia
Giulia

Balaton

Danubio
Danube

SLOVENIA

Sava

Lago Maggiore
Lake Maggiore

Lago di Como
Lake Como

Bergamo

Lago di Garda
Lake Garda

Lombardia
Lombardy

Trento

Udine

Trieste

Adige

Drava

FRANCIA
FRANCE

Valle d'Aosta
Aosta
Aosta Valley

Piemonte
Piedmont

Torino
Turin

Milano
Milan

Alessandria

Veneto

Verona

Padova
Padua

Venezia
Venice

C
R
O
A
Z
I
A

Po

BOSNIA
ERZEGOVINA

BOSNIA AND
HERZEGOVINA

Po

Parma

Reggio
Emilia

Modena

Emilia-Romagna

Bologna

Ravenna

FRANCIA
FRANCE

Liguria

Genova
Genoa

La Spezia

Rimini

SAN MARINO

MONACO

Arno

Prato

Firenze
Florence

Pisa

Toscana
Tuscany

Marche

Ancona

M
a
r

A
d
r
i
a
t
i
c
o

Mar Ligure
Ligurian Sea

Elba

Perugia

Umbria

Terni

L'Aquila

Abruzzo
Abruzzi

Corsica
(FRANCIA)
(FRANCE)

CITTÀ DEL VATICANO
VATICAN CITY

Roma
Rome

L
a
z
i
o

Molise

Campobasso

Foggia

Bari

A
d
r
i
a
t
i
c
o

S
e
a

Isole Ponziane/
Isole Pontine

Pontini Islands

Napoli
Naples

Ischia

Salerno

Capri

Campania

Puglia
Apulia

Potenza

Taranto

Lecce

Basilicata

Golfo di Taranto
Gulf of Taranto

Sassari

Sardegna
Sardinia

Cagliari

M a r   T i r r e n o

T y r r h e n i a n

S e a

Cosenza

Catanzaro

Ustica

Stromboli

Isole Lipari
Lipari Is.

Messina

Reggio Calabria

C
a
l
a
b
r
i
a

Mar Ionio

Ionian Sea

Stretto di Messina
Strait of Messina

M

e

d

i

t

Palermo

Sicilia
Sicily

Catania

Siracusa

Isole Egadi
Egadi Is.

Canale di Sicilia
Strait of Sicily

ALGERIA

TUNISIA

Pantelleria

e

r

r

a

n

e

o

Linosa

MALTA

Lampedusa

M
e
d
i
t
e
r
r
a
n
e
a
n

S
e
a

Italia
Italy

7 000 000

<u>Roma</u> Capitale di Stato
<u>Rome</u> National capital
<u>Bologna</u> Capoluogo di regione
  Capitol of region

```
0    50   100   150   200 km
0        50        100    150 mi
```

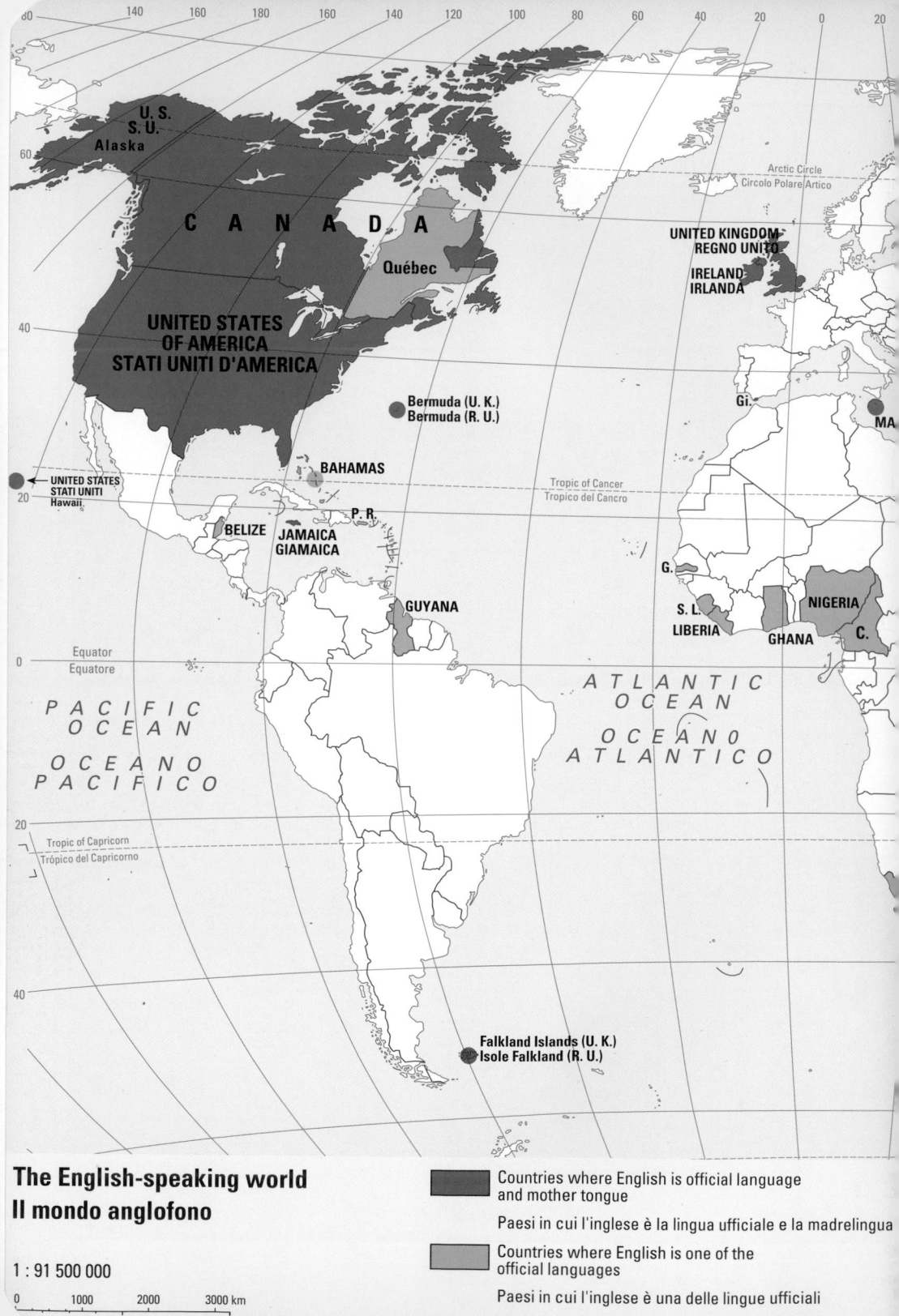

The English-speaking world
Il mondo anglofono

1 : 91 500 000

0   1000   2000   3000 km

1000   2000 mi

Countries where English is official language and mother tongue

Paesi in cui l'inglese è la lingua ufficiale e la madrelingua

Countries where English is one of the official languages

Paesi in cui l'inglese è una delle lingue ufficiali

U. S.
S. U.
Alaska

CANADA

Québec

UNITED STATES
OF AMERICA
STATI UNITI D'AMERICA

UNITED KINGDOM
REGNO UNITO

IRELAND
IRLANDA

Gi.

MA

Bermuda (U. K.)
Bermuda (R. U.)

BAHAMAS

UNITED STATES
STATI UNITI
Hawaii

Tropic of Cancer
Tropico del Cancro

BELIZE

P. R.

JAMAICA
GIAMAICA

GUYANA

G.

S. L.
LIBERIA

GHANA

NIGERIA

C.

Equator
Equatore

PACIFIC
OCEAN

OCEANO
PACIFICO

ATLANTIC
OCEAN

OCEANO
ATLANTICO

Tropic of Capricorn
Trópico del Capricorno

Falkland Islands (U. K.)
Isole Falkland (R. U.)

Arctic Circle
Circolo Polare Artico

| 60 | 80 | 100 | 120 | 140 | 160 | 180 | 160 | 140 | 120 | 100 | 80 | 60 |

CANADA

U. S.
S. U.
Alaska

40

PAKISTAN

PACIFIC
OCEAN

INDIA

HONG KONG

OCEANO
PACIFICO

20

N.

Gu.

SRI
LANKA

PALAU

UGANDA   KENYA

S.

Equator
Equatore   0

TANZANIA

SEYCHELLES

I N D I A N
O C E A N

P.

3
4
S. I.

ZAMBIA   MALAWI

O C E A N O
I N D I A N O

VANUATU

5

Z.

6

MAURITIUS
MAURIZIO

7

A.   SW.

8

AUSTRALIA

9

NEW ZEALAND
NUOVA ZELANDA

40

Legend:

B.	BOTSWANA
C.	CAMEROON CAMERUN
G.	THE GAMBIA GAMBIA
Gi.	Gibraltar (U. K.) Gibilterra (R. U.)
Gu.	Guam (U.S./S. U.)
L.	LESOTHO

N.	Northern Mariana Is. (U. S.) Marianne Settentrionali (S. U.)
P.	PAPUA NEW GUINEA PAPUASIA-NUOVA GUINEA
P. R.	Puerto Rico (U. S./S. U.)
S.	SINGAPORE
SW.	SWAZILAND

S. A.	SOUTH AFRICA SUDAFRICA
S. I.	SOLOMON ISLANDS ISOLE SALOMONE
S. L.	SIERRA LEONE
Z.	ZIMBABWE

Countries in the Pacific Ocean:
Paesi nell'Oceano Pacifico:

1	Midway (U. S./S. U.)
2	MARSHALL ISLANDS ISOLE MARSHALL
3	NAURU
4	KIRIBATI
5	TUVALU

6	Western Samoa Samoa Occidentali
7	American Samoa Samoa Americane
8	FIJI FIGI
9	TONGA

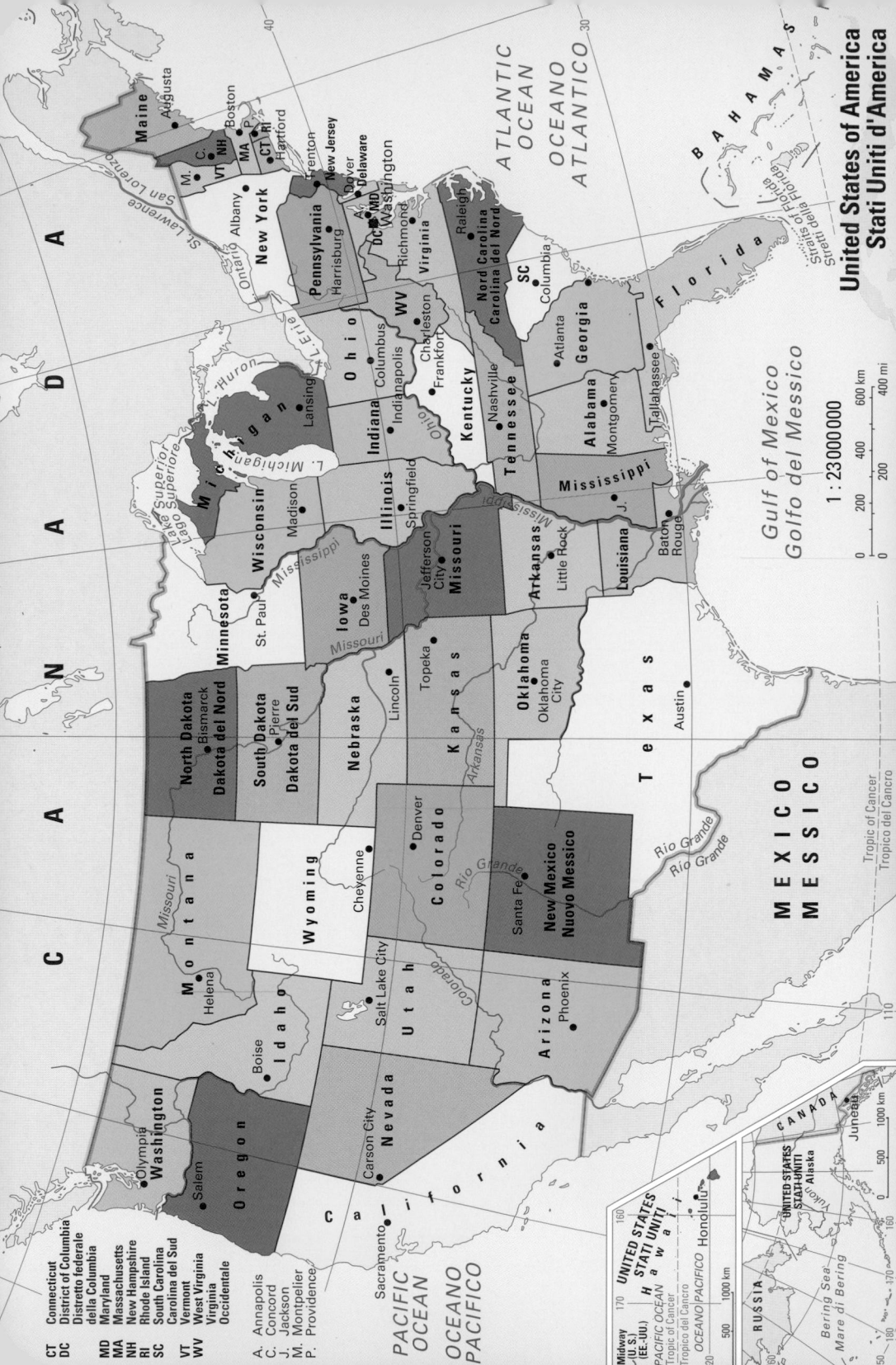

United States of America
Stati Uniti d'America

CT Connecticut
DC District of Columbia
    Distretto federale
    della Columbia
MD Maryland
MA Massachusetts
NH New Hampshire
RI Rhode Island
SC South Carolina
    Carolina del Sud
VT Vermont
WV West Virginia
    Virginia
    Occidentale

A. Annapolis
C. Concord
J. Jackson
M. Montpelier
P. Providence

1 : 23000000

0   200   400   600 km
0   200   400 mi

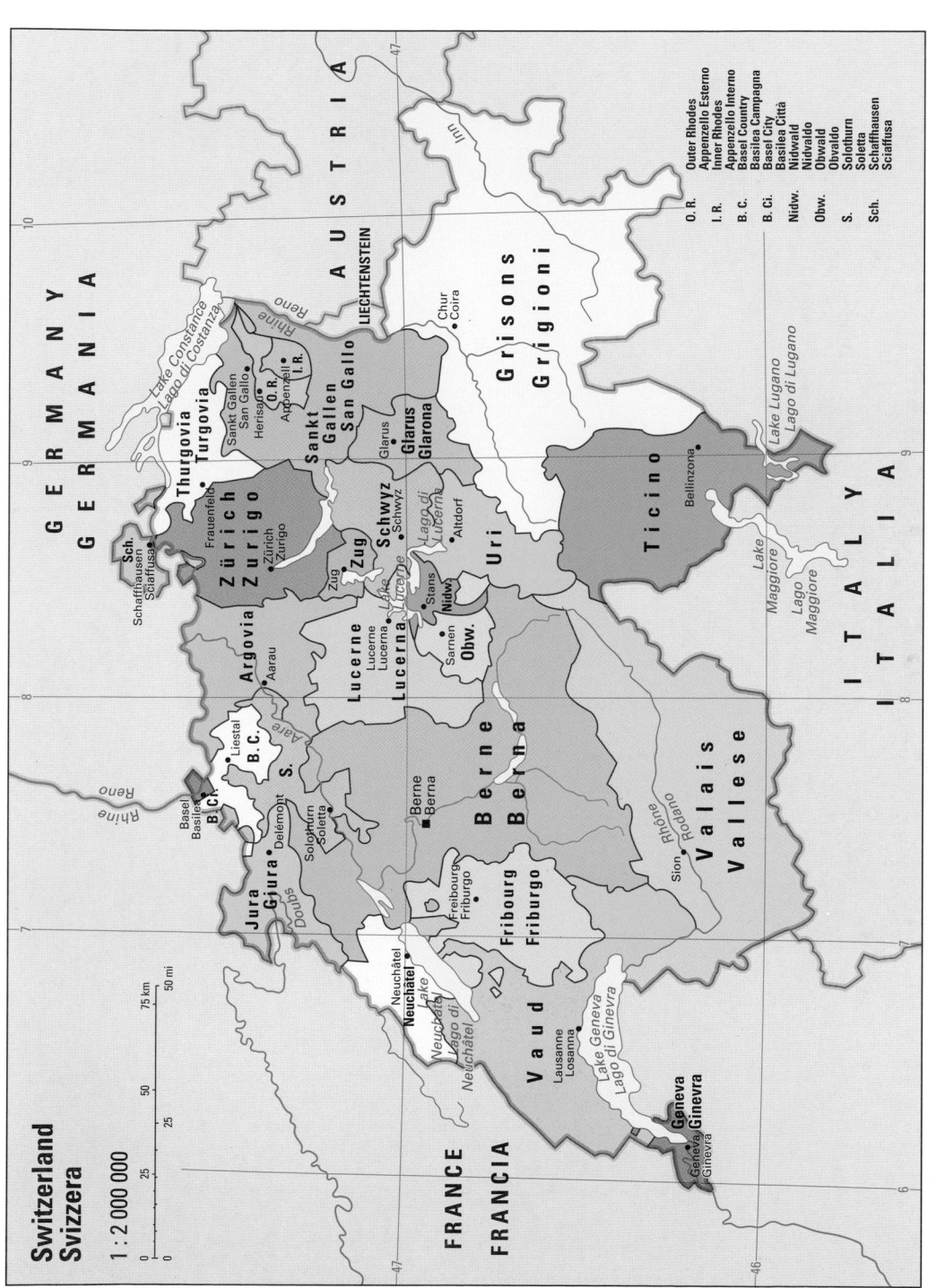

Switzerland
Svizzera

1 : 2 000 000

0   25   50   75 km
0   25   50 mi

GERMANY
GERMANIA

AUSTRIA

LIECHTENSTEIN

FRANCE
FRANCIA

ITALY
ITALIA

Rhine
Reno

Lake Constance
Lago di Costanza

Schaffhausen
Sciaffusa

Sch.
Sciaffusa

Thurgovia
Turgovia

Frauenfeld

Zürich
Zurigo

Zürich
Zurigo

Sankt Gallen
San Gallo

Herisau

O. R.
Appenzell
I. R.

Sankt
Gallen
San Gallo

Glarus

Glarus
Glarona

Chur
Coira

Grisons
Grigioni

Argovia

Aarau

Zug

Zug

Schwyz
Svitto

Lago di
Lucerna

Altdorf

Uri

Ticino

Bellinzona

Basel
Basilea

Liestal

B. C.

B. Ci.

S.

Delémont

Solothurn
Soletta

Lucerne
Lucerna

Lucerne
Lucerna

Lake
Lucerne

Stans

Sarnen

Nidw.

Obw.

Lake
Maggiore

Lago
Maggiore

Lake
Maggiore

Jura
Giura

Doubs

Aare

Fribourg
Friburgo

Fribourg
Friburgo

Berne
Berna

Berne
Berna

Valais
Vallese

Sion

Rhône
Rodano

Lake Lugano
Lago di Lugano

Neuchâtel

Neuchâtel

Lake
di
Neuchâtel

Lago di
Neuchâtel

Vaud

Lausanne
Losanna

Lake Geneva
Lago di Ginevra

Geneva
Ginevra

Geneva
Ginevra

O. R.   Outer Rhodes
            Appenzello Esterno
I. R.   Inner Rhodes
            Appenzello Interno
B. C.   Basel Country
            Basilea Campagna
B. Ci.   Basel City
            Basilea Città
Nidw.   Nidwald
            Nidvaldo
Obw.   Obwald
            Obvaldo
S.   Solothurn
            Soletta
Sch.   Schaffhausen
            Sciaffusa

ICELAND
ISLANDA

G r o e n l a n d i a
Groenlandia
(Denm.)
(Danim.)

Arctic Circle
Circolo Polare Artico

ATLANTIC OCEAN
OCEANO
ATLANTICO

Labrador Sea
Mare del Labrador

Labrador Sea

Baffin Bay
Baia di Baffin

Baffin Island
Isola Baffin

Iqaluit

Saint John's

St. Pierre and
Miquelon (Fr.)
Saint-Pierre e
Miquelon (Fr.)

Newfoundland and Labrador
Terranova e Labrador

Charlottetown

Halifax

P. E. I.

N. B.   New Brunswick
         Nuova Brunswick
N. S.   Nova Scotia
         Nuova Scozia
P. E. I. Prince Edward Island
         I. Pr. Edoardo

Fredericton

N. B.   N. S.

St. Lawrence River
San Lorenzo

Québec

Québec
Quebec

Ottawa

Lake Ontario
Lago Ontario

Lake Erie
Lago Erie

Toronto

Lake Huron
Lago Huron

Lake Superior
Lago Superiore

Lake Michigan
Lago Michigan

Hudson Bay
Baia
di Hudson

N u n a v u t

C   A   N   A   D   A

Ontario

Manitoba

Lake Winnipeg
Lago Winnipeg

Nelson

Winnipeg

Saskatchewan

Regina

Lake Athabasca
Lago Athabasca

Athabasca

Great Bear Lake
Gran Lago degli Orsi

Gt. Slave L.
Gran Lago
degli Schiavi

Yellowknife

Northwest Territories
Territori del Nord-Ovest

Mackenzie River
F. Mackenzie

Alberta

Edmonton

Peace

Columbia

British
Columbia
Columbia
Britannica

Victoria

Missouri

Mississippi

UNITED STATES
STATI UNITI

U N I T E D   S T A T E S
S T A T I   U N I T I

Yukon
Territory
Territori
dello Yukon

Whitehorse

Yukon

Beaufort Sea
Mare di Beaufort

UNITED STATES
STATI UNITI

A l a s k a

Gulf of Alaska
Golfo dell'Alaska

RUSSIA

Bering
Sea
Mare di
Bering

PACIFIC OCEAN
OCEANO PACIFICO

Canada

1 : 30 000 000

0   500   1000 mi

0   500   1000   1500 km

A

A, a [eɪ] *n* **1.** (*letter*) A, a *f o m inv; ~* **as in Abel** A come Ancona; **to get from ~ to B** andare da un posto all'altro; **from ~ to Z** dalla A alla Z **2.** MUS (*note*) la *m* **3.** SCHOOL *voto massimo*

a [ə, *stressed:* eɪ] *indef art before consonant,* **an** [ən, *stressed:* æn] *before vowel* **1.** (*in general*) un, uno, una; ~ **car** un'automobile; ~ **house** una casa; **in ~ day or two** in un paio di giorni **2.** (*not translated*) **do you have ~ car?** hai la macchina?; **he is an American** è americano; **she is ~ teacher** è insegnante; **a hundred days** cento giorni **3.** (*to express prices, rates*) **$2 ~ dozen** 2 dollari la dozzina; **$6 ~ week** 6 dollari a settimana **4.** (*before person's name*) ~ **Mr. Robinson** un certo sig. Robinson

a. *abbr of* **answer** risposta

AA [ˌeɪˈeɪ] *abbr of* **Alcoholics Anonymous** AA *f*

AAA 1. AUTO *abbr of* **American Automobile Association** ≈ ACI *m* **2.** *abbr of* **Amateur Athletic Association** *associazione dell'atletica dilettantistica*

aback [əˈbæk] *adv* **to take sb ~** cogliere qn di sorpresa; **to be taken ~** (**by sth**) essere colto alla sprovvista (da qc)

abacus [ˈæ·bə·kəs] *n* abaco *m*

abandon [əˈbæn·dən] **I.** *vt* **1.** (*vehicle, place, person*) abbandonare; **to ~ ship** abbandonare la nave **2.** (*give up: plan*) rinunciare a; (*game*) sospendere **3.** (*lose self-control*) **to ~ oneself to sth** abbandonarsi a qc **II.** *n* abbandono *m*; **with** (**wild**) ~ con (grande) trasporto

abandoned [əˈbæn·dənd] *adj* abbandonato, -a

abashed [əˈbæʃt] *adj* imbarazzato, -a; **to be ~ at sth** essere imbarazzato da [*o* per] qc

abate [əˈbeɪt] *vi* **1.** (*noise*) attenuarsi; (*anger*) placarsi **2.** (*wind*) calmarsi

abatement *n* riduzione *f*

abattoir [ˈæ·bət·wɑːr] *n* mattatoio *m*

abbess [ˈæ·bəs] *n* REL badessa *f*

abbey [ˈæ·bi] *n* abazia *f*

abbot [ˈæ·bət] *n* REL abate *m*

abbreviate [əˈbriː·vi·eɪt] *vt* abbreviare

abbreviation [əˌbriː·vɪˈeɪ·ʃən] *n* abbreviazione *f*

ABC¹ [ˌeɪ·biːˈsiː] *n pl* **1.** (*alphabet*) alfabeto *m* **2.** (*rudiments*) abbiccì *m*

ABC² [ˌeɪ·biːˈsiː] *n* TV *abbr of* **American Broadcasting Company** *emittente televisiva americana*

abdicate [ˈæb·dɪ·keɪt] **I.** *vi* abdicare **II.** *vt* (*right*) rinunciare a; (*throne*) abdicare (a)

abdication [ˌæb·dɪˈkeɪ·ʃən] *n* **1.** (*of right*) rinuncia *f* **2.** (*of throne*) abdicazione *f*

abdomen [ˈæb·də·mən] *n* ANAT addome *m*

abdominal [æbˈdɑː·mə·nl] *adj* addominale

abduct [æbˈdʌkt] *vt* rapire

abduction [æbˈdʌk·ʃən] *n* rapimento *m*

aberration [ˌæ·bəˈreɪ·ʃən] *n* aberrazione *f*

abet [əˈbet] <-tt-> *vt* istigare; **to aid and ~ sb** rendersi complice di qn

abeyance [əˈbeɪ·əns] *n* **to fall into ~** cadere in disuso

abhor [æbˈhɔːr] <-rr-> *vt* aborrire

abhorrence [æbˈhɔː·rəns] *n* ripugnanza *f*

abhorrent *adj* ripugnante

abide [əˈbaɪd] <-d *o* abode, -d *o* abode> *vt* sopportare; **I can't ~ her** non la sopporto

◆**abide by** *vt* **1.** (*rule, decision*) attenersi a **2.** (*promise*) mantenere

abiding *adj* duraturo, -a

ability [əˈbɪ·lə·t̬i] <-ies> *n* **1.** (*capability*) capacità *f;* **to the best of one's ~** al meglio delle proprie capacità **2.** (*talent*) talento *m* **3.** *pl* (*skills*) doti *fpl*

abject [ˈæb·dʒekt] *adj* **1.** (*wretched*) abietto, -a **2.** (*absolute: poverty*) estremo, -a; (*failure*) totale

ablaze [əˈbleɪz] *adj* in fiamme; *fig* splendente

able [ˈeɪ·bl] *adj* (*capable: person*) capace; **to be ~ to do sth** (*have ability, manage*) essere in grado di fare qc; (*have knowledge*) saper fare qc

able-bodied *adj* di sana e robusta costituzione; ~ **seaman** marinaio *m* scelto

ABM *n abbr of* **antiballistic missile** missile *m* antimissile *inv*

abnormal [æbˈnɔːr·ml] *adj* **1.** (*feature*) anomalo, -a **2.** (*person*) anormale

abnormality [ˌæb·nɔːrˈmæ·lə·t̬i] <-ies> *n* **1.** (*abnormal feature*) anomalia *f* **2.** (*unusualness*) anormalità *f*

aboard [əˈbɔːrd] **I.** *adv* a bordo; **all ~!** FERR in vettura!; NAUT tutti a bordo! **II.** *prep* a bordo di; **to go ~ a boat** salire a bordo di una nave; **to go ~ a plane** salire a bordo di un aereo

abode [əˈboʊd] **I.** *vi pt, pp of* **abide II.** *n form* dimora *f*

abolish [əˈbɑː·lɪʃ] *vt* abolire

abolition [ˌæ·bəˈlɪ·ʃən] *n* abolizione *f*

abominable [əˈbɑː·mɪ·nə·bl] *adj* abominevole

abominate [əˈbɑː·mɪ·neɪt] *vt* avere in abominio

abomination [əˌbɑː·mɪˈneɪ·ʃən] *n* **1.** (*abominable thing*) abominio *m* **2.** (*disgust*) avversione *f*

aboriginal [ˌæ·bəˈrɪ·dʒə·nl] **I.** *adj* aborigeno, -a **II.** *n* aborigeno (, -a d'Australia) *m*

Aborigine [ˌæ·bəˈrɪ·dʒɪ·ni] *n* aborigeno, -a (d'Australia) *m*

abort [əˈbɔːrt] **I.** *vt* **1.** MED fare abortire **2.** *a.* INFOR interrompere **II.** *vi* **1.** MED abortire **2.** (*fail*) fallire

abortion [əˈbɔːr·ʃən] *n* MED aborto (*m* provocato); **to have an ~** abortire

abortive [əˈbɔːr·t̬ɪv] *adj* fallito, -a

abound [əˈbaʊnd] *vi* abbondare

about [əˈbaʊt] **I.** *prep* **1.** (*on subject of*) su; **a**

book ~ **football** un libro sul calcio; **what is the film ~?** di cosa parla il film? **2.** (*characteristic of*) **that's what I like ~ him** è questo che mi piace di lui **3.** (*surrounding*) intorno a; **the garden ~ the house** il giardino intorno alla casa **4.** (*in and through*) per; **to go ~ the streets** girare per le strade ▶ **how ~ that!** però!; **how ~ a drink?** che ne dici di bere qualcosa?; **what ~ it?** (*suggestion*) che ne dici?; (*so what?*) e allora? **II.** *adv* **1.** (*approximately*) pressapoco; **~ my size** più o meno della mia statura; **~ 5 lbs.** circa 5 libbre; **~ here** più o meno qui; **~ 5 years ago** circa 5 anni fa; **~ twenty** una ventina; **to have had just ~ enough of sth** averne avuto abbastanza di qc; **that's ~ it for today** è tutto per oggi **2.** (*almost*) quasi; **to be** (**just**) **~ ready** essere quasi pronto **3.** (*on the point of*) **to be ~ to do sth** stare (proprio) per fare qc **4.** (*around*) **all ~** in giro; **to be somewhere ~** essere nei paraggi; **is Paul ~?** c'è Paul da queste parti? **5.** (*willing to*) **not to be ~ to do sth** non avere nessuna intenzione di fare qc

about-face *n* MIL, A. FIG dietrofront *m inv*

above [ə-ˈbʌv] **I.** *prep* **1.** (*on the top of*) sopra **2.** (*over*) al di sopra; **~ suspicion** al di sopra di ogni sospetto **3.** (*greater than, superior to*) oltre; **~ 3** più di 3; **those ~ the age of 70** quelli con più di 70 anni; **he is not ~ lying** non si fa scrupolo di mentire; **~ all** soprattutto; **to shout ~ the noise** gridare per sovrastare il rumore; **it's ~ me** va al di là della mia comprensione **4.** GEO (*upstream*) a monte di; (*north of*) a nord di **II.** *adv* di sopra; **the floor ~** il piano di sopra; **up ~ sth** sopra qc; **from ~** dall'alto; **see ~** (*in text*) vedi sopra **III.** *adj* summenzionato, -a **IV.** *n* **the ~** il suddetto

aboveboard *adj* chiaro, -a

above-mentioned *adj* suddetto, -a

abrasion [ə-ˈbreɪ·ʒən] *n* MED abrasione *f*

abrasive [ə-ˈbreɪ·sɪv] **I.** *adj* **1.** (*rough*) abrasivo, -a **2.** (*in manner*) brusco, -a **II.** *n* abrasivo *m*

abreast [ə-ˈbrest] *adv* **1.** (*side by side*) **two/three ~** in fila per due/tre **2.** (*up to date*) **to be/keep ~ of sth** essere/tenersi al corrente di qc

abridge [ə-ˈbrɪdʒ] *vt* abbreviare; **an ~d version** una versione ridotta

abridgement *n*, **abridgment** [ə-ˈbrɪdʒ·mənt] *n* **1.** (*version*) compendio *m* **2.** (*action*) riduzione *f*

abroad [ə-ˈbrɑːd] *adv* **1.** (*in foreign country*) all'estero; **from ~** dall'estero; **to be ~** essere all'estero; **to go ~** andare all'estero; **at home and ~** in patria e all'estero **2.** *form* (*outside*) in circolazione; **the news quickly spread ~** la notizia si diffuse rapidamente

abrupt [ə-ˈbrʌpt] *adj* **1.** (*sudden*) repentino, -a; (*change*) brusco, -a; (*end*) improvviso, -a **2.** (*brusque*) brusco, -a

ABS [ˌeɪ·biːˈes] *n abbr of* **antilock braking system** ABS *m*

abscess [ˈæb·ses] *n* ascesso *m*

abscond [əb-ˈskɑːnd] *vi* fuggire; **to ~ with sb/sth** fuggire con qn/qc

absence [ˈæb·səns] *n* **1.** (*not being present: of person, thing*) assenza *f*; **in the ~ of** in assenza di; **on leave of ~** MIL in permesso **2.** (*lack of: of money, information*) mancanza *f*; **in the ~ of** in mancanza di

absent[1] [ˈæb·sənt] *adj* **1.** (*not present*) assente; **without leave** MIL assente senza permesso **2.** (*lacking*) mancante; **to be ~ in sth** mancare di qc **3.** (*distracted*) assente

absent[2] [əb-ˈsent] *vt form* **to ~ oneself** (**from sth**) assentarsi (da qc)

absentee [ˌæb·sən-ˈtiː] *n* assente *mf*

absentee ballot *n* voto *m* per corrispondenza

absenteeism *n* assenteismo *m*

absentee owner *n* proprietario, -a assenteista *m*

absentee voting *n* voto *m* per corrispondenza

absent-minded *adj* distratto, -a

absolute [ˈæb·sə·luːt] **I.** *adj* **1.** (*total, not relative*) *a.* POL assoluto, -a; (*denial*) categorico, -a; (*trust, power, confidence*) pieno, -a; (*disaster*) totale **2.** CHEM assoluto, -a **II.** *n* **the ~** PHILOS l'assoluto

absolutely *adv* **1.** (*comprehensively*) assolutamente; **~!** *inf* sicuramente!; **~ not!** assolutamente no! **2.** (*very*) totalmente

absolution [ˌæb·sə·ˈluː·ʃən] *n* REL assoluzione *f*

absolutism [ˈæb·sə·luː·ˌtɪ·zəm] *n* POL assolutismo *m*

absolve [əb-ˈzɑːlv] *vt* assolvere

absorb [əb-ˈsɔːrb] *vt* **1.** (*liquid*) assorbire; (*shock*) attutire **2.** (*understand*) assimilare **3.** (*engross*) **to get ~ed in sth** essere assorto in qc; **to be ~ed in one's thoughts** essere assorto nei propri pensieri

absorbent [əb-ˈsɔːr·bənt] *adj* assorbente

absorbing *adj* (*book*) avvincente; (*appassionante*)

absorption [əb-ˈsɔːrp·ʃən] *n* **1.** (*of liquid*) assorbimento *m* **2.** (*in book, story*) interesse *m* **3.** (*in work*) coinvolgimento *m*

abstain [əb-ˈsteɪn] *vi a.* POL astenersi; **to ~ from** (**doing**) **sth** astenersi da (l fare) qc

abstemious [əb-ˈstiː·mi·əs] *adj* morigerato, -a

abstention [əb-ˈsten·ʃən] *n a.* POL astensione *f*

abstinence [ˈæb·stɪ·nəns] *n* astinenza *f*

abstract[1] [ˈæb·strækt] **I.** *adj* astratto, -a; **~ art/painting** arte/pittura astratta **II.** *n* **1.** (*not concrete*) astratto *m;* **in the ~** in astratto **2.** (*summary*) riassunto *m*

abstract[2] [əb-ˈstrækt] *vt* **1.** *a.* CHEM estrarre **2.** (*summarize*) riassumere **3.** (*steal*) sottrarre

abstracted [æb-ˈstræk·tɪd] *adj* distratto, -a

abstraction [əb-ˈstræk·ʃən] *n* **1.** (*abstract concept*) astrazione *f* **2.** (*abstracted state*) distrazione *f*

abstruse [əb-ˈstruːs] *adj* astruso, -a

absurd [əb-ˈsɜːrd] *adj* assurdo, -a

absurdity [əb-ˈsɜːr·də·ti] <**-ies**> *n* assurdità *f*

abundance [ə-ˈbʌn·dəns] *n* abbondanza *f*

abundant [ə·'bʌn·dənt] *adj* abbondante

abuse¹ [ə·'bju:s] *n* **1.** (*insults*) insulti *mpl;* **to hurl ~ at sb** insultare qn **2.** (*mistreatment*) maltrattamenti *mpl* **3.** (*misuse*) abuso *m;* **sexual ~** violenza *f* sessuale

abuse² [ə·'bju:z] *vt* **1.** (*insult*) insultare **2.** (*mistreat*) maltrattare **3.** (*sexually*) abusare di **4.** (*misuse*) abusare di

abusive [ə·'bju:·sɪv] *adj* **1.** (*language*) offensivo, -a **2.** (*person*) violento, -a

abut [ə·'bʌt] <-tt-> **I.** *vt* confinare con **II.** *vi* **to ~ on** confinare con

abysmal [ə·'bɪz·məl] *adj* pessimo, -a

abyss [ə·'bɪs] *n a. fig* abisso *m*

AC [ˌeɪ·'si:] *n abbr of* **alternating current** CA

a/c [ˌeɪ·'si:] **1.** *abbr of* **account** c.to **2.** *abbr of* **air conditioning** aria *f* condizionata

academic [ˌæ·kə·'de·mɪk] **I.** *adj* **1.** UNIV academico, -a; SCHOOL scolastico, -a **2.** (*intellectual*) erudito, -a **3.** (*theoretical*) teorico, -a **4.** (*irrelevant*) irrilevante **II.** *n* accademico, -a *m, f*

academy [ə·'kæ·də·mi] <-ies> *n* **1.** (*for special training*) accademia *f* **2.** (*prep school*) scuola *f* secondaria privata **3.** CINE **the Academy Awards** gli Oscar

accede [æk·'si:d] *vi* **1.** (*agree*) **to ~ to sth** acconsentire a qc **2.** (*to a position*) accedere; **to ~ to the throne** salire al trono

accelerate [ək·'se·lə·reɪt] **I.** *vi* (*car*) accelerare; (*growth*) accelerarsi **II.** *vt* accelerare

acceleration [ək·ˌse·lə·'reɪ·ʃən] *n* accelerazione *f*

accelerator [ək·'se·lə·reɪ·tə·] *n* **1.** AUTO (*gas pedal*) acceleratore *m* **2.** *a. PHYS* acceleratore *m*

accent ['æk·sent] **I.** *n* **1.** LING accento *m* **2.** LIT, MUS enfasi *f inv* **II.** *vt* **1.** LIT, MUS accentare **2.** (*emphasize*) mettere in evidenza

accentuate [ək·'sen·tʃʊ·eɪt] *vt* accentuare

accept [ək·'sept] **I.** *vt* **1.** (*take when offered*) accettare **2.** (*approve*) approvare **3.** (*believe*) credere in **4.** (*acknowledge*) riconoscere **5.** (*include socially*) accogliere **II.** *vi* accettare

acceptable *adj* (*behavior, suggestion*) accettabile; (*explanation*) soddisfacente

acceptance [ək·'sep·təns] *n* **1.** (*of gift, help*) accettazione *f* **2.** (*approval*) approvazione *f* **3.** (*social*) accettazione *f*

accepted *adj* accettato, -a; **the ~ procedure** la solita prassi

access ['æk·ses] **I.** *n a.* INFOR accesso *m;* **~ road** strada *f* d'accesso; **Internet ~** INFOR accesso a Internet; **to gain ~ to sth** accedere a qc; **to have ~ to sth** avere accesso a qc; **with easy ~ to the sea** con accesso al mare **II.** *vt* INFOR accedere a

accessibility [æk·ˌse·sə·'bɪ·lə·t̬i] *n* **1.** accessibilità *f* **2.** *fig* disponibilità *f*

accessible [æk·'se·sə·bl] *adj* **1.** (*place, work of art*) accessibile **2.** (*person*) disponibile

accession [æk·'se·ʃən] *n* ascesa *f*

accessory [ək·'se·sə·ri] <-ies> *n* **1.** (*for outfit, machine, toy*) accessorio *m* **2.** LAW complice *mf*

access road *n* (strada *f* d') accesso *m*

accident ['æk·sɪ·dənt] *n* incidente *m;* **~ insurance** assicurazione *f* contro gli infortuni; **by ~** (*unintended*) senza volere; (*by chance*) per caso; **more by ~ than design** più per caso che per altro; **~s will happen** son cose che capitano

accidental [ˌæk·sɪ·'den·t̬əl] *adj* **1.** (*unintentional*) casuale; LAW (*death*) accidentale **2.** (*discovery*) fortuito, -a

accident-prone *adj* soggetto, -a agli incidenti

acclaim [ə·'kleɪm] **I.** *vt* acclamare; **critically ~ed** acclamato dalla critica **II.** *n* acclamazione *f*

acclamation [ˌæk·lə·'meɪ·ʃən] *n* acclamazione *f*

acclimate ['æk·lə·meɪt] **I.** *vi* acclimatarsi **II.** *vt* acclimatare

acclimation [ˌæk·laɪ·'meɪ·ʃən] *n* acclimatazione *f*

accolade ['æ·kə·leɪd] *n* riconoscimento *m*

accommodate [ə·'kɑ:·mə·deɪt] *vt* **1.** (*give place to stay*) ospitare; (*have room for*) sistemare **2.** *form* (*adapt*) adattarsi a; **to ~ oneself to sth** adattarsi a qc **3.** (*satisfy*) soddisfare

accommodating [ə·'kɑ:·mə·deɪ·t̬ɪŋ] *adj* accomodante

accommodation [ə·ˌkɑ:·mə·'deɪ·ʃən] *n* **1.** *pl* (*lodgings*) alloggio *m* **2.** (*on vehicle, plane*) posti *mpl* **3.** *form* (*compromise*) accordo *m*

accompaniment [ə·'kʌm·pə·nɪ·mənt] *n a.* MUS accompagnamento *m*

accompanist [ə·'kʌm·pə·nɪst] *n* MUS accompagnatore, -trice *m, f*

accompany [ə·'kʌm·pə·ni] <-ie-> *vt a.* MUS (*go with*) accompagnare; **to ~ sb on the violin** accompagnare qn al violino

accomplice [ə·'kɑ:m·plɪs] *n* complice *mf*

accomplish [ə·'kɑ:m·plɪʃ] *vt* **1.** (*achieve*) compiere **2.** (*finish*) portare a termine; **to ~ a task** portare a termine un compito

accomplished [ə·'kɑ:m·plɪʃt] *adj* provetto, -a

accomplishment *n* **1.** (*achievement*) risultato *m* **2.** (*completion*) realizzazione *f;* **~ of a task** realizzazione di un compito **3.** (*skill*) talento *m*

accord [ə·'kɔ:rd] **I.** *n* **1.** (*treaty*) accordo *m* **2.** (*agreement, harmony*) accordo *m;* **on** [*o* **of**] **one's own ~** spontaneamente; **to be in ~ with** concordare con **II.** *vt form* concedere **III.** *vi* **to ~ with sth** concordare con qc

accordance [ə·'kɔ:r·dəns] *n* **in ~ with** in conformità con

accordingly *adv* **1.** (*appropriately*) conformemente **2.** (*therefore*) di conseguenza

according to [ə·'kɔ:r·dɪŋ·tə] *prep* **1.** (*as told by*) secondo; **~ her/what I read** secondo lei/quanto ho letto; **to go ~ plan** andare secondo il previsto **2.** (*as basis*) in conformità con; **~ the law** secondo la legge; **~ the recipe** secondo la ricetta

accordion [ə·'kɔ:r·di·ən] *n* MUS fisarmonica *f*

accost [ə·'kɑ:st] *vt* accostare

account [ə·'kaʊnt] I. n 1. (*with bank*) conto m 2. (*bill*) fattura f; **to settle an ~** saldare un conto 3. pl (*financial records*) contabilità f; **to keep ~s** tenere la contabilità; **to keep an ~ of sth** tenere il conto di qc 4. (*customer*) cliente mf 5. (*description*) resoconto m; **an ~ of sth** un resoconto di qc; **to give an ~ of sth** fare un resoconto di qc; **by all ~s** a dire di tutti; **by her own ~** a quanto dice lei stessa 6. (*consideration*) **to take sth into ~** prendere [o tenere] in considerazione qc; **to take no ~ of sth** non tener conto di qc; **on ~ of sth** a causa di qc; **on no ~** in nessun caso 7. form (*importance*) **of little/no ~** di poca/nessuna importanza 8. (*responsibility*) responsabilità f; **on one's own ~** per conto proprio; **on sb's ~** per conto di qn ▸ **to be** called **to ~** (**for sth**) dover rendere conto di qc; **to settle ~s with sb** regolare i conti con qn; **to turn sth to ~** trarre profitto da qc II. vt form considerare
◆ **account for** vt 1. (*explain*) spiegare 2. (*constitute*) rappresentare
accountability [ə·ˌkaʊn·tə·'bɪ·lɪ·t̬i] n responsabilità f
accountable [ə·'kaʊn·tə·bl] adj responsabile
accountancy [ə·'kaʊn·tən·si] n contabilità f
accountant [ə·'kaʊn·tənt] n contabile mf
account book n libro m contabile
accredit [ə·'kre·dɪt] vt 1. (*recognize: school*) riconoscere 2. POL accreditare 3. (*attribute to*) attribuire
accrue [ə·'kruː] vi (*increase*) aumentare; (*interest*) maturare
accumulate [ə·'kjuː·mjʊ·leɪt] I. vt accumulare II. vi accumularsi
accumulation [ə·ˌkjuː·mjʊ·'leɪ·ʃən] n 1. (*process*) accumulazione f 2. (*quantity*) cumulo m
accuracy ['æ·kjɚ·ə·si] n accuratezza f
accurate ['æ·kjɚ·ət] adj 1. (*on target*) preciso, -a 2. (*correct*) esatto, -a 3. (*careful*) accurato, -a
accusation [ˌæ·kjuː·'zeɪ·ʃən] n accusa f
accusative [ə·'kjuː·zə·t̬ɪv] LING I. n accusativo m II. adj accusativo, -a
accusatory [ə·'kjuː·zə·tɔː·ri] adj form accusatorio, -a
accuse [ə·'kjuːz] vt accusare; **she is ~d of ...** è accusata di ...
accused [ə·'kjuːzd] n **the ~** l'imputato, -a m, f
accustom [ə·'kʌs·təm] vt abituare
accustomed [ə·'kʌs·təmd] adj 1. (*in habit of*) abituato, -a; **to be ~ to doing sth** essere abituato a fare qc; **to grow ~ to doing sth** abituarsi a fare qc 2. (*usual*) solito, -a
AC/DC [ˌeɪ·siː·'diː·siː] n 1. ELEC abbr of **alternating current/direct current** c.a./c.c. 2. sl (*bisexual*) bisessuale mf
ace [eɪs] I. n 1. (*playing card*) asso m 2. inf (*expert*) asso m ▸ **to have an ~ up one's** sleeve avere un asso nella manica; **to come** within **an ~ of doing sth** essere a un soffio dal fare qc II. adj inf (*expert*) provetto, -a III. vt sl (*perform well*) superare brillantemente

acetate ['æ·sɪ·teɪt] n acetato m
acetic [ə·'siː·t̬ɪk] adj acetico, -a
acetone ['æ·sɪ·ˌtoʊn] n acetone m
acetylene [ə·'se·t̬ə·liːn] n acetilene m
ache [eɪk] I. n dolore m; **~s and pains** acciacchi mpl II. vi fare male; **I am aching to see her again** muoio dalla voglia di rivederla
achieve [ə·'tʃiːv] vt (*goal, objective*) raggiungere; (*task*) portare a termine; (*victory*) conseguire; (*success*) ottenere
achievement n 1. (*feat*) impresa f; (*success*) successo m 2. (*achieving*) realizzazione f
acid ['æ·sɪd] I. n 1. CHEM acido m 2. sl (*LSD*) acido m II. adj 1. CHEM acido, -a 2. (*sarcastic*) caustico, -a
acid house n MUS acid house f inv
acidic [ə·'sɪ·dɪk] adj acido, -a
acidify [ə·'sɪ·dɪ·faɪ] <-ie-> I. vt acidificare II. vi acidificarsi
acidity [ə·'sɪ·də·t̬i] n 1. CHEM acidità f 2. fig causticità f
acid rain n pioggia f acida
acid rock n MUS rock m psichedelico inv
acid test n prova f del fuoco
acid-washed adj (*jeans, denim*) stone-washed inv
acknowledge [ək·'nɑː·lɪdʒ] vt 1. (*admit*) ammettere 2. (*recognize*) riconoscere; (*letter*) accusare ricevuta di; (*favor*) ringraziare per 3. (*reply to: person, smile*) **he acknowledged my smile with a wave** ha risposto al mio sorriso con un cenno di saluto
acknowledg(e)ment n 1. (*admission*) ammissione f 2. (*recognition*) riconoscimento m 3. (*reply*) avviso m di ricevimento 4. pl (*in book*) ringraziamenti mpl
ACLU [ˌeɪ·siː·el·'juː] n abbr of **American Civil Liberties Union** Unione Americana per i Diritti Civili
acne ['æk·ni] n acne f
acorn ['eɪ·kɔːrn] n BOT ghianda f
acorn squash n zucca verde a forma di ghianda
acoustic(al) [ə·'kuː·s·tɪk(əl)] I. adj acustico, -a II. npl acustica f
acoustic guitar n chitarra f acustica
acoustic nerve n ANAT nervo m acustico
acquaint [ə·'kweɪnt] vt 1. (*know*) **to be/become ~ed with sb/sth** conoscere qn/qc 2. (*familiarize*) familiarizzare; **to ~ oneself with sth** familiarizzarsi con qc; **to be ~ed with sth** essere al corrente di qc
acquaintance [ə·'kweɪn·təns] n 1. (*person*) conoscente mf 2. (*relationship*) conoscenza f; **to make sb's ~** conoscere qn 3. (*knowledge*) conoscenza f
acquiesce [ˌæ·kwɪ·'es] vi form **to ~ in sth** acconsentire a qc
acquiescence [ˌæ·kwɪ·'e·sns] n form acquiescenza f
acquiescent [ˌæ·kwɪ·'e·snt] adj form aquiescente
acquire [ə·'kwa·ɪɚ] vt (*by buying*) acquistare;

(*by effort*) acquisire; **to ~ a taste for sth** cominciare ad apprezzare qc

acquired immunity deficiency syndrome *n* sindrome *f* da immunodeficienza acquisita

acquisition [ˌæ·kwɪ·'zɪ·ʃən] *n* (*by buying*) acquisto *m;* (*of knowledge, skill*) acquisizione *f*

acquisitive [ə·'kwɪ·zə·t̬ɪv] *adj* avido, -a

acquit [ə·'kwɪt] <-tt-> *vt* **1.** LAW assolvere; **to ~ sb of a charge** prosciogliere qn da un'accusa **2. to ~ oneself well/badly** cavarsela bene/ male

acquittal [ə·'kwɪ·t̬əl] *n* LAW assoluzione *f*

acre ['eɪ·kɚ] *n* acro *m* (*4840 iarde quadrate; 4047 metri quadrati*); **~s of space** *inf* un sacco di spazio

acreage ['eik·rədʒ] *n* superficie *f* in acri

acrid ['æ·krɪd] *adj* **1.** (*smell, taste*) acre **2.** *fig* aspro, -a

acrimonious [ˌæ·krɪ·'moʊ·ni·əs] *adj* (*remark*) astioso, -a; (*debate*) acrimonioso, -a

acrimony ['æ·krɪ·moʊ·ni] *n form* acrimonia *f*

acrobat ['æ·krə·bæt] *n* acrobata *mf*

acrobatic [ˌæ·krə·'bæ·t̬ɪk] *adj* acrobatico, -a

acronym ['æ·krə·nɪm] *n* acronimo *m*

acrophobia [æ·krə·'foʊ·biə] *n* acrofobia *f*

across [ə·'krɑːs] **I.** *prep* **1.** (*on other side of*) dall'altro lato di; **just ~ the street** proprio dall'altra parte della strada; **~ from sb/sth** di fronte a qn/qc **2.** (*from one side to other*) attraverso; **to walk ~ the bridge** attraversare il ponte a piedi; **the bridge ~ the river** il ponte sul fiume; **to go ~ the ocean to France** attraversare l'oceano per andare in Francia **II.** *adv* **1.** (*in distance*) da un lato all'altro; **to run/swim ~** attraversare di corsa/a nuoto; **to be 10 feet ~** essere largo 10 piedi **2.** (*in contact with*) **to come ~ sth** imbattersi in qc **3.** (*conveying meaning*) **to get a point ~** far capire qc

across-the-board *adj* generale

acrylic *n* acrilico *m*

acrylic paint *n* colore *m* acrilico

act [ækt] **I.** *n* **1.** (*action*) atto *m;* **~ of charity** atto di carità; **an ~ of God** LAW una calamità naturale; **the Acts of the Apostles** REL gli Atti degli Apostoli; **to catch sb in the ~** cogliere qn sul fatto **2.** (*performance*) numero *m;* **a hard ~ to follow** un numero difficile da eguagliare **3.** (*pretence*) scena *f* **4.** THEAT atto *m* **5.** LAW legge *f* ▸ **to get one's ~ together** *inf* organizzarsi; **to get in on the ~** approfittare della situazione **II.** *vi* **1.** (*take action*) agire; **to ~ for sb** agire per conto di qn **2.** (*behave*) comportarsi **3.** (*take effect*) agire **4.** THEAT recitare **5.** (*pretend*) fingere **III.** *vt* THEAT recitare; **to ~ the part of sb** recitare la parte di qn; **to ~ the fool** fare lo stupido
◆ **act on** *vt* agire sulla base di
◆ **act out** *vt* (*scene*) rappresentare
◆ **act up** *vi inf* **1.** (*person*) fare capricci **2.** (*machine*) funzionare male

acting ['æk·tɪŋ] **I.** *adj* facente funzione di **II.** *n* THEAT recitazione *f*

action ['æk·ʃən] *n* **1.** (*activeness*) azione *f;* **to be out of ~** (*person*) essere fuori combattimento; (*machine*) non funzionare; **to put sth out of ~** mettere qc fuori uso; **to spring into ~** entrare in azione; **to take ~** agire; **to take no ~** non fare nulla **2.** MIL azione *f;* **to see ~** combattere; **to go into ~** entrare in azione; **killed in ~** morto in combattimento **3.** (*mechanism*) meccanismo *m* **4.** (*motion*) movimento *m* **5.** LAW (*azione legale*) **civil ~** causa *f* civile; **to bring an ~ against sb** fare causa a qn **6.** *inf* (*exciting events*) vita *f;* (*fun*) movimento *m* ▸ **~s speak louder than** <u>words</u> *prov* valgon più i fatti delle parole *prov*

action-packed *adj* pieno, -a d'azione

activate ['æk·tɪ·veɪt] *vt a.* CHEM attivare

active ['æk·tɪv] *adj* (*lively, not passive*) attivo, -a; **to be ~ in sth** partecipare a qc; **to take an ~ part in sth** partecipare attivamente a qc

actively *adv* **1.** (*in a lively manner*) attivamente **2.** (*intentionally*) seriamente

activist ['æk·tɪ·vɪst] *n* POL attivista *mf*

activity [æk·'tɪ·və·t̬i] <-ies> *n* **1.** (*state*) attività *f* **2.** *pl* (*pursuits*) attività *fpl*

actor ['æk·tɚ] *n* attore *m*

actress ['æk·trɪs] *n* attrice *f*

actual ['æk·tʃʊ·əl] *adj* **1.** (*real*) effettivo, -a; **in ~ fact** in realtà **2.** (*precise*) esatto, -a; **what were her ~ words?** quali sono state le sue precise parole?

actually ['æk·tʃʊ·li] *adv* **1.** (*in fact*) effettivamente **2.** (*by the way*) **~ I saw her yesterday** a proposito, l'ho vista ieri

actuate ['æk·tʃʊ·eɪt] *vt* **1.** (*set going: mechanism*) azionare **2.** *form* (*motivate*) motivare

acumen [ə·'kju:·mən] *n* acume *m;* **business ~** senso *m* degli affari

acupuncture ['æ·kjʊ·pʌŋk·tʃɚ] *n* agopuntura *f*

acute [ə·'kju:t] **I.** *adj* **1.** (*serious*) acuto, -a; (*anxiety*) intenso, -a; (*embarrassment*) grande; (*difficulties*) serio, -a; (*shortage*) grave **2.** (*shrewd*) perspicace **3.** MAT (*angle*) acuto, -a **II.** *n* LING accento *m* acuto

acutely *adv* estremamente; **to be ~ aware of sth** essere pienamente cosciente di qc

ad [æd] *n inf abbr of* **advertisement** pubblicità *f*

A.D. [ˌeɪ·'diː] *abbr of* anno Domini d.C.

adage ['æ·dɪdʒ] *n* adagio *m*

adagio [ə·'dɑː·dʒoʊ] MUS **I.** *adv* adagio **II.** *n* adagio *m*

Adam ['æ·dəm] *n* Adamo *m* ▸ **not to** <u>know</u> **sb from ~** non conoscere affatto qn

adamant ['æ·də·mənt] *adj* categorico, -a

Adam's apple *n* ANAT pomo *m* d' Adamo

adapt [ə·'dæpt] **I.** *vt* adattare; **to ~ oneself** adattarsi **II.** *vi* adattarsi

adaptable *adj* adattabile

adaptation [ˌæ·dæp·'teɪ·ʃən] *n* **1.** THEAT, MUS, CINE, LIT adattamento *m* **2.** (*act of adapting*) adattamento *m*

adapter *n*, **adaptor** [ə·'dæp·tɚ] *n* ELEC adattatore *m;* (*for several plugs*) presa *f* multipla

ADD *n abbr of* **Attention Deficit Disorder** disturbo *m* da deficit di attenzione

add [æd] *vt* **1.** (*put with*) aggiungere **2.** (*say*) aggiungere **3.** MAT sommare
◆ **add up** I. *vi* sommare; **to ~ to ...** ammontare a ...; **it doesn't ~ to much** *fig* non significa molto II. *vt* sommare

addendum [ə·'den·dəm] <-da> *n* aggiunta *f*

adder ['æ·dəʳ] *n* vipera *f*

addict ['æ·dɪkt] *n* **1.** MED **drug ~** tossicodipendente *mf* **2.** *fig* fanatico, -a *m, f;* **to be a movie ~** essere un fanatico del cinema

addicted [ə·'dɪk·tɪd] *adj* dipendente; **~ to drugs** tossicodipendente; **to be ~ to sth** essere dipendente da qc; *fig* essere fanatico di qc

addiction [ə·'dɪk·ʃən] *n* dipendenza *f;* **drug ~** tossicodipendenza *f*

addictive [ə·'dɪk·tɪv] *adj* che dà dipendenza

addition [ə·'dɪ·ʃən] *n* **1.** MAT addizione *f* **2.** (*act of adding*) aggiunta *f;* **in ~** inoltre; **in ~ to ...** oltre a ... **3.** (*added thing*) acquisizione *f;* **an ~ to the family** un nuovo arrivo in famiglia

additional [ə·'dɪ·ʃə·nl] *adj* supplementare

additionally [ə·'dɪ·ʃə·nə·li] *adv* inoltre; **and ~** e più

additive ['æ·də·t̮ɪv] *n* additivo *m*

address¹ ['æ·dres] *n* **1.** *a.* INFOR indirizzo *m* **2.** (*speech*) discorso *m*

address² [ə·'dres] I. *vt* **1.** (*write address on*) indirizzare; **to ~ sth wrong** scrivere l'indirizzo sbagliato su qc **2.** (*speak to*) parlare a **3.** (*use title*) **to ~ sb** (**as sth**) rivolgersi a qn usando il titolo di **4.** (*deal with: issue*) affrontare II. *n* **1.** (*speech*) discorso *m* **2.** (*title*) **form of ~** titolo *m*

addressee [,æ·dre·'si:] *n* destinatario, -a *m, f*

adenoids ['æd·nɔ·ɪdz] *npl* ANAT adenoidi *fpl*

adept [ə·'dept] *adj* esperto, -a; **to be ~ at sth** essere esperto in qc

adequacy ['æ·dɪ·kwə·si] *n* **1.** (*being enough*) sufficienza *f* **2.** (*being good enough*) adeguatezza *f*

adequate ['æ·dɪk·wət] *adj* **1.** (*sufficient*) sufficiente **2.** (*good enough*) adeguato, -a

ADHD [,eɪ·di:·eɪtʃ·'di:] *abbr of* **attention deficit hyperactivity disorder** disturbo *m* da deficit di attenzione e iperattività

adhere [əd·'hɪr] *vi* **1.** *form* (*stick to*) aderire **2.** (*follow*) **to ~ to sth** (*rule*) osservare; (*belief*) aderire a; (*plan*) attenersi a

adherence [əd·'hɪ·rəns] *n* (*to rule*) osservanza *f;* (*to belief*) fedeltà *f*

adherent [əd·'hɪ·ə·rənt] *n form* seguace *mf*

adhesive [əd·'hi:·sɪv] I. *adj* adesivo, -a II. *n* adesivo *m*

ad hoc [,æd·'hɑːk] I. *adj* ad hoc II. *adv* ad hoc

ad infinitum [æd ɪn·,fə·'naɪ·təm] *adv* all'infinito

adipose tissue [,æ·dɪ·poʊs·'tɪ·ʃu:] *n* tessuto *m* adiposo

adjacent [ə·'dʒeɪ·snt] *adj* attiguo, -a; MAT adiacente

adjectival [,æ·dʒɪk·'ti:·vl] *adj* aggettivale

adjective ['æ·dʒɪk·tɪv] *n* LING aggettivo *m*

adjoin [ə·'dʒɔɪn] I. *vt* confinare con II. *vi* confinare

adjoining *adj* attiguo, -a

adjourn [ə·'dʒɜːrn] I. *vt* sospendere II. *vi* **1.** (*pause: meeting*) sospendere **2.** *form* (*go to*) **to ~ to another room** spostarsi in un'altra stanza

adjudicate [ə·'dʒuː·dɪ·keɪt] I. *vt* giudicare II. *vi* fare da arbitro

adjust [ə·'dʒʌst] I. *vt* **1.** *a.* TECH regolare **2.** (*rearrange*) sistemare **3.** (*change*) modificare **4.** (*adapt*) adattare II. *vi* adattarsi; **to ~ to sth** adattarsi a qc

adjustable *adj* regolabile

adjustable-rate mortgage *n* mutuo *m* ipotecario a tasso variabile

adjustable wrench *n* chiave *f* a rullino

adjustment *n* **1.** (*mechanical*) modifica *f* **2.** (*mental*) adattamento *m*

adjutant ['æ·dʒu·tənt] *n* aiutante *mf*

ad lib [,æd·'lɪb] *adv* a braccio

ad-lib [,æd·'lɪb] <-bb-> *vi, vt* improvvisare

adman ['æd·mæn] <-men> *n* ECON pubblicitario, -a *m, f*

admin [əd·'mɪn] *abbr of* **administration** amministrazione *f*

administer [əd·'mɪ·nɪs·təʳ] *vt* **1.** *a.* POL (*manage: funds, estate*) amministrare **2.** (*dispense: punishment*) infliggere; (*medicine*) somministrare; **to ~ aid to sb** assistere qn; **to ~ first aid to sb** prestare i primi soccorsi a qn; **to ~ a severe blow to sb** infliggere un severo colpo a qn; **to ~ an oath** presenziare a un giuramento

administration [əd·,mɪ·nɪs·'treɪ·ʃən] *n* **1.** (*organization*) amministrazione *f;* (*management*) gestione *f;* **the ~** l'amministrazione **2.** POL (*time in power*) mandato *m* **3.** POL (*government*) governo *m* **4.** (*dispensing: of medicine*) somministrazione *f*

administrative [əd·'mɪ·nɪs·trə·tɪv] *adj* amministrativo, -a

administrator [əd·'mɪ·nɪs·treɪ·təʳ] *n* **1.** (*of organization, institution*) amministratore, -trice *m, f* **2.** LAW curatore, -trice *m, f*

admirable ['æd·mə·rə·bl] *adj* ammirevole

admiral ['æd·mə·rəl] *n* MIL ammiraglio *m*

admiration [,æd·mə·'reɪ·ʃən] *n* ammirazione *f;* **in ~** con ammirazione

admire [əd·'ma·ɪəʳ] *vt* ammirare; **to ~ sb for sth** ammirare qn per qc; **to ~ sb from afar** avere una passione nascosta per qn

admirer [əd·'ma·ɪə·əʳ] *n* ammiratore, -trice *m, f*

admissible [əd·'mɪ·sə·bl] *adj* ammissibile

admission [əd·'mɪ·ʃən] *n* **1.** (*entry: to place, building*) ingresso *m;* (*to college, organization*) ammissione *f* **2.** (*entrance fee*) (prezzo *m* di)ingresso *m* **3.** (*acknowledgement*) ammissione *f;* **by** [*o* **on**] **his own ~, ...** per sua stessa ammissione, ... **4.** *pl* UNIV ufficio *m* ammissioni

admit [əd·'mɪt] <-tt-> I. *vt* 1. (*acknowledge: error*) riconoscere; (*crime*) confessare; **to ~ that ...** ammettere che ... 2. (*allow entrance to*) lasciar entrare 3. (*permit*) ammettere II. *vi* **to ~ to sth** riconoscere qc

admittance [əd·'mɪ·tns] *n* ingresso *m;* **to refuse sb ~** rifiutare l'ingresso a qn; **no ~** vietato l'ingresso

admittedly [əd·'mɪ·t̬ɪd·li] *adv* **~, ...** va riconosciuto che ...

admonish [əd·'mɑː·nɪʃ] *vt* ammonire

admonishment *n*, **admonition** [ˌæd·mə·'nɪ·ʃən] *n* ammonizione *f*

ado [ə·'duː] *n* 1. (*commotion*) trambusto *m* 2. (*delay*) indugio *m;* **without further ~** senza indugiare oltre ▸ **much ~ about nothing** molto rumore per nulla

adobe [ə·'dou·bi] *n* adobe *m inv*

adolescence [ˌæ·də·'le·sns] *n* adolescenza *f*

adolescent [ˌæ·də·'le·snt] I. *adj* 1. (*relating to adolescence*) adolescente 2. (*immature*) puerile II. *n* adolescente *mf*

adopt [ə·'dɑːpt] *vt* 1. (*child, strategy*) adottare 2. (*candidate*) scegliere

adoption [ə·'dɑːp·ʃən] *n* 1. (*of child, strategy*) adozione *f* 2. (*of candidate*) scelta *f*

adorable [ə·'dɔː·rə·bl] *adj* adorabile; **just ~** semplicemente incantevole

adoration [ˌæ·də·'reɪ·ʃən] *n* adorazione *f;* **the ~ of the Virgin Mary** REL il culto della Vergine Maria

adore [ə·'dɔːr] *vt* adorare

adoring [ə·'dɔː·rɪŋ] *adj* adorante

adorn [ə·'dɔːrn] *vt form* adornare

adornment *n form* ornamento *m*

adrenaline [ə·'dre·nə·lɪn] *n* adrenalina *f*

Adriatic [ˌeɪ·dri·'æ·tɪk] *n* **the ~ (Sea)** il (mare) Adriatico

adrift [ə·'drɪft] *adv* alla deriva; **to cut sth ~** lasciar andare alla deriva; **to go ~** *fig* fallire

adroit [ə·'drɔɪt] *adj* abile; **to be ~ at sth** essere abile in qc; **to be ~ at doing sth** essere abile nel fare qc

adulation [ˌæ·dʒə·'leɪ·ʃən] *n* adulazione *f*

adult [ə·'dʌlt] I. *n* adulto, -a *m, f* II. *adj* 1. (*fully grown*) adulto, -a 2. (*mature*) maturo, -a; **let's try to be ~ about this problem** cerchiamo di essere ragionevoli riguardo a questo problema 3. (*sexually explicit*) per adulti

adult education *n* educazione *f* permanente

adulterate [ə·'dʌl·tə·reɪt] *vt* adulterare

adulterer [ə·'dʌl·tə·ɚ] *n* adultero *m*

adulteress [ə·'dʌl·trɪs] <-es> *n* adultera *f*

adulterous [ə·'dʌl·tə·əs] *adj* (*person*) adultero, a; (*relationship*) adulterino, -a

adultery [ə·'dʌl·tə·i] <-ies> *n* adulterio *m;* **to commit ~** commettere adulterio

adulthood ['æ·dʌlt·hʊd] *n* età *f* adulta

advance [əd·'væns] I. *vi* avanzare; **to ~ on sb/sth** avanzare verso qn/qc II. *vt* 1. (*cause to move forward*) far avanzare; (*interest*) favorire; (*cause*) promuovere 2. (*pay in advance*)

anticipare III. *n* 1. (*forward movement*) avanzata *f;* progresso *m;* **in ~** in anticipo 2. FIN anticipo *m* 3. *pl* (*sexual flirtation*) avances *fpl;* **unwelcome ~s** molestie *fpl;* **to reject sb's ~s** rifiutare le avances di qn IV. *adj* anticipato, -a; **without ~ warning** senza preavviso

advanced [əd·'vænst] *adj* (*country, course, stage*) avanzato, -a; (*student*) di livello avanzato

advancement [əd·'væns·mənt] *n* 1. (*improvement*) avanzamento *m* 2. (*promotion*) promozione *f;* **an opportunity for ~** un'opportunità per migliorare

advance notice *n* preavviso *m*

advance payment *n* anticipo *m*

advantage [əd·'væn·tɪdʒ] *n a.* SPORTS vantaggio *m; ~* **Jackson** vantaggio a Jackson; **to have an ~ over sb** essere in vantaggio su qn; **to take ~ of sb/sth** approfittare di qn/qc

advantageous [ˌæd·væn·'teɪ·dʒəs] *adj* vantaggioso, -a

advent ['æd·vənt] *n* 1. (*coming*) avvento *m* 2. REL **Advent** Avvento *m*

adventure [əd·'ven·tʃɚ] *n* avventura *f;* **to look for ~** essere in cerca d'avventure

adventurer *n* 1. (*seeker of excitement*) amante *mf* dell'avventura 2. (*opportunist*) avventuriero, -a *m, f*

adventurous [əd·'ven·tʃə·əs] *adj* (*person*) avventuroso, -a; (*decision*) rischioso, -a

adverb ['æd·vɜːrb] *n* LING avverbio *m*

adverbial [æd·'vɜːr·bi·əl] *adj* avverbiale

adversary ['æd·və·se·ri] <-ies> *n* avversario, -a *m, f*

adverse ['æd·vɜːrs] *adj* (*decision, criticism, effect*) sfavorevole; (*conditions*) avverso, -a; (*reaction*) ostile

adversity [əd·'vɜːr·sə·t̬i] <-ies> *n* avversità *f;* **in (the face of) ~** nelle avversità

advertent [æd·'vɜːr·tənt] *adj* attento, -a

advertise [əd·'və·taɪz] I. *vt* rendere noto II. *vi* fare pubblicità

advertisement [ˌæd·və·'taɪz·mənt] *n* COM pubblicità *f;* **to be a good/bad ~ for sth** *fig* essere una buona/cattiva pubblicità per qc; **job ~** annuncio *m* di lavoro

advertiser ['æd·və·taɪ·zə] *n* inserzionista *mf*

advertising ['æd·və·ˌtaɪ·zɪŋ] *n* pubblicità *f*

advertising agency <-ies> *n* agenzia *f* pubblicitaria

advertising campaign *n* campagna *f* pubblicitaria

advice [əd·'vaɪs] *n* 1. (*suggestion, opinion*) consiglio *m;* **a piece of ~** un consiglio; **to ask for ~** chiedere consiglio; **to ask sb for ~ on sth** chiedere (un) consiglio a qn su qc; **to give some good ~** dare buoni consigli; **on sb's ~** su consiglio di qn 2. COM avviso *m*

advisable [əd·'vaɪ·zə·bl] *adj* consigliabile; **it is (not) ~** (non) è consigliabile

advise [əd·'vaɪz] I. *vt* consigliare; (*specialist*) offrire consulenze a; **to ~ sb against sth** sconsigliare qc a qn; **to ~ sb on sth** consigliare qn

su qc; **to ~ sb of sth** informare qn di qc **II.** *vi*
to ~ against sth sconsigliare qc; **to ~ on sth**
consigliare su qc
adviser *n*, **advisor** [əd·'vaɪ·zɚ] *n* consulente
mf
advisory [əd·'vaɪ·zɚ·ri] *adj* **1.** consultivo, -a; **in**
an ~ capacity in qualità di consulente; **~ com-**
mittee comitato consultivo **2.** (*warning*) **hur-**
ricane ~ allarme *m* uragani
advocacy *n* perorazione *f*
advocate¹ ['æd·və·keɪt] *vt* sostenere; **to ~**
doing sth raccomandare di fare qc
advocate² ['æd·və·kət] *n* **1.** (*supporter*) sostenitore, -trice *m*, *f* **2.** (*lawyer*) avvocato (difensore) *m*
AEC *n abbr of* **Atomic Energy Commission**
commissione per l'energia atomica
Aegean [i:·'dʒi:·ən] *n* **the ~** (**Sea**) il mar Egeo,
l'Egeo
aegis ['i:·dʒɪs] *n* **under the ~ of ...** sotto
l'egida di ...
eon ['i:·ɑːn] *n* **1.** (*period of time*) eone *m* **2.** *fig*
eternità *f*
aerate ['e·reɪt] *vt* **1.** (*expose to air*) areare
2. (*drink*) gassare
aerial ['e·ri·əl] **I.** *adj* aereo, -a; **~ photography**
fotografia *f* aerea **II.** *n* antenna *f*
aerobatic [ˌe·rə·'bæ·t̬ɪk] *adj* di acrobazie aeree
aerobatics *npl* acrobazie *f* aeree *pl*
aerobics [e·'roʊ·bɪks] *n + sing/pl vb*
aerobica *f*; **to do ~** fare aerobica
aerodynamic [ˌe·roʊ·daɪ·'næ·mɪk] *adj* aerodinamico, -a
aerodynamics *n + sing vb* aerodinamica *f*
aeronautic ['e·rə·nɑː·t̬ik] *adj* aeronautico, -a
aeronautics *n + sing vb* aeronautica *f*
aerosol ['e·rə·sɑːl] *n* aerosol *m inv*
aerospace industry ['e·roʊ·speɪs 'ɪn·dəs·tri]
n industria *f* aerospaziale
aesthetic [es·'θe·t̬ɪk] *adj* estetico, -a
aesthetics *n + sing vb* estetica *f*
afar [ə·'fɑːr] *adv* lontano; **from ~** da lontano
affable ['æ·fə·bl] *adj* affabile
affair [ə·'fer] *n* **1.** (*matter*) affare *m*; **~s of state**
affari di stato; **financial ~s** questioni finanzi-
arie; **to meddle in sb's ~s** intromettersi negli
affari di qn; **it's his own ~** sono affari suoi
2. (*controversial situation*) questione *f*; (*scandal*) caso *m* **3.** (*sexual relationship*) relazione
(*f* amorosa); **to have an ~** (**with sb**) avere
una relazione (con qn) **4.** (*event, occasion*)
vicenda *f*
affect [ə·'fekt] *vt* **1.** (*have effect on*) colpire; **to**
be ~ed by sth (*be moved*) essere toccato da
qc **2.** (*influence: decision*) influire su **3.** (*simulate*) fingere
affectation [ˌæ·fek·'teɪ·ʃən] *n* affettazione *f*
affected [ə·'fek·t̬ɪd] *adj* (*behavior, accento*)
affettato, -a; (*smile, emotion*) falso, -a; (*style*)
artificioso, -a
affection [ə·'fek·ʃən] *n* affetto *m*; **to have a**
deep ~ for sb provare un grande affetto per
qn

affectionate [ə·'fek·ʃə·nət] *adj* affettuoso, -a
affidavit [ˌæ·fɪ·'deɪ·vɪt] *n* affidavit *m inv*
affiliate¹ [ə·'fɪ·li·eɪt] *vt* affiliare; **to be ~d with**
sth essere affiliato a qc
affiliate² [ə·'fɪ·li·ət] *n a.* ECON filiale *f*
affiliation [ə·ˌfɪ·li·'eɪ·ʃən] *n* affiliazione *f*
affinity [ə·'fɪ·nə·t̬i] <-ies> *n* affinità *f*
affirm [ə·'fɜːrm] *vt* affermare
affirmation [ˌæ·fɚ·'meɪ·ʃən] *n* affermazione *f*
affirmative [ə·'fɜːr·mə·t̬ɪv] **I.** *adj* affermativo,
-a **II.** *n* **to answer** [*o* **reply**] **in the ~** rispondere affermativamente; **~ action** discrimina-
zione *f* positiva
affix¹ [ə·'fɪks] *vt* (*signature*) apporre; (*stamp*)
attaccare
affix² ['æ·fɪks] *n* <-es> LING affisso *m*
afflict [ə·'flɪkt] *vt* affliggere; **to be ~ed with**
sth essere afflitto da qc
affliction [ə·'flɪk·ʃən] *n* afflizione *f*
affluence ['æ·flu·əns] *n* ricchezza *f*
affluent ['æ·flu·ənt] *adj* ricco, -a; **an ~ life-**
style una vita agiata; **the ~ society** la società
del benessere
afford [ə·'fɔːrd] *vt* **1.** (*have money, time for*)
permettersi; **to be able to ~ sth** potersi permettere qc; **he can hardly ~ it** se lo può permettere a malapena **2.** (*provide*) fornire; **to ~**
protection offrire protezione
affordable [ə·'fɔːr·də·bl] *adj* (*price, purchase*)
abbordabile
afforest [ə·'fɔː·rəst] *vt* imboschire
afforestation [ə·ˌfɔː·rəs·'teɪ·ʃən] *n* imboschi-
mento *m*
affront [ə·'frʌnt] **I.** *n* affronto *m;* **an ~ to sb's**
dignity un affronto [*o* insulto] alla dignità di qn
II. *vt* fare un affronto a; **to be ~ed at** [*o* **by**]
sth offendersi per qc
Afghan ['æf·gæn] **I.** *n* **1.** (*person*) afgano,
-a *m*, *f* **2.** LING afgano *m* **3.** (*dog*) levriero *m*
afgano **4.** (*blanket*) coperta (*o* scialle) *lavorata*
ai ferri o all'uncinetto **II.** *adj* afgano, -a
Afghanistan [æf·'gæ·nɪs·tæn] *n* Afganistan *m*
afield [ə·'fiːld] *adv* **far/farther ~** molto/più
lontano
afloat [ə·'floʊt] *adj* a galla; **to keep** [*o* **stay**] **~**
a. fig rimanere a galla
afoot [ə·'fʊt] *adj* **there's sth ~** si sta tramando qc
aforementioned [ə·ˌfɔːr·'men·ʃnd], **afore-**
said [ə·ˌfɔːr·sed] *form* **I.** *adj* (*in text*) summenzionato,-a; (*in conversation*) suddetto, -a
II. *n inv* **the ~** il summenzionato/la summen-
zionata; (*person mentioned in conversation*)
il suddetto/la suddetta
afraid [ə·'freɪd] *adj* **1.** (*scared*) **to be ~** aver
paura; **to be ~ of doing** [*o* **to do**] **sth** aver
paura di fare qc; **to be ~ of sb/sth** aver paura
di qn/qc **2.** (*sorry*) **I'm ~ so** temo proprio di sì;
I'm ~ not purtroppo no; **I'm ~ I haven't got**
the time mi dispiace, ma non ho tempo
afresh [ə·'freʃ] *adv* da capo; **to start ~** ricominciare da capo
Africa ['æf·rɪ·kə] *n* Africa *f*

African ['æf·rɪ·kən] I. *n* africano, -a *m, f* II. *adj* africano, -a

African American I. *adj* afroamericano, -a II. *n* afroamericano, -a *m, f*

Afrikaans [ˌæf·rɪ·'kɑːns] *n* LING afrikaans *m inv*

Afro-American *adj, n s.* **African-American**

Afro-Caribbean [ˌæf·rou·ke·rɪ·'biː·ən] I. *adj* afrocaraibico -a II. *n* afrocaraibico, -a *m, f*

aft [æft] *n* NAUT poppa *f*

after ['æf·tə·] I. *prep* 1. (*at later time*) dopo; ~ **two days** dopo due giorni; (**shortly**) ~ **breakfast** (poco) dopo colazione 2. (*behind*) dietro; **to run ~ sb** correre dietro a qn 3. (*following*) dopo; **D comes ~ C** la D viene dopo la C; **to have argument ~ argument** avere continue discussioni 4. (*about*) **to ask ~ sb** chiedere (notizie) di qn 5. (*despite*) ~ **all** dopotutto 6. (*in the style of*) **a drawing ~ Picasso** un disegno alla maniera di Picasso 7. (*in honor of*) **to name sth/sb ~ sb** chiamare qc/qn come qn II. *adv* dopo; **soon ~** poco dopo; **the day ~** il giorno dopo III. *conj* dopo che +*subj;* **he spoke ~ she went out** parlò dopo che lei fu uscita; **I'll call him** (**right**) ~ **I've taken a shower** lo chiamerò subito dopo aver fatto la doccia

afterbirth *n* MED placenta *f*, e *membrane fetali espulse dopo il parto*

aftercare ['æf·tə·ker] *n* MED assistenza *f* postoperatoria

after-dinner *adj* dopocena

aftereffects ['æf·tə·ɪ·fektz] *npl* (*of drugs, treatment*) effetti *m pl* secondari; (*of accident*) postumi *mpl*

afterglow *n* 1. (*after sunset*) luce del sole dopo il tramonto 2. PHYS luminescenza *f* residua

after-hours *adj* al termine della giornata lavorativa

afterlife ['æf·tə·laɪf] *n* vita *f* ultraterrena; **the ~** l'aldilà *m*

after-market *n* mercato *m* dei ricambi

aftermath ['æf·tə·mæθ] *n* conseguenze *fpl*

afternoon [ˌæf·tə·'nuːn] I. *n* pomeriggio *m;* **this ~** oggi pomeriggio; **in the ~** nel [*o* di] pomeriggio; **all ~** tutto il pomeriggio; **tomorrow/yesterday ~** domani/ieri pomeriggio; **4 o'clock in the ~** le 4 del pomeriggio; **good ~!** buongiorno! II. *adj* pomeridiano, -a; ~ **nap** sonnellino (*m* pomeridiano)

after-sales service *n* servizio *m* assistenza clienti

after-shave ['æf·tə·ʃeɪv] *n* dopobarba *m inv*

aftershock *n* GEO scossa *f* di assestamento

aftertaste ['æf·tə·teɪst] *n a. fig* retrogusto *m*

after-tax *adj* al netto

afterthought ['æf·tə·θɑːt] *n* ripensamento *m*

afterward *adv*, **afterwards** ['æf·tə·wə·dz] *adv* (*later*) più tardi; (*after something*) dopo; **shortly ~** poco dopo

again [ə·'gen] *adv* 1. (*as a repetition*) ancora; (*one more time*) di nuovo; **never ~** mai più; **once ~** ancora una volta; **then ~** d'altra parte;

yet ~ di nuovo; ~ **and** ~ tante volte 2. (*anew*) di nuovo

against [ə·'genst] I. *prep* 1. (*in opposition to*) contro; **to be ~ sth/sb** essere contro qc/qn; ~ **my will** contro la mia volontà 2. (*as protection from*) contro; **to protect oneself ~ rain** proteggersi dalla pioggia 3. (*in contact with*) contro; **to lean ~ a tree** appoggiarsi a un albero; **to run ~ a wall** finire contro un muro 4. (*in front of*) ~ **the light** in controluce 5. (*in competition with*) contro; ~ **time/the clock** contro il tempo 6. (*in comparison with*) **the dollar rose/fell ~ the euro** il dollaro è salito/sceso rispetto all'euro II. *adv a.* POL contro; **there were 10 votes ~** c'erano 10 voti contro

agate ['æ·gət] *n* agata *f*

age [eɪdʒ] I. *n* 1. (*of person, object*) età *f;* **old ~** vecchiaia *f;* ~ **of consent** età del consenso; **what is your ~?** quanti anni hai?; **when I was her ~** quando avevo la sua età; **to be seven years of ~** avere sette anni; **to be under ~** essere minorenne; **to come of ~** diventare maggiorenne; **to improve with ~** migliorare con [*o* l'età] gli anni 2. (*era*) era *f;* **in this day and ~** ai giorni nostri 3. (*long time*) secoli *mpl;* **I haven't seen her in ~s** è una vita che non la vedo II. *vi* 1. (*become older*) invecchiare 2. GASTR (*wine*) far invecchiare; (*cheese*) far stagionare III. *vt* 1. (*make older*) invecchiare 2. GASTR (*wine*) invecchiare; (*cheese*) stagionare

age bracket *n s.* **age group**

aged[1] [eɪdʒd] *adj* 1. (*wine*) invecchiato, -a; (*cheese*) stagionato, -a 2. (*with age of*) dell'età di; **this game is for children ~ 8 to 12** questo gioco è adatto a bambini di età compresa tra gli 8 e i 12 anni

aged[2] ['eɪ·dʒɪd] I. *adj* (*old*) anziano, -a II. *n* **the ~** gli anziani

age group *n* fascia *f* d'età

ageless ['eɪdʒ·lɪs] *adj* eterno, -a

age limit *n* limite *m* di età

agency ['eɪ·dʒən·si] <-ies> *n* 1. COM agenzia *f;* **travel ~** agenzia di viaggi 2. ADMIN organismo *m;* **government ~** ente governativo 3. *form* **through the ~ of** per opera di

agenda [ə·'dʒen·də] *n* (*for meeting*) ordine *m* del giorno; **to be at the top of the ~** *fig* avere la massima priorità

agent ['eɪ·dʒənt] *n* agente *mf;* **secret ~** agente segreto

Age of Aquarius *n* età *f* dell'Acquario

Agent Orange *n* agente *m* arancio, *defogliante utilizzato durante la guerra del Vietnam*

age-old *adj* antichissimo, -a

agglomerate [ə·'glɑː·mə·eɪt] *n*, **agglomeration** [ə·ˌglɑː·mə·'reɪ·ʃən] *n* agglomerato *m*

aggravate ['æ·grə·veɪt] *vt* 1. (*make worse*) aggravare 2. *inf* (*annoy*) irritare

aggravating *adj* (*annoying*) irritante

aggravation [ˌæ·grə·'veɪ·ʃən] *n inf* seccatura *f*

aggregate[1] ['æ·grɪ·gɪt] I. *n* 1. FIN, ECON aggregato *m;* (*sum total*) somma *f* totale; (*total* *value*) valore *m* totale **2.** MAT somma *f* **II.** *adj* FIN, ECON totale

aggregate² ['æ·ɡrɪ·ɡeɪt] *vt* FIN, ECON sommare

aggression [ə·'ɡre·ʃən] *n* **1.** (*feelings*) aggressività *f* **2.** (*violence*) aggressione *f;* **an act of ~** un'aggressione

aggressive [ə·'ɡre·sɪv] *adj* aggressivo, -a

aggressor [ə·'ɡre·sə·] *n* aggressore, aggreditrice *m, f*

aggrieved [ə·'ɡriːvd] *adj* risentito, -a

aghast [ə·'ɡæst] *adj* inorridito, -a; **to be ~ at sth** essere inorridito di fronte a qc

agile ['æ·dʒl] *adj* agile

agility [ə·'dʒɪ·lə·t̬i] *n* agilità *f*

aging I. *adj* che invecchia **II.** *n* invecchiamento *m;* **the process of ~** il processo di invecchiamento

agitate ['æ·dʒɪ·teɪt] **I.** *vt* **1.** (*make nervous*) mettere in agitazione; **to become ~d** agitarsi **2.** TECH (*shake*) agitare **II.** *vi* **to ~ for/against sth** mobilitarsi per/contro qc

agitation [ˌæ·dʒɪ·'teɪ·ʃən] *n a.* POL agitazione *f*

agitator ['æ·dʒɪ·teɪ·t̬ə·] *n* agitatore, -trice *m, f*

agnostic [æɡ·'nɑːs·tɪk] **I.** *n* agnostico, -a *m, f* **II.** *adj* agnostico, -a

ago [ə·'ɡoʊ] *adv* **a minute/a year ~** un minuto/un anno fa; **a long time ~, long ~** molto tempo fa; **how long ~ was that?** da quanto tempo è successo?

agog [ə·'ɡɑːɡ] *adj* **to watch/listen ~** guardava/ascoltava con interesse

agonize ['æ·ɡə·naɪz] *vi* angustiarsi; **to ~ about whether to do sth** angustiarsi rispetto al fare o non fare qc; **an ~d cry** un grido d'angoscia

agonizing ['æ·ɡə·naɪ·zɪŋ] *adj* **1.** (*pain*) atroce; **to die an ~ death** fare una morte atroce **2.** (*delay, decision*) angoscioso, -a

agony ['æ·ɡə·ni] <-ies> *n* agonia *f;* **to be in ~** avere dolori atroci; **to prolong the ~** (of sth) prolungare l'agonia (di qc)

agony column *n* PUBL *rubrica di annunci per la ricerca di persone scomparse*

agoraphobia [ə·ˌɡɔː·rə·'fɔː·biə] *n* agorafobia *f*

agrarian [ə·'ɡre·ri·ən] *adj* agrario, -a

agree [ə·'ɡriː] **I.** *vi* **1.** (*hold same opinion*) essere d'accordo; **to ~ on sth** (*be in agreement*) essere d'accordo su qc; (*reach agreement*) accordarsi su qc; **to ~ to do sth** (*reach agreement*) accordarsi per fare qc; (*consent*) accettare di fare qc; **to ~ to a suggestion** accettare un suggerimento; **we don't ~ on many things** non ci troviamo d'accordo su molte cose; **they can't ~** non riescono a mettersi d'accordo; **to ~ to disagree** rimanere ognuno della propria opinione **2.** (*be good for*) **to ~ with sb** andare bene per qn **3.** (*match up*) concordare **4.** LING concordare **II.** *vt* (*concur*) essere d'accordo; **it is ~d that ...** è stato deciso che ...; **at the ~d time** all'ora fissata

agreeable *adj* **1.** (*pleasant*) gradevole; **he's quite an ~ guy** è una persona molto piacevole **2.** (*consenting*) **to be ~** (**to sth**) essere d'accordo (con qc) **3.** (*acceptable*) accettabile; **is

that ~ to you?** sei d'accordo?

agreement *n* **1.** (*contract, arrangement*) accordo *m;* **to break an ~** rompere un accordo **2.** (*shared opinion*) accordo *m;* **to be in ~ with sb/sth** essere d'accordo con qn/qc; **to reach an ~** raggiungere un accordo **3.** LING concordanza *f*

agribusiness ['æɡ·rɪ·ˌbɪz·nɪs] *n* agribusiness *m inv*

agricultural [ˌæɡ·rɪ·'kʌl·tʃə·rəl] *adj* agricolo, -a; **~ science** scienza agraria *f*

agriculture ['æɡ·rɪ·kʌl·tʃə·] *n* agricoltura *f*

agritourism [æɡ·roʊ·'tʊ·rɪ·zəm] *n* agriturismo *m*

aground [ə·'ɡraʊnd] *adv* NAUT **to run ~** incagliarsi; *fig* arenarsi

ah [ɑː] *interj* ah

aha [ɑː·'hɑː] *interj* ah ah

ahead [ə·'hed] *adv* **1.** (*in front*) davanti; **the road ~ was blocked** più avanti la strada era bloccata **2.** (*advanced position, forwards*) avanti; **to go ~** andare avanti; **to move ~ quickly** avanzare rapidamente; **to press ~ with the plan** andare avanti con il progetto **3.** (*in the future*) **to look ~** guardare al futuro; **to plan ~** pianificare per tempo

ahead of *prep* **1.** (*in front of*) davanti a; **to walk ~ sb** camminare davanti a qn; (**way**) **~ sb/sth** (molto) più avanti di qn/qc **2.** (*before*) prima di; **to decide/arrive ~ time** decidere/arrivare in anticipo **3.** (*more advanced than*) **to be a minute ~ sb** avere un minuto di vantaggio su qn; **to be ~ one's time** precorrere i tempi **4.** (*informed about*) **to keep ~ sth** tenersi al passo con qc

ahem [ə·'həm] *interj* ehm

ahoy [ə·'hɔɪ] *interj* **land/ship ~!** terra/nave in vista!; **~ there!** ehi della nave!

AI [ˌeɪ·'aɪ] *n* **1.** INFOR *abbr of* **artificial intelligence** IA *f* **2.** MED, BIO *abbr of* **artificial insemination** inseminazione *f* artificiale

aid [eɪd] **I.** *n* **1.** (*assistance, support*) aiuto *m;* **to come/go to the ~ of sb** venire/andare in aiuto di qn; **with the ~ of sb/sth** con l'aiuto di qn/qc **2.** POL, ECON aiuto *m;* **emergency ~** primi aiuti; **financial ~** sovvenzione *f* **3.** (*device*) aiuto *m;* **hearing ~** apparecchio *m* acustico; **visual ~** sussidio *m* audiovisivo **II.** *vt* aiutare; **to ~ and abet sb** LAW essere complice di qn

aid convoy *n* convoglio *m* umanitario

aide [eɪd] *n* assistente *mf*

AIDS [eɪdz] *n abbr of* **Acquired Immune Deficiency Syndrome** AIDS *m*

ail [eɪl] *form* **I.** *vi* essere malato, -a **II.** *vt* affliggere; **what ~s you?** *a. iron* cosa ti succede?

ailing ['eɪ·lɪŋ] *adj* **1.** (*person*) malato, -a **2.** (*company, economy*) in crisi

ailment ['eɪl·mənt] *n* disturbo *m*

aim [eɪm] **I.** *vi* **1.** (*point: weapon*) mirare; **to ~ at sb/sth** mirare a qn/qc **2.** (*plan to achieve*) **to ~ at** [*o* **for**] **sth** puntare a qc; **to ~ to do sth** mirare a fare qc **II.** *vt* **1.** (*point a weapon*) pun-

tare; **to ~ sth at sb/sth** puntare qc su [*o* contro] qn/qc **2.**(*direct at*) **to ~ sth at sb** rivolgere qc a qn **3.**(*intend to*) **to be ~ed at doing sth** essere inteso a fare qc **III.** *n* **1.**(*ability to shoot*) mira *f;* **to take ~** mirare **2.**(*goal*) scopo *m;* **his ~ was to make fun of us** il suo intento era quello di burlarsi di noi; **sb's ~ in life** lo scopo di qn nella vita; **with the ~ of doing sth** col proposito di fare qc
aimless ['eɪm·lɪs] *adj* senza scopo
ain't [eɪnt] *inf* **1.**(*to be*) *s.* **am not, are not, is not 2.**(*to have*) *s.* **have not, has not**
air [er] **I.** *n* **1.**(*earth's atmosphere*) aria *f* **2.**(*space overhead, sky*) aria *f;* **to fire into the ~** sparare in aria; **to be up in the ~** *fig* essere ancora in alto mare **3.**AVIAT **by ~ in** aereo; **to travel by ~** viaggiare in aereo **4.**TV, RADIO, CINE **to be on the ~** essere in onda; **to be taken off the ~** non essere più mandato in onda **5.**(*aura, quality*) aria *f;* **to have an ~ of confidence/danger** avere un aspetto sicuro/pericoloso **6.**MUS aria *f* ▶**out of thin ~** dal nulla; **to disappear into thin ~** svanire nel nulla **II.** *adj* aereo, -a **III.** *vt* **1.**TV, RADIO trasmettere; **the program will be ~ed on Saturday** il programma andrà in onda sabato **2.**(*expose to air*) arieggiare **3.**(*publicize*) **to ~ one's grievances** esternare il proprio malcontento **IV.** *vi* **1.**TV, RADIO andare in onda **2.**(*be exposed to air*) prendere aria
air bag *n* airbag *m inv*
air ball *n* (*in basketball*) tiro *m* sbagliato
air base *n* base *f* aerea
airborne ['er·bɔːrn] *adj* **1.**(*transported by aircraft*) aerotrasportato, -a **2.**(*in the air*) **to be ~** essere in volo
air brake *n* freno *m* pneumatico
airbrush I. *n* aerografo *m* **II.** *vt* dipingere con l'aerografo
air bubble *n* bolla *f* d'aria
airbus *n* AVIAT airbus *m inv*
air-conditioned *adj* climatizzato, -a
air conditioner *n* climatizzatore *m*
air conditioning *n* climatizzazione *f*
air-cooled *adj* raffreddato, -a ad aria
air corridor *n* corridoio *m* aereo
aircraft ['er·kræft] *n* (*airplane*) aereo *m;* (*in general*) velivolo *m*
aircraft carrier *n* portaerei *f inv*
aircraft industry *n* industria *f* aerea
aircrew *n* + *sing/pl vb* equipaggio (*m* di volo)
air cushion *n* cuscinetto *m* d'aria
airdrome ['er·droʊm] *n* aerodromo *m*
air-dry *vt* essiccare all'aria
airfare *n* (costo *m* del) biglietto *m* aereo
airfield *n* campo *m* d'aviazione
air filter *n* filtro *m* dell'aria
air force *n* aeronautica *f* militare
airframe *n* cellula; (*of rocket*) struttura *f*
airfreight *n* merci *f pl* trasportate per via aerea
air gun *n* pistola *f* ad aria compressa
airhead *n inf* testa *f* vuota
air hole *n* fornello *m* di ventilazione

air lane *n* corridoio *m* aereo
airless ['er·ləs] *n* (*room*) mal ventilato, -a; (*day*) senza vento
airlift I. *n* ponte *m* aereo **II.** *vt* aerotrasportare
airline *n* compagnia *f* aerea
airliner *n* aereo *m* di linea
airmail I. *n* posta *f* aerea **II.** *vt* spedire per posta aerea
airman <-men> *n* **1.**(*pilot*) aviatore *m;* (*crew member*) membro *m* dell'equipaggio **2.**MIL aviere *m*
air mass *n* METEO massa *f* d'aria
air mattress *n* materassino *m* gonfiabile
air piracy *n* pirateria *f* aerea
airplane *n* aeroplano *m*
air pocket *n* vuoto *m* d'aria
air pollutant *n* agente *m* inquinante (dell'aria)
air pollution *n* inquinamento *m* atmosferico
airport *n* aeroporto *m*
airport terminal *n* terminal (*m* dell'aeroporto) *inv*
air quality *n* qualità *f* dell'aria
air pump *n* pompa *f* per l'aria
air raid *n* incursione *f* aerea
air rifle *n* fucile *m* ad aria compressa
airship *n* dirigibile *m*
air show *n* manifestazione *f* aerea
airsick *adj* **to get ~** soffrire di mal d'aereo
airspace *n* spazio *m* aereo
airstrip *n* pista *f* d'atterraggio
plane ticket *n* biglietto *m* aereo
air taxi *n* aerotaxi *m inv*
airtight *adj* ermetico, -a
airtime *n* TV spazio *m* televisivo
air traffic *n* traffico *m* aereo
air-traffic controller *n* controllore *m* di volo
airway ['er·weɪ] *n* **1.**ANAT via *f* respiratoria **2.**(*route of aircraft*) rotta *f* aerea
airworthy ['er·ˌwɜːr·ði] *adj* in condizione di poter volare
airy ['e·ri] *adj* **1.**ARCHIT arioso, -a **2.**(*light*) leggero, -a; **with an ~ step** con passo leggero **3.**(*lacking substance*) etereo, -a
aisle [aɪl] *n* corridoio *m;* (*in church*) navata *f* laterale ▶**to have sb rolling in the ~s** far ridere qn a crepapelle; **to take sb down the ~** portare all'altare qn
ajar [ə·'dʒɑːr] *adj* socchiuso, -a
AK [ə·'læs·kə] *n abbr of* **Alaska** Alaska
AKA, aka *abbr of* **also known as** alias
akimbo [ə·'kɪm·boʊ] *adj* (**with**) **arms ~** (con) le mani sui fianchi
akin [ə·'kɪn] *adj* **~ to** simile a
AL [æ·lə·'bæ·mə] *n*, **Ala.** *n abbr of* **Alabama** Alabama *m*
à la carte [ɑː·lə·'kɑːrt] *adj, adv* alla carta
alacrity [ə·'læk·rə·ṭi] *n* alacrità *f*
à la mode [ˌɑː·lə·'moʊd] *adj* con gelato
alarm [ə·'lɑːrm] **I.** *n* **1.**(*worry*) apprensione *f;* **to cause sb ~** allarmare qn **2.**(*warning*) allarme *m;* **fire ~** allarme antincendio; **burglar ~** allarme antifurto; **a false ~** un falso allarme; **to give** [*o* **sound**] **the ~** *a. fig* dare

Jane lo può fare ▶let ~ ... figuriamoci ... II. *adv* solo

along [ə·'lɑːŋ] I. *prep* lungo; **all ~ the river** lungo tutto il fiume; **~ the road** lungo la strada; **I lost it ~ the way** l'ho perso per strada; **it's ~ here** è per di qua II. *adv* **all ~** fin dall'inizio; **to bring/take sb ~** portare qn (con sé); **to go ~** andare avanti; **he will be ~ in an hour** sarà qui tra un'ora; **come ~!** vieni anche tu!

alongside [ə·'lɑːŋ·saɪd] I. *prep* 1. (*next to*) accanto a; **to draw up ~ sb/sth** accostarsi a qn/qc; **~ each other** uno accanto all'altro; **to fight ~ sb** lottare a fianco di qn 2. NAUT sottobordo II. *adv* accanto; NAUT accostato

aloof [ə·'luːf] *adj* distante; **to remain ~ from sth** tenersi lontano da qc

aloud [ə·'laʊd] *adv* ad alta voce; **to think ~** pensare ad alta voce

alpha ['æl·fə] *n* alfa *f*

alphabet ['æl·fə·bet] *n* alfabeto *m*

alphabetical [ˌæl·fə·'be·tɪ·kl] *adj* alfabetico, -a; **in ~ order** in ordine alfabetico

alphabetize *vt* mettere in ordine alfabetico

alphanumeric [ˌæl·fə·nuː·'me·rɪk] *adj* alfanumerico, -a

alpha particle *n* particella *f* alfa

alpha ray *n* raggio *m* alfa

alpine ['æl·paɪn] *adj* alpino, -a

Alps [ælps] *npl* **the ~** le Alpi

already [ɔːl·'re·di] *adv* già

alright [ɔl·'raɪt] *adv s.* **all right**

Alsace ['æl·sæs] *n* Alsazia *f*

Alsatian [æl·'seɪ·ʃən] I. *n* 1. (*person*) alsaziano, -a *m, f* 2. (*dog*) pastore *m* tedesco II. *adj* alsaziano, -a

also ['ɔːl·soʊ] *adv* anche

altar ['ɔːl·tə·] *n* altare *m*

altar boy *n* chierichetto *m*

altar girl *n* chierichetta *f*

alter ['ɔːl·tə·] I. *vt* 1. (*change: text, plan*) modificare; (*option*) cambiare; (*paint*) ritoccare 2. FASHION (*dress, suit*) apportare modifiche a 3. (*castrate: dog, cat*) sterilizzare II. *vi* cambiare

alterable ['ɔːl·tə·ə·bl] *adj* modificabile

alteration [ˌɔːl·tə·'reɪ·ʃən] *n* 1. (*change*) alterazione *f;* (*in house*) ristrutturazione *f* 2. (*act of changing*) modifica *f*

altercation [ˌɔːl·tə·'keɪ·ʃən] *n* alterco *m*

alter ego ['ɑː·tə·ˌiː·goʊ] *n* 1. (*second identity*) alter ego *mf inv* 2. (*close friend*) amico, -a intimo *m*

alternate¹ ['ɔːl·tə·neɪt] I. *vt* alternare II. *vi* alternarsi

alternate² [ɔːl·'tɜːr·nət] *adj* 1. (*by turns*) alterno, -a; **on ~ days** a giorni alterni 2. (*alternative*) alternativo, -a

alternating ['ɔːl·tə·neɪ·tɪŋ] *adj* alterno, -a

alternating current *n* ELEC corrente *f* alternata

alternative [ɔːl·'tɜːr·nə·tɪv] I. *n* alternativa *f;* **to have no ~ but to do sth** non avere altra scelta se non fare qc II. *adj* alternativo, -a

alternatively *adv* 1. (*on the other hand*) altrimenti 2. (*as a substitute*) in alternativa

alternator ['ɔːl·tə·neɪ·tə·] *n* alternatore *m*

although [ɔːl·'ðoʊ] *conj* nonostante; **he is stingy ~ he is rich** nonostante sia ricco è avaro; **~ it's snowing ...** sebbene nevichi ...

altimeter [æl·'tɪ·mə·tə·] *n* AVIAT altimetro *m*

altitude ['æl·tə·tuːd] *n* altitudine *f*

alto ['æl·toʊ] *n* 1. (*woman*) contralto *m* 2. (*man*) controtenore *m*

altogether [ˌɔːl·tə·'ge·ðə·] I. *adv* 1. (*completely*) completamente; **not ~** non del tutto 2. (*in total*) complessivamente II. *n* **in the ~** completamente nudo

alto saxophone *n* sassofono *m* contralto

altruism ['æl·truː·ɪ·zəm] *n* altruismo *m*

altruist ['æl·truː·ɪst] *n* altruista *mf*

altruistic [ˌæl·truː·'ɪs·tɪk] *adj* altruistico, -a

aluminum [ə·'luː·mɪ·nəm] *n* alluminio *m*

aluminum foil *n* carta *f* stagnola

aluminum oxide *n* allumina *f*

always ['ɔːl·weɪz] *adv* 1. (*at all times*) sempre 2. (*alternatively*) sempre

Alzheimer's disease ['ɑːlts·haɪ·mərz] *n* morbo *m* di Alzheimer

am [əm, *stressed:* æm] *vi* 1. pers sing *of* be

A.M. [ˌeɪ·'em], **a.m.** *abbr of* ante meridiem a.m.

amalgam [ə·'mæl·gəm] *n* amalgama *m*

amalgamate [ə·'mæl·gə·meɪt] I. *vt* 1. (*metals*) amalgamare 2. COM fondere II. *vi* 1. (*metals*) amalgamarsi 2. COM fondersi

amalgamation [ə·ˌmæl·gə·'meɪ·ʃən] *n* 1. (*process*) amalgamazione *f* 2. COM fusione *f*

amass [ə·'mæs] *vt* (*money*) ammassare; (*information*) accumulare

amateur ['æ·mə·tʃə·] I. *n a. pej* dilettante *mf* II. *adj* dilettantistico, -a; **~ sport** sport *m* dilettantistico *inv*

amateurish [ˌæ·mə·'tʃɜːr·rɪʃ] *adj* da dilettante

amaze [ə·'meɪz] *vt* 1. (*astound*) stupire; **to be ~d that ...** essere stupito che ...; **to be ~d by sth** essere stupito da qc 2. (*surprise*) sorprendere; **to be ~d by sth** essere sorpreso da qc

amazement *n* stupore *m;* **to stare at sth in ~** fissare qc per lo stupore; **to my ~** con mio grande stupore

amazing *adj* sorprendente; **truly ~** davvero incredibile

Amazon ['æ·mə·zɑːn] *n* 1. (*river*) **the ~** il Rio delle Amazzoni 2. (*female warrior*) amazzone *f*

ambassador [æm·'bæ·sə·də·] *n* ambasciatore, -trice *m, f*

amber ['æm·bə·] I. *n* ambra *f* II. *adj* ambrato, -a

ambidextrous [ˌæm·bɪ·'deks·trəs] *adj* ambidestro, -a

ambient ['æm·bɪənt] *adj* circostante

ambiguity [ˌæm·bə·'gjuː·ə·t̬i] <-ies> *n* ambiguità *f*

ambiguous [æm·'bɪg·juː·əs] *adj* ambiguo, -a

ambition [æm·'bɪ·ʃən] *n* ambizione *f;* **she has**

no ~ non ha nessuna ambizione

ambitious [æm·'bɪ·ʃəs] *adj* ambizioso, -a; **to be ~ for sth** avere ambizioni per qc; **to be ~ to do sth** avere l'ambizione di fare qc

ambivalent [æm·'bɪ·və·lənt] *adj* ambivalente; **to feel ~ about** [*o* **towards**] **sth/sb** provare sentimenti contrastanti nei confronti di qc/qn

amble ['æm·bl] **I.** *vi* camminare senza fretta **II.** *n* **1.**(*stroll*) passeggiata *f* **2.**(*of horse*) ambio *m*

ambulance ['æm·bjʊ·ləns] *n* ambulanza *f*

ambush ['æm·bʊʃ] **I.** *vt* **to ~ sb** tendere un'imboscata a qn **II.** *n* <-es> imboscata *f;* **to lie in ~ for sb** stare in agguato in attesa di qn

ameba <-bas *o* -bae> *n s.* **amoeba**

amebiasis *n* amebiasi *f inv*

amebic *adj s.* **amoebic**

ameliorate [ə·'mi:·li·ə·reɪt] *vt form* migliorare

amelioration [ə·ˌmi:·li·ə·'reɪ·ʃən] *n form* miglioramento *m*

amen [eɪ·'men] *interj* amen; **~ to that!** sono assolutamente d'accordo!

amenable [ə·'mi:·nə·bl] *adj* disponibile; **to be ~ to sth** essere ben disposto nei confronti di qc; **to be ~ to reason** mostrarsi ragionevole

amend [ə·'mend] *vt* **1.**(*constitution*) emendare; (*text, plan*) correggere **2.** BOT (*soil*) arricchire

amendment *n* **1.**(*to constitution*) emendamento *m;* (*to text, plan*) correzione *f* **2.**(*to soil*) arricchimento *m*

amends *npl* **to make ~ for sth** farsi perdonare per qc

amenities [ə·'me·nə·ṭi·z] *npl* strutture *f pl* ricreative

America [ə·'me·rɪ·kə] *n* America *f;* **the ~s** le Americhe

American [ə·'me·rɪ·kən] **I.** *n* **1.**(*person*) americano, -a *m, f* **2.** LING (inglese *m*) americano *m* **II.** *adj* americano, -a

American Indian *n* indiano , -a *m, f* d'America

Americanism *n* americanismo *m*

Americanize *vt* americanizzare

amethyst ['æ·mɪ·θɪst] **I.** *n* **1.**(*stone*) ametista *f* **2.**(*color*) ametista *m* **II.** *adj* ametista

amiability [ˌeɪ·mi·ə·'bɪ·lə·ṭi] *n* amabilità *f*

amiable ['eɪ·mi·ə·bl] *adj* amabile

amicable ['æ·mɪ·kə·bl] *adj* amichevole; **to reach an ~ settlement** arrivare a un accordo amichevole

amid(st) [ə·'mɪd(st)] *prep* in mezzo a, fra

amino acid [ə·'mi:·noʊ·'æ·sɪd] *n* aminoacido *m*

amiss [ə·'mɪs] **I.** *adj* **there's something ~** c'è qualcosa che non va **II.** *adv* **to take sth ~** prendersela a male; **a little courtesy would not go ~** un po' di cortesia non ci starebbe male

ammeter ['æ·mɪ·ṭə˞] *n* ELEC amperometro *m*

ammonia [ə·'moʊn·jə] *n* ammoniaca *f*

ammunition [ˌæm·jə·'nɪ·ʃən] *n* **1.**(*for guns*) munizioni *fpl* **2.** *fig* argomenti *mpl*

ammunition depot *n* deposito *m* di munizioni

amnesia [æm·'ni:z·ʒə] *n* amnesia *f*

amnesty ['æm·nəs·ti] <-ies> *n* amnistia *f*

amoeba [ə·'mi:·bə] <-bas *o* -bae> *n* ameba *f*

amoebic [ə·'mi:·bɪk] *adj* amebico, -a

amok [ə·'mʌk] *adv s.* **amuck**

among(st) [ə·'mʌŋ(st)] *prep* tra; **~ friends** tra amici; **(just) one ~ many** (solo) uno fra tanti; **~ Canadians** tra canadesi; **to divide sth up ~ us** dividere qc tra di noi; **~ the flowers/the pupils** tra i fiori/gli alunni; **~ other things** fra le altre cose

amoral [ˌeɪ·'mɔ:·rəl] *adj* amorale

amorous ['æ·mə·rəs] *adj* amoroso, -a

amorphous [ə·'mɔ:r·fəs] *adj* amorfo, -a

amortization [æ·ˌmɔ:r·tə·ˈzeɪ·ʃən] *n* ammortamento *m*

amortize [æ·'mɔ:r·taɪz] *vt* ammortizzare

amount [ə·'maʊnt] **I.** *n* **1.**(*quantity*) quantità *f;* **a certain ~ of difficulty** varie difficoltà **2.**(*very much*) **any ~ of** grandi quantità di; **any ~ of people** molte persone **3.**(*of money*) somma *f;* (*of bill*) importo *m;* **a check in the ~ of ...** un assegno per il valore di ...; **~ carried forward** somma riportata **II.** *vi* **1.**(*add up to*) **to ~ to sth** ammontare a qc; **that ~s to a refusal** questo equivale a un rifiuto **2.**(*be successful*) **to ~ to sth** arrivare a qc; **he will never ~ to much** non combinerà mai granché

amp 1. *abbr of* **ampere** ampere *m inv* **2.** MUS *abbr of* **amplifier** amplificatore *m*

ampere ['æm·pɪr] *n* ampere *m inv*

amphetamine [æm·'fe·tə·mi:n] *n* anfetamina *f*

amphibian [æm·'fɪb·iən] **I.** *adj* anfibio, -a **II.** *n* ZOOL, AUTO anfibio *m*

amphibious [æm·'fɪb·iəs] *adj* anfibio, -a

amphitheater ['æmp·fə·ˌθi:·ə·ṭə˞] *n* anfiteatro *m*

ample ['æm·pl] *adj* **1.**(*plentiful*) abbondante **2.**(*large*) ampio, a **3.**(*enough*) sufficiente

amplification [ˌæmp·lɪ·fɪ·'keɪ·ʃən] *n* **1.** MUS amplificazione *f* **2.**(*increased detail*) approfondimento *m*

amplifier ['æmp·lɪ·fa·ɪə˞] *n* amplificatore *m*

amplify ['æmp·lɪ·faɪ] <-ie-> **I.** *vt* **1.** MUS amplificare **2.**(*enlarge upon: statement*) ampliare; (*idea*) sviluppare **II.** *vi* **to ~ upon sth** approfondire qc

amplitude ['æmp·lɪ·tu:d] *n* ampiezza *f*

ampoule *n*, **ampule** ['æm·pu:l] *n* MED fiala *f*

amputate ['æmp·jʊ·teɪt] *vt* amputare

amputation [ˌæmp·jʊ·'teɪ·ʃən] *n* amputazione *f*

amputee [ˌæmp·jʊ·'ti:] *n* mutilato, -a *m, f*

amuck [ə·'mʌk] *adv* fuori controllo; **to run ~** scatenarsi

amulet ['æm·jʊ·lɪt] *n* amuleto *m*

amuse [ə·'mju:z] *vt* **1.**(*entertain*) divertire; **to ~ oneself** distrarsi; **to keep sb ~d** intrattenere qn **2.**(*cause laughter*) divertire; **I'm not ~d** non lo trovo divertente

amusement [ə·'mju:z·mənt] *n* **1.**(*entertainment*) divertimento *m;* **for one's own ~** per svago **2.**(*mirth*) divertimento *m;* (*much*) **to**

my ~ con mio gran divertimento; **he looked on in** ~ guardò divertito **3.** (*laughter*) risata *f;* **to conceal one's** ~ trattenersi dal ridere

amusement park *n* luna park*m inv*

amusing *adj* divertente

an [ən, *stressed:* æn] *indef art before vowel s.* **a**

anabolic steroid [æ·nə·ˈbɒ·lik·ˈsteˈrɔid] *n* steroide *m* anabolizzante

anachronism [ə·ˈnæ·krə·nɪ·zəm] *n* anacronismo *m*

anachronistic [ə·ˌnæ·krə·ˈnɪs·tik] *adj* anacronistico, -a

anaconda [ˌæ·nə·ˈkɑːn·də] *n* anaconda *m inv*

anagram [ˈæ·nə·græm] *n* anagramma *m*

anal [ˈeɪ·nəl] *adj* anale

analgesic [ˌæ·næl·ˈdʒiː·sik] **I.** *adj* analgesico, -a **II.** *n* analgesico *m*

analog [ˈæ·nə·lɑːg] *n* equivalente *m*

analog computer *n* computer *m* analogico *inv*

analogous [ə·ˈnæ·lə·gəs] *adj* analogo, -a; **to be** ~ **to sth** essere analogo a qc

analogy [ə·ˈnæ·lə·dʒi] <-ies> *n* analogia *f;* **to draw an** ~ **between** fare un'analogia tra; **by** ~ **with sth** per analogia con qc

analysis [ə·ˈnæ·lə·sis] <-ses> *n* **1.** (*examination*) analisi *f inv* **2.** (*psychoanalysis*) (psic)analisi *f inv;* **to be in** ~ essere in analisi ▶ **in the** **final** [*o* **last**] ~ in ultima analisi

analyst [ˈæ·nə·list] *n* **1.** (*analyzer*) analista *mf;* **food** ~ analista alimentare; **financial** ~ analista finanziario **2.** PSYCH (psic)analista *mf*

analytic(al) [ˌæ·nə·ˈlɪ·t̬ɪ·k(əl)] *adj* analitico, -a

analyze [ˈæ·nə·laɪz] *vt* analizzare; PSYCH psicanalizzare

anarchic(al) [æ·ˈnɑːr·kɪ·k(əl)] *adj* anarchico, -a

anarchism [ˈæ·nɚ·kɪ·zəm] *n* anarchismo *m*

anarchist [ˈæ·nɚ·kɪst] **I.** *adj* anarchico, -a **II.** *n* anarchico, -a *m, f*

anarchistic [ˌæ·nɚ·ˈkɪs·tik] *adj* anarchico, -a

anarchy [ˈæ·nɚ·ki] *n* anarchia *f*

anathema [ə·ˈnæ·θə·mə] *n* **1.** REL anatema *m* **2.** *fig* **the very idea was** ~ **to her** odiava anche solo l'idea

anatomical [ˌæ·nə·ˈtɑː·mɪ·kl] *adj* anatomico, -a

anatomy [ə·ˈnæ·t̬ə·mi] <-ies> *n* **1.** BIO anatomia *f* **2.** *iron* (*body*) corpo *m* **3.** (*analysis*) analisi *f inv*

ancestor [ˈæn·ses·tɚ] *n* **1.** (*of person*) antenato, -a *m, f* **2.** (*of idea, organization*) prototipo *m*

ancestral [æn·ˈses·trəl] *adj* ancestrale; **the** ~ **home** la casa avita

ancestry [ˈæn·ses·tri] <-ies> *n* ascendenza *f;* **she is of Polish** ~ è di stirpe polacca

anchor [ˈæn·kɚ] **I.** *n* **1.** NAUT ancora *f;* **to be at** ~ essere ancorato; **to drop/weigh** ~ gettare/levare l'ancora **2.** *fig* sostegno *m* **3.** (*news* ~) anchorman, -woman *m, f inv* **II.** *vt* **1.** NAUT ancorare **2.** (*rope, tent*) fissare **3.** RADIO, TV **to** ~ **a radio/TV program** condurre un programma radiofonico/televisivo **III.** *vi* NAUT get-

tare l'ancora

anchorage [ˈæŋ·kə·rɪdʒ] *n* ancoraggio *m*

anchorman [ˈæŋ·kɚ·mæn] <-men> *n* **1.** RADIO, TV anchorman *m inv* **2.** *fig* figura *f* cruciale

anchorwoman [ˈæŋ·kɚ·ˌwʊ·mən] <-men> *n* **1.** RADIO, TV anchorwoman *f inv* **2.** *fig* figura *f* cruciale

anchovy [ˈæn·tʃoʊ·vi] <-ies> *n* acciuga *f*

ancient [ˈeɪn·ʃənt] **I.** *adj* **1.** *a.* HIST antico, -a; **since** ~ **times** da tempi remoti; ~ **history** storia antica; **to be** ~ **history** *fig* essere storia vecchia **2.** *inf* (*very old*) decrepito, -a; **I feel pretty** ~ mi sento vecchissimo **II.** *n* **the** ~**s** gli antichi

ancillary [ˈæn·sə·le·ri] *adj* **1.** (*staff*) ausiliario, -a **2.** (*road*) secondario, -a; **to be** ~ **to sth** essere subordinato a qc

and [ən, ənd, *stressed:* ænd] *conj* **1.** (*also*) e; (*before 'i' or 'hi'*) ed; **black** ~ **white** bianco e nero; **food** ~ **drink** cibo e bevande; **parents** ~ **children** genitori e figli **2.** MAT **2** ~ **3 is 5** 2 più 3 fa 5; **four hundred** ~ **twelve** quattrocentododici **3.** (*then*) **he left** ~ **everybody was relieved** quando se n'è andato tutti han tirato un respiro di sollievo **4.** (*increase*) **more** ~ **more** sempre più; **better** ~ **better** sempre meglio **5.** (*repetition*) **I tried** ~ **tried** ho provato e riprovato **6.** (*continuation*) **he cried** ~ **cried** continuava a piangere ▶ ~ **so on** [*o* **forth**] e così via

Andalusia [ˌæn·də·ˈluː·ʒə] *n* Andalusia *f*

Andalusian **I.** *adj* andaluso, -a **II.** *n* **1.** (*person*) andaluso, -a *m, f* **2.** LING andaluso *m*

Andean [ˈæn·di·ən] *adj* andino, -a

Andes [ˈæn·diːz] *npl* Ande *fpl*

Andorra [æn·ˈdɔː·rə] *n* Andorra *f*

Andorran **I.** *adj* andorrano, -a **II.** *n* andorrano, -a *m, f*

androgynous [æn·ˈdrɑː·dʒə·nəs] *adj* androgino, -a

android [ˈæn·drɔid] *n* androide *m*

anecdotal [ˌæ·nik·ˈdoʊ·t̬əl] *adj* anedddotico, -a

anecdote [ˈæ·nik·doʊt] *n* aneddoto *m*

anemia [ə·ˈniː·mi·ə] *n* anemia *f*

anemic [ə·ˈniː·mik] *adj* anemico, -a

anemone [ə·ˈne·mə·ni] *n* anemone *m*

anesthesia [ˌæ·nis·ˈθiː·ʒə] *n* anestesia *f*

anesthetic [ˌæ·nis·ˈθe·tik] **I.** *adj* anestetico, -a **II.** *n* anestetico *m;* **to be under** ~ essere sotto anestesia; **to give sb an** ~ anestetizzare qn

anesthetist [ə·ˈnis·ˈθe·tist] *n* anestesista *mf*

anesthetize [ə·ˈnis·θə·taɪz] *vt* anestetizzare

anew [ə·ˈnuː] *adv* di nuovo; **to begin** ~ ricominciare da capo

angel [ˈeɪn·dʒl] *n* angelo *m;* ~ **of death** angelo della morte; **to be no** ~ non essere proprio un angelo

angelic [æn·ˈdʒe·lik] *adj* angelico, -a

anger [ˈæŋ·gɚ] **I.** *n* rabbia *f;* (*stronger*) collera *f;* **to speak in** ~ parlare con rabbia **II.** *vt* far arrabbiare

angina [æn·'dʒaɪ·nə] *n* angina *f;* ~ **pectoris** angina pectoris

angle¹ ['æŋ·gl] I. *n* 1. *a.* MAT angolo *m;* **at an ~ of 90 degrees, at a 90-degree** ~ a un angolo di 90 gradi; **to be at an ~ (to sth)** formare un angolo (con qc); **the picture was hanging at an ~** il quadro pendeva da un lato; **he wore his hat at an ~** portava il cappello inclinato da un lato 2. (*perspective*) prospettiva *f;* **to see sth from a different ~** vedere qc da un altro punto di vista; **what is the best news ~ for this story?** qual è il taglio migliore per presentare questa notizia? 3. (*opinion*) punto *m* di vista; **what's your ~ on this issue?** lei come vede la questione? II. *vt* 1. (*turn at an angle: shot*) angolare 2. (*information*) rivolgere; **this article is ~d towards teenagers** questo articolo è rivolto agli adolescenti

angle² ['æŋ·gl] *vi* 1. (*to fish*) pescare (con la lenza); **to go ~** andare a pescare 2. *fig* **to ~ for sth** *inf* andare a caccia di qc

angler ['æŋ·glɚ] *n* pescatore , -trice (con la lenza) *m*

Anglican ['æŋ·glɪ·kən] I. *adj* anglicano, -a II. *n* anglicano, -a *m, f*

Anglican Church *n* Chiesa *f* anglicana

Anglicist ['æŋ·glɪ·sɪst] *n* anglista *mf*

Anglicize ['æŋ·glɪ·saɪz] *vt* anglicizzare

Anglo-American [ˌæŋ·glou·ə·'me·rɪ·kən] I. *n* angloamericano, -a *m, f* II. *adj* angloamericano, -a

Anglophile [ˌæŋ·glə·faɪl] *n* anglofilo, -a *m, f*

Anglophobe [ˌæŋ·glə·'foub] *n* anglofobo, -a *m, f*

Anglo-Saxon [ˌæŋ·glou·'sæk·sən] I. *adj* anglosassone II. *n* 1. (*person*) anglosassone *mf* 2. LING anglosassone *m*

Angola [æŋ·'gou·lə] *n* Angola *m*

Angolan I. *adj* angolano, -a II. *n* angolano, -a *m, f*

angora [æŋ·'gɔː·rə] *n* 1. (*fabric*) angora *f* 2. (*cat*) gatto *m* d'angora

angry ['æŋ·gri] *adj* 1. (*person*) arrabbiato, -a; (*crowd*) inferocito, -a; (*sky*) minaccioso, -a; (*sea*) tempestoso, -a; **to make sb ~** far arrabbiare qn; **to get ~ with sb** arrabbiarsi con qn; **to get ~ about sth** arrabbiarsi per qc; **to exchange ~ words** scambiarsi parole di fuoco 2. MED infiammato, -a

angst [æŋst] *n* angoscia *f*

anguish ['æŋ·gwɪʃ] *n* angoscia *f;* **to be in ~ (over sth)** essere angosciato (da qc); **to cause sb ~** angosciare qn

angular ['æŋ·gjʊ·lɚ] *adj* (*shape*) angolare; (*face*) spigoloso, -a

animal ['æ·nɪ·ml] I. *n* 1. ZOOL animale *m;* ~ **fat** grasso *m* animale 2. *fig* (*person*) animale *m* II. *adj* (*instincts, desires*) animale

animal cracker *n* CULIN *biscotto a forma di animale*

animal husbandry *n* allevamento *m* di animali

animal kingdom *n* regno *m* animale

animal rights *npl* diritti *m pl* degli animali

animate¹ ['æ·nɪ·meɪt] *vt* animare

animate² ['æ·nɪ·mɪt] *adj* animato, -a

animated *adj* animato, -a; **to become ~** animarsi

animation [ˌæ·nɪ·'meɪ·ʃən] *n* animazione *f;* **computer ~** animazione al computer

animator ['æ·nɪ·meɪ·tɚ] *n* animatore, -trice *m, f*

animosity [ˌæ·nɪ·'mɑː·sə·t̬i] *n* animosità *f*

anise ['æ·nɪs] *n* anice *m*

anise seed *n,* **aniseed** ['æ·nɪ·siːd] *n* semi *m pl* di anice

ankle ['æŋ·kl] *n* caviglia *f*

anklebone ['æŋ·kl·boun] *n* astragalo *m*

ankle-deep *adj* **to be ~ in sth** affondare fino alle caviglie in qc

anklet ['æŋ·klɪt] *n* 1. (*chain*) cavigliera *f* 2. (*short sock*) calzino *m*

annals ['æ·nlz] *npl* annali *mpl*

annex ['æ·neks] I. *n* <-es> 1. (*of building*) annesso *m* 2. (*of document*) allegato *m* II. *vt* 1. (*territory*) annettere 2. (*document, clause*) allegare

annexation [ˌæ·nek·'seɪ·ʃən] *n* annessione *f*

annihilate [ə·'naɪ·ə·leɪt] *vt a. fig* annientare

annihilation [ə·ˌnaɪ·ə·'leɪ·ʃən] *n a. fig* annientamento *m*

anniversary [ˌæ·nɪ·'vɜːr·sə·ri] <-ies> *n* anniversario *m*

annotate ['æ·nə·teɪt] *vt* annotare; ~ **d edition** edizione *f* commentata

annotation [ˌæ·nə·'teɪ·ʃən] *n* 1. (*act of writing*) annotazione *f* 2. (*note*) nota *f*

announce [ə·'nauns] *vt* annunciare; (*result*) comunicare

announcement *n* annuncio *m;* **official ~** comunicato *m* ufficiale; **to make an ~ about sth** annunciare qc

announcer [ə·'naun·sɚ] *n* annunciatore, -trice *m, f*

annoy [ə·'nɔɪ] *vt* infastidire; **to get ~ed with sb** essere arrabbiato con qn

annoyance [ə·'nɔ·ɪəns] *n* 1. (*irritation*) irritazione *f;* **much to my ~, she won** con mia grande rabbia, ha vinto 2. (*irritating thing*) fastidio *m*

annoying *adj* (*noise, habit*) fastidioso, -a; (*person, fact*) irritante; **it's ~ to think that ...** fa rabbia pensare che ...; **how ~!** che seccatura!

annual ['æn·jʊ·əl] I. *adj* annuale II. *n* 1. (*book*) annuario *m* 2. BOT pianta *f* annuale

annually ['æn·jʊ·ə·li] *adv* annualmente

annuity [ə·'nuː·ə·t̬i] <-ies> *n* rendita *f* annuale

annul [ə·'nʌl] <-ll-> *vt* annullare

annulment [ə·'nʌl·mənt] *n* annullamento *m*

Annunciation [ə·ˌnʌn·sɪ·'eɪ·ʃən] *n* **the ~** l'Annunciazione *f*

anode ['æ·noud] *n* anodo *m*

anodyne ['æ·nou·daɪn] I. *adj* anodino, -a II. *n* MED analgesico *m*

anoint [ə·'nɔɪnt] *vt* ungere

anointing *n* unzione *f*

anomalous [ə·'nɑː·mə·ləs] *adj* anomalo, -a

anomaly [ə·'nɑː·mə·li] <-ies> *n* anomalia *f*

anonymity [ˌæ·nə·'nɪ·mə·t̬i] *n* anonimato *m*

anonymous [ə·'nɑː·nə·məs] *adj* anonimo, -a; ~ **letter** lettera anonima; **to remain** ~ mantenere l'anonimato

anorexia [ˌɑ·nə·'rek·sɪ·ə] *n* anoressia *f*

anorexia nervosa *n* anoressia *f* nervosa

anorexic [ˌæ·nə·'rek·sɪk] *adj* anoressico, -a

another [ə·'nʌ·ðɚ] I. *pron* 1. (*one more*) un altro, un'altra; **it's always one thing or** ~ ce n'è sempre una 2. (*mutual*) **one** ~ l'un l'altro; **they love one** ~ si amano II. *adj* un altro, un'altra; ~ **pastry?** un altro pasticcino?; ~ **$30** altri 30 dollari; **could he be** ~ **Mozart?** che sia un altro Mozart?

answer ['æn·sɚ] I. *n* 1. (*reply*) risposta *f*; **in** ~ **to your question** in risposta alla tua domanda; **I called but there was no** ~ ho chiamato, ma non hanno risposto; **the short** ~ **is 'no'** in poche parole: no 2. (*solution*) soluzione *f* 3. LAW replica *f* 4. (*equivalent*) **to be the French** ~ **to the Beatles** essere la risposta francese ai Beatles II. *vt* 1. (*respond to*) rispondere a; **to** ~ **the telephone** rispondere al telefono; **to** ~ **the door** andare ad aprire la porta 2. (*fit, suit: description*) rispondere a; (*need*) soddisfare; (*prayers*) esaudire III. *vi* rispondere

◆**answer back** *vi* rispondere (male); **don't** ~! non rispondere!

◆**answer for** *vt* (*action, situation*) rispondere di; (*person*) rispondere di; **to** ~ **oneself** rispondere delle proprie azioni; **to have a lot to** ~ dover render conto di molte cose

◆**answer to** *vt* 1. (*obey*) obbedire a 2. (*fit: description*) rispondere a 3. (*be named*) **to** ~ **the name of Billy** rispondere al nome di Billy

answerable ['æn·sə·rə·bl] *adj* 1. (*responsible*) **to be** ~ **for sth** essere responsabile di qc 2. (*accountable*) **to be** ~ **to sb** dover rendere conto a qn; **to be** ~ **to nobody** non dover render conto a nessuno

answering machine *n* segreteria *f* telefonica

answering service *n* servizio *m* di segreteria telefonica

ant [ænt] *n* formica *f* ▸ **to have** ~**s in one's pants** <ins>*inf*</ins> non star fermo un attimo

antagonism [æn·'tæ·gə·nɪ·zəm] *n* 1. (*towards sb*) antagonismo *m*; (*between people*) rivalità *f* 2. (*of ideas, systems*) antagonismo *m*

antagonistic [æn·ˌtæ·gə·'nɪs·tɪk] *adj* 1. (*person, attitude*) antagonistico, -a 2. ANAT antagonista

antagonize [æn·'tæ·gə·naɪz] *vt* inimicarsi

Antarctic [ænt·'ɑːrk·tɪk] I. *adj* antartico, -a II. *n* **the** ~ l'Antartico *m*

Antarctica [ænt·'ɑːrk·tɪ·kə] *n* Antartide *m*

Antarctic Circle *n* Circolo *m* polare antartico

Antarctic Ocean *n* Oceano *m* antartico

ante ['æn·t̬i] *n* posta *f*; **to raise the** ~ alzare la posta

anteater ['æn·ˌtiː·t̬ɚ] *n* formichiere *m*

antecedent [ˌæn·t̬ɪ·'siː·dnt] I. *n* 1. (*forerunner*) antecedente *m* 2. *pl* (*past history*) antecedenti *mpl* II. *adj* antecedente

antechamber ['æn·t̬ɪ·tʃeɪm·bɚ] *n* anticamera *f*

antediluvian [ˌæn·t̬ɪ·də·'luː·vi·ən] *adj a. fig* antidiluviano, -a

antelope ['æn·t̬ɪ·loʊp] <-(s)> *n* antilope *f*

antenna [æn·'te·nə] <-nae *o* -s> *n* antenna *f*

anterior [æn·'tɪ·ri·ɚ] *adj* anteriore

anteroom ['æn·t̬ɪ·ruːm] *n* anticamera *f*

anthem ['æn·θəm] *n* inno *m*

anthill ['ænt·hɪl] *n* formicaio *m*

anthology [æn·'θɑː·lə·dʒi] <-ies> *n* antologia *f*

anthracite ['æn·θrə·saɪt] *n* antracite *f*

anthropoid ['æn·θrə·pɔɪd] I. *n* antropoide *mf* II. *adj* antropoide

anthropological [ˌæn·θrə·pə·'lɑː·dʒɪ·kl] *adj* antropologico, -a

anthropologist [ˌæn·θrə·'pɑː·lə·dʒɪst] *n* antropologo, -a *m, f*

anthropology [ˌæn·θrə·'pɑː·lə·dʒi] *n* antropologia *f*

anti ['æn·ti] I. *adj* contro; **to be** ~ esser contro II. *prep* contro

antiabortion [ˌæn·ti·ə·'bɔːr·ʃən] *adj* antiabortista

antiaging cream *n* crema *f* antietà

antiaircraft [ˌæn·t̬ɪ·'er·kræft] *adj* antiaereo, -a

anti-American *adj* antiamericano, -a

antibiotic [ˌæn·t̬ɪ·baɪ·'ɑː·t̬ɪk] I. *n* antibiotico *m* II. *adj* antibiotico, -a

antibody ['æn·t̬ɪ·bɑː·di] <-ies> *n* anticorpo *m*

anticipate [æn·'tɪ·sə·peɪt] *vt* 1. (*expect, foresee*) prevedere; **to** ~ **doing/being sth** prevedere di fare/essere qc 2. (*look forward to*) pregustare 3. (*act in advance of*) anticipare; **to** ~ **one's inheritance** spendere in anticipo l'eredità

anticipation [æn·ˌtɪ·sə·'peɪ·ʃən] *n* 1. (*foresight*) previsione *f*; **in** ~ **of** in previsione di 2. (*funds*) anticipo *m* 3. (*excitement*) trepidazione *f*; **to wait in** ~ aspettare con impazienza

anticipatory [æn·'tɪ·sɪ·pə·tɔː·ri] *adj* preventivo, -a

anticlerical [ˌæn·t̬ɪ·'kle·rɪ·kl] *adj* anticlericale

anticlimactic [ˌæn·t̬ɪ·klɪ·'mæk·tɪk] *adj* deludente

anticlimax [ˌæn·t̬ɪ·'klaɪ·mæks] <-es> *n* delusione *f*

anticoagulant [ˌæn·t̬ɪ·koʊ·'æg·jə·lənt] I. *n* anticoagulante *m* II. *adj* anticoagulante

antics ['æn·tɪks] *npl* 1. (*foolish behavior*) stravaganze *fpl* 2. (*tricks*) scherzetti *mpl*

antidepressant [ˌæn·t̬ɪ·dɪ·'pre·snt] I. *adj* antidepressivo, -a II. *n* antidepressivo *m*

antidote ['æn·t̬ɪ·doʊt] *n* antidoto *m*; **an** ~ **to sth** un antidoto a qc

antiestablishment *adj* contro l'establishment

antifreeze ['æn·t̬ɪ·friːz] *n* antigelo *m*

antigen ['æn·t̬ɪ·dʒən] *n* antigene *m*

Antigua and Barbuda [æn·'tiː·gə ən bɑːr·

'buː·də] *n* Antigua *f* e Barbuda *f*
Antiguan [æn·'tiː·gən] I. *adj* antiguano, -a II. *n* antiguano, -a *m, f*
antihero [æn·ʈɪ·'hɪ·roʊ] <-es> *n* antieroe *m*
antihistamine [ˌæn·tɪ·'hɪs·tə·ˌmiːn] *n* MED antistaminico *m*
anti-inflammatory [ˌæn·tɪn·'flæ·mə·tɔː·ri] *adj* MED antinfiammatorio, -a
antiknock ['æn·tɪ·'nɑːk] *adj* antidetonante
Antilles [æn·'tɪ·liːz] *npl* the ~ le Antille
antilock braking system *n* AUTO sistema *m* antibloccaggio delle ruote
antimatter ['æn·tɪ·mæ·ʈə·] *n* antimateria *f*
antimissile [ˌæn·tɪ·'mɪ·sɪl] *adj* antimissile
antioxidant [ˌæn·tɪ·'ɑːk·sɪ·dənt] *n* antiossidante *m*
antipasto *n* antipasto *m*
antipathy [æn·'tɪ·pə·θi] <-ies> *n* antipatia *f*
antiperspirant [ˌæn·tɪ·'pɜːr·spə·ənt] *n* antitraspirante *m*
antipodes [æn·'tɪ·pə·diːz] *npl* antipodi *mpl*
antipollution *adj* (*filter, law*) antinquinamento *inv*
antiquarian [ˌæn·tɪ·'kwe·ri·ən] I. *n* (*dealer*) antiquario, -a *m, f;* (*collector*) collezionista *mf* di antichità II. *adj* antiquario, -a
antiquary ['æn·tɪ·kwə·ri] <-ies> *n s.* **antiquarian**
antiquated ['æn·tɪ·kwei·ʈɪd] *adj* antiquato, -a
antique [æn·'tiːk] I. *n* (*object, piece of furniture*) pezzo *f* d'antiquariato; (*old-fashioned*) anticaglia *f* II. *adj* antico, -a; (*old-fashioned*) antiquato, -a
antique dealer *n* antiquario, -a *m, f*
antique shop *n* negozio *m* d'antiquariato
antiquity [æn·'tɪ·kwə·ti] <-ies> *n* 1. (*ancient times*) antichità *f* 2. *pl* (*relics*) antichità *fpl*
antirust [ˌæn·tɪ·'rʌst] *adj* antiruggine
anti-Semite [ˌæn·tɪ·'se·mait] *n* antisemita *mf*
anti-Semitic [ˌæn·tɪ·sə·'mɪ·ʈɪk] *adj* antisemita
anti-Semitism [æn·tɪ·'se·mə·tɪ·sm] *n* antisemitismo *m*
antiseptic [ˌæn·tə·'sep·tɪk] I. *n* antisettico *m* II. *adj* 1. MED antisettico, -a 2. *fig, pej* asettico, -a
antisocial [ˌæn·tɪ·'soʊ·ʃl] *adj* antisociale
antistatic [ˌæn·tɪ·'stæ·ʈɪk] *adj* antistatico, -a
antitank [ˌæn·tɪ·'tæŋk] *adj* anticarro *inv*
antiterrorist *adj* (*measures*) antiterrorismo *inv*
antithesis [æn·'tɪ·θə·sɪs] <-ses> *n* antitesi *f inv*
antithetic(al) [ˌæn·tɪ·'θe·ʈɪ·k(əl)] *adj* antitetico, -a
antitoxin [ˌæn·tɪ·'tɑːk·sɪn] *n* antitossina *f*
antivirus [ˌæn·tɪ·'vai·rəs] *adj* COMPUT antivirus *inv;* ~ **program** (programma *m*) antivirus *m inv*
antiwar [ˌæn·tɪ·'wɔːr] *adj* contrario, -a alla guerra
antiwrinkle cream [ˌæn·tɪ·'rɪŋ·kl·ˌkriːm] *n* crema *f* antirughe
antler ['ænt·lə·] *n* corno ramificato *m;* ~ **s** palchi
antonym ['æn·tə·nɪm] *n* antonimo *m*

Antwerp ['ænt·wɜːrp] *n* Anversa *f*
anus ['ei·nəs] *n* ano *m*
anvil ['æn·vɪl] *n a.* ANAT incudine *f*
anxiety [æŋ·'za·ɪə·ʈi] *n* 1. (*concern*) preoccupazione *f;* PSYCH ansia *f;* **a source of** ~ una fonte di preoccupazione 2. (*desire*) smania *f;* ~ **to do sth** smania di fare qc; ~ **for sth** smania di qc
anxiety attack *n* attacco *m* d'ansia
anxious ['æŋk·ʃəs] *adj* 1. (*concerned*) preoccupato, -a; (*look*) pieno, -a d'ansia; **to keep an** ~ **eye on sth** tenere d'occhio qc con apprensione; **to be** ~ **about sth** essere in ansia per qc; **an** ~ **moment** un momento di tensione 2. *inf* (*eager*) impaziente; **to be** ~ **to do sth** essere impaziente di fare qc
any ['e·ni] I. *adj* 1. (*some*) del, della; ~ **books** dei libri; **do they have** ~ **money?** hanno soldi?; **do you want** ~ **more soup?** vuoi ancora un po' di zuppa? 2. (*not important which*) qualsiasi; **come at** ~ **time** vieni quando vuoi; **in** ~ **case** in ogni caso 3. (*in negatives*) I **don't have** ~ **money** non ho soldi; **there aren't** ~ **cars** non ci sono macchine II. *adv* 1. (*not*) ~ **more** non più; **she doesn't come here** ~ **more** non viene più qui 2. (*at all*) **does she feel** ~ **better?** si sente un po' meglio?; **that doesn't help him** ~ *inf* non l'aiuta per niente III. *pron* 1. (*some*) chiunque; ~ **of you** chiunque di voi; ~ **but him would have gone** chiunque altro sarebbe andato 2. (*in negatives*) nessuno, -a; **not** ~ nessuno; **he ate two pastries and I didn't eat** ~ lui ha mangiato due paste e io nessuna
anybody ['e·nɪ·bɑː·di] *pron indef* 1. (*someone*) nessuno, -a 2. (*not important which*) chiunque; ~ **but him** tutti tranne lui; ~ **else would have done it** chiunque altro l'avrebbe fatto; **she's not just** ~ non è una qualunque 3. (*no one*) nessuno, -a; **I've never seen** ~ **like that** non ho mai visto nessuno così; **more than** ~ più di chiunque altro
anyhow ['e·nɪ·haʊ] *adv* 1. (*in any case*) in ogni caso; (*nevertheless*) comunque 2. (*well*) comunque; ~, **as I was saying ...** comunque, come stavo dicendo ... 3. (*in a disorderly way*) in qualche modo; **she dumped the tools into the box just** ~ ha buttato gli attrezzi a casaccio nella scatola
anyone ['e·nɪ·wʌn] *pron indef s.* **anybody**
anyplace ['e·nɪ·pleis] *adv* 1. (*interrogative*) da qualche parte; **have you seen my glasses** ~? hai visto da qualche parte i miei occhiali? 2. (*in or at any location*) dovunque; I **can sleep** ~ posso dormire in qualsiasi posto 3. (*in negatives*) in nessun luogo; **you won't see this** ~ questo non lo vedrai in nessun posto
anything ['e·nɪ·θɪŋ] *pron indef* 1. (*something*) qualcosa; ~ **else?** nient'altro?; **is there** ~ **new?** ci sono novità? 2. (*each thing*) qualsiasi cosa; **it is** ~ **but funny** è tutto tranne che divertente; ~ **and everything** qualsiasi cosa;

to be as fast as ~ *inf* essere rapidissimo **3.**(*nothing*) niente; **hardly** ~ quasi niente; **I didn't find** ~ **better** non ho trovato niente di meglio; **I was afraid, if** ~ se mai, avevo paura; **for** ~ (**in the world**) per niente al mondo

anytime ['e·ni·taɪm] *adv* (*ready*) in qualsiasi momento; (*come*) a qualsiasi ora

anyway ['e·ni·weɪ] *adv,* **anyways** ['e·ni·weɪz] *adv sl* **1.**(*in any case*) in ogni modo **2.**(*well*) insomma; ~**, as I was saying ...** insomma, come stavo dicendo ...

anywhere ['e·ni·wer] *adv* **1.**(*interrogative*) da qualche parte; **have you seen my glasses** ~? hai visto da qualche parte i miei occhiali?; **are we** ~ **near finished yet?** *inf* ci manca molto per finire? **2.**(*positive sense*) dovunque; **I can sleep** ~ posso dormire in qualsiasi posto; **its value is** ~ **between $25 and $30** vale tra i 25 e i 30 dollari; **to live miles from** ~ *inf* abitare a casa del diavolo; ~ **else** in qualsiasi altro posto; (*in negatives*) in nessun altro posto **3.**(*in negatives*) in nessun posto; **you won't see this** ~ questo non lo vedrai in nessun posto; **he isn't** ~ **near as popular as he used to be** *inf* non è più famoso come una volta

aorta [eɪ·'ɔːr·tə] *n* <-s *o* -tae> aorta *f*

apace [ə·'peɪs] *adv* rapidamente

apart [ə·'pɑːrt] *adv* **1.**(*separated*) distanti; **to be 20 miles** ~ stare a 20 miglia di distanza; **far** ~ molto lontani; **to move** ~ separarsi **2.**(*aside*) **to be** ~ **from sth** essere separato da qc; **to set sth** ~ mettere da parte qc; **to stand** ~ stare in disparte **3.**(*into pieces*) **to come** ~ cadere a pezzi; **to take sth** ~ smontare qc **4.**(*except for*) **you and me** ~ tranne te e me; **all joking** ~ scherzi a parte

apart from *prep* **1.**(*except for*) a parte; ~ **that** a parte questo **2.**(*in addition to*) oltre a **3.**(*separate from*) **to live** ~ **sb** vivere separato da qn; **to live** ~ **each other** vivere separati

apartheid [ə·'pɑːr·teɪt] *n* apartheid *f inv*

apartment [ə·'pɑːrt·mənt] *n* appartamento *m*

apartment building *n,* **apartment house** *n* condominio *m*

apathetic [ˌæ·pə·'θe·ṭɪk] *adj* apatico, -a

apathy ['æ·pə·θi] *n* apatia *f;* ~ **about sth** apatia nei confronti di qc

ape [eɪp] **I.** *n* scimmia *f* ▶ **to go** ~ *inf* dare fuori di matto **II.** *vt* scimmiottare

aperitif [ə·ˌpe·rə·'tiːf] *n* aperitivo *m*

aperture ['æ·pə·tʃʊr] *n* **1.**(*crack*) spiraglio *m* **2.** PHOT apertura *f*

apex ['eɪ·peks] <-es *o* apices> *n* **1.**(*top*) apice *m* **2.** *fig* apice *m* **3.** MAT vertice *m*

aphid ['eɪ·fɪd] *n* afide *m*

aphorism ['æ·fə·ɪ·zəm] *n* aforisma *m*

aphrodisiac [ˌæf·rə·'dɪ·zi·æk] **I.** *n* afrodisiaco *m* **II.** *adj* afrodisiaco, -a

apiarist ['eɪ·piə·rɪst] *n* apicoltore, -trice *m, f*

apiary ['eɪ·pɪe·ri] <-ies> *n* apiario *m*

apiculture ['eɪ·pɪ·kʌl·tʃə] *n* apicoltura *f*

apiece [ə·'piːs] *adv* ciascuno, -a; (*per person*) a testa; (*per item*) l'uno, -a; **they cost $5** ~ cost-

ano 5 dollari l'uno

aplenty [ə·'plen·ti] *adv* in abbondanza

aplomb [ə·'plɑːm] *n* aplomb *m inv*

apnea *n* apnea *f;* **sleep** ~ apnea del sonno

APO *n abbr of* **Army Post Office** *ufficio postale per i militari americani all'estero*

apocalypse [ə·'pɑː·kə·lɪps] *n* apocalisse *f;* **the Apocalypse** REL l'Apocalisse

apocalyptic [ə·ˌpɑː·kə·'lɪp·tɪk] *adj* apocalittico, -a

apocryphal [ə·'pɑː·krə·fəl] *adj* fittizio, -a

apogee ['æ·pə·dʒi:] *n a.* ASTR apogeo *m*

apologetic [ə·ˌpɑː·lə·'dʒe·ṭɪk] *adj* (*tone, look, smile*) di scusa; **to be** ~ **about sth** scusarsi per qc

apologetically *adv* per scusarsi; **to say sth** ~ dire qc per scusarsi

apologize [ə·'pɑː·lə·dʒaɪz] *vi* chiedere scusa; **to** ~ **to sb for sth** scusarsi con qn per qc; **I** (**do**) ~ **if ...** chiedo scusa se ...

apology [ə·'pɑː·lə·dʒi] <-ies> *n* scuse *fpl;* **to make an** ~ scusarsi; **please accept my apologies** la prego di accettare le mie scuse

apoplectic [ˌæ·pə·'plek·tɪk] *adj* **1.** MED apoplettico, -a **2.** *fig* (*angry*) furibondo, -a; **to be** ~ **about sth** essere furibondo per qc

apoplectic stroke *n* colpo *m* apoplettico

apostle [ə·'pɑː·sl] *n* apostolo *m*

apostolic [ˌæ·pəs·'tɑː·lɪk] *adj* apostolico, -a

apostrophe [ə·'pɑː·s·trə·fi] *n* apostrofo *m*

Appalachian Mountains [ˌæ·pə·'leɪ·ʃən-] *npl* monti *m pl* Appalachi

> **i** Gli (**Appalachian Mountains**) si estendono su 1.600 miglia (2.270 km) nella parte orientale dell'America del Nord: dal Québec/Canada all'Alabama/USA. Più antiche, dunque più erose, delle Montagne Rocciose nella fascia orientale dell'America settentrionale, queste montagne sono incredibilmente ricche di foreste e attraversate da strade e sentieri come quelli del *Blue Ridge,* del *Parkway* e dello *Skyline Drive,* caratterizzate da paesaggi magnifici, o ancora da una pista da trekking (l'*Appalachian Trail*) lunga 2.050 miglia (3.299 km), che si estende dal Maine fino alla Georgia.

appall [ə·'pɔːl] *vt* sconvolgere; **to be** ~ **led at sth** essere sconvolto da qc

appalling *adj* **1.**(*shocking: behavior*) spaventoso, -a **2.**(*terrible: conditions*) terribile

apparatus [ˌæ·pə·'ræ·ṭəs] *n* **1.**(*equipment*) attrezzatura *f* **2.**(*organization*) apparato *m*

apparel [ə·'pe·rəl] *n* FASHION abbigliamento *m;* **sports** ~ abbigliamento sportivo

apparent [ə·'pe·rənt] *adj* **1.**(*clear*) evidente; **to become** ~ **that ...** diventare chiaro che ...; **it is** ~ **to me that ...** mi pare ovvio che ... +*subj* **2.**(*seeming*) apparente; **for no** ~ **reason** senza alcun motivo apparente

apparition [ˌæ·pə·'rɪ·ʃən] *n* apparizione *f*
appeal [ə·'piːl] I. *vi* 1. (*attract*) attirare; **the idea doesn't ~ to me** non mi attira l'idea 2. LAW ricorrere in appello 3. (*plead*) **to ~ to sb for sth** far appello a qn per ottenere qc; **to ~ for donations/help** fare richiesta di donazioni/aiuto; **she ~ed to his sense of honor** fece appello al suo senso dell'onore II. *n* 1. (*attraction*) fascino *m;* **to have ~** avere fascino *inf* 2. LAW appello *m;* **court of ~s** corte *f* d'appello; **to file an ~** (**against sth**) fare ricorso (contro qc) 3. (*request*) richiesta *f;* **an ~ to sb for sth** una richiesta di qc a qn; **to launch an ~ to do sth** lanciare un appello per fare qc 4. (*authority of: to reason, justice, sense of humanity*) appello *m*
appealing [ə·'piː·lɪŋ] *adj* 1. (*attractive: smile*) affascinante; (*idea*) attraente 2. (*beseeching: eyes*) supplichevole
appealingly *adv* 1. (*dress*) con stile 2. (*look*) in modo supplichevole; (*speak*) con tono supplichevole
appear [ə·'pɪr] *vi* 1. (*be seen*) apparire 2. (*newspaper*) uscire; (*book*) essere pubblicato; (*film*) apparire 3. LAW **to ~ in court/before a judge** presentarsi in tribunale/davanti a un giudice 4. (*seem*) **to ~ to be ...** sembrar essere ...; **it ~s to me that ...** mi sembra che ...; **it ~s so** così sembra; **it would ~ that ...** sembrerebbe che ...
appearance [ə·'pɪ·rəns] *n* 1. (*instance of appearing*) apparizione *f;* **to make an ~** apparire 2. LAW comparizione *f* 3. (*looks*) aspetto *m* 4. *pl* (*outward signs*) apparenze *fpl;* **from all ~s** dalle apparenze; **to keep up ~s** salvare le apparenze 5. (*performance*) comparsa *f;* **stage ~** comparsa in scena ▸**~s can be** deceptive *prov* l'apparenza inganna *prov*
appease [ə·'piːz] *vt form* 1. (*pacify*) rabbonire 2. (*relieve: hunger, suspicion, pain*) placare
appeasement *n* 1. (*conciliation*) pacificazione *f;* **policy of ~** POL politica *f* conciliatoria 2. (*relief: of anger*) acquietamento *m;* (*of pain*) sollievo *m*
appellant [ə·'pe·lənt] *n* appellante *mf*
appellation [ˌæ·pə·'leɪ·ʃən] *n* appellativo *m;* (*of wine*) denominazione *f* di origine
append [ə·'pend] *vt* (*document, note*) aggiungere; (*signature*) apporre
appendage [ə·'pen·dɪdʒ] *n* appendice *f*
appendicitis [ə·ˌpen·dɪ·'saɪ·tɪs] *n* MED appendicite *f*
appendix [ə·'pen·dɪks] *n* 1. <-es> ANAT appendice *f* 2. <-dices *o* -es> TYPO appendice *f*
appertain [ˌæ·pər·'teɪn] *vi* **to ~ to** (*person*) riferirsi a; (*matter*) essere pertinente a
appetite ['æ·pə·taɪt] *n* 1. (*for food*) appetito *m* 2. *fig* (*for gambling, adventure*) voglia *f*
appetite suppressant *n* inibitore *m* dell'appetito
appetizer ['æ·pə·taɪ·zə] *n* 1. (*first course*) antipasto *m* 2. (*snack*) salatino *m*
appetizing ['æ·pə·taɪ·zɪŋ] *adj* appetitoso, -a

applaud [ə·'plɑːd] I. *vi* applaudire II. *vt a. fig* approvare
applause [ə·'plɑːz] *n* applauso *m;* **a round of ~ for the singer** un applauso per il cantante; **loud ~** forte applauso
apple ['æ·pl] *n* mela *f* ▸**to be the ~ of sb's eye** stravedere per qn; **the Big Apple** *inf* la Grande Mela
applecart *n* **to upset the ~** rovinare i piani
apple juice *n* succo *m* di mela
apple pie *n* torta *f* di mele; **to be as American as ~** essere americano al 100%
apple polisher *n* leccapiedi *mf inv*
applesauce *n* salsa *f* di mele
apple tree *n* melo *m*
appliance [ə·'plaɪ·əns] *n* apparecchio *m;* **electrical ~** elettrodomestico *m*
applicability [ˌæ·plɪ·kə·'bɪ·lə·t̬i] *n* applicabilità *f*
applicable [ə·'plɪ·kə·bl] *adj* applicabile; **delete where not ~** cancellare le parti non pertinenti; **those rules are not ~ anymore** queste norme non sono più in vigore
applicant ['æ·plɪ·kənt] *n* 1. (*for job*) candidato, -a *m, f* 2. (*for money, support*) richiedente *mf*
application [ˌæ·plɪ·'keɪ·ʃən] *n* 1. (*form: for job, credit card, loan*) domanda *f* 2. (*coating*) applicazione *f* 3. (*use*) impiego *m;* INFOR ALSO applicazione *f* 4. (*perseverance*) applicazione *f* 5. (*request*) richiesta *f;* **on ~** su richiesta
application form *n* (modulo *m* di) domanda *f*
applicator *n* applicatore *m*
applied [ə·'plaɪd] *adj* applicato, -a
appliqué [ˌæ·plɪ·'keɪ] I. *vt* 1 FASHION applicazione *f*
apply [ə·'plaɪ] I. *vi* 1. (*request*) fare domanda; **to ~ to a college/a company** fare domanda ad un'università/una compagnia; **to ~ to sb for sth** rivolgersi a qn per qc; **to ~ for a job** fare domanda di lavoro; **to ~ in writing** fare domanda scritta 2. (*be relevant*) **to ~ to sb** riguardare qn II. *vt* 1. (*glue, paint*) applicare 2. (*use*) applicare; **to ~ force** usare la forza; **to ~ pressure to sth** esercitare una pressione su qc; **to ~ sanctions** applicare sanzioni; **to ~ common sense** usare il buonsenso 3. (*work hard*) **to ~ oneself to sth** dedicarsi a qc
appoint [ə·'pɔɪnt] *vt* 1. (*select*) nominare; **to ~ sb as heir** nominare qn erede 2. *form* (*designate*) **to ~ a date** fissare una data; **at the ~ed time** all'ora stabilita
appointee [ə·pɔɪn·'tiː] *n* persona *f* designata
appointment *n* 1. (*to office, position*) nomina *f* 2. (*meeting*) appuntamento *m;* **dentist's ~** appuntamento dal dentista; **to have an ~ at the hairdresser's** avere un appuntamento dal parrucchiere; **to keep an ~** non mancare ad un appuntamento; **by ~ only** solo su appuntamento
appointment book *n* agenda *f* per appuntamenti
apportion [ə·'pɔːr·ʃən] *vt* ripartire

apposite ['æ·pə·zɪt] *adj form* appropriato, -a; (*observation*) pertinente

apposition [ˌæ·pə·ˈzɪ·ʃən] *n* apposizione *f*

appraisal [ə·ˈpreɪ·zl] *n* **1.** (*evaluation*) valutazione *f* **2.** (*estimation*) stima *f*

appraise [ə·ˈpreɪz] *vt* **1.** (*evaluate*) valutare; **to ~ sb's needs** valutare i bisogni di qn **2.** (*estimate*) fare una stima di

appreciable [ə·ˈpriː·ʃə·bl] *adj* apprezzabile; (*change*) notevole; (*progress*) considerevole

appreciate [ə·ˈpriː·ʃi·eɪt] **I.** *vt* **1.** (*value*) apprezzare **2.** (*understand*) rendersi conto di **3.** (*be grateful for*) apprezzare **II.** *vi* FIN (*in price*) aumentare; (*in value: property, shares*) rivalutarsi

appreciation [ə·ˌpriː·ʃi·ˈeɪ·ʃən] *n* **1.** (*gratitude*) gratitudine *f* **2.** (*understanding*) comprensione *f*; **she has no ~ of my work** non apprezza il mio lavoro **3.** FIN (*in price*) aumento *m*; (*in value: of property, shares*) rivalutazione *f*

appreciative [ə·ˈpriː·ʃi·ə·tɪv] *adj* riconoscente; **an ~ audience** un pubblico entusiasta

apprehend [ˌæ·prɪ·ˈhend] *vt form* **1.** (*arrest*) arrestare **2.** (*comprehend*) comprendere; **to ~ the importance of doing sth** comprendere l'importanza di fare qc

apprehensible [æ·prə·ˈhen·sə·bl] *adj* comprensibile

apprehension [ˌæ·prɪ·ˈhen·ʃən] *n* **1.** (*of a criminal*) arresto *m* **2.** (*fear*) apprensione *f*; **~ about sth** apprensione per qc **3.** *form* (*comprehension*) comprensione *f*

apprehensive [ˌæ·prɪ·ˈhen·sɪv] *adj* apprensivo, -a; **to be ~ about sth** essere preoccupato per qc; **to be ~ that** temere che +*subj*

apprentice [ə·ˈpren·tɪs] *n* apprendista *mf*

apprenticeship [ə·ˈpren·tə·ʃɪp] *n* apprendistato *m*

approach [ə·ˈproʊtʃ] **I.** *vt* **1.** (*get close to*) avvicinarsi a **2.** (*ask*) rivolgersi a; **to ~ sb** (**about sth**) rivolgersi a qn (per qc) **3.** (*deal with*) affrontare **II.** *vi* avvicinarsi **III.** *n* **1.** (*coming*) l'avvicinarsi *m*; **at the ~ of winter** all'avvicinarsi dell'inverno **2.** (*access: to highway, bridge*) accesso *m* **3.** (*proposition*) proposta *f*; (*for help*) richiesta *f*; **to make ~es to sb** contattare qn **4.** (*methodology*) approccio *m*

approachable [ə·ˈproʊ·tʃə·bl] *adj* (*person, place*) accessibile

appropriate¹ [ə·ˈproʊ·pri·ət] *adj* appropriato, -a; **~ to the occasion** adatto all'occasione

appropriate² [ə·ˈproʊ·pri·eɪt] *vt form* **1.** (*take*) appropriarsi di **2.** FIN assegnare; **to ~ funds (for sth)** destinare fondi (a qn)

appropriation [ə·ˌproʊ·pri·ˈeɪ·ʃən] *n* **1.** (*taking*) appropriazione *f* **2.** FIN assegnazione *f*

approval [ə·ˈpruː·vl] *n* approvazione *f*; **to meet with sb's ~** ottenere l'approvazione di qn; **to nod one's ~** assentire con un cenno del capo; **on ~** ECON in prova

approve [ə·ˈpruːv] **I.** *vi* essere d'accordo; **to ~ of sth** approvare qc; **she doesn't ~ of smoking** disapprova che si fumi **II.** *vt* approvare

approved *adj* **1.** (*agreed*) approvato, -a **2.** (*authorized*) autorizzato, -a; **an ~ qualification** un titolo riconosciuto

approving [ə·ˈpruː·vɪŋ] *adj* d'approvazione

approvingly [ə·ˈpruː·vɪŋ·li] *adv* con approvazione; **to smile ~** sorridere in segno d'approvazione

approx. [ə·ˈprɑːks] *n abbr of* **approximately** approssimativamente

approximate¹ [ə·ˈprɑːk·sɪ·mət] *adj* approssimativo, -a

approximate² [ə·ˈprɑːk·sɪ·meɪt] **I.** *vt* avvicinarsi a **II.** *vi form* **to ~ to sth** avvicinarsi a qc

approximately *adv* approssimativamente

approximation [ə·ˌprɑːk·sɪ·ˈmeɪ·ʃən] *n* approssimazione *f*

APR [ˌeɪ·pi·ˈɑːr] *n abbr of* **annual percentage rate** *tasso di interesse annuo*

Apr. *n abbr of* **April** apr.

apricot ['eɪ·prɪ·kɑːt] **I.** *n* **1.** (*fruit*) albicocca *f* **2.** (*tree*) albicocco *m* **3.** (*color*) (color *m*) albicocca *m inv* **II.** *adj* (di color) albicocca *inv*

April ['eɪ·prəl] *n* aprile *m*; **in ~** in aprile; **every ~** ogni mese di aprile; **the month of ~** il mese di aprile; **at the beginning/end of ~** all'inizio/alla fine di aprile; **on ~ (the) fourth** il quattro aprile

April Fools' Day *n* il primo d'aprile, *giorno del pesce d'aprile*

a priori [ˌeɪ·priː·ˈɔː·ri] *adv* a priori

apron ['eɪ·prən] *n* **1.** (*clothing*) grembiule *m* **2.** AVIAT area *f* di stazionamento **3.** THEAT proscenio *m*

apron strings *n pl* lacci *m pl* del grembiule ▶ **to be tied to one's mother's ~** essere attaccato alle sottane della madre

apropos, a propos [ˌæ·prə·ˈpoʊ] **I.** *prep* a proposito di **II.** *adv* a proposito **III.** *adj* appropriato, -a

apse [æps] *n* ARCHIT abside *f*

apt [æpt] *adj* **1.** (*appropriate*) appropriato, -a; (*comment*) opportuno, -a; (*description*) indovinato, -a **2.** (*clever*) capace **3.** (*likely*) **to be ~ to do sth** avere la tendenza a fare qc

apt. *n abbr of* **apartment** app.to

aptitude ['æp·tɪ·tuːd] *n* attitudine *f*

aquacize ['æk·wə·saɪz] *n* acquagym *f inv*

aquaculture ['ɑːk·wə·ˌkʌl·tʃər] *n* acquacoltura *f*

Aqua-Lung® ['æk·wə·lʌŋ] autorespiratore *m*

aquamarine [ˌɑːk·wə·mə·ˈriːn] **I.** *n* **1.** (*stone*) acquamarina *f* **2.** (*color*) (color *m*) acquamarina *f inv* **II.** *adj* (di color) acquamarina *inv*

aquaplaning [ˌɑːk·wə·ˈpleɪ·nɪŋ] *n* **1.** SPORTS acquaplano *m* **2.** AUTO aquaplaning *m inv*

Aquarian [ə·ˈkwe·ri·ən] *n* Acquario *m*

aquarium [ə·ˈkwe·ri·əm] <-s *o* -ria> *n* acquario *m*

Aquarius [ə·ˈkwe·ri·əs] *n* Acquario *m*

aquatic [ə·ˈkwæ·tɪk] *adj* acquatico, -a

aquatics *npl* SPORTS sport *m pl* acquatici

aqueduct ['æ·kwɪ·dʌkt] *n* acquedotto *m*

A

aquifer ['æ·kwɪ·fə̆] *n* falda *f* acquifera
aquiline ['æ·kwɪ·lən] *adj* aquilino, -a; ~ **nose** naso aquilino
Arab ['æ·rəb] I. *adj* arabo, -a; **the (United)** ~ **Emirates** gli Emirati Arabi (Uniti) II. *n* arabo, -a *m, f*
arabesque [ˌæ·rə·'besk] *n* arabesco *m*
Arabia [ə·'reɪ·biə] *n* Arabia *f*
Arabian *adj* arabo, -a
Arabic ['æ·rə·bɪk] *n* LING arabo *m*
arable ['æ·rə·bl] *adj* coltivabile
arachnid [ə·'ræk·nɪd] *n* aracnide *m*
arbiter ['ɑːr·bɪ·ţə̆] *n* arbitro *m*
arbitrage [ˌɑːr·bɪ·tra·ʒ] *n* FIN arbitraggio *m*
arbitrariness ['ɑːr·bɪ·tre·rɪ·nɪs] *n* arbitrarietà *f*
arbitrary ['ɑːr·bə·tre·ri] *adj* arbitrario, -a
arbitrate ['ɑːr·bə·treɪt] I. *vt* arbitrare; **to** ~ **an argument** fare da arbitro in una discussione II. *vi* arbitrare
arbitration [ˌɑːr·bə·'treɪ·ʃən] *n* arbitrato *m; to go to* ~ andare in arbitrato
arbitrator ['ɑːr·bə·treɪ·ţə̆] *n* arbitro *m*
arbor ['ɑːr·bə̆] *n* pergolato *m*

ℹ️ Negli USA è costume piantare degli alberi in occasione dell'**Arbor Day**. Questa tradizione, volta ad incrementare il numero degli alberi, proviene dal Nebraska, dove è stata celebrata per la prima volta nel 1872. Lo scopo è quello di rendere omaggio all'albero per il ruolo primordiale che riveste nella natura. Questo giorno è festivo in alcuni stati. La data esatta dell'**Arbor Day** cambia da uno stato all'altro in funzione del periodo più adatto a piantare degli alberi, che varia secondo la posizione geografica.

---

arboriculture ['ɑːr·bə̆·ɪ·ˌkʌl·tʃə̆] *n* arboricoltura *f*
arc [ɑːrk] I. *n* arco *m* II. *vi* formare un arco
arcade [ɑːr·'keɪd] *n* **1.** (*of shops*) centro *m* commerciale **2.** (*around square*) portici *mpl* **3.** (*with games*) sala *f* giochi
arcane [ær·'keɪn] *adj* arcano, -a
arch[1] [ɑːrtʃ] I. *n* arco *m* II. *vi* inarcarsi III. *vt* inarcare; **to** ~ **one's eyebrows** inarcare le sopracciglia
arch[2] [ɑːrtʃ] <-er, -est> *adj* malizioso, -a
archaeology [ˌɑːr·ki·'ɑː·lə·dʒi] *n* archeologia *f*
archaic [ɑːr·'keɪ·ɪk] *adj* arcaico, -a
archangel ['ɑːrk·eɪn·dʒl] *n* arcangelo *m*
archbishop [ˌɑːrtʃ·'bɪ·ʃəp] *n* arcivescovo *m*
archdeacon [ˌɑːrtʃ·'diː·kən] *n* arcidiacono *m*
archdiocese [ˌɑːrtʃ·'da·ɪə·sɪs] *n* arcidiocesi *f inv*
archenemy <-ies> *n* acerrimo, -a nemico, -a *m, f*
archeological [ˌɑːr·ki·ə·'lɑː·dʒɪ·kəl] *adj* archeologico, -a
archeologist [ˌɑːr·ki·'ɑː·lə·dʒɪst] *n* archeologo, -a *m, f*

archeology [ˌɑːr·ki·'ɑː·lə·dʒi] *n s.* archaeology
archer ['ɑːr·tʃə̆] *n* arciere *m*
archery ['ɑːr·tʃə·ri] *n* tiro *m* con l'arco
archetype ['ɑːr·kɪ·taɪp] *n* archetipo *m*
archipelago [ˌɑːr·kə·'pe·lə·goʊ] <-(e)s> *n* arcipelago *m*
architect ['ɑːr·kə·tekt] *n* **1.** (*of building*) architetto *m* **2.** *fig* artefice *mf*
architecture ['ɑːr·kə·tek·tʃə̆] *n* architettura *f*
archive ['ɑːr·kaɪv] *n a.* INFOR archivio *m*
archivist ['ɑːr·kə·vɪst] *n* archivista *mf*
archway ['ɑːrtʃ·weɪ] *n* arco *m*
arc lamp *n*, **arc light** *n* lampada *f* ad arco
Arctic ['ɑːrk·tɪk] I. *n* the ~ l'Artico *m* II. *adj* artico, -a
arctic *adj* (*extremely cold*) polare
Arctic Circle *n* Circolo *m* Polare Artico
Arctic Ocean *n* Mare *m* Glaciale Artico
arc welding *n* saldatura *f* ad arco
ardent ['ɑːr·dnt] *adj* fervente; (*desire, plea*) ardente
ardor ['ɑːr·də̆] *n* ardore *m*
arduous ['ɑːr·dʒu·əs] *adj* arduo, -a
are [ə̆, *stressed:* ɑːr] *vi s.* be
area ['e·ɪ·ə] *n* **1.** *a.* MAT, SPORTS area *f; in the* ~ *of* intorno a **2.** (*field*) campo *m;* ~ *of competence/knowledge* ambito *m* di competenza/conoscenza
area code *n* prefisso *m*
area rug *n* tappeto *m*
arena [ə·'riː·nə] *n a. fig* arena *f*
aren't [ɑːrnt] = **are not**
Argentina [ˌɑːr·dʒən·'tiː·nə] *n* Argentina *f*
Argentine ['ɑːr·dʒən·taɪn], **Argentinean** [ˌɑːr·dʒən·'tɪ·ni·ən] I. *adj* argentino, -a II. *n* argentino, -a *m, f*
argon ['ɑːr·gɑːn] *n* argo *m*
arguable ['ɑːr·gju·ə·bl] *adj* discutibile
arguably *adv* probabilmente
argue ['ɑːr·gjuː] I. *vi* **1.** (*disagree*) litigare **2.** (*reason*) argomentare; **to** ~ **for/against sth** portare argomenti a favore di/contro qc II. *vt* **1.** (*debate*) sostenere; **to** ~ **that ...** sostenere che ... **2.** (*persuade*) **to** ~ **sb into doing sth** persuadere qn a fare qc; **to** ~ **sb out of doing sth** dissuadere qn dal fare qc
argument ['ɑːr·gjə·mənt] *n* **1.** (*disagreement*) discussione *f* **2.** (*reasoning*) ragionamento *m; for the sake of* ~, *suppose that ...* tanto per discutere, supponiamo che ... **3.** LAW argomentazioni *fpl* **4.** MAT argomento *m*
argumentative [ˌɑːr·gjə·'men·tə·ţɪv] *adj* polemico, -a
argyle ['ɑːr·gaɪl] *n* motivo *m* a rombi
aria ['ɑː·ri·ə] *n* MUS aria *f*
Arian ['e·ri·ən] *n* Ariete *m*
arid ['æ·rɪd] *adj* arido, -a
Aries ['e·riːz] *n* Ariete *m*
arise [ə·'raɪz] <arose, arisen> *vi* **1.** (*come about*) sorgere; **to** ~ **from** derivare da; **should the need** ~ se fosse necessario; **should doubt** ~ dovesse sorgere il dubbio **2.** *form* (*rise*

up) alzarsi

arisen [ə·'rɪ·zn] *pp of* **arise**

aristocracy [ˌæ·rɪs·'tɑː·krə·si] <-ies> *n* + *sing/pl vb* aristocrazia *f*

aristocrat [ə·'rɪs·tə·kræt] *n* aristocratico, -a *m, f*

aristocratic [e·ˌrɪs·tə·'kræ·t̬ɪk] *adj* aristocratico, -a

arithmetic [ə·'rɪθ·mɪ·tɪk] I. *n* aritmetica *f* II. *adj* aritmetico, -a

arithmetical [ˌæ·rɪθ·'me·t̬ɪ·kl] *adj* aritmetico, -a

Ariz. [æ·rɪ·zoʊ·nə] *n abbr of* **Arizona** Arizona

Arizona [æ·rɪ·zoʊ·nə] *n* Arizona *f*

ark [ɑːrk] *n* arca *f;* **Noah's ~** l'arca di Noè

Arkansas ['ɑːr·kən·sɑː] *n s.* **Arkansas** Arkansas *m*

arm[1] [ɑːrm] *n* **1.** ANAT, GEO braccio *m;* **to put one's ~s around sb** abbracciare qn; **to hold sb in one's ~s** tenere qn tra le braccia; **~ in ~** sottobraccio **2.** (*sleeve*) manica *f* **3.** (*division*) ramo *m* ▶ **to welcome sth with open ~s** accogliere qc con entusiasmo; **the** (**long**) **~ of the law** il braccio della legge; **to cost an ~ and a leg** *inf* costare un occhio della testa; **to keep sb at ~'s length** *fig* tenere qn a distanza

arm[2] [ɑːrm] MIL I. *vt* **1.** (*supply with weapons*) armare; **to ~ oneself against sth** armarsi contro qc **2.** (*prepare for detonation*) armare II. *n* (*weapon*) arma *f;* **under ~s** in armi; **to bear ~s** portare armi; **to lay down one's ~s** deporre le armi; **to take up ~s** (**against sb/ sth**) insorgere (contro qn/qc) ▶ **to be up in ~s about ...** essere sul piede di guerra per ...

armadillo [ɑːrˌmə·'dɪ·loʊ] *n* armadillo *m*

armaments ['ɑːr·mə·mənts] *npl* armamenti *mpl*

armature ['ɑːr·mə·tʃə] *n* **1.** TECH, ZOOL, BOT armatura *f* **2.** ELEC indotto *m*

armband ['ɑːrm·bænd] *n* bracciale *m*

armchair ['ɑːrm·tʃer] *n* poltrona *f*

armed [ɑːrmd] *adj* armato, -a

armed forces *npl* the ~ le forze armate

Armenia [ɑːr·'miː·niə] *n* Armenia *f*

Armenian I. *n* **1.** (*person*) armeno, -a *m, f* **2.** LING armeno *m* II. *adj* armeno, -a

armful ['ɑːrm·fʊl] *n* bracciata *f*

armhole ['ɑːrm·hoʊl] *n* giromanica *m*

arming ['ɑːr·mɪŋ] *n* approvvigionamento *m* d'armi

armistice ['ɑːr·məs·tɪs] *n* armistizio *m*

armload *n* bracciata *f*

armor ['ɑːr·mə] *n* **1.** (*protective covering*) armatura *f* **2.** *a.* MIL, ZOOL corazza *f* **3.** (*tanks*) mezzi *m pl* blindati

armored *adj* blindato, -a

armor-plated *adj* blindato, -a

armpit ['ɑːrm·pɪt] *n* ascella *f*

armrest ['ɑːrm·rest] *n* bracciolo *m*

arms control *n*, **arms limitation** *n* MIL controllo *m* degli armamenti

arms race *n* the ~ la corsa agli armamenti

arms reduction *n* riduzione *f* degli armamenti

arm wrestling *n* braccio *m* di ferro

army ['ɑːr·mi] <-ies> *n* **1.** MIL esercito *m;* **to join the ~** arruolarsi **2.** *fig* esercito *m*

army brat *n inf* figlio, -a *m, f* di militare

aroma [ə·'roʊ·mə] *n* aroma *m*

aromatherapy [əˌroʊ·mə·'θe·rə·pi] *n* aromaterapia *f*

aromatic [ˌæ·rə·'mæ·t̬ɪk] *adj* aromatico, -a

arose [ə·'roʊz] *pt of* **arise**

around [ə·'raʊnd] I. *prep* **1.** (*surrounding*) intorno a; **all ~ sth** tutto intorno a qc; **the earth goes ~ the sun** la terra gira intorno al sole; **to go ~ the corner** girare l'angolo **2.** (*move within sth*) per; **to drive ~ France** girare in macchina per la Francia; **to go ~ a museum** girare per un museo; **to sit ~ the room** sedersi in modo sparso in una stanza **3.** (*approximately*) intorno a; **~ May 10th** intorno al 10 maggio; **somewhere ~ here** qui vicino II. *adv* **1.** (*all over*) tutto intorno; **all ~** dappertutto; **for 50 miles ~** per un raggio di 50 miglia; **for miles ~** nel raggio di miglia; **to be the other way ~** essere esattamente al contrario **2.** (*aimlessly*) **to walk ~** andare in giro; **to stand/hang ~** starsene/andare in giro; **to have been ~** conoscere il mondo; (*be experienced*) avere una grande esperienza **3.** (*nearby*) nelle vicinanze; **is Mark ~?** c'è Mark?; **to be still ~** essere ancora in circolazione

arouse [ə·'raʊz] *vt* **1.** (*stir*) suscitare; (*anger*) provocare **2.** (*sexually excite*) eccitare

arraign [ə·'reɪn] *vt* LAW chiamare in giudizio

arrange [ə·'reɪndʒ] I. *vt* **1.** (*organize*) organizzare; **to ~ a date** fissare una data **2.** (*put in order*) sistemare; MUS arrangiare II. *vi* dare disposizioni; **to ~ for sth** dare disposizioni per qc; **to ~ to do sth** prendere accordi per fare qc

arrangement *n* **1.** *pl* (*preparations*) preparativi *mpl;* **to make ~s** (**for sth**) fare i preparativi (di qc) **2.** (*agreement*) accordo *m;* **to have an ~ with sb** essere d'accordo con qn **3.** (*method of organizing sth*) sistemazione *f;* MUS arrangiamento *m*

array [ə·'reɪ] I. *n* **1.** (*display*) assortimento *m* **2.** *form* (*clothes*) abbigliamento *m* elegante **3.** MIL schieramento *m* II. *vt* **1.** (*display*) disporre **2.** *form* (*dress finely*) abbigliare in modo elegante **3.** MIL spiegare

arrears [ə·'rɪrz] *npl* FIN arretrati *mpl;* **to be in ~ on sth** essere in arretrato con qc; **to pay in ~** pagare posticipatamente

arrest [ə·'rest] I. *vt* **1.** LAW arrestare **2.** *form* (*put a stop to*) fermare, arrestare **3.** (*attract*) **to ~ sb's attention** catturare l'attenzione di qn II. *n* arresto *m;* **to be under ~** essere in (stato di) arresto; **to put sb under ~** mettere qn agli arresti

arresting *adj* che colpisce; (*account*) accattivante; (*performance*) impressionante

arrival [ə·'raɪ·vl] *n* **1.** (*at destination*) arrivo *m;* **on his ~** al suo arrivo **2.** (*person*) arrivato, -a *m, f;* **new ~** nuovo arrivo

A

arrive [ə·'raɪv] *vi* **1.** (*come*) arrivare; **to ~ at a conclusion** giungere a una conclusione **2.** *inf* (*establish one's reputation*) arrivare **3.** (*be born*) nascere

arriviste [ˌæ·riː·'viːst] *n* arrivista *mf*

arrogance ['æ·rə·gəns] *n* arroganza *f*

arrogant ['æ·rə·gənt] *adj* arrogante

arrow ['æ·roʊ] *n* freccia *f*

arrowhead *n* punta *f* di freccia

arrowroot *n fecola ricavata dalla radice di una pianta tropicale americana utilizzata in cucina per addensare le salse*

arsenal ['ɑːr·sə·nl] *n* arsenale *m*

arsenic ['ɑːrs·nɪk] *n* arsenico *m*

arson ['ɑːr·sn] *n* incendio *m* doloso

art [ɑːrt] *n* arte *f*

art collection *n* collezione *f* d'arte

art critic *n* critico *m* d'arte

art dealer *n* mercante *m* d'arte

arterial [ɑːr·'tɪ·ri·əl] *adj* **1.** ANAT arterioso, -a **2.** AUTO, RAIL principale

arteriosclerosis [ɑːrˌtɪ·ri·oʊs·klə·'roʊ·səs] *n* MED arteriosclerosi *f*

artery ['ɑːr·tə·i] <-ies> *n* arteria *f*

artesian well [ɑːr·'tiː·ʒən·'wel] *n* pozzo *m* artesiano

artful ['ɑːrt·fəl] *adj* abile

art gallery *n* galleria *f* d'arte

arthritic [ɑːr·'θrɪ·t̬ɪk] *adj* artritico, -a

arthritis [ɑːr·'θraɪ·t̬əs] *n* MED artrite *f*

artichoke ['ɑːr·tə·tʃoʊk] *n* FOOD carciofo *m*

article ['ɑːr·tɪ·kl] *n* **1.** (*object*) articolo *m;* **~ of clothing** articolo di vestiario **2.** *a.* LAW, LING, TYPO articolo *m*

articulate¹ [ɑːr·'tɪk·jə·lət] *adj* **1.** (*person*) che si esprime con chiarezza; (*speech*) chiaro, -a **2.** TECH, ANAT articolato, -a

articulate² [ɑːr·'tɪk·jə·leɪt] *vt form* **1.** (*express*) esprimere chiaramente; **to ~ an idea** esprimere chiaramente un'idea **2.** (*pronounce*) pronunciare distintamente

tractor trailer *n* autoarticolato *m*

articulation [ɑːrˌtɪk·jə·'leɪ·ʃən] *n* (*pronunciation*) pronuncia *f;* (*of idea, feeling*) espressione *f*

artifact ['ɑːr·tə·fækt] *n* manufatto *m*

artifice ['ɑːr·tə·fɪs] *n form* artificio *m*

artificial [ˌɑːr·tə·'fɪ·ʃl] *adj* artificiale

artificial insemination *n* inseminazione *f* artificiale

artificial intelligence *n* intelligenza *f* artificiale

artificial respiration *n* respirazione *f* artificiale

artillery [ɑːr·'tɪ·lə·ri] *n* artiglieria *f*

artilleryman [ɑːr·'tɪl·ri·men] *n* artigliere *m*

artisan ['ɑːr·tɪ·zən] *n* artigiano, -a *m, f*

artist ['ɑːr·təst] *n* artista *m*

artiste [ɑːr·'tiːst] *n* THEAT artista *mf*

artistic [ɑːr·'tɪs·tɪk] *adj* artistico, -a

artistry ['ɑːr·təs·tri] *n* arte *f*

artless ['ɑːrt·lɪs] *adj* **1.** (*natural*) semplice **2.** (*clumsy*) goffo, -a

arts and crafts *n a.* SCHOOL attività *f pl* creative

manuali

artsy ['ɑːrt·si] *n inf: persona con tendenze artistiche*

artwork ['ɑːrt·wɜːrk] *n* materiale *m* illustrativo

arty ['ɑːr·t̬i] <-ier, -iest> *adj inf* (*person*) con pretese artistiche; (*film*) pretenzioso, -a

as [əz, *stressed:* æz] **I.** *prep* da; **dressed ~ a clown** vestito da clown; **the king, ~ such** il re come tale; **~ a baby, I was ...** da bambino io ero ...; **to use sth ~ a lever** utilizzare qc come leva **II.** *conj* **1.** (*in comparison*) come; **the same name ~ sth/sb** lo stesso nome di qc/qn; **~ fast ~ sth/sb** (così) rapido come qc/qn; **to eat ~ much ~ sb** mangiare (tanto) quanto qn; **~ soon ~ possible** il più presto possibile **2.** (*like*) (così) come; **~ it is** così com'è; **I came ~ promised** son venuto, come promesso; **she was dressed just ~ he was** era vestita esattamente come lui; **~ if it were true** come se fosse vero **3.** (*because*) poiché; **~ he is here,** I'm going visto che c'è lui, io vado **4.** (*while*) mentre **5.** (*although*) **~ nice ~ the day is, ...** per quanto sia una bella giornata ...; **try ~ I might, I couldn't** malgrado tutti gli sforzi, non ho potuto ▶ **~ far ~** (*to the extent that*) fino a; (*concerning*) quanto a; **~ for her/him/me/them ...** quanto a lei/lui/me/loro ... **III.** *adv* **~ well** anche; **~ long as** purché +*subj;* **~ much as** tanto quanto; **~ soon as** non appena

ASAP [ˌeɪ·es·eɪ·'piː] *abbr of* **as soon as possible** il più presto possibile

asbestos [æz·'bes·təs] *n* asbesto *m*

asbestosis [ˌæs·bes·'toʊ·sɪs] *n* asbestosi *f inv*

ascend [ə·'send] **I.** *vt form* (*steps*) salire; (*mountain*) scalare; **to ~ the throne** salire [*o* ascendere] al trono **II.** *vi* salire; **in ~ing order** in ordine crescente

ascendancy [ə·'sen·dən·tsi] *n* ascendente *m*

ascendant [ə·'sen·dənt] **I.** *n form* **1.** (*position of power*) **to be in the ~** essere in auge **2.** ASTR ascendente *m* **II.** *adj* in auge

ascendency [ə·'sen·dən·tsi] *n s.* **ascendancy**

ascendent [ə·'sen·dənt] *n, adj s.* **in auge**

ascension [ə·'sen·ʃən] *n* **1.** (*going up*) ascensione *f* **2.** REL **the Ascension** l'Ascensione *f*

Ascension Day *n* il giorno dell'Ascensione

ascent [ə·'sent] *n* **1.** *form* (*climb*) ascesa *f* **2.** (*slope*) salita *f*

ascertain [ˌæ·sə·'teɪn] *vt* **1.** (*find out*) verificare **2.** (*make sure*) accertare

ascetic [ə·'se·t̬ɪk] **I.** *n* asceta *mf* **II.** *adj* ascetico, -a

asceticism [ə·'se·t̬ə·sɪ·zəm] *n* ascetismo *m*

ASCII ['æs·kiː] *abbr of* **American Standard Code for Information Interchange** ASCII *m*

ascot ['æs·kət] *n* FASHION *larga sciarpa annodata sul davanti in modo che i lembi combacino*

ascribe [ə·'skraɪb] *vt* **to ~ sth to sb** attribuire qc a qn

ascription [ə·'skrɪp·ʃən] *n* attribuzione *f*

ASE *n abbr of* **American Stock Exchange**

borsa valori statunitense

asexual [ˌeɪˈsekˈʃuˈəl] *adj* **1.**(*reproduction*) asessuale **2.**(*person*) asessuato, -a

ash[1] [æʃ] *n* (*from fire*) cenere *f*

ash[2] [æʃ] *n* **1.** BOT (*tree*) frassino *m* **2.**(*wood*) (legno *m* di) frassino *m*

ashamed [əˈʃeɪmd] *adj* **to feel** ~ vergognarsi; **to be** ~ **of oneself** vergognarsi di se stesso

ashore [əˈʃɔːr] I. *adj* a terra II. *adv* a riva; **to go** ~ sbarcare; **to run** ~ arenarsi

ashtray [ˈæʃˌtreɪ] *n* posacenere *m inv*

Ash Wednesday *n* mercoledì *m inv* delle ceneri

Asia [ˈeɪʒə] *n* Asia *f*

Asia Minor *n* Asia *f* Minore

Asian [ˈeɪʒən] I. *n* asiatico, -a *m, f* II. *adj* asiatico, -a

Asian American *n* cittadino americano di origine asiatica

Asiatic [ˌeɪʒiˈæˌtɪk] I. *adj* asiatico, -a II. *n pej* asiatico, -a *m, f*

aside [əˈsaɪd] I. *n* **1.**(*in a speech*) digressione *f*; (*in a conversation*) commento *m* a parte **2.** THEAT a parte *m inv* II. *adv* da parte; **to stand** [*o* step] ~ farsi da parte; **to leave sth** ~ lasciar qc da parte

aside from *prep* a parte

ask [æsk] I. *vt* **1.**(*request information*) chiedere, domandare; **to** ~ **sb sth** chiedere qc a qn; **to** ~ (**sb**) **a question about sth** fare (a qn) una domanda su qc; **don't** ~ **me** non chiederlo a me; **if you** ~ **me** ... secondo me ... **2.**(*request*) chiedere; **to** ~ **sb's advice/a favor** chiedere consiglio a qn/un favore **3.**(*invite*) invitare; **to** ~ **sb to do sth** invitare qn a fare qc **4.**(*demand a price*) chiedere; **to** ~ **100 dollars for sth** chiedere 100 dollari per qc **5.**(*expect*) **to** ~ **too much of sb** pretendere troppo da qn II. *vi* **1.**(*request information*) chiedere **2.**(*make a request*) chiedere

◆**ask for** *vt* **1.**(*request*) chiedere **2.**(*inquire about*) chiedere di **3.**(*deserve*) **to** ~ **trouble** andarsela a cercare

askance [əsˈkæns] *adv* di traverso; **to look** ~ (**at sb/sth**) guardare storto (qn/qc)

askew [əˈskjuː] *adj* sbilenco, -a

asking [ˈæsˈkɪŋ] *n* **it's yours for the** ~ è tuo se lo vuoi

asking price *n* prezzo *m* richiesto

asleep [əˈsliːp] *adj* addormentato, -a; **to be** ~ dormire; **to fall** ~ addormentarsi

asocial [eɪˈsouˈʃəl] *adj* (*not sociable*) asociale; (*antisocial*) antisociale

asparagus [əˈspeˈrəˈgəs] *n* **1.** FOOD (*vegetable*) asparagi *mpl* **2.**(*plant*) asparago *m*

aspartame [ˈæsˈpərˈteɪm] *n* aspartame *m*

ASPCA [ˌeɪˈesˌpiːˈsiːˈeɪ] *n abbr of* **American Society for Prevention of Cruelty to Animals** ≈ ENPA

aspect [ˈæsˈpekt] *n* **1.**(*point of view*) punto *m* di vista **2.**(*feature*) aspetto *m* **3.**(*direction*) esposizione *f* **4.**(*appearance*) aspetto *m*

5. ASTR aspetto *m* **6.** LING aspetto *m*

aspen [ˈæsˈpən] *n* BOT pioppo *m* tremulo

aspersion [əsˈpɜːrˈʒən] *n form* calunnia *f*; **to cast** ~ **s on sb** calunniare qn

asphalt [ˈæsˈfaːlt] I. *n* asfalto *m* II. *vt* asfaltare

asphalt jungle *n* giungla *f* d'asfalto

asphyxia [æsˈfɪkˈsiə] *n* asfissia *f*

asphyxiate [əsˈfɪkˈsiˈeɪt] I. *vi form* asfissiare II. *vt* asfissiare

asphyxiation [əsˌfɪkˈsɪˈeɪˈʃən] *n* asfissia *f*

aspic [ˈæsˈpɪk] *n* aspic *m inv*

aspirant [ˈæsˈpəˈrənt] *n form* aspirante *mf*

aspiration [ˌæsˈpəˈreɪˈʃən] *n* aspirazione *f*

aspire [əˈspaɪˈə] *vi* **to** ~ **to sth** aspirare a qc

aspirin [ˈæsˈprɪn] *n* aspirina *f*

aspiring [əˈspaˈɪəˈɪŋ] *adj* aspirante

ass [æs] <-es> *n* **1.** *vulg* (*bottom*) culo *m* **2.**(*donkey*) asino *m* **3.** *inf* (*idiot*) stupido, -a *m, f*; **to make an** ~ **of oneself** rendersi ridicolo ▶**get your** ~ **in gear!** alza le chiappe!; **move your** ~! datti una mossa!; **to work one's** ~ **off** farsi un culo così

assail [əˈseɪl] *vt* **1.**(*attack*) assalire **2.**(*torment*) assalire

assailant *n* assalitore, -trice *m, f*

assassin [əˈsæˈsən] *n* assassino, -a *m, f*; **paid** ~ sicario *m*

assassinate [əˈsæˈsɪˈneɪt] *vt* assassinare

assassination [əˌsæˈsɪˈneɪˈʃən] *n* assassinio *m*

assault [əˈsɔːlt] I. *n* (*attack*) aggressione *f*; **to make an** ~ **on sth/sb** aggredire qc/qn II. *vt* assalire

assault and battery *n* aggressione *f* e lesioni *f pl*

assault course *n* percorso *m* di guerra

assemble [əˈsemˈbl] I. *vi* radunarsi II. *vt* **1.**(*collect: people, things*) radunare **2.**(*put together*) assemblare

assembly [əˈsemˈbli] <-ies> *n* **1.**(*meeting*) assemblea *f* **2.** TECH assemblaggio *m*; "~ **required**" (*on toy package*) "da assemblare"

assembly line *n* catena *f* di montaggio

assent [əˈsent] I. *n form* assenso *m* II. *vi* **to** ~ **to sth** acconsentire a qc

assert [əˈsɜːrt] *vt* asserire; **to** ~ **oneself** farsi valere

assertion [əˈsɜːrˈʃən] *n* asserzione *f*

assertive [əˈsɜːrˈtɪv] *adj* che sa farsi valere

assertiveness *n* capacità *f* di farsi valere

assess [əˈses] *vt* **1.**(*evaluate*) valutare **2.**(*tax*) calcolare

assessment *n* **1.**(*calculation*) calcolo *m* **2.**(*evaluation*) valutazione *f* **3.**(*taxation*) calcolo *m* del valore imponibile

assessor [əˈseˈsə] *n* **1.**(*tax evaluator*) ispettore, -trice fiscale *m* **2.**(*legal advisor*) consulente *mf* legale; **legal** ~ perito *m* legale **3.**(*evaluator*) valutatore, -trice *m, f*

asset [ˈæsˈset] *n* **1.**(*benefit*) vantaggio *m*; (*person*) elemento *m* valido; **he is an** ~ **to the team** è un punto di forza per la squadra **2.** *pl*

FIN attivo *m;* **liquid ~s** attività *f pl* liquide
assiduous [ə·'sɪ·dʒu·əs] *adj* **1.** (*hardworking*) diligente **2.** (*keen*) assiduo, -a
assign [ə·'saɪn] *vt* **1.** (*task, resources*) assegnare; **to ~ sb to a position** destinare qn a una carica; **to ~ sb to do sth** incaricare qn di fare qc; **to ~ the blame for sth to sb** attribuire la colpa di qc a qn **2.** LAW cedere
assignment *n* **1.** (*task*) incarico *m;* **foreign ~** incarico all'estero; **diplomatic ~** missione *f* diplomatica; **to send sb on an ~** mandare qn in missione; **an ~ to do sth** un incarico di fare qc **2.** (*attribution*) assegnazione *f*
assimilate [ə·'sɪ·mə·leɪt] **I.** *vt* assimilare **II.** *vi* assimilarsi
assimilation [ə·ˌsɪ·mə·'leɪ·ʃən] *n* assimilazione *f*
assist [ə·'sɪst] **I.** *vt* aiutare; **to ~ sb with sth** aiutare qn in qc **II.** *vi* aiutare; **to ~ with sth** aiutare in qc
assistance [ə·'sɪs·təns] *n* aiuto *m;* **to be of ~** esser d'aiuto; **can I be of any ~?** posso aiutarla?
assistant [ə·'sɪs·tənt] *n* **1.** (*helper*) aiutante *mf* **2.** INFOR assistente *m*
assistant manager *n* vicedirettore, -trice *m, f*
assn. *n abbr of* **association** ass.ne
associate¹ [ə·'soʊ·ʃi·ɪt] **I.** *n* persona *f* vicina; **business ~** socio, -a in affari *m* **II.** *adj* UNIV associato, -a
associate² [ə·'soʊ·ʃi·eɪt] **I.** *vt* associare; **to ~ oneself with sth** avere a che fare con qc **II.** *vi* associarsi
associate professor *n* professore *m* associato
associate's degree *n* UNIV *diploma universitario rilasciato al termine di un corso biennale*
association [ə·ˌsoʊ·si·'eɪ·ʃən] *n* **1.** (*organization*) associazione *f* **2.** (*involvement*) collaborazione *f* **3.** (*mental connection*) associazione *f*
assorted [ə·'sɔːr·tɪd] *adj* (*mixed*) assortito, -a
assortment [ə·'sɔːrt·mənt] *n* assortimento *m;* **a rich ~** un ricco assortimento
asst. *n abbr of* **assistant** assistente *mf*
assuage [ə·'sweɪdʒ] *vt* (*pain*) alleviare; (*anger*) placare
assume [ə·'suːm] *vt* **1.** (*regard as true*) presumere; **let's ~ that ...** supponiamo che ... **2.** (*adopt: alias, identity*) assumere **3.** (*undertake*) assumere; (*power*) prendere
assumed [ə·'suːmd] *adj* presunto, -a; **under an ~d name** sotto falso nome
assumption [ə·'sʌmp·ʃən] *n* **1.** (*supposition*) presupposto *m;* **on the ~ that ...** supponendo che ...; **to act on the ~ that ...** agire supponendo che ... **2.** (*hypothesis*) ipotesi *f inv* **3.** (*of office, power*) assunzione *f* **4.** REL **the Assumption** l'Assunzione *f*
assurance [ə·'ʃʊ·rəns] *n* **1.** (*self-confidence*) sicurezza *f;* **to have ~** aver fiducia **2.** (*promise*) assicurazione *f;* **to give an ~ of sth** garantire qc
assure [ə·'ʃʊr] *vt* **1.** (*guarantee*) assicurare

2. (*promise*) assicurare; **to ~ sb of sth** assicurare qc a qn
assured *adj* sicuro, -a
assuredly *adv* **1.** (*confidently*) con sicurezza **2.** (*certainly*) senza dubbio
asterisk ['æs·tə·rɪsk] *n* TYPO asterisco *m*
astern [ə·'stɜːrn] *adv* **1.** NAUT a poppa; **to go ~** andare indietro **2.** (*behind*) **~ of** dietro a **3.** (*backwards*) indietro
asteroid ['æs·tə·rɔɪd] *n* asteroide *m*
asthma ['æz·mə] *n* MED asma *f*
asthma attack *n* attacco *m* d'asma
asthmatic [æz·'mæ· t̬ɪk] **I.** *n* asmatico, -a *m, f* **II.** *adj* asmatico, -a
astigmatism [ə·'stɪg·mə·tɪ·zəm] *n* astigmatismo *m*
astonish [ə·'staː·nɪʃ] *vt* sorprendere; **to be ~ed** essere sorpreso
astonishing *adj* sorprendente
astonishment *n* sorpresa *f;* **to her ~** con sua grande sorpresa
astound [ə·'staʊnd] *vt* sbalordire; **to be ~ed** essere sbalordito
astounding *adj* sbalorditivo, -a
astray [ə·'streɪ] *adv* **to go ~** (*letter*) andare perso; (*person*) smarrirsi; **to lead sb ~** portare qn sulla cattiva strada
astride [ə·'straɪd] **I.** *prep* a cavallo di **II.** *adv* a cavalcioni
astringent [ə·'strɪn·dʒənt] **I.** *n* astringente *m* **II.** *adj* **1.** MED astringente **2.** *fig* caustico, -a
astrologer [əs·'traː·lə·dʒɚ] *n* astrologo, -a *m, f*
astrological [ˌæs·trə·'laː·dʒɪ·kl] *adj* astrologico, -a
astrology [əs·'traː·lə·dʒi] *n* astrologia *f*
astronaut ['æs·trə·naːt] *n* astronauta *mf*
astronomer [əs·'traː·nə·mɚ] *n* astronomo, -a *m, f*
astronomical [ˌæs·trə·'naː·mɪ·kl] *adj* a. *fig* astronomico, -a
astronomy [əs·'traː·nə·mi] *n* astronomia *f*
AstroTurf® ['æs·troʊ·ˌtɜːrf] *n tappeto erboso artificiale usato specialmente per campi sportivi*
Asturian [əs·'tʊ·ri·ən] **I.** *adj* asturiano, -a **II.** *n* (*person*) asturiano, -a *m, f*
astute [əs·'tuːt] *adj* astuto, -a
astuteness *n* astuzia *f*
asylum [ə·'saɪ·ləm] *n* **1.** (*protection*) asilo *m* **2.** (*institution*) casa *f* di ricovero; **insane ~** manicomio *m*
asylum seeker *n chi chiede asilo politico*
asymmetrical [ˌeɪ·sɪ·'me·trɪ·kəl] *adj* asimmetrico, -a
at¹ [ət, æt] *prep* **1.** (*place*) a; **~ the dentist's** dal dentista; **~ home/school** a casa/scuola; **~ the table** a tavola; **~ the office** in ufficio; **~ the window** alla finestra **2.** (*time*) **~ Christmas** a Natale; **~ night** di notte; **~ once** subito; **all ~ once** all'improvviso; **~ present** in questo momento; **~ the time** in quel momento; **~ the same time** nello stesso momento; **~ three o'clock** alle tre; **while I am ~ it** già che ci

sono **3.** (*towards*) **to laugh ~ sb** ridere di qn; **to look ~ sth/sb** guardare qc/qn; **to aim ~ sth/sb** mirare a qc/qn; **to point ~ sb** indicare qn; **to rush ~ sb/sth** avventarsi su qn/qc **4.** (*in reaction to*) **~ sb's request** su richiesta di qn; **to be astonished/annoyed ~ sth** essere sbalordito/irritato da qc; **to be mad ~ sb** essere arrabbiato con qn; **to be unhappy ~ sth** essere scontento di qc **5.** (*in amount of*) **~ all** per niente; **to sell sth ~ $10 a pound** vendere qc a 10 dollari alla libbra; **~ 120 mph** a 120 miglia orarie **6.** (*in state of*) **~ best/worst** nel migliore/peggiore dei casi; **~ first** all'inizio; **~ least** almeno; **~ war/peace** in guerra/pace; **~ 20** a vent'anni; **I feel ~ ease** mi sento a mio agio; **to be ~ a loss** essere un po' perso; **a child ~ play** un bimbo che gioca **7.** (*in ability to*) **to be good/bad ~ French** andare bene/male in francese; **to be ~ an advantage** essere in vantaggio **8.** (*repeatedly do*) **to pull ~ sb's hair** tirare i capelli a qn; **to tug ~ the rope** tirare la fune; **to wear ~ sb's nerves** dare sui nervi a qn **► ~ all** assolutamente; **did you know the film ~ all?** conoscevi il film?; **not ~ all!** per niente!, niente affatto!; (*as answer to thanks*) (di) niente; **nobody ~ all** assolutamente nessuno

at² [æt] (*in email address*) chiocciola *f*
at bat *n* (*in baseball*) turno *m* di battuta
ate [eɪt] *pt of* eat
atheism ['eɪ·θi·ɪ·zəm] *n* ateismo *m*
atheist ['eɪ·θi·ɪst] **I.** *n* ateo, -a *m, f* **II.** *adj* ateo, -a
Athens ['æ·θənz] *n* Atene *f*
athlete ['æθ·li:t] *n* atleta *mf*
athletic [æθ·'le·t̬ɪk] *adj* atletico, -a
athletics *npl* atletica *f*
Atlanta [æt·'læn·t̬ə] *n* Atlanta *f*
Atlantic [ət·'læn·t̬ɪk] **I.** *n* the ~ (**Ocean**) l'(oceano) Atlantico *m* **II.** *adj* atlantico, -a
atlas ['æt·ləs] <-es> *n* atlante *m*
ATM [ˌeɪ·ti:·'em] *n abbr of* **automated teller machine** ≈ Bancomat® *m inv*
atmosphere ['æt·məs·fɪr] *n* **1.** *a.* PHYS atmosfera *f* **2.** *fig* atmosfera *f*
atmospheric [ˌæt·məs·'fe·rɪk] *adj* **1.** METEO atmosferico, -a **2.** *fig* pieno, -a d'atmosfera
atoll ['æ·tɔ:l] *n* atollo *m*
atom ['æ·t̬əm] *n* **1.** PHYS atomo *m* **2.** *fig* (*small amount*) briciolo *m*
atom bomb *n* bomba *f* atomica
atomic [ə·'tɑ:·mɪk] *adj* atomico, -a
atomic energy *n* energia *f* atomica
atomize ['æ·t̬ə·maɪz] *vt* atomizzare; *fig* polverizzare
atomizer ['æ·t̬ə·maɪ·zɚ] *n* atomizzatore *m*
atone for [ə·'toʊn] *vt* (*sin*) espiare; (*mistake*) riparare a
atonement *n* espiazione *f*
atrocious [ə·'troʊ·ʃəs] *adj* atroce
atrocity [ə·'trɑ:·sə·t̬i] <-ies> *n* atrocità *f*
atrophy ['æ·trə·fi] <-ies> **I.** *n* atrofia **II.** *vi* atrofizzarsi

at sign *n* INFOR chiocciola *f*
attach [ə·'tætʃ] **I.** *vt* **1.** (*fix onto*) fissare; (*label*) attaccare; **to ~ sth to sth** attaccare qc a qc **2.** (*connect*) legare **3.** INFOR (*to email*) allegare **4.** (*join*) unire; **to ~ oneself to sb** unirsi a qn; **to be** (**very**) **~ed to one's family/car** essere molto attaccato alla propria famiglia/automobile **5.** (*assign*) assegnare; **to be ~ed to sth** essere assegnato a qc **6.** (*associate*) attribuire; **to ~ importance to sth** dare importanza a qc **II.** *vi form* **no blame ~es to you** tu non hai nessuna colpa
attaché [ˌæ·t̬ə·'ʃeɪ] *n* attaché *mf inv*
attaché case *n* ventiquattrore *f inv*
attachment [ə·'tætʃ·mənt] *n* **1.** (*fondness*) attaccamento *m;* **to form an ~ to sb** legarsi (affettivamente) a qn **2.** (*support*) adesione *f* **3.** (*union*) fissaggio *m* **4.** (*attached device*) accessorio *m* **5.** LAW sequestro *m* di beni **6.** INFOR allegato *m*
attack [ə·'tæk] **I.** *n* attacco *m;* **to be on the ~** andare all'attacco; **to come under ~** essere attaccato **II.** *vt* **1.** (*use violence*) attaccare **2.** (*tackle: problem*) affrontare **3.** (*eat greedily*) divorare **III.** *vi* attaccare
attain [ə·'teɪn] *vt* raggiungere; (*independence*) ottenere
attainable *adj* raggiungibile
attainment *n* raggiungimento *m*
attempt [ə·'tempt] **I.** *n* **1.** (*try*) tentativo *m;* **to make an ~ at doing sth** tentare di fare qc **2.** (*attack*) attentato *m* **II.** *vt* tentare
attempted murder *n* tentato omicidio *m*
attend [ə·'tend] **I.** *vt* (*be present at*) partecipare a **II.** *vi* **1.** (*be present*) essere presente **2.** (*take care of*) **to ~ to sb/sth** occuparsi di qn/qc **3.** *form* (*listen carefully*) ascoltare
attendance [ə·'ten·dəns] *n* **1.** (*presence*) presenza *f;* **to be in ~** essere presente **2.** (*people present*) affluenza *f*
attendant [ə·'ten·dənt] **I.** *n* **1.** (*helper*) aiutante *mf* **2.** (*servant*) assistente *mf* **II.** *adj* relativo, -a
attention [ə·'ten·ʃən] *n* **1.** (*maintenance*) attenzione *f* **2.** (*care, notice*) attenzione *f;* **Attention: John Smith** (*on envelope*) all'attenzione di John Smith; **to pay ~** prestare attenzione; **to turn one's ~s to sth** rivolgere la propria attenzione a qc **3.** MIL **to stand at ~** stare sull'attenti; **~!** attenti!
attention deficit disorder *n* disturbo *m* da deficit di attenzione
attention deficit hyperactivity disorder *n* disturbo *m* da deficit di attenzione e iperattività
attention span *n* capacità *f* di concentrazione
attentive [ə·'ten·tɪv] *adj* attento, -a; **to be ~ to sb** essere premuroso con qn; **to be ~ to sb's needs** preoccuparsi delle esigenze di qn
attenuate [ə·'ten·ju·eɪt] *vt form* attenuare
attest [ə·'test] **I.** *vt* **1.** (*demonstrate*) attestare **2.** (*authenticate*) autenticare **II.** *vi* attestare
Att. Gen. [ˌæt·'dʒen] *n abbr of* **Attorney Gen-**

eral Procuratore *m* Generale
attic ['æ·ṭɪk] *n* soffitta *f*
attire [ə·'ta·ɪə·] *n* abbigliamento *m*
attitude ['æ·ṭə·tu:d] *n* 1.(*opinion*) atteggiamento *m;* **a change of ~** un cambiamento d'atteggiamento; **to have the ~ that ...** essere dell'opinione che ...; **an ~ towards sb/sth** un atteggiamento nei confronti di qn/qc 2.(*position*) posa *f;* **to adopt an ~** assumere una posa 3. ART posa *f*
attorney [ə·'tɜ:r·ni] *n* avvocato *m;* **criminal ~** avvocato penalista; **legal ~** procuratore *m* legale
attorney-at-law *n* <attorneys-at-law> procuratore *m* legale
attract [ə·'trækt] *vt* attrarre; **to ~ attention/ support** attirare l'attenzione/ottenere l'appoggio; **to ~ sb's notice** attirare l'attenzione di qn; **to be ~ed by sb/sth** essere attratto da qn/qc
attraction [ə·'træk·ʃən] *n* 1.(*force, place of enjoyment*) attrazione *f;* **tourist ~** attrazione turistica 2.(*appeal*) fascino *m;* **to feel an ~ to sb** provare un'attrazione per qn
attractive [ə·'træk·tɪv] *adj* attraente
attribute[1] [ə·'trɪb·ju:t] *vt* 1.(*ascribe*) attribuire; **to ~ the blame to sb** attribuire la colpa a qn; **to ~ importance to sth** dare importanza a qc 2.(*give credit for*) **to ~ sth to sb** attribuire qc a qn
attribute[2] ['æ·trɪb·ju:t] *n* attributo *m*
attributive [ə·'trɪb·jə·ṭɪv] *adj* attributivo, -a
attrition [ə·'trɪ·ʃən] *n* 1.(*wearing down*) logoramento *m;* **war of ~** guerra *f* di logoramento 2. ECON riduzione *f* del personale, *ottenuta tramite la sospensione di nuove assunzioni* 3. REL attrizione *f*
ATV [eɪ·ti:·'vi:] *n abbr of* **all terrain vehicle** ≈ fuoristrada *m inv*
auburn ['ɔ:·bə·n] *adj* castano ramato *inv*
auction ['ɔ:k·ʃən] I. *n* asta *f;* **to be sold at ~** essere venduto all'asta; **to put sth up for ~** mettere qc all'asta II. *vt* **to ~ sth (off)** mettere qc all'asta
auctioneer [ˌɔ:k·ʃə·'nɪr] *n* banditore, -trice *m, f*
audacious [ɔ:·'deɪ·ʃəs] *adj* 1.(*bold*) audace 2.(*impudent*) sfacciato, -a
audacity [ɔ:·'dæ·sə·ṭi] *n* 1.(*boldness*) audacia *f* 2.(*impudence*) sfacciataggine *f*
audible ['ɔ:·də·bl] I. *adj* udibile II. *n* (*in football*) audible *m inv, cambio di tattica di gioco chiamato dal quarterback*
audience ['ɔ:·di·əns] *n* 1.(*spectators*) pubblico *m;* RADIO ascoltatori *mpl;* TV telespettatori *mpl;* (*of book*) lettori *mpl* 2.(*formal interview*) udienza *f*
audio ['ɔ:·dɪ·oʊ] I. *adj inv* audio; *inv;* **~ cassette** audiocassetta *f* II. *n* audio *m*
audio-visual *adj* audiovisivo, -a
audit[1] ['ɔ:·dɪt] FIN I. *n* revisione *f* dei conti II. *vt* sottoporre a revisione
audit[2] ['ɔ:·dɪt] *vt* UNIV **to ~ a course** seguire un corso come uditore

audition [ɔ:·'dɪ·ʃən] THEAT I. *n* audizione *f* II. *vi* fare un'audizione III. *vt* **to ~ sb** sottoporre a un'audizione qn
auditor ['ɔ:·də·ṭə·] *n* 1. COM revisore *m* dei conti 2. UNIV uditore, -trice *m, f*
auditorium [ˌɔ:·də·'tɔ:·ri·əm] <-s *o* auditoria> *n* auditorium *m inv*
Aug. [ɑ:·'ɡʌst] *n abbr of* **August** ag.
augment [ɔ:ɡ·'ment] *vt form* aumentare; **to ~ one's income** aumentare le entrate
au gratin [oʊ·ɡrɑ:·tən] *adj* gratinato, -a
augur ['ɔ:·ɡə·] I. *vi* **to ~ badly/well** essere di cattivo/buon augurio II. *vt* far presagire
august [ɔ:·'ɡʌst] *adj form* augusto, -a
August ['ɔ:·ɡəst] *n* agosto *m; s.a.* **April**
aunt [ænt] *n* zia *f*
au pair [oʊ·'per] I. *n* au pair *mf inv* II. *adj* **~ girl** ragazza alla pari
aura ['ɔ:·rə] *n* aura *f*
aural ['ɔ:·rəl] *adj* uditivo, -a
auricle ['ɔ:·rɪ·kl] *n* (*of ear*) padiglione *m* auricolare; (*of heart*) auricola *f*
auricular [ɔ:·'rɪk·jə·lə·] *adj* 1.(*relating to hearing*) auricolare 2.(*concerning the heart*) auricolare
aurora [ɔ:·'rɔ:·rə] *n* aurora *f*
aurora borealis [ɔ:·'rɔ:·rə ˌbɔ:·ri·'æ·lɪs] <aurora borealises *o* aurorae borealis> *n* ASTRON aurora *f* boreale
auspices ['ɔ:s·pɪ·sɪz] *n pl* auspici *mpl;* **under the ~ of** sotto gli auspici di
auspicious [ɔ:s·'pɪ·ʃəs] *adj form* di buon auspicio
austere [ɔ:s·'tɪr] *adj* austero, -a
austerity [ɔ:s·'te·rə·ṭi] <-ies> *n* austerità *f;* **~ program** ECON programma *m* d'austerità
Australia [ɔ:s·'treɪ·ljə] *n* Australia *f*
Australian I. *n* australiano, -a *m, f* II. *adj* australiano, -a
Austria ['ɔ:s·tri·ə] *n* Austria *f*
Austrian I. *n* austriaco, -a *m, f* II. *adj* austriaco, -a
authentic [ɔ:·'θen·ṭɪk] *adj* autentico, -a; **~ leather** vera pelle; **an ~ Goya painting** un Goya autentico
authenticate [ɔ:·'θen·tɪ·keɪt] *vt* autenticare
authentication [ɔ:·θen·tɪ·'keɪ·ʃən] *n* autenticazione *f*
authenticity [ˌɔ:·θən·'tɪ·sə·ṭi] *n* autenticità *f*
author ['ɔ:·θə·] I. *n* 1.(*writer*) autore, -trice *m, f* 2. *fig* artefice *mf* II. *vt* scrivere
authoritarian [ə·ˌθɔ:·rə·'te·ri·ən] I. *n* persona *f* autoritaria II. *adj* autoritario, -a
authoritative [ə·'θɔ:·rə·teɪ·ṭɪv] *adj* 1.(*assertive*) autoritario, -a 2.(*reliable*) autorevole
authority [ə·'θɔ:·rə·ṭi] <-ies> *n* 1.(*right to control*) autorità *f;* **to be in ~** avere autorità 2.(*permission*) autorizzazione *f* 3.(*control*) controllo *m* 4.(*knowledge*) **with ~** con cognizione di causa; **to be an ~ on sth** essere un'autorità in qc 5.(*organization*) autorità *f;* **the authorities** le autorità ▶**to have sth on good ~** sapere qc da fonte sicura; **to have sth**

on sb's ~ sapere qc da fonte autorevole
authorization [ˌɔːθəˈɹɪˈzeɪˈʃən] *n* autorizzazione *f*
authorize [ˈɔːθəˈɹaɪz] *vt* autorizzare; **to ~ sb to do sth** autorizzare qn a fare qc
authorship [ˈɔːθəˈʃɪp] *n* paternità *f;* **the article is of unknown ~** non si conosce l'autore dell'articolo
autistic [ɔːˈtɪsˈtɪk] *adj* autistico, -a
auto [ˈɔːˈto̞u] *n* auto *f*
autobiographical [ˌɔːˈtə·ba·ɪəˈgræ·fɪ·kl] *adj* autobiografico, -a
autobiography [ˌɔːˈtə·baɪˈɑːˈgɹə·fi] *n* autobiografia *f*
autocracy [ɔːˈtɑːˈkɹə·si] *n* autocrazia *f*
autocrat [ˈɔːˈtə·kɹæt] *n* autocrate *mf*
autocratic [ˌɔːˈtə·ˈkɹæ·tɪk] *adj* autocratico, -a
autocross *n* autocross *m*
autograph [ˈɔːˈtə·gɹæf] I. *n* autografo *m* II. *vt* autografare
automate [ˈɔːˈtə·meɪt] *vt* automatizzare
automated *adj* automatizzato, -a
automated teller machine *n* ≈ Bancomat® *m inv*
automatic [ˌɔːˈtə·ˈmæ·tɪk] I. *n* 1. (*car*) automobile *f* con cambio automatico 2. (*pistol*) pistola *f* automatica; (*rifle*) fucile *m* automatico II. *adj* automatico, -a
automatic pilot *n* pilota *m* automatico
automation [ˌɔːˈtə·ˈmeɪ·ʃən] *n* automatizzazione *f*
automaton [ɔːˈtɑːˈmə·tən] <automata> *n a. fig* automa *m*
automobile [ˈɔːˈtə·mo̞u·biːl] *n* automobile *f;* **~ accident** incidente *m* automobilistico
automotive [ˌɔːˈtə·ˈmo̞u·tɪv] *adj inv* automobilistico, -a
autonomous [ɔːˈtɑːˈnə·məs] *adj* autonomo, -a
autonomy [ɔːˈtɑːˈnə·mi] *n* autonomia *f*
autopsy [ˈɔːˈtɑːp·si] <-ies> *n* autopsia *f*
autumn [ˈɔːˈtəm] *n* autunno *m;* **in** (**the**) ~ in autunno; **~ colors** colori autunnali
autumnal [ɔːˈtʌm·nəl] *adj* autunnale
auxiliary [ɔːɡˈzɪlˈjə·ri] <-ies> I. *n* 1. (*aid in hospital*) ausiliario, -a *m, f* 2. LING ausiliare *m* 3. HIST (*soldier*) ausiliario *m* II. *adj* ausiliario, -a; **~ staff** personale ausiliario
AV *abbr of* **audiovisual** audiovisivo
av. 1. *abbr of* **average** media *f* 2. *abbr of* **avenue** V.le
avail [əˈveɪl] I. *n* **to no ~** inutilmente II. *vt* **to ~ oneself of sth** avvalersi di qc
available [əˈveɪ·lə·bl] *adj* 1. (*obtainable*) disponibile; **to make sth ~ to sb** mettere qc a disposizione di qn 2. (*free*) libero, -a; **to be ~ to do sth** avere tempo a disposizione per fare qc 3. (*free for romantic involvement*) **to be ~** essere disponibile
avalanche [ˈæ·və·læntʃ] *n a. fig* valanga *f*
avant-garde [ˌɑː·vɑːntˈgɑːrd] I. *n* avanguardia *f* II. *adj* d'avanguardia
avarice [ˈæ·və·ɹɪs] *n form* avidità *f*

avaricious [ˌæ·və·ˈɹɪ·ʃəs] *adj form* avido, -a
Ave. *n abbr of* **Avenue** V.le
avenge [əˈvendʒ] *vt* vendicare; **to ~ oneself** vendicarsi
avenue [ˈæ·və·nuː] *n* 1. (*street*) viale *m* 2. (*possibility*) strada *f;* **to explore every ~** tentare ogni strada
average [ˈæ·və·ɹɪdʒ] I. *n* MAT media *f;* **above/ below ~** sopra/sotto la media; **on ~** in media II. *adj* 1. MAT medio, -a; **~ rainfall** precipitazioni *f* medie *pl* 2. (*mediocre*) mediocre 3. (*ordinary*) **~ Joe** un tipo ordinario III. *vt* 1. (*have mean value*) avere una media di 2. (*calculate mean value of*) calcolare la media di
averse [əˈvɜrs] *adj* **to be ~ to sth** essere contrario a qc; **I'm not ~ to an occasional glass of wine** non mi dispiace bere un bicchiere di vino di tanto in tanto
aversion [əˈvɜːrˈʒən] *n* 1. (*dislike*) avversione *f;* **to have an ~ to sth/sb** provare avversione per qc/qn 2. (*object of dislike*) fobia *f*
avert [əˈvɜːrt] *vt* 1. (*prevent*) prevenire 2. (*turn away*) **to ~ one's eyes from sth** distogliere lo sguardo da qc; **to ~ one's thoughts from sth** allontanare il pensiero da qc
aviary [ˈeɪ·vie·ri] *n* voliera *f*
aviation [ˌeɪ·vi·ˈeɪ·ʃən] *n* aviazione *f*
aviation industry *n* industria *f* aeronautica
avid [ˈæ·vɪd] *adj* avido, -a
avidity [əˈvɪ·də·ti] *n* avidità *f*
avocado [ˌæ·və·ˈkɑː·do̞u] <-s *o* -es> *n* FOOD avocado *m inv*
avoid [əˈvɔɪd] *vt* (*person, thing*) evitare; (*when moving*) schivare; **to ~ doing sth** evitare di fare qc
avoidable *adj* evitabile
avoidance *n* l'evitare *m*
avow [əˈvaʊ] *vt form* 1. (*admit*) ammettere 2. (*declare*) dichiarare
avowal [əˈvaʊ·əl] *n form* dichiarazione *f*
avowedly [əˈvaʊ·ɪd·li] *adv* dichiaratamente
AWACS [ˈeɪ·wæks] *n abbr of* **Airborne Warning and Control System** sistema *m* AWACS
await [əˈweɪt] *vt* attendere; **eagerly ~ed** atteso con ansia
awake [əˈweɪk] I. <awoke *o* awaked, awoken *o* awaked> *vi* svegliarsi; **to ~ to sth** *fig* rendersi conto di qc II. *vt* svegliare III. *adj* 1. (*not sleeping*) sveglio, -a; **to stay ~** stare sveglio; **to keep sb ~** tenere sveglio qn; **to lie ~** rimanere (a letto) sveglio 2. *fig* conscio, -a; **to be ~ to sth** essere conscio di qc
awaken [əˈweɪ·kən] I. *vt form* svegliare; **to ~ sb to sth** *fig* aprire gli occhi a qn su qc II. *vi fig* rendersi conto di
awakening [əˈweɪ·kə·nɪŋ] *n* risveglio *m;* **she's in for a rude ~** l'attende un brusco risveglio
award [əˈwɔːrd] I. *n* 1. (*prize*) premio *m* 2. (*reward*) ricompensa *f* 3. MIL decorazione *f* II. *vt* assegnare; **to ~ sth to sb** assegnare qc a qn; **to ~ damages** liquidare i danni; **to ~ sb a**

grant assegnare a qn una borsa di studio
aware [ə·'wer] *adj* **1.** (*knowing*) **to be ~ that ...** sapere che ...; **as far as I'm ~ ...** per quel che ne so ...; **not that I'm ~ of** non che io sappia **2.** (*sense*) **to be ~ of sth** rendersi conto di qc
awareness [ə·'wer·nɪs] *n* coscienza *f*
awash [ə·'wɑːʃ] *adj* inondato, -a; **to be ~ with money** esser pieno di soldi
away [ə·'weɪ] *adv* **1.** (*distant*) **10 miles ~ a** 10 miglia; **as far ~ as possible** il più lontano possibile; **to be miles ~** *fig* non prestare attenzione **2.** (*absent*) via; **to be ~ on vacation** essere in vacanza **3.** (*in future time*) **to be only a week ~** mancare solo una settimana da; **right ~!** subito! **4.** (*continuously*) **to read/eat/write ~** leggere/mangiare/scrivere in continuazione
away from *prep* **1.** (*at distance from*) **~ the town** lontano dalla città; **~ each other** lontani l'uno dall'altro; **to stay ~ sth/sb** tenersi lontano da qc/qn **2.** (*in other direction from*) **to go ~ sth** allontanarsi da qc
away game *n* partita *f* fuori casa
awe [ɔː] *n* rispetto *m;* **to hold sb in ~** nutrire un grande rispetto per qn; **to stand in ~ of sb** avere soggezione di qn
awe-inspiring *adj* imponente
awesome ['ɔː·səm] *adj* **1.** (*impressive*) impressionante **2.** *inf* (*very good*) fantastico, -a **3.** (*fearsome*) terribile **4.** (*daunting*) sconfortante
awestricken ['ɔː·ˌstrɪ·kən] *adj*, **awestruck** ['ɔː·strʌk] *adj* impressionato, -a
awful ['ɔː·fəl] *adj* **1.** (*bad*) terribile **2.** (*as intensifier*) **an ~ lot** moltissimo
awfully ['ɔː·fə·li] *adv* **1.** (*badly*) terribilmente **2.** (*very*) **~ smart/stupid** molto intelligente/stupido; **I'm ~ sorry** mi dispiace infinitamente; **not to be ~ good at sth** non essere molto bravo in qc
awhile [ə·'hwaɪl] *adv* **to wait ~** aspettare un po'
awkward ['ɔːk·wəd] *adj* **1.** (*difficult*) difficile; **an ~ customer** *inf* un tipo difficile; **to make things ~ for sb** rendere le cose difficili a qn **2.** (*embarrassed*) imbarazzato, -a; **an ~ silence** un silenzio imbarazzante; **an ~ question** una domanda imbarazzante; **to feel ~** sentirsi a disagio **3.** (*inconvenient*) **an ~ time** un momento poco opportuno **4.** (*clumsy*) goffo, -a
awl [ɑːl] *n* punteruolo *m*
awning ['ɔː·nɪŋ] *n* tenda *f*
awoke [ə·'wouk] *pt of* **awake**
awoken [ə·'wou·kən] *pp of* **awake**
AWOL ['eɪ·wɔːl] MIL *abbr of* **absent without leave** assente senza permesso; **to go ~** *inf* sparire nel nulla
awry [ə·'raɪ] *adj* **to go ~** andare storto
ax *n*, **axe** [æks] **I.** *n* ascia *f* ▶ **to get the ~** *inf* (*worker*) essere licenziato; (*project*) essere annullato; **to have an ~ to grind** avere un interesse personale **II.** <axing> *vt* tagliare dras-

ticamente; **to ~ jobs** ridurre drasticamente i posti di lavoro
axiom ['æk·siəm] *n* assioma *m*
axis ['æk·sɪs] *n a.* MAT, POL asse *m*
axle ['æk·sl] *n* assale *m;* **back/front ~** assale posteriore/anteriore
ayatollah [ˌaɪ·ə·'tou·lə] *n* ayatollah *m inv*
aye [aɪ] *n* POL **the ~s** i voti a favore
AZ [æ·rɪ·zou·nə] *n abbr of* **Arizona** Arizona
azalea [ə·'zeɪl·jə] *n* BOT azalea *f*
Azerbaijan [ˌæ·zə·baɪ·'dʒɑːn] *n* Azerbaigian *m*
Azerbaijani **I.** *adj* azerbaigiano, -a **II.** *n* azerbaigiano, -a *m, f*
Aztec ['æz·tek] **I.** *adj* azteco, -a **II.** *n* azteco, -a *m, f*
azure ['æ·ʒɚ] **I.** *n* azzurro *m* **II.** *adj* azzurro, -a

B

B, b [biː] *n* **1.** (*letter*) B, b *m o f;* **~ as in Baker** B come Bologna **2.** MUS si *m*
b & b *n*, **B & B** [ˌbiː·ənd·'biː] *n abbr of* **bed and breakfast** bed and breakfast *m*
BA [ˌbiː·'eɪ] *n abbr of* **Bachelor of Arts** *laureato in lettere e filosofia con laurea breve*
baa [bæ] **I.** *n* belato *m* **II.** <-ed> *vi* belare
babble ['bæ·bl] **I.** *n* **1.** (*of a baby*) balbettio *m* **2.** (*of a stream*) mormorio *m* **II.** *vi* (*baby*) balbettare; (*adult*) chiacchierare
babe [beɪb] *n* **1.** (*baby*) bebè *m inf* **2.** *pej, sl* (*young woman*) pupa *f* **3.** (*term of endearment*) cara *f*
babel ['bæ·bl] *n* babele *f*
baboon [bæ·'buːn] *n* babbuino *m*
baby ['beɪ·bi] **I.** *n* **1.** (*child*) bebè *m;* **to expect/have a ~** aspettare/avere un bambino **2.** (*youngest person*) piccolo, -a *m, f;* **the ~ of the family** il piccolo di famiglia **3.** *inf* (*term of endearment*) caro, -a *m, f* **4.** (*personal interest*) **her ~** la sua creatura ▶ **to throw out the ~ with the bathwater** esagerare **II.** *adj* **1.** (*person*) infantile **2.** (*carrots*) baby **III.** *vt* coccolare come un bebè
baby carriage *n* carrozzina *f*
baby food *n* alimenti *m* per bambini *pl*
babyhood ['beɪ·bɪ·hʊd] *n* infanzia *f*
babyish ['beɪbɪʃ] *adj* infantile
babysitter ['beɪ·bɪ·ˌsɪ·t̬ɚ] *n* baby-sitter *mf inv*
bachelor ['bæ·tʃə·lɚ] *n* **1.** (*man*) scapolo *m* **2.** UNIV *laureato con laurea breve;* **Bachelor of Arts** *laureato in lettere e filosofia con laurea breve;* **Bachelor of Science** *laureato in materie scientifiche con laurea breve*

 Un **Bachelor's degree** è nella maggior parte dei casi un diploma universitario di primo o secondo ciclo che si consegue dopo un corso di studi di quattro anni. I principali sono il *Bachelor of Arts (BA)* per le discipline umanistiche e il *Bachelor of Science (BS)* per le scienze naturali.

back [bæk] I. *n* 1. (*opposite of front*) dietro *m;* (*of a hand*) dorso *m;* (*of a chair*) schienale *m;* (*of fabric*) rovescio *m;* (*of a piece of paper, envelope*) retro *m;* ~ **to front** al contrario; **to know sth ~ to front** sapere qc a menadito 2. (*end: of a book*) fine *m* 3. ANAT schiena *f;* (*of an animal*) dorso *m;* **to be on one's** ~ stare a pancia in su; **to break one's** ~ *inf* spaccarsi la schiena; **to do sth behind sb's** ~ *a. fig* fare qc alle spalle di qu; **to turn one's** ~ **on sb** girare le spalle a qu; *fig* abbandonare qu 4. SPORTS difesa *f* ► **to know sth like the** ~ **of one's hand** conoscere qc a menadito *inf;* **to have one's** ~ **against the** wall essere con le spalle al muro; **you** scratch **my** ~ **and I'll scratch yours** una mano lava l'altra; **to** stab **sb in the** ~ pugnalare qc alle spalle II. *adj* (*rear*) posteriore III. *adv* 1. **to be** ~ essere di ritorno; **to come** ~ tornare; **to want sb** ~ desiderare che qu torni; **I want the money** ~ rivoglio i miei soldi; **to bring** ~ **memories** far venire in mente ricordi 2. (*to the rear, behind*) dietro; ~ **and forth** avanti e indietro; **to look** ~ pensare al passato; **to sit** ~ rilassarsi 3. (*in return*) indietro 4. (*into the past*) fa IV. *vt* appoggiare
♦**back away** *vi* prendere le distanze da
♦**back down** *vi* far marcia indietro
♦**back off** *vi* (*physically*) farsi da parte; *fig* lasciar perdere
♦**back out of** *vt* uscire da; *fig* ritirarsi da
♦**back up** *vt* 1. (*reverse*) fare marcia indietro 2. COMPUT **to** ~ **data/files** fare il back-up dei dati/dei file 3. (*support*) appoggiare
backbone *n* 1. (*spine*) spina *f* dorsale 2. *fig* pilastro *m* 3. (*strength of character*) fegato *m*
back door *n* porta *f* di dietro
backdrop *n a. fig* fondale *m*
backer ['bæ·kɚ] *n* sostenitore, -trice *m, f;* **financial** ~ finanziatore *m*
backfire ['bæk·ˌfa·ɪɚ] *vi* 1. (*go wrong*) avere un effetto inverso a quello previsto; **his plans** ~ **d** i suoi piani si sono ripercossi contro di lui 2. AUTO avere un ritorno di fiamma
backgammon ['bæk·gæ·mən] *n* backgammon *m*
background ['bæk·graʊnd] *n* 1. (*rear view*) sfondo *m;* **in the** ~ *fig* in secondo piano 2. (*education, family*) origini *f pl* 3. (*training*) formazione *f;* **to have a** ~ **in sciences** avere una formazione scientifica 4. (*circumstances*) contesto *m*
background music *n* musica *f* di sottofondo
backhand ['bæk·hænd] *n* rovescio *m*
backing ['bæ·kɪŋ] *n* 1. (*support, aid*) suporto *m* 2. FASHION rinforzo *m* 3. MUS accompagnamento *m*
backlash *n* reazione *f* brutale

backlog *n* atraso *m;* **a** ~ **of work** un cumulo *m* di lavoro arretrato; ~ **of orders** ordini *m* inevasi *pl*
backpack ['bæk·pæk] I. *n* zaino *m* II. *vi* viaggiare con lo zaino
backpacker *n* turista *mf* con lo zaino
back pay *n* arretrati *mpl*
back seat *n* sedile *m* posteriore
backside *n inf* deretano *m*
backslash *n* barra *f* inversa
backspace (**key**) *n* tasto *m* backspace, tasto *m* ritorno unitario
backstabbing ['bæk·ˌstæ·bɪŋ] *n* pugnalata *f* alle spalle
backstage [bæk·'steɪdʒ] I. *adj* 1. THEAT (*pass*) per dietro le quinte 2. *fig* (*of organization*) interno, -a II. *adv* THEAT dietro le quinte
backstroke *n* dorso *m*
back talk *n* risposte *f* insolenti *pl*
backtrack ['bæk·træk] *vi* 1. (*go back*) far marcia indietro; (*to previous topic*) risalire 2. *fig* far marcia indietro; **to** ~ **on one's statement** ritrattare quanto si è detto
backup ['bæk·ʌp] *n* 1. COMPUT copia *f* di sicurezza, backup *m* 2. (*support*) sostegno *m*
backward ['bæk·wɚd] I. *adj* 1. (*to the rear*) indietro 2. (*slow in learning*) ritardato, -a 3. (*underdeveloped*) arretrato, -a II. *adv* all'indietro
backwards ['bæk·wɚdz] *adv* 1. (*towards the back*) all'indietro 2. (*in reverse order*) all'incontrario 3. (*from better to worse*) di male in peggio 4. (*into the past*) indietro
backwater *n* 1. (*river*) braccio *m* morto 2. *pej* luogo *m* arretrato
backwoods *npl* **the** ~ zone *f* più remote *pl*
backyard *n* giardino *m* sul retro della casa
bacon ['beɪ·kən] *n* pancetta *f* ► **to bring** home **the** ~ *inf* guadagnarsi il pane
bacteria [bæk·'tɪ·riə] *n pl of* **bacterium**
bacteriologist [bæk·ˌtɪ·ri·'ɑː·lə·dʒɪst] *n* batteriologo, -a *m, f*
bacterium [bæk·'tɪ·ri·əm] *n* <-ria> batterio *f*
bad [bæd] <worse, worst> I. *adj* 1. (*not good*) cattivo, a; **to have a** ~ **marriage** avere un matrimonio difficile; **to feel** ~ sentirsi male; **to look** ~ avere una brutta cera; **too** ~! peccato!; ~ **habits** cattive abitudini; **to use** ~ **language** dire parolacce; ~ **luck** sfortuna *f;* **a** ~ **name** una cattiva reputazione; **in** ~ **taste** di cattivo gusto; **to have a** ~ **temper** avere un cattivo carattere; ~ **times** tempi *m pl* duri 2. (*harmful*) nocivo, -a; **to be** ~ **for sth/sb** nuocere a qc/qu 3. (*spoiled*) andato, -a a male; **to go** ~ andare a male 4. (*unhealthy*) malato, -a; **to have a** ~ **heart/back** soffrire di mal di cuore/di schiena 5. (*serious: accident, mistake*) grave 6. (*severe: pain*) forte ► **to go from** ~ **to** worse andare di male in peggio II. *adv inf* male III. *n* **the** ~ la cosa brutta
bad dream *n* incubo *m*
badge [bædʒ] *n* distintivo *m*
badger ['bæ·dʒɚ] I. *n* tasso *m* II. *vt* importu-

nare

badly ['bæd·li] <worse, worst> *adv* **1.** (*poorly*) male **2.** (*in a negative way*) male; **to think ~ of sb** pensar male di qu **3.** (*very much*) disperatamente; **to be ~ in need of sth** aver disperato bisogno di qc; **he was ~ defeated** subire una sconfitta strepitosa

badminton ['bæd·mɪn·tən] *n* badminton *m inv*

baffle ['bæ·fl] **I.** *vt* **1.** (*confuse*) sconcertare **2.** (*hinder*) impedire **II.** *n* TECH deflettore *m*

baffling *adj* sconcertante

bag [bæg] **I.** *n* **1.** (*container*) borsa *f;* (*handbag*) borsetta *f;* (*sack*) sacchetto *m;* **to pack one's ~s** *a. fig* fare le valigie **2.** (*under eyes*) **to have ~s under one's eyes** avere le occhiaie **3.** *inf* (*ugly woman*) racchia *f* **4.** (*in hunting: catch*) preda *f* ▶ **to be a ~ of bones** *inf* essere pelle e ossa; **the whole ~ of tricks** *inf* tutto il repertorio; **a mixed ~** una mistura **II.** *vt* <-gg-> **1.** (*put in bag*) insacchettare **2.** *inf* (*obtain*) appropriarsi **3.** (*capture*) prendere

bagel ['beɪ·gəl] *n panino a forma di ciambella*

baggage ['bæ·gɪdʒ] *n* **1.** (*luggage*) bagaglio *m;* **excess ~** bagaglio in eccedenza **2.** (*army equipment*) equipaggiamento *m* militare **3.** *pej* (*unpleasant woman*) racchia *f*

baggage allowance *n* bagaglio *m* consentito

baggage car *n* bagagliaio *m*

baggage check *n* tagliando *m* del bagaglio

baggage claim *n* ritiro *m* bagagli

baggy ['bæ·gi] *adj* abbondante

bag lady *n inf* barbona *f*

bagpipes *npl* cornamusa *f*

baguette [bæ·'get] *n* CULIN baguette *f*

Bahamas [bə·'hɑ:·məz] *npl* **the ~** le Bahamas

Bahamian [bə·'hæ·mi·ən] **I.** *adj* delle Bahamas **II.** *n* abitante *mf* delle Bahamas

Bahrain [bɑ:·'reɪn] *n* Bahrein *m*

bail [beɪl] **I.** *n* cauzione *f;* **on ~** su cauzione; **to post ~ for sb** pagare la cauzione per qu **II.** *vi* NAUT sgottare **III.** *vt* **1.** (*remove: water*) sgottare **2.** (*guarantee*) garantire

◆ **bail out** *vt* **to bail sb out** far uscire qu di prigione, pagando la cauzione; *fig;* **to bail sb out of trouble** tirare qu fuori dai guai

bailiff ['beɪ·lɪf] *n* usciere *m* del tribunale

bait [beɪt] **I.** *n* **1.** (*for fish*) esca *m* **2.** *fig* lusinga *f;* **to swallow the ~** *inf* abboccare all'amo **II.** *vt* **1.** (*put bait on: hook*) amo **2.** (*harass: person*) tormentare

bake [beɪk] **I.** *vi* **1.** (*cook*) cuocere (nel forno) **2.** *inf* (*be hot*) arroventarsi **II.** *vt* **1.** (*cook*) cuocere al forno **2.** (*harden*) cuocere

baker ['beɪ·kɚ] *n* panettiere, -a *m, f*

bakery ['beɪ·kə·ri] *n* panetteria *f*

baking *adj* **it's ~ hot** fa un caldo allucinante

baking powder *n* lievito *m* in polvere

baking soda *n* bicarbonato *m* di soda

balance ['bæ·lənts] *n* **1.** (*device*) bilancia *f* **2.** *a. fig* equilibrio *m;* **to lose one's ~** perdere l'equilibrio **3.** (*in bank account*) saldo *m* **4.** (*amount to be paid*) saldo *m* **II.** *vi* equili-

brarsi **III.** *vt* **1.** (*compare*) soppesare; **to ~ sth against sth** confrontare qc con qc **2.** (*keep in a position*) tenere in equilibrio **3.** (*achieve equilibrium*) equilibrare; **to ~ the books** far quadrare i conti; **how do you ~ working and having a family?** come fai a conciliare lavoro e famiglia?

balanced *adj* equilibrato, -a

balance of trade *n* bilancia *f* commerciale

balance sheet *n* balancio *m*

balcony ['bæl·kə·ni] *n* balcone *m*

bald [bɔːld] *adj* **1.** (*lacking hair*) calvo, -a; **to go ~** perdere i capelli **2.** (*plain: assertion*) sintetico, -a

baldness ['bɔːld·nɪs] *n* calvizie *f*

bale [beɪl] **I.** *n* balla *f* **II.** *vt* imballare

Balearic Islands *n* **the ~** le (Isole) Baleari

Balearics [ˌbɑː·li·'æ·rɪks] *n* **the ~** le Baleari

baleen whale [bə·'liːn hweɪl] *n* misticeto *m*

baleful [·beɪl·fʊl] *adj* sinistro, -a

balk [bɔːk] **I.** *n* (*beam*) trave *f* **II.** *vi* **to ~ at sth** opporsi a qc

Balkans ['bɔːl·kəns] *n* **the ~** i Balcani

ball [bɔːl] *n* **1.** (*for golf, tennis*) palla *f;* (*for soccer, basketball*) pallone *m;* (*for football*) pallone *m* ovale; **to play ~** giocare a palla; *fig* cooperare **2.** (*round form*) palla *f* **3.** (*dance*) ballo *m* ▶ **to have a ~** divertirsi; **to get the ~ rolling** far partire le cose

ballad ['bæ·ləd] *n* ballata *f*

balladeer [ˌbæ·lə·'dɪr] *n* cantante *mf* di ballate

ballast ['bæ·ləst] *n* **1.** NAUT zavorra *f* **2.** (*gravel*) pietrisco *m*

ball bearing *n* cuscinetto *m* a sfere

ballerina [ˌbæ·lə·'riː·nə] *n* ballerina *f*

ballet dancer *n* ballerino, ina *m, f* classico, -a

ball game *n* partita *f* di baseball ▶ **it's a whole new ~** è un altro paio di maniche

ballistic [bə·'lɪs·tɪk] *adj* balistico, -a ▶ **to go ~** *inf* dar fuori di matto

balloon [bə·'luːn] **I.** *n* palloncino *m* ▶ **to go over like a lead ~** fallire clamorosamente **II.** *vi* gonfiarsi

balloonist *n* pilota *mf* di mongolfiere

ballot ['bæ·lət] **I.** *n* **1.** (*paper*) scheda *f* (elettorale) **2.** (*election*) votazione *f* (a scrutinio segreto) **II.** *vi* votare (a scrutinio segreto) **III.** *vt* consultare tramite votazione

ballot box *n* urna *f* (elettorale)

ballot paper *n* scheda *f* (elettorale)

ballpark *n* **1.** stadio *m* di baseball **2.** *fig* **a ~ figure** una cifra approssimativa

ballplayer *n* giocatore, trice *m, f* di baseball

ballpoint (pen) *n* penna *f* a sfera, biro *f*

ballroom *n* sala *f* da ballo

ballroom dancing *n* ballo *m* liscio

balm [bɑːm] *n a. fig* (*ointment*) balsamo *m*

balmy ['bɑː·mi] <-ier, -iest> *adj* (*weather*) mite; (*breeze*) odoroso, -a

Baltic ['bɔːl·tɪk] *n* **the ~** (**Sea**) il (Mar) Baltico

balustrade ['bæ·ləs·treɪd] *n* balaustra *f*

bamboo [bæm·'buː] *n* bambù *m*

bamboozle [bæm·'buː·zl] *vt inf* **1.** (*confuse*)

disorientare **2.** (*trick*) infinocchiare

ban [bæn] I. *n* divieto *m;* **to put** [*o* **place**] **a ~ on sth** proibire qc II. *vt* <-nn-> proibire; **she was ~ned from driving** le hanno ritirato la patente

banal [bə·'nɑːl] *adj* banale

banality [bə·'næ·lə·ṭi] *n* <-ies> banalità *f*

banana [bə·'næ·nə] *n* banana *f* ▶ **to go ~s** *inf* dare i numeri

banana republic *n pej* repubblica *f* delle banane

band[1] [bænd] *n* **1.** (*strip: of cloth, metal*) banda *f* **2.** (*stripe*) sriscia *f* **3.** (*ribbon*) nastro *m;* **head ~** fascetta *f* (da fronte); **waist ~** busto *m* **4.** (*range*) *a.* TEL banda *f* **5.** (*ring*) anello *m;* **wedding ~** fede *f* (nuziale)

band[2] [bænd] *n* **1.** MUS complesso *m;* **brass ~** banda *f* di ottoni **2.** (*of friends*) cricca *f;* (*of robbers*) banda *f*

◆**band together** *vi* unirsi

bandage ['bæn·dɪdʒ] I. *n* benda *f* II. *vt* bendare

Band-Aid® *n* cerotto *m*

bandit ['bæn·dɪt] *n* bandito *m*

bandsman ['bændz·mən] *n* <-men> bandista *mf*

bandstand *n* palco *m* della banda

bandwagon *n* **to jump on the ~** *fig* salire sul carrozzone

bandwidth *n* INFOR larghezza *f* di banda

bandy ['bæn·di] I. <-ier, -iest> *adj* (*bent: legs*) storto, -a II. *vt* <-ies, -ied> (*insults, words*) scambiarsi

◆**bandy about** *vt* (*story*) far circolare; **it was bandied about that ...** è stata messa in giro la voce che ...

bang [bæŋ] I. *n* **1.** (*noise, blow*) colpo *m* **2. ~s** (*hair*) frangia *f* ▶ **to go** (**off**) **with a ~** *inf* essere un gran successo II. *adv* **1.** *inf* (*exactly*) proprio; **smack ~ in the middle of the road** proprio nel mezzo della strada **2.** (*make noise*) **to go ~** scoppiare III. *interj* bang IV. *vi* (*make noise*) far rumore; (*exploding noise*) scoppiare; (*slam: porta*) sbattere; **to ~ on sth** dare colpi a qc V. *vt* (*hit*) sbattere; **to ~ one's head against** [*o* **on**] **sth** sbattere la testa contro qc

Bangladesh [bæŋ·glə·'deʃ] *n* Bangladesh *m*

Bangladeshi [bæŋ·glə·'deʃi] I. *n* abitante del Bangladesh *mf* II. *adj* del Bangladesh

bangle ['bæŋ·gl] *n* braccialetto *m* rigido

banish ['bæ·nɪʃ] *vt* **1.** (*make noise*) esiliare **2.** *fig* (*dispel*) eliminare; **to ~ sth from one's mind** bandire qc dalla mente

banishment *n* esilio *m*

banister ['bæ·nəs·tə·] *n* **1.** (*handrail*) corrimano *m* **2.** (*baluster*) balaustra *f*

banjo ['bæn·ʒoʊ] *n* <-(oe)s> banjo *m inv*

bank[1] [bæŋk] I. *n* **1.** FIN banca *m;* (*in games*) banco *f;* **to break the ~** far saltare il banco **2.** (*storage place*) banca *m;* **blood ~** banca *f* del sangue; **data ~** banca *f* dati ▶ **to laugh all the way to the ~** *inf* fare un mucchio di soldi II. *vi* **1.** (*do banking*) **to ~ with Citibank**

avere un conto alla Citybank **2.** (*rely on*) **to ~ on sb/sth** contare su qu/qc III. *vt* depositare

bank[2] [bæŋk] I. *n* (*edge: of river*) sponda *f* II. *vi* AVIAT inclinarsi

bank[3] [bæŋk] *n* (*of earth*) terrapieno *m;* (*of fog*) banco *m;* (*of cloud*) ammasso *m;* (*of switches*) serie *f*

◆**bank up** I. *vi* ammassarsi II. *vt* ammassare

bank account *n* conto *m* in banca

bank balance *n* saldo *m* del conto

bankbook *n* libretto *m* bancario

bank charges *n* spese *f pl* bancarie

bank clerk *n* impiegato, -a *m, f* di banca

banker ['bæŋ·kə·] *n* banchiere, -a *m, f*

bank holiday *n periodo ufficiale di chiusura delle banche*

banking *n* attività *f pl* bancarie

banking hours *npl* orario *m* di apertura (delle banche)

bank manager *n* direttore *m* di banca

bank note *n* banconota *f*

bank rate *n* tasso *m* d'interesse

bank robber *n* rapinatore *m*

bankrupt ['bæŋ·krʌpt] I. *n* bancarotta *f* II. *vt* far fallire III. *adj* (*bust*) insolvente; **to be ~** aver fatto fallimento; **to go ~** far fallimento; *fig;* **to be morally ~** essere privo di moralità

bankruptcy ['bæŋ·krəp·si] *n* <-ies> bancarotta *f*

bank statement *n* estratto *m* conto

bank transfer *n* bonifico *f* bancario

banner ['bæ·nə·] *n* **1.** (*flag*) stendardo *m;* **under the ~ of ...** sotto la bandiera di ... **2.** (*placard*) striscione *m* **3.** (*in Internet*) banner *m inv*

banquet ['bæn·kwət] I. *n* banchetto *m* II. *vi* banchettare

banter ['bæn·tə·] I. *n* spiritosaggini *fpl* II. *vi* scherzare

baptism ['bæp·tɪ·zəm] *n* battesimo *m;* **~ of fire** battesimo del fuoco

baptismal ['bæp·tɪz·məl] *adj* di battesimo

baptismal font *n* fonte *f* battesimale

Baptist ['bæp·tɪst] *n* battista *mf;* **John the ~** Giovanni Battista; **the Baptist Church** la chiesa battista

baptize ['bæp·taɪz] *vt* battezzare; **I was ~d Clara** mi hanno battezzato con il nome di Clara

bar[1] [bɑːr] I. *n* **1.** (*of cage, prison*) sbarra *f;* (*of chocolate*) tavoletta *f;* (*of gold*) lingotto *m;* **a ~ of soap** saponetta *f;* **to be behind ~s** *inf* stare dietro le sbarre **2.** (*band of color*) striscia *f* **3.** MUS battuta *f* **4.** MIL gallone *m* **5.** (*sandbank*) banco *m* di sabbia **6.** (*restriction*) sbarra *f* **7.** (*nightclub*) night *m;* (*counter*) bancone *m* **8.** INFOR barra *f;* **task/scroll ~** barra delle applicazioni/di scorrimento; **space ~** barra spaziatrice II. *vt* <-rr-> **1.** (*fasten: door, window*) sprangare **2.** (*obstruct*) sbarrare; **to ~ sb's way** [*o* **path**] sbarrare la strada a qu **3.** (*prohibit*) proibire; **to ~ sb from doing sth** proibire a qu di fare qc **4.** (*exclude*) escludere

bar² [bɑːr] *prep* ad eccezione di; ~ **none** senza eccezioni

Bar [bɑːr] *n* the ~ (*group of lawyers*) l'Ordine degli Avvocati; (*profession*) l'avvocatura

barb [bɑːrb] *n* 1. (*of hook*) barbiglio *m* 2. ZOOL (*of feather*) barba *f* 3. (*insult*) cattiveria *f*

Barbadian [bɑːrˈbeɪ·di·ən] I. *adj* di Barbados II. *n* abitante *mf* di Barbados

Barbados [bɑːrˈbeɪ·doʊs] *n* Barbados *fpl*

barbarian [bɑːrˈbe·ri·ən] *n* barbaro, -a *m, f*

barbaric [bɑːrˈbe·rɪk] *adj* barbaro, -a

barbarity [bɑːrˈbe·rə·ţi] *n* <-ies> barbarie *f inv*

barbarous [ˈbɑːr·bə·rəs] *adj* barbaro, -a

barbecue *n* 1. (*grill*) griglia *f* 2. (*event*) grigliata *f*

barbed [bɑːrbd] *adj* 1. (*with barbs*) con barbigli 2. *fig* (*comment, criticism*) mordace

barbed wire *n* filo *m* spinato

barber [ˈbɑːr·bɚ] *n* barbiere *m*

barbershop *n* negozio *m* di barbiere

barbiturate [bɑːrˈbɪ·tʃə·rət] *n* barbiturico *m*

bar code *n* codice *m* a barre

bard [bɑːrd] *n* bardo *m;* **the Bard** Shakespeare

bare [ber] I. *adj* 1. (*without clothes*) nudo, -a; (*uncovered*) scoperto, -a; **with one's ~ hands** con le proprie mani; **to fight with one's ~ hands** combattere a mani nude 2. (*empty*) vuoto, -a; (*without plants, leaves*) spoglio, -a; **to be ~ of sth** essere privo di qc 3. (*unadorned*) **to tell sb the ~ facts** [*o* **truth**] dire la verità nuda e cruda a qu 4. (*little*) **the ~ minimum** il minimo indispensabile; **the ~ necessities** lo stretto necessario II. *vt* desnudar; **to ~ one's teeth** mostrare i denti; **to ~ one's heart** [*o* **soul**] **to sb** aprire il proprio cuore a qu

bareback [ˈber·bæk] *adv* a pelo

barefaced [ˈber·feɪst] *adj* spudorato, a

barefoot [ˈber·fʊt] *adv,* **barefooted** [ˌber·ˈfʊ·tɪd] *adv* scalzo, -a

barely [ˈber·li] *adv* 1. (*hardly*) a malapena 2. (*scantily*) scarsamente

barf [bɑːrf] *vi sl* vomitare

barf bag *n sl* sacchetto *m* per il vomito

bargain [ˈbɑːr·gɪn] I. *n* 1. (*agreement*) patto *m;* **to drive a hard** ~ saper trattare; **to strike a** ~ concludere un affare 2. (*item*) affare *f* ▶ **into the** ~ per di più II. *vi* (*negotiate*) contrattare; (*haggle*) tirare sul prezzo; **to ~ sth away** vendere male qc

◆ **bargain for** *vi,* **bargain on** *vi* aspettarsi; **to get more than one bargained for** *fig* ottenere più di quanto ci si aspettasse

bargain basement *n* angolo *f* delle occasioni

bargain sale *n* saldi *mpl*

barge [bɑːrdʒ] I. *n* chiatta *f* II. *vt inf* **to ~ one's way through the crowd** aprirsi un varco tra la folla spintonando

◆ **barge in** *vi* 1. (*intrude*) irrompere 2. *fig* (*interrupt*) intromettersi; **sorry to** ~ scusatemi [*o* scusami] se mi intrometto

◆ **barge into** *vi* **to ~ sb** sbattere contro qu

◆ **barge through** *vi* attraversare come una furia

bar graph *n* grafico *m* a barre

baritone [ˈbe·rə·toʊn] I. *n* baritono *m* II. *adj* baritono, -a

bark¹ [bɑːrk] I. *n* (*of a dog*) latrato *m* ▶ **his ~ is worse than his bite** can che abbaia non morde *prov* II. *vi* abbaiare III. *vt* urlare

◆ **bark out** *vt* urlare

bark² [bɑːrk] *n* (*of a tree*) corteccia *f*

barkeeper [ˈbɑːr·kiː·pɚ] *n* (*bartender*) barista *mf*

barley [ˈbɑːr·li] *n* orzo *m*

barman [ˈbɑːr·mən] *n* <-men> barista *mf*

barn [bɑːrn] *n* fienile *m*

barnacle [ˈbɑːr·nə·kl] *n* dente *m* di cane

barnyard *n* aia *f*

barometer [bəˈrɑː·mə·tɚ] *n* barometro *m*

baron [ˈbæ·rən] *n a. fig* barone *m*

baroness [ˈbæ·rə·nəs] *n* baronessa *f*

baronet [ˈbæ·rə·nɪt] *n* baronetto *m*

baronial [bəˈroʊ·ni·əl] *adj* 1. (*of a baron*) baronale 2. (*statley: room*) signorile

baroque [bəˈroʊk] *adj a. fig* barroco, -a

barracks [ˈbæ·rəks] *npl* caserma *f*

barrage [bəˈrɑːʒ] *n* 1. MIL fuoco *m* di sbarramento 2. *fig* (*of questions, complaints*) raffica *f*

barrel [ˈbæ·rəl] I. *n* 1. (*container*) botte *m* 2. (*measure: of oil*) barile *m* 3. (*of a gun*) canna *f* ▶ **to be a ~ of fun** [*o* **laughs**] essere divertente; **to have sb over a ~** tenere qu in pugno; **to scrape (the bottom of) the ~** accontentarsi di ciò che resta II. *vi* <-l-> *inf* correre; **to ~ along** (*vehicle, person in vehicle*) andare a tutta birra; **he was barreling along at 80 miles per hour** sfrecciava a 80 miglia all'ora III. *vt* <-l-> mettere in botte [*o* barile]

barren [ˈbæ·rən] *adj* 1. (*infertile*) sterile; (*landscape*) arido, -a 2. (*unproductive*) improduttivo, -a; ~ **years** anni delle vacche magre

barricade [ˈbæ·rə·keɪd] I. *n* barricata *f* II. *vt* barricare; **she ~d herself into her room** si è barricata in camera

barrier [ˈbæ·ri·ɚ] *n* barrera *f;* **language** ~ barriera linguistica

barring [ˈbɑː·rɪŋ] *prep* (*except for*) ad eccezione di; (*if there are no*) salvo +*subj;* ~ **accidents** a Dio piacendo; ~ **complications** salvo complicazioni; ~ **delays** salvo ritardi

barrow [ˈbæ·roʊ] *n* (*wheelbarrow*) carriola *f;* (*cart*) carretto *m*

bartender [ˈbɑːr·ten·dɚ] *n* barista *mf*

barter [ˈbɑːr·ţɚ] I. *n* baratto *m* II. *vi* fare baratti III. *vt* **to ~ sth for sth** barattare qc con qc

basalt [bəˈsɔːlt] *n* basalto *m*

base¹ [beɪs] I. *n* 1. (*lower part, support*) base *f* 2. (*bottom*) fondo *m* 3. (*basis*) fondamento *m* 4. MIL base *f* 5. (*of a company*) sede *f* ▶ **to be off ~** *inf* sragionare; **to touch ~ with sb** riprendere contatto con qu II. *vt* 1. (*found*) basare; **to be ~d on** basarsi su 2. MIL stazionare **3.**(*stay*) **to be ~d in Florida** (*company*) avere la propria sede in Florida; (*person*) lavorare in Florida; **which hotel are you ~d at?** in quale albergo stai?

base² [beɪs] *adj* **1.**(*not honorable*) ignobile, vile **2.**(*not pure: metal*) vile

baseball ['beɪs·bɔːl] *n* baseball *m*

> **i** Il **baseball** è lo sport nazionale negli Stati Uniti. Due squadre passano alternativamente all'*up* (battuta o attacco), cioè, cercano di segnare dei *runs* (punti). Per far ciò, i giocatori devono toccare una dopo l'altra le tre basi situate in un quadrato. Il *pitcher* (lanciatore) della squadra avversaria lancia la palla e un giocatore dell'attacco, il *batter* (battitore), tenta di colpirla con la *bat* (mazza). Se colpisce la palla, corre per raggiungere la prima base "salvo", cioè prima che l'avversario riprenda possesso della palla.

base camp *n* campo *m* base
Basel ['bɑː·zl] *n* Basilea *f*
baseless ['beɪs·lɪs] *adj* (*accusation*) infondato, -a
base pay *n* stipendio *m* base
bash [bæʃ] **I.** *n* **1.**(*blow*) botta *f* **2.** *inf* (*party*) festa *f* **II.** *vt* (*hit hard: thing*) colpire; (*person*) picchiare; **to have a ~ at doing sth** *inf* provare a fare qc
◆**bash into** *vi insep* schiantarsi contro
◆**bash up** *vt inf* sfasciare
bashful ['bæʃ·fəl] *adj* timido, -a
basic ['beɪ·sɪk] **I.** *adj* fondamentale; **~ idea** idea *f* di fondo; **~ requirements** requisiti minimi; **to have a ~ command of sth** avere nozioni rudimentali di qc **II.** *npl* **the ~s** l'essenziale
BASIC ['beɪ·sɪk] *n* INFOR *abbr of* **Beginner's All-purpose Symbolic Instruction Code** BASIC *m*
basically *adv* sostanzialmente
basil ['beɪ·zəl] *n* basilico *m*
basilica [bə·'sɪ·lɪ·kə] *n* ARCHIT basilica *f*
basin ['beɪ·sn] *n* **1.**(*large container*) bacinella *f*; (*sink*) lavandino *m* **2.** GEO bacino *m*
basis ['beɪ·sɪs] *n* <bases> base *f*; **on a weekly ~** settimanalmente; **to be the ~ for sth** essere il punto di partenza per qc; **on the ~ of sth** in base a qc
bask [bæsk] *vi* **to ~ in the sun** crogiolarsi al sole; **to ~ in sb's favor** godere del favore di qu
basket ['bæs·kət] *n* cesto
basketball ['bæs·kət·bɔːl] *n* pallacanestro *f inv*
basket case *n inf* **to be a ~** essere un disastro
Basque [bæsk] **I.** *adj* basco, -a; **~ Country** Paesi *m* Baschi *pl* **II.** *n* **1.** basco, -a *m, f* **2.**(*language*) basco *m*
bass¹ [beɪs] *n* MUS **1.**(*voice*) basso *m* **2.**(*instrument: classical*) contrabbasso *m*; (*electric*) basso *m*

bass² [bæs] *n* ZOOL spigola *f*
bass clef *n* chiave *f* di basso
bass drum *n* grancassa *f*
bassoon [bə·'suːn] *n* fagotto *m*
bastard ['bæs·təd] *n a. vulg* bastardo, -a *m, f*
baste [beɪst] *vt* **1.** GASTR bagnare con il grasso di cottura **2.**(*sew loosely*) imbastire
bastion ['bæs·tʃən] *n a. fig* baluardo *m*
bat¹ [bæt] *n* ZOOL pipistrello *m* ▶ **to have ~s in the belfry** *inf* essere suonato; **to be as blind as a ~** essere cieco come una talpa
bat² [bæt] *vt* (*blink*) **to ~ one's eyelashes** battere le ciglia; **to ~ one's eyelashes at sb** far l'occhiolino a qu; **he/she didn't ~ an eyelash when …** *fig* non ha battuto ciglio quando …
bat³ [bæt] **I.** *n* **1.**(*in baseball*) mazza *f*; **he is be up at ~** è il suo turno di battuta **2.**(*blow*) colpo *m* ▶ **right off the ~** all'istante **II.** *vt, vi* <-tt-> SPORTS battere
batch [bætʃ] *n* <-es> pila *f*; COM, INFOR lotto *m*; (*of cookies*) sfornata *f*
batch file *n* INFOR file *m* batch *inv*
batch processing *n* INFOR batch *m* processing *inv*
bated ['beɪ·tɪd] *adj* **with ~ breath** con il fiato sospeso
bath [bæθ] *n* **1.**(*action*) bagno; **to give a child/dog a ~** fare il bagno al bambino; **to take a ~** fare il bagno **2.**(*bathtub*) vasca *f* da bagno **3.**(*bathroom*) bagno **4.** CHEM bagno
bathe [beɪð] **I.** *vi* fare il bagno **II.** *vt* (*person, animal*) fare il bagno a; (*wound, eyes*) lavare; **to be ~d in sweat** essere madido di sudore; **to be ~d in tears** essere coperto di lacrime; **the living room was ~d in sunlight** la sala era inondata di luce
bathing *n* balneazione *f*; **~ prohibited** divieto di balneazione
bathing cap *n* cuffia *m* da bagno
bathing suit *n* costume *m* da bagno
bathing trunks *npl* calzoncini *m pl* da bagno
bath mat *n* tappetino *m* da bagno
bathrobe *n* accappatoio *m*
bathroom *n* **1.**(*room with bath*) bagno *m* **2.**(*lavatory*) gabinetto *m*
bath towel *n* telo *m* da bagno
bathtub *n* vasca *f* da bagno
baton [bə·'tɑːn] *n* **1.** MUS bacchetta *f*; (*billy club*) manganello *m* **2.** SPORTS testimone *m*; **~ change** passaggio *m* del testimone
batsman ['bæts·mən] <-men> *n* SPORTS battitore *m*
battalion [bə·'tæl·jən] *n* battaglione *m*
batten ['bæ·tn] **I.** *n* NAUT (*for a sail*) stecca *m*; (*for a hatch*) listello *m* **II.** *vt* rinforzare con listelli **III.** *vi* **to ~ on sb** vivere a spese di qu
◆**batten down** *vt* **to ~ the hatches** *fig* prepararsi al peggio
batter¹ ['bæ·t̬ɚ] **I.** *n* GASTR pastella *f* **II.** *vt* GASTR passare nella pastella
batter² ['bæ·t̬ɚ] **I.** *n* SPORTS battitore *m* **II.** *vt* **1.**(*assault*) maltrattare **2.**(*hit*) colpire; **to ~**

the door in [*o* **down**] abbattere la porta III. *vi* to ~ at the door battere con violenza alla porta; **the waves ~ed against the rocks** le onde si frangevano sulle rocce

battered ['bæ·t̬ə·d] *adj* 1.(*injured*) maltrattato, -a 2.(*damaged: hat, clothes*) sformato, -a; (*reputation, image*) rovinato, -a 3. GASTR fritto, -a nella pastella

battering ['bæ·t̬ə·ɪŋ] *n* bastonata *f;* **to give sb a ~** prendere qu a bastonate

battery ['bæ·t̬ə·ri] <-ies> *n* 1.(*for a radio, flashlight*) pila *f;* (*for a car*) batteria *f* 2.(*large number*) batteria *f;* **a ~ of questions** una raffica di domande 3. MIL batteria *f* 4. LAW aggressione *f*

battery charger *n* caricapile *m inv;* AUTO caricabatterie *m inv*

battle ['bæ·t̬l] I. *n* 1. MIL battaglia *f* 2.(*struggle*) lotta *f* ▶ **that's half the ~** il più è fatto; **to fight a losing ~** lottare per una causa persa II. *vi* (*fight*) combattere; (*nonviolently*) lottare III. *vt* combattere

battle-ax(e) ['bæ·t̬l·æks] *n* 1. HIST ascia *f* da guerra 2. *pej, inf*(*woman*) generalessa *f*

battle cry *n* grido *m* di battaglia

battlefield *n*, **battleground** *n* campo *m* di battaglia

battlements ['bæ·t̬l·mənts] *npl* merli *mpl*

battleship *n* corazzata *f*

batty ['bæ·t̬i] *adj sl* picchiato, -a; **to go ~** dare i numeri

baud [bɑːd] *n* INFOR baud *m*

baud rate *n* INFOR velocità *f* di trasmissione

bawdy ['bɑː·di] <-ier, -iest> *adj* (*scene*) piccante; (*joke*) salace

bawl [bɑːl] I. *vi* 1.(*yell at*) urlare a squarciagola 2.(*weep*) piangere gridando II. *vt* gridato; **to ~ sb out** dare una lavata di testa a qu; **to ~ one's eyes out** sgolarsi

bay[1] [beɪ] *n* GEO baia *f*

bay[2] [beɪ] *n* BOT lauro *m*

bay[3] [beɪ] *n* ARCHIT (*between columns*) camapta *m;* (*in a house*) saliente *m;* (*for car, boat*) parcheggio *m;* (*for boat*) posto *m* barca; (*for bus*) pensilina *f*

bay[4] [beɪ] *n* ZOOL baio *m*

bay[5] [beɪ] I. *vi* (*dog, wolf*) ululare II. *n* (*howling*) ululato *m* ▶ **to be at ~** essere ridotto agli estremi; **to bring sth/sb to ~** mettere alle strette; **to hold sth/sb at ~** tenere a bada qc/qu

bay leaf *n* foglia *f* di lauro

Bay of Biscay *n* Golfo *m* di Biscaglia

bayonet [ˌbeɪ·ə·'net] I. *n* baionetta *f* II. *vt* (*wound*) ferire con la baionetta; (*kill*) uccidere con la baionetta

bayou *n* palude *f*

bay window *n* bovindo *m*

bazaar [bə·'zɑːr] *n* 1.(*market*) bazar *m* 2.(*event*) vendita *f* di beneficenza

BB gun *n* fucile *m* ad aria compressa

BBQ ['bɑːr·bɪ·kjuː] *n abbr of* **barbecue** (*event*) grigliata *f*

BC [ˌbiː·'siː] *abbr of* **British Columbia** Columbia *f* Britannica

B.C. [ˌbiː·'siː] *adv abbr of* **before Christ** a.C.

BCG (**vaccine**) *abbr of* **bacillus of Calmette and Guérin** vaccino *m* antitubercolosi

be [biː] <was, been> I. *vi* 1. + *n/adj* (*permanent state, quality, identity*) essere; **she's a cook** fa la cuoca; **she's Spanish** è spagnola; **to ~ good** essere buono; **to ~ able to do sth** essere capace di far qc; **what do you want to ~ when you grow up?** cosa vuoi fare da grande?; **to ~ married** essere sposato; **to ~ single** essere celibe [*o* nubile]; **to ~ a widow** essere vedovo 2. + *adj* (*mental and physical states*) essere; **to ~ fat/happy** essere grasso/contento; **to ~ hungry** aver fame 3.(*age*) avere; **I'm 21 (years old)** ho 21 anni 4.(*indicates sb's opinion*) **to ~ for/against sth** essere a favore/contro qc 5.(*calculation, cost*) **two and two is four** due più due fa quattro; **these glasses are $2 each** i bicchieri costano 2$ l'uno; **how much is that?** qunat'è? 6.(*measurement*) essere; (*weight*) pesare; **to ~ 2 feet long** è lungo due piedi 7.(*exist, live*) **there is/are ...** c'è/ci sono...; **to let sth ~** lasciare stare qc; **to let sb ~** lasciare in pace qu; **I think, therefore I am** penso e dunque esisto; **to ~ or not to ~** essere o non essere 8.(*location, situation*) essere, trovarsi; **to ~ in Rome** essere a Roma; **to ~ in a bad situation** essere in una brutta situazione 9. *pp* (*go, visit*) **I've never ~en to Mexico** non sono mai stato in Messico; **the plumber hasn't ~en here yet** l'idraulico non è ancora venuto 10.(*take place*) essere, tenersi; **the meeting is next Tuesday** la riunione è [*o* si terrà] martedì prossimo 11.(*circumstances*) **to ~ on the pill** prendere la pillola; **to ~ on vacation** essere in vacanza; **to ~ on a diet** essere a dieta 12.(*in time expressions*) **I won't ~ too long** non mi dilungherò 13.(*expressing possibility*) **could it ~ that ...?** *form* è possibile che ...? + *subj;* **what are we to do?** cosa dobbiamo fare? ▶ **~ that as it may** sia come sia; **so ~ it** così sia II. *impers vb* (*expressing conditions, circumstances*) **it's cloudy** è nuvolo; **it's sunny** c'è sole; **it's two o'clock** sono le due; **it's ~en so long!** quanto tempo!; **it's ten minutes by bus to the market** il mercato è a dieci minuti di autobus; **it was Anne who drank it** è stata Anne a berlo III. *aux vb* 1.(*expressing continuation*) stare; **to ~ doing sth** star facendo qc; **don't sing while I'm reading** non cantare mentre leggo; **you're always complaining** non fai altro che lamentarti 2.(*expressing the passive*) venire; **to ~ discovered by sb** venir scoperto da qu; **he was left speechless** è rimasto senza parole; **he was asked ...** gli hanno chiesto ... 3.(*expressing future*) **we are to visit Peru in the winter** andiamo in Perù quest'inverno; **she's leaving tomorrow** parte domani 4.(*expressing future in past*) **she was never**

to see her brother David again non avrebbe mai più visto suo fratello David **5.** (*expressing the subjunctive in conditionals*) **if he were to work harder, he'd get better grades** se facesse di più, prenderebbe voti migliori; **were I to refuse, they'd ~ very annoyed** se rifiutassi, si offenderebbero molto **6.** (*expressing obligation*) **you are to come here right now** devi venir qui subito **7.** (*in tag questions*) **she is tall, isn't she?** è alta, vero?

beach [biːtʃ] **I.** *n* spiaggia *f* **II.** *vt* far arenare

beach ball *n* pallone *m* da spiaggia

beachhead *n* testa *f* di ponte

beachwear *n* moda *f* da spiaggia

beacon ['biː·kən] *n* **1.** NAUT (*signal*) meda *f* **2.** NAUT (*lighthouse*) fanale *m* **3.** (*fire*) fuoco *m* di segnalazione **4.** *fig* (*guide*) guida *f*

bead [biːd] *n* **1.** (*out of glass*) perla *f;* (*out of wood*) pallina *f* **2.** (*drop*) goccia *f;* **~s of sweat** gocce *f pl* di sudore **3.** *pl* (*necklace*) collana *f* di perle **4.** *pl* REL rosario *m* **5.** (*on a gun*) mirino *m;* **to draw a ~ on sb/sth** puntare qu/qc **6.** (*on a tire*) tallone *m*

beading ['biː·dɪŋ] *n* ARCHIT modanatura *f*

beady ['biː·di] <-ier, -iest> *adj* **~ eyes** *occhi piccoli e brillanti;* **to cast a ~ eye on** [*o* **over**] **sth** tenere qc sotto osservazione

beak [biːk] *n* **1.** ZOOL becco *m* **2.** *inf* naso *m*

beaker ['biː·kɚ] *n* **1.** CHEM bicchiere *m* da laboratorio **2.** (*cup*) tazzone *m*

be-all *n* **the ~** (**and end-all**) l'unica cosa che importa

beam [biːm] **I.** *n* **1.** (*ray*) raggio *m;* (*light*) fascio *m* di luce; **high ~** AUTO abbaglianti *mpl;* **low ~** anabbaglianti *mpl* **2.** ARCHIT trave *f* **3.** SPORTS trave *f* **4.** NAUT (*width of a ship*) baglio *m,* larghezza *f* massima **II.** *vt* (*broadcast*) trasmettere; (*send*); **to ~ a smile at sb** fare un gran sorriso a qu **III.** *vi* brillare; (*smile*) sorridere

beaming *adj* **to be ~** essere raggiante

bean [biːn] **I.** *n* **1.** BOT, CULIN fagiolo *m;* (**broad**) **~** fava *f;* **green ~** fagiolino *m;* **baked ~s** fagioli *m pl* in salsa di pomodoro **2.** (*seed, pod*) **coffee ~** grano *m* di caffè; **vanilla ~** bacello *m* di vaniglia ▶ **to be full of ~s** *inf* avere il fuoco addosso; **to not have a ~** *inf* non avere un soldo in tasca; **to spill the ~s** *inf* spifferare tutto **II.** *vt sl* **to ~ sb** (**on the head**) dare un colpo in testa a qu

beanbag *n* (*chair*) poltrona *f* sacco

bean sprout *n* germoglio *m* di soia

bear[1] [ber] *n* **1.** ZOOL orso, -a *m, f* **2.** FIN ribassista *mf* **3.** *sl* (*sth difficult*) lavoraccio *m*

bear[2] [ber] <bore, borne> **I.** *vt* **1.** (*carry*) portare **2.** (*display*) **to ~ a resemblance to …** somigliare a … **3.** (*have, possess*) avere; **to ~ a scar** avere una cicatrice **4.** (*conduct*) **to ~ oneself** comportarsi **5.** (*support: weight*) sostenere **6.** (*accept: cost*) sostenere; (*responsibility*) assumere **7.** (*endure: hardship, pain*) sopportare; (*blame*) portare **8.** (*be fit for*) **what might have happened doesn't ~**

thinking about meglio non pensare a ciò che sarebbe successo **9.** (*tolerate*) sopportare **10.** (*harbor*) **to ~ sb a grudge** serbare rancore a qu; **she ~s him no ill will** non ce l'ha con lui **11.** (*keep*) **to ~ sth/sb in mind** tener presente qc/qu **12.** (*give birth to*) dare la luce a; **she bore him a daughter** gli ha dato una bambina **13.** AGR, BOT (*fruit*) dare; **to ~ fruit** *fig* dare dei frutti **14.** FIN, ECON (*interest*) fruttare **15.** (*give*) **to ~ testimony** [*o* **witness**] **to sth** testimoniare qc **II.** *vi* (*tend*) **to ~ east** dirigersi a est; **to ~ left/right** prendere a sinistra/destra ◆ **bear down on** *vt* dirigersi contro; **the train was bearing down on her** il treno le stava andando addosso

◆ **bear on** *vt* **1.** (*be relevant to*) avere a vedere con **2.** (*have effect on*) riguardare **3.** (*pressurize*) far pressione su

◆ **bear up** *vi* non lasciarsi abbattere

◆ **bear with** *vi* sopportare pazientemente

bearable ['be·rə·bl] *adj* sopportabile

beard [bɪrd] **I.** *n* **1.** (*facial hair*) barba *f;* **to shave off one's ~** farsi la barba **2.** ZOOL barba *f* **II.** *vt* HIST affrontare

bearded *adj* barbuto, -a

beardless ['bɪrd·ləs] *adj* imberbe

bearer ['be·rə] *n* portatore, -trice *m, f*

bearing ['be·rɪŋ] *n* **1.** NAUT rilevamento *m;* **to get one's ~s** *a. fig* orientarsi; **to lose one's ~s** *a. fig* perdere l'orientamento **2.** (*behavior*) comportamento *m* **3.** (*posture*) portamento *m* **4.** TECH cuscinetto *m* ▶ **to have some ~ on sth** influire su qc

bearskin ['ber·skɪn] *n* **1.** (*bear fur*) pelle *f* d'orso **2.** (*military hat*) colbacco *m*

beast [biːst] *n* **1.** (*animal*) bestia *f;* **~ of burden** animale *m* da soma **2.** *inf* (*person*) bruto *m;* **to be a ~ to sb** comportarsi come un animale con qu

beastly ['biːst·li] <-ier, -iest> *adj inf* tremendo, -a; **to be ~ to sb** comportarsi in modo abominevole con qu

beat [biːt] <beat, beaten> **I.** *n* **1.** (*pulsation: of the heart*) battito *m;* (*of the pulse*) polso *m;* (*of a hammer*) colpo *m* **2.** MUS (*stress*) tempo *m;* (*stroke of the hand*) battuta *f;* (*rhythm*) ritmo *m* **3.** (*of a police officer*) ronda *f;* **to walk one's ~** fare la ronda **II.** *adj inf* (*worn out*) sfinito, -a **III.** *vt* **1.** (*strike*) colpire; (*metal*) battere; (*carpet*) sbattere; **to ~ sb black and blue** dare una manica di botte a qu; **to ~ a confession out of sb** estorcere una confessione a qu picchiandolo; **to ~ sb to death** picchiare qu a morte **2.** (*wings*) battere **3.** GASTR sbattere **4.** (*cut through*) **to ~ a path through sth** aprirsi un varco in qc **5.** (*defeat*) battere; **Mary always ~s me at chess** Mary mi batte sempre a scacchi **6.** (*surpass: record*) battere **7.** (*arrive before*) **she ~ me to the door** è arrivata prima di me alla porta **8.** (*be better than*) superare; **to ~ sb in** [*o* **at**] **sth** superare qu in qc; **taking the bus sure ~s walking there** *inf* è meglio andarci in autobus che non a piedi

B

9. MUS (*drum*) suonare ▶ **if you can't ~ them, join them** *prov* se non puoi batterli, unisciti a loro; **that ~s everything** *inf* è il colmo!; **~ it!** *sl* vattene!, smamma!; **it ~s me how/why ...** non riesco a capire come/perché ... **IV.** *vi* **1.** (*pound: rain, sea*) battere; (*person*) dar colpi **2.** (*pulsate, vibrate: heart, pulse*) battere; (*wings*) sbattere; (*drum*) rullare

◆**beat around** *vi* **to ~ the bush** menare il can per l'aia

◆**beat back** *vt* respingere

◆**beat down I.** *vi* (*rain*) piovere a dirotto; (*sun*) picchiare **II.** *vt* **1.** (*haggle*) **to beat the price down** far scendere il prezzo; **I managed to beat him down to 50 cents** sono riuscito a farlo arrivare a 50 centesimi **2.** (*flatten: door*) derribar

◆**beat off** *vt* respingere

◆**beat up I.** *vt* pestare **II.** *vi* **to ~ on sb** pestare

beaten ['biːtn] **I.** *pp of* beat **II.** *adj* **1.** (*metal*) battuto, -a **2. to be off the ~ track** [*o* **path**] (*isolated*) essere isolato

beater ['biːtə'] *n* **1.** CULIN frullino *m*; (*for carpets*) battipanni *m inv* **2.** (*in hunting*) battitore, -trice *m, f*

beatific [biːəˈtɪfɪk] *adj* (*smile*) di beatitudine

beatification [bɪˌæˑtəˑfɪˈkeɪˑʃən] *n* beatificazione *f*

beatify [bɪˈæˑtəˑfaɪ] *vt* beatificare

beating ['biːtɪŋ] *n* **1.** (*assault*) botte *fpl*; **to give sb a ~** dare una manica di botte a qu **2.** (*defeat*) sconfitta *f*; **to take a ~** prendersi una batosta **3.** (*of the heart*) battito *m*

beautician [bjuːˈtɪˑʃən] *n* estetista *mf*

beautiful ['bjuːˑtəˑfəl] *adj* bello, -a; (*sight, weather*) stupendo, -a

beautify ['bjuːˑtəˑfaɪ] *vt* abbellire

beauty ['bjuːˑṭi] <-ies> *n* **1.** (*property*) bellezza *f* **2.** (*beautiful woman*) bellezza *f* **3.** *inf* (*specimen*) chicca *f* **4.** *inf* (*advantage*) **the ~ of ...** il bello è che ... ▶ **~ is in the eye of the beholder** *prov* non è bello ciò che è bello ma è bello ciò che piace; **~ is only skin-deep** *prov* la bellezza è superficiale

beauty contest *n*, **beauty pageant** *n* concorso *m* di bellezza

beauty parlor *n*, **beauty salon** *n*, **beauty shop** *n* istituto *m* di bellezza

beauty spot *n* **1.** (*location*) luogo *m* pittoresco **2.** (*on the skin*) neo *m*

beaver ['biːˑvə'] **I.** *n* **1.** ZOOL castoro *m* **2.** (*fur*) castoro *m* **3.** *fig, inf* (*person*) (**eager**) **~** stacanovista *mf* **4.** *vulg* (*female genitals*) figa *f* **II.** *vi* *inf* **to ~ away** lavorare di grn lena

becalmed [bɪˈkɑːmd] *adj* **to be ~** essere immobile (per mancanza di vento)

became [bɪˈkeɪm] *pt of* become

because [bɪˈkɑːz] **I.** *conj* perché; **just ~ he's smiling doesn't mean he is in love** *inf* solo perché sorride non significa che è innamorato; **~ I said that, I had to leave** ho dovuto andarmene perché ho detto quella cosa; **not ~ I am sad but ...** non perché sia triste ma ... **II.** *prep*

~ of a causa di; **~ of me** per colpa mia; **~ of illness** a causa della malattia; **~ of the fine weather** grazie al buon tempo

beck [bek] *n* **to be at sb's ~ and call** essere a completa disposizione di qu

beckon ['beˑkən] **I.** *vt* chiamare con un cenno; **to ~ sb over** fare segni a qu perché si avvicini; **I ~ed her to follow (me)** gli ho fatto cenno di seguirmi **II.** *vi* **to ~ to sb** fare segni a qu; **I have to go because work ~s** devo andarmene perché il lavoro mi chiama

become [bɪˈkʌm] <became, become> **I.** *vi* **1.** diventare; **to ~ angry** arrabbiarsi; **to ~ famous/old** diventare famoso/vecchio; **to ~ sad/happy** intristirsi/rallegrarsi; **to ~ convinced that ...** convincersi che ... **2.** (*happen to*) **what ever became of her?** che cosa ne è stato di lei? **II.** *vt* **1.** (*look good*) star bene **2.** (*be appropriate*) addirsi

becoming [bɪˈkʌˑmɪŋ] *adj* **1.** (*clothes, haircut*) che dona **2.** (*behavior*) adatto, -a

becquerel [bəˈkrel] *n* becquerel *m*

bed [bed] **I.** *n* **1.** (*furniture*) letto *m*; **to get out of ~** alzarsi; **to go to ~** andare a letto; **to go to ~ with sb** andare a letto con qu; **to make the ~** (ri)fare il letto; **to put sb to ~** mettere ɖu a letto; **always brush your teeth before ~** (*bedtime*) lavati sempre i denti prima di andare a letto **2.** (*for vegetables, flowers*) aiuola *f*; (*of clams, oysters*) banco *m* **3.** (*base*) base *f* **4.** (*bottom: of the ocean*) fondo *m*; (*of a river*) letto *m* **5.** (*layer*) strato *m* ▶ **a ~ of nails** un calvario; **life is not a ~ of roses** la vita non è tutte rose e fiori; **to get up on the wrong side of the ~** alzarsi con il piede sbagliato; **you have made your ~ and now you have to lie in it** bisogna accettare le conseguenze delle proprie azioni **II.** <-dd-> *vt* **1.** *form* (*have sex with*) fare l'amore con **2.** (*embed: plants*) piantare

◆**bed down** *vi* andare a dormire

BEd [biːˈed] *abbr of* **Bachelor of Education** laureato, -a *m, f* in Scienze dell'educazione

bed and breakfast *n* pensione *f* familiare

bedbug *n* cimice *f*

bedclothes *npl* lenzuola *f* e coperte *pl*

bedding ['beˑdɪŋ] *n* **1.** (*blankets and sheets*) lenzuola *f* e coperte *pl* **2.** (*for an animal*) lettiera *f*

bedecked [bɪˈdekt] *adj* **to be ~ with ...** essere adornato con ...

bedevil [bɪˈdeˑvəl] <-l-> *vt* **to be ~ed with** [*o* **by**] **problems** essere afflitto da problemi

bedfellow *n* **to make strange ~s** formare una strana coppia

bedlam ['bedˑləm] *n* baraonda *m*

bed linen *n* lenzuola *fpl*

Bedouin ['beˑdʊɪn] **I.** *adj* beduino, -a **II.** <-(s)> *n* beduino, -a *m, f*

bedraggled [bɪˈdræˑgld] *adj* **1.** (*wet*) fradicio, -a **2.** (*disheveled: person, appearance*) trasandato, -a; (*hair*) spettinato, -a

bedridden ['bedˑrɪˑdn] *adj* inchiodato, -a a

letto
bedrock ['bed·rɑ:k] *n* 1.GEO basamento *m*
2. *fig* base *f*
bedroom ['bed·ru:m] *n* camera *f* da letto
bedside ['bed·saɪd] *n* capezzale *f*
bedside lamp *n* lampada *f* da comodino
bedside rug *n* scendiletto *m*
bedside table *n* comodino *m*
bedsore ['bed·sɔ:r] *n* piaga *f* da decubito
bedspread ['bed·spred] *n* copriletto *m*
bedstead ['bed·sted] *n* struttura *f* del letto
bedtime ['bed·taɪm] *n* ora *f* di andare a letto;
it's (way) past your ~ a quest'ora dovresti
essere a letto (da un pezzo)
bee [bi:] *n* 1.ZOOL ape *f* 2.(*group*) gruppo *m;*
they have a sewing ~ on Fridays si trovano
a cucire tutti i venerdì; **spelling ~** gara orale *f*
di ortografia ▶to have a ~ in one's <u>bonnet</u>
about sth avere la fissazione di qc; to be a
<u>busy</u> ~ *iron* essere molto indaffarato
beech [bi:tʃ] *n* BOT faggio *m*
beechnut ['bi:tʃ·nʌt] *n* BOT faggina *f*
beef [bi:f] I. *n* 1.GASTR carne *f* di manzo;
ground ~ carne di manzo tritata; **roast ~**
roast-beef *m* 2. *inf* (*complaint*) lamentela;
what's your ~? di che cosa ti lamenti? *f* II. *vi*
inf to ~ about sth lamentarsi di qc
◆**beef up** *vt* rimpolpare
beefcake *n inf* (*man*) mister *m* muscolo *inv*
beefsteak *n* bistec *m,* bistecca *f* di manzo
beefy ['bi:·fi] <-ier, -iest> *adj inf* muscoloso, -a
beehive ['bi:·haɪv] *n* arnia *f*
beekeeper ['bi:·ˌki:·pɚ] *n* apicoltore, -trice *m, f*
beeline ['bi:·laɪn] *n inf* to make a ~ for sth/
sb dirigersi dritto verso qc/qu
been [bɪn] *pp of* be
beep [bi:p] I. *n* (*of horn*) suono *m;* (*of electronic device*) segnale *m* acustico II. *vi* (*horn*)
suonare; (*electronic device*) fare bip
beeper ['bi:·pɚ] *n* cercapersone *m inv*
beer [bɪr] *n* birra *f*
beer belly *n* pancia *f* da bevitore
beer garden *n* birreria *f* all'aperto
beery ['bɪ·ri] *adj* (*kiss, breath*) che sa di birra
beeswax ['bi:z·wæks] *n* cera *f* d'api
beet [bi:t] *n* 1.(*vegetable*) barbabietola *f;* to
turn as red as a ~ diventare rosso come un
peperone 2.(*sugar beet*) barbabietola *f* da zucchero
beetle ['bi:·ţl] *n* coleottero *m;* **black ~** scarafaggio *m*
beet sugar *n* zucchero *m* da barbabietola
befit [bɪ·'fɪt] <-tt-> *vt form* confarsi a; **as ~s a
princess** come si confà a una principessa
befitting *adj form* conveniente
before [bɪ·'fɔ:r] I. *prep* 1.(*earlier*) prima di; to
leave ~ sb partire prima di qu; ~ doing sth
prima di far qc; to wash one's hands ~ lunch
lavarsi le mani prima di pranzo 2.(*in front of*)
davanti a; ~ my house davanti a casa mia; to
bow ~ sb inchianarsi davanti a qc; ~ our
(very) eyes sotto i nostri occhi 3.(*preceding*)
C comes ~ D la C precede la D; **just ~ the**

bus stop proprio prima della fermata dell'autobus 4.(*having priority*) prima di; ~ everything prima di tutto; to put sth ~ sth else
anteporre qc a qc 5.(*as future task*) to have
sth ~ one avere qc davanti a sé II. *adv* 1.(*previously*) prima; I've seen it ~ l'ho già visto;
the day ~ il giorno prima; two days ~ due
giorni prima; as ~ come prima 2.(*in front*)
this word and the one ~ questa parola e
quella prima III. *conj* prima che +*subj;* he
spoke ~ she went out parlò prima che lei se
ne andasse; he had a glass ~ he went ha
bevuto un bicchiere prima di andarsene; it
was a week ~ he came passò una settimana
prima che arrivasse; he'd die ~ he'd tell the
truth preferirebbe morire piuttosto che dire la
verità
beforehand [bɪ·'fɔ:r·hænd] *adv* in anticipo
befriend [bɪ·'frend] *vt* diventare amico di
beg [beg] <-gg-> I. *vt* (*request*) supplicare; to
~ sb to do sth supplicare qu di fare qc; to ~
sb's pardon supplicare il perdono di qu; I ~
your pardon! scusi! II. *vi* 1.(*seek charity*) to
~ (for money) mendicare 2.(*request*) implorare; I ~ of you ti imploro; to ~ for mercy
implorare pietà; I ~ to differ *form* non sono
d'accordo 3.(*sit up and request: dog*) sedersi
sulle zampe posteriori per ottenere qualcosa
◆**beg off** *vi* scusarsi; to ~ from sth disdire qc
scusandosi
began [bɪ·'gæn] *pt of* begin
beget [bɪ·'get] <begot, begotten> *vt form* generare
beggar ['be·gɚ] I. *vt* to ~ belief essere incredibile; to ~ description essere al di là di ogni
descrizione II. *n* (*poor person*) mendicante *mf*
▶~s can't be <u>choosers</u> *prov* o mangiare
questa minestra o saltare dalla finestra *prov*
begin [bɪ·'gɪn] <began, begun> I. *vt* cominciare, incominciare; to ~ a conversation intavolare una conversazione; to ~ doing sth
incominciare a fare qc; to ~ work incominciare a lavorare II. *vi* cominciare, incominciare;
the film ~s at eight il film comincia alle otto;
to ~ with ... per cominciare ...; "well" he
began ... "bene", esordì ...
beginner [bɪ·'gɪ·nɚ] *n* principiante *mf;* ~s'
class corso *m* per principianti; ~'s luck la fortuna del principiante
beginning I. *n* 1.(*start*) inizio *m;* at [*o* in]
the ~ all'inizio; from ~ to end dall'inizio alla
fine 2.(*origin*) origine *f;* the ~s of humanity
le origini dell'umanità II. *adj* iniziale; ~ stage
fase *f* iniziale
begonia [bɪ·'goʊn·jə] *n* BOT begonia *f*
begot [bɪ·'gɑt] *pt, pp of* beget
begotten [bɪ·'gɑ:·ţn] *pp of* beget
begrudge [bɪ·'grʌdʒ] *vt* 1.(*envy*) invidiare a
2.(*resent*) to ~ doing sth fare qc controvoglia
begun [bɪ·'gʌn] *pp of* begin
behalf [bɪ·'hæf] *n* on ~ of sb/sth (*for*) a nome
di qu/qc; (*from*) per conto di qu/qc
behave [bɪ·'heɪv] *vi* 1.(*act*) comportarsi; (*in a*

proper manner) comportarsi bene; **to ~ badly/well** comportarsi bene/male; **~ yourself!** comportati bene! **2.**(*function*) funzionare

behavior [bɪ·ˈheɪv·jər] *n* comportamento *m;* **to be on one's best ~** comportarsi al meglio

behavioral *adj* comportamentale

behaviorism [bɪ·ˈheɪv·jə·rɪ·zəm] *n* comportamentismo *m*

behead [bɪ·ˈhed] *vt* decapitare

behind [bɪ·ˈhaɪnd] **I.** *prep* **1.**(*to the rear of*) dietro; **right ~ sb/sth** proprio dietro qu/qc; **he's walking ~ me** sta camminando dietro di me; **~ the wheel** al volante; **a face ~ a mask** il volto dietro la maschera **2.** *fig* **who is ~ that plan?** chi c'è dietro quel piano?; **there is somebody ~ this** c'è qualcuno dietro a tutto questo; **~ the scenes** dietro le quinte **3.**(*in support of*) **to be ~ sb/sth** (**all the way**) appoggiare qu/qc (fino alla fine) **4.**(*late for*) **~ time** in ritardo; **to be ~ schedule** essere in ritardo **5.**(*less advanced*) **to be ~ sb/the times** essere indietro rispetto aqu/ai tempi **II.** *adv* **1.**(*at the back*) dietro; **to fall ~** (*be slower*) restare indietro; **to come from ~** venire da dietro; **a blow from ~** un colpo da dietro; **to leave sb ~** lasciare qu indietro; **to stay ~** fermarsi **2.**(*overdue*) **to be ~** ritardare; **to be ~** (**in sth**) essere in ritardo (con qc) **III.** *n inf* didietro *m;* **to get off one's ~** darsi una smossa

behindhand [bɪ·ˈhaɪnd·hænd] *adv* indietro; **to be ~** essere indietro

behold [bɪ·ˈhoʊld] *vt* vedere

beige [beɪʒ] *adj* beige

being [ˈbiː·ɪŋ] **I.** *n* **1.**(*creature*) essere *m* **2.**(*life*) vita *f;* **to come into ~** nascere **3.**(*soul*) anima *f* **II.** *pres p of* **be III.** *adj after n* **for the time ~** per il momento

Belarus [be·lə·ˈruːs] *n* Bielorussia *f*

Belarusian [be·lə·ˈruː·si·ən] **I.** *adj* bielorusso, -a **II.** *n* **1.**(*person*) bielorusso, -a *m, f* **2.** LING bielorusso *m*

belated [bɪ·ˈleɪ·ṭɪd] *adj* tardivo, -a

belch [beltʃ] **I.** *n inf* rutto *m* **II.** *vi inf* ruttare **III.** *vt fig* **to ~ clouds of smoke** sputare nuvole di fumo

beleaguered [bɪ·ˈliː·gərd] *adj* (*city*) assediato, -a; (*person, government*) assillato, -a da problemi

belfry [ˈbel·fri] *n* campanile *m*

Belgian [ˈbel·dʒən] **I.** *adj* belga **II.** *n* belga *mf*

Belgium [ˈbel·dʒəm] *n* Belgio *m*

belie [bɪ·ˈlaɪ] *irr vt* **1.**(*conceal*) nascondere **2.**(*contradict*) smentire

belief [bɪ·ˈliːf] *n* **1.** REL fede *f* **2.**(*conviction*) convinzione *f;* **it is my firm ~ that ...** sono fermamente convinto che ...; **to be beyond ~** essere incredibile; **in the ~ that ...** nella convinzione che ...

believable [bɪ·ˈliː·və·bl] *adj* credibile

believe [bɪ·ˈliːv] **I.** *vt* credere; **~ (you) me!** credimi!; **would you ~ it?** figurati!; **she**

couldn't ~ her eyes/ears non poteva credere ai suoi occhi/alle sue orecchie; I can't ~ how ... non riesco a capacitarmi di come ...; I'll ~ it when I see it! se non lo vedo non ci credo!; ~ it or not, ... che tu ci creda o meno ... **II.** *vi* credere; **to ~ in sth** credere a qc; (*support*) essere sostenitore di qc; **to ~ in sb** credere in qu

believer [bɪ·ˈliː·vər] *n* **1.** REL credente *mf* **2.**(*supporter*) sostenitore, -trice *m, f;* **to be a ~ in sth** essere sostenitore di qc

belittle [bɪ·ˈlɪ·ṭl] *vt* disprezzare

Belize [bə·ˈliːz] *n* Belize *m*

Belizean [bə·ˈliː·zi·ən] **I.** *adj* del Belize **II.** *n* abitante del Belize *mf*

bell [bel] *n* **1.**(*of a church*) campana *f;* (*hand bell*) campanella *f;* (*on a hat, cat*) sonaglio *m;* (*of a bicycle, door*) campanello *m* **2.**(*signal*) suoneria *f* ▶ **as clear as a ~** chiaro come il sole; **his name/face rings a ~** il suo nome/volto mi dice qualcosa

belladonna [ˌbe·lə·ˈdɑː·nə] *n* belladonna *f*

bellboy *n* fattorino *m* dell'albergo

bellicose [ˈbe·lɪ·koʊs] *adj* bellicoso, -a; **to be in a ~ mood** aver voglia di litigare

belligerent [bɪ·ˈlɪ·dʒə·rənt] *adj* **1.**(*at war*) belligerante **2.**(*quarrelsome*) bellicoso, -a

bellhop *n* fattorino *m* dell'albergo

bellow [ˈbe·loʊ] **I.** *vt* gridare **II.** *vi* muggire **III.** *n* grido *m*

bellows [ˈbe·loʊz] *npl* mantice *m;* **a pair of ~** un mantice

bell pepper *n* peperone *m*

belly [ˈbe·li] <-ies> *n* **1.** *inf* (*stomach*) pancia *f* **2.**(*of a ship*) ventre *m* ▶ **to have fire in one's ~** avere il fuoco addosso; **to go ~ up** *inf* fallire

bellyache *inf* **I.** *n* mal *m* di pancia; **to have a ~** avere mal di pancia **II.** *vi* lamentarsi

bellybutton *n* ombelico *m*

belly dancer *n* ballerina *f* del ventre

belly flop *n inf* panciata, spanciata *f*

belong [bɪ·ˈlɑːŋ] *vi* **1.**(*be property of, be from*) **to ~ to sb/sth** appartenere a qu/qc **2.**(*have a place*) **where do these spoons ~?** dove vanno questi cucchiai?; **this doesn't ~ here** questo non è il suo posto; **I feel I don't ~ here** non mi sento a mio agio qui **3.**(*be a member of*) **to ~ to** (*club*) essere socio di; (*political party*) essere membro di **4.**(*should be*) **a book that belongs in every home** un libro che ogni famiglia dovrebbe avere **5.**(*match*) **they ~ together** sono fatti l'uno per l'altra

belongings *npl* averi *mpl;* **personal ~** effetti *m* personali *pl*

Belorussian [be·lə·ˈrʌ·ʃən] *adj, n s.* **Belarusian**

beloved[1] [bɪ·ˈlʌ·vɪd] *n* amato, -a *m, f*

beloved[2] [bi·ˈlʌvd] *adj* amato, -a; **her ~ brother** il suo amato fratello; **to be ~ by sb** essere amato da qu

below [bɪ·ˈloʊ] **I.** *prep* **1.**(*lower than, underneath*) sotto; **~ the table/surface** sotto la tavola/la superficie; ~ **us** sotto di noi; ~ **sea level** sotto il livello del mare; **the sun sank ~ the horizon** il sole è sceso sotto l'orizzonte **2.** GEO **San Diego is ~ Los Angeles** San Diego è a sud di Los Angeles; **the river is ~ the town** il fiume è a valle della città **3.** (*less than*) ~ **average** al di sotto della media; ~ **freezing** sotto zero; **it's 4 degrees ~ zero** sono 4 gradi sotto (lo) zero; **children ~ the age of twelve** bambini al di sotto dei dodic'anni **4.** (*inferior to*) **to be ~ sb in rank** essere di rango inferiore a qu; **to work ~ sb** lavorare sotto [*o* agli ordini di] qu; **to work ~ him** lavorare sotto di lui **5.** (*of a lower standard than*) **to be ~ sb** non essere degno di qu; **to marry ~ one-self** sposare qu al di sotto della propria condizione **II.** *adv* (di) sotto; **the family (in the apartment)** ~ la famiglia del piano di sotto; **from** ~ da sotto; **see** ~ (*in a text*) vedi sotto

belt [belt] **I.** *n* **1.** FASHION cintura *m;* **to fasten one's** ~ allacciarsi la cintura **2.** TECH cinghia *f* **3.** (*area: industrial, green*) cintura *f* **4.** inf (*punch*) sventola *f* ▸ **to tighten one's** ~ tirare la cinghia; **to have some experience under one's** ~ avere un po' di esperienza alle spalle **II.** *vt* **1.** (*secure with a belt*) fissare (con una cinghia) **2.** inf (*hit*) picchiare **III.** *vi* inf correre a tutta velocità
◆ **belt out** *vt* inf to ~ **a song** cantare una canzone a pieni polmoni
◆ **belt up** *vi* **1.** AUTO allacciare la cintura di sicurezza **2.** inf ~! chiudi il becco!

bemoan [bɪˈmoʊn] *vt form* lamentare

bemused [bɪˈmjuːzd] *adj* perlesso, -a

bench [bentʃ] *n* **1.** (*seat*) panchina *f* **2.** SPORTS **the** ~ la panchina **3.** LAW **the** ~ la corte; **to serve on the** ~ fare il giudice **4.** (*worktable*) banco *m* di lavoro

benchmark [ˈbentʃˌmɑːrk] *n* parametro *m* di riferimento, benchmark *m* inv

bend [bend] <bent, bent> **I.** *n* **1.** (*in a river, road*) curva *f;* (*in a pipe*) gomito *m* **2.** *pl, inf* (*illness*) malattia *f* da decompressione ▸ **to go/be around the** ~ inf diventare/essere matto **II.** *vi* **1.** (*move*) piegarsi **2.** (*change direction: road*) fare una curva **III.** *vt* **1.** (*move: arms, legs*) piegare; (*head*) inclinare **2.** (*change*) **to** ~ **sb to one's will** piegare qu alla propria volontà **3.** (*not follow strictly*) **to** ~ **the rules** cambiare le regole a proprio piacimento ▸ **to** ~ **sb's ear** inf attaccare un bottone a qu
◆ **bend back** *vt* piegare all'indietro
◆ **bend down** *vi* piegarsi
◆ **bend over** *vi* chinarsi ▸ **to** ~ **backwards** (**to help sb**) farsi in quattro (per aiutare qu)

bended [ˈbenˌdɪd] *adj form* **on** ~ **knee** sulle ginocchia; **to go down on** ~ **knee** inginocchiarsi

beneath [bɪˈniːθ] **I.** *prep* **1.** (*lower than, underneath*) sotto; ~ **the table/surface** sotto la tavola/superficie; ~ **us** sotto di noi; **the sun sank ~ the horizon** il sole è sceso sotto l'oriz-

zonte **2.** (*inferior to*) **to be ~ sb in rank** essere di rango inferiore a qu **3.** (*lower standard than*) **to marry ~ oneself** sposare qu al di sotto della propria condizione; **to be ~ sb** non essere degno di qu **II.** *adv* sotto, di sotto

benediction [ˌbenɪˈdɪkʃən] *n form* benedizione *f*

benefactor [ˈbenəˌfæktər] *n* benefattore *m*

benefactress [ˈbenɪˌfæktrɪs] *n* benefattrice *f*

beneficence [bɪˈnefɪsns] *n* beneficenza *f*

beneficent [bɪˈnefɪsnt] *adj form* benefico, -a

beneficiary [ˌbenɪˈfɪʃiəri] *n* <-ies> beneficiario, -a *m, f*

benefit [ˈbenɪfɪt] **I.** *n* **1.** (*profit*) beneficio *m;* **to derive** (**much**) ~ **from sth** trarre (molto) vantaggio da qc; **to be of ~ to sb** giovare a qu; **for the ~ of sb** a beneficio di qu; **to the ~ of sth/sb** a beneficio di qc/qu; **to give sb the ~ of the doubt** concedere a qu il beneficio del dubbio **2.** (*welfare payment*) sussidio *m* **II.** <-t-*o* -tt-> *vi* **to ~ from sth** trarre profitto da qc **III.** <-t-*o* -tt-> *vt* giovare a

Benelux [ˈbenɪˌlʌks] *n* **the ~ countries** i paesi del Benelux

Bengali [beŋˈɡɔːli] **I.** *adj* bengali **II.** *n* bengali *mf*

Benin [beˈniːn] *n* Benin *m*

Beninese [ˌbenɪˈniːz] **I.** *adj* del Benin **II.** *n* abitante *mf* del Benin

bent [bent] **I.** *pt, pp* of **bend II.** *n* (*tendency*) inclinazione *f;* **to have a ~ for sth** avere una predisposizione per qc; **to follow one's ~** seguire le proprie inclinazioni **III.** *adj* **1.** (*not straight*) storto, -a **2.** (*determined*) **to be ~ on** (**doing**) **sth** essere deciso a fare qc ▸ **to get all ~ out of shape** inf infuriarsi

bequeath [bɪˈkwiːð] *vt form* lasciare in eredità

bequest [bɪˈkwest] *n form* lascito *m*

berate [bɪˈreɪt] *vt form* redarguire

bereaved [bɪˈriːvd] *n* **the ~** la famiglia del defunto

bereavement [bɪˈriːvmənt] *n* lutto *f* (per la morte di un familiare); **to suffer a ~** subire la perdita di un familiare

bereft [bɪˈreft] *adj form* **to be ~ of sth** essere privo di qc; **to feel ~** essere afflitto

beret [bəˈreɪ] *n* berretto *m*

Bermuda [bəˈmjuːdə] *n* le Bermuda

Bermuda shorts *n* bermuda *mpl*

berry [ˈberi] <-ies> *n* bacca *f*

berserk [bəˈsɜːrk] *adj* (*angry*) pazzo furioso, -a; **to go ~** (**over sth**) andare su tutte le furie (per qc); (*be enthusiastic*) impazzire per qc

berth [bɜːrθ] **I.** *n* **1.** (*on train, ship*) cuccetta *f* **2.** (*in a harbor*) posto *m* barca **3.** *fig* **to give sb a wide ~** evitare qu **II.** *vt, vi* NAUT ormeggiare

beseech [bɪˈsiːtʃ] <beseeched, besought> *vt form* **to ~ sb to do sth** implorare qu di fare qc

beseeching *adj* implorante

beset [bɪˈset] <beset, beset> *vt* assalire; **to be ~ by sth** venir assalito da qc; ~ **by worries** assillato dalle preoccupazioni

beside [bɪˈsaɪd] *prep* **1.** (*next to*) accanto a;

right ~ **sb/sth** proprio accanto a qu/qc **2.** (*together with*) ~ **sb** insieme a qu **3.** (*in comparison to*) in confronto a **4.** (*overwhelmed*) **to be ~ oneself** essere fuori di sé **5.** (*irrelevant to*) **to be ~ the point** essere irrilevante

besides [bɪ·ˈsaɪdz] **I.** *prep* **1.** (*in addition to*) oltre a **2.** (*except for*) tranne **II.** *adv* **1.** (*in addition*) inoltre **2.** (*else*) **nothing ~** nient'altro

besiege [bɪ·ˈsiːdʒ] *vt* **1.** (*city*) assediare **2.** *fig* **to ~ with** (*questions, complaints*) tempestare di

besmirch [bɪ·ˈsmɜːrtʃ] *vt liter* macchiare; **to ~ sb's good name** macchiare il buon nome di qu

besotted [bɪ·ˈsɑː·tɪd] *adj* infatuato, -a; **to be ~ with sth** essere preso da qc; **to be ~ with sb** essere cotto di qu *inf*

besought [bɪ·ˈsɑːt] *pt, pp of* beseech

best [best] **I.** *adj superl of* good migliore; **the ~** il/la migliore; **the ~ days of my life** i giorni migliori della mia vita; **the ~ part** (*the majority*) la maggior parte; **may the ~ man win** che vinca il migliore; **~ wishes!** auguri! **II.** *adv superl of* well meglio; **~** il meglio; **as ~ (as) you can** meglio che puoi; **do what you think is ~** fai ciò che credi meglio; **at ~** al meglio **III.** *n* **1.** (*the finest*) **all the ~!** *inf* auguri!; **to be the ~ of friends** essere i migliori amici del mondo; **to bring out the ~ in sb** tirare fuori il meglio da qu; **to turn out for the ~** andare per il meglio; **to the ~ of my knowledge** che io sappia **2.** SPORTS record *m inv* **IV.** *vt form* battere

bestial [ˈbes·tʃl] *adj* bestiale

bestiality [ˌbes·tʃiˈæ·lə·ti] *n* **1.** (*behavior*) bestialità *f* **2.** LAW (*sexual*) zoofilia *f*

best man *n* testimone *m* di nozze

bestow [bɪ·ˈstoʊ] *vt form* **to ~ sth on sb** conferire qc a qu; **to ~ a favor on sb** concedere un favore a qu

bestowal [bɪ·ˈstoʊ·əl] *n form* conferimento *m*

best-seller *n* best-seller *m inv*

bet [bet] <bet *o* -ted, bet *o* -ted> **I.** *n* scommessa *f*; **it is a fair** [*o* safe] **~ that ...** è quasi sicuro che ... +*subj*; **to be the best ~** è la cosa migliore; **to place a ~ on sth** scommettere su qc **II.** *vt* scommettere; **I ~ you don't!** scommetto che non lo fai! **III.** *vi* scommettere; **to ~ on sth** scommettere su qc; **I wouldn't ~ on it** non contarci troppo ▶ **I'll ~!** certo!; **you ~!** *inf* ne puoi star certo!

beta [ˈbeɪ·tə] *n* beta *f*

beta-blocker [ˈbeɪ·tə·ˈblɑː·kər] *n* MED betabloccante *m*

beta testing *n* INFOR test *m pl* beta

beta version *n* INFOR versione *f* beta

betray [bɪ·ˈtreɪ] *vt* **1.** (*be disloyal to*) tradire; **to ~ a promise** rompere una promessa; **to ~ sb's trust** tradire la fiducia di qu; **to be ~ed by sb** essere tradito da qu; **he ~ed his wife** ha tradito sua moglie **2.** (*reveal: nature, feelings*) tradire; **to ~ sth to sb** rivelare qc a qu

betrayal [bɪ·ˈtre·ɪəl] *n* **1.** (*disloyalty*) tradimento *m*; **an act of ~** un tradimento **2.** (*revelation*) rivelazione *f*

better¹ [ˈbe·tər] **I.** *adj comp of* good migliore; **to be ~** MED star meglio; **~ than nothing** meglio di niente; **to appeal to sb's ~ nature** appellarsi alla bontà di qu; **~ luck next time** andrà meglio la prossima volta; **it's ~ that way** è meglio così **II.** *adv comp of* well meglio; **I like this ~** questo mi piace di più; **there is nothing I like ~ than ...** non c'é nulla che mi piaccia di più di ...; **we'd ~ stay here** faremmo meglio a fermarci qui; **It would be ~ to tell him** sarebbe meglio dirglielo; **you had ~ go** faresti meglio ad adartene; **to think ~ of sth** cambiare idea su qc; **or ~ yet ...** o meglio ... **III.** *n* **1. not to have seen ~** non conoscere di meglio; **to change for the ~** cambiare in meglio; **the sooner, the ~** prima è, meglio è; **so much the ~** tanto meglio **2.** *pl* **my ~s i** miei superiori ▶ **for ~ or (for) worse** che ci piaccia o meno; **to get the ~ of sb** battere qu **IV.** *vt* migliorare; **to ~ oneself** migliorare la propria condizione

better² [ˈbe·tər] *n s.* bettor

betterment [ˈbe·tər·mənt] *n* miglioramento *m*

betting *n* scommesse

betting office *n* agenzia *f* di scommesse

bettor [ˈbe·tər] *n* scommettitore, -trice *m, f*

between [bɪ·ˈtwiːn] **I.** *prep* tra; **to eat ~ meals** mangiare tra un pasto e l'altro; **~ now and tomorrow** prima di domani; **~ the two of us** tra noi; **a misunderstanding ~ the couple** un'incomprensione di coppia; **nothing will come ~ them** tra loro non si potrà intromettere nulla; **the 3 children have $10 ~ them** i 3 bambini hanno in tutto $10 **II.** *adv* (**in**) **~** in mezzo; (*time*) nel frattempo

bevel [ˈbe·vl] **I.** <-l-> *vt* smussare **II.** *n* smusso *m*

beverage [ˈbe·və·rɪdʒ] *n* bevanda *f*; **alcoholic ~s** bevande alcoliche

bevy [ˈbe·vi] *n* (*of birds*) stormo *m*; (*of people*) gruppo *m*

bewail [bɪ·ˈweɪl] *vt form* lamentare

beware [bɪ·ˈwer] *vi* stare attento; **~!** stai attento!; **~ of pickpockets!** attenti ai borseggiatori!

bewilder [bɪ·ˈwɪl·dər] *vt* sconcertare

bewildered *adj* sconcertato, -a

bewildering *adj* sconcertante

bewilderment *n* sconcerto *m*

bewitch [bɪ·ˈwɪtʃ] *vt* **1.** (*place magic charm on*) stregare **2.** (*fascinate*) affascinare

bewitching *adj* affascinante

beyond [bɪ·ˈjɑːnd] **I.** *prep* **1.** (*on the other side of*) al di là di; **~ the mountain** dall'altra parte della montagna; **don't go ~ the line!** non oltrepassare la linea!; **~ the wall** al di là del muro; **from ~ the grave** dall'aldilà **2.** (*after*) dopo; (*more than*) più di; **~ 8:00** dopo le 8:00; **to stay ~ a week** fermarsi più di una settimana; **~ lunchtime** dopo pranzo **3.** (*further* *than*) oltre; **to see/go** (**way**) **~ sth** vedere/andare (molto) oltre qc; **it goes ~ a joke** non è più uno scherzo; **~ the reach of sb** fuori della portata di qu; **~ belief** incredibile; **~ hope** senza speranza; **he is ~ help** *a. iron* è un caso senza speranza; **~ the shadow of a doubt** senza l'ombra di un dubbio; **to go ~ the point of no return** andare oltre al punto di non ritorno **4.** (*too difficult for*) **to be ~ sb** (*theory, idea*) essere troppo difficile per qu; **that's ~ me** io non ci arrivo; **this is ~ my abilities** è al di sopra delle mie capacità **5.** (*more than*) al di sopra; **to live ~ one's means** vivere al di sopra delle proprie possibilità; **to value sth above and ~ all else** stimare qc sopra tutto **6.** *with neg or interrog* (*except for*) tranne **II.** *adv* **1.** (*past*) **the house ~** la casa più avanti **2.** (*future*) **the next ten years and ~** i prossimi dieci anni e oltre **III.** *n* **the ~** REL l'aldilà

biannual [ˌbaɪˈæn·ju·əl] *adj* semestrale

bias [ˈbaɪ·rəs] **I.** *n* **1.** (*prejudice*) pregiudizio *m;* **to have ~es against sb/sth** essere prevenuto nei confronti di qu/qc **2.** (*one-sidedness*) parzialità *f;* **without ~** imparziale **3.** (*tendency*) preferenza *f;* **to have a ~ towards sth** avere una preferenza per qc **4.** (*in sewing*) sbieco *m;* **on the ~** di sbieco **II.** <-s-> *vt* influenzare; **to ~ sb towards/against sb** influenzare qu positivamente/negativamente nei confronti di qu

biased *adj* parziale; **~ in sb's favor** essere bendisposto nei confronti di qu; **~ opinions** opinioni parziali

bib [bɪb] *n* bavaglino *m*

Bible [ˈbaɪ·bl] *n* **the ~** la Bibbia

biblical [ˈbɪb·lɪ·kl] *adj* biblico, -a

bibliographer [ˌbɪb·lɪˈɑː·grə·fɚ] *n* bibliografo, -a *m, f*

bibliographic(al) [ˌbɪb·lɪ·əˈgræ·fɪ·k(l)] *adj* bibliografico, -a

bibliography [ˌbɪb·liˈɑː·grə·fi] <-ies> *n* bibliografia *f*

bibliophile [ˈbɪb·lɪ·ə·faɪl] *n form* bibliofilo, -a *m, f*

bicarbonate [ˌbaɪˈkɑːr·bə·nət] *n* bicarbonato *m*

bicarbonate of soda *n* bicarbonato *m* di soda

bicentenary [baɪˈsent·ne·ri] <-ies> *n,* **bicentennial** [baɪ·senˈte·ni·əl] **I.** *n* bicentenario *m* **II.** *adj* bicentenario, -a; **~ celebration** celebrazione *f* del bicentenario

biceps [ˈbaɪ·seps] *n inv* bicipite *m*

bicker [ˈbɪ·kɚ] *vi* litigare

bickering *n* litigi *mpl*

bicycle [ˈbaɪ·sɪ·kl] *n* bicicletta *f;* **to ride a ~** andare in bicicletta; **by ~** in bicicletta

bicycle lane *n* pista *f* ciclabile

bid[1] [bɪd] <bid *o* bade, bid *o* bidden> *vt form* **1.** (*greet*) **to ~ sb farewell** dire addio a qu; **to ~ sb good morning** augurare il buongiorno a qu; **to ~ sb welcome** dare il benvenuto a qu **2.** (*command*) ingiungere **3.** (*invite*) invitare

bid[2] [bɪd] **I.** *n* **1.** (*offer*) offerta *f;* **hostile takeover ~** COM offerta ostile (di acquisto); **to make a ~ for sth** fare un'offerta per qc **2.** (*attempt*) tentativo *m;* **to make a ~ to do sth** tentare di fare qc **II.** <bid, bid> *vi* **1.** (*at an auction*) pujar **2.** COM fare un'offerta; **to ~ for a contract** partecipare ad una gara di appalto **III.** <bid, bid> *vt* rilanciare

bidden [ˈbɪ·dn] *pp of* **bid**[1]

bidder [ˈbɪ·dɚ] *n* postor, -a *m, f;* **to the highest ~** al miglior offerente

bidding [ˈbɪ·dɪŋ] *n* **1.** FIN rilancio *m* **2.** (*command*) ordine *m;* **to do sb's ~** fare ciò che vuole qu; **at sb's ~** agli ordini di qu

bide [baɪd] *vt* **to ~ one's time** aspettare il momento opportuno

bidet [bɪˈdeɪ] *n* bidè *m*

biennial [baɪˈe·ni·əl] **I.** *adj a.* BOT biennale **II.** *n* pianta *f* biennale

bier [bɪr] *n* catafalco *m*

bifocal [ˈbaɪ·foʊ·kl] *adj* bifocale

bifocals [ˈbaɪ·foʊ·klz] *npl* occhiali *m pl* bifocali

big [bɪg] <-ger, -gest> *adj* **1.** (*in size, amount*) grande; **a ~ book** un libro grande; **a ~ budget film** un film ad alto budget; **a ~ house** una casa grande; **~ letters** maiuscole *fpl;* **to be a ~ spender** *inf* essere uno spendaccione; **~ words** *inf* parole *f pl* altisonanti; **the ~ger the better** più grande è, meglio è **2.** (*older*) più grande; **~ boy/girl** bambino/bambina più grande; **~ sister/brother** fratello/sorella maggiore **3.** (*significant*) grande; **a ~ day** *inf* un gran giorno; **a ~ decision** una decisione importante; **this group is ~ in Italia** questo gruppo è famoso in Italia **4.** (*on a large scale*) su larga scala ▸ **to have a ~ heart** essere una persona di cuore; **to have a ~ mouth** *inf* parlare troppo; **to make it ~** *inf* avere un successo pazzesco; **to think ~** avere grandi idee

bigamist [ˈbɪ·gə·mɪst] *n* bigamo, -a *m, f*

bigamy [ˈbɪ·gə·mi] *n* bigamia *f*

Big Apple *n* **the ~** New York, Nuova York *f*

---

i Il **Big Ben** era, originariamente, il soprannome dato a una campana di grandi dimensioni, fusa nel 1856, posta in cima alla torre delle **Houses of Parliament**. A battezzarla con questo nome è stato Sir Benjamin Hall, **Chief Commissioner of Works**. Oggigiorno **Big Ben** viene usato per indicare sia la campana che la torre. I rintocchi del **Big Ben** vengono trasmessi da alcune stazioni radio e televisive per annunciare il radiogiornale o il telegiornale.

---

big business *n* grandi aziende

Big Easy *n* **the ~** New Orleans *f*

big game *n* selvaggina *f* grossa

bigot [ˈbɪ·gət] *n* intollerante *mf*

bigoted *adj* intollerante

bigotry [ˈbɪ·gət·ri] *n* intolleranza *f*

big shot *n inf* pezzo *m* grosso

big toe *n* alluce *m*

big top *n* circo *m*

bigwig *n inf* pezzo *m* grosso

bike [baɪk] *n inf* **1.** (*bicycle*) bici *f* **2.** (*motorcycle*) moto *f*

biker ['baɪ·kɚ] *n inf* motociclista *mf*

bikini [bɪ·'kiː·ni] *n* bikini *m inv*

bilateral [ˌbaɪ·'læ· t̬ɚl] *adj* bilaterale

bile [baɪl] *n a. fig* ANAT bile *f*

bilingual [baɪ·'lɪŋ·gwəl] *adj* bilingue

bilious ['bɪl·jəs] *adj* **1.** MED bilioso, -a **2.** *fig* (*angry*) collerico, -a

bill¹ [bɪl] I. *n* **1.** (*invoice*) fattura *f;* **phone ~** bolletta *f* del teléfono; **to foot the ~** pagare il conto; **the ~, please** il conto, per favore **2.** (*bank note*) banconota *m* **3.** POL, LAW disegno *m* di legge; **to pass a ~** approvare un disegno di legge **4.** (*poster*) cartellone *m* ▶ **to give sth/sb a clean ~ of** health approvare qc/qn; **to fit the ~** rispondere ai requisiti II. *vt* **to ~ sb** presentare il conto a qu; **to ~ sb for sth** fatturare qc a qu

bill² [bɪl] I. *n* (*of a bird*) becco *m* II. *vi* **to ~ and coo** *inf* tubare

billboard *n* tabellone *m* pubblicitario

billet ['bɪ·lət] MIL I. *n* accantonamento *m* II. *vt* accantonare

billfold *n* portafoglio *m*

billiard ball *n* palla *f* da biliardo

billiards ['bɪl·jɚdz] *n* biliardo *m*

billiard table *n* tavolo *m* da biliardo

billing *n* **to be given top ~** essere in testa al cartellone

billion ['bɪl·jən] *n* miliardo *m*

billow ['bɪ·loʊ] I. *vi* (*clothes*) svolazzare; (*sails*) gonfiarsi II. *n* **a ~ of smoke** una nube di fumo

billowy *adj* (*waves, clouds*) grosso, -a; (*sail*) gonfio, -a di vento

billposter *n* attacchino *m*

billy club *n* manganello *m*

billy goat *n inf* becco *m*, caprone *m*

bimbo ['bɪm·boʊ] <-(e)s> *n* **1.** *pej, inf* ochetta *f* **2.** *pej, vulg* (*prostitute*) prostituta *f*

bimonthly [ˌbaɪ·'mʌnθ·li] I. *adj* **1.** (*twice a month*) quindicinale **2.** (*every two months*) bimestrale II. *adv* **1.** (*twice a month*) quindicinalmente **2.** (*once every two months*) bimestralmente

bin [bɪn] *n* recipiente *m;* **trash ~** pattumiera *f*

binary ['baɪ·nə·ri] *adj* COMPUT binario, -a

binary code *n* INFOR codice *m* binario

bind [baɪnd] I. *n inf* difficoltà *fpl;* **to be in a ~** avere delle difficoltà II. <bound, bound> *vi* unirsi III. <bound, bound> *vt* **1.** (*tie together*) legare; **to be bound hand and foot** avere mani e piedi legati **2.** (*unite*) **to ~** (**together**) unire; **to be bound to sb** essere legato a qu **3.** (*commit*) vincolare **4.** (*sew*) bordare **5.** (*book*) rilegare **6.** (*oblige*) **to ~ sb to do sth** obbligare qu a fare qc; **to ~ sb to a contract** obbligare qu contrattualmente

binder ['baɪn·dɚ] *n* (*notebook*) classificatore *m*

binding ['baɪn·dɪŋ] I. *n* **1.** TYPO rilegatura *f* **2.** FASHION bordo *m* II. *adj* vincolante

binge [bɪndʒ] *inf* I. *n* (*of drinking*) sbronza *f;* (*of eating*) abbuffata *f;* **to go on a ~** far baldoria II. *vi* (*on food*) abbuffarsi

bingo ['bɪŋ·goʊ] I. *n* bingo *m inv* II. *interj inf* eureka

binoculars [bɪ·'nɑː·kjə·lɚz] *npl* binocolo *m;* **a pair of ~** un binocolo

binomial [baɪ·'noʊm·iəl] I. *n* MAT binomio *m* II. *adj* MAT binomiale

biochemical [ˌba·ɪoʊ·'ke·mɪ·kl] *adj* biochimico, -a

biochemist [ˌba·ɪoʊ·'ke·mɪst] *n* biochimico, -a *m, f*

biochemistry [ˌba·ɪoʊ·'ke·mɪs·tri] *n* biochimica *f*

biodegradable [ˌba·ɪoʊ·dɪ·'grei·də·bl] *adj* biodegradabile

biodegrade [ˌba·ɪoʊ·dɪ·'greid] *vi* biodegradarsi

biodiversity [ˌba·ɪoʊ·dɪ·'vɜːr·sə·t̬i] *n* biodiversità *f*

bioengineering [ˌba·ɪoʊ·en·dʒɪ·'nɪ·rɪŋ] *n* bioingegneria *f*

biofeedback [ˌba·ɪoʊ·'fiːd·bæk] *n* PSYCH biofeedback *m inv*

biofuel ['ba·ɪoʊ·ˌfjuːl] *n* biocarburante *m*

biogas ['ba·ɪoʊ·ɡæs] *n* biogas *m*

biographer [baɪ·'ɑː·grə·fɚ] *n* biografo, -a *m, f*

biographical [ˌba·ɪoʊ·'græ·fɪ·kəl] *adj* biografico, -a

biography [baɪ·'ɑː·grə·fi] <-ies> *n* biografia *f*

biological [ˌba·ɪə·'lɑː·dʒɪ·kəl] *adj* biologico, -a; **~ cycle/rhythm** ciclo/ritmo biologico; **~ parents** genitori *m* naturali *pl*

biological clock *n* orologio *m* biologico

biological control *n* controllo *m* biologico

biological indicator *n* indicatore *m* biologico

biologist [baɪ·'ɑː·lə·dʒɪst] *n* biologo, -a *m, f*

biology [baɪ·'ɑː·lə·dʒi] *n* biologia *f*

biomass ['ba·ɪoʊ·ˌmæs] *n* BIO biomassa *f*

biopsy ['ba·ɪɑːp·si] *n* MED biopsia *f*

biorhythm ['ba·ɪoʊ·ri·ðəm] *n* bioritmo *m*

biosphere ['ba·ɪəs·fir] *n* biosfera *f*

biotechnology [ˌba·ɪoʊ·tek·'nɑː·lə·dʒi] *n* biotecnologia *f*

biotope ['ba·ɪə·toʊp] *n* biotopo *m*

bipartisan [ˌbaɪ·'pɑːr·t̬ə·zən] *adj* POL bipartisan

biped ['baɪ·ped] *n* BIO bipede *m*

biplane ['baɪ·plein] *n* biplano *m*

bipolar [ˌbaɪ·'poʊ·lə] *adj* ELEC, PHYS bipolare

birch [bɜːrtʃ] *n* BOT betulla *f*

bird [bɜːrd] *n* **1.** ZOOL uccello *m;* **a flock of ~s** uno stormo di uccelli **2.** *inf* (*person*) **a strange** [*o* queer] **~** un tipo strano ▶ **~s of a** feather **flock together** *prov* Dio li fa e poi li accoppia *prov;* **to kill two ~s with one** stone prendere due piccioni con una fava *prov;* **the early ~ catches the** worm *prov* chi dorme non piglia pesci *prov;* **for the ~s** invano

birdbath *n* vaschetta *f* per gli uccelli

B

birdcage *n* gabbietta *f* per gli uccelli

birdie ['bɜːr·di] *n* **1.** (*in golf*) birdie *m* **2.** (*in badminton*) volano *m* **3.** *childspeak* uccellino *m;* **watch the** ~ PHOT guarda l'uccellino!

birdseed *n* becchime *m*

bird's-eye view *n* vista *f* a volo d'uccello

bird watching *n* osservazione *f* degli uccelli

birth [bɜːrθ] *n* **1.** nascita *f;* MED parto *m;* **at** ~ alla nascita; **by** ~ di nascita; **from** ~ dalla nascita; **date/place of** ~ data/luogo di nascita; **to give** ~ **to a child** dare alla luce un figlio **2.** (*descent, beginning*) origine *m;* **to be of low/noble** ~ essere di umili/nobili origini

birth certificate *n* certificato *m* di nascita

birth control *n* controllo *m* delle nascite

birthday ['bɜːrθ·deɪ] *n* compleanno *m;* **happy** ~! buon compleanno!

birthday cake *n* torta *f* di compleanno

birthday card *n* biglietto *m* di auguri di compleanno

birthday party *n* festa *f* di compleanno

birthday present *n* regalo *m* di compleanno

birthday suit *n* *inf* **in one's** ~ come mamma l'ha fatto

birthmark *n* voglia *f*

birthplace *n* luogo *m* di nascita

birthrate *n* tasso *f* di natalità; **falling/rising** ~ natalità in diminuzione/aumento

birthright *n* diritto *m* di nascita

Biscay ['bɪs·keɪ] *n* Biscaglia *f*

biscuit ['bɪs·kɪt] *n* FOOD *piccolo panino piatto lievitato con il bicarbonato*

---

i I **biscuits and gravy**, piatto originario degli Stati Uniti del sud, sono spesso consumati per la prima colazione negli USA. I *biscuits* sono una sorta di panini piatti serviti con *gravy* (un sugo di arrosto). In alcune regioni, i **biscuits and gravy** si trovano solo nei *truck stops* (i ristoranti lungo le strade).

---

bisect ['baɪ·sekt] *vt* MAT bisecare

bisection [baɪ·'sek·ʃən] *n* MAT bisezione *f*

bisexual [ˌbaɪ·'sek·ʃʊ·əl] **I.** *n* bisessuale *mf* **II.** *adj* bisessuale

bishop ['bɪ·ʃəp] *n* **1.** REL vescovo *m* **2.** (*chess piece*) alfiere *m*

bishopric ['bɪ·səp·rɪk] *n* vescovado *m*

bison ['baɪ·sən] *n* bisonte *m*

bit¹ [bɪt] *n* **1.** *inf* (*small piece*) pezzo *m;* (*of glass*) scheggia *f;* **a** ~ **of paper** un pezzo di carta; **little** ~**s** pezzettini *mpl;* **to smash sth to** ~**s** mandare in pezzi qc **2.** (*some*) **a** ~ **of** un po' di; **a** ~ **of news** una notizia; **a** ~ **of trouble** un problemino **3.** (*part*) parte *f;* ~ **by** ~ poco a poco; **to do one's** ~ *inf* fare la propria parte **4.** *inf* (*short time*) momento *m;* **for a** ~ per un momento; **hold on a** ~ aspetta un momento **5.** (*somewhat*) **a** ~ un po'; **a** ~ **stupid** un po' stupido; **quite a** ~ un bel po'; **not a** ~ per nulla

bit² [bɪt] *n* **1.** (*for horses*) morso *m* **2.** (*for drill*) punta *f* del trapano ▸ **to chomp at the** ~ mordere il freno

bit³ [bɪt] *n* COMPUT bit *m*

bit⁴ [bɪt] *pt of* **bite**

bitch [bɪtʃ] **I.** *n* **1.** ZOOL cagna *f* **2.** *pej, sl* (*woman*) puttana *f;* **you** ~! puttana! **3.** *sl* (*difficult matter*) casino; **life's a** ~ la vita è una merda **II.** *vi inf* lamentarsi; **to** ~ **about sb/sth** lamentarsi di qu/qc

bitchy ['bɪt·ʃi] *adj* maligno, -a

bite [baɪt] **I.** <bit, bitten> *vt* mordere; (*insect*) pungere; **to** ~ **one's nails** mangiarsi le unghie; **to** ~ **one's lips** mordersi le labbra **II.** <bit, bitten> *vi* (*dog, person*) mordere; (*insect*) pungere; (*fish*) abboccare ▸ **once bitten twice shy** *prov* se ci si scotta una volta non si gioca più col fuoco **III.** *n* **1.** (*of a dog, person*) morso *m;* (*of an insect*) puntura *f;* ~ **mark** impronta *f* dei denti; (*of an insect*) puntura *f;* **a dog's** ~ il morso di un cane; **to give sb a** ~ dare un morso a qu **2.** (*mouthful*) boccone *m;* **to take a** ~ **of sth** mangiare un boccone di qc **3.** *fig* (*sharpness*) mordente *m;* **to have** (**real**) ~ avere mordente

biting ['baɪ·tɪŋ] *adj* (*wind*) pungente; (*criticism*) mordace

bitten ['bɪ·tn] *pp of* **bite**

bitter ['bɪ·t̮ɚ] **I.** *adj* <-er, -est> **1.** (*in taste*) amaro, -a; (*fruit*) aspro, -a **2.** (*painful*) amaro, -a; **to be** ~ **about sth** essere amareggiato da qc; **to carry on to the** ~ **end** continuare fino all'ultimo **3.** (*intense*) acerrimo, -a; (*dispute*) aspro, -a; (*disappointment*) amaro, -a; (*wind*) pungente **II.** *n* ~**s** (*in cocktails*) amaro *m*

bitterly *adv* **1.** (*resentfully*) amaramente; **to weep** ~ piangere amaramente **2.** (*intensely*) aspramente; **to condemn sth** ~ condannare aspramente qc

bitterness *n* **1.** (*animosity*) amarezza *f;* (*resentment*) risentimento *m;* ~ **towards sb** risentimento contro qu **2.** (*taste*) amaro *m*

bitumen [bɪ·'tuː·mən] *n* bitume *m*

bituminous [bɪ·'tuː·mɪ·nəs] *adj* bituminoso, -a

bivalve ['baɪ·vælv] *n* bivalve *m*

bivouac ['bɪ·vu·æk] **I.** *n* bivacco *m* **II.** <-k-> *vi* bivaccare

biweekly [ˌbaɪ·'wiːk·li] **I.** *adj* **1.** (*every two weeks*) quindicinale **2.** (*twice a week*) bisettimanale **II.** *adv* **1.** (*every two weeks*) quindicinalmente **2.** (*twice a week*) bisettimanalmente

bizarre [bɪ·'zɑːr] *adj* bizzarro, -a

blab [blæb] <-bb-> *vi inf* **1.** (*reveal secret*) spifferare un segreto **2.** (*talk too much*) far andare la lingua

blabber ['blæ·bɚ] *vi* far andare la lingua

blabbermouth *n* **1.** (*revealer of secret*) spifferone, -a *m, f;* **he's a** ~ non sa tenere la bocca chiusa **2.** (*talkative person*) chiacchierone, -a *m, f*

black [blæk] **I.** *adj* **1.** (*color*) nero, -a; ~ **man** nero *m;* ~ **woman** nera *f* **2.** *fig* (*extreme*) nero, -a; ~ **despair** disperazione nera **3.** (*dark*) oscuro, -a; *fig;* **to give sb a ~ look** lanciare un'occhiataccia a qu **4.** (*very dirty: hands*) nero, -a ►**to beat sb ~ and blue** *inf* riempire di botte qu **II.** *vt* (*make black*) annerire; **to ~ one's face** annerirsi il viso **III.** *n* **1.** (*color*) nero *m;* **in ~** di nero; **in ~ and white** CINE, PHOT in bianco e nero **2.** (*person*) nero, -a *m, f* **3.** FIN **to be in the ~** essere in nero [*o* in attivo] ♦**black out I.** *vi* perdere conoscenza **II.** *vt* **1.** (*make illegible*) oscurare **2.** (*censure*) censurare

blackball *vt* (*vote*) votare contro; (*reject*) mettere al bando

blackberry ['blæk·ˌbe·ri] <-ies> *n* (*fruit*) mora *f;* (*plant*) rovo *m*

blackbird *n* merlo *m*

blackboard *n* lavagna *f*

black book *n* **to <u>be</u> in sb's ~(s)** essere sulla lista nera di qu

black box *n* AVIAT scatola *f* nera

blacken ['blæ·kən] **I.** *vt* **1.** (*make black*) annerire; **to ~ sb's eye** fare un occhio nero a qu **2.** (*slander*) infangare; **to ~ sb's name** infangare il nome di qu **II.** *vi* (*sky*) farsi scuro

black eye *n* occhio *m* nero

blackguard *n* canaglia *f*

blackhead ['blæk·hed] *n* punto *m* nero

black hole *n* buco *m* nero

black ice *n* ghiaccio *m* invisibile

blackish ['blæ·kɪʃ] *adj* tendente al nero

blackjack *n* **1.** GAMES blackjack *m* **2.** (*weapon*) manganello *m*

black light *n* luce [*o* ultravioletta] nera *f*

blacklist ['blæk·lɪst] **I.** *vt* mettere sulla lista nera **II.** *n* lista *f* nera

blackmail ['blæk·meɪl] **I.** *n* ricatto *m* **II.** *vt* ricattare; **to ~ sb into doing sth** constringere qu a fare qc con un ricatto

blackmailer ['blæk·meɪ·lɚ] *n* ricattatore, -trice *m, f*

black mark *n* voto *m* negativo

black market *n* mercato *m* nero

black markete(e)r *n* borsanerista *mf*

blackness ['blæk·nɪs] *n* (*color*) nero *m;* (*darkness*) oscurità *f*

blackout ['blæk·aʊt] *n* **1.** (*faint*) svenimento *m;* **to have a ~** avere uno svenimento **2.** ELEC blackout *m inv* **3.** (*censorship*) **news ~** silenzio *m* stampa

Black Sea *n* Mar *m* Nero

black sheep *n a. fig* pecora *f* nera

blacksmith *n* fabbro *m*

bladder ['blæ·dɚ] *n* ANAT vescica *f*

blade [bleɪd] **I.** *n* (*of a tool, weapon*) lama *f;* (*of an oar*) pala *f;* **~ of grass** filo *f* d'erba **II.** *vi inf* pattinare (in-line)

blah [blɑː] **I.** *adj inf* (*boring*) noioso, -a **II.** *interj inf* ~ **, ~, (~)** bla bla

blame [bleɪm] **I.** *vt* incolpare; **to ~ sb for sth, to ~ sth on sb** dare la colpa di qc a qu; **to be to ~ for sth** essere responsabile di qc; **I don't ~ you** hai tutta la mia comprensione **II.** *n* colpa *f;* **to carry the ~** essere responsabile; **to**

lay the ~ for sth on sb attribuire la colpa di qc a qu; **to take the ~** assumersi la colpa

blameless ['bleɪm·lɪs] *adj* innocente; **~ life** vita *f* irreprensibile

blameworthy ['bleɪm·ˌwɜːr·ði] *adj form* deplorevole

blanch [blænʃ] **I.** *vi* (*become pale*) sbiancare **II.** *vt* **1.** (*whiten*) sbiancare **2.** GASTR sbollentare; **~ed almonds** mandorle mondate

bland [blænd] *adj* **1.** (*mild*) insipido, -a **2.** (*dull*) insulso, -a

blandishments ['blæn·dɪʃ·mənts] *npl* lusinghe *fpl*

blank [blæŋk] **I.** *adj* **1.** (*empty*) bianco, -a; **~ page** pagina *f* bianca; **~ space** spazio *m* vuoto; **~ tape** cinta *f* vergine; **~ check** assegno *m* in bianco; **my mind went ~** ho avuto un vuoto; **the screen went ~** il monitor si è oscurato **2.** (*without emotion: look*) privo di espressione **3.** (*complete*) assoluto, -a; (*despair*) totale; **to be met by a ~ refusal** trovarsi di fronte ad un totale rifiuto **II.** *n* **1.** (*space*) vuoto *m;* (*on form*) spazio *m* vuoto **2.** (*cartridge*) cartuccia *m* a salve ►**to <u>draw</u> a** (*complete*) ~ fare un buco nell'acqua

blanket ['blæŋ·kɪt] **I.** *n* **1.** (*cover*) coperta *f* **2.** (*of snow*) coltre *f* **II.** *vt* coprire; **to ~ sth in sth** coprire qc con qc **III.** *adj* general; LING (*term*) generico, -a

blankly *adv* (*without expression*) con l'aria assente; (*without understanding*) senza capire

blare [bler] **I.** *vi* risuonare *m* frastuono *m;* (*of a trumpet*) strombettio *m*

blaspheme ['blæs·fiːm] *vi* bestemmiare

blasphemous ['blæs·fə·məs] *adj* blasfemo, -a

blasphemy ['blæs·fə·mi] *n* bestemmia *f*

blast [blæst] **I.** *vt* **1.** (*with an explosive*) far saltare in aria **2.** *inf* (*criticize*) criticare duramente **II.** *n* **1.** (*detonation*) splosione *f* **2.** (*gust of wind*) raffica *f* **3.** (*noise*) colpo *m* **4.** *inf* (*party*) festa *f;* (*lots of fun*); **to have a ~** divertirsi un mondo ►(**at**) <u>full</u> ~ (*volume*) a tutto volume; (*speed*) a tutto gas **III.** *interj inf* maledizione; **~ it!** maledetto!

blasted *adj inf* (*damned*) maledetto, -a

blastoff ['blæst·ɑːf] *n* lancio *m*

blatant ['bleɪ·tnt] *adj* spudorato, -a

blaze[1] [bleɪz] **I.** *vi* (*fire*) divampare; **to ~ with anger** dare in escandescenze **II.** *vt* **to ~ a trail** tracciare una pista **III.** *n* **1.** (*fire*) incendio *m;* (*flames*) fiammata *f* **2.** (*of light*) bagliore *m;* (*a ~ of color*) un'esplosione di colore *m* **3.** (*display*) **a ~ of glory** un'aureola di gloria; **in a ~ of publicity** con grande battage pubblicitario; **~ of anger** accesso *m* d'ira ♦**blaze up** *vi* infiammarsi

blaze[2] [bleɪz] *n* (*on horse*) stella *f*

blazer ['bleɪ·zɚ] *n* blazer *m inv*

blazing ['bleɪ·zɪŋ] *adj* splendente; (*heat, sunshine*) cocente; (*light*) sfolgorante; (*fire*) ardente; **in a ~ temper** infuriato

bleach [bliːtʃ] **I.** *vt* (*clothing*) candeggiare; (*hair*) decolorare **II.** *n* candeggina *f;* (*for hair*) decolorante *m*

bleachers ['bli:·tʃəz] *n pl* gradinate *fpl*

bleak [bli:k] *adj* (*future*) avvilente; (*weather*) uggioso, -a; (*landscape*) desolato, -a; (*smile*) triste

bleary ['blɪ·ri] *adj* <-ier, -iest> (*person*) stanco, -a; (*eyes*) annebbiato, -a

bleary-eyed *adj* con gli occhi annebbiati

bleat [bli:t] I. *vi* 1. (*sheep, goat*) belare 2. (*complain*) lagnarsi II. *n* 1. (*of sheep*) belato *m* 2. (*complaint*) lamento *m*

bled [bled] *pt, pp of* **bleed**

bleed [bli:d] <bled, bled> I. *vi* 1. (*from a wound*) sanguinare; **to ~ to death** morire dissanguato; **my heart ~s for ...** soffrire per ... 2. (*colors: in the laundry*) stingere II. *vt* 1. salassare; **to ~ sb dry** *inf* lasciare qu senza un soldo 2. TECH, AUTO (*drain*) spurgare

bleep [bli:p] I. *n* (*sound*) pitido *m* II. *vi* (*emit sound*) fare bip III. *vt* (*censor*) coprire (con un bip)

blemish ['ble·mɪʃ] I. *n a. fig* macchia *f;* **a reputation without ~** una reputazione senza macchia II. *vt a. fig* mancchiare

blemish-free *adj* senza difetti

blench [blentʃ] *vi* indietreggiare; **to ~ at the thought** impallidire al pensiero

blend [blend] I. *n* mescolanza *f* II. *vt* mescolare III. *vi* fondersi; **the colors ~ in well** i colori stanno bene insieme

blender ['blen·də] *n* frullatore *m*

bless [bles] *vt* benedire ▸ ~ **him/**her! che Dio lo benedica!; (**God**) ~ **you!** (*after a sneeze*) salute!

blessed ['ble·sɪd] *adj* 1. (*holy*) benedetto, -a; (*ground*) santo, -a; **the Blessed Virgin** la Santissima Vergine; ~ **are the meek ...** benedetti siano gli umili ... 2. *inf* (*as intensifier*) benedetto, -a; **the whole ~ day** tutto il santo giorno

blessing ['ble·sɪŋ] *n* 1. (*benediction*) benedizione *f;* **to give one's ~ to sth** dare la propria approvazione a qc 2. (*advantage*) vantaggio *m* ▸ **it's a ~ in** disguise non tutto il male vien per nuocere *prov;* **to** count **one's ~s** apprezzare ciò che si ha

blew [blu:] *pt of* **blow**

blight [blaɪt] I. *vt a. fig* AGR rovinare II. *n* 1. AGR *malattia delle piante che ne causa l'avvizzimento* 2. *fig* rovine *f;* **to cast a ~ on sth** rovinare qc

blimp [blɪmp] *n* (*airship*) *piccolo dirigibile da ricognizione;* (*obese person*) pallone *m*

blind [blaɪnd] I. *n* 1. *pl* (*person*) **the ~** i ciechi, i nonvedenti 2. (*window shade*) persiana *f* 3. (*for hunters*) palchetto *m* II. *vt* 1. ANAT, MED accecare 2. (*dazzle*) abbagliare III. *adj* 1. (*unable to see*) cieco, -a; **to be ~ in one eye** essere cieco da un occhio; **to be ~ to sth** non accorgersi di qc 2. (*hidden: corner*) senza visibilità 3. (*without reason: acceptance, devotion*) cieco, -a 4. (*without knowledge*) cieco, -a; **a ~ wine test** degustazione cieca di vini

IV. *adv* 1. (*without sight*) senza vederci 2. (*as intensifier*) **to be ~ drunk** essere ubriaco perso

blind alley <-s> *n a. fig* vicolo *m* cieco

blind date *n* appuntamento *m* al buio [*o* con uno sconosciuto]

blinders ['blaɪn·dəz] *n pl* SPORTS paraocchi *mpl*

blindfold ['blaɪnd·foʊld] I. *n* venda *f* II. *vt* bendare gi occhi a III. *adj* con gli occhi bendati; **to be able to do sth ~ed** riuscire a fare qc ad occhi chiusi

blinding *adj* (*dazzling: light, color, hate*) accecante

blindman's buff *n* moscacieca *f*

blindness *n* cecità *f*

blind spot *n* AUTO angolo *m* cieco

blink [blɪŋk] I. *vt* **to ~ one's eyes** sbattere le palpebre II. *vi* sbattere le palpebre; **to ~ back one's tears** contenere le lacrime; **she didn't even ~** non ha battuto ciglio III. *n* battito *m* di ciglia ▸ **in the ~ of an** eye in un battito d'occhio; **to be** on **the ~** *inf* essere rotto

blinker ['blɪŋ·kə] *n* AUTO freccia *f;* **to turn on the ~** accendere le frecce

blinkered *adj* con i paraocchi

bliss [blɪs] *n* beatitudine *f;* **marital ~** felicità *f* coniugale

blissful ['blɪs·fəl] *adj* (*enjoyable*) meraviglioso, -a; ~ **ignorance** beata ignoranza

blister ['blɪs·tə] I. *n* 1. ANAT vescica *f* 2. (*bubble*) bolla *f* II. *vt* far venire le vesciche a III. *vi* riempirsi di vesciche

blistering *adj* (*very hot*) torrido, -a

blithering ['blɪ·ðə·ɪŋ] *adj* ~ **idiot!** pezzo d'idiota!

blizzard ['blɪ·zəd] *n* tempesta *f* di neve

bloated ['bloʊ·t̬ɪd] *adj* 1. (*swollen*) gonfio, -a 2. (*excessive*) smisurato, -a

blob [blɑːb] *n* grossa goccia *f*

block [blɑːk] I. *n* 1. (*solid lump*) blocco *m* 2. (*city block*) isolato *m* 3. (*of traffic*) ingorgo *m* 4. (*physiological, psychological*) blocco *m* 5. (*child's toy*) cubo *m* 6. (*for executions*) ceppo *m;* **to be sent to the ~** essere condannato alla decapitazione 7. *inf* (*head*) **to knock sb's ~ off** spaccare la faccia a qu; **to be a chip off the old ~** tale padre tale figlio 8. SPORTS blocco *m* di partenza 9. COMPUT selezione *f* II. *vt* 1. (*road, pipe*) bloccare; (*sb's progress*) ostacolare 2. COMPUT **to ~ and copy** seleziona e copia

◆ **block off** *vt* bloccare

◆ **block out** *vt* 1. (*censor*) cancellare 2. (*repress: memory*) rimuovere

◆ **block up** I. *vt* ostruire II. *vi* otturarsi

blockade [blɑː·'keɪd] I. *n* blocco *m* II. *vt* bloccare

blockage ['blɑː·kɪdʒ] *n* ostruzione *f*

block letters *n* stampatello *m*

blond(e) [blɑːnd] I. *adj* (*hair*) biondo, -a II. *n* biondo, -a *m, f*

blood [blʌd] *n* sangue *f;* **to be of the same ~** essere imparentati ▸ **to have ~ on one's**

hands *fig* avere le mani sporche di sangue; ~ **is thicker than** water il sangue non è acqua; *prov;* bad ~ cattivo sangue; **in** cold ~ a sangue freddo; **her** ~ **ran** cold le si è gelato il sangue nelle vene; **it makes my** ~ boil mi fa ribollire il sangue; **to make sb's** ~ curdle far gelare il sangue nelle vene a qu; **to** smell ~ fiutare il sangue; **to** sweat ~ sudare sangue; **to be** after **sb's** ~ avercela con qu

blood bank *n* banca *f* del sangue

bloodbath *n* bagno *m* di sangue

blood clot *n* coagulo *m*, grumo *m* di sangue

bloodcurdling *adj* agghiacciante

blood donor *n* donatore, -trice *m, f* di sangue

blood group *n* gruppo *m* sanguigno

bloodhound *n* segugio *m*

bloodless ['blʌd·lɪs] *adj* **1.** (*face, lips*) esangue **2.** (*coup*) incruento, -a **3.** (*emotionless: film*) insulso, -a

blood poisoning *n* setticemia *f*

blood pressure *n* pressione *f* arteriosa

blood relation *n*, **blood relative** *n* consanguineo, -a *m, f*

bloodshed *n* spargimento *m* di sangue

bloodshot ['blʌd·ʃɑːt] *adj* (*eyes*) iniettato, -a di sangue

blood sport *n* (*hunting*) sport *m* cruento

bloodstained ['blʌd·steɪnd] *adj* macchiato, -a di sangue

bloodstock *n* purosangue *m inv*

bloodstream *n* sistema *m* sanguigno

bloodsucker *n* sanguisuga *f*

blood sugar *n* zucchero *m* nel sangue

blood test *n* analisi *m inv* del sangue

bloodthirsty ['blʌd·ˌθɜːrs·ti] *adj* sanguinario, -a

blood transfusion *n* trasfusione *f* di sangue

blood type *n* gruppo *m* sanguigno

blood vessel *n* vaso *m* sanguigno

bloody ['blʌd·i] <-ier, -iest> *adj* (*with blood*) insanguinato, -a; **to have a** ~ **nose** avere il sangue dal naso; (*fight, battle*) sanguinoso, -a

bloom [bluːm] **I.** *n a. fig* fiore *f;* **to come into** ~ fiorire; **in the full** ~ **of youth** nel fiore della gioventù **II.** *vi* **1.** (*produce flowers*) fiorire **2.** (*peak*) prosperare

blooming ['bluːmɪŋ] *adj* fiorente

blossom ['blɑː·səm] **I.** *n* fiore *f;* **in** ~ in fiore; **orange** ~ zagara *f,* fiore *m* d'arancio **II.** *vi* **1.** (*flower*) fiorire **2.** (*develop*) diventare

blot [blɑːt] **I.** *n a. fig* (*mark*) macchia *f* **II.** *vt* **1.** (*make mark on*) macchiare **2.** (*dry*) asciugare

blotch [blɑːtʃ] *n* macchia *f*

blotchy ['blɑː·tʃi] <-ier, -iest> *adj* pieno, -a di macchie

blotter ['blɑː·tə̆] *n* folglio *f* di carta assorbente

blotting paper *n* carta *f* assorbente

blotto ['blɑː·t̬ou] *adj sl* **to be** ~ essere sbronzo

blouse [blaus] *n* camicetta *f*

blow¹ [blou] *n* **1.** (*hit*) colpo *m;* (*with the fist*) pugno *m;* **to come to** ~**s** venire alle mani **2.** *fig* (*setback*) colpo *m*

blow² [blou] **I.** <blew, blown> *vi* **1.** (*expel air*) soffiare **2.** (*fuse*) saltare **3.** (*tire*) scoppiare ▶ **to** ~ hot **and** cold fare la banderuola **II.** *vt* **1.** (*instrument*) suonare **2.** (*clear*) **to** ~ **one's** nose soffiarsi il naso **3.** (*burst: tire*) far scoppiare **4.** *inf* (*spend*) sperperare **5.** (*mess up, fail: test*) essere respinto [*o* bocciato] a; (*interview*) giocarsi; **to** ~ **one's chances at doing** sth giocarsi la possibilità di fare qc; **it blew my** mind! *sl* mi ha sconvolto; **to** ~ **one's** top [*o* lid] *inf* infuriarsi

◆ **blow away** *vt* **1.** (*doubt*) dissipare **2.** *sl* (*kill*) liquidare

◆ **blow down I.** *vi* (*fall down*) essere abbattuto dal vento **II.** *vt* (*knock down*) abbattere

◆ **blow off** *vt* (*wind*) portar via; **to** ~ **off** steam sfogarsi

◆ **blow out I.** *vt* (*candle*) spegnere **II.** *vi* spegnersi

◆ **blow over** *vi* (*scandal*) finire nel dimenticatoio; (*argument, dispute*) calmarsi

◆ **blow up I.** *vi* **1.** (*storm, gale*) alzarsi **2.** (*bomb*) esplodere **II.** *vt* **1.** (*fill with air: balloon*) gonfiare **2.** PHOT (*enlarge*) ingrandire **3.** (*explode*) far saltare in aria

blow-by-blow *adj* **a** ~ **account** un resoconto dettagliato

blow-dry *vt* asciugare con il phon

blow dryer *n* phon *m inv*

blowfly <-ies> *n* mosca *f* della carne

blowgun *n* (*weapon*) cerbottana *f*

blowhole *n* (*in whale, dolphin*) sfiatatoio *m*

blowjob *n vulg* pompino *m*

blown [bloun] *vt, vi pp of* **blow**

blowout *n inf* **1.** (*burst tire*) scoppio *m* **2.** *sl* (*party*) **to have a** ~ far bisboccia

blowtorch *n* cannello *m* per saldatura

blowup *n* PHOT ingrandimento *m*

blubber¹ ['blʌ·bə̆] *vi* (*cry*) piangere come un vitello

blubber² ['blʌ·bə̆] *n* (*whale fat*) grasso *m* (di balena)

bludgeon ['blʌ·dʒən] **I.** *n* manganello *m* **II.** *vt* prendere a manganellate

blue [bluː] **I.** *adj* **1.** (*color*) blu; **light** ~ azzurro; **dark** ~ blu scuro; **pale** ~ azzurro pallido; **deep** ~ blu intenso **2.** (*sad*) triste; **to feel** ~ sentirsi triste **II.** *n* (*light*) azzurro *m;* (*dark*) blu *m inv;* **sky** ~ azzurro cielo; **the door is painted** ~ la porta è dipinta di blu ▶ out of **the** ~ quando meno ce lo si aspetta

bluebell *n* BOT campanula *f*

blueberry ['bluː·be·ri] <-ies> *n* mirtillo *m*

bluebottle *n* moscone *m*

blue chip *adj* di prim'ordine

blue collar *adj* (*union, background*) operaio, -a; (*job*) manuale

blueprint *n* plano *m;* (*plan of action*) progetto *m*

blues [bluːz] *npl* **1.** (*sadness*) malinconia *f* **2.** MUS blues *m inv*

blue whale *n* balena *f* blu

bluff¹ [blʌf] **I.** *vi* bluffare **II.** *vt* ingannare **III.** *n*

B

bluff *m inv;* **to call sb's** ~ far mettere le carte in tavola a qu

bluff² [blʌf] *n* (*steep bank*) rupe *m;* (*cliff*) scogliera *f*

bluff³ [blʌf] <-er, -est> *adj* (*in manner*) diretto, -a

bluffer ['blʌ·fə] *n* bluffatore, -trice *m, f*

bluish ['bluːɪʃ] *adj* bluastro, -a

blunder ['blʌn·də] I. *n* gaffe *f* II. *vi* 1. (*make a mistake*) fare una gaffe 2. (*move clumsily*) **to** ~ **into sth** inciampare in qc

blunt [blʌnt] I. *adj* 1. (*not sharp*) non affilato, -a 2. (*direct*) brusco, -a II. *vt a. fig* smussare

bluntly *adv* senza giri di parole; **to put it** ~, ... per dirlo senza giri di parole,...

bluntness *n fig* (*directness*) franchezza *f*

blur [blɜːr] I. *vi* <-rr-> velarsi II. *vt* <-rr-> velare; (*picture*) sfuocare III. *n* (*shape*) massa *f* indistinta; (*memory*) ricordo *m* confuso

blurb [blɜːrb] *n inf* frase *f* pubblicitaria

blurred [blɜːrd] *adj* confuso, -a; (*photograph, picture*) sfuocato, -a

blurt out [blɜːrt·'aʊt] *vt* lasciarsi sfuggire

blush [blʌʃ] I. *vi* arrossire II. *n* 1. (*natural color*) rossore *m* 2. (*makeup*) fard *m inv*

blusher ['blʌ·ʃə] *n* fard *m inv*

blushing *adj* che arrossisce facilmente

bluster ['blʌs·tə] I. *vi* 1. (*speak*) dire fanfaronate 2. (*blow*) soffiare a raffiche II. *n* fanfaronate *fpl*

BO [ˌbiːˈoʊ] *n abbr of* **body odor** odori *m pl* corporali

boa ['boʊ·ə] *n* zool boa *m*

boar [bɔːr] *n* (*male pig*) verro *m;* (**wild**) ~ cinghiale *m*

board [bɔːrd] I. *n* 1. (*wood*) tavola *f* 2. (*blackboard*) lavagna *f;* (*notice board*) tabellone *m* 3. games scacchiera *f* 4. admin consiglio *m;* ~ (**of directors**) consiglio di amministrazione; ~ **of trade** camera *f* di commercio; ~ **of education** consiglio d'Istituto 5. (*in a hotel*) **room and** ~ pensione *f* completa 6. naut **on** ~ a bordo ▸**to sweep the** ~ avere un successo assoluto; (*in gambling*) fare man bassa; **to take sth on** ~ adottare qc; **to tread the** ~**s** theat calcare le scene; **across the** ~ a tutti i livelli II. *vt* (*get on: airplane, ship*) salire a bordo di; (*bus, train*) salire su III. *vi* (*stay*) alloggiare; (*in school*) essere interno; **to** ~ **with sb** alloggiare in casa di qu

♦**board up** *vt* chiudere con tavole di legno

boarder ['bɔːr·də] *n* (*in a rooming house*) pensionante *mf;* (*at a school*) convittore, -trice *m, f*

board game *n* gioco *m* da tavolo

boarding house *n* pensione *f*

boarding pass *n* carta *f* di imbarco

boarding school *n* collegio *m*

board meeting *n* riunione *f* del consiglio di amministrazione

boardroom *n* sala *f* del consiglio

boardwalk *n passeggiata a mare realizzata con tavole di legno*

boast [boʊst] I. *vi* fare sfoggio; **to** ~ **about** [*o* **of**] **sth** vantarsi di qc II. *vt* (*be proud of*) vantare; **this house** ~**s 10 rooms** questa casa ha 10 stanze III. *n* vanto *m*

boastful ['boʊst·fəl] *adj* borioso, -a

boat [boʊt] *n* barca *f;* **to go by** ~ andare in barca ▸**to be in the same** ~ essere nella stessa barca; **to miss the** ~ perdere il treno; **to rock the** ~ *inf* agitare le acque

boat hook *n* mezzo *m* marinaio

boathouse *n* rimessa *f* per le barche

boating ['boʊ·tɪŋ] *n* **to go** ~ andare in barca

boatman *n* barcaiolo *m*

boat people *npl* profughi *m pl* delle barche

boat race *n* regata *f*

boatswain ['boʊ·sən] *n* nostromo *m*

boat train *n* treno *m* che garantisce la coincidenza con un traghetto

boat trip *n* viaggio *m* in barca

bob [bɑːb] <-bb-> I. *vi* **to** ~ (**up and down**) ondeggiare II. *n* 1. (*hairstyle*) caschetto *m* 2. (*movement*) dondolio *m*

bobbin ['bɑː·bɪn] *n* bobina *f*

bobby pin *n* molletta *f* per capelli

bobsled ['bɑːb·sled] *n* sports bob *m inv*

bobtail ['bɑːb·teɪl] *n* 1. (*docked tail*) coda *f* tagliata 2. (*animal*) animale *m* con la coda tagliata

bode [boʊd] I. *vi* **to** ~ **well/ill** essere di buon/cattivo augurio II. *vt* presagire

bodice ['bɑː·dɪs] *n* (*of a dress*) corpetto *m*

bodily ['bɑːd·li] I. *adj* (*functions, injury*) corporale; (*needs*) materiale II. *adv* (*in person*) di persona; (*as a whole*) nel complesso

body ['bɑː·di] <-ies> *n* 1. *a.* anat, astr, chem, mus corpo *m;* (*dead*) cadavere *m; fig* (*person*); **a cheerful old** ~ un tipo allegro 2. admin, pol ente *m;* (*governing*) organismo *m;* **in a** ~ in blocco 3. (*amount*) quantità *f;* (*of water*) massa *f* 4. auto carrozzeria *f* 5. (*of wine*) corpo *m* ▸**to keep** ~ **and soul together** sopravvivere; **to throw oneself** ~ **and soul into sth** gettarsi anima e corpo in qc; **over my dead** ~ dovrai passare sul mio cadavere; **to sell one's** ~ prostituirsi

body bag *n* sacco *m* per cadaveri

bodybuilding *n* culturismo *m*

bodyguard *n* guardia *f* del corpo

body language *n* linguaggio *m* del corpo

body lotion *n* lozione *f* per il corpo

body politic *n* pol estado *m*

body search *n* perquisizione *f* personale

body suit *n* body *m inv*

bodywork *n* carrozzeria *f*

bog [bɑːg] *n* (*wet ground*) pantano *m;* **peat** ~ torbiera *f*

♦**bog down** <-gg-> *vt* **to get bogged down in sth** *fig* impantanarsi in qc

bogey ['boʊ·gi] *n* (*golf score*) bogey *m inv*

boggle ['bɑː·gl] I. *vi* restare attonito II. *vt* **to** ~ **the mind** essere incredibile

boggy ['bɑː·gi] <-ier, -iest> *adj* pantanoso, -a

bogus ['boʊ·gəs] *adj* (*document*) falso, -a
bohemian [boʊ·'hiː·mi·ən] I. *n* bohémien *mf inv* II. *adj* bohémien
boil [bɔɪl] I. *vi, vt a. fig* bollire II. *n* **1. to bring sth to a** ~ portare a ebollizione; **to be at a** ~ stare bollende **2.** MED forunculo *m*
◆**boil away** *vi* evaporare
◆**boil down** I. *vi* ridursi cuocendo; *fig;* **it all boils down to …** ridursi a … II. *vt* **1.** CULIN (*sauce*) far ridurre **2.** *fig* (*text*) ridurre
◆**boil over** *vi* **1.** CULIN traboccare **2.** (*person*) perdere il controllo
◆**boil up** *vt* (*milk*) montare
boiler ['bɔɪ·lɚ] *n* caldaia *f*
boiler room *n* locale *m* delle caldaie
boiling *adj* **1.** (*liquid*) bollente **2.** *fig* (*day, weather*) torrido, -a; (*angry: person*) furente; **to be** ~ **mad** essere fuori di sé dalla rabbia; **I am** ~ (*feeling hot*) sto morendo di caldo; **it's** ~ (**hot**) **today** fa un caldo allucinante
boiling point *n* punto *m* di ebollizione; **the situation has reached the** ~ la situazione sta per precipitare
boisterous ['bɔɪs·tə·rəs] *adj* **1.** (*person*) turbolento, -a; (*party*) movimentato, -a **2.** (*sea*) infuriato, -a
bold [boʊld] <-er, -est> *adj* **1.** (*brave, audacious*) audace **2.** (*not shy*) sfacciato, -a **3.** (*strong: color*) sgargiante **4.** COMPUT, TYPO ~ (**type**) grassetto *m;* **in** ~ in grassetto
boldness *n* audacia *f*
bole [boʊl] *n* (*of tree*) tronco *m*
bolero [bə·'le·roʊ] <-s> *n* **1.** (*short jacket*) bolero *m* **2.** MUS bolero *m*
Bolivia [bə·'lɪ·vi·ə] *n* Bolivia *f*
Bolivian [bə·'lɪ·vi·ən] I. *adj* boliviano, -a II. *n* boliviano, -a *m, f*
bolster ['boʊl·stɚ] I. *n* capezzale *m* II. *vt* **1.** (*support*) rinforzare **2.** (*spirits*) sollevare
bolt [boʊlt] I. *vi* (*run away*) fuggire II. *vt* **1.** (*lock*) chiudere con il chiavistello **2.** (*fasten down*) imbullonare III. *n* **1.** (*on a door*) chiavistello *m* **2.** (*screw*) bullone *m* **3.** (*lightning*) fulmine *m* **4.** (*roll: of cloth*) rotolo *m* **5.** (*arrow*) freccia *f* ▶ **to make a** ~ **for it** fuggire; **a** ~ **from the blue** un fulmine a ciel sereno IV. *adv* ~ **upright** dritto come un fuso
◆**bolt down** *vt* (*food*) ingurgitare
bomb [baːm] I. *n* **1.** (*explosive*) bomba *f;* (*for killing insects*) bomboletta *f;* **the** ~ la bomba atomica **2.** *fig, inf* (*failure*) fiasco *m* II. *vt* bombardare III. *vi inf* essere un fiasco
bombard [baːm·'baːrd] *vt* bombardare; **to** ~ **sb with questions** bombardare qu di domande
bombardment [baːm·'baːrd·mənt] *n* bombardamento *m*
bombast ['baːm·bæst] *n* magniloquenza *f*
bombastic [baːm·'bæs·tɪk] *adj* magniloquente
bomb crater *n* cratere *m* di una bomba
bombed [baːmd] *adj* **1.** bombardato, -a **2.** *sl* (*on alcohol*) ubriaco, -a perso, -a; (*on drugs*)

fatto, -a
bomber ['baː·mɚ] *n* **1.** AVIAT bombardiere *m* **2.** (*terrorist*) dinamitardo, -a *m, f*
bombing *n* **1.** MIL bombardamento *m* **2.** (*by terrorists*) attentato *m* dinamitardo
bombproof *adj* a prova di bomba
bomb scare *n* allarme *m* bomba
bombshell ['baːm·ʃel] *n* **1. a.** *fig* MIL bomba *f* **2.** (*woman*) **a blonde** ~ una bionda esplosiva
bona fide [ˌboʊ·nə·'faɪ·di] *adj* **1.** (*genuine*) genuino, -a; (*agreement, alibi*) autentico, -a **2.** (*serious*) serio, -a
bonanza [bə·'næn·zə] *n* **1.** (*large deposit*) immenso giacimento *m* **2.** *fig* boom *m inv*
bond [baːnd] I. *n* **1.** (*connection*) vincolo *m;* (*of friendship, love*) legame *m;* **to break one's** ~ rompere i ponti *fig* **2.** (*obligation*) impegno *m* **3.** FIN obbligazione *f;* **to place goods in** ~ depositare le merci presso il magazzino doganale **4.** LAW garanzia *f;* (*bail*) cauzione *f* **5.** *pl, liter* (*chains*) catene *fpl* II. *vt* **1.** (*stick*) far aderire **2.** (*unite emotionally*) **to** ~ (**together**) unire **3.** COM depositare presso il magazzino doganale III. *vi* aderire
bondage ['baːn·dɪdʒ] *n* **1.** *liter* (*slavery*) schiavitù *f* **2.** (*for sexual pleasure*) *legare o farsi legare*
bonded *adj* COM depositato, -a presso il magazzino doganale
bonded debt *n* FIN debito *m* consolidato
bonded warehouse *n* COM magazzino *m* doganale
bondholder *n* FIN obbligazionista *mf*
bone [boʊn] I. *n* ANAT osso *m;* (*of a fish*) lisca *f* ▶ ~ **of contention** pomo *m* della discordia; **to work one's fingers to the** ~ lavorare come un cane; **close to the** ~ fuori luogo; **to cut sth to the** ~ ridurre qc all'essenziale; **to feel sth in one's** ~**s** sentirsi qc; **to make no** ~**s about sth** non far segreto di qc; **to have a** ~ **to pick with sb** *inf* dover regolare un conto con qu II. *adj* d'osso III. *adv* (*as intensifier*) ~ **lazy** pigrissimo, -a; ~ **tired** stanchissimo, -a IV. *vt* (*chicken, meat*) disossare; (*fish*) spinare
◆**bone up for** *vt* (*prepare for*) fare una secchiata *inf*
bonehead *n inf* testa *f* di rapa
bone marrow *n* midollo *m* osseo
bone meal *n* farina *f* d'ossa
bonfire ['baːn·fa·ɪɚ] *n* falò *m*
bonk [baːŋk] *inf* I. *vt* (*hit on head*) dare un colpo in testa a II. *n* colpo *m* in testa
bonkers ['baːŋ·kɚz] *adj inf* matto, -a; **to go** ~ ammattire
bonnet ['baː·nɪt] *n* (*hat*) berretto *m;* (*baby's*) cuffia *f*
bonus ['boʊ·nəs] I. *n* **1.** (*money*) gratifica *f;* **Christmas** ~ tredicesima *f;* **productivity** ~ premio *m* di produttività **2.** (*advantage*) vantaggio *m* II. *adj* (*additional*) gratuito, -a
bony ['boʊ·ni] *adj* <-ier, -iest> **1.** (*with prominent bones*) ossuto, -a; (*fish*) pieno, -a di lische **2.** (*like bones*) osseo, -a

B

boo [bu:] I. *interj inf* bu II. *vi* fischiare III. *vt* fischiare; **he was ~ed off the stage** lo hanno fischiato fino a fargli abbandonare la scena

boob [bu:b] *n* 1. *vulg* (*breast*) tetta *f* 2. *sl* (*fool*) scemo, -a *m*, *f*

boob tube *n sl* tele *f inv*

booby ['bu:·bi] *n* scemo, -a *m*, *f*

booby prize *n* premio *m* all'ultimo classificato

booby trap *n* MIL trappola *f* esplosiva

booger ['bʊ·gə·] *n sl* 1. (*dried mucus*) croste *f* del naso *pl* 2. (*person*) disgraziato, -a *m*, *f*

book [bʊk] I. *n* 1. libro *m*; **the Good Book** la Bibbia 2. (*of stamps*) carnet *m inv*; (*of tickets*) blocchetto *m*; (*of matches*) bustina *f* 3. COM, FIN **the ~s** contabilità; **to cook the ~s** *inf* manipolare la contabilità ▶ **to be a closed ~** (**to sb**) essere un mistero (per qu); **to bring sb to ~** obbligare qu a rendere conto; **to know sb like a ~** conoscere qu come se stessi; **to be able to read sb like a ~** conoscere qu a fondo; **to throw the ~ at sb** punire duramente qu; **in my ~** secondo me; **by the ~** secondo i canoni II. *vt* 1. (*reserve*) prenotare 2. (*register*) registrare 3. (*file charges against*) schedare III. *vi* prenotare

◆**book up** *vt* **to be booked up** (*hotel*) essere al completo

bookbinder *n* rilegatore, -trice *m*, *f*

bookbinding *n* rilegatura *f*

bookcase *n* libreria *f*

book club *n* club *m* del libro

bookend *n* reggilibro *m inv*

bookie ['bʊ·ki] *n inf* bookmaker *m inv*

booking ['bʊ·kɪŋ] *n* prenotazione *f*; **to make/cancel a ~** fare/annullare una prenotazione

bookish ['bʊ·kɪʃ] *adj* libresco, -a; *pej* pedante

bookkeeper *n* contabile *mf*

bookkeeping *n* contabilità *f*

booklet ['bʊk·lɪt] *n* opuscolo *m*

bookmaker *n* bookmaker *m inv*

bookmark *n a.* COMPUT segnalibro *m*

bookplate *n* ex libris *m inv*

book review *n* critica *f* letteraria

book reviewer *n* critico, -a *m*, *f* letterario

bookseller *n* (*person*) libraio, -a *m*, *f*; (*shop*) libreria *f*

bookshelf <-shelves> *n* mensola *m* per i libri

bookshop *n* libreria *f*

bookstore *n* libreria *f*

bookworm *n* topo *m* di biblioteca

boom¹ [bu:m] ECON I. *vi* vivere un periodo di boom II. *n* boom *m inv* III. *adj* **a ~ time** un periodo di sviluppo economico; **a ~ town** una città in pieno sviluppo

boom² [bu:m] I. *n* (*sound*) rimbombo *m* II. *vi to* ~ (*out*) rimbombare; (*voice*) risuonare III. *vt* dire con voce tonante

boom³ [bu:m] *n* 1. NAUT boma *m inv* 2. (*floating barrier*) barriera *f* 3. (*for a microphone*) giraffa *f*

boom box *n* ghetto blaster *m inv*, stereo portatile con forte amplificazione

boomerang ['bu:·mə·ræŋ] I. *n* bumerang *m* *inv* II. *vi* it ~ed on her/him gli/le è tornato indietro come un boomerang

boon [bu:n] *n* benedizione *f*; **to be a ~** (**to sb**) essere una benedizione (per qu); **~ companion** *liter* compagno, -a *m*, *f* di bisbocce

boondocks *n pl* **the ~** a casa del diavolo

boonies *n pl, inf s.* **boondocks**

boor [bʊr] *n* cafone, -a *m*, *f*

boorish ['bʊ·rɪʃ] *adj* villano, -a

boost [bu:st] I. *n* 1. (*lift*) **to give sb a ~** tirare su qu 2. (*increase*) **to give a ~ to sth**, **to give sth a ~** stimolare qc; **a ~ in sales** incremento delle vendite; (*incentive*) incentivo *m* II. *vt* 1. (*help go higher*) tirare su 2. (*increase*) incrementare; (*morale*) tirare su; (*process*) stimolare 3. *inf* (*promote: product, image*) promuovere

booster ['bu:·stə·] *n* MED (vaccino di) richiamo *m*

booster rocket *n* TECH razzo *m* propulsore

booster seat *n* AUTO rialza bimbo *m*, *seggiolino auto per bambini dai 4 agli 11 anni*

boot [bu:t] I. *n* 1. (*footwear*) stivale *m*; **ankle ~** stivaletto *m*; **rubber ~** stivale *m* di gomma 2. *inf* (*kick*) pedata *f*; *fig* (*dismissal from job*); **to get the ~** essere messo alla porta; **to give sb the ~** mettere qu alla porta 3. COMPUT avvio *m*, inizializzazione *f*; **warm/cold ~** avvio a caldo/a freddo ▶ **to be too big for one's ~s** *inf* montarsi la testa; **to lick sb's ~s** leccare i piedi a qu; **to shake in one's ~s** *inf* tremare come una foglia II. *vt inf* 1. (*kick*) dare una pedata a 2. *fig, inf* (*fire from job*) mettere alla porta 3. COMPUT avviare, inizializzare ▶ **to ~** per di più

◆**boot out** *vt inf* buttar fuori qu a pedate

bootblack ['bu:t·blæk] *n* lustrascarpe *mf inv*

bootee ['bu:·ti] *n* (*for babies*) scarpetta *f*; (*for women*) stivaletto *m*

booth [bu:ð] *n* 1. (*cubicle*) cabina *f*; **telephone ~** cabina telefonica; **polling ~** cabina elettorale 2. (*at a fair, market*) bancarella *f*

bootlace ['bu:t·leɪs] *n* laccio *m*

bootleg ['bu:t·leg] <-gg-> *adj* 1. (*alcohol, cigarettes*) di contrabbando 2. (*recording, software*) pirata

bootlicker ['bu:t·lɪ·kə·] *n inf* leccapiedi *mf inv*

booty ['bu:·ti] *n* bottino *m*

booze [bu:z] I. *n inf* bevande *f* alcoliche *pl*; **to be on the ~** alzare il gomito II. *vi inf* alzare il gomito

boozer ['bu:·zə·] *n inf* ubriacone, -a *m*, *f*

boozy ['bu:·zi] <-ier, -iest> *adj inf* brillo, -a

border ['bɔ:r·də·] I. *n* 1. (*between states, countries*) frontiera *f* 2. (*edge, boundary*) margine *m*; (*of lake*) riva *f* 3. FASHION bordo *m* 4. (*in a garden*) aiuola *f* II. *adj* di confine III. *vt* confinare con

◆**border on** *vt* 1. (*share border with*) confinare con 2. *fig* rasentare

bordering *adj* confinante

borderland ['bɔ:r·də·lænd] *n* zona *f* di confine

borderline ['bɔ:r·də·laɪn] I. *n* linea *f* di confine **II.** *adj* (*candidate, case*) limite

bore[1] [bɔːr] **I.** *n* **1.** (*thing*) noia *f;* **what a ~!** che noia! **2.** (*person*) persona *f* noiosa **II.** <bored> *vt* annoiare; **to ~ sb to death** *inf* annoiare qu a morte

bore[2] [bɔːr] **I.** *n* (*of a gun*) calibro *m* **II.** *vt* perforare; **to ~ a hole** fare un buco

bore[3] [bɔːr] *pp of* **bear**

bored *adj* annoiato, -a

boredom ['bɔːr·dəm] *n* noia *f*

boric ['bɔː·rɪk] *adj* borico, -a; **~ acid** acido borico

boring ['bɔː·rɪŋ] *adj* noioso, -a; **to find sth ~** trovare qc noioso

born [bɔːrn] *adj* **1.** (*brought into life*) nato, -a; **to be ~** nascere; **where were you ~?** dove sei nato?; **he was ~ in** (**the year**) **1975** è nato nel 1975; **he was ~ blind** è cieco dalla nascita **2.** (*ability*) nato, -a; (*quality, sympathy*) innato, -a; **to be ~ to do sth** è nato per fare qc ▶ **I wasn't ~** <u>yesterday</u> *inf* non sono nato ieri

born-again *adj* rinato, -a; **~ Christian** cristiano rinato

borne [bɔːrn] *pt of* **bear**

borough ['bɜː·roʊ] *n* comune *m*

borrow ['baː·roʊ] *vt* **1.** (*be given temporarily*) prendere in prestito; **may I ~ your bag?** mi presti la tua borsa? **2.** MAT riportare **3.** LING prendere (a prestito)

borrower *n* persona *f* che prende in prestito

borrowing *n* prestito *m*

Bosnia ['baːz·niə] *n* Bosnia *f*

Bosnia-Herzegovina ['baːz·niə·ˌhert·sə·goʊ·viː·nə] *n* Bosnia *f* Erzegovina

Bosnian ['baːz·ni·ən] **I.** *adj* bosniaco, -a **II.** *n* bosniaco, -a *m, f*

bosom ['bʊ·zəm] *n* **1.** (*chest*) petto *m*, seno *m* **2.** *fig* seno *m;* **in the ~ of one's family** in seno alla famiglia

bosom buddy *n* amico *m* del cuore

boss [baːs] **I.** *n* **1.** (*supervisor*) capo, -a *m, f;* (*owner*) principale *mf;* **to be one's own ~** lavorare in proprio **2.** (*bossy person*) prepotente *mf* **II.** *vt inf* **to ~ sb around** comandare a bacchetta **III.** *adj inf* (*terrific*) eccezionale

bossy ['baː·si] <-ier, -iest> *adj* prepotente

botanical [bə·'tæ·nɪ·kəl] *adj* botanico, -a

botanist ['baːt·nɪst] *n* botanico, -a *m, f*

botany ['baːt·ni] *n* botanica *f*

botch [baːtʃ] **I.** *n* pasticcio *m;* **to make a ~ of sth** raffazzonare qc **II.** *vt* **to ~ sth** (**up**) raffazzonare qc

botch-up *s.* botch **I.**

both [boʊθ] **I.** *adj, pron* entrambi, -e; **~ of them** tutti, -e e due; **~ of us** tutti, -e e due; **~** (**the**) **brothers** entrambi i fratelli; **on ~ sides** su entrambi i lati **II.** *adv* **~ David and Peter** sia David che Peter; **to be ~ sad and pleased** essere tristi e soddisfatti al tempo stesso

bother ['baː·ðɚ] **I.** *n* seccatura *f;* **not to want to be a ~** non voler dar fastidio; **it is not worth the ~** non vale la pena **II.** *vi* scomodarsi; **to** (**not**) **~ to do sth** (non) scomodarsi a fare qc; **why ~?** a che pro? **III.** *vt* **1.** (*annoy*) dar fastidio a **2.** (*worry*) preoccupare; **he doesn't seem to be ~ed by this** non sembra che ciò lo preoccupi; **what ~s me is ...** ciò che mi preoccupa è ... **3.** (*give pain*) far male a; **my back has been ~ing me lately** ho sofferto di mal di schiena negli ultimi tempi

bothersome ['baː·ðɚ·səm] *adj* fastidioso, -a

Botswana [ˌbaːt·'swaː·nə] *n* Botswana *f*

Botswanan [ˌbaːt·'swaː·nən] **I.** *adj* del Botswana **II.** *n* abitante *mf* del Botswana

bottle ['baː·t̬l] **I.** *n* **1.** (*container*) bottiglia *f;* (*of perfume*) flacone *m;* (*of ink*) boccetta *m;* (*baby's*) biberon *m inv* **2.** *inf* (*alcohol*) **the ~** l'alcol; **to hit the ~** darsi all'alcol **II.** *vt* imbottigliare; *fig;* **to ~ one's emotions up** reprimere le proprie emozioni

bottlebrush *n* spazzola *f* per bottiglie

bottled ['baː·t̬ld] *adj* imbottigliato, -a; (*beer*) in bottiglia; (*gas*) in bombole

bottle-feeding *n* allattamento *m* artificiale

bottle green *adj* verde bottiglia

bottleneck ['baː·t̬l·nek] **I.** *n* (*narrow route*) strettoia *m;* (*traffic*) ingorgo *m; fig* (*standstill*) impasse *f inv* **II.** *vi* (*traffic*) ingorgarsi

bottle opener *n* apribottiglie *m inv*

bottom ['baː·t̬əm] **I.** *n* **1.** (*of sea, street, glass, page*) fondo *m;* (*of chair*) sedile *m;* **to touch ~** *fig* toccare il fondo **2.** (*lower part*) parte *f* inferiore; **from top to ~** da cima a fondo **3.** (*buttocks*) sedere *m* ▶ **from the ~ of one's** <u>heart</u> con tutto il cuore; **~s up!** cin cin!; **to get to the ~ of sth** andare in fondo a qc; **at ~** in fondo; **to be at the ~ of sth** essere alla radice di qc **II.** *adj* (*lower*) più in basso; **the ~ half of society** la classe medio-bassa

bottomless ['baː·t̬əm·ləs] *adj* **1.** (*without limit*) illimitato, -a **2.** (*very deep*) senza fondo; **he is a ~ pit** *fig* mangia per quattro

bottom line *n* **the ~ line is that ...** *fig* il succo della questione è che ...

botulism ['baː·tʃə·lɪ·zəm] *n* botulismo *m*

bough [baʊ] *n liter* ramo *m*

bought [baːt] *vt pt of* **buy**

boulder ['boʊl·dɚ] *n* masso *m*

boulevard ['bʊ·lə·vaːrd] *n* viale *m*

---

i Il **Boston Tea party** fu nel 1773 un atto di sfida nei confronti del dominio coloniale britannico in America. Dei colonialisti vestiti da Amerindi, tra i quali Samuel Adams e Paul Revere, salirono a bordo di alcune navi inglesi e gettarono in mare centinaia di casse di tè per protestare contro l'assoggettamento delle colonie a tassazione da parte della Gran Bretagna, pur non essendo rappresentate nel parlamento inglese. Si trattò di uno degli avvenimenti chiave che condussero alla guerra di indipendenza degli USA contro l'Inghilterra.

bounce [baʊnts] I. *vi* 1. (*rebound*) rimbalzare; **to ~ against sth** rimbalzare contro qc 2. (*jump or spring up and down*) saltellare 3. *inf* COM (*check*) essere scoperto II. *vt* 1. (*cause to rebound*) far rimbalzare; **to ~ a baby** far fare il cavallino al bambino; **to ~ an idea off sb** chiedere il parere di qu; **to ~ sb into doing sth** spingere qu a fare qc 2. *inf* COM **to ~ a check** respingere un assegno scoperto III. *n* 1. (*rebound*) rimbalzo *m* 2. (*spring*) salto *m* 3. (*vitality*) vitalità *f;* (*energy*) energia *f* 4. *inf* **to give sb the ~** buttar qu fuori a pedate
◆**bounce back** *vi* riprendersi velocemente
bouncer ['baʊn·tsɚ] *n inf* buttafuori *m inv*
bouncing *adj* robusto, -a
bouncy ['baʊn·tsi] *adj* 1. (*ball*) che rimbalza 2. (*lively*) pieno, -a di vita
bound[1] [baʊnd] I. *vi* 1. (*leap*) saltare 2. (*bounce: ball*) rimbalzare II. *n* salto *m;* **in leaps and ~s** a passi da gigante
bound[2] [baʊnd] *vt* (*confine*) **to be ~ed by sth** essere circondato da qc
bound[3] [baʊnd] *adj* (*showing direction*) **to be ~ for ...** essere diretto a ...; **where is this ship ~ for?** dov'è diretta questa nave?; **north/ south-bound traffic** il traffico diretto a nord/ sud
bound[4] [baʊnd] I. *pt, pp of* **bind** II. *adj* 1. (*sure*) **she's ~ to come** viene di sicuro; **it's ~ to be very expensive** è certamente molto caro; **it was ~ to happen sooner or later** prima o poi doveva succedere 2. (*obliged*) **to be ~ to do sth** essere obbligato a fare qc
boundary ['baʊn·dri] <-ies> *n* 1. *a. fig* (*line*) limite *m* 2. (*border*) confine *m;* **to cross a ~** attraversare il confine; **to mark a ~** (**between two places**) segnare il confine (tra due luoghi) 3. SPORTS limite *m*
boundless ['baʊnd·lɪs] *adj* (*love, patience*) sconfinato, -a; (*energy*) inesauribile; (*universe*) infinito, -a
bounds [baʊndz] *n pl a.* SPORTS limiti *mpl;* **to know no ~** non conoscere limiti; **to be beyond the ~ of possibility** rasentare l'impossibile; **to be outside the ~ of acceptable behavior** essere al di fuori di un comportamento accettabile; **this area is out of ~ to unauthorized personnel** l'accesso a questa zona è proibito ai non addetti ai lavori; **within ~** entro certi limiti; **to be within the ~ of the law** essere nei limiti della legalità
bounty ['baʊn·ti] <-ies> *n* 1. (*reward*) ricompensa *f* 2. (*gift*) regalo *m* 3. *liter* (*generosity*) generosità *f*
bouquet [boʊ·'keɪ] *n* 1. (*of flowers*) bouquet *m inv* 2. (*of wine*) bouquet *m inv*
bourbon ['bɜːr·bən] *n* bourbon *m inv*
bourgeois ['bʊr·ʒwɑ:] *adj* borghese
bout [baʊt] *n* 1. SPORTS (*in boxing, wrestling*) incontro *m* 2. (*of illness*) attacco *m; ~* **of coughing** attacco *m* di tosse; **drinking ~** sbronza *f*
boutique [bu:·'ti:k] *n* boutique *f inv*

bovine ['boʊ·vaɪn] *adj a. fig* bovino, -a
bow[1] [boʊ] *n* 1. (*weapon*) arco *m* 2. MUS archetto *m* 3. (*knot*) fiocco *m*
bow[2] [baʊ] *n* NAUT prua *f*
bow[3] [baʊ] I. *vi* 1. (*as greeting*) fare un inchino 2. (*yield*) **to ~ to sth** rassegnarsi a qc ▸**to ~ and scrape** leccare i piedi II. *vt* (*one's head*) chinare; (*body*) piegare III. *n* inchino *m;* **to take a ~** salutare con un inchino
◆**bow out** *vi* ritirarsi
bowdlerize ['boʊ·dlə·raɪz] *vt* espurgare
bowel ['baʊ·əl] *n* 1. MED intestino *m* 2. *pl* (*of a ship*) ventre *m*
bowel movement *n* evacuazione *f;* **to have a ~** andare di corpo
bowl[1] [boʊl] *n* 1. (*dish*) scodella *f;* **fruit ~** coppetta *f* per la frutta; **salad ~** insalatiera *f* 2. (*of toilet*) tazza *f;* (*for washing*) catino *m;* (*of pipe*) fornello *m* 3. (*stadium*) stadio *m* 4. GEO (*hollow*) bacino *m*
bowl[2] [boʊl] SPORTS I. *vi* 1. (*go bowling*) giocare a bowling 2. (*throw bowling ball*) lanciare la palla II. *vt* lanciare; **to ~ a strike/7** fare strike/7 III. *n* (*throw of the ball*) lancio *m*
◆**bowl out** *vt* eliminare
◆**bowl over** *vt* 1. (*knock over*) far cadera 2. (*astonish*) stupire; **to be bowled over** restare a bocca aperta
bow-legged [ˌboʊ·'legd] *adj* (*person*) con le gambe storte
bowler ['boʊ·lɚ] *n* 1. (*in bowling*) giocatore, -trice *m, f* 2. (*hat*) bombetta *f*
bowling *n* (*game*) bowling *m inv*
bowling alley *n* bowling *m inv*
bowling ball *n* palla *f* da bowling
bowman ['boʊ·mən] *n* arciere *m*
bowstring ['boʊ·strɪŋ] *n* MUS corda *f* dell'arco
bow tie *n* farfallino *m*
bow window *n* bovindo *m*
box[1] [bɑ:ks] I. *vi* SPORTS fare pugilato II. *vt* 1. SPORTS combattere contro 2. **to ~ sb's ears** dare un ceffone a qu III. *n* ceffone *m;* **to give sb a ~ on the ears** dare un ceffone a qu
box[2] [bɑ:ks] I. *n* 1. (*container*) scatola *f;* **cardboard ~** scatola di cartone; **tool ~** cassetta degli attrezzi 2. (*rectangular space*) casella *f;* (*in soccer, baseball*) area *f;* (**penalty**) *~* (*in soccer*) area di rigore; (*in ice hockey*) panchina *f* 3. THEAT palco *m;* (*booth*) cabina *f* 4. *inf* (*television*) **the ~** la tivù 5. (*mailbox*) cassetta *f* delle lettere 6. COMPUT **dialog ~** finestra *f* di dialogo ▸**to think outside of the ~** pensare fuori dagli schemi II. *vt* mettere in una scatola
◆**box in** *vt* bloccare; **to ~ a car** bloccare una macchina; **to feel boxed in** *fig* sentirsi soffocato
◆**box off** *vt* recingere
◆**box up** *vt* mettere in una scatola
boxer ['bɑ:k·sɚ] *n* 1. (*person*) pugile *mf* 2. (*dog*) boxer *m inv*
boxer shorts *npl* boxer *mpl*
boxing ['bɑ:k·sɪŋ] *n* boxe *f inv,* pugilato *m*

B

---

i Il 26 di dicembre in alcuni Paesi del Commonwealth si celebra **Boxing Day**. Questa festività prende il nome dal fatto che un tempo il giorno dopo Natale gli apprendisti di un mestiere raccoglievano in **boxes** (scatole) i regali che venivano loro fatti dai clienti dell'officina in cui lavoravano. Anticamente si chiamava **Christmas box** la gratifica natalizia che veniva data agli impiegati.

---

boxing glove *n* guantone *m* da boxe

boxing match *n* incontro [*o* pugilato] di boxe *m*

boxing ring *n* ring *m inv*

box lunch *n* cestino *m* pranzo

box office *n* botteghino *m*

boy [bɔɪ] I. *n* 1. (*child*) bambino *m* 2. (*young man*) ragazzo *m;* **country/city ~** ragazzo di campagna/città 3. (*son*) figlio *m* 4. *pej* (*servant*) servo *m* 5. (*boyfriend*) ragazzo *m* ▶ **the old ~ network** rete di interessi che lega gli ex alunni di una scuola privata; **the ~s in blue** *inf* la polizia; **~s will be ~s** i maschi son fatti così II. *interj* (**oh**) **~!** capperi!

boycott ['bɔɪ·kɑːt] I. *vt* boicottare II. *n* boicottaggio *m*

boyfriend ['bɔɪ·frend] *n* ragazzo *m*

boyhood ['bɔɪ·hʊd] *n* infanzia *f*

boyish ['bɔɪ·ɪʃ] *adj* (*woman*) androgino, -a; (*enthusiasm*) da ragazzino

Boy Scout *n* boy scout *m inv*

Bq PHYS *abbr of* **becquerel** Bq

bra [brɑː] *n* reggiseno *m*

brace [breɪs] I. *vt* 1. (*prepare*) **to ~ oneself for sth** prepararsi a qc 2. (*support: wall*) rinforzare II. *n* 1. *pl* (*for teeth*) apparecchio *m* per i denti 2. (*for the back*) corsetto *m* ortopedico 3. (*clamp*) graffa *f;* (*for drilling*) trapano *m* a mano 4. TYPO (*curly brackets*) graffa *f*

bracelet ['breɪs·lɪt] *n* braccialetto *m*

bracket ['bræ·kɪt] I. *n* 1. *pl* TYPO (*round*) parentesi *f inv;* **curly ~** graffa *f;* **square ~** parentesi quadra *m;* **in ~s** tra parentesi 2. (*category*) categoría *f;* **age ~** fascia *f* d'età; **income ~** fascia *f* di reddito; **tax ~** scaglione *m* di reddito (ai fini fiscali) 3. (*for a shelf*) staffa *f* II. *vt* 1. TYPO mettere tra parentesi 2. (*include*) mettere nello stessa categoria; **to ~ sb with sb else** paraganoare qu con qualcun altro

brackish ['bræ·kɪʃ] *adj* salmastro, -a

brag [bræg] <-gg-> *inf* I. *vi* vantarsi; **to ~ about sth** vantarsi di qc II. *vt* **they ~ that they have done sth** si vantano di aver fatto qc III. *n* 1. (*instance*) vanteria *f* 2. (*person*) sbruffone, -a *m, f*

braid [breɪd] I. *n* 1. (*in hair*) treccia *f* 2. FASHION passamano *m* II. *vt* (*hair*) intrecciare

Braille [breɪl] *n* braille *m inv*

brain [breɪn] I. *n* 1. (*organ*) cervello *m* 2. *pl* (*substance*) cervella *fpl* 3. (*intelligence*) cervello *m;* **to have ~s** essere intelligente 4. *inf* (*intelligent person*) cervello *m;* **the best ~s** i migliori cervelli ▶ **to beat one's ~s out** *inf* farsi saltare le cervella; **to blow sb's ~s out** *inf* freddare qu; **to have sth on the ~** *inf* avere la fissa di qc; **to pick sb's ~s** *inf* consultare qu; **to rack one's ~** lambiccarsi il cervello II. *vt inf* spaccare la testa a

brainchild *n* creatura *f*

brain damage *n* lesione *f* cerebrale

brain-dead *adj* 1. MED clinicamente morto, -a 2. *fig* balordo, -a

brain death *n* morte *f* clinica

brain drain *n* fuga *f* di cervelli

brainless ['breɪn·ləs] *adj* stupido, -a

brain scan *n* scansione *f* del cervello

brainstorm ['breɪn·stɔːrm] I. *vi* fare un brainstorming II. *vt* fare un brainstorming su III. *n* (*great idea*) lampo *m* di genio

brainstorming ['breɪn·ˌstɔːr·mɪŋ] *n* brainstorming *m inv*

brain trust *n* trust *m* dei cervelli *inv*

brain tumor *n* tumore *m* cerebrale

brainwash ['breɪn·wɑːʃ] *vt* fare il lavaggio del cervello a

brainwashing ['breɪn·wɑː·ʃɪŋ] *n* lavaggio *m* del cervello

brainwave ['breɪn·weɪv] *n inf* 1. ANAT onda *f* cerebrale 2. *fig* idea *f* geniale; **she had a ~** ha avuto un'idea geniale

brainwork *n* lavoro *m* intellettuale

brainy ['breɪ·ni] <-ier, -iest> *adj* intelligente

braise [breɪz] *vt* estofar

brake [breɪk] I. *n* freno *m;* **to put on the ~s** frenare; **to put a ~ on sth** *fig* porre freno a qc II. *vi* frenare

brake block *n* pastiglia *f* del freno

brake fluid *n* AUTO olio *m* dei freni

brake shoe *n* AUTO ganascia *f*

braking *n* frenata *f*

braking distance *n* distanza *f* di frenata

bramble ['bræm·bl] *n* (*bush*) rovo *m*

bran [bræn] *n* crusca *f*

branch [bræntʃ] I. *n* 1. (*of a tree*) ramo *m* 2. (*of railroad, river*) ramo *m;* (*of road*) diramanzione *f* 3. (*office: of a company, bank, library*) filiale *f;* (*of a union*) rappresentanza *f* 4. (*subdivision*) branca *f;* **the ~es of learning** le branche del sapere II. *vi* 1. (*tree*) ramificare 2. (*river, road*) biforcarsi

◆**branch off** *vi* 1. (*start*) diramarsi 2. (*digress*) **to ~ from a subject** allontanarsi da un argomento

◆**branch out** *vi* estendere le proprie attività; **to ~ on one's own** mettersi in proprio

branch office *n* filiale *f*

brand [brænd] I. *n* 1. COM marca *f* 2. *fig* genere *m;* **do you like his ~ of humor?** ti piace il suo umorismo? 3. (*mark*) marchio *m* II. *vt* 1. (*label*) **to ~ sb (as) sth** bollare qu come qc; **to ~ sb a liar** dare del bugiardo a qu 2. (*cattle*) marchiare

brandish ['bræn·dɪʃ] *vt* brandire

brand name *n* marca *f*

brand-new *adj inv* nuovo, -a di zecca; ~ **baby** bambino appena nato

brandy ['bræn·di] <-ies> *n* brandy *m inv;* French ~ cognac *m inv*

brash [bræʃ] *adj* 1. (*cocky: attitude*) arrogante 2. (*gaudy: colors*) sgargiante

brass [bræs] *n* 1. (*metal*) ottone *m* 2. + *sing/ pl vb* MUS the ~ gli ottoni 3. (*plaque: in a church*) targa *f* commemorativa (*di ottone*)

brass band *n* fanfara *f*

brass plate *n* targa *f* commemorativa (*di ottone*)

brass section *n* MUS the ~ gli ottoni

brassware *n* oggetti *m* d'ottone *pl*

brassy ['bræ·si] <-ier, -iest> *adj* 1. (*of brass*) d'ottone; ~ **color** colore *m* giallastro 2. (*voice*) stridente 3. (*cocky*) vistoso, -a

brat [bræt] *n inf* moccioso, -a *m, f;* **he is a spoiled** ~ è un bambino viziato

bravado [brə·'vɑ:·doʊ] *n* spavalderia *f*

brave [breɪv] I. *adj* coraggioso, -a II. *vt* sfidare III. *n* (*Native American warrior*) guerriero *m* indiano

bravery ['breɪ·və·ri] *n* coraggio *m*

brawl [brɑːl] I. *n* zuffa *f* II. *vi* azzuffarsi

brawling *n* zuffa *f*

brawn [brɑːn] *n* (*physical strength*) forza *f* fisica

brawny ['brɑː·ni] <-ier, -iest> *adj* muscoloso, -a

bray [breɪ] I. *vi* (*donkey*) ragliare; ~**ing laugh** risata *f* stridente II. *n* raglio *m*

brazen ['breɪ·zn] *adj* spudorato, -a; ~ **lie** menzogna *f* spudorata

◆**brazen out** *vt* **to brazen it out** far finta di niente

brazier ['breɪ·zɚ] *n* braciere *m*

Brazil [brə·'zɪl] *n* Brasile *m*

Brazilian [brə·'zɪl·jən] I. *n* brasiliano, -a *m, f* II. *adj* brasiliano, -a

Brazil nut *n* noce *m* dele Brasile

breach [briːtʃ] I. *n* 1. (*infraction: of a regulation*) infrazione *f;* (*of an agreement*) violazione *f;* (*of confidence*) abuso *m;* (*of a contract*) inadempimento *m;* **to be in ~ of the law** infrangere la legge 2. (*opening*) breccia *f* II. *vt* 1. (*break: law*) infrangere; (*agreement*) violare; (*contract*) non adempiere a; (*security*) non rispettare 2. (*infiltrate*) aprire una breccia in

breach of promise *n* rottura *f* della promessa di matrimonio

breach of the peace *n* attentato *m* all'ordine pubblico

bread [bred] I. *n* 1. pane *m;* **a loaf of** ~ una pagnotta 2. *sl* (*money*) grana *f* ▶ **to cast one's** ~ **upon the** <u>waters</u> *form* agire in modo disinteressato; **to** <u>earn</u> **one's** (**daily**) ~ *form* guadagnarsi il pane (quotidiano) II. *vt* CULIN (*fish, chicken*) impanare

bread and butter *n* fonte *m* di guadagno; ~ **issues** temi *m pl* fondamentali

breadbasket *n* 1. (*container*) cestino *f* del pane 2. (*farming area*) ~ **region** granaio *m*

breadbox *n* cassetta *f* per il pane

breadcrumb *n* 1. (*small fragment*) briciola *f* (di pane) 2. *pl* GASTR pangrattato *m*

breadth [bretθ] *n a. fig* larghezza *f;* **to be 5 feet in** ~ essere largo 5 piedi

breadwinner *n* sostegno *m* della famiglia

break [breɪk] I. *n* 1. (*crack, gap*) crepa *f* 2. (*escape*) fuga *f;* **to make a ~ for** [*o* **towards**] **sth** lanciarsi verso qc 3. (*interruption*) interruzione *f;* (*commercial*) break *m inv* 4. (*rest period*) pausa *f;* **coffee** ~ pausa per il caffè; **lunch** ~ pausa pranzo 5. (*vacation*) vacanza *fpl;* **spring** ~ *vacanze scolastiche di primavera* 6. (*first light*) **at the** ~ **of day** [*o* **dawn**] all'alba 7. (*divergence*) rottura *f* 8. (*opportunity*) opportunità *f* 9. SPORTS break *m inv* ▶ **to make a** <u>clean</u> ~ voltar pagina; <u>give</u> **me a** ~! lasciami in pace! II. <broke, broken> *vt* 1. (*shatter, damage, fracture*) rompere; **to ~ sth** (**in**)**to pieces** mandare qc in pezzi 2. (*interrupt: circuit*) interrompere 3. (*put an end to: deadlock, impasse*) uscire da; (*silence*) rompere; (*strike*) porre fine a; (*give up: habit*) perdere; **to ~ sb of a habit** far perdere un vizio a qu 4. (*in tennis*) **to ~ sb's service** strappare il servizio a 5. (*violate: agreement, treaty*) violare; (*date*) non presentarsi a; (*promise*) non mantenere 6. (*decipher: code*) decifrare 7. (*make public*) rivelare 8. (*tell*) dire; **to ~ the news to sb** dare la notizia a qu; ~ **it to me gently!** *iron* dimmelo con tatto! 9. (*make change for*) cambiare; **to ~ a 100 dollar bill** cambiare una banconota da 100 dollari 10. **to ~ a sweat** cominciare a sudare; *fig* (*become nervous*) cominciare a sudar freddo 11. MIL **to ~ formation** rompere le righe III. <broke, broken> *vi* 1. (*shatter or separate: leg, chair, glass, TV*) rompersi; **to ~ into pieces** andare a pezzi 2. (*interrupt*) **shall we ~ for lunch?** facciamo una pausa per il pranzo? 3. (*hit the shore: wave*) frangersi 4. (*change of voice*) **the boy's voice is ~ing** il ragazzo sta cambiando voce; (*under strain*); **her voice broke** (**with emotion**) le si ruppe la voce (per l'emozione) 5. (*come to end: fever*) finire 6. METEO (*weather*) cambiare; (*dawn, day*) spuntare 7. (*in pool, snooker*) aprire il gioco 8. (*giving birth*) **her water broke on the way to hospital** le si sono rotte le acque mentre stava andando all'ospedale ▶ **to ~** <u>even</u> rientrare delle spese; **to ~** <u>free</u> liberarsi

◆**break away** *vi* (*piece*) staccarsi; (*from friends*) allontanarsi; (*boat*) rompere gli ormeggi; POL (*faction, region*) scindersi

◆**break down** I. *vi* 1. (*stop working: machine*) smettere di funzionare; (*car*) avere un guasto 2. (*marriage*) fallire; **before negotiations broke down** prima della rottura dei negoziati 3. (*physically, psychologically*) avere un crollo 4. (*decompose*) decomporsi II. *vt* 1. (*door*) forzare 2. (*opposition, resistance*) stroncare **3.** CHEM decomporre **4.** (*separate into parts: sentence*) scomporre

◆**break in I.** *vi* **1.** (*enter: burglar*) entrare (per rubare) **2.** (*interrupt*) interrompere; **to ~ on sb** interrompere qu **II.** *vt* **1.** (*make comfortable: shoes*) **it took a couple of weeks to ~ my new shoes** ci sono volute un paio di settimane prima che le scarpe nuove mi andassero bene **2.** AUTO fare il rodaggio di **3.** (*tame: animal*) domare

◆**break into** *vi* **1.** (*enter: car*) scassinare **2.** (*start doing*) **to ~ laughter/tears** scoppiare a ridere/a piangere; **to ~ song** mettersi a cantare **3.** (*get involved in: business*) intraprendere

◆**break off I.** *vt* **1.** (*detach*) staccare **2.** (*end: relationship*) troncare **II.** *vi* **1.** (*become detached*) staccarsi **2.** (*stop speaking*) interrompersi

◆**break out** *vi* **1.** (*escape: of a prison*) scappare **2.** (*begin: war, storm*) scoppiare **3. to ~ in a sweat** incominciare a sudare; **she broke out in a rash** le è venuta un'eruzione cutanea; **he broke out in spots** si è riempito di macchie

◆**break through I.** *vi* penetrare; (*sun*) spuntare **II.** *vt* forzare; **to ~ a crowd** aprirsi un varco tra la folla

◆**break up I.** *vt* **1.** (*end: meeting, strike*) porre fine a; **break it up, you two!** *inf* voi due smettetela! **2.** (*split up: coalition, union*) sciogliere; (*collection*) dividere; (*family*) separare; (*monopoly, cartel*) smantellare **3.** (*make laugh*) **to break sb up** far morire dal ridere **II.** *vi* **1.** (*end a relationship*) separarsi **2.** (*come to an end: marriage*) sfasciarsi; (*meeting*) terminare **3.** (*fall apart: coalition*) sciogliersi; (*ship*) colare a picco

breakable ['breɪ·kə·bl] *adj* fragile

breakage ['breɪ·kɪdʒ] *n* rotture *fpl*

breakaway ['breɪk·ə·weɪ] *adj* POL dissidente

breakdown ['breɪk·daʊn] *n* **1.** (*collapse: in negotiations, relationship*) rottura *f* **2.** TECH guasto *m* **3.** (*division*) resoconto *m* dettagliato; **give me a ~ of the situation** fammi un quadro della situazione **4.** (*decomposition*) decomposizione *f* **5.** PSYCH (**nervous**) ~ esaurimento *m* nervoso

breaker ['breɪ·kə] *n* **1.** (*wave*) frangente *m* **2.** *inf* RADIO radioamatore, -trice *m, f*

breakfast ['brek·fəst] **I.** *n* colazione *m;* **to have ~** fare colazione **II.** *vi form* fare colazione

---

ℹ️ Negli USA, il **breakfast** è un momento importante della giornata. Oltre alla prima colazione tradizionale, vengono spesso servite abbondanti porzioni di uova strapazzate, pancetta o salsicce alla griglia e patate saltate in padella. Durante il fine settimana, si mangiano anche dei *pancakes*, una sorta di crêpe dolci spesse, o un *French toast*, una fetta di pane inzuppata nell'uovo sbattuto e cotta in

---

padella. I *French toasts* sono accompagnati da sciroppo d'acero, miele o marmellata.

---

breaking and entering *n* violazione *f* di domicilio con effrazione

breaking point *n* limite *m;* **to reach the ~** arrivare al punto di rottura

breakneck ['breɪk·nek] *adj* vertiginoso, -a; **drive at ~ speed** guidare a rotta di collo

breakout ['breɪk·aʊt] *n* evasione *f*

breakthrough ['breɪk·θruː] *n* **1.** (*in science*) scoperta *f* decisiva **2.** MIL penetrazione *f*

breakup ['breɪk·ʌp] *n* (*of marriage, talks*) fallimento *m;* (*of group*) scioglimento *m;* (*of empire*) crollo *m;* (*of family, physical structure*) disintegrazione *f*

breakwater ['breɪk·wɑː·t̬ə] *n* frangiflutti *m inv*

breast [brest] *n* **1.** ANAT (*of woman*) seno *m;* (*of man*) petto *m* **2.** CULIN petto *m*

breastbone ['brest·boʊn] *n* **1.** ANAT sterno *m* **2.** CULIN forcella *f*

breast cancer *n* cancro *m* del seno

breastfeed ['brest·fiːd] *vt* allattare

breast pocket *n* taschino *m*

breaststroke ['brest·stroʊk] *n* (nuoto *m*) a rana; **to do (the) ~** nuotare a rana

breath [breθ] *n* fiato *m;* **to be out of ~** essere senza fiato; **to be short of ~** avere il fiatone; **to catch one's ~** (*stop breathing*) trattenere il respiro; (*return to normal breathing*) riprendere a respirare normalmente; **to draw ~** riprendere fiato; **to hold one's ~** *a. fig* trattenere il respiro; **to mutter sth under one's ~** dire qc sotto voce; **to take a deep ~** respirare a fondo; **to go out for a ~ of fresh air** uscire a prendere una boccata d'aria fresca ▶**in the same ~** un momento dopo; **to take sb's away** mozzare il fiato a qu

breathalyze ['bre·θə·laɪz] *vt* fare la prova del palloncino a, fare il test dell'etilometro a

Breathalyzer® *n* etilometro *m*, alcolimtero *m*

breathe [briːð] **I.** *vi* respirare; **to ~ again** [*o easily*] riprendere a respirare; **to ~ through one's nose** respirare dal naso; **to let a wine ~** far respirare il vino **II.** *vt* **1.** (*exhale*) **to ~ smoke on sb** soffiare il fumo addosso a qu **2.** (*whisper*) sussurrare; **don't ~ a word of this to anyone!** non farne parola a nessuno! **3.** (*let out: sigh*) emettere

breather ['briː·ðə] *n* pausa *f;* **to take a ~** fare una pausa

breathing *n* respirazione *f*

breathing room *n*, **breathing space** *n* pausa *f*

breathless ['breθ·lɪs] *adj* (*person*) senza fiato; (*words*) soffocato, -a

breathtaking *adj* mozzafiato

breath test *n* alcoltest *m inv*

bred [bred] *pt, pp of* **breed**

breech [briːtʃ] *n* culatta *f*

breeches ['brɪ·tʃɪz] *npl* **1.** (*knee-length pants*)

knickerbockers *mpl;* **riding** ~ pantaloni *m pl* da equitazione **2.** *inf* (*pants*) pantaloni *mpl*

breed [bri:d] **I.** *vt* <bred, bred> **1.** (*animals, plants*) allevare **2.** (*disease, violence*) causare **II.** *vi* <bred, bred> riprodursi; (*violence*) nascere **III.** *n* **1.** ZOOL razza *f;* BOT varietà *f* **2.** *inf* (*type of person*) tipo *m;* **a dying** ~ una specie in via d'estinzione

breeder ['bri:·də·] *n* (*of animals*) allevatore, -trice *m, f;* (*of plants*) coltivatore, -trice *m, f*

breeding *n* **1.** (*of animals*) allevamento *m* **2.** *fig* (*upbringing*) educazione *f*

breeding ground *n fig* terreno *m* fertile

breeze [bri:z] **I.** *n* **1.** (*wind*) brezza *f* **2.** *inf* (*easy task*) **to be a** ~ essere un gioco da ragazzi **3.** (*cinders*) ceneri *m pl* di carbone ▶ **to shoot the** ~ chiacchierare **II.** *vi* **to** ~ **into the room** entrare con nonchalance in una stanza

breezy ['bri:·zi] <-ier, -iest> *adj* **1.** (*windy*) ventoso, -a; **it is** ~ c'è brezza **2.** (*lively*) allegro

breve [bri:v] *n* MUS breve *f*

brevity ['bre·və·ţi] *n* **1.** (*shortness*) brevità *f* **2.** (*conciseness*) concisione *f*

brew [bru:] **I.** *n* **1.** (*mixture*) beveraggio *m* **2.** *inf* (*beer*) birra *f* **II.** *vi* **1.** (*beer*) fermentare **2.** (*tea*) farsi; **to let the tea** ~ lasciare in infusione il tè **3.** (*storm, trouble*) avvicinarsi; **there's something** ~**ing** qualcosa bolle in pentola **III.** *vt* (*beer*) produrre; (*tea*) fare ◆ **brew up I.** *vi* (*storm, trouble*) avvicinarsi **II.** *vt inf* **to** ~ **a story/an excuse** inventare una storia/una scusa

brewer ['bru:·ə·] *n* birraio, -a *m, f*

brewery ['bru:·ə·i] <-ies> *n* fabbrica *f* di birra

brewski ['bru:s·ki] <-ies *o* -s> *n sl* birra *f*

briar ['bra·ɪə·] *n* (*bush*) rovo *m*

bribe [braɪb] **I.** *vt* corrompere; **to** ~ **sb into doing sth** corrompere qu affinché faccia qc **II.** *n* tangente *f;* **to take a** ~ lasciarsi corrompere

bribery ['braɪ·bə·ri] *n* corruzione *f*

bric-a-brac ['brɪ·kə·bræk] *n* cianfrusaglie *fpl*

brick [brɪk] *n* mattone *m* ◆ **brick in** *vt* murare ◆ **brick up** *vt* murare

bricklayer *n* muratore *m*

brick wall *n* muro *m* (di mattoni) ▶ **to be banging one's head against a** ~ *inf* parlare al muro

brickwork *n* mattoni *mpl*

brickyard *n* mattonificio *m*

bridal ['braɪ·dəl] *adj* (*suite*) nuziale; (*shop*) di abiti da sposa; (*gown*) da sposa

bridal shower *n* festa *f* di addio al nubilato

bride [braɪd] *n* sposa *f*

bridegroom ['braɪd·gru:m] *n* sposo *m*

bridesmaid ['braɪdz·meɪd] *n* damigella *f* d'onore

bridge [brɪdʒ] **I.** *n* **1.** **a.** ARCHIT, MED ponte *m* **2.** MUS ponticello *m* **3.** ANAT dorso *m* (del naso) **4.** NAUT ponte *m* (di comando) **5.** GAMES bridge *m inv* ▶ **to burn** one's ~s bruciarsi i

ponti alle spalle **II.** *vt* **1.** (*build a bridge over*) costruire un ponte sopra **2.** (*decrease the difference*) colmare

bridge loan *n* credito *m* ponte

bridle ['braɪ·dl] **I.** *n* briglia *f* **II.** *vt* (*horse*) imbrigliare **III.** *vi* **to** ~ **at sth** risentirsi per qc

bridle path *n* pista *f* per cavalli

brief [bri:f] **I.** *adj* **1.** (*short*) breve **2.** (*skirt*) corto, -a **3.** (*concise*) breve, conciso, -a; **be** ~! sii breve!; **in** ~ in breve **II.** *n* **1.** (*instructions*) istruzioni *fpl;* **her** ~ **is to** ... ha l'incarico di ... **2.** LAW fascicolo *m,* dossier *m inv* **3.** *pl* (*underwear: men's*) mutande *fpl;* (*women's*) mutandine *fpl* **III.** *vt* (*give instructions to*) dare istruzioni a

briefcase ['bri:f·keɪs] *n* ventiquattrore *f inv*

briefing *n* **1.** (*instructions*) istruzioni *fpl* **2.** (*information session*) briefing *m inv;* (*for reporters*) conferenza *f* stampa

briefly *adv* **1.** (*for short time*) per poco tempo **2.** (*concisely*) brevemente; ~, ... in breve, ...

briefness *n* brevità *f*

brigade [brɪ·'geɪd] *n* MIL brigata *f*

brigadier general [ˌbrɪ·gə·dɪr·'dʒe·nə·rəl] *n* MIL generale *m* di brigata

bright [braɪt] **I.** *adj* **1.** (*light*) forte; (*room*) luminoso, -a; (*star*) brillante; **a** ~ **day** una giornata luminosa **2.** (*color*) vivace; **to go** ~ **red** diventare rosso come un peperone **3.** (*intelligent: person*) intelligente; (*idea*) brillante **4.** (*cheerful, happy*) vivace **5.** (*promising: future*) promettente ▶ **to look on the** ~ **side of sth** cogliere il lato buono di qc [*o* verl]; **to get up** ~ **and early** alzarsi di buon'ora **II.** *n pl* AUTO abbaglianti *mpl*

brighten ['braɪ·tən] **I.** *vt* **1.** (*make brighter*) **to** ~ **sth** (**up**) illuminare qc **2.** (*become cheerful*) **to** ~ **sth** (**up**) allietare qc **II.** *vi* **1.** (*become brighter*) **to** ~ (**up**) (*weather*) migliorare **2.** (*become cheerful*) **to** ~ (**up**) rallegrarsi; (*eyes, face*) illuminarsi **3.** (*become more promising*) **to** ~ (**up**) (*future*) diventare più promettente

brightness *n* **1.** (*lightness*) luminosità *f;* (*of sound*) chiarezza *f* **2.** (*cheerfulness*) allegria *f* **3.** (*cleverness*) intelligenza *f*

brilliance ['brɪl·jəns] *n* **1.** (*cleverness*) genialità *f* **2.** (*brightness*) splendore *m*

brilliant ['brɪl·jənt] *adj* **1.** (*shining: color*) brillante; (*sunlight*) splendente; (*smile*) smagliante; (*water*) luccicante **2.** (*clever*) brillante; (*idea*) geniale **3.** *inf* (*excellent*) fantastico, -a; ~ **success** successo strepitoso

brim [brɪm] **I.** *n* **1.** (*of a hat*) tesa *f* **2.** (*of a vessel*) orlo *m;* **to fill sth to the** ~ riempire qc fino all'orlo **II.** *vi* <-mm-> **to** ~ **with happiness/energy** traboccare di felicità/d'energia ◆ **brim over** *vi a. fig* traboccare

brimful [ˌbrɪm·'fʊl] *adj* colmo, -a; (*of life, confidence*) traboccante

brine [braɪn] *n* CULIN salamoia *f;* (*sea water*) acqua *f* di mare

bring [brɪŋ] <brought, brought> *vt* **1.** (*come*

with, carry) portare; ~ **her here!** portala qui!;
to ~ sb in far entrare qu; **to ~ sth in** portar
dentro qc; **to ~ news** portare notizie **2.**(*take*)
portare; **this subject ~s me to the second
part** questo tema mi porta alla seconda parte;
to ~ sth with oneself portare qc con sé
3.(*cause to come or happen*) portare, causare;
to ~ poverty/fame to a town portare pov-
ertà/fama a una città; **to ~ sb luck** portar fortuna a qu **4.**LAW intentare; **to ~ a lawsuit
(against sb)** fare causa a qu; **to ~ a complaint against sb** sporgere querela contro qu
5.(*force*) **to ~ oneself to do sth** trovare il coraggio di fare qc **6.**FIN dare
◆**bring about** *vt* (*cause to happen*) provocare
◆**bring along** *vt* portare
◆**bring around** *vt* **1.**MED rianimare **2.**(*persuade*) persuadere
◆**bring back** *vt* **1.**(*reintroduce*) reintrodurre
2.(*call to mind*) ricordare **3.**(*return*) riportare
◆**bring down** *vt* **1.**(*reduce: benefits, level*)
ridurre; (*temperature*) far abbassare **2.**(*fell:
tree*) abbattere; (*dictator, government*) far
cadere **3.**(*make sad*) deprimere
◆**bring forth** *vt insep, form* dare alla luce
◆**bring forward** *vt* **1.**(*reschedule for an earlier date*) anticipare **2.**(*present: evidence*)
produrre **3.** FIN (*carry over*) riportare
◆**bring in** *vt* **1.**(*introduce*) introdurre; (*bill*)
presentare **2.**(*call in*) far entrare **3.**FIN (*guadagnare*) **to ~ a profit** fruttare un utile **4.**(*reap*)
raccogliere **5.**LAW (*emettere*) **to ~ a verdict of
not guilty** pronunciare un verdetto di non colpevolezza
◆**bring off** *vt inf* accaparrarsi
◆**bring on** *vt* (*cause to occur*) provocare;
(*shame, dishonor*) acarreare; **to bring sth on
oneself** tirarsi addosso qc
◆**bring out** *vt* **1.**COM lanciare; (*book*) pubblicare **2.**(*reveal*) **to ~ sth in sb** mettere in evidenza qc di qu; **to ~ the best/worst in sb**
tirar fuori il meglio/peggio di qu
◆**bring over** *vt* **1.**(*person*) convincere
2.(*take with*) portare
◆**bring to** *vt always sep* far rinvenire
◆**bring up** *vt* **1.**(*child*) allevare; **to bring sb
up to be/to do sth** formare qu perché
diventi/faccia qc **2.**(*mention*) citare **3.***inf*
(*vomit*) rigettare
brink [brɪŋk] *n* orlo *m;* **to drive sb to the ~ of
sth** portare qu sull'orlo di qc; **to be on the ~
of bankruptcy** stare per fare bancarotta; **to be
on the ~ of civil war** essere arrivati all'orlo
della guerra civile
briny ['braɪ·ni] <-ier, -iest> *adj liter* salmastro, -a
briquet(te) [brɪ·'ket] *n* mattonella *f* di carbone
brisk [brɪsk] *adj* **1.**(*fast: pace*) rapido, -a;
(*walk*) spedito, -a **2.**(*refreshing: breeze*)
fresco, -a **3.**(*manner, voice*) energico, -a
briskness *n* (*of pace*) sveltezza *f;* (*of trading*)
vivacità *f;* (*of business*) dinamismo *m*

bristle ['brɪ·sl] I. *n* (*of an animal*) setola *f;* (*on
the face*) barba *f;* (*of a brush*) setole *fpl* II. *vi*
1.(*fur, hair*) rizzarsi **2.**fig **to ~ with anger**
infuriarsi
bristly ['brɪs·li] <-ier, -iest> *adj* ispido, -a
Brit [brɪt] *n inf* britannico, -a *m, f*
Britain ['brɪ·tən] *n* Gran Bretagna *f*
British ['brɪ·tɪʃ] I. *adj* britannico, -a; ~ **English**
inglese *m* britannico II. *n pl* **the ~** i britannici
British Columbia *n* Columbia *f* Britannica
British Isles *n* **the ~** le Isole Britanniche
Briton ['brɪ·tn] *n* britannico, -a *m, f*
Brittany ['brɪ·tə·ni] *n* Bretagna *f*
brittle ['brɪt] *adj* **1.**(*fragile*) fragile **2.**(*irritable*)
irascibile
broach [broʊtʃ] I. *vt* (*mention*) affrontare II. *n*
(*pin*) spilla *f*
broad [brɑːd] I. *adj* **1.**(*wide*) largo, -a
2.(*spacious*) ampio, -a **3.**(*obvious*) **a ~ hint**
un'evidente allusione **4.**(*general*) generale
5.(*wide-ranging*) vasto, -a; ~ **interests** vasti
interessi **6.**(*liberal*) aperto, -a; **a ~ mind** una
mente aperta **7.**(*strong: accent*) marcato, -a
II. *n inf* (*woman*) donna *f*
broadcast ['brɑːd·kæst] I. *n* RADIO, TV trasmissione *f* II. *vi,vt* <broadcast *o* broadcasted,
broadcast *o* broadcasted> trasmettere
broadcaster *n* (*person*) conduttore , -trice
televisivo *m;* (*station*) emittente *f*
broadcasting *n* TV trasmissioni *fpl*
broadcasting station *n* emittente *f*
broaden ['brɑː·dn] I. *vi* (*interests, valley*)
allargarsi II. *vt* (*street*) allargare; (*horizons*)
ampliare; **to ~ the mind** allargare la mente
broadly ['brɑːd·li] *adv* **1.**(*generally*) in linea di
massima **2.**(*widely: smile*) da un orecchio
all'altro
broad-minded *adj* di mentalità aperta
broadside ['brɑːd·saɪd] *n* **1.**NAUT, MIL bordata *f* **2.**(*verbal attack*) bordata *f* **3.**(*paper*)
giornale *di formato grande*

i **Broadway** è una grande via di New York.
È lì che si trova il famoso quartiere dei teatri
che porta lo stesso nome. **Broadway** è
sinonimo del grande teatro americano e
praticamente tutte le opere teatrali di una
certa importanza vi sono state rappresentate.
Quelle che non vi sono state rappresentate
sono spesso produzioni sperimentali o a
basso costo, che vengono chiamate *off-
Broadway plays.*

brocade [broʊ·'keɪd] *n* broccato *m*
broccoli ['brɑː·kli] *n* broccoli *mpl*
brochure [broʊ·'ʃʊr] *n* opuscolo *m*
brogue [broʊg] *n* LING accento *m* irlandese
broil [brɔɪl] I. *vt* grigliare II. *n* (*argument*)
rissa *f*
broiler ['brɔɪ·lə] *n* **1.**(*grill*) grill *m* superiore
inv **2.**(*chicken*) pollo *m* da fare alla griglia

broke [broʊk] I. *pt of* **break** II. *adj inf* al verde ▶ **to go ~** *inf* fallire; **to go for ~** *inf* rischiare il tutto per tutto

broken ['broʊ·kən] I. *pp of* **break** II. *adj* 1. (*damaged: TV, radio, toy*) rotto, -a; (*marriage, family, home*) distrutto, -a; (*spirit*) a pezzi; **~ heart** cuore spezzato 2. LING **to speak in ~ English** parlare un inglese sgrammaticato 3. (*interrupted*) interrotto, -a

broken-down *adj* 1. TECH guasto, -a 2. (*dilapidated: building*) fatiscente

broken-hearted *adj* affranto, -a; **to die ~** morire di dolore

broker ['broʊ·kɚ] I. *n* 1. FIN agente *mf* di borsa 2. (*of an agreement, marriage*) intermediario, -a *m, f;* (*of marriage*) agente *mf* II. *vt* (*agreement*) mediare

brokerage ['broʊ·kə·rɪdʒ] *n* FIN (*commission*) commissione *f* di borsa

bromide ['broʊ·maɪd] *n* 1. CHEM bromuro *m* 2. (*cliché*) luogo *m* comune

bromine ['broʊ·miːn] *n* bromo *m*

bronchial ['brɑːŋ·ki·əl] *adj* bronchiale

bronchial tubes *npl* bronchi *mpl*

bronchitis [brɑːŋ·'kaɪ·t̬ɪs] *n* bronchite *f*

bronze [brɑːnz] I. *n* bronzo *m* II. *adj* di bronzo; (*hair*) ramato, -a; (*skin*) abbronzato, -a

Bronze Age I. *n* **the ~** l'età del Bronzo II. *adj* dell'età del Bronzo

bronze medal *n* medaglia *f* di bronzo

brooch [broʊtʃ] *n* spilla *f*

brood [bruːd] I. *n* 1. (*of mammals*) nidiata *f;* (*of birds*) covata *f* 2. iron (*children*) prole *f* II. *vi* 1. **to ~ over sth** (*reflect at length*) rimuginare qc; (*worry about*) preoccuparsi per qc 2. (*hatch*) covare

broody ['bruː·di] <-ier, -iest> *adj* 1. (*hen*) covaticcio, -a; **a ~ hen** una chioccia 2. (*gloomy*) malinconico, -a

brook¹ [brʊk] *n* ruscello *m*

brook² [brʊk] *vt form* (*tolerate*) tollerare

broom [bruːm] *n* 1. (*for sweeping*) scopa *f* 2. BOT ginestra *f*

broomstick ['bruːm·stɪk] *n* manico *m* della scopa

broth [brɑːθ] *n* brodo *m*

brothel ['brɑː·θl] *n* bordello *m*

brother ['brʌ·ðɚ] *n* fratello *m*

brotherhood ['brʌ·ðɚ·hʊd] *n* + *sing/pl vb* 1. (*fellowship*) fratellanza *f* 2. (*organization*) confraternità *f*

brother-in-law <brothers-in-law *o* brother-in-laws> *n* cognato *m*

brotherly ['brʌ·ðɚ·li] *adj* fraterno, -a

brought [brɑːt] *pp, pt of* **bring**

brow [braʊ] *n* 1. *liter* (*forehead*) fronte *f* 2. (*of a hill*) cima *f*

browbeat ['braʊ·biːt] <browbeat, browbeaten> *vt* intimidire; **to ~ sb into doing sth** costringere qu a fare qc

brown [braʊn] I. *n* marrone *m* II. *adj* marrone; (*eyes, hair*) castano, -a III. *vi* (*leaves*) ingiallire; (*person*) abbronzarsi; CULIN dorarsi IV. *vt* abbronzare; CULIN far dorare

brown bread *n* pane *m* integrale

brownie ['braʊ·ni] *n* 1. (*sweet*) dolcetto *m* di cioccolato e noci 2. (*young girl scout*) coccinella *f*

brownish ['braʊ·nɪʃ] *adj* tendente al marrone

brownnose ['braʊn·noʊz] *vt inf* leccare i piedi a

brownout ['braʊn·aʊt] *n* ELEC abbassamento *m* di elettricità

brown rice *n* riso *m* integrale

brownstone ['braʊn·stoʊn] *n* 1. (*sandstone*) arenaria *f* rossastra 2. (*house*) casa *f* con la facciata rivestita di arenaria rossastra

browse [braʊz] I. *vi* 1. (*skim*) **to ~ through sth** dare un'occhiata a qc; (*book, magazine*) sfogliare qc 2. (*look around*) curiosare 3. (*graze*) brucare II. *n* 1. (*act of looking around*) **to go for a ~ around the shops** fare un giro per i negozi 2. (*act of skimming*) occhiata *f;* **to have a ~ through sth** dare un'occhiata a qc; (*book, magazine*) dare una sfogliata a qc

browser ['braʊ·zɚ] *n* COMPUT browser *m inv,* navigatore *m*

bruise [bruːz] I. *n* livido *m;* (*on fruit*) ammaccatura *f;* **to be covered in ~s** essere pieno di lividi II. *vt* (*person*) farsi un livido a; (*fruit*) ammaccare; *fig* (*hurt*) ferire; **to ~ one's arm** farsi un livido al braccio; **to ~ sb's feelings** ferire i sentimenti di qu III. *vi* (*fruit*) ammaccarsi; **she ~s easily** le vengono i lividi con facilità

bruiser ['bruː·zɚ] *n inf* bestione *m*

brunch [brʌntʃ] *n* brunch *m inv,* pasto da consumare in tarda mattinata che unisce la colazione al pranzo

Brunei ['bruː·naɪ] *n* Brunei *m*

brunette [bruː·'net] *n* morena *f,* bruna *f*

brunt [brʌnt] *n* (*impact*) impatto *m;* **to bear the ~ of the work** fare il grosso del lavoro; **to bear the ~ of the expense** far fronte alla maggior parte delle spese

brush [brʌʃ] I. *n* 1. (*for hair*) spazzola *f* 2. (*broom*) scopa *f* 3. (*for painting*) pennello *m* 4. (*action*) spazzolata *f* 5. (*stroke*) pennellata *f* 6. (*encounter*) sfiorata *f;* **a ~ with death** sfuggire per un pelo alla morte; **a ~ with the law** avere dei guai con la giustizia 7. (*brushwood*) sottobosco *m* 8. (*fox's tail*) coda *f* di volpe II. *vt* 1. (*hair*) spazzolare; **to ~ one's teeth** pulirsi i denti 2. (*remove*) **to ~ sth off** togliere qc con una spazzola 3. (*graze, touch lightly*) sfiorare

◆**brush against** *vt* sfiorare

◆**brush aside** *vt* 1. (*push to one side*) allontanare 2. (*disregard*) ignorare

◆**brush away** *vt* togliere con una spazzola

◆**brush off** *vt* (*dust*) togliere con una spazzola; (*person*) non far caso a; (*criticism*) ignorare

◆**brush up** I. *vt* rinfrescare II. *vi* **to ~ on sth** dare una ripassata a qc

brush-off *n inf* **to give sb the ~** dare il due di picche a qn

B

brushwood ['brʌʃ·wʊd] n sottobosco m
brusque [brʌsk] adj brusco, -a
brusqueness n rudezza f
Brussels ['brʌ·səlz] n Bruxelles f
Brussels sprout n cavolino m di Bruxelles
brutal ['bruː·təl] adj 1.(cruel, savage) brutale 2.(harsh: honesty, truth) spietato, -a
brutality [bruː·'tæ·lə·t̬i] n (cruelty) brutalità f; (harshness) spietatezza f
brutalize ['bruː·t̬ə·laɪz] vt 1.(treat cruelly) brutalizzare 2.(make brutal) abbruttire
brute [bruːt] I. n 1.(person) bruto m 2.(animal) bestia f II. adj ~ **force** forza f bruta
brutish ['bruː·t̬ɪʃ] adj 1.(cruel) brutale 2.(like an animal) da animale
BSc [ˌbiː·es·'siː] abbr of **Bachelor of Science**
BSE [ˌbiː·es·'iː] n abbr of **bovine spongiform encephalopathy** BSE m, mucca f pazza
bubble ['bʌ·bl] I. n 1.bolla f; (in cartoons) fumetto m, nuvoletta f; **to blow a** ~ fare una bolla 2.fig, inf (protective environment) **to live in a** ~ vivere sotto una campana di vetro ▸ **to** burst **sb's** ~ far tornare con i piedi per terra; **the** ~ **has** burst l'incanto si è rotto II. vi 1.(boil) bollire 2.(make boiling sound) gorgogliare
◆**bubble over with** vi **to** ~ **joy** sprizzare di gioia
bubble bath n bagnoschiuma m inv
bubblegum n chewing-gum m
bubble-jet printer n INFOR stampante f a getto d'inchiostro
bubbly ['bʌb·li] I. n infchampagne m invII. adj a. fig effervescente
bubonic plague [bjuː·ˌbaː·nɪk·'pleɪg] n peste f bubbonica
buccaneer [ˌbʌ·kə·'nɪr] n bucaniere m
buck[1] [bʌk] <-(s)> I. n 1.(male: of deer, rabbit, hare) maschio m 2.liter (man) bell'uomo m II. vi sgroppare III. vt ir contra; **to** ~ **the trend** invertire la tendenza
buck[2] [bʌk] n inf(dollar) dollare m; **to make a fast** ~ fare soldi facili
buck[3] [bʌk] n inf **to pass the** ~ scaricare la responsabilità agli altri; **the** ~ **stops here** prov me la vedo io
◆**buck up** vt inf1.(cheer up) **to buck sb up** rincuorare qu 2.**to** ~ **one's ideas** darsi una scrollata
bucket ['bʌ·kɪt] n (pail) secchio m ▸ **a drop in the** ~ una goccia nell'oceano; **to** kick **the** ~ inftirare le cuoia
bucketful ['bʌ·kɪt·fʊl] <-s o bucketsful> n secchio m

bucket truck n camion con gru a cestello m inv
buckle ['bʌ·kl] I. n fibbia f II. vt 1.(fasten: belt, shoes) allacciare 2.(bend) piegare III. vi 1.(fasten) allacciarsi 2.(bend) torcersi; (knees) piegarsi; (metal) deformarsi
◆**buckle down** vi mettersi d'impegno
◆**buckle up** vi allaccaire la cintura di sicurezza
buckshot n pallettoni mpl
buckskin I. n pelle f di daino II. adj di pelle di daino
buckwheat n grano m saraceno
bud [bʌd] I. n (of leaf, branch) gemma f; (of a flower) bocciolo m; **to be in** ~ essere in boccio II. vi <-dd-> gettare
Buddhism ['buː·dɪ·zəm] n buddismo m
Buddhist I. n buddista mf II. adj buddista
budding ['bʌ·dɪŋ] adj in erba; fig (romance, relationship) che sta nascendo
buddy ['bʌ·di] n infamico m
budge [bʌdʒ] I. vi 1.(move) spostarsi 2.(change opinion) **to not** ~ **(from sth)** non smuoversi (da qc) II. vt 1.(move) spostare 2.(cause to change opinion) smuovere
budgerigar ['bʌ·dʒə·rɪ·gaːr] n parrocchetto m
budget ['bʌ·dʒɪt] I. n budget m inv, bilancio [o di previsione] preventivo m II. vt preventivare; (wages, time) amministrare III. vi **to** ~ **for sth** mettere nel bilancio preventivo m per qc IV. adj (travel) low-cost; (prices) stracciato, -a
budgetary ['bʌ·dʒɪ·te·ri] adj di bilancio
budget deficit n deficit m di bilancio inv
budgie ['bʌ·dʒi] n infparrocchetto m
buff [bʌf] I. n 1.(leather) pelle f di bufalo 2.inf (person) appassionato, -a f; film ~ cinefilo, -a m, f ▸ **in the** ~ infnudo, -a II. adj 1.giallognolo, -a 2.sl (muscular: athlete) muscoloso, -a III. vt (metal, shoes) lucidare
buffalo ['bʌ·fə·loʊ] <-(es)> n bisonte m
buffer ['bʌ·fər] I. n 1.(of a train) respingente m; fig (intermediary) cuscinetto m 2.COMPUT buffer m; inv 3.CHEM tampone m II. vt attutire
buffer zone n zona f cuscinetto
buffet[1] [bə·'feɪ] n buffet m inv
buffet[2] ['bʌ·fɪt] vt (hit repeatedly) sferzare
buffet lunch n buffet m inv
buffoon [bə·'fuːn] n buffone, -a m, f; **to play the** ~ fare il buffone
bug [bʌg] I. n 1.ZOOL cimice f; (any insect) insetto m 2.MED virus m inv 3.COMPUT baco m 4.TEL cimice m 5.inf(enthusiasm) passione f; **she's caught the travel** ~ le è venuta la passione per i viaggi ▸ **to be snug as a** ~ **in a** rug star comodo come un pascià II. vt <-gg-> 1.(tap: telephone) mettere sotto controllo; (conversation) intercettare; (room) installare microspie in 2.inf(annoy) rompere inf
bugaboo ['bʌ·gə·buː] n incubo m
bugger ['bʌ·gə] I. n 1.vulg (sodomite) cullattone m 2.sl (contemptible person) stronzo, -a m, f; **poor** ~ povero disgraziato II. vt vulg inculare

buggery ['bʌ·gə·ri] *n* sodomia *f*
buggy ['bʌ·gi] *n* <-ies> **1.** (*stroller*) passeggino *m* **2.** (*carriage*) calesse *f*
bugle ['bju:·gl] *n* tromba *f*
bugler ['bju:g·lə*] *n* trombettiere *m*
build [bɪld] **I.** *vt* <built, built> **1.** (*make: house*) costruire; (*fire*) fare; (*car*) fabbricare **2.** (*establish: trust*) fondare; (*relationship*) impiantare; (*support*) ottenere; (*a following*) creare **II.** *vi* <built, built> **1.** (*construct*) costruire **2.** (*increase*) aumentare **III.** *n* costituzione *f*
◆**build in** *vt* incassare
◆**build on** *vt* basare su; **to build sth on sth** basare qc su qc
◆**build up I.** *vt* **1.** (*increase*) aumentare **2.** (*accumulate*) accumulare **3.** (*strengthen*) consolidare **4.** (*develop*) potenziare **5.** (*praise*) **to build sth up** promuovere qc **II.** *vi* **1.** (*increase*) aumentare **2.** (*accumulate*) accumularsi
builder ['bɪl·də*] *n* (*owner*) costruttore *m* edile; (*worker*) muratore *m*
building *n* edificio *m*
building contractor *n* imprenditore *m* edile
building site *n* cantiere *m* edile
build-up *n* **1.** (*accumulation*) accumulo *m;* (*of pressure*) aumento *m* **2.** (*publicity*) battage *m* pubblicitario *inv*
built [bɪlt] **I.** *pp, pt of* **build II.** *adj* **1.** (*house*) **well ~** ben costruito, -a **2.** (*person*) **slightly ~** minuto, -a; **well ~** ben piantato, -a **3.** (*have nice body*) **he's/she's (really) built!** che fisico!
built-in *adj* **1.** (*cabinets*) a muro **2.** (*feature*) incorporato, -a **3.** (*advantage*) intrinseco, -a
built-up *adj* **1.** (*area*) edificato, -a **2.** (*shoes*) rialzato, -a
bulb [bʌlb] *n* **1.** BOT bulbo *m* **2.** (*of a thermometer*) bulbo *m* **3.** ELEC lampadina *f*
bulbous ['bʌl·bəs] *adj* (*nose*) grosso, -a
Bulgaria [bʌl·'ge·ri·ə] *n* Bulgaria *f*
Bulgarian [bʌl·'ge·ri·ən] **I.** *adj* bulgaro, -a **II.** *n* **1.** (*person*) bulgaro, -a *m, f* **2.** LING bulgaro *m*
bulge [bʌldʒ] **I.** *vi* sporgere; **her eyes ~d in surprise** aveva gli occhi fuori dalle orbite per la sorpresa; **to ~ (with sth)** essere gonfio (de qc) **II.** *n* **1.** (*swelling*) rigonfiamento *m* **2.** (*a statistical trend*) impennata *f*
bulging *adj* gonfio, -a; (*bag, box*) pieno, -a; **~ eyes** occhi *m pl* sporgenti
bulimia [bu:·'li:·miə] *n* MED bulimia *f*
bulk [bʌlk] **I.** *n* **1.** (*magnitude*) volume *m* **2.** (*mass*) massa *f* **3.** (*quantity*) **to ~ buy sth, to buy (sth) in ~** comprare (qc) in grandi quantità; ECON comprare (qc) all'ingrosso **4.** (*largest part*) **the ~ of** la maggior parte di **II.** *vi* **to ~ large** invadere **III.** *adj* (*large in quantity: mailing*) a larga diffusione; (*order*) in gran quantità; (*discount*) quantità; (*apples, canned goods, paper goods*) all'ingrosso
bulk buying *n* ECON acquisti *m pl* all'ingrosso
bulkhead ['bʌlk·hed] *n* NAUT paratia *f*

bulky ['bʌl·ki] <-ier, iest> *adj* (*large*) voluminoso, -a; (*heavy*) pesante; (*person*) corpulento, -a
bull [bʊl] *n* **1.** (*male bovine*) toro *m* **2.** (*male animal*) macho *m;* **~ elephant** elefante *m* maschio; **~ whale** ballena *f* maschio ▶ **to take the ~ by the horns** prendere il toro per le corna; **to be like a red rag to a ~ to sb** essere per qu come drappo rosso per i tori **4.** *inf* (*nonsense*) stronzate *fpl* **5.** FIN toro *m;* **~ market** mercato *m* rialzista
bulldog ['bʊl·da:g] *n* bulldog *m inv*
bulldoze ['bʊl·doʊz] *vt* **1.** ARCHIT spianare **2.** *fig* **to ~ sth through** ottenere qc con la forza; **to ~ sb into doing sth** costringere qu a fare qc
bulldozer ['bʊl·doʊ·zə*] *n* bulldozer *m inv*
bullet ['bʊ·lɪt] *n* MIL proiettile *f;* **to fire a ~** sparare un proiettile ▶ **to bite the ~** *inf* farsi forza
bulletin ['bʊ·lə·t̬ɪn] *n* bollettino *m;* (**news**) **~** TV, CINE notiziario *m*
bulletin board *n* bacheca *f;* COMPUT bacheca *m* informatica
bulletproof ['bʊ·lɪt·pru:f] *adj* antiproiettile; **~ glass** vetro [*o* corazzato] antiproiettile *m*
bulletproof vest *n* giubbotto *m* antiproiettile
bullfight ['bʊl·faɪt] *n* corrida *f*
bullfighter ['bʊl·faɪ·t̬ə*] *n* torero *m*
bullfinch ['bʊl·fɪntʃ] *n* ciuffolotto *m*
bullion ['bʊl·jən] *n* **gold/silver ~** oro *m/* argento *m* in lingotti
bullock ['bʊ·lək] *n* (*castrated bull*) manzo *m;* (*young bull*) vitelllone *m*
bullring ['bʊl·rɪŋ] *n* arena *f*
bull's-eye *n* blanco *f;* **to hit the ~** *a. fig* far centro
bullshit ['bʊl·ʃɪt] **I.** *n sl* stronzate *fpl vulg;* **don't give me that ~!** non venirmi a raccontare stronzate! *vulg* **II.** *interj sl* e che cazzo! *vulg* **III.** <-tt-> *vi sl* dire stronzate
bully ['bʊ·li] **I.** <-ies> *n* (*person*) prepotente *mf* **II.** <-ie-> *vt* intimidar; **to ~ sb into doing sth** costringere qu a fare qc **III.** *interj inf* **~ for you!** ben fatto!; *iron* bravo!
bulrush ['bʊl·rʌʃ] <-es> *n* lisca *f* lacustre
bulwark ['bʊl·wə*k] *n* **1.** (*fortification*) baluardo *m* **2.** NAUT (*of ship*) murate *f*
bum [bʌm] **I.** *n* **1.** (*lazy person*) fannullone, -a *m, f* **2.** (*homeless person*) vagabondo, -a *m, f* **3.** Cana (*buttocks*) culo *m* ▶ **to give sb the ~'s rush** *inf* mandare qu a quel paese **II.** *adj inf* (*bad, useless*) schifoso, -a; **a ~ job** un lavoro schifoso **III.** <-mm-> *vt inf* **to ~ sth off sb** scroccare qc a qu **IV.** *vi inf* **1.** **to ~ around** (*live as a bum*) vagabondare; (*laze around*) bighellonare **2.** (*cadge*) **to ~ off sb** vivere alle spalle di qu
bumble ['bʌm·bl] *vi* brancolare
bumblebee ['bʌm·bl·bi:] *n* bombo *m*
bumbling *adj* maldestro
bummed out *adj sl* depresso, -a
bump [bʌmp] **I.** *n* **1.** (*lump*) protuberanza *f;* (*on head*) bernoccolo *m;* (*on road*) cunetta *f* **2.** *inf* (*blow*) colpo *m* **3.** (*thud*) tonfo *m* **II.** *vt*

sbattere contro; **to ~ one's head on** [*o against*] **sth** sbattere con la testa contro qc
◆**bump into** *vt insep* **1.**(*collide with*) sbattere contro **2.**(*meet accidentally*) imbattersi in
◆**bump off** *vt sl* **to bump sb off** far fuori qu
bumper ['bʌm·pɚ] **I.** *n* AUTO paraurti *m inv;* **the traffic is ~ to ~** le macchine procedono incollate l'una all'altra **II.** *adj* **1.**(*crop*) abbondante **2.**(*edition*) speciale
bumper car *n* autoscontro *m*
bumper sticker *n* autoadesivo *m* per paraurti
bumpkin ['bʌmp·kɪn] *n inf*(**country**) ~ buzzurro, -a *m, f*
bumptious ['bʌmp·ʃəs] *adj* presuntuoso, -a
bumpy ['bʌm·pi] <-ier, iest> *adj* (*surface*) scabro, -a; (*road*) accidentato, -a; (*journey*) pieno, -a di scossoni
bun [bʌn] *n* **1.**(*roll*) panino *m* al latte **2.**(*knot of hair*) chignon *m inv* **3.** *pl, sl* (*buttocks*) culo *vulg*
bunch [bʌntʃ] <-es> **I.** *n* **1.**(*of grapes*) grappolo *m;* (*of bananas*) casco *m;* (*of carrots, radishes, keys*) mazzetto *m;* (*of flowers*) mazzo *m* **2.**(*group: of people, friends*) gruppo *m* **3.**(*a lot*) **a** (**whole**) **~ of problems** un mucchio di problemi ▶**to be the best of the ~** essere il migliore **II.** *vt* raggruppare **III.** *vi* **to ~** (**together**) raggrupparsi
bundle ['bʌn·dl] **I.** *n* (*of clothes*) fagotto *m;* (*of money*) mazzetta *f;* (*of sticks*) fascio *m* ▶**to be a ~ of joy** *inf* essere sempre allegro; **to be a ~ of nerves** essere nervosissimo **II.** *vt* **to ~ sb into a car** spingere qu dentro una macchina
◆**bundle up I.** *vt* legare **II.** *vi* (*dress warmly*) infagottarsi
bung [bʌŋ] **I.** *n* (*stopper*) tappo *m* **II.** *vt* (*close*) tappare
bungalow ['bʌŋ·gə·loʊ] *n* bungalow *m inv*
bungee jumping ['bʌn·dʒi·,dʒʌm·pɪŋ] *n* bungee jumping *m inv*
bungle ['bʌŋ·gl] *vt* fare pasticci
bungler *n* pasticcione, -a *m, f*
bungling *adj* ~ **idiot** cretino patentato
bunk [bʌŋk] *n a.* NAUT cuccetta *f*
◆**bunk down** *vi inf* dormire
bunk bed *n* letto *m* a castello
bunker ['bʌŋ·kɚ] *n* bunker *m inv*
bunkum ['bʌŋ·kəm] *n* fesserie *fpl*
bunny (**rabbit**) ['bʌ·ni ('ræ·bɪt)] *n childspeak* coniglietto *m*
Bunsen burner ['bʌn·tsɪn·,bɜːr·nɚ] *n* becco *m* Bunsen
bunting ['bʌn·tɪŋ] *n* bandierine *fpl*
buoy [bɔɪ] *n* boa *f*
◆**buoy up** *vt* **1.**(*cause to float*) tenere a galla **2.** *fig* (*cause to rise*) far aumentare **3.** *fig* (*cheer up*) **to buoy sb up** rincuorare qu
buoyancy ['bɔɪ·jən·si] *n* **1.** capacità *f* di stare a galla; NAUT galleggiamento *m* **2.** (*cheerfulness*) ottimismo *m*
buoyant ['bɔɪ·jənt] *adj* **1.**(*able to float*) che galleggia **2.** (*cheerful*) ottimista; **to be in a ~ mood** essere di buonumore

burble ['bɜːr·bl] *vi* **1.**(*make burbling noise*) borbottare **2.**(*talk nonsense*) parlottare
burden ['bɜːr·dən] **I.** *n* **1.**(*load*) carico *m* **2.** *fig* peso *m;* (*responsibility*) responsabilità *f;* **tax ~** ECON peso *m* tributario; **the ~ of proof** LAW l'onere della prova; **to be a ~ on** [*o* **to**] **sb** essere un onere per qu **II.** *vt* **1.**(*load*) caricare **2.** *fig* opprimere; **I don't want to ~ you with my problems** non voglio oberarti con i miei problemi
burdensome ['bɜːr·dən·səm] *adj form* oneroso, -a
bureau ['bjʊ·roʊ] <-s> *n* **1.**(*government department*) dipartimento *m* **2.**(*chest of drawers*) comò *m inv*
bureaucracy [bjʊ·'rɑː·krə·si] *n* burocrazia *f*
bureaucrat ['bjʊ·rə·kræt] *n* burocrate *mf*
bureaucratic [,bjʊ·rə·'kræ·ṭɪk] *adj* burocratico, -a
burgeoning ['bɜːr·dʒə·nɪŋ] *adj* (*tourism*) in pieno sviluppo; (*tourist industry, economy*) fiorente; (*demand*) crescente; (*talent*) in crescita
burger ['bɜːr·gɚ] *n inf abbr of* **hamburger** hamburger *m inv*
burglar ['bɜːr·glɚ] *n* scassinatore, -trice *m, f*
burglar alarm *n* allarme *m* antifurto
burglarize ['bɜːr·glə·raɪz] *vt* svaligiare
burglary ['bɜːr·glə·ri] <-ies> *n* furto *m* con scasso
burgle ['bɜːr·gl] *vt s.* **burglarize**
burial ['be·ri·əl] *n* sepoltura *f*
burial ground *n* cimitero *m*
burial service *n* funerale *m*
Burkinabe ['bɜːr·ki··neɪb] **I.** *adj* del Burkina Faso **II.** *n* abitante *mf* del Burkina Faso
Burkina Faso [bɜːr·,ki··nə·'fæ·soʊ] *n* Burkina *m* Faso
burlesque [bɜːr·'lesk] **I.** *n* parodia *f* **II.** *adj* burlesco, -a
burly ['bɜːr·li] <-ier, -iest> *adj* (*man*) corpulento, -a
Burma ['bɜːr·mə] *n* Birmania *f*
burn [bɜːrn] **I.** <burnt *o* -ed, burnt *o* -ed> *vi* **1.**(*be in flames: house*) bruciare; (*coal, wood*) ardere **2.**(*be hot*) scottare; **his forehead was ~ing** gli scottava la fronte **3.**(*be switched on*) essere acceso, -a; **he left all the lights ~ing** ha lasciato tutte le luci accese **4.**(*want*) **to be ~ing to do sth** bruciare dalla volgia di fare qc **5.**(*feel emotion strongly*) **to ~ with sth** arder di qc **6.**(*be red*) **his face ~ed with anger/shame** è diventato rosso per la rabbia/vergogna **II.** <burnt *o* -ed, burnt *o* -ed> *vt* (*paper, garbage, food*) bruciare; (*building*) incendiare; **to ~ one's finger/tongue** scottarsi un dito/la lingua; **to be ~ed** (*by the sun*) avere una scottatura; (*injured*) avere delle bruciature; **to ~ calories/fat** bruciare le calorie/il grasso; **this machine ~s electricity** questo macchinario va a elettricità **III.** *n* bruciatura *f,* scottatura *f;* **severe/minor ~s** bruciature gravi/lievi
◆**burn away I.** *vi* (*forest*) bruciare; (*candle*) consumarsi **II.** *vt* bruciare

◆**burn down** I. *vt* incendiare II. *vi* (*house*) essere distrutto da un incendio; (*fire, candle*) abbassarsi

◆**burn out** I. *vi* (*engine*) bruciarsi; (*fire, candle*) spegnersi; (*light bulb*) saltare II. *vt* **to burn oneself out** esaurirsi

◆**burn up** I. *vt* 1.(*fuel*) consumare; (*calories*) bruciare 2. *inf* (*make angry*) far infuriare II. *vi* incendiarsi; **you're burning up!** *inf* (*have fever*) scotti!

burner ['bɜːr·nə] *n* TECH bruciatore *m*

burning ['bɜːr·nɪŋ] *adj* 1.(*hot*) in fiamme; (*sun*) infuocato, -a; **it is ~ hot** fa un caldo allucinante; **a ~ sensation** un bruciore 2.(*issue, question*) scottante; (*desire, hatred*) ardente

---

i Il 25 di gennaio si celebra la **Burns Night** per commemorare la nascita del poeta scozzese Robert Burns (1759–1796). Questo anniversario viene celebrato dagli ammiratori di Burns non solo in Scozia ma nel mondo intero. In quest'occasione viene servito il **Burns Supper** composto da **haggis** (un insaccato fatto con le frattaglie della pecora, tritate e mescolate con grasso e farina d'avena leggermente tostata e chiuso in uno stomaco di pecora che viene fatto bollire per almeno 3 ore), **neeps** (rape) e **mashed tatties** (puré di patate).

---

burnt [bɜːrnt] I. *pt, pp of* **burn** II. *adj* bruciato; **a ~ smell/taste** un odore/sapore di bruciato

burp [bɜːrp] I. *n* rutto *m;* (*of baby*) ruttino *m;* **to let out a ~** fare un rutto; (*baby*) fare un ruttino II. *vi* ruttare; (*baby*) fare un ruttino III. *vt* **to ~ a baby** far fare il ruttino al bambino

burr [bɜːr] *n* LING erre *f* arrotata

burrow ['bɜː·roʊ] I. *n* tana *f* II. *vi* scavare una tana; (*dig a hole*) scavare un buco; (*dig a tunnel*) scavare una galleria; **to ~ into sth** *a. fig* rovistare in qc III. *vt* scavare

bursar ['bɜːr·sə] *n* economo, -a *m, f*

burst [bɜːrst] I. *n* 1.(*explosion*) esplosione *f* 2. MIL (*of fire*) raffica *f* 3.(*brief period*) **a ~ of laughter** uno scoppio di riso; **a ~ of applause** uno scroscio di applausi; **a ~ of anger** un accesso di collera II. <burst, burst> *vi* 1.(*balloon, tire, scoppiare*) scoppiare; **to ~ into tears** scoppiare a piangere 2.(*move suddenly*) **to ~ into a place** irrompere in un luogo; **to ~ open** aprirsi di colpo 3. *fig* **to be ~ing to do sth** morire dalla voglia di fare qc; **to be ~ing with health** scoppiare di salute; **to be ~ing with curiosity** morire di curiosità III. <burst, burst> *vt* far scoppiare; **to ~ its banks** (*river*) esondare

◆**burst forth** *vi* sgorgare

◆**burst in** *vi* irrompere

◆**burst out** *vi* 1.(*exclaim*) esclamare 2.(*break out*) **to ~ laughing/crying** scoppiare e ridere/piangere

Burundi [bʊ·'rʊn·di] *n* Burundi *m*

bury ['be·ri] <-ie-> *vt* 1.(*put underground*) sotterrare 2.(*hide*) nascondere; **to ~ oneself in sth** immergersi in qc; **to be buried in thought** essere immerso nei propri pensieri; **to ~ one's head in one's hands** coprirsi il viso con le mani

bus [bʌs] I. <-es> *n* autobus *m inv;* **school ~** scuolabus *m inv;* **to catch/miss the ~** prendere/perdere l'autobus; **to go by ~** [*o* **to take the ~**] andare in autobus ▸ **to miss the ~** perdere il autobus II. <-ss-> *vt* 1.(*travel by bus*) portare in autobus 2.(*in restaurant*) **to ~ tables** sparecchiare i tavoli III. <-ss-> *vi* viaggiare in autobus

busboy *n* sparecchiatavoli *m inv*

bus driver *n* conducente *m* di autobus

bush [bʊʃ] <-es> *n* 1. BOT cespuglio *m;* **a ~ of hair** un ciuffo di capelli 2.(*land*) **the ~** la boscaglia ▸ **to beat around the ~** menare il can per l'aia; **to beat the ~es for sth** cercare qc dappertutto

bushel ['bʊ·ʃl] *n* fanega *f* (*misure che in Gran Bretagna equivale a 36,4 l; mentre negli Stati Uniti equivale a 35,2 l.*) ▸ **to hide one's light under a ~** nascondere le proprie qualità

bushman ['bʊʃ·mən] <-men> *n* boscimano *m*

bushy ['bʊ·ʃi] <-ier, -iest> *adj* (*hair, beard, eyebrows*) folto, -a

busily *adv* alacremente

business ['bɪz·nɪs] *n* 1.(*trade, commerce*) affari *mpl;* **to be away on ~** essere in viaggio d'affari; **to do ~ with sb** fare affari con qu; **to get down to ~** incominciare a lavorare; **to go out of ~** cessare l'attività; **to set up a ~** mettere su un impresa; **to set up ~ as a lawyer** aprire uno studio legale; **~ is booming** gli affari vanno bene; **once we get the computer installed, we'll be in ~** *inf* una volta che abbiamo installato il computer, possiamo iniziare 2. <-es> (*sector*) settore *m;* **the frozen food ~** il settore dei surgelati; **what line of ~ are you in?** in che settore lavori? 3. <-es> (*company*) impresa *f;* **to start up/run a ~** metter su/gestire un impresa 4.(*matter*) affare *m;* **an unfinished ~** una questione in sospeso; **it's none of your ~!** *inf* non sono fatti tuoi!; **mind your own ~!** *inf* fatti i fatti tuoi!; **to have no ~ doing sth** non avere alcun diritto di fare qc; **I make it my ~ to do that** me ne occupo io; **it's a time-consuming ~** è una cosa che richiede molto tempo ▸ **~ before pleasure** *prov* prima il dovere poi il piacere; **~ as usual** *prov* continua tutto come prima; **to (not) be in the ~ of doing sth** (non) avere l'abitudine di fare qc; **to give sb the ~** dare una lavata di testa a; **to mean ~** parlare sul serio; **like nobody's ~** *inf* come un matto

business address *n* indirizzo *m* dell'ufficio

business card *n* biglietto *f* da visita

business class *n* AVIAT business class *f inv*
business expenses *npl* spese *fpl*
business hours *n* orario *m* d'ufficio
business letter *n* lettera *f* commerciale
businesslike ['bɪz·nɪs·laɪk] *adj* **1.**(*serious*) serio, -a **2.**(*efficient*) efficiente
businessman <-men> *n* uomo *m* d'affari
business park *n* parco *m* tecnologico
business trip *n* viaggio *m* d'affari
businesswoman <-women> *n* donna *f* d'affari
busk [bʌsk] *vi* fare il suonatore ambulante
busker ['bʌs·kə] *n* sounatore, -trice *m*, *f* ambulante
busload ['bʌs·loʊd] *n* ~s of tourists pullman *m* carichi di turisti *inv*
bus service *n* servizio *m* di autobus
bus station *n* stazione *f* delle corriere
bus stop *n* fermata *f* dell'autobus
bust¹ [bʌst] *n* ART busto *m*
bust² [bʌst] **I.** *adj inf* **1.**(*broken*) rotto, -a **2.**(*bankrupt*) fallito, -a; **to go ~** far fallimento **II.** *vt inf* **1.**(*break*) spaccare **2.**(*raid*) fare una retata in ▶**to ~ one's** <u>butt</u> (**doing sth/to do sth**) spaccarsi la schiena (per fare qc)
bustle ['bʌ·sl] **I.** *vi* **to ~ around** affacendarsi; **to ~ with activity** essere molto animato **II.** *n* viavai *m*; **hustle and ~** trambusto *m*
bustling *adj* (*town, street*) animato, -a
busy ['bɪ·zi] **I.**<-ier, -iest> *adj* **1.**(*occupied*) occupato, -a; **to be ~ doing sth** star facendo qc; **to be ~ with sth** occuparsi di qc; **to get ~** darsi da fare **2.**(*full of activity*) animato, -a; **~ street** strada *f* affollata; **seaport** *m* pieno di trambusto; **a ~ time** un periodo di grande attività; **I've had a ~ day** ho avuto una giornata molto piena **3.** TEL occupato, -a **4.**(*pattern, wallpaper*) che dà fastidio agli occhi **II.**<-ie-> *vt* **to ~ oneself with sth** occuparsi di qc
busybody ['bɪ·zi·ˌbɑ:·di] <-ies> *n inf* ficcanaso *mf inv*
but [bʌt] **I.** *prep* tranne; **all ~ one** tutti tranne uno; **anything ~ ...** qualsiasi cosa tranne ...; **nothing ~ ...** nient'altro che ...; **no one ~ him** solo lui; **~ for him ...** se non fosse stato per lui ... **II.** *conj* ma; **I'm not quitting ~ taking time off** non mi sto licenziando mi sto solo prendendo una vacanza; **he has paper ~ no pen** ha la carta ma non ha la penna; **it is not red ~ pink** non è rosso ma rosa **III.** *adv* solo; **he is ~ a baby** è solo un bebè; **I can't help ~ cry** non posso far altro che piangere; **I can ~ hope she wins** posso solo sperare che vinca **IV.** *n* pero *m*; **there are no ~s about it!** non ci sono ma che tengano
butane ['bju:·teɪn] *n* butano *m*
butch [bʊtʃ] *adj* **1.**(*man*) macho **2.**(*woman*) mascolino, -a
butcher ['bʊ·tʃə] **I.** *n* macellaio, -a *m*, *f* **II.** *vt* **1.**(*meat*) macellare **2.**(*murder*) massacrare **3.** *fig* **to ~ a language** massacrare una lingua
butchery ['bʊ·tʃə·ri] *n* **1.**(*of an animal*) macel-

lazione *f* **2.**(*killing*) massacro *m*
butler ['bʌt·lə] *n* maggiordomo *m*
butt [bʌt] **I.** *n* **1.**(*of rifle*) calcio *m* **2.**(*of cigarette*) mozzicone *m* **3.**(*blow: with the head*) testata *f* **4.**(*target*) **to be the ~ of sth** essere oggetto di qc **5.**(*container*) botte *f* **6.** *inf* (*buttocks*) culo *m vulg* **II.** *vt* (*with the horns*) dare una cornata testata; (*with the head*) dare una testata
butter ['bʌ·tə] **I.** *n* burro *m* ▶**he/she looks as if ~ wouldn't melt in his/her** <u>mouth</u> fare il santarellino/la santarellina **II.** *vt* imburrare
◆**butter up** *vt* lisciare qu
buttercup *n* BOT ranuncolo *m*
butter dish *n* portaburro *m inv*
butterfingers *n inv* mani di ricotta *fpl*
butterfly ['bʌ·tə·flaɪ] <-ies> *n* **1.** ZOOL farfalla *f*; *fig* (*person*) farfallone, -a *m*, *f* **2.** SPORTS nuoto *m* a farfalla ▶**to have butterflies in one's** <u>stomach</u> essere emozionato
buttermilk ['bʌ·tə·mɪlk] *n* latticello *m*
buttery ['bʌ·tə·ri] <-ier, -iest> *adj* di burro
buttock ['bʌ·tək] *n* natica *f*
button ['bʌ·tən] **I.** *n* **1.** bottone *m* **2.**(*with slogan*) distintivo *m* **3.** COMPUT, TECH tasto *m*; **start ~** tasto di start; **right/left mouse ~** tasto destro/sinistro del mouse; **to push a ~** premere un tasto; **at the** <u>push</u> **of a ~** senza far fatica; **to be** <u>right</u> **on the ~** avere ragione **II.** *vi* abbottonarsi **III.** *vt* abbottonare ▶**~ it!** *inf* stai zitto!
◆**button up** *vt* abbottonare
buttonhole ['bʌ·tən·hoʊl] **I.** *n* FASHION asola *f* **II.** *vt* attaccare bottone con
buttress ['bʌ·trɪs] <-es> *n* ARCHIT contrafforte *m*; *fig* sostegno *m*
buxom ['bʌk·səm] *adj* formoso, -a
buy [baɪ] **I.** *n* acquisto *m*; **a good ~** un buon acquisto **II.**<bought, bought> *vt* **1.**(*purchase*) comprare; **to ~ sth from** [*o inf* **off**] **sb** comprare qc da qu; **to ~ sb's silence** comprare il silenzio di qu **2.** *inf* (*believe*) credere; **the teacher did not ~ your excuse** il maestro non ha creduto alle tue scuse **3.**(*bribe*) corrompere
◆**buy back** *vt* ricomprare
◆**buy into** *vt* (*in business*) acquisire una partecipazione in; (*accept as valid*) credere a
◆**buy off** *vt always sep* comprare
◆**buy out** *vt* COM rilevare
◆**buy up** *vt insep* rastrellare
buyer ['ba·ɪə] *n* **1.**(*in store*) compratore, -trice *m*, *f* **2.**(*as work*) buyer *m inv*
buyout ['baɪ·aʊt] *n* FIN acquisizione *f* (*della totalità delle azioni*); **management/worker ~** acquisizione di un'azienda da parte dei dirigenti/dei lavoratori
buzz [bʌz] **I.** *vi* **1.**(*hum*) ronzare; (*bell*) suonare; **my ears were ~ing** mi ronzavano le orecchie; **the town was ~ing with rumors** la città era un brusio di suoni **2.** *inf* (*be tipsy*) essere sbronzo **II.** *vt inf* **1.** TEL telefonare a; (*sig-*

nal to) chiamare con il cicalino **2.** AVIAT (*fly low over*) volare radente a **III.** *n* **1.** (*humming noise*) ronzio *m;* (*low noise*) brusio *m;* (*of a doorbell*) suono *m;* **the ~ of conversation** brusio della conversazione **2.** *inf* (*telephone call*) colpo *m* di telefono; **to give sb a ~** dare un colpo di telefono a qu **3.** *inf* (*feeling*) euforia *f;* (*from alcohol*) sbornia *f;* **I get a ~ from** [*o* **out of**] **surfing** fare surf mi fa sballare; **sb gets a ~ from sth** qc fa sballare qu; **I get a ~ from champagne** lo champagne mi dà alla testa

◆ **buzz off** *vi inf* smammare

buzzard ['bʌ·zɚd] *n* (*turkey vulture*) avvoltoio *m*

buzzer ['bʌ·zɚ] *n* cicalino *m*

buzz word *n* parola *f* di moda

by [baɪ] **I.** *prep* **1.** (*near*) vicino a; **close** [*o* **near**] **~ ...** vicino a ...; **to be/stand ~ ...** essere/stare vicino a ...; **~ the sea** sul mare **2.** (*at*) presso; **to remain ~ sb for two days** restare presso qu per due giorni **3.** (*during*) **~ day/night** durante il giorno/la notte; **~ moonlight** al chiaro di luna **4.** (*at the latest time*) entro; **~ tomorrow/midnight** entro domani/la mezzanotte; **~ now** [*o* **then**] ormai **5.** (*cause*) da; **a novel ~ Joyce** un romanzo di Joyce; **to be killed ~ sth/sb** essere uccisio da qc/qu; **surrounded ~ dogs** circondato da cani **6.** (*through means of*) **~ train/plane/ bus** in treno/aereo/autobus; **made ~ hand** fatto a mano; **to hold sb ~ the arm** tenere qu per il braccio; **to be doing sth** facendo qc **7.** (*through*) **~ chance/mistake** per caso/ sbaglio **8.** (*under*) **to call sb/sth ~ their/its name** chiamare qu/qc per nome; **what does he mean ~ that?** che cosa vuol dire con ciò? **9.** (*alone*) **to be ~ oneself** da solo; **to do sth ~ oneself** fare qc da solo **10.** (*as promise to*) **to swear ~ God/sth** giurare su Dio/qc **11.** (*in measurement, arithmetic*) **to buy ~ the kilo/dozen** comprare a chili/dozzine; **to divide ~ 6** dividere per 6; **to increase ~ 10%** aumentare del 10%; **to multiply ~ 4** moltiplicare per 4; **paid ~ the hour/day** pagato a ore/a giornata; **4 feet ~ 6** 4 piedi per 6; **one ~ one** uno a uno **12.** (*from the perspective of*) **to judge ~ appearances** giudicare dalle apparenze; **all right ~ me** *inf* per me, va bene **II.** *adv* **1.** (*aside*) vicino; **to put** [*o* **lay**] **sth ~** mettere qc da parte **2.** (*in a while*) **~ and ~** fra poco **3.** (*past*) **to go/pass ~** passare ▶ **~ and large** in generale

bye [baɪ] *interj,* **bye-bye** [ˌbaɪ·'baɪ] *interj inf* ciao

Byelorussian [bje·lə·'rʌ·ʃən] *adj, n s.* **bielorusso, -a**

by-election ['baɪ·ɪə·lek·ʃən] *n* elezione *f* parziale

bygone ['baɪ·gɑːn] **I.** *adj inv* passato, -a **II.** *n* let **~ s be ~ s** il passato è passato

bylaw *n* **1.** (*regional law*) ordinanza *l* **2.** (*organization's rule*) statuto *m*

---

i	I **BYO-restaurants** (Bring Your Own) sono tipici dell'Australia. Sono ristoranti che non possono vendere alcolici. Per cui chi voglia bere alcolici deve portarseli da casa.

bypass ['baɪ·pæs] **I.** *n* **1.** AUTO circonvallazione *f* **2.** ELEC derivatore *m* **3.** MED by-pass *m inv* **II.** *vt* **1.** (*make a detour*) evitare **2.** *fig* (*act without permission of*) **to ~ sb** scavalcare qu **3.** *fig* (*avoid*) evitare

by-play *n* THEAT azione *f* secondaria

byproduct ['baɪ·prɑː·dəkt] *n* sottoprodotto *m; fig* conseguenza *f*

byroad ['baɪ·roʊd] *n* strada *f* secondaria

bystander ['baɪ·stæn·də] *n* spettatore, -trice *m, f*

byte [baɪt] *n* byte *m; inv*

byway ['baɪ·weɪ] *n* strada *f* secondaria

byword ['baɪ·wɜːrd] *n* sinonimo *m;* **to be a ~ for sth** essere sinonimo di qc

C

C, c [siː] *n* **1.** (*letter*) C, c *f;* **~ as in Charlie** C come Como **2.** MUS do *m* **3.** SCHOOL ≈ sufficiente *m*

C *after int abbr of* **Celsius** C

c. **1.** *abbr of* **circa** (*by numbers*) c.; (*by dates*) ca. **2.** *abbr of* **cent** centesimo *m* **3.** *abbr of* **century** sec.

ca. *abbr of* **circa** **1.** (*by numbers*) c. **2.** (*by dates*) ca.

CA [ˌkæ·lə·'fɔːrn·jə] *n abbr of* **California** California *f*

cab [kæb] *n* **1.** (*taxi*) taxi *m inv;* **by ~** in taxi **2.** (*of truck, locomotive*) cabina *f*

cabaret [ˌkæ·bə·'reɪ] *n* cabaret *m*

cabbage ['kæ·bɪdʒ] *n* **1.** CULIN cavolo *m* **2.** ZOOL **~ white** cavolaia *f*

cabbie *n,* **cabby** ['kæ·bi] *n,* **cabdriver** *n* tassista *mf*

cabin ['kæ·bɪn] *n* **1.** (*house*) bungalow *m inv* **2.** (*in ship, airplane*) cabina *f*

cabin class *n* NAUT classe *f* tra la turistica e la prima

cabin cruiser *n* cabinato *m*

cabinet ['kæ·bɪ·nɪt] *n* **1.** (*storage place*) armadietto *m;* (*glass-fronted*) vetrina *f;* **filing ~** archivio *m* **2.** + *sing/pl vb* POL consiglio *m* dei ministri

cabinet maker *n* ebanista *mf*

cable ['keɪ·bl] **I.** *n* **1.** (*wire rope*) cavo *m* **2.** TV televisione *f* via cavo **3.** HIST (*electrically transmitted message*) cablogramma *m;* **to send sth by ~** cablare qc **II.** *vt* HIST cablare

cable car *n* teleferica *f*

cable network *n* rete *f* via cavo

cable railway *n* funicolare *f*
cable stitch *n* punto *m* a treccia
cable television *n*, **cable TV** *n* televisione *f* via cavo
caboodle [kə·'buː·dl] *n inf* **the whole (kit and)** ~ tutto quanto
cabriolet [ˌkæ·bri·ə·'leɪ] *n* cabriolet *m inv*
cacao [kə·'kɑː·oʊ] *n* cacao *m;* ~ **(bean)** (seme *m* di) cacao *m*
cache [kæʃ] *n* **1.** (*hiding place*) nascondiglio *m;* (*secret stockpile*) scorta *f* segreta; **weapons** ~ deposito *m* segreto di armi **2.** COMPUT cache *f;* ~ **memory** memoria *f* cache
cachet [kæʃ·'eɪ] *n* prestigio *m*
cackle ['kæ·kl] **I.** *vi* **1.** (*hen*) fare coccodè **2.** *fig* (*laugh*) ridacchiare **3.** (*talk*) chiacchierare **II.** *n* **1.** (*of hen*) coccodè *m* **2.** (*laugh*) risata *f*
cacophony [kə·'kɑː·fə·ni] *n* (*loud discord*) cacofonia *f;* (*noise*) strepitio *m*
cactus ['kæk·təs] <-es *o* cacti> *n* cactus *m inv*
CAD [kæd] *n abbr of* **Computer-Aided Design** CAD *m*
cadaver [kə·'dæ·vɚ] *n* MED cadavere *m*
CAD/CAM ['kæd·kæm] *n abbr of* **computer-aided design/computer-aided manufacturing** CAD/CAM *m*
caddie, caddy ['kæ·di] <-ies> **I.** *n* caddie *m inv* **II.** <caddied, caddied, caddying> *vi* **to** ~ **for sb** essere il caddie di qu
cadence ['keɪ·dns] *n* cadenza *f*
cadet [kə·'det] *n a.* MIL cadetto *m*
cadmium ['kæd·mjəm] *n* cadmio *m*
cadre ['kæd·riː] *n* **1.** (*elite trained group*) élite *f* **2.** (*group member*) membro *m* dell'élite
Caesar ['siː·zɚ] *n* Cesare *m;* **Julius** ~ HIST Giulio Cesare
caesarean [si·'ze·ri·ən] *n* ~ **(section)** (taglio *m*) cesareo *m*
cafe *n*, **café** [kæ·'feɪ] *n* caffè *m*
cafeteria [ˌkæ·fɪ·'tɪ·riə] *n* self-service *m inv*
caffeine [kæ·'fiːn] *n* caffeina *f*
cage [keɪdʒ] **I.** *n* gabbia *f* **II.** *vt* mettere in gabbia [*o* tenere]
cagey ['keɪ·dʒi] <-ier, -iest> *adj inf* riservato, -a; **to be** ~ **about sth** mostrarsi reticente su qc
cahoots [kə·'huːts] *npl inf* **to be in** ~ **(with sb)** essere in combutta (con qu)
cairn [kern] *n* cairn *m inv*
Cairo ['kɪ·roʊ] *n* il Cairo
cajole [kə·'dʒoʊl] *vt* blandire; **to** ~ **sb into/out of doing sth** blandire qu affinché faccia/non faccia qc
cake [keɪk] **I.** *n* **1.** CULIN torta *f;* (*small*) pasta *f*, pasticcino *m;* **frosted** ~ torta glassata; **sponge** ~ pan di Spagna *m* **2.** (*of soap*) pezzo *m;* (*of chocolate*) barra *f* ▶ **to sell like hot** ~ **s** andare a ruba; **to want to have one's** ~ **and eat it, too** volere la botte piena e la moglie ubriaca; **to take the** ~ (*outdo in a positive sense*) essere il massimo; (*outdo in a negative sense*) essere il colmo **II.** *vt* (*cover with*) **his boots were** ~ **d with mud** aveva gli stivali incrostati di fango **III.** *vi* (*form into*

mass) incrostarsi
cal. *n abbr of* **calorie** cal *f*
calamity [kə·'læ·mə·ti] <-ies> *n* calamità *f*
calciferous [kæl·'sɪ·fə·rəs] *adj* calcifico, -a
calcify ['kæl·sɪ·faɪ] <-ie-> **I.** *vt* calcificare **II.** *vi* calcificarsi
calcium ['kæl·si·əm] *n* calcio *m*
calculable ['kæl·kjə·lə·bl] *adj* MATH, ECON calcolabile; **the total damage is** ~ **at $15,000** il totale dei danni ammonta a 15.000 dollari
calculate ['kæl·kjə·leɪt] **I.** *vt* calcolare; **to** ~ **sth at ...** calcolare che qc ammonta a ... **II.** *vi* calcolare
calculated *adj* **1.** (*likely*) **it's** ~ **to do sth** è molto probabile che faccia qc **2.** MATH calcolato, -a; **a** ~ **risk** un rischio calcolato **3.** (*deliberate*) deliberato, -a
calculating *adj* calcolatore, -trice
calculation [ˌkæl·kjə·'leɪ·ʃən] *n* **1.** MATH calcolo *m;* (*figures*) calcoli *mpl* **2.** (*foreseeing*) valutazione *f* **3.** (*selfish planning*) calcolo *m*
calculator ['kæl·kjə·leɪ·t̬ɚ] *n* calcolatrice *f*
calculus ['kæl·kjə·ləs] *n* calcolo *m*
calendar ['kæ·lɪn·dɚ] *n* calendario *m*
calendar month <-es> *n* mese *m* civile
calendar year *n* anno *m* civile
calf¹ [kæf] <calves> *n* **1.** (*young cow or bull*) vitello *m;* **to be in** ~ essere gravida **2.** (*leather*) pelle *f* di vitello ▶ **to kill the** fatted ~ ammazzare il vitello grasso
calf² [kæf] <calves> *n* (*lower leg*) polpaccio *m*
caliber ['kæ·lə·bɚ] *n* calibro *m;* **to be of** (**a**) **high** ~ essere un grosso calibro
calibrate ['kæ·lɪ·breɪt] *vt* calibrare
calico ['kæ·lɪ·koʊ] *n* cotonina *f*
California [ˌkæ·lə·'fɔːrn·jə] *n* California *f*
call [kɔːl] **I.** *n* **1.** (*telephone*) chiamata *f;* **to give sb a** ~ telefonare a qu **2.** (*visit*) visita *f;* **to be on** ~ essere di guardia; **to pay a** ~ **on sb** fare visita a qu **3.** (*shout*) grido *m;* **a** ~ **for help** una richiesta d'aiuto **4.** (*animal cry*) richiamo *m* **5.** *a.* POL appello *m* **6.** *a.* ECON richiesta *f;* **money on** ~ denaro *m* a vista; **there is not much** ~ **for sth** non c'è molta richiesta di qc **7.** *form* (*need*) **there's no** ~ **for sth** non c'è bisogno di qc; **you had no** ~ **to say that** non c'era alcun bisogno che tu lo dicessi **8.** (*decision*) decisione *f;* **you make the** ~ sta a te decidere **9.** (*attraction*) richiamo *m;* **the** ~ **of the wild** il richiamo della natura ▶ **to have a close** ~ scamparla per un pelo **II.** *vt* **1.** (*name, address as*) chiamare; **to** ~ **sb names** insultare qu; **what's that actor** ~**ed?** come si chiama quell'attore?; **what's his new film** ~**ed?** come si intitola il suo ultimo film?; **she's** ~**ed by her middle name, Jane** sì la chiamare col suo secondo nome, Jane **2.** (*telephone*) chiamare; **to** ~ **sb collect** chiamare qu a carico del destinatario **3.** (*make noise to attract*) **to** ~ **sb's attention** attirare l'attenzione di qu; **I** ~**ed you to come to eat ten minutes ago** ti ho chiamato per dirti di venire a tavola dieci minuti fa **4.** (*ask to*

come) convocare; **she was ~ed to a meeting in Denver** è stata convocata a Denver per una riunione **5.** (*ask for quiet*) **to ~ for order** richiamare all'ordine **6.** (*reprimand*) ammonire; **to ~ sth to mind** (*recall, remember*) ricordare qc **7.** (*regard as*) **to ~ sth one's own** considerare qc suo; **you ~ this a party?** questa la chiami festa?; **I'm not ~ing you a liar** non ti sto dando del bugiardo; **I don't know exactly how much you owe me, but let's ~ it an even $10** non so esattamente quanto mi devi, diciamo 10 dollari tondi?; **he has very few ideas that he can genuinely ~ his own** ha poche idee che può dire veramente sue **8.** (*decide to have*) **to ~ a meeting** (to order) convocare una riunione; **to ~ a halt to sth** sospendere qc; **to ~ a strike** indire uno sciopero **III.** *vi* **1.** (*telephone*) chiamare **2.** (*drop by*) passare **3.** (*shout*) gridare
◆ **call away** *vt* **he was called away** è dovuto andare via
◆ **call back** **I.** *vt* **1.** (*telephone*) richiamare **2.** (*ask to return*) far tornare **3.** ECON ritirare dal mercato; **the company has called back a type of toy** la ditta ha ritirato dal mercato un tipo di giocattolo **II.** *vi* (*phone again*) richiamare
◆ **call for** *vt insep* **1.** (*come to get*) passare a prendere **2.** (*ask*) chiedere **3.** (*demand, require*) richiedere; **this calls for a celebration** qui bisogna festeggiare
◆ **call forth** *vt form* suscitare
◆ **call in** *vt* **1.** (*ask to come*) chiamare **2.** FIN **to ~ a loan** richiedere il pagamento di un prestito
◆ **call off** *vt* **1.** (*cancel*) annullare **2.** (*order back*) **he called off his dog** ha richiamato il cane
◆ **call on** *vt insep* **1.** (*appeal to*) **to ~ sb** (to do sth) fare appello a qu (affinché faccia qc); **to ~ a witness** convocare un testimone; **I now ~ everyone to raise a glass to our friend** *form* adesso invito tutti a fare un brindisi al nostro amico **2.** (*visit*) fare visita a
◆ **call out** **I.** *vt* (*shout*) gridare **II.** *vi* **1.** (*shout*) gridare **2.** *fig* (*demand*) **to call out for sth** richiedere qc
◆ **call up** *vt* **1.** (*telephone*) chiamare **2.** COMPUT **to ~ sth** richiamare qc a video **3.** (*order to join the military*) **to call up the reserves** richiamare le riserve **4.** (*conjure up*) rievocare
caller ['kɔː·lə·] *n* **1.** (*person on the telephone*) persona *f* che fa una telefonata; **hold the line please,** ~ attenda in linea, per favore **2.** (*announcer*) (*at bingo game*) persona *f* che legge i numeri estratti
call girl *n* prostituta *f*
calligraphy [kə·'lɪ·grə·fi] *n* calligrafia *f*
call-in *n* RADIO, TV *programma televisivo o radiofonico con chiamate del pubblico in diretta*
calling ['kɔː·lɪŋ] *n form* vocazione *f*
calling card *n* scheda *f* telefonica
callous ['kæ·ləs] *adj* (*heartless*) crudele;

(*insensitive*) insensibile
call sign ['kɔːl·saɪn] *n* segnale *m* di chiamata
callus ['kæ·ləs] <-es> *n* MED callo *m*
calm [kɑːm] **I.** *adj* **1.** (*not nervous*) tranquillo, -a; **to keep ~** mantenere la calma **2.** (*peaceful, not wavy*) calmo, -a **3.** (*not windy*) senza vento **II.** *n* calma *f*, tranquillità *f*; **the ~ before the storm** *fig* la calma che precede la tempesta **III.** *vt* calmare; **to ~ oneself** calmarsi
calmness *n* **1.** (*lack of agitation*) tranquillità *f*, calma *f* **2.** (*of the sea*) calma *f*
caloric [kə·'lɔː·rɪk] *adj* calorico, -a
calorie ['kæ·lə·ri] *n* caloria *f*
calorific [ˌkæ·lə·'rɪ·fək] *adj* calorifico, -a
calumny ['kæ·ləm·ni] *n form* calunnia *f*
calve [kæv] *vi* figliare
Calvinism ['kæl·vɪ·nɪ·zəm] *n* REL Calvinismo *m*
Calvinist ['kæl·vɪ·nɪst] REL **I.** *n* calvinista *mf* **II.** *adj* calvinista
CAM [kæm] *n abbr of* **computer assisted manufacturing** CAM *m*
cam [kæm] *n* TECH camma *f*
camaraderie [ˌkæ·mə·'ræ·də·ri] *n* cameratismo *m*
camber ['kæm·bə·] *n* (*of road*) pendenza *f* trasversale
Cambodia [kæm·'boʊ·diə] *n* Cambogia *f*
Cambodian [kæm·'boʊ·di·ən] **I.** *adj* cambogiano, -a **II.** *n* cambogiano, -a *m, f*
camcorder ['kæm·kɔ·də·] *n* videocamera *f*
came [keɪm] *vi pt of* **come**
camel ['kæ·ml] **I.** *n* **1.** ZOOL cammello *m* **2.** (*color*) color *m* cammello **II.** *adj* **1.** (*camel-hair*) di cammello **2.** (*color*) color cammello
camel-hair ['kæ·məl·her] *n* (pelo *m* di) cammello
cameo ['kæm·ioʊ] *n* **1.** (*jewelry*) cammeo *m* **2.** CINE, TV piccolo ruolo *m*
camera ['kæ·mə·rə] *n* **1.** PHOT macchina *f* fotografica; CINE cinepresa *f*; **to be on ~** essere in onda **2.** LAW **in ~** a porte chiuse
camera angle *n* angolatura *f*
cameraman <-men> *n* cameraman *m inv*
camera-ready copy <-ies> *n* TYPO copia *f* pronta per la fotoincisione
camera shot *n* CINE ripresa *f*
camera-shy *adj* **to be ~** non amare farsi fotografare
camerawoman <-women> *n* cameraman *f inv*
Cameroon [ˌkæ·mə·'ruːn] *n* Camerun *m*
Cameroonian [ˌkæ·mə·'roʊː·ni·ən] **I.** *adj* camerunese **II.** *n* camerunese *mf*
camomile ['kæ·mə·miːl] *n* camomilla *f*; **~ tea** camomilla
camouflage ['kæ·mə·ˌflɑːʒ] **I.** *n* mimetizzazione *f* **II.** *vt* mimetizzare; **to ~ oneself** mimetizzarsi
camp¹ [kæmp] **I.** *n* **1.** (*encampment*) accampamento *m*, campo *m*; **army ~** accampamento militare; **summer ~** colonia *f* estiva; **to break ~** levare le tende; **to set up ~** accamparsi **2.** (*group*) gruppo *m*; **to go over to the**

other ~ passare all'altra parte; **to have a foot in both** ~**s** tenere il piede in due staffe **II.** *vi* accamparsi; **to** ~ **out** accamparsi; **to go** ~**ing** andare in campeggio

camp² [kæmp] **I.** *n* (**high**) ~ leziosaggine *m* **II.** *adj* (*affected*) affettato, -a; (*effeminate*) effeminato, -a **III.** *vt* **to** ~ **it up** fare il gigione

campaign [kæm·'peɪn] **I.** *n* campagna *f;* ~ **trail** campagna elettorale **II.** *vi* condurre una campagna; **to** ~ **for sth/sb** condurre una campagna a favore di qc/qu

campaigner [kæm·'peɪ·nə·] *n* **1.** (*election worker*) persona *f* che collabora a una campagna elettorale **2.** (*person who campaigns*) persona *f* che porta avanti una campagna; **a** ~ **for sth** un sostenitore di qc

camper ['kæm·pə·] *n* **1.** (*person*) campeggiatore, -trice *m, f* **2.** AUTO camper *m inv*

campfire *n* falò *m* (in accampamento); ~ **song** canzone *f* da cantare intorno al falò

camp follower *n* (*supporter*) simpatizzante *mf*

campground *n* campeggio *m*

camphor ['kæm·fə·] *n* MED canfora *m*

camping ['kæm·pɪŋ] *n* campeggio *m;* **to go** ~ andare in campeggio

campsite ['kæmp·saɪt] *n* campeggio *m;* (*for one tent*) piazzola *f*

campus ['kæm·pəs] <-es> *n* campus *m inv*

camshaft ['kæm·ʃæft] *n* TECH albero *m* a camme

can¹ [kæn] **I.** *n* **1.** (*container: of food*) scatola *f,* barattolo *m;* (*of drink*) lattina *f;* (*of oil*) bidone *m* **2.** *inf* (*toilet*) cesso *m* **3.** *inf* (*prison*) galera *f* ▶ **to open** (**up**) **a** ~ **of worms** sollevare un vespaio **II.** <-nn-> *vt* **1.** (*put in cans*) inscatolare **2.** *inf* (*stop*) ~ **it!** basta!

can² [kən] <could, could> *aux* **1.** (*be able to*) potere, essere in grado di; **if I could** se potessi; **I think she** ~ **help you** penso che lei possa aiutarti; **I could have kissed her** avrei potuto baciarla **2.** *inf* (*be permitted to*) potere; **you can't go** non puoi andare; **could I look at it?** potrei vederlo? **3.** (*know how to*) sapere, essere capace di; ~ **you swim?** sai nuotare?

Canada ['kæ·nə·də] *n* Canada *m*

Canadian [kə·'neɪ·di·ən] **I.** *n* canadese *mf* **II.** *adj* canadese

canal [kə·'næl] *n* canale *m*

canalization [ˌkæ·nə·lɪ·'zeɪ·ʃən] *n* canalizzazione *f*

canalize ['kæ·nə·laɪz] *vt* canalizzare

canary [kə·'ne·ri] **I.** <-ies> *n* canarino *m* **II.** *adj* ~ **yellow** giallo canarino

Canary Islands *n* Canarie *fpl*

canary seed *n* seme *m* di scagliola

canasta [kə·'næs·tə] *n* GAMES canasta *f*

cancel ['kæn·sl] <-ll-, -l-> **I.** *vt* **1.** (*reservation, meeting, flight*) cancellare; (*license*) revocare; (*contract*) disdire **2.** MATH **to** ~ **each other out** elidersi **3.** COMPUT annullare **II.** *vi* cancellare

cancellation [ˌkæn·sə·'leɪ·ʃən] *n* (*of reservation, meeting, flight*) cancellazione; (*of license*) revoca; (*of contract*) disdetta

cancer ['kæn·sə·] *n* MED cancro *m;* ~ **specialist** oncologo, -a *m, f;* ~ **cell** cellula *f* cancerogena

Cancer ['kæn·sə·] *n* Cancro *m*

cancer clinic *n* MED clinica *f* oncologica

cancerous ['kæn·sə·rəs] *adj* MED canceroso, -a

cancer research *n* MED ricerca *f* sul cancro

candelabra [ˌkæn·də·'lɑː·brə] <-(s)> *n* candelabro *m*

candid ['kæn·dɪd] *adj* sincero, -a; (*picture*) naturale

candidacy ['kæn·dɪ·də·si] *n,* **candidature** ['kæn·də·də·tʃʊr] *n* candidatura *f*

candidate ['kæn·dɪ·dət] *n* (*competitor*) (*possible choice*) candidato, -a *m, f*

candid camera *n* candid camera *f inv*

candied ['kæn·dɪd] *adj* candito, -a

candle ['kæn·dl] *n* (*light*) candela *f* ▶ **to burn one's** ~ **at both ends** ammazzarsi di lavoro; **she can't hold a** ~ **to him** non è degna di legargli le scarpe

candlelight ['kæn·dl·laɪt] *n* lume *f* di candela; **to do sth by** ~ fare qc a lume di candela

Candlemas ['kæn·dl·məs] *n* REL Candelora *f*

candlepower ['kæn·dl·pa·ʊə·] *n* candelaggio *m*

candlestick ['kæn·dl·stɪk] *n* portacandele *m inv*

candlewick ['kæn·dl·wɪk] *n* (*textile*) ciniglia *f*

candor ['kæn·də·] *n form* candore *m*

candy ['kæn·di] **I.** <-ies> *n* (*sweets*) caramelle *fpl* **II.** *vt* candire

candy bar *n* barretta *f* al cioccolato

candy store *n* negozio *m* di caramelle

cane [keɪn] **I.** *n* **1.** (*dried plant stem*) canna *f* **2.** (*furniture*) giunco *m* **3.** (*stick*) bastone *m;* (*for punishment*) bacchetta *f* **II.** *vt* punire con la bacchetta

cane sugar *n* zucchero *m* di canna

canine ['keɪ·naɪn] **I.** *n* **1.** ZOOL canide *m* **2.** (*tooth*) canino *m* **II.** *adj* canino, -a

canister ['kæ·nəs·tə·] *n* barattolo *m,* scatola *f;* (*for gas*) candelotto *m*

cannabis ['kæ·nə·bɪs] *n* (*plant*) canapa *f* indiana; (*drug*) hascisc *m*

canned [kænd] *adj* **1.** (*food, fruit, meat*) in scatola; (*beer*) in lattina **2.** MUS, TV registrato, -a

cannery ['kæ·nə·ri] <-ies> *n* conservificio *m*

cannibal ['kæ·nɪ·bl] *n* cannibale *m*

cannibalism ['kæ·nɪ·bə·lɪ·zəm] *n* cannibalismo *m*

cannibalize ['kæ·nɪ·bə·laɪz] *vt* AUTO cannibalizzare

canning ['kæ·nɪŋ] *n* inscatolamento *m;* ~ **factory** conservificio *m*

cannon ['kæ·nən] *n* cannone *m*

cannon ball *n* palla *f* di cannone

cannon fodder *n* carne *f* da cannone

cannot ['kæ·nɑːt] *aux* = **can not** *s.* **can²**

canny ['kæ·ni] <-ier, -iest> *adj* (*clever*) astuto, -a

canoe [kə·'nuː] *n* canoa *f* ▶ **to paddle one's own** ~ essere autonomo

canoeing *n* canottaggio *m*

canoeist [kə·'nuː·ɪst] *n* canoista *mf*
canon ['kæ·nən] *n* **1.** REL, MUS canone *m* **2.** (*person*) canonico *m* **3.** LIT bibliografia *f*
canonization [ˌkæ·nə·nɪ·'zeɪ·ʃən] *n* canonizzazione *f*
canonize ['kæ·nə·naɪz] *vt* canonizzare
can opener ['kæn·ˌoʊp·nə·] *n* apriscatole *m inv*
canopy ['kæ·nə·pi] <-ies> *n* **1.** (*roof-like covering*) tettoia *f* **2.** OF COCKPIT tettuccio *m* **3.** OF SEAT, BED baldacchino *m* **4.** *form* (*sky*) volta *f* celeste
cant¹ [kænt] *n* **1.** (*insincere talk*) ipocrisie *fpl* **2.** LING gergo *m*
cant² [kænt] **I.** *n* pendenza *f* **II.** *vt* inclinare **III.** *vi* inclinarsi
can't [kænt] = **cannot**
cantankerous [kæn·'tæŋ·kə·rəs] *adj* intrattabile
cantata [kən·'tɑː·ʈə] *n* MUS cantata *f*
canteen [kæn·'tiːn] *n* **1.** (*cafeteria*) mensa *f* **2.** MIL (*drink container*) borraccia *f*
canter ['kæn·ʈə·] **I.** *n* piccolo galoppo *m* **II.** *vi* andare al piccolo galoppo
cantilever ['kæn·ʈə·liː·və·] *n* trave *f* a mensola; ~ **bridge** ponte *m* a sbalzo
Cantonese [ˌkæn·tə·'niːz] **I.** *adj* cantonese **II.** *n* **1.** (*language*) cantonese *m* **2.** (*person*) cantonese *mf*
canvas ['kæn·vəs] <-es> *n* **1.** (*cloth*) tela *f*; **under** ~ (*in a tent*) in tenda; NAUT a vele spiegate **2.** ART tela *f*
canvass ['kæn·vəs] **I.** *vt* **1.** (*gather opinion*) sondare; **to** ~ **sth** (*proposal*) fare un sondaggio d'opinione su qc **2.** POL (*votes*) sollecitare **II.** *vi* POL fare propaganda
canvasser ['kæn·və·sə·] *n* POL *appartenente a un partito politico che fa propaganda porta a porta*
canvassing *n* POL propaganda *f* elettorale porta a porta
canyon ['kæn·jən] *n* canyon *m inv*
CAP [ˌsiː·eɪ·'piː] *n abbr of* **Civil Air Patrol** soccorso *m* aereo civile
cap¹ [kæp] **I.** *n* **1.** (*without peak*) cuffia *f* **2.** (*with peak*) berretto *m;* ~ **and gown** UNIV toga e tocco **3.** (*cover*) tappo *m;* PHOT copriobiettivo *f;* **screw-on** ~ tappo a vite **4.** (*of tooth, in toy gun*) capsula *f* **5.** (*limit*) limite *m;* **salary** ~ tetto *m* salariale **6.** (*contraceptive*) diaframma *m* ▶**to put on one's** thinking ~ *inf* mettere in moto il cervello **II.** <-pp-> *vt* **1.** (*limit*) limitare **2.** (*cover*) tappare; (*tooth*) incapsulare **3.** (*outdo*) coronare; **to** ~ **it all** per coronare il tutto
cap² [kæp] *n abbr of* **capital** (**letter**) maiuscola *f*
capability [ˌkeɪ·pə·'bɪ·lə·ti] <-ies> *n* **1.** (*ability*) capacità *f;* (*power*) potenziale *m* **2.** (*skill*) capacità *f inv*
capable ['keɪ·pə·bl] *adj* **1.** (*competent*) competente **2.** (*able*) capace; **to be** ~ **of doing sth** essere capace di fare qc

capacity [kə·'pæ·sə·ti] <-ies> *n* **1.** (*volume, amount*) capacità *f,* capienza *f;* **to be full to** ~ essere completamente pieno; **filled to** ~ completamente pieno; **seating** ~ **of fifty** cinquanta posti a sedere **2.** (*ability*) capacità *f,* attitudine *f* **3.** (*output*) capacità *f;* **to work at full** ~ operare a pieno regime **4.** (*role*) qualità *f*
cape¹ [keɪp] *n* GEO capo *m*
cape² [keɪp] *n* (*cloak*) mantella *f*
caper¹ ['keɪ·pə·] **I.** *n* **1.** (*joyful leaping movement*) capriola *f;* **to cut** ~**s** fare le capriole **2.** (*dubious activity*) intrallazzo *m* **II.** *vi* saltellare
caper² ['keɪ·pə·] *n* BOT cappero *m*
Cape Town ['keɪp·taʊn] *n* Città *f* del Capo
Cape Verde ['keɪp·vɜːrd] *n* Capo *m* Verde
capillary ['kæ·pə·le·ri] <-ies> *n* capillare *m*
capital ['kæ·pə·tl] **I.** *n* **1.** (*principal city*) capitale *f* **2.** TYPO maiuscola *f;* **to write in** ~**s** scrivere in stampatello **3.** ARCHIT capitello *m* **4.** FIN capitale *m;* **to make** ~ (**out**) **of sth** *fig* trarre vantaggio da qc **II.** *adj* **1.** (*principal*) capitale; ~ **city** capitale *f* **2.** TYPO (*letter*) maiuscolo, -a **3.** LAW capitale; ~ **punishment** pena *f* capitale
capital assets *npl* FIN capitale *m* fisso
capital crime *n* LAW reato *m* punibile con la pena capitale
capital gains tax <-es> *n* imposta *f* sulle plusvalenze
capital investment *n* FIN investimento *m* di capitale
capital investment company <-ies> *n* società *f* d'investimento
capitalism ['kæ·pə·tə·lɪ·zəm] *n* capitalismo *m*
capitalist ['kæ·pə·tə·lɪst] **I.** *n* capitalista *mf* **II.** *adj* capitalista
capitalistic [ˌkæ·pə·tə·'lɪs·tɪk] *adj* capitalistico, -a
capitalization [ˌkæ·pət·lɪ·'zeɪ·ʃən] *n* capitalizzazione *f*
capitalize ['kæ·pə·tə·laɪz] *vt* **1.** TYPO scrivere in maiuscolo **2.** *a.* FIN capitalizzare
capital letter ['kæ·pə·tl·'le·ʈə·] *n* maiuscola *f;* **in** ~**s** in stampatello
capital punishment *n* pena *f* capitale
capitulate [kə·'pɪt·ʃə·leɪt] *vi* capitolare; **to** ~ **to sth/sb** capitolare di fronte a qc/qu
capitulation [kə·'pɪt·ʃə·'leɪ·ʃən] *n* capitolazione *f;* ~ **to sb/sth** capitolazione di fronte a qu/qc
cappuccino [ˌkæ·pə·'tʃiː·noʊ] *n* cappuccino *m*
caprice [kə·'priːs] *n liter* capriccio *m*
capricious [kə·'prɪ·ʃəs] *adj* capriccioso, -a
Capricorn ['kæp·rə·kɔːrn] *n* Capricorno *m*
caps. *n abbr of* **capital letters** maiuscole *fpl*
capsize ['kæp·saɪz] **I.** *vt* NAUT *fig* capovolgere **II.** *vi* NAUT *fig* capovolgersi
capstan ['kæps·tən] *n* NAUT cabestano *m*
capsule ['kæp·sl] *n* capsula *f*
captain ['kæp·tɪn] **I.** *n* capitano, -a *m, f* **II.** *vt* (*team*) capitanare; (*ship*) comandare
captaincy ['kæp·tɪn·si] *n* posto *m* di capitano
caption ['kæp·ʃən] *n* **1.** (*of picture*) didascalia *f*

2. CINE sottotitolo *m*

captivate ['kæp·tə·veɪt] *vt* accattivare

captive ['kæp·tɪv] **I.** *n* (*person*) prigioniero, -a *m, f;* (*animal*) animale *m* in cattività **II.** *adj* (*person*) prigioniero, -a; (*animal*) in cattività; **to hold sb ~** tenere prigioniero qu

captivity [kæp·'tɪ·və·ti] *n* prigionia *f;* **to be in ~** (*animal*) essere in cattività

capture ['kæp·tʃɚ] **I.** *vt* **1.** (*take prisoner*) catturare **2.** (*city, votes, market*) conquistare; (*ship*) catturare **3.** ART cogliere; **to ~ sth on film** cogliere qc sullo schermo **4.** COMPUT inserire **II.** *n* cattura *f;* (*of city, ship*) presa *f*

car [kɑːr] *n* **1.** AUTO macchina *f,* auto *f inv* **2.** RAIL vagone *m* **3.** (*in airship, balloon*) navicella *f*

carafe ['kæ·rəf] *n* caraffa *f*

caramel ['kɑ·r·ml] **I.** *n* **1.** (*burnt sugar*) caramello *m* **2.** (*sweet*) dolciume tipo *caramella mou* **II.** *adj* di caramello; **~ cream** crème caramel *m inv*

carat <-(s)> *n* carato *m*

caravan ['ke·rə·væn] *n* (*group of travelers*) carovana *f*

caravansary [ˌke·rə·'væn·sə·ri] *n,* **caravanserai** [ˌkerə'vænsəraɪ] *n* caravanserraglio *m*

caraway ['ke·rə·weɪ] *n* cumino *m*

caraway seed *n* seme *m* di cumino

carbide ['kɑːr·baɪd] *n* carburo *m*

carbine ['kɑːr·biːn] *n* carabina *f*

car body ['kɑːr·bɑːˌdi] <-ies> *n* carrozzeria *f*

carbohydrate [ˌkɑːr·boʊ·'haɪ·dreɪt] *n* carboidrato *m*

carbolic [kɑːr·'bɑːˌlɪk] *adj* **~ acid** acido *m* fenico

car bomb ['kɑːr·bɑːm] *n* autobomba *f*

carbon ['kɑːr·bən] **I.** *n* **1.** CHEM carbonio *m* **2.** (*copy*) copia *f* carbone **3.** (*paper*) carta *f* carbone **II.** *adj* di carbonio

carbon copy <-ies> *n* copia *f* carbone

carbon dating *n* datazione *f* al carbonio

carbon dioxide *n* diossido *m* di carbonio

carbonic [kɑːr·'bɑːˌnɪk] *adj* **~ acid** acido *m* carbonico

carbonize ['kɑːr·bə·naɪz] **I.** *vt* carbonizzare **II.** *vi* carbonizzarsi

carbon monoxide *n* monossido *m* di carbonio

carbon paper *n* carta *f* carbone

carbuncle ['kɑːr·bʌŋ·kl] *n* **1.** MED foruncolo *m* **2.** (*gem*) carbonchio *m*

carburet ['kɑː·bjʊ·ˌret] *vt* arricchire un gas combustibile con vapori di idrocarburi liquidi

carburetor ['kɑːr·bə·reɪ·ˌtɚ] *n* carburatore *m*

carcass ['kɑːr·kəs] <-es> *n* **1.** (*of animal, vehicle*) carcassa *f* **2.** (*of cooked chicken*) resti *mpl*

carcinogen [kɑːr·'si·nə·ˌdʒen] *n* MED (agente *m*) cancerogeno *m*

carcinogenic [ˌkɑːr·sə·noʊ·'dʒe·nɪk] *adj* MED cancerogeno, -a

carcinoma [kɑːrs·'noʊ·mə] *n* MED carcinoma *m*

card¹ [kɑːrd] **I.** *n* **1.** (*birthday, Christmas, etc.*) biglietto *m* (d'auguri) **2.** GAMES *a.* FIN carta *f;*

pack of ~s mazzo *m* di carte; **to play ~s** giocare a carte **3.** (*proof of identity*) documento *m;* **membership ~** tessera *f* dei soci **4.** *a.* COMPUT scheda *f* **5.** SPORTS (*program*) programma *m* **6.** (*index ~*) scheda *f* **7.** *inf* tipo *m* bizzarro ► **to have a ~ up one's sleeve** avere un asso nella manica; **to put one's ~s on the table** mettere le carte in tavola; **to play one's ~s right** giocare bene le proprie carte; **to be in the ~s** essere destino **II.** *vt inf* chiedere i documenti

card² [kɑːrd] **I.** *n* cardatrice *f* **II.** *vt* cardare

cardboard ['kɑːrd·bɔːrd] *n* cartone *m*

cardiac ['kɑːr·dɪ·æk] *adj* MED cardiaco, -a

cardigan ['kɑːr·dɪ·gən] *n* cardigan *m inv*

cardinal ['kɑːr·dɪ·nl] **I.** *n* cardinale *m* **II.** *adj* (*important: rule*) fondamentale; (*error, sin*) capitale

cardinal number *n* numero *m* cardinale

cardinal points *npl* punti *m pl* cardinali

card index ['kɑːrd·ˌɪn·deks] <-es> *n* schedario *m*

cardiogram ['kɑːr·dɪoʊ·græm] *n* MED cardiogramma *m*

card reader *n* lettore *m* di schede perforate

card table *n* tavolo *m* da gioco

care [ker] **I.** *n* **1.** (*attention*) cura *f;* **to take ~ of** prendersi cura di; (*object*) fare attenzione a; (*situation*) occuparsi di; **take ~** (*of yourself*) riguardati!; **to do sth with ~** fare qc con cura; **that takes ~ of that!** questo è sistemato!; **handle with ~** maneggiare con cura **2.** (*worry*) preoccupazione *f;* **to not have a ~ in the world** essere spensierato, -a **II.** *vi* **1.** (*be concerned*) preoccuparsi; **to ~ about sb/sth** preoccuparsi per qu/qc; **as if I ~d!** e a me che m'importa?; **for all I ~** (*as far as I'm concerned*) per me; **who ~s?** chi se ne frega? **2.** (*feel affection*) **to ~ about sb** voler bene a qu, tenere a qu **3.** (*want*) **to ~ to do sth** essere disposto a fare qc

CARE [ker] *n abbr of* **Cooperative for American Relief Everywhere** *cooperativa statunitense di soccorso nel mondo*

career [kə·'rɪr] *n* **1.** (*profession*) professione *f* **2.** (*working life*) carriera *f* (professionale)

career counselor *n* consulente *mf* per l'orientamento professionale

careerist [kə·'rɪ·rɪst] **I.** *n* carrierista *mf* **II.** *adj* carrierista

career woman <-women> *n* donna *f* in carriera

carefree ['ker·friː] *adj* spensierato, -a

careful ['ker·fəl] *adj* (*cautious, meticulous*) attento, -a; **to be ~ of sth** fare attenzione a qc; **to be ~ to do sth** fare attenzione a fare qc

carefulness *n* attenzione *f,* cura *f*

careless ['ker·lɪs] *adj* **1.** (*lacking attention, unthinking, not painstaking*) distratto, -a **2.** (*carefree*) spensierato, -a

carelessness *n* **1.** (*lack of attention*) distrazione *f* **2.** (*lack of concern*) menefreghismo *m*

carer *n* badante *mf,* persona che si prende cura

di una persona anziana, malata o disabile
caress [kə·'res] I. <-es> *n* carezza *f* II. *vi* fare una carezza III. *vt* accarezzare
caretaker ['ker·ˌteɪ·kə*] *n* (*of building, property*) custode *mf*
careworn ['ker·wɔːrn] *adj* segnato, -a dalle preoccupazioni
car ferry <-ies> *n* NAUT traghetto *m* per auto
cargo ['kɑːr·goʊ] <-(e)s> *n* 1. (*goods*) carico *m* 2. (*load*) carico *m*
cargo aircraft *n* aereo *m* da carico
cargo boat *n* cargo *m inv,* nave *f* da carico
cargo plane *n* aereo *m* da carico
cargo ship *n* cargo *m inv,* nave *f* da carico
cargo vessel *n* cargo *m inv,* nave *f* da carico
Caribbean [ˌkerɪ·'biː·ən] I. *n* the ~ i Caraibi; (*sea*) il Mar dei Caraibi II. *adj* caraibico, -a
caricature ['ke·rə·kə·tjʊr] I. *n a.* ART caricatura *f* II. *vt* LIT fare la caricatura di
caricaturist ['kæ·rə·kə·tʃʊ·rɪst] *n* ART caricaturista *mf*
caries ['ke·riːz] *n* MED carie *f inv*
caring *adj* premuroso, -a
car insurance *n* assicurazione *f* della macchina
carjacking *n* furto *m* d'auto
carnage ['kɑːr·nɪdʒ] *n* massacro *m*
carnal ['kɑːr·nl] *adj* carnale
carnation [kɑːr·'neɪ·ʃən] I. *n* 1. BOT garofano *m* 2. (*color*) rosa *m* carne II. *adj* rosa carne *inv*
carnival ['kɑːr·nə·vl] *n* carnevale *m*
carnivore ['kɑːr·nə·vɔːr] *n* carnivoro, -a *m, f*
carnivorous [kɑːr·'nɪ·və·rəs] *adj* carnivoro, -a
carol ['ke·rəl] *n* canto *m* (di Natale)
carol singer *n* cantante *mf* di canti di Natale
carotene ['kæ·rə·tiːn] *n* BIO carotene *m*
carousel [ˌkæ·rə·'sel] *n* 1. (*merry-go-round*) giostra *f* 2. (*baggage return*) nastro *m* trasportatore
carp¹ [kɑːrp] <-(s)> *n* ZOOL carpa *f*
carp² [kɑːrp] *vi* avere sempre da ridire
carpenter ['kɑːr·pn·ˌtə*] *n* falegname *m*
carpentry ['kɑːr·pn·tri] *n* falegnameria *f*
carpet ['kɑːr·pət] I. *n* (*fitted*) moquette *f inv;* (*not fitted*) tappeto *m* ▶ **to sweep sth under the ~** nascondere qc sotto il tappeto II. *vt* 1. (*cover floor*) mettere la moquette in 2. *lit* (*cover sth*) ricoprire
carpetbag ['kɑːr·pət·bæg] *n* borsa *f* in tessuto di tappeto
carpetbagger ['kɑːr·pət·ˌbæ·gə*] *n* POL *politico che cerca di farsi eleggere in un collegio in cui non è conosciuto;* HIST *in America, nordista che alla fine della Guerra di Secessione andava negli stati sudisti per trarre profitto o conquistare potere politico*
carpeting ['kɑːr·pə·ˌtɪŋ] *n* moquette *f*
carpool ['kɑːr·puːl] *n condivisione della stessa auto da parte di un gruppo di persone che lavorano nello stesso luogo*
car rental *n* autonoleggio *m*
carriage ['ke·rɪdʒ] *n* 1. (*horse-drawn vehicle*)

carrozza *f* 2. (*part of typewriter*) carrello *m*
carriage return *n* TYPO ritorno *m* carrello
carrier ['kæ·rɪ·ə*] *n* 1. (*person who carries*) corriere *m* 2. MIL (*vehicle*) veicolo *m* da trasporto; **aircraft ~** portaerei *f inv* 3. MED portatore, -trice *m, f* 4. (*transport company*) spedizioniere *m*
carrion ['ke·ri·ən] *n* carogna *f*
carrion crow *n* cornacchia *f*
carrot ['ke·rət] *n* 1. (*vegetable*) carota *f* 2. *inf* (*reward*) incentivo *m;* **the ~-and-stick approach** la tecnica del bastone e della carota
carroty ['ke·rə·ˌti] <-ier, -iest> *adj* color carota *inv*
carry ['ke·ri] <-ies, -ied> I. *vt* 1. (*transport in hands or arms*) portare 2. (*transport*) trasportare 3. (*have on one's person*) avere con sé 4. MED (*transmit*) trasmettere 5. (*support*) sostenere 6. (*sell*) vendere 7. (*win: position*) conquistare 8. (*approve*) approvare 9. PUBL **to ~ an article** pubblicare un articolo 10. (*develop*) **to ~ consequences** avere conseguenze; **to ~ an argument to its (logical) conclusion** arrivare alla conclusione logica di un ragionamento 11. (*be pregnant*) **to ~ a child** aspettare un bambino II. *vi* (*be audible*) arrivare
♦**carry along** *vt* portarsi dietro; (*water*) portare via
♦**carry away** *vt* 1. (*remove*) portare via 2. **to be carried away (by sth)** (*be overcome by*) lasciarsi sopraffare (da qc); (*be enchanted by*) entusiasmarsi (per qc); **to get carried away** esaltarsi
♦**carry forward** *vt* FIN trasferire
♦**carry off** *vt* 1. (*remove*) **to carry sb off** portarsi via qu 2. (*succeed*) **to carry it off** farcela
♦**carry on** I. *vt insep* continuare; ~ **(with) the good work!** bravo, continua così! II. *vi* 1. (*continue*) continuare; **to ~ doing sth** continuare a fare qc 2. *inf* (*make a fuss*) non finirla più
♦**carry out** *vt* eseguire
♦**carry over** I. *vt* 1. (*bring forward*) riportare; FIN trasferire 2. (*postpone*) rimandare II. *vi* 1. **to ~ into sth** (*have an effect on*) influire su qc 2. (*remain*) permanere
♦**carry through** *vt* 1. (*support*) sostenere 2. (*complete successfully*) portare a termine
carryall ['kæ·ri·ɔːl] *n* borsone *m*
carrying capacity <-ies> *n* capacità *f* di carico
carrying-on <carryings-on> *n inf* 1. (*dubious affair*) tresca *f* 2. (*dubious activity*) tresca *f*
carryover *n* 1. FIN riporto *m* 2. (*remnant*) rimanenze *fpl*
cart [kɑːrt] I. *n* 1. (*vehicle*) carro *m* 2. (*supermarket trolley*) carrello *m* ▶ **to put the ~ before the horse** mettere il carro davanti ai buoi II. *vt* (*transport*) portare
carte blanche [ˌkɑːrt·'blɑːnʃ] *n* carta *f* bianca
cartel [kɑːr·'tel] *n* cartello *m*
cartilage ['kɑːr·ʈ·lɪdʒ] *n* cartilagine *f*

cartload ['kɑːrt·loʊd] *n* carrettata *f;* ~ **s of garbage** montagne *f pl* di spazzatura
cartographer [kɑːr·'tɑː·grə·fər] *n* cartografo, -a *m, f*
cartography [kɑːr·'tɑː·grə·fi] *n* cartografia *f*
carton ['kɑːr·tn] *n* (*box*) scatola *f* di cartone; (*of juice, milk*) cartone *m*
cartoon [kɑːr·'tuːn] *n* 1. ART vignetta *f* 2. CINE cartone *m* animato
cartoonist *n* fumettista *mf*
cartridge ['kɑːr·trɪdʒ] *n* 1. (*for ink, ammunition*) cartuccia *m* 2. (*for record player*) testina *f*
cartwheel ['kɑːrt·hwiːl] I. *n* ruota *f;* **to do a** ~ fare la ruota II. *vi* fare le ruote
carve [kɑːrv] I. *vt* 1. (*cut*) ritagliare; **to** ~ (**out**) **a name for oneself** *fig* farsi un nome 2. (*stone, wood*) intagliare 3. (*cut meat*) tagliare II. *vi* ritagliare
carver ['kɑːr·vər] *n* 1. ART intagliatore, -trice *m, f* 2. *pl* CULIN trinciante *m*
carvery ['kɑːr·və·i] <-ies> *n* *ristorante specializzato in carni arrosto*
carving *n* ART intaglio *m*
carving knife <knives> *n* trinciante *m*
car wash <-es> *n* autolavaggio *m*
cascade [kæs·'keɪd] I. *n* cascata *f* II. *vi* **to** ~ **from sth** ricadere a cascata da qc
case[1] [keɪs] *n* 1. *a.* MED, LING caso *m;* **in any** ~ in ogni caso; **just in** ~ per precauzione; **in** ~ **it rains** in caso piova; **as the** ~ **may be** a seconda dei casi 2. LAW causa *f,* caso *m;* **to close the** ~ chiudere il caso; **to lose one's** ~ perdere la causa 3. (*argument*) **to make a** ~ **for sth** argomentare in favore di qc
case[2] [keɪs] *n* (*container*) cassa *f;* (*for jewels*) astuccio *m;* (*for eyeglasses, musical instrument*) custodia *f;* **a** ~ **of beer/soft drinks** una cassa di birra/bevande analcoliche; **glass** ~ vetrina *f*
casebook *n* registro *m*
case law *n* LAW giurisprudenza *f*
case study <-ies> *n* casistica *f*
cash [kæʃ] I. *n* (denaro *m*) contante *m;* ~ **in advance** pagamento *m* anticipato; **to be strapped for** ~ *inf* essere al verde II. *vt* incassare; **to** ~ **sth in** riscuotere qc; **to** ~ **in** (**one's chips**) *inf* (*die*) morire
♦ **cash in** I. *vt insep* riscuotere II. *vi* **to** ~ **on sth** trarre profitto da qc
cash-and-carry [‚kæʃ·ənd·'ke·ri] I. <-ies> *n* cash and carry *m inv,* negozio *m* all'ingrosso II. *adj* all'ingrosso
cash cow *n sl: settore di un'azienda che realizza stabilmente grossi profitti*
cash crop *n* prodotto agricolo coltivato per la vendita anziché per il consumo diretto
cashew ['kæ·ʃuː] *n,* **cashew nut** *n* anacardio *m*
cash flow ['kæʃ‚floʊ] *n* FIN flusso *m* di cassa
cashier [kæʃ·'ɪr] *n* cassiere, -a *m, f*
cash machine *n* Bancomat® *m inv*
cashmere ['kæʒ·mɪr] *n* cachemire *m inv*

cash register *n* registratore *m* di cassa
casing ['keɪ·sɪŋ] *n* involucro *m;* (*of cable*) rivestimento *m* isolante
casino [kə·'siː·noʊ] *n* casinò *m, inv*
cask [kæsk] *n* barile *m;* (*of wine*) botte *f*
casket ['kæs·kɪt] *n* 1. (*box*) cofanetto 2. (*coffin*) bara *f*
Caspian Sea ['kæs·pi·ən] *n* Mar *m* Caspio
casserole ['kæ·sə·roʊl] *n* 1. (*cooking vessel*) casseruola *f* 2. CULIN piatto *m* di carne e verdure in casseruola
cassette [kə·'set] *n* cassetta *f;* **video** ~ videocassetta *f*
cassette deck *n* piastra *f* di registrazione
cassette player *n,* **cassette recorder** *n* registratore *m* a cassetta
cast [kæst] I. *n* 1. THEAT, CINE cast *m inv;* **supporting** ~ attori *m pl* non protagonisti 2. (*mold*) stampo *m* 3. MED ingessatura *f* 4. (*of worm*) escrementi *mpl* II. <cast, cast> *vt* 1. (*throw*) lanciare 2. (*direct*) **to** ~ **doubt on sth** mettere in dubbio qc; **to** ~ **a shadow on sth** fare ombra su qc; *fig* gettare un'ombra su qc; **to** ~ **light on sth** illuminare qc; *fig* fare luce su qc 3. (*allocate roles*) **to** ~ **sb as sb/sth** assegnare a qu la parte di qu/qc; **to** ~ **sb in a role** scegliere qu per una parte 4. (*give*) dare 5. (*make in a mold*) fondere
♦ **cast aside** *vt,* **cast away** *vt* (*rid oneself of*) sbarazzarsi di; (*free oneself of*) liberarsi di
♦ **cast off** I. *vt* 1. (*get rid of*) disfarsi di 2. (*stitch*) chiudere II. *vi* 1. NAUT salpare 2. (*in knitting*) chiudere le maglie
♦ **cast on** I. *vt* (*in knitting: stitch*) avviare II. *vi* (*in knitting*) avviare le maglie
♦ **cast out** *vt* (*cacciare*) (*ideas*) respingere; *form* (*person*) espellere
castanets [kæs·tə·'nets] *npl* nacchere *fpl*
castaway ['kæst·ə·weɪ] *n* (*survivor from a ship*) naufrago, -a *m, f*
caste [kæst] *n* (*social class*) casta *f;* ~ **system** sistema *m* delle caste
caster ['kæs·tə] *n* rotella *f*
castigate ['kæs·tə·geɪt] *vt form* **to** ~ **sb for sth** criticare duramente qu per qc
castigation [‚kæs·tə·'geɪ·ʃən] *n* critica *f*
casting ['kæs·tɪŋ] *n* 1. (*forming in a mold*) gettata *f,* colata *f* 2. THEAT casting *m inv*
cast iron [‚kɑːst·'a·ɪən] *n* ghisa *f*
cast-iron *adj* 1. (*made of cast iron*) in ghisa 2. *fig* (*evidence*) irrefutabile; (*alibi*) di ferro; (*promise*) fermo, -a
castle ['kæ·sl] I. *n* 1. (*building*) castello *m* 2. (*chess piece*) torre *f* ▶ **to build** ~**s in the air** fare castelli in aria II. *vi* (*in chess*) arroccare
castoff [‚kæst·ɑːf] I. *n* (*garment*) ~**s** abiti *m pl* smessi II. *adj* (*clothes, shoes*) vecchio, -a
castor ['kæs·tə] *n* rotella *f*
castor oil *n* olio *m* di ricino
castrate [kæs·'streɪt] *vt* castrare
casual ['kæ·ʒuː·əl] *adj* 1. (*relaxed*) disinvolto, -a 2. (*not permanent*) occasionale 3. (*not*

serious) noncurante; (*glance*) casuale; (*remark*) alla leggera; (*meeting*) fortuito, -a **4.** (*informal*) informale; (*clothes*) casual *inv*

casually *adv* in modo informale

casualty ['kæ·ʒuː·əl·ti] <-ies> *n* **1.** (*accident victim*) vittima *f;* (*dead person*) morto, -a *m, f* **2.** (*injured person*) ferito, -a *m, f;* ~ **s** MIL (*dead people*) perdite *fpl* **3.** (*sth eliminated*) **to be a** ~ **of the recession** scomparire in seguito alla recessione

cat [kæt] *n* gatto, -a *m, f* ▶ **to let the** ~ **out of the bag** rivelare un segreto; **to fight like** ~**s and dogs** fare come cane e gatto; **to rain** ~**s and dogs** piovere a catinelle; **to play** ~ **and mouse with sb** giocare come il gatto col topo con qu; **has the** ~ **got your tongue?** ti sei fatto mangiare la lingua dal gatto?

CAT [kæt] *n* **1.** COMPUT *abbr of* **computer-assisted translation** traduzione *f* assistita dal computer **2.** MED *abbr of* **computerized axial tomography** TAC *f inv;* ~ **scan** TAC

cataclysmic [ˌkæ·tə·ˈklɪz·mɪk] *adj* disastroso, -a

catacombs ['kæ·tə·koʊmz] *npl* catacombe *fpl*

Catalan ['kæ·tə·læn] I. *adj* catalano, -a II. *n* **1.** (*habitant*) catalano, -a *m, f* **2.** (*language*) catalano *m*

catalog ['kæ·tə·lɑːg] I. *n* catalogo *m;* (*repeated events*) serie *f;* **a** ~ **of mistakes** *fig* un errore dietro l'altro II. *vt* catalogare

catalysis [kə·ˈtæ·lə·sɪs] *n* catalisi *f inv*

catalyst ['kæ·tə·lɪst] *n a. fig* catalizzatore *m*

catalytic [kæ·tə·ˈlɪ·tɪk] *adj* catalitico, -a; ~ **converter** AUTO catalizzatore *m*

catamaran [ˌkæ·tə·mə·ˈræn] *n* catamarano *m*

catapult ['kæ·tə·pʌlt] I. *n* catapulta *f* II. *vt* catapultare

cataract[1] ['kæ·tə·rækt] *n* MED cateratta *f*

cataract[2] ['kæ·tə·rækt] *n lit* (*waterfall*) cateratta *f*

catarrh [kə·ˈtɑːr] *n* catarro *m*

catastrophe [kə·ˈtæs·trə·fi] *n* catastrofe *f*

catastrophic [ˌkæ·tə·ˈstrɑː·fɪk] *adj* catastrofico, -a

catcall ['kæt·kɔːl] *n* fischio *m*

catch [kætʃ] <-es> I. *n* **1.** (*fish caught*) pesca *f* **2.** (*fastening device*) chiusura *f;* (*on window*) fermo *m* **3.** *inf* (*suitable partner*) **he's a good** ~ è un buon partito **4.** (*trick*) tranello *m* II. <caught, caught> *vt* **1.** (*hold moving object*) afferrare; (*person*) prendere, catturare; **to** ~ **sb at a bad moment** cogliere qu in un momento poco opportuno **2.** (*entangle*) **to get caught in sth** rimanere incastrato in qc; **to get caught up in sth** rimanere coinvolto in qc; **to get caught on sth** rimanere impigliato in qc **3.** (*collect*) raccogliere **4.** (*capture an expression*) percepire; (*hear*) sentire **5.** (*attract*) attirare **6.** (*get*) prendere; **to** ~ **the bus** prendere l'autobus **7.** (*understand*) capire **8.** (*notice*) rendersi conto di; (*by chance*) notare (per caso) **9.** (*discover by surprise*) **to** ~ **sb doing sth** cogliere qu mentre fa qc; **to** ~ **sb**

red-handed *fig* cogliere qu in flagrante; **to** ~ **sb with their pants down, to** ~ **sb napping** *fig* cogliere qu alla sprovvista **10.** MED (*become infected*) prendere **11.** (*start burning: fire*) prendere

♦ **catch on** *vi* **1.** (*become popular*) prendere piede **2.** *inf* (*understand*) capire

♦ **catch up** I. *vi* **to** ~ **with sb** raggiungere qu; **to** ~ **with sth** (*make up lost time*) recuperare qc; (*equal the standard*) mettersi in pari con qc II. *vt* **to catch sb up** mettersi in pari con qu

catchall ['kæ·tʃɔːl] *adj* generico, -a

catcher ['kæ·tʃɚ] *n* SPORTS catcher *m inv*

catch phrase ['kætʃ·freɪz] *n* slogan *m inv*

catchup ['kæ·tʃəp] *n s.* **ketchup**

catchword ['kætʃ·ˌwɜːrd] *n* slogan *m inv*

catchy ['kæ·tʃi] <-ier, -iest> *adj* (*tune*) orecchiabile

catechism ['kæ·tɪ·kɪ·zəm] *n* catechismo *m*

categorical [ˌkæ·tə·ˈgɔː·rɪ·kl] *adj* (*denial, refusal*) categorico, -a

categorize ['kæ·tə·gə·raɪz] *vt* classificare

category ['kæ·tə·gɔː·ri] <-ies> *n* categoria *f*

cater ['keɪ·tɚ] *vi* preparare da mangiare

caterer ['keɪ·tə·ɚ] *n* incaricato, -a *m, f* del servizio catering

catering ['keɪ·tə·rɪŋ] *n* catering *m inv*

Caterpillar® ['kæ·tə·pɪ·lɚ] *n* cingolato *m*

caterpillar ['kæ·tə·pɪ·lɚ] *n* ZOOL bruco *m*

caterwaul ['kæ·tə·wɔːl] I. *n* verso *m* stridulo II. *vi* fare versi striduli

catfish *n* pesce *m* gatto

catgut ['kæt·gʌt] *n* corda *f* in budello; MED catgut *m inv*

cathartic [kə·ˈθɑːr·tɪk] *adj* catartico, -a

cathedral [kə·ˈθiː·drəl] *n* cattedrale *f;* ~ **city** città *f* vescovile

catheter ['kæ·θə·tɚ] *n* MED catetere *m*

cathode ['kæ·θoʊd] *n* ELEC catodo *m*

cathode ray *n* raggio *m* catodico

Catholic ['kæ·θə·lɪk] REL I. *n* cattolico, -a *m, f* II. *adj* cattolico, -a

catholic ['kæ·θə·lɪk] *adj* eclettico, -a

Catholicism [kə·ˈθɑː·lə·sɪ·zəm] *n* Cattolicesimo *m*

cat litter *n* lettiera *f* per gatti

catnap ['kæt·ˌnæp] I. *n inf* pisolino *f;* **to have a** ~ fare un pisolino II. <-pp-> *vi inf* fare un pisolino

cat's cradle [ˌkæts·ˈkreɪ·dl] *n* ripiglino *m*

catsup ['kæt·səp] *n s.* **ketchup**

cattle ['kæ·tl] *npl* (*bovines*) bestiame *m;* **beef** ~ bovini *m pl* da carne; **dairy** ~ vacche da *f pl* latte

cattle breeder *n* allevatore, -trice *m, f* di bestiame

cattle breeding *n* allevamento *m* del bestiame

cattle car *n* RAIL carro *m* bestiame

cattle thief <thieves> *n* ladro *m* di bestiame

catty ['kæ·ti] <-ier, -iest> *adj* (*hurtful*) maligno, -a

catwalk ['kæt·ˌwɑːk] *n* THEAT FASHION passerella *f*

Caucasian [kɑː·ˈkeɪ·ʒən] *form* I. *n* **1.** (*white*)

persona *f* di razza bianca **2.** (*European*) europoide *mf* **3.** (*languages*) caucasico *m* **II.** *adj* **1.** (*white*) di razza bianca **2.** (*European*) europoide **3.** (*of the Caucasus: person, language*) caucasico, -a

caucus ['kɑː·kəs] **I.** *n* <-es> **1.** (*group*) (*members*) vertici *m pl* del partito **2.** (*meeting*) riunione *f* dei vertici del partito **II.** *vi* fare una riunione dei vertici del partito

caught [kɑːt] *pt, pp of* **catch**

cauldron ['kɑːl·drən] *n* calderone *m*

cauliflower ['kɑː·lɪˌflaˌʊəˠ] *n* cavolfiore *m*

caulk [kɑːk] *vt* stuccare; NAUT calafatare

causal ['kɑː·zl] *adj a.* LING causale; (*relationship*) di causa-effetto

causality [kɑː·'zæ·lə·ti] *n form* causalità *f*

causative ['kɑː·zə·tɪv] *adj form* (*acting as a cause*) LING causativo, -a

cause [kɔːz] **I.** *n* **1.** (*a reason for*) (*principle*) LAW causa *f;* **he is the ~ of all her woes** è lui la causa di tutti i suoi mali; **this is no ~ for ...** ciò non giustifica ...; **to do sth in the ~ of sth** fare qc per qc **2.** (*objective*) causa *f* **II.** *vt* causare; (*an accident*) provocare; **to ~ sb/sth to do sth** far sì che qu/qc faccia qc; **to ~ sb harm** recare danno a qu; **this medicine may ~ dizziness and nausea** il farmaco può provocare vertigini e nausea

causeway ['kɑːzˌweɪ] *n* **1.** (*road bridge*) strada *f* rialzata **2.** (*pathway*) passaggio *m* rialzato

caustic ['kɑːs·tɪk] *adj a. fig* (*lime*) caustico, -a; (*tongue*) di vipera

cauterize ['kɑː·ʈə·raɪz] *vt* cauterizzare

caution ['kɑː·ʃən] **I.** *n* **1.** (*carefulness*) cautela *f;* **~ is advised** si raccomanda di procedere con prudenza; **to throw ~ to the winds** gettare la prudenza alle ortiche **2.** (*warning*) avvertimento *m;* **a note of ~** un avvertimento; **~!** attenzione! **II.** *vt form* **to ~ sb about sth** avvertire qu di qc; **to ~ sb not to do sth** diffidare qu dal fare qc

cautionary ['kɑː·ʃə·ne·ri] *adj* di avvertimento; **a ~ tale** un racconto con una morale

cautious ['kɑː·ʃəs] *adj* cauto, -a; (*optimism*) moderato, -a

cavalcade [ˌkæ·vlˈkeɪd] *n* **1.** (*procession*) sfilata *f* **2.** (*succession*) serie *f;* (*of memories*) carrellata *f*

cavalier [ˌkæ·vəˈlɪr] **I.** *n* HIST cavaliere *m* **II.** *adj* menefreghista

cavalry ['kæ·vəl·ri] *n pl vb* MIL cavalleria *f*

cavalryman ['kæ·vəl·ri·mən] <-men> *n* soldato *m* di cavalleria

cave [keɪv] **I.** *n* grotta *f,* caverna *f* **II.** *vi* **1.** (*hollow out*) scavare **2.** SPORTS praticare speleologia
♦**cave in** *vi* cedere

caveat ['kæ·vi·æt] *n* **1.** (*warning*) ammonimento *m* **2.** LAW *avvertimento che indica la necessità di tenere presente qualcosa prima di poter prendere una decisione finale*

cave dweller *n* cavernicolo *m*

cave-in *n* cedimento *m*

caveman ['keɪv·mæn] <-men> *n* **1.** (*prehistoric man*) uomo *m* delle caverne **2.** *inf* (*socially underdeveloped*) troglodita *m*

cave painting *n* pittura *f* rupestre

caver ['keɪ·vəˠ] *n* speleologo, -a *m, f*

cavern ['kæ·vən] *n* caverna *f*

cavernous ['kæ·vəˠ·nəs] *adj* enorme; (*hole, room*) scuro, -a; (*pit*) profondo, -a; (*eyes*) infossato, -a

caviar(e) ['kæ·vɪ·ɑːr] *n* caviale *m*

cavity ['kæ·vɪ·ti] <-ies> *n* **1.** *a.* ANAT cavità *f* **2.** MED carie *f inv*

caw [kɑː] **I.** *n* gracchio *m* **II.** *vi* gracchiare

cayenne [kaɪ·'en] *n,* **cayenne pepper** *n* pepe *m* di Caienna

Cayman Islands ['keɪ·mən·ˌaɪ·ləndz] *n* Isole *f pl* Cayman

CB [ˌsiː·'biː] *n abbr of* **Citizen's Band** banda *f* cittadina

CBW *n abbr of* **chemical and biological warfare** guerra *f* biochimica

cc [ˌsiː·'siː] *abbr of* **cubic centimeter** cc

CCTV [ˌsiː·siː·tiː·'viː] *n abbr of* **closed-circuit television** televisione *f* a circuito chiuso

ccw. *adj, adv abbr of* **counterclockwise** in senso antiorario

CD [ˌsiː·'diː] *n abbr of* **compact disc** CD *m inv*

CD-R *n abbr of* **compact disc-recordable** CD-R *m inv*

CD-ROM [ˌsiː·diː·'rɑːm] *n abbr of* **compact disc read-only memory** CD-ROM *m inv;* **on ~** su CD-ROM

CD-RW *n abbr of* **compact disc-rewritable** CD-RW *m inv*

cease [siːs] *form* **I.** *vi* cessare; **to ~ to do sth** cessare di fare qc **II.** *vt* cessare; **it never ~s to amaze me** non finisce mai di stupirmi; **~ fire!** MIL cessate il fuoco! **III.** *n* **without ~** senza sosta

cease-fire [ˌsiːs·'fa·ɪəˠ] *n* MIL cessate *m* il fuoco *inv*

ceaseless ['siːs·lɪs] *adj* incessante

cedar ['siː·dəˠ] *n* **1.** (*tree*) cedro *m* **2.** (*wood*) (legno *m* di) cedro *m*

cede [siːd] *vt form* cedere

ceiling ['siː·lɪŋ] *n* **1.** ARCHIT soffitto *m* **2.** AVIAT plafond *m inv* **3.** (*upper limit*) tetto *m* massimo; (*on prices*) limite *m;* **to impose a ~ on sth** imporre un limite a qc **4.** METEO ceiling *m*
▶ **to hit the ~** *inf* andare su tutte le furie

celebrate ['se·lɪ·breɪt] **I.** *vi* festeggiare; **let's ~!** bisogna festeggiare! **II.** *vt* celebrare; **they ~d him as a hero** lo accolsero come un eroe

celebrated *adj* celebre

celebration [ˌse·lɪ·'breɪ·ʃən] *n* **1.** (*party*) festeggiamento *m* **2.** (*of an occasion, event*) celebrazione *f;* **to throw a party in ~ of sth** dare una festa per festeggiare qc; **this calls for (a) ~!** qui bisogna festeggiare!

celebratory ['se·lə·brə·tɔː·ri] *adj* **we went for a ~ dinner** siamo andati a cena per festeggiare

celebrity [sə·'le·brə·ʈi] *n* **1.** <-ies> (*person*) famoso, -a *m, f* **2.** (*fame*) celebrità *f*

celeriac [sə·'le·rɪ·æk] *n* sedano *m* rapa

celery ['se·lə·ri] *n* sedano *m*

celestial [sɪ·'les·tʃl] *adj a. fig* celestiale

celestial body <-ies> *n* corpo *m* celeste

celibacy ['se·lɪ·bə·si] *n* 1. *a.* REL castità *f* 2. (*being single*) celibato *m*

celibate ['se·lɪ·bət] I. *n* 1. *a.* REL persona *f* che ha fatto voto di castità 2. (*single man*) celibe *m;* (*single woman*) nubile *f* II. *adj* 1. *a.* REL (*refraining from sex*) casto, -a 2. (*unmarried man*) celibe *m;* (*unmarried woman*)

cell [sel] *n* 1. (*in prison*) cella *f* 2. BIO, POL cellula *f;* **a single-~ animal** un organismo animale unicellulare; **grey ~s** materia *f* grigia *inf* 3. ELEC cellula *f*

cellar ['se·lə] *n* 1. cantina *f* 2. SPORTS ultimo posto *m*

cellist ['tʃe·lɪst] *n* MUS violoncellista *mf*

cell nucleus ['sel·ˌnuː·kli·əs] <-clei *o* -es> *n* nucleo *m* cellulare

cello ['tʃe·loʊ] <-s *o* -li> *n* MUS violoncello *m*

cellophane® ['se·lə·feɪn] *n* cellophane *m*

cellular ['sel·ju·lə] *adj* 1. BIO cellulare 2. (*porous*) poroso, -a

cellular phone *n,* **cell phone** ['sel·foʊn] *n* cellulare *m*

cellulite ['sel·jə·laɪt] *n* cellulite *f*

celluloid ['sel·ju·lɔɪd] I. *n* celluloide *m* II. *adj* di celluloide

cellulose ['sel·ju·loʊs] *n* cellulosa *f*

Celsius ['sel·si·əs] *adj* PHYS Celsius

Celt [kelt, selt] *n* HIST celta *mf*

Celtic ['kel·tik, 'sel·tik] I. *adj* celtico, -a II. *n* (*language*) celtico *m*

cement [sɪ·'ment] I. *n* 1. ARCHIT, MED cemento *m* 2. (*glue*) colla *f;* **rubber ~** mastice *m* 3. (*uniting idea*) cemento *m* II. *vt* 1. (*cover with cement, stablize*) cementare; **to ~ over sth** rivestire qc di cemento 2. MED otturare

cemetery ['se·mə·te·ri] <-ies> *n* cimitero *m*

censer ['sen·sə] *n* REL incensiere *m*

censor ['sen·sə] I. *n* 1. (*official*) censore *m* 2. PSYCH censura *f* II. *vt* censurare

censorious [sen·'sɔː·ri·əs] *adj* censurador(a); (*comments*) molto critico, -a

censorship ['sen·tsə·ʃɪp] *n* censura *f*

censure ['sen·tʃə] *vt* censurare

census ['sen·səs] <-es> *n* censimento *m*

cent [sent] *n* centesimo *m* ▶ **to not have a red ~** *inf* non avere un soldo

centenarian [ˌsent·ne·ri·ən] *n* centenario, -a *m, f*

centenary ['sent·ne·ri] I. <-ies> *n* centenario *m* II. *adj* (*once every century*) centenario, -a; **~ year** centenario *m*

centennial [sen·'ten·iəl] I. *n* centenario *m* II. *adj* centennale

center ['sen·tə] I. *n* 1. centro *m* 2. SPORTS (*in football*) centravanti *m inv* II. *vt* 1. *a.* SPORTS, TYPO centrare 2. (*efforts*) concentrare
   ◆**center around** *vi* incentrarsi attorno a
   ◆**center on** *vi* concentrarsi su

centerpiece ['sen·tə·piːs] *n* fulcro *m*

centigrade ['sen·tə·greɪd] *adj* centigrado, -a

centigram ['sen·tə·græm] *n* centigrammo *m*

centimeter ['sen·tə·ˌmiː·tə] *n* centimetro *m*

centipede ['sen·tə·piːd] *n* centopiedi *m inv*

central ['sen·trəl] *adj* 1. (*at the middle*) centrale; **in ~ Boston** nel centro di Boston 2. (*important: issue*) fondamentale; **to be ~ to sth** essere fondamentale per qc; **to be of ~ importance** (**to sb**) essere di fondamentale importanza (per qu); **the ~ character** il personaggio principale 3. (*from a main point: bank, air conditioning*) centrale; **~ processing unit** COMPUT unità *f* centrale di elaborazione

Central African I. *adj* centroafricano, -a II. *n* centroafricano, -a *m, f*

Central African Republic *n* Repubblica *f* Centroafricana

centralization [ˌsen·trə·lɪ·'zeɪ·ʃən] *n* centralizzazione *m*

centralize ['sen·trə·laɪz] *vt* centralizzare

centrifugal [sen·'trɪ·fjə·gl] *adj* PHYS centrifugo, -a

centrifuge ['sen·trə·fjuːdʒ] *n* MED, TECH centrifuga *f*

centripetal [sen·'trɪ·pə·tl] *adj* PHYS centripeto, -a

century ['sen·tʃə·ri] <-ies> *n* (*100 years*) secolo *m;* **the twentieth ~** il ventesimo; **a centuries-old custom** una tradizione secolare

CEO [ˌsiː·iː·'oʊ] *n abbr of* **chief executive officer** direttore, -trice *m, f* generale

ceramic [sə·'ræ·mɪk] *adj* di ceramica

ceramics *n pl* ceramiche *fpl*

cereal ['sɪ·ri·əl] I. *n* 1. (*cultivated grass*) cereale *m* 2. (*breakfast food*) cereali *mpl* II. *adj* di cereali

cerebellum [ˌse·rə·'be·ləm] <-s *o* -la> *n* cervelletto *m*

cerebral [ˌse·rə·brəl] *adj* cerebrale; **~ palsy** paralisi *f inv* cerebrale

cerebrum [ˌse·rə·brəm] <-(bra)> *n* cervello *m*

ceremonial [ˌse·rə·'moʊn·iəl] I. *n form* cerimoniale *m* II. *adj* formale; (*event*) solenne; **~ uniform** gran uniforme *f*

ceremonious [ˌse·rə·'moʊn·iəs] *adj* cerimonioso, -a

ceremony ['se·rə·moʊ·ni] <-ies> *n* cerimonia *f;* **to go through the ~ of sth** *fig* seguire tutta la procedura di qc

certain ['sɜːr·tn] I. *adj* 1. (*sure*) certo, -a, sicuro, -a; **it is quite ~** (**that**) ... è molto probabile che ... +*subj;* **to be ~ about sb** avere fiducia in qu; **to be ~ about sth** essere convinto di qc; **to make ~ of sth** assicurarsi di qc; **it is not yet ~ ...** non è ancora certo ...; **to feel ~** (**that ...**) essere sicuro (che ...); **to make ~** (**that ...**) assicurarsi (che ...); **please make ~ that he has answered** per favore, si assicuri che abbia risposto; **I don't know yet for ~** non lo so ancora con certezza; **one thing is** (**for**) **~ ...** quel che è certo è che ...; **for ~ con**

certezza **2.**(*undeniable*) certo, -a; **it is ~ that ...** sicuramente ...; **the disaster seemed ~** il disastro pareva inevitabile **3.**(*specified*) **a ~ Steve Rukus** un certo Steve Rukus; **to a ~ extent** in parte **II.** *pron* certo, -a

certainly *adv* certamente; **she ~ is a looker, isn't she?** indubbiamente è una bella ragazza, no?; **she ~ had a friend called Mark** di sicuro aveva un amico che si chiamava Mark; **~, Sir!** certo, signore!; **~ not!** assolutamente no!

certainty ['sɜːr·tən·ti] <-ies> *n* certezza *f*; **Joan is a ~ to win** di sicuro vincerà Joan; **with ~** con certezza

certifiable ['sɜːr·tə·'fa·ɪə·bl] *adj* **1.**(*declared*) attestabile **2.** PSYCH (*mentally ill*) incapace; **he is ~!** *inf* è matto!

certificate [sə·'tɪ·fɪ·kət] *n* **1.**(*document*) certificato *m* **2.** SCHOOL diploma *m*

certification [‚sɜːr·tə·fɪ·'keɪ·ʃən] *n* **1.**(*process*) certificazione *f* **2.**(*document*) certificato *m*

certify ['sɜːr·tə·faɪ] <-ie-> *vt* certificare; **certified copy** copia *f* autenticata; **this is to ~ that ...** *form* con la presente si certifica che ...; **he is certified to practice medicine** è abilitato a esercitare la professione medica

certitude ['sɜːr·tə·tuːd] *n* certezza *f*

cervical ['sɜːr·vɪ·kl, sɜː·'vaɪ·kl] *adj* **1.**(*neck*) cervicale; **~ collar** collare *m* cervicale **2.**(*cervix*) del collo dell'utero

cervix ['sɜːr·vɪks] <-es *o* -vices> *n* **1.**(*neck*) cervice *f* **2.**(*womb*) collo *m* dell'utero

cesarean [sə·'ze·ri·ən] *n* **a ~ section** un taglio cesareo

cesium ['siː·zi·əm] *n* cesio *m*

cessation [se·'seɪ·ʃən] *n form* (*end*) cessazione *f*

cesspit ['ses·pɪt] *n* pozzo *m* nero

cesspool ['ses·puːl] *n* **1.**(*for excrements*) pozzo *m* nero **2.**(*unpleasant area*) cloaca *f*

Ceylon [sɪ·'lɑːn] *n* **1.** HIST (*Sri Lanka*) Ceylon *m* **2.**(*Ceylon tea*) tè *m* di Ceylon

Ceylonese [‚siː·lə·'niːz] **I.** *n* singalese *mf* **II.** *adj* HIST singalese

cf. *abbr of* **confer** (**compare**) cfr.

CFC [‚siː··ef·'siː] *n abbr of* **chlorofluorocarbon** CFC *m*

Chad [tschæd] *n* Chad *m*

Chadian I. *adj* ciadiano, -a **II.** *n* ciadiano, -a *m, f*

chafe [tʃeɪf] **I.** *vi* **1.**(*become sore*) irritarsi; (*become worn*) consumarsi **2.** *fig* (*feel irritated*) irritarsi; **to ~ at sth** irritarsi per qc **II.** *vt* **1.**(*rub sore*) irritare **2.**(*rub*) sfregare **3.** *fig* irritare

chafer ['tʃeɪ·fə·] *n* coleottero *m*

chaff[1] [tʃæf] *n* AGR **1.**(*husks*) pula *f* **2.**(*cut grass*) fieno *m* **3.**(*worthless material*) robetta *f*

chaff[2] [tʃæf] **I.** *n* scherzo *m* **II.** *vt* tosare

chaffinch ['tʃæ·fɪntʃ] <-es> *n* fringuello *m*

chagrin [ʃə·'grɪn] **I.** *n* irritazione *f* **II.** *vt* irritare

chain [tʃeɪn] **I.** *n* **1.** catena *f*; **~ gang** gruppo di prigionieri incatenati insieme impegnati in

lavori forzati; **to be in ~s** essere incatenato **2.**(*series*) serie *f inv* **II.** *vt* incatenare; **to ~ sth/sb** (**up**) **to sth** incatenare qc/qu a qc; **to be ~ed to a desk** *fig* essere incollato alla scrivania

chain letter *n* lettera *di una catena di Sant'Antonio*

chain mail *n* cotta *f* di maglia

chain reaction *n* reazione *f* a catena; **to set off a ~** innescare una reazione a catena

chain saw *n* motosega *f*

chain smoker *n* fumatore, -trice *m, f* accanito, -a

chain store *n* negozio *f* che fa parte di una catena

chair [tʃer] **I.** *n* **1.**(*seat*) sedia *f* **2.**(*head*) presidente *mf*; **to be ~ of a department** essere il/la capodipartimento **3.** UNIV cattedra *f* **4.** *sl* (*electric chair*) sedia *f* elettrica **II.** *vt* (*a meeting*) presiedere

chairlift *n* seggiovia *f*

chairman ['tʃer·mən] <-men> *n* presidente *m*

chairmanship ['tʃer·mən·ʃɪp] *n* presidenza *f*

chairperson ['tʃer·‚pɜːr·sən] *n* presidente *mf*

chairwoman <-women> *n* presidente *f*

chalet [ʃæ·'leɪ] *n* chalet *m inv*

chalk [tʃɔːk] **I.** *n* gesso *m* **II.** *vt* (*write*) scrivere col gesso; (*draw*) disegnare col gesso

◆**chalk up** *vt* **1.**(*ascribe*) attribuire; **to ~ sth to sb/sth** attribuire qc a qu/qc; **they won, and you can chalk that up to experience** hanno vinto loro e puoi attribuirlo all'esperienza **2.**(*achieve*) raggiungere

chalkboard ['tʃɔːk·bɔːrd] *n* lavagna *f*

chalky ['tʃɔː·ki] <-ier, -iest> *adj* **1.**(*made of chalk*) (*chalk-like*) gessoso, -a; (*water*) calcareo, -a **2.**(*dusty*) **to be all ~** essere impolverato di gesso **3.**(*pale*) pallido, -a

challenge ['tʃæ·lɪndʒ] **I.** *n* **1.**(*a call to competition*) sfida *f*; **to be faced with a ~** trovarsi di fronte a una sfida; **to present sb** (**with**) **a ~** costituire una sfida per qu; **to pose a ~ to sth** rappresentare un problema per qc **2.** *a.* MIL alt *m inv* **3.** LAW contestazione *f* **II.** *vt* **1.**(*ask to compete*) sfidare; **to ~ sb to a duel** sfidare qu a duello **2.**(*question*) mettere in discussione **3.**(*test*) mettere alla prova; **that's a matter that ~s attention** è una questione che richiede attenzione **4.** *a.* MIL intimare l'alt; **I was ~d by the security guard** sono stato fermato dalla guardia giurata **5.** LAW contestare

challenger ['tʃæ·lɪn·dʒə·] *n* sfidante *mf*; (*for a title*) aspirante *mf* a un titolo

challenging *adj* (*book, idea*) stimolante; (*course, task*) impegnativo, -a

chamber ['tʃeɪm·bə·] *n* **1.**(*room*) sala *f*; **torture ~** stanza *f* della tortura **2.** ANAT, ECON, POL camera *f*; **~ of commerce** camera di commercio **3.** *pl* LAW (*judge's office*) gabinetto *m* **4.** TECH (*of a gun*) camera *f*; **combustion ~** camera di combustione

chambermaid ['tʃeɪm·bə·meɪd] *n* cameriera *f* (d'albergo)

chamber music *n* musica *f* da camera
chamber pot *n* vaso *m* da notte
chameleon [kə·'miː·li·ən] *n a. fig* camaleonte *m*
chamois ['ʃæ·mi] <- *o* chamoix> *n inv* camoscio *m*
champ [tʃæmp] I. *n inf* campione, -essa *m, f* II. *vi* masticare III. *vt* masticare
champagne [ʃæm·'peɪn] I. *n* champagne *m* II. *adj* 1. (*color*) champagne 2. (*expensive*) he has ~ tastes ha gusti costosi
champion ['tʃæm·pi·ən] I. *n* 1. SPORTS campione, -essa *m, f* 2. (*supporter*) difensore *m;* to be a ~ of sth essere un paladino di qc II. *vt* sostenere; to ~ a cause sostenere una causa III. *adj* SPORTS campione, -essa
championship ['tʃæm·piən·ʃɪp] *n* 1. (*competition*) campionato *m* 2. (*advocacy*) difesa *f*
chance [tʃæns] I. *n* 1. (*random force*) caso *m;* a ~ encounter un incontro fortuito; a game of ~ un gioco d'azzardo; to leave nothing to ~ non lasciare nulla al caso; by ~ per caso 2. (*likelihood*) probabilità *f;* there's not much of a ~ that I'll go to the party è improbabile che vada alla festa; the ~s are that she's already gone è molto probabile che se ne sia già andata; to do sth on the off ~ that ... fare qc sperando che ...; to stand a ~ of doing sth *inf* avere qualche possibilità di fare qc; to not stand a ~ with sb non avere alcuna possibilità di fare qc; not a ~! *inf* neanche per sogno! 3. (*opportunity*) opportunità *f inv;* the ~ of a lifetime un'occasione unica; to give sb a ~ (to do sth) dare a qu l'opportunità (di fare qc); given half a ~ ... alla prima occasione ...; to have the ~ (to do sth) avere l'opportunità (di fare qc); to jump at the ~ cogliere la palla al balzo; to miss one's ~ (to do sth) perdere l'opportunità (di fare qc); to not have a ~ in hell non avere alcuna possibilità; you have to take your ~s when they arise si deve cogliere l'occasione quando si presenta 4. (*hazard*) rischio *m;* to take a ~ rischiare II. *vt* rischiare; to ~ it correre il rischio III. *vi* arrischiarsi
chancellor ['tʃæn·sə·ləʳ] *n* 1. POL (*head of state*) cancelliere *m* 2. (*head of a university*) rettore *m*
chancellory ['tʃæn·səl·ri] <-ies> *n* cancelleria *f*
chancy ['tʃæn·si] <-ier, -iest> *adj* rischioso, -a
chandelier [ʃæn·də·'lɪr] *n* lampadario *m*
change [tʃeɪndʒ] I. *n* 1. (*alteration*) cambio *m,* cambiamento *m;* a ~ of clothes un cambio di abiti; for a ~ per cambiare; that would be a nice ~ sarebbe un piacevole diversivo; we could use a ~ of pace ci farebbe bene prendercela con più calma 2. (*coins*) spiccioli *m;* a dollar in ~ un dollaro in monete; have you got ~ for a twenty-dollar bill? ha da cambiare 20 dollari?; how much do you have in ~? quanto hai in spiccioli? 3. (*money returned*) resto *m;* no ~ given non dà resto 4. (*exact amount*) to have exact ~ avere l'im-

porto esatto II. *vt* 1. (*exchange*) cambiare; to ~ places with sb *fig* cambiare di posto con qu; to ~ sth/sb into sth cambiare qc/qu in qc 2. (*get off a train/plane and board another*) to ~ trains cambiare treno 3. (*alter speed*) to ~ gear(s) cambiare marcia III. *vi* 1. (*alter*) cambiare; to ~ into sth trasformarsi in qc; the traffic light ~d back to red il semaforo è tornato rosso 2. (*get off a train/plane and board another*) cambiare 3. (*put on different clothes*) cambiarsi
changeable ['tʃeɪn·dʒə·bl] *adj* mutevole
changeover ['tʃeɪndʒ·ˌou·vəʳ] *n* 1. (*transition*) passaggio *m* 2. (*in a race*) passaggio *m* del testimone
changing ['tʃeɪn·dʒɪŋ] *adj* ~ room SPORTS spogliatoio *m;* (*in a shop*) camerino *m*
channel ['tʃæ·nl] I. *n* canale *m;* The English Channel il Canale della Manica II. <-ll-, -l-> *vt* canalizzare
Channel Islands *n* Isole *f pl* Normanne
Channel Tunnel *n* tunnel *m* della Manica *inv*
chant [tʃænt] I. *n* 1. REL canto *m;* Gregorian ~ canto gregoriano 2. (*utterance*) coro *m* II. *vi* 1. REL (*intone*) salmodiare 2. (*repeat*) ripetere in coro III. *vt* 1. REL (*sing*) cantare; (*speak in a monotone*) salmodiare 2. (*repeat*) ripetere in coro
Chanukah ['haː·nə·kə] *n* REL Chanukah *m*
chaos ['keɪ·ɑːs] *n* caos *m*
Chaos Theory *n* PHYS teoria *f* del caos
chaotic [keɪ·'ɑː·t̬ɪk] *adj* caotico, -a
chap [tʃæp] <-pp-> I. *vi* screpolarsi II. *vt* screpolare
chap. *n abbr of* chapter cap. *m*
chapel ['tʃæ·pl] *n* 1. cappella *f;* funeral ~ camera ardente 2. (*religious service*) funzione *f* religiosa
chaperon(e) ['ʃæ·pə·roun] *n* chaperon *m inv;* (*supervisor*) accompagnatore, -trice *m, f*
chaplain ['tʃæp·lɪn] *n* REL cappellano *m*
chapter ['tʃæp·təʳ] *n* 1. *a. fig* capitolo *m* 2. (*local branch*) sezione *f*
chapter house *n* 1. (*fraternity*) sala *f* riunioni 2. (*chapter*) capitolo *m*
char [tʃɑːr] <-rr-> I. *n* carbone *m* di legna II. *vi* (*be burned black*) carbonizzarsi III. <-rr-> *vt* (*burn black*) carbonizzare
character ['ke·rək·t̬əʳ] *n* 1. (*qualities*) carattere *m;* to be in/out of ~ with sb/sth essere/non essere tipico di qu/qc 2. (*moral integrity*) reputazione *f;* ~ reference referenze *fpl;* to be a bad ~ avere una cattiva reputazione 3. (*unique person*) (*representation*) personaggio *m;* in the ~ of ... nel ruolo di ... 4. TYPO carattere *m*
character actor *n* caratterista *mf*
characteristic [ˌke·rək·tə·'rɪs·tɪk] I. *n* caratteristica *f* II. *adj* caratteristico, -a; with her ~ dignity con la sua tipica dignità
characteristically [ˌke·rək·tə·'rɪs·tɪk·li] *adv* tipicamente
characterization [ˌke·rək·tə·rɪ·'zeɪ·ʃən] *n* car-

atterizzazione *f*

characterize ['ke·rək·tə·raɪz] *vt* **1.** *a.* CINE, THEAT caratterizzare **2.** (*outline*) descrivere; **to ~ sth/sb as sth** descrivere qc/qu come qc

charade [ʃə·'reɪd] *n* **1.** *pl* GAMES sciarada *f* **2.** (*pretence*) farsa *f*

charcoal ['tʃɑːr·koʊl] **I.** *n* **1.** (*fuel*) carbone *m* **2.** ART (*for drawing*) carboncino *m;* **to draw in ~** disegnare a carboncino **II.** *adj* **1.** (*of charcoal*) **~ drawing** disegno *m* a carboncino **2.** (*dark grey*) **~ grey** grigio *m* antracite

charge [tʃɑːrdʒ] **I.** *n* **1.** (*cost*) spese *fpl;* **admission ~** prezzo *m* d'ingresso; **at no extra ~** senza costi aggiuntivi; **free of ~** gratis **2.** LAW (*accusation*) accusa *f;* **to bring ~s against sb** denunciare qc **3.** (*attack*) carica *f;* SPORTS attacco *m* **4.** (*authority*) responsabilità *f;* **in the ~ of sb** sotto la responsabilità di qu; **to be in ~ of sb/sth** essere responsabile di qu/qc; **who is in ~ here?** chi è il responsabile qui? **5.** ELEC carica *f* **6.** (*load*) carico *m* **II.** *vi* **1.** FIN far pagare **2.** (*attack*) **to ~ at sb/sth** caricare qu/qc; **~!** carica! **3.** ELEC caricarsi **III.** *vt* **1.** FIN (*ask a price*) far pagare; **to ~ sth to sb's account** addebitare qc sul conto di qu **2.** LAW (*accuse*) imputare; **she's been ~d with murder** l'hanno accusata di omicidio; **the crimes with which he is ~d** i reati di cui è stato imputato *form* **3.** MIL, ELEC caricare

chargeable ['tʃɑːr·dʒə·bl] *adj* FIN **~ to the customer** a carico del cliente; **to be ~ to tax** essere imponibile

charge account *n* conto *m* di credito

charge card *n* carta *f* di credito

charged *adj* carico, -a

chargé d'affaires [ˌʃɑːr·ʒeɪ·də·'fer] <chargés d'affaires> *n* incaricato, -a *m, f* d'affari

chariot ['tʃæ·ri·ət] *n* HIST carro *m*

charisma [kə·'rɪz·mə] *n* carisma *m*

charitable ['tʃe·rɪ·tə·bl] *adj* **1.** (*with money, kindness*) generoso, -a **2.** (*concerning charity*) di beneficenza; (*donation, organization*) benefico, -a

charity ['tʃe·rə·ti] <-ies> *n* **1.** beneficenza *f* **2.** (*generosity of spirit*) carità *f* **3.** (*organization*) ente *m* di beneficenza

charlatan ['ʃɑːr·lə·tən] *n* ciarlatano *m*

Charlie [tʃɑːr·li] *n* *inf* stupido, -a

charm [tʃɑːrm] **I.** *n* **1.** (*quality*) fascino *m* **2.** (*ornament*) ciondolo *m* **3.** (*talisman*) amuleto *m* **II.** *vt* incantare; **to ~ sb into doing sth** convincere qu a fare qc usando il proprio fascino ▶ **to ~ the pants off (of) sb** *inf* sedurre qu

charmed *adj* **to lead a ~ life** fare una vita privilegiata

charmer ['tʃɑːr·mər] *n* persona *f* affascinante

charming ['tʃɑːr·mɪŋ] *adj* incantevole

charred *adj* carbonizzato, -a

chart [tʃɑːrt] **I.** *n* **1.** (*display of information*) tabella *f;* **weather ~** carta *f* meteorologica **2.** *pl* MUS **the ~s** la classifica; **to top the ~s** arrivare in cima alla classifica **II.** *vt* **1.** *a. fig*

riportare; **the map ~s the course of the river** la cartina riporta il corso del fiume **2.** (*observe*) seguire attentamente

charter ['tʃɑːr·tər] **I.** *n* **1.** statuto *m*, carta *f* **2.** (*exclusive right*) concessione *f* **3.** COM noleggio *m* **II.** *vt* **1.** (*sign founding papers*) riconoscere (lo statuto di) **2.** COM noleggiare

charter company <-ies> *n* compagnia *f* di voli charter

chartered ['tʃɑːr·tərd] *adj* COM noleggiato, -a

charterer ['tʃɑːr·tə·rər] *n* COM noleggiatore *m*

charter flight *n* volo *m* charter

chase [tʃeɪs] **I.** *n* **1.** (*pursuit*) inseguimento *m;* **to give ~** mettersi all'inseguimento **2.** *a. fig* (*hunt*) caccia *f* **II.** *vi* (*rollick about*) **they ~ed after her** le dettero la caccia **III.** *vt* **1.** (*pursue: dreams*) inseguire; (*women*) andare dietro a **2.** (*scare away*) **to ~ away sb/sth** cacciar via qc

chasm ['kæ·zəm] *n a. fig* abisso *m;* **to bridge a ~** colmare la differenza

chassis ['ʃæ·si] *n inv* chassis *m inv*

chaste [tʃeɪst] *adj form* casto, -a

chasten ['tʃeɪ·sn] *vt* **1.** (*admonish*) rimproverare **2.** (*punish*) castigare

chastise ['tʃæs·taɪz] *vt* rimproverare

chastity ['tʃæs·tə·ti] *n* castità *f;* **vow of ~** voto *m* di castità

chat [tʃæt] **I.** *n* **1.** chiacchierata *f* **2.** COMPUT chat *f inv* **II.** *vi* <-tt-> **1.** chiacchierare **2.** COMPUT chattare

chateau [ʃæt·'oʊ] *n* castello *m*

chatroom *n* chat room *f inv*

chatter ['tʃæ·tər] **I.** *n* **1.** chiacchiere *fpl;* (*of birds*) cinguettio *m* **II.** *vi* **1.** (*converse superficially*) **to ~ about sth** chiacchierare di qc; **they ~ed about everything and nothing** chiacchierarono del più e del meno **2.** (*make clacking noises: machines*) vibrare; (*birds*) cinguettare; **his teeth were chattering** batteva i denti

chatty ['tʃæ·ti] <-ier, -iest> *adj inf* **1.** (*friendly person*) chiacchierone, -a **2.** LIT (*informal*) informale

chauffeur ['ʃoʊ·fər] **I.** *n* autista *mf* **II.** *vt* **to ~ sb around** *a. fig* fare da autista a qu

chauvinism ['ʃoʊ·vɪ·nɪ·zəm] *n* sciovinismo *m*

chauvinist *n* sciovinista *mf*

chauvinistic [ˌʃoʊ·vɪ·'nɪs·tɪk] *adj* sciovinista

cheap [tʃiːp] *adj* **1.** (*inexpensive*) economico, -a, conveniente; **dirt ~** regalato, -a **2.** (*exploited*) **~ labor** manodopera *f* a basso costo **3.** (*worthless, inexpensive but bad quality*) scadente **4.** (*miserly*) taccagno, -a

cheapen ['tʃiː·pən] *vt* **1.** (*lower price of*) ribassare **2.** (*reduce morally*) degradare

cheaply *adv* a buon mercato

cheapness ['tʃiːp·nɪs] *n* **1.** (*low price*) convenienza *f* **2.** (*low quality*) bassa qualità *f*

cheapskate ['tʃiːp·skeɪt] *inf* **I.** *n* taccagno, -a *m, f* **II.** *adj* taccagno, -a

cheat [tʃiːt] **I.** *n* **1.** (*dishonest person*) imbroglione, -a *m, f* **2.** (*trick*) imbroglio *m* **II.** *vi* **to ~ at sth** imbrogliare in qc; **to ~ on a test** copiare a un esame **III.** *vt* ingannare; **to ~ the taxman** frodare il fisco

check [tʃek] **I.** *n* **1.** controllo *m;* **security ~** controllo di sicurezza; **to keep sth in ~** tenere qc sotto controllo; **to run a ~** fare un controllo **2.** (*deposit receipt*) scontrino *m;* **coat ~** guardaroba *m* **3.** (*mark*) segno *m* di spunta, visto *m* **4.** (*paper money*) assegno *m;* **to make out a blank ~** fare un assegno in bianco; *fig* dare carta bianca; **to pay by ~** pagare con un assegno **5.** (*bill for food*) conto *m* **6.** (*textile*) tessuto *m* a quadri **7.** GAMES **to be in ~** essere in scacco **II.** *adj* a quadri **III.** *vt* **1.** controllare **2.** (*prevent*) frenare **3.** lasciare in consegna; AVIAT (*baggage*) consegnare **4.** (*make a mark*) fare un segno in **5.** GAMES dare scacco a **IV.** *vi* **1.** controllare **2.** (*be in accordance with*) coincidere

◆**check in** *vi* **1.** (*at airport*) fare il check-in **2.** (*at hotel*) registrarsi

◆**check off** *vt* spuntare

◆**check out I.** *vi* **to ~ of a room** lasciare libera una stanza **II.** *vt* **1.** (*investigate*) controllare **2.** *sl* (*look at*) guardare; **wow! ~ the legs on that chick!** accidenti! guarda un po' che gambe quella ragazza!

◆**check up on** *vt* controllare; (*person*) tenere sotto controllo

checkbook ['tʃek·bʊk] *n* libretto *m* degli assegni

checked *adj* a quadri

checkerboard ['tʃe·kɚ·bɔːrd] *n* (*chessboard for checkers*) scacchiera *f*

checkered ['tʃe·kɚd] *adj* **1.** (*patterned with squares*) a quadri **2.** (*inconsistent*) con alti e bassi; **to have a ~ past** avere un passato caratterizzato da alti e bassi

checkers ['tʃe·kɚz] *n + sing vb* GAMES dama *f*

check-in ['tʃek·ɪn] *n* check-in *m*

check-in counter *n*, **check-in desk** *n* banco *m* del check-in

checking account *n* conto *m* corrente

check-in time *n* orario *f* del check-in

checklist ['tʃek·lɪst] *n* lista *f*

checkmate I. *n* **1.** GAMES scacco *m* matto **2.** (*defeat*) smacco *m* **II.** *vt* **1.** GAMES dare scacco matto a **2.** (*win a victory over*) vincere

checkout ['tʃek·aʊt] *n* cassa *f*

checkout counter *n* cassa *f*

checkpoint ['tʃek·pɔɪnt] *n* posto *m* di blocco

checkroom *n* **1.** (*for coats*) guardaroba *m* **2.** (*for luggage*) deposito *m* bagagli

checkup ['tʃek·ʌp] *n* visita *f* di controllo

cheddar ['tʃe·dɚ] *n* formaggio *m* cheddar

cheek [tʃiːk] *n* **1.** (*soft skin connecting jaws*) guancia *f;* **to turn the other ~** porgere l'altra guancia **2.** (*impertinence*) faccia *f* tosta; **to have the ~ to do sth** avere la faccia tosta di fare qc

cheekbone ['tʃiːk·boʊn] *n* zigomo *m*

cheeky ['tʃiː·ki] <-ier, -iest> *adj* sfacciato, -a; **to be ~ to sb** essere sfacciato con qu

cheep [tʃiːp] **I.** *n* (*of bird*) pigolio *m;* **to not get**

a ~ out of sb non cavare una parola di bocca a qu **II.** *vi* pigolare

cheer [tʃɪr] **I.** *n* **1.** (*exuberant shout*) acclamazione *f;* **three ~s for the champion!** tre urrà il campione!; **to give a ~** acclamare **2.** (*joy*) allegria *f;* **to be of good ~** essere felice **II.** *interj pl* (*said when drinking*) salute **III.** *vi* **to ~ for sb** acclamare qu

cheerful ['tʃɪr·fʊl] *adj* **1.** (*happy*) allegro **2.** (*color*) vivace **3.** (*encouraging*) confortante

cheerfulness *n* allegria *f*

cheeriness *n* **1.** (*happiness*) allegria *f* **2.** (*brightness*) vivacità *f*

cheering I. *n* applausi *mpl* **II.** *adj* confortante

cheerleader ['tʃɪr·liː·dɚ] *n* ragazza *f* pompon

cheery ['tʃɪ·ri] <-ier, -iest> *adj* allegro, -a

cheese [tʃiːz] *n* formaggio *m;* **hard ~** formaggio a pasta dura; **melted ~** formaggio fuso ▶**say ~!** dite cheese!

cheeseburger ['tʃiːz·bɜːr·gɚ] *n* hamburger *m* al formaggio *inv*

cheesecake ['tʃiːz·keɪk] *n* cheesecake *m inv* (*torta a base di formaggio fresco*)

cheesecloth ['tʃiːz·klɑːθ] <-es> *n* garza *f* (per formaggio)

cheese-paring ['tʃiːz·pe·rɪŋ] *n* taccagno, -a *m, f*

cheesy ['tʃiː·zi] <-ier, -iest> *adj* **1.** (*like cheese*) di formaggio **2.** *inf* (*cheap and shoddy*) di cattivo gusto

cheetah ['tʃiː·ʈə] *n* ghepardo *m*

chef [ʃef] *n* chef *mf*

chemical ['ke·mɪ·kl] **I.** *n* (*atoms*) sostanza *f* chimica; (*additive*) additivo *m* **II.** *adj* chimico, -a

chemist ['ke·mɪst] *n* chimico, -a *m, f*

chemistry ['ke·mɪs·tri] *n* chimica *f*

chemotherapy [ˌkiː·moʊ·'θe·rə·pi] *n* chemioterapia *f;* **to undergo ~** fare la chemioterapia

cherish ['tʃe·rɪʃ] *vt* (*hold dear*) tenere molto a; (*remember fondly*) ricordare con affetto

cheroot [ʃə·'ruːt] *n* sigaro *m* (*spuntato da ambo le parti*)

cherry ['tʃe·ri] <-ies> **I.** *n* **1.** (*fruit*) ciliegia *f* **2.** (*tree*) ciliegio *m* **II.** *adj* (rosso) ciliegia

cherry blossom *n* fiore *m* di ciliegio

cherry brandy *n* acquavite *f* di ciliegie

cherub ['tʃe·rəb] <-s *o* -im> *n* cherubino *m*

chervil ['tʃɜːr·vɪl] *n* cerfoglio *m*

chess [tʃes] *n* scacchi *mpl*

chessboard ['tʃes·bɔːrd] *n* scacchiera *f*

chess piece ['tʃes·mæn] <-men> *n* pezzo *m* degli scacchi

chest [tʃest] *n* **1.** (*human torso*) petto *m*, torace *m;* **~ pains** dolori *m pl* al petto; **to fold one's arms across one's ~** incrociare le braccia **2.** (*breasts*) petto *m*, seno *m* **3.** (*trunk*) baule *m;* **medicine ~** armadietto *m* dei medicinali ▶**to get sth off one's ~** togliersi un peso dallo stomaco

chestnut ['tʃes·nʌt] **I.** *n* **1.** (*fruit*) castagna *f* **2.** (*tree, wood*) castagno *m* **3.** (*color*) cast-

ano *m* **4.**(*horse*) sauro, castagno *m* **II.** *adj* castano, -a
chesty ['tʃes·ti] <-ier, -iest> *adj inf* procace
chew [tʃuː] **I.** *n* **1.**(*tobacco plug*) mozzicone *m* **2.**(*candy*) caramella *f* **II.** *vt* masticare
◆**chew out** *vt sl* fare una parte a
chewing gum ['tʃuː·ɪŋ·gʌm] *n* gomma *f* da masticare
chewy ['tʃuː·i] <-ier, -iest> *adj* da masticare per bene; (*meat*) tiglioso, -a
chic [ʃiːk] **I.** *n* chic *m* **II.** *adj* chic
chicane [ʃɪˈkein] *n* chicane *f inv*
chicanery [ʃɪˈkei·nə·ri] *n* raggiri *fpl*
chick [tʃɪk] *n* **1.**(*baby chicken, young bird*) pulcino *m* **2.** *inf*(*young woman*) ragazza *f*
chicken ['tʃɪ·kɪn] *n* **1.**(*farm bird*) pollo *m* **2.**(*meat*) pollo *m;* **fried/roasted** ~ pollo fritto/arrosto; **grilled** ~ pollo alla griglia **3.** *inf* (*person*) coniglio *m* ▶ **it's a** ~ **and egg situation** è come la storia dell'uovo e la gallina; **to not be a (spring)** ~ non essere più un giovincello
chicken broth *n* brodo *m* di pollo
chicken farm *n* allevamento *m* di polli
chicken feed *n* **1.**(*food*) mangime *m* per polli **2.**(*small amount of money*) spiccioli *mpl*
chicken-hearted *adj* fifone, -a
chickenpox *n* varicella *f*
chicken run *n* pollaio *m*
chickpea ['tʃɪk·piː] *n* cece *m*
chicory ['tʃɪ·kə·ri] *n* **1.** BOT indivia *f* **2.**(*in coffee*) cicoria *f*
chief [tʃiːf] **I.** *n* capo *m* **II.** *adj* **1.**(*top*) capo *inv* **2.**(*major*) principale
chief executive *n*, **chief executive officer** *n* direttore, -trice *m, f* generale
chief justice *n* presidente *mf* della Corte Suprema
chiefly *adv* principalmente
chieftain ['tʃiːf·tən] *n* capo [*o* tribù] di clan *m*
chiffon [ʃɪˈfɑːn] *n* chiffon *m inv*
child [tʃaɪld] <children> *pl n* **1.**(*person who's not fully grown*) bambino, -a *m, f* **2.**(*offspring*) figlio, -a *m, f;* **to be a** ~ **of the eighties** *fig* essere un prodotto degli anni Ottanta ▶ **spare the rod and spoil the** ~ *prov* il medico pietoso uccide l'ammalato *prov*
child abuse ['tʃaɪld·ə·bjuːs] *n* abuso *m* di minori
childbearing **I.** *n* maternità *f* **II.** *adj* **women of** ~ **age** donne in età fertile *fpl*
childbirth *n* parto *m*
child-care *n* assistenza *f* ai bambini
childhood *n* infanzia *f*
childish ['tʃaɪl·dɪʃ] *adj pej* infantile; **don't be** ~! non fare il bambino!
childless ['tʃaɪld·lɪs] *adj* senza figli
childlike ['tʃaɪld·laɪk] *adj* infantile
childproof *adj* a prova di bambino; ~ **lock** chiusura *f* di sicurezza per bambini
children ['tʃɪl·drən] *n pl of* **child**
child-resistant *adj form* a prova di bambino
child's play *n fig* gioco *m* da ragazzi

child support *n* assegno *m* di maternità
Chile ['tʃɪ·li] *n* Cile *m*
Chilean [tʃɪˈli·ən] **I.** *adj* cileno, -a **II.** *n* cileno, -a *m, f*
chili ['tʃɪ·li] <-es> *n*, **chile** ['tʃɪ·li] *n* peperoncino *m*
chill [tʃɪl] **I.** *n* **1.**(*coldness*) freddo *m;* **to catch a** ~ prendere il raffreddore; **to take the** ~ **off of something** riscaldare qc **2.**(*shiver*) brivido *m;* **to send a** ~ **down someone's spine** far venire i brividi a qu **II.** *adj* (*cold*) freddo, -a; (*frightening*) agghiacciante **III.** *vt* (*thing*) raffreddare; (*person*) infreddolire; **to be** ~**ed to the bone** avere un freddo cane
chill(i)ness *n* freddo *m; fig* freddezza *f*
chilling *adj* agghiacciante
chilly ['tʃɪ·li] <-ier, -iest> *adj a. fig* freddo, -a; **to feel** ~ avere freddo
chime [tʃaɪm] **I.** *n* rintocco *m;* **wind** ~**s** campane *f pl* eoliche **II.** *vi* suonare **III.** *vt* **to** ~ **eleven** suonare le undici
chimney ['tʃɪm·ni] *n* camino *m*
chimney pot *n* comignolo *m*
chimney sweep *n*, **chimneysweeper** *n a.* HIST spazzacamino *m*
chimpanzee [tʃɪm·ˈpæn·ziː] *n* scimpanzé *m inv*
chin [tʃɪn] *n* mento *m* ▶ **to keep one's** ~ **up** non buttarsi giù
china ['tʃaɪ·nə] *n* **1.**(*porcelain*) porcellana *f* **2.**(*crockery*) vasellame *m*
China ['tʃaɪ·nə] *n* Cina *f*
chinchilla [tʃɪn·ˈtʃɪ·lə] *n* cincillà *f 5nv*
Chinese [tʃaɪ·ˈniːz] **I.** *adj* cinese **II.** *n* **1.**(*person*) cinese *mf* **2.** LING cinese *m*
Chinese cabbage *n* cavolo *m* cinese
Chinese lantern *n* lanterna *f* cinese
chink [tʃɪŋk] **I.** *n* **1.**(*thin opening*) fessura *f;* **the** ~ **in sb's armor** *fig* il punto debole di qu **2.**(*clinking noise*) tintinnio *m* **II.** *vi* tintinnare
chintz [tʃɪnts] *n* chintz *m inv*
chip [tʃɪp] **I.** *n* **1.**(*flake*) frammento *m;* (*stone*) scheggia, wood *f* **2.** COMPUT chip *m inv* **3.**(*money token for gambling*) fiche *f inv;* **bargaining** ~ moneta *f* di scambio **4.** FOOD patatina *f;* **chocolate** ~ scaglia *f* di cioccolato ▶ **he's a** ~ **off the old block** *inf* ha preso dal padre [*o* dalla madre]; **to have a** ~ **on one's shoulder** *inf* avere la coda di paglia; **when the** ~**s are down** *inf* alla resa dei conti **II.** *vt* <-pp-> scheggiare **III.** *vi* <-pp-> scheggiarsi
chipmunk ['tʃɪp·mʌŋk] *n* scoiattolo *m* striato
chipped [tʃɪpt] *adj* scheggiato, -a
chiropractic ['kaɪ·rə·præk·tɪk] *n* chiropratica *f*
chiropractor [ˌkaɪ·roʊ·præk·tər] *n* chiropratico, -a *m, f*
chirpy ['tʃɜːr·pi] <-ier, -iest> *adj* allegro, -a
chirrup ['tʃɪ·rəp], **chirp** **I.** *n* cinguettio *m* **II.** *vi* cinguettare **III.** *vt* dire allegramente
chisel ['tʃɪ·zl] **I.** *n* cesello *m* **II.**<-ll-, -l-> *vt* **1.**(*cut*) cesellare **2.** *inf*(*get by trickery*) fregare
chit [tʃɪt] *n* **1.**(*note*) nota *f* **2.**(*voucher*) buono *m*

chitchat ['tʃɪt‚tʃæt] **I.** *n inf* chiacchiere *fpl* **II.** *vi inf* **to ~ about sth** chiacchierare di qc
chivalrous ['ʃɪ‧vl‧rəs] *adj* cavalleresco, -a
chivalry ['ʃɪ‧vl‧ri] *n* cavalleria *f*
chives [tʃaɪvz] *npl* erba *f* cipollina
chloride ['klɔː‧raɪd] *n* cloruro *m*
chlorinate ['klɔː‧rɪ‧neɪt] *vt* clorare
chlorine ['klɔː‧riːn] *n* cloro *m*
chlorofluorocarbon [‚klɔː‧rou‧flɔː‧rou‧‚kɑːrbən] *n* clorofluorocarburo *m*
chloroform ['klɔː‧rə‧fɔːrm] **I.** *n* cloroformio *m* **II.** *vt* cloroformizzare
chlorophyll ['klɔː‧rə‧fɪl] *n* clorofilla *f*
chlorous ['klɔː‧rəs] *adj* cloroso, -a
chock [tʃɑːk] *n* cuneo *m*
chock-a-block [‚tʃɑː‧kə‧'blɑːk] *adj* **~ with people** pieno zeppo di gente
chock-full *adj* **to be ~ of sth** essere pieno zeppo di qc; **to be ~ of calories** essere pieno di calorie
chocolate ['tʃɑː‧k‧lət] *n* **1.** (*sweet*) cioccolato *m;* **dark ~** cioccolato fondente; **a bar of ~** una barretta di cioccolato **2.** (*piece of chocolate candy*) cioccolatino *m*
choice [tʃɔɪs] **I.** *n* **1.** (*possibility of selection, selection*) scelta *f;* **to make a ~** scegliere; **to have no ~** non avere scelta; **a wide ~ of sth** un'ampia scelta di qc **2.** (*selected person or thing*) scelta *f;* **he wouldn't be my ~ as a friend** non lo sceglierei come amico **II.** *adj* (*top quality*) di prima scelta
choir ['kwa‧ɪə-] *n* coro *m*
choirmaster ['kwa‧ɪə-‚mæs‧tə-] *n* maestro, -a *m, f* del coro
choke [tʃouk] **I.** *vi* soffocare; **to ~ to death** morire soffocato **II.** *n* AUTO starter *m* **III.** *vt* **1.** (*deprive of air*) soffocare **2.** (*block*) intasare; **~d with leaves** intasato dalle foglie
◆**choke back** *vt* soffocare; **to ~ tears** trattenere le lacrime
◆**choke off** *vt* diminuire; **to choke sb off** *inf* mettere a tacere qu
◆**choke up** *vt* intasare
choker ['tʃou‧kə-] *n* collarino *m*
cholera ['kɑː‧lə-‧ə] *n* colera *m inv*
choleric ['kɑː‧lə-‧ɪk] *adj* irascibile
cholesterol [kə‧'les‧tə‧rɑːl] *n* colesterolo *m*
choose [tʃuːz] <chose, chosen> **I.** *vt* scegliere **II.** *vi* scegliere; **to have to ~ between** dover scegliere tra
choos(e)y ['tʃuː‧zi] <-ier, -iest> *adj inf* difficile
chop [tʃɑːp] **I.** *vt* <-pp-> tagliare; (*wood*) spaccare **II.** *vi* <-pp-> cambiare direzione **III.** *n* **1.** CULIN braciola *f* **2.** (*blow*) colpo *m*
◆**chop away** *vt* tagliare
◆**chop down** *vt* abbattere
◆**chop off** **I.** *vt* mozzare **II.** *vi* (*wind*) cambiare improvvisamente direzione
chop-chop [‚tʃɑː‧p‧'tʃɑːp] *interj inf* su, svelti!
chopper ['tʃɑː‧pə-] *n* **1.** (*tool*) scure *f* **2.** *inf* AVIAT elicottero *m*
choppy ['tʃɑː‧pi] <-ier, -iest> *adj* **1.** NAUT mosso, -a **2.** (*words, sentences*) frammenta-

rio, -a
chopsticks ['tʃɑːp‧stɪks] *npl* bacchette*f pl* (cinesi)
chop suey [‚tʃɑː‧p‧'suːi] *n* chop suey *m inv*
choral ['kɔː‧rəl] *adj* corale; **~ society** corale *f*
chord [kɔːrd] *n* MUS accordo *m* ▶ **to strike a ~ (with sb)** riuscire a toccare la sensibilità di (qu)
chore [tʃɔːr] *n* **1.** (*routine job*) lavoro *m;* **household ~s** faccende*f pl* domestiche **2.** (*tedious task*) lavoraccio *m*
choreograph ['kɔː‧ri‧ə‧græf] *vi, vt* coreografare
choreographer [‚kɔː‧rɪ‧'ɑː‧grə‧fə-] *n* coreografo, -a *m, f*
choreography [‚kɔː‧rɪ‧'ɑː‧grə‧fi] *n* coreografia *f*
chorus ['kɔː‧rəs] **I.** <-es> *n* **1.** (*refrain*) ritornello *m;* **to join in the ~** cantare in coro il ritornello **2.** + *sing/pl vb* (*group of singers*) coro *m* **3.** + *sing/pl vb* (*supporting singers*) coro *m;* **~ girl** corista *f;* **in ~** in coro **II.** *vi, vt* cantare in coro
chose [tʃouz] *pt of* **choose**
chosen ['tʃou‧zn] *pp of* **choose**
chow [tʃau] *n inf* (*food*) sbobba *f*
chow chow *n* chow-chow *m inv*
chowder ['tʃau‧də-] *n zuppa di pesce e verdure*
Christ [kraɪst] **I.** *n* Cristo *m* **II.** *interj inf* Cristo santo!
christen ['krɪ‧sən] *vt* **1.** (*baptize*) battezzare **2.** (*give name to*) **they ~ed their second child Jeff** il secondo figlio l'hanno chiamato Jeff **3.** (*use for first time*) inaugurare
Christendom ['krɪ‧sən‧dəm] *n* HIST cristianità *f*
christening ['krɪ‧sə‧nɪŋ] *n,* **christening ceremony** *n* battesimo *m*
Christian ['krɪst‧ʃən] **I.** *n* cristiano, -a *m, f* **II.** *adj* **1.** (*of Christ's teachings*) cristiano, -a **2.** (*kind*) caritatevole **3.** (*decent*) degno, -a
Christian burial *n* sepoltura *f* cristiana
Christianity [‚krɪs‧tʃi‧'æ‧nə‧ti] *n* Cristianesimo *m*
Christianize ['krɪs‧tʃə‧naɪz] *vt* cristianizzare
Christmas ['krɪs‧məs] <-es *o* -ses> *n* Natale *m;* **at ~** a Natale; **Merry ~!** Buon Natale!; **Father ~** Babbo *m* Natale; **~ card** biglietto *m* d'auguri natalizio
Christmas carol *n* canto *m* di Natale
Christmas Day *n* (giorno *m* di) Natale *m*
Christmas Eve *n* vigilia *f* di Natale
Christmas tree *n* albero *m* di Natale
Christopher ['krɪs‧tə‧fə-] *n* Cristoforo *m;* **~ Columbus** HIST Cristoforo Colombo
chromatic [krou‧'mæ‧t̬ɪk] *adj* cromatico, -a
chrome [kroum] *n* cromo *m*
chrome-plated *adj* cromato, -a
chromosome ['krou‧mə‧soum] *n* cromosoma *m*
chronic ['krɑː‧nɪk] *adj* **1.** (*lasting a long time*) cronico, -a **2.** (*habitual: liar*) inguaribile
chronicle ['krɑː‧nɪ‧kl] **I.** *vt* descrivere **II.** *n* cronaca *f*
chronicler ['krɑː‧nɪk‧lə-] *n* cronista *mf,*

storico *m*
chronological [ˌkrɑːnəˈlɑːdʒɪkl] *adj* cronologico, -a; **in ~ order** in ordine cronologico
chronology [krəˈnɑːlədʒi] *n* cronologia *f*
chrysalis [ˈkrɪsəlɪs] <-es> *n* crisalide *f*
chrysanthemum [krɪˈsænθəməm] *n* crisantemo *m*
chubby [ˈtʃʌbi] <-ier, -iest> *adj* cicciottello, -a
chuck¹ [tʃʌk] I. *vt* 1. *inf* (*throw*) tirare 2. *inf*
(*discard*) buttare II. *n* *inf* tiro *m*
chuck² [tʃʌk] *n* 1. (*cut of beef*) bistecca di
manzo della parte della spalla 2. (*device for
holding tool*) mandrino *m*
chuckle [ˈtʃʌkl] I. *n* risata *f* II. *vi* ridacchiare
chug [tʃʌg] I. <-gg-> *vi* sbuffare II. *n* sbuffo *m*
chum¹ [tʃʌm] *n* *inf* amicone, -a *m, f*
chum² [tʃʌm] *n* (*bait*) esca *f*
chummy [ˈtʃʌmi] <-ier, -iest> *adj* *inf*
(*friendly*) simpatico, -a; **to get ~ with sb**
diventare amicone con qu
chump [tʃʌmp] *n* *inf* tonto, -a *m, f*
chump change *n* *sl* spiccioli *m pl*
chunk [tʃʌŋk] *n* 1. (*thick lump: of cheese,
bread, meat*) pezzo *m* 2. *inf* (*large part*) bella
fetta *f*
chunky [ˈtʃʌŋki] <-ier, -iest> *adj* (*person*) ben
piantato, -a; (*peanut butter*) non cremoso, -a;
(*soup*) con verdura a pezzi
church [tʃɜːrtʃ] I. *n* chiesa *f*; **to go to ~** andare
in chiesa; **to enter the ~** farsi prete; (*become a
nun*) farsi suora II. *adj* 1. (*of the organization:
parade, celebration*) religioso, -a 2. (*of a building*) della chiesa
churchgoer [ˈtʃɜːrtʃˌgoʊər] *n* praticante *mf*
churchyard [ˈtʃɜːrtʃjɑːrd] *n* cimitero *m*
churlish [ˈtʃɜːrlɪʃ] *adj* maleducato, -a
churn [tʃɜːrn] I. *n* 1. (*for milk*) bidone *m* 2. (*for
butter*) zangola *f* II. *vt* agitare III. *vi* (*liquid*)
frullare; (*wheels*) girare rapidamente; **my
stomach was ~ing** mi si rivoltava lo stomaco
chute [ʃuːt] *n* 1. (*sloping tube*) rampa *f*; **garbage ~** botola *f* per i rifiuti 2. (*swimming pool
slide*) scivolo *m* 3. *inf* AVIAT paracadute *m*
chutney [ˈtʃʌtni] *n* chutney *m inv*
CIA [ˌsiːaɪˈeɪ] *n* *abbr of* **Central Intelligence
Agency** CIA *f*
cider [ˈsaɪdər] *n* (*unfermented apple juice*)
sweet ~ sidro *m*
cigar [sɪˈgɑːr] *n* sigaro *m*
cigar box <-es> *n*, **cigar case** *n* portasigari *m
inv*
cigar cutter *n* tagliasigari *m inv*
cigarette [ˌsɪgəˈret] *n* sigaretta *f*; **to light a ~**
accendere una sigaretta
cigarette butt *n* mozzicone *m* di sigaretta
cigarette case *n* portasigarette *m inv*
cigarette holder *n* bocchino *m*
cigarette paper *n* cartina *f* (per sigarette)
cigarillo [ˌsɪgəˈrɪloʊ] *n* piccolo sigaro *m*
cilantro [sɪˈlɑntroʊ] *n* coriandolo *m*
cinch [sɪntʃ] <-es> *n* **it's a ~** *inf* è una bazzecola
cinder [ˈsɪndər] *n* 1. (*burnt residue*) brace *f*; **to**

burn sth to a ~ ridurre qc in cenere 2. *pl*
(*ashes*) ceneri *fpl*
Cinderella [ˌsɪndəˈrelə] *n* Cenerentola *f*
cinema [ˈsɪnəmə] *n* cinema *m inv*
cinemagoer [ˈsɪnəməˌgoʊər] *n* cinefilo,
-a *m, f*
cinematic [ˌsɪnəˈmæt̬ɪk] *adj* cinematografico, -a
cinnamon [ˈsɪnəmən] *n* cannella *f*; **a ~ stick**
un bastoncino di cannella
CIO *n* *abbr of* **Congress of Industrial Organizations** Associazione *f* delle Organizzazioni
Industriali
cipher *n*, **cypher** [ˈsaɪfər] *n* codice *m;* **in ~** in
codice
circa [ˈsɜːrkə] *prep* circa; **~ 1850** 1850 circa
circle [ˈsɜːrkl] I. *n* 1. *a.* MATH cerchio *m;* **to go
around in ~s** girare attorno; **to run around
in ~s** *fig* non riuscire a combinare niente; **to
have ~s under one's eyes** avere le occhiaie
2. THEAT galleria *f* ▶ **to come full ~** chiudere il
cerchio; **to square the ~** quadrare il cerchio
II. *vt* cerchiare; (*move in a circle around*)
girare attorno a III. *vi* (*aircraft*) girare in tondo
circuit [ˈsɜːrkɪt] *n* 1. circuito *m* 2. (*district
under circuit judge*) distretto *m* giurisdizionale
circuit board *n* circuito *m* stampato
circuit breaker *n* salvavita *m inv*
circuitous [səˈkjuːətəs] *adj* (*route*) tortuoso, -a
circular [ˈsɜːrkjələr] I. *adj* circolare II. *n* circu-
lare *f*
circular saw *n* sega *f* circolare
circulate [ˈsɜːrkjəleɪt] I. *vt* far circolare II. *vi*
circolare
circulating library <-ies> *n* biblioteca *f* itinerante
circulation [ˌsɜːrkjuˈleɪʃən] *n* 1. circolazione *f*; **to be out of ~** essere fuori circolazione
2. (*of publication*) tiratura *f*
circulatory [ˈsɜːrkjələˌtɔːri] *adj* circolatorio, -a
circumcise [ˈsɜːrkəmsaɪz] *vt* circoncidere
circumcision [ˌsɜːrkəmˈsɪʒən] *n* circoncisione *f*
circumference [səˈkʌmfərəns] *n* 1. (*circle's
boundary line*) circonferenza *f* 2. (*perimeter*)
perimetro *m*
circumlocution [ˌsɜːrkəmləˈkjuːʃən] *n* *form*
1. (*expression*) circonlocuzione *f* 2. (*way of
speaking*) sproloqui *mpl*
circumnavigate [ˌsɜːrkəmˈnævɪgeɪt] *vt*
form circumnavigare; (*cape*) doppiare
circumnavigation [ˌsɜːrkəmˌnævɪˈgeɪʃən]
n *form* circumnavigazione *f*
circumscribe [ˈsɜːrkəmskraɪb] *vt* *form* circoscrivere
circumscription [ˌsɜːrkəmˈskrɪpʃən] *n*
1. circoscrizione *f* 2. (*on coin*) iscrizione *f*
circumspect [ˈsɜːrkəmspekt] *adj* *form* circospetto, -a
circumstance [ˈsɜːrkəmstæns] *n* circostanza *f*; **under no ~s** in nessun caso

circumstantial [ˌsɜːr·kəm·'stæn·ʃl] *adj* indiziario, -a

circumvent [ˌsɜːr·kəm·'vent] *vt form* (*laws*) eludere; (*obstacle*) aggirare

circus ['sɜːr·kəs] I.<-es> *n* circo *m* II. *adj* del circo

cirrhosis [sə·'roʊ·sɪs] *n* cirrosi *f inv;* ~ of the liver cirrosi epatica

cirrus ['sɪ·rəs] *n* METEO cirro *m*

CIS [ˌsiː·aɪ·'es] *n abbr of* Commonwealth of Independent States CSI *f, Comunità di Stati Indipendenti*

cistern ['sɪs·tən] *n* cisterna *f*

citadel ['sɪ·tə·dəl] *n* cittadella *f*

citation [saɪ·'teɪ·ʃən] *n* 1.(*written quotation*) citazione *f* 2. MIL menzione *f* 3.(*ticket*) multa *f*

cite [saɪt] *vt form* citare

citizen ['sɪ·tɪ·zn] *n* 1.(*subject*) cittadino, -a *m, f* 2.(*resident of town*) abitante *mf*

citizens' band *n s.* CB banda *f* cittadina

citizenship ['sɪ·tɪ·zən·ʃɪp] *n* cittadinanza *f*

citric ['sɪt·rɪk] *adj* citrico, -a

citrus ['sɪt·rəs] <citrus *o* citruses> I. *n* agrume *m* II. *adj* citrico, -a

city ['sɪ·ti] <-ies> I. *n* città *f* II. *adj* (*landscape*) urbano, -a; (*life*) di città

city hall *n* municipio *m*

civic ['sɪ·vɪk] <inv> *adj* (*authorities*) civile; (*education*) civico, -a

civies ['sɪ·viz] *npl* abiti *m* civili *pl*

civil ['sɪ·vl] *adj* 1.civile 2.(*courteous*) cortese; to not have a ~ word to say about sb parlar male di qu

civil action *n* procedimento *m* civile

civil court *n* tribunale *m* civile

civil defense *n* protezione *f* civile

civil disobedience *n* resistenza *f* passiva

civil engineer *n* ingegnere *m* civile

civilian [sɪ·'vɪl·jən] <inv> I. *n* civile *mf* II. *adj* (*clothes*) civile

civility [sɪ·'vɪ·lə·ti] <-ies> *n* 1.(*formality*) civiltà *f* 2.(*formal remarks*) convenevoli *mpl*

civilization [ˌsɪ·və·lɪ·'zeɪ·ʃən] *n* civiltà *f inv*

civilize ['sɪ·və·laɪz] *vt* civilizzare

civil law ['sɪ·vl·'lɑː] *n* diritto *m* civile

civil liberties *npl* diritti *m pl* civili

civil marriage *n* matrimonio *m* civile

civil rights *npl* diritti *m pl* civili

civil servant *n* funzionario, -a *m, f* statale

civil service *n* Amministrazione *f* Pubblica

civil war *n* guerra *f* civile

civvies ['sɪ·viz] *npl inf* in ~ in abiti civili

clack [klæk] I. *vi* 1.(*heels, typewriter*) produrre un ticchettio 2.(*talk rapidly*) parlottare II. *n* 1.(*with heels*) ticchettio *m* 2.(*continual rapid talk*) parlottio *m*

clad [klæd] *adj a. iron* vestito, -a

claim [kleɪm] I. *n* 1.(*assertion*) affermazione *f* 2.(*written demand*) richiesta *f;* insurance ~ richiesta di risarcimento 3.(*right*) rivendicazione *f;* to lay ~ to sth rivendicare qc II. *vt* 1.(*assert*) affermare; (*right, responsibility*) rivendicare 2.(*declare ownership*) recla-

mare; (*reward, title*) rivendicare; (*diplomatic immunity*) chiedere 3.(*require: time*) richiedere 4.(*demand in writing*) fare richiesta di; to ~ damages chiedere il risarcimento dei danni III. *vi* to ~ for sth reclamare qc

claimant ['kleɪ·mənt] *n* richiedente *mf;* (*to a throne*) pretendente *mf*

clairvoyance [ˌkler·'vɔ·rənts] *n* chiaroveggenza *f*

clairvoyant [ˌkler·'vɔ·rən] I. *n* chiaroveggente *mf* II. *adj* paranormale; to be ~ essere chiaroveggente

clam [klæm] *n* vongola *f* ▶ to be happy as a ~ essere felice come una pasqua

◆ clam up <-mm-> *vi* (*not say anything*) non aprire (più) bocca

clamber ['klæm·bə] I. *vi* arrampicarsi II. *n* arrampicata *f*

clam chowder ['klæm·ˌtʃaʊ·də] *n* zuppa *f* di vongole

clammy ['klæ·mi] <-ier, -iest> *adj* (*feet*) sudato, -a; (*weather*) appiccicoso, -a

clamor ['klæ·mə] I. *vi* (*demand loudly*) to ~ for sth chiedere a gran voce qc II. *n* clamore *m*

clamorous ['klæ·mə·rəs] *adj* chiassoso, -a

clamp [klæmp] I. *n* TECH morsetto *m* II. *vt* 1.(*fasten together*) stringere 2.(*impose forcefully*) imporre

◆ clamp down *vi* to ~ on sth mettere freno a qc

clan [klæn] *n* clan *m inv*

clandestine [klæn·'des·tɪn] *adj form* clandestino, -a

clang [klæŋ] I. *vi* (*bells*) suonare II. *vt* to ~ sth shut chiudere qc con fragore III. *n* forte suono *m* metallico; the ~ of the bell il clangore della campana

clangor ['klæŋ·gə] *n* forte suono *m* metallico

clank [klæŋk] I. *vi* produrre un rumore metallico II. *vt* far risuonare III. *n* rumore *m* metallico

clap¹ [klæp] I.<-pp-> *vt* 1.(*applaud*) applaudire 2.(*slap palms together*) to ~ one's hands (together) battere le mani II.<-pp-> *vi* 1.(*applaud*) applaudire 2.(*slap palms together*) battere le mani III. *n* 1.(*slap*) pacca *f* 2.(*applause*) applauso *m;* to give sb a ~ applaudire qu 3.(*noise*) a ~ of thunder un tuono

clap² [klæp] *n sl* the ~ gonorrea

clapper ['klæ·pə] *n* battaglio *m*

claptrap ['klæp·træp] *n inf* scemenze *fpl*

claret ['kle·rət] *n* 1.(*wine*) bordeaux *m* rosso *inv* 2.(*color*) bordeaux *m*

clarification [ˌkle·rɪ·fɪ·'keɪ·ʃən] *n* chiarimento *m*

clarify ['kle·rɪ·faɪ] <-ie-> *vt* 1.(*make clearer, explain*) chiarire 2.(*purify*) chiarificare

clarinet [ˌkle·rɪ·'net] *n* clarinetto *m*

clarity ['kle·rə·ti] *n* chiarezza *f*

clash [klæʃ] I. *vi* 1.(*fight*) scontrarsi; to ~ over sth scontrarsi su qc 2.(*compete against*)

C

affrontarsi **3.**(*contradict: views*) contraddirsi **4.**(*not match: colors*) non intonarsi **5.**(*make loud noise*) far rumore **II.** *vt* sbattere rumorosamente **III.**<-es> *n* **1.**(*hostile encounter, contest*) scontro *m* **2.**(*conflict, incompatibility*) conflitto *m* **3.**(*loud harsh noise*) fragore *m*

clasp [klæsp] **I.** *n* **1.**(*firm grip: of hands*) stretta *f* **2.**(*fastening device*) fermaglio *m*, fibbia *f* **II.** *vt* **1.**(*grip*) serrare; **to ~ one's hands** stringersi la mano; **to ~ sb in one's arms** stringere qu tra le braccia **2.**(*fasten: belt*) allacciare

clasp knife <knives> *n* coltello *m* a serramanico

class [klæs] **I.**<-es> *n* **1.**classe *f* **2.**(*lesson*) lezione *f*, corso *m* **II.** *vt* classificare; **to ~ sb as sth** classificare qu come qc; **to ~ sb among sth** considerare qu qc

class-conscious [ˈklæs‧kɑːnˈtʃəs] *adj* con coscienza di classe; (*classist*) classista

classic [ˈklæ‧sɪk] **I.** *adj* **1.**classico, -a **2.** *inf* (*joke, story*) memorabile **II.** *n* classico *m*

classical [ˈklæ‧sɪ‧kl] *adj* classico, -a

classicism [ˈklæ‧sɪ‧sɪ‧zəm] *n* classicismo *m*

classicist [ˈklæ‧sɪ‧sɪst] *n* classicista *mf*

classics [ˈklæ‧sɪks] *n* **1.** *pl* **the ~** (*great literature*) i classici **2.** + *sing vb* (*Greek and Roman studies*) studi *m pl* classici

classification [ˌklæ‧sə‧fɪˈkeɪ‧ʃən] *n* classificazione *f*

classified [ˈklæ‧sɪ‧faɪd] <inv> *adj* classificato, -a; (*confidential*) riservato, -a

classify [ˈklæ‧sɪ‧faɪ] <-ie-> *vt* classificare; (*designate as secret*) dichiarare di carattere riservato

classless [ˈklæs‧lɪs] *adj* (*society*) senza classi

classmate *n* compagno, -a *m, f* di classe

classroom *n* aula *f*, classe *f*

class struggle *n*, **class war** *n* lotta *f* di classe

classy [ˈklæ‧si] <-ier, -iest> *adj* raffinato, -a

clatter [ˈklæ‧t̬ər] **I.** *vi* **1.**(*make rattling noise*) fare fracasso **2.**(*walk noisily*) scalpicciare **II.** *n* fracasso *m*; (*of hooves*) scalpiccio *m*

clause [klɑːz] *n* clausola *f*; LING proposizione *f*

claustrophobia [ˌklɑːs‧trə‧ˈfoʊ‧biə] *n* claustrofobia *f*

claustrophobic *adj* claustrofobico, -a

clavicle [ˈklæ‧vɪ‧kl] *n* clavicola *f*

claw [klɑː] **I.** *n* artiglio *m*; (*of sea creatures*) chela *f*; **to show one's ~s** *fig* tirar fuori le unghie **II.** *vt* graffiare

clay [kleɪ] **I.** *n* **1.**argilla *f* **2.** SPORTS terra *f* battuta **II.** *adj* di argilla

clay pigeon *n* piattello *m*

clean [kliːn] **I.** *adj* **1.**(*free of dirt, fair*) pulito, -a; (*as*) **~ as a whistle** pulitissimo **2.**(*free from bacteria*) disinfettato, -a **3.**(*morally acceptable*) onesto, -a; (*reputation*) senza macchia; (*driving license*) con tutti i punti; **~ police record** fedina *f* penale pulita **4.**(*smooth: cut*) netto, -a; (*design*) elegante **5.**(*complete*) **to make a ~ break with sth** dare un taglio netto a qc **6.**(*blank: piece of paper*) bianco, -a **II.** *n* pulita *f* **III.** *adv* completamente; **to ~ forget that ...** dimenticarsi completamente che ... **IV.** *vt* pulire **V.** *vi* pulirsi; **the coffee stain ~ed off easily** la macchia di caffè è venuta via facilmente

♦**clean out** *vt* **1.**(*clean thoroughly*) pulire; (*with water*) lavare **2.** *sl* (*make penniless*) ripulire

♦**clean up I.** *vt* **1.**(*make clean*) pulire; (*tidy up*) riordinare; **to clean oneself up** darsi una ripulita **2.**(*eradicate*) ripulire da **II.** *vi* **1.**(*make clean*) pulire **2.** *inf* (*make profit*) guadagnare

clean-cut [ˌkliːnˈkʌt] *adj* (*straight*) netto, -a; (*person*) dall'aspetto curato

cleaner [ˈkliː‧nər] *n* **1.**(*person*) addetto, -a *m, f* alle pulizie **2.**(*substance*) prodotto *m* detergente

cleaning [ˈkliː‧nɪŋ] *n* pulizia *f*

cleaning lady <-ies> *n*, **cleaning woman** <women> *n* donna *f* delle pulizie

cleanliness [ˈklen‧lɪ‧nɪs] *n* pulizia *f*

cleanly [ˈklen‧li] *adv* (*cut*) di netto; (*honestly*) onestamente

cleanse [klenz] *vt* **1.**(*make clean*) pulire **2.**(*make morally pure*) purificare

cleanser [ˈklen‧zər] *n* latte *m* detergente

clean-shaven [ˈkliːn‧ˈʃeɪ‧vn] *adj* sbarbato, -a

cleansing cream *n* crema *f* detergente

cleansing tissue *n* fazzolettino *m* struccante

cleanup [ˈkliːn‧ʌp] *n* pulita *f*

clear [klɪr] **I.** *n* **to be in the ~** essere fuori pericolo **II.** *adv* **to get ~ of sth** togliersi da qc; **to stand ~ (of sth)** tenersi lontano (da qc) **III.** *adj* **1.**(*transparent*) trasparente; (*picture*) nitido, -a; **to make oneself ~** spiegarsi bene; **as ~ as day** chiaro come il giorno **2.**(*obvious*) evidente **3.**(*free from guilt: conscience*) a posto; **to be ~ of debt** non avere debiti **4.**(*net*) netto, -a **IV.** *vt* **1.**(*remove obstacles*) sgombrare; (*empty*) liberare **2.**(*remove blockage*) stasare; **to ~ the way** sgombrare la strada **3.**(*remove doubts*) chiarire; **to ~ one's head** chiarirsi le idee **4.**(*acquit*) scagionare **5.**(*net*) guadagnare **6.**(*jump*) saltare **7.**(*give official permission*) autorizzare **V.** *vi* (*water, weather*) schiarirsi

♦**clear away I.** *vt* mettere via **II.** *vi* andarsene

♦**clear off I.** *vi inf* filarsela **II.** *vt* mandare via

♦**clear out I.** *vt* ripulire; (*throw away*) sbarazzarsi di **II.** *vi* andarsene

♦**clear up I.** *vt* risolvere; (*tidy*) riordinare **II.** *vi* schiarire

clearance [ˈklɪr‧rəns] *n* **1.**(*act of clearing*) rimozione *f* **2.**(*space*) spazio *m* libero **3.**(*permission*) autorizzazione *f*

clearance sale *n* liquidazione *f*

clear-cut [ˌklɪrˈkʌt] **I.** *adj* ben definito, -a **II.** *vt* tagliare in modo netto

clearheaded *adj* lucido, -a

clearing [ˈklɪr‧rɪŋ] *n* radura *f*

clearing-house *n* camera *f* di compensazione

clearly [ˈklɪr‧li] *adv* chiaramente

clearness [ˈklɪr‧nɪs] *n* chiarezza *f*

clear-sighted [ˌklɪə·ˈsaɪ·tɪd] *adj* perspicace

cleavage [ˈkliː·vɪdʒ] *n* **1.** (*in a dress*) scollatura *f* **2.** *form* (*division*) spaccatura *f*

cleave [kliːv] <-ed *o* cleft *o* clove, -ed *o* cleft *o* cloven> **I.** *vi liter* fendersi **II.** *vt* fendere

cleaver [ˈkliː·və] *n* mannaia *f*

clef [klef] *n* chiave *f*

cleft [kleft] **I.** <inv> *adj* solcato, -a; (*lip*) leporino, -a **II.** *n* crepaccio *f*

clematis [ˈkle·mə·təs] *n inv* clematide *f*

clemency [ˈkle·mən·si] *n form* clemenza *f*

clement [ˈkle·mənt] *adj* **1.** *form* (*mild*) mite **2.** *form* (*merciful*) clemente

clench [klentʃ] *vt* stringere

clergy [ˈklɜ·r·dʒi] *n* + *sing/pl vb* clero *m*

clergyman [ˈklɜ·r·dʒɪ·mən] <-men> *n* sacerdote *m;* (*protestant*) pastore *m*

clergywoman [ˈklɜ·r·dʒɪ·ˌwʊ·mən] <-women> *n* pastore *m* donna

cleric [ˈkle·rɪk] *n* ecclesiastico *m*

clerical [ˈkle·rɪ·kl] *adj* **1.** (*of the clergy*) clericale **2.** (*of offices*) d'ufficio; ~ **worker** impiegato, -a *m, f*

clerical error *n* errore *m* burocratico

clerical staff *n* personale *m* d'ufficio

clerical work *n* lavoro *m* d'ufficio

clerk [klɑːrk] *n* **1.** (*in office*) impiegato, -a *m, f* **2.** (*in hotel*) receptionist *mf inv;* (*in shop*) commesso, -a *m, f;* **sales** ~ addetto , -a alle vendite *m*

clever [ˈkle·və] *adj* **1.** (*intelligent*) intelligente **2.** (*skillful*) abile; (*invention*) ingegnoso, -a **3.** *pej* furbo, -a; **to be too** ~ **by half** voler fare il furbo

cleverness *n* **1.** (*intelligence*) intelligenza *f* **2.** (*skill*) abilità *f*

cliché [kliː·ˈʃeɪ] *n* cliché *m inv*

click [klɪk] **I.** *n* clic *m inv;* (*of one's heels*) ticchettio *m;* (*of one's tongue*) schiocco *m* **II.** *vi* **1.** (*make short, sharp sound*) fare un rumore secco **2.** COMPUT fare clic **3.** (*become friendly*) andare subito d'accordo; (*become popular*) avere successo **4.** (*become clear*) tornare **III.** *vt* **1.** (*make short, sharp sound: tongue*) schioccare; (*heels*) battere **2.** (*press button on mouse*) cliccare

client [ˈklaɪ·ənt] *n* cliente *mf*

clientele [ˌklaɪ·ən·ˈtel] *n* clientela *f*

cliff [klɪf] *n* dirupo *m;* (*on coast*) scogliera *f*

cliffhanger *n* situazione *f* carica di suspense

climacteric [klaɪ·ˈmæk·tə·rɪk] *n form* climaterio *m*

climactic [ˌklaɪ·ˈmæk·tɪk] *adj* culminante

climate [ˈklaɪ·mɪt] *n* clima *m;* **the** ~ **of opinion** l'opinione generale

climatic [klaɪ·ˈmæ·tɪk] *adj* climatico, -a

climatologist [ˌklaɪ·mə·ˈtɑː·lə·dʒɪst] *n* climatologo, -a *m, f*

climatology [ˌklaɪ·mə·ˈtɑː·lə·dʒi] *n* climatologia *f*

climax [ˈklaɪ·mæks] **I.** <-es> *n* culmine *m;* (*sexual*) orgasmo *m* **II.** *vi* arrivare al culmine; (*sexual*) raggiungere l'orgasmo

climb [klaɪm] **I.** *n* scalata *f* **II.** *vt* (*stairs*) salire; (*tree*) arrampicarsi su; (*mountain*) scalare **III.** *vi* salire; **to** ~ **to a height of ...** AVIAT raggiungere una quota di ...

◆**climb down** *vi* scendere; *fig* fare marcia indietro

climb-down [ˈklaɪm·daʊn] *n* marcia *f* indietro

climber [ˈklaɪ·mə] *n* **1.** (*of mountains*) alpinista *mf;* (*of rock faces*) scalatore, -trice *m, f* **2.** (*plant*) rampicante *m* **3.** *inf* (*striver for higher status*) arrampicatore , -trice *m, f* sociale

climbing [ˈklaɪ·mɪŋ] **I.** *n* **1.** (*ascending mountains*) alpinismo *m* **2.** (*ascending rock faces*) arrampicata *f* **II.** *adj* (*plant*) rampicante; (*boots*) da montagna

climbing iron *n s.* **crampon**

clinch [klɪntʃ] **I.** <-es> *n* stretta *f* **II.** *vt* **1.** (*settle decisively*) risolvere; (*a deal*) concludere **2.** *inf* (*embrace*) abbracciarsi **3.** (*secure a nail*) ribadire **4.** (*in boxing*) SPORTS chiudere in clinch

clincher [ˈklɪn·tʃə] *n inf* argomento *m* decisivo

cling [klɪŋ] <clung, clung> *vi* **1.** (*embrace*) abbracciarsi **2.** (*hold*) aggrapparsi **3.** (*stick*) aderire **4.** (*stay close*) stare addosso **5.** (*follow closely*) seguire

clinging *adj* **1.** (*clothes*) attillato, -a **2.** (*person*) appiccicoso, -a

clingy [ˈklɪ·ŋi] <-ier, -iest> *adj* aderente

clinic [ˈklɪ·nɪk] *n* clinica *f*

clinical [ˈklɪ·nɪ·kl] *adj* **1.** clinico, -a **2.** (*emotionless*) freddo, -a

clinician [klɪ·ˈnɪ·ʃən] *n* specialista *mf*

clink [klɪŋk] **I.** *vt* far tintinnare; (*glasses*) ; **to** ~ **glasses** fare cin cin **II.** *vi* tintinnare **III.** *n* **1.** tintinnio *m;* (*of glasses*) rumore *m* dei bicchieri quando si brinda **2.** *inf* (*prison*) gattabuia *f*

clinker [ˈklɪŋ·kə] *n* scorie *fpl*

clip[1] [klɪp] **I.** *n* **1.** (*fastener*) clip *f inv;* (*for paper*) graffetta *f;* (*for hair*) fermaglio *m* **2.** (*gun part*) caricatore *m* **3.** (*jewelry*) spillina *f* **II.** <-pp-> *vt* attaccare

clip[2] [klɪp] <-pp-> **I.** *vt* **1.** (*cut*) tagliare; (*sheep*) tosare; (*ticket*) forare **2.** (*reduce*) accorciare **3.** (*attach*) attaccare **4.** (*hit*) colpire **II.** *n* **1.** (*trim*) spuntata *f* **2.** (*extract*) frammento *m* **3.** (*hit*) colpetto *m*

clipboard [ˈklɪp·bɔːrd] *n* portablocco *m* a molla

clipped *adj* tagliato, -a

clipper [ˈklɪ·pə] *n* NAUT clipper *m*

clipping [ˈklɪ·pɪŋ] *n* ritaglio *m*

clique [kliːk] *n* combriccola *f*

cliquey [ˈkliː·ki] <cliquier, cliquiest> *adj*, **cliquish** [ˈkliː·kɪʃ] *adj* esclusivo, -a

clitoris [ˈklɪ·tə·əs] <-es> *n* clitoride *m*

cloak [kloʊk] **I.** *n* **1.** *a. fig* mantello *m* **2.** (*covering*) manto *m;* **under the** ~ **of darkness** col favore delle tenebre **II.** *vt* avvolgere

cloakroom [ˈkloʊk·ruːm] *n* guardaroba *m inv*

clobber [ˈklɑː·bə] *vt inf* prendere a bastonate

clock [klɑːk] I. n 1. (for time) orologio m; **alarm** ~ sveglia f; **around the** ~ 24 ore su 24; **to run against the** ~ essere in corsa contro il tempo 2. (speedometer) cronometro m; (odometer) contachilometri m inv II. vt 1. (take amount of time) cronometrare 2. (measure time) **this car can** ~ **150 mph** questa macchina fa 150 miglia all'ora

◆**clock in** vi 1. (record time) timbrare il cartellino (all'arrivo) 2. inf (arrive) arrivare a lavoro

◆**clock out** vi 1. (record time) timbrare il cartellino (all'uscita) 2. inf (leave work) uscire dal lavoro

◆**clock up** vt insep (attain) ottenere; (travel) percorrere

clock face n quadrante m

clock radio n radiosveglia f

clockwise adj, adv in senso orario

clockwork n meccanismo m; **to go like** ~ andare tutto liscio; **as regular as** ~ preciso come un orologio

clod [klɑːd] n 1. (earth) zolla f 2. (person) idiota mf

clog [klɑːg] I. n zoccolo m II. <-gg-> vi intasarsi III. <-gg-> vt intasare

◆**clog up** vt intasare

cloister ['klɔɪs·tə] n pl chiostro m

clone [kloʊn] I. n BIO, COMPUT clone m II. vt clonare

cloning ['kloʊ·nɪŋ] n clonazione f

close¹ [kloʊs] I. adj 1. (near in location, almost even) vicino, -a; ~ **combat** combattimento m corpo a corpo 2. (intimate) intimo, -a; ~ **relatives** parenti m pl stretti 3. (similar) simile 4. (unwilling to be frank) riservato, -a 5. (airless) chiuso, -a II. adv vicino; **to move** ~ avvicinarsi

close² [kloʊz] I. n (end) fine f; (finish) finale m; **to bring sth to a** ~ terminare qc II. vt 1. (shut) chiudere 2. (end) terminare, chiudere; (bring to an end) concludere; **to** ~ **a deal** concludere un accordo III. vi 1. (shut) chiudersi 2. (end) terminare, chiudersi

◆**close down** I. vi chiudere (definitivamente) II. vt chiudere (definitivamente)

◆**close in** vi 1. (surround) **to** ~ **on sth** circondare qc 2. (get shorter) accorciarsi

◆**close off** vt chiudere

◆**close up** I. vi 1. (people) chiudersi 2. (wound) cicatrizzarsi II. vt chiudere

closed adj chiuso, -a; **behind** ~ **doors** a porte chiuse

closed-door adj a porte chiuse

closedown n chiusura f

close-knit adj unito, -a

closely ['kloʊs·li] adv 1. (near) da vicino 2. (intimately) estremamente 3. (carefully) attentamente

closeness ['kloʊs·nɪs] n 1. (nearness,) vicinanza f 2. (intimacy) intimità f 3. (airlessness) mancanza f d'aria

closet ['klɑː·zɪt] I. n (cupboard) armadio m

▶**to come out** of the ~ dichiararsi apertamente omosessuale II. adj segreto, -a III. vt to be ~ed with sb avere un colloquio privato con qc

close to I. prep 1. (near) vicino a; **to be** ~ **the beginning/end of sth** essere prossimi all'inizio/alla fine di qc; **to live** ~ **the airport** abitare vicino all'aeroporto 2. (almost) ~ **tears** sul punto di piangere; **to be** ~ **doing sth** stare per fare qc; ~ **three feet** circa tre piedi 3. (in friendship with) **to be** ~ **sb** essere vicino a qu II. adv (almost) ~ **finished/complete** quasi finito/completo

close-up ['kloʊs·ʌp] n CINE primo piano m

closing I. adj ultimo, -a; (speech) di chiusura II. n chiusura f

closing date n ultimo giorno m

closing time n orario m di chiusura

closure ['kloʊ·ʒə] n chiusura f

clot [klɑːt] I. n grumo m; **blood** ~ coagulo m di sangue II. <-tt-> vi raggrumarsi; (blood) coagularsi

cloth [klɑːθ] I. n 1. (material) tela f; (for cleaning) panno m 2. (clergy) clero m; **a man of the** ~ un ecclesiastico II. adj di tela

clothe [kloʊð] vt vestire; fig rivestire di

clothes [kloʊðz] npl abiti mpl

clothes hanger n gruccia f (appendiabiti)

clotheshorse n stenditoio m

clothesline n corda f per il bucato

clothespin n molletta f (per il bucato)

clothing ['kloʊ·ðɪŋ] n abbigliamento f; **article of** ~ capo m d'abbigliamento

clothing industry <-ies> n industria f dell'abbigliamento

cloud [klaʊd] I. n nube f ▶**every** ~ **has a silver lining** prov non tutto il male vien per nuocere prov; **to be on** ~ **nine** essere al settimo cielo; **to be under a** ~ essere in cattiva luce II. vt a. fig offuscare

◆**cloud over** vi 1. METEO rannuvolarsi 2. (become gloomy) rabbuiarsi 3. (become misty: eyes) offuscarsi

cloud bank n banco m di nubi

cloudburst n nubifragio m

cloud-capped adj avvolto, -a di nubi

cloud chamber n PHYS camera f a nebbia

clouded ['klaʊ·dɪd] adj 1. (cloudy) nuvoloso, -a 2. (not transparent: liquid) torbido, -a 3. (confused: mind) confuso, -a

cloudless ['klaʊd·lɪs] adj sereno, -a

cloudy ['klaʊ·di] <-ier, -iest> adj 1. (overcast) nuvoloso, -a 2. (not transparent: liquid) torbido, -a

clout [klaʊt] I. n 1. inf (hit) botta f 2. (power) influenza f II. vt inf dare una botta a

clove¹ [kloʊv] n FOOD chiodo m di garofano; (of garlic) spicchio m

clove² [kloʊv] pt of **cleave**

cloven ['kloʊ·vn] I. pp of **cleave** II. adj spaccato, -a

clover ['kloʊ·və] n trifoglio m

cloverleaf n <-leaves> foglia f di trifoglio

clown [klaʊn] I. *n* pagliaccio *m* II. *vi* to ~ around fare il pagliaccio
clownish ['klaʊ·nɪʃ] *adj* da pagliaccio
cloying ['klɔɪ·ɪŋ] *adj* stucchevole
cloyingly *adv* in modo stucchevole
club [klʌb] I. *n* 1.(*group*) associazione *f*, circolo *m* 2.(*team*) club *m inv*, squadra *f* 3.SPORTS mazza *f* da golf 4.(*weapon*) randello *m* 5.(*playing card*) carta *f* di fiori; (*in Spanish cards*) 6.(*disco*) locale *m* notturno II.<-bb-> *vt* bastonare
clubbing *vi* to go ~ andare a ballare
club car *n* carrozza *f* bar
clubfoot <feet> *n* piede *m* equino
clubhouse *n* sede *f* di un circolo
club sandwich <-es> *n* tramezzino *m*
club soda *n* seltz *m inv*
cluck [klʌk] *vi* chiocciare
clue [kluː] *n* 1.(*evidence, hint*) indizio *m* 2.(*secret*) chiave *f* 3.(*idea*) idea *f*; I don't have a ~ *inf* non ne ho la più pallida idea
♦**clue in** *vt* to clue sb in (on sth) informare qu (di qc)
clueless ['kluː·lɪs] *adj inf* to be ~ (about sth) non sapere niente (di qc)
clump [klʌmp] I. *vt* to ~ sth together raggruppare qc II. *vi* 1.(*group*) to ~ together unirsi 2.(*walk noisily*) camminare facendo rumore III. *n* 1.(*thick group: of trees*) gruppo *m*; (*of flowers*) cespo *m* 2.(*lump*) pezzo *m*
clumsiness ['klʌm·zɪ·nɪs] *n* goffaggine *f*
clumsy ['klʌm·zi] <-ier, -iest> *adj* maldestro, -a; (*object*) scomodo, -a
clung [klʌŋ] *pp, pt of* **cling**
clunk [klʌŋk] *n* suono *m* metallico
cluster ['klʌs·tə˞] I. *n* (*of people*) gruppo *m*; (*of fruits*) grappolo *m* II. *vi* raggrupparsi
cluster bomb *n* bomba *f* a grappolo
clutch [klʌtʃ] I. *vi* to ~ at sth aggrapparsi a qc II. *vt* stringere III. *n* 1.AUTO frizione *f* 2.(*set: of eggs*) covata *f* 3.(*control*) to be in the ~es of sb/sth essere nelle grinfie di qu/qc 4.(*crucial situation*) situazione *f* critica
clutch bag *n* pochette *f inv*
clutch hitter *n* clutch-hitter *m inv*
clutter ['klʌ·t̮ə˞] I. *n* disordine *m* II. *vt* ingombrare
♦**clutter up** *vt* ingombrare
cluttered *adj* disordinato, -a; *fig* confuso, -a; to be ~ with essere ingombro di
cm *inv abbr of* **centimeter** cm
c'mon *inf* = come on
CO¹ [ˌkɑː·lə·'ræ·doʊ] *n abbr of* **Colorado** Colorado *m*
CO² [ˌsiː·'oʊ] *n*, **C.O.** [ˌsiː·'oʊ] *n* 1.*abbr of* **Commanding Officer** ufficiale *m* in comando 2.*abbr of* **conscientious objector** obiettore, -trice *m, f* di coscienza
Co *n abbr of* **cobalt** Co
co. [koʊ] 1.*abbr of* **company** C. 2.GEO *abbr of* **county** contea *f*
c/o *abbr of* **care of** c/o
coach [koʊtʃ] I.<-es> *n* 1.(*private bus*) pull-

man *m inv* 2.(*horse-drawn carriage*) carrozza *f*, diligenza *f* 3.(*railway car*) carrozza *f* 4.(*teacher*) insegnante *mf* privato; SPORTS allenatore, -trice *m, f* II. *vt* to ~ sb (in sth) insegnare (qc) a qu; SPORTS allenare qu (a qc) III. *vi* dare lezioni private
coaching *n* lezioni *f pl* private
coaching staff *n* + *sing/pl vb* personale *m* docente
coagulate [koʊ·'æg·jə·leɪt] I. *vi* (*blood*) coagularsi; (*sauce*) rapprendersi II. *vt* (*blood*) coagulare; (*sauce*) far rapprendere
coagulation [koʊ·ˌæg·jə·'leɪ·ʃən] *n* coagulazione *f*
coal [koʊl] *n* carbone *m;* piece of ~ pezzo *f* di carbone
coal bed *n* strato *m* di carbone
coal black *adj* nero, -a come il carbone
coalesce [koʊ·ə·'les] *vi form* (*to merge*) fondersi; (*to unite in coalition*) coalizzarsi
coalescence [koʊ·ə·'le·snts] *n form* (*merger*) fusione *f;* (*coalition*) coalizione *f*
coalfield *n* giacimento *m* di carbone
coal-fired *adj* a carbone
coalition [ˌkoʊ·ə·'lɪ·ʃən] *n* coalizione *f*
coal mine *n* miniera *f* di carbone
coal miner *n* minatore *m*
coal mining *n* estrazione *f* carbonifera
coal tar *n* catrame *m* di carbone
coarse [kɔrs] <-r, -st> *adj* 1.(*rough*) grezzo, -a; (*sand*) grosso, -a; (*skin*) ruvido, -a 2.(*vulgar*) grossolano, -a
coarsely *adv* grossolanamente
coarsen ['kɔr·sn] I. *vt* irruvidire II. *vi* irruvidirsi
coarseness ['kɔrs·nɪs] *n* 1.(*roughness*) ruvidità *f* 2.(*rudeness*) grossolanità *f*
coast [koʊst] I. *n* costa *f* ▶ the ~ is clear *inf* la via è libera II. *vi* (*car*) procedere in folle
coastal ['koʊs·tl] *adj* costiero, -a
coaster ['koʊs·tə˞] *n* 1.(*for glasses*) sottobicchiere *m* 2. *inf* (*roller coaster*) montagne *f pl* russe
coast guard ['koʊst·gɑːrd] *n*, **Coast Guard** ['koʊst·gɑːrd] *n* guardacoste *m inv*
coastline *n* litorale *m*
coast-to-coast *adj* da costa a costa
coat [koʊt] I. *n* 1.(*overcoat*) cappotto *m;* (*jacket*) giaccone *m*, giacca *f* 2.(*animal's skin*) manto *m*, pelo *m* 3.(*layer*) strato *m;* (*of paint*) mano *f* ▶ to cut one's ~ according to one's cloth vivere secondo i propri mezzi II. *vt* to ~ sth in sth ricoprire qc di qc
coated ['koʊ·t̮ɪd] *adj* ricoperto, -a
coat hanger *n* gruccia *f*
coat hook *n* attaccapanni *m inv*
coati [kəʊ·'ɑ·ti] *n* coati *m*
coating ['koʊ·t̮ɪŋ] *n s.* coat
coat of arms <coats of arms> *n* stemma *m*
coattails *npl* falde *fpl* (*di un frac, ecc.*) ▶ to ride on sb's ~ fare strada grazie a qu
coauthor [koʊ·'ɑː·θə˞] I. *n* coautore, -trice *m, f* II. *vt* scrivere a quattro mani

coax [koʊks] *vt* persuadere; **to ~ sth out of sb** riuscire ad ottenere qc da qu

coaxing I. *n* persuasione *f* **II.** *adj* persuasivo, -a

coaxingly *adv* in modo persuasivo

cobalt ['koʊ·bɔːlt] *n* cobalto *m*

cobalt blue *n* blu *m* cobalto *inv*

cobble[1] ['kɑː·bl] **I.** *n* ciottolo *m* (*per pavimentazione*) **II.** *vt* acciottolare

cobble[2] ['kɑː·bl] *vt* (*repair*) riparare
  ◆**cobble together** *vt* improvvisare

cobbled *adj* **~ streets** strade*f pl* acciottolate

cobbler ['kɑː·b·lə] *n* calzolaio *m*

cobblestone ['kɑː·bl·stoʊn] *n* acciottolato *m*

cobnut ['kɑː·b·nʌt] *n* nocciola *f*

Cobol *n*, **COBOL** ['koʊ·bɔːl] *n* COMPUT *abbr of* **common business-oriented language** COBOL *m*

cobra ['koʊ·brə] *n* cobra *m inv*

cobweb ['kɑː·b·web] *n* ragnatela *f*

coca ['koʊ·kə] *n* coca *f*

Coca-Cola® [ˌkoʊ·kə·'koʊ·lə] *n* Coca-Cola® *f*

cocaine [koʊ·'keɪn] *n* cocaina *f*

coccyx ['kɑː·k·sɪks] <-es *o* coccyges> *n* coccige *m*

cochineal ['kɑː·tʃə·niːl] *n* cocciniglia *f*

cochlea ['kɑː·k·li·ə] <-e *o* -s> *n* coclea *f*

cock [kɑːk] **I.** *n* **1.**(*male chicken*) gallo *m* **2.** *vulg* (*penis*) uccello *m* **II.** *vt* **1.**(*turn*) piegare **2.**(*ready gun*) armare **III.** *adj* (*in ornitology*) maschio

cockade [kɑː·'keɪd] *n* coccarda *f*

cock-a-doodle-doo [ˌkɑː·kə·ˌduː·dl·'duː] *n* *childspeak* chicchirichì *m inv*

cock-a-leekie *n* zuppa *f* di pollo e porri

cock-and-bull story <-es> *n* panzana *f*

cockatoo ['kɑː·kə·'tuː] <-(s)> *n* cacatua *m inv*

cockchafer ['kɑː·k·tʃeɪ·fə] *n* maggiolino *m*

cockcrow ['kɑː·k·kroʊ] *n* canto *m* del gallo; **at ~** al canto del gallo

cocked *adj* **~ hat** tricorno *m*

cocker ['kɑː·kə] *n*, **cocker spaniel** *n* cocker *m inv*

cockerel ['kɑː·kə·əl] *n* galletto *m*

cockeyed ['kɑː·k·aɪd] *adj* **1.** *inf* (*not straight*) storto, -a **2.**(*ridiculous*) assurdo, -a

cockfight *n* combattimento *m* di galli

cockiness ['kɒ·kɪ·nɪs] *n* sfacciataggine *f*

cockle ['kɑː·kl] *n* cardio *m*

cockpit ['kɑː·k·pɪt] *n* (*pilot's area*) cabina *f* di pilotaggio; (*of car*) abitacolo *m*; (*of boat*) pozzetto *m*

cockroach ['kɑː·k·roʊtʃ] <-es> *n* scarafaggio *m*

cockscomb ['kɑː·ks·koʊm] *n* cresta *f* di gallo

cocksure [ˌkɑː·k·'ʃʊr] *adj inf* sfacciato, -a

cocktail ['kɑː·k·teɪl] *n* cocktail *m inv*

cocktail dress <-es> *n* abito *m* da cocktail

cocktail lounge *n* bar *m inv* (*di un hotel*)

cocky ['kɑː·ki] <-ier, -iest> *adj inf* sfacciato, -a

cocoa ['koʊ·koʊ] *n* **1.**(*chocolate powder*) cacao *m* **2.**(*hot drink*) cioccolata *f* calda

cocoa butter *n* burro *m* di cacao

coconut ['koʊ·kə·nʌt] *n* cocco *m*, noce *f* di cocco

coconut butter *n* burro *m* di cocco

coconut matting *n* stuoia *f* di (fibra di) cocco

coconut milk *n* latte *m* di cocco

coconut oil *n* olio *m* di cocco

coconut palm *n* palma *f* di cocco

cocoon [kə·'kuːn] **I.** *n* bozzolo *m* **II.** *vt a. fig* proteggere

cod [kɑːd] *n inv* merluzzo *m*

COD [ˌsi·oʊ·'diː] *abbr of* **cash on delivery** pagamento *m* alla consegna

coda ['koʊ·də] *n* MUS coda *f*

coddle ['kɑː·dl] *vt* **1.**(*cook gently*) cuocere a fuoco lento **2.**(*treat tenderly*) vezzeggiare

code [koʊd] **I.** *n* codice *m* **II.** *vt* cifrare

coded *adj* cifrato, -a

codeine [koʊ·di·n] *n* codeina *f*

code name *n* nome *m* in codice

code-named *adj* **the mission is ~ 'David'** il nome in codice della missione è 'David'

code number *n* prefisso *m*

code of conduct *n* codice *m* etico

codetermination [ˌkoʊ·dɪ·tɜːr·mɪ·'neɪ·ʃən] *n* codeterminazione *f*

code word *n* parola *f* in codice

codex ['koʊ·deks] <codices> *n* codice *m*

codger ['kɒ·dʒəʳ] *n iron* (vecchio) pazzo *m*

codices ['koʊ·də·siːz] *n pl of* **codex**

codicil ['kɒʊ·dɪ·sɪl] *n* codicillo *m*

codify ['kɑː·ʊ·dɪ·faɪ] <-ie-> *vt* codificare

codling ['kɑː·d·lɪŋ] *n* merluzzetto *m*

codling moth *n* carpocapsa *f*

cod-liver oil *n* olio *m* di fegato di merluzzo

codpiece ['kɑː·d·piːs] *n* brachetta *f*

coed ['koʊ·ed] **I.** *adj inf* misto, -a **II.** *n inf* studentessa *f* (*di un college misto*)

coeducation [ˌkoʊ·ed·ʒʊ·'keɪ·ʃən] *n* istruzione *f* mista

coeducational [ˌkoʊ·ed·ʒə·'keɪ·ʃə·nəl] *adj* misto, -a

coefficient [ˌkoʊ·ɪ·'fɪ·ʃnt] *n* coefficiente *m*

coequal [ˌkoʊ·'iː·kwl] **I.** *n form* uguale *mf* **II.** *adj form* uguale

coerce [koʊ·'ɜːrs] *vt form* costringere

coercion [koʊ·'ɜːr·ʒən] *n* coercizione *f*

coercive [koʊ·'ɜːr·sɪv] *adj* coatto, -a

coeval [koʊ·'iː·vl] *form* **I.** *n* contemporaneo, -a *m, f* **II.** *adj* contemporaneo, -a

coexist [ˌkoʊ·ɪg·'zɪst] *vi* coesitire

coexistence [ˌkoʊ·ɪg·'zɪs·təns] *n* coesistenza *f*

coexistent [ˌkoʊ·ɪg·'zɪs·tənt] *adj* coesistente

coffee ['kɑː·fi] *n* caffè *m inv*

coffee bar *n* bar *m inv*, caffè *m inv*

coffee bean *n* chicco *m* di caffè

coffee break *n* pausa *f* caffè

coffeecake *n* sorta di pan di spagna con noci e frutta secca

coffee-colored *adj* color caffè

coffee cup *n* tazzina *f* da caffè

coffee grinder *n* macinacaffè *m inv*

coffee grounds *n pl* fondi *m pl* di caffè

coffeehouse *n* caffè *m inv*

coffee klatch <-es> *n* incontro tra amici per un caffè e quattro chiacchiere

coffee machine n 1. (in bar, kitchen) macchina f del caffè 2. (vending machine) distributore m del caffè
coffee mill n macinacaffè m inv
coffeepot n caffettiera f
coffee shop n 1. (café) bar m inv, caffè m inv 2. (shop) negozio m di caffè
coffee table n tavolino m basso
coffee-table book n grande libro m illustrato
coffer ['kɑ·fə] n 1. (storage place) cassa f 2. pl (money reserves) casse fpl
coffin ['kɔ·fɪn] n bara f
cog [kɑg] n TECH dente m; (wheel) ruota f dentata; **to be a ~ in a machine** essere un pezzo dell'ingranaggio
cogency ['koʊ·dʒən·tsi] n form forza f
cogent ['koʊ·dʒənt] adj form convincente
cogently adv form in modo convincente
cogitate ['kɑ·dʒə·teɪt] vi riflettere
cogitation [ˌkɑ·dʒə·'teɪ·ʃən] n riflessione f
cognac ['koʊn·jæk] n cognac m
cognate ['kɑg·neɪt] adj affine
cognition [kɑg·'nɪ·ʃən] n form cognizione f
cognitive ['kɑg·nə·tɪv] adj cognitivo, -a
cognitive psychology n psicologia f cognitiva
cognitive therapy <-ies> n terapia f cognitiva
cognizance ['kɑg·nə·znts] n LAW competenza f; **to take ~ of sth** prendere atto di qc
cognizant ['kɑg·nə·znt] adj **to be ~ of sth** essere al corrente di qc; LAW competente
cognomen [kɑg·'noʊ·mən] n 1. (nickname) soprannome m 2. HIST cognome m
cognoscenti [ˌkɑg·nə·'ʃen·ti] npl esperti mpl
cogwheel ['kɑg·wiːl] n ruota f dentata
cohabit [koʊ·'hæ·bɪt] vi coabitare
cohabitant [koʊ·'hæ·bɪ·tænt] n coinquilino m
cohabitation [koʊ·ˌhæ·bɪ·'teɪ·ʃən] n coabitazione f
cohabitee [ˌkoʊ·hæ·bɪ·'tiː] n form s. **cohabitant**
cohere [koʊ·'hɪr] vi essere coerente
coherence [koʊ·'hɪ·rəns] n coerenza f
coherent [koʊ·'hɪ·rənt] adj coerente
coherently adv coerentemente
cohesion [koʊ·'hiː·ʒən] n coesione f
cohesive [koʊ·'hiː·sɪv] adj coesivo, -a
cohesiveness n coesione f
cohort ['koʊ·hɔːrt] n coorte f
coil [kɔɪl] I. n 1. (spiral) rotolo m 2. ELEC bobina f 3. MED spirale f (intrauterina) II. vi arrotolarsi III. vt arrotolare
coiled adj arrotolato, -a
coin [kɔɪn] I. n moneta f; **to toss a ~** fare testa o croce II. vt coniare ▸ **to ~ a phrase** ... come si suol dire ...
coinage ['kɔɪ·nɪdʒ] n 1. (system) sistema m monetario 2. (act) coniazione f
coincide [ˌkoʊ·ɪn·'saɪd] vi coincidere; (agree) trovarsi d'accordo
coincidence [koʊ·'ɪn·sɪ·dəns] n coincidenza f
coincident [koʊ·'ɪn·sɪ·dənt] adj coincidente
coincidental [koʊ·ˌɪn·sɪ·'den·təl] adj coincidente

coincidentally adv per pura coincidenza
coitus ['koʊ·ə·təs] n form coito m
coitus interruptus n coito m interrotto
coke [koʊk] n 1. (fuel) coke m 2. inf coca f
Coke® [koʊk] n Coca-Cola® f
col. [kɑːl] n abbr of **column** col.
Col. n abbr of **colonel** Col.
cola ['koʊ·lə] n Coca-Cola® f
colander ['kʌ·lən·də] n scolapasta m inv
cold [koʊld] I. adj freddo, -a; **to be ~** (person) avere freddo; **to go ~** (soup, coffee) raffreddarsi; **to get ~** (person) infreddolirsi; **it's bitterly ~** fa un freddo cane ▸ **to leave sb** non fare né caldo né freddo a qu II. n 1. METEO **the ~** il freddo m 2. MED raffreddore m; **to catch a ~** prendere il raffreddore; **to have a ~** avere il raffreddore ▸ **to leave sb out in the ~** lasciare qu in disparte
cold-blooded adj (animal) a sangue freddo; (person) crudele
cold call n stile di vendita consistente nel telefonare o far visita al potenziale cliente senza preavviso
cold comfort n magra consolazione f
cold cream n cold cream f
cold cuts npl carni f pl arrosto a fette
cold feet n pl, sl paura f
cold frame n cassone m
cold front n fronte m freddo
cold-hearted adj insensibile
coldish ['koʊl·dɪʃ] adj freddino, -a
coldness ['koʊld·nɪs] n freddezza f
cold snap n ondata f di freddo
cold sore n MED febbre f sorda
cold start n AUTO, COMPUT partenza m a freddo
cold storage n conservazione f in cella frigorifera
cold store n cella f frigorifera
cold sweat n sudore m freddo
cold truth n **the ~** la cruda verità
cold turkey I. n inf crisi f d'astinenza II. adv **to quit smoking ~** smettere di fumare di brutto
cold war n guerra f fredda
cold wave n ondata f di freddo
coleslaw ['koʊl·slɑː] n insalata f a base di cavolo e maionese
colic ['kɑː·lɪk] n colica f
collaborate [kə·'læ·bə·reɪt] vi collaborare
collaboration [kə·ˌlæ·bə·'reɪ·ʃən] n collaborazione f
collaborationist [kə·ˌlæ·bə·'reɪʃ·nɪst] adj collaborazionista mf
collaborative [kə·'læ·bə·rə·tɪv] adj in collaborazione; (effort) comune
collaborator [kə·'læ·bə·reɪ·tə] n 1. collaboratore, -trice m, f 2. pej collaborazionista mf
collage ['kə·lɑːʒ] n collage m inv
collagen ['kɑː·lə·dʒən] n collagene m
collagen implant n, **collagen injection** n iniezione f di collagene
collapse [kə·'læps] I. vi 1. MED collassare 2. (fall down: building) crollare; (person) svenire 3. (fail) fallire II. n 1. MED colasso m 2. (act

of falling down) crollo *m;* (*of people*) svenimento *m* **3.** (*failure*) fallimento *m*

collapsible [kə·'læp·sɪ·bl] *adj* pieghevole

collar ['kɑː·lə·] I. *n* **1.** FASHION collo *m* **2.** (*of a
dog, cat*) collare *m* ▶ **to get** (**all**) **hot under
the ~** (*angry*) accaldarsi II. *vt inf* acciuffare

collarbone *n* clavicola *f*

collate [kə·'leɪt] *vt* **1.** (*arrange in order*) ordinare **2.** (*analyze*) mettere a confronto

collateral [kə·'læ·ṭə·rəl] I. *n* FIN garanzia *f* collaterale II. *adj* collaterale

collateral damage *n* danni *m pl* collaterali

collateral loan *n* FIN prestito *m* garantito

collaterally [kə·'læ·ṭə·rə·li] *adv* collateral-
mente

colleague ['kɑː·liːg] *n* collega *mf*

collect¹ [kə·'lekt] I. *vt* **1.** (*gather*) raccogliere;
(*stamps*) collezionare **2.** *form* (*regain control*)
to ~ oneself ricomporsi; **to ~ one's thoughts**
riordinare le proprie idee II. *vi* **1.** (*gather*) raccogliersi **2.** (*money: contributions*) fare una
colletta; (*money: payments due*) riscuotere
III. *adj* TEL (*call*) a carico del destinatario
IV. *adv* TEL (*call*) a carico del destinatario

collect² [kə·'lekt] *n* REL colletta *f*

collectable [kə·'lek·tə·bl] I. *adj* da collezione
II. *n* articolo *m* da collezione

collect call *n* telefonata *f* a carico del destinatario; **to place** [*o* **make**] **a ~** fare una telefonata
a carico del destinatario

collected [kə·'lek·tɪd] *adj* composto, -a

collectible [kə·'lek·tə·bl] I. *adj* da collezione
II. *n* articolo *m* da collezione

collection [kə·'lek·ʃən] *n* **1.** (*money gathered*)
REL colletta *f* **2.** (*objects collected, large
number*) collezione *f* **3.** (*act of getting*) raccolta *f*

collective [kə·'lek·tɪv] I. *adj* collettivo, -a II. *n*
collettivo *m*

collective bargaining *n* contrattazione *f*
collettiva

collective farm *n* fattoria *f* collettiva

collectively *adv* collettivamente

collective noun *n* nome *m* collettivo

collectivism [kə·'lek·tə·vɪ·zm] *n* collettiv-
ismo *m*

collector [kə·'lek·tə·] *n* **1.** (*one who gathers
objects*) collezionista *mf* **2.** (*one who collects
payments*) esattore *m*

collector's item *n,* **collector's piece** *n*
pezzo *m* da collezione

college ['kɑː·lɪdʒ] *n* **1.** (*school*) istituto *m*
superiore **2.** (*university*) università *f inv*

college graduate *n* diplomato, -a *m, f,* laureato, -a *m, f*

collegiate [kə·'liː·dʒɪt] *adj* universitario, -a

collide [kə·'laɪd] *vi* scontrarsi

collie ['kɑː·li] *n* collie *m inv*

collier ['kɑːl·jə·] *n form* **1.** MIN minatore *m* (in
miniera di carbone) **2.** (*ship*) carboniera *f*

colliery ['kɑːl·jə·i] <-ies> *n* miniera *f* di carbone

collision [kə·'lɪ·ʒən] *n* collisione *f*

collocate ['kɑː·ləʊ·keɪt] I. *vi* LING **to ~ with
sth** essere usato come collocatore di qc II. *n*
LING collocatore *m*

collocation [ˌkɑː·lə·'keɪ·ʃən] *n* collocazione *f*

colloquial [kə·'loʊ·kwi·əl] *adj* colloquiale

colloquialism *n* espressione *f* colloquiale

colloquy ['kɑː·lə·kwi] *n* coloquio *m*

collude [kə·'luːd] *vi form* colludere

collusion [kə·'luː·ʒən] *n form* collusione *f*

collusive [kə·'luː·sɪv] *adj form* collusivo, -a

cologne [kə·'loʊn] *n* (*perfume*) colonia *f*

Colombia [kə·'lʌm·biə] *n* Colombia *f*

Colombian [kə·'lʌm·bi·ən] I. *adj* colombiano,
-a II. *n* colombiano, -a *m, f*

colon ['koʊ·lən] *n* **1.** ANAT colon *m* **2.** LING due
punti *mpl*

colon cancer *n* cancro *m* del colon

colonel ['kɜːr·nl] *n* colonnello *m*

colonial [kə·'loʊ·ni·əl] I. *adj* coloniale II. *n*
coloniale *mf*

colonialism [kə·'loʊ·ni·ə·lɪ·zəm] *n* colonialismo *m*

colonialist I. *n* colonialista *mf* II. *adj* colonialista

colonial mentality *n* mentalità *f* coloniale

colonist ['kɑː·lə·nɪst] *n* **1.** (*foreigner*) colonizzatore, -trice *m, f,* **2.** (*former inhabitant*) colono, -a *m, f*

colonization [ˌkɑː·lə·nɪ·'zeɪ·ʃən] *n* colonizzazione *f*

colonize ['kɑː·lə·naɪz] *vt* colonizzare

colonizer ['kɑː·lə·naɪ·zə·] *n* colonizzatore,
-trice *m, f*

colony ['kɑː·lə·ni] <-ies> *n a.* ZOOL colonia *f*

color ['kʌ·lə·] I. *n* **1.** colore *m;* **primary ~**
colore primario; **what ~ is your dress?** di che
colore è il tuo vestito?; **to have ~ in one's
cheeks** avere le guance colorite **2.** *pl* POL, MIL
(*official flag*) bandiera *f* **3.** (*character*) **to
show one's true ~s** mostrare il proprio vero
volto II. *vt* **1.** (*change color of*) colorare; **to ~ a
room blue** dipingere una stanza d'azzurro
2. (*dye*) colorare, tingere **3.** (*distort*) alterare
III. *vi* arrossire

Colorado beetle [ˌkɑː·lə·'ræ·doʊ·'biː·ṭl] *n,*
Colorado potato beetle *n* dorifora *f*

coloration [ˌkʌ·lə·'reɪ·ʃən] *n* colore *m*

colorblind *adj* daltonico, -a

colorblindness *n* daltonismo *m*

colored *adj* colorato, -a; (*picture*) a colori;
(*people*) di colore

colorfast ['kʌ·lə··fæst] *adj* che non stinge

color filter *n* PHOT filtro *m* colorato

colorful ['kʌ·lə·fəl] *adj* vivace

coloring ['kʌ·lə·rɪŋ] *n* **1.** (*complexion*)
colorito *m* **2.** (*chemical*) colorante *m*

colorless ['kʌ·lə·lɪs] *adj* **1.** (*having no color*)
incolore **2.** (*bland*) scialbo, -a

color line *n* barriera *f* razziale

color scheme *n* accostamento *m* cromatico

color slide *n* diapositiva *f* a colori

color television *n* televisione *f* a colori

colossal [kə·'lɑː·sl] *adj* colossale

C

colossus [kə·'lɒ·səs] *n* <-es *o* colossi> colosso *m*

cols *n abbr of* **columns** colonne *fpl*

colt [koʊlt] *n* puledro *m*

Columbia [kə·'lʌm·biə] *n* **the District of** ~ il Distretto di Columbia

Columbus Day [kə·'lʌm·bəs·ˌdeɪ] *n* anniversario *m* della scoperta dell'America

column ['kɑː·ləm] *n a.* ARCHIT, ANAT, TYPO colonna *f;* **spinal** ~ colonna vertebrale

columnist ['kɑː·ləm·nɪst] *n* autore , -trice di rubrica *m*

coma ['koʊ·mə] *n* coma *m;* **to go into a** ~ entrare in coma; **to wake up out of one's** ~ uscire dal coma

comatose ['koʊ·mə·toʊs] *adj* comatoso, -a; ~ **state** stato *m* di coma

comb [koʊm] I. *n* 1. (*hair device*) pettine *m* 2. ZOOL cresta *f* II. *vt* 1. (*tidy with a comb*) **to** ~ **one's hair** pettinarsi (i capelli) 2. (*search thoroughly*) **to** ~ **an apartment for clues** perquisire l'appartamento in cerca di prove

◆**comb out** *vt* (*a knot, tangles*) sciogliere

combat ['kɑː·m·bæt] I. *n* 1. (*wartime fighting*) combattimento *m;* **hand-to-hand** ~ combattimento corpo a corpo 2. (*battle*) lotta *f* II. *vt* combattere

combat aircraft *n* aereo *m* da combattimento

combatant [kəm·'bæ·tənt] *n* combattente *mf*

combative [kəm·'bæ·t̬ɪv] *adj* combattivo, -a

combination [ˌkɑː·m·bə·'neɪ·ʃən] *n* combinazione *f;* **in** ~ (*together*) in associazione

combine [kəm·'baɪn] I. *vt* combinare; **to** ~ **forces against sb/sth** unire le forze contro qu/qc II. *vi* associarsi

combined [kəm·'baɪnd] *adj* combinato, -a; (*efforts*) congiunto, -a

combine harvester *n* mietitrebbia *f*

combustible [kəm·'bʌs·tə·bl] *adj form* 1. (*highly flammable*) combustibile 2. (*easily angry*) irascibile

combustion [kəm·'bʌs·tʃən] *n* combustione *f*

combustion chamber *n* camera *f* di combustione

come [kʌm] <came, come, coming> *vi* 1. (*move towards*) venire; **to** ~ **towards sb** venire verso qu; **are you coming to the game with us?** vieni alla partita con noi?; **January** ~s **before February** gennaio viene prima di febbraio; **the year to** ~ l'anno prossimo; **to** ~ **to an agreement/a decision** raggiungere un accordo/una decisione; **to** ~ **home** tornare a casa; **to** ~ **to sb's rescue** venire in aiuto di qu; **to** ~ **first/second/third** arrivare primo/secondo/terzo 2. (*happen*) succedere; **to** ~ **to pass** succedere; ~ **what may** qualunque cosa capiti; **how** ~? *inf* come mai?; **nothing came of it** finì tutto lì 3. (*become*) diventare; **my dream has** ~ **true** il mio sogno si è avverato; **I like it as it** ~s mi piace così com'è; **to** ~ **open** aprirsi ► ~ **again?** *inf* come?; **to** ~ **clean** (**about sth**) dire la verità (riguardo a qc); **good things** ~ **to those**

who wait *prov* diamo tempo al tempo *prov;* **to have it coming** meritarselo

◆**come about** *vi* succedere

◆**come across** I. *vt insep* incappare in II. *vi* 1. (*be evident*) emergere 2. (*create an impression*) dare l'impressione

◆**come along** *vi* 1. (*hurry*) sbrigarsi 2. (*go too*) **do you want to** ~? vuoi venire anche tu? 3. (*progressing*) procedere

◆**come apart** *vi* staccarsi

◆**come around** *vi* 1. (*change one's mind*) cambiare idea; **to** ~ **to sb's point of view** finire per condividere il punto di vista di qu 2. MED riprendere coscienza 3. (*visit sb's home*) passare

◆**come at** *vt insep* aggredire

◆**come away** *vi* venire via

◆**come back** *vi* 1. ritornare 2. (*be remembered*) tornare alla mente 3. SPORTS contrattaccare

◆**come by** I. *vt insep* trovare II. *vi* passare

◆**come down** *vi* 1. (*move down*) scendere 2. (*drop: roof*) venir giù 3. (*land*) atterrare 4. (*fall: rain, snow*) cadere 5. (*become less: prices, cost, inflation*) calare

◆**come forward** *vi* farsi avanti; **to** ~ **to do sth** offrirsi di fare qc

◆**come from** *vt* essere di; **where do you** ~? di dove sei?; **to** ~ **a good family** essere di buona famiglia

◆**come in** *vi* 1. (*enter*) entrare 2. (*arrive*) arrivare 3. (*become fashionable*) diventare di moda 4. (*be useful*) servire 5. (*be*) risultare 6. (*participate in*) prender parte a 7. (*be positioned*) **to** ~ **first** piazzarsi al primo posto

◆**come into** *vt insep* 1. (*enter*) entrare in; (*power*) andare al; **to** ~ **office** entrare in carica; **to** ~ **fashion** diventare di moda; **to** ~ **sb's life** entrare nella vita di qu 2. (*inherit*) ereditare

◆**come off** I. *vi* 1. *inf* (*succeed*) funzionare 2. (*end up*) uscirne 3. (*become detached*) venir via 4. (*fall*) cadere II. *vt insep* (*complete*) uscire da; **to** ~ **an injury** MED riprendersi da una lesione ► ~ **it!** *inf* finiscila!

◆**come on** *vi* 1. (*improve*) fare progressi 2. THEAT, CINE (*actor, performer*) entrare in scena 3. (*begin: film, program*) iniziare; **what time does the news** ~? a che ora inizia il telegiornale? 4. (*start gradually*) **I've got a headache coming on** mi sta venendo il mal di testa II. *vt insep* incontrare III. *interj* (*hurry*) sbrigati!; (*encouragement, annoyance*) dai!

◆**come on to** *vt sl* **to** ~ **sb** fare delle avance a qu

◆**come out** *vi* 1. (*express opinion*) **to** ~ **in favor of/against sth** dichiararsi a favore di/contro qc 2. (*end up*) **how did your painting** ~? com'è venuto il tuo quadro? 3. + *n* **to** ~ **a mess** (*person*) uscirne a pezzi 4. + *adj* **to** ~ **wrong/right** venire fuori male/bene 5. (*go out socially*) entrare in società 6. (*become known*) venire fuori; **to** ~ **that ...** è emerso che

... **7.** (*reveal one's homosexuality*) dichiararsi omosessuale **8.** (*be removed*) venire via **9.** (*become available: stamp, book, magazine*) uscire **10.** (*appear in sky: moon, stars, sun*) spuntare **11.** (*open: flowers*) sbocciare

◆**come over** I. *vi* **1.** (*come nearer*) avvicinarsi **2.** (*visit sb's home*) passare **3.** (*feel*) sentirsi II. *vt* **I don't know what came over me!** non so cosa mi è preso!

◆**come through** I. *vi* **1.** (*show: one's nervousness, excitement, charm*) trasparire **2.** (*arrive: results, visa, call*) arrivare **3.** (*survive*) sopravvivere II. *vt insep* superare

◆**come to** I. *vt insep* **1.** (*reach*) arrivare a; **to ~ rest** fermarsi; **to ~ nothing** non approdare a nulla **2.** (*amount to*) ammontare a II. *vi* MED rinvenire

◆**come under** *vt* **1.** (*be listed under*) comparire nella categoria **2.** (*be dealt with*) essere competenza di **3.** (*be subjected to*) **to ~ criticism** essere oggetto di critiche

◆**come up** *vi* **1.** (*be mentioned*) venire fuori **2.** (*happen*) capitare **3.** (*arrive: a holiday*) avvicinarsi

◆**come upon** *vt* imbattersi in

comeback ['kʌm·bæk] *n* **1.** ritorno *m* **2.** (*retort*) replica *f*

comedian [kə'mi:·di·ən] *n* **1.** (*person telling jokes*) comico, -a *m, f* **2.** (*funny person*) tipo *m* divertente

comedienne [kə·ˌmi:·di·'ən] *n* **1.** (*female comedian*) comica *f* **2.** (*funny female*) tipo *m* divertente

comedown ['kʌm·daʊn] *n inf* passo *m* indietro

comedy ['ka:·mə·di] <-ies> *n* **1.** CINE, THEAT, LIT commedia *f* **2.** (*funny situation*) comicità *f*

comeliness ['kʌm·lɪ·nɪs] *n* avvenenza *f*

comely ['kʌm·li] <-ier, -iest> *adj* (*woman*) avvenente

come-on ['kʌm·a:n] *n inf* **1.** (*expression of sexual interest*) invito *m* **2.** (*enticement*) slogan *m inv*

comet ['ka:·mɪt] *n* cometa *f*

comeuppance [kʌm·'ʌ·pənts] *n* **he got his ~ in the end** alla fine ha avuto quello che si meritava

comfort ['kʌm·fət] I. *n* **1.** comfort *m inv*, comodità *f inv*; **the ~ s of life** le comodità della vita **2.** (*consolation*) conforto *m;* **to be a ~ to sb** essere di conforto a qu II. *vt* confortare

comfortable ['kʌm·fə·tə·bl] *adj* **1.** (*offering comfort*) comodo, -a; **to make oneself ~** mettersi comodo **2.** (*financially stable*) agiato, -a *f* **3.** SPORTS (*substantial*) sicuro, -a

comfortably ['kʌm·fə·təb·li] *adv* **1.** (*in a comfortable manner: sit, lie*) comodamente **2.** (*easily*) facilmente **3.** (*in financially stable manner*) **to live ~** vivere agiatamente

comforter ['kʌm·fə·tə] *n* (*duvet*) piumone *m*

comforting ['kʌm·fə·tɪŋ] *adj* (*thought, words*) confortante

comfortless ['kʌm·fət·lɪs] *adj form* scomodo, -a

comfy ['kʌm·fi] <-ier, -iest> *adj inf* (*furniture, clothes*) comodo, -a

comic ['ka:·mɪk] I. *n* **1.** (*cartoon magazine*) fumetti *mpl* **2.** (*person*) comico, -a *m, f* II. *adj* comico, -a; **~ play** commedia *f* brillante

comical ['ka:·mɪ·kl] *adj* comico, -a; (*idea*) divertente

comic book *n* (*comic*) fumetti *mpl*

comic strip *n* fumetti *mpl*

coming ['kʌ·mɪŋ] I. *adj* prossimo, -a; **the ~ year** l'anno prossimo II. *n* venuta *f;* **~ s and goings** viavai *m*

comma ['ka:·mə] *n* virgola *f*

command [kə·'mænd] I. *vt* **1.** (*order*) **to ~ sb to do sth** ordinare a qu di fare qc; **to ~ that** ordinare che +*subj* **2.** (*have command over*) comandare **3.** (*have at one's disposal*) disporre di **4.** (*overlook: view*) avere **5.** (*respect, sympathy*) suscitare II. *n* **1.** (*order*) ordine *m*, comando *m;* **to obey a ~** eseguire un ordine; **under sb's ~** agli ordini di qu **2.** (*control*) MIL, COMPUT comando *m;* **to be in ~ of sth** essere al comando di qc; **to take ~ of** assumere il comando di; **to have ~ over a fleet** essere al comando di una flotta; **at sb's ~** ai comandi di qu **3.** (*knowledge*) padronanza *f*

commandant ['ka:·mən·dænt] *n* MIL comandante *m*

commandeer [ˌka:·mən·'dɪr] *vt* requisire

commander [kə·'mæn·də] *n* **1.** MIL (*officer in charge*) comandante *m* **2.** MIL, NAUT (*naval officer*) capitano *m* di fregata

commanding [kə·'mæn·dɪŋ] *adj* **1.** (*authoritative*) autoritario, -a **2.** (*dominant: position*) dominante

command key *n* COMPUT tasto *m* di comando

commandment [kə·'mænd·mənt] *n liter* ordine *m*

Commandment [kə·'mænd·mənt] *n* **the Ten ~ s** REL i dieci Comandamenti

command module *n* AVIAT modulo *m* di comando

commando [kə·'mæn·doʊ] <-s *o* -es> *n* MIL **1.** (*group of soldiers*) commando *m inv* **2.** (*member of commando*) membro *m* di un commando

command post *n* MIL posto *m* di comando

command prompt *n* COMPUT prompt *m inv* di comando

commemorate [kə·'me·mə·reɪt] *vt* commemorare

commemoration [kə·ˌme·mə·'reɪ·ʃən] *n* commemorazione *f; in ~ of ...* in memoria di ...

commemorative [kə·'me·mə·rə·tɪv] *adj* commemorativo, -a

commence [kə·'ments] *vi form* iniziare; **to ~ speaking** iniziare a parlare

commencement [kə·'ments·mənt] *n form* **1.** (*beginning*) inizio *m* **2.** SCHOOL, UNIV cerimonia *f* di consegna del diploma

commend [kə·'mend] *vt* **1.** (*praise*) elogiare; **to ~ sth/sb (on sth)** elogiare qc/a qu (per qc) **2.** (*entrust*) affidare; **to ~ sth to sb** affidare qc

a qu **3.** (*recommend*) raccomandare
commendable [kə·'men·də·bl] *adj* encomiabile; ~ **bravery** coraggio *m* encomiabile
commendation [ˌkɑ··men·'deɪ·ʃən] *n* encomio *m*
commendatory [kə·'men·də·tɔ:·ri] *adj* encomiabile
commensurable [kə·'men·sə·ə·bl] *adj* commensurabile
commensurate [kə·'men·sə·ət] *adj form* proporzionato, -a
comment ['kɑ:·ment] I. *n* commento *m,* osservazione *f;* **no** ~ no comment; **to make a** ~ fare un'osservazione II. *vi* commentare; **to** ~ **that** ... osservare che ...
commentary ['kɑ:·mən·te·ri] <-ies> *n* cronaca *f;* **color** ~ reportage *m inv* a colori; **literary** ~ commento *f* letterario
commentate ['kɑ:·mən·teɪt] *vi* TV, RADIO **to** ~ **on sth** fare la cronaca di qc
commentator ['kɑ:·mən·teɪ·ṭə] *n* TV, RADIO commentatore, -trice *m, f,* cronista *mf*
commerce ['kɑ:·mɜːrs] *n* commercio *m*
commercial [kə·'mɜːr·ʃl] I. *adj* commerciale II. *n* RADIO, TV pubblicità *f inv*
commercialism [kə·'mɜːr·ʃə·lɪ·zəm] *n* spirito *m* commerciale
commercialization [kə·ˌmɜːr·ʃə·laɪ·'zeɪ·ʃən] *n* commercializzazione *f*
commercialize [kə·'mɜːr·ʃə·laɪz] *vt* commercializzare
commercialized *adj* commercializzato, -a
commiserate [kə·'mɪ·zə·reɪt] *vi* mostrare commiserazione
commiseration [kə·ˌmɪ·zə·'reɪ·ʃən] *n* commiserazione *f*
commission [kə·'mɪ·ʃən] I. *vt* **1.** (*order*) commissionare **2.** MIL (*appoint*) **to** ~ **sb as sth** nominare qu qc; ~**ed officer** ufficiale *m* II. *n* **1.** commissione *m;* **to be on** ~ lavorare a provvigione **2.** MIL (*appointment*) nomina *m;* **to resign one's** ~ dimettersi dall'incarico **3.** NAUT, AVIAT **out of** ~ in disarmo
commissioned officer *n* ufficiale *m*
commissioner [kə·'mɪ·ʃə·nə] *n* commissario *m*
commit [kə·'mɪt] <-tt-> *vt* **1.** (*carry out*) commettere; **to** ~ **an error** commettere un errore; **to** ~ **suicide** suicidarsi **2.** (*bind*) **to** ~ **oneself** (**to sth**) impegnarsi (in qc); **to** ~ **soldiers to the defense of a region** inviare soldati a difendere la regione **3.** (*institutionalize*) **to** ~ **sb to prison** incarcerare qu; **to** ~ **sb to a hospital** fare internare qu in ospedale **4.** (*entrust*) **to** ~ **sth to memory** memorizzare qc; **to** ~ **sth to paper** mettere qc per iscritto
commitment [kə·'mɪt·mənt] *n* impegno *m;* **to make a** ~ prendersi un impegno
committed *adj* impegnato, -a
committee [kə·'mɪ·ṭi] *n* comitato *m;* **to appoint a** ~ nominare un comitato; **to be** [*o* **sit**] **on a** ~ far parte di un comitato
commode [kə·'moʊd] *n* **1.** (*chest of drawers*)

cassettone *m* **2.** (*toilet*) comoda *f*
commodious [kə·'moʊ·di·əs] *adj* ampio, -a
commodity [kə·'mɑ:·də·ti] <-ies> *n* **1.** (*product*) merce *f;* ~ **markets** borsa *f* delle materie prime **2.** *pl* (*raw material*) materia *f* prima
commodore ['kɑ:·mə·dɔ:r] *n* commodoro *m*
common ['kɑ:·mən] I. *adj* **1.** comune; **to be** ~ **knowledge** essere risaputo; **by** ~ **assent** all'unanimità; **for the** ~ **good** per il bene di tutti **2.** (*vulgar*) grossolano, a II. *n* **1.** (*land*) parco *m* pubblico **2.** *pl* UNIV refettorio *m*
common denominator *n* denominatore *m* comune
commoner ['kɑ:·mə·nə] *n* plebeo, -a *m, f*
common ground *n* punti *m pl* in comune; **to be on** ~ **with sb** concordare con qu
common law *n* diritto *m* consuetudinario
common-law marriage *n* matrimonio *m* di fatto
common-law wife <wives> *n* convivente *f*
commonly *adv* (*often*) comunemente
commonplace ['kɑ:·mən·pleɪs] I. *adj* comune II. *n* luogo *m* comune
common room *n* sala *f* professori
common sense *n* buon senso *m;* **a** ~ **solution** una soluzione logica
common stock *n* FIN azioni *f pl* ordinarie
commonwealth ['kɑ:·mən·welθ] *n* **the** ~ il Commonwealth
commotion [kə·'moʊ·ʃən] *n* trambusto *m*
communal [kə·'mju:·nl] *adj* comune
commune ['kɑ:m·ju:n] *n* comune *f*
communicable [kə·'mju:·ni·kə·bl] *adj* **1.** (*information*) comunicabile **2.** MED trasmissibile
communicate [kə·'mju:·nɪ·keɪt] I. *vt* **1.** (*information*) comunicare **2.** MED trasmettere II. *vi* comunicare
communication [kə·ˌmju:·nɪ·'keɪ·ʃən] *n* **1.** (*process*) comunicazione *f* **2.** (*missive*) comunicazione *f* **3.** *pl* (*means*) comunicazioni *fpl*
communicative [kə·'mju:·nə·keɪ·tɪv] *adj* comunicativo, -a
communion [kə·'mju:n·jən] *n* comunione *f;* **to take** ~ fare la comunione
communiqué [kə·ˌmju:·nɪ·'keɪ] *n* comunicato *m*
communism ['kɑ:m·jə·nɪ·zəm] *n* comunismo *m*
Communist ['kɑ:m·jə·nɪst] I. *n* comunista *mf* II. *adj* comunista
community [kə·'mju:·nə·ti] <-ies> *n* **1.** (*of people*) comunità *f inv;* **the local** ~ il vicinato **2.** (*of animals, plants*) colonia *f*
community center *n* centro *m* sociale
community service *n* servizio *m* civile
commutable [kə·'mju:·ṭə·bl] *adj* convertibile
commutation [ˌkɑ:m·jə·'teɪ·ʃən] *n* commutazione *f*
commutation ticket *n* abbonamento *m*
commute [kə·'mju:t] I. *vi* fare il pendolare II. *n inf* viaggio *m* (quotidiano) per andare e tornare

dal lavoro **III.** *vt* commutare
commuter [kə·'mju:·ʈəˑ] *n* pendolare *mf*
commuter train *n* treno *m* dei pendolari
Comoran ['kɑ:·mə·rən] **I.** *adj* comoriano, -a
II. *n* comoriano, -a *m, f*
Comoros ['kɑ:·mə·roʊz] *npl* **the** ~ le Isole
Comore
compact[1] ['kɑ:m·pækt] **I.** *adj* (*small*) compatto, -a **II.** *vt* compattare **III.** *n* **1.** AUTO utilitaria *f* **2.** (*powder*) portacipria *f inv*
compact[2] ['kɑ:m·pækt] *n* (*agreement*)
patto *m*
compact disk *n* compact disc *m inv*
compact disk player *n* lettore *m* di compact
disc
compactness [kəm·'pækt·nəs] *n* compattezza *f*
companion [kəm·'pæn·jən] *n* **1.** (*person, animal*) compagno, -a *m, f;* **traveling** ~ compagno di viaggio **2.** (*guidebook*) manuale *m*
companionable [kəm·'pæn·jə·nə·bl] *adj* simpatico, -a
companionship *n* compagnia *f*
companionway [kəm·'pæn·jən·weɪ] *n* NAUT
scaletta *f*
company ['kʌm·pə·ni] <-ies> *n* **1.** (*firm, enterprise*) società *f inv;* ~ **union** sindacato *m*
aziendale **2.** (*companionship*) compagnia *f;*
you are in good ~ sei in buona compagnia; **to keep sb** ~ fare compagnia a qu; **he's been keeping bad** ~ frequenta cattive compagnie;
Margaret stayed for a week as ~ **for my mother** Margaret è rimasta una settimana a
fare compagnia a mia madre **3.** (*group*) *a.* MIL
compagnia *f*
comparable ['kɑ:m·pə·rə·bl] *adj* paragonabile; ~ **to** paragonabile a
comparative [kəm·'pe·rə·tɪv] **I.** *n* comparativo *m* **II.** *adj* comparativo, -a; ~ **literature** letteratura *f* comparata
comparatively *adv* relativamente
compare [kəm·'per] **I.** *vt* paragonare; **to** ~
sth/sb to [*o* **with**] **sth/sb** paragonare qc/qu a
qc/qu; **instant coffee can't be** ~**d with an expresso** il caffè istantaneo non è paragonabile a quello espresso; **to** ~ **notes on sth**
scambiare le proprie impressioni su qc **II.** *vi*
essere paragonabile; **to** ~ **favorably with sth**
risultare al confronto migliore di qc; **last year's weather just doesn't** ~ il tempo dell'anno
scorso non ha niente a che vedere
comparison [kəm·'pe·rɪ·sn] *n* paragone *m,*
confronto *m;* **to make a** ~ fare un paragone;
by ~ **with sb/sth** a paragone di qu/qc;
there's no ~ **between the two restaurants**
non c'è paragone tra i due ristoranti
compartment [kəm·'pɑːrt·mənt] *n* **1.** RAIL
scompartimento *m* **2.** (*section*) scomparto *m*
compass ['kʌm·pəs] <-es> *n* **1.** *a.* NAUT bussola *f* **2.** *form* (*range*) gamma *f;* (*area*)
ambito *m;* **to be beyond the** ~ **of sb's knowledge** andare al di là delle conoscenze di
qu

compassion [kəm·'pæ·ʃən] *n* compassione *f*
compassionate [kəm·'pæ·ʃə·nət] *adj* compassionevole
compatibility [kəm·ˌpæ·ʈə·'bɪ·lə·ti] *n* compatibilità *f*
compatible [kəm·'pæ·ʈə·bl] *adj* compatibile
compatriot [kəm·'peɪt·ri·ət] *n* **1.** (*countryman*) compatriota *mf* **2.** (*companion*) collega
mf
compel [kəm·'pel] <-ll-> *vt* **1.** (*force*) obbligare **2.** (*produce*) imporre
compelling *adj* convincente
compendium [kəm·'pen·di·əm] <-s *o* -dia> *n*
compendio *m*
compensate ['kɑ:m·pən·seɪt] **I.** *vt* (*make up for*) compensare; (*for loss, damage*) risarcire
II. *vi* **to** ~ **for sth** (*reward*) ricompensare
per qc
compensation [ˌkɑ:m·pen·'seɪ·ʃən] *n* ricompensa *f;* (*for loss, damage*) risarcimento *m;* **to claim** ~ chiedere il risarcimento; **in** ~ **for sth**
come ricompensa di qc
compete [kəm·'pi:t] *vi* **1.** (*strive*) competere;
to ~ **for sth** competere per qc; **the new shop will have a tough time competing with the two supermarkets** per il nuovo negozio sarà
dura fare concorrenza ai due supermercati;
turn the music down — I'm not competing with that noise abbassa la musica — non
voglio urlare per farmi sentire **2.** (*take part*)
partecipare; **to** ~ **in an event** partecipare a un
evento
competence ['kɑ:m·pɪ·təns] *n,* **competency** *n* competenza *f*
competent ['kɑ:m·pɪ·ʈənt] *adj* competente;
to be ~ **at sth** essere competente in qc
competition [ˌkɑ:m·pə·'tɪ·ʃən] *n* **1.** (*state of competing*) competizione *f* **2.** (*rivalry*) concorrenza *f* **3.** (*contest*) gara *m;* **beauty** ~ concorso *m* di bellezza; **to enter a** ~ presentarsi in
gara
competitive [kəm·'pe·ʈə·tɪv] *adj* competitivo,
-a; ~ **spirit** spirito *m* di competizione;
~ **sports** sport *m inv* competitivi; **their prices are very** ~ hanno prezzi molto competitivi
competitiveness [kəm·'pe·ʈə·tɪv·nəs] *n* competitività *f*
competitor [kəm·'pe·ʈə·ʈəˑ] *n* **1.** *a.* ECON concorrente *mf* **2.** SPORTS avversario, a *m, f;* (*participant*) concorrente *mf*
compilation [ˌkɑ:m·pə·'leɪ·ʃən] *n* **1.** (*act of compiling*) compilazione *f* **2.** (*collection*) raccolta *f*
compile [kəm·'paɪl] *vt* **1.** *a.* COMPUT compilare
2. (*collect*) raccogliere
compiler [ˌkɒm·'pɪ·lə] *n* **1.** (*person*) compilatore, -trice *m, f* **2.** *a.* COMPUT compilatore *m*
complacence [kəm·'pleɪ·sn·s(i)] *n,* **complacency** *n* eccessivo compiacimento *m*
complacent [kəm·'pleɪ·sənt] *adj* eccessivamente soddisfatto, -a
complain [kəm·'pleɪn] *vi* lamentarsi; **to** ~
about [*o* **of**] **sth** lamentarsi di qc

complainant [kəmˈpleɪ·nənt] *n* LAW querelante *mf*

complaint [kəmˈpleɪnt] *n* **1.** (*expression of displeasure*) lamentela *f;* **to have cause for ~** avere motivo di lamentarsi; **to make a ~ about sb/sth** lamentarsi di qu/qc **2.** LAW reclamo *m* **3.** (*illness*) disturbo *m*

complaisance [kəmˈpleɪ·səns] *n form* compiacenza *f*

complaisant [kəmˈpleɪ·sənt] *adj form* compiacente

complement [ˈkɑːm·plɪ·mənt] *vt* complementare

complementary [ˌkɑːm·pləˈmen·t̬ə·i] *adj* complementare

complete [kəmˈpliːt] **I.** *vt* **1.** (*add what is missing*) completare **2.** (*finish*) terminare; **to ~ doing sth** terminare di fare qc **3.** (*fill out entirely*) riempire **II.** *adj* completo, -a, intero, -a; **~ coverage** copertura *f* totale; **in ~ darkness** nella completa oscurità; **~ paralysis** paralisi*f inv* totale; **the man's a ~ fool!** quell'uomo è un vero cretino!

completely *adv* completamente, totalmente

completeness *n* totalità *f*

completion [kəmˈpliː·ʃən] *n* ultimazione *f;* **to be nearing ~** essere quasi ultimato; **you'll be paid upon ~ of the project** verrete pagati a progetto ultimato

complex [ˈkɑːm·pleks] **I.** *adj* complesso, -a **II.** <-es> *n* complesso *m;* **guilt ~** senso di colpa; **inferiority ~** complesso di inferiorità; **to have a ~ about sth** essere complessato per qc; **to give sb a ~** far complessare qu; **I've got a real ~ about spiders** ho una vera fobia dei ragni

complexion [kəmˈplek·ʃən] *n* **1.** (*skin*) carnagione *f;* (*color*) colorito *m;* **a healthy ~** un colorito sano **2.** (*character*) aspetto *m;* **that puts a different ~ on things** ciò dà una sfumatura nuova alle cose

complexity [kəmˈplek·sə·t̬i] *n* complessità *f*

compliance [kəmˈpla·rənts] *n* osservanza *f;* (*agreement*) conformità *f;* **in ~ with the law** in conformità con la legge; **to act in ~ with sth** agire conformemente a qc

compliant [kəmˈpla·rənt] *adj form* (*obedient*) obbediente; (*overly obedient*) sottomesso, -a

complicate [ˈkɑːm·plə·keɪt] *vt* complicare

complicated *adj* complicato, -a

complication [ˌkɑːm·pləˈkeɪ·ʃən] *n* complicazione *f*

complicity [kəmˈplɪ·sə·t̬i] *n* complicità *f*

compliment [ˈkɑːm·plə·mənt] **I.** *n* **1.** (*expression of approval*) complimento *m; to* **pay sb a ~** fare un complimento a qu; **to repay a ~** ricambiare un complimento; **I take it as a ~ that ...** mi lusinga che ... **2.** *pl* omaggi *mpl;* **to present one's ~s** *form* porgere i propri omaggi; **to send ~s** inviare i saluti; **with ~s** con i nostri migliori auguri ▶ **to fish for ~s** andare in cerca di lodi **II.** *vt* **to ~ sb on sth** complimentarsi con qu per qc

complimentary [ˌkɑːm·pləˈmen·t̬ə·i] *adj* **1.** (*praising*) lusinghiero, -a; **to be ~ about sth** dare un giudizio lusinghiero su qc **2.** (*free*) omaggio *inv*

comply [kəmˈplaɪ] <-ie-> *vi* conformarsi; **to refuse to ~** rifiutarsi di obbedire; **to ~ with the law/the rules** conformarsi alla legge/alle normative

component [kəmˈpoʊ·nənt] *n* componente *m;* **key ~** parte *f* chiave

compose [kəmˈpoʊz] **I.** *vi* (*write music, poetry*) comporre **II.** *vt* **1.** comporre **2.** (*write*) redigere **3.** (*make up*) **to be ~d of** essere composto di qc; **the committee is ~d of experts** il comitato è composto di esperti **4.** (*calm*) **to ~ oneself** ricomporsi; **to ~ one's thoughts** raccogliere le idee

composed [kəmˈpoʊzd] *adj* tranquillo, -a

composer [kəmˈpoʊ·zɚ] *n* compositore, -trice *m, f*

composite [kəmˈpɑː·zɪt] *adj* composito, -a

composition [ˌkɑːm·pəˈzɪ·ʃən] *n* **1.** composizione *f* **2.** (*make-up: of a group*) composizione *f*

compositor [kəmˈpɑː·zɪ·tɚ] *n* TYPO compositore *m*

compost [ˈkɑːm·poʊst] **I.** *n* concime *m* organico **II.** *vt* **1.** (*turn into fertilizer*) trasformare in concime **2.** (*fertilize*) concimare

composure [kəmˈpoʊ·ʒɚ] *n* calma *f;* **to lose/regain one's ~** perdere/ritrovare la calma

compound[1] [ˌkɑːmˈpaʊnd] *vt* **1.** (*make worse*) aggravare **2.** (*mix*) combinare **3.** (*make up*) **to be ~ed of sth** constare di qc

compound[2] [ˈkɑːm·paʊnd] *n* **1.** composto *m* **2.** (*enclosure*) recinto *m*

compound fracture *n* frattura *f* multipla

compound interest *n* interesse *m* composto

comprehend [ˌkɑːm·prɪˈhend] *vi, vt* comprendere

comprehensible [ˌkɑːm·prɪˈhen·sə·bl] *adj* comprensibile

comprehension [ˌkɑːm·prɪˈhen·ʃən] *n* comprensione *f;* **beyond ~** incomprensibile; **he has no ~ of the size of the problem** non è consapevole della portata del problema

comprehensive [ˌkɑːm·prəˈhen·sɪv] *adj* esauriente; (*global*) totale; **~ coverage** copertura *f* globale; **~ list** lista *f* completa

compress [kəmˈpres] **I.** *vt* **1.** *a.* COMPUT comprimere **2.** (*make shorter*) condensare **II.** <-es> *n* impacco *m*

compressed [kəmˈprest] *adj* compresso, -a

compression [kəmˈpre·ʃən] *n a.* COMPUT compressione *f*

compressor [kəmˈpre·sɚ] *n* compressore *m*

comprise [kəmˈpraɪz] *vt* comprendere

compromise [ˈkɑːm·prə·maɪz] **I.** *n* compromesso *m;* **to agree to a ~** accettare un compromesso; **to reach a ~** arrivare a un compromesso **III.** *vt* **1.** (*betray*) tradire; **to ~ one's beliefs** tradire le proprie convinzioni **2.** (*endanger*) compromettere; **to ~ one's reputation** compromettere la propria reputazione

compromising *adj* compromettente

comptroller [kən·'trou·lə·] *n* controllore *m* (finanziario)

compulsion [kəm·'pʌl·ʃən] *n* obbligo *m;* **to be under no ~ to do sth** non avere l'obbligo di fare qc; **he seems to have a constant ~ to eat** sembra che abbia un continuo impulso a mangiare

compulsive [kəm·'pʌl·sɪv] *adj* **he's a ~ gambler** ha il vizio del gioco; **she's a ~ eater** non riesce a controllare l'irrefrenabile impulso a mangiare

compulsory [kəm·'pʌl·sə·ri] *adj* obbligatorio, -a; **~ education** istruzione *f* obbligatoria; **~ by law** obbligatorio per legge

compunction [kəm·'pʌŋk·ʃən] *n* rimorso *m;* **to have no ~ about sth** non avere rimorso per qc

computation [ˌkɑːm·pjə·'teɪ·ʃən] *n* calcolo *m*

compute [kəm·'pjuːt] *vt* calcolare

computer [kəm·'pjuː·tə·] *n* computer *m inv;* **to do sth by ~** fare qc con il computer

computer-aided *adj* assistito, -a dal computer

computer center *n* centro *m* di informatica

computer game *n* videogioco *m*

computer graphics *n + sing/pl vb* grafica *f* al computer

computerization [kəm·ˌpjuː·tə·ɪ·'zeɪ·ʃən] *n* **1.** (*computer storage*) computerizzazione *f* **2.** (*equipping with computers*) informatizzazione *f*

computerize [kəm·'pjuː·tə·raɪz] I. *vt* **1.** (*store on computer*) computerizzare **2.** (*equip with computers*) informatizzare II. *vi* informatizzarsi

computer network *n* rete *f* informatica

computer program *n* programma *m* informatico

computer programer *n* programmatore, -trice *m, f*

computer science *n* informatica *f;* **~ course** corso *m* di informatica

computer scientist *n* informatico, -a *m, f*

computer search <-es> *n* ricerca *f* computerizzata

computer virus <-es> *n* virus *m inv* informatico

computer workstation *n* stazione *f* di lavoro

computing *n* informatica *f*

comrade ['kɑːm·ræd] *n* compagno, -a *m, f*

comradeship ['kɑːm·ræd·ʃɪp] *n* cameratismo *m*

Comsat ['kɑːm·sæt] *n abbr of* **communications satellite** satellite *m* di telecomunicazione

con¹ [kɑːn] <-nn-> *vt inf* fregare; **to ~ sb into doing sth** indurre qu a fare qc con l'inganno; **to ~ sb into believing that ...** far credere a qu che ...; **to ~ sb out of sth** sottrarre qc a qu con l'inganno

con² [kɑːn] *n* (*against*) contro *m inv;* **the pros and ~s of sth** i pro e i contro di qc

con³ [kɑːn] *n sl* (*convict*) carcerato, -a *m, f*

con artist [ˌkɑːn·'ɑːr·ṭəst] *n inf* imbroglione, -a *m, f*

concatenation [kən·ˌkæ·ṭə·'neɪ·ʃən] *n* concatenazione *f*

concave [kɑːn·keɪv] *adj* concavo, -a

concavity [kɑːn·'kæ·və·ti] <-ies> *n* concavità *f*

conceal [kən·'siːl] *vt* nascondere; (*a surprise*) contenere

concealment [kən·'siːl·mənt] *n* (*of information, evidence*) occultamento *m;* (*of feelings*) dissimulazione *f;* **to watch sth from a place of ~** osservare qc da un nascondiglio

concede [kən·'siːd] I. *vt* **1.** (*acknowledge*) ammettere **2.** (*surrender, permit*) concedere **3.** (*allow to score*) **to ~ a goal** regalare un gol II. *vi* darsi per vinto

conceit [kən·'siːt] *n* **1.** (*vanity*) presunzione *f;* **to be full of ~** essere presuntuoso **2.** *liter* (*elaborate comparison*) concetto *m*

conceited [kən·'siː·ṭɪd] *adj* presuntuoso, -a; **without wishing to sound ~** senza voler sembrare presuntuoso

conceivable [kən·'siː·və·bl] *adj* concepibile; **it's ~** è plausibile

conceive [kən·'siːv] I. *vt* concepire II. *vi* concepire; **to ~ of sb/sth** concepire qu/qc; **other people may influence how we ~ of ourselves** gli altri possono influenzare l'idea che abbiamo di noi stessi

concentrate ['kɑːn·sən·treɪt] I. *vi* concentrarsi; **to ~ on sth** concentrarsi su qc II. *vt* concentrare III. *n* concentrato *m*

concentrated *adj* concentrato, -a; (*attack*) intenso, -a

concentration [ˌkɑːn·sn·'treɪ·ʃən] *n* concentrazione *f;* **to lose (one's) ~** perdere la concentrazione

concentration camp *n* campo *m* di concentramento

concentric [kən·'sen·trɪk] *adj* concentrico, -a

concept ['kɑːn·sept] *n* concetto *m;* **to grasp a ~** afferrare un concetto

conception [kən·'sep·ʃən] *n* **1.** concezione *f* **2.** BIO concepimento *m*

conceptual [kən·'sep·tʃu·əl] *adj* concettuale

conceptualize [kən·'sep·tʃu·ə·laɪz] *vt* concettualizzare

concern [kən·'sɜːrn] I. *vt* **1.** (*apply to*) riguardare; **to ~ oneself about sth** occuparsi di qc; **to whom it may ~** a chi di dovere; **as far as I'm ~ed** per quanto mi riguarda; **I'd like to thank everyone ~ed** vorrei ringraziare tutti coloro che sono stati coinvolti; **I'm not very good where money is ~ed** non sono molto abile per quanto riguarda i soldi; **her job is something ~ed with computers** il suo lavoro ha a che vedere con i computer **2.** (*worry*) preoccuparsi; **to be ~ed about sth** essere preoccupati per qc II. *n* **1.** (*matter of interest*) interesse *m;* **it's no ~ of mine** non mi riguarda;

what's happening? — **that's none of your** ~ cosa succede? — non ti riguarda; **to be of** ~ **to sb** riguardare qu **2.** (*worry*) preoccupazione *f;* **a matter of** ~ motivo di preoccupazione **3.** (*company*) azienda *f;* **a going** ~ un'azienda attiva

concerning *prep* riguardo (a)

concert ['kɑːn·sət] *n* **1.** (*musical performance*) concerto *m;* ~ **hall** sala *f* concerti; ~ **pianist** pianista *mf* **2. in** ~ (*performing live*) in concerto; *form* (*all together*) insieme; **in** ~ **with sb** insieme a qu; **to act in** ~ agire di comune accordo

concerted [kən·'sɜː·tɪd] *adj* **1.** (*joint*) comune, concertato, -a **2.** (*resolute*) determinato, -a

concert grand ['kɑːn·sət grænd] *n* pianoforte *m* a coda

concertina [ˌkɑːn·sə·'tiː·nə] *n* concertina *f*

concertina wire *n* filo *m* spinato arrotolato

concertmaster [ˌkɑːn·sət·'mæs·tə] *n* primo violino *m*

concerto [kən·'tʃer·toʊ] <-s *o* -ti> *n* concerto *m*

concert pitch *n* MUS diapason *m inv* ▶ **to be at** ~ essere preparato

concession [kən·'se·ʃən] *n* **1.** (*tax compensation*) sgravio *m* (fiscale) **2.** (*compromise*) concessione *f;* ~ **to sell goods** licenza *f* per la vendita di prodotti

conciliate [kən·'sɪ·li·eɪt] **I.** *vi* fare da mediatore **II.** *vt* **1.** (*placate*) placare **2.** (*reconcile*) conciliare

conciliation [kən·ˌsɪ·li·'eɪ·ʃən] *n form* conciliazione *f*

conciliatory [kən·'sɪ·li·ə·tɔː·ri] *adj* conciliatorio, -a

concise [kən·'saɪs] *adj* conciso, -a

conciseness *n*, **concision** [kən·'sɪ·ʒən] *n* concisione *f*

conclave ['kɑːn·kleɪv] *n form* **1.** (*private meeting*) riunione *f* a porte chiuse **2.** REL (*gathering of cardinals*) conclave *m*

conclude [kən·'kluːd] **I.** *vi* terminare; **to** ~ **by doing sth** terminare facendo qc **II.** *vt* concludere; **to** ~ (**from sth**) **that ...** concludere (da qc) che ...

concluding *adj* finale

conclusion [kən·'kluː·ʒən] *n* conclusione *f;* **to come to a** ~ arrivare a una conclusione; **in** ~, **I would like to say that ...** a conclusione, vorrei dire che ...

conclusive [kən·'kluː·sɪv] *adj* **1.** (*convincing*) convincente; ~ **arguments** argomentazioni *f pl* irrefutabili **2.** (*decisive*) decisivo, -a

concoct [kən·'kɑːkt] *vt* **1.** (*create by mixing ingredients: a dish*) preparare **2.** (*devise*) tramare **3.** (*fabricate*) inventare

concoction [kən·'kɑːk·ʃən] *n* (*dish, drink*) miscuglio *m;* **is this dish one of your** ~**s, Paul?** *iron* questo piatto è una delle tue invenzioni, Paul?

concourse ['kɑːn·kɔːrs] *n* atrio *m*

concrete ['kɑːn·kriːt] **I.** *n* calcestruzzo *m,*

cemento *m* **II.** *adj* di calcestruzzo **III.** *vt* ricoprire di calcestruzzo

concrete mixer *n* betoniera *f*

concubine ['kɑːŋ·kju·baɪn] *n* HIST concubina *f*

concur [kən·'kɜːr] <-rr-> *vi form* **1.** (*agree*) concordare; **to** ~ **with sb** (**in sth**) concordare con qu (su qc) **2.** (*happen simultaneously*) coincidere

concurrence [kən·'kʌ·rəns] *n form* **1.** (*agreement*) accordo *m* **2.** (*simultaneous occurrence*) concorso *m*

concurrent [kən·'kʌ·rənt] *adj* simultaneo, -a

concuss [kən·'kʌs] *vt* **to be** ~**ed** avere una commozione cerebrale

concussed *adj* con una commozione cerebrale

concussion [kən·'kʌ·ʃən] *n* commozione *f* cerebrale; **to suffer** (**from**) **a** ~ avere una commozione cerebrale

condemn [kən·'dem] *vt* **1.** (*reprove, sentence*) condannare; **to** ~ **sb for sth** condannare qu per qc; **to be** ~**ed to death** essere condannato a morte **2.** (*pronounced unsafe: building*) dichiarare inagibile

condemnation [ˌkɑːn·dem·'neɪ·ʃən] *n* **1.** (*reproof*) condanna *f* **2.** (*reason to reprove*) motivo *m* di critica

condensation [ˌkɑːn·den·'seɪ·ʃən] *n* **1.** (*process of changing to liquid*) condensazione *f* **2.** (*reducing in size*) abbreviazione *f*

condense [kən·'dens] **I.** *vt* condensare; **to** ~ **a liquid** condensare un liquido **II.** *vi* condensarsi

condenser [kən·'den·sə] *n* condensatore *m*

condescend [ˌkɑːn·dɪ·'send] *vi* **to** ~ **to do sth** abbassarsi a fare qc

condescending [ˌkɑːn·dɪ·'sen·dɪŋ] *adj* con aria di superiorità

condescension [ˌkɑːn·dɪ·'sen·ʃən] *n* aria *f* di superiorità

condiment ['kɑːn·də·mənt] *n form* condimento *m*

condition [kən·'dɪ·ʃən] **I.** *n* **1.** (*state*) condizione *f;* **in perfect** ~ in perfetto stato; **in peak** ~ in ottime condizioni; **in terrible** ~ in pessime condizioni; **to be out of** ~ (*person*) non essere in forma; (*thing*) essere in cattivo stato; **to be in no** ~ **to do sth** non essere in condizioni di fare qc; **for a man of sixty-three, Jim's in pretty good** ~ per un uomo di sessantatré anni Jim è in forma **2.** (*mental or physical state*) stato *m;* **heart** ~ malattia *f* cardiaca **3.** (*circumstances*) ~**s** pl condizioni *fpl* **4.** (*stipulation*) condizione *f;* **to make a** ~ mettere una condizione; **on the** ~ **that ...** a condizione che ... +*subj;* **under the** ~**s of sth** secondo i termini di qc **II.** *vt* **1.** (*train*) preparare; (*influence*) condizionare **2.** (*treat hair*) trattare (con balsamo)

conditional [kən·'dɪ·ʃə·nl] **I.** *adj* (*provisional*) ~ **on sth** condizionato da qc **II.** *n* LING **the** ~ il condizionale

conditionally [kən·'dɪ·ʃə·nə·li] *adv* con riserve

conditioned [kən·'dɪ·ʃənd] *adj* (*trained*) preparato, -a; (*air*) condizionato, -a; (*place*) con aria condizionata; ~ **reflex** riflesso *m* condizionato

conditioner [kən·'dɪ·ʃə·nə] *n* **1.** (*for hair*) balsamo *m* **2.** (*for soil*) concime *m* curativo

conditioning *n* condizionamento *m*

condo [ˌkɑːn·doʊ] *n inf s.* **condominium**

condolence [kən·'doʊ·ləns] *n* ~**s** condoglianze *fpl;* **to offer one's** ~**s** (**to sb**) *form* fare le proprie condoglianze (a qu)

condom ['kɑːn·dəm] *n* preservativo *m*

condominium [ˌkɑːn·də·'mɪ·ni·əm] *n* **1.** (*apartment building*) condominio *m* **2.** (*unit*) appartamento *m* **3.** POL condominio *m* internazionale

condone [kən·'doʊn] *vt* **1.** (*approve*) approvare **2.** (*forgive*) condonare

conducive [kən·'duː·sɪv] *adj* propizio, -a; **to be** ~ **to sth** giovare a qc

conduct[1] [ˌkɑːn·'dʌkt] **I.** *vt* **1.** condurre; **to** ~ **a religious service** officiare una funzione religiosa **2.** (*behave*) **to** ~ **oneself** comportarsi **II.** *vi* MUS dirigere

conduct[2] ['kɑːn·dʌkt] *n* **1.** (*management*) conduzione *f* **2.** (*behavior*) condotta *f;* **sb's** ~ **towards sb** il comportamento di qu verso qu

conductive [kən·'dʌk·tɪv] *adj* ELEC, PHYS conduttore, -trice

conductor [kən·'dʌk·tə] *n* **1.** (*director*) direttore *m* d'orchestra **2.** PHYS, ELEC conduttore *m* **3.** (*fare collector*) bigliettaio *m;* (*of train*) capotreno *m*

conductress [kən·'dʌk·trɪs] <-es> *n* direttrice *f* d'orchestra; (*of train*) capotreno *f*

conduit ['kɑːn·duɪt] *n* condotto *m*

cone [koʊn] *n* **1.** cono *m* **2.** BOT pigna *f*

confection [kən·'fek·ʃən] *n form* **1.** COM confezione *f* **2.** CULIN dolce *m;* (*sweet*) dolcetto *m*

confectioner [kən·'fekʃ·nə] *n* confettiere, -a *m, f*

confectionery [kən·'fek·ʃə·ne·ri] *n* confetteria *f*

confederacy [kən·'fe·də·rə·si] <-ies> *n* **1.** + *sing/pl vb* (*union*) confederazione *f;* **the Confederancy** HIST la Confederazione **2.** (*plot*) complotto *m*

confederate [kən·'fe·də·rət] **I.** *n* complice *mf* **II.** *adj* POL, HIST confederato, -a

confederation [kən·ˌfe·də·'reɪ·ʃən] *n* + *sing/pl vb* POL confederazione *f*

confer [kən·'fɜːr] <-rr-> **I.** *vi* consultarsi **II.** *vt* conferire

conference ['kɑːn·fə·əns] *n* **1.** (*meeting*) conferenza *f;* **to be in a** ~ (**with sb**) essere in riunione (con qu) **2.** SPORTS lega *f* sportiva universitaria

confess [kən·'fes] **I.** *vi* **1.** **to** ~ **to a crime** confessare un reato **2.** REL confessarsi **II.** *vt* confessare

confessedly *adv* con franchezza

confession [kən·'fe·ʃən] *n* confessione *f;* **I have a** ~ **to make** devo fare una confessione; ~ **of faith** professione di fede

confessional [kən·'fe·ʃə·nl] *n* confessionale *m*

confessor [kən·'fe·sə] *n* confessore *m*

confetti [kən·'fe·ti] *n* coriandoli *mpl;* **to shower sb in** ~ tirare i coriandoli a qu

confidant [ˌkɑːn·fə·'dænt] *n* confidente *m*

confidante [ˌkɑːn·fə·'dænt] *n* confidente *f*

confide [kən·'faɪd] *vt* confidare; **to** ~ (**to sb**) **that ...** confidare (a qu) che ...

confidence ['kɑːn·fə·dəns] *n* **1.** (*trust*) fiducia *f;* **to have every** ~ **in sb** avere piena fiducia in qu; **to place one's** ~ **in sb/sth** riporre la propria fiducia in qu/qc; **to take sb into one's** ~ confidarsi con qu; **to win sb's** ~ guadagnarsi la fiducia di qu; **he certainly doesn't lack** ~ non gli manca certo la fiducia in se stesso **2.** (*secrecy*) ~**s** confidenze *fpl*

confident ['kɑːn·fə·dənt] *adj* **1.** (*sure*) sicuro, -a; **to be** ~ **about oneself** avere fiducia in se stessi; **to be** ~ **about sth** essere sicuro di qc **2.** (*self-assured*) sicuro, -a di sé

confidential [ˌkɑːn·fə·'den·ʃl] *adj* confidenziale

confidentially [ˌkɑːn·fə·'den·ʃə·li] *adv* in via confidenziale

confiding [kən·'faɪ·dɪŋ] *adj* fiducioso, -a

configuration [kən·ˌfɪg·jə·'reɪ·ʃən] *n a.* COMPUT configurazione *f*

confine [kən·'faɪn] **I.** *vt* **1.** (*limit*) **to** ~ **sth to sth** limitare qc a qc; **to be** ~**d to doing sth** limitarsi a fare qc **2.** (*imprison*) mettere al confino **3.** (*shut in*) rinchiudere; **to be** ~**d to quarters** MIL essere messo in consegna **II.** *n pl* **the** ~**s** i confini; **beyond the** ~**s of sth** oltre i confini di qc

confined *adj* (*prisoner*) recluso, -a; (*space*) ridotto, -a

confinement [kən·'faɪn·mənt] *n* (*act of being confined*) reclusione *f;* (*state of being confined*); **his** ~ **to bed really annoyed him** essere costretto a letto lo seccava molto

confines *n pl* limiti *mpl*

confirm [kən·'fɜːrm] **I.** *vt* **1.** (*verify*) confermare **2.** REL cresimare **II.** *vi* fare la cresima

confirmation [ˌkɑːn·fə·'meɪ·ʃən] *n a.* REL cresima *f*

confirmed [kən·'fɜːrmd] *adj* **1.** convinto, -a **2.** (*chronic*) ~ **alcoholic** alcolizzato *m* recidivo **3.** (*proved*) confermato, -a

confiscate ['kɑːn·fəs·keɪt] *vt* confiscare

conflict[1] ['kɑːn·flɪkt] *n* conflitto *m;* **to come into** ~ **with sb** entrare in conflitto con qu

conflict[2] [kən·'flɪkt] *vi* (*differ*) **to** ~ **with sth** scontrarsi con qc

conflicting [kən·'flɪk·tɪŋ] *adj* contrastante; (*evidence*) contraddittorio, -a

confluence ['kɑːn·flu·əns] *n* confluenza *f*

conform [kən·'fɔːrm] *vi* conformarsi; **to** ~ **to the law** essere conforme alla legge

conformist [kən·'fɔːr·mɪst] **I.** *n* conformista *mf* **II.** *adj* conformista

conformity [kən·'fɔːr·mə·ti] *n* conformità *f;* **in** ~ **with sth** conforme a qc

confound [kən·'faʊnd] *vt* confondere

confounded *adj inf* maledetto, -a

confront *vt* affrontare

confrontation [ˌkaːn·frən·'teɪ·ʃən] *n* scontro *m*

confrontational [ˌkaːn·frən·'teɪʃ·nəl] *adj* polemico, -a

confuse [kən·'fjuːz] *vt* confondere

confused [kən·'fjuːzd] *adj* confuso, -a

confusing [kən·'fjuː·zɪŋ] *adj* confuso, -a

confusion [kən·'fjuː·ʒən] *n* confusione *f*

congeal [kən·'dʒiːl] *vi* (*sauce*) rapprendersi; (*blood*) coagulare

congenial [kən·'dʒiː·n·jəl] *adj* piacevole

congenital [kən·'dʒe·nə·ṭəl] *adj* congenito, -a

congested [kən·'dʒes·tɪd] *adj* congestionato, -a

congestion [kən·'dʒest·ʃən] *n* congestione *f*

conglomerate [kən·'glɑː·mə·ət] *n* conglomerato *m*

conglomeration [kən·ˌglɑː·mə·'reɪ·ʃən] *n* conglomerazione *f*

Congo ['kɑː·ŋ·goʊ] I. *n* the ~ il Congo II. *adj* congolese

Congolese [ˌkɑː·ŋ·gə·'liːz] I. *adj* congolese II. *n* congolese *mf*

congratulate [kən·'græt·ʃə·leɪt] *vt* to ~ sb (on sth) congratularsi con qu (per qc)

congratulation [kən·ˌgræt·ʃə·'leɪ·ʃən] *n* ~ s! congratulazioni! *fpl;* a note of ~ un biglietto di congratulazioni

congregate ['kɑː·ŋ·grɪ·geɪt] *vi* congregarsi

congregation [ˌkɑː·ŋ·grɪ·'geɪ·ʃən] *n* assemblea *f* dei fedeli

congregational [ˌkɑː·ŋ·grɪ·'geɪ·ʃə·nl] *adj* dei fedeli

congress ['kɑː·ŋ·gres] *n* congresso *m*

congressional [kən·'gre·ʃə·nəl] *adj* del congresso

congressman ['kɑː·ŋ·gres·mən] *n* <-men> membro *m* del Congresso

congresswoman *n* <-women> membro *m* (donna) del Congresso

congruence ['kɑː·ŋ·grʊ·əns] *n a.* MATH congruenza *f*

congruent ['kɑː·ŋ·grʊ·ənt] *adj a.* MATH congruente

conical ['kɑː·nɪ·kl] *adj* conico, -a

conifer ['kɑː·nə·fə·] *n* conifera *f*

coniferous [koʊ·'nɪ·fə·rəs] *adj* (*tree*) conifero, -a

conjectural [kən·'dʒek·tʃə·rəl] *adj* congetturale

conjecture [kən·'dʒek·tʃə·] I. *n* congettura *f* II. *vi* congetturare

conjugal ['kɑː·n·dʒə·gl] *adj form* coniugale; ~ visit visita *f* del coniuge

conjugate ['kɑː·n·dʒə·geɪt] *vt* coniugare

conjugation [ˌkɑː·n·dʒə·'geɪ·ʃən] *n* coniugazione *f*

conjunction [kən·'dʒʌŋk·ʃən] *n a.* LING congiunzione *f;* in ~ with insieme a [*o* con]

conjunctivitis [kən·ˌdʒʌŋk·tə·'vaɪ·ṭɪs] *n* congiuntivite *f*

conjure ['kʌn·dʒə·] I. *vi* fare una magia II. *vt* far apparire; *fig* evocare

◆conjure up *vt* far apparire; to ~ an image evocare un'immagine

conjurer ['kʌn·dʒə·ə·] *n*, conjuror ['kʌn·dʒə·ə·] *n* mago, -a *m, f*

conk [kɑː·ŋk] I. *n* colpo *m* in testa II. *vt inf* to ~ sb on the head dare un colpo in testa a qc

◆conk out *vi inf* 1. (*break down: machine, vehicle*) guastarsi 2. (*become exhausted*) crollare

con man ['kɑː·n·ˌmæn] *n abbr of* confidence man truffatore *m*

connect [kə·'nekt] I. *vi* collegarsi; to ~ to the Internet collegarsi a Internet II. *vt* collegare; to ~ sth/sb with sth collegare qc/qu a qc

connected *adj* 1. (*joined together*) connesso, -a 2. (*having ties*) to be ~d to sb avere legami con qu

connecting *adj* comunicante; ~ link connessione *f*

connection [kə·'nek·ʃən] *n* 1. *a.* ELEC, COMPUT collegamento *m* 2. (*relation*) connessione *f*

connector *n* connettore *m*

connivance [kə·'naɪ·vənts] *n* connivenza *f*

connive [kə·'naɪv] *vi* to ~ with sb essere connivente con qu

connoisseur [ˌkɑː·nə·'sɜːr] *n* intenditore, -trice *m, f;* art/wine ~ intenditore, -trice *m, f* d'arte/di vini

connotation [ˌkɑː·nə·'teɪ·ʃən] *n* connotazione *f*

conquer ['kɑː·ŋ·kə·] *vt* 1. *a.* HIST conquistare 2. (*a problem*) superare

conqueror ['kɑː·ŋ·kə·ə·] *n* 1. *a.* HIST conquistatore, -trice *m, f* 2. (*in a competition*) vincitore, -trice *m, f*

conquest ['kɑː·nk·west] *n a. iron* conquista *f*

conscience ['kɑː·n·ʃəns] *n* coscienza *f;* a clear ~ la coscienza pulita; a guilty ~ rimorsi *m pl* di coscienza; to prey on sb's ~ *fig* pesare sulla coscienza di qu; in all [*o* good] ~ in tutta coscienza

conscientious [ˌkɑː·n·tʃi·'en·tʃəs] *adj* scrupoloso, -a

conscientiousness *n* scrupolosità *f*

conscientious objector *n* obiettore, -trice *m, f* di coscienza

conscious ['kɑː·n·ʃəs] *adj* 1. (*deliberate*) conscio, -a 2. (*aware*) cosciente; fashion ~ attento alla moda; to be ~ of sth essere cosciente di qc; to become ~ of sth prendere coscienza di qc

consciousness ['kɑː·n·ʃəs·nɪs] *n* coscienza *f;* political/social ~ coscienza politica/sociale; to raise one's ~ prendere coscienza

conscript[1] ['kɑː·n·'skrɪpt] I. *n* MIL recluta *mf* II. *adj* MIL reclutato, -a

conscript[2] [ˌkə·n·'skrɪpt] *vt* MIL reclutare

conscription [kən·'skrɪp·ʃən] *n* MIL servizio *m* militare

consecrate ['kɑː·n·sə·kreɪt] *vt* consacrare

consecration [ˌkɑː·n·sə·'kreɪ·ʃən] *n* REL consacrazione *f*

consecutive [kən-'sek-jə-t̬ɪv] *adj* consecutivo, -a
consecutively *adv* consecutivamente
consensus [kən-'sen-səs] *n* consenso *m*
consent [kən-'sent] I. *n form* consenso *m; by common* ~ di comune accordo II. *vi* (*accon-sentire*) **to** ~ **to do sth** acconsentire a fare qc
consequence ['kɑːn-tsɪ-kwənts] *n* conseguenza *f;* **as a** ~ come conseguenza; **in** ~ di conseguenza; **nothing of** ~ niente di importante
consequent ['kɑːn-tsɪ-kwənt] *adj,* **consequential** [ˌkɑːn-tsɪ-'kwen-tʃəl] *adj* conseguente
consequently *adv* di conseguenza
conservation [ˌkɑːn-tsɚ-'veɪ-ʃən] *n* conservazione *f;* **environmental** ~ tutela *f* dell'ambiente
conservationist [ˌkɑːn-tsɚ-'veɪ-ʃə-nɪst] *n* ambientalista *mf*
conservatism [kən-'sɜːr-və-tɪ-zəm] *n* conservatorismo *m*
conservative [kən-'sɜːr-və-tɪv] *adj* 1. *a.* POL (*opposed to change*) conservatore, trice 2. (*cautious*) cauto, a; ~ **estimate** stima prudente
conservatory [kən-'sɜːr-və-tɔː-ri] *n* conservatorio *m*
conserve [kən-'sɜːrv] *vt* preservare; **to** ~ **energy/strength** risparmiare energia/le forze
consider [kən-'sɪ-dɚ] *vt* considerare; **to be** ~**ed to be the best** essere considerato il migliore
considerable [kən-'sɪ-də-rə-bl] *adj* considerevole
considerate [kən-'sɪ-də-rət] *adj* carino, -a
consideration [kən-ˌsɪ-də-'reɪ-ʃən] *n* considerazione *f;* **to take sth into** ~ prendere qc in considerazione; **the project is under** ~ il progetto è all'esame; **for a small** ~ *iron* per una modica somma
considered [kən-'sɪ-dɚd] *adj* ponderato, -a; **highly** ~ assai reputato
considering [kən-'sɪ-də-rɪŋ] I. *prep* considerando; ~ **the weather** visto il tempo II. *adv* tutto considerato III. *conj* ~ (**that**) ... considerato che ...
consignment [kən-'saɪn-mənt] *n* 1. (*instance of consigning*) spedizione *f* 2. ECON partita *f;* **goods on** ~ merce *f* in conto deposito
consist [kən-'sɪst] *vi* **to** ~ **of sth** consistire di qc
consistency [kən-'sɪs-tən-tsi] *n* 1. (*degree of firmness*) consistenza *f* 2. (*being coherent*) coerenza *f*
consistent [kən-'sɪs-tənt] *adj* 1. (*keeping to same principles*) coerente; **to be** ~ **with sth** essere coerente con qc 2. (*not varying*) stabile
consolation [ˌkɑːn-sə-'leɪ-ʃən] *n* consolazione *f;* **it was no** ~ **to him to know that ...** non gli è stato di alcun conforto sapere che ...; **if it's of any** ~ ... se ti consola ...
consolation prize *n* premio *m* di consolazione

consolatory [kən-'sɑː-lə-tɔː-ri] *adj* consolatorio, -a; ~ **words** parole *f pl* di conforto
console[1] [kən-'soʊl] *vt* (*comfort*) consolare
console[2] ['kɑːn-soʊl] *n* (*switch panel*) console *f*
consolidate [kən-'sɑː-lə-deɪt] I. *vi* 1. (*reinforce*) consolidarsi 2. (*unite*) fondersi II. *vt* consolidare
consolidated *adj* consolidato, -a
consolidation [kən-ˌsɑː-lə-'deɪ-ʃən] *n* 1. (*becoming stronger*) consolidamento *m* 2. ECON fusione *f*
consommé [ˌkɑːn-sə-'meɪ] *n* consommé *m inv*
consonance ['kɑːn-sə-nəns] *n* MUS consonanza *f*
consonant ['kɑːn-sə-nənt] *n* consonante *f*
consort [kən-'sɔːrt] I. *vi* **to** ~ **with sb** frequentare qu II. *n* consorte *mf;* **prince** ~ principe *m* consorte
consortium [kən-'sɔːr-t̬i-əm] *n* <consortiums *o* consortia> consorzio *m*
conspicuous [kən-'spɪk-ju-əs] *adj* vistoso, -a; **to be** ~ **by one's absence** *iron* brillare per la propria assenza
conspiracy [kən-'spɪ-rə-si] <-ies> *n* cospirazione *f;* **a** ~ **against sb** una cospirazione contro qu
conspirator [kən-'spɪ-rə-t̬ɚ] *n* cospiratore, -trice *m, f*
conspire [kən-'spa-ɪɚ] *vi* cospirare; **to** ~ **to do sth** cospirare per fare qc; **to** ~ **against sb** cospirare contro qu
constancy ['kɑːn-stən-tsi] *n form* costanza *f*
constant ['kɑːn-stənt] I. *n* costante *f* II. *adj* costante; (*noise*) continuo, -a; **to be in** ~ **trouble** essere costantemente nei guai
constantly *adv* costantemente
constellation [ˌkɑːn-stə-'leɪ-ʃən] *n* costellazione *f*
consternation [ˌkɑːn-stɚ-'neɪ-ʃən] *n* costernazione *f*
constipate ['kɑːn-stə-peɪt] *vt* MED dare stitichezza a
constipated *adj* stitico, -a
constipation ['kɑːn-stə-'peɪ-ʃən] *n* MED stitichezza *f*
constituency [kən-'stɪ-tʃu-ən-tsi] *n* 1. (*electoral district*) collegio *m* elettorale 2. (*body of voters in this area*) elettorato *m* 3. (*seat*) seggio *m*
constituent [kən-'stɪ-tʃu-ənt] I. *n* 1. (*voter*) elettore, -trice *m, f* 2. CHEM, PHYS (*component*) componente *m* II. *adj* costituente
constitute ['kɑːn-stə-tuːt] *vt* costituire
constitution [ˌkɑːn-stə-'tuː-ʃən] *n* costituzione *f*
constitutional [ˌkɑːn-stə-'tuː-ʃə-nl] I. *adj* costituzionale II. *n iron* salutare passeggiata *f*
constrain [kən-'streɪn] *vt* 1. (*restrict*) limitare 2. (*oblige*) **to be** [*o* **feel**] ~**ed to do sth** essere [*o* sentirsi] costretto a fare qc
constraint [kən-'streɪnt] *n* 1. (*compulsion*)

C

costrizione *f;* **he confessed under** ~ ha confessato perché costretto **2.** (*limit*) restrizione *f;* **to impose** ~**s on sb/sth** imporre delle restrizioni a qu/su qc

constrict [kən·'strɪkt] *vt* comprimere

constriction [kən·'strɪk·ʃən] *n* costrizione *f*

constrictor *n* costrittore *m*

construct [kən·'strʌkt] **I.** *n* costruzione *f* **II.** *vt* costruire

construction [kən·'strʌk·ʃən] *n* **1.** (*act of making or building*) costruzione *f* **2.** (*building*) edificio *m* **3.** LING costruzione *f* **4.** *form* (*interpretation*) interpretazione *f;* **to put a** ~ **on sth** interpretare qc

constructional [kən·'strʌk·ʃnl] *adj* strutturale

constructive [kən·'strʌk·tɪv] *adj* costruttivo, -a

constructor [kən·'strʌk·tə·] *n* costruttore, -trice *m, f*

construe [kən·'struː] *vt* interpretare

consul ['kɑːn·sl] *n* console *m*

consular ['kɑːn·sjʊ·lə·] *adj* consolare

consulate ['kɑːn·sjʊ·lət] *n* consolato *m*

consulate general *n* consolato *m* generale

consul general *n* console *m* generale

consult [kən·'sʌlt] **I.** *vi* consultarsi **II.** *vt* **1.** (*seek information or advice*) consultare **2.** (*examine*) tener conto di; **to** ~ **one's feelings** tener conto dei propri sentimenti

consultancy [kən·'sʌl·tən·tsi] <-ies> *n* **1.** (*company*) società *f* di consulenza **2.** (*activity*) consulenza *f*

consultant [kən·'sʌl·tənt] *n* ECON consulente *mf;* **management** ~ consulente di gestione; **tax** ~ consulente fiscale

consultation [ˌkɑːn·sʌl·'teɪ·ʃən] *n* consultazione *f*

consultative [kən·'sʌl·tə·tɪv] *adj* consultivo, -a

consulting [kən·'sʌl·tɪŋ] *adj* ~ **fee** onorario *m* per la consulenza

consume [kən·'suːm] *vt* **1.** consumare; **to be** ~**d by sth** essere consumato da qc; **to be** ~**d by anger/by envy** essere roso dalla rabbia/dall'invidia

consumer [kən·'suː·mə·] *n* consumatore, -trice *m, f;* ~ **credit** credito *m* al consumo; ~ **demand** domanda *f* dei consumatori; ~ **society** associazione *f* di consumatori

consumerism [kən·'suː·mə·ɪ·zəm] *n* **1.** (*protection*) difesa *f* dei consumatori **2.** *pej* (*exaggerated purchasing*) consumismo *m*

consummate ['kɑːn·sə·meɪt] **I.** *adj form* consumato, -a; ~ **happiness** felicità totale; ~ **skill** somma abilità **II.** *vt* **1.** (*complete*) **to** ~ **a marriage** consumare un matrimonio **2.** *form* (*conclude*) **to** ~ **a deal** concludere un accordo

consummation [ˌkɑːn·sə·'meɪ·ʃən] *n form* consumazione *f*

consumption [kən·'sʌmp·ʃən] *n* **1.** consumo *m* **2.** HIST, MED consunzione *f*

consumptive [kən·'sʌmp·tɪv] *adj* HIST, MED tisico, -a

contact ['kɑːn·tækt] **I.** *n* contatto *m;* **to have** ~**s** avere conoscenze; **physical** ~ contatto

fisico; **to come into** ~ **with sth** entrare in contatto con qc **II.** *vt* contattare

contact lens *n* lente *f* a contatto

contact man *n* intermediario *m*

contact print *n* provino *m* a contatto

contagion [kən·'teɪ·dʒən] *n form* contagio *m*

contagious [kən·'teɪ·dʒəs] *adj a. fig* contagioso, -a

contain [kən·'teɪn] *vt* contenere

container [kən·'teɪ·nə·] *n* **1.** (*vessel*) contenitore *m* **2.** (*for transport*) container *m inv*

containerize [kən·'teɪ·nə·raɪz] *vt* mettere in container

container ship *n* portacontainer *f inv*

containment [kən·'teɪn·mənt] *n* contenimento *m*

contaminate [kən·'tæ·mɪ·neɪt] *vt* contaminare

contamination [kən·ˌtæ·mɪ·'neɪ·ʃən] *n* contaminazione *f*

contemplate ['kɑːn·ṭem·pleɪt] *vt* **1.** (*intend*) **to** ~ **doing sth** avere intenzione di fare qc; **to** ~ **suicide** pensare al suicidio **2.** (*consider, gaze at*) contemplare

contemplation [ˌkɑːn·ṭem·'pleɪ·ʃən] *n* contemplazione *f*

contemplative [kən·'tem·plə·tɪv] *adj* contemplativo, -a

contemporary [kən·'tem·pə·re·ri] **I.** *n* contemporaneo, -a *m, f* **II.** *adj* contemporaneo, -a

contempt [kən·'tempt] *n* disprezzo *m;* **to hold sth/sb in** ~ disprezzare qc/qu; **she's beneath** ~ non la rispetto assolutamente

contemptible [kən·'temp·tə·bl] *adj* spregevole

contemptuous [kən·'temp·tʃu·əs] *adj* sprezzante; (*look*) di disprezzo; **to be** ~ **of sb** mostrare disprezzo per qu

contend [kən·'tend] **I.** *vi* **1.** (*compete*) competere; **to** ~ **for sth** contendere per qc **2.** (*struggle*) lottare; **to have sb/sth to** ~ **with** dover lottare con qu/qc; **to** ~ **against sb/sth** lottare contro qu/qc **II.** *vi* **to** ~ **that ...** sostenere che ...

contender *n* aspirante *mf*

content[1] ['kɑːn·tent] *n* contenuto *m*

content[2] [kən·'tent] **I.** *vt* soddisfare; **to** ~ **oneself with sth** accontentarsi di qc **II.** *adj* contento, -a; **to be** ~ **with sth** essere soddisfatto di qc; **to be** ~ **to do sth** essere contento di fare qc

contented *adj* soddisfatto, -a

contention [kən·'ten·ʃən] *n* **1.** (*disagreement*) controversia *f;* **teams in** ~ gruppi *m pl* rivali **2.** (*opinion*) opinione *f* **3.** (*competition*) **to be in** ~ **for sth** contendersi qc; **to be out of** ~ **for sth** non avere alcuna chance di ottenere qc

contentious [kən·'ten·ʃəs] *adj* controverso, -a

contentment [kən·'tent·mənt] *n* appagamento *m*

contents ['kɑːn·tents] *n pl* contenuto *m;* (*index*) sommario *m*

contest I. ['kɑːn·test] *n* **1.** (*competition*) concorso *m;* **beauty** ~ concorso di bellezza; **sports** ~ gara *f* sportiva **2.** (*dispute*) controversia *f* **II.** [kən'test] *vt* **1.** (*challenge: claims, a decision*) contestare; (*a will*) impugnare **2.** (*compete for*) disputare

contestant [kən'tes·tənt] *n* (*in a match, contest*) concorrente *mf;* (*in an election*) candidato, -a *m, f*

context ['ka:n·tekst] *n* contesto *m*

contextual [kən'teks·tʃu·əl] *adj form* contestuale

contextualize [kən'teks·tʃu·ə·laɪz] *vt* contestualizzare

continent[1] ['ka:nt·nənt] *n* GEO continente *m*

continent[2] ['ka:nt·nənt] *adj a.* MED continente

continental [,ka:nt̬·'nen·t̬l] **I.** *adj* **1.** (*relating to a continent*) continentale; ~ **drift** deriva *f* dei continenti; ~ **shelf** piattaforma *f* continentale **2.** (*of the mainland*) ~ **Europe** Europa *f* continentale; **the** ~ **United States** gli Stati Uniti *m pl* continentali **II.** *n* continentale *mf*

continental breakfast *n* colazione *f* continentale

contingency [kən'tɪn·dʒən·tsi] <-ies> *n form* eventualità *f*

contingent [kən'tɪn·dʒənt] **I.** *n* contingente *m* **II.** *adj* **1.** (*liable to happen*) eventuale **2.** (*dependent*) **to be** ~ **on** [*o* **upon**] sth dipendere da qc **3.** (*incidental*) **risks** ~ **to a profession** rischi contingenti a una professione

continual [kən'tɪn·ju·əl] *adj* continuo, -a

continually *adv* continuamente

continuation [kən·,tɪn·ju·'eɪ·ʃən] *n* continuazione *f*

continue [kən'tɪn·ju:] **I.** *vi* continuare; **he** ~**d by saying that ...** ha proseguito dicendo che ...; **to** ~ **to do** [*o* **doing**] sth continuare a fare qc; **to** ~ (**on**) **one's way** continuare per la propria strada; **to be** ~**d** continua **II.** *vt* continuare

continued *adj* **to be** ~ continua

continuity [,ka:n·tə·'nu:·ə·ti] *n* **1.** (*fact of continuing*) continuità *f* **2.** CINE, TV (*scenario*) continuity *f*

continuous [kən'tɪn·ju·əs] *adj* continuo, -a

contort [kən·'tɔ:rt] **I.** *vi* contorcersi; **his face had** ~**ed with rage** aveva il volto contorto per la rabbia **II.** *vt* contorcere; **to** ~ **the truth** distorcere la verità

contortion [kən·'tɔ:r·ʃən] *n* contorsione *f;* **bodily** ~**s** contorsioni *fpl;* **a** ~ **of reality** una distorsione della realtà

contortionist [kən·'tɔ:r·ʃə·nɪst] *n a. fig* contorsionista *mf*

contour ['ka:n·tʊr] **I.** *n* contorno *m;* (*face*) profilo *m* **II.** *vt* tracciare i contorni di

contour line *n* GEO curva *f* di livello

contour map *n* GEO carta *m* topografica

contraband ['ka:n·trə·bænd] **I.** *n* contrabbando *m* **II.** *adj* di contrabbando

contraception [,ka:n·trə·'sep·ʃən] *n* contraccezione *f*

contraceptive [,ka:n·trə·'sep·tɪv] *n* anticoncezionale *m*

contract[1] [kən·'trækt] **I.** *vi* contrarsi **II.** *vt* contrarre; **to** ~ **smallpox/AIDS/a cold** contrarre il vaiolo/l'Aids/il raffreddore

contract[2] ['ka:n·trækt] **I.** *n* contratto *m;* ~ **of employment** contratto di lavoro; **temporary** ~ contratto temporaneo; **to sign/enter into a** ~ firmare/stipulare un contratto **II.** *vi* **to** ~ **with sb** stipulare un contratto con qu **III.** *vt* contrattare

♦**contract out** *vt* appaltare

contraction [kən·'træk·ʃən] *n* contrazione *f*

contractor ['ka:n·træk·tə·] *n* appaltatore, -trice *m, f*

contractual [kən·'træk·tʃu·əl] *adj* contrattuale; ~ **conditions** condizioni *f pl* contrattuali; ~ **terms** termini *m pl* del contratto; **to be under a** ~ **obligation to sb** avere un contratto con qu

contradict [,ka:n·trə·'dɪkt] **I.** *vi* contraddirsi **II.** *vt* contraddire; **to** ~ **oneself** contraddirsi; **everything I say you want to** ~ devi contraddire tutto quello che dico; **don't** ~ **me!** non mi contraddire!

contradiction [,ka:n·trə·'dɪk·ʃən] *n* contraddizione *f;* **a** ~ **in terms** un controsenso

contradictory [,ka:n·trə·'dɪk·tə·ri] *adj* contraddittorio, -a

contralto [kən·'træl·t̬ou] *n* MUS contralto *m*

contraption [kən·'træp·ʃən] *n* aggeggio *m*

contrary ['ka:n·trə·i] **I.** *n* **on the** ~ al contrario; **quite the** ~! proprio il contrario!; **to the** ~ del contrario **II.** *adj* contrario, -a; **to be** ~ **to ...** essere contrario a...

contrary to *prep* al contrario di, contrariamente a; ~ **what he says** contrariamente a quanto dice; ~ **all our expectations** contro ogni pronostico

contrast [kən·'træst] **I.** *n* contrasto *m;* **to be quite a** ~ **to sb/sth** contrastare spiccatamente con qu/qc; **by** [*o* **in**] ~ per contrasto; **in** ~ **to** [*o* **with**] **sb/sth** a differenza di qu/qc **II.** *vt* contrastare

contrast control *n* TV controllo *m* del contrasto

contrasting *adj* contrastante

contravene [,ka:n·trə·'vi:n] *vt* contravvenire a

contravention [,ka:n·trə·'ven·ʃən] *n* contravvenzione *f;* **to act in** ~ **of the regulations** contravvenire alle norme

contribute [kən·'trɪ·bju:t] **I.** *vi* contribuire; ~ **towards sth** contribuire a qc; **to** ~ **to a fund** sovvenzionare un fondo **II.** *vt* **1.** (*money*) contribuire; **to** ~ (**sth**) **to sth** contribuire (qc) a qc; **to** ~ **sth towards ...** dare qc a ... **2.** (*article*) scrivere; (*information*) dare

contribution [,ka:n·trɪ·'bju:·ʃən] *n* **1.** contributo *m;* **a** ~ **to a charitable organization** una donazione a un ente di beneficenza **2.** (*text or article for publication*) collaborazione *f;* **a** ~ **for the Fall issue of a magazine** un articolo per il numero autunnale di una rivista

contributor [kən·ˈtrɪb·jə·tɚ] *n* **1.** (*for charity*) donatore, -trice *m, f* **2.** (*of publication*) collaboratore, -trice *m, f*

contributory [kən·ˈtrɪb·jə·tɔː·ri] *adj* contributivo, -a

contrite [kən·ˈtraɪt] *adj* contrito, -a; **~ expression** espressione *f* contrita

contrition [kən·ˈtrɪ·ʃən] *n* contrizione *f*

contrivance [kən·ˈtraɪ·vəns] *n* **1.** (*act of contriving*) calcolo *m* **2.** (*device*) congegno *m* **3.** (*inventive capacity*) inventiva *f*

contrive [kən·ˈtraɪv] *vt* **1.** (*plan*) congegnare; (*a meeting*) organizzare **2.** (*manage*) **to ~ to do sth** escogitare il modo di fare qc; **she ~d to make it happen** è riuscita a far sì che succedesse

contrived *adj* artificioso, -a

control [kən·ˈtroʊl] **I.** *n* **1.** controllo *m;* **to bring sth under ~** controllare qc; **spam is out of ~** lo spamming dilaga; **to have ~ over sb** controllare qu; **to lose ~ over sth** perdere il controllo di qc; **to lose ~ of oneself** perdere il controllo (di sé) **2.** (*leadership*) comando *m;* **to be in ~** essere al comando; **to be under the ~ of sb** essere dominato da qu **3.** AVIAT stazione *f* di controllo **4.** *pl* TECH comandi *mpl;* **to be at the ~s** stare ai comandi **II.** *vt* <-ll-> controllare; (*vehicle*) manovrare

control board *n* comitato *m* di controllo

control center *n* centrale *f* di controllo

control column *n* cloche *f*

control desk *n* pannello *m* di controllo

controllable *adj* controllabile

controlled [kən·ˈtroʊld] *adj* controllato, -a

controller [kən·ˈtroʊ·lɚ] *n* (*person in charge*) direttore, -trice *m, f;* FIN, ECON ispettore, -trice *m, f* finanziario, -a

control panel *n* quadro *m* dei comandi

control point *n* punto *m* di controllo

control tower *n* torre *f* di controllo

control unit *n* COMPUT unità *f* di controllo

controversial [ˌkɑːn·trə·ˈvɜːr·ʃəl] *adj* polemico, -a

controversy [ˈkɑːn·trə·vɜːr·si] *n* <-ies> polemica *f;* **to be beyond ~** essere incontestabile

contusion [kən·ˈtuː·ʒən] *n* contusione *f*

conundrum [kə·ˈnʌn·drəm] *n* rompicapo *m*

conurbation [ˌkɑːn·ɜːr·ˈbeɪ·ʃən] *n* conurbazione *f*

convalesce [ˌkɑːn·və·ˈles] *vi* essere in convalescenza; **to ~ from sth** riprendersi da qc

convalescence [ˌkɑːn·və·ˈle·sns] *n* convalescenza *f*

convalescent [ˌkɑːn·və·ˈle·snt] **I.** *n* convalescente *mf* **II.** *adj* convalescente; **a long ~ period** un lungo periodo di convalescenza; **~ hospital** centro ospedaliero riabilitativo

convection [kən·ˈvek·ʃən] *n* convezione *f*

convection oven *n* forno *m* a convezione

convector [kən·ˈvek·tɚ] *n*, **convector heater** *n* termoconvettore *m*

convene [kən·ˈviːn] **I.** *vi form* riunirsi **II.** *vt form* riunire; (*meeting*) convocare

convener [kən·ˈviː·nɚ] *n* convocatore, -trice *m, f*

convenience [kən·ˈviː·n·jəns] *n* comodità *f;* **for ~'s sake** per comodità; **at your ~** quando le torna più comodo

convenience store *n emporio che apre presto e chiude tardi*

convenient [kən·ˈviː·ni·ənt] *adj* comodo, -a

convenor [kən·ˈviː·nɚ] *n s.* **convener**

convent [ˈkɑːn·vənt] *n* convento *m*

convention [kən·ˈven·ʃən] *n* **1.** convenzione *f;* **~ dictates that** è usanza **2.** (*large meeting*) congresso *m*

conventional [kən·ˈven·tʃə·nəl] *adj* convenzionale; (*wisdom*) ortodosso, -a; (*medicine*) tradizionale

conventionally *adv* convenzionalmente

converge [kən·ˈvɜːrdʒ] *vi a. fig* convergere; (*persons*) riunirsi

convergence [kən·ˈvɜːr·dʒəns] *n* convergenza *f*

convergent [kən·ˈvɜːr·dʒent] *adj* convergente

conversant [kən·ˈvɜːr·snt] *adj* pratico, -a; **to be ~ with sth** essere pratico di qc

conversation [ˌkɑːn·vɚ·ˈseɪ·ʃən] *n* (*word exchange*) conversazione *f;* **to strike up a ~ with sb** mettersi a parlare con qu

conversational [ˌkɑːn·vɚ·ˈseɪ·ʃə·nəl] *adj* (*tone*) colloquiale; (*skills*) di conversazione

conversationally *adv* in tono colloquiale

converse[1] [kən·ˈvɜːrs] *vi form* **to ~ with sb** conversare con qu

converse[2] [ˈkɑːn·vɜːrs] **I.** *n* **the ~** il contrario **II.** *adj form* contrario, -a

conversely *adv* al contrario

conversion [kən·ˈvɜːr·ʒən] *n* conversione *f*

conversion rate *n* tasso *m* di cambio

convert [kən·ˈvɜːrt] **I.** *n* convertito, -a *m, f* **II.** *vi* convertirsi **III.** *vt* convertire

converter [kən·ˈvɜːr·tɚ] *n* **1.** (*person*) convertitore, -trice *m, f* **2.** ELEC trasformatore *m* **3.** TECH convertitore *m*

convertible [kən·ˈvɜːr·ṭə·bl] **I.** *n* AUTO decappottabile *m* **II.** *adj a.* FIN, ECON convertibile; **~ sofa** divano *m* letto

convex [ˈkɑːn·veks] *adj* convesso, -a

convey [kən·ˈveɪ] *vt* **1.** (*transport*) trasportare; (*electricity*) condurre **2.** (*communicate*) trasmettere; **to ~ how ...** comunicare come ...; **to ~ sth to sb** trasmettere qc a qu

conveyance [kən·ˈveɪ·ənts] *n* **1.** (*act of carrying*) trasporto *m* **2.** (*communication*) trasmissione *f* **3.** (*vehicle*) veicolo *m;* **form of ~** mezzo *m* di trasporto **4.** LAW cessione *f;* (*document*) atto *m* di cessione

conveyancing *n* LAW cessione *f* di proprietà; (*document*) redazione *f* di atto cessione di proprietà

conveyor [kən·ˈve·ɪɚ] *n* trasportatore *m;* (*belt*) nastro *m* trasportatore

convict[1] [ˈkɑːn·vɪkt] *n* detenuto, -a *m, f*

convict[2] [kə·ˈn·ˈvɪkt] *vt* condannare

conviction [kən·'vɪk·ʃən] *n* **1.** LAW condanna *f* **2.** (*firm belief*) convinzione *f;* **to have a ~ about sth** essere convinto di qc

convince [kən·'vɪnts] *vt* convincere; **I'm not ~ d** non ne sono convinto

convincing [kən·'vɪnt·sɪŋ] *adj* convincente

convoluted *adj* contorto, -a

convoy ['ka:n·vɔɪ] **I.** *n* convoglio *m;* **in ~** in convoglio **II.** *vt* scortare

convulse [kən·'vʌls] **I.** *vi* contorcersi; **to ~ in laughter** contorcersi dalle risa; **to ~ in pain** torcersi dal dolore **II.** *vt* far contorcere; **to be ~ d with anger** agitarsi in modo convulso per la rabbia

convulsion [kən·'vʌl·ʃən] *n* convulsione *f;* **she went into ~s** le vennero le convulsioni; (*uncontrolled laughter*) si mise a ridere convulsamente

convulsive [kən·'vʌl·sɪv] *adj* convulsivo, -a

coo [ku:] **I.** *vi* tubare **II.** *vt* dire amorevolmente

cook [kʊk] **I.** *n* cuoco, -a *m, f* **II.** *vi* cuocere; **how long does pasta take to ~?** quanto ci mette a cuocere la pasta?; **can you ~?** sai cucinare? ▶ what's ~ing? *inf* cosa c'è? **III.** *vt* cuocere; **to ~ lunch** preparare il pranzo

cookbook ['kʊk·bʊk] *n* libro *m* di cucina

cooker ['kʊ·kə] *n* cucina *f*

cookery ['kʊ·kə·ri] *n* cucina *f*

cookie ['kʊ·ki] *n* **1.** (*biscuit*) biscotto *m* **2.** *inf* (*person*) tipo *m;* **a tough ~** un tipo tosto **3.** COMPUT cookie *m* ▶ that's the way the ~ crumbles *inf* è la vita!

cooking ['kʊ·kɪŋ] *n* **to do the ~** far da mangiare

cool [ku:l] **I.** *adj* **1.** (*slightly cold*) fresco, -a **2.** (*calm*) tranquillo, -a; **keep ~** mantieni la calma **3.** *inf* (*impudent*) sfacciato, -a; **to be a ~ one** essere uno sfacciato **4.** (*unfriendly*) freddo, -a **5.** *inf* (*fashionable*) **to be ~** essere trendy **II.** *interj* *inf* grande! **III.** *n* **1.** (*coolness*) fresco *m* **2.** (*calm*) calma *f* **IV.** *vt* rinfrescare; **just ~ it** *inf* calma! **V.** *vi* (*become colder*) rinfrescare; **to ~ down** [*o* **off**] (*become cooler*) rinfrescare; (*food*) freddarsi; (*become calmer*) calmarsi

cooler ['ku:·lə] *n* **1.** (*box*) borsa *f* termica **2.** (*drink*) bevanda *f* rinfrescante

cool-headed [ˌku:l·'he·dɪd] *adj* calmo, -a

cooling ['ku:·lɪŋ] *adj* rinfrescante; (*breeze*) fresco, -a

cooling tower *n* torre *f* di raffreddamento

coolly ['ku:·li] *adv* **1.** (*calmly*) con calma **2.** (*coldly*) freddamente

coolness ['ku:l·nɪs] *n* **1.** METEO fresco *m* **2.** (*unfriendliness*) freddezza *f*

coop [ku:p] **I.** *n* stia *f* **II.** *vt* rinchiudere ◆**coop up** *vt* rinchiudere

co-op ['koʊ·a:p] *n abbr of* **cooperative** cooperativa *f*

cooper ['ku:·pə] **I.** *n* barilaio, -a *m, f* **II.** *vi* (*make barrels*) fabbricare barili; (*repair barrels*) riparare barili

cooperate [koʊ·'a:·pə·reɪt] *vi* cooperare; **to ~ with sb** collaborare con qu

cooperation [koʊˌa:·pə·'reɪ·ʃən] *n* cooperazione *f*

cooperative [koʊ·'a:·pə·ə·tɪv] **I.** *n* ECON cooperativa *f* **II.** *adj* cooperativo, -a; **~ society** società *f* cooperativa

co-opt [koʊ·'a:pt] *vt* **1.** (*adopt as own*) adottare **2.** (*absorb into larger unit*) **to be ~ed into sth** essere incorporato in qc

coordinate [ˌkoʊ·'ɔ:r·dɪ·neɪt] **I.** *n* coordinata *f* **II.** *vi* **1.** (*work together effectively*) operare insieme **2.** (*match*) essere coordinato **III.** *vt* coordinare **IV.** *adj* **1.** (*equal*) egalitario, -a **2.** (*involving coordination*) coordinato, -a

coordination [ˌkoʊˌɔ:r·də·'neɪ·ʃən] *n* coordinazione *f*

coordinator *n* coordinatore, -trice *m, f*

coot [ku:t] *n* **1.** ZOOL folaga *f* **2.** *inf* (*rather dim person*) cretino, -a *m, f*

cop [ka:p] **I.** *n inf* (*police officer*) sbirro *m;* **to play ~s and robbers** giocare a guardie e ladri **II.** <-pp-> *vt* **1.** (*grab*) prendere; **to ~ a** (**quick**) **look at sth** dare un'occhiata a qc **2.** LAW **to ~ a plea** dichiararsi colpevole

copartner [koʊ·'pa:rt·nə] *n* socio, -a *m, f*

copartnership ['koʊˌpa:rt·nə·ʃɪp] *n* compartecipazione *f*

cope [koʊp] *vi* **1.** (*master a situation*) farcela **2.** (*deal with*) **to ~ with sth** (*problem*) far fronte a qc; (*pain*) sopportare qc

copier ['ka:·piə] *n* fotocopiatrice *f*

copilot ['koʊˌpaɪ·lət] *n* copilota *m*

copious ['koʊ·pi·əs] *adj* copioso, -a

copper ['ka:·pə] **I.** *n* **1.** (*metal*) rame *m* **2.** *inf* (*police officer*) sbirro *m* **II.** *adj* (*color*) color rame

copper beech <-es> *n* faggio *m* rosso

copper ore *n* minerale *m* di rame

copperplate **I.** *n* **1.** (*handwriting*) bella calligrafia *f* **2.** (*metal plaque*) lastra *f* di rame **II.** *adj* in bella calligrafia

coppersmith *n* calderaio, -a *m, f*

coppice ['ka:·pɪs] **I.** *n* bosco *m* ceduo **II.** *vt* tagliare

copulate ['ka:p·jə·leɪt] *vi* copulare

copulation [ˌka:p·jə·'leɪ·ʃən] *n* copulazione *f*

copy ['ka:·pi] **I.** <-ies> *n* **1.** (*facsimile*) copia *f;* **to be a carbon ~ of sb** essere la fotocopia di qu; **an exact ~** una copia esatta **2.** COMPUT copia *f;* **hard ~** copia cartacea; **to make a ~** fare una copia **3.** (*text to be published*) testo *m;* (*advertisement text*) testo *m* di pubblicità **4.** (*topics for articles*) tema *m* **II.** <-ie-> *vt* **1.** *a.* COMPUT, MUS copiare **2.** (*imitate*) imitare **III.** *vi* SCHOOL copiare

copybook ['ka:·pi·bʊk] **I.** *adj* **1.** (*exemplary*) modello **2.** (*unoriginal*) convenzionale **II.** *n* quaderno *m*

copycat **I.** *n childspeak, inf* copione, -ona *m, f* **II.** *adj* **~ version** imitazione *f;* **a ~ crime** un reato ispirato a un altro

copy desk *n* tavolo *m* della redazione

copy editor *n* redattore, -trice *m, f*

copy protection *n* COMPUT protezione *f* anticopia

copyright *n* diritti *m pl* d'autore; **to hold the ~ of sth** possedere i diritti d'autore di qc

copywriter *n* copywriter *mf*

coral ['kɔː·rəl] I. *n* corallo *m;* **made of ~** di corallo II. *adj* (*reddish color*) (color) corallo

coral island *n* isola *f* corallina

coral reef *n* barriera *f* corallina

cord [kɔːrd] *n* (*rope*) corda *f;* ELEC filo *m;* **spinal ~** midollo *m* spinale; **umbilical ~** cordone *m* ombelicale

cordial ['kɔːr·dʒəl] I. *adj* **1.** (*friendly*) cordiale **2.** *form* (*strong*) intenso, -a II. *n* bevanda *f* alla frutta

cordiality [ˌkɔːr·dʒɪ·'æ·lə·ti] <-ies> *n form* cordialità *f*

cordless ['kɔːrd·ləs] *adj* senza fili

cordon ['kɔːr·dn] I. *n* cordone *m;* **police ~** cordone di polizia II. *vt* fare cordone attorno a

cords *npl* pantaloni *m pl* di velluto a coste

corduroy ['kɔːr·də·ˌrɔɪ] *n* velluto *m* a coste

core [kɔːr] I. *n* **1.** (*center*) centro *m;* **to the ~** *fig* fino al midollo; **to be rotten to the ~** *fig* essere corrotto fino al midollo; **the ~ of a problem** il nocciolo della questione **2.** (*center with seeds*) torsolo *m* **3.** PHYS nucleo *m* **4.** ELEC anima *f* II. *adj* **the ~ issue** la questione principale III. *vt* togliere il torsolo

CORE [kɔːr] *n abbr of* **Congress of Racial Equality** associazione *m* per l'uguaglianza razziale

core subject *n* tema *m* centrale

coriander ['kɔː·ri·æn·dəˀ] *n* coriandolo *m*

cork [kɔːrk] I. *n* **1.** sughero *m* **2.** (*stopper*) tappo (di sughero) *m* II. *vt* **1.** (*put stopper in*) tappare **2.** (*restrain*) **to ~ one's anger** soffocare la propria rabbia **3.** (*blacken*) **to ~ one's face** annerirsi il viso

corkage ['kɔːr·kədʒ] *n*, **cork charge** *n tariffa che alcuni ristoranti fanno pagare per stappare bottiglie di vino portate dai clienti*

corkscrew ['kɔːrk·skruː] I. *n* cavatappi *m inv* II. *adj* a spirale; **~ curls** boccoli *mpl*

corn[1] [kɔːrn] *n* **1.** (*crop*) granturco *m;* **~ on the cob** pannocchia *f* di granturco **2.** *inf* (*something trite*) roba *f* sdolcinata

corn[2] [kɔːrn] *n* MED callo *m* ▸ **to** <u>tread</u> **on sb's ~s** pestare i calli a qu

corn bread *n* pane *m* di granturco

corncob *n* pannocchia *f* di granturco

cornea ['kɔːr·niə] *n* cornea *f*

corner ['kɔːr·nəˀ] I. *n* **1.** angolo *m;* **to cut a ~** svicolare; **to be around the ~** essere girato l'angolo; **to turn the ~** girare l'angolo; *fig* essere al giro di boa; **a distant ~ of the globe** un angolo remoto della terra; **the four ~s of the world** da ogni parte del mondo **2.** (*kick or shot*) corner *m* **3.** (*difficult position*) **to be in a tight ~** trovarsi in una posizione difficile; **to drive sb into a** (**tight**) **~** mettere qu con le spalle al muro **4.** (*domination*) **to have a ~ of the market** controllare una fetta di mercato

5. (*periphery*) **out of the ~ of one's eye** con la coda dell'occhio; **out of the ~ of sb's mouth** all'angolo della bocca ▸ **to cut ~s** fare le cose tirate via II. *vt* **1.** (*hinder escape*) intrappolare; **to get sb ~ed** *fig* intrappolare qu **2.** ECON **to ~ the market** monopolizzare il mercato III. *vi* (*auto*) curvare

cornered ['kɔːr·nəˀd] *adj* intrappolato, -a

corner house *n* casa *f* all'angolo

corner seat *n* posto *m* d'angolo

corner shop *n* piccolo emporio *m*

cornerstone *n a. fig* pietra *f* angolare

cornet [kɔːr·'net] *n* **1.** (*brass instrument*) cornetta *f* **2.** (*wafer cone*) cornetto *m*

cornflakes ['kɔːrn·fleɪks] *npl* cornflakes *mpl*

cornflower ['kɔːrn·fla·ʊəˀ] I. *n* fiordaliso *m* II. *adj* **~ blue** azzurro fiordaliso

cornice ['kɔːr·nɪs] *n* ARCHIT cornice *f*

corn poppy <-ies> *n* papavero *m*

cornstarch *n* farina *f* di mais

corny ['kɔːr·ni] <-ier, -iest> *adj* **1.** *inf* vecchio, -a; (*joke*) trito, -a **2.** (*emotive*) sdolcinato, -a

corollary ['kɔːr·rə·le·ri] <-ies> *n form* corollario *m*

coronary ['kɔːr·rə·ne·ri] I. *n* infarto *m* del miocardio; **when he got the bill he nearly had a ~ iron** quando gli hanno portato il conto per poco non gli è venuto un infarto II. *adj* coronario, -a; (*bypass*) coronarico, -a

coronation [ˌkɔːr·rə·'neɪ·ʃən] I. *n* incoronazione *f* II. *adj* dell'incoronazione

coroner ['kɔːr·rə·nəˀ] *n magistrato incaricato di investigare morti non naturali*

corp. *abbr of* **corporation** società *f*

corpl. *n* MIL *abbr of* **corporal** caporale *m*

corporal ['kɔːr·pə·rəl] I. *n* MIL caporale *m* II. *adj form* corporale; **a ~ oath** HIST giuramento *m* alla corona

corporate ['kɔːr·pə·rət] *adj* **1.** (*shared by group*) collettivo, -a **2.** (*of corporation*) aziendale; **~ capital** capitale *m* societario; **~ law** diritto *m* aziendale

corporation [ˌkɔːr·pə·'reɪ·ʃən] *n + sing/pl vb* **1.** (*business*) società *f;* **multinational ~** multinazionale *f;* **a public ~** una impresa pubblica **2.** (*local council*) **municipal ~** autorità *f* comunale

corporation tax <-es> *n* imposta *f* sulle società

corps [kɔːr] *n + sing/pl vb* corpo *m*

corps de ballet [ˌkɔːr·də·'bæ·leɪ] *n* corpo *m* di ballo

corpse [kɔːrps] *n* cadavere *m*

corpus ['kɔːr·pəs] <-pora *o* -es> *n* **1.** LIT, LING corpus *m inv* **2.** ECON capitale *m*

Corpus Christi [ˌkɔːr·pəs·'krɪs·ti] *n* REL Corpus Domini *m*

corpuscle ['kɔːr·pʌ·sl] *n* corpuscolo *m*

corral [kə·'ræl] I. *n* recinto *m* II. <-ll-> *vt* recintare

correct [kə·'rekt] I. *vt* (*put right*) correggere; **~ me if I'm wrong, but ...** correggimi se sbaglio, ma... II. *adj* corretto, -a; **that is ~ form**

esatto
correction [kə·'rek·ʃən] *n* correzione *f*
correction fluid *n* bianchetto *m*
corrective [kə·'rek·tɪv] I. *adj* correttivo, -a II. *n* chiarimento *m*
correctly [kə·'rekt·li] *adv* correttamente
correctness [kə·'rekt·nɪs] *n* correttezza *f*
correlate ['kɔː·rə·leɪt] I. *vt* correlare II. *vi* essere in correlazione
correlation [ˌkɔː·rə·'leɪ·ʃən] *n* correlazione *f;* there is a ~ between smoking and lung cancer c'è una correlazione tra il fumo e il cancro ai polmoni
correspond [ˌkɔː·rə·'spɒnd] *vi* corrispondere
correspondence [ˌkɔː·rə·'spɑːn·dəns] *n* corrispondenza *f;* business ~ corrispondenza commerciale; to enter into ~ with sb *form* entrare in corrispondenza con qu
correspondent [ˌkɔː·rə·'spɑːn·dənt] *n* corrispondente *mf;* special ~ inviato, -a *m, f* speciale
corresponding [ˌkɔː·rə·'spɒn·dɪŋ] *adj* corrispondente
corridor ['kɔː·rə·də·] *n* corridoio *m*
corroborate [kə·'rɑː·bə·reɪt] *vt* corroborare
corroboration [kə·ˌrɑː·bə·'reɪ·ʃən] *n* corroborazione *f;* in ~ of sth a corroborazione di qc
corroborative [kə·'rɑː·bə·ə·tɪv] *adj* a corroborazione
corrode [kə·'roʊd] I. *vi* corrodersi II. *vt* corrodere
corrosion [kə·'roʊ·ʒən] *n* 1. corrosione *f* 2. *fig* (*deterioration*) deterioramento *m*
corrosive [kə·'roʊ·sɪv] I. *adj* 1. (*destructive*) corrosivo, -a 2. *fig* (*harmful*) distruttivo, -a; ~ attack *fig* attacco *m* al vetriolo II. *n* corrosivo *m*
corrugated ['kɒ·rə·geɪ·ţɪd] *adj* (*furrowed*) ondulato, -a
corrupt [kə·'rʌpt] I. *vt* 1. corrompere 2. (*document*) danneggiare II. *vi* corrompere III. *adj* 1. (*influenced by bribes*) corrotto, -a; ~ practices pratiche*f pl* corrotte 2. (*document*) danneggiato, -a
corruption [kə·'rʌp·ʃən] *n* corruzione *f*
corset ['kɔːr·sɪt] *n* corsetto *m*
cos [kɑːs] MATH *abbr of* **cosine** cos
cosec ['koʊ·sek] MATH *abbr of* **cosecant** cosec
cosignatory [ˌkoʊ·'sɪg·nə·tɔː·ri] <-ies> *n* cofirmatario, -a *m, f*
cosine ['koʊ·saɪn] *n* coseno *m*
cosmetic [kɑːz·'me·ţɪk] I. *n* cosmetico *m;* ~s cosmetici *mpl* II. *adj* 1. cosmetico, -a; ~ cream crema *f* di bellezza 2. (*superficial*) superficiale
cosmetician [ˌkɒz·mə·'tɪ·ʃən] *n* estetista *mf*
cosmic ['kɑːz·mɪk] *adj fig* cosmico, -a; of ~ proportions di enorme portata
cosmology [kɑːz·'mɑː·lə·dʒi] *n* cosmologia *f*
cosmonaut ['kɑːz·mə·nɑːt] *n* cosmonauta *mf*
cosmopolitan [ˌkɑːz·mə·'pɑː·lɪ·tən] I. *adj* cosmopolita II. *n* cosmopolita *mf*
cosmos ['kɑːz·moʊs] *n* cosmo *m*

cost [kɑːst] I. *vt* 1. <cost, cost> (*amount to, cause the loss of*) costare; to ~ a fortune *inf* costare un patrimonio; to ~ sb dearly costare caro a qu 2. <costed, costed> (*calculate price*) calculare il costo di II. *n* 1. (*price*) costo *m,* prezzo *m;* at no extra ~ compreso nel prezzo; to cut the ~ ridurre i costi; to defray the ~ of sth *form* coprire i costi di qc 2. *pl* (*expense*) costi *mpl;* LAW spese *fpl;* to cut ~s ridurre le spese 3. (*cost price*) to purchase sth at ~ acquistare qc a prezzo di costo 4. *fig* (*sacrifice*) (only) at the ~ of doing sth (solo) facendo qc; at all ~(s) a tutti i costi
costar ['koʊ·stɑːr] I. *n* coprotagonista *mf* II. <-rr-> *vt* avere come coprotagonista III. <-rr-> *vi* to ~ with sb interpretare insieme a qu
costly ['kɑːst·li] <-ier, -iest> *adj* costoso, -a; (*mistake*) che costa caro, -a; to prove ~ *a. fig* risultare molto caro
cost price ['kɑːst·ˌpraɪs] *n* at ~ a prezzo di costo
costume ['kɑːs·tuːm] *n* costume *m*
cot [kɑːt] *n* 1. (*baby's bed*) culla *f* 2. (*camp bed*) brandina *f*
cotangent [ˌkoʊ·'tæn·dʒənt] *n* cotangente *f*
cottage ['kɑː·ţɪdʒ] *n* country ~ casetta *f* di campagna; thatched ~ casetta col tetto di paglia
cottage cheese *n* fiocchi*m pl* di formaggio
cottage industry <-ies> *n* lavoro *m* a domicilio
cot(an) MATH *abbr of* **cotangent** ctg
cotton ['kɑː·tn] *n* 1. (*plant*) cotone *m* 2. (*material*) cotone *m* 3. (*thread*) filo *m*
cotton candy *n* zucchero *m* filato
cotton gin *n* sgranatrice *f* da cotone
cotton-picking *adj inf* del cavolo
cottonseed *n* seme *m* di cotone
couch [kaʊtʃ] <-es> I. *n* divano *m;* psychiatrist's ~ lettino *m* dello psicanalista II. *vt* esprimere
couchette [ku·'ʃet] *n* cuccetta *f*
couch potato <- -es> *n* pantofolaio, -a *m, f* teledipendente
cough [kɑːf] I. *n* tosse *f* II. *vi* tossire III. *vt* to ~ blood tossire sangue
◆**cough up** I. *vi inf* sganciare II. *vt inf* 1. (*bring up: blood*) tossire; MED espettorare 2. *sl* (*pay*) sganciare; (*divulge reluctantly*) tirar fuori
cough drop *n* caramella *f* per la tosse
cough medicine *n* medicinale *m* per la tosse
could [kʊd] *pt, pp* **can**[2]
council ['kaʊn·tsəl] *n* ADMIN, MIL consiglio *m;* city ~ consiglio comunale; local ~ autorità*f pl* locali; the United Nations Security Council il Consiglio di Sicurezza delle Nazioni Unite
council(l)or ['kaʊn·tsə·lə·] *n* consigliere *m*
counsel ['kaʊn·tsəl] I. <-ll-, -l-> *vt* (*advise*) consigliare; to ~ sb against sth *form* sconsigliare qc a qu II. *n* 1. *form* (*advice*) consiglio *m;* to seek ~ chiedere consiglio 2. (*lawyer*) avvo-

cato *m;* ~ **for the defense** avvocato difensore; ~ **for the prosecution** pubblico ministero *m* ▶**to keep one's own** ~ non parlare

counsel(l)ing I. *n* assistenza *f* II. *adj* di assistenza

counsel(l)or ['kaʊn·tsə·lə] *n* consulente *mf;* **marriage guidance** ~ consulente matrimoniale

count[1] [kaʊnt] *n* conte *m*

count[2] [kaʊnt] I. *n* 1. conto *m;* **final** ~ cifra definitiva; **to keep** ~ **of sth** tenere il conto di qc; **to lose** ~ **of sth** perdere il conto di qc *f* 2. (*measured amount*) livello *m* 3. LAW capo *m* d'accusa 4. (*opinion*) punto *m;* **to be angry with sb on several** ~**s** essere arrabbiato con qu per vari motivi ▶**to be out for the** ~ dormire della grossa II. *vt* 1. (*number*) contare; **to** ~ **one's change** controllare il resto; **to** ~ **heads/noses** contare uno ad uno 2. (*consider*) considerare; **to** ~ **sth a success/failure** considerare qc un successo/fallimento; **to** ~ **sb as a friend** considerare qu un amico III. *vi* contare; **that's what** ~**s** questo è ciò che conta; **this doesn't** ~ **for anything** questo non conta nulla; **to not** ~ non contare

◆**count down** *vi* fare il conto alla rovescia

◆**count out** *vt always sep* 1. (*money*) contare 2. *inf* (*leave out*) **to count sb out** escludere qu

countdown ['kaʊnt·daʊn] *n* conto *m* alla rovescia

countenance ['kaʊn·tə·nəns] I. *n* 1. *form* (*facial expression*) espressione *f* (del volto); **to be of noble** ~ avere tratti nobili 2. (*approval*) approvazione *f;* **to give** ~ **to sth** approvare qc II. *vt form* approvare

counter ['kaʊn·tə] I. *n* 1. (*service point*) banco *m;* **over the** ~ senza ricetta; **under the** ~ *fig* sottobanco 2. (*person who counts*) cassiere, -a *m, f* 3. (*machine*) cassa *f;* TECH contatore *m* 4. (*disc*) fiche *f inv* II. *vt* controbattere III. *vi* 1. (*oppose*) opporsi 2. (*react by scoring*) contrattacare IV. *adv* contro; **to act** ~ **to sth** agire contrariamente a qc; **to run** ~ **to sth** andare contro a qc

counteract [ˌkaʊn·tə·ˈækt] *vt* neutralizzare; **to** ~ **the effects of sth** neutralizzare gli effetti di qc; ~ **inflation** combattere l'inflazione

counteractive [ˌkaʊn·tə·ˈæk·tɪv] *adj* 1. (*working against*) contrario, -a 2. (*neutralizing*) neutralizzante

counterattack ['kaʊn·tə·ə·tæk] I. *n* contrattacco *m* II. *vt* contrattaccare III. *vi* (*attack in return*) contrattaccare

counterbalance ['kaʊn·tə·bæ·ləns] I. *n* contrappeso *m* II. *vt* (*balance out*) controbilanciare

countercharge ['kaʊn·tə·tʃɑːrdʒ] I. *n* LAW controaccusa *f* II. *vt* LAW rispondere a

countercheck ['kaʊn·tə·tʃek] I. *n* riscontro *m* II. *vt* riscontrare

counterclockwise [ˌkaʊn·tə·ˈklɑːk·waɪz] *adj* in senso antiorario

counterespionage [ˌkaʊn·tə·ˈes·piə·nɑːʒ] *n*

controspionaggio *m*

counterfeit ['kaʊn·tə·fɪt] I. *adj* contraffatto, -a; (*money*) falso, -a II. *vt* contraffare III. *n* contraffazione *f*

counterintelligence [ˌkaʊn·tə·ɪn·ˈte·lɪ·dʒəns] *n* controspionaggio *m*

countermand [ˌkaʊn·tə·ˈmænd] *vt* revocare

countermeasure ['kaʊn·tə·me·ʒə] *n* contromisura *f*

counterpart ['kaʊn·tə·pɑːrt] *n* controparte *f;* POL omologo *m*

counterpoint ['kaʊn·tə·pɔɪnt] *n* MUS contrappunto *m*

counterpoise ['kaʊn·tə·pɔɪz] *form* I. *n* contrappeso *m* II. *vt* controbilanciare

counterproductive [ˌkaʊn·tə·prə·ˈdʌk·tɪv] *adj* controproducente

counterrevolution [ˌkaʊn·tə·ˌre·və·ˈluː·ʃən] *n* controrivoluzione *f*

countersign ['kaʊn·tə·saɪn] *vt* controfirmare

countersink ['kaʊn·tə·sɪŋk] *irr vt* svasare

countersue *vt* fare causa a propria volta a

counterterrorism [ˌkaʊn·tə·ˈte·rə·ɪ·zəm] *n* controterrorismo *m*

countess ['kaʊn·tɪs] *n* contessa *f*

countless ['kaʊnt·lɪs] *adj* innumerevole

country ['kʌn·tri] I. *n* 1. (*rural area*) campagna *f* 2. <-ies> (*political unit*) paese *m;* (*native land*) patria *f* 3. (*area of land*) territorio *m* 4. MUS country *m* II. *adj* 1. (*rural*) di campagna 2. MUS (*music*) country

country bumpkin *n* contadino, -a *m, f*

country club *n* circolo esclusivo per attività sportive o ricreative situato in campagna

country-dance *n* danza *f* folkloristica

country folk *n* + *pl vb* gente *f* di campagna

country house *n* residenza *f* di campagna

countryman ['kʌn·tri·mən] <-men> *n* 1. (*same nationality*) compatriota *m* 2. (*from rural area*) contadino *m*

country music *n* musica *f* country

country road *n* strada *f* di campagna

countryside ['kʌn·tri·saɪd] *n* campagna *m*

countrywide ['kʌn·tri·waɪd] *adj* su scala nazionale

countrywoman ['kʌn·tri·wʊ·mən] <-women> *n* 1. (*same nationality*) compatriota *f* 2. (*from rural area*) contadina *f*

county ['kaʊn·ti] <-ies> *n* contea *f*

county fair *n* festa *f* della contea

county seat *n* capoluogo *m* della contea

coup [kuː] <coups> *n* golpe *m inv*

coup de grâce [ˌkuː·də·ˈɡrɑːs] *n* colpo *m* di grazia

coup d'état <coups d'état> *n* colpo *m* di stato

coupé ['kuː·peɪ] *n* coupé *m*

couple ['kʌ·pl] I. *n* 1. (*a few*) paio *m;* **the first** ~ **of weeks** le prime due settimane 2. I *sing/pl vb* (*two people*) coppia *f* II. *vt* 1. RAIL, AUTO attaccare 2. (*connect, link*) collegare III. *vi* HIST accoppiarsi

couplet ['kʌp·lɪt] *n* distico *m*

coupling ['kʌp·lɪŋ] *n* 1. RAIL, AUTO agganciamento *m* **2.**(*linking*) collegamento *f* **3.**(*sexual intercourse*) accoppiamento *m*

coupon ['kuː·pɑːn] *n* **1.**(*voucher*) buono *m* **2.**(*order form*) tagliando *m*

courage ['kʌ·rɪdʒ] *n* coraggio *m;* **to show great ~** dimostrare grande coraggio; **to take one's ~ in both hands** prendere il coraggio a quattro mani

courageous [kə·'reɪ·dʒəs] *adj* coraggioso, -a

courier ['kʊ·ri·ɚ] I. *n* (*messenger*) messaggero, -a *m, f* II. *adj* **~ service** servizio *m* corriere

course [kɔːrs] I. *n* **1.**(*direction*) rotta *f;* (*of a river*) corso *m;* **to be off ~** *a. fig* deviare; **to set ~ for sth** fare rotta verso qc; **your best ~ of action would be ...** la cosa migliore da fare sarebbe... **2.**(*development*) sviluppo *m; over the ~ of time* col tempo **3.**(*treatment*) ciclo *m* **4.** SPORTS (*area*) pista *f;* (*golf*) campo *m* **5.**(*part of meal*) portata *f* **6.**(*layer*) corso *m* ► **to let sth run its ~** lasciare che qc faccia il suo corso; **to stay the ~** rimanere fino alla fine; **of ~** certo; **of ~ not** certo che no II. *vi* scorrere

courseware *n* COMPUT software *m* didattico

court [kɔːrt] I. *n* **1.**(*room for trials*) tribunale *m*, aula *f* **2.**(*judicial body*) tribunale *m*, corte *f* **3.**(*playing area*) cortile *m;* (*for tennis, basketball*) campo *m* **4.**(*road*) via *f* **5.** HIST palazzo *m* **6.**(*sovereign*) corte *f* ► **to hold ~** fare salotto; **to laugh sb out of ~** ridicolizzare qu II. *vt* (*woman*) corteggiare; (*danger*) esporsi a III. *vi* (*couple*) stare insieme

courteous ['kɜːr·t̬i·əs] *adj* cortese

courtesy ['kɜːr·t̬ə·si] <-ies> *n* cortesia *f*

courtesy light *n* AUTO luce *f* di cortesia

courtesy title *n* trattamento *m* di cortesia

court hearing *n* udienza *f*

courthouse ['kɔːrt·haʊs] *n* tribunale *m*

courtier ['kɔːr·t̬iɚ] *n* cortigiano, -a *m, f*

court-martial I.<courts-martial> *n* corte *f* marziale II.<-ll-, -l-> *vt* sottoporre alla corte marziale

court of appeals *n* corte *f* d'appello

Court of Justice *n* Tribunale *m* di Giustizia

courtroom ['kɔːrt·ruːm] *n* aula *f* di tribunale

courtship *n* corteggiamento *m*

courtyard *n* cortile *m*

cousin ['kʌ·zn] *n* cugino, -a *m, f*

couture [kuː·'tʊr] *n* FASHION moda *f;* **haute ~** alta moda

cove [koʊv] *n* cala *f*

covenant ['kʌ·və·nənt] I. *n* vincolo *m* II. *vt* versare (per contratto)

cover ['kʌ·vɚ] I. *n* **1.**(*top*) rivestimento *m* **2.**(*outer sheet*) copertina *f* **3.**(*bedding*) copriletto *m* **4.**(*concealment*) copertura *f;* **to break ~** uscire allo scoperto **5.**(*shelter*) riparo *m;* **to take ~** ripararsi **6.**(*insurance*) copertura *f* **7.**(*provision*) sostituzione *f* **8.**(*envelope*) **first day ~** busta col timbro del primo giorno d'emissione del francobollo **9.** MUS cover *f* II. *vt* **1.**(*hide: eyes, ears*) tappare; (*head*) coprire **2.**(*put over*) coprire; (*book*) rivestire **3.**(*keep warm*) coprire

4.(*travel*) percorrere **5.**(*deal with*) riguardare **6.**(*include*) includere **7.**(*report on*) fare un servizio su **8.**(*insure*) assicurare **9.**(*give armed protection*) coprire **10.** MUS (*song*) fare una cover di **11.** *sl* **to ~ one's ass** pararsi il culo *vulg* III. *vi* sostituire

◆**cover over** *vt* coprire

◆**cover up** I. *vt* (*protect*) coprire II. *vi* **to ~ for sb** coprire qu

coverage ['kʌ·və·rɪdʒ] *n* **1.**(*reporting*) servizio *m* **2.**(*dealing with*) trattamento *m*

coveralls ['kʌ·və·rɔːlz] *npl* tuta *f*

cover charge ['kʌ·vɚ·tʃɑːrdʒ] *n* coperto *m*

covered *adj* **1.**(*roofed over*) coperto -a **2.**(*insured*) asegurado, -a

cover girl ['kʌ·vɚ·gɜːrl] *n* ragazza *f* copertina

covering *n* rivestimento *m*

cover letter *n* lettera *f* d'accompagnamento

covers ['kʌ·vɚz] *n* coperte *fpl*

cover story <-ies> *n* notizia *f* di prima pagina

covert¹ ['koʊ·vɜːrt] *adj* segreto, -a

covert² ['kʌ·vɚt] *n* (*thicket*) cespuglio *m*

cover-up ['kʌ·və·rʌp] *n* occultamento *m*

covet ['kʌ·vɪt] *vt* agognare

cow¹ [kaʊ] *n* **1.**(*female ox*) mucca *f* **2.**(*female mammal*) femmina *f* ► **until the ~s come home** all'infinito

cow² [kaʊ] *vt* intimidire

coward ['kaʊ·əd] *n* vigliacco, -a *m, f*

cowardice ['kaʊ·ə·dɪs] *n* vigliaccheria *f*

cowardly ['kaʊ·əd·li] *adj* **1.**(*fearful*) vigliacco, -a **2.**(*nasty*) meschino, -a

cowboy ['kaʊ·bɔɪ] I. *n* **1.**(*cattlehand*) mandriano *m*, cowboy *m* **2.** *inf* (*dishonest tradesperson*) mascalzone *m* II. *adj* di/da cowboy

cower ['ka·ʊɚ] *vi* rannicchiarsi per la paura

cowherd ['kaʊ·hɜːrd] *n* mandriano, -a *m, f*

cowhide I. *n* cuoio *m* II. *adj* di cuoio

cowl [kaʊl] *n* **1.**(*hood*) cappuccio *m* **2.**(*hood on chimney*) mitra *f* **3.**(*engine hood*) cofano *f*

cowling *n* cappottatura *f*

cowman ['kaʊ·mən] <-men> *n* mandriano *m*

coworker ['koʊ·ˌwɜːr·kə] *n* collega *mf*

cowshed ['kaʊ·ʃed] *n* stalla *f*

cowslip ['kaʊ·slɪp] *n* primula *f*

cox [kɑːks] <-es> *n*, **coxswain** ['kɑːk·sən] *n form* timoniere *m*

coy [kɔɪ] <-er, -est> *adj* **1.**(*secretive*) timido, -a **2.**(*flirtatiously shy*) civettuolo, -a

coyote [kaɪ·'oʊ·t̬i] *n* coyote *m inv*

coziness ['koʊ·zɪ·nɪs] *n* intimità *f*

cozy ['koʊ·zi] I.<-ier, -iest> *adj* **1.**(*comfortable*) comodo, -a; (*place*) accogliente **2.** *pej* (*convenient*) di convenienza II.<-ies> *n* copriteiera *f*

CPA *n abbr of* **certified public accountant** ragioniere *m* qualificato

CPR *n abbr of* **cardiopulmonary resuscitation** rianimazione *f* cardiorespiratoria

CPU [ˌsiː·piː·'juː] *n* COMPUT *abbr of* **central processing unit** CPU *f*

crab¹ [kræb] *n* **1.**(*sea animal*) granchio *m* **2.** ASTR Cancro *m*

C

crab² [kræb] <-bb-> *vi* brontolare

crab (apple) ['kræb·ˌæ·pl] *n* **1.** (*fruit*) mela *f* selvatica **2.** (*tree*) melo *m* selvatico

crabby ['kræ·bi] <-ier, -iest> *adj inf* brontolone, -ona

crab louse *n* piattola *f*

crack [kræk] I. *n* **1.** (*fissure*) crepa *f* **2.** (*sharp sound: of a rifle*) scoppio *m;* (*of a breaking branch*) scricchiolio *m;* (*of a whip*) schiocco *m* **3.** *inf* (*drug*) crack *m* **4.** *inf* (*attempt*) tentativo *m* ▶**the ~ of dawn** all'alba II. *adj* di prim'ordine III. *vt* **1.** (*break*) rompere **2.** (*open: an egg*) spaccare; (*nuts*) aprire; (*safe*) forzare; (*code*) decifrare **3.** (*resolve*) risolvere **4.** (*hit*) battere; (*knuckles*) far scrocchiare; (*whip*) far schioccare; **to ~ a joke** raccontare una barzelletta IV. *vi* **1.** (*break*) rompersi; (*paintwork*) creparsi **2.** (*break down*) crollare **3.** (*make a sharp noise*) schioccare ▶**to get ~ing** mettersi al lavoro

◆**crack down** *vi* **to ~ on sb/sth** prendere dure misure contro qu/qc

◆**crack up** *vi* (*laugh*) scoppiare a ridere

crackdown ['kræk·daʊn] *n* offensiva *f*

cracked [krækt] *adj* (*having fissures*) crepato, -a; (*lips*) screpolato, -a

cracker ['kræ·kə] *n* **1.** (*dry biscuit*) cracker *m* **2.** COMPUT cracker *mf*

crackle ['kræ·kl] I. *vi* scricchiolare; (*telephone line*) gracchiare; (*burning logs*) crepitare II. *vt* far scricchiolare III. *n* (*of paper*) scricchiolio *m;* (*of a telephone line*) gracchiare *m;* (*of burning wood*) crepitio *m*

crackling ['kræk·lɪŋ] *n* **1.** (*sound: of a fire*) crepitio *m;* (*of a radio*) gracchiare *m* **2.** *pl* (*pork skin*) cotenna di maiale arrostita *f*

crackpot ['kræk·pɑːt] I. *n inf* matto, -a *m, f* II. *adj inf* matto, -a

cradle ['kreɪ·dl] I. *n* **1.** (*baby's bed*) culla *f;* **from the ~ to the grave** per tutta la vita **2.** (*framework*) intelaiatura *f* II. *vt* cullare

craft [kræft] I. *n* **1.** (*means of transport*) imbarcazione *f* **2.** (*special skill*) arte *m* **3.** (*trade*) mestiere *m* **4.** (*ability*) maestria *f* II. *vt* fare

craftiness *n* astuzia *f*

craftsman ['kræfts·mən] <-men> *n* artigiano *m*

craft store *n* negozio *m* di artigianato

crafty ['kræf·ti] <-ier, -iest> *adj* astuto, -a

crag [kræg] *n* rupe *f*

craggy ['kræ·gi] <-ier, -iest> *adj* scosceso, -a; (*features*) marcato, -a

cram [kræm] <-mm-> I. *vt* stipare; **to ~ sth with sth** stipare qc di qc II. *vi* sgobbare

cramp [kræmp] I. *vt* ostacolare; **to ~ sb's style** essere di peso a qu II. *n* crampo *m*

cramped *adj* ristretto, -a

crampon ['kræm·pɑːn] *n* rampone *m*

cranberry ['kræn·ˌbe·ri] <-ies> *n* mirtillo *m* rosso

crane [kreɪn] I. *n* gru *f* II. *vt* **to ~ one's neck** alungare il collo III. *vi* **to ~ forward** sporgersi in avanti allungando il collo

crane fly <-ies> *n* tipula *f*

cranium ['kreɪ·ni·əm] <craniums *o* crania> *n* cranio *m*

crank¹ [kræŋk] I. *n inf* tipo, -a strano, -a *m* II. *adj* **a ~ call** una telefonata molesta

crank² [kræŋk] *n* TECH manovella *f*

crankcase ['kræŋk·keɪs] *n* carter *m inv*

crankshaft ['kræŋk·ʃæft] *n* albero *m* a gomiti

cranky ['kræn·ki] <-ier, -iest> *adj inf* strano, -a

cranny ['kræ·ni] <-ies> *n* fessura *f;* **in every nook and ~** in ogni buco

crap [kræp] I. <-pp-> *vi vulg* cacare II. *n vulg* **1.** (*excrement*) merda *f* **2.** (*nonsense*) stronzata *f* III. *adj* di merda

crape [kreɪp] *n* crespo *m*

crappy ['kræ·pi] <-ier, -iest> *adj inf* di merda

crash [kræʃ] I. *n* <-es> **1.** (*accident*) scontro *m* **2.** (*noise*) fracasso *m* **3.** COM crollo *m* **4.** COMPUT blocco *m* (del sistema) II. *vi* **1.** (*have an accident*) scontrarsi; (*plane*) precipitare **2.** (*make loud noise*) fare fracasso **3.** (*break noisily*) fracassarsi **4.** COM crollare **5.** COMPUT piantarsi III. *vt* (*damage in accident*) schiantare ▶**to ~ a party** infilarsi a una festa

crash barrier *n* barriera *f* di sicurezza

crash course *n* corso *m* intensivo

crash diet *n* dieta *f* lampo

crash helmet *n* casco *m*

crash-land ['kræʃ·lænd] *vi* eseguire un atterraggio di fortuna

crash landing *n* atterraggio *m* di fortuna

crash-test *vt* eseguire un crash test

crass [kræs] *adj* grossolano, -a

crate [kreɪt] I. *n* cassa *f* II. *vt* mettere in casse

crater ['kreɪ·tə] *n* cratere *m*

cravat [krə·ˈvæt] *n* foulard *m*

crave [kreɪv] *vt* desiderare ardentemente

craving ['kreɪ·vɪŋ] *n* gran desiderio *m*

crawl [krɑːl] I. *vi* **1.** (*go on all fours*) gattonare **2.** (*move slowly*) procedere lentamente **3.** *inf* (*be obsequious*) **to ~ (up) to sb** strisciare davanti a qu **4.** *inf* (*become infested*) **to be ~ing with sth** brulicare di qc II. *n* **1.** (*go very slowly*) **at a ~** a passo d'uomo **2.** (*style of swimming*) stile *m* libero; **to do the ~** nuotare a stile libero

crawler ['krɑː·lə] *n* **1.** TECH mezzo *m* lento **2.** (*baby*) bambino *m* piccolo

crayfish ['kreɪ·fɪʃ] *n inv* **1.** (*Astacus*) gambero *m* d'acqua dolce **2.** CULIN (*in sea*) aragosta *f*

crayon ['kre·ɪɑːn] I. *n* pastello *m* II. *vt* disegnare coi pastelli III. *vi* disegnare coi pastelli

craze [kreɪz] *n* mania *f*

crazed [kreɪzd] *adj* impazzito, -a; (*expression*) da pazzo, -a

craziness *n* pazzia *f*

crazy ['kreɪ·zi] <-ier, -iest> *adj* pazzo, -a; **to go ~** impazzire

creak [kriːk] I. *vi* (*door*) cigolare; (*bones*) scricchiolare II. *n* (*of door*) cigolio *m;* (*of bones*) scricchiolio *m*

creaky ['kriː·ki] <-ier, -iest> *adj* **1.** (*squeaky*) cigolante; (*chair*) che scricchiola **2.** (*decrepit*) che cade a pezzi

cream [kri:m] **I.** *n* **1.** (*milk fat*) panna *f* **2.** (*cosmetic product*) crema *f* **3.** (*the best*) fior fiore *m* **II.** *adj* **1.** (*containing cream*) cremoso, -a **2.** (*off-white color*) color crema **III.** *vt* (*butter*) amalgamare; (*milk*) scremare

cream cheese *n* formaggio *m* cremoso

cream-colored *adj* color crema

creamery ['kri:·mə·ri] <-ies> *n* latteria *m*

creamy ['kri:·mi] <-ier, -iest> *adj* **1.** (*smooth*) cremoso, -a **2.** (*off-white*) color crema

crease [kri:s] **I.** *n* **1.** (*fold*) piega *f* **2.** (*in ice hockey*) area *f* di porta **II.** *vt* piegare **III.** *vi* piegarsi

create [kri:·'eɪt] *vt* creare

creation [kri:·'eɪ·ʃən] *n* creazione *f*

creative [kri:·'eɪ·ţɪv] *adj* creativo, -a; (*imagination*) fervido, -a

creator [kri:·'eɪ·ţə] *n* creatore, -trice *m, f*

creature ['kri:·tʃə] *n* **1.** (*being*) essere *m* (vivente), organismo *m* **2.** (*person being discussed*) persona *f*; **to be a ~ of habit** essere un abitudinario; **poor ~!** poveretto! **3.** (*pawn*) creazione *f*

creature comforts *npl inf* comodità *fpl*

creche [kreɪʃ] *n* REL presepe *m*

credence ['kri:·dns] *n form* credito *m*

credentials [krɪ·'den·ʃlz] *npl* credenziali *fpl*

credibility [ˌkre·də·'bɪ·lə·ti] *n* credibilità *f*

credible ['kre·də·bl] *adj* credibile

credit ['kre·dɪt] **I.** *n* **1.** (*belief*) credito *m;* **to give ~ to sth/sb** dar credito a qc/qu **2.** (*honor*) onore *m;* (*recognition*) merito *m;* **to be a ~ to sb** fare onore a qu; **to sb's ~ a** merito di qu; **to take (the) ~ for sth** prendersi il merito di qc **3.** FIN credito *m;* **to buy sth on ~** comprare qc a credito; **to give sb ~** fare credito a qu **4.** COM attivo *m* **5.** *pl* CINE titoli[*o coda*] *m* di testa *pl* **II.** *vt* **1.** (*believe*) credere **2.** FIN **to ~ sb with 2000 dollars** accreditare 2000 dollari a qu **3.** (*attribute*) **he is ~ed with ... gli si atribuisce ...**

creditable ['kre·dɪ·ţə·bl] *adj* **1.** (*believable*) credibile **2.** (*commendable*) meritevole

credit card *n* carta *f* di credito

credit limit *n* limite *m* di credito

creditor ['kre·dɪ·ţə] *n* creditore, -trice *m, f*

credit rating *n* posizione *f* creditizia

credits *npl* CINE titoli [*o coda*] *m* di testa *pl*

credit slip *n* ricevuta *f* della carta di credito

credit terms *npl* condizioni *f pl* di credito

credit union *n* cooperativa *f* di credito

creditworthy ['kre·dɪt·ˌwɜ:r·ði] *adj* solvibile

credulity [krə·'du:·lə·ti] *n* credulità *f*

credulous ['kred·jə·ləs] *adj* credulo, -a

creed [kri:d] *n* credo *m;* **the Creed** il Credo

creek [kri:k] *n* (*stream*) ruscello *m* ▶ **to be up the ~** (**without a paddle**) *inf* essere nei pasticci

creep [kri:p] **I.** *n* <crept, crept> *vi* **1.** strisciare; (*baby*) gattonare; (*plant*) arrampicarsi **2.** (*move imperceptibly*) avanzare furtivamente **3.** (*move slowly*) avanzare lentamente **II.** *n* **1.** (*act of creeping*) avanzamento *m* furtivo **2.** *inf* (*sycophant*) leccapiedi *mf* **3.** (*pervert*) persona *f* viscida ▶ **to give sb the ~s** *inf* far accapponare la pelle a qu

◆**creep into** *vt insep* entrare furtivamente in
◆**creep up** *vi* **to ~ on sb** avvicinarsi furtivamente a qu

creeper ['kri:·pə] *n* **1.** (*rope*) liana *f* **2.** BOT rampicante *m*

creeping *adj* strisciante

creepy ['kri:·pi] <-ier, -iest> *adj inf* repellente

creepy-crawly *n a. childspeak, inf* insetto *m* che striscia

cremate [kri:·'meɪt] *vt* cremare

cremation [krɪ·'meɪ·ʃən] *n* cremazione *f*

crematorium [ˌkri:·mə·'tɔ:·ri·əm] <-s *o* -ria> *n* crematorio *m*

crematory ['kre·mə·tə·ri] **I.** *n* (*crematorium*) crematorio *m* **II.** *adj* crematorio, -a

crème de la crème [ˌkrem·də·lɑ:·'krem] *n* **the ~** la crème de la crème

crepe [kreɪp] *n* **1.** (*food*) crêpe *f* **2.** (*cloth*) crespo *m* **3.** (*rubber*) para *f*

crept [krept] *pp, pt of* **creep**

crescendo [krɪ·'ʃen·doʊ] *n* crescendo *m*

crescent ['kre·snt] **I.** *n* **1.** (*shape*) mezzaluna *f* **2.** (*curved street*) strada *f* semicircolare **II.** *adj* crescente

cress [kres] *n* crescione *m*

crest [krest] **I.** *n* **1.** (*peak*) cima *f;* (*of wave, bird*) cresta *f* **2.** (*helmet decoration*) cimiero *m* **II.** *vt* ornare con una cresta **III.** *vi* (*wave*) incresparsi

crestfallen ['krest·ˌfɔ:·lən] *adj* abbattuto, -a

Crete [kri:t] *n* Creta *f*

cretin ['kri:·tn] *n inf* cretino, -a *m, f*

crevasse [krə·'væs] *n* crepaccio *m*

crevice ['kre·vɪs] *n a. fig* crepa *f*

crew [kru:] **I.** *n* + *sing/pl vb* **1.** NAUT, AVIAT (*sport of rowing*) equipaggio *m;* RAIL personale *m;* **ground/flight ~** personale di terra/di volo **2.** *inf* (*gang*) banda *f* **II.** *vt* **to ~ a boat** far parte dell'equipaggio di una imbarcazione **III.** *vi* **to ~ for sb** far parte dell'equipaggio di qu

crew cut *n* taglio *m* a spazzola

crewman <-men> *n* membro *m* dell'equipaggio

crewmember *n* membro *m* dell'equipaggio

crib [krɪb] *n* **1.** (*baby's bed*) lettino *f* **2.** *sl* (*home*) casa *f* **3.** *inf* SCHOOL scopiazzata *f*

cribbage ['krɪ·bɪdʒ] *n* GAMES gioco a carte per due, tre o quattro giocatori

crick [krɪk] **I.** *n* (*in the neck*) torcicollo *m;* (*in the back*) mal *m* di schiena; **to have a ~ in one's neck/back** avere il torcicollo/mal di schiena **II.** *vt* **I have ~ed my neck/back** mi è venuto il torcicollo/il mal di schiena

cricket¹ ['krɪ·kɪt] *n* SPORTS cricket *m*

cricket² ['krɪ·kɪt] *n* ZOOL grillo *m*

cricket bat *n* mazza *f* da cricket

cricketer ['krɪ·kɪ·ţə] *n* giocatore, -trice *m, f* di

cricket

cricket field *n*, **cricket ground** *n* campo *m* di cricket

crier ['kra·ɪɚ] *n* banditore *m*

crime [kraɪm] *n* **1.** LAW (*illegal act*) reato *m;* (*more serious*) crimine *m;* **a ~ against humanity** un crimine contro l'umanità; **~ of passion** delitto *m* passionale; **to accuse sb of a ~** accusare qu di un reato; **to commit a ~** commettere un reato; **the scene of the ~** la scena del reato; **it would be a ~** *inf* sarebbe un peccato **2.** (*criminal activity*) delinquenza *f*, criminalità *f;* **~ rate** tasso *m* di criminalità; **organized ~** crimine organizzato

crime prevention *n* prevenzione *f* della criminalità

crime-ridden *adj* con un alto tasso di criminalità

crime wave *n* ondata *f* di criminalità

criminal ['krɪ·mɪ·nl] **I.** *n* (*offender*) delinquente *mf;* (*more serious*) criminale *mf* **II.** *adj* **1.** (*illegal*) illegale; (*more serious*) criminale **2.** LAW penale; **~ court** tribunale *m* penale; **~ lawyer** penalista *mf;* **~ record** precedenti *m pl* penali **3.** *fig* (*shameful*) vergognoso, -a; **to be ~ to do sth** essere una vergogna fare qc

criminality [ˌkrɪ·mə·'næ·lə·ti] *n* criminalità *f*

criminologist [krɪ·mɪ·'nɑː·lə·dʒɪst] *n* criminologo, -a *m, f*

criminology [ˌkrɪ·mɪ·'nɑː·lə·dʒi] *n* criminologia *f*

crimp [krɪmp] *vt* **1.** (*press into folds, frill*) ripiegare **2.** (*make wavy*) ondulare; (*make curly*) arricciare

crimson ['krɪm·zn] **I.** *n* cremisi *m inv* **II.** *adj* **1.** (*color*) cremisi **2.** (*red-faced*) paonazzo, -a

cringe [krɪndʒ] *vi* **1.** *inf* (*shrink*) rannicchiarsi; **to ~ with embarrassment at sth** sprofondare di vergogna per qc **2.** (*lower*) umiliarsi; **to ~ before sb** umiliarsi di fronte a qu

crinkle ['krɪŋ·kl] **I.** *vt* (*wrinkle*) raggrinzire; (*nose*) arricciare; (*wave*) increspare **II.** *vi* **to ~ (up)** (*wrinkle*) corrugarsi; (*ripple*) incresparsi **III.** *n* grinza *f;* (*in hair*) riccio *m*

crinkly ['krɪŋ·kli] <-ier, -iest> *adj* **1.** (*wrinkled*) grinzoso, -a **2.** (*wavy*) ondulato, -a; (*curly*) riccio, -a

cripple ['krɪ·pl] **I.** *n* zoppo, -a *m, f* **II.** *vt* **1.** (*disable*) menomare; (*machine, object*) danneggiare **2.** (*paralyze*) paralizzare

crippling *adj fig* paralizzante

crisis ['kraɪ·sɪs] <crises> *n* crisi *f inv;* **a ~ over sth** una crisi provocata da qc; **to go through a ~** attraversare una crisi

crisis management *n* gestione *f* della crisi

crisp [krɪsp] **I.** <-er, -est> *adj* **1.** (*bacon*) croccante; (*snow*) friabile, -a **2.** (*apple, lettuce*) fresco, -a **3.** (*shirt, pants*) pulito, -a; (*banknote*) nuovissimo, -a **4.** (*air*) tonificante **5.** (*sharp*) nitido, -a **6.** (*lively*) animato, -a **7.** (*manner, style*) secco, -a **II.** *vt* **1.** (*make crisp*) tostare leggermente **2.** (*curl*) increspare

crispy ['krɪs·pi] <-ier, -iest> *adj* croccante

crisscross ['krɪs·krɑːs] **I.** *vt* attraversare **II.** *vi* attraversare **III.** *adj* incrociato, -a **IV.** <-es> *n* incrocio *m*

criterion [kraɪ·'tɪ·ri·ən] <-ria> *n* criterio *m*

critic ['krɪ·ṭɪk] *n* critico, -a *m, f*

critical ['krɪ·ṭɪ·kl] *adj* **1.** (*disapproving*) critico, -a; **to be ~ of sth/sb** criticare qc/qu; **to be highly ~ of sth** criticare aspramente qc **2.** (*decisive*) fondamentale; **to be ~ to sth** essere di vitale importanza per qc; **to be in ~ condition** *a.* MED essere in condizioni critiche

criticism ['krɪ·ṭɪ·sɪ·zəm] *n* critica *f;* **to take ~** accettare le critiche; **I have a few ~s about what you said** ho alcuni commenti su quello che ha detto

criticize ['krɪ·ṭɪ·saɪz] *vt, vi* criticare

critique [krɪ·'tiːk] *n* critica *f*

croak [kroʊk] **I.** *vi* **1.** gracchiare; (*frog*) gracidare **2.** *inf* (*die*) tirare le cuoia **II.** *vt* gracchiare **III.** *n* gracchiare *m;* (*frog*) gracidare *m*

Croat ['kroʊ·æt] *n* croato, -a *m, f*

Croatia [kroʊ·'eɪ·ʃə] *n* Croazia *f*

Croatian [kroʊ·'eɪ·ʃi·ən] **I.** *adj* croato, -a **II.** *n* croato, -a *m, f*

crochet [kroʊ·'ʃeɪ] **I.** *n* lavoro *m* all'uncinetto **II.** *vi* fare l'uncinetto **III.** *vt* fare all'uncinetto

crochet hook *n*, **crochet needle** *n* uncinetto *m*

crock [krɑːk] *n* **1.** (*clay container*) vaso *m* di coccio **2.** *sl* **a ~ of shit** (*nonsense*) delle stronzate **3.** *iron old* **~** catorcio *m inf*

crockery ['krɑː·kɚ·i] *n* vasellame *f*

crocodile ['krɑː·kə·daɪl] <-(s)> *n* ZOOL coccodrillo *m*

crocodile tears *npl* lagrime *f pl* di coccodrillo; **to shed ~** piangere lacrime di coccodrillo

crocus ['kroʊ·kəs] <-es> *n* croco *m*

croissant [kwɑ·'sɑŋ] *n* cornetto *m*

crony ['kroʊ·ni] <-ies> *n iron, inf* amicone, -a *m, f*

crook [krʊk] **I.** *n* **1.** (*criminal*) delinquente *mf* **2.** *inf* (*rogue*) imbroglione, -a *m, f* **3.** (*of elbow*) piega *f* **4.** (*curve*) angolo *m* **5.** (*staff: of shepherd*) bastone *m;* (*of bishop*) pastorale *m* **II.** *vt* piegare

crooked ['krʊ·kɪd] *adj* **1.** (*not straight: nose, legs*) storto, -a; (*back*) ricurvo, -a; (*path*) tortuoso, -a **2.** *inf* (*dishonest*) disonesto, -a

croon [kruːn] **I.** *vt, vi* cantilenare **II.** *n* canto *m* melodioso

crooner ['kruː·nɚ] *n iron, inf* cantante *mf* melodico, -a

crop [krɑːp] **I.** *n* **1.** AGR (*plant*) coltura *f;* (*harvest*) raccolto *m* **2.** (*group*) mucchio *m;* **a ~ of lies** un mucchio di bugie **3.** (*haircut*) taglio *m* cortissimo; **to wear one's hair in a ~** portare i capelli tagliati cortissimi **4.** (*of bird*) gozzo *m* **5.** (*whip*) frusta *f* **II.** <-pp-> *vt* **1.** AGR coltivare **2.** (*cut*) tagliare; (*hair*) tagliare cortissimi; (*plant*) potare **3.** (*graze*) brucare **III.** *vi* AGR dare frutti; (*land*) rendere

◆ **crop out** *vi* GEO affiorare

◆ **crop up** *vi* saltar fuori

crop-duster *n aereo per spargere di pesticidi*

cropper ['krɑ:·pə·] *n* agricoltore, -trice *m, f*

crop rotation *n* rotazione *f* delle colture

croquet [krou·'keɪ] *n* croquet *m inv*

cross [krɑ:s] **I.** *vt* **1.** (*go across, lie across*) attraversare; (*threshold*) superare; **the bridge ~es the river** il ponte passa sul fiume **2.** (*place crosswise*) **to ~ one's legs** accavallare le gambe, incrociare le gambe; **to ~ one's arms** incrociare le braccia; **to ~ one's fingers** incrociare le dita; *fig* tenere le dita incrociate **3.** BIO (*crossbreed*) incrociare **4.** REL **to ~ oneself** farsi il segno della croce **5.** (*oppose*) fare arrabbiare **6.** (*mark with a cross*) mettere una crocetta in **7.** (*draw a line across*) barrare ▶ **I'll ~ that bridge when I come to it** ci penserò quando sarà il momento; **~ my heart and hope to die** giuro; **to ~ swords with sb** discutere con qu **II.** *vi* **1.** (*intersect*) incrociarsi **2.** (*go across*) fare una traversata **III.** *n* **1. a.** REL croce *f;* **the sign of the ~** il segno della croce; **to bear one's ~** portare la propria croce; **Maltese ~** croce di Malta **2.** (*crossing: of streets, roads*) attraversamento *m,* incrocio *m* **3.** BIO (*mixture*) incrocio *m* **IV.** *adj* arrabbiato, -a; **to be ~ about sth** essere arrabbiato per qc; **to get ~ with sb** arrabbiarsi con qu

◆ **cross off** *vt,* **cross out** *vt* depennare

◆ **cross over** *vi, vt* attraversare

crossbar ['krɑ:s·bɑ:r] *n* sbarra *f;* (*of goal*) traversa *f;* (*of bicycle*) canna *f*

crossbeam *n* trave *f* trasversale

cross-border *adj* internazionale

crossbow *n* balestra *f*

crossbreed *n* BIO ibrido *m*

crosscheck I. *n* (*verification*) controllo *m* incrociato **II.** *vt* (*verify*) fare un controllo incrociato

cross-country I. *adj* che passa per la campagna; **~ race** campestre *f;* **~ skiing** sci *m* di fondo *inv* **II.** *adv* attraverso la campagna **III.** *n* campestre *f*

cross-cultural *adj* interculturale

crosscurrent *n* controcorrente *f*

cross-dress *vi* travestirsi (*da uomo o da donna*)

cross-dresser *n* travestito *m*

cross-examination *n* LAW controinterrogatorio *m*

cross-examine *vt* controinterrogare

cross-eyed *adj* strabico, -a

cross-fertilization *n* BIO ibridazione *f*

crossfire *n* fuoco *m* incrociato; **to be caught in the ~** *fig* trovarsi tra due fuochi

cross-grained *adj* (*wood*) con venature non regolari

crossing ['krɑ:·sɪŋ] *n* **1.** (*place to cross*) passaggio *m* pedonale; **level ~** RAIL passaggio *m* a livello; **border ~** valico *m* di frontiera; **pedestrian ~** passaggio pedonale **2.** (*crossroads*) incrocio *m* **3.** ARCHIT crociera *f* **4.** (*journey*) traversata *f*

cross-legged [ˌkrɑ:s·'legəd] *adj* a gambe incrociate

crossover *n* passaggio *m;* **a ~ of popular and classical music** una fusione tra musica popolare e classica

cross-purposes *npl* **to be talking at ~** fraintendersi

cross-reference *n* rimando *m*

crossroads *n inv* **1.** incrocio *m* **2.** *fig* crocevia *f;* **to be at a ~** essere a un bivio

cross section *n* **1.** sezione *f* trasversale **2.** *fig* campione *m*

crosstown I. *adj* che attraversa la città **II.** *adv* attraverso la città

crosswalk *n* (*pedestrian crossing*) passaggio *m* pedonale

crossways *adv* trasversalmente

crosswind *n* vento *m* laterale

crosswise *adv* trasversalmente

crossword (**puzzle**) *n* cruciverba *m inv*

crotch [krɑ:tʃ] <-es> *n* (*of body*) inforcatura *f;* (*of trousers*) cavallo *m*

crotchet ['krɑ:t·ʃət] *n* MUS semiminima *f*

crotchety ['krɑ:t·ʃə·ti] *adj inf* (*bad-tempered*) irritabile

crouch [krautʃ] **I.** *vi* **to ~ (down)** accovacciarsi; **to be ~ing** stare accovacciato **II.** *n* **to lower oneself into a ~** accovacciarsi

croup [kru:p] *n* **1.** (*rump*) groppa *f* **2.** MED crup *m*

croupier ['kru:·piə·] *n* crupier *mf*

crow[1] [krou] *n* ZOOL corvo *m,* cornacchia *f* ▶ **to eat ~** *inf* dover ammettere un errore; **as the ~ flies** in linea d'aria

crow[2] [krou] <crowed, crowed> **I.** *n* **1.** (*call of a cock*) canto *m* del gallo **2.** (*cry of pleasure*) gridolino *m* di gioia; (*of baby*) verso *m* **II.** *vi* **1.** (*cock*) cantare **2.** (*cry out happily*) fare gridolini di gioia; (*baby*) fare i versi **3.** (*boast*) vantarsi; **to ~ over sth** vantarsi di qc

crowbar ['krou·bɑ:r] *n* palanchino *m*

crowd [kraud] **I.** *n* + *sing/pl vb* **1.** (*throng*) folla *f;* **there was quite a ~** c'era parecchia gente **2.** *inf* (*group*) gruppo *m;* **the usual ~** la solita gente **3.** *inf* (*large number*) sacco *m;* **a ~ of things** un sacco di cose **4.** (*common people, masses*) massa *fpl;* **to stand out from the ~** *fig* distinguersi dalla massa; **to follow the ~** *fig* seguire la massa **5.** (*audience*) pubblico *m* **II.** *vi* ammassarsi **III.** *vt* **1.** (*fill*) affollare; **to ~ the streets/a stadium** gremire le strade/uno stadio **2.** (*cram*) stipare **3.** *inf* (*pressure*) fare pressione su

◆ **crowd out** *vt* **1.** (*exclude*) escludere **2.** (*fill*) **to be crowded out** essere gremito

crowded *adj* pieno, -a; **the bar was ~** il bar era affollato

crowd pleaser *n inf:* qualcuno o qualcosa che piace alla massa

crown [kraun] **I.** *n* **1.** corona *f;* **the Crown** (*monarchy*) la Corona **2.** (*top part*) cima *f;* (*of head*) cocuzzolo *m;* (*of road*) colmo *m* **3.** ZOOL (*of bird*) cresta *f* **4.** (*culmination*) culmine *m* **5.** (*of tooth*) corona *f* **II.** *vt* **1.** (*coronate*) incoronare; **to ~ sb queen** incoronare qu regina **2.** (*complete*) coronare; **the church is ~ed by a golden dome** la chiesa termina con una cupola dorata; **the prize ~ed his career** il premio ha segnato il culmine della sua carriera **3.** *inf* (*hit on head*) dare un colpo in testa **4.** MED (*tooth*) incapsulare

crown colony <-ies> *n* colonia *f* della Corona

crowning *adj* supremo, -a

crown jewels *n* gioielli *f pl* della Corona

crown prince *n* principe *m* ereditario

crow's feet ['krooz·fi:t] *npl* zampe *f pl* di gallina

crow's nest *n* NAUT coffa *f*

CRT [ˌsiː·ɑːr·'tiː] *n abbr of* **cathode-ray tube** TRC *m*

crucial ['kruː·ʃl] *adj* (*decisive*) decisivo, -a; (*moment*) crucial; **to be ~ to sth** essere cruciale per qc; **it is ~ that ...** è di vitale importanza che ... +*subj*

crucible ['kruː·sɪ·bl] *n* **1.** (*container*) crogiolo *m* **2.** *fig* dura prova *f*

crucifix [ˌkruː·sɪ·'frks] <-es> *n* crocifisso *m*

crucifixion [ˌkruː·sɪ·'frk·ʃən] *n* crocifissione *f*

crucify ['kruː·sɪ·faɪ] <-ie-> *vt* **1.** (*execute*) crocifiggere **2.** *fig* stroncare; **if she ever finds out, she'll ~ me** se se ne accorge mi ammazza

cruddy ['krʌ·di] <-ier, -iest> *adj inf* schifoso, -a; **a ~ book** una schifezza di libro

crude [kruːd] **I.** *adj* **1.** (*rudimentary*) rudimentale **2.** (*unrefined*) grezzo, -a; (*oil*) greggio, -a **3.** (*unfinished, undeveloped*) rozzo, -a **4.** (*vulgar*) volgare **II.** *n* greggio *m*

cruel ['kru·əl] <-(l)ler, -(l)lest> *adj* crudele; **to be ~ to sb** essere crudele con qu ▶ **to be ~ to be kind** *prov* far soffrire qu per il suo bene

cruelty ['kru·əl·ti] <-ies> *n* crudeltà *f;* **~ to sb** crudeltà verso qu; **society for the prevention of ~ to animals** lega *f* per la protezione degli animali

cruise [kruːz] **I.** *n* crociera *f;* **~ ship** transatlantico *m;* **to go on a ~** fare una crociera **II.** *vi* **1.** NAUT (*take a cruise*) fare una crociera **2.** (*travel at constant speed*) viaggiare a velocità di crociera; (*airplane*) volare a velocità di crociera **3.** (*police car*) pattugliare **4.** *inf* (*drive around aimlessly*) fare un giro (in macchina)

cruise control *n* regolazione *f* di crociera

cruise missile *n* MIL cruise *m inv*

cruiser ['kruː·zɚ] *n* **1.** (*warship*) incrociatore *m* **2.** (*pleasure boat*) cabinato *m* **3.** (*squad car*) autopattuglia *f*

cruise ship *n* transatlantico *m*

cruising *adj* (*speed*) di crociera

crumb [krʌm] *n* **1.** (*of bread*) briciola *f* **2.** (*small amount*) briciolo *m; ***a small ~ of ...** un pochino di...; **a ~ of hope** un barlume di speranza

crumble ['krʌm·bl] **I.** *vt* **1.** (*bread, biscuit*) sbriciolare **2.** (*stone*) sgretolare **II.** *vi* sgretolarsi

crumbly ['krʌm·bli] <-ier, -iest> *adj* (*bread, cake*) friabile; (*house, wall*) che cade a pezzi

crummy ['krʌ·mi] <-ier, -iest> *adj inf* scadente; **a ~ salary** uno stipendio da fame

crumple ['krʌm·pl] **I.** *vt* (*clothes, paper*) spiegazzare; (*metal*) accartocciare; **to ~ a piece of paper into a ball** appallottolare un foglio **II.** *vi* **1.** (*become wrinkled: fabric*) spiegazzarsi; (*face*) coprirsi di rughe **2.** (*collapse*) accasciarsi

crunch [krʌntʃ] **I.** *vt* **1.** (*in the mouth*) sgranocchiare **2.** (*grind*) schiacciare **II.** *vi* scricchiolare **III.** <-es> *n* **1.** (*sound*) scricchiolio *m* **2.** (*crisis*) crisi *f* **3.** (*a sit-up*) esercizio *m* per gli addominali

crunchy ['krʌn·tʃi] <-ier, -iest> *adj* croccante

crusade [kruː·'seɪd] **I.** *n* **1.** REL, HIST cruciata *f* **2.** *fig* campagna *f;* **a ~ for/against sth** una campagna a favore di/contro qc **II.** *vi* **1.** HIST, REL partecipare alle crociate **2.** *fig* fare una campagna; **to ~ for sth** fare una campagna a favore di qc

crusader [kruː·'seɪ·dɚ] *n* **1.** REL, HIST crociato *m* **2.** *fig* sostenitore, -trice *m, f;* **a ~ against sth** un detrattore di qc

crush [krʌʃ] **I.** *vt* schiacciare; **to be ~ed to death** morire schiacciato; (*ice*) triturare; (*rumor*) mettere a tacere **II.** <-es> *n* **1.** (*act of crushing*) aplastamento *m* **2.** (*throng*) calca *f;* **there was a great ~** c'era una gran calca **3.** *inf* (*temporary infatuation*) cotta *f;* **to have a ~ on sb** avere una cotta per qu **4.** (*crushed ice drink*) orange **~** spremuta *f* d'arancia
◆**crush up** *vt* triturare

crushing **I.** *n* schiacciamento *m* **II.** *adj* (*defeat, argument*) schiacciante; (*reply*) umiliante

crust [krʌst] **I.** *n* **1.** crosta *f;* **~ of the Earth** GEO crosta terrestre; **a ~ of ice/dirt** una crosta di ghiaccio/sporcizia **2.** (*deposit from wine*) gromma *f* **II.** *vi* incrostarsi **III.** *vt* **to be ~ed with mud** essere incrostato di fango

crustacean [krʌ·'steɪ·ʃən] *n* crostaceo *m*

crusty ['krʌs·ti] <-ier, -iest> *adj* **1.** CULIN croccante **2.** (*grumpy, surly*) scontroso, -a

crutch [krʌtʃ] <-es> *n* **1.** MED stampella *f;* **to be on ~es** avere le stampelle **2.** *fig* (*source of support*) appoggio *m*

crux [krʌks] *n* **the ~ of the matter** il nocciolo *m* della questione

cry [kraɪ] **I.** <-ie-> *vi* **1.** (*weep*) piangere; **to ~ for joy** piangere di gioia **2.** (*shout*) gridare; (*animal*) emettere gridi; **to ~ for help** gridare aiuto **II.** <-ie-> *vt* **1.** (*shed tears*) piangere **2.** (*shout*) gridare **3.** (*announce publicly*) dichiarare ▶ **to ~ one's eyes out** piangere a dirotto; **to ~ foul at sth** denunciare qc; **to ~ wolf** gridare al lupo; **to ~ over spilled milk** piangere sul latte versato **III.** *n* **1.** (*weeping*) pianto *m;* **to have a ~** farsi un bel pianto **2.** (*shout*) grido *m;* **to give a ~** gridare; **a ~ for help** un grido d'aiuto **3.** (*slogan*) slogan *m inv* **4.** ZOOL verso *m* ▶ **to be a far ~ from sth** essere ben diverso da qc
◆**cry down** *vt* **1.** (*decry*) denigrare **2.** (*disparage*) sminuire
◆**cry for** *vt insep* chiedere

◆**cry off** *vi inf* tirarsi indietro; **to ~ a deal** rompere un accordo

◆**cry out** I. *vi* gridare; **to ~ against sth** protestare contro qc; **to ~ for sth** chiedere qc a gran voce; **for crying out loud!** *inf* madonna santa! II. *vt* gridare

crying ['kraɪ·ɪŋ] I. *n* grida *fpl* II. *adj* (*need*) urgente; (*injustice*) vero, -a; **a ~ shame** *inf* una vera indecenza

crypt [krɪpt] *n* cripta *f*

cryptic ['krɪp·tɪk] *adj* criptico, -a; (*comment, remark*) ambiguo, -a; (*smile*) enigmatico, -a

crystal ['krɪs·tl] I. *n* cristallo *m* II. *adj* **1.** cristallino, -a **2.** (*made of crystal*) di cristallo

crystal ball *n* sfera *f* di cristallo

crystal clear *adj* **1.** (*transparent: water*) cristallino, -a; (*image*) nitido, -a **2.** (*obvious*) evidente

crystalline ['krɪs·tə·laɪn] *adj* cristallino, -a

crystallization [ˌkrɪs·tə·lɪ·ˈzeɪ·ʃən] *n* cristallizzazione *f*

crystallize ['krɪs·tə·laɪz] I. *vi* cristallizzarsi II. *vt* **1.** cristalizar; (*plan, thought*) chiarire **2.** CULIN candire

ct. **1.** *abbr of* **cent** centesimo *m* **2.** *abbr of* **carat** carato *m*

CT *n* **1.** GEO *abbr of* **Connecticut** Connecticut *m* **2.** MED *abbr of* **computerized tomography** TAC *f*

cub [kʌb] *n* ZOOL cucciolo *m*

Cuba ['kjuː·bə] *n* Cuba *f*

Cuban ['kjuː·bən] I. *adj* cubano, -a II. *n* cubano, -a *m, f*

cubbyhole ['kʌ·bɪ·hoʊl] *n* sgabuzzino *m*

cube [kjuːb] I. *n* cubo *m;* (*of cheese*) cubetto *m;* (*of sugar*) zolletta *f;* **ice ~** cubetto *m* di ghiaccio; **~ root** MATH radice *f* cubica II. *vt* **1.** CULIN tagliare a cubetti **2.** MATH elevare al cubo; **2 ~d** 2 (elevato) al cubo

cubic ['kjuː·bɪk] *adj* **1.** (*cube-shaped*) cubico, -a; (*feet, yards*) cubo, -a **2.** MATH di terzo grado; **~ equation** equazione *f* di terzo grado

cubicle ['kjuː·bɪ·kl] *n* **1.** (*changing room*) cabina *m* **2.** (*sleeping compartment*) cuccetta *f*

Cub Scout *n* lupetto *m*

cuckoo ['kuː·kuː] I. *n* cuculo *m* II. *adj inf* matto, -a

cuckoo clock *n* orologio *m* a cucù

cucumber ['kjuː·kʌm·bə*] *n* cetriolo *m* ▶ (**as**) **cool as a ~** *inf* incredibilmente calmo

cud [kʌd] *n* **to chew the ~** *a. fig, inf* ruminare

cuddle ['kʌ·dl] I. *vt* abbracciare II. *vi* abbracciarsi III. *n* abbraccio *m;* **to give sb a ~** abbracciare qu

cuddly <-ier, -iest> *adj* tenerissimo, -a; **~ toy** giocattolo *m* di peluche

cudgel ['kʌ·dʒəl] I. *n* **1.** (*short thick stick*) bastone *m* **2.** (*weapon*) randello *f* II. <-ll-, -l-> *vt* (*with a cudgel*) bastonare; (*with a weapon*) prendere a randellate

cue [kjuː] *n* **1.** THEAT battuta *f* d'entrata; **to miss one's ~** non entrare in scena al momento

giusto **2.** MUS attacco *m* **3.** (*billiards*) stecca *f;* **~ ball** pallino *m* ▶ **to take** one's **~ from sb** seguire l'imbeccata di qu; (*right*) **on ~** al momento giusto

cuff [kʌf] I. *n* **1.** (*end of sleeve*) polsino *m* **2.** (*turned-up trouser leg*) risvolto *m* **3.** *pl, inf* (*handcuffs*) manette *fpl* ▶ **off the ~** improvvisato, -a II. *vt inf* ammanettare

cuff links *npl* gemelli *m*

cuisine [kwɪ·ˈziːn] *n* cucina *f*

cul-de-sac ['kʌl·də·sæk] <-s *o* culs-de-sac> *n a. fig* vicolo *m* cieco

culinary ['kʌ·lə·ne·ri] *adj* culinario, -a

cull [kʌl] I. *vt* **1.** ZOOL decimare (*come forma di controllo delle specie*) **2.** (*choose*) raccogliere; **to ~ sth from sth** raccogliere qc da qc II. *n* decimazione *f* (selettiva)

culminate ['kʌl·mɪ·neɪt] *vi* culminare; **to ~ in sth** culminare in qc

culmination [ˌkʌl·mɪ·ˈneɪ·ʃən] *n* culmine *m*

culottes ['kuː·lɑːts] *npl* gonna *f* pantalone; **a pair of ~** una gonna pantalone

culpable ['kʌl·pə·bl] *adj form* colpevole; **to hold sb ~ for sth** ritenere qu colpevole di qc

culprit ['kʌl·prɪt] *n* colpevole *mf*

cult [kʌlt] *n* **1.** (*sect*) setta *f* **2.** (*worship*) culto *m*

cult figure *n* idolo *m*

cultivate ['kʌl·tə·veɪt] *vt a. fig* coltivare

cultivated *adj* **1.** AGR coltivato, -a **2.** (*person*) colto, -a

cultivation [ˌkʌl·tə·ˈveɪ·ʃən] *n* **1.** AGR coltivazione *f;* **to be under ~** essere coltivato **2.** (*of a person*) cultura *f*

cultivator ['kʌl·tə·veɪ·tə*] *n* AGR **1.** (*tool, machine*) coltivatore *m* **2.** (*person*) coltivatore, -trice *m, f*

cultural ['kʌl·tʃə·rəl] *adj* culturale

culture ['kʌl·tʃə*] I. *n* **1.** (*way of life*) cultura *f* **2.** (*arts*) cultura *f* **3.** AGR coltura *f* II. *vt* cultivare

cultured ['kʌl·tʃə*d] *adj* **1.** AGR, BIO coltivato, -a **2.** (*intellectual*) colto, -a; (*taste*) raffinato, -a

culture shock *n* shock *m* culturale

cumbersome ['kʌm·bə*·səm] *adj* **1.** (*unwieldly*) ingombrante **2.** (*awkward*) strano, -a

cumin ['kʌ·mɪn] *n* cumino *m*

cumulative ['kjuːm·jə·lə·tɪv] *adj* **1.** (*increasing*) cumulativo, -a **2.** (*accumulated*) accumulato, -a

cumulus ['kjum·jə·ləs] <-li> *n* cumulo *m*

cunning ['kʌ·nɪŋ] I. *adj* **1.** (*ingenious: person*) astuto, -a; (*device, idea, plan*) ingegnoso, -a **2.** (*sly*) scaltro, -a II. *n* astuzia *f*

cunt [kʌnt] *n* **1.** *vulg* fica *m* **2.** *vulg* (*despicable person*) testa *mf* di cazzo

cup [kʌp] I. *n* **1.** (*container*) tazza *f;* **coffee/ tea ~** tazza da caffè/tè; **egg ~** portauovo *m inv;* **a ~ of flour/sugar** una tazza di farina/ zucchero **2.** SPORTS (*trophy*) coppa *f;* **the World Cup** la Coppa del Mondo **3.** BOT, REL calice *m* **4.** (*part of bra*) coppa *f;* **a C ~** una coppa di taglia C ▶ **it's not my ~ of** <u>tea</u> non è il mio genere **II.** <-pp-> *vt* **to ~ one's hands** mettere le mani a coppa

cupboard ['kʌ·bəd] *n* armadio *m;* **built-in ~** armadio a muro; **kitchen ~** armadio di cucina

cupful ['kʌp·fʊl] *n* tazza *f;* **a ~ of sugar** una tazza di zucchero

cupola ['kju:·pə·lə] *n* ARCHIT cupola *f*

cur [kɜ:r] *n* **1.** (*dog*) cagnaccio *m* bastardo **2.** (*person*) carogna *f*

curable ['kjʊ·rə·bl] *adj* curabile

curate ['kjʊ·rət] *n* curato *m*

curator ['kjʊ·reɪ·t̬ər] *n* direttore, -trice *m, f* (*di museo o galleria*)

curb [kɜ:rb] **I.** *vt* tenere a freno **II.** *n* **1.** (*control*) freno *m;* **to keep a ~ on sth** tenere a freno qc; **to put a ~ on sth** mettere freno a qc **2.** (*obstacle*) ostacolo *m* **3.** (*at roadside*) bordo *m* del marciapiede

curb bit *n* morso *m*

curbstone ['kɜ:rb·stoʊn] *n* bordo del marciapiede *m*

curd [kɜ:rd] *n* cagliata *f;* **~ cheese** formaggio *m* a fiocchi

curdle ['kɜ:r·dl] **I.** *vi* cagliare; (*sauce*) rapprendersi **II.** *vt* far cagliare; (*sauce*) far rapprendere

cure [kjʊr] **I.** *vt* **1.** MED guarire, curare **2.** CULIN (*with smoke*) affumicare; (*with salt*) salare **3.** (*problem*) rimediare a **4.** (*leather*) conciare **II.** *n* **1.** MED cura *f;* (*return to health*) guarigione *f* **2.** CULIN affumicatura *f,* salatura *f* **3.** (*solution*) rimedio *m* **4.** (*of leather*) conciatura *f*

cure-all ['kjʊr·ɑ:l] *n* panacea *f;* **a ~ for sth** una panacea per qc

curfew ['kɜ:r·fju:] *n* coprifuoco *m*

curiosity [ˌkjʊ·rɪ·'ɑ:·sə·t̬i] <-ies> *n* **1.** (*desire to know*) curiosità *f* **2.** (*strange thing*) curiosità *f* ▶ **~ killed the** <u>cat</u> *prov* tanto va la gatta al lardo che ci lascia lo zampino

curious ['kjʊ·ə·ri·əs] *adj* curioso, -a; **to be ~ to see sth/sb** essere curioso di vedere qc/qu; **to be ~ about sth** essere curioso di qc; **it is ~ that ...** è curioso che ... +*subj*

curl [kɜ:rl] **I.** *n* **1.** (*loop of hair, sinuosity*) ricciolo *m* **2.** (*spiral*) spirale *f;* **~ of smoke** anello *m* di fumo **3.** (*of the lips*) smorfia *f* di disprezzo **II.** *vi* (*hair*) arricciarsi; (*paper*) arrotolarsi; (*path*) snodarsi; (*smoke*) formare spirali **III.** *vt* (*hair*) arricciare; **to ~ oneself up** arannicchiarsi ▶ **to ~ one's** <u>lip</u> fare una smorfia di disprezzo

curler ['kɜ:r·lə] *n* bigodino *m*

curling ['kɜ:r·lɪŋ] *n* **1.** (*of hair*) arricciatura *f* **2.** SPORTS curling *m*

curling iron *n* arricciatore *m*

curly ['kɜ:r·li] <-ier, -iest> *adj* (*hair*) riccio, -a; (*paper*) che si arrotola

currant ['kɜ:·rənt] *n* **1.** (*dried grape*) uvetta *f* **2.** (*berry*) ribes *m*

currency ['kɜ:·rən·si] <-ies> *n* **1.** FIN moneta *f;* **foreign ~** valuta *f* estera; **~ conversion** conversione *f* monetaria; **~ market** mercato *m*

valutario; **~ unit** unità *f* monetaria **2.** (*acceptance*) diffusione *f;* **to enjoy wide ~** essere ampiamente diffuso; **to gain ~** diffondersi

current ['kɜ:·rənt] **I.** *adj* **1.** (*present*) attuale; (*year, month*) corrente; **in ~ use** di uso corrente **2.** (*latest*) ultimo, -a; **the ~ issue** (*of magazine*) l'ultimo numero; **the ~ craze** l'ultima moda **3.** (*prevalent*) comune **4.** (*valid*) vigente **II.** *n* **1.** *a.* ELEC corrente *f* **2.** (*tendency: of fashion*) tendenza *f* ▶ **to** <u>drift</u> **with the ~** seguire la corrente; **to** <u>swim</u> **against the ~** nuotare controcorrente

current affairs *npl,* **current events** *npl* attualità *f*

current expenses *npl* spese *f pl* correnti

currently *adv* **1.** (*at present*) attualmente **2.** (*commonly*) comunemente

current opinion *n* opinione *f* corrente

current rate *n* tasso *m* corrente

curry[1] ['kɜ:·ri] **I.** <-ies> *n* curry *m;* **chicken ~** pollo *m* al curry; **vegetable ~** verdure *f pl* al curry **II.** *vt* cucinare al curry

curry[2] ['kɜ:·ri] *vt* **1.** (*groom: horse*) strigliare **2.** (*leather*) conciare ▶ **to ~** <u>favor</u> **with sb** cercare il favore di qu

curse [kɜ:rs] **I.** *n* **1.** (*bad word*) bestemmia *m* **2.** (*evil spell*) maledizione *f;* **to put a ~ on sb** maledire qu **3.** (*affliction*) **the ~ of racism** la piaga del razzismo; **to be the ~ of sb's life** essere la croce di qu **II.** *vt* **1.** (*swear at*) insultare **2.** (*wish evil on*) maledire **III.** *vi* (*swear*) bestemmiare

cursed ['kɜ:r·sɪd] *adj* maledetto, -a

cursor ['kɜ:r·sə] *n* COMPUT cursore *m*

cursory ['kɜ:r·sə·ri] *adj* superficiale

curt [kɜ:rt] *adj* **1.** (*brief*) conciso, -a **2.** (*laconic*) laconico, -a **3.** (*rudely brief*) secco, -a

curtail [kə·'teɪl] *vt* **1.** (*limit, reduce: rights, freedom*) limitare; (*expenses*) ridurre **2.** (*shorten*) abbreviare

curtailment *n* **1.** (*of spending, freedom*) riduzione *f* **2.** (*cutting short*) accorciamento *m*

curtain ['kɜ:r·tn] **I.** *n* **1.** tenda *f;* **lace ~** tenda di pizzo; **to draw the ~s** chiudere le tende **2.** *fig* cortina *f* **3.** THEAT sipario *m;* **to raise/lower the ~** alzare/abbassare il sipario ▶ **it's ~s for you** per te è finita **II.** *vt* mettere le tende in; **to ~ off** separare con una tenda

curtain call *n* THEAT chiamata *f* alla ribalta

curtain raiser *n* THEAT pezzo *m* d'apertura

curts(e)y ['kɜ:rt·si] **I.** *vi* fare una riverenza **II.** *n* riverenza *f;* **to make a ~ to sb** fare una riverenza a qu

curvature ['kɜ:r·və·tʃər] *n* curvatura *f;* MED deviazione *f*

curve [kɜ:rv] **I.** *n* curva *f* **II.** *vi* piegarsi; (*path, road*) fare una curva; **to ~ around to the left** (*path*) fare una curva a sinistra **III.** *vt* curvare

cushion ['kʊ·ʃən] **I.** *n* **1.** cuscino *m* **2.** TECH **a ~ of air** un cuscino d'aria **3.** (*in billiards*) sponda *f* **II.** *vt* **1.** (*furnish with cushions*) mettere dei cuscini in [*o* per] **2.** (*pad*) imbottire **3.** (*ease the effects of*) attutire **4.** (*protect*) proteggere

cushy ['kʊ·ʃi] <-ier, -iest> *adj inf* facile; **a ~ job** un lavoro di tutto comodo

cuss [kʌs] *inf* I. *vi* imprecare II. *n* imprecazione *f*

custard ['kʌs·tə·d] *n* crema *f* pasticcera

custodial [kʌs·'toʊ·di·əl] *adj* 1. LAW detentivo, -a 2. (*care: parent*) che ha la custodia

custodian [kʌs·'toʊ·di·ən] *n* 1. custode *mf* 2. (*of a museum*) responsabile *mf*

custody ['kʌs·tə·di] *n* custodia *f*; **in the ~ of sb** in custodia a qu; **to award ~ of sb to sb** affidare a qu la custodia di qu; **to take sb into ~** mettere qu agli arresti

custom ['kʌs·təm] *n* 1. (*tradition*) costume *f*; **an ancient ~** un'antica usanza; **according to ~** secondo la tradizione; **it is his ~ to do sth** ha l'abitudine di fare qc 2. LAW diritto *m* consuetudinario 3. *pl* (*place, tax*) dogana *f*; **to get through ~s** passare la dogana; **to pay ~s (on sth)** pagare la dogana (su qc)

customary ['kʌs·tə·me·ri] *adj* 1. (*traditional*) tradizionale; **it is ~ to +***infin* è tradizione +*infin* 2. (*usual*) abituale

custom-built ['kʌs·təm·ˌbɪlt] *adj* (*car*) fatto, -a su commissione

custom clothes *npl* abiti *f pl* fatti su misura

customer ['kʌs·tə·mə·] *n* COM, ECON 1. (*buyer, patron*) cliente, -a *m, f*; **regular ~** cliente abituale 2. *inf* (*person*) tipo, -a *m, f*

customer service *n* assistenza *f* clienti

customize ['kʌs·tə·maɪz] *vt* adattare (alle esigenze del cliente); *a.* COMPUT personalizzare

customized *adj* personalizzato, -a

custom-made ['kʌs·təm·ˌmeɪd] *adj* (*clothes*) fatto, -a su misura; (*furniture*) fatto, -a su commissione

customs declaration *n* dichiarazione *f* doganale

customs dues *npl*, **customs duties** *npl* dazi *m pl* doganali; **to pay ~** pagare la dogana

custom(s)house *n* dogana *f*

customs officer *n*, **customs official** *n* doganiere *m*

customs union *n* unione *f* doganale

cut [kʌt] I. *n* 1. taglio *m;* **to make a ~** tagliare; **the ~ of a shirt** il taglio di una camicia; **a deep ~** un taglio profondo; **to get a ~** tagliarsi; **a ~ in production/staff** una riduzione della produzione/del personale; **wage/budget ~** tagli salariali/del budget; **to make a ~ in a film** tagliare una scena di un film 2. (*slice, part*) fetta *f*; **to take one's ~ of sth** *inf* prendersi la propria fetta di qc; **cold ~s** carne *f* fredda affettata 3. GAMES **who's ~ is it?** a chi tocca tagliare? 4. *inf* (*absence*) assenza *f* 5. (*swing in baseball*) colpo tagliato ▸ **the ~ and thrust** la battaglia; **to be a ~ above sb/ sth** avere una marcia in più rispetto a qu/qc II. *adj* tagliato, -a III. <cut, cut, -tt-> *vt* 1. tagliare; **to ~ oneself** tagliarsi; **to ~ sth open** aprire qc con un taglio; **to ~ sth in half** tagliare qc a metà; **to ~ sth to pieces** tagliare qc a

pezzetti; **to have one's hair ~** tagliarsi i capelli; **to ~ the lawn** tagliare l'erba; **who's going to ~ the cards?** GAMES chi taglia? 2. (*cause moral pain*) ferire 3. (*decrease size, amount, length*) tagliare, ridurre 4. (*divide: benefits*) ripartire 5. (*hollow out*) **to ~ a hole** fare un buco 6. shorten; (*speech*) tagliare; CINE, TV montare 7. *inf* (*skip: school, class*) saltare 8. MUS (*a record, CD*) incidere IV. <cut, cut, -tt-> *vi* 1. (*slice*) tagliare, tagliarsi; **this knife ~s well** questo coltello taglia bene; **this cheese ~s easily** questo formaggio si taglia bene 2. GAMES tagliare il mazzo; **let's ~ to see who starts** tagliamo il mazzo per vedere a chi tocca dare le carte 3. CINE **~!** stop! 4. (*change direction suddenly*) **to ~ to the right** sterzare a destra 5. (*morally wound: remark, words*) ferire ▸ **to ~ both ways** essere un'arma a doppio taglio

◆ **cut across** *vt insep* 1. (*take shortcut*) tagliare attraverso 2. (*transcend*) oltrepassare

◆ **cut away** *vt* tagliare via

◆ **cut back** I. *vt* 1. (*trim down*) scorciare; (*bushes, branches*) potare 2. (*reduce: production*) tagliare; **to ~ (on) sth** ridurre qc; **to ~ (on) costs** ridurre i costi II. *vi* CINE **to ~ to ...** tornare a ...

◆ **cut down** I. *vt* 1. (*tree*) tagliare 2. (*reduce: production*) ridurre; **to ~ expenses** ridurre le spese 3. (*destroy, kill*) distruggere; **David was ~ in his prime** David è morto nel fiore degli anni 4. (*remodel, shorten: garment*) accorciare II. *vi* **to ~ on sth** ridurre qc; **to ~ on smoking** fumare meno

◆ **cut in** I. *vi* 1. (*interrupt*) **to ~ (on sb)** interrompere (qu); **to ~ on a conversation** interrompere una conversazione; **may I ~?** (*in dance*) permette? 2. AUTO sorpassare; **to ~ on sb** tagliare la strada a qu II. *vt* 1. (*divide profits with*) **to cut sb in on sth** spartire qc con qu 2. (*include when playing*) **to cut sb in on the game** far partecipare qu al gioco

◆ **cut into** *vt insep* 1. (*start cutting: cake*) (iniziare a) tagliare 2. (*interrupt*) interrompere 3. AUTO sorpassare

◆ **cut off** *vt* 1. (*sever*) *a.* ELEC, TEL staccare 2. (*amputate*) tagliare 3. (*stop talking*) interrompere 4. (*separate, isolate*) isolare; **to cut oneself off (from sb)** isolarsi (da qu); **to be ~ by the snow** rimanere isolato a causa della neve

◆ **cut out** I. *vt* 1. (*slice out of*) tagliare, ritagliare 2. (*suppress: sugar, fatty food*) eliminare; **to cut a scene out of a film** tagliare una scena da un film; **to cut sb out of one's will** diseredare qu 3. *inf* (*stop*) eliminare; **to ~ smoking** smettere di fumare; **~ all this nonsense!** smettila con queste stupidaggini!; **cut it out!** smettila! II. *vi* TECH (*engine*) fermarsi; (*machine*) bloccarsi

◆ **cut short** *vt* abbreviare

◆ **cut up** I. *vt* 1. (*slice into pieces*) tagliare a pezzetti; (*meat*) tritare 2. (*hurt*) ferire; **to be**

badly ~ essere ferito gravemente **II.** *vi* (*laugh*) ridere

cut-and-dried [ˌkʌt·ən·'draɪd] *adj* **1.** (*fixed in advance*) definitivo, -a **2.** (*not original*) fisso, -a

cut-and-paste [ˌkʌt·ənd·'peɪst] *adj a.* COMPUT di taglia e incolla

cutback ['kʌt·bæk] *n* **1.** (*reduction*) riduzione *f;* ~ **in expenditures** riduzione delle spese **2.** CINE flashback *m inv*

cute [kjuːt] *adj* **1.** (*sweet: baby*) carino, -a *inf* **2.** (*remark, idea*) ingegnioso, -a

cutey ['kjuː·ţi] <-ies> *n inf s.* **cutie**

cuticle ['kjuː·ţə·kl] *n* cuticola *f*

cutie ['kjuː·ţi] *n,* **cutiepie** ['kjuː·ţi·paɪ] *n inf* (*woman*) bambola *f;* (*child*) birba *f*

cutlass ['kʌt·ləs] <-es> *n* MIL sciabola *f*

cutlery ['kʌt·lə·ri] *n* posate *fpl*

cutlet ['kʌt·lɪt] *n* cotoletta *f*

cutoff ['kʌţ·ɑːf] *n* **1.** TECH otturatore *m;* ~ **date** termine *m;* ~ **point** limite *m* massimo **2.** (*end of supply*) disconnessione *f* **3.** (*baseball player*) difensore *m* interno

cutout *n* **1.** (*design prepared for cutting*) modello *m* **2.** ELEC interruttore *m* automatico

cut-rate *adj* ridotto, -a

cutter ['kʌ·ţə·] *n* **1.** (*tool which cuts*) taglierina *f,* tagliatrice *f;* (*for glass*) tagliavetro *m inv* **2.** (*person*) tagliatore, -trice *m, f* **3.** NAUT cutter *m inv*

cutthroat ['kʌt·θroʊt] **I.** *n* **1.** (*murderer*) assassino, -a *m, f* **2.** (*razor*) rasoio *m* da barbiere **II.** *adj* spietato, -a

cutting ['kʌ·ţɪŋ] **I.** *n* **1.** (*act*) taglio *m* **2.** (*piece*) ritaglio *m* **3.** BOT talea *f* **4.** (*for road, railway*) trincea *f* **5.** CINE montaggio *m* **II.** *adj a. fig* tagliente

cutting-edge *adj* d'avanguardia

cuttlefish ['kʌ·ţl·fɪʃ] *n inv* seppia *f*

cyanide ['sa·ɪə·naɪd] *n* cianuro *m*

cybercafé ['saɪ·bə·ˌkæ·feɪ] *n* Internet caffè *m*

cybercash ['saɪ·bə·ˌkæʃ] *n* cybercash *m,* denaro *m* virtuale

cybernaut [ˌsaɪ·bə·'nɔːt] *n* cibernauta *mf*

cybernetics [ˌsaɪ·bə·'ne·ţɪks] *n + sing vb* cibernetica *f*

cybersex ['saɪ·bə·seks] *n* sesso *m* virtuale

cyberspace *n* ciberspazio *m*

cyclamen ['saɪ·klə·mən] *n* ciclamino *m*

cycle[1] ['saɪ·kl] **I.** *n* bicicletta *f* **II.** *vi* andare in bicicletta

cycle[2] ['saɪ·kl] *n* **1.** (*of life, seasons*) ciclo *m* **2.** ASTR orbita *f*

cyclic ['saɪk·lɪk] *adj,* **cyclical** *adj* ciclico, -a

cycling I. *n* SPORTS ciclismo *m* **II.** *adj* ~ **shorts** pantaloncini *m pl* da ciclista

cyclist ['saɪk·lɪst] *n* SPORTS ciclista *mf*

cyclone ['saɪ·kloʊn] *n* METEO ciclone *m*

cygnet ['sɪg·nɪt] *n* cigno *m* giovane

cylinder ['sɪ·lɪn·də·] *n* **1.** MATH, AUTO, TECH cilindro *m* **2.** (*container: of gas*) bombola *f*

cylinder block *n* TECH blocco *m* motore

cylinder capacity *n* TECH cilindrata *f*

cylinder head *n* TECH testata *f*

cylindrical [sɪ·'lɪn·drɪ·kl] *adj* cilindrico, -a

cymbal ['sɪm·bl] *n* MUS piatto *m*

cynic ['sɪ·nɪk] **I.** *n* cinico, -a *m, f* **II.** *adj* cinico, -a

cynical ['sɪ·nɪ·kl] *adj* cinico, -a

cynicism ['sɪ·nɪ·sɪ·zəm] *n* cinismo *m*

cypher ['saɪ·fə·] *n s.* **cipher**

cypress ['saɪ·prəs] <-es> *n* cipresso *m*

Cypriot ['sɪ·pri·ət] **I.** *adj* cipriota **II.** *n* cipriota *mf*

Cyprus ['saɪ·prəs] *n* GEO Cipro *m*

cyst [sɪst] *n* MED ciste *f*

cystitis [sɪs·'taɪ·ţɪs] *n* MED cistite *f*

czar [zɑːr] *n* zar *m*

czarina ['zɑː·'riː·nə] *n* zarina *f*

Czech [tʃek] **I.** *n* **1.** (*person*) ceco, -a *m, f* **2.** (*language*) ceco *m* **II.** *adj* ceco, -a

Czech Republic *n* Repubblica *f* Ceca

D

D, d [diː] *n* **1.** (*letter*) D, d *f o m inv;* ~ **as in David** D come Domodossola **2.** MUS re *m* **3.** *s.* **day** g.

d *abbr of* **diameter** d.

d. 1. *abbr of* **date** data **2.** *abbr of* **died** morto

DA [ˌdiː·'eɪ] *n abbr of* **District Attorney** ≈ procuratore, -trice distrettuale *m*

dab [dæb] **I.** <-bb-> *vt* tamponare; **to** ~ **one's eys with a handkerchief** asciugarsi gli occhi con un fazzoletto **II.** <-bb-> *vi* **to** ~ **at sth** tamponare qc; **he** ~ **ed at his bleeding lip** si tamponava il labbro sanguinante **III.** *n* **1.** (*pat*) tocco *m;* **to give sth a** ~ (**with sth**) dare a qc un tocco (di qc) **2.** (*tiny bit*) (*of liquid*) goccia *f;* **a** ~ **of paint** un velo di pittura

dabble ['dæ·bl] **I.** <-ling> *vi* **1.** (*play in water*) sguazzare **2.** (*work*) **to** ~ **in sth** dilettarsi di qc **II.** <-ling> *vt* immergere; **to** ~ **sth** (**in sth**) immergere qc (in qc)

dad [dæd] *n inf* papà *m inv*

daddy ['dæ·di] *n childspeak, inf* papà *m inv*

daddy longlegs [ˌdæ·dɪ·'lɔː·ŋ·legz] *n* ZOOL opilione *m*

daemon ['diː·mən] *n* COMPUT daemon *m inv*

daffodil ['dæ·fə·dɪl] *n* giunchiglia *f*

dagger ['dæ·gə·] *n* pugnale *m* ▶ **to look** ~ **s at sb** guardare qn in cagnesco

dahlia ['dæl·jə] *n* dalia *f*

daily ['deɪ·li] **I.** *adj* giornaliero, -a; **on a** ~ **basis** quotidianamente; **to earn one's** ~ **bread** *inf* guadagnarsi il pane quotidiano **II.** *adv* quotidianamente; **twice** ~ due volte al giorno **III.** <-ies> *n* PUBL quotidiano *m*

daintiness *n* (*delicacy*) delicatezza *f*

dainty ['deɪn·ti] <-ier, -iest> *adj* **1.** (*delicate: flowers, painting*) delicato, -a; (*manners*) raffinato, -a **2.** (*delicious*) prelibato, -a **3.** (*scrupu-*

lous) scrupoloso, -a

dairy ['deˑri] **I.** *n* **1.** (*farm*) caseificio *m* **2.** (*shop*) latteria *f* **II.** *adj* **1.** (*made from milk*) fatto, -a con il latte **2.** (*producing milk*) che produce latte; **~ industry** industria casearia

dairy cattle *npl* mucche *f pl* da latte

dairy farm *n* caseificio *m*

dairyman *n* casaro *m*

dairy products *npl* prodotti *m pl* caseari

dais ['deɪˑɪs] *n* ARCHIT palco *m*

daisy ['deɪˑzi] <-ies> *n* margherita *f* ▶ **to be as** fresh **as a ~** essere fresco come una rosa; **to be** pushing **up daisies** *inf* essere morto e sepolto

daisy wheel *n* margherita *f;* **~ printer** stampante *f* a margherita

dally ['dæˑli] <-ie-> *vi* **1.** (*dawdle*) perder tempo; **to ~ around** ciondolare; **to ~ over sth** indugiare su qc **2.** (*play*) giocare; **to ~ with sb/sth** flirtare con qn/qc; **to ~ with an idea** trastullarsi con un'idea

dam [dæm] **I.** *n* **1.** (*barrier*) diga *f* **2.** (*reservoir*) bacino *m* **II.** <-mm-> *vt* (*river*) arginare; *fig* (*emotions, feelings*) trattenere

damage ['dæˑmɪdʒ] **I.** *vt* **1.** (*harm, hurt: building, objects*) danneggiare; (*environment, health, reputation*) nuocere a; **to be badly ~d** subire danni considerevoli **2.** (*ruin*) rovinare **II.** *n* **1.** (*harm: to objects*) danno *m;* **to do ~ to sb/sth** nuocere a qn/qc; **to cause serious ~ to sb's reputation** compromettere la reputazione di qn **2.** *pl* LAW danni *mpl* ▶ **the ~ is** done *inf* il danno è fatto; what's **the ~?** *inf* quanto devo?

damage control *n* POL *tattica per minimizzare l'impatto negativo di una decisione*

Damascus [dəˑ'mæsˑkəs] *n* Damasco *f*

damask ['dæˑməsk] **I.** *n* damasco *m* **II.** *adj* damascato, -a

dame [deɪm] *n pej, sl* (*woman*) donna *f*

damn [dæm] *sl* **I.** *interj* accidenti **II.** *adj* **1.** (*expressing irritation*) maledetto, -a **2.** (*for emphasis*) **to be a ~ fool** essere un cretino patentato; **it's a ~ mess!** è un bel casino! *vulg* **III.** *vt* **1.** (*expressing irritation*) (**God** *vulg*) **~ it!** maledizione! *inf;* **~ him!** he took my bike without asking! ha preso la mia bici senza chiedermelo! *vulg* **2.** REL dannare ▶ well, I'll be **~ed!** mi venisse un colpo!; I'll be **~ed if I know** non ne so proprio niente! **IV.** *adv* molto; **to be ~ lucky** avere una fortuna sfacciata; **you know ~ well that ... sai** benissimo che ... **V.** *n* **I don't give a ~ what he says!** non me ne frega niente di quello che dice!

damnable ['dæmˑnəˑbl] *adj sl* maledetto, -a

damnation [dæmˑ'neɪˑʃən] **I.** *n* dannazione *f* **II.** *interj* maledizione

damned I. *adj sl* **1.** (*expressing irritation*) maledetto, -a **2.** (*for emphasis*) maledetto, -a **II.** *npl* REL **the ~** i dannati

damning *adj* **~ evidence** prova *f* schiacciante

damp [dæmp] **I.** *adj* umido, -a; (*clothing*) bag-

nato, -a **II.** *vt* **1.** (*moisten*) inumidire **2.** *a. fig* PHYS, TECH, MUS smorzare **3.** (*extinguish*) **to ~** (**down**) (*flames, fire*) soffocare; (*enthusiasm*) smorzare; **to ~ down sb's spirits** scoraggiare qn

dampen ['dæmˑpən] *vt* **1.** (*make wet*) inumidire **2.** (*lessen*) diminuire; **to ~ sb's enthusiasm** raffreddare l'entusiasmo di qn; **to ~ sb's expectations** scoraggiare le speranze di qn **3.** PHYS, TECH, MUS attutire

damper ['dæmˑpəʳ] *n* **1.** (*on fireplace*) valvola *f* di tiraggio **2.** *inf* **to put a ~ on things** guastare le feste; **to put a ~ on sb's enthusiasm** raffreddare l'entusiasmo di qn

dampness *n* umidità *f*

dance [dænts] **I.** <-cing> *vi* **1.** (*move to music*) ballare; **to ~ to sth** ballare al ritmo di qc; **shall we ~?** balliamo?; **to go dancing** andare a ballare **2.** (*move energetically*) saltare; **to ~ with joy** saltare di gioia **3.** (*twinkle*) **his eyes ~d with pleasure** i suoi occhi brillavano di piacere; (*bob*) agitarsi; **the daffodils were dancing in the breeze** i narcisi ondeggiavano al vento ▶ **to ~ to sb's** tune fare ciò che vuole qn; **she makes him dance to her tune** gli fa fare quello che vuole **II.** <-cing> *vt* ballare; **to ~ the night away** ballare tutta la notte **III.** *n* ballo *m;* **to have a ~ with sb** ballare con qn; **the band played a slow ~** l'orchestra suonava un lento ballo

dance band *n* orchestra *f* da ballo

dance music *n* musica *f* da ballo

dancer ['dænt·səʳ] *n* ballerino, -a *m, f*

dancing *n* ballo *m*

dancing partner *n* compagno, -a di ballo *m*

dancing shoes *npl* scarpette *f* da ballo *pl*

dandelion ['dæn·də·la·iən] *n* BOT dente *m* di leone

dandruff ['dæn·drəf] *n* forfora *f*

dandy ['dæn·di] **I.** <-ies> *n* dandy *m inv* **II.** <-ier, -iest> *adj* fantastico, -a

Dane [deɪn] *n* danese *mf*

danger ['deɪn·dʒəʳ] *n* **1.** (*peril*) pericolo *m;* **to be in ~** essere in pericolo; **to be out of ~** esser fuori pericolo; **a ~ to sth/sb** un pericolo per qc/qn; **there's no ~ of him finding out** non c'è pericolo che venga a saperlo **2.** (*perilous aspect*) rischio *m;* **the ~s of sth** i rischi di qc

danger pay *n* indennità *f* di rischio

danger zone *n* zona *f* pericolosa

dangerous ['deɪn·dʒə·rəs] *adj* pericoloso, -a

dangle ['dæŋ·gl] **I.** <-ling> *vi* **1.** (*hang down*) penzolare; **to ~ from sth** penzolare da qc **2.** (*follow*) **to ~ after sb** seguire qn **II.** <-ling> *vt* **1.** (*cause to hang down*) far penzolare **2.** (*tempt with*) **to ~ sth in front of sb** tentare qn con qc

Danish ['deɪ·nɪʃ] **I.** *adj* danese **II.** *n* **1.** (*person*) danese *mf* **2.** LING danese *m* **3.** FOOD **~** (**pastry**) *brioche di pasta sfoglia e frutta*

dank [dæŋk] *adj* (*air, building*) umido, -a

Danube ['dæn·ju:b] *n* GEO Danubio *m*

dapper ['dæ·pəʳ] *adj* (*man*) agghindato, -a; **a ~**

D

appearance un aspetto curato

dapple ['dæ·pl] *vt* screziare

dare [der] I. <-ring> *vt* 1. (*risk doing*) osare 2. (*challenge*) sfidare; **to ~ sb** (**to do sth**) sfidare qn (a fare qc) II. <-ring> *vi* (*risk doing*) osare; **to ~ to do sth** osare fare qc; **I don't ~ go there** non oso andar lì; **just you ~!** provaci, se ne hai il coraggio!; **how ~ you ...** come osi ... ▸**don't** you **~!** non azzardarti! III. *n* sfida *f*; **to take a ~** accettare una sfida

daredevil ['der·ˌde·vəl] *inf* I. *n* scavezzacollo *mf* II. *adj* temerario, -a

daresay ['der·seɪ] *vt* osar dire

daring ['de·rɪŋ] I. *adj* 1. (*courageous*) temerario, -a 2. (*provocative: dress*) audace II. *n* audacia *f*

dark [dɑːrk] I. *adj* 1. (*without light, black*) scuro, -a; **~ blue** blu scuro; **~ chocolate** cioccolato fondente 2. (*not pale: complexion, hair*) scuro, -a 3. (*tragic, depressing*) cupo, -a; **a ~ chapter** un capitolo nero; **to have a ~ side** avere un lato negativo; **to look on the ~ side of things** vedere solo il lato negativo delle cose 4. (*evil*) tenebroso, -a 5. (*unknown, secret*) nascosto, -a; **the ~ side of sth** il lato nascosto di qc II. *n* 1. (*darkness*) oscurità *f*; **to be in the ~** essere al buio; **to be afraid of the ~** aver paura del buio 2. (*time of day*) **at ~** quando fa buio; **to do sth before/after ~** far qc prima che faccia buio/col buio ▸**to keep sb in the ~ about sth** tener qn all'oscuro di qc

Dark Ages *npl* HIST **the ~** l'alto Medioevo; *fig* la preistoria

darken ['dɑːr·kən] I. *vi* oscurarsi; (*sky*) rannuvolarsi; *fig* rabbuiarsi II. *vt* (*make darker*) oscurare; *fig* rabbuiare

dark horse *n* POL outsider *mf, inv*

darkly *adv* 1. (*mysteriously*) misteriosamente 2. (*gloomily*) tristemente; **to look at sb ~** guardare con aria triste qn

darkness *n* 1. (*dark*) oscurità *f*; **to plunge sth into ~** far piombare qc nel buio 2. *fig* (*lack of knowledge*) ignoranza *f*

darkroom *n* PHOT camera *f* oscura

dark-skinned *adj* di pelle scura

darling ['dɑːr·lɪŋ] I. *n* 1. (*beloved person*) tesoro *m* 2. (*term of endearment*) amore *m* II. *adj* 1. (*beloved*) caro, -a 2. (*cute*) delizioso, -a; **a ~ little room** una stanzetta deliziosa

darn¹ [dɑːrn] I. *vt* (*sock*) rammendare II. *n* rammendo *m*

darn² [dɑːrn] *vt inf* **~ it!** maledizione!; **well, I'll be ~!** (*in surprise*) mi venisse un colpo!; **I'll be ~ed if I'll do it!** manco morto lo faccio!

darning *n* rammendo *m*

darning needle *n* ago *m* da rammendo

dart [dɑːrt] I. *n* 1. (*type of weapon*) freccia *f*; **to fire a ~ at sb/sth** scagliare una freccia contro qn/qc 2. *pl* (*game*) freccette *fpl*; **to play ~s** giocare a freccette; **a game of ~s** una partita a freccette 3. (*quick run*) guizzo *m* 4. FASHION pince *f inv* II. *vi* **to ~ (for sth)** precipitarsi (verso qc); **to ~ away** sfrecciare via; **I ~ed**

behind the sofa corsi a nascondermi dietro il divano III. *vt* 1. (*send quickly: look*) lanciare 2. (*move quickly*) **the lizard ~ed out its tongue** la lucertola fece scattare la lingua

dartboard ['dɑːrt·bɔːrd] *n* bersaglio *m*

dash [dæʃ] I. <-es> *n* 1. (*rush*) corsa *f*; **to make a ~ for** precipitarsi verso; **to make a ~ for it** fare una corsa 2. (*pinch*) pochino *m*; (*of salt*) pizzico *m*; **a ~ of color** una punta di colore 3. (*flair*) brio *m* 4. TYPO lineetta *f* 5. (*in Morse code*) linea *f* II. *vi* 1. (*hurry*) correre 2. (*slam into*) **to ~ against sth** sbattere contro qc III. *vt* 1. (*shatter*) rompere 2. (*hopes*) infrangere 3. (*to ~ off a letter/note*) buttar giù una lettera/un appunto

dashboard ['dæʃ·bɔːrd] *n* AUTO cruscotto *m*

dashing ['dæ·ʃɪŋ] *adj* affascinante

dastardly ['dæs·tə·d·li] *adj liter* (*crime, act*) efferato, -a

DAT [dæt] *n abbr of* **digital audio tape** DAT *m*

data ['deɪ·tə] *npl + sing/pl vb a.* COMPUT dati *mpl*

data bank *n*, **databank** *n* banca *f* dati

database *n* database *m inv*

data file *n* file *m* dati *inv*

dataglove *n* COMPUT guanto *m* virtuale

data processing *n* elaborazione *f* dei dati

date¹ [deɪt] I. *n* 1. (*calendar day*) data *f*; **expiration ~** data di scadenza; **what ~ is it today?** quanti ne abbiamo oggi?; **to be out of ~** FASHION esser fuori moda 2. (*appointment*) appuntamento *m*; **to have a ~** avere un appuntamento; **to make a ~ with sb** fissare un appuntamento con qn 3. *inf* (*person*) ragazzo, -a *m, f*, con cui si esce II. *vt* 1. (*recognize age of*) far risalire; **to ~ sth at ...** far risalire qc al ... 2. (*give date to sth*) datare 3. *inf* (*have relationship with*) **to ~ sb** uscire con qn III. *vi* 1. (*go back to*) **to ~ back to** risalire a 2. (*go out of fashion*) passare di moda 3. (*go on dates*) uscire con qn

date² [deɪt] *n* 1. (*fruit*) dattero *m* 2. (*tree*) palma *f* da datteri

dated ['deɪ·tɪd] *adj* datato, -a

dateline ['deɪt·laɪn] *n* linea *f* del cambiamento di data

date rape *n* *stupro commesso durante un appuntamento*

i Con riferimento a un **dating**, negli Stati Uniti si usano diverse espressioni a seconda del tipo di relazione tra una ragazza e un ragazzo. *Seeing each other* significa che due persone si frequentano regolarmente ma sono libere di uscire con altri partner. *Going out* indica che la relazione è seria.

dative ['deɪ·tɪv] I. *n* dativo *m*; **to be in the ~** essere al dativo II. *adj* dativo, -a

daub [dɔːb] I. *vt* 1. (*smear*) **to ~ sth with sth** spalmare qc di qc 2. (*paint unskillfully*) imbrattare II. *n* 1. (*smear*) macchia *f* 2. (*painting*) crosta *f*

daughter ['dɔ:·t̬ɚ] *n* figlia *f*

daughter-in-law <daughters-in-law> *n* nuora *f*

daunt [dɔ:nt] *vt* 1.(*discourage*) scoraggiare 2.(*intimidate*) intimidire

daunting *adj* scoraggiante

dauntless ['dɑ:nt·ləs] *adj* intrepido, -a

dawdle ['dɔ:·dl] *vi* ciondolare

dawdler ['dɔ:d·lɚ] *n* persona *f* lenta

dawn [dɔ:n] I. *n* 1.(*time of day*) alba *f;* from ~ to dusk dall'alba al tramonto; at ~ all'alba 2.*fig* (*beginning*) albori *mpl* II. *vi* spuntare; *fig* (*era*) nascere; it ~ed on him that ... si rese conto che ...

day [deɪ] *n* 1. giorno *m;* ~ after ~ giorno dopo giorno; ~ by ~ giorno per giorno; all ~ (long) tutto il giorno; any ~ now da un giorno all'altro; by ~ di giorno; by the ~ giornalmente; for a few ~s per qualche giorno; from that ~ on(wards) da quel giorno; from this ~ forth da oggi in poi; from one ~ to the next da un giorno all'altro; one ~ un giorno; two ~s ago due giorni fa; the ~ before yesterday l'altro ieri; the ~ after tomorrow dopodomani; in the (good) old ~s ai bei tempi; the exam is ten ~s from now [*o* in ten ~s] l'esame è fra dieci giorni 2.(*working period*) giornata *f;* to take a ~ off prendere un giorno di vacanza ▶ in this ~ and age al giorno d'oggi; to have seen <u>better</u> ~s aver conosciuto tempi migliori; to <u>call</u> it a ~ smettere; to <u>carry</u> the ~ uscire vittorioso; ~ <u>in</u> ~ out tutti i santi giorni

day bed *n* divano *m* letto

daybreak ['deɪ·breɪk] *n* alba *f*

day camp *n* campo *m* estivo

daycare ['deɪ·ker] *n* 1.(*for children*) asilo *m* nido 2.(*for the elderly*) assistenza *f* diurna per anziani

daydream ['deɪ·dri:m] I. *vi* sognare ad occhi aperti II. *n* sogno *m* ad occhi aperti

daylight ['deɪ·laɪt] *n* luce *f* del giorno; in broad ~ in pieno giorno ▶ to scare the <u>living</u> ~s out of sb *inf* spaventare a morte qn

day shift *n* turno *m* di giorno

daytime ['deɪ·taɪm] *n* giorno *m;* in the ~ di giorno

day-to-day *adj* quotidiano, -a

day trip *n* gita *f* (di un giorno)

daze [deɪz] I. *n* stordimento *m;* to be in a ~ essere stordito II. *vt* stordire

dazed *adj* stordito, -a

dazzle ['dæ·zl] I. *vt* abbagliare II. *n* bagliore *m*

dazzled *adj* abbagliato, -a

dB *n* abbr of decibel dB

DC [ˌdi:·'si:] *n* 1. abbr of direct current c.c. 2. abbr of District of Columbia DC

DD [ˌdi:·'di:] *n* abbr of Doctor of Divinity dottore, -essa *m, f* in Teologia

D-Day ['di:·deɪ] *n* D-day *m, il giorno dello sbarco degli alleati in Normandia*

DDT [ˌdi:·di:·'ti:] *n* abbr of dichlorodiphenyl-trichloroethane DDT *m*

deacon ['di:·kən] *n* diacono *m*

deaconess ['di:·kə·nəs] *n* diaconessa *f*

dead [ded] I. *adj* 1.(*no longer alive*) morto, -a; to be ~ on arrival giungere cadavere (all'ospedale); she wouldn't be seen ~ wearing that *inf* neanche morta lo indosserebbe 2. *inf* (*inactive: battery*) scarico, -a; (*fire*) spento, -a; the line went ~ è caduta la linea 3. *inf* (*quiet, boring*) morto, -a; (*town*) deserto, -a 4.(*numb*) addormentato, -a 5.(*complete: silence*) di tomba; to be a ~ loss essere un disastro totale; to come to a ~ stop fermarsi di colpo ▶ as ~ as a <u>doornail</u> morto stecchito; ~ <u>men</u> tell no tales *prov* i morti non parlano II. *n* the ~ i morti ▶ in the ~ of <u>night</u>/<u>winter</u> nel cuore della notte/dell'inverno III. *adv* 1. *inf* (*totally*) completamente; to be ~ set on doing sth essere assolutamente determinato a fare qc; to be ~ set against sth essere assolutamente contrario a qc 2.(*directly*) proprio; ~ ahead sempre dritto

deadbeat [ˌded·'bi:t] *adj inf* restio, -a a pagare debiti; ~ dad *padre divorziato che non paga gli alimenti per il mantenimento dei figli*

dead center *n* punto *m* morto

deaden ['de·dən] *vt* (*pain*) alleviare; (*noise*) attutire

dead end *n* vicolo *m* cieco

dead-end *adj* senza uscita; ~ job lavoro *m* senza prospettive

dead heat *n* risultato *m* di parità

deadline ['ded·laɪn] *n* scadenza *f;* to meet/miss the ~ rispettare/non rispettare la scadenza

deadlock ['ded·lɑ:k] *n* punto *m* morto

deadly ['ded·li] I. <-ier, -iest> *adj* 1.(*capable of killing*) mortale 2. *inf* (*boring*) noiosissimo, -a II. <-ier, -iest> *adv* estremamente; ~ pale pallido come un cadavere

deadpan *adj* impassibile

Dead Sea *n* mar *m* Morto

deadwood ['ded·wʊd] *n a. fig* rami *m pl* secchi

deaf [def] I. *adj* sordo, -a; to go ~ diventare sordo; to be ~ to sth *fig* fare orecchi da mercante a qc II. *npl* the ~ i sordi

deafen ['de·fən] *vt* assordare

deafening *adj* assordante

deaf-mute [ˌdef·'mju:t] *n* sordomuto, -a *m, f*

deafness *n* sordità *f*

deal¹ [di:l] *n* (*large amount*) quantità *f;* a great ~ una gran quantità; a great ~ of effort grande sforzo

deal² [di:l] <dealt, dealt> I. *n* 1. COM affare *m;* a big ~ un affare importante 2.(*agreement*) accordo *m;* to do a ~ (with sb) fare un patto (con qn) 3. GAMES (*of cards*) turno *m, di dare le carte;* it's your ~ tocca a te dare le carte ▶ big ~! *iron, inf* sai che roba!; it's no big ~! *inf* non è niente di eccezionale! II. *vi* 1.(*do business*) fare affari; to ~ with sb fare affari con qn; to ~ in sth trattare qc 2. GAMES dare le carte 3. *sl* (*accept situation, cope*) to ~ (with sth) farcela (con qc) **III.** *vt* **1.** GAMES (*cards*) distribuire **2.** (*give*) dare; **to ~ sb a blow** assestare un colpo a qn

◆ **deal out** *vt* distribuire

◆ **deal with** *vt* **1.** (*take care of: problem*) affrontare; (*person*) occuparsi di **2.** (*be about: book*) trattare di **3.** (*punish*) fare i conti con

dealer ['diː·lə] *n* **1.** COM commerciante *mf;* **drug ~** spacciatore, ·trice *m, f;* **antique ~** antiquario, ·a *m, f* **2.** GAMES (*in cards*) persona *f* che dà le carte

dealership ['diː·lə·ʃɪp] *n* COM concessione *f*

dealing ['diː·lɪŋ] *n* **1.** COM commercio *m* **2.** *pl* FIN transazione *f* **3.** *pl* (*relations*) rapporti *mpl;* **to have ~s with sb** avere a che fare con qn **4.** GAMES il dare le carte *m*

dealt [delt] *pt, pp of* **deal**

dean [diːn] *n* **1.** UNIV preside *mf* di facoltà **2.** REL decano *m*

dean's list *n* UNIV *la lista degli studenti migliori di un'università*

dear [dɪr] **I.** *adj* **1.** (*much loved*) caro, ·a; **it is ~ to me** mi è molto caro **2.** (*in letters*) **Dear David** caro David; **Dear Sir** Egregio Signor **3.** (*expensive*) caro, ·a **II.** *adv* caro **III.** *interj inf* **oh ~!** oddio! **IV.** *n* tesoro *m;* **she is a ~** è un tesoro; **be a ~ and ...** sii gentile e ...

dearly *adv* **1.** molto; **I love her ~** l'amo molto **2.** *fig* caro; **he paid ~ for his success** ha pagato caro il suo successo

dearth [dɜːrθ] *n* penuria *f;* **to suffer from a ~ of sth** risentire della mancanza di qc

death [deθ] *n* morte *f;* **to die a natural ~** morire di morte naturale; **to put sb to ~** giustiziare qn; **to be bored to ~ with sth** *inf* annoiarsi a morte con qc; **scared to ~** *inf* spaventato a morte; **to catch one's ~ of cold** prendersi un malanno ▸ **to be at ~'s <u>door</u>** essere in punto di morte; **to <u>be</u> the ~ of sb** essere la rovina di qn; **to <u>be</u> the ~ of sth** essere la fine di qc

deathbed ['deθ·bed] *n* letto *m* di morte

deathblow *n* colpo *m* mortale

death certificate *n* certificato *m* di grazia

deathly ['deθ·li] **I.** *adv* mortalmente; **~ pale** di un pallore mortale **II.** *adj* mortale

death penalty *n* pena *f* di morte

death rate *n* tasso *m* di mortalità

death row *n* braccio *m* della morte

death sentence *n* pena *f* di morte

death squad *n* squadrone *m* della morte

death trap *n* trappola *f* mortale

debacle [dɪ·'bɑː·kl] *n* débâcle *f inv*

debar [dɪ·'bɑːr] <-rr-> *vt* escludere; **to ~ sb from doing sth** impedire a qn di fare qc

debase [dɪ·'beɪs] *vt* (*degrade*) degradare; ECON svalutare

debatable [dɪ·'beɪ·tə·bl] *adj* discutibile

debate [dɪ·'beɪt] **I.** *n* **1.** (*argument*) dibattito *m;* **a ~ over sth** un dibattito su qc **2.** (*consideration*) esame *m* approfondito **II.** *vt* **1.** (*argue*) dibattere **2.** (*consider*) considerare **III.** *vi* **to ~ about sth** discutere di qc

debater [dɪ·'beɪ·tə] *n* chi partecipa a un dibattito

debauch [dɪ·'bɔːtʃ] **I.** *vt* corrompere **II.** *n* dissolutezza *f*

debauchery [dɪ·'bɔː·tʃə·ri] *n* dissolutezza *f*

debenture [dɪ·'ben·tʃə] *n* FIN obbligazione *f*

debilitate [dɪ·'bɪ·lɪ·teɪt] *vt* debilitare

debilitating *adj* debilitante

debility [dɪ·'bɪ·lə·ti] *n* debolezza *f*

debit ['de·bɪt] **I.** *n* debito *m* **II.** *vt* **the bank ~ed my account for the rent** la banca mi ha addebitato l'affitto in conto

debit card *n* carta *f* d'addebito

debit column *n* colonna *f* del dare

debonair(e) [ˌde·bə·'ner] *adj form* raffinato, ·a

debris [də·'briː] *n* macerie *fpl*

debt [det] *n* debito *m;* **to be in ~** essere in debito; **to pay off a ~** pagare un debito; **to be out of ~** essersi liberato dai debiti

debt collector *n* agente *mf* di recupero crediti

debtor ['de·tə] *n* debitore, ·trice *m, f*

debtor country *n,* **debtor nation** *n* paese *m* debitore

debug [ˌdiː·'bʌg] <-gg-> *vt* COMPUT effettuare il debugging di

debunk [diː·'bʌŋk] *vt* sfatare

debut [deɪ·'bjuː] **I.** *n* **1.** (*first public appearance*) debutto *m;* **to make one's ~** debuttare **2.** (*introduction into society*) debutto *m* in società **II.** *vi* debuttare; **to ~ in/as sth** debuttare come

debutante ['de·bju·tɑːnt] *n* debuttante *mf*

decade ['de·keɪd] *n* decennio *m*

decadence ['de·kə·dəns] *n* decadenza *f*

decadent ['de·kə·dənt] *adj* decadente

decaf ['diː·kæf] *adj, n inf abbr of* **decaffeinated** decaffeinato *m*

decaffeinated [ˌdiː·'kæ·fɪ·neɪ·tɪd] *adj* decaffeinato, ·a

decamp [dɪ·'kæmp] *vi* (*leave*) andarsene; (*secretly*) svignarsela

decant [dɪ·'kænt] *vt* decantare

decanter [dɪ·'kæn·tə] *n* decanter *m inv*

decapitate [dɪ·'kæ·pɪ·teɪt] *vt* decapitare

decapitation [dɪ·ˌkæ·pɪ·'teɪ·ʃən] *n* decapitazione *f*

decathlete [dɪ·'kæθ·liːt] *n* decatleta *mf*

decathlon [dɪ·'kæθ·lɑːn] *n* decathlon *m*

decay [dɪ·'keɪ] **I.** *n* (*of food*) deperimento *m;* (*of building, intellect*) deterioramento *m;* (*dental*) carie *f inv;* (*of civilization*) decadenza *f* **II.** *vi* (*food*) deperire; (*building, intellect*) deteriorarsi; (*teeth*) cariarsi **III.** *vt* far deperire

decease [dɪ·'siːs] *n* decesso *m*

deceased [dɪ·'siːst] **I.** *n* defunto, ·a *m, f* **II.** *adj* defunto, ·a

deceit [dɪ·'siːt] *n* inganno *m*

deceitful [dɪ·'siːt·fəl] *adj* ingannevole

deceive [dɪ·'siːv] *vt* ingannare; **to ~ oneself** ingannarsi ▸ **<u>appearances</u> can ~** *prov* l'apparenza inganna *prov*

deceiver [dɪ·'siː·və] *n* impostore, ·a *m, f*

decelerate [diː·'se·lə·reɪt] I. *vi* decelerare; (*vehicle, driver*) rallentare II. *vt* decelerare

December [dɪ·'sem·bə·] *n* dicembre *m; s.a.* **April**

decency ['diː·sənt·si] *n* 1. (*respectability*) decenza *f* 2. *pl* (*approved behavior*) regole *f* del buon vivere civile *pl*

decent ['diː·sənt] *adj* 1. (*socially acceptable*) decente; **are you ~?** *fig* sei presentabile? 2. *inf* (*kind*) gentile 3. *inf* (*adequate: salary, living, wage*) adeguato, -a

decentralization [diː·ˌsen·trə·lɪ·'zeɪ·ʃən] *n* decentramento *m*

decentralize [diː·'sen·trə·laɪz] *vt* decentrare

decentralized *adj* decentrato, -a

deception [dɪ·'sep·ʃən] *n* inganno *m;* **to practice ~ on sb** ingannare qn

deceptive [dɪ·'sep·tɪv] *adj* ingannevole

decibel ['de·sɪ·bel] *n* decibel *m inv*

decide [dɪ·'saɪd] I. *vi* decidere; **to ~ on sth** scegliere qc II. *vt* decidere

decided [dɪ·'saɪ·dɪd] *adj* 1. (*obvious: improvement*) netto, -a 2. (*resolute: person, manner*) deciso, -a

deciduous [dɪ·'sɪd·ʒʊ·əs] *adj* deciduo, -a

decimal ['de·sɪ·ml] I. *n* decimale *m* II. *adj* decimale

decimalize ['de·sɪ·mə·laɪz] *vt* decimalizzare

decimate ['de·sɪ·meɪt] *vt* decimare

decipher [dɪ·'saɪ·fə·] *vt* decifrare

decision [dɪ·'sɪ·ʒən] *n* 1. (*choice, resolution*) decisione *f;* **to make a ~** prendere una decisione 2. LAW decisione *f* 3. (*resoluteness*) risolutezza *f*

decision-making *adj* **~ process** processo *m* decisionale

decisive [dɪ·'saɪ·sɪv] *adj* 1. (*factor*) decisivo, -a 2. (*resolute: manner*) risoluto, -a 3. (*beyond doubt: victory, defeat, change*) determinante

deck [dek] I. *n* 1. (*of ship*) ponte *m;* **to go below** ~ scendere sottocoperta 2. (*back porch*) piattaforma di legno costruita sul retro di una casa 3. (*of cards*) mazzo *m* 4. MUS, ELEC piastra *f* ▶ **to clear the ~** *inf* sgombrare il campo; **to hit the ~** *inf* cadere a terra II. *vt* **to ~ sth out** decorare qc; **to ~ oneself out** mettersi in ghingheri; **to be all ~ed out** essere in ghingheri

deck chair *n* sdraio *f inv*

declaim [dɪ·'kleɪm] *vi, vt* declamare

declamation [ˌde·klə·'meɪ·ʃən] *n* declamazione *f*

declamatory [dɪ·'klæ·mə·tɔː·ri] *adj form* declamatorio, -a

declaration [ˌde·klə·'reɪ·ʃən] *n* dichiarazione *f;* **the D~ of Independence** la Dichiarazione d'Indipendenza

---

i   Nella **Declaration of Independence**, la Dichiarazione di Indipendenza, le 13 colonie dell'America del Nord si proclamarono indipendenti dalla Gran Bretagna e si attribui-

rono il nome di Stati Uniti d'America, fornendo le motivazioni che le portarono ad una tale azione. La dichiarazione fu ratificata il 4 luglio 1776 dal *Continental Congress* e tale data, chiamata *Independence Day*, viene celebrata ogni anno negli Stati Uniti.

---

declare [dɪ·'kler] I. *vt* dichiarare; **to ~ war on sb** dichiarare guerra a qn; **to ~ oneself (to be) bankrupt** dichiarare fallimento II. *vi* dichiararsi

decline [dɪ·'klaɪn] I. *vi* 1. (*price*) calare; (*power, influence*) diminuire; (*civilization*) decadere; **to ~ in value** diminuire di valore 2. MED deperire 3. (*refuse*) declinare II. *vt* 1. (*refuse*) declinare 2. LING declinare III. *n* 1. (*in price, power, influence*) diminuzione *f;* (*of civilization*) declino *m;* **to be in ~** essere in declino 2. MED deperimento *m*

decode [ˌdiː·'koʊd] *vi, vt* decodificare

decoder *n* decoder *m inv*

decolonization [ˌdiː·ˌkɑː·lə·nɪ·'zeɪ·ʃən] *n* decolonizzazione *f*

decompose [ˌdiː·kəm·'poʊz] I. *vi* decomporsi II. *vt* decomporre

decomposition [ˌdiː·kɑːm·pə·'zɪ·ʃən] *n* decomposizione *f*

decompress [ˌdiː·kəm·'pres] *vt* decomprimere

decompression [ˌdiː·kəm·'pre·ʃən] *n* decompressione *f*

decompression chamber *n* camera *f* di decompressione

decontaminate [ˌdiː·kən·'tæ·mɪ·neɪt] *vt* decontaminare

decontamination [ˌdiː·kən·ˌtæ·mɪ·'neɪ·ʃən] *n* decontaminazione *f*

decontrol [ˌdiː·kən·'troʊl] <-ll-> *vt* liberalizzare

decor ['deɪ·kɔːr] *n* arredamento *m*

decorate ['de·kə·reɪt] I. *vt* 1. (*adorn*) decorare; (*by painting*) pitturare; (*by wallpapering*) tappezzare 2. (*honor*) decorare II. *vi* 1. (*paint*) pitturare 2. (*wallpaper*) tappezzare

decoration [ˌde·kə·'reɪ·ʃən] *n* decorazione *f*

decorative ['de·kə·rə·tɪv] *adj* decorativo, -a

decorator ['de·kə·reɪ·tə·] *n* imbianchino *m;* (*with wallpaper*) tappezziere *m*

decorous ['de·kə·əs] *adj form* decoroso, -a

decorum [dɪ·'kɔː·rəm] *n form* decoro *m*

decoy ['diː·kɔɪ] I. *n a. fig* esca *f;* **to act as a ~** fare da esca II. *vt* attirare con un tranello

decrease¹ [dɪ·'kriːs] I. *vi* diminuire; (*prices*) calare II. *vt* diminuire

decrease² ['diː·kriːs] *n* diminuzione *f*

decree [dɪ·'kriː] I. *n* 1. (*command*) decreto *m;* **to issue a ~** emanare un decreto 2. LAW sentenza *f* II. *vt* decretare

decrepit [dɪ·'kre·pɪt] *adj* decrepito, -a; (*house*) fatiscente

decrepitude [dɪ·'kre·pɪ·tuːd] *n* decrepitezza *f*

decriminalize [ˌdiːˈkrɪ·mɪ·nə·laɪz] *vt* depenalizzare

decry [dɪˈkraɪ] *vt* condannare

dedicate [ˈde·dɪ·keɪt] *vt* **1.** (*devote*) **to ~ oneself to sth** dedicarsi a qc; **to ~ one's life to sth** dedicare la propria vita a qc **2.** (*book, poem, song*) **to ~ sth to sb** dedicare qc a qn **3.** (*formally open*) inaugurare; (*a church*) dedicare

dedicated *adj* coscienzioso, -a

dedication [ˌde·dɪˈkeɪ·ʃən] *n* **1.** (*devotion*) dedizione *f* **2.** (*inscription*) dedica *f* **3.** (*official opening*) inaugurazione *f*; (*of a church*) dedica *f*

deduce [dɪˈduːs] *vt* dedurre

deducible [dɪˈduː·sə·bl] *adj* deducibile

deduct [dɪˈdʌkt] *vt* dedurre

deductible *adj* deducibile

deduction [dɪˈdʌk·ʃən] *n* detrazione *f*; **$1000 after ~s** 1000 dollari netti

deductive [dɪˈdʌk·tɪv] *adj* deduttivo, -a

deed [diːd] *n* **1.** (*act*) azione *f*; (*remarkable*) impresa *f*; **in word and ~** di nome e di fatto **2.** LAW atto *m*

deejay [ˈdiː·dʒeɪ] *n inf* deejay *mf inv*

deem [diːm] *vt form* considerare; **he was ~ed to be of sound mind** è stato giudicato capace di intendere e di volere

deep [diːp] **I.** *adj* **1.** (*not shallow*) profondo, -a **2.** (*full*) **to take a ~ breath** respirare a fondo **3.** (*extending back*) profondo, -a; **the drawer is 2 feet ~** il cassetto è largo 2 piedi **4.** (*extreme: love, disappointment*) profondo, -a; **in ~ mourning** in lutto stretto; **to be in ~ trouble** esser nei guai fino al collo *inf* **5.** (*absorbed by*) **to be in ~ thought** esser immerso nei propri pensieri **6.** *inf* (*hard to understand*) complesso, -a **7.** (*low in pitch*) grave **8.** (*dark*) intenso, -a; **~ red** rosso scuro **II.** *adv* **1.** (*far down*) in profondità; **~ in the forest** nel cuore della foresta **2.** (*extremely*) profondamente; **to be ~ in debt** essere nei debiti fino al collo ▶ **to dig ~** scavare in profondità; **to go ~ into sth** andare a fondo di qc **III.** *n liter* **the ~** il mare; **in the ~ of winter** nel cuore dell'inverno

deepen [ˈdiː·pən] **I.** *vt* **1.** (*make deeper*) rendere più profondo **2.** (*increase*) aumentare; (*knowledge*) approfondire **II.** *vi* **1.** (*become deeper*) farsi più profondo **2.** (*increase*) aumentare **3.** (*become lower in pitch*) diventare più profondo **4.** (*color*) intensificarsi

deep freeze *n* congelatore *m*

deep-frozen *adj* surgelato, -a

deep-fry *vt* friggere in olio abbondante

deeply *adv* profondamente; **to be ~ interested in sth** avere un forte interesse per qc

deepness *n* profondità *f*

deep-rooted *adj* (*well-established*) profondamente radicato, -a

deep-sea *adj* d'alto mare

deep-seated *adj* profondamente radicato, -a

deep space *n* AVIAT spazio *m* profondo

deer [dɪr] *n inv* cervo *m*

deerstalker [ˈdɪr·ˌstɔː·kə·] *n* berretto *m* alla Sherlock Holmes

deface [dɪˈfeɪs] *vt* deturpare; (*a wall*) imbrattare; (*a stamp*) annullare

defamation [ˌde·fə·ˈmeɪ·ʃən] *n* diffamazione *f*

defamatory [dɪˈfæ·mə·tɔː·ri] *adj* diffamatorio, -a

defame [dɪˈfeɪm] *vt* diffamare

default [dɪˈfɔːlt] **I.** *vi* **1.** FIN essere inadempiente; **to ~ on a loan** non restituire un prestito **2.** LAW essere contumace **3.** SPORTS abbandonare **II.** *n* **1.** (*failure to do sth*) inadempienza *f* **2.** LAW **judgement by ~** sentenza *f* contumaciale; **to win a case by ~** vincere in contumacia **3.** (*pre-selected option*) **by ~** automaticamente **4.** *form* (*absence*) **in ~ of any better alternative ...** in assenza di migliori alternative ...

default value *n* COMPUT valore *m* di default

defeat [dɪˈfiːt] **I.** *vt* sconfiggere; (*hopes*) deludere; (*a proposal*) respingere **II.** *n* **1.** (*loss*) sconfitta *f*; **to admit ~** darsi per vinto **2.** (*of plans*) fallimento *m*

defeatism [dɪˈfiː·ˌtɪ·zəm] *n* disfattismo *m*

defeatist *adj* disfattista

defecate [ˈde·fə·keɪt] *vi* MED defecare

defecation [ˌde·fə·ˈkeɪ·ʃən] *n* MED defecazione *f*

defect[1] [ˈdiː·fekt] *n a.* TECH, MED difetto *m*

defect[2] [dɪˈfekt] *vi* POL (*from a country*) fuggire; (*from the army*) disertare

defection [dɪˈfek·ʃən] *n* POL defezione *f*; MIL diserzione *f*

defective [dɪˈfek·tɪv] *adj* difettoso, -a

defend [dɪˈfend] **I.** *vt* **1.** (*protect*) difendere; **to ~ oneself (from sb/sth)** difendersi (da qn/qc) **2.** *a.* LAW difendere **3.** SPORTS (*a title*) difendere **II.** *vi* **1.** LAW **who is ~ing in that case?** chi è l'avvocato difensore in quella causa? **2.** SPORTS (*play defense*) difendere

defendant [dɪˈfen·dənt] *n* LAW (*in a civil case*) convenuto, -a *m, f*; (*in a criminal case*) imputato, -a *m, f*

defense [dɪˈfents] *n* **1.** (*against attack*) difesa *f*; **to rush to sb's ~** accorrere in difesa di qn; MED; **the body's ~s** le difese dell'organismo **2.** LAW **the ~** la difesa; **counsel for the ~** avvocato *m* difensore **3.** SPORTS **to play ~** giocare in difesa

defenseless [dɪˈfents·ləs] *adj* indifeso, -a

defense mechanism *n* PSYCH meccanismo *m* di difesa

defensible [dɪˈfen·tsə·bl] *adj* **1.** (*against attack*) difendibile **2.** (*justifiable*) giustificabile

defensive [dɪˈfent·sɪv] **I.** *adj* difensivo, -a; **she's very ~ about her family background** si mette subito sulla difensiva quando si parla della sua situazione familiare **II.** *n* **to be/go on the ~** essere/mettersi sulla difensiva

defer [dɪˈfɜːr] <-rr-> *vt* rinviare

deference [ˈde·fə·rənts] *n* deferenza *f*

deferential [ˌde·fə·ˈren·tʃəl] *adj* deferente

deferred *adj* (*exam*) rinviato, -a; (*annuity, interest*) differito, -a; **~ payment** pagamento dilazionato

defiance [dɪ·'fa·ɪənts] *n* sfida *f;* **in ~ of sth** a dispetto di qc

defiant [dɪ·'fa·ɪənt] *adj* **1.** (*person*) ribelle **2.** (*attitude*) di sfida

deficiency [dɪ·'fɪ·ʃənt·si] *n* (*shortage*) scarsità *f;* (*of funds*) mancanza *f;* (*of nutrients*) carenza *f*

deficient [dɪ·'fɪ·ʃənt] *adj* carente; **to be ~ in sth** essere carente di qc

deficit ['de·fɪ·sɪt] *n* deficit *m inv*

defile [dɪ·'faɪl] **I.** *vt* *form* **1.** (*spoil*) rovinare; (*reputation*) macchiare **2.** (*desecrate*) profanare **II.** *n* gola *f*

define [dɪ·'faɪn] *vt* **1.** (*give definition of*) definire **2.** (*explain*) definire; (*rights*) stabilire **3.** (*characterize*) caratterizzare **4.** (*clearly show*) **the outline of the skyscraper castle was clearly ~d against the sky** il grattacielo si stagliava nettamente contro il cielo

definite ['de·fɪ·nət] *adj* **1.** (*certain*) sicuro, a; (*date*) stabilito, -a; (*opinion*) chiaro, -a; **to be ~ about sth** essere chiaro in merito a qc; **it's ~ that ...** non c'è dubbio che ... **2.** (*clearly defined*) definitivo, -a

definite article *n* articolo *m* determinativo

definitely *adv* di sicuro

definition [ˌde·fɪ·'nɪ·ʃən] *n* **1.** definizione *f* **2. her ideas lack ~** le sue idee non sono molto chiare

definitive [dɪ·'fɪ·nə·t̬ɪv] *adj* **1.** (*final*) definitivo, -a **2.** (*best*) autorevole

definitively *adv* definitivamente

deflate [dɪ·'fleɪt] **I.** *vt* **1.** (*let air out of*) sgonfiare **2.** (*reduce*) ridurre; (*hopes*) distruggere **3.** (*cause to lose confidence*) avvilire **4.** ECON, FIN deflazionare **II.** *vi* sgonfiarsi

deflation [dɪ·'fleɪ·ʃən] *n* **1.** (*act of deflating*) sgonfiamento *m* **2.** ECON, FIN deflazione *f* **3.** (*reduction*) caduta *f*

deflationary *adj* deflazionistico, -a

deflect [dɪ·'flekt] **I.** *vt* far deviare **II.** *vi* (*change direction of*) **to ~ off sth** deviare da qc

deflection [dɪ·'flek·ʃən] *n* deviazione *f*

defog [ˌdi·'fɔːg] *vt* (*window*) sbrinare

defogger [ˌdi·'fɔː·gɚ] *n* AUTO sbrinatore *m*

defoliant [ˌdi·'foʊ·li·ənt] *n* defogliante *m*

defoliate [ˌdi·'foʊ·li·eɪt] *vt* defogliare

deforest [ˌdi·'fɔː·rɪst] *vt* disboscare

deforestation [di·ˌfɔː·rɪ·'steɪ·ʃən] *n* disboscamento *m*

deform [dɪ·'fɔːrm] **I.** *vt* deformare; (*person*) sfigurare **II.** *vi* deformarsi; (*person*) rimanere sfigurato

deformation [ˌdi·fɔːr·'meɪ·ʃən] *n* deformazione *f;* (*of a person*) deformità *f*

deformed *adj* deforme

deformity [dɪ·'fɔːr·mə·t̬i] *n* deformità *f*

defraud [dɪ·'frɔːd] *vt* defraudare; **to ~ sb (of sth)** defraudare qn (di qc)

defray [dɪ·'freɪ] *vt form* (*costs, expenses*) rim-

borsare

defrost [ˌdi·'frɔːst] **I.** *vt* (*food*) scongelare; (*fridge, windshield*) sbrinare **II.** *vi* (*food*) scongelarsi; (*fridge*) sbrinarsi

deft [deft] *adj* abile; **to be ~ at sth** essere abile in qc

defunct [dɪ·'fʌŋkt] *adj* (*dead*) defunto, -a; (*idea*) superato, -a; (*institution*) non più in esistenza

defy [dɪ·'faɪ] *vt* **1.** (*challenge: gravity, authority*) sfidare **2.** (*resist*) resistere a; **it defies description** è indescrivibile **3.** (*disobey*) disobbedire a

deg. *abbr of* **degree** grado *m*

degenerate[1] [dɪ·'dʒe·nə·reɪt] *vi* degenerare; **to ~ into sth** degenerare in qc

degenerate[2] [dɪ·'dʒe·nə·rət] **I.** *adj* degenerato, -a **II.** *n* degenerato, -a *m, f*

degeneration [dɪ·ˌdʒe·nə·'reɪ·ʃən] *n* degenerazione *f*

degrade [dɪ·'greɪd] **I.** *vt* **1.** *a.* CHEM degradare; **to ~ oneself** degradarsi **2.** (*decompose: leaves, garbage*) degradare **II.** *vi* deteriorarsi

degree [dɪ·'griː] *n* **1.** MATH, METEO grado *m;* **5 ~s below zero** 5 gradi sotto zero; **first/second ~ murder** LAW omicidio di primo/secondo grado; **first/second ~ burns** MED ustioni di primo/secondo grado **2.** (*amount*) livello *m* **3.** (*extent*) **I agree with you to some ~** son d'accordo con te fino a un certo punto; **by ~s** gradualmente; **to the last ~** al massimo **4.** UNIV laurea *f;* **to have a ~ in sth** essere laureato in qc; **she's got a physics ~ from UCLA** si è laureata in fisica alla UCLA; **to have a master's ~ in sth** avere un master in qc; **to do a ~ in chemistry** prendere una laurea in chimica

dehumanize [ˌdi·'hjuː·mə·naɪz] *vt* disumanizzare

dehydrate [ˌdi·haɪ·'dreɪt] **I.** *vt* disidratare **II.** *vi* MED disidratarsi

dehydrated *adj* disidratato, -a; (*milk*) in polvere; **to become ~** disidratarsi

dehydration [ˌdi·haɪ·'dreɪ·ʃən] *n* MED disidratazione *f*

deice [ˌdi·'aɪs] *vt* liberare dal ghiaccio

deign [deɪn] *vi* **to ~ to do sth** degnarsi di fare qc

deism ['di·ɪ·zəm] *n* deismo *m*

deity ['di·ə·t̬i] *n* divinità *f*

deject [dɪ·'dʒekt] *vt* avvilire

dejected *adj* avvilito, -a

dejection [dɪ·'dʒek·ʃən] *n* avvilimento *m*

delay [dɪ·'leɪ] **I.** *vt* rimandare; **to be ~ed** subire un ritardo; **to ~ doing sth** tardare a fare qc **II.** *vi* ritardare; **to ~ in doing sth** tardare a fare qc; **don't ~!** non perder tempo! **III.** *n* ritardo *m;* **without ~** senza perder tempo; **a two-hour ~** un ritardo di due ore

delayed-action *adj* a scoppio ritardato

delaying tactics *npl* tattiche *f pl* dilatorie

delectable [dɪ·'lek·tə·bl] *adj* dilettevole; (*food, taste, person*) delizioso, -a

delectation [ˌdiː·lek·ˈteɪ·ʃən] *n form* diletto *m;* **for the public's** ~ per la gioia del pubblico

delegate[1] [ˈde·lɪ·gət] *n a.* POL delegato, -a *m, f*

delegate[2] [ˈde·lɪ·geɪt] *vt* delegare

delegation [ˌde·lɪ·ˈgeɪ·ʃən] *n* delegazione *f*

delete [dɪ·ˈliːt] *vt* 1.(*erase*) cancellare 2. COMPUT cancellare

deletion [dɪ·ˈliː·ʃən] *n* 1.(*act of erasing*) cancellazione *f* 2.(*removal*) soppressione *f*

deli [ˈde·li] *n inf* s. **delicatessen**

deliberate[1] [dɪ·ˈlɪ·bə·rət] *adj* 1.(*intentional*) deliberato, -a 2.(*cautious: decision*) ponderato, -a 3.(*unhurried*) posato, -a

deliberate[2] [dɪ·ˈlɪ·bə·reɪt] I. *vi* to ~ **on sth** riflettere su qc; **to ~ on a case** deliberare su un caso II. *vt* deliberare

deliberately *adv* 1.(*intentionally*) deliberatamente 2.(*unhurriedly*) posatamente

deliberation [dɪ·ˌlɪ·bə·ˈreɪ·ʃən] *n* 1.(*formal discussion*) discussione *f* 2.(*consideration*) riflessione *f;* **after due** ~ dopo lunga riflessione 3.(*unhurried manner*) posatezza *f*

delicacy [ˈde·lɪ·kə·si] *n* 1.(*tact*) tatto *m* 2.(*trickiness*) **the ~ of the situation** la delicatezza della situazione 3.(*food*) manicaretto *m*

delicate [ˈde·lɪ·kət] *adj* 1.(*fragile*) delicato, -a; **to be in ~ health** essere delicato di salute 2.(*fine*) raffinato, -a; (*balance*) delicato, -a 3.(*soft: aroma, color*) delicato, -a 4.(*tricky: situation*) delicato, -a 5.(*highly sensitive*) sensibile

delicatessen [ˌde·lɪ·kə·ˈte·sən] *n* gastronomia *f*

delicious [dɪ·ˈlɪ·ʃəs] *adj* delizioso, -a

delight [dɪ·ˈlaɪt] I. *n* piacere *m;* **to do sth with** ~ far qc con piacere; **to take ~ in sth** trarre piacere da qc II. *vt* deliziare; **to be ~ed with sth** essere contentissimo di qc
◆**delight in** *vi* to ~ **doing sth** dilettarsi nel fare qc

delighted *adj* felicissimo, -a

delightful [dɪ·ˈlaɪt·fəl] *adj* delizioso, -a; (*person*) incantevole

delimit [dɪ·ˈlɪ·mɪt] *vt* delimitare

delineate [dɪ·ˈlɪ·ni·eɪt] *vt* 1.(*draw*) delineare 2.(*describe: plan*) tracciare; (*character*) delineare

delinquency [dɪ·ˈlɪŋ·kwənt·si] *n* delinquenza *f*

delinquent [dɪ·ˈlɪŋ·kwənt] I. *n* LAW delinquente *mf;* **juvenile ~** delinquente minorile II. *adj* 1.(*behavior*) delinquenziale 2.(*account*) insoluto, -a

delirious [dɪ·ˈlɪ·ri·əs] *adj* **to be ~** delirare; *fig, inf;* **to be ~ with joy** essere pazzo, -a di gioia

deliriously *adv* 1. MED delirantemente; **she raves ~** farnetica in delirio 2.*fig, inf* follemente; **she was ~ happy** era pazza di gioia *inf*

delirium [dɪ·ˈlɪ·ri·əm] *n* delirio *m*

deliver [dɪ·ˈlɪ·vɚ] I. *vt* 1.(*hand over*) consegnare; (*mail, letter, package*) recapitare 2.(*recite: lecture, speech*) tenere; (*verdict*) pronunciare 3.(*direct*) **to ~ a blow to sb's**

head assestare un colpo sulla testa a qn; **he ~ed a sharp rebuke to his son** ha fatto un aspro rimprovero al figlio 4. SPORTS (*throw*) lanciare 5.(*give birth to*) **to ~ a baby** (*mother*) dare alla luce un bambino; (*doctor*) far nascere un bambino 6.(*save*) liberare 7.(*produce*) **to ~ a promise** tener fede a una promessa; **to ~ the goods** mantenere la parola II. *vi* 1. COM **we ~** si fanno consegne a domicilio 2.*inf* (*make good on*) **to ~ on sth** mantenere qc 3.(*give birth*) partorire
◆**deliver of** *vt* **to deliver oneself of sth** esprimere qc

deliverance [dɪ·ˈlɪ·və·rənts] *n* liberazione *f*

deliverer *n* liberatore, -trice *m, f*

delivery [dɪ·ˈlɪ·və·ri] *n* 1.(*distribution*) consegna *f;* ~ **charges** spese *f pl* di consegna; ~ **man** fattorino *m;* ~ **woman** fattorina *f;* **to pay on** ~ pagare alla consegna; **to take ~ of sth** ricevere qc 2.(*manner of speaking*) dizione *f* 3. SPORTS lancio *m* 4.(*birth*) parto *m*

delivery room *n* sala *f* parto

delivery service *n* servizio *m* di consegne a domicilio

delivery truck *n* furgone *m* per le consegne

delta [ˈdel·tə] *n* GEO delta *m inv*

delta wing *n* AVIAT ala *f* a delta

delude [dɪ·ˈluːd] *vt* illudere; **to ~ sb into believing sth** indurre qn a credere qc

deluge [ˈde·ljuːdʒ] I. *n a. fig* diluvio *m* II. *vt a. fig* inondare; **to be ~d with tears** essere inondato di lacrime; **she is ~d with offers** è sommersa dalle offerte

delusion [dɪ·ˈluː·ʒən] *n* 1.(*wrong idea*) illusione *f;* **to labor under a ~** essere vittima di un'illusione 2. PSYCH allucinazione *f;* ~**s of grandeur** manie *f pl* di grandezza 3.(*deceit*) inganno *m*

deluxe [dɪ·ˈlʌks] *adj* di lusso

delve [delv] *vi* 1.(*explore*) **to ~ into sth** scavare a fondo in qc 2.(*rummage*) rovistare

demagog *n* s. **demagogue**

demagogic [ˌde·mə·ˈgaː·dʒɪk] *adj* demagogico, -a

demagogue [ˈde·mə·gaːg] *n* demagogo, -a *m, f*

demagoguery [ˌde·mə·ˈgaː·dʒə·i] *n*, **demagogy** [ˈde·mə·gaː·dʒi] *n* demagogia *f*

demand [dɪ·ˈmænd] I. *vt* 1.(*ask for forcefully*) esigere; (*a right*) rivendicare; **to ~ that...** esigere che ... +*subj;* **she demanded to see the person in charge** ha preteso di vedere un responsabile 2.(*require*) richiedere II. *n* 1.(*insistent request*) richiesta *f;* ~ **for independence** richiesta di indipendenza; **to make a ~ on sth** richiedere qc; **to make a ~ that ...** richiedere che ... +*subj;* **to make heavy ~s on sb's time** portar via gran parte del tempo di qn; **to meet a ~ for sth** soddisfare le richieste di qn; **by popular ~** richiesta a furor di popolo; **on ~** su richiesta 2. COM domanda *f;* **payable on ~** pagabile a vista; **to be in ~** (*object, person*) essere richiesto

demanding *adj* esigente
demand note *n* cambiale *f* a vista
demarcate [di:'mɑːr·keɪt] *vt* demarcare
demarcation [ˌdi:·mɑːr·'keɪ·ʃən] *n* demarcazione *f*
demarcation line *n* MIL, POL linea *f* di demarcazione
demean [dɪ'miːn] *vt* degradare; **to ~ oneself** abbassarsi
demeaning *adj* degradante
demeanor [dɪ'miː·nəʳ] *n* (*behavior*) condotta *f*; (*bearing*) portamento *m*
demented [dɪ'men·tɪd] *adj* MED demente; *fig, inf* pazzo, -a
dementia [dɪ'men·ʃə] *n* MED demenza *f*
demerit [dɪ'me·rɪt] *n* **1.** SCHOOL nota *f* di biasimo **2.** (*fault*) demerito *m*
demesne [dɪ'meɪn] *n* **1.** LAW proprietà *f* **2.** (*domain*) dominio *m*
demigod ['de·mi·gɑːd] *n* semidio *m*
demilitarize [ˌdi:·'mɪ·lɪ·tə·raɪz] *vt* demilitarizzare
demise [dɪ'maɪz] *n* **1.** (*death*) decesso *m* **2.** *fig* (*end*) fine *f*; (*of a company*) chiusura *f*
demo ['de·moʊ] *n inf s.* **demonstration 1.** (*act of showing*) dimostrazione *f* **2.** (*protest*) manifestazione *f*
demobilize [ˌdi:·'moʊ·bə·laɪz] **I.** *vt* smobilitare **II.** *vi* smobilitare
democracy [dɪ'mɑː·krə·si] *n* democrazia *f*
democrat ['de·mə·kræt] *n* democratico, -a *m, f*
democratic [ˌde·mə·'kræ·t̬ɪk] *adj* democratico, -a
democratization [dɪ·ˌmɑː·krə·t̬ɪ·'zeɪ·ʃən] *n* democratizzazione *f*
democratize [dɪ'mɑː·krə·taɪz] *vt* democratizzare
demolish [dɪ'mɑː·lɪʃ] *vt a. fig* demolire
demolition [ˌde·mə·'lɪ·ʃən] *n* demolizione *f*
demon ['di:·mən] *n* **1.** (*evil spirit*) demonio *m* **2.** (*destructive force*) demone *m* ▶ **to be a ~ at sth** *inf* essere un asso in qc; **to work like a ~** lavorare come un matto
demoniac [dɪ'moʊ·ni·æk] *adj*, **demonic** [dɪ'mɑː·nɪk] *adj* **1.** (*devilish*) demoniaco, -a **2.** (*evil*) diabolico, -a
demonstrable [dɪ'mɑːnts·trə·bl] *adj* dimostrabile
demonstrate ['de·məns·treɪt] **I.** *vt* (*show clearly*) mostrare; (*prove*) dimostrare; **to ~ that ...** dimostrare che ... **II.** *vi* POL manifestare
demonstration [ˌde·mən·'streɪ·ʃən] *n* **1.** (*act of showing*) dimostrazione *f*; **she gave him a kiss as a ~ of her affection** gli ha dato un bacio in segno d'affetto **2.** (*march*) manifestazione *f*; **to hold a ~** tenere una manifestazione
floor model *n* modello *m* per dimostrazione
demonstrative [dɪ'mɑːns·trə·t̬ɪv] *adj* **1.** (*illustrative*) dimostrativo, -a **2.** (*expressing feelings*) espansivo, -a
demonstrator ['de·məns·treɪ·t̬əʳ] *n* **1.** (*of a product*) dimostratore, -trice *m, f* **2.** (*protester*) dimostrante *mf*

demoralize [dɪ'mɔː·rə·laɪz] *vt* demoralizzare
demote [dɪ'moʊt] *vt* retrocedere; MIL degradare
demure [dɪ'mjʊr] *adj* **1.** (*modest, shy*) schivo, -a **2.** (*affectedly modest*) vezzoso, -a
den [den] *n* **1.** (*animal habitation*) tana *f* **2.** *a. iron* (*place for vice*) covo *m*; **a ~ of thieves** un covo di ladri **3.** (*small room*) soggiorno *m* **4.** (*in cub scouts*) tana *f*
denationalize [ˌdi:·'næ·ʃə·nə·laɪz] *vt* denazionalizzare
denial [dɪ'na·ɪəl] *n* **1.** (*act of refuting*) negazione *f* **2.** (*refusal*) rifiuto *m* **3.** (*of a right*) negazione *f* **4.** (*rejection*) smentita *f*; **to issue a ~ of sth** smentire qc
denigrate ['de·nɪ·greɪt] *vt* denigrare
denim ['de·nɪm] *n* **1.** (*cloth*) tela *f* jeans **2.** *pl, inf* (*clothes*) jeans *mpl*
denim jacket *n* giubbotto *m* di jeans
denim shirt *n* camicia *f* jeans
Denmark ['den·mɑːrk] *n* Danimarca *f*
denomination [dɪ·ˌnɑː·mə·'neɪ·ʃən] *n* **1.** (*religious group*) confessione *f* **2.** (*unit of value*) valore *m*
denominational [dɪ·ˌnɑː·mə·'neɪ·ʃə·nl] *adj* confessionale
denominator [dɪ'nɑː·mə·neɪ·t̬əʳ] *n* denominatore *m*
denotation [ˌdi:·noʊ·'teɪ·ʃən] *n* denotazione *f*
denote [dɪ'noʊt] *vt* **1.** (*indicate*) denotare **2.** (*show: displeasure*) mostrare
denouement [deɪ·'nu:·mãːn] *n* epilogo *m*
denounce [dɪ'naʊnts] *vt* **1.** (*condemn*) condannare **2.** (*give information against*) denunciare
dense [dents] *adj* **1.** (*thick*) fitto, -a **2.** (*closely packed*) denso, -a; (*compact*) compatto, -a **3.** (*complex*) complesso, -a **4.** *inf* (*stupid*) ottuso, -a
densely *adv* densamente
density ['den·tsə·t̬i] *n* **1.** (*compactness*) densità *f*; **to be high/low in ~** essere ad alta/bassa densità **2.** (*complexity*) spessore *m*
dent [dent] **I.** *n* **1.** (*mark*) ammaccatura *f* **2.** (*adverse effect*) tacca *f* **II.** *vt* **1.** (*put a dent in*) ammaccare **2.** (*have adverse effect on: confidence*) intaccare
dental ['den·təl] *adj* (*treatment, care*) dentistico, -a; (*problem, disease*) dentario, -a; **a ~ appointment** un appuntamento dal dentista
dental floss *n* filo *m* interdentale
dentist ['den·tɪst] *n* dentista *mf*
dentistry ['den·tɪst·ri] *n* odontoiatria *f*
dentition [den·'tɪ·ʃən] *n* dentizione *f*
dentures ['den·tʃəʳz] *npl* protesi *f* dentaria *inv*
denude [dɪ'nu:d] *vt* (*surface*) denudare
denunciation [dɪ·ˌnʌn·tsi·'eɪ·ʃən] *n* **1.** (*condemnation*) condanna *f* **2.** (*accusation*) denuncia *f*
deny [dɪ'naɪ] *vt* **1.** (*declare untrue*) negare; (*report*) smentire; **to ~ having done sth** negare di aver fatto qc; **she denies that she saw it** nega di averlo visto **2.** (*refuse*) rifiutare;

to ~ **oneself sth** privarsi di qc; **to ~ sb a privilege** negare a qn un privilegio; **to ~ sb a right** negare a qn un diritto **3.** (*disown*) rinnegare

deodorant [di·'oʊ·də·rənt] *n* deodorante *m*

deodorize [di·'oʊ·də·raɪz] *vt* deodorare

dep. 1. *abbr of* **department** dip. **2.** *abbr of* **deputy** deputato

depart [dɪ·'pɑːrt] **I.** *vi* partire **II.** *vt* **to ~ this life** lasciare questa vita

◆**depart from** *vi* allontanarsi da

departed I. *adj* **1.** (*dead*) defunto, -a **2.** (*past: era, triumph*) passato, -a **II.** *n pl* **the ~** i defunti; **to mourn the ~** piangere i morti

department [dɪ·'pɑːrt·mənt] *n* **1.** (*division: of a university, company*) dipartimento *m*; (*of a shop*) reparto *m* **2.** ADMIN, POL ministero *m*; **~ of Health and Human Services** ≈ Ministero *m* della Sanità **3.** *inf* (*domain*) ramo *m*

departmental [ˌdiː·pɑːrt·'men·təl] *adj* dipartimentale

department store *n* grandi *m pl* magazzini

departure [dɪ·'pɑːr·tʃə·] *n* **1.** (*act of leaving*) partenza *f*; **~ from politics** allontanamento *m* dalla politica; **to make one's ~** allontanarsi **2.** (*deviation*) svolta *f*; (*new undertaking*) nuova fase *f*; **to be a new ~ for sb/sth** essere una nuova fase per qn/qc

departure gate *n* AVIAT uscita *f*

departure lounge *n* AVIAT sala *f* d'imbarco

departure time *n* orario *m* di partenza

depend [dɪ·'pend] *vi* **1.** (*be determined by*) **to ~ on sth** dipendere da qc; **to ~ on sb** dipendere da qn; **~ing on the weather...** a seconda del tempo ... **2.** (*rely on for aid*) **she depends on her father for money** dipende economicamente dal padre **3.** (*trust*) **to ~ on sb/sth** contare su qn/qc

dependability [dɪˌpen·də·'bɪ·lə·t̬i] *n* affidabilità *f*

dependable [dɪ·'pen·də·bl] *adj* (*thing*) affidabile; (*person*) fidato, -a

dependence [dɪ·'pen·dənts] *n* dipendenza *f*

dependency *n* **1.** (*overreliance*) dipendenza *f* **2.** (*dependent state*) possedimento *m*; **Puerto Rico is a U.S. ~** Portorico è un possedimento statunitense

dependent [dɪ·'pen·dənt] **I.** *adj* **1.** (*conditional*) **to be ~ on sb/sth** dipendere da qn/qc **2.** (*in need of*) dipendente; **to be ~ on sth** dipendere da qc; **to be ~ on drugs** essere farmacodipendente; **she has two ~ children** ha due figli a carico **II.** *n* persona *f* a carico

depict [dɪ·'pɪkt] *vt* rappresentare

depiction [dɪ·'pɪk·ʃən] *n* rappresentazione *f*

depilatory [dɪ·'pɪ·lə·tɔː·ri] **I.** *n* depilatorio *m* **II.** *adj* depilatorio, -a

depilatory cream *n* crema *f* depilatoria

deplete [dɪ·'pliːt] *vt* ridurre

depleted *adj* esaurito, -a; (*soil*) impoverito, -a

depletion [dɪ·'pliː·ʃən] *n* (*of resources*) esaurimento *m*; (*of money*) dissipazione *f*; (*of nutrients*) impoverimento *m*; **~ of the ozone layer** assottigliamento *m* dello strato d'ozono

deplorable [dɪ·'plɔː·rə·bl] *adj* deplorevole

deplore [dɪ·'plɔːr] *vt* deplorare

deploy [dɪ·'plɔɪ] *vt* (*resources*) impiegare; (*troops*) schierare; (*skills*) utilizzare

deployment [dɪ·'plɔɪ·mənt] *n* impiego *m*; (*of troops*) schieramento *m*

depopulate [ˌdiː·'pɑː·p·jə·leɪt] *vt* spopolare

deport [dɪ·'pɔːrt] *vt* espellere

deportation [ˌdiː·pɔːr·'teɪ·ʃən] *n* espulsione *f*

deportee [ˌdiː·pɔːr·'tiː] *n* deportato, -a *m, f*

deportment [dɪ·'pɔːrt·mənt] *n* portamento *m*

depose [dɪ·'pɔːrt·mənt] *vt* deporre

deposit [dɪ·'pɑː·zɪt] **I.** *vt* **1.** (*leave*) depositare; (*eggs*) deporre; **the bus ~ed me in the middle of nowhere** l'autobus mi ha lasciato a casa di nessuno **2.** FIN (*store, pay into account*) depositare; **to ~ $1000** depositare 1000 dollari **II.** *n* **1.** (*sediment*) deposito *m* **2.** GEO giacimento *m* **3.** (*first payment*) acconto *m*; **to make a ~** effettuare un versamento; **to leave a ~** lasciare un acconto; **to leave sth as a ~** lasciare qc in acconto; **on ~** in deposito

money market account *n* conto *f* a termine

deposition [ˌde·pə·'zɪ·ʃən] *n* **1.** (*removal from power*) deposizione *f* **2.** LAW deposizione *f*; **to file a ~** dare una deposizione

depositor [dɪ·'pɑː·zə·t̬ə·] *n* depositante *mf*

depot ['diː·poʊ] *n* **1.** (*station*) stazione *f* **2.** (*storehouse*) magazzino *m*; (*for vehicles*) deposito *m*

deprave [dɪ·'preɪv] *vt* depravare

depraved *adj* depravato, -a

depravity [dɪ·'præ·və·t̬i] *n* depravazione *f*

deprecate ['de·prə·keɪt] *vt* **1.** (*disapprove of*) deprecare **2.** (*belittle*) denigrare

deprecating *adj* **1.** (*disapproving*) che disapprova **2.** (*belittling*) denigratorio, -a

deprecation [ˌde·prə·'keɪ·ʃən] *n* **1.** (*disapproval*) disapprovazione *f* **2.** (*belittlement*) denigrazione *f*

deprecatory ['de·prə·kə·tɔː·ri] *adj s.* **deprecating**

depreciate [dɪ·'priː·ʃi·eɪt] **I.** *vi* svalutarsi **II.** *vt* svalutare

depreciation [dɪˌpriː·ʃi·'eɪ·ʃən] *n* svalutazione *f*

depredation [ˌde·prə·'deɪ·ʃən] *n* depredazione *f*

depress [dɪ·'pres] *vt* **1.** (*sadden*) deprimere; **it ~es me that ...** mi deprime che ... +*subj* **2.** (*reduce activity of*) ridurre; (*the economy*) deprimere; (*prices*) far abbassare **3.** (*press down*) premere

depressant I. *n* sedativo *m* **II.** *adj* deprimente

depressed *adj* **1.** (*sad*) depresso, -a; **to feel ~** sentirsi depresso **2.** (*impoverished: period*) di depressione; (*area*) depresso, -a; (*economy*) in crisi

depressing *adj* deprimente

depression [dɪ·'pre·ʃən] *n* **1.** *a.* METEO, FIN depressione *f* **2.** (*hollow*) avvallamento *m*

depressive [dɪ·'pre·sɪv] **I.** *n* depresso, -a *m, f*

II. *adj* depressivo, -a
deprivation [ˌde·prɪ·'veɪ·ʃən] *n* privazioni *fpl*
deprive [dɪ·'praɪv] *vt* privare; (*of dignity*) spogliare; **to ~ sb of sth** privare qn di qc
deprived *adj* svantaggiato, -a
depth [depθ] *n* 1. *a. fig* profondità *f;* **in the ~s of her heart** nel profondo del cuore; **in the ~ of winter** in pieno inverno; **in the ~s of the forest** nel cuore della foresta; **in the ~s of solitude** nella più profonda solitudine 2. (*intensity*) intensità *f* 3. (*low sound*) gravità *f* ▶ **in ~** a fondo
depth charge *n* carica *f* di profondità
deputation [ˌdep·jə·'teɪ·ʃən] *n* + *sing/pl vb* delegazione *f*
depute [dɪ·'pjuːt] *vt* 1. (*appoint*) assegnare 2. (*delegate*) **to ~ sth to sb** delegare qc a qn
deputize ['dep·jə·taɪz] *vi* **to ~ for sb** sostituire qn
deputy ['dep·jə·ṭi] *n* (*assistant*) vice *mf;* (*in police department*) vicesceriffo *m*
derail [dɪ·'reɪl] I. *vt a. fig* far deragliare II. *vi* deragliare
derailment [dɪ·'reɪl·mənt] *n a. fig* deragliamento *m*
derange [dɪ·'reɪndʒ] *vt* disturbare
deranged *adj* squilibrato, -a
derangement *n* squilibrio *m* mentale
derby ['dɜːr·bi] *n* 1. derby *m inv* 2. (*hat*) bombetta *f*
deregulation [ˌdi·reg·jə·'leɪ·ʃən] *n* deregolamentazione *f*
derelict ['de·rə·lɪkt] I. *adj* (*building*) fatiscente; (*site*) abbandonato, -a II. *n* (*person*) vagabondo, -a *m, f*
dereliction [ˌde·rə·'lɪk·ʃən] *n* 1. (*dilapidation*) abbandono *m* 2. (*deliberate neglect*) negligenza *f*
deride [dɪ·'raɪd] *vt* deridere; **to ~ sb for doing sth** deridere qn perché fa qc
derision [dɪ·'rɪ·ʒən] *n* derisione *f;* **to meet sth with ~** accogliere qc con derisione
derisive [dɪ·'raɪ·sɪv] *adj* derisorio, -a
derisory [dɪ·'raɪ·sə·ri] *adj* (*amount*) irrisorio, -a
derivation [ˌde·rɪ·'veɪ·ʃən] *n* 1. (*origin*) origine *f* 2. (*process of evolving*) derivazione *f*
derivative [dɪ·'rɪ·və·tɪv] I. *adj* derivato, -a; *pej* poco originale II. *n* derivato *m*
derive [dɪ·'raɪv] I. *vt* **to ~ sth from sth** trarre qc da qc; **I ~ a lot of pleasure from working with children** il lavoro con i bambini mi dà grande gioia II. *vi* **to ~ from sth** derivare da qc
dermatitis [ˌdɜːr·mə·'taɪ·ṭəs] *n* dermatite *f*
dermatologist *n* dermatologo, -a *m, f*
dermatology [ˌdɜːr·mə·'tɑː·lə·dʒi] *n* dermatologia *f*
derogate ['de·rə·geɪt] *vi* **to ~ from sth** sminuire qc
derogation [ˌde·rə·'geɪ·ʃən] *n* disprezzo *m*
derogatory [dɪ·'rɑː·gə·tɔː·ri] *adj* sprezzante
derrick ['de·rɪk] *n* 1. (*crane*) gru *f inv* 2. (*framework*) derrick *m inv,* torre *f* di trivel-

lazione
desalinate [ˌdiː·'sæ·lɪ·neɪt] *vt* desalinizzare
desalination [diː·ˌsæ·lɪ·'neɪ·ʃən] *n* desalinizzazione *f*
desalination plant *n* impianto *m* di desalinizzazione
descale [ˌdiː·'skeɪl] *vt* disincrostare
descant ['des·kænt] *n* MUS discanto *m*
descend [dɪ·'send] I. *vi* 1. (*go down*) scendere; (*fall*) calare 2. (*lower oneself*) **to ~ to stealing** abbassarsi a rubare 3. (*come from*) **to ~ from sb/sth** discendere da qn/qc II. *vt* scendere; (*a ladder*) scendere
descendant [dɪ·'sen·dənt] *n* discendente *mf*
descent [dɪ·'sent] *n* 1. AVIAT discesa *f;* (*way down*) discesa *f* 2. (*decline*) caduta *f* 3. (*ancestry*) discendenza *f;* **of Irish ~** di origine irlandese
describe [dɪ·'skraɪb] *vt* 1. (*tell in words*) descrivere; **to ~ sb as stupid** definire qn uno stupido 2. (*draw*) tracciare
description [dɪ·'skrɪp·ʃən] *n* 1. (*account*) descrizione *f;* **to answer a ~ of sb/sth** corrispondere a una descrizione di qn/qc 2. (*sort*) sorta *f;* **of every ~** d'ogni tipo
descriptive [dɪ·'skrɪp·tɪv] *adj* descrittivo, -a
desecrate ['de·sɪ·kreɪt] *vt* profanare
desecration [ˌde·sɪ·'kreɪ·ʃən] *n* profanazione *f*
desegregate [ˌdiː·'se·grɪ·geɪt] *vt* desegregare
desegregation [diː·ˌse·grɪ·'geɪ·ʃən] *n* desegregazione *f*
desensitize [ˌdiː·'sen·sɪ·taɪz] *vt a.* MED desensibilizzare
desert[1] [dɪ·'zɜːrt] I. *vi* MIL disertare II. *vt* abbandonare; (*one's post*) lasciare; **to ~ sb** (**for sb else**) lasciare qn (per un'altra persona)
desert[2] ['de·zət] *n* deserto *m;* **~ plant/animal** pianta/animale del deserto
deserted *adj* 1. (*place*) deserto, -a 2. (*person*) abbandonato, -a
deserter *n* MIL disertore *m;* POL transfuga *mf*
desertification [dɪ·ˌzɜːr·ṭə·fɪ·'keɪ·ʃən] *n* desertificazione *f*
desertion [dɪ·'zɜːr·ʃən] *n* MIL diserzione *f;* (*act of leaving*) abbandono *m*
deserts [dɪ·'zɜːrts] *npl* **to get one's just ~** avere ciò che ci si merita
deserve [dɪ·'zɜːrv] *vt* meritare; **what have I done to ~** (**all**) **this?** cos'ho fatto per meritare (tutto) questo?
deservedly *adv* meritatamente
deserving *adj* meritevole; **to be ~ of sth** esser degno, -a di qc
design [dɪ·'zaɪn] I. *vt* 1. (*plan*) **to ~ sth** (**for sb**) progettare qc (per qn) 2. (*intend*) **to ~ sth for sb/sth** concepire qc per qn/qc; **this dictionary is ~ed for advanced learners** questo dizionario è rivolto a studenti di livello avanzato; **these measures are ~ed to reduce criminality** questi provvedimenti hanno come obiettivo la riduzione della criminalità II. *vi* fare il designer III. *n* 1. (*plan*) progetto *m* 2. (*sketch*) schizzo *m* 3. (*pattern*)

motivo *m* **4.**(*intention*) proposito *m;* **to do sth by** ~ far qc di proposito **5.** *pl, inf*(*dishonest intentions*) cattive*f pl* intenzioni; **to have ~s on a championship title** ambire a vincere un campionato **IV.** *adj* di progetto

designate[1] ['de·zɪg·neɪt] *vt* **1.**(*appoint*) designare; **to ~ sb to do sth** designare qn a fare qc **2.**(*indicate*) contrassegnare

designate[2] ['de·zɪg·nɪt] *adj* designato, -a; **the ambassador ~** l'ambasciatore designato

designated driver *n* autista *mf* designato, -a, *che rimane sobrio per portare gli altri a casa dopo una festa*

designation [,de·zɪg·'neɪ·ʃən] *n* **1.**(*appointment*) designazione *f* **2.**(*act of indicating*) indicazione *f* **3.**(*title*) titolo *m*

designedly *adv* di proposito

designer [dɪ·'zaɪ·nɚ] **I.** *n* designer *mf inv* **II.** *adj* firmato, -a

designing *adj pej* intrigante

desirable [dɪ·'za·ɪə·rə·bl] *adj* **1.**(*necessary*) utile; **it is ~ that ...** sarebbe opportuno che ... *+subj* **2.**(*sexually attractive*) desiderabile **3.**(*popular or fashionable: area, job*) interessante

desire [dɪ·'za·ɪə] **I.** *vt* **1.**(*request*) **to ~ that ...** desiderare che ... *+subj* **2.**(*want*) desiderare; **I ~ you to leave** ti prego di andartene **3.**(*be sexually attracted to*) **to ~ sb** desiderare qn **II.** *n* **1.**(*craving*) desiderio *m* **2.**(*request*) desiderio *m* **3.**(*sensual appetite*) desiderio *m* sessuale; **to be the object of sb's ~** essere l'oggetto del desiderio di qn

desired *adj* desiderato, -a

desirous [dɪ·'zaɪ·rəs] *adj* desideroso, -a

desist [dɪ·'sɪst] *vi form* desistere

desk [desk] *n* **1.**(*table*) scrivania *f* **2.**(*service counter*) banco *m* **3.**(*department of a newspaper*) redazione *f*

desk lamp *n* lampada *f* da tavolo

desktop *n* COMPUT ~ (**computer**) computer *m inv* da tavolo

desktop publishing *n* desktop publishing *m inv*

desolate[1] ['de·sə·lət] *adj* **1.**(*barren*) desolato, -a; (*prospect*) triste **2.**(*sad*) sconsolato, -a; **to feel ~** sentirsi sconsolato

desolate[2] ['de·sə·'leɪt] *vt* affliggere

desolation [,de·sə·'leɪ·ʃən] *n* **1.**(*barrenness*) desolazione *f* **2.**(*sadness*) desolazione *f*

despair [dɪs·'per] **I.** *n* disperazione *f;* **to be in ~ about sth** essere disperato per qc; **to drive sb to ~** portare qn alla disperazione ▶ **to be the ~ of sb** essere la disperazione di qn **II.** *vi* disperare; **to ~ of sth** disperare di qc

despairing *adj* disperato, -a

despatch [dɪs·'pætʃ] *n, vt s.* **dispatch**

desperado [,des·pə·'rɑː·dou] <-(e)s> *n* criminale *mf* pericoloso

desperate ['des·pə·rət] *adj* **1.**(*as last chance*) disperato, -a; (*measure, solution*) estremo, -a; (*violent*) pronto, -a a tutto **2.**(*serious*) grave; (*poverty*) estremo, -a; (*situation*) disperato, -a

3.(*great*) estremo, -a; **to be in a ~ hurry** avere una fretta terribile **4.**(*having great need*) **to be ~ for sth** avere assolutamente bisogno di qc

desperation [,des·pə·'reɪ·ʃən] *n* disperazione *f;* **in ~** in preda alla disperazione; **to drive sb to ~** portare qn alla disperazione

despicable [dɪs·'pɪ·kə·bl] *adj* ignobile

despise [dɪs·'paɪz] *vt* disprezzare; **to ~ sb for sth** disprezzare qn per qc

despite [dɪs·'paɪt] *prep* nonostante

despoil [dɪs·'pɔɪl] *vt* saccheggiare

despondent [dɪs·'pɑːn·dənt] *adj* demoralizzato, -a; **to feel ~ about sth** sentirsi avvilito per qc

despot ['des·pət] *n* despota *mf*

despotic [des·'pɑː·t̬ɪk] *adj* dispotico, -a

despotism ['des·pə·tɪ·zəm] *n* dispotismo *m*

dessert [dɪ·'zɜːrt] *n* dolce *m,* dessert *m inv*

dessertspoon [dɪ·'zɜːrt·,spuːn] *n* **1.**(*spoon*) cucchiaio *m* da dessert **2.**(*amount*) cucchiaiata *f*

destabilization [,diː·'steɪ·bə·lɪ·'zeɪ·ʃən] *n* destabilizzazione *f*

destabilize [,diː·'steɪ·bə·laɪz] *vt* destabilizzare

destination [,des·tɪ·'neɪ·ʃən] *n* destinazione *f*

destine ['des·tɪn] *vt* **1.**(*be certain*) destinare; **to be ~d to fail/succeed** essere destinato a fallire/avere successo **2.**(*intend*) **to be ~d for sth** essere destinato a qc **3.**(*have as destination*) **the plane is ~d for Paris** l'aereo è diretto a Parigi

destiny ['des·tɪ·ni] *n* destino *m;* **to fight one's ~** lottare contro il destino; **to shape one's ~** essere artefice del proprio destino

destitute ['des·tɪ·tuːt] **I.** *adj* in miseria **II.** *n* **the ~** *pl* gli indigenti

destitution [,des·tɪ·'tuː·ʃən] *n* indigenza *f*

destroy [dɪs·'trɔɪ] *vt* **1.**(*demolish*) distruggere **2.**(*kill: animal*) abbattere **3.**(*ruin*) distruggere

destroyer [dɪs·'trɔ·ɪɚ] *n* NAUT cacciatorpediniere *m*

destructible [dɪs·'trʌk·tə·bl] *adj* distruttibile

destruction [dɪs·'trʌk·ʃən] *n* distruzione *f;* **mass ~** distruzione di massa; **to leave a trail of ~** lasciare una scia di distruzione

destructive [dɪs·'trʌk·tɪv] *adj* distruttivo, -a

destructiveness *n* potere *m* distruttivo

desulphurization [diː·,sʌl·fə·rɪ·'zeɪ·ʃən] *n* desolforazione *f*

desultory ['des·əl·tɔː·ri] *adj* (*disconnected*) sconnesso, -a; (*lacking plan*) disordinato, -a

detach [dɪ·'tætʃ] *vt* staccare

detachable *adj* staccabile

detached *adj* **1.**(*separated*) separato, -a; **~ house** villetta unifamiliare **2.**(*aloof*) distante **3.**(*impartial*) imparziale

detachment [dɪ·'tætʃ·mənt] *n* **1.**(*separation*) distacco *m* **2.**(*disinterest*) disinteresse *m* **3.**(*of soldiers*) distaccamento *m*

detail [dɪ·'teɪl] **I.** *n* **1.**(*item of information*) dettaglio *m;* **in ~** in modo dettagliato; **to go into ~** entrare nei dettagli **2.**(*unimportant* *item*) minuzia *f;* **the gory ~s** *iron* i particolari più intimi **3.**(*small feature*) particolare *m* **4.**MIL (*group*) distaccamento *m* **II.** *vt* **1.**(*explain fully*) specificare dettagliatamente **2.**(*tell, mention*) elencare dettagliatamente **3.**(*assign a duty to*) **to ~ sb to sth** assegnare qn a qc

detailed *adj* dettagliato, -a

detain [dɪ·'teɪn] *vt* **1.**(*hold as prisoner*) detenere **2.**(*delay*) trattenere

detainee [‚di:·teɪ·'ni:] *n* detenuto, -a *m, f*

detect [dɪ·'tekt] *vt* **1.**(*note*) notare; (*sense presence of*) percepire; (*a mine*) trovare **2.**(*discover*) scoprire

detectable [dɪ·'tek·tə·bl] *adj* (*discernible*) percepibile; (*able to be found*) rilevabile

detection [dɪ·'tek·ʃən] *n* (*of disease*) scoperta *f;* (*of plane*) individuazione *f*

detective [dɪ·'tek·tɪv] *n* **1.**(*private investigator*) detective *mf inv* **2.**(*police officer*) agente *mf* investigativo

detective novel *n,* **detective story** *n* romanzo *m* poliziesco

detector [dɪ·'tek·tə-] *n* detector *m inv*

detention [dɪ·'ten·ʃən] *n* **1.**(*act*) detenzione *f* **2.**(*as a prisoner*) detenzione *f* **3.**SCH *castigo consistente nell'essere trattenuti a scuola al termine delle lezioni*

detention home *n* istituto *m* di detenzione

deter [dɪ·'tɜ:r] <-rr-> *vt* dissuadere

detergent [dɪ·'tɜ:r·dʒənt] *n* detergente *m*

deteriorate [dɪ·'tɪ·rɪ·ə·reit] *vi* **1.**(*wear out*) deteriorarsi **2.**(*become worse*) peggiorare

deterioration [dɪ·‚tɪ·ri·ə·'rei·ʃən] *n* **1.**(*wearing out*) deterioramento *m* **2.**(*worsening*) peggioramento *m*

determinable [dɪ·'tɜ:r·mɪ·nə·bl] *adj* determinabile

determinant [dɪ·'tɜ:r·mɪ·nənt] **I.** *n* determinante *m* **II.** *adj* determinante

determinate [dɪ·'tɜ:r·mɪ·nət] *adj* **1.**(*limited*) definitivo, -a **2.**(*of specific scope*) determinato, -a

determination [dɪ·‚tɜ:r·mɪ·'nei·ʃən] *n* **1.**(*firmness of purpose*) risoluzione *f* **2.**(*decision*) determinazione *f*

determine [dɪ·'tɜ:r·mɪn] **I.** *vi* **1.**(*decide*) **to ~ on sth** decidersi per qc **2.**LAW estinguersi **II.** *vt* **1.**(*decide*) decidere; (*settle*) definire **2.**(*find out*) stabilire **3.**(*influence*) determinare **4.**LAW (*terminate*) rescindere

determined [dɪ·'tɜ:r·mɪnd] *adj* determinato, -a; **to be ~ to do sth** essere determinato a fare qc

deterrence [dɪ·'te·rəns] *n* dissuasione *f*

deterrent [dɪ·'te·rənt] **I.** *n* freno *m;* **to act as a ~ to sb** agire da deterrente **II.** *adj* deterrente

detest [dɪ·'test] *vt* detestare

detestable [dɪ·'tes·tə·bl] *adj* odioso, -a

detestation [‚di:·tes·'tei·ʃən] *n* odio *m*

dethrone [dɪ·'θroʊn] *vt* detronizzare

detonate ['de·tə·neɪt] **I.** *vi* detonare **II.** *vt* far detonare

detonation [‚de·tə·'nei·ʃən] *n* detonazione *f*

detonator ['de·tə·nei·t̬ə-] *n* detonatore *m*

detour ['di:·tʊr] *n* deviazione *f;* **to make a ~** fare una deviazione

detoxify [di:·'tɑ:k·sɪ·fai] *vt* disintossicare

detract [dɪ·'trækt] *vi* **1.**(*devalue*) **to ~ from sth** sminuire qc **2.**(*take away*) distogliere

detractor [dɪ·'træk·tə-] *n* detrattore, -trice *m, f*

detriment ['de·trɪ·mənt] *n* detrimento *m;* **to the ~ of sth** a detrimento [*o* scapito] di qn/qc; **without ~ to sth** senza danno per qc

detrimental [‚de·trɪ·'men·təl] *adj* nocivo, -a

detritus [dɪ·'trai·t̬əs] *n* **1.**(*small fragments*) detrito *m* **2.**(*debris*) detriti *mpl*

deuce [du:s] *n* **1.**(*in cards*) due *m* **2.**(*in tennis*) parità *f*

devaluate [‚di:·'væ·lu·eɪt] *vt s.* **devalue**

devaluation [‚di:·væl·ju·'ei·ʃən] *n* svalutazione *f*

devalue [‚di:·'væl·ju:] *vt* svalutare

devastate ['de·vəs·teɪt] *vt* (*land, city*) devastare; (*person*) distruggere

devastating *adj* **1.**(*causing destruction*) devastante; (*powerful*) devastatore, -trice **2.**(*stunning*) impressionante; (*beauty*) sconvolgente; (*charm*) irresistibile

devastation [‚de·vəs·'tei·ʃən] *n* devastazione *f*

develop [dɪ·'ve·ləp] **I.** *vi* (*grow*) svilupparsi; (*become more advanced*) progredire; **to ~ into sth** trasformarsi in qc **II.** *vt* **1.**(*expand*) sviluppare; (*improve*) ampliare **2.**(*create*) creare **3.**(*begin to show*) rivelare; (*catch*) prendere; (*an illness*) contrarre **4.**(*build*) costruire; (*build on*) sviluppare **5.**PHOT sviluppare

developed *adj* sviluppato, -a; **~ countries** paesi sviluppati

developer [dɪ·'ve·lə·pə-] *n* **1.**(*person*) imprenditore, -trice *m, f* immobiliare; (*company*) immobiliare *f* **2.**PHOT rivelatore *m*

developing *adj* in via di sviluppo; **~ countries** paesi in via di sviluppo

development [dɪ·'ve·ləp·mənt] *n* **1.**(*process*) sviluppo *m;* (*growth*) crescita *f* **2.**(*growth stage*) sviluppo *m;* (*of skills*) acquisizione *f* **3.**(*progress*) progresso *m;* (*of products*) ideazione *f* **4.**(*event*) sviluppo *m* **5.**(*building of*) costruzione *f;* **housing ~** complesso *m* abitativo **6.**(*building on: of land*) sviluppo *m* **7.**(*industrialization*) industrializzazione *f*

deviant ['di:·vi·ənt] *adj* (*behavior*) deviante; (*sexually*) da pervertito, -a

deviate ['di:·vi·eɪt] *vi* deviare; **to ~ from sth** deviare da qc

deviation [‚di:·vi·'ei·ʃən] *n* deviazione *f*

device [dɪ·'vais] *n* **1.**(*mechanism*) dispositivo *m;* **input/output ~** COMPUT unità *f* di entrata/uscita **2.**(*method*) stratagemma *m;* **literary/rhetorical ~** artificio *m* letterario/retorico **3.**(*bomb*) ordigno *m;* **nuclear ~** ordigno *m* nucleare ►**to leave sb to their own ~s** abbandonare qn al proprio destino

devil ['de·vəl] *n* **1.**(*Satan*) diavolo *m;* **to be possessed by the D~** essere posseduto dal demonio **2.**(*evil spirit*) demone *m* **3.**inf (*wicked person*) diavolo *m* **4.**(*mischievous person*) he's a little ~ è una peste; **lucky ~**! fortunato mortale!; **the poor ~**! povero diavolo! **5.**(*difficult thing*) **to have a ~ of a time doing sth** fare una fatica del diavolo a fare qc **6.**(*feisty energy*) audacia *f* ▶ ~ **take the hindmost** ognuno per sé e Dio per tutti *prov;* **between the ~ and the deep blue sea** tra l'incudine e il martello; **to sell one's soul to the ~** vendere l'anima al diavolo; **to go to the ~** andare all'inferno; **there'll be the ~ to pay** saranno guai seri; **to play the ~ with sth** sconvolgere qc; **speak of the ~** si parla del diavolo (e ne spuntano le corna); **how/who/what/where the ~ ...?** come/chi/cosa/dove diavolo ...?; **like the ~** come un dannato

devilish ['de·və·lɪʃ] *adj* **1.**(*evil*) diabolico, -a **2.**(*mischievous*) malizioso, -a **3.**(*extreme*) molto difficile; (*terrible*) terribile **4.**(*very clever*) diabolico, -a

devil-may-care *adj* irresponsabile

devilment ['de·vəl·mənt] *n*, **devilry** ['de·vəl·ri] *n* cattiveria *f*

devil's advocate *n* **to play the ~** fare l'avvocato del diavolo

devil's food cake *n* dolce *m* al cioccolato

devious ['di:·vi·əs] *adj* **1.**(*dishonest*) sleale **2.**(*winding*) tortuoso, -a

devise [dɪ·'vaɪz] **I.** *n* LAW legato *m* **II.** *vt* **1.**(*plan, think out*) escogitare; (*a plot*) ideare; (*a scheme*) concepire **2.**LAW legare

devoid [dɪ·'vɔɪd] *adj* **to be ~ of sth** esser privo di qc

devolution [ˌde·və·'lu:·ʃən] *n* **1.**(*progression through stages*) trasferimento *m* **2.**(*transference of wealth*) trapasso *m* **3.**POL (*decentralization of power*) devoluzione *f inv*

devolve [dɪ·'va:lv] **I.** *vi* ricadere **II.** *vt* (*transfer: powers*) trasferire

devote [dɪ·'vout] *vt* dedicare; **to ~ oneself to sth** dedicarsi a qc

devoted [dɪ·'vou·t̮ɪd] *adj* dedicato, -a; (*husband, mother*) devoto, -a; (*couple*) fedele; **to be ~ to sb** essere affezionato a qn; **to be ~ to sth** dedicarsi a qc

devotee [ˌde·və·'ti:] *n* (*supporter*) sostenitore, -trice *m, f;* (*admirer*) appassionato, -a *m, f*

devotion [dɪ·'vou·ʃən] *n* **1.**(*loyalty*) lealtà *f;* (*affection*) affetto *m;* (*great attachment*) dedizione *f;* **to inspire ~** ispirare devozione **2.**REL devozione *f* **3.**(*devoutness*) pietà *f*

devotional [dɪ·'vou·ʃə·nəl] *adj* (*attitude*) devoto, -a; (*music, practices*) religioso, -a

devour [dɪ·'va·ʊə] *vt* divorare; **to be ~ed by jealousy** essere divorato dalla gelosia

devouring *adj* divorante

devout [dɪ·'vaut] *adj* **1.**REL devoto, -a **2.**(*compulsive*) fervido, -a

dew [du:] *n* rugiada *f*

dewdrop ['du:·dra:p] *n* goccia *f* di rugiada

dewy ['du:·i] *adj* coperto, -a di rugiada

dexterity [ˌdeks·'te·rə·t̮i] *n* destrezza *f*

dexterous ['deks·tə·rəs] *adj* abile; (*movement*) agile

dextrose ['deks·trous] *n* destrosio *m*

dextrous ['deks·trəs] *adj s.* **dexterous**

diabetes [ˌda·ɪə·'bi:·t̮iz] *n* diabete *m*

diabetic [ˌda·ɪə·'be·t̮ɪk] **I.** *n* diabetico, -a *m, f* **II.** *adj* diabetico, -a

diabolic(al) [ˌda·ɪə·'ba:·lɪ·k(əl)] *adj* **1.**(*of the Devil*) diabolico, -a **2.**(*evil*) diabolico, -a **3.**inf (*very bad*) terribile

diadem ['da·ɪə·dem] *n* diadema *m*

diagnose [ˌda·ɪəg·'nous] **I.** *vi* fare una diagnosi **II.** *vt* diagnosticare

diagnosis [ˌda·ɪəg·'nou·sɪs] <-ses> *n* **1.**(*process*) diagnosi *f inv* **2.**(*result*) diagnosi *f inv*

diagnostic [ˌda·ɪəg·'na:s·tɪk] **I.** *n* diagnosi *f inv* **II.** *adj* diagnostico, -a

diagonal [daɪ·'æ·gə·nl] **I.** *n* diagonale *f* **II.** *adj* diagonale

diagram ['da·ɪə·græm] **I.** *n* **1.**(*drawing*) diagramma *m;* (*plan*) schema *m* **2.**(*chart*) grafico *m* **II.** <-mm-> *vt* rappresentare con un diagramma

dial ['da·ɪəl] **I.** *n* **1.**(*face of clock*) quadrante *m* **2.**(*on telephone*) disco (*m* combinatore) **3.**(*on radio*) manopola *f* di sintonizzazione **II.** <-l- *o* -ll-, -l- *o* -ll-> *vi* fare un numero; **to ~ direct** chiamare direttamente **III.** *vt* **1.**(*phone number*) chiamare **2.**(*radio station*) sintonizzarsi su

◆**dial in** *vi* **to ~ (to sth)** telefonare (a qc)

dialect ['da·ɪə·lekt] *n* dialetto *m*

dialectal [ˌda·ɪə·'lek·təl] *adj* dialettale

dialectical [ˌda·ɪə·'lek·tɪ·kəl] *adj* dialettico, -a

dialog *n*, **dialogue** ['da·ɪə·la:g] *n* **1.**(*conversation*) dialogo *m* **2.**POL dialogo *m;* **to engage in ~** dialogare

dial tone *n* segnale *m* di libero

dial-up service *n* COMPUT servizio *m* dialup

dialysis [daɪ·'æ·lə·sɪs] *n* dialisi *f inv*

diameter [daɪ·'æ·mə·t̮ə] *n* diametro *m*

diametrically [ˌda·ɪə·'met·rɪ·kə·li] *adv* diametralmente

diamond ['da·ɪə·mənd] *n* **1.**(*gemstone*) diamante *m;* **the ace/king of ~s** GAMES l'asso/il re di quadri **2.**(*rhombus*) rombo *m* **3.**(*for cutting glass*) (punta *f* di) diamante *m* **4.**(*baseball field*) campo *m;* (*infield*) diamante *m* ▶**a ~ in the rough** un diamante grezzo

diamond cutter *n* tagliatore *m* di diamanti

diaper ['da·ɪə·pə] *n* pannolino *m*

diaphanous [daɪ·'æ·fə·nəs] *adj liter* diafano, -a; (*cloth*) trasparente

diaphragm ['da·ɪə·fræm] *n* diaframma *m*

diarist ['da·ɪə·rɪst] *n* diarista *mf*

diarrhea [ˌda·ɪə·'ri:·ə] *n* diarrea *f*

diary ['da·ɪə·ri] *n* diario *m*

diatonic [ˌda·ɪə·'ta:·nɪk] *adj* MUS diatonico, -a

diatribe ['da·ɪə·traɪb] *n* diatriba *f*

dice [daɪs] **I.** *n pl* **1.**(*cubes*) dadi *mpl;* **to roll the ~** tirare i dadi **2.**(*game*) gioco *m* dei dadi **3.**(*food cut in cubes*) dadini *mpl* ▶**no ~** *sl* non se ne parla nemmeno **II.** *vi* giocare a dadi **III.** *vt* tagliare a dadini

dicey ['daɪ·si] <-ier, -iest> *adj inf* rischioso, -a

dichotomy [daɪ·'kɑː·t̬ə·mi] *n* dicotomia *f*

dick [dɪk] *n vulg* **1.** (*penis*) cazzo *m* **2.** (*stupid person*) cazzone, -a *m, f*

dickens ['dɪ·kɪnz] *npl sl* **what the ~ ...?** che cavolo ...?; **to scare the ~ out of sb** spaventare a morte qn

dicky ['dɪ·ki] *n inf* **a ~ heart** un cuore debole

dictaphone® ['dɪk·tə·foʊn] *n* dittafono® *m*

dictate ['dɪk·teɪt] **I.** *n* dettame *m* **II.** *vi* **1.** (*command*) dare ordini **2.** (*to a typist*) **to ~ to sb** dettare a qn **III.** *vt* **1.** (*give orders*) dare ordini a; (*terms*) dettare **2.** (*make necessary*) rendere necessario; (*state exactly*) imporre **3.** (*to a typist*) dettare

dictation [dɪk·'teɪ·ʃən] *n* SCHOOL dettato *m*

dictator ['dɪk·teɪ·t̬ə] *n* POL dittatore, -trice *m, f*

dictatorial [ˌdɪk·tə·'tɔː·ri·əl] *adj* dittatoriale

dictatorship [dɪk·'teɪ·t̬ə·ʃɪp] *n* dittatura *f*

diction ['dɪk·ʃən] *n* dizione *f*

dictionary ['dɪk·ʃə·ne·ri] *n* dizionario *m*

did [dɪd] *pt of* **do**

didactic [daɪ·'dæk·tɪk] *adj* didattico, -a

diddle ['dɪ·dl] *vt sl* (*swindle*) imbrogliare; **to ~ sb out of sth** fregare qc a qn

♦ **diddle around** *vi* (*hang around*) ciondolare

didn't ['dɪ·dənt] = **did not** *s.* **do**

die¹ [daɪ] *n* **1.** dado *m* **2.** TECH stampo *m* ▶ **the ~ is cast** il dado è tratto

die² [daɪ] <dying, died> *vi* **1.** (*cease to live*) morire; **to ~ a violent/natural death** morire di morte violenta/naturale; **to ~ by one's own hand** morire di propria mano **2.** (*end*) finire; **the secret will ~ with her** si porterà il segreto nella tomba **3.** (*stop functioning: appliance*) smettere di funzionare; (*battery*) scaricarsi; **the engine just ~d on me** il motore mi ha abbandonato **4.** (*go out, fade away*) spegnersi ▶ **to ~ hard** essere duro a morire; **never say ~!** dai, non arrenderti!; **to do or ~** vincere o morire; **to be dying to do sth** morire dalla voglia di fare qc; **I'm dying for a cup of tea** muoio dalla voglia di bere una tazza di tè

♦ **die away** *vi* (*sobs, anger, wind*) calmarsi; (*enthusiasm*) spegnersi; (*sound*) smorzarsi

♦ **die back** *vi* seccarsi, *della parte apicale della pianta*

♦ **die down** *vi* (*wind, gossip*) placare; (*enthusiasm, applause, laughter*) smorzarsi

♦ **die off** *vi* (*species*) estinguersi; (*customs*) scomparire

♦ **die out** *vi* estinguersi

dieback ['daɪ·bæk] *n* mal *m* secco

die-hard *n* intransigente *mf;* **a ~ conservative** un irriducibile conservatore

diesel ['diː·zəl] *n* diesel *m inv*

diesel engine *n* motore *m* diesel

diet¹ ['da·ɪət] **I.** *n* dieta *f;* **to be on a ~** essere a dieta; **to put sb on a ~** mettere qn a dieta; **to go on a ~** seguire una dieta **II.** *vi* essere a dieta

III. *vt* **to ~ sb** mettere qn a dieta

diet² ['da·ɪət] *n* (*legislative body*) dieta *f*

dietary ['da·ɪə·te·ri] *adj* (*food*) dietetico, -a

dietary fiber *n* fibra *f* alimentare

dietetic [ˌda·ɪə·'te·t̬ɪk] *adj* dietetico, -a

dietetics *n* dietetica *f*

dietician *n,* **dietitian** [ˌda·ɪə·'tɪ·ʃən] *n* dietologo, -a *m, f*

differ ['dɪ·fə] *vi* **1.** (*be unlike*) differire; **to ~ from sth** essere diverso da qc **2.** (*disagree*) non essere d'accordo; **to ~ about sth** discordare su qc

difference ['dɪ·fə·rənts] *n* **1.** (*state of being different*) differenza *f* **2.** (*distinction*) diversità *f; that makes all the ~* questo cambia tutto; **to make a ~** fare una bella differenza; **to not make any ~** non fare alcuna differenza **3.** (*new feature*) differenza *f* **4.** (*remaining amount*) **to pay the ~** pagare la differenza **5.** (*disagreement*) divergenza *f;* **to put aside ~s** accantonare le divergenze; **to settle ~s** mettersi d'accordo

different ['dɪ·fə·rənt] *adj* diverso, -a; **to do something ~** far qualcosa di diverso; **to be as ~ as night and day** essere diversi come il giorno e la notte

differential [ˌdɪ·fə·'ren·tʃəl] **I.** *n* **1.** *a.* MATH differenziale *m* **2.** (*difference in pay*) **pay ~s** differenzialif *pl* salariali **II.** *adj* **1.** (*different*) differenziale; (*access*) differenziato, -a **2.** MATH differenziale

differentiate [ˌdɪ·fə·'ren·tʃi·eɪt] **I.** *vi* distinguere **II.** *vt* distinguere

differentiation [ˌdɪ·fə·ren·tʃi·'eɪ·ʃən] *n* differenziazione *f*

difficult ['dɪ·fɪ·kəlt] *adj* **1.** (*not easy*) difficile; **she is said to be a very ~ person** si dice che sia una persona molto difficile **2.** (*troublesome*) duro, -a

difficulty ['dɪ·fɪ·kəl·ti] <-ies> *n* **1.** (*being difficult*) difficoltà *f;* **with ~** difficilmente **2.** (*problem*) difficoltà *f;* **to have difficulties with sb** avere dei problemi con qn; **to have ~ doing sth** avere difficoltà a fare qc; **to encounter difficulties** incontrare delle difficoltà

diffident ['dɪ·fɪ·dənt] *adj* (*shy*) timido, -a; (*modest*) modesto, -a

diffract [dɪ·'frækt] *vt* diffrangere

diffuse¹ [dɪ·'fjuːz] **I.** *vi* diffondersi **II.** *vt* diffondere

diffuse² [dɪv'fjuːs] *adj* **1.** (*spread out*) diffuso, -a **2.** (*verbose*) verboso, -a **3.** (*imprecise*) vago, -a

diffusion [dɪ·'fjuː·ʒən] *n* **1.** (*process of diffusing*) diffusione *f* **2.** CHEM, PHYS diffusione *f*

dig [dɪg] **I.** *n* **1.** (*poke*) gomitata *f* **2.** (*excavation*) scavo *m* **3.** (*sarcastic remark*) frecciata *f* **II.** <-gg-, dug, dug> *vi* **1.** (*turn over ground*) scavare; **to ~ deeper** *fig* approfondire **2.** (*poke*) conficcarsi **III.** *vt* **1.** (*move ground*) scavare; (*garden*) zappare **2.** (*excavate*) scavare **3.** (*stab, poke*) conficcare; **to ~ one's elbow into sb's ribs** dare di gomito a qn; **to ~**

D

one's spurs into a horse speronare il cavallo **4.** *sl* (*like*) piacere ▶ **to** ~ **one's own grave** scavarsi la fossa

◆ **dig in** I. *vi inf* (*start eating*) come on, everybody - ~! forza, cominciate! II. *vt* (*bury*) interrare ▶ **to dig oneself in** (*dig trenches*) trincerarsi; (*establish oneself*) piazzarsi; (*settle in*) sistemarsi

◆ **dig into** I. *vi* conficcarsi ▶ **to dig** (**deeper**) **into one's pockets** frugare nelle tasche II. *vt always sep inf* cominciare ▶ **to dig oneself into a hole** mettersi in una situazione difficile

◆ **dig out** *vt* (*hole*) scavare; (*buried object*) estrarre

◆ **dig up** *vt* **1.** (*from ground*) dissotterrare **2.** (*excavate*) scavare **3.** *fig* (*find out*) scovare

digest[1] ['daɪ-dʒest] *n* **1.** (*of essays*) sunto *m* **2.** (*of laws*) raccolta *f*

digest[2] [daɪ-'dʒest] I. *vi* digerire II. *vt* **1.** (*break down: food*) essere digerito **2.** *inf* (*understand*) assimilare **3.** (*classify*) classificare

digestible [daɪ-'dʒes-tə-bl] *adj* digeribile

digestion [daɪ-'dʒest-ʃən] *n* digestione *f*

digestive [daɪ-'dʒes-tɪv] *adj* digestivo, -a

digger ['dɪ-gə] *n* **1.** (*machine*) escavatrice *f* **2.** (*person*) sterratore, -trice *m, f* **3.** *inf* (*Australian soldier*) australiano, -a *m, f*

digit ['dɪ-dʒɪt] *n* **1.** (*number*) cifra *f* **2.** (*finger, toe*) dito *m*

digital ['dɪ-dʒɪ-t̩l] *adj* digitale; ~ **audio tape** audiocassetta numerica a nastro

digitalize ['dɪ-dʒɪ-tə-laɪz] *vt* digitalizzare

digitize ['dɪ-dʒɪ-taɪz] *vt* COMPUT digitalizzare

digitizer ['dɪ-dʒɪ-taɪ-zə] *n* COMPUT digitalizzatore *m*

dignified ['dɪg-nɪ-faɪd] *adj* **1.** (*honorable*) dignitoso, -a **2.** (*solemn*) solenne

dignify ['dɪg-nɪ-faɪ] <-ie-> *vt* nobilitare

dignitary ['dɪg-nə-te-ri] <-ies> *n* dignitario, -a *m, f*

dignity ['dɪg-nə-t̩i] *n* **1.** (*state worthy of respect*) dignità *f* **2.** (*respect*) rispetto *m;* **to be beneath sb's** ~ non esser degno di qn **3.** (*composed style*) decoro *m*

digress [daɪ-'gres] *vi* **1.** (*wander from topic*) fare una digressione **2.** (*deviate*) divagare; **to** ~ **from sth** divagare da qc

digressive [daɪ-'gre-sɪv] *adj* digressivo, -a

dike [daɪk] *n* **1.** *a. fig* diga *f* **2.** (*channel*) canale *m* di scolo

dilapidated [dɪ-'læ-pɪ-deɪ-t̩ɪd] *adj* (*house*) fatiscente; (*car*) scassato, -a

dilate ['daɪ-leɪt] I. *vi* dilatarsi II. *vt* dilatare

dilation [daɪ-'leɪ-ʃən] *n* dilatazione *f*

dilatory ['dɪ-lə-tɔː-ri] *adj* **1.** (*slow*) lento, -a **2.** LAW dilatorio, -a

dilemma [dɪ-'le-mə] *n* dilemma *m;* **to be in a** ~ esser di fronte a un dilemma; **to face a** ~ trovarsi di fronte a un dilemma

dilettante [ˌdɪ-lə-'taːnt] *n* <-s *o* -ti> dilettante *mf*

diligence ['dɪ-lɪ-dʒəns] *n* diligenza *f*

diligent ['dɪ-lɪ-dʒənt] *adj* diligente

dill [dɪl] *n* aneto *m*

dilly-dally ['dɪ-li-dæ-li] *vi inf* **1.** (*waste time*) perder tempo **2.** (*be indecisive*) tentennare

dilute [daɪ-'luːt] I. *vt* **1.** (*liquid*) diluire **2.** *fig* attenuare II. *adj* diluito, -a

dilution [daɪ-'luː-ʃən] *n* **1.** (*of liquid*) diluizione *f* **2.** *fig* attenuazione *f*

dim [dɪm] I. <-mm-> *vi* (*lights*) affievolirsi II. *vt* abbassare III. <-mm-> *adj* **1.** (*not bright*) tenue **2.** (*unclear, faint*) vago, -a **3.** (*stupid*) ottuso, -a **4.** (*unfavorable*) cupo, -a

dime [daɪm] *n* moneta *f* da dieci centesimi ▶ **a** ~ **a dozen** di poco valore

dimension [dɪ-'men-tʃən] *n* dimensione *f*

dimensional [dɪ-'men-tʃə-nəl] *adj* dimensionale

diminish [dɪ-'mɪ-nɪʃ] I. *vi* diminuire; **to** (**greatly**) ~ **in value** perdere molto valore II. *vt* **1.** (*make less*) diminuire **2.** (*damage sb's reputation*) screditare

diminution [dɪ-mə-'nuː-ʃən] *n* diminuzione *f*

diminutive [dɪ-'mɪn-jə-t̩ɪv] I. *n* LING diminutivo *m* II. *adj* minuto, -a

dimmer ['dɪ-mə] *n* dimmer *m inv*

dimness *n* oscurità *f*

dimple ['dɪm-pl] I. *n* fossetta *f* II. *vt* formare le fossette su

din [dɪn] *n* strepito *m*

dine [daɪn] *vi* cenare

diner ['daɪ-nə] *n* **1.** (*person*) cliente *mf* **2.** (*restaurant*) *piccolo ristorante aperto tutto il giorno con tavoli fissi disposti come in un vagone ristorante*

i Negli USA, un **diner** è una sorta di ristorante dove i clienti si siedono al banco invece che ai tavoli. Originariamente, i **diners** degli anni '50 proponevano nel menu hamburgers, patate fritte e altri piatti rapidi. Oggi sono famosi per i loro menu, che sembrano quasi dei romanzi. Vi si possono consumare, tra le altre cose, panini, bistecche, pollo e piatti a base di uova. Molti **diners** sono gestiti da immigrati greci e propongono pertanto anche delle specialità greche.

dinghy ['dɪŋ-gi] *n* <-ies> (*on larger boat*) tender *m inv;* (*small rowing boat*) piccola imbarcazione *f* a remi

dingy ['dɪn-dʒi] <-ier, -iest> *adj* tetro, -a

dining car *n* vagone *m* ristorante

dining room *n* sala *f* da pranzo

dink [dɪŋk] *n abbr of* **dual income no kids** *coppia con doppio stipendio e senza figli*

dinky ['dɪn-ki] *adj* **1.** (*insignificant*) misero, -a **2.** (*shabby*) squallido, -a

dinner ['dɪ-nə] *n* cena *f;* (**Sunday**) ~ (*meal served in early to mid-afternoon*) pranzo *m;* **to make** ~ preparare la cena

dinner jacket *n* smoking *m inv*

dinner party *n* cena *f* (tra amici)

dinner service *n* servizio *m* da tavola
dinner table *n* tavolo *m* da pranzo
dinnertime *n* ora *f* di cena
dinnerware *n* stoviglie *fpl*
dinosaur ['daɪ·nə·sɔːr] *n a. fig* dinosauro *m*
dint [dɪnt] *n* **by ~ of sth** a forza di qc
diocese ['da·ɪə·sɪs] *n* diocesi *f inv*
dioxide [daɪ·'ɑːk·saɪd] *n* diossido *m*
dioxin [daɪ·'ɑːk·sɪn] *n* diossina *f*
dip [dɪp] I. *n* 1. (*dunking*) bagno *m* 2. (*sudden drop*) calo *m;* (*in the road*) dosso *m* 3. (*cold sauce*) salsetta *f* 4. (*brief swim*) nuotata *f* 5. (*depression in ground*) avvallamento *m* 6. (*magnetic*) inclinazione *f* II. *vi* 1. (*drop down: prices*) diminuire; (*road*) essere in discesa 2. (*slope down*) inclinarsi 3. (*into a liquid*) immergersi III. *vt* 1. (*immerse*) immergere; *a.* CULIN inzuppare 2. (*put into*) infilare 3. (*dye*) tingere 4. (*wash*) disinfettare 5. (*lower*) abbassare
 ◆**dip into** *vt* 1. *always sep* (*put*) infilare 2. **to ~ into one's savings** attingere ai propri risparmi 3. (*look casually*) dare un'occhiata a
diphtheria [dɪf·'θɪ·ri·ə] *n* MED difterite *f*
diphthong ['dɪf·θɑːŋ] *n* LING dittongo *m*
diploma [dɪ·'ploʊ·mə] *n* diploma *m*
diplomacy [dɪ·'ploʊ·mə·si] *n* 1. (*between countries*) diplomazia *f* 2. (*tact*) tatto *m*
diplomat ['dɪp·lə·mæt] *n* 1. (*of country*) diplomatico, -a *m, f* 2. (*tactful person*) persona *f* diplomatica
diplomatic [ˌdɪp·lə·'mæ·t̬ɪk] *adj* diplomatico, -a
dippy ['dɪ·pi] *adj sl* sciocco, -a
dipsomania [ˌdɪp·sə·'meɪ·niə] *n* MED dipsomania *f*
dipsomaniac [ˌdɪp·sə·'meɪ·ni·æk] *n* MED dipsomane *mf*
dipstick ['dɪp·stɪk] *n* astina *f* dell'olio
dire ['da·ɪə] *adj* 1. (*terrible*) terribile 2. (*serious*) grave; **to be in ~ straits** essere in gravi difficoltà 3. (*extreme*) estremo, -a
direct [dɪ·'rekt] I. *vi* MUS dirigere II. *vt* 1. (*point, intend*) rivolgere; **to ~ sth at sb** destinare qc a qn 2. (*command*) dirigere 3. (*indicate*) **to ~ sb to a place** indicare la strada a qn 4. (*film, play*) dirigere III. *adj* 1. (*straight*) diretto, -a 2. (*exact*) esatto, -a; **the ~ opposite of sth** l'esatto contrario di qc 3. (*frank*) franco, -a IV. *adv* 1. (*with no intermediary*) direttamente 2. (*by a direct way*) dritto
direct action *n* azione *f* diretta
direct current *n* corrente *f* continua
direct hit *n* centro *m*
direction [dɪ·'rek·ʃən] *n* 1. (*supervision*) direzione *f* 2. (*movement*) **in the ~ of sth** in direzione di qc; **sense of ~** senso dell'orientamento *m* 3. *pl* (*information*) istruzioni *fpl;* **can you give me directions?** mi può dare delle indicazioni? 4. (*of film, play*) regia *f*
directional [dɪ·'rek·ʃə·nəl] *adj* direzionale
directive [dɪ·'rek·tɪv] *n* direttiva *f*

directly [dɪ·'rekt·li] *adv* 1. (*without deviation*) direttamente; **go ~ home** va' dritto a casa 2. (*immediately*) immediatamente 3. (*shortly*) subito 4. (*exactly*) esattamente 5. (*frankly*) francamente
direct object *n* oggetto *m* diretto
director [dɪ·'rek·tə·] *n* 1. ECON (*manager*) dirigente *mf* 2. (*board member*) membro *m* del consiglio; **board of ~s** consiglio *m* di amministrazione
directorate [dɪ·'rek·tə·rət] *n* 1. (*board of directors*) consiglio *m* d'amministrazione 2. (*department*) direzione *f*
directorship [dɪ·'rek·tə·ʃɪp] *n* direzione *f*
directory [dɪ·'rek·tə·ri] *n* 1. (*book*) guida *f* 2. COMPUT directory *f inv*
directory assistance *n* servizio *m* informazioni elenco abbonati
dirt [dɜːrt] *n* 1. (*earth, soil*) terra *f* 2. (*unclean substance*) sporco *m* 3. (*excrement*) escrementi *mpl* 4. *inf* (*worthless thing*) schifezza *f;* (*person*) merda *f;* **to treat sb like ~** trattare qn come una pezza da piedi 5. (*foul language*) oscenità *f* 6. *inf* (*scandal, gossip*) pettegolezzi *mpl fig;* **to get the ~ on sb** sapere tutto su qn
 ▶ **to eat ~** ingoiare il rospo
dirt cheap *adj inf* a prezzo stracciato
dirt road *n* strada *f* sterrata
dirty ['dɜːr·t̬i] I. *vt* sporcare; **to ~ one's hands** sporcarsi le mani II. <-ier, -iest> *adj* 1. (*not clean*) sporco, -a 2. (*mean, nasty*) **a ~ look** un'occhiataccia 3. (*lewd*) osceno, -a; (*joke*) spinto, -a; **~ old man** vecchio sporcaccione 4. (*unpleasant*) sporco, -a; **to do the ~ work** fare il lavoro sporco III. *adv* in modo sporco; **to play ~** giocare sporco
disability [ˌdɪs·ə·'bɪ·lə·t̬i] *n* 1. (*handicap*) handicap *m inv* 2. (*condition of incapacity*) disabilità *f*
disable [dɪs·'eɪ·bl] *vt* 1. mettere fuori uso 2. MED rendere invalido, -a
disabled I. *npl* **the ~** i disabili II. *adj* disabile
disablement *n* disabilità *f;* MED invalidità *f*
disabuse [ˌdɪs·ə·'bjuːz] *vt* **to ~ sb of sth** disilludere qn su qc
disadvantage [ˌdɪs·əd·'væn·tɪdʒ] I. *n* svantaggio *m;* **to be at a ~** essere svantaggiato II. *vt* svantaggiare
disadvantaged *adj* svantaggiato, -a
disadvantageous [ˌdɪs·ˌæd·væn·'teɪ·dʒəs] *adj* svantaggioso, -a
disaffected [ˌdɪs·ə·'fek·tɪd] *adj* 1. (*disloyal*) scontento, -a 2. (*estranged*) disaffezionato, -a
disaffection [ˌdɪs·ə·'fek·ʃən] *n* disaffezione *f*
disagree [ˌdɪs·ə·'griː] *vi* 1. (*not agree*) non essere d'accordo; **to ~ on sth** non essere d'accordo su qc 2. (*differ*) differire; **the answers ~** le risposte non concordano 3. (*have bad effect*) **spicy food ~s with me** il cibo piccante mi fa star male
disagreeable [ˌdɪs·ə·'griː·ə·bl] *adj* sgradevole
disagreement [ˌdɪs·ə·'griː·mənt] *n* 1. (*lack of agreement*) disaccordo *m* 2. (*argument*) dis-

cussione *f* **3.** (*discrepancy*) discordanza *f*

disallow [ˌdɪs·ə·'laʊ] *vt* respingere; *a.* LAW, SPORTS annullare

disappear [ˌdɪs·ə·'pɪr] *vi* scomparire; **to ~ from sight** sparire alla vista; **to ~ without a trace** scomparire senza lasciare traccia; **to have all but ~ed** esser quasi scomparso

disappearance [ˌdɪs·ə·'pɪ·rənts] *n* scomparsa *f*

disappoint [ˌdɪs·ə·'pɔɪnt] *vt* deludere

disappointed *adj* deluso, -a; **I'm really ~ed in you** mi deludi profondamente

disappointing *adj* deludente

disappointment [ˌdɪs·ə·'pɔɪnt·mənt] *n* delusione *f*

disapprobation [ˌdɪs·ˌæ·prə·'beɪ·ʃən] *n* disapprovazione *f*

disapproval [ˌdɪs·ə·'pruː·vəl] *n* disapprovazione *f*

disapprove [ˌdɪs·ə·'pruːv] *vi* disapprovare; **to ~ of sth** disapprovare qc

disarm [dɪs·'ɑːrm] **I.** *vi* deporre le armi **II.** *vt* **1.** (*take weapons away*) disarmare **2.** (*remove fuse: bomb*) disattivare **3.** (*win over*) disarmare

disarmament [dɪs·'ɑːr·mə·mənt] *n* disarmo *m*

disarming [dɪs·'ɑːr·mɪŋ] *adj* (*person, smile*) disarmante

disarrange [ˌdɪs·ə·'reɪndʒ] *vt* mettere in disordine

disarray [ˌdɪs·ə·'reɪ] *n* (*disorder*) caos *m*

disaster [dɪ·'zæs·tə˞] *n* **1.** (*great misfortune*) disastro *m*; **~ area** zona *f* disastrata **2.** (*failure*) fiasco *m*

disastrous [dɪ·'zæs·trəs] *adj* **1.** (*causing disaster*) disastroso, -a **2.** (*unsuccessful*) catastrofico, -a

disband [dɪs·'bænd] *vt* sciogliere

disbelief [ˌdɪs·bɪ·'liːf] *n* incredulità *f*

disbelieve [ˌdɪs·bɪ·'liːv] *vt* non credere a

disbeliever *n* incredulo, -a *m, f*

disburse [dɪs·'bɜːrs] *vt* sborsare

disbursement [dɪs·'bɜːrs·mənt] *n* sborso *m*

disc [dɪsk] *n* disco *m*

discard[1] [dɪs·'kɑːrd] *n* scarto *m*

discard[2] [dɪs·'kɑːrd] *vt* **1.** (*get rid of*) scartare **2.** *a.* GAMES scartare

disc brake *n* freno *m* a disco

discern [dɪ·'sɜːrn] *vt* **1.** (*perceive*) percepire; (*distinguish*) distinguere **2.** (*make out*) discernere

discernible [dɪ·'sɜːr·nə·bl] *adj* (*with senses*) percepibile; (*mentally*) discernibile

discerning [dɪ·'sɜːr·nɪŋ] *adj* (*discriminating*) esigente; (*acute*) perspicace

discernment [dɪ·'sɜːrn·mənt] *n* (*good judgment*) giudizio *m*; (*clear perception*) discernimento *m*

discharge[1] ['dɪs·tʃɑːrdʒ] *n* **1.** (*from hospital*) dimissione *f*; (*from army*) congedo *m*; (*from jail*) rilascio *m* **2.** (*firing off*) scarica *f* **3.** (*emission*) emissione *f*; (*of liquid*) secrezione *f* **4.** (*debt payment*) estinzione *f* **5.** (*per-*

forming of a duty) adempimento *m* **6.** (*energy release*) scarica *f*

discharge[2] [dɪs·'tʃɑːrdʒ] **I.** *vi* **1.** (*ship*) scaricare **2.** (*produce liquid: wound*) suppurare **II.** *vt* **1.** *a.* LAW (*release*) liberare **2.** (*dismiss*) MIL congedare; ECON licenziare **3.** (*let out*) emettere **4.** (*utter*) gridare **5.** (*perform*) **to ~ one's duty** compiere il proprio dovere **6.** (*pay: debt*) estinguere **7.** (*cancel*) cancellare **8.** (*shoot*) scaricare

disciple [dɪ·'saɪ·pl] *n* **1.** (*follower*) seguace *mf* **2.** *a.* REL (*student*) discepolo, -a *m, f*

disciplinary ['di·sə·plɪ·ne·ri] *adj* disciplinario, -a

discipline ['dɪ·sə·plɪn] **I.** *n* **1.** (*obedience, self-control*) disciplina *f* **2.** (*punishment*) punizione *f* **3.** (*field*) disciplina *f* **II.** *vt* **1.** (*punish*) punire; **to ~ oneself to do sth** imporsi di fare qc **2.** (*train*) educare

disciplined *adj* disciplinato, -a

disc jockey *n* disc jockey *mf inv*

disclaim [dɪs·'kleɪm] *vt* (*deny*) negare; (*responsibility*) declinare

disclaimer [dɪs·'kleɪ·mə˞] *n* **1.** (*denial*) diniego *m* di responsabilità **2.** (*repudiating a claim*) smentita *f* **3.** LAW esonero *m* da responsabilità

disclose [dɪs·'kloʊz] *vt* **1.** (*make public*) divulgare **2.** (*uncover*) rivelare

disclosure [dɪs·'kloʊ·ʒə˞] *n* **1.** (*act of making public*) divulgazione *f* **2.** (*revelation*) rivelazione *f*

disco ['dɪs·koʊ] *n* **1.** (*music*) disco-music *f inv* **2.** (*place*) discoteca *f*

discolor [dɪs·'kʌ·lə˞] **I.** *vi* scolorirsi **II.** *vt* scolorire; **my blue shirt has ~d the curtains** la mia camicia blu ha macchiato le tende

discomfit [dɪs·'kʌmp·fɪt] *vt* sconcertare

discomfiture [dɪs·'kʌmp·fɪ·tʃə˞] *n* (*uneasiness*) turbamento *m*; (*confusion*) sconcerto *m*

discomfort [dɪs·'kʌmp·fət] *n* **1.** (*uneasiness*) fastidio *m*; **~ at sth** fastidio rispetto a qc **2.** (*inconvenience*) disagio *m*

disconcert [ˌdɪs·kən·'sɜːrt] *vt* sconcertare

disconnect [ˌdɪs·kə·'nekt] *vt* **1.** (*phone*) **I've been ~ed** è caduta la linea **2.** (*customer*) staccare **3.** (*unfasten*) staccare

disconnected *adj* **1.** (*cut off*) staccato, -a **2.** (*incoherent*) sconnesso, -a

disconsolate [dɪs·'kɑːn·tsə·lət] *adj* sconsolato, -a

discontent [ˌdɪs·kən·'tent] **I.** *n* malcontento *m* **II.** *adj* scontento, -a

discontented *adj* scontento, -a

discontentment *n* malcontento *m*

discontinue [ˌdɪs·kən·'tɪn·juː] *vt* sospendere; **that item's been ~ed** quell'articolo è fuori produzione

discontinuity [ˌdɪs·kɑːn·tə·'nuː·ə·ti] <-ies> *n* **1.** (*lack of continuity*) discontinuità *f* **2.** (*gap*) lacuna *f*

discontinuous [ˌdɪs·kən·'tɪn·ju·əs] *adj* (*without continuity*) discontinuo, -a; (*broken*) interrotto, -a

discord ['dɪs·kɔːrd] *n* **1.**(*disagreement*) discordia *f* **2.**(*clashing noise*) discordanza *f* **3.**(*lack of harmony*) dissonanza *f*

discordant [dɪs·'kɔːr·dənt] *adj* **1.**(*disagreeing*) discordante **2.**(*not in harmony*) dissonante

discotheque ['dɪs·kə·tek] *n* discoteca *f*

discount¹ ['dɪs·kaʊnt] *n* sconto *m;* **at a** ~ a prezzo ridotto

discount² [dɪs·'kaʊnt] *vt* **1.**(*reduce price*) scontare **2.**(*disregard*) non far caso a **3.**(*leave out*) scartare

discount store *n* discount *m inv*

discourage [dɪs·'kɜː·rɪdʒ] *vt* **1.**(*dishearten*) scoraggiare **2.**(*dissuade*) **to ~ sb from doing sth** dissuadere qn dal fare qc

discouragement [dɪs·'kɜː·rɪdʒ] *n* **1.**(*feeling*) scoraggiamento *m* **2.**(*deterrent*) impedimento *m*

discouraging *adj* scoraggiante

discourse¹ ['dɪs·kɔːrs] *n* discorso *m;* (*written*) trattato *m; a ~ about* [*o* **on**] **sth** un discorso su qc; (*written*) un trattato su qc

discourse² [dɪs·'kɔːrs] *vi* dissertare; **to ~ on sth** dissertare di qc

discourteous [dɪs·'kɜːr·ṭi·əs] *adj* scortese

discourtesy [dɪs·'kɜːr·ṭə·si] <-ies> *n* **1.**(*rudeness*) maleducazione *f* **2.**(*act of rudeness*) scortesia *f*

discover [dɪs·'kʌ·və] *vt* **1.**(*find out*) scoprire **2.**(*find*) trovare

discoverer *n* scopritore, -trice *m, f*

discovery [dɪs·'kʌ·və·ri] <-ies> *n* scoperta *f*

Discovery Day *n Can: anniversario della scoperta dell'America*

discredit [dɪs·'kre·dɪt] **I.** *n* **1.**(*disrepute*) discredito *m* **2.**(*disgrace*) disonore *m; she is a ~ to her school* è il disonore della scuola **3.**(*doubt*) dubbio *m* **II.** *vt* screditare

discreditable [dɪs·'kre·dɪ·ṭə·bl] *adj* disonorevole

discreet [dɪs·'kriːt] *adj* discreto, -a

discrepancy [dɪs·'kre·pənt·si] <-ies> *n* discrepanza *f*

discrete [dɪs·'kriːt] *adj* distinto, -a

discretion [dɪs·'kre·ʃən] *n* **1.**(*discreet behavior*) discrezione *f* **2.**(*good judgment*) giudizio *m;* **to leave sth to sb's ~** lasciare qc alla discrezione di qn **3.** LAW (*of court*) arbitrio *m*

discriminate [dɪs·'krɪ·mɪ·neɪt] **I.** *vi* **1.**(*see a difference*) distinguere **2.**(*treat unfairly*) **to ~ against sb** discriminare qn **II.** *vt* distinguere

discriminating *adj* **1.**(*able to discern*) perspicace **2.**(*palate, taste*) raffinato, -a

discrimination [dɪs·ˌkrɪ·mɪ·'neɪ·ʃən] *n* **1.**(*unfair treatment*) discriminazione *f* **2.**(*good judgement*) discernimento *m* **3.**(*ability to differentiate*) capacità di discriminare *m*

discriminatory [dɪs·'krɪ·mɪ·nə·tɔː·ri] *adj* discriminatorio, -a

discursive [dɪs·'kɜːr·sɪv] *adj* discorsivo, -a

discus ['dɪs·kəs] *n* SPORTS disco *m*

discuss [dɪs·'kʌs] *vt* **1.**(*exchange ideas about*) discutere **2.**(*consider*) trattare di

discussion [dɪs·'kʌ·ʃən] *n* discussione *f;* **~ group** gruppo *m* di discussione

disdain [dɪs·'deɪn] **I.** *n* disdegno *m* **II.** *vt* disdegnare; **to ~ to do sth** non degnarsi di fare qc

disdainful [dɪs·'deɪn·fəl] *adj* sprezzante

disease [dɪ·'ziːz] *n a. fig* malattia *f*

diseased *adj a. fig* malato, -a

disembark [ˌdɪs·ɪm·'baːrk] *vi* sbarcare

disembarkation [ˌdɪs·ˌɪm·baːr·'keɪ·ʃən] *n* sbarco *m*

disembodied [ˌdɪs·ɪm·'baː·did] *adj* incorporeo, -a

disenchant [ˌdɪs·ɪn·'tʃænt] *vt* disincantare

disenchanted *adj* disincantato, -a

disenfranchise [ˌdɪs·ɪn·'fræn·tʃaɪz] *vt* (*of vote*) privare del voto; (*of rights*) privare dei diritti

disengage [ˌdɪs·ɪn·'geɪdʒ] **I.** *vi* **1.**(*become detached*) staccarsi **2.**(*in fencing*) eseguire una cavazione **II.** *vt* **1.**(*uncouple*) separarsi **2.**(*detach*) scollegare; (*a clutch*) disinnestare **3.** MIL disimpegnare

disengagement [ˌdɪs·ɪn·'geɪdʒ·mənt] *n* sganciamento *m*

disentangle [ˌdɪs·ɪn·'tæŋ·gl] **I.** *vi* districarsi **II.** *vt* **1.**(*release*) sganciare; **to ~ oneself from sb/sth** sganciarsi da qn/qc **2.**(*untangle*) districare **3.** *fig* (*unravel*) sbrogliare

disfavor [ˌdɪs·'feɪ·və] **I.** *n* disapprovazione *f; to* **fall into ~** cadere in disgrazia **II.** *vt* disapprovare

disfigure [dɪs·'fɪ·gə] *vt* sfigurare

disfigurement *n* deturpazione *f*

disfranchise [dɪs·'fræn·tʃaɪz] *s.* **disenfranchise**

disgorge [dɪs·'gɔːrdʒ] *vt* riversare; *fig* vomitare

disgrace [dɪs·'greɪs] **I.** *n* **1.**(*loss of honor*) disonore *m* **2.**(*sth or sb shameful*) vergogna *f* **II.** *vt* disonorare

disgraced *adj* caduto, -a in disgrazia

disgraceful [dɪs·'greɪs·fəl] *adj* vergognoso, -a

disgruntled [dɪs·'grʌn·tld] *adj* insoddisfatto, -a; **to be ~ at sth** esser scontento di qc

disguise [dɪs·'gaɪz] **I.** *n* travestimento *m;* **to be in ~** esser travestito **II.** *vt* **1.**(*change appearance*) travestire; **to ~ oneself as sth** travestirsi da qc **2.**(*hide*) nascondere

disgust [dɪs·'gʌst] **I.** *n* **1.**(*repugnance*) disgusto *m;* **to turn away from sth in ~** allontanarsi disgustato da qc **2.**(*indignation*) indignazione *f; ~* **at sth** indignazione per qc **II.** *vt* **1.**(*sicken*) disgustare, ripugnare **2.**(*be offensive*) indignare

disgusted *adj* **1.**(*sickened*) disgustato, -a **2.**(*indignant*) indignato, -a

disgusting *adj* **1.**(*repulsive*) disgustoso, -a **2.**(*unacceptable*) vergognoso, -a

dish [dɪʃ] **I.** <-es> *n* **1.**(*for food*) piatto *m;* **to do the ~es** lavare i piatti **2.** TEL antenna *f* parabolica **3.** *inf* (*attractive person*) bocconcino *m*

II. *vi inf* (*gossip*) spettegolare
◆**dish out** *vt* 1. (*give too liberally*) distribuire liberamente 2. (*serve*) servire
◆**dish up** *vt inf* 1. (*serve*) servire 2. *inf* (*offer*) offrire
dish antenna *n* antenna *f* parabolica
disharmonious [ˌdɪs·hɑːr·ˈmoʊ·ni·əs] *adj* discordante
disharmony [dɪs·ˈhɑːr·mə·ni] *n* disaccordo *m*
dishcloth [ˈdɪʃ·klɑːθ] *n* panno, *per lavare i piatti*
dishearten [dɪs·ˈhɑːr·tən] *vt* demoralizzare
disheveled *adj*, **dishevelled** [dɪ·ˈʃe·vəld] *adj* in disordine; **with ~ hair** spettinato
dishonest [dɪ·ˈsɑː·nɪst] *adj* disonesto, -a; **to be ~ about sth** non essere onesto su qc
dishonesty [dɪ·ˈsɑː·nəs·ti] *n* 1. (*lack of honesty*) disonestà *f* 2. (*dishonest act*) frode *f*
dishonor [dɪ·ˈsɑː·nə] I. *n* disonore *m;* **to bring ~ on sb** gettare il disonore su qn II. *vt* 1. (*disgrace*) disonorare 2. (*not keep: agreement*) venir meno a 3. (*not pay: a check, bill*) non onorare
dishonorable [dɪ·ˈsɑː·nə·ə·bl] *adj* disonorevole
dishtowel *n* strofinaccio *m*
dishwasher *n* 1. (*machine*) lavastoviglie *f inv;* **to run the ~** far andare la lavastoviglie *m* 2. (*person*) lavapiatti *mf inv*
dishwater *n* acqua *f* dei piatti
disillusion [ˌdɪs·ɪ·ˈluː·ʒən] I. *vt* disilludere II. *n* disillusione *f*
disillusioned *adj* disilluso, -a; **to be ~ with sth/sb** non farsi illusioni su qc/qn
disillusionment *n* disillusione *f*
disinclination [ˌdɪs·ɪn·klɪ·ˈneɪ·ʃən] *n* resistenza *f*
disinclined [ˌdɪs·ɪn·ˈklaɪnd] *adj* riluttante; **to be ~ to do sth** esser restio a fare qc
disinfect [ˌdɪs·ɪn·ˈfekt] *vt* disinfettare
disinfectant [ˌdɪs·ɪn·ˈfek·tənt] I. *n* disinfettante *m* II. *adj* disinfettante
disinfection [ˌdɪs·ɪn·ˈfek·ʃən] *n* disinfezione *f*
disingenuous [ˌdɪs·ɪn·ˈdʒen·ju·əs] *adj* insincero, -a
disinherit [ˌdɪs·ɪn·ˈhe·rɪt] *vt* diseredare
disintegrate [dɪs·ˈɪn·tə·greɪt] I. *vi* disintegrarsi II. *vt* disintegrare
disintegration [dɪs·ˌɪn·tə·ˈgreɪ·ʃən] *n* disintegrazione *f*
disinterested [dɪs·ˈɪn·trɪs·tɪd] *adj* 1. (*impartial*) imparziale 2. (*not interested*) disinteressato, -a
disjointed [dɪs·ˈdʒɔɪn·tɪd] *adj* sconnesso, -a
disk [dɪsk] *n* COMPUT disco *m;* **hard ~** disco *m* rigido; **floppy ~** dischetto *m;* **start-up ~** disco di avvio; **high density ~** disco ad alta densità
disk drive *n* unità *f* disco *inv*
diskette [dɪs·ˈket] *n* dischetto *m*
dislike [dɪs·ˈlaɪk] I. *vt* **I really ~ her** mi sta proprio antipatica; **I ~ walking** non mi piace camminare II. *n* avversione *f;* **to take a ~ to sb/sth** prendere in antipatia qn/qc

dislocate [dɪs·ˈloʊ·keɪt] *vt* 1. MED (*shoulder, hip*) lussare 2. *fig* (*disturb the working of*) scombussolare
dislocation [ˌdɪs·loʊ·ˈkeɪ·ʃən] *n* 1. MED lussazione *f* 2. *fig* (*disturbance*) scombussolamento *m*
dislodge [dɪs·ˈlɑːdʒ] *vt* rimuovere
disloyal [dɪs·ˈlɔ·ɪəl] *adj* sleale; **to be ~ to sb/ sth** essere sleale nei confronti di qn/qc
dismal [ˈdɪz·məl] *adj* 1. (*depressing*) deprimente 2. *inf* (*awful*) terribile; (*truth*) triste
dismantle [dɪs·ˈmæn·tl] *vt* smontare; (*system*) smantellare
dismay [dɪs·ˈmeɪ] I. *n* costernazione *f;* **to sb's (great) ~** con (grande) costernazione di qn II. *vt* costernare
dismayed *adj* costernato, -a
dismember [dɪs·ˈmem·bə] *vt a. fig* smembrare
dismiss [dɪs·ˈmɪs] *vt* 1. (*allow to leave*) congedare 2. (*from job*) licenziare; **to be ~ed from one's job** essere licenziato 3. (*not consider*) non tener conto di 4. LAW archiviare
dismissal [dɪs·ˈmɪ·səl] *n* 1. (*from school*) permesso *m* di uscire; (*from job*) licenziamento *m* 2. (*disregarding*) rifiuto *m* di considerare
dismissive [dɪs·ˈmɪ·sɪv] *adj* **she was ~ of the idea** non ha preso sul serio l'idea
dismount [dɪs·ˈmaʊnt] *vi* smontare
disobedience [ˌdɪs·ə·ˈbiː·di·ənts] *n* disubbidienza *f*
disobedient [ˌdɪs·ə·ˈbiː·di·ənt] *adj* disubbidiente
disobey [ˌdɪs·ə·ˈbeɪ] I. *vi* disubbidire II. *vt* disubbidire a
disoblige [ˌdɪs·ə·ˈblaɪdʒ] *vt* 1. (*act contrary to*) non andare incontro a 2. (*offend*) offendere
disobliging *adj* poco disponibile
disorder [dɪs·ˈɔːr·də] *n* 1. (*lack of order*) disordine *m* 2. MED disturbo *m*
disordered *adj* disordinato, -a
disorderly [dɪs·ˈɔːr·dər·li] *adj* 1. (*untidy*) disordinato, -a 2. (*unruly*) turbolento, -a; **~ conduct** turbamento *m* dell'ordine pubblico
disorganized [dɪs·ˈɔːr·gə·naɪzd] *adj* disorganizzato, -a
disorient [dɪs·ˈɔː·ri·ent] *vt* disorientare; **to become** [*o* **get**] **~ed** disorientarsi
disoriented *adj* disorientato, -a
disown [dɪs·ˈoʊn] *vt* ripudiare
disparage [dɪs·ˈpe·rɪdʒ] *vt* sminuire
disparagement *n* disprezzo *m*
disparaging *adj* (*disdainful*) sprezzante
disparate [ˈdɪs·pə·rət] *adj* disparato, -a
disparity [dɪs·ˈpe·rə·t̬i] *n* disparità *f*
dispassionate [dɪs·ˈpæ·ʃə·nət] *adj* spassionato, -a
dispatch [dɪs·ˈpætʃ] I. <-es> *n* 1. (*news item*) comunicato *m;* **the latest ~ from our war correspondent** l'ultimo servizio dal nostro corrispondente di guerra 2. (*delivery*) spedizione *f* II. *vt* 1. (*to send*) inviare 2. *a. fig* (*to*

kill) ammazzare

dispel [dɪs·'pel] <-ll-> *vt* (*fears, doubts*) dissipare; (*a rumor*) smentire

dispensable [dɪs·'pen·sə·bl] *adj* superfluo, -a

dispensary [dɪs·'pen·sə·ri] *n* dispensario *m*

dispensation [ˌdɪs·pen·'seɪ·ʃən] *n* 1. (*act of distributing*) amministrazione *f* 2. (*special permission*) dispensa *f*

dispense [dɪs·'pens] *vt* 1. (*give out*) dispensare 2. MED (*medicine*) distribuire

♦**dispense with** *vt* fare a meno di

dispenser [dɪs·'pen·sɚ] *n* 1. (*device*) distributore *m* automatico 2. (*container*) dispenser *m inv*

dispersal [dɪs·'pɜːr·sl] *n* dispersione *f*

disperse [dɪs·'pɜːrs] I. *vt* disperdere II. *vi* disperdersi

dispersion [dɪs·'pɜːr·ʒən] *n* dispersione *f*

dispirited [dɪs·'pɪ·rɪ·t̬ɪd] *adj* demoralizzato, -a

displace [dɪs·'pleɪs] *vt* 1. (*force to leave*) spostare 2. (*take the place of*) rimpiazzare

displacement [dɪs·'pleɪs·mənt] *n* spostamento *m;* NAUT dislocamento *m*

display [dɪs·'pleɪ] I. *vt* 1. (*arrange for showing*) esporre; **to ~ sth in a store window** esporre qc in vetrina 2. (*express*) mostrare II. *n* 1. (*arrangement*) esposizione *f;* **firework ~** spettacolo *m* pirotecnico 2. (*demonstration*) dimostrazione *f* 3. COMPUT display *m inv;* **liquid crystal ~** schermo *m* a cristalli liquidi

display case *n* vetrinetta *f*

display window *n* vetrina *f*

displease [dɪs·'pliːz] *vt* contrariare; **to be ~d by sth** essere seccato per qc

displeasing *adj* spiacevole

displeasure [dɪs·'ple·ʒɚ] *n* disappunto *m*

disposable [dɪs·'poʊ·zə·bl] *adj* usa e getta

disposable income *n* reddito *m* disponibile

disposal [dɪs·'poʊ·zl] *n* 1. (*getting rid of*) eliminazione *f* 2. (*garbage disposal*) smaltimento *m* ▸**to be at sb's ~** essere a disposizione di qn

dispose [dɪs·'poʊz] I. *vt* 1. (*place*) disporre 2. (*incline*) predisporre II. *vi* **to ~ of sth** (*throw away*) eliminare qc; (*get rid of*) sbarazzarsi di qc; **to ~ of sb** *fig* eliminare qn

disposed *adj* **to be well ~ towards sb** esser ben disposto verso qn

disposition [ˌdɪs·pə·'zɪ·ʃən] *n* temperamento *m;* **to have a happy ~** avere un carattere allegro

dispossess [ˌdɪs·pə·'zes] *vt* espropriare

disproportionate [ˌdɪs·prə·'pɔːr·ʃə·nət] *adj* sproporzionato, -a

disprove [dɪs·'pruːv] *vt* smentire

disputable [dɪs·'pjuː·t̬ə·bl] *adj* discutibile

disputation [ˌdɪs·pju·'teɪ·ʃən] *n* disputa *f*

disputatious [ˌdɪs·pju·'teɪ·ʃəs] *adj* polemico, -a

dispute [dɪs·'pjuːt] I. *vt* 1. (*argue*) discutere 2. (*doubt*) mettere in discussione II. *vi* **to ~ (with sb) over sth** discutere (con qn) di qc

III. *n* disputa *f;* **a ~ over sth** una disputa su qc

disqualification [dɪs·ˌkwɑː·lə·fɪ·'keɪ·ʃən] *n* 1. SPORTS squalifica *f* 2. (*incapacity*) incapacità *f*

disqualify [dɪs·'kwɑː·lə·faɪ] <-ie-> *vt* squalificare; **to ~ sb from an event** squalificare qn da una gara

disquiet [dɪs·'kwa·ɪət] I. *n* inquietudine *f;* **~ over sth** inquietudine riguardo a qc II. *vt* inquietare

disquieting *adj* inquietante

disregard [ˌdɪs·rɪ·'gɑːrd] I. *vt* ignorare II. *n* indifferenza *f*

disrepair [ˌdɪs·rɪ·'per] *n* cattivo stato *m;* **to be in a state of ~** essere in cattivo stato

disreputable [dɪs·'re·pjə·t̬ə·bl] *adj* poco raccomandabile

disrepute [ˌdɪs·rɪ·'pjuːt] *n* discredito *m*

disrespect [ˌdɪs·rɪ·'spekt] *n* mancanza *f* di rispetto; **to show ~** mancare di rispetto

disrespectful [ˌdɪs·rɪ·'spekt·fəl] *adj* irrispettoso, -a

disrupt [dɪs·'rʌpt] *vt* (*disturb*) scombussolare; (*interrupt*) interrompere

disruption [dɪs·'rʌp·ʃən] *n* (*disturbance*) scombussolamento *m; fig* (*disorder*) scompiglio *m;* (*interruption*) interruzione *f*

disruptive [dɪs·'rʌp·tɪv] *adj* che crea scompiglio

dissatisfaction [dɪs·ˌsæ·t̬ɪs·'fæk·ʃən] *n* insoddisfazione *f*

dissatisfied [dɪs·'sæ·t̬ɪs·faɪd] *adj* insoddisfatto, -a

dissect [dɪ·'sekt] *vt* 1. (*cut open*) sezionare 2. *fig* (*examine*) esaminare attentamente

dissection [dɪ·'sek·ʃən] *n* dissezione *f*

dissemble [dɪ·'sem·bl] *vi, vt* dissimulare

disseminate [dɪ·'se·mɪ·neɪt] *vt* divulgare

dissemination [dɪ·ˌse·mɪ·'neɪ·ʃən] *n* divulgazione *f*

dissension [dɪ·'sent·ʃən] *n* dissenso *m;* **to sow ~** seminare zizzania

dissent [dɪ·'sent] I. *n* dissenso *m* II. *vi* 1. (*disagree with*) dissentire; **to ~ from sth** dissentire da qc 2. (*reject a doctrine*) essere dissidente

dissenter *n* dissidente *mf*

dissertation [ˌdɪ·sɚ·'teɪ·ʃən] *n* UNIV tesi *f inv*

disservice [ˌdɪs·'sɜːr·vɪs] *n* danno *m;* **to do sb a ~** rendere un cattivo servizio a qn

dissident ['dɪ·sɪ·dənt] I. *n* dissidente *mf* II. *adj* dissidente

dissimilar [dɪ·'sɪ·mɪ·lɚ] *adj* dissimile; **to be ~ to sb/sth** essere diverso, -a da qn/qc

dissimilarity [ˌdɪ·ˌsɪ·mɪ·'le·rə·t̬i] <-ies> *n* dissimilarità *f*

dissimulation [ˌdɪ·ˌsɪm·jə·'leɪ·ʃən] *n* dissimulazione *f*

dissipate ['dɪ·sɪ·peɪt] I. *vi* 1. (*disperse*) dispersersi 2. *fig* (*indulge in pleasures*) condurre una vita dissoluta II. *vt* dissipare

dissipated *adj* dissoluto, -a

dissipation [ˌdɪ·sɪ·'peɪ·ʃən] *n* 1. (*dispersion*) dispersione *f* 2. (*frivolous waste*) dissipazione *f* **3.** (*indulgence in pleasure*) dissolutezza *f*

dissociate [dɪˈsoʊ·ʃi·eɪt] *vt a.* CHIM dissociare; **to ~ oneself from sb/sth** dissociarsi da qn/qc

dissociation [dɪˌsoʊ·ʃiˈeɪ·ʃən] *n* dissociazione *f*

dissolute [ˈdɪ·sə·luːt] *adj liter* dissoluto, -a

dissolution [ˌdɪ·səˈluː·ʃən] *n* scioglimento *m*

dissolve [dɪˈzɑːlv] I. *vi* **1.** (*in a liquid*) dissolversi **2.** *fig* (*collapse*) **to ~ into tears** sciogliersi in lacrime; **to ~ into laughter** scompisciarsi dal ridere **3.** *fig* (*disappear*) svanire II. *vt* sciogliere; **to ~ a business** sciogliere un'impresa

dissonance [ˈdɪ·sə·nənts] *n* dissonanza *f*

dissonant [ˈdɪ·sə·nənt] *adj* dissonante; *fig* discordante

dissuade [dɪˈsweɪd] *vt* dissuadere

distance [ˈdɪs·tənts] I. *n* **1.** (*space*) distanza *f*; **his house is within walking ~** casa sua è a due passi da qui; **to keep one's ~** tenersi a distanza **2.** (*space far away*) lontananza *f*; **in the ~** in lontananza II. *vt* **to ~ oneself from sb/sth** prendere le distanze da qn/qc

distant [ˈdɪs·tənt] *adj* **1.** (*far away*) distante **2.** (*relative, cousin*) lontano, -a

distantly *adv* **1.** (*in the distance*) lontano **2.** *fig* (*in unfriendly manner*) con distacco

distaste [dɪsˈteɪst] *n* antipatia *f*

distasteful [dɪsˈteɪst·fəl] *adj* sgradevole

distemper [dɪsˈtem·pəˈ] *n* (*animal disease*) cimurro *m*

distend [dɪsˈtend] *vi* dilatarsi

distension [dɪsˈtent·ʃən] *n* dilatazione *f*

distill [dɪsˈtɪl] *vt* distillare

distillation [ˌdɪs·təˈleɪ·ʃən] *n* distillazione *f*

distiller [dɪsˈtɪ·ləˈ] *n* **1.** (*company*) distilleria *f* **2.** (*person*) distillatore, -trice *m, f*

distillery [dɪsˈtɪ·lə·ri] *n* distilleria *f*

distinct [dɪsˈtɪŋkt] *adj* **1.** (*separate*) distinto, -a **2.** (*marked*) definito, -a **3.** (*noticeable*) netto, -a

distinction [dɪsˈtɪŋk·ʃən] *n* **1.** (*difference*) distinzione *f* **2.** (*eminence*) eminenza *f*; **of great ~** di grande rilievo **3.** (*honors*) riconoscimento *m*

distinctive [dɪsˈtɪŋk·tɪv] *adj* caratteristico, -a

distinguish [dɪsˈtɪŋ·gwɪʃ] I. *vi* distinguere II. *vt* **1.** (*tell apart*) distinguere **2.** (*be excellent in*) **to ~ oneself in sth** distinguersi in qc

distinguishable *adj* distinguibile

distinguished *adj* **1.** (*celebrated*) eminente **2.** (*stylish*) distinto, -a

distort [dɪsˈtɔːrt] *vt* distorcere; (*facts*) travisare; (*the truth*) falsare

distortion [dɪsˈtɔːr·ʃən] *n* (*of the truth, facts*) distorsione *f*; (*of a face*) alterazione *f*

distract [dɪsˈtrækt] *vt* distrarre

distracted *adj* distratto, -a

distraction [dɪsˈtræk·ʃən] *n* **1.** (*disturbance*) distrazione *f* **2.** (*confused agitation*) sconvolgimento *m* **3.** (*pastime*) diversivo *m*

distraught [dɪsˈtrɔːt] *adj* sconvolto, -a

distress [dɪsˈtres] I. *n* **1.** (*emotional*) angoscia *f* **2.** (*extreme pain*) sofferenza *f* **3.** (*state of danger*) pericolo *m* II. *vt* angosciare

distressed *adj* **1.** (*unhappy*) angosciato, -a **2.** (*in difficulties*) in difficoltà **3.** FASHION scolorito, -a

distressful *adj*, **distressing** *adj* **1.** (*causing worry*) angosciante **2.** (*painful*) doloroso, -a

distribute [dɪsˈtrɪ·bjuːt] *vt* distribuire; **to be evenly ~d** essere distribuito uniformemente

distribution [ˌdɪs·trɪˈbjuː·ʃən] *n* distribuzione *f*

distribution area *n* ECON area *f* di distribuzione

distribution channel *n* ECON canale *m* di distribuzione

distribution rights *npl* diritti *m pl* di distribuzione

distributive [dɪsˈtrɪb·jə·tɪv] *adj* distributivo, -a

distributor [dɪsˈtrɪb·jə·təˈ] *n* **1.** (*person*) distributore, -trice *m, f* **2.** AUTO spinterogeno *m*

district [ˈdɪs·trɪkt] *n* **1.** (*defined area*) distretto *m* **2.** (*region*) regione *f*

i Il **District of Columbia** (o D.C.) non è uno stato federale, ma un distretto autonomo nel quale si trova "Washington D.C.", la capitale federale degli Stati Uniti. È stato creato nel 1791 dal primo presidente americano, George Washington, che desiderava fondare la capitale americana in un territorio neutro, non appartenente ad alcuno stato. Il progetto iniziale della città è opera dell'architetto e ingegnere franco-americano Pierre Charles L'Enfant. La Casa Bianca, la Corte Suprema e il Campidoglio, sede del Congresso, si trovano a "Washington D.C."

district attorney *n* procuratore *m* distrettuale

district court *n* corte *f* distrettuale federale

distrust [dɪsˈtrʌst] I. *vt* diffidare di II. *n* diffidenza *f*

distrustful [dɪsˈtrʌst·fəl] *adj* diffidente

disturb [dɪsˈtɜːrb] *vt* **1.** (*interrupt*) disturbare **2.** (*worry*) turbare **3.** (*move around*) scompigliare

disturbance [dɪsˈtɜːr·bənts] *n* **1.** (*interruption*) disturbo *m* **2.** (*public incident*) disordini *mpl*

disturbed *adj* **1.** (*mentally ill*) affetto, -a da turbe mentali **2.** (*restless*) inquieto, -a **3.** (*moved around*) in disordine

disturbing *adj* **1.** (*annoying*) inquietante **2.** (*worrying*) allarmante

disunite [ˌdɪs·juːˈnaɪt] *vt* disunire

disunity [dɪsˈjuː·nə·ti] *n* disunione *f*

disuse [dɪsˈjuːs] *n* disuso *m*

disused [dɪsˈjuːzd] *adj* in disuso

ditch [dɪtʃ] I. <-es> *n* **1.** (*trench*) fosso *m*; (*by* *a road*) cunetta *f;* **irrigation** ~ canale *m* d'irrigazione **2.** (*for defense*) fossato *m* **II.** *vt* **1.** *sl* (*discard*) disfarsi di; (*car*) abbandonare; (*idea*) scartare **2.** *sl* (*escape from*) liberarsi di **3.** *sl* (*end a relationship*) mollare **4.** (*land in water*) **to ~ a plane** fare un ammaraggio di fortuna **III.** *vi* scavare fossi

dither ['dɪ·ðə] **I.** *n* **to be in a ~** esser nel pallone **II.** *vi inf* **1.** (*be indecisive*) tentennare **2.** (*behave nervously*) essere in agitazione

ditsy ['dɪt·si] *adj sl* svampito, -a

ditto ['dɪ·ţou] **I.** *n* (*mark indicating repetition*) virgolette *fpl* **II.** *adv* (*so do I*) idem; (*same for me*) lo stesso

ditty ['dɪ·ţi] <-ies> *n* canzonetta *f*

diurnal [daɪ·'ɜːr·nəl] *adj* diurno, -a

divan [dɪ·'vɑːn] *n* divano *m, privo di spalliera o braccioli*

dive [daɪv] **I.** *n* **1.** (*in swimming*) tuffo *m* **2.** (*submerge*) immersione *f* **3.** *a. fig* (*sudden decline*) caduta *f* repentina; **to take a ~** precipitare **4.** (*leap*) **to make a ~ for sth** lanciarsi verso qc **5.** *sl* (*undesirable establishment*) bettola *f* **II.** *vi* <dived *o* dove, dived *o* dove> **1.** (*in swimming*) tuffarsi **2.** (*submerge*) immergersi; **to ~ under sth** passare sotto qc, *a nuoto;* **to ~ to a depth of ...** immergersi a una profondità di ... **3.** (*go sharply downwards*) scendere in picchiata **4.** (*move towards*) precipitarsi; **to ~ for cover** buttarsi al riparo

diver ['daɪ·və] *n* **1.** (*sb who dives*) tuffatore, -trice *m, f* **2.** (*sb working under water*) sommozzatore, -trice *m, f*

diverge [dɪ·'vɜːrdʒ] *vi* divergere; **to ~ from sth** divergere da qc

divergence [dɪ·'vɜːr·dʒəns] *n* divergenza *f*

divergent [dɪ·'vɜːr·dʒənt] *adj* divergente

diverse [dɪ·'vɜːrs] *adj* **1.** (*varied*) vario, -a **2.** (*not alike*) diverso, -a

diversification [dɪ·ˌvɜːr·sɪ·fɪ·'keɪ·ʃən] *n* diversificazione *f*

diversify [dɪ·'vɜːr·sɪ·faɪ] <-ie-> **I.** *vi* diversificarsi **II.** *vt* diversificare

diversion [dɪ·'vɜːr·ʃən] *n* **1.** (*changing of direction*) deviazione *f* **2.** (*distraction*) distrazione *f* **3.** (*activity*) diversivo *m*

diversity [dɪ·'vɜːr·sə·ţi] *n* diversità *f*

divert [dɪ·'vɜːrt] *vt* **1.** (*change direction*) deviare **2.** (*distract*) distrarre **3.** (*amuse*) divertire

diverting [dɪ·'vɜːr·ţɪŋ] *adj* divertente

divest [dɪ·'vest] **I.** *vt* spogliare **II.** *vi* **1.** ECON (*sell off*) vendere **2.** (*renounce*) **to ~ from sth** rinunciare a qc

◆**divest of** *vt fig* **to divest oneself of sth** liberarsi di qc

divide [dɪ·'vaɪd] **I.** *n* **1.** (*separating line*) divisione *f* **2.** (*watershed*) spartiacque *m inv* **II.** *vt* **1.** *a.* MATH dividere; **to ~ sth into three groups** dividere qc in tre gruppi; **the party is ~d** *fig* il partito è diviso **2.** (*allot*) ripartire **III.** *vi* (*split*) dividersi; **their paths ~d** le loro strade si divisero ▶ **~ and** conquer divide et

impera
◆**divide off** *vt always sep* separare
◆**divide out**, **divide up** *vt always sep* distribuire

divided *adj* **1.** (*not in agreement*) diviso, -a **2.** (*separated*) separato, -a **3.** (*undecided*) **to be ~ between two options** essere indeciso, -a tra due possibilità

dividend ['dɪ·vɪ·dend] *n* MATH, FIN dividendo *m*

dividing line *n* linea *f* di demarcazione

divination [ˌdɪ·vɪ·'neɪ·ʃən] *n* divinazione *f*

divine [dɪ·'vaɪn] **I.** *adj* **1.** (*of or from God*) divino, -a **2.** (*wonderful*) sublime **II.** *vt* (*guess correctly*) indovinare; (*the future*) predire **III.** *vi* far pronostici

diviner [dɪ·'vaɪ·nə] *n* indovino, -a *m, f;* (*of future events*) veggente *mf*

diving *n* **1.** (*jumping*) tuffi *mpl* **2.** (*swimming*) immersione *f*

diving bell *n* campana *f* subacquea

diving board *n* trampolino *m*

diving suit *n* muta *f*

divining rod *n* bacchetta *f* da rabdomante

divinity [dɪ·'vɪ·nə·ţi] <-ies> *n* **1.** (*state*) divinità *f* **2.** **the D~** (*God*) la Divinità **3.** (*study*) teologia *f*

divisible [dɪ·'vɪ·zə·bl] *adj* divisibile

division [dɪ·'vɪ·ʒən] *n* **1.** *a.* MIL, MATH, SPORTS divisione *f* **2.** (*splitting up*) ripartizione *f* **3.** (*disagreement*) disaccordo *m* **4.** (*separating point*) separazione *f* **5.** COM (*branch of company*) divisione *f*

divisive [dɪ·'vaɪ·sɪv] *adj* che crea divisioni

divorce [dɪ·'vɔːrs] **I.** *n* divorzio *m; fig* separazione *f* **II.** *vt* **1.** (*break marriage*) **to get ~d** (*from sb*) divorziare (da qn); **he ~d her for infidelity** ha ottenuto il divorzio da lei per adulterio **2.** *fig* (*separate*) separare **III.** *vi* divorziare

divorced *adj* divorziato, -a

divorcé [dɪ·ˌvɔːr·'seɪ] *n* divorziato *m*

divorcée [dɪ·ˌvɔːr·'seɪ] *n* divorziata *f*

divulge [dɪ·'vʌldʒ] *vt* divulgare

DIY [ˌdiː·aɪ·'waɪ] *abbr of* **do-it-yourself** fai da te *m inv*

dizziness *n* capogiro *m;* (*because of height*) vertigini *fpl*

dizzy ['dɪ·zi] <-ier, -iest> *adj* **1.** (*having vertigo*) che ha le vertigini **2.** (*causing vertigo*) vertiginoso, -a **3.** *inf* (*silly*) tonto, -a

DJ ['diː·dʒeɪ] *n abbr of* **disc jockey** DJ *m inv*

Djibouti [dʒɪ·'buː·ti] *n* Gibuti *m*

Djiboutian [dʒɪ·'buː·tiən] **I.** *adj* del Gibuti **II.** *n* abitante *mf* del Gibuti

DMV [ˌdiː·em·'viː] *n abbr of* **Department of Motor Vehicles** Ufficio *m* Motorizzazione Civile

DNA [ˌdiː·en·'eɪ] *n abbr of* **deoxyribonucleic acid** DNA *m*

do [duː] **I.** *n* **1.** **the ~s and don'ts** ciò che si deve e ciò che non si deve fare **2.** *inf* (*party*) festa *f* **3.** *inf* (*hairdo*) acconciatura *f* **4.** *sl* (*excrement*) cacca *f; dog* ~ cacca di cane; (*e*)

II. <does, did, done> *aux* **1.** (*in questions*) **~ you own a dog?** hai un cane? **2.** (*in negatives*) **Frida ~esn't like olives** a Frida non piacciono le olive **3.** (*in imperatives*) **~ your homework!** fa i compiti!; **~ come in!** entrate, prego! **4.** (*for emphasis*) **~ go to the party!** andateci alla festa!; **he ~es get on my nerves** mi dà proprio ai nervi; **he did ~ it** sì che l'ha fatto **5.** (*replacing a repeated verb*) **so ~ I** anch'io; **neither ~ I** nemmeno io; **she speaks more fluently than he ~es** parla con maggior scioltezza di lui **6.** (*requesting affirmation*) non è vero?; **you ~n't want to answer, ~ you?** non vuoi rispondere, vero? III. <does, did, done> *vt* **1.** (*carry out*) fare; **to ~ nothing but ...** non fare altro che ...; **to ~ one's best** fare del proprio meglio; **to ~ justice** rendere giustizia; **to ~ everything possible** fare tutto il possibile; **what on earth are you ~ing** (there)? che cavolo stai facendo (lì)?; **what is to be ~ne about that?** cosa si può fare in proposito?; **~n't just stand there, ~ something!** non startene lì impalato, fa qualcosa! **2.** (*undertake*) realizzare **3.** (*help*) **to ~ something for sb/sth** far qualcosa per qn/qc **4.** (*act*) agire; **to ~ as others ~** fare come fanno gli altri **5.** (*deal with*) incaricarsi di; **if you ~ the washing up, I'll ~ the drying** se tu lavi i piatti, io li asciugo **6.** (*learn: math, English*) studiare **7.** (*figure out: puzzle, math problem*) risolvere **8.** (*finish*) terminare **9.** (*put in order*) ordinare; (*clean*) pulire; **to ~ one's nails** (*with nail polish*) mettere lo smalto alle unghie; (*cut*) tagliarsi le unghie; **to do one's hair/face** pettinarsi/lavarsi il viso **10.** (*make neat: the bathroom, one's room*) pulire **11.** (*tour: Europe, California*) visitare **12.** (*go at a speed of*) **to ~ Milan to Rome in five hours** fare Milano-Roma in cinque ore **13.** (*be satisfactory*) **"I only have beer — will that ~ you?"** "ho solo birra — ti va bene?" **14.** (*sell*) vendere; **the shop does fancy kitchen equipment** il negozio vende utensili da cucina un po' particolari; (*offer*) servire **15.** (*cook*) cucinare; **to ~ sth for sb** preparare qc per qn **16.** (*cause*) **to ~ sb credit** fare onore a qn; **to ~ sb a good turn** fare un favore a qn; **to ~ sb good** far bene a qn **17.** (*perform: a play*) rappresentare; (*a song*) eseguire; (*imitate: an accent, bird call*) imitare **18.** *inf* (*serve prison sentence: time, life, 10 years*) scontare **19.** *inf* (*burglarize*) scassinare **20.** *inf* (*swindle*) truffare **21.** *inf* (*drugs*) farsi; (*cocaine, heroin*) farsi di **22.** *sl* (*have sex*) **to ~ it** farlo ▶ **just ~ it!** fallo e basta!; **what's ~ne is ~ne** quel che è fatto è fatto; **that ~es it** adesso basta IV. <does, did, done> *vi* **1.** (*behave, act*) fare **2.** (*manage*) andare; **mother and baby are ~ing well** sia la mamma che il bambino stanno bene; **many stores are ~ing well** molti negozi stanno andando bene; **how are you ~ing?** come va?; **to ~ well for oneself** trattarsi bene **3.** (*finish*

with) **to be ~ne with sb/sth** aver chiuso con qn/qc **4.** (*be satisfactory*) **this behavior just won't ~!** questo comportamento non è tollerabile! **5.** (*function as*) **it'll ~ for a spoon** può fare da cucchiaio **6.** *inf* (*going on*) **to be ~ing** succedere **7.** (*treat*) **to ~ badly/well by sb** trattar bene/male qn ▶ **that will never ~** non se ne parla nemmeno; **~ unto others as you would have them ~ unto you** *prov* non fare agli altri quel che non vorresti venisse fatto a te; **that will ~!** adesso basta!

♦**do away with** *vi* **1.** (*dispose of*) eliminare **2.** *inf* (*kill*) **to ~ sb** far fuori qn

♦**do in** *vt always sep* **1.** (*murder*) **to do sb in** far fuori qn **2.** (*ruin*) rovinare **3.** *fig* (*make exhausted*) sfinire

♦**do out** *vt always sep* **1.** (*adorn*) decorare **2.** (*cheat*) **to do sb out of sth** derubare qn di qc

♦**do over** *vt always sep* **1.** *inf* (*redo*) **to do sth over again** rifare qc **2.** *inf* (*redecorate*) ridecorare **3.** *inf* (*beat up*) **to do sb over** pestare qn

♦**do up** *vt* **1.** (*fasten: button*) abbottonare; (*tie*) fare il nodo a; (*shoes*) allacciare; (*zipper*) tirar su **2.** (*make attractive: one's hair*) raccogliere; **to do oneself up** farsi bello **3.** (*wrap*) avvolgere

♦**do with** *vi* **1.** (*be related to*) **to have to do with sth** (*book*) trattare di qc; (*person*) avere a che fare [*o* vedere] con qn; **to not have anything to do with sb** non aver niente a che vedere con qn **2.** *inf* (*need*) **I could do with a drink** mi ci vorrebbe un bicchierino

♦**do without** *vi* fare a meno di

DOA [ˌdiːˌoʊˈeɪ] *abbr of* **dead on arrival** giunto, -a cadavere

doable [ˈduːəbl] *n inf* fattibile

docile [ˈdɑːsəl] *adj* docile

docility [dɑːˈsɪləˌti] *n* docilità *f*

dock[1] [dɑːk] I. *n* **1.** (*wharf*) banchina *f*; (*pier*) molo *m* **2.** (*enclosed part of port*) bacino *m* II. *vi* **1.** NAUT attraccare **2.** (*spacecraft*) agganciarsi III. *vt* NAUT attraccare

dock[2] [dɑːk] *n* **to be in the ~** essere sul banco degli imputati; *fig* finire nei guai

dock[3] [dɑːk] *vt* **1.** (*take away: sb's pay, salary*) decurtare **2.** (*cut off: tail*) mozzare

dock[4] [dɑːk] *n* BOT romice *f*

docker [ˈdɑːkɚ] *n inf* portuale *m*

docket [ˈdɑːkɪt] I. *n* **1.** LAW (*list of cases*) ruolo *m* delle cause **2.** (*business agenda*) agenda *f* **3.** (*documentation*) distinta *f* II. *vt* LAW registrare

docking [ˈdɑːkɪŋ] *n* **1.** NAUT attracco *m* **2.** (*joining of spacecraft*) aggancio *m* **3.** (*cutting*) riduzione *f*; (*of wages*) decurtazione *f*

dockyard [ˈdɑːkjɑːrd] *n* cantiere *m* navale

doctor [ˈdɑːktɚ] I. *n* **1.** (*physician*) dottore, -essa *m, f*; **to be at the ~'s** essere dal medico; **to go to the ~'s** andare dal medico; **this hot bath is just what the ~ ordered** *fig* questo bagno caldo è proprio quello che ci voleva

2. UNIV dottore, -essa *m, f* **II.** *vt* **1.** (*fix temporarily*) **to ~ sth (up)** riparare qc **2.** (*change*) modificare; (*illegally*) falsare **3.** (*improve taste*) correggere

doctorate ['dɑ:k·tə·rət] *n* dottorato *m*

> ℹ️ Il **doctorate** o *doctor's degree* in una disciplina è il titolo accademico più alto che viene rilasciato dalle università a chi presenta una tesi di ricerca. I **doctorates** più diffusi sono il *Ph.D.* e il *D.Phil. (Doctor of Philosophy)* per una tesi di terzo ciclo; ne esistono altri, quali il *D.Mus. (Doctor of Music)*, l'*MD (Doctor of Medicine)*, l'*LLD (Doctor of Laws)*. Il *D.Litt. (Doctor of Letters)*, ad esempio, o il *D.Sc. (Doctor of Science)* possono essere conferiti ad honorem da un'università a una personalità per le sue pubblicazioni di articoli o altri lavori degni di nota.

doctrinaire [ˌdɑ:k·trə·'ner] *adj* dottrinario, -a
doctrine ['dɑ:k·trɪn] *n* dottrina *f*; **military ~** dottrina *f* militare
docudrama *n* film *m* verità *inv*
document ['dɑ:k·jə·mənt] **I.** *n* documento *m* **II.** *vt* documentare
documentary [ˌdɑ:k·jə·'men·tə·i] **I.** <-ies> *n* documentario *m* **II.** *adj* documentario, -a
documentation [ˌdɑ:k·jə·men·'teɪ·ʃən] *n* documentazione *f*
DOD *n abbr of* **Department of Defense** Ministero *m* della Difesa
dodge [dɑ:dʒ] **I.** *vt* schivare; *fig* (*a question, the press*) eludere; **to ~ doing sth** evitare di fare qc **II.** *vi* SPORTS schivare **III.** *n inf* trucco *m*
dodger ['dɑ:·dʒɚ] *n* imbroglione, -a *m, f*; **a tax ~** un evasore fiscale
doe [doʊ] *n* **1.** (*female deer*) cerva *f* **2.** (*female rabbit*) coniglia *f*
DOE *n abbr of* **Department of Energy** Ministero *m* delle Risorse Energetiche
doer ['du:·ɚ] *n* **1.** (*person acting*) persona *f* che agisce **2.** (*active person*) persona *f* dinamica
does [dʌz] *vt, vi, aux 3. pers sing of* **do**
doeskin ['doʊ·skɪn] *n* pelle *f* di daino
doesn't ['dʌ·znt] = **does not** *s.* **do**
dog [dɔ:g] **I.** *n* **1.** cane, cagna *m, f*; **hunting ~** cane da caccia; **my pet ~** il mio cagnolino **2.** *inf* (*unattractive person*) cesso *m*; (*mean person*); **the (dirty) ~!** che bastardo!; (*failure: movie, product*) fallimento *m* ►**he doesn't have a ~'s** <u>chance</u> *inf* non ha la benché minima possibilità; **every ~ has its** <u>day</u> *prov* ognuno ha il suo momento di gloria; **to lead a ~'s** <u>life</u> fare una vita da cani; **to be a ~ in the** <u>manger</u> essere una persona che, pur non volendo una cosa, non permette ad altri di averla; **to give a ~ a bad** <u>name</u> *prov* attribuire una cattiva reputazione (a qn); **it's a ~** <u>eat</u> **~ world** è una giungla; **to** <u>go</u> **to the ~s** andare in

malora **II.** <-gg-> *vt a. fig* (*pursue*) perseguitare
dog biscuit *n* biscotto *m* per cani
dog collar *n* collare *m* per cani; *iron* colletto *m* da prete
dog days *n pl* canicola *f*
dog-eared *adj* (*book*) **to be ~** avere le orecchie
dogged ['dɔ:·gɪd] *adj* ostinato, -a
doggerel ['dɔ:·gə·əl] *n* poesia *f* scadente
doggy bag *n inf*: pacchetto *con* gli avanzi di un pasto consumato al ristorante
doghouse *n* canile *m*; **to be in the ~** essere caduto in disgrazia
dogma ['dɔ:g·mə] *n* dogma *m*
dogmatic [dɔ:g·'mæ·tɪk] *adj* dogmatico, -a
dogmatism ['dɔ:g·mə·tɪ·zəm] *n* dogmatismo *m*
do-gooder *n inf* benefattore, -trice *m, f, non richiesto*
dog-tired *adj inf* sfinito, -a
doing ['du:·ɪŋ] *n* **1.** *pl* (*activities*) imprese *fpl* **2.** (*action*) **to be (of) sb's ~** essere opera di qn; **to take some ~** non essere facile
do-it-yourself *n* fai da te *m inv*
doldrums ['doʊl·drəmz] *npl* GEO zona *f* delle calme equatoriali; **to be in the ~** (*person*) esser depresso; (*business*) esser in stallo
dole out *vt* (*money, food*) distribuire
doleful ['doʊl·fəl] *adj* (*person*) triste; (*expression, cry*) addolorato, -a
doll [dɑ:l] *n* **1.** (*toy*) bambola *f* **2.** *inf* tesoro *m* **3.** *inf* (*term of address*) bellezza *f*
♦**doll up** *vt* agghindare; **to ~ oneself up** mettersi in ghingheri
dollar ['dɑ:·lə] *n* dollaro *m* ►**to feel like a** <u>million</u> **~s** sentirsi una meraviglia; **to look like a** <u>million</u> **~s** avere un aspetto fantastico
dollhouse *n* casa *f* delle bambole
dollop ['dɑ:·ləp] *n* (*amount*) piccola quantità *f*; (*spoonful*) cucchiaiata *f*
dolly ['dɑ:·li] <-ies> *n* **1.** *childspeak* (*doll*) bambola *f* **2.** (*for transporting*) carrello *m*
dolphin ['dɑ:l·fɪn] *n* delfino *m*
dolt [doʊlt] *n* imbecille *mf*
domain [doʊ·'meɪn] *n* **1.** POL, COMPUT dominio *m*; (*lands*) proprietà *f* **2.** (*sphere of activity*) ambito *m*; **to be in the public ~** essere di dominio pubblico; **that is outside my ~** la cosa esula dalla mia sfera
dome [doʊm] *n* **1.** (*rounded roof*) cupola *f* **2.** (*rounded ceiling*) volta *f* **3.** *inf* (*bald head*) testa *f* calva
domestic [də·'mes·tɪk] **I.** *adj* **1.** (*of the house*) domestico, -a **2.** (*home-loving*) casalingo, -a **3.** *a.* ECON, FIN, POL (*produce, flight*) nazionale; (*market, trade, policy*) interno, -a; **~ news** notizie dall'interno; **gross ~ product** prodotto *m* interno lordo **II.** *n* domestico, -a *m, f*
domestic appliance *n* elettrodomestico *m*
domesticate [də·'mes·tɪ·keɪt] *vt* (*animal*) addomesticare; (*plant*) acclimatare; (*person*); **he is a very ~d man** è un uomo molto casal-

ingo
domesticated *adj* addomesticato, -a
domesticity [ˌdoʊ·mes·'tɪ·sə·ti] *n* vita *f* familiare
domestic science *n* economia *f* domestica
domicile ['dɑː·mə·saɪl] I. *n* domicilio *m* II. *vt* fissare la residenza di; **to be ~d in** risiedere in
dominance ['dɑː·mə·nənts] *n* 1. (*rule*) predominio *m* 2. MIL supremazia *f*
dominant ['dɑː·mə·nənt] *adj* dominante
dominate ['dɑː·mə·neɪt] *vi, vt* dominare
domination [ˌdɑː·mə·'neɪ·ʃən] *n* dominazione *f*
domineer [ˌdɑː·mə·'nɪr] *vi* dominare; **to ~ over sb** tiranneggiare qn
domineering *adj* dominante; **a ~ management style** uno stile manageriale autoritario
Dominica [ˌdɑː·mɪ·'niː·kə] *n* Dominica *f*
Dominican [doʊ·'mɪr·nɪ·kən] I. *adj* dominicano, -a II. *n* 1. (*nationality*) dominicano, -a *m, f* 2. REL domenicano, -a *m, f*
Dominican Republic *n* Repubblica *f* Dominicana
dominion [də·'mɪn·jən] *n* dominio *m;* **to have ~ over sb/sth** avere potere su qn/qc
domino ['dɑː·mə·noʊ] <-es> *n* 1. *pl* (*game*) domino *m;* **to play ~es** giocare a domino 2. (*piece*) tessera *f* del domino
domino effect *n* effetto *m* domino
don [dɑːn] *vt* (*clothing*) indossare
donate ['doʊ·neɪt] *vt* donare
donation [doʊ·'neɪ·ʃən] *n* 1. (*contribution*) donazione *f* 2. (*act*) donazione *f*
done [dʌn] *pp of* **do**
donkey ['dɑː·ŋ·ki] *n a. fig* asino *m*
donkey work *n inf* lavoro *m* pesante
donor ['doʊ·nɚ] *n* donatore, -trice *m, f*
don't [doʊnt] = **do not** *s.* **do**
donut ['doʊ·nʌt] *n* bombolone *m*
doodle ['duː·dl] I. *vi* scarabocchiare II. *n* scarabocchio *m*
doom [duːm] I. *n* 1. (*destiny*) destino *m* 2. (*death*) morte *f* II. *vt* condannare
doomed *adj* condannato, -a; **to be ~ to failure** esser destinato a fallire; **~ to die** destinato a morire
doomsday ['duːmz·deɪ] *n* giorno *m* del giudizio universale
door [dɔːr] *n* 1. porta *f;* **front/back ~** porta principale/di servizio; **revolving/sliding ~** porta girevole/scorrevole; **to knock at** [*o* **on**] **the ~** bussare alla porta; **there's someone at the ~** bussano alla porta; **to answer the ~** aprire la porta; **to see sb to the ~** accompagnare qn alla porta; **to live next ~** (**to sb**) abitare vicino (a qn); **to show sb the ~** mettere qn alla porta; **out of ~s** all'aria aperta; **behind closed ~s** a porte chiuse; **to close the ~ on sb** chiudere le porte a qn; **to leave the ~ open to sb** lasciare la porta aperta a qn 2. (*doorway*) entrata *f* ▶ **to slam the ~ in sb's face** sbattere la porta in faccia a qn; **to never darken sb's ~s again** *liter* non osare mettere

piede in casa di qn; **to lay sth at sb's ~** dar la colpa di qc a qn
doorbell *n* campanello *m*
doorjamb *n* stipite *m* della porta
doorkeeper *n s.* **doorman**
doorknob *n* maniglia *f* della porta
doorman <-men> *n* portiere *m*
doormat *n* zerbino *m*
doornail *n inf* **dead as a ~** morto stecchito
doorstep *n* gradino *m, della porta d'ingresso* ▶ **to be right on sb's ~** essere a due passi da casa di qn
door-to-door I. *adj* porta a porta *inv;* **~ selling** vendita *f* a domicilio II. *adv* porta a porta
doorway *n* entrata *f*
dope [doʊp] I. *n inf* 1. (*drugs*) droga *f* illegale; (*marijuana*) erba *f* 2. SPORTS doping *m inv;* **~ test** controllo *m* antidoping 3. (*stupid person*) idiota *mf* 4. (*information*) informazioni *fpl;* **to give sb the ~ on** [*o* **about**] **sth** fare una soffiata a qn su qc II. *vt* (*drug*) drogare; SPORTS dopare
dope dealer *n,* **dope pusher** *n inf* spacciatore, -trice *m, f*
dopey *adj,* **dopy** ['doʊ·pi] *adj* <-ier, -iest> *inf* 1. (*drowsy*) intontito, -a 2. (*stupid*) tonto, -a
dormant ['dɔːr·mənt] *adj* (*volcano*) inattivo, -a; (*animal*) in letargo; (*law*) in quiescenza; (*idea*) latente; **to lie ~** rimanere latente
dormer *n* lucernario *m*
dormitory ['dɔːr·mə·tɔː·ri] <-ies> *n* 1. (*room*) dormitorio *m;* **~ town** città *f* dormitorio 2. UNIV pensionato *m* per studenti
dormouse ['dɔːr·maʊs] <-mice> *n* ghiro *m*
dorsal ['dɔːr·səl] *adj* dorsale
DOS [dɑːs] *n abbr of* **disk operating system** DOS *m inv*
dosage ['doʊ·sɪdʒ] *n* dose *f*
dose [doʊs] I. *n a. fig* dose *f;* **a ~ of bad news** una brutta notizia; **a nasty ~ of the flu** una brutta influenza II. *vt* somministrare una dose a; **to ~ oneself with** imbottirsi di
dossier ['dɑː·s·ieɪ] *n* dossier *m inv;* **to keep a ~ on sb/sth** tenere un dossier su qn/qc
dot [dɑːt] I. *n* 1. puntino *m;* **on the ~** in punto; **she arrived at half past three on the ~** arrivò alle tre e mezza in punto 2. *pl* TYPO puntini *m pl* di sospensione; **120 ~s per inch** 120 punti per pollice II. <-tt-> *vt* 1. (*mark with a dot*) punteggiare 2. (*put a dot on*) mettere il puntino a 3. (*scatter*) sparpagliare ▶ **to ~ one's i's and cross one's t's** mettere i puntini sulle 'i'
dote on [ˌdoʊt̬·'ɑːn] *vt* adorare
doting *adj* **a ~ father** un padre che stravede per i figli
dot-matrix printer *n* stampante *f* ad aghi
dotty ['dɑː·t̬i] *adj* <-ier, -iest> (*person*) suonato, -a; (*idea*) balzano, -a
double ['dʌ·bl] I. *adj* 1. (*twice as much/many*) doppio, -a; **a ~ door** una porta a due ante; **a ~ whiskey** un doppio whisky; **it is ~ that** è due volte quello; **to have a ~ meaning** avere un

doppio senso; **to lead a ~ life** condurre una doppia vita **2.** (*composed of two*) **in ~ digits** a due cifre; **the number of deaths has now reached double digits** i morti ormai si contano a decine; **a ~ 's' esse doppia 3.** (*for two*) **~ mattress** materasso *m* matrimoniale; **~ room** camera *f* doppia **II.** *adv* doppio; **to see ~** vedere doppio; **to fold sth ~** piegare qc a metà; **he's ~ your age** ha il doppio dei tuoi anni; **to be bent ~** essere piegato in due **III.** *vt* (*increase*) raddoppiare; **we have ~d our profits** abbiamo raddoppiato i profitti **IV.** *vi* raddoppiare; **to ~ for sb** CINE fare la controfigura di; THEAT fare anche la parte di; **to ~ as sth** fare anche da qc **V.** *n* **1.** (*double quantity*) doppio *m* **2.** (*person*) sosia *mf inv;* **sb's ~** il [*o* la] sosia di qn **3.** *pl* SPORTS doppio *m;* **to play ~s** giocare un doppio ▸ **on** [*o* **at**] **the ~** immediatamente

◆**double back** *vi* (*person, animal*) tornare sui propri passi; (*path, river*) descrivere una curva

◆**double up** *vi* **1.** (*bend over*) **to ~ with pain/laughter** piegarsi in due per il dolore/dalle risate **2.** (*share room*) dividere la stanza

double-barreled *adj* **1.** (*shotgun*) a due canne **2.** (*having two purposes*) a doppio effetto

double bass <-es> *n* contrabbasso *m*

double bed *n* letto *m* matrimoniale

double-breasted *adj* (*jacket*) a doppio petto

double-check *vt* ricontrollare

double chin *n* doppio mento *m*

double-click *vi* COMPUT fare doppio clic; **to ~ on the left mouse button** cliccare due volte sul tasto sinistro del mouse

double-cross I. *vt* fare il doppio gioco con **II.** <-es> *n* doppio gioco *m*

double-crosser *n* doppiogiochista *mf*

double-dealer *n* doppiogiochista *mf*

double-dealing *n* doppio gioco *m*

double-decker *n* **1.** (*bus*) autobus *m* a due piani *inv* **2.** (*sandwich*) sandwich *m* doppio *inv*

double-edged *adj a. fig* a doppio taglio

double-entry bookkeeping *n* contabilità *f* a partita doppia

double feature *n* programma *m* con due spettacoli

double-glaze *vt* **to ~ a window** mettere i doppi vetri a una finestra

double-jointed *adj* snodato, -a

double-park *vi, vt* parcheggiare in doppia fila

double-quick I. *adv* a passo accelerato; **to get home ~** arrivare a casa in un baleno **II.** *adj* (*step*) leggero, -a; **in ~ time** in un attimo

doublespeak ['dʌ·bl·spiːk] *n s.* **double-talk**

double standard *n* **to have ~s** usare due pesi e due misure

double take *n* reazione *f* a scoppio ritardato; **to do a ~** reagire a scoppio ritardato

double talk *n* discorsi *m pl* ambigui

doublethink *n* accettazione *f* di principi contraddittori

double time *n* **1.** COM, ECON retribuzione *f* dop-

pia, *per lavoro straordinario* **2.** MIL passo *m* di corsa

double vision *n* diplopia *f*

doubly ['dʌb·li] *adv* doppiamente; **to make ~ sure that ...** assicurarsi bene che ... +*subj*

doubt [daʊt] **I.** *n* dubbio *m;* **to be in ~ whether to ...** essere in dubbio se ...; **without a shadow of a ~** senza ombra di dubbio; **no ~** senza dubbio; **without a ~** senza alcun dubbio; **he will no ~ come at Christmas** sicuramente verrà a Natale; **there is no ~ about it** non c'è alcun dubbio a riguardo; **to have one's ~s about sth** avere dei dubbi riguardo a qc; **the future of the project is in ~** il futuro del progetto è incerto; **beyond all reasonable ~** al di là di qualsiasi dubbio; **to raise ~s about sth** sollevare dubbi su qc; **to cast ~ on sth** mettere in dubbio qc **II.** *vt* **1.** (*be unwilling to believe*) dubitare di; **to ~ sb's word** dubitare della parola di qn **2.** (*call into question: abilities, sincerity*) mettere in dubbio **3.** (*feel uncertain*) nutrire dubbi su; **to ~ that** dubitare che ... +*subj;* **to ~ if** [*o* **whether**] **...** dubitare che ... +*subj;* **I ~ it very much** ne dubito molto **III.** *vi* dubitare

doubtful ['daʊt·fəl] *adj* **1.** (*uncertain, undecided*) dubbioso, -a; **to be ~ whether to ...** non essere sicuro, -a se ...; **to be ~ about going** essere indeciso, -a se andare o no **2.** (*unlikely*) incerto, -a **3.** (*questionable*) dubbio, -a

doubtless ['daʊt·lɪs] *adv* indubbiamente

dough [doʊ] *n* **1.** CULIN impasto *m* **2.** *inf* (*money*) grana *f*

doughnut ['doʊ·nʌt] *n* bombolone *m*

doughy ['doʊ·i] *adj* pastoso, -a

dour [dʊr] *adj* (*manner*) arcigno, -a; (*appearance*) austero, -a

douse [daʊs] *vt* **1.** (*throw liquid on*) bagnare; **to ~ sth in gas** cospargere qc di benzina **2.** (*extinguish: light, candle*) spegnere

dove[1] [dʌv] *n* ZOOL colomba *f*

dove[2] [doʊv] *pt of* **dive**

dovecot(e) ['dʌv·koʊt] *n* colombaia *f*

dovetail ['dʌv·teɪl] **I.** *n* TECH incastro *m* a coda di rondine **II.** *vi* combaciare **III.** *vt* **1.** TECH unire con un incastro a coda di rondine **2.** (*fit*) **to ~ sth into/with sth** far combaciare qc con qc

dowager ['daʊ·ə·dʒɚ] *n* vedova *f* di un nobile

dowdy ['daʊ·di] *adj* <-ier, -iest> sciatto, -a; **to wear ~ clothes** vestire in modo trasandato

dowel ['da·ʊəl] *n* TECH caviglia *f*

down[1] [daʊn] *n* (*feathers*) piumino *m;* (*hairs*) peluria *f*

down[2] [daʊn] **I.** *adv* **1.** (*movement*) giù; **to fall ~** cadere; **to lie ~** stendersi **2.** (*from another point*) **to go ~ to Washington/the lake** andare a Washington/al lago; **~ South** a sud **3.** (*less in volume or intensity*) **to be worn ~** essere consumato; **the wind died ~** il vento si è calmato; **the sun is ~** il sole è tramontato; **the fire is burning ~** il fuoco si sta consumando; **the price is** ~ il prezzo è sceso **4.** (*temporal*) **from 1900** ~ **to the present** dal 1900 fino ai nostri giorni; ~ **through the ages** attraverso i secoli **5.** (*in writing*) **to write/get sth** ~ scrivere/annotare qc **6.** (*not functioning: computer, server, telephone lines*) **to be** ~ non funzionare **7.** (*as deposit*) **to put $100/10%** ~ **on sth** versare un anticipo di 100 dollari/del 10% per qc ▶ **to be** ~ **on sb** avercela con qn; ~ **with the dictator!** abbasso il dittatore! **II.** *prep* **1.** (*lower*) **to go** ~ **the stairs** scendere le scale; **to run** ~ **the slope** correre giù per la discesa **2.** (*along*) **to go** ~ **the street** camminare per strada

down and out, down-and-out I. *adj* **to be** ~ essere uno spiantato **II.** *n* vagabondo, -a *m, f*

downcast ['daʊn·kæst] *adj* avvilito, -a

downfall ['daʊn·fɔːl] *n* (*of government*) caduta *f;* (*of organization, firm*) crollo *m;* (*of person*) rovina *f;* **that will be his** ~ questa sarà la sua rovina

downgrade [ˌdaʊn·'greɪd] **I.** *vt* **1.** (*lower category of*) declassare **2.** (*disparage*) sminuire; **to** ~ **the importance of sth** sminuire l'importanza di qc **II.** *n* pendenza *f;* **to be on the** ~ *fig* essere in declino

downhearted [ˌdaʊn·'hɑːr·t̬ɪd] *adj* scoraggiato, -a

downhill [ˌdaʊn·'hɪl] **I.** *adv* in discesa; **to go** ~ andare in discesa; *fig* andare sempre peggio **II.** *adj* (*path*) in discesa; **it's all** ~ **from now on** *fig* da adesso è tutta discesa *inf*

download ['daʊn·loʊd] *vt* COMPUT scaricare

down-market I. *adj* (*neighborhood, newspaper*) popolare; (*shop, store*) a buon mercato; (*program*) mediocre **II.** *adv* **to move** ~ perder prestigio; (*intentionally*) rivolgersi a un settore poco esigente del mercato

down payment *n* acconto *m;* **to make a** ~ **on sth** versare un acconto per qc

downplay ['daʊn·pleɪ] *vt* minimizzare

downpour ['daʊn·pɔːr] *n* acquazzone *m*

downright ['daʊn·raɪt] **I.** *adj* (*refusal*) categorico, -a; (*disobedience, lie, liar*) bell'e buono, -a; (*fool*) vero, -a; **it is a** ~ **disgrace** è proprio una vergogna; **that's** ~ **stupid** è una vera stupidaggine **II.** *adv* completamente; **to be** ~ **difficult** essere difficilissimo; **to refuse** ~ rifiutare categoricamente

downside ['daʊn·saɪd] *n* svantaggio *m;* **on the** ~**, it's far from town** lo svantaggio è che è lontano dalla città

downsize ['daʊn·saɪz] *vt* ridimensionare

downsizing *n* ridimensionamento *m*

downstairs [ˌdaʊn·'sterz] **I.** *adv* giù; **to go** ~ andare di sotto; **to run** ~ precipitarsi di sotto **II.** *adj* al piano di sotto **III.** *n* (*ground floor*) pianterreno *m;* (*lower floors*) piani*m pl* inferiori

downstream [ˌdaʊn·'striːm] *adv* a valle; **it is another few miles** ~ **from here** è a qualche miglio più a valle

Down syndrome *n* sindrome *f* di Down

downtime ['daʊn·taɪm] *n* **1.** COMPUT, TECH tempo *m* di inattività **2.** (*rest*) momento *m* di riposo

down-to-earth *adj* (*explanation*) realistico, -a; (*person*) pratico, -a

downtown [ˌdaʊn·'taʊn] **I.** *n* centro (*m* città) **II.** *adv* **to go** ~ andare in centro; **to live** ~ vivere in centro **III.** *adj* del centro; ~ **Los Angeles** il centro di Los Angeles

downtrodden ['daʊn·trɑː·dn] *adj* (*grass*) calpestato, -a; (*person*) oppresso, -a

downturn ['daʊn·tɜːrn] *n* peggioramento *m;* **a** ~ **in sth** un calo in qc; **an economic** ~ un peggioramento della situazione economica

downward ['daʊn·wɚd] **I.** *adj* (*movement*) discendente; (*direction*) verso il basso; (*path*) in discesa; (*tendency, prices*) al ribasso; **inflation is on a** ~ **trend** l'inflazione ha una tendenza al ribasso **II.** *adv* verso il basso

downwards ['daʊn·wɚdz] *adv* verso il basso

downy ['daʊ·ni] *adj* lanuginoso, -a

dowry ['da·ʊə·ri] <-ies> *n* dote *f*

dowse[1] [daʊz] *vi* cercare con la bacchetta da rabdomante; **to** ~ **for water** cercare l'acqua con la bacchetta da rabdomante

dowse[2] [daʊs] *vt s.* **douse**

dowser *n* **1.** (*tool*) bacchetta *m* da rabdomante **2.** (*person*) rabdomante *mf*

dowsing *n* rabdomanzia

dowsing rod *n* bacchetta *f* da rabdomante

doyen ['dɔ·ɪən] *n* decano *m*

doyenne ['dɔ·ɪen] *n* decana *f*

doz. *abbr of* **dozen** dozzina *f*

doze [doʊz] **I.** *vi* sonnecchiare; **to** ~ **off** appisolarsi **II.** *n* sonnellino *m;* **to have a** ~ schiacciare un pisolino

dozen ['dʌ·zn] *n* **1.** (*twelve*) dozzina *f;* **half a** ~ mezza dozzina; **two** ~ **eggs** due dozzine di uova **2.** (*many*) ~**s of times** moltissime volte; **by the** ~ a dozzine ▶ **it's six of one and half a** ~ **of the other** è la stessa cosa

dozy ['doʊ·zi] *adj* <-ier, -iest> sonnolento, -a

DP 1. *abbr of* **data processing** elaborazione *f* dati **2.** *abbr of* **displaced person** profugo, -a *m, f*

DPh *n*, **DPhil** *n abbr of* **Doctor of Philosophy** *titolo di chi possiede un dottorato di ricerca*

Dr. 1. *abbr of* **Doctor** Dott. *m*, Dott.ssa *f* **2.** *abbr of* **Drive** viale *m*

drab [dræb] *adj* <drabber, drabbest> **1.** (*dull: food*) insipido, -a; (*color*) smorto, -a; (*existence*) piatto, -a **2.** (*khaki colored*) grigioverde

draconian [drə·'koʊn·ɪən] *adj* draconiano, -a

draft [dræft] **I.** *n* **1.** (*current of air*) corrente *f* d'aria **2.** (*drawing*) schizzo *m* **3.** (*preliminary version*) bozza *f;* (*of novel, speech*) prima stesura *f;* (*of contract*) minuta *f;* ~ **bill** LAW progetto *m* di legge **4. the** ~ MIL la leva **5.** NAUT pescato *m* **6.** MED dose *f* **7.** (*drink*) sorso *m* **8.** (*beer from tap*) birra *f* alla spina; **on** ~ alla spina **II.** *vt* **1.** (*prepare first version*) preparare una bozza di; (*novel*) redigere la prima stesura di; (*plan*) tracciare; (*contract*) stendere una

bozza di **2.**MIL chiamare alle armi **III.** *adj*
1.(*beer*) alla spina **2.**(*horse*) da tiro
draft board *n* scacchiera *f*
draft dodger *n* MIL renitente *m* alla leva
draftee [dræf·'tiː] *n* MIL recluta *f*
draftsman ['dræfts·mən] <-men> *n* TECH disegnatore, -trice *m, f*
drafty ['dræf·ti] *adj* <-ier, -iest> pieno, -a di
correnti d'aria; **it's ~ here with the door**
open con la porta aperta c'è corrente
drag [dræg] **I.** <-gg-> *vt* **1.**(*pull*) trascinare; **to**
~ oneself somewhere trascinarsi in qualche
posto; **to ~ one's heels** [*o* **feet**] strascicare i
piedi; *fig* tirarla per le lunghe; **to ~ sb's name**
through the mud trascinare il nome di qn nel
fango **2.**(*in water*) dragare **3.**COMPUT trascinare **II.** <-gg-> *vi* **1.**(*trail along*) strascicare
2.(*time*) non passare mai; (*meeting, conver-*
sation) trascinarsi **3.**(*lag behind*) restare
indietro **III.** *n* **1.**(*device*) draga *f* **2.**PHYS resistenza *f;* AVIAT resistenza *f* aerodinamica **3.**(*hin-*
drance) ostacolo *m;* **to be a ~ on sb** essere un
peso per qn **4.** *inf*(*boring person*) noia *f;* (*bor-*
ing experience) rottura *f;* **what a ~!** che rottura! **5.** *inf* (*women's clothes*) vestitim *pl* da
donna; **to be in ~** travestirsi da donna **6.** *inf*
(*inhalation*) tiro *m;* **to take a ~** fare un tiro
▶ **the main ~** *inf* la strada principale
♦**drag along** *vt* trascinare, *controvoglia*
♦**drag away** *vt* trascinare via
♦**drag behind** *vi* seguire per ultimo
♦**drag down** *vt* **1.**(*lower forcefully*) trascinare verso il basso **2.**(*make depressed*) avvilire; (*make weak*) buttare giù
♦**drag in** *vt* (*person*) coinvolgere; (*subject*)
tirare in ballo
♦**drag on** *vi* (*meeting, film*) prolungarsi
♦**drag out** *vt* (*meeting, conversation*) tirare
per le lunghe
♦**drag up** *vt* ritirare fuori
draglift *n* skilift, m *inv*
dragon ['dræ·gən] *n* **1.**(*mythical creature*)
drago *m* **2.** *fig* (*fierce woman*) arpia *f*
dragonfly ['dræ·gən·flaɪ] <-ies> *n* libellula *f*
dragoon [drə·'guːn] *n* MIL dragone *m*
drain [dreɪn] **I.** *vt* **1.**AGR, MED drenare; (*river,*
pond) prosciugare; (*food*) scolare; (*machine*)
spurgare **2.**(*empty by drinking: glass, cup*)
svuotare; (*bottle*) scolare **3.**(*exhaust, tire out:*
person) sfinire; (*resources*) esaurire; **to ~ sb's**
energy prosciugare le energie di qn; **war ~ s**
the nation of its youth la guerra priva il paese
della sua gioventù **II.** *vi* (*dishes*) scolare **III.** *n*
1.(*channel*) canale *m* di scolo; (*pipe*) tubo *m*
di scarico **2.**(*sewer*) fognatura *f* **3.**(*in sink*)
scarico *m; fig;* **to throw sth down the ~** buttare qc dalla finestra; **to throw** [*o* **pour**]
money down the ~ buttare i soldi dalla finestra; **to go down the ~** finire in fumo **4.**(*con-*
stant outflow) fuga *f;* **brain ~** fuga di cervelli;
to be a ~ on sb's resources essere un salasso
per qn
♦**drain away** *vi* (*water*) defluire; (*energy*)

esaurirsi; (*tension*) sciogliersi
♦**drain off** *vt* (*liquid*) vuotare
drainage ['dreɪ·nɪdʒ] *n* **1.**AGR, MED drenaggio *m* **2.**TECH scarico *m; ~* **system** rete *f* fogna-
ria
drainage basin *n* bacino *m* di drenaggio
drainboard *n* sgocciolatoio *m*
drainpipe *n* tubo *m* di scarico
drake [dreɪk] *n* anatra *f* maschio
dram [dræm] *n* (*of whiskey, brandy*) bicchierino *m*
drama ['drɑː·mə] *n* **1.**LIT, CINE dramma *m*
2.THEAT arte *f* drammatica; *~* **teacher** insegnante *mf* di recitazione **3.** *inf* (*emotional situ-*
ation) dramma *m;* **a night of high ~** una notte
drammatica
drama school *n* scuola *f* d'arte drammatica
dramatic [drə·'mæ·ṭɪk] *adj* **1.**THEAT drammatico, -a; (*artist, production*) teatrale; (*res-*
cue, events, escape) drammatico, -a **2.**(*very*
noticeable: rise) spettacolare; (*effect, dis-*
covery) straordinario, -a
dramatics [drə·'mæ·ṭɪks] *npl* **1.** + *sing vb*
THEAT arte *f* drammatica; **amateur ~** filodram-
matica *f* **2.** *pej* (*behavior*) teatralità *f*
dramatis personae [ˌdræ·mə·ṭɪs·pə·'sou·niː]
npl THEAT personaggi *mpl, di un'opera teatrale*
dramatist ['dræ·mə·ṭɪst] *n* THEAT drammaturgo, -a *m, f*
dramatization [ˌdræ·mə·ṭɪ·'zeɪ·ʃən] *n* drama-
tizzazione *f*
dramatize ['dræ·mə·taɪz] *vt* **1.**THEAT adattare
per il teatro **2.**(*exaggerate*) drammatizzare
drank [dræŋk] *pt of* **drink**
drape [dreɪp] **I.** *vt* **1.**(*hang*) coprire; **to ~ sth**
(**in a flag**) avvolgere qc (in una bandiera)
2.(*place*) mettere; **she ~ d the scarf around**
her shoulders si avvolse le spalle nello scialle;
to ~ one's arms/legs over sth far penzolare
le braccia/le gambe da qc **II.** *vi* ricadere; **to ~**
well (*clothes*) cadere bene **III.** *n* **1.** *pl* (*cur-*
tains) tende *fpl* **2.**MED tendina *f* **3.**(*how sth*
hangs) drappeggio *m*
drapery ['dreɪ·pə·ri] <-ies> *n* **1.**(*hangings*)
drappeggio *m* **2.** *pl* (*curtains*) tendaggi *mpl*
3.(*cloths, fabrics*) tessuti *mpl*
drastic ['dræs·tɪk] *adj* (*measure*) drastico, -a;
(*change*) radicale
drat [dræt] *interj* accidenti
draw [drɔː] **I.** <drew, drawn> *vt* **1.**ART disegnare; (*line*) tracciare; (*character*) delineare; **to**
~ sth to scale riprodurre qc su scala **2.**(*pull,*
haul: cart, wagon) trainare; **to ~ the curtains**
tirare le tende; **to ~ sb aside** prendere da parte
qn; **to ~ sb into a trap** attirare qn in una trappola; **I was soon drawn into the argument**
sono stato subito trascinato nella discussione
3.(*attract*) attirare; **to ~ applause** scatenare
l'applauso; **to be ~n toward(s) sb** sentirsi
attratto da qn; **to ~ attention to** richiamare
l'attenzione su; **to ~ criticism** suscitare
critiche **4.**(*elicit, evoke*) **to ~ sth** (**from sb/**
sth) ottenere qc (da qn/qc); **to ~ a confession**

from sb strappare una confessione a qn; **to ~ a reply** ottenere una risposta; **to ~ laughter** provocare delle risate **5.** (*formulate, perceive*) **to ~ an analogy** stabilire un'analogia; **to ~ a conclusion** arrivare a una conclusione; **to ~ an inference** trarre una conclusione **6.** (*take out: gun*) estrarre; **to ~ a card** (**from the deck**) GAMES pescare una carta (dal mazzo); **to ~ blood** *fig* toccare un nervo scoperto **7.** (*obtain*) ottenere; (*salary*) guadagnare; (*pension*) prendere **8.** (*pay with*) **to ~ a check** emettere un assegno; (*withdraw: money*) prelevare **9.** (*lottery*) tirare a sorte; **to ~ straws** tirare a sorte, *con le pagliuzze* **10.** SPORTS, GAMES pareggiare **11.** CULIN **to ~ a beer** spillare una birra **12.** NAUT **the boat ~s 7 feet** la barca pesca 7 piedi **13.** SPORTS **to ~ a bow** tendere un arco **II.** <drew, drawn> *vi* **1.** ART disegnare **2.** (*move, procede*) **to ~ ahead** andare avanti; **to ~ away** allontanarsi; **~ up here and he'll get into the car** accosta qui così può scendere dalla macchina **3.** (*approach*) avvicinarsi; **to ~ to a close** volgere al termine; **to ~ to an end** avvicinarsi alla fine **4.** (*chimney*) tirare **5.** (*draw lots*) estrarre a sorte **6.** SPORTS, GAMES pareggiare **III.** *n* **1.** (*attraction*) attrazione *f* **2.** SPORTS, GAMES pareggio *m* **3.** (*drawing of lots*) sorteggio *m* **4.** (*act of drawing a gun*) **to be quick on the ~** esser veloce nell'estrarre la pistola; *fig* avere la risposta pronta **5.** (*of a chimney*) tiraggio *m*

◆**draw apart** *vi* allontanarsi

◆**draw aside** *vt always sep* (*person*) prendere da parte; (*curtain*) scostare

◆**draw away I.** *vi* **1.** (*move off*) allontanarsi **2.** (*move ahead*) **to ~ from sb** portarsi in vantaggio su qn **3.** (*move away*) allontanarsi **II.** *vt* allontanare

◆**draw down** *vt* abbassare; **to wear a hat drawn down over one's ears** portare un cappello calato sulle orecchie

◆**draw in I.** *vi* **1.** (*car, bus, train*) arrivare **2.** (*days*) accorciarsi **II.** *vt* **1.** (*breath*) tirare **2.** (*attract*) attirare

◆**draw off** *vt* (*boots*) togliersi; (*liquid*) estrarre

◆**draw on I.** *vt* **1.** (*make use of*) fare ricorso a; **to ~ sb's own resources** attingere alle proprie risorse; **to ~ the stocks** ricorrere alle scorte **2.** (*put on*) mettersi **II.** *vi* **1.** (*continue: time, day*) avanzare **2.** (*approach*) avvicinarsi

◆**draw out I.** *vt* **1.** (*prolong*) prolungare **2.** (*elicit*) tirar fuori; **to ~ information from sb** strappare delle informazioni a qn; **to ~ feelings and memories** far affiorare sentimenti e ricordi; **to draw sb out** (**of himself**) far uscire dal guscio qn **3.** FIN, ECON, COM prelevare **II.** *vi* **1.** (*car, bus, train*) partire **2.** (*day*) allungarsi

◆**draw together I.** *vt* unire **II.** *vi* riavvicinarsi

◆**draw up I.** *vt* **1.** (*draft*) stendere; (*list*) compilare; (*guidelines, plan*) preparare; **to ~ a constitution** LAW redigere una costituzione

2. (*pull toward one*) avvicinare **3.** (*raise*) alzare; **to draw oneself up** tirarsi su **II.** *vi* (*vehicle*) fermarsi

drawback *n* svantaggio *m*

drawbridge *n* ponte *m* levatoio

drawer ['drɔ:r] *n* cassetto *m*

drawing *n* ART disegno *m*

drawing board *n* tavolo *m* da disegno; **back to the ~!** si ricomincia da capo!

drawing room *n* salotto *m*

drawl [drɔ:l] **I.** *n* parlata *f* strascicata **II.** *vi* parlare staras ciccando le vocali

drawn [drɔ:n] **I.** *pp of* **draw II.** *adj* **1.** (*face*) tirato, -a; **you look tired and ~** hai un aspetto stanco e tirato **2.** (*butter*) chiarificato, -a

dread [dred] **I.** *vt* temere; **I ~ to think ...** non oso pensare ... **II.** *n* terrore *m;* **to fill sb with ~** terrorizzare qn **III.** *adj* terribile

dreadful ['dred·fəl] *adj* **1.** (*terrible*) terribile; (*storm, weather*) orribile; **I feel ~ about it** è una cosa che mi fa stare malissimo **2.** (*of bad quality*) orrendo, -a **3.** (*very great*) spaventoso, -a; (*atrocity*) terribile

dreadfully ['dred·fə·li] *adv* **1.** (*in a terrible manner*) terribilmente **2.** (*very poorly*) malissimo **3.** (*extremely*) estremamente

dream [dri:m] **I.** *n* **1.** sogno *m;* **a bad ~** un brutto sogno **2.** (*daydream*) sogno *m* (ad occhi aperti); (*fantasy*) fantasticheria *f;* **to be in a ~** esser con la testa tra le nuvole; **like a ~** benissimo; **he cooks like a ~** cucina meravigliosamente; **to go like a ~** funzionare perfettamente; **a ~ come true** un sogno fatto realtà; **in your ~s!** *inf* col cavolo! **II.** <dreamed *o* dreamt, dreamed *o* dreamt> *vi* sognare; **to ~ of** (**doing**) **sth** sognare (di fare) qc; **~ on!** *inf* sogna, sogna!; **I wouldn't ~ of** (**doing**) **that** non mi sognerei mai (di fare) una cosa del genere **III.** <dreamed *o* dreamt, dreamed *o* dreamt> *vt* sognare; **I never ~ed that ...** non avrei mai immaginato che ... +*conditional* **IV.** *adj* ideale; **his ~ house** la casa dei suoi sogni; **to be** (**living**) **in a ~ world** vivere nel mondo dei sogni

◆**dream away** *vt* **to ~ the day** passare la giornata a fantasticare

◆**dream up** *vt* ideare

dreamer ['dri:·mər] *n* sognatore, -trice *m, f*

dreamland *n* paese *m* dei sogni

dreamless *adj* senza sogni

dreamlike *adj* irreale

dreamt [dremt] *pt, pp of* **dream**

dreamy ['dri:·mi] *adj* <-ier, -iest> **1.** (*dreamlike*) irreale **2.** (*as in daydream*) sognante **3.** *inf* (*wonderful*) fantastico, -a

dreary ['drɪ·ri] *adj* <-ier, -iest> (*life*) monotono, -a; (*place*) desolato, -a; (*weather*) uggioso, -a

dredge[1] [dredʒ] **I.** *n* TECH draga *f* **II.** *vt* TECH dragare

dredge[2] [dredʒ] *vt* CULIN spolverizzare

dredger[1] ['dre·dʒər] *n* TECH draga *f*

dredger[2] ['dre·dʒər] *n* CULIN *vasetto con coper-*

chio dotato di piccoli fori, utilizzato per spolverizzare zucchero, farina, sale ecc.

dregs [dregz] *npl* 1.(*sediment*) fondo *m* 2.(*undesirable part*) **the ~ of society** la feccia della società

drench [drentʃ] *vt* infradiciare; **to be ~ed in sweat** esser madido di sudore

dress [dres] I. *n* <-es> abito *m;* **strapless/ sleeveless ~** abito senza spalline/maniche II. *vi* vestirsi; **to ~ in blue** vestirsi di blu; **to ~ for sth** vestirsi per qc III. *vt* 1.(*put clothes on*) vestire 2.CULIN (*greens, salad*) condire 3.MED (*wound*) medicare 4.(*decorate*) decorare; (*hair*) pettinare; **to ~ shop windows** allestire vetrine IV. *adj* di gala; **a ~ suit** completo *m* da sera

◆**dress down** I. *vi* vestire in modo informale II. *vt* **to dress sb down** fare una ramanzina a qn

◆**dress up** I. *vi* vestirsi in modo elegante; **to ~ as** travestirsi da II. *vt* 1.(*put on formal clothes*) vestire in modo elegante 2.(*disguise*) travestire; **to dress sb up as** travestire qn da 3.(*embellish*) abbellire

dress circle *n* THEAT prima galleria *f*

dresser ['dre·sər] *n* 1.FASHION **to be a very stylish ~** vestire con molto stile 2.THEAT assistente *mf* di camerino 3.(*chest of drawers*) cassettiera *f;* (*sideboard*) credenza *f*

dressing ['dre·sɪŋ] *n* 1.FASHION modo *m* di vestire 2.CULIN condimento *m* 3.MED medicazione *f*

dressing-down *n* rimprovero *m*

dressing gown *n* (*bathrobe*) vestaglia *f*

dressing room *n* vestidor *m;* THEAT camerino *m*

dressing table *n* toilette *f inv*

dressmaker ['dres·ˌmeɪ·kər] *n* sarto, -a *m, f*

dress rehearsal *n* prova *f* generale

dress shirt *n* camicia *f* da sera, *maschile*

dress suit *n* completo *m* da sera, *maschile*

dress uniform *n* alta uniforme *f*

dressy ['dre·si] *adj* <-ier, -iest> (*clothing*) elegante

drew [druː] *pt of* **draw**

dribble ['drɪ·bl] I. *vi* 1.(*person*) sbavare 2.(*water*) sgocciolare 3.SPORTS dribblare; **to ~ past a defender** dribblare un difensore II. *vt* 1.(*water*) far gocciolare 2.SPORTS dribblare III. *n* 1.(*saliva*) bava *f* 2.(*water*) goccio *m* 3.SPORTS dribbling, m *inv*

driblet ['drɪb·lɪt] *n* goccio *m;* **in ~s** in piccole quantità

dried [draɪd] I. *pt, pp of* **dry** II. *adj* secco, -a; **~ meat** carne secca; **~ milk** latte *m* in polvere

dried-up *adj*, **dried up** *adj* essiccato, -a

drier ['dra·ɪər] *adj comp of* **dry**

drift [drɪft] I. *vi* 1.(*on water*) lasciarsi trasportare dalla corrente; (*in air*) lasciarsi trasportare dal vento; **to ~ out to sea** andare alla deriva 2.(*move aimlessly*) vagare 3.(*progress aimlessly*) scivolare verso 4.METEO (*sand, snow*) accumularsi II. *n* 1.NAUT deriva *f* 2.*fig* (*move-*

ment) movimento *m* 3.(*trend*) tendenza *f* 4.METEO cumulo *m;* **a sand ~** un cumulo di sabbia 5. *inf* (*sense*) significato *m;* **to catch sb's ~** cogliere il senso di ciò che qn dice

◆**drift apart** *vi* (*people*) allontanarsi (progressivamente)

◆**drift off** *vi* scivolare nel sonno

drifter ['drɪf·tər] *n* vagabondo, -a *m, f*

drift ice *n* banchi *m pl* di ghiaccio

driftwood *n* *legname galleggiante trasportato dalla corrente del mare*

drill [drɪl] I. *n* 1.TECH, MED trapano *m;* **~ bit** punta *f* da trapano 2.MIL, SCHOOL esercitazione *fpl;* **spelling ~** esercizio ortografico II. *vt* 1.TECH trapanare; **to ~ a hole** fare un buco con il trapano 2.SCHOOL far esercitare; **to ~ sth into sb** inculcare qc a qn 3.MIL addestrare III. *vi* 1.TECH fare perforazioni 2.(*go through exercise*) fare esercizi 3.MIL fare esercitazioni IV. *adj* MIL da esercitazione

drilling rig *n* impianto *m* di trivellazione

drink [drɪŋk] I. <drank, drunk> *vi* bere; **to ~ heavily** bere come una spugna; **to ~ in moderation** bere con moderazione; **to ~ to sb** bere alla salute di qn II. <drank, drunk> *vt* bere; **to ~ a toast** (**to sb/sth**) brindare (a qn/ qc); **to ~ sb under the table** battere qn nel bere, *reggendo meglio l'alcol;* **to ~ one's troubles away** bere per dimenticare III. *n* 1.(*drinkable liquid*) bibita *f;* (*alcoholic beverage*) bicchierino *m;* **to have a ~** bere qualcosa; **to drive sb to ~** spingere qn al bere; **the ~** *sl* il mare

◆**drink in** *vt* assaporare; (*words*) bere

drinkable ['drɪŋ·kə·bl] *adj* potabile

drinker *n* bevitore, -trice *m, f*

drinking *n* (*act*) il bere *m;* (*drunkenness*) il bere alcolici *m;* **no ~ allowed on these premises** vietato il consumo di bevande alcoliche

drinking fountain *n* fontanella *f*

drinking song *n* canzone *f* da osteria

drinking water *n* acqua *f* potabile

drip [drɪp] I. <-pp-> *vi* gocciolare; (*pipe, faucet*) perdere; (*person, animal*) grondare II. <-pp-> *vt* far gocciolare; **to ~ paint/ water/blood on the floor** far gocciolare la pittura/l'acqua/il sangue sul pavimento III. *n* 1.(*act of dripping*) gocciolio *m* 2.(*drop*) goccia *f* 3.MED flebo(clisi) *f inv* 4. *inf* (*person*) inetto, -a *m, f*

drip-dry <-ie-> *adj* che non si stira

dripping ['drɪ·pɪŋ] I. *adj* 1.(*faucet, pipe*) che gocciola 2.(*extremely wet*) fradicio, -a II. *adv* **to be ~ wet** esser bagnato fradicio III. *n pl* sugo *m* d'arrosto

drive [draɪv] I. <drove, driven> *vt* 1.AUTO guidare; (*race car*) pilotare; **to ~ a sports car** guidare un'auto sportiva; **to ~ sb home** accompagnare a casa qn (in macchina) 2.(*urge*) spingere; **to ~ sb to (do) sth** spingere qn a (fare) qc 3.(*cattle*) condurre 4.(*render, make*) ridurre a; **to ~ sb crazy** far diventar matto qn 5.(*ball*) colpire; (*tunnel*) aprire; (*nail,*

stake) conficcare **6.** TECH azionare **II.**<drove, driven> *vi* AUTO **1.** (*operate vehicle*) guidare; **the car ~s well** un'auto bella da guidare **2.** (*travel*) andare in auto **3.** (*function*) funzionare **III.** *n* **1.** AUTO giro *m;* (*journey*) viaggio *m;* **to go for a ~** andare a fare un giro in macchina **2.** (*in street names*) **Broadview D~** viale Broadview **3.** (*driveway*) vialetto *m* d'accesso **4.** TECH trasmissione *f;* **front-wheel ~** trazione *f* anteriore; **all-wheel** [*o* **four-wheel**] **~** trazione *f* a quattro ruote motrici **5.** PSYCH impulso *m;* **to have ~** avere grinta; **sex ~** impulso *m* sessuale **6.** (*campaign*) campagna *f;* **a fund-raising ~** campagna per raccogliere fondi **7.** SPORTS colpo *m* forte **8.** COMPUT drive *m inv*
  ◆**drive at** *vt inf* insinuare
  ◆**drive in I.** *vi* entrare (in auto) **II.** *vt* (*nail*) piantare
  ◆**drive off I.** *vt always sep* costringere ad allontanarsi **II.** *vi* andarsene (in auto)
  ◆**drive out** *vt* cacciare
  ◆**drive up** *vt* **to ~** (**somewhere**) avvicinarsi (a qualche posto)
drive-in ['draɪv·ɪn] *n* (*restaurant, cinema*) *drive-in inv*
drive-in bank *n* banca *f* drive-in
drive-in movie *n*, **drive-in theater** *n* cinema *m inv* drive-in
drivel ['drɪ·vəl] *n* stupidaggini *fpl*
driven ['drɪ·vən] *pp of* **drive**
driver ['draɪ·vɚ] *n* **1.** AUTO conducente *mf;* **truck ~** camionista *mf;* **taxi ~** tassista *mf;* **to be in the ~'s seat** *fig* essere al comando di qc **2.** COMPUT driver *m inv*
driver's license *n* patente *f* di guida
drive-through *adj*, **drive-thru** *adj* per automobilisti
driveway ['draɪv·weɪ] *n* vialetto *m* d'accesso
driving I. *n* guida *f* **II.** *adj* **1.** AUTO, TECH di guida **2.** METEO (*rain*) scrosciante **3.** (*powerful: ambition, force*) trainante
driving force *n* forza *f* motrice
driving instructor *n* istruttore, -trice di (scuola) guida *m*
driving lessons *npl* lezioni *f pl* di guida
driving school *n* scuola *f* guida
driving test *n* esame *m* di guida
drizzle ['drɪ·zl] METEO **I.** *n* pioggerellina *f* **II.** *vi* piovigginare
drizzly ['drɪz·li] *adj* **it was a grey ~ afternoon** era un pomeriggio grigio e piovigginoso
droll [droʊl] *adj* buffo, -a
dromedary ['drɑ·mə·de·ri] <-ies> *n* dromedario *m*
drone [droʊn] **I.** *n* **1.** ZOOL fuco *m* **2.** (*sb who does no work*) fannullone, -a *m, f;* (*sb who does menial work*) schiavo, -a del lavoro *m* **3.** (*sound*) ronzio *m* **4.** AVIAT aereo *m* spia **II.** *vi* **1.** (*hum*) ronzare **2.** (*speak in monotonous tone*) parlare in modo monotono
drool [druːl] **I.** *vi* sbavare; **to ~ over sth/sb** *fig* sbavare per qn/qc **II.** *n* bava *f*

droop [druːp] **I.** *vi* **1.** (*fall*) penzolare; (*eyes*) chiudersi **2.** (*flowers*) afflosciarsi **3.** (*person*) abbattersi; (*mood, spirits*) precipitare **II.** *vt* piegare
drop [drɑːp] **I.** *n* **1.** (*of liquid*) goccia *f;* **~ by ~** goccia a goccia **2.** *inf* (*small amount: of drink*) goccio *m;* **just a ~** solo un goccio; **to have had a ~ too much** (**to drink**) bere un bicchiere di troppo **3.** *fig* (*trace*) briciolo *m* **4.** (*vertical distance*) dislivello *m;* **a sheer ~** uno strapiombo **5.** (*decrease*) diminuzione *f;* (*in temperature*) abbassamento *m* **6.** (*fall*) caduta *f;* (*distribution by aircraft*) lancio *m;* **~ of food supplies** lancio *m* di viveri **7.** (*secret collection point*) posto *m* di consegna **8.** (*sweet*) **lemon/peppermint ~s** caramelle *f pl* al limone/alla menta ► **it's a ~ in the** bucket è una goccia nel mare; **at the ~ of a** hat all'istante **II.** <-pp-> *vt* **1.** (*allow to fall*) lasciar cadere; **to ~ anchor** gettare l'ancora; **to ~ a bomb** lanciare una bomba **2.** (*lower*) abbassare; **to ~ prices** ridurre i prezzi; **to ~ one's voice** abbassare la voce **3.** *inf* (*send*) mandare; **to ~ a letter into a mailbox** imbucare una lettera; **to ~ sb a line** [*o* **note**] scrivere due righe a qn **4.** *inf* (*express*) accennare; **to ~ a hint** fare un'allusione; **to ~ names** fare dei nomi **5.** (*dismiss*) mollare **6.** (*abandon, give up*) rinunciare a; **to ~ a demand** ritirare una richiesta; **to ~ a class** abbandonare un corso; **to ~ sb** rompere con qn **7.** (*leave out*) omettere; **let's ~ the subject** lasciamo perdere **III.** <-pp-> *vi* **1.** (*descend*) lasciarsi cadere **2.** (*go to*) **to ~ into a bar/a store** andare in un bar/in un negozio **3.** (*go lower: prices*) diminuire **4.** *inf* (*become exhausted*) **to ~ with exhaustion** crollare dalla stanchezza; **he is ready to ~** non farcela più dalla stanchezza; **to ~ dead** morire di colpo; **~ dead!** *inf* crepa! ► **to** let **it ~** lasciar perdere qc; **to** let **it ~ that ...** lasciar intendere che ...
  ◆**drop across** *vt insep, inf* incontrarsi con
  ◆**drop behind** *vi* restare indietro; **to ~ in sth** rimanere indietro in qc
  ◆**drop by** *vi* passare
  ◆**drop down** *vi* cadere
  ◆**drop in** *vi inf* **to ~ on sb** passare a trovare qn
  ◆**drop off I.** *vt inf* (*passenger*) lasciare **II.** *vi* **1.** (*decrease*) diminuire **2.** *inf* (*fall asleep*) addormentarsi **3.** (*become separated*) staccarsi
  ◆**drop out** *vi* (*person*) ritirarsi; **to ~ of school/college/a club** abbandonare la scuola/l'università/un club
drop-down menu *n* COMPUT menu *m* a tendina *inv*
drop kick *n* SPORTS calcio *m* di rimbalzo
droplet ['drɑːp·lət] *n* gocciolina *f*
dropout ['drɑːp·aʊt] *n* **1.** UNIV, SCHOOL persona *f* che ha abbandonato gli studi **2.** (*from society*) emarginato, -a *m, f*
dropper ['drɑː·pɚ] *n* contagocce *m inv*
droppings ['drɑː·pɪŋz] *npl* escrementi *mpl*

drop shot *n* SPORTS palla *f* smorzata
dross [drɑːs] *n* scoria *f*
drought [draʊt] *n* siccità *f*
drove[1] [droʊv] *n* **1.** (*of animals*) mandria *f* **2.** *pl, inf* (*of people*) folla *f*; **in ~s** in massa **3.** (*chisel*) scalpello *m*
drove[2] [droʊv] *pt of* **drive**
drover ['droʊ·vɚ] *n* mandriano, -a *m, f*
drown [draʊn] I. *vt* **1.** (*die in water*) affogare; **to look like a ~ed rat** *inf* esser bagnato come un pulcino **2.** (*engulf in water*) affogare **3.** (*make inaudible*) soffocare; **the music drowned out her voice** la musica copriva la sua voce ▶ **to ~ one's sorrows in** <u>drink</u> affogare i propri dispiaceri nell'alcol II. *vi* **1.** (*die*) annegare **2.** *fig, inf* (*have too much*) **to be ~ing in work** essere sommerso dal lavoro
drowning *n* annegamento *m*
drowse [draʊz] *vi* sonnecchiare
drowsy ['draʊ·zi] <-ier, -iest> *adj* sonnolento, -a
drudge [drʌdʒ] I. *n* uomo, donna di fatica *m* II. *vi* sgobbare
drudgery ['drʌ·dʒə·ri] *n* sgobbata *f*
drug [drʌg] I. *n* **1.** MED farmaco *m* **2.** (*narcotic*) droga *f*; **to take ~s** drogarsi II. <-gg-> *vt* drogare
drug abuse *n* uso *m* di droghe
drug addict *n* tossicodipendente *mf*
drug addiction *n* tossicodipendenza *f*
drug bust *n* sequestro *m* di droga
drug dealer *n* spacciatore, -trice *m, f*
drug manufacturer *n* fabbricante *mf* di droga
drug pusher *n* *inf* spacciatore, -trice *m, f*
drugstore *n* farmacia *f*, *che vende anche prodotti cosmetici, tabacco, giornali, etc.*
drug traffic *n* traffico *m* di droga
drug trafficker *n* narcotrafficante *mf*
drug trafficking *n* narcotraffico *m*
druid ['druː·ɪd] *n* druido *m*
drum [drʌm] I. *n* **1.** MUS, TECH tamburo *m* **2.** *pl* (*in a band*) batteria *f* **3.** (*for oil*) bidone *m* **4.** ANAT timpano *m* II. <-mm-> *vi* (*play percussion*) suonare il tamburo; (*with fingers*) tamburellare con le dita; **to ~ on sth** tamburellare con le dita su qc III. <-mm-> *vt* *inf* **to ~ sth into sb** ficcare in testa qc a qn
drumbeat *n* colpo *m* di tamburo
drum brake *n* freno *m* a tamburo
drumhead *n* pelle *f* di tamburo
drum major *n* tamburo *m* maggiore
drummer ['drʌ·mɚ] *n* (*in a band*) tamburo *m*; (*in a group*) batterista *mf*
drumstick *n* **1.** MUS bacchetta *f* **2.** CULIN coscia *f*
drunk [drʌŋk] I. *vt, vi pp of* **drink** II. *adj* **1.** (*inebriated*) ubriaco, -a; **to be ~** essere ubriaco; **to get ~** ubriacarsi; **~ driving** guida *f* in stato di ebbrezza **2.** *fig* (*very much affected*) **to be ~ with joy** esser ebbro di gioia III. *n* ubriaco, -a *m, f*
drunkard ['drʌŋ·kɚd] *n* ubriacone, -a *m, f*
drunken ['drʌŋ·kən] *adj* da ubriaco, -a; **a ~ brawl** una rissa tra ubriachi; **~ driving** guida *f*

in stato di ebbrezza
drunkenness ['drʌŋ·kə·nɪs] *n* ubriachezza *f*
dry [draɪ] I. <-ier *o* -er, -iest *o* -est> *adj* **1.** (*not wet*) asciutto, -a; **to go ~** asciugarsi; **~ red wine** vino rosso secco **2.** (*climate, soil*) arido, -a **3.** (*bread, toast*) asciutto, -a; (*without alcohol: state, county*) proibizionista **4.** (*uninteresting*) noioso, -a **5.** (*brief*) laconico, -a; **~ (sense of) humor** (senso dell')umorismo pungente ▶ **to run ~** prosciugarsi II. <-ie-> *vt* asciugare; (*tears*) asciugarsi III. <-ie-> *vi* asciugare; **to put sth out to ~** metter qc fuori ad asciugare
◆**dry up** I. *vi* **1.** (*become dry*) prosciugarsi **2.** (*dry the dishes*) asciugare i piatti **3.** *inf* (*become silent*) ammutolire; (*on stage*) dimenticare la battuta **4.** (*run out*) finire II. *vt* asciugare
dryad ['draɪ·æd] *n* driade *f*
dry cell *n* ELEC elemento *m* a secco
dry cell battery *n* pila *f* a secco
dry-clean *vt* lavare a secco
dry cleaner's *n* tintoria *f*
dry cleaning *n* lavaggio *m* a secco
dry dock *n* bacino *m* di carenaggio
dryer ['dra·ɪɚ] *n* **1.** (*for hair*) asciugacapelli *m inv* **2.** (*for clothes*) asciugabiancheria *f inv*
dry goods *npl* mercerie *fpl*
dry ice *n* ghiaccio *m* secco
dry land *n* (*not sea*) terraferma *f*
dry measure *n* misura *f* di capacità per aridi
dryness ['draɪ·nəs] *n a. fig* aridità *f*
dry rot *n* malattia *f* del legno
dry run *n* prova *f*
dry wall *n* muro *m* a secco
DSc *abbr of* **Doctor of Science** titolo di chi possiede un dottorato di ricerca in materie scientifiche
DTP [ˌdiː·tiːˈpiː] *n abbr of* **desktop publishing** DTP *m*
dual ['duː·əl] *adj inv* doppio, -a
dual citizenship *n* doppia cittadinanza *f*
dualism ['duː·ə·lɪ·zəm] *n* dualismo *m*
dub[1] [dʌb] <-bb-> *vt* **1.** (*confer knighthood*) fare cavaliere **2.** (*give sb/sth a nickname*) soprannominare
dub[2] [dʌb] <-bb-> *vt* (*film*) doppiare; **to be ~bed into English/French** essere doppiato in inglese/francese
dubbing ['dʌ·bɪŋ] *n* doppiaggio *m*
dubious ['duː·bi·əs] *adj* **1.** (*doubtful*) dubbioso, -a **2.** (*untrustworthy*) dubbio, -a
duchess ['dʌ·tʃɪs] *n* duchessa *f*
duchy ['dʌ·tʃi] *n* ducato *m*
duck [dʌk] I. *n* **1.** (*bird*) anatra *f* **2.** (*lowering of head*) schivata *f*, *abbassando la testa* ▶ **to take to sth like a ~ to** <u>water</u> *inf* imparare qc con grande naturalezza II. *vi* **1.** (*dip head*) abbassare la testa **2.** (*go under water*) tuffarsi **3.** (*hide*) nascondersi; **to ~ out of sth** *inf* schizzar fuori da qc III. *vt* **1.** (*lower suddenly*) **to ~ one's head** abbassare la testa; **to ~ one's head under water** andare sott'acqua con la

testa **2.** (*avoid*) schivare; *fig* eludere; **to ~ an issue** eludere un tema

duckboards ['dʌk·bɔːrdz] *npl* passerella *f*

duckling ['dʌk·lɪŋ] *n* anatroccolo *m*

ducky ['dʌ·ki] *adj inf* fantastico, -a

duct [dʌkt] *n* **1.** (*pipe*) condotto *m;* **air ~** condotto d'aria **2.** ANAT canale *m;* **ear ~** canale uditivo

dud [dʌd] *n* **1.** (*person*) inetto, -a *m, f* **2.** (*bomb*) bomba *f* inesplosa **3.** (*failure*) fallimento *m* **4.** *pl* (*clothing*) abiti *mpl*

dude [duːd] *n inf* (*guy*) tipo *m;* (*smartly dressed*) figurino *m*

due [duː] **I.** *adj* **1.** (*payable*) pagabile; (*owing*) dovuto, -a; **~ date** scadenza *f;* **the loan is now ~** (*for repayment*) il prestito deve essere rimborsato; **to fall ~** scadere **2.** (*appropriate*) debito, -a; **in ~ course** a tempo debito; **with all ~ respect** col dovuto rispetto; **to treat sb with the respect ~ to him/her** trattare qn col rispetto che gli è dovuto **3.** (*expected*) atteso, -a; **I'm ~ in Mexico City this evening** devo essere a Città del Messico stanotte **4.** (*owing to, because of*) **~ to** a causa di; **~ to circumstances beyond our control** per motivi che esulano dalla nostra volontà ... **II.** *n* **1.** (*fair treatment*) dovuto *m;* **to give sb his ~** dare a qn ciò che gli spetta **2.** *pl* (*debts*) debiti *m; pl* (*obligations*) doveri *mpl;* **to pay one's ~s** (*meet obligations/duties*) fare il proprio dovere; (*meet debts*) pagare i debiti **3.** *pl* (*regular payment*) quota *f* **III.** *adv before adv* **~ north/south** dritto verso nord/sud

duel ['duː·əl] **I.** *n* duello *m;* **to fight a ~** battersi in duello **II.** *vi* <-l- *o* -ll-, -l- *o* -ll-> battersi in duello

duet [du·'et] *n* duetto *m;* **to play a ~** suonare un duetto

duffer ['dʌ·fə·] *n* imbranato, -a *m*

duffle bag ['dʌ·fəl·ˌbæg] *n* sacca *f* da marinaio

duffle coat *n* montgomery *m inv*

dug[1] [dʌg] *pt, pp of* **dig**

dug[2] [dʌg] *n* mammella *f*

dugout ['dʌg·aʊt] *n* **1.** MIL rifugio *m* sotterraneo **2.** SPORTS panchina *m* **3.** NAUT piroga *f*

duke [duːk] *n* duca *m*

dull [dʌl] **I.** *adj* **1.** (*boring*) noioso, -a; (*life*) monotono, -a **2.** (*not bright: surface*) opaco, -a; (*sky*) grigio, -a; (*weather*) uggioso, -a; (*color*) spento, -a; (*light*) pallido, -a **3.** (*ache, noise*) sordo, -a **4.** (*not sharp: knife, ax*) non affilato, -a **II.** *vt* **1.** (*alleviate*) alleviare **2.** (*desensitize*) intorpidire **3.** (*make blunt*) rovinare il filo di

dullard ['dʌ·lə·d] *n* tonto, -a *m, f*

dullness ['dʌl·nɪs] *n* **1.** (*lack of excitement*) monotonia *f* **2.** (*tediousness*) tedio *m*

duly ['duː·li] *adv* **1.** (*appropriately*) debitamente **2.** (*on time*) come previsto

dumb [dʌm] *adj* **1.** (*mute*) muto, -a; **deaf and ~** sordomuto, -a; **to be struck ~** ammutolire di colpo **2.** *inf* (*stupid*) stupido, -a; **to play ~** fare il finto tonto

dumbbell ['dʌm·bel] *n* **1.** (*weight*) manu-

brio *m* **2.** *inf* (*person*) citrullo, -a *m, f*

dumbfound ['dʌm·faʊnd] *vt* sbalordire

dumbfounded *adj* sbalordito, -a

dumbstricken ['dʌm·ˌstrɪ·kən] *adj*, **dumbstruck** ['dʌm·strʌk] *adj* senza parole

dumb waiter *n* montavivande *m inv*

dumfound *vt s.* **dumbfound**

dummy ['dʌ·mi] **I.** <-ies> *n* **1.** (*mannequin*) manichino *m* **2.** (*duplicate*) riproduzione *f* **3.** (*fool*) tonto, -a **II.** *adj* (*false*) finto, -a **III.** *vi sl* **to ~ up** tacere

dump [dʌmp] **I.** *n* **1.** (*for waste*) discarica *f* **2.** *fig, sl* (*dirty place*) tugurio *m* **3.** MIL deposito *m;* **ammunition ~** deposito *m* di munizioni **II.** *vt* **1.** (*drop carelessly*) metter giù; (*get rid of*) disfarsi di **2.** (*abandon*) abbandonare **3.** *inf* (*end relationship with*) piantare **4.** COMPUT riversare **III.** *vi sl* **to ~ on sb** prendersela con qn

dumper ['dʌm·pə·] *n* autocarro *m* ribaltabile

dumping *n* scarico *m*

dumping ground *n* discarica *f*

dumpling ['dʌmp·lɪŋ] *n* gnocco *di* pasta *ripieno di carne o frutta*

dumpy ['dʌm·pi] <-ier, -iest> *adj* tracagnotto, -a

dun[1] [dʌn] *adj* bigio, -a

dun[2] [dʌn] **I.** <-nn-> *vt* **to ~ sb** sollecitare il pagamento di un debito da parte di qn **II.** *n* sollecito *m* di pagamento

dunce [dʌns] *n* somaro *m*

dune [duːn] *n* duna *f*

dung [dʌŋ] *n* sterco *m*

dungarees [ˌdʌŋ·gə·'riːz] *npl* salopette *f inv*

dungeon ['dʌn·dʒən] *n* prigione *f* sotterranea

dunghill ['dʌŋ·hɪl] *n* letamaio *m*

dunk [dʌŋk] *vt* inzuppare

duo ['duː·oʊ] *n* duo *m;* **comedy ~** duo comico

duodenum [ˌduː·ə·'diː·nəm] <-na *o* -s> *n* duodeno *m*

dup. *n abbr of* **duplicate** duplicato *m*

dupe [duːp] **I.** *n* grullo, -a *m, f* **II.** *vt* **to be ~d** essere imbrogliato

duplex ['duː·pleks] **I.** *n* **1.** (*house*) villetta *f* bifamiliare **2.** (*apartment*) appartamento *m* su due piani **II.** *adj* doppio, -a

duplicate[1] ['duː·plɪ·kət] **I.** *adj inv* duplicato, -a; **~ key** copia *f* di una chiave **II.** *n* duplicato *m*

duplicate[2] ['duː·plɪ·keɪt] *vt* **1.** (*replicate*) duplicare; (*repeat*) ripetere **2.** (*copy*) copiare; **to ~ a device** copiare un dispositivo

duplicator ['duː·plɪ·keɪ·t̬ə·] *n* duplicatore *m*

duplicity [duː·'plɪ·sə·t̬i] *n* doppiezza *f*

durability [ˌdʊ·rə·'bɪ·lə·t̬i] *n* **1.** (*permanence, persistence*) durabilità *f* **2.** (*life of a product*) durata *f*

durable ['dʊ·rə·bl] *adj* **1.** (*hard-wearing*) resistente **2.** (*long-lasting*) duraturo, -a

duration [dʊ·'reɪ·ʃən] *n* durata *f;* **for the ~ of sth** per l'intera durata di qc

duress [dʊ·'res] *n* costrizione *f;* **under ~** sotto coercizione

during ['dʊ·rɪŋ] *prep* durante; **~ work/the**

week durante il lavoro/la settimana

dusk [dʌsk] *n* crepuscolo *m;* **at ~** al crepuscolo

dusky ['dʌs·ki] <-ier, iest> *adj* **1.** (*almost dark*) scuro, -a **2.** *a. pej* (*dark-skinned*) di pelle scura

dust [dʌst] **I.** *n* polvere *f;* **coal ~** polvere di carbone *m* ▶ **to** <u>bite</u> **the ~** mordere la polvere; **to** <u>leave</u> **sb in the ~** far mangiare la polvere a qn; **to wait till the ~ has** <u>settled</u> lasciare che si rischiari l'atmosfera; **to** <u>turn</u> **to ~** *liter* trasformarsi in polvere **II.** *vt* **1.** (*clean*) spolverare **2.** (*spread over*) spargere; **to ~ sth with insecticide** cospargere di insetticida la superficie di qc **III.** *vi* spolverare

dust bunny *n inf* lanìccio *m*

dust cover *n* **1.** (*for furniture*) protezione *f* antipolvere **2.** (*on book*) sovraccoperta *f*

duster ['dʌs·tɚ] *n* straccio *m* per la polvere

dust jacket *n* (*on book*) sovraccoperta *f*

dust mite *n* acaro *m* della polvere

dustpan *n* paletta *f;* **~ and brush** paletta e scopetta

dust storm *n* tempesta *f* di polvere

dust-up *n inf* (*fistfight*) zuffa *f;* (*argument*) lite *f*

dusty ['dʌs·ti] <-ier, -iest> *adj* **1.** (*covered in dust*) polveroso, -a **2.** (*grayish*) polvere; **~ blue** azzurro polvere

Dutch [dʌtʃ] **I.** *adj* olandese **II.** *n* **1.** *pl* (*people*) **the ~** gli olandesi **2.** LING olandese ▶ **to go ~** pagare alla romana

Dutchman ['dʌtʃ·mən] <-men> *n* olandese *m*

Dutchwoman ['dʌtʃ·wʊ·mən] <-women> *n* olandese *f*

dutiable ['du:·t̬iə·bl] *adj* soggetto, -a a dazio dogananle

dutiful ['du:·t̬ɪ·fəl] *adj* obbediente

duty ['du:·t̬i] <-ies> *n* **1.** (*moral*) dovere *m;* (*obligation*) obbligo *m;* **it's my ~** è mio dovere; **to do sth out of ~** far qc solo per dovere; **to do one's ~** fare il proprio dovere **2.** (*task, function*) funzione *f* **3.** (*work*) servizio *m;* **to do ~ for sb** sostituire qn; **to be suspended from ~** essere sospeso dal servizio; **to be on/off ~** essere in/fuori servizio **4.** (*tax*) imposta *f;* (*revenue on imports*) dirittim *pl* doganali; **customs duties** dazio *m* doganale; **to pay ~ on sth** pagare il dazio su qc

duty call *n* visita *f* di dovere

duty-free *adj* esente da dazio

duty roster *n* lista *f* dei turni di guardia

duvet [du:·'veɪ] *n* piumino *m*

DVD *n inv* COMPUT *abbr of* **Digital Video Disk** DVD, m *inv*

dwarf [dwɔːrf] **I.** <-s *o* -ves> *n* nano, -a *m, f* **II.** *vt* far scomparire

dwell [dwel] <dwelt *o* -ed, dwelt *o* -ed> *vi* **1.** (*live*) dimorare **2.** (*give attention to*) **to ~ on sth** soffermarsi su qc; **to ~ on a subject** dilungarsi su un tema

dweller *n* abitante *m*

dwelling ['dwe·lɪŋ] *n* dimora *f*

dwelt [dwelt] *pp, pt of* **dwell**

dwindle ['dwɪn·dl] *vi* ridursi

dye [daɪ] **I.** *vt* tingere **II.** *n* tinta *m*

dyed-in-the-wool *adj* convinto, -a; **~ opinions** ferme opinioni

dye-works ['daɪ·wɜːrks] *n* tintoria *f*

dying ['daɪ·ɪŋ] *adj* **1.** (*approaching death*) moribondo, -a **2.** (*words, wishes*) ultimo, -a

dyke¹ [daɪk] *n s.* **dike**

dyke² [daɪk] *n inf* (*lesbian*) lesbica *f*

dynamic [daɪ·'næ·mɪk] *adj* dinamico, -a

dynamics [daɪ·'næ·mɪks] *n* **1.** PHYS dinamica *f;* (*development*) sviluppo *m* **2.** MUS (*alterations of volume*) dinamica *f*

dynamite ['daɪ·nə·maɪt] **I.** *n* dinamite *f* **II.** *vt* far saltare con la dinamite

dynamo ['daɪ·nə·moʊ] <-s> *n* dinamo *f inv*

dynasty ['daɪ·nəs·ti] <-ies> *n* dinastia *f*

dysentery ['dɪ·sən·te·ri] *n* MED dissenteria *f*

dysfunctional [dɪs·'fʌŋk·ʃə·nəl] *adj* disfunzionale

dyslexia [dɪs·'lek·si·ə] *n* dislessia *f*

dyslexic [dɪs·'lek·sɪk] *adj* dislessico, -a

dyspepsia [dɪs·'pep·si·ə] *n* MED dispepsia *f*

E

E, e [iː] *n* **1.** (*letter*) E, e *f o m inv;* **~ as in Eric** E come Empoli **2.** MUS mi *m inv*

E *abbr of* **east** E

each [iːtʃ] **I.** *adj* ogni; **~ one of you** ognuno di voi; **~ and every house** ogni casa senza eccezione **II.** *pron* ciascuno, -a; **~ of them could beat you** ciascuno di loro potrebbe batterti; **$70 ~** $70 ciascuno; **he gave us $10 ~** ci ha dato 10 dollari ciascuno; **I'll take a pound of ~** ne prendo una libbra di ognuno

each other *pron* l'un l'altro, -a; **they are always arguing with ~** litigano sempre tra di loro; **to help ~** si aiutano l'un l'altro; **to be made for ~** essere fatti l'uno per l'altro

eager ['iː·gɚ] *adj* desideroso, -a; **to be ~ for sth** essere desideroso di qc; **to be ~ for revenge** essere assetato di vendetta; **to be ~ to start** essere impaziente di cominciare; **to be ~ to please** far di tutto per compiacere gli altri

eager beaver *n inf* **he is an ~** è un lavoratore instancabile

eagerness *n* entusiasmo *m*

eagle ['iː·gl] *n* aquila *f*

eagle eye *n* **1.** (*keen eyesight*) vista *f* d'aquila **2.** (*observe attentively*) **she monitors the expenses with an ~** controlla le spese con occhio attento

eagle-eyed ['iː·gl·aɪd] *adj* **to be ~** avere occhi di lince

ear¹ [ɪr] *n* ANAT orecchio *m;* **~, nose and throat specialist** otorinolaringoiatra *mf;* **to have a good ~** avere orecchio; **to have an ~ for music** avere orecchio per la musica; **to**

smile from ~ to ~ sorridere da un orecchio all'altro ►to be up to one's ~s in <u>debt</u> *inf* essere indebitato fino al collo; to have [*o* keep] an [*o* one's] ~ to the <u>ground</u> *inf* stare in campana; to be <u>all</u> ~s *inf* essere tutto orecchi; to keep one's eyes and ~s <u>open</u> *inf* tenere gli occhi e le orecchie ben aperti; to fall on <u>deaf</u> ~s rimanere inascoltato; to turn a <u>deaf</u> ~ (to sth) fare orecchie da mercante (riguardo a qc); he'll be <u>out</u> on his ~ *inf* si ritroverà per strada; to be <u>wet</u> behind the ~s puzzare ancora di latte; it <u>goes</u> in one ~ and out the other *inf* entra da un orecchio ed esce dall'altro; to <u>lend</u> sb an ~ prestare ascolto a qn; to <u>play</u> it by ~ *inf* decidere al momento

ear² [ɪr] *n* BOT spiga *f*
earache ['ɪ·reɪk] *n* mal *m* d'orecchi
eardrum *n* timpano *m*
ear infection *n* infezione *f* dell'orecchio
earl [ɜːrl] *n* conte *m*
earlobe ['ɪr·loʊb] *n* lobo *m* dell'orecchio
early ['ɜːr·li] I. <-ier, -iest> *adj* 1. (*ahead of time, near the beginning*) to be ~ essere in anticipo; ~ **retirement** prepensionamento *m;* to take ~ **retirement** andare in prepensionamento; **an ~ death** una morte prematura; **the ~ hours** le prime ore del mattino; **in the ~ morning** di primo mattino; **in the ~ afternoon** nel primo pomeriggio; **at an ~ age** da piccolo; **he is in his ~ twenties** è poco più che ventenne; **in the ~ 15th century** all'inizio del XV secolo; ~ **education** istruzione *f* primaria; **to make it an ~ night** andare a letto presto; **the ~ stages** le prime fasi; **the ~ days/ years of sth** gli esordi di qc; **to die an ~ death** morire prematuramente 2. *form* (*prompt: reply*) sollecito, -a; **at your earliest (possible) convenience** non appena possibile 3. (*first*) primo, -a II. *adv* 1. (*ahead of time*) presto; **to get up ~** alzarsi presto; ~ **in the morning** di mattino presto; ~ **in the year** all'inizio dell'anno; **to be half an hour ~** essere in anticipo di mezz'ora 2. (*soon*) prima; **as ~ as possible** prima possibile; **reply ~** rispondete il prima possibile; **book your tickets ~** prenotate i biglietti il prima possibile 3. (*prematurely*) prematuramente; **to die ~** morire giovane

earmark ['ɪr·mɑːrk] I. *vt* 1. (*animal*) marchiare (sull'orecchio); (*document*) contrassegnare 2. (*put aside*) riservare; (*funds*) destinare II. *n* marchio (*m* sull'orecchio); *fig* marchio *m* distintivo

earmuffs ['ɪr·mʌfs] *npl* copriorecchie *m inv*
earn [ɜːrn] I. *vt* 1. (*be paid*) guadagnare; **to ~ one's daily bread** guadagnarsi il pane; **to ~ a living** guadagnarsi da vivere 2. (*bring in*) rendere; (*interest*) fruttare 3. (*obtain*) **to ~ money from sth** ottenere denaro da qc; **coffee exports ~ Brazil millions of dollars** l'esportazione di caffè frutta milioni di dollari al Brasile 4. (*deserve*) guadagnarsi; **his decision ~ed him the confidence/respect of his**

boss con quella decisione si è guadagnato la fiducia/il rispetto del suo capo II. *vi* guadagnare

earned income ['ɜːrnd·'ɪn·kʌm] *n* reddito *m* da lavoro
earner *n* salariato, -a *m, f*
earnest ['ɜːr·nɪst] I. *adj* 1. (*serious*) serio, -a 2. (*sincere*) sincero, -a; (*desire*) ardente II. *n* **in ~** sul serio; **school has now begun in ~** ora la scuola è iniziata sul serio
earnestly *adv* 1. (*speak*) seriamente 2. (*desire*) profondamente
earning power *n* capacità *f* di produrre reddito
earnings ['ɜːr·nɪŋz] *npl* 1. (*of a person*) entrate *fpl* 2. (*of a company*) utili *mpl*
earnings-related *adj* rapportato alle entrate
earphones ['ɪr·foʊnz] *npl* cuffie *fpl*
earpiece ['ɪr·piːs] *n* 1. (*of a phone*) ricevitore *m* 2. (*of glasses*) stanghetta *f*
earplug ['ɪr·plʌg] *n pl* tappo *m* per le orecchie
earring ['ɪ·rɪŋ] *n* orecchino *m;* **a pair of ~s** un paio di orecchini
earshot ['ɪr·ʃɑːt] *n* **in/out of ~** a portata/fuori portata d'orecchio; **within ~** a portata d'orecchio
earth [ɜːrθ] *n* 1. (*planet*) terra *f;* **on ~** al mondo; **you look like nothing (else) on ~** hai un aspetto terribile 2. (*soil*) terra *f* ►to **bring sb back (down) to ~** riportare qn coi piedi per terra; **to <u>come back</u> (down) to ~** tornare coi piedi per terra; **what/who/ where/why <u>on</u> ~ ...?** *inf* cosa/chi/dove/ perchè diavolo ...?
earthbound ['ɜːrθ·baʊnd] *adj* 1. incapace di sollevarsi da terra 2. *fig* (*ordinary*) prosaico, -a
earthenware ['ɜːr·θn·wer] I. *n* vasellame *m* di terracotta II. *adj* di terracotta
earthiness ['ɜːr·θɪ·nɪs] *n* 1. (*directness*) franchezza *f* 2. (*coarseness*) grossolanità *f*
earthling ['ɜːrθ·lɪŋ] *n* terrestre *mf*
earthly ['ɜːrθ·li] *adj* 1. (*concerning life on earth*) terreno, -a; (*paradise*) in terra; **her ~ belongings** *form* i suoi beni terreni; **~ remains** resti *m pl* mortali 2. *inf* (*possible*) **to be of no ~ use** non servire assolutamente a niente
earthquake ['ɜːrθ·kweɪk] *n* terremoto *m*
earth-shattering *adj* sconvolgente
earthwork *n* 1. *pl* MIL terrapieno *m* 2. (*work*) lavori *m pl* di sterro
earthworm *n* lombrico *m*
earthy ['ɜːr·θi] <-ier, -iest> *adj* 1. (*soil-like: color*) della terra; (*smell*) di terra 2. (*coarse: joke, person*) grossolano, -a 3. (*simple*) un semplice spezzatino fatto in casa
earwax ['ɪr·wæks] *n* cerume *m*
earwig ['ɪr·wɪg] *n* forbicina *f*
ease [iːz] I. *n* 1. (*without much effort*) facilità *f;* **for ~ of access** per comodità d'accesso; **to do sth with ~** fare qc con facilità 2. (*comfort, uninhibitedness*) agio *m;* **to live a life of ~** fare una vita agiata; **to feel at ~** sentirsi a proprio agio; **to be ill at ~** essere a disagio; **to be**

at ~ essere a proprio agio; **to put sb at** (**his/her**) ~ mettere qn a proprio agio; (**stand**) **at** ~! MIL riposo! **II.** *vt* **1.** (*relieve: pain*) attenuare; (*tension*) allentare; **to** ~ **one's conscience** alleggerirsi la coscienza; **to** ~ **sb's mind** tranquillizzare qn **2.** (*burden*) alleggerire **III.** *vi* (*pain*) attenuarsi; (*tension*) allentarsi; (*prices*) calare

◆**ease off** *vi*, **ease up** *vi* (*pain*) attenuarsi; (*fever, wind*) abbassarsi; (*sales, rain*) diminuire; (*tension*) allentarsi; (*person*) rilassarsi; ~ **or you will have a nervous breakdown** rallenta il ritmo o ti verrà un esaurimento nervoso

easel ['i:·zl] *n* cavalletto *m*

easily ['i:·zə·li] *adv* **1.** (*without difficulty*) facilmente; **to be** ~ **impressed** lasciarsi impressionare facilmente; **to win** ~ vincere con facilità; **I get tired very** ~ mi stanco facilmente **2.** + *superl* (*clearly*) **to be** ~ **the best** è indubbiamente il migliore **3.** (*probably*) con ogni probabilità; **his guess could** ~ **be wrong** è facile che si sbagli

easiness ['i:·zɪ·nɪs] *n* facilità *f*

east [i:st] **I.** *n* est *m;* **to lie 5 miles to the** ~ **of Boston** trovarsi a 5 miglia a est di Boston; **to go/drive to the** ~ andare/guidare verso est; **further** ~ più a est; **in the** ~ **of France** a est della Francia; **Far East** Estremo *m* Oriente; **Middle East** Medio *m* Oriente **II.** *adj* orientale; ~ **wind** vento *m* dell'est; ~ **coast** costa *f* orientale; **East Indies** Indie *f pl* Orientali

eastbound ['i:st·baʊnd] *adj* diretto, -a a est

Easter ['i:s·tə·] *n* Pasqua *f;* **during** ~ a Pasqua

Easter Bunny *n* Coniglietto *m* pasquale

Easter Day *n*, **Easter Sunday** *n* domenica *f* di Pasqua

Easter egg *n* uovo *m* di Pasqua

Easter holidays *npl* vacanze *f pl* di Pasqua

Easter Island *npl* isola *f* di Pasqua

easterly ['i:s·tə·li] **I.** *adj* (*wind*) dell'est; **in an** ~ **direction** in direzione est **II.** *adv* **1.** (*towards the east*) verso est **2.** (*from the east*) da est **III.** *n* vento *m* dell'est

Easter Monday *n* lunedì *m* dell'Angelo

eastern ['i:s·tən] *adj* orientale

easterner ['i:s·tə·nə·] *n* abitante *mf* dell'est degli Stati Uniti

easternmost ['i:s·tən·moʊst] *adj* più orientale; **the** ~ **time zone** il fuso orario più orientale

East Germany [ˌi:st·'dʒɜ:·mə·ni] *n* HIST Germania *f* dell'Est

eastward ['i:st·wə·d] **I.** *adj* **in an** ~ **direction** in direzione est **II.** *adv* verso est

eastwards ['i:st·wə·dz] *adv* verso est

easy ['i:·zi] (<-ier, -iest> **I.** *adj* **1.** (*simple*) facile; ~ **money** *inf* denaro *m* facile; **the hotel is within** ~ **reach of the beach** l'albergo è a poca distanza dalla spiaggia; **to be far from** ~ essere tutt'altro che facile; **she's** ~ **to get along with** è facile andare d'accordo con lei; **to take the** ~ **way out** scegliere la via d'uscita

più facile; **to be as** ~ **as anything** [*o* **can be**] *inf* essere facilissimo; **to be the easiest thing in the world** essere la cosa più facile del mondo; **that's** ~ **said than done** *inf* è più facile a dirsi che a farsi **2.** (*relaxed*) tranquillo, -a; **to have an** ~ **manner** avere modi spigliati; **at an** ~ **pace** senza fretta; **to be on** ~ **terms with sb** essere in confidenza con qn **3.** (*pleasant*) ~ **on the ear/eye** piacevole da ascoltare/guardare; **an** ~ **disposition** un carattere accomodante **4.** (*undemanding*) indulgente; **to be** ~ **on sb** non essere troppo severo con qn **5.** (*exploitable*) **an** ~ **target** un bersaglio facile **6.** (*financially secure*) agiato, -a; **to live the** ~ **life** fare una vita agiata **7.** *pej, sl* (*sexually promiscuous*) facile; **she's an** ~ **lay** è una che ci sta ►**to be** (**as**) ~ **as pie** essere facile come bere un bicchier d'acqua **II.** *adv* **1.** (*cautiously*) con calma; ~ **does it** *inf* piano! **2.** (*lenient*) **to go** ~ **on sb** *inf* andarci piano con qn **3.** *inf* (*less actively*) **to take things** ~ prendere le cose con calma; **take it** ~! (prenditela con) calma! ►~ **come,** ~ **go** *inf* tanti presi, tanti spesi

easy-care *adj* che non necessita stiratura

easy chair *n* poltrona *f*

easy-going *adj* (*person*) accomodante; (*attitude*) tollerante

eat [i:t] **I.** <ate, eaten> *vt* mangiare; **to** ~ **breakfast** fare colazione; **to** ~ **lunch/dinner** pranzare/cenare; **to** ~ **one's fill** mangiare a sazietà ►~ **your heart out!** mangiati il fegato!; **to** ~ **one's words** rimangiarsi ciò che si è detto; **what is** ~**ing him?** *inf* cos'è che lo rode? **II.** *vi* mangiare

◆**eat away** *vt* (*acid*) corrodere; (*termites*) rosicchiare

◆**eat away at** *vt*, **eat into** *vt* intaccare

◆**eat in** *vi* mangiare a casa

◆**eat out I.** *vi* mangiare fuori **II.** *vt vulg* leccarla a

◆**eat up** *vt* mangiare tutto

eaten ['i:·tən] *pp of* **eat**

eater ['i:·tə·] *n* **to be a big** ~ essere una buona forchetta [*o* un mangione]; **to be a small** ~ non mangiare molto

eatery ['i:·tə·i] *n inf* ristorante *m*

eating disorder *n* disturbo *m* dell'alimentazione

eating habits *npl* abitudini *f pl* alimentari

eats *npl sl* roba *f* da mangiare; **good** ~ cibo *m* appetitoso

eau de Cologne [ˌoʊ də kə·'loʊn] *n* acqua *f* di colonia

eaves [i:vz] *npl* ARCHIT gronda *f*

eavesdrop ['i:vz·drɑ:p] <-pp-> *vi* **to** ~ **on sth/sb** ascoltare qc/qn di nascosto

eavesdropper ['i:vz·drɑ:·pə·] *n* chi origlia

eaves spout *n reg*, **eaves trough** *n reg* (*gutter*) grondaia *f*

ebb [eb] **I.** *vi* **1.** (*tide*) abbassarsi **2.** *fig* diminuire **II.** *n* **1.** (*tide*) riflusso *m;* **the tide is on the** ~ c'è bassa marea **2.** *fig* **the** ~ **and flow of**

sth gli alti e bassi di qc; **to be at a low ~** andare male; (*person*) essere a terra
ebb tide *n* bassa marea *f*
ebony ['e·bə·ni] *n* ebano *m*
ebullient [ɪ·'bʊl·jənt] *adj* entusiasta; **to be in an ~ mood** essere (d'umore) euforico
EC [ˌi:·'si:] *n abbr of* **European Community** CE *f*
eccentric [ɪk·'sent·rɪk] I. *n* eccentrico, -a *m, f* II. *adj* eccentrico, -a
eccentricity [ˌek·sen·'trɪ·sə·ti] *n* <-ies> eccentricità *f*
ecclesiastic [ɪ·ˌkli:·zɪ·'æs·tɪk] I. *n form* ecclesiastico *m* II. *adj form* ecclesiastico, -a
ecclesiastical [ɪ·ˌkli:·zɪ·'æs·tɪ·kl] *adj form* ecclesiastico, -a
ECG [ˌi:·si:·'dʒi:] *n abbr of* **electrocardiogram** ECG *m*
echelon ['e·ʃə·lɑ:n] *n* 1. (*strata*) rango *m*; (*of society*) strato *m*; **the highest ~s of sth** i livelli più alti di qc 2. MIL scaglione *m*
echo ['e·koʊ] I. <-es> *n* eco *f o m* II. <-es, -ing, -ed> *vi* echeggiare III. <-es, -ing, -ed> *vt* 1. (*reflect*) ripetere; **the mountains ~ed his howls** le montagne rimandavano l'eco dei suoi ululati 2. (*repeat*) fare eco a 3. (*imitate*) richiamare
echo chamber *n* camera *f* di riverberazione
echo sounder *n* ecoscandaglio *m*
eclectic [ek·'lek·tɪk] I. *n form* eclettico, -a *m, f* II. *adj form* eclettico, -a
eclipse [ɪ·'klɪps] I. *n* eclissi *f inv*; **solar/lunar ~** eclissi solare/lunare; **total/partial ~ of the sun** eclissi solare totale/parziale; **to be in ~** essere in eclissi; *fig* essere in declino II. *vt* eclissare
ecological [ˌi:·kə·'lɑ:·dʒɪ·kl] *adj* ecologico, -a
ecologically [ˌi:·kə·'lɑ:·dʒɪk·li] *adv* dal punto di vista ecologico; **~ friendly** attento all'aspetto ecologico; **~ harmful** nocivo all'ambiente
ecologist [i:·'kɑ:·lə·dʒɪst] *n* 1. (*expert*) ecologo, -a *m* 2. POL ecologista *mf*
ecology [i:·'kɑ:·lə·dʒi] *n* ecologia *f*
ecology movement *n* movimento *m* ecologista
e-commerce ['i:·kɑ:·mɜ:rs] *n* e-commerce *m*
economic [ˌi:·kə·'nɑ:·mɪk] *adj* 1. POL, ECON economico, -a 2. (*profitable*) redditizio, -a
economical [ˌi:·kə·'nɑ:·mɪ·kl] *adj* economico, -a
economics [ˌi:·kə·'nɑ:·mɪks] *npl* 1. + *sing vb* (*discipline*) economia *f*; **School of Economics** Facoltà *f* di Scienze Economiche 2. + *pl vb* (*matter*) aspetti *m pl* economici; **the ~ of the agreement** gli aspetti economici dell'accordo
economist [ɪ·'kɑ:·nə·mɪst] *n* economista *mf*
economize [ɪ·'kɑ:·nə·maɪz] *vi* economizzare; **to ~ on sth** fare economia su qc
economy [ɪ·'kɑ:·nə·mi] <-ies> *n* 1. (*frugality*) risparmio *m*; **for the purposes of ~** per ragioni economiche; **to make economies** risparmiare; **to practice ~** economizzare 2. (*monetary assets*) economia *f*; **the state of the ~** la situazione economica; **capitalist/market/planned ~** economia capitalista/di mercato/pianificata
economy class *n* AVIAT classe *f* turistica
economy size *n* formato *m* risparmio
ecosystem *n* ecosistema *m*
ecotourism *n* ecoturismo *m*
ecotourist *n* ecoturista *mf*
eco-warrior *n* ecologista *mf* militante
ecstasy ['eks·tə·si] <-ies> *n* 1. (*psychological state*) estasi *f inv* 2. *inf* (*MDMA*) ecstasy *f inv*
ecstatic [ek·'stæ·tɪk] *adj* estatico, -a; (*rapturous*) entusiasta; **to be ~ about sth** essere entusiasta di qc
ECT [ˌi:·si:·'ti:] *n abbr of* **electroconvulsive therapy** elettroshockterapia *f*
Ecuador ['ek·wə·dɔ:r] *n* Ecuador *m*
Ecuadorian [ˌek·wə·'dɔ:·ri·ən] I. *n* ecuadoriano, -a *m, f* II. *adj* ecuadoriano, -a
ecumenical [ˌek·jʊ·'me·nɪ·kl] *adj* ecumenico, -a
eczema ['ek·sə·mə] *n* eczema *m*
ed. 1. *abbr of* **editor** redattore, -trice *m, f* 2. *abbr of* **edition** ed. 3. *abbr of* **edited** a cura di
eddy ['e·di] I. <-ie-> *vi* mulinare II. <-ies> *n* mulinello *m*
Eden ['i:·dn] *n* Eden *m*; **the garden of ~** il giardino dell'Eden
edge [edʒ] I. *n sing* 1. (*limit*) bordo *m*; (*of a lake, pond*) sponda *f*; (*of a mountain*) cresta *f*; (*of a page*) margine *m*; **to bring sth to the ~ of disaster** portare qc sull'orlo del disastro; **to take the ~ off one's appetite/hunger** placare l'appetito/la fame; **to take the ~ off an argument** sottrarre forza a un argomento 2. (*cutting part*) filo *m*; **to put an ~ on sth** affilare qc 3. (*anger*) **to be on ~** avere i nervi a fior di pelle; **there's a definite ~ in her voice** ha un tono decisamente irritato 4. SPORTS **to have the ~ over sb** essere avvantaggiato rispetto a qn ▶ **to be (balanced) on a razor's ~** stare sul filo del rasoio; **to set sb's teeth on ~** dare sui nervi a qn; **to live on the ~** vivere pericolosamente II. *vt* 1. (*border*) delimitare 2. (*in sewing*) orlare 3. (*move slowly*) **to ~ one's way through sth** farsi strada tra qc; **she's edging her party towards extremism** a poco a poco sta spingendo il suo partito verso l'estremismo 4. (*skis*) mettere di taglio III. *vi* **to ~ closer to sth** accostarsi a qc; **to ~ away from danger** allontanarsi dal pericolo; **to ~ forward** avanzare progressivamente
edgeways ['edʒ·weɪz] *adv*, **edgewise** *adv* di fianco
edging ['e·dʒɪŋ] *n* bordo *m*
edgy ['e·dʒi] <-ier, -iest> *adj inf* teso, -a
edible ['e·dɪ·bl] I. *adj* commestibile II. *n pl* (*food*) commestibili *mpl*
edict ['i:·dɪkt] *n* 1. HIST editto *m* 2. (*order*) decreto *m*

edification [ˌe·dɪ·fɪ·'keɪ·ʃən] *n form* edificazione *f*

edifice ['e·dɪ·fɪs] *n* **1.** *form* (*building*) edificio *m* **2.** *fig* (*of ideas*) struttura *f*

edify ['e·dɪ·faɪ] <-ie-> *vt form* edificare

edifying *adj form* edificante

edit ['e·dɪt] *vt* **1.** (*correct*) correggere; (*articles*) rivedere **2.** (*newspaper*) dirigere **3.** CINE montare **4.** INFOR editare

♦ **edit out** *vt* tagliare

edition [ɪ·'dɪ·ʃən] *n* edizione *f*; (*set of books*) tiratura *f*; **paperback** ~ edizione *f* economica; **limited** ~ edizione a tiratura limitata; **collector's** ~ edizione per collezionisti

editor ['e·dɪ·tə·] *n* **1.** (*of book*) curatore, -trice *m, f*; (*of article*) redattore, -trice *m, f*; (*of newspaper*) direttore, -trice *m, f*; **chief** ~ redattore, -trice capo *m*; **sports** ~ redattore, -trice sportivo *m* **2.** CINE addetto, -a *m, f* al montaggio **3.** INFOR editor *m inv*

editorial [ˌe·də·'tɔ:·ri·əl] **I.** *n* editoriale *m* **II.** *adj* editoriale; ~ **staff** redazione *f*

editor-in-chief [ˌe·dɪ·tə·ɪn·'tʃi:f] *n* redattore, -trice *m, f* capo

EDP [ˌi:·di:·'pi:] *n abbr of* **electronic data processing** EDP *m*

EDT [ˌi:·di:·'ti:] *n abbr of* **Eastern Daylight Time** *ora legale adottata negli Stati Uniti orientali*

educate ['ed·ʒʊ·keɪt] *vt* **1.** (*bring up*) educare **2.** (*teach*) istruire; **to ~ the ear** educare l'udito **3.** (*inform*) informare; **to ~ sb in sth** informare qn su qc

educated ['ed·ʒʊ·keɪ·tɪd] *adj* istruito, -a; **highly** ~ colto

education [ˌed·ʒʊ·'keɪ·ʃən] *n* **1.** SCHOOL istruzione *f*; **primary/secondary** ~ istruzione *f* primaria/secondaria; **Education Secretary** [*o* **Secretary of Education**] Ministro *m* della Pubblica Istruzione **2.** (*training*) formazione *f*; **science/literary** ~ formazione scientifica/letteraria **3.** (*teaching*) insegnamento *m*; (*study of teaching*) pedagogia *f* **4.** (*culture*) cultura *f*

educational [ˌed·ʒʊ·'keɪ·ʃə·nl] *adj* **1.** SCHOOL (*system, establishment*) educativo, -a; (*method*) pedagogico, -a; **for ~ purposes** a fini educativi **2.** (*instructive*) istruttivo, -a **3.** (*raising awareness*) formativo, -a

educationist, educationalist *n* pedagogista *mf*

educator ['ed·ʒʊ·keɪ·tə·] *n* educatore, -trice *m, f*

EEC [ˌi:·i·'si:] *n abbr of* **European Economic Community** CEE *f*

EEG [ˌi:·i·'dʒi:] *n abbr of* **electroencephalogram** EEG *m*

eel [i:l] *n* anguilla *f* ► **to be as slippery as an** ~ essere viscido come un'anguilla

eerie ['ɪ·ri] *adj*, **eery** <-ier, -iest> *adj* inquietante

efface [ɪ·'feɪs] *vt* **1.** *a. fig* cancellare **2.** (*be humble*) **to ~ oneself** cercare di passare inosservato

effect [ɪ·'fekt] **I.** *n* **1.** (*consequence*) effetto *m*; **to have an ~ on sth** avere effetto su qc; **to have a disastrous ~ on** [*o* **upon**] **sth** avere un effetto disastroso su qc; **to have no ~ on sb** non avere alcun effetto su qn **2.** (*result*) risultato *m*; **to have little/no ~** dare scarsi risultati/non dare risultati; **to take ~** dare risultati; (*medicine, alcohol*) fare effetto; **to the ~ that** ... con lo scopo di ...; **to no ~** senza risultato **3.** LAW **to come into** [*o* **to take**] ~ entrare in vigore; **to remain/be in ~** rimanere/essere in vigore **4.** (*gist*) **to the same ~** in quel senso; **he disapproved of our idea and wrote to us to that ~** era in disaccordo con la nostra idea e ci ha scritto in tal senso **5.** (*impression*) impressione *f*; **the overall ~** l'impressione generale; **for ~** per creare un effetto **6.** *pl* (*belongings*) effetti *mpl*; **personal ~s** effetti personali ► **in** ~ in pratica **II.** *vt* effettuare

effective [ɪ·'fek·tɪv] *adj* **1.** (*giving result*) efficace; **he was an ~ speaker** era un oratore di grande abilità **2.** (*real*) reale; ~ **control** controllo effettivo **3.** (*operative*) in vigore; **to become** ~ entrare in vigore **4.** (*striking*) d'effetto

effectively *adv* **1.** (*giving result*) efficacemente **2.** (*really*) di fatto **3.** (*strikingly*) con grande effetto

effectiveness *n* **1.** (*efficiency*) efficacia *f* **2.** (*of a rule*) validità *f*

effectual [ɪ·'fek·tʃu:·əl] *adj* **1.** (*efficient*) efficace **2.** (*operative*) valido, -a

effectuate [ɪ·'fek·tʃu:·eɪt] *vt* effettuare

effeminacy [ɪ·'fe·mɪ·nə·si] *n* effeminatezza *f*

effeminate [ɪ·'fe·mɪ·nət] **I.** *adj* effeminato, -a **II.** *n* effeminato *m*

effervesce [ˌe·fə·'ves] *vi* **1.** (*bubble*) frizzare **2.** *fig* (*person*) essere effervescente

effervescence [ˌe·fə·'ve·sns] *n* effervescenza *f*

effervescent [ˌe·fə·'ve·snt] *adj a. fig* effervescente

effete [ɪ·'fi:t] *adj* **1.** (*enfeebled*) infiacchito, -a **2.** (*decadent*) decadente **3.** (*effeminate*) effeminato, -a

efficacious [ˌe·fɪ·'keɪ·əs] *adj form* (*solution, suggestion*) efficace; **an ~ medicine** un farmaco efficace

efficacy ['e·fɪ·kə·si] *n form* efficacia *f*

efficiency [ɪ·'fɪ·ʃn·si] *n* **1.** (*of a person*) efficienza *f*; (*of a method*) efficacia *f* **2.** (*of a machine*) rendimento *m*

efficient [ɪ·'fɪ·ʃnt] *adj* (*person*) efficiente; (*machine, system*) ad alto rendimento

effigy ['e·fɪ·dʒi] *n* effigie *f*

effluent ['e·flʊ·ənt] *n* **1.** emissario *m* **2.** (*liquid waste*) effluente *m*

effort ['e·fə·t] *n* **1.** *a.* PHYS sforzo *m*; **to be worth the** ~ valerne la pena; **to make an ~ to do sth** sforzarsi [*o* fare lo sforzo] di fare qc; **to spare no** ~ non risparmiarsi; **without** ~ senza fatica **2.** (*attempt*) tentativo *m*; **please make an ~ to** ... per favore, cerca di ... **3.** (*work*) impresa *f*

E

effortless ['e·fət·ləs] *adj* facile; **an ~ movement** un movimento senza sforzo apparente; **an ~ grace** una grazia naturale

effrontery [e·'frʌn·tə·ri] *n form* sfrontatezza *f;* **to have the ~ to do sth** avere la sfacciataggine di fare qc

effusion [ɪ·'fjuː·ʒən] *n a. fig* effusione *f*

effusive [ɪ·'fjuː·sɪv] *adj form* (*person*) espansivo, -a; (*welcome*) caloroso, -a

eft [eft] *n* tritone *m*

EFTS *abbr of* **electronic funds transfer system** servizio *m* di trasferimento elettronico di fondi

e.g. [ˌiː·'dʒiː] *abbr of* **exempli gratia** (= **for example**) ad es.

egalitarian [ɪ·ˌgæ·lɪ·'te·ri·ən] *adj* egualitario, -a

e-generation [iː·ˌdʒe·nə·'reɪ·ʃən] *n* generazione *f* di Internet

egg [eg] *n* uovo *m;* **fried/boiled ~s** uova fritte/alla coque; **hard-boiled ~** uovo sodo; **scrambled ~s** uova strapazzate ▶ **to put all one's ~s in one** basket puntare tutto su una carta sola; **they had ~ on their** faces *inf* hanno fatto una figuraccia; **to be a** bad **~** *inf* essere un cattivo elemento

◆ **egg on** *vt* incitare

egg cell *n* ovulo *m*

eggcup *n* portauovo *m*

egghead *n inf* testa *f* d'uovo

eggnog *n* bevanda *a base di uova, latte e panna e zucchero, spesso con aggiunta di rum o brandy, che si beve tradizionalmente a Natale*

eggplant *n* melanzana *f*

egg roll *n* involtino *m* primavera

eggshell *n* guscio *m* d'uovo

egg timer *n* clessidra *f* da tre minuti

egg yolk *n* tuorlo *m*

ego ['iː·goʊ] *n* <-s> **1.** PSYCH ego *m;* **to bolster sb's ~** rafforzare l'ego di qn **2.** (*self-esteem*) amor *m* proprio

egocentric [ˌiː·goʊ·'sent·rɪk] *adj* egocentrico, -a

egoism ['iː·goʊ·ɪ·zəm] *n* egoismo *m*

egoist ['iː·goʊ·ɪst] *n* egoista *mf*

egoistic(al) [ˌiː·goʊ·'ɪs·tɪ·k(l)] *adj* egoista

egotism ['iː·goʊ·tɪ·zəm] *n* egotismo *m*

egotist ['iː·goʊ·tɪst] *n* egotista *mf*

egotistic(al) [ˌiː·goʊ·'tɪs·tɪ·k(l)] *adj* **1.** (*selfish*) egoista **2.** (*self-important*) egotista

ego trip ['iː·goʊ·trɪp] *n* **to be on an ~** gasarsi

egregious [ɪ·'griː·dʒəs] *adj* madornale

Egypt ['iː·dʒɪpt] *n* Egitto *m*

Egyptian [ɪ·'dʒɪp·ʃən] **I.** *n* egiziano, -a *m, f* **II.** *adj* egiziano, -a

eh [e:] *interj* **1.** (*what did you say?*) eh? **2.** *Can* (*isn't it; aren't you/they/we*) **it's cold outside, ~?** fa freddo fuori, eh?

eider ['aɪ·də] *n* edredone *m*

eiderdown ['aɪ·də·daʊn] *n* piumino *m*

eight [eɪt] **I.** *adj* otto *inv;* **there are ~ of us** siamo (in) otto; **~ and a quarter/half** otto e un quarto/mezzo; **~ o'clock** le otto; **it's ~**

o'clock sono le otto; **it's half past ~** sono le otto e mezza; **at ~ twenty/thirty** alle otto e venti/mezza **II.** *n* otto *m*

eighteen [ˌeɪ·'tiːn] **I.** *adj* diciotto **II.** *n* diciotto *m; s.a.* **eight**

eighteenth [ˌeɪ·'tiːnθ] **I.** *adj* diciottesimo, -a **II.** *n* **1.** (*order*) diciottesimo, -a *m, f* **2.** (*date*) diciotto *m* **3.** (*fraction*) diciottesimo *m;* (*part*) diciottesima parte *f; s.a.* **eighth**

eighth [eɪtθ] **I.** *adj* ottavo, -a; **~ note** croma *f* **II.** *n* **1.** (*order*) ottavo, -a *m, f;* **to be ~ in a race** arrivare ottavo in una corsa **2.** (*date*) otto *m;* **the ~ of December; the ~ of December** (**the**) **~**] l'otto dicembre **3.** (*fraction*) ottavo *m;* (*part*) ottava parte *f* **III.** *adv* (*in lists*) ottavo

eight-hour day *n* giornata *f* di otto ore

eightieth ['eɪ·ti·əθ] **I.** *adj* ottantesimo, -a **II.** *n* (*order*) ottantesimo, -a *m, f;* (*fraction*) ottantesimo *m;* (*part*) ottantesima parte *f; s.a.* **eighth**

eighty ['eɪ·ti] **I.** *adj* ottanta *inv;* **he is ~** (**years old**) ha ottant'anni; **a man of about ~ years of age** un uomo di circa ottant'anni **II.** *n* <-ies> **1.** (*number*) ottanta *m;* **to do ~** *inf* andare a 80 miglia all'ora **2.** (*age*) **a woman in her eighties** una donna tra gli ottanta e i novant'anni **3.** (*decade*) **the eighties** gli anni *m* ottanta *pl*

either ['iː·ðə] **I.** *adj* **1.** (*one of two*) **I'll do it ~ way** lo farò in un modo o nell'altro; **I don't like ~ dress** non mi piace né un vestito, né l'altro **2.** (*each*) ciascun(o), -a; **on ~ side of the river** su entrambi i lati del fiume **II.** *pron* l'uno, -a o l'altro, -a; **which one? — ~** quale? — l'uno o l'altro **III.** *adv* neppure; **if he doesn't go, I won't go ~** se lui non ci va, non ci vado neanch'io **IV.** *conj* **~ ... or ...** o ... o ...; **~ buy it or rent it** o lo compri o lo noleggi; **I can ~ stay or leave** posso rimanere o andarmene

ejaculate¹ [ɪ·'dʒæ·kju·leɪt] **I.** *vt* **1.** (*semen*) espellere **2.** *lit* (*blurt out*) esclamare **II.** *vi* ANAT eiaculare

ejaculate² [ɪ·'dʒæk·ju·lət] *n* sperma *m*

ejaculation [ɪ·ˌdʒæ·kjʊ·'leɪ·ʃən] *n* **1.** (*of semen*) eiaculazione *f* **2.** *lit* (*sudden outburst*) esclamazione *f*

eject [ɪ·'dʒekt] **I.** *vt* buttare fuori, espellere; (*liquid, gas*) emettere **II.** *vi* lanciarsi con il seggiolino eiettabile

ejector seat [ɪ·'dʒek·tə siːt] *n* seggiolino *m* eiettabile

eke out [iːk aʊt] *vt* (*money, food*) far bastare; **to ~ one's salary** farsi bastare lo stipendio *inf;* **to ~ a living** sbarcare il lunario

EKG [ˌiː·keɪ·'dʒiː] *n abbr of* **electrocardiogram** elettrocardiogramma *m*

elaborate¹ [ɪ·'læ·bə·rət] *adj* (*complicated*) elaborato, -a; (*very detailed: plan*) minuzioso, -a; (*style*) ornato, -a; (*excuse*) macchinoso, -a

elaborate² [ɪ·'læ·bə·reɪt] **I.** *vt* elaborare; (*plan*) sviluppare **II.** *vi* fornire dettagli; **to refuse to ~**

rifiutarsi di fornire dettagli; **to ~ on an idea** sviluppare un'idea

elaboration [ɪ·ˌlæ·bə·ˈreɪ·ʃən] <-(s)> *n* **1.** (*of a theory*) elaborazione *f*; (*of texts*) spiegazione *f*; **without** ~ senza entrare in troppi dettagli **2.** (*complexity*) complessità *f*

elapse [ɪ·ˈlæps] *vi form* trascorrere

elastic [ɪ·ˈlæs·tɪk] **I.** *adj* elastico, -a **II.** *n* **1.** (*material*) elastico *m* **2.** (*garter*) giarrettiera *f*

elasticity [ˌe·læ·ˈstɪ·sə·ti] *n a. fig* elasticità *f*

elate [ɪ·ˈleɪt] *vt* esaltare; **to be ~d about sth** essere esultante per qc

elated *adj* esultante

elation [ɪ·ˈleɪ·ʃən] *n* esultanza *f*

elbow [ˈel·boʊ] **I.** *n* **1.** (*of people*) gomito *m* **2.** (*in a pipe*) gomito *m*; (*in a road, river*) curva *f*; (*in a river*) ansa *f* ▶ **to** <u>rub</u> **~s with sb** essere in confidenza con qn **II.** *vt* dare una gomitata a; **to ~ one's way through the crowd** farsi largo a gomitate tra la folla

elbow grease *n inf* olio *m* di gomito; **to put some ~ into sth** mettere impegno in qc

elbow room *n* **1.** (*space*) spazio *m* **2.** (*freedom*) libertà *f* d'azione

elder[1] [ˈel·dɚ] **I.** *n* **1.** (*older person*) maggiore *mf*; **she is my ~ by three years** è maggiore di me di tre anni **2.** (*senior person*) anziano, -a *m, f* **3.** (*in Mormon Church*) anziano *m* **II.** *adj* maggiore; **~ statesman/stateswoman** POL veterano, -a della politica *m*

elder[2] [ˈel·dɚ] *n* BOT sambuco *m*

elderberry [ˈel·dɚ·be·ri] <-ies> *n* **1.** (*berry*) bacca *f* di sambuco **2.** BOT sambuco *m*

elderly [ˈel·dɚ·li] **I.** *adj* anziano, -a; **an ~ woman** una signora anziana **II.** *n* **the ~** gli anziani

eldest [ˈel·dɪst] *adj superl of* **old** maggiore; **the ~** il/la maggiore; **her ~** (**child**) **is nearly 14** il suo primogenito ha quasi 14 anni

elect [ɪ·ˈlekt] **I.** *vt* **1.** (*by vote*) eleggere **2.** (*not by vote*) decidere; **to ~ to resign** optare per le dimissioni **II.** *n* REL **the ~** gli eletti **III.** *adj* **the president ~** il presidente eletto

election [ɪ·ˈlek·ʃən] *n* **1.** (*event*) elezioni *fpl;* **to call/hold an ~** indire le elezioni; **to run for ~** presentarsi alle elezioni **2.** (*action*) elezione *f*

election campaign *n* campagna *f* elettorale

Election Day *n* giornata *f* elettorale

election defeat *n* sconfitta *f* elettorale

electioneer [ɪ·ˌlek·ʃə·ˈnɪr] *vi* fare propaganda elettorale

electioneering [ɪ·ˌlek·ʃə·ˈnɪ·rɪŋ] *n* propaganda *f* elettorale; *pej* promesse *f pl* elettorali

election platform *n*, **election program** *n* piattaforma *f* elettorale

election results *npl*, **election returns** *npl* risultati *m pl* elettorali

election speech *n* discorso *m* elettorale

elective [ɪ·ˈlek·tɪv] **I.** *adj* **1.** *form* (*appointed by election*) elettivo, -a; (*based on voting*) elettorale **2.** (*optional*) facoltativo, a **3.** (*selective*) **~ affinity** affinità elettiva **II.** *n* SCHOOL, UNIV corso *m* facoltativo

elector [ɪ·ˈlek·tɚ] *n* **1.** (*voter*) elettore, -trice *m, f* **2.** (*member of Electoral College*) membro *m* dell'Electoral College

electoral [ɪ·ˈlek·tə·rəl] *adj* elettorale; **Electoral College** *collegio elettorale incaricato di eleggere il presidente e il vicepresidente degli Stati Uniti;* ~ **register** [*o* **roll**] lista *f* elettorale

electorate [ɪ·ˈlek·tə·rət] *n* elettorato *m*

electric [ɪ·ˈlek·trɪk] *adj* **1.** ELEC elettrico, -a; (*fence*) elettrificato, -a; ~ **blanket** termocoperta *f*; ~ **stove** fornello *m* elettrico; ~ **current** corrente *f* elettrica; ~ **heater** stufetta *f* elettrica; ~ **shock** scossa *f* elettrica **2.** *fig* elettrizzante; (*atmosphere*) carico, -a di elettricità

electrical [ɪ·ˈlek·trɪ·kl] *adj* elettrico, -a; ~ **tape** nastro *m* isolante; ~ **engineering** (ingegneria *f*) elettrotecnica

electric chair *n* sedia *f* elettrica; **he was sentenced to death in the ~** è stato condannato alla sedia elettrica

electric guitar *n* chitarra *f* elettrica

electrician [ɪ·ˌlek·ˈtrɪ·ʃən] *n* elettricista *mf*

electricity [ɪ·ˌlek·ˈtrɪ·sə·ti] *n* elettricità *f*; **powered by ~** azionato dall'elettricità; **to run on ~** funzionare a elettricità

electrification [ɪ·ˌlek·trɪ·fɪ·ˈkeɪ·ʃən] *n* elettrificazione *f*

electrify [ɪ·ˈlek·trɪ·faɪ] *vt* elettrificare; *fig* elettrizzare

electroanalysis [ɪ·ˌlek·trəʊ·ə·ˈnæ·lɪ·sɪs] *n* elettroanalisi *f*

electrocardiogram [ɪ·ˌlek·troʊ·ˈkɑːr·dɪəʊ·græm] *n* elettrocardiogramma *m*

electroconvulsive therapy [ɪ·ˌlek·troʊ·kən·ˈʌl·sɪv ˈθe·rə·pi] *adj* elettroshockterapia *f*

electrocute [ɪ·ˈlek·trə·kjuːt] *vt* folgorare

electrocution [ɪ·ˌlek·trə·ˈkjuː·ʃən] *n* elettrocuzione *f*

electrode [ɪ·ˈlek·troʊd] *n* elettrodo *m*

electroencephalogram [ɪ·ˌlek·troʊ·en·ˈse·fə·loʊ·ˌgræm] *n* elettroencefalogramma *m*

electrolysis [ɪ·ˌlek·ˈtrɑː·lə·sɪs] *n* elettrolisi *f*

electromagnet [ɪ·ˈlek·troʊ·ˈmæg·nɪt] *n* elettromagnete *m*

electromagnetic [ɪ·ˌlek·troʊ·mæg·ˈne·ţɪk] *adj* elettromagnetico, -a

electron [ɪ·ˈlek·trɑːn] *n* elettrone *m*

electronic [ɪ·ˌlek·ˈtrɑː·nɪk] *adj* elettronico, -a

electronic data processing *n* elaborazione *f* elettronica dei dati

electronic fund transfer *n* trasferimento *m* elettronico di fondi

electronic mail *n* posta *f* elettronica

electronic music *n* musica *f* elettronica

electronics [ɪ·ˌlek·ˈtrɑː·nɪks] *n + sing vb* elettronica *f*; **the ~ industry** l'industria elettronica

electron microscope *n* microscopio *m* elettronico

electroplate [ɪ·ˈlek·troʊ·pleɪt] *vt* galvanizzare

electroscope [ɪ·ˈlek·troʊ·ˌskoʊp] *n* elettroscopio *m*

electrotherapy *n* elettroterapia *f*

elegance [ˈe·lɪ·gəns] *n* eleganza *f*

elegant ['e·lɪ·gənt] *adj* elegante
elegiac [ˌe·lɪ·'dʒa·ɪək] I. *adj* elegiaco, -a II. *n pl* versi *m pl* elegiaci
elegy ['e·lə·dʒi] *n* elegia *f*
element ['e·lɪ·mənt] *n* 1. *a.* CHEM, MAT elemento *m;* **the four ~s** i quattro elementi; **he's in his ~** si trova nel suo elemento 2. *(factor)* fattore *m;* **an ~ of luck** un pizzico di fortuna; **the ~ of surprise** il fattore sorpresa; **there's an ~ of truth in what they say** c'è del vero in quello che dicono 3. ELEC resistenza *f* 4. *pl (rudiments)* rudimenti *mpl* 5. *pl* METEO **the ~s** gli elementi
elemental [ˌe·lə·'men·t̩l] *adj* degli elementi; *(forces)* della natura; *(feelings, needs)* primario, -a
elementary [ˌe·lə·'men·t̩ə·i] *adj* elementare; *(course)* di base
elementary school *n* scuola *f* elementare
elephant ['e·lɪ·fənt] *n* elefante *m*
elephantiasis [ˌe·lɪ·fən·'taɪ·ə·sɪs] *n* MED elefantiasi *f inv*
elephantine [ˌe·lɪ·'fæn·taɪn] *adj* 1. *(huge)* elefantesco, -a 2. *(clumsy)* goffo, -a
elevate ['e·lɪ·veɪt] *vt* 1. *(raise)* elevare; *(prices)* aumentare; **to ~ the mind** elevare la mente 2. REL innalzare 3. *(in rank)* promuovere
elevated ['e·lɪ·veɪ·t̩ɪd] *adj* 1. *(raised: part)* sopraelevato, -a 2. *(important)* elevato, -a; *(position)* di prestigio
elevation [ˌel·ɪ·'veɪ·ʃən] *n* 1. *(rise)* elevazione *f;* *(of person)* ascesa *f* 2. *(height)* altezza (sul livello del mare) *f* 3. GEO altura *f* 4. ARCHIT prospetto *m*
elevator ['e·lɪ·veɪ·t̩ə] *n (for people)* ascensore *m;* *(for goods)* montacarichi *m inv*
eleven [ɪ·'le·vn] I. *adj* undici II. *n* undici *m;* *s.a.* **eight**
eleventh [ɪ·'le·vnθ] I. *adj* undicesimo, -a II. *n* 1. *(order)* undicesimo, -a *m, f* 2. *(date)* undici *m* 3. *(fraction)* undicesimo *m;* *(part)* undicesima parte *f; s.a.* **eighth**
elf [elf] <elves> *n (folklore)* folletto *m;* *(mythology)* elfo *m*
elicit [ɪ·'lɪ·sɪt] *vt* 1. *(obtain)* ottenere 2. *(provoke: criticism, response)* suscitare
eligibility [ˌe·lɪ·dʒə·'bɪ·lə·ti] *n* idoneità *f*
eligible ['e·lɪ·dʒə·bl] *adj* 1. idoneo, -a; **~ to vote** con diritto di voto 2. *(desirable)* adatto, -a; **to be ~ for the job** avere i requisiti necessari a un posto di lavoro; **an ~ bachelor** uno scapolo ambito; **an ~ young man/woman** un buon partito
eliminate [ɪ·'lɪ·mɪ·neɪt] *vt* 1. *(eradicate)* eliminare 2. *(exclude from consideration)* scartare
elimination [ɪ·ˌlɪ·mɪ·'neɪ·ʃən] *n* eliminazione *f;* **by (a) process of ~** (andando) per eliminazione
elite [eɪ·'liːt] I. *n* élite *f inv* II. *adj* d'élite
elitism [eɪ·'liː·tɪ·sm] *n* elitismo *m*
elitist [eɪ·'liː·tɪst] *adj* elitario, -a
elixir [ɪ·'lɪk·sə] *n* elisir *m inv*
elk [elk] <-(s)> *n (European)* alce *m;* *(Ameri-*

can) wapiti *m inv*
ellipse [ɪ·'lɪps] *n* ellisse *f*
elliptic(al) [ɪ·'lɪp·tɪ·k(l)] *adj* ellittico, -a
elm [elm] *n* olmo *m*
elocution [ˌe·lə·'kjuː·ʃən] *n* dizione *f;* *(art)* elocuzione *f*
elongate [ɪ·'lɑːŋ·geɪt] I. *vt* allungare II. *vi* allungarsi
elongated *adj* allungato, -a
elope [ɪ·'loʊp] *vi* fuggire (per sposarsi)
elopement [ɪ·'loʊp·mənt] *n* fuga *f* d'amore
eloquent ['e·lək·wənt] *adj* eloquente
El Salvador *n* El Salvador *m*
El Salvadorian I. *adj* salvadoregno, -a II. *n* salvadoregno, -a *m, f*
else [els] *adv* 1. *(in addition)* altro; **anyone/ anything ~** chiunque altro/qualsiasi altra cosa; **anywhere ~** in qualsiasi altro posto; **anyone ~?** nessun altro?; **anything ~?** (nient')altro?; **everybody ~** tutti gli altri; **I can't remember anything/anybody ~** non ricordo nient'altro/nessun altro; **everything ~** tutto il resto; **if all ~ fails** se tutto il resto andasse male; **someone/something ~** qualcun altro/qualcos'altro; **it's something ~!** è tutta un'altra cosa!; **how ~?** in che altro modo?; **what/who ~?** cos'/chi altro? 2. *(otherwise)* **or ~** altrimenti; **come here or ~!** vieni qui, se no vedi!; **shut up, or else!** zitto, altrimenti ...!
elsewhere ['els·wer] *adv* altrove; **let's go ~!** andiamo in un altro posto!
elucidate [ɪ·'luː·sɪ·deɪt] *form* I. *vt* delucidare; *(mystery)* chiarire II. *vi* **I don't understand, you'll have to ~** non capisco, me lo dovrai spiegare
elude [ɪ·'luːd] *vt* eludere; *(blow)* schivare
elusive [ɪ·'luː·sɪv] *adj* 1. *(evasive)* elusivo, -a; *(personality)* schivo, -a; **memory** fugace 2. *(slippery)* sfuggevole 3. *(difficult to obtain)* irraggiungibile
elves [elvz] *n pl of* **elf**
emaciated [ɪ·'meɪ·ʃi·eɪ·t̩ɪd] *adj form* emaciato, -a
e-mail ['iː·meɪl] *n abbr of* **electronic mail** e-mail *f inv*
e-mail address *n* indirizzo *m* di posta elettronica
emanate ['e·mə·neɪt] I. *vi form (originate)* provenire da; *(radiate)* emanare da II. *vt* emanare
emancipate [ɪ·'mæn·sɪ·peɪt] *vt* emancipare
emancipated *adj* emancipato, -a; *(ideas)* progressista
emancipation [ɪ·ˌmæn·sɪ·'peɪ·ʃən] *n* emancipazione *f*
embalm [em·'bɑːm] *vt* imbalsamare
embankment [em·'bæŋk·mənt] *n (of a road)* massicciata *f;* *(by river)* argine *m*
embargo [em·'bɑːr·goʊ] I. <-goes> *n* embargo *m;* **trade ~** embargo commerciale; **to be under ~** essere soggetto a embargo; **to put an ~ on a country** imporre l'embargo a un

paese **II.** *vt* mettere l'embargo su

embark [em·'bɑːrk] **I.** *vi* imbarcarsi; **to ~ on** [*o* **upon**] **a journey** iniziare un viaggio **II.** *vt* imbarcare

embarkation [ˌem·bɑ·r·'keɪ·ʃən] *n* imbarco *m*

embarrass [em·'be·rəs] *vt* **1.** (*make feel uncomfortable*) mettere in imbarazzo **2.** (*disconcert*) sconcertare

embarrassed *adj* imbarazzato, -a; **to be ~** essere in imbarazzo; **I felt ~ about saying that** mi imbarazzava dirlo

embarrassing *adj* imbarazzante; (*silence*) sconcertante

embarrassment [em·'be·rəs·ment] *n* **1.** (*shame*) imbarazzo *m* **2.** (*trouble, nuisance*) motivo *m* di imbarazzo; **to be an ~ (to sb)** essere motivo di imbarazzo (per qn)

embassy ['em·bə·si] <-ies> *n* ambasciata *f*

embed [em·'bed] <-dd-> *vt* (*fix*) conficcare; (*in rock*) incassare; (*in memory*) imprimere

embellish [em·'be·lɪʃ] *vt* abbellire

embers ['em·bəz] *npl* brace *f*

embezzle [ɪm·'be·zl] <-ing> *vt* appropriarsi indebitamente di

embezzlement [ɪm·'be·zl·mənt] *n* appropriazione *f* indebita; **~ of public funds** appropriazione indebita di fondi pubblici

embezzler [em·'bez·lə·] *n* malversatore, -trice *m, f*

embitter [em·'bɪ·ţə·] *vt* amareggiare

emblem ['em·bləm] *n* emblema *m*

embodiment [em·'bɑː·dɪ·mənt] *n* **1.** (*personification*) incarnazione *f*; **the ~ of virtue** la virtù personificata **2.** (*inclusion*) realizzazione *f* concreta

embody [em·'bɑː·dɪ] <-ied> *vt* **1.** (*convey: theory, idea*) esprimere **2.** (*personify*) incarnare **3.** (*include*) incorporare

embolism ['em·bə·lɪ·sm] *n* MED embolia *f*

emboss [em·'bɑːs] *vt* **1.** (*design, letters*) stampare in rilievo **2.** (*metal*) lavorare a sbalzo; (*leather*) goffrare; **~ed writing paper** carta da lettera con intestazione in rilievo

embrace [em·'breɪs] **I.** *vt* **1.** (*hug*) abbracciare **2.** (*accept: offer*) accettare; (*ideas, religion*) abbracciare **3.** (*include*) comprendere **II.** *vi* abbracciarsi **III.** *n* abbraccio *m*

embrocation [ˌem·brou·'keɪ·ʃən] *n* linimento *m*

embroider [em·'brɔɪ·də·] **I.** *vi* ricamare **II.** *vt* ricamare; *fig* ricamare su

embroidery [em·'brɔɪ·də·ri] *n* **1.** ricamo *m;* **~ frame** telaio *m* da ricamo **2.** *fig* ricami *mpl*

embroil [ɪm·'brɔɪl] *vt* invischiare

embryo ['em·bri·ou] *n* embrione *m*

embryonic [ˌem·bri·'ɑː·nɪk] *adj* embrionale; *fig* allo stato embrionale

emcee [em·'siː] **I.** *n* presentatore, -trice *m, f* **II.** *vt* presentare **III.** *vi* presentare

emend [ɪ·'mend] *vt form* emendare

emerald ['e·mə·rəld] **I.** *n* smeraldo *m* **II.** *adj* di smeraldi; (*color*) smeraldo *inv*

emerge [ɪ·'mɜːrdʒ] *vi* (*come out*) spuntare;

(*secret*) rivelarsi; (*ideas*) emergere; **they ~d from the bushes** spuntarono fuori dai cespugli; **new ideas ~d from the meeting** dalla riunione sono emerse nuove idee

emergence [ɪ·'mɜːr·dʒəns] *n* uscita *f;* (*of a secret*) rivelazione *f;* (*appearance*) comparsa *f*

emergency [ɪ·'mɜːr·dʒən·si] **I.** <-ies> *n* **1.** (*dangerous situation*) emergenza *f;* **in an** [*o* **in case of**] **~** in caso d'emergenza; **to be ready for an ~** tenersi pronti per qualsiasi emergenza **2.** MED urgenza *f;* **~ room** (reparto *m* di) pronto soccorso *m* **3.** POL emergenza *f;* **national ~** emergenza nazionale; **to declare a state of ~** dichiarare lo stato di emergenza **II.** *adj* (*brake*) a mano; (*rations*) di sopravvivenza; **~ exit** uscita di sicurezza; **~ landing** atterraggio d'emergenza; **~ services** servizi di pronto intervento

emergency room *n* (reparto *m* di) pronto soccorso

emergent [ɪ·'mɜːr·dʒənt] *adj* emergente; (*democracy*) giovane

emerging *adj* emergente

emery ['e·mə·ri] *n* smeriglio *m*

emery board *n* limetta *f* per unghie (di cartone smerigliato)

emetic [ɪ·'me·ţɪk] **I.** *adj* emetico, -a **II.** *n* emetico *m*

emigrant ['e·mɪ·grənt] *n* emigrante *mf*

emigrate ['e·mɪ·greɪt] *vi* emigrare

emigration [ˌe·mɪ·'greɪ·ʃən] *n* emigrazione *f*

eminence ['e·mɪ·nəns] *n* eminenza *f;* **Your Eminence** REL Sua Eminenza

eminent ['e·mɪ·nənt] *adj* eminente

eminently *adv* assolutamente

emissary ['e·mɪ·se·ri] <-ies> *n* emissario, -a *m, f*

emission [ɪ·'mɪ·ʃn] *n* emissione *f*

emit [ɪ·'mɪt] <-tt-> *vt* (*radiation, light, smoke*) emettere; (*heat, odor*) emanare; (*cry*) lanciare

emoticon *n* INFOR emoticon *m inv*

emotion [ɪ·'mou·ʃən] *n* **1.** (*feeling*) sentimento *m* **2.** (*affective state*) emozione *f*

emotional [ɪ·'mou·ʃə·nl] *adj* **1.** (*relating to the emotions*) emotivo, -a; (*involvement, link*) affettivo, -a **2.** (*moving*) commovente **3.** (*governed by emotion*) emozionato, -a; **to get ~** emozionarsi **4.** (*determined by emotion: decision*) impulsivo, -a

emotionless *adj* impassibile

emotive [ɪ·'mou·ţɪv] *adj* che suscita reazioni

empathy ['em·pə·θi] *n* empatia *f*

emperor ['em·pə·ə·] *n* imperatore *m*

emphasis ['em·fə·sɪs] <emphases> *n a.* LING enfasi *f inv;* **to put** [*o* **place**] **great ~ on punctuality** dare particolare importanza alla puntualità

emphasize ['em·fə·saɪz] *vt* **1.** (*insist on*) sottolineare; (*fact*) enfatizzare **2.** LING porre l'enfasi su

emphatic [em·'fæ·ţɪk] *adj* (*forcibly expressive*) enfatico, -a; (*strong*) veemente; (*assertion, refusal*) categorico, -a; **to be ~ about sth**

essere categorico su qc

emphatically *adv* (*expressively*) con enfasi; (*strongly*) con veemenza; (*forcefully*) categoricamente

empire ['em·pa·ɪə] *n* impero *m*

empirical [em·'pɪ·rɪ·kl] *adj* empirico, -a

employ [em·'plɔɪ] *vt* 1. (*give a job to*) impiegare; **to ~ sb to do sth** assumere qn per fare qc 2. (*put to use*) utilizzare

employee ['em·plɔɪ·'iː] *n* impiegato, -a *m, f*

employer [em·'plɔ·ɪə] *n* datore, -trice di lavoro *m*

employment ['em·plɔɪ·mənt] *n* 1. (*of a person*) impiego *m* 2. (*of an object*) utilizzo *m*

employment agency *n* agenzia *f* di collocamento

employment equity *n Can* pari opportunità *f pl* di lavoro

emporium [em·'pɔ:·ri·əm] <-s *o* emporia> *n* emporio *m*

empower [em·'paʊ·ə·] *vt* **to ~ sb to do sth** (*give ability to*) mettere in grado qn di fare qc; (*authorize*) dare a qn il potere di fare qc

empowerment [em·'paʊ·ə·mənt] *n* acquisizione *f* del potere

empress ['em·prɪs] *n* imperatrice *f*

emptiness ['emp·tɪ·nɪs] *n* vuoto *m; fig* vacuità *f*

empty ['emp·ti] I. <-ier, -iest> *adj* 1. (*with nothing inside*) vuoto, -a; (*truck, ship*) senza carico; (*house*) disabitato, -a 2. (*insincere: promise, threat*) vuoto, -a 3. (*useless*) vano, -a; **~ phrase** frase senza significato II. <-ie-> *vt* (*pour*) versare; (*deprive of contents*) svuotare III. <-ie-> *vi* svuotarsi; (*river*) sfociare; **to ~ into the Mississippi** sfociare nel Mississippi IV. <-ies> *n pl* vuoti *m* (*di bottiglie, bicchieri, ecc.*)

◆**empty out** *vt* svuotare

empty-handed [ˌemp·tɪ·'hæn·dɪd] *adj* a mani vuote

empty-headed *adj* scriteriato, -a

empty nester *n* genitore i cui figli sono cresciuti e vivono fuori casa

empty-nest syndrome *n* sindrome *f* del nido vuoto

EMT [ˌiː·em·'tiː] *n abbr of* **emergency medical technician** assistente *mf* medico d'emergenza

emu ['iː·m·juː] *n* emù *m*

emulate ['em·ju·leɪt] *vt* emulare

emulation [ˌem·ju·'leɪ·ʃən] *n* emulazione *f;* **~ of sb** emulazione di qn

emulsifier [ɪ·'mʌl·si·fa·ɪə] *n* emulsionante *m*

emulsify [ɪ·'mʌl·si·faɪ] <-ie-> I. *vt* emulsionare II. *vi* emulsionarsi

emulsion [ɪ·'mʌl·ʃən] *n* 1. *a.* PHOT emulsione *f* 2. (*paint*) pittura *f* a emulsione

enable [ɪ·'neɪ·bl] *vt* 1. **to ~ sb to do sth** consentire a qn di fare qc 2. INFOR predisporre

enact [ɪ·'nækt] *vt* 1. (*carry out*) mettere in pratica 2. THEAT rappresentare 3. (*law*) promulgare; **to ~ that ...** decretare che ...

enactment *n* 1. (*carrying out*) messa *f* in atto;

(*of legislation*) promulgazione *f* 2. THEAT rappresentazione *f*

enamel [ɪ·'næ·ml] I. *n* smalto *m* II. <-ll-, -l-> *vt* smaltare

enamored [ɪ·'næ·məd] *adj* **to be ~ of sb** essere innamorato di qn; **to be ~ with sth** essere entusiasta di qc

enc. *s.* enc(l).

encamp [en·'kæmp] *vi* accamparsi

encampment *n* accampamento *m*

encapsulate [ɪn·'kæps·jə·leɪt] *vt* incapsulare; *fig* sintetizzare

encase [en·'keɪs] *vt* racchiudere

encephalitis [en·ˌse·fə·'laɪ·tɪs] *n* encefalite *f*

enchant [en·'tʃænt] *vt* 1. (*charm*) incantare 2. (*bewitch*) stregare

enchanted *adj* 1. (*charmed*) incantato, -a 2. (*bewitched*) stregato, -a

enchanter *n* (*sorcerer*) mago *m*

enchanting *adj* incantevole

enchantment *n* 1. (*charm*) incanto *m* 2. (*spell*) incantesimo *m*

enchantress *n* (*charming woman*) ammaliatrice *f;* (*witch*) maga *f*

enchilada [ˌen·tʃɪ·'lɑː·də] *n* tortilla messicana ripiena di carne o formaggio e ricoperta di salsa piccante; **the whole ~** *fig* l'intera faccenda

encipher [en·'saɪ·fə] *vt* cifrare

encircle [en·'sɜːr·kl] *vt* circondare; **to ~ the enemy** accerchiare il nemico

encirclement *n* cerchio *m;* MIL accerchiamento *m*

enc(l). *abbr of* **enclosure** allegato *m*

enclave ['en·kleɪv] *n* enclave *f inv*

enclose [en·'kloʊz] *vt* 1. (*surround*) circondare; **to ~ sth in brackets** mettere qc tra parentesi; (*field*) recintare 2. (*include*) allegare

enclosed [en·'kloʊzd] *adj* 1. (*confined*) chiuso, -a; (*garden*) recintato, -a 2. (*included*) allegato, -a

enclosure [en·'kloʊ·ʒə] *n* 1. (*enclosed area*) area *f* delimitata; (*for animals*) recinto *m* 2. (*action*) recinzione *f* 3. (*letter*) allegato *m*

encode [en·'koʊd] *vt a.* INFOR, LING codificare

encompass [en·'kʌm·pəs] *vt* 1. (*surround*) racchiudere 2. (*include*) abbracciare

encore ['ɑːn·kɔːr] I. *n* bis *m inv;* **as** [*o* **for**] **an ~** come bis II. *interj* bis

encore marriage *n* matrimonio *m* successivo

encore performance *n* rappresentazione *f* successiva

encounter [en·'kaʊn·tə] I. *vt* incontrare; **to ~ sb** imbattersi in qn II. *n* incontro *m;* **a close ~** un incontro ravvicinato

encourage [en·'kɜː·rɪdʒ] *vt* 1. (*give confidence, hope*) incoraggiare; **to ~ sb to do sth** incoraggiare qn a fare qc 2. (*support*) favorire

encouragement [en·'kɜː·rɪdʒ·mənt] *n* incoraggiamento *m;* **to give ~ to sth** favorire qc; **to give ~ to sb** incoraggiare qn

encouraging *adj* incoraggiante; **an ~ prospect** una prospettiva incoraggiante

encroach [en·ˈkroʊtʃ] *vi* **to ~ on** [*o* **upon**] **sth** (*intrude*) invadere qc; *fig* usurpare qc

encroachment *n* **1.** (*intrusion*) invasione *f* **2.** *fig* usurpazione *f;* **an ~ on human rights** una violazione dei diritti umani

encryption [ɪn·ˈkrɪp·ʃən] *n* INFOR criptaggio *m*

encumber [en·ˈkʌm·bɚ] *vt* **to be ~ed with sth** essere carico di qc; (*impede*) essere intralciato da qc

encyclopedia [en·ˌsaɪ·klə·ˈpiː·diə] *n* enciclopedia *f*

encyclopedic [en·ˌsaɪ·klə·ˈpiː·dɪk] *adj* enciclopedico, -a

end [end] **I.** *n* **1.** (*finish*) fine *f* **2.** (*extremity*) estremità *f* **3.** (*boundary*) limite *m* estremo **4.** (*stop*) termine *m* **5.** *pl* (*goal*) fine *m;* (*purpose*) scopo *m;* **to achieve one's ~s** raggiungere i propri scopi **6.** (*phone line*) capo *m;* **who is on the other ~?** chi c'è all'altro capo? **7.** (*death*) fine *f;* **he is nearing his ~** si avvicina alla fine **8.** (*piece remaining*) avanzo *m* **9.** (*obligation*) parte *f;* **to uphold one's ~ of the deal** [*o* **bargain**] fare la propria parte (in un accordo) **10.** SPORTS capo *m* **11.** INFOR tasto *m* di fine ►**to reach the ~ of the line** [*o* **road**] arrivare agli sgoccioli; **the ~s justify the means** *prov* il fine giustifica i mezzi *prov;* **~ of story** punto e basta; **you deserved to be punished, ~ of story** meritavi di essere punito, punto e basta; **to be at the ~ of one's rope** non poterne più; **it's not the ~ of the world** non è la fine del mondo; **to be the ~** *sl* essere il massimo; **to go off the deep ~** *inf* dare in escandescenze; **to make ~s meet** far quadrare il bilancio; **to meet one's ~** incontrare la morte; **to play both ~s against the middle** mettere l'uno contro l'altro a proprio vantaggio; **to put an ~ to oneself** [*o* **it all**] mettere fine alla propria vita; **in the ~** alla fine; **to this ~** a questo scopo **II.** *vt* **1.** (*finish*) finire **2.** (*bring to a stop: reign, war*) porre fine a **III.** *vi* finire; **to ~ in sth** finire in qc
◆**end up** *vi* finire; **to ~ in love with sb** finire coll'innamorarsi di qn; **to ~ a rich man** finire col diventare ricco; **to ~ penniless** finire col ritrovarsi senza un centesimo; **to ~ in prison** finire in prigione; **to ~ doing sth** finire col fare qc

endanger [en·ˈdeɪn·dʒɚ] *vt* mettere a repentaglio; **an ~ed species** una specie a rischio d'estinzione

endear [en·ˈdɪr] *vt* **to ~ oneself to sb** farsi benvolere da qn

endearing *adj* accattivante; **an ~ smile** un sorriso accattivante

endearment *n* affettuosità *fpl;* **terms of ~** termini *m pl* affettuosi

endeavor [en·ˈde·vɚ] **I.** *vi* **to ~ to do sth** sforzarsi di fare qc **II.** *n* sforzo *m;* **to make every ~ to do sth** fare l'impossibile per fare qc

endemic [en·ˈde·mɪk] *adj* endemico, -a

ending [ˈen·dɪŋ] *n* finale *m;* LING desinenza *f*

endive [ˈen·daɪv] *n* indivia *f*

endless [ˈend·lɪs] *adj* infinito, -a, interminabile

endorse [en·ˈdɔːrs] *vt* **1.** (*declare approval for*) approvare; (*product*) promuovere; (*candidate*) appoggiare **2.** FIN girare

endorsee [ɪn·ˌdɔːr·ˈsiː] *n* giratario, -a *m, f*

endorsement *n* **1.** (*support: of a plan*) approvazione *f;* (*of a candidate*) appoggio *m;* (*recommendation*) promozione *f* **2.** FIN girata *f*

endorser *n* girante *mf*

endow [en·ˈdaʊ] *vt* sovvenzionare; **to be ~ed with sth** essere dotato di qc

endowment *n* **1.** FIN sovvenzione *f* **2.** (*talent*) dote *f* **3.** BIO **genetic ~** corredo *m* genetico

endpaper [ˈend·peɪ·pɚ] *n* risguardo *m*

end product *n* prodotto *m* finale

end result *n* risultato *m* finale

end table *n* tavolino *m*

endurable [en·ˈdʊ·rə·rə·bl] *adj* sopportabile

endurance [en·ˈdʊ·rəns] *n* resistenza *f*

endurance athlete *n* atleta *mf* di discipline di resistenza

endurance sports *n* sport *m pl* di resistenza

endure [en·ˈdʊr] **I.** *vt* **1.** (*tolerate*) sopportare **2.** (*suffer*) resistere a **II.** *vi form* durare

enduring *adj* duraturo, -a

ENE *abbr of* **east-northeast** ENE

enema [ˈe·nə·mə] <-s *o* enemata> *n* clistere *m*

enemy [ˈe·nə·mi] **I.** *n* nemico, -a *m, f* **II.** *adj* nemico, -a

energetic [ˌe·nɚ·ˈdʒe·t̬ɪk] *adj* energico, -a; (*active*) attivo, -a

energize [ˈe·nɚ·dʒaɪz] *vt* **1.** ELEC alimentare **2.** *fig* dare vigore a

energy [ˈe·nɚ·dʒi] <-ies> *n* energia *f;* **to be full of ~** essere pieno d'energia; **to have the ~ to do sth** avere l'energia per fare qc

energy crisis *n* crisi *f inv* energetica

energy resources *npl* risorse *f pl* energetiche

energy-saving *adj* a risparmio energetico

enervate [ˈe·nɚ·veɪt] *vt liter* snervare

enervating *adj liter* snervante

enfeeble [en·ˈfiː·bl] *vt form* indebolire

enforce [en·ˈfɔːrs] *vt* imporre; (*law*) far osservare; (*law, regulation*) far rispettare

enforceable *adj* che si può imporre; (*law*) esecutivo

enforcement [en·ˈfɔːrs·mənt] *n* imposizione *f;* (*of a law, regulation*) applicazione *f*

enfranchise [en·ˈfræn·tʃaɪz] *vt form* concedere il diritto di voto a

engage [en·ˈgeɪdʒ] **I.** *vt* **1.** *form* (*hold interest*) attirare; **to ~ sb's attention** catturare l'attenzione di qn **2.** (*put into use*) ingaggiare **3.** TECH (*cogs*) ingranare; **to ~ the clutch** innestare la frizione **4.** MIL (*enemy*) attaccare; **to ~ the enemy** ingaggiare il nemico **II.** *vi* **1.** MIL ingaggiare battaglia **2.** TECH ingranare

engaged *adj* **1.** (*to be married*) fidanzato, -a; **to get ~ (to sb)** fidanzarsi (con qn) **2.** (*occupied*) occupato, -a **3.** (*in battle*) impegnato, -a in combattimento

engagement [en·ˈgeɪdʒ·mənt] *n* **1.** (*appoint-

ment) impegno *m* **2.**(*marriage*) fidanzamento *m* **3.**MIL combattimento *m*

engagement ring *n* anello *m* di fidanzamento

engaging *adj* affascinante

engender [en·ˈdʒen·dəʳ] *vt form* generare

engine [ˈen·dʒɪn] *n* **1.**(*motor*) motore *m;* **diesel/gasoline** ~ motore diesel/a benzina; **jet** ~ motore a reazione **2.**RAIL locomotiva *f*

engineer [ˌen·dʒɪ·ˈnɪr] I. *n* **1.**(*with a degree*) ingegnere *m;* **civil** ~ ingegnere civile **2.**(*technician*) tecnico *m* **3.**RAIL macchinista *mf* II. *vt* costruire; *fig* macchinare

engineering [ˌen·dʒɪ·ˈnɪ·rɪŋ] *n* ingegneria *f*

England [ˈɪŋ·glənd] *n* Inghilterra *f*

English [ˈɪŋ·glɪʃ] I. *n inv* **1.**(*language*) inglese *m* **2.** *pl* (*people*) **the** ~ gli inglesi II. *adj* inglese; **a movie in** ~ un film in inglese; **an** ~ **class** una lezione di inglese

English breakfast *n* colazione *f* all'inglese

English Canada *n* Canada *m* inglese

English Canadian *n* inglese *mf* canadese

English Channel *n* canale *m* della Manica

Englishman <-men> *n* inglese *m*

English muffin *n* focaccina tonda e schiacciata, generalmente tostata, tagliata a metà orizzontalmente e mangiata calda con burro

English speaker *n* anglofono, -a *m, f*

English-speaking *adj* anglofono, -a

Englishwoman <-women> *n* inglese *f*

engrave [en·ˈgreɪv] *vt* incidere; **to be** ~**d in the memory** essere scolpito nella memoria

engraver [en·ˈgreɪ·vəʳ] *n* incisore *m*

engraving [en·ˈgreɪ·vɪŋ] *n* incisione *f*

engross [en·ˈgroʊs] *vt* assorbire; **to be** ~**ed in sth** essere assorto in qc

engulf [en·ˈgʌlf] *vt* inghiottire

enhance [ɪn·ˈhæns] *vt* migliorare; (*improve or intensify: chances*) aumentare; (*memory*) rafforzare; (*photo*) ritoccare

enigma [ɪ·ˈnɪg·mə] *n* enigma *m*

enigmatic(al) [ˌe·nɪg·ˈmæ·t̬ɪ·k(əl)] *adj* enigmatico, -a

enjoy [en·ˈdʒɔɪ] I. *vt* **1.**(*get pleasure from*) trovare piacevole; **to** ~ **doing sth** provare piacere a fare qc; ~ **yourselves!** buon divertimento! **2.**(*have: health*) godere di; **to** ~ **sb's confidence** godere della fiducia di qn; **to** ~ **good health** godere di buona salute II. *vi* divertirsi

enjoyable [en·ˈdʒɔ·ɪə·bl] *adj* piacevole; (*film, book, play*) divertente

enjoyment [en·ˈdʒɔɪ·mənt] *n* piacere *m;* **to get real** ~ **out of doing sth** trarre un vero piacere dal fare qc

enlarge [en·ˈlɑːrdʒ] I. *vt* **1.**(*make bigger*) ingrandire; (*expand*) espandere; **to** ~ **one's vocabulary** ampliare il proprio lessico **2.** PHOT ingrandire II. *vi* ingrandire

enlargement *n* ampliamento *m;* (*expanding*) espansione *f;* PHOT ingrandimento *m*

enlighten [en·ˈlaɪ·tn] *vt* **1.**REL illuminare **2.**(*explain*) chiarire; **to** ~ **the public about sth** informare il pubblico di qc

enlightened *adj* (*person*) progressista; REL

illuminato, -a; (*age*) illuminato, -a

enlightenment [en·ˈlaɪ·tn·mənt] *n* **1.**REL illuminazione *f* **2.**PHILOS **the** (**Age of**) **Enlightenment** l'Illuminismo **3.**(*explanation*) chiarimento *m;* **to give sb** ~ **about sth** dare chiarimenti a qn su qc

enlist [en·ˈlɪst] I. *vi* MIL arruolarsi II. *vt* **1.**MIL arruolare **2.**(*support*) ottenere; **to** ~ **sb's help** assicurarsi l'aiuto di qn

enliven [en·ˈlaɪ·vn] *vt* ravvivare; (*person*) rianimare

en masse [ɑːnm·ˈmæs] *adv* in massa

enmesh [en·ˈmeʃ] *vt* intrappolare (in una rete); **to be** ~**ed in sth** *a. fig* essere invischiato in qc; **to get** ~**ed in sth** *a. fig* rimanere invischiato in qc

enmity [ˈen·mə·t̬i] <-ies> *n* inimicizia *f*

ennoble [e·ˈnoʊ·bl] *vt* nobilitare

enormity [ɪ·ˈnɔːr·mə·t̬i] <-ies> *n* (*of damage*) gravità *f;* (*of a task, mistake*) enormità *f;* (*of a crime*) atrocità *f*

enormous [ɪ·ˈnɔːr·məs] *adj* enorme; ~ **difficulties** enormi difficoltà

enough [ɪ·ˈnʌf] I. *adj* (*sufficient*) sufficiente II. *adv* abbastanza; **to be experienced** ~ (**to do sth**) avere abbastanza esperienza (per fare qc); **to have seen** ~ aver visto abbastanza; **she was kind** [*o* **friendly**] ~ **to help me** è stata così gentile da aiutarmi; **oddly** [*o* **strangely**] ~ per quanto possa sembrare strano III. *interj* basta IV. *pron* abbastanza; **to have** ~ **to eat and drink** avere da mangiare e bere a sufficienza; **I know** ~ **about it** ne so abbastanza; **that should be** ~ questo dovrebbe bastare; **more than** ~ più che a sufficienza; **it is** ~ **for me to know ...** mi basta sapere ...; **to have had** ~ (**of sb/sth**) averne abbastanza (di qn/qc); **as if that weren't** ~ come se non bastasse; **that's** (**quite**) ~**!** adesso basta!; ~ **is** ~ adesso basta!

enquire [en·ˈkwa·ɪəʳ] *vi, vt s.* **inquire**

enquiry [en·ˈkwaɪ·ri] <-ies> *n* **1.**(*question*) domanda *f;* **to make an** ~ **into sth** indagare su qc **2.**(*investigation*) inchiesta *f;* **an** ~ **into sth** un'inchiesta su qc; **to hold an** ~ svolgere un'inchiesta

enrage [en·ˈreɪdʒ] *vt* far infuriare

enraged [en·ˈreɪdʒd] *adj* infuriato, -a

enrapture [en·ˈræp·tʃəʳ] *vt* rapire

enrich [en·ˈrɪtʃ] *vt* arricchire

enroll <-ll-> *vt,* **enrol** [en·ˈroʊl] I. *vi* iscriversi; **to** ~ **for/in a course** iscriversi a un corso II. *vt* iscrivere

enrollment *n,* **enrolment** [en·ˈroʊl·mənt] *n* iscrizione *f*

en route [ɑːn·ˈruːt] *adv* in viaggio

ensemble [ɑːn·ˈsɑːm·bl] *n* **1.**MUS, THEAT gruppo *m* **2.**FASHION completo *m*

ensign [ˈen·sən] *n* MIL **1.**bandiera *f* **2.**(*standard-bearer*) portabandiera *m*

enslave [en·ˈsleɪv] *vt* rendere schiavo; **to be** ~**d by sb/sth** essere reso schiavo da qn/qc

ensnare [en·ˈsner] *vt liter* intrappolare; **to be**

~**d in sth** essere intrappolato in qc

ensue [en·'suː] *vi form* seguire; **to ~ from sth** derivare da qc

ensuing *adj* seguente

en suite bathroom [ˌɑːn·swiːt·'bæθ·ruːm] *n* bagno *m* annesso

ensure [en·'ʃʊr] *vt* assicurare; (*guarantee*) garantire

ENT *abbr of* **ear, nose and throat** ORL *m*

entail [en·'teɪl] *vt* **1.** (*involve*) comportare; **to ~ some risk** comportare dei rischi **2.** (*necessitate*) **to ~ doing sth** richiedere che si faccia qc

entangle [en·'tæŋ·gl] *vt* impigliare; **to ~ oneself** impigliarsi; **to get ~d in sth** rimanere impigliato in qc; *fig* rimanere coinvolto in qc; **to get ~d with sb** essere coinvolto sentimentalmente con qn

entanglement *n* groviglio *m;* (*situation*) complicazione *f;* **emotional ~s** legami *m pl* sentimentali

enter ['en·t̬ə] **I.** *vt* **1.** (*go into*) entrare in; (*penetrate*) penetrare in **2.** (*insert*) inserire; (*into a register*) iscrivere; **to ~ data** COMPUT inserire dati **3.** (*compete in*) partecipare a; **to ~ a competition** partecipare a una gara **4.** (*begin*) entrare in; **to ~ politics** entrare in politica; **to ~ adulthood** diventare adulto **5.** (*make known*) rendere noto; (*claim, plea*) presentare **II.** *vi* THEAT entrare in scena

◆**enter into** *vi* (*form part of*) prendere parte a; **to ~ marriage** contrarre matrimonio; **to ~ conversation** intavolare una conversazione; **to ~ discussion** partecipare a una discussione; **to ~ negotiations** dare avvio ai negoziati

enter key *n* INFOR tasto *m* di invio

enterprise ['en·t̬ə·praɪz] *n* **1.** (*business firm*) impresa *f;* **to start an ~** avviare un'impresa **2.** (*initiative*) iniziativa *f*

enterprising *adj* intraprendente

entertain [ˌen·t̬ə·'teɪn] **I.** *vt* **1.** (*amuse*) intrattenere **2.** (*guests*) ricevere **3.** (*consider*) prendere in considerazione; **to ~ doubts** nutrire dubbi; **to ~ an idea/a plan** valutare un'idea/un piano **II.** *vi* (*invite guests*) ricevere

entertainer [ˌen·t̬ə·'teɪ·nə] *n* intrattenitore, -trice *m, f*

entertaining *adj* divertente

entertainment [ˌen·t̬ə·'teɪn·mənt] *n* **1.** (*amusement*) intrattenimento *m;* **to provide some ~** fornire intrattenimento **2.** (*show*) spettacolo *m*

enthrall [en·'θrɔːl] *vt* incantare

enthrone [en·'θroʊn] *vt form* mettere sul trono

enthuse [en·'θuːz] **I.** <-sing> *vi* **to ~ about sth** entusiasmarsi per qc **II.** <-sing> *vt* **to ~ sb (with sth)** entusiasmare qn (con qc)

enthusiasm [en·'θuː·zi·æ·zəm] *n* entusiasmo *m;* **~ for sth** entusiasmo per qc

enthusiast [ɪn·'θjuː·zi·æst] *n* appassionato, -a *m, f*

enthusiastic [en·ˌθuː·zi·'æs·tɪk] *adj* entusiasta; **to be ~ about sth** essere entusiasta per qc

entice [en·'taɪs] *vt* attrarre; **to ~ sb to do sth** indurre (con lusinghe) qn a fare qc; **to ~ sb away from sth** persuadere qn a lasciare qc

enticement *n* attrattiva *f*

enticing *adj* allettante; (*smile*) seducente

entire [en·'ta·ɪə] *adj* **1.** (*whole: life*) tutto, -a; **the ~ day** tutto il giorno; **the ~ world** il mondo intero **2.** (*total: commitment, devotion*) totale **3.** (*complete*) intero, -a

entirely *adv* completamente; **he's ~ to blame** è tutta colpa sua; **to agree ~** essere totalmente d'accordo; **to disagree ~** non essere assolutamente d'accordo

entirety [en·'taɪ·rə·t̬i] *n* **in its ~** nella sua totalità

entitle [en·'taɪ·t̬l] *vt* **1.** (*give right*) dare diritto a; **to ~ sb to act** autorizzare qn ad agire; **to ~ sb to a holiday** dare diritto a qn a una vacanza **2.** (*book*) intitolare

entitled *adj* **1.** (*person*) autorizzato, -a **2.** (*book*) intitolato, -a

entitlement [en·'taɪ·t̬l·mənt] *n* diritto *m*

entity ['en·t̬ə·ti] <-ies> *n form* entità *f;* **legal ~** persona *f* giuridica; **a single/separate ~** un ente singolo/separato

entomology [ˌen·t̬ə·'mɑː·lə·dʒi] *n* entomologia *f*

entourage [ˌɑːn·tu·'rɑːʒ] *n* entourage *m inv*

entrails ['en·treɪlz] *npl* interiora *fpl*

entrance[1] ['en·trəns] *n* **1.** (*act of entering*) entrata *f* **2.** (*way in*) entrata *f;* **front ~** ingresso *m* principale; **the ~ to sth** l'accesso *m* a qc; **to refuse sb ~** [*o* **to refuse ~ to sb**] negare l'accesso a qn **3.** THEAT entrata *f* in scena

entrance[2] [en·'træns] *vt* (*cast spell*) incantare

entrance exam(ination) [en·'trəns ɪg·ˌzæ·m(ɪ·'neɪ·ʃən)] *n* esame *m* d'ammissione

entrance fee *n* (biglietto *m* di)ingresso *m*

entrance hall *n* atrio *m*

entrance requirement *n* requisiti *m pl* di ammissione

entrant ['en·trənt] *n* concorrente *mf*

entreat [en·'triːt] *vt* **to ~ sb to do sth** supplicare qn di fare qc

entreaty [en·'triː·t̬i] <-ies> *n* supplica *f*

entrée ['ɑːn·treɪ] *n* piatto *m* principale

entrench [en·'trentʃ] *vt passive* **1. to become ~ed** (*idea*) radicarsi **2. to ~ oneself** MIL trincerarsi

entrenched *adj* **1.** (*idea*) radicato, -a **2.** MIL trincerato, -a

entrepreneur [ˌɑːn·trə·prə·'nɜːr] *n* imprenditore, -trice *m, f*

entrepreneurial spirit [ˌɑːn·trə·prə·'nɜː·ri·əl 'spɪ·rɪt] *n* spirito *m* imprenditoriale

entrust [en·'trʌst] *vt* affidare; **to ~ sth to sb** [*o* **to ~ sb with sth**] affidare qc a qn; **to ~ sth into sb's care** affidare qc alle cure di qn

entry ['en·tri] <-ies> *n* **1.** (*act of entering*) entrata *f;* (*joining an organization*) adesione *f* **2.** (*right to enter*) ammissione; **to refuse sb ~** negare a qn l'accesso **3.** (*entrance*) entrata *f* **4.** (*in dictionary*) voce *f*

E

entry fee *n* quota *f* di ammissione

entry-level job *n* lavoro di primo livello

entwine [en·'twaɪn] *vt* (*weave*) intrecciare; (*twist*) attorcigliare; **to be ~d** (**together**) *fig* essere unito inestricabilmente

enumerate [ɪ·'nuː·mə·reɪt] *vt* enumerare

enumeration [ɪ·ˌnuː·mə·'reɪ·ʃən] *n* enumerazione *f*

enunciate [ɪ·'nʌn·si·eɪt] *vt* **1.** (*sound*) articolare **2.** (*theory*) enunciare

envelop [en·'ve·ləp] *vt* avviluppare

envelope ['en·və·loʊp] *n* busta *f*

enviable ['en·vɪ·ə·bl] *adj* invidiabile

envious ['en·vi·əs] *adj* invidioso, -a; **to be ~ of sb/sth** essere invidioso di qn/qc

environment [en·'vaɪ·ə·rən·mənt] *n* ambiente *m;* **the ~** ECOL l'ambiente; **home/ professional ~** ambiente familiare/professionale; **working ~** ambiente di lavoro

environmental [en·ˌvaɪ·rən·'men·t̬l] *adj* ambientale; **~ damage** danni*m pl* ambientali; **~ impact** impatto *m* sull'ambiente; **~ pollution** inquinamento *m* ambientale; **~ stress** stress *m* ambientale

environmentalist [en·ˌvaɪ·rən·'men·t̬ə·lɪst] *n* ambientalista *mf*

environmentally-friendly [en·ˌvaɪ·rən·'men·t̬ə·li·'frend·li] *adj* ecologico, -a

environs [en·'vaɪ·ə·rənz] *npl form* dintorni *mpl*

envisage [en·'vɪ·zɪdʒ] *vt,* **envision** [en·'vɪ·ʒən] *vt* **1.** (*expect*) prevedere **2.** (*imagine*) immaginare; **to ~ that ...** prevedere che ...

envoy ['ɑːn·vɔɪ] *n* inviato, -a *m, f*

envy ['en·vi] **I.** *n* invidia *f;* **this car is the ~ of my brother** quest'auto è l'invidia di mio fratello; **she feels ~ towards her sister** è invidiosa della sorella ▸ **to be green with ~** essere verde d'invidia **II.** <-ie-> *vt* invidiare

enzyme ['en·zaɪm] *n* enzima *m*

EOF *n* INFOR *abbr of* **end of file** fine *f* del file

EP [ˌiː·'piː] **1.** *abbr of* **extended play** extended play *m inv* **2.** *abbr of* **European plan** tariffa alberghiera che include solo il prezzo della camera senza pasti

EPA [ˌiː·piː·'eɪ] *abbr of* **Environmental Protection Agency** Agenzia *f* di Protezione dell'Ambiente

ephemeral [ɪ·'fe·mə·əl] *adj a.* BIO effimero, -a

epic ['e·pɪk] **I.** *n* epopea *f* **II.** *adj* epico, -a; **~ poetry** poesia epica; **an ~ journey** un viaggio epico

epicenter ['e·pɪ·sen·t̬ə] *n* epicentro *m*

epicycle ['e·pə·saɪ·kl] *n* MAT, ASTR epiciclo *m*

epidemic [ˌe·pə·'de·mɪk] **I.** *n* epidemia *f* **II.** *adj* epidemico, -a; **~ proportions** proporzioni gigantesche

epidermis [ˌe·pə·'dɜːr·mɪs] <-mes> *n* epidermide *f*

epidural *n* MED epidurale *f*

epigram ['e·pə·græm] *n* epigramma *m*

epilepsy ['e·pɪ·lep·si] *n* epilessia *f*

epileptic [ˌe·pɪ·'lep·tɪk] **I.** *n* epilettico, -a *m, f*

II. *adj* epilettico, -a; **~ seizure** attacco *m* epilettico

epilog ['e·pə·lɑːg] *n* epilogo *m*

Epiphany [ɪ·'pɪ·fə·ni] <-ies> *n* Epifania *f*

episcopacy [ɪ·'pɪs·kə·pə·si] <-ies> *n* episcopato *m*

episcopal [ɪ·'pɪs·kə·pl] *adj* episcopale

Episcopalian [ɪ·ˌpɪs·kə·'peɪ·li·ən] **I.** *adj* episcopaliano, -a **II.** *n* episcopaliano, -a *m, f*

episiotomy *n* MED episiotomia *f*

episode ['e·pə·soʊd] *n* episodio *m*

episodic [ˌe·pə·'sɑː·dɪk] *adj* **1.** (*occasional*) episodico, -a **2.** LIT (*consisting of episodes*) a episodi

epistle [ɪ·'pɪ·sl] *n* epistola *f*

epistolary [ɪ·'pɪs·tə·le·ri] *adj* epistolare

epitaph ['e·pə·tæf] *n* epitaffio *m*

epithet ['e·pɪ·θet] *n* LING epiteto *m*

epitome [ɪ·'pɪ·t̬ə·mi] *n* **1.** (*embodiment*) personificazione *f* **2.** (*example*) classico esempio *m;* **the ~ of poor taste** il massimo del cattivo gusto

epitomize [ɪ·'pɪ·t̬ə·maɪz] *vt* incarnare

epoch ['e·pək] *n form* epoca *f;* **historical ~** epoca storica

epoch-making ['e·pək·ˌmeɪ·kɪŋ] *adj* **~ discovery** una scoperta che fa epoca

eponymous [ɪ·'pɑː·nə·məs] *adj* eponimo, -a

epoxy *n* resina *f* epossidica

equable ['ek·wə·bl] *adj* (*temperament*) equilibrato, -a; (*climate*) mite; **to have an ~ disposition** avere un carattere tranquillo

equal ['iː·k·wəl] **I.** *adj* **1.** (*the same*) uguale; (*treatment*) equo, -a; **to have ~ reason to do sth** avere le stesse ragioni per fare qc; **of ~ size** della stessa misura; **on ~ terms** alla pari **2.** (*able to do*) **to be ~ to a task** essere all'altezza di un compito **II.** *n* pari *mf inv;* **it has no ~** non ha pari **III.** *vt* **1.** *pl* MAT essere uguale a **2.** (*match*) uguagliare

equality [ɪ·'kwɑː·lə·ti] *n* parità *f*

equalization [ˌiː·kwə·lɪ·'zeɪ·ʃən] *n* livellamento *m*

equalize ['iː·kwə·laɪz] *vt* livellare

equalizer ['iː·kwə·laɪ·zə] *n* **1.** MUS equalizzatore *m* **2.** SPORTS punto *m* del pareggio

equally ['iː·kwə·li] *adv* ugualmente; **to contribute ~ to sth** contribuire in parti uguali a qc; **to divide sth ~** dividere qc equamente

equal opportunity *n* pari opportunità *fpl*

equal(s) sign *n* MAT segno *m* d'uguaglianza

equanimity [ˌe·kwə·'nɪ·mə·ti] *n* equanimità *f;* **to receive sth with ~** ricevere qc con serenità

equate [ɪ·'kweɪt] **I.** *vt* equiparare **II.** *vi* **to ~ to sth** equivalere a qc

equation [ɪ·'kweɪ·ʒən] *n* equazione *f*

equator [ɪ·'kweɪ·t̬ə] *n* equatore *m*

equatorial [ˌe·kwə·'tɔː·ri·əl] *adj* equatoriale

Equatorial Guinea *n* Guinea *f* equatoriale

equestrian [ɪ·'kwes·tri·ən] **I.** *adj* equestre; **~ events** gare*f pl* d'equitazione; **~ statue** statua *f* equestre **II.** *n* (*man*) cavaliere *m;* (*woman*) amazzone *f*

equidistant [ˌiː·kwɪ·'dɪs·tənt] *adj* equidistante

equilateral [ˌiː·kwɪ·'læ·ṭə·rəl] *adj* MAT equilatero, -a

equilibrium [ˌiː·kwɪ·'lɪ·bri·əm] *n* equilibrio *m*

equinoctial [ˌiː·kwɪ·'nɑːk·ʃl] *adj* equinoziale

equinox ['iː·kwɪ·nɑːks] <-es> *n* equinozio *m;* **fall** ~ equinozio d'autunno; **spring** ~ equinozio di primavera

equip [ɪ·'kwɪp] <-pp-> *vt* **1.** (*fit out*) equipaggiare; **to** ~ **sb with sth** equipaggiare qn di qc; **to** ~ **sth with sth** attrezzare qc con qc **2.** (*prepare*) preparare

equipment [ɪ·'kwɪp·mənt] *n* equipaggiamento *m;* **camping** ~ attrezzatura *f* da campeggio; **office** ~ arredo *m* per l'ufficio

equitable ['e·kwɪ·ṭə·bl] *adj* equo, -a

equity ['e·kwə·ti] <-ies> *n* **1.** (*fairness*) equità *f* **2.** *pl* FIN azioni *f pl* ordinarie

eq(uiv). *abbr of* **equivalent** equivalente

equivalence [ɪ·'kwɪ·və·ləns] *n* equivalenza *f*

equivalent [ɪ·'kwɪ·və·lənt] **I.** *adj* equivalente; **to be** ~ **to sth** essere equivalente a qc **II.** *n* equivalente *m*

equivocal [ɪ·'kwɪ·və·kl] *adj* equivoco, -a

equivocate [ɪ·'kwɪ·və·keɪt] *vi form* esprimersi in modo equivoco

equivocation [ɪ·ˌkwɪ·və·'keɪ·ʃən] *n* ambiguità *f*

ER *n abbr of* **emergency room** DEA *m inv*

era ['ɪ·rə] *n* era *f;* **communist** ~ era comunista; **postwar** ~ il periodo del dopoguerra; **to usher in a new** ~ inaugurare una nuova era

eradicate [ɪ·'ræ·dɪ·keɪt] *vt* debellare

erase [ɪ·'reɪs] *vt a.* INFOR cancellare; **to** ~ **a deficit** eliminare un deficit

eraser [ɪ·'reɪ·sɚ] *n* gomma *f*

erasure [ɪ·'reɪ·ʃɚ] *n* cancellazione *f*

ere [eəɹ] **I.** *prep liter* prima di; ~ **long** in breve tempo **II.** *conj liter* prima che

erect [ɪ·'rekt] **I.** *adj a.* ANAT eretto, -a **II.** *vt* erigere; (*construct*) costruire; (*put up*) montare

erectile [ɪ·'rek·təl] *adj* ANAT erettile

erectile dysfunction *n* disfunzione *f* erettile

erection [ɪ·'rek·ʃən] *n* **1.** ANAT erezione *f* **2.** ARCHIT costruzione *f*

erg [ɜːrg] *n* PHYS erg *m*

ergo ['er·goʊ] *adv* dunque

ergonomic [ˌɜːr·gə·'nɑː·mɪk] *adj* ergonomico, -a

ergonomics *n* ergonomia *f*

ermine ['ɜːr·mɪn] *n* ermellino *m*

erode [ɪ·'roʊd] **I.** *vt* erodere **II.** *vi* corrodersi

erogenous [ɪ·'rɑː·dʒɪ·nəs] *adj* erogeno, -a

erogenous zone *n* zona *f* erogena

erosion [ɪ·'roʊ·ʒən] *n* erosione *f*

erotic [ɪ·'rɑː·ṭɪk] *adj* erotico, -a

eroticism [ɪ·'rɑː·ṭə·sɪ·zəm] *n* erotismo *m*

err [ɜːr] *vi* errare; **to** ~ **on the side of sth** peccare per eccesso di qc; **to** ~ **on the side of caution** peccare per eccesso di cautela ▶ **to** ~ **is** **human** *prov* errare è umano *prov*

errand ['e·rənd] *n* commissione *f;* **to run an** ~ andare a fare una commissione; **an** ~ **of**

mercy *form* una missione di soccorso

errand boy *n* fattorino *m*

errant ['e·rənt] *adj* **1.** (*off course*) vagante **2.** (*deviant: youngster*) dal comportamento deviante

erratic [ɪ·'ræ·ṭɪk] *adj* **1.** (*inconsistent: heartbeat*) irregolare; (*behavior*) imprevedibile **2.** (*off-line: course*) discontinuo, -a **3.** GEO erratico, -a

erratum [e·'rɑː·ṭəm] <-ta> *n form* errore *m* di stampa

erroneous [ə·'roʊ·ni·əs] *adj* erroneo, -a; ~ **assumption** supposizione errata

error ['e·rɚ] *n* errore *m;* **to do sth in** ~ far qc per errore; **human** ~ errore umano ▶ **to see the** ~ **of one's** <u>ways</u> riconoscere i propri errori; **to show sb the** ~ **of his/her** <u>ways</u> mostrare a qn dove sbaglia

error message *n* INFOR messaggio *m* di errore

error-prone *adj* soggetto, -a a errori

ersatz ['er·zɑːts] *adj* ~ **coffee** surrogato *m* di caffè

erudite ['er·jə·daɪt] *adj* erudito, -a

erudition [ˌer·ju·'dɪ·ʃən] *n* erudizione *f*

erupt [ɪ·'rʌpt] *vi* **1.** (*explode: volcano*) essere in eruzione; *fig* scoppiare **2.** MED spuntare

eruption [ɪ·'rʌp·ʃən] *n* eruzione *f; fig* scoppio *m*

escalate ['es·kə·leɪt] **I.** *vi* (*increase*) aumentare; (*incidents*) intensificarsi; **to** ~ **into sth** trasformarsi in qc (*di più grave*) **II.** *vt* intensificare

escalation [ˌes·kə·'leɪ·ʃən] *n* escalation *f inv;* ~ **of tension** escalation della tensione

escalator ['es·kə·leɪ·ṭɚ] *n* scala *f* mobile

escalope [ˌes·kə·'loʊp] *n* scaloppina *f*

escapade [ˌes·kə·'peɪd] *n* avventura *f;* (*mischievous*) bravata *f*

escape [ɪ·'skeɪp] **I.** *vi* scappare; (*person*) fuggire; **to** ~ **from** scappare da; **to** ~ **from a program** INFOR uscire da un programma **II.** *vt* sfuggire a; (*avoid*) evitare; **to** ~ **sb('s attention)** sfuggire all'attenzione di qn; **nothing** ~**s his attention** non gli sfugge nulla; **the word** ~**s me** mi sfugge il nome; **a cry** ~**d him** gli sfuggì un grido **III.** *n* **1.** (*act*) fuga *f;* **to make a narrow** ~ salvarsi per un pelo **2.** (*outflow*) fuga *f* **3.** LAW ~ **clause** clausola *f* di recesso da un contratto

escapee [ɪ·ˌskeɪ·'piː] *n* fuggiasco, -a *m, f*

escapism [ɪ·'skeɪ·pɪ·zəm] *n* evasione *f* dalla realtà

escapist **I.** *n* persona *che tende a evadere dalla realtà* **II.** *adj* d'evasione; ~ **literature** letteratura *f* d'evasione

escarole *n* scarola *f*

escarpment [ɪ·'skɑːr·mənt] *n* scarpata *f*

eschew [es·'stʃuː] *vt form* evitare

escort ['es·kɔːrt] **I.** *vt* accompagnare; (*politician*) scortare **II.** *n* **1.** (*companion, paid companion*) accompagnatore, -trice *m, f* **2.** (*guard*) scorta *f*

ESE *n abbr of* **east-southeast** ESE *m*

E

Eskimo ['es·kə·mou] <Eskimo *o* -s> *n* 1.(*person*) eschimese *mf* 2. LING eschimese *m*

Eskimo pie® *n* pinguino *m* (*gelato alla vaniglia ricoperto di cioccolato*)

ESL [ˌiː·esˈel] *n* abbr of **English as a second language** inglese *m* come seconda lingua

ESOL ['iː·saːl] English for speakers of other languages

esophagus [ɪˈsaː·fə·gəs] *n* esofago *m*

esoteric [ˌe·səˈte·rɪk] *adj* esoterico, -a

ESP [ˌiː·esˈpiː] *n* abbr of **extrasensory perception** percezione *f* extrasensoriale

esp. abbr of **especially** spec.

espadrille ['es·pə·drɪl] *n* espadrille *f inv*

especial [ɪˈspe·ʃl] *adj* speciale

especially [ɪˈspe·ʃə·li] *adv* 1.(*particularly*) specialmente; **I bought this ~ for you** l'ho comprato espressamente per te 2.(*in particular*) particolarmente

espionage ['es·piə·naːʒ] *n* spionaggio *m;* **industrial ~** spionaggio industriale

esplanade ['es·plə·naːd] *n* lungomare *m*

espousal [ɪˈspau·zl] *n form* adesione *f*

espouse [ɪˈspauz] *vt* sposare

espresso [esˈpre·sou] <-s> *n* (caffè *m*) espresso *m*

Esq. abbr of **Esquire** Sig.

essay[1] ['e·seɪ] *n* 1. LIT saggio *m* 2. SCHOOL tema *m;* **an ~ about sth** un tema su qc

essay[2] [e·ˈseɪ] *vt* 1.(*try*) tentare 2.(*test*) provare

essayist *n* saggista *mf*

essence ['e·sns] *n* 1.essenza *f;* **in ~** in sostanza; **time is of the ~** è essenziale fare presto 2.(*in food*) essenza *f*

essential [ɪˈsen·ʃl] I. *adj* essenziale; (*difference*) fondamentale; **to be ~ to sb/sth** essere essenziale per qn/qc II. *n pl* **the ~s** gli elementi essenziali; **the bare ~s** lo stretto necessario

essentially [ɪˈsen·ʃə·li] *adv* essenzialmente

essential oil *n* olio *m* essenziale

est. 1. abbr of **estimated** stimato 2. abbr of **established** fondato

establish [ɪˈstæb·lɪʃ] I. *vt* 1.(*found*) fondare; (*commission, hospital*) creare; (*dictatorship*) instaurare 2.(*begin: relationship*) instaurare 3.(*set: precedent*) creare; (*priorities, norm*) stabilire 4.(*secure*) affermare; (*order*) imporre; **he ~ed his authority over the workers** affermò la sua autorità sugli operai; **to ~ a reputation as a pianist** farsi un nome come pianista 5.(*demonstrate*) **to ~ sb as sth** imporre qn come qc 6.(*determine*) stabilire; (*facts*) accertare; (*truth*) provare; **to ~ whether/where ...** determinare se/dove ...; **to ~ that ...** dimostrare che ... 7. ADMIN **to ~ residence** fissare la residenza II. *vi* stabilirsi

established [ɪˈstæb·lɪʃt] *adj* 1.(*founded*) fondato, -a 2.(*fact*) provato, -a; (*procedures*) consolidato, -a

establishment [ɪˈstæb·lɪʃ·mənt] *n* 1.(*business*) impresa *f;* **family ~** impresa familiare *f*

2.(*organization*) istituto *m;* **educational ~** istituto *m* d'istruzione; **financial ~** istituto *m* finanziario; **the Establishment** POL l'establishment *m; inv*

estate [ɪˈsteɪt] *n* 1.(*piece of land*) tenuta *f;* **country ~** tenuta di campagna *f* 2. LAW (*possessions after death*) patrimonio *m;* **industrial ~** zona *f* industriale

estate tax *n* imposta *f* di successione

esteem [ɪˈstiːm] I. *n* stima *f;* **to fall/rise in sb's ~** perdere/guadagnare la stima di qn; **to hold sb in high/low ~** stimare molto/poco qn II. *vt* 1.(*respect*) stimare 2.(*consider*) ritenere; **to ~ it an honor to do sth** considerare un onore fare qc

esteemed *adj* stimato, -a; **highly ~** stimatissimo

esthetic [esˈθe·tɪk] *adj* estetico, -a

esthetics *n* estetica *f*

estimable ['es·tɪ·mə·bl] *adj form* stimabile

estimate[1] ['es·tɪ·meɪt] *vt* stimare; **to ~ that ...** calcolare che ...

estimate[2] ['es·tɪ·mɪt] *n* stima *f;* **a rough ~** *inf* un calcolo approssimativo

estimated ['es·tɪ·meɪ·tɪd] *adj* stimato, -a

estimation [ˌes·tɪˈmeɪ·ʃən] *n* opinione *f;* **in my ~** a mio avviso

Estonia [esˈtou·ni·ə] *n* Estonia *f*

Estonian [esˈtou·ni·ən] I. *adj* estone II. *n* 1.(*person*) estone *mf* 2. LING estone *m*

estrange [ɪˈstreɪndʒ] *vt* **to ~ sb from sb/sth** estraniare qn da qn/qc

estranged *adj* (*distance*) estraniato, -a; (*state*) separato, -a

estrangement [ɪˈstreɪndʒ·mənt] *n* estraniazione *f*

estrogen ['es·trə·dʒən] *n s.* **oestrogen**

estuary ['es·tʃuː·e·ri] <-ies> *n* estuario *m*

ETA [ˌiː·tiːˈeɪ] abbr of **estimated time of arrival** ora *f* di arrivo prevista

et al. [etˈæl] abbr of **et alii** et al.

etc. abbr of **et cetera** ecc.

et cetera [ɪtˈse·tə·ə] *adv* eccetera

etch [etʃ] *vt* 1.incidere (all'acquaforte) 2. *fig* **to be ~ed in sb's memory** essere impresso nella memoria di qn

etcher *n* acquafortista *mf*

etching *n* acquaforte *f*

ETD abbr of **estimated time of departure** ora *f* prevista di partenza

eternal [ɪˈtɜːr·nl] *adj* 1.(*lasting forever: life*) eterno, -a 2.(*constant: complaints*) continuo, -a

eternally [ɪˈtɜːr·nə·li] *adv* 1.(*forever*) eternamente 2.(*constantly*) continuamente

eternity [ɪˈtɜːr·nə·ti] *n* eternità *f;* **to seem like an ~** sembrare un'eternità; **to wait an ~ for sb** aspettare qn una vita

ether ['iː·θəʳ] *n* etere *m*

ethereal [ɪˈθɪ·ri·əl] *adj* etereo, -a

ethic ['e·θɪk] *n* **work ~** etica *f* del lavoro

ethical *adj* etico, -a

ethics *n + sing vb* etica *f*

Ethiopia [ˌiːˈθɪˈouˈpiˈə] *n* Etiopia *f*
Ethiopian [ˌiːˈθɪˈouˈpiˈən] I. *n* etiope *mf*
II. *adj* etiope
ethnic ['eθˈnɪk] *adj* etnico, -a; ~ **cleansing** pulizia etnica; ~ **costumes** costumi etnici
ethnology [eθˈnɑːˈləˈdʒi] *n* etnologia *f*
ethos ['iːˈθɑːs] *n* ethos *m;* **the working-class** ~ i valori della classe operaia
ethyl alcohol ['eˈθəl ˈælˈkəˈhɑːl] *n* alcol *m* etilico; *inv*
etiquette ['eˈtɪˈkɪt] *n* etichetta *f;* **court** ~ etichetta di corte
etymological [ˌeˈtɪˈməˈlɑːˈdʒɪˈkl] *adj* etimologico, -a
etymology [ˌeˈtɪˈmɑːˈləˈdʒi] *n* etimologia *f*
EU [ˌiːˈjuː] *n abbr of* **European Union** UE *f*
eucalyptus [juːˈkəˈlɪpˈtəs] <-es *o* -ti> *n* eucalipto *m*
eucalyptus oil *n* olio *m* essenziale di eucalipto
Eucharist ['juːˈkəˈrɪst] *n* REL **the** ~ l'Eucaristia *f*
euchre ['juːˈkəˈ] *n gioco di carte, che si basa sulle 32 carte più alte.*
eulogize ['juːˈləˈdʒaɪz] I. *vt form* elogiare II. *vi form* **to** ~ **over sth/sb** fare l'elogio di qc/qn
eulogy ['juːˈləˈdʒi] <-ies> *n form* 1. *(high praise)* elogio *m* 2. LIT panegirico *m;* **to deliver a** ~ fare un panegirico
eunuch ['juːˈnək] *n* eunuco *m*
euphemism ['juːˈfəˈmɪˈzəm] *n* eufemismo *m*
euphemistic [ˌjuːˈfəˈmɪsˈtɪk] *adj* eufemistico, -a
euphony ['juːˈfəˈni] *n form* eufonia *f*
euphoria [juːˈfɔːˈriˈə] *n* euforia *f*
euphoric [juːˈfɔːˈrɪk] *adj* euforico, -a
EUR *n abbr of* **Euro** EUR *m*
Eurasia [jʊˈreɪˈʒə] *n* Eurasia *f*
Eurasian [jʊˈreɪˈʒən] I. *adj* euroasiatico, -a II. *n* euroasiatico, -a *m, f*
eurhythmics [jʊˈrɪðˈmɪks] *n*, **eurythmics** *n* + *sing vb* euritmia *f*
euro ['jʊˈrou] *n* euro *m; inv*
Eurocrat ['jʊˈrəʊˈkræt] *n* eurocrate *mf*
Europe ['jʊˈrəp] *n* Europa *f*
European [jʊˈrəˈpiˈən] I. *adj* europeo, -a II. *n* europeo, -a *m, f*
European Community *n* Comunità *f* Europea
European Union *n* Unione *f* Europea
euthanasia [ˌjuːˈθəˈneɪˈʒə] *n* eutanasia *f*
evacuate [ɪˈvækˈjuˈeɪt] *vt (people)* evacuare; *(building)* sgombrare
evacuation [ɪˈvækˈjuˈeɪˈʃən] *n* evacuazione *f;* ~ **of the bowels** MED evacuazione *f* dell'intestino
evacuee [ɪˈvækˈjuːˈiː] *n* sfollato, -a *m, f*
evade [ɪˈveɪd] *vt (responsibility, person)* eludere; *(police)* sfuggire a; *(taxes)* evadere; **to** ~ **doing sth** evitare di fare qc
evaluate [ɪˈvælˈjuˈeɪt] *vt (value)* valutare
evaluation [ɪˈvælˈjuˈeɪˈʃən] *n* valutazione *f;* *(of a book)* critica *f*
evangelical [ˌiːˈvænˈdʒeˈlɪˈkl] I. *n* evangelico, -a *m, f* II. *adj* evangelico, -a
evangelist [ɪˈvænˈdʒəˈlɪst] *n* evangelista *mf*

evangelize [ɪˈvænˈdʒəˈlaɪz] I. *vt* evangelizzare II. *vi* predicare il vangelo
evaporate [ɪˈvæˈpəˈreɪt] I. *vt* far evaporare II. *vi* evaporare; *fig* svanire
evaporated milk *n* latte *m* condensato
evaporation [ɪˈvæˈpəˈreɪˈʃən] *n* evaporazione *f*
evasion [ɪˈveɪˈʒən] *n* 1. *(of tax, responsibility)* evasione *f* 2. *(avoidance)* risposta *f* evasiva
evasive [ɪˈveɪˈsɪv] *adj* evasivo, -a
eve [iːv] *n* vigilia *f;* **on the** ~ **of** alla vigilia di; **Christmas Eve** la vigilia di Natale; **New Year's Eve** la notte di Capodanno
Eve [iːv] *n* Eva *f*
even ['iːvn] I. *adj* 1. *(level)* piano, -a; *(surface)* liscio, -a 2. *(equalized)* alla pari; **the chances are about** ~ le possibilità sono più o meno le stesse; **to be on** ~ **terms** essere nelle stesse condizioni; **to get** ~ **with sb** pareggiare i conti con qn 3. *(of same size, amount)* uguale 4. *(constant, regular)* regolare; *(rate)* costante 5. *(fair)* equo, -a 6. MAT pari II. *vt* 1. *(make level)* livellare; *(surface)* appianare 2. *(equalize)* pareggiare III. *adv* 1. *(indicates the unexpected)* perfino; **not** ~ neppure 2. *(despite)* ~ **if** ... anche se ...; ~ **so** ... nonostante ciò ...; ~ **though** ... nonostante ... 3. *(used to intensify)* addirittura 4. + *comp (all the more)* ancora; **it will be** ~ **colder** farà ancora più freddo
◆**even out** I. *vi (prices)* livellarsi II. *vt* pareggiare
◆**even up** *vt* pareggiare
evening ['iːvˈnɪŋ] *n* sera *f;* **good** ~! buonasera!; **in the** ~ di sera; **that** ~ quella sera; **the previous** ~ la sera prima; **every Monday** ~ tutti i lunedì sera; **on Monday** ~ lunedì sera; **during the** ~ di sera; **one July** ~ una sera di luglio; **8 o'clock in the** ~ le 8 di sera; **at the end of the** ~ alla fine della serata; **all** ~ **(long)** tutta la sera
evening class *n* corso *m* serale
evening dress *n* abito *m* da sera; **to wear** ~ vestirsi in abito da sera
evening edition *n* edizione *f* della sera
evening gown *n* vestito *m* da sera
evening (news)paper *n* giornale *m* della sera
evening prayer *n* preghiera *f* della sera
evening star *n* stella *f* vespertina
evenly ['iːvˈnˈli] *adv* 1. *(calmly)* pacatamente; **to state sth** ~ dire qc in modo pacato 2. *(equally)* equamente; **to divide sth** ~ dividere qc in parti uguali
evenness ['iːvˈnˈnɪs] *n* 1. uniformità *f* 2. *(calmness)* serenità *f*
even-steven *adj*, **even-Steven** *adj inf* 1. *(settled up: transaction)* ben equilibrato, -a; **to be** ~ essere pari 2. SPORTS perfettamente pari
event [ɪˈvent] *n* 1. *(happening)* evento *m;* **sports** ~ avvenimento *m* sportivo; **to be swept along by the tide of** ~**s** essere travolto dagli eventi 2. *(case)* caso *m;* **in any** [*o* **either**] ~ in qualsiasi caso [*o* nell'uno o

E

nell'altro caso]; **in the ~ (that) it rains** nel caso piovesse

even-tempered ['iː·vən·'tem·pəd] *adj* placido, -a

eventful [ɪ·'vent·fəl] *adj* movimentato, -a

eventual [ɪ·'ven·tʃʊ·əl] *adj* finale

eventuality [ɪ·ˌven·tʃʊ·'æ·lə·ti] <-ies> *n inv* eventualità *f*

eventually [ɪ·'ven·tʃʊ·ə·li] *adv* 1.(*finally*) alla fine 2.(*some day*) col tempo

ever ['e·vəʳ] *adv* 1.(*on any occasion*) mai; **have you ~ been to Hawaii?** sei mai stato alle Hawaii?; **for the first time ~** per la prima volta in assoluto; **the hottest day ~** il giorno più caldo; **better than ~** meglio che mai; **have you ~ seen such a thing!** s'è mai vista una cosa simile?; **would you ~ dye your hair?** ti tingeresti mai i capelli? 2.(*in negative statements*) mai; **nobody has ~ heard of him** nessuno ha mai sentito parlare di lui; **never ~** mai; **hardly ~** quasi mai; **nothing ~ happens** non succede mai niente; **don't you ~ do that again!** non farlo mai più! 3.(*always*) **~ after** per sempre; **as ~** come sempre; **~ since ...** da quando ...; **~ since** (*since then*) da allora 4.(*used to intensify*) **who ~ was that woman?** chi mai era quella donna?; **all he ~ does is +***infin* tutto quello che sa fare è +*infin;* **don't you ~ come here again!** non venire mai più qui!

everglade ['e·vəʳ·gleɪd] *n terreno basso paludoso coperto di erba alta*

evergreen ['e·vəʳ·griːn] I. *n* sempreverde *mf* II. *adj* sempreverde; *fig* evergreen

everlasting [ˌe·vəʳ·'læs·tɪŋ] *adj* 1.(*undying*) imperituro, -a; (*gratitude, love*) eterno, -a *f* 2.(*incessant*) interminabile

evermore [ˌe·vəʳ·'mɔːr] *adv liter* eternamente; **for ~** per sempre

every ['ev·ri] *adj* 1.(*each*) ogni; **~ time** ogni volta; **her ~ wish** ogni suo minimo desiderio; **not ~ book can be borrowed** non tutti i libri possono essere presi in prestito 2.(*all*) tutto, -a; **~ one of them** tutti loro senza eccezione; **in ~ way** in tutti i sensi 3.(*repeated*) **~ other week** ogni due settimane; **~ now and then** [*o* **again**] di tanto in tanto ▶ **~ little bit helps** *prov* tutto fa brodo *prov*

everybody ['ev·ri·ˌbɑː·di] *pron indef, sing* tutti, -e *pl;* **~ but Paul** tutti meno Paul; **~ who agrees** tutti quelli che sono d'accordo

everybody else *pron* tutti gli altri

everyday ['ev·ri·deɪ] *adj* di tutti i giorni; (*event*) ordinario, -a; (*language*) comune; (*life*) quotidiano, -a

everyone ['ev·ri·wʌn] *pron s.* **everybody**

everything ['ev·ri·θɪŋ] *pron indef, sing* tutto; **is ~ all right?** va tutto bene?; **~ they drink** tutto quello che bevono; **to be ~ to sb** essere tutto per qn; **to do ~ necessary/one can** fare tutto il necessario/il possibile; **time is ~** il tempo è di vitale importanza; **money isn't ~** i soldi non son tutto

everywhere ['ev·ri·wer] *adv* dappertutto; **~ else** in qualsiasi altro posto; **to look ~ for sth** cercare qc dappertutto; **to travel ~** viaggiare dovunque

evict [ɪ·'vɪkt] *vt* sfrattare

eviction [ɪ·'vɪk·ʃən] *n* sfratto *m*

evidence ['e·vɪ·dəns] *n* 1.(*sign*) segno *m* evidente 2.(*proof*) prova *f* 3.(*testimony*) deposizione *f;* **based on the ~** basato sulle prove; **to turn state's ~ against sb** diventare testimone d'accusa contro qn 4.(*view*) evidenza *f;* **to be in ~** essere visibile

evident ['e·vɪ·dənt] *adj* evidente; **to be ~** essere evidente; **to be ~ to sb** essere chiaro per qn; **to be ~ in sth** essere evidente da qc; **it is ~ that ...** è chiaro che ...

evidently *adv* evidentemente

evil ['iː·vl] I. *adj* malvagio, -a; **~ spirit** spirito maligno; **to have an ~ tongue** essere una malalingua II. *n* male *m;* **social ~** piaga *f* sociale; **an aura of ~** un'aura di malvagità; **good and ~** il bene e il male; **the lesser of two ~s** il minore dei mali

evildoer [ˌiː·vl·'duː·əʳ] *n* malfattore, -trice *m, f*

evil eye *n* malocchio *m;* **to give sb the ~ eye** fare il malocchio a qn

evil-minded *adj* malintenzionato, -a

evil-tempered *adj* che ha un pessimo carattere; **to be ~** avere un pessimo carattere

evince [ɪ·'vɪns] *vt form* mostrare; **to ~ interest** mostrare interesse

evocation [ˌe·vəʳ·'keɪ·ʃən] *n form* evocazione *f*

evocative [ɪ·'vɑː·kə·t̬ɪv] *adj* evocativo, -a; **an ~ image** un'immagine suggestiva; **to be ~ of sth** evocare qc

evoke [ɪ·'voʊk] *vt* evocare

evolution [ˌe·və·'luː·ʃən] *n a. fig* evoluzione *f*

evolutionary theory *n* teoria *f* dell'evoluzione

evolve [ɪ·'vɑːlv] I. *vi* (*gradually develop*) svilupparsi; (*animals*) evolversi; **to ~ into sth** trasformarsi in qc II. *vt* sviluppare; **to ~ new forms of life** creare nuove forme di vita

ewe [juː] *n* pecora (femmina) *f*

ewer ['juː·əʳ] *n* brocca *f*

ex [eks] <-es> *n inf* ex *mf*

exacerbate [ɪg·'zæ·səʳ·beɪt] *vt* esacerbare

exact [ɪg·'zækt] I. *adj* esatto, -a; **to be ~ in one's reporting** essere molto preciso nell'informare; **the ~ opposite** l'esatto contrario II. *vt* esigere; **to ~ sth from sb** esigere qc da qn

exacting *adj* esigente

exactitude [ɪg·'zæk·tə·tuːd] *n* esattezza *f*

exactly [ɪg·'zækt·li] *adv* esattamente; **~ like ...** proprio come ...; **how/what/where ~ ...** come/che cosa/dove esattamente; **I don't ~ agree with that** non sono del tutto d'accordo su questo; **not ~** non proprio; **~!** esatto!

exactness [ɪg·'zækt·nɪs] *n* esattezza *f*

exaggerate [ɪg·'zæ·dʒə·reɪt] *vi, vt* esagerare; **let's not ~!** non esageriamo!

exaggerated [ɪg·'zæ·dʒə·reɪ·t̬ɪd] *adj* esagerato, -a; **greatly ~** molto esagerato

exaggeration [ɪgˌzæ·dʒə·'reɪ·ʃən] *n* esagerazione *f;* **it's no ~ to say that ...** non è esagerato dire che ...

exalt [ɪg·'zɔːlt] *vt* **1.** (*praise*) esaltare; (*honor*) elevare; **to ~ sth as a virtue** esaltare qc come una virtù **2.** (*raise rank*) innalzare

exaltation [ˌeg·zɔːl·'teɪ·ʃən] *n* esaltazione *f*

exalted [ɪg·'zɔːl·tɪd] *adj* **1.** (*elevated*) elevato, -a; **~ rank** alto rango **2.** (*jubilant*) esaltato, -a

exam [ɪg·'zæm] *n* esame *m*

examination [ɪgˌzæ·mɪ·'neɪ·ʃən] *n* **1.** (*exam*) esame *m* **2.** (*investigation*) indagine *f;* **medical ~** visita *f* medica **3.** LAW interrogatorio *m*

examine [ɪg·'zæ·mɪn] *vt* **1.** (*study*) esaminare; **to ~ the effects of sth** esaminare gli effetti di qc **2.** MED visitare **3.** LAW interrogare

examinee [ɪgˌzæ·mɪ·'niː] *n* esaminando, -a *m, f*

examiner [ɪg·'zæ·mɪ·nɚ] *n* esaminatore, -trice *m, f*

example [ɪg·'zæm·pl] *n* **1.** (*sample, model*) esempio *m;* **for ~** per esempio; **to be a shining ~ of sth** essere un chiaro esempio di qc; **to follow sb's ~** seguire l'esempio di qn; **to give (sb) an ~ (of sth)** dare (a qn) un esempio (di qc); **to set a good ~** dare il buon esempio **2.** (*copy*) esemplare *m*

exasperate [ɪg·'zɑːs·pə·reɪt] *vt* esasperare; **he ~s me** mi esaspera

exasperating [ɪg·'zɑːs·pə·reɪ·t̬ɪŋ] *adj* esasperante

exasperation [ɪgˌzæs·pə·'reɪ·ʃən] *n* esasperazione *f*

ex-boyfriend *n* ex ragazzo *m*

ex-girlfriend *n* ex ragazza *f*

excavate ['eks·kə·veɪt] I. *vt* **1.** (*expose*) portare alla luce **2.** (*hollow*) scavare II. *vi* scavare

excavation [ˌeks·kə·'veɪ·ʃən] *n* scavo *m*

excavator ['eks·kə·veɪ·t̬ɚ] *n* scavatore *m,* scavatrice *f*

exceed [ɪk·'siːd] *vt* eccedere; (*outshine*) superare

exceedingly *adv* estremamente

excel [ɪk·'sel] <-ll-> I. *vi* eccellere; **to ~ at** [*o* in] sth eccellere in qc II. *vt* **to ~ oneself** superare sé stesso; **to ~ all others** eccellere su tutti

excellence ['ek·sə·ləns] *n* eccellenza *f*

Excellency ['ek·sə·lən·si] *n* Eccellenza *f;* **His ~** Sua Eccellenza; (**Your**) **~** (Sua/Vostra) Eccellenza

excellent ['ek·sə·lənt] *adj* eccellente

except [ɪk·'sept] I. *prep* **~ (for)** tranne; **to do nothing ~ wait** non fare altro che aspettare II. *vt form* escludere; **to ~ sth/sb from sth** escludere qc/qn da qc; **children under the age of 14 are ~ed** esclusi i ragazzi sotto i 14 anni

excepting *prep* eccetto

exception [ɪk·'sep·ʃən] *n* eccezione *f;* **to be an ~** essere un'eccezione; **to make an ~** fare un'eccezione; **with the ~ of ...** a eccezione di ...; **to take ~ (to sth)** offendersi (per qc); **I**

take great ~ to your last comment mi ha dato molto fastidio il tuo ultimo commento
▶ **the ~ proves the rule** *prov* l'eccezione conferma la regola *prov*

exceptional [ɪk·'sep·ʃə·nl] *adj* eccezionale

exceptionally [ɪk·'sep·ʃnə·li] *adv* eccezionalmente; **to be ~ clever** essere straordinariamente intelligente

excerpt ['ek·sɜːrpt] *n* brano (tratto da qc) *m*

excess [ɪk·'ses] <-es> *n* eccesso *m; to eat* **to ~** mangiare eccessivamente; **to carry sth to ~** portare qc all'eccesso; **in ~ of** più di

excess baggage *n,* **excess luggage** *n* bagaglio *m* in eccedenza

excessive [ɪk·'se·sɪv] *adj* eccessivo, -a; (*claim*) esagerato, -a; (*violence*) gratuito, -a

excess supply *n* offerta *f* eccedente

exchange [ɪks·'tʃeɪndʒ] I. *vt* **1.** (*trade for the equivalent*) cambiare **2.** (*interchange*) scambiare; **to ~ blows** picchiarsi; **to ~ words** litigare II. *n* **1.** (*interchange, trade*) scambio *m;* **in ~ for sth** in cambio di qc; **~ of (gun)fire** scambio di colpi (d'arma da fuoco) **2.** FIN, ECON cambio *m;* **foreign ~** cambio estero **3.** (*verbal interchange*) **~ of threats** scambio *m* di minacce

exchangeable *adj* scambiabile; (*goods*) che si può cambiare; **~ currency** valuta *f* scambiabile; **to be ~ for sth** poter essere cambiato con qc

exchange rate *n* tasso *m* di cambio

exchange student *n* studente, -essa *m, f* che partecipa a uno scambio culturale

exchange teacher *n* insegnante *mf* che partecipa a uno scambio culturale

excise [ek·'saɪz] *vt form* **1.** recidere; (*tumor*) asportare **2.** *fig* eliminare

excise tax *n* dazio *m*

excitable [ɪk·'saɪ·t̬ə·bl] *adj* eccitabile

excite [ɪk·'saɪt] *vt* **1.** (*move*) entusiasmare; **to ~ an audience** entusiasmare il pubblico; **to be ~d about an idea** essere eccitato all'idea di qc **2.** (*stimulate*) suscitare; **to ~ sb's curiosity** suscitare la curiosità di qn

excited [ɪk·'saɪ·t̬ɪd] *adj* eccitato, -a

excitement [ɪk·'saɪt·mənt] *n* eccitazione *f;* **to be in a state of ~** essere molto agitato; **what ~!** che emozione!

exciting [ɪk·'saɪ·t̬ɪŋ] *adj* eccitante

excl. 1. *abbr of* **excluding** eccetto **2.** *abbr of* **exclusive** esclusivo

exclaim [ɪks·'kleɪm] *vi, vt* esclamare; **to ~ in delight** gridare di gioia

exclamation [ˌeks·klə·'meɪ·ʃən] *n* esclamazione *f*

exclamation mark *n,* **exclamation point** *n* punto *m* esclamativo

exclude [ɪks·'kluːd] *vt* **1.** (*keep out*) escludere; **to ~ sb from a group** escludere qn da un gruppo **2.** (*possibility*) scartare

excluding [ɪks·'kluː·dɪŋ] *prep* eccetto

exclusion [ɪks·'kluː·ʒən] *n* esclusione *f*

exclusive [ɪks·'kluː·sɪv] I. *adj* esclusivo, -a;

E

~ **interview** intervista *f* esclusiva; **in** ~ **circles** in circoli esclusivi; **to be** ~ **to sb** essere esclusivo per qn; ~ **of** escluso; **to be** ~ **of** non includere **II.** *n* esclusiva *f*

exclusively *adv* esclusivamente

excommunicate [ˌeks·kə·ˈmjuː·nɪ·keɪt] *vt* scomunicare

excommunication [ˌeks·kə·ˌmjuː·nɪ·ˈkeɪ·ʃən] *n* scomunica *f*

excrement [ˈeks·krə·mənt] *n* escremento *m*

excreta [ɪks·ˈkriː·tə] *n form* escrementi *mpl*

excrete [ɪks·ˈkriːt] *vi, vt form* espellere

excretion [ɪks·ˈkriː·ʃən] *n form* escrezione *f*

excruciating [ɪks·ˈkruː·ʃi·eɪ·tɪŋ] *adj* **1.** straziante; (*pain*) atroce **2.** (*intense: accuracy*) estremo, -a

excursion [ɪks·ˈkɜːr·ʒən] *n* escursione *f;* **to go on an** ~ fare un'escursione

excusable [ɪks·ˈkjuː·zə·bl] *adj* perdonabile

excuse[1] [ɪks·ˈkjuːz] *vt* **1.** (*justify: behavior*) giustificare; (*lateness*) scusare; **to** ~ **sb for sth** perdonare qn per qc **2.** (*forgive*) scusare; ~ **me!** mi scusi! **3.** (*allow not to attend*) **to** ~ **sb from sth** dispensare qn da qc **4.** (*leave*) **after an hour she** ~**d herself** dopo un'ora si è scusata e se n'è andata

excuse[2] [ɪks·ˈkjuːs] *n* **1.** (*explanation*) scusa *f* **2.** (*pretext*) pretesto *m;* **poor** ~ misera scusa; **to make** ~**s for sb** giustificare qn; **be there on time** — **no** ~**s!** sii puntuale — niente scuse!

exec *n inf abbr of* **executive** dirigente *mf*

execute [ˈek·sɪ·kjuːt] *vt* **1.** (*carry out*) eseguire; (*maneuver*) effettuare; (*plan*) attuare; **to** ~ **sb's will** dare esecuzione al testamento di qn **2.** (*put to death*) giustiziare

execution [ˌek·sɪ·ˈkjuː·ʃən] *n* **1.** (*carrying out*) esecuzione *f;* **to put a plan into** ~ attuare un piano **2.** (*putting to death*) esecuzione *f*

executioner [ˌek·sɪ·ˈkjuː·ʃ·nə] *n* boia *m inv*

executive [ɪg·ˈze·kjʊ·tɪv] **I.** *n* **1.** (*senior manager*) dirigente *mf* **2.** + *sing/pl vb* POL (potere *m*) esecutivo *m;* ECON organo *m* esecutivo **II.** *adj* esecutivo, -a; ~ **branch** organo esecutivo

executive assistant *n* assistente *mf* alla direzione

executive order *n* provvedimento *m* esecutivo

executive producer *n* produttore *m* esecutivo

executor [ɪg·ˈze·kjʊ·tə] *n* esecutore, -trice testamentario, -a *m*

exemplary [ɪg·ˈzemp·lə·ri] *adj* esemplare

exemplification [ɪg·ˌzemp·lə·fɪ·ˈkeɪ·ʃən] *n* esemplificazione *f*

exemplify [ɪg·ˈzemp·lɪ·faɪ] <-ie-> *vt* esemplificare; (*strategy*) mostrare

exempt [ɪg·ˈzempt] **I.** *vt* esentare **II.** *adj* esente; **to be** ~ **from** (**doing**) **sth** essere esentato da qc (dal fare qc)

exemption [ɪg·ˈzemp·ʃən] *n* esenzione *f*

exercise [ˈek·sə·saɪz] **I.** *vt* **1.** (*muscles*) esercitare; (*dog*) portare a passeggio; (*horse*) far fare esercizio a; **to** ~ **one's muscles/memory**

esercitare i muscoli/la memoria **2.** (*apply: authority, control*) esercitare; **to** ~ **caution** usare cautela; **to** ~ **common sense** usare un po' di buonsenso; **to** ~ **discretion** usare discrezione; **to** ~ **self-discipline** esercitare l'autodisciplina **II.** *vi* fare esercizio **III.** *n* **1.** (*physical training*) esercizio *m;* **physical** ~ esercizio fisico; **to do** ~**s** fare un po' di esercizio **2.** SCHOOL, UNIV esercizio *m;* **written** ~**s** esercizi scritti **3.** MIL esercitazione *f* **4.** (*action, achievement*) operazione *f* **5.** (*use*) esercizio *m* **6.** *pl* cerimonia *f;* **graduation** ~**s** cerimonia di laurea

exercise bike *n* cyclette *f inv*

exercise book *n* quaderno *m*

exerciser [ˈek·sə·saɪ·zə] *n* estensore *m*

exert [ɪg·ˈzɜːrt] *vt* esercitare; (*apply*) applicare; **to** ~ **oneself** sforzarsi

exertion [ɪg·ˈzɜːr·ʃən] *n* **1.** (*application*) esercizio *m* **2.** (*physical effort*) sforzo *m*

exfoliant [ɪks·ˈfəʊ·li·ənt] *n* esfoliante *m*

exfoliating cream [eks·ˌfoʊ·lɪ·ˈeɪ·tɪŋ·kriːm] *n* crema *f* esfoliante

exfoliation [eks·ˌfoʊ·li·ˈeɪ·ʃən] *n* esfoliazione *f*

exhalation [ˌeks·hə·ˈleɪ·ʃən] *n* esalazione *f*

exhale [eks·ˈheɪl] **I.** *vt* espirare; (*gases*) emettere; (*scents*) emanare **II.** *vi* espirare

exhaust [ɪg·ˈzɑːst] **I.** *vt a. fig* esaurire; **to** ~ **oneself** sfinirsi **II.** *n* **1.** AUTO (*gas*) gas *m pl* di scarico **2.** (*pipe*) tubo *m* di scappamento

exhausted *adj* esausto, -a

exhaust fumes *npl* gas *m pl* di scarico

exhausting *adj* estenuante

exhaustion [ɪg·ˈzɑːs·tʃən] *n* sfinimento *m;* **to suffer from** ~ essere esausto

exhaustive [ɪg·ˈzɑːs·tɪv] *adj* esauriente

exhaust pipe *n* tubo *m* di scappamento

exhaust system *n* sistema *m* di scarico

exhibit [ɪg·ˈzɪ·bɪt] **I.** *n* **1.** (*display*) oggetto *m* esposto **2.** LAW prova *f* **II.** *vt* **1.** (*show*) esporre; (*work*) presentare **2.** (*display character traits*) mostrare

exhibition [ˌek·sɪ·ˈbɪ·ʃən] *n* (*display*) esposizione *f;* (*performance*) esibizione *f* ▶**to make an** ~ **of oneself** rendersi ridicolo

exhibitionism [ˌek·sɪ·ˈbɪʃ·nɪ·zəm] *n* esibizionismo *m*

exhibitionist [ˌek·sɪ·ˈbɪʃ·nɪst] *n* esibizionista *mf*

exhibitor [ɪg·ˈzɪ·bɪ·tə] *n* espositore, -trice *m, f*

exhilarating [ɪg·ˈzɪ·lə·reɪ·tɪŋ] *adj* esaltante; **an** ~ **performance** una performance entusiasmante

exhilaration [ɪg·ˈzɪ·lə·reɪ·ʃən] *n* euforia *f;* **the** ~ **of liberty/speed** la sensazione inebriante della libertà/velocità; **the** ~ **of doing sth** l'euforia di fare qc

exhort [ɪg·ˈzɔːrt] *vt form* **to** ~ **sb to do sth** esortare qn a fare qc; **she** ~**ed him to keep working** lo esortò a proseguire il lavoro

exhortation [ˌek·zɔːr·ˈteɪ·ʃən] *n* esortazione *f*

exhumation [ˌeks·hjuː·ˈmeɪ·ʃən] *n* esumazione *f*

exhume [ekz·'u:m] *vt* esumare

ex-husband *n* ex marito *m*

exigence ['ek·sɪ·dʒəns] *n*, **exigency** ['ek·zɪ·dʒən·si] <-ies> *n* **1.** (*extreme urgency*) emergenza *f* **2.** *pl* (*urgent demands*) esigenze *fpl*

exigent ['ek·sɪ·dʒənt] *adj form* **1.** (*urgent*) urgente; **an ~ issue** una questione urgente; **an ~ environmental problem** un problema ambientale impellente **2.** (*demanding*) esigente

exiguous [eg·'zɪ·gjʊ·əs] *adj form* esiguo, -a

exile ['ek·saɪl] **I.** *n* **1.** (*banishment*) esilio *m*; **political ~** esilio politico; **to be in ~** essere in esilio; **to go into ~** andare in esilio **2.** (*person*) esiliato, -a *m, f* **II.** *vt* esiliare; **to ~ sb to Siberia** esiliare qn in Siberia

exist [ɪg·'zɪst] *vi* **1.** (*be*) esistere **2.** (*live*) vivere; **to ~ on sth** vivere di qc; **to ~ without sth** sopravvivere senza qc

existence [ɪg·'zɪs·təns] *n* **1.** (*being*) esistenza *f*; **to be in ~** esistere; **to come into ~** nascere **2.** (*life*) vita *f*

existent [ˌeg·'zɪs·tent] *adj* esistente; **the only ~ copy** l'unica copia esistente

existential [ˌeg·zɪ·'sten·ʃl] *adj* esistenziale

existentialism [ˌeg·zɪ·'sten·ʃə·lɪ·zəm] *n* esistenzialismo *m*

existing [ɪg·'zɪs·tɪŋ] *adj* esistente; **the ~ laws** l'attuale legislazione

exit ['ek·sɪt] **I.** *n* uscita *f*; **to make an ~** uscire **II.** *vt* uscire da **III.** *vi* **1.** *a.* INFOR (*leave*) uscire **2.** THEAT uscire di scena

exit visa *n* visto *m* d'uscita

exodus ['ek·sə·dəs] *n* esodo *m*

ex officio [ˌeks ə·'fɪ·ʃi·oʊ] **I.** *adv* ADMIN di diritto; **to act ~** agire d'ufficio **II.** *adj* ADMIN di diritto

exonerate [ɪg·'zɑː·nə·reɪt] *vt form* prosciogliere

exoneration [ɪg·ˌzɑː·nə·'reɪ·ʃən] *n form* proscioglimento *m*

exorbitance [ɪg·'zɔːr·bə·təns] *n* esorbitanza *f*

exorbitant [ɪg·'zɔːr·bə·tənt] *adj* esorbitante; (*demand*) eccessivo, -a

exorcism ['ek·sɔːr·sɪ·zəm] *n* esorcismo *m*

exorcist ['ek·sɔːr·sɪst] *n* esorcista *mf*

exorcize ['ek·sɔːr·saɪz] *vt* esorcizzare

exotic [ɪg·'zɑː·t̬ɪk] *adj* esotico, -a; **~ fruit** frutta esotica

expand [ɪk·'spænd] **I.** *vi* **1.** (*increase*) espandersi; (*trade*) svilupparsi **2.** (*spread*) estendersi **3.** PHYS dilatarsi **II.** *vt* **1.** (*make larger*) ampliare; (*wings*) spiegare; (*trade*) sviluppare **2.** PHYS dilatare **3.** (*elaborate*) sviluppare

expandable [ɪk·'spæn·də·bl] *adj* espansibile

expanse [ɪk·'spæns] *n* **1.** (*large area*) distesa *f* **2.** (*expansion*) espansione *f*

expansion [ɪk·'spæn·ʃən] *n* **1.** (*spreading out*) espansione *f*; (*of a metal*) dilatazione *f* **2.** (*elaboration*) sviluppo *m*

expansionism [ɪk·'spæn·ʃə·nɪ·zəm] *n* espansionismo *m*; **policy of ~** politica *f* espansionistica

expansive [ɪk·'spæn·sɪv] *adj* **1.** (*sociable*) espansivo, -a **2.** (*broad, vast*) ampio, -a **3.** (*elaborated*) elaborato, -a

ex-partner *n* ex partner *mf*

expat [ˌeks·'pæt] *n abbr of* **expatriate** residente *mf* all'estero

expatriate[1] [eks·'peɪ·tri·ət] *n* residente *mf* all'estero

expatriate[2] [eks·'peɪ·tri·eɪt] *vt* mandare in esilio

expect [ɪk·'spekt] *vt* aspettarsi; (*imagine*) immaginare; **to ~ to do sth** pensare di fare qc; **to ~ sb to do sth** aspettarsi che qn faccia qc; **you are ~ed to return books on time** devi restituire i libri per tempo; **to ~ sth of sb** aspettarsi qc da qn; **to be ~ing (a baby)** aspettare (un bambino); **I ~ed as much** me l'aspettavo; **I ~ed better of you than that** mi aspettavo di meglio da te; **I ~ you are hungry** immagino che tu sia affamato; **I ~ so** penso di sì; **to ~ that** penso che +*subj*

expectancy [ɪk·'spek·tən·tsi] *n* speranza *f*; **life ~** aspettativa *f* di vita

expectant [ɪks·'pek·tənt] *adj* pieno, -a d'attesa; (*look*) speranzoso, -a; **~ mother** futura mamma

expectation [ˌeks·pek·'teɪ·ʃən] *n* **1.** (*hope*) speranza *f* **2.** (*anticipation*) aspettativa *f*; **in ~ of sth** nella speranza di qc

expectorate [ɪks·'pek·tə·reɪt] *vi form* espettorare

expedience *n*, **expediency** [ɪks·'pi:·di·ən·tsi] *n* **1.** (*advisability*) convenienza *f*; **as a matter of ~, we will not be hiring any new staff members this year** per una questione di convenienza, quest'anno non assumeremo altri membri del personale **2.** (*self-interest*) opportunismo *m*; **to operate on the basis of ~** agire per convenienza

expedient [ɪks·'pi:·di·ənt] **I.** *adj* **1.** (*advantageous*) conveniente; **it is ~ to do sth** è opportuno fare qc *form* **2.** (*necessary*) necessario, -a; (*measure*) opportuno, -a; **to be ~ that** essere opportuno che +*subj* **II.** *n* espediente *m*; **they took the ~ of asking advice** hanno preso l'accorgimento di informarsi

expedite ['eks·pɪ·daɪt] *vt form* accelerare

expedition [ˌeks·pɪ·'dɪ·ʃən] *n* spedizione *f*; **to be on an ~** partecipare a una spedizione; **to go on an ~** partire per una spedizione; **to go on a shopping ~** *iron* andare a fare spese

expeditious [ˌeks·pɪ·'dɪ·ʃəs] *adj form* rapido, -a

expel [ɪks·'pel] <-ll-> *vt* espellere; **to ~ sb from school** espellere qn da scuola

expend [ɪks·'pend] *vt form* impiegare; (*money*) spendere; **to ~ time on sth** dedicare tempo a qc

expenditure [ɪks·'pen·dɪt·ʃər] *n* (*money*) spesa *f*; **public ~s** spesa pubblica; **cleaning ~s** spese di pulizia

expense [ɪks·'pens] *n* spesa *f*; **all ~(s) paid** tutto spesato; **at great ~** con forte spesa; **at**

sb's ~ *a. fig* a spese di qn; **at the ~ of sth** *a. fig* a spese di qc; **to go to ~** sostenere delle spese; **to go to the ~ of** sobbarcarsi le spese di; **to spare no ~** non badare a spese

expense account *n* conto *m* spese

expensive [ɪks·'pen·sɪv] *adj* caro, -a; **that was an ~ mistake for him to make** quell'errore gli è costato caro

experience [ɪks·'pɪ·ri·əns] I. *n* esperienza *f;* **to have translating ~** avere esperienza di traduzione; **from ~** per esperienza; **to know sth from ~** sapere qc per esperienza; **to learn by ~** imparare con l'esperienza II. *vt* provare; **to ~ happiness/pain** provare felicità/dolore; **please do not adjust your television set — we're experiencing technical difficulties** per favore non regolate il vostro apparecchio televisivo — stiamo incontrando difficoltà tecniche; **to ~ a loss** subire una perdita

experienced [ɪks·'pɪ·ri·ənst] *adj* esperto, -a; **to be ~ at organizing large events** essere esperto nell'organizzare grandi eventi

experiment [ɪks·'pe·rɪ·mənt] I. *n* esperimento *m;* **as an ~** come esperimento; **by ~** sperimentando II. *vi* sperimentare; **to ~ on a patient** sperimentare su un paziente; **to ~ with mice** sperimentare sui topi

experimental [eks·ˌpe·rɪ·'men·tl] *adj* sperimentale; **~ psychology** psicologia sperimentale; **to be still at the ~ stage** essere ancora in fase sperimentale

experimentation [ɪks·ˌpe·rɪ·men·'teɪ·ʃən] *n* sperimentazione *f*

expert ['eks·pɜːrt] I. *n* esperto, -a *m, f;* **to be a computer ~** essere un esperto di informatica II. *adj* 1. (*skilful*) esperto, -a; **she's an ~ swimmer** è un'esperta nuotatrice 2. LAW del perito; **~ report** relazione del perito

expert advice *n* **to seek ~** chiedere il parere di un esperto

expertise [ˌeks·pɜːr·'tiːz] *n* maestria *f;* (*knowledge*) competenza *f*

expert knowledge *n* competenza *f* specialistica

expert opinion *n* parere *m* di un esperto

expert witness *n* perito *m* chiamato come testimone

expiate ['eks·pi·eɪt] *vt form* espiare

expiation [ˌeks·pɪ·'eɪ·ʃən] *n form* espiazione *f*

expiration [ˌeks·pə·'reɪ·ʃən] *n* scadenza *f*

expiration date *n* (*of a contract*) scadenza *f;* (*of food or medicine*) data *f* di scadenza

expire [ɪks·'pa·ɪə] I. *vi* 1. (*terminate*) scadere 2. (*die*) spirare II. *vt* espirare

expiry [ɪks·'paɪ·ri] *n s.* **expiration**

explain [ɪks·'pleɪn] I. *vt* spiegare; **to ~ how/ what/where/why ...** spiegare come/cosa/dove/perché ...; **to ~ oneself** spiegarsi; **that ~s everything!** questo spiega tutto! II. *vi* spiegare

◆**explain away** *vt* giustificare

explanation [ˌeks·plə·'neɪ·ʃən] *n* spiegazione *f;* **to give an ~ for an incident** dare la spiegazione di un incidente; **to offer no ~ for the delay** non dare alcuna spiegazione per il ritardo; **by way of ~** come spiegazione

explanatory [ɪks·'plæ·nə·tɔː·ri] *adj* esplicativo, -a

expletive ['əks·plə·t̬ɪv] *n* imprecazione *f;* **to unleash a string of ~s** se n'è uscito con una sfilza di imprecazioni

explicable [eks·'plɪ·kə·bl] *adj* spiegabile

explicate ['eks·plɪ·keɪt] *vt form* spiegare

explicit [ɪks·'plɪ·sɪt] *adj* 1. (*exact*) esplicito, -a; **~ directions** istruzioni precise; **he was very ~ about the plans** è stato molto franco riguardo ai piani 2. (*vulgar*) esplicito, -a; **~ language** linguaggio esplicito

explode [ɪks·'ploʊd] I. *vi* 1. (*blow up*) esplodere; (*tire*) scoppiare; **to ~ with anger** scoppiare di rabbia 2. (*grow rapidly*) espandersi II. *vt* 1. (*blow up: bomb*) far esplodere; (*ball*) far scoppiare 2. (*discredit: theory*) demolire; (*myth*) distruggere

exploit ['eks·plɔɪt] I. *vt* sfruttare II. *n* impresa *f*

exploitation [ˌeks·plɔɪ·'teɪ·ʃən] *n* sfruttamento *m*

exploration [ˌeks·plɔː·'reɪ·ʃən] *n* 1. *a.* MED esplorazione *f;* **voyage of ~** viaggio d'esplorazione; **to make an ~ of sth** esplorare qc 2. (*examination*) esame *m*

exploratory [ɪks·'plɔː·rə·tɔː·ri] *adj* (*voyage, test*) esplorativo, -a; (*meeting*) preliminare; **~ foreign language class** corso preliminare di lingua straniera

explore [ɪks·'plɔːr] I. *vt* 1. *a.* MED, INFOR esplorare 2. (*examine*) esaminare; **to ~ sb's past** investigare sul passato di qn II. *vi* esplorare

explorer [ɪks·'plɔː·rə] *n* esploratore, -trice *m, f*

explosion [ɪks·'ploʊ·ʒən] *n* esplosione *f;* **gas ~** esplosione di gas; **population ~** esplosione demografica; **there has been an ~ in demand for computers in the last few years** la domanda di computer ha visto un aumento vertiginoso negli ultimi anni

explosive [ɪks·'ploʊ·sɪv] I. *adj* esplosivo, -a; **~ device** ordigno esplosivo; **an ~ situation** una situazione delicata; **an ~ issue** un tema spinoso; **to have an ~ temper** avere un carattere irascibile II. *n* esplosivo *m*

exponent [ɪks·'poʊ·nənt] *n* 1. (*person*) esponente *mf;* **a leading ~ of neoclassicism** un esponente di punta del neoclassicismo 2. MAT esponente *m*

export I. [ɪks·'pɔːrt] *vt* esportare II. ['eks·pɔːrt] *n* 1. (*product*) prodotto *m* d'esportazione 2. (*selling*) esportazione *f;* **~ taxes** tasse *f pl* d'esportazione

exportable [ɪks·'pɔːr·t̬ə·bl] *adj* esportabile

exportation [ˌeks·pɔːr·'teɪ·ʃən] *n* esportazione *f*

export business *n* 1. (*business which sells abroad*) impresa *f* d'esportazione 2. (*special branch*) esportazione *f;* **to be in the ~** occuparsi di esportazione

exporter [ɪks·'pɔːr·t̬ə·] *n* esportatore, -trice *m, f*

export goods *npl* prodotti*m pl* d'esportazione

export license *n* licenza *f* d'esportazione

export regulations *npl* disposizioni*f pl* sull'esportazione

export surplus *n* eccedenza *f* delle esportazioni

export trade *n* commercio *m* con l'estero

expose [ɪks·'poʊz] *vt* 1.(*uncover*) mettere a nudo 2.(*leave vulnerable to*) esporre; **to ~ sb to ridicule** mettere qn in ridicolo 3.(*reveal: person*) mostrare (per quello che è); (*plot*) smascherare; (*secret*) svelare; **to ~ a business as a fraud** smascherare una frode (*che si nasconde sotto un affare, o un'impresa, ecc.*)

exposé [ˌeks·poʊ·'zeɪ] *n* rivelazioni *fpl*

exposed [ɪks·'poʊzd] *adj* 1.(*vulnerable*) esposto, -a 2.(*uncovered*) scoperto, -a 3.(*unprotected*) non riparato, -a

exposition [ˌeks·pə·'zɪ·ʃən] *n* esposizione *f*

expostulate [ɪks·'pɑ:s·tʃə·leɪt] *vi form* fare rimostranze; **to ~ with the waiter about the bill** protestare con il cameriere per il conto

exposure [ɪks·'poʊ·ʒɚ] *n* 1.(*contact*) esposizione *f;* **~ to the sun** esposizione al sole; **~ to new ideas** contatto *m* con nuove idee 2. MED assideramento *m;* **to die of ~** morire assiderato 3. *a.* PHOT esposizione *f* 4.(*revelation*) rivelazione *f* 5.(*media coverage*) pubblicità *f*

exposure meter *n* PHOT esposimetro *m*

expound [ɪks·'paʊnd] **I.** *vi form* **to ~ (at length) on** [*o* **about**] **sth** fare un'esposizione dettagliata su qc **II.** *vt form* esporre

express [ɪks·'pres] **I.** *vt* 1.(*convey: thoughts, feelings*) esprimere; **to ~ oneself** esprimersi; **to ~ oneself through music** esprimersi attraverso la musica; **I would like to ~ my thanks for ...** vorrei esprimere il mio ringraziamento per ... 2. *inf* (*send quickly*) spedire per espresso; **to ~ sth to sb** spedire per espresso qc a qn 3. *form* (*squeeze out*) spremere **II.** *adj* 1.(*rapid*) rapido, -a; **by ~ delivery** per posta celere; **~ train** (treno) espresso; **~ mail** posta celere 2.(*precise*) esplicito, -a; **by ~ order** per ordine espresso; **these are her ~ wishes** questi sono i suoi espressi desideri **III.** *n* (*train*) espresso *m* **IV.** *adv* **to send sth ~** spedire qc per espresso

expression [ɪks·'pre·ʃən] *n* espressione *f;* (*of love, solidarity*) manifestazione *f;* **as an ~ of thanks** in segno di ringraziamento; **to give ~ to sth** dare voce a qc; **to find ~ in music** trovare espressione nella musica

expressionism [ɪks·'pre·ʃə·nɪ·zəm] *n* espressionismo *m*

expressionist [ɪks·'pre·ʃə·nɪst] *n* espressionista *mf*

expressionless [ɪks·'pre·ʃən·lɪs] *adj* inespressivo, -a

expressive [ɪks·'pre·sɪv] *adj* espressivo, -a; **to be ~ of sadness** *form* denotare tristezza

expressly [ɪks·'pres·li] *adv* 1.(*clearly*) chiaramente 2.(*especially*) espressamente

expressway [ɪks·'pres·weɪ] *n* autostrada *f*

ex-prisoner *n* ex prigioniero, -a *m, f*

expropriate [eks·'proʊ·pri·eɪt] *vt* espropriare

expropriation [eks·'proʊ·pri·eɪ·ʃən] *n* espropriazione *f*

expulsion [ɪks·'pʌl·ʃən] *n* espulsione *f*

exquisite ['eks·kwɪ·zɪt] *adj* 1.(*delicate*) squisito, -a; **an ~ piece of china** un raffinato oggetto in porcellana 2.(*intense*) intenso, -a

ex-serviceman [ˌeks·'sɜːr·vɪs·mən] <-men> *n* ex militare *m*

ext. TEL *abbr of* **extension** interno

extant ['eks·tənt] *adj form* (ancora) esistente; **to be still ~** esistere ancora

extemporaneous [eks·ˌtem·pə·'reɪ·ni·əs] *adj form* estemporaneo, -a

extempore [eks·'tem·pə·ri] *form* **I.** *adj* estemporaneo, -a **II.** *adv* estemporaneamente; **to perform ~** improvvisare; **to speak ~** improvvisare un discorso

extemporize [ɪks·'tem·pə·raɪz] *vi form* improvvisare

extend [ɪks·'tend] **I.** *vt* 1.(*enlarge: house*) ampliare; (*street*) allargare 2.(*prolong: deadline*) prorogare; (*holiday*) prolungare 3.(*offer*) offrire; **to ~ an invitation to sb** rivolgere un invito a qn; **to ~ one's hand as a greeting** tendere la mano per salutare; **to ~ one's thanks to sb** esprimere il proprio ringraziamento a qn; **to ~ a warm welcome to sb** dare un caloroso benvenuto a qn 4. FIN (*credit*) concedere **II.** *vi* estendersi; **to ~ beyond the river** estendersi oltre il fiume; **to ~ to a discussion** arrivare a una discussione

extended *adj* esteso, -a; **~ family** famiglia *f* allargata; **an ~ holiday** una vacanza prolungata

extension [ɪks·'ten·ʃən] *n* 1.(*increase*) estensione *f;* (*of rights*) ampliamento *m;* **by ~** per estensione 2.(*of a deadline*) proroga *f* 3.(*appendage*) annesso *m* 4. TEL interno *m*

extension cord *n* prolunga *f*

extension ladder *n* scala *f* allungabile

extensive [ɪks·'ten·sɪv] *adj* 1. *a. fig* esteso, -a; (*knowledge*) approfondito, -a; (*experience*) vasto, -a 2.(*large: repair*) considerevole; **~ damage** danni *m* ingenti *pl* 3. AGR (*farming*) estensivo, -a

extensively *adv* ampiamente

extent [ɪks·'tent] *n* 1.(*size*) estensione *f;* **to its fullest ~** in tutta la sua estensione 2.(*degree*) portata *f;* **to go to the ~ of hitting sb** arrivare fino al punto di picchiare qn; **to a great ~** in gran parte; **to the same ~ as ...** nella stessa misura in cui ...; **to some ~** in parte; **to such an ~ that ...** al punto che ...; **to that ~** fino a questo punto; **to what ~ ...?** fino a che punto ...?

extenuate [ɪks·'ten·ju·eɪt] *vt form* attenuare

extenuating *adj form* attenuante; **~ circumstances** circostanze attenuanti

extenuation [ɪks·ˌten·ju·'eɪ·ʃən] *n form* attenuazione *f;* **in ~ of sth** come attenuante di qc

exterior [ɪks·'tɪ·ri·ɚ] **I.** *adj* esterno, -a **II.** *n*

E

1. (*outside surface*) esterno *m* 2. (*outward appearance*) aspetto *m* 3. CINE esterni *mpl*

exterminate [ɪks·ˈtɜːr·mɪ·neɪt] *vt* sterminare

extermination [ɪks·ˌtɜːr·mɪ·ˈneɪ·ʃən] *n* sterminio *m*

external [ɪks·ˈtɜːr·nl] I. *adj* 1. (*exterior*) esterno, -a; **to be ~ to the problem** essere estraneo al problema 2. (*foreign*) estero, -a 3. MED esterno, -a II. *npl* apparenze *fpl*

externalize [ɪks·ˈtɜːr·nə·laɪz] *vt* esternare

external world *n* mondo *m* esterno

exterritorial [ˌeks·ˌte·rɪ·ˈtɔː·ri·əl] *adj* extraterritoriale

extinct [ɪks·ˈtɪŋkt] *adj* (*practice*) estinto, -a; (*volcano*) spento, -a; **to become ~** estinguersi

extinction [ɪks·ˈtɪŋk·ʃən] *n* estinzione *f*

extinguish [ɪks·ˈtɪŋ·gwɪʃ] *vt* (*candle, cigar*) spegnere; (*love, passion*) consumare; (*memory*) cancellare; (*debt, life*) estinguere

extinguisher [ɪks·ˈtɪŋ·gwɪ·ʃər] *n* estintore *m*

extol <-ll-> *vt*, **extoll** [ɪks·ˈtoʊl] *vt* decantare; **to ~** (**upon**) **the virtues of yoga** decantare le virtù dello yoga

extort [ɪks·ˈtɔːrt] *vt* estorcere; (*confession*) strappare

extortion [ɪks·ˈtɔːr·ʃən] *n* estorsione *f*; **that's sheer ~**! questo è un furto!

extortionate [ɪks·ˈtɔːr·ʃə·nət] *adj* eccessivo, -a; **~ demands** richieste smodate; **~ prices** prezzi esorbitanti

extra [ˈeks·trə] I. *adj* in più; **to work an ~ two hours** lavorare due ore in più; **~ clothes** abiti di riserva; **it costs an ~ $2** costa due dollari in più; **meals are ~** i pasti sono a parte II. *adv* (*more*) di più; (*extraordinarily*) particolarmente; **they pay her ~ to work nights** le danno di più per il lavoro notturno; **I'll try ~ hard this time** questa volta ci metterò il massimo dell'impegno; **$10 ~** dieci dollari in più; **to charge ~ for sth** far pagare un supplemento per qc III. *n* 1. ECON extra *m inv*; AUTO optional *m inv* 2. CINE comparsa *f*

extract [ɪks·ˈtrækt] I. *vt* 1. (*remove*) estrarre 2. (*obtain: information*) strappare 3. MAT (*square root*) estrarre II. *n* 1. (*concentrate*) estratto *m* 2. (*excerpt*) brano *m*

extraction [ɪks·ˈtræk·ʃən] *n* 1. (*removal*) estrazione *f* 2. (*descent*) origine *f*; **he's of Irish ~** è di origine irlandese

extracurricular [ˌeks·trə·kə·ˈrɪk·jə·lər] *adj* extracurricolare; **~ activities** attività extracurricolari; **are you involved in any ~ activities?** sei coinvolto in attività extracurricolari?; *fig* sei coinvolto in avventure extraconiugali?

extradite [ˈeks·trə·daɪt] *vt* estradare

extradition [eks·trə·ˈdɪ·ʃən] *n* estradizione *f*

extramarital [ˌeks·trə·ˈme·rə·tl] *adj* extraconiugale

extraneous [ɪks·ˈtreɪ·ni·əs] *adj* estraneo, -a; **to be ~ to sth** essere estraneo a qc

extranet [ˈeks·trə·net] *n* INFOR extranet *f*

extraordinary [ɪks·ˈtrɔːr·də·ne·ri] *adj* 1. *a.* POL straordinario, -a 2. (*astonishing*) incredibile

extrapolate [eks·ˈtræ·pə·leɪt] I. *vt form* estrapolare II. *vi form* **to ~ from sth** fare un'estrapolazione da qc

extrasensory [ˌeks·trə·ˈsen·sə·ri] *adj* extrasensoriale; **~ perception** percezione *f* extrasensoriale

extraterrestrial [ˈeks·trə·tə·ˈres·tri·əl] *adj* extraterrestre

extraterritorial [ˌeks·trə·ˌte·rɪ·ˈtɔː·ri·əl] *adj* extraterritoriale

extravagance [ɪks·ˈtræ·və·gəns] *n* 1. (*wastefulness*) sperpero *m* 2. (*luxury*) lusso *m* 3. (*elaborateness*) esagerazione *f*

extravagant [ɪks·ˈtræ·və·gənt] *adj* 1. (*wasteful*) eccessivamente dispendioso, -a 2. (*luxurious*) dispendioso, -a; **an ~ lifestyle** uno stile di vita dispendioso 3. (*exaggerated: praise*) sperticato, -a; **~ price** prezzo esorbitante 4. (*elaborate*) esagerato, -a

extravaganza [ɪks·ˌtræ·və·ˈgæn·zə] *n* (*spectacle*) **a film ~** un film spettacolare

extreme [ɪks·ˈtriːm] I. *adj* estremo, -a; **an ~ case** un caso estremo; **with ~ caution** con estrema cautela; **~ difficulties** enormi difficoltà; **~ pain** dolore lancinante; **in the ~ north** all'estremo nord; **~ sport** sport estremo; **to be ~ in sth** essere estremista in qc II. *n* estremo *m*; **a man of ~s** un estremista; **at the ~** *fig* nel peggiore dei casi; **in the ~** estremamente; **to go from one ~ to the other** andare da un estremo all'altro; **to go to ~s** arrivare agli estremi

> [i] Negli Stati Uniti vengono chiamati **extreme sports** o *alternative sports* gli sport non tradizionali quali il salto con l'elastico, il parapendio o la scalata libera. Altri sport, come ad esempio l'elisci, il canyoning, il wakeboard e lo street luge fanno ugualmente parte degli **extreme sports**. Si tratta di sport di velocità molto in voga perché considerati più percolosi e più eccentrici rispetto a sport come il calcio o il tennis.

extremely *adv* estremamente; **to be ~ sorry** essere immensamente dispiaciuto

extremism [ɪks·ˈtriː·mɪ·zəm] *n* estremismo *m*

extremist [ɪks·ˈtriː·mɪst] I. *adj* estremista; **~ tendencies** tendenze estremiste II. *n* estremista *mf*

extremity [ɪks·ˈtre·mə·ti] *n* 1. (*furthest point*) estremità *f* 2. (*greatest degree*) grado *m* estremo; **at the ~ of his endurance** al limite della resistenza 3. (*situation*) caso *m* estremo 4. *pl* ANAT estremità *fpl*

extricate [ˈeks·trɪ·keɪt] *vt form* districare; **to ~ oneself from sth** districarsi da qc

extrovert [ˈeks·trə·vɜːrt] *adj* estroverso, -a

extroverted *adj* estroverso, -a

extrude [eks·ˈtruːd] *vt* 1. TECH estrudere 2. (*force out*) spingere fuori

exuberance [ɪɡ·'zuː·bə·rəns] *n* **1.** (*abundance*) sovrabbondanza *f* **2.** (*liveliness*) esuberanza *f*

exuberant [ɪɡ·'zuː·bə·rənt] *adj* **1.** (*luxuriant*) abbondante **2.** (*energetic*) esuberante; **young and** ~ giovane ed esuberante

exude [ɪɡ·'zuːd] **I.** *vt* **1.** trasudare; **to** ~ **pus** arrivare a suppurazione **2.** *fig* emanare; **to** ~ **confidence** emanare un'aria di fiducia in sé **II.** *vi* trasudare

exult [ɪɡ·'zʌlt] *vi form* esultare; **to** ~ **at** [*o* **in**] **the prize** esultare per il premio

exultant [ɪɡ·'zʌl·tənt] *adj form* esultante; ~ **shout** grido *m* d'esultanza

exultation [ˌek·sʌl·'teɪ·ʃən] *n form* esultanza *f;* ~ **at sth** esultanza per qc

ex-wife *n* ex moglie *f*

eye [aɪ] **I.** *n* **1.** ANAT occhio *m;* **to blink one's** ~**s** battere le palpebre; **to keep an** ~ **on sth/ sb** *inf* tenere d'occhio qc/qn; **to roll one's** ~**s** roteare gli occhi; **to rub one's** ~**s** sfregarsi gli occhi; **to set** ~**s on sb/sth** mettere gli occhi su qn/qc; **visible to the naked** ~ visibile a occhio nudo; **her** ~**s flashed with anger** i suoi occhi sprizzavano lampi di collera; **his** ~**s (nearly) popped (out of his head)** (a momenti) gli uscivano gli occhi dalle orbite; **he couldn't take his** ~**s off the girl** *inf* non riusciva a staccare gli occhi di dosso alla ragazza **2.** BOT gemma *f* ▶ **to have** ~**s in the back of one's head** *inf* avere cento occhi; **an** ~ **for an** ~, **a tooth for a tooth** *prov* occhio per occhio, dente per dente *prov;* **to be all** ~**s** essere tutt'occhi; **to give sb a black** ~ fare un occhio nero a qn; **to turn a blind** ~ (**to sth**) far finta di non vedere (qc); **as far as the** ~ **can see** fin dove si riesce a vedere; **to have a good** ~ **for sth** avere occhio per qc; **there's more to this than meets the** ~ le cose non sono così semplici come appaiono; **to keep one's** ~**s open** tenere gli occhi aperti; **to do sth with one's** ~**s open** *inf* fare qc con piena consapevolezza; **to keep one's** ~**s peeled for sth** *inf* tenere gli occhi ben aperti per qc; **to go around with one's** ~**s closed** *inf* andare in giro con la testa tra le nuvole; **to be able to do sth with one's** ~**s closed** *inf* saper fare qc a occhi chiusi; **(right) before** [*o* **under**] **my very** ~**s** proprio davanti ai miei occhi; **to not believe one's** ~**s** non credere ai propri occhi; **to catch sb's** ~ catturare l'attenzione di qn; **to give sb the** ~ *inf* lanciare occhiate seducenti a qn; **to make** ~**s at sb** *inf* cercare di sedurre qn con gli sguardi; **to open sb's** ~**s** aprire gli occhi a qn; **to run one's** ~ **over sth** dare un'occhiata a qc; **to (not) see** ~ **to** ~ **with sb** (non) trovarsi d'accordo con qn; **in my** ~**s** a parer mio; **in the public** ~ sotto l'occhio del pubblico **II.** <-ing> *vt* guardare; (*observe*) osservare; **to** ~ **sb up and down** esaminare qn da capo a piedi

eyeball ['aɪ·bɔːl] **I.** *n* bulbo *m* oculare ▶ **to meet** ~ **to** ~ **with sb** *inf* affrontarsi faccia a faccia con qn **II.** *vt inf* guardare con aria di sfida

eyebrow *n* sopracciglio *m;* **bushy** ~**s** sopracciglia cespugliose; **to raise one's** ~**s at sth** alzare le ciglia di fronte a qc

eyebrow pencil *n* matita *f* per le sopracciglia

eye-catching ['aɪ·ˌkæt·ʃɪŋ] *adj* che attira lo sguardo

eye contact *n* contatto *m* visivo; **to establish** ~ guardare dritto negli occhi

eyedrops *npl* gocce *f pl* per gli occhi

eyeful *n* **to be an** ~ *inf* essere uno spettacolo da vedere; **get an** ~ **of this!** *inf* dagli un'occhiata!; **I got an** ~ **of dust** mi è andata della polvere in un occhio

eyeglass *n* **1.** monocolo *m* **2.** *pl* occhiali *mpl*

eyelash <-es> *n* ciglio *m;* **false** ~**es** ciglia *f pl* finte

eyelet *n* occhiello *m*

eyelid *n* palpebra *f*

eyeliner *n* eyeliner *m*

eye opener *n* *inf* rivelazione *f; ;* **it was quite an** ~ **for me** mi ha aperto gli occhi

eyepiece *n* oculare *m*

eye shadow *n* ombretto *m*

eyesight *n* vista *f;* **keen** ~ vista acuta; **his** ~ **is failing** la sua vista si sta indebolendo

eyesore *n* **to be an** ~ offendere la vista

eyestrain *n* affaticamento *m* della vista; **to cause** ~ affaticare la vista

eyewitness <-es> *n* testimone *mf* oculare

e-zine ['iː·ziːn] *n* e-zine *f inv* (*rivista via Internet*)

F

F, f [ef] *n* **1.** (*letter*) F, f *f;* ~ **as in Fox** F di Firenze **2.** MUS fa *m inv*

f *abbr of* **feminine** f.

f. *abbr of* **folio** libro *m* in folio

F *abbr of* **Fahrenheit** F

fable ['feɪ·bl] *n* **1.** (*story*) favola *f* **2.** (*lie*) fandonia *f*

fabled ['feɪ·bld] *adj* leggendario, -a

fabric ['fæ·brɪk] *n* **1.** (*cloth, textile*) stoffa *f;* **cotton/woolen** ~ tessuto *m* di cotone/di lana **2.** (*of building*) struttura *f;* **the** ~ **of society** il tessuto *m* sociale

fabricate ['fæ·brɪ·keɪt] *vt* **1.** (*manufacture*) fabbricare **2.** *fig* (*invent: excuse*) inventare; (*alibi, evidence*) fabbricare **3.** (*forge*) falsificare

fabulous ['fæb·jə·ləs] *adj* favoloso, -a; **to look absolutely** ~ essere stupendo, -a

façade [fə·'sɑːd] *n a. fig* facciata *f*

face [feɪs] **I.** *n* **1.** *a.* ANAT faccia *f,* viso *m;* **a happy/sad** ~ una faccia allegra/triste; **a smiling** ~ un viso sorridente; **to dare (to) show one's** ~ osare farsi vedere; **to have a puzzled expression on one's** ~ avere un aria per-

plessa; **to keep a smile on one's** ~ non perdere il sorriso; **to keep a straight** ~ rimanere serio; **to laugh in sb's** ~ ridere in faccia a qu; **to make a** ~ (**at sb**) fare le boccacce (a qu); **to tell sth to sb's** ~ dire qc in faccia a qu; **you should have seen her** ~ avresti dovuto vedere la sua faccia **2.** (*front: of building*) facciata *f*; (*of coin*) faccia *f*; (*of clock*) quadrante *m*; (*of mountain*) parete *f* **3.** (*respect, honor*) **to lose/save** ~ perdere/salvare la faccia ▶ **to put a** brave ~ **on sth** far buon viso a cattivo gioco; **to be** brought ~ **to** ~ **with sth** trovarsi faccia a faccia con qc; **to make a** long ~ mettere il muso; **his** ~ fell **when he opened the letter** ha cambiato espressione quando ha aperto la lettera; **to** fly **in the** ~ **of logic/reason** sfidare la logica/la ragione; **on the** ~ **of it** a giudicare dalle apparenze **II.** *vt* **1.** (*turn towards*) guardare verso; **to** ~ **the audience** essere rivolti verso il pubblico; **please** ~ **me when I'm talking to you** quando ti parlo guardami in faccia, per cortesia **2.** (*confront*) affrontare; **the two teams will** ~ **each other next week** le due squadre si affronteranno la prossima settimana; **to** ~ **the facts** guardare in faccia la realtà; **to** ~ **one's fears/problems** guardare in faccia le proprie paure/i propri problemi; **to be** ~**d with sth** trovarsi di fronte a qc; **I can't** ~ **doing that** non ho il coraggio di farlo; **we are** ~**d with financial problems** dobbiamo affrontare dei problemi finanziari; **she can't** ~ **seeing him so soon after their breakup** non se la sente di rivederlo così presto dopo la separazione **3.** ARCHIT rivestire **4.** FASHION bordare ▶ **to** ~ **the** music *inf* accettare le conseguenze **III.** *vi* **to** ~ **towards the street** dare sulla strada; **about** ~! dietro front!
◆**face up to** *vt* **to** ~ **sth** affrontare qc; **you must** ~ **the fact that** ... devi accettare il fatto che...

facecloth *n* manopola *f* per il viso
face cream *n* crema *f* per il viso
facelift *n* lifting *m inv*
face pack *n* maschera *f* per il viso
face powder *n* cipria *f*
facet ['fæ·sɪt] *n* (*on gemstone*) faccetta *f*; *fig* sfaccettatura *f*
facetious [fə·'siː·ʃəs] *adj* spiritoso, -a; **stop being so** ~ smettila di fare lo spiritoso
face to face [ˌfeɪs·tə·'feɪs] *adv* faccia a faccia; **to come** ~ **with sth/sb** trovarsi faccia a faccia con qc/qu; **to discuss sth** ~ **with sb** discutere qc con qu faccia a faccia
face value *n* **1.** ECON valore *m* nominale **2.** *fig* **to take sth at** ~ prender qc alla lettera; **to take sb at** ~ fidarsi di qu
facial ['feɪ·ʃl] **I.** *adj* (*plastic*) facciale; (*cream*) per il viso; (*hair*) del viso **II.** *n* pulizia *f* del viso
facile ['fæ·sɪl] *adj* **1.** (*remark, argument*) semplicistico, -a **2.** (*victory*) facile
facilitate [fə·'sɪ·lɪ·teɪt] *vt* facilitare
facilitator [fə·'sɪ·lɪ·teɪ·tɚ] *n* facilitatore, -trice *m, f*

facility [fə·'sɪ·lə·t̬i] *n* <-ies> **1.** (*services*) servizio *m*; **transport facilities** mezzi *m pl* di trasporto **2.** (*ability*) facilità *f*; (*feature*) funzione *f*; ~ **for doing sth** facilità a fare qu **3.** (*building for a special purpose*) complesso *m*; **research** ~ centro *m* di ricerca; **sports** ~ impianto *m* sportivo
facing ['feɪ·sɪŋ] *n* **1.** ARCHIT rivestimento *m* **2.** (*cloth strip*) fettuccia *f*
facsimile [fæk·'sɪ·mə·li] *n* **1.** (*exact copy*) facsimile *m inv* **2.** (*fax*) fax *m inv*
facsimile machine *n* fax *m inv*
fact [fækt] *n* fatto *m*; **the bare** ~**s** i fatti nudi e crudi; **to stick to the** ~**s** attenersi ai fatti ▶ ~**s and** figures *inf* fatti e numeri *mpl*; **a** ~ **of** life un dato di fatto; **to know the** ~**s of life** sapere come si fanno i bambini; **as a** matter **of** ~ ... a dir il vero...; **the** ~ **of the** matter **is that** ... la verità è che...; in ~ anzi
fact-finding ['fækt·faɪn·dɪŋ] *adj* investigativo, -a; ~ **committee** commissione *f* di inchiesta
faction ['fæk·ʃən] *n* POL fazione *f*
factor ['fæk·t̬ɚ] *n* fattore *m*; **to be a contributing** ~ **in sth** contribuire a qc; **to be a crucial** ~ **in sth** essere un fattore cruciale per qc; **rhesus** ~ fattore *m* Rh
factory ['fæk·t̬ə·ri] <-ies> *n* fabbrica *f*; **car** ~ fabbrica automobilistica
factory farm *n* allevamento *m* industriale
factory worker *n* operaio, -a *m, f* di fabbrica
factotum [fæk·'toʊ·t̬əm] *n form* factotum *m inv*
factual ['fæk·tʃu·əl] *adj* basato, -a sui fatti; **a** ~ **error** un errore di fatto
faculty ['fæ·kl·t̬i] <-ies> *n* **1.** (*teachers*) corpo *m* docente **2.** UNIV facoltà *f* **3.** (*ability*) facoltà *f*; **to have a** ~ **for doing sth** avere la capacità di fare qc
fad [fæd] *n inf* **1.** (*fashion*) moda *f*; **a passing** ~ una moda passeggera **2.** (*obsession*) mania *f*
faddish ['fæ·dɪʃ] *adj inf s.* **faddy**
faddy ['fæ·di] *adj inf* schizzinoso, -a
fade [feɪd] **I.** *vi* **1.** (*lose color*) sbiadire **2.** (*lose intensity: light, sound*) affievolirsi; (*smile, life*) spegnersi; (*interest*) scemare; (*hope, optimism, memory*) svanire; (*plant, beauty*) appassire **3.** (*disappear*) scomparire; **to** ~ **sight/view** sparire alla vista; **to** ~ **from the scene** sparire di scena **4.** CINE, TV chiudere o aprire in dissolvenza **II.** *vt* scolorire
◆**fade away** *vi* (*hope, memory, love, grief*) svanire; (*sound*) affievolirsi; (*beauty*) appassire; (*person*) consumarsi
◆**fade in I.** *vi* (*picture*) apparire gradualmente; (*sound*) aumentare gradualmente **II.** *vt* (*picture*) far apparire gradualmente; (*sound*) far aumentare gradualmente
◆**fade out** *vi* (*picture*) sparire gradualmente; (*sound*) sfumare
fag [fæg] *n pej* (*homosexual*) checca *f*
faggot ['fæ·gət] *n pej* (*homosexual*) checca *f*
fagot ['fæ·gət] *n* (*bundle of sticks*) fascio *m* di legna

Fahrenheit ['fæ·rən·haɪt] *n* Fahrenheit *m*
fail [feɪl] I. *vi* 1. (*not succeed*) fallire; **if all else
~s** come ultima spiaggia; **to ~ to do sth** non
riuscire a fare qc; **to never ~ to do sth** non
scordarsi mai di fare qc; **to ~ to appreciate
sth** non saper apprezzare qc; **to ~ in one's
duty** venir meno al proprio dovere; **I ~ to see
why that matters** non vedo che importanza
abbia 2. SCHOOL, UNIV essere bocciato 3. TECH,
AUTO (*brakes, steering, engine*) guastarsi
4. (*eyesight, hearing*) abbassarsi; **his heart
failed** ha avuto un attacco di cuore 5. FIN, COM
(*go bankrupt*) fallire 6. AGR, BOT andare perso
II. *vt* 1. (*not pass: exam*) non superare; (*pupil*)
bocciare 2. (*not help*) **her courage ~ed her**
le è mancato il coraggio; **his nerve ~ed him**
gli mancò il coraggio III. *n* SCHOOL, UNIV insufficienza *f* ► **without ~** (*definitely*) senza eccezioni; (*always*) immancabilmente
failing ['feɪ·lɪŋ] I. *adj* (*health*) debole II. *n* (*of
mechanism*) difetto *m;* (*of person*) debo-
lezza *f* III. *prep* in mancanza di
fail-safe ['feɪl·seɪf] *adj* di sicurezza
fail-safe device *n* meccanismo *m* di sicurezza
failure ['feɪl·jə˞] *n* 1. (*lack of success*) fallimento *m;* **crop ~** AGR perdita *f* del raccolto; **to
be doomed to ~** essere destinato al fallimento; **his ~ to answer** il fatto che non abbia
risposto 2. TECH, ELEC (*breakdown*) guasto *m*
3. COM fallimento *m*
faint [feɪnt] I. *adj* 1. (*scent, odor, taste*) leggero, -a; (*sound, light, smile*) debole; (*line,
outline, scratch*) appena abbozzato, -a; (*memory*) vago, -a 2. (*slight: resemblance, sign, suspicion, chance, hope*) vago, -a; **not to make
the ~est attempt to do sth** non mostrare la
minima intenzione di voler fare qc; **not to
have the ~est idea** *inf* non avere la più pallida idea 3. (*weak*) **to be ~ with hunger** non
reggersi in piedi dalla fame; **to feel ~** sentirsi
mancare II. *vi* svenire III. *n* svenimento *m;* **to
fall down in a faint** cadere svenuto
faint-hearted [,feɪnt·'hɑːr·t̬ɪd] *adj* (*person*)
pauroso, -a
faintly *adv* (*barely perceptibly: smile, shine*)
debolmente; (*remember*) vagamente
fair¹ [fer] I. *adj* 1. (*just: society, trial, wage,
price*) giusto, -a; **a ~ share** una buona dose;
~ enough mi sembra giusto; **it's only ~ that
she should be told** è giusto dirglielo 2. *inf*
(*quite large: amount*) discreto, -a; **it's a ~ size**
è della grandezza giusta 3. (*reasonably good:
chance, prospect*) buono, -a 4. (*not bad*) discreto, -a 5. (*light in color: skin*) chiaro, -a;
(*hair*) biondo, -a 6. METEO **~ weather** tempo *m*
bello ► **by ~ means or foul** o con le buone o
con le cattive; **~'s ~** *inf* quel che è giusto è
giusto II. *adv* **to play ~** giocare pulito ► **~ and
square** (*following the rules*) lealmente;
(*directly*) in pieno
fair² [fer] *n* fiera *f;* **trade ~** fiera commerciale
fair game *n fig* bersaglio *m* legittimo
fairground ['fer·graʊnd] *n* luna park *m inv*

fair-haired [,fer·'herd] *adj* biondo, -a
fairly ['fer·li] *adv* 1. (*quite*) abbastanza
2. (*justly*) in modo imparziale 3. *liter* (*almost*)
praticamente
fair-minded [,fer·'maɪn·dɪd] *adj* imparziale
fairness *n* 1. (*justice*) imparzialità *f;* **in** (**all**)
~ ... in tutta onestà... 2. (*of skin*) bianchezza *f;*
(*of hair*) biondo *m*
fair play *n* fair play *m inv*
fairway ['fer·weɪ] *n* 1. (*in golf*) fairway *m inv,*
zona di prato con erba corta fra il tee e il green
2. NAUT canale *m* navigabile
fairy ['fe·ri] <-ies> *n* 1. (*creature*) fata *f* 2. *pej,
inf* (*homosexual*) checca *f*
fairy tale *n a.fig* fiaba *f;* **a ~ ending** un finale da
favola
faith [feɪθ] *n* fede *f;* **to have/lose ~ in sb/sth**
avere/perdere la fede in qu/qc; **to put one's ~
in sb/sth** confidare in qu/qc; **to renounce
one's ~** rinnegare la propria fede; **to keep
the ~** conservare la fiducia
faithful ['feɪθ·fəl] I. *adj* fedele II. *n* **the ~** i
fedeli
faithfully *adv* 1. (*loyally: serve*) fedelmente; **to
promise ~ to do sth** promettere solenne-
mente di fare qc 2. (*exactly: copy, translate*)
fedelmente
faith healer *n* guaritore, -trice *m, f*
faithless ['feɪθ·ləs] *adj* REL infedele; (*disloyal*)
sleale
fake [feɪk] I. *n* 1. (*painting, jewel*) falso *m*
2. (*person*) impostore, -a *m, f* II. *adj* **~ fur** pelliccia finta; **~ jewel** gioiello falso; **a ~ tan**
un'abbonzatura artificiale III. *vt* 1. (*counterfeit*) falsificare 2. (*pretend to feel*) fingere
IV. *vi* fingere
falcon ['fæl·kən] *n* falcone *m*
Falkland Islands ['fɔːk·ləd·,aɪ·ləndz] *npl*
the ~ le (isole) Falkland *fpl*
fall [fɔːl] <fell, fallen> I. *vi* 1. (*drop down: rain,
snow*) scendere; (*tree*) cadere; THEAT (*curtain*)
calare; **to ~ flat** (*joke*) non far ridere; (*plan*)
fallire; (*suggestion*) cadere nel vuoto; **to ~
down the stairs** cadere dalle scale; **to ~
(down) dead** cadere morto; **to ~ flat on
one's face** cadere faccia a terra 2. **to ~ to
one's knees** cadere in ginocchio 3. (*land:
bomb, missile*) cadere 4. (*decrease: prices,de-
mand*) scendere; **to ~ sharply** calare bruscamente 5. (*temperature*) scendere 6. (*accent,
stress*) cadere 7. (*in rank, on charts*) scendere
8. (*be defeated*) cadere; **to ~ under sb's
power** cadere sotto il dominio di qu; **the
prize fell to him** il premio toccò a lui
9. *liter* (*die in battle*) cadere 10. REL peccare
11. (*occur*) **to ~ on a Monday** cadere di lunedì 12. (*darkness, silence*) calare; **night was
~ing** stava calando la notte 13. (*belong*) **to ~
into a category** rientrare in una categoria
14. (*hang down: hair, cloth*) ricadere 15. (*go
down: cliff, ground, road*) scendere 16. + *adj*
(*become*) **to ~ asleep** addormentarsi; **to ~
due** scadere; **to ~ afoul of the law** avere

problemi con la legge; **to ~ ill** ammalarsi **17.** (*enter a particular state*) **to ~ madly in love** (**with sb/sth**) innamorarsi perdutamente (di qu/qc); **to ~ out of favor** cadere in disgrazia; **to ~ under the influence of sb/sth** cadere sotto l'influenza di qu/qc; **to ~ to pieces** *fig* (*person*) crollare; (*plan, relationship*) andare in pezzi **II.** *n* **1.** (*drop from a height*) caduta *f* **2.** (*decrease*) calo *m;* **~ in temperature** calo della temperatura **3.** (*defeat*) caduta *f* **4.** (*autumn*) autunno *m* **5.** *pl* (*waterfall*) cascata *f;* **Niagara Falls** le cascate *pl* del Niagara **6.** REL **the Fall** il peccato *m* originale **III.** *adj* autunnale

◆**fall apart** *vi* (*thing*) cadere a pezzi; (*emotionally: person*) crollare

◆**fall away** *vi* **1.** (*become detached: plaster, rock*) staccarsi **2.** (*slope downward*) digradare **3.** (*decrease: attendance, support*) diminuire; **to ~ sharply** diminuire drammaticamente **4.** (*disappear: feeling*) svanire

◆**fall back** *vi* **1.** (*move backwards: crowd*) restare indietro **2.** (*retreat: army*) ripiegare **3.** SPORTS (*runner*) perdere posizioni **4.** (*decrease: production, prices*) diminuire

◆**fall back on** *vt*, **fall back upon** *vt* ripiegare su

◆**fall behind** *vi* **1.** (*become slower*) rimanere indietro **2.** (*achieve less: team, country*) rimanere indietro **3.** (*fail to do sth on time*) essere in ritardo **4.** SPORTS farsi distanziare

◆**fall down** *vi* **1.** (*person*) cadere; (*building*) crollare; **our school is falling down** la nostra scuola sta cadendo a pezzi **2.** (*be unsatisfactory: plan*) fare acqua; (*person*) non essere all'altezza; **to ~ on the job** *inf* non essere all'altezza

◆**fall for** *vt* **to ~ sb** prendersi una cotta per qu; **to ~ a trick** cadere in uno scherzo

◆**fall in** *vi* **1.** (*into water, hole*) cadere **2.** (*collapse: roof, ceiling*) venire giù **3.** MIL mettersi in riga

◆**fall in with** *vt insep* **1.** (*agree to*) adeguarsi a **2.** (*become friendly with*) **to ~ sb** mettersi a frequentare

◆**fall off** *vi* **1.** (*become detached*) staccarsi **2.** (*decrease*) diminuire

◆**fall on** *vt insep* **1.** (*day or date*) cadere il **2.** (*attack*) gettarsi su; **to ~ sb** (*cuts*) ricadere su qu ▶ **to ~ hard times** cadere in miseria

◆**fall out** *vi* **1.** (*drop out*) cadere **2.** *inf* (*argue*) litigare **3.** MIL rompere le righe

◆**fall over I.** *vi insep* cadere **II.** *vt* inciampare in; **to ~ oneself to do sth** *inf* farsi in quattro per fare qc

◆**fall through** *vi* andare a monte

◆**fall to** *vt insep* (*be responsibility of*) toccare a

◆**fall upon** *vt s.* **fall on**

fallacious [fə·'leɪ·ʃəs] *adj form* fallace

fallacy ['fæ·lə·si] <-ies> *n* convinzione *f* errata

fallen ['fɔː·lən] *adj* caduto, -a; **~ arches** MED piedi *m pl* piatti; **a ~ dictator** un dittatore

deposto; **a ~ woman** una donna perduta

fall guy *n inf* capro *m* espiatorio

fallible ['fæ·lə·bl] *adj* fallibile; **we are all ~** tutti possono sbagliare

falling star *n* stella *f* cadente

falloff ['fɔːl·ɑːf] *n* COM calo *m*

Fallopian tube [fə·'loʊ·pi·ən·'tuːb] *n* tromba *f* di Fallopio

fallout ['fɔːl·aʊt] *n* **1.** PHYS fallout *m inv, pioggia di polvere radioattiva* **2.** *fig* ripercussioni *mpl*

fallout shelter *n* rifugio *m* antiatomico

fallow ['fæ·loʊ] **I.** *adj* **1.** (*ground, field*) a maggese **2.** (*period, time*) improduttivo, -a **II.** *adv* **to let a field lie ~** tenere il campo a maggese

fallow deer *n inv* daino *m*

false [fɔːls] **I.** *adj* **1.** (*untrue: idea, information*) falso, -a; **a ~ dawn** un falso allarme *m;* **~ economy** finto risparmio *m;* **~ move** mossa *f* falsa; **to take a ~ step** fare un passo falso; **a ~ pregnancy** MED, PSYCH gravidanza *f* isterica; **to give a ~ impression** fare un'impressione sbagliata; **to raise ~ hopes** suscitare false speranze **2.** (*artificial: beard, eyelashes*) finto, -a; **a ~ bottom** un doppio fondo *m* **3.** (*name, address, identity*) falso, -a; **to give ~ evidence in court** LAW testimoniare il falso in tribunale; **~ accounting** LAW, FIN falso *m* in bilancio; **under ~ colors** *liter* sotto mentite spoglie; **under ~ pretenses** con l'inganno **4.** (*insincere: smile, laugh, manner*) falso, -a; **to put on a ~ front** fingere; **~ modesty** falsa modestia *f* **5.** *liter* (*disloyal*) **a ~ friend** un falso amico **II.** *adv* **to play sb ~** ingannare qu

false alarm *n* falso allarme *m*

false friend *n* LING falso amico *m*

falsehood ['fɔːls·hʊd] *n* **1.** (*untruth*) falsità *f* **2.** (*lie*) menzogna *f*

false imprisonment *n* detenzione *f* illegale

falseness *n* **1.** (*inaccuracy*) inesattezza *f* **2.** (*insincerity*) falsità *f*

false start *n* SPORTS falsa partenza *f*

false teeth *npl* denti *m pl* finti

falsetto [fɔːl·'se·toʊ] **I.** *n* falsetto *m;* **~ voice** voce *f* di falsetto **II.** *adv* **to sing ~** cantare in falsetto

falsification [ˌfɔːl·sɪ·fɪ·'keɪ·ʃən] *n* falsificazione *f;* **~ of evidence** falsificazione *f* delle prove

falsify ['fɔːl·sɪ·faɪ] *vt* falsificare

falsity ['fɔːl·sə·ti] *n* **1.** (*inaccuracy*) inesattezza *f* **2.** (*insincerity*) falsità *f*

falter ['fɔːl·tə] *vi* **1.** (*move uncertainly*) barcollare **2.** (*lose strength: conversation*) languire; (*courage, negotiations*) vacillare

faltering ['fɔːl·tə·rɪŋ] *adj* (*voice, speech*) esitante; (*steps*) incerto, -a

fame [feɪm] *n* fama *f;* **to rise to ~** diventare famoso

famed *adj* famoso, -a

familiar [fə·'mɪl·jə] *adj* **1.** (*well-known*) familiare **2.** (*acquainted*) **to be ~ with sth** conoscere qc **3.** (*friendly*) familiare; **~ form of**

address LING modo informale di rivolgersi a qu *f;* **to be on ~ terms** (**with sb**) essere in (rapporti di) confidenza (con qu)

familiarity [fə·ˌmɪ·li·ˈe·rə·ţi] *n* **1.** (*intimacy*) familiarità *f;* (*inappropriate friendliness*) troppa confidenza *f* **2.** (*knowledge*) familiarità *f*

familiarize [fə·ˈmɪl·jə·raɪz] *vt* (far)familiarizzare; **to ~ oneself with sth** familiarizzarsi con qc

family [ˈfæ·mə·li] <-ies> **I.** *n* famiglia *f;* **to be ~** essere una famiglia; **to be** (**like**) **one of the ~** essere come uno di famiglia; **to run in the ~** essere un vizio di famiglia; **to start a ~** metter su famiglia **II.** *adj* (*jewels, dinner*) di famiglia; (*life*) familiare; (*entertainment*) per tutta la famiglia

family allowance *n* Can assegni *m pl* familiari

family doctor *n* medico *m* di famiglia

family man *n* (*enjoying family life*) uomo *m* tutto casa e famiglia; (*with wife and family*) padre *m* di famiglia

family name *n* cognome *m*

family planning *n* pianificazione *f* familiare

family tree *n* albero *m* genealogico

famine [ˈfæ·mɪn] *n* carestia *f*

famished [ˈfæ·mɪʃt] *adj inf* **to be ~** essere morto, -a di fame

famous [ˈfeɪ·məs] *adj* famoso, -a; **to become ~ for sth** diventare famoso per qc

famously *adv* **to get on ~** andare perfettamente d'accordo

fan[1] [fæn] **I.** *n* **1.** (*hand-held*) ventaglio *m* **2.** (*electrical*) ventilatore *m* **II.** <-nn-> *vt* **1.** (*cool with fan*) sventolare; **to ~ oneself** sventolarsi **2.** *fig* (*heighten: passion, interest*) alimentare; **to ~ the flames** *fig* soffiare sul fuoco

fan[2] [fæn] *n* (*admirer: of person*) ammiratore, -trice *m, f;* (*of team*) tifoso, -a *m, f;* (*of classical music*) appassionato, -a *m, f;* (*of pop star*) fan *mf inv*

fanatic [fə·ˈnæ·ţɪk] *n* **1.** fanatico, -a *m, f* **2.** *pej* fondamentalista *mf*

fanatical *adj* fanatico, -a; **to be ~ about sth** essere un fanatico di qc

fanaticism [fə·ˈnæ·ţɪ·sɪ·zəm] *n* fanatismo *m*

fan belt *n* AUTO cinghia *f* del ventilatore

fancier [ˈfæn·tsɪ·ɚ] *n* **pigeon ~** allevatore , -trice di piccioni *m*

fanciful [ˈfæn·tsɪ·fəl] *adj* **1.** (*idea, notion*) stravagante **2.** (*design, style*) fantasioso, -a

fan club *n* fan club *m inv*

fancy [ˈfæn·tsi] **I.** *adj* <-ier, -iest> **1.** (*elaborate: decoration, frills*) fantasioso, -a; **the speech was all ~ phrases** il discorso era infarcito di frasi elaborate **2.** *inf* (*expensive*) costoso, -a; **~ hotel** hotel *m* di lusso; **~ prices** prezzi *m pl* esorbitanti **3.** (*whimsical: ideas, notions*) stravagante **II.** *n* <-ies> **1.** (*liking*) **to take a ~ to sth/sb** invaghirsi di qc/qu; **to take sb's ~** attirare qu; **it tickled his ~** ha stuzzicato la sua fantasia **2.** (*imagination*) fan-

tasia *f* **3.** (*whimsical idea*) capriccio *m;* **whenever the ~ takes you** tutte le volte ti gira III. <-ie-> *vt* **1.** (*want, like*) **to ~ doing sth** aver voglia di fare qu; **he fancies you** gli piaci; **to ~ oneself** credersi chissà cosa **2.** (*imagine*) **to ~ oneself as sth** immaginare di essere qc; **to ~** (**that**) ... immaginare (che)...; **~** (**that**)! ma pensa un po'!; **~ shouting at him!** come ti è venuto in mente di sgridarlo!; **~ meeting here!** che combinazione incontrarsi proprio qui!

fancy-free [ˌfæ·tsi·ˈfriː] *adj* libero, -a, *da legami sentimentali*

fancy goods *npl* articoli *m pl* da regalo

fanfare [ˈfæn·fer] *n* fanfara *f*

fang [fæŋ] *n* (*of dog, lion*) zanna *f;* (*of snake*) dente *m*

fan mail *n* lettere *f pl* degli ammiratori

fanny [ˈfæ·ni] *n inf* sedere *m*

fantasize [ˈfæn·tə·saɪz] *vi* **to ~ about sth** fantasticare su qc

fantastic [fæn·ˈtæs·tɪk] *adj* **1.** (*excellent*) fantastico, -a **2.** (*unbelievable: coincidence*) incredibile; (*notion, plan*) fantasioso, -a

fantasy [ˈfæn·tə·si] <-ies> *n* fantasia *f*

fanzine [ˈfæn·ziːn] *n* fanzina *f*

FAQ *n* COMPUT *abbr of* **frequently asked questions** FAQ *f inv*

far [fɑːr] <farther, farthest *o* further, furthest> **I.** *adv* **1.** (*a long distance*) lontano; **how ~ is it from Boston to Maine?** quanto dista Boston dal Maine?; **~ away** (molto) lontano; **~ from doing sth** lungi dal fare qc; **~ from it** al contrario **2.** (*distant in time*) **as ~ back as I remember ...** per quanto riesco a ricordare ...; **to be not ~ off sth** non essere molto lontano da qc; **so ~** finora **3.** (*in progress*) **to not get very ~ with sth** non andare molto lontano con qc; **he will go ~** farà molta strada; **to go too ~** esagerare **4.** (*much*) **~ better** molto meglio; **~ nicer** assai più carino; **to be the best by ~** essere di gran lunga il [*o* la] migliore; **to be ~ too expensive** essere troppo caro **5.** (*connecting adverbial phrase*) **as ~ as I know ...** per quanto ne so...; **as ~ as you can** più che puoi; **as ~ as possible** per quanto possibile; **as ~ as I'm concerned ...** per quel che mi riguarda...; **the essay is OK as ~ as it goes** il tema a grandi linee va bene ▶ **so ~ so good** per ora tutto bene; **~ and wide** in lungo e in largo **II.** *adj* **1.** (*distant*) lontano, -a; **in the ~ distance** in lontananza; **a ~ country** *liter* un paese lontano **2.** (*further away*) **the ~ bank of the river** l'altra riva del fiume; **the ~ left/ right** (**of a political party**) l'estrema sinistra/ destra (di un partito)

faraway [ˈfɑːr·ə·weɪ] *adj* **a ~ land** una terra lontana; **to have a ~ expression** avere un'espressione assente

farce [fɑːrs] *n* **1.** THEAT farsa *f* **2.** *fig* farsa *f*

farcical [ˈfɑːr·sɪ·kl] *adj* farsesco, -a

fare [fer] **I.** *n* **1.** (*for journey*) tariffa *f*, per viaggio; **one way/round trip ~** costo del biglietto di sola andata/andata e ritorno **2.** (*taxi passenger*) passeggero, -a *m, f, di taxi* **3.** CULIN cibo *m;* **simple home-style** ~ cucina *f* casalinga **II.** *vi* **to** ~ **badly/well** andare male/bene; **how did you** ~ **at the interview?** come te la sei cavata al colloquio?

Far East *n* **the** ~ l'Estremo Oriente *m*

farewell [ˌferˈwel] **I.** *interj form* addio; **to bid** ~ **to sb/sth** accomiatarsi da qu/qc **II.** *n* addio *m* **III.** *adj* d'addio

far-fetched [ˌfɑːrˈfetʃt] *adj* esagerato, -a

far-flung [ˌfɑːrˈflʌŋ] *adj liter* **1.** (*spread over wide area*) molto esteso, -a **2.** (*remote*) remoto, -a

farm [fɑːrm] **I.** *n* (*small*) fattoria *f* **II.** *vt* (*land*) coltivare; (*sheep*) allevare **III.** *vi* fare l'agricoltore

◆**farm out** *vt* **to** ~ **work** dare un lavoro in appalto

farmer [ˈfɑːrˌmɚ] *n* (*land*) agricoltore, -trice *m, f;* (*animal*) allevatore, -trice *m, f*

farm hand *n* bracciante *mf* agricolo, -a

farmhouse *n* <-s> casa *f* colonica

farmland *n* terreno *m* agricolo

farmstead *n* casa *f* colonica

farmyard *n* aia *f*

far-off [ˌfɑːrˈɑːf] *adj* (*place, country, time*) lontano, -a

far-reaching [ˌfɑːrˈriːˌtʃɪŋ] *adj* di grande portata

farseeing [ˌfɑːrˈsiːˌɪŋ] *adj* (*decision, policy*) di largo respiro; (*person*) lungimirante

farsighted [ˌfɑːrˈsaɪˌtɪd] *adj* (*decision, policy*) di largo respiro; (*person*) lungimirante

fart [fɑːrt] *inf* **I.** *n* scorreggia *f;* **to do/lay a** ~ fare una scorreggia **II.** *vi* scorreggiare

farther [ˈfɑːrˌðɚ] **I.** *adv comp of* **far 1.** (*distance*) più lontano; ~ **away from ...** più lontano da...; ~ **down/up** più in basso/in alto **2.** (*time*) ~ **back in time** più indietro nel tempo **II.** *adj comp of* **far** più lontano, -a

farthest [ˈfɑːrˌðɪst] **I.** *adv superl of* **far** più lontano **II.** *adj superl of* **far** (*distance, time*) più lontano, -a

fascia [ˈfeɪˌʃə] <fasciae> *n* **1.** ANAT guaina *f* **2.** (*board above shop window*) insegna *f* **3.** ARCHIT fascia *f*

fascinate [ˈfæˌsəˌneɪt] *vt* affascinare

fascinating [ˈfæˌsɪˌneɪˌtɪŋ] *adj* affascinante

fascination [ˌfæˌsəˌneɪˌʃən] *n* fascino *m;* **to listen in** ~ ascoltare affascinato

fascism *n*, **Fascism** [ˈfæˌʃɪˌzəm] *n* fascismo *m*

fascist, Fascist [ˈfæˌʃɪst] **I.** *n* fascista *mf* **II.** *adj* fascista

fashion [ˈfæˌʃən] **I.** *n* **1.** (*popular style*) moda *f;* **to be in** ~ essere di moda; **to be out of** ~ essere fuori moda; **to come into** ~ diventare di moda; **to be all the** ~ essere molto di moda; **the latest** ~ l'ultima moda **2.** (*manner*) modo *m;* **in the usual** ~ al solito modo; **after a** ~ in un certo senso **II.** *vt* fare

fashionable [ˈfæˌʃəˌnəˌbl] *adj* (*nightclub, restaurant, style, person*) alla moda; (*clothes*) di moda

fashion designer *n* stilista *mf*

fashion show *n* sfilata *f* di moda

fast[1] [fæst] **I.** <-er, -est> *adj* **1.** (*quick*) veloce; **the** ~ **lane** la corsia *f* di sorpasso; ~ **train** (treno) rapido *m;* **to be a** ~ **worker** essere uno che va subito al sodo **2.** (*clock*) **to be** ~ andare avanti **3.** (*firmly fixed*) ben saldo, -a; **to make** ~ NAUT ormeggiare; **to make sth** ~ (**to sth**) fissare qc (a qc) **4.** (*immoral*) ~ **woman** donna *f* dissoluta **II.** *adv* **1.** (*quickly*) velocemente; **not so** ~! non così forte! **2.** (*firmly*) saldamente; **to hold** ~ **to sth** tenersi bene a qc; **to stand** ~ non cedere **3.** (*deeply*) profondamente; **to be** ~ **asleep** dormire profondamente

fast[2] [fæst] **I.** *vi* (*go without food*) digiunare **II.** *n* (*period without food*) digiuno *m*

fasten [ˈfæsən] *vt* **1.** (*do up: dress*) allacciare; (*bag*) chiudere **2.** (*fix securely*) fissare; **to** ~ **one's seatbelt** allacciare la cintura di sicurezza **3. to** ~ **sth onto sth** attacare qc a qc; **to** ~ **one's eyes on sth** fissare lo sguardo su qc; **to** ~ **sth together** (*with paper clip*) appuntare qc; (*with string*) legare qc

◆**fasten down** *vt* fermare

◆**fasten on I.** *vt* fissarsi su; **to** ~ **an idea** fissarsi su un'idea **II.** *vi* **to** ~ **to sb** attaccarsi a qu

◆**fasten up** *vt* allacciare

fastener [ˈfæˌsəˌnɚ] *n* chiusura *f;* **snap** ~ bottone *m* automatico

fast food *n* fast food *m inv*

fast-forward [ˌfæstˈfɔːrˌwɚd] **I.** *vt* far andare avanti velocemente **II.** *vi* avanzare velocemente **III.** *n* tasto di avanzamento *m* veloce

fastidious [fəˈstɪˌdiˌəs] *adj* pignolo, -a

fastness [ˈfæstˌnɪs] <-es> *n* **1.** MIL fortezza *f* **2.** *liter* (*stronghold*) rifugio *m*

fat [fæt] **I.** *adj* **1.** grasso, -a; **to get** ~ ingrassare **2.** (*thick*) grosso, -a **3.** (*large*) grosso, -a; **a** ~ **check** un grosso assegno ►~ **chance!** *inf* aspetta e spera! **II.** *n* **1.** (*body tissue*) grasso *mpl* **2.** (*fatty substance*) grasso *m;* **vegetable** ~ grasso vegetale ►**the** ~ **is in the fire** la frittata è fatta; **to live off the** ~ **of the land** fare una vita da nababbo; **to chew the** ~ **with sb** *inf* chiacchierare con qu

fatal [ˈfeɪˌtəl] *adj* fatale

fatalism [ˈfeɪˌtəˌlɪˌzəm] *n* fatalismo *m*

fatalist *n* fatalista *mf*

fatality [fəˈtæˌləˌti] <-ies> *n* vittima *f*

fatally *adv* **1.** (*causing death*) mortalmente; ~ **ill** gravemente malato **2.** (*disastrously*) irrimediabilmente; ~ **damaged** danneggiato irrimediabilmente

fate [feɪt] *n* (*destiny*) fato *m;* (*one's end*) destino *m;* **to leave sb to his** ~ abbandonare qu al suo destino; **to meet one's** ~ andare incontro al proprio destino; **to seal sb's** ~ decidere la sorte di qu; **to share the same** ~ avere lo stesso destino; **to tempt** ~ sfidare la sorte; **a** ~ **worse than death** un destino peggiore della morte; **it must be** ~ deve essere il destino

fated [ˈfeɪˌtɪd] *adj* destinato, -a; **to be** ~ **to do**

F

sth essere destinato a fare qc; **it was ~ that ...** era destino che...

fateful ['feɪt·fəl] *adj* fatidico, -a

fat-free *adj* senza grassi

fathead ['fæt·hed] *n inf* imbecille *mf*

father ['fɑː·ðəʳ] **I.** *n* **1.** (*parent*) padre *m;* **from ~ to son** di padre in figlio; **to be like a ~ to sb** essere come un padre per qu; **on your ~'s side** da parte di padre **2.** (*founder*) padre *m* **3.** *pl, liter* (*ancestors*) antenati *mpl* ▶ **like ~, like son** tale padre, tale figlio **II.** *vt* (*child*) diventare padre di; (*idea*) concepire

Father Christmas *n* Babbo *m* Natale

father figure *n* figura *f* paterna

fatherhood ['fɑː·ðəʳ·hʊd] *n* paternità *f*

father-in-law ['fɑː·ðəʳ·ɪn·lɑː] <fathers-in-law *o* father-in-laws> *n* suocero *m*

fatherland ['fɑː·ðəʳ·lænd] *n* madre *f* patria

fatherless ['fɑː·ðəʳ·ləs] *adj* orfano, -a di padre

fatherly ['fɑː·ðəʳ·li] *adj* paterno, -a

Father's Day *n* Festa *f* del Papà

fathom ['fæ·ðəm] **I.** *n* NAUT braccio *m* **II.** *vt* (*mystery*) penetrare

fathomless *adj liter* **1.** (*too deep to measure*) insondabile **2.** (*impossible to understand*) incomprensibile

fatigue [fə·'tiːg] **I.** *n* **1.** (*tiredness*) fatica *f;* **to suffer from ~** essere affaticato, -a **2.** TECH fatica *f* **3.** MIL corvée *f inv;* (*uniform*) tuta *m* da fatica **II.** *vt form* (*tire*) affaticare

fatigues *npl* MIL tuta *f* da fatica

fatten ['fæ·tən] *vt* ingrassare

fattening *adj* che fa ingrassare

fatty ['fæ·t̮i] **I.** *adj* **1.** (*food*) grasso, -a **2.** (*tissue*) adiposo, -a **II.** <-ies> *n inf* grassone, -a *m, f*

fatuous ['fæ·tʃu·əs] *adj* fatuo, -a

faucet ['fɑː·sɪt] *n* rubinetto *m;* **to turn the ~ on/off** aprire/chiudere il rubinetto

fault [fɔːlt] **I.** *n* **1.** (*responsibility*) colpa *f;* **it's not my ~** non è colpa mia; **to be sb's ~** (**that ...**) essere colpa di qu (se ...); **to find ~ with sb** trovare da ridire su qu **2.** (*character weakness*) difetto *m;* **to have its ~s** avere i suoi difetti; **to be generous to a ~** essere fin troppo generoso **3.** (*defect*) difetto *m;* **electrical/technical ~** problema *f* elettrico/tecnico **4.** GEO faglia *f* **5.** SPORTS fallo *m;* **double ~** doppio fallo; **foot ~** fallo di piede; **to call a ~** fischiare un fallo **II.** *vt* criticare

faultfinding ['fɔːlt·faɪn·dɪŋ] **I.** *n* (*criticism*) tendenza a cercare il pelo nell'uovo *f* **II.** *adj* criticone, -a

faultless ['fɔːlt·ləs] *adj* impeccabile

faulty ['fɔːl·ti] *adj* difettoso, -a; **~ logic** logica *f* difettosa

faun [fɑːn] *n* fauno *m*

fauna ['fɑː·nə] *n* fauna *f*

favor ['feɪ·vəʳ] **I.** *n* **1.** (*approval*) favore *m;* **to be in ~ of sb/sth** essere a favore di qu/qc; **to decide/vote in ~ of** (**doing**) **sth** decidere/votare a favore di (fare) qc; **to come down in**

~ of (**doing**) **sth** schierarsi a favore di (fare) qc; **to be in ~** essere di moda; **to be in ~ with sb** godere dell'appoggio di qu; **to be out of ~** non riscuotere più consenso; **to reject sth in ~ of sth else** respingere qc a favore di qc altro; **to find in ~ of sb** LAW emettere una sentenza a favore di qu; **to find ~ with sb** essere nelle grazie di qu; **to gain** [*o* **win**] **sb's ~** guadagnarsi il favore di; **to show ~ to sb** *form* favorire qu **2.** (*advantage*) **to be in sb's ~** essere a vantaggio di qu; **to have sth in one's ~** avere qc che va a vantaggio di qu; **to have the wind in one's ~** avere il vento a favore **3.** (*helpful act*) favore *m;* **to ask sb a ~** chiedere un favore a qu; **to do sb a ~** fare un favore a qu; **do me a ~!** *inf* ma fammi il piacere! **4.** (*small gift*) pensierino *m* **II.** *vt* **1.** (*prefer*) preferire **2.** (*give advantage to*) privilegiare **3.** (*show partiality towards*) favorire **4.** *form* (*graciously give*) **to ~ sb with sth** onorare qu di qc

favorable ['feɪ·və·ə·bl] *adj* **1.** (*approving*) favorevole; **to make a ~ impression** (**on sb**) fare un'impressione positiva (a qu) **2.** (*advantageous*) vantaggioso, -a; **~ to sth/sb** vantaggioso per qu/qc

favored ['feɪ·vəʳd] *adj* (*preferred*) favorito, -a; (*child*) prediletto, -a

favorite ['feɪ·və·ɪt] **I.** *adj* (*most liked*) preferito, -a; **~ son** POL candidato alle elezioni presidenziali americane designato dal suo Stato natale **II.** *n* preferito, -a *m, f*

favoritism *n* favoritismo *m*

fawn[1] [fɑːn] **I.** *n* **1.** (*young deer*) cerbiatto *m* **2.** (*color*) fulvo *m* chiaro *inv* **II.** *adj* fulvo chiaro

fawn[2] [fɑːn] *vi* (*be eager to please*) **to ~ on sb** adulare qu

fawning ['fɑː·nɪŋ] *adj* adulatore, -trice

fax [fæks] **I.** *n* fax *m inv;* **to send something by ~** inviare qc per fax **II.** *vt* mandare per fax; **to ~ sth through to sb** inviare qc a qu per fax

fax machine *n* fax *m inv*

FBI [ˌef·biː·'aɪ] *n abbr of* **Federal Bureau of Investigation** FBI *f*

i L' **FBI**, *the Federal Bureau of Investigation*, è la polizia giudiziaria federale. I suoi funzionari sono chiamati *FBI agents* o *federal agents. Central Intelligence Agency (CIA)* è il nome dei servizi segreti internazionali degli Stati Uniti. Oltre alla CIA, esistono numerosissimi altri servizi segreti.

FDA *n abbr of* **Food and Drug Administration** FDA, *organismo governativo statunitense incaricato del controllo di alimenti e medicinali*

fear [fɪr] **I.** *n* paura *m;* **to have a ~ of sth** avere paura di qc; **~ of heights** paura dell'altezza; **for ~ of doing sth** per paura di fare qc; **for ~ that** per paura che; **to be in ~ of sth** temere qc; **to go in ~ of sth** temere per qc; **to put the**

~ of God into sb spaventare qu a morte; without ~ or favor in modo imparziale II. *vt* 1.(*be afraid of*) temere; to have nothing to ~ non aver nulla da temere; to ~ to do sth aver paura di fare qc 2. *form* (*feel concern*) to ~ (that ...) temere (che ...) III. *vi liter* temere; to ~ for one's life temere per la propria vita; never ~! *iron* niente paura!

fearful ['fɪr·fəl] *adj* 1.(*anxious*) timoroso, -a; ~ of doing sth timoroso di fare qc 2.(*terrible: pain*) tremendo; (*accident*) terrible 3. *inf*(*very bad: noise, mess*) tremendo, -a

fearless ['fɪr·ləs] *adj* impavido, -a

fearsome ['fɪr·səm] *adj* terrificante

feasibility [ˌfiː·zə·'bɪ·lə·t̬i] *n* fattibilità *f*

feasibility study *n* studio *m* di fattibilità

feasible ['fiː·zə·bl] *adj* 1.(*plan*) fattibile 2.(*story*) plausibile; (*solution*) possibile

feast [fiːst] I. *n* 1.(*meal*) banchetto *m;* a ~ for the eye una festa per gli occhi; a ~ for the ear musica per le orecchie 2. REL festa *f* II. *vi* to ~ on sth festeggiare con qc III. *vt* organizzare un banchetto per ▶ to ~ one's eyes on sth rifarsi gli occhi con qc

feat [fiːt] *n* impresa *f;* ~ of agility prova *f* di agilità; ~ of engineering capolavoro *m* di ingegneria

feather ['fe·ðɚ] I. *n* piuma *f* ▶ to be a ~ in sb's cap esere un fiore all'occhiello di qu; as light as a ~ leggero come una piuma; to ruffle sb's ~s dare fastidio a qu II. *vt* to ~ one's own nest ingrassare le proprie tasche

featherbed ['fe·ðɚ·bed] *vt* (*child*) crescere nella bambagia

featherbrained ['fe·ðɚ·breɪnd] *adj* tonto, -a

featherweight ['fe·ðɚ·weɪt] *n* SPORTS peso *m* piuma

feathery ['fe·ðɚ·ri] *adj* (*clouds, leaves*) leggero, -a (come una piuma); (*feel, texture*) soffice

feature ['fiː·tʃɚ] I. *n* 1.(*distinguishing attribute*) caratteristica *f;* sb's/sth's best ~ la caratteristica migliore di qu/qc; a distinguishing ~ un tratto distintivo; a physical ~ una caratteristica fisica; to make a ~ of sth valorizzare qc 2. *pl* (*of face*) lineamento *mpl;* to have regular/strong ~s avere dei lineamenti regolari/molto marcati 3.(*in newspaper, magazine*) articolo *m* 4. CINE film *m* II. *vt* 1.(*have as performer, star*) a film featuring sb as ... un film con qu nel ruolo di... 2.(*give special prominence to*) offrire (come attrazione principale); to ~ sth (*article, report*) contenere 3.(*include*) includere III. *vi* 1.(*appear*) apparire; to ~ in ... apparire in ... 2.(*be an actor in*) recitare; to ~ in ... recitare in...

feature film *n* film *m, lungometraggio*

featureless *adj* senza tratti caratteristici

feature story *n* reportage *m inv*

febrile ['fiː·brɪl] *adj liter* (*excitement, convulsion*) febbrile; (*child*) febbricitante

February ['fe·bru·e·ri] *n* febbraio *m; s.a.* April

feces ['fiː·siːz] *npl* feci *fpl*

feckless ['fek·lɪs] *adj form* irresponsabile

fed [fed] *pt, pp of* feed

fed. *abbr of* federal federale

federal ['fe·də·rəl] *adj* federale; ~ republic repubblica *f* federale

federalism ['fe·də·rə·lɪ·zəm] *n* federalismo *m*

federalist ['fe·də·rə·lɪst] *n* federalista *mf*

federate ['fe·də·reɪt] I. *vt* federare II. *vi* federarsi

federation [ˌfe·də·'reɪ·ʃən] *n* federazione *f*

fed up *adj inf* stufo, -a; to be ~ with sth/sb essere stufo di qc/qu

fee [fiː] *n* (*for doctor, lawyer*) onorario *m;* (*for membership*) quota *f* di iscrizione; (*for school, university*) tasse *f pl* (scolastiche o universitarie); to charge/receive a ~ for sth far pagare/ricevere un onorario per qc e

feeble ['fiː·bl] *adj* (*person, attempt*) debole; (*performance*) poco convincente

feeble-minded [ˌfiː·bl·'maɪn·dɪd] *adj* (*stupid*) deficiente

feebleness *n* debolezza *f*

feed [fiːd] <fed> I. *vt* 1.(*give food to: person, animal*) dar da mangiare; (*plant*) nutrire; (*baby*) allattare; to ~ the fire ravvivare il fuoco 2.(*provide food for: family, country*) sfamare 3.(*supply*) inserire; to ~ the data from a scanner into the computer travasare i dati da uno scanner in un computer; to ~ sb a line THEAT suggerire una battuta a qu II. *vi* nutrirsi; (*baby*) poppare III. *n* 1.(*for farm animals*) mangime *m;* cattle ~ foraggio *m* per bestiame; to be off its ~ non aver fame 2. *inf* (*meal*) mangiata *f* 3. TECH tubo *m* d'alimentazione

◆**feed back** *vt* restituire

◆**feed in** *vt* alimentare; (*information*) introdurre

◆**feed on** *vt insep, a. fig* nutrirsi di

◆**feed up** *vt* (*person, animal*) ingozzare

feedback ['fiːd·bæk] *n* 1.(*evaluation*) feedback *m inv;* positive/negative ~ feedback positivo/negativo 2. ELEC feedback *m inv*

feeder *n* 1. TECH alimentatore *m* 2.(*river*) affluente *m;* ~ road strada *f* secondaria

feel [fiːl] <felt> I. *vi* 1.+ *adj/n* (*sensation or emotion*) sentirsi; to ~ well sentirsi bene; to ~ hot/cold sentire caldo/freddo; to ~ hungry/thirsty avere fame/sete; to ~ certain/convinced essere sicuro/convinto; to ~ as if ... sentirsi come se... +*subj;* to ~ like a cup of coffee/something sweet aver voglia di ua tazza di caffè/di qualcosa di dolce; to ~ like a walk aver voglia di fare una passeggiata; to ~ free to do sth sentirsi libero di fare qc; to ~ one's age sentire il peso degli anni; it ~s wonderful/awful mi sembra meraviglioso/terribile; how do you ~ about him? che idea ti sei fatta di lui?; how would you ~ if ...? che ne diresti se...? 2.+ *adj* (*seem*) sembrare 3.(*search*) to ~ for sth cercare qc, *tastando;* to ~ (around) somewhere muoversi a tastoni II. *vt* 1.(*experience*) sentire; not to ~ a thing non provare nulla; **to ~ the cold/heat** sentire il freddo/il caldo; **to ~ something/nothing for sb** provare qualcosa/non provare niente per qu; **to ~ it in one's bones** (that ...) sentirsela (che...) **2.** (*think, believe*) **to ~** (that) ... credere (che)...; **to ~ it appropriate/necessary to do sth** ritenere (che) sia giusto/necessario fare qc **3.** (*touch*) sentire; (*pulse*) prendere **III.** *n* **1.** (*texture*) **I can't stand the ~ of wool** non sopporto la lana al tatto **2.** (*act of touching*) **to have a ~ of sth** toccare qc **3.** (*character, atmosphere*) atmosfera *f;* **a ~ of mystery** un'atmosfera misteriosa **4.** (*natural talent*) talento *m* naturale; **to have a ~ for sth** avere un talento naturale per qc; **to get the ~ of sth** abituarsi a qc

◆**feel around** *vi* cercare, *a tastoni;* **to ~ for sth** cercare qc a tastoni

◆**feel for** *vt* **to ~ sb** dispiacersi per qu

feeler ['fiː·ləʳ] *n* ZOOL antenna *f* ▶ **to put out one's ~s** mettere fuori le antenne

feel-good ['fiːl·gʊd] *adj* che fa sentire bene; **~ factor** sensazione *f* di benessere

feeling ['fiː·lɪŋ] *n* **1.** (*emotion*) sentimento *m;* **mixed ~s** sentimenti contrastanti; **to hurt sb's ~s** ferire i sentimenti di qu **2.** (*sensation*) sensazione *f;* **a dizzy ~** un senso di vertigine **3.** (*impression*) sensazione *f;* **to have the ~** (that) ... avere la sensazione (che)...; **to have a bad ~ about sth/sb** avere un brutto presentimento su qc/qu **4.** (*opinion*) opinione *f;* **to have strong ~s about sth** avere idee ben precise su qc **5.** (*strong emotion*) sentimento *m;* **to say sth with ~** dire qc con trasporto **6.** (*physical sensation*) sensibilità *f;* **to lose the ~ in one's leg** perdere la sensibilità ad una gamba **7.** (*natural talent*) **to have a ~ for sth** avere un talento innato per qc

feet [fiːt] *n pl of* **foot**

feign [feɪn] *vt liter* fingere; **to ~ madness** fingere di essere pazzo

feigned [feɪnd] *adj liter* finto, -a

feint [feɪnt] **I.** *vi* fare una finta; **to ~ left** fare una finta a sinistra; **to ~ to do sth** fingere di fare qc **II.** *n* SPORTS finta *f*

felicitous [fə·'lɪ·sɪ·təs] *adj* indovinato, -a

felicity [fə·'lɪ·sə·t̬i] <-ies> *n liter* (*happiness*) felicità *f*

feline ['fiː·laɪn] **I.** *adj* **1.** ZOOL felino, -a **2.** (*cat-like*) da gatto **II.** *n* felino *m*

fell¹ [fel] *pt of* **fall**

fell² [fel] *vt* **1.** (*cut down*) abbattere **2.** (*knock down*) buttare a terra

fell³ [fel] *adj* HIST feroce ▶ **at** [*o* **in**] **one ~ swoop** in un colpo solo

fellow ['fe·loʊ] **I.** *n* **1.** *inf* (*man*) tizio *m;* **an odd ~** un tipo strano **2.** UNIV docente *mf* **3.** *form* (*colleague*) collega *mf* **II.** *adj* **~ student** compagno, -a *m, f* di studi

fellow citizen *n* concittadino, -a *m, f*

fellow countryman *n* compatriota *mf*

fellow feeling *n* cameratismo *m*

fellow member *n* consocio, -a *m, f*

fellowship ['fe·loʊ·ʃɪp] *n* **1.** (*comradely feeling*) cameratismo *m* **2.** (*group*) associazione *f* **3.** UNIV **research ~** borsa *f* di studio per ricercatori

fellow traveler *n* compagno, -a *m, f* di viaggio

fellow worker *n* compagno, -a *m, f* di lavoro

felon ['fe·lən] *n* criminale *mf*

felonious [fə·'loʊ·ni·əs] *adj* criminale

felony ['fe·lə·ni] <-ies> *n* crimine *m*

felt¹ [felt] *pt, pp of* **feel**

felt² [felt] **I.** *n* (*material*) feltro *m* **II.** *adj* di feltro

felt-tip (pen) [ˌfel·t'tɪp (pen)] *n* pennarello *m*

female ['fiː·meɪl] **I.** *adj* femminile; ZOOL, TECH femmina **II.** *n* (*woman*) donna *f;* ZOOL femmina *f*

feminine ['fe·mə·nɪn] **I.** *adj* femminile **II.** *n* LING **the ~** il femminile *m*

femininity [ˌfe·mə·'nɪ·nə·t̬i] *n* femminilità *f*

feminism ['fe·mɪ·nɪ·zəm] *n* femminismo *m*

feminist ['fe·mɪ·nɪst] **I.** *n* femminista *mf* **II.** *adj* femminista

femur ['fiː·məʳ] <-s *o* -mora> *n* femore *m*

fence [fens] **I.** *n* **1.** (*barrier*) recinto *f* **2.** *inf* (*person*) ricettatore, -trice *m, f* ▶ **to mend one's ~s** ricucire i rapporti; **to sit on the ~** restare alla finestra **II.** *vi* **1.** SPORTS giocare a scherma **2.** *form* **to ~** (**with sb**) duellare (con qu) **III.** *vt* (*enclose*) recintare

fencer *n* schermitore, -trice *m, f*

fencing *n* scherma *f*

fend for *vt* (*go without help*) **to ~ oneself** badare a se stesso

◆**fend off** *vt* (*defend against*) schivare; **to ~ a question** schivare una domanda

fender ['fen·dəʳ] *n* **1.** AUTO parafango *m inv* **2.** (*around fireplace*) parafuoco *m* **3.** NAUT parabordo *m*

fennel ['fe·nl] *n* finocchio *m*

ferment¹ [fəʳ·'ment] **I.** *vt* **1.** CHEM far fermentare **2.** *form* (*stir up*) fomentare **II.** *vi* **1.** CHEM fermentare **2.** *form* (*develop*) essere in fermento

ferment² ['fɜːr·ment] *n* **1.** *form* (*state of excitement*) fermento *m;* **to be in ~** essere in (grande) fermento **2.** (*fermentation*) fermentazione *f*

fermentation [ˌfɜːr·men·'teɪ·ʃən] *n* fermentazione *f*

fern [fɜːrn] *n* felce *f*

ferocious [fə·'roʊ·ʃəs] *adj* (*battle, criticism, competition*) feroce; (*heat*) tremendo, -a; (*temper*) violento, -a

ferocity [fə·'rɑː·sə·t̬i] *n* (*of animal, person*) ferocia *f;* (*of attack*) ferocia *f;* (*of storm, wind*) violenza *f*

ferret ['fe·rɪt] **I.** *n* furetto *m* **II.** *vi* **1.** (*search*) **to ~ around for sth** frugare in cerca di qc **2.** (*hunt with ferrets*) **to go ~ing** andare a caccia con i furetti

Ferris wheel ['fe·rɪs·ˌhwiːl] *n* ruota *f* panoramica

ferrous ['fe·rəs] *adj* ferroso, -a

ferry ['feˑri] <-ies> **I.** n (*ship*) nave *f* traghetto; **car** ~ traghetto *m* (per automobili) **II.** *vt* **1.** (*in boat*) traghettare **2.** *inf* (*by car*) portare con la macchina

ferryboat *n* ferry-boat *m inv*

ferryman <-men> *n* traghettatore *m*

fertile ['fɜːrˑt̬l] *adj a. fig* fertile; **to be ~ ground for sth** *fig* essere terreno fertile per qc

fertility [fəˑ'tɪˑləˑt̬i] *n* fertilità *f*

fertilization [ˌfɜːrˑt̬əˑlɪˑ'zeɪˑʃən] *n* fertilizzazione *f*

fertilize ['fɜːrˑt̬əˑlaɪz] *vt* **1.** BIO fertilizzare **2.** AGR fertilizzare

fertilizer ['fɜːrˑt̬əˑlaɪˑzər] *n* fertilizzante *m*

fervent ['fɜːrˑvənt] *adj*, **fervid** ['fɜːrˑvɪd] *adj form* fervente

fervor ['fɜːrˑvəˑ] *n* fervore *m*

fester ['fesˑtəˑ] *vi* (*wound, anger*) incancrenirsi

festival ['fesˑtɪˑvəl] *n* **1.** (*special event*) festa *m;* **a film/music ~** un festival del cinema/della musica **2.** REL festività *f inv*

festive ['fesˑtɪv] *adj* festivo, -a; **to be in ~ mood** essere d'umore allegro

festivity [fesˑ'tɪˑvəˑt̬i] <-ies> *n* **1.** *pl* (*festive activities*) festeggiamenti *mpl* **2.** (*festival*) festa *f*

festoon [feˑ'stuːn] **I.** *n* festone *m* **II.** *vt* adornare con festoni

fetal ['fiːˑt̬l] *adj* BIO fetale

fetch [fetʃ] **I.** *vt* **1.** (*bring back*) andare a prendere; **to ~ the police** andare a chiamare la polizia; **to ~ sb sth** (*from somewhere*) andare a prendere qc per qn (in qualche posto) **2.** (*be sold for*) fruttare **II.** *vi* (*dog*) rincorrere, afferrare e riportare un oggetto

fetching ['fetˑʃɪŋ] *adj* attraente

fête [feɪt] **I.** *n* (*festival, party*) festa *f* **II.** *vt* festeggiare

fetid ['feˑt̬ɪd] *adj form* fetido, -a

fetish ['feˑt̬ɪʃ] *n* feticcio *m;* **to make a ~ of sth** trasformare qc in un feticcio

fetishism ['feˑt̬ɪˑʃɪˑzəm] *n* feticismo *m*

fetter ['feˑt̬əˑ] *vt* **1.** (*chain up*) **to ~ sb** (**to sth**) incatenare qu (a qc); **to ~ a horse** impastoiare un cavallo **2.** *liter* (*restrict freedom*) impastoiare

fetus ['fiːˑt̬əs] *n* feto *m*

feud [fjuːd] **I.** *n* faida *f;* **a ~ between sb and sb** una faida fra qu e qu; **a ~ over sth** una faida per qc; **a family ~** una faida familiare **II.** *vi* essere in lotta

feudal ['fjuːˑdəl] *adj* HIST feudale

feudalism ['fjuːˑdəˑlɪˑzəm] *n* feudalesimo *m*

fever ['fiːˑvəˑ] *n* **1.** MED febbre *f;* **to have** [*o* **run**] **a ~** avere la febbre **2.** (*excited state*) febbre *f;* **a ~ of excitement** uno stato di febbrile eccitazione; **baseball ~** febbre del baseball

feverish ['fiːˑvəˑrɪʃ] *adj* **1.** MED febbricitante **2.** (*frantic*) febbrile

few [fjuː] <-er, -est> **I.** *adj det* **1.** (*small number*) pochi, poche; **there are ~ things that please him** sono poche le cose che gli piacciono; **one of her ~ friends** uno dei suoi

pochi amici; **quite a ~ people** abbastanza gente; **not ~er than 100 people** non meno di 100 persone; **the pickings are ~** i guadagni sono scarsi; **to be ~ and far between** contarsi sulla punta della dita **2.** (*some*) qualche; **they left a ~ boxes** hanno lasciato alcune scatole **II.** *pron* pochi, poche; **a ~** alcuni, alcune; **I'd like a ~ more** ne vorrei degli altri; **the ~ who have the book** i pochi che hanno il libro; **the happy/lucky ~** i pochi felici/fortunati

fewer ['fjuːˑəˑ] *adj, pron* meno; **no ~ than** non meno di

fewest ['fjuːˑɪst] *adj, pron* il minor numero di

ff. *abbr of* **the following** seg.

fiancé [ˌfiːˑɑːnˑ'seɪ] *n* fidanzato *m*

fiancée [ˌfiːˑɑːnˑ'seɪ] *n* fidanzata *f*

fiasco [fiˑ'æsˑkoʊ] <-cos *o* -coes> *n* fiasco *m*

fib [fɪb] <-bb-> *inf* **I.** *vi* raccontare balle; **to ~** (**to sb**) **about sth** raccontare balle (a qu) su qc **II.** *n* frottola *f;* **to tell a ~** (**about sth/sb**) raccontare una frottola (su qc/qu)

fibber ['fɪbˑəˑ] *n* contaballe *mf inv*

fiber ['faɪˑbəˑ] *n a. fig* fibra *f*

fiberglass ['faɪˑbəˑˌglæs] *n* fibra *f* di vetro

fiber optic cable *n* cavo *m* a fibre ottiche

fiber optics *n + sing vb* trasmissione *f* su fibre ottiche

fibula ['fɪbˑjəˑlə] <-s *o* -ae> *n* fibula *f*

fickle ['fɪˑkl] *adj* volubile

fiction ['fɪkˑʃən] *n* **1.** LIT narrativa *f;* **~ writer** scrittore, -trice *m, f* di romanzi **2.** (*false statement*) finzione *f*

fictional ['fɪkˑʃəˑnl] *adj* immaginario, -a

fictitious [fɪkˑ'tɪˑʃəs] *adj* **1.** (*false, untrue*) falso, -a **2.** (*imaginary*) fittizio, -a; **~ character** personaggio *m* fittizio

fiddle ['fɪˑdl] **I.** *vi* **1.** *inf* (*play the violin*) suonare il violino **2. to ~** (**around**) **with sth** (*fidget with*) giocherellare con qc; (*try to repair*) armeggiare con qc **II.** *vt inf* (*falsify*) falsificare **III.** *n inf* **1.** (*violin*) violino *m;* **to play the ~** suonare il violino **2.** (*fraud*) truffa *f;* **to be on the ~** truffare ▶ **to be** (**as**) **fit as a ~** *inf* essere sano come un pesce; **to play second ~** avere un ruolo secondario

fiddler ['fɪdˑləˑ] *n inf* **1.** (*violinist*) violinista *mf* **2.** (*swindler*) imbroglione, -a *m, f*

fiddling ['fɪdˑlɪŋ] **I.** *adj* di poco conto; **~ restrictions** restrizioni *f pl* insignificanti **II.** *n* imbrogli *mpl*

fiddly ['fɪdˑli] <-ier, -iest> *adj inf* rognoso, -a

fidelity [fɪˑ'deˑləˑt̬i] *n* fedeltà *f*

fidget ['fɪˑdʒɪt] **I.** *vi* agitarsi **II.** *n* persona *f* irrequieta; **to have the ~s** stare sulle spine

fidgety ['fɪˑdʒɪˑt̬i] *adj* irrequieto, -a

fiefdom ['fiːfˑdəm] *n* feudo *m*

field [fiːld] **I.** *n* **1.** *a.* ELEC, AGR, SPORTS campo *m;* (*meadow*) prato *m* **2.** + *sing/pl vb* (*contestants*) concorrenti *mpl;* **to lead the ~** essere in testa; **to play the ~** *fig* tastare il terreno **3.** (*sphere of activity*) campo *m;* **to be outside sb's ~** esulare dal campo di qu; **it's not my ~** non è il mio campo **4.** COMPUT campo *m* **II.** *vt*

1. (*return*) **to ~ the ball** raccogliere la palla; **to ~ a question** schivare una domanda 2. (*candidate*) presentare

field day *n* 1. SPORTS giornata *f* dello sport 2. MIL manovre *fpl* ▸ **to have a ~** divertirsi un mondo

fielder ['fi:l·də] *n* SPORTS fielder *mf inv*, nel cricket, il giocatore che recupera le palle battute

field event *n* SPORTS incontro *m* di atletica

field glasses *n* binocolo *m*

field mouse *n* topo *m* di campagna

fieldwork ['fi:ld·wɜ:rk] *n* ricerca *f* sul campo

fieldworker *n* ricercatore, -trice *m*, *f* sul campo

fiend [fi:nd] *n* 1. (*brute*) demonio *m* 2. *inf* (*enthusiast*) fanatico -a; **a chess ~** un fanatico degli scacchi

fiendish ['fi:n·dɪʃ] *adj* (*cruel*) diabolico, -a

fierce [fɪrs] *adj* <-er, -est> 1. (*animal*) feroce 2. feroce; (*love*) sconvolgente; (*wind*) forte 3. *inf* (*hard*) tosto, -a

fierceness ['fɪrs·nɪs] *n* 1. (*wildness*) ferocia *f* 2. (*of competition, opposition*) ferocia *f*; (*of emotions*) impetuosità *f* 3. (*of wind*) furia *f*

fiery ['faɪ·ri] <-ier, -iest> *adj* 1. (*heat*) infuocato, -a 2. (*passionate*) infuocato, -a 3. (*very spicy*) piccante

FIFA ['fi:·fə] *n abbr of* **Fédération Internationale de Football Association** FIFA *f*

fife [faɪf] *n* piffero *m*

fifteen [ˌfɪf·'ti:n] I. *adj* quindici II. *n* quindici *m*; *s.a.* **eight**

fifteenth I. *adj* quindicesimo, -a II. *n* 1. (*order*) quindicesimo, -a *m*, *f* 2. (*date*) quindici *m* 3. (*fraction*) quindicesimo *m*; (*part*) quindicesimo *m*; *s.a.* **eighth**

fifth [fɪfθ] I. *adj* quinto, -a II. *n* 1. (*order*) quinto, -a *m*, *f* 2. (*date*) cinque *m* 3. (*fraction*) quinto *m*; (*part*) quinto *m*; *s.a.* **eighth**

fiftieth ['fɪf·ti·əθ] I. *adj* cinquantesimo, -a II. *n* (*order*) cinquantesimo, -a *m*, *f*; (*fraction*) cinquantesimo *m*; (*part*) cinquantesimo *m*; *s.a.* **eighth**

fifty ['fɪf·ti] I. *adj* cinquanta II. <-ies> *n* cinquanta *m*; *s.a.* **eighty**

fig [fɪg] *n* 1. (*fruit*) fico *m* 2. (*tree*) fico *m* ▸ **I don't give [*o* care] a ~ about it!** non me ne importa un fico secco!; **to be not worth a ~** non valere un fico secco

fig. I. *n abbr of* **figure** fig. II. *adj abbr of* **figurative** fig.

fight [faɪt] I. *n* 1. (*physical*) rissa *f*; (*argument*) lite *f*; **to put up a ~** lottare 2. MIL combattimento *m* 3. (*struggle*) lotta *f*; **the ~ against AIDS** la lotta contro l'AIDS 4. (*spirit*) combattività *f*; **to show some ~** tirar fuori le unghie II. <fought, fought> *vi* 1. (*exchange blows*) lottare; MIL combattere; **to ~ with each other** bisticciarsi; **to ~ with sb** (*against*) combattere contro qu; (*on same side*) combattere al fianco di qu 2. (*dispute*) litigare; **to ~ over/about sth** litigare per qc 3. (*struggle to overcome*) lottare; **to ~ for/against sth** lottare per/con-

tro qc III. *vt* 1. (*exchange blows with, argue with*) lottare contro 2. (*wage war, do battle*) combattere contro; **to ~ a battle** combattere una battaglia; **to ~ a duel** battersi in duello 3. (*struggle to overcome*) combattere; **to ~ a case** LAW difendere una causa 4. (*struggle to obtain*) **to ~ one's way through the crowd** farsi largo a fatica fra la folla; **to ~ one's way to the top** lottare per arrivare in alto

◆**fight back** I. *vi* (*defend oneself*) difendersi; (*counterattack*) contrattaccare II. *vt* **to ~ one's tears** trattenere le lacrime

◆**fight off** *vt* (*repel*) respingere; (*master, resist*) resistere; **to ~ the cold/depression** lottare contro il freddo/la depressione

◆**fight on** *vi* continuare a lottare

fighter ['faɪ·t̬ə] *n* 1. (*person*) persona *f* combattiva 2. AVIAT caccia *m*

fighting ['faɪ·t̬ɪŋ] I. *n* (*in the street*) rissa *f*; (*battle*) combattimenti *mpl* II. *adj* combattivo, -a; **~ spirit** spirito *m* combattivo ▸ **there's a ~ chance that ...** ci sono buone possibiltà che... +*subj*

figment ['fɪg·mənt] *n* **a ~ of the imagination** un frutto *m* della fantasia

figurative ['fɪg·jə·ə·t̬ɪv] *adj* 1. LING figurato, -a 2. ART figurativo, -a

figuratively *adv* in senso figurato

figure ['fɪg·jə] I. *n* 1. (*shape*) figura *f*; **mother ~** figura materna; **a fine ~ of a man** un uomo di bell'aspetto; **to cut a fine ~** fare una bella figura; **to cut a sorry ~** fare una bruta figura; **to keep one's ~** mantenere la linea 2. ART figura *f* 3. (*digit*) cifra *f*; (*numeral*) numero *m*; **column of ~s** colonna *f* di numeri; **to have a head for ~s** essere bravo con i numeri; **to be good at ~s** essere bravo con i numeri; **in round ~s** cifra tonda 4. (*price*) cifra *f*; **a high ~** una cifra esorbitante 5. (*diagram, illustration*) figura *f* II. *vt* 1. (*think*) immaginare; **to ~ that ...** figurarsi che... 2. (*in diagram*) raffigurare 3. (*calculate*) calcolare III. *vi* (*feature*) figurare; **to ~ in sth** figurare in qc; **to ~ as sth/sb** figurare come qc/qu; **that ~s!** lo sapevo!

◆**figure out** *vt* (*comprehend*) capire; (*work out*) risolvere; **to ~ why ...** spiegarsi perchè...

figurehead ['fɪg·jə·hed] *n* 1. NAUT polena *f* 2. *fig* prestanome *mf inv*

figure skater *n* pattinatore, -trice *m*, *f* artistico, -a

figure skating *n* pattinaggio *m* artistico

Fiji ['fi:·dʒi:] *n* **the ~ Islands** le Isole Figi

Fijian [fɪ·'dʒi:·ən] I. *adj* delle Figi II. *n* abitante *mf* delle Figi

filament ['fɪ·lə·mənt] *n* filamento *m*

filch [fɪltʃ] *vt inf* fregare

file[1] [faɪl] I. *n* 1. (*folder*) cartella *f* 2. (*record*) pratica *f*; **to open a ~** aprire una pratica; **to keep sth on ~** tenere qc in archivio 3. COMPUT file *m inv* 4. (*row*) fila *f*; **in single ~** in fila indiana II. *vt* 1. (*record*) archiviare 2. (*present: claim, complaint*) inoltrare; **to ~ a petition**

presentare una petizione III. *vi* 1. LAW to ~ for **bankruptcy** dichiarare bancarotta; to ~ for **divorce** chiedere il divorzio 2. (*move in line*) muoversi in fila
◆**file away** *vt* archiviare
◆**file in** *vi* entrare in fila
◆**file out** *vi* uscire in fila
file [faɪl] I. *n* (*tool*) lima *f* II. *vt* limare; to ~ **one's nails** limarsi le unghie III. *vi* to ~ sth **down** limare qc; to ~ **through sth** tagliare qc con una lima
file manager *n* file manager *m inv*
file name *n* nome *m* del file
filial ['fɪ·li·əl] *adj form* filiale
filibuster ['fɪ·lɪ·bʌs·tə·] *vi* POL fare ostruzionismo
filigree ['fɪ·lɪ·griː] *n* filigrana *f*
filing ['faɪ·lɪŋ] *n* 1. (*archiving*) schedatura *f* 2. LAW presentazione *f, di un'istanza* 3. *pl* (*bits of metal*) limatura *f*
filing cabinet *n* schedario *m*
Filipino [fɪ·lɪ·ˈpiː·noʊ] I. *adj* filippino, -a II. *n* filippino, -a *m, f*
fill [fɪl] I. *vt* 1. (*make full*) riempire; (*space*) occupare; to ~ **a vacancy** coprire un posto vacante; to ~ **a vacuum** riempire un vuoto; to ~ **a need** soddisfare un bisogno; to ~ **a need in the market** soddisfare la domanda del mercato 2. (*seal*) otturare 3. CULIN farcire 4. (*fulfill: order*) espletare; (*requirement*) soddisfare II. *vi* riempirsi III. *n* to drink/eat one's ~ bere/mangiare a sazietà; to have one's ~ of sth averne abbastanza di qc
◆**fill in** I. *vt* 1. (*seal opening*) riempire; to ~ a **hole** tappare un buco 2. (*document*) compilare 3. (*color in*) colorare 4. (*inform*) informare; to fill sb in on the details mettere qu al corrente dei particolari 5. (*time*) riempire II. *vi* to ~ (for sb) sostituire (qu)
◆**fill out** I. *vt* (*document*) compilare II. *vi* (*put on weight*) arrotondarsi
◆**fill up** I. *vt* riempire; (*completely*) colmare; to fill oneself up rimpinzarsi II. *vi* riempirsi
filler ['fɪ·lə·] *n* 1. (*sealing material*) stucco *m* 2. TV *materiale usato come riempitivo in un giornale o in un programma radiofonico o televisivo*
fillet ['fɪ·lɪt] I. *n* filetto *m* II. *vt* sfilettare; to ~ a **fish** tagliare un pesce a filetti
fillet steak *n* filetto *m*
filling I. *n* 1. (*substance*) ripieno *m* 2. (*in tooth*) otturazione *f* II. *adj* sostanzioso, -a; to be ~ riempire
filling station *n* stazione *f* di servizio
fillip ['fɪ·lɪp] *n* stimolo *m;* to provide a ~ to sb incoraggiare qu; to give sb a (big) ~ essere di (grande) stimolo a qu
film [fɪlm] I. *n* 1. PHOT, CINE film *m;* to make a ~ fare un film; to see [*o* watch] a ~ vedere un film 2. (*fine coating*) pellicola *f; a* ~ of oil un velo d'olio II. *vt* filmare III. *vi* filmare
film buff *n* cinefilo, -a *m, f*
film camera *n* macchina *f* da presa

film director *n* regista *mf* cinematografico, -a
film star *n* stella *f* del cinema
film studio *n* studio *m* cinematografico
filter ['fɪl·tə·] I. *n* filtro *m* II. *vt* filtrare III. *vi* filtrare
◆**filter out** I. *vi* filtrare II. *vt* eliminare
◆**filter through** *vi* filtrare
filter bed *n* letto *m* filtrante
filter paper *n* carta *f* filtro, *per il caffè*
filter tip *n* filtro *m*
filth [fɪlθ] *n* 1. (*dirt*) sudiciume *m;* (*excrement*) sterco *m* 2. (*obscenity*) oscenità *f inv*
filthy ['fɪl·θi] I. *adj* 1. (*very dirty*) sudicio, -a; (*weather*) schifoso, -a 2. *inf* (*obscene*) osceno, -a II. *adv inf* to be ~ rich essere ricco sfondato
filtration [fɪl·ˈtreɪ·ʃən] *n* filtrazione *f*
fin [fɪn] *n* pinna *f*
final ['faɪ·nl] I. *adj* 1. (*last*) finale; ~ installment ultima rata *f* 2. (*irrevocable*) definitivo, -a; to have the ~ say (on sth) avere l'ultima parola (su qc); and that's ~ *inf* e basta II. *n* 1. SPORTS finale *f;* to get (through) to the ~s arrivare in finale 2. *pl* UNIV esame *m, di fine corso;* to take one's ~s dare gli esami finali
finale [fɪ·ˈnæ·li] *n* finale *m;* grand ~ gran finale
finalist ['faɪ·nə·lɪst] *n* finalista *mf*
finality [faɪ·ˈnæ·lə·t̬i] *n* 1. (*irreversibility*) definitività *f* 2. (*determination*) perentorietà *f*
finalize ['faɪ·nə·laɪz] *vt* ultimare
finally ['faɪ·nə·li] *adv* 1. (*at long last*) finalmente 2. (*in conclusion*) infine 3. (*irrevocably*) definitivamente
finance ['faɪ·nænts] *vt* finanziare
finance company *n*, **finance house** *n* compagnia *f* finanziaria
finances ['faɪ·nænt·sɪz] *npl* finanze *fpl*
financial [faɪ·ˈnænt·ʃəl] *adj* finanziario, -a; sb's ~ affairs le questioni finanziarie di qu
financial adviser *n* consulente *m* finanziario
financial year *n* anno *m* fiscale
financier [fɪ·ˈnænt·siə·] *n* finanziatore, -trice *m, f*
finch [fɪntʃ] *n* fringuello *m*
find [faɪnd] I. <found, found> *vt* 1. (*lost object, person*) trovare 2. (*locate*) trovare; to ~ support trovare appoggio; to ~ happiness with sb trovare la felicità con qu; to ~ oneself somewhere ritrovarsi da qualche parte; to be nowhere to be found non trovarsi da nessuna parte; to ~ no reason why ... non vedere alcun motivo per cui; to ~ (the) time trovare il tempo; to ~ excuses trovare scuse; to ~ the strength (to do sth) trovare la forza (di fare qc); to ~ (enough) money trovare (abbastanza) denaro 3. (*experience*) provare; to ~ oneself alone ritrovarsi da solo 4. (*conclude*) to ~ sb guilty/innocent riconoscere qu colpevole/innocente 5. (*discover*) scoprire II. *n* scoperta *f*
◆**find out** I. *vt* scoprire; (*dishonesty*) smascherare; to ~ when/where/who ... scoprire quando/dove/chi... II. *vi* to ~ about sth/sb informarsi su qc/qu

finder ['faɪn·dər] *n* (*of sth unknown*) scopritore, -trice *m, f;* (*of sth lost*) persona *f* che trova
finding ['faɪn·dɪŋ] *n* 1. LAW verdetto *m* 2. (*recommendation*) conclusione *f* 3. (*discovery*) ritrovamento *m*
fine¹ [faɪn] I. *adj* 1. (*slender, light*) sottile; (*feature*) delicato, -a; (*nuance*) sottile 2. (*clothes, words*) bello, -a; **a ~ man** una brava persona; **to be ~** andare bene; **~ weather** tempo *m* bello; **how are you? — I'm ~, thanks** come stai? — Bene, grazie; **to be ~ by sb** andare bene per qu; **that's all very ~, but ...** va bene, però... 3. (*excellent*) eccellente; **the ~st wines in the world** i vini più pregiati del mondo; **to have a ~ time doing sth** divertirsi a fare qc; **to appeal to sb's ~r feelings** fare appello ai migliori sentimenti di qu II. *adv* 1. (*all right*) bene; **to feel ~** sentirsi bene; **to work ~** funzionare bene 2. (*fine-grained*) fine
fine² [faɪn] I. *n* (*penalty*) multa *f* II. *vt* (*order to pay penalty*) multare
fine arts *n* belle arti *fpl*
fineness *n* (*lightness*) finezza *f;* (*delicacy, ornateness*) delicatezza *f*
finery ['faɪ·nə·ri] *n* **in all one's ~** tutto in ghingheri
finesse [fɪ·'nes] *n* 1. (*elegance*) finezza *f* 2. (*skill*) delicatezza *f*
fine-tooth comb [ˌfaɪn·tu:θ·'koʊm] *n* **to go through sth with a ~** analizzare qc nei minimi dettagli
finger ['fɪŋ·gər] I. *n* dito *m;* **little/middle ~** dito mignolo/medio ▶**to be able to be counted on the ~s of one hand** potersi contare sulla dita di una mano; **to have a ~ in every pie** avere le mani in pasta dappertutto; **to have one's ~ on the pulse** avere il polso della situazione; **to put one's ~ on the spot** mettere il dito nella piaga; **to catch sb with their ~s in the till** cogliere qu con le mani nel sacco; **to get/have one's ~s burned** scottarsi le dita *fig;* **to have sb wrapped around one's little ~** fare su qu come si vuole; **to keep one's ~s crossed** incrociare le dita; **to lay a ~ on sb** sfiorare qu con un dito; **to not lift a ~** non muovere un dito II. *vt* 1. (*touch*) palpare 2. *inf* (*reveal*) denunciare; **to ~ sb to the police** denunciare qu alla polizia
fingering ['fɪŋ·gə·rɪŋ] *n* diteggiatura *f*
finger mark ['fɪŋ·gər·mɑːrk] *n* ditata *f*
fingernail *n* unghia *f*
fingerprint I. *n* impronta *f* digitale II. *vt* **to ~ sb** prendere le impronte digitali di qu
fingertip *n* punta *f* del dito; **to have sth at one's ~s** avere qc a portata di mano; *fig* conoscere qc a menadito
finicky ['fɪ·nɪ·ki] *adj* 1. (*person*) schizzinoso, -a 2. (*job*) minuzioso, -a
finish ['fɪ·nɪʃ] I. *n* 1. (*end*) fine *f;* SPORTS finale *f;* **to be in at the ~** essere presente alla conclusione 2. (*sealing, varnishing: of fabric*) appretto *m;* (*of furniture*) finitura *f* II. *vi* finire, terminare; **to ~ doing sth** finire di fare qc; **to**

~ by saying that ... concludere dicendo che... III. *vt* 1. (*bring to end*) finire; **to ~ school** finire gli studi; **to ~ a sentence** finire una frase 2. (*make final touches to*) rifinire
◆**finish off** I. *vt* 1. (*end*) finire 2. (*defeat*) distruggere 3. *inf* (*murder*) finire II. *vi* finire
◆**finish up** I. *vi* **to ~ at** ritrovarsi a II. *vt* (*food, drink*) finire
◆**finish with** *vt* finire con; **to ~ sb** rompere con qu; **to ~ politics** chiudere con la politica
finished *adj* 1. (*product*) finito, -a 2. *inf* (*tired*) sfinito, -a
finishing line *n*, **finishing post** *n* (linea *f* del) traguardo *m*
finite ['faɪ·naɪt] *adj a.* LING finito, -a
Finland ['fɪn·lənd] *n* Finlandia *f*
Finn [fɪn] *n* finlandese *mf*
Finnish ['fɪ·nɪʃ] I. *adj* finlandese II. *n* finlandese *mf*
fiord [fjɔːrd] *n* fiordo *m*
fir [fɜːr] *n* abete *m*
pine cone *n* pigna *f*
fire ['fa·ɪə] I. *n* 1. (*flames*) fuoco *m;* (*in fireplace*) fuoco *f;* (*accidental*) incendio *m;* **to set sth on ~** dare fuoco a qc; **to catch ~** incendiarsi; **forest ~** incendio forestale 2. (*stove*) stufa *f* 3. MIL **to open ~ on sb** aprire il fuoco su qu; **to be under ~** MIL essere sotto il fuoco (nemico); *fig* essere sotto tiro 4. (*passion*) fuoco *m* ▶**there's no smoke without ~** *prov* non c'è fumo senza arrosto *prov;* **to go through ~ and water** farsi in quattro; **to set the world on ~** fare fuoco e fiamme; **to hang ~** attendere; **to play with ~** giocare col fuoco II. *vt* 1. (*burn*) incendiare; (*ceramics*) cucinare 2. (*weapon*) sparare; **to ~ questions at sb** bombardare qu di domande 3. *inf* (*dismiss*) licenziare 4. (*inspire*) accendere III. *vi* 1. (*with gun*) sparare; **to ~ at sb** sparare a qu 2. AUTO accendersi
◆**fire away** *vi inf* sparare
◆**fire off** *vt* (*letter, reply*) scrivere in tutta fretta
fire alarm *n* allarme *m* antincendio
firearm *n* arma *f* da fuoco
fireball *n* palla *f* di fuoco
firebrand *n* 1. (*torch*) tizzone *m* 2. *fig* agitatore, -trice *m, f*
firebreak *n* tagliafuoco *m inv*
firebrick *n* mattone *m* refrattario
firecracker *n* petardo *m*
fire department *n* vigili *m* del fuoco *pl*
fire-eater *n* mangiatore, -trice di fuoco *m*
fire engine *n* autopompa *f*
fire escape *n* scala *f* antincendio
fire exit *n* uscita *f* di sicurezza
fire extinguisher *n* estintore *m*
firefighter *n* vigile, -essa del fuoco *m*
firefly *n* lucciola *f*
fireguard *n* parafuoco *m*
fire house *n* caserma *f* dei vigili del fuoco
fire insurance *n* assicurazione *f* antincendio
fire irons *npl* accessori *m pl* per caminetto

F

fireman <-men> *n* vigile *m* del fuoco
fireplace *n* caminetto *m*
fireproof *adj* ignifugo, -a
fireside *n* focolare *m*
fire station *n* caserma *m* dei vigili del fuoco
firewall *n* parete *m* tagliafuoco
firewater *n* *inf* liquore *m* forte
firewoman <-women> *n* vigilessa *f* del fuoco
firewood *n* legna *f*
firework *n* 1. fuochi *m* d'artificio *pl* 2. *pl, fig* scoppio *m* d'ira
firing ['fa·ɪə·ɪŋ] *n* 1. MIL spari *mpl* 2. (*of ceramic*) cottura *f*
firing line *n* linea *f* del fuoco
firing squad *n* plotone *m* d'esecuzione
firm¹ [fɜːrm] I. *adj* 1. (*secure: ladder*) stabile; (*base*) saldo, -a; (*strong*) solido, -a; **a ~ offer** un'offerta definitiva 2. (*dense, solid*) sodo, -a 3. (*resolute*) fermo, -a 4. (*strict*) rigido, -a II. *adv* saldamente; **to stand ~** tener duro
firm² [fɜːrm] *n* (*company*) ditta *f*; **~ of lawyers** studio *m* legale
firmament ['fɜːr·mə·mənt] *n* firmamento *m*
firmness ['fɜːrm·nɪs] *n* 1. (*hardness*) durezza *f* 2. (*strictness*) fermezza *f*
first [fɜːrst] I. *adj* (*earliest*) primo, -a; **for the ~ time** per la prima volta; **at ~ sight** a prima vista; **the ~ of December/December ~** il primo dicembre ▸**~ and foremost** anzitutto II. *adv* per primo; (*firstly*) in primo luogo; **~ of all** prima di tutto; **at ~** all'inizio; **to go head ~** buttarsi a capofitto ▸**~ come ~ served** *inf* chi tardi arriva male alloggia III. *n* the ~ il/i primo,-i, la/le prima, -e; **from the (very) ~** fin dall'inizio
first aid *n* pronto soccorso *m*
first aid box *n* cassetta *f* del pronto soccorso
firstborn ['fɜːrst·bɔːrn] I. *adj* primogenito, -a II. *n* primogenito, -a *m, f*
first class I. *n* prima classe *f* II. *adv* **to travel ~** viaggiare in prima (classe)
first-class *adj* di prim'ordine
first cousin *n* cugino, -a di primo grado *m*
first floor *n* primo piano *m*
firsthand [ˌfɜːrst·'hænd] I. *adj* di prima mano II. *adv* in prima persona
first lady, First Lady *n* the ~ la first lady *f inv*
firstly ['fɜːrst·li] *adv* in primo luogo
first name *n* nome *m* (di battesimo)
first night *n* prima *f*
first offender *n* incensurato, -a *m, f*
first person *n* LING prima persona *f*
first-rate [ˌfɜːrst·'reɪt] *adj* di prim'ordine
first strike *n* primo colpo *m*
fiscal ['fɪs·kl] *adj* fiscale
fish [fɪʃ] *n* 1. ZOOL pesce *m* 2. CULIN pesce *m* ▸**to be a big ~ in a small pond** essere importante o potente solo perchè gli altri non sono validi avversari; **there are plenty more ~ in the sea** morto un papa se ne fa un altro; (**like**) **a ~ out of water** (come) un pesce fuor d'acqua; **to have bigger ~ to fry** avere cose più importanti da fare; **an odd ~**

un tipo strano II. *vi* pescare; **to ~ for information** andare a caccia di informazioni; **to ~ for compliments** andare in cerca di complimenti III. *vt* pescare
fishbone ['fɪʃ·boʊn] *n* lisca *f* di pesce
fishcake ['fɪʃ·keɪk] *n* polpetta *f* di pesce
fisherman ['fɪ·ʃə·mən] <-men> *n* pescatore *m*
fishery ['fɪ·ʃə·ri] *n* vivaio *m* di pesce
fishhook *n* amo *m*
fishing I. *n* pesca *f* II. *adj* da pesca
fishing grounds *npl* zona *f* di pesca
fishing line *n* lenza *f*
fishing rod *n*, **fishing pole** *n* canna *f* da pesca
fishing tackle *n* attrezzatura *f* da pesca
fishnet *n* rete *f* da pesca
fishpond ['fɪʃ·pɑːnd] *n* vasca *f* dei pesci
fish stick *n* bastoncino *m* di pesce
fishy ['fɪ·ʃi] <-ier, -iest> *adj* 1. (*taste, smell*) di pesce 2. *inf* (*dubious*) equivoco, -a ▸**to smell ~** puzzare
fissile ['fɪ·sɪl] *adj* fissile
fission ['fɪ·ʃən] *n* PHYS fissione *f*; BIO scissione *f*
fissure ['fɪ·ʃə·] *n* fessura *f*
fist [fɪst] *n* pugno *m*; **to clench one's ~s** stringere i pugni; **to shake one's ~ at sb** minacciare qu con un pugno
fit¹ [fɪt] I. <-tt-> *adj* 1. (*apt, competent*) adatto, -a; **~ to eat** buono, -a da mangiare; **it's not ~ to eat** non è commestibile 2. (*ready*) pronto, -a 3. SPORTS in forma 4. MED sano, -a ▸**to be ~ to be tied** essere fuori di sè II. <-tt-> *vt* 1. (*adapt*) adattare; **to ~ the key in the lock** mettere la chiave nella serratura 2. (*clothes*) andare bene a 3. (*facts*) corrispondere a 4. TECH entrare in III. *vi* <-tt-> 1. (*be correct size*) andare bene 2. (*correspond*) corrispondere IV. *n* (*of clothes*) **to be a good fit** stare a pennello; **to be a tight fit** stare stretto
◆**fit in** I. *vi* 1. (*conform*) adattarsi 2. (*get along well*) andare d'accordo II. *vt* trovare il tempo per
◆**fit out** *vt* attrezzare
◆**fit together** *vi* incastrarsi
◆**fit up** *vt* attrezzare
fit [fɪt] *n* 1. MED attacco *m*; **coughing ~** attacco *m* di tosse 2. *inf* (*outburst of rage*) scatto *m*; **they were in ~s of laughter** ridevano a crepapelle; **in ~s and starts** a sbalzi
fitful ['fɪt·fəl] *adj* (*breath, sleep*) irregolare; (*gusts*) intermittente
fitness ['fɪt·nɪs] *n* 1. (*good condition*) forma *f* fisica; (*health*) (buona) salute *f*; **physical ~** efficienza *f* fisica 2. (*competence, suitability*) idoneità *f*
fitted ['fɪ·tɪd] *adj* (*adapted, suitable*) idoneo, -a; (*tailor-made*) su misura
fitter ['fɪ·tə·] *n* installatore, -trice *m, f*
fitting ['fɪ·tɪŋ] I. *n* 1. *pl* (*fixtures*) arredi *mpl* 2. (*of clothes*) prova *f* II. *adj* appropriato, -a
five [faɪv] I. *adj* cinque II. *n* cinque *m*; **gimme ~!** *inf* dammi un cinque!; *s.a.* **eight**
fivefold *adj* quintuplo, -a
fiver ['faɪ·və·] *n* *inf* biglietto *m* da 5 dollari

fix [fɪks] I. *vt* 1. (*repair*) aggiustare 2. (*fasten*) fissare; **to ~ sth in one's mind** fissarsi qc nella mente; **to ~ one's eyes on sb** fissare gli occhi su qu 3. (*determine*) fissare; **to ~ a date** fissare una data 4. (*arrange*) sistemare; **to ~ one's face** *inf* aggiustarsi il trucco 5. *inf* (*lunch, dinner*) preparare 6. *inf* (*manipulate: election, result*) truccare 7. *inf* (*take revenge on*) fare i conti con; **I'll ~ him** lo aggiusto io 8. PHYS, PHOT (*color*) fissare II. *vi* **to be ~ing to do sth** stare per fare qc III. *n* 1. (*dilemma*) casino *m*; **to be in a ~** trovarsi nei casini 2. *inf* (*dose of heroin*) pera *f* 3. AVIAT, AUTO posizione *f*
◆**fix on** *vt* 1. (*choose*) scegliere 2. (*make definite*) fissare
◆**fix up** *vt* 1. (*supply with*) **to fix sb up** (**with sth**) procurare qc a qu 2. (*arrange a date*) **to fix sb up** (**with sb**) organizzare un combino (con qu) 3. (*arrange*) organizzare 4. (*repair*) aggiustare
fixation [fɪkˈseɪ·ʃən] *n* fissazione *f*
fixed *adj* fisso, -a; **to be of no ~ abode** LAW essere senza fissa dimora
fixedly [ˈfɪk·sɪd·li] *adv* fissamente
fixer *n inf* traffichino, -a *m, f*
fixity [ˈfɪk·sə·ti] *n form* fissità *f*
fixture [ˈfɪks·tʃɚ] *n* (*in bathroom and kitchen*) *impianti sanitari ed elettrici e infissi di una casa;* **light ~s** *lampadari e lampade a muro*
fizz [fɪz] I. *vi* frizzare II. *n* 1. (*bubble, frothiness*) effervescenza *f* 2. *inf* (*champagne*) champagne *m inv* 3. (*soda*) bibita *f* gassata
fizzle [ˈfɪ·zl] *vi* frizzare
fizzy [ˈfɪ·zi] <-ier, -iest> *adj* (*bubbly*) frizzante; (*carbonated*) gassato, -a
fjord [fjɔːrd] *n* fiordo *m*
flabbergast [ˈflæ·bɚ·gæst] *vt inf* **to be flabbergasted** restare a bocca aperta
flabby [ˈflæ·bi] <-ier, -iest> *adj pej* 1. (*body*) floscio, -a 2. (*weak*) fiacco, -a
flaccid [ˈflæ·sɪd] *adj* flaccido, -a; *fig* fiacco, -a
flag[1] [flæg] I. *n* 1. (*national*) bandiera *f*; (*pennant*) stendardo *m*; **to raise a ~** issare una bandiera; **to fly the ~ for one's country** *fig* difendere i colori del proprio paese; **to keep the ~ flying** *fig* tenere alta la bandiera 2. (*marker*) bandierina *f* II. <-gg-> *vt* (*mark*) mettere un segno su; (*label computer data*) mettere un flag III. <-gg-> *vi* affievolirsi
flag[2] [flæg] *n* (*stone*) lastra *f* di pietra
Flag Day *n* giorno *m* della bandiera, *il 14 giugno, giorno in cui negli Stati Uniti si celebrano la bandiera nazionale e i suoi creatori*

---

i Il **Flag Day** è la commemorazione del 14 giugno 1777, data in cui il *Continental Congress* ha dichiarato la *Stars and Stripes* bandiera nazionale. Non si tratta però di un giorno festivo nazionale. Gli americani considerano la bandiera il simbolo più importante del loro paese.

---

flagellate [ˈflæ·dʒə·leɪt] *vt* flagellare
flagon [ˈflæ·gən] *n* brocca *f*
flagpole [ˈflæg·poʊl] *n* asta *f* della bandiera
flagrant [ˈfleɪ·grənt] *adj* flagrante
flagship [ˈflæg·ʃɪp] *n* nave *f* ammiraglia
flagstaff [ˈflæg·stæf] *n s.* flagpole
flail [fleɪl] I. *vt* 1. (*horse*) frustare 2. **to ~ one's arms** agitare le braccia II. *vi* (*arms*) agitare
flair [fler] *n* 1. (*genius*) talento *m*; **to have a ~ for sth** avere una particolare predisposizione per qc 2. (*style*) stile *m*
flak [flæk] *n* 1. MIL fuoco *m* antiaereo 2. (*criticism*) critiche *fpl*; **to give sb ~** criticare qu
flake [fleɪk] I. *vi* (*skin*) squamarsi; (*paint, plaster, wood*) sfaldarsi II. *n* (*shaving, sliver*) truciolo *m*; (*of paint, plaster*) scaglia *f*; (*of wood*) scheggia *f*; (*of skin*) squama *f*; (*of snow*) fiocco *m*
◆**flake out** *vi inf* crollare per la stanchezza
flaky [ˈfleɪ·ki] <-ier, -iest> *adj* 1. (*skin*) squamoso, -a; (*paint*) scrostato, -a 2. *inf* (*strange*) strambo, -a
flaky pastry *n* pasta *f* sfoglia
flamboyant [flæmˈbɔ·ɪənt] *adj* (*manner, person*) stravagante; (*air, clothes*) vistoso, -a
flame [fleɪm] I. *n* 1. fiamma *f*; **to be in ~s** essere in fiamme; **to go up in ~s** andare in fiamme; **to burst into ~** prendere fuoco 2. (*lover*) (*old*) ~ (vecchia) fiamma *f* II. *vi* (*blaze, burn*) ardere; (*glare*) risplendere
flaming [ˈfleɪ·mɪŋ] *adj* 1. (*burning*) in fiamme 2. *fig* (*quarrel*) acceso, -a 3. *inf* (*as intensifier*) totale
flamingo [fləˈmɪŋ·goʊ] <-(e)s> *n* fenicottero *m*
flammable [ˈflæ·məbl] *adj* infiammabile
flan [flæn] *n* torta *f*, di frutta, vedura o formaggio
Flanders [ˈflæn·dɚz] *n* Fiandre *fpl*
flange [flændʒ] *n* flangia *f*
flank [flæŋk] I. *n a.* MIL fianco *m*; (*of animal*) lombata *f* II. *vt* fiancheggiare
flannel [ˈflæ·nl] *n* 1. (*material*) flanella *f* 2. *pl* (*trousers*) pantaloni *m pl* di flanella
flap [flæp] I. <-pp-> *vt* (*wings*) battere; (*shake*) agitare II. <-pp-> *vi* 1. (*wings*) battere; (*sails*) sbattere; (*flag*) sventolare 2. *inf* (*become nervous*) agitarsi; **don't ~!** stai calmo! III. *n* 1. (*of skin*) lembo *m*; (*of pocket*) patta *f*; (*of envelope*) linguetta *f*; (*of table*) ribalta *f* 2. AVIAT flap *m inv* 3. (*of wing*) battito *m* 4. *inf* (*commotion*) agitazione *f*; **to cause a ~** creare un po' di trambusto
flapjack [ˈflæp·dʒæk] *n* (*pancake*) *frittella dolce o salata servita con marmellata, sciroppo d'acero o salse*
flare [fler] I. *n* 1. (*blaze*) fiammata *f*; (*of light*) chiarore *m* 2. (*signal*) razzo *m* di segnalazione 3. MIL bengala *m inv* 4. (*of clothes*) svasatura *f* II. *vi* 1. (*blaze*) bruciare; (*light*) brillare 2. (*trouble*) scoppiare 3. (*skirt*) essere svasato III. *vt* **to ~ one's nostrils** dilatare le narici
flare-up *n fig* (*anger*) scoppio *m* d'ira

flash [flæʃ] I. *vt* **1.** (*shine: light*) far lampeggiare; **to ~ a light in sb's eyes** puntare una luce sugli occhi di qu **2.** (*show quickly*) mostrare velocemente; **to ~ sth on the screen** proiettare qc sullo schermo molto rapidamente **3.** (*communicate*) trasmettere velocemente; (*smile, look*) lanciare II. *vi* **1.** (*lightning*) lampeggiare; *fig* (*eyes*) brillare **2.** *inf* (*expose genitals*) fare esibizionismo **3.** (*move swiftly*) **to ~ by** (*car*) passare a gran velocità; (*time*) volare III. *n* **1.** (*burst*) lampo *m;* **~ of inspiration** momento *m* di ispirazione; **~ of lightning** lampo *m;* **~ of light** lampo di luce **2.** PHOT flash *m* ▶ **a ~ in the pan** un fuoco di paglia; **like a ~** come un lampo; **in a ~** in un baleno IV. <-er, -est> *adj inf* vistoso, -a
♦**flash back** *vi* ritornare

flashback ['flæʃ·bæk] *n* CINE, LIT, THEAT flashback *m inv*

flashbulb ['flæʃ·bʌlb] *n* lampadina *f* per il flash

flasher ['flæ·ʃə] *n inf* esibizionista *m*

flashgun ['flæʃ·gʌn] *n* flash *m inv*

flashlight ['flæʃ·laɪt] *n* torcia *f* (elettrica)

flash point *n* **1.** CHEM punto *m* di infiammabilità **2.** *fig* punto *m* critico

flashy ['flæ·ʃi] <-ier, -iest> *adj inf* vistoso, -a

flask [flæsk] *n* CHEM beuta *f;* (*thermos*) termos *m inv;* **hip ~** fiaschetta *f*

flat¹ [flæt] I. *adj* <-tt-> **1.** (*surface*) piatto, -a; (*land*) pianeggiante; **~ as a pancake** *inf* piatto come una frittata **2.** (*unexciting*) piatto, -a **3.** (*drink*) sgasato, -a **4.** (*tire*) a terra **5.** (*absolute: refusal, rejection*) categorico, -a; **and that's ~** e non se ne parli più **6.** COM (*not changing*) fisso, -a **7.** MUS (*note*) bemolle; (*string*) scordato, -a II. <-tt-> *adv* **1.** (*level*) lungo disteso; **to lie ~ on one's back** stare a pancia in su **2.** *inf* (*absolutely*) completamente ▶ **to be ~ broke** essere completamente al verde; **to fall ~** essere un fiasco; **in five minutes ~** *inf* in cinque minuti esatti III. *n* **1.** (*level surface: of sword, knife*) piatto *m;* **the ~ of one's hand** il palmo *m* della mano **2.** (*low level ground*) pianura *f;* **salt ~s** saline *fpl* **3.** (*flat tire*) foratura *f* **4.** MUS bemolle *m inv*

flat² [flæt] *n* (*apartment*) appartamento *m*

flat feet *npl* piedi *m pl* piatti

flatfish ['flæt·fɪʃ] <-(es)> *n* pesce *m* piatto

flat-footed [‚flæt·'fʊ·tɪd] *adj* con i piedi piatti

flatly *adv* (*deny, refuse*) categoricamente

flatness *n* piattezza *f*

flatten ['flæ·tn] *vt* **1.** (*make level*) appiattire; **to ~ oneself against sth** appiattirsi contro qc **2.** MUS abbassare di un tono

flatter ['flæ·tə] *vt* **1.** (*gratify vanity*) adulare **2.** (*make attractive*) donare **3.** (*be proud of*) **to ~ oneself on sth** andare orgoglioso di qc

flatterer *n* adulatore, -trice *m, f*

flattering *adj* **1.** (*clothes, portrait*) che dona [*o* donano] **2.** (*remark, description*) lusinghiero, -a

flattery ['flæ·tə·ri] *n* adulazione *f;* **~ will get you nowhere** con l'adulazione non otterrai nulla

flatulence ['flæ·tʃə·ləns] *n form* flatulenza *f*

flaunt [flɑːnt] *vt* ostentare

flautist ['flɑː·tɪst] *n* flautista *mf*

flavor ['fleɪ·və] I. *n* **1.** (*taste*) sapore *m;* (*ice cream, fizzy drink*) gusto *m* **2.** *fig* sapore *m;* **a novel with a romantic ~** un romanzo dal sapore romantico II. *vt* insaporire

flavoring ['fleɪ·və·ɪŋ] *n* aroma *m;* (*in industry*) aromatizzante *m*

flaw [flɑː] I. *n* (*in machine, cloth, character*) difetto *m;* (*in argument*) errore *m* II. *vt* guastare

flawless ['flɑː·lɪs] *adj* perfetto, -a; **~ performance** esecuzione *f* impeccabile

flax [flæks] *n* lino *m*

flaxen ['flæk·sn] *adj liter* biondo chiaro *inv*

flay [fleɪ] *vt* **1.** (*animal*) scuoiare **2.** *fig* stroncare

flea [fliː] *n* pulce *f* ▶ **to send sb away with a ~ in his/her ear** mandare via qu in malo modo

fleabite ['fliː·baɪt] *n* morso *m* di pulce

flea-bitten *adj inf* pidocchioso, -a

flea market *n* mercato *m* delle pulci

fleck [flek] I. *n* (*of color*) macchiolina *f;* (*of paint*) schizzo *m* II. *vt* chiazzare

fled [fled] *pp of* **flee**

fledged [fledʒd] *adj* coperto, -a di piume

fledgeling, fledgling ['fledʒ·lɪŋ] I. *n* (*young bird*) uccellino *m* II. *adj* (*inexperienced*) alle prime armi

flee [fliː] <fled> I. *vt* (*run away from*) fuggire da II. *vi* (*run away*) fuggire; *liter* svanire

fleece [fliːs] I. *n* **1.** (*of sheep*) vello *m* **2.** (*clothing*) pile *m inv* II. *vt* **1.** (*a sheep*) tosare **2.** *inf* (*cheat*) spellare

fleet¹ [fliːt] *n* **1.** NAUT flotta *f* **2.** (*of airplanes*) flotta *f* aerea; **car ~** parco *m* macchine

fleet² [fliːt] <-er, -est> *adj* (*quick*) veloce

fleeting ['fliː·tɪŋ] *adj* fugace; (*visit*) breve

Flemish ['fle·mɪʃ] *adj* fiammingo, -a

flesh [fleʃ] *n* (*body tissue*) carne *f;* (*pulp*) polpa *f;* **to put ~ on an argument/idea** dar corpo ad un ragionamento/un'idea ▶ **to be (only) ~ and blood** essere fatto di carne ed ossa; **it made my ~ crawl** mi ha fatto accapponare la pelle; **in the ~** in carne ed ossa

skin-colored *adj* color carne

fleshpot ['fleʃ·pɑːt] *n* luogo *m* di perdizione

flesh wound *n* ferita *f* superficiale

fleshy ['fle·ʃi] <-ier, -iest> *adj* (*voluminous: person*) in carne; (*fruit*) carnoso, -a

flew [fluː] *pp, pt of* **fly**

flex [fleks] I. *vt* flettere ▶ **to ~ one's muscles** mostrare i muscoli II. *n* ELEC flessibile *m*

flexibility [‚flek·sə·'bɪ·lə·ti] *n* **1.** (*of material*) flessibilità *f* **2.** (*of person, approach*) flessibilità *f*

flexible ['flek·sə·bl] *adj* flessibile

flextime ['fleks·taɪm] *n* orario *m* flessibile

flick [flɪk] I. *vt* (*with finger*) lanciare con le dita; **to ~ out one's tongue** tirare fuori la lingua; **to ~ the light switch on/off** accendere/spegnere la luce; **to ~ channels** fare zapping **II.** *n* **1.** (*sudden movement, strike*) colpetto *m* **2.** *inf* (*movie*) film *m inv;* **the ~s** (*cinema*) il cinema *m*

flicker [ˈflɪ·kə˕] **I.** *vi* tremolare **II.** *n* tremolio *m*

switchblade *n* coltello *m* a serramanico

flier [ˈflaˑɪ˕] *n* **1.** (*leaflet*) volantino *m* **2.** (*in airplane*) aviatore, -trice *m, f*

flight [flaɪt] *n* **1.** (*movement through air*) volo *m;* **the ~ of time** il passare del tempo **2.** (*group: of birds, of aircrafts*) stormo *m* **3.** (*retreat*) fuga *f;* **~ of investment** fuga *f* degli investimenti; **to take ~** darsi alla fuga; **to put sb to ~** mettere qu in fuga **4.** (*series: of stairs*) rampa *f* ▸**a ~ of fancy** un volo della fantasia

flight attendant *n* assistente *mf* di volo

flight controller *n* controllore *m* di volo

flight deck *n* **1.** (*cockpit*) cabina *f* di pilotaggio **2.** (*on aircraft carrier*) ponte *m* di volo

flight engineer *n* tecnico *m* di volo

flightless *adj* che non sa volare

flight number *n* numero *m* di volo

flight path *n* traiettoria *f* di volo

flight recorder *n* scatola *f* nera, registratore *m* di volo

flighty [ˈflaɪ·t̬i] <-ier, -iest> *adj pej* (*woman*) irresponsabile

flimsiness [ˈflɪm·zɪ·nɪs] *n* **1.** (*of dress*) leggerezza *f* **2.** (*of construction*) fragilità *f* **3.** (*of argument, excuse*) debolezza *f*

flimsy [ˈflɪm·zi] <-ier, -iest> *adj* **1.** (*light: dress, blouse*) leggero, -a **2.** (*construction*) fragile **3.** (*argument, excuse*) debole

flinch [flɪntʃ] *vi* (*from pain*) sobbalzare; **to ~ from sth** tirarsi indietro davanti a qc; **to ~ from doing sth** tirarsi indietro quando si tratta di fare qc

fling [flɪŋ] <flung> **I.** *vt* (*throw*) lanciare; **to ~ oneself in front of a train** lanciarsi contro un treno; **to ~ sb into prison** gettare qu in prigione; **to ~ accusations at sb** lanciare accuse contro qu **II.** *n inf* **1.** (*short pleasant time*) **to have a ~** spassarsela per un po' *m* **2.** (*relationship*) avventura *f* **3.** (*try*) **to have a ~ at sth** provare qc

◆**fling away** *vt* gettare via

◆**fling off** *vt* **to ~ one's clothes** spogliarsi in tutta fretta

◆**fling on** *vt inf* **to ~ one's clothes** vestirsi in tutta fretta

◆**fling open** *vt* spalancare

◆**fling out** *vt inf* (*throw out*) gettare via

flint [flɪnt] *n* (*for tools*) selce *f;* (*in lighter*) pietrina *f*

flip [flɪp] <-pp-> **I.** *vt* (*pancake*) rigirare; (*pages*) sfogliare; **to ~ a coin** fare a testa e croce ▸**to ~ one's lid** andare fuori dai gangheri **II.** *vi* **1.** **to ~ over** (*car*) ribaltarsi **2.** *inf* (*go crazy*) perdere la testa **III.** *n* (*toss in the air*) **~ of a coin** lancio *m* di una moneta

flip chart *n* lavagna *f* a fogli mobili

flip-flop [ˈflɪp·flɑːp] *n* infradito *m inv*

flippancy [ˈflɪ·pənt·si] *n* frivolezza *f*

flippant [ˈflɪ·pənt] *adj* (*attitude*) irriverente; (*remark*) spiritoso, -a

flipper [ˈflɪ·pə˕] *n* pinna *f*

flip side *n* **1.** MUS (*of record*) lato *m* B **2.** (*of policy, situation*) **the ~** l'altra faccia *f*

flirt [flɜːrt] **I.** *n* (*woman*) civetta *f;* (*man*) farfallone *m* **II.** *vi* **1.** (*be sexually attracted*) flirtare **2.** (*toy with*) **to ~ with sth** giocare con qc

flirtation [flɜːr·ˈteɪ·ʃən] *n* (*love affair*) flirt *m inv*

flirtatious [flɜːr·ˈteɪ·ʃəs] *adj* (*woman*) civettuolo, -a; (*man*) donnaiolo, -a

flit [flɪt] <-tt-> *vi* **to ~** (**around**) (*bats, bees*) svolazzare; (*people*) muoversi

float [floʊt] **I.** *vi* **1.** (*in liquid*) galleggiare; (*air*) fluttuare; **to ~ to the surface** venire a galla **2.** (*move aimlessly*) ciondolare **3.** ECON fluttuare **II.** *vt* **1.** (*keep afloat*) far galleggiare **2.** ECON, FIN **to ~ a business/company** quotare in borsa un'azienda/una società **3.** (*suggest*) **to ~ an idea/a plan** lanciare una idea/un piano **III.** *n* **1.** NAUT galleggiante *m;* (*for people*) salvagente *m inv* **2.** (*vehicle*) carro *m*

◆**float around** *vi inf* (*people*) bighellonare; (*rumor*) circolare

◆**float off** *vi* andare alla deriva

floatation [floʊ·ˈteɪ·ʃən] *n s.* **flotation**

floating [ˈfloʊ·t̬ɪŋ] *adj* (*interest rate*) variabile; (*bridge*) galleggiante

flock [flɑːk] **I.** *n* **1.** (*group: of goats, sheep*) gregge *m;* (*of birds*) stormo *m;* (*of people*) stuolo *m* **2.** REL congregazione *f* **II.** *vi* affluire; **people ~ to the mall at Christmas** a Natale il centro commerciale è stato preso d'assalto

floe [floʊ] *n* banchisa *f*

flog [flɑːg] <-gg-> *vt* **1.** (*punish*) frustare; *fig* flagellare **2.** *inf* (*sell*) rifilare ▸**to ~ sth to death** *inf* ripetere sempre la stessa cosa

flogging *n* fustigazione *f*

flood [flʌd] **I.** *vt* inondare; **the calls for tickets ~ed the switchboard** il centralino è stato sommerso di chiamate per i biglietti; **to ~ an engine** AUTO ingolfare un motore **II.** *vi* METEO (*town*) allagarsi; (*river*) esondare; *fig;* **refugees have been ~ing in** i rifugiati sono affluiti in massa **III.** *n* **1.** METEO inondazione *f* **2.** REL **the Flood** il diluvio *m* universale **3.** *fig* (*outpouring*) marea *f;* **~ of tears** mare *m* di lacrime; **~ of products/complaints** valanga *f* di prodotti/di reclami; **~ of abuse** valanga *f* di insulti; **to let out a ~ of abuse** coprire di insulti

floodgate [ˈflʌd·geɪt] *n fig* **to open the ~s to sth** aprire le porte a qc

floodlight [ˈflʌd·laɪt] **I.** *n* riflettore *m* **II.** *vt irr* illuminare con i riflettori

floor [flɔːr] **I.** *n* **1.** (*of room*) pavimento *m;* **dance ~** pista *f* da ballo; **to take the ~** (*in debate*) prendere la parola; (*start dancing*) scendere in pista **2.** (*level in building*) piano *m;* **first ~** (*floor on ground level*) piano terra; **sea ~** fondo *m* del mare **3.** FIN (*lowest limit*) livello *m* minimo ▸to **wipe** the ~ with sb (*defeat*) annientare qu; **to go through** the ~ (*prices*) crollare **II.** *vt* (*knock down*) stendere; **the question** ~**ed her** la domanda l'ha spiazzata

floorboard ['flɔr·bɔːrd] *n* trave *f* di legno, *del pavimento*

flooring *n* pavimentazione *f*; **wooden** ~ pavimentazione in legno

floor lamp *n* lampada *f* a stelo

floor polish *n* cera *f* per pavimenti

floorshow *n* spettacolo *m* di varietà

floorwalker *n* capo *m* reparto

flop [flɑːp] <-pp-> **I.** *vi* **1.** (*on bed, chair*) buttarsi **2.** *inf* (*fail*) fare fiasco **II.** *n inf* (*failure*) fiasco *m*

floppy ['flɑː·pi] **I.** <-ier, -iest> *adj* (*ears*) cadente; (*hat*) floscio, -a **II.** <-ies> *n* dischetto *m*

floppy disk *n* dischetto *m*

flora ['flɔː·rə] *n* flora *f*; ~ **and fauna** flora e fauna

floral ['flɔː·rəl] *adj* floreale

florid ['flɔː·rɪd] *adj* **1.** (*style, prose, rhetoric*) ornato, -a **2.** *form* (*ruddy*) rubicondo, -a

Florida ['flɔː·rɪ·də] *n* Florida *f*

florist ['flɔː·rɪst] *n* fioraio, -a *m, f*; **the ~'s** il fioraio

flotation [floʊ·'teɪ·ʃən] *n* ECON, FIN (*of shares*) emissione *m*

flotilla [floʊ·'tɪ·lə] *n* MIL, NAUT flottiglia *f*

flotsam ['flɑːt·səm] *n* relitti *mpl*, *galleggianti o arenati*; ~ **and jetsam** (*people*) relitti *m* umani *pl*

flounce¹ [flaʊnts] *vi* (*in lively manner*) **to** ~ **around** dimenarsi; (*emotionally*); **to** ~ **in/out** entrare/uscire nervosamente

flounce² [flaʊnts] *n* (*decoration*) balza *f*

flounder¹ ['flaʊn·dɚ] *vi* **1.** (*in mud, water*) annaspare **2.** (*economy, firm*) annaspare **3.** (*while speaking*) impappinarsi

flounder² ['flaʊn·dɚ] *n* (*flatfish*) passera *f* di mare

flour ['flaʊ·ɚ] **I.** *n* farina *f* **II.** *vt* infarinare

flourish ['flɜː·rɪʃ] **I.** *vi* (*business, trade*) fiorire; (*plant*) crescere rigoglioso, -a **II.** *vt* agitare **III.** *n* **with a** ~ con un gesto cerimonioso

flourishing *adj* (*garden, plant*) rigoglioso, -a; (*business, market, trade*) fiorente

flour mill *n* mulino *m*

floury ['flaʊ·ə·ri] <-ier, -iest> *adj* (*hands*) infarinato, -a; (*like flour*) farinoso, -a

flout [flaʊt] *vt* **to** ~ **a law/rule** violare una legge/regola; **to** ~ **tradition** sfidare la tradizione

flow [floʊ] **I.** *vi* fluire, scorrere **II.** *n* (*of water, ideas, goods*) flusso *m*; **to cut the** ~ **of oil/water** interrompere le forniture *f* di petrolio/acqua ▸**in full** ~ nel bel mezzo di un discorso; **to go against** the ~ andare contro corrente; **to go with** the ~ seguire la corrente

flowchart *n*, **flow diagram** *n* diagramma *m* di

flusso

flower ['fla·ʊ·ɚ] **I.** *n* **1.** (*plant, bloom*) fiore *m*; **to be in** ~ essere in fiore **2.** *liter* (*best*) **the** ~ il fior fiore **II.** *vi* fiorire

flower arrangement *n* composizione *f* floreale

flowerbed *n* aiuola *f*

flower garden *n* giardino *m* ornamentale

flower girl *n la damigella che porta i fiori in una cerimonia nuziale*

flowerpot *n* vaso *f* (da fiori)

flowery ['fla·ʊ·ə·ri] <-ier, -iest> *adj* **1.** (*material*) a fiori **2.** (*style, language*) fiorito, -a

flowing *adj* (*hair*) fluente; (*robes*) morbido, -a

flown [floʊn] *pp of* **fly¹**

flu [fluː] *n* influenza *f*

fluctuate ['flʌk·tʃʊ·eɪt] *vi* fluttuare

fluctuation [ˌflʌk·tʃʊ·'eɪ·ʃən] *n* fluttuazione *f*

flue [fluː] *n* canna *f* fumaria

fluency ['fluː·ənt·si] *n* scioltezza *f*

fluent ['fluː·ənt] *adj* (*style*) scorrevole; (*movement*) sciolto, -a; **to speak** ~ **English** paralare l'inglese correntemente

fluff [flʌf] **I.** *n* **1.** (*on young animals*) peluria *f*; (*dust*) laniccio *m* **2.** (*unimportant matter*) banalità *f* **II.** *vt* **I.to** ~ (**up**) **a pillow** scuotere un cuscino **2.** *inf* (*exam*) andare male in; (*line*) sbagliare

fluffy ['flʌ·fi] <-ier, -iest> *adj* (*furry: animal*) morbido, -a; (*toy*) di peluche; (*clothes*) soffice; CULIN (*light*) spumoso, -a

fluid ['fluː·ɪd] **I.** *n* liquido *m* **II.** *adj* **1.** (*liquid*) liquido, -a **2.** (*situation*) fluido, -a

fluid ounce *n* oncia *f* fluida, *unità di capacità di misura equivalente a 29,57 millilitri*

flung [flʌŋ] *pp, pt of* **fling**

flunk [flʌŋk] *vt inf* (*student*) segare; (*math, history*) cannare

fluorescence [flɔː·'re·sns] *n* fluorescenza *f*

fluorescent [flɔː·'re·snt] *adj* fluorescente; ~ **tube** tubo *m* fluorescente

fluoride ['flɔː·raɪd] *n* fluoruro *m*

fluorine ['flɔː·riːn] *n* fluoro *m*

fluorocarbon [ˌflɔː·rə·'kɑːr·bən] *n* fluorocarburo *m*

flurry ['flɜː·ri] <-ies> *n* (*of snow*) spruzzata *f*; (*of wind*) folata *f*; **a** ~ **of excitement** un leggero trambusto *m*; **a** ~ **of speculation** un'ondata *f* di speculazioni

flush¹ [flʌʃ] **I.** *vi* (*blush*) arrossire **II.** *vt* **to** ~ **the toilet** tirare l'acqua **III.** *n* **1.** (*blush*) rossore *m*; ~ **of anger** accesso *m* di rabbia **2.** (*toilet*) sciacquone *m*

◆**flush out** *vt* stanare

flush [flʌʃ] *adj* **1.** (*level*) ben allineato, -a **2.** *inf* (*rich*) **to be** ~ **with money** essere pieno di soldi

flushed [flʌʃt] *adj* arrossato, -a; ~ **with anger** rosso, -a per la rabbia; ~ **with joy** raggiante di gioia; ~ **with success** emozionato, -a per il successo

fluster ['flʌs·tɚ] **I.** *vt* **to** ~ **sb** fare agitare qu **II.** *n* **to be in a** ~ essere agitato, -a

flute [fluːt] *n* MUS flauto *m*
fluting *n* scanalatura *f*
flutist [ˈfluːˌtɪst] *n s.* **flautist**
flutter [ˈflʌˌtə] I. *n* 1.(*of wings*) battito *m* 2.*fig* (*nervousness*) agitazione *f;* **to put sb in a ~** fare agitare qu; **to be all in a ~** essere tutto agitato II. *vi* 1.(*quiver*) tremare; **to make hearts ~** *fig* far battere il cuore 2.(*flag*) sventolare; (*leaves*) volteggiare III. *vt* (*wings, eyeleshes*) sbattere; **to ~ one's eyelashes** *fig* fare gli occhi dolci
fluvial [ˈfluːˌviˌəl] *adj* fluviale
flux [flʌks] *n* 1.(*change*) cambiamento *m* continuo; **to be in a state of ~** essere soggetto a frequenti mutamenti 2. MED flusso *m*
fly¹ [flaɪ] <flew, flown> I. *vi* 1.(*bird, airplane*) volare 2.(*travel by aircraft*) volare; **to ~ to New York** andare a new York in aereo 3.(*move rapidly*) precipitarsi; **to ~ at sb** lanciarsi su qu 4. *inf* (*leave*) scappare ▶ **to ~ high** (*very happy*) essere al settimo cielo II. *vt* 1.(*aircraft*) pilotare 2.(*make move through air*) far volare; **to ~ a flag** sventolare una bandiera; **to ~ a kite** far volare un aquilone
◆**fly away** *vi* volare via
◆**fly in** *vi* **to ~ from somewhere** arrivare (in aereo) da qualche parte
◆**fly off** *vi* volare via
fly [flaɪ] *n* (*insect*) mosca *f* ▶ **he wouldn't harm a ~** non farebbe del male a una mosca; **to drop** (**off**) [*o* **die**] **like flies** *inf* cadere come le mosche; **the only ~ in the ointment** l'unico neo
flyaway [ˈflaɪˌəˌweɪ] *adj* (*hair*) ribelle
fly-by-night [ˈflaɪˌbaɪˌnaɪt] *adj inf* poco serio, -a
flycatcher [ˈflaɪˌkætˌʃə] *n* pigliamosche *m*
flyer [ˈflaɪə] *n* 1.(*leaflet*) volantino *m* 2.(*airplane pilot*) aviatore, -trice *m, f*
flying [ˈflaɪɪŋ] I. *n* volare II. *adj* **to pass an exam with ~ colors** superare un esame brillantemente
flying boat *n* idrovolante *m* a scafo
flying fish *n* pesce *m* volante
flying fox *n* rossetta *f*
flying saucer *n* disco *m* volante
flying start *n* SPORTS partenza *f* lanciata; **to get off to a ~** partire bene
flying time *n* durata *f* del volo
flyleaf [ˈflaɪˌliːf] <flyleaves> *n* risguardo *m*
flyover [ˈflaɪˌoʊˌvə] *n* (*bridge*) cavalcavia *m*
flypaper [ˈflaɪˌpeɪˌpə] *n* carta *f* moschicida
flyby *n* ASTRON flyby *m inv, passaggio di un veicolo spaziale vicino a un corpo terrestre*
flysheet *n* doppio telo *m, di una tenda da campeggio*
fly swatter *n* acchiappamosche *m inv*
flytrap *n* trappola *f* per mosche
flyweight [ˈflaɪˌweɪt] *n* SPORTS peso *m* mosca
flywheel [ˈflaɪˌhwiːl] *n* TECH volano *m*
FM [ˌefˈem] PHYS *abbr of* **frequency modulation** FM
foal [foʊl] I. *n* puledro, -a *m, f;* **to be in ~**

essere gravida II. *vi* partorire
foam [foʊm] I. *n* (*bubbles, foam rubber*) schiuma *f* II. *vi* **to ~ with rage** schiumare di rabbia
foam rubber *n* gommapiuma *f inv*
foamy [ˈfoʊˌmi] <-ier, -iest> *adj* (*shampoo, washing-up liquid*) schiumoso, -a; (*sea*) spumeggiante
focal [ˈfoʊˌkl] *adj* centrale; **~ point** punto *m* focale
focus [ˈfoʊˌkəs] <-es *o* foci> I. *n* 1.fuoco *m;* **to be in/out of ~** essere a fuoco/sfocato, -a 2.(*center*) centro *m;* **~ of interest** centro d'interesse; **the ~ of a program** il fulcro di un programma; **to bring sth into ~** *fig* mettere qc a fuoco II. <-s- *o* -ss-> *vi* mettere a fuoco; **to ~ on sth** (*concentrate*) focalizzare qc III. *vt* focalizzare; **to ~ one's attention on sth** focalizzare la propria attenzione su qc
fodder [ˈfɑːˌdə] *n* 1.(*animal food*) foraggio *m;* **~ crop** foraggio *m* 2.*fig, inf* materiale *m*
foe [foʊ] *n* nemico, -a *m, f*
fog [fɑːɡ] *n* nebbia *f;* **to be in a ~** *fig* essere confuso
◆**fog up** *vi* (*glasses, window*) appannarsi
fog bank *n* banco *m* di nebbia
fogbound [ˈfɑːɡˌbaʊnd] *adj* bloccato, -a dalla nebbia
fogey [ˈfoʊˌɡi] <-ies> *n pej, inf s.* **fogy**
foggy [ˈfɑːˌɡi] <-ier, -iest> *adj* (*weather*) nebbioso, -a; (*memory*) vago, -a ▶ **to not have the foggiest** (**idea**) non avere la più pallida idea
foghorn [ˈfɑːɡˌhɔːrn] *n* sirena *f* da nebbia; **to have a voice like a ~** avere un vocione
fog light *n* faro *m* antinebbia
fogy [ˈfoʊˌɡi] <-ies> *n pej, inf* parruccone, -a *m, f*
foible [ˈfɔɪˌbl] *n* (*weakness*) debolezza *f;* (*habit*) mania *f*
foil¹ [fɔɪl] *n* 1.(*metal sheet*) carta *f* d'alluminio 2.(*sword*) fioretto *m* 3.*fig* **to act as a ~ to sth** mettere in risalto qc
foil² [fɔɪl] *vt* (*cause to fail*) sventare
foist (**up**)**on** [ˌfɔɪstˌ(ə)ˈpɑːn] *vt* **to foist sth** (**up**)**on sb** (*values*) imporre qc a qn; (*old apples*) rifilare qc a qu
fold¹ [foʊld] I. *vt* 1.(*bend*) piegare; **to ~ sth back/down** ripiegare qc 2.(*wrap*) **to ~ sth** (**in sth**) avvolgere qc (in qc) II. *vi* 1.(*chair, table*) ripiegarsi 2.(*fail, go bankrupt*) chiudere i battenti III. *n* (*crease*) piega *f*
◆**fold up** *vt* piegare
fold [foʊld] *n* (*sheep pen*) ovile *m;* **to return to the ~** *fig* tornare all'ovile
folder [ˈfoʊlˌdə] *n a.* COMPUT cartella *f*
folding [ˈfoʊlˌdɪŋ] *adj* pieghevole; **~ door** porta *f* pieghevole; **~ money** soldi *m pl* di carta
foliage [ˈfoʊˌliˌɪdʒ] *n* fogliame *m*
folio [ˈfoʊˌliˌoʊ] *n* libro *m* in folio
folk [foʊk] *n* 1. *pl* gente *f;* **farming ~** agricoltori *mpl;* **the old ~** i vecchi *pl;* **ordinary ~** gente comune; (**~ memory**) memoria *f* collettiva; **~ wisdom** saggezza *f* popolare 2. *pl* (*par-*

ents) genitori *mpl*

folk dance *n* danza *f* popolare

folklore ['foʊk·lɔːr] *n* folklore *m*

folk music *n* musica *f* folk

folk song *n* canzone *f* popolare

folksy ['foʊk·si] <-ier, -iest> *adj* (*friendly*) alla buona

folktale *n* racconto *m* popolare

follow ['fɑ·loʊ] I. *vt* 1.(*take same route as*) seguire 2.(*happen next*) **to ~ sth** seguire a qc 3.**to ~ sb's example/advice** seguire l'esempio/il consiglio di qu 4.(*understand*) **to ~ sb/ sth** seguire qu/qc 5.(*have an interest in*) **to ~ sth** seguire qc II. *vi* 1.(*take same route as*) seguire 2.(*happen next*) seguire 3.(*result*) conseguire; **to ~ from sth** derivare da qc

◆**follow on** *vi* conseguire

◆**follow through** I. *vt* 1.(*study*) approfondire 2.(*see through to end*) portare a termine II. *vi* SPORTS accompagnare la palla

◆**follow up** *vt* 1.(*consider, investigate*) esaminare a fondo 2.(*do next*) **to ~ sth by** [*o* with] **sth** far seguire qc a qc

follower *n* seguace *mf*

following I. *n inv* 1.**I'd say the ~** direi così; **my idea was the ~** la mia idea era la seguente 2.(*supporters: of idea*) sostenitori, -trici *m, f pl*; (*of doctrine*) seguaci *mfpl* II. *adj* 1.(*next*) seguente; **the ~ ideas** le idee seguenti 2.(*from behind*) **~ wind** vento *m* di spalle III. *prep* dopo; **~ dinner** dopo cena; **~ your letter** facendo seguito alla Sua lettera

follow-up *n* seguito *m*

folly ['fɑː·li] *n* (*foolishness*) follia *f;* **it's sheer ~!** è pura follia!

fond [fɑːnd] <-er, -est> *adj* 1.(*with liking for*) **to be ~ of sb** essere affezionato, -a a qu; **he is ~ of ...** gli piace [*o* piacciono]... 2.(*loving*) affettuoso, -a; **~ memories** cari ricordi *mpl* 3.(*hope*) vano, -a

fondle ['fɑːn·dl] <-ling> *vt* accarezzare

fondness ['fɑːnd·nɪs] *n* affetto *m;* **to have a ~ for sth** avere una passione per qc

font [fɑːnt] *n* 1.TYPO carattere *m* 2.(*receptacle*) fonte *f* battesimale

food [fuːd] *n* cibo *m* ▶**to give sb ~ for thought** dare da pensare a qu; **to be off one's ~** non aver voglia di mangiare, *perché non ci si sente molto bene*

food chain *n* catena *f* alimentare

food poisoning *n* avvelenamento *m* alimentare

food processor *n* robot *m* da cucina *inv*

food stamps *n* buoni *m* alimentari *pl*

foodstuff *n* generi *m* alimentari *pl*

fool [fuːl] I. *n* sciocco, -a *m, f;* **to be a big enough ~ to do sth** essere così stupido da fare qc; **to act like a ~** comportarsi da stupido, -a; **to make a ~ of sb** rendersi ridicolo, -a; **any ~** chiunque II. *vt* ingannare; **you could have ~ed me!** *inf* non l'avrei mai detto! III. *vi* (*joke around*) scherzare IV. *adj inf* (*silly*) sciocco, -a

◆**fool around** *vi* (*waste time*) perdere tempo

foolhardy ['fuːl·hɑːr·di] *adj* sconsiderato, -a

foolish ['fuː·lɪʃ] *adj* sciocco, -a

foolproof ['fuːl·pruːf] *adj* infallibile

fool's cap *n* carta *f* protocollo

foot [foʊt] I.<feet> *n* 1.(*of person*) piede *m;* (*of animal*) zampa *f* 2.(*unit of measurement*) piede *m, 30,48 cm* 3.(*bottom or lowest part*) **at the ~ of one's bed** ai piedi del letto; **at the ~ of the page** a piè di pagina ▶**to get a ~ in the** <u>door</u> mettere un piede dentro; **to have one ~ in the** <u>grave</u> avere un piede nella tomba; **to have both feet on the** <u>ground</u> avere i piedi per terra; **to set ~ on dry** <u>land</u> mettere piede sulla terra ferma; **to be** <u>back</u> **on one's feet** essere di nuovo in piedi; **to have/ get** <u>cold</u> **feet** avere fifa; **to get off on the** <u>wrong</u> **~** partire col piede sbagliato; **to** <u>fall</u> **on one's feet** cadere in piedi; **to** <u>find</u> **one's feet** ambientarsi; **to** <u>put</u> **one's ~** <u>down</u> puntare i piedi; **to** <u>put</u> **one's ~ in it** [*o* **in one's mouth**] fare una gaffe; **to** <u>set</u> **~ in sth** metter piede in qc; **I'll never set ~ in his house again** non metterò mai più piede a casa sua; **to be** <u>under</u> **sb's feet** stare sempre in mezzo a piedi a qu II. *vt inf* **to ~ the bill** pagare il conto

footage ['foʊ·t̬ɪdʒ] *n* CINE, TV sequenze *fpl*

foot-and-mouth disease *n* afta *f* epizootica

football ['foʊt·bɔːl] *n* 1.(*American football*) calcio *m* americano 2.(*ball*) palla *f* ovale

football player *n* calciatore, -trice *m, f*

footboard *n* AUTO predellino *m*

footbridge ['foʊt·brɪdʒ] *n* ponte *m* pedonale

footer ['foʊ·t̬ə] *n* nota *f* a piè di pagina

foothills ['foʊt·hɪlz] *n* colline *f* pedemontane *pl*

foothold ['foʊt·hoʊld] *n* punto *m* d'appoggio; **to gain a ~** *fig* prendere piede

footing ['foʊ·t̬ɪŋ] *n* 1.**to lose one's ~** perdere l'equilibrio 2.(*basis*) piano *m;* **on an equal ~** su un piano di parità

footlights ['foʊt·laɪts] *npl* luci *f* della ribalta *pl*

footling ['fuːt·lɪŋ] *adj* stupido, -a

footloose ['foʊt·luːs] *adj* libero, -a ▶**to be ~ and** <u>fancy-free</u> essere libero e senza legami

footman ['foʊt·mən] <-men> *n* valletto *m*

footnote ['foʊt·noʊt] *n* nota *f* a piè di pagina

footpath ['fʊt·pæθ] *n* sentiero *m*

footprint ['fʊt·prɪnt] *n* orma *f*

footrest ['fʊt·rest] *n* poggiapiedi *m inv*

footsie ['fʊt·si] *n inf* **to play ~ with sb** fare piedino a qu

footslog ['fʊt·slɑ:g] <-gg-> *vi inf* camminare faticosamente

footsore ['fʊt·sɔ:r] *adj liter* **to be ~** avere male ai piedi

footstep ['fʊt·step] *n* passo *m*

footstool ['fʊt·stu:l] *n* poggiapiedi *m inv*

footwear ['fʊt·wer] *n* calzature *fpl*

footwork ['fʊt·wɜ:rk] *n* gioco *m* di gambe

for [fɔ:r] I. *prep* 1. (*destined for*) per; **this is ~ you** questo è per te; **a present ~ my mother** un regalo è mia madre 2. (*in order to help*) per; **to do sth ~ sb** fare qc per qu 3. (*intention, purpose*) **~ sale/rent** in vendita/affitto; **sth ~ a headache** qc per il mal di testa; **it's time ~ lunch** è ora di pranzo; **to invite sb ~ dinner** invitare qu a cena; **to wait ~ sb** aspettare qu; **to go ~ a walk** andare a fare una passeggiata; **fit ~ nothing** buono a nulla; **what ~?** per quale motivo?; **what's that ~?** a cosa serve?; **it's ~ cutting cheese** serve per tagliare il formaggio; **~ this to be possible** perché ciò sia possibile; **to look ~ a way to do sth** cercare il modo di fare qc 4. (*to acquire*) **eager ~ power** avido, -a di potere; **to search ~ sth** cercare qc; **to ask/hope ~ news** chiedere/ aspettare notizie; **to apply ~ a job** fare domanda di lavoro; **to shout ~ help** gridare aiuto 5. (*towards*) **the train ~ Boston** il treno per Boston; **to make ~ home** dirigersi verso casa; **to run ~ safety** correre in salvo 6. (*distance*) **to walk ~ 8 miles** camminare per 8 miglia 7. (*time*) **~ now** per ora; **~ a while/a time** per un po'/un periodo; **to last ~ hours** durare ore e ore; **I'm going to be here ~ three weeks** starò qui per tre settimane; **I haven't been there ~ three years** sono tre anni che non ci vado; **I have known her ~ three years** la conosco da tre anni 8. (*on date of*) **to have sth finished ~ Sunday** finire qc per domenica; **to set the wedding ~ May 4th** fissare il matrimonio per il 4 maggio 9. (*in support of*) **is he ~ or against it?** lui è a favore o contrario?; **to fight ~ sth** lottare per qc 10. (*employed by*) **to work ~ a company** lavorare per una compagnia 11. (*the task of*) **it's ~ him to say/do ...** deve essere lui a dire/ fare... 12. (*in substitution*) **the substitute ~ the teacher** il supplente dell'insegnante; **say hello ~ me** saluta da parte mia 13. (*price*) **a check ~ $100** un assegno di $100; **I paid $10 ~ it** l'ho pagato $10 14. (*concerning*) **as ~ me/that** riguardo a me/quello; **two are enough ~ me** a me ne bastano due; **sorry ~ doing that** scusami per quello che ho fatto; **the best would be ~ me to go** farei meglio ad andarmene 15. (*in reference to*) **what's Chinese ~ 'book'?** come si dice 'libro' in cinese? 16. (*cause*) **excuse me ~ being late**

scusami per il ritardo; **as the reason ~ one's behavior** a motivo del proprio comportamento 17. (*because of*) **to do sth ~ love** fare qc per amore; **~ fear of doing sth** per paura di fare qc; **to cry ~ joy** piangere di gioia; **he can't talk ~ laughing** non riuscire a parlare per le risate 18. (*despite*) **~ all that/her money** malgrado tutto quello/i suoi soldi; **~ all I know** per quanto ne so 19. (*as*) **~ example** per esempio; **he ~ one** lui per primo ▶ **she's ~ it!** sono guai per lei!; **that's kids ~ you!** i bambini sono così! II. *conj form* perché

forage ['fɔ:·rɪdʒ] I. *vi* **to ~ for sth** andare alla ricerca di qc II. *n* (*fodder*) foraggio *m*

foray ['fɔ:·reɪ] *n* (*raid*) incursione *m;* **to make a ~** (**into sth**) fare un incursion (in qc)

forbad(e) [fə·'bæd] *pt of* **forbid**

forbear [fɔ:r·'ber] <forbore, forborne> *vi form* (*abstain, refrain*) trattenersi; **to ~ from doing sth** astenersi dal fare qc

forbearance [fɔ:r·'be·rəns] *n form* 1. (*patience*) pazienza *f* 2. (*self-control*) autocontrollo *m*

forbid [fə·'bɪd] <forbade, forbidden> *vt* proibire; **to ~ sb from doing sth** proibire a qu di fare qc; **to ~ sb sth** *form* proibire qc a qu

forbidden [fə·'bɪ·dn] *pp of* **forbid**

forbidding [fə·'bɪ·dɪŋ] *adj* 1. (*threatening*) minaccioso, -a 2. (*disapproving: frown, look*) severo, -a; (*bearing rain: sky, clouds*) minaccioso, -a

forbore [fɔ:r·'bɔ:r] *pt of* **forbear**

forborne [fɔ:r·'bɔ:rn] *pp of* **forbear**

force [fɔ:rs] I. *n* 1. (*power*) forza *f;* **by sheer ~ of numbers** solo grazie alla superiorità numerica; **~ of gravity** PHYS forza di gravità; **to combine ~s** unire le forze 2. (*large numbers*) **in ~** in gran numero 3. (*influence*) forza *f;* **by ~ of circumstance** per cause di forza maggiore; **by ~ of habit** per abitudine; **the ~s of nature** le forze della natura 4. (*validity*) **to come into ~** entrare in vigore 5. MIL **police ~** forze *f* di polizia *pl;* **Air Force** aeronautica *f* militare; **the armed ~s** le forze *f pl* armate II. *vt* 1. (*use power*) forzare; **to ~ a door** forzare una porta 2. (*oblige to do*) costringere; **to ~ sb to do sth** obbligare qu a fare qc; **to ~ sb into (doing)** sth costringere qu a fare qc; **to ~ sth on sb** imporre qc a qu; **to ~ a smile** sorridere forzatamente; **to ~ words out of sb** costringere qu a parlare 3. (*cause to grow faster*) forzare

♦**force out** *vt* costringere ad uscire

forced *adj* (*smile, friendliness*) forzato, -a; **~ landing** atterraggio *m* forzato

force-feed ['fɔ:rs·fi:d] *vt* alimentare forzatamente

forceful ['fɔ:rs·fəl] *adj* (*person, character*) energico, -a; (*argument*) convincente

forceps ['fɔ:r·seps] *npl* MED forcipe *m;* **a pair of ~** un paio di forcipi

forcible ['fɔ:r·sə·bl] *adj* (*entry, return*) forzato, -a; (*reminder*) efficace

forcibly *adv* con la forza

ford [fɔːrd] I. *n* guado *m* II. *vt* guadare

fore [fɔːr] I. *adj* anteriore; ~ **and aft** da prua a poppa II. *n* **to be to the** ~ essere d'attualità; **to come to the** ~ diventare d'attualità III. *interj* (*in golf*) ~! *urlo lanciato quando la pallina rischia di colpire i giocatori che precedono*

forearm¹ [ˈfɔːr·ɑːrm] *n* (*body part*) avambraccio *m*

forearm² [ˌfɔːr·ˈɑːrm] *vt liter* (*prepare for battle*) **to** ~ **oneself** (**against sth**) premunirsi (contro qc)

forebears [ˈfɔːr·berz] *npl form* antenati *mpl*

forebode [fɔːr·ˈboʊd] *vt liter* presagire

foreboding [fɔːr·ˈboʊ·dɪŋ] *n liter* presentimento *m;* **to have a** ~ (**that**) ... avere un presentimento (che)...

forecast [ˈfɔːr·kæst] <forecast *o* forecasted> I. *n* previsione *f;* **weather** ~ previsioni *m* del tempo *pl* II. *vt* prevedere

forecaster *n* ECON analista *mf;* **weather** ~ meteorologo, -a *m, f*

foreclose [fɔːr·ˈkloʊz] I. *vt* **to** ~ **a possibility** escludere una possibilità II. *vi* FIN pignorare un bene ipotecato; **to** ~ **on a loan** pignorare un bene ipotecato

forecourt [ˈfɔːr·kɔːrt] *n* piazzale *f* anteriore

forefathers [ˈfɔːr·ˌfɑː·ðərz] *npl liter* antenati *mpl*

forefinger [ˈfɔːr·fɪŋ·gər] *n* indice *m*

forefront [ˈfɔːr·frʌnt] *n* primo piano *m;* **to be at the** ~ **of sth** essere all'avanguardia in qc

forego [fɔːr·ˈgoʊ] <forewent, foregone> *vt s.* **forgo**

foregoing [ˈfɔːr·goʊ·ɪŋ] I. *adj form* suddetto, -a II. *n* **the** ~ *form* quanto precedentemente detto

foregone [fɔːr·ˈgɑːn] *pp of* **forego**

foreground [ˈfɔːr·graʊnd] I. *n a.* ART **the** ~ primo piano; **in the** ~ in primo piano; **to put oneself in the** ~ mettersi in vista II. *vt* mettere in primo piano

forehand [ˈfɔːr·hænd] *n* (*tennis shot*) diritto *m*

forehead [ˈfɔːr·ed] *n* fronte *f*

foreign [ˈfɔː·rɪn] *adj* 1.(*from another country*) straniero, -a; ~ **soil** *form* terra *f* straniera 2.(*involving other countries*) estero, -a; ~ **relations** rapporti *m pl* con l'estero; ~ **trade** commercio *m* estero 3.(*unknown, uncharacteristic*) estraneo, -a; **to be** ~ **to sb** essere estraneo a qu; **to be** ~ **to one's nature** non fare parte della natura di qu 4.(*not belonging*) estraneo, -a; **a** ~ **body** un corpo estraneo

foreign affairs *npl* affari *m pl* esteri

foreign aid *n* aiuti *m pl* ai paesi esteri

foreign correspondent *n* corrispondente *mf* estero

foreign currency *n* valuta *f* estera

foreigner [ˈfɔː·rɪ·nər] *n* straniero, -a *m, f*

foreign exchange *n* 1.(*system*) cambio *m* (estero) 2.(*currency*) valuta *f* estera

foreign minister *n* ministro, -a *m, f* degli esteri

foreign policy *n* politica *f* estera

foreknowledge [ˌfɔːr·ˈnɑː·lɪdʒ] *n* precogni-

zione *f;* **to have** ~ **of sth** prevedere qc

foreman [ˈfɔːr·mən] <-men> *n* 1.(*in factory*) caposquadra *m* 2. LAW (*head of jury*) capo *m* della giuria

foremost [ˈfɔːr·moʊst] *adj* 1.(*most important*) maggiore; **to be** ~ **among ...** essere in prima fila fra... 2.(*farthest forward*) più avanti

forename [ˈfɔːr·neɪm] *n form* nome *m* (di battesimo)

forensic [fə·ˈren·sɪk] *adj* ~ **experts** esperti *m pl* della (Polizia) Scientifica; ~ **evidence** risultati *m pl* della perizia medico-legale; ~ **medicine** medicina *f* legale; ~ **science** scienze *f pl* forensi

foreordain [ˌfɔːr·ɔːr·ˈdeɪn] *vt form* predestinare; **to be** ~**ed** (**to do sth**) essere predestinato (a fare qc)

foreplay [ˈfɔːr·pleɪ] *n* preliminari *mpl, in rapporto sessuale*

forerunner [ˈfɔːr·ˌrʌ·nər] *n* precursore, precorritrice *m, f*

foresail [ˈfɔːr·seɪl] *n* NAUT vela *f* di trinchetto

foresee [fɔːr·ˈsiː] *irr vt* prevedere

foreseeable *adj* prevedibile; **in the** ~ **future** nell'immediato futuro

foreshadow [fɔːr·ˈʃæ·doʊ] *vt* preannunciare

foresight [ˈfɔːr·saɪt] *n* lungimiranza *f;* **lack of** ~ mancanza *f* di lungimiranza

foreskin [ˈfɔːr·skɪn] *n* prepuzio *m*

forest [ˈfɔː·rɪst] I. *n* (*woods*) bosco *m;* (*tropical*) foresta *f* II. *adj* forestale

forestall [fɔːr·ˈstɔːl] *vt* prevenire; **to** ~ **criticism** prevenire le critiche

forester [ˈfɔː·rɪs·tər] *n* guardia *f* forestale

forest fire *n* incendio *m* boschivo

forest ranger *n* guardia *f* forestale

forestry [ˈfɔː·rɪs·tri] *n* selvicoltura *f*

foretaste [ˈfɔːr·teɪst] *n* assaggio *m*

foretell [fɔːr·ˈtel] <foretold> *vt* predire

forever [fɔːr·ˈe·vər] *adv* 1.(*for all time*) per sempre 2. *inf* (*continually*) continuamente; **to be** ~ **doing sth** fare qc in continuazione

forewarn [fɔːr·ˈwɔːrn] *vt* avvisare ▶ ~**ed is forearmed** *prov* uomo avvisato mezzo salvato

forewent [fɔːr·ˈwent] *pp of* **forego**

foreword [ˈfɔːr·wɜːrd] *n* prefazione *f*

forfeit [ˈfɔːr·fɪt] I. *vt* 1.(*lose*) perdere 2.(*renounce*) rinunciare II. *n* 1.(*fine*) ammenda *f;* **to pay a** ~ pagare una multa 2. *pl* (*game*) **to play** ~**s** giocare ai pegni 3. *form* (*penalty*) penale *f* III. *adj* **her property was** ~ i suoi beni sono stati confiscati

forfeiture [ˈfɔːr·fə·tʃər] *n* confisca *f*

forgather [fɔːr·ˈgæ·ðər] *vi form* riunirsi

forgave [fə·ˈgeɪv] *n pt of* **forgive**

forge [fɔːrdʒ] I. *vt* 1.(*make illegal copy*) falsificare 2.(*metal*) forgiare 3. *fig* **to** ~ **a bond** forgiare un legame; **to** ~ **a career** forgiare una carriera II. *vi* **to** ~ **into the lead** conquistare un buon vantaggio III. *n* 1.(*furnace*) forgia *f* 2.(*smithy*) fucina *f*

◆**forge ahead** *vi* 1.(*make progress*) fare rapidi progressi 2.(*move into lead*) passare in

testa
forger ['fɔːr·dʒɚ] *n* falsario, -a *m, f*
forgery ['fɔːr·dʒə·ri] <-ies> *n* contraffazione *f*
forget [fə·'get] <forgot, forgotten> I. *vt*
1. (*not remember*) dimenticare; **to ~ to do sth**
dimenticare di fare qc; **to ~ (that)** ... dimenticare (che)... **2.** (*leave behind*) **to ~ sth**
dimenticare qc; **to ~ one's keys** dimenticare
le chiavi **3.** (*stop thinking about*) **to ~ sth/sb**
dimenticare qc/qu; **to ~ one's dignity** mettere da parte la propria dignità; **it's best forgotten** meglio scordarselo **4.** (*give up*) **to ~
sth** lasciar perdere; **~ it** lascia perdere **5. to ~
oneself** (*behave badly*) perdere il controllo di
sè II. *vi* **1.** (*not remember*) dimenticarsi; **to ~
about sth/sb** dimenticarsi di qc/qu; **to ~
about doing sth** dimenticarsi di fare qc
2. (*stop thinking about*) **to ~ about sth/sb**
scordarsi di qc/qu; **to ~ about a plan** lasciar
perdere un piano; **let's ~ about it!** lasciamo
perdere! **3. ~ it!** (*no*) te lo puoi scordare!
forgetful [fə·'get·fəl] *adj* smemorato, -a
forget-me-not *n* nontiscordardimé *m inv*
forgive [fə·'gɪv] <forgave, forgiven> I. *vt*
1. (*pardon*) perdonare; **to ~ sb for sth** perdonare qc a qu; **to ~ sb for doing sth** perdonare a
qu di aver fatto qc **2.** (*pardon*) **~ me** perdon-
ami; **~ my ignorance/language** perdoni l'ig-
noranza/il linguaggio; **~ me for mentioning
it** scusa se ne parlo II. *vi* perdonare; **to ~ and
forget** perdonare e dimenticare
forgiven *pp of* **forgive**
forgiveness *n* perdono *m*
forgiving *adj* indulgente
forgo [fɔːr·'goʊ] *irr vt* rinunciare a
forgot [fə·'gɑːt] *pt of* **forget**
forgotten [fə·'gɑː·tn] I. *pp of* forget II. *adj*
dimenticato, -a
fork [fɔːrk] I. *n* **1.** (*cutlery*) forchetta *f* **2.** (*tool*)
forca *f* **3.** (*in road*) biforcazione *f* **4.** *pl* (*on
bicycle*) forcella *f* II. *vt* (*a pattern*) disegnare
con la forchetta; (*food*) prendere con la forchetta III. *vi* (*road*) biforcarsi
forked *adj* (*tongue, tail, branch*) biforcuto, -a;
(*road*) che si biforca
forklift [ˌfɔːrk·'lɪft] *n* elevatore *m* a forca
forlorn [fɔːr·'lɔːrn] *adj* (*person*) sconsolato, -a;
(*place*) desolato, -a; (*hope*) vano, -a
form [fɔːrm] I. *n* **1.** (*type, variety*) forma *f*; **~ of
exercise** forma d'esercizio; **~ of government**
sistema *f* di governo; **~ of transportation**
mezzo *m* di trasporto; **~ of persuasion** strumento *m* di persuasione; **a ~ of disease** un
tipo di malattia; **in any way, shape or ~** in
nessun modo; **in the ~ of sth** sotto forma di
qc; **to take the ~ of sth** prendere la forma di
qc **2.** (*outward shape*) forma *f*; **to take ~**
prender forma; **in liquid/solid ~** allo stato
liquido/solido **3.** LING (*of word*) forma *f*; **the
singular ~** la forma singolare **4.** (*document*)
modulo *m*; **an application/entry ~** un
modulo di domanda/di iscrizione; **to fill in a ~**
compilare un modulo **5.** SPORTS forma *f*; **to be**

in ~ essere in forma; **to be out of ~** essere
fuori forma **6.** (*correct procedure*) **in due ~**
come si conviene; **a matter of ~** una questione
di forma; **for ~'s sake** per salvare la forma; **to
be bad ~** essere cattiva educazione **7.** (*mold*)
forma *f* II. *vt* **1.** (*make*) formare; **to ~ part of
sth** far parte di qc; **to ~ the basis of sth** costituire le basi di qc; **to ~ a line** mettersi in coda;
to ~ the impression that ... farsi l'idea che...;
to ~ an opinion formarsi un'opinione; **to ~ a
habit** prendere un'abitudine **2.** (*shape*) **to
form the clay into a ball** formare una palla di
argilla **3.** (*set up*) formare; **to ~ a committee/
government** formare un comitato/governo;
to ~ a relationship allacciare una relazione;
to ~ an alliance with sb formare un'alleanza
con qu III. *vi* formarsi
formal ['fɔːr·məl] *adj* (*official, ceremonious*)
formale; **~ dress** abito *m* da cerimonia; **~ procedures** procedure *f pl* formali; **~ interest**
interesse *m* formale
formaldehyde [fɔːr·'mæl·dɪ·haɪd] *n* formaldeide *f*
formality [fɔːr·'mæ·lə·t̬i] <-ies> *n* formalità *f*;
to be merely a ~ essere una pura formalità
formalize ['fɔːr·mə·laɪz] *vt* formalizzare; **to ~
one's thoughts** dare forma ai propri pensieri
formally *adv* formalmente
format ['fɔːr·mæt] I. *n* formato *m* II. <-tt-> *vt*
COMPUT formattare
formation [fɔːr·'meɪ·ʃən] *n* formazione *f*;
rock ~ formazione delle rocce; **in ~** in formazione; **in battle ~** in assetto da combattimento
formation flying *n* volo *m* in formazione
formative ['fɔːr·mə·t̬ɪv] *adj* formativo, -a; **the
~ years** gli anni della formazione
formatting *n* COMPUT formattazione *f*
former ['fɔːr·mɚ] *adj* **1.** (*previous*) precedente;
in a ~ life in un'altra vita **2.** (*first of two*)
primo, -a
formerly *adv* precedentemente; **~ known as**
una volta conosciuto, -a come
form feed *n* COMPUT *funzione di una stampante
che permette, grazie al tasto FF, di far avanzare la carta*
formic acid [ˌfɔːr·mɪk·'æ·sɪd] *n* acido *m* formico
formidable ['fɔːr·mə·də·bl] *adj* (*person*) formidabile; (*opponent, task*) difficile
formless ['fɔːrm·lɪs] *adj* informe
formula ['fɔːrm·jʊ·lə] <-s *o* -lae> *n* **1.** *a. fig*
MAT, COM formula *f*; **the ~ for success** la formula del successo **2.** (*form of words*) formula *f*
3. (*baby milk*) latte *f* per bebè
formulate ['fɔːrm·jʊ·leɪt] *vt* formulare
formulation [ˌfɔːrm·jʊ·'leɪ·ʃən] *n* formulazione *f*
fornicate ['fɔːr·nɪ·keɪt] *vi* fornicare
forsake [fɔːr·'seɪk] <forsook, forsaken> *vt*
abbandonare
forsaken [fɔːr·'seɪ·kən] I. *pp of* **forsake** II. *adj*
abbandonato, -a

F

forsook [fɔːrˈsʊk] *pt of* **forsake**

forswear [fɔːrˈswer] <forswore, forsworn> *vt liter* rinunciare a

fort [fɔːrt] *n* forte *m*

forte¹ [ˈfɔːˌteɪ, fɔːrt] *n* (*strong point*) forte *m*

forte² [ˈfɔːˌteɪ] *adv* MUS forte *m*

forth [fɔːrθ] *adv* **to go ~** andarsene; **back and ~** avanti e indietro; **from that day ~** da quel giorno in poi

forthcoming [ˌfɔːrθˈkʌ·mɪŋ] *adj* **1.** (*happening soon*) prossimo, -a; (*book*) di prossima pubblicazione; (*film*) di prossima uscita **2.** (*available*) disponibile; **to be ~** (*from sb*) venire (da qu) **3.** (*informative*) **to be ~** (*about sth*) essere disposto, -a a parlare (di qc)

forthright [ˈfɔːrθ·raɪt] *adj* schietto, -a

forthwith [ˌfɔːrθ·ˈwɪθ] *adv form* immediatamente

fortieth [ˈfɔːr·ṭɪ·əθ] **I.** *adj* quarantesimo, -a **II.** *n* (*order*) quarantesimo, -a *m, f;* (*fraction*) quarantesimo *m;* (*part*) quarantesimo *m; s.a.* **eighth**

fortification [ˌfɔːr·ṭə·fɪ·ˈkeɪ·ʃən] *n* fortificazione *f*

fortify [ˈfɔːr·ṭə·faɪ] <-ie-> *vt* **1.** MIL fortificare **2. to ~ oneself** (**with sth**) rinvigorirsi (con qc); **fortified with vitamins and minerals** con l'aggiunta di vitamine e minerali

fortitude [ˈfɔːr·ṭə·tuːd] *n form* forza *f* d'animo

fortnight [ˈfɔːrt·naɪt] *n* due settimane *fpl*

fortress [ˈfɔːr·trɪs] *n* fortezza *f*

fortuitous [fɔːrˈtuː·ə·ṭəs] *adj form* fortuito, -a

fortunate [ˈfɔːr·tʃə·nət] *adj* fortunato, -a; **to be ~ to do sth** avere la fortuna di fare qc; **to be ~ in sth** essere fortunato in qc; **it is ~ for her that ...** è una fortuna che lei...

fortunately *adv* fortunatamente

fortune [ˈfɔːr·tʃən] *n* **1.** (*money*) fortuna *f;* **a small ~** una piccola fortuna; **to be worth a ~** valere una fortuna; **to cost a ~** costare una fortuna; **to make a ~** guadagnare una fortuna **2.** *form* (*good luck*) fortuna *f;* (*destiny*) sorte *f;* **good/ill ~** buona/cattiva sorte; **to have the good ~ to do sth** avere la fortuna di fare qc; **to tell sb's ~** predire il futuro a qu **3.** *liter* (*luck personified*) **~ smiled on him** la fortuna gli sorrise **4.** *pl* (*fate*) (alterne) vicende *fpl*

fortune cookie *n* biscotto *m* della fortuna

fortune hunter *n* cacciatore, -trice di dote *m*

fortune teller *n* indovino, -a *m, f*

forty [ˈfɔːr·ṭi] **I.** *adj* quaranta **II.** <-ies> *n* quaranta *m; s.a.* **eighty**

forum [ˈfɔː·rəm] *n* forum *m inv*

forward [ˈfɔːr·wəd] **I.** *adv* **1.** (*towards the front*) avanti; **to lean ~** sporgersi in avanti; **a step ~** *fig* un passo avanti **2.** (*in time*) avanti; **from that day/time ~** da quel giorno/quel momento in poi; **to set one's watch/the clock ~** rimettere l'orologio/la sveglia avanti; **to look ~ to sth** aspettare qc con impazienza **II.** *adj* **1.** (*towards the front*) in avanti; **~ movement** movimento *m* in avanti; **~ gear** AUTO marcia *f* avanti **2.** (*in a position close to*

front) avanti; **to be ~ of sth** trovarsi davanti a qc **3.** (*near front of plane*) davanti; (*ship*) di prua **4.** (*relating to the future*) **~ buying** acquisto *m* a termine; **~ look** sguardo *m* verso il futuro; **~ planning** programmazione a lungo termine **5.** (*bold, not modest*) sfrontato, -a **III.** *n* SPORTS attaccante *mf;* **center ~** centravanti *m inv* **IV.** *vt* **1.** (*letter, e-mail*) inoltrare; **please ~** si prega di inoltrare **2.** (*help to progress*) promuovere

forwarding address *n* nuovo indirizzo *m,* dove inoltrare la posta

forward-looking *adj* progressista

forwardness *n* sfacciataggine *f*

forwards [ˈfɔːr·wədz] *adv* **1.** (*towards the front*) avanti **2.** (*in time*) avanti

forwent [fɔːr·ˈwent] *pt of* **forgo**

fossil [ˈfɑː·səl] *n a. fig* GEO fossile *m*

fossil fuel *n* combustibile *m* fossile

fossilized [ˈfɑː·sə·laɪzd] *adj* **1.** GEO fossilizzato, -a **2.** *fig, inf* (*outdated*) fossilizzato, -a

foster [ˈfɑː·s·tə·] *vt* **1.** (*look after*) prendere in affidamento **2.** (*encourage*) coltivare

foster brother *n* fratello *m* adottivo

foster child *n* bambino, -a *m, f* in affidamento

foster father *n* padre *m* affidatario

foster home *n* famiglia *f* affidataria

foster mother *n* madre *f* affidataria

foster sister *n* sorella *f* adottiva, sorella *f* affidataria

fought [fɑːt] *pt, pp of* **fight**

foul [faʊl] **I.** *adj* **1.** (*disagreeable: mood, temper*) pessimo, -a; (*air*) viziato, -a; (*weather*) orribile **2.** (*rotten: taste, smell*) disgustoso, -a **3.** (*vulgar: language*) sconcio, -a **II.** *n* SPORTS fallo *m* **III.** *vt* **1.** (*pollute*) inquinare; (*dog*) sporcare **2.** SPORTS **to ~ sb** commettere un fallo su qu **3.** (*tangle*) impigliare

♦**foul up** *vt* rovinare

foulmouthed *adj* sboccato, -a

foulness [ˈfaʊl·nəs] *n* **1.** (*dirtiness*) sporcizia *f* **2.** (*unpleasantness*) sgradevolezza *f* **3.** (*coarseness*) volgarità *f*

foul play *n* **1.** SPORTS gioco *m* irregolare **2.** (*crime*) delitto *m*

found¹ [faʊnd] *pt, pp of* **find**

found² [faʊnd] *vt* **1.** (*establish*) fondare **2.** (*base*) fondare; **to ~ a statement/a case on sth** fondare una dichiarazione/un caso su qc **3.** (*build*) **to be ~ed on sth** essere fondato su qc

found³ [faʊnd] *vt* MIN fondere

foundation [faʊn·ˈdeɪ·ʃən] *n* **1.** *pl* (*of building*) fondamenta *fpl;* **to lay the ~(s)** (**of sth**) gettare le fondamenta (di qc) **2.** *fig* (*basis*) fondamenta *fpl;* **to lay the ~(s) of sth** gettare le fondamenta (di qc) **3.** (*evidence*) fondamento *m;* **to have no ~** non avere nessun fondamento **4.** (*act of establishing*) fondazione *f* **5.** (*organization*) fondazione *f* **6.** (*make-up*) fondotinta *m inv*

foundation cream *n* fondotinta *m inv*

foundation stone *n* prima pietra *f*

founder¹ [ˈfaʊn·də·] *n* (*of organization*) fondatore, -trice *m, f*

founder² ['faʊn·dər] *vi* **1.** (*sink*) affondare **2.** *fig* (*fail*) naufragare; **to ~ on sth** fallire a causa di qc

Founding Fathers *npl* the ~ i padri *m* fondatori *pl, della nazione americana*

foundry ['faʊn·dri] <-ries> *n* fonderia *f*

fount [faʊnt] *n a. fig, form* fonte *f;* **to be the ~ of all knowledge/wisdom** essere un pozzo di conoscenze/di saggezza

fountain ['faʊn·tən] *n* fontana *f*

fountain pen *n* penna *f* stilografica

four [fɔːr] **I.** *adj* quattro **II.** *n* **1.** quattro *m* **2.** (*group of four*) quattro *m* ▶ **to go on** all **~ s** camminare carponi; *s.a.* **eight**

four-by-four *n* AUTO veicolo *m* a quattro ruote motrici

four-door car *n* cinque porte *f inv*

fourfold ['fɔːr·foʊld] **I.** *adj* quadruplice **II.** *adv* **to increase ~** aumentare di quattro volte

four-footed *adj* quadrupede

fourhanded *adj* **1.** (*involving four people: bridge, checkers, poker*) che si gioca in quattro **2.** (*for two pianists*) a quattro mani

four-leaf clover *n* quadrifoglio *m*

four-letter word *n* parolaccia *f*

foursome ['fɔːr·səm] *n* gruppo *m* di quattro persone; **to make up a ~** formare un gruppo di quattro

foursquare [ˌfɔːr·'skwer] *adj* **1.** (*building*) squadrato, -a **2.** (*person*) risoluto, -a; **to stand ~ behind sb** appoggiare totalmente qu

fourteen [ˌfɔːr·'tiːn] **I.** *adj* quattordici **II.** *n* quattordici *m; s.a.* **eight**

fourteenth I. *adj* quattordicesimo, -a **II.** *n* **1.** (*order*) quattordicesimo, -a *m, f* **2.** (*date*) quattordici *m* **3.** (*fraction*) quattordicesimo *m;* (*part*) quattordicesimo *m; s.a.* **eighth**

fourth [fɔːrθ] **I.** *adj* quarto, -a **II.** *n* **1.** (*order*) quarto, -a *m, f* **2.** (*date*) quattro *m* **3.** (*fraction*) quarto *m;* (*part*) quarto *m* **4.** MUS quarto *m; s.a.* **eighth**

fourth gear *n* AUTO quarta *f*

Fourth of July *n* the ~ il quattro luglio, *festa dell'indipendenza degli Stati Uniti*

---

i Il **Fourth of July** o *Independence Day* è una festa laica molto importante negli Stati Uniti che commemora la *Declaration of Independence* (Dichiarazione di Indipendenza), attraverso la quale le colonie americane si sono sottratte al dominio britannico. È tradizione festeggiare questa ricorrenza in famiglia, con un picnic o andando a vedere una partita di baseball professionistico. Per concludere la festa, vengono organizzati dei grandi fuochi d'artificio in tutto il paese.

---

four-wheel drive *n* trazione *f* a quattro ruote

fowl [faʊl] <-(s)> *n* pollo *m*

fox [fɑːks] **I.** *n* **1.** (*animal, fur*) volpe *f* **2.** *inf*

(*cunning person*) **an old ~** una vecchia volpe **3.** *inf* (*sexy woman*) bona *f* **II.** *vt* **1.** (*mystify*) confondere **2.** (*trick*) ingannare

foxglove ['fɑːks·glʌv] *n* BOT digitale *m*

foxhunt ['fɑːks·hʌnt] *n* caccia *f* alla volpe

fox terrier *n* fox terrier *m inv*

foxtrot ['fɑːks·trɑːt] <-tt-> **I.** *n* fox-trot *m inv* **II.** *vi* ballare un fox-trot

foxy ['fɑːk·si] <-ier, -iest> *adj* **1.** (*crafty*) scaltro, -a **2.** *inf* (*sexy*) sexy

foyer ['fɔ·ɪə˞] *n* **1.** (*in house*) ingresso *m* **2.** (*in hotel*) hall *f inv;* (*in theater*) foyer *m inv*

fracas ['freɪ·kəs] <-(ses)> *n* lite *f*

fractal ['fræk·tl] *n* MATH frattale *m*

fraction ['fræk·ʃən] *n* frazione *f;* **at a ~ of the cost** a una frazione del costo

fractional ['fræk·ʃə·nl] *adj* **1.** MATH frazionario, -a **2.** (*difference*) minimo, -a

fractious ['fræk·ʃəs] *adj* permaloso, -a

fracture ['fræk·tʃə˞] **I.** *vt* **1.** MED fratturare; **to ~ one's leg** fratturarsi la gamba **2.** (*break*) rompere; **to ~ an agreement** rompere un accordo **II.** *vi* (*leg*) fratturarsi **III.** *n* MED frattura *f*

fragile ['fræ·dʒəl] *adj* (*emotionally*) fragile; (*object, peace*) fragile; (*health*) delicato, -a; **to feel ~** sentirsi debole

fragility [frə·'dʒɪ·lə·t̬i] *n* fragilità *f*

fragment ['fræg·mənt] **I.** *n* frammento *m* **II.** *vi* (*a. fig*) frammentarsi **III.** *vt* (*a. fig*) frammentare

fragmentary ['fræg·mən·tri] *adj* frammentario, -a

fragrance ['freɪ·grəns] *n* fraganza *f*

fragrant ['freɪ·grənt] *adj* fragrante

frail [freɪl] *adj* (*person*) gracile; (*thing*) fragile

frailty ['freɪl·ti] <-ies> *n* **1.** (*weakness: of person*) gracilità *f;* (*of thing*) fragilità *f* **2.** (*moral flaw*) debolezza *f*

frame [freɪm] **I.** *n* **1.** (*for picture*) cornice *f;* (*for door*) telaio *m* **2.** COMPUT frame *m inv* **3.** *pl* (*spectacles*) montatura *f* **4.** (*of building*) struttura *f* **5.** (*body*) struttura (fisica) *f;* **a slight/sturdy ~** una corporatura esile/robusta **6.** CINE, TV fotogramma *m* **II.** *vt* **1.** (*picture, face*) incorniciare **2.** (*conceive: proposal*) elaborare; (*put into words: reply*) formulare **3.** *inf* (*falsely incriminate*) incastrare

frame-up ['freɪm·ʌp] *n inf* montatura *f*

framework ['freɪm·wɜːrk] *n* **1.** (*supporting structure*) struttura *f* **2.** *fig* (*set of rules, principles*) base *f*

franc [fræŋk] *n* franco *m*

France [fræns] *n* Francia *f*

franchise ['fræn·tʃaɪz] **I.** *n* COM concessione *f* in franchising **II.** *vt* dare in franchising

Franciscan [fræn·'sɪs·kən] **I.** *n* REL francescano, -a *m, f* **II.** *adj* REL francescano, -a

Franco- ['fræn·koʊ] *in compounds* franco-

frank [fræŋk] **I.** *adj* franco, -a; **to be ~, ...** ad essere sinceri,... **II.** *vt* (*letter*) affrancare; (*stamp*) annullare

frankfurter ['fræŋk·fɜːr·t̬ə˞] *n* würstel *m inv*

frankincense ['fræn·kɪn·sents] *n* incenso *m*

frankly *adv* francamente

frantic ['fræn·tɪk] *adj* (*hurry, activity*) frenetico, -a; **to be ~ with rage** essere furibondo, -a; **to be ~ with worry** essere disperato, -a; **to drive sb ~** mandare qu fuori di testa

fraternal [frə·'tɜ:r·nl] *adj* (*relationship, feeling*) fraterno, -a

fraternity   [frə·'tɜ:r·nə·t̬i]   <-ies>   *n* **1.** (*brotherly feeling*) fratellanza *f* **2.** (*group of people*) comunità *f* **3.** UNIV *associazione studentesca maschile nelle università americane.*

fraternize ['fræ·t̬ə· naɪz] *vi* fraternizzare

fratricide ['fræ·trə·saɪd] *n* (*crime*) fratricidio *m*

fraud [frɑ:d] *n* **1.** a. LAW frode *f* **2.** (*trick*) imbroglio *m* **3.** (*person*) impostore, -a *m, f*

fraudulence ['frɑ:·dʒə·ləns] *n* **1.** (*financial dishonesty*) frode *f* **2.** (*of claim, behavior*) fraudolenza *f*

fraudulent ['frɑ:·dʒə·lənt] *adj* fraudolento, -a

fraught [frɑ:t] *adj* teso, -a; **to be ~ with difficulties/problems** essere pieno, -a di difficoltà/problemi

fray¹ [freɪ] *vi* (*rope, cloth*) sfilacciarsi; **tempers were beginning to ~** la gente comiciava a spazientirsi

fray² [freɪ] *n* (*fight*) lotta *f;* **to enter the ~** entrare in lotta

freak [fri:k] I. *n* **1.** (*abnormal person, thing*) mostro *m;* **a ~ of nature** uno scherzo *m* della natura **2.** (*enthusiast*) fanatico, -a *m, f* II. *adj* anomalo, -a III. *vi s.* **freak out** I

♦**freak out** I. *vi* restare sconvolto, -a II. *vt* to **freak sb out** mandare qu fuori di testa

freckle ['fre·kl] *n pl* lentiggine *f*

freckled ['fre·kld] *adj* lentigginoso, -a

free [fri:] I. <-r, -est> *adj* **1.** (*not constrained: person, country, elections*) libero, -a; **to break ~ (of sth/sb)** liberarsi (da qc); **to go ~** essere liberato, -a; **to set sb ~** mettere in libertà qu; **to be ~ to do sth** essere libero di fare qc **2.** (*not affected by*) **to be ~ of sth** essere libero da qc; **to be ~ of a disease** essere guarito, -a da una malattia **3.** (*not attached*) **to get sth ~** liberare qc **4.** (*not busy*) **to be ~ to do sth** essere libero di fare qc; **to leave sb ~ to do sth** lasciare qu libero di fare qc **5.** (*not occupied*) libero, -a; **to leave sth ~** lasciare qu libero **6.** (*costing nothing*) gratuito, -a; **~ ticket** biglietto *m* gratuito; **~ of charge** gratis; **~ sample** campione *m* gratuito; **to be ~ of customs/tax** essere esente da dazio/imposte; **to be ~ to sb** essere gratis per qu **7.** (*generous*) **to be ~ with sth** essere prodigo, -a di qc; **to make ~ with sth** *pej* usare liberamente qc, *che non ci appartiene* **8.** (*translation, verse*) libero, -a ▶ **~ and easy** rilassato, -a e informale II. *adv* gratuitamente; **~ of charge** gratis; **for ~** *inf* gratis III. *vt* **1.** (*release: person*) liberare **2.** (*make available*) liberare; **to ~ sb to do sth** lasciare a qu la libertà di fare qc

freebie ['fri:·bi] *n* omaggio *m*

freebooter ['fri:·bu:·t̬ər] *n* filibustiere *m*

freedom ['fri:·dəm] *n* **1.** (*of person, country*) libertà *f;* **to have the ~ to do sth** avere la libertà di fare qc; **~ of action/movement** libertà di azione/movimento; **~ of the press** libertà di stampa; **~ of speech/thought** libertà di espressione/pensiero; **to have ~ from interference** non avere interferenze **2.** (*right*) libertà *f* **3.** (*room for movement*) **~ of movement** libertà di movimento **4.** (*unrestricted use*) **to have the ~ of sb's house** poter usare liberamente la casa di qu

free enterprise *n* iniziativa *f* privata

free fall *n* caduta *f* libera; **to go into ~** FIN precipitare

free-for-all *n* (*brawl*) rissa *f*

freehold ['fri:·hoʊld] I. *n* piena proprietà *f* II. *adj* **a ~ house** in Gran Bretagna, casa di cui si possiede o si può acquistare la piena proprietà III. *adv* **to sell ~** vendere la piena proprietà

freeholder *n* in Gran Bretagna, chi ha la piena proprietà di un immobile o di un terreno

free kick *n* SPORTS calcio *m* di punizione

freelance ['fri:·læns] I. *n* freelance *mf inv* II. *adj* freelance III. *adv* come freelance IV. *vi* lavorare come freelance

freeload ['fri:·loʊd] *vi pej* scroccare; **to ~ off sb** scroccare a qu

freeloader *vi pej* scroccone, -a *m, f*

freely *adv* **1.** (*unrestrictedly*) **to be ~ available** trovarsi facilmente **2.** (*without obstruction*) liberamente **3.** (*frankly: speak, criticize*) liberamente; (*admit*) apertamente **4.** (*generously*) generosamente

freeman ['fri:·mən] <-men> *n* **1.** HIST (*not slave*) uomo *m* libero **2.** (*honorary citizen*) cittadino *m* onorario

free market *n* libero mercato *m*

Freemason ['fri:·ˌmeɪ·sən] *n* massone *m*

free port *n* porto *m* franco

free press *n* stampa *f* indipendente

free-range [ˌfri:·'reɪndʒ] *adj* ruspante

free-range chicken *n* pollo *m* allevato a terra

free-range egg *n* uovo *m* di galline allevate a terra

free speech *n* libertà *f* di espressione

free-spoken [ˌfri:·'spoʊ·kən] *adj* che non ha peli sulla lingua

freestanding [ˌfri:·'stæn·dɪŋ] *adj* independente

freestyle ['fri:·staɪl] *n* stile *m* libero

freethinker [ˌfri:·'θɪŋ·kər] *n* libero,-a pensatore, -trice *m, f*

freethinking *adj* libero, -a pensatore,- trice

free trade *n* libero scambio *m*

freeware *n* freeware *m inv, software fornito gratuitamente, specialmente su Internet*

freeway *n* autostrada *f*

freewheel ['fri:·hwi:l] *vi* (*car*) andare in folle; (*bicycle*) andare a ruota libera

free will *n* libero arbitrio *m*

freeze [fri:z] <froze, frozen> I. *vi* **1.** (*liquid*) gelare; (*food*) congelarsi **2.** (*become totally still*) rimanere di ghiaccio II. *vt* (*liquid, food,* *prices*) congelare **III.** *n* **1.** METEO ondata *f* di gelo **2.** ECON congelamento *m;* **to place a ~ on prices/hiring** bloccare i prezzi/le assunzioni ◆**freeze up** *vi* gelarsi

freezer *n* congelatore *m*

freezing I. *adj* (*temperatures*) sotto zero; (*rain*) ghiacciato, -a; **it's ~** si gela; **I'm ~** sto morendo di freddo **II.** *n* congelamento *m*

freezing point *n* punto *m* di congelamento

freight [freɪt] **I.** *n* **1.** (*type of transportation*) trasporto *m* **2.** (*goods*) merci *fpl* **3.** (*charge*) nolo *m* **II.** *vt* trasportare

freight car *n* RAIL vagone *m* merci

freighter ['freɪ·t̬ə] *n* **1.** (*ship*) nave *f* da carico **2.** (*plane*) aereo *m* da carico **3.** RAIL treno *m* merci

freight train *n* treno *m* merci

French [frentʃ] **I.** *adj* francese; **~ speaker** francofono, -a *m, f* **II.** *n* **1.** (*person*) francese *mf* **2.** (*language*) francese *m*

French bread *n* pane *m* francese

French chalk *n* gessetto *m* da sarto

French doors *npl* portafinestra *f*

French dressing *n* olio e aceto, *Come condimento per insalata*

French fried potatoes *npl*, **French fries** *npl* patatine*f pl* fritte

French horn *n* corno *m* da caccia

French kiss *n* bacio *m* alla francese

Frenchman <-men> *n* francese *m*

French toast *n* toast *m* francese, *fetta di pane passata in latte e uova e poi fritta*

French windows *npl s.* **French doors**

Frenchwoman <-women> *n* francese *f*

frenetic [frə·'ne·t̬ɪk] *adj* frenetico, -a

frenzied *adj* frenetico, -a

frenzy ['fren·zi] *n* frenesia *f*

frequency ['friː·kwən·tsi] <-cies> *n* frequenza *f*

frequency band *n* banda *f* di frequenza

frequency modulation *n* modulazione *f* di frequenza

frequent[1] ['friː·kwənt] *adj* (*occurring often*) frequente

frequent[2] [frɪ·'kwent] *vt* (*visit regularly*) frequentare

frequently ['friː·kwənt·li] *adv* di frequente

fresco ['fres·koʊ] <-s o -es> *n* affresco *m*

fresh [freʃ] *adj* **1.** (*not stale: air, water, food*) fresco, -a **2.** (*new*) fresco, -a; **to make a ~ start** ricominciare da zero; **~ from the oven/the factory** appena sfornato, -a; **~ from the factory** fresco, -a di fabbrica **3.** (*cool: breeze*) fresco, -a **4.** (*not tired*) fresco, -a **5.** *inf* (*disrespectful*) sfacciato, -a

freshen ['fre·ʃən] **I.** *vt* rinfrescare; **can I ~ your drink?** posso versartene un altro po'? **II.** *vi* (*wind*) rinforzare

freshman ['freʃ·mən] <-men> *n* UNIV matricola *f*

ⓘ Un **Freshman** negli USA è uno studente al primo anno delle scuole medie superiori,

---

un *Sophomore* uno studente del secondo anno, un Junior, uno studente del terzo e un *Senior* uno studente del quarto e ultimo anno. Sono i termini utilizzati per gli studenti della *High School*. Gli stessi termini sono utilizzati per designare gli studenti dei primi quattro anni del *College*.

---

freshness *n* freschezza *f*

fresh water *n* acqua *f* dolce

fret[1] [fret] **I.** <-tt-> *vi* (*worry*) agitarsi **II.** *n* **to be in a ~** essere molto agitato

fret[2] [fret] *n* MUS tasto *m, di strumento a corda*

fretful ['fret·fəl] *adj* (*person, tone*) agitato -a

fret saw ['fret·sɑː] *n* seghetto *m* da traforo

fretwork ['fret·wɜːrk] *n* lavoro *m* di intaglio

friar ['fra·ɪə] *n* frate *m*

fricative ['frɪ·kə·t̬ɪv] LING **I.** *adj* fricativo, -a **II.** *n* fricativa *f*

friction ['frɪk·ʃən] *n* (*a. fig*) attrito *m*

Friday ['fraɪ·di] *n* venerdì *m inv;* **on ~s** di venerdì; **every ~** tutti i venerdì; **this (coming) ~** questo venerdì; **on ~ mornings** di venerdì mattina; **on ~ night** venerdì notte; **last/next ~** venerdì scorso/prossimo; **every other ~** un venerdì sì e uno no; **on ~ we are going on vacation** partiamo per le vacanze venerdì

fridge [frɪdʒ] *n* frigorifero *m*

fried [fraɪd] *adj* fritto, -a

fried chicken *n* pollo *m* fritto

fried egg *n* uovo *m* fritto

friend [frend] *n* **1.** amico, -a *m, f;* **to be ~s** essere amici; **to make ~s** (**with sb**) fare amicizia (con qu); **a ~ of mine/his/hers/yours** un mio/suo/tuo amico **2.** (*supporter*) sostenitore, -trice *m, f*

friendless ['frend·ləs] *adj* senza amici

friendly ['frend·li] <-ier, -iest> *adj* (*person*) socievole; (*look, manner*) amichevole; (*house, environment*) accogliente; (*nation*) amico, -a; **to be on ~ terms with sb** essere in rapporti di amicizia con qu; **to be ~ towards sb** mostrarsi gentile con qu; **to be ~ with sb** essere amico di qu

friendly fire *n* fuoco *m* amico

friendship ['frend·ʃɪp] *n* amicizia *f*

fries [fraɪz] *npl inf* patatine*f pl* fritte

frigate ['frɪ·gət] *n* fregata *f*

fright [fraɪt] *n* **1.** (*feeling of fear*) spavento *m;* **to take ~** (**at sth**) spaventarsi (per qc) **2.** (*frightening experience*) spavento *m;* **to get a ~** prendersi uno spavento; **to give sb a ~** far prendere uno spavento a qu **3.** *inf* (*unattractive sight*) obbrobrio *m;* **to look a ~** fare paura

frighten ['fraɪ·tən] **I.** *vt* spaventare **II.** *vi* spaventarsi ◆**frighten away** *vt* far scappare, spaventando

frightened *adj* spaventato, -a

frightening *adj* spaventoso, -a

frightful ['fraɪt·fəl] *adj* spaventoso, -a

frigid ['frɪ·dʒɪd] *adj* 1.(*very cold*) molto freddo, -a 2.(*sexually*) frigido, -a 3.(*unfriendly*) freddo, -a

frigidity [frɪ·'dʒɪ·də·t̬i] *n* 1.(*sexual*) frigidità *f* 2.(*unfriendliness*) freddezza *f*

frill [frɪl] *n* 1.(*cloth*) balza *f inv* 2.**no ~s** *compagnie aeree e viaggi a basso costo*

frilly ['frɪ·li] *adj* (*dress*) con balze; (*style*) infiorettato, -a

fringe [frɪndʒ] I. *n* 1.(*decorative edging*) frangia *fpl* 2.(*edge*) margine *m; fig;* **the ~ of society** i margini della società; **the lunatic ~** la frangia estremista 3.(*fringe benefit*) beneficio *m* accessorio II. *vt* contornare III. *adj* marginale

fringe benefits *npl* ECON beneficio *m* accessorio, *bene o servizio corrisposto in aggiunta alla normale busta paga*

fringe group *n* gruppo *m* minoritario

frippery ['frɪ·pə·ri] <-ies> *n pl* fronzoli *mpl*

frisk [frɪsk] I. *vi* saltellare II. *vt* perquisire

frisky ['frɪs·ki] <-ier, -iest> *adj* 1.(*lively, energetic*) vispo, -a; (*horse*) focoso, -a 2.*inf* (*sexually*) arrapato, -a

fritter¹ ['frɪ·t̬ə·] *n* FOOD frittella *f*

fritter² ['frɪ·t̬ə·] *vt* (*reduce*) **to ~ (away)** (*money*) sperperare; (*time*) sprecare

frivolity [frɪ·'vɑ·lə·t̬i] <-ties> *n* frivolezza *f*

frivolous ['frɪ·və·ləs] *adj* frivolo, -a

frizzy ['frɪ·zi] *adj* (*hair*) crespo, -a

fro [froʊ] *adv* **to and ~** avanti e indietro

frock [frɑːk] *n* abito *m*

frog¹ [frɑːg] *n* ZOOL rana *f* ► **to have a ~ in one's throat** avere un raspino (in gola)

frog² [frɑːg] *n pej* (*French person*) mangiarane *mf, francese*

frogman ['frɑː·g·mən] <-men> *n* uomo *m* rana

frog-march ['frɑː·g·mɑːrtʃ] *vt* trascinare via con la forza, *dopo aver legato le braccia dietro la schiena*

frolic ['frɑː·lɪk] I. <-ck-> *vi* divertirsi II. *n* scherzo *m*

frolicsome ['frɑː·lɪk·səm] *adj* scherzoso, -a

from [frɑːm] *prep* 1.(*as starting point*) da; **where is he ~?** di dov'è?; **the flight ~ Boston** il volo da Boston; **to fly ~ New York to Tokyo** volare da New York a Tokio; **to appear ~ among the trees** spuntare fra gli alberi; **shirts ~ $10** camice (a partire) da $10; **~ inside** da dentro; **to drink ~ a cup/the bottle** bere da una tazza/dalla bottiglia 2.(*temporal*) **~ day to day** di giorno in giorno; **~ time to time** di quando in quando; **~ his childhood** dall'infanzia; **~ that date on(wards)** a partire da quella data 3.(*at distance to*) **100 miles ~ the river** 100 miglia dal fiume; **far ~ doing sth** lungi dal fare qc 4.(*one to another*) **to go ~ door to door** andare di porta in porta; **to tell good ~ evil** distinguere il bene dal male 5.(*originating in*) **a card ~ Paul/Corsica** una cartolina da Paul/dalla Corsica; **~ my point of view** dal mio punto di vista 6.(*in reference to*) **~ what I**

heard da quello che ho sentito; **translated ~ English** tradotto dall'inglese; **quotations ~ Joyce** citazioni da Joyce; **~ 'War and Peace'** da 'Guerra e Pace'; **to judge ~ appearances** giudicare dalle apparenze; **different ~ the others** diverso, -a dagli altri 7.(*caused by*) **~ experience** per esperienza; **weak ~ hunger** debole per la fame; **to die ~ thirst** morire di sete 8.(*removed*) **to steal/take sth ~ sb** rubare/prendere qc a qu; **to prevent sb ~ doing sth** impedire a qu di fare qc; **to keep sth ~ sb** nascondere qc a qu; **to protect ~ the sun** proteggere dal sole; **4 ~ 7 equals 3** 7 meno quattro fa 3

front [frʌnt] I. *n* 1.(*forward-facing part*) davanti *m inv;* (*of building*) facciata *f* 2.JOURN, LIT (*outside cover*) copertina *f;* (*first pages*) inizio *m* 3.(*front area*) parte *f* davanti; **in ~** davanti; **in ~ of** davanti a 4.THEAT sala *f* 5.(*deceptive appearance*) facciata *fpl;* **to put on a bold ~** fare mostra di coraggio 6.MIL fronte *m; fig;* **on the domestic/work ~** sul fronte domestico/lavorativo 7.POL fronte *m;* **a united ~** un fronte comune 8.(*promenade*) lungomare *m* 9.METEO fronte *m* II. *adj* 1.(*at the front*) davanti *inv* 2.(*first*) primo, -a III. *vt* 1.(*be head of*) capeggiare 2.TV presentare IV. *vi* guardare a; **the apartment ~s north** l'appartamento guarda a nord; **to ~ for** servire da copertura a

frontage ['frʌn·tɪdʒ] *n* facciata *f*

frontal ['frʌn·təl] *adj* ANAT, METEO frontale; (*attack*) frontale

front door *n* porta *f* d'ingresso

front-end *n* COMPUT front end *m, inv, termine utilizzato per caratterizzare le interfacce che hanno come destinatario un utente*

frontier [frʌn·'tɪr] *n a. fig* (*border*) frontiera *f*

frontiersman <-men> *n* HIST pioniere *m*

frontier station *n* posto *m* di confine

frontispiece ['frʌn·tɪs·piːs] *n* frontespizio *m*

front line *n* MIL linea *f* del fronte; *fig* prima linea *f*

front page *n* prima pagina *f*

front-page *adj* di prima pagina

front-runner *n* favorito, -a *m, f*

front-wheel drive *n* trazione *f* anteriore

front yard *n* giardino *m, davanti alla casa*

frost [frɑːst] I. *n* (*crystals*) brina *f;* (*weather*) gelata *f* II. *vt* 1.(*cover with frost*) gelare 2.(*cover with icing: cake*) glassare

frostbite ['frɑːst·baɪt] *n* congelamento *m*

frostbitten *adj* congelato, -a

frost-bound *adj* ghiacciato, -a

frosted *adj* 1.(*covered with icing*) glassato, -a 2.(*opaque: glass*) smerigliato, -a

frosting *n* (*on cake*) glassa *f*

frosty ['frɑː·sti] <-ier, -iest> *adj* 1.(*pavement*) ghiacciato, -a; (*morning*) gelido, -a 2.(*unfriendly*) gelido, -a

froth [frɑːθ] I. *n* 1.(*bubbles*) schiuma *f* 2.*fig* frivolezze *fpl* II. *vi* fare schiuma III. *vt* coprire di schiuma

frothy ['frɑː·θi] <-ier, -iest> *adj* schiumoso, -a

frown [fraʊn] **I.** *vi* **1.** aggrottare le sopracciglia; **to ~ at sb/sth** guardare qu/qc in cagnesco **2.** *fig* (*disapprove of*) **to ~ on sth** non veder di buon occhio qc **II.** *n* cipiglio *m*

frowsy *adj*, **frowzy** ['fraʊ·zi] <-ier, -iest> *adj inf* (*dirty*) sudicio, -a; (*messy*) trasandato, -a; (*room*) che sa di chiuso

froze [froʊz] *pt of* **freeze**

frozen ['froʊ·zn] **I.** *pp of* **freeze II.** *adj* (*water*) ghiacciato, -a; (*food*) surgelato, -a

frugal ['fruː·gl] *adj* frugale

frugality [fruː·'gæ·lə·t̬i] *n* frugalità *f*

fruit [fruːt] **I.** *n* **1.** (*for eating*) frutta *f*; (*on tree, product*) frutto *m* **2.** (*results*) frutto *m* ▶ **to bear ~** portare frutti; **to bear ~** (*fig*) dare frutti **II.** *vi* dare frutti

fruitcake ['fruːt·keɪk] *n* **1.** (*cake*) torta *f* di frutta secca **2.** *inf* (*crazy person*) svitato, -a *m, f*

fruitful ['fruːt·fəl] *adj* **1.** (*discussion*) fruttuoso, -a **2.** *liter* (*fertile*) fecondo, -a

fruition [fruː·'ɪ·ʃən] *n* **to bring sth to ~** portare qc a compimento; **to come to ~** realizzarsi

fruit knife *n* coltello *m* da frutta

fruitless ['fruːt·ləs] *adj* infruttuoso, -a

fruit salad *n* macedonia *f* (di frutta)

fruity ['fruː·t̬i] <-ier, -iest> *adj* **1.** fruttato, -a **2.** *inf* (*crazy*) svitato, -a

frumpish ['frʌm·pɪʃ] *adj pej* sciatto, -a

frustrate ['frʌs·treɪt] <-ting> *vt* frustrare

frustrated *adj* frustrato, -a

frustrating *adj* frustrante

frustration [frʌs·'treɪ·ʃən] *n* frustrazione *f*

fry[1] [fraɪ] <-ie-> **I.** *vt* friggere **II.** *vi* **1.** (*be cooked*) friggere **2.** *inf* (*get burned*) friggere **III.** *n* **fish ~** <f=> grigliata = di pesce

fry[2] [fraɪ] *n* **small ~** (*unimportant person*) pesce *m* piccolo; (*young person*) bambino, -a *m, f*

frying pan *n* padella *f* ▶ **to jump out of the ~ into the fire** cascare dala padella alla brace

ft. *abbr of* **foot, feet** piede *m*

FT [ˌef·'tiː] *abbr of* **full-time** tempo *m* pieno

fuchsia ['fjuː·ʃə] **I.** *n* fucsia *f* **II.** *adj* fucsia

fuck [fʌk] *vulg* **I.** *vt* scopare; **~ you!** fottiti!; **~ that idea** è un'idea di merda! **II.** *vi* scopare **III.** *n* scopata *f* **IV.** *interj* cazzo

◆**fuck off** *vi* ~! vaffanculo!

fucked up *adj vulg* (*drunk*) sbronzo, -a; (*messed up*) di merda

fucker ['fʌ·kə*r*] *n vulg* testa *f* di cazzo

fuddled ['fʌ·dld] *adj* **1.** (*confused*) confuso, -a **2.** (*drunk*) brillo, -a

fuddy-duddy ['fʌ·di·ˌdʌ·di] **I.** <-ies> *n pej, inf* persona *f* all'antica **II.** *adj pej, inf* all'antica

fudge [fʌdʒ] **I.** *n* **1.** (*candy*) caramella *f* mou **2.** (*nonsense*) sciocchezze *fpl* **II.** <-ging> *vt* (*issue*) aggirare; (*numbers, figures*) ritoccare **III.** <-ging> *vi* essere evasivo, -a

fuel ['fjuː·əl] **I.** *n* carburante *m* **II.** <-l-> *vt* **1.** (*provide with fuel*) rifornire di carburante **2.** (*increase: tension, controversy*) alimentare

fuel consumption *n* AUTO consumo *m* di car-

burante

fuel gauge *n* indicatore *m* di livello di carburante

fuel injection *n* iniezione *f, di carburante*

fuel pump *n* pompa *f* della benzina

fuel rod *n* barra *f* combustibile

fug [fʌg] *n* aria *f* viziata

fuggy ['fʌ·gi] <-ier, -iest> *adj* pieno, -a di aria viziata

fugitive ['fjuː·dʒə·t̬ɪv] **I.** *n* fuggitivo, -a *m, f* **II.** *adj* (*escaping*) fuggitivo, -a

fugue [fjuːg] *n* MUS fuga *f*

fulfil <-ll-> *vt*, **fulfill** [fʊl·'fɪl] *vt* (*ambition*) realizzare; (*task*) adempiere; (*condition, requirement*) soddisfare; (*need*) rispondere a; (*function, role*) adempiere; **to ~ oneself** realizzarsi

fulfilment *n*, **fulfillment** *n* (*of condition, requirement*) soddisfacimento *m;* (*of function, role*) adempimento *m;* (*satisfaction*) soddisfazione *f*

full [fʊl] **I.** <-er, -est> *adj* **1.** (*container, space*) pieno, -a; (*vehicle*) completo, -a **2.** (*total: support*) pieno, -a; (*recovery*) completo, -a; (*member*) a pieno titolo; **to be in ~ dress** essere in abito da cerimonia; **to be in ~ flow** essere nel bel mezzo di un discorso; **to be in ~ swing** essere in pieno svolgimento **3.** (*maximum: employment*) pieno, -a; **~ of mistakes** pieno di errori; **at ~ speed** a tutta velocità; **at ~ stretch** al massimo **4.** (*busy and active*) intenso, -a **5.** (*plump*) rotondetto, -a; **~ lips** labbra *f* carnose *pl* **6.** (*wide*) ampio, -a **7.** (*wine*) corposo, -a **8.** (*not hungry*) **to be ~** essere sazio, -a **9.** (*conceited*) **to be ~ of oneself** essere pieno, -a di sé **II.** *adv* **1.** (*completely*) completamente **2.** (*directly*) direttamente **3.** (*very*) molto; **to know ~ well** (**that** ...) sapere perfettamente (che...) **III.** *n* **in ~** per esteso; **to the ~** appieno

fullback ['fʊl·bæk] *n* SPORTS terzino *m*

full-blooded [ˌfʊl·'blʌ·dɪd] *adj* **1.** (*wholehearted*) vigoroso, -a **2.** (*animal*) di razza pura

full-blown [ˌfʊl·'bloʊn] *adj* (*disaster, scandal*) autentico, -a

full board *n* pensione *f* completa

full-bodied [ˌfʊl·'bɑː·dɪd] *adj* (*taste, wine*) corposo, -a

full-fledged [ˌfʊl·'fledʒd] *adj* **1.** (*doctor, architect*) a tutti gli effetti **2.** (*bird*) che ha messo tutte le penne

full-frontal I. *adj* (*attack*) frontale **II.** *n* nudo *m* frontale

full-grown *adj* adulto, -a

full-length *adj* **1.** (*for entire body: gown*) lungo, -a fino ai piedi; (*mirror*) a figura intera **2.** (*not short: film, book*) in versione integrale

full moon *n* luna *f* piena

fullness *n* **1.** (*being full*) pienezza *f;* **in the ~ of time** a tempo debito **2.** (*roundedness*) rotondità *f* **3.** (*richness*) ricchezza *f*

full-page *adj* a tutta pagina

full-scale *adj* **1.** (*original size*) a grandezza naturale **2.** (*all-out*) su vasta scala

full stop I. *n* punto *m;* **to come to a** ~ *fig* bloccarsi II. *adv* punto e basta

full-time *adj* a tempo pieno

fully ['fʊ·li] *adv* **1.** (*completely*) completamente **2.** (*in detail*) dettagliatamente **3.** (*at least*) almeno

fulminate ['fʌl·mɪ·neɪt] *vi* **to** ~ (**against sth**) tuonare (contro qu)

fulsome ['fʊl·səm] *adj pej* (*praise*) sperticato, -a; (*person, manner*) stucchevole

fumble ['fʌm·bl] I. *vi* **to** ~ **around for sth** frugare alla ricerca di qc; **to** ~ **for words** farfugliare II. *vt* SPORTS **to** ~ **the ball** lasciarsi sfuggire la palla

fumbler ['fʌm·blə] *n* persona *f* maldestra

fume [fjuːm] *vi* **1.** (*be angry*) essere furibondo; **to** ~ **at sb** inveire contro qu **2.** (*emit fumes*) fumare

fumigate ['fjuː·mɪ·geɪt] *vt* disinfestare, irrorando

fun [fʌn] I. *n* divertimento *m;* **it was a lot of** ~ è stato molto divertente; **full of** ~ divertente; **to do sth for** [*o* **in**] ~ fare qc per divertimento; **to do sth in** ~ fare qc per scherzo; **to have** (**a lot of**) ~ divertirsi (molto); **have** ~ **on your weekend!** buon fine settimana!; **have** ~! divertiti!; **to have** ~ **at sb's expense** ridersela alle spalle di qu; **to get a lot of** ~ **out of** [*o* **from**] **sth** spassarsela con qc; **to make** ~ **of sb, to poke** ~ **at sb** prendere in giro qu; **what** ~! che divertimento! ▸ ~ **and games** *pej* odissea *f;* **it's not all** ~ **and games** non è tutto rose e fiori II. *adj* **1.** (*enjoyable*) simpatico, -a **2.** (*funny*) divertente; **she's a real** ~ **person** *inf* è una persona molto divertente

function ['fʌŋk·ʃən] I. *n* **1.** (*of brain, tool*) funzione *f;* (*of person*) ruolo *m;* **in my** ~ **as mayor, ...** in qualità di sindaco,... **2.** MATH funzione *f* **3.** (*formal ceremony*) cerimonia *f;* (*formal social event*) ricevimento *m* II. *vi* funzionare

functional ['fʌŋk·ʃə·nl] *adj* **1.** *a.* LING funzionale **2.** (*working*) funzionante; (*operational*) operativo, -a

functionary ['fʌŋk·ʃə·ne·ri] <-ies> *n* funzionario, -a *m, f*

function key *n* COMPUT tasto *m* funzione

fund [fʌnd] I. *n* fondo *m;* **to be short of** ~**s** essere a corto di fondi; **to have a** ~ **of knowledge about sth** essere un pozzo di sapienza su qc II. *vt* finanziare

fundamental [ˌfʌn·də·'men·təl] I. *adj* fondamentale; **to be of** ~ **importance** essere di importanza fondamentale II. *n* **the** ~**s** le basi

fundamentalism [ˌfʌn·də·'men·tə·lɪ·zəm] *n* fondamentalismo *m*

fundamentalist I. *n* fondamentalista *mf* II. *adj* fondamentalista

fundamentally *adv* fondamentalmente

funding *n* (*act*) finanziamento *m;* (*resources*) fondi *mpl*

fund-raising *n* raccolta *f* di fondi

funeral ['fjuː·nə·rəl] *n* funerale *m;* **to attend a** ~ partecipare a un funerale ▸ **that's your/his** ~ *inf* tanto peggio per te/lui

funeral director *n* impresario, -a *m, f* di pompe funebri

funeral home *n* camera *f* mortuaria

funeral march <-es> *n* marcia *f* funebre

funeral parlor *n* camera *f* mortuaria

funeral pyre *n* pira *f*

funereal [fjuː·'nɪ·ri·əl] *adj* funereo, -a

fungicide ['fʌn·dʒɪ·saɪd] *n* fungicida *m*

fungus ['fʌŋ·gəs] *n* (*wild mushroom*) fungo *m;* (*mold*) muffa *f*

fun house *n* castello *m* delle streghe

funicular [fjuː·'nɪk·ju·lə] *n*, **funicular railway** *n* funicolare *f*

funk [fʌŋk] *n* **1.** (*depression*) **to be in a** ~ essere molto giù *fig* **2.** *inf* (*fear*) paura *f* **3.** (*music*) funk *m inv*

funky ['fʌŋ·ki] <-ier, -iest> *adj inf* **1.** (*musty*) **a** ~ **taste/smell** un odore/sapore di muffa **2.** (*cool*) fico, -a **3.** (*music*) funky

fun-loving *adj* che ama il divertimento

funnel ['fʌ·nəl] I. *n* **1.** (*tool*) imbuto *m* **2.** NAUT fumaiolo *m* II. <-l-> *vt* (*with funnell*) versare con l'imbuto; (*with tube, pipe*) canalizzare

funnies ['fʌ·niz] *npl* **the** ~ strisce *f pl* comiche

funny ['fʌ·ni] <-ier, -iest> *adj* **1.** (*amusing*) divertente; **to see the** ~ **side of a situation** vedere il lato comico di una situazione **2.** *inf* (*witty*) spiritoso, -a; **to try to be** ~ *inf* fare lo spiritoso **3.** (*odd, peculiar*) strano, -a; **to have a** ~ **feeling that ...** avere lo strano presentimento che...; **to have** ~ **ideas** avere idee strambe **4.** (*slightly ill*) **to feel** ~ sentirsi strano, -a

funny bone *n inf:* osso del gomito che, se urtato, provoca una sensazione di scossa elettrica

fur [fɜːr] *n* **1.** (*animal hair*) pelo *m* **2.** (*garment*) pelliccia *f*

fur coat *n* pelliccia *f*

furious ['fjʊ·ri·əs] *adj* **1.** (*very angry*) furioso, -a; **to be** ~ **about sth** essere furioso per qc; **a** ~ **outburst** un accesso di collera **2.** (*intense, violent*) violento, -a; **at a** ~ **pace** a un ritmo vertiginoso

furl [fɜːrl] *vt* (*flag, sail*) piegare

furlong ['fɜːr·lɑːŋ] *n* unità di misura equivalente a circa 200 metri, usata soprattutto nelle corse dei cavalli

furlough ['fɜːr·loʊ] *n* MIL permesso *m;* **to be on** ~ essere in pemesso

furnace ['fɜːr·nɪs] *n* (*in factory*) fornace *f;* (*for heating*) caldaia *f; fig* forno *m*

furnish ['fɜːr·nɪʃ] *vt* **1.** (*supply*) fornire; **to** ~ **sb with sth** fornire qc a qu; **to be** ~ **ed with sth** essere provvisto, -a di qc **2.** (*provide furniture for*) arredare

furnished ['fɜːr·nɪʃt] *adj* arredato, -a

furnishings ['fɜːr·nɪ·ʃɪŋz] *npl* mobili *mpl*

furniture ['fɜːr·nɪ·tʃə] *n* mobili *mpl;* **piece of** ~ mobile *m*

furniture van *n* camion *m* dei traslochi

furor ['fjʊ·rɔːr] *n* scalpore *m*

furrier ['fɜː·riə˞] *n* pellicciaio, -a *m, f*

furrow ['fɜː·roʊ] I. *n* 1.(*groove*) solco *m* 2.(*wrinkle*) ruga *f* II. *vt* corrugare; **to ~ one's brow** corrugare la fronte

furry ['fɜː·ri] <-ier, -iest> *adj* 1.peloso, -a 2.(*looking like fur*) peloso, -a; **~ toy** peluche *m inv*

further ['fɜːr·ðə˞] I. *adj comp of* **far** 1.(*greater distance*) più lontano, -a; **nothing could be ~ from his mind** non ci pensa neanche lontanamente 2.(*additional*) altro, -a; **if you have any ~ problems ...** se hai altri problemi...; **until ~ notice** fino a nuovo avviso II. *adv comp of* **far** 1.(*greater distance*) più lontano; **we didn't get much ~** non siamo arrivati tanto più avanti; **~ on** più avanti; **~ and ~** sempre più lontano; **to go ~ with sth** andare avanti con qc 2.(*more*) in più; **I have nothing ~ to say** non ho nient'altro da aggiungere ▸ **to not go** any **~** non spingersi oltre; **this can't go on** any **~** così non può continuare III. *vt* promuovere; **to ~ sb's interests** favorire gli interessi di qu

furtherance ['fɜːr·ðə·rəns] *n form* avanzamento *m*

furthermore ['fɜːr·ðə˞·mɔːr] *adv* inoltre

furthermost ['fɜːr·ðə˞·moʊst] *adj* più lontano, -a

furthest ['fɜːr·ðɪst] I. *adj* 1.*superl of* **far** 2.(*at the greatest distance*) più lontano, -a; **the ~ island from the mainland** l'isola più lontana dalla terra ferma II. *adv* 1.*superl of* **far** 2.(*greatest distance*) più lontano; **that's the ~ I can go** non posso spingermi più in là di così 3.(*greatest*) maggiormente; **prices have fallen/risen ~ in the south** i prezzi sono scesi/cresciuti di più al sud

furtive ['fɜːr·t̬ɪv] *adj* furtivo, -a

furtiveness *n* furtività *f*

fury ['fjʊ·ri] *n* furia *f;* **fit of ~** attacco *m* d'ira

fuse [fjuːz] I. *n* 1.ELEC fusibile *m;* **the ~ has blown** è saltato il fusibile 2.(*ignition device, detonator*) detonatore *m;* (*string*) miccia *f* ▸ **to have a** short **~** saltare per niente; **to** light **the ~** accendere la miccia II. *vi* 1.ELEC saltare 2.(*join together*) fondersi III. *vt* 1.ELEC far saltare 2.(*join*) fondere

fuse box <-es> *n* cassetta *f* dei fusibili

fuselage ['fjuː·sə·lɑːʒ] *n* AVIAT fusoliera *f*

fusion ['fjuː·ʒən] *n* 1.(*joining together*) fusione *f* 2.PHYS fusione *f;* **nuclear ~** fusione nucleare

fusion bomb *n* bomba *f* a fusione

fusion reactor *n* reattore *m* a fusione

fuss [fʌs] I. *n* trambusto *m;* **it's a lot of ~ about nothing** tanto rumore per nulla; **to make a ~** fare storie II. *vi* agitarsi; **to ~ over sth** preoccuparsi per qc; **to ~ over sb** soffocare qu di attenzioni

fusspot ['fʌs·pɑːt] *n inf* schizzinoso, -a *m, f*

fussy ['fʌ·si] <-ier, -iest> *adj* 1.(*overparticular*) esigente 2.(*quick to criticize*) criticone, -a

3.(*overdone, overdecorated*) troppo elaborato, -a 4.(*baby*) piagnucolone, -a

fusty ['fʌs·ti] <-ier, -iest> *adj pej* 1.(*smell*) di muffa; (*room*) che puzza di chiuso 2.(*old-fashioned*) antiquato, -a

futile ['fjuː·t̬əl] *adj* inutile; **~ attempt** vano tentativo *m;* **~ question** domanda *f* futile

futility [fjuː·'t̬ɪ·lə·t̬i] *n* inutilità *f*

future ['fjuː·tʃə˞] I. *n* 1. *a.* LING futuro *m;* **to have plans for the ~** avere progetti per il futuro; **in the ~ tense** al futuro; **in the distant/near ~** in un lontano/prossimo futuro; **what the ~ will bring** quello che porterà il futuro 2.(*prospects*) futuro *m;* **she has a great ~ ahead of her** ha un brillante avvenire avanti a sé II. *adj* futuro, -a

future perfect *n* LING futuro *m* anteriore

futures market *n* mercato *m* dei futures

futuristic [ˌfjuː·tʃə·'rɪs·tɪk] *adj* futuristico, -a

fuze [fjuːz] I. *n* (*ignition device, detonator*) detonatore *m;* (*string*) miccia *f* II. *vt* munire di miccia

fuzz [fʌz] *n* 1.(*fluff*) peluria *f* 2.(*fluffy hair*) capelli *m* crespi *pl* 3.(*short growing hair*) peluria *m;* **peach ~** *fig* pelle *f* della pesca 4. *inf* (*police*) **the ~** la polizia *f*

fuzzy ['fʌ·zi] *adj* 1.(*unclear*) sfuocato, -a 2.(*with short soft hair*) lanuginoso, -a; (*curly*) riccio, -a; (*frizzy*) crespo, -a

fuzzy logic *n* logica *f* sfumata

f-word ['ef·ˌwɜːrd] *n espressione usata per evitare di dire 'fuck'*

G

G, g [dʒiː] *n* G, g *f;* **~ as in George** G come Genova

g *abbr of* **gram** g.

GA, Ga. *n abbr of* **Georgia** GA

gab [gæb] I.<-bb-> *vi inf* ciarlare II. *n* parlantina *f;* **to have the gift of the ~** avere una bella parlantina

gabardine ['gæ·bə˞·diːn] *n* gabardine *f inv*

gabble ['gæ·bl] I. *vi* cianciare II. *vt* blaterare III. *n* ciance *fpl*

gable ['geɪ·bl] *n* ARCHIT timpano *m;* **~ roof** tetto *m* spiovente

Gabon [gæ·'boʊn] *n* Gabon *m*

Gabonese [ˌgæ·boʊ·'niːz] I. *adj* gabonese II. *n* gabonese *mf*

gad [gæd] <-dd-> *vi inf* **to ~ about** bighellonare

gadabout ['gæ·də·baʊt] *n* bighellone, -a *m, f*

gadfly ['gæd·flaɪ] <-flies> *n* tafano *m*

gadget ['gæ·dʒɪt] *n* gadget *m inv*

gadgetry ['gæ·dʒɪt·ri] *n* gadget *m inv*

Gaelic ['geɪ·lɪk] I. *n* gaelico *m* II. *adj* gaelico, -a

gaff[1] [gæf] *n* gaffa *f*

gaff² [gæf] *n s.* **gaffe**
gaffe [gæf] *n* gaffe *f inv*
gaffer ['gæ·fɚ] *n* caposquadra *mf* elettricisti
gag [gæg] I. *n* 1. (*cloth*) bavaglio *m* 2. (*joke*) battuta *f* 3. THEAT gag *f inv* II. <-gg-> *vt* (*silence*) imbavagliare III. <-gg-> *vi inf* (*to almost vomit*) avere conati di vomito
gaga ['gɑː·gɑː] *adj inf* rimbambito, -a; **to go ~** rimbambire
gage [geɪdʒ] *n, vt s.* **gauge**
gaggle ['gæ·gl] *n a. iron* manipolo *m*
gag order *n inf* silenzio *m* stampa
gaiety ['geɪ·ə·ti] *n* gaiezza *f*
gaily ['geɪ·li] *adv* gaiamente
gain [geɪn] I. *n* 1. (*increase*) aumento *m;* **~ in weight** aumento di peso 2. ECON, FIN (*profit*) guadagno *m;* **net ~** utile *m* netto 3. *fig* (*advantage*) vantaggio *m* II. *vt* 1. (*obtain*) guadagnare; **to ~ success** conseguire il successo 2. (*increase: velocity*) acquistare; **to ~ weight** ingrassare ▶ **to ~ the upper hand** prendere il sopravvento; **to ~ ground** guadagnare terreno III. *vi* 1. (*benefit*) guadagnare 2. (*increase*) aumentare; **to ~ in experience** acquistare esperienza 3. (*put on weight*) ingrassare; **when she quit her diet, she started ~ing** quando ha interrotto la dieta ha cominciato a ingrassare 4. (*clock, watch*) andare avanti
◆ **gain on** *vt* guadagnare terreno su
gainful ['geɪn·fəl] *adj* rimunerativo, -a; **~ employment** lavoro rimunerativo
gait [geɪt] *n a.* SPORTS passo *m*
gaiter ['geɪ·tɚ] *n pl* ghette *fpl*
gal [gæl] *n inf* ragazza *f*
gal. *abbr of* **gallon** gal.
gala ['geɪ·lə] I. *n* (*celebration*) (gran) gala *m inv* II. *adj* (*festive*) di gala; **~ night** serata *f* di gala
galactic [gə·'læk·tɪk] *adj* galattico, -a
Galapagos Islands [gə·'læ·pə·gəs 'aɪ·ləndz] *npl* isole *f pl* Galapagos
galaxy ['gæ·læk·si] <-ies> *n* 1. (*space*) galassia *f* 2. *fig* parata *f;* **a ~ of film stars** una parata di star del cinema
gale [geɪl] *n* burrasca *f;* **a ~-force wind** un vento di burrasca
gale warning *n* avviso *m* di burrasca
gall [gɔːl] I. *n* 1. (*bile*) bile *f* 2. (*impertinence*) sfrontatezza *f;* **to have the ~ to do sth** avere la faccia tosta di fare qc II. *vt* esasperare
gallant ['gæ·lənt] *adj* 1. (*chivalrous*) galante 2. (*brave*) valoroso, -a
gallantry ['gæ·lən·tri] *n* 1. (*chivalry*) galanteria *f* 2. (*courage*) valore *m* 3. <-tries> (*act of courtly politeness*) galanterie *fpl*
gall bladder *n* cistifellea *f*
galleon ['gæ·li·ən] *n* galeone *m*
gallery ['gæ·lə·ri] <-ries> *n a.* ARCHIT, THEAT galleria *f*
galley ['gæ·li] *n* 1. (*kitchen*) cucina *f* di bordo 2. (*ship*) galera *f*
galley proof *n* bozza *f* in colonna
gallivant [ˌgæ·lə·'vænt] *vi inf* **to ~ around** andare a zonzo
gallon ['gæ·lən] *n* gallone *m* (*3,79 l*)
gallop ['gæ·ləp] I. *vi* galoppare II. *vt* (*cause to gallop*) far galoppare III. *n* galoppo *m;* **to break into a ~** rompere al galoppo; **at a ~** *fig* a gran velocità
gallows ['gæ·loʊz] *npl* **the ~** la forca; **to send sb to the ~** mandare qu al patibolo
gallstone ['gɔːl·stoʊn] *n* calcolo *m* biliare
Gallup poll ['gæ·ləp poʊl] *n* sondaggio *m* d'opinione
galore [gə·'lɔːr] *adj* a volontà
galoshes [gə·'lɑː·ʃɪz] *npl* galosce *fpl*
galvanize ['gæl·və·naɪz] *vt a. fig* galvanizzare
Gambia ['gæm·biə] *n* Gambia *m*
Gambian I. *adj* gambiano, -a II. *n* gambiano, -a *m, f*
gambit ['gæm·bɪt] *n* 1. (*tactic*) tattica *f;* **opening ~** mossa *f* iniziale 2. (*chess move*) gambetto *m*
gamble ['gæm·bl] I. *n* scommessa *f;* **to take a ~** rischiare II. *vi* giocare d'azzardo; **to ~ on sth** scommettere su qc; **to ~ on the stock market** giocare in borsa III. *vt* (*money*) scommettere; (*one's life*) rischiare; **to ~ one's fortune/future** giocarsi il patrimonio/il futuro
gambler ['gæmb·lɚ] *n* giocatore, -trice *m, f* d'azzardo
gambling *n* gioco *m* d'azzardo
gambol ['gæm·bl] <-ll-, -l-> *vi liter* saltellare
game¹ [geɪm] I. *n* 1. (*entertaining activity*) gioco *m;* **board ~** gioco da tavolo; **~ of chance** gioco d'azzardo; **the Olympic Games** le Olimpiadi 2. (*match*) partita *f;* **a ~ of chess** una partita a scacchi 3. SPORTS (*skill level*) **to be off one's ~** *a. fig* essere fuori forma 4. (*tactic*) **the ~ is up** il giochetto è finito; **what's your ~?** a che gioco stai giocando? ▶ **to give the ~ away** scoprire gli altarini; **two can play at that ~** chi la fa l'aspetti; **to beat sb at his/her own ~** battere qu con le sue stesse armi II. *adj inf* (*willing*) pronto, -a; **to be ~ (to do sth)** starci (a fare qc); **to be ~ for anything** essere pronto a tutto
game² [geɪm] *n* (*in hunting*) cacciagione *f;* **big ~** caccia grossa
gamecock ['geɪm·kɑːk] *n* gallo *m* da combattimento
gamekeeper *n* guardacaccia *mf inv*
game show *n* gioco *m* a premi
gaming ['geɪ·mɪŋ] *n* 1. (*gambling*) gioco *m* d'azzardo 2. COMPUT videogiochi *minv*
gamma radiation *n*, **gamma rays** *npl* raggi *m pl* gamma
gammon ['gæ·mən] *n* prosciutto *m*
gamut ['gæ·mət] *n* gamma *f*
gander ['gæn·dɚ] *n* 1. (*male goose*) maschio *m* dell'oca 2. *inf* (*look*) **to take a ~** dare un'occhiata
gang [gæŋ] *n* 1. (*criminal group*) banda *f* 2. (*group of workers*) squadra *f;* **chain ~** gruppo *m* di detenuti incatenati 3. *inf* (*group of friends*) gruppo *m*

G

◆**gang up on** *vt* coalizzarsi contro

gangling ['gæŋg·lɪŋ] *adj* dinoccolato, -a

gangly ['gæŋ·gli] <-ier, -iest> *adj* dinoccolato, -a

gangplank ['gæŋ·plæŋk] *n* passerella *f*

gangrene ['gæŋ·gri:n] *n* cancrena *f*

gangrenous ['gæŋ·grə·nəs] *adj* cancrenoso, -a

gangster ['gæŋs·tɚ] *n* gangster *m inv*

gang warfare *n* guerra *f* fra bande rivali

gangway ['gæŋ·weɪ] I. *n* 1. (*gangplank*) passerella *f* 2. (*passage*) corridoio *m* II. *interj inf* pista

gantry ['gænt·ri] <-ies> *n* (*metal frame*) incastellatura *f*; AVIAT torre *f* di lancio

gap [gæp] *n* 1. (*opening*) apertura *f*; (*empty space*) spazio *m* (vuoto); **to fill a ~** colmare un vuoto 2. (*break in time*) intervallo *m* 3. (*difference*) divario *m*; **age ~** differenza *f* d'età

gape [geɪp] I. *vi* (*jacket*) aprirsi; (*person*) restare a bocca aperta II. *n* (*look*) sguardo *m* allibito; (*yawn*) sbadiglio *m*

gaping *adj* (*hole*) enorme; (*wound*) aperto, -a

garage [gə·'rɑːʒ] I. *n* 1. (*of house*) garage *m inv* 2. (*for repair*) officina *f* II. *vt* **to ~ a car** tenere la macchina in garage

garage sale *n vendita di roba usata che si tiene in garage o nel prato di fronte a casa*

garb [gɑːrb] I. *n* abiti *mpl* II. *vt* **to be ~ed as** essere vestito di

garbage ['gɑː·r·bɪdʒ] *n* spazzatura *f*; **to take** [*o* **throw**] **out the ~** buttare la spazzatura

garbage can *n* bidone *m* della spazzatura

garbage disposal *n* tritarifiuti *m inv*

garbage dump *n* discarica *f*

garbage man *n* netturbino *m*

garbage truck *n* camion *m* della nettezza urbana *inv*

garble ['gɑː·r·bl] *vt* 1. (*confuse: facts*) confondere 2. (*distort: message*) rendere indecifrabile

garbled *adj* 1. (*confused: facts*) confuso, -a 2. (*distorted: message*) indecifrabile

garden ['gɑː·r·dn] I. *n* 1. (*giardino m*; **vegetable ~** orto *m*; **~ furniture** mobili*m pl* da giardino 2. *pl* (*ornamental grounds*) giardini *mpl*; **botanical ~** orto *m* botanico II. *vi* fare del giardinaggio

gardener ['gɑːrd·nɚ] *n* giardiniere *m*

gardenia [gɑ·r·'diː·niə] *n* gardenia *f*

gardening ['gɑːrd·nɪŋ] *n* giardinaggio *m*

garden party <-ies> *n* garden-party *m inv*

gargantuan [gɑː·r·'gæn·tʃu·ən] *adj liter* gigantesco, -a

gargle ['gɑː·r·gl] I. *vi* fare gargarismi II. *n* gargarismi *mpl*

gargoyle ['gɑː·r·gɔɪl] *n* gargouille *f inv*

garish ['ge·rɪʃ] *adj* sgargiante

garland ['gɑː·r·lənd] I. *n* ghirlanda *f* II. *vt* inghirlandare

garlic ['gɑː·r·lɪk] *n* aglio *m*; **clove of ~** spicchio *m* d'aglio; **~ sauce** salsa *f* aioli

garlic press <-es> *n* spremiaglio *m inv*

garment ['gɑː·r·mənt] *n* capo *m* di vestiario

garnet ['gɑː·r·nɪt] *n* granato *m*

garnish ['gɑː·r·nɪʃ] I. *vt* guarnire II. <-es> *n* guarnizione *f*

garrison ['ge·rə·sn] I. *n* guarnigione *f* II. *vt* (*troops*) assegnare a una guarnigione; (*place*) presidiare

garrulous ['ge·rə·ləs] *adj* garrulo, -a

garter ['gɑː·r·tɚ] *n* giarrettiera *f*

garter belt *n* reggicalze *m inv*

garter stitch <-es> *n* punto *m* legaccio

gas [gæs] I. <-s(s)es> *n* 1. *a.* MED, CHEM gas *m inv*; **natural ~** gas naturale; **to cut off the ~** chiudere il gas 2. (*fuel*) benzina *f*; **unleaded ~** benzina senza piombo; **to step on the ~** accelerare 3. (*flatulence*) flatulenza *f* II. <-ss-> *vt* gassare

gas chamber *n* camera *f* a gas

gaseous ['gæ·si·əs] *adj* gassoso, -a

gas field *n* giacimento *m* di gas

gas gauge *n* indicatore *m* del livello di benzina

gas-guzzler *n inf: macchina che succhia molta benzina*

gash [gæʃ] I. <-es> *n* (*wound*) sfregio *m* II. *vt* (*wound*) sfregiare

gas heater *n* stufa *f* a gas

gas heating *n* riscaldamento *m* a gas

gasholder *n* gasometro *m*

gasket ['gæs·kɪt] *n* guarnizione *f*

gas lamp *n* lampada *f* a gas

gas lighter *n* accendino (*m* a gas)

gas mask *n* maschera *f* antigas

gas meter *n* contatore *m* del gas

gasoline ['gæ·sə·liːn] *n* benzina *f*

gasoline tank *n*, **gas tank** *n* serbatoio (*m* della benzina)

gasometer *n* gasometro *m*

gas oven *n* forno *m* a gas

gasp [gæsp] I. *vi* 1. (*breathe with difficulty*) ansimare; **to ~ for air** [*o* **breath**] boccheggiare 2. (*in shock*) rimanere senza fiato; **to ~ed in amazement** sono rimasto senza fiato per lo stupore II. *vt* **to ~ sth out** dire qc con voce soffocata III. *n* grido *m* soffocato; **he gave a ~ of astonishment** stupito, lanciò un grido soffocato ▶ **to be at one's <u>last</u> ~** essere arrivato all'ultimo respiro; **to do sth at the <u>last</u> ~** fare qc all'ultimo momento

gas pedal *n* acceleratore *m*

gas pipe *n* tubatura *f* del gas

gas pump *n* pompa *f* di benzina

gas station *n* distributore *m* di benzina

gas station attendant *n* benzinaio, -a *m, f*

gas stove *n* cucina *f* a gas

gassy ['gæ·si] <-ier, -iest> *adj* 1. (*full of gas*) gasato, -a 2. (*gas-like*) gassoso, -a

gastric ['gæs·trɪk] *adj* gastrico, -a

gastritis [gæ·'straɪ·təs] *n* gastrite *f*

gastroenteritis [ˌgæs·troʊ·en·tə·'raɪ·təs] *n* gastroenterite *f*

gastronomic [ˌgæs·trə·'nɑː·mɪk] *adj* gastronomico, -a

gastronomy [gæ·'strɑː·nə·mi] *n* gastronomia *f*

gastroscopy [ˌgæs·'troʊ·skɒ·pi] <-ies> *n* MED

gastroscopia *f*

gate [geɪt] *n* **1.** (*entrance*) cancello *m* **2.** AVIAT uscita *f* d'imbarco **3.** SPORTS (*in skiing*) porta *f* **4.** RAIL barriera *f*

gatecrash ['geɪt·kræʃ] **I.** *vt* imbucarsi a; **to ~ a party** imbucarsi a una festa **II.** *vi* imbucarsi

gatecrasher *n* imbucato, -a *m, f*

gatehouse *n* casa *f* del guardiano

gatekeeper *n* guardiano, -a *m, f*

gatepost *n* pilastro *m* ▶**between** you and me and the ~ detto tra noi

gate receipts *n pl* affluenza *f* allo stadio

gateway *n* **1.** (*entrance*) entrata *f* **2.** (*means of access*) porta *f*

gateway drug *n droga di passaggio a sostanze più pesanti*

gather ['gæ·ðɚ] **I.** *vt* **1.** (*convene: people*) radunare **2.** (*collect: flowers, information*) raccogliere **3.** (*increase*) **to ~ speed** acquistare velocità **4.** (*muster*) **to ~ one's strength** raccogliere le forze; **to ~ one's courage** trovare il coraggio **5.** (*infer*) dedurre; **to ~ that ...** dedurre che... **II.** *vi* **1.** (*convene*) radunarsi **2.** (*accumulate*) accumularsi

gathering *n* riunione *f*

GATT [gæt] *n abbr of* **General Agreement on Tariffs and Trade** GATT *m*

gaudy ['gɑː·di] <-ier, -iest> *adj* sgargiante

gauge [geɪdʒ] **I.** *n* **1.** (*measure: of bullet*) calibro *m;* (*of wire*) spessore *m;* (*of rails*) scartamento *m* **2.** (*instrument*) indicatore *m;* **rain ~** pluviometro *m;* **tyre ~** manometro *m* **3.** *fig* misura *f* **II.** *vt* **1.** (*measure*) misurare **2.** (*assess*) valutare; **it's difficult to ~ what his response will be** è difficile prevedere come reagirà

gaunt [gɑːnt] *adj* **1.** (*very thin*) emaciato, -a **2.** (*desolate*) desolato, -a

gauntlet ['gɑːnt·lɪt] *n* guanto *m* di protezione; **to take up/throw down the ~** *fig* raccogliere/lanciare il guanto (di sfida) ▶**to run the ~ of sth** *fig* esporsi a qc

gauze [gɑːz] *n a.* MED garza *f*

gauzy ['gɑː·zi] <-ier, -iest> *adj* diafano, -a

gave [geɪv] *pt of* **give**

gavel ['gæ·vl] **I.** *n* martelletto *m, del giudice, del banditore d'aste* **II.** <-ll-, -l-> *vt* riportare all'ordine, *battendo il martelletto*

gawk [gɑːk] *vi inf* stare come un salame; **to ~ at** guardare a bocca aperta

gawky ['gɑː·ki] *adj* (*tall, awkward*) allampanato, -a

gay [geɪ] **I.** *adj* **1.** (*homosexual*) gay **2.** (*cheerful*) gaio, -a **II.** *n* gay *mf inv*

gaze [geɪz] **I.** *vi* guardare; **to ~ at sth** rimirare qc **II.** *n* sguardo *f* fisso; **exposed to the public ~** rivelato al pubblico

gazelle [gə·'zel] *n* gazzella *f*

gazette [gə·'zet] *n* gazzetta *f*

gazetteer [ˌgæ·zə·'tɪr] *n* dizionario *m* geografico

GB [ˌdʒiː·'biː] *n* **1.** COMPUT *abbr of* **gigabyte** GB **2.** *abbr of* **Great Britain** GB

GDP [ˌdʒiː·diː·'piː] *n abbr of* **gross domestic product** PIL *m*

gear [gɪr] *n* **1.** TECH ingranaggio *m* **2.** AUTO marcia *f* **3.** (*equipment*) attrezzatura *f*

gearbox ['gɪr·bɑːks] <-es> *n* scatola *f* de cambios

gearshift ['gɪr·ʃɪft] *n* leva *f* del cambio

gearwheel *n* ruota *f* dentata

gee whiz ['dʒiː] *interj inf* caspita

geez [dʒiːz] *interj inf* madonna

geezer ['giː·zə] *n sl* tipo *m;* **old ~** vecchietto *m*

geisha (**girl**) ['geɪ·ʃə] *n* geisha *f*

gel [dʒel] *n* gel *m*

gelatin(**e**) ['dʒe·lə·tɪn] *n* gelatina *f*

gelatinous [dʒɪ·'læ·tə·nəs] *adj* gelatinoso, -a

geld [geld] *vt* castrare

gelding ['gel·dɪŋ] *n* castrone *m*

gem [dʒem] *n* **1.** (*jewel*) pietra *f* preziosa **2.** (*person*) perla *f fig*

Gemini ['dʒe·mɪ·ni] *n* Gemelli *mf*

gen. [dʒen] *n abbr of* **general** gener.

gender ['dʒen·də] *n* **1.** (*sexual identity*) sesso *m* **2.** LING genere *m*

gene [dʒiːn] *n* gene *m*

genealogical [ˌdʒiː·ni·ə·'lɑː·dʒɪ·kl] *adj* genealogico, -a

genealogist [ˌdʒiː·nɪ·'æ·lə·dʒɪst] *n* genealogista *mf*

genealogy [ˌdʒiː·nɪ·'æ·lə·dʒi] *n* genealogia *f*

gene bank *n* banca *f* genetica

general ['dʒen·rəl] **I.** *adj* generale; **of ~ interest** di interesse generale; **as a ~ rule** di regola; **to talk in ~ terms** parlare in termini generali **II.** *n* MIL generale *m;* **major ~** generale di divisione; **lieutenant ~** generale di corpo d'armata; **four-star ~** generale d'armata

general admission *n* posto *m* unico non numerato

general anesthetic *n* anestesia *f* generale

general assembly <-ies> *n* assemblea *f* generale

general director *n* direttore, -trice *m, f* generale

general election *n* elezioni *f pl* politiche

general hospital *n* ospedale *m* generale

generality [ˌdʒe·nə·'ræ·lə·ti] <-ies> *n* generalità *f*

generalization [ˌdʒe·nə·rə·lɪ·'zeɪ·ʃn] *n* generalizzazione *f*

generalize ['dʒe·nə·rə·laɪz] *vi, vt* generalizzare

generally ['dʒen·rə·li] *adv* **1.** (*usually*) generalmente **2.** (*widely, extensively*) in generale; **~ speaking** (parlando) in generale

general management *n* direzione *f* generale

general manager *n* direttore, -trice *m, f* generale

general partnership *n* società *f* in nome collettivo

general practitioner *n* medico *m* generico

general store *n* emporio *m*

general view *n* opinione *f* diffusa; **I do not subscribe to the ~ that ...** non sono d'accordo sull'opinione diffusa che...

generate ['dʒe·nə·reɪt] *vt* **1.**(*cause: interest*) suscitare; (*jobs*) creare; (*revenue*) produrre **2.** ELEC generare

generating station ['dʒe·nə·reɪ·tɪŋ ˌsteɪ·ʃən] *n* centrale *f* elettrica

generation [ˌdʒe·nə·'reɪ·ʃən] *n* generazione *f;* **for ~s** per generazioni

generative ['dʒe·nə·rə·tɪv] *adj* generativo, -a

generator ['dʒe·nə·reɪ·t̬ə·] *n a.* ELEC generatore *m*

generic [dʒɪ·'ne·rɪk] I. *adj* generico, -a II. *n* generico *m*

generosity [ˌdʒe·nə·'rɑː·sə·t̬i] *n* generosità *f*

generous ['dʒe·nə·rəs] *adj* generoso, -a

genesis ['dʒe·nə·sɪs] *n* genesi *f*

gene therapy [ˌdʒiːn·'θe·rə·pi] *n* terapia *f* genica

genetic [dʒɪ·'ne·t̬ɪk] *adj* genetico, -a; **~ disease** malattia *f* genetica

geneticist [dʒɪ·'ne·t̬ə·sɪst] *n* genetista *mf*

genetics *n + sing vb* genetica *f*

genial ['dʒiː·ni·əl] *adj* cordiale

geniality [ˌdʒiː·nɪ·'æ·lə·t̬i] *n* cordialità *f*

genie ['dʒiː·ni] <-nii *o* -ies> *n* genio *m*

genitalia [dʒe·nɪ·'teɪ·liə] *npl form*, **genitals** ['dʒe·nə·t̬əlz] *npl* genitali *mpl*

genitive ['dʒe·nə·t̬ɪv] I. *adj* genitivo, -a II. *n* genitivo *m*

genius ['dʒiː·ni·əs] *n* <-ses> genio *m*

genocide ['dʒe·nə·saɪd] *n* genocidio *m*

genre ['ʒɑːn·rə] *n a.* LIT genere *m*

genre painting *n* pittura *f* di genere

gent [dʒent] *n inf abbr of* **gentleman** signore *m*

genteel [dʒen·'tiːl] *adj* distinto, -a

Gentile ['dʒen·taɪl] I. *adj* gentile II. *n* gentile *mf*

gentle ['dʒen·tl] *adj* **1.**(*person*) gentile; **to be as ~ as a lamb** essere mite come un agnello **2.**(*breeze, tap on the door*) leggero, -a; (*slope*) dolce **3.**(*upper-class*) **of ~ birth** di buona famiglia

gentlefolk ['dʒen·t̬l·foʊk] *npl* gente *f* di buona famiglia

gentleman ['dʒen·t̬l·mən] <-men> *n* **1.**(*man*) signore *m;* **ladies and ~** signore e signori **2.**(*well-behaved man*) gentiluomo *m;* **he is a true ~** è un vero gentiluomo

gentlemanly ['dʒen·t̬l·mən·li] *adj* signorile

gentleman's agreement *n* gentleman's agreement *m inv, accordo basato solo sulla parola d'onore*

gentleness ['dʒen·tl·nɪs] *n* gentilezza *f*

gentlewoman ['dʒen·t̬l·wʊ·mən] <-women> *n* gentildonna *f*

gentry ['dʒent·ri] *n* aristocrazia *f*

genuine ['dʒe·nju·ɪn] *adj* **1.**(*not fake: leather, pearls*) vero, -a; (*work of art*) autentico, -a **2.**(*sincere: person, emotion*) sincero, -a

genus ['dʒiː·nəs] <-nera> *n* BIO genere *m*

geocentric [ˌdʒiː·oʊ·'sen·trɪk] *adj* geocentrico, -a

geodesic [ˌdʒɪ·ə·'de·sɪk] *adj* geodesico, -a

geographer [dʒi·'ɑː·grə·fə·] *n* geografo, -a *m, f*

geographic(al) [ˌdʒi·ə·'græ·fɪ·k(l)] *adj* geografico, -a

geography [dʒi·'ɑː·grə·fi] *n* geografia *f*

geological [ˌdʒi·ə·'lɑː·dʒɪ·kəl] *adj* geologico, -a

geologist [dʒi·'ɑː·lə·dʒɪst] *n* geologo, -a *m, f*

geology [dʒi·'ɑː·lə·dʒi] *n* geologia *f*

geometric(al) [ˌdʒi·ə·'met·rɪ·k(l)] *adj* geometrico, -a

geometry [dʒi·'ɑː·mət·ri] *n* geometria *f*

geophysical [ˌdʒi·oʊ·'fɪ·zɪ·kl] *adj* geofisico, -a

geophysics [ˌdʒi·oʊ·'fɪ·zɪks] *n + sing vb* geofisica *f*

Georgia ['dʒɔː·r·dʒə] *n* Georgia *f*

geothermal [ˌdʒi·oʊ·'θɜː·r·məl] *adj* geotermico, -a

geranium [dʒi·'reɪ·ni·əm] *n* geranio *m*

geriatric [ˌdʒe·ri·'æ·trɪk] *adj* geriatrico, -a

geriatrician [ˌdʒe·ri·ə·'trɪ·ʃən] *n* geriatra *mf*

geriatrics *n + sing vb* geriatria *f*

germ [dʒɜːrm] *n* germe *m*

German ['dʒɜː·r·mən] I. *n* **1.**(*person*) tedesco, -a *m, f* **2.**(*language*) tedesco *m* II. *adj* tedesco, -a

germane [dʒɚ·'meɪn] *adj form* pertinente

Germanic [dʒɚ·'mæ·nɪk] *adj* germanico, -a

German measles *n + sing vb* rosolia *f*

German shepherd *n* pastore *m* tedesco

Germany ['dʒɜː·r·mə·ni] *n* Germania *f*

germfree *adj* sterile

germicidal [ˌdʒɜː·r·mə·'saɪ·dəl] *adj* germicida

germicide ['dʒɜː·r·mə·saɪd] *n* germicida *m*

germinal ['dʒɜː·r·mə·nəl] *adj* germinale

germinate ['dʒɜː·r·mə·neɪt] I. *vi* germinare II. *vt* far germinare

germination [ˌdʒɜː·r·mə·'neɪ·ʃən] *n* germinazione *f*

germ warfare *n* guerra *f* batteriologica

gerontologist [ˌdʒɜ·rn·'tɑː·lə·dʒɪst] *n* gerontologo *m*

gerontology [ˌdʒɜ·rn·'tɑː·lə·dʒi] *n* gerontologia *f*

gerrymander ['dʒe·rɪ·mæn·dɚ] *vt* manipolare *i confini di una circoscrizione elettorale per favorire un partito*

gerund ['dʒe·rənd] *n* gerundio *m*

gestation [dʒe·'steɪ·ʃən] *n* gestazione *f*

gesticulate [dʒe·'stɪk·jə·leɪt] *vi form* gesticolare

gesticulation [dʒe·ˌstɪk·jə·'leɪ·ʃən] *n form* gesticolazione *f*

gesture ['dʒest·ʃə·] I. *n* gesto *m;* **a ~ towards sb** un gesto verso qu II. *vi* fare un gesto III. *vt* indicare con un gesto

get [get] I. <got, gotten> *vt inf* **1.**(*obtain, catch*) prendere; **to ~ a taxi/bus** prendere un taxi/autobus; **to ~ the impression that ...** avere l'impressione che...; **to ~ a glimpse of sb/sth** intravedere qu/qc; **to ~ the flu** prendere l'influenza **2.**(*receive*) ricevere; **to ~ sth from sb** ricevere qc da qu; **to ~ a surprise** avere una sorpresa; **we don't ~ much rain** qui non piove molto; **do you ~ channel 4?**

prendi canale 4? **3.**(*hear, understand*) capire; **to ~ a joke** capire una battuta; **to ~ sth/sb wrong** fraintendere qc/qn; **I don't ~ it** non capisco **4.**(*answer*) **to ~ the door** *inf* aprire (la porta); **to ~ the phone** *inf* rispondere (al telefono) **5.**(*buy*) comprare; **to ~ sth for sb** comprare qc a qn; **to ~ food/drinks** *inf* mangiare/bere qc **6.**(*cause to be*) **to ~ sb to do sth** far fare qc a qn; **to ~ sb/sth doing sth** far fare qc a qn/qc; **to ~ sb ready** preparare qu; **to ~ sth finished/typed** finire/battere a macchina qc **7.** *inf* **that really ~s me** (*irk*) mi secca proprio; (*make emotional*) mi fa effetto **II.** *vi* **1.** + *n/adj* (*become*) diventare; **to ~ rich** arricchirsi; **to ~ married** sposarsi; **to ~ upset** prendersela; **to ~ used to sth** abituarsi a qc; **to ~ to be sth** diventare qc; **to ~ better** migliorare; **~ better soon!** tanti auguri di pronta guarigione! **2.**(*have opportunity*) **to ~ to do sth** riuscire a fare qc; **to ~ to see sb** riuscire a vedere qu **3.**(*travel*) arrivare; **to ~ home** arrivare a casa; **to ~ to the restaurant/station** arrivare al ristorante/alla stazione **4.** *inf* (*begin*) iniziare; **to ~ to like sth** iniziare ad apprezzare qc; **to ~ cracking** mettersi all'opera; **to ~ going** darsi una mossa

◆**get across** *vt* far capire

◆**get after** *vt* inseguire

◆**get along** *vi* **1.**(*have a good relationship*) andare d'accordo **2.**(*manage*) cavarsela

◆**get around I.** *vt insep* (*avoid*) aggirare **II.** *vi* **1.**(*spread*) spargersi; **word eventually got around that ...** si è sparsa la voce che... **2.**(*travel*) viaggiare molto

◆**get at** *vt insep, inf* **1.**(*reach*) arrivare a **2.**(*suggest*) alludere a

◆**get away** *vi* andarsene

◆**get away with** *vt* cavarsela con; **to ~ murder** *fig* passarla liscia

◆**get back** *vt* ricuperare

◆**get back at** *vt* vendicarsi di

◆**get back to** *vt* ritornare a

◆**get behind** *vi* rimanere indietro

◆**get by** *vi* (*manage*) cavarsela

◆**get down I.** *vt always sep* (*disturb*) deprimere **II.** *vi* **1.**(*descend*) scendere **2.**(*dance*) scatenarsi

◆**get down to** *vt* mettersi a (fare) qc

◆**get in I.** *vi* **1.**(*arrive*) arrivare **2.**(*enter*) entrare **3.**(*become member*) essere ammesso **II.** *vt* **1.**(*say*) dire **2.**(*bring inside*) portare dentro **3.**(*accomplish*) effettuare

◆**get into** *vt insep* **1.**(*become interested in*) interessarsi a **2.**(*involve*) mettere; **to get sb into trouble** mettere qu nei guai

◆**get off I.** *vi* **1.**(*avoid punishment*) cavarsela **2.**(*leave work*) staccare **3.**(*have audacity*) osare **4.**(*have orgasm*) venire **II.** *vt always sep* **1.**(*shoot*) sparare **2.**(*help avoid punishment*) fare assolvere **3.**(*send*) spedire

◆**get on I.** *vi* **1.**(*manage*) cavarsela **2.**(*have relationship*) andare d'accordo **3.**(*age*) invecchiare **II.** *vt sl* **let's get it on** diamoci da fare

◆**get out I.** *vi* **1.**(*leave home*) uscire **2.**(*spread*) circolare **3.**(*escape*) scappare **II.** *vt* **1.**(*make leave*) fare uscire **2.**(*make spread*) far circolare

◆**get over** *vt insep* **1.**(*recover from*) riprendersi da; (*difficulty*) superare **2.**(*forget about*) **to ~ sb/sth** dimenticarsi di qu/qc

◆**get through I.** *vt* **1.**(*succeed*) passare **2.**(*finish*) finire **3.**(*make understood*) **to get it through to sb that ...** far capire a qu che ... **II.** *vi* **to ~ to sth/sb** mettersi in comunicazione con qc/qu

◆**get together I.** *vi* incontrarsi **II.** *vt* **1.**(*gather*) raccogliere **2.**(*organize*) **get it together before it's too late!** datti una mossa prima che sia troppo tardi!

◆**get up I.** *vt* **1.** *always sep, inf* (*wake*) svegliare **2.**(*muster*) trovare **3.** *insep* (*climb*) salire **4.** *inf* (*dress*) **to get sb/oneself up as** travestire qu/travestirsi da **II.** *vi* **1.**(*get out of bed*) alzarsi **2.**(*rise*) alzarsi in piedi

◆**get up to** *vt* arrivare a

get-at-able [ˌgeṯˈæˈṯəbl] *adj inf* accessibile

getaway [ˈgeṯˈəˈweɪ] *n inf* fuga *f;* **to make a** (**clean**) ~ darsi alla fuga

get-together [ˈgetˈtəˈgeˈðɚ] *n inf* festicciola *f*

get-up [ˈgeṯˈʌp] *n inf* tenuta *m*

geyser [ˈgiːˈzɚ] *n* geyser *m inv*

Ghana [ˈgɑːˈnə] *n* Ghana *m*

Ghanaian [gɑːˈniːˈən] **I.** *adj* ghanense **II.** *n* ghanense *mf*

ghastly [ˈgæsˈtli] <-ier, -iest> *adj inf* **1.**(*frightful*) spaventoso, -a **2.**(*unpleasant*) terribile **3.** *liter* (*pallid*) spettrale; **~ white/pale** bianco, -a/pallido, -a come un fantasma

gherkin [ˈgɜːrˈkɪn] *n* cetriolino *m*

ghetto [ˈgeˈṯoʊ] <-s *o* -es> *n* ghetto *m*

ghetto blaster *n inf* radione *m*

ghost [goʊst] **I.** *n a. fig* (*spirit*) fantasma *m;* **to believe in ~s** credere ai fantasmi; **haunted by ~s** infestato dai fantasmi; **the ~ of the past** i fantasmi del passato ▶ **to give up the ~** *lit* (*to die*) esalare l'ultimo respiro; *inf* (*to stop working*) smettere di funzionare **II.** *vt inf* redigere per conto di altri; **his speech was ~ed** il discorso era stato preparato da qualcun altro **III.** *vi* redigere testi per conto di altri

ghostly [ˈgəʊsˈtli] <-ier, -iest> *adj* spettrale

ghost story *n* racconto *m* di fantasmi

ghost town *n* città *f* fantasma

ghost-write *vt* redigere per conto di altri

ghost-writer *n* scrittore, -trice *m, f* fantasma

ghoul [guːl] *n* (*evil spirit*) spirito *m* demoniaco

GHz *n s.* **gigahertz** GHz

GI [ˌdʒiːˈaɪ] *n inf* soldato *m* dell'esercito USA

GI *abbr of* **government issue** proprietà *f* dello Stato

giant [ˈdʒaɪˈənt] **I.** *n* gigante *m;* **a political ~** un gigante della politica **II.** *adj* gigantesco, -a

giantess [ˈdʒaɪˈənˈtəs] *n* gigante *f*

gibberish [ˈdʒɪˈbəˈrɪʃ] *n* parole *f* senza senso *pl*

gibbon [ˈgɪˈbən] *n* gibbone *m*

gibe [dʒaɪb] I. *vi* to ~ at sb/sth schernirsi di qu/qc II. *vt* schernire III. *n* scherno *m*

giblets ['dʒɪb·lɪts] *npl* rigaglie *fpl*

giddy ['gɪ·di] <-ier, -iest> *adj* to feel ~ avere le vertigini

gift [gɪft] *n* 1. (*present*) regalo *m;* to bear ~s portare regali; to be a ~ from the Gods essere un dono caduto dal cielo 2. *inf* (*bargain*) $100 for this bicycle! it's a ~! 100 dollari per questa bici? è regalata! 3. (*talent*) dono *m;* to have a ~ for languages avere il dono delle lingue; to have the ~ of the gab *inf* avere una bella parlantina

gift certificate *n* buono *m* regalo

gifted *adj* 1. (*talented: musician*) di (gran) talento 2. (*intelligent*) ~ child bambino, -a prodigio *m*

gift horse *n* never look a ~ in the <u>mouth</u> *prov* a caval donato non si guarda in bocca *prov*

gift shop *n* gift shop *m inv*

gig[1] [gɪg] I. *n inf* (*musical performance*) concerto *m;* to do a ~ fare un concerto II. *vi* <-gg-> (*do a gig*) fare un concerto

gig[2] [gɪg] *n* COMPUT *abbr of* **gigabyte** giga

gigabyte ['gɪ·gə·baɪt] *n* gigabyte *m inv*

gigantic [dʒaɪ·'gæn·tɪk] *adj* gigantesco, -a

giggle ['gɪ·gl] I. *vi* ridacchiare II. *n* 1. (*laugh*) risolino *m* 2. *pl* the ~s ridarella *f;* to get the ~s avere la ridarella

gild [gɪld] *vt* 1. (*cover with gold*) dorare 2. (*light up*) illuminare ► to ~ the <u>lily</u> voler strafare

gilded *adj* dorato, -a

gill [gɪl] *n* (*of a fish*) branchia *f* ► to be <u>green</u> around [*o* about] the ~s *inf* essere pallido come un cencio; <u>to</u> the ~s *inf* completamente; to be <u>stuffed</u> to the ~s *inf* essere pieno come un uovo

gilt [gɪlt] I. *adj* dorato, -a II. *n* doratura *f*

gilt-edged [ˌgɪlt·'edʒd] *adj* ~ securities titoli *m pl* di Stato

gimcrack ['dʒɪm·kræk] *n* gingillo *m*

gimlet ['gɪm·lɪt] *n* 1. (*alcoholic drink*) cocktail a base di succo di lime, zucchero, gin o vodka 2. (*tool*) succhiello *m*

gimlet-eyed *adj* to be ~ avere la vista acuta

gimmick ['gɪ·mɪk] *n* 1. (*trick*) trucco *m* 2. (*attention-getter*) trovata *f;* sales ~ trovata *f* commerciale

gimmicky ['gɪ·mɪ·ki] *adj* d'effetto

gin[1] [dʒɪn] *n* gin *m inv;* ~ and tonic gin tonic *m inv*

gin[2] [dʒɪn] *n* AGR a cotton ~ sgranatrice *f*

gin[3] [dʒɪn] *n* (*card game*) gin rummy *m*

ginger ['dʒɪn·dʒɚ] I. *n* 1. (*root spice*) zenzero *m* 2. (*color*) rossiccio *m* II. *adj* rossiccio, -a

ginger ale *n* ginger ale *m,* analcolico *m* a base di zenzero

gingerbread ['dʒɪn·dʒɚ·bred] *n* pan *m* di zenzero

gingerly ['dʒɪn·dʒɚ·li] *adv* con cautela

ginger snap *n* biscotto *m* allo zenzero

gingivitis [ˌdʒɪn·dʒə·'vaɪ·t̬əs] *n* gengivite *f*

ginseng ['dʒɪn·seŋ] *n* ginseng *m*

gip [dʒɪp] *vt, n s.* **gyp**

gipsy ['dʒɪp·si] *n s.* **gypsy**

giraffe [dʒə·'ræf] *n* <-(s)> giraffa *f*

girder ['gɜːr·dɚ] *n* trave *f* (*di metallo o cemento*)

girdle ['gɜːr·dl] I. *n* 1. a. *fig* (*belt*) fascia *f* 2. (*corset*) busto *m* II. *vt a. fig* (*surround*) circondare

girl [gɜːrl] *n* 1. (*child*) bambina *f;* (*young woman*) ragazza *f* 2. (*daughter*) figlia *f* 3. the ~s *pl* (*at work*) le colleghe; (*friends*) le amiche

girl Friday *n* impiegata *f* factotum

girlfriend ['gɜːrl·frend] *n* 1. (*of man*) ragazza *f* 2. (*of woman*) amica *f*

girlhood ['gɜːrl·hʊd] *n* infanzia *f*

girlie ['gɜːr·li] *adj* senza veli

girlie magazine *n* rivista *f* di donne nude

girlish ['gɜːr·lɪʃ] *adj* da ragazza

Girl Scout *n* Giovane Esploratrice *f*

girth [gɜːrθ] *n* 1. (*circumference*) circonferenza *f* 2. *iron* (*obesity*) pancetta *f* 3. (*strap around horse*) sottopancia *m*

gist [dʒɪst] *n* to get the ~ of sth capire il succo di qc; to give sb the ~ of sth riassumere qc a qn

give [gɪv] I. *vt* <gave, given> 1. (*offer, organize*) dare; to ~ sb an excuse for sth dare a qu la scusa buona per (fare) qc; given the choice ... potendo scegliere...; to ~ sb something to eat/drink dare a qu qualcosa da mangiare/bere; to not ~ much for sth *fig* non dare molta importanza a qc; to ~ sb life in prison dare l'ergastolo a qu; don't ~ me that! *inf* ma che storie racconti!; ~ me a break! lasciami in pace!; I don't ~ a damn *inf* non me ne importa un cavolo; to ~ (it) one's all [*o* best] dare il meglio di sé; to ~ anything for sth/to do sth dare qualunque cosa per qc/per fare qc; to ~ one's life to sth sacrificare la (propria) vita a qc; to ~ birth partorire; to ~ sb a call dare un colpo di telefono a qu; to ~ sth a go provare (a fare) qc; to ~ sb to understand sth *form* dare a intendere qc a qu 2. (*cause*) far venire; (*headache, appetite*); to ~ sb the creeps far venire i brividi a qu 3. (*pass on*) to ~ sb sth contagiare qc a qu II. *vi* <gave, given> 1. (*offer*) dare; to ~ as good as one gets sapersi difendere; to ~ of one's money fare una donazione; to ~ of one's best dare il meglio di sé 2. (*stretch*) cedere; something will have to ~ *fig* bisogna che qualcosa cambi 3. what ~s? *inf* come va? ► it is better to ~ than to <u>receive</u> *prov* è più bello donare che ricevere *prov* III. *n* elasticità *f*

♦**give away** *vt* 1. (*for free*) regalare 2. (*reveal*) revelare 3. (*betray*) to give sb away tradire qu 4. *form* (*bride*) dare in matrimonio

♦**give back** *vt* restituire

♦**give in** I. *vi* 1. (*agree*) cedere; to ~ to sth

cedere a qc 2.(*admit defeat*) arrendersi II. *vt* consegnare

♦**give off** *vt* emettere

♦**give out** I. *vt* 1.(*distribute*) distribuire 2.(*announce*) annunciare 3.(*emit*) emettere II. *vi* 1.(*run out*) esaurirsi 2.(*machine*) fermarsi; (*legs*) cedere

♦**give up** I. *vt* 1.(*renounce*) rinunciare a; **to ~ candy for a month** rinunciare alla cioccolata per un mese; **to ~ doing sth** smettere di fare qc; **to ~ smoking** smettere di fumare 2.(*hand over: seat*) cedere 3.(*lose hope*) **to give sb up for dead** dare qu per spacciato; **to give sb up as lost** dare qu per scomparso 4.(*surrender*) **to give oneself up** arrendersi; **to give oneself up to the police** costituirsi II. *vi* 1.(*quit*) rinunciare 2.(*cease trying to guess*) arrendersi

give-and-take [ˌgɪv·ən·ˈteɪk] *n* (*compromise*) elasticità *f fig*

giveaway [ˈgɪv·ə·weɪ] *n* 1. *inf*(*free gift*) omaggio *m* 2. *inf*(*exposure*) prova *f* lampante

given [ˈgɪ·vn] I. *pp of* **give** II. *adj* 1.(*specified*) stabilito, -a, dato, -a; **at a ~ time and place** all'ora e nel luogo stabiliti 2. **to be ~ to** (**doing**) **sth** essere dedito a (fare) qc III. *prep ~* **that** dato che +*subj;* **~ the chance, I would go to Japan** se ne avessi la possibilità andrei in Giappone IV. *n* dato *m* di fatto; **to take sth as a ~** dare qc per scontato; **that's a ~** va da sé

giver [ˈgɪ·vɚ] *n* donatore, -trice *m*

glacé [glæs·ˈeɪ] *adj*, **glacéed** *adj inv* candito, -a; **~ fruit** frutta *f* candita

glacial [ˈgleɪ·ʃəl] *adj a. fig* glaciale

glacier [ˈgleɪ·ʃɚ] *n* ghiacciaio *m*

glad [glæd] <gladder, gladdest> *adj* contento, -a; **to be ~ about sth** essere contento di qc; **I'd be ~ to go with you** verrei volentieri con te

gladden [ˈglæ·dn] *vt* rallegrare

glade [gleɪd] *n* radura *f*

gladiator [ˈglæ·di·eɪ·t̬ɚ] *n* gladiatore *m*

gladiolus [ˌglæ·dɪ·ˈoʊ·ləs] <-es *o* -li> *n* gladiolo *m*

gladly [ˈglæd·li] *adv* volentieri

gladness [ˈglæd·nɪs] *n* contentezza *f*

glad rags *n pl, sl* **to put on one's ~** mettersi in ghingheri

glamor [ˈglæ·mɚ] *n s.* **glamour**

glamorize [ˈglæ·mə·raɪz] *vt* esaltare; **this film ~s violence** questo film esalta la violenza

glamorous [ˈglæ·mə·rəs] *adj* prestigioso, -a; (*outfit*) chic *inv*

glamour [ˈglæ·mɚ] *n* glamour *m inv,* fascino *m*

glamour-puss *n* donna *f* seducente

glance [glæns] I. *n* occhiata *f;* **to take a ~ at sth** dare un'occhiata [*o* uno sguardo] a qc; **at first ~** a prima vista; **at a ~** a colpo d'occhio II. *vi* 1.(*look cursorily*) **to ~ up** (**from sth**) sollevare lo sguardo (da qc); **to ~ around sth** dare un'occhiata intorno a qc; **to ~ over sth** dare uno sguardo a qc 2.(*shine*) brillare

♦**glance off** *vi* rimbalzare

gland [glænd] *n* ghiandola *f*

glandular [ˈglæn·dʒə·lɚ] *adj* ghiandolare

glare [gler] I. *n* 1.(*mean look*) occhiata *f* fulminante; **to give sb a ~** fulminare qu con lo sguardo 2.(*reflection*) bagliore *m;* **to be dazzled by the ~ of sth** restare abbagliato da qc II. *vi* 1.(*look*) fulminare con lo sguardo 2.(*shine*) sfolgorare; **the sun ~s down on my eyes** il sole mi sta abbagliando

glaring *adj* 1.(*obvious*) palese 2.(*sun*) sfolgorante 3.(*hostile: eyes*) minaccioso, -a

glass [glæs] <-es> *n* 1.(*material*) vetro *m;* **pane of ~** lastra *f* di vetro 2.(*container, glassful*) bicchiere *m;* **a ~ of wine** un bicchiere di vino; **a wine ~** un bicchiere da vino 3. *pl* occhiali *mpl* 4.(*glassware*) cristalleria *f*

glass blower [ˈglæs·ˌbloʊ·ɚ] *n* soffiatore, -trice di vetro *m*

glass cutter *n* tagliavetro *minv*

glassful [ˈglæs·fʊl] *n* bicchiere *m;* **a ~ of orange juice** un bicchiere di succo d'arancia

glasshouse [ˈglæs·haʊs] *n* serra *m*

glassware *n* cristalleria *f*

glassworks *npl* vetreria *f*

glassy [ˈglæ·si] <-ier, -iest> *adj* 1. *liter* (*as glass: sea, lake*) come uno specchio 2.(*eyes*) vitreo, -a

glaucoma [glɑ·ˈkoʊ·mə] *n* glaucoma *m*

glaucous [ˈglɑ·kəs] *adj* glauco, -a

glaze [gleɪz] I. *n* CULIN glassa *f;* (*pottery*) vernice *f* II. *vt* 1.(*pottery*) invetriare; (*donut*) glassare 2.(*window*) mettere i vetri a

glazier [ˈgleɪ·zi·ɚ] *n* vetraio, -a *m, f*

gleam [gliːm] I. *n* bagliore *m;* **~ of hope** raggio *m* di speranza II. *vi* luccicare

glean [gliːn] *vt* (*information*) raccogliere

gleanings *npl* informazioni *f* raccolte *pl*

glee [gliː] *n* gioia *f;* **to do sth with ~** fare qc con gioia

gleeful [ˈgliː·fəl] *adj* (*smile, shout*) di gioia

glen [glen] *n* valle *f*

glib [glɪb] <glibber, glibbest> *adj* disinvolto, -a

glide [glaɪd] I. *vi* 1.(*move smoothly*) scivolare 2. AVIAT planare II. *n* 1.(*sliding movement*) passo *m* scivolato 2. AVIAT volo *m* planato

glider [ˈglaɪ·dɚ] *n* aliante *m*

glider pilot *n* pilota *mf* di aliante

gliding [ˈglaɪ·dɪŋ] *n* volo *m* a vela

glimmer [ˈglɪ·mɚ] I. *vi* baluginare II. *n* (*light*) baluginio *m;* **~ of hope** barlume *m* di speranza

glimpse [glɪmps] I. *vt* intravedere II. *n* **to catch a ~ of** intravedere

glint [glɪnt] I. *vi* scintillare; **to ~ with sth** brillare di qc II. *n* scintillio *m*

glisten [ˈglɪ·sn] *vi* scintillare

glitch [glɪtʃ] <-es> *n inf* intoppo *m*

glitter [ˈglɪ·t̬ɚ] I. *vi* luccicare II. *n* 1.(*sparkling*) luccichio *m* 2.(*excitement*) sfolgorio *m* 3.(*shiny material*) brillantini *mpl*

glittering *adj* 1.(*sparkling*) luccicante 2.(*exciting, impressive*) sfolgorante

glitz [glɪts] *n* sfarzo *m*

glitzy [ˈglɪ·tsi] <-ier, -iest> *adj inf* sfarzoso, -a

gloat [gloʊt] I. *vi* gongolare; **to ~ over/at sth** gongolare per qc II. *n* gongolamento *m*

global [ˈgloʊ·bl] *adj* globale

global warming *n* riscaldamento *m* globale

globe [gloʊb] *n* **1.**(*world*) mondo *m* **2.**(*object*) mappamondo *m*

globetrotter [ˈgloʊb·ˌtra:·tə·] *n* giramondo *mf inv*

globule [ˈglɑːb·juːl] *n* globulo *m*

gloom [gluːm] *n* **1.**(*hopelessness*) disperazione *f;* **~ and doom** pessimismo *m* **2.**(*darkness*) oscurità *f*

gloominess [ˈgluː·mɪ·nəs] *n* **1.**(*hopelessness*) disperazione *f* **2.**(*darkness*) oscurità *f*

gloomy [ˈgluː·mi] <-ier, -iest> *adj* **1.**(*dismal*) deprimente; **to be ~ about sth** essere pessimista rispetto a qc; **to feel ~** sentirsi depresso, -a **2.**(*dark*) tetro, -a

glorification [ˌglɔː·rə·fə·ˈkeɪ·ʃən] *n* glorificazione *f*

glorify [ˈglɔː·rə·faɪ] <-ie-> *vt* glorificare; **to ~ God** REL glorificare Dio

glorious [ˈglɔː·ri·əs] *adj* **1.**(*honorable, illustrious*) glorioso, -a **2.**(*splendid: day, weather*) splendido, -a

glory [ˈglɔː·ri] I. *n* **1.**(*honor, adoration*) gloria *f;* **to bathe in reflected ~** brillare di luce riflessa; **to cover oneself in ~** coprirsi di gloria; **~ be!** (*thank God!*) grazie a Dio! **2.**(*splendor*) splendore *m;* **in all her ~** in tutto il suo splendore **3.**(*state of delight*) **to be in one's ~** essere all'apice II. <-ie-> *vi* gloriarsi; **to ~ in sth** gloriarsi di qc

gloss¹ [glɑːs] *n* **1.**(*shine*) lucentezza *f;* **high ~** alta lucentezza **2.**(*shiny substance*) vernice *f* **3.**(*shiny finish*) verniciatura *f* **4.**(*shiny paint*) smalto *m* **5.**(*lip moisturizer*) lipgloss *m inv*

gloss² [glɑːs] I. <-es> *n* glossa *f* II. *vt* glossare
 ◆**gloss over** *vt* glissare su

glossary [ˈglɑː·sə·ri] <-ies> *n* PUBL, LIT glossario *m*

glossy [ˈglɑː·si] I. <-ier, -iest> *adj* **1.**(*shiny*) lucido, -a **2.** *inf* (*superficially attractive*) patinato, -a II. <-ies> *n* PHOT fotografia *f* patinata

glottal stop [ˈglɑː·təl·ˈstɑːp] *n* LING occlusiva *f* glottale

glottis [ˈglɑː·təs] <-es> *n* ANAT, MED glottide *f*

glove [glʌv] I. *n* guanto *m;* **leather/wool ~s** guanti di pelle/lana; **a pair of ~s** un paio di guanti; **to put on/take off one's ~s** mettersi/togliersi i guanti ▶ **to fit like a ~** calzare come un guanto II. *vt* **1.**(*dress in gloves*) **to ~ one's hands** mettersi i guanti **2.**(*catch*) agguantare

glove box *n*, **glove compartment** *n* AUTO vano *m* portaoggetti

glow [gloʊ] I. *n* **1.**(*light*) bagliore *m* **2.**(*warmth and redness*) calore *m* **3.**(*good feeling*) (piacevole) sensazione *f;* **~ of happiness** sensazione *f* di felicità; **~ of pride** sentimento *m* di orgoglio; **~ of satisfaction** senso *m* di soddisfazione II. *vi* **1.**(*produce light*) brillare **2.**(*be red and hot*) ardere **3.**(*look radiant*) (ri)splendere

glower [ˈglaʊ·ə·] I. *vi* guardare torvo; **to ~ at sb** guardare torvo qu II. *n* sguardo *m* torvo

glowing *adj* (*embers*) ardente; (*report, praise*) entusiastico, -a

glow-worm *n* lucciola *f*

glucose [ˈgluː·koʊs] *n* glucosio *m;* **~ syrup** sciroppo *m* di glucosio

glue [gluː] I. *n* colla *f;* **to sniff ~** sniffare colla II. *vt* incollare; **to ~ sth together** incollare qc; **to ~ sth on** incollare qc; **to be ~d to sth** *fig* stare incollato a qc; **to keep one's eyes ~d to sth/sb** *fig* tenere gli occhi incollati a qc/qu

glue stick *n* colla *f* stick

glum [glʌm] <glummer, glummest> *adj* **1.**(*morose, downcast*) abbattuto, -a; **to be/feel ~** (*about sth*) abbattersi (per qc) **2.**(*drab*) tetro, -a

glut [glʌt] I. *n* ECON eccedenza *f;* **a ~ of sth** un'eccedenza di qc II. <-tt-> *vt* ECON saturare

gluten [ˈgluː·tən] *n* glutine *m*

glutinous [ˈgluː·t·nəs] *adj* colloso, -a

glutton [glʌtn] *n* **1.**(*overeater*) goloso, -a *m, f* **2.** *inf* (*enthusiast*) **to be a ~ for sth** essere appassionato di qc

gluttonous [ˈglʌ·tə·nəs] *adj* avido, -a

gluttony [ˈglʌ·tə·ni] *n* gola *f,* golosità *f*

glycerin [ˈglɪ·sə·rɪn] *n*, **glycerine** [ˈglɪ·sə·riːn] *n*, **glycerol** [ˈglɪ·sə·rɑːl] *n* glicerina *f*

glycol [ˈglaɪ·kɑːl] *n* glicol *m*

gnarled [nɑːrld] *adj* nodoso, -a

gnash [næʃ] *vt* **to ~ one's teeth** digrignare i denti

gnat [næt] *n* BIO zanzara *f*

gnaw [nɑː] I. *vi* **1.**(*chew*) **to ~ at** [*o* on] **sth** rosicchiare qc **2.** *fig* (*deplete*) **to ~ away at sth** erodere qc **3.**(*bother*) **to ~ at sb** assillare qu II. *vt* **1.**(*chew*) rosicchiare **2.** *fig* (*pursue*) **to be ~ed by doubt/guilt** essere assillato dal dubbio/dal senso di colpa

gnawing *adj* assillante

gnome [noʊm] *n* gnomo *m*

GNP [ˌdʒiː·enˈpiː] *abbr of* **Gross National Product** PNL

gnu [nuː] <-(s)> *n* ZOOL gnu *m inv*

go¹ [goʊ] I. <went, gone> *vi* **1.**(*proceed*) andare; **to ~** (**and**) **do sth** andare a fare qc; **to ~ home** andare a casa **2.**(*travel*) andare; **to ~ on a cruise** andare in crociera; **to ~ on a holiday** andare in vacanza; **to ~ on a trip** fare un viaggio; **to ~ abroad** andare all'estero **3.**(*adopt position*) **when I ~ like this, my back hurts** quando faccio così mi duole la schiena **4.**(*leave*) partire; **to have to ~** dover andare; **when does the bus ~?** quando parte l'autobus? **5.**(*do*) **to ~ biking** andare in bicicletta; **to ~ camping/fishing/shopping** andare in campeggio/a pesca/a fare spese; **to ~ jogging** fare jogging; **to ~ swimming** andare in piscina **6.**(*attend*) andare; **to ~ to a concert** andare a un concerto; **to ~ to a movie** andare al cinema; **to ~ to a party** andare a una festa **7.** + *adj or n* (*become*) diventare; **to ~ senile** rimbambire; **to ~ bank-**

rupt fare fallimento; **to ~ public** rendere pubblico; **to ~ communist** diventare comunista; **to ~ adrift** andare alla deriva; **to ~ bald** diventare calvo; **to ~ haywire** andare in tilt; **to ~ to sleep** addormentarsi; **to ~ wrong** andare storto **8.** + *adj* (*exist*) **to ~ hungry/thirsty** soffrire la fame/sete; **to ~ unsolved** restare irrisolto; **to ~ unnoticed** passare inosservato; **as prices ~ ...** considerando i prezzi ... **9.** (*happen*) **to ~ badly/well** andare male/bene; **to ~ from bad to worse** andare di male in peggio; **the way things are ~ing** visto come stanno andando le cose **10.** (*pass*) passare; **time seems to ~ faster** il tempo sembra passare più in fretta **11.** (*begin*) cominciare; **ready, set, ~** pronti, attenti, via **12.** (*fail*) **to ~ downhill** andare peggiorando **13.** (*belong*) andare; **where does this ~?** dove va questo? **14.** (*fit*) stare; **that picture would ~ well on that wall** quel quadro starebbe bene su quella parete **15.** (*lead*) condurre; **this highway ~es all the way to California** questa autostrada va fino in California **16.** (*extend*) andare; **those numbers ~ from 1 to 10** questi numeri vanno dall'1 al 10 **17.** (*function*) funzionare; **to ~ slow** rallentare; **to get sth to ~** far funzionare qc; **to keep a conversation ~ing** mantenere viva una conversazione; **the ambulance had sirens ~ing** l'ambulanza andava a sirene spiegate **18.** (*be sold*) essere venduto; **the painting went for a lot more than was expected** il dipinto fu venduto a una cifra superiore a quella stimata; **to ~ for $50** essere in vendita a 50 dollari; **to ~ like hot cakes** *fig* vendersi come il pane **19.** (*contribute*) contribuire; **love and friendship ~ to make a lasting relationship** amore e amicizia contribuiscono a consolidare una relazione **20.** (*be told*) **as the saying ~es** come dice il proverbio **21.** GAMES toccare, spettare; **I ~ now** ora tocca a me **22.** *inf* (*use the toilet*) **do any of the kids have to ~?** qualcuno dei bambini deve andare al bagno? **23.** (*express annoyance*) **~ climb a rock!** *inf* vai al diavolo! ▸ **what he says ~es** la sua parola è legge; **anything ~es** tutto è ammesso; **here ~!** stiamo a vedere! **II.** <went, gone> *vt* **1.** *inf* (*say*) fare; **and then he goes, "Knock it off!"** e poi fa "Smettila!"; **ducks ~ 'quack'** le anatre fanno 'qua' **2.** (*make*) fare; **to ~ it alone** farlo da solo **III.** <-es> *n* **1.** (*attempt*) tentativo *m*; **all in one ~** tutto in una volta; **to have a ~ at sth** provare a fare qc; **to have a ~ at sb about sth** prendersela con qu per qc **2.** (*a success*) **to be no ~** essere impossibile; **to make a ~ of sth** riuscire in qc **3.** (*activity*) dinamismo *m*; **to be on the ~** essere sempre attivo; **from the word** ~ dall'inizio **IV.** *adj* AVIAT pronto, -a
go² [gəʊ] *n* (*game*) go *m*

◆**go about I.** *vt insep* **1.** (*proceed with*) occuparsi di; **to ~ one's business** occuparsi delle proprie faccende **2.** (*perform a task*) procedere; **how does one ~ it?** qual è la prassi? **II.** *vi* andare in giro

◆**go after** *vt insep* **1.** (*follow*) seguire; **to ~ sb** andare dietro a qu **2.** (*chase*) inseguire **3.** (*try to get*) cercare di ottenere

◆**go against** *vt insep* **1.** (*contradict*) andare contro a **2.** (*oppose*) opporsi a **3.** (*be unfavorable*) essere sfavorevole a

◆**go ahead** *vi* **1.** (*begin*) iniziare; **all preparations have finished but they can't ~** i preparativi sono finiti ma non si può iniziare **2.** (*happen*) aver luogo; **the meeting will ~ as planned** la riunione si terrà come previsto **3.** (*give permission*) **~!** fai pure!

◆**go along** *vi* procedere

◆**go around** *vi* **1.** (*be enough*) bastare; **are there enough pens to ~?** le penne bastano per tutti? **2.** (*visit*) **to ~ to sb's** passare da qu; **to ~ and see sb** passare a trovare qu **3.** (*spin*) ruotare **4.** (*be in circulation*) girare; **it's going around that ...** gira voce che...

◆**go at** *vt insep* **1.** (*attack*) avventarsi su **2.** (*work hard*) **to ~ it** darci dentro

◆**go away** *vi* **1.** (*travel*) viaggiare **2.** (*leave*) andarsene **3.** (*disappear*) sparire

◆**go back** *vi* **1.** (*move backwards*) retrocedere **2.** (*return*) ritornare **3.** (*date back*) risalire

◆**go between** *vi* fare da intermediario

◆**go beyond** *vt* **1.** (*proceed past*) oltrepassare **2.** (*exceed*) superare

◆**go by** *vi* **1.** (*move past*) passare **2.** (*pass*) trascorrere; **in days gone by** *form* in passato; **to let sth ~** lasciarsi scappare qc

◆**go down I.** *vt insep* scendere in; **to ~ a mine** calarsi in miniera **II.** *vi* **1.** (*sun*) calare; (*ship*) affondare; (*plane*) precipitare; **to ~ on all fours** mettersi a quattro zampe **2.** (*become lower*) diminuire; (*become worse*) peggiorare; **to ~ in sb's estimation** scendere nella stima di qu **3.** *sl* (*happen*) succedere **4.** (*lose*) perdere; **to ~ to sb/sth** essere battuto da qu/qc; **to ~ without a fight** arrendersi senza lottare **5.** (*be received*) essere accolto; **to ~ well/badly (with sb)** essere accolto bene/male (da qu) **6.** (*be remembered*) essere ricordato; **to ~ in history** passare alla storia **7.** *vulg* (*give oral sex to*) **to ~ on sb** fare sesso orale con qu

◆**go far** *vi* **1.** (*have success*) andare lontano **2.** (*contribute*) **to ~ towards sth** contribuire in maniera significativa a qc

◆**go for** *vt insep* **1.** (*fetch*) andare a prendere; **could you ~ oranges?** puoi andare a prendere delle arance? **2.** (*try to achieve*) cercare di ottenere; (*try to grasp*) cercare di prendere; **~ it!** buttati! *fig* **3.** (*choose*) scegliere **4.** (*attack*) aggredire; **to ~ sb with sth** aggredire qu con qc **5.** (*sell for*) essere in vendita a **6.** *inf* (*like*) amare; **I don't ~ for war movies** non mi piacciono i film di guerra

◆**go in** *vi* **1.** (*enter*) entrare **2.** (*belong in*) andare; **the forks ~ that drawer** le forchette vanno in quel cassetto

◆**go into** *vt insep* **1.** (*enter*) entrare in **2.** (*fit into*) stare in; **two goes into eight four times**

MATH il due nell'otto sta quattro volte **3.** (*begin*) entrare; **to ~ a coma** entrare in coma; **to ~ a trance** andare in trance; **to ~ action** passare all'azione; **to ~ effect** entrare in vigore; **to ~ politics** entrare in politica; **to ~ production** entrare in produzione; **to ~ the military** entrare nelle forze armate **4.** (*examine and discuss*) parlare di; **to ~ detail** entrare nei particolari **5.** (*be used in*) essere impiegato in **6.** (*crash into*) sbattersi contro

◆**go off** *vi* **1.** (*explode: bomb*) esplodere **2.** (*make sound: alarm clock, siren*) suonare **3.** (*proceed*) andare; **to ~ badly/well** andare male/bene **4.** (*leave*) andarsene **5.** (*stop working*) spegnersi **6.** (*digress*) divagare; **to ~ the subject** uscire dall'argomento ▶**to ~ the deep end** partire per la tangente

◆**go on** I. *vi* **1.** (*move on*) andare avanti **2.** (*continue*) continuare; (*continue speaking*) continuare a parlare; **the show must ~** lo spettacolo deve continuare **3.** (*go further*) andare oltre; **to ~ ahead** avanzare **4.** (*pass*) passare **5.** (*happen*) succedere **6.** (*start*) accendersi II. *vt insep* basarsi su III. *interj* (*as encouragement*) dai; (*express disbelief*) ma dai

◆**go out** *vi* **1.** (*leave*) uscire; **to ~ to dinner** andare a cena fuori; **to ~ with sb** uscire con qu **2.** (*stop working*) spegnersi **3.** (*recede*) calare **4.** (*become unfashionable*) passare di moda

◆**go over** I. *vt insep* **1.** (*examine*) controllare **2.** (*cross*) attraversare; **to ~ a border** passare una frontiera; **to ~ a river** guadare un fiume **3.** (*exceed*) superare; **to ~ a budget** sforare un budget II. *vi* **to ~ to** (*visit*) passare da; (*change party*) passare a

◆**go through** *vt insep* **1.** (*pass*) attraversare **2.** (*experience*) attraversare; (*operation*) subire **3.** (*practice, review*) ripassare **4.** (*be approved*) essere approvato **5.** (*use up*) consumare **6.** (*look through*) frugare in

◆**go to** *vt insep* andare a; **to ~ the country** indire le elezioni politiche; **to ~ court** andare in tribunale

◆**go together** *vi* **1.** (*harmonize*) **to ~** (**with sth**) stare bene (con qc) **2.** (*date*) stare insieme

◆**go under** *vi* **1.** NAUT (*sink*) affondare **2.** (*move below*) andare sotto **3.** (*fail*) andare in fallimento

◆**go up** *vi* **1.** (*move higher*) salire **2.** (*increase*) aumentare **3.** (*approach*) **to ~ to sb/sth** avvicinarsi a qu/qc **4.** (*be built*) sorgere **5.** (*explode*) esplodere; **to ~ in flames** andare in fiamme

◆**go with** *vt insep* **1.** (*accompany*) accompagnare **2.** (*match*) abbinarsi con **3.** (*agree with*) approvare; **to ~ sb on sth** concordare con qu su qc **4.** (*follow*) essere collegato a **5.** (*date*) andare con

◆**go without** *vt insep* fare a meno di
goad [goʊd] I. *vt* **1.** (*spur*) incitare **2.** (*tease*) punzecchiare II. *n* **1.** (*motivating factor*) sti-

molo *m* **2.** AGR pungolo *m*
go-ahead ['goʊ·ə·hed] *n* (*permission*) **to give/receive the ~** dare/ricevere l'OK
goal [goʊl] *n* **1.** (*aim*) obiettivo *m;* **to achieve/set a ~** raggiungere/prefiggersi un obiettivo **2.** SPORTS (*scoring area*) porta *f;* **to play in ~** giocare in porta **3.** SPORTS (*point*) gol *m inv,* rete *f;* **to score a ~** segnare un gol
goalie ['goʊ·li] *n inf,* **goalkeeper** ['goʊl·ˌki·pə'] *n* SPORTS portiere *m*
goal line *n* SPORTS linea *f* di porta
goalpost *n* SPORTS palo *m* della porta
goat [goʊt] *n* **1.** ZOOL capra *f;* **~'s milk** latte *m* di capra; **~'s cheese** caprino *m;* **mountain ~** capra delle nevi **2.** *inf* (*man*) caprone *m* ▶**to get sb's ~** *inf* fare imbestialire qu
goatee [goʊ·'ti:] *n* pizzo *m, barba*
gobble ['gɑː·bl] I. *vi* **1.** *inf* (*eat*) ingozzarsi **2.** (*make turkey noise*) fare glu glu II. *vt inf* ingozzarsi di III. *n* glu glu *m*
gobbledegook, gobbledygook ['gɑː·bl·di·ˌguːk] *n inf* linguaggio *m* incomprensibile
go-between ['goʊ·bət·wiːn] *n* intermediario, -a *m, f;* **to act as a ~** fare da intermediario
goblet ['gɑːb·lət] *n* calice *m*
goblin ['gɑːb·lɪn] *n* folletto *m*
go-cart ['goʊ·kɑːrt] *n* AUTO, SPORTS go-kart *m inv*
god [gɑːd] *n* **1.** REL God Dio; **God bless you** Dio ti/vi benedica; **God forbid** Dio non voglia; **God** (**only**) **knows** Dio (solo lo) sa; **please God!** se Dio vuole!; **for God's sake!** per amor di Dio! **2.** REL **Greek/Roman ~s** dei *m pl* greci/romani **3.** (*idolized person*) dio *m*
God-awful *adj sl* horrible; **the ~ truth** la tremenda verità
godchild *n* figlioccio, -a *m, f*
goddamn(ed) *adj sl* maledetto, -a
goddaughter *n* figlioccia *f*
goddess ['gɑː·dɪs] <-es> *n* dea *f*
godfather *n* padrino *m*
God-fearing *adj* timorato, -a di Dio
godforsaken *adj* dimenticato, -a da Dio
godless ['gɑːd·lɪs] *adj* **1.** (*without God*) senza Dio **2.** (*evil*) empio, -a
godlike ['gɑːd·laɪk] *adj* divino, -a
godly ['gɑːd·li] *adj* pio, -a
godmother *n* madrina *f*
godparents *npl* padrino *m* e madrina *f*
godsend *n inf* dono *m* del cielo; **to be a ~** (**to sb**) essere una manna (per qu)
godson *n* figlioccio *m*
goes [goʊz] *3rd pers sing of* go
go-getter [ˌgəʊ·'ge·tə'] *n inf* persona *f* intraprendente
goggle ['gɑː·gl] I. *n pl* (*glasses*) occhiali *mpl;* **safety/ski/swim ~s** occhiali di protezione/da sci/nuoto II. *vi inf* **to ~ at sb/sth** guardare con occhi sgranati qu/qs
goggle-eyed ['gɑː·gl·aɪd] *adj inf* con gli occhi sgranati
go-go dancer ['goʊ·goʊ·'dæn·sə'] *n* cubista *mf*

go-go dancing *n* animazione *f* nei locali notturni

going ['goʊ·ɪŋ] I. *n* 1.(*departure*) partenza *f* 2.(*conditions*) (condizioni *f pl* del) terreno *m*; **while the ~ is good** finché le cose vanno bene 3.(*progress*) **it's hard/heavy ~** è difficile/pesante ▶ **when the ~ gets** <u>tough</u> (**the tough get ~**) quando il gioco si fa duro (i duri entrano in gioco) II. *adj* 1.(*available*) in circolazione 2.(*in action*) in moto; **to get sth ~** mettere in moto qc 3.(*current*) attuale; **~ price** prezzo *m* di mercato III. *vi aux* **to be ~ to do sth** stare per fare qc; **it's ~ to rain** sta per piovere

going-away party *n* festa *f* d'addio

goings-on [ˌgoʊ·ɪŋz·'ɑːn] *npl* (*events*) **strange/odd ~** fatti *m* strani *pl*

goiter ['gɔɪ·ṭə] *n* MED gozzo *m*

go-kart ['goʊ·kɑːrt] *n s.* go-cart

gold [goʊld] I. *n* 1.(*metal*) oro *m;* **to pan for ~** lavare (col setaccio) le sabbie aurifere; **to strike ~** trovare l'oro; **to be dripping with ~** *fig* essere carico d'oro 2.SPORTS medaglia *f* d'oro; **to win the ~** vincere l'oro; **to go for ~** inseguire l'oro ▶ **to be worth one's** <u>weight</u> **in ~** valere tanto oro quanto si pesa; **to be** <u>good</u> **as ~** essere un angelo; **all that** <u>glitters</u> **is not ~** *prov* non è tutto oro quello che luccica *prov* II. *adj* d'oro; **a ~ ring** un anello d'oro

gold bullion *n* lingotti *m* d'oro *pl*

gold digger *n* 1.(*gold miner*) cercatore, -trice *m, f* d'oro 2.(*money-seeker*) avventuriera *f*

gold dust *n* oro *m* in polvere; **to be like ~** *fig* essere una mosca bianca

golden ['goʊl·dən] *adj* 1.d'oro; **~ anniversary** nozze *f pl* d'oro 2.(*color*) dorato, -a 3.(*very good*) d'oro; **~ oldies** MUS canzoni *f pl* d'altri tempi

golden age *n* epoca *f* d'oro

golden goose *n* gallina *f* dalle uova d'oro

golden mean *n* giusto mezzo *m*

golden triangle *n* **the ~** il Triangolo d'Oro

golden wedding *n* nozze *f pl* d'oro

goldfinch ['goʊld·fɪntʃ] <-es> *n* cardellino *m*

goldfish *n inv* pesce *m* rosso

gold leaf *n* foglia *f* d'oro

gold medal *n* SPORTS medaglia *f* d'oro

goldmine *n a. fig* miniera *f* d'oro

gold nugget *n* pepita *f* d'oro

gold plating *n* placcatura *f* d'oro

gold reserve *n* riserva *f* aurea

goldsmith *n* orefice *m*

gold standard *n* FIN sistema *m* aureo

golf [gɑːlf] I. *n* golf *m;* **to play ~** giocare a golf; **miniature ~** minigolf *m* II. *vi* giocare a golf

golf ball *n* pallina *f* da golf

golf-ball typewriter *n* macchina *f* da scrivere a testina rotante

golf club *n* (*stick*) mazza *f* da golf

golf course *n* campo *m* da golf

golfer ['gɑːl·fə] *n* golfista *mf*

Goliath [gə·'laɪ·əθ] *n* Golia; **a David and ~**

battle *fig* una battaglia tra Davide e Golia

golliwog *n*, **golliwogg** ['gɑː·lɪ·wɔːg] *n* bambolotto negro di pezza, *espressione offensiva*

golly ['gɑː·li] *interj inf* (**by**) ~ perbacco

gondola ['gɑːn·də·lə] *n* gondola *f*

gondolier [ˌgɑːn·də·'lɪr] *n* gondoliere *m*

gone [gɑːn] I. *pp of* go II. *adj* 1.(*absent*) andato, -a, partito, -a 2.(*used up*) finito, -a 3. *inf* (*dead*) morto, -a 4.(*lost*) perduto, -a

goner ['gɑː·nə] *n sl* **to be a ~** essere spacciato, -a

gong [gɑːŋ] *n* gong *m inv*

gonorrhea [ˌgɑː·nə·'ri·ə] *n* gonorrea *f*

goo [guː] *n inf* 1.(*substance*) sostanza *f* appiccicosa 2.(*sentimentality*) sentimentalismo *m*

goober *n reg* nocciolina *f* americana

good [gʊd] I.<better, best> *adj* 1.(*of high quality*) buono, -a; **~ ears** udito buono; **~ thinking!** buona idea!; **to be a ~ catch** essere un buon partito; **to do a ~ job** fare un buon lavoro; **to have the ~ sense to do sth** avere il buon senso di fare qc; **to be in ~ shape** essere in (ottima) forma; **to be/to be not ~ enough** andare/non andare bene 2.(*skilled*) bravo, -a; **to be ~ at** [*o* in] **sth/ doing sth** essere bravo in [*o* a] qc/a fare qc; **to be ~ with one's hands** essere bravo nei lavori manuali 3.(*pleasant*) bello, -a; **to have a ~ evening** passare una bella serata; **to have a ~ time** divertirsi; **it's so ~ to see you!** che piacere rivederti!; **she's ~ company** è molto simpatica 4.(*appealing to senses*) **to feel ~** sentirsi bene; **to look ~** stare bene; **to smell ~** avere un buon odore 5.(*favorable, beneficial*) buono, -a; **~ luck (in sth)** buona fortuna (per qc); **a ~ omen** un buon auspicio; **the ~ life** la bella vita; **it's a ~ thing that ...** meno male che...; **to be/sound too ~ to be true** essere/ sembrare troppo bello per essere vero; **a ~ habit** una buona abitudine; **to be ~ for sb/ sth** far bene a qu/qc; **to be ~ for business** essere buono per gli affari 6.(*appropriate*) giusto, -a; **to be in a ~ position to do sth** essere nella posizione giusta per fare qc; **a ~ time to do sth** il momento buono per fare qc 7.(*moral*) **the Good Book** la Bibbia; **a ~ name/reputation** un buon nome/una buona reputazione; **~ deeds/work** opere buone; **to be as ~ as one's word** mantenere la parola (data) 8.(*well-behaved*) buono, -a; **~ manners** buone maniere; **to be on ~ behavior** comportarsi bene 9.(*thorough*) bello, -a; **a ~ beating** una (bella) batosta; **have a ~ cry and you'll feel better** fatti un bel pianto e starai meglio 10.(*valid*) valido, -a; (*not forged*) autentico, -a; (*useable*) buono, -a; **to make sth ~** (*pay for*) compensare per qc; (*do successfully*) portare a termine qc; **to be ~ for nothing** non servire a niente 11.(*substantial*) buono, -a; **a ~ chance** buone probabilità; **a ~ few/many** un bel po'; **a ~ 10%** un buon 10% 12.(*almost, virtually*) **it's as ~ as done** è praticamente finito; **to be as ~ as new** essere come nuovo

13. (*said to emphasize*) **to be ~ and ready** essere pronto **14.** (*said to express affection*) **the ~ old days** i bei tempi (andati) ▶ **to give as ~ as one gets** sapersi difendere **II.** *n* **1.** (*moral force, not evil*) bene *m;* **to be no ~** non servire a nulla; **to be up to no ~** star tramando qc **2.** (*profit, benefit*) bene *m;* **this will do you ~** questo ti farà bene; **for your own ~** per il tuo bene; **to do ~** fare del bene; **to do more harm than ~** fare più male che bene **3.** *pl* (*moral people*) **the ~** i buoni ▶ **for ~** definitivamente **III.** *adv inf* (*well*) bene **IV.** *interj* **1.** (*to express approval*) bene **2.** (*to express surprise, shock*) **~ God!** santo Dio! **3.** (*said as greeting*) **~ afternoon, ~ evening** buonasera; **~ morning** buongiorno; **~ night** buonanotte

goodbye I. *interj* arrivederci **II.** *n* **1.** (*departing word*) arrivederci *m,* addio *m;* **to say ~** (to sb) salutare (qu) **2.** *inf* (*loss*) **to say ~ to sth/to kiss sth ~** dire addio a qc

good-for-nothing ['gʊd·fə·ˌnʌ·θɪŋ] **I.** *n* buono, -a a nulla *m* **II.** *adj* buono, -a a nulla

Good Friday *n* Venerdì *m* Santo

good-humored [ˌgʊd·'hju:·məd] *adj* cordiale

good-looking [ˌgʊd·'lʊ·kɪŋ] <better-looking, best-looking> *adj* bello, -a

good looks *n* bellezza *f*

goodly ['gʊd·li] <-ier, -iest> *adj* considerevole

good-natured <better-natured, best-natured> *adj* **1.** (*pleasant*) amichevole **2.** (*inherently good*) bonario, -a

goodness ['gʊd·nɪs] **I.** *n* **1.** (*moral virtue, kindness*) bontà *f* **2.** (*quality*) (buona) qualità *f* **3.** (*said for emphasis*) **my ~!** santo cielo!; **for ~' sake** per amor del cielo!; **thank ~!** grazie al cielo! **II.** *interj* **~ gracious!** mamma mia!

goods [gʊdz] *npl* **1.** (*wares*) articoli *mpl,* merci *fpl;* **frozen ~** surgelati *mpl;* **manufactured ~** manufatti *mpl* **2.** (*personal belongings*) effetti *m* personali *pl* **3. to deliver the ~** *fig* mantenere le promesse

good-sized [ˌgʊd·'saɪzd] <better-sized, best-sized> *adj* spazioso, -a

good-tempered [ˌgʊd·'tem·pəd] <better-tempered, best-tempered> *adj irr* bonario, -a

goodwill [ˌgʊd·'wɪl] *n* buona volontà *f;* **~ towards sb** benevolenza *f* nei confronti di qu; **a gesture of ~** un segno di buona volontà

goody ['gʊ·di] **I.** <-ies> *n* CULIN caramella *f* **II.** *interj childspeak* che bello

goody two-shoes *n inf* santerellino, -a *m, f*

gooey ['gu:·i] <gooier, gooiest> *adj* appiccicoso, -a

goof [gu:f] **I.** *vi inf* cannare **II.** *n inf* **1.** (*mistake*) cannata *f* **2.** (*silly person*) buffone, -a *m, f*

goofball *n sl* imbranato, -a *m, f*

goofy ['gu:·fi] <-ier, -iest> *adj inf* goffo, -a

goon [gu:n] *n sl* **1.** (*stupid person*) svitato, -a *m, f* **2.** (*thug*) criminale *m* prezzolato

goose [gu:s] <geese> *n* oca *f* ▶ **to kill the ~ that lays the golden eggs** uccidere la gallina dalle uova d'oro; **to cook someone's ~** *inf* rompere le uova nel paniere a qu

gooseberry ['gu:s·be·ri] <-ies> *n* uva *f* spina

goose bumps *npl* pelle *f* d'oca

goose step *n* passo *m* dell'oca

goose-step <-pp-> *vi* marciare col passo dell'oca

gore¹ [gɔːr] *n* (*blood*) sangue *m* (rappreso); **blood and ~** violenza e sangue

gore² [gɔːr] *vt* (*pierce*) incornare

gorge [gɔːrdʒ] **I.** *n* GEO, ANAT gola *f;* **my ~ rises** mi dà il voltastomaco **II.** *vt* **to ~ oneself on sth** ingozzarsi di qc **III.** *vi* ingozzarsi

gorgeous ['gɔːr·dʒəs] **I.** *adj* splendido, -a **II.** *n* **hello, ~!** ciao bella!

gorilla [gə·'rɪ·lə] *n* gorilla *m*

gory ['gɔː·ri] <-ier, -iest> *adj* (*bloody*) truculento, -a **2. the ~ details about sth** i particolari piccanti di qc

gosh [gɑ:ʃ] *interj inf* caspita

gosling ['gɑːz·lɪŋ] *n* papero, -a *m, f*

gospel ['gɑːs·pl] *n* vangelo *m;* **~ singer** cantante *mf* di gospel

gossamer ['gɑː·sə·mə·] **I.** *n* seta *f* di ragno **II.** *adj* diafano, -a

gossip ['gɑː·səp] **I.** *n* **1.** (*rumor*) pettegolezzi *mpl,* gossip *m inv;* **idle ~** pettegolezzi; **~ columnist** cronista *mf* mondano, -a **2.** (*person*) pettegolo, -a *m, f* **II.** *vi* **1.** (*spread rumors*) spettegolare; **to ~ about sb** spettegolare su qu **2.** (*chatter*) chiacchierare

gossip column *n* cronaca *f* mondana

gossipy ['gɑː·sə·pi] *adj* **1.** (*rumor-spreading: neighbor*) pettegolo, -a **2.** (*containing gossip: article*) di gossip

got [gɑːt] *pt of* get

Gothic ['gɑː·θɪk] **I.** *adj a.* ARCHIT, LIT gotico, -a; **~ architecture** architettura *f* gotica; **~ script** caratteri *m* gotici *pl* **II.** *n* gotico *m*

gotten ['gɑː·tən] *pp of* get

gouge [gaʊdʒ] **I.** *vt* **1.** (*pierce*) scavare; **to ~ a hole into sth** scavare un buco in qc **2.** *inf* (*overcharge*) spennare **II.** *n* buca *f*

goulash ['gu:·lɑːʃ] *n* gulash *m inv*

gourd [gɔːrd] *n* zucca *f* da vino

gourmand ['gʊr·mɑːnd] *n* buongustaio, -a *m, f*

gourmet ['gʊr·meɪ] CULIN **I.** *n* gourmet *m inv* **II.** *adj* gourmet

gout [gaʊt] *n* gotta *f*

Gov. *abbr of* **Governor** governatore, -trice *m, f*

govern ['gʌ·vən] **I.** *vt* **1.** *a.* POL, ADMIN governare **2.** (*regulate*) regolare; **to ~ how/when/what ...** determinare come/quando/che...; **to be ~ed by sth** essere determinato da qc **3.** (*control*) controllare **4.** LING reggere **II.** *vi* POL, ADMIN governar; **fit/unfit to ~** capace/incapace di governare

governess ['gʌ·və·nəs] <-es> *n* governante *f*

governing *adj* direttivo, -a

government ['gʌ·vən·mənt] *n* (*ruling body*) governo *m;* **local ~** amministrazione *f* locale; **~ policy** politica *f* governativa; **~ securities** FIN titoli *m pl* statali; **to form a ~** formare il governo; **to be in ~** essere al governo

governmental [ˌgʌ·vən·'men·t̬l] *adj* governativo, -a

governor ['gʌ·vɚ·nɚ] *n* **1.**POL governatore *m* **2.**(*of organization*) direttore *m;* **the board of ~s** il consiglio di amministrazione **3.**TECH regolatore *m*

govt. *abbr of* **government** gov.

gown [gaʊn] *n* **1.**(*evening dress*) abito *m* da sera; **ball** ~ abito da ballo **2.**MED camice *m;* **surgical** ~ camice da chirurgo **3.**UNIV toga *f;* **cap and** ~ tocco e toga

grab [græb] I.<-bb-> *vt* **1.**(*snatch*) prendere; **to** ~ **sth** (**away**) **from sb** strappare qc a qn; **to** ~ **sth out of sb's hands** strappare qc di mano a qu **2.**(*take hold of*) afferrare; **to** ~ **hold of sth** afferrare qc **3.** *inf*(*get, acquire*) **to** ~ **some sleep** schiacciare un pisolino; **to** ~ **a chance** afferrare al volo un'opportunità; **to** ~ **sb's attention** attrarre l'attenzione di qu; **how does this** ~ **you?** *inf* che te ne pare? II.<-bb-> *vi* cercare di prendere III. *n* **to make a** ~ **for sth** cercare di afferrare qc; **to be up for ~s** *inf* essere in palio

grace [greɪs] I. *n* **1.**(*movement, elegant proportions*) grazia *f* **2.**REL grazia *f;* **divine** ~ grazia divina; **by the** ~ **of God** per grazia di Dio; **to be in a state of** ~ essere in stato di grazia; **the year of** ~ *form* l'anno di grazia **3.**(*favor*) benevolenza *f;* **to be in/get into sb's good ~s** entrare nelle buone grazie di qu; **to fall from** ~ cadere in disgrazia **4.**(*politeness*) cortesia *f;* **to do sth with good/bad** ~ fare qc con buonagrazia/di malagrazia; **to have the** (**good**) ~ **to do sth** avere la cortesia di fare qc **5.**(*prayer*) preghiera *f* di ringraziamento; **to say** ~ dire la preghiera di ringraziamento **6.**(*leeway*) proroga *f* **7.**(*Highness*) **Your/His/Her Grace** Vostra/Sua Grazia **8.**(*sister goddesses*) **the Graces** le (tre) Grazie II. *vt* **1.**(*honor*) onorare **2.**(*make beautiful*) abbellire

graceful ['greɪs·fəl] *adj* **1.**(*elegant*) aggraziato, -a **2.**(*polite*) garbato, -a

graceless ['greɪs·lɪs] *adj* **1.**(*lacking elegance*) sgraziato, -a **2.**(*impolite*) sgarbato, -a

grace period *n* periodo *m* di grazia

gracious ['greɪ·ʃəs] I. *adj* **1.**(*kind*) cortese **2.**(*comfortable*) agiato, -a **3.**(*tactful*) garbato, -a **4.**(*merciful*) clemente II. *interj* **goodness** ~ mamma mia

gradation [grəɪ·'deɪ·ʃən] *n* gradazione *f*

grade [greɪd] I. *n* **1.**SCHOOL classe *f,* anno (*m* scolastico); **to skip a** ~ saltare un anno **2.**(*mark*) voto *m;* **good/bad ~s** bei/brutti voti **3.**(*level of quality*) qualità *f;* **high/low** ~ buona/scarsa qualità **4.**GEO pendenza *f;* **gentle/steep** ~ pendenza leggera/forte **5.**(*rank*) grado *m* ▶**to make the** ~ essere all'altezza II. *vt* **1.**(*evaluate*) valutare **2.**(*categorize*) classificare

grade school *n* SCHOOL scuola *f* primaria

gradient ['greɪ·di·ənt] *n* GEO, AUTO gradiente *m*

grading ['greɪ·dɪŋ] *n* **1.**(*gradation*) gradazione *f* **2.**(*classification*) classificazione *f*

gradual ['græ·dʒʊ·əl] *adj* **1.**(*not sudden*) graduale **2.**(*not steep*) dolce

gradually ['græ·dʒʊ·li] *adv* **1.**(*not suddenly*) gradualmente **2.**(*not steeply*) dolcemente

graduate[1] ['græ·dʒʊ·ət] *n* **1.**UNIV laureato, -a *m, f m* **2.**HIGH-SCHOOL diplomato, -a *m, f*

graduate[2] ['græ·dʒʊ·eɪt] I. *vi* **1.**UNIV laurearsi; SCHOOL diplomarsi; **to** ~ **cum laude** laurearsi summa cum laude **2.**(*move to a higher level*) avanzare; **to** ~ **from... to ...** avanzare da ... a ... **3.**(*calibrate*) graduare II. *vt* graduare

graduated *adj* graduato, -a

graduate school *n* scuola *f* di specializzazione postlaurea

graduation [ˌgræ·dʒʊ·'eɪ·ʃən] *n* **1.**UNIV laurea *f* **2.**SCHOOL diploma *m* **3.**(*marks of calibration*) calibratura *f*

graffiti [grə·'fi:·ţi] *npl* graffiti *m*

graffiti artist *n* graffitista *mf*

graft [græft] I. *n* **1.**BOT, AGR, MED innesto *m;* **a skin** ~ un innesto di pelle **2.**POL tangenti *fpl* II. *vt a.* BOT, AGR, MED innestare III. *vi* POL estorcere

grafter ['græf·tɚ] *n* innestatore *m*

Grail [greɪl] *n* **the Holy** ~ il Sacro Graal

grain [greɪn] I. *n* **1.**(*cereal*) cereali *mpl* **2.**(*of wheat, rice*) chicco *m* **3.**(*of sand, salt*) granello *m* **4.** *fig* briciolo *m;* **a** ~ **of hope** un briciolo di speranza; **a** ~ **of truth** un briciolo di verità **5.**(*direction of fibers*) venatura *f* ▶**to take sth with a** ~ **of** salt prendere qc con un grano di sale; **to go against the** ~ andare controcorrente *inf* II. *vt* (*granulate*) granulare

grain elevator *n* silo *m* per cereali

grammar ['græ·mɚ] *n* grammatica *f*

grammar book *n* (libro *m* di) grammatica *f*

grammarian [grə·'me·ri·ən] *n* grammatico *m*

grammar school *n* scuola secondaria a indirizzo umanistico

grammatical [grə·'mæ·ţɪ·kl] *adj* grammaticale

gram [græm] *n* grammo *m*

gramophone ['græ·mə·foʊn] *n* grammofono *m*

granary ['græ·nə·ri] AGR I.<-ies> *n* granaio *m* II. *adj* del granaio

grand [grænd] I. *adj* **1.**(*splendid*) magnifico, -a; **in** ~ **style** in grande stile **2.** *inf*(*excellent*) benissimo **3.**(*noble*) nobile; **a** ~ **purpose** un nobile proposito **4.**(*solemn, sumptuous*) grandioso, -a; **on a** ~ **scale** su larga scala; **a** ~ **opening** un'inaugurazione ufficiale; **to make a** ~ **entrance** fare un'entrata trionfale **5.**(*over-*

all) **the ~ total** il totale generale **II.** *n* **1.** *inv, inf* (*dollars*) mille dollari *mpl* **2.** MUS pianoforte *m* a coda; **baby ~** pianoforte a mezzacoda

grandchild <-children> *n* nipote *m o f, di nonni*

grand(d)ad *n inf* nonno *m*

granddaughter *n* nipote *f, di nonni*

grandeur ['græn·dʒəˠ] *n* **1.** (*imposing splendor*) grandiosità *f* **2.** (*nobility*) nobiltà *f*

grandfather *n* nonno *m*

grandiloquent [græn·'dɪ·lək·wənt] *adj* magniloquente

grandiose ['græn·di·oʊs] *adj* **1.** (*ideas, plans*) grandioso, -a **2.** (*façade of building*) imponente

grand jury <- -ies> *n* LAW Gran Giurì *m*

grand larceny *n* reato *m* grave

grandly *adv* grandiosamente

grandma *n inf* nonna *f*

grandmaster *n* GAMES (*chess pro*) Gran Maestro *m*

grandmother *n* nonna *f*

grandpa *n inf* nonno *m*

grandparents *npl* nonni *mpl*

grand piano *n* pianoforte *m* a coda

grandson *n* nipote *m, di nonni*

grandstand *n* tribuna *f;* **~ seat** posto *m* in tribuna; **~ ticket** biglietto *m* di tribuna; **a ~ view** *fig* un posto in prima fila

granite ['græ·nɪt] *n* granito *m*

grannie, granny ['græ·ni] *n inf* **1.** nonna *f* **2.** *inf* (*fussy person*) pignolo, -a *m, f* **3.** *reg* (*midwife*) ostetrica *f*

grant [grænt] **I.** *n* **1.** UNIV borsa *f* di studio; **to give sb a ~** concedere una borsa di studio a qu **2.** (*funds*) sovvenzione *f;* **federal ~** sovvenzioni statali; **research ~** sovvenzioni alla ricerca **3.** LAW concessione *f* **II.** *vt* **1.** (*allow*) concedere; **to ~ sb a permit/visa** concedere un permesso/visto a qu; **to ~ a pardon** concedere l'indulto; **to ~ a request** acconsentire a una richiesta; **to ~ a wish** esaudire un desiderio **2.** (*admit to*) riconoscere, ammettere; **~ed** d'accordo; **~ed, it's not easy ...** d'accordo, non è facile ...; **I ~ you that ...** ammetto che ... ▶ **to take sth for ~ed** dare qc per scontato; **to take sb for ~ed** non apprezzare qu come merita

granular ['græn·jə·ləˠ] *adj* granulare

granulated ['græn·jə·leɪ·t̬ɪd] *adj* granulato, -a; **~ sugar** zucchero *m* semolato

granule ['græn·ju:l] *n* granulo *m*

grape [greɪp] *n* **1.** (*fruit*) uva *f;* **a bunch of ~ s** un grappolo d'uva **2.** *iron* (*wine*) **the ~** il vino ▶ **it's just** sour **~s** è tutta invidia

grapefruit ['greɪp·fru:t] *n inv* pompelmo *m*

grape juice *n* succo *m* d'uva

grapevine *n* vite *f* ▶ **to** hear **sth on the ~** sentir dire qc

graph[1] [græf] *n* grafico *m;* **temperature ~** grafico delle temperature

graph[2] [græf] *n* LING grafia *f*

graphic ['græ·fɪk] *adj* grafico, -a; **to describe sth in ~ detail** descrivere qc con dovizia di

particolari; **~ works** (**of an artist**) opere grafiche (di un artista)

graphic design *n* graphic design *m,* progettazione *f* grafica

graphics *n* + *sing vb* (*a. comput*) grafica *f;* **computer ~** computer grafica

graphics card *n* scheda *f* grafica

graphite ['græ·faɪt] *n* grafite *f*

graphologist [grə·'fɑː·lə·dʒɪst] *n* grafologo, -a *m, f*

graphology [grə·'fɑː·lə·dʒi] *n* grafologia *f*

grapple ['græ·pl] *vi* **to ~ for sth** azzuffarsi per qc; **to ~ with sth** essere alle prese con qc

grappling iron *n,* **grappling hook** *n* rampino *m*

grasp [græsp] **I.** *n* **1.** (*grip*) presa *f* **2.** (*attainability*) portata *f;* **to be beyond sb's ~** essere fuori della portata di qu **3.** (*understanding*) comprensione *f;* (*knowledge*) conoscenza *f* **II.** *vt* **1.** (*take firm hold*) afferrare; **to ~ sb by the arm/hand** afferrare qu per il braccio/la mano **2.** (*understand*) afferrare **III.** *vi* **1.** (*try to hold*) cercare di afferrare **2.** *fig* (*take advantage*) **to ~ at** approfittare di; **to ~ at the chance** approfittare dell'opportunità

grasping *adj* avido, -a

grass [græs] **I.** <-es> *n* **1.** erba *f;* **wild ~es** erbe selvatiche **2.** (*area of grass*) prato *m* **3.** *inf* (*marijuana*) erba *f* ▶ **to let the ~ grow under one's** feet perdere tempo; **the ~ is** (**always**) **greener on the other** side (**of the fence**) *prov* l'erba del vicino è sempre più verde **II.** *vt* coprire d'erba

grasshopper ['græs·hɑː·pəˠ] *n* cavalletta *f*

grassland *n* prateria *f*

grassroots I. *npl* base *f fig* **II.** *adj* di base; **a ~ movement** un movimento politico di base

grass snake *n* biscia *f* dal collare

grass widow *n* vedova *f* bianca

grassy ['græ·si] <-ier, -iest> *adj* erboso, -a

grate[1] [greɪt] *n* grata *f*

grate[2] [greɪt] **I.** *vi* **1.** (*annoy*) infastidire; **to ~ on sb** dare sui nervi a qu **2.** (*scrape*) stridere **II.** *vt* **1.** CULIN grattugiare **2.** (*one's teeth*) digrignare

grateful ['greɪt·fəl] *adj* grato, -a; **to be ~** (**to sb**) **for sth** essere grato (a qu) per qc; **I'd be most ~ if you ...** *form* le sarei grato se ... +*subj*

grater ['greɪ·t̬əˠ] *n* grattugia *f*

gratification [ˌgræ·t̬ə·fɪ·'keɪ·ʃən] *n* soddisfazione *f;* **sexual ~** piacere *m* sessuale

gratify ['græ·t̬ə·faɪ] <-ie-> *vt* soddisfare; **to be gratified at sth** essere soddisfatto di qc

gratifying *adj* gratificante

grating ['greɪ·t̬ɪŋ] **I.** *n* grata *f* **II.** *adj* **1.** (*scraping*) stridente **2.** (*annoyingly harsh*) stridulo, -a; **~ voice** voce *f* stridula

gratis ['græ·t̬əs] **I.** *adj* gratuito, -a **II.** *adv* gratis

gratitude ['græ·t̬ə·tu:d] *n form* gratitudine *f;* **as a token of my ~** in segno di gratitudine

gratuitous [grə·'tu:·ət̬·əs] *adj* gratuito, -a

gratuity [grə·'tu:·ə·t̬i] <-ies> *n form* mancia *f*

grave[1] [greɪv] *n* tomba *f;* **mass ~** fossa *f*

comune; **beyond the** ~ dopo la morte; **from beyond the** ~ d'oltretomba

grave² [greɪv] *adj* **1.** (*serious*) grave **2.** (*solemn*) solenne; **a** ~ **ceremony** una cerimonia solenne

gravedigger ['greɪv·ˌdɪ·gə] *n* becchino *m*

gravel ['græ·vəl] *n* ghiaia *f*; **a** ~ **path** un vialetto di ghiaia

gravel pit *n* cava *f* di ghiaia

grave robber *n* ladro, -a *m*, *f* di tombe

gravestone *n* lapide *f* (sepolcrale)

graveyard *n* cimitero *m*

graving dock ['greɪ·vɪŋ·ˌdɑːk] *n* bacino *m* di carenaggio

gravitate ['græ·vɪ·teɪt] *vi* gravitare; **to** ~ **towards sth/sb** gravitare intorno a qc/qu

gravitation [ˌgræ·vɪ·'teɪ·ʃən] *n* gravitazione *f*

gravitational [ˌgræ·vɪ·'teɪ·ʃə·nl] *adj* gravitazionale; ~ **force** forza *f* gravitazionale

gravity ['græ·və·ti] *n* gravità *f*; **the law of** ~ la legge di gravità

gravure [grə·'vjʊr] *n* calcografia *f*

gravy ['greɪ·vi] *n* **1.** CULIN sugo *m* d'arrosto **2.** *sl* (*easy money*) cuccagna *f*

gravy boat *n* salsiera *f*

gravy train *n* cuccagna *f*

gray [greɪ] **I.** *adj* **1.** *a.* *fig* grigio; **dressed in** ~ vestito di grigio; **to go** ~ ingrigire; **he has started to go** ~ ha incominciato a ingrigire **2.** (*pale*) smorto, -a **II.** *n* grigio *m* **III.** *vi* invecchiare

graybeard ['greɪ·ˌbɪrd] *n* vecchio *m*

graying *adj* brizzolato, -a

grayish ['greɪ·ɪʃ] *adj* grigiastro, -a

gray matter *n* *inf* materia *f* grigia

graze¹ [greɪz] **I.** *n* scalfittura *f* **II.** *vt* scalfire; **the bullet just** ~**d his arm** la pallottola gli scalfì il braccio

graze² [greɪz] AGR **I.** *vi* pascolare **II.** *vt* far pascolare

grease [griːs] **I.** *n* **1.** (*fat*) grasso *m* **2.** (*lubricant*) lubrificante *m* **II.** *vt* (*in cooking*) ungere; (*in mechanics*) lubrificare

grease gun *n* ingrassatore *m*

grease monkey *n* *sl* meccanico *m*

greasepaint *n* cerone *m*

grease pencil *n* matita *f* dermografica

greasy ['griː·si] <-ier, -iest> *adj* (*hair*) grasso, -a; (*hands*) unto, -a; (*food*) untuoso, -a

greasy spoon *n* ristorantino economico che serve per lo più cibi fritti

great [greɪt] **I.** *n* grande *mf*; **Alexander the** ~ Alessandro Magno **II.** *adj* **1.** (*very big, very good*) grande; **a** ~ **amount** una gran quantità; **a** ~ **deal of time/money** moltissimo tempo/denaro; **a** ~ **many people** moltissima gente; **the** ~ **majority of people** la stragrande maggioranza (de la gente); **it gives me** ~ **pleasure to announce ...** *form* è con immenso piacere che annuncio ...; **it is with** ~ **sorrow that I tell you of ...** mi dispiace immensamente comunicarvi che ...; **the** ~**est boxer ever** il più grande pugile di tutti i tempi; ~ **minds**

think alike i geni pensano allo stesso modo **2.** (*wonderful*) fantastico, -a; **to be** ~ **at doing sth** *inf* essere bravissimo in qc; **she's** ~ **at playing tennis** *inf* gioca benissimo a tennis; **to be a** ~ **one for doing sth** essere bravissimo a fare qc; **it's** ~ **to be back home again** che bello essere di nuovo a casa; **the** ~ **thing about sth/sb is** (**that**) il bello di qc/qu è (che); **I had a** ~ **time** mi sono divertita moltissimo; ~**!** bene!; **to feel** ~ stare benissimo; **they're** ~ **friends** sono molto amici; **he's a** ~ **big ...** è un grandissimo...

great-aunt *n* prozia *f*

greatcoat *n* cappotto *m*

Great Depression *n* Grande Depressione *f*

great-grandchild *n* bisnipote *mf*

great-grandparents *npl* bisnonni *mpl*, bisavoli *pl*

great-great-grandparents *npl* trisnonni *mpl*, trisavoli *pl*

Great Lakes *n* Grandi Laghi *mpl*

---

i I **Great Lakes**, i grandi laghi, situati lungo il confine tra gli Stati Uniti e il Canada, rappresantano il più grande gruppo di laghi di acqua dolce sulla terra e, con la via d'acqua del San Lorenzo, il più grande sistema di acqua dolce del mondo. I laghi che costituisco questo mare interno sono, da ovest verso est: il lago Superiore, il lago Michigan, il lago Huron, il lago Erie e il lago Ontario. Tra il lago Erie e il lago Ontario si trovano le magnifiche cascate del Niagara, delle quali una parte è situata negli USA, l'altra in Canada.

---

greatly ['greɪt·li] *adv* *form* notevolmente; **to improve** ~ migliorare notevolmente; **to be** ~ **impressed** essere notevolmente colpito; **I** ~ **regret not having told him** mi rincresce moltissimo non avergielo detto

great-nephew *n* pronipote *m*

greatness ['greɪt·nɪs] *n* grandezza *f*

great-niece *n* pronipote *f*

---

i Le **Great Plains** erano un tempo delle vaste steppe (praterie) delle province di Alberta e Saskatchewan, nel Canada orientale. La coltivazione di queste steppe ne ha fatto una delle più importanti regioni di produzione cerealicola del mondo.

---

great-uncle *n* prozio *m*

Greece [griːs] *n* Grecia *f*

greed [griːd] *n* (*for food*) ingordigia *f*; (*for money*) avidità *f*; (*for power*) sete *f*

greediness ['griː·dɪ·nɪs] *n* *s.* greed

greedy ['griː·di] <-ier, -iest> *adj* (*wanting food*) ingordo, -a; (*wanting money, things*) avido, -a; ~ **for success** avido di successi

Greek [griːk] I. *n* 1.(*person*) greco, -a *m, f* 2.(*language*) greco *m* II. *adj* greco, -a ▸ it's all ~ to me per me è arabo

green [griːn] I. *n* 1.(*color*) verde *m* 2. *pl* (*green vegetables*) verdure *fpl* 3.(*lawn*) prato *m* 4. SPORTS campo *m;* **bowling** ~ campo da bocce; **putting** ~ green *m inv* 5. ECOL, POL **Green** verde *mf* II. *adj* 1.(*green-colored*) verde; **to turn** ~ (*traffic lights*) diventare verde 2.(*not ripe*) verde, acerbo, -a 3.(*inexperienced*) inesperto, -a 4. *fig* (*jealous*) ~ **with envy** verde d'invidia 5. ECOL, POL verde

greenback *n inf* banconota *f*

green belt *n* cintura *f* verde

green card *n* permesso *m* di soggiorno

greenery ['griː·nə·ri] *n* vegetazione *f*

green-eyed [ˌgriː·n·aɪd] *adj* 1.(*with green eyes*) con gli occhi verdi 2. *fig* (*jealous*) invidioso, -a

greenhorn *n* novellino, -a *m, f*

greenhouse *n* serra *f*

greenhouse effect *n* the ~ l'effetto serra

greenish ['griː·nɪʃ] *adj* verdognolo, -a

Greenland ['griː·n·lənd] *n* Groenlandia *f*

greenness ['griː·n·nɪs] *n* verde *m*

green pepper [ˌgriː·n·'pe·pə·] *n* peperone *m* verde

green politics *n* + *sing vb* politica *f* ambientalista

green tea *n* tè *m* verde *inv*

green thumb *n* **to have a** ~ avere il pollice verde

greet [griːt] *vt* 1.(*welcome*) salutare; **to** ~ **each other** salutarsi; **to** ~ **sb by shaking hands/with a smile** salutare qu con una stretta di mano/con un sorriso 2.(*receive*) accogliere; **to** ~ **sth with applause** accogliere qc con un applauso; **to** ~ **sth with delight** accogliere qc con gioia 3. *fig* (*make itself noticeable*) presentarsi; **a scene of joy** ~ **ed us** ci si presentò una scenetta gioiosa

greeting *n* saluto *m*

gregarious [grɪ·'ge·ri·əs] *adj* 1.(*liking company*) socievole 2. ZOOL gregario, -a

grenade [grɪ·'neɪd] *n* granata *f;* **hand** ~ bomba *f* a mano

grenadier [ˌgre·nə·'dɪr] *n* granatiere *m*

grew [gruː] *pt of* **grow**

grey [greɪ] *adj, n, s.* **gray**

greyhound *n* levriero *m*

grid [grɪd] *n* griglia *f*

griddle ['grɪ·dl] I. *n* CULIN piastra *f* II. *vt* cuocere alla piastra

gridiron ['grɪ·daɪ·ə·n] *n* 1.(*American football field*) campo *m* di football americano 2.(*metal grid*) graticola *f*

gridlock *n* paralisi *f* del traffico; *fig* situazione *f* di stallo

grid square *n* griglia *f*

grief [griːf] *n* (*extreme sadness*) dolore *m;* **to cause** ~ *inf* rompere; **to cause sb** ~ dare delle noie a qu; **to give sb** (**a lot of**) ~ criticare (aspramente) qu ▸ **to come to** ~ avere un inci-

dente; **good** ~! *inf* santo cielo!

grievance ['griː·vns] *n* 1.(*complaint*) lagnanza *f;* **to harbor a** ~ **against sb** covare risentimento contro qu 2.(*sense of injustice*) ingiustizia *f*

grieve [griːv] I. *vi* soffrire; **to** ~ **for sth/sb** piangere la perdita di qc/qu II. *vt* 1.(*make sad*) rattristare; **it** ~ **s me to see your situation** mi rattrista vederti così 2.(*mourn*) **to** ~ **the death of ...** piangere la scomparsa di ...

grievous ['griː·vəs] *adj form* (*loss, wound, danger*) grave; (*news*) doloroso, -a; (*pain, crime*) atroce

grievous bodily harm *n* lesioni *f pl* personali gravi

griffin ['grɪ·fən] *n*, **griffon** *n* grifone *m*

grill [grɪl] I. *n* 1.(*part of oven*) grill *m inv*; (*for barbecue*) griglia *f* 2.(*informal restaurant*) grill *m inv* II. *vt* cuocere alla griglia

grille [grɪl] *n* (*of windows*) grata *f*; (*of car*) griglia *f*

grilling ['grɪ·lɪŋ] *n inf* interrogatorio *m;* **to give sb a** (**good**) ~ fare il terzo grado a qu

grim [grɪm] *adj* 1.(*very serious: expression*) severo, -a 2.(*ghastly*) desagradable; (*gloomy*) deprimente; **to feel** ~ stare malissimo 3.(*without hope*) grigio, -a *fig*; **the future looks** ~ il futuro è grigio ▸ **to hang on like** ~ death aggrapparsi a qc con le unghie e coi denti

grimace ['grɪ·məs] I. *n* (*facial expression*) smorfia *f;* **to make a** ~ **of disgust/pain** fare una smorfia di disgusto/dolore II. *vi* fare una smorfia; **to** ~ **with pain** fare una smorfia di dolore

grime [graɪm] I. *n* sporcizia *f* II. *vt* **to be** ~ **d with soot** essere sporco di fuliggine

Grim Reaper *n lit* Tristo Mietitore *m*

grimy ['graɪ·mi] <-ier, -iest> *adj* sporco, -a

grin [grɪn] I. *n* gran sorriso *m* II. *vi* sorridere; **to** ~ **impishly at sb** sorridere maliziosamente a qu ▸ **to** ~ **and** bear **it** fare buon viso a cattivo gioco

grind [graɪnd] I. *n inf* sgobbata *f;* **to be a real** ~ essere una bella sgobbata; **the daily** ~ il trantran quotidiano II. <ground, ground> *vt* 1.(*crush*) pestare; (*mill*) macinare; **to** ~ **sth** (**in**)**to a powder** ridurre in polvere qc 2.(*chop finely*) tritare 3.(*press firmly and twist*) **to** ~ **a cigarette into an ashtray** schiacciare una sigaretta nel posacenere 4.(*sharpen*) molare III. *vi* 1.(*grate*) stridere 2. *inf* (*devote oneself to*) sgobbare; **to** ~ **away at sth** sgobbare su qc 3. *inf* (*dance seductively*) ballare ruotando il bacino 4.(*in skateboarding*) grindare

◆**grind down** *vt* 1.(*file*) levigare 2.(*mill*) macinare 3.(*wear*) logorare 4.(*oppress*) schiacciare; **to grind sb down** schiacciare qu

◆**grind out** *vt* (*produce continuously*) sfornare *fig*

grinder ['graɪn·də·] *n* 1.(*for coffee, grains*) macinino *m;* (*for meat*) tritacarne *m inv* 2.(*sharpener*) affilacoltelli *m inv*

grindstone ['graɪnd·stoʊn] *n* mola *f* ▸ to

keep one's <u>nose</u> **to the ~** *inf* lavorare come un somaro

grip [grɪp] I. *n* 1. (*hold*) presa *f;* **to keep a firm ~ on sth** tenere ben stretto qc; **to be in the ~(s) of sth** (*emotion*) essere in preda a qc; (*crisis*) essere nella morsa di qc 2. (*bag*) borsa da viaggio *m* ▸ **to** <u>get</u> **to ~s with sth** affrontare qc; **to** <u>get</u> **a ~ on oneself** darsi una calmata II. <-pp-> *vt* 1. (*hold firmly*) afferrare 2. (*overwhelm*) **to be ~ped by emotion/fear** essere preso dall'emozione/paura 3. (*interest deeply*) avvincere III. *vi* aderire

gripe [graɪp] I. *n* *inf* lamentela *f* II. *vi* *inf* lamentarsi

gripping ['grɪ·pɪŋ] *adj* (*story*) avvincente

grisly ['grɪz·li] <-ier, -iest> *adj* raccapricciante; **a ~ discovery** una macabra scoperta

grist [grɪst] *n* **it's all ~ for one's** [*o* the] <u>mill</u> tutto fa brodo

gristle ['grɪ·sl] *n* cartilagine *f*

grit [grɪt] I. *n* 1. (*small stones*) sabbia *f* 2. *inf* (*courage*) fegato *m* II. <-tt-> *vt* 1. (*press together*) **to ~ one's teeth** *a. fig* stringere i denti 2. **to ~ a road** spargere sabbia sulla strada

grits [grɪts] *n pl* farina *f* di mais

gritty ['grɪ·t̮i] <-ier, -iest> *adj* (*sandy*) sabbioso; (*brave*) coraggioso, -a

grizzly ['grɪz·li] I. <-ier, iest> *adj* grigio, -a II. <-ies> *n* grizzly *m inv*

groan [groʊn] I. *n* gemito *m* II. *vi* 1. (*make a noise*) gemere; **to ~ in pain** gemere di dolore 2. (*complain*) lamentarsi; **to ~ about sth** lamentarsi di qc; **she's always moaning and ~ing about it** se ne lamenta in continuazione

grocer ['groʊ·sɚ] *n* 1. (*store owner*) negoziante *mf* 2. (*food store*) negozio *f* di (generi) alimentari

groceries ['groʊ·sə·riz] *n pl* generi *m* alimentari *pl*

grocery store *n* negozio *m* di (generi) alimentari

grog [grɑ:g] *n* grog *m inv*

groggy ['grɑ:·gi] <-ier -iest> *adj* intontito, -a

groin [grɔɪn] *n* inguine *m;* (*male sex organs*) basso ventre *m*

groom [gru:m] I. *n* 1. (*for horses*) mozzo *m* di stalla 2. (*bridegroom*) sposo *m* II. *vt* 1. (*clean: an animal*) pulire; (*a horse*) strigliare 2. (*prepare: a person*) preparare

groove [gru:v] *n* scanalatura *f;* MUS solco *m; fig* routine *f* ▸ **to** <u>be</u> **stuck in a ~** essersi fossilizzato, -a

groovy ['gru:·vi] <-ier, -iest> *adj* *inf* figo, -a

grope [groʊp] I. *vi* andare a tentoni; **to ~ for sth** cercare qc a tentoni; **to ~ for the right words** cercare le parole giuste II. *vt* 1. *inf* (*touch sexually*) palpare 2. **to ~ one's way** andare a tentoni

gropingly ['groʊ·pɪŋ·li] *adv* a tentoni

gross [groʊs] I. *adj* 1. (*vulgar*) volgare 2. LAW grave 3. (*revolting*) schifoso, -a 4. (*total*) lordo, -a II. *n* <-es> grossa *f;* **by the ~** alla grossa

III. *vt* FIN (*earn before taxes*) realizzare un incasso lordo di; **the film has grossed over $200 million** il film ha realizzato un incasso di oltre 200 milioni di dollari

gross domestic product *n* prodotto *m* interno lordo

gross income *n* reddito *m* lordo

grossly *adv* (*in a gross manner*) volgarmente; (*extremely*) estremamente

gross national product *n* prodotto *m* nazionale lordo

gross negligence *n* colpa *f* grave

gross pay *n* stipendio *f* lordo

gross profit *n* guadagno *m* lordo

gross tonnage *n* stazza *f* lorda

gross weight *n* peso *m* lordo

grotesque [groʊ·'tesk] *n a.* ART, LIT grottesco, -a

grotto ['grɑ:·t̮oʊ] <-oes *o* -os> *n* grotta *f*

grouch [graʊtʃ] I. *n* (*grumpy person*) brontolone, -a *m, f* II. *vi* brontolare; **to ~ about sth/ sb** lamentarsi di qc/qu

grouchy ['graʊ·tʃi] <-ier, -iest> *adj* brontolone

ground¹ [graʊnd] I. *n* 1. (*the Earth's surface*) terra *f;* **above/below ~** in superficie/sottoterra 2. (*soil*) suolo *m* 3. (*area of land*) terreno *m;* **breeding ~** zona *f* di riproduzione; **waste ~** terreno *m* abbandonato 4. (*reason*) motivo *m;* **to have ~s to do sth** avere validi motivi per fare qc; **on the ~s that ...** perché ... 5. (*area of knowledge*) argomento *m;* **to be on one's own ~** essere nel proprio elemento; **to give ~** cedere terreno; **to stand one's ~** tenere duro II. *vt* 1. AVIAT tenere a terra; **to be ~ed** non poter decollare 2. (*unable to move*) **to be ~ed** essere incagliato, -a 3. *fig, inf* non fare uscire (*per punizione*)

ground² [graʊnd] I. *vt pt of* grind II. *adj* (*glass*) tritato, -a III. *n pl* sedimenti *mpl*

ground ball *n* SPORTS palla *f* rimbalzante

groundbreaking ['graʊnd·ˌbreɪ·kɪŋ] *adj* rivoluzionario, -a

ground crew *n* personale *m* di terra

ground control *n* torre *f* di controllo

ground floor *n* pianterreno *m;* **on the ~** a pianterreno; **~ apartment** appartamento a pianterreno *m* ▸ **to** <u>get in</u> **on the ~** cominciare dal basso

ground forces *npl* MIL esercito *m*

i Negli Stati Uniti, il 2 febbraio è chiamato **Groundhog Day**. È in tale data che si può prevedere se la primavera sarà precoce o tardiva osservando il comportamento del *groundhog* (la marmotta) quando esce dalla tana nella quale ha trascorso l'inverno. Se vede la sua ombra, la marmotta si spaventa e ritorna nella tana, il che sta a significare che l'inverno durerà ancora sei settimane. Ma se il cielo è coperto e non scorge la sua ombra, rimane fuori perché la primavera è in arrivo.

groundless ['graʊnd·lɪs] *adj* infondato, -a

ground rule double *n* SPORTS doppio *m* per regola di campo

ground rules *npl* **1.** (*guidelines*) principi *m* di base *pl* **2.** (*in baseball*) regole *f* del gioco *pl*

grounds crew *n* personale *m* di terra

groundskeeper *n* custode *mf* del campo di gioco

ground speed *n* velocità *f* a terra

groundswell *n* **1.** (*opinion*) ondata *f* **2.** NAUT mareggiata *f*

ground-to-air missile *n* missile *m* terra-aria

ground water *n* acque *f pl* freatiche

groundwork ['graʊnd·wɜːrk] *n* lavoro *m* di preparazione; **to lay the ~ for sth** *fig* stabilire le basi di qc

group [gruːp] **I.** *n* gruppo *m;* **~ photo** foto *f* di gruppo; **in ~s** a gruppi; **to get into ~s** formare dei gruppi **II.** *vt* raggruppare **III.** *vi* raggrupparsi

group discount *n* sconto *m* comitiva

group dynamics *npl* dinamica *f* di gruppo

groupie ['gruː·pi] *n inf* groupie *mf*

grouping ['gruː·pɪŋ] *n* raggruppamento *m*

group rate *n* tariffa *f* comitiva

group therapy <-ies> *n* terapia *f* di gruppo

grouse¹ [graʊs] *n* **black ~** fagiano *m* di monte

grouse² [graʊs] **I.** *n* **1.** (*complaint*) lamentela *f* **2.** (*complaining person*) brontolone, -a *m, f* **II.** *vi* brontolare

grove [groʊv] *n* (*group of trees*) boschetto *m;* **olive ~** oliveto *m;* **orange ~** aranceto *m*

grow [groʊ] <grew, grown> **I.** *vi* **1.** (*increase*) crescere; **to ~ taller** crescere di statura; **to ~ by 2%** crescere del 2% **2.** (*develop*) svilupparsi **3.** (*become*) diventare; **to ~ old** diventare vecchio, invecchiare; **to ~ to like sth** cominciare ad apprezzare qc **II.** *vt* **1.** (*cultivate*) coltivare **2.** (*let grow*) farsi crescere; **to ~ a beard** farsi crescere la barba; **some animals ~ a thicker coat in winter** la pelliccia di alcuni animali s'infoltisce durante l'inverno

◆**grow into** *vt insep* diventare; *fig* abituarsi a

◆**grow on** *vt* (*become pleasing*) **it's an album that ~s on you** è un album che più l'ascolti e più ti piace

◆**grow out of** *vt insep* **1.** (*become too big*) **she has grown out of her clothes** è cresciuta e i vestiti non le stanno più **2.** (*habit*) perdere

◆**grow up** *vi* **1.** (*become adult*) crescere; **oh, ~!** smettila di fare il bambino!; **when I grow up I'd like to ...** da grande voglio ... **2.** (*develop*) svilupparsi

grower ['groʊ·ɚ] *n* **1.** (*gardener*) coltivatore, -trice *m, f;* **fruit ~** frutticoltore, -trice *m, f* **2.** (*plant*) **this plant is a good ~** questa pianta cresce rapidamente

growing ['groʊ·ɪŋ] **I.** *n* crescita *f* **II.** *adj* **1.** (*developing*) **a ~ boy/girl** un bambino/una bambina che sta crescendo **2.** ECON que se espande **3.** (*increasing*) crescente

growing pains *npl* **1.** (*pains in the joints*) dolori *m pl* della crescita **2.** (*adolescent emo-*

tional problems) problemi *m pl* dell'adolescenza

growl [graʊl] **I.** *n* ringhio *m* **II.** *vi* ringhiare

grown [groʊn] **I.** *adj* adulto, -a **II.** *pp of* **grow**

grown-up ['groʊn·ʌp] *n a.* *childspeak* grande *m,* adulto, -a *m, f*

growth [groʊθ] *n* **1.** (*increase in size*) crescita *f* **2.** (*stage of growing*) maturità *f;* **to reach full ~** raggiungere la piena maturità **3.** (*increase*) crescita *f;* **rate of ~** tasso *m* di crescita **4.** (*something grown*) **he had three days ~ of beard on his chin** aveva la barba di tre giorni **5.** (*growing part of plant*) germoglio *m* **6.** MED escrescenza *f*

growth hormone *n* ormone *m* della crescita

growth industry *n* industria *f* in crescita

growth rate *n* ECON tasso *m* di crescita

growth stock *n* ECON azioni *f pl* di società ad elevato potenziale di crescita

grub [grʌb] **I.** *n* **1.** *sl* (*food*) roba *f* da mangiare **2.** (*larva*) larva *f* **II.** <-bb-> *vi* scavare; **to ~ about** (**for sth**) scavare (cercando qc) **III.** *vt* **to ~ up** estirpare

grubby ['grʌ·bi] <-ier, -iest> *adj inf* sporco, -a

grudge [grʌdʒ] **I.** *n* rancore *m;* **to have** [*o* **hold**] **a ~ against sb** serbare rancore a qu **II.** *vt* **to ~ sb sth** invidiare qc a qu

grudge match *n* grudge match *m inv*

grudging *adj* riluttante

grudgingly ['grʌ·dʒɪŋ·li] *adv* con riluttanza

gruel ['gruː·əl] *n* pappa *f* d'avena

grueling ['gruː·lɪŋ] *adj* faticoso, -a

gruesome ['gruː·səm] *adj* agghiacciante

gruff [grʌf] *adj* (*reply*) brusco, -a; **a ~ voice** una voce burbera

grumble ['grʌm·bl] **I.** *n* (*complaint*) lamentela *f* **II.** *vi* (*person*) lamentarsi; (*stomach*) borbottare; **to ~ about sth/sb** lamentarsi di qc/qu

grumpy ['grʌm·pi] <-ier, -iest> *adj inf* (*bad tempered*) brontolone, -a; (*annoyed*) scorbutico, -a

grunt [grʌnt] **I.** *n* **1.** (*snort*) grugnito *m* **2.** *sl* (*soldier*) soldato *m* di fanteria **II.** *vi* grugnire

gryphon *n s.* **griffin**

G-string ['dʒiː·strɪŋ] *n* tanga *m inv*

GU *n abbr of* **Guam** GU

Guam *n* Guam *m*

Guamanian **I.** *adj* del Guam **II.** *n* abitante *mf* del Guam

guarantee [ˌge·rən·'tiː] **I.** *n* **1.** (*certainty, warranty*) garanzia *f;* **there's no ~ that ...** non ci sono garanzie che ... **+***subj* **2.** (*security*) pegno *m* **II.** *vt* garantire; **to be ~d for three years** avere una garanzia di tre anni; **to ~ that** garantire che **+***subj*

guarantor [ˌge·rən·'tɔːr] *n* garante *mf*

guaranty ['ge·rən·ti] <-ies> *n* **1.** (*acceptance of debt*) fideiussione *f* **2.** (*thing offered as security*) pegno *m*

guard [gɑːrd] **I.** *n* **1.** (*a. sport*) guardia *mf;* **prison ~** secondino, -a *m, f;* **security ~** guardia giurata; **to be on ~** essere di guardia;

to be on one's ~ (against sth/sb) stare in guardia (contro qc/qu); **to be under ~** essere sotto vigilanza; **to drop one's ~** abbassare la guardia; **to keep ~ over sth/sb** vigilare su qc/qu **2.** (*protective device*) **fire ~** parascintille *m inv;* **shin ~** parastinchi *m inv* **3.** MIL **the National Guard** la Guardia Nazionale **II.** *vt* **1.** (*protect*) difendere **2.** (*prevent from escaping*) fare la guardia a **3.** (*keep secret*) custodire
◆**guard against** *vt always sep* (*protect from*) **to guard sth/sb against sth/sb** proteggere qc/qu da qc/qu

guard dog *n* cane *m* da guardia

guard duty <-ies> *n* turno *m* di guardia

guarded ['gɑːr·dɪd] *adj* guardingo, -a

guardhouse *n* corpo *m* di guardia

guardian ['gɑːr·di·ən] *n* **1.** (*responsible person*) tutore, -trice *m, f* **2.** *form* (*protector*) difensore *m*

guardian angel *n a. fig* angelo *m* custode

guardianship *n form* tutela *f;* **to be in the ~ of sb** essere sotto la tutela di qu

guardrail ['gɑːrd·reɪl] *n* guardrail *m inv*

guardroom *n* cella *f* di detenzione

guardsman <-men> *n* soldato *m* della guardia

Guatemala [ˌgwɑː·tə·'mɑː·lə] *n* Guatemala *m*

Guatemalan [ˌgwɑː·tə·'mɑː·lən] **I.** *adj* guatemalteco, -a **II.** *n* guatemalteco, -a *m, f*

guerilla *n*, **guerrilla** [gə·'rɪ·lə] *n* guerriglia *f*

guerrilla warfare *n* guerriglia *f*

guess [ges] **I.** *n* congettura *f;* **to take a ~** tirare a indovinare; **to take a wild ~** azzardare un'ipotesi; **that was a lucky ~** è stata tutta fortuna; **your ~ is as good as mine!** ne so quanto te ▸**it's anybody's ~** Dio solo lo sa **II.** *vi* **1.** (*conjecture*) indovinare; **to ~ right/wrong** indovinare/non indovinare; **~ what I'm doing now?** indovina cosa sto facendo ora?; **how did you ~?** come hai fatto a indovinare? **2.** (*believe, suppose*) supporre; **to ~ that ...** immaginare che...; **I ~ you're right** immagino che tu abbia ragione **III.** *vt* indovinare ▸**to keep sb ~ing** tenere qu sulle spine; **~ what?** indovina?

guessing game ['ge·sɪŋ·ˌgeɪm] *n a. fig* indovinello *f*

guesstimate ['ges·tɪ·mət] *n inf* ipotesi *f*

guesswork ['ges·wɜːrk] *n* congetture *fpl*

guest [gest] **I.** *n* **1.** (*invited person*) ospite *mf;* **paying ~** (*lodger*) pensionante *mf* **2.** (*hotel customer*) cliente *mf* ▸**be my ~** *inf* fai pure **II.** *vi a.* TV apparire come ospite d'onore

guesthouse *n* pensione *f*

guestroom *n* stanza *f* degli ospiti

guffaw [gə·'fɑː] **I.** *n* risata *f* sguaiata **II.** *vi* ridere sguaiatamente

guidance ['gaɪ·dns] *n* (*help and advice*) guida *f;* (*for students*) orientamento *m;* **~ system** *a.* MIL sistema *m* di guida

guide [gaɪd] **I.** *n* **1.** (*person*) guida *f;* **tour/mountain ~** guida turistica/alpina **2.** (*book*) guida *f* **3.** (*indication*) indicazione *f* **II.** *vt* guidare; **to be ~d by one's emotions** lasciarsi

guidare dai sentimenti

guidebook *n* guida *f*

guided ['gaɪd·ɪd] *adj* **1.** (*led by a guide*) guidato, -a; **~ed tour** visita *f* guidata **2.** (*automatically steered*) teleguidato, -a; **~ missile** MIL missile *m* teleguidato

guide dog *n* cane *m* guida

guidelines *npl* linee *f* guida *pl*

guiding hand ['gaɪ·dɪŋ 'hænd] *n fig* guida *f*

guiding light *n* guida *f*

guiding principle *n* principio *m* guida

guild [gɪld] *n* (*medieval*) corporazione *f;* (*modern*) associazione *f;* **Writers' Guild** Unione *f* Nazionale Scrittori

guilder ['gɪl·dɚ] *n* fiorino *m* olandese

guile [gaɪl] *n form* scaltrezza *f*

guileful ['gaɪl·fəl] *adj form* scaltro, -a

guileless ['gaɪl·lɪs] *adj* innocente

guillotine ['gɪ·lə·tiːn] *n* ghigliottina *f*

guilt [gɪlt] *n* **1.** (*feeling*) senso *m* di colpa **2.** (*blame*) colpa *f;* **to admit one's ~** ammettere le proprie colpe **3.** (*responsibility for crime*) colpevolezza *f;* **to establish sb's ~** determinare la colpevolezza di qu

guiltless ['gɪlt·ləs] *adj* innocente

guilt-ridden *adj* tormentato, -a dal senso di colpa

guilty ['gɪl·ti] <-ier, -iest> *adj* colpevole; **to be ~ of a murder** essere colpevole di omicidio; **to have a ~ conscience** avere la coscienza sporca; **to feel ~ about sth** sentirsi in colpa per qc; **to plead ~ to a crime** dichiararsi colpevole di qc; **to prove sb ~** dimostrare la colpevolezza di qu

Guinea ['gɪ·ni] *n* Guinea *f*

guinea fowl *n* faraona *f*

Guinean I. *adj* guineano, -a **II.** *n* guineano, -a *m, f*

guinea pig *n* porcellino *m* d'India, cavia *f*

guise [gaɪz] *n* sembianze *fpl;* **under the ~ of sth** sotto le sembianze di qc; **it's an old idea in a new ~** sotto le sembianze nuove si cela un'idea vecchia

guitar [gɪ·'tɑːr] *n* chitarra *f;* **to play the ~** suonare la chitarra

guitarist [gɪ·'tɑː·rɪst] *n* chitarrista *mf*

gulf [gʌlf] *n* **1.** (*area of sea*) golfo *m;* **the Gulf of Mexico** il Golfo del Messico; **the Persian Gulf** il Golfo Persico; **the Gulf of Suez** il Golfo di Suez **2.** (*chasm*) abisso *m;* **to bridge a ~** colmare la distanza

gull¹ [gʌl] *n* ZOOL gabbiano *m*

gull² [gʌl] *vt* **to ~ sb** imbrogliare qu; **I was ~ed into believing that ...** mi hanno imbrogliato facendomi credere che ...

gullet ['gʌ·lɪt] *n* **1.** (*food pipe*) esofago *m* **2.** (*throat*) gola *f*

gullible ['gʌ·lə·bl] *adj* credulone, -a

gully ['gʌ·li] <-ies> *n* (*channel*) gola *f*

gulp [gʌlp] **I.** *n* **in one ~** tutto d'un fiato; **a ~ of water** un sorso d'acqua; **a ~ of air** una boccata d'aria **II.** *vt* inghiottire **III.** *vi* **1.** (*swallow with emotion*) deglutire **2.** (*breath*) **to ~ for**

air prendere (il) fiato

gum¹ [gʌm] I. *n* 1. (*soft sticky substance*) gomma *f;* BOT resina *f* 2. (*adhesive*) colla *f* 3. **chewing ~** gomma *f* da masticare; **fruit gum** caramella *f* gommosa alla frutta II. *vt* incollare

gum² [gʌm] *n* ANAT gengiva *f*
♦**gum up** *vt* appiccicare ▶ **to ~ the works** mettere i bastoni tra le ruote

gumball *n* pallina *f* di gomma da masticare

gumbo *n reg* gombo *m*

gum disease *n* gengivite *f*

gumdrop ['gʌm·drɑːp] *n* caramella *f* gommosa

gummed *adj* gommato, -a

gummy ['gʌ·mi] <-ier, -iest> *adj* (*sticky*) appiccicoso, -a

gumption ['gʌmp·ʃən] *n inf* 1. (*courage*) coraggio *m;* **to have the ~ to do sth** avere il coraggio di fare qc 2. (*intelligence*) buonsenso *m*

gumshoe ['gʌm·ʃuː] *n inf* detective *mf*

gum tree ['gʌm·triː] *n* albero *m* della gomma

gun [gʌn] I. *n* 1. (*weapon*) arma *f* da fuoco; (*cannon*) cannone *m;* (*pistol*) pistola *f;* (*revolver*) revolver *m;* (*rifle*) fucile *m;* **to carry a ~** portare la pistola 2. SPORTS pistola *f* da starter; **to jump the ~** partire prima del segnale 3. (*device*) pistola *f;* **grease ~** pistola ingrassatrice 4. (*person*) sicario *m;* **a hired ~** assassino *m* prezzolato ▶ **to stick to one's ~s** proseguire sulla propria strada II. <-nn-> *vi* accelerare a fondo
♦**gun down** *vt* freddare

gunboat *n* cannoniera *f*

gunboat diplomacy *n* politica *f* della cannoniera

gun control *n* controllo *m* delle armi (da fuoco)

gunfight *n* scontro *m* a fuoco

gunfire *n* 1. (*gunfight*) scontro *m* a fuoco; (*shots*) spari *mpl* 2. (*cannon fire*) cannonate *fpl*

gung-ho ['gʊŋ·hoʊ], **gung ho** *adj sl* fanatico, -a

gunk [gʊŋk] *n inf* sostanza *f* vischiosa

gunman <-men> *n* bandito *m*

gunner ['gʌ·ɚ] *n* artigliere *m*

gunpoint *n* **at ~** sotto la minaccia di un'arma

gunpowder *n* polvere *f* da sparo

gunrunner *n* trafficante *mf* d'armi

gunrunning *n* traffico *m* d'armi

gunship *n* elicottero *m* da guerra

gunshot ['gʌn·ʃɑːt] *n* sparo *m*

gunshot wound *n* ferita *f* da arma da fuoco

gunslinger ['gʌn·ˌslɪ·ŋɚ] *n* HIST pistolero, -a *m, f*

gurgle ['gɜːr·gl] I. *n* gorgoglio *m* II. *vi* gorgogliare

guru ['guː·ruː] *n* guru *m inv*

gush [gʌʃ] I. <-es> *n* fiotto *m; fig* slancio *f;* **a ~ of water** un getto d'acqua II. *vi* 1. (*any liquid*) zampillare 2. *inf* (*praise excessively*) spericarsi in elogi III. *vt* zampillare

gusher ['gʌ·ʃɚ] *n* pozzo *m* petrolifero

gushing *adj* (*praise*) sperticato, -a

gushy ['gʌ·ʃi] <-ier, -iest> *adj* sdolcinato, -a

gusset ['gʌ·sɪt] *n* tassello *m*

gust [gʌst] I. *n* (*of wind*) raffica *f;* (*of rain*) scroscio *m* II. *vi* soffiare

gusto ['gʌs·toʊ] *n* entusiasmo *m*

gusty ['gʌs·ti] <-ier -iest> *adj* a raffiche

gut [gʌt] I. *n* 1. (*intestine*) intestino *m;* **a ~ feeling/reaction** un instinto/una reazione viscerale 2. (*string from animal intestine*) budello *m* 3. *pl, inf* (*bowels*) budella *fpl* 4. *pl* (*courage*) coraggio *m;* **it takes ~s** ci vuole coraggio ▶ **to bust a ~** *inf* farsi il mazzo II. <-tt-> *vt* 1. (*remove the innards*) sventrare 2. (*destroy*) distruggere

gutless [gʌt·lɪs] *adj inf* codardo, -a

gutsy ['gʌt·si] <-ier, -iest> *adj* 1. (*brave*) coraggioso, -a 2. (*powerful*) vigoroso, -a

gutter ['gʌ·tɚ] *n* (*on the roadside*) canale *m* di scolo; (*on the roof*) grondaia *f; fig* bassifondi *mpl*

guttural ['gʌ·tə·rəl] *adj a.* LING gutturale

guy [gaɪ] *n inf* 1. (*man*) tipo *m;* **hi ~s** ciao ragazzi 2. (*for tent: guy rope*) tirante *m*

Guyana [gaɪ·ˈæ·nə] *n* Guyana *f*

Guyanese [ˌgaɪ·ə·ˈnɪːz] I. *adj* guianese II. *n* guyanese *mf*

guzzle ['gʌ·zl] I. *vt inf* (*of person: alcohol*) tracannare; (*of car: gas*) bere II. *vi* gozzovigliare

gym [dʒɪm] *n inf* palestra *f*

gymnasium [dʒɪm·ˈneɪ·zi·əm] *n* palestra *f*

gymnast ['dʒɪm·næst] *n* ginnasta *mf*

gymnastic [dʒɪm·ˈnæs·tɪk] *adj* ginnico, -a

gymnastics [dʒɪm·ˈnæs·tɪks] *npl* ginnastica *f*

gym shoes *n* scarpe *f pl* da tennis

gynecological [ˌgaɪ·nə·kə·ˈlɑː·dʒɪ·kəl] *adj* ginecologico, -a

gynecologist *n* ginecologo, -a *m, f*

gynecology [ˌgaɪ·nə·ˈkɑː·lə·dʒi] *n* ginecologia *f*

gyp [dʒɪp] *sl* I. *vt* truffare II. *n* 1. (*swindler*) truffatore, -trice *m, f* 2. (*swindle*) truffa *f*

gypsum ['dʒɪp·səm] *n* gesso *m*

gypsy ['dʒɪp·si] <-ies> I. *n* zingaro, -a *m, f* II. *adj* da zingaro, -a; **~ encampment** accampamento *m* di zingari

gyrate [ˌdʒaɪ·ˈreɪt] *vi* ruotare

gyration [ˌdʒaɪ·ˈreɪ·ʃən] *n* rotazione *f*

gyrocompass ['dʒaɪ·roʊ·ˌkʌm·pəs] *n* girobussola *f*

gyroscope ['dʒaɪ·rəs·koʊp] *n* NAUT, AVIAT giroscopio *m*

G

H

H, h [eɪtʃ] *n* H, h *f;* ~ **as in How** H come Hotel
ha [hɑː] *interj a. iron* ah!
habeas corpus [ˌheɪ·bɪ·əs·ˈkɔːr·pəs] *n* LAW habeas corpus *m inv*
haberdasher [ˈhæ·bə·dæ·ʃə·] *n* sarto , -a da uomo *m*
haberdashery [ˈhæ·bə·dæ·ʃə·i] <-ies> *n* 1.(*clothing*) abbigliamento *m* maschile 2.(*shop*) negozio *m* di abbigliamento maschile
habit [ˈhæ·bɪt] *n* 1.(*customary practice*) abitudine *f;* **to be in the** ~ **of doing sth** avere l'abitudine di fare qc; **by** (**sheer**) **force of** ~ per pura abitudine; **to do sth out of** ~ fare qc per abitudine; **to get into the** ~ (**of doing sth**) abituarsi (a fare qc); **to get out of the** ~ **of doing sth** perdere l'abitudine di fare qc; **a bad** ~ una cattiva abitudine; **to break a** ~ perdere l'abitudine; **don't make a** ~ **of it** non prenderci l'abitudine 2.(*dress*) abito *m;* **riding** ~ tenuta *f* da equitazione 3.(*addiction*) assuefazione *f;* **to have a heroin** ~ essere eroinomane
habitable [ˈhæ·bɪ·ṭə·bl] *adj* abitabile
habitat [ˈhæ·bɪ·tæt] *n* habitat *m inv*
habitation [ˌhæ·bɪ·ˈteɪ·ʃən] *n* 1.(*occupancy*) **unfit for human** ~ inabitabile 2.(*dwelling*) abitazione *f*
habitual [hə·ˈbɪt·ʃu·əl] *adj* 1.(*usual*) abituale; ~ **drug use** regolare uso di droga 2.(*describing person: liar*) impenitente
habituate [həv·ˈbɪt·ʃu·eɪt] *vt* abituare; **to be** ~**d to doing sth** essere abituato a fare qc
hack¹ [hæk] I. *vt* 1.(*chop violently*) tagliare a pezzi; **to** ~ **sth to pieces** fare qc a pezzi 2.*sl* (*cope with*) **she can't** ~ **it** non ce la fa II. *vi* 1.(*chop*) **to** ~ **at sth** fare a pezzi qc 2.(*cough*) tossire III. *n* (*writer*) scribacchino, -a *m, f;* (*journalist*) giornalista *mf* di bassa leva
hack² [hæk] *vt* COMPUT **to** ~ (**into**) **a system** entrare illecitamente in un sistema
hack³ [hæk] I. *vi* andare a cavallo II. *n* 1.(*horse*) cavallo *m* 2.*inf* (*taxi cab*) taxi *m inv*
hacker [ˈhæ·kə·] *n* COMPUT hacker *mf inv*
hackles [ˈhæ·klz] *npl* (*on back of dog*) peli *m pl* del collo; (*on neck of bird*) piume *f pl* del collo ▸ **to get one's** ~ **up** arrabbiarsi; **to make sb's** ~ **rise** fare arrabbiare qu
hackney [ˈhæk·ni] *n,* **hackney carriage** *n* 1.(*horse*) cavallo *m* da nolo 2.(*carriage*) carrozza *f* da nolo
hackneyed [ˈhæk·nɪd] *adj* (*argument, theme*) trito, -a e ritrito, -a
hacksaw [ˈhæk·sɑː] *n* sega *f* per metalli
had [hæd, *unstressed:* həd] *pt, pp of* **have**
haddock [ˈhæ·dək] *n* eglefino *m*
hadn't [ˈhæ·dnt] = **had not** *s.* **have**
haft [hæft] *n* (*of a knife*) manico *m;* (*of a sword*) impugnatura *f*
hag [hæg] *n* (*woman*) megera *f*

haggard [ˈhæ·gə·d] *adj* sciupato, -a
haggle [ˈhæ·gl] *vi* contrattare; **to** ~ **over sth** contrattare il prezzo di qc
Hague [heɪg] *n* **the** ~ L'Aia
ha-ha [ˈhɑː·hɑː] *interj iron* ah, ah!
hail¹ [heɪl] I. *n* METEO grandine *f;* (*of stones*) scarica *f;* (*of insults*) pioggia *f* II. *vi* grandinare; **to** ~ **down on sb/sth** *a. fig* piovere addosso a qu/qc
hail² [heɪl] I. *vt* 1.(*call*) chiamare; **to** ~ **a taxi** fermare un taxi 2.(*acclaim*) acclamare 3.(*welcome*) accogliere; **she** ~**ed the news with joy** ha accolto la notizia con gioia II. *vi* **to** ~ **from** (*person*) essere di; (*thing*) venire da III. *interj* ~! cavolo!
hail-fellow(-well-met) *n* (troppo) cordiale
hair [her] *n* 1.(*on head*) capello *m,* capelli *mpl;* (*on chest, armpits, legs*) pelo *m;* **to do one's** ~ farsi i capelli; **to have one's** ~ **cut** tagliarsi i capelli; **to wash one's** ~ lavarsi la testa; **to wear one's** ~ **up/down** avere i capelli raccolti/sciolti 2.(*on animal*) pelo *m* 3.(*on plant*) peluzzo *m* ▸ **that'll put** ~ **on your chest** *inf* questo ti rimetterà; **to make sb's** ~ **curl** *inf* far rizzare i capelli a qu; **to get in sb's** ~ seccare qu (*standogli troppo tra i piedi;* **to not harm a** ~ **on sb's head** non torcere un capello a qu; **to split** ~**s** spaccare il capello in quattro
hairbrush <-es> *n* spazzola (*f* per capelli)
hairclip *n* mollettina *f*
hair conditioner *n* balsamo *m*
curling iron *n* arricciacapelli *m inv*
haircut *n* taglio (*m* di capelli); **to get a** ~ tagliarsi i capelli
hairdo *n inf* pettinatura *f*
hairdresser *n* parrucchiere, -a *m, f;* **at the** ~**'s** dal parrucchiere
hairdressing *n* (*profession*) a ~ **salon** *un negozio di parrucchiere*
hair dryer *n* asciugacapelli *m inv*
hairless [ˈher·lɪs] *adj* (*head*) calvo, -a, pelato, -a; (*body*) senza peli; (*face*) glabro, -a; (*animal*) senza pelo
hairline *n* 1.(*edge of the hair*) attaccatura *f* di capelli; **he has a receding** ~ è stempiato 2.(*fine line*) linea *f* finissima
hairline crack *n,* **hairline fracture** *n* incrinatura *f* finissima
hairnet *n* retina *f*
hairpiece *n* parrucchino *m*
hairpin *n* forcina *f*
hairpin curve *n,* **hairpin turn** *n* curva *f* a gomito
hair-raising *adj inf* da far rizzare i capelli
hair remover *n* prodotto *m* depilatorio
hair restorer *n* prodotto *m* per rinfoltire i capelli
hairsplitting I. *n* cavillosità *f* II. *adj* cavilloso, -a
hair spray *n* lacca (*f* per capelli)
hairstyle *n* acconciatura *f*
hairy [ˈhe·ri] <-ier, -iest> *adj* 1.(*having much*

hair) peloso, -a **2.** *sl* (*difficult, dangerous*) rischioso, -a

Haiti ['heɪ·ṭi] *n* Haiti *f*

Haitian ['heɪ·ʃən] **I.** *n* haitiano, -a *m, f* **II.** *adj* haitiano, -a

hake [heɪk] <-(s)> *n* nasello *m*

hale [heɪl] *adj* robusto, -a

half [hæf] **I.**<halves> *n* (*equal part*) metà *f inv;* ~ **an apple** mezza mela; **in** ~ a metà; **to cut sth into halves** tagliare qc metà; **a pound and a** ~ una libbra e mezzo; **to go halves (on sth)** *inf* pagare (qc) a metà; **to go halves with sb** fare a metà con qu; **my better** ~ *fig* la mia dolce metà; **first/second** ~ SPORTS primo/secondo tempo; **the first/second** ~ **of a century** la prima/seconda metà di un secolo **II.** *adj* mezzo, -a; ~ **a pint** mezza pinta; ~ **an hour** [*o* **a** ~ **hour**] mezz'ora; **she's** ~ **the player she used to be** non è più la giocatrice di un tempo **III.** *adv* **1.** (*almost*) quasi; **to be** ~ **sure** essere quasi sicuro **2.** (*partially*) mezzo; ~ **asleep** mezzo addormentato; ~ **cooked** mezzo crudo; ~ **dead** *fig* mezzo morto; (*exhausted*); **only** ~ **done** fatto solo a metà; ~ **naked** mezzo nudo; ~ **empty/full** mezzo vuoto/pieno **3.** (*by fifty percent*) ~ **as many/much** la metà; ~ **as much again** ancora la metà **4.** *inf* (*most*) la maggior parte; ~ (**of**) **the time** la metà del tempo **5.** (*thirty minutes after*) ~ **past three** le tre e mezzo; (**at**) ~ **past nine** alle nove e mezzo; **at** ~ **past** ai 30 **IV.** *pron* la metà; **only** ~ **of them came** soltanto metà di loro sono venuti

half and half *adj* **to split sth** ~ dividere qc a metà

half-and-half *n* miscela di panna e latte

halfback *n* SPORTS mediano *m*

half-baked *adj* **1.** (*food*) mezzo crudo, -a **2.** *inf* (*plan*) stupido, -a

half boot *n* stivaletto *m*

half-breed *n* meticcio, -a *m, f*

half brother *n* fratellastro *m*

half-caste *n pej* meticcio, -a *m, f*

half-dollar *n* mezzo dollaro *m*

half-dozen *adj* mezza dozzina *f*

half-empty *adj* (*glass*) mezzo, -a vuoto, -a

halfhearted *adj* poco entusiasta; **a** ~ **attempt** un mezzo tentativo

half-life *n* PHYS periodo *m* di semitrasformazione

half-mast *n* **at** ~ a mezz'asta

half-moon *n* mezzaluna *f;* ~ **shaped** a (forma di) mezzaluna

half note *n* MUS minima *f*

half-price *n* **at** ~ a metà prezzo

half sister *n* sorellastra *f*

midterm *n* **1.** (*between semesters*) vacanze *f pl* di metà trimestre **2.** *pl* (*exams*) esami *m pl* di metà trimestre

half-timbered *adj* con travatura in legno visibile

halftime *n* SPORTS intervallo *m* tra il primo e il secondo tempo; **at** ~ alla fine del primo tempo

half title *n* occhiello *m*

halftone *n* mezzatinta *f*

half-truth *n* mezza verità *f inv*

halfway ['hæf·weɪ] **I.** *adj* **1.** (*midway*) a metà strada; ~ **stage** fase intermedia **2.** (*partial*) parziale **II.** *adv* **1.** (*half the distance*) a metà strada; **to be** ~ **between ... and ...** essere a metà strada tra... e...; **to be** ~ **through sth** essere a metà di qc; ~ **through the year** a metà anno; ~ **up** a metà salita; **to meet sb** ~ *fig* incontrare qu a metà strada **2.** (*nearly, partly*) **to go** ~ **toward (doing) sth** fare qc in parte; **the proposals only went** ~ **toward meeting their demands** le proposte hanno risposto solo in parte alle loro richieste

halfway house *n* struttura *f* per il reinserimento sociale di malati mentali o ex-detenuti

half-wit *n* deficiente *mf*

semiyearly I. *adj* semestrale **II.** *adv* semestralmente

halibut ['hæ·lɪ·bət] <-(s)> *n* halibut *m inv*

Haligonian I. *n* abitante *mf* di Halifax (Nuova Scozia) **II.** *adj* di Halifax (Nuova Scozia)

halitosis [ˌhæ·lɪ·'toʊ·sɪs] *n* alitosi *f*

hall [hɔːl] *n* **1.** (*corridor*) corridoio *m* **2.** (*entrance room*) atrio *m,* ingresso *m* **3.** (*large public room*) sala *f;* (*in schools*) mensa *f;* **concert** ~ sala *f* concerti; **town** [*o* **city**] ~ municipio *m* **4.** UNIV collegio *m;* **residence** ~ casa *f* dello studente

hallelujah [ˌhæ·lɪ·'luː·jə] **I.** *interj* alleluia! **II.** *n* alleluia *m*

hallmark ['hɔːl·mɑːrk] **I.** *n* **1.** (*identifying symbol*) segno *m* distintivo; **her** ~ il suo segno distintivo; **to bear all the** ~**s of ...** *fig* avere tutte le caratteristiche di... **2.** (*engraved mark*) marchio *m* **II.** *vt* contraddistinguere

hallow ['hæ·loʊ] *vt* **1.** (*sanctify*) santificare; (*consecrate*) consacrare **2.** (*venerate*) venerare

hallowed *adj* sacro, -a

Halloween *n,* **Hallowe'en** [ˌhæ·lə·'wiːn] *n* Halloween *m*

> **i** **Halloween** si festeggia il 31 ottobre, la vigilia di *All Saint's Day* o *All Hallows* (Ognissanti). Da tempo immemorabile, questa festa è associata agli spiriti e alle streghe. I bambini fanno delle *jack-o-lanterns* (lanterne ricavate da zucche). Di sera i bambini mascherati ne approfittano per bussare alle porte delle case e chiedere "Trick or Treat!" "Dolcetto o scherzetto?": o si dà loro un dolciume, (*treat*), oppure si deve subire uno scherzo (*trick*). Ai giorni nostri, gli scherzi sono divenuti sempre più rari perché i bambini vanno solo nelle case illuminate dalle zucche in segno di benvenuto.

hallucinate [hə·'luː·sɪ·neɪt] *vi a. fig* avere le allucinazioni

hallucination [həvˌluː·sɪ·'neɪ·ʃən] *n* allucinazione *f*

hallucinogen [hə·'luː·sɪ·nə·'dʒen] *n* allucinogeno *m*

hallucinogenic *adj* allucinogeno, -a

halo ['heɪ·loʊ] <-s *o* -es> *n* **1.** *a. fig* REL aureola *f* **2.** *a. fig* ASTR alone *m*

halogen ['hæ·lə·dʒen] *n* alogeno *m*

halogen bulb *n* lampadina *f* alogena

halogen lamp *n* lampada *f* alogena

halt [hɔːlt] **I.** *n* **1.** (*standstill, stop*) fermata *f;* **to bring sth/sb to a ~** fermare qc/qu; **to call a ~ to sth** porre fine a qc; **to come** [*o* **grind**] **to a ~** fermarsi **2.** (*interruption*) interruzione *f* **II.** *vt* fermare **III.** *vi* fermarsi **IV.** *interj* **~!** alt!

halter ['hɔːl·tə·] *n* **1.** (*on animal*) cavezza *f* **2.** (*for criminal*) capestro *m* **3.** (*top*) top *m* con scollo all'americana *inv*

halter-top *n* top *m* con scollo all'americana *inv*

halting *adj* (*speech, movement*) esitante

halve [hæv] **I.** *vt* **1.** (*lessen*) dimezzare; (*number*) dividere per due **2.** (*cut in half*) dividere a metà **II.** *vi* dimezzarsi

ham [hæm] **I.** *n* **1.** prosciutto *m;* **a slice of ~** una fetta di prosciutto **2.** (*actor*) gigione *m* **3.** (*radio*) radioamatore, -trice *m, f* **II.** *vi* recitare in modo gigionesco

◆**ham up** *vt* recitare in modo gigionesco; **to ham it up** recitare in modo gigionesco

hamburger ['hæm·bɜːr·gə·] *n* **1.** (*patty*) hamburger *m inv* **2.** (*meat*) carne *f* tritata

ham-fisted *adj*, **ham-handed** *adj* goffo, -a

hamlet ['hæm·lət] *n* borgo *m*

hammer ['hæ·mə·] **I.** *n* **1.** (*tool*) martello *m;* **~ blow** martellata *f;* **the ~ and sickle** POL, HIST la falce e il martello; **to go under the ~** *a. fig* (*painting*) essere messo all'asta **2.** (*of gun*) cane *m* ▶ **to go at it ~ and tongs** *inf* (*argue*) discutere animatamente; (*fight*) lottare con tutte le proprie forze **II.** *vt* **1.** (*hit with tool: metal*) prendere a martellate; (*nail*) piantare; **to ~ sth** (**into sth**) piantare qc (in qc); **to ~ sth into sb** *fig* inculcare qc in testa a qu **2.** *inf* SPORTS (*beat easily*) battere **3.** (*criticize: book, film*) stroncare; **to ~ sb for sth** criticare duramente qu per qc **4.** *inf* (*become very drunk*) **to get ~ed** (**on sth**) prendersi una sbornia (di qc) **III.** *vi* **1.** (*use a hammer*) martellare; **to ~ at sth** dare martellate a qc **2.** (*beat heavily*) battere; (*heart*) battere forte; (*head*) martellare; **to ~ on sth** insistere su qc

◆**hammer in** *vt* piantare

◆**hammer out** *vt* **1.** (*correct: dent*) riaggiustare a martellate **2.** (*find solution*) **to ~ a settlement** raggiungere un accordo

hammer drill *n* martello *m* pneumatico

hammerhead *n* **1.** (*on hammer*) testa *f* del martello **2.** ZOOL **~ shark** pesce *m* martello

hammock ['hæ·mək] *n* amaca *f*

hamper[1] ['hæm·pə·] *vt* (*hinder*) **to ~ sb/sth** ostacolare qu/qc

hamper[2] ['hæm·pə·] *n* **1.** (*picnic basket*) cestino *f* da picnic **2.** (*for dirty laundry*) cesto *m*

della biancheria

hamster ['hæm·stə·] *n* criceto *m*

hamstring ['hæm·strɪŋ] **I.** *n* ANAT tendine *m* del ginocchio; ZOOL tendine *m* del garretto **II.** *vt irr* **1.** (*cut the hamstring*) sgarrettare **2.** (*render powerless*) paralizzare; **to be hamstrung** essere legato mani e piedi

hand [hænd] **I.** *n* **1.** ANAT mano *f;* **to be good with one's ~s** avere le mani d'oro; **to deliver a letter by ~** consegnare a mano una lettera; **to do sth by ~** fare qc a mano; **to keep one's ~s off** non toccare; **to shake ~s with sb** stringere la mano a qu; **to take sb by the ~** prendere qu per mano; **to tie ~ and foot** *a. fig* legare mani e piedi; **~ in ~** mano nella mano; **get your ~s off!** giù le mani!; **~s up!** mani in alto!; **to ask for sb's ~** (**in marriage**) chiedere la mano di qu **2.** (*handy, within reach*) **at ~** a portata di mano; **to keep sth close at ~** tenere qc a portata di mano; **to be at ~** essere vicino; **on ~** (*available to use*) disponibile; **to be on ~** (*object*) essere a portata di mano; (*person*) essere a disposizione **3.** (*what needs doing now*) **the problem at ~** il problema in questione; **in ~** (*being arranged*) **preparations are in ~** i preparativi sono in corso **4.** *pl* (*responsibility, authority, care*) **to be in good ~s** essere in buone mani; **to fall into the ~s of sb** cadere nelle mani di qu; **to put sth into sb's ~s** mettere qc in mano a qu; **at the ~s of sb** (*because of*) per mano di qu **5.** (*assistance*) **to give** (**sb**) **a ~** (**with sth**) dare (a qu) una mano (con qc); **to keep one's ~ in** non perdere la mano a qu **6.** (*control*) **to get out of ~** (*things, situation*) sfuggire di mano; **to have sth in ~** avere qc per le mani; **to have sth well in ~** avere qc sotto controllo; **to have a ~ in sth** intervenire in qc; **to take sb in ~** far rigare dritto qu **7.** GAMES **to have a good/ poor ~** avere delle belle/brutte carte; **to show one's ~s** *a. fig* scoprire le proprie carte; **a ~ of poker** una mano a poker **8.** (*on clock*) lancetta *f;* **the hour/the minute ~** la lancetta delle ore/dei minuti **9.** (*manual worker*) operaio, -a *m, f;* (*sailor*) marinaio *m;* **farm ~** bracciante *mf* **10.** (*skillful person*) **old ~** veterano, -a *m, f;* **to be an old ~ at sth** avere molta pratica in qc; **to try one's ~ at sth** provare qc; **to be able to turn one's ~ to anything** sapere fare un po' di tutto **11.** (*applause*) applauso *m;* **let's have a big ~ for ...** un applauso per... **12.** (*measurement for horses*) spanna *f* **13.** (*handwriting*) calligrafia *f;* **in his own ~** di suo pugno ▶ **to make money ~ over <u>fist</u>** fare soldi rapidamente; **to lose money ~ over <u>fist</u>** perdere soldi rapidamente; **to be ~ in <u>glove</u> with sb** essere pappa e ciccia con qu; **to put one's ~ in one's <u>pocket</u>** mettere mano alla borsa; **with a <u>firm</u> ~** con mano dura; **at <u>first</u> ~** personalmente; **to have one's ~s <u>full</u>** essere molto impegnato; **with a <u>heavy</u>** [*o* **an <u>iron</u>**] **~** con mano dura; **to play a <u>lone</u> ~** agire da solo; **on**

the <u>one</u> ~ ... **on the other** (~) ... da un lato..., dall'altro (lato)...; **to have one's ~s** <u>tied</u> avere le mani legate; **to** <u>force</u> **sb's** ~ forzare la mano a qu; **to** <u>get</u> **one's** ~**s on sb** acciuffare qu; **to** <u>lay</u> **one's** ~**s on sth** trovare qc; **to not** <u>soil</u> **one's** ~**s with sth** non sporcarsi le mani con qc; **to** <u>throw in</u> **one's** ~ darsi per vinto II. vt 1. (give) passare; **will you** ~ **me my bag?** mi passi la borsa? 2. (give credit to) **you've got to** ~ **it to him** gli va riconosciuto

◆**hand around** vt far circolare

◆**hand back** vt restituire

◆**hand down** vt 1. (knowledge, tradition) trasmettere; (objects) lasciare in eredità 2. LAW (judgment) pronunciare

◆**hand in** vt (document) consegnare; **to** ~ **one's resignation** presentare le dimissioni

◆**hand on** vt (knowledge) trasmettere; (object) passare; **to hand sth on to sb** passare qc a qu

◆**hand out** vt 1. (distribute) distribuire 2. (give) dare

◆**hand over** I. vt 1. (give, submit: money, prisoner) consegnare 2. (pass: power, authority) trasferire; (property) cedere 3. TEL passare; **to hand sb over to sb** passare qu a qu II. vi to ~ **to sb** passare le consegne a qu; TV passare la linea a qu

handbag n borsa f

handball n SPORTS pallamano f

handbill n volantino m

handbook n manuale m

hand brake n AUTO freno m a mano

handcart n carretto m

handcuff vt ammanettare

handcuffs npl manette fpl; **a pair of** ~ un paio di manette

handful ['hænd·fʊl] n 1. a. fig (small amount) manciata f; **a** ~ **of people** un gruppetto di persone 2. (person) **to be a real** ~ (child) essere una peste; (adult) essere una persona che da' da fare

hand grenade n granata f

handgun n pistola f

handicap ['hæn·dɪ·kæp] I. n (disability, disadvantage) SPORTS handicap m inv; **mental/physical** ~ handicap mentale/fisico II. <-pp-> vt ostacolare; **to be ~ped** essere in svantaggio

handicapped I. adj **physically/mentally** ~ fisicamente/mentalmente disabile II. n **the** ~ i disabili

handicraft ['hæn·dɪ·kræft] n 1. (work) lavoro m artigianale 2. (product) articolo m artigianale

handiwork ['hæn·dɪ·wɜrk] n 1. (work) lavoro m fatto a mano 2. (product) prodotto m fatto a mano; **this must be Peter's** ~ iron questo dev'essere opera di Peter

handkerchief ['hæŋ·kə·tʃɪf] n fazzoletto m

handle ['hæn·dl] I. n 1. (of pot, basket, bag, knife) manico m; (of drawer) maniglia f 2. (knob) pomello m; (lever) leva f 3. inf RADIO

(name) titolo m ▶ **to fly** <u>off</u> **the** ~ inf perdere le staffe; **to get a** ~ **on sth** capire qc II. vt 1. (touch) toccare 2. (move, transport) maneggiare; ~ **with care** fragile 3. (machine) manovrare; (tool, weapon) maneggiare; (chemicals) manipolare; **to** ~ **a situation well** gestire bene una situazione; **she ~s light expertly in her paintings** nei suoi dipinti usa la luce con maestria 4. (direct) occuparsi di; **I'll** ~ **this** me ne occupo io; **he doesn't know how to** ~ **other people** (business) non sa dirigere le persone; (socially) non sa come prendere le persone 5. (control) gestire; **to** ~ **an increase in prices** far fronte a un aumento dei prezzi 6. (discuss, portray: subject) trattare 7. (operate) manovrare III. vi + adv/prep rispondere (ai comandi); **to** ~ **poorly** non rispondere bene

handlebar moustache n baffi m pl a manubrio

handlebars npl manubrio m

handler n addestratore, -trice m, f

handling n 1. (management) gestione f; (of goods) manipolazione f; (of subject) trattazione f; (of person) trattamento m; (of car) conduzione f 2. COM (fee) trasporto m

hand luggage n bagaglio m a mano

handmade adj fatto, -a a mano

hand-me-down n abiti m pl usati

hand-operated adj manuale

handout ['hænd·aʊt] n 1. (money) elemosina f 2. (leaflet) volantino m 3. (press release) comunicato m stampa 4. (written information) appunti mpl

hand-picked adj selezionato, -a

handrail n (on stairs) corrimano m; (on bridge) parapetto m

handsaw n sega f

handshake n stretta f di mano

handsome ['hæn·səm] adj bello, -a; **the most** ~ **man** un uomo bellissimo; **by a** ~ **margin** con un bel vantaggio

hands-on adj 1. (practical) pratico, -a; ~ **approach** approccio pratico 2. COMPUT manuale

handspring n salto m mortale; **backward** ~ salto mortale all'indietro

handstand n verticale f; **to do a** ~ fare la verticale

hand-to-mouth adj (salary) precario, -a; **to lead a** ~ **existence** vivere precariamente

handwork n lavoro m fatto a mano

handwriting n calligrafia f

handwritten adj scritto, -a a mano

handy ['hæn·di] <-ier, -iest> adj 1. (convenient) comodo, -a; (available) disponibile; (nearby) vicino, -a; **to keep sth** ~ tenere qc a portata di mano; **to be** ~ **for sth** essere comodo per qc; **to come in** ~ (for sb) tornare utile (a qu) 2. (user-friendly) maneggevole; (form, guide) utile 3. (skillful) abile; **to be** ~ **with sth** avere pratica di qc; **to be** ~ **around the house** essere bravo nei lavoretti fai da te

handyman ['hæn·dɪ·mæn] <-men> n

operaio *m* tuttofare

hang [hæŋ] I.<hung, hung> *vi* 1.(*be suspended*) pendere; (*picture*) essere appeso, -a; **to ~ by/on/from sth** pendere per/da qc; **to ~ in a gallery** essere esposto in una galleria 2.(*lean over or forward*) pendere 3.(*float*) essere sospeso, a; **to ~ above sb/sth** incombere sopra qu/qc 4.(*die*) morire sulla forca 5.(*fit, drape: clothes, fabrics*) cadere; **to ~ well** cadere bene 6. *inf*(*be friendly with*) **to ~ with sb** frequentare qu; (*spend time at*) bighellonare ▸**~ in there!** non mollare! II.<hung, hung> *vt* 1.(*attach*) appendere; (*laundry*) stendere; (*door*) mettere; **to ~ wallpaper (on a wall)** attaccare la carta da parati (a un muro); **to ~ the curtains** attaccare le tende; **the gallery will ~ many of his paintings** la galleria esporrà molti dei suoi dipinti 2.(*lights, ornaments, decorations*) appendere 3.(*one's head*) chinare 4.(*execute*) impiccare ▸**to ~ it up** smettere III. *n* FASHION *modo in cui cade un tessuto o un abito* ▸**to get the ~ of sth** *inf* capire come qc funziona; **I don't give a ~** *inf* non me ne importa nulla

◆**hang around** I. *vi* 1. *inf* (*waste time*) perdere tempo 2.(*wait*) aspettare 3.(*idle*) bighellonare 4.(*be friendly with*) **to ~ with sb** frequentare qu II. *vt insep* gironzolare per; **I had to ~ the bus station for an hour** ho dovuto girellare per la stazione degli autobus per un'ora

◆**hang back** *vi* 1.(*be reluctant to move forward*) rimanere indietro 2.(*hesitate*) tirarsi indietro

◆**hang behind** *vi* rimanere indietro

◆**hang on** I. *vi* 1.(*wait briefly*) aspettare; **to keep sb hanging on** fare aspettare qu; **~!** *inf* aspetta un attimo!; **she's on the other phone — would you like to ~?** è sull'altra linea, vuole attendere? 2.(*hold on to*) **to ~ to sth** tenersi a qc; **~ tight** tenersi forte 3.(*persevere, resist*) tenere duro II. *vt insep* 1.(*depend upon*) dipendere da 2.(*give attention*) **to ~ sb's every word** pendere dalle labbra di qu

◆**hang out** I. *vt* (*laundry*) stendere; (*tongue*) tirare fuori; (*flag*) alzare II. *vi* 1.(*dangle*) sporgere; **let it all ~!** *inf* lasciati andare! 2. *inf* (*spend time at*) bazzicare; **where does he ~ these days?** dove bazzica ultimamente? 3. *inf* (*reside*) abitare

◆**hang over** *vt insep* essere sospeso sopra; *fig* incombere su

◆**hang together** *vi* 1.(*make sense*) essere coerente 2.(*remain associated*) rimanere compatto, -a

◆**hang up** I. *vi* 1. riagganciare; **to ~ on sb** mettere giù il telefono a qu 2. *inf* to get hung up on sth (*have trouble with*) bloccarsi su qc II. *vt* 1.(*curtains*) attaccare; (*receiver*) mettere giù 2.(*give up*) **to ~ one's cleats/boxing gloves** *fig* appendere al chiodo le scarpette/i guantoni 3. *inf*(*delay*) rallentare

hangar ['hæŋ·ɚ] *n* hangar *m inv*

hangdog ['hæŋ·dɑːg] *adj* 1.(*defeated*) abbattuto, -a 2.(*ashamed*) pieno, -a di vergogna

hanger ['hæŋ·ɚ] *n* (*clothes*) gruccia *f*

hanger-on <hangers-on> *n a. fig* parassita *mf*

hang glider *n* SPORTS deltaplano *m*

hang-gliding *n* SPORTS deltaplano *m*

hanging ['hæŋ·ɪŋ] I. *n* 1.(*act of execution*) impiccagione *f* 2.(*system of execution*) impiccagione *f* 3. *pl* (*curtains*) tende *fpl* II. *adj* 1.(*bridge*) sospeso, -a 2.(*crime*) punibile con l'impiccagione

hangman <-men> *n* 1.(*person*) boia *m* 2. GAMES impiccato *m*

hangnail *n* pepita *f*

hangout *n inf* ritrovo *m;* **a favorite ~ of artists** un posto frequentato dagli artisti

hangover *n* 1.(*after drinking*) postumi *m pl* di sbronza 2.(*left-over*) conseguenze *fpl*

hang-up *n inf* complesso *m;* **to have a ~ about sth** essere complessato per qc

hank [hæŋk] *n* matassa *f*

◆**hanker after** *vt*, **hanker for** *vt* anelare a; **to ~ the past** rimpiangere il passato

hankering *n* desiderio *m;* **to have a ~ for sth** anelare a qc

hankie *n*, **hanky** ['hæŋ·ki] *n inf abbr of* **handkerchief** fazzoletto *m*

hanky-panky [ˌhæŋ·ki·'pæŋ·ki] *n inf* intrallazzi *mpl*

Hanukkah ['hɑː·nə·kə] *n* Hanukah *m*

haphazard [hæp·'hæ·zɚd] *adj* a casaccio

hapless ['hæp·ləs] *adj* disgraziato, -a

happen ['hæ·pən] *vi* 1.(*occur*) succedere; **if anything ~s to me ...** se mi succede qualcosa...; **these things ~** [*o sl* **shit ~s**] sono cose che succedono; **whatever ~s** qualunque cosa succeda; **what ~ed to your hand?** cosa ti sei fatto alla mano?; **something amazing ~ed to her that day** quel giorno le è capitata una cosa straordinaria 2.(*chance*) **it ~ed (that) ...** il caso ha voluto che...; **I ~ed to be at home** per puro caso mi trovavo a casa; **as it ~s ...** come succede...; **how does it ~ that ...?** com'è che...?; **he ~s to be my best friend** è il mio migliore amico

happening ['hæ·pə·nɪŋ] *n* 1.(*events*) avvenimento *m* 2.(*performance*) happening *m inv*

happily ['hæ·pɪ·li] *adv* 1.(*contentedly*) felicemente; **they lived ~ ever after** vissero sempre felici e contenti 2.(*willingly*) molto volentieri 3.(*fortunately*) fortunatamente

happiness ['hæ·pɪ·nɪs] *n* felicità *f;* **I wish you every ~** ti auguro di essere felice

happy ['hæ·pi] <-ier, -iest> *adj* 1.(*feeling very good, fortunate, suitable*) felice; **to be ~ that ...** essere contento che...; **to be ~ to know that ...** essere felice di sapere che...; **I'm so ~ for you** sono felice per te; **to be ~ to do sth** essere contento di fare qc; **I'll be ~ to see you tomorrow morning** la vedrò volentieri domani mattina; **~ birthday!** buon compleanno!; **many ~ returns (of the day)!** cento di questi giorni!; **a ~ coincidence** una felice coincidenza **2.**(*satisfied*) contento, -a; **to be ~ about sb/sth** essere contento di qu/qc; **to be ~ doing sth** non avere problemi a fare qc; **are you ~ with the idea?** ti piace l'idea?

happy-go-lucky *adj* spensierato, -a

happy medium *n* giusto mezzo *m*

harass [hə·'ræs] *vt* **1.**(*persistently annoy, torment*) tormentare; **to ~ sb with questions** tempestare qu di domande; (*sexually*) molestare **2.**(*attack continually*) attaccare ripetutamente

harassed [hə·'ræst] *adj* tormentato, -a

harassment [hə·'ræs·mənt] *n* **1.**(*pestering*) molestia *f;* **sexual ~** molestie sessuali **2.**(*attack*) vessazioni *fpl*

harbinger ['hɑːr·bɪn·dʒə·] *n liter* (*person*) messaggero, -a *m, f;* (*thing*) presagio *m;* **a ~ of doom** un cattivo presagio

harbor ['hɑːr·bə·] I. *n* **1.**(*port*) porto *m* **2.** *fig* (*shelter*) rifugio *m* II. *vt* **1.**(*give shelter to*) dare rifugio a **2.**(*keep: feelings*) nutrire; **to ~ suspicions** covare dei sospetti; **to ~ a grudge (against sb)** serbare rancore (a qu) **3.**(*keep in hiding*) aiutare a nascondersi **4.**(*contain*) contenere

hard [hɑːrd] I. *adj* **1.**(*firm, rigid, hostile, unkind*) duro, -a; (*rule*) severo, -a; (*fate*) crudele; **~ times** tempi duri; **to have a ~ time** attraversare un brutto periodo; **to give sb a ~ time** rendere le cose difficili a qu; **to have ~ luck** avere sfortuna; **a ~ heart** un cuore di pietra; **to be ~ on sb/sth** essere duro con qu/qc **2.**(*intense, concentrated*) **to take a (good) ~ look at sth** guardare bene qc; **a ~ fight** una lotta accanita; **to be a ~ worker** lavorare sodo **3.**(*forceful*) forte **4.**(*difficult, complex*) difficile; **to be ~ work for sb to do sth** essere duro per qu fare qc; **to be ~ to please** essere difficile da accontentare; **to get ~** diventare difficile; **a ~ bargain** un affare poco vantaggioso; **to learn the ~ way** *fig* imparare a proprie spese **5.**(*severe*) severo, -a **6.**(*extremely cold*) rigido, -a **7.**(*solid: evidence*) inconfutabile **8.**(*fact*) innegabile; **~ and fast information** informazioni certe **9.**(*with alcohol*) **~ cider/punch** sidro/punch forte **10.** CHEM (*water*) duro, -a II. *adv* **1.**(*forcefully*) con forza; **to hit sb ~** colpire qu con forza; **to press/pull ~** premere/tirare forte **2.**(*rigid*) **frozen ~** ghiacciato, -a **3.**(*energetically, vigorously*) **to fight ~** *fig* lottare duramente; **to study/work ~** studiare/lavorare sodo; **to try ~ to do sth** sforzarsi di fare qc; **he was ~ at it** era tutto impegnato; **think ~** concentrati; **to die ~** *fig* essere duro a morire **4.**(*intently*) intensamente; **to look ~ at sth** osservare intensamente qc **5.**(*closely*) vicino; **to be ~ up** essere al verde **6.**(*heavy*) forte; **it rained ~** ha piovuto forte; **to take sth ~** prendere male qc; **I would be ~ pressed to choose one** sarebbe duro per me sceglierne uno

hardback ['hɑːrd·bæk] I. *n* (*book*) libro *m* in brossura; **in ~** in brossura II. *adj* in brossura

hardball *n* **1.**(*baseball*) baseball *m* **2.** *inf* uso *m* di qualsiasi mezzo

hard-bitten *adj* indurito, -a

hardboard *n* cartone *m* di fibra compressa

hard-boiled *adj* (*egg*) sodo, -a; *inf* (*person*) indurito, -a

hard cash *n* denaro *m* contante

hard copy <-ies> *n* COMPUT copia *f* stampata

hard core *n* **1.**(*inner circle within group*) nucleo *m* irriducibile **2.**(*pornography*) pornografia *f* hard

hard court *n* campo *m* (da tennis) in terra battuta

hardcover *n* (*book*) libro *m* in brossura

hard currency <-ies> *n* FIN moneta *f* forte

hard disk *n* COMPUT disco *m* duro

hard drive *n* COMPUT hard drive *m inv*

hard drug *n* droga *f* pesante

hard-earned *adj* (*money*) guadagnato, -a col sudore della fronte; (*rest, vacation*) meritato, -a

harden ['hɑːr·dn] I. *vt* **1.**(*make more solid, firmer*) indurire; (*steel*) temprare **2.**(*make tougher*) rafforzare; **to ~ oneself to sth** fare il callo a qc; **to become ~ed** indurirsi; **life has ~ed his personality** la vita lo ha reso duro; **to ~ one's heart** *fig* diventare duro **3.**(*opinions*) irrigidire; (*character*) temprare II. *vi* **1.**(*become firmer: character*) indurirsi **2.**(*become accustomed to*) **to ~ to sth** fare il callo a qc **3.**(*attitude*) irrigidirsi **4.**(*become confirmed*) rafforzarsi

hardening *n* **~ of the arteries** ispessimento *m*

hard feelings *npl* rancore *m;* **no ~!** senza rancore!

hard-fought *adj* combattuto, -a

hardhat *n* casco *m*

hardheaded *adj* **1.**(*stubborn*) testardo, -a **2.**(*realistic*) realista

hardhearted *adj* duro, -a

hard-hit *adj* duramente colpito, -a; **to be ~ by sth** essere duramente colpito da qc

hard-hitting *adj* aspramente critico, -a

hard labor *n* LAW lavori *m pl* forzati

hard line *n* POL linea *f* dura

hard-liner *n* POL radicale

hard liquor *n* superalcolico *m*

hardly ['hɑːrd·li] *adv* **1.**(*barely*) appena; **~ anything** quasi niente; **~ ever** quasi mai; **she can ~ walk** riesce appena a camminare; **she can ~ wait until tomorrow** non vede l'ora di arrivare a domani **2.**(*certainly not*) **it's ~ my fault that it's raining** cosa c'entro io se piove?; **you can ~ expect him to do that** non puoi certo aspettarti che lo faccia; **~!** è improbabile! *inf*

hardness ['hɑːrd·nɪs] *n* **1.**(*solidity, unfeelingness*) durezza *f* **2.**(*difficulty*) difficoltà *f* **3.**(*of winter*) rigidità *f*

hard-nosed *adj* duro, -a

hard-pressed *adj* in difficoltà

hard rock *n* MUS hard rock *m*

hard sell *n* vendita *f* aggressiva
hardship ['hɑːrd·ʃɪp] *n* (*suffering, adversity, deprivation*) stenti *mpl;* **to suffer great ~** avere molte privazioni; **to live in ~** vivere di stenti
shoulder *n* (*on road*) corsia *f* d'emergenza
hardtop *n* AUTO auto *f* non decappottabile *inv*
hardware *n* **1.** (*household articles*) ferramenta *f inv;* **a ~ store** un negozio di ferramenta; (*home improvement center*) un centro di fai-da-te **2.** COMPUT hardware *m* **3.** MIL armamenti *mpl*
hard-wearing *adj* resistente
hardwood *n* legno *m* duro
hard-working *adj* laborioso, -a
hardy ['hɑːr·di] <-ier, -iest> *adj* (*person, animal*) forte; (*plant*) resistente
hare [her] *n* BIO lepre *f*
harebrained ['her·breɪnd] *adj* strambo, -a
harelip *n* MED labbro *m* leporino
harem ['he·rəm] *n* harem *m inv*
hark [hɑːrk] *vi* ~! ascolta!; **to ~ back to sth** *fig* evocare qc
harm [hɑːrm] **I.** *n* male *m;* **to do ~ to sb/sth** fare del male a qu/qc, danneggiare qu/qc; **to do more ~ than good** fare più male che bene; (**to put**) **out of ~'s way** (mettere) al sicuro; **to see no ~ in sth** non vedere niente di male in qc; **I meant no ~** non intendevo fare del male; **you will come to no ~** non ti succederà niente; **there's no ~ in trying** non si perde niente a provare **II.** *vt* **1.** (*hurt*) fare del male a; (*reputation*) danneggiare; **it wouldn't ~ you to stay at home** non ti farebbe male restare a casa **2.** (*ruin, spoil*) rovinare
harmful ['hɑːrm·fəl] *adj* nocivo, -a; **to be ~ to sth** nuocere a qc
harmless ['hɑːrm·lɪs] *adj* (*animal, person*) inoffensivo, -a; (*thing*) innocuo, -a; (*fun, joke*) innocente
harmonic [hɑːr·'mɑː·nɪk] *adj* armonico, -a
harmonica [hɑːr·'mɑː·nɪ·kə] *n* MUS armonica *f*
harmonious [hɑːr·'moʊn·iəs] *adj* armonioso, -a
harmonium [hɑːr·'moʊn·iəm] *n* MUS armonium *m inv*
harmonization [ˌhɑːr·mə·nɪ·'zeɪ·ʃən] *n* armonizzazione *f*
harmonize ['hɑːr·mə·naɪz] **I.** *vt* armonizzare **II.** *vi* **to ~** (**with sb/sth**) armonizzarsi (con qu/qc)
harmony ['hɑːr·mə·ni] <-ies> *n* armonia *f;* **in ~** (**with sb/sth**) in armonia (con qu/qc)
harness ['hɑːr·nɪs] **I.** *n* **1.** (*for animals*) finimenti *mpl;* (*for children*) briglie *fpl* **2.** (*cooperation*) **to work in ~** lavorare insieme **3.** (*everyday life*) **to get back in ~** *fig* tornare alla routine **II.** *vt* **1.** (*secure: horse*) mettere i finimenti a; **to ~ a horse/donkey to a carriage** attaccare un cavallo/asino a un carro **2.** (*exploit: resources*) sfruttare
harp [hɑːrp] **I.** *n* MUS arpa *f* **II.** *vi* **to ~ on about sth** (*talk about*) insistere su qc; (*com-*

plain) lamentarsi di qc
harpoon [hɑːr·'puːn] **I.** *n* arpione *m* **II.** *vt* arpionare
harpsichord ['hɑːrp·sɪ·kɔːrd] *n* MUS clavicembalo *m*
harrow ['hæ·roʊ] **I.** *n* erpice *f* **II.** *vt* **1.** AGR erpicare **2.** (*distress*) tormentare
harrowing *adj* (*story, experience*) sconvolgente; (*prospect*) tremendo, -a
harsh [hɑːrʃ] *adj* **1.** (*severe: parents*) severo, -a; (*punishment*) duro, -a **2.** (*unfair: criticism, words, reality*) duro, -a **3.** (*unfriendly*) brusco, -a **4.** (*uncomfortable: light*) troppo forte; (*climate, winter*) rigido, -a; (*contrast*) violento, -a **5.** (*rough*) aspro, -a **6.** (*unaesthetic: color*) vistoso, -a **7.** (*unpleasant to the ear*) stridente
harum-scarum [ˌhe·rəm·'ske·rəm] **I.** *adv* irresponsabilmente **II.** *adj* irresponsabile
harvest ['hɑːr·vɪst] **I.** *n* (*of crops*) raccolto *m;* (*of grapes*) vendemmia *f;* (*of vegetables*) raccolta *f;* **the apple ~** la raccolta delle mele; **a good ~ of potatoes** una buona produzione di patate **II.** *vt a. fig* raccogliere; (*crops*) mietere; **to ~ grapes** vendemmiare **III.** *vi* fare il raccolto
harvester *n* **1.** (*machine*) **combine ~** mietitrebbiatrice *f* **2.** (*person: of fruits*) raccoglitore, -trice *m, f;* (*of grain*) mietitore, -trice *m, f;* (*of grapes*) vendemmiatore, -trice *m, f*
harvest moon *n* luna *f* piena intorno all'equinozio d'autunno
has [hæz, *unstressed:* həz] *3rd pers sing of* **have**
has-been *n inf* vecchia gloria *f;* **to be a ~** aver fatto il proprio tempo
hash[1] [hæʃ] **I.** *vt* CULIN tritare **II.** *n* **1.** CULIN *piatto a base di carne, patate e verdure tritate e cotte al forno o in padella* **2.** *inf* pasticcio *m;* **to make a ~ of sth** rovinare qc
◆**hash up** *vt* rovinare
hash[2] [hæʃ] *n inf* fumo *m*
hash browns *npl* crocchette *f pl* di patate
hashish ['hæ·ʃiːʃ] *n* hashish *m*
hasn't ['hæ·znt] = **has not** *s.* **have**
hassle ['hæ·sl] **I.** *n inf* (*trouble*) scocciatura *f;* **to give sb a ~** scocciare qu; **it's such a ~ è** una bella scocciatura **II.** *vt inf* scocciare; **to ~ sb to do sth** scocciare qu perché faccia qc
hassock ['hæ·sək] *n* **1.** (*for kneeling*) cuscino *m* (per inginocchiarsi) **2.** (*tuft of grass*) ciuffo *m* d'erba
haste [heɪst] *n* fretta *f;* **to make ~** affrettarsi; **in ~** di fretta
hasten ['heɪ·sn] **I.** *vt* affrettare; **to ~ sb along** dire a qu di fare in fretta; **to ~ one's steps** affrettare il passo **II.** *vi* affrettarsi; **to ~ to do sth** affrettarsi a fare qc
hasty ['heɪs·ti] <-ier, -iest> *adj* **1.** (*fast*) rapido, -a; **to beat a ~ retreat** *a. fig* ritirarsi in tutta fretta **2.** (*not thought out*) frettoloso, -a; **to make ~ decisions** prendere decisioni affrettate; **to be ~ in doing sth** essere troppo frettoloso a fare qc

hat [hæt] *n* cappello *m;* **to pass around the ~** fare una colletta ▶ **at the drop of a ~** in men che non si dica; **I'll eat my ~ if...** ci scommetterei che non...; **to hang one's ~ somewhere** fermarsi da qualche parte; **to keep sth under one's ~** non dire una parola su qc; **to talk through one's ~** *inf* parlare a vanvera

hatch¹ [hætʃ] I. *vi* uscire dal guscio II. *vt* 1. (*egg*) far schiudere 2. (*devise in secret*) tramare; **to ~ a plan** tramare un piano

hatch² [hætʃ] <-es> *n* portello *m;* NAUT osteriggio *m* ▶ **down the ~!** alla salute!

hatch³ [hætʃ] *vt* ART ombreggiare

hatchback ['hætʃ·bæk] *n* AUTO auto *f* a tre/cinque porte *inv*

hatchet ['hæt·ʃɪt] *n* accetta *f* ▶ **to bury the ~** seppellire l'ascia di guerra

hatchet-faced *adj inf* dai lineamenti decisi

hatchet man *n inf* 1. (*employee*) uomo che si occupa dei lavori sgradevoli 2. (*thug*) sicario *m*

hatching ['hæt·ʃɪŋ] *n* uscita *f* dal guscio

hate [heɪt] I. *n* odio *m;* **to feel ~ for sb/sth** odiare qu/qc II. *vt* odiare; **to ~ sb's guts** *inf* odiare qu a morte

hate crime *n* reato scatenato dall'odio religioso, razziale ecc

hateful ['heɪt·fəl] *adj* odioso, -a

hatpin ['hæt·pɪn] *n* spillone *m* da cappello

hatred ['heɪ·trɪd] *n* odio *m*

hat trick *n* SPORTS tripletta *f;* **to score a ~** fare una tripletta

haughty ['hɑ:·t̬i] <-ier, iest> *adj* altero, -a

haul [hɑ:l] I. *vt* 1. (*pull with effort*) tirare; **to ~ up the sail** issare la vela; **to ~ a boat out of the water** tirare in secco una barca 2. *inf* (*force to go*) trascinare 3. (*transport goods*) trasportare II. *n* 1. (*distance*) tragitto *m;* **long ~ flight** volo *m* intercontinentale; **in** [*o* over] **the long ~** *fig* alla lunga 2. (*quantity caught: of fish, shrimp*) pesca *f;* (*of stolen goods*) refurtiva *f* 3. (*tug*) strattone *m*

◆**haul down** *vt* (*flag, sail*) ammainare

◆**haul off** *vi* NAUT orzare

◆**haul up** *vt inf* to haul sb up before sb trascinare qu davanti a qu

haulage ['hɑ:·lɪdʒ] *n* 1. (*transportation*) trasporto *m* 2. (*costs*) spese *f pl* di trasporto

hauler ['hɑ:·lɚ] *n* (*business*) ditta *f* di autotrasporti; (*person*) autotrasportatore, -trice *m, f*

haunch [hɑ:ntʃ] <-es> *n* 1. ANAT anca *f;* **to sit on one's ~es** accucciarsi 2. (*of meat*) coscia *f*

haunt [hɑ:nt] I. *vt* 1. (*ghost*) infestare 2. (*bother, torment*) perseguitare; **to be ~ed by memories of an unhappy childhood** essere perseguitato dai ricordi di un'infanzia infelice; **to be ~ed by sth** essere ossessionato da qc 3. (*frequent*) bazzicare; **to ~ a place** bazzicare un posto II. *n* ritrovo *m* preferito; **a student ~** un posto frequentato dagli studenti

haunted *adj* 1. (*by ghosts*) infestato, -a dai fantasmi, stregato, -a 2. (*troubled: look*) preoccupato, -a

haunting *adj* 1. (*disturbing*) **a ~ fear/mem-**

ory una paura/un ricordo ricorrente e inquietante 2. (*memorable*) **to have a ~ beauty** avere una bellezza non comune; **a ~ melody** una melodia che rimane in testa

Havana [hə·'væ·nə] *n* L'Avana

have [hæv, *unstressed:* həv] I.<has, had, had> *vt* 1. (*own*) avere; **I have two brothers** ho due fratelli; **~ you got a cold? — no, I ~ a headache** hai il raffreddore? — no, ho mal di testa; **to ~ sth to do** avere qc da fare 2. (*engage in*) **to ~ a talk with sb** parlare con qu; **to ~ a game of sth** fare una partita a qc 3. (*eat*) **to ~ lunch** pranzare; **I ~n't had shrimp in ages!** sono secoli che non mangio gamberetti!; **to ~ a coffee** prendere un caffè 4. (*give birth to*) **to ~ a child** avere [*o* fare] un bambino 5. (*receive*) avere, ricevere; **to ~ news about sb/sth** avere notizie di qu/qc; **to ~ visitors** avere visite 6. (*show trait*) **to ~ patience/mercy** avere pazienza/pietà; **to ~ doubts/second thoughts** avere dubbi/ripensamenti 7. (*cause to occur*) **to ~ dinner ready by seven** la cena sarà pronta per le sette; **I'll ~ Bob give you a ride home** ti farò dare un passaggio da Bob; **I won't ~ you doing that** non te lo lascerò fare ▶ **to ~ it in for sb** *inf* avercela con qu; **to ~ it in one to do sth** essere capace di fare qc; **I didn't think she had it in her!** non pensavo che ne fosse capace!; **to ~ had it with sb/sth** *inf* averne (avuto) abbastanza di qu/qc II.<has, had, had> *aux* 1. (*indicates perfect tense*) **he has never been to California** non è mai stato in California; **we had been swimming** eravamo stati a nuotare; **had I known you were coming, ...** *form* se avessi saputo che venivi,... 2. (*must*) **to ~ (got) to do sth** dover fare qc; **what time ~ we got to be there?** a che ora dobbiamo essere lì?; **do we ~ to finish this today?** dobbiamo finirlo oggi? III. *n pl* **the ~s and the have-nots** i ricchi e i poveri

◆**have around** *vt always sep* (*gadget*) avere a portata di mano

◆**have back** *vt always sep* **can I have it back?** posso riaverlo?; **they solved their problems and she had him back** hanno risolto i problemi e lei se lo è ripreso

◆**have in** *vt always sep* invitare; **they had some experts in** hanno chiamato degli esperti

◆**have on** *vt always sep* 1. (*wear: clothes*) indossare; **he didn't have any clothes on** era completamente nudo 2. (*carry*) **to have sth on oneself** avere con sé; **have you got any money on you?** hai dei soldi con te?

◆**have out** *vt always sep* 1. (*remove*) togliersi 2. *inf* (*argue*) **to have it out with sb** mettere le cose in chiaro con qu

◆**have over** *vt always sep* invitare

◆**have up** *vt always sep* denunciare

haven ['heɪ·vn] *n* rifugio *m*

have-nots *npl* **the ~** i poveri

haven't ['hæ·vnt] = **have not** *s.* **have**

havoc ['hæ·vək] *n* caos *m;* **the ~ of the fire/**

the storm il caos dell'incendio/del temporale; **to play ~ with sth** creare il caos in qc; **to wreak ~ on sth** rovinare qc

haw [hɑ:] I. *interj* (*to horse*) ah! II. *vi* **to hem and ~** esitare (nel parlare)

Hawaii [həˈwaːɪ·iː] *n* Hawaii *fpl*

Hawaiian [həˈwaːɪ·jən] I. *n* 1. (*person*) hawaiano, -a *m, f* 2. LING hawaiano *m* II. *adj* hawaiano, -a

hawk [hɑ:k] I. *n* falco *m* II. *vt* (*wares*) vendere per strada III. *vi* raschiarsi la gola

hawker *n* venditore, -trice *m, f* ambulante

hawk-eyed *adj* **to be ~** avere occhi di lince

hawkmoth *n* atropo *m*

hawser [ˈhɔː·zə·] *n* NAUT gomenetta *f*

hawthorn [ˈhɑː·θɔːrn] *n* BOT biancospino *m*

hay [heɪ] *n* fieno *m* ▶ **to hit the ~** *inf* andare a nanna

hay fever *n* raffreddore *m* da fieno

haystack *n* pagliaio *m*

haywire *adj inf* **to go/be ~** (*person*) dare i numeri; (*machine*) andare in tilt

hazard [ˈhæ·zəd] I. *n* 1. (*danger*) pericolo *m* 2. (*risk*) rischio *m;* **fire ~** pericolo di incendio; **health ~** rischio per la salute II. *vt* 1. (*dare*) azzardare; **to ~ a guess at sth** provare a indovinare qc 2. (*endanger*) mettere a rischio

hazardous [ˈhæ·zə·dəs] *adj* (*dangerous*) pericoloso, -a; (*risky*) rischioso, -a

hazard lights *npl* AUTO blinker *m inv*

haze [heɪz] I. *n* 1. (*mist*) foschia *f;* (*smog*) nebbiolina *f* 2. (*mental*) stordimento *m* II. *vt* ESP. UNIV fare scherzi a

hazel [ˈheɪ·zl] I. *adj* (*eyes*) castano, -a II. *n* BOT nocciolo *m*

hazelnut [ˈheɪ·zl·nʌt] *n* BOT nocciola *f*

hazy [ˈheɪ·zi] <-ier, -iest> *adj* 1. (*with bad visibility*) nebbioso, -a 2. (*confused, unclear*) vago, -a

HDTV [ˌeɪtʃ·diː·tiːˈviː] *n* TV *abbr of* **high-definition television** televisione *f* ad alta definizione

he [hiː] I. *pron pers* 1. (*male person or animal*) egli, lui; **~'s** [*o* **~ is**] **my father** (lui) è mio padre; **~'s gone away but ~'ll be back soon** è partito ma tornerà presto; **here ~ comes** eccolo 2. (*unspecified sex*) **if somebody comes, ~ will buy it** se qualcuno viene, lo comprerà; **~ who ...** *form* colui che... II. *n* (*of baby, animal*) maschio *m*

head [hed] I. *n* 1. ANAT testa *f;* **to nod one's ~** fare sì con la testa; **to go straight to sb's ~** (*alcohol, wine*) andare subito alla testa di qu 2. (*unit*) testa *f;* **a** [*o* **per**] **~ a testa; a hundred ~ of cattle** cento capi di bestiame; **to be a ~ taller than sb** essere più alto di qu di tutta una testa 3. (*mind*) **to clear one's ~** chiarirsi le idee; **to get sth/sb out of one's ~** togliersi qc/qu dalla testa; **to have a good ~ for numbers** essere bravo con i numeri; **to need a clear ~ to do sth** dover essere lucido per fare qc 4. (*top: of line, page, column*) cima *f;* (*of bed*) testata *f;* **at the ~ of the table** a capo-

tavola 5. BOT (*of garlic*) testa *f;* **a ~ of lettuce** un cespo d'insalata 6. *pl* FIN (*face of coin*) testa *f;* **~s or tails?** testa o croce? 7. (*beer foam*) spuma *f* 8. GEO (*of river*) sorgenti *fpl* 9. (*boss*) capo *m;* **the department ~** il capodipartimento; **~ of a company** il direttore di un'azienda; **~ of a committee** il presidente del comitato 10. TECH (*device*) testa *f;* (*for recording*) testina *f* 11. COMPUT **read/write ~** testina *f* di lettura/scrittura 12. NAUT (*toilet*) gabinetto *m* ▶ **to have one's ~ in the clouds** avere la testa tra le nuvole; **to be ~ over heels in love** essere innamorato pazzo; **to fall ~ over heels in love with sb** innamorarsi pazzamente di qu; **to bury one's ~ in the sand** fare come lo struzzo; **to not be able to make ~ (n)or tail of sth** non capire un'acca di qc; **~s I win, tails you lose** vinco comunque; **to bang one's ~ against a wall** sbattere la testa contro il muro; **to keep one's ~ above water** tenersi a galla; **to keep one's ~ down** (*avoid attention*) tenersi in disparte; (*work hard*) impegnarsi; **to hold one's ~ high** andare a testa alta; **~s up!** attenzione!; **to be soft in the ~** essere un po' tonto; **to have one's ~ screwed on right** avere la testa sulle spalle; **to bite sb's ~ off** trattare male qu; **to bring sth to a ~** portare qc a un punto critico; **to give sb his/her ~** lasciare fare a qu di testa sua; **to laugh one's ~ off** schiantarsi dalle risate; **~s will roll** cadrà qualche testa II. *vt* 1. (*lead*) capeggiare; (*a company, organization*) dirigere; (*team*) capitanare 2. PUBL intitolare 3. SPORTS (*ball*) colpire di testa III. *vi* **to ~** (*for*) **home** dirigersi verso casa

◆ **head back** *vi* tornare indietro

◆ **head for** *vt insep* essere diretto a; **to ~ the exit** dirigersi verso l'uscita; **to ~ disaster** rischiare di finire male

◆ **head off** I. *vt* bloccare II. *vi* **to ~ toward** andare verso

◆ **head up** *vt* dirigere

headache [ˈhed·eɪk] *n* mal *m* di testa *inv*

headband *n* fascia *f* per la testa

headbanger *n inf* metallaro, -a *m, f*

headboard *n* testata *f*

head cold *n* raffreddore *m*

head cook *n* capocuoco, -a *m, f*

headdress <-es> *n* copricapo *m*

header [ˈhe·də·] *n* 1. SPORTS colpo *m* di testa 2. COMPUT intestazione *f*

headfirst [ˈhed·ˈfɜːrst] *adv* di testa; **to fall ~** cadere a testa in giù

headhunt *vt* ECON reclutare

headhunter *n* ECON (*warrior*) cacciatore *m* di teste

heading [ˈhe·dɪŋ] *n* (*of chapter*) titolo *m;* (*letterhead*) intestazione *f*

headland [ˈhed·lænd] *n* promontorio *m*

headless *adj* senza testa

headlight *n*, **headlamp** *n* faro *m*

headline I. *n* titolo *m* ▶ **to hit the ~s** fare notizia II. *vt* intitolare

headlong I. *adv* a capofitto; **to rush ~ into sth** buttarsi in qc II. *adj* precipitoso, -a

headmaster *n* direttore *m* di scuola

headmistress <-es> *n* direttrice *f* di scuola

head of state <heads of state> *n* capo *m* di stato

head-on I. *adj* (*collision*) frontale II. *adv* frontalmente

headphones *npl* cuffie *fpl*

headquarters *n+ sing/pl vb* MIL quartiere *m* generale; (*of company*) sede *f* centrale; (*of political party*) sede *f;* (*of the police*) comando *m* di polizia

headrest *n* poggiatesta *m inv*

headroom *n* altezza *f*

headscarf <-scarves> *n* fazzoletto *m* (per la testa)

headset *n* cuffie *fpl*

headship *n* ADMIN direzione *f*

headshrinker *n inf* (*psychiatrist*) strizzacervelli *mf inv*

head start *n* vantaggio *f;* **to give sb a ~** dare un vantaggio a qu

headstone *n* lapide *f*

headstrong *adj* testardo, -a

heads-up *adj* (*baseball, player*) competente

headwaiter *n* capo *m* cameriere

headwaters *npl* GEO sorgenti *fpl*

headway *n* progresso *m;* **to make ~** fare progressi

headwind *n* vento *m* contrario; NAUT vento *m* di prua

headword *n* lemma *m*

heady ['he·di] <-ier, -iest> *adj* 1.(*intoxicating*) inebriante 2.(*exciting*) emozionante

heal [hi:l] I. *vt* (*wound*) guarire; (*differences*) sanare II. *vi* (*wound, injury*) guarire

health [helθ] *n* salute *f;* **to be in good/bad ~** godere/non godere di buona salute; **to drink to sb's ~** bere alla salute di qu

health care *n* assistenza *f* sanitaria

health center *n* poliambulatorio *m*

health certificate *n* certificato *m* medico

health club *n* (centro *m*) fitness *m inv*

health food *n* alimenti *m pl* naturali

health food shop *n*, **health food store** *n* negozio *m* di prodotti naturali

health hazard *n* rischio *m* per la salute

health insurance *n* assicurazione *f* sanitaria

health maintenance organization *n* assicurazione *f* sanitaria di categoria

health resort *n*, **health spa** *n* stazione *f* termale

healthy ['hel·θi] <-ier, -iest> *adj* 1. MED sano, -a 2. FIN (*strong*) prospero, -a; (*profit*) sostanzioso, -a 3.(*positive: attitude*) positivo, -a

heap [hi:p] I. *n* (*pile*) mucchio *m*, pila *f;* **to collapse in a ~** *fig* (*person*) accasciarsi; **a** (**whole**) **~ of work** *inf* (tutta) una montagna di lavoro II. *vt* ammucchiare; **to ~ sth with sth** riempire qc di qc

hear [hɪr] <heard, heard> I. *vt* 1.(*perceive, be told*) sentire; **to ~ that ...** sentire [*o* sapere]

che... 2.(*listen*) ascoltare; **Lord, ~ our prayers** REL ascoltaci, Signore 3. LAW (*witness, arguments*) ascoltare; (*case*) esaminare II. *vi* (*perceive, get news*) sentire; **to ~ of** [*o* about] **sth** sentire [*o* sapere] di qc ▶ **~, ~!** senti, senti!

heard [hɜːrd] *pt, pp of* **hear**

hearing ['hɪ·rɪŋ] *n* 1.(*sense*) udire *m;* **to be hard of ~** avere problemi d'udito 2.(*act*) ascolto *m* 3.(*range*) **in sb's ~** in presenza di qu 4. LAW udienza *f*

hearing aid *n* apparecchio *m* acustico

hearsay ['hɪr·seɪ] *n* dicerie *fpl;* **by ~** per sentito dire

hearse [hɜːrs] *n* carro *m* funebre

heart [hɑːrt] *n* 1. ANAT cuore *m* 2.(*center of emotions*) **to break sb's ~** spezzare il cuore a qu; **to have a cold ~** avere il cuore di pietra; **to have a change of ~** cambiare idea; **to have a good** [*o* **kind**] **~** essere una persona generosa; **to lose ~** scoraggiarsi; **to lose one's ~** (**to sb/sth**) innamorarsi (di qu/qc); **to pour one's ~ out to sb** sfogarsi con qu; **to take ~** farsi coraggio; **her ~ sank** si sentì mancare 3.(*core*) centro *m;* **to get to the ~ of the matter** arrivare al nocciolo della questione 4. CULIN (*of lettuce, artichoke*) cuore *m* 5. *pl* (*card suit*) cuori *mpl* ▶ **to one's ~'s content** finché uno vuole; **to have a ~ of gold/stone** avere il cuore d'oro/di pietra; **to have one's ~ in the right place** non voler fare del male; **to wear one's ~ on one's sleeve** essere franco; **with all one's ~** con tutta l'anima; **she is a girl after my own ~** è una ragazza di quelle che piacciono a me; **to not have the ~ to do sth** non sentirsela di fare qc; **by ~** a memoria; **in one's ~ of ~s** dentro di sé, in fondo al cuore

heartache ['hɑːrt·eɪk] *n* sofferenza *f*

heart attack *n* infarto *m*

heartbeat *n* battito *m* cardiaco

heartbreak *n* dolore *m*

heartbreaking *adj* struggente

heartbroken *adj* col cuore infranto

heartburn *n* MED acidità *f* di stomaco

heart disease *n* disturbo *m* cardiaco

heartening ['hɑːr·tə·nɪŋ] *adj* incoraggiante

heart failure *n* arresto *m* cardiaco

heartfelt *adj* sincero, -a; **my ~ condolences** le mie più sentite condoglianze; **~ relief** gran sollievo

hearth [hɑːrθ] *n* focolare *m;* **to leave ~ and home** lasciare il focolare domestico

hearth rug *n* tappeto *m* (davanti al caminetto)

heartily *adv* con entusiasmo; **to dislike sth/sb ~** detestare qc/qu; **to eat ~** mangiare di gusto

heartland ['hɑːrt·lænd] *n* centro *m;* **the economic ~** il centro economico

heartless ['hɑːrt·ləs] *adj* senza cuore

heart murmur *n* MED soffio *m* al cuore

heart rate *n* frequenza *f* cardiaca

heart-rending *adj* straziante

heart-searching *n* esame *m* di coscienza

heartstrings *npl* **to pull at sb's ~** *fig* toccare

H

profondamente qu

heartthrob *n inf* idolo *m*

heart-to-heart I. *n* chiacchierata *f* franca II. *adj* franco, -a

heart transplant *n* trapianto *m* di cuore

heartwarming *adj* rincuorante

hearty ['hɑːrˌt̬i] *adj* <-ier, -iest> 1. (*enthusiastic*) entusiasta; ~ **congratulations** congratulazione di tutto cuore; ~ **welcome** accoglienza calorosa 2. (*large, strong*) robusto, -a; ~ **appetite** bell'appetito; **a** ~ **breakfast** una colazione sostanziosa; **to have a** ~ **dislike for sth** detestare davvero qc

heat [hiːt] I. *n* 1. (*warmth, high temperature*) calore; **in the** ~ **of the day** quando fa più caldo; **to cook sth on a high/low** ~ cuocere qc a ad alta/bassa temperatura 2. (*heating system*) riscaldamento *m;* **to turn down the** ~ abbassare il riscaldamento 3. (*emotional state*) eccitazione *f;* **in the** ~ **of the argument** nel fervore della discussione 4. (*sports race*) eliminatoria *f* 5. ZOOL calore *m;* **to be in** ~ essere in calore ▸ **to put the** ~ **on sb** mettere qu sotto pressione; **to take the** ~ **off sb** dar un po' di respiro a qu II. *vt* 1. (*make hot*) scaldare 2. (*excite*) accalorare III. *vi* (*become hot*) scaldarsi; *fig* (*inflame*) accalorarsi

◆ **heat up** I. *vi* scaldarsi II. *vt* scaldare

heated *adj* 1. (*window*) termico, -a; (*pool, room*) riscaldato, -a 2. (*argument*) acceso, -a

heatedly *adv* con veemenza; **to** ~ **deny sth** negare qc con veemenza

heater ['hiːˌt̬ɚ] *n* termosifone *m,* stufa *f;* **water** ~ scaldaacqua *m inv*

heat exchanger *n* radiatore *m*

heat exhaustion *n* MED colpo *m* di calore

heat gauge *n* termostato *m*

heath [hiːθ] *n* BOT erica *f*

heathen ['hiːˌðn] I. *n* pagano, -a *m, f;* **the** ~ i pagani II. *adj* pagano, -a

heather ['heˌðɚ] *n* BOT erica *f*

heating *n* riscaldamento *m*

heating system *n* impianto *m* di riscaldamento

heat pump *n* pomba *f* termica

heat rash <-es> *n* eruzione *f* cutanea da calore

heat-resistant *adj*, **heat-resisting** *adj* termoresistente

heat-seeking *adj* MIL termoguidato, -a

heat shield *n* scudo *m* termico

heat stroke *n* MED insolazione *f*

heat treatment *n* termoterapia *f*

heat wave *n* ondata *f* di caldo

heave [hiːv] I. *vi* 1. (*pull*) tirare; (*push*) spingere 2. (*move up and down*) alzare e abbassare; **to** ~ **into view** [*o* **sight**] NAUT apparire all'orizzonte 3. (*vomit*) vomitare II. *vt* 1. (*pull*) tirare; (*push*) spingere; **he** ~**d the door open** aprì la porta con una spinta; **to** ~ **a sigh of relief** tirare un sospiro di sollievo; **to** ~ **sth at sb** lanciare qc a qu 2. (*lift*) sollevare III. *n* 1. (*push*) spinta *f;* (*pull*) strattone *m* 2. (*great*

effort) grande sforzo *m*

◆ **heave to** *vi* <hove to, hoved to> NAUT mettersi in panna

◆ **heave up** *vt* vomitare

heaven ['heˌvən] *n* cielo *m,* paradiso *m;* **to go to** ~ andare in paradiso; **it's** ~ *fig, inf* è fantastico; **to be** ~ **on earth** *fig* (*place*) essere un paradiso; **to be in** (**seventh**) ~ *a. fig* essere al settimo cielo; **the** ~**s** (*sky*) il cielo ▸ **to move** ~ **and earth** muovere mari e monti; **what/where/when/who/why in** ~**'s name ...?** cosa/dove/quando/chi/perché diavolo...?; **for** ~**s sake!** per l'amor del cielo!; **good** ~**s!** santo cielo!; **to stink to high** ~ puzzare tremendamente; ~ **only knows** Dio solo lo sa; ~ **help us** che il cielo ci aiuti; **thank** ~**s** grazie al cielo

heavenly ['heˌvənˌli] *adj* <-ier, -iest> 1. (*of heaven*) celestiale; ~ **body** corpo *m* celeste 2. (*wonderful*) divino, -a

heavens *npl liter* firmamento *m*

heaven-sent *adj* capitato, -a a proposito

heavy ['heˌvi] I. *adj* <-ier, -iest> 1. (*weighing a lot*) pesante; ~ **food** cibi pesanti 2. (*difficult*) difficile; **the book was rather** ~ **going** il libro era piuttosto difficile da leggere 3. (*strong*) forte; ~ **fall** *a.* ECON forte calo 4. (*not delicate, coarse*) poco delicato, -a; (*features*) marcato, -a 5. (*severe*) severo, -a; (*responsibility, sea*) grosso, -a; ~ **casualties** un elevato numero di vittime 6. (*abundant*) abbondante; (*investment*) grosso, -a; ~ **rain** forti rovesci; **to go** ~ **on fuel** consumare molto carburante; **the tree was** ~ **with fruit** l'albero era carico di frutti 7. (*excessive: drinker, smoker*) accanito, -a 8. (*thick: fog*) denso, -a; (*beard*) folto, -a II. *n* <-ies> *inf* gorilla *m inv*

heavy drinker *n* gran bevitore, -trice *m, f*

heavy-duty *adj* resistente; (*machine*) per uso industriale

heavy going *adj* difficile

heavy-handed *adj* 1. (*clumsy*) maldestro, -a 2. (*harsh*) duro, -a

heavy-hearted *adj* afflitto, -a

heavy hitter *n* persona *f* chiave

heavy industry *n* industria *f* pesante

heavy metal *n* 1. (*lead, cadmium*) metallo *m* pesante 2. MUS heavy metal *m*

heavy water *n* acqua *f* pesante

heavyweight I. *adj* 1. SPORTS di pesi massimi 2. (*cloth*) resistente 3. (*important*) serio, -a e importante II. *n* peso *m* massimo; *fig* personaggio *m* di spicco

Hebrew ['hiːˌbruː] I. *n* 1. (*person*) ebreo, -a *m, f* 2. LING ebraico *m* II. *adj* ebreo, -a

Hebrides ['heˌbrɪˌdiːz] *n* **the** ~ le Ebridi

heck [hek] *interj inf* **where the** ~ **have you been?** dove cavolo eri?; **what the** ~**!** chi se ne frega!

heckle ['heˌkl] *vi, vt* interrompere

heckler ['hekˌlɚ] *n* persona *f* che interrompe

hectare ['hekˌteɚ] *n* ettaro *m*

hectic ['hekˌtɪk] *adj* febbrile; ~ **pace** ritmo febbrile

he'd [hiːd] = **he had, he would** *s.* **have, will**

hedge [hedʒ] I. *n* 1. (*row of bushes*) siepe *m* 2. FIN (*protection*) copertura *f* II. *vi* (*avoid action*) essere evasivo, -a; FIN coprirsi III. *vt* recintare (con una siepe)

hedge fund *n* FIN *fondo comune d'investimento spregiudicato*

hedgehog ['hedʒ·haːg] *n* porcospino *m*

hedgerow *n* siepe *f*

hedging ['hed·ʒɪŋ] *n* FIN copertura *f*

heebie-jeebies ['hiː·bɪ·'dʒiː·bɪz] *npl sl* **to give sb the ~** far accapponare la pelle

heed [hiːd] I. *vt form* prestare attenzione a II. *n* **to pay (no) ~ to sth, to take (no) ~ of sth** (non) prestare attenzione a qc

heedful ['hiːd·fəl] *adj* **to be ~ of sb's advice** seguire i consigli di qu

heedless ['hiːd·lɪs] *adj* irresponsabile; **~ of sth** noncurante di qc; **to be ~ of the risk** non preoccuparsi del rischio

hee-haw ['hiː·haː] I. *n* raglio *m* II. *vi* (*donkey*) ragliare

heel [hiːl] I. *n* 1. (*of foot*) tallone *m;* **to be at sb's ~s** stare alle calcagna di qu 2. (*of shoe*) tacco *m* 3. (*of the hand*) base *f* della mano 4. (*of loaf of bread*) cantuccio *m* 5. *inf* (*unfair person*) carogna *f* ▸ **to be down** at the **~s** essere male in arnese; **to follow close** on the **~s of sth** seguire immediatamente qc; **to be hard** on sb's **~s** stare alle calcagna a qu; **under** the **~ of sb/sth** sotto a qu/qc; **to bring sb to ~** ridurre all'obbedienza qu; **to come to ~** finire per obbedire; **to dig one's ~s in** puntare i piedi; **to take to one's ~s** *inf* alzare i tacchi; **to turn on one's ~** girare sui tacchi II. *interj* (*to dogs*) vieni III. *vi* (*dog*) **this dog won't heel** il cane non viene quando si chiama

hefty ['hef·ti] *adj* <-ier, -iest> (*person*) corpulento, -a; (*profit, amount*) sostanzioso, -a; (*book*) massiccio, -a

heifer ['he·fɚ] *n* giovenca *f*

height [haɪt] *n* 1. (*of person*) statura *f,* altezza *f;* (*of thing*) altezza *f* 2. *pl* (*high places*) alture *fpl;* **to be afraid of ~s** soffrire di vertigini; **to attain great ~s** *fig* arrivare in alto; **to scale (new) ~s** *fig* affrontare (nuove) sfide 3. *pl* (*hill*) cime *fpl* 4. (*strongest point*) culmine *m;* **to be at the ~ of one's career** essere all'apice della carriera; **the ~ of fashion** l'ultimo grido 5. (*the greatest degree*) colmo *m;* **the ~ of stupidity/patience** il colmo della stupidità/pazienza; **the ~ of kindness/** il massimo della generosità

heighten ['haɪ·tn] I. *vi* aumentare II. *vt* aumentare; **to ~ the effect of sth** intensificare l'effetto di qc

heinous ['heɪ·nəs] *adj form* atroce

heir [er] *n* erede *mf;* **to be (the) ~ to sth** essere l'erede di qc; **~ apparent** erede in linea diretta; **~ to the throne** erede al trono

heiress ['e·rɪs] *n* ereditiera *f*

heirloom ['er·luːm] *n* family **~** cimelio di famiglia

heist [haɪst] *n inf* rapina *m* a mano armata

held [held] *pt, pp of* **hold**

helicopter ['he·lɪ·kaːp·tɚ] *n* elicottero *m*

Hel(i)goland ['he·lɪ·goʊ·lænd] *n* Helgoland *f*

helipad ['he·lɪ·pæd] *n* piattaforma *f* per elicotteri

heliport ['he·lɪ·pɔːrt] *n* eliporto *m*

helium ['hiː·li·əm] *n* elio *m*

hell [hel] I. *n* 1. (*place of punishment*) inferno *m;* **~ on earth** un inferno; **to be (pure) ~** essere un (vero) inferno; **to go to ~** andare all'inferno; **to go through ~** soffrire le pene dell'inferno; **to make sb's life ~** *inf* rendere la vita impossibile a qu 2. *inf* (*as intensifier*) **as cold as ~** un freddo cane; **as hot as ~** un caldo infernale; **as hard as ~** durissimo; **to beat the ~ out of sb** ammazzare di botte qu; **to frighten the ~ out of sb** spaventare a morte qu; **to hurt like ~** fare un male cane; **to run like ~** correre a gambe levate; **a ~ of a decision** una decisione veramente importante ▸ **the road to ~ is paved with good intentions** *prov* la via dell'inferno è lastricata di buone intenzioni; **come ~ or high water** ad ogni costo; **to have been to ~ and back** aver passato l'inferno; **all ~ broke loose** si è scatenato l'inferno; **to catch ~** prendersi una bella tirata d'orecchie; **to do sth for the ~ of it** fare qc per il gusto di farlo; **to give sb ~** non perdonarla a qu; **go to ~!** *inf* (*leave me alone*) levati di torno!; (*stronger*) vaffanculo! *vulg;* **to hope to ~** *inf* sperare vivamente; **to have ~ to pay** *inf* pagarla cara; **like ~** *inf* un cavolo; **what the ~** *inf* chi se ne frega II. *interj* (*emphasis*) cavolo! ▸ **~'s bells!** per Dio!; **what the ~ ...!** che cavolo...!

he'll [hiːl] = **he will** *s.* **will**

hellacious [he·'leɪ·ʃəs] *adj* (*awful*) tremendo, -a

hell-bent *adj* **to be ~ on doing sth** essere decisissimo a fare qc

hellfire *n* fuoco *m* dell'inferno

hellhole *n inf* postaccio *m*

hellish ['he·lɪʃ] *adj* infernale; (*experience*) orrendo, -a

hellishly *adv* tremendamente

hello [hə·'loʊ] I. <hellos> *n* saluto *m* II. *interj* 1. (*greeting*) salve; **to say ~ to sb** salutare qu 2. (*beginning of phone call*) pronto 3. (*to attract attention*) scusi 4. (*surprise*) scusa; **~,~** senti, senti

helm [helm] *n* timone *m;* **to be at the ~** stare al timone; *fig* (*lead*) essere al comando; **to take the ~** *a.fig* (*control*) assumere il comando

helmet ['hel·mɪt] *n* casco *m;* **crash ~** casco (di sicurezza)

helmsman ['helmz·mən] *n* <-men> timoniere *m*

help [help] I. *vi* aiutare II. *vt* 1. (*assist*) aiutare; **nothing can ~ him now** non si può fare più niente per aiutarlo; **can I ~ you?** (*in shop*) desidera?; **to ~ sb with sth** aiutare qu con qc; **to ~ sb with his homework** aiutare qu a fare i compiti **2.** (*improve*) migliorare; **this medicine will ~ your headache** questo farmaco ti allevierà il mal di testa **3.** (*contribute to a condition*) contribuire a **4.** (*prevent*) evitare; **it can't be ~ed** non c'è altro da fare; **to not be able to ~ doing sth** non poter fare a meno di fare qc; **I can't ~ it** è più forte di me; **he can't ~ the way he is** è fatto così; **to not be able to ~ but ...** non poter fare a meno di... **5.** (*take sth*) **to ~ oneself to sth** (*at table*) servirsi di qc; (*steal*) prendersi **III.** *n* **1.** (*assistance*) aiuto *m;* **to be a ~** essere d'aiuto **2.** (*servant*) uomo, donna delle pulizie *m;* (*in a shop*) aiutante *mf* **IV.** *interj* **~!** aiuto!; **so ~ me God** e che Dio m'assista

♦ **help out** *vt* aiutare

helper ['hel·pɚ] *n* aiutante *mf*

helpful ['help·fəl] *adj* **1.** (*willing to help*) disponibile **2.** (*useful*) utile

helping ['hel·pɪŋ] **I.** *n* (*food*) porzione *f* **II.** *adj* **to give sb a ~ hand** dare una mano a qu

helpless ['help·lɪs] *adj* impotente; (*baby*) indifeso, -a

helpline ['help·laɪn] *n* servizio *m* di assistenza

helter-skelter [ˌhel·tɚ·'skel·tɚ] **I.** *adj* caotico, -a **II.** *adv* in fretta e furia

hem [hem] **I.** *n* orlo *m;* **to take the ~ up/down** accorciare/allungare l'orlo **II.** *vt* fare l'orlo a **III.** *vi* <-mm-> **to ~ and haw** esitare (nel parlare) **IV.** *interj* mmmh

♦ **hem in** *vt* (*surround*) accerchiare

he-man ['hi:·mæn] <-men> *n* *inf* macho *m inv*

hematite ['he·mə·taɪt] *n* MIN ematite *f*

hemisphere ['he·mɪs·fɪr] *n* emisfero *m*

hemline ['hem·laɪn] *n* orlo *m*

hemlock ['hem·lɑːk] *n* cicuta *f*

hemoglobin ['hiː·mə·gloʊ·bɪn] *n* emoglobina *f*

hemophilia [ˌhiː·moʊ·'fɪl·iə] *n* emofilia *f*

hemophiliac [ˌhiː·moʊ·'fɪ·li·æk] *n* emofiliaco, -a *m, f*

hemorrhage ['he·mə·ɪdʒ] **I.** *n* emorragia *f;* **brain ~** emorragia *m* cerebrale **II.** *vi* MED avere una emorragia

hemorrhoids ['he·mə·ɔɪdz] *npl* emorroidi *fpl*

hemp [hemp] *n* canapa *m*

hen [hen] *n* (*female chicken*) gallina *f;* (*female bird*) femmina *f*

hence [hens] *adv* **1.** (*therefore*) donde **2.** *after n* (*from now*) **two years ~** da qui a due anni

henceforth [ˌhens·'fɔːrθ] *adv*, **henceforward** [ˌhens·'fɔːr·wɚd] *adv* da ora in avanti

henchman ['hentʃ·mən] <-men> *n* tirapiedi *m inv*

hencoop ['hen·kuːp] *n*, **henhouse** ['hen·haʊs] *n* gabbia *f* per galline

henna ['he·nə] **I.** *n* henné *m* **II.** *vt* tingere con l'henné

hennery ['he·nɚ·i] *n* <-ies> gabbia *f* per galline

henpecked ['hen·pekt] *adj* **a ~ husband** un uomo che fa quel che dice la moglie

HEPA ['he·pə] *abbr of* high-efficiency particulate arresting **~ filter** filtro *m* HEPA

hepatitis [ˌhe·pə·'taɪ·tɪs] *n* epatite *f*

heptathlon [hep·'tæθ·lɑːn] *n* eptatlon *m*

her [hɜːr] **I.** *adj pos* il suo *m,* la sua *f,* i suoi *mpl,* le sue *fpl;* **~ dress** il suo vestito; **~ house** la sua casa; **~ children** i suoi figli; **~ sisters** le sue sorelle **II.** *pron pers* **1.** (*she*) lei; **it's ~** è lei; **younger than ~** più giovane di lei; **if I were ~** se fossi in lei **2.** *direct object* la; *indirect object* le; **look at ~** guardala; **I see ~** la vedo; **he told ~ that ...** le ha detto che...; **he gave ~ the pencil** le ha dato la matita [*o* ha dato la matita a lei] **3.** *after prep* lei; **it's for ~** è per lei

herald ['he·rəld] **I.** *vt* annunciare; **to ~ a new era** annunciare una nuova era; **the much ~ed** il tanto acclamato **II.** *n* **1.** (*sign*) presagio *m;* **to be a ~ of sth** essere un segnale di qc **2.** HIST (*bringer of news*) araldo *m*

heraldic [hə·'ræl·dɪk] *adj* araldico, -a

heraldry ['he·rəld·ri] *n* araldica *f*

herb [hɜːrb] *n* erba *f* aromatica

herbaceous [hɚ·'beɪ·ʃəs] *adj* erbaceo, -a

herbalism ['hɜːr·bə·lɪ·zəm] *n* fitoterapia *f,* erboristeria *f*

herbalist ['hɜːr·bə·lɪst] *n* erborista *mf*

herbal medicine *n* fitoterapia *f*

herbicide ['hɜːr·bɪ·saɪd] *n* erbicida *m*

herbivore ['hɜːr·bɪ·vɔːr] *n* erbivoro *m*

herbivorous [hɜːr·'bɪ·və·rəs] *adj* erbivoro, -a

Herculean [ˌhɜːrk·ju·'liː·ən] *adj* herculeo, -a; **~ task** impresa *f* erculea

Hercules ['hɜːrk·jə·li:z] *n* Ercole *m*

herd [hɜːrd] **I.** *n* + *sing/pl vb* **1.** (*of animals*) mandria *f;* (*of sheep*) gregge *m;* (*of pigs*) branco *m* **2.** (*of people*) massa *f;* **to follow the ~** seguire la massa **II.** *vt* (*animals*) radunare; (*sheep*) guidare; (*people*) ammassare

♦ **herd together** *vt* (*animals*) radunare

herd instinct *n* istinto *m* gregale

herdsman ['hɜːrdz·mən] *n* <-men> (*of cattle*) mandriano *m;* (*of sheep*) pastore *m*

here [hɪr] **I.** *adv* **1.** (*in, at, to this place*) qui; **over ~** qui; **give it ~** *inf* dammelo; **~ and there** qui e là **2.** (*in introductions*) **here is ...** ecco... **3.** (*show arrival*) **they are ~** sono arrivati **4.** (*next to*) **my colleague ~** il mio collega **5.** (*now*) ora; **~ you are, ~ you go** (*giving sth*) tieni; **the ~ and now** il presente; **~ goes** *inf* pronti, via; **~ we go** e ci risiamo; **where do we go from ~?** dove andiamo a finire? **II.** *interj* (*in roll call*) presente

hereabouts [ˌhɪ·rə·'baʊts] *adv* da queste parti

hereafter [hɪr·'æf·tɚ] **I.** *adv* in seguito **II.** *n* **the ~** l'aldilà

hereby [hɪr·'baɪ] *adv form* con la presente

hereditary [hə·'re·dɪ·te·ri] *adj* ereditario, -a

heredity [hə·'re·dɪ·ţi] *n* eredità *f*

herein [ˌhɪr·'ɪn] *adv form* qui

hereof [hɪr·'ɑːv] *adv form* del presente

heresy ['he·rə·si] <-ies> *n* eresia *f*

heretic ['he·rə·tɪk] *n* eretico, -a *m, f*
heretical [hə·'re·t̬ɪ·kl] *adj* eretico, -a
hereupon [ˌhɪ·rə·'pɑːn] *adv form* a questo punto
herewith [ˌhɪr·'wɪð] *adv form* **I enclose three documents** ~ accludo tre documenti
heritage ['he·rɪ·t̬ɪdʒ] *n* patrimonio *m*
hermaphrodite [hə·'mæ·frou·daɪt] **I.** *n* ermafrodita *m* **II.** *adj* ermafrodito
hermetic [hə·'me·t̬ɪk] *adj* ermetico, -a; ~ **seal** chiusura *f* ermetica
hermit ['hɜ:r·mɪt] *n* eremita *mf*
hermitage ['hɜ:r·mɪ·t̬ɪdʒ] *n* eremo *m*
hermit crab *n* paguro *m* bernardo
hernia ['hɜ:r·niə] *n* MED ernia *f*
hero ['hɪ·rou] <heroes> *n* **1.**(*brave man*) eroe *m* **2.**(*main character*) protagonista *m;* **the ~ of a film** il protagonista di un film **3.**(*idol*) idolo *m* **4.**(*sandwich*) panino con carne fritta, formaggio e lattuga
heroic [hɪ·'rou·ɪk] *adj* **1.**(*brave, bold*) eroico, -a; ~ **attempt** tentativo eroico; ~ **deed** gesto *f* eroico **2.**(*epic*) eroico, -a
heroics *n pl* **1.**(*action*) impresa *f* spericolata **2.**(*language*) linguaggio *m* magniloquente
heroin ['he·rou·ɪn] *n* eroina *f, droga*
heroin addict *n* MED eroinomane *mf*
heroine ['he·rou·ɪn] *n* (*brave woman*) eroina *f;* (*of film*) protagonista *f*
heroism ['he·rou·ɪ·zəm] *n* eroismo *m*
heron ['he·rən] <-(s)> *n* airone *m*
herpes ['hɜ:r·piːz] *n* herpes *m*
herring ['he·rɪŋ] <-(s)> *n* aringa *f*
herringbone ['he·rɪŋ·boun] FASHION **I.** *n* spigato *m* **II.** *adj* spigato, -a
herring gull *n* gabbiano *m* reale
hers [hɜ:rz] *pron pos* (il) suo *m,* (la) sua *f,* (i) suoi *mpl,* (le) sue *fpl;* **it's not my bag, it's ~** non è la mia borsa, è la sua; **this house is ~** questa casa è sua; **this glass is ~** questo bicchiere è suo; **a book of ~** uno dei suoi libri
herself [hə·'self] *pron* **1.** *reflexive* si; *after prep* sé; **she lives by ~** vive sola **2.** *emphatic* lei stessa
hertz [hɜ:rts] *n inv* hertz *m inv*
he's [hiːz] **1.** = **he is** *s.* **be 2.** = **he has** *s.* **have**
hesitant ['he·zɪ·tənt] *adj* esitante; **to be ~ about doing sth** esitare a fare qc
hesitantly *adv* con esitazione
hesitate ['he·zɪ·teɪt] *vi* esitare; **to (not) ~ to do sth** (non) esitare a fare qc
hesitation [ˌhe·zɪ·'teɪ·ʃən] *n* esitazione *f;* **without ~** senza esitazione; **to have no ~ in doing sth** non esitare affatto a fare qc
heterogeneous [ˌhe·t̬ə·rou·'dʒiː·ni·əs] *adj* eterogeneo, -a
heterosexual [ˌhe·t̬ə·rou·'sek·ʃu·əl] **I.** *n* eterosessuale *mf* **II.** *adj* eterosessuale
hew [hjuː] <hewed, hewed *o* hewn> **I.** *vt* **1.**(*cut away*) tagliare **2.**(*cut into shape*) **to ~ stone/wood** intagliare la pietra/il legno **II.** *vi* (*conform*) **to ~ to sth** attenersi a qc

hewn [hjuːn] *pp of* **hew**
hex [heks] *n inf* maleficio *m;* **to put a ~ on sb/ sth** fare un maleficio a qu/qc
hexagon ['hek·sə·gɑːn] *n* esagono *m*
hexagonal [hek·'sæ·gə·nl] *adv* esagonale
hexameter [hek·'sæ·mə·t̬ə·] *n* esametro *m*
hey [heɪ] *interj inf* ehi
heyday ['heɪ·deɪ] *n* apogeo *m;* **in his/her/ its ~** al suo apogeo
hi [haɪ] *interj* ciao
hiatus [haɪ·'eɪ·t̬əs] <-es> *n* (*pause*) LING iato *m*
hibernate ['haɪ·bə··neɪt] *vi* andare in letargo
hibernation [ˌhaɪ·bə·'neɪ·ʃən] *n* **to go into ~** andare in letargo
hibiscus [hɪ·'bɪs·kəs] <-es> *n* BOT ibisco *m*
hiccup, hiccough ['hɪk·ʌp] **I.** *n* singhiozzo *m;* **to have the ~s** avere il singhiozzo **II.** *vi* <-p(p)-> avere il singhiozzo
hid [hɪd] *pt of* **hide²**
hidden ['hɪ·dn] **I.** *pp of* **hide²** **II.** *adj* nascosto, -a; ~ **assets** ECON attività *f* occulta *inv;* ~ **economy** economia sommersa
hide¹ [haɪd] *n* (*of an animal*) pelle *f* ▸ **to see neither ~ nor hair of sb** non vedere qu
hide² [haɪd] <hid, hidden> **I.** *vi* (*be out of sight*) nascondersi **II.** *vt* (*conceal: person, thing*) nascondere; (*emotion, information*) tenere nascosto, -a; **to ~ one's face** coprirsi il volto
◆**hide away** *vt* nascondere
◆**hide out** *vi,* **hide up** *vi* nascondersi
hide-and-seek to play ~ giocare a nascondino
hideaway ['haɪ·də·weɪ] *n* nascondiglio *m*
hideous ['hɪ·di·əs] *adj* tremendo, -a
hideout ['haɪd·aut] *n* nascondiglio *m*
hiding¹ ['haɪ·dɪŋ] *n* **a real ~** un sacco di botte; **to get a real ~** (*defeat*) essere stroncato
hiding² ['haɪ·dɪŋ] *n* **to be in ~** essere nascosto; **to go into ~** nascondersi
hierarchic(al) [ˌhaɪ·'rɑ:r·kɪ·k(l)] *adj* gerarchico, -a
hierarchy ['haɪ·rɑ:r·ki] <-ies> *n* **1.**(*system*) gerarchia *f* **2.**(*upper levels of organization*) dirigenza *f*
hieroglyph [ˌhaɪ·rou·'glɪf] *n* geroglifico *m*
hieroglyphics *npl* geroglifici *mpl*
hi-fi ['haɪ·faɪ] **I.** *n abbr of* **high-fidelity** alta fedeltà *f* **II.** *adj abbr of* **high-fidelity** hi-fi; ~ **equipment** impianto *m* stereo
higgledy-piggledy [ˌhɪ·gl·dɪ·'pɪ·gl·di] *adj inf* alla rinfusa
high [haɪ] **I.** *adj* **1.** alto, -a; **one meter ~ and three meters wide** alto una iarda e largo tre; **knee/waist-~** fino al ginocchio/alla cintura; **to fly at ~ altitude** volare ad alta quota; ~ **cheekbones** zigomi alti; **to do a ~ dive** fare un tuffo dall'alto; **to have ~ hopes for sb/sth** riporre molte aspettative in qu/qc; **to have a ~ opinion of sb** stimare molto qu; **to have ~ praise for sb/sth** parlare molto bene di qu/ qc; **of the ~est caliber** del migliore livello; ~ **blood-pressure/fever** pressione/febbre

alta; **a ~ caliber gun** un'arma di grosso calibro; **of ~ rank** di alto rango; **to have friends in ~ places** avere amicizie che contano; **an order from on ~** un ordine dall'alto; **to be ~ and mighty** credersi chissacchì; **with a ~ neckline/waistline** a collo alto/vita alta **2.**(*under influence of drugs*) fatto, -a **3.**(*of high frequency, shrill: voice*) acuto, -a; **a ~ note** una nota alta **4.**(*at peak, maximum*) **~ noon** mezzogiorno in punto; **~ priority** massima importanza ▶ **to leave sb ~ and <u>dry</u>** lasciare qu abbandonato a se stesso **II.** *adv* **1.**(*at or to a great point or height*) (in) alto **2.**(*rough or strong*) intensamente; **the sea runs ~** il mare è agitato ▶ **to search for sth ~ and <u>low</u>** cercare qc in lungo e in largo **III.** *n* **1.**(*high*(*est*) *point*) massimo *m;* **an all-time ~** un picco massimo; **to reach a ~** raggiungere un picco massimo **2.** *inf*(*from drugs*) **to be on a ~** essere fatto **3.**(*heaven*) **on ~** in cielo

highball *n* whisky *m* e soda *inv*

high beam *n* abbagliante *m*

highboy *n cassettone alto e stretto, con zampe alte*

highbrow I. *adj* intellettuale **II.** *n* intellettuale *mf*

highchair *n* seggiolone *m*

high-class *adj* d'alta classe

high court *n* corte *f* suprema

high-definition television *n* televisione *f* ad alta definizione

high-density *adj a.* INFOR ad alta densità

high-end *adj* per le fasce più abbienti

higher education *n* istruzione *f* a livello universitario

higher-up *n inf* superiore *m*

highfalutin [ˌhaɪ·fə·'luː·tɪn] *adj inf* presuntuoso, -a

high-fiber [ˌhaɪ·'faɪ·bɚ] *adj* ricco, -a di fibre

high fidelity *n* alta fedeltà *f*

high-five *n gesto di saluto o congratulazioni consistente nell'alzare le braccia e battere i palmi delle mani contro quelli di un'altra persona*

highflier *n* persona *f* di talento

high-flown *adj* altisonante

high frequency *adj* ad/di alta frequenza

high-grade *adj* di alto livello

highhanded *adj* dispotico, -a

highhandedness *n* dispotismo *m*

high heels *npl* tacchi *m pl* alti

high horse *n* **to get** (**down**) **off one's ~** scendere dal piedistallo

high-income *adj* ad alto reddito

highjack *vt s.* **hijack**

high jinks *npl* baldoria *f*

high jump *n* salto *m* in alto

Highlands *npl* Highlands *fpl*

high-level *adj* di alto livello

highlife *n* bella vita *f;* **to live the ~** fare la bella vita

highlight I. *n* **1.**(*most interesting part*) parte *f* più interessante **2.** *pl* (*in hair*) colpi *m* di sole

pl **II.** *vt* evidenziare

highlighter *n* evidenziatore *m*

highly ['haɪ·li] *adv* **1.**(*very*) molto **2.**(*very well*) **to speak ~ of sb** parlare molto bene di qu; **to think ~ of sb** avere un'alta opionione di qu

highly-educated *adj* di livello culturale alto

highly-skilled *adj* qualificato, -a

High Mass [ˌhaɪ·'mæs] *n* REL messa *f* solenne

highness ['haɪ·nɪs] <-es> *n* **1.**(*level*) altezza *f* **2.**(*prince or princess*) **His/Her/Your Highness** Sua Altezza

high noon *n* mezzogiorno *m* in punto

high-octane *n* **~ gasoline** benzina *f* ad alto numero di ottani

high-performance *adj a.* AUTO di buona prestazione

high-pitched *adj* **1.**(*sloping steeply*) **~ roof** tetto *m* spiovente **2.**(*sound, voice*) acuto, -a

high point *n* **the ~** il culmine

high-powered *adj* **1.**(*powerful*) di grande potenza **2.**(*influential, important*) potente **3.**(*advanced*) avanzato, -a

high pressure *n* METEO alta pressione *f*

high-pressure I. *adj* **1.** METEO **a ~ area** una zona di alta pressione **2.**(*aggressive*) **~ sales techniques** ECON tecniche di vendita aggressive **3.**(*stressful: job*) stressante **II.** *vt* fare pressione su

high priest *n* REL sommo sacerdote *m*

high priestess *n* REL sacerdotessa *f*

high-profile *adj* noto, -a

high-protein *adj* ricco, -a di proteine

high-ranking *adj* di alto livello

high-resolution *adj* COMPUT (*image, screen, shot*) ad alta risoluzione

high-rise I. *adj* molto alto, -a; **~ building** edificio *m* molto alto **II.** *n* edificio *m* molto alto

high-risk *adj* ad alto rischio; (*investment*) rischioso, -a

high roller *n sl* spendaccione, -a *m, f*

high school *n* scuola *f* media superiore; **junior ~** scuola media inferiore

high seas *npl* alto mare *m*

peak season *n* alta stagione *f;* **at ~** in alta stagione

high-security *adj* di massima sicurezza

high sign *n inf* segnale *m* convenuto

high society *n* alta società *f*

high-sounding *adj* altisonante

high-speed *adj* ad alta velocità

high-spirited *adj* (*cheerful, lively*) vivace; (*fiery: horse*) focoso, -a

high spirits *npl* buon umore *m*

high-stick *vt* (*in ice hockey*) colpire tenendo la mazza più alta del consentito

high-strung *adj* tesissimo, -a

high summer *n* piena estate *f*

hightail I. *vi inf* darsela a gambe **II.** *vt* **to ~ it home** filare a casa

high-tech *adj* ad/di alta tecnologia; (*architecture*) all'avanguardia

high technology *n* alta tecnologia *f*

high-tension *adj* ELEC (*cable*) dell' alta tensione

high tide *n* **1.** (*of ocean*) alta marea *f* **2.** *fig* (*most successful point*) apogeo *m*

high-tops *npl* scarpe *f pl* da ginnastica alte

high treason *n* alto tradimento *m*

high-up I. *adj* importante II. *n* pezzo *m* grosso

high water *n* alta marea *f*

high-water mark *n* **1.** (*showing water level*) livello *m* di guardia **2.** (*most successful point*) apogeo *m*

highway ['haɪ·weɪ] *n* superstrada *f*

highway patrol *n* polizia *f* stradale

highway robbery <-ies> *n* **1.** HIST assalto (a scopo di rapina) *m* **2.** *fig, inf* (*too expensive*) furto *m*

hijack ['haɪ·dʒæk] I. *vt* **1.** (*take over by force: plane*) dirottare **2.** *fig* (*adopt as one's own*) to ~ sb's ideas/plans appropriarsi delle idee/dei progretti di qu II. *n* dirottamento *m*

hijacker ['haɪ·dʒæ·kɚ] *n* dirottatore, -trice *m, f*

hijacking ['haɪ·dʒæ·kɪŋ] *n* dirottamento *m*

hike [haɪk] I. *n* **1.** (*long walk*) escursione *f*; to go on a ~ fare un'escursione; **take a ~!** *inf* vattene! **2.** *inf* (*increase*) aumento *m* II. *vi* fare escursioni (a piedi) III. *vt inf* (*prices, taxes*) aumentare

hiker ['haɪ·kɚ] *n* escursionista *mf*

hiking ['haɪ·kɪŋ] *n* escursionismo *m*

hilarious [hɪ·'le·ri·əs] *adj* **1.** (*very funny*) troppo divertente **2.** (*high-spirited*) allegro, -a

hilarity [hɪ·'le·rə·t̬i] *n* ilarità *f*

hill [hɪl] *n* **1.** (*in landscape*) collina *f* **2.** (*in road*) pendio *m* **3.** (*small heap*) monticello *m* **4.** POL The Hill il Congresso ▸it ain't [*o* it's not] worth a ~ of **beans** *inf* non ha alcuna importanza; as **old** as the ~s vecchio come il cucco; to be **over** the ~ *inf* essere troppo vecchio

hillbilly ['hɪl·bɪ·li] <-ies> *n* montanaro, -a *m, f*

hillock ['hɪ·lək] *n* collinetta *f*

hillside ['hɪl·saɪd] *n* fianco *m* della collina

hilltop ['hɪl·tɑːp] I. *n* cima *f* della collina II. *adj* in cima alla collina

hilly ['hɪl·li] <-ier, -iest> *adj* collinare

hilt [hɪlt] *n* (*of a weapon*) impugnatura *f* ▸to the ~ completamente; to be **mortgaged to** the ~ essere indebitato fino al collo

him [hɪm] *pron pers* **1.** (*he*) lui; it's ~ è lui; younger **than** ~ più giovane di lui; **if I were** ~ se fossi in lui **2.** *direct object* lo; *indirect object* gli; **she gave** ~ **the pencil** gli ha dato la matita [*o* ha dato la matita a lui] **3.** *after prep* lui; it's **for** ~ è per lui **4.** (*unspecified sex*) if **somebody comes, tell** ~ **that** ... se viene qualcuno, digli che...

Himalayas [ˌhɪ·mə·'le·rəz] *npl* l'Himalaia

himself [hɪm·'self] *pron* **1.** *reflexive* si; *after prep* sé; **for** ~ per sé; **he lives by** ~ vive solo **2.** *emphatic* lui stesso

hind [haɪnd] I. *adj* posteriore II. <-(s)> *n* cerva *f*

hinder ['hɪn·dɚ] *vt* **1.** (*obstruct*) intralciare; to

~ **progress** rallentare il progresso **2.** (*prevent*) to ~ sb **from doing sth** impedire a qu di fare qc

Hindi ['hɪn·diː] *n* hindi *m*

hind legs *npl* zampe *f pl* posteriori ▸to talk the ~ **off a donkey** *inf* parlare incessantemente

hindmost ['haɪnd·moʊst] *adj* **1.** (*last*) ultimo, -a **2.** (*rear*) posteriore

hindquarters ['haɪnd·ˌkwɔːr·t̬ɚz] *npl* ZOOL parte *f* posteriore

hindrance ['hɪn·drəns] *n* ostacolo *m*; to **allow** sb to **enter without** ~ far entrare qu senza impedimenti

hindsight ['haɪnd·saɪt] *n* **in** ~ in retrospettiva; **with the benefit of** ~ col senno di poi

Hindu ['hɪn·duː] I. *n* indù *mf inv* II. *adj* indù

Hinduism ['hɪn·duː·ɪ·zəm] *n* REL induismo *m*

hinge [hɪndʒ] I. *n* cerniera *f* II. *vi* to ~ **on/ upon sb/sth** dipendere da qu/qc

hint [hɪnt] I. *n* **1.** (*trace*) indizio *m*; (*of anger, suspicion, salt, curry*) pizzico *m* **2.** (*allusion*) allusione *f*; to **drop a** ~ fare un'allusione; to **take a** ~ capire l'antifona **3.** (*practical tip*) indicazione *f*; **a handy** ~ una dritta II. *vt* to ~ **sth to sb** accennare qc a qu III. *vi* fare allusioni; to ~ **at sth** fare allusioni a qc

hip [hɪp] I. *n* **1.** ANAT anca *f*; to **stand with one's hands on (one's)** ~**s** stare in piedi con le mani sui fianchi **2.** BOT cinorrodo *m* II. *adj sl* (*fashionable*) moderno, -a

hipbone ['hɪp·boʊn] *n* osso *m* iliaco

hip flask *n* fiaschetta *f* tascabile

hippie ['hɪ·pi] *n* hippy *mf inv*

hippo ['hɪ·poʊ] *n* *inf abbr of* **hippopotamus** ippopotamo *m*

hippopotamus [ˌhɪ·pə·'pɑː·t̬ə·məs] <-es *o* -mi> *n* ippopotamo *m*

hippy ['hɪ·pi] <-ies> *n* hippy *mf inv*

hire ['haɪr] I. *n* **1.** (*rental*) noleggio *m* **2.** *inf* (*employee*) **a new** ~ una persona appena assunta II. *vt* **1.** (*rent*) noleggiare; to ~ **sth by the hour/day/week** noleggiare qc a ore/ giornalmente/settimanalmente **2.** (*employ*) assumere; to ~ **more staff** assumere altro personale

♦**hire out** *vt* noleggiare; to ~ **sth by the hour/day/week** noleggiare qc a ore/giornalmente/settimanalmente; to ~ **oneself out as sth** offrirsi come qc

hired hand *n* (*employee*) dipendente *mf*; (*on ranch, farm*) bracciante *mf*

his [hɪz] I. *adj pos* il suo *m*, la sua *f*, i suoi *mpl*, le sue *fpl*; ~ **car** la sua auto; ~ **coat** il suo cappotto; ~ **children** i suoi figli; ~ **sisters** le sue sorelle II. *pron pos* (il) suo *m*, (la) sua *f*, (i) suoi *mpl*, (le) sue *fpl*; it's **not my bag, it's** ~ non è la mia borsa, è la sua; **this house is** ~ questa casa è sua; **this glass is** ~ questo bicchiere è suo; **a book of** ~ uno dei suoi libri

Hispanic [hɪs·'pæ·nɪk] I. *adj* ispanico, -a, ispanoamericano, -a II. *n* ispanico, -a *m, f*, ispanoamericano, -a *m, f*

hiss [hɪs] I. *vi* sibilare; (*crowd*) fischiare II. *vt* sibilare; (*crowd*) fischiare III. *n* sibilo *m*, fischio *m*

histamine ['hɪs·tə·miːn] *n* MED istamina *f*

historian [hɪs·'tɔː·ri·ən] *n* storico, -a *m*, *f*

historic [hɪ·'stɔː·rɪk] *adj* storico, -a

historical *adj* storico, -a; **the ~ present** il presente storico

history ['hɪs·tə·i] *n* storia *f*; **a ~ book** un libro di storia; **sb's life ~** la vita di qu; **to make ~** fare epoca

histrionic [ˌhɪs·trɪ·'aː·nɪk] *adj* istrionico, -a

hit [hɪt] I. *n* 1.(*blow, stroke*) colpo *m* 2.*inf* (*shot*) centro *m* 3.(*bomb*) impatto *m* 4.SPORTS punto *m*; **to score a ~** segnare un punto 5.(*success*) successo *m* 6.*inf*(*murder*) omicidio *m* II.<-tt-, hit, hit> *vt* 1.colpire; **to ~ sb hard** colpire qc con forza; *fig* colpire qc duramente; **to ~ sb where it hurts** toccare qu nel vivo 2.(*crash into*) sbattere contro; **to ~ one's head on a shelf** sbattere la testa nella mensola; **to ~ a reef/a sandbank** incagliarsi/ arenarsi 3.(*arrive at, reach target*) raggiungere; (*reach*) toccare; **to ~ rock bottom** *fig* toccare il fondo; **to ~ 100 mph** *inf* fare 100 m/h 4.(*encounter*) trovare; **to ~ a lot of resistance** trovare grande opposizione; **to ~ a traffic jam** rimanere intrappolato in un ingorgo III. *vi* 1.(*strike*) colpire; **to ~ against sth** scontrarsi con qc; **to ~ at sb/sth** dare un colpo a qu/qc 2.(*attack*) **to ~ at sth** attaccare qc

◆**hit back** *vi* contrattaccare; **to ~ at sb** restituire il colpo a qu

◆**hit off** *vt* **to hit it off (with sb)** andare d'accordo (con qu)

◆**hit on** *vt* 1.(*show sexual interest*) cercare di rimorchiare 2.(*think of*) avere

◆**hit out** *vi* lanciare un attacco; **to ~ at sb** colpire qu; *fig* criticare qu

◆**hit up** *vi always sep* **to hit sb up for sth** chiedere qc a qu

hit-and-run *adj* **~ accident** incidente stradale con omissione di soccorso; **~ attack** MIL raid; **~ driver** pirata della strada

hitch [hɪtʃ] I.<-es> *n* 1.(*obstacle*) contrattempo *m*; **technical ~** problema *m* tecnico; **to go off without a ~** andare tutto liscio 2.(*sudden pull*) strattone *m* 3.(*for a trailer*) gancio *m* II. *vt* 1.(*fasten*) attaccare; **to ~ sth to sth** attaccare qc a qc; **to ~ an animal to sth** legare un animale a qc 2.*inf*(*hitchhike*) **to ~ a lift** [*o ride*] farsi dare un passaggio III. *vi inf* fare l'autostop

◆**hitch up** *vt* 1.(*fasten*) **to hitch sth up to sth** attaccare qc a qc; **to ~ an animal to sth** legare un animal a qc 2.(*pull up quickly: clothes*) tirare su

hitcher ['hɪt·ʃə] *n* autostoppista *mf*

hitchhike ['hɪtʃ·haɪk] *vi* fare l'autostop

hitchhiker ['hɪtʃ·haɪ·kə] *n* autostoppista *mf*

hitch-hiking *n* autostop *m*

hi-tech [ˌhaɪ·'tek] *adj* ad/di alta tecnologia; (*architecture*) all'avanguardia

hither ['hɪ·ðə] *adv form* qui; **~ and thither** [*o yon*] qui e là

hitherto [ˌhɪ·ðə·'tuː] *adv form* fino ad ora [*o ad allora*]; **~ unpublished** fino ad ora non pubblicato

hit list *n* lista nera

hit man ['hɪt·mæn] <-men> *n* sicario *m*

hit-or-miss *adj* casuale

hit parade *n* HIST (*top forty*) hit parade *f*; **to be at the top of the ~** essere in testa alla classifica

HIV [ˌeɪtʃ·aɪ·'viː] *abbr of* **human immunodeficiency virus** HIV *m*; **to be ~ positive/ negative** essere sieropositivo/sieronegativo

hive [haɪv] I. *n* 1.(*beehive*) alveare *m* 2.**+** *sing/pl vb* (*swarm of bees*) sciame *m* 3.(*busy place*) **it was a ~ of activity** c'era una grande attività II. *vt* **to ~ sth off** (*separate*) separare qc

◆**hive off** *vi* separarsi

hives [haɪvz] *n* MED orticaria *f*

HMO [ˌeɪtʃ·em·'oʊ] *abbr of* **health maintenance organization** assicurazione *f* sanitaria di categoria

ho [hoʊ] *interj inf* (*expressing scorn, surprise*) oh; (*attracting attention*) oh; **land ~!** NAUT terra!

hoagie ['hoʊ·giː] *n panino con carne fritta, formaggio e lattuga*

hoard [hɔːrd] I. *n* scorta *f* II. *vt* accumulare; (*food*) fare scorta di

hoarding ['hɔːr·dɪŋ] *n* palizzata *f*

hoarfrost [ˌhɔːr·'frɑːst] *n* brina *f*

hoarse [hɔːrs] *adj* rauco, -a

hoarseness *n* MED raucedine *f*

hoary ['hɔː·ri] <-ier, -iest> *adj* 1.*liter* (*hair*) bianco, -a 2.*fig* (*old*) **~ old joke** vecchia barzelletta *m*; **~ old excuse** scusa *f* di sempre

hoax [hoʊks] I.<-es> *n* (*joke*) burla *f*; (*fraud*) imbroglio *m* II. *vt* imbrogliare

hoaxer *n* (*joker*) burlone, -a *m*, *f*; (*fraudster*) imbroglione, -a *m*, *f*

hobble ['haː·bl̩] I. *vi* zoppicare; **to ~ around** zoppicare II. *vt* 1.*liter* (*hinder*) intralciare 2.(*tie legs: animal*) impastoiare

hobby ['haː·bi] <-ies> *n* hobby *m inv*

hobbyhorse *n* 1.(*toy*) cavallino *m* giocattolo 2.(*topic*) argomento *m* di conversazione preferito

hobgoblin ['haːb·ˌgaː·blɪn] *n* folletto *m*

hobnailed ['haːb·neɪld] *adj* **~ boots** scarponcini con bullette

hobnob ['haːb·naːb] <-bb-> *vi inf* **to ~ with the rich and famous** frequentare gente ricca e famosa

hobo ['hoʊ·boʊ] <-s *o* -es> *n* 1.(*tramp*) vagabondo, -a *m*, *f* 2.(*migrant worker*) lavoratore, -trice stagionale *m*

hock[1] [haːk] *inf* I. *vt* (*pawn off*) impegnare II. *n* **to be in ~** (*object*) essere impegnato; **my car is in ~** ho impegnato l'auto; **to be in ~ (to sb)** (*person*) essere in debito (con qu)

hock[2] [haːk] *n* ANAT garretto *m*

hockey ['haː·ki] *n* hockey *m*; **field ~** hockey su

prato; **ice** ~ hockey su ghiaccio
hockey stick *n* SPORTS mazza *f* da hockey
hocus-pocus [ˌhoʊ·kəs·ˈpoʊ·kəs] *n* raggiro *m*
hodgepodge [ˈhɑːdʒ·pɑːdʒ] *n* miscuglio *m*
hoe [hoʊ] I. *n* zappa *f* II. *vt* zappare
hoedown *n* quadriglia *f*
hog [hɑːg] I. *n* 1. (*pig*) porco *m* 2. *inf* (*person*) ingordo, -a *m, f* ▸ **to live high on the** ~ fare una vita da nababbo II. <-gg-> *vt inf* (*keep for oneself*) monopolizzare; **to** ~ **sb/sth all to oneself** tenersi qu/qc tutto per sé
hog heaven *n inf* to be in ~ essere al settimo cielo
hogshead [ˈhɑːgz·hed] *n* 1. (*barrel*) barile *m* 2. (*measurement*) *misura di capacità pari a circa 240 litri*
hogwash [ˈhɑːg·wɑːʃ] *n inf* scemenze *fpl*
ho-hum [ˈhoʊ·hʌm] *adj inf* noioso, -a
hoi polloi [ˌhɔɪ·pəˈlɔɪ] *npl inf* **the** ~ la plebe
hoist [hɔɪst] *vt* (*raise up*) alzare; (*flag*) issare
hoity-toity [ˌhɔɪ·t̮iˈtɔɪ·t̮i] *adj inf* presuntuoso, -a
hold [hoʊld] I. *n* 1. (*grasp, grip*) presa *f;* **to take** ~ **of sb/sth** afferrare qu/qc; **to catch** ~ **of sb/sth** afferrare qu/qc; **to keep** ~ **of sth** tenersi a qc 2. (*thing to hold by*) appiglio *m* 3. (*wrestling*) presa *f;* **no** ~s **barred** *fig* senza restrizioni 4. (*control*) influenza *f;* **to have a** (**strong/powerful**) ~ **over sb** avere (molta/grande) influenza su qu 5. NAUT, AVIAT stiva *f* 6. (*delayed*) **to be on** ~ essere rimandato; TEL essere in attesa; **to put sb on** ~ mettere qu in attesa 7. (*understand*) **to get** ~ **of sth** afferrare qc; **to have a** ~ **of sth** avere un'idea di qc; **to get** ~ **of the wrong idea** sbagliarsi; **I don't know where you got** ~ **of that idea** non so da dove ti sia venuta un'idea del genere 8. (*prison cell*) guardina *f* II. <held, held> *vt* 1. (*keep*) tenere; (*grasp*) afferrare; **to** ~ **a gun** impugnare una pistola; **to** ~ **hands** tenersi per mano; **to** ~ **sth in one's hand** tenere qc in mano; **to** ~ **sb in one's arms** stringere qu tra le braccia; **to** ~ **sb/sth** (**tight**) stringere (forte) qu/qc; **to** ~ **the door open for sb** tenere la porta aperta a qu 2. (*support*) reggere; **to** ~ **one's head high** tenere alta la testa 3. (*cover up*) **to** ~ **one's ears/nose** turarsi le orecchie/il naso 4. (*keep, retain*) mantenere; **to** ~ **sb's attention** tenere viva l'attenzione di qu; **to** ~ **sb in custody** LAW trattenere qu in custodia cautelare; **to** ~ **sb hostage** tenere qu in ostaggio; **to** ~ (**on to**) **the lead** mantenere il vantaggio 5. (*maintain*) **to** ~ **oneself in readiness** tenersi pronto; **to** ~ **oneself well** tenersi in forma 6. (*make keep to*) **to** ~ **sb to his/her word** [*o* **promise**] far mantenere a qu la parola [*o* la promessa] 7. (*control*) **to** ~ **sth at the present/last year's level** mantenere qc al livello attuale/dell'anno scorso; **to** ~ **a note** MUS tenere una nota 8. (*delay, stop*) fermare; ~ **it!** un attimo!; **to** ~ **one's breath** trattenere il respiro; **to** ~ **one's fire** MIL non fare fuoco; **to** ~ **sb's phone calls** TEL non passare alcuna

chiamata a qu 9. (*contain*) contenere; **what the future** ~**s** ciò che ci riserva il futuro 10. (*possess, own*) possedere; (*land, town*) occupare; **to** ~ **an account** (**with a bank**) avere un conto (presso una banca); **to** ~ **the** (**absolute**) **majority** avere la maggioranza (assoluta); **to** ~ **a position** (**as sth**) ricoprire un incarico (di qc); **to** ~ (**down**) **the fort** MIL resistere; *fig* badare a tutto 11. (*make happen*) **to** ~ **a conversation** (**with sb**) avere una conversazione (con qu); **to** ~ **a meeting/a news conference** tenere una riunione/una conferenza stampa; **the election will be held in November** le elezioni si terranno a novembre 12. (*believe*) considerare; **to be held in great respect** essere assai rispettato; **to** ~ **sb responsible for sth** ritenere qu responsabile di qc; **to** ~ **sb/sth in contempt** disprezzare qu/qc III. *vi* 1. (*continue*) mantenere; (*good weather, luck*) durare; **to** ~ **still** stare fermo; **to** ~ **true** continuare ad essere valido; ~ **tight!** tieni duro! 2. (*stick*) tenere 3. (*believe*) sostenere

◆**hold against** *vt always sep* **to hold sth against sb** volerne a qu per qc

◆**hold back** I. *vt* (*keep*) trattenere; **to** ~ **information** non dare informazioni; (*stop*) fermare; (*impede development*) frenare; **to** ~ **tears** trattenere le lacrime ▸ **there's no holding me back** non mi trattiene niente II. *vi* 1. (*be unforthcoming*) essere reticente 2. (*refrain*) **to** ~ **from doing sth** trattenersi dal fare qc

◆**hold down** *vt* tenere fermo; (*control, suppress*) reprimere; **to** ~ **a job** riuscire a tenersi un impiego

◆**hold forth** *vi* **to** ~ (**about sth**) blaterare (di qc)

◆**hold in** *vt* (*emotion*) contenere

◆**hold off** I. *vt* (*enemy*) resistere a; (*reporters*) tenere a bada II. *vi* (*wait*) aspettare; **to** ~ **off on project** rimandare (la realizzazione di) un progetto

◆**hold on** *vi* 1. (*attach*) tenersi stretto; **to be held on by/with sth** essere tenuto da/con qc 2. (*manage to keep going*) **to** ~ (**tight**) tenere duro 3. (*wait*) aspettare

◆**hold onto** *vt insep* 1. (*grasp*) tenersi stretto a 2. (*keep*) tenere

◆**hold out** I. *vt* tendere II. *vi* 1. resistere; **to** ~ **for sth** tener duro fino a qc 2. (*refuse to give sth*) **to** ~ **on sb** non cedere a qu

◆**hold over** *vt* 1. (*defer*) rinviare 2. (*extend*) prolungare

◆**hold to** *vt insep* attenersi a

◆**hold together** I. *vi* restare unito; **to be held together with glue** essere tenuto insieme dalla colla II. *vt* restare unito

◆**hold up** I. *vt* 1. (*raise*) alzare; **to** ~ **one's hand** alzare la mano; **to be held up by** (**means of**)/**with sth** essere sorretto da/con qc; **to hold one's head up high** *fig* andare a testa alta 2. (*delay*) trattenere 3. (*rob with viol-*

ence) rapinare **4.** (*offer as example*) **to hold sb up as an example of sth** portare qu come un esempio di qc **II.** *vi* (*weather*) reggere; (*material*) durare

◆**hold with** *vt insep* approvare

holdall [ˈhoʊlˑdɔːl] *n* borsone *m* da viaggio

holder [ˈhoʊlˑdəˑ] *n* **1.** (*device*) supporto *m;* **cigarette** ~ bocchino *m* **2.** (*person: of shares, of account*) titolare *mf;* (*of title*) detentore, -trice *m, f;* **world record** ~ detentore del record mondiale

holding *n* **1.** *pl* (*tenure*) tenuta *f* **2.** ECON partecipazione *f*

holding company *n* holding *f inv*

holdup [ˈhoʊldˑʌp] *n* **1.** (*robbery*) rapina *f* **2.** (*delay*) ritardo *m*

hole [hoʊl] **I.** *n* **1.** (*hollow space*) buco *m; fig* (*in an argument, sb's reasoning*) punto *m* debole **2.** (*in golf*) buca *f* **3.** (*of mouse, rabbit*) tana *f* **4.** *inf* (*jam*) guaio *m;* **to be in a** ~ essere nei guai ▶**to be a round peg in a square** ~ essere [*o* sentirsi] fuori posto; **to be in the** ~ essere indebitato **II.** *vt* **1.** (*perforate*) bucare, fare un buco in **2.** (*in golf*) mettere in buca

◆**hole up** *vi inf* nascondersi

holiday [ˈhɑːˑləˑdeɪ] *n* (*public day off*) giorno *m* festivo ▶**a busman's** ~ giorno festivo passato a lavorare

summer camp *n* campeggio *m* estivo

vacation house *n* casa *f* delle vacanze

holiday resort *n* località *f* turistica *inv*

holiness [ˈhoʊˑlɪˑnɪs] *n* santità *f;* **His/Your Holiness** Sua Santità

holism [ˈhoʊˑlɪˑzəm] *n* olismo *m*

holistic [hoʊˑˈlɪsˑtɪk] *adj* olistico, -a

Holland [ˈhɑːˑlənd] *n* Olanda *f*

holler [ˈhɑːˑləˑ] **I.** *vi inf* strillare **II.** *n inf* strillo *m*

hollow [ˈhɑːˑloʊ] **I.** *adj* **1.** (*empty*) vuoto, -a **2.** (*worthless, empty: promise, victory*) vano, -a; (*laughter*) falso, -a **3.** (*sound*) sordo, -a **II.** *n* vuoto *m;* (*valley*) vallata *f* **III.** *vt* **to** ~ (*out*) (*pumpkin*) vuotare; (*tree trunk*) scavare **IV.** *vi* (*become hollow*) scavarsi

holly [ˈhɑːˑli] *n* BOT agrifoglio *m*

hollyhock [ˈhɑːˑlɪˑhɑːk] *n* BOT malvarosa *f*

holocaust [ˈhɑːˑləˑkɑːst] *n* olocausto *m*

hologram [ˈhɑːˑləˑgræm] *n* ologramma *m*

holster [ˈhoʊlsˑtəˑ] *n* fondina *f*

holy [ˈhoʊˑli] <-ier, -iest> *adj* **1.** (*sacred*) santo, -a; (*water*) benedetto, -a **2.** *fig* **to be a** ~ **terror** essere una peste

Holy Communion *n* (Santa) Comunione *f*

Holy Father *n* Santo Padre *m*

Holy Ghost *n* Spirito *m* Santo

Holy Scripture *n* **the** ~ le Sacre Scritture

Holy See *n* Santa Sede *f*

Holy Spirit *n* Spirito *m* Santo

Holy Week *n* Settimana *f* Santa

homage [ˈhɑːˑmɪdʒ] *n* omaggio *m;* **to pay** ~ **to sb** rendere omaggio a qu

home [hoʊm] **I.** *n* **1.** (*residence*) casa *f;* **at** ~ a [*o* in] casa; **to leave** ~ uscire di casa; (*stop living with one's parents*) andarsene di casa; **to**

be away from ~ essere via; **I live in Seattle but my** ~ **is in Napoli** abito a Seattle ma sono di Napoli; **make yourself at** ~ fai come fossi a casa tua **2.** (*family*) famiglia *f* **3.** (*institution*) istituto *m;* **children's** ~ orfanotrofio *m* **II.** *adv* **1.** (*one's place of residence*) **to be** ~ essere a casa; **to go/come** ~ andare/venire a casa; **to take work** ~ portarsi il lavoro a casa **2.** (*understanding*) **to bring sth** ~ **to sb** far capire qc a qu; **to hit** ~ colpire da vicino ▶**to be** ~ **free** avere la vittoria assicurata; **this is nothing to write** ~ **about** non è niente di straordinario **III.** *adj* **1.** (*from own country*) nazionale **2.** (*from own area*) locale; (*team*) che gioca in casa; (*game*) in casa; **the** ~ **ground** terreno conosciuto

◆**home in on** *vt insep, inf* **1.** MIL puntare su **2.** (*locate*) localizzare e dirigersi verso

home address *n* indirizzo *m* (privato)

internal affairs *n* POL affari *m pl* interni

home banking *n* telebanking *m*

homebody *n* persona *f* casalinga

homeboy *n sl* (*from the same area*) compaesano *m;* (*from the same gang*) compagno *m*

homebrew *n* birra fatta in casa

homecoming *n* ritorno *m* (a casa)

i **Homecoming** negli USA è una festa importante nelle *High Schools* e università. Si tratta del giorno in cui la squadra di football rientra per giocare una partita "in casa". Nel corso del gala annuale che si tiene in occasione di questa partita viene anche eletta la *homecoming queen* (reginetta scolastica).

home computer *n* personal *m inv* (computer) *m inv*

home cooking *n* cucina *f* casalinga

home ec *n,* **home economics** *n* + *sing vb* economia *f* domestica

home-equity loan *n* FIN mutuo *m* casa

home fries *npl* FOOD patate *f pl* fritte

homegirl *n sl* (*from neighborhood*) compaesana *f;* (*from same gang*) compagna *f*

homegrown *adj* **1.** (*vegetables*) del proprio orto **2.** (*not foreign*) del paese **3.** (*local*) locale

home-helper *n* badante *mf*

homeland *n* (*country of birth*) terra *f* natale; (*of cultural heritage*) madrepatria *f*

Homeland Security *n* dipartimento governativo statunitense per la sicurezza nazionale

homeless **I.** *adj* senza casa **II.** *n* + *pl vb* **the** ~ **i** senzatetto

homelike *adj* familiare, casereccio, -a

homely [ˈhoʊmˑli] <-ier, -iest> *adj* (*ugly*) brutto, -a

homemade *adj* fatto, -a in casa

homemaker *n* casalinga *f*

domestic market *n* mercato *m* interno

homeopath [ˈhoʊˑmioʊˑpæθ] *n* omeopata *mf*

homeopathic [ˌhoʊˑmioʊˑˈpæˑθɪk] *adj* omeopatico, -a

homeopathy [ˌhoʊ·mi·ˈɑː·pə·θi] *n* homeopatia *f*

homeowner [ˈhoʊm·ˌoʊ·nɚ] *n* proprietario, -a di una casa *m*

homepage *n* homepage *f inv*

home plate *n* SPORTS base *f* del battitore

homeroom *n* SCH *aula in cui si fa l'appello*

home rule *n* governo *m* autonomo

Secretary of the Interior *n* ministro *m* dell'Interno

homeschool *vt* istruire a casa

homesick [ˈhoʊm·sɪk] *adj* **to be ~** avere nostalgia di casa; **to feel ~** (**for**) avere nostalgia (di)

homesickness *n* nostalgia *f* (di casa)

homespun [ˈhoʊm·spʌn] *adj* (*wisdom*) popolare; (*cloth*) tessuto, -a in casa

homestead *n* fattoria *f*

homestretch <-es> *n* dirittura *f* d'arrivo

home team *n* squadra *f* locale [*o* che gioca in casa]

hometown *n* città *f* natale *inv*

home truth *n* **to tell sb a few ~s** dire a qu come stanno veramente le cose

home video *n* homevideo *m inv*

homeward [ˈhoʊm·wɚd] **I.** *adv* verso casa **II.** *adj* (*journey*) di ritorno

homewards *adv s.* **homeward I.**

homework [ˈhoʊm·wɜːrk] *n* SCHOOL compiti *mpl*

homey [ˈhoʊ·mi] <-ier, -iest> *adj* **1.** (*cozy*) intimo, -a **2.** *sl* (*boy or girl from neighborhood*) compagno, -a di quartiere *m*; (*from same gang*) fratello, sorella *m, f*

homicidal [ˌhɑː·mə·ˈsaɪ·dl̩] *adj* LAW omicida

homicide [ˈhɑː·mə·saɪd] **I.** *n* **1.** (*crime*) omicidio *m* **2.** (*criminal*) omicida *mf* **II.** *adj* **the ~ squad** la omicidi

homing [ˈhoʊ·mɪŋ] *adj* (*device*) autoguida; **birds have a strong ~ instict** gli uccelli per istinto sanno ritrovare la strada di casa

homing pigeon *n* piccione *m* viaggiatore

hominy grits *npl* chicchi di granturco bolliti e soffritti mangiati nel sud degli USA a colazione o come contorno

homogeneous *adj*, **homogenous** [ˌhoʊ·moʊ·ˈdʒiː·ni·əs] *adj* omogeneo, -a

homogenize [hə·ˈmɑː·dʒə·naɪz] *vt* omogeneizzare

homograph [ˈhɑː·mə·græf] *n* omografo *m*

homonym [ˈhɑː·mə·nɪm] *n* omonimo *m*

homophobia [ˌhoʊ·mə·ˈfoʊ·biə] *n* omofobia *f*

homophone [ˈhɑː·mə·foʊn] *n* omofono *m*

homosexual [ˌhoʊ·mə·ˈsek·ʃu·əl] **I.** *adj* omosessuale **II.** *n* omosessuale *mf*

homosexuality [ˌhoʊ·moʊ·sek·ʃu·ˈæ·lə· t̬i] *n* omosessualità *f*

Hon. *abbr of* **Honorable**

Honduran [hɑː·n·ˈdʊ·rən] **I.** *adj* honduregno, -a **II.** *n* honduregno, -a *m, f*

Honduras [hɑː·n·ˈdʊ·rəs] *n* Honduras *m*

hone [hoʊn] *vt* (*sharpen*) affilare; *fig* (*refine*) affinare

◆**hone in on** *vt* **1.** (*move toward target*) avvicinarsi a **2.** (*focus on*) concentrarsi

honest [ˈɑː·nɪst] *adj* **1.** (*trustworthy, fair*) onesto, -a **2.** (*truthful*) sincero, -a; **to be ~ with oneself** essere sincero con se stesso; **~** (**to God**) *inf* lo giuro (su Dio)

honestly *adv* onestamente

honest-to-goodness *adj* vero, -a

honesty [ˈɑː·nɪs·ti] *n* **1.** (*trustworthiness*) onestà *f* **2.** (*sincerity*) sincerità *f*; **in all ~** a esser sincero

honey [ˈhʌ·ni] *n* **1.** CULIN miele *f* **2.** (*term of endearment, sweet person*) tesoro *m* **3.** (*sweet thing*) gioiello *f*

honeybee *n* ape *f*

honeycomb **I.** *n* favo *m* **II.** *adj* (*pattern*) a nido d'ape

honeydew (**melon**) *n* melone invernale *m*

honeymoon **I.** *n* luna *f* di miele **II.** *vi* passare la luna di miele

honeysuckle *n* BOT madreselva *f*

honk [hɑːŋk] **I.** *vi* **1.** ZOOL starnazzare **2.** AUTO suonare (il clacson) **II.** *n* **1.** ZOOL starnazzare *m* **2.** AUTO colpo *m* di clacson

honor [ˈɑː·nɚ] **I.** *n* **1.** (*respect*) onore *m*; **in ~ of sb/sth** in onore di qu/qc; **to be** (**in**) **~ bound to ...** essere moralmente obbligato a... **2.** LAW **Your Honor** Vostro onore **3.** *pl* (*distinction*) **final ~s** onori *m pl* funebri; **to graduate with ~s** laurearsi con lode **II.** *vt* onorare; **to be ~ed** sentirsi onorato

ⓘ I nomi degli studenti che hanno riportato ottimi voti sono pubblicati nei giornali scolastici e universitari, talvolta persino nei quotidiani. Questa lista si chiama **honor roll** o, soprattutto nelle università, *dean's list*. Gli studenti che fanno parte di questa lista hanno maggiori possibilità quando fanno domanda di iscrizione all'università o quando cercano lavoro presso un'azienda.

honorable *adj* **1.** (*worthy of respect: person*) degno, -a di rispetto; (*agreement*) onorevole **2.** (*honest*) onesto, -a **3.** JUR **the Honorable John Thompson** il giudice John Thompson

honorary [ˈɑː·nə·re·ri] *adj* **1.** (*conferred as an honor: title*) onorifico, -a; (*president*) onorario, -a **2.** (*without pay*) onorifico, -a

hood[1] [hʊd] *n* **1.** (*covering for head*) cappuccio *m* **2.** AUTO cofano *m* **3.** (*on machine*) coperchio *m*; (*on cooker*) cappa *f*

hood[2] [hʊd] *n* **1.** *inf* (*gangster*) teppista *mf* **2.** *sl* (*urban neighborhood*) quartiere *m*

hoodlum [ˈhuː·d·ləm] *n* teppista *mf*

hoodwink [ˈhʊd·wɪŋk] *vt inf* fregare

hoof [hʊf] **I.** <hooves *o* hoofs> *n* zoccolo *m*; **on the ~** (*cattle*) ancora vivo **II.** *vt inf* **to ~ it** andare a piedi

hoo-ha [ˈhuː·hɑː] *n inf* pandemonio *m*

hook [hʊk] **I.** *n* **1.** (*for holding sth*) gancio *m*;

H

(*fish*) amo *m;* **to leave the phone off the ~** lasciare il ricevitore staccato **2.**SPORTS tiro *m* a gancio; (*in boxing*) gancio *m* ▶**by ~ or by crook** ad ogni costo; **to fall for it ~, line and sinker** berla; **to be off the ~** essere fuori dai guai **II.** *vt* **1.**(*fasten*) agganciare **2.**(*fish*) prendere all'amo **3.**(*capture attention*) attirare **III.** *vi* agganciarsi

◆**hook on I.** *vi* agganciarsi **II.** *vt* agganciare

◆**hook up I.** *vt* **1.**(*hang: curtains*) attaccare **2.**(*link up*) agganciare; (*connect*) collgare; **to hook sb up with sb** *sl* (*arrange date*) combinare a qu un appuntamento con qu **II.** *vi* **1.**(*connect*) collegarsi **2.**(*clothes*) agganciarsi

hooked [hʊkt] *adj* **1.**(*nose*) aquilino, -a **2.**(*fascinated*) **I read the first page of the book and was ~** ho letto la prima pagina e sono stato completamente preso dal libro **3.**(*addicted*) assuefatto, -a

hooker ['hʊ·kə·] *n inf*prostituta *f*

hooky ['hʊ·ki] *n inf* **to play ~** marinare la scuola

hooligan ['huː·lɪ·gən] *n* teppista *mf*

hooliganism *n* teppismo *m*

hoop [huːp] *n* cerchio *m; sl* (*in basketball*) canestro *m;* **to shoot some ~s** fare qualche tiro ▶**to put sb through the ~s** far dannare qu

hoot [huːt] **I.** *vi* (*owl*) ululare; (*with horn*) suonare il clacson; **to ~ with laughter** schiantarsi dalle risate **II.** *vt* **to ~ sb** suonare il clacson a qu **III.** *n* (*of owl*) ululato *m;* (*of horn*) colpo *m;* (*of train*) fischio *m;* **to give a ~ of laughter** fare una risata; **I don't give a ~ (about sth)** non m'importa niente (di qc)

◆**hoot down** *vt* fischiare

hooter ['huː·tə·] *n* **1.**(*siren*) sirena *f* **2.** *inf* (*nose*) naso *m*

hop¹ [hɑːp] *n* **1.**BOT luppolo *m* **2.** *pl* (*dried*) luppolo *m*

hop² [hɑːp] <-pp-> **I.** *vi* **1.**(*on one foot*) saltare; *fig;* **to ~ to it** *inf*mettersi a lavoro **2.** *inf* (*be busy*) **to be ~ping** essere in piena attività **II.** *vt inf* (*bus, train*) saltare su **III.** *n* **1.**(*leap*) salto *m;* (*using only one leg*) salto *m* su una gamba **2.** *inf* (*informal dance*) ballo *m* **3.**(*short flight*) volo *m* breve ▶**a ~, skip and a jump** *inf*due passi

◆**hop around** *vi* saltellare; **to ~ from one subject to another** saltare da un argomento all'altro

◆**hop in** *vt insep* salire su; **to ~ a taxi** *inf* salire su un taxi

◆**hop out** *vi* saltare giù; **to ~ of bed** saltare giù dal letto

hope [hoʊp] **I.** *n* speranza *f;* **to give up ~** perdere le speranze; **to pin all one's ~s on sb/ sth** riporre tutte le speranze in qu/qc; **there is still ~** si può ancora sperare ▶**to not have a ~ in hell** non avere alcuna speranza; **to hope against ~** sperare con tutto il cuore **II.** *vi* (*wish*) sperare; **to ~ for the best** sperare bene

hopeful ['hoʊp·fəl] **I.** *adj* **1.**(*person*) speran-

zoso, -a; **to be ~** essere ottimista **2.**(*promising*) di belle speranze **II.** *n pl* aspirante *mf;* **young ~s** giovani speranze *fpl*

hopefully *adv* **1.**(*in a hopeful manner*) speranzosamente **2.**(*one hopes*) **~!** speriamo!; **~ we'll be in Sweden at six** se tutto va bene siamo in Svezia alle sei

hopeless ['hoʊp·ləs] *adj* (*situation, effort*) disperato, -a; **to be ~** *inf*(*person, service*) essere un disastro; **to be ~ at sth** essere negato in qc

hopelessly *adv* **1.**(*without hope*) disperatamente **2.**(*totally, completely*) **~ lost** completamente perso

hopper ['hɑː·pə·] *n* tramoggia *f*

hopping mad *adj inf*furioso, -a

hopscotch ['hɑːp·skɑːtʃ] *n* **to play ~** giocare a campana

horde [hɔːrd] *n* orda *f*

horizon [hə·'raɪ·zn] *n a. fig* orizzonte *m*

horizontal [ˌhɔː·rɪ·'zɑː·n·tl] **I.** *adj* orizzontale **II.** *n* orizzontale *f*

hormone ['hɔː·r·moʊn] *n* ormone *m*

horn [hɔːrn] *n* **1.**ZOOL, MUS corno *m* **2.**AUTO clacson *m inv* **3.**(*material*) corno *m* ▶**to be on the ~s of a dilemma** trovarsi fra l'incudine e il martello; **to draw in one's ~s** stringere la cinghia; **to lock ~s (over sth)** scontrarsi (su qc); **to toot** [*o* **blow**] **one's own ~** darsi delle arie

◆**horn in** *vi* **to ~ on sth** intromettersi in qc

hornet ['hɔːr·nɪt] *n* calabrone *m*

horn-rimmed *adj* (*glasses*) con montatura di corno

horny ['hɔːr·ni] <-ier, -iest> *adj* **1.**(*made of horn*) corneo, -a **2.** *inf* (*sexually aroused*) arrapato, -a

horoscope ['hɔː·rəs·koʊp] *n* oroscopo *m*

horrendous [hɔːr·'ren·dəs] *adj* **1.**(*crime*) orrendo, -a **2.**(*losses*) tremendo, -a

horrible ['hɔː·rə·bl] *adj* orribile

horrid ['hɔː·rɪd] *adj* (*unpleasant*) orribile; (*unkind*) antipatico, -a

horrific [hɔːr·'rɪ·fɪk] *adj* terribile

horrify ['hɔː·rɪ·faɪ] <-ie-> *vt* sconvolgere

horror ['hɔː·rə·] *n* orrore *m;* **~ film** film*m inv* dell'orrore

horror-stricken *adj,* **horror-struck** *adj* terrorizzato, -a, inorridito, -a

hors d'"uvre [ɔːr·'dɜːrv] <hors d'oeuvre *o* hors d'oeuvres> *n* FOOD antipasto *m*

horse [hɔːrs] *n* **1.**ZOOL cavallo *m;* **to ride a ~** andare [*o* montare] a cavallo; **to eat like a ~** mangiare come un lupo **2.**SPORTS cavallo *m* ▶**to change ~s (in) midstream** cambiare idea a metà strada; **to get sth straight from the ~'s mouth** sapere qc da fonti dirette; **don't look a gift ~ in the mouth** *prov;* **to flog a dead ~** perdere tempo (tentando qc); **to hold one's ~s** *inf*non essere impaziente

◆**horse around** *vi* fare il pagliaccio

horseback ['hɔːrs·bæk] **I.** *n* **on ~** a cavallo **II.** *adj* **~ riding** equitazione *f*

horse chestnut *n* (*tree*) ippocastano *m;* (*nut*) castagna *f* d'India

horse-drawn *adj* a cavalli

horsefly <-ies> *n* tafano *m*

horsehair *n* crine *m* (di cavallo)

horseman ['hɔːrs·mən] <-men> *n* cavallerizzo *m*

horsemanship *n* equitazione *f*

horseplay ['hɔːrs·pleɪ] *n* giochi *m pl* scatenati

horsepower *inv n* cavallo *m* (vapore)

horserace *n* corsa *f* di cavalli

horseracing *n* ippica *f*

horseradish *n* rafano *m*

horse sense *n inf* buonsenso *m*

horseshoe *n* ferro *m* di cavallo

horse-trading *n* attività *f pl* losche

horse van *n* rimorchio *m* per il trasporto dei cavalli

horsewhip ['hɔːrs·wɪp] I. <-pp-> *vt* frustare II. *n* frustino *m*

horsewoman ['hɔːrs·wʊ·mən] <-women> *n* amazzone *f*

hors(e)y ['hɔːr·si] <-ier, -iest> *adj* 1. (*interested in horses*) appassionato, -a di cavalli 2. (*like a horse: face*) cavallino, -a

horticultural [ˌhɔːr·ţə·'kʌl·tʃə·əl] *adj* orticolo, -a

horticulture ['hɔːr·ţə·kʌl·tʃə·] *n* orticultura *f*

hose [hoʊz] *n* 1. (*flexible tube*) tubo *m;* (*in motor*) manicotto *m* 2. (*pantyhose*) collant *mpl*

hosiery ['hoʊ·zə·i] *n* (*shop*) negozio *m* di calzetteria; (*goods*) calzetteria *f*

hospice ['hɑːs·pɪs] *n* 1. (*hospital*) centro *m* per malati terminali 2. (*house of shelter*) ospizio *m*

hospitable ['hɑːs·pɪ·ţə·bl] *adj* ospitale

hospital ['hɑːs·pɪ·ţəl] *n* ospedale *m*

hospitality [ˌhɑːs·pɪ·'tæ·lə·ţi] *n* ospitalità *f*

hospitalization [ˌhɑːs·pɪ·ţə·lɪ·'zeɪ·ʃən] *n* ricovero *m* ospedaliero

hospitalize ['hɑːs·pɪ·ţə·laɪz] *vt* ricoverare in ospedale

host¹ [hoʊst] I. *n* 1. (*person who receives guests*) ospite *m,* padrone *m* di casa 2. (*presenter*) presentatore *m* 3. *BIO* ospite *m* 4. *COMPUT* host *m inv* II. *vt* 1. (*party*) dare; (*event*) ospitare 2. *TV, RADIO* (*program*) presentare

host² [hoʊst] *n* mollitudine *f;* **a whole ~ of reasons** tutto un insieme di ragioni

Host [hoʊst] *n REL* ostia *f*

hostage ['hɑːs·tɪdʒ] *n* ostaggio *m;* **to take/hold sb ~** prendere/tenere qu in ostaggio

host country <-ies> *n* paese *m* ospite

hostel ['hɑːs·tl] *n* (*inexpensive hotel*) ostello *m;* **student ~** casa *f* dello studente; **youth ~** ostello della gioventù

hosteler ['hɑːs·tə·lə·] *n* albergatore, -trice *m, f*

hostess ['hoʊs·tɪs] <-es> *n* 1. (*woman who receives guests*) ospite *f,* padrona *f* di casa 2. (*presenter*) presentatrice *f* 3. (*in restaurant*) cameriera *f*

hostile ['hɑːs·tl] *adj* ostile; **~ aircraft** aereo nemico

hostility [hɑːs·'tɪ·lə·ţi] <-ies> *n* ostilità *f inv*

hot [hɑːt] I. *adj* 1. (*very warm*) caldo, -a; **it's ~** fa caldo 2. (*spicy*) piccante 3. *inf* (*skillful*) bravo, -a; **to be ~ stuff** essere un asso 4. *inf* (*demanding*) **to be ~ for sth** dare molta importanza a qc 5. (*dangerous*) rischioso, -a; **to be too ~ to handle** *fig* essere troppo difficile da gestire 6. *inf* (*sexually attractive*) **to be ~** essere sexy 7. (*exciting: music, party*) animato, -a; **~ news** notizie fresche 8. *sl* (*stolen*) **to be ~** scottare ▶ **to be all ~ and bothered** essere agitato II. *n* **he has the ~s for her** gli piace un sacco

◆ **hot up** <-tt-> *vi inf* (*situation*) farsi sempre più agitato

hot air *n fig* discorsi *m pl* campati in aria; **to be full of ~** essere campato in aria

hot-air balloon *n* mongolfiera *f*

hotbed ['hɑːt·bed] *n fig* (*of vice, crime*) covo *m;* (*of disease*) focolaio *m*

hot-blooded *n* (*easy to anger*) irascibile; (*passionate*) focoso, -a

hotcake *n* pancake *m inv;* **to sell like ~s** andare a ruba

hot dog *n CULIN* hotdog *m inv*

hotel [hoʊ·'tel] *n* hotel *m inv,* albergo *m*

hotel accommodations *npl* alberghi *mpl*

hotel bill *n* conto *f* dell'albergo

hotelier [ˌhoʊ·tel·'jeɪ] *n* (*owner*) albergatore, -trice *m, f;* (*manager*) direttore, -trice *m, f* d'albergo

hotel industry *n* settore *m* alberghiero

hotel staff *n* personale *m* d'albergo

hotfoot ['hɑːt·fʊt] I. *adv* di corsa II. *vt* **to ~ it somewhere** *inf* andare di corsa da qualche parte

hothead ['hɑːt·hed] *n* testa *f* calda

hotheaded *adj* impulsivo, -a

hothouse ['hɑːt·haʊs] I. *n* serra *f* II. *adj* di serra

hot line *n TEL* linea *f* diretta

hotly *adv* appassionatamente

hot metal *n TYPO* composizione *f* a caldo

hot plate *n* piastra *f*

hot potato <-oes> *n fig* patata *f* bollente

hot rod *n inf AUTO* auto *f* col motore truccato *inv*

hot seat *n* 1. (*difficult position*) **to be in the ~** avere un posto che scotta 2. (*electric chair*) sedia *f* elettrica

hotshot *n inf* pezzo *m* grosso; **to be a (real) ~ at sth** *fig* essere un (vero) asso di qc

hot spot *n inf* 1. (*popular place*) posto *m* molto popolare 2. (*nightclub*) locale *m* notturno

hot stuff *n* 1. (*good*) **to be ~ at sth** essere grande a qc 2. (*sexy*) **to be ~** essere molto sexy

hot-tempered *adj* irascibile

hot tub *n* vasca *f* in legno per più persone

hot-water bottle *n* borsa *f* dell'acqua calda

hound [haʊnd] I. *n* cane *m* da caccia II. *vt* perseguitare

hour ['aʊ·r] *n* 1. (*60 minutes*) ora *f;* **to be paid**

by the ~ essere pagato all'ora **2.** (*time of day*) **at all ~s of the day and night** notte e giorno; **ten minutes to the ~** ai 50; **till all ~s** fino a tardi; **after ~s** fuori orario **3.** (*time for an activity*) **lunch ~** ora di pranzo; **at the agreed ~** all'ora convenuta; **opening ~s** orario *m* d'apertura **4.** (*period of time*) momento *m;* **at any ~** in qualsiasi momento; **to spend long ~s doing sth** passare molto tempo a fare qc; **to change from ~ to ~** cambiare ogni ora; **to keep irregular/regular ~s** avere orari irregolari/regolari; **to work long ~s** lavorare molto; **~ after ~** per ore (ed ore)

hour hand *n* lancetta *f* delle ore

hourly *adv* (*every hour*) ogni ora; (*pay*) a ore

house¹ [haʊs] *n* **1.** (*inhabitation*) casa *f;* **to set one's ~ in order** *fig* sistemare le proprie cose **2.** (*family*) famiglia *f* **3.** (*business*) ditta *f;* **it's on the ~** offre la casa **4.** UNIV (*fraternity*) associazione *f* **5.** (*legislative body*) camera *f* **6.** (*audience*) pubblico *m;* **a full ~** il tutto esaurito; **to bring the ~ down** *inf* essere un successo

house² [haʊz] *vt* **1.** (*give place to live*) alloggiare **2.** (*contain*) ospitare

house arrest *n* arresti *m pl* domiciliari

houseboat *n* house boat *f inv*

housebreaker ['haʊs·ˌbreɪ·kɚ] *n* ladro, -a d'appartamento *m*

housebreaking *n* violazione *f* di domicilio a scopo di furto

housebroken *adj* addestrato, -a

housecleaning *n* pulizie *f pl* di casa

housecoat ['haʊs·koʊt] *n* vestaglia *f*

housefly <-ies> *n* mosca *f*

household ['haʊs·hoʊld] **I.** *n* famiglia *m* **II.** *adj* domestico, -a

householder *n* (*owner*) proprietario, -a *m, f* di una casa; (*head*) capo *m* famiglia

house-hunt *vi inf* cercare casa

househusband *n* marito *m* che sta a casa

housekeeper ['haʊs·ˌki·pɚ] *n* governante *f*

housekeeping *n* gestione *f* della casa

housekeeping money *n* soldi *m pl* per le spese domestiche

housemaid ['haʊs·meɪd] *n* domestica *f*

housemate *n* persona con cui si divide la casa

House of Representatives *n* POL Camera *f* dei Rappresentanti

house physician *n* medico *m* interno

houseplant *n* pianta *f* da appartamento

house rules *npl* regole *f pl* della casa

house sitter *n* persona che bada alla casa in assenza del proprietario

house-to-house *adj* porta a porta

housewarming *n*, **house-warming party** *n* festa *f* per inaugurare l'arrivo in casa nuova

housewife <-wives> *n* casalinga *f*

housework *n* faccende *f pl* domestiche

housing ['haʊ·zɪŋ] *n* **1.** (*for living*) alloggio *f* **2.** (*for machinery*) alloggiamento *m*

housing association *n* cooperativa *f* edilizia

housing conditions *npl* condizioni *f pl* degli

alloggi

housing development *n* complesso *m* edilizio

housing project *n* complesso di case popolari *m*

hove [hoʊv] *vi* NAUT *pp of* **heave**

hovel ['hʌ·vl] *n* tugurio *m*

hover ['hʌ·vɚ] *vi* **1.** (*stay in air*) stare sospeso a mezz'aria **2.** (*wait near*) aspettare **3.** (*be in an uncertain state*) oscillare **4.** (*hesitate*) indugiare; **to ~ on the brink of accepting sth** essere lì per accettare qc

hovercraft ['hʌ·vɚ·kræft] <-(s)> *n* hovercraft *m inv*

HOV lane *n* *abbr of* **High Occupancy Vehicle lane** *corsia preferenziale per veicoli con a bordo due o più persone*

how [haʊ] **I.** *adv* **1.** (*in this way, in which way?*) come; **~ are you?** come stai?; **~ do you do?** piacere **2.** (*for what reason?*) **~ come ...?** *inf* come mai...? **3.** (*suggestion*) **~ about ...?** che ne dici di...?; **~ about that!** senti un po'!; **~'s that for an offer?** che ne dice? **4.** (*intensifier*) **~ pretty she looked!** come stava bene!; **and ~!** eccome! **II.** *n* modo *m;* **to know the ~(s) and why(s) of sth** sapere il come e il perché di qc

howdy *interj inf* salve

however [haʊ·ˈe·vɚ] **I.** *adv* **1.** (*no matter how*) per quanto +*subj;* **~ hard she tries ...** per quanto ci provi... **2.** (*in whichever way*) come; **do it ~ you like** fallo come ti pare **II.** *conj* (*nevertheless*) comunque

howl [haʊl] **I.** *vi* **1.** ululare; **to ~ in** [*o* with] **pain** urlava dal dolore **2.** (*cry*) urlare **3.** *inf* (*laugh*) ridere a crepapelle **II.** *n* **1.** (*person, animal*) ululato *m* **2.** (*cry*) urlo *m;* **to give a ~ of pain** cacciare un urlo di dolore **3.** (*funny person*) **to be a ~** essere uno schianto

◆**howl down** *vt* fischiare

howler ['haʊ·lɚ] *n sl* errore *m* madornale; **to make a ~** fare una gaffe

howling *adj* urlante

hp [ˌeɪtʃ·ˈpi:] *abbr of* **horsepower** CV

HP [ˌeɪtʃ·ˈpi:] *abbr of* **high pressure** AP

HQ [ˌeɪtʃ·ˈkju:] *abbr of* **headquarters** QG

HRT [ˌeɪtʃ·ɑːr·ˈtiː] *abbr of* **hormone replacement therapy** terapia *f* ormonale di sostituzione

ht *abbr of* **height** a

HTML [ˌeɪtʃ·tiː·em·ˈel] COMPUT *abbr of* **Hypertext Markup Language** HTML

http, HTTP COMPUT *abbr of* **hypertext transfer protocol** http

hub [hʌb] *n* **1.** (*of wheel*) mozzo *m* **2.** *fig* (*center*) centro *m*

hubbub ['hʌ·bʌb] *n* trambusto *m*

hubcap ['hʌb·kæp] *n* cerchione *m*

huckleberry ['hʌ·kl·be·ri] <-ies> *n* BOT mirtillo *m*

huckster ['hʌks·tɚ] *n* imbonitore, -trice *m, f*

HUD [hʌd] *abbr of* **Department of Housing and Urban Development** *Dipartimento della Casa e dello Sviluppo Urbano*

huddle ['hʌ·dl] I. *vi* rannicchiarsi II. *n* (*close group*) gruppetto *f;* **to go into a ~** fare gruppetto

◆**huddle down** *vi* accovacciarsi
◆**huddle together** *vi* stringersi l'uno all'altro
◆**huddle up** *vi* rannicchiarsi

hue [hju:] *n* **1.** (*shade*) colore *m;* **all ~s of ...** *fig* ogni tipo di... **2.** (*disapproval*) **~ and cry** protesta *f*

huff [hʌf] I. *vi* **to ~ and puff** (*breathe loudly*) ansimare; *inf* (*complain*) sbuffare II. *vt* dire in malo modo III. *n inf* sbuffo *m;* **to be in a ~** essere impermalito; **to get into a ~** prendersela; **to go off in a ~** andarsene impermalito

huffy ['hʌ·fi] <-ier, -iest> *adj* **1.** (*offended*) impermalito, -a **2.** (*touchy*) permaloso, -a

hug [hʌg] I. <-gg-> *vt* **1.** *a.fig* (*embrace*) abbracciare **2.** (*not slide on*) **these tires ~ the road** questi pneumatici hanno buona tenuta di strada II. *n* abbraccio *m*

huge [hju:dʒ] *adj* (*extremely big, impressive*) enorme

hugely *adv* enormemente

hugeness *n* enormità *f*

hulk [hʌlk] *n* **1.** (*of car, ship*) carcassa *f* **2.** (*mass*) mole *f*

hulking *adj* enorme

hull [hʌl] I. *n* **1.** NAUT scafo *m* **2.** (*shell*) guscio *m;* (*of strawberry*) picciolo *m* II. *vt* pulire

hullabaloo [ˌhʌ·lə·bə·'lu:] *n* baccano *m;* **to make a real ~** fare un gran baccano

hum [hʌm] <-mm-> I. *vi* **1.** (*bee*) ronzare **2.** (*sing*) canticchiare (a bocca chiusa) **3.** (*be full of activity*) essere molto animato, -a II. *vt* canticchiare (a bocca chiusa) III. *n* ronzio *m*

human ['hju:·mən] I. *n* essere *m* umano II. *adj* umano, -a

human being *n* essere *m* umano

humane [hju:·'meɪn] *adj* umano, -a

humanism ['hju:·mə·nɪ·zəm] *n* umanesimo *m*

humanistic [ˌhju:·mə·'nɪs·tɪk] *adj* umanistico, -a

humanitarian [hju:ˌmæ·nə·'te·ri·ən] I. *n* umanitario, -a *m, f* II. *adj* umanitario, -a; **~ aid** aiuti umanitari

humanities [hju:·'mæ·nə·tiz] *npl* ESP. UNIV materie *f pl* umanistiche

humanity [hju:·'mæ·nə·ţi] *n* umanità *f*

humanize ['hju:·mə·naɪz] *vt* umanizzare

humanly *adv* umanamente

human nature *n* natura *f* umana

human race *n* razza *f* umana

human resources *npl* risorse *f pl* umane

human rights *npl* diritti *m pl* dell'uomo

humble ['hʌm·bl] I. *adj* umile; **in my ~ opinion, ...** a mio modesto parere,... II. *vt* umiliare

humbleness *n* umiltà *f*

humbug ['hʌm·bʌg] *n* (*fraud*) imbroglio *m;* (*nonsense*) scemenze *fpl*

humdrum ['hʌm·drʌm] *adj* monotono, -a

humid ['hju:·mɪd] *adj* umido, -a

humidifier [hju:·'mɪ·dɪ·fa·ɪə'] *n* umidificatore *m*

humidify [hju:·'mɪ·dɪ·faɪ] *vt* umidificare

humidity [hju:·'mɪ·də·ţi] *n* umidità *f*

humiliate [hju:·'mɪ·li·eɪt] *vt* umiliare

humiliating *adj* umiliante

humiliation [hju:ˌmɪ·li·'eɪ·ʃən] *n* umiliazione *f*

humility [hju:·'mɪ·lə·ţi] *n* umiltà *f*

hummingbird ['hʌ·mɪŋ·bɜːrd] *n* colibrì *m inv*

humor ['hju:·məʳ] *n* **1.** (*capacity for amusement*) umorismo *m;* **sense of ~** senso *m* dell'umorismo **2.** *form* (*mood*) umore *m;* **in (a) good/bad ~** di buon/cattivo umore

humorist ['hju:·mə·ɪst] *n* **1.** (*writer*) umorista *mf* **2.** (*funny person*) comico, -a *m, f*

humorless ['hju:·məʳ·lɪs] *adj* privo, -a di umorismo; **a ~ smile** un sorriso forzato

humorous ['hju:·məʳ·əs] *adj* (*speech*) umoristico, -a; (*situation*) divertente

hump [hʌmp] I. *n* gobba *f* ▶ **we are over the ~** il più è fatto II. *vt* **1.** *inf* (*lug, carry*) portare **2.** *vulg* (*have sex*) scopare *vulg*

humpback ['hʌmp·bæk] *n* gobba *f*

humpbacked ['hʌmp·bækt] *adj* gobbo, -a; **~ bridge** ARCHIT ponte a schiena d'asino

humph [hʌmpf, mm] *interj* ah!

hunch [hʌntʃ] I. <-es> *n* presentimento *m;* **to have a ~ that ...** avere la sensazione che...; **to act on a ~** agire per intuito II. *vi* piegarsi III. *vt* curvare

hunchback ['hʌntʃ·bæk] *n* (*person*) gobbo, -a *m, f*

hundred ['hʌn·drəd] <-(s)> I. *n* cento *m;* **~s of times** centinaia di volte II. *adj* cento

hundredfold ['hʌn·drəd·foʊld] *n* centuplo *m*

hundredth ['hʌn·drədθ] I. *n* centesimo *m* II. *adj* centesimo, -a

hundredweight ['hʌn·drəd·weɪt] <-(s)> *n* unità di peso equivalente a 45,36 kg negli USA e a 50,80 kg in Gran Bretagna

hung [hʌŋ] I. *pt, pp* of **hang** II. *adj* diviso, -a; **~ jury** LAW giuria che non riesce a raggiungere la maggioranza necessaria per decidere il verdetto

Hungarian [hʌŋ·'ge·ri·ən] I. *adj* ungherese II. *n* **1.** (*person*) ungherese *mf* **2.** LING ungherese *m*

Hungary ['hʌŋ·gə·ri] *n* Ungheria *f*

hunger ['hʌŋ·gəʳ] I. *n* **1.** fame *f* **2.** *fig* (*desire*) desiderio *m;* **to have a ~ for sth** desiderare qc II. *vi fig* **to ~ after** [*o* **for**] desiderare intensamente

hungry ['hʌŋ·gri] <-ier, -iest> *adj* **1.** (*desiring food*) affamato, -a; **to be ~** aver fame; **to go ~** soffrire la fame **2.** *fig* (*wanting badly*) desideroso, -a; **to be ~ for sth** desiderare qc

hung up *adj* **1.** (*delayed*) trattenuto, -a **2.** (*not able to continue*) bloccato, -a **3.** (*obsessed with*) fissato, -a

hunk [hʌŋk] *n* **1.** (*piece*) pezzo *m* **2.** *inf* (*man*) gran figo *m*

hunky dory [ˌhʌŋ·ki·'dɔ:·ri] *adj inf* **everything is ~** va tutto benone

H

hunt [hʌnt] I. *vt* **1.**(*chase to kill*) cacciare **2.**(*search for*) dare la caccia a II. *vi* **1.**(*chase to kill*) cacciare; **to go ~ing** andare a caccia **2.**(*search*) **to ~ for** cercare III. *n* **1.**(*chase*) caccia *f;* **to go on a ~** andare a caccia **2.**(*search*) ricerca *f*

hunter *n* **1.**(*person*) cacciatore, -trice *m, f* **2.**(*dog*) cane *m* da caccia **3.**(*horse*) cavallo *m* per la caccia alla volpe

hunting *n* caccia *f*

hunting ground *n* terreno *m* di caccia

hunting license *n* licenza *f* di caccia

hunting season *n* stagione *f* della caccia

huntress ['hʌn·trɪs] *n* cacciatrice *f*

huntsman ['hʌnts·mən] <-men> *n* cacciatore *m*

hurdle ['hɜːr·dl] I. *n* ostacolo *m* II. *vi* SPORTS gareggiare in una corsa ad ostacoli III. *vt* SPORTS saltare

hurdler *n* SPORTS ostacolista *mf*

hurdle race *n* SPORTS corsa *f* ad ostacoli

hurdy-gurdy [ˌhɜːr·di·'gɜːr·di] <-ies> *n* organetto *m*

hurl [hɜːrl] *vt* lanciare

hurly-burly ['hɜːr·li·bɜːr·li] *n* trambusto *m*

hurrah [hə·'rɑː] *interj*, **hurray** [hə·'reɪ] *interj* urrà

hurricane ['hɜːr·rɪ·keɪn] *n* uragano *m*

hurricane lamp *n* lampada *f* controvento

hurried ['hɜːr·rɪd] *adj* affrettato, -a

hurry ['hɜːr·ri] <-ie-> I. *vi* affrettarsi, sbrigarsi II. *vt* **1.**(*rush*) mettere fretta a; (*process*) affrettare **2.**(*take quickly*) **he was hurried to the hospital** lo portarono di corsa all'ospedale III. *n* fretta *f;* **to leave in a ~** andarsene in fretta e furia; **to do sth in a ~** fare qc in fretta; **what's (all) the ~?** perché tanta fretta?

◆**hurry along** I. *vi* sbrigarsi II. *vt always sep* mettere fretta a

◆**hurry away, hurry off** I. *vi* andarsene in fretta II. *vt* (*person*) fare andare via in fretta; (*object*) fare partire in fretta

◆**hurry on** *vi* continuare rapidamente

◆**hurry up** I. *vi* sbrigarsi II. *vt* mettere fretta a

hurt [hɜːrt] I. <hurt, hurt> *vi* far male II. *vt* **1.**(*wound, offend*) ferire **2.**(*cause pain*) fare male a; **it ~s me** mi fa male **3.**(*damage*) danneggiare III. *adj* ferito, -a IV. *n* **1.**(*pain*) dolore *m* **2.**(*injury, offence*) ferita *f* **3.**(*damage*) danno *m*

hurtful ['hɜːrt·fəl] *adj* che ferisce

hurtle ['hɜːr·tl] I. *vi* lanciarsi II. *vt* lanciare

husband ['hʌz·bənd] I. *n* marito *m* II. *vt* risparmiare

husbandry ['hʌz·bənd·ri] *n* **1.**(*care, management*) gestione *f* oculata **2.** AGR agricoltura *f;* **animal ~** cura *f* degli animali

hush [hʌʃ] I. *n* silenzio *m* II. *interj* **~!** silenzio! III. *vi* tacere IV. *vt* (*make silent*) zittire; (*soothe*) calmare

◆**hush up** *vt* mettere a tacere

hush-hush *adj inf* secreto, -a

hush money *n inf:* denaro per comprare il silenzio di qu

husk [hʌsk] I. *n* (*outside covering*) buccia *f* II. *vt* sbucciare

husky[1] ['hʌs·ki] <-ier, -iest> *adj* **1.**(*low, rough: voice*) roco, -a **2.**(*big, strong*) robusto, -a

husky[2] ['hʌs·ki] <-ies> *n* husky *m inv*

hussy ['hʌ·si] *n inf* svergognata *f*

hustings ['hʌs·tɪŋz] *npl* campagna *f* elettorale

hustle ['hʌ·sl] I. *vt* **1.**(*hurry, push*) spingere **2.**(*achieve*) rimediare II. *vi* **1.**(*push for*) insistere **2.**(*practice prostitution*) battere *inf* III. *n* raggiro *m*

hustler ['hʌs·lə·] *n* **1.**(*persuader*) imbonitore, -trice *m, f* **2.**(*swindler*) imbroglione, -a *m, f* **3.**(*prostitute*) prostituto, -a *m, f*

hustling ['hʌs·lɪŋ] *n* raggiri *mpl*

hut [hʌt] *n* capanna *f*

hutch [hʌtʃ] <-es> *n* **1.**(*box for animals*) gabbia *f* **2.**(*cupboard*) credenza a vetrina

hyacinth ['ha·ɪə·sɪnθ] *n* BOT giacinto *m*

hybrid ['haɪ·brɪd] *n* ibrido *m*

hydrangea [haɪ·'dreɪn·dʒə] *n* BOT ortensia *f*

hydrant ['haɪ·drənt] *n* idrante *m*

hydrate ['haɪ·dreɪt] *n* idrato *m*

hydraulic [haɪ·'drɑː·lɪk] *adj* idraulico, -a

hydraulics [haɪ·'drɑː·lɪks] *n* idraulica *f*

hydrocarbon [ˌhaɪ·drou·'kɑːr·bən] I. *n* idrocarburo *m* II. *adj* di idrocarburo

hydrochloric acid [ˌhaɪ·drou·klɔː·rɪk·'æ·sɪd] *n* acido *m* cloridrico

hydroelectric [ˌhaɪ·drou·ɪ·'lek·trɪk] *adj* idroelettrico, -a

hydrofoil ['haɪ·drə·fɔɪl] *n* aliscafo *m*

hydrogen ['haɪ·drə·dʒən] *n* idrogeno *m*

hydrogen bomb *n* bomba *f* all'idrogeno

hydrophobia [ˌhaɪ·drə·'fou·biə] *n* idrofobia *f*

hydroponics [ˌhaɪ·drə·'pɑː·nɪks] *n + sing vb* idroponica *f*

hyena [haɪ·'iː·nə] *n* iena *f*

hygiene ['haɪ·dʒiːn] *n* igiene *f*

hygienic [ˌhaɪ·dʒiˈe·nɪk] *adj* igienico, -a

hygroscope ['haɪ·grəs·koup] *n* igroscopio *m*

hymn [hɪm] *n* inno *m*

hymnal ['hɪm·nəl] *n*, **hymnbook** *n* libro *m* degli inni

hype [haɪp] I. *n* COM gran pubblicità *f* II. *vt* superpubblicizzare

hyperactive [ˌhaɪ·pə·'æk·tɪv] *adj* iperattivo, -a

hyperbola [haɪ·'pɜːr·bə·lə] *n* MATH iperbole *f*

hyperbole [haɪ·'pɜːr·bə·li] *n* LIT iperbole *f*

hyperbolic [ˌhaɪ·pə·'bɑː·lɪk] *adj* LIT iperbolico, -a

hyperlink [ˌhaɪ·pə·'lɪŋk] *n* COMPUT collegamento *m* ipertestuale

hypermarket ['haɪ·pə·mɑːr·kɪt] *n* ipermercato *m*

hypersensitive [ˌhaɪ·pə·'sen·sə·ṭɪv] *adj* ipersensibile

hypertension *n* ipertensione *f*

hypertext [ˌhaɪ·pə·'tekst] *n* COMPUT ipertesto *m*

hyphen ['haɪ·fn] *n* TYPO trattino *m*

hyphenate ['haɪ·fə·neɪt] *vt* (*compound*) scrivere col trattino

hypnosis [hɪp·'noʊ·sɪs] *n* ipnosi *f inv;* **to be under ~** essere in stato d'ipnosi

hypnotherapy [ˌhɪp·noʊ·'θe·rə·pi] *n* ipnoterapia *f*

hypnotic [hɪp·'nɑː·t̬ɪk] *adj* ipnotico, -a

hypnotist ['hɪp·nə·tɪst] *n* ipnotizzatore, -trice *m, f*

hypnotize ['hɪp·nə·taɪz] *vt* ipnotizzare

hypochondria [ˌhaɪ·pə·'kɑːn·dri·ə] *n* ipocondria *f*

hypochondriac [ˌhaɪ·pə·'kɑːn·dri·æk] I. *n* ipocondriaco, -a *m, f* II. *adj* ipocondriaco, -a

hypocrisy [hɪ·'pɑː·krə·si] *n* ipocrisia *f*

hypocrite ['hɪ·pə·krɪt] *n* ipocrita *mf*

hypocritical [ˌhɪ·pə·'krɪ·t̬ɪ·kl] *adj* ipocrita

hypodermic [ˌhaɪ·pə·'dɜːr·mɪk] *adj* ipodermico, -a

hypotenuse [ˌhaɪ·'pɑ·t̬ə·nuːs] *n* MATH ipotenusa *f*

hypothermia [ˌhaɪ·poʊ·'θɜːr·miə] *n* ipotermia *f*

hypothesis [haɪ·'pɑː·θə·sɪs] *n* <-es> ipotesi *f inv*

hypothetical [ˌhaɪ·pə·'θe·t̬ɪ·kl] *adj* ipotetico, -a

hysterectomy [ˌhɪs·tə·'rek·tə·mi] *n* MED isterectomia *f*

hysteria [hɪ·'ste·riə] *n* isterismo *m*

hysteric [hɪ·'ste·rɪk] I. *adj* isterico, -a II. *n* isterico, -a *m, f*

hysterical *adj* isterico, -a

I

I, i [aɪ] *n* I, i *f; ~* **as in Irene** I di Imola

I [aɪ] *pron pers* (*1st person sing*) io; *~*'**m coming** arrivo; *~*'**ll do it** lo faccio io; **am ~ late?** sono in ritardo?; **she and ~** lei ed io; **it was ~ who did that** sono stato io a farlo

IA ['aɪ·ə·wə] *n abbr of* **Iowa** IA

IAEA *n abbr of* **International Atomic Energy Agency** AIEA *f*

IATA [ˌaɪ·ˌeɪ·ˌtiː·'eɪ] *n abbr of* **International Air Transport Association** IATA *f*

ibex ['aɪ·beks] <-es> *n* stambecco *m*

ibid. [ɪ·'bɪd] *adv abbr of* **ibidem** ibid.

IC [ˌaɪ·'siː] *n abbr of* **integrated circuit** IC, *circuito integrato*

ICBM [ˌaɪ·siː·biː·'em] *n abbr of* **intercontinental ballistic missile** ICBM *m, missile balistico intercontinentale*

ice [aɪs] I. *n* (*frozen water*) ghiaccio *m* ▶ **to be skating on** <u>thin</u> *~* camminare su un campo minato; **to** <u>break</u> **the** *~ inf* rompere il ghiaccio; **to** <u>put</u> **sth on** *~* accantonare II. *vt* 1. (*chill a drink*) mettere in ghiaccio 2. (*put icing on*) glassare

◆**ice over** *vi* ghiacciare

Ice Age *n* era *f* glaciale

ice ax <-es> *n* piccozza *f* (da ghiaccio)

iceberg *n* iceberg *m inv;* **the tip of the** *~ fig* la punta dell' iceberg

iceberg lettuce *n* lattuga *f* iceberg

icebound *adj* bloccato, -a dal ghiaccio

icebox <-es> *n* 1. (*freezer*) ghiacciaia *f* 2. (*fridge*) frigorifero *m*

icebreaker *n* rompighiaccio *m inv*

ice cap *n* calotta *f* glaciale

ice-cold *adj* gelato, -a

ice cream *n* gelato *m*

ice-cream cone *n* 1. (*only wafer*) cono *m* (per gelato) 2. (*wafer plus scoops*) cono *m* (gelato)

ice-cream parlor *n* gelateria *f*

ice cube ['aɪs·kjuːb] *n* cubetto *m* di ghiaccio

iced [aɪst] *adj* 1. (*with ice*) con ghiaccio; (*very cold*) ghiacciato, -a 2. (*covered with icing*) glassato, -a

ice floe ['aɪs·floʊ] *n* blocco *m* di ghiaccio galleggiante

ice hockey *n* hockey *m* su ghiaccio

Iceland ['aɪs·lənd] *n* Islanda *f*

Icelander ['aɪs·lən·dɚ] *n* islandese *mf*

Icelandic [aɪs·'læn·dɪk] I. *adj* islandese II. *n* islandese *mf*

ice pack *n* borsa *f* del ghiaccio

ice rink *n* pista *f* di pattinaggio

ice skate *n* pattino *m* da ghiaccio

ice-skate *vi* pattinare sul ghiaccio

ice skater *n* pattinatore, -trice *m, f* sul ghiaccio

ice-skating *n* pattinaggio *m* su ghiaccio

icicle ['aɪ·sɪ·kl] *n* ghiacciolo *m*

icing ['aɪ·sɪŋ] *n* 1. glassa *f* 2. (*in ice hockey*) pista da hockey ▶ **to be the** *~* **on the** <u>cake</u> essere la ciliegina sulla torta

icon ['aɪ·kɑːn] *n* icona *f*

iconoclast [aɪ·'kɑː·nə·klæst] *n* iconoclasta *mf*

iconoclastic [aɪ·ˌkɑː·nə·'klæs·tɪk] *adj* iconoclasta

ICU [ˌaɪ·siː·'juː] *n abbr of* **intensive care unit** reparto *m* di terapia intensiva

icy ['aɪ·si] <-ier, -iest> *adj* 1. (*with ice*) ghiacciato, -a; (*very cold*) gelido, -a 2. (*unfriendly*) gelido, -a

ID[1] [ˌaɪ·'diː] I. *n abbr of* **identification** documento *m* d'identità II. *vt inf abbr of* **identify** identificare; **to positively** *~* **sb** identificare qu con certezza

ID[2] [ˌaɪ·'diː] *n abbr of* **Idaho** ID

I'd [aɪd] 1. = I would *s.* would 2. = I had *s.* have

Idaho ['aɪ·də·hoʊ] *n* Idaho *m*

ID card [aɪ·'diː·ˌkɑːd] *n s.* **identity card** carta *f* d'identità

idea [aɪ·'diːə] *n* idea *f;* **to get an** *~* **of sth** farsi un'idea di qc

ideal [aɪ·'diː·əl] I. *adj* ideale II. *n* ideale *m*

idealism [aɪ·'diː·ə·lɪ·zəm] *n* idealismo *m*

idealist [aɪ·'diː·ə·lɪst] *n* idealista *mf*

idealistic [ˌaɪ·dɪ·ə·'lɪs·tɪk] *adj* idealistico, -a

idealize [aɪˈdiː·ə·laɪz] *vt* idealizzare

ideally [aɪˈdiː·li] *adv* **1.** (*in an ideal way*) idealmente **2.** ~, **we could catch the train** l'ideale sarebbe prendere il treno

identical [aɪˈden·t̬ə·kl] *adj* identico, -a

identifiable [aɪˌden·t̬ə·ˈfa·ɪə·bl] *adj* identificabile

identification [aɪˌden·t̬ə·fɪˈkeɪ·ʃən] *n* identificazione *f*

identification papers *npl* documentim *pl* d'identità

identifier [aɪˈden·t̬ə·fa·ɪə·] *n* COMPUT identificatore *m*

identify [aɪˈden·t̬ə·faɪ] <-ie-> *vt* identificare

identity [aɪˈden·t̬ə·ti] <-ies> *n* identità *f*

identity card *n* carta *f* d'identità

ideological [ˌaɪ·di·ə·ˈlɑː·dʒɪ·kl] *adj* ideologico, -a

ideologist [ˌaɪ·di·ˈɑː·lə·dʒɪst] *n* ideologo, -a *m, f*

ideology [ˌaɪ·di·ˈɑː·lə·dʒi] <-ies> *n* ideologia *f*

idiocy [ˈɪ·dɪə·si] <-ies> *n* idiozia *f*

idiom [ˈɪ·di·əm] *n* LING **1.** (*phrase*) espressione *f* idiomatica **2.** (*style of expression*) linguaggio *m*

idiomatic [ˌɪ·di·ə·ˈmæ·t̬ɪk] *adj* idiomatico, -a

idiosyncrasy [ˌɪ·di·oʊ·ˈsɪn·krə·si] <-ies> *n* idiosincrasia *f*

idiosyncratic [ˌɪ·di·oʊ·sɪn·ˈkræ·t̬ɪk] *adj* idiosincratico, -a

idiot [ˈɪ·di·ət] *n* idiota *mf*

idiotic [ˌɪ·di·ˈɑː·t̬ɪk] *adj* idiota

idle [ˈaɪ·dl] **I.** *adj* **1.** (*lazy*) pigro, -a **2.** (*not busy*) inoperoso, -a; (*machine*) inattivo, -a **3.** (*frivolous: pleasures*) futile **4.** (*unfounded: promise*) vano, -a; (*gossip*) ozioso, -a; (*fear*) infondato, -a **5.** (*ineffective: threat*) inconsistente **6.** FIN (*capital*) infruttifero, -a **II.** *n* AUTO minimo *m* **III.** *vi* (*machine*) girare al minimo; (*person*) oziare

idleness [ˈaɪ·dl·nɪs] *n* pigrizia *f*

idler [ˈaɪd·lə·] *n* pigro, -a *m, f*

idol [ˈaɪ·dl] *n* idolo *m*

idolatrous [aɪˈdɑː·lət·rəs] *adj* REL idolatra

idolatry [aɪˈdɑː·lət·ri] *n* idolatria *f*

idolize [ˈaɪ·də·laɪz] *vt* idolatrare

idyll [ˈaɪ·dəl] *n* idillio *m*

idyllic [aɪˈdɪ·lɪk] *adj* idilliaco, -a

i.e. [ˌaɪˈiː] *abbr of* **id est** cioè

if [ɪf] **I.** *conj* **1.** (*supposing that*) se; ~ **it snows** se nevica; ~ **not** se non; **as** ~ **it were true** come se fosse vero; ~ **they exist at all** se esistono davvero; ~ **A is right, then B is wrong** se A è giusto, allora B è sbagliato; **I'll stay,** ~ **only for a day** mi fermo, anche se solo per un giorno **2.** (*every time that*) ~ **he needs me, I'll help him** se avrà bisogno di me, lo aiuterò **3.** (*whether*) **I wonder** ~ **he'll come** mi chiedo se verrà **4.** (*although*) anche se; **cold** ~ **sunny weather** tempo freddo, ma soleggiato **II.** *n* se *m;* **no** ~**s, ands, or buts!** niente se o ma!

iffy [ˈɪ·fi] <-ier, -iest> *adj inf* (*weather*) incerto,

-a; (*person*) insicuro, -a

igloo [ˈɪg·luː] *n* iglù *m inv*

igneous [ˈɪg·ni·əs] *adj* igneo, -a

ignite [ɪgˈnaɪt] **I.** *vi* prendere fuoco **II.** *vt form* dare fuoco a

ignition [ɪgˈnɪ·ʃən] *n* **1.** AUTO accensione *f;* **to switch on the** ~ accendere il motore **2.** *form* (*causing to burn*) accensione *f*

ignition coil *n* bobina *f* d'accensione

ignition key *n* chiave *f* d'accensione

ignition switch <-es> *n* interruttore *m* d'accensione

ignoble [ɪgˈnoʊ·bl] *adj liter* ignobile

ignominious [ˌɪg·nə·ˈmɪ·ni·əs] *adj liter* ignominioso, -a

ignominy [ˈɪg·nə·mɪ·ni] *n* ignominia *f*

ignoramus [ˌɪg·nə·ˈreɪ·məs] *n* ignorante *mf*

ignorance [ˈɪg·nə·rəns] *n* ignoranza *f;* **to be left in** ~ **of sth** restare all'oscuro di qc ▶~ **is bliss** occhio non vede cuore non duole

ignorant [ˈɪg·nə·rənt] *adj* ignorante; **to be** ~ **about sth** essere ignorante in materia di qc; **to be** ~ **of sth** ignorare qc

ignore [ɪgˈnɔːr] *vt* ignorare

iguana [ɪˈgwɑː·nə] *n* iguana *f*

IL [ˌɪ·lə·ˈnɔɪ] *n abbr of* **Illinois** Il

ilk [ɪlk] *n liter* specie *f*

ill [ɪl] **I.** *adj* **1.** (*sick*) malato, -a; **to fall** ~ ammalarsi **2.** (*bad*) cattivo, -a; (*harmful*) nocivo, -a; (*unfavorable*) avverso, -a; **an** ~ **omen** un cattivo presagio **II.** *adv form* (*badly*) male; **to bode** ~ essere di cattivo augurio; **to speak** ~ **of sb** parlare male di qu

I'll [aɪl] = **I will** *s.* **will**

ill-advised [ˌɪl·əd·ˈvaɪzd] *adj* imprudente

ill at ease *adj* a disagio

ill-bred *adj* maleducato, -a

ill-conceived *adj* mal concepito, -a

illegal [ɪˈliː·gəl] *adj* illegale

illegal immigrant *n* immigrato, -a clandestino, -a *m*

illegality [ˌɪ·lɪ·ˈgæ·lə·ti] <-ies> *n* illegalità *f*

illegible [ɪˈle·dʒə·bl] *adj* illeggibile

illegitimate [ˌɪ·lɪ·ˈdʒɪ·t̬ə·mət] *adj* illegittimo, -a

ill-equipped [ˌɪl·ɪ·ˈkwɪpt] *adj* mal equipaggiato, -a

ill-fated *adj* (*having bad luck*) sfortunato, -a; (*bringing bad luck*) malaugurato, -a; **an** ~ **hour** un'ora infausta

ill-favored *adj* sgradevole

ill-fitting *adj* ~ **clothes** abiti*f inv* che vestono male

ill-gotten *adj* (*gains*) illecito, -a

illiberal [ɪˈlɪ·bə·rəl] *adj* illiberale

illicit [ɪˈlɪ·sɪt] *adj* illecito, -a

illimitable [ɪˈlɪ·mɪ·t̬ə·bl] *adj* illimitato, -a

ill-informed [ˈɪl·ɪn·ˌfɔːrmd] *adj* **1.** (*wrongly informed*) male informato, -a **2.** (*ignorant*) ignorante

Illinois [ˌɪ·lə·ˈnɔɪ] *n* Illinois *m*

illiteracy [ɪˈlɪ·t̬ə·rə·si] *n* analfabetismo *m*

illiterate [ɪˈlɪ·t̬ə·rət] **I.** *adj* analfabeta; *pej, fig* ignorante **II.** *n* analfabeta *mf*

ill-mannered [ˌɪlˈmæ·nəd] *adj* maleducato, -a
ill-natured *adj* bisbetico, -a
illness [ˈɪl·nɪs] <-es> *n* malattia *f*
illogical [ɪ·ˈlɑː·dʒɪ·kl] *adj* illogico, -a
illogicality [ɪ·ˌlɑː·dʒɪ·ˈkæ·lə·ti] *n* illogicità *f*
ill-omened [ˌɪlˈou·mend] *adj* malaugurato, -a
ill-starred *adj* nato, -a sotto una cattiva stella
ill-tempered *adj* irritabile
ill-timed *adj* inopportuno, -a
ill-treat [ˌɪlˈtriːt] *vt* maltrattare
ill-treatment [ˌɪlˈtriːt·mənt] *n* maltrattamento *m*
illuminate [ɪ·ˈluː·mə·neɪt] *vt a. fig* illuminare
illuminating [ɪ·ˈluː·mɪ·neɪ·ṭɪŋ] *adj form* illuminante
illumination [ɪ·ˌluː·mɪ·ˈneɪ·ʃən] *n* illuminazione *f*; ART miniatura *f*
illus. *abbr of* **illustrated, illustration** ill.
illusion [ɪ·ˈluː·ʒən] *n* illusione *f*; **to have no ~ s (about sth)** non farsi delle illusioni(su qc); **to be under the ~ that ...** illudersi che...
illusionist [ɪ·ˈluː·ʒə·nɪst] *n* illusionista *mf*
illusive [ɪ·ˈluː·sɪv] *adj*, **illusory** [ɪ·ˈluː·sə·ri] *adj* illusorio, -a
illustrate [ˈɪ·ləs·treɪt] *vt a. fig* illustrare
illustration [ˌɪ·ləs·ˈtreɪ·ʃən] *n* 1.(*drawing*) illustrazione *f* 2.(*example*) esemplificazione *f*; **by way of ~** a modo di esempio
illustrative [ɪ·ˈlʌs·trə·ṭɪv, ˈɪ·ləs·treɪ·ṭɪv] *adj form* illustrativo, -a
illustrator [ˈɪ·ləs·treɪ·ṭəʳ] *n* illustratore, -trice *m, f*
illustrious [ɪ·ˈlʌs·tri·əs] *adj form* illustre
ill will *n* animosità *f*
I'm [aɪm] = **I am** *s.* **am**
image [ˈɪ·mɪdʒ] *n* 1.(*likeness*) immagine *f*; **to be the living ~ of sb** essere il ritratto vivente di qu 2.(*picture*) immagine *f* 3.(*reputation*) immagine *f*
imagery [ˈɪ·mɪ·dʒə·ri] *n* LIT immagini *fpl*
imaginable [ɪ·ˈmæ·dʒɪ·nə·bl] *adj* immaginabile
imaginary [ɪ·ˈmæ·dʒə·ne·ri] *adj* immaginario, -a
imagination [ɪ·ˌmæ·dʒɪ·ˈneɪ·ʃən] *n* immaginazione *f*
imaginative [ɪ·ˈmæ·dʒɪ·nə·ṭɪv] *adj* (*solution, use, way*) creativo, -a
imagine [ɪ·ˈmæ·dʒɪn] *vt* 1.(*form mental image*) immaginare 2.(*suppose*) imaginare; **~ that!** pensa un po'!
imaging *n* COMPUT imaging *m inv, processi di produzione e riproduzione dell'immagine*
imbalance [ˌɪm·ˈbæ·ləns] *n* squilibrio *m*
imbecile [ˈɪm·bə·sɪl] *n* imbecille *mf*
imbecility [ˌɪm·bə·ˈsɪ·lə·ti] *n form* imbecillità *f*
imbibe [ɪm·ˈbaɪb] *vt* bere; *fig* imbeversi di
imbroglio [ɪm·ˈbrou·liou] *n liter* imbroglio *m*
imbue [ɪm·ˈbjuː] *vt form* 1.(*fill, inspire*) **to ~ sb with sth** imbevere qu di qc; **to be ~d with** essere impregnato, -a di 2.(*soak*) imbevere
IMF [ˌaɪ·em·ˈef] *n abbr of* **International Monetary Fund** FMI *m*

imitate [ˈɪ·mɪ·teɪt] *vt* imitare
imitation [ˌɪ·mɪ·ˈteɪ·ʃən] I. *n* 1.(*mimicry*) imitazione *f*; **in ~ of sb/sth** a imitazione di qu/qc 2.(*copy*) imitazione *f* II. *adj* finto, -a; **~ jewels** bigiotteria *f*
imitative [ˈɪ·mɪ·teɪ·ṭɪv] *adj* imitativo, -a
imitator [ˈɪ·mɪ·tə·ṭəʳ] *n* imitatore, -trice *m, f*
immaculate [ɪ·ˈmæ·kjʊ·lət] *adj* 1.(*spotless, neat*) immacolato, -a 2.(*flawless*) perfetto, -a
immanence [ˈɪ·mə·nəns] *n* PHILOS immanenza *f*
immanent [ˈɪ·mə·nənt] *adj* immanente
immaterial [ˌɪ·mə·ˈtɪ·ri·əl] *adj* 1.(*not important*) irrilevante 2.(*intangible*) immateriale
immature [ˌɪ·mə·ˈtʊr] *adj* 1.(*young*) immaturo, -a 2.(*childish*) immaturo, -a
immaturity [ˌɪ·mə·ˈtʊ·rə·ti] *n* immaturità *f*
immeasurable [ɪ·ˈme·ʒə·rə·bl] *adj* incommensurabile
immediacy [ɪ·ˈmiː·di·ə·si] *n* immediatezza *f*
immediate [ɪ·ˈmiː·di·ɪt] *adj* immediato, -a; **the ~ family** parenti *m* diretti *pl*; **in the ~ area** nelle immediate vicinanze; **in the ~ future** nell'immediato futuro
immediately *adv* 1.(*time*) immediatamente; **~ after ...** subito dopo... 2.(*place*) **my flat is the one ~ above yours** il mio appartamento è quello subito sopra il tuo
immemorial [ˌɪ·mə·ˈmɔː·ri·əl] *adj liter* immemorabile
immense [ɪ·ˈmens] *adj* immenso, -a
immensely *adv* immensamente
immensity [ɪ·ˈmen·sə·ti] *n* immensità *f*
immerse [ɪ·ˈmɜːrs] *vt* immergere; **to ~ d in sth** *fig* essere assorto, -a in qc; **to ~ oneself in sth** *fig* immergersi in qc
immersion [ɪ·ˈmɜː·rʃən] *n* 1.(*putting under water*) immersione *f* 2.(*absorption*) **his immersion in his studies was total** era completamente immerso negli studi
immersion heater *n* scaldabagno *m* elettrico
immigrant [ˈɪ·mɪ·grənt] *n* immigrante *mf*
immigrate [ˈɪ·mɪ·greɪt] *vi* immigrare
immigration [ˌɪ·mɪ·ˈgreɪ·ʃən] *n* immigrazione *f*
imminence [ˈɪ·mɪ·nəns] *n* imminenza *f*
imminent [ˈɪ·mɪ·nənt] *adj* imminente
immobile [ɪ·ˈmou·bl] *adj* 1.(*not moving*) immobile 2.(*rigid*) immobilizzato, -a
immobilize [ɪ·ˈmou·bə·laɪz] *vt* immobilizzare
immobility [ˌɪ·mou·ˈbɪ·lə·ti] *n* immobilità *f*
immoderate [ɪ·ˈmɑː·də·ət] *adj* smodato, -a
immodest [ɪ·ˈmɑː·dɪst] *adj* 1.(*conceited*) presuntuoso, -a 2.(*slightly indecent*) indecente
immolate [ˈɪ·mə·leɪt] *vt form* immolare
immoral [ɪ·ˈmɔː·rəl] *adj* immorale
immortal [ɪ·ˈmɔːr·tl] I. *adj* immortale II. *n* immortale *mf*
immortalize [ɪ·ˈmɔːr·tə·laɪz] *vt* immortalare
immortality [ˌɪ·mɔːr·ˈtæ·lə·ti] *n* immortalità *f*
immovable [ɪ·ˈmuː·və·bl] *adj* 1.(*not moveable*) inamovibile 2.(*not changeable*) irremovibile
immune [ɪ·ˈmjuːn] *adj* MED, POL, LAW immune

I

immune system *n* sistema *m* immunitario

immunity [ɪ·'mju:·nə·ti] *n* **1.** MED, LAW immunità *f*; **diplomatic** ~ immunità diplomatica **2.** (*lack of susceptibility*) insensibilità *f*

immunize ['ɪm·jə·naɪz] *vt* immunizzare

immunological [ˌɪm·jə·noʊ·'lɑː·dʒɪ·kl] *adj* immunologico, -a

immunologist [ˌɪm·jʊ·'nɑː·lə·dʒɪst] *n* immunologo, -a *m, f*

immure [ɪ·'mjʊr] *vt liter* imprigionare

immutable [ɪ·'mju:·ţə·bl] *adj form* **1.** (*unchangeable: fact, set of rules*) immutabile **2.** COMPUT (*file, image*) non modificabile

imp [ɪmp] *n* **1.** (*mischievous child*) diavoletto, -a *m, f* **2.** (*small evil spirit*) folletto *m*

impact ['ɪm·pækt] **I.** *n* **1.** (*contact*) impatto *m*; **on** ~ all'impatto **2.** (*effect*) impatto *m* **II.** *vt* avere un impatto su **III.** *vi* **to** ~ **on sb/sth** avere un impatto su qu/qc

impacted [ɪm·'pæk·tɪd] *adj* (*tooth*) incluso, -a

impair [ɪm·'per] *vt* (*hearing*) indebolire; (*health*) danneggiare; (*one's performance, chances*) compromettere; (*communications*) ostacolare

impaired *adj* (*vision, hearing*) debole; (*health*) malfermo, -a; (*speech*) disturbato, -a; ~ **driving** guida in stato di alterazione dovuta a alcol o stupefacenti; **to be visually** ~ essere debole di vista

impale [ɪm·'peɪl] *vt* **to** ~ **sb on** trafiggere qu con; **to** ~ **oneself on** trafiggersi con

impalpable [ɪm·'pæl·pə·bl] *adj liter* impalpabile; (*change*) impercettibile

impart [ɪm·'pɑːrt] *vt form* (*information, wisdom*) impartire; (*flavor, tranquillity*) conferire; (*secret*) svelare

impartial [ɪm·'pɑːr·ʃl] *adj* imparziale

impartiality [ˌɪm·ˌpɑːr·ʃɪ·'æ·lə·ti] *n* imparzialità *f*

impassable [ɪm·'pæ·sə·bl] *adj* (*road*) intransitabile; *fig* (*problem*) insormontabile

impasse ['ɪm·pæs] *n a. fig* vicolo *m* cieco; **to have reached an** ~ essere arrivato ad un punto morto

impassioned [ɪm·'pæ·ʃnd] *adj form* appassionato, -a; **an** ~ **appeal for help** un'accalorata richiesta d'aiuto

impassive [ɪm·'pæ·sɪv] *adj* impassibile

impatience [ɪm·'peɪ·ʃns] *n* impazienza *f*

impatient [ɪm·'peɪ·ʃnt] *adj* impaziente; **to be** ~ **to do sth** essere impaziente di fare qc

impeach [ɪm·'pi:tʃ] *vt* mettere in stato di accusa

impeachment [ɪm·'pi:tʃ·mənt] *n* impeachment *m inv*, incriminazione *del Presidente*

impeccable [ɪm·'pe·kə·bl] *adj* impeccabile

impecunious [ˌɪm·pɪ·'kju:·ni·əs] *adj form* indigente

impede [ɪm·'pi:d] *vt* ostacolare

impediment [ɪm·'pe·dɪ·mənt] *n* **1.** (*hindrance*) ostacolo *m* **2.** MED difetto *m*; **a speech** ~ un disturbo del linguaggio

impel [ɪm·'pel] <-ll-> *vt* spingere

impend [ɪm·'pend] *vi* avvicinarsi

impending *adj* imminente

impenetrable [ɪm·'pe·nɪ·trə·bl] *adj* **1.** (*substance*) impenetrabile **2.** (*incomprehensible*) incomprensibile

impenitent [ɪm·'pe·nə·tənt] *adj form* impenitente

imperative [ɪm·'pe·rə·tɪv] **I.** *adj* **1.** (*urgently essential*) **silence is** ~ il silenzio è d'obbligo; **it is** ~ **that** ... bisogna assolutamente ... **2.** LING imperativo, -a **II.** *n a.* LING imperativo *m*

imperceptible [ˌɪm·pə·'sep·tə·bl] *adj* impercettibile

imperfect [ɪm·'pɜːr·fɪkt] **I.** *adj* (*world*) imperfetto, -a; (*flawed*) difettoso, -a **II.** *n* LING imperfetto *m*

imperfection [ˌɪm·pə·'fek·ʃən] *n* imperfezione *f*

imperial [ɪm·'pɪ·ri·əl] *adj* imperiale

imperialism [ɪm·'pɪ·ri·ə·lɪ·zəm] *n* imperialismo *m*

imperialist [ɪm·'pɪ·ri·ə·lɪst] **I.** *n* imperialista *mf* **II.** *adj* imperialista

imperil [ɪm·'pe·rəl] <-ll-, -l-> *vt form* mettere a repentaglio

imperious [ɪm·'pɪ·ri·əs] *adj* imperioso, -a

imperishable [ɪm·'pe·rɪ·ʃə·bl] *adj* (*memory*) imperituro, -a; (*food*) non deteriorabile; (*material*) indistruttibile

impermanent [ɪm·'pɜːr·mə·nənt] *adj* (*job*) precario, -a; (*change*) temporaneo, -a

impermeable [ɪm·'pɜːr·mi·ə·bl] *adj* impermeabile

impersonal [ˌɪm·'pɜːr·sə·nl] *adj a.* LING impersonale

impersonate [ɪm·'pɜːr·sə·neɪt] *vt* (*to trick people*) spacciarsi per; (*imitate*) imitare

impersonator *n* (*job*) imitatore, -trice *m, f*

impertinent [ɪm·'pɜːr·ţ·nənt] *adj* impertinente

imperturbable [ˌɪm·pə·'tɜːr·bə·bl] *adj form* imperturbabile

impervious [ɪm·'pɜːr·vi·əs] *adj* **1.** (*to substance*) impermeabile **2.** (*not affected*) insensibile

impetuous [ɪm·'pet·ʃu·əs] *adj* precipitoso, -a

impetus ['ɪm·pɪ·təs] *n* **1.** (*push*) impeto *m* **2.** (*driving force*) slancio *m*

impiety [ɪm·'pa·ɪə·ti] *n* empietà *f*

impinge [ɪm·'pɪndʒ] *form* **I.** *vt* influire su **II.** *vi* **to** ~ **on sb/sth** influire su qu/qc

impious ['ɪm·pi·əs] *adj* empio, -a

impish ['ɪm·pɪʃ] *adj* **1.** (*mischievous*) malizioso, -a **2.** (*impudent*) impertinente; (*grin*) birichino, -a

implacable [ɪm·'plæ·kə·bl] *adj form* implacabile

implacably *adv form* implacabilmente

implant [ɪm·'plænt] **I.** *n* impianto *m* **II.** *vt* **1.** (*add surgically*) impiantare **2.** (*put in the mind*) inculcare

implausible [ɪm·'plɑː·zɪ·bl] *adj* inverosimile

implement ['ɪm·plɪ·mənt] **I.** *n* (*tool*) attrezzo *m*; (*small tool*) utensile *m* **II.** *vt* implementare

implementation [ˌɪm·plɪ·men·ˈteɪ·ʃən] *n* (*of tools, devices*) messa *f* a punto; (*of measures, policies*) attuazione *f*

implicate [ˈɪm·plɪ·keɪt] *vt* **1.**(*show sb's involvement*) implicare **2.**(*involve*) implicare

implication [ˌɪm·plɪ·ˈkeɪ·ʃən] *n* **1.**(*hinting at*) insinuazione *f*; **by ~** implicitamente **2.**(*effect*) implicazione *f* **3.**(*showing of involvement*) implicazione *f*

implicit [ɪm·ˈplɪ·sɪt] *adj* **1.**(*suggested*) implicito, -a **2.**(*total*) assoluto, -a

implied [ɪm·ˈplaɪd] *adj* implicito, -a

implode [ɪm·ˈploʊd] *vi* implodere

implore [ɪm·ˈplɔːr] *vt* implorare; **to ~ sb to do sth** implorare qu di fare qc

imploring [ɪm·ˈplɔː·rɪŋ] *adj* supplichevole

implosion [ɪm·ˈploʊ·ʒən] *n* implosione *f*

imply [ɪm·ˈplaɪ] <-ie-> *vt* **1.**(*suggest*) insinuare **2.** *form* (*imply*) implicare

impolite [ˌɪm·pə·ˈlaɪt] *adj* maleducato, -a; (*rude*) scortese

impoliteness *n* maleducazione *f*

impolitic [ɪm·ˈpɑː·lə·tɪk] *adj form* sconveniente

imponderable [ɪm·ˈpɑːn·də·rə·bl] **I.** *adj* imponderabile **II.** *n* imponderabile *m*

import I. [ɪm·ˈpɔːrt] *vt* **1.** ECON, COMPUT importare **2.** *form* (*signify*) comportare **II.** [ˈɪm·pɔːrt] *n* **1.**(*product*) prodotto *m* d'importazione **2.** *form* (*significance*) importanza *f*

importance [ɪm·ˈpɔːr·tns] *n* importanza *f*

important [ɪm·ˈpɔːr·tənt] *adj* importante

importantly *adv* (*to behave*) con aria di superiorità; (*to emphasize importance*) cosa assai importante

importation [ˌɪm·pɔːr·ˈteɪ·ʃən] *n* ECON importazione *f*

import duty <-ies> *n* dazio *m* di importazione

importunate [ɪm·ˈpɔːr·tʃə·nɪt] *adj form* importuno, -a

importune [ˌɪm·pɔːr·ˈtuːn] *vt form* importunare

impose [ɪm·ˈpoʊz] **I.** *vt* imporre **II.** *vi* disturbare; **to ~ on sb** approfittare di qu; **I don't want to ~** non vorrei disturbare

imposing [ɪm·ˈpoʊ·zɪŋ] *adj* imponente

imposition [ˌɪm·pə·ˈzɪ·ʃən] *n* **1.**(*forcing, application*) imposizione *f* **2.**(*inconvenience*) disturbo *m*

impossibility [ɪm·ˌpɑː·sə·ˈbɪ·lə·ti] *n* impossibilità *f*

impossible [ɪm·ˈpɑː·sə·bl] **I.** *adj* impossibile **II.** *n* **the ~** l'impossibile

impossibly *adv* (*very*) incredibilmente

imposter *n*, **impostor** [ɪm·ˈpɑːs·tə-] *n* impostore, -a *m, f*

imposture [ɪm·ˈpɑːs·tʃə-] *n* impostura *f*

impotence [ˈɪm·pə·təns] *n* impotenza *f*

impotent [ˈɪm·pə·tənt] *adj* impotente

impound [ɪm·ˈpaʊnd] *vt* sequestrare

impoverish [ɪm·ˈpɑː·və·rɪʃ] *vt* **1.**(*make poor*) impoverire **2.**(*deplete*) depauperare

impoverished *adj* **1.**(*made poor*) impoverito, -a **2.**(*depleted*) depauperato, -a

impracticable [ɪm·ˈpræk·tɪ·kə·bl] *adj* (*scheme, idea, plan*) impraticabile; (*person*) intrattabile

impractical [ɪm·ˈpræk·tɪ·kl] *adj* (*person*) privo, -a di senso pratico; (*scheme, idea, plan*) impraticabile

imprecation [ˌɪm·prɪ·ˈkeɪ·ʃən] *n form* imprecazione *f*

imprecise [ˌɪm·prɪ·ˈsaɪs] *adj* impreciso, -a

impregnable [ɪm·ˈpreg·nə·bl] *adj* **1.**(*unable to be taken*) inespugnabile **2.**(*undefeatable*) imbattibile

impregnate [ɪm·ˈpreg·neɪt] *vt* **1.**(*inseminate*) fecondare **2.**(*saturate*) impregnare

impresario [ˌɪm·prə·ˈsɑː·ri·oʊ] *n* impresario, -a *m, f*

impress [ɪm·ˈpres] **I.** *vt* **1.**(*affect*) colpire **2.**(*stamp*) imprimere; **to ~ sth on** [*o* **upon**] **sb** far capire qc a qu **II.** *vi* fare una buona impressione

impression [ɪm·ˈpre·ʃən] *n* **1.**(*general opinion*) impressione *f*; **to be of** [*o* **under**] **the ~ that ...** avere l'impressione che... **2.**(*feeling*) impressione *f*; **to make an ~ on sb** fare impressione su qu **3.**(*imitation*) imitazione *f* **4.** *a. fig* impronta *f*

impressionable [ɪm·ˈpre·ʃə·nə·bl] *adj* impressionabile

impressionism [ɪm·ˈpreʃ·nɪ·zəm] *n* impressionismo *m*

impressionist [ɪm·ˈpreʃ·nɪst] **I.** *n* **1.** ART impressionista *mf* **2.**(*imitator*) imitatore, -trice *m, f* **II.** *adj* impressionista

impressionistic [ɪm·ˌpre·ʃə·ˈnɪs·tɪk] *adj* impressionistico

impressive [ɪm·ˈpre·sɪv] *adj* impressionante

imprint I. [ɪm·ˈprɪnt] *vt* **1.**(*stamp*) stampare **2.**(*in memory*) imprimere **II.** [ˈɪm·prɪnt] *n* **1.** *a. fig* (*mark*) impronta *f* **2.** TYPO sigla *f* editoriale

imprison [ɪm·ˈprɪ·zən] *vt* imprigionare

imprisonment [ɪm·ˈprɪ·zən·mənt] *n* carcerazione *f*; **life ~** carcere *m* a vita

improbability [ˌɪm·prɑː·bə·ˈbɪ·lə·ti] *n* improbabilità *f*

improbable [ɪm·ˈprɑː·bə·bl] *adj* improbabile

impromptu [ɪm·ˈprɑːm·tuː] *adj* improvvisato, -a

improper [ɪm·ˈprɑː·pə-] *adj* **1.**(*incorrect*) scorretto, -a; (*showing bad judgment*) improprio, -a **2.**(*not socially decent*) sconveniente; (*immoral*) indecente **3.**(*dishonest*) improprio, -a

impropriety [ˌɪm·prə·ˈpraɪ·ə·ti] <-ies> *n* **1.**(*improper doings*) scorrettezza *f*; (*language*) improprietà *f* **2.**(*indecency*) indecenza *f*

improve [ɪm·ˈpruːv] **I.** *vt* migliorare **II.** *vi* **1.** migliorare **2.**(*price*) aumentare

◆**improve on** *vi* migliorare

improvement [ɪm·ˈpruːv·mənt] *n* **1.**(*better-*

ment, progress) miglioramento *m* **2.** (*of illness*) miglioramento *m* **3.** (*increase in value*) aumento *m*

improvident [ɪm·ˈprɑː·və·dənt] *adj form* **1.** (*not planning*) imprevidente **2.** (*imprudent*) sconsiderato, -a

improvisation [ɪm·ˌprɑː·vɪ·ˈzeɪ·ʃən] *n* improvvisazione *f*

improvise [ˈɪm·prə·vaɪz] *vi, vt* improvvisare

imprudent [ɪm·ˈpruː·dnt] *adj form* imprudente

impudence [ˈɪm·pjʊ·dəns] *n* impudenza *f*

impudent [ˈɪm·pjʊ·dənt] *adj* sfacciato, -a

impugn [ɪm·ˈpjuːn] *vt form* screditare

impulse [ˈɪm·pʌls] *n* **1.** *a.* ELEC, PHYS, BIO impulso *m;* **to do sth on** (**an**) ~ fare qc d'impulso **2.** (*motive*) impulso *m*

impulsion [ɪm·ˈpʌl·ʃən] *n* **1.** (*urge*) impulso *m;* **to have** [*o* **feel**] **the** ~ **to do sth** sentire l'impulso di fare qc **2.** (*force*) impulso *m*

impulsive [ɪm·ˈpʌl·sɪv] *adj* impulsivo, -a

impunity [ɪm·ˈpjuː·nə·ti] *n* impunità *f*

impure [ɪm·ˈpjʊr] *adj* impuro, -a

impurity [ɪm·ˈpjʊ·rə·ti] <-ies> *n* impurità *f*

imputation [ˌɪm·pjʊ·ˈteɪ·ʃən] *n form* accusa *f*

impute [ɪm·ˈpjuːt] *vt* imputare

in [ɪn] **I.** *prep* **1.** (*inside, into*) dentro; **to be ~ bed** essere a letto; **there is sth ~ the drawer** c'è qc nel cassetto; **to put sth ~ sb's hands** mettere qc nelle mani di qu; ~ **town/jail** in città/carcere; ~ **the country/hospital** in campagna/ospedale; ~ **Canada/Mexico** in Canada/Messico **2.** (*within*) ~ **sb's face** in faccia a qu; ~ **the picture** nella forografia; ~ **the snow** sotto la neve; ~ **the sun** al sole; **the best** ~ **New England/town** il migliore del New England/della città; **to find a friend ~ sb** trovare un amico in qu **3.** (*position of*) ~ **the beginning** all'inizio; ~ **end** alla fine; **right** ~ **the middle** proprio in mezzo **4.** (*during*) ~ **the twenties** negli anni venti; **to be ~ one's thirties** essere sulla trentina; ~ **May** in maggio; ~ **the spring** in [*o* a] primavera; ~ **the afternoon** nel pomeriggio **5.** (*at later time*) ~ **a week/three hours** fra una settimana/tre ore; ~ (**the**) **future** in futuro **6.** (*in less than*) **to do sth ~ 4 hours** fare qc in 4 ore **7.** (*for*) **he hasn't done that ~ years/a week** non lo fa da anni/una settimana **8.** (*in situation, state of*) ~ **fashion** di moda; ~ **search of sth/sb** in cerca di qc/qu; ~ **this way** in questo modo; **when** ~ **doubt** in caso di dubbio; ~ **anger** con rabbia; ~ **fun** per scherzo; ~ **earnest** sul serio; **to be ~ a hurry** essere di fretta; **to be ~ love** (**with sb**) essere innamorato (di qu); ~ **alphabetical order** in ordine alfabetico; **written ~ black and white** *fig* messo nero su bianco; **dressed** ~ **red** vestido di rosso **9.** (*concerning*) **deaf** ~ **one ear** sordo da un orecchio; **to be interested** ~ **sth** interessarsi di qc; **to have faith** ~ **God** avere fede in Dio; **to have confidence** ~ **sb** avere fiducia in qu; **to have a say** ~ **the matter** aver voce in capitolo; **a**

change ~ **attitude** un cambio d'atteggiamento; **a rise** ~ **prices** un aumento dei prezzi **10.** (*by*) ~ **saying sth** nel dire qc; **to spend one's time** ~ **doing sth** passare il tempo a fare qc **11.** (*taking the form of*) **to speak** ~ **French** parlare in francese; ~ **the form of a request** sotto forma di richiesta **12.** (*made of*) ~ **wood/stone** di legno/pietra **13.** (*sound of*) ~ **a whisper** sussurrando; **to speak** ~ **a loud/low voice** parlare a voce alta/bassa **14.** (*aspect of*) **6 feet** ~ **length/height** lungo/alto 2 metri; ~ **every respect** sotto ogni aspetto **15.** (*ratio*) **two** ~ **six** due su sei; **to buy sth** ~ **twos** comprare qc due alla volta; **10** ~ **number** 10 di numero; ~ **part** in parte; ~ **tens** in gruppi di dieci **16.** (*substitution of*) ~ **your place** al posto tuo; ~ **lieu of sth** *form* invece di qc **17.** (*as consequence of*) ~ **return** in cambio; ~ **reply** in risposta ▸ ~ **all** in tutto; **all** ~ **all** tutto sommato **II.** *adv* **1.** (*inside, into*) dentro; **to go** ~ entrare; **to put sth** ~ mettere qc dentro **2.** (*to a place*) **to be** ~ *inf* essere in casa; **to hand sth** ~ consegnare **3.** (*popular*) **to be** ~ essere di moda **4.** (*up*) **the tide is coming** ~ la marea sta salendo ▸ **to be** ~ **for sth** *inf* doversi aspettare; **to be** ~ **on sth** essere al corrente di qc **III.** *adj* di moda **IV.** *n* **the** ~ **s and outs** gli annessi e connessi *mpl*

IN [ɪn·di·ˈæ·nə] *n abbr of* **Indiana** IN

in. *abbr of* **inch** pollice *m*

inability [ˌɪn·ə·ˈbɪ·lə·ti] *n* incapacità *f*

inaccessible [ˌɪn·æk·ˈse·sə·bl] *adj* inaccesibile

inaccuracy [ɪn·ˈæk·jə·ə·si] <-ies> *n* **1.** (*fact*) inesattezza *m* **2.** (*quality*) imprecisione *f*

inaccurate [ɪn·ˈæk·jə·ət] *adj* **1.** (*inexact*) inesatto, -a **2.** (*wrong*) errato, -a

inaction [ɪn·ˈæk·ʃən] *n* inazione *f*

inactive [ɪn·ˈæk·tɪv] *adj* inattivo, -a

inactivity [ˌɪn·æk·ˈtɪ·və·ti] *n* inattività *f*

inadequacy [ɪn·ˈæ·dɪ·kwə·si] <-ies> *n* **1.** (*insufficiency*) insufficienza *f* **2.** (*quality of being inadequate*) inadeguatezza *f*

inadequate [ɪn·ˈæ·dɪ·kwət] *adj* inadeguato, -a

inadmissible [ˌɪn·əd·ˈmɪ·sə·bl] *adj* inammissibile

inadvertent [ˌɪn·əd·ˈvɜːr·tənt] *adj* involontario, -a

inadvisable [ˌɪn·əd·ˈvaɪ·zə·bl] *adj* sconsigliabile

inalienable [ɪn·ˈeɪ·li·ən·ə·bl] *adj form* inalienabile

inane [ɪ·ˈneɪn] *adj* (*person, remark*) stupido, -a; (*hope*) vano, -a

inanimate [ɪn·ˈæ·nɪ·mət] *adj* inanimato, -a

inanity [ɪ·ˈnæ·nə·ti] <-ies> *n* inanità *f*

inapplicable [ɪn·ˈæp·lɪ·kə·bl] *adj* inapplicabile

inappropriate [ˌɪn·ə·ˈprou·pri·ət] *adj* (*incorrect*) inadeguato, -a; (*not suitable*) fuori luogo

inapt [ɪn·ˈæpt] *adj* (*remark, behavior*) poco appropriato, -a; (*not skillful*) incapace

inaptitude [ɪn·ˈæp·tə·tuːd] *n* inettitudine *f*

inarticulate [ˌɪn·ɑːr·ˈtɪk·jʊ·lət] *adj* **1.** (*unable to express*) incapace di esprimersi **2.** (*unclear*) incomprensibile

inartistic [ˌɪn·ɑːr·'tɪs·tɪk] *adj* (*work*) poco artistico, -a; (*person*) privo, -a di senso artistico

inasmuch as [ˌɪn·əz·'mʌtʃ əz] *conj form* **1.** (*because*) poichè **2.** (*to the extent that*) nella misura in cui +*subj*

inattention [ˌɪn·ə·'ten·ʃən] *n* disattenzione *f*

inattentive [ˌɪn·ə·'ten·ʈɪv] *adj* disattento, -a; **to be ~ to sb/sth** trascurare qu/qc

inaudible [ɪn·'ɑː·də·bl] *adj* impercettibile

inaugural [ɪ·'nɑː·gjʊ·rəl] *adj* inaugurale

inaugurate [ɪ·'nɑː·gjʊ·reɪt] *vt* inaugurare

inauguration [ɪˌnɑː·gjʊ·'reɪ·ʃən] *n* inaugurazione *f*

inauspicious [ˌɪn·ɑː·'spɪ·ʃəs] *adj* poco propizio, -a

in-between *adj* intermedio, -a

inboard ['ɪn·bɔːrd] *adj* entrobordo

inborn ['ɪn·bɔːrn] *adj* innato, -a

inbred ['ɪn·bred] *adj* **1.** (*too closely related*) endogamico, -a **2.** (*inherent*) innato, -a

inbreeding ['ɪn·briː·dɪŋ] *n* endogamia *f*

inbuilt ['ɪn·bɪlt] *adj* (*built in*) incorporato, -a; *fig* intrinseco, -a

Inc. [ɪŋk] *abbr of* **incorporated** Inc.

incalculable [ɪn·'kæl·kjʊ·lə·bl] *adj* incalcolabile

incandescent [ˌɪn·ken·'de·snt] *adj* incandescente

incantation [ˌɪn·kæn·'teɪ·ʃən] *n* incantesimo *m*

incapability [ɪn·ˌkeɪ·pə·'bɪl·ə·ti] *n* incapacità *f*

incapable [ɪn·'keɪ·pə·bl] *adj* incapace; **to be ~ of doing sth** non essere in grado di fare qc

incapacitate [ˌɪn·kə·'pæ·sɪ·teɪt] *vt* rendere inabile

incapacity [ˌɪn·kə·'pæ·sə·ti] *n* incapacità *f*

incarcerate [ɪn·'kɑːr·sə·reɪt] *vt* incarcerare

incarnate [ɪn·'kɑːr·nət] *adj* (*goodness*) personificato, -a; **the devil ~** il diavolo incarnato

incarnation [ˌɪn·kɑːr·'neɪ·ʃən] *n* incarnazione *f*; **to be the ~ of sth** essere la personificazione di qc

incautious [ɪn·'kɑː·ʃəs] *adj form* malaccorto, -a

incendiary [ɪn·'sen·die·ri] *adj a. fig* incendiario, -a

incense¹ ['ɪn·sents] *n* incenso *m*

incense² [ɪn·'sents] *vt* fare infuriare

incensed *adj* infuriato, -a

incentive [ɪn·'sen·ʈɪv] *n* incentivo *m*

incentive plan *n* piano *m* incentivi

inception [ɪn·'sep·ʃən] *n* inizio *m*

incertitude [ɪn·'sɜːr·ʈɪ·tuːd] *n* incertezza *f*

incessant [ɪn·'se·snt] *adj* incessante

incest ['ɪn·sest] *n* incesto *m*

incestuous [ɪn·'ses·tʃu·əs] *adj a. fig* incestuoso, -a

inch [ɪntʃ] I. <-es> *n* pollice *m, 2,54 cm;* **she knows every ~ of Miami** conosce Miami come le sue tasche ▶ **give someone an ~ and they'll take a mile** *prov* dai a qualcuno un dito e ti prendono il braccio *prov;* **to do sth ~ by ~** fare qualcosa per gradi II. *vi* muoversi lentamente

◆ **inch forward** *vi* avanzare lentamente

incidence ['ɪn·tsɪ·dənts] *n* incidenza *f;* **there is a higher ~ of left-handedness amongst boys than girls** ci sono più mancini fra i ragazzi che fra le ragazze

incident ['ɪn·tsɪ·dənt] *n* incidente *m;* **an isolated ~** un incidente isolato

incidental [ˌɪn·tsɪ·'den·ʈəl] *adj* **1.** (*related, of lesser importance*) secondario, -a **2.** (*occurring by chance*) accidentale

incidentally *adv* (*by the way*) a proposito

incinerate [ɪn·'sɪ·nə·reɪt] *vt* incenerire

incinerator [ɪn·'sɪ·nə·reɪ·ʈɚ] *n* inceneritore *m*

incipient [ɪn·'sɪ·pi·ənt] *adj* incipiente; **at an ~ stage** ad uno stato incipiente

incise [ɪn·'saɪz] *vt* incidere

incision [ɪn·'sɪ·ʒən] *n* MED incisione *f*

incisive [ɪn·'saɪ·sɪv] *adj* **1.** (*clear*) incisivo, -a; (*penetrating*) penetrante **2.** (*keen, acute: mind*) acuto, -a; (*person*) perspicace

incisor [ɪn·'saɪ·zɚ] *n* incisivo *m*

incite [ɪn·'saɪt] *vt* istigare

incitement [ɪn·'saɪt·mənt] *n* istigazione *f*

incivility [ˌɪn·sɪ·'vɪ·lə·ti] *n form* inciviltà *f*

inclement [ɪn·'kle·mənt] *adj* inclemente

inclination [ˌɪn·klɪ·'neɪ·ʃən] *n* **1.** (*tendency*) propensione *f;* **to have an ~ to do sth** avere voglia di fare qc **2.** (*slope*) inclinazione *f*

incline¹ ['ɪn·klaɪn] *n* inclinazione *f;* (*of hill, mountain*) pendenza *f*

incline² [ɪn·'klaɪn] I. *vi* **1.** (*tend*) essere incline **2.** (*lean*) pendere II. *vt* **1.** (*make sth tend*) propendere; **to ~ (sb) to do sth** indurre(qu) a fare qc **2.** (*make lean*) inclinare

inclined [ɪn·'klaɪnd] *adj* incline; **to be ~ to do sth** essere incline a fare qc

inclose [ɪn·'kloʊz] *vt* (*letter*) allegare

include [ɪn·'kluːd] *vt* includere; (*in a letter*) allegare; **do you ~ that in the service?** è incluso nel servizio?

including [ɪn·'kluː·dɪŋ] *prep* incluso; **~ tax** tasse incluse *fpl;* **not ~ tax, up to and ~ June 6th** fino al 6 giugno compreso

inclusion [ɪn·'kluː·ʒən] *n* inclusione *f*

inclusive [ɪn·'kluː·sɪv] *adj* compreso, -a

incognito [ˌɪn·kɑːg·'niː·toʊ] *adv* in incognito

incoherent [ˌɪn·koʊ·'hɪ·rənt] *adj* incoerente

income ['ɪn·kʌm] *n* reddito *m*

income tax *n* imposta *f* sul reddito; **graduated ~** imposta proporzionale sul reddito

incoming ['ɪn·kʌ·mɪŋ] *adj* (*calls, mail*) in entrata; (*president*) entrante

incommensurate [ˌɪn·kə·'men·sə·ət] *adj* sproporzionato, -a; **to be ~ to** essere sproporzionato

incommunicado [ˌɪn·kə·ˌmjuː·nɪ·'kɑː·doʊ] *adj* irreperibile; **we wanted to invite you to the party, but you were ~** volevamo invitarti alla festa, ma eri sparito

incomparable [ɪn·'kɑːm·prə·bl] *adj* incomparabile

incompatibility [ˌɪn·kəm·ˌpæ·ʈə·'bɪ·lə·ti] <-ies> *n* incompatibilità *f;* **~ with sth** incompatibilità con qc; **Laura left the firm because of her ~ with her colleagues** Laura ha lasciato la ditta perchè non andava d'accordo con i colleghi

incompatible [ˌɪn·kəm·'pæ·ṭə·bl] *adj* incompatibile

incompetence [ɪn·'kɑːm·pə·tənts] *n*, **incompetency** *n* incompetenza *f*

incompetent [ɪn·'kɑːm·pə·tənt] I. *adj* incompetente; **mentally ~** incapace di intendere e di volere; **she was mentally ~ when she wrote the will** non era nel pieno delle sue facoltà quando ha scritto il testamento II. *n* incompetente *mf*

incomplete [ˌɪn·kəm·'pliːt] *adj* incompleto, -a; (*not finished*) incompiuto, -a

incomprehensible [ˌɪn·kɑːm·prɪ·'hen·sə·bl] *adj* incomprensibile

inconceivable [ˌɪn·kən·'siː·və·bl] *adj* inconcepibile

inconclusive [ˌɪn·kən·'kluː·sɪv] *adj* (*result, discussion, evidence*) inconcludente

incongruous [ɪn·'kɑːŋ·grʊ·əs] *adj* 1. (*unsuitable*) poco adatto, -a 2. (*strange*) fuori luogo

inconsequent [ɪn·'kɑːn·sɪ·kwənt] *adj form* (*not important*) irrilevante

inconsequential [ɪn·ˌkɑːn·sɪ·'kwen·ʃl] *adj* 1. (*illogical*) incongruente 2. (*unimportant*) irrilevante

inconsiderable [ˌɪn·kən·'sɪ·drə·bl] *adj* **a not ~ amount** una somma affatto trascurabile

inconsiderate [ˌɪn·kən·'sɪ·də·rət] *adj* (*action, reply*) irriguardoso, -a; **to be inconsiderate to sb** mancare di rispetto a qu

inconsistency [ˌɪn·kən·'sɪs·tən·tsi] <-ies> *n* 1. (*lack of consistency*) incoerenza *f* 2. (*discrepancy*) contraddizione *f*

inconsistent [ˌɪn·kən·'sɪs·tənt] *adj* 1. (*changeable*) incoerente 2. (*lacking agreement*) in contraddizione

inconsolable [ˌɪn·kən·'soʊ·lə·bl] *adj* inconsolabile

inconspicuous [ˌɪn·kən·'spɪ·kjʊ·əs] *adj* poco appariscente; **to be highly ~** passare del tutto inosservato, -a; **to try to look ~** cercare di non farsi notare

inconstant [ɪn·'kɑːns·tənt] *adj* incostante

incontestable [ˌɪn·kən·'tes·tə·bl] *adj form* incontestabile; **it is ~ that ...** è incontestabile che...

incontinent [ɪn·'kɑːn·tə·nənt] *adj* MED incontinente

incontrovertible [ˌɪn·ˌkɑːn·trə·'vɜːr·ṭə·bl] *adj* incontrovertibile; **her logic is ~** la sua logica è incontrovertibile; **~ proof** prova *f* incontrovertibile; **it is ~ that ...** è incontrovertibile che...

inconvenience [ˌɪn·kən·'viː·ni·əns] I. *n* disturbo *m* II. *vt* disturbare

inconvenient [ˌɪn·kən·'viː·ni·ənt] *adj* scomodo, -a; (*time*) inopportuno, -a; **it's a very ~ place to hold the party** è un luogo poco adatto per una festa

incorporate [ɪn·'kɔːr·pə·reɪt] *vt* 1. (*integrate*)

incorporare; (*work into*) incorporare; (*add*) annettere 2. (*include*) includere 3. LAW, ECON costituire; **to ~ a company** costituire una società

incorporation [ɪn·ˌkɔːr·pə·'reɪ·ʃən] *n* 1. (*integration*) incorporazione *f*; (*working into*) incorporamento *m* 2. LAW, ECON costituzione *f*

incorrect [ˌɪn·kə·'rekt] *adj* 1. (*wrong, untrue*) errato, -a; **it would be ~ to say that ...** non sarebbe del tutto corretto dire che... 2. (*improper: behavior*) scorretto, -a

incorrigible [ɪn·'kɔː·rə·dʒə·bl] *adj* incorreggibile

incorruptible [ˌɪn·kə·'rʌp·tə·bl] *adj* incorruttibile

increase¹ ['ɪn·kriːs] *n* aumento *m;* **to be on the ~** essere in aumento

increase² [ɪn·'kriːs] I. *vi* (*become more*) aumentare; (*grow*) crescere; **to ~ dramatically** aumentare notevolmente; **to ~ tenfold/ threefold** aumentare di dieci/tre volte II. *vt* (*make more, larger*) aumentare; (*make stronger*) intensificare

increasing *adj* crescente

increasingly *adv* sempre più

incredible [ɪn·'kre·dɪ·bl] *adj* incredibile

incredibly *adv* (*in an incredible way*) incredibilmente; **~, nobody was hurt** incredibilmente, nessuno è rimasto ferito

incredulity [ˌɪn·krɪ·'duː·lə·ti] *n* incredulità *f*

incredulous [ɪn·'kre·dʒʊ·ləs] *adj* incredulo, -a

increment ['ɪŋ·krə·mənt] *n* incremento *m;* **salary ~** incremento salariale

incremental [ˌɪŋ·krə·'mən·ṭəl] *adj* ECON incrementale

incriminate [ɪn·'krɪ·mɪ·neɪt] *vt* incriminare; **to ~ oneself** autoaccusarsi

incriminating *adj* incriminante

incubate ['ɪn·kjʊ·beɪt] I. *vt* (*eggs, disease*) covare II. *vi* (*eggs*) essere in cova

incubation [ˌɪn·kjʊ·'beɪ·ʃən] *n* incubazione *f*

incubation period *n* periodo *m* di incubazione

incubator ['ɪŋ·kjʊ·beɪ·ṭɚ] *n* incubatrice *f*

inculcate ['ɪn·kʌl·keɪt] *vt* inculcare

incumbent [ɪŋ·'kʌm·bənt] I. *adj* **it is ~ on sb to do sth** è compito di qu fare qc II. *n* titolare *m*

incur [ɪn·'kɜːr] <-rr-> *vt* 1. FIN, ECON (*debt*) contrarre; (*costs*) incorrere in; (*losses*) soffrire 2. (*bring upon oneself*) tirarsi addosso; **to ~ the anger of sb** attirarsi l'ira di qu

incurable [ɪn·'kjʊ·rə·bl] *adj* incurabile; *fig* incorreggibile; **he is an ~ romantic** è un inguaribile romantico

incursion [ɪn·'kɜːr·ʃən] *n* 1. MIL incursione *f* 2. (*intrusion*) irruzione *f*

indebted [ɪn·'de·ṭɪd] *adj* 1. (*obliged*) in debito; **to be ~ to sb** (**for sth**) essere in debito con qu (per qc) 2. (*having debt*) indebitato, -a

indebtedness *n* 1. (*state of obligation*) debito *m* 2. (*state of debt*) indebitamento *m*

indecency [ɪn·'diː·sən·tsi] *n* 1. (*impropriety*) indecenza *f* 2. LAW abuso *m*

indecent [ɪn·'diː··sənt] *adj* indecente
indecipherable [ˌɪn·dɪ·'saɪ·frə·bl] *adj* indecifrabile
indecision [ˌɪn·dɪ·'sɪ·ʒən] *n* indecisione *f*
indecisive [ˌɪn·dɪ·'saɪ·sɪv] *adj* **1.** (*unable to make decisions*) indeciso, -a **2.** (*not clear*) incerto, -a
indeclinable [ɪn·dɪ·'klaɪ·nə·bl] *adj* LING indeclinabile
indecorous [ɪn·'de·kə·rəs] *adj form* (*unsuitable*) sconveniente; (*undignified*) indecoroso, -a
indeed [ɪn·'diːd] **I.** *adv* **1.** (*really*) davvero; **this is good news ~!** questa si che è una buona notizia!; **many people here are very rich ~** molte persone qui sono veramente ricche **2.** (*expresses affirmation*) certamente; **yes, he did ~ say that** si, lo ha proprio detto **II.** *interj* (*to express surprise*) veramente; **she said she won't come! — Won't she, ~!** ha detto che non verrà! — veramente!
indefatigable [ˌɪn·dɪ·'fæ·t̬ɪ·gə·bl] *adj form* instancabile
indefensible [ˌɪn·dɪ·'fen·sə·bl] *adj* (*theory*) insostenibile; (*crime*) ingiustificabile; (*behavior, argument*) MIL indifendibile
indefinable [ˌɪn·dɪ·'faɪ·nə·bl] *adj* indefinibile
indefinite [ɪn·'de·fə·nət] *adj* indefinito, -a; **for an ~ period** per un periodo indefinito
indefinite article *n* LING articolo *m* indeterminativo
indefinitely *adv* (*put off, suspend*) indefinitamente
indelible [ɪn·'de·lə·bl] *adj* indelebile
indemnify [ɪn·'dem·nɪ·faɪ] <-ie-> *vt* **1.** (*insure against damage*) assicurare **2.** (*compensate for damage*) risarcire
indemnity [ɪn·'dem·nə·ti] <-ies> *n form* **1.** (*insurance for damage*) assicurazione *f* **2.** (*compensation*) indennizzo *m* **3.** (*exemption*) esenzione *f*
indent [ɪn·'dent] **I.** *vi* TYPO (*make a space*) rientrare **II.** *vt* intaccare; TYPO far rientrare; **his footsteps ~ed the sand** i suoi passi hanno lasciato impronte sulla sabbia **III.** *n* TYPO rientro *m*
indentation [ˌɪn·den·'teɪ·ʃən] *n* **1.** TYPO rientro *m* **2.** (*notch*) tacca *f*; (*cut*) solco *m*
independence [ˌɪn·dɪ·'pen·dəns] *n* independenza *f*
Independence Day *n* Festa *f* dell'Indipendenza, *il 4 luglio, giorno in cui negli Stati uniti si celebra l'indipendenza delle colonie americane dall'Inghilterra nel 1776*
independent [ˌɪn·dɪ·'pen·dənt] **I.** *adj* indipendente; **to be financially ~** essere economicamente indipendente **II.** *n* POL deputato, -a *m, f* indipendente
in-depth ['ɪn·depθ] *adj* approfondito, -a
indescribable [ˌɪn·dɪ·'skraɪ·bə·bl] *adj* indescrivibile
indestructible [ˌɪn·dɪ·'strʌk·tə·bl] *adj* indistruttibile; **~ waste products** rifiuti *m pl* non

smaltibili
indeterminable [ˌɪn·dɪ·'tɜːr·mɪ·nə·bl] *adj* indeterminabile
indeterminate [ˌɪn·dɪ·'tɜːr·mɪ·nət] *adj* indefinito, -a; **to take an ~ stance** non prendere posizione
index ['ɪn·deks] **I.** *n* **1.** <-es> (*in book*) indice *m*; (*in library*) catalogo *m* **2.** <-ices *o* -es> ECON indice *m*; **the Dow Jones Index** l'indice Dow Jones; **consumer price ~** indice dei prezzi al consumo **3.** <-ices *o* -es> (*indication*) indicazione *f* **4.** <-ices> MATH esponente *m* **II.** *vt* **1.** (*provide with a list*) fornire d'indice **2.** (*enter in a list: word*) inserire in un indice; (*book*) catalogare **3.** ECON indicizzare; **to ~ wages to inflation** adeguare i salari all'inflazione
indexation [ˌɪn·dek·'seɪ·ʃən] *n* ECON indicizzazione *f*
index card *n* scheda *f*
indexer ['ɪn·dek·sə·] *n* classificatore, -trice *m, f*
index finger *n* dito *m* indice
India ['ɪn·di·ə] *n* India *f*
India ink *n* inchiostro *m* di china
Indian ['ɪn·di·ən] **I.** *adj* **1.** (*of India*) indiano, -a **2.** (*of America*) indiano, -a (d'America) **II.** *n* **1.** (*of India*) indiano, -a *m, f* **2.** (*of America*) indiano (d'America), -a *m, f*
Indiana [ˌɪn·di·'æ·nə] *n* Indiana *f*
Indian Ocean *n* Oceano *m* Indiano
Indian summer *n* estate *f* di San Martino
India rubber *n* (*substance*) caucciù *m inv*
indicate ['ɪn·dɪ·keɪt] *vt* indicare; **to ~ (to sb) that ...** fare segno (a qu) che...
indication [ˌɪn·dɪ·'keɪ·ʃən] *n* **1.** (*evidence*) indicazione *f*; **an ~ of willingness** un segnale della volontà **2. a.** MED indicazione *f*
indicative [ɪn·'dɪ·kə·tɪv] **I.** *adj* indicativo, -a **II.** *n* indicativo *m*
indicator ['ɪn·dɪ·keɪ·t̬ə·] *n* indicatore *m*
indices ['ɪn·dɪ·siːz] *n pl of* **index**
indict [ɪn·'daɪt] *vt* **to ~ sb for sth** LAW accusare qu di qc
indictment [ɪn·'daɪt·mənt] *n* **1.** LAW atto *m* d'accusa **2.** *fig* accusa *f*
indie ['ɪn·di] *adj inf* (*album, record company*) indipendente
Indies ['ɪn·diz] *npl* Indie *fpl*; **the West ~** le Indie Occidentali
indifference [ɪn·'dɪf·rəns] *n* indifferenza *f*
indifferent [ɪn·'dɪf·rənt] *adj* **1.** (*not interested*) indifferente **2.** (*neither good nor bad*) mediocre
indigenous [ɪn·'dɪ·dʒɪ·nəs] *adj* indigeno, -a
indigestible [ˌɪn·dɪ·'dʒəs·tə·bl] *adj* **1.** (*food*) indigesto, -a **2.** *fig* incomprensibile
indigestion [ˌɪn·dɪ·'dʒəst·ʃən] *n* indigestione *f*; **to give oneself ~** farsi venire l'indigestione
indignant [ɪn·'dɪg·nənt] *adj* indignato, -a; **to become ~** indignarsi; **to be/feel ~ about sth** essere/sentirsi indignato per qc
indignation [ˌɪn·dɪg·'neɪ·ʃən] *n* indignazione *f*
indignity [ɪn·'dɪg·nə·ti] <-ies> *n* **1.** (*humili-*

ation) umiliazione *f* **2.**(*sth that humiliates*) affronto *m*

indirect [ˌɪn·dɪ·'rekt] *adj* indiretto, -a

indirect object *n* LING complemento *m* indiretto

indiscernible [ˌɪn·dɪ·'sɜː·r·nə·bl] *adj* (*change*) impercettibile; (*reason*) incomprensibile; ~ **to the naked eye** invisibile a occhio nudo

indiscreet [ˌɪn·dɪ·'skriːt] *adj* indiscreto, -a; (*tactless*) privo, -a di tatto

indiscretion [ˌɪn·dɪ·'skre·ʃən] *n* (*lack of discretion, tactfulness*) mancanza *f* indiscrezione; (*act*) indiscrezione *f*

indiscriminate [ˌɪn·dɪ·'skrɪ·mɪ·nət] *adj* indiscriminato, -a

indispensable [ˌɪn·dɪ·'spen·sə·bl] *adj* indispensabile

indisposed [ˌɪn·dɪ·'spoʊzd] *adj* contrario, -a; **to be/feel ~ to do sth** non essere/sentirsi disposto a fare qc

indisposition [ˌɪn·dɪs·pə·'zɪ·ʃən] *n form* **1.**(*illness*) indisposizione *f* **2.**(*disinclination*) indisponibilità *f*

indisputable [ˌɪn·dɪs·'pjuː·tə·bl] *adj* (*skill*) indiscutibile; (*evidence*) inconfutabile

indistinct [ˌɪn·dɪs·'tɪŋkt] *adj* (*shape, voice, words*) indistinto, -a; (*memory, recollection*) confuso, -a

indistinguishable [ˌɪn·dɪ·'stɪŋ·gwɪ·ʃə·bl] *adj* indistinguibile

individual [ˌɪn·dɪ·'vɪ·dʒu·əl] **I.** *n* individuo *m* **II.** *adj* (*separate*) individuale; (*single*) singolo, -a; (*particular*) originale; **an ~ style** uno stile personale

individualize [ˌɪn·dɪ·'vɪ·dʒu·ə·laɪz] *vt* individualizzare

individualism [ˌɪn·dɪ·'vɪ·dʒu·ə·lɪ·zəm] *n* individualismo *m*

individualist *n* individualista *mf*

individualistic [ˌɪn·dɪ·ˌvɪ·dʒu·ə·'lɪs·tɪk] *adj* individualistico, -a

individuality [ˌɪn·dɪ·ˌvɪ·dʒu·'æ·lə·ti] *n* individualità *f*

individually *adv* individualmente

indivisible [ˌɪn·dɪ·'vɪ·zə·bl] *adj* indivisibile

Indochina [ˌɪn·doʊ·'tʃaɪnə] *n* Indocina *f*

indoctrinate [ɪn·'dɑːk·trɪ·neɪt] *vt* indottrinare; **to ~ children in sth** indottrinare i bambini a qc

indoctrination [ɪn·ˌdɑːk·trɪ·'neɪ·ʃən] *n* indottrinamento *m*

indolent ['ɪn·də·lənt] *adj* indolente

indomitable [ɪn·'dɑː·mə·tə·bl] *adj* indomito, -a; **an ~ strength of character** un'indomita forza di carattere

Indonesia [ˌɪn·də·'niː·ʒə] *n* Indonesia *f*

Indonesian **I.** *adj* indonesiano, -a **II.** *n* indonesiano, -a *m, f*

indoor [ˌɪn·'dɔːr] *adj* SPORTS indoor; (*pool*) coperto, -a; ~ **plant** pianta *f* da appartamento

indoors [ˌɪn·'dɔːrz] *adv* dentro (casa)

indubitable [ɪn·'duː·bɪ·tə·bl] *adj form* indubitabile

indubitably [ɪn·'duː·bɪ·tə·b·li] *adv form* indubitabilmente

induce [ɪn·'duːs] *vt* **1.**(*persuade*) a. ELEC, PHYS indurre **2.**(*cause*) provocare

inducement [ɪn·'duːs·mənt] *n* incentivo *m*

induct [ɪn·'dʌkt] *vt* **1.**(*install*) insediare **2.**(*initiate*) iniziare **3.**(*recruit*) arruolare

induction [ɪn·'dʌk·ʃən] *n* **1.**(*installation*) investitura *f*; (*into organization*) insediamento *m* **2.**(*initiation*) avviamento *m* **3.**(*of labor at childbirth*) induzione *f* del parto **4.** PHILOS, ELEC induzione *f*

inductive [ɪn·'dʌk·tɪv] *adj* induttivo, -a

indulge [ɪn·'dʌldʒ] *vt* (*allow*) assecondare; (*desire*) soddisfare; **to ~ oneself in ...** concedersi...

indulgence [ɪn·'dʌl·dʒəns] *n* **1.**(*treat*) lusso *m*; (*satisfaction*) piacere *m*; ~ **in** esagerare con **2.**(*tolerance*) indulgenza *f* **3.** REL indulgenza *f*

indulgent [ɪn·'dʌl·dʒənt] *adj* indulgente

industrial [ɪn·'dʌs·tri·əl] **I.** *adj* industriale; **for ~ use** per uso industriale **II.** *npl* FIN titoli *m pl* industriali

industrialism [ɪn·'dʌs·tri·ə·lɪ·zəm] *n* industrialismo *m*

industrialist *n* industriale *mf*

industrialization [ɪn·ˌdʌs·tri·ə·lɪ·'zeɪ·ʃən] *n* industrializzazione *f*

industrialize [ɪn·'dʌs·tri·ə·laɪz] **I.** *vi* industrializzarsi **II.** *vt* industrializzare

industrial park *n* poligono *m* industriale

Industrial Revolution *n* Rivoluzione *f* Industriale

industrious [ɪn·'dʌs·tri·əs] *adj* laborioso, -a

industry ['ɪn·dəs·tri] *n* **1.**(*manufacturing production*) industria *f*; **heavy/light ~** industria pesante/leggera **2.**<-ies> (*branch*) industria *f* **3.**(*diligence*) laboriosità *f*

inebriate [ɪ·'niː·bri·eɪt] *vt form* inebriare

inedible [ɪn·'e·də·bl] *adj* **1.**(*unsuitable as food*) non commestibile **2.**(*extremely unpalatable*) immangiabile

ineducable [ɪn·'e·dʒʊ·kə·bl] *adj* ineducabile

ineffable [ɪn·'e·fə·bl] *adj* ineffabile

ineffective [ˌɪn·ɪ·'fek·tɪv] *adj* inefficace

ineffectual [ˌɪn·ɪ·'fek·tʃʊ·əl] *adj* (*person*) incapace; (*measures*) inefficace

inefficiency [ˌɪn·ɪ·'fɪ·ʃən·si] *n* inefficenza *f*

inefficient [ˌɪn·ɪ·'fɪ·ʃnt] *adj* inefficente

inelegant [ɪn·'e·lɪ·gənt] *adj* **1.**(*unattractive*) inelegante **2.**(*unrefined*) rozzo, -a; (*gesture, movement*) inelegante

ineligible [ɪn·'e·lɪ·dʒə·bl] *adj* non idoneo, -a; **to be ~ for sth** non avere diritto a qc; **to be ~ to do sth** non essere idoneo a fare qc

inept [ɪ·'nept] *adj* (*unskilled*) inetto, -a; (*inappropriate*) inopportuno, -a; **to be ~ at sth** non avere attitudine per qc; **to be socially ~** non avere abilità sociali

inequality [ˌɪn·ɪ·'kwɑː·lə·ti] <-ies> *n* diseguaglianza *f*

inequitable [ɪn·'ek·wə·tə·bl] *adj* iniquo, -a

inequity [ɪn·ˈek·wə·ti] <-ies> *n* iniquità *f*
ineradicable [ˌɪn·ɪ·ˈræ·dɪ·kə·bl] *adj* inestirpabile
inert [ɪ·ˈnɜːrt] *adj* **1.** *a. fig* (*not moving*) inerte **2.** PHYS inerte
inertia [ɪn·ˈɜːr·ʃə] *n a. fig* inerzia *f*
inescapable [ˌɪn·ɪ·ˈskeɪ·pə·bl] *adj* ineludibile
inessential [ˌɪn·ɪ·ˈsen·ʃl] **I.** *adj* non essenziale **II.** *n* cosa *f* futile
inestimable [ɪn·ˈes·tɪ·mə·bl] *adj* inestimabile; **to be of ~ value** avere un valore inestimabile
inevitable [ɪn·ˈe·vɪ·tə·bl] **I.** *adj* inevitabile **II.** *n* **the ~** l'inevitabile
inexact [ˌɪn·ɪg·ˈzækt] *adj* inesatto, -a
inexcusable [ˌɪn·ɪk·ˈskjuː·zə·bl] *adj* imperdonabile
inexhaustible [ˌɪn·ɪg·ˈzɔːs·tə·bl] *adj* inesauribile
inexorable [ˌɪn·ˈek·sə·rə·bl] *adj form* inesorabile
inexpedient [ˌɪn·ɪk·ˈspiː·di·ənt] *adj form* inopportuno, -a
inexpensive [ˌɪn·ɪk·ˈspen·sɪv] *adj* economico, -a; **to be ~ to do sth** essere poco costoso fare qc
inexperience [ˌɪn·ɪk·ˈspɪ·ri·ənts] *n* inesperienza *f*
inexperienced [ˌɪn·ɪk·ˈspɪ·ri·ənst] *adj* inesperto, -a; **to be ~ with relationships** non avere esperienza di rapporti sentimentali
inexpert [ɪn·ˈeks·pɜːrt] *adj* inesperto, -a; (*attempt*) maldestro, -a
inexplicable [ˌɪn·ək·ˈsplɪ·kə·bl] **I.** *adj* inspiegabile **II.** *n* **the ~** l'inspiegabile
inextricable [ˌɪn·ɪk·ˈstrɪ·kə·bl] *adj* inestricabile
infallible [ɪn·ˈfæ·lə·bl] *adj* infallibile
infamous [ˈɪn·fə·məs] *adj* (*notorious: reputation*) infame; (*person*) famigerato, -a; (*place*) malfamato, -a
infamy [ˈɪn·fə·mi] *n* **1.** <-ies> (*shocking act*) infamia *f* **2.** (*notoriety*) ignominia *f*
infancy [ˈɪn·fən·tsi] *n* infanzia *f*; **from ~** fin da piccolo; **to be in its ~** *fig* essere agli inizi
infant [ˈɪn·fənt] *n* (*very young child*) bambino, -a *m, f*; **a newborn ~** un neonato
infanticide [ɪn·ˈfæn·tə·saɪd] *n* infanticidio *m*
infantile [ˈɪn·fən·taɪl] *adj* infantile
infant mortality *n* mortalità *f* infantile
infantry [ˈɪn·fən·tri] *n* + *sing/pl vb* MIL fanteria *f*
infantryman <-men> *n* MIL soldato *m* di fanteria
infatuated [ɪn·ˈfæ·tʃu·eɪt·ɪd] *adj* infatuato, -a; **to become ~ with sb/sth** infatuarsi di qu/qc
infect [ɪn·ˈfekt] *vt* infettare; *a. fig* (*person*) contagiare
infection [ɪn·ˈfek·ʃən] *n* infezione *f*; *fig* contagio *m*; **risk of ~** rischio *m* di contagio
infectious [ɪn·ˈfek·ʃəs] *adj* (*disease*) infettivo, -a; *a. fig* contagioso, -a
infelicitous [ˌɪn·fɪ·ˈlɪ·sə·təs] *adj iron* (*choice, remark*) infelice
infer [ɪn·ˈfɜːr] <-rr-> *vt* dedurre

inference [ˈɪn·fə·rəns] *n form* **1.** (*conclusion*) conclusione *f*; **to draw the ~ that ...** trarre la conclusione che... **2.** (*process of inferring*) deduzione *f*; **by ~** per deduzione
inferior [ɪn·ˈfɪ·ri·ɚ] **I.** *adj* inferiore **II.** *n* inferiore *mf*
inferiority [ɪn·ˌfɪ·ri·ˈɔː·rə·ti] *n* inferiorità *f*
inferiority complex <-es> *n* complesso *m* di inferiorità
infernal [ɪn·ˈfɜːr·nəl] *adj* infernale
inferno [ɪn·ˈfɜːr·noʊ] *n* (*situation*) inferno *m*; (*fire*) incendio *m* infernale; **the building was an ~** l'edificio era un inferno di fiamme
infertile [ɪn·ˈfɜːr·t̬l] *adj* sterile
infertility [ˌɪn·fɚ·ˈtɪ·lə·ti] *n* sterilità *f*
infest [ɪn·ˈfest] *vt* infestare
infestation [ˌɪn·fes·ˈteɪ·ʃən] *n* infestazione *f*
infidel [ˈɪn·fə·del] *n* infedele *mf*
infidelity [ˌɪn·fə·ˈde·lə·ti] *n* infedeltà *f*
infighting [ˈɪn·faɪ·tɪŋ] *n* lotta *f* intestina
infiltrate [ɪn·ˈfɪl·treɪt] *vt* infiltrarsi in
infiltration [ˌɪn·fɪl·ˈtreɪ·ʃən] *n* infiltrazione *f*
infiltrator *n* infiltrato, -a *m, f*
infinite [ˈɪn·fə·nɪt] *adj* infinito, -a; **with ~ patience** con una pazienza infinita; **to take ~ care** prendersi grande cura
infinitely *adv* infinitamente
infinitesimal [ˌɪn·fɪ·nɪ·ˈte·sɪ·ml] *adj form* infinitesimale
infinitive [ɪn·ˈfɪ·nə·tɪv] LING **I.** *n* infinito *m* **II.** *adj* infinito, -a
infinity [ɪn·ˈfɪ·nə·ti] <-ies> *n* **1.** MATH infinito *m*; **to ~** all' infinito **2.** (*huge amount*) infinità *f*
infirm [ɪn·ˈfɜːrm] *adj* (*ill*) infermo, -a; (*weak*) debole
infirmary [ɪn·ˈfɜːr·mə·ri] <-ies> *n* **1.** (*hospital*) ospedale *m* **2.** (*room*) infermeria *f*
infirmity [ɪn·ˈfɜːr·mə·ti] <-ies> *n* **1.** (*illness*) infermità *f* **2.** (*weakness*) infermità *f*
inflame [ɪn·ˈfleɪm] *vt* **1.** *a.* MED infiammare **2.** (*stir up: anger*) fomentare; (*desire, enthusiasm*) accendere; **to ~ sb with passion** accendere la passione di qu
inflammable [ɪn·ˈflæ·mə·bl] *adj* (*liquid*) infiammabile; (*situation*) esplosivo, -a
inflammation [ˌɪn·flə·ˈmeɪ·ʃən] *n* MED infiammazione *f*
inflammatory [ɪn·ˈflæ·mə·tɔː·ri] *adj* **1.** MED infiammatorio, -a **2.** (*speech*) incendiario, -a
inflatable [ɪn·ˈfleɪ·t̬ə·bl] **I.** *adj* gonfiabile **II.** *n* gommone *m*
inflate [ɪn·ˈfleɪt] **I.** *vt a.* ECON gonfiare **II.** *vi* gonfiarsi
inflated [ɪn·ˈfleɪ·t̬ɪd] *adj* gonfiato, -a
inflation [ɪn·ˈfleɪ·ʃən] *n* inflazione *f*
inflationary *adj* FIN inflazionistico, -a
inflect [ɪn·ˈflekt] *vt* (*verb*) coniugare; (*noun*) declinare; **to ~ one's voice** modulare la propria voce
inflection [ɪn·ˈflek·ʃən] *n* inflessione *f*
inflexibility [ɪn·ˌflek·sə·ˈbɪ·lə·ti] *n* (*of attitude*) inflessibilità *f*; (*of system*) rigidità *f*

I

inflexible [ɪn·'flek·sə·bl] *adj* inflessibile

inflict [ɪn·'flɪkt] *vt* (*wound, damage, punishment*) infliggere

infliction [ɪn·'flɪk·ʃən] *n* inflizione *f*

influence ['ɪn·flʊ·əns] I. *n* influenza *f;* **to exert one's ~** esercitare la propria influenza; **to bring one's ~ to bear on sb** fare pressioni su qu; **to be under the ~** *fig* essere sbronzo; **to drive under the ~** *fig* guidare ubriaco II. *vt* influenzare

influential [ˌɪn·flʊ·'en·ʃl] *adj* influente

influenza [ˌɪn·flʊ·'en·zə] *n* influenza *f*

influx ['ɪn·flʌks] *n* afflusso *m*

inform [ɪn·'fɔːrm] I. *vt* informare; **I'm happy to ~ you that ...** sono lieto di informarLa [*o* informarVi] che...; **to be ~ed about sth** essere informato di qc II. *vi* **to ~ against sb** denunciare qu

informal [ɪn·'fɔːr·ml] *adj* (*tone, manner*) informale; (*person*) alla mano

informality [ˌɪn·fɔːr·'mæ·lə·ti] *n* 1. (*lack of formality*) informalità *f* 2. (*unofficial character*) carattere *m* informale

informant [ɪn·'fɔːr·mənt] *n* informatore, -trice *m, f;* **a reliable ~** una fonte attendibile

information [ˌɪn·fə·'meɪ·ʃən] *n* 1. (*data*) informazioni *fpl;* **a lot of/a little ~** molte/poche informazioni; **to ask for ~** chiedere informazioni; **for further ~** per ulteriori informazioni 2. COMPUT dati *mpl* 3. (*knowledge*) informazioni *fpl* 4. (*inquiry desk*) banco *m* informazioni 5. LAW denuncia *f*

information age *n* era *f* informatica

information science *n* scienze *f pl* dell'informazione

information superhighway *n* autostrada *f* informatica

information technology *n* informatica *f*

informative [ɪn·'fɔːr·mə·tɪv] *adj* istruttivo, -a

informed *adj* informato, -a

informer [ɪn·'fɔːr·mə*] *n* informatore, -trice *m, f*

infotainment ['ɪn·foʊ·teɪn·mənt] *n* infotainment *m inv, l'industria dell'informazione e dell'intrattenimento*

infraction [ɪn·'fræk·ʃən] *n* infrazione *f*

infrared ['ɪn·frə·'red] *adj* infrarosso, -a

infrastructure ['ɪn·frə·ˌstrʌk·tʃə*] *n* infrastruttura *f*

infrequent [ɪn·'friː·k·wənt] *adj* raro, -a

infringe [ɪn·'frɪndʒ] I. *vt* LAW violare; **to ~ sb's right** ledere un diritto di qu II. *vi* **to ~ on** [*o* **upon**] **sth** violare qc

infringement [ɪn·'frɪndʒ·mənt] *n* LAW violazione *f;* (*of a rule*) infrazione *f;* **copyright ~** violazione del copyright; **~ of a law** violazione di una legge

infuriate [ɪn·'fjʊ·ri·eɪt] *vt* fare infuriare

infuse [ɪn·'fjuːz] *vt* 1. (*fill*) infondere; **to ~ sb with courage** infondere coraggio a qu 2. (*tea, herbs*) fare un infuso di

infusion [ɪn·'fjuː·ʒən] *n a.* MED (*drink*) infuso *m;* (*procedure*) infusione; ECON inie-

zione *f*

ingenious [ɪn·'dʒiːn·jəs] *adj* (*creatively inventive*) dotato, -a di inventiva; (*idea, method, plan*) ingegnoso, -a

ingenuity [ˌɪn·dʒɪ·'njuː·ə·ti] *n* ingegnosità *f;* **to use one's ~** usare l'ingegno

ingenuous [ɪn·'dʒen·jʊ·əs] *adj form* 1. (*naive*) ingenuo, -a 2. (*openly honest*) franco, -a

ingest [ɪn·'dʒest] *vt form* ingerire

inglenook ['ɪŋ·gl·nʊk] *n* ARCHIT cantuccio *m* del focolare

inglorious [ɪn·'glɔː·ri·əs] *adj* inglorioso, -a

ingoing ['ɪn·goʊ·ɪŋ] *adj* in entrata

ingot ['ɪŋ·gət] *n* lingotto *m*

ingrained [ˌɪn·'greɪnd] *adj* 1. (*embedded: dirt*) incrostato, -a; **dirt had become ~ in his skin** aveva la pelle incrostata di sporco 2. (*deep-seated*) radicato, -a

ingratiate [ɪn·'greɪ·ʃi·eɪt] *vt* **to ~ oneself with sb** ingraziarsi qu

ingratitude [ɪn·'græ·tə·tuːd] *n* ingratitudine *f*

ingredient [ɪn·'griː·di·ənt] *n* 1. CULIN ingrediente *m* 2. (*component*) *a.* MED componente *m*

ingrowing ['ɪn·groʊ·ɪŋ] *adj* che cresce verso l'interno; **~ toenail** unghia *f* incarnita

ingrown ['ɪn·groʊn] *adj* cresciuto, -a verso l'interno; **~ toenail** unghia *f* incarnita; (*innate*) **~ habits** abitudini *f pl* innate

inhabit [ɪn·'hæ·bɪt] *vt* abitare

inhabitable *adj* abitabile

inhabitant [ɪn·'hæ·bɪ·tənt] *n* abitante *mf*

inhale [ɪn·'heɪl] I. *vt* inspirare; MED inalare II. *vi* inspirare

inhaler [ɪn·'heɪ·lə*] *n* inalatore *m*

inharmonious [ˌɪn·hɑːr·'moʊ·ni·əs] *adj* disarmonico, -a

inhere [ɪn·'hɪr] *vi form* **to ~ in sth/sb** essere inerente a qc/qu

inherent [ɪn·'hɪ·rənt] *adj* inerente; PHILOS intrinseco, -a; **to be ~ in sth** essere inerente a qc

inherit [ɪn·'he·rɪt] I. *vt* ereditare II. *vi* ereditare

inheritable *adj* (*disease*) ereditario, -a

inheritance [ɪn·'he·rɪ·təns] *n a. fig* eredità *f;* **to come into an ~** ereditare

inhibit [ɪn·'hɪ·bɪt] *vt* (*hinder*) impedire; (*impair*) inibire; **to ~ sb from doing sth** impedire a qu di fare qc

inhibition [ˌɪn·ɪ·'bɪ·ʃən] *n* inibizione *f*

inhospitable [ɪn·'hɑːs·pɪ·tə·bl] *adj* (*attitude, place*) inospitale

in-house ['ɪn·haʊs] COM I. *adj* interno, -a II. *adv* in sede

inhuman [ɪn·'hjuː·mən] *adj* (*not human*) inumano, -a

inhumane [ˌɪn·hjuː·'meɪn] *adj* (*cruel*) disumano, -a

inhumanity [ˌɪn·hjuː·'mæ·nə·ti] *n* disumanità *f*

inimical [ɪ·'nɪ·mɪ·kl] *adj form* 1. (*hostile*) ostile; **to be ~ to sth** essere ostile a qc 2. (*harmful*) dannoso, -a

inimitable [ɪ·'nɪ·mɪ·tə·bl] *adj* inimitabile

iniquitous [ɪ·'nɪk·wɪ·təs] *adj* iniquo, -a

iniquity [ɪˈnɪk·wə·t̬i] <-ies> *n* iniquità *f inv*

initial [ɪˈnɪ·ʃəl] **I.** *n* iniziale *f;* **one's ~s** le proprie iniziali **II.** *adj* iniziale; **in the ~ phases** nelle fasi iniziali **III.** <-ll-, -l-> *vt (document)* siglare

initialize [ɪˈnɪ·ʃə·laɪz] *vt* COMPUT inizializzare

initially [ɪˈnɪ·ʃə·li] *adv* all'inizio

initiate [ɪˈnɪ·ʃi·eɪt] **I.** *vt* **1.** *(start)* avviare **2.** *(admit to group)* ammettere **II.** *n* iniziato, -a *m, f*

initiation [ɪˌnɪ·ʃiˈeɪ·ʃən] *n* **1.** *(starting)* avvio *m* **2.** *(introducing)* iniziazione *f;* *(as a member)* ammissione *f*

initiative [ɪˈnɪ·ʃə·t̬ɪv] *n* iniziativa *f;* **to take the ~ in sth** prendere l'iniziativa in qc; **to show ~** mostrare iniziativa; **to use one's ~** usare la propria iniziativa

inject [ɪnˈdʒekt] *vt* **1.** *a.* MED iniettare **2.** *(introduce)* introdurre; *(enthusiasm)* infondere; *(funds, money)* immettere; *(invest)* investire

injection [ɪnˈdʒek·ʃən] *n* iniezione *f*

injudicious [ˌɪn·dʒuːˈdɪ·ʃəs] *adj* sconsiderato, -a

injunction [ɪnˈdʒʌŋk·ʃən] *n a.* LAW ingiunzione *f*

injure [ˈɪn·dʒɚ] *vt* **1.** *(wound)* ferire **2.** *(damage)* danneggiare **3.** *(do wrong to)* offendere

injured *adj* **1.** *(wounded)* ferito, -a **2.** *(damaged)* danneggiato, -a **3.** *(wronged)* offeso, -a

injury [ˈɪn·dʒə·ri] <-ies> *n* **1.** *(physical)* lesione *f,* ferita *f;* **a knee/back ~** una ferita al ginocchio/alla schiena; **to receive an ~** restare ferito **2.** *(psychological)* ferita *f*

injustice [ɪnˈdʒʌs·tɪs] *n* ingiustizia *f;* **you do me an ~** sei ingiusto con me

ink [ɪŋk] **I.** *n* inchiostro *m;* **to write in ~** scrivere con l'inchiostro **II.** *vt* **1.** TYPO inchiostrare **2.** *inf (to sign)* firmare

ink-jet printer *n* stampante *f* a getto d'inchiostro

inkling [ˈɪŋk·lɪŋ] *n* **1.** *(suspicion)* sospetto *m;* **to have an ~ that ...** avere il sospetto che ... **2.** *(hint)* indizio *m*

inkpad [ˈɪŋk·pɑːt] *n* tampone *m* per inchiostro

inky [ˈɪŋ·ki] <-ier, -iest> *adj* **1.** *(stained)* macchiato, -a d'inchiostro **2.** *(black)* nero, -a come l'inchiostro

inlaid [ˈɪn·leɪd] **I.** *vt pt, pp of* **inlay II.** *adj* intarsiato, -a; **~ work** intarsio *m*

inland [ˈɪn·lənd] **I.** *adj* *(not coastal: sea, shipping)* interno, -a; *(town, village)* dell'interno *m* **II.** *adv* **1.** *(direction)* verso l'interno **2.** *(place)* all'interno

in-laws [ˈɪn·lɑːz] *npl* suoceri *mpl*

inlay [ˌɪnˈleɪ] **I.** *n a.* MED intarsio *m* **II.** <inlaid, inlaid> *vt* intarsiare

inlet [ˈɪn·let] *n* **1.** GEO insenatura *f* **2.** TECH entrata *f;* *(pipe)* tubo *m* di entrata

in-line skate *n* pattinaggio *m* in linea

inmate [ˈɪn·meɪt] *n* *(in mental hospital)* paziente *mf;* *(in prison)* detenuto, -a *m, f*

inn [ɪn] *n* locanda *f*

innards [ˈɪn·ɚdz] *npl inf* **1.** *(entrails)* viscere

fpl **2.** TECH ingranaggi *mpl*

innate [ɪˈneɪt] *adj* innato, -a

inner [ˈɪ·nɚ] *adj* **1.** *(located in the interior)* interno, -a **2.** *(deep)* intimo, -a; *(secret)* nascosto, -a; **one's ~ feelings** i sentimenti più intimi di qu

inner city *n* il centro degradato di una città, abitato da poveri ed emarginati

innermost [ˈɪ·nɚ·moʊst] *adj* più intimo, -a; **in his/her ~ being** nel suo intimo

inner tube *n* camera *f* d'aria

inning [ˈɪ·nɪŋ] *n* SPORTS *(part of baseball game)* inning *m inv*

innocence [ˈɪ·nə·sns] *n* innocenza *f;* **to plead one's ~** dichiararsi innocente; **in all ~** in tutta innocenza

innocent [ˈɪ·nə·snt] **I.** *adj* innocente; **to be ~ of a crime** essere innocente di un delitto; **an ~ bystander** un testimone innocente **II.** *n* *(child)* innocente *mf;* *(inexperienced)* sprovveduto, -a *m, f*

innocuous [ɪˈnɑːk·ju·əs] *adj* innocuo, -a

innovate [ˈɪ·nə·veɪt] *vi* innovare

innovation [ˌɪ·nəˈveɪ·ʃən] *n* innovazione *f*

innovative [ˈɪ·nə·veɪ·t̬ɪv] *adj* *(model, product)* innovativo, -a; *(person)* innovatore, -trice

innovator *n* innovatore, -trice *m, f*

innuendo [ˌɪn·juːˈen·doʊ] <-(e)s> *n* **1.** *(insinuation)* insinuazione *f;* **to make an ~ (about sth)** fare un'insinuazione (su qu) **2.** *(suggestive remark)* allusione *f*

innumerable [ɪˈnuː·mə·rə·bl] *adj* innumerabile

innumerate [ɪˈnuː·mə·ət] *adj* **to be ~** non saper far di conto

inoculate [ɪˈnɑːk·jə·leɪt] *vt* **to ~ sb (against sth)** vaccinare qu (contro qc)

inoculation [ɪˌnɑːk·jəˈleɪ·ʃən] *n* vaccinazione *f*

inoffensive [ˌɪn·əˈfen·sɪv] *adj* inoffensivo, -a

inoperable [ˌɪnˈɑː·pɚ·ə·bl] *adj* MED inoperabile; *(law)* inapplicabile

inoperative [ˌɪnˈɑː·pɚ·ə·t̬ɪv] *adj* *(machine)* non funzionante; *(law)* inapplicabile

inopportune [ˌɪn·ˌɑː·pɚˈtuːn] *adj* inopportuno, -a

inordinate [ɪˈnɔːr·dɪ·nət] *adj* smisurato, -a; **an ~ amount of sth** una quantità smisurata di qc

inorganic [ˌɪn·ɔːrˈgæ·nɪk] *adj* inorganico, -a

inpatient [ˈɪn·peɪ·ʃnt] *n* paziente *mf* interno, -a

input [ˈɪn·pʊt] **I.** *n* **1.** *(contribution)* contributo *m* **2.** COMPUT input *m inv* **3.** *(of energy)* **power ~** potenza assorbita **4.** FIN input *m inv* **II.** <-tt-> *vt* COMPUT immettere; *(with a scanner)* acquisire

inquest [ˈɪn·kwest] *n A.LAW* inchiesta *f;* **to hold an ~ (into sth)** svolgere un'inchiesta (su qc)

inquire [ɪnˈkwaɪr] **I.** *vi* **1.** *(ask)* chiedere; **to ~ about sb/sth** chiedere informazioni su qu/qu **2.** *(investigate)* indagare; **to ~ into a matter** indagare su una questione **II.** *vt* chiedere; **to ~ the reason** informarsi sul perchè

inquiry [ɪnˈkwaɪ·ri] *n* **1.**(*question*) domanda *f* **2.**(*investigation*) indagine *f;* **a judicial** ~ un'inchiesta giudiziaria

inquisition [ˌɪn·kwɪˈzɪ·ʃən] *n* **1.**(*questioning*) terzo grado *m inv;* **to subject sb to an** ~ sottoporre qu a un terzo grado **2.** HIST **the Inquisition** l' Inquisizione *f*

inquisitive [ɪnˈkwɪ·zə·tɪv] *adj* **1.**(*curious*) curioso, -a; **to be** ~ **about sth/sb** avere curiosità per qc/qu **2.**(*prying*) ficcanaso

inroad [ˈɪn·roʊd] *n* MIL incursione *f; fig* invasione *f;* **to make** ~**s into sth** (*economy, market*) invadere qc; (*savings*) intaccare qc

inrush [ˈɪn·rʌʃ] <-es> *n* afflusso *m*

insalubrious [ˌɪn·səˈlu:·bri·əs] *adj* insalubre; **an** ~ **climate** un clima insalubre

ins and outs *npl* retroscena *m inv*

insane [ɪnˈseɪn] *adj* (*crazy*) malato, -a di mente; *fig* pazzo, -a; **to be/go** ~ essere/andare fuori di testa

insanitary [ɪnˈsæ·nɪ·te·ri] *adj* antigenico, -a

insanity [ɪnˈsæ·nə·ti] *n* **1.**(*mental illness*) infermità *f* mentale **2.** *a. fig* (*craziness*) follia *f*

insatiable [ɪnˈseɪ·ʃə·bl] *adj* insaziabile

inscribe [ɪnˈskraɪb] *vt* (*write*) iscrivere; (*engrave*) incidere

inscription [ɪnˈskrɪp·ʃən] *n* (*on stone, metal*) iscrizione *f;* (*dedication*) dedica *f*

inscrutable [ɪnˈskru:·t̬ə·bl] *adj* (*look, smile, person*) enigmatico, -a

insect [ˈɪn·sekt] *n* insetto *m;* ~ **bite** puntura *f* d'insetto

insecticide [ɪnˈsek·tɪ·saɪd] *n* insetticida *m*

insecure [ˌɪn·sɪˈkjʊr] *adj* (*person*) insicuro, -a; (*future*) incerto, -a; (*job*) precario, -a; (*structure*) malsicuro, -a

insecurity [ˌɪn·sɪˈkjʊ·rə·ti] <-ies> *n* insicurezza *f*

inseminate [ɪnˈse·mɪ·neɪt] *vt* inseminare

insemination [ɪn·se·mɪˈneɪ·ʃən] *n* inseminazione *f*

insensible [ɪnˈsen·sə·bl] *adj form* **1.**(*unfeeling, indifferent*) insensibile; **to be** ~ **to sth** essere insensibile a qc **2.**(*unaware*) incosciente; **to be** ~ **of sth** non essere cosciente di qc

insensitive [ɪnˈsen·sə·tɪv] *adj* insensibile

inseparable [ɪnˈsep·rə·bl] *adj* inseparabile

insert¹ [ˈɪn·sɜ:rt] *n* **1.**(*page*) inserto *m* **2.**(*piece of material*) inserto *m*

insert² [ɪnˈsɜ:rt] *vt* **1.**(*put into*) inserire **2.**(*add within a text, fill in*) inserire

insertion [ɪnˈsɜ:rˈʃən] *n* **1.**(*act of inserting*) inserimento *m* **2.**(*thing inserted*) inserto *m* **3.**(*in a newspaper*) inserto *m*

in-service [ˈɪn·sɜ:r·vɪs] *adj* (*training*) in servizio

inshore [ˌɪnˈʃɔ:r] **I.** *adj* costiero, -a; ~ **waters** acque *f pl* costiere **II.** *adv* verso la costa

inside [ɪnˈsaɪd] **I.** *adj* **1.**(*internal*) interno, -a; **the** ~ **door** la porta interna **2.**(*from within: information*) confidenziale; **the robbery was an** ~ **job** la rapina è stata realizzata con l'aiuto di un basista **II.** *n* **1.**(*internal part or side*) interno *m;* **on the** ~ all'interno; **to turn sth** ~ **out** rivoltare qc; **to turn the whole room** ~ **out** *fig* mettere una stanza sottosopra; **to know a place** ~ **out** conoscere un posto a menadito; **to know the** ~ **of sth** conoscere i retroscena di qc **2.** *pl, inf* (*entrails*) pancia *f* **III.** *prep* (*within*) ~ (**of**) dentro; **to play** ~ **the house** giocare dentro casa; **to go** ~ **the house** entrare in casa **IV.** *adv* **1.**(*within something*) dentro; **to go** ~ entrare **2.**(*internally*) internamente

insider [ˈɪn·saɪ·də] *n* insider *mf inv*

insidious [ɪnˈsɪ·di·əs] *adj* insidioso, -a

insight [ˈɪn·saɪt] *n* **1.**(*capacity*) perspicacia *f* **2.**(*instance*) intuizione *f;* **to gain** ~ **into sth/sb** capire meglio qc/qu; **the exhibition gave us** ~ **into the 19th century** la mostra ci ha dato un'idea del 19° secolo

insignia [ɪnˈsɪg·ni·ə] *n* insegna *f*

insignificance [ˌɪn·sɪgˈnɪ·fɪ·kəns] *n* insignificanza *f;* **to fade into** ~ perdere importanza

insignificant [ˌɪn·sɪgˈnɪ·fɪ·kənt] *adj* insignificante

insincere [ˌɪn·sɪnˈsɪr] *adj* falso, -a

insinuate [ɪnˈsɪn·ju·eɪt] **I.** *vt* (*imply sth unpleasant*) insinuare **II.** *vr* **to** ~ **oneself into** insinuarsi in

insinuation [ɪn·sɪn·ju·ˈeɪ·ʃən] *n* insinuazione *f*

insipid [ɪnˈsɪ·pɪd] *adj* insipido, -a

insist [ɪnˈsɪst] **I.** *vi* insistere; **to** ~ **on doing sth** ostinarsi a fare qc; **if you** ~ se insisti [*o* se insiste] **II.** *vt* **1.**(*state*) insistere **2.**(*demand*) esigere

insistence [ɪnˈsɪs·təns] *n* insistenza *f;* **her** ~ **on ...** la sua insistenza in ...; **to do sth at sb's** ~ fare qc dietro insistenza di qu

insistent [ɪnˈsɪs·tənt] *adj* insistente; **to be** ~ (**that**) ... insistere (che)...

insofar as [ˌɪn·soʊˈfɑ:r əz] *adv form* per quanto +*subj*

insole [ˈɪn·soʊl] *n* soletta *f*

insolence [ˈɪn·sə·ləns] *n* insolenza *f*

insolent [ˈɪn·sə·lənt] *adj* insolente

insoluble [ɪnˈsɑ:l·jə·bl] *adj* insolubile

insolvency [ɪnˈsɑ:l·vənt·si] *n* insolvenza *f*

insolvent [ɪnˈsɑ:l·vənt] **I.** *adj* insolvente **II.** *n* insolvente *mf*

insomnia [ɪnˈsɑ:m·ni·ə] *n* insonnia *m;* **to suffer from** ~ soffrire d'insonnia

insomniac [ɪnˈsɑ:m·nɪ·æk] *n* insonne *mf*

insomuch as [ˌɪn·soʊˈmʌtʃ] *conj form* **1.**(*because*) dal momento che **2.**(*to the extent that*) tanto che +*subj*

inspect [ɪnˈspekt] *vt* **1.**(*examine carefully*) ispezionare **2.**(*examine officially*) ispezionare; (*tickets, passport*) controllare; **to** ~ **the books** ispezionare i libri contabili **3.** MIL **to** ~ **the troops** passare in rassegna le truppe

inspection [ɪnˈspek·ʃən] *n* ispezione *f;* MIL rassegna *f*

inspector [ɪnˈspek·tər] *n* ispettore, -trice *m, f;*

ticket ~ controllore, -a *m, f*
inspiration [ˌɪn·spə·ˈreɪ·ʃən] *n* **1.** MED inspirazione *f* **2.** (*source*) ispirazione *f;* **to provide the ~ for sth** servire da ispirazione per qc; **to lack ~** essere privo, -a di ispirazione
inspire [ɪn·ˈspaɪr] *vt* **1.** (*stimulate*) ispirare; **to ~ sb with hope** infondere speranza a qu **2.** (*cause, lead to*) stimolare
inspired *adj* ispirato, -a
instability [ˌɪn·stə·ˈbɪ·lə·ti] *n* instabilità *f*
instal <-ll->, **install** [ɪn·ˈstɔːl] I. *vt* **1.** *a.* TECH, COMPUT installare **2. to ~ sb** insediare qu II. *vr* **to ~ oneself** piazzarsi
installation [ˌɪn·stə·ˈleɪ·ʃən] *n* installazione *f*
installment *n*, **instalment** [ɪn·ˈstɔːl·mənt] *n* **1.** RADIO, TV puntata *f* **2.** COM rata *f;* **to pay (for sth) in ~s** pagare (qc) a rate; **to be payable in monthly ~s** essere pagabile in rate mensili
installment plan *n* pagamento *m* rateale
instance [ˈɪn·stəns] I. *n* **1.** (*case*) caso *m;* **in this ~** in questo caso; **for ~** per esempio; **in the first ~** in primo luogo; **in the second ~** in secondo luogo **2.** *form.* (*request*) istanza *f;* (*order*) richiesta *f;* **to do sth at sb's ~** fare qualcosa su richiesta di qu II. *vt* portare l'esempio
instant [ˈɪn·stənt] I. *n* istante *m;* **at the same ~** contemporaneamente; **for an ~** per un momento; **in an ~** in un istante; **to do sth this ~** fare qc immediatamente II. *adj* **1.** (*immediate*) immediato, -a **2.** CULIN istantaneo, -a; **~ coffee** caffè *m* istantaneo; **~ soup** minestra *f* pronta **3.** *liter.* (*urgent*) urgente
instantaneous [ˌɪn·stən·ˈteɪ·ni·əs] *adj* istantaneo, -a
instantaneously *adv* istantaneamente
instantly [ˈɪn·stənt·li] *adv* all'istante
instant replay *n* (*action replay*) replay *m inv*
instead [ɪn·ˈsted] I. *adv* invece II. *prep* **~ of** invece di; **~ of him** al posto suo; **~ of doing sth** invece di fare qc
instep [ˈɪn·step] *n* (*part of foot, shoe*) collo
instigate [ˈɪn·stɪ·geɪt] *vt* (*laws, proceedings*) promuovere; (*rebellion*) istigare a
instigation [ˌɪn·stɪ·ˈgeɪ·ʃən] *n* istigazione *f;* **to do sth at the ~ of sb** fare qc su istigazione di qu
instil [ɪn·ˈstɪl] <-ll-> *vt*, **instill** *vt* **to ~ sth (into sb)** instillare qc (in qu)
instinct [ˈɪn·stɪŋkt] *n* istinto *m;* **to do sth by ~** fare qc d'istinto; **a business/political ~** istinto per gli affari/la politica
instinctive [ɪn·ˈstɪŋk·tɪv] *adj* istintivo, -a
institute [ˈɪn·stɪ·tuːt] I. *n* istituto *m* II. *vt form.* **1.** (*establish: system, reform*) istituire **2.** (*initiate: steps, measures*) intraprendere; (*legal action*) intentare
institution [ˌɪnt·stɪ·ˈtuː·ʃən] *n* **1.** (*act*) istituzione *f* **2.** (*society*) istituzione *f* **3.** (*home*) istituto *m* **4.** *inf* (*person*) istituzione *f*
institutional [ˌɪnt·stɪ·ˈtuː·ʃə·nəl] *adj* istituzionale
institutionalize [ˌɪnt·stɪ·ˈtuː·ʃə·nə·laɪz] *vt*

(*procedure*) istituzionalizzare; (*person*) mettere in un istituto
in-store [ˌɪn·ˈstɔːɐ] *adj* all'interno di un grande magazzino; **~ detective** addetto, -a alla sicurezza in un grande magazzino *m*
instruct [ɪn·ˈstrʌkt] *vt* **1.** (*teach*) istruire **2.** (*order*) dare ordini; (*give instructions*) dare istruzioni; **to ~ sb (to do sth)** ordinare a qu (di fare qc) **3.** LAW dare l'incarico a
instruction [ɪn·ˈstrʌk·ʃən] *n* **1.** (*teaching*) istruzione *f;* **to give sb ~ in sth** insegnare qc a qu **2.** (*order*) istruzione *f;* **to give sb ~s** dare istruzioni a qu; **to act on ~s** agire dietro istruzioni; **to carry out ~s** eseguire le istruzioni **3.** *pl* (*information on method*) istruzioni *fpl*
instruction manual *n* manuale *m* di istruzioni
instructive [ɪn·ˈstrʌk·tɪv] *adj* istruttivo, -a
instructor [ɪn·ˈstrʌk·tɚ] *n* **1.** (*teacher*) istruttore, -trice *m, f;* **driving ~** istruttore, -trice *m, f* di scuola guida; **ski ~** maestro, -a *m, f* di sci **2.** UNIV assistente *mf*
instrument [ˈɪn·strə·mənt] *n* **1.** MUS strumento *m* **2.** (*tool*) strumento *m* **3.** LAW (*document*) atto *m*
instrumental [ˌɪn·strə·ˈmen·t̬l] I. *adj* **1.** MUS strumentale **2.** (*greatly influential*) **to be ~ to sth** contribuire fattivamente a qc; **to be ~ in doing sth** giocare un ruolo chiave in qc **3.** (*relating to tools*) strumentale II. *n* MUS pezzo *m* strumentale
instrumentation [ˌɪn·strə·men·ˈteɪ·ʃən] *n* MUS strumentazione *f*
instrument board *n*, **instrument panel** *n* AUTO quadro *m* strumenti; AVIAT, NAUT pannello *m* dei comandi
insubordinate [ˌɪn·sə·ˈbɔːr·də·nɪt] *adj* insubordinato, -a; **~ behavior** comportamento *m* insubordinato
insubstantial [ˌɪn·səb·ˈstæn·ʃl] *adj* **1.** (*lacking substance: meal*) poco sostanzioso, -a; (*structure*) poco solido, -a **2.** (*lacking significance*) insignificante **3.** (*not real: vision*) incorporeo, -a
insufferable [ɪn·ˈsʌf·rə·bl] *adj* (*person*) insopportabile; (*behavior*) intollerabile; **to be ~** insopportabile
insufficiency [ˌɪn·sə·ˈfɪ·ʃən·tsi] <-ies> *n* insufficienza *f*
insufficient [ˌɪn·sə·ˈfɪ·ʃənt] *adj* insufficiente
insular [ˈɪnt·sə·lɚ] *adj* **1.** GEO insulare **2.** (*person*) provinciale
insularity [ˌɪnt·sə·ˈle·rə·ti] *n* **1.** GEO insularità *f* **2.** (*of person*) provincialismo *m*
insulate [ˈɪnt·sə·leɪt] *vt* isolare; **to ~ sth (against sth)** isolare qc (contro qc)
insulating [ˈɪn·sju·leɪ·t̬ɪŋ] *adj* isolante
insulation [ˌɪnt·sə·ˈleɪ·ʃən] *n* isolamento *m*
insulin [ˈɪnt·sə·lɪn] *n* insulina *f*
insult I. [ɪn·ˈsʌlt] *vt* insultare II. [ˈɪn·sʌlt] *n* insulto *m* ► **to add ~ to injury ... ...:** oltre al danno anche la beffa ...
insuperable [ɪn·ˈsuː·pə·rə·bl] *adj* insuperabile
insupportable [ˌɪn·sə·ˈpɔːr·t̬ə·bl] *adj form.*

insopportabile

insurance [ɪn·ˈʃʊ·rəns] *n* **1.** (*financial protection*) assicurazione *f;* **life** ~ assicurazione sulla vita; **to have** ~ (**against sth**) avere un'assicurazione (contro qc); **to take out** ~ (**against sth**) assicurarsi (contro qc) **2.** (*payment*) assicurazione *f;* (*premium*) assicurazione *f* **3.** (*measure*) protezione *f*

insurance policy <-ies> *n* polizza *f* d'assicurazione

insure [ɪn·ˈʃʊr] *vt* assicurare

insured [ɪn·ˈʃʊrd] **I.** *adj* assicurato, -a **II.** *n* **the** ~ l'assicurato, -a *m, f*

insurer [ɪn·ˈʃʊ·rɚ] *n* **1.** (*agent*) assicuratore, -trice *m, f* **2.** (*company*) assicurazione *f*

insurmountable [ˌɪn·sɚ·ˈmaʊn·t̬ə·bl] *adj* insormontabile

insurrection [ˌɪn·sə·ˈrek·ʃən] *n* insurrezione *f;* **to crush the** ~ soffocare un'insurrezione

intact [ɪn·ˈtækt] *adj* intatto, -a

intake [ˈɪn·teɪk] *n* **1.** TECH (*mechanical aperture*) aspirazione *f;* **fuel** ~ presa del carburante **2.** (*action of taking in: of water*) entrata *f;* (*of air*) aspirazione *f* **3.** (*amount taken in*) consumo *m;* **the recommended daily** ~ **of fiber** il consumo giornaliero raccomandato di fibre; **food** ~ razione *f* di cibo

intangible [ɪn·ˈtæn·dʒə·bl] **I.** *adj* impalpabile; ~ **assets** attività *f pl* immateriali **II.** *n* cosa *f* intangibile

integer [ˈɪn·t̬ɪ·dʒɚ] *n* MATH numero *m* intero

integral [ˈɪn·t̬əg·rəl] *adj* **1.** (*central, essential*) **to be** ~ **to sth/sb** essere parte integrante di qc; **to be** ~ **to sb** essere di vitale importanza per qu **2.** (*complete*) integrale **3.** MATH ~ **calculus** calcolo *m* integrale

integrate [ˈɪn·t̬ə·ɡreɪt] **I.** *vt* (*cause to merge socially*) **to** ~ **sb/sth into sth** integrare qu/qc in qc; **to** ~ **oneself into sth** integrarsi in qc; **to** ~ **learning with playing** combinare apprendimento e gioco **II.** *vi* integrarsi

integrated [ˈɪn·t̬ɪ·ɡreɪ·t̬ɪd] *adj* **1.** (*coordinating different elements*) integrato, -a **2.** (*with different ethnic groups*) ~ **school** scuola *f* multietnica

integration [ˌɪn·t̬ə·ˈɡreɪ·ʃən] *n a.* MAT integrazione *f*

integrity [ɪn·ˈte·ɡrə·t̬i] *n* **1.** (*incorruptibility, uprightness*) integrità *f;* **a man of** ~ un uomo integro; **professional** ~ integrità professionale *f* **2.** *form* (*unity, wholeness*) integrità *f*

intellect [ˈɪn·t̬ə·lekt] *n* **1.** (*faculty*) inteletto *m;* **a man/woman of** ~ un uomo/una donna di grande intelligenza; **powers of** ~ capacità *f* intellettuali **2.** (*thinker, intellectual*) intellettuale *mf*

intellectual [ˌɪn·t̬ə·ˈlek·tʃʊ·əl] **I.** *n* intellettuale *mf* **II.** *adj* intellettuale

intelligence [ɪn·ˈte·lɪ·dʒəns] *n* **1.** (*cleverness*) intelligenza *f;* **artificial** ~ intelligenza artificiale **2.** (*information*) intelligence *f inv;* **the** ~ **community** i servizi segreti, *agenzie e organizzazioni governative che espletano attività di*

intelligence *per il governo degli Stati Uniti;* ~ **sources** fonti *f pl* dell'intelligence

intelligence quotient *n* quoziente *m* d'intelligenza

intelligence test *n* esame *m* d'intelligenza

intelligent [ɪn·ˈte·lɪ·dʒənt] *adj* intelligente

intelligentsia [ɪn·ˌte·lɪ·ˈdʒen·tsi·ə] *n* **the** ~ l'intellighenzia *f*

intelligible [ɪn·ˈte·lɪ·dʒə·bl] *adj* intellegibile; **this text is hardly** ~ questo testo si capisce a mala pena

intend [ɪn·ˈtend] *vt* **1.** (*aim for, plan*) **to** ~ **to do sth** avere l'intenzione di fare qc; **I'm sure that remark was** ~**ed for me** sono sicuro che quell'osservazione era diretta a me; **I** ~**ed no harm** non volevo fare del male **2.** (*mean*) intendere **3.** (*earmark, destine*) **to be** ~**ed for sth** essere destinato a qc; **to be** ~**ed to do sth** essere destinato a fare qc; **this film is not** ~**ed for children** questo non è un film per bambini

intended [ɪn·ˈten·dɪd] **I.** *adj* **1.** (*planned, intentional*) programmato, -a; (*sought*) voluto, -a **2.** (*husband, wife*) futuro, -a **II.** *n inf* promesso sposo *m,* promessa sposa *f*

intense [ɪn·ˈtents] *adj* **1.** (*acute, concentrated, forceful*) intenso, -a **2.** (*demanding*) impegnativo, -a

intensify [ɪn·ˈten·tsɪ·faɪ] <-ie-> **I.** *vt* (*fighting*) intensificare; (*joy, sadness*) aumentare; (*pain*) acuire **II.** *vi* (*fighting*) intensificarsi; (*joy, sadness*) aumentare; (*pain*) acuirsi

intensity [ɪn·ˈten·tsə·t̬i] *n* intensità *f*

intensive [ɪn·ˈtent·sɪv] *adj* intensivo, -a

intensive care *n* terapia *f* intensiva

intent [ɪn·ˈtent] **I.** *n* intento *m;* **a declaration of** ~ una dichiarazione di intenti; **to all** ~**s and purposes** a tutti gli effetti; **with** ~ **to** con lo scopo di; **with good/evil** ~ con buone/cattive intenzioni **II.** *adj* **1.** (*absorbed, concentrated, occupied*) intento, -a; **to be** ~ **on sth** essere intento a qc **2.** (*decided, set*) intenzionato, -a; **to be/seem** ~ **on doing sth** essere/sembrare intenzionato a fare qc

intention [ɪn·ˈtent·ʃən] *n* intenzione *f;* **it is my** ~ **to ...** ho intenzione di...; **to have no** ~ **of doing sth** non avere nessuna intenzione di fare qc; **with the best of** ~**s** con le migliori intenzioni

intentional [ɪn·ˈtent·ʃə·nəl] *adj* intenzionale; (*insult*) deliberato, -a

interact [ɪn·t̬ɚ·ˈækt] *vi* interagire

interaction [ˌɪn·t̬ɚ·ˈæk·ʃən] *n* interazione *f;* **nonverbal** ~ comunicazione *f* non verbale

interactive [ˌɪn·t̬ɚ·ˈæk·tɪv] *adj* interattivo, -a

interactive TV [ˌɪn·t̬ɚ·æk·tɪv·tiː·ˈviː] *n* televisione *f* interattiva

interbreed [ˌɪn·t̬ɚ·ˈbriːd] *irr* **I.** *vt* incrociare **II.** *vi* incrociarsi

intercede [ˌɪn·t̬ɚ·ˈsiːd] *vi* intercedere; **to** ~ **for/on behalf of sb** intercedere per/a favore di qu

intercept [ˌɪn·t̬ɚ·ˈsept] *vt a.* MAT intercettare; **to** ~ **sb** bloccare la strada a qu

interception [ˌɪn·t̬ə·'sep·ʃən] *n* **1.**(*act of intercepting*) intercettazione *f;* MATH intersezione *f* **2.** SPORTS (*football play*) intercettazione

interceptor [ˌɪn·t̬ə·'sep·t̬ə] *n* MIL intercettore *m*

intercession [ˌɪn·t̬ə·'se·ʃən] *n* intercessione *f;* **through the ~ of sb/sth** grazie all'intercessione di qu/qc; **the ~ of human rights organizations** la mediazione delle organizzazioni per i diritti umani

interchange [ˌɪn·t̬ə·'tʃeɪndʒ] I. *n* **1.**(*exchange*) interscambio *m;* **~ of ideas** interscambio *m* d'idee **2.** (*of roads*) svincolo *m* II. *vt* **1.**(*exchange: ideas, knowledge*) scambiarsi; COMPUT (*data*) scambiare **2.**(*switch one for another: player*) sostituire; (*product*) scambiare **3.**(*alternate*) alternare; **to ~ terms** utilizzare termini in maniera interscambiabile

interchangeable [ˌɪn·t̬ə·'tʃeɪn·dʒə·bl] *adj* intercambiabile

interchangeably *adv* in modo intercambiabile

intercom ['ɪn·t̬ə·kɑːm] *n* (*on a plane or ship*) interfono *m;* (*in a building*) citofono *m;* **through** (**an**) **~** per interfono; **to speak over the ~** parlare all'interfono

intercommunicate [ˌɪn·t̬ə·kə·'mjuː·nɪ·keɪt] *vi* essere intercomunicante

intercontinental [ˌɪn·t̬ə·ˌkɑːn·t̬ə·'nen·t̬l] *adj* intercontinentale; **~ flight** volo *m* intercontinentale

intercourse ['ɪn·t̬ə·kɔːrs] *n* **1.** **sexual ~** rapporti *m* sessuali *pl;* **to have sexual ~ with sb** avere rapporti sessuali con qu **2.** *form* **social ~** rapporti *m* sociali *pl;* **commercial ~** relazioni *f pl* commerciali

interdenominational [ˌɪn·t̬ə·dɪ·ˌnɑː·mə·'neɪ·ʃə·nl] *adj* interconfessionale

interdepartmental ['ɪn·t̬ə·ˌdiː·pɑːrt·'men·t̬l] *adj* interdipartimentale

interdependence [ˌɪn·t̬ə·diː·'pen·dəns] *n* interdipendenza *f*

interdependent [ˌɪn·t̬ə·diː·'pen·dənt] *adj* interdipendente

interdict [ˌɪn·t̬ə·'dɪkt] *n* LAW interdizione *f*

interest ['ɪn·trɪst] I. *n* **1.**(*hobby*) interesse *m;* **to take an ~ in sth** interessarsi a qc **2.**(*curiosity*) **just out of ~** *inf* per curiosità; **to lose ~ in sb/sth** perdere interesse in qu/qc; **to take no further ~ in sth** perdere interesse in qc **3.** *pl* (*profit, advantage*) interesse *m;* **a conflict of ~ s** un conflitto di interessi; **to look after the ~ s of sb** badare agli interessi di qu; **to pursue one's own ~ s** fare i propri interessi; **in the ~ of liberty** nell'intersse della libertà; **it's in your own ~ to do it** è nel tuo interesse farlo **4.**(*power to excite attentiveness*) interesse *m;* **to be of ~ for sb** interessare qu; **this might be of ~ to you** questo potrebbe interessarti; **this is of no ~ to me** questo non mi interessa **5.** FIN interesse *m;* **~ rate** tasso *m* di interesse; **at 5% ~** con un interesse del 5%; **to bear ~** maturare interessi; **to earn/pay ~ on sth** percepire/pagare gli interessi su qc; **to pay back with ~** *a.fig* restituire con gli interessi **6.**(*legal right*) partecipazione *f;* **to have an ~ in sth** avere una partecipazione in qc; **to have a controlling ~ in a firm** avere una partecipazione di controllo in un'impresa; **business ~ s** interessi *m pl* commerciali; **crude oil ~ s** interessi *m pl* petroliferi; **vested ~ s** interessi *m pl* acquisiti II. *vt* interessare; **may I ~ you in this encyclopedia?** potrebbe interessarLe questa enciclopedia?

interested ['ɪn·trɪs·tɪd] *adj* interessato, -a; **to be ~ in sth/sb** interessarsi a qc/qu; **I am ~ to know more about it** mi interesserebbe saperne di più; **the ~ parties** le parti interessate

interest-free *adj* FIN senza interessi

interesting ['ɪn·trəs·'tɪŋ] *adj* interessante; **it is ~ to do sth** è interessante fare qc

interface [ˌɪn·t̬ə·feɪs] I. *n a.* PHYS, INFOR interfaccia *f;* **user ~** interfaccia utente; **graphic/parallel/serial ~** interfaccia grafica/parallelo/seriale II. *vi* COMPUT **to ~ with sth** connettersi con III. *vt* COMPUT interfacciare

interfere [ˌɪn·t̬ə·'fɪr] *vi* **1.**(*become involved*) immischiarsi; **to ~ between two people** intromettersi fra due persone; **to ~ in sth** intromettersi in qc **2.**(*disturb*) disturbare **3.** **to ~ with sth** (*touch*) armeggiare con qc; **someone has been interfering with my papers** qualcuno ha toccato le mie carte **4.** RADIO, TECH (*hamper signals*) interferire **5.** SPORTS (*get in way*) effettuare un intervento

interference [ˌɪn·t̬ə·'fɪ·rəns] *n* **1.**(*hindrance*) intromissione *f* **2.** RADIO, TECH interferenza *f* **3.** SPORTS intervento *m;* (*in American football*) interferenza *f*

interim ['ɪn·t̬ə·ɪm] I. *n* interim *m inv* II. *adj* (*administration, government*) provvisorio, -a; (*payment*) intermedio, -a; **~ dividend** FIN dividendo *m* provvisorio; **~ coach/manager** allenatore/direttore ad interim

interior [ɪn·'tɪ·ri·ə] I. *adj* **1.**(*inner, inside, internal*) interno, -a; (*lighting*) d'interni **2.**(*central, inland, remote*) dell'interno II. *n* **1.**(*inside*) interno *m;* **the ~ of the country** l'interno del paese **2.** POL (*home affairs*) **the U.S. Department of the Interior** il Ministero degli Interni degli Stati Uniti

interior decoration *n* decorazione *f* d'interni

interior designer *n* arredatore, -trice d'interni *mf*

interject [ˌɪn·t̬ə·'dʒekt] *vt form* interloquire; **to ~ a few remarks** interrompere con delle osservazioni

interjection [ˌɪn·t̬ə·'dʒek·ʃən] *n* **1.** *form* (*verbal interruption*) interruzione *f;* **~ s from the audience** interruzioni *f pl* del pubblico **2.** LING interiezione *f*

interlace [ˌɪn·t̬ə·'leɪs] I. *vt* intrecciare II. *vi* intrecciarsi

interlibrary loan [ɪn·t̬ə·'laɪ·brə·rɪ·ˌləʊn] *n* prestito *m* interbibliotecario

interlocutor [ˌɪn·t̬ə·'lɑːk·jə·t̬ə] *n form* interlocutore, -trice *m, f*

interloper ['ɪn·tə·lou·pə] *n* intruso, -a *m, f*

interlude ['ɪn·tə·lu:d] *n* **1.** (*interval*) intervallo *m;* **a romantic** ~ un interludio romantico **2.** THEAT (*intermission*) intervallo *m;* (*short play*) interludio *m* **3.** MUS interludio *m*

intermarry ['ɪn·tə·me·ri] <-ie-> *vi* sposarsi, *con un consanguineo o con persona di diversa razza, religione o ceto sociale*

intermediary [ˌɪn·tə·'mi:·die·ri] **I.** *adj* (*between persons*) intermediario, -a; (*intermediate*) intermedio, -a **II.**<-ies> *n* intermediario, -a *m, f*

intermediate [ˌɪn·tə·'mi:·di·ət] **I.** *adj* intermedio, -a; ~ **course** corso *m* intermedio; ~ **students** studenti *m pl* di scuola media; ~ **memory** COMPUT memoria *f* intermedia **II.** *n* intermediario, -a *m, f*

intermezzo [ˌɪn·tə·'met·sou] <-s *o* -zi> *n* MUS intermezzo *m*

interminable [ɪn·'tɜ:r·mɪ·nə·bl] *adj* interminabile

intermission [ˌɪn·tə·'mɪ·ʃən] *n* **1.** interruzione *m;* **without** ~ senza pausa **2.** CINE, THEAT intervallo *m*

intermittent [ˌɪn·tə·'mɪ·tnt] *adj* intermittente; ~ **fever** febbre *f* intermittente

intern[1] ['ɪn·tɜ:rn] *n* tirocinante *mf;* **hospital** ~ medico *m* tirocinante; **she worked for the Washington Post as a summer** ~ durante l'estate ha lavorato come stagista presso il Washington Post

intern[2] [ɪn·'tɜ:rn] **I.** *vt* internare **II.** *vi* SCHOOL fare il tirocinio; MED fare l'internato

internal [ɪn·'tɜ:r·nl] *adj a.* MED interno, -a; **for use only** solo per uso interno; **Internal Revenue Service** *Agenzia delle Entrate del Ministero delle Finanze degli Stati Uniti*

international [ˌɪn·tə·'næʃ·nəl] **I.** *adj a.* LAW internazionale **II.** *n* POL Internazionale *f*

international date line *n* linea *f* del cambiamento di data

internationalize [ˌɪn·tə·'næ·ʃə·nə·laɪz] *vt* internazionalizzare

International Monetary Fund *n* Fondo *m* Monetario Internazionale

International Olympic Committee *n* Comitato *m* Olimpico Internazionale

internee [ˌɪn·tɜ:r·'ni:] *n* internato, -a *m, f*

Internet ['ɪn·tə·net] *n* COMPUT Internet *f;* **to access the** ~ entrare in Internet; **to do business over the** ~ fare affari in Internet

Internet café *n* Internet caffè *m*

Internet service provider *n* provider *m inv*

internist [ɪn·'tɜ:r·nɪst] *n* internista *mf*

internment [ɪn·'tɜ:rn·mənt] *n* internamento *m*

internment camp *n* campo *m* di internamento

internship *n* internato *m*

interoffice *adj* interno (all'ufficio); ~ **memo** promemoria interno

interpersonal *adj* interpersonale

interplanetary [ˌɪn·tə·'plæ·nə·te·ri] *adj* interplanetario, -a

interplay ['ɪn·tə·pleɪ] *n* interazione *f*

Interpol ['ɪn·tə·pɑ:l] *n abbr of* **International Criminal Police Organization** Interpol *f*

interpret [ɪn·'tɜ:r·prət] **I.** *vt* **1.** (*decode, construe*) interpretare **2.** (*translate*) tradurre **II.** *vi* fare da interprete; **to** ~ **from English into Spanish** tradurre dall'inglese allo spagnolo

interpretation [ɪn·ˌtɜ:r·prə·'teɪ·ʃən] *n* interpretazione *f;* **to give an** ~ **of sth** dare un'interpretazione di qc; **the rules are open to** ~ le regole possono essere interpretate in modi diversi

interpreter [ɪn·'tɜ:r·prə·tə] *n* **1.** *a.* MUS, THEAT interprete *mf* **2.** COMPUT interprete *m*

interpreting [ɪn·'tɜ:r·prə·tɪŋ] *n* interpretazione *f*

interrelate [ˌɪn·tə·ɪ·'leɪt] *vi* essere collegato; **to** ~ **with each other** essere in correlazione

interrogate [ɪn·'te·rə·geɪt] *vt* interrogare

interrogation [ɪn·ˌte·rə·'geɪ·ʃən] *n* **1.** *a.* INFOR interrogazione *f* **2.** LAW interrogatorio *m;* **police** ~ interrogatorio di polizia; ~ **room** sala *f* interrogatoria

interrogative [ˌɪn·tə·'rɑ:·gə·tɪv] **I.** *n* LING (*word*) parola *f* interrogativa; (*sentence*) frase *f* interrogativa **II.** *adj* **1.** *liter* (*having questioning form*) interrogativo, -a **2.** LING interrogativo, -a

interrogator [ɪn·'te·rə·geɪ·tər] *n* interrogatore, -trice *m, f*

interrogatory [ˌɪn·tə·'rɑ:·gə·tɔ:·ri] **I.** *adj* interrogatorio, -a **II.**<-ies> *n* interrogatorio *m*

interrupt [ˌɪn·tə·'rʌpt] *vi, vt* interrompere

interrupter [ˌɪn·tə·'rʌp·tə] *n* ELEC interruttore *m*

interruption [ˌɪn·tə·'rʌp·ʃən] *n* interruzione *f;* **without** ~ senza interruzioni

intersect [ˌɪn·tər·'sekt] **I.** *vt* (*cross at a junction*) incrociare; (*lines*) intersecare **II.** *vi* **1.** (*cut, divide*) intersecare *form;* (*cross at a junction*) incrociarsi; ~**ing roads** strade *f pl* che si intersecano **2.** MATH (*sets*) intersecarsi

intersection [ˌɪn·tər·'sek·ʃən] *n* **1.** (*crossing of lines*) intersezione *f* **2.** AUTO incrocio *m*

intersession *n* UNIV pausa *f* tra il primo e il secondo semestre, *all'università*

intersperse [ˌɪn·tə·'spɜ:rs] *vt* inframmezzare; **to** ~ **sth with sth** inframmezzare qc di qc; **to** ~ **sth between sth** cospargere qc fra qc; **to** ~ **anecdotes throughout a speech** costellare un discorso di aneddoti

interstate ['ɪn·tə·steɪt] *adj* interestatale, *che attraversa vari stati degli USA;* ~ **trade** commercio *m* interstatale, *fra vari stati americani*

interstate (**highway**) *n* autostrada *f* interstatale

interstellar [ˌɪn·tə·'ste·lə] *adj form* interestellare

interstice [ɪn·'tɜ:r·stɪs] *n form* interstizio *m*

intertwine [ˌɪn·tə·'twaɪn] **I.** *vt* intrecciare **II.** *vi* (*flowers, hands*) intrecciarsi; (*paths*) incrociarsi

interurban [ˌɪn·tə·'ɜ:r·bən] *adj* interurbano, -a

interval ['ɪn· t̬ə·ˌvl] *n a.* MUS intervallo *m;* **at ~s of five minutes** a intervalli di cinque minuti; **at two-inch ~s** a intervalli di cinque centimetri; **at regular ~s** a intervalli regolari; **sunny ~s** METEO intervalli soleggiati

intervene [ˌɪn· t̬ə·ˈviːn] *vi* **1.** (*involve oneself to help*) intervenire; **to ~ militarily/personally** intervenire militarmente/personalmente; **to ~ on sb's behalf** intervenire a favore di qu **2.** (*meddle unhelpfully*) **to ~ in sth** intromettersi in qc **3.** (*elapse*) trascorrere; **six months ~d before the opening of the swimming pool** passarono sei mesi prima dell'inaugurazione della piscina

intervening *adj* **in the ~ period** nel frattempo; **in the ~ days** nei giorni di intervallo

intervention [ˌɪn· t̬ə·ˈven·ʃən] *n* intervento *m;* **military ~** MIL intervento militare; **~ price** ECON prezzo *m* di intervento

interventionist [ˌɪn· t̬ə·ˈven·ʃə·nɪst] **I.** *n* POL, ECON interventista *mf* **II.** *adj* interventista

interview ['ɪn· t̬ə·ˌvjuː] **I.** *n* **1.** (*formal conversation*) intervista *f;* **telephone ~** intervista telefonica; **to have a job ~** avere un colloquio di lavoro; **to give an ~** rilasciare un'intervista **2.** *inf* (*person being interviewed*) intervistato, -a *m, f* **II.** *vt* intervistare; **to ~ sb about sth** intervistare qu su qc

interviewee [ˌɪn· t̬ə·vjuːˈiː] *n* intervistato, -a *m, f*

interviewer ['ɪn· t̬ə·vjuː·ə] *n* intervistatore, -trice *m, f*

interweave [ˌɪn· t̬ə·ˈwiːv] *irr* **I.** *vt* intrecciare; **to be interwoven with sth** essere strettamente legato a qc **II.** *vi* (*threads*) intrecciarsi; (*paths*) incrociarsi

intestate [ɪnˈtes·teɪt] *adj* intestato, -a

intestine [ɪnˈtes·tɪn] *n* intestino *m*

intimacy ['ɪn· t̬ə·mə·si] <-ies> *n* **1.** (*familiarity*) intimità *f;* **to be on terms of ~ with sb** essere in intimità con qu **2.** (*sexual relations*) rapporti *m pl* intimi

intimate¹ ['ɪn· t̬ə·mət] **I.** *adj* **1.** (*close, sexual*) intimo, -a; **~ relationship** rapporto *m* intimo; **to be on ~ terms with sb** essere intimo, -a di qu; **to become ~ with sb** diventare intimo di qu; **to be ~ with sb** avere rapporti intimi con qu **2.** (*personal: letter*) intimo, -a **3.** (*very detailed: knowledge*) profondo, -a **4.** (*link*) stretto, -a **II.** *n* amico, -a *m, f* intimo, -a

intimate² ['ɪn· t̬ə·meɪt] *vt form* far trasparire; **to ~ to sb** (**that**) ... far capire a qu (che)...

intimation [ˌɪn· t̬ə·ˈmeɪ·ʃən] *n form* (*hint*) indizio *m;* (*sign*) segno *m;* **~s** segnali *mpl*

intimidate [ɪnˈtɪ·mɪ·deɪt] *vt* intimidire; **to ~ sb into doing sth** costringere qu (con le minacce) a fare qc

intimidating *adj* (*manner*) intimidatorio, -a

intimidation [ɪnˌtɪ·mɪ·ˈdeɪ·ʃən] *n* intimidazione *f*

into ['ɪn· t̬ə] *prep* **1.** (*to the inside of*) in; (*towards*) verso; **to walk ~ a place** entrare in un posto; **to get ~ bed** mettersi a letto; **shall we walk ~ the park?** entriamo nel parco?; **~ the future** (*walk*) verso il futuro **2.** (*indicating an extent in time or space*) **deep ~ the forest** nel cuore della foresta; **to work late ~ the evening** lavorare fino a tarda sera **3.** (*against*) contro; **to drive ~ a tree** andare a sbattere (con la macchina) contro un albero; **to bump ~ a friend** imbattersi in un amico **4.** (*to the state or condition of*) **to burst ~ tears** scoppiare in lacrime; **to grow ~ a woman** diventare donna; **to translate from Italian ~ English** tradurre dall'italiano in inglese; **to turn sth ~ sth** trasformare qc in qc **5.** *inf* (*interested in*) **she's really ~ her new job** è davvero presa dal suo nuovo lavoro; **I think they are ~ drugs** credo che facciano uso di droga **6.** MATH **two goes ~ five two and a half times** il due sta nel cinque due volte e mezzo

intolerable [ɪnˈtɑː·lə·ə·bl] *adj* intollerabile

intolerance [ɪnˈtɑː·lə·əns] *n* intolleranza *f*

intolerant [ɪnˈtɑː·lə·ənt] *adj* intollerante; **to be ~ of different opinions** essere intollerante verso chi la pensa diversamente; **to be ~ of sb** essere intollerante verso qu; **to be ~ of alcohol** MED non sopportare l'alcol

intonation [ˌɪn·toʊ·ˈneɪ·ʃən] *n* LING, MUS intonazione *f*

intone [ɪnˈtoʊn] *vt form* intonare

intoxicant [ɪnˈtɑː·k·sɪ·kənt] *n* MED (*alcohol*) bevanda *f* alcolica; (*drug*) stupefacente *m*

intoxicate [ɪnˈtɑː·k·sɪ·keɪt] **I.** *vt* **1.** *a. fig* (*induce inebriation*) inebriare **2.** MED intossicare **II.** *vi* **1.** *a. fig* (*cause intoxication*) ubriacare **2.** MED intossicare

intoxicating [ɪnˈtɑː·k·sɪ·keɪ·t̬ɪŋ] *adj* **1.** (*exhilarating, stimulating*) inebriante **2.** (*substance*) stupefacente; (*causing drunkenness*) alcolico, -a; **~ drink** bevanda *f* alcolica

intoxication [ɪnˌtɑː·k·sɪ·ˈkeɪ·ʃən] *n* **1.** (*drunkenness*) ubriachezza *f; fig* ebbrezza *f;* **in a state of ~** in stato di ebbrezza **2.** MED intossicazione *f*

intractable [ˌɪn·ˈtræk·tə·bl] *adj form* **1.** (*temperament*) intrattabile **2.** (*problem*) irrisolvibile; **an ~ situation** una situazione irrisolvibile **3.** MED incurabile

intramural [ˌɪn·trə·ˈmjʊ·rəl] *adj* **1.** (*within a city or institution*) intramurale **2.** SCHOOL scolastico, -a; UNIV universitario, -a; **~ sports** attività *f* sportiva scolastica [*o* universitaria]

Intranet [ˌɪn·trəˈnet] *n* intranet *f inv*

intransigence [ɪnˈtræn·sə·dʒəns] *n form* intransigenza *f*

intransigent [ɪnˈtræn·sə·dʒənt] *adj form* intransigente

intransitive [ɪnˈtræn·sə·tɪv] *adj* LING, MAT intransitivo, -a

intrauterine [ˌɪn·trə·ˈjuː·t̬ə·ɪn] *adj* MED intrauterino, -a; **~ device** dispositivo *m* intrauterino, spirale *f*

intravenous [ˌɪn·trə·ˈviː·nəs] *adj* MED endovenoso, -a; **~ feeding** alimentazione *f* (per via) endovenosa

intrepid [ɪn·'tre·pɪd] *adj* intrepido, -a
intricacy ['ɪn·trɪ·kə·si] <-ies> *n* complessità *f*
intricate ['ɪn·trɪ·kət] *adj* **1.** (*detailed*) dettagliato, -a **2.** (*complicated: mechanism, problem*) intricato, -a
intrigue I. [ɪn·'triːg] *vt* intrigare; **to be ~d by sth** essere intrigato da qc II. *vi* (*plot*) tramare III. ['ɪn·triːg] *n* intrigo *m*
intriguing [ɪn·'triː·gɪŋ] *adj* intrigante
intrinsic [ɪn·ˠtrɪn·sɪk] *adj* intrinseco, -a; **the ~ value of a coin** il valore intrinseco di una moneta; **this is ~ to ...** è parte essenziale di...
introduce [ɪn·trə·'duːs] *vt* **1.** (*acquaint*) presentare; **allow me to ~ myself** permetta che mi presenti; **may I ~ you to my husband?** posso presentarLe mio marito?; **they were ~d to each other** vennero presentati l'uno all'altro **2.** (*raise interest in subject*) **to ~ sb to sth** introdurre qu a qc **3.** (*bring in*) introdurre; (*question*) fare; (*subject*) introdurre; (*bill*) presentare; **to ~ a product into the market** introdurre un prodotto sul mercato **4.** (*insert*) **to ~ sth into sth** introdurre qc in qc **5.** (*begin, present: book*) presentare; **the second movement is ~d by ...** il secondo movimento è introdotto da...; **the director will ~ the film personally** il regista in persona presenterà il film
introduction [ɪn·trə·'dʌk·ʃən] *n* **1.** (*making first acquaintance*) presentazione *f*; **letter of ~** lettera *f* di presentazione; **to do the ~s** fare le presentazioni **2.** (*first contact with sth*) introduzione *f*; **my holidays served as an ~ to sailing** le mie vacanze sono servite per un primo contatto con la vela **3.** (*establishment*) introduzione *f*; (*of a bill*) presentazione *f*; **~ into the market** introduzione *f* sul mercato **4.** (*insertion*) introduzione *f* **5.** *a.* MUS (*preface*) introduzione *f*
introductory [ɪn·trə·'dʌk·tə·ri] *adj a.* COM introduttivo, -a; **~ chapter** capitolo *m* introduttivo; **~ remarks** dichiarazioni *f pl* introduttive
introspection [ɪn·troʊ·'spek·ʃən] *n* introspezione *f*
introspective [ɪn·troʊ·'spek·tɪv] *adj* introspettivo, -a
introvert [ɪn·troʊ·'vɜːrt] *n* introverso, -a *m, f*
introverted *adj* introverso, -a
intrude [ɪn·'truːd] I. *vi* **1.** (*meddle*) intromettersi; **to ~ into sth** immischiarsi in qc; **to ~ upon sb's privacy** violare la privacy di qu **2.** (*disturb*) disturbare; **to ~ on sb** disturbare qu; **am I intruding?** disturbo? II. *vt* **to ~ sth on sb** importunare qu con qc
intruder [ɪn·'truː·dəˠ] *n* intruso, -a *m, f*
intrusion [ɪn·'truː·ʒən] *n* **1.** (*encroachment, infringement*) intrusione *f* **2.** (*meddling*) intromissione *f*
intrusive [ɪn·'truː·sɪv] *adj* (*noise*) molesto, -a; (*question*) indiscreto, -a; (*person*) invadente
intuition [ɪn·tuː·'ɪ·ʃən] *n* intuizione *f*; **to have an ~** (**that**) ... avere l'intuizione (che)...

intuitive [ɪn·'tjuː·ɪ·tɪv] *adj* intuitivo, -a; **an ~ feeling** una percezione intuitiva
inundate ['ɪn·ən·deɪt] *vt a. fig* inondare; **to ~ sb with sth** inondare qu di qc; **to be ~d with letters** essere sommerso di lettere; **to be ~d with presents** ricevere una montagna di regali
inundation [ɪn·ən·'deɪ·ʃən] *n a. fig* inondazione *f*
inure [ɪ·'njʊr] *vt form* (*become familiar with*) assuefarsi; **to ~ sb to sth** abituare qu a qc; **to ~ oneself against sth** diventare immune a qc
invade [ɪn·'veɪd] I. *vt* invadere; **to ~ sb's privacy** invadere la privacy di qu II. *vi* invadere
invader [ɪn·'veɪ·dəˠ] *n* (*aggressive trespasser*) invasore, -ditrice *m, f*
invalid¹ ['ɪn·və·lɪd] I. *n* invalido, -a *m, f* II. *adj* invalido, -a III. *vt* dichiarare inabile
invalid² [ɪn·'væ·lɪd] *adj* **1.** LAW (*not legally binding: marriage*) nullo, -a; (*ticket*) non valido, -a; **legally ~** privo, -a di validità legale; **to become ~** non essere più valido **2.** (*unsound*) inefficace; **technically ~** tecnicamente non valido, -a
invalidate [ɪn·'væ·lɪ·deɪt] *vt* **1.** (*argument, decision, results*) invalidare **2.** LAW invalidare; **to ~ a judgment** invalidare una sentenza
invalidism [ɪn·və·'lɪ·dɪ·zəm] *n* invalidità *f*
invalidity [ɪn·və·'lɪ·də·ti] *n* **1.** (*inadmissibility: of a contract*) invalidità *f*; (*of evidence*) invalidità *f* **2.** (*faultiness: of a theory*) inefficacia *f*
invaluable [ɪn·'væl·ju·ə·bl] *adj* inestimabile; (*help*) prezioso, -a; **to be ~ to sb** avere un valore inestimabile per qu
invariable [ɪn·'ve·ri·ə·bl] *adj form* (*answer, temperature*) invariabile; (*smile, attitude*) immutabile
invariably *adv* invariabilmente; **he would ~ be sitting at the bar** lo si poteva vedere sempre seduto al bar
invasion [ɪn·'veɪ·ʒən] *n* **1.** MIL invasione *f*; **~ by enemy forces** invasione da parte di forze nemiche **2.** (*interference*) violazione *f*; **~ of privacy/of a right** violazione della privacy/di un diritto
invective [ɪn·'vek·tɪv] *n form* invettiva *f*; **a stream of ~** una valanga di improperi
inveigle [ɪn·'veɪ·gl] *vt* **to ~ sb into doing sth** indurre qu a fare qc, *con lusinghe o imbrogli*
invent [ɪn·'vent] *vt* inventare
invention [ɪn·'ven·ʃən] *n* **1.** (*gadget*) invenzione *f* **2.** (*creativity*) inventiva *f* **3.** (*falsehood*) invenzione *f*
inventive [ɪn·'ven·tɪv] *adj* inventivo, -a
inventiveness [ɪn·'ven·tɪv·nɪs] *n* inventiva *f*
inventor [ɪn·'ven·təˠ] *n* inventore, -trice *m, f*
inventory ['ɪn·vən·tɔː·ri] <-ies> I. *n* **1.** (*catalog*) inventario *m*; **to draw up an ~** fare l'inventario **2.** (*stock*) scorte *mpl* II. *vt* inventariare III. *adj* (*audit, level*) delle scorte; (*number*) di inventario
inverse [ɪn·'vɜːrs] I. *adj* inverso, -a II. *n* **the ~**

l' inverso; **the ~ of sth** l'inverso di qc
inversion [ɪn·'vɜːr·ʒən] *n* inversione *f*
invert [ɪn·'vɜːrt] *vt* invertire
invertebrate [ɪn·'vɜːr·tə·brɪt] I. *n* invertebrato *m* II. *adj* invertebrato, -a
invest [ɪn·'vest] I. *vt* 1. (*put in*) investire; **to ~ time and effort in sth** investire tempo ed energie in qc 2. (*bestow attributes*) investire; **to ~ sb with sth** investire qu di qc II. *vi* investire; **to ~ in sth** investire in qc
investigate [ɪn·'ves·tɪ·geɪt] *vt* indagare su
investigation [ɪn·ˌves·tɪ·'geɪ·ʃən] *n* indagine *f*
investigative [ɪn·'ves·tɪ·geɪ·ţɪv] *adj* investigativo, -a; **~ journalism** giornalismo *m* investigativo
investigator [ɪn·'ves·tɪ·geɪ·ţɚ] *n* investigatore, -trice *m, f*
investment [ɪn·'vest·mənt] I. *n a. fig* investimento *m;* **to be a good ~** essere un buon investimento; **long-term ~s** investimenti *m pl* a lungo termine II. *adj* (*bank, company*) d'investimento
investor [ɪn·'ves·tɚ] *n* investitore, -trice *m, f*
inveterate [ɪn·'ve·ţə·rət] *adj* (*hatred, habit*) inveterato, -a; (*gambler*) accanito, -a; (*smoker*) incallito, -a; (*liar*) inguaribile
invidious [ɪn·'vɪ·di·əs] *adj* (*task*) ingrato, -a; (*choices*) impopolare; (*comparisons*) ingiusto, -a; **to be in an ~ position** trovarsi in una posizione poco invidiabile
invigorate [ɪn·'vɪ·gə·reɪt] *vt* rinvigorire
invigorating [ɪn·'vɪ·gə·reɪ·ţɪŋ] *adj* (*shower, walk*) rigenerante; (*swim*) tonificante
invincible [ɪn·'vɪn·sə·bl] *adj* invincibile
invisible [ɪn·'vɪ·zə·bl] *adj* invisibile; **~ to sth** invisibile a qc
invitation [ˌɪn·vɪ·'teɪ·ʃən] *n* invito *m;* **an ~ to sth** un invito a qc
invite¹ ['ɪn·vaɪt] *n inf* invito *m*
invite² [ɪn·'vaɪt] *vt* 1. (*request to attend*) invitare; **to ~ sb for/to sth** invitare qu per/a qc 2. (*request*) invitare; **to ~ offers** sollecitare offerte; **they ~d readers to send in their views** invitare i lettori a far pervenire le loro opinioni; **to ~ questions** sollecitare domande 3. (*provoke*) provocare; **to ~ trouble** andare in cerca di guai
inviting [ɪn·'vaɪ·ţɪŋ] *adj* invitante
in vitro [ɪn·'viː·t·roʊ] *adj, adv* in vitro
in vitro fertilization *n* fecondazione *f* in vitro
invocation [ˌɪn·və·'keɪ·ʃən] *n* invocazione *f*
invoice ['ɪn·vɔɪs] I. *vt* fatturare II. *n* fattura *f;* **~ for sth** fattura per qc
invoke [ɪn·'voʊk] *vt* invocare
involuntary [ɪn·'vɑː·lən·te·ri] *adj* involontario, -a
involve [ɪn·'vɑːlv] *vt* 1. (*implicate*) coinvolgere; **to be ~d in sth** essere coinvolto, -a in qc; **to get ~d in sth** immischiarsi in qc; **to ~ sb in an argument** coinvolgere qu in una discussione 2. (*entail*) implicare; **to ~ great expense** comportare grosse spese
involved [ɪn·'vɑːlvd] *adj* 1. (*implicated*) coin-

volto, -a 2. (*complicated*) complicato, -a
involvement [ɪn·'vɑːlv·mənt] *n* (*being involved*) coinvolgimento *m*
invulnerable [ɪn·'vʌl·nə·ə·bl] *adj* invulnerabile; **to be ~ to sth** essere invulnerabile a qc
inward ['ɪn·wəd] *adj* 1. (*inner*) interiore 2. (*moving in*) verso l'interno 3. (*in the mind: doubts*) intimo, -a
inwardly *adv* interiormente
inwardness *n* interiorità *f*
inwards ['ɪn·wəds] *adv* verso l'interno
I/O COMPUT *abbr of* **input/output** I/O, *input/output*
IOC *n abbr of* **International Olympic Committee** CIO *m*
iodine ['aɪ·ə·daɪn] *n* iodio *m*
ion ['aɪ·ən] *n* ione *m*
Ionic [aɪ·'ɑː·nɪk] *adj* ionico, -a
Iowa ['aɪ·ə·wə] *n* Iowa *m*
iota [aɪ·'oʊ·ţə] *n* 1. pizzico *m;* **there is not one ~ of truth in that** non c'è un briciolo di verità 2. (*letter*) iota *m*
IOU [ˌaɪ·oʊ·'juː] *n inf abbr of* **I owe you** pagherò *m inv*
IQ [ˌaɪ·'kjuː] *n abbr of* **intelligence quotient** QI *m*
IRA [ˌaɪ·ɑːr·'eɪ] *n abbr of* **Irish Republican Army** IRA *f*
Iran [ɪ·'ræn] *n* Iran *m*
Iranian [ɪ·'reɪ·ni·ən] I. *n* iraniano, -a *m, f* II. *adj* iraniano, -a
Iraq [ɪ·'rɑːk] *n* Iraq *m*
Iraqi [ɪ·'rɑː·ki] I. *n* iracheno, -a *m, f* II. *adj* iracheno, -a
irascible [ɪ·'ræ·sə·bl] *adj* irascibile
irate [aɪ·'reɪt] *adj* adirato, -a
Ireland ['aɪr·lənd] *n* Irlanda *f;* **Republic of ~** Repubblica *f* di Irlanda; **Northern ~** Irlanda del Nord
iridescent [ˌɪ·rɪ·'de·snt] *adj* iridescente
iris ['aɪ·rɪs] <-es> *n* 1. BOT iris *m inv* 2. ANAT iride *m*
Irish ['aɪ·rɪʃ] I. *adj* irlandese II. *n* 1. *pl* (*people*) **the ~** gli irlandesi 2. LING irlandese *m;* **~ Gaelic** gaelico *m* irlandese
Irishman ['aɪ·rɪʃ·mən] <-men> *n* irlandese *m*
Irishwoman ['aɪ·rɪʃ·wʊ·mən] <-women> *n* irlandese *f*
irk [ɜːrk] *vt* infastidire
irksome ['ɜːrk·səm] *adj* fastidioso, -a
iron ['aɪ·ən] I. *n* 1. (*metal*) ferro *m* 2. (*for pressing clothes*) ferro *m* (da stiro); **steam ~** ferro da stiro a vapore 3. SPORTS (*golf club*) ferro *m* 4. *pl* (*shackles*) ferri *mpl* ► **to have many ~s in the fire** avere molta carne al fuoco II. *vt* stirare; *fig* appianare III. *vi* stirare IV. *adj* di ferro; (*discipline*) ferreo, -a
Iron Age I. *n* età *f* del ferro II. *adj* dell'età del ferro
ironclad ['aɪ·ən·ˌklæd] *adj* 1. (*solid: rule, job security*) inviolabile 2. (*covered with iron*) corazzato, -a
Iron Curtain *n* HIST, POL cortina *f* di ferro

I

iron fist *n* pugno *m* di ferro; **to rule with an ~** governare col pugno di ferro

ironic(al) [aɪ·'rɑː·nɪ·k(el)] *adj* ironico, -a

ironing ['aɪ·ə·nɪŋ] *n* (*clothes*) roba *f* da stirare; **to do the ~** stirare

ironing board *n* asse *f* da stiro

iron lung *n* polmone *m* d'acciaio

ironman *n* SPORTS *atleta maschile di straordinaria potenza e resistenza*

ironman triathlon *n* triathlon *m* ironman *inv*

ironwork *n* lavori *m* in ferro *pl*

ironworks *n inv* stabilimento *m* siderurgico

irony ['aɪ·rə·ni] <-ies> *n* ironia *f;* **~ of fate** ironia del destino

irradiate [ɪr·'reɪ·di·eɪt] *vt* irradiare

irrational [ɪ·'ræ·ʃə·nəl] *adj* irrazionale

irrational number *n* MATH numero *m* irrazionale

irreconcilable [ɪ·ˌre·kən·'saɪ·lə·bl] *adj* (*differences, positions*) inconciliabile

irrecoverable [ˌɪ·rɪ·'kʌ·və·rə·bl] *adj* irrecuperabile

irredeemable [ˌɪ·rɪ·'diː·mə·bl] *adj* (*loss*) irreparabile; (*stupidity*) incurabile; (*debt*) irredimibile

irrefutable [ɪ·'re·fjə·tə·bl] *adj* inconfutabile

irregular [ɪ·'reg·jə·lə] *adj* irregolare; **~ soldiers** soldati *m pl* irregolari

irregularity [ɪ·ˌreg·jə·'le·rə·ti] <-ies> *n* irregolarità *f*

irrelevance [ɪr·'re·lə·vəns] *n,* **irrelevancy** <-ies> *n* irrilevanza *f;* **to fade into ~** perdere importanza

irrelevant [ɪr·'re·lə·vənt] *adj* irrilevante; **to be ~ to sth** non essere rilevante per qc

irremediable [ˌɪ·rɪ·'miː·diə·bl] *adj* irremediabile

irreparable [ɪ·'re·pə·rə·bl] *adj* irreparabile

irreplaceable [ˌɪ·rɪ·'pleɪ·sə·bl] *adj* insostituibile

irrepressible [ˌɪ·rɪ·'pre·sə·bl] *adj* irrefrenabile, irrefrenabile

irreproachable [ˌɪ·rɪ·'prou·tʃə·bl] *adj* irreprensibile

irresistible [ˌɪ·rɪ·'zɪs·tə·bl] *adj* irresistibile

irresolute [ɪ·'re·zə·luːt] *adj* irresoluto, -a; (*reply*) incerto, -a

irrespective [ˌɪ·rɪ·'spek·tɪv] *prep* **~ of** indipendentemente da; **~ of whether he agrees or not** indipendentemente dal fatto che lui sia d'accordo o no; **~ of sth/sb** a prescindere da qc/qu

irresponsible [ˌɪ·rɪ·'spɑːn·sə·bl] *adj* irresponsabile

irretrievable [ˌɪ·rɪ·'triː·və·bl] *adj* irrecuperabile; (*mistake*) irreparabile

irreverence [ɪ·'re·və·rəns] *n* irriverenza *f*

irreverent [ɪ·'re·və·rənt] *adj* irriverente

irreversible [ˌɪ·rɪ·'vɜːr·sə·bl] *adj* (*movement*) irreversibile; (*decision*) irrevocabile

irrevocable [ɪ·'re·və·kə·bl] *adj* irrevocabile

irrigate ['ɪ·rɪ·geɪt] *vt* AGR, MED irrigare; **to ~ land** irrigare il terreno

irrigation [ˌɪ·rɪ·'geɪ·ʃən] **I.** *n* AGR, MED irrigazione *f* **II.** *adj* di irrigazione; **~ canal** canale *m* di irrigazione

irrigation plant *n* impianto *m* di irrigazione

irritable ['ɪ·rɪ·tə·bl] *adj* (*person*) irritabile; (*voice*) irritato, -a

irritant ['ɪ·rɪ·tənt] *n* irritante *m*

irritate ['ɪ·rɪ·teɪt] *vt a.* MED irritare

irritated *adj* irritato, -a

irritating *adj* irritante

irritation [ˌɪ·rɪ·'teɪ·ʃən] *n* irritazione *f*

IRS [ˌaɪ·ɑːr·'es] *n abbr of* **Internal Revenue Service** Agenzia *f* delle Entrate, *negli Stati Uniti*

is [ɪz] *vt, vi 3rd pers sing of* **to be**

ISBN [ˌaɪ·es·biː·'en] *n abbr of* **International Standard Book Number** ISBN *m*

ISDN *n abbr of* **integrated services digital network** ISDN *f*

Islam [ɪz·'lɑːm] *n* Islam *m*

Islamic [ɪz·'lɑː·mɪk] *adj* islamico, -a; **~ law** legge *f* islamica

island ['aɪ·lənd] *n* isola *f;* **~ of calm** *fig* isola di pace

islander ['aɪ·lən·də] *n* isolano, -a *m, f*

isle *n,* **Isle** [aɪl] *n* isola *f*

islet ['aɪ·lɪt] *n liter* isoletta *f*

isn't ['ɪ·znt] = **is not**

isobar ['aɪ·sou·bɑːr] *n* METEO isobara *f*

isolate ['aɪ·sə·leɪt] *vt* isolare

isolated ['aɪ·sə·leɪ·t̬ɪd] *adj* isolato, -a

isolation [ˌaɪ·sə·'leɪ·ʃən] *n* isolamento *m*

isolationism [ˌaɪ·sə·'leɪʃ·nɪ·zəm] *n* isolazionismo *m*

isosceles triangle [aɪ·'sɑːs·liːz·ˌtraɪ·æŋ·gl] *n* MATH triangolo *m* isoscele

isotherm ['aɪ·sou·θɜːrm] *n* METEO, PHYS isoterma *f*

isotope ['aɪ·sə·toup] *n* PHYS, ELEC isotopo *m*

Israel ['ɪz·ri·əl] *n* Israele *m*

Israeli [ɪz·'re·ɪ·li] **I.** *n* israeliano, -a *m, f* **II.** *adj* israeliano, -a

Israelite ['ɪz·ri·ə·laɪt] *n* israelita *mf*

issue ['ɪ·ʃuː] **I.** *n* **1.** (*problem, topic*) questione *f;* **family ~s** questioni familiari; **side ~** questione secondaria; **a burning ~** *fig* una questione scottante; **the real ~s** le questioni fondamentali; **the point at ~** il punto in discussione; **to force an ~** premere per una decisione; **to make an ~ of sth** fare un caso di qc; **at ~** in discussione **2.** PUBL (*copy*) numero *m;* **latest ~** l'ultimo numero **3.** FIN, ECON (*of shares, stamps, checks*) emissione *f* **4.** *form* (*offspring, children*) prole *f* **II.** *vt* **1.** (*supply*) distribuire; (*passport, patent*) rilasciare **2.** (*announce*) **to ~ a statement** rilasciare una dichiarazione; **to ~ a call for sth** lanciare un appello per qc; (*ultimatum*) lanciare **3.** (*publish*) pubblicare **III.** *vi* **to ~ from** (*be born out of*) nascere da; (*come out of*) provenire da

isthmus ['ɪs·məs] <-es> *n* istmo *m*

it [ɪt] **I.** *pron dem* esso, essa (*in many cases 'it' is omitted*)*;* **who was ~?** chi era?; **~ 's in my**

bag è nella mia borsa; ~ **'s Paul who did that** è stato Paul a farlo; ~ **was in Chicago that ...** fu a Chicago che ... **II.** *pron pers* **1.** esso, essa; *direct object:* lo, la; *indirect object:* gli, le (*in many cases 'it' is omitted*); **where is your pencil/notebook?** ~ **is on my desk** dov'è la tua matita/il tuo quaderno? è sulla mia scrivania; ~ **went off badly** è andato a male; **your purse? I took** ~ il tuo borsellino? l'ho preso io; ~ **'s your cat, give** ~ **something to eat** il gatto è tuo, dagli qualcosa da mangiare; **I'm afraid of** ~ mi fa paura; **I fell into** ~ ci sono cascata **2.** (*time*) **what time is** ~**?** che ore sono? **3.** (*weather*) ~ **'s cold** fa freddo; ~ **'s snowing** nevica **4.** (*distance*) ~ **'s 5 miles to town from here** la città è a 5 miglia da qui **5.** (*empty subject*) ~ **seems that ...** sembra che... **6.** (*passive subject*) ~ **is said/hoped that ...** si dice/spera che...

IT [ˌaɪˈtiː] *n* COMPUT *abbr of* **Information Technology** Informatica *f*

Italian [ɪˈtæl·jən] **I.** *adj* italiano, -a **II.** *n* **1.** (*person*) italiano, -a *m, f* **2.** LING italiano *m*

italicize [ɪˈtæ·lɪ·saɪz] *vt* mettere in corsivo

italics [ɪˈtæ·lɪks] *npl* corsivo *m;* **in** ~ in corsivo

Italy [ˈɪ·tə·li] *n* Italia *f*

itch [ɪtʃ] **I.** *vi* **1.** MED (*arm, leg*) prudere; (*person*) avere prurito **2.** *fig, inf* **to be** ~**ing to do sth** morire dalla voglia di fare qc **II.** *n* **1.** MED prurito *m* **2.** *fig, inf* smania *f*

itchy [ˈɪt·ʃi] <-ier, -iest> *adj* che prude; **my arm feels** ~ ho prurito al braccio; **I've got an** ~ **feeling** ho prurito

item [ˈaɪ·təm] *n* **1.** (*thing*) articolo *m;* **luxury** ~ articoli di lusso; ~ **of clothing** capo *m* di abbigliamento **2.** (*topic*) argomento *m;* ~ **on the agenda** punto *m* all'ordine del giorno; ~ **by** ~ punto per punto **3.** COM ~ **of expenditure** voce *f* di spesa **4.** PUBL notizia *f;* **news** ~ notizia *f* **5.** *inf* (*couple*) coppia *f*

itemize [ˈaɪ·tə·maɪz] *vt* dettagliare

itinerant [aɪˈtɪ·nə·rənt] **I.** *n* lavoratore, -trice itinerante *mf* **II.** *adj* itinerante; (*merchant*) ambulante

itinerary [aɪˈtɪ·nə·re·ri] <-ies> *n* itinerario *m*

it'll [ˈɪ·tl̩] = **it will**

its [ɪts] *adj pos* il suo, la sua, i suoi, le sue; ~ **color/weight** il suo colore/peso; ~ **mountains** le sue montagne; **the cat hurt** ~ **head** il gatto si è fatto male alla testa

it's [ɪts] **1.** = **it is 2.** = **it has**

itself [ɪtˈself] *pron* **1.** *reflexive* si; **the cat licks** ~ il gatto si lecca; **the government got** ~ **into trouble** il governo si è cacciato nei pasticci **2.** *emphatic* **the place** ~ il posto stesso; **she is beauty** ~ è la personificazione della bellezza; **by** ~ da solo

IUD [ˌaɪ·juːˈdiː] *n abbr of* **intrauterine device** IUD *m*

IV <IVs> *abbr of* **intravenous** endovenosa *f*

I've [aɪv] = **I have** *s.* have

IVF [ˌaɪ·viːˈef] *n* MED *abbr of* **in vitro fertilization** fecondazione *f* in vitro

---

ivory [ˈaɪ·və·ri] <-ies> *n* **1.** avorio *m* **2.** *pl, inf* MUS tasti *f pl* (del pianoforte); **to tickle the ivories** *fig* suonare il piano **3.** *pl, sl* ANAT denti *mpl*

Ivory Coast *n* Costa *f* d'Avorio

ivory tower *n fig* torre *f* d'avorio

ivy [ˈaɪ·vi] <-ies> *n* edera *f*

Ivy League *n* UNIV *associazione molto esclusiva che comprende colleges e università di altissimo livello e prestigio nel Nord est degli Stati Uniti*

J

J, j [dʒeɪ] *n* J, j *f;* ~ **as in Jack** J di Jolly

J *n* PHYS *abbr of* **joule** J

jab [dʒæb] **I.** *n* **1.** (*with a pin*) puntura *f;* (*with an elbow*) gomitata *f* **2.** (*in boxing*) jab *m inv* **II.** <-bb-> *vt* **to** ~ **a needle into sth** conficcare un ago in qc; **to** ~ **a finger at sth** indicare qc con un dito; **to** ~ **sb in the eye with sth** colpire qu in un occhio con qc **III.** <-bb-> *vi* **to** ~ **at sb/sth** (**with sth**) colpire qu/qc (con qc)

jabber [ˈdʒæ·bɚ] *vi, vt* farfugliare

jabbering *n* chiaccherio *m*

jack [dʒæk] *n* **1.** AUTO cric *m inv* **2.** (*in cards*) jack *m inv,* fante *m* **3.** *sl* (*anything*) **you don't know** ~**!** tu non sai un accidenti!

♦**jack off** *vi vulg* farsi una sega

♦**jack up** *vt* **1.** (*object*) sollevare **2.** *inf* (*prices*) aumentare

jackal [ˈdʒæ·kəl] *n* **1.** ZOOL sciacallo *m* **2.** *pej, inf* (*person*) sciacallo *m*

jackass [ˈdʒæ·kæs] *n* **1.** ZOOL asino *m* **2.** *pej, inf* (*idiot*) somaro, -a *m, f*

jackboot [ˈdʒæk·buːt] *n* stivale *m, militare in pelle*

jackdaw [ˈdʒæk·dɑː] *n* taccola *f*

jacket [ˈdʒæ·kɪt] *n* **1.** (*short coat*) giacca *f* **2.** (*of a book*) sovraccoperta *f;* (*of a record*) copertina *f*

jacket potato *n* patata *f* al forno (*cotta intera con la buccia*)

jack-in-the-box [ˈdʒæ·kɪn·ðə·bɑːks] <-xes> *n* pupazzo *m* a molla che fuoriesce aprendo una scatola

jackknife [ˈdʒæk·naɪf] **I.** *n* **1.** (*knife*) coltello *m* a serramanico **2.** (*dive*) tuffo *m* avanti carpiato **II.** *vi* ripiegarsi su se stesso

jack-o'-lantern [ˈdʒæ·kə·ˌlæn·tən] *n* lanterna *fatta con una zucca vuota*

jackpot [ˈdʒæk·pɑːt] *n* monte *m* premi ▸ **to hit the** ~ *inf* avere un colpo di fortuna

Jacuzzi® [dʒəˈkuː·zi] *n* vasca *f* idromassaggio

jade [dʒeɪd] *n* **1.** (*precious green stone*) giada *f* **2.** (*color*) verde *m* giada

jaded [ˈdʒeɪ·dɪd] *adj* **to be** ~ **with sth** essere stufo, -a di qc

jagged ['dʒæ·gɪd] *adj* (*coastline, rocks*) frastagliato, -a; (*cut, tear*) dentellato, -a

jaggy ['dʒæ·gi] <-ier, -iest> *adj* irregolare

jaguar ['dʒæg·wɑːr] *n* giaguaro *m*

jail [dʒeɪl] I. *n* carcere *m*, prigione *f*; **to be in ~** (**for sth**) essere in carcere (per qc); **to put sb in ~** mettere qu in carcere II. *vt* incarcerare; **she was ~ed for life** è stato condannato al carcere a vita

jailbird ['dʒeɪl·bɜːrd] *n inf* avanzo *m* di galera

jailbreak *n* evasione *f*

jailer *n*, **jailor** ['dʒeɪ·lə·] *n* carceriere, -a *m, f*

jalopy [dʒə·'lɑː·pi] *n inf* macinino *m*

jam¹ [dʒæm] *n* CULIN marmellata *f*

jam² [dʒæm] I. *n* 1. *inf* (*awkward situation*) pasticcio *m*; **to get into a ~** cacciarsi in un pasticcio 2. (*blockage*) **traffic ~** ingorgo *m* stradale; **paper ~** COMPUT inceppamento *m* carta II.<-mm-> *vt* 1. (*cause to become stuck*) far inceppare; (*door*) bloccare; **to ~ sth into sth** ficcare qc in qc 2. (*a wheel*) bloccare 3. RADIO disturbare con interferenze III.<-mm-> *vi* 1. (*become stuck*) bloccarsi; (*rifle*) incepparsi 2. (*play music*) improvvisare

Jamaica [dʒə·'meɪ·kə] *n* Giamaica *f*

Jamaican I. *adj* giamaicano, -a II. *n* giamaicano, -a *m, f*

jamb [dʒæm] *n* montante *m*

jamboree [ˌdʒæm·bə·'riː] *n* 1. (*celebration*) kermesse *f inv* 2. (*scouts' meeting*) jamboree *m inv* (*raduno internazionale degli scout*)

jammies ['dʒæ·miːz] *npl inf* pigiama *m*

jammy ['dʒæ·mi] <-ier, -iest> *adj* coperto, -a di marmellata

jam-packed [ˌdʒæm·'pækt] *adj inf* **to be ~** (**with sth**) essere stracolmo, -a (di qc); **the streets were ~ with people** le strade erano piene zeppe di gente

jam session *n inf* jam session *f inv*

Jane Doe *n* soggetto *m* da identificare

jangle ['dʒæŋ·gl] I. *vt* (*coins, keys*) far tintinnare; **to ~ sb's nerves** far saltare i nervi di qu II. *vi* tintinnare; **to make sb's nerves ~** far saltare i nervi a qu III. *n* (*of coins, keys*) tintinnio *m*

janitor ['dʒæ·nə·tə·] *n* (*in school*) bidello, -a *m, f*

January ['dʒæn·ju·e·ri] <-ies> *n* gennaio *m*; *s.a.* **April**

Jap [dʒæp] *abbr of* **Japanese** I. *n pej, inf* giapponese *mf* II. *adj pej, inf* giapponese

japan [dʒə·'pæn] *n* lacca *f* giapponese

Japan [dʒə·'pæn] *n* Giappone *m*

Japanese [ˌdʒæ·pə·'niːz] I. *adj* giapponese II. *n* 1. (*person*) giapponese *mf* 2. LING giapponese *m*

jar¹ [dʒɑːr] *n* barattolo *m*

jar² [dʒɑːr] I.<-rr-> *vt* (*shake*) scuotere II.<-rr-> *vi* 1. (*cause unpleasant feelings*) **to ~ on sb's nerves** dare ai nervi a qu 2. (*make unpleasant sound*) stridere 3. (*clash: colors, design*) stonare; **to ~ on the eye** essere un

pugno in un occhio III. *n* 1. (*shake*) scossa *f* 2. (*shock*) colpo *m*

jargon ['dʒɑːr·gən] *n* gergo *m*

jasmine ['dʒæs·mɪn] *n* gelsomino *m*

jaundice ['dʒɑːn·dɪs] *n* MED itterizia *f*

jaundiced ['dʒɑːn·dɪst] *adj* 1. MED itterico, -a 2. (*bitter*) cinico, -a; **to look on sth with a ~ eye** guardare qc con occhio cinico

jaunt [dʒɑːnt] *n* gita *f*; **to go on a ~** andare a fare una gita

jaunty ['dʒɑːn·ti] <-ier, -iest> *adj* (*smile, air*) sbarazzino, -a; **~ step** passo *m* disinvolto

Java ['dʒɑː·və] *n* Giava *f*

java ['dʒɑː·və] *n inf* caffè *m*

javelin ['dʒæv·lɪn] *n* 1. (*spear*) giavellotto *m* 2. (*competition*) lancio *m* del giavellotto

jaw [dʒɑː] I. *n* 1. ANAT mascella *f* 2. *pl, a. fig* fauci *fpl* 3. *pl* TECH ganasce *fpl* II. *vi inf* chiacchierare; **to ~ away at sb** dare una lavata di capo a qu

jawbone ['dʒɑː·bəʊn] *n* mandibola *f*

jawbreaker ['dʒɑː·breɪ·kə·] *n* 1. (*sweet*) caramella *f* spaccadenti 2. *inf* (*tongue twister*) scioglilingua *m inv*

jay [dʒeɪ] *n* ghiandaia *f*

jaywalk ['dʒeɪ·wɑːk] *vi* attraversare la strada senza prestare attenzione

jaywalker ['dʒeɪ·wɑː·kə·] *n* pedone *m* indisciplinato

jaywalking *n* attraversare la strada senza prestare attenzione

jazz [dʒæz] *n* jazz *m inv*; **~ band** orchestra *f* jazz; **~ club** locale *m* jazz ► **and all that ~** *inf* e compagnia bella

♦ **jazz up** *vt inf* (*party*) vivacizzare; (*dress*) ravvivare

jazzy ['dʒæ·zi] <-ier, -iest> *adj* 1. MUS jazzato, -a 2. *inf* (*flashy*) chiassoso, -a

jealous ['dʒe·ləs] *adj* 1. (*envious*) invidioso, -a; **to be ~ of sb** essere invidioso di qu 2. (*of unfaithfulness*) geloso, -a; **to feel/be ~** diventare/essere geloso; **a ~ rage** un attacco di gelosia 3. (*fiercely protective*) geloso, -a; **to be ~ of sth** essere geloso di qc

jealousy ['dʒe·lə·si] <-ies> *n* 1. (*possessiveness*) gelosia *f*; **to be consumed by ~** essere consumato dalla gelosia 2. (*envy*) invidia *f*

jeans [dʒiːnz] *npl* jeans *mpl*; **a pair of ~** un paio di jeans

jeep [dʒiːp] *n* jeep *m inv*

jeer [dʒɪr] I. *vt* sbeffeggiare II. *vi* dire con tono di scherno; **to ~ at sb** sbeffeggiare qu III. *n* scherno *m*

jeez [dʒiːz] *interj inf* (*expressing surprise*) Gesù; (*expressing annoyance*) Cristo

Jehovah [dʒɪ·'hoʊ·və] *n* Geova; **~'s Witness** testimone *mf* di Geova

jell [dʒel] *vi s.* **gel**

jellied ['dʒe·lid] *adj* in gelatina

Jell-O® ['dʒe·loʊ] *n* budino *m* di frutta in gelatina

jelly ['dʒe·li] <-ies> *n* 1. (*soft transparent substance*) gelatina *f* 2. (*jam*) marmellata *f* ► **my**

legs turned to ~ *inf* mi sentii mancare le gambe

jellybean *n* gelatina *f* alla frutta (*caramella*)

jellyfish <-es> *n* medusa *f*

jeopardize ['dʒe·pə·daɪz] *vt* mettere a repentaglio

jeopardy ['dʒe·pə·di] *n* pericolo *m;* **to put sth in** ~ mettere qc in pericolo

jerk [dʒɜːrk] I. *n* **1.** (*jolt*) scossone *m;* **with a** ~ di soprassalto **2.** (*movement*) strattone *m;* **to give sth a** ~ dare una strattonata a qc **3.** *pej, inf* (*person*) cretino, -a *m, f;* **to feel like such a** ~ sentirsi un imbecille II. *vi* muoversi a scatti; **to** ~ **to a halt** fermarsi con un sobbalzo III. *vt* **1.** (*shake*) scuotere **2.** (*pull*) tirare bruscamente

◆**jerk off** *vi vulg* farsi una sega

jerkin ['dʒɜːr·kɪn] *n* farsetto *m*

jerky¹ ['dʒɜːr·ki] <-ier, -iest> *adj* (*not smooth: ride*) con sobbalzi continui

jerky² ['dʒɜːr·ki] *n* **beef** ~ carne *di manzo essiccata*

jersey ['dʒɜːr·zi] *n* **1.** (*garment*) maglione *m* **2.** (*sports shirt*) maglietta *f* **3.** (*cloth*) jersey *m inv* **4.** (*type of cow*) mucca *f* Jersey

jest [dʒest] I. *n form* scherzo *m;* **to say sth in** ~ dire qc per scherzo ▶ **many a true word is spoken in** ~ *prov* burlando si dice il vero *prov* II. *vi form* scherzare; **to** ~ **about sth** scherzare su qc

jester ['dʒes·tə] *n* HIST buffone *m*

jesting I. *n* scherzo *m* II. *adj* scherzoso, -a

Jesuit ['dʒez·ju·ɪt] I. *n* gesuita *mf* II. *adj* gesuitico, -a

Jesus ['dʒi:·zəs] I. Gesù II. *interj inf* Gesù!

Jesus Christ I. *n* Gesù Cristo *m* II. *interj inf* Gesù Cristo

jet¹ [dʒet] I. *n* **1.** (*aircraft*) jet *m inv* **2.** (*stream*) getto *m* **3.** (*nozzle*) ugello *m* II. <-tt-> *vi* viaggiare in aereo; **to** ~ **off** andare in aereo

jet² [dʒet] *n* (*stone*) giaietto *m*

jet-black *adj* corvino, -a; ~ **eyes/hair** occhi/ capelli corvini

jet engine *n* motore *m* a reazione

jet fighter *n* caccia *f* a reazione

jetfoil *n* aliscafo *m*

jet lag *n* jet lag *m inv*

jetliner *n* jet *m inv*

jet plane *n* jet *m inv*

jet-propelled *adj* a reazione

jet propulsion *n* propulsione *f* a reazione

jetsam ['dʒet·səm] *n s.* flotsam

jet set *n inf* **the** ~ il jet-set *m*

Jet Ski® I. *n* acquascooter *m inv,* moto *f* d'acqua II. *vi* andare in acquascooter

jet stream *n* corrente *f* a getto

jettison ['dʒe·tə·sən] *vt* **1.** NAUT buttare in mare **2.** (*get rid of: person*) mandar via; (*plan*) abbandonare

jetty ['dʒe·t̬i] *n* imbarcadero *m*

Jew [dʒu:] *n* ebreo, -a *m, f*

jewel ['dʒu:·əl] *n* **1. a.** *fig* (*piece of jewelry*) gioiello *m;* (*precious stone*) pietra *f* preziosa

2. (*watch part*) rubino *m*

jeweler ['dʒu:·ə·lə] *n,* **jeweller** ['dʒu:·ə·lə] *n* gioielliere, -a *m, f*

jewelry ['dʒu:·əl·ri] *n* gioielli *mpl;* **a piece of** ~ un gioiello

Jewess ['dʒu:·ɪs] *n* ebrea *f*

Jewish ['dʒu:·ɪʃ] *adj* (*person*) ebreo, -a; (*law*) ebraico, -a

Jewry ['dʒu:·ri] *n form* gli ebrei *mpl*

Jew's harp *n* scacciapensieri *m inv*

jib¹ [dʒɪb] *n* (*sail*) fiocco *m*

jib² [dʒɪb] *n* (*of a crane*) braccio *m*

jibe [dʒaɪb] *vi inf* (*agree*) combaciare

jiffy ['dʒɪ·fi] *n inf* **in a** ~ in un batter d'occhi

jig [dʒɪg] I. <-gg-> *vi* **1.** (*dance a jig*) ballare una giga **2.** (*move around*) saltellare II. *n* **1.** (*dance*) giga *f* **2.** TECH (*device*) maschera *f* di montaggio

jigger ['dʒɪ·gə] *n* jigger *m inv* (*unità di misura usata per dosare gli alcolici*)

jiggle ['dʒɪ·gl] I. *vt* muovere; **to** ~ **sth about** scuotere qc II. *vi* muoversi III. *n* scrollata *f*

jigsaw ['dʒɪg·sɑ:] *n* seghetto *m* da traforo

jigsaw puzzle *n* puzzle *m inv*

jilt [dʒɪlt] *vt* piantare

Jim Crow [ˌdʒɪm·'kroʊ] *n pej* razzismo *m*

jimmy ['dʒɪ·mi] I. *n* piede *m* di porco II. *vt* scassinare

jingle ['dʒɪŋ·gl] I. *vt* far tintinnare II. *vi* tintinnare III. *n* **1.** (*noise*) tintinnio *m* **2.** (*in advertisements*) jingle *m inv*

jingoism ['dʒɪŋ·goʊ·ɪ·zəm] *n pej* sciovinismo *m*

jingoistic [ˌdʒɪŋ·goʊ·'ɪs·tɪk] *adj pej* sciovinista

jinx [dʒɪŋks] I. *vt* portare iella a II. *n* malocchio *m;* **to put a** ~ **on sb/sth** gettare il malocchio su qu/qc

jitterbug ['dʒɪ·t̬ə·bʌg] I. *n* **1.** (*dance*) jitterbug *m* (*ballo di coppia popolare negli Stati Uniti negli anni trenta e quaranta*) **2.** (*nervous person*) persona *f* nervosa II. <-gg-> *vi* ballare il jitterbug

jitters ['dʒɪ·t̬əz] *npl inf* (*nervousness*) nervosismo *m;* **he got the** ~ gli è venuta fifa

jittery ['dʒɪ·t̬ə·ri] <-ier, -iest> *adj inf* nervoso, -a; **he felt** ~ aveva la tremarella; **he got** ~ gli è venuta fifa

jiujitsu [ˌdʒu:·'dʒɪt·su:] *n s.* **jujitsu**

jive [dʒaɪv] I. *n* (*dance*) jive *m inv* (*ballo veloce in voga negli anni quaranta e cinquanta*) II. *vi* ballare il jive

job [dʒɑ:b] *n* **1.** (*piece of work, employment*) lavoro *m;* **to apply for a** ~ fare domanda di lavoro **2.** (*duty*) dovere *m;* **to do one's** ~ compiere il proprio dovere; **it's not her** ~ non tocca a lei farlo **3.** *inf* (*robbery*) **a bank** ~ un colpo in banca *m*

job description *n* descrizione *f* delle mansioni

jobholder *n* occupato, -a *m, f*

job interview *n* colloquio *m* di lavoro

jobless ['dʒɑ:b·lɪs] I. *adj* disoccupato, -a II. *npl* **the** ~ i disoccupati *mpl;* ~ **figures** numero *m* di disoccupati

J

job market *n* mercato *m* del lavoro
job rating *n* (*of president, prime minister*) tasso *m* di popolarità
jobseeker *n* persona *f* che cerca lavoro
jock [dʒɑːk] *n* **1.** *sl* (*athlete*) atleta *mf* **2.** (*jockstrap*) sospensorio *m*
jockey ['dʒɑːˑki] **I.** *n* fantino, -a *m, f* **II.** *vi* to ~ for sth competere per qc; **to ~ for position** lottare per ottenere il miglior piazzamento
jockstrap *n* sospensorio *m*
jocose [dʒoʊˑ'koʊs] *adj form* giocoso, -a
jocular ['dʒɑːk·jə·lə] *adj* giocoso, -a
jocund ['dʒɑːˑkənd] *adj* giocondo, -a
jodhpurs ['dʒɑːd·pə·z] *npl* pantaloni *m pl* da cavallerizzo
Joe Blow *n inf* uomo *m* della strada
jog [dʒɑːg] **I.** *n* **1.** (*run*) corsa *f* lenta; **to go for a ~** andare a fare jogging **2.** (*nudge*) colpetto *m;* **to give sth a ~** dare una gomitata a qc **II.** <-gg-> *vi* fare jogging **III.** <-gg-> *vt* to ~ sb's memory rinfrescare la memoria a qu
 ◆**jog along** *vi inf* (*vehicle*) procedere lentamente; (*person*) tirare avanti
jogger ['dʒɑːˑgə] *n* persona *f* che fa jogging
jogging ['dʒɑːˑgɪŋ] *n* jogging *m inv;* **to go** (**out**) ~ andare a fare jogging
joggle ['dʒɑːˑgl] **I.** *vt* scuotere **II.** *n* leggera scossa *f*
john [dʒɑːn] *n inf* (*toilet*) gabinetto *m*
John Bull *n inf* John Bull *m* (*personificazione dell'inglese medio*)
John Doe *n* soggetto *m* da identificare
John Hancock *n inf* firma *f*
join [dʒɔɪn] **I.** *vt* **1.** (*connect*) unire; **to ~ hands** prendersi per mano; **to ~ sb** (**together**) **in marriage** *form* unire qu in matrimonio **2.** (*come together with sb*) unirsi a; **they'll ~ us after dinner** ci raggiungeranno dopo cena **3.** (*become member of: club, society*) iscriversi a; (*army*) arruolarsi a **4.** (*begin to work with*) unirsi a **II.** *vi* **1.** (*unite*) unirsi **2.** (*become member*) iscriversi **3.** (*participate*) to ~ in sth partecipare a qc **III.** *n* giuntura *f*
joiner ['dʒɔɪˑnə] *n* falegname *m*
joinery ['dʒɔɪˑnə·ri] *n* falegnameria *f*
joint [dʒɔɪnt] **I.** *adj* (*effort, investigation, communiqué*) congiunto, -a; (*current account*) cointestato, -a **II.** *n* **1.** ANAT articolazione *f;* **out of ~** slogato, -a; **to come out of ~** slogarsi **2.** (*connection*) unione *f* **3.** TECH giuntura *f* **4.** *sl* (*nightclub*) locale *m* **5.** *inf* (*jail*) galera *f* **6.** *inf* (*marijuana*) spinello *m*
jointed *adj* (*doll*) snodabile; (*rod*) smontabile
joint effort *n* sforzo *m* congiunto
jointly *adv* congiuntamente
joint ownership *n* comproprietà *f*
joint stock *n* capitale *m* sociale
joint-stock company *n* società *f* per azioni
joint venture *n* joint venture *f inv*
joist [dʒɔɪst] *n* trave *f*
joke [dʒoʊk] **I.** *n* **1.** (*amusing story*) barzelletta *f;* (*trick, remark*) scherzo *m;* **to play a ~ on sb** fare uno scherzo a qu; **to not be able to** take a ~ non saper stare allo scherzo; **to do sth as a ~** fare qc per scherzo **2.** *inf* (*easy thing*) **to be no ~** non essere uno scherzo **3.** *inf* (*ridiculous thing*) cosa *f* ridicola; (*ridiculous person*) zimbello *m;* **what a ~!** questa sì che è bella! ▶**the ~ was on me** sono passato io per fesso *inf* **II.** *vi* scherzare; **to ~ about sth** scherzare su qc; **you must be joking!** stai scherzando?
joker ['dʒoʊˑkə] *n* **1.** (*one who jokes*) burlone, -a *m, f* **2.** *inf* (*annoying person*) idiota *mf* **3.** (*playing card*) jolly *m inv* ▶**to be the ~ in the pack** essere la grande incognita
joking I. *adj* scherzoso, -a **II.** *n* scherzi *mpl*
jokingly *adv* scherzosamente
jolly ['dʒɑːˑli] **I.** <-ier, -iest> *adj* **1.** (*happy: tune*) allegro, -a **2.** (*enjoyable*) **we're having a ~ time** ci stiamo divertendo molto **II.** *npl a.* *vulg* (*amusement*) **to get one's jollies** divertirsi
jolt [dʒoʊlt] **I.** *n* **1.** (*sudden jerk*) sobbalzo *m* **2.** (*shock*) colpo *m* **II.** *vt a.fig* scuotere **III.** *vi* (*vehicle*) sobbalzare
Jordan ['dʒɔːr·dn] *n* **1.** (*country*) Giordania *f* **2.** (*river*) Giordano *m*
Jordanian [dʒɔːr·'deɪ·niən] **I.** *adj* giordano, -a **II.** *n* giordano, -a *m, f*
josh [dʒɑːʃ] **I.** *vt inf* prendere in giro **II.** *vi* scherzare
jostle ['dʒɑːˑsl] **I.** *vt* spingere **II.** *vi* **1.** (*push*) spintonare **2.** (*compete*) **to ~ for position** contendersi il primato
jot [dʒɑːt] **I.** <-tt-> *vt* to ~ sth down annotare qc **II.** *n* there's not a ~ of truth in it non c'è un briciolo di verità
jottings *npl* appunti *mpl*
joule [dʒuːl] *n* PHYS joule *m*
journal ['dʒɜːr·nəl] *n* **1.** (*periodical*) rivista *f* (specializzata) **2.** (*diary*) diario *m*
journalism ['dʒɜːrn·lɪ·zəm] *n* giornalismo *m*
journalist ['dʒɜːrn·lɪst] *n* giornalista *mf*
journalistic [ˌdʒɜːr·nə·'lɪs·tɪk] *adj* giornalistico, -a
journey ['dʒɜːr·ni] **I.** *n* viaggio *m* **II.** *vi liter* viaggiare
journeyman ['dʒɜːr·nɪ·mən] <-men> *n* operaio, -a specializzato, -a *m*
joust [dʒaʊst] **I.** *vi* giostrare **II.** *n* giostra *f*
jovial ['dʒoʊ·viəl] *adj* gioviale
joviality [ˌdʒoʊ·vi·'æ·lə·ti] *n* giovialità *f*
jowl [dʒaʊl] *n* mascella *f*
joy [dʒɔɪ] *n* gioia *f;* **to jump for ~** fare salti di gioia
joyful ['dʒɔɪ·fəl] *adj* gioioso, -a
joyless ['dʒɔɪ·ləs] *adj* (*marriage*) infelice; (*expression*) triste
joyous ['dʒɔɪ·əs] *adj liter* gioioso, -a
joy ride ['dʒɔɪ·raɪd] *n* giro *m* in un auto rubata
joystick ['dʒɔɪ·stɪk] *n* **1.** AVIAT cloche *f inv* **2.** COMPUT joystick *m inv*
JPEG ['dʒeɪ·peg] *n* COMPUT immagine *f* JPEG
Jr., jr. *abbr of* **Junior** jr.
jubilant ['dʒuː·bɪ·lənt] *adj* giubilante

jubilation [,dʒuː·bɪ·'leɪ·ʃən] *n* giubilo *m*
jubilee ['dʒuː·bɪ·liː] *n* **1.** (*anniversary*) anniversario *m* **2.** REL giubileo *m*
Judaism ['dʒuː·deɪ·ɪ·zəm] *n* giudaismo *m*
Judas ['dʒuː·dəs] *n* Giuda *m inv*
judge [dʒʌdʒ] **I.** *n* **1.** LAW giudice *mf* **2.** (*referee*) giudice *mf* di gara; (*in a jury*) membro *m* della giuria; **panel of ~s** giuria *f* **II.** *vi a.* LAW giudicare **III.** *vt* **1.** *a.* LAW giudicare; (*question*) decidere; (*assess*) valutare; (*consider*) considerare; **to ~ that ...** ritenere che... **2.** (*as a referee*) fare da arbitro in; (*in a jury*) fare da giudice in
judg(e)ment ['dʒʌdʒ·mənt] *n* **1.** LAW sentenza *f* **2.** (*opinion*) giudizio *m* **3.** (*discernment*) (capacità *f* di) giudizio
judgmental [dʒʌdʒ·'men·təl] *adj* sentenzioso, -a
judicature ['dʒuː·dɪ·kə·tʃə] *n* ordinamento *m* giudiziario
judicial [dʒuː·'dɪ·ʃl] *adj* (*system, enquiry*) giudiziario, -a
judiciary [dʒuː·'dɪ·ʃie·ri] *n form* **the ~** (*branch of government*) il potere giudiziario; (*judges*) la magistratura
judicious [dʒuː·'dɪ·ʃəs] *adj form* giudizioso, -a
judo ['dʒuː·doʊ] *n* judo *m inv*
jug [dʒʌg] *n* **1.** (*container*) caraffa *f*; (*small: for milk, cream*) bricco *m* **2.** *pl vulg* (*breasts*) tette *fpl*
juggernaut ['dʒʌ·gə·nɑːt] *n* mostro *m*; **a ~ of industry** un gigante dell'industria
juggle ['dʒʌ·gl] **I.** *vi* giocolare; *fig* giocare **II.** *vt* giocolare con; *fig* (*do many things at once*) destreggiarsi fra; (*figures*) manipolare
juggler *n* giocoliere, -a *m, f*
jugular ['dʒʌg·jə·lə] *n* (vena *f*) giugulare ▶**to go for the ~** *inf* pungere sul vivo
jugular vein *n* vena *f* giugulare
juice [dʒuːs] *n* **1.** (*drink*) succo *m* **2.** (*of meat*) succo *m* **3.** *inf* (*electricity*) corrente *f*; (*fuel*) benzina *f* ▶**to stew in one's own ~** cuocersi nel proprio brodo
juiced *adj sl* bevuto, -a
juicy ['dʒuː·si] <-ier, -iest> *adj* **1.** (*fruit, steak*) succoso, -a **2.** *inf* (*profit*) sostanzioso, -a; (*role*) interessante **3.** *inf* (*details*) piccante
jujitsu [,dʒuː·'dʒɪt·suː] *n* jujitsu *m inv*
jukebox ['dʒuːk·bɑːks] *n* jukebox *m inv*
julep ['dʒuː·ləp] *n* (*drink*) julep *m inv*, bevanda alla menta
July [dʒuː·'laɪ] *n* luglio *m*; *s.a.* **April**
jumble ['dʒʌm·bl] **I.** *n* guazzabuglio *m* **II.** *vt* mescolare
jumbo ['dʒʌm·boʊ] **I.** *adj* gigante *m* **II.** *n inf* jumbo jet *m inv*
jumbo jet *n* jumbo jet *m inv*
jump [dʒʌmp] **I.** *vi* **1.** (*leap*) saltare; **to ~ up and down** saltare su e giù **2.** (*skip*) saltare alla corda; **to ~ for joy** fare salti di gioia **3.** (*jerk*) trasalire **4.** (*increase suddenly*) salire di colpo ▶**go ~ in the lake!** *inf* va a farti friggere! **II.** *vt* **1.** (*leap across or over*) saltare **2.** (*attack*) sal-

tare addosso a **3.** (*disregard*) saltare ▶**to ~ the gun** agire impulsivamente **III.** *n* **1.** (*leap*) salto *m* **2.** (*hurdle*) ostacolo *m*
♦**jump about** *vi* saltellare qua e là
♦**jump at** *vt* (*an opportunity, an offer*) cogliere al volo
♦**jump down** *vi* saltare giù
♦**jump in** *vi* saltare dentro
♦**jump on** *vt* (*criticize*) rimproverare
♦**jump up** *vi* scattare in piedi
jumper ['dʒʌm·pə] *n* **1.** (*person, animal*) saltatore, -trice *m, f* **2.** (*dress*) maglione *m*
jumper cables *npl* AUTO cavi *m pl* con morsetti, *per batterie*
jump jet *n* aereo *m* a decollo verticale
jump-start *vt* **1.** AUTO far partire (*facendo ponte con i cavi*) **2.** *inf* (*reinvigorate: a career*) rinvigorire
jumpsuit *n* **1.** (*for parachutist*) tuta *f* da lancio **2.** FASHION tuta *f* intera
jumpy ['dʒʌm·pi] <-ier, -iest> *adj inf* nervoso, -a
junction ['dʒʌŋ·kʃən] *n* incrocio *m*
juncture ['dʒʌŋ·ktʃə] *n form* congiuntura *f*; **at this ~** in questo frangente
June [dʒuːn] *n* giugno *m*; *s.a.* **April**
jungle ['dʒʌŋ·gl] *n a. fig* giungla *f*
junior ['dʒuː·n·jə] **I.** *adj* **1.** (*younger*) più giovane **2.** SPORTS juniores **3.** (*lower in rank*) subalterno, -a; (*partner*) più giovane **II.** *n* **1.** (*younger person*) **he is five years my ~** è più giovane di me di cinque anni **2.** (*low-ranking person*) subalterno, -a *m, f* **3.** UNIV, SCH negli USA, studente del penultimo anno di scuola superiore o università
junior college *n* negli USA, scuola che offre i primi due anni di un corso di studi universitario
junior high school *n* negli USA, scuola per studenti dai 12 ai 15 anni
juniper ['dʒuː·nɪ·pə] *n* ginepro *m*
junk¹ [dʒʌŋk] **I.** *n* **1.** (*objects of no value*) cianfrusaglie *fpl* **2.** *sl* (*heroin*) eroina *f* **II.** *vt inf* sbarazzarsi di
junk² [dʒʌŋk] *n* (*boat*) giunca *f*
junk bond *n* obbligazione *f* ad alto rischio
junk food *n* porcherie *fpl*
junkie ['dʒʌŋ·ki] *n* **1.** *sl* (*addict*) tossico, -a *m, f* **2.** *inf* (*fanatic*) fanatico, -a *m, f*
junk mail *n* posta *f* spazzatura
junkyard *n* deposito *m* di robivecchi
junta ['hʊn·tə] *n* governo *m* dittatoriale; (*military*) ~ giunta *f* militare
Jupiter ['dʒuː·pɪ·tə] *n* Giove *m*
juridical [dʒʊ·'rɪ·dɪ·kəl] *adj* giuridico, -a
jurisdiction [,dʒʊ·rɪs·'dɪk·ʃən] *n* giurisdizione *f*; **to have ~ in sth** avere giurisdizione su qc
jurisprudence [,dʒʊ·rɪs·'pruː·dənts] *n* giurisprudenza *f*
jurist ['dʒʊ·rɪst] *n* giurista *mf*
juror ['dʒʊ·rə] *n* giurato, -a *m, f*
jury ['dʒʊ·ri] *n* giuria *f*

J

jury-rig *vt* realizzare con mezzi di fortuna
just [dʒʌst] **I.** *adv* **1.** (*very soon*) subito; **we're ~ about to leave** stiamo per partire **2.** (*now*) giusto; **to be ~ doing sth** stare giusto facendo qc **3.** (*very recently*) appena; **~ after 10 o'clock** subito dopo le 10; **she's ~ turned 15** ha appena compiuto 15 anni **4.** (*exactly, equally*) proprio; **~ like that** proprio così; **~ as I expected** proprio come mi aspettavo; **~ now** proprio adesso; **not ~ yet** non ancora **5.** (*only*) solo; **~ a minute** aspetta un attimo **6.** (*simply*) soltanto; **~ in case it rains** in caso piovesse **7.** (*barely*) **~** (**about**), (**only**) **~** appena; **we** (**only**) **~ caught the bus** abbiamo fatto appena in tempo a prendere l'autobus; **~ in time** appena in tempo **8.** (*very*) proprio; **you look ~ wonderful!** sei semplicemente fantastica! **9.** **~ about** (*nearly*) quasi **10.** **it's ~ as well that ...** tanto vale che... ▸ **~ my luck!** tutte a me! **II.** *adj* (*fair*) giusto, -a ▸ **to get one's ~ deserts** avere quel che uno si merita
justice ['dʒʌs·tɪs] *n* **1.** giustizia *f;* **to bring sb to ~** assicurare qu alla giustizia **2.** (*judge*) giudice *mf*
Justice of the Peace *n* giudice *mf* di pace
justifiable [ˌdʒʌs·tə·'faɪ·ə·bl] *adj* giustificabile
justification [ˌdʒʌs·tə·fɪ·'keɪ·ʃən] *n* giustificazione *f*
justify ['dʒʌs·tɪ·faɪ] *vt* giustificare; **to ~ oneself** giustificarsi; **to ~ oneself to sb** giustificarsi con qu
justly ['dʒʌs·tli] *adv* giustamente
jut [dʒʌt] <-tt-> *vi* **to ~ out** sporgere
jute [dʒuːt] *n* iuta *f*
juvenile ['dʒuː·vən·aɪl] *adj* **1.** *form* (*young*) giovanile **2.** *pej* (*childish*) infantile
juvenile court *n* tribunale *m* dei minori
juvenile delinquency *n* criminalità *f* minorile
juvenile delinquent *n* delinquente *mf* minorenne
juxtapose ['dʒʌks·tə·poʊz] *vt* giustapporre
juxtaposition [ˌdʒʌks·tə·pə·'zɪ·ʃən] *n* giustapposizione *f*

K

K, k [keɪ] *n* K, k *f;* **~ as in King** K di Kursaal
K 1. COMPUT *abbr of* **kilobyte** kbyte *m* **2.** (*thousand*) **$30~** mille dollari
kaiser roll ['kaɪ·zə ˌroʊl] *n* panino tondo e croccante
kale [keɪl] *n*, *n* cavolo *m* riccio
kaleidoscope [kə·'laɪ·dəs·koʊp] *n* caleidoscopio *m*
kamik ['kɑː·mɪk] *n Can: stivale indossato dagli Inuit*
kamikaze [ˌkɑ·mɪ·'kɑː·zi] *adj* kamikaze *m inv*
kamikaze attack *n* attacco *m* kamikaze

Kampuchea [ˌkæm·pu·'tʃiː·ə] *n* Cambogia *f*
Kampuchean I. *adj* cambogiano, -a **II.** *n* cambogiano, -a *m, f*
kangaroo [ˌkæŋ·gə·'ruː] <-(s)> *n* canguro *m*
kangaroo court *n* tribunale *m* illegale
Kans. *n abbr of* **Kansas** Kan., Kansas *m*
kaolin ['keɪ·ə·lɪn] *n* MIN caolino *m*
kaput [kɑ·'puːt] *adj inf* kaput; **to go ~** finire kaput
Kaposi's sarcoma [kə·'pəʊ·ziz sɑːr·'kəʊ·mə] *n* MED sarcoma *m* di Kaposi
karaoke [kæ·ri·'əʊ·ki] *n* karaoke *m inv*
karat ['ke·rət] <-(s)> *n* carato *m*
karate [kə·'rɑː·ti] *n* karate *m inv*
karate chop *n* colpo *m* di karate
karma ['kɑːr·mə] *n* karma *m inv*
katydid ['keɪ·ti·dɪd] *n* cavalletta *f* verde
kayak ['kaɪ·æk] *n* kayak *m*
kayaking *n* **I love ~** mi piace moltissimo andare in kayak
kazoo [kə·'zuː] *n* MUS kazoo *m inv* (*strumento musicale di origine africana*)
Kb, KB [ˌkeɪ·'biː] COMPUT *abbr of* **kilobyte** kB *m*
kbyte COMPUT *abbr of* **kilobyte** kbyte *m*
kc *abbr of* **kilocycle** kc *m*
kebab [kə·'bab] *n* kebab *m inv*
keel [kiːl] *n* NAUT chiglia *f*
◆ **keel over** *vi* (*boat*) scuffiare; (*person*) cadere a terra
keen [kiːn] **I.** *adj* **1.** (*intent, eager*) entusiasta; (*student*) appassionato, -a; **to be ~ to do sth** avere voglia di fare qc; **to be ~ on sth** essere appassionato di qc **2.** (*perceptive: intelligence*) acuto, -a; (*ear*) fine; **to have ~ eyesight** avere una vista acuta; **to have a ~ sense of smell** avere un olfatto sviluppato **3.** (*extreme*) forte; **a ~ interest** un vivo interesse; **to have a ~ appetite** avere un appetito robusto **4.** *liter* (*sharp*) affilato, -a; (*wind*) tagliente **5.** (*shrill, piercing*) penetrante **II.** *n* lamento *m* funebre **III.** *vi* piangere; **to ~ for sb** piangere la morte di qu
keep [kiːp] **I.** *n* **1.** (*livelihood*) sostentamento *m;* **to earn one's ~** guadagnarsi da vivere **2.** HIST (*castle tower*) maschio *m* ▸ **for ~s** per sempre **II.** <kept, kept> *vt* **1.** (*have: shop*) avere; (*guesthouse*) gestire; (*animals*) allevare; (*children*) prendersi cura di **2.** (*store: silence, secret*) mantenere; **~ my seat** tienimi il posto; **~ the change** tenga il resto **3.** (*maintain*) tenere; **to ~ sb under observation** tenere qu sotto osservazione; **to ~ one's eyes fixed on sth/sb** non staccare gli occhi da qc/qu; **to ~ sb awake** tenere sveglio qu; **to ~ sth going** (*conversation, fire*) mantenere vivo **4.** (*detain*) **to ~ sb waiting** fare aspettare qu; **to ~ sb in prison** tenere qu in prigione; **he was kept at the hospital** è stato trattenuto in ospedale; **what kept you?** cosa ti ha trattenuto? **5.** (*guard*) **to ~ one's temper** mantenere la calma **6.** (*fulfill*) **to ~ an appointment** rispettare un appuntamento; **to ~ one's word** mantenere la parola (data) **7.** (*record: diary,*

accounts) tenere **8.**(*person's expenses*) mantenere; **to earn enough to ~ oneself** guadagnare abbastanza per mantenersi; **to ~ a mistress** mantenere un'amante **9.**(*obey, respect: law*) rispettare **10.**(*remain involved*) **to ~ one's hand in** non perdere la mano ▸**to ~ one's** <u>balance</u> mantenersi in equilibrio; **to ~** <u>time</u> tenere il tempo **III.**<kept, kept> *vi* **1.** *a. fig* (*stay fresh*) conservarsi **2.**(*stay*) mantenersi; **to ~ fit** mantenersi in forma; **to ~ silent** (*about sth*) mantenere il silenzio (su qc); **to ~ to the left** tenere la sinistra; **~ quiet!** silenzio!; **~ still!** state fermi! **3.**(*continue*) **to ~ going** (*person*) andare avanti; (*machine*) continuare a funzionare; **to ~ doing sth** continuare a fare qc; **he ~s losing his keys** perde sempre le chiavi

◆**keep ahead** *vi* conservare il vantaggio; **to ~ of the others** mantenere il vantaggio sugli altri

◆**keep at I.** *vi* perseverare; **to ~ work** continuare a lavorare; **~ it!** tieni duro! **II.** *vt* **to keep sb at sth** spingere qu a continuare a fare qc

◆**keep away I.** *vi* stare alla larga; **keep medicines away from children** tenere i medicinali fuori della portata dei bambini; **he can't ~ from it** non riesce a staccarsene; **~!** non avvicinarti! **II.** *vt always sep* tenere lontano

◆**keep back I.** *vi* (*stay away*) **to ~ from sth/ sb** non avvicinarsi a qc/qu **II.** *vt* **1.to ~ one's tears** trattenere le lacrime **2.**(*hide*) nascondere; **to keep the truth back from sb** nascondere la verità a qu **3.**(*retain sth*) **to keep sth back** trattenere qc; (*slow down*) tenere a freno qc

◆**keep down** *vt* **1.to keep one's voice down** non alzare la voce; **to keep prices down** contenere i prezzi **2.**(*suppress*) **to keep sb down** reprimere qu **3.**(*not vomit*) trattenere

◆**keep from I.** *vt always sep* **1.**(*prevent*) impedire; **to keep sb from doing sth** impedire a qu di fare qc **2.**(*retain information*) **to keep sth from sb** nascondere qc a qu **II.** *vi* evitare; **I couldn't ~ laughing** non ho potuto trattenermi dal ridere

◆**keep in I.** *vt* (*person*) tenere dentro; (*emotions*) trattenere; **to keep a pupil in** *trattenere un alunno a scuola per punizione* **II.** *vi* **to ~ line** stare al proprio posto; **to ~ with sb** rimanere in buoni rapporti con qu

◆**keep off I.** *vi* (*stay off*) tenersi lontano; '**~**' 'vietato avvicinarsi'; '**~ the grass**' vietato calpestare l'erba' **II.** *vt* **1.**tenere lontano; **to keep the rain off sth/sb** proteggere qc/qu dalla pioggia; **keep your hands off!** non toccare! **2.**(*avoid*) evitare; **to ~ a subject** non toccare un argomento

◆**keep on I.** *vi* **1.**(*continue*) continuare; **to ~ doing sth** continuare a fare qc **2.**(*pester*) **to ~ about sb/sth** non fare altro che parlare di qu/ qc; **to ~ at sb** stare sempre addosso a qu **II.** *vt*

always sep **1.**(*not to dismiss*) tenere **2.**(*not to get rid of*) non togliersi

◆**keep out I.** *vi* no entrare; **~!** vietato l'ingresso!; **to ~ of sth** non intromettersi in qc; **to ~ of trouble** tenersi fuori dai guai **II.** *vt* **to keep sth/sb out** (of sth) non far entrare qc/ qu (in qc); **to keep the rain/cold out** non far passare la pioggia/il freddo

◆**keep to I.** *vt always sep* (*remain private*) **to keep sth to oneself** tenersi qc per sé; **to keep to oneself** starsene in disparte **II.** *vi* **1.**(*stay in*) **~ the right** tenere la destra; **to ~ one's bed** rimanere a letto **2.**(*respect*) **to ~ sth** rispettare qc; **to keep sb to his/her word** fare rispettare a qu la parola data

◆**keep together I.** *vt* tenere unito **II.** *vi* restare insieme; **please, ~** per favore, non allontanatevi dal gruppo

◆**keep up I.** *vt* **1.**(*trousers*) tenere su; (*ceiling*) reggere; (*prices*) tenere alto **2.**(*continue*) continuare; **to ~ the payments** rispettare i pagamenti; **~ the good work!** continua così!; **keep it up!** continua così! **3.**(*maintain*) **to ~ appearances** mantenere le apparenze; **to ~ traditions** conservare le tradizioni **4.**(*stop sb sleeping*) tenere sveglio **II.** *vi* **1.**(*prices*) mantenersi stabile; (*moral*) mantenersi alto, -a **2.**(*continue*) continuare; **the rain kept up all night** ha continuato a piovere tutta la notte **3.**(*to stay level with*) **to ~** (with sb/sth) stare al passo (con qu/qc); **wages are failing to ~ with inflation** i salari non riescono a stare al passo con l'inflazione; **I cannot ~ with their conversations** non riesco a seguire le loro conversazioni; **to ~ with the Joneses** *fig* non essere da meno dei propri vicini **4.**(*maintain contact with*) **to ~ with sb** mantenere i contatti con qu **5.**(*remain informed*) **to ~ with sth** tenersi aggiornato su qc; **to ~ with the times** stare al passo coi tempi

keeper ['kiː·pə] *n* **1.**(*in charge*) guardiano, -a *m, f;* (*museum*) curatore, -trice *m, f;* (*jail*) guardia *f* **2.**SPORTS portiere *m*

keeping ['kiː·pɪŋ] *n* **1.**(*guarding*) custodia *f;* **to leave sth/sb in sb's ~** affidare qc/qu in custodia di qu; **to leave sth/sb in safe ~** lasciare qc/qu in buone mani **2.in ~ with sth** in linea con qc; **to be out of ~ with sth** non essere adatto a qc

keepsake ['kiːp·seɪk] *n* ricordo *m*

kefir [kə·'fiːr] *n* bevanda cremosa fatta con latte di mucca

keg [keg] *n* barilotto *m*

keister ['kiː·s·tə] *n* *sl* (*buttocks*) chiappe *fpl;* (*anus*) culo *m*

kelp [kelp] *n* laminaria *f* (*tipo di alga bruna*)

ken [ken] *n* **to be beyond sb's ~** andare oltre la propria comprensione

Ken. *n abbr of* **Kentucky** Ken., Kentucky *m*

kennel ['ke·nl] *n* **1.**(*doghouse*) cuccia *f* **2.** *pl* (*boarding*) pensione *f* per cani; (*breeding*) allevamento *m* di cani

Kentucky [kən·'tʌ·ki] *n* Kentucky *m*

Kenya ['ken·jə] *n* Kenia *m*

Kenyan ['ken·jən] I. *n* keniota *mf* II. *adj* keniota

Keogh plan ['ki:·oʊ plæn] *n piano di pensionamento per i lavoratori autonomi statunitensi*

kept [kept] I. *pt, pp of* **keep** II. *adj* mantenuto, -a; **a ~ woman** un'amante; **a ~ man** un gigoló

kerchief ['kɜ:r·tʃɪf] *n fazzoletto per il collo o per la testa*

kernel ['kɜ:r·nl] *n* **1.** (*center of fruit*) mandorla *f;* (*of nut*) gheriglio *m* **2. corn ~** chicco *m* di grano **3.** (*essential part*) nocciolo *m;* **a ~ of truth** un fondo di verità

kerosene ['ke·rə·si:n] *n* cherosene *m*

ketchup ['ke·tʃəp] *n* ketchup *m inv*

kettle ['ke·t̬l] *n* bollitore *m;* **to put the ~ on** mettere a bollire l'acqua ▶ **that's a different ~ of fish** è un altro paio di maniche; **to get into a pretty ~ of fish** cacciarsi in un bel guaio

kettledrum ['ke·t̬l·drʌm] *n* MUS timpano *m*

key¹ [ki:] I. *n* **1.** (*doors*) chiave *f;* **master ~** passe-partout *m inv* **2. a.** COMPUT tasto *m;* **caps lock ~** tasto delle maiuscole; **to hit a ~** premere un tasto **3.** (*essential topic*) chiave *f;* **the ~ to a mystery** la chiave di un mistero; **a ~ factor/role** un fattore/ruolo chiave **4.** (*list*) legenda *f;* (*exercises*) soluzioni *fpl* **5.** MUS tonalità *f;* **change of ~** cambio *m* di tonalità; **in the ~ of C major** in (tonalità di) Do maggiore; **to go off ~** stonare ▶ **to hold the ~ to** avere la chiave di qc II. *adj* chiave III. *vt* **1.** (*type*) **to ~** (**in**) (*data*) immettere **2.** (*make appropriate*) adattare

♦ **key in** *vt* COMPUT (*data*) immettere

♦ **key up** *vt* emozionare; **to be keyed up** essere emozionato; **to be keyed up for sth** essere agitato per qc

key [ki:] *n* (*island*) isolotto *m*

keyboard ['ki:·bɔ:rd] I. *n* tastiera *f* II. *vi* digitare III. *vt* (*data*) immettere

keyboarding *n* digitazione *f*

keyboard instrument *n* strumento *m* a tastiera

keycard *n* keycard *f inv*

keyhole ['ki:·hoʊl] *n* buco *m* della serratura

key money *n* cauzione *f;* **as ~** a titolo cauzionale

keynote ['ki:·noʊt] *n* **1.** MUS dominante *f* **2.** (*central idea*) idea *f* fondamentale; **to be the ~ of sth** essere la nota dominante di qc *fig*

keynote address *n* discorso *m* principale

keynoter *n* oratore, -trice *m, f* principale

keynote speech *n* discorso *m* principale

keypad ['ki:·pæd] *n* COMPUT tastiera *f*

key ring *n* portachiavi *m inv*

keystone *n* **a.** ARCHIT (*center stone*) chiave *f* di volta

keystroke *n* battuta *f* di tasto

keyword *n* parola *f* chiave

kg *abbr of* **kilogram** kg

khaki ['kæ:·ki] I. *n* (*color*) cachi *m;* (*cloth*) tessuto *m* cachi; **~s** pantaloni *m pl* di tessuto cachi II. *adj* cachi

kHz *n abbr of* **kilohertz** KHz

KIA *adj abbr of* **killed in action** ucciso, -a in azione

kibble ['kɪ·bl] *n* croccantini *mpl*

kibbutz [kɪ·'bʊts] *n* kibbutz *m inv*

kibosh ['kaɪ·bɑ:ʃ] *n* **to put the ~ on sth** mettere fine a qc

kick [kɪk] I. *n* **1.** (*of person, horse*) calcio *m;* (*in football*) tiro *m;* (*in swimming*) battuta *f* delle gambe **2.** (*exciting feeling*) piacere *m;* **to do sth for ~s** fare qc per divertimento; **to get a ~ out of sth** trarre un immenso piacere da qc; **this drink has a ~ to it** questa bevanda ti stende **3.** (*craze*) **he is on an exercise ~ at the moment** adesso ha la fissa della ginnastica **4.** (*gun jerk*) rinculo *m* ▶ **a ~ in the teeth** un calcio sui denti II. *vt* **1.** dare un calcio a; **to ~ sth open** aprire qc con un calcio; **to ~ a ball** dare un calcio a una palla; **to ~ oneself** *fig* prendersi a schiaffi da solo **2.** (*stop*) smettere; **to ~ a habit** perdere un vizio III. *vi* **1.** (*person*) dare un calcio; (*horse*) scalciare; SPORTS tirare un calcio **2.** (*gun*) rinculare **3.** (*complain*) protestare; **to ~ about sth** lamentarsi di qc; **to ~ against sth** opporsi a qc **4. to be alive and ~ing** *inf* essere vivo e vegeto

♦ **kick about, kick around** I. *vi inf* (*hang about*) gironzolare; (*thing*) rotolare II. *vt* **1.** (*a ball*) palleggiare **2.** (*treat badly*) maltrattare

♦ **kick against** *vt insep* ribellarsi a

♦ **kick around** *vt inf* **1.** (*treat badly*) prendere a calci **2.** (*ponder: idea*) esaminare **3.** *insep* (*person*) andarsene in giro; (*object*) essere in giro da qualche parte

♦ **kick at** *vt* prendere a calci

♦ **kick away** *vt* allontanare con un calcio

♦ **kick back** I. *vt* (*football*) restituire II. *vi inf* **1.** (*recoil: gun*) rinculare **2.** *inf* (*relax*) rilassarsi **3.** *sl* (*give a kickback*) corrompere

♦ **kick in** *vt* sfondare a calci; **to kick sb's teeth in** spaccare la faccia a qu

♦ **kick off** I. *vi* (*begin*) cominciare; (*in football*) battere il calcio d'inizio II. *vt* togliersi con un calcio

♦ **kick out** I. *vt* **to kick sb out** cacciare via qu a pedate *inf;* **he was kicked out of the party** lo hanno buttato fuori a calci dalla festa II. *vi* (*person, horse*) tirare calci

♦ **kick over** *vi* **to ~ the traces** perdere ogni controllo

♦ **kick up** *vt* **to ~ dust** *a. fig* sollevare polvere; **to ~ a fuss/row** piantare un casino ▶ **to ~ one's heels** darsi alla pazza gioia

♦ **kick upstairs** *vt* promuovere (*allo scopo di sbarazzarsi di una persona*)

kickback ['kɪk·bæk] *n inf* bustarella *f*

kicker ['kɪ·kɚ] *n* **1.** (*person who kicks*) tiratore, -trice *m, f* **2.** *fig* **to be a ~** avere coraggio **3.** (*surprise*) **it was a real ~ for me** mi lasciò di stucco *inf* **4.** (*sth disadvantageous*) tranello *m*

kickoff ['kɪk·ɑ:f] *n* **1.** SPORTS calcio *m* d'inizio

2. *inf* (*beginning*) inizio *m*
kick starter *n* AUTO pedale *m* d'avviamento
kid [kɪd] **I.** *n* **1.** (*child*) bambino, -a *m, f;* (*young person*) ragazzo, -a *m, f;* ~ **brother** fratello *m* piccolo; **as a** ~ ... da ragazzo...; *sl* (*term of address*) ragazzo, -a *m, f* **2.** ZOOL (*young goat*) capretto *m* **3.** (*goat leather*) capretto *m* ▸ **to treat sb with** ~ **gloves** trattare qu con i guanti (bianchi); **that's** ~ **'s stuff** è roba da bambini *inf* **II.** <-dd-> *vi* scherzare; **are you** ~**ding?** stai scherzando?; **just** ~ **ding** stavo scherzando; **no** ~**ding!** davvero! **III.** *vt* **to** ~ **sb** (**about sth**) prendere in giro qu (per qc) **IV.** *vr* **to** ~ **oneself that** ... illudersi che...; **stop** ~**ding yourself!** smettila di illuderti!
kiddie *n,* **kiddy** ['kɪ·di] *n inf* bimbo, -a *m, f*
kidnap ['kɪd·næp] **I.** <-pp-> *vt* rapire **II.** *n* sequestro *m* di persona
kidnapper ['kɪd·næ·pə·] *n* sequestratore, -trice *m, f*
kidnapping *n* sequestro *m* di persona
kidney ['kɪd·ni] *n* rene *m;* ~ **disease** malattia *f* renale
kidney bean *n* fagiolo *m* rosso
kidney donor *n* donatore, -trice di reni *m*
kidney failure *n* MED blocco *m* renale
kidney machine *n* MED rene *m* artificiale
kidney stone *n* MED calcolo *m* renale
kill [kɪl] **I.** *n* **1.** (*slaughter*) uccisione *f* **2.** (*hunting*) preda *f* ▸ **to be in at the** ~ essere presente al momento cruciale; **to go in for the** ~ assestare il colpo di grazia **II.** *vi* uccidere; **thou shalt not** ~ (*Bible*) non uccidere ▸ **to be dressed to** ~ essere tutto in ghingheri **III.** *vt* **1.** (*cause to die*) uccidere; **to** ~ **oneself** uccidersi; **to** ~ **oneself with laughter** *fig* morire dalle risate; **this will** ~ **you!** *fig* questa ti farà morire dalle risate!; **not to** ~ **oneself trying** *fig, inf* non sforzarsi troppo **2.** (*destroy*) distruggere; **to** ~ **the flavor of sth** uccidere il sapore di qc; **my feet are** ~**ing me!** i piedi mi fanno male da morire!; **to** ~ **sb with kindness** sommergere qu di attenzioni
◆ **kill off** *vt* sterminare; (*a disease*) eradicare
killer ['kɪ·lə·] *n* **1.** (*sb who kills*) assassino, -a *m, f;* **to be a** ~ (*person*) essere un assassino; (*disease*) fare tante vittime; **the test was a real** ~ *fig, inf* il compito era proprio tosto **2.** *inf* (*talented*) **to be a** ~ essere geniale; (*amusing*); **this joke is a** ~ questa barzelleta fa morire dalle risate
killer disease *n* malattia *f* mortale
killer whale *n* orca *f*
killing ['kɪ·lɪŋ] **I.** *n* (*of a person*) assassinio *m;* (*of an animal*) uccisione *f* ▸ **to make a** ~ *inf* fare una fortuna **II.** *adj* **1.** (*murderous*) mortale **2.** (*exhausting*) micidiale **3.** (*funny*) esilarante
killjoy ['kɪl·dʒɔɪ] *n* guastafeste *mf inv*
kiln [kɪln] *n* forno *m* per ceramica
kilo ['kiː·loʊ] *n* chilo *m,* kilo *m*
kilobyte ['kɪ·lə·baɪt] *n* COMPUT kilobyte *m inv*
kilocycle ['kɪ·lə·ˌsaɪ·kl] *n* kilociclo *m*
kilogram ['kɪ·lə·græm] *n* kilogrammo *m*

kilohertz *n* kilohertz *m inv*
kilojoule ['kɪ·lə·dʒuːl] *n* kilojoule *m inv*
kilometer [kɪ·'lɑː·mə·t̬ə·] *n* chilometro *m,* kilometro *m*
kilowatt ['kɪ·lə·wɑːt] *n* kilowatt *m inv*
kilowatt-hour *n* kilowattora *m inv*
kilt [kɪlt] *n* kilt *m inv*
kimono [kə·'mɔʊ·nə] *n* chimono *m*
kin [kɪn] *n* **next of** ~ parenti *m pl* stretti
kind[1] [kaɪnd] *adj* gentile; **to be** ~ **to sb** essere gentile con qu; **he was** ~ **enough to** ... è stato così gentile da...; **would you be** ~ **enough/so** ~ **as to** ...? può essere così gentile da...?; **with** ~ **regards** (*in a letter*) distinti saluti
kind[2] [kaɪnd] **I.** *n* **1.** (*type*) tipo *f;* **sth of the** ~ qualcosa del genere; **he is not that** ~ (*of person*) non è quel genere di persona; **what** ~ **of** ...? che tipo di...?; **all** ~**s of** ... tutti i tipi di...; **the first of its** ~ il primo nel suo genere; **to hear/say nothing of the** ~ non sentire/dire niente del genere; **they are two of a** ~ sono tali e quali **2.** (*sth similar to*) specie *f;* **a** ~ **of soup** una specie di minestra **3.** (*sth equal to*) **to do sth in** ~ fare qc allo stesso modo; **he swore at me so I answered in** ~ mi insultò, così gli riposi per le rime; **he repaid her betrayal in** ~ ripagò il suo tradimento con la stessa moneta **4.** (*limited*) **in a** ~ **of way** in un certo senso; **she has found happiness of a** ~ **with him** con lui ha trovato una qualche forma di felicità **5.** (*payment*) **to pay sb in** ~ pagare qu in natura **II.** *adv inf* **I** ~ **of like it** in un certo senso mi piace; **he was** ~ **of sad** era piuttosto triste; **"do you like it?" — "~ of"** "ti piace?" — "abbastanza"
kindergarten ['kɪn·də·gɑːr·dn] *n* asilo *m* infantile
kindhearted [ˌkaɪnd·'hɑːr·t̬ɪd] *adj* di cuore; **he is very** ~ è molto generoso
kindle ['kɪn·dl] **I.** *vt a. fig* accendere; **to** ~ **sb's interest** suscitare l'interesse di qu; **to** ~ **sb's desire** accendere il desiderio in qu **II.** *vi a. fig* accendersi
kindling ['kɪnd·lɪŋ] *n* **1.** (*firewood*) legna *f* da ardere **2.** (*act of lighting*) accensione *f*
kindly ['kaɪnd·li] **I.** <-ier, -iest> *adj* gentile **II.** *adv* **1.** (*in a kind manner*) gentilmente **2.** (*please*) **you are** ~ **requested to leave the building** siete pregati di abbandonare l'edificio; ~ **put that book away!** metti via quel libro, per piacere! **3.** (*favorably*) **to take** ~ **to sth** accettare qc di buon grado
kindness ['kaɪnd·nɪs] <-es> *n* **1.** (*act of being kind*) gentilezza *f* **2.** (*kind act*) gentilezza *f;* **to do sb a** ~ fare una gentilezza a qu
kindred ['kɪnd·rɪd] **I.** *n* + *pl vb* familiari *mpl* **II.** *adj* affine; ~ **spirits** anime *f pl* gemelle
kinetic [kɪ·'ne·t̬ɪk] *adj* PHYS cinetico, -a
kinfolk ['kɪn·foʊk] *n* + *pl vb, Am* familiari *mpl*
king [kɪŋ] *n* **1. a.** GAMES re *m;* **the** ~ **of beasts** il re della foresta **2.** (*in checkers*) dama *f*
kingdom ['kɪŋ·dəm] *n* regno *m;* **animal/plant** ~ regno animale/vegetale; **the** ~ **of**

God REL il regno di Dio ►**to blow** sth **to ~ come** distruggere qc; **(un)til ~ come** fino al Giorno del Giudizio

kingfisher ['kɪŋ·fɪ·ʃə] *n* martin *m* pescatore *inv*

kingly ['kɪŋ·li] *adj* regale

kingpin ['kɪŋ·pɪn] *n* 1. (*in bowling*) birillo centrale 2. TECH perno *m;* **to be the ~** (*person, thing*) essere il perno

king-size ['kɪŋ·saɪz] *adj* gigante; **~ bed** letto *m* doppio

kink [kɪŋk] *n* 1. (*twist: in a pipe, rope*) attorcigliamento *m;* (*in hair*) riccio *m* 2. (*sore muscle*) contrattura *f* (muscolare); **to have a ~ in one's neck** avere il torcicollo 3. (*problem*) difficoltà *m;* **to iron out** (**a few**) **~s** appianare (del)le difficoltà 4. (*strange habit*) stramberia *f*

kinky ['kɪŋ·ki] <-ier, -iest> *adj* 1. (*twisted*) attorcigliato, -a 2. (*with tight curls*) crespo, -a 3. (*unusual*) bizzarro, -a; (*involving unusual sexual acts*) pervertito, -a

kinsfolk ['kɪnz·fʊk] *n* HIST + *pl vb* parentado *m*

kinship *n* (*family relationship*) parentela *f;* (*similarity*) affinità *f;* **to feel a ~ with sb** sentire affinità con qu

kinsman <-men> *n* HIST parente *m*

kinswoman <-women> *n* HIST parente *f*

kiosk ['kiː·ɑːsk] *n* (*stand, pavilion*) chiosco *m*

kipper ['kɪ·pə] *n* aringa *f* affumicata

Kiribati [kɪ·rə·'bɑː·ti, -'bæs] *n* Kiribati *m*

kiss [kɪs] I. <-es> *n* bacio *m;* **~ of life** respirazione *f* bocca a bocca; **~ of death** *fig* colpo *m* di grazia; **to blow sb a ~** mandare un bacio a qu; **love and ~es** (*at the end of a letter*) tanti baci II. *vi* baciarsi III. *vt* baciare; **to ~ sb goodnight/goodbye** dare il bacio della buonanotte/dell'arrivederci a qu

kisser ['kɪ·sə] *n* 1. (*person*) **he's a wonderful ~!** bacia molto bene! 2. *sl* (*mouth*) bocca *f;* (*face*) faccia *f*

kiss-off ['kɪs·ɑːf] *n inf* **to give the ~** dare il benservito

kissproof *adj* indelebile

kit [kɪt] *n* 1. (*set*) attrezzatura *f;* **first aid ~** cassetta *f* di pronto soccorso; **sewing ~** kit *m* per cucire *inv;* **tool ~** cassetta *f* degli attrezzi 2. (*parts to put together*) kit *m inv*

kitchen ['kɪt·ʃɪn] *n* cucina *f*

kitchen cabinet *n* gruppo *di consulenti non ufficiali di un capo di governo*

kitchenette [ˌkɪt·ʃɪ·'net] *n* (*room*) cucinino *m;* (*part of room*) angolo *m* cottura

kitchen foil *n* carta *f* stagnola

kitchen garden *n* orto *m*

kitchen paper *n* carta *f* da cucina

kitchen range *n*, **kitchen stove** *n* cucina *f* economica

kitchen sink *n* lavello *m* ►**to take everything but the ~** portarsi appresso tutta la casa

kitchen towel *n* (*dishtowel*) strofinaccio *m* da cucina

kitchen unit *n* modulo *m* di cucina componi-bile

kitchenware *n* stoviglie *fpl*

kite [kaɪt] *n* 1. ZOOL nibbio *m* 2. FIN assegno *m* a vuoto 3. (*toy*) aquilone *m;* **to fly a ~** far volare un aquilone; *fig* tastare il terreno ►**go fly a ~!** *inf* va a farti friggere!

kitsch [kɪtʃ] I. *n* kitsch *m inv* II. *adj* kitsch

kitten ['kɪ·tn] *n* gattino, -a *m, f* ►**I nearly had ~s** mi è quasi preso un colpo

kittenish ['kɪ·tə·nɪʃ] *adj* che fa la gatta morta

kitty ['kɪ·ti] <-ies> *n* 1. *childspeak* (*kitten or cat*) micio, -a *m, f* 2. (*money*) cassa *f* comune

kiwi ['kiː·wiː] *n* 1. ZOOL, BOT kiwi *m* 2. *inf* (*New Zealander*) neozelandese *mf*

kJ *abbr of* **kilojoule** kJ *inv*

KKK [ˌkeɪ·keɪ·'keɪ] *n abbr of* **Ku Klux Klan** KKK, Ku Klux Klan *m*

Klaxon® ['klæk·sn] *n* clacson *m inv*

Kleenex® ['kliː·neks] *n* kleenex® *m inv*

kleptomania [ˌklep·toʊ·'meɪ·niə] *n* cleptomania *f*

kleptomaniac [ˌklep·toʊ·'meɪ·nɪ·æk] *n* cleptomane *mf*

klick [klɪk] *n inf* (*kilometer*) kilometro *m;* **the speed limit is 100 ~s** il limite di velocità è 100 kilometri

klutz [klʌts] *n sl* imbranato, -a *m, f*

km *abbr of* **kilometer** km

km/h, kmph *abbr of* **kilometers per hour** km/h

knack [næk] *n* abilità *f;* **to have a ~ for sth** aver una straordinaria capacità per qc; **to get the ~ of doing sth** prenderci la mano a fare qc

knapsack ['næp·sæk] *n* zaino *m*

knead [niːd] *vt* 1. CULIN impastare; (*clay*) modellare 2. (*massage*) massaggiare

knee [niː] I. *n* ginocchio *m;* **to be on one's ~s** *a. fig* essere in ginocchio; **to get down on one's ~s** inginocchiarsi; **on your ~s!** in ginocchio! ►**to bring sb to their ~s** mettere qu in ginocchio II. *vt* **to ~ sb** dare una ginocchiata a qu

kneecap ['niː·ˌkæp] I. *n* rotula *f* II. <-pp-> *vt* gambizzare

knee-deep *adj* **to be ~ in sth** (*work, problems*) essere sommerso da qc; **I was ~ in water/snow** l'acqua/la neve mi arrivava alle ginocchia

knee-high *adj* **to be ~** alto, -a fino al ginocchio

knee-jerk ['niː·dʒɜːrk] *adj sl* impulsivo, -a

kneel [niːl] <knelt *o* kneeled, knelt *o* kneeled> *vi* inginocchiarsi

knee pad *n* SPORTS ginocchiera *f*

knee sock *n* calzino *m* lungo

knell [nel] *n* campana *f* a morto; **to sound the ~ for sth** *fig* annunciare la fine di qc

knelt [nelt] *pt of* **kneel**

knew [nuː] *pt of* **know**

knickers ['nɪ·kəz] *npl* (*panties*) mutandine *fpl;* (*trousers*) pantaloni alla zuava

knickknack ['nɪk·næk] *n inf* ninnolo *m*

knife [naɪf] <knives> I. *n* 1. coltello *m* 2. (*dagger*) pugnale *m;* **to wield a ~** brandire un coltello *elev* **3.** (*in a machine*) lama *f* ► to **turn the** ~ (**in the wound**) rigirare il coltello nella piaga; **to be <u>under</u> the** ~ MED essere sotto i ferri **II.** *vt* accoltellare

knife-edge *n* filo *m* del coltello; **to be (balanced) on a** ~ *fig* essere appeso a un filo

knife sharpener *n* affilacoltelli *m inv*

knifing ['naɪ·fɪŋ] *n* accoltellamento *m*

knight [naɪt] **I.** *n* **1.** (*man given honorable rank*) cavaliere *m* **2.** HIST (*man of high social position*) cavaliere *m* **3.** (*chess figure*) cavallo *m* ► ~ **in shining <u>armor</u>** principe *m* azzurro; (*salvatore*) cavaliere *m* senza macchia (e senza paura) **II.** *vt* HIST investire cavaliere; (*give a honorable title*) nominare cavaliere

knight-errant [ˌnaɪt·ˈe·rənt] <knights-errant> *n* cavaliere *m* errante

knighthood *n* titolo *m* di cavaliere; **to give sb a** ~ nominare qu cavaliere

knightly ['naɪt·li] *adj liter* cavalleresco, -a

knit [nɪt] **I.** *vi* (*wool*) lavorare a maglia; (*with a machine*) tessere **II.** *vt* (*wool*) fare ai ferri ► to ~ **one's <u>brows</u>** aggrottare le sopracciglia

♦**knit together I.** *vi* **1.** (*combine or join*) unirsi **2.** (*mend*) saldarsi **II.** *vt* **1.** (*bones*) saldare **2.** *fig* (*join*) unire

knitter ['nɪ·t̬ɚ] *n* **Tabitha is a wonderful** ~ Tabitha è molto brava a lavorare a maglia

knitting *n* **1.** (*the product of knitting*) lavoro *m* a maglia **2.** (*material being knitted*) lavoro *f* a maglia **3.** (*action of knitting*) **she likes** ~ le piace lavorare a maglia

knitting needle *n* ferro *m* da calza

knitting yarn *n* filato *m* di lana

knitwear ['nɪt̬·wer] *n* maglieria *f*

knives *n pl of* **knife**

knob [nɑːb] *n* **1.** (*round handle: of a door, a drawer*) pomello *m;* (*of switch*) manopola *f* **2.** (*small amount*) pezzetto *m;* (*of butter*) noce *f* **3.** (*lump*) zolletta *f*

knobby ['nɑː·bi] <-ier, -iest> *adj* nodoso, -a

knock [nɑːk] **I.** *n* **1.** (*blow*) colpo *m* **2.** (*sound*) colpo *m;* **to give a** ~ **at the door** bussare alla porta **3.** *fig, inf* (*criticism*) strigliata *f;* **to take a** ~ (*damage*) ricevere una mazzata **II.** *vi* **1.** (*hit*) urtare; **to** ~ **on the window/at the door** bussare alla finestra/porta **2.** TECH (*engine*) battere in testa **III.** *vt* **1.** (*hit*) colpire; **to** ~ **sb** colpire qu; **to** ~ **a hole into the wall** fare un buco nella parete; **to** ~ **the bottom out of sth** sfondare qc; *fig* mettere in crisi qc **2.** *inf* (*criticize*) dare addosso a

♦**knock about** *vi, vt s.* **knock around**

♦**knock around I.** *vi inf* vagabondare; **to** ~ **in town** andarsene in giro per la città **II.** *vt* (*person*) picchiare; (*ball*) colpire

♦**knock back** *vt inf* **1.** (*drink quickly*) bere tutto d'un sorso; **to knock a beer back** scolarsi una birra **2.** (*surprise*) lasciare di stucco

♦**knock down** *vt* **1.** (*cause to fall*) buttare a terra; (*with a car*) investire **2.** (*demolish*) buttar giù; **to** ~ **every argument** *fig* smontare punto per punto un ragionamento **3.** (*reduce*)

abbassare; **to knock the price down** farsi fare uno sconto **4.** (*sell at auction*) aggiudicare; **the picture was knocked down to David** David si è aggiudicato il quadro

♦**knock into** *vt* (*make understand*) inculcare; **to knock some sense into sb** ficcare un po' di buon senso nell zucca di qu

♦**knock off I.** *vt* **1.** (*cause to fall off*) far cadere; **to knock sb off his pedestal** *fig* far scendere qu dal piedistallo **2.** (*reduce*) abbassare; **to knock \$5 off the price** fare uno sconto di 5 dollari **3.** *inf* (*steal*) fregare **4.** *inf* (*murder*) ammazzare **5.** (*produce easily*) sfornare; **to** ~ **some copies** sfornare alcune copie **6.** (*stop*) **to knock it off** smetterla; **knock it off!** smettila! **II.** *vi inf* staccare; **to** ~ **work at 3 p.m.** smontare alle tre dal lavoro; **to** ~ **for lunch** fare la pausa pranzo

♦**knock on** *vi* **to be knocking on 40** avvicinarsi ai 40

♦**knock out** *vt* **1.** (*render unconscious*) far perdere i sensi; SPORTS mettere K.O.; (*cause to sleep*) far dormire; (*exhaust*) sfiancare **2.** (*remove*) vuotare; (*contents in text*) togliere **3.** (*eliminate*) eliminare; **to be knocked out of a competition** essere eliminato da una gara **4.** (*produce quickly*) sfornare **5.** *inf* (*astonish*) sbalordire; **to knock sb out** lasciare qu di stucco

♦**knock over** *vt* (*person*) investire; (*object*) rovesciare

♦**knock together** *vt* montare alla meno peggio; **to** ~ **something to eat** mettere insieme qualcosa da mangiare

♦**knock up I.** *vt inf* (*make pregnant*) mettere incinta; **to get knocked up** rimanere incinta **II.** *vi* SPORTS palleggiare

knockabout ['nɑː·kə·baʊt] *adj* **1.** (*rowdy*) grossolano, -a **2.** (*sturdy: overcoat, toy*) da battaglia

knockdown *adj* **1.** (*very cheap*) bassissimo, -a; ~ **price** prezzo *m* di saldo; (*at auction*) prezzo *m* iniziale **2.** (*violent: blow*) duro, -a; (*argument*) schiacciante; (*fight*) violento, -a

knockdown-dragout *adj* senza esclusione di colpi

knocker ['nɑː·kɚ] *n* (*on door*) battente *m*

knock-kneed ['nɑː·k·niːd] *adj* con le gambe ad X; *fig* debole

knockoff *n inf* oggetto *m* contraffatto

knockout I. *n* **1.** (*competition*) gara *f* a eliminazione diretta **2.** SPORTS (*boxing*) K.O. *m;* **to win sth by a** ~ vincere qc per K.O. **3.** *inf* (*person*) schianto *m* **II.** *adj* **1.** (*competition*) a eliminazione diretta **2.** (*boxing*) ~ **blow** colpo *m* da K.O.; *fig* duro colpo *m;* **to deal sb's hopes a** ~ **blow** dare un duro colpo alle speranze di qu **3.** *inf* (*attractive*) da schianto

knoll [noʊl] *n* collinetta *f*

knot [nɑːt] **I.** *n* **1.** *a.* NAUT nodo *m;* **to tie/untie a** ~ fare/disfare un nodo **2.** (*bow*) fiocco *m* **3.** (*chignon*) chignon *m inv*, chongo **4.** (*small group*) capannello *m* **5.** (*in a wooden board*)

K

nodo *m* ▶ **to tie the ~** *inf* sposarsi **II.** <-tt-> *vt* annodare; **to ~ sth together** legare qc insieme con un nodo **III.** <-tt-> *vi* (*stomach*) chiudersi
knotty ['nɑːt̬i] <-ier, -iest> *adj* **1.** (*full of knots: lumber, wood*) nodoso, -a; (*hair*) pieno, -a di nodi **2.** (*difficult*) spinoso, -a
knotty pine *n* pino *m* nodoso
know [noʊ] **I.** <knew, known> *vt* **1.** (*have information*) sapere; **to ~ a bit of English** sapere un po' di inglese; **she ~s all of their names** conosce tutti i loro nomi; **to ~ how to do sth** saper fare qc; **to ~ all there is to ~ about sth** sapere tutto quello che c'è da sapere su qc; **to ~ what one is talking about** sapere ciò che si dice; **to ~ sth by heart** sapere qc a memoria; **not to ~ the first thing about sth/ sb** non sapere un bel niente di qc/qu; **to ~ all the answers** conoscere tutte le risposte; **if you ~ what I mean** sai di cosa parli; **do you ~ what I mean?** sai cosa voglio dire?; **to ~ that ...** sapere che...; **to want to ~ sth** voler sapere qc; **do you ~ ...?** sai...?; **you ~ what?** *inf* sai una cosa? **2.** (*be acquainted with*) conoscere; **to ~ sb by sight/by name/personally** conoscere qu di vista/di nome/personalmente; **(not) to ~ sb to speak to** (non) conoscere qualcuno con cui parlare; **~ing sb, ...** conoscendo qu,...; **to get to ~ sb** cominciare a conoscere qu; **to get to ~ each other** cominciare a conoscersi (bene); **to have ~n sth** aver conosciuto qc; **to ~ sth like the back of one's hand** *fig* conoscere qc come le proprie tasche **3.** (*recognize*) riconoscere; **to ~ sb/sth by sth** riconoscere qu/qc da qc; **to ~ sb for sth** riconoscere qu per qc **II.** <knew, known> *vi* **1.** (*be informed*) sapere; **as far as I ~** per quanto ne so; **to ~ better (than sb)** sapere meglio (di qu); **to ~ of** [*o* about] **sth** sapere di qc; **you ~** (*you remember*) lo sai; (*you understand*) sai; **(well) what do you ~!** *iron* indovina un po'!; **I ~!** (*I've got an idea!*) ho un'idea!; (*said to agree with sb*) lo so! **2.** (*be certain*) essere sicuro; **there's no ~ing** chissà; **one never ~s** non si sa mai **3.** *inf* (*understand*) capire **III.** *n* **to be in the ~** essere informato; **to be in the ~ about sth** essere al corrente di qc
know-how *n* know-how *m inv;* **to have ~ about sth** avere il know-how di qc
knowing ['noʊ·ɪŋ] **I.** *adj* astuto, -a; (*grins, look, smile*) d'intesa **II.** *n* **there's no ~** non c'è modo di saperlo
knowingly *adv* **1.** (*look, smile*) con complicità **2.** (*with full awareness*) deliberatamente
know-it-all ['noʊ·ɪt̬·ɔːl] *n inf* sapientone, -a *m, f*
knowledge ['nɑː·lɪdʒ] *n* **1.** (*body of learning*) conoscenza *m;* **to have (some) ~ of sth** avere (una qualche) conoscenza di qc; **to have a thorough ~ of sth** conoscere qc a fondo **2.** (*acquired information*) sapere *m;* **to have (no) ~ about sth/sb** non sapere (niente) di qc/qu; **to my ~** che io sappia; **to be common ~** essere di dominio pubblico **3.** (*aware-*

ness) conoscenza *m;* **to bring sth to sb's ~** mettere qu a conoscenza di qc; **to do sth without sb's ~** fare qc all'insaputa di qu; **to deny all ~ (of sth)** negare di sapere qualsiasi cosa (di qc)
knowledgeable ['nɑː·lɪ·dʒə·bl] *adj* bene informato, -a; **to be ~ about sth** conoscere qc molto bene
known [noʊn] **I.** *vt, vi pp of* **know II.** *adj* (*expert*) riconosciuto, -a; (*criminal*) noto, -a; **for no ~ reason** per nessun motivo conosciuto; **to make sth ~** rivelare qc; **to make oneself ~ to sb** farsi riconoscere da qu
knuckle ['nʌ·kl] *n* nocca *f* ▶ **to rap sb's ~s** *inf* dare una strigliata a qu
◆**knuckle down** *vi* darci dentro; **to ~ to work** mettersi sotto a lavorare
◆**knuckle under** *vi* piegarsi
knuckle-duster ['nʌ·kl·dʌs·tə] *n sl* (*weapon*) pugno *m* di ferro
knucklehead *n inf* stupido, -a
knuckle sandwich *n sl* pugno *m* in faccia
KO [ˌkeɪ·'oʊ] *abbr of* **knockout** K.O. *m inv*
koala [koʊ·'ɑː·lə] *n,* **koala bear** *n* koala *m inv*
kooky ['kuː·ki] <-ier, -iest> *adj inf* strampalato, -a
Koran [kə·'ræn] *n* **the ~** il Corano
Korea [kə·'ri·ə] *n* Corea *f;* **North/South ~** Corea del Nord/Sud
Korean [kə·'ri·ən] **I.** *adj* coreano, -a **II.** *n* **1.** (*person*) coreano, -a *m, f* **2.** LING coreano *m*
kosher ['koʊ·ʃə] *adj* kosher
kowtow [ˌkaʊ·'taʊ] *vi inf* inchinarsi fino a terra; **to ~ to sb** essere servile verso qu
kraft (paper) *n* carta *f* kraft
Kremlin ['krem·lɪn] *n* **the ~** il Cremlino
KS *n abbr of* **Kansas** KS, Kansas *m*
kudos ['kuː·doʊz] *n* fama *f;* **to get ~ for sth** conquistare la fama per qc
Ku Klux Klan ['kuː·'klʌks·'klæn] *n* **the ~** il Ku Klux Klan *m*
kumquat ['kʌm·kwɑːt] *n* kumquat *m inv* (*frutto simile al mandarino*)
kung fu [ˌkʊŋ·'fuː] *n* kung fu *m inv*
Kurd [kɜːrd] *n* curdo, -a *m, f*
Kurdish I. *adj* curdo, -a **II.** *n* **1.** (*person*) curdo, -a *m, f* **2.** LING curdo *m*
Kurdistan [ˌkɜːr·dɪ·'stæn] *n* Kurdistan *m*
Kuwait [kʊ·'weɪt] *n* Kuwait *m*
Kuwaiti I. *adj* kuwaitiano, -a **II.** *n* (*person*) kuwaitiano, -a *m, f*
kw *abbr of* **kilowatt** KW *m*
Kwanzaa ['kɑːn·zə] *n ricorrenza celebrata negli Stati Uniti all'interno della comunità afro americana durante la settimana che va dal 26 dicembre al primo gennaio.*
kWh *abbr of* **kilowatt hour** kWh
KWIC [kwɪk] COMPUT *abbr of* **key word in context** KWIC
KWOC COMPUT *abbr of* **key word out of context** KWOC
Ky. *n abbr of* **Kentucky** Ky, Kentucky *m*
KY *n abbr of* **Kentucky** Ky, Kentucky *m*

L

L, l [el] *n* L, l *f;* **~ as in Love** L come Livorno
l *abbr of* **liter** l.
L. *abbr of* **lake** L.
LA [ˌel·'eɪ] *n* **1.** *abbr of* **Los Angeles** Los
Angeles **2.** *abbr of* **Louisiana** Louisiana
lab [læb] *n abbr of* **laboratory** laboratorio *m*
lab coat *n* camice *m*
label ['leɪ·bəl] **I.** *n* **1.** etichetta *f* **2.** (*brand
name*) marca *f* **II.** <-l- *o* -ll-, -l- *o* -ll-> *vt*
1. (*affix label*) mettere l'etichetta su **2.** (*categorize*) etichettare
labelling *n*, **labeling** *n* etichettatura *f*
labor ['leɪ·bɚ] **I.** *n* **1.** (*work*) lavoro *m;* **manual ~** lavoro manuale; **to be a ~ of love** essere
un cosa fatta per passione **2.** ECON (*workers*)
manodopera *f;* **skilled ~** manodopera qualificata **3.** MED (*childbirth*) travaglio *m;* **to be in ~**
avere le doglie **II.** *vi* **1.** (*work*) lavorare **2.** (*do
sth with effort*) sforzarsi, faticare; **to ~ over
sth** sforzarsi per/in qc **3.** (*act at a disadvantage*) **to ~ under a delusion** illudersi **III.** *vt*
insistere su; **to ~ a point** insistere su un punto
laboratory ['læb·rə·ˌtɔː·ri] <-ies> *n* laboratorio *m*
laboratory assistant *n* assistente *mf* di laboratorio
laboratory test *n* test *m* di laboratorio *inv*
labor camp *n* campo *m* di lavoro
labor costs *npl* costo *m* della manodopera
Labor Day *n* festa *f* del lavoro

> **i** Il **Labor Day**, la festa del lavoro ameri-
> cana, non è celebrata il primo maggio, ma il
> primo lunedì di settembre. Il **Labor Day** è
> stato istituito a seguito di uno sciopero di fer-
> rovieri a Kensington, nel Maryland, nel corso
> del quale l'intervento di truppe dell'esercito
> causò la morte di due persone. Questa gior-
> nata in onore dei lavoratori è un giorno fes-
> tivo riconosciuto in tutto il paese.

labor dispute *n* conflitto *m* col datore di lavoro
laborer *n* manovale *mf*
labor force *n* forza *f* lavoro
labor-intensive *adj* che richiede molta manodopera
laborious [lə·'bɔː·ri·əs] *adj* laborioso, -a
labor pains *npl* MED dolori *m pl* del parto
labor relations *npl* rapporti *m pl* tra datore di
lavoro e dipendenti
laborsaving *adj* che fa risparmiare lavoro
labor shortage *n* carenza *f* di manodopera
labor union *n* sindacato *m*
Labrador (**retriever**) ['læb·rə·dɔːr (rɪ·'triː·
vɚ)] *n* labrador *m inv*
labyrinth ['læ·bə·rɪnθ] *n* labirinto *m*
lace [leɪs] **I.** *n* **1.** (*cloth*) pizzo *m;* (*edging*)

merletto *m* **2.** (*cord*) laccio *m;* **shoe ~s** lacci
delle scarpe **II.** *vt* **1.** (*fasten*) allacciare **2.** (*add
alcohol to*) correggere **3. she ~d her speech
with humorous remarks** inframmezzò il suo
discorso di battute
◆ **lace into** *vt* **to ~ sb** aggredire qu
◆ **lace up** *vt* allacciare
lacerate ['læ·sə·raɪt] *vt* lacerare
laceration [ˌlæ·sə·'reɪ·ʃən] *n* lacerazione *f*
lachrymose ['læk·rɪ·moʊs] *adj liter* **1.** (*given
to crying*) piagnone, -a **2.** (*sad*) lacrimoso, -a
lack [læk] **I.** *n* mancanza *f,* carenza *f;* **~ of
funds** mancanza di fondi; **for ~ of ...** per
mancanza di... **II.** *vt* mancare di; **she ~s tal-
ent/experience** le manca il talento/l'esperienza; **to ~ the energy to do sth** non avere la
forza per fare qc
lackadaisical [ˌlæ·kə·'deɪ·zɪ·kl] *adj* apatico, -a
lackey ['læ·ki] *n a. fig* lacché *m inv*
lacking ['læ·kɪŋ] *adj* **he is ~ in talent/experi-
ence** gli manca il talento/l'esperienza
lackluster ['læk·ˌlʌs·tɚ] *adj* **1.** (*not shiny*)
opaco, -a **2.** (*dull*) spento, -a
laconic [lə·'kɑː·nɪk] *adj* laconico, -a
lacquer ['læ·kɚ] **I.** *n* lacca *f* **II.** *vt* laccare
lacrosse [lə·'krɑːs] *n* SPORTS lacrosse *m*
lactose ['læk·toʊs] *n* lattosio *m;* **to be ~ intolerant** avere l'intolleranza al lattosio
lad [læd] *n inf* ragazzo *m*
ladder ['læ·dɚ] *n* **1.** (*for climbing*) scala *f* a
pioli **2.** (*hierarchy*) scala *f;* **to move up the ~**
farsi strada; (*in company*) fare carriera; **to
climb the social ~** avanzare nella scala sociale
laden ['leɪ·dn] *adj* carico, -a; **to be ~ with ...**
essere carico di...
la-di-da [ˌlɑː·di·'dɑː] *adj inf* pretenzioso, -a
ladies' room *n inf* bagno *m* delle signore
lading ['leɪ·dɪŋ] *n* NAUT carico *m*
ladle ['leɪ·dl] **I.** *n* mestolo *m;* **soup ~**
ramaiolo *m* **II.** *vt* **1.** (*soup*) servire (*con il
ramaiolo*) **2.** (*advice*) offrire generosamente
lady ['leɪ·di] <-ies> *n* signora *f;* (*aristocratic*)
dama *f;* **young ~** signorina *f;* **the ~ of the
house** la padrona di casa; **to be a real ~**
essere una vera signora; **cleaning ~** donna *f*
delle pulizie; **ladies and gentlemen!** signore
e signori!
ladybug ['leɪ·di·bʌg] *n* coccinella *f*
lady in waiting <-ies> *n* dama *f* di compagnia
lady-killer *n inf* dongiovanni *m inv*
ladylike *adj* da signora
ladyship *n form* **her ~** Sua Signoria
lady's maid *n* cameriera *f* personale
lady's man *n inf* uomo *m* che ci sa fare con le
donne
LAFTA *n abbr of* **Latin American Free Trade
Association**
lag [læg] **I.** *n* (*lapse*) intervallo *m* **II.** <-gg-> *vi*
to ~ behind sb/sth essere indietro rispetto a
qu/qc
lager ['lɑː·gɚ] *n* birra *f* chiara
lagging ['læ·gɪŋ] *n* rivestimento *m*
lagoon [lə·'guːn] *n* laguna *f*

L

laid [leɪd] *pt, pp of* **lay**[1]
laid-back *adj inf* rilassato, -a
lain [leɪn] *pp of* **lie**[2]
lair [ler] *n* **1.** (*of animal*) tana *f* **2.** (*of criminal*) covo *m*
laissez faire ['le·seɪ·'fer] *n* laissez-faire *m;* ~ **attitude** atteggiamento *m* permissivo
laity ['le·ɪə·t̬i] *n* **the** ~ il laicato
lake [leɪk] *n* lago *m*
lam [læm] **I.** *n inf* **to be on the** ~ essere latitante **II.** <-mm-> *vt inf* pestare
lama ['lɑː·mə] *n* REL lama *m inv*
lamb [læm] **I.** *n* **1.** (*animal*) agnello *m* **2.** (*meat*) (carne *f* di) agnello *m* **II.** *vi* figliare
lambaste [læm·'beɪst] *vt inf* attaccare duramente
lamb chop *n* costoletta *f* d'agnello
lambskin *n* (pelle *f* di) agnello *m*
lamb's wool *n* lambswool *m*
lame [leɪm] *adj* **1.** (*person, horse*) zoppo, -a; **to go** ~ azzopparsi **2.** *inf* (*argument, excuse*) debole
lameness *n* **1.** (*of person, horse*) zoppia *f* **2.** *inf* (*of argument, excuse*) debolezza *f*
lament [lə·'ment] **I.** *n* MUS, LIT lamento *m* **II.** *vt* lamentare; **to** ~ **sb** piangere qu **III.** *vi* **to** ~ **over sth** lamentarsi di qc
lamentable [lə·'mən·t̬ə·bl] *adj* deplorevole
lamentation [ˌlæ·mən·'teɪ·ʃən] *n* **1.** (*mourning*) lamentazioni *fpl* **2.** (*regrets*) lamenti *mpl*
laminate[1] ['læ·mɪ·nət] *n* TECH laminato *m*
laminate[2] ['læ·mɪ·neɪt] *vt* (*document*) plastificare; (*glass, wood*) laminare
laminated ['læ·mɪ·neɪ·t̬ɪd] *adj* (*document*) plastificato, -a; (*glass, wood*) laminato, -a
lamp [læmp] *n* lampada *f*; **bedside** ~ lampada *f* da comodino; **street** ~ lampione *m*
lampoon [læm·'puːn] **I.** *n* satira *f* **II.** *vt* fare la satira di
lamppost ['læmp·poʊst] *n* lampione *m*
lamprey ['læmp·ri] *n* lampreda *f*
lampshade ['læmp·ʃeɪd] *n* paralume *m*
LAN [læn] *n* INFOR *abbr of* **local area network** LAN *f*
lance [læns] **I.** *n* MIL lancia *f* **II.** *vt* MED incidere
lancet ['læn·sɪt] *n* MED lancetta *f*
land [lænd] **I.** *n* **1.** GEO, AGR terra *f*; **on** ~ sulla terraferma; **to travel by** ~ viaggiare via terra; **to work (on) the** ~ lavorare la terra; **to have dry** ~ **under one's feet** essere sulla terraferma **2.** (*for building*) terreno *m* **3.** *a.fig* (*country*) paese *m* ▶ **to see how the** ~ **lies** tastare il terreno **II.** *vi* **1.** (*plane, bird*) atterrare; **to** ~ **on the moon** allunare **2.** (*arrive by boat*) sbarcare **3.** (*set down, fall on*) posarsi **4.** (*person, ball*) finire; **if they catch you, you'll** ~ **in trouble** se ti scoprono, finisci nei guai **III.** *vt* **1.** (*bring onto land: aircraft*) far atterrare; (*boat*) approdare **2.** (*unload*) sbarcare **3.** (*obtain*) ottenere; (*fish*) prendere; **to** ~ **a job** beccarsi un impiego **4.** (*cause*) **to** ~ **sb with a problem** creare un problema a qu; **to** ~ **sb in trouble** mettere qu nei guai

landed ['læn·dɪd] *adj* che possiede terreni; **a** ~ **family** una famiglia di proprietari terrieri; **the** ~ **gentry** i proprietari terrieri
landfall ['lænd·fɔːl] *n* avvistamento *m* della terraferma; **to make** ~ vedere terra
landfill ['lænd·fɪl] *n* interramento *m* di immondizia
landholder *n* proprietario, -a *m, f* terriero, -a
landing ['læn·dɪŋ] *n* **1.** AVIAT atterraggio *m;* **to make a** ~ compiere un atterraggio **2.** NAUT sbarco *m* **3.** (*on staircase*) pianerottolo *m*
landing card *n* carta *f* di sbarco
landing craft *n* MIL mezzo *m* da sbarco
landing field *n* campo *m* d'atterraggio
landing gear *n* AVIAT carrello *m*
landing net *n* retino *m*
landing stage *n* pontile *m*
landing strip *n* pista *f* d'atterraggio
landlady ['lænd·ˌleɪ·di] <-ies> *n* padrona *f* di casa
landless *adj* senza terra
landlocked *adj* senza accesso al mare; **a** ~ **country** un paese senza accesso al mare
landlord *n* padrone *m* di casa
landlubber *n inf* marinaio *m* d'acqua dolce
landmark **I.** *n* **1.** punto *m* di riferimento **2.** (*monument*) monumento *m* **3.** (*event*) pietra *f* miliare **II.** *adj* (*significant: decision, ruling*) decisivo, -a
land mine *n* mina *f* terrestre
land office *n* HIST ufficio *f* del catasto; **to do a land-office business** *inf* fare un buon affare
landowner *n* proprietario, -a *m, f* terriero, -a
land reform *n* riforma *f* agraria
landscape ['lænd·skeɪp] **I.** *n* **1.** (*scenery, painting*) paesaggio *m;* **urban** ~ paesaggio urbano **2.** *fig* panorama *m;* **the political** ~ il panorama politico **3.** INFOR orientamento *m* orizzontale **II.** *vt* allestire spazi verdi
landscape architect *n*, **landscape gardener** *n* architetto *m* di giardini
landscape architecture *n*, **landscape gardening** *n* architettura *f* di giardini
landscape painter *n* paesaggista *mf*
landslide ['lænd·slaɪd] *n* **1.** GEO frana *f* **2.** POL vittoria *f* schiacciante; **to win by a** ~ vincere in modo schiacciante
property tax <-es> *n* imposta *f* sulla proprietà
landward **I.** *adj* verso terra; **the** ~ **side** il lato di terra **II.** *adv* verso terra
lane [leɪn] *n* **1.** (*marked strip*) corsia *f*; **bus/bike** ~ corsia degli autobus/ciclabile; **to change** ~**s** cambiare corsia **2.** (*small road*) vicolo *m* **3.** AVIAT rotta *f* aerea; NAUT rotta *f* marittima
language ['læŋ·gwɪdʒ] *n* **1.** (*system of communication*) linguaggio *m;* **bad** ~ parolacce *fpl;* **formal/spoken/written** ~ lingua formale/orale/scritta **2.** (*of particular community*) lingua *f*; **native** ~ madrelingua *f*; **the English** ~ la lingua inglese **3.** (*jargon*) linguaggio *m;* **computer programming** ~ linguaggio di programmazione informatica; **legal** ~

gergo *m* giuridico ▸ **to speak the** <u>same</u> **~** parlare la stessa lingua

language arts *n discipline quali lettura, scrittura, ortografia ecc.*

language lab *n,* **language laboratory** *n* laboratorio *m* linguistico

language learning *n* apprendimento *m* linguistico

languid [ˈlæŋ·gwɪd] *adj* languido, -a

languish [ˈlæŋ·gwɪʃ] *vi* languire; **he ~ed in bed for weeks** fu costretto a letto per settimane

languor [ˈlæŋ·gɚ] *n liter* languore *m*

languorous [ˈlæŋ·gɚ·əs] *adj liter* languido, -a

lank [læŋk] *adj* (*hair*) piatto, -a

lanky [ˈlæŋ·ki] *adj* allampanato, -a

lanolin [ˈlæ·nə·lɪn] *n* lanolina *f*

lantern [ˈlæn·tən] *n* lanterna *f*

lanyard [ˈlæn·jəd] *n* **1.** (*short rope or cord*) cordoncino *m* **2.** NAUT corridore *m*

Laos [laʊs] *n* Laos *m*

lap¹ [læp] *n* grembo *m* ▸ **to live in the ~ of** <u>luxury</u> vivere nel lusso

lap² [læp] SPORTS **I.** *n* giro *m;* **~ of honor** giro d'onore **II.** <-pp-> *vt* doppiare

lap³ [læp] <-pp-> **I.** *vt* **1.** (*drink*) leccare **2.** (*waves*) lambire **II.** *vi* (*hit gently*) **to ~ against sth** lambire qc

◆**lap up** *vt* **1.** (*drink*) leccare **2.** *fig, inf* accettare con entusiasmo; **he lapped up the praise** si beò delle lusinghe

lap dog *n* cagnolino *m* da salotto

lapel [lə·ˈpel] *n* risvolto *m;* **to grab sb by the ~s** prendere qu per il colletto

lapis lazuli [ˌlæ·pɪs·ˈlæ·zə·li] *n* **1.** (*blue gemstone*) lapislazzuli *m inv* **2.** (*blue color*) azzurro *m* intenso

Lapland [ˈlæp·lænd] *n* Lapponia *f*

Laplander [ˈlæp·læn·də] *n,* **Lapp** [læp] *n* lappone *mf*

lapse [læps] **I.** *n* **1.** (*failure*) errore *m;* **~ in judgment** errore di giudizio; **~ of memory** vuoto di memoria **2.** (*period*) intervallo *m* **II.** *vi* **1.** (*deteriorate*) deteriorarsi **2.** (*end*) terminare; (*contract, subscription*) scadere **3.** (*revert to*) **to ~ into sth** ripiombare in qc; **to ~ into one's native dialect** riprendere a parlare nel proprio dialetto; **to ~ into silence** tacere

lapsed [læpst] *adj* (*membership, subscription*) scaduto, -a; (*Catholic*) non praticante

laptop (**computer**) [ˈlæp·tɑːp] *n* (computer *m*) portatile *m*

lapwing [ˈlæp·wɪŋ] *n* pavoncella *f*

larceny [ˈlɑːr·sə·ni] <-ies> *n* furto *m*

larch [lɑːrtʃ] *n* larice *m*

lard [lɑːrd] **I.** *n* lardo *m* **II.** *vt* lardellare

larder [ˈlɑːr·də] *n* (*pantry*) dispensa *f;* (*supply of food*) provviste *fpl*

large [lɑːrdʒ] *adj* grande; **a ~ number of people** un gran numero di persone; **a ~ family** una famiglia numerosa ▸ **to be** <u>at</u> **~** essere a piede libero; <u>by and</u> **~** nel complesso

largely [ˈlɑːrdʒ·li] *adv* in gran parte

largeness *n* ampiezza *f*

large-scale *adj* su grande scala

largess(e) [lɑːr·ˈdʒes] *n* generosità *f*

lariat [ˈle·ri·ət] *n* laccio *m*

lark¹ [lɑːrk] *n* (*bird*) allodola *f* ▸ **to be** <u>up</u> **with the ~** alzarsi all'alba

lark² [lɑːrk] **I.** *n inf* **1.** (*joke*) gioco *m;* **for a ~** per gioco **2.** (*adventure*) faccenda *f* **II.** *vi inf* **to ~ about** spassarsela

larkspur [ˈlɑːrk·spɜːr] *n* BOT speronella *f*

larva [ˈlɑːr·və] <-vae> *n* larva *f*

laryngitis [ˌle·rɪn·ˈdʒaɪ·t̬ɪs] *n* laringite *f*

larynx [ˈle·rɪŋks] <-ynxes *o* -ynges> *n* ANAT laringe *f*

lasagna [lə·ˈzɑːn·jə] *n* lasagne *fpl*

lascivious [lə·ˈsɪ·vi·əs] *adj* lascivo, -a

laser [ˈleɪ·zə] *n* laser *m inv*

laser beam *n* raggio *m* laser

laser printer *n* stampante *f* laser

laser show *n* spettacolo *m* laser

lash¹ [læʃ] <-es> *n* (*eyelash*) ciglio *m*

lash² [læʃ] **I.** <-es> *n* **1.** (*whip*) frusta *f* **2.** (*stroke of whip*) frustata *f;* **he felt a ~ of conscience** ebbe un rimorso di coscienza ▸ **to feel the ~ of sb's** <u>tongue</u> ricevere critiche sferzanti da qu **II.** *vt* **1.** (*whip*) frustare; (*rain*) sferzare **2.** (*criticize*) criticare aspramente

◆**lash about** *vi,* **lash around** *vi* menar colpi a destra e a manca

◆**lash down** *vt* legare stretto

◆**lash out** *vi* **to ~ at sb** attaccare qu

lashing [ˈlæ·ʃɪŋ] *n* frustate *fpl;* **to give sb a tongue ~** fare una ramanzina a qu

lass [læs] <-es> *n inf* (*girl*) ragazza *f*

lassitude [ˈlæ·sɪ·tuːd] *n form* lassitudine *f*

lasso [ˈlæ·soʊ] **I.** <-os *o* -oes> *n* lazo *m inv* **II.** *vt* prendere al lazo

last¹ [læst] *n* (*for shoes*) forma *f*

last² [læst] **I.** *adj* **1.** (*final: time, opportunity*) ultimo, -a; **to have the ~ word** avere l'ultima parola; **to wait till the ~ minute** (**to do sth**) aspettare fino all'ultimo minuto (per fare qc); **this will be the ~ time** questa sarà l'ultima volta **2.** (*most recent*) scorso, -a; **~ week** la settimana scorsa; **~ night** ieri notte **II.** *adv* **1.** (*at the end*) per ultima cosa; **but not least** infine, ma non per ultimo meno importante **2.** (*most recently*) l'ultima volta **III.** *n* **the ~ to do sth** l'ultimo a fare qc; **the second to ~** il penultimo; **that was the ~ of the cake** era tutto quello che rimaneva della torta ▸ <u>at</u> (**long**) **~** alla fine; <u>to the</u> **~** *form* fino all'ultimo

last³ [læst] **I.** *vi* durare **II.** *vt* **this coat has ~ed me five years** questo cappotto mi è durato cinque anni

last-ditch *adj* disperato, -a

lasting [ˈlæs·tɪŋ] *adj* duraturo, -a

lastly [ˈlæst·li] *adv* infine

last minute *adj* dell'ultimo minuto

last name *n* cognome *m*

latch [lætʃ] <-es> *n* chiavistello *m*

◆**latch on** *vi inf* **1.** (*attach oneself*) **to ~ to**

L

sb/sth aggrapparsi a qu/qc **2.**(*obtain*) **to ~ to sth** afferrare qc

latchkey ['læt∫·kiː] *n* chiave *f* (di casa)

latchkey child *n* bambino che dopo la scuola sta in casa da solo perché i genitori lavorano

late [leɪt] **I.** *adj* **1.**(*after appointed time*) in ritardo; **you're ~!** sei in ritardo!; **the train was an hour ~** il treno aveva un'ora di ritardo **2.**(*after the usual time*) tardivo, -a **3.**(*towards end of*) **~ night TV show** programma *m* in tarda serata; **in the ~ nineteenth century** alla fine del secolo XIX; **in ~ summer** alla fine dell'estate **4.**(*recent: development*) recente; **~est news** ultime notizie*f pl* **5.**(*deceased*) defunto, -a **II.** *adv* **1.**(*after usual time*) tardi; **too little, too ~** troppo poco, troppo tardi; **to work ~** lavorare fino a tardi; **it's kind of ~ in the day to do sth** è un po' tardi per fare qc **2.**(*towards end of*) **~ in the day** a fine giornata; **~ at night** a tarda notte; **he got his driver's license ~ in life** ha preso la patente in età avanzata **3.**(*recently*) **as ~ as the 1980s** fino ancora negli anni ottanta; **of ~** ultimamente ▶ **better ~ than never** *prov* meglio tardi che mai *prov*

late-breaking *adj* di grande attualità

latecomer ['leɪt·kʌ·məʳ] *n* ritardatario, -a *m, f*

lately ['leɪt·li] *adv* (*recently*) ultimamente, recentemente; **until ~** fino a poco tempo fa

lateness ['leɪt·nɪs] *n* ritardo *m*

late-night *adj* notturno, -a

latent ['leɪ·tnt] *adj* latente

later ['leɪ·təʳ] **I.** *adj comp of* **late** successivo, -a; (*version*) più recente **II.** *adv comp of* **late** più tardi; **no ~ than nine o'clock** non più tardi delle nove; **~ on** dopo, in seguito; **see you ~!** a dopo!

lateral ['læ·tə·əl] *adj* laterale; **~ thinking** pensiero *m* laterale

latest ['leɪ·tɪst] **I.** *adj superl of* **late** ultimo, -a; **the ~ ...** il più recente...; **his ~ movie** il suo ultimo film; **at the ~** al più tardi **II.** *n* **the ~** le ultime notizie; **have you heard the ~ about Gerry?** la sai l'ultima di Gerry?; **the ~ in art/physics** l'ultima in fatto di arte/fisica; **at the** (**very**) **~** al più tardi

latex ['leɪ·teks] *n* lattice *m*

lath [læθ] <-es> *n* listello *m*

lathe [leɪð] *n* tornio *m*

lathe operator *n* tornitore, -trice *m, f*

lather ['læ·ðəʳ] **I.** *n* **1.**(*fine bubbles*) schiuma *f* **2.**(*sweat*) sudore *m;* **to be in a ~ over sth** *fig* essere in grande agitazione per qc **II.** *vi* fare la schiuma **III.** *vt* insaponare

Latin ['læ·tən] **I.** *adj* latino, -a **II.** *n* **1.**LING latino *m* **2.**(*person*) abitante degli USA di origine latinoamericana

Latina [lə·'tiː·nə] *n* (*person*) abitante degli USA di origine latinoamericana

Latin America *n* America *f* Latina

Latin American I. *adj* latinoamericano, -a **II.** *n* (*person*) latinoamericano, -a *m, f*

Latino [lə·'tiː·noʊ] *n* (*person*) abitante degli USA di origine latinoamericana

latish ['leɪ·tɪʃ] **I.** *adj* sul tardi **II.** *adv* un po' tardino

latitude ['læ·tə·tuːd] *n* **1.**GEO latitudine *f* **2.**(*freedom*) libertà *f* d'azione

latrine [lə·'triːn] *n* latrina *f*

latter ['læ·təʳ] *adj* **1.**(*second of two*) **the ~** il secondo; **in the ~ half of the year** nella seconda metà dell'anno **2.**(*near the end*) ultimo, -a

Latter-day Saint *n* mormone

latterly *adv* ultimamente

lattice ['læ·tɪs] *n* (*framework*) reticolo *m;* **~ window** finestra *f* con vetri piombati

Latvia ['læt·vi·ə] *n* Lettonia *f*

Latvian I. *adj* lettone **II.** *n* **1.**(*person*) lettone *mf* **2.**LING lettone *m*

laudable ['lɔː·də·bl] *adj form* lodevole

laudanum ['lɔː·də·nəm] *n* laudano *m*

laudatory ['lɔː·də·tɔː·ri] *adj form* laudatorio, -a

laugh [læf] **I.** *n* **1.**(*sound*) riso *m;* **to get a ~** far ridere; **to do sth for a ~** [*o* for ~s] fare qc per ridere **2.** *inf* (*activity*) divertimento *m* **3.** *inf* (*funny thing*) scherzo *m;* (*sth absurd*) barzelletta *f* **II.** *vi* ridere; **to ~ aloud** ridere a crepapelle; **to make sb ~** far ridere qu; **to ~ at sb/sth** *a. fig* ridere di qu/qc; **to ~ until one cries** piangere dalle risate; **don't make me ~!** *inf* non farmi ridere! ▶ **he who ~s last ~s best** *prov* ride bene chi ride ultimo *prov*

◆ **laugh off** *vt* ridere su

laughable ['læ·fə·bl] *adj* ridicolo, -a

laughing I. *n* risate *fpl* **II.** *adj* **this is no ~ matter** non è una cosa da ridere

laughing gas *n inf* gas esilarante

laughingstock *n* zimbello *m*

laughter ['læf·təʳ] *n* riso *m;* **to roar with ~** ridere fragorosamente

launch [lɔːnt∫] **I.** <-ches> *n* **1.**(*boat*) lancia *f* **2.**(*of a boat*) varo *m* **3.**(*of a missile*) lancio *m* **4.**(*introduction: of exhibition*) inaugurazione *f;* (*of book*) presentazione *f* **II.** *vt* **1.**(*set in the water*) varare **2.**(*set in motion: missile*) lanciare **3.**(*introduce: book*) presentare **4.**(*start: investigation*) avviare; (*exhibition*) inaugurare **5.to ~ oneself at sb** lanciarsi su qu

◆ **launch into** *vt* lanciarsi in

◆ **launch out** *vi* lanciarsi

launching ['lɔːnt∫·∫ɪŋ] *n* **1.**(*of boat*) varo *m* **2.**(*of missile, campaign*) lancio *m* **3.**(*of exhibition, campaign*) inaugurazione *f* **4.**(*of book*) presentazione *f*

launching pad *n*, **launch pad** *n* rampa *f* di lancio

launder ['lɔːn·dəʳ] *vt* **1.**(*clothing*) lavare e stirare **2.** *fig* (*money*) riciclare

launderette [lɔːn·də·'ret] *n*, **laundromat** ['lɔːn·drə·mæt] *n* lavanderia *f* (automatica)

laundry ['lɔːn·dri] *n* **1.**(*dirty clothes*) panni*m pl* sporchi; **to do the ~** fare il bucato **2.**(*washed clothes*) bucato *m* **3.**<-ies> (*place*) lavanderia *f* ▶ **to wash one's dirty ~**

in <u>public</u> lavare i propri panni sporchi in pubblico

laundry basket *n* cesto *m* della biancheria

laundry service *n* servizio *m* di lavanderia

laureate ['lɔːˑriˑɪt] *n* **Nobel ~** premio *m* Nobel; **Poet Laureate** poeta *m* laureato (*in Gran Bretagna, poeta scelto dalla regina per il componimento di poesie per occasioni speciali*)

laurel ['lɔːˑrəl] *n* alloro *m* ▶ **to** <u>rest</u> **on one's ~ s** dormire sugli allori

lava ['lɑːˑvə] *n* lava *f*

lavatory ['læˑvəˑtɔːˑri] <-ies> *n* toilette *f inv*

toilet seat *n* ciambella *f* del water

lavender ['læˑvənˑdɚ] I. *n* BOT lavanda *f* II. *adj* (di/alla) lavanda

lavish ['læˑvɪʃ] I. *adj* (*banquet, reception*) fastoso, -a; (*party*) splendido, -a; (*praise*) grande II. *vt* **to ~ sth on sb** [*o* **to ~ sb with sth**] prodigare qc a qu

law [lɔː] *n* **1.** *a.* PHYS legge *f*; **the ~ of supply and demand** la legge della domanda e dell'offerta; **the ~ s governing the export of paintings** le leggi che regolano l'esportazione dei dipinti; **his word is ~** è lui che detta legge; **the first ~ of sth** il principio base di qc **2.** (*legal system*) diritto *m*; (*body of laws*) legislazione *f*; **~ -and-order** la legge e l'ordine pubblico; **to be against the ~** essere illegale; **to take the ~ into one's own hands** farsi giustizia da sé **3.** (*the police*) giustizia *f* **4.** (*trial*) **to go to ~** andare in tribunale ▶ **the ~ of the** <u>jungle</u> la legge della giungla

law-abiding *adj* che rispetta la legge

lawbreaker *n* trasgressore, -ditrice *m, f* (della legge)

court of law *n* tribunale *m*

law enforcement *n* applicazione *f* della legge

lawful ['lɔːˑfəl] *adj* **1.** (*legal*) legale; (*demands*) legitttimo, -a **2.** (*law-abiding*) che rispetta la legge

lawgiver ['lɔːˌgɪˑvɚ] *n* legislatore *m*

lawless ['lɔːˑlɪs] *adj* senza legge; (*country*) anarchico, -a

lawmaker ['lɔːˌmeɪˑkɚ] *n* legislatore *m*

lawn [lɔːn] *n* prato *m*

lawn mower *n* tosaerba *m inv*

law school *n* facoltà *f inv* di giurisprudenza

law student *n* studente, -essa *m, f* di giurisprudenza

lawsuit *n* causa *f;* **to bring a ~ against sb** fare causa a qu

lawyer ['lɔːˑjɚ] *n* avvocato *m*

lax [læks] *adj* **1.** (*lacking care*) negligente; **~ security** sicurezza *f* poco rigorosa; **to be ~ in doing sth** essere negligente nel fare qc **2.** (*not tense*) non teso, -a **3.** (*lenient*) indulgente; (*rules*) poco severo, -a

laxative ['lækˑsəˑt̬ɪv] I. *n* lassativo *m* II. *adj* lassativo, -a

laxity ['lækˑsəˑt̬i] *n*, **laxness** *n* lassismo *m*

lay¹ [leɪ] I. *n* **1.** (*situation*) situazione *f;* **the ~ of the land** la configurazione del terreno; *fig* il panorama attuale **2.** *vulg* **to be a good ~**

saperci fare a letto II. <laid, laid> *vt* **1.** (*place*) porre; **to ~ sth on/over sth** porre qc su/sopra qc; **to ~ sth flat** stendere qc; **to ~ stress on sth** enfatizzare qc; **to ~ the blame on sb** addossare la colpa a qu **2.** (*install*) mettere; **to ~ the foundations for sth** *a. fig* gettare le fondamenta di qc **3.** (*prepare*) allestire; **to ~ a plan** preparare un piano **4.** (*egg*) deporre **5.** *vulg* (*have sex with*) scopare **6.** (*gamble*) puntare; **to ~ an amount on sth** puntare una cifra su qc **7.** (*state*) presentare; **to ~ sth before sb** mettere qc di fronte a qu; **to ~ one's case before sb** presentare il proprio caso a qu/qc; **to ~ a charge against sb** muovere una accusa contro qu; **to ~ claim to sth** reclamare qc III. <laid, laid> *vi* deporre le uova

◆ **lay about** *vt* **to ~ sb** colpire qu

◆ **lay aside** *vt* mettere da parte; **to ~ one's differences** mettere da parte le proprie differenze

◆ **lay away** *vt* **1.** (*save*) mettere da parte **2.** (*at department store*) tenere da parte

◆ **lay back** *vt* rilassarsi

◆ **lay by** *vt* mettere da parte

◆ **lay down** *vt* **1.** (*put down*) mettere via; (*arms*) deporre; (*life*) sacrificare **2.** (*establish*) stabilire; (*law*) dettare; **it is laid down that ...** è stabilito che...

◆ **lay in** *vt* fare provviste di

◆ **lay into** *vt inf* **1.** (*assault, criticize*) aggredire **2.** (*eat*) buttarsi su

◆ **lay off** I. *vt* (*employee*) lasciare a casa II. *vi inf* smettere; **to ~ sb** lasciare in pace qu; **to ~ smoking** smettere di fumare

◆ **lay on** *vt* **1.** (*provide: food, drink*) offrire **2.** *sl* (*reveal*) **to ~ sth on sb** dire qc a qu

◆ **lay open** *vt* **1.** (*uncover*) scoprire **2.** (*expose*) esporre; **to lay oneself open** esporsi

◆ **lay out** *vt* **1.** (*organize*) organizzare **2.** (*explain*) presentare **3.** (*spread out*) estendere **4.** (*prepare for burial*) preparare **5.** *inf* (*knock unconscious*) far perdere conoscenza a **6.** *inf* (*money*) spendere

◆ **lay over** *vi* fare una sosta

◆ **lay to** *vi* NAUT gettare l'ancora

◆ **lay up** *vt* **1.** (*store: food*) fare scorta di; (*money*) accumulare **2.** (*ship*) disarmare; (*car*) rottamare **3.** *inf* (*in bed*) **to be laid up** rimanere a letto

lay² [leɪ] *adj* **1.** (*not professional*) non specializzato, -a; **in ~ terms** in parole povere **2.** REL laico, -a

lay³ [leɪ] *pt of* **lie²**

layabout ['leɪˑəˌbaʊt] *n inf* fannullone, -a *m, f*

layaway ['leɪˑəˑweɪ] *n* **to buy on ~** comprare a rate ottenendo il prodotto solo dopo l'ultimo pagamento

layer¹ ['leˑɪɚ] I. *n* strato *m* II. *vt* disporre a strati

layer² ['leˑɪɚ] *n* (*hen*) gallina *f* ovaiola

layer cake *n* torta *f* a strati

L

layered *adj* a strati

layette [leɪˈet] *n* corredino *m*

layman [ˈleɪˌmən] <-men> *n* laico *m*

layoff [ˈleɪˌɔːf] *n* licenziamento (per mancanza di lavoro) *m*

layout [ˈleɪˌaʊt] *n* **1.** (*of letter, magazine*) impaginazione *f*; (*of town, building*) pianta *f*; (*of factory*) lay-out *m* **2.** TYPO lay-out *m inv*

layover [ˈleɪˌoʊˌvəˈ] *n* (*on journey*) sosta *f*; AVIAT scalo *m*

laywoman [ˈleɪˌwʊˌmən] <-women> *n* laica *f*

laze [leɪz] <-zing> *vi* oziare

laziness [ˈleɪˌzɪˌnɪs] *n* pigrizia *f*

lazy [ˈleɪˌzi] <-ier, -iest> *adj* (*person*) pigro, -a; (*day*) tranquillo, -a

lb. *abbr of* **pound** libbra *f* (= 0,45 kg)

LCD [ˌelˌsiːˈdiː] *n abbr of* **liquid crystal display** display *m* a cristalli liquidi *inv*

lead¹ [liːd] I. *n* **1.** **to be in the ~** essere in testa; **to hold the ~** rimanere in testa; **to lose one's ~** perdere il vantaggio; **to move into the ~** andare in testa; **to take the ~** assumere il comando **2.** (*example*) esempio *m*; (*guiding*) iniziativa *f*; **to follow sb's ~** seguire l'esempio di qu **3.** THEAT ruolo *m* principale; **to play the ~** essere il/la protagonista **4.** (*clue, tip*) pista *f*; **to get a ~ on sth** ricevere un indizio su qc; **to give a ~** dare una dritta **5.** (*connecting wire*) cavo *m* **6.** (*dog leash*) guinzaglio *m* II. <led, led> *vt* **1.** (*be in charge of*) guidare; (*discussion, inquiry*) condurre **2.** (*conduct*) condurre, portare; **to ~ the way** fare strada; *fig* indicare la strada **3.** (*induce*) indurre; **to ~ sb to do sth** portare qu a fare qc; **to ~ sb to believe that ...** far credere a qu che ...; LAW; **to ~ a witness** fare domande tendenziose a un testimone **4.** COM, SPORTS (*be ahead of*) essere in vantaggio su; **to ~ the field** *fig* essere il primo **5.** (*live a particular way: life*) condurre; **to ~ a life of luxury** vivere nel lusso; **to ~ a quiet/hectic life** fare una vita tranquilla/frenetica ▶ **to ~ sb (around) by the nose** *inf* far fare a qu ciò che si vuole III. <led, led> *vi* **1.** (*be in charge*) dirigere **2.** (*guide followers*) essere alla guida **3.** (*conduct*) portare; **to ~ to/into sth** *a. fig* portare a qc **4.** (*be ahead*) essere in vantaggio; **to ~ by 2 laps** essere in vantaggio di due giri

♦ **lead along** *vt* condurre

♦ **lead aside** *vt* portare in disparte

♦ **lead astray** *vt* fuorviare

♦ **lead away** *vt* portare via

♦ **lead back** *vt* riportare

♦ **lead off** I. *vt* (*person*) mettere fuori strada; (*room*) comunicare con II. *vi* cominciare

♦ **lead on** *vt* (*trick, fool*) imbrogliare; (*encourage*) incoraggiare; **she doesn't want to lead him on** non vuole dargli false speranze

♦ **lead to** *vt* portare a/in

♦ **lead up to** *vi* **1.** (*cause, slowly introduce*) portare a **2.** (*precede*) precedere

lead² [led] *n* **1.** (*metal*) piombo *m* **2.** (*in pencil*) mina *f* **3.** NAUT scandaglio *m*

leaded [ˈleˌdəd] I. *adj* impiombato, -a; **~ fuel** benzina *f* con piombo II. *n* benzina *f* con piombo

leaden [ˈleˌdn] *adj* **1.** (*heavy*) pesante **2.** (*dull*) scialbo, -a **3.** (*dark*) plumbeo, -a

leader [ˈliːˌdəˈ] *n* **1.** (*of group*) leader *mf inv* **2.** (*guide*) guida *f* **3.** MUS (*conductor*) direttore *m* **4.** MUS (*in section of orchestra*) musicista *mf* principale

leadership [ˈliːˌdəˈˌʃɪp] *n* **1.** (*ability to lead*) **~ qualities** doti *f pl* di leader **2.** (*leaders*) direzione *f* **3.** (*guidance*) comando *m*; **to be under sb's ~** essere al comando di qu

lead-free [ˈledˌfriː] *adj* senza piombo

lead guitar *n* **to play ~** essere il primo chitarrista

leading [ˈliːˌdɪŋ] I. *adj* (*main, principle: cause, factor*) primario, -a; (*candidate, manager*) di punta II. *n* comando *m*

leading-edge *adj* di punta; **~ technology** tecnologia *f* d'avanguardia

leading lady *n* protagonista *f*

leading light *n inf* **to be a ~ in sth** essere un luminare in qc

leading man *n* protagonista *m*

leading question *n* domanda *f* tendenziosa

lead pencil *n* matita *f* (di grafite)

lead poisoning *n* saturnismo *m*

lead singer *n* cantante *mf* solista

lead story *n* PUBL notizia *f* in prima pagina

lead-time *n* tempo *m* di consegna

lead-up *n* fase *f* preparatoria

leaf [liːf] <leaves> *n* **1.** (*of plant*) foglia *f* **2.** (*foliage*) fogliame *m*; **to be in** [*o* **come into**] **~** mettere le foglie **3.** (*piece of paper*) foglio *m*; **~ of paper** foglio di carta **4.** (*thin layer*) **gold/silver ~** foglia *f* d'oro/d'argento **5.** (*of table*) prolunga *f* ▶ **to take a ~ from sb's book** seguire l'esempio di qu; **to shake like a ~** tremare come una foglia; **to turn over a new ~** voltare pagina

♦ **leaf through** *vt* sfogliare

leafless [ˈliːfˌləs] *adj* spoglio, -a

leaflet [ˈliːfˌlɪt] *n* dépliant *m inv*

leafy [ˈliːfˌfi] <-ier, -iest> *adj* frondoso, -a

league [liːg] *n* **1.** *a.* SPORTS lega *f*; **to be/to not be in the same ~ as sb/sth** *fig* essere/non essere al livello di qu/qc; **to be out of sb's ~** non essere alla portate di qu **2.** (*measurement*) lega *f* ▶ **to be in ~ with sb** essere in combutta con qu

leak [liːk] I. *n* (*of gas, information*) fuga *f*; (*of water*) perdita *f*; (*in boat*) falla *f* II. *vi* **1.** (*gas, water*) fuoriuscire; (*hose, bucket, faucet*) perdere; (*tire*) perdere aria **2.** (*information*) trapelare; **news had ~ed out** c'era stata una fuga di notizie III. *vt* **1.** (*let escape*) far fuoriuscire; **to ~ water** fare acqua **2.** (*information*) far trapelare

leakage [ˈliːˌkɪdʒ] *n* **1.** (*leak*) perdita *f* **2.** (*of information*) fuga *f*

leaky [ˈliːˌki] <-ier, -iest> *adj* che perde

lean¹ [liːn] I. <-ed, -ed> *vi* pendere; **to ~**

against sth appoggiarsi a qc **II.** <-ed, -ed> *vt* appoggiare; **to ~ sth against sth** appoggiare qc a qc
♦ **lean back** *vi* appoggiarsi all'indietro
♦ **lean forward** *vi* piegarsi in avanti
♦ **lean on** *vt* **1.** (*rely on*) appoggiarsi a **2.** *sl* (*pressure*) mettere sotto pressione
♦ **lean out** *vi* sporgersi
♦ **lean over I.** *vt* piegarsi su **II.** *vi* piegarsi
lean² [li:n] *adj* **1.** (*thin*) magro, -a **2.** (*efficient: company*) efficiente
leaning ['li:·nɪŋ] *n* inclinazione *f;* **political ~s** tendenze *f pl* politiche
lean-to ['li:n·tu:] *n* **1.** (*building extension*) costruzione annessa ad un edificio più grande **2.** (*shack*) capanno *m*
leap [li:p] **I.** <leaped *o* leapt, leaped *o* leapt> *vi* saltare; **to ~ forward** fare un salto in avanti; **to ~ with joy** saltare dalla gioia; **to ~ to do sth** precipitarsi a fare qc; **to ~ to sb's defense** lanciarsi in difesa di qu; **his heart ~ed** ebbe un tuffo al cuore; **to ~ to mind** venire in mente **II.** <leaped *o* leapt, leaped *o* leapt> *vt* saltare **III.** *n* salto *m;* **to take a ~** fare un salto ▶ **by ~s and bounds** a passi da gigante; **a ~ in the dark** un salto nel buio
♦ **leap at** *vt* **1.** (*jump*) buttarsi su **2.** *inf* (*accept*) non lasciarsi sfuggire; **to ~ the chance to do sth** non lasciarsi sfuggire l'occasione di fare qc
♦ **leap out** *vi* saltare fuori
♦ **leap up** *vi* **1.** (*jump up*) scattare in piedi; **to ~ to do sth** scattare a fare qc **2.** (*rise quickly*) alzarsi di scatto
leapfrog [ˌli:p·frɑ:g] **I.** *n* cavallina *f;* **to play a game of ~** giocare alla cavallina **II.** <-gg-> *vt* superare con un salto
leapt [lept] *vt, vi pt, pp of* **leap**
leap year *n* anno *m* bisestile
learn [lɜ:rn] **I.** <learned, learned> *vt* imparare; **to ~ that** enire a sapere che **II.** <learned, learned> *vi* imparare; **to ~ to do sth** imparare a fare qc; **to ~ from one's mistakes** imparare dai propri errori
learned ['lɜ:r·nɪd] *adj* erudito, -a
learner ['lɜ:r·nɚ] *n* principiante *mf;* **to be a quick ~** imparare alla svelta
learning ['lɜ:r·nɪŋ] *n* **1.** (*acquisition of knowledge*) apprendimento *m* **2.** (*extensive knowledge*) cultura *f*
learning disability *n* <-ies> difficoltà *f* di apprendimento *inv*
lease [li:s] **I.** *vt* (*building*) dare in locazione **II.** *n* (*act*) locazione *f;* (*contract*) contratto *m* di locazione; **to take sth on ~** prendere qc in locazione ▶ **a new ~ on life** una nuova opportunità
leasehold ['li:s·hoʊld] COM, FIN, ECON **I.** *n* possesso *m* immobiliare **II.** *adj* **1.** (*kept by lease*) in locazione **2.** (*dealing with leases*) di locazione
leaseholder ['li:s·hoʊl·dɚ] *n* locatario, -a *m, f*
leash [li:ʃ] *n* guinzaglio *m* ▶ **to keep sb on a**

tight ~ tenere qu al guinzaglio
leasing ['li:·sɪŋ] *n* locazione *f*
least [li:st] **I.** *adj* minore **II.** *adv* meno; **the ~ possible** il meno possibile **III.** *n* at (**the very**) **~** almeno; **not in the ~!** affatto!; **to say the ~** per lo meno
leather ['le·ðɚ] *n* cuoio *m*
leatherneck ['le·ðɚ·nek] *n sl* marine *m inv*
leathery ['le·ðɚ·i] *adj* (*skin*) coriaceo, -a; (*meat*) duro, -a
leave¹ [li:v] **I.** <left, left> *vt* **1.** (*depart from*) partire da; (*school, work*) lasciare; **to ~ home** uscire di casa **2.** (*not take away with*) lasciare; **to ~ sth to sb** lasciare qc a qu; **to ~ sth at home** lasciare qc a casa; **to ~ a note/message (for sb)** lasciare un biglietto/un messaggio (per qu) **3.** (*put in a situation*) **to ~ sb alone** lasciare in pace qu; **to be left homeless** ritrovarsi senza casa; **to ~ sth open** lasciare qc aperto ▶ **to ~ a lot to be desired** lasciare molto a desiderare; **to ~ it at that** finirla qui **II.** <left, left> *vi* andare via **III.** *n* congedo *m;* **to take (one's) ~ (of sb)** congedarsi (da qu); **to take (complete) ~ of one's senses** perdere (completamente) la testa
♦ **leave behind** *vt* **1.** (*not take along, forget*) lasciare **2.** (*progress beyond*) lasciarsi dietro
♦ **leave off I.** *vt* **1.** (*give up*) smettere **2.** (*omit*) omettere **II.** *vi* smettere
♦ **leave on** *vt* lasciare; (*light*) lasciare acceso
♦ **leave out** *vt* **1.** (*omit*) omettere **2.** (*exclude*) escludere
♦ **leave over** *vt* lasciare; **there's nothing left over** non è rimasto niente
leave² [li:v] *n* permesso *m;* **to have/get sb's ~ (to do sth)** avere/ottenere il permesso di qu (per fare qc); **with/without sb's ~** con/senza il permesso di qu; **to go/be on ~** MIL andare/essere in licenza
leaven ['le·vn] **I.** *n* lievito *m* **II.** *vt* far lievitare; *fig;* **to ~ a speech with jokes** alleggerire un discorso con battute
leaves [li:vz] *n pl of* **leaf**
leave-taking *n* commiato *m*
leaving ['li:·vɪŋ] *n* **1.** (*departure*) partenza *f,* commiato *m* **2.** *pl* (*remaining things, leftovers*) avanzi *mpl*
Lebanese [ˌle·bə·'ni:z] **I.** *adj* libanese **II.** *n* libanese *mf*
Lebanon ['le·bə·nɑn] *n* (**the**) **~** il Libano
lech [letʃ] *n,* **lecher** ['le·tʃɚ] *n* sporcaccione *m*
lecherous ['le·tʃɚ·əs] *adj* lascivo, -a
lechery ['le·tʃɚ·i] *n* lascivia *f*
lectern ['lek·tɚn] *n* leggio *m;* REL pulpito *m*
lecture ['lek·tʃɚ] **I.** *n* conferenza *f;* UNIV lezione *f;* **a ~ on sth** una conferenza su qc; **to give sb a ~** *fig* fare la predica a qu **II.** *vi* (*give a lecture*) tenere una conferenza; (*teach*) fare lezione **III.** *vt* **1.** (*give a lecture*) fare una conferenza per; (*teach*) fare lezione a **2.** *fig* (*criticize*) fare la predica a
lecture hall *n* aula *f* (universitaria)
lecture notes *npl* appunti *m pl* della lezione

L

lecturer ['lek·tʃɚ·ɚ] *n* conferenziere, -a *m, f;* UNIV professore, -essa *m, f* universitario, -a

lecture tour *n* giro *m* di conferenze

led [led] *pt, pp of* **lead**[1]

LED [ˌel·iː·'diː] *n abbr of* **light-emitting diode** LED *m*

ledge [ledʒ] *n (shelf)* mensola *f; (on building)* cornicione *m; (on cliff)* cengia *f;* **window ~** davanzale *m*

ledger ['le·dʒɚ] *n* COM libro *m* mastro

lee [liː] *n* lato *m* sottovento

leech [liːtʃ] <-es> *n* sanguisuga *f;* **he stuck to her like a ~** le stava appiccicato come una sanguisuga

leek [liːk] *n* FOOD porro *m*

leer [lɪr] I. *vi* lanciare occhiate maliziose II. *n* occhiata *f* maliziosa

leery ['lɪ·ri] *adj* diffidente

leeward ['liː·wɚd] METEO I. *adj* sottovento II. *adv* sottovento

Leeward Islands *n* Isole *f pl* Sottovento

leeway ['liː·weɪ] *n* libertà *f* di manovra

left [left] *pt, pp of* **leave**[1]

left[2] [left] I. *n* 1. A.POL sinistra *f;* **the ~** la sinistra; **to turn to the ~** girare a sinistra; **on/to the/her ~** a/alla sua sinistra 2. *a.* POL di sinistra II. *adj* sinistro, -a, di sinistra III. *adv* a sinistra; **to turn ~** girare a sinistra

left field *n (in baseball)* left field *m inv; fig, sl;* **to be out in ~** essere un tipo particolare

left hand *n* sinistra *f;* **on the ~** a sinistra

left-hand *adj* sinistro, -a, di/a sinistra; **~ side** lato *m* sinistro; **~ turn** curva *f* a sinistra

left-handed *adj* mancino, -a; **~ scissors** forbici *f pl* per mancini

left-hander *n* mancino, -a *m, f*

leftist ['lef·tɪst] POL I. *adj* di sinistra II. *n* persona *f* di sinistra

leftovers ['left·ˌoʊ·vɚz] *npl* 1. *(food)* avanzi *mpl* 2. *(remaining things)* resti *mpl*

left wing *n* POL sinistra *f*

left-wing *adj* POL di sinistra

left-winger *n* POL persona *f* di sinistra

lefty *n* mancino, -a *m, f*

leg [leg] I. *n* 1. *(of person, pants)* gamba *f; (of animal, furniture)* zampa *f* 2. GASTR *(of lamb, chichen)* coscio *m* 3. *(segment of journey)* tappa *f* ► **to be on one's last ~s** averne per poco; **to give sb a ~ up** *inf* dare una mano a qu; **break a ~!** in bocca al lupo!; **to pull sb's ~** *inf* prendere in giro qu; **to shake a ~** *inf* darsi una mossa II. *vt* <-gg-> *info* **to ~ it** *(go by foot)* camminare; *(run fast)* correre

legacy ['le·gə·si] <-ies> *n* lascito *m; (inheritance)* retaggio *m*

legal ['liː·gl] *adj* 1. *(in accordance with law)* legale 2. *(concerning the law)* legale, giuridico, -a

legal advice *n* consulenza *f* legale

legal age *n* maggiore età *f*

legal aid *n* diritto ad avere un avvocato d'ufficio

legal fee *n* parcella *m* dei legali

legality [liː·'gæ·lə·ti] *n* legalità *f*

legalization [ˌliː·gə·lɪ·'zeɪ·ʃən] *n* legalizzazione *f*

legalize ['liː·gə·laɪz] *vt* legalizzare

legally ['liː·gə·li] *adv* legalmente

legal system *n* sistema *m* giuridico

legate ['le·gɪt] *n* legato *m*

legation [lɪ·'geɪ·ʃən] *n* legazione *f*

legend ['le·dʒənd] *n* leggenda *f;* **~ has it that ...** secondo la leggenda...; **he was a ~ in his own time** era una leggenda vivente

legendary ['le·dʒən·de·ri] *adj* leggendario, -a

legerdemain [ˌle·dʒɚ·də·'meɪn] *n* giochi *m pl* di prestigio

leggings ['le·gɪŋz] *npl* fuseaux *mpl*

leggy ['le·gi] <-ier, -iest> *adj* con le gambe lunghe

legible ['le·dʒɚ·bl] *adj* leggibile

legion ['liː·dʒən] *n* 1. *(national organization)* associazione *f* 2. *(many)* schiera *f* II. *adj form* **the difficulties are ~** le difficoltà sono innumerevoli

legionary ['liː·dʒə·ne·ri] I. *adj* legionario, -a II. *n* <-ies> legionario *m*

legionnaire [ˌliː·dʒə·'ner] *n* legionario *m*

Legionnaires' disease *n* MED legionellosi *f*

legislate ['le·dʒɪs·leɪt] *vi* legislare

legislation [ˌle·dʒɪs·'leɪ·ʃən] *n* legislazione *f*

legislative ['le·dʒɪs·leɪ·tɪv] *adj* legislativo, -a

legislator ['le·dʒɪs·leɪ·tɚ] *n* legislatore *m*

legislature ['le·dʒɪs·leɪ·tʃɚ] *n* assemblea *f* legislativa

legit [lə·'dʒɪt] *adj sl* legale

legitimacy [lə·'dʒɪ·tə·mə·si] *n* legalità *f*

legitimate[1] [lə·'dʒɪ·tə·mət] *adj* 1. *(legal)* legale 2. *(reasonable)* valido, -a 3. *(born in wedlock)* legittimo, -a

legitimate[2] [lə·'dʒɪ·tə·meɪt] *vt* legittimare

legitimize [lə·'dʒɪ·tə·maɪz] *vt* legittimare

legroom ['leg·ruːm] *n* spazio *m* per le gambe

legume [lə·'gjuːm] *n* FOOD legume *m*

leguminous [lə·'gjuː·mɪ·nəs] *adj* con frutto a baccello

leisure ['liː·ʒɚ] *n* tempo *m* libero ► **at one's ~** con comodo; **call me at your ~** chiamami con comodo

leisure activities *n* attività *f pl* ricreative

leisured *adj (comfortable)* comodo, -a

leisurely I. *adj* rilassato, -a II. *adv* in modo rilassato

leisure time *n* tempo *m* libero

leisure wear *n* abbigliamento *m* per il tempo libero

lemming ['le·mɪŋ] *n* lemming *m inv*

lemon ['le·mən] *n* 1. *(fruit)* limone *m;* **a slice of ~** una fettina di limone 2. *(color)* giallo *m* limone 3. *inf (defective object)* catorcio *inv*

lemonade [ˌle·mə·'neɪd] *n* limonata *f*

lemon juice *n* succo *m* di limone

lemon peel *n* scorza *f* di limone

lend [lend] <lent, lent> I. *vt* 1. *(give temporarily)* prestare; **to ~ money to sb** prestare soldi a qu 2. *(impart, provide)* dare; **to ~ color**

to sth avvalorare qc; **to ~ support to a view** appoggiare un'idea ▶**to ~ an ear** prestare attenzione; **to ~ an ear to sb** dare ascolto a qu; **to ~ a hand to sb** dare una mano a qu; **to ~ one's name to sth** appoggiare pubblicamente qc **II.** *vi* fare prestiti

lender ['len·də] *n* FIN prestatore, -trice *m, f*

lending ['len·dɪŋ] *n* prestito *m*

lending library *n* biblioteca *f* che fa prestiti a domicilio

length [leŋθ] *n* **1.** (*measurement*) lunghezza *f;* it's 3 yards in ~ è lungo 3 iarde; (**along**) **the ~ of sth** per la lunghezza di qc **2.** (*piece: of pipe, rope*) pezzo *m* **3.** (*of swimming pool*) vasca *f* **4.** (*duration*) durata *f;* (**for**) **any ~ of time** (per) un periodo qualsiasi; **at ~** finalmente; **to speak at ~** parlare a lungo; **at great ~** con dovizia di particolari ▶**to go to great ~s to do sth** darsi un gran daffare per fare qc

lengthen ['leŋ·θən] **I.** *vt* **1.** (*in time*) prolungare **2.** (*physically*) allungare **II.** *vi* **1.** (*in time*) prolungarsi **2.** (*physically*) allungarsi

lengthways ['leŋθ·weɪz] *adv, adj,* **lengthwise** ['leŋθ·waɪz] *adv, adj* per lungo

lengthy ['leŋ·θi] <-ier, -iest> *adj* lungo, -a; (*speech*) prolisso, -a; **a ~ wait** una lunga attesa

lenience ['liː·ni·ənts] *n,* **leniency** *n* indulgenza *f*

lenient ['liː·ni·ənt] *adj* (*judge*) indulgente; (*punishment*) poco severo, -a

lens [lenz] <-es> *n* **1.** (*of glasses*) lente *f;* **contact ~es** lenti a contatto **2.** (*of camera*) obiettivo *m;* **zoom ~** zoom *m inv* **3.** ANAT cristallino *m*

lent [lent] *pt, pp of* **lend**

Lent [lent] *n* Quaresima *f*

lentil ['len·tl] *n* lenticchia *f*

Leo ['liː·oʊ] *n* Leone *m, nello zodiaco*

leonine ['lɪ·ə·naɪn] *adj form* leonino, -a

leopard ['le·pəd] *n* leopardo *m* ▶**a ~ can't change its spots** *prov* il lupo perde il pelo ma non il vizio *prov*

leotard ['liː·ə·taːrd] *n* body *m inv*

leper ['le·pə] *n* **1.** MED lebbroso, -a *m, f* **2.** *fig* appestato, -a *m, f*

leprosy ['lep·rə·si] *n* lebbra *f*

leprous ['lep·rəs] *adj* lebbroso, -a

lesbian ['lez·bi·ən] **I.** *n* lesbica *f* **II.** *adj* lesbico, -a

lesbianism *n* lesbismo *m*

lesion ['liː·ʒən] *n* lesione *f*

Lesotho [lə·'soʊ·toʊ] *n* Lesotho *m*

less [les] *comp of* **little I.** *adj* meno; **sth of ~ value** qc di minor valore; **~ wine/fat** meno vino/grasso **II.** *adv* meno; **to drink ~** bere meno; **to see sb ~** vedere meno qu; **~ than 10** meno di 10; **to grow** [*o* **become**] **~** diminuire; **not him, much ~ her** lui no, e ancora meno lei **III.** *pron* meno; **~ than ...** meno di ...; **~ and ~** sempre meno; **to cost ~ than ...** costare meno di ...; **the ~ you eat, the ~ you get fat** meno mangi, meno ingrassi **IV.** *prep*

meno; **a month, ~ two days** un mese meno due giorni

lessen ['le·sn] **I.** *vi* (*danger*) ridurre; (*fever, pain*) diminuire **II.** *vt* (*diminish*) diminuire; (*risk, pain*) ridurre

lesser ['le·sə] *adj comp of* **less** minore; **to a ~ extent** in grado minore

lesson ['le·sn] *n a.fig* lezione *f;* **to draw a ~** (**from sth**) imparare la lezione (da qc); **to learn one's ~** imparare la lezione; **to teach sb a ~** dare una lezione a qu

lest [lest] *conj liter* **1.** (*for fear that*) per timore che +*subj,* per timore di +*inf;* **I didn't do it ~ he should come** non lo feci per timore che venisse **2.** (*if*) nel caso che +*subj*

let¹ [let] *n* SPORTS net *m inv* ▶**without ~ or hindrance** LAW senza nessun impedimento

let² [let] *vt* <let, let> **1.** (*allow*) lasciare; **to ~ sb do sth** lasciar fare qc a qu; **to ~ sb know sth** far sapere qc a qu; **to ~ sth pass** far passare qc; **to ~ sb alone** lasciare in pace qu; **~ him be!** lascialo stare! **2.** (*in suggestions*) **~'s go!** andiamo!; **~'s say ...** diciamo ...; **~ us pray** preghiamo! **3.** *inf* (*filler while thinking*) **~'s see** vediamo; **~ me think** fammi pensare **4.** MAT **~ x be y** sia x uguale a y ▶**~ alone ...** tanto meno ...; **to ~ sb have it** farla vedere a qu; **to ~ sth lie** lasciar perdere qc; **to ~ rip** scatenarsi

♦**let by** *vt* lasciar passare

♦**let down** *vt* **1.** (*disappoint*) deludere **2.** (*lower*) abbassare; (*hair*) sciogliere; **to let one's hair down** *a. fig* rilassarsi **3.** FASHION allungare

♦**let in** *vt* (*person*) far entrare; (*light*) lasciar passare ▶**to let oneself in for sth** andarsi a cercare qc; **to let sb in on sth** rivelare qc a qu

♦**let off** *vt* **1.** (*forgive*) lasciarla passare a; **to be let off with a fine** cavarsela con una multa **2.** (*fire: gun*) fare fuoco con; (*bomb, firework*) far esplodere

♦**let on** *vi inf* (*divulge*) **to ~ about sth** rivelare qc; **to not ~ about sth** non dire niente di qc

♦**let out I.** *vi* finire **II.** *vt* **1.** (*release*) far uscire; (*prisoner*) mettere in libertà; **to ~ a laugh** scoppiare a ridere; **to ~ a scream** emettere un grido **2.** FASHION allargare **3.** (*reveal: secret*) rivelare

♦**let up** *vi* **1.** (*become weaker, stop: rain*) cessare; (*cold*) diminuire; (*fog*) svanire **2.** (*relent*) demordere; **to ~ on sb** essere meno duro con qu; **to ~ on the gas** rallentare

lethal ['liː·θl] *adj* letale; **this brandy's ~!** *inf* questo brandy è letale!

lethargic [lɪ·'θaːr·dʒɪk] *adj* **1.** (*lacking energy*) apatico, -a **2.** (*drowsy*) insonnolito, -a

lethargy ['le·θə·dʒi] *n* **1.** (*lack of energy*) apatia *f* **2.** (*drowsiness*) torpore *m*

letter ['le·tə] *n* (*message, symbol*) lettera *f;* **~ of recommendation** lettera di raccomandazione; **~ of credit** lettera di credito ▶**to stick to the ~ of the law** attenersi rigorosamente

alla legge; <u>**to the**</u> ~ alla lettera
letter bomb *n* lettera *f* esplosiva
letterbox *n* cassetta *f* delle lettere
letterhead *n* (*logo*) intestazione *f;* (*paper*) carta *f* intestata
lettering [ˈleˑ.tə.ɪŋ] *n* caratteri *mpl*
letterpress *n* TYPO stampa *f* rilievografica
lettuce [ˈleˑ.tɪs] *n* insalata *f,* lattuga *f*
leucocyte *n* s. **leukocyte**
leukemia [luːˈkiː.mi.ə] *n* leucemia *f*
leukocyte [ˈluː.koʊ.saɪt] *n* MED leucocita *m*
level [ˈleˑ.vəl] **I.** *adj* **1.** (*horizontal*) orizzontale; (*flat*) piatto, -a; (*spoonful*) raso, -a **2.** (*having same height*) **to be ~ with sth** essere allo stesso livello di qc **3.** (*in same position*) **to be ~ with sb/sth** essere alla pari con qu/qc **4.** (*of same amount*) uguale **5.** (*calm*) sereno, -a; (*look*) sincero, -a; (*tone, voice*) misurato, -a; **to keep a ~ head** restare lucido **6.** (*uniform*) uniforme ▶ **to do one's ~** <u>**best**</u> *inf* fare del proprio meglio **II.** *adv* alla pari **III.** *n* **1.** (*position, amount, height*) livello *m;* **above sea ~** sopra il livello del mare; **at ground ~** al pianoterra **2.** (*position in hierarchy*) livello *m;* **at a higher ~** a un livello alto; **at the** (**very**) **highest ~** a livello più alto; **to be on a ~ with sb/sth** essere alla pari con qu/qc; **to find one's** (**own**) **~** *inf* trovare il proprio posto nel mondo **3.** (*quality of performance*) livello *m;* **intermediate ~ students** studenti*m pl* di livello intermedio **4.** (*meaning*) **on one ~ ... on another ~** da un lato ... dall'altro; **on a serious ~** in modo serio ▶ **to** <u>**be**</u> **on the ~** (*business, person*) essere serio **IV.** <-l- *o* -ll-> *vt* **1.** (*smoothen, flatten*) livellare, spianare **2.** (*demolish completely*) radere al suolo **3.** (*point*) **to ~ sth at sb** (*gun*) puntare qc contro qu
◆**level down** *vt* spianare
◆**level off** *vi*, **level out** *vi* (*aircraft*) disporsi in assetto orizzontale; (*inflation*) stabilizzarsi
◆**level up** *vt* livellarsi
◆**level with** *vt inf* essere sincero, -a con
levelheaded *adj* sensato, -a
lever [ˈleˑ.və] **I.** *n* leva *f* **II.** *vt* fare leva su; **to ~ sth open** aprire qc facendo leva
leverage [ˈleˑ.və.ɪdʒ] *n* **1.** (*using lever*) azione *f* di leva **2.** *fig* influenza *f*
leviathan [lɪˈva.ɪə.θən] *n* A.REL leviatano *m*
levitate [ˈleˑ.vɪ.teɪt] **I.** *vt* far levitare **II.** *vi* levitare
levity [ˈleˑ.və.ti] *n* leggerezza *f*
levy [ˈleˑ.vi] **I.** <-ies> *n* tassa *f* **II.** <-ie-> *vt* imporre; **to ~ a tax on sth** imporre una tassa su qc
lewd [luːd] *adj* (*person*) libidinoso, -a; (*gesture, remark*) osceno, -a
lewdness *n* (*behavior*) libidine *f;* (*of gesture, remark*) oscenità *f*
lexical [ˈlek.sɪ.kl] *adj* lessicale
lexicographer [ˌlek.sɪˈkɑː.grə.fə] *n* lessicografo, -a *m, f*
lexicography [ˌlek.sɪˈkɑː.grə.fi] *n* lessicogra-

fia *f*
lexicology [ˌlek.sɪˈkɑː.lə.dʒi] *n* lessicologia *f*
lexicon [ˈlek.sɪ.kɑːn] *n* **1.** (*vocabulary*) lessico *m* **2.** (*dictionary*) dizionario *m*
lexis [ˈlek.sɪs] *n* LING vocabolario *m*
LF *abbr of* **low frequency** BF
liability [ˌla.ɪəˈbɪ.lə.ti] *n* **1.** FIN, LAW responsabilità *f;* **to accept ~ for sth** assumersi la responsabilità di qc **2.** FIN **liabilities** debiti *mpl* **3.** *inf* **he's a ~!** lui è un peso!
liable [ˈla.ɪə.bl] *adj* **1.** (*prone*) soggetto, -a; **to be ~ to do sth** tendere a fare qc **2.** LAW responsabile; **to be ~ for sth** essere responsabile di qc
liaise [lɪˈeɪz] *vi* **to ~ with sb/sth** fare da collegamento con qu/qc
liaison [ˈliː.ə.zɑːn] *n* **1.** (*contact*) comunicazione *f;* (*coordination*) coordinazione *f* **2.** LING liaison *f* **3.** (*person*) contatto *mf;* MIL ufficiale *m* di collegamento **4.** (*sexual affair*) avventura *f*
liar [ˈla.ɪə] *n* bugiardo, -a *m, f*
lib [lɪb] *n inf abbr of* **liberation** liberazione *f*
libel [ˈla.ɪ.bl] **I.** *n* LAW libello *m;* PUBL diffamazione *f;* **to sue sb for ~** fare causa a qu per diffamazione **II.** <-l- *o* -ll-> *vt* LAW, PUBL diffamare
libellous *adj*, **libelous** [ˈla.ɪ.bə.ləs] *adj* LAW, PUBL diffamatorio, -a
liberal [ˈlɪ.bə.rəl] **I.** *adj* **1.** (*tolerant*) *a.* POL liberale **2.** (*generous, plentiful*) generoso, -a **3.** (*not strict: interpretation*) libero, -a **II.** *n* liberale *mf*
liberal arts *n* materie *f pl* umanistiche
liberalism [ˈlɪ.bə.rə.lɪ.zəm] *n* liberalismo *m*
liberality [ˌlɪ.bəˈræ.lə.ti] *n* **1.** (*tolerance*) liberalità *f* **2.** (*generosity*) generosità *f*
liberalization [ˌlɪ.bə.rə.lɪˈzeɪ.ʃən] *n* liberalizzazione *f*
liberalize [ˈlɪ.bə.rə.laɪz] *vt* liberalizzare
liberate [ˈlɪ.bə.reɪt] *vt* **1.** (*free*) liberare; **to ~ oneself from sth/sb** liberarsi di qc/qu **2.** *fig, iron, sl* (*steal*) portare via
liberation [ˌlɪ.bəˈreɪ.ʃən] *n* liberazione *f*
liberator [ˈlɪ.bə.reɪ.tə] *n* liberatore, -trice *m, f*
Liberia [laɪˈbɪ.ri.ə] *n* Liberia *f*
Liberian **I.** *adj* liberiano, -a **II.** *n* liberiano, -a *m, f*
libertine [ˈlɪ.bə.tiːn] *n* libertino, -a *m, f*
liberty [ˈlɪ.bə.ti] *n form* **1.** (*freedom*) libertà *f;* **to be at ~** essere in libertà; **to be at ~ to do sth** avere il diritto di fare qc; **to take the ~ of doing sth** prendersi la libertà di fare qc; **to take liberties with sb** prendersi delle libertà verso qu **2. liberties** *pl* (*rights*) diritti *mpl*
libidinous [ləˈbɪd.nəs] *adj form* libidinoso, -a
libido [lɪˈbiː.doʊ] *n* libido *f*
Libra [ˈliː.brə] *n* Bilancia *f*
Libran [ˈliːb.rən] **I.** *n* Bilancia *f* **II.** *adj* della Bilancia
librarian [laɪˈbre.ri.ən] *n* bibliotecario, -a *m, f*
library [ˈlaɪ.bre.ri] *n* <-ies> **1.** (*place*) biblioteca *f;* **film ~** cineteca *f;* **newspaper ~** emeroteca *f* **2.** (*collection*) archivio *m*

libretto [lɪˈbreˌt̬oʊ] *n* libretto *m*
Libya [ˈlɪbiə] *n* Libia *f*
Libyan I. *adj* libico, -a II. *n* libico, -a *m, f*
lice [laɪs] *npl s.* louse
license [ˈlaɪsənts] I. *n* 1. (*document*) licenza *f*, permesso *m*; **driver's ~** patente *f* di guida; **gun ~** portom *inv* d'armi 2. (*freedom*) licenza *f*; **artistic ~** licenza artistica II. *vt* autorizzare
licensed *adj* autorizzato, -a
licensed practical nurse *n* infermiere non qualificato per dispensare farmaci
licensee [ˌlaɪsəntˈsiː] *n* concessionario, -a *m, f*
license plate *n* AUTO targa *f*
license plate number *n* AUTO numero *m* di targa
licensing [ˈlaɪsəntˌsɪŋ] *n* licenza *f*, permesso *m*
licentious [laɪˈsenˌʃəs] *adj* licenzioso, -a
lichen [ˈlaɪkən] *n* lichene *m*
lick [lɪk] I. *n* 1. (*with tongue*) leccata *f* 2. (*light coating*) **a ~ of paint** una mano di tinta 3. *inf* (*try*) **to give it a ~** provarci 4. MUS chorus *m inv* ▶ **a ~ and a promise** *inf* una ripassatina II. *vt* 1. (*with tongue*) leccare 2. (*lightly touch*) lambire 3. *inf* (*defeat*) battere 4. *sl* (*beat up*) pestare
licking *n* 1. *sl* (*physical beating*) pestata *f* 2. SPORTS (*defeat*) sconfitta *f*
licorice [ˈlɪkɚɪʃ] *n* liquorizia *f*
lid [lɪd] *n* 1. (*for container*) tappo *m*, coperchio *m* 2. *fig* (*limit*) freno *m* 3. (*eyelid*) palpebra *m* ▶ **to keep the ~ on sth** controllare qc; **that puts the ~ on it** questa è la fine
lie¹ [laɪ] I. <-y-> *vi* mentire; **to ~ about sth** mentire su qc II. <-y-> *vt* **to ~ oneself out of sth** tirarsi fuori da qc mentendo III. *n* menzogna *f*, bugia *f*; **to be an outright ~** essere tutta una menzogna; **to live a ~** vivere nella menzogna; **don't tell me ~s!** non mentirmi!
lie² [laɪ] I. <lay, lain> *vi* 1. (*be lying down: person*) giacere, stare disteso; **to ~ in bed** giacere a letto; **to ~ on the ground** giacere a terra; **to ~ awake** stare a letto sveglio; **to ~ still** giacere immobile 2. (*be positioned*) trovarsi; **to ~ off the coast** (*boat*) trovarsi al largo; **to ~ on the route to ...** trovarsi sulla strada per ...; **to ~ to the east of ...** essere situato a est di ...; **to ~ in ruins** essere in rovina; **to ~ in wait** stare in attesa 3. *form* (*be buried*) giacere 4. **to ~ with sb/sth** (*be responsibility of*) spettare a qu/qc; (*be the reason for sth*) essere colpa di qu/qc 5. SPORTS posizionarsi II. *n* posizione *f*
◆ **lie around** *vi* 1. (*be somewhere*) essere in giro 2. (*be lazy*) bighellonare
◆ **lie back** *vi* appoggiarsi (all'indietro)
◆ **lie down** *vi* 1. (*act*) sdraiarsi 2. *inf* (*do nothing*) **to ~ on the job** prendersela comoda al lavoro; **to take sth lying down** accettare qc senza protestare
◆ **lie to** *vi* NAUT essere alla cappa
lie detector *n* macchina *f* della verità
lien [liːn] *n* diritto *m* di pegno

lieu [luː] *n* **in ~ of** al posto di
lieutenant [luːˈteˌnənt] *n* 1. MIL tenente *m* 2. (*assistant*) luogotenente *m*
life [laɪf] <lives> *n* 1. vita *f*; **~ after death** vita ultraterrena; **intelligent ~** (*formef pl* di) vita intelligente; **plant ~** vita vegetale; **private ~** vita privata; **to be full of ~** essere pieno di vita; **to lose one's ~** perdere la vita; **to take sb's ~** togliere la vita a qu; **to take one's (own) ~** togliersi la vita 2. (*existence*) vita *f*; **to want sth out of ~** volere qc dalla vita; **to be sb's (whole) ~** essere tutto per qu 3. (*duration*) durata *f* 4. *inf* (*prison sentence*) ergastolo *m*; **to get ~** essere condannato all'ergastolo ▶ **a ~ and death struggle** una lotta tra la vita e la morte; **to be a matter of ~ and death** essere una questione di vita o di morte; **to take one's ~ in one's hands** rischiare la vita; **to risk ~ and limb (to do sth)** rischiare la vita (per fare qc); **to lay one's ~ on the line** mettere a rischio la propria vita; **to be the ~ of the party** essere l'anima della festa; **to do sth for dear ~** fare qc disperatamente; **to live the good ~** fare la bella vita; **~ is hard!** *iron, inf* che vitaccia!; **as large as ~** in carne ed ossa; **to breathe new ~ into sth** dare nuova vita a qc; **to bring sth to ~** vivacizzare qc; **to come to ~** diventare vivo; **to frighten the ~ out of sb** spaventare a morte qu; **to give one's ~ for sb/sth** dare la vita per qu/qc; **to make a new ~** cominciare una nuova vita; **for ~** per tutta la vita; **I'm not able for the ~ of me to ...** non sono assolutamente capace di ...; **not on your ~!** *inf* nemmeno per idea!; **that's ~!** così è la vita!; **this is the ~ (for me)!** questa sì che è vita!
life annuity <-ies> *n* vitalizio *m*
life belt *n* salvagente *m inv*
lifeboat *n* scialuppa *f* di salvataggio
life buoy *n* salvagente *m inv*
life cycle *n* ciclo *m* vitale
life expectancy <-ies> *n* durata *f* (media) della vita
life form *n* forma *f* di vita
lifeguard *n* bagnino, -a *m, f*
life insurance *n* assicurazione *f* sulla vita
life jacket *n* giubbotto *m* di salvataggio
lifeless [ˈlaɪfˌləs] *adj* 1. (*dead*) senza vita 2. *fig* spento, -a
lifelike [ˈlaɪfˌlaɪk] *adj* naturale
lifeline *n* 1. NAUT cima *f* di salvataggio 2. *fig* ancora *f* di salvezza
lifelong [ˌlaɪfˈlɑːŋ] *adj* che dura tutta la vita
life preserver *n* salvagente *m inv*
lifer [ˈlaɪfɚ] *n sl* ergastolano, -a *m, f*
life raft *n* zattera *f* di salvataggio
lifesaver *n* bagnino, -a *m, f*
life sentence *n* condanna *f* all'ergastolo
life-size *adj*, **life-sized** *adj* a grandezza naturale
life span *n* (*of animals, people*) durata *f* della vita; (*of machines*) durata *f*
lifestyle *n* stile *m* di vita

L

life-support system n respiratore m artificiale

life-threatening adj potenzialmente letale

lifetime n 1. (of person) vita f; **in my** ~ nella mia vita; **the chance of a** ~ (**for sb**) un'occasione unica (per qu); **to happen once in a** ~ succedere una volta nella vita; **to see sth during one's** ~ vedere qc prima di morire 2. inf (eternity) vita f; **to seem like a** ~ sembrare un'eternità

lifework n lavoro m di tutta una vita

lift [lɪft] I. n 1. (upward motion) sollevamento m; **to give sth a** ~ sollevare qc 2. AVIAT portanza f 3. fig (positive feeling) **to give sb a** ~ tirare un po' su qu 4. (hoisting device) montacarichi m inv 5. inf (help) mano f 6. inf (car ride) passaggio m; **to give sb a** ~ dare un passaggio a qu II. vi sollevarsi III. vt 1. (move upwards) sollevare, alzare; **to** ~ **fingerprints from sth** rilevare le impronte digitali da qc; **to** ~ **one's eyes** alzare gli occhi; **to** ~ **one's head** alzare la testa; **to** ~ **one's voice** alzare la voce; **to** ~ **one's voice to sb** (yell at) urlare a qu; (argue with) discutere con qu 2. (stop) togliere; **to** ~ **restrictions** togliere le restrizioni 3. (encourage) **to** ~ **sb's spirits** sollevare il morale di qu 4. (move by air) trasportare (per via aerea) 5. inf (steal) fregare; (plagiarize) copiare; **to** ~ **a tune** copiare una melodia

◆**lift down** vt tirare giù

◆**lift off** vi AVIAT decollare

◆**lift up** vt alzare; **to** ~ **one's head** alzare la testa; **to** ~ **one's voice** alzare la voce

liftoff n AVIAT, TECH decollo m

ligament ['lɪ·gə·mənt] n legamento m

ligature ['lɪ·gə·tʃər] n 1. MED filo m per legatura 2. MUS, TYPO legatura f

light [laɪt] I. n 1. (energy, brightness) luce f; **by the** ~ **of the moon** al chiaro di luna 2. (daytime) luce f (del giorno); **first** ~ prime luci 3. (source of brightness, lamp) luce f; **to turn a** ~ **off/on** spegnere/accendere una luce; ~**s out** inf (bedtime) ora f di dormire 4. (traffic light) semaforo m 5. (flame) fuoco m; **to catch** ~ prendere fuoco; **to set** ~ **to sth** dare fuoco a qc; **do you have a** ~? hai da accendere? 6. (clarification, insight) luce f; **to bring sth to** ~ portare alla luce; **to cast** [o **shed**] ~ **on sth** far luce su qc; **to come to** ~ venire alla luce, emergere 7. (perspective) luce f; **to see things in a new** ~ vedere le cose sotto una luce diversa 8. fig (joy, inspiration) luce f; **you are the** ~ **of my life** sei la luce dei miei occhi ►**to see the** ~ **at the end of the** tunnel vedere la luce in fondo al tunnel; **to go out like a** ~ inf (fall asleep quickly) addormentarsi di colpo; (faint suddenly) svenire II. adj 1. (not heavy) leggero, -a; **a** ~ **touch** un tocco leggero 2. (not dark: color) chiaro, -a; (room) luminoso, -a 3. (not serious) leggero, -a; ~ **opera** operetta f 4. (not intense: breeze, rain) lieve; **to be a** ~ **sleeper** avere il sonno leggero; **to be** ~ **on sth** essere a corto di qc 5. GASTR leggero, -a; **a** ~ **meal** un pasto leggero 6. (with

few calories) light III. adv leggermente ►**to make** ~ **of sth** prendere qc alla leggera IV. vt <lit o lighted> 1. (illuminate) illuminare; **to** ~ **the way** indicare la strada 2. (start burning) accendere; **to** ~ **a cigarette** accendere una sigaretta V. vi <lit o lighted> (catch fire) prendere fuoco

◆**light into** vt inf fare una sfuriata a

◆**light up** I. vt 1. illuminare 2. (cigarette) accendere II. vi 1. (become bright) illuminarsi 2. (become animated) animarsi; **his face lit up** gli si illuminò il volto 3. (start smoking) accendersi una sigaretta [o accendersi un sigaro]

◆**light upon** vi imbattersi in; (suddenly see) posarsi su

lightbulb n lampadina f, foco

lighten ['laɪ·tən] I. vi 1. (become brighter) schiarire 2. (become less heavy) alleggerirsi; (mood) sollevarsi II. vt 1. (make less heavy) alleggerire; **to** ~ **sb's burden** [o **load**] alleggerire il peso che qu ha sulle spalle 2. (bleach, make paler) schiarire

◆**lighten up** vi rilassarsi

lighter ['laɪ·tər] n accendino m

light-footed adj agile, veloce

lightheaded adj stordito, -a

lighthearted adj (carefree) spensierato, -a; (happy) allegro, -a

lighthouse n faro m

lighting ['laɪ·tɪŋ] n illuminazione f

lightly ['laɪt·li] adv leggermente; **to sleep** ~ dormire non profondamente; **to take sth** ~ prendere qc alla leggera; **to get off** ~ cavarsela con poco

light meter n PHOT esposimetro m

lightness ['laɪt·nɪs] n 1. (of thing, touch) leggerezza f 2. (brightness) luminosità f

lightning ['laɪt·nɪŋ] n lampo m; **a bolt of** ~ un lampo; **thunder and** ~ tuoni e fulmini; **quick as** ~ come un fulmine

lightning bug n lucciola f

lightning rod n parafulmine m

light pen n penna f ottica

light pollution n inquinamento m luminoso

lightship n battello-faro m

lightweight I. adj (clothing, material) leggero, -a II. n 1. SPORTS peso m leggero 2. sl (unimpressive person) persona f da poco

light-year n anno m luce; **to be** ~**s away** inf essere lontano anni luce

likable ['laɪ·kə·bl] adj simpatico, -a

like[1] [laɪk] I. vt 1. (find good) I ~ **it** mi piace; **she** ~**s apples** le piacciono le mele; I ~ **swimming** mi piace nuotare; I ~ **Sarah** Sarah mi piace; **he** ~**s classical music** gli piace la musica classica; I ~ **it when/how ...** mi piace quando/come...; **well, how do you** ~ **that?** (expressing surprise) allora, che te ne pare? 2. (desire, wish) volere; I **would** ~ **to go to ...** vorrei andare...; **would you** ~ **a cup of tea?** vuoi un tè?; I **would** ~ **a little bit more time** vorrei un po' più di tempo; I'**d** ~ **to know ...**

vorrei sapere...; **I'd ~ a steak** vorrei una bistecca **II.** *n pl* preferenze *fpl;* **sb's ~s and dislikes** le preferenze di qu

like² [laɪk] **I.** *adj* simile; **to be of ~ mind** pensare allo stesso modo **II.** *prep* **1.to be ~ sb/ sth** essere come qu/qc; **what was it ~?** com'era?; **what does it look ~?** che aspetto ha?; **to work ~ crazy** *inf* lavorare come un mulo; **there's nothing ~ ...** non c'è niente di meglio di/che ... **2.** *sl* **be ~** (*say*) fare, dire ▶ ~ **anything** a più non posso **III.** *conj inf* come se +*subj;* **he speaks ~ he was drunk** parla come se fosse ubriaco; **he doesn't do it ~ I do** lui non lo fa come me **IV.** *n* **1.** (*similar things*) **toys, games and the ~** giocattoli, giochi e simili **2.** *inf* **the ~s of that/him** roba/gente del genere **V.** *interj sl* (*as filler*) **I'm ~ kind of tired** sono, beh, un po' stanco; (*for emphasis*); **just ~ get out of here!** vattene!

likeable *adj* s. **likable**

likelihood ['laɪk·li·hʊd] *n* probabilità *f;* **in all ~** molto probabilmente; **there is every/little ~ that ...** è molto/poco probabile che ... +*subj*

likely ['laɪk·li] **I.** <-ier, -iest> *adj* probabile; **it is ~ (that ...)** è probabile (che ... +*subj*); **to be quite/very ~** essere abbastanza/molto probabile; **to be a ~ story** *iron* essere bella; **not ~!** *inf* neanche per idea! **II.** *adv* probabilmente; **as ~ as not** probabilmente; **most/very ~** molto probabilmente

like-minded *adj* con la stessa mentalità

liken ['laɪ·kən] *vt* paragonare; **to ~ sb to sb** paragonare qu a qu

likeness ['laɪk·nɪs] <-es> *n* **1.** (*similarity*) somiglianza *f;* **to bear a ~ to sb** assomigliare a qu **2.** (*painting*) ritratto *m*

likewise ['laɪk·waɪz] *adv* allo stesso modo; **to do ~** fare altrettanto; **thank you for your help — ~** grazie dell'aiuto altrettanto

liking ['laɪ·kɪŋ] *n* predilezione *f;* (*for particular person*) simpatia *f;* **to develop a ~ for sth** prendere gusto a qc; **to develop a ~ for sb** prendere qu in simpatia; **to be to sb's ~** *form* essere di gradimento di qu; **it's too sweet for my ~** è troppo dolce per i miei gusti

lilac ['laɪ·læk] **I.** *n* **1.** (*bush*) lillà *m inv* **2.** (*color*) lilla *m* **II.** *adj* lilla

lilt [lɪlt] *n* cadenza *f*

lily ['lɪ·li] <-ies> *n* giglio *m;* **water ~** ninfea *f*

lily-livered *adj liter* codardo, -a

lily pad *n* foglia *f* di ninfea

lima bean *n* fagiolo *m* americano

limb [lɪm] *n* **1.** BOT ramo *m* **2.** ANAT arto *m* ▶ **to be/go out on a ~** (to do sth) essere/mettersi nei guai (per fare qc); **to tear sb ~ from ~** fare a pezzi qu

limber ['lɪm·bɚ] *adj* (*person*) sciolto, -a; (*material*) flessibile

♦**limber up** *vi* fare esercizi di riscaldamento

limbo ['lɪm·boʊ] *n* **1.** a. *fig* limbo *m;* **to be in ~** essere in un limbo **2.** (*dance*) limbo *m;* **to do the ~** ballare il limbo

lime¹ [laɪm] **I.** *n* **1.** (*fruit, tree*) limetta *f*

2. (*juice*) succo *m* di limetta **3.** (*color*) verde *m* acido **II.** *adj* verde acido

lime² [laɪm] **I.** *n* CHEM calce *f* **II.** *vt* calcinare

lime³ [laɪm] *n* (*linden tree*) tiglio *m*

limelight ['laɪm·laɪt] *n* **to be in the ~** essere alla ribalta; **to steal the ~** rubare la scena

limerick ['lɪ·mə·ɹɪk] *n* limerick *m inv*

limestone ['laɪm·stoʊn] *n* calcare *m*

limit ['lɪ·mɪt] **I.** *n* limite *m;* (*border*) confine *m;* **speed ~** AUTO limite *m* di velocità; **to put a ~ on sth** porre un limite a qc; **to overstep the ~** oltrepassare i limiti; **to know one's ~s** conoscere i propri limiti; **to know no ~s** non avere limiti; **within ~s** entro certi limiti; **to be off ~s** (to sb) essere divieto d'accesso (per qu) **II.** *vt* limitare; **to ~ oneself to sth** limitarsi a qc

limitation [ˌlɪ·mɪ·'teɪ·ʃən] *n* **1.** (*lessening*) limitazione *f;* (*of pollution*) riduzione *f* **2.** *pl* limiti *mpl;* **she knows her ~s** conosce i suoi limiti **3.** LAW decadenza *f*

limited ['lɪ·mɪ·t̬ɪd] *adj* limitato, -a; **to be ~ to sth** arrivare solo a qc

limitless ['lɪ·mɪt·lɪs] *adj* illimitato, -a

limousine ['lɪ·mə·ziːn] *n* limousine *f inv*

limp¹ [lɪmp] **I.** *vi* zoppicare **II.** *n* **to walk with a ~** zoppicare

limp² [lɪmp] *adj* floscio, -a; **to have a ~ handshake** dare la mano in modo poco energico

limpet ['lɪm·pɪt] *n* patella *f*

limpid ['lɪm·pɪd] *adj liter* limpido, -a; (*prose*) chiaro, -a

limy ['laɪ·mi] *adj* calcareo, -a

linchpin ['lɪntʃ·pɪn] *n* **1.** TECH acciarino *m* (di ruota) **2.** *fig* perno *m*

linden ['lɪn·dən] *n* BOT tiglio *m*

line¹ [laɪn] <-ning> *vt* rivestire; (*clothes*) foderare

line² [laɪn] **I.** *n* **1.** (*mark*) *a.* MAT linea *f;* **dividing ~** linea divisoria; **to be in a ~** essere allineato; **to form a ~** formare una linea **2.** (*for waiting*) fila *f,* coda *f;* **to get in ~** mettersi in fila; **to stand/wait in ~** fare la fila **3.** (*chronological succession*) serie *f;* **a (long) ~ of disasters/kings** una (lunga) serie di catastrofi/re **4.** (*cord*) corda *f;* **clothes ~** corda per il bucato **5.** TEL linea *f;* **~s will be open from ...** le linee saranno aperte da ...; **to be/stay on the ~** essere/restare in linea; **hold the ~!** resti in linea! **6.** INFOR **on ~** on line; **on/off ~** collegato/scollegato **7.** (*defense*) fronte *m,* linea *f;* **front ~** linea del fronte; **to be the last ~ of defense** *fig* essere l'ultimo baluardo; **to be behind enemy ~s** trovarsi oltre le linee nemiche **8.** (*set of tracks*) binari *m inv;* (*train route*) linea *f;* **the end of the ~** il capolinea; **to be at** [*o* **to reach**] **the end of the ~** *fig* toccare il fondo **9.** (*transport company*) linea *f* **10.** (*of text*) riga *f;* (*of poem*) verso *m;* **to drop sb a ~** *inf* mandare due righe qu **11.** MUS rigo *m* **12.** (*comment*) uscita *f;* **to come up with a ~ about sb/sth** uscirsene con un commento su qu/qc **13.** (*position, attitude*) linea *f;*

~ of reasoning ragionamento *m;* to be divided along ethnic ~s non trovarsi d'accordo riguardo alle questioni etniche; the official ~ (on sth) la posizione ufficiale (su qc); to take a ~ on sth prendere posizione riguardo a qc 14. (*field, pursuit, interest*) specialità *f inv;* what ~ are you in? di che cosa si occupa? 15. (*product type*) linea *f;* to come out with a new ~ produrre una nuova linea 16. *inf* (*of cocaine*) striscia *f;* to do a ~ of cocaine farsi una striscia ▶ somewhere along the ~ a un certo punto; to cross the ~ superare il limite; to get a ~ on sb informarsi su qu; to give sb a ~ on sb dare a qu informazioni su qu; to be in ~ for sth essere vicino a qc; to be in ~ with sb/sth concordare con qu/qc; to be out of ~ essere fuori luogo; to be out of ~ with sb/sth non concordare con qu/qc II. <-ning> *vt* to ~ the streets (*people*) essere lungo le strade; (*trees*) fiancheggiare

◆line up I. *vt* allineare; (*support, customers*) assicurarsi; (*appointment, job*) avere in programma II. *vi* 1. (*stand in row*) allinearsi 2. (*wait for sth*) fare la fila 3. (*oppose*) to ~ against sb/sth schierarsi contro qu/qc

lineage ['lɪ·ni·ɪdʒ] *n* lignaggio *m*

lineal ['lɪ·ni·əl] *adj* in linea diretta

linear ['lɪ·niə] *adj* lineare

linear equation *n* equazione *f* lineare

line backer *n* (*in football*) linebacker *m inv*

line dancing *n* line dancing *m*

linen ['lɪ·nɪn] *n* lino *m;* bed ~s biancheria *f* da letto; table ~s biancheria *f* da tavola

liner ['laɪ·nə] *n* 1. (*lining*) fodera *f;* (*garbage bag*) sacchetto *m* della spazzatura 2. (*ship*) transatlantico *m*

linesman ['laɪnz·mən] <-men> *n* SPORTS guardalinee *m inv;* TENNIS giudice *m* di linea

line-up ['laɪn·ʌp] *n* 1. SPORTS (*team*) formazione *f* 2. (*for identifying criminals*) confronto *m* all'americana

linger ['lɪŋ·gə] *vi* 1. trattenersi; to ~ in one's memory restare impresso nella memoria; to ~ over sth soffermarsi su qc 2. (*die slowly*) to ~ on continuare a vivere

lingerie [ˌlɑːn·ʒə·'reɪ] *n* biancheria *f* intima

lingering ['lɪŋ·gə·ɪŋ] *adj* persistente

lingo ['lɪŋ·goʊ] <-es> *n inf* 1. (*unfamiliar language*) lingua *f* (straniera) 2. (*jargon*) gergo *m*

linguist ['lɪŋ·gwɪst] *n* linguista *mf*

linguistic [lɪŋ·'gwɪs·tɪk] *adj* linguistico, -a

linguistics [lɪŋ·'gwɪs·tɪks] *n* linguistica *f*

liniment ['lɪ·nɪ·mənt] *n* linimento *m*

lining ['laɪ·nɪŋ] *n* 1. (*of coat, jacket*) fodera *f;* (*of boiler, pipes*) rivestimento *m* 2. ANAT parete *f*

link [lɪŋk] I. *n* 1. (*in chain*) maglia *f* 2. (*connection*) collegamento *m;* rail ~ nodo *m* ferroviario 3. INFOR collegamento *m*, link *m inv* II. *vt* collegare; to ~ arms prendersi sottobraccio; to be ~ed (together) essere legato (assieme)

links [lɪŋks] *n* SPORTS campo *m* di golf

linkup *n* collegamento *m;* satellite ~ collega-

mento via satellite

linnet ['lɪ·nɪt] *n* fanello *m*

linoleum [lɪ·'nou·li·əm] *n* linoleum *m*

Linotype® ['laɪ·nə·taɪp] *n* linotype® *f*

linseed ['lɪn·siːd] *n* semi *m pl* di lino

linseed oil *n* olio *m* di semi di lino

lint [lɪnt] *n* lanugine *f*

lintel ['lɪn·tl] *n* architrave *m*

lion ['la·ɪən] *n* leone *m* ▶ the ~'s share la parte del leone

lioness [la·ɪə·'nes] <-sses> *n* leonessa *f*

lionhearted *adj* coraggioso, -a

lionize ['la·ɪə·naɪz] *vt* trattare da vip

lip [lɪp] *n* 1. ANAT labbro *m; my* ~s are sealed sarò una tomba 2. (*rim: of cup, jug*) orlo *m* 3. *inf* (*impudence*) insolenza *f*

lip balm *n* crema *f* per le labbra

lip-gloss *n* lucidalabbra *m*

liposuction ['lɪ·pou·ˌsʌk·ʃən] *n* liposuzione *f*

lip-read I. *vi* leggere le labbra II. *vt* leggere le labbra a

lip service *n inf* to pay ~ to sth appoggiare qc soltanto a parole

lipstick *n* rossetto *m*

liquefy ['lɪk·wə·faɪ] <-ie-> I. *vt* liquefare II. *vi* liquefarsi

liqueur [lɪ·'kɜːr] *n* liquore *m*

liquid ['lɪk·wɪd] I. *n* liquido *m* II. *adj* liquido, -a

liquidate ['lɪk·wɪ·deɪt] *vt a. fig* liquidare

liquidation [ˌlɪk·wɪ·'deɪ·ʃən] *n* liquidazione *f;* to go into ~ ECON andare in liquidazione

liquidity [lɪk·'wɪ·də·ţi] *n* liquidità *f*

liquidize ['lɪk·wɪ·daɪz] *vt* frullare

liquidizer ['lɪk·wɪ·daɪ·zə] *n* frullatore *m*

liquor ['lɪ·kə] *n* alcolico *m*

liquor laws *n* leggi *f pl* sul controllo degli alcolici

liquor license *n* licenza *f* per vendita o servizio di alcolici

Lisbon ['lɪz·bən] *n* Lisbona *f*

lisp [lɪsp] I. *n* pronuncia *f* blesa II. *vi* avere la pronuncia blesa III. *vt* dire con pronuncia blesa

lissom(e) ['lɪ·səm] *adj liter* agile

list[1] [lɪst] I. *n* lista *f;* ~ price listino *m* prezzi; shopping ~ lista della spesa; to make a ~ (of sth) fare la lista (di qc) II. *vt* 1. (*make a list*) fare la lista di 2. (*enumerate*) elencare 3. (*have list price*) to ~ at $100 avere un prezzo di listino di

list[2] [lɪst] NAUT I. *vi* inclinarsi II. *n* inclinazione *f*

listen ['lɪ·sən] I. *n inf* to have a ~ (to sth) *inf* ascoltare (qc) II. *vi* 1. (*hear*) ascoltare; to ~ to sth/sb ascoltare qc/qu; to ~ to reason intendere ragioni 2. (*pay attention*) stare in ascolto; ~ for the phone stai attento se suona il telefono

◆listen in *vi* origliare; to ~ on sth origliare qc

listener ['lɪs·nə] *n* ascoltatore, -trice *m, f*

listeria [lɪs·'tɪ·ri·ə] *npl* listeria *f*

listing ['lɪs·tɪŋ] *n* 1. (*list*) lista *f*, elenco *m* 2. (*entry in list*) voce *f*

listless ['lɪst·lɪs] *adj* fiacco, -a

lit [lɪt] *pt, pp of* **light**

litany ['lɪ·tə·ni] <-ies> *n* litania *f*
litchi ['li:·tʃi:] *n* litchi *m inv*
liter ['li:·tə·] *n* litro *m*
literacy ['lɪ·tə·ə·si] *n* alfabetismo *m; ~* **rate** tasso *m* di alfabetismo
literal ['lɪ·tə·əl] *adj* letterale; **to take sth in the ~ sense of the word** prendere qc alla lettera
literally ['lɪ·tə·ə·li] *adv* letteralmente; **to take sth/sb ~** prendere qc/qu alla lettera; **quite ~** letteralmente
literary ['lɪ·tə·e·ri] *adj* letterario, -a
literary criticism *n* critica *f* letteraria
literate ['lɪ·tə·ət] *adj* 1. (*able to read and write*) **to be ~** saper leggere e scrivere 2. (*well-educated*) colto, -a
literature ['lɪ·tə·ə·tʃə·] *n* 1. (*novels, poems*) letteratura *f;* **nineteenth-century ~** letteratura dell'800 2. (*promotional material*) materiale *m* illustrativo
lithe [laɪð] *adj* agile
lithium ['lɪ·θi·əm] *n* litio *m*
lithograph ['lɪ·θə·græf] I. *n* litografia *f* II. *vi* fare litografie
lithography [lɪ·'θɑː·grə·fi] *n* litografia *f*
Lithuania [ˌlɪ·θʊ·'eɪ·niə] *n* Lituania *f*
Lithuanian I. *n* 1. (*person*) lituano, -a *m, f* 2. LING lituano *m* II. *adj* lituano, -a
litigant ['lɪ·tɪ·gənt] *n* parte *f* in causa
litigate ['lɪ·tɪ·geɪt] *vi* fare causa
litigation [ˌlɪ·tɪ·'geɪ·ʃən] *n* controversia *f*
litigious [lɪ·'tɪ·dʒəs] *adj* incline a intentare cause
litmus ['lɪt·məs] *n* tornasole *m*
litmus paper *n* cartina *f* di tornasole
litmus test *n* prova *m* del tornasole; *fig* prova *f* del fuoco
litter ['lɪ·tə·] I. *n* 1. (*refuse*) immondizia *f* 2. ZOOL figliata *f* 3. (*bedding for animals*) lettiera *f* 4. MED barella *f* II. *vt* 1. (*make untidy*) sporcare 2. *inf* (*scatter*) ricoprire di; **the floor was ~ed with clothes** il pavimento era ricoperto di vestiti
litter box *n* vaschetta *f* per la sabbia (del gatto)
litter bug *n inf: persona que getta rifiuti per terra*
little ['lɪ·t̬l] I. *adj* 1. (*in size, age*) piccolo, -a; **a ~ old man/woman** un vecchietto/una vecchietta; **the ~ ones** *inf* i bambini; **my ~ brother/sister** il mio fratellino/la mia sorellina 2. (*in amount*) poco, -a; **a ~ bit** (**of sth**) un pochino (di qc); **a ~ something** qualcosina; (*to eat or drink*) qualcosina (da mangiare o da bere); **~ hope** poche speranze; **~ by ~** poco a poco 3. (*in distance, duration*) breve; **a ~ way** poco distante; **for a ~ while** per un po'; **to have a ~ word with sb** dire due parole a qu II. *n* poco *m;* **a ~** un poco; **to know ~** sapere poco; **we see ~ of him** lo vediamo poco; **to have ~ to say** aver poco da dire III. *adv* poco; **~ less than ...** poco meno che ...; **~ more than an hour** poco più di un'ora; **to make ~ of sth** non fare una questione di qc

liturgical [lɪ·'tɜː·r·dʒɪ·kl] *adj* liturgico, -a
liturgy ['lɪ·tə·dʒi] <-ies> *n* REL liturgia *f*
live¹ [laɪv] I. *adj* 1. (*living*) vivo, -a 2. RADIO, TV in diretta; MUS dal vivo 3. ELEC sotto tensione; **to be a** (**real**) **~ wire** *fig* essere pieno di energie 4. (*cartridge*) carico, -a; (*bomb*) inesploso, -a II. *adv* RADIO, TV in diretta; MUS dal vivo
live² [lɪv] I. *vi* vivere; **to ~ above one's means** vivere al di sopra dei propri mezzi; **to ~ in sb's memory** essere vivo nella memoria di qu; **long ~ the king!** lunga vita al re!; **to ~ off sth/sb** vivere alle spalle di qc/qu; **to ~ on sth** (*eat*) mangiare qc ► **to ~ and let ~** vivere e lasciar vivere II. *vt* vivere; **to ~ a happy life** avere una vita serena
◆**live down** *vt* far dimenticare
◆**live in** *vi* vivere nel luogo di lavoro o di studio
◆**live on** *vi* sopravvivere
◆**live out** *vt* vivere; (*dreams*) realizzare
◆**live through** *vt* (*experience*) vivere
◆**live together** *vi* vivere insieme
◆**live up** *vt* **to live it up** fare la bella vita
◆**live up to** *vt* rispondere a; **to ~ expectations** essere all'altezza delle aspettative
◆**live with** *vt* 1. (*share home, couple*) convivere con; (*friends*) abitare con 2. (*accept*) convivere con
livelihood ['laɪv·li·hʊd] *n* sostentamento *m;* **to earn one's ~** guadagnarsi da vivere
liveliness ['laɪv·li·nɪs] *n* vivacità *f*
lively ['laɪv·li] *adj* vivace; (*imagination, interest*) vivo, -a
liven up ['laɪ·vən ʌp] I. *vi* animarsi II. *vt* animare
liver ['lɪ·və·] *n* fegato *m*
liverish ['lɪ·və·rɪʃ] *adj* 1. (*ill*) con disturbi di fegato 2. (*grumpy*) bilioso, -a
liverwurst ['lɪ·və·wɜːrst] *n* salsiccia *f* di fegato
livery ['lɪ·və·ri] *n* 1. FASHION livrea *f* 2. (*for horses*) stallaggio *m*
livestock ['laɪv·staːk] *n* bestiame *m*
livid ['lɪ·vɪd] *adj* 1. (*discolored*) livido, -a 2. (*furious*) livido, -a di rabbia
living ['lɪ·vɪŋ] I. *n* 1. (*livelihood*) vita *f;* **to work for one's ~** lavorare per vivere; **to make a ~** guadagnarsi da vivere 2. (*way of life*) (stile *m* di) vita *f* 3. *pl* (*people*) **the ~** i vivi II. *adj* vivo, -a; (*creature*) vivente
living conditions *npl* condizioni *f pl* di vita
living quarters *npl* alloggi *mpl*
living room *n* soggiorno *m*
living space *n a. fig* spazio *m*
living wage *n* salario *m* sufficiente per vivere
lizard ['lɪ·zə·d] *n* lucertola *f*
llama ['lɑː·mə] *n* lama *m inv*
load [loʊd] I. *n* 1. carico *m;* **take a ~ off** (**your feet**) *inf* (*sit down*) sedersi; **that took a ~ off my mind!** mi sono tolto un peso! 2. (*amount of work*) carico *m* (di lavoro); **a heavy/light ~** molto/poco lavoro 3. *inf* (*lots*) mucchio *m;* **~s** [*o* **a ~**] **of ...** un mucchio di... ► **to get a ~ of sth** *sl* stare a vedere/sentire qc II. *vt* **a.** AUTO,

PHOT, INFOR caricare III. *vi* caricarsi
◆**load down** *vt a.fig* caricare
◆**load up** I. *vt* caricare II. *vi* caricarsi
loaded ['loʊ·dɪd] *adj* 1.(*filled*) carico, -a
2.(*unfair: question*) tendenzioso, -a; ~ **dice**
dadi *m pl* truccati 3. *inf*(*rich*) straricco, -a 4. *inf*
(*drunk*) sbronzo, -a
loadstone *n s.* **lodestone**
loaf[1] [loʊf] <loaves> *n* pane *m;* **a ~ of bread**
una pagnotta ▶ **half a ~ is** better **than none**
prov meglio di niente
loaf[2] [loʊf] *vi* **to ~** (**around**) oziare
loafer ['loʊ·fɚ] *n* 1.(*lazy person*) fannullone,
-a *m, f* 2.(*shoe*) mocassino *m*
loam [loʊm] *n* terra *f* grassa
loan [loʊn] I. *vt* prestare II. *n* prestito *m*
loan shark *n* strozzino, -a *m, f*
loan-word ['loʊn·wɜːrd] *n* LING prestito *m*
loath [loʊθ] *adj form* riluttante; **to be ~ to do**
sth essere riluttante a fare qc
loathe [loʊð] *vt* detestare
loathing *n* odio *m;* **to have a ~ for sb/sth**
detestare qu
loathsome ['loʊð·səm] *adj* odioso, -a
loaves [loʊvz] *n pl of* **loaf**[1]
lob [lɑːb] I. <-bb-> *vt* lanciare; SPORTS lanciare
(a parabola) II. *n* SPORTS lob *m inv*
lobby ['lɑː·bi] I. <-ies> *n* 1. ARCHIT ingresso *m*
2. POL gruppo *m* di pressione II. <-ie-> *vi* **to ~**
to have sth done fare pressione perché si faccia qc; **to ~ against/for sth** fare pressioni con-
tro/a favore di qc III. <-ie-> *vt* fare pressioni su
lobbyist ['lɑː·bi·ɪst] *n* membro *m* di un gruppo
di pressione
lobe [loʊb] *n* lobo *m*
lobster ['lɑːbs·tɚ] *n* (*with claws*) aragosta *f*
lobster pot *n* nassa *f*
local ['loʊ·kəl] I. *adj* local; (*people*) del posto;
(*official, police*) municipale; TEL urbano, -a
II. *n* 1.(*inhabitant*) abitante *mf* del posto
2.(*bus*) autobus *m inv;* (*train*) treno *m* locale
local anesthetic *n* anestesia *f* locale
local authority *n* comune *m,* circoscrizione *f*
local call *n* chiamata *f* urbana
locale [loʊ·'kæl] *n* ambientazione *f*
local elections *npl* elezioni *f pl* amministrative
local government *n* amministrazione *f* comunale
locality [loʊ·'kæ·lə·t̬i] <-ies> *n* località *f inv*
localization [ˌloʊ·kə·lɪ·'zeɪ·ʃən] *n* localizzazione *f*
localize ['loʊ·kə·laɪz] *vt* localizzare
local paper *n* giornale *m* locale
local time *n* ora *f* locale
local train *n* treno *m* locale
locate ['loʊ·keɪt] *vt* 1.(*find*) localizzare, trovare 2.(*situate*) trovarsi; **to be ~d near sth**
essere situato presso qc
location [loʊ·'keɪ·ʃən] *n* 1.(*place*) posizione *f,*
luogo *m* 2.(*act of locating*) localizzazione *f*
3. CINE esterni *mpl;* **to film sth on ~** girare qc
in esterni

loc. cit. [ˌlɑːk·'sɪt] *abbr of* **loco citato** loc. cit.
loch [lɑːk] *n Scot* 1.(*lake*) lago *m* 2.(*inlet*)
insenatura *f* stretta e profonda
lock[1] [lɑːk] *n* (*of hair*) ricciolo *m*
lock[2] [lɑːk] I. *n* 1.(*fastening device*) serratura *f* 2.(*on canal*) chiusa *f* 3.(*in wrestling*)
chiave *f* ▶ **~, stock and** barrel completamente; **to be under ~ and** key essere sotto
chiave II. *vt* 1.(*fasten with lock*) chiudere a
chiave; (*confine safely: thing*) tenere sotto
chiave; (*person*) rinchiudere 2.(*make immovable*) bloccare; **be ~ed** essere bloccato; **to be**
~ed in(to) discussions impegnarsi in discussioni III. *vi* chiudersi (a chiave)
◆**lock away** *vt* (*jewels, document*) tenere
sotto chiave; (*person*) rinchiudere
◆**lock in** *vt* rinchiudere
◆**lock on** *vi,* **lock onto** *vi* MIL localizzare
◆**lock out** *vt* bloccare; **to lock oneself out**
chiudersi fuori
◆**lock up** *vt* (*jewels, document*) tenere sotto
chiave; (*person*) rinchiudere
locker ['lɑː·kɚ] *n* (*at train station*) (armadietto *m* per) deposito *m* bagagli; (*at school*)
armadietto *m*
locker room *n* spogliatoio *m*
locket ['lɑː·kɪt] *n* medaglione *m*
lockjaw ['lɑːk·dʒɑː] *n* MED tetano *m*
lockout ['lɑːk·aʊt] *n* serrata *f*
locksmith ['lɑːk·smɪθ] *n* fabbro *m*
lockup ['lɑːk·ʌp] *n inf* 1.(*cell*) guardina *f*
2.(*storage space*) magazzino *m*
locomotion [ˌloʊ·kə·'moʊ·ʃən] *n* locomozione *f*
locomotive [ˌloʊ·kə·'moʊ·t̬ɪv] I. *n* locomotiva *f* II. *adj* locomotore, -trice; (*force*)
motrice
locus ['loʊ·kəs] <-ci> *n* 1.(*exact place*)
luogo *m* 2. MAT luogo *m* geometrico 3. BIO
locus *m*
locust ['loʊ·kəst] *n* locusta *f*
locution [loʊ·'kju·ʃən] *n* locuzione *f*
lode [loʊd] *n* MIN filone *m*
lodestar ['loʊd·stɑːr] *n* stella *f* polare
lodestone ['loʊd·stoʊn] *n* magnetite *f*
lodge [lɑːdʒ] I. *vi* 1.(*stay in rented room*)
alloggiare 2.(*become fixed*) incastrarsi II. *vt*
1.(*accommodate*) alloggiare 2.(*place*) collocare 3.(*insert*) mettere 4.(*deposit*) depositare
5.(*register officially*) presentare III. *n* 1.(*for
hunters*) padiglione *m* di caccia; (*inn*) pensione *f;* **ski ~** rifugio (*m* per sciatori) 2.(*gate-
keepers house*) casa *f* del custode 3.(*of
organizations*) loggia *f* 4.(*of beaver*) tana *f*
lodger ['lɑː·dʒɚ] *n* persona *cui si affitta una
camera;* **to take in ~s** affittare camere
lodging ['lɑː·dʒɪŋ] *n* 1.(*accomodations*) alloggio *m* 2. *pl* (*room to rent*) camera *f* in affitto
lodging house *n* pensione *f*
loft [lɑːft] I. *n* 1.(*space under roof*) solaio *m;*
hay ~ fienile *m* 2.(*upstairs living space*) mansarda *f* II. *vt* (*ball*) lanciare in alto
lofty ['lɑːf·ti] <-ier, -iest> *adj* 1.(*tall*) alto, -a

2. (*noble: aims, ideals*) nobile **3.** (*haughty*) altero, -a

log¹ [lɑ:g] **I.** *n* **1.** (*tree trunk*) tronco *m* **2.** (*firewood*) ciocco *m* ▶ **to sleep like a** ~ dormire come un ghiro **II.** <-gg-> *vt* tagliare **III.** <-gg-> *vi* abbattere alberi (per il legname)

log² [lɑ:g] *inf abbr of* **logarithm** log.

log³ [lɑ:g] **I.** *n* registro *m;* **ship's** ~ diario *m* di bordo **II.** *vt* **1.** (*record*) annotare **2.** (*achieve, attain*) raggiungere

◆**log in** *vi* INFOR entrare nel sistema

◆**log off** *vi* INFOR uscire dal sistema

◆**log on** *vi s.* **log in**

◆**log out** *vi s.* **log off**

loganberry ['loʊ·gən·be·ri] <-ies> *n* bacca tra la mora e il lampone

logarithm ['lɑ:·gə·rɪ·ðəm] *n* logaritmo *m*

logarithmic [ˌlɑ:·gə·'rɪð·mɪk] *adj* logaritmico, -a

log book *n* NAUT, AVIAT diario *m* di bordo

log cabin *n* casetta *f* di tronchi d'albero

logger ['lɑ:·gə·] *n* taglialegna *m inv*

loggerheads ['lɑ:·gə·hedz] *npl inf* **to be at** ~ (**with sb/over sth**) non trovarsi d'accordo (con qu/su qc)

logic ['lɑ:·dʒɪk] *n* logica *f*

logical ['lɑ:·dʒɪ·kl] *adj* logico, -a

login [lɑ:·gɪn] *n* INFOR inizio *m* della sessione

logistics [loʊ·'dʒɪs·tɪks] *n* logistica *f*

logjam *n* ostruzione *f* causata da tronchi

logo ['loʊ·goʊ] *n* logo *m inv*

logoff [lɑ:g·ɑ:f] *n* INFOR fine *m* della sessione

logon *n s.* **login**

logrolling ['lɑ:g·roʊ·lɪŋ] *n* scambio *m* di favori tra politici

loin [lɔɪn] **I.** *n* **1.** *pl* (*body area*) reni *fpl* **2.** *pl, liter* **the fruit of his** ~**s** suo figlio/figlio **3.** GASTR lombata *f* **II.** *adj* di lombata

loincloth ['lɔɪn·klɔ:θ] *n* perizoma *m inv*

loiter ['lɔɪ·t̬ə·] *vi* **1.** (*linger*) attardarsi **2.** *a.* LAW vagabondare

loiterer ['lɔɪ·t̬ə·ə·] *n* **1.** *inf* fannullone, -a *m, f* **2.** LAW vagabondo, -a *m, f*

loll [lɑ:l] *vi* **to** ~ (**about**) ciondolare

lollipop ['lɑ:·li·pɑ:p] *n* lecca lecca *m inv*

crossing guard *n* persona che ferma il traffico per far attraversare la strada agli scolari

lollop ['lɑ:·ləp] *vi* avanzare a balzi

London ['lʌn·dən] *n* Londra *f*

Londoner I. *adj* londinese **II.** *n* londinese *mf*

lone [loʊn] *adj* solitario, -a

loneliness ['loʊn·lɪ·nɪs] *n* solitudine *f*

lonely ['loʊn·li] <-ier, -iest> *adj* (*person*) solo, -a; (*life, place*) solitario, -a

loner ['loʊ·nə·] *n* solitario, -a *m, f*

lonesome ['loʊn·səm] *adj* (*person*) solo, -a; (*place*) solitario, -a

long¹ [lɔ:ŋ] **I.** *adj* (*distance, time, shape*) lungo, -a; **to have a** ~ **way to go** aver molta strada da fare; **it's been a** ~ **time since ...** è molto che ...; ~ **time no see!** *inf* quanto tempo (che non ci vedevamo)! **II.** *adv* **1.** (*a long time*) molto (tempo); ~ **after/before**

molto dopo/prima; ~ **ago** molto tempo fa; **to take** ~ (**to do sth**) metterci molto (a fare qc); **to be not** ~ **in doing sth** *form* non tardare a fare qc; ~ **live the king!** lunga vita al re! **2.** (*for the whole duration*) **all day** ~ tutto il giorno; **as** ~ **as I live** finché vivo; **so** ~ **as** finché **3.** *in comparisons* **as** ~ **as** lungo quanto; **to no** ~**er do sth** non fare più qc ▶ **so** ~ *inf* ciao! **III.** *n* molto (tempo *m*) *m* ▶ **the** ~ **and the short of it is that ...** in breve...

long² [lɔ:ŋ] *vi* **to** ~ **for sb** desiderare qu; **to** ~ **for sth** aver voglia di qc; **to** ~ **to do sth** aver vogli di fare qc

long. *abbr of* **longitude** long.

longboat *n* scialuppa *f*

long-distance I. *adj* (*flight*) lungo, -a; (*race, runner*) di fondo; (*negotiations, relationship*) a distanza; ~ **call** chiamata *f* interurbana, chiamata *f* internazionale **II.** *adv* **to phone** ~ fare una chiamata interurbana [*o* fare una chiamata internazionale]

longevity [lɑ:n·'dʒe·və·t̬i] *n* longevità *f*

longhaired *adj* (*person*) con i capelli lunghi; (*animal*) dal pelo lungo

longhand *n* scrittura *f* a mano (*per esteso*)

long-haul *adj* AVIAT su lunga distanza

longing ['lɔ:ŋ·ɪŋ] **I.** *n* **1.** (*nostalgia*) nostalgia *f;* **to feel a** ~ **for sb** sentire la nostalgia di qu **2.** (*strong desire*) desiderio *m* ardente; **to have a** ~ **to do sth** desiderare ardentemente di fare qc **II.** *adj* pieno, -a di desiderio

longish ['lɔ:ŋ·ɪʃ] *adj inf* lunghetto, -a

longitude ['lɑ:n·dʒə·tu:d] *n* longitudine *f*

longitudinal [ˌlɑ:n·dʒə·'tu:d·nl] *adj* longitudinale

long johns *npl inf* mutandoni *m pl* da uomo

long jump *n* salto *m* in lungo

long-lived *adj* **1.** (*person*) longevo, -a **2.** (*feud*) annoso, -a

long-lost *adj* (*friend*) perso, -a di vista da molto tempo; (*object*) perso, -a da molto tempo

long-range *adj* (*missile*) a lungo raggio; (*aircraft*) transcontinentale; (*policy*) a lungo termine

longship *n* nave *f* vikinga

long shot *n* **1.** (*not likely*) **to be a** ~ essere una possibilità remota **2.** (*at all*) **not by a** ~ affatto

long-sighted *adj* **1.** (*far-sighted*) presbite **2.** (*having foresight*) lungimirante

long-standing *adj* di lunga data

long-suffering *adj* paziente

long-term *adj* a lungo termine

long wave *n* onda *f* lunga

long-wave *adj* a onde lunghe

longwise *adv s.* **lengthwise**

long-winded *adj* prolisso, -a

loofa(h) ['lu:·fə] *n* spugna *f* naturale

look [lʊk] **I.** *n* **1.** (*act of looking, examination*) sguardo *m*, occhiata *f;* **to take** [*o* **have**] **a** ~ **at sth** dare un'occhiata a qc; **to take a** ~ **for sth/ sb** cercare qc/qu **2.** (*appearance*) aspetto *m;* **good** ~**s** bellezza *f;* **to have the** ~ **of sb/sth** assomigliare a qu/qc; **by the** ~ **of things** a

L

quanto pare 3. (*style*) look *m inv* II. *vi* 1. (*use sight*) guardare; **to ~ at sth/sb** guardare qc/qu; **to ~ at a book** dare un'occhiata a un libro; **to ~ out (of) the window** guardare dalla finestra; **oh, ~!** guarda!; **~ here** ehi tu! 2. (*search*) cercare; **to ~ for sth/sb** cercare qc/qu 3. (*appear, seem*) sembrare; **to ~ like sb/sth** sembrare qu/qc; **to ~ bad/good** avere/non avere un bell'aspetto; **to ~ tired** avere l'aria stanca; **to ~ as if ...** sembrare che ... +*subj* 4. (*face*) dare; **to ~ north** essere esposto a nord III. *vt* 1. (*examine*) guardare; **to ~ sb in the eye** guardare qc negli occhi 2. (*seem*) sembrare; **to ~ one's age** dimostrare la propria età; **to ~ the part** THEAT calarsi nel personaggio ▶ **to ~ the other way** voltarsi dall'altra parte

◆ **look about** *vi* guardarsi intorno
◆ **look after** *vi* occuparsi di
◆ **look ahead** *vi* guardare in avanti
◆ **look around** I. *vi* 1. (*look behind oneself*) voltarsi 2. (*look in all directions*) guardarsi intorno 3. (*search*) **to ~ for** cercare II. *vt* (*inspect*) ispezionare
◆ **look away** *vi* volgere lo sguardo
◆ **look back** *vi* 1. (*look behind oneself*) guardarsi indietro 2. (*remember*) ricordare
◆ **look down** *vi* 1. (*from above*) guardare verso il basso; (*lower eyes*) abbassare lo sguardo 2. (*feel superior*) **to ~ on sth/sb** disprezzare qc/qu
◆ **look for** *vt* 1. (*search for*) cercare 2. (*expect*) sperare
◆ **look forward** *vi* **to ~ to sth** aspettare impazientemente qc; **to ~ to doing sth** non vedere l'ora di fare qc; **I ~ to hearing from you** spero di ricevere presto tue notizie
◆ **look in** *vi* **to ~ on sb** passare da qu; **to ~ at the office** passare dall'ufficio
◆ **look into** *vi* esaminare
◆ **look on** *vi* (*watch*) guardare
◆ **look onto** *vi* dare su
◆ **look out** *vi* 1. (*face a particular direction*) **to ~ on** (*window*) dare su 2. (*watch out*) fare attenzione; **~!** attento!; **to ~ for** fare attenzione a; (*look for*) cercare
◆ **look over** *vt* (*report*) rivedere; (*house*) ispezionare
◆ **look through** *vt* 1. (*look*) guardare da 2. (*examine*) rivedere 3. (*peruse*) **to ~ sth** dare un'occhiata a qc
◆ **look to** *vi* 1. (*attend to*) occuparsi di 2. (*depend on, count on*) contare su
◆ **look up** I. *vt* 1. (*consult*) cercare 2. (*visit*) andare a trovare II. *vi* 1. (*raise one's eyes upward*) guardare in su; **to ~ to sb** *fig* ammirare qu 2. (*improve*) migliorare; **things are looking up!** le cose vanno meglio!
◆ **look upon** *vi s.* look on
look-alike ['lʊk·ə·ˌlaɪk] *n* (*person*) sosia *m;* (*thing*) imitazione *f*
looker ['lʊ·kə·] *n sl* **to be a (real) ~** essere molto bello, -a

looking glass <-es> *n* specchio *m*
lookout ['lʊk·ˌaʊt] *n* 1. (*observation post*) posto *m* di osservazione 2. (*person*) vedetta *mf;* **to be on the ~** stare all'erta 3. *dial* (*panorama view*) vista *f* panoramica 4. (*concern*) problema *m;* **that's his/your ~** è un problema suo/tuo
lookover ['lʊk·əʊ·və·] *n* occhiata *f;* **to give sth a ~** dare un'occhiata a qc
loom[1] [luːm] *n* (*for weaving*) telaio *m*
loom[2] [luːm] *vi* 1. (*come into view*) apparire 2. (*threaten*) incombere; **to ~ large** assumere grande importanza
loony ['luː·ni] *sl* I. <-ier, -iest> *adj* strambo, -a II. <-ies> *n* matto, -a *m, f*
loop [luːp] I. *n* 1. (*bend*) curva *f;* (*of string*) cappio *f;* (*of river*) ansa *f* 2. ELEC circuito *m* chiuso 3. INFOR ciclo *m* 4. (*contraceptive coil*) spirale *f* ▶ **to throw sb for a ~** *inf* lasciare qu di sale II. *vi* serpeggiare III. *vt* legare con un laccio; **to ~ sth around ...** passare qc intorno a... ▶ **to ~ the loop** AVIAT effettuare una gran volta
loophole ['luːp·hoʊl] *n fig* scappatoia *f;* **legal ~** scappatoia legale
loose [luːs] I. *adj* 1. (*not tight: clothing*) comodo, -a; (*knot, rope, screw*) non ben stretto, -a; (*skin*) flaccido, -a 2. (*not confined*) libero, -a; **~ change** spiccioli *m pl* 3. (*not exact: instructions*) vago, -a; (*translation*) libero, -a 4. (*not strict or controlled: discipline*) non rigoroso, -a; **~ tongue** bocca *f* larga 5. (*sexually immoral*) dissoluto, -a II. *n* **to be on the ~** essere a piede libero III. *vt* sciogliere
loose cannon *n sl* mina *f* vagante
loose-leaf notebook *n* quaderno *m* con gli anelli
loosely ['luːs·li] *adv* 1. (*not tightly*) senza stringere 2. (*not exactly: translate*) liberamente; (*speak*) genericamente 3. (*not strictly: organized*) non rigidamente
loosen ['luː·sn] I. *vt* (*belt*) allentare; (*tongue*) sciogliere II. *vi* allentarsi
loot [luːt] I. *n* 1. (*plunder*) bottino *m* 2. *inf* (*money*) grana *f* II. *vt, vi* saccheggiare
looting *n* saccheggio *m*
lop [lɑːp] *vt s.* lop off
◆ **lop off** <-pp-> *vt* 1. (*branch*) potare; (*limb*) amputare 2. (*pages*) tagliare
lope [loʊp] *vi* (*person, animal*) procedere a grandi falcate
lopsided [ˌlɑːp·ˈsaɪ·dɪd] *adj* 1. (*leaning to one side*) storto, -a 2. (*biased*) di parte
loquacious [loʊ·ˈweɪ·ʃəs] *adj* loquace
lord [lɔːrd] *n* signore *m*
lordly ['lɔːrd·li] <-ier, -iest> *adj* 1. (*suitable to a lord*) signorile 2. (*arrogant*) arrogante
lordship ['lɔːrd·ʃɪp] *n form* **His Lordship** Sua Signoria
lore [lɔːr] *n* folklore *m*
lose [luːz] <lost, lost> I. *vt* perdere; **to get lost** (*person*) perdersi; (*object*) andare smarrito II. *vi* perdere

loser ['luː·zɚ] *n* perdente *mf*

losing ['luː·zɪŋ] *adj* perdente

loss [lɔːs] <-es> *n* perdita *f;* **to be at a ~** essere spiazzato, -a; **to be at a ~ for words** non avere parole

loss leader *n* articolo *m* civetta

loss-making *adj* in perdita

lost [lɔːst] **I.** *pt, pp of* **lose II.** *adj* **1.** perduto, -a; (*object*) smarrito, -a; **to get ~** perdersi; **to give sth/sb up for ~** dare qc/qu per disperso; **to be ~ in a book** essere totalmente immerso nella lettura **2.** (*preoccupied*) perplesso, -a

lost and found *n* ufficio *m* oggetti smarriti

lot [lɑːt] *n* **1.** (*for deciding*) **to cast ~s** tirare a sorte **2.** (*destiny*) destino *m;* (*fate*) sorte *f* **3.** (*plot of land, in auction*) lotto *m* **4.** *inf* (*large quantity*) **a ~ of, lots of** un sacco di; **a ~ of wine** molto vino; **~s of houses** molte case; **I like it a ~** mi piace molto; **the whole ~** tutto

loth [louθ] *adj s.* **loath**

lotion ['lou·ʃən] *n* lozione *f*

lottery ['lɑː·tɚ·i] <-ies> *n* lotteria *f*

lottery number *n* numero *m* della lotteria

lotus ['lou·təs] <-es> *n* loto *m*

lotus position *n* posizione *f* del loto

loud [laʊd] **I.** *adj* **1.** (*voice*) alto, -a; (*shout*) forte **2.** (*noisy*) rumoroso, -a **3.** (*vigorous: complaint*) energico, -a **4.** *fig* (*color*) vistoso, -a **II.** *adv* forte; **to laugh out ~** ridere a crepapelle

loudmouth ['laʊd·maʊθ] *n inf:* persona che parla troppo e con linguaggio offensivo

loudness *n* **1.** (*volume*) volume *m;* (*of explosion*) intensità *f* **2.** (*of color*) vistosità *f*

loudspeaker [ˌlaʊd·'spiː·kɚ] *n* altoparlante *m*

Louisiana [luˌiː·ziː·'æ·nə] *n* Louisiana *f*

lounge [laʊndʒ] **I.** *n* **1.** (*room*) sala *f* **2.** (*bar*) bar *m inv* **II.** *vi* **1.** (*recline*) appoggiarsi all'indietro **2.** (*be idle*) oziare

◆**lounge around** *vt* bighellonare

lounge chair *n* poltrona *f*

lounge lizard *n* frequentatore di bar e salotti alla moda

loungewear *n* abbigliamento *m* per il tempo libero

louse [laʊs] *n* **1.** <lice> (*insect*) pidocchio *m* **2.** <-es> *sl* (*person*) verme *m*

◆**louse up** *vt sl* rovinare

lousy ['laʊ·zi] <-ier, -iest> *adj inf* **1.** (*infested with lice*) pidocchioso, -a **2.** (*of poor quality*) schifoso, -a; **to feel ~** stare male **3.** (*nasty*) brutto, -a ▶ **to be ~ with money** essere uno spilorcio

lout [laʊt] *n* teppistello *m*

loutish ['laʊ·t̬ɪʃ] *adj* da teppistello

louver ['luː·vɚ] *n* persiana *f*

louvred door *n* porta *f* con persiane

lovable ['lʌ·və·bl] *adj* adorabile

love [lʌv] **I.** *vt* amare; (*friend*) voler bene a; **I ~ swimming, I ~ to swim** adoro nuotare **II.** *n* **1.** (*affection*) amore *m;* **to be in ~ (with sb)** essere innamorato (di qu); **to fall in ~ (with sb)** innamorarsi (di qu); **to make ~ to sb** fare l'amore con qu **2.** *inf* (*darling*) tesoro *m* **3.** (*in tennis*) zero *m* ▶ **not for ~ or money** per niente al mondo; **there is no ~ lost between the two** non si sopportano **III.** *vi* amare

love affair *n* storia *f* d'amore, relazione *f*

lovebird *n* piccioncino *m*

love handles *npl inf* maniglie *f pl* dell'amore

love-hate relationship *n* rapporto *m* d'amore e odio

loveless [lʌv·lɪs] *adj* senza amore

love letter *n* lettera *f* d'amore

love life *n* vita *f* sentimentale

loveliness ['lʌv·li·nɪs] *n* (*of scenery, person*) bellezza *f*

lovely ['lʌv·li] <-ier, -iest> *adj* (*house, present, weather*) bello, -a; (*person*) carino, -a; **to have a ~ time** divertirsi

lovemaking *n* rapporti *m pl* sessuali

lover ['lʌ·vɚ] *n* amante *mf*

love seat *n* divano *m* a due posti

lovesick ['lʌv·sɪk] *adj* pazzo, -a d'amore

love song *n* canzone *f* d'amore

love story *n* storia *f* d'amore

loving ['lʌ·vɪŋ] *adj* affettuoso, -a

low¹ [lou] **I.** *adj* **1.** (*not high, not loud*) basso, -a; **to be ~ on gas/coffee/chips** aver poca benzina/poco caffè/poche patatine; **to cook sth on ~ heat** cuocere qc a fuoco lento **2.** (*poor: opinion, quality*) cattivo, -a; (*self-esteem, visibility*) scarso, -a; **a ~ trick** un tiro mancino **II.** *adv* basso, -a; **to feel ~** essere giù; **stocks are running ~** le provviste cominciano a scarseggiare; **the batteries are running ~** le batterie si stanno scaricando **III.** *n* **1.** METEO zona *f* di bassa pressione **2.** (*minimum*) minimo *m*

low² [lou] **I.** *vi* (*cow*) muggire **II.** *n* muggito *m*

low-alcohol *adj* a basso tasso alcolico

lowborn *adj* di umili origini

lowbrow *adj* non certo intellettuale

low-cal *adj*, **low-calorie** *adj* a basso contenuto calorico

low-cost *adj* economico, -a

low-cut *adj* scollato, -a

lowdown *n inf* **to give sb the ~ on sth** aggiornare qu su qc

low-down *adj inf* vile; **a ~ trick** un tiro mancino

lower¹ ['lou·ɚ] **I.** *vt* abbassare; (*flag, sails*) ammainare; (*lifeboat*) calare; **to ~ one's eyes** abbassare lo sguardo; **to ~ oneself to do sth** abbassarsi a fare qc **II.** *vi* abbassarsi **III.** *adj* inferiore

lower² [laur] *vi* **1.** (*person*) accigliarsi **2.** (*sky*) oscurarsi

lower-case *adj* minuscolo, -a

low-fat *adj* a basso contenuto calorico; (*milk*) scremato, -a

low frequency *n* bassa frequenza *f*

low-grade *n* voto *m* basso

low-key *adj* (*affair*) discreto, -a; (*debate, discussion*) contenuto, -a

lowlands *npl* pianure *fpl*

low-level *adj* **1.** (*discussion*) di basso livello

L

2. (*radiation*) leggero, -a
lowly ['loʊ·li] <-ier, -iest> *adj* umile
low-minded *adj* volgare
lowness *n* **1.** (*state of being low*) la scarsa altezza **2.** MUS gravità *f* **3.** (*baseness*) bassezza *f,* viltà *f* **4.** (*humbleness*) umiltà *f*
low-pitched *adj* (*voice*) grave
low-pressure *n* bassa pressione *f*
low profile *n* **to keep a ~** non mettersi in vista
low season *n* bassa stagione *f*
low-spirited *adj* depresso, -a
low-tech *adj* tecnologicamente arretrato, -a
low tide *n,* **low water** *n* bassamarea *f*
lox [lɑːks] *n* salmone *m* affumicato
loyal ['lɔ·ɪəl] *adj* leale; **to remain ~ to sb/sth** rimanere fedele a qu/qc
loyalist ['lɔ·ɪə·lɪst] *n* lealista *mf*
loyalty ['lɔ·ɪəl·ti] <-ies> *n* lealtà *f*
lozenge ['lɑː·zəndʒ] *n* pastiglia *f*
LP [,el·'piː] *n* *abbr of* **long-playing record** LP *m inv*
LPG *n* *abbr of* **liquefied petroleum gas** GPL *m*
LPN *n* *abbr of* **licensed practical nurse** *infermiere non qualificato per dispensare farmaci*
LSD [,el·es·'diː] *n* *abbr of* **lysergic acid diethylamide** LSD *m*
LT *n,* **Lt.** *n* *abbr of* **Lieutenant 1.** MIL tenente *m* **2.** (*assistant*) luogotenente *m*
Ltd. ['lɪ·mɪ·t̬ɪd] *abbr of* **Limited** S.r.l
lubricant ['luː·brɪ·kənt] *n* lubrificante *m*
lubricate ['luː·brɪ·keɪt] *vt* lubrificare
lubrication [,luː·brɪ·'keɪ·ʃən] *n* lubrificazione *f*
lubricator ['luː·brɪ·keɪ·t̬ə] *n* lubrificante *m*
lucid ['luː·sɪd] *adj* **1.** (*rational*) lucido, -a **2.** (*easily understood*) chiaro, -a
luck [lʌk] *n* fortuna *f;* (*chance*) sorte *f;* **good/ bad ~** fortuna/sfortuna; **a stroke of ~** un colpo di fortuna; **to bring sb ~** portare fortuna a qu; **to wish sb** (**good**) **~** augurare buona fortuna a qu; **with any ~** con un po' di fortuna; **with no ~** senza successo; **as ~ would have it ...** la sorte ha voluto che... +*subj;* **to be down on one's ~** attraversare un periodo sfortunato ▸ **to be the ~ of the** <u>draw</u> essere questione di fortuna; **no** <u>such</u> **~!** *inf* purtroppo no!; **to press one's ~** sfidare la sorte
luckless ['lʌk·ləs] *adj* sfortunato, -a
lucky ['lʌ·ki] <-ier, -iest> *adj* fortunato, -a; **to be ~ in love** essere fortunato in amore; **to make a ~ guess** indovinare; **~ day** giorno *m* fortunato; **~ number** numero *m* portafortuna
lucrative ['luː·krə·t̬ɪv] *adj* vantaggioso, -a
lucre ['luː·kə] *n* lucro *m;* (**filthy**) **~** *iron* (vile) denaro *m*
ludicrous ['luː·dɪ·krəs] *adj* assurdo, -a
lug [lʌg] I. *vt* <-gg-> *inf* trascinare II. *n* *inf* omaccione *m*
luggage ['lʌ·gɪdʒ] *n* bagaglio *m*
luggage rack *n* portabagagli *m inv*
lugger ['lʌ·gə] *n* NAUT lugger *m inv*
lug nut *n* dado *m*
lugubrious [lə·'guː·bri·əs] *adj* lugubre

lukewarm [,luː·k·'wɔːrm] *adj a.fig* tiepido, -a
lull [lʌl] I. *vt* **1.** (*soothe*) calmare; **to ~ sb to sleep** far addormentare qu (cullandolo) **2.** (*deceive*) **to ~ sb into believing that ...** far credere a qu che... II. *n* **1.** (*temporary stillness*) periodo *m* di tregua **2.** (*in conversation*) pausa *f* **3.** (*in fighting*) tregua *f*
lullaby ['lʌ·lə·baɪ] <-ies> *n* ninnananna *f*
lumbago [lʌm·'beɪ·goʊ] *n* lombaggine *f*
lumbar ['lʌm·bɑːr] *adj* ANAT lombare
lumbar puncture *n* MED iniezione *f* lombare
lumber¹ ['lʌm·bə] *vi* avanzare pesantemente
lumber² ['lʌm·bə] I. *n* legname *m* II. *vi* tagliare legname
lumberjack *n* taglialegna *m inv*
lumber room *n* ripostiglio *m*
lumber trade *n* industria *f* del legname
lumberyard *n* deposito *m* di legname
luminary ['luː·mə·ne·ri] <-ies> *n* *fig* luminare *m*
luminosity [,luː·mə·'nɑː·sə·t̬i] *n* luminosità *f*
luminous ['luː·mə·nəs] *adj* luminoso, -a
lump [lʌmp] I. *n* **1.** (*solid mass*) massa *f;* (*of sauce*) grumo *m;* (*of coal*) pezzo *m;* (*of sugar*) zolletta *f;* **~ sum** cifra *f* forfettaria **2.** (*swelling: in breast*) nodulo *m;* (*on head*) bozzo *m* **3.** *inf* (*person*) zoticone *m* ▸ **to have a ~ in one's** <u>throat</u> avere un nodo alla gola II. *vt* <to ~ (together)> raggruppare
lump-sum payment *n* pagamento *m* unico
sugar cube *n* zolletta *f* di zucchero
lumpy ['lʌm·pi] <-ier, -iest> *adj* (*custard, sauce*) grumoso, -a; (*surface*) non uniforme
lunacy ['luː·nə·si] *n* pazzia *f*
lunar ['luː·nə] *adj* lunare
lunatic ['luː·nə·tɪk] I. *n* pazzo, -a *m, f* II. *adj* lunatico, -a
lunatic fringe *n* frangia *f* estremista
lunch [lʌntʃ] I. *n* pranzo *m;* **to have ~** pranzare ▸ **to be** <u>out</u> **to ~** *inf* essere fuori di testa II. *vi* pranzare
lunch break *n* pausa *f* pranzo
luncheon ['lʌn·tʃən] *n* *form* pranzo *m*
luncheon meat *n* carne *f* in scatola
lunch hour *n* pausa *f* pranzo
lunchtime I. *n* ora *f* di pranzo II. *adj* (*concert*) di mezzogiorno
lung [lʌŋ] *n* polmone *m;* **to shout at the top of one's ~s** urlare a squarciagola
lung cancer *n* cancro *m* al polmone
lunge [lʌndʒ] I. *vi* **to ~ at sb** scagliarsi contro qu II. *n* affondo *m*
lupin(e) ['luː·pɪn] *n* lupesco, -a *m*
lurch [lɜːrtʃ] I. *vi* (*people*) barcollare; (*car, train*) sbandare II. <-es> *n* sobbalzo *m* ▸ **to** <u>leave</u> **sb in the ~** *inf* lasciare qu nelle peste
lure [lʊr] I. *n* **1.** (*attraction*) fascino *m* **2.** (*bait*) esca *f;* (*decoy*) richiamo *m* II. *vt* attirare; **to ~ sb into a trap** attirare qu in una trappola
lurid ['lʊ·rɪd] *adj* **1.** (*gruesome: details*) scabroso, -a; (*language*) osceno, -a **2.** (*sensationalist*) clamoroso, -a **3.** (*extremely bright*) sgargiante

lurk [lɜːrk] *vi* nascondersi
luscious ['lʌ·ʃəs] *adj* 1.(*fruit*) polposo, -a 2.*inf* (*girl*) appetitoso, -a; (*curves*) voluttuoso, -a; (*lips*) carnoso, -a
lush [lʌʃ] I. *adj* 1.(*vegetation*) lussureggiante 2.(*luxurious*) opulento, -a II. *n* <-es> *sl* ubriacone, -a *m, f*
lust [lʌst] *n* 1.(*sexual desire*) lussuria *f* 2.(*strong desire*) brama *f;* ~ **for sth** brama di qc; ~ **for life** voglia *f* di vivere
luster ['lʌs·tər] *n* lustro *m*
lustful ['lʌst·fəl] *adj* lussurioso, -a
lusty ['lʌs·ti] <-ier, -iest> *adj* (*person*) sano, -a; (*voice*) potente
lute [luːt] *n* liuto *m*
Lutheran ['luː·θə·rən] I. *adj* luterano, -a II. *n* luterano, -a *m, f*
Luxembourg ['lʌk·səm·bɜːrg] *n* Lussemburgo *m*
Luxembourger *n* lussemburghese *mf*
luxuriant [lʌg·'ʒʊ·ri·ənt] *adj* (*hair*) folto, -a; (*vegetation*) lussureggiante
luxuriate [lʌg·'ʒʊ·ri·eɪt] *vi* 1.(*person*) **to ~ in sth** godersi qc 2.(*plant*) crecere rigoglioso, -a
luxurious [lʌg·'ʒʊ·ri·əs] *adj* lussuoso, -a
luxury ['lʌk·ʃəʳ·i] <-ies> *n* lusso *m;* ~ **appartment** appartamento *m* di lusso
LW *n abbr of* **long wave** OL *f*
lychee ['liː·tʃiː] *n* litchi *m inv*
Lycra® ['laɪ·krə] *n* lycra® *f*
lye [laɪ] *n* lisciviɑ *f*
lying ['laɪ·ɪŋ] I. *n* menzogne *fpl* II. *adj* bugiardo, -a
Lyme disease *n* malattia *f* di Lyme
lymph [lɪmpf] *n* linfa *f*
lymphatic [lɪm·'fæ·t̬ɪk] *adj* linfatico, -a
lymph node *n* linfonodo *m*
lynch [lɪntʃ] *vt* linciare
lynx [lɪŋks] <-(es)> *n* lince *f*
lynx-eyed *adj* con gli occhi di lince
lyre ['la·ɪr] *n* lira *f*
lyric ['lɪ·rɪk] I. *adj* lirico, -a II. *n* 1.(*poem*) lirica *f* 2. *pl* (*words for song*) testo *m* (di canzone)
lyrical ['lɪ·rɪ·kl] *adj* lirico, -a; **to get ~ about sth** *fig* entusiasmarsi per qc
lyricism ['lɪ·rɪ·ˌsɪ·zəm] *n* LIT, MUS lirismo *m*
lyricist ['lɪ·rɪ·sɪst] *n* paroliere *m*

M

M, m [em] *n* M, m *f;* ~ **as in Mary** M come Milano
m 1.*abbr of* **mile** miglio *m* 2.*abbr of* **million** milione *m* 3.*abbr of* **minutes** min 4.*abbr of* **meter** m 5.*abbr of* **married** coniugato, -a
M *n* 1.*abbr of* **male** M 2.*abbr of* **medium** M
MA [ˌem·'eɪ] *n* 1.*abbr of* **Master of Arts**

laurea *f* (*in discipline umanistiche*)*;* **he has an ~ in linguistics** è laureato in linguistica; **Louie Sanders, MA** Dott. Louie Sanders 2. *abbr of* **Massachusetts** Massachusetts
ma [mɑː] *n inf* mamma *f*
ma'am [mæm] = **madam** (*form of address*) signora *f*
Mac [mæk] *n* COMPUT *abbr of* **Macintosh** Mac(intosh) *m*
macabre [mə·'kɑː·brə] *adj* macabro, -a
macadam [mə·'kæ·dəm] *n* macadam *m*
macaroni [ˌmæ·kə·'roʊ·ni] *n* maccheroni *mpl*
macaroni and cheese *n* maccheroni *m pl* al formaggio
mace[1] [meɪs] *n* (*club*) mazza *f*
mace[2] [meɪs] *n* (*spice*) macis *f o m inv*
Mace® [meɪs] *n* aerosol *m* lacrimogeno *inv*
Macedonia [ˌmæ·sə·'doʊ·niə] *n* Macedonia *f*
Macedonian I. *adj* macedone II. *n* 1.(*person*) macedone *mf* 2. LING macedone *m*
Mach [mɑːk] *n* PHYS mach *m inv*
machete [mə·'ʃe·t̬i] *n* machete *m inv*
machine [mə·'ʃiːn] *n* 1.(*mechanical device*) macchina *f* 2.(*system*) apparato *m*
machine gun *n* mitragliatrice *f*
machine-made *adj* fatto, -a a macchina
machine-readable *adj* COMPUT in linguaggio macchina
machinery [mə·'ʃiː·nə·ri] *n* 1.(*machines*) macchinari *mpl*, macchine *fpl* 2. *fig* (*organization, structure*) macchina *f* 3.(*mechanism*) ingranaggi *mpl*
machine tool *n* macchina *f* utensile
machine-wash *vt* lavare in lavatrice
machine-washable *adj* lavabile in lavatrice
machinist [mə·'ʃiː·nɪst] *n* macchinista *mf*
macho ['mɑːt·ʃoʊ] I. *n* macho *m* II. *adj* macho *inv*
mackerel ['mæ·krəl] <-(s)> *n* sgombro *m*
macro ['mæ·kroʊ] *n* COMPUT macro(istruzione) *f inv*
macrobiotic [ˌmæ·kroʊ·baɪ·'ɑː·t̬ɪk] *adj* macrobiotico, -a
macrocosm ['mæ·kroʊ·kɑː·zəm] *n* macrocosmo *m*
macroeconomics [ˌmæ·kroʊ·ˌe·kə·'nɑː·mɪks] *n* macroeconomia *f*
mad [mæd] *adj* 1.(*upset*) arrabbiato, -a 2.(*frantic*) frenetico, -a 3.(*insane: person*) pazzo, -a, matto, -a; **to go ~** impazzire, diventare matto; **to drive sb ~** fare impazzire qu 4.(*enthusiastic*) **to be ~ about sb** essere pazzo di qc; **she's ~ about chocolate** andare pazzo per qc
Madagascar [ˌmæ·də·'gæs·kə] *n* Madagascar *m*
madam ['mæ·dəm] *n* signora *f*
mad cow disease *n* (morbo *m* della) mucca pazza *f*
madden ['mæ·dən] *vt* fare infuriare
maddening *adj* esasperante
made [meɪd] *pp, pt of* **make**
made-to-order [ˌmeɪd·tə·'me·ʒəʳ] *adj* 1.(*cus-*

tom-made) fatto, -a su ordinazione **2.** (*perfect*) fatto, -a apposta

made-up ['meɪd·ʌp] *adj* **1.** (*wearing make-up*) truccato, -a **2.** (*invented*) inventato, -a

madhouse ['mæd·haʊs] *n inf* manicomio *m*

madly ['mæd·li] *adv* **1.** (*frantically*) furiosamente **2.** (*intensely*) terribilmente; **she's ~ in love with him** è follemente innamorata di lui

madman ['mæd·mən] <-men> *n* pazzo *m*

madness ['mæd·nɪs] *n* pazzia *f,* follia *f*

madwoman ['mæd·ˌwʊ·mən] <-women> *n* pazza *f*

maelstrom ['meɪl·strəm] *n a. fig* vortice *m*

maestro ['maɪs·troʊ] *n* maestro *m*

Mafia ['mɑː·fiə] *n* mafia *f*

mag [mæg] *n inf abbr of* **magazine** rivista *f*

magazine ['mæ·gə·ziːn] *n* **1.** (*periodical publication*) rivista *f* **2.** MIL (*of gun*) caricatore *m* **3.** MIL (*storage place on ship*) santabarbara *f*

maggot ['mæ·gət] *n* verme *m*

Magi ['meɪ·dʒaɪ] *npl* **the ~** i (Re) Magi

magic ['mæ·dʒɪk] **I.** *n* magia *f;* **as if by ~** come per incanto **II.** *adj* magico, -a

magical *adj* **1.** (*power*) magico, -a **2.** (*extraordinary, wonderful*) favoloso, -a

magically *adv* per magia

magic carpet *n* tappeto *m* volante

magician [mə·'dʒɪ·ʃən] *n* mago, -a *m, f*

magisterial [ˌmæ·dʒɪ·'stɪ·ri·əl] *adj form* **1.** (*having complete authority*) autorevole **2.** (*imperious: tone, way*) autoritario, -a

magistrate ['mæ·dʒɪs·treɪt] *n giudice di cause di minore entità*

magnanimity [ˌmæg·nə·'nɪ·mə·ti] *n form* magnanimità *f*

magnanimous [mæg·'næ·nə·məs] *adj form* magnanimo, -a

magnate ['mæg·neɪt] *n* magnate *mf*

magnesia [mæg·'niː·ʒə] *n* magnesia *f*

magnesium [mæg·'niː·zi·əm] *n* magnesio *m*

magnet ['mæg·nɪt] *n* calamita *f,* magnete *m;* **to act as a ~ for sth** *fig* attrarre qc come una calamita

magnetic [mæg·'ne·t̬ɪk] *adj* **1.** (*force*) magnetico, -a **2.** (*personality*) affascinante

magnetic field *n* campo *m* magnetico

magnetic pole *n* polo *m* magnetico

magnetism ['mæg·nə·t̬ɪ·zəm] *n* magnetismo *m*

magnetize ['mæg·nə·taɪz] *vt* magnetizzare; **to ~ sb** affascinare qu

magneto [mæg·'niː·t̬oʊ] *n* TECH, AUTO magnete *m*

magnification [ˌmæg·nɪ·fɪ·'keɪ·ʃən] *n* (*lens*) ingrandimento *m;* (*photograph*) ingrandimento *m*

magnificence [mæg·'nɪ·fɪ·səns] *n* magnificenza *f*

magnificent [mæg·'nɪ·fɪ·snt] *adj* magnifico, -a

magnify ['mæg·nɪ·faɪ] <-ie-> *vt* **1.** (*make larger*) ingrandire; (*voice*) amplificare **2.** (*make worse: problem*) esasperare

magnifying glass *n* lente *f* d'ingrandimento

magnitude ['mæg·nɪ·tuːd] *n* **1.** (*importance*) importanza *f* **2.** (*large size*) grandezza *f*

magnolia [mæg·'noʊl·jə] *n* magnolia *f*

magnum opus [ˌmæg·nəm·'oʊ·pəs] *n form* capolavoro *m*

magpie ['mæg·paɪ] *n* (*bird*) gazza *f*

maharajah *n,* **maharaja** [ˌmɑː·hə·'rɑː·dʒə] *n* HIST maharajah *m inv,* maragià *m inv*

mahogany [mə·'hɑː·gə·ni] **I.** *n* mogano *m* **II.** *adj* di mogano

maid [meɪd] *n* **1.** (*female servant*) donna *f* (di servizio); (*in hotel*) cameriera *f* **2.** *liter* (*girl, young woman*) fanciulla *f*

maiden ['meɪ·dən] **I.** *n liter* fanciulla *f* **II.** *adj* **1.** (*unmarried*) nubile **2.** (*first: voyage*) inaugurale

maidenhair fern [ˌmeɪ·dən·her·'fɜːrn] *n* capelvenere *m*

maiden name *n* (cog)nome *m* da ragazza

maid of honor *n* damigella *f* d'onore

mail¹ [meɪl] **I.** *n a.* COMPUT posta *f;* **electronic ~** COMPUT posta elettronica; **incoming/outgoing ~** COMPUT posta in arrivo/in partenza; **to send sth through the ~** inviare [*o* spedire] qc per posta [*o* mandare] **II.** *vt* inviare [*o* spedire] per posta [*o* mandare]

mail² [meɪl] *n* (*armor*) maglia *f*

mailbox *n* **1.** (*for postal deliveries*) casella *f* postale **2.** COMPUT (**electronic**) ~ casella *f* (di posta elettronica)

mailing list *n* mailing list *f inv*

mailman *n* postino *m*

mail order *n* vendita *f* per corrispondenza

maim [meɪm] *vt* mutilare

main [meɪn] **I.** *adj* (*problem, reason, street*) principale **II.** *n* **1.** (*pipe*) tubatura *f* principale; **the water/gas ~** la conduttura dell'acqua/del gas **2.** (*cable*) cavo *m* principale ►**in the ~** in generale

mainframe ['meɪn·freɪm] *n* COMPUT elaboratore *m* centrale

mainland ['meɪn·lənd] **I.** *n* continente *m* **II.** *adj* **~ China** Cina continentale

mainline ['meɪn·laɪn] *vi, vt inf* bucarsi

mainly ['meɪn·li] *adv* soprattutto; **I ~ go to bed at midnight** di solito vado a letto a mezzanotte

main office *n* ufficio *f* principale

main road *n* strada *f* principale

mainsail *n* NAUT randa *f*

mainspring *n* movente *m* principale

mainstay *n fig* base *f;* (*of economy, organization*) pilastro *m*

mainstream **I.** *n* corrente *f* dominante **II.** *adj* **1.** (*ideology*) dominante **2.** (*film, novel*) convenziale; (*jazz*) mainstream

maintain [meɪn·'teɪn] *vt* **1.** (*preserve, provide for*) mantenere **2.** (*claim*) sostenere

maintenance ['meɪn·tə·nəns] *n* **1.** (*repair work*) manutenzione *f* **2.** (*keeping, preservation*) mantenimento *m*

Maj. *abbr of* **Major** maggiore *mf*

majestic [mə·'dʒes·tɪk] *adj* maestoso, -a

majesty ['mæ·dʒəs·ti] <-ies> *n* maestà *f;* **Her/His/Your Majesty** Sua/Vostra Maestà; **the Alps, in all their** ~ le Alpi, in tutta la loro maestosità

major ['meɪ·dʒɚ] **I.** *adj* **1.** (*important, significant*) principale, significativo; **a** ~ **problem** un problema serio **2.** (*serious: illness*) grave **3.** MUS maggiore; **in C** ~ in do maggiore **II.** *n* **1.** MIL maggiore *mf* **2.** UNIV (*subject*) materia *f* principale

Majorca [mə·'jɔːr·kə] *n* Maiorca *f*

Majorcan **I.** *adj* maiorchino, -a **II.** *n* maiorchino, -a *m, f*

major general [ˌmeɪ·dʒɚ 'dʒe·nə·rəl] *n* generale *m* di divisione

majorette *n* majorette *f inv*

majority [mə·'dʒɔː·rə·ti] <-ies> *n* **1.** (*greater part/number*) maggioranza *f;* **he won by a narrow/large** ~ POL ha vinto di stretta/larga misura **2.** (*most powerful group*) maggioranza *f* **3.** (*full legal age*) maggiore età *f;* **to reach the age of** ~ diventare maggiorenne

make [meɪk] **I.** *vt* <made, made> **1.** (*produce: coffee, soup, dinner*) fare, preparare; (*product*) fare, produrre; (*clothes*) fare, confezionare; (*record*) incidere; (*film*) girare; **to make sth out of sth** fare qc con qc; **to** ~ **time** trovare il tempo **2.** (*cause: trouble*) fare; **to** ~ **noise/a scene** fare rumore/una scenata; **to** ~ **oneself look ridiculous** rendersi ridicolo; **to** ~ **a wonderful combination** formare un insieme fantastico **3.** (*cause to be*) **to** ~ **sb sad** rendere triste qu; **to** ~ **sb happy** fare felice qu; **to** ~ **oneself heard** farsi sentire; **to** ~ **oneself understood** farsi capire; **to** ~ **sth easy** rendere facile qc; **to** ~ **something of oneself** arrivare a essere qualcuno **4.** (*perform, carry out*) **to** ~ **a call** fare una chiamata; **to** ~ **a decision** prendere una decisione; **to** ~ **a reservation** fare una prenotazione **5.** (*force*) obligar; **to** ~ **sb do sth** far fare qc a qu **6.** (*amount to, total*) fare; **two plus two** ~**s four** due più due fa quattro **7.** (*earn, get*) **to** ~ **friends** fare amicizia; **to** ~ **money** fare [*o* guadagnare] soldi; **to** ~ **a profit** ricavare un profitto; **to** ~ **a loss** subire una perdita; **to** ~ **a living** guadagnarsi da vivere **8.** *inf* (*get to, reach*) **to** ~ **it to somewhere** arrivare da qualche parte; **to** ~ **it** farcela, riuscirci **9.** (*make perfect*) **that made my day!** questo mi ha fatto felice! ▶ **to** ~ **or break** sth determinare il successo o l'insuccesso di qc; **to** ~ **do** (**with sth**) cavarsela (con qc) **II.** *vi* (*amount to, total*) **today's earthquake** ~**s five since the beginning of the year** con quello di oggi siamo al quinto terremoto di quest'anno ▶ **to** ~ **as if to do sth** fare come per fare qc **III.** *n* **1.** (*brand*) marca *f* **2.** (*identification*) **to get a** ~ **on sb** scoprire l'identità di qu ▶ **to be on the** ~ *sl* (*for money, power*) essere un arrivista; (*sexually*) cercare di cuccare

◆**make for** *vt insep* **1.** (*head for*) dirigersi verso **2.** (*lead to*) **to** ~ **sth** contribuire a qc

◆**make of** *vt* **what do you** ~ **this book?** cosa ne pensi di questo libro?

◆**make off with** *vt* **to** ~ **sth** scappare con qc

◆**make out** **I.** *vi* **1.** (*succeed, cope: person*) cavarsela **2.** *sl* (*kiss passionately*) **to** ~ **with sb** pomiciare con qu **II.** *vt* **1.** (*discern: writing, numbers*) decifrare; (*sth in the distance*) scorgere **2.** (*pretend*) **he made himself out to be rich** si fece passare per ricco **3.** (*write out*) **to** ~ **a check for $100** emettere un assegno per 100 dollari

◆**make over** *vt* **1.** LAW (*transfer: ownership*) trasferire **2.** (*alter, convert*) **to make sth over into sth** trasformare qc in qc

◆**make up** **I.** *vt* **1.** (*invent*) inventare **2.** (*prepare*) preparare **3.** (*compensate*) **to** ~ **for sth** compensare qc **4.** (*constitute*) costituire **5.** (*decide*) **to** ~ **one's mind** decidersi **6.** SCH **to** ~ **an exam** (*take again*) ripetere un esame; (*take at a later time*) rimandare un esame **II.** *vi* riconciliarsi

◆**make up to** *vt* **to make it up to sb** sdebitarsi con qu

make-believe ['meɪk·bɪˌliːv] **I.** *n* (*pretense*) finta *f,* finzione *f;* **a world of** ~ un mondo immaginario **II.** *adj* immaginario, -a; (*weapon*) per finta; **a** ~ **world** un mondo immaginario

make-or-break *adj* **this is a** ~ **situation** qui o la va o la spacca

maker ['meɪ·kɚ] *n* **1.** (*manufacturer*) produttore, -trice *m, f,* fabbricante *mf* **2.** (*God*) il Creatore; **to meet one's Maker** andare al Creatore

makeshift ['meɪk·ʃɪft] *adj* di fortuna

make-up ['meɪk·ʌp] *n* **1.** (*cosmetics*) trucco *m;* **to put on** ~ truccarsi; **to wear** ~ essere truccato **2.** (*structure*) composizione *f* **3.** (*character*) natura *f*

make-up artist *n* truccatore, -trice *m, f*

making ['meɪ·kɪŋ] *n* **1.** (*production*) produzione *m;* (*of clothes*) confezione *f;* (*of meals*) preparazione *f* **2.** *pl* (*essential qualities*) **to have the** ~**s of sth** avere la stoffa di qc ▶ **to be the** ~ **of sb** essere decisivo per qu

maladjusted [ˌmæl·ə·'dʒʌs·tɪd] *adj* PSYCH disadattato, -a

maladroit ['mæl·ə·drɔɪt] *adj form* maldestro, -a

Malagasy [ˌmæ·lə·'gæ·si] **I.** *adj* malgascio, -a **II.** *n* *a.* LING malgascio *m*

malaise [mæ·'leɪz] *n* malessere *m*

malapropism ['mæ·lə·prɑː·pɪˌzəm] *n* LING malapropismo *m*

malaria [mə·'le·ri·ə] *n* malaria *f*

Malawi [mə·'lɑː·wi] *n* Malawi *m*

Malawian **I.** *adj* malawiano, -a **II.** *n* malawiano, -a *m, f*

Malaysia [mə·'leɪ·ʒə] *n* Malaysia *f*

Malaysian [mə·'leɪ·ʒən] **I.** *adj* malese **II.** *n* malese *mf*

malcontent ['mæl·kən·tənt] *n form* malcontento, -a *m, f*

Maldives ['mæl·daɪvz] *npl* Maldive *fpl*

male [meɪl] **I.** *adj* (*person, hormone*)

M

maschile; (*animal*) maschio; ~ **chauvinism** maschilismo *m* **II.** *n* (*person*) maschio *m;* (*animal*) maschio *m*

malediction [ˌmæl·ə·ˈdɪk·ʃən] *n* maledizione *f*

malevolent [mə·ˈle·və·lnt] *adj liter* (*malicious*) malevolo, -a; (*deity, powers*) maligno, -a

malformation [ˌmæl·fɔː·ˈmeɪ·ʃən] *n* MED malformazione *f*

malfunction [ˌmæl·ˈfʌŋk·ʃən] **I.** *vi* **1.** (*not work properly*) funzionare male **2.** (*stop functioning*) smettere di funzionare **II.** *n* **1.** (*defective functioning*) funzionamento *m* imperfetto **2.** (*sudden stop*) arresto *m* improvviso

Mali [ˈmɑː·li] *n* Mali *m*

Malian I. *adj* malinese **II.** *n* malinese *mf*

malice [ˈmæ·lɪs] *n* malevolenza *f;* **with ~ aforethought** con premeditazione

malicious [mə·ˈlɪ·ʃəs] *adj* maligno, -a

malign [mə·ˈlaɪn] **I.** *adj form* maligno, -a **II.** *vt* denigrare

malignancy [mə·ˈlɪg·nən·si] <-ies> *n a.* MED malignità *f*

malignant [mə·ˈlɪg·nənt] *adj* maligno, -a

malinger [mə·ˈlɪŋ·gɚ] *vi* fingersi malato

malingerer [mə·ˈlɪŋ·gə·ɚ] *n* chi si finge malato

mall [mɔːl] *n* centro *m* commerciale

mallard [ˈmæ·lɚd] <-(s)> *n* germano *m* reale, anatra *f* selvatica

malleable [ˈmæ·lɪ·ə·bl] *adj* (*material*) malleabile; (*person*) docile

mallet [ˈmæ·lɪt] *n* mazzuolo *m*

mallow [ˈmæ·loʊ] *n* malva *f*

malnutrition [ˌmæl·nuː·ˈtrɪ·ʃən] *n* malnutrizione *f*

malodorous [ˌmæl·ˈoʊ·də·rəs] *adj form* maleodorante

malpractice [ˌmæl·ˈpræk·tɪs] *n* negligenza *f* professionale; **medical ~** negligenza *f* professionale (in campo medico)

malt [mɔːlt] **I.** *n* malto *m* **II.** *vt* trasformare in malto

Malta [ˈmɔː·l·tə] *n* Malta *f; s.a.* **Republic of Malta**

Maltese [ˌmɔː·l·ˈtiːz] **I.** *adj* maltese; **~ cross** croce *f* di Malta **II.** *n* maltese *mf*

maltreat [ˌmæl·ˈtriːt] *vt form* maltrattare

maltreatment *n* maltrattamenti *mpl*

mamma [mə·ˈmɑː] *n* mamma *f*

mammal [ˈmæ·məl] *n* mammifero *m*

mammary gland [ˈmæ·mə·rɪ·ˌglænd] *n* ghiandola *f* mammaria

mammography [mə·ˈmɑː·grə·fi] <-ies> *n* mammografia *f*

mammoth [ˈmæ·məθ] **I.** *adj* mastodontico, -a **II.** *n* mammut *m inv*

man [mæn] **I.** *n* <men> **1.** (*male human*) uomo *m* **2.** (*the human race*) genere *m* umano **3.** (*in games*) pedina *f*, pezzo *m* ▶ **to talk** (as) **~ to ~** parlare da uomo a uomo; **as one ~** come un sol uomo **II.** *vt* <-nn-> (*operate: ship*) equipaggiare; **to ~ a factory** dotare di personale uno stabilimento; **some volunteers**

~ the phones alcuni volontari sono addetti ai telefoni **III.** *interj* **~**, **was that cake good!** accidenti, se era buono il dolce!

manage [ˈmæ·nɪdʒ] **I.** *vt* **1.** *a.* ECON (*control, be in charge of*) dirigere; (*money, time*) gestire; (*a baseball team*) dirigere **2.** (*accomplish*) riuscire; **to ~ to do sth** riuscire a fare qc **3.** (*fit into one's schedule*) **to not ~ the time** non (riuscire a) trovare il tempo **II.** *vi* **to ~ on a few dollars a day** (riuscire a) farcela con pochi dollari al giorno

manageable [ˈmæ·nɪ·dʒə·bl] *adj* (*vehicle*) maneggevole; (*person, animal*) docile; (*amount*) ragionevole

management [ˈmæ·nɪdʒ·mənt] *n* **1.** (*direction*) gestione *f*, direzione *f* **2.** *a.* ECON gestione *f;* **to study business ~** studiare gestione aziendale

management consultant *n* consulente *mf* aziendale

management information system *n* management information system *m inv*

manager [ˈmæ·nɪ·dʒɚ] *n* **1.** COM (*administrator*) amministratore, -trice *m, f*, direttore, -trice *m, f;* (*of business unit*) gestore, -trice *m, f* **2.** (*of performer, artist*) agente *mf*, manager *mf inv;* (*of a baseball team*) manager *mf inv*

managerial [ˌmæ·nə·ˈdʒɪ·ri·əl] *adj* (*relating to a manager*) manageriale, direttivo; **~ position** posizione direttiva; **~ skills** abilità *f pl* manageriali

managing director *n* amministratore *m/f* delegato

mandarin [ˈmæn·də·rɪn] *n* (*person*) mandarino *m*

Mandarin *n* LING mandarino *m*

mandarin orange *n* mandarino *m*

mandate [ˈmæn·deɪt] **I.** *n* **1.** *a.* POL mandato *m* **2.** (*territory*) territorio *m* sotto mandato internazionale **II.** *vt* approvare ufficialmente

mandatory [ˈmæn·də·tɔː·ri] *adj form* obbligatorio, -a; **to make sth ~** rendere obbligatorio qc

mandible [ˈmæn·dɪ·bl] *n* mandibola *f*

mandolin(e) [ˈmæn·də·lɪn] *n* MUS mandolino *m*

mandrake [ˈmæn·dreɪk] *n* mandragola *f*, mandragora *f*

mandrill [ˈmæn·drɪl] *n* mandrillo *m*

mane [meɪn] *n* criniera *f*

man-eater [ˈmæn·iː·tɚ] *n* *inf* (*of woman*) divoratrice *f* di uomini; (*of animal*) mangiatore, -trice *m, f* di uomini

maneuver [mə·ˈnuː·vɚ] **I.** *n* *a.* MIL manovra *f;* **army ~s** manovre militari **II.** *vt* manovrare; **to ~ sb into doing sth** indurre qu a fare qc **III.** *vi* manovrare

maneuverability [mə·ˌnuː·və·rə·ˈbɪ·lə·ti] *n* manovrabilità *f*

maneuverable [mə·ˈnuː·və·rə·bl] *adj* manovrabile

manfully [ˈmæn·fʊ·li] *adv* valorosamente

manganese [ˈmæŋ·gə·niːz] *n* manganese *m*

manger ['meɪn·dʒə-] *n* mangiatoia *f*

mangle ['mæŋ·gl] *vt* (*body*) maciullare; (*text*) fare scempio di

mango ['mæŋ·goʊ] *n* <-(e)s> mango *m*

mangrove ['mæn·groʊv] *n* mangrovia *f*

manhandle ['mæn·hæn·dl] *vt* **1.** (*treat roughly: person*) maltrattare **2.** (*move by hand: heavy object*) spostare a mano

manhole ['mæn·hoʊl] *n* tombino *m*, pozzetto *m*

manhole cover *n* chiusino *m*

manhood ['mæn·hʊd] *n* **1.** (*adulthood*) età *f* virile **2.** (*masculinity*) virilità *f*

man-hour ['mæn·aʊ·ə-] *n* ECON ora-uomo *f*

manhunt ['mæn·hʌnt] *n* caccia *f* all'uomo

mania ['meɪ·niə] *n a.* PSYCH mania *f*

maniac ['meɪ·ni·æk] *n* maniaco, -a *m, f*

maniacal [mə·'na·iə·kl] *adj inf* demenziale

manic ['mæ·nɪk] *adj* frenetico, -a

manic depression *n* mania *f* depressiva

manic depressive *adj* maniaco-depressivo, -a

manic psychosis *n* PSYCH psicosi *f inv* maniaco-depressiva

manicure ['mæ·nɪ·kjʊr] **I.** *n* manicure *f inv* **II.** *vt* **to ~ one's fingernails** farsi la manicure

manicurist ['mæ·nɪ·kjʊ·rɪst] *n* manicure *mf inv*

manifest ['mæ·nɪ·fest] **I.** *adj form* manifesto, -a; **to make sth ~** rendere manifesto qc **II.** *vt form* manifestare; **to ~ symptoms of sth** manifestare i sintomi di qc

manifestation [ˌmæ·nɪ·fe·'steɪ·ʃən] *n form* manifestazione *f*

manifestly ['mæ·nɪ·fest·li] *adv form* palesemente

manifesto [ˌmæ·nɪ·'fes·toʊ] <-stos *o* -stoes> *n* manifesto *m*

manifold ['mæ·nɪ·foʊld] **I.** *adj liter* molteplice **II.** *n* TECH, AUTO collettore *m;* **exhaust ~** collettore di scarico

manikin ['mæ·nɪ·kɪn] *n* **1.** (*model*) manichino *m* **2.** (*dwarf*) nano, -a *m, f*

manila envelope [mə·'nɪ·lə 'en·və·loʊp] *n* busta *m* manil(l)a

manioc ['mæ·ni·ɑːk] *n* **1.** (*cassava*) manioca *f*, cassava *f* **2.** (*flour*) tapioca *f*

manipulate [mə·'nɪp·jə·leɪt] *vt* manipolare

manipulation [mə·ˌnɪp·jə·'leɪ·ʃən] *n* manipolazione *f*

manipulative [mə·ˌnɪp·jə·'le·tɪv] *adj* manipolatorio, -a

manipulator [mə·'nɪp·jə·leɪ·tə-] *n* manipolatore, -trice *m, f*

mankind [ˌmæn·'kaɪnd] *n* umanità *f*

manliness ['mæn·lɪ·nəs] *n* mascolinità *f*

manly ['mæn·li] <-ier, -iest> *adj* (*of man*) virile, maschile

man-made ['mæn·meɪd] *adj* (*lake*) artificiale; (*fiber*) sintetico, -a

manna ['mæ·nə] *n* manna *f*

manned [mænd] *adj* AVIAT con equipaggio umano

mannequin ['mæ·nɪ·kɪn] *n* **1.** (*dummy*) mani-

chino *m* **2.** (*person*) indossatore, -trice *m, f*

manner ['mæ·nə-] *n* **1.** (*way, fashion*) maniera *f*, modo *m;* **in the ~ of sb** alla maniera di qc, nello stile; **in a ~ of speaking** per così dire; **a ~ of speech** un modo di dire **2.** (*behavior*) **~s** buone *f pl* maniere; **to teach sb ~s** insegnare a qu l'educazione; **it's bad ~s to ...** è da maleducati ... **3.** *form* (*kind, type*) tipo *m;* **what ~ of man is he?** che razza di uomo è?; **all ~ of ...** ogni sorta di ... ▶ **as if to the ~ born** con la massima naturalezza

mannered *adj* manierato, -a

mannerism ['mæ·nə·rɪ·zəm] *n* manierismo *m*

mannikin ['mæ·nɪ·kɪn] *n s.* **manikin**

mannish ['mæ·nɪʃ] *adj* mascolino, -a

manometer [mə·'nɑː·mə·tə-] *n* manometro *m*

manor ['mæ·nə-] *n* **1.** (*house*) maniero *m* **2.** HIST (*territory*) feudo *m*

manpower ['mæn·pa·ʊə-] *n* manodopera *f*

manservant ['mæn·sɜːr·vənt] *n* servitore *m*

mansion ['mæn·ʃən] *n* dimora *f*

man-sized *adj* grande

manslaughter ['mæn·slɑː·tə-] *n* omicidio *m* colposo

mantelpiece ['mæn·tl·piːs] *n* mensola *f* del caminetto

mantis ['mæn·tɪs] *n* mantide *f* (religiosa)

mantle ['mæn·tl] *n* **1.** *liter* (*cloak, layer*) mantello *m;* **a ~ of snow** un manto di neve **2.** (*of gas lamp*) reticella *f*

man-to-man *adj* franco, -a, da uomo a uomo

mantra ['mæn·trə] *n* mantra *m inv*

manual ['mæn·ju·əl] **I.** *adj* manuale; **~ dexterity** abilità manuale **II.** *n* manual *m;* **instruction ~** manuale di istruzioni

manual labor *n* lavoro *m* manuale

manually ['mæn·ju·ə·li] *adv* manualmente, a mano

manual transmission *n* AUTO trasmissione *f* manuale

manufacture [ˌmæn·ju·'fæk·tʃə-] **I.** *vt* **1.** (*produce*) fabbricare; **~d goods** prodotti finiti **2.** (*invent*) inventare; **to ~ an excuse/a story** inventare una scusa/una storia **II.** *n* **1.** (*production*) manufactura *f* **2.** (*product*) prodotto *m* (industriale)

manufacturer [ˌmæn·ju·'fæk·ʃə·ə-] *n* produttore *m*, azienda *f* produttrice; **~'s label** etichetta *f* del produttore; **to send sth back to the ~** rispedire qc alla fabbrica

manufacturing [ˌmæn·jə·'fæk·tʃə·rɪŋ] *adj* (*region, company*) industriale; **~ industry** industria *f* manifatturiera

manure [mə·'nʊr] *n* letame *m*

manuscript ['mæn·jʊs·krɪpt] *n* manoscritto *m*

many ['me·ni] <more, most> **I.** *adj* molti, -e, tanti, -e; **how ~ bottles?** quante bottiglie?; **too/so ~ people** troppa/tanta gente; **one too ~** uno di troppo; **~ times** molte/tante volte; **as ~ as** tanti quanti **II.** *pron* molti, molte, tanti, tante; **~ think that ...** molti [*o* tanti] pensano che ...; **so ~** tanti, -e; **too ~** troppi, -e **III.** *n* **a good ~** moltissimi, -e

M

many-sided [ˌme·nɪˈsaɪ·dɪd] *adj* poliedrico, -a

Maoism [ˈmaʊ·ɪ·zm] *n* maoismo *m*

Maoist [ˈmaʊ·ɪzt] I. *n* maoista *mf* II. *adj* maoista

Maori [ˈmaʊ·ri] I. *n* maori *mf* II. *adj* maori

map [mæp] I. *n* 1.(*of region, stars*) carta *f* (geografica); (*of town*) pianta *f*; ~ **of the world** carta geografica del mondo; **road** ~ carta stradale 2.(*simple diagram*) piantina *f* ▶ **to** <u>blow</u> [*o* <u>wipe</u>] **sth off the** ~ cancellare qc dalla faccia della terra; **to** <u>put</u> **a town on the** ~ far conoscere una città II. <-pp-> *vt* mappare ◆ **map out** *vt* pianificare, progettare; **to** ~ **a route** pianificare un itinerario; **to** ~ **a plan/a strategy** delineare un piano/una strategia; **his future is all mapped out for him** la sua vita è stata pianificata

maple [ˈmeɪ·pl] *n* 1.(*tree*) acero *m* 2.(*wood*) (legno *m* di) acero

maple leaf *n* foglia *f* d'acero

maple sugar *n* zucchero *m* d'acero

maple syrup *n* sciroppo *m* d'acero

map maker *n* cartografo, -a *m, f*

map making *n* cartografia *f*

mar [mɑːr] <-rr-> *vt* (*ruin*) guastare; (*the fun, the day*) rovinare

Mar. *n abbr of* **March** marzo *m*

maraschino cherry [ˌme·rəˈʃiː·noʊ-] *n* ciliegia *f* al maraschino

marathon [ˈme·rə·θɑːn] *n a. fig* maratona *f*

marathon runner *n* maratoneta *mf*

maraud [məˈrɑːd] *vi* razziare

marauder *n* (*animal*) predatore, -trice *m, f*; (*person*) predone, -a *m, f*

marauding *adj* (*animal*) predatore, -trice; (*person*) che saccheggia

marble [ˈmɑːr·bl] *n* 1.(*stone*) marmo *m*; ~ **table** tavolo *m* di marmo 2.(*glass ball*) bilia *f*, pallina *f*; **to play** ~**s** giocare a bilie ▶ **to** <u>lose</u> **one's** ~**s** *inf* perdere la testa

marble cake *n* ciambella al cioccolato

march [mɑːrtʃ] I.<-es> *n a.* MIL marcia *f*; **funeral** ~ marcia funebre; **a 20 mile** ~ una marcia di 32 km; **to be on the** ~ essere in marcia; **to be within a day's** ~ essere a un giorno di cammino II. *vi a.* MIL marciare; (*parade*) sfilare; **to** ~ **into a country** invadere un paese III. *vt* (*compel to walk*) **to** ~ **sb off** fare marciare qu

March [mɑːrtʃ] *n* marzo *m; s.a.* **April**

marching orders [ˈmɑːr·tʃɪŋ·ˌɔːr·dəz] *n* 1. MIL **to get one's** ~ ricevere il proprio ruolino di marcia 2. *inf* **to give sb his** ~ licenziare qu

Mardi Gras [ˈmɑːr·di·ˌɡrɑː] *n* martedì *m* grasso

mare [mer] *n* giumenta *f*

mare's nest *n* buco *m* nell'acqua

margarine [ˈmɑːr·dʒə·rɪn] *n* margarina *f*

margin [ˈmɑːr·dʒɪn] *n a.* TYPO margine *m*; **profit** ~ margine di profitto; **narrow** [*o* **tight**] ~ margine esiguo; ~ **of error** margine di errore

marginal [ˈmɑːr·dʒɪ·nl] *adj* marginale; **to be of** ~ **interest** essere di interesse marginale; ~ **land** terreno *f* marginale

marginalize [ˈmɑːr·dʒɪ·nə·laɪz] *vt* marginalizzare

marigold [ˈme·rɪ·ɡoʊld] *n* calendula *f*

marihuana *n*, **marijuana** [ˌme·rɪˈwɑː·nə] *n* marihuana *f*, marijuana *f*

marina [məˈriː·nə] *n* porticciolo *m* sportivo

marinade [ˌme·rɪˈneɪd] *n* marinata *f*

marinate [ˈme·rɪ·neɪt] *vt* marinare

marine [məˈriːn] I. *adj* (*of the sea*) marino, -a; NAUT nautico, -a; MIL navale II. *n* marine *mf inv*

marine biologist *n* biologo, -a *m, f* marino, -a

Marine Corps *n* Corpo *m* dei Marine

mariner [ˈme·rɪ·nəʳ] *n liter* marinaio, -a *m, f*

marionette [ˌme·rɪ·əˈnet] *n* marionetta *f*

marital [ˈme·rɪ·təl] *adj* coniugale; ~ **bliss** felicità *f* coniugale; ~ **problems** problemi *m pl* coniugali

marital status *n form* stato *m* civile

maritime [ˈme·rɪ·taɪm] *adj form* marittimo, -a

maritime law *n* diritto *m* marittimo

marjoram [ˈmɑːr·dʒə·əm] *n* maggiorana *f*

mark¹ [mɑːrk] I. *n* 1.(*spot, stain*) macchia *f*; (*scratch*) graffio *m*; (*trace*) traccia *f*; **to leave one's** ~ **on sth/sb** *fig* lasciare il segno su qc/qu 2.(*written sign*) segno *m* 3.(*required standard*) livello *m;* **to be up to the** ~ essere all'altezza; **to not feel up to the** ~ non sentirsi in forma 4.(*target*) bersaglio *m;* **to hit the** ~ colpire il bersaglio 5.(*starting line*) linea *f* di partenza; **on your** ~, **get set, go!** pronti, via! 6. LING segno *m;* **punctuation** ~ segno di interpunzione ▶ **to be** <u>wide</u> **of the** ~ *fig* essere fuori strada II. *vt* 1.(*make a spot, stain*) macchiare 2.(*make written sign, indicate*) marcare; **I've** ~**ed the route on the map** ho segnato l'itinerario sulla carta; **the bottle was** ~**ed 'poison'** sulla bottiglia c'era la scritta 'veleno' 3.(*characterize*) contraddistinguere; **to** ~ **sb as sth** etichettare qu come qc 4.(*commemorate*) commemorare; **to** ~ **the beginning/end of sth** segnare l'inizio/la fine di qc; **to** ~ **the 10th anniversary** commemorare il 10° anniversario

◆**mark down** *vt* **1.**(*reduce prices*) ribassare **2.**(*jot down*) annotare **3.**SCHOOL **to mark sb down** abbassare il voto a qu **4.***fig* (*assess*) **to mark sb down as sth** etichettare qu come qc

◆**mark off** *vt* **1.**(*divide land*) delimitare **2.**(*cross off*) spuntare

◆**mark out** *vt* tracciare i contorni di

◆**mark up** *vt* aumentare

mark [mɑːrk] *n* FIN marco *m*

marked [mɑːrkt] *adj* **1.**(*improvement, difference*) notevole; (*contrast*) netto, -a **2.**(*with distinguishing marks*) marcato, -a **3.**(*liable to be attacked*) **to be a ~ man/woman** essere una vittima designata

markedly ['mɑːr·kəd·li] *adv* notevolmente

marker ['mɑːr·kə] *n* **1.**(*sign, symbol*) segno *m* **2.**(*pen*) evidenziatore *m* **3.**SPORTS (*indicator*) segnapunti *m inv;* **the first-down ~** la linea del primo down (nel football americano) **4.** *sl* (*IOU*) cambiale *f*

market ['mɑːr·kɪt] **I.***n* mercato *m;* **the coffee ~** il mercato del caffè; **the housing ~** il mercato immobiliare; **the job ~** il mercato del lavoro; **the stock ~** la borsa valori *f;* **to put sth on the ~** mettere in vendita qc; **on the ~** sul mercato **II.** *vt* commercializzare

marketable *adj* commerciabile; **~ commodities** beni *m pl* commerciabili

market forces *npl* forze *f pl* di mercato

marketing *n* **1.**(*discipline*) marketing *m* **2.**(*commercialization*) commercializzazione *f*

marketing strategy *n* strategia *f* di mercato

market leader *n* leader *mf* di mercato *inv*

marketplace *n* **1.**ECON mercato *m* **2.**(*square*) piazza *f*

market price *n* prezzo *m* di mercato

market research *n* ricerca *f* [*o* analisi] di mercato *f inv*

market researcher *n* analista *mf* di mercato

market trader *n* commerciante *mf*

marking *n* (*identification*) segno *f;* (*on animal*) marchio *m*

marksman ['mɑːrks·mən] <-men> *n* tiratore (scelto)

marksmanship ['mɑːrks·mən·ʃɪp] *n* abilità *f* di tiro

markswoman ['mɑːrks·wʊ·mən] <-women> *n* tiratrice (scelta) *f*

markup ['mɑːrk·ʌp] *n* margine *m* di utile lordo

marmalade ['mɑːr·mə·leɪd] *n* marmellata *f* (*di agrumi*)*;* **orange ~** marmellata di arance

marmoset ['mɑːr·mə·zet] *n* uistitì *mf inv*

maroon[1] [mə·'ruːn] **I.***n* marrone *m* rossiccio **II.** *adj* marrone rossiccio *inv*

maroon[2] [mə·'ruːn] *vt* abbandonare

marquee [mɑːr·'kiː] **I.***n* (*rooflike structure*) pensilina *f* **II.** *adj* (*of performer*) da cartellone

marriage ['me·rɪdʒ] *n* **1.**(*wedding*) matrimonio *m*, nozze *fpl* **2.**(*relationship, state*) matrimonio *m;* **arranged ~** matrimonio combinato; **related by ~** imparentato per matrimonio; **he is a relative by ~** è un parente acquisito **3.** *fig* (*of organizations*) unione *f*

marriageable *adj* maritabile

marriage license *n* licenza *f* di matrimonio

marriage of convenience *n* matrimonio *m* di convenienza

married *adj* (*person*) sposato, -a, coniugato, -a; **~ couple** una coppia sposata; **~ life** la vita coniugale; **to be ~ to sth** *fig* avere sposato qc

married name *n* nome *m* da sposata

marrow ['me·roʊ] *n* MED midollo *m*

marrowbone *n* ossobuco *m*

marry ['me·ri] <-ie-> **I.** *vt* **1.**(*become husband or wife*) **to ~ sb** sposarsi con qu; **to get married (to sb)** sposare qu, sposarsi (con qu) **2.**(*priest*) sposare **II.** *vi* sposarsi; **to ~ above/beneath oneself** sposarsi con qu di ceto superiore/inferiore; **to ~ into a wealthy family** imparentarsi con una famiglia ricca

Mars [mɑːrz] *n* Marte *m*

marsh [mɑːrʃ] <-es> *n* palude *f*

marshal ['mɑːr·ʃl] **I.**<-ll-, -l-> *vt* ordinare **II.** *n* **1.**LAW ufficiale *mf* giudiziario **2.**(*police officer*) capo *m* della polizia locale; (*fire officer*) capo *m* dei vigili del fuoco **3.**MIL maresciallo *m;* **field ~** feldmaresciallo **4.**(*honoree*) **the grand ~** il cerimoniere

marshland ['mɑːrʃ·lænd] *n* terreno *m* paludoso

marshmallow ['mɑːrʃ·mæ·ləʊ] *n* **1.**(*sweet*) dolce a pasta soffice **2.**(*plant*) altea *f*

marshy ['mɑːr·ʃi] <-ier, -iest> *adj* paludoso, -a

marsupial [mɑːr·'suː·piəl] **I.***n* marsupiale *m* **II.** *adj* (*of the marsupium*) marsupiale

marten ['mɑːr·tn] *n* mustelide *m;* **pine ~** martora *f*

martial ['mɑːr·ʃəl] *adj* marziale

martial arts *n* SPORTS arti *f pl* marziali

martial law *n* legge *f* marziale; **to impose ~ on a country** imporre la legge marziale in un paese

Martian ['mɑːr·ʃən] **I.** *adj* marziano, -a **II.** *n* marziano, -a *m, f*

martin ['mɑːr·tn] *n* balestruccio *m*

martinet [ˌmɑːr·tə·'net] *n form* rigorista *mf*

Martinique [ˌmɑːr·tə·'niːk] *n* Martinica *f*

martyr ['mɑːr·ţə] **I.** *n* martire *mf;* **to be a ~ to a disease** *fig* essere tormentato da una malattia **II.** *vt* martirizzare; **~ed saint** (santo) martire

martyrdom ['mɑːr·ţə·dəm] *n* martirio *m;* **to suffer ~** subire il martirio

marvel ['mɑːr·vl] **I.** *n* **1.**(*thing*) meraviglia *f;* **it's a ~ to me how ...** mi meraviglia come ... **2.**(*person*) persona *f* meravigliosa **II.**<-ll-, -l-> *vi* **to ~ that ...** meravigliarsi che ... +*subj;* **to ~ at sb/sth** meravigliarsi di qu/qc

marvelous *adj*, **marvellous** ['mɑːr·və·ləs] *adj* meraviglioso, -a; **to feel ~** sentirsi in gran forma

Marxism ['mɑːrk·sɪ·zm] *n* marxismo *m*

Marxist ['mɑːrk·sɪst] **I.** *n* marxista *mf* **II.** *adj* marxista

marzipan ['mɑːr·zɪ·pæn] *n* marzapane *m*

masc. *adj abbr of* **masculine**

M

mascara [mæ·'ske·rə] *n* mascara *m*

mascot ['mæs·ka:t] *n* mascotte *f*

masculine ['mæs·kjə·lɪn] *adj a.* LING maschile

masculinity [ˌmæs·kjə·'lɪ·nə·ti] *n* mascolinità *f*

MASH [mæʃ] *n abbr of* **mobile army surgical hospital** ospedale (militare) da campo

mash [mæʃ] **I.** *n* **1.** AGR (*animal feed*) pastone *m* **2.** (*fermentable mixture*) infuso *m* di malto (per fare la birra) **II.** *vt* ridurre a purè; **to ~ potatoes** passare le patate; **~ ed potatoes** purè *m* di patate *inv*
♦ **mash up** *vt* CULIN schiacciare (per farne un purè)

mask [mæsk] **I.** *n a. fig* maschera *f;* (*only covering eyes*) mascherina *f;* **oxygen ~** maschera di ossigeno **II.** *vt* mascherare; **to ~ sth with sth** nascondere qc con qc; **to ~ the statistics** occultare le statistiche
♦ **mask out** *vt* PHOT, TYPO mascherare

masked *adj* mascherato, -a

masked ball *n* ballo *m* in maschera

masking tape *n* nastro *m* adesivo per mascheratura

masochism ['mæ·sə·kɪ·zəm] *n* masochismo *m*

masochist ['mæ·sə·kɪst] *n* masochista *mf*

masochistic ['mæ·sə·kɪs·tik] *adj* masochistico, -a

mason ['meɪ·sn] *n* **1.** (*stonecutter*) scalpellino, -a *m, f* **2.** (*bricklayer*) muratore, -trice/-a *m, f* **3.** (*Freemason*) massone, -ona *m, f*

Masonic [mə·'sɑ:·nɪk] *adj* massonico, -a

Masonic Temple *n* tempio *m* massonico

masonry ['meɪ·sn·ri] *n* **1.** (*occupation*) arte *f* muraria **2.** (*stonework*) muratura *f* **3.** (*Freemasonry*) massoneria *f*

masquerade [ˌmæs·kə·'reɪd] **I.** *n* mascherata *f* **II.** *vi* **to ~ as sth** camuffarsi da qc

masquerade ball *n* ballo *m* mascherato

mass [mæs] **I.** *n* **1.** *a.* PHYS massa *f* **2.** (*formless substance*) massa *f* **3.** (*large quantity*) massa *f;* **to be a ~ of contradictions** essere pieno di contraddizioni; **the ~ of the people** la folla; **the ~ of the population** la maggior parte della popolazione **II.** *vi* (*gather*) ammassarsi **III.** *adj* di massa

Mass [mæs] *n* messa *f;* **to attend ~** andare a messa; **to celebrate a ~** celebrare una messa

Mass. *n abbr of* **Massachusetts** Massachusetts *m*

massacre ['mæ·sə·kə] **I.** *n* **1.** (*killing*) massacro *f* **2.** *fig* (*defeat*) pesante sconfitta *f* **II.** *vt* **1.** (*kill*) massacrare **2.** *fig* (*defeat*) annientare

massage [mə·'sɑ:dʒ] **I.** *n* massaggio *m;* **to give sb a ~** fare un massaggio a qu; **water ~** idromassaggio *m* **II.** *vt* **1.** massaggiare **2.** *fig* manipolare

massage parlor *n* (*for treatment*) salone *m* massaggi

masseur [mæ·'sɜ:r] *n* massaggiatore *m*

masseuse [mæ·'sɜ:z] *n* massaggiatrice *f*

mass grave *n* fossa *f* comune

massif ['mæ·sɪv] *n* GEO massiccio *m*

massive ['mæ·sɪv] *adj* massiccio, -a, enorme; **~ amounts of money** enormi quantità di denaro

mass market *n* mercato *m* di massa

mass-market *adj* di largo consumo

mass media *n* **the ~** i mezzi di comunicazione di massa, i (mass) media

mass murder *n* uccisione *f* di massa

mass murderer *n* massacratore, -trice *m, f*

mass-produce *vt* produrre su vasta scala

mass production *n* produzione *f* su vasta scala

mass tourism *n* turismo *m* di massa

mass unemployment *n* disoccupazione *m* massiccia

mast [mæst] *n* **1.** NAUT albero *m* **2.** (*flag pole*) asta *f;* **at half ~** a mezz'asta **3.** RADIO, TV antenna *f*

mastectomy [ˌmæs·'te·kə·mi] <-ies> *n* mastectomia *f*

master ['mæs·tə] **I.** *n* **1.** (*of house*) padrone *m;* (*of slave, dog*) padrone *m* **2.** (*one who excels*) maestro *m;* **~ craftsman** maestro artigiano; **to be a ~ of sth** essere un esperto di [*o* in] qc **3.** (*instructor*) insegnante *m;* **dancing/singing ~** maestro di ballo/canto; **fencing ~** maestro di scherma **4.** (*master copy*) originale *m*, master *m inv* ▶ **to be one's own ~** non avere padroni; **jack of all trades, ~ of none** sa fare di tutto, ma non eccelle in niente **II.** *vt* **1.** (*cope with*) controllare; **to ~ one's fear of flying** dominare la propria paura di volare **2.** (*become proficient at*) padroneggiare

ℹ️ Negli USA, il **Master's degree** è per lo più un titolo accademico conseguito al termine di un corso di studi che prevede la redazione di una tesi di ricerca scientifica *(thesis)*. I **Master's degree** più noti sono: *MA (Master of Arts)* e *MS (Master of Science)*.

master bedroom *n* camera *f* da letto principale

master copy <-ies> *n* originale *m*, master *m*

masterful ['mæs·tə·fəl] *adj* **1.** (*authoritative*) autoritario, -a **2.** (*skillful*) magistrale

master key *n* passe partout *m inv*

masterly ['mæs·tə·li] *adj* magistrale

mastermind ['mæs·tə·maɪnd] **I.** *n* (*person*) cervello *m* **II.** *vt* (*activity*) orchestrare; (*crime*) essere il cervello di

Master of Arts *n* (*person*) laureato, -a in lettere *m*

Master of Ceremonies *n* maestro *m* di cerimonia

masterpiece *n* capolavoro *m*

master plan *n* piano *m* generale

master race *n* razza *f* superiore

Master's *n*, **Master's degree** *n* laurea (di secondo grado) *f*

masterstroke *n* colpo *m* da maestro

master switch <-es> *n* interruttore *m* principale

masterwork *n s.* **masterpiece**

mastery ['mæs·tə·i] *n* (*skill*) maestria *f;* (*sway*) padronanza *f*

masticate ['mæs·tɪ·keɪt] *vt* masticare

mastication [ˌmæs·tɪ·'keɪ·ʃən] *n* masticazione *f*

mastitis [mæ·'staɪ·ṭɪs] *n* mastite *f*

masturbate ['mæs·tə·beɪt] I. *vi* masturbarsi II. *vt* masturbare

masturbation [ˌmæs·tə·'beɪ·ʃən] *n* masturbazione *f*

mat[1] [mæt] *n* 1. (*on floor*) tappeto *m*, stuoia *f;* (*doormat*) zerbino *m;* **bath ~** tappetino *m* da bagno 2. (*on table*) sottopiatto *m* 3. SPORTS (*in gymnastics*) materassino *m* 4. (*thick layer: of grass*) (folto) tappeto *m;* (*of hair*) (folto) groviglio *m*

mat[2] *adj,* **matte** [mæt] *adj* opaco, -a

matador ['mæ·tə·dɔːɛ] *n* matador *m inv,* torero *m*

match[1] [mætʃ] <-es> *n* (*for making fire*) fiammifero *m;* **box of ~ es** scatola di fiammiferi

match[2] [mætʃ] I. *n* 1. (*competitor*) pari *mf;* **to be a good ~ for sb** essere un degno avversario per qu; **to be no ~ for sb** non essere all'altezza di qu; **to meet one's ~** trovare pane per i propri denti 2. (*similarity*) **to be a good ~** essere bene accoppiati 3. (*in marriage*) **to make a good ~** fare una bella coppia 4. SPORTS partita *f;* **wrestling ~** incontro di lotta [*o* wrestling] II. *vi* (*harmonize: design, color*) armonizzare, coordinare; (*description*) corrispondere III. *vt* 1. (*have same color*) intonarsi a 2. (*equal*) uguagliare

◆**match against** *vt always sep* contrapporre

◆**match up** I. *vi* 1. (*make sense*) concordare 2. (*align*) combaciare 3. **to ~ to sth** essere all'altezza di qc II. *vt* (*put together*) abbinare

matchbox ['mætʃ·bɑːks] <-es> *n* scatola *f* di fiammiferi

matching ['mæt·ʃɪŋ] *adj* intonato, -a

matchless ['mætʃ·lɪs] *adv* incomparabile

matchmaker ['mætʃ·meɪ·kə] *n* pronubo, -a *m, f*

match point *n* SPORTS punto *m* decisivo, match *m* point *inv*

matchstick ['mætʃˌstɪk] *n* fiammifero *m*

mate[1] [meɪt] I. *n* 1. (*spouse*) compagno, -a *m, f* 2. ZOOL (*male*) maschio *m;* (*female*) femmina *f* 3. NAUT secondo *m;* **first/second ~** primo/secondo ufficiale 4. (*one of a pair*) compagno, -a, -a *m, f* II. *vi* accoppiarsi III. *vt* accoppiare

mate[2] [meɪt] I. *n* GAMES (scacco) *m* matto II. *vt* dare scacco matto a

material [mə·'tɪ·ri·əl] I. *n* 1. PHILOS, PHYS materia *f* 2. (*physical substance*) materiale *m;* **raw ~** materia *f* prima 3. (*information*) **publicity ~** materiale *m* pubblicitario 4. (*cloth*) stoffa *f* 5. (*textile*) tessuto *m* 6. *pl* (*equipment*) attrezzatura *mpl;* **writing ~(s)** necessario *m* per scrivere II. *adj* 1. (*physical*) materi-

ale; **~ damage** danno materiale 2. (*important*) importante; **to be ~ to sth** essere importante per qc

materialism [mə·'tɪ·ri·ə·lɪ·zəm] *n* materialismo *m*

materialist *n* materialista *mf*

materialistic [mə·ˌtɪ·ri·ə·'lɪs·tɪk] *adj* materialista, materialistico, -a

materialize [mə·'tɪ·ri·ə·laɪz] *vi* 1. (*take physical form*) materializzarsi 2. (*hope, idea*) realizzarsi 3. (*appear*) comparire

material witness <-es> *n* testimone *mf* oculare

maternal [mə·'tɜːr·nl] *adj* 1. (*feeling*) materno, -a 2. (*relative*) materno, -a

maternity [mə·'tɜːr·nə·ti] *n* maternità *f*

maternity clothes *npl* indumenti *m* prémaman

maternity leave *n* congedo *m* di maternità, maternità *f*

maternity ward *n* reparto *m* maternità

math [mæθ] *n inf abbr of* **mathematics** matematica *fsing*

mathematical [ˌmæ·θə·'mæ·ṭɪ·kl] *adj* matematico, -a

mathematician [ˌmæ·θə·mə·'tɪ·ʃən] *n* matematico, -a *m, f*

mathematics [ˌmæ·θə·'mæ·ṭɪks] *n* matematica *fsing*

matinée ['mæ·tə·neɪ] *n* CINE, THEAT matinée *f inv*

mating *n* accoppiamento *m*

mating season *n* stagione *f* degli amori

matriarch *n* matriarca *f*

matrices ['meɪ·trɪ·siːz] *n pl of* **matrix**

matriculate [mə·'trɪk·jə·leɪt] I. *vi* immatricolarsi, iscriversi II. *vt* immatricolare, iscrivere

matriculation [mə·ˌtrɪk·jə·'leɪ·ʃən] *n* (*enrollment*) immatricolazione *f;* (*exam*) ammissione *f* all'università

matrimonial [ˌmæ·trə·'moʊn·i·əl] *adj form* matrimoniale

matrimony ['mæ·trə·moʊ·ni] *n* matrimonio *m*

matrix ['meɪ·trɪks] <-ices> *n a.* MAT matrice *f*

matrix printer *n* COMPUT stampante *f* a matrice

matron ['meɪ·trən] *n* 1. (*middle-aged woman*) matrona *f* 2. (*prison guard*) guardia carceraria *f*

matronly ['meɪ·trən·li] *adj iron* matronale; **a ~ figure** una matrona

matron of honor *n* dama d'onore (nelle cerimonie nuziali)

matted *adj* aggrovigliato, -a

matter ['mæ·tə] I. *n* 1. (*subject*) argomento *m;* (*question, affair*) questione *f;* **that's another ~ altogether** questo è un altro discorso [*o* questo non c'entra] *fig;* **that's no laughing ~** non è uno scherzo; **to do sth as a ~ of course** fare qc naturalmente; **the ~ at hand** la faccenda in questione; **it's a ~ of life or death** è una questione di vita o di morte; **money ~s** questioni di soldi; **a ~ of opinion** questione di punti di vista; **the truth of the ~** la verità (dei

fatti); **personal** ~ questione [*o* faccenda] privata **2.** *pl* (*situation*) situazione *f;* **to make ~s worse** come se non bastasse; **to help** ~s migliorare le cose **3.** (*wrong*) problema *m;* **what's the ~ with you?** cosa c'è che non va?; **what's the ~ with asking for a pay raise?** che problema c'è a chiedere un aumento di stipendio? **4.** (*material*) materiale *m;* **advertising** ~ materiale pubblicitario **5.** (*amount*) **a ~ of ...** una questione di ...; **in a ~ of seconds** in pochi secondi **6.** (*substance*) sostanza *f* **II.** *vi* importare; **it really ~s to me** mi importa molto; **no ~ what they say** non mi importa (di) quello che dicono, dicano quello che vogliono; **it doesn't ~ if ...** non importa se ...; **it ~s that ...** importa che ... +*subj;* **what ~s now is that ...** l'importante adesso è che ...
matter-of-fact [ˌmæ·tə·əv·ˈfækt] *adj* **1.** (*practical*) pratico, -a **2.** (*emotionless*) prosaico, -a
matter-of-factly *adv* **1.** (*practically*) in modo pratico **2.** (*emotionlessly*) prosaicamente
matting [ˈmæ·tɪŋ] *n* **1.** (*floor covering*) stuoia *f* **2.** (*tangling*) garbuglio *m*
mattress [ˈmæ·trɪs] *n* materasso *m*
mature [mə·ˈtʊr] **I.** *adj* **1.** (*person, attitude*) maturo, -a; (*animal*) adulto, -a; **to be ~ beyond one's years** essere maturo per la propria età; **after ~ reflection** dopo lunga riflessione **2.** (*wine*) invecchiato, -a; (*cheese*) stagionato, -a; (*fruit*) maturo, -a **3.** FIN maturato, -a **II.** *vi* **1.** *a. fig* maturare **2.** FIN maturare **III.** *vt* **1.** (*cheese, ham*) fare stagionare; (*wine*) fare invecchiare **2.** (*person*) fare maturare
maturity [mə·ˈtʊ·rə·ti] *n* <-ies> **1.** (*of person, attitude*) maturità *f;* **to come to** ~ raggiungere la maturità **2.** FIN maturazione *f;* **to reach** ~ giungere a scadenza
maudlin [ˈmɑːd·lɪn] *adj* **1.** (*sentimental*) sentimentale **2.** (*tearful*) lacrimoso, -a
maul [mɑːl] *vt* **1.** (*wound*) dilaniare **2.** (*criticize*) stroncare
Mauritania [ˌmɔː·rɪ·ˈteɪn·iə] *n* Mauritania *f*
Mauritanian I. *n* mauritano, -a *m, f* **II.** *adj* mauritano, -a
Mauritian I. *n* mauriziano, -a *m, f* **II.** *adj* mauriziano, -a
Mauritius [mɔː·ˈrɪ·ʃi·əs] *n* Maurizio *m*
mausoleum [ˌmɑː·sə·ˈliː·əm] *n* mausoleo *m*
mauve [moʊv] *adj* malva
maverick [ˈmæ·və·rɪk] *n* **1.** ZOOL vitello *m* non marchiato **2.** (*person*) nonconformista *mf*
mawkish [ˈmɑː·kɪʃ] *adj* (*sentimental*) sdolcinato, -a *fig*
max. *inf abbr of* **maximum** massimo
maxim [ˈmæk·sɪm] *n* massima *f*
maximal [ˈmæk·sɪ·məl] *adj form* massimo, -a
maximize [ˈmæk·sɪ·maɪz] *vt* massimizzare
maximum [ˈmæk·sɪ·məm] **I.** *n* massimo *m;* **to do sth to the** ~ fare qc al massimo; **to reach a** ~ raggiungere un massimo **II.** *adj* massimo, -a; **this car has a ~ speed of 100 mph** questa auto ha una velocità massima di 100 miglia all'ora

maximum security prison *n* carcere *m* di massima sicurezza
may¹ [meɪ] <might, might> *aux* **1.** *form* (*be allowed*) potere; ~ **I come in?** (è) permesso?; ~ **I ask you a question?** posso farti una domanda? **2.** (*possibility*) essere possibile; **it ~ rain** può darsi che piova; **be that as it ~** in ogni modo **3.** (*hope, wish*) ~ **she rest in peace** riposi in pace
may² [meɪ] *n* (*bush*) biancospino *m;* (*flower*) fiori *m pl* di biancospino
May [meɪ] *n* maggio; *s.a.* **April**
maybe [ˈmeɪ·biː] **I.** *adv* **1.** (*perhaps*) forse **2.** (*approximately*) pressappoco; ~ **as many as two hundred people** più o meno duecento persone **II.** *n* forse *m;* **a definite** ~ un forse definitivo
mayday [ˈmeɪ·deɪ] *n* mayday *m inv, segnale radiotelefonico internazionale di soccorso*
May Day *n* il primo *m* maggio
mayfly [ˈmeɪ·flaɪ] *n* <-ies> effimera *f,* efemera *f*
mayhem [ˈmeɪ·hem] *n* caos *m inv;* **it was utter ~** era una baraonda infernale
mayo [ˈmeɪ·oʊ] *n inf abbr of* **mayonnaise** maionese *f*
mayonnaise [ˌme·ɪə·ˈneɪz] *n* maionese *f*
mayor [ˈmeɪ·ə·] *n* sindaco *m*
maypole [ˈmeɪ·poʊl] *n palo ornato di nastri intorno a cui si danzava il primo maggio*
may've *inf =* **may have** *s.* **may**
maze [meɪz] *n* labirinto *m*
MB [ˌem·ˈbiː] *abbr of* **megabyte** Mb
MBA [ˌem·biː·ˈeɪ] *n abbr of* **Master of Business Administration** laurea *f* in amministrazione aziendale
MC [ˌem·ˈsiː] *n* **1.** *abbr of* **Master of Ceremonies** maestro, -a *m, f* di cerimonie **2.** *abbr of* **Member of Congress** deputato, -a (negli Stati Uniti) *m*
MD [ˌem·ˈdiː] *n* **1.** *abbr of* **Doctor of Medicine** dott. *mf* **2.** *abbr of* **Maryland** Maryland *m* **3.** *abbr of* **muscular dystrophy** distrofia muscolare
ME *n abbr of* **Maine** Maine *m*
me [miː] *pron* **1.** mi; **look at** ~ guardami; **she saw** ~ mi ha visto; **he told** ~ **that ...** mi ha detto che ...; **give** ~ **the pencil** dammi la matita **2.** (*in comparisons*) **she is older than** ~ è più vecchia di me **3.** (*after verb 'to be'*) io; **it's** ~ sono io; **she is older than** ~ è più vecchia di me **4.** (*after prep*) me; **is this for** ~? è per me?
meadow [ˈme·doʊ] *n* prato *m*
meager *adj,* **meagre** [ˈmiː·gə·] *adj* scarso, -a
meal¹ [miːl] *n* pasto *m;* **a heavy/light** ~ un pasto abbondante/leggero; **to go out for a** ~ andare fuori a pranzo/cena; ~**s on wheels** *distribuzione di pasti caldi a domicilio ad anziani o invalidi* ► **to make a** ~ **of sth** essere troppo zelanti in qc
meal² [miːl] *n* (*flour*) farina *f*
meal ticket *n* **1.** (*lunch voucher*) buono *m*

pasto **2.** *fig* (*means of living*) fonte *f* di sostentamento; **he's her latest ~** è lui che la mantiene ultimamente

mealtime ['mi:l·taɪm] *n* ora *f* dei pasti

mean[1] [mi:n] *adj* **1.** (*unkind*) sgarbato; **to be ~ to sb** trattare male qu; **to have a ~ streak** avere una vena di perfidia **2.** *inf* (*excellent*) eccellente; **he is one ~ cook** *inf* è un cuoco con i fiocchi

mean[2] [mi:n] <meant, meant> *vt* **1.** (*signify: word, event*) significare; **does that name ~ anything to you?** ti dice niente quel nome? **2.** (*express, indicate: person*) volere dire; **what do you ~?** che cosa vuoi dire?; **what do you ~ it was my fault?** vuoi dire che era colpa mia?; **I ~ what I say** non sto scherzando **3.** (*intend for particular purpose*) destinare; **to be meant for sth** essere destinato a qu; **to be meant for each other** essere fatti l'uno per l'altro [*o* l'altra]; **it was meant to be** doveva accadere **4.** (*intend*) intendere; **to ~ to do sth** avere intenzione di fare qc; **to ~ well** avere buone intenzioni; **I ~ to say ...** intendo [*o* voglio] dire ...; **what do you ~ by arriving so late?** perché diavolo sei così in ritardo? ▶ **to ~ business** *inf* fare sul serio

meander [mɪ·'æn·dɚ] **I.** *n* meandro *m* **II.** *vi* **1.** (*flow*) snodarsi **2.** *fig* (*wander*) vagare; (*digress*) divagare

meandering [mɪ·'æn·dɚ·rɪŋ] *adj* **1.** (*river*) sinuoso, -a **2.** (*explanation*) incoerente

meanie ['mi:·ni] *n inf* perfido, -a *m, f*

meaning ['mi:·nɪŋ] *n* significato *m;* **to give sth a whole new ~** dare un senso completamente nuovo a qc; **what is the ~ of this?** e questo cosa vuol dire?; **the full ~ of sth** il pieno significato di qc; **to have ~ for sb** essere importante per qu

meaningful ['mi:·nɪŋ·fəl] *adj* **1.** (*difference, change*) significativo, -a **2.** (*look, smile*) eloquente **3.** (*relationship*) importante, -a

meaningless ['mi:·nɪŋ·ləs] *adj* senza senso

meanness ['mi:n·nɪs] *n* bassezza *f*

means [mi:nz] *n* **1.** (*instrument, method*) mezzo *m*, metodo *m;* **~ of communication/transport** mezzo di comunicazione/trasporto **2.** *pl* (*resources*) mezzi *mpl;* **~ of support** mezzi di sostentamento; **ways and ~** modi e maniere; **by ~ of sth** mediante qc; **to try by all (possible) ~ to do sth** cercare in tutti i modi di fare qc; **to use all the ~ at one's disposal** usare tutti i mezzi a propria disposizione **3.** *pl* (*income*) mezzi (economici) *mpl;* **a person of ~** una persona facoltosa; **private ~** rendita *f;* **to be without ~** *form* non avere mezzi; **to live beyond one's ~** vivere al disopra delle proprie possibilità ▶ **by all ~!** ma certo!; **by no ~** niente affatto

meant [ment] *pt, pp of* **mean**

meantime ['mi:n·taɪm] **I.** *adv* frattempo **II.** *n* **in the ~** nel frattempo

meanwhile ['mi:n·waɪl] *adv* nel frattempo

meany ['mi:·ni] *n inf s.* **meanie**

measles ['mi:·zlz] *n* morbillo *m*

measly ['mi:z·li] *adj* <-ier, -iest> miserabile

measurable ['me·ʒə·rə·bl] *adj* **1.** (*quantifiable*) misurabile **2.** (*perceptible*) apprezzabile

measure ['me·ʒɚ] **I.** *vt* misurare; **to ~ sth in feet and inches** misurare qc in piedi e pollici **II.** *vi* misurare; **the box ~s 4 in. by 4 in. by 6 in.** la scatola misura 4 pollici [*o* 10 cm] per 4 pollici [*o* 10 cm] per 6 pollici [*o* 15 cm] **III.** *n* **1.** (*size*) misura *f* **2.** (*measuring instrument*) metro *m;* (*ruler*) righello *m* **3.** (*amount of alcohol*) dose *f* **4.** *pl* (*action*) misurazione *f;* **to take ~s to do sth** prendere i provvedimenti per fare qc **5.** (*degree, amount*) grado *m;* **there was some ~ of truth in what he said** c'era del vero in quello che diceva; **in some ~** in parte **6.** LIT metro *m* **7.** MUS battuta *f* ▶ **for good ~** per buona misura; **beyond ~** oltre la giusta misura

♦ **measure off** *vt* **1.** (*for cutting*) misurare **2.** (*mark limits*) delimitare

♦ **measure up** *vi* avere i requisiti (per); **to not ~ to sth** non essere all'altezza di qc

measured *adj* (*response*) misurato, -a; (*voice, tone*) cadenzato, -a

measurement ['me·ʒɚ·mənt] *n* **1.** (*size*) misura *f* **2.** (*dimension of body*) misura *f;* **to take sb's ~s** prendere le misure a qu **3.** (*act of measuring*) misurazione *f*

measuring cup *n* misurino *m*

measuring spoon *n* cucchiaio *m* dosatore

meat [mi:t] *n* **1.** carne *f* **2.** *fig* (*essence*) essenza *f* **3.** *fig* (*target*) **this guy is fresh ~** questo ce lo mangiamo in un boccone ▶ **one man's ~ is another man's poison** *prov* ciò che giova a uno è veleno per un altro

meat-and-potatoes [ˌmi:t·ənd·pə·'teɪ·t̪ouz] *n inf* essenziale *m*

meatball *n* polpetta *f*

meat cleaver *n* mannaia *f* (da macellaio)

meat grinder *n* tritacarne *m inv*

meat hook *n* gancio *m* da macellaio

meat loaf *n* polpettone *m* di carne

meat market *n sl* mercato *m* delle carni

Mecca ['me·kə] *n* REL la Mecca *f*

mecca ['me·kə] *n* (*center*) mecca *f*

mechanic [mɪ·'kæ·nɪk] *n* meccanico, -a *m, f*

mechanical *adj* **1.** (*relating to machines*) meccanico, -a **2.** (*without thinking*) automatico, -a

mechanical engineer *n* ingegnere *m* meccanico

mechanical engineering *n* ingegneria *f* meccanica

mechanical pencil *n* portamina *f*, matita *f* automatica

mechanics [mɪ·'kæ·nɪks] *npl* **1.** AUTO, TECH meccanica *f* **2.** *inf* (*how things are organized*) meccanismi *m*

mechanism ['me·kə·nɪ·zəm] *n* meccanismo *m*

mechanize ['me·kə·naɪz] *vt* meccanizzare

MEd *n abbr* **Master of Education** laurea *f* in pedagogia

M

med. *adj abbr of* **medium** medio, -a

medal ['me·dl] *n* medaglia *f*

medalist ['me·də·lɪst] *n* vincitore, -trice di medaglia *m;* **he was a gold ~ at the Olympic Games** è stato medaglia d'oro alle olimpiadi

medallion [mə·'dæl·jən] *n* medaglione *m*

meddle ['me·dl] *vi* **to ~ in sth** intromettersi

meddlesome ['me·dl·səm] *adj* invadente

media ['miː·di·ə] *n* **1.** *pl of* **medium 2. the ~** i media; **the mass ~** i mezzi di comunicazione di massa; **a ~ event** un evento mediatico

mediaeval [ˌme·di·'iː·vəl] *adj s.* **medievale**

median ['miː·di·ən] *adj* mediano, -a

median strip *n* AUTO spartitraffico *m inv*

mediate ['miː·di·eit] **I.** *vi* mediare; **to ~ between two groups** mediare tra due gruppi; **to ~ in sth** fare da mediatore in qc **II.** *vt* **to ~ a settlement** mediare un accordo

mediation [ˌmiː·dɪ·'ei·ʃən] *n* mediazione *f*

mediator ['miː·di·ei·ʈə·] *n* mediatore, -trice *m, f*

medic ['me·dɪk] *n* medico, -a *m, f*

Medicaid ['me·dɪ·keid] *n servizio sanitario gratuito statunitense per i meno abbienti*

medical ['me·dɪ·kəl] **I.** *adj* medico, -a **II.** *n inf* visita *f* medica

medical examination *n* visita *f* medica

medical history *n* anamnesi *f inv*

medicament [mɪ·'dɪ·kə·mənt] *n* medicamento *m*

Medicare ['me·dɪ·ker] *n servizio sanitario statunitense per anziani e disabili*

medicate ['me·dɪ·keit] *vt* (*treat medically*) medicare

medicated *adj* (*soap, shampoo*) medicato, -a

medication [ˌme·dɪ·'kei·ʃən] <-(s)> *n* medicinale *m*

medicinal [mə·'dɪ·sɪ·nəl] *adj* medicinale

medicine ['me·dɪ·sən] *n* **1.** (*substance*) medicinale *m;* **to take (one's) ~** prendere le medicine **2.** (*medical knowledge*) medicina *f* **3.** (*remedy*) rimedio *m* ▶ **to give sb a** taste **of his/her own ~** ripagare qu con la stessa moneta

medicine ball *n* palla *f* medica

medicine cabinet *n,* **medicine chest** *n* armadietto *m* delle medicine

medicine man *n* <-men> stregone *m*

medieval [ˌmiː·di·'iː·vl] *adj* medievale

mediocre [ˌmiː·di·'ou·kə·] *adj* mediocre

mediocrity [ˌmiː·di·'ɑː·krə·ti] *n* **1.** (*quality*) mediocrità *f* **2.** (*person*) mediocre *mf*

meditate ['me·dɪ·teit] **I.** *vi* **1.** (*engage in contemplation*) meditare **2.** (*think deeply*) riflettere; **to ~ on sth** riflettere su qc **II.** *vt* (*plan: revenge*) meditare

meditation [ˌme·dɪ·'tei·ʃən] *n* meditazione *f*

Mediterranean [ˌme·dɪ·tə·'rein·iən] **I.** *n* (mare) Mediterraneo *m* **II.** *adj* mediterraneo, -a

Mediterranean Sea *n* mar(e) *m* Mediterraneo

medium ['miː·di·əm] **I.** *adj* **1.** (*not big or small*) medio, -a **2.** FOOD cotto, -a **II.** *n*

1. <media *o* -s> (*method*) mezzo *m;* **through the ~ of** per mezzo di **2.** COMPUT supporto *m;* **data ~** supporto (di) dati **3.** <-s> (*spiritualist*) medium *mf inv*

medium-dry *adj* semisecco, -a

medium-rare *adj* CULIN poco cotto, -a

medium-sized *adj* di taglia media

medley ['med·li] *n* **1.** (*mixture*) miscuglio *f* **2.** MUS medley *m inv*

meek [miːk] *adj* (*person*) mite; (*animal*) docile

meet [miːt] <met, met> **I.** *vt* **1.** (*encounter*) incontrare; (*intentionally*) incontrarsi con; (*for first time*) conoscere; **to arrange to ~ sb** decidere di vedersi con qu **2.** (*collect: at train station, airport*) andare a prendere **3.** (*confront: opponent*) incontrare; (*problem*) affrontare **4.** (*fulfill*) fare al caso; (*cost*) sostenere; (*demand*) soddisfare; (*obligation*) rispettare **II.** *vi* **1.** (*encounter*) incontrarsi; (*intentionally*) trovarsi; (*for first time*) conoscersi; **to arrange to ~** decidere di vedersi **2.** (*join: lines*) incontrarsi; (*rivers*) confluire **3.** SPORTS incontrarsi **III.** *n* (*sporting event*) riunione *f;* **a track ~** una riunione di atletica

♦ **meet with** *vt insep* incontrarsi con; **to ~ success** avere successo; **to meet force with force** rispondere alla forza con la forza

meeting ['miː·ʈɪŋ] *n* **1.** (*gathering*) riunione *f,* assemblea *f;* **to call a ~** indire una riunione **2.** POL riunione *f* **3.** (*casual*) incontro *m*

meeting point *n* punto *m* di incontro

megabyte ['me·gə·bait] *n* COMPUT megabyte *m inv*

megahertz ['me·gə·hɜːrts] *n* ELEC megahertz *m inv*

megalomania [ˌme·gə·lou·'mein·iə] *n* megalomania *f*

megalomaniac [ˌme·gə·lou·'mein·iæk] *n* megalomane *mf*

megaphone ['me·gə·foun] *n* megafono *m*

megastore ['me·gə·stɔːr] *n* megastore *m inv*

megawatt ['me·gə·waːt] *n* megawatt *m inv*

melancholic [ˌme·lən·'kɑː·lɪk] *adj* malinconico, -a

melancholy ['me·lən·kɑː·li] **I.** *n* malinconia *f* **II.** *adj* malinconico, -a

melee ['mei·lei] *n* **1.** (*fight*) mischia *f* **2.** (*crowd*) mischia *m*

mellow ['me·lou] **I.** *adj* <-er, -est> **1.** (*light: voice*) pastoso, -a; (*flavor*) dolce **2.** (*mature: wine*) maturo, -a **3.** (*relaxed*) rilassato, -a **II.** *vi* (*person, fruit*) maturare; (*voice, color*) addolcirsi **III.** *vt* **1.** (*wine*) fare invecchiare **2.** (*make less severe*) attenuare

melodic [mə·'lɑː·dɪk] *adj* melodico, -a

melodious [mə·'loud·iəs] *adj* melodioso, -a

melodrama ['me·lou·drɑː·mə] *n* melodramma *m*

melodramatic [ˌme·lou·drə·'mæ·ʈɪk] *adj* melodrammatico, -a

melody ['me·lə·di] <-ies> *n* melodia *f*

melon ['me·lən] *n* melone *m;* (*watermelon*) anguria *f,* cocomero *m*

melt [melt] **I.** *vt* (*metal*) fondere; (*ice, chocolate*) sciogliere **II.** *vi* **1.** (*metal*) fundersi; (*ice, chocolate*) sciogliersi **2.** *fig* intenerirsi
meltdown ['melt·daʊn] *n* fusione *f*
melting point *n* punto *m* di fusione
melting pot *n a. fig* crogiolo *m*
member ['mem·bɚ] *n* membro *mf*; (*of society, club*) socio, -a *m, f*
membership *n* **1.** (*state of belonging*) appartenenza *f*; **to apply for ~ to a club** fare domanda di iscrizione a un club; **~ dues** quote *f* sociali *pl* **2.** (*number of members*) numero *m* di membri/iscritti
membership card *n* tessera *f* (di iscrizione)
membrane ['mem·breɪn] *n* membrana *f*
memento [mə·'men·toʊ] <-s *o* -es> *n* ricordo *m*
memo ['me·moʊ] *n abbr of* **memorandum 1.** (*message*) promemoria *m inv* **2.** (*note*) nota *f*
memoir ['mem·wɑːr] *n* **1.** (*record of events*) memoria *f* **2.** *pl* (*autobiography*) memorie *fpl*
memorabilia [ˌme·mə·rə·'bɪl·iə] *npl* cimeli *mpl*
memorable ['me·mə·rə·bl] *adj* memorabile
memorandum [ˌme·mə·'ræn·dəm] <-s *o* -anda> *n form* **1.** (*message*) promemoria *m inv* **2.** (*note*) nota *f*
memorial [mə·'mɔː·ri·əl] **I.** *n* monumento *m* commemorativo **II.** *adj* commemorativo, -a
Memorial Day *n giorno della commemorazione dei caduti negli Stati Uniti*

> **i** Il **Memorial Day** viene celebrato negli USA l'ultimo lunedì di maggio. È un giorno festivo riconosciuto nella quasi totalità degli stati americani (con la sola eccezione di qualche stato del sud). In questa giornata si commemorano i caduti delle guerre americane.

memorize ['me·mə·raɪz] *vt* memorizzare
memory ['me·mə·ri] <-ies> *n* **1.** (*ability to remember*) memoria *f*; **to recite sth from ~** recitare qc a memoria; **if my ~ serves me correctly** se la memoria non mi inganna **2.** (*remembered event*) ricordo *m*; **to bring back memories** riportare alla mente ricordi **3.** COMPUT memoria *f*; **internal/external/core ~** memoria interna/esterna/a nuclei magnetici; **cache ~** memoria cache; **read only ~** memoria a sola lettura; **random access ~** memoria ad accesso casuale
memory lane *n* **to take a walk down ~** ripercorrere il viale dei ricordi
men [men] *n pl of* **man**
menace ['me·nəs] **I.** *n* **1.** (*threat*) minaccia *f* **2.** (*child*) peste *f* **II.** *vt* minacciare
menacing *adj* minaccioso, -a
menacingly *adv* minacciosamente
ménage à trois *n* <ménages à trois> ménage *m* a tre *inv*

menagerie *n* serraglio *m*
mend [mend] **I.** *n* **1.** (*repair*) riparazione *f* **2.** (*patch*) rattoppo *m* **3.** *inf* **to be on the ~** essere in via di guarigione **II.** *vt* **1.** (*repair*) riparare **2.** (*darn: socks*) rammendare **III.** *vi* (*improve*) migliorare; (*broken bone*) saldarsi
mending ['men·dɪŋ] *n* **1.** (*repair work*) riparazione *f* **2.** (*darning*) rammendo *m* **3.** (*clothes*) cose *f pl* da rammendare
menial ['miː·ni·əl] *adj* umile; **~ labor** lavoro umile
meningitis [ˌme·nɪn·'dʒaɪ·ṭɪs] *n* meningite *f*
menopause ['me·nə·pɑːz] *n* menopausa *f*
men's room ['menz·ˌruːm] *n* bagno *m* degli uomini
menstrual ['mens·trəl] *adj* mestruale
menstruate ['men·stru·eɪt] *vi* mestruare
menstruation [ˌmen·stru·'eɪ·ʃən] *n* mestruazione *f*
mental ['men·ṭəl] *adj* **1.** (*of the mind*) mentale **2.** *inf* (*crazy*) pazzo, -a
mental arithmetic *n* calcolo *m* mentale
mental hospital *n* ospedale *m* psichiatrico
mental illness *n* <-es> malattia *f* mentale
mentality [men·'tæ·lə·ti] <-ies> *n* mentalità *f*
mentally *adv* mentalmente; **~ disturbed** affetto, -a da turbe psichiche
mentally handicapped *adj* **to be ~** essere un handicappato mentale
menthol ['men·θɔːl] *n* mentolo *m*
mention ['men·ʃən] **I.** *n* menzione *f*; **to receive a** (**special**) **~** ricevere una menzione (speciale); **to make ~ of sth** accennare a qc; **honorable ~** menzione d'onore **II.** *vt* menzionare; **don't ~ it!** prego, non c'è di che; **not to ~ ...** per non parlare di ...
mentor ['men·tɚ] *n* mentore *mf*
menu ['men·juː] *n* **1.** (*list of dishes, fixed meal*) menu *m inv* **2.** COMPUT menu *m inv*; **context/pull-down ~** menu contestuale/a tendina
menu bar *n* barra *f* del menu
menu-driven *adj* COMPUT guidato, -a dal menu
mercenary ['mɜːr·sə·ne·ri] **I.** *n* <-ies> mercenario, -a *m, f* **II.** *adj* mercenario, -a
merchandise ['mɜːr·tʃən·daɪz] *n* merce *f*
merchant ['mɜːr·tʃənt] *n* commerciante *mf*
merchantman <-men> *n* mercantile *m*
merchant marine *n* marina *f* mercantile
merchant ship *n* nave *f* mercantile
merciful ['mɜːr·sɪ·fəl] *adj* misericordioso, -a
merciless ['mɜːr·sɪ·lɪs] *adj* spietato, -a
mercurial [mɜːr·'kjʊ·ri·əl] *adj* **1.** CHEM mercuriale **2.** (*changeable*) imprevedibile **3.** (*lively*) vivace, -a
mercury ['mɜːr·kjə·ri] *n* mercurio *m*
Mercury ['mɜːr·kjə·ri] *n* Mercurio *m*
mercy ['mɜːr·si] *n* **1.** (*compassion*) pietà *f*; **to have ~ on sb** avere pietà di qu **2.** (*forgiveness*) misericordia *f*; **to be at the ~ of sb** essere alla mercè di qu; **to throw oneself upon sb's ~** rimettersi alla clemenza di qu; **to plead for ~** chiedere clemenza
mere [mɪr] *adj* mero, -a, semplice; **a ~ formal-**

M

ity una mera formalità
merely ['mɪr·li] *adv* semplicemente
merge [mɜːrdʒ] **I.** *vi* unirsi; ECON, POL fondersi; **to ~ into sth** fondersi con qc **II.** *vt* unir; ECON, POL, COMPUT fondere
merger ['mɜːr·dʒɚ] *n* ECON fusione *f*
meridian [mə·'rɪ·diən] *n* meridiano *m*
meringue [mə·'ræŋ] *n* meringa *m*
merit ['me·rɪt] **I.** *n* **1.** (*virtue*) valore *m* **2.** (*advantage*) pregio *m* **3.** *pl* (*commendable quality or act*) merito *m;* **to achieve sth on one's own ~s** ottenere qc per merito proprio **II.** *vt* meritare; **this ~s another look** vale la pena di dargli un'altra occhiata
meritocracy [ˌme·rə·'tɑː·krə·si] <-ies> *n* meritocrazia *f*
mermaid ['mɜːr·meɪd] *n* sirena *f*
merriment ['me·rɪ·mənt] *n* **1.** (*laughter and joy*) allegria *f* **2.** (*amusement*) divertimento *m*
merry ['me·ri] <-ier, -iest> *adj* allegro; **Merry Christmas!** Buon Natale!
merry-go-round ['me·ri·goʊ·ˌraʊnd] *n* giostra *f*
mesh [meʃ] **I.** *n* rete *f;* (*of net*) maglia *f;* **wire ~** rete *f* metallica **II.** *vi* ingranare **III.** *vt* fare ingranare
mesmerism ['mez·mə·rɪ·zəm] *n* mesmerismo *m*
mesmerize ['mez·mə·raɪz] *vt* mesmerizzare, magnetizzare
mesmerizing [mez·'me·rɪk] *adj* magnetizzante
mess [mes] <-es> *n* **1.** (*confusion*) confusione *f;* (*disorganized state*) disordine *m;* **to be in a ~** essere sottosopra; **to make a ~ of sth** fare un pasticcio di qc; (*things*) scompigliare qc **2.** (*trouble*) guaio *m;* **this is a fine ~ you've gotten me into!** mi hai cacciato proprio in un bel guaio! **3.** (*disheveled person*) disastro *m;* **just look at him — he's a ~!** ma guarda com'è conciato! **4.** (*dining hall*) (sala) *f* mensa
◆**mess around** *vi* **1.** (*joke*) scherzare; **to ~ with sb** fare lo stupido [*o* la stupida] con qu **2.** (*waste time*) gingillarsi **3.** *sl* (*have sex*) **to ~ with sb** farsela con qu
◆**mess up** **I.** *vt inf* **1.** (*make untidy*) incasinare **2.** (*dirty*) insozzare **3.** (*screw up*) scombinare **II.** *vi* rovinare tutto, far casino *inf*
◆**mess with** *vi inf* **to ~ sb** impegolarsi con qu; **to ~ sth** interferire con qc
message ['me·sɪdʒ] *n* messaggio *m;* **error ~** COMPUT messaggio *m* di errore; **a ~ in a bottle** un messaggio nella bottiglia
messenger ['me·sɪn·dʒə] *n* messaggero, -a *m, f*
messenger boy *n* fattorino *m*
messiah [mə·'sa·ɪə] *n* messia *m inv*
mess-up ['mes·ʌp] *n inf* casino *m*
messy ['me·si] <-ier, -iest> *adj* **1.** (*untidy*) disordinato, -a **2.** (*dirty*) sporco, -a **3.** (*unpleasant*) sgradevole; **~ business** faccenda *f* complicata

Met *n* **1.** *s.* **Metropolitan Museum of Art** (in New York) Metropolitan *m* Museum of Art (a New York) **2.** *s.* **Metropolitan Opera House** (in New York) Metropolitan Opera House *f* (a New York)
met [met] *vi, vt pt of* **meet**
metabolic [ˌme·ṭə·'bɑː·lɪk] *adj* metabolico, -a
metabolism [mɪ·'tæ·bə·lɪ·zəm] *n* metabolismo *m*
metal ['me·ṭl] **I.** *n* (*element*) metallo *m* **II.** *adj* metallico, -a
metal detector *n* cercametalli *m inv*
metallic [mə·'tæ·lɪk] *adj* metallico, -a
metallurgy ['mə·ṭə·lɜːr·dʒi] *n* metallurgia *f*
metalwork ['me·ṭəl·wɜːrk] *n* lavorazione *f* dei metalli
metalworker *n* metallurgico, -a *m, f*
metamorphosis [ˌme·ṭə·'mɔːr·fə·sɪs] <-es> *n* metamorfosi *f inv*
metaphor ['me·ṭə·fɔːr] *n* metafora *f*
metaphorical [ˌme·ṭə·'fɔː·rɪ·kl] *adj* metaforico, -a
metaphysical [ˌme·ṭə·'fɪ·zɪ·kl] *adj* metafisico, -a
metaphysics [ˌme·ṭə·'fɪ·zɪks] *n* metafisica *f*
metastasis [mə·'tæ·stə·sɪs] <-ses> *n* metastasi *f inv*
mete [miːt] *vt* **to ~ out** (*punishment*) infliggere
meteor ['miː·ṭiə] *n* meteora *f*
meteoric [ˌmiː·ṭi·'ɔː·rɪk] *adj a. fig* fulmineo, -a
meteorite ['miː·ṭi·ə·raɪt] *n* meteorite *m*
meteorological [ˌmiː·ṭiə·ə·'lɑː·dʒɪ·kəl] *adj* meteorologico, -a
meteorologist [ˌmiː·ṭiə·'rɑː·lə·dʒɪst] *n* meteorologo, -a *m, f*
meteorology [ˌmiː·ṭiə·'rɑː·lə·dʒi] *n* meteorologia *f*
meter[1] ['miː·ṭə] *n* contatore *m;* (**parking**) ~ parchimetro *m;* (**taxi**) ~ tassametro *m*
meter[2] ['miː·ṭə] *n* metro *m*
methane ['meθ·eɪn] *n* metano *m*
methanol *n* metanolo *m*
method ['me·θəd] *n* metodo *m;* **there's a ~ to his madness** non è così pazzo come sembra
methodical [mə·'θɑː·dɪ·kl] *adj* metodico, -a
Methodism ['me·θə·dɪ·zəm] *n* metodismo *m*
Methodist **I.** *n* metodista *mf* **II.** *adj* metodista
methodology [ˌme·θə·'dɑː·lə·dʒi] *n* metodologia *f*
Methuselah [mə·'θuː·zə·lə] *n* Matusalemme ▶ **as old as ~** vecchio come il cucco
meticulous [mɪ·'tɪkjʊləs] *adj* meticoloso, -a
metric ['met·rɪk] *adj* metrico, -a
metrical ['met·rɪ·kl] *adj* metrico, -a
metro ['met·roʊ] *n* RAIL metro(politana) *f inv*
metronome ['met·rə·noʊm] *n* metronomo *m*
metropolis [mə·'trɑː·pə·lɪs] <-es> *n* metropoli *f*
metropolitan [ˌme·trə·'pɑː·lə·tən] *adj* metropolitano, -a
mettle ['me·ṭl] *n form* tempra *m;* **to show one's ~** dare buona prova di sé; **to be on**

one's ~ mettercela tutta
mew [mju:] I. *n* miagolio *m* II. *vi* miagolare
Mexican ['mek·sɪ·kən] I. *n* messicano, -a *m, f*
II. *adj* messicano, -a
Mexico ['mek·sɪ·koʊ] *n* Messico *m;* **New ~**
New Mexico *m*
Mexico City *n* Città *f* del Messico
Mg *abbr of* **magnesium** Mg
mg *n abbr of* **milligram** mg
MH *abbr of* **Marshall Islands** MH, *sigla auto-mobilistica internazionale delle isole Marshall*
Mhz *abbr of* **megahertz** MHz
MI *n abbr of* **Michigan** Michigan *m*
MIA *abbr of* **missing in action** *disperso in battaglia*
miaow [mi:·'aʊ] I. *n* miao *m* II. *vi* miagolare
mic [maɪk] *n inf abbr of* **microphone** microfono *m*
mica ['maɪ·kə] *n* mica *f*
mice [maɪs] *n pl of* **mouse**
mickey ['mɪ·ki] *n sl* bevanda alcolica cui è stato aggiunto furtivamente un sedativo; **to slip sb a ~** mettere furtivamente un forte sedativo nella bevanda di qu
Mickey Mouse [ˌmɪ·ki·'maʊs] *n* Topolino *m*
microbe ['maɪ·kroʊb] *n* microbo *m*
microbiology [ˌmaɪ·kroʊ·baɪ·'ɑ:·lə·dʒi] *n* microbiologia *f*
microbrewery *n* piccola fabbrica *f* di birra
microchip ['maɪ·kroʊ·ˌtʃɪp] *n* microchip *m inv*
microclimate ['maɪ·kroʊ·ˌklaɪ·mɪt] *n* microclima *m*
microcomputer ['maɪ·kroʊ·kəm·ˌpju:·tə·] *n* microcomputer *m inv*
microcosm ['maɪ·kroʊ·ˌkɑ:·zəm] *n* microcosmo *m*
microeconomics *n* microeconomia *f*
microelectronics [ˌmaɪ·kroʊ·ɪ·ˌlek·'trɑ:·nɪks] *n* microelettronica *f*
microfiche ['maɪ·kroʊ·fi:ʃ] *n* microfiche *f inv*
microfilm ['maɪ·kroʊ·fɪlm] *n* microfilm *m inv*
Micronesia [ˌmaɪ·kroʊ·'ni·ʒə] *n* Micronesia *f*
microorganism [ˌmaɪ·kroʊ·'ɔ:r·gə·nɪ·zəm] *n* microorganismo *m*
microphone ['maɪ·krə·foʊn] *n* microfono *m;* **to speak into a ~** parlare al microfono
microprocessor [ˌmaɪ·kroʊ·ˌprɑ:·se·sə·] *n* microprocessore *m*
microscope ['maɪ·krə·skoʊp] *n* microscopio *m*
microscopic [ˌmaɪ·krə·'skɑ:·pɪk] *adj* microscopico, -a
microwave ['maɪ·kroʊ·weɪv] I. *n* 1. (*wave*) microonda *f* 2. (*oven*) microonde *m inv* II. *vt* cuocere nel microonde
microwave oven *n* forno *m* a microonde
mid [mɪd] *prep* nel mezzo di
midday [ˌmɪd·'deɪ] I. *n* mezzogiorno *m;* **at ~** a mezzogiorno; **~ meal** pasto *m* di mezzogiorno II. *adj* di mezzogiorno
middle ['mɪ·dl] I. *n* 1. (*center*) centro *m;* **in the ~ of sth** in mezzo a qc; **in the ~ of the night** nel cuore della notte; **to be in the ~ of**

doing sth essere impegnato a fare qc; (**in**) **the ~ of nowhere** in capo al mondo 2. *inf* (*waist*) vita *f* II. *adj* 1. (*equidistant*) centrale 2. (*medium*) medio, -a
middle age *n* mezza età *f*
middle-aged *adj* di mezza età
Middle Ages *npl* Medioevo *m*
middle class *n* ceto *m* medio
middle-class *adj* del ceto medio
Middle East *n* Medio Oriente *m*
middleman ['mɪ·dl·mæn] <-men> *n* intermediario *m*
middle name *n* secondo nome *m*
middle-of-the-road *adj* moderato, -a
middleweight ['mɪ·dl·weɪt] *n* SPORTS peso *m* medio
middling ['mɪd·lɪŋ] I. *adj inf* 1. (*average*) discreto, -a 2. (*not very good*) mediocre II. *adv* abbastanza
Mideast *n* Medio Oriente *m*
midget ['mɪ·dʒɪt] I. *n* nano, -a *m, f* II. *adj* minuscolo, -a
midlife crisis [ˌmɪd·'laɪf 'kraɪ·sɪs] *n* crisi *f inv* della mezza età
midnight ['mɪd·naɪt] I. *n* mezzanotte *f* II. *adj* di mezzanotte
midpoint ['mɪd·pɔɪnt] *n a.* MAT punto *m* medio
midriff ['mɪd·rɪf] *n* ANAT diaframma *m*
midshipman ['mɪd·ʃɪp·mən] <-men> *n* cadetto *m* (di marina)
midst [mɪdst] *n* **in the ~ of** nel mezzo di
midsummer [ˌmɪd·'sʌ·mə·] *n* piena estate *f*
Midsummer Day *n* giorno *m* di san Giovanni Battista
midterm [ˌmɪd·'tɜːrm] I. *n* UNIV esame *m* di metà trimestre II. *adj* di metà trimestre
midway [ˌmɪd·'weɪ] I. *adv* a metà strada II. *n* viale *m* centrale di un luna park
midweek [ˌmɪd·'wi:k] *adv* a metà settimana
midwife ['mɪd·waɪf] <-wives> *n* ostetrica *f*
miffed *adj* offeso, -a; **to be ~ at sb** essere offeso per qc
might[1] [maɪt] *pt of* **may it ~ be that ...** potrebbe essere che ... +*subj*; **how old ~ she be?** quanti anni avrà?
might[2] [maɪt] *n* 1. (*power*) potere *m* 2. (*strength*) forza *f;* **military ~** forza *f* militare; **with all one's ~** con tutte le proprie forze
mightily ['maɪ·t̮ɪ·li] *adv liter* fortemente
mighty ['maɪ·t̮i] I. <-ier, -iest> *adj* 1. (*powerful*) potente 2. (*great*) imponente II. *adv inf* enormemente; **that's ~ fine, indeed** è davvero incredibilmente bello
migraine ['maɪ:·greɪn] <-(s)> *n* emicrania *f*
migrant ['maɪ·grənt] I. *n* 1. (*person*) emigrante *mf* 2. ZOOL migratore, -trice *m, f* II. *adj* migratorio, -a
migrant worker *n* lavoratore, -trice *m, f* migratore
migrate ['maɪ·greɪt] *vi* migrare
migration [maɪ·'greɪ·ʃən] <-(s)> *n* migrazione *f*
migratory ['maɪ·grə·tɔ:·ri] *adj* migratorio, -a

M

mike [maɪk] *n inf abbr of* **mic**

mild [maɪld] <-er, -est> *adj* **1.** (*climate, nature*) mite; (*criticism*) moderato, -a; (*penalty*) lieve **2.** (*not strong tasting*) delicato, -a **3.** METEO temperato, -a **4.** MED (*not serious*) leggero, -a

mildew ['mɪl·duː] *n* muffa *f*

mildly ['maɪld·li] *adv* **1.** (*gently*) dolcemente; **to punish sb** ~ punire qualcuno in modo non troppo severo **2.** (*slightly*) leggermente ▸ **to put it** ~, **that's putting it** ~ a dir poco

mildness ['maɪld·nɪs] *n* **1.** (*placidity*) mitezza *f* **2.** (*softness*) dolcezza *f*

mile [maɪl] *n* miglio *m* (*1,6093 km*); **to walk for** ~**s** (**and** ~**s**) camminare per chilometri e chilometri; **to be** ~**s away** *fig* essere distratto ▸ **to smell sth a** ~ **away** accorgersi di qc lontano un miglio

mileage ['maɪ·lɪdʒ] *n* AUTO chilometraggio *m*

milepost ['maɪl·poʊst] *n* pietra *f* miliare

milestone ['maɪl·stoʊn] *n* **1.** (*marker*) pietra *f* miliare **2.** *fig* pietra *f* miliare

militant ['mɪ·lɪ·tənt] **I.** *adj* militante **II.** *n* militante *mf*

militarism ['mɪ·lɪ·tə·ɪ·zəm] *n* militarismo *m*

militarist ['mɪ·lɪ·tə·ɪst] *n* militarista *mf*

militaristic [ˌmɪ·lɪ·tə·'rɪs·tɪk] *adj* militarista, militaristico, -a

militarize ['mɪ·lɪ·tə·raɪz] *vt* militarizzare

military ['mɪ·lɪ·te·ri] **I.** *n* **the** ~ le forze armate **II.** *adj* militare

military academy *n* accademia *f* militare

military police *n* polizia *f* militare

military service *n* servizio *m* militare

militia [mɪ·'lɪ·ʃə] *n* milizia *f*

milk [mɪlk] **I.** *n* latte *m* ▸ **there's no use crying over spilt** ~ è inutile piangere sul latte versato **II.** *vt* **1.** ZOOL **to** ~ **a cow** mungere una mucca **2.** *fig, inf* (*exploit*) **to** ~ **sb dry** dissanguare qu

milk chocolate *n* cioccolato *m* al latte

milkmaid *n* lavoratrice *f* di un caseificio

milkman <-men> *n* lattaio *m*

milkshake *n* frullato *m*

milk tooth *n* dente *m* da latte

milky ['mɪl·ki] <-ier, -iest> *adj* **1.** (*skin*) latteo, -a; (*color*) bianco latte **2.** (*tea, coffee*) con molto latte

Milky Way *n* **the** ~ la Via Lattea

mill [mɪl] **I.** *n* **1.** (*machine: for grain*) mulino *m;* (*for coffee*) macinino *m* **2.** (*factory*) fabbrica *f* **II.** *vt* **1.** (*grain, coffee*) macinare **2.** (*metal*) fresare

♦ **mill about** *vi*, **mill around** *vi* muoversi confusamente

millennium [mɪ·'len·iəm] <-s *o* -ennia> *n* millennio *m*

miller ['mɪ·lər] *n* mugnaio, -a *m, f*

millet ['mɪ·lət] *n* miglio *m*

millibar ['mɪ·lɪ·bɑːr] *n* millibar *m*

milligram ['mɪ·lɪ·græm] *n* milligrammo *m*

milliliter ['mɪ·lɪ·ˌliː·t̬ər] *n* millilitro *m*

millimeter ['mɪ·lɪ·ˌmiː·t̬ər] *n* millimetro *m*

milliner ['mɪ·lɪ·nər] *n* modista *f*

millinery ['mɪ·lɪ·ne·ri] *n* modisteria *f*

million ['mɪl·jən] <-(s)> *n* milione *m;* **two** ~ **people** due milioni di persone; **a** ~ **times** *inf* un milione di volte; **to be one in a** ~ essere unico

millionaire [ˌmɪl·ɪə·'ner] *n* milionario, -a *m, f*

millipede ['mɪl·lɪ·piːd] *n* millepiedi *m inv*

mill wheel *n* ruota *f* del mulino

milt [mɪlt] *n* (*fish sperm*) latte *m* (di pesce); (*spleen*) milza *f*

mime [maɪm] **I.** *n* THEAT pantomima *f* **II.** *vi* esprimersi a gesti **III.** *vt* mimare

mimic ['mɪ·mɪk] **I.** *vt* <-ck-> imitare **II.** *n* imitatore, -trice *m, f*

mimicry ['mɪ·mɪk·ri] *n* **1.** (*art*) mimica *f;* (*imitation*) imitazione *f* **2.** BIO mimetismo *m*

mimosa [mɪ·'moʊ·sə] *n* mimosa *f*

min. **1.** *abbr of* **minute** min **2.** *abbr of* **minimum** minimo

minaret [ˌmɪ·nə·'ret] *n* minareto *m*

mince [mɪns] **I.** *vt* **1.** (*shred*) macinare, tritare **2.** (*use tact*) **to not** ~ **words** non usare mezzi termini **II.** *vi* camminare in modo affettato **III.** *n* carne *f* tritata

mincemeat *n* **1.** (*meat*) carne *f* macinata **2.** (*fruit*) frutta secca macinata (per ripieno) *m* ▸ **to make** ~ **of sb/sth** *sl* fare a pezzi qu/qc

mince pie *n* pasticcino *m* con ripieno di frutta secca

mind [maɪnd] **I.** *n* **1.** (*brain*) mente *f;* **to be in one's right** ~ avere la testa a posto; **to be out of one's** ~ essere impazzito **2.** (*thought*) mente *f;* **to bear sth in** ~ tenere presente qc; **to bring sth to** ~ richiamare qc alla mente **3.** (*intention*) intenzione *f;* **to change one's** ~ cambiare idea; **to have sth in** ~ avere in mente qc; **to have half a** ~ **to ...** avere una mezza intenzione di ...; **to know one's own** ~ sapere quello che si vuole; **to make up one's** ~ decidersi; **to set one's** ~ **on doing sth** mettersi in testa di fare qc; **to set one's** ~ **on sth** dedicare tutto sé stesso a qc; **to set one's** ~ **at ease** tranquillizzarsi **4.** (*consciousness*) coscienza *f;* **her mother is on her** ~ è preoccupata per sua madre; **this will take your** ~ **off** (**of**) **it** così distoglierai la mente da quello **5.** (*opinion*) opinione *f;* **to be of the same** ~ essere d'accordo; **to give sb a piece of one's** ~ dirne quattro a qu; **to be in two** ~**s** essere indeciso ▸ **in my** ~**'s eye** nella mia immaginazione; **through** ~ **over matter** grazie alla forza di volontà; **to have a** ~ **like a sewer** pensare solo alle porcherie **II.** *vt* **1.** (*be careful of*) fare attenzione a; ~ **what you're doing!** (stai) attento a quello che fai!; ~ **the step!** attenzione al gradino! **2.** (*look after*) badare a; **don't** ~ **me** non preoccuparti per me **3.** (*bother*) dare fastidio a; **I don't** ~ **the cold** il freddo non mi dà fastidio; **do you** ~ **my smoking?** ti dispiace se fumo?; **would you** ~ **opening the window?** le dispiacerebbe aprire la finestra?; **I wouldn't** ~ **a beer** una birra non mi dispiacerebbe ▶ to ~ one's P͟s and Q͟s sforzarsi di essere educato III. *vi* **never ~!** non fa niente!; **I don't ~ sì,** va bene; **if you don't ~, I prefer ...** se non ti dispiace, preferisco ...; **would you ~ if ...** ti dispiacerebbe se ...?

mind-bending ['maɪnd·ben·dɪŋ] *adj* allucinante

mind-blowing *adj inf* stupefacente

mind-boggling *adj* allucinante

mindful ['maɪnd·fəl] *adj form* conscio, -a; **to be ~ of sth** essere conscio di qc

mind game *n* manovra *f* psicologica; **to play ~s** mettere in atto manovre psicologiche

mindless ['maɪnd·lɪs] *adj* 1. (*job*) meccanico, -a 2. (*violence*) gratuito, -a 3. (*heedless*) scriteriato, -a

mind reader *n* chi legge nel pensiero

mine¹ [maɪn] *pron pos* (il) mio *m*, (la) mia *f*, (i) miei *mpl*, (le) mie *fpl*; **it's not his bag, it's ~** non è la sua borsa, è la mia; **this glass is ~** questo bicchiere è mio; **these are his shoes and those are ~** queste sono le sue scarpe e queste sono le mie; **she is a friend of ~** è una mia amica

mine² [maɪn] I. *n* 1. MIN miniera *f*; **a ~ of information** *fig* una miniera di notizie 2. MIL mina *f* II. *vt* 1. MIN estrarre 2. MIL minare III. *vi* MIN estrarre; **to ~ for silver/gold** estrarre l'argento/l'oro

mine detector *n* cercamine *m inv*

minefield ['maɪn·fiːld] *n a. fig* campo *m* minato

miner ['maɪ·nə˞] *n* minatore, -trice *m, f*

mineral ['mɪ·nə·rəl] I. *n* minerale *m* II. *adj* minerale

mineralogical [ˌmɪ·nə·rə·'lɑː·dʒɪ·kl] *adj* mineralogico, -a

mineralogist [ˌmɪ·nə·'rɑː·lə·dʒɪst] *n* mineralogista *mf*

mineralogy [ˌmɪ·nə·'rɑː·lə·dʒi] *n* mineralogia *f*

mineral water *n* acqua *f* minerale

minestrone *n* minestrone *m*

minesweeper ['maɪn·ˌswiː·pə˞] *n inf* dragamine *m inv*

mingle ['mɪŋ·gl] I. *vi* mescolarsi; **to ~ with the crowd** mescolarsi tra la folla; **to ~ with the guests** socializzare con gli invitati II. *vt* mescolare

miniature ['mɪ·niə·tʃə˞] I. *adj* in miniatura II. *n* miniatura *f*

miniature golf *n* minigolf *m inv*

minibus ['mɪ·nɪ·bʌs] *n* minibus *m inv*

minimal ['mɪ·nɪ·ml] *adj* minimo, -a

minimize ['mɪ·nɪ·maɪz] *vt* minimizzare; *fig* sminuire

minimum ['mɪ·nɪ·məm] I. <-s *o* minima> *n* minimo *m;* **to reduce sth to a ~** ridurre qc al minimo II. *adj* minimo, -a; **~ requirements** requisiti indispensabili

mining ['maɪ·nɪŋ] *n* attività *f* mineraria; **copper ~** estrazione del rame

mining engineer *n* ingegnere *m* minerario

minion ['mɪn·jən] *n* tirapiedi *mf inv*

miniskirt ['mɪ·nɪ·skɜːrt] *n* minigonna *f*

minister ['mɪ·nɪ·stə˞] *n* POL, REL ministro, -a *m, f*

ministerial [ˌmɪ·nɪ·'stɪ·ri·əl] *adj* ministeriale

ministrations [ˌmɪ·nɪ·'streɪ·ʃən] *n pl, liter* attenzioni *fpl*

ministry ['mɪ·nɪs·tri] <-ies> *n* 1. REL sacerdozio *m;* **to enter the ~** (*Catholic*) diventare sacerdote; (*Protestant*) diventare ministro del culto 2. POL ministero *m*

minivan *n* monovolume *m o f inv*

mink [mɪŋk] *n* visone *m*

minor ['maɪ·nə˞] I. *adj* (*not great*) minore; (*role*) secondario, -a; (*detail*) di secondaria importanza; **~ offense** reato *m* minore; **B ~** MUS si *m* minore II. *n* 1. (*person*) minorenne *mf* 2. UNIV materia *f* complementare

Minorca [mɪ·'nɔːr·kə] *n* Minorca *f*

Minorcan I. *adj* minorchino, -a II. *n* minorchino, -ina *m, f*

minority [maɪ·'nɔː·rə·ti] I. <-ies> *n* minoranza *f;* **to be in the ~** essere in minoranza; **to be a ~ of one** essere l'unico a pensarla così II. *adj* minoritario, -a; **~ sport** sport minoritario

mint¹ [mɪnt] *n* 1. (*herb*) menta *f* 2. (*sweet*) (caramella *f* di) menta

mint² [mɪnt] I. *n* (*coin factory*) zecca *f* II. *vt* coniare III. *adj* (*coin*) fior di conio; (*stamp*) non usato; **in ~ condition** in perfette condizioni

mint julep *n* mint julep *m inv, cocktail a base di bourbon*

minuet [ˌmɪn·ju·'et] *n* minuetto *m*

minus ['maɪ·nəs] I. *prep* 1. *a.* MAT meno; **5 ~ 2 equals 3** 5 meno 2 fa 3; **~ ten degrees Celsius** dieci gradi sotto zero 2. *inf* (*without*) senza II. *adj* MATH negativo, -a; **~ figures** numeri negativi III. *n* 1. MATH segno *m* meno 2. (*negative amount*) quantità *f* negativa

minuscule ['mɪ·nɪs·kju:l] *adj* minuscolo, -a

minute¹ ['mɪ·nɪt] *n* 1. (*sixty seconds*) minuto *m* 2. (*moment*) momento *m*, attimo *m;* **any ~** da un momento all'altro; **at the last ~** all'ultimo momento [*o* minuto]; **in a ~** tra un attimo; **this very ~** in questo istante; **to the ~** precisamente; **wait a ~** aspetta un attimo [*o* momento] 3. *pl* (*of meeting*) verbale *m*

minute² [maɪ·'nu:t] *adj* minuto, -a

minute hand *n* lancetta *f* dei minuti

minutely *adv* minuziosamente

minuteman *n durante la rivoluzione americana, volontario pronto a prestare immediato servizio militare*

minutiae [mɪ·'nu:·ʃɪ·i:] *npl* minuzie *fpl*

miracle ['mɪ·rə·kl] *n* miracolo *m;* **by a ~** per miracolo

miracle drug *n* farmaco *m* miracolo

miraculous [mɪ·'ræk·jə·ləs] *adj* miracoloso, -a

mirage [mə·'rɑːʒ] *n* miraggio *m*

mire [maɪr] I. *vt* **to become ~d in sth** impantanarsi in qc II. *n* 1. (*swamp*) pantano *m* 2. *fig* pasticcio *m*

M

mirror ['mɪ·rə·] I. *n* specchio *m* II. *vt* riflettere

mirror image *n* immagine *f* speculare

mirth [mɜːrθ] *n* ilarità *f*

mirthful ['mɜːrθ·fəl] *adj* giulivo, -a

mirthless ['mɜːrθ·ləs] *adj* 1. (*joyless*) triste 2. (*unhappy*) infelice

misadventure [ˌmɪs·əd·'vent·ʃə·] *n* disavventura *f*

misalliance [ˌmɪs·ə·'la·rəns] *n* 1. (*alliance*) unione *f* sbagliata 2. (*marriage*) mésalliance *f inv*

misanthrope ['mɪ·sn·θroʊp] *n* misantropo, -a *m, f*

misanthropic [ˌmɪ·sən·'θrɑː·pɪk] *adj* misantropico, -a

misanthropy [mɪs·'æn·θrə·pi] *n* misantropia *f*

misapply [ˌmɪs·ə·'plaɪ] <-ie-> *vt* to ~ sth fare un uso improprio di qc

misapprehend [ˌmɪs·æ·prɪ·'hend] *vt* fraintendere

misapprehension [ˌmɪs·æprɪ·'hen·ʃən] *n* fraintendimento *m*, malinteso *m;* to be under a ~ cadere in un equivoco

misappropriate [ˌmɪs·ə·'proʊ·pri·eɪt] *vt* FIN malversare

misappropriation [ˌmɪs·ə·ˌproʊ·prɪ·'eɪ·ʃən] *n* FIN malversazione *f*

misbehave [ˌmɪs·bɪ·'heɪv] *vi* comportarsi male

misbehavior [ˌmɪs·bɪ·'heɪv·jə·] *n* cattiva condotta *f*

misc. *adj abbr of* **miscellaneous** miscellaneo, -a

miscalculate [ˌmɪs·'kæl·kjə·leɪt] *vt, vi* calcolare male

miscalculation [ˌmɪs·ˌkæl·kjə·'leɪ·ʃən] *n* errore *m* di calcolo

miscarriage ['mɪs·ˌke·rɪdʒ] *n* 1. MED aborto *m* spontaneo 2. *form* (*failure*) fallimento *m;* a ~ of justice un errore giudiziario

miscarry ['mɪs·ˌke·ri] <-ied, -ying> *vi* 1. MED abortire spontaneamente 2. *fig* fallire

miscellaneous [ˌmɪ·sə·'leɪ·ni·əs] *adj* miscellaneo, -a, di vario genere; ~ expenses spese varie

miscellany ['mɪ·sə·leɪ·ni] <-ies> *n* miscellanea *f*

mischance [ˌmɪs·'tʃæns] *n* (*bad luck*) sfortuna *f;* (*unlucky event*) disavventura *f;* by some ~ per sfortuna

mischief ['mɪs·tʃɪf] *n* 1. (*naughtiness*) birichinata *f;* to keep sb out of ~ distogliere qu dal fare marachelle 2. to get (oneself) into ~ cacciarsi nei guai; to make ~ for sb amareggiare l'esistenza a qu 3. (*wickedness*) malizia *f*

mischievous ['mɪs·tʃə·vəs] *adj* 1. (*naughty*) birichino, -a 2. (*malicious*) maligno, -a; ~ rumors pettegolezzi *m pl* malevoli

misconceive [ˌmɪs·kən·'siːv] *vt form* fraintendere

misconceived *adj* progettato, -a male

misconception [ˌmɪs·kən·'sep·ʃən] *n* idea *f* sbagliata; a popular ~ un'errata credenza popolare

misconduct [ˌmɪs·'kɑːn·dʌkt] I. *n* 1. (*misbehavior*) cattiva condotta *f* 2. (*mismanage*) cattiva gestione *f* II. *vt* 1. (*behave badly*) to ~ oneself comportarsi male 2. (*organize badly*) gestire male

misconstruction [ˌmɪs·kən·'strʌk·ʃən] *n form* fraintendimento *m*

misconstrue [ˌmɪs·kən·'struː] *vt* fraintendere

misdeed [ˌmɪs·'diːd] *n form* misfatto *m*

misdemeanor [ˌmɪs·dɪ·'miː·nə·] *n* 1. LAW infrazione *f* 2. (*bad behavior*) cattiva condotta *f*

misdirect [ˌmɪs·də·'rekt] *vt* 1. (*letter*) indirizzare erroneamente; (*person*) dare indicazioni sbagliate a 2. LAW dare istruzioni sbagliate a

miser ['maɪ·zə·] *n* avaro, -a *m, f*

miserable ['mɪz·rə·bl] *adj* 1. (*unhappy*) infelice; to make life ~ for sb rendere la vita un inferno a qu 2. (*unpleasant*) deprimente 3. (*inadequate*) miserabile; a ~ amount una miseria

miserably *adv* 1. (*unhappily*) tristemente 2. (*completely*) to fail ~ fallire miseramente

miserly *adj* taccagno, -a

misery ['mɪ·zə·ri] *n* 1. (*unhappiness*) infelicità *f* 2. (*suffering*) sofferenza *f;* to make sb's life a ~ rendere la vita un inferno a qu 3. (*extreme poverty*) miseria *f;* to be born into ~ essere nato poverissimo

misfire [ˌmɪs·'fa·ɪə·] *vi* 1. (*weapon*) fare cilecca 2. *fig* (*joke*) andare a vuoto 3. (*engine*) perdere colpi

misfit ['mɪs·fɪt] *n* disadattato, -a *m, f*

misfortune [ˌmɪs·'fɔːr·tʃən] *n* sventura *m;* to suffer ~ subire una disgrazia

misgiving [ˌmɪs·'gɪ·vɪŋ] *n* preoccupazione *f*, timore *m;* to have ~s about sth avere dubbi su qc; to be filled with ~s essere pieno di dubbi

misgovern [mɪs·'gʌ·və·n] *vt* (*country*) governare male; (*business*) gestire male

misgovernment *n* (*of country*) malgoverno *m;* (*of company*) cattiva gestione *f*

misguided [mɪs·'gaɪ·dɪd] *adj* incauto, -a; ~ idea idea fuorviante

mishandle [ˌmis·'hæn·dl] *vt* 1. (*handle without care*) maneggiare sbadatamente 2. (*maltreat*) maltrattare 3. (*deal badly with*) trattare senza le dovute attenzioni

mishap ['mɪs·hæp] *n form* incidente *m;* a series of ~s una serie di incidenti

mishear [ˌmɪs·'hɪr] *vt irr* udire male

mishmash ['mɪʃ·mæʃ] *n* accozzaglia *f;* a ~ of sth un'accozzaglia di qc

misinform [ˌmɪs·ɪn·'fɔːrm] *vt* informare male, disinformare

misinformation *n* disinformazione *f*

misinterpret [ˌmɪs·ɪn·'tɜːr·prɪt] *vt* interpretare male

misinterpretation [ˌmɪs·ɪn·ˌtɜːr·prɪ·'teɪ·ʃən] *n* interpretazione *f* sbagliata

misjudge [ˌmɪs·'dʒʌdʒ] *vt* giudicare male

misjudgment [mɪs·'dʒʌdʒ·mənt] *n* giudizio *m* errato

mislay [ˌmɪsˈleɪ] *vt irr, form* fuorviare
mislead [ˌmɪsˈliːd] *vt irr* **1.** (*deceive*) ingannare; **to ~ sb about sth** ingannare qu su qc; **to ~ sb into doing sth** indurre con l'inganno qu a fare qc **2.** (*lead into error*) indurre in errore; **to let oneself be misled** farsi fuorviare **3.** (*corrupt*) corrompere
misleading *adj* fuorviante
mismanage [ˌmɪsˈmæ·nɪdʒ] *vt* amministrare [*o* gestire] male; **to ~ a business** amministrare [*o* gestire] male un'azienda
mismanagement *n* cattiva amministrazione [*o* gestione] *f*
misname [ˌmɪsˈneɪm] *vt* **to ~ sth** chiamare qc con il nome sbagliato
misnomer [ˌmɪsˈnoʊ·mə·] *n* nome *m* sbagliato
misogynist [mɪˈsɑː·dʒə·nɪst] I. *n* misogino *m* II. *adj* misogino, -a
misogynistic *adj* misogino, -a
misplace [ˌmɪsˈpleɪs] *vt* **1.** (*lose*) mettere fuori posto **2.** *fig* (*confidence*) riporre male
misprint [ˈmɪs·ˌprɪnt] *n* errore *m* di stampa
mispronounce [ˌmɪs·prə·ˈnaʊns] *vt* pronunciare male
mispronunciation [ˌmɪs·prə·ˌnʌn·sɪ·ˈeɪ·ʃən] *n* pronuncia *f* errata
misread [ˌmɪsˈriːd] *vt irr* **1.** (*read badly*) leggere male **2.** (*interpret badly*) interpretare male
misrepresent [ˌmɪs·ˌre·prɪˈzent] *vt* falsare
misrepresentation [ˌmɪs·ˌre·prɪ·zen·ˈteɪ·ʃən] *n* dichiarazione *f* falsa
miss¹ [mɪs] *n* (*form of adress*) signorina *f;* **Miss America** miss America
miss² [mɪs] I. <-es> *n* colpo *m* mancato II. *vi* **1.** fallire III. *vt* **1.** (*not hit*) mancare **2.** (*not catch*) perdere; **to ~ the bus/train** perdere il bus/il treno; **to ~ a deadline** non rispettare una scadenza **3.** (*avoid*) evitare **4.** (*not notice*) non accorgersi di; **to ~ sb** non incontrare qu; **you didn't ~ much** non hai perso molto; **you can't ~ it** non puoi perderlo **5.** (*not hear*) non sentire **6.** (*overlook*) saltare; **to ~ a meeting** saltare una riunione **7.** (*not take advantage*) perdere; **to ~ an opportunity** perdere un'occasione **8.** (*regret absence*) sentire la mancanza di; **we ~ you** ci manchi **9.** (*notice loss*) accorgersi della mancanza di
◆**miss out** *vi* essere svantaggiato
◆**miss out on** *vt* **to ~ sth** lasciarsi sfuggire qc
misshapen [ˌmɪsˈʃeɪ·pən] *adj* (*malformed: limb*) deforme
missile [ˈmɪ·səl] *n* (*rocket*) missile *m;* (*projectile*) proiettile *m*
missile base *n* base *f* missilistica
missile defense system *n* sistema *m* missilistico di difesa
missile launcher *n* lanciamissili *m inv*
missing [ˈmɪ·sɪŋ] *adj* **1.** (*lost: person*) scomparso, -a; (*thing or object*) introvabile; **~ in action** disperso, -a; **to report sth ~** denunciare la perdita di qc **2.** (*absent*) assente

missing link *n* anello *m* mancante
missing person *n* scomparso, -a *m, f*
mission [ˈmɪ·ʃən] *n* **1.** *a.* REL (*task*) missione *f;* **peace ~** missione di pace; **rescue ~** operazione *f* di salvataggio; **his ~ in life** la sua missione (nella vita); **~ accomplished** missione compiuta **2.** (*space project*) missione *f* spaziale **3.** POL missione *f* **4.** (*building*) missione
missionary [ˈmɪ·ʃə·ne·ri] I. <-ies> *n* missionario, -a *m, f* II. *adj* missionario, -a
missionary position *n iron* posizione *f* del missionario
mission control *n* sala *f* di controllo
missis [ˈmɪ·sɪz] *n inf s.* **missus**

> **i** Il **Mississipi River** o Mississippi in italiano, è la terza via fluviale del mondo dopo il Rio delle Amazzoni e il Congo. Dalla sua sorgente, nel lago Itasca/Minnesota alla sua foce, nel Golfo del Messico nei pressi di New Orleans/Louisiana, percorre 2.320 miglia (3.733 km). Scorre su 1.245.000 miglia quadrate (3.225.000 km²) di terra, attraversa 31 stati e due province canadesi. Una goccia di pioggia caduta nel lago Itasca impiegherà tre mesi per raggiungere il Golfo del Messico.

misspell [ˌmɪsˈspel] *vt irr* scrivere scorrettamente
misspelling *n* errore *m* di ortografia
misspent [ˌmɪsˈspent] *adj* sprecato, -a; **a ~ youth** una gioventù dissipata
misstate [ˌmɪsˈsteɪt] *vt* esporre in modo inesatto
missus [ˈmɪ·sɪz] *n inf* (*wife*) moglie *f*
mist [mɪst] *n* **1.** (*light fog*) foschia *f;* **to be shrouded in ~** essere avvolto nella foschia **2.** (*condensation*) condensa *f*
◆**mist up** *vi* appannarsi
mistakable [mɪˈsteɪ·kə·bl] *adj* confondibile
mistake [mɪˈsteɪk] I. *n* errore *m,* sbaglio *m;* **typing ~** errore *m* di battitura; **to learn from one's ~s** trarre esperienza dai propri errori; **to make a ~** commmettere [*o* fare] un errore; **make no ~ about it** puoi scommetterci!; **to repeat past ~s** rifare gli stessi errori [*o* sbagli]; **there must be some ~** ci dev'essere un errore [*o* sbaglio]; **by ~** per sbaglio [*o* errore] II. *vt irr* confondere
mistaken [mɪˈsteɪ·kən] I. *pp of* **mistake** II. *adj* (*belief*) errato, -a; **~ identity** errore di persona; **to be** (**very much**) **~** sbagliarsi (di grosso); **unless I'm very much ~ ...** a meno che non mi sbagli di grosso ...
Mister [ˈmɪ·stə·] *n* signore *m*
mistime [ˌmɪsˈtaɪm] *vt* fare [*o* dire] nel momento sbagliato
mistletoe [ˈmɪ·sl·toʊ] *n* vischio *m*
mistook [mɪsˈtʊk] *pt of* **mistake**
mistranslate [ˌmɪsˈtrænz·leɪt] *vt* tradurre in

M

modo errato

mistreat [ˌmɪs·ˈtriːt] *vt* maltrattare

mistress [ˈmɪs·trɪs] *n* **1.** (*sexual partner*) amante *f* **2.** (*owner, woman in charge*) padrona *f;* **the ~ of the house** la padrona di casa

mistrial [ˈmɪs·ˌtra·ɪəl] *n* procedimento *m* giudiziario nullo

mistrust [ˌmɪs·ˈtrʌst] **I.** *n* sfiducia *f,* diffidenza *f;* **to have a ~ of sb** provare diffidenza verso qu; **to have a ~ of sth** non avere fiducia in qc **II.** *vt* **to ~ sb** diffidare di qu; **to ~ sth** non fidarsi di qc

mistrustful [ˌmɪs·ˈtrʌst·fəl] *adj* diffidente; **to be ~ of sb/sth** essere diffidente di qu/qc

misty [ˈmɪs·ti] <-ier, -iest> *adj* **1.** (*foggy*) brumoso, -a; (*window, glasses*) appannato, -a **2.** *fig* indistinto, -a

misunderstand [ˌmɪs·ˌʌn·dɚ·ˈstænd] *vt irr* capire male

misunderstanding *n* **1.** (*failure to understand*) equivoco *m;* **there must be some ~** ci dev'essere un equivoco **2.** (*disagreement*) malinteso *m*

misuse[1] [ˌmɪs·ˈjuːs] *n* **1.** (*wrong use*) cattivo uso *m* **2.** (*excessive consumption*) abuso *m*

misuse[2] [ˌmɪs·ˈjuːz] *vt* **1.** (*handle wrongly*) trattare male **2.** (*consume to excess*) abusare di

mite[1] [maɪt] *n* (*insect*) acaro *m*

mite[2] [maɪt] *n* (*small amount*) briciolo *m*

miter [ˈmaɪ·t̬ɚ] *n* mitr(i)a *f*

mitigate [ˈmɪ·t̬ɪ·geɪt] *vt form* mitigare

mitigation [ˌmɪ·t̬ɪ·ˈgeɪ·ʃən] *n* attenuazione *f;* **in ~** come attenuante

mitten [ˈmɪ·tn] *n* muffola *f,* manopola *f*

mix [mɪks] **I.** *n* misto *m,* mistura *f;* **a cake ~** un preparato per torte; **a ~ of people** un insieme di persone **II.** *vt* **1.** CULIN mischiare; (*ingredients*) mescolare; (*cocktails*) preparare **2.** (*combine*) unire; **to ~ business with pleasure** unire il lavoro al piacere; **religion and politics don't ~** religione e politica non vanno d'accordo **III.** *vi* **1.** (*combine*) unirsi **2.** (*socially*) **to ~ with sb** socializzare con qu; **to ~ well** legare bene con gli altri

◆**mix in I.** *vi* convivere **II.** *vt* **to mix sth in with sth** incorporare qc a qc

◆**mix up** *vt* **1.** (*confuse*) confondere **2.** (*put in wrong order*) mettere in disordine **3.** CULIN mescolare ▶**to mix it up with sb** *sl* attaccar briga con qu

◆**mix up in** *vt* **to be mixed up in sth** essere invischiato in qc

◆**mix up with** *vt* **to mix up sth with sth** incorporare qc a qc; **to be mixed up with sth** essere invischiato in qc

mixed *adj* **1.** (*containing various elements*) misto, -a; **~ marriage** matrimonio misto; **person of ~ race** meticcio, -a *m, f* **2.** (*contradictory*) contraddittorio, -a; **~ emotions** sentimenti contrastanti; **to be a ~ blessing** essere una benedizione ma anche una maledizione

mixed doubles *npl* SPORTS doppio *m sing* misto

mixed message *n* messaggio contraddittorio; **to send ~s** mandare messaggi poco chiari

mixer [ˈmɪk·sɚ] *n* **1.** (*machine*) CULIN frullatore **2.** (*drink*) *bevanda analcolica per diluire alcolici o preparare cocktail*

mixture [ˈmɪks·tʃɚ] *n* miscuglio *m*

mix-up [ˈmɪks·ʌp] *n* pasticcio *m*

ml *n abbr of* **milliliter** ml

mm *abbr of* **millimeter** mm

MN *n abbr of* **Minnesota** Minnesota *m*

mnemonic [nɪ·ˈmɑː·nɪk] *adj* mnemonico, -a

mo. [moʊ] *n abbr of* **month** mese *m*

MO *n* **1.** *abbr of* **modus operandi** modus operandi *m* **2.** *abbr of* **Missouri** Missouri *m* **3.** *abbr of* **money order** vaglia *m inv*

moan [moʊn] **I.** *n* **1.** (*sound*) gemito *m* **2.** (*complaint*) lamentela *f* **II.** *vi* **1.** (*make a sound*) gemere; **to ~ with pain** gemere per il dolore **2.** (*complain*) lamentarsi; **to ~ about sth** lamentarsi di qc; **to ~ that ...** lamentarsi che ...

moat [moʊt] *n* fossato *m*

mob [mɑːb] **I.** *n + sing/pl vb* **1.** (*crowd*) folla *f;* **angry ~** turba *f* inferocita **2.** *inf* **the Mob** la mafia **II.** <-bb-> *vt* accalcarsi intorno a; **he was ~bed by his fans** i suoi fan gli si sono affollati intorno

mobile [ˈmoʊ·bəl] **I.** *n* **1.** (*work of art*) mobile *m inv* **2.** TEL cellulare *m,* telefonino *m* **II.** *adj* **1.** (*able to move*) in grado di muoversi; (*shop, canteen*) ambulante; **to be ~** *inf* disporre di un mezzo di trasporto **2.** (*movable*) mobile

mobile home *n* casa *f* mobile

mobility [moʊ·ˈbɪ·lə·ti] *n* mobilità *f;* **social ~** mobilità sociale

mobilization [ˌməʊ·bə·lɪ·ˈzeɪ·ʃən] *n a.* MIL mobilizzazione *f*

mobilize [ˈməʊ·bə·laɪz] *vt* mobilizzare

mobster *n* gangster *mf inv*

moccasin [ˈmɑː·kə·sən] *n* moccassino *m*

mocha [ˈmoʊ·kə] *n* (caffè) *m* moca; **~ ice cream** gelato *m* al caffè

mock [mɑːk] **I.** *adj* **1.** (*imitation*) finto, -a; **~ baroque** che imita lo stile barocco **2.** (*fake*) finto, -a; **~ battle** battaglia simulata; **~ approval/disapproval** falsa approvazione/disapprovazione *m* **II.** *vi* prendersi gioco; **to ~ at sb** prendersi gioco di qu **III.** *vt* **1.** (*ridicule*) canzonare **2.** (*imitate*) parodiare

mockery [ˈmɑː·kɚ·i] *n* **1.** (*ridicule*) derisione *f* **2.** (*subject of derision*) zimbello *m;* **to make a ~ of sb/sth** mettere in ridicolo qu/qc **3.** (*ridiculous imitation*) parodia *f*

mocking *n* burla *f*

mockingbird [ˈmɑː·kɪŋ·ˌbɜːrd] *n* mimo *m*

mock-up [ˈmɑːk·ʌp] *n* modello *m* in scala

modal [ˈmoʊ·dəl] *adj* modale

modal verb *n* verbo *m* servile

mode [moʊd] *n* **1.** *a.* LING, PHILOS (*manner*) modo *m;* **~ of transportation** mezzo *m* di trasporto; **~ of travel** mezzo *m* di trasporto;

~ of operation modo di funzionamento; **~ of expression** modo di esprimersi **2.** *form* (*fashion*) moda *f;* **to be all the ~** essere di gran moda; **in ~** di moda

model ['mɑː·dəl] **I.** *n* (*version, example*) *a.* ART modello *m;* (*of car*) modellino *f;* **to be the very ~ of sth** essere un autentico esempio di **II.** *adj* esemplare; **a ~ student** uno studente modello **III.** <-ll-> *vt* **1.** (*make figure, representation*) modellare; **to ~ sth in clay** modellare qc in creta **2.** (*show clothes*) sfilare **3. to ~ oneself on sb** prendere qu a modello **IV.** *vi* fare l'indossatore, -trice

modem ['moʊ·dəm] *n* COMPUT modem *m inv*

moderate¹ ['mɑː·də·ət] **I.** *adj* **1.** (*neither large nor small*) medio, -a **2.** *a.* POL (*not extreme: speed*) moderato, -a; (*increase, means*) modesto, -a; (*price*) modico, -a **II.** *n* POL moderato, -a *m, f*

moderate² ['mɑː·də·reɪt] **I.** *vt* moderare; **to ~ a debate** moderare un dibattito; **to ~ a meeting** presiedere una riunione **II.** *vi* **1.** (*act as moderator*) moderare **2.** (*become less extreme*) moderarsi

moderation [ˌmɑː·də·'reɪ·ʃən] *n* moderazione *f;* **to drink in ~** non eccedere nel bere

moderator ['mɑː·də·eɪ·tə] *n form* **1.** (*mediator*) mediatore, -trice *m, f* **2.** (*of discussion*) moderatore, -trice *m, f*

modern ['mɑː·dən] *adj* moderno, -a

modernization [ˌmɑː·də·nɪ·'zeɪ·ʃən] *n* modernizzazione *f*

modernize ['mɑː·də·naɪz] *vt* modernizzare

modest ['mɑː·dɪst] *adj* **1.** (*not boastful*) modesto, -a; **to be ~ about sth** non vantarsi di qc **2.** (*moderate*) moderato, -a; **a ~ wage increase** un modesto aumento di stipendio

modesty ['mɑː·dɪs·ti] *n* modestia *f*

modicum ['mɑː·dɪ·kəm] *n* briciolo *m;* **a ~ of truth** un briciolo di verità

modifiable ['mɑː·dɪ·fa·ɪə·bl] *adj* modificable

modification [ˌmɑː·dɪ·fɪ·'keɪ·ʃən] *n* modifica *f*

modifier ['mɑː·dɪ·fa·ɪə] *n* LING modificatore *m*

modify ['mɑː·dɪ·faɪ] <-ie-> *vt a.* LING modificare

modular ['mɑː·d·ʒə·lə] *adj* modulare

modulate ['mɑː·d·ʒə·leɪt] *vt a.* ELEC, RADIO, TV modulare

modulation [ˌmɑː·d·ʒə·'leɪ·ʃən] *n* modulazione *f*

module ['mɑː·d·ʒuːl] *n* modulo *m*

mohair ['moʊ·her] *n* mohair *m inv*

moist [mɔɪst] *adj* umido, -a

moisten ['mɔɪ·sn] **I.** *vt* inumidire **II.** *vi* inumidirsi

moisture ['mɔɪs·tʃə] *n* umidità *f*

moisturize ['mɔɪs·tʃə·raɪz] *vt* idratare

moisturizer *n* idratante *m*

molar¹ ['moʊ·lə] *n* molare *m*

molar² ['moʊ·lə] *adj* CHEM molare

molasses [moʊ·'læ·sɪz] *n* melassa *f*

mold¹ [moʊld] **I.** *n* (*for metal, clay, jelly*) stampo *m* ► **to be cast in the** same **~** essere

dello stesso stampo **II.** *vt* modellare

mold² [moʊld] *n* BOT muffa *f*

Moldavia [mɑːl·'deɪ·viə] *n s.* **Moldova**

Moldavian I. *adj* moldavo, -a **II.** *n* **1.** (*person*) moldavo, -a *m, f* **2.** LING moldavo *m*

molder ['moʊl·də] *vi* sgretolarsi; *fig* disgregarsi

molding ['moʊl·dɪŋ] *n* ARCHIT modanatura *f*

Moldova [mɑːl·'doʊ·və] *n* Moldavia *f*

Moldovan I. *adj* moldavo, -a **II.** *n* moldavo, -a *m, f*

moldy ['moʊl·di] <-ier, -iest> *adj a.* CULIN ammuffito, -a

mole¹ [moʊl] *n* ANAT neo *m*

mole² [moʊl] *n* **1.** ZOOL talpa *f* **2.** (*spy*) spia *mf*

mole³ [moʊl] *n* CHEM, PHYS mole *f*

molecular [mə·'lek·jə·lə] *adj* molecolare

molecule ['mɑː·lɪ·kjuːl] *n* molecola *f*

molehill ['moʊl·hɪl] *n* monticello *m* di terra accumulato da una talpa

molest [mə·'lest] *vt* **1.** (*pester*) importunare **2.** (*sexually*) abusare (sessualmente) di

moll [mɑːl] *n inf* pupa *f* di un gangster

mollify ['mɑː·lə·faɪ] <-ie-> *vt* **1.** (*pacify*) ammansire **2.** (*reduce effect*) placare

mollusc, mollusk ['mɑː·ləsk] *n* mollusco *m*

mollycoddle ['mɑː·lɪ·kɑː·dl] *vt inf* tenere nella bambagia

Molotov cocktail [ˌmɑː·lə·tɔːf 'kɑːk·teɪl] *n* molotov *f inv*

molt [moʊlt] ZOOL **I.** *vi* (*lose feathers*) fare la muda; (*lose hair*) fare la muta **II.** *vt* (*lose feathers*) perdere le penne (durante la muda); (*lose hair*) perdere il pelo (durante la muta) **III.** *n* (*of feathers*) muda *f;* (*of hair*) muta *f*

molten ['moʊl·tən] *adj* fuso, -a

mom [mɑːm] *n inf* mamma *f*

moment ['moʊ·mənt] *n* momento *m;* **at the ~** per il momento; **at any ~** da un momento all'altro; **at the last ~** all'ultimo momento; **in a ~** tra un momento, a momenti; **not to believe for a ~** non crederci affatto; **the ~ that ...** (non) appena ...; **the ~ of truth** il momento della verità; **at the** (**precise**) **~ when ...** nel (preciso) istante in cui ...; **to choose one's ~** scegliere il momento giusto; **to leave sth until the last ~** aspettare a fare qc all'ultimo momento

momentarily [ˌmoʊ·mən·'ter·li] *adv* **1.** (*very briefly*) momentaneamente **2.** (*very soon*) tra un momento

momentary ['moʊ·mən·te·ri] *adj* momentaneo, -a

momentous [moʊ·'men·təs] *adj* (*fact*) molto importante; (*day*) memorabile

momentum [moʊ·'men·təm] *n* PHYS momento *m; fig* impeto *m;* **to gather ~** acquistare velocità

momma ['mɑː·mə] *n,* **mommy** ['mɑː·mi] *n inf* mamma *f*

Monacan ['mɑː·nə·kən] **I.** *adj* monegasco, -a **II.** *n* monegasco, -a *m, f*

Monaco ['mɑː·nə·koʊ] *n* Monaco *m*

monarch ['mɑː·nək] *n* monarca *mf*

M

monarchic(al) [mə·'nɑː·kɪ·k(l)] *adj* monarchico, -a

monarchism ['mɑː·nə·kɪ·zəm] *n* monarchismo *m*

monarchist ['mɑː·nə·kɪst] *n* monarchista *mf*

monarchy ['mɑː·nə·ki] <-ies> *n* monarchia *f*

monastery ['mɑː·nəs·te·ri] <-ies> *n* monastero *m*

monastic [mə·'næs·tɪk] *adj* 1. REL monastico, -a 2. (*ascetic*) monacale

Monday ['mʌn·di] *n* lunedì *m inv;* **Easter** [*o* Whit] ~ lunedì dell'Angelo, lunedì di Pasqua; *s.a.* **Friday**

Monegasque [mɑː·nə·'gask] I. *adj* monegasco, -a II. *n* monegasco, -a *m, f*

monetary ['mɑː·nə·te·ri] *adj* monetario, -a

monetary fund *n* fondo *m* monetario

monetary policy *n* politica *f* monetaria

Monetary Union *n* unione *f* monetaria

money ['mʌ·ni] *n* denaro *m,* soldi *mpl;* **to be short of** ~ essere a corto di soldi; **to change** ~ cambiare i soldi; **to make** ~ fare soldi; **to raise** ~ raccogliere fondi; **to throw** ~ **at sth** sperperare denaro in qc ▶ ~ **is the root of all evil** *prov* il denaro è la radice di tutti i mali; **put your** ~ **where your mouth is** dimostralo a fatti, non solo a parole; ~ **doesn't grow on trees** *prov* i soldi non piovono dal cielo *prov;* **to be made of** ~ nuotare nell'oro; **he has** ~ **to burn** ha soldi da buttar via; **she married into** ~ si è sposata con uno ricco; ~ **talks** *prov* il denaro apre tutte le porte *prov;* **to be in the** ~ avere soldi a palate; **for my** ~ secondo me

moneybags ['mʌ·ni·bægz] *npl inf* riccone, -ona *m, f*

moneychanger *n* cambiavalute *mf*

moneyed *adj form* benestante

moneymaker *n* miniera *f* d'oro *fig*

moneymaking I. *adj* lucrativo, -a II. *n* lucro *m*

money market *n* mercato *m* monetario

money order *n* vaglia *m inv*

Mongol ['mɑː·ŋ·gəl] I. *adj* mongolo, -a II. *n* 1. (*person*) mongolo, -a *m, f* 2. LING mongolo *m*

Mongolia [mɑː·ŋ·'gou·liə] *n* Mongolia *f*

Mongolian [mɑː·ŋ·'goul·iən] I. *adj* mongolo, -a, mongolico, -a II. *n* 1. (*person*) mongolo, -a *m, f* 2. LING mongolo *m*

mongolism ['mɑː·ŋ·gə·lɪ·zəm] *n* mongolismo *m*

mongrel ['mɑː·ŋ·grəl] *n, n* bastardo, -a *m*

monitor ['mɑː·nɪ·tə·] I. *n* 1. COMPUT monitor *m inv;* **15-inch** ~ monitor da 15 pollici 2. (*person*) osservatore, -trice *m, f* II. *vt* monitorare; **to** ~ **sb/sth closely** controllare da vicino qu/qc

monk [mʌŋk] *n* monaco *m*

monkey ['mʌŋ·ki] *n* scimmia *f* ▶ **to have a** ~ **on your back** (*desire for drugs*) avere la scimmia; (*a big problem*) avere un problema
    ◆ **monkey around** *vi inf* giocherellare

monkey bars *n pl* struttura *f* per arrampicarsi, per bambini

monkey business *n* 1. (*improper conduct*) intrallazzi *mpl* 2. (*mischief*) birichinate *fpl*

monkey wrench *n* <-es> chiave *f* inglese

mono¹ ['mɑː·nou] I. *n* mono(fonia) *f* II. *adj* mono(fonico, -a)

mono² ['mɑː·nou] *n inf* MED *abbr of* (**infectious**) **mononucleosis** mononucleosi *f* (infettiva) *inv*

monochrome ['mɑː·nou·kroum] *adj* monocromo, -a

monocle ['mɑː·nə·kl] *n* monocolo *m*

monogamous [mə·'nɑː·gə·məs] *adj* monogamo, -a

monogamy [mə·'nɑː·gə·mi] *n* monogamia *f*

monogram ['mɑː·nə·græm] *n* monogramma *m*

monolingual [ˌmɑː·nou·'lɪŋ·gwəl] *adj* monolingue

monolith ['mɑː·nə·lɪθ] *n* monolito *m*

monolithic [ˌmɑː·nə·'lɪ·θɪk] *adj* monolitico, -a

monolog *n,* **monologue** ['mɑː·nə·la:g] *n* monologo *m*

monopolize [mə·'nɑː·pə·laɪz] *vt* monopolizzare

monopoly [mə·'nɑː·pə·li] <-ies> *n* monopolio *m*

monorail ['mɑː·nou·reɪl] *n* (ferrovia)*f* monorotaia *f*

monosyllabic [ˌmɑː·nə·sɪ·'læ·bɪk] *adj* monosillabico, -a

monotone ['mɑː·nə·toun] *n* tono *m* uniforme

monotonous [mə·'nɑː·tə·nəs] *adj* monotono, -a

monotony [mə·'nɑː·tə·ni] *n* monotonia *f*

monoxide [mə·'nɑːk·saɪd] *n* monossido *m*

monsoon [mɑː·n·'suːn] *n* monsone *m;* ~**s** piogge *fpl* monsoniche

monster ['mɑː·n·stə·] I. *n* mostro *m* II. *adj inf* gigantesco, -a

monstrosity [mɑː·n·'strɑː·sə·ti] <-ies> *n* mostruosità *f*

monstrous ['mɑː·n·strəs] *adj* mostruoso, -a

montage ['mɑː·n·ta:ʒ] *n* montaggio *m*

month [mʌnθ] *n* mese *m*

monthly ['mʌnθ·li] I. *adj* mensile II. *adv* mensilmente III. *n* mensile *m*

monument ['mɑː·n·jə·mənt] *n* monumento *m*

monumental [ˌmɑː·n·jə·'men·t̬l] *adj* monumentale

moo [muː] I. <-s> *n* muggito *m* II. *vi* muggire

mood¹ [muːd] *n* umore *m;* **in a good/bad** ~ di buonumore/malumore; **the public** ~ l'umore generale; **to be in a talkative** ~ essere in vena di parlare; **to not be in the** ~ **to do sth** non aver voglia di fare qc

mood² [muːd] *n* LING modo *m*

moodiness ['muː·dɪ·nəs] *n* malumore *m*

moody ['muː·di] <-ier, -iest> *adj* 1. (*changeable*) lunatico, -a 2. (*bad-tempered*) di cattivo umore

moon [muːn] I. *n* luna *f;* **full/new** ~ luna piena/nuova ▶ **once in a blue** ~ a ogni morte di papa; **to be <u>over</u> the** ~ non stare in sé dalla gioia **II.** *vt inf* **to** ~ **sb** scoprire il sedere per esibirlo a qu

moonbeam ['mu:n·bi:m] *n* raggio *m* di luna

moonboots *npl* doposci *mpl*

moonlight I. *n* chiaro *m* di luna **II.** *vi inf* svolgere un secondo lavoro

moonlit *adj* illuminato, -a dalla luna

moonshine *n* **1.** *inf* (*alcoholic drink*) liquore *distillato illegalmente* **2.** (*moonlight*) chiaro *m* di luna

moonwalk I. *n* **1.** (*on moon*) passeggiata *f* lunare **2.** (*glide*) moonwalk *m inv* **II.** *vi* **1.** (*on moon*) camminare sulla luna **2.** (*glide*) fare il moonwalk

moor[1] [mʊr] *n* (*area*) brughiera *f*

moor[2] [mʊr] *vt* NAUT ormeggiare

moorhen ['mʊr·hen] *n* gallinella *f* d'acqua

mooring ['mʊ·rɪŋ] *n* ormeggio *m*

moose [mu:s] *n* alce *m*

moot [mu:t] **I.** *adj* discutibile; **the point is** ~ il punto è discutibile **II.** *vt* **it has been** ~**ed that ...** è stato proposto che ...

mop [mɑ:p] **I.** *n* **1.** (*cleaning device*) mocio *m* **2.** (*mass*) **a** ~ **of hair** una massa (incolta) di capelli **II.** <-pp-> *vt* **1.** (*wash*) lavare (con il mocio); **to** ~ **the floor** passare lo straccio **2.** (*dry*) asciugare

mope [moʊp] *vi* essere depresso

◆**mope about** *vi*, **mope around** *vi* gironzolare senza scopo

moped ['moʊ·ped] *n* motorino *m*

moral ['mɔ:·rəl] **I.** *adj* morale; **to give sb** ~ **support** dare un sostegno morale a qu **II.** *n* **1.** (*message*) morale *f*; **the** ~ **of the story** la morale della favola **2.** *pl* (*standards*) principi *m* morali; *pl*

morale [mə·'ræl] *n* morale *f*

moralist ['mɔ:·rə·lɪst] *n* moralista *mf*

morality [mɔ:·'ræ·lə·ti] <-ies> *n* moralità *f*

moralize ['mɔ:·rə·laɪz] *vi* moralizzare

morass [mə·'ræs] *n* **1.** (*boggy area*) pantano *m* **2.** *fig* (*complicated situation*) guazzabuglio *m*

moratorium [ˌmɔ:·rə·'tɔ:·ri·əm] <-s *o* -ria> *n* form moratoria *f*

morbid ['mɔ:r·bɪd] *adj* A.MED morboso, -a

morbidity [mɔ:r·'bɪ·də·ti] *n* morbosità *f*

more [mɔ:r] *comp of* **much, many I.** *adj* più; ~ **coins** più monete; **a few** ~ **coins** qualche moneta in più; **no** ~ **money at all** niente più soldi; **some** ~ **coffee** un po' più di caffè **II.** *adv* più; ~ **beautiful than me** più bello di me; **to drink** (**a bit/much**) ~ bere (un po'/molto) di più; **once** ~ ancora una volta; **never** ~ mai più; **to see** ~ **of sb** vedere più spesso qu; ~ **than 10** più di 10 **III.** *pron* più; ~ **and** ~ sempre più; **to have** ~ **than sb** avere di più di qu; **to cost** ~ **than sth** costare di più di qc; **the** ~ **you try it, the** ~ **you'll like it** più lo provi e più ti piace; **what** ~ **does he want?** cosa vuole di più?; **many do it but** ~ **don't** lo fanno in tanti, ma la maggioranza non lo fa ▶**all the** ~ tanto più

moreover [mɔ:r·'oʊ·vɚ] *adv form* inoltre

morgue [mɔ:rg] *n* obitorio *m*

moribund ['mɔ:·rɪ·bʌnd] *adj form* moribondo, -a

Mormon ['mɔ:r·mən] **I.** *n* mormone *mf* **II.** *adj* mormone

morning ['mɔ:r·nɪŋ] *n* mattina *f*, mattino *m*; **good** ~! buon giorno!; **in the** ~ al mattino; **that** ~ quella mattina; **the** ~ **after** la mattina dopo; **every** ~ ogni mattina, tutte le mattine; **every Monday** ~ il lunedì mattina; **to come in the** ~ arrivare la mattina; **one July** ~ una mattina di luglio; **early in the** ~ la mattina presto; **6 o'clock in the** ~ alle 6 del mattino; **from** ~ **until night** dal mattino/dalla mattina alla sera

morning-after pill [ˌmɔ:r·nɪŋ·'æf·tɚ·ˌpɪl] *n* pillola *f* del giorno dopo

Morning Prayer *n* mattutino *m*

morning sickness *n* nausea mattutina *f*

morning star *n* stella *f* del mattino

Moroccan [mə·'rɑ:·kən] **I.** *n* marocchino, -a *m, f* **II.** *adj* marocchino, -a

Morocco [mə·'rɑ:·koʊ] *n* Marocco *m*

moron ['mɔ:·rɑ:n] *n inf* deficiente *mf*

moronic [mɔ:·'rɑ:·nɪk] *adj inf* da deficiente

morose [mə·'roʊs] *adj* (*person, mood*) scontroso, -a; (*expression*) immusonito, a

morpheme ['mɔ:r·fi:m] *n* LING morfema *m*

morphia ['mɔ:r·fiə] *n*, **morphine** ['mɔ:r·fi:n] *n* morfina *f*

morphological [ˌmɔ:r·fə·'lɑ:·dʒɪ·kl] *adj* morfologico, -a

morphology [mɔ:r·'fɑ:·lə·dʒi] *n* morfologia *f*

Morse (**code**) [mɔ:rs] *n* (alfabeto) *m* morse

morsel ['mɔ:r·sl] *n* (*of food*) boccone *m;* (*of hope*) briciolo *f*

mortal ['mɔ:r·ţl] **I.** *adj* mortale; ~ **danger** pericolo *m* di morte/di vita; **to be in** ~ **fear** avere una grande paura **II.** *n liter* mortale *mf*

mortality [mɔ:r·'tæ·lə·ti] *n form* mortalità *f*

mortar ['mɔ:r·ţɚ] *n a.* MIL, TECH mortaio *m*

mortarboard ['mɔ:r·ţɚ·bɔ:rd] *n* tocco *m*

mortgage ['mɔ:r·gɪdʒ] **I.** *n* ipoteca *m* **II.** *vt* ipotecare

mortician [mɔ:r·'tɪ·ʃən] *n* impresario, -a *m, f* di pompe funebri

mortification [ˌmɔ:r·ţə·fɪ·'keɪ·ʃən] *n a.* REL mortificazione *f*

mortify ['mɔ:r·ţə·faɪ] *vt* <-ie-> mortificare

mortuary ['mɔ:r·tʃu·e·ri] *n* obitorio *m*

mosaic [moʊ·'zeɪ·ɪk] *n* mosaico *m*

Moscow ['mɑ:s·kaʊ] *n* Mosca *f*

Moses ['moʊ·zɪz] *n* Mosè *m*

Moslem ['mɑ:z·lem] **I.** *adj* mus(s)ulmano, -a **II.** *n* mus(s)ulmano, -a *m, f*

mosque [mɑ:sk] *n* moschea *f*

mosquito [mə·'ski:·ţoʊ] <-(e)s> *n* zanzara *f*

mosquito net *n* zanzariera *f*

moss [mɑ:s] <-es> *n* muschio *m*

mossy ['mɑ:·si] <-ier, -iest> *adj* muschioso, -a

most [moʊst] *superl of* **many, much I.** *adj* la maggior parte di; ~ **people** la maggior parte della gente; **to have the ~ friends** avere il maggior numero di amici; **for the ~ part** per lo più [o la maggior parte] **II.** *adv* più; **she's the ~ beautiful** è la più bella; **a ~ beautiful evening** una serata bellissima; **what I want ~** quello che desidero di più; **~ of all** soprattutto; **~ likely** molto probabilmente **III.** *pron* la maggior parte; **at the (very) ~** al massimo; **~ of them** la maggior parte di loro, quasi tutti loro; **~ of the time** la maggior parte del tempo, quasi tutto il tempo; **to make the ~ of sth/of oneself** ricavare il massimo da qc/da sé stesso; **the ~ you can have is ...** il massimo che puoi avere è ...

mostly ['moʊst·li] *adv* **1.** (*mainly*) per lo più **2.** (*usually*) di solito

motel [moʊ·'tel] *n* motel *m inv*

moth [mɑ:θ] *n* **1.** (*nocturnal*) falena *f* **2.** of clothes, tarma *f*

mothball ['mɑ:θ·bɑ:l] **I.** *n* pallina *f* di naftalina **II.** *vt* (*idea, plan*) mettere in naftalina

moth-eaten ['mɑ:θ·ˌi:·tn] *adj* tarmato, -a

mother ['mʌ·ðə˞] **I.** *n* **1.** (*woman*) madre *f* **2.** (*biggest thing*) madre; **that was the ~ of all wars** quella fu la madre di tutte le guerre **3.** *sl* (*sth bad*) **that was a real ~ of a problem** è stato un vero casino **II.** *vt* coccolare

mother country *n* madrepatria *f*

motherhood *n* maternità *f*

mother-in-law *n* suocera *f*

motherly ['mʌ·ðə˞·li] *adj* materno, -a

mother-of-pearl *n* madreperla *f*

Mother's Day *n* giornata *m* della mamma

mother tongue *n* lingua *f* materna

motif [moʊ·'ti:f] *n* ART motivo *m*

motion ['moʊ·ʃən] **I.** *n* **1.** (*movement*) movimento *m*, moto *m*; **in slow ~** al rallentatore, al ralenti; **to put sth in ~** mettere in moto qc **2.** (*proposal*) mozione *f* ▶ **to go through the ~s of doing sth** fare qc senza interesse **II.** *vt* fare cenno a; **to ~ sb to do sth** fare cenno a qu di fare qc **III.** *vi* fare cenno

motionless *adj* immobile

motion picture *n* film *m inv*

motivate ['moʊ·tə·veɪt] *vt* **1.** (*cause*) motivare **2.** (*arouse interest of*) stimolare

motivation [ˌmoʊ·tə·'veɪ·ʃən] *n* **1.** (*reason*) motivo *m* **2.** (*ambition, drive*) motivazione *f*

motive ['moʊ·tɪv] **I.** *n* motivo *m* **II.** *adj* PHYS, TECH motore, -trice

motley ['mɑ:t·li] <-ier, -iest> *adj pej* eterogeneo, -a

motor ['moʊ·tə˞] **I.** *n a. fig* motore *m* **II.** *adj a.* PHYS motore, -trice **III.** *vi* **1.** *form* (*drive*) andare in auto **2.** *inf* (*run quickly*) andare forte

motorbike *n inf* moto *f inv*

motorboat *n* motoscafo *m*

motorcycle *n* motocicletta *f*

motorcycling *n* motociclismo *m*

motorcyclist *n* motociclista *mf*

motor home *n* motorhome *m inv*

motorist ['moʊ·tə˞·ɪst] *n* automobilista *mf*

motorize ['moʊ·tə˞·raɪz] *vt* motorizzare

motor racing *n* automobilismo *m*

motor scooter *n* scooter *m inv*

motor vehicle *n form* automobile *f*

mottled ['mɑ:·tld] *adj* (*leaf, marble*) variegato, -a; (*skin*) a chiazze

motto ['mɑ:·toʊ] <-(e)s> *n* motto *m*

mound [maʊnd] *n* **1.** (*elevation*) monticello *m* **2.** (*heap*) mucchio *m* **3.** (*in baseball*) **the pitcher's ~** monte *m* di lancio

mount [maʊnt] **I.** *n* **1.** (*horse*) cavalcatura *f* **2.** (*frame*) montatura *f* **II.** *vt* **1.** (*get on: horse*) montare; **to ~ a ladder** salire su una scala; **to ~ the throne** *form* salire al trono **2.** (*organize*) organizzare; **to ~ an attack** lanciare un attacco; **to ~ a rescue** organizzare un salvataggio **3.** (*fix for display*) fissare; (*stamps*) sistemare **4.** ZOOL montare **III.** *vi* salire

> **i** Scolpite tra il 1927 e il 1941 nei massicci granitici del **Mount Rushmore** o Monte Rushmore/Dakota del Sud, i busti, alti 60 piedi (18 m), dei presidenti George Washington, Thomas Jefferson, Theodore Roosevelt e Abraham Lincoln rappresentano i primi 150 anni della storia americana e sono un omaggio alla nascita e allo sviluppo degli Stati Uniti d'America.

mountain ['maʊn·tən] *n* **1.** GEO montagna *f* **2.** *inf* (*amount*) mucchio *m* ▶ **to make a ~ out of a molehill** perdersi in un bicchier d'acqua; **to move ~s** muovere mari e monti

mountain bike *n* mountain bike *f inv*

mountain chain *n* GEO catena *f* montuosa

mountaineer [ˌmaʊn·tən·'ɪr] *n* alpinista *mf*

mountaineering *n* alpinismo *m*

mountainous ['maʊnt·nəs] *adj* **1.** GEO montuoso, -a **2.** (*large and high*) gigantesco, -a

mountain range *n* GEO catena *f* montuosa

mounted ['maʊn·tɪd] *adj* a cavallo; **~ police** polizia *f* a cavallo

mounting *n* (*of machine*) base *f*; (*in frame*) montaggio *m*

mourn [mɔ:rn] **I.** *vi* lamentare; **to ~ for sb** piangere la morte di qu **II.** *vt* lamentare

mourner ['mɔ:r·nə˞] *n* chi accompagna un funerale

mournful ['mɔ:rn·fəl] *adj* **1.** (*grieving*) afflitto, -a **2.** (*gloomy*) triste

mourning ['mɔ:r·nɪŋ] *n* lutto *m*; **to be in ~** essere in lutto

mouse [maʊs] <mice> *n* ZOOL topo *m*; COMPUT mouse *m inv* ▶ **to be as poor as a church ~** essere povero in canna

mouse pad *n* COMPUT tappetino *m* del mouse

mousetrap *n* trappola *f* per topi

mousse [mu:s] *n* mousse *f inv*

moustache ['mʌs·tæʃ] *n* baffi *mpl*

mousy ['maʊ·si] *adj* **1.** (*shy*) timido, -a; **she is very ~** è timida e insignificante **2.** (*brown*) **~ hair** capelli scialbi

mouth[1] [mauθ] *n* **1.**(*of person, animal*) bocca *f;* **to shut one's** ~ *inf* stare zitto, tacere **2.**(*opening*) apertura *f;* (*of bottle, jar*) bocca *f;* (*of cave*) imboccatura *f;* (*of river*) foce *f* ► **to be born with a** silver spoon **in one's** ~ essere nato con la camicia; **it made her** ~ water le ha fatto venire l'acquolina in bocca; **to be** down **in the** ~ essere depresso; **to** shoot off **one's** ~ **about sth** *inf* (*indiscreetly*) raccontarne delle belle; (*brag*) spararne delle grosse

mouth[2] [mauð] *vt* **1.**(*form words silently*) muovere le labbra senza articolare le parole **2.**(*say insincerely*) dire senza sincerità; **to** ~ **an excuse** tirare fuori la solita scusa

◆**mouth off** *vi sl* **1.**(*rant*) sproloquiare **2.**(*talk back*) rispondere in modo villano

mouthful ['mauθ·fʊl] *n* **1.**(*of food*) boccone *m;* (*of drink*) sorso *m* **2.**(*word*) parolona *f* (difficile da pronunciare)

mouthpiece *n* **1.** TEL microfono *m* **2.**(*of pipe*) bocchino *m;* (*of instrument*) imboccatura *m* **3.**(*person*) portavoce *mf*

mouth-to-mouth resuscitation *n* rianimazione *f* bocca a bocca

mouthwash *n* collutorio *m*

mouthwatering *adj* appetitoso, -a

movable ['mu:·və·bl] *adj* mobile

move [mu:v] **I.** *n* **1.**(*movement*) movimento *m;* **to be on the** ~ (*traveling*) essere in viaggio; (*very busy*) essere in movimento; **to get a** ~ **on** spicciarsi **2.**(*change of abode*) trasloco *m;* (*change of job*) trasferimento *m* **3.** GAMES mossa *f;* **it's your** ~ tocca a te **4.**(*action*) mossa *f;* **to make the first** ~ fare la prima mossa **II.** *vi* **1.**(*change position*) muoversi, spostarsi; (*advance fast*) correre; (*make progress*) progredire **2.**(*in games*) muovere **3.**(*change abode*) traslocare; (*change job*) trasferirsi ► ~ **it!** *inf* muoviti! **III.** *vt* **1.**(*change position*) spostare; (*make sb change their mind*) fare cambiare idea; (*reschedule*) spostare la data **2.**(*cause emotions*) commuovere; **to be ~d by sth** commuoversi per qc **3.**(*propose*) proporre

◆**move along I.** *vt* spostare **II.** *vi* spostarsi

◆**move away I.** *vi* allontanarsi; (*move house*) traslocare **II.** *vt* allontanare

◆**move back I.** *vi* spostarsi all'indietro **II.** *vt* spostare all'indietro

◆**move down I.** *vi* scendere **II.** *vt* abbassare

◆**move forward I.** *vi* avanzare **II.** *vt* spostare in avanti; (*date*) posticipare

◆**move in I.** *vi* **1.**(*move into abode*) andare ad abitare, traslocare **2.**(*intervene*) intervenire **3.**(*advance to attack*) attaccare; **to** ~ **on enemy territory** invadere il nemico **II.** *vt* portare

◆**move on** *vi* **1.**(*leave*) andarsene **2.**(*continue to move*) circolare; **to** ~ **to another subject** passare a un altro argomento

◆**move out** *vi* **1.**(*stop inhabiting*) andare via (da una casa), traslocare **2.**(*depart*) andarsene

◆**move over I.** *vi* **1.**(*make room*) spostarsi; (*on seat*) farsi da parte **2.**(*switch*) **to** ~ **towards sth** passare a qc **II.** *vt* spostare da una parte

◆**move up I.** *vi* **1.**(*make room*) fare posto; (*on seat*) farsi da parte **2.**(*increase*) aumentare **3.**(*advance*) avanzare; **he's slowly but surely moving up in the company** sta pian piano facendo carriera nell'azienda **II.** *vt* spostare in alto

movement ['mu:v·mənt] *n* **1.** *a.* MUS (*act*) movimento *m* **2.** FIN, COM attività *f* **3.**(*tendency*) tendenza *f*

movie ['mu:·vi] *n* film *m inv;* **the ~s** il cinema

movie camera *n* cinepresa *f*

moviegoer *n* cinefilo, -a *m, f*

movie star *n* stella *f* del cinema

movie theater *n* cinema *m inv*

moving ['mu:·vɪŋ] **I.** *adj* **1.**(*that moves*) mobile; ~ **stairs** scala mobile **2.**(*motivating*) ispiratore, -trice; **the** ~ **force** l'ispirazione **3.**(*causing emotion*) commovente, toccante **II.** *n* trasloco *m*

mow [mou] <mowed, mown *o* mowed> *vt* (*grass*) tosare; (*hay*) tagliare

◆**mow down** *vt* **1.**(*kill*) falciare **2.**(*overwhelm*) sopraffare

mower ['mo·uə·] *n* (*for lawn*) tosaerba *m inv*

mown [moun] *pp of* **mow**

moxie *n sl* grinta *f*

MP [ˌem·'pi:] *n abbr of* **Military Police** polizia *f* militare

mpg *n abbr of* **miles per gallon** miglia *fpl* con un gallone

mph [ˌem·pi:·'eɪtʃ] *abbr of* **miles per hour** miglia all'ora

Mr. ['mɪs·tə·] *n abbr of* **Mister** Signor

Mrs. ['mɪ·sɪz] *n* Signora

Ms. [mɪz] *n titolo che evita la distinzione tra donna nubile e sposata*

MS [ˌem·'es] **1.** *abbr of* **multiple sclerosis** sclerosi *finv* multipla **2.** *abbr of* **Mississippi** Mississippi *m* **3.** *abbr of* **Master of Science** laurea *f* (*in discipline scientifiche*)*;* **Louie Sanders, MS, he has an** ~ **in geology** è laureato in geologia; **Louie Sanders, MS** Dott. Louie Sanders

MSG *abbr of* **monosodium glutamate** glutammato *m* monosodico

MT *n* **1.** *abbr of* **Montana** Montana *m* **2.** *abbr of* **Mountain Time** *ora legale nella zona delle Montagne Rocciose*

Mt. *abbr of* **Mount** monte

much [mʌtʃ] <more, most> **I.** *adj* molto, molta; **too** ~ **wine** troppo vino; **how** ~ **milk?** quanto latte?; **too/so** ~ **water** troppa/tanta acqua; **as** ~ **as** tanto quanto; **three times as** ~ tre volte tanto **II.** *adv* molto; ~ **better** molto meglio; **thank you very** ~ molte grazie; **to be very** ~ **surprised** essere molto sorpreso; ~ **to my astonishment** con mia grande sorpresa; **not him,** ~ **less her** non lui, e tanto meno lei **III.** *pron* molto; ~ **of the day** gran parte della

M

giornata; **I don't think ~ of it** non gli dò grande importanza; **to make ~ of sb/sth** dare importanza a qu/qc

muck [mʌk] *n inf* **1.** (*dirt*) sporcizia *f* **2.** (*manure*) letame *m* ▶ **to be stuck in the ~** essere nella merda *vulg*

◆**muck up** *vt inf* rovinare

muckheap *n* letamaio *m*

muckraker ['mʌk·reɪ·kɚ] *n* scandalista *mf*

mucky ['mʌ·ki] <-ier, -iest> *adj inf* sudicio, -a

mucous ['mjuː·kəs] *adj* MED muco *m*

mucous membrane *n* (membrana) *f* mucosa *f*

mucus ['mjuː·kəs] *n* MED muco *m*

mud [mʌd] *n* **1.** (*wet earth*) fango *m;* **to wallow in ~** rivoltarsi nel fango **2.** (*insult*) **to hurl ~ at sb** gettare fango su qu ▶ **here's ~ in your eye** *inf* beviamoci sopra!; **to drag sb's name through the ~** infangare il nome di qu

muddle ['mʌ·dl] **I.** *vt* **1.** (*mix up*) mettere in disordine **2.** (*confuse*) confondere **II.** *vi* **to ~ along** tirare avanti **III.** *n* desordine *m;* **to get into a ~** fare una gran confusione

muddle-headed ['mʌ·dl·ˌhe·dɪd] *adj* che ha le idee confuse

muddy ['mʌ·di] **I.** <-ier, -iest> *adj* (*dirty*) infangato, -a; (*water*) torbido, -a; (*ground*) fangoso, -a **II.** *vt* **1.** (*make dirty*) infangare **2.** (*confuse*) confondere ▶ **to ~ the waters** intorbidire

mud flap *n,* **mudguard** ['mʌd·gɑːrd] *n* parafango *m*

mudslide *n* (*flow*) colata *f* di fango

mudslinging *n inf* calunnia *f*

muff¹ [mʌf] **I.** *vt* **1.** (*screw up: opportunity*) lasciarsi sfuggire; THEAT (*one's lines*) dire male **2.** SPORTS mancare **II.** *n* sport presa *f* mancata

muff² [mʌf] *n* FASHION manicotto *m*

muffin ['mʌ·fɪn] *n* tortina ai mirtilli o al cioccolato

muffle ['mʌ·fl] *vt* smorzare

muffler ['mʌf·lɚ] *n* AUTO marmitta *f*

mug¹ [mʌg] *n* (*for tea, coffee*) tazzone *m;* (*for beer*) boccale *m*

mug² [mʌg] **I.** *n inf* muso *m,* grugno *m* **II.** <-gg-> *vt* aggredire e rapinare **III.** *vi* **to ~ for the camera** fare le facce per essere fotografati

mugger ['mʌ·gɚ] *n* rapinatore, -trice *m, f*

mugging ['mʌ·gɪŋ] *n* aggressione e rapina *m*

muggy ['mʌ·gi] <-ier, -iest> *adj* afoso, -a

mulberry ['mʌl·be·ri] *n* **1.** (*fruit*) mora *f* **2.** (*tree*) gelso *m*

mule [mjuːl] *n* (*animal*) mulo, -a *m, f* ▶ **as stubborn as a ~** testardo come un mulo

mull [mʌl] *vt* **to ~ sth over** pensarci su

mulled wine [mʌld waɪn] *n* vin *m* brulé

mullion ['mʌl·jən] *n* ARCHIT piantone *m*

multicolored [ˌmʌl·ti·ˈkʌ·lɚd] *adj* variopinto, -a

multicultural [ˌmʌl·ti·ˈkʌl·tʃə·rəl] *adj* multiculturale

multifarious [ˌmʌl·tə·ˈfe·ri·əs] *adj form* molteplice

multifunctional [ˌmʌl·ti·ˈfʌnk·ʃə·nəl] *adj* multifunzionale

multilateral [ˌmʌl·ti·ˈlæ·t̬ə·rəl] *adj* POL multilaterale

multilingual [ˌmʌl·ti·ˈlɪŋ·gwəl] *adj* multilingüe

multimedia [ˌmʌl·ti·ˈmiː·diə] *adj* multimediale

multimillionaire [ˌmʌl·ti·mil·jə·ˈner] *n* multimilionario, -a *m, f*

multinational [ˌmʌl·ti·ˈnæʃ·nəl] **I.** *n* multinazionale *f* **II.** *adj* multinazionale

multiple ['mʌl·t̬ə·pl] *adj* multiplo

multiplex ['mʌl·tə·pleks] *n* (cinema) *m* multisala *pl*

multiplication [ˌmʌl·tə·plɪ·ˈkeɪ·ʃən] *n* moltiplicazione *f*

multiplicity [ˌmʌl·tə·ˈplɪ·sə·ti] *n form* molteplicità *f*

multiplier ['mʌl·tə·pla·ɪɚ] *n* MATH multiplo *m*

multiply ['mʌl·tə·plaɪ] <-ie-> **I.** *vt* moltiplicare **II.** *vi* moltiplicarsi

multipurpose [ˌmʌl·ti·ˈpɜːr·pəs] *adj* multiuso

multiracial [ˌmʌl·ti·ˈreɪ·ʃl] *adj* multirazziale

multistage [ˌmʌl·ti·ˈsteɪdʒ] *adj* multistadio

multistory [ˌmʌl·ti·ˈstɔː·ri] *adj* a più piani

multitasking [ˌmʌl·ti·ˈtɑːs·kɪŋ] *n* COMPUT multitasking *m inv*

multitude ['mʌl·tə·tuːd] *n* **1.** (*of things, problems*) massa *f* **2.** (*crowd*) folla *f;* **the ~s** *liter* le folle

multitudinous [ˌmʌl·tə·ˈtuː·d·nəs] *adj* innumerevole

mum [mʌm] *adj* **to keep ~** *inf* restare in silenzio ▶ **~'s the word** acqua in bocca!

mumble ['mʌm·bl] *vi* borbottare

mumbo jumbo [ˌmʌm·boʊ·ˈdʒʌm·boʊ] *n inf* linguaggio *m* esoterico

mummify ['mʌ·mə·faɪ] <-ie-> *vt* mummificare

mummy ['mʌ·mi] <-ies> *n* mummia *f*

mumps [mʌmps] *n* MED orecchioni *mpl;* **he's got the ~** ha gli orecchioni

munch [mʌntʃ] *vi, vt* sgranocchiare

mundane [mʌn·ˈdeɪn] *adj* banale

municipal [mjuː·ˈnɪ·sə·pl] *adj* municipale

municipality [mjuː·ˌnɪ·sə·ˈpæ·lə·ti] *n* <-ies> **1.** (*city, town*) comune *m* **2.** (*local government*) municipalità *f*

munitions [mjuː·ˈnɪ·ʃənz] *npl* munizioni *fpl*

mural ['mjʊ·rəl] *n* murale *m*

murder ['mɜːr·dɚ] **I.** *n* (*killing*) assassinio *m;* LAW omicidio (volontario/premeditato) *m;* **to commit ~** commettere un omicidio; **this job is ~** *fig* questo lavoro è infernale; **he gets away with ~** *fig* riesce a cavarsela sempre ▶ **to scream bloody ~** fare il diavolo a quattro **II.** *vt* (*kill*) assassinare; *fig* (*music, play*) massacrare

murderer ['mɜː·r·də·ɚ] *n* (*killer*) assassino, -a *m, f;* LAW omicida *mf*

murderous ['mɜːr·də·rəs] *adj* **1.** (*capable of murder*) capace di uccidere; **~ dealer/gangster** trafficante/gangster assassino **2.** (*capable of causing death: look*) assassino, -a; (*instinct*) omicida; (*plan*) criminale **3.** *inf* (*difficult: heat*) bestiale; (*traffic*) infernale

murky ['mɜːr·ki] <-ier, -iest> *adj* (*water*) torbido, -a; (*past*) losco, -a; (*night*) tenebroso, -a

murmur ['mɜːr·mə·] I. *vi, vt* mormorare II. *n* mormorio *m*

muscle ['mʌ·sl] *n* 1. ANAT muscolo *m* 2. *fig* forza *f*
 ♦ **muscle in** *vi* to ~ (on sth) intromettersi (in qc)

muscle-bound ['mʌ·sl·ˌbaʊnd] *adj* molto muscoloso, -a

muscle car *n* muscle car *f inv, coupé supermotorizzata*

muscleman ['mʌ·sl·mæn] <-men> *n* uomo *m* muscoloso

Muscovite I. *adj* moscovita II. *n* moscovita *mf*

muscular ['mʌs·kjə·lə·] *adj* 1. (*pain, contraction*) muscolare 2. (*arms, legs*) muscoloso, -a

muse [mju:z] I. *vi* to ~ (on sth) meditare (su qc) II. *vt* to ~ that ... dire tra sé e sé che ... III. *n* musa *f*

museum [mju:·'zi:·əm] *n* museo *m*; ~ **piece** pezzo *f* da museo

mush[1] [mʌʃ] *n* 1. *inf* (*food*) pappa *f* 2. (*in a film, book*) sentimentalismo *m* sdolcinato

mush[2] [mʌʃ] I. *interj* comando di incitamento dato ai cani da traino di una slitta II. *vt* guidare una slitta trainata da cani III. *vi* viaggiare su una slitta trainata da cani IV. *n* viaggio *m* su slitta trainata da cani

mushroom ['mʌʃ·ru:m] I. *n* (*wild*) fungo *m*; (*button mushroom*) fungo *m* coltivato II. *vi* (*population, prices*) aumentare rapidamente; (*town*) spuntare all'improvviso [*o* come i funghi]

mushy ['mʌ·ʃi] *adj* <-ier, -iest> 1. (*soft: food*) ridotto, -a a pappetta 2. (*film, book*) sdolcinato, -a

music ['mju:·zɪk] *n* 1. (*art*) musica *f; it was ~* to her ears era musica per le sue orecchie 2. (*notes*) partitura *f,* spartito *m;* to read ~ leggere la musica

musical ['mju:·zɪ·kəl] I. *adj* musicale II. *n* musical *m inv*

music box *n* carillon *m inv*

music hall *n* teatro *m* di varietà, music hall *m inv*

musician [mju:·'zɪ·ʃən] *n* musicista *mf*

music stand *n* leggio *m*

musk [mʌsk] *n* muschio *m*

musket ['mʌs·kɪt] *n* moschetto *m*

musketeer [ˌmʌs·kə·'tɪr] *n* moschettiere *m*

muskrat ['mʌs·kræt] *n* ondatra *f,* topo *m* muschiato

Muslim ['mʌz·ləm] I. *adj* mus(s)ulmano, -a II. *n* mus(s)ulmano, -a *m, f*

muslin ['mʌz·lɪn] *n* mussola *f*

muss [mʌs] *vt* scompigliare

mussel ['mʌ·sl] *n* cozza *f,* muscolo *m*

must [mʌst] I. *aux* 1. (*obligation*) dovere; ~ you leave so soon? devi proprio andar via così presto?; you ~n't do that non devi fare questo 2. (*probability*) dovere; I ~ have lost it

devo averlo perso; you ~ be hungry (immagino che) avrai fame; you ~ be joking! vuoi scherzare! II. *n* must *m inv;* this book is an absolute ~ leggere questo libro è un must

mustache ['mʌs·tæʃ] *n* baffi *mpl*

mustang ['mʌs·tæn] *n* mustang *m inv*

mustard ['mʌs·tə·d] *n* senape *f*

muster ['mʌs·tə·] I. *vt* 1. (*gather*) radunare; to ~ the courage to do sth armarsi di coraggio per fare qc 2. MIL adunare II. *vi* radunarsi III. *n* to pass ~ superare l'esame

mustn't ['mʌ·snt] *must not* must

musty ['mʌs·ti] <-ier, -iest> *adj* (*room*) che ha odore di umido e di chiuso; (*book*) ammuffito, -a

mutant ['mju:·tənt] I. *adj* mutante II. *n* mutante *mf*

mutation [mju:·'teɪ·ʃən] *n* mutazione *f*

mute [mju:t] I. *n* 1. (*person*) muto, -a *m, f* 2. MUS sordina *f* II. *vt* MUS mettere la sordina a III. *adj* muto, -a; to remain ~ restare in silenzio

muted *adj* smorzato, -a

mutilate ['mju:·tə·leɪt] *vt* mutilare

mutilation [ˌmju:·tl·'leɪ·ʃən] *n* mutilazione *f*

mutineer [ˌmju:t·'nɪr] *n* ammutinato, -a *m, f*

mutinous ['mju:·t̬·nəs] *adj* ammutinato, -a

mutiny ['mju:·tɪ·ni] I. *n* <-ies> ammutinamento *m* II. *vi* <-ie-> ammmutinarsi

mutter ['mʌ·tə·] I. *vi* 1. (*talk*) sussurrare [*o* borbottare] 2. (*complain*) brontolare; to ~ about sth brontolare per qc II. *vt* sussurrare [*o* borbottare] III. *n* mormorio *m,* brontolio *m*

mutton ['mʌ·tən] *n* carne *f* di montone

muttonchops *n pl,* **muttonchop whiskers** *n pl* scopettoni *mpl*

mutual ['mju:·t·ʃu·əl] *adj* (*understanding*) mutuo, -a; (*friend, interest*) comune

mutual fund *n* fondo *m* comune di investimento a capitale variabile

mutually *adv* a vicenda; it was ~ agreed lo si è deciso di comune accordo

muzak® ['mju:·zæk] *n* musica *f* di sottofondo

muzzle ['mʌ·zl] I. *n* 1. (*of horse, dog*) muso *m* 2. (*for dog*) museruola *f* 3. (*of gun*) bocca *f* II. *vt* 1. (*dog*) mettere la museruola a 2. *fig* (*person, newspaper*) imbavagliare

MVP *n abbr of* most valuable player giocatore, -trice *m, f* di maggior valore

MW *abbr of* megawatt MW

my [maɪ] I. *adj pos* (il) mio *m,* (la) mia *f,* (i) miei *mpl,* (le) mie *fpl; ~* dog/house il mio cane/la mia casa; ~ father/sister mio padre/mia sorella; ~ children i miei figli; this car is ~ own quest'auto è mia; I hurt ~ foot/head mi sono fatto male a un piede/alla testa II. *interj* santo cielo!

myopia [maɪ·'oʊp·iə] *n* miopia *f*

myopic [maɪ·'ɑ:·pɪk] *adj a. fig, form* miope

myriad ['mɪ·ri·əd] *n* miriade *f*

myrrh [mɜːr] *n* mirra *f*

myrtle ['mɜːr·tl] *n* mirto *m*

myself [maɪ·'self] *pron reflexive* 1. (*direct,*

indirect object) mi; **I hurt** ~ mi sono fatto male; **I deceived** ~ mi sono illuso; **when I express/exert** ~ quando mi esprimo/sforzo; **I bought** ~ **a bag** mi sono comprato una borsa **2.** *emphatic* me (stesso, stessa), io (stesso, stessa); **my brother and** ~ mio fratello e io; **I'll do it** ~ lo farò io (stesso); **I did it** (**all**) **by** ~ l'ho fatto da solo/da me **3.** *after prep* me (stesso/stessa); **I said to** ~ mi sono detto; **I am ashamed of** ~ mi vergogno di me stesso; **I live by** ~ vivo da solo [*o* per conto mio]

mysterious [mɪ·'stɪ·ri·əs] *adj* misterioso, -a

mystery ['mɪs·tə·ri] <-ies> *n* mistero *m*

mystic ['mɪs·tɪk] **I.** *n* mistico, -a *m, f* **II.** *adj* mistico, -a

mystical ['mɪs·tɪ·kl] *adj* mistico, -a

mysticism ['mɪs·tɪ·sɪ·zəm] *n* misticismo *m*

mystification [,mɪs·tɪ·fɪ·'keɪ·ʃən] *n* **1.** (*mystery*) mistero *m* **2.** (*confusion*) perplessità *f*

mystify ['mɪs·tɪ·faɪ] *vt* <-ie-> disorientare

mystique [mɪs·'tiːk] *n* mistica *f*

myth [mɪθ] *n* mito *m*

mythical ['mɪ·θɪ·kl] *adj* **1.** (*legendary*) mitico, -a **2.** (*supposed*) ipotetico, -a

mythological [,mɪ·θə·'lɑː·dʒɪ·kl] *adj* mitologico, -a

mythology [mɪ·'θɑː·lə·dʒi] *n* <-ies> mitologia *f*

N

N, n [en] *n* N, n *f;* ~ **as in Nancy** N di Napoli

n *abbr of* **noun** s.

N *abbr of* **north** N

nab [næb] <-bb-> *vt inf* (*person*) beccare; (*thing*) sgraffignare

nadir ['neɪ·dɚ] *n* nadir *m inv*

nag[1] [næg] *n* (*horse*) ronzino *m*

nag[2] [næg] **I.** <-gg-> *vi* rompere *inf;* **to** ~ **at sb** tormentare qu **II.** <-gg-> *vt* seccare **III.** *n inf* seccatore, -trice *m, f*

nagging ['næ·gɪŋ] **I.** *n* lamentele *fpl* **II.** *adj* **1.** (*criticizing*) assillante **2.** (*pain, ache*) fastidioso, -a

nail [neɪl] **I.** *n* **1.** (*tool*) chiodo *m* **2.** ANAT unghia *f* ▶ **to hit the** ~ **on the** <u>head</u> cogliere nel segno **II.** *vt* **1.** (*fasten*) inchiodare **2.** *inf* (*catch: police*) beccare; (*lie*) scoprire

nail-biting *adj fig* snervante

nail brush <-es> *n* spazzolino *m* per unghie

nail clippers *npl* tronchesina *f*

nail file *n* limetta *f* per le unghie

nail polish *n* smalto *m* per unghie

nail polish remover *n* acetone *m*

nail scissors *npl* forbicine *fpl* per unghie

naive, naïve [nɑː·'iːv] *adj* ingenuo, -a

naivety [,nɑː·iːv·'teɪ], **naïveté** [nɑː·'iː·və·t̬i] *n* ingenuità *f*

naked ['neɪ·kɪd] *adj* **1.** (*unclothed*) nudo, -a **2.** (*uncovered: blade*) sguainato, -a; (*aggression*) manifesto, -a; (*ambition*) palese; **to the** ~ **eye** a occhio nudo

nakedness *n* nudità *f*

namby-pamby [,næm·bɪ·'pæm·bi] *adj inf* (*person*) rammollito, -a; (*poem*) sdolcinato, -a

name [neɪm] **I.** *n* **1.** nome *m;* **by** ~ di nome; **to know sb by** ~ conoscere qu di nome; **to go by the** ~ **of ...** *form* essere noto con il nome di ...; **in** ~ **only** solo di nome; **under the** ~ **of ...** sotto lo pseudonimo di ...; **in God's** ~ in nome di Dio; **in the** ~ **of freedom and justice** in nome della libertà e della giustizia; **to call sb** ~**s** coprire qu di insulti; **in all but** ~ di fatto **2.** (*reputation*) fama *f;* **a good** ~ una buona reputazione; **his** ~ **is mud** *fig* il suo nome non vale una cicca; **to make a** ~ **for oneself** farsi un nome ▶ **the** ~ **of the** <u>game</u> la cosa essenziale; **not to have a** <u>penny</u> **to one's** ~ non avere il becco di un quattrino **II.** *vt* **1.** (*call*) chiamare **2.** (*list*) dire il nome di **3.** (*choose*) **to** ~ **the time and the place** fissare il posto e l'ora

name day *n* onomastico *m*

name-dropping ['neɪm·drɑː·pɪŋ] *n abitudine di vantarsi di conoscere persone importanti per impressionare l'interlocutore*

nameless ['neɪm·lɪs] *adj* anonimo, -a

namely ['neɪm·li] *adv* vale a dire

nameplate ['neɪm·pleɪt] *n* targa *f* con il nome

namesake ['neɪm·seɪk] *n* omonimo, -a *m, f*

Namibia [nə·'mɪb·iə] *n* Namibia *f*

Namibian I. *adj* namibiano, -a **II.** *n* namibiano, -a *m, f*

nanny ['næ·ni] <-ies> *n* bambinaia *f*

nanny goat ['næ·ni·goʊt] *n* capra *f*

nanosecond ['nɑː·noʊ·,se·kənd] *n* nanosecondo *m*

nap[1] [næp] (*sleep*) **I.** *n* pisolino *m; (after lunch)* pennichella *f;* **to take a** ~ fare un pisolino [*o* una pennichella] **II.** <-pp-> *vi* schiacciare un pisolino

nap[2] [næp] *n* (*on fabric*) pelo *m*

napalm ['neɪ·pɑːm] *n* napalm *m*

nape [neɪp] *n* nuca *f*

napkin ['næp·kɪn] *n* tovagliolo *m*

narc [nɑːrk] *n sl abbr of* **narcotics agent** agente *mf* della narcotici

narcissism ['nɑːr·sə·sɪ·zəm] *n* narcisismo *m*

narcissus [nɑːr·'sɪ·səs] <-es *o* narcissi> *n* narciso *m*

narcosis [nɑːr·'koʊ·sɪs] *n* narcosi *f inv*

narcotic [nɑːr·'kɑː·t̬ɪk] **I.** *n* narcotico *m* **II.** *adj* narcotico, -a

narrate ['ne·reɪt] *vt* **1.** (*tale, story*) narrare **2.** TV commentare

narration [ner·'eɪ·ʃən] *n* (*tale*) narrazione *f;* TV commento *m* parlato

narrative ['ne·rə·t̬ɪv] *n* narrazione *f*

narrator ['ne·reɪ·t̬ɚ] *n* narratore, -trice *m, f;* TV voce *f* narrante

narrow ['ne·roʊ] **I.** <-er, -est> *adj* **1.** (*thin*) stretto, -a **2.**(*limited*) limitato, -a **3.**(*small: margin*) scarso, -a **II.** *vi* (*road, field*) restringersi; (*gap*) ridursi **III.** *vt* (*field*) restringere; (*gap*) ridurre

narrowly *adv* **1.**(*barely*) per poco **2.**(*meticulously*) attentamente

narrow-minded [ˌneˑroʊˈmaɪnˑdɪd] *adj* (*person*) di vedute ristrette; (*opinions, views*) ristretto, a

NASA [ˈnæˑsə] *n abbr of* **National Aeronautics and Space Administration** NASA *f*

ℹ️ La *National Aeronautics and Space Administration*, di solito chiamata **NASA**, è un organismo governativo dedicato alle ricerche in ambito areonautico e spaziale. Creata il 29 luglio del 1958, ha organizzato la celebre *mission Apollo 11*, grazie alla quale Neil Armstrong fu il primo uomo a camminare sulla Luna, il 21 luglio 1969. Tra le missioni più recenti della NASA, si possono ricordare la missione *Mars Exploration Rovers*, lanciata nel 2003 con l'obiettivo di esplorare la superficie del pianeta Marte grazie all'aiuto di due robot, Spirit e Opportunity, e la missione *Deep Impact*, lanciata il 12 gennaio 2005 verso la cometa 9P/Tempel 1 per studiare, a partire dalla sonda, il cratere provocato da un "impattatore" e i materiali scagliati intorno dall'impatto prodottosi, come previsto, il 4 luglio 2005.

nasal [ˈneɪˑzl] *adj* nasale

nascent [ˈnæˑsənt] *adj* nascente

nastiness [ˈnæsˑtɪˑnəs] *n* **1.**(*wickedness*) cattiveria *f* **2.**(*of accident*) gravità *f* **3.**(*of odor*) pestilenza *f* **4.**(*dirtiness*) sudiciume *f*

nasturtium [nəˈstɜːrˑʃəm] *n* BOT nasturzio *m*

nasty [ˈnæsˑti] <-ier, -iest> *adj* **1.**(*bad*) cattivo, -a; (*surprise*) brutto, -a **2.**(*dangerous, serious*) brutto, -a

natal [ˈneɪˑtl] *adj* (*place, day*) di nascita

natality [nəˈtæˑlɪˑti] *n* natalità *f*

nation [ˈneɪˑʃən] *n* **1.**(*country, state*) nazione *f*, paese *m*; **to serve the** ~ servire il proprio paese **2.**(*people living in a state*) nazione *f*; **the Jewish** ~ la nazione ebraica

national [ˈnæˑʃəˑnəl] **I.** *adj* nazionale; **at the** ~ **level** a livello nazionale **II.** *n* cittadino, -a *m, f*; **foreign** ~ cittadino straniero

national anthem *n* inno *m* nazionale

national assembly <-ies> *n* assemblea *f* nazionale

national bank *n* banca *f* nazionale

national costume *n* costume *m* nazionale

national currency <-ies> *n* valuta *f* nazionale

national debt *n* debito *m* pubblico

national emblem emblema *f* nazionale

National Guard *n* Guardia *f* Nazionale, *negli Stati Uniti, milizia di volontari che interviene*

in questioni di ordine pubblico o di protezione civile

national holiday *n* festa *f* nazionale

national income *n* reddito *m* nazionale

nationalism [ˈnæʃˑnəˑlɪˑzəm] *n* nazionalismo *m*

nationalist [ˈnæʃˑnəˑlɪst] **I.** *adj* nazionalista **II.** *n* nazionalista *mf*

nationalistic [ˌnæʃˑnəˈlɪsˑtɪk] *adj* nazionalistico, -a

nationality [ˌnæˑʃəˈnæˑləˑti] <-ies> *n* nazionalità *f*; **to adopt American/Spanish** ~ prendere la nazionalità americana/spagnola

nationalization [ˌnæˑʃəˑnəˑlaɪˈzeɪˑʃən] *n* nazionalizzazione *f*

nationalize [ˈnæˑʃəˑnəˑlaɪz] *vt* nazionalizzare

national park *n* parco *m* nazionale

national product *n* prodotto *m* nazionale

national security *n* sicurezza *f* nazionale

national service *n* (*community service*) servizio volontario espletato in enti di pubblica utilità

national socialism *n* nazionalsocialismo *m*

national unity *n* unità *f* nazionale

nation state *n* stato *m* nazione

nationwide [ˌneɪˑʃənˈwaɪd] **I.** *adv* a livello nazionale **II.** *adj* su scala nazionale

native [ˈneɪˑtɪv] **I.** *adj* **1.**(*indigenous*) indigeno, -a; **to be** ~ **to the United States** (*plant, animal*) essere originario degli Stati Uniti **2.**(*of place of origin*) nativo, -a; ~ **country** paese *m* nativo **3.**(*indigenous, aboriginal, primitive*) indigeno, -a **4.**(*original*) originario, -a; (*innate*) innato, -a; (*language*) materno, -a **II.** *n* (*indigenous inhabitant*) indigeno, -a *m, f*; **a** ~ **of Italy** un italiano di nascita; **to speak English like a** ~ parlare inglese come un madrelingua

native American I. *n* indiano, -a d'America *m* **II.** *adj* amerindio, -a

ℹ️ La maggior parte degli specialisti concordano nel dire che i **Native Americans**, gli indiani del Nordamerica, sono emigrati dall'Asia attraversando lo stretto di Bering e si sono dispersi in direzione del Canada meridionale e degli USA ben prima della scoperta del Nuovo Mondo da parte degli esploratori europei. Si suddividono in sette aree culturali, che vanno dagli Esquimesi nel Grande Nord ai Seminoli delle Everglades in Florida e i loro stili di vita riflettono un legame molto stretto con l'ambiente in cui vivono.

native-born *adj* nativo, -a; **is he a** ~ **person or did he move there?** è nativo di lì o viene da fuori?; ~ **citizen of New York** nativo di New York

native speaker *n* madrelingua *mf*

nativity [nəˈtɪˑvəˑti] <-ies> *n* natività *f*; **the Nativity** la Natività

N

nativity play *n* rappresentazione *f* della natività

NATO ['neɪ·t̬oʊ] *n abbr of* **North Atlantic Treaty Organization** NATO *f*

natter ['næ·t̬ɚ] *vi inf* to ~ (**away**) chiacchierare

natural ['næt·ʃɚ·əl] I. *adj* 1. (*not artificial, inherent*) naturale; ~ **causes** cause *fpl* naturali; **to die of** ~ **causes** morire per cause naturali; ~ **disaster** calamità *f* naturale; **to be a** ~ **blonde** essere bionda naturale; ~ **father** padre *m* naturale 2. (*usual, to be expected*) naturale; **a** ~ **explanation** una spiegazione naturale II. *n* 1. *inf* **to be a** ~ **for sth** avere un talento naturale per qc 2. MUS nota *f* naturale

natural childbirth *n* parto *m* naturale

natural gas *n* gas *m* naturale

natural history *n* storia *f* naturale; ~ **museum** museo *m* di Storia Naturale

naturalism ['næ·tʃɚ·ə·lɪ·zəm] *n* naturalismo *m*

naturalist ['næ·tʃɚ·ə·lɪst] I. *n* naturalista *mf* II. *adj* naturalista

naturalistic [ˌnæ·tʃɚ·əl·'ɪs·tɪk] *adj* naturalista

naturalization [ˌnæ·tʃɚ·ə·lɪ·'zeɪ·ʃən] *n* naturalizzazione *f*

naturalize ['næ·tʃɚ·ə·laɪz] *vt* naturalizzare

naturalized *adj* naturalizzato, -a; ~ **citizen** cittaddino, -a *m*, *f* naturalizzato, -a

natural language *n* linguaggio *m* naturale

naturally *adv* naturalmente

natural resources *npl* risorse *fpl* naturali; **to be rich/poor in** ~ essere ricco/povero di risorse naturali

natural science *n*, **natural sciences** *npl* scienze *fpl* naturali

natural selection *n* selezione *f* naturale

nature ['neɪ·tʃɚ] *n* 1. (*the environment, natural forces*) natura *f;* **to get back to** ~ ritornare alla natura; **to let** ~ **take its course** lasciare che la natura faccia il suo corso 2. (*essential or innate qualities*) natura *f;* **things of this** ~ cose di questa natura; **in the** ~ **of things** nella natura delle cose; **to be in sb's** ~ essere nella natura di qn ▶ **second** ~ seconda natura

nature conservation *n* tutela *f* della natura

nature lover *n* amante *mf* della natura

nature reserve *n* riserva *f* naturale

nature study *n* storia *f* naturale

nature trail *n* percorso *m* naturalistico

nature worship *n* culto *m* della natura

naturism ['neɪ·tʃə·rɪ·zəm] *n* naturismo *m*

naturist ['neɪ·tʃə·rɪst] *n form* naturista *mf*

naught [nɑːt] *pron lit* niente *m;* **to be all for** ~ essere del tutto inutile

naughty ['nɑː·t̬i] <-ier, -iest> *adj* 1. (*badly behaved: children*) birichino, a 2. *iron* (*adults*) birbante 3. *iron, inf* (*sexually stimulating*) piccante

nausea ['nɑː·ziə] *n a. fig* nausea *f;* **feeling of** ~ senso *m* di nausea; **to suffer from** ~ avere la nausea

nauseate ['nɑː·zɪ·eit] *vt form* nauseare; **to be** ~**d by sth** essere nauseato da qc

nauseating ['nɑː·zɪ·eɪ·tɪŋ] *adj* nauseante

nauseous ['nɑː·ʃəs] *adj* nauseante; **she is** ~ ha la nausea

nautical ['nɑː·t̬ɪ·kəl] *adj* nautico, -a; ~ **chart** carta *f* nautica

nautical mile *n* miglio *m* marino

naval ['neɪ·vəl] *adj* (*battle, engagement, force*) navale; ~ **commander** ufficiale *m* di marina

naval academy <-ies> *n* accademia *f* navale

naval base *n* base *f* navale

naval power *n* potenza *f* navale

naval warfare *n* guerra *f* navale

nave [neɪv] *n* navata *f*

navel ['neɪ·vl] *n* 1. ombelico *m* 2. *fig* **to contemplate one's** ~ contemplare il proprio ombelico

navel orange *n* arancia *f* navel

navigable ['næ·vɪ·gə·bl] *adj* navigabile; ~ **waters** acque *fpl* navigabili

navigate ['næ·vɪ·geɪt] I. *vt* 1. (*steer*) governare; AVIAT pilotare; AUTO guidare 2. (*sail*) navigare; **to** ~ **the ocean/a river** navigare l'oceano/un fiume 3. (*cross*) attraversare 4. COMPUT **to** ~ **the Internet** navigare in Internet II. *vi* NAUT, AVIAT navigare; AUTO fare da navigatore

navigation [ˌnæ·vɪ·'geɪ·ʃən] *n* navigazione *f*

navigational [ˌnæ·vɪ·'geɪʃ·nəl] *adj* di navigazione; ~ **error** errore *m* di navigazione

navigator ['næ·vɪ·geɪ·t̬ɚ] *n* AUTO navigatore, -trice *m*, *f*

navy ['neɪ·vi] I. <-ies> *n* (*country's military fleet and servicemen*) **the Navy** la Marina *f;* **to be in the Navy** essere in Marina; **to serve in the** ~ servire in Marina II. *adj* (*dark blue*) blu marino

navy bean *n* fagiolo *m* bianco

nay [neɪ] I. *adv form* no II. *n* (*negative vote*) voto *m* contrario

Nazi ['nɑː·tsi] *n* nazista *mf*

Naziism *n*, **Nazism** ['nɑː·tsɪ·zəm] *n* nazismo *m*

NB [ˌen·'biː] 1. *abbr of* **nota bene** N.B. 2. *abbr of* **New Brunswick** New Brunswick

NBA [ˌen·biː·'eɪ] *n abbr of* **National Basketball Association** NBA *f*

NC *n abbr of* **North Carolina** NC

NCO [ˌen·siː·'oʊ] *n abbr of* **noncommissioned officer** sottufficiale *m*

ND *n abbr of* **North Dakota** ND

NE [ˌen·'iː] 1. *abbr of* **Nebraska** NB 2. *abbr of* **New England** NE 3. *abbr of* **northeast** NE

neap tide ['niːp·ˌtaɪd] *n* marea *f* delle quadrature

near [nɪr] I. *adj* 1. (*spatial*) vicino, -a 2. (*temporal*) vicino, -a; **in the** ~ **future** nel prossimo futuro 3. (*dear*) **a** ~ **and dear friend** un amico intimo 4. (*similar: portrait*) simile; **the** ~**est thing to sth** la cosa che più assomiglia a qc 5. (*almost true*) **to have a** ~ **accident** fare quasi un incidente; **that was a** ~ **miss** [*o* **thing**] c'è mancato poco II. *adv* 1. (*spatial or temporal*) vicino; **to be** ~ essere vicino; **to**

come ~ avvicinarsi; **to live quite** ~ vivere abbastanza vicino; ~ **at hand** a portata di mano; **to come** ~**er to sb/sth** avvicinarsi di più a qu/qc **2.** (*almost*) ~ **to tears** sul punto di piangere; **as** ~ **as I can guess** per quanto ne so **III.** *prep* **1.** (*in proximity to*) ~ (**to**) vicino (a); ~ (**to**) **the house** vicino alla casa; ~ **the end of the film** verso la fine del film **2.** (*almost*) **it's** ~ **midnight** è quasi mezzanotte; **it's nowhere** ~ **enough** non è neanche lontanamente sufficiente **3.** (*about ready to*) **to be** ~ **to doing sth** essere sul punto di fare qc **4.** (*like*) **the copy is** ~ **to the original** la copia è simile all'originale **IV.** *vt* avvicinarsi a; **it is** ~**ing completion** è quasi finito; **he is** ~**ing his goal** si sta avvicinando alla meta

nearby [ˌnɪrˈbaɪ] **I.** *adj* vicino, -a **II.** *adv* vicino; **is it** ~? è vicino?

Near East *n* **the** ~ il Vicino oriente *m*

nearly [ˈnɪrˌli] *adv* quasi; ~ **certain** quasi certo; **to be not** ~ **as bad** essere assai meno peggio; **to be** ~ **there** essere quasi arrivato; **I very** ~ **bought that car** per poco non compravo quella macchina; **to be** ~ **sth** essere quasi qc; **that wall is** ~ **ten feet high** quella parete è alta quasi tre metri; **she's** ~ **as tall as her father** è alta quasi come suo padre

near-sighted [ˌnɪrˈsaɪˌʈɪd] *adj a. fig* miope

nearsightedness [ˌnɪrˈsaɪˌʈɪdˌnɪs] *n a. fig* miopia *f*

neat [niːt] *adj* **1.** (*orderly, well-ordered*) ordinato, -a; (*appearance, beard*) curato, -a; **to be** ~ **in one's habits** essere ordinato; ~ **and tidy** ordinato **2.** (*deft*) buono, -a; ~ **solution** buona soluzione *f* **3.** (*undiluted, pure*) puro, -a; **I'll have a** ~ **gin please** io prendo un gin liscio **4.** *inf* (*fine, good, excellent*) fantastico, -a *inf;* **a** ~ **guy** un tipo figo

neaten [niːˌtən] *vt* (*dress*) sistemare; **to** ~ **one's hair** sistemarsi i capelli

neatly *adv* **1.** (*with care*) con cura **2.** (*in orderly fashion*) in modo ordinato **3.** (*deftly*) abilmente

neatness [ˈniːtˌnəs] *n* ordine *m*

Nebraska [nəˈbræsˌkə] *n* Nebraska *m*

nebula [ˈnebˌjəˌlə] <-lae *o* -las> *n* ASTR nebulosa *f*

nebulae *n pl of* **nebula**

nebular *adj* nebulare

nebulous [ˈnebˌjʊˌləs] *adj* nebuloso, -a; ~ **promise** vaga promessa *f*

necessarily [ˌneˌsəˈserəˌli] *adv* necessariamente; **not** ~ non necessariamente

necessary [ˈneˌsəˌseˌri] *adj* necesario, -a; **to make the** ~ **arrangements** fare i preparativi necessari; **a** ~ **evil** un male necesario; **strictly** ~ strettamente necessario; **to be** ~ essere necessario; **that won't be** ~ non sarà necessario; **was it really** ~ **for you to say that?** dovevi proprio dirlo?; **to do what is** ~ fare ciò che è necessario; **if** ~ se necessario

necessitate [nəˈseˌsɪˌteɪt] *vt form* rendere necessario; **to** ~ **doing sth** richiedere che si

faccia qc

necessity [nəˈseˌsəˌti] <-ies> *n* (*need*) necessità *f;* **in case of** ~ in caso di necessità; **when the** ~ **arises** quando se ne presenta la necessità; ~ **of doing sth** necessità di fare qc; ~ **for sb to do sth** bisogno che qu faccia qc; **there's no** ~ **to pay in advance** non c'è bisogno di pagare in anticipo; **by** ~ per necessità; **the bare** ~ lo stretto indispensabile ▶ ~ **is the mother of** invention *prov* la necessità aguzza l'ingegno *prov*

neck [nek] **I.** *n* **1.** ANAT collo *m;* **to fling one's arms around sb's** ~ gettare le braccia al collo di qu **2.** FASHION scollo *m;* **round** ~ **sweater** maglione (a) girocollo **3.** (*of bottle, violin*) collo *m* ▶ **to be up to one's** ~ **in sth** *inf* essere dentro fino al collo in qc; **to be breathing down sb's** ~ stare alle costole di qu **II.** *vi inf* pomiciare

neckerchief [ˈneˌkəˌtʃɪf] <neckerchieves> *n* fazzoletto *m* da collo

necklace [ˈnekˌlɪs] *n* collana *f*

neckline [ˈnekˌlaɪn] *n* scollatura *f*

necktie *n* cravatta *f*

nectar [ˈnekˌtə] *n* nettare *m*

nectarine [ˌnekˌtəˈriːn] *n* nettarina *f*

née [neɪ] *adj* nata

need [niːd] **I.** *n* **1.** bisogno *m;* **in** ~ bisognoso, -a; ~ **for sb/sth** bisogno di qu/qc; **to be in** ~ **of sth** aver bisogno di qc; **to have no** ~ **of sth** non avere alcun bisogno di qc; **as the** ~ **arises** al bisogno; **if** ~(**s**) **be** se fosse necessario; **no** ~ **to be sth** nessun bisogno di essere qc; **there's no** ~ **to shout so loud** non c'è bisogno di gridare così forte; **in sb's hour of** ~ (*emergency, crisis*) nel momento di maggior bisogno di qu **2.** *pl* **basic** ~**s** bisogni primari **II.** *vt* **1.** (*require*) avere bisogno di; **to** ~ **sb to do sth** aver bisogno che qu faccia qc **2.** (*ought to have*) necessitare di; **to not** ~ **sth** non esserci bisogno di qc; **to** ~ **sth** richiedere qc; **the house needs cleaning** la casa ha bisogno di una pulita; **I** ~ **it like** (**I** ~) **a hole in my head** *iron* non ne ho assolutamente bisogno **3.** (*must, have*) **to** ~ **to do sth** dover fare qc; ~ **we/I/you?** dobbiamo/devo/devi proprio?; **there was no** ~ **to do sth** non c'era bisogno di fare qc

needed *adj* necessario, -a

needle [ˈniːˌdl] **I.** *n* ago *m;* **hypodermic** ~ siringa *f* (ipodermica); **knitting** ~ ferro *m* da calza; ~ **and thread** ago e filo; **to thread a** ~ infilare l'ago ▶ **a** ~ **in a** haystack un ago in un pagliaio; **to look for a** ~ **in a haystack** cercare un ago in un pagliaio **II.** *vt* punzecchiare

needless [ˈniːdˌlɪs] *adj* inutile; ~ **to say** ... inutile dire...; ~ **to say, I didn't reply** naturalmente non ho risposto

needlework [ˈniːˌdlˌwɜːrk] *n* (*sewing*) cucito *m;* (*embroidery*) ricamo *m*

needn't [ˈniːˌdənt] = **need not** *s.* **need**

needy [ˈniːˌdi] **I.** <-ier, -iest> *adj* bisognoso, -a **II.** *npl* **the** ~ i bisognosi

nefarious [nə·'fe·ri·əs] *adj pej, form* nefando, -a

negate [nɪ·'geɪt] *vt* annullare

negation [nɪ·'geɪ·ʃən] *n* negazione *f*

negative ['ne·gə·tɪv] I. *adj a.* LING, MED negativo, -a; ~ **answer** risposta *f* negativa; ~ **form** forma *f* negativa; ~ **pole** polo *m* negativo; ~ **number** numero *m* negativo; **to be ~ about sth/sb** avere un atteggiamento negativo nei confronti di qu/qc II. *n* 1.(*rejection*) risposta *f* negativa 2.(*making use of negation*) negazione *f* 3.PHOT negativo *m* III. *vt* (*veto: application, plan*) respingere

negatively *adv* negativamente

negativity [ˌne·gə·'tɪ·və·ti] *n* negatività *f*

neglect [nɪ·'glekt] I. *vt* trascurare; **to ~ one's duties** trascurare i propri doveri; **to ~ to do sth** dimenticarsi di fare qc; **I'd ~ed to write to him** mi ero dimenticato di scrivergli II. *n* (*poor state, unrepaired state*) abbandono *m;* **to be in a state of ~** essere in uno stato di abbandono; **to fall into a state of ~** andare in rovina

neglected *adj* (*person, thing*) trascurato, -a

neglectful [nɪ·'glekt·fəl] *adj* negligente; ~ **parents** genitori *mpl* negligenti; **to be ~ of sth/ sb** venir meno ai propri doveri nei confronti di qc/qu

negligée *n,* **negligee** [ˌne·glə·'ʒeɪ] *n* négligé *m; inv*

negligence ['ne·glɪ·dʒənts] *n* 1.(*lack of care, inattention, indifference*) negligenza *f* 2.LAW **gross ~** colpa *f* grave

negligible ['ne·glɪ·dʒə·bl] *adj* trascurabile

negotiable [nɪ·'gou·ʃiə·bl] *adj* negoziabile; ~ **securities** FIN titoli *mpl* trasferibili; **non ~** non trasferibile

negotiate [nɪ·'gou·ʃi·eɪt] I. *vt* 1.(*discuss*) negoziare; **to ~ a loan/treaty** negoziare un prestito/accordo 2.(*check, securities*) negoziare II. *vi* negoziare; **to ~ on sth** negoziare qc; **to ~ with sb** negoziare con qu

negotiating committee *n* comitato *m* di negoziazione

negotiating table *n fig* tavolo *m* di negoziazione

negotiation [nɪ·ˌgou·ʃi·'eɪ·ʃən] *n* negoziato *m;* ~ **for sth** negoziato per qc

negotiator [nɪ·'gou·ʃi·eɪ·tə·] *n* negoziatore, -trice *m, f*

Negress ['niː·grɪs] *n pej* negra *f*

Negro ['niː·grou] <-es> *n pej* negro *m*

Negroid [niː·grɔ·ɪd] *adj* negroide

neigh [neɪ] I. *n* nitrito *m* II. *vi* nitrire

neighbor ['neɪ·bə·] I. *n* vicino, -a *m, f* ▶ love your ~ as you love yourself ama il prossimo tuo come te stesso II. *vi* **to ~ on sth** confinare con qc

neighborhood ['neɪ·bə·hʊd] *n* 1.(*smallish localized community*) quartiere *m;* (*people*) vicinato *m;* **a closed/friendly ~** vicini chiusi/ socievoli; **the whole ~ is talking about it** ne parla tutto il vicinato 2.(*vicinity*) vicinanze *fpl,* dintorni *mpl;* **in the ~** nei paraggi; **I wouldn't like to live in the ~ of the airport** non mi piacerebbe vivere vicino all'aeroporto 3.**in the ~ of** intorno a; **we're hoping to get something in the ~ of $125,000 for the house** per la casa speriamo di riuscire a prendere intorno ai 125.000 dollari

neighborhood watch *n vigilanza organizzata dagli stessi abitanti di un quartiere per prevenire e combattere episodi di criminalità*

neighboring ['neɪ·bə·rɪŋ] *adj* (*nearby, bordering*) vicino, -a; ~ **house** casa *f* vicina; ~ **country** paese *m* vicino

neighborliness *n* cordialità e disponibilità nei confronti dei vicini; **an act of ~** un atto di buon vicinato; **good ~** buon vicinato *m*

neighborly ['neɪ·bə·li] *adj* cordiale

neither ['niː·ðə·] I. *pron* nessuno, -a; **which one? — ~ (of them)** quale? — nessuno dei due II. *adv* né; ~ **... nor ...** né... né...; **he is ~ wounded nor dead** non è né ferito né morto III. *conj* nemmeno; **if he won't eat, ~ will I** se lui non mangia, non mangio nemmeno io IV. *adj* nessuno, -a; **in ~ case** in nessun caso; ~ **book is good** nessuno dei due libri va bene

nemesis ['ne·mə·sɪs] <-ses> *n a. fig* nemesi *f*

neoclassical [ˌniː·ou·'klæ·sɪ·kəl] *adj* neoclassico, -a

neocolonialist [ˌniː·ou·kə·'lou·niə·lɪst] *adj* neocolonialista

Neolithic [ˌniː·ou·'lɪ·θɪk] *adj* neolitico, -a; ~ **Period** periodo *m* neolitico

neologism [niː·'ɑː·lə·dʒɪ·zəm] *n form* neologismo *m*

neon ['niː·ɑːn] *n* neon *m*

neo-Nazi [ˌnɪː·əʊ·'nɑː·tsi] I. *n* neonazista *mf* II. *adj* neonazista

neon lamp *n,* **neon light** *n* lampada *f* al neon

neon sign *n* insegna *f* al neon

nephew ['nef·juː] *n* nipote *m*

nephritis [nɪ·'fraɪ·təs] *n* MED nefrite *f*

nepotism ['ne·pə·tɪ·zəm] *n* nepotismo *m*

Neptune ['nep·tjuːn] *n* Nettuno *m*

nerd [nɜːrd] *n* sfigato, -a *m, f*

nerdy <-ier, -iest> *adj inf* sfigato, -a

nerve [nɜːrv] *n* 1. ANAT nervo *m* 2.(*high nervousness*) ~ **s** nervi *mpl;* **to be in a state of ~ s** essere nervoso; **to be a bundle of ~ s** *fig* avere i nervi a fior di pelle; **to calm one's ~ s** calmarsi; **to get on sb's ~ s** *inf* dare sui nervi a qu 3.(*courage, bravery*) coraggio *m;* **to lose one's ~** perdersi d'animo 4.(*apprehension*) ~ **s** nervosismo *m* 5.(*temerity*) sfacciataggine *f;* **to have the ~ to do sth** *inf* avere la faccia tosta di fare qc; **of all the ~!** *inf* che faccia tosta ▶ ~ **s of** steel nervi *mpl* d'acciaio; **to** expose [*o* to hit] a (raw) ~ toccare un nervo scoperto

nerve cell *n* cellula *f* nervosa

nerve center *n* 1.(*nerve cells*) centro *m* nervoso 2. *fig* (*center of control*) centro *m* nevralgico

nerve gas <-es> *n* gas *m* nervino

nerveless ['nɜːrv·lɪs] *adj* **1.** (*calm*) padrone di sé **2.** (*lacking courage*) senza nerbo

nerve-racking ['nɜːrv·ræ·kɪŋ] *adj* snervante

nervous ['nɜːr·vəs] *adj* (*jumpy*) nervoso, -a; (*edgy*) teso, -a; **of a ~ disposition** facilmente impressionabile; **to be ~ in sb's presence** essere nervoso in presenza di qu; **you look like a ~ wreck!** devi avere i nervi a pezzi!; **to make sb ~** far innervosire qu; **to be ~ about sth** essere nervoso per qc

nervous breakdown *n* esaurimento *m* nervoso; **to have a ~** avere un esaurimento nervoso

nervously *adv* nervosamente

nervousness *n* (*nervous condition or state, excitement*) nervosismo *m*; (*fearfulness*) paura *f*; **~ about sth** paura per qc

nervous system *n* sistema *f* nervoso

nervy ['nɜːr·vi] <-ier, -iest> *adj* **1.** (*rude*) sfrontato, -a **2.** (*courageous*) coraggioso, -a

nest [nest] **I.** *n* **1.** (*of insects, birds and small animals*) nido *m* **2.** (*cozy domicile*) nido *m*; **to leave the ~** lasciare il nido **3.** *pej* (*den*) covo *m* **4.** (*location that swarms with sth bad*) covo *m* **5.** (*set, cluster, assemblage*) set *m* **II.** *vi* fare il nido

nest egg *n* **1.** (*egg in a nest*) endice *m* **2.** (*money saved*) gruzzolo *mpl*

nesting *adj* **1.** (*of sets fitting together*) che si incastrano **2.** (*concerning nests*) **~ time** nidificazione *f*

nestle ['ne·sl] **I.** *vt* appoggiare; **to ~ sth on sth** appoggiare qc contro qc **II.** *vi* **1.** (*snuggle up*) accoccolarsi; **to ~ up to sb** rannicchiarsi contro qc **2.** (*be in sheltered position*) essere annidato, -a

nestling ['nest·lɪŋ] *n* nidiace *m*

net¹ [net] **I.** *n* **1.** (*material with spaces*) rete *f*; (*fine netted fabric*) tulle *m inv*; **mosquito ~** zanzariera *f* **2.** (*device for trapping fish*) rete *f*; **to haul in a ~** ritirare una rete; **to fall** [*o* **slip**] **through the ~** *fig* sfuggire alle maglie di qu/qc **3.** SPORTS rete *f* **II.** <-tt-> *vt* (*catch: fish*) prendere (con la rete); (*criminals*) catturare

net² [net] **I.** *adj* **1.** ECON netto, -a; **~ assets** patrimonio *m* netto; **~ income** [*o* **earnings**] reddito *m* netto **2.** (*excluding package: weight*) netto, -a; **~ tonnage** tonnellaggio *m* netto **II.** *vt* **to ~ 10,000 dollar** guadagnare 10.000 dollari netti

Net [net] *n* COMPUT **the ~** la rete; **~ surfer** navigatore, -trice *m, f* della rete

nether ['ne·θəɾ] *adj iron, liter* inferiore; **~ regions** *fig* (*hell*) inferi *mpl*; (*of building*) seminterrato *m*

Netherlands ['ne·ðəɾ·ləndz] *n* **the ~** i Paesi *m pl* Bassi

netiquette ['ne·tɪ·ket] *n* COMPUT netiquette *f inv, norme per il corretto comportamento nell'uso di Internet e della posta elettronica*

Netspeak ['net·spiːk] *adj* COMPUT linguaggio *m* di Internet

nett [net] *adj, vt s.* **net¹** **II.**, **net²**

netting ['ne·tɪŋ] *n* **1.** (*net*) rete *f*; **you should get some ~ for those windows** dovresti comprare una zanzariera per quelle finestre **2.** SPORTS rete *f*

nettle ['ne·tl] **I.** *n* ortica *f* **II.** *vt* irritare; **to be ~d by sth** essere infastidito da qc

nettle rash <-es> *n* orticaria *f*

net weight *n* peso *m* netto

network ['net·wɜːrk] **I.** *n* **1.** COMPUT, TEL rete *f*; **cable ~** cablaggio *m*; **computer ~** rete informatica; **telephone ~** rete telefonica **2.** TV network *m inv* **II.** *vt* **1.** (*link together*) collegare in rete **2.** (*broadcast*) trasmettere a reti unificate **III.** *vi* crearsi una rete di contatti

networking *n* COMPUT collegamento *m* in rete

neural ['nʊ·rəl] *adj* neurale

neuralgia [nʊ·ˈræl·dʒə] *n* nevralgia *f*

neuralgic [nʊ·ˈræl·dʒɪk] *adj* nevralgico, -a

neural network *n* COMPUT rete *f* neurale

neurasthenia [nʊ·ræs·ˈθiː·niə] *n* nevrastenia *f*

neuritis [nʊ·ˈrai·təs] *n* MED nevrite *f*

neurological [nʊ·rə·ˈlɑ·dʒɪ·kəl] *adj* neurologico, -a; **~ disorder** disturbo *m* neurologico

neurologist [nʊ·ˈrɑː·lə·dʒɪst] *n* neurologo, -a *m, f*

neurology [nʊ·ˈrɑː·lə·dʒi] *n* neurologia *f*

neuron ['nʊ·rɑːn] *n*, **neurone** ['nʊ·roʊn] *n* neurone *m*

neuroscience [ˌnʊ·roʊ·ˈsai·ənts] *n* neuroscienza *f*

neurosis [nʊ·ˈroʊ·sɪs] <-es> *n* nevrosi *f inv*

neurosurgeon [ˌnʊ·roʊ·ˈsɜːr·dʒən] *n* neurochirurgo *m*

neurosurgery [ˌnʊ·roʊ·ˈsɜːr·dʒə·ri] *n* neurochirurgia *f*

neurotic [nʊ·ˈrɑː·tɪk] **I.** *n* nevrotico, -a *m, f* **II.** *adj* nevrotico, -a

neurotransmitter [ˌnʊ·roʊ·træns·ˈmɪ·təɾ] *n* MED neurotrasmettitore *m*

neuter ['nuː·təɾ] **I.** *adj* neutro, -a; **~ noun** LING sostantivo *m* neutro **II.** *vt* **1.** (*castrate: male*) castrare **2.** (*sterilize: female*) sterilizzare **3.** (*neutralize*) neutralizzare

neutral ['nuː·trəl] **I.** *adj* **1.** (*uninvolved, unemotional*) neutrale; **~ country** POL paese *m* neutrale; **to remain ~** rimanere neutrale **2.** *a.* CHEM, ELEC neutro, -a **II.** *n* **1.** (*non-combatant in war*) paese *m* neutrale **2.** (*part of gear system*) posizione *f* di folle; **in ~** in folle

neutrality [nuː·ˈtræ·lə·ti] *n* neutralità *f*

neutralization [ˌnuː·trə·lɪ·ˈzei·ʃən] *n* neutralizzazione *f*

neutralize ['nuː·trə·laiz] *vt* neutralizzare; **the bomb was ~d by the specialists** la bomba fu dissinnescata dagli specialisti

neutron ['nuː·trɑːn] *n* neutrone *m*

neutron bomb *n* bomba *f* al neutrone

Nevada [nə·ˈvɑː·də] *n* Nevada *f*

never ['ne·vəɾ] *adv* **1.** (*at no time, on no occasion*) non...mai; **I ~ forget a face** non dimentico mai un volto **2.** (*under no circumstances*) mai; **~ again!** mai più!; **~ fear!** niente paura!; **well I ~ (did)** chi l'avrebbe mai detto!; **it's ~ too late to do sth** non è mai troppo tardi per fare qc; **~ before had I had so much money** non avevo mai avuto tanti soldi in vita mia; **as ~ before** come mai prima; **~ ever** mai e poi mai; **~ mind** non importa; **~ say die** *fig* non gettare la spugna

never-ending ['ne·və·'en·dɪŋ] *adj* infinito, -a

never-failing *adj* infallibile

nevermore *adv* mai più

never-never land *n fig, inf* mondo *m* dei sogni

nevertheless [ˌne·və·ðə·'les] *adv* ciò nonostante, tuttavia

new [nu:] I. *adj* **1.** (*latest, recent*) nuovo, -a; (*word*) nuovo, -a; **~ technology** nuova tecnologia *f;* **to be the ~est fad** [*o* **craze**] *inf* essere l'ultima moda **2.** (*changed*) nuovo, -a; **~ boy** SCHOOL nuovo alunno; **~ girl** SCHOOL nuova alunna; **the ~ kid on the block** l'ultimo arrivato **3.** (*inexperienced*) nuovo, -a; **to be a ~ one on sb** essere una novità per qu; **she's ~ to the job** è nuova del mestiere **4.** (*in new condition*) nuovo, -a; **brand ~** nuovo di zecca **5.** (*fresh*) fresco, -a; **~ blood** *fig* forze *f pl* fresche; **to feel like a ~ man/woman** sentirsi rinato, -a **6.** (*freshly found or made public*) fresco, -a II. *n* **the ~** il nuovo

New Age *n* **1.** (*movement*) New Age *f* **2.** (*music*) new age *f*

New Ager *n* seguace *mf* della New Age

New-Agey *adj* new age

newbie *n* COMPUT newbie *mf inv, nuovo arrivato in un blog, un forum, un newsgroup online*

newborn I. *adj* appena nato, -a; **~ democracy** democrazia *f* appena nata; **~ science** scienza *f* recente; **~ baby** neonato, -a *m, f* II. *n* **the ~** i neonati

New Brunswick *n* Nuovo Brunswick *m*

New Caledonia *n* Nuova Caledonia *f*

newcomer *n* **1.** (*person who has just arrived*) nuovo arrivato, -a *m, f* **2.** (*stranger*) nuovo, -a *m, f;* **I'm a ~ to Phoenix** sono nuovo di Phoenix **3.** (*beginner, recent starter*) novellino, -a *m, f*

newel ['nu:·əl] *n* **1.** (*of a circular staircase*) montante *m* centrale **2.** (*supporting banister*) montante *m*

New England *n* New England *m*

newfangled *adj* ultramoderno, -a

new-fashioned *adj* moderno, -a, all'ultima moda

new-found [ˌnu:·'faʊnd] *adj* nuovo; **a ~ friend** un nuovo amico

Newfoundland¹ ['nu:·fənd·lənd] *n* Terranova *f*

Newfoundland² ['nu:·fənd·lənd], **Newfoundland dog** *n* ZOOL terranova *m inv*

New Hampshire *n* New Hampshire *m*

newish ['nu:·ɪʃ] *adj inf* abbastanza nuovo, -a

New Jersey *n* New Jersey *m*

new-laid ['nu:·'leɪd] *adj* **~ eggs** uova *fpl* fresche di giornata

newly ['nu:·li] *adv* **1.** (*recently*) di recente; **~ married** appena sposati **2.** (*shaved, painted*)

di fresco **3.** (*done differently than before*) in modo nuovo

newlywed ['nu:·lɪ·wed] I. *npl* sposini *mpl* II. *adj* appena sposato, -a

New Mexico *n* Nuovo Messico *m*

new moon *n* luna *f* nuova

New Orleans *n* New Orleans *f*

new potatoes *npl* patate *fpl* novelle

New Right *n* Nuova Destra *f*

news [nu:z] *n + sing vb* **1.** (*fresh information*) notizie *fpl;* **the ~ media** i mezzi di informazione; **bad/good ~** buone/cattive notizie; **he's bad ~ for the company** porterà solo grane alla società; **to break the ~ to sb** dare la notizia a qu; **when the ~ broke** quando la cosa si venne a sapere; **really! that's ~ to me** davvero? non ne sapevo niente **2.** TV telegiornale *m,* notiziario *m;* RADIO giornale *m* radio, notiziario *m;* **to be ~** fare notizia ▶ **no ~ is good ~** *prov* nessuna nuova, buona nuova *prov*

news agency <-ies> *n* agenzia *f* di stampa

newsboy *n* **1.** (*seller*) ragazzo che vende i giornali **2.** (*sb delivering papers*) ragazzo che consegna i giornali

newscast *n* notiziario *m*

newscaster *n* conduttore, -trice *m, f* (di telegiornale o giornale radio)

news conference *n* conferenza *f* stampa

news dealer *n* giornalaio, -a *m, f*

newsflash <-es> *n* notiziario *m* flash

newsgroup *n* COMPUT gruppo *m* di discussione

newshound *n fig, inf* cronista *mf* d'assalto

news item *n* notizia *f*

newsletter *n* bollettino *m* di informazione

newsmonger *n* (*sb given to gossiping*) pettegolo, -a *m, f*

newspaper *n* giornale *m;* **~ clipping** ritaglio *m* di giornale

newspeak *n pej* politichese *m*

newsprint *n* carta *f* da giornale

newsreel *n* cinegiornale *m*

news release *n* comunicato *m* stampa

news report *n* notizia *f*

newsroom *n* redazione *f*

newsstand *n* edicola *f*

newsvendor *n* giornalaio, -a *m, f*

newsworthy *adj* che fa notizia

newsy ['nu:·zi] <-ier, -iest> *adj* ricco, -a di notizie; **a ~ letter** una lettera piena di notizie

newt [nu:t] *n* tritone *m*

New Testament *n* REL Nuovo Testamento *m*

new town *n centro urbano creato per ridistribuire la popolazione*

new wave *n fig* **1.** (*music*) new wave *f inv* **2.** (*fresh outbreak*) nuova ondata *f;* **a ~ of layoffs/violence** una nuova ondata di licenziamenti/violenza

new world order *n,* **New World Order** *n* nuovo ordine *m* mondiale

New Year *n* **1.** anno *m* nuovo; **Happy ~** felice anno nuovo; **to celebrate ~** festeggiare l'anno nuovo **2.** (*opening weeks of year*) inizio *m*

dell'anno
New Year's *n inf* (*New Year's Day*) capodanno *m;* (*New Year's Eve*) ultimo *m* dell'anno
New Year's Day *n* capodanno *m*
New Year's Eve *n* ultimo *m* dell'anno
New York I. *n* New York *f* II. *adj* newyorkese
New Yorker *n* newyorkese *mf*
New Zealand I. *n* Nuova Zelanda *f* II. *adj* neozelandese
New Zealander *n* neozelandese *mf*
next [nekst] I. *adj* 1. (*nearest in location*) accanto, -a 2. (*following in time*) prossimo, -a; **the ~ day** il giorno seguente; **~ month** il mese prossimo; **the ~ thing** il passo successivo; (**the**) **~ time** la prossima volta 3. (*following in order*) successivo, a; **to be ~** venire dopo; **to be** (**the**) **~ to do sth** fare qc subito dopo; **~ to sth/sb** vicino a qc/qu II. *adv* 1. (*afterwards, subsequently*) dopo 2. (*almost as much*) **~ to** subito dopo; **cheese is my favorite food and ~ to cheese I like chocolate best** dopo il formaggio, la cioccolata è il mio cibo preferito 3. (*again, once more*) di nuovo; **when I saw him ~ he had transformed** quando lo rividi era molto cambiato; **when are you going to New York ~?** quando vai a New York la prossima volta ? 4. (*almost*) quasi; **~ to impossible** quasi impossibile; **~ to nothing** quasi niente 5. (*second*) **the ~ best thing** in alternativa, la cosa migliore III. *prep* 1. (*beside*) **~ to** accanto a; **~ to the skin** a contatto con la pelle; **my room is ~ to yours** la mia stanza è accanto alla tua 2. (*almost*) quasi; **to cost ~ to nothing** non costare quasi niente 3. (*second to*) **~ to last** penultimo; **~ to Bach, I like Mozart best** dopo Bach, Mozart è quello che mi piace di più
next door [ˌnekst·'dɔːr] *adv* accanto; **we live ~ to the airport** abitiamo vicino all'aeroporto
next-door neighbor *n* vicino, -a *m, f* di casa
next of kin *n* parente *mf* stretto, -a
nexus ['nek·səs] *n inv* nesso *m*
NF [ˌen·'ef] *n abbr of* **Newfoundland** Terranova
NFL [ˌen·ef·'el] *n abbr of* **National Football League** NFL *f*
NH *n abbr of* **New Hampshire** NH
NHL [ˌen·eɪtʃ·'el] *n abbr of* **National Hockey League** NHL *f*
Niagara Falls [naɪ·ˌæ·gə·rə·'fɔːlz] *n* (**the**) ~ le cascate *f pl* del Niagara
nib [nɪb] *n* (*of a pen*) punta *f*
nibble ['nɪ·bl] I. *n* (*a small bite/peck*) boccone *m;* **to take a ~** (**at sth**) dare un morso (a qc) II. *vt* 1. (*bite*) sgranocchiare; (*rat*) rosicchiare 2. (*pick at*) mangiucchiare III. *vi* 1. (*eat*) mangiucchiare; *fig* interessarsi 2. (*deplete slowly*) **to ~ away at sth** erodere qc
Nicaragua [ˌnɪ·kə·'rɑːg·wə] *n* Nicaragua *m*
Nicaraguan I. *n* nicaraguense *mf* II. *adj* nicaraguense
nice [naɪs] I. *adj* 1. (*pleasant, agreeable*) bello,

-a; **~ one!, ~ work!** *inf* ben fatto!; **~ weather** bel tempo *m;* **~ work** *inf* buon lavoro *m;* **far ~r** molto più bello; **it is ~ to do sth** è bello fare qc 2. (*amiable*) simpatico, -a; (*kind*) gentile; **to be ~ to sb** essere gentile con qu; **it is/was ~ of sb to do sth** è/è stato gentile da parte di qu fare qc; **~ boys** bravi ragazzi 3. *iron, inf* (*unpleasant*) **that's a ~ thing to say to your brother** bel modo di rivolgerti a tuo fratello 4. (*subtle*) sottile; (*fine*) raffinato, -a II. *adv* bene
nice-looking *adj* attraente
nicely ['naɪs·li] *adv* 1. (*well, satisfactorily*) bene; **to do very ~** caversela bene 2. (*having success*) splendidamente 3. (*in healthy state*) **the princess and the baby were both doing ~** la principessa e il bambino erano entrambi in buona salute 4. (*pleasantly, politely*) gentilmente
nicety ['naɪ·sə·ti] <-ies> *n* 1. (*subtle distinction*) sottigliezza *f;* **~ of an argument** sottigliezze *fpl* di un ragionamento 2. (*precision*) precisione *f* 3. (*precise differentiations*) **niceties** sfumature *fpl;* (*in negative sense*) convenevoli *mpl*
niche [nɪtʃ] *n* 1. (*alcove*) nicchia *f* 2. (*desired job*) buon posto *m;* (*suitable position*) bella posizione *f* 3. (*place suiting a particular group*) **ecological ~** nicchia ecologica
niche market *n* ECON mercato *m* di nicchia
nick [nɪk] I. *n* (*chip in surface*) intaccatura *f* ►**in the ~ of** <u>time</u> appena in tempo II. *vt* 1. (*chip*) scheggiare; (*cut*) intaccare 2. *sl* (*trick*) fregare
nickel ['nɪ·kl] *n* 1. CHEM nichel *m* 2. (*coin*) moneta *f* da cinque centesimi (di dollaro)
nickel-plated *adj* nichelato, -a
nicknack ['nɪk·næk] *n s.* **knickknack**
nickname ['nɪk·neɪm] I. *n* soprannome *m* II. *vt* soprannominare
nicotine ['nɪ·kə·tiːn] *n* nicotina *f*
nicotine patch <-es> *n* cerotto *m* alla nicotina
niece [niːs] *n* nipote *f*
nifty ['nɪf·ti] <-ier, -iest> *adj inf* (*stylish, smart*) elegante; (*skilful*) abile
Niger ['naɪ·dʒɚ] *n* Niger *m*
Nigeria [naɪ·'dʒɪ·ri·ə] *n* Nigeria *f*
Nigerian I. *adj* nigeriano, -a II. *n* nigeriano, -a *m, f*
niggardly ['nɪ·gɚd·li] *adj* (*stingy*) taccagno, -a; (*meager*) misero, -a
nigger ['nɪ·gɚ] *n pej* negro, -a *m, f*
niggle ['nɪ·gl] I. *vi* spaccare i capelli in quattro II. *vt* (*nag pettily*) tormentare
niggling ['nɪg·lɪŋ] *adj* 1. (*doubt, worry*) assillante 2. (*needing very precise work*) di precisione
nigh [naɪ] *adj liter* vicino, -a
night [naɪt] *n* notte *f*, sera *f;* **good ~!** buona notte!; **last ~** la notte scorsa; **10** (**o'clock**) **at ~** le dieci di sera; **the ~ before** la sera prima; **open at ~** aperto di notte; **~ and day** giorno e notte; **during the ~** durante la notte; **during**

Tuesday ~ durante la notte di martedì; **far into the** ~ a tarda notte; **in the dead of (the)** ~ nel cuore della notte; **wedding** ~ prima notte di nozze; **the Arabian Nights** le mille e una notte; **Twelfth Night** notte dell'Epifania; **to work ~s** lavorare di notte

night bird [naɪt·bɜːrd] *n* uccello *m* notturno; *s.* **night owl**

night blindness *n* cecità *f* notturna

nightcap *n* **1.** (*cap*) berretto *m* da notte **2.** (*drink*) bicchierino che si beve prima di andare a dormire

nightclothes *npl* biancheria *f* da notte

nightclub *n* nightclub *m inv*

nightdress <-es> *n* camicia *f* da notte

nightfall *n* crepuscolo *m*

nightgown *n* camicia *f* da notte

nightie *n inf* camicia *f* da notte

nightingale *n* usignolo *m*

night life *n* vita *f* notturna

nightlight *n* lampada *f* da notte

nightlong *liter* **I.** *adv* per tutta la notte **II.** *adj* che dura tutta la notte

nightly [ˈnaɪt·li] **I.** *adv* ogni sera **II.** *adj* **1.** (*done or happening each night*) di tutte le sere **2.** (*nocturnal*) notturno, -a

nightmare [ˈnaɪt·mer] *n* incubo *m*

nightmarish [ˈnaɪt·me·rɪʃ] *adj* (*like a horrible dream, very distressing*) da incubo

night-night [ˈnaɪt·ˌnaɪt] *interj inf* notte

night-nurse *n* infermiere, -a di notte *m*

night owl *n* (*person*) nottambulo, -a *m, f*

night porter *n* portiere, -a di notte *m*

nights *adv* di notte

night school *n* scuola *f* serale

night shift *n* turno *m* di notte

nightshirt *n* camicia *f* da notte (da uomo)

nightspot *n inf* nightclub *m inv*

nightstand *n* comodino *m*

nightstick *n* manganello *m*

night table *n* comodino *m*

nighttime *n* notte *f;* **at** ~ di notte

night watch <-es> *n* vigilanza *f* notturna

night watchman *n* guardia *f* notturna

nightwear *n* biancheria *f* da notte

nihilism [ˈnaɪ·ə·lɪ·zəm] *n* nichilismo *m*

nihilist [ˈnaɪ·ə·lɪst] *n* nichilista *mf*

nihilistic [ˌnaɪ·ə·ˈlɪs·tɪk] *adj* nichilista

Nikkei [ˈniː·keɪ] *n,* **Nikkei Index** *n* FIN indice *m* Nikkei

nil [nɪl] *n* zero *m*

Nile [naɪl] *n* **the** ~ il Nilo *m*

nimble [ˈnɪm·bl] *adj* (*feet, fingers*) agile; (*quick-thinking*) pronto, -a; ~ **mind** mente *f* sveglia

nimbus [ˈnɪm·bəs] *n* nembo *m*

NIMBY, nimby [ˈnɪm·bi] *n abbr of* **not in my backyard** *persona pronta a mobilitarsi contro la realizzazione di grandi opere nei pressi della propria città o del proprio paese*

nincompoop [ˈnɪn·kəm·puːp] *n inf* sciocco, -a *m, f*

nine [naɪn] **I.** *adj* nove *inv* ▶**a** ~ **days'**

wonder un fuoco di paglia; ~ **times out of ten** nove volte su dieci **II.** *n* nove *m* ▶**to be dressed** to the ~**s** *inf* mettersi in tiro; *s.a.* **eight**

nineteen [ˌnaɪn·ˈtiːn] **I.** *adj* diciannove **II.** *n* diciannove *m; s.a.* **eight**

nineteenth **I.** *adj* diciannovesimo, -a **II.** *n* **1.** (*order*) diciannovesimo, -a *m, f* **2.** (*date*) diciannove *m* **3.** (*fraction, part*) diciannovesimo *m; s.a.* **eighth**

nineteenth hole *n inf* bar *m* (in un circolo di golf)

nineties *npl* **the** ~ gli anni *m pl* novanta

ninetieth [ˈnaɪn·tɪ·əθ] **I.** *adj* novantesimo, -a **II.** *n* (*order*) novantesimo, -a *m, f;* (*fraction, part*) novantesimo *m; s.a.* **eighth**

nine-to-five **I.** *adv* dalle nove alle cinque **II.** *adj* dalle nove alle cinque; ~ **schedule** orario *m* d'ufficio

ninety [ˈnaɪn·ti] **I.** *adj* novanta **II.** <-ies> *n* novanta *m; s.a.* **eighty**

ninja [ˈnɪn·dʒə] *n* ninja *mf*

ninjutsu *n* ninjutsu *m*

ninny [ˈnɪ·ni] <-ies> *n inf* babbeo, -a *m, f*

ninth [naɪnθ] **I.** *adj* nono, -a **II.** *n* **1.** (*order*) nono, -a *m, f* **2.** (*date*) nove *m* **3.** (*fraction, part*) nono *m; s.a.* **eighth**

nip¹ [nɪp] **I.** <-pp-> *vt* **1.** (*bite*) mordicchiare **2.** (*pinch, squeeze: pliers*) pizzicare **3.** (*remove: dead leaves*) strappare ▶**to** ~ **sth in the bud** *fig* stroncare qc sul nascere **II.** *n* **1.** (*of brandy*) goccio *m* **2.** (*pinch, tight squeeze*) pizzicotto *m* **3.** (*bite*) morso *m* **4.** (*coldness*) gelo *m*

nip² [nɪp] *n inf* (*alcohol*) bicchierino *m*

nipple [ˈnɪ·pl] *n* ANAT capezzolo *m;* (*teat*) tettarella *f*

nippy [ˈnɪ·pi] <-ier, -iest> *adj inf* gelido, -a

nirvana [nɪr·ˈvɑ·nə] *n a. fig* nirvana *m*

Nissen hut [ˈnɪ·sn·hʌt] *n* baracca *f* Nissen, *fatta di metallo e cemento*

nit [nɪt] *n* ZOOL lendine *m*

niter [ˈnaɪ·tə] *n* nitrato *m* di potassio

nitpick [ˈnɪt·pɪk] *vi* cercare il pelo nell'uovo

nitpicker [ˈnɪt·pɪ·kə] *n* (*quibbler*) sofista *mf;* (*petty fault-finder*) pignolo, -a *m, f*

nitpicking [ˈnɪt·pɪ·kɪŋ] **I.** *adj inf* pignolo, -a; ~ **criticism** critica *f* puntigliosa **II.** *n inf* pedanteria *f*

nitrate [ˈnaɪ·treɪt] *n* nitrato *m*

nitric [ˈnaɪ·trɪk] *adj* nitrico, -a

nitric acid *n* acido *m* nitrico

nitrite [ˈnaɪ·traɪt] *n* nitrito *m*

nitrogen [ˈnaɪ·trə·dʒən] *n* nitrogeno *m*

nitroglycerin(e) [ˌnaɪ·troʊ·ˈglɪ·sə·riːn] *n* nitroglicerina *f*

nitrous [ˈnaɪ·trəs] *adj* nitroso, -a; ~ **acid** acido *m* nitroso

nitty-gritty [ˌnɪ·ṭi·ˈgrɪ·ṭi] *n inf* **the** ~ il succo *m;* **to get down to the** ~ venire al sodo

nitwit [ˈnɪt·wɪt] *n inf* idiota *mf*

nix **I.** *vt sl* bocciare **II.** *adv inf* no **III.** *n sl* niente *m*

NJ *n abbr of* New Jersey NJ
NLP [ˌen·el·ˈpiː] *n abbr of* Neuro-Linguistic Programming programmazione *f* neurolinguistica
NM *n abbr of* New Mexico NM
NNE *abbr of* north-northeast NNE *m*
NNW *abbr of* north-northwest NNO *m*
no [noʊ] I. *adj* 1.(*not to any degree*) nessuno, -a; ~ **parking** divieto di sosta; ~ **way** in nessun modo; ~ **can do** *inf* non posso farlo; ~ **less than sth/sb** non meno di qc/qu 2.(*equivalent to a negative sentence*) no; (*emphasizes previous statement's falsity*) no, anzi II. *n* <-(e)s>, *n* (*denial, refusal*) no *m;* to **not take** ~ **for an answer** non accettare un no come risposta III. *interj* (*word used to deny*) no; (*emphasizes distress*) questa poi!
no., No. *abbr of* number no.
Noah's ark [ˌnoʊ·əz·ˈɑːrk] *n* arca *f* di Noé
Nobel prize [ˌnoʊ·bel·ˈpraɪz] *n* premio *m* Nobel
Nobel prize winner *n* vincitore, - trice *m, f* del premio Nobel
nobility [noʊ·ˈbɪ·lə·ti] *n* 1. + *sing/pl vb* (*aristocracy*) **the** ~ la nobiltà *f* 2.(*nobleness of character, selflessness*) nobiltà *f*
noble [ˈnoʊ·bl] I. *adj* 1.(*of aristocratic birth*) nobile 2.(*person, action, ideas*) nobile; ~ **act** gesto *m* nobile 3.(*splendid*) maestoso, -a 4.(*excellent*) magnifico, -a; (*horse*) nobile II. *n* nobile *mf*
nobleman [ˈnoʊ·bl·mən] <-men> *n* nobiluomo *m*
noble-minded *adj* magnanimo, -a
noblewoman <-women> *n* nobildonna *f*
nobly [ˈnoʊb·li] *adv* nobilmente
nobody [ˈnoʊ·ba·di] I. *pron indef, sing* nessuno; ~ **speaks** nessuno parla; **we saw** ~ (**else**) non abbiamo visto nessuno (altro); **he told** ~ non l'ha detto a nessuno II. *n inf* nessuno *m inv;* **those people are nobodies** quelle persone non valgono niente
nocturnal [nɑːk·ˈtɜːr·nəl] *adj form* notturno, -a
nocturnally *adv* di notte
nod [nɑːd] I. *n* cenno *m* (del capo) II. <-dd-> *vt* **to** ~ **one's head** far cenno di sì con la testa; **to** ~ **one's head to do sth** fare cenno con la testa di fare qc; **to** ~ **one's head at sth** indicare qc con un cenno della testa; **to** ~ **farewell to sb** congedarsi da qu con un cenno del capo III. <-dd-> *vi* 1.(*incline head in agreement*) assentire col capo; **to** ~ **to sb** salutare qu con un cenno del capo; **to** ~ **at sth** indicare qc con un cenno del capo 2. *inf* (*start sleeping, drift off*) addormentarsi
♦ **nod off** *vi* appisolarsi
nodding [ˈnɑː·dɪŋ] *adj* ~ **acquaintance** conoscenza *f* superficiale; **to have only a** ~ **acquaintance with sth** conoscer qu solo di vista
node [noʊd] *n* nodo *m*
nodule [ˈnɑː·djuːl] *n a.* ANAT, BOT nodulo *m*
no-fault [ˈnoʊ·fɔːlt] *adj* (*insurance*) con inden-

nizzo diretto
noggin [ˈnɑː·gɪn] *n* 1.(*small measure*) bicchierino *m* 2. *inf* (*head, mind*) zucca *f*
no-go area [noʊ·goʊ·ˈe·ri·ə] *n* MIL zona *f* off limits
nohow [ˈnoʊ·haʊ] *adv inf* in nessun modo
noise [nɔɪz] *n* 1.(*sound*) rumore *m;* **to make a** ~ fare rumore 2.(*loud, unpleasant sounds*) rumore *m* 3. ELEC interferenze *f pl* ▶ **to make** ~ **about sth** *inf* fare molto baccano per qc; **to make** (**the right**) ~**s** (*to go along with*) dire quello che va detto; (*be polite*) dire parole di circostanza
noise barrier *n* barriera *f* del suono
noiseless [ˈnɔɪz·ləs] *adj* silenzioso, -a
noise pollution *n* inquinamento *m* acustico
noise prevention *n* prevenzione *f* del rumore
noisome [ˈnɔɪ·səm] *adj form* (*sight, smell*) ripugnante, -a
noisy [ˈnɔɪ·zi] <-ier, -iest> *adj* 1.(*child*) chiassoso, -a; (*protest, street*) rumoroso, -a; **to be** ~ fare rumore 2. ELEC (*signal*) acustico, -a 3. *fig* (*clothes*) chiassoso, -a
no-jump [ˌnəʊ·ˈdʒʌmp] *n* SPORTS salto *m* nullo
nomad [ˈnoʊ·mæd] *n* nomade *mf*
nomadic [noʊ·ˈmæ·dɪk] *adj* nomade
no man's land [ˈnoʊ·mænz·lænd] *n* terra *f* di nessuno
nomenclature [ˈnoʊ·men·kleɪ·tʃɚ] *n* nomenclatura *f*
nominal [ˈnɑː·mə·nl] *adj* 1.(*in name*) nominale 2.(*small: sum*) simbolico, -a
nominally [ˈnɑː·mə·nə·li] *adv* nominalmente
nominate [ˈnɑː·mə·neɪt] *vt* 1.(*propose*) designare; (*for an award*) candidare 2.(*appoint*) nominare
nomination [ˌnɑː·mə·ˈneɪ·ʃən] *n* 1.(*proposal*) designazione *f* 2.(*appointment*) nomina *f;* (*for an award*) candidatura *f* 3.(*action of proposing*) designazione *f*
nominative [ˈnɑː·mə·nə·tɪv] I. *n* nominativo *m* II. *adj* nominativo, -a
nominee [ˌnɑː·mə·ˈniː] *n* (*person chosen*) persona *f* designata; (*person suggested: for an award*) candidato, -a *m, f*
nonacceptance [ˌnɑː·nək·ˈsep·təns] *n* 1.(*failure to accept*) non accettazione *f* 2. FIN mancata accettazione *f*
nonagenarian [ˌnɑː·nə·dʒə·ˈne·ri·ən] I. *n* nonagenario, -a *m, f* II. *adj* nonagenario, -a
nonaggression [ˌnɑː·nə·ˈgre·ʃən] *n* non aggressione *f*
nonaggression pact, nonaggression treaty <-ies> *n* patto *m* di non aggressione
nonalcoholic [ˌnɑː·næl·kə·ˈhɑː·lɪk] *adj* analcolico, -a
nonaligned [ˌnɑː·nə·ˈlaɪnd] *adj* non allineato, -a
nonalignment [ˌnɑː·nə·ˈlaɪn·mənt] *n* non-allineamento *m*
nonappearance [ˌnɑː·nə·ˈpɪ·rənts] *n* LAW contumacia *f*
nonattendance [ˌnɑː·nə·ˈten·dənts] *n*

assenza *f*

nonbelligerent [ˌnɑːnˈbəˈlɪˈdʒəˈrənt] *adj* non belligerante

nonce word [ˈnɑːnsˈwɜːrd] *n* parola coniata *per un occasione speciale*

nonchalant [ˌnɑːnˈʃəˈlɑːnt] *adj* noncurante; **to appear ~** mostrarsi indifferente; **to be ~ about sth** non mostrare interesse verso qc

noncom [ˈnɑːnˈkɑːm] *adj inf abbr of* **noncommissioned officer** sottufficiale *m*

noncombatant [ˌnɑːnˈkəmˈbæˈtənt] *n* MIL non combattente *mf*

noncombustible [ˌnɑːnˈkəmˈbʌsˈtəˈbl] *adj* incombustibile

noncommissioned officer [ˌnɑːnˈkəˈmɪˈʃəndˈaːˈfɪˈsɚ] *n* MIL sottufficiale *m*

noncommittal [ˌnɑːnˈkəˈmɪˈt̬əl] *adj* evasivo, -a

noncompliance [ˌnɑːnˈkəmˈplaɪˈənts] *n* inadempienza *f*

non compos mentis [ˌnɑːnˌkɑːmˈpoʊsˈmenˈt̬ɪs] *adj* LAW incapace di intendere e di volere

nonconformist [ˌnɑːnˈkənˈfɔːrˈmɪst] I. *adj* nonconformista II. *n* nonconformista *mf*

nonconformity [ˌnɑːnˈkənˈfɔːrˈməˈti] *n* nonconformismo *m*

noncontributory [ˌnɑːnˈkənˈtrɪˈbjuːˈtɔːˈri] *adj* non contributivo, -a; **~ pension plan** pensione *f* non contributiva

noncooperation [ˌnɑːnˈkoʊˌaːˈpəˈreɪˈʃən] *n* non cooperazione *f*

non-deposit bottle [ˌnɒnˈdɪˈpɒˈzɪtˌbɒˈtl] *n* bottiglia *f* con vuoto a perdere

nondescript [ˈnɑːnˈdɪsˈkrɪpt] *adj* (*person*) insignificante; (*color*) indefinito, -a

nondurables [ˌnɒnˈdjʊəˈrəˈblz] *npl* prodotti *mpl* deperibili

none [nʌn] I. *pron* 1. (*nobody*) nessuno, -a; **~ of them** nessuno di loro; **~ but he saw it** l'ha visto solo lui; **~ of you helped me** nessuno di voi mi ha aiutato 2. (*not any*) nessuno, -a; **~ of my letters arrived** nessuna delle mie lettere è arrivata 3. (*not any*) **nuts/wine? I've ~** (*at all*) frutta secca/vino? Non ne ho (neanche un po'); **~ of your speeches!** basta con i tuoi discorsi!; **~ of that!** smettila! II. *adv* 1. (*not*) **~ the less** ciononostante; **to be ~ the wiser** non saperne più di prima 2. (*not very*) **it's ~ too soon** non è mai troppo presto; **it's ~ too warm** fa tutt'altro che caldo

nonentity [nɑːˈnenˈt̬əˈti] <-ies> *n* 1. (*person*) nullità *f* 2. (*insignificance*) anonimato *m*

nonessential [nɑːnɪˈsenˈtʃəl] I. *adj* non essenziale II. *n* cosa *f* non essenziale

nonevent [ˌnɑːnɪˈvent] *n inf* fiasco *m*

nonexistence *n* inesistenza *f*

nonexistent [ˌnɑːnˈnɪɡˈzɪsˈtənt] *adj* inesistente

nonfiction [ˌnɑːnˈfɪkˈʃən] *n* non fiction *f*

nonflammable [ˌnɑːnˈflæˈməˈbl] *adj* non infiammabile

noninfectious [ˌnɑːnɪnˈfekˈʃəs] *adj* non infettivo, -a

non-iron [ˌnɑːnˈnaɪˈəˈn] *adj* no stiro *inv*

nonmember country [ˌnɑːnˈmemˈbɚˈkʌnˈtri] <-ies> *n* POL stato *m* non membro

nonnegotiable [ˌnɑːnɪˈɡoʊˈʃiəˈbl] *adj* LAW, FIN non negoziabile

nonpareil [ˌnɑːnˈpəˈrel] I. *adj liter* impareggiabile II. *n liter* persona [*o* cosa] *f* senza pari

nonplus [ˌnɑːnˈplʌs] <-ss-> *vt* disorientare; **to be ~sed** restare disorientato

nonpolluting [ˌnɑːnˈpəˈluːˈtɪŋ] *adj* non inquinante

nonproductive [ˌnɑːnˈprəˈdʌkˈtɪv] *adj* improduttivo, -a

nonprofit, non-profit-making [ˌnɑːnˈpraːˈfɪtˌmeɪˈkɪŋ] *adj* non profit

nonproliferation [ˌnɑːnˈprəˌlɪˈfəˈreɪˈʃən] I. *n* POL non proliferazione *f* II. *adj* POL di non proliferazione

nonproliferation treaty <-ies> *n* POL trattato *m* di non proliferazione

nonrefundable [ˌnɑːnˈrɪˈfʌnˈdəˈbl] *adj* non rimborsabile; **~ down payment** acconto *m* non rimborsabile

nonresident [ˌnɑːnˈreˈzɪˈdənt] I. *adj* non residente II. *n* non residente *mf*

nonreturnable [ˌnɑːnˈrɪˈtɜːrˈnəˈbl] *adj* non restituibile; (*bottle*) a perdere

nonscheduled [ˌnɑːnˈskedˈʒuːld] *adj* non programmato, -a

nonsense [ˈnɑːnˈsents] I. *n* assurdità *fpl*; **to make ~ of sth** ridicolizzare qc; **to talk ~** *inf* dire sciocchezze II. *adj* 1. LIT (*invented for amusement*) senza senso 2. (*without meaning*) inventato, -a III. *interj* sciocchezze

nonsensical [ˌnɑːnˈsenˈtsɪˈkl] *adj* assurdo, -a

nonshrink [ˌnɑːnˈʃrɪŋk] *adj* irrestringibile

nonskid [ˌnɑːnˈskɪd] *adj* antisdrucciolevole

nonsmoker [ˌnɑːnˈsmoʊˈkɚ] *n* non fumatore, -trice *m, f*

nonsmoking *adj* non fumatori

nonstarter [ˌnɑːnˈstɑːrˈt̬ɚ] *n inf* that proposal is a ~ quella proposta è destinata al fallimento

nonstick [ˌnɑːnˈstɪk] *adj* antiaderente

nonstop [ˌnɑːnˈstɑːp] I. *adj* 1. (*without stopping, direct*) diretto, -a 2. (*uninterrupted*) ininterrotto, -a II. *adv* ininterrottamente

nonswimmer [ˌnɑːnˈswɪˈmɚ] *n* non nuotatore, -trice *m, f*

nontaxable [ˌnɒnˈtækˈsəˈbl] *adj* non tassabile

nontoxic [ˌnɒnˈtɒkˈsɪk] *adj* non tossico, -a

nonverbal [ˌnɑːnˈvɜːrˈbl] *adj* non verbale

nonviolent [ˌnɑːnˈvaɪˈəˈlənt] *adj* non violento, -a

nonvoting [ˌnɒnˈvəʊˈtɪŋ] *adj* senza diritto di voto

noodle[1] [ˈnuːˈdl] I. *n* spaghetto *m*; (*with eggs*) tagliatella *m* II. *adj* con la pasta

noodle[2] [ˈnuːˈdl] *n inf* 1. (*head*) testa *f* 2. (*person*) idiota *mf*

noodle[3] [ˈnuːˈdl] *vi inf* MUS strimpellare

nook [nʊk] *n liter* angolo *m*; **~s and crannies** angolini

noon [nu:n] *n* mezzogiorno *m;* **at** ~ a mezzogiorno; **about** ~ intorno a mezzogiorno
no one ['noʊ·wʌn] *pron s.* **nobody**
noose [nu:s] *n* **1.**(*loop of rope*) cappio *m* **2.**(*for catching*) laccio *m* **3.**fig (*problem*) **the** ~ **of poverty** il fantasma della povertà; **a way to escape the** ~ **of poverty** un modo di spezzare le catene della povertà ▶**to have a** ~ **around one's** neck avere l'acqua alla gola
nope [noʊp] *adv inf* no
nor [nɔːr] *conj* **1.**(*and also not*) nemmeno; ~ (do) I nemmeno io **2.**(*not either*) né
Nordic ['nɔːr·dɪk] *adj* nordico, -a
norm [nɔːrm] *n* norma *f*
normal ['nɔːr·ml] *adj* **1.**(*not out of the ordinary*) normale **2.**(*usual*) normale; **as** (**is**) ~ come al solito
normalcy ['nɔːr·məl·si], **normality** [nɔːr·'mæ·lə·ti] *n* normalità *f*
normalize ['nɔːr·mə·laɪz] *a.* COMPUT **I.** *vt* normalizzare **II.** *vi* normalizzarsi
normally ['nɔːr·mə·li] *adv* normalmente
Normandy ['nɔːr·mən·di] *n* Normandia *f*
north [nɔːrθ] **I.** *n* **1.**(*cardinal point*) nord *m;* **to lie 3 miles to the** ~ **of sth** trovarsi a 5 km a nord di qc; **to go/drive to the** ~ andare/viaggiare verso nord; **further** ~ più a nord **2.** GEO nord *m;* **in the** ~ **of France** nel nord della Francia; **the Far North** il Grande Nord **II.** *adj* del nord, settentrionale; ~ **wind** vento *m* del nord; ~ **coast** costa *f* nord; **the North Sea** il Mare del Nord; **North Star** stella *f* polare; **the North Pole** il Polo *m* Nord
North Africa *n* Africa *f* del Nord
North African I. *n* nordafricano, -a *m, f* **II.** *adj* nordafricano, -a
North America *n* America *f* del Nord
North American I. *n* nordamericano, -a *m, f* **II.** *adj* nordamericano, -a
North Carolina *n* Carolina *f* del Nord
North Dakota *n* Nord Dakota *m*
northeast [ˌnɔːrθ·'iːst] **I.** *n* nordest *m* **II.** *adj* del nordest
northeastern [ˌnɔːrθ·'iːs·tərn] *adj* nordorientale
northerly ['nɔːr·ðər·li] *adj* del nord; ~ **direction** direzione *f* nord
northern ['nɔːr·ðərn] *adj* del nord, settentrionale; ~ **hemisphere** emisfero *m* boreale; **the** ~ **part of the country** la parte nord del paese; ~ **lights** aurora *f* boreale
northerner ['nɔːr·ðər·nər] *n* abitante *mf* del nord
Northern Marianas *n* Marianne *fpl* del Nord
northernmost *adj* più a nord
Northern Territory *n* Territorio *m* del Nord
North Pole ['nɔːrθ·poʊl] *n* **the** ~ il Polo *m* Nord
North Sea I. *n* Mare *m* del Nord **II.** *adj* del Mare del Nord
North-South divide *n* ECON divario *m* Nord-Sud
northward ['nɔːrθ·wərd] *adv* verso nord

northwest [ˌnɔːrθ·'west] **I.** *n* nordovest *m;* **to the** ~ (of) a nordovest(di) **II.** *adj* del nordovest; ~ **Texas** il Texas nordoccidentale **III.** *adv* in direzione nordest
northwesterly [ˌnɔːrθ·'wes·tər·li] *adj* nordoccidentale; (*from the northwest*) del nordovest; ~ **part** settore *m* nordoccidentale
Northwest Territories *n pl* Territori *mpl* del Nordovest
Norway ['nɔːr·weɪ] *n* Norvegia *f*
Norwegian [nɔːr·'wiː·dʒən] **I.** *adj* norvegese **II.** *n* **1.**(*person*) norvegese *mf* **2.** LING norvegese *m*
nose [noʊz] **I.** *n* **1.** ANAT naso *m;* **to blow one's** ~ soffiarsi il naso **2.** AVIAT (*front*) muso *m* **3.**(*smell of wine*) bouquet *m inv* ▶**with one's** ~ **in the** air con aria di superiorità; **to put one's** ~ **to the** grindstone *inf* lavorare sodo; **to put sb's** ~ **out of** joint *inf* far storcere il naso a qu; **to keep one's** ~ clean *inf* tenersi fuori dai guai; **to** follow **one's** ~ *inf* (*trust instincts*) andare a naso; (*go straight ahead*) andare sempre dritto; **to** have **a** (**good**) ~ **for sth** avere (un buon) fiuto per qc; **to** keep **one's** ~ **out of sth** *inf* non immischiarsi in qc no; **to** poke **one's** ~ **into sth** *inf* ficcare il naso in qc; **to** rub **sb's** ~ **in it** rimestare il coltello nella piaga; **to** thumb **one's** ~ **at sb** fare marameo a qu; (**from**) under **sb's** (**very**) ~ *inf,* right out from under sb's ~ *inf* sotto il naso di qc **II.** *vi* ficcare il naso **III.** *vt* **to** ~ **one's way in/out/up** entrare/uscire/superare lentamente; **to** ~ (**its way**) **through sth** farsi strada attraverso qc
◆**nose about, nose around** *vi inf* curiosare
◆**nose out I.** *vt* scovare **II.** *vi* avanzare con cautela
nosebag ['noʊz·bæg] *n* musetta *f*
nosebleed *n* emorragia *f* nasale
nose cone *n* AVIAT ogiva *f*
nosedive I. *n* **1.** AVIAT picchiata *f* **2.** FIN crollo *m* **II.** *vi* **1.** AVIAT scendere in picchiata **2.** FIN crollare
nosegay *n* mazzolino *m* di fiori
nose job *n inf* **to have a** ≈ rifarsi il naso
nose wheel *n* carrello *m* anteriore
nosey ['noʊ·zi] <-ier, -iest> *adj s.* **nosy**
nosh [nɑːʃ] **I.** *n inf* (*snack*) spuntino *m* **II.** *vi* fare uno spuntino
nostalgia [nɑː·'stæl·dʒə] *n* nostalgia *f*
nostalgic [nɑː·'stæl·dʒɪk] *adj* nostalgico, -a
no-strike agreement [ˌnoʊ·straɪk·ə·'griː·mənt] *n* accordo per la regolamentazione del diritto di sciopero
nostril ['nɑːs·trəl] *n* narice *f*
nosy ['noʊ·zi] <-ier, -iest> *adj* ficcanaso, -a; **to be** ~ *pej* essere invadente
Nosy Parker ['noʊ·zi·'pɑːr·kər] *n inf* ficcanaso, -a *m, f*
not [nɑːt] *adv* non; **it's a woman,** ~ **a man** è una donna, non un uomo; **he's asked me** ~ **to do it** mi ha chiesto di non farlo; ~ **all the children like singing** non a tutti i bambini

piace cantare; ~ **me!** io no!; **why ~?** perchè no?; **he is ~ ugly** non è brutto; **or** ~ o no; ~ **at all** (*nothing*) affatto; (*no need to thank*) di niente; ~ **only ... but also ...** non solo ... ma anche; ~ **just** [*o* simply] non solo; ~ **much** non tanto

notable ['noʊ·ṭə·bl] I. *adj* 1. (*remarkable*) notevole 2. (*eminent*) eminente II. *n* notabile *mf*

notably ['noʊ·ṭə·bli] *adv* particolarmente

notary ['noʊ·ṭəi] <-ies> *n* ~ (**public**) notaio *m*

notation [noʊ·'teɪ·ʃən] *n* MATH, MUS notazione *f*

notch [nɑːtʃ] <-es> I. *vt* 1. (*cut*) intaccare 2. *inf* (*achieve*) ottenere II. *n* 1. (*cut*) tacca *f*; (*hole*) intaglio *m* 2. (*degree*) gradino *m* 3. (*narrow valley*) valle *m*

note [noʊt] I. *n* 1. (*annotation*) appunto *m*; **to take** ~ prendere nota 2. LIT nota *f* 3. MUS nota *f*; **to strike the right** ~ *fig* toccare la corda giusta 4. (*piece of paper money*) banconota *f* 5. (*importance*) **of** ~ *form* degno di nota; **nothing of** ~ nulla di importante II. *vt form* notare; (*mention*); **to** ~ (**that**) **...** far notare (che) ...

notebook ['noʊt·bʊk] *n* taccuino *m*

noted ['noʊ·ṭɪd] *adj* celebre; **to be ~ for sth** essere noto, -a per qc

notepad ['noʊt·pæd] *n* blocchetto *m* per gli appunti

notepaper ['noʊt·ˌpeɪ·pə] *n* carta *f* da lettera

noteworthy ['noʊt·ˌwɜːr·ði] *adj form* notevole; **nothing/something** ~ nulla/qualcosa di rilevante

nothing ['nʌ·θɪŋ] I. *pron indef, sing* 1. (*no objects*) niente; ~ **happens** non succede niente; **we saw** ~ (**else/more**) non abbiamo visto niente (altro); ~ **new** niente di nuovo; **next to** ~ quasi niente 2. (*not anything*) ~ **came of it** non ha portato a niente; ~ **doing!** *inf* niente da fare!; **fit for** ~ buono a nulla; **to make** ~ **of it** non dargli importanza; **there is** ~ **to laugh at** non c'è niente da ridere 3. (*not important*) **that's ~!** non è niente!; **time is ~ to me** il tempo per me non conta 4. (*only*) ~ **but** solo; **she is ~ if not patient** è a dir poco paziente; ~ **much** niente di importante II. *adv* ~ **less than** né più né meno che; ~ **daunted, I went on** per nulla scoraggiato, andai avanti III. *n* 1. niente *m* 2. MATH, SPORTS zero *m*; **three to** ~ tre a zero 3. (*person*) nessuno *m*

nothingness ['nʌ·θɪŋ·nɪs] *n* (*emptiness*) vuoto *m*; (*worthlessness*) nulla *m*

notice ['noʊ·ṭɪs] I. *vt* 1. (*see*) vedere; (*perceive*) notare; **to** ~ (**that**) **...** accorgersi (che) ... 2. (*recognize*) notare II. *vi* accorgersi III. *n* 1. (*attention*) attenzione *f*; **to take** ~ **of sb/ sth** prestare attenzione a qc/qc; **to come to sb's** ~ (**that ...**) venire a sapere (che...); **to escape one's** ~ sfuggire a qu; **to escape sb's** ~ **that ...** sfuggire a qu che ... 2. (*display*) cartello *m*; (*in a newspaper, magazine*) annuncio *m* 3. (*warning*) avviso *m*; **to give sb** ~ (**of**

sth) avvisare qu (di qc); **at short** ~ con poco preavviso; **at a moment's** ~ su due piedi; **until further** ~ fino a nuovo avviso 4. LAW preavviso *m*; **to give** (**in**) **one's** ~ dare le dimissioni; **to give sb their** ~ licenziare qu

noticeable ['noʊ·ṭɪ·sə·bl] *adj* evidente; (*difference*) notevole

notifiable ['noʊ·ṭə·faɪ·ə·bl] *adj* (*disease*) da notificare alle autorità competenti

notification [ˌnoʊ·ṭə·fɪ·'keɪ·ʃən] *n* notificazione *f*

notify ['noʊ·ṭə·faɪ] <-ie-> *vt* informare; **to** ~ **sb of sth** informare qu di qc

notion ['noʊ·ʃən] *n* 1. (*idea*) idea *f*; **to have some** ~ **of sth** avere una qualche idea di qc; **to have no** ~ **of sth** non avere la minima idea di qc 2. (*silly idea*) ghiribizzo *m*; **to have a** ~ **to do sth** avere voglia di fare qc

notional ['noʊ·ʃə·nl] *adj form* teorico, -a

notoriety [ˌnoʊ·ṭə·'raɪ·ə·ti] *n* notorietà *f* negativa

notorious [noʊ·'tɔː·ri·əs] *adj* notorio, -a; (*thief*) famigerato, -a; **she's a** ~ **liar** è famosa per le sue bugie; **to be** ~ **for sth** essere famoso, -a per qc

notwithstanding [ˌnɑːt·wɪθ·'stæn·dɪŋ] *form* I. *prep* nonostante II. *adv* ciononostante

nougat ['nuː·gət] *n* nougat *m inv*

nought [nɑːt] *pron s.* **naught**

noun [naʊn] I. *n* nome *m*; LING sostantivo *m* II. *adj* nominale

nourish ['nɜː·rɪʃ] *vt* 1. (*provide with food*) nutrire; **to** ~ **oneself on sth** nutrirsi di qc 2. *fig, form* (*cherish*) nutrire

nourishing ['nɜː·rɪ·ʃɪŋ] *adj* nutriente

nourishment *n* 1. (*food*) nutrimento *m* 2. (*providing with food*) nutrizione *f*

Nova Scotia [ˌnoʊ·və·'skoʊ·ʃə] *n* Nuova Scozia *f*

novel¹ ['nɑː·vl] *n* LIT romanzo *m*

novel² ['nɑː·vl] *adj* (*new*) nuovo, -a

novelette [ˌnɑː·və·'let] *n* romanzetto *m* rosa

novelist ['nɑː·və·lɪst] *n* romanziere, -a *m, f*

novelty ['nɑː·vl·ti] I. <-ies> *n* 1. (*newness, innovation*) novità *f* 2. (*cheap trinket*) giocattolino *m* II. *adj* 1. (*new*) novità 2. (*cheap*) economico, -a

November [noʊ·'vem·bə] *n* novembre *m*; *s.a.* **April**

novice ['nɑː·vɪs] *n a.* REL novizio, -a *m, f*

now [naʊ] I. *adv* 1. (*at the present time*) ora; **just** ~ in questo momento 2. (*currently*) attualmente 3. (*then*) allora; **any time** ~ da un momento all'altro; (**every**) ~ **and then** di tanto in tanto 4. (*give emphasis*) ~, **where did I put her book?** dunque, vediamo, dove ho messo il suo libro?; ~ **then** allora ▶ (**it's**) ~ **or never** (è) ora o mai più II. *n* (*present*) **now isn't a good time...** questo non è il momento...; **before** ~ prima d'ora; **by** ~ ormai; **for** ~ per ora; **as of** ~ a partire da adesso III. *conj* ~ (**that**) **...** ora che ...

nowadays ['naʊ·ə·deɪz] *adv* al giorno d'oggi
nowhere ['noʊ·wer] *adv* da nessuna parte; **to appear out of** ~ spuntare fuori dal nulla; **to be going** ~ *a. fig* non portare da nessuna parte
noxious ['nɑ:k·ʃəs] *adj form* (*smoke, habit, influence*) nocivo, -a
nozzle ['nɑ:·zl] *n* ugello *m;* (*of a gas pump*) erogatore *m;* (*of a gun*) bocca *f*
NT 1. *abbr of* **New Testament** Nuovo Testamento *m* 2. *abbr of* **Northwest Territories** Territori *m* del Nord Ovest *pl*
nuance ['nu:·ɑ:ns] *n* sfumatura *f*
nub [nʌb] *n* 1. (*point*) nòcciolo *m* 2. (*piece*) pezzetto *m*
nubile ['nu:·bɪl] *adj* nubile
nuclear ['nu:·kliə] *adj* nucleare
nuclear medicine *n* medicina *f* nucleare
nuclear nonproliferation treaty <-ies> *n* POL, MIL trattato *m* di non proliferazione nucleare
nuclear power station *n* centrale *f* nucleare
nuclear reactor *n* reattore *m* nucleare
nucleic acid [nu:·'kli:·ɪk·æ·sɪd] *n* acido *m* nucleico
nucleus ['nu:·kli·əs] <-ei *o* -es> *n* nucleo *m*
nude [nu:d] I. *adj* nudo, -a II. *n* 1. ART, PHOT nudo *m* 2. (*naked*) **in the** ~ nudo, -a
nude beach *n* spiaggia *f* nudista
nudge [nʌdʒ] I. *vt* dare una gomitata a; *fig* spronare; **to** ~ **sb into doing sth** spronare qu a fare qc II. *vi* spingersi lentamente III. *n* 1. (*push*) gomitata *f* 2. (*encouragement*) spinta *f*
nudism ['nu:·dɪ·zəm] *n* nudismo *m*
nudist ['nu:·dɪst] I. *n* nudista *mf* II. *adj* nudista
nudist camp *n* campo *m* nudista
nudity ['nu:·də·ti] *n* nudità *f*
nugatory ['nu:·gə·tɔ:·ri] *adj form* irrisorio, -a
nugget ['nʌ·gɪt] *n* MIN pepita *f*
nuisance ['nu:·sns] *n* 1. (*thing*) seccatura *f;* (*person*) seccatore, -trice *m, f;* **to make a** ~ **of oneself** rompere le scatole 2. LAW turbativa *f*
nuke [nu:k, nju:k] *vt inf* 1. MIL bombardare con armi atomiche 2. *inf* (*cook*) cucinare al microonde
null [nʌl] *adj* nullo, -a; ~ **and void** nullo
nullification [ˌnʌ·lɪ·fɪ·'keɪ·ʃən] *n* annullamento *m*
nullify ['nʌ·lɪ·faɪ] <-ie-> *vt* annullare
nullity ['nʌ·lə·ti] *n* nullità *f*
numb [nʌm] I. *adj* intorpidito, -a; **to go** ~ intorpidirsi II. *vt* (*fear, terror*) paralizzare; (*desensitize*) intorpidire
number ['nʌm·bə] I. *n* 1. MATH numero *m;* **house** ~ numero di casa; **telephone** ~ numero di telefono 2. (*amount*) numero *m;* (**a**) **small/large** ~(**s**) (**of children**) pochi/tanti(bambini); **for a** ~ **of reasons** per una serie di motivi; **to be 3 in** ~ essere in 3; **to be few in** ~ essere in pochi 3. (*magazine, newspaper*) numero *m;* THEAT numero *m;* MUS pezzo *m* ▶ ~ **one** se stesso *-a;* **to look after** ~ **one** pensare prima a se stesso, -a; **to be** (**the**) ~ **one** essere il numero uno; **to have sb's** ~ inquadrare qu; **to be beyond** ~ essere una quantità innumerevole II. *vt* 1. (*assign a number to*) numerare; **to** ~ **sth from ... to ...** numerare qc da ... a ... 2. (*count*) contare 3. (*amount to*) contare; **each group** ~**s 10 members** ciascun gruppo conta 10 membri
numbering *n* numerazione *f*
numberless *adj* innumerevole
numbness ['nʌm·nɪs] *n* 1. (*on part of body*) intorpidimento *m* 2. (*lack of feeling*) torpore *f*
numeracy ['nu:·mə·rə·si] *n* capacità *f* di calcolo *pl*
numeral ['nu:·mə·rəl] *n* numero *m*
numerate ['nu:·mə·rət] *adj* MATH che sa fare di conto
numeration [ˌnu:·mə·'reɪ·ʃən] *n form* numerazione *f*
numerical [nu:·'me·rɪ·kl] *adj* numerico, -a; **in** ~ **order** in ordine numerico
numeric keypad [nu:·me·rɪk·'ki:·pæd] *n* COMPUT tastiera *f* numerica
numerous ['nu:·mə·rəs] *adj* numeroso, -a
numismatics [ˌnu:·mɪz·'mæ·tɪks] *n + sing vb* numismatica *f*
numskull ['nʌms·kʌl] *n* idiota *mf*
nun [nʌn] *n* suora *f*
nuncio ['nʌn·sioʊ] *n* REL nunzio *m* apostolico
nunnery ['nʌ·nə·ri] <-ies> *n* convento *m* di suore
nuptial ['nʌp·ʃl] *adj* nuziale
nurse [nɜːrs] I. *n* 1. MED infermiere, -a *m, f* 2. (*nanny*) bambinaia *f;* (*wet nurse*) balia *f* II. *vt* 1. (*care for*) curare 2. (*nurture*) coltivare 3. (*harbor*) nutrire 4. (*drink*) sorseggiare 5. (*hold a child*) cullare 6. (*breastfeed*) allattare III. *vi* poppare
nursery ['nɜːr·sə·ri] I. <-ies> *n* 1. (*school*) asilo *m* nido 2. (*bedroom*) camera *f* dei bambini 3. BOT vivaio *m* II. *adj* ~ **education** istruzione *f* prescolare
nursery rhyme *n* filastrocca *f*
nursery school *n* scuola *f* materna
nursing I. *n* professione *f* infermieristica II. *adj* infermieristico, -a
nursing home *n* casa *f* di riposo
nurture ['nɜːr·tʃə] I. *vt* (*children*) crescere; (*plant*) coltivare II. *n* allevamento *m*
nut [nʌt] *n* 1. BOT noce *f* 2. TECH dado *m* 3. *inf* (*madman*) svitato, -a *m, f;* (*enthusiast*) fanatico, -a *m, f* 4. *inf* (*person's head*) testa *f;* **to be off one's** ~ essere fuori di testa ▶ **the** ~**s and bolts of sth** la pratica di qc; **a hard** ~ **to crack** (*situation*) una situazione difficile; (*person*) un osso duro
nutcracker ['nʌt·ˌkræ·kə] *n* schiaccianoci *m inv*
nuthatch <-es> *n* picchio *m* muraiolo
nuthouse <-s> *n inf* manicomio *m*
nutmeg *n* noce *f* moscata
nutrient ['nu:·tri·ənt] I. *n* sostanza *f* nutriente II. *adj* nutritivo, -a
nutrition [nu:·'trɪ·ʃən] I. *n* nutrizione *f* II. *adj*

della nutrizione

nutritionist [nuː'trɪ·ʃə·nɪst] *n* nutrizionista *mf*

nutritious [nuː'trɪ·ʃəs] *adj*, **nutritive** ['nuː·trə·tɪv] *adj* nutriente

nuts [nʌts] I. *npl vulg* coglioni *mpl* II. *adj* **to be** ~ essere fuori di testa; **to go** ~ diventare pazzo; **to be** ~ **about sb** essere pazzo di qn; **to be** ~ **about sth** andare matto per qc

nutshell ['nʌt·ʃel] *n* guscio *m* di noce ▶ **to put sth in a** ~ dire qc in due parole; **in a** ~ in poche parole

nutty ['nʌ·ti̩] <-ier, -iest> *adj* **1.** (*cake*) alle noci; (*ice cream*) alla nocciola; (*taste*) di nocciola **2.** *inf* (*crazy*) svitato, -a; **to be** (**as**) ~ **as a fruitcake** essere fuori come un balcone

nuzzle ['nʌ·zl] I. *vt* (*dog*) strofinare il muso contro; (*person*) strofinare il naso contro II. *vi* accoccolarsi; **to** ~ **closer** (**to sb**) stringersi forte (a qn); **to** ~ (**up**) **against sb/sth** accoccolarsi contro qu/qc

NV *abbr of* **Nevada** NV

NW [ˌen·'dʌbl·juː] *abbr of* **northwest** NO

NY [ˌen·'waɪ] *abbr of* **New York** NY

nylon ['naɪ·lɑːn] I. *n* nylon *m* II. *adj* di nylon

nymph [nɪmf] *n* ninfa *f*

nymphomania [ˌnɪm·fou·'meɪ·ni·ə] *n* ninfomania *f*

nymphomaniac [ˌnɪm·fou·'meɪ·ni·æk] *n* ninfomane *f*

NZ [ˌen·'ziː] *abbr of* **New Zealand** NZ

O

O, o [əʊ] *n* **1.** (*letter*) O, o *f;* ~ **as in Oscar** O come Otranto **2.** (*zero*) zero *m*

oaf [oʊf] *n inf* (*uncultured*) zoticone, -a *m, f;* (*clumsy*) goffo, -a *m, f*

oafish ['oʊ·fɪʃ] *adj inf* (*uncultured*) zotico, -a; (*clumsy*) goffo, -a

oak [oʊk] *n* (*tree, wood*) quercia *f* ▶ **mighty** ~ **s from little acorns grow** *prov* i piccoli ruscelli fanno i grandi fiumi *prov*

oar [ɔːr] *n* remo *m*

oarsman ['ɔːrz·mən] <-men> *n* rematore *m*

oarswoman ['ɔːrz·wʊ·mən] <-women> *n* rematrice *f*

OAS [ˌoʊ·eɪ·'es] *n abbr of* **Organization of American States** OSA *f*

oasis [oʊ·'eɪ·sɪs] <-es> *n* oasi *f inv*

oatcake ['oʊt·keɪk] *n* biscotto *m* di avena

oath [oʊθ] *n* giuramento *m;* **to take an** ~ prestare giuramento; **under** ~ sotto giuramento; ~ **of allegiance** giuramento di fedeltà

oatmeal ['oʊt·miːl] *n* farina *f* di avena

oats [oʊts] *n pl* avena *f* ▶ **to sow one's wild** ~ correre la cavallina *inf;* **to feel one's** ~ sentirsi in piena forma

obduracy ['ɑː·b·dʊ·rə·si] *n* ostinazione *f*

obdurate ['ɑː·b·dʊ·rɪt] *adj form* ostinato, -a

obedience [oʊ·'biː·di·əns] *n* ubbidienza *f;* **in** ~ **to** secondo

obedient [oʊ·'biː·di·ənt] *adj* ubbidiente; **to be** ~ **to sb/sth** ubbidire a qu/qc

obelisk ['ɑː·bə·lɪsk] *n* obelisco *m*

obese [oʊ·'biːs] *adj* obeso, -a

obesity [oʊ·'biː·sə·ti] *n* obesità *f*

obey [oʊ·'beɪ] *vt* (*person, order*) ubbidire a; (*instincts, advice*) seguire; (*the law*) rispettare

obituary [oʊ·'bɪ·tʃu·e·ri] <-ies> *n*, **obituary notice** *n* necrologio *m*

object[1] ['ɑː·b·dʒɪkt] *n* **1.** (*unspecified thing*) oggetto *m* **2.** (*purpose, goal*) scopo *m;* **the** ~ **of the exercise is ...** lo scopo dell'esercizio è... **3.** (*obstacle*) **money is no** ~ i soldi non sono un problema **4.** LING complemento *m*

object[2] [əb·'dʒekt] I. *vi* avere obiezioni II. *vt* obiettare; **to** ~ **that ...** obiettare che...

objection [əb·'dʒek·ʃən] *n* obiezione *f;* **to raise** ~ **s** sollevare obiezioni; **to raise** ~ **s to sth** opporsi a qc; **if there is no** ~ **...** se non c'è nulla in contrario

objectionable [əb·'dʒek·ʃən·əbl] *adj form* (*smell*) sgradevole; (*person*) insopportabile; (*conduct*) deplorevole

objective [əb·'dʒek·tɪv] I. *n* obiettivo *m* II. *adj* obiettivo, -a

objectivity [ˌɑː·b·dʒek·'tɪ·və·ti] *n* obiettività *f*

object lesson *n* dimostrazione *f*

objector *n* obiettore, -trice *m, f*

obligate ['ɑː·b·lɪ·geɪt] *vt* obbligare; **to** ~ **sb to do sth** obbligare qu a fare qc

obligation [ˌɑː·b·lə·'geɪ·ʃən] *n* obbligo *m;* **to be under an** ~ **to do sth** avere l'obbligo di fare qc; **to have an** ~ **to sb** doverlo a qu

obligatory [əb·'lɪ·gə·tɔː·ri] *adj* obbligatorio, -a

oblige [əb·'laɪdʒ] I. *vt* **1.** (*force*) obbligare **2.** (*perform service for*) **to** ~ **sb** fare un favore a qu II. *vi* **to be happy to** ~ essere felice di poter essere d'aiuto

obliging [əb·'laɪ·dʒɪŋ] *adj* servizievole

oblique [oʊb·'liːk] I. *adj* **1.** (*indirect*) indiretto, -a **2.** (*slanting*) obliquo, -a II. *n* **1.** (*thing*) barra *f* obliqua **2.** (*muscle*) muscolo *m* obliquo

obliterate [əb·'lɪ·tə·reɪt] *vt* cancellare; (*town*) rasare al suolo

obliteration [ə,b·lɪ·tə·'reɪ·ʃən] *n* cancellazione *f;* (*of town*) totale distruzione *f*

oblivion [əb·'lɪ·vi·ən] *n* oblio *m;* **to fall into** ~ cadere nell'oblio

oblivious [əb·'lɪ·vi·əs] *adj* ignaro, -a; ~ **of sth** ignaro di qc

oblong ['ɑː·b·lɑː·ŋ] I. *n* rettangolo *m* II. *adj* rettangolare

obnoxious [əb·'nɑː·k·ʃəs] *adj* insopportabile

OBO [ˌoʊ·en·'əʊ] *adv abbr of* **or best offer** negoziabile

oboe ['oʊ·boʊ] *n* oboe *m*

oboist ['oʊ·boʊ·ɪst] *n* oboista *mf*

obscene [əb·'siːn] *adj* **1.** (*indecent*) osceno, -a **2.** (*scandalous*) scandaloso, -a

obscenity [əb·'se·nə·ti] <-ies> *n* oscenità *f*

obscure [əb·'skjʊr] I. *adj* oscuro, -a II. *vt* **1.**(*make difficult to see*) oscurare **2.**(*make difficult to understand, hide*) occultare

obscurity [əb·'skjʊ·rə·ti] *n* oscurità *f*

obsequious [əb·'si:·kwi·əs] *adj* servile

observable [əb·'zɜ:r·və·bl] *adj* evidente

observance [əb·'zɜ:r·vəns] *n* **1.**(*of laws, rules*) osservanza *f*, rispetto *m* **2.** REL (*practice*) pratica *f*

observant [əb·'zɜ:r·vənt] *adj* **1.**(*quick to notice things*) dotato, -a di spirito d'osservazione **2.**(*respectful: of rules, laws*) osservante

observation [ˌɑ:b·zə·'veɪ·ʃən] *n* **1.**(*act of seeing*) osservazione *f;* **to keep sth/sb under ~** (*police*) sorvegliare qc/qu; **under ~** MED in osservazione; **to escape ~** passare inosservato **2.**(*remark*) osservazione *f;* **to make an ~** (**about sb/sth**) fare un'osservazione (su qu/qc)

observation car *n* RAIL vagone *m* panoramico

observation post *n* MIL osservatorio *m*

observation tower *n* torre *f* d'avvistamento

observatory [əb·'zɜ:r·və·tɔ:·ri] *n* osservatorio *m*

observe [əb·'zɜ:rv] *vt* osservare; **to ~ sb doing sth** osservare qu fare qc; **to ~ a minute of silence** osservare un minuto di silenzio; **to ~ Passover** celebrare la Pasqua (ebraica)

observer [əb·'zɜ:r·və] *n* osservatore, -trice *m, f*

obsess [əb·'ses] *vt* ossessionare; **to be ~ed by sb/sth** essere ossessionato da qu/qc; **he is ~ed with being the best** si è fissato che deve essere il migliore

obsession [əb·'se·ʃən] *n* ossessione *f;* **to have an ~ with sb/sth** avere la fissazione di qu/qc

obsessive [əb·'se·sɪv] *adj* (*person, jealousy*) ossessivo, -a; (*memory*) ossessionante; **to be ~ about sth** avere l'ossessione di qc; **to become ~ about sth** fissarsi su qc

obsolescence [ˌɑ:b·sə·'le·sənts] *n* obsolescenza *f*

obsolescent [ˌɑ:b·sə·'le·snt] *adj* superato, -a

obsolete [ˌɑ:b·sə·li:t] *adj* obsoleto, -a

obstacle ['ɑ:b·stə·kl] *n* ostacolo *m;* **an insurmountable ~** un ostacolo insormontabile; **to overcome an ~** superare un ostacolo; **to put ~s in the way of sb/sth** ostacolare qu/qc; **to be an ~ to sth** essere d'ostacolo a qc

obstacle course *n* percorso *m* di guerra

obstetrician [ˌɑ:b·stə·'trɪ·ʃən] *n* MED (medico) ostetrico *m*

obstetrics [əb·'stet·rɪks] I. *npl* MED ostetricia *f* II. *adj* MED ostetrico, -a

obstinacy ['ɑ:b·stə·nə·si] *n* ostinazione *f*

obstinate ['ɑ:b·stə·nət] *adj* **1.**(*person, attitude*) ostinato, -a; **an ~ refusal** un rifiuto ostinato **2.**(*disease, problem*) persistente

obstreperous [əb·'stre·pə·rəs] *adj form* turbolento, -a

obstruct [əb·'strʌkt] *vt* **1.**(*block*) ostruire; (*view*) impedire; **to ~ the traffic** bloccare il traffico **2.**(*hinder: course of justice, progress*) ostacolare

obstruction [əb·'strʌk·ʃən] *n* **1.**(*action*) *a.* MED, POL ostruzione *f* **2.**(*impediment*) ostacolo *m;* **an ~ to sth** un ostacolo a qc; **to cause an ~** essere d'ostacolo; AUTO ostruire il passaggio

obstructive [əb·'strʌk·tɪv] *adj* (*tactic, attitude*) ostruzionista; (*person*) che crea difficoltà; **don't be so ~** non mettermi i bastoni tra le ruote

obtain [əb·'teɪn] I. *vt* ottenere; **to ~ sth from sb/sth** ottenere qc da qu/qc; **to ~ sth for sb** procurare qc a qu II. *vi form* esistere

obtainable [əb·'teɪ·nə·bl] *adj* disponibile; **it is not ~ in this country** non si trova in questo paese

obtrude [əb·'tru:d] I. *vt form* (*force*) imporre; **to ~ one's opinion(s) (up)on sb** imporre a qu la propria opinione II. *vi form* **to ~ upon sth** intromettersi in qc

obtrusive [əb·'tru:·sɪv] *adj form* (*question, presence*) invadente; (*noise*) molesto, -a; (*smell*) penetrante; (*color, design*) vistoso, -a

obtuse [ɑ:b·'tu:s] *adj* ottuso, -a

obviate ['ɑ:b·vi·eɪt] *vt* (*necessity, difficulty*) ovviare a; (*danger*) evitare

obvious ['ɑ:b·vi·əs] *adj* ovvio, -a, chiaro, -a; **a sign of ~ displeasure** un segno di chiaro disgusto; **for ~ reasons** per ovvi motivi; **it is ~ what/where ...** è chiaro cosa/dove ...; **it is ~ to me that ...** mi sembra ovvio che ...; **to make sth ~ to sb** chiarire qc a qu; **the ~ thing to do** la cosa più ovvia da fare

obviously *adv* ovviamente, chiaramente; **~, ...** ovviamente,...

occasion [ə·'keɪ·ʒən] I. *n* **1.**(*particular time, event, opportunity*) occasione *f;* **on ~** talvolta; **on one ~** una volta; **on several ~s** in varie occasioni; **on the ~ of ...** in occasione di...; **to dress to suit the ~** vestirsi in modo adatto all'occasione; **to rise to the ~** dimostrarsi all'altezza della situazione; **should the ~ arise** se si presentasse l'occasione; **to have ~ to do sth** avere occasione di fare qc **2.**(*reason*) motivo; **to give ~ to sth** dare luogo a qc II. *vt* creare

occasional [ə·'keɪ·ʒə·nəl] *adj* occasionale; **to pay sb an ~ visit** andare a trovare qu di tanto in tanto; **I smoke an ~ cigarette** fumo una sigaretta di tanto in tanto

occasionally *adv* occasionalmente, di tanto in tanto

Occident ['ɑ:k·sə·dənt] *n* **the ~** l'Occidente

occidental [ˌɑ:k·sə·'den·t̬əl] *adj* occidentale

occult [ə·'kʌlt] I. *adj* occulto, -a II. *n* **the ~** le scienze occulte

occultism [ə·'kʌl·tɪ·zəm] *n* occultismo *m*

occupancy ['ɑ:·kjə·pən·tsi] *n* (*of building*) occupazione *f*

occupancy rate *n* indice *m* di occupazione

occupant ['ɑ:·kjə·pənt] *n form* **1.**(*of building, vehicle*) occupante *mf;* (*tenant*) inquilino, -a *m, f* **2.**(*of post*) titolare *mf*

occupation ['ɑ:·kjə·peɪ·ʃən] *n* occupazione *f;*

O

~ forces forze *f pl* di occupazione; **what's your favorite ~?** cosa fai nel tempo libero?

occupational [ˌɑːkjəˈpeɪʃənəl] *adj* professionale

occupational disease *n* malattia *f* professionale

occupational hazard *n* rischio *m* sul lavoro

occupational therapy *n* ergoterapia *f*

occupier [ˈɑːkjəpaɪɚ] *n* (*of territory, building*) occupante *mf;* (*tenant*) inquilino, -a *m, f*

occupy [ˈɑːkjuːpaɪ] <-ie-> *vt* **1.** occupare; **to ~ space** occupare spazio; **the bathroom's occupied** il bagno è occupato; **~ing forces** forze *f pl* di occupazione; **to be occupied with doing sth** essere occupato a fare qc; **to keep sb occupied** tenere occupato qu; **to keep one's mind occupied** tenersi la mente occupata; **to ~ a post** ricoprire una carica; **the house hasn't been occupied for a long time** la casa è disabitata da molto tempo **2.** (*employ*) dare lavoro a

occur [əˈkɜːr] <-rr-> *vi* **1.** (*happen*) avvenire; **don't let it ~ again!** che non succeda più!; **consult your doctor if any of these symptoms ~** consultare il proprio medico se dovessero comparire alcuni di questi sintomi; **to ~ once every two years** verificarsi ogni due anni **2.** (*exist*) esistere; **the disease does not ~ in this area** la malattia non si manifesta in questa zona **3.** (*come into mind*) **to ~ to sb** venire in mente a qu; **it ~d to me that ...** mi è venuto in mente che ...; **did it ever ~ to you that ...?** non hai mai pensato che ...?

occurrence [əˈkɜːrəns] *n* **1.** (*event*) avvenimento *m;* **an unexpected ~** un avvenimento inatteso; **to be an everyday ~** accadere tutti i giorni; **to be of frequent/rare ~** essere/non essere frequente **2.** (*case*) caso *m* **3.** (*incidence: of disease*) insorgenza *f*

ocean [ˈoʊʃən] *n* oceano *m* ▶ **~s of ...** un sacco di ... *inf*

oceangoing [ˈoʊʃnˌgoʊɪŋ] *adj* transatlantico, -a

Oceania [ˌoʊʃiˈeɪniə] *n* Oceania *f*

oceanic [ˌoʊʃiˈænɪk] *adj* oceanico, -a

ocean liner *n* NAUT transatlantico *m*

oceanography [ˌoʊʃəˈnɑːgrəfi] *n* oceanografia *f*

ocelot [ˈɑːsəlɑːt] *n* ocelot *m*

ocher, ochre [ˈoʊkɚ] **I.** *n* **1.** (*color*) ocra *m* **2.** (*mineral*) ocra *f* **II.** *adj* ocra *inv*

o'clock [əˈklɑːk] *adv* **it's one ~** è l'una; **it's two/seven ~** sono le due/le sette

octagon [ˈɑːktəgɑːn] *n* ottagono *m*

octagonal [ɑːkˈtægənəl] *adj* ottagonale

octane [ˈɑːkteɪn] *n* ottano *m*

octave [ˈɑːktɪv] *n* LIT, MUS ottava *f*

octet [ɑːkˈtet] *n* MUS ottetto *m*

October [ɑːkˈtoʊbɚ] *n* ottobre *m; s.a.* **April**

octogenarian [ˌɑːktoʊdʒɪˈneriən] **I.** *adj* ottuagenario, -a **II.** *n* ottuagenario, -a *m, f*

octopus [ˈɑːktəpəs] <-es *o* -pi> *n* polpo *m*

oculist [ˈɑːkjəlɪst] *n* oculista *mf*

OD [ˌoʊˈdiː] **I.** *n abbr of* **overdose** overdose *f inv* **II.** *vi* **to ~ on sth** (*sleeping pills*) prendere una dose eccessiva di qc; (*heroin*) fare overdose di qc; *fig* farsi un'overdose di qc

odd [ɑːd] *adj* **1.** (*strange*) strano, -a; **an ~ person/thing** una persona/cosa strana; **how (very) ~!** che strano!; **it is ~ that ...** è strano che ... +*subj;* **to look ~** avere un aspetto strano **2.** (*not even: number*) dispari **3.** (*approximately*) **30 ~ people** poco più di 30 persone **4.** (*occasional*) sporadico, -a; **at ~ times** alcune volte; **she does the ~ teaching job** occasionalmente insegna **5.** (*unmatched: glove, sock*) spaiato, -a **6.** (*left over*) rimanente; **to feel the ~ one out** sentirsi escluso

oddball [ˈɑːdbɔːl] **I.** *n inf* tipo *m* strano **II.** *adj inf* (*sense of humor*) strano, -a; (*idea*) stravagante

oddity [ˈɑːdəti] <-ies> *n* (*person*) eccentrico, -a *m, f;* (*thing, characteristic*) stranezza *f*

odd-job man [ˈɑːdˌdʒɑːbˌmæn] *n* tuttofare *m inv*

oddly *adv* stranamente; **~ enough** per quanto strano sembri

odds [ɑːdz] *npl* (*probability*) probabilità *fpl;* **the ~ against/in favor of sth** le probabilità che qc non avvenga/avvenga; **to shorten/lengthen the ~** diminuire/aumentare le probabilità; **the ~ are against us** tutto gioca a nostro sfavore; **the ~ are in his favor** tutto gioca a suo favore; **the ~ are that ...** è molto probabile che ... +*subj* ▶ **~ and ends** *inf* (*bits*) cianfrusaglie *fpl;* **against all (the) ~** contrariamente alle previsioni; **to be at ~ with sb** non essere d'accordo con qu

odds-on [ˌɑːdzˈɑːn] *adj* molto probabile; **it's ~ that ...** la cosa più probabile è che ... +*subj;* **the ~ favorite to win the race** il favorito della gara

ode [oʊd] *n* ode *f*

odious [ˈoʊdiəs] *adj* odioso, -a

odometer [oʊˈdɑːmətɚ] *n* contachilometri *m inv*

odor [ˈoʊdɚ] *n* (*smell*) odore *m;* (*fragrance*) profumo *m*

odorless *adj form* inodore

odyssey [ˈɑːdɪsi] *n* odissea *f*

OECD [ˌoʊiːsiːˈdiː] *n abbr of* **Organization for Economic Cooperation and Development** OCSE *f*

of [əv, *stressed:* ɒv] *prep* **1.** di **2.** (*belonging to*) di; **the works ~ Twain** le opere di Twain; **a friend ~ mine/theirs** un mio/loro amico **3.** (*done by*) **it's kind ~ him** è gentile da parte sua **4.** (*representing*) di; **a drawing ~ Paul/ the sun** un disegno di Paul/del sole **5.** (*without*) **a tree bare ~ leaves** un albero spoglio; **free ~ charge** gratis; **free ~ tax** non soggetto a imposta; **to cure sb ~ a disease** guarire qu da una malattia **6.** (*with*) **a man ~ courage** un uomo coraggioso; **a man ~ no importance** un uomo senza importanza; **a city ~ wide avenues** una città dai grandi viali **7.** (*away* *from*) **to be north ~ Atlanta** essere a nord di Atlanta **8.** (*temporal*) **the 4th ~ May** il 4 (di) maggio; **in May ~ 2005** nel maggio del 2005 **9.** (*to*) **it is ten/(a) quarter ~ two** sono le due meno dieci/un quarto **10.** (*consisting of*) di; **a ring ~ gold** un anello d'oro; **to smell/to taste ~ cheese** sapere di formaggio; **to consist ~ six parts** essere composto di sei parti **11.** (*characteristic*) **with the patience ~ a saint** con la pazienza di un santo; **this idiot ~ a plumber** questo idiota di idraulico; **doctor ~ medicine** dottore in medicina **12.** (*concerning*) **his love ~ jazz** la sua passione per il jazz; **to know sth ~ sb's past** sapere qc del passato di qu; **to approve ~ sb's idea** essere d'accordo con l'idea di qu; **what has become ~ him?** che cosa ne è stato di lui?; **what do you think ~ him?** cosa pensi di lui? **13.** (*cause*) **because ~ sth/sb** a causa di qc/qu; **to die ~ grief** morire di dolore; **it happened ~ itself** è accaduto da sé **14.** (*a portion of*) **there's a lot ~ it** ce n'è molto; **one ~ the best** uno dei migliori; **the best ~ friends** grandi amici; **many ~ them came** molti di loro sono venuti; **there are five ~ them** ce ne sono cinque; **he knows the five ~ them** conosce tutti e cinque; **two ~ the five** due dei cinque; **he ~ all people knows that** lui dovrebbe saperlo meglio di tutti; **today ~ all days** proprio oggi **15.** (*to amount of*) **80 years ~ age** 80 anni

off [ɑːf] **I.** *prep* **1.** (*near*) **to be just ~ the main road** essere vicinissimo alla strada principale **2.** (*away from*) **to take sth ~ the shelf** prendere qc dallo scaffale; **keep ~ the grass** non calpestare l'erba **3.** (*down from*) **to fall/jump ~ a ladder** cadere/saltare da una scala; **to get ~ the train** scendere dal treno **4.** (*from*) **to eat ~ a plate** mangiare nel piatto; **to cut a piece ~ the cheese** tagliare un pezzetto di formaggio; **to take 10 dollars ~ the price** scontare di 10 dollari **5.** (*stop using*) **to be ~ caffeine** aver eliminato la caffeina; **to be ~ drugs** aver smesso di drogarsi **6.** (*as source of*) **to run ~ batteries** funzionare a batteria **II.** *adv* **1.** (*not on*) **to switch/turn sth ~** spegnere qc; (*tap, water*) chiudere qc; **it's ~ between them** *fig* tra loro è finita **2.** (*away*) **the town is 5 miles ~ to the east** la cittadina è a 5 miglia in direzione est; **not far ~** poco lontano; **a way's ~** parecchio lontano; **to drive/run ~** partire/correre via; **~ with you** vattene; **it's time I was ~** è ora che vada **3.** (*removed*) **the lid is ~** senza il tappo; **with one's coat ~** senza cappotto; **~ with that hat!** togliti il cappello! **4.** (*free from work*) **to get ~ at 4:00 p.m.** finire di lavorare alle 4 del pomeriggio; **to get a day ~** prendersi un giorno libero **5.** (*completely*) **to kill ~** sterminare; **to pay sth ~** finire di pagare **6.** COM **5% ~** 5% di sconto **7.** (*until gone*) **to walk ~ the dinner** fare una passeggiata per digerire (la cena); **to sleep ~ the wine** dormire per smaltire gli effetti del vino **8.** (*separating*) **to fence sth ~** recintare

qc ▶ **straight** [*o* **right**] **~ the bat** subito; **~ and on, on and ~** a periodi; **it rained ~ and on** piovve intermittentemente **III.** *adj* **1.** (*not on: light*) spento, -a; (*faucet*) chiuso, -a; (*water supply*) tolto, -a **2.** (*canceled: engagement, wedding, deal*) annullato, -a **3.** (*free from work*) **to be ~ at 5:00 p.m.** finire di lavorare alle 5 del pomeriggio; **I'm ~ on Mondays** il lunedì è il mio giorno libero **4.** (*provided for*) **to be well ~** essere abbiente; **to be not well ~** non essere abbiente **5.** (*substandard*) **to be ~ one's game** SPORTS non essere in forma **6.** *inf* **I've gone ~ on him** non mi interessa più **IV.** *vt inf* **to ~ sb** far fuori qu

offal [ˈɑːfəl] *n* (*of animal*) frattaglie *fpl*

offbeat [ˌɑːfˈbiːt] *adj* poco convenzionale

off-center *adj* **1.** (*diverging from the center*) non centrale **2.** (*unconventional*) alternativo, -a

off chance [ˈɑːfˌtʃænts] *n* **on the ~** sperando nella sorte

off-color [ˌɑːfˈkʌlɚ] *adj Brit* **1.** (*unwell*) **to feel ~** non sentirsi bene; **to look ~** avere una brutta cera **2.** (*somewhat obscene: joke*) sconcio, -a

off day *n* **to have an ~** avere una giornata no

off-duty *adj* fuori servizio

offend [əˈfend] **I.** *vi* **1.** (*cause displeasure*) offendere **2.** (*violate*) **to ~ against sth** andare contro a qc; **his remarks ~ against common sense** i suoi commenti fanno torto al buon senso **3.** LAW infrangere la legge; (*commit a crime*) commettere un reato **II.** *vt* **1.** (*upset sb's feelings*) offendere; **to be ~ed by sth** essere offeso da qc; **to be easily ~ed** essere molto suscettibile; **she was ~ed that she had not been invited** si è offesa perché non è stata invitata **2.** (*affect disagreeably*) **to ~ the eye** essere un pugno in un occhio; **to ~ good taste** essere un'offesa al buongusto

offender [əˈfenˌdɚ] *n* trasgressore, ditrice *m, f;* (*guilty of crime*) criminale *mf,* delinquente *mf;* **first ~** colpevole di reato senza precedenti penali; **previous** [*o* **repeat**] **~** recidivo; **young ~** delinquente minorile

offense [əˈfents] *n* **1.** (*crime*) reato *m;* **minor ~** reato *m* minore; **second ~** recidiva *f;* **traffic ~** infrazione *f* del codice stradale **2.** (*affront*) offesa *f;* **an ~ against sth** un'offesa a qc; **it is an ~ to the eye** *fig* essere un pugno in un occhio **3.** (*upset feeling*) offesa *f;* **to cause ~** (**to sb**) offendere (qu); **to take ~** (**at sth**) offendersi (di qc); **no ~** (**intended**) *inf* senza offesa **4.** REL peccato *m* **5.** SPORTS attacco *m*

offensive [əˈfenˌsɪv] **I.** *adj* **1.** (*remark, language, tone*) offensivo, -a; **to be ~ to sb** insultare qu **2.** (*disagreeable: smell*) ripugnante **3.** MIL **~ weapon** arma *f* offensiva **II.** *n* MIL offensiva *f;* **to go on the ~** passare all'offensiva; **to launch an ~** (**against sth**) lanciare l'offensiva (contro qc); **to take the ~** attaccare

O

per primi

offer ['ɑːfə] I. *vt* 1.(*proffer: help, money*) off-rire; (*chance, advice*) dare; **to ~ sb sth** offrire qc a qu; **to ~ an apology** chiedere scusa; **to ~ congratulations to sb** congratularsi con qu; **can I ~ you a drink?** le [*o* ti] va qualcosa da bere?; **to ~ a good price for sth** fare una buona offerta per (comprare) qc; **to ~ information** dare informazioni; **to ~ a reward** offrire una ricompensa; **to ~ an explanation** dare una spiegazione; **to ~ shelter** dare riparo; **to have much to ~** avere molto da offrire; **to ~ oneself for a position** presentarsi per un impiego 2.(*give: gift*) dare 3.(*volunteer*) **to ~ to do sth** offrirsi di fare qc 4.(*propose: plan*) proporre; (*excuse*) presentare; (*opinion*) esprimere; **to ~ a suggestion** fare un suggerimento 5.(*show*) **to ~ resistance** opporre resistenza II. *vi* (*present itself: opportunity*) presentarsi III. *n* (*proposal*) proposta *f*; (*of help, of a job*) offerta *f*; **an ~ of marriage** una proposta di matrimonio; **to make sb an ~ they can't refuse** fare a qu un'offerta molto allettante; **that's my last ~** è la mia ultima offerta; **to make** [*o* **put in**] **an ~ of $1000 for sth** offrire 1000 dollari per qc

offering ['ɑːfə·rɪŋ] *n* offerta *f*; **as an ~ of thanks** in segno di gratitudine

offhand [ˌɑːf·'hænd] I. *adj* 1.(*without previous thought*) istintivo, -a 2.(*uninterested*) brusco, -a II. *adv* su due piedi; **to judge sb/sth ~** giudicare qu/qc alla leggera; **Offhand, I'd say ...** Così su due piedi direi ...

office ['ɑːfɪs] *n* 1.(*of a company*) ufficio *m*; (*room in house*) studio *m*; **they've got ~s in Los Angeles and Miami** hanno uffici a Los Angeles e Miami; **to stay at the ~** rimanere in ufficio; **architect's/lawyer's ~** studio di archi-tetto/avvocato; **doctor's ~** ambulatorio *m* 2. POL (*authoritative position*) carica *f*; **to hold ~ as** ricoprire la carica di; **to be in ~** (*person*) essere in carica; (*party*) essere al potere; **to be out of ~** aver lasciato la carica; **to take ~** assu-mere una carica 3. *pl* (*assistance*) servigi *mpl*; **through the ~s of** grazie all'intervento di 4. REL rito *m*

office building *n* palazzo *m* di uffici

office hours *npl* orario *f* d'ufficio; **to do sth after ~** fare qc fuori dall'orario d'ufficio

officer ['ɑːfɪ·sə] *n* 1. MIL ufficiale *m*; **naval ~** ufficiale di marina 2.(*policeman*) agente *mf*; **police ~** agente di polizia 3.(*in organization*) funzionario *m*; (*in political party*) dirigente *mf*

office staff *n* personale *m* amministrativo

office supplies *npl* articoli *mpl* per l'ufficio

office worker *n* impiegato, -a *m, f*

official [ə·'fɪʃl] I. *n* 1. POL dirigente *mf* 2.(*civil servant*) funzionario, -a *m, f* II. *adj* ufficiale

officialdom [ə·'fɪʃ·l·dəm] *n pej* burocrazia *f*

officialese [ə·ˌfɪ·ʃə·'liːz] *n* gergo *m* burocratico

officially [ə·'fɪʃ·ə·li] *adv* ufficialmente

officiate [ə·'fɪ·ʃi·eɪt] *vi form* officiare; **to ~ at a wedding/funeral** celebrare un matrimonio/funerale

officious [ə·'fɪ·ʃəs] *adj pej* petulante

offing ['ɑːfɪŋ] *n* **to be in the ~** *fig* esserci in vista; **good news is in the ~** ci saranno presto buone notizie

off-key MUS I. *adv* **to play/sing ~** stonare II. *adj* stonato, -a, fuori tono

off-limits *adj* con divieto di accesso

offline [ˌɑːf·'laɪn] *adj* COMPUT non in linea

offload ['ɑːf·loud] *vt* 1.(*unload*) scaricare 2.(*get rid of*) **to ~ sth** sbarazzarsi di qc; **to ~ sth onto sb** sbolognare qc a qu; **to ~ work onto sb** scaricare il lavoro a qu

off-peak [ˌɑːf·'piːk] *adj* (*fare, rate*) fuori dalle ore di punta; (*phone call*) a tariffa ridotta

off-piste [ˌɑːf·'piːst] *adj* SPORTS fuoripista; **~ skiing** sci fuoripista

off-putting ['ɑːf·ˌpʊt̬·ɪŋ] *adj* 1.(*smell, manner, appearance*) sgradevole; (*person*) antipatico, -a 2.(*experience*) scoraggiante

off-ramp *n* rampa *f* di svincolo

off-road vehicle *n* fuoristrada *m inv*

off-season ['ɑːf·ˌsiː·zən] I. *n* bassa stagione *f* II. *adj* di bassa stagione

offset ['ɑːf·set] I. *n* 1.(*compensation*) com-pensazione *f* 2. BOT germoglio *m* 3. TYPO off-set *m* II.<offset, offset> *vt* 1.(*compensate*) compensare; **in order to ~ the cost/loss ...** per compensare i costi/le perdite 2. TYPO stam-pare offset

offset printing *n* stampa *f* offset

offshore [ˌɑːf·'ʃɔːr] I. *adj* 1.(*from the shore: breeze, wind*) di terra 2.(*at sea*) vicino alla costa; **~ fishing** pesca *f* costiera; **~ oilfield** giacimento *m* petrolifero off-shore 3.(*in foreign country*) off-shore *inv* II. *adv* vicino alla costa; **to anchor ~** ormeggiare a un certa distanza alla costa

offside [ˌɑːf·'saɪd], **offsides** SPORTS I. *adv* in fuorigioco II. *adj* (*rule*) del fuorigioco III. *n* fuorigioco *m inv*; **he was called for an ~** gli è stato fischiato il fuorigioco

offspring ['ɑːf·sprɪŋ] *n inv* 1.(*animal young*) piccoli *mpl* 2. *pl* (*children*) prole *f*

offstage [ˌɑːf·'steɪdʒ] I. *adj* dietro le quinte II. *adv* dietro le quinte

off-street parking [ˌɑːf·striːt·'pɑːr·kɪŋ] *n* posto *m* auto

off-the-cuff [ˌɑːf·ðə·'kʌf] I. *adj* spontaneo, -a II. *adv* spontaneamente

off-the-rack [ˌɑːf·ðə·'ræk] *adj* confezionato, -a

off-white [ˌɑːf·'hwaɪt] *adj* bianco sporco *inv*

often ['ɑːf·ən] *adv* spesso; **we ~ go there** ci andiamo spesso; **as ~ as not** il più delle volte; **every so ~** di tanto in tanto; **how ~?** ogni quanto?; **it's not ~ that ...** non accade di fre-quente che ... +*subj;* **more ~ than not** il più delle volte

ogle ['oʊ·gl] *vt* **to ~ sb** mangiarsi qu con gli occhi

ogre ['oʊ·gə] *n* orco *m*

ogress ['oʊg·res] *n* orchessa *f*

oh [oʊ] *interj* 1.(*expressing surprise, disap-*

pointment, pleasure) oh; ~ **dear!** oddio!; ~ **no!** oh no!; ~ **well** pazienza; ~ **yes?** ah sì? **2.**(*by the way*) ah

OH *n abbr of* **Ohio** Ohio *m*

Ohio *n* Ohio *m*

oil [ɔɪl] **I.** *n* **1.**(*lubricant*) olio *m;* **sunflower ~** olio di girasole **2.**(*petroleum*) petrolio *m;* **to strike ~** trovare il petrolio; *fig* trovare una miniera d'oro **3.** *pl* (*oil-based paint*) colori *m pl* a olio; **to paint in ~s** dipingere a olio ▸ **to burn the** <u>midnight</u> **~** lavorare fino a tarda notte; **to pour ~ on troubled** <u>waters</u> placare le acque **II.** *vt* oliare

oilcan *n* oliera *f*

oilcloth *n* tela *f* cerata

oil consumption *n* consumo *m* petrolifero

oil crisis *n* crisi *f* petrolifera *inv*

oil-exporting *adj* esportatore, -trice *m, f* di petrolio

oil field *n* giacimento *m* petrolifero

oil-fired *adj* a gasolio; ~ **heating system** riscaldamento *m* a gasolio

oiliness ['ɔɪ·lɪ·nɪs] *n* **1.**(*greasiness: of food*) oleosità *f;* (*of material, skin*) untuosità *f* **2.** *fig* untuosità *f*

oil lamp *n* lampada *f* a olio

oil level *n* TECH livello *m* dell'olio

oil painting *n* **1.**(*picture*) dipinto *m* a olio **2.**(*art*) pittura *f* a olio ▸ **to be no ~** *Aus, Brit, iron* non essere una gran bellezza

oil pipeline *n* oleodotto *m*

oil-producing *adj* produttore, -trice *m, f* di petrolio

oil-producing country *n* paese *m* produttore di petrolio

oil production *n* produzione *f* di petrolio

oil rig *n* piattaforma *f* petrolifera

oil sheik *n* magnate *m* del petrolio

oilskin *n* **1.**(*cloth*) tela *f* cerata **2.** *pl* (*clothing*) cerata *fsing*

oil slick *n* marea *f* nera

oil tanker *n* NAUT petroliera *f*

oil well *n* pozzo *m* di petrolio

oily ['ɔɪ·li] <-ier, -iest> *adj* **1.**(*oil-like*) oleoso, -a **2.**(*greasy*) unto, -a **3.**(*manner*) untuoso, -a

ointment ['ɔɪnt·mənt] *n* MED pomata *f*

OK¹, okay [ˌoʊ·'keɪ] *inf* **I.** *adj* **1.**(*acceptable*) **is it ~ with you if ...?** ti va bene se ...?; **it's ~ with me** per me va bene; **to be ~ for money/work** avere abbastanza soldi/lavoro **2.**(*not bad*) **to be ~** non essere male; **her voice is ~, but it's nothing special** la sua voce non è male, ma niente di speciale **II.** *interj* ok *inf* **III.** <OKed, okayed> *vt* **to ~ sth** dare l'ok a qc **IV.** *n* ok *m;* **to give (sb/sth) the ~** dare l'ok (a qu/qc) **V.** *adv* abbastanza bene

OK² *n abbr of* **Oklahoma** Oklahoma, f

Oklahoma *n* Oklahoma *f*

okra ['oʊ·krə] *n* abelmosco *m*

old [oʊld] **I.** *adj* **1.**(*not young, not new*) vecchio, -a; ~ **people** i vecchi; **to be a bit ~ to be doing sth** (*adult*) essere troppo vecchio per fare qc; (*child*) essere ormai grande per fare qc;

to grow ~er invecchiare **2.**(*wine*) invecchiato, -a; (*furniture, house*) antico, -a **3.**(*denoting an age*) **how ~ are you?** quanti anni hai?; **he's five years ~** ha cinque anni; **she's three years ~er than I** ha tre anni più di me; **Ted is fifteen, she's ~er** Ted ha 15 anni, lei è più grande; **to be ~ enough to do sth** essere grande abbastanza per fare qc **4.**(*former*) ~ **boyfriend** ex fidanzato *m;* ~ **English** antico inglese *m* **5.**(*long known*) ~ **friend** vecchio amico; **the same ~ faces** le stesse facce di sempre **6.** *inf* (*expression of affection*) **I heard poor ~ Frank has lost his job** ho sentito che il povero Frank ha perso il lavoro **II.** *n* **1.**(*elderly people*) **the ~** i vecchi; **young and ~** grandi e piccini **2.** *liter* (*past*) **of ~** anticamente; **to know sb of ~** conoscere qu da molto tempo

old age *n* vecchiaia *f;* **to reach ~** arrivare alla vecchiaia

old-fashioned [ˌoʊld·'fæ·ʃənd] *adj pej* **1.**(*not modern: clothes*) fuori moda *inv;* (*views*) antiquato, -a; **to be ~** essere all'antica **2.**(*traditional*) tradizionale; **it has an ~ charm** ha un fascino antico

oldie *n* **1.**(*person*) vecchio, -a *m, f* **2.**(*song, film*) vecchio successo *m*

old lady *n inf* **my ~** (*mother*) mia mamma; (*wife*) mia moglie

old man *n inf* **my ~** (*father*) mio padre; (*husband*) mio marito

old master *n* ART **1.**(*artist*) grande maestro *m* **2.**(*painting*) opera *f* di un grande maestro

old school I. *adj* della vecchia scuola **II.** *n fig* vecchia scuola *f*

Old Testament *n* Antico Testamento *m*

old-timer ['oʊld·ˌtaɪ·mɚ] *n inf* **1.**(*old man*) vecchio, -a *m, f* **2.**(*longtime worker, resident*) veterano, -a *m, f*

old wives' tale [ˌoʊld·'waɪvz·ˌteɪl] *n* credenza *f* popolare

oleander [ˌoʊ·li·'æn·dɚ] *n* oleandro *m*

olfactory [ɑːl·'fæk·tə·ri] *adj* olfattivo, -a

olive ['ɑː·lɪv] *n* **1.**(*fruit*) oliva *f* **2.**(*tree*) olivo *m* **3.**(*color*) verde *m* oliva

olive branch *n* ramo *m* d'olivo ▸ **to hold out the ~ to sb** porgere a qu il ramo d'olivo

olive grove *n* oliveto *m*

olive oil *n* olio *m* d'oliva

Olympiad [oʊ·'lɪm·pi·æd] *n* SPORTS olimpiade *f*

Olympian [oʊ·'lɪm·pi·ən] *adj* olimpico, -a

Olympic [oʊ·'lɪm·pɪk] *adj* olimpico, -a; **the Olympic Games** SPORTS i Giochi Olimpici

Oman [oʊ·'mɑːn] *n* Oman *m*

Omani [oʊ·'mɑː·ni] **I.** *adj* omanita **II.** *n* omanita *mf*

ombudsman ['ɑːm·bədz·mən] <-men> *n* POL difensore *m* civico

omelet(te) ['ɑːm·lət] *n* frittata *f*

omen ['oʊ·men] *n* presagio *m;* **to be a good/bad ~ for sth** essere di buon/cattivo auspicio per qc

ominous ['ɑː·mə·nəs] *adj* (*news, silence*)

O

inquietante; (*implications*) funesto, -a

omission [oʊ·'mɪ·ʃən] *n* omissione *f*

omit [oʊ·'mɪt] <-tt-> *vt* (*information, paragraph*) omettere; (*person*) escludere; **to ~ any reference to sb/sth** evitare qualsiasi riferimento a qu/qc; **to ~ to do sth** (*neglect*) tralasciare di fare qc; (*forget*) dimenticarsi di fare qc

omnibus ['ɑːm·nɪ·bəs] **I.** <-es> *n* **1.** (*bus*) autobus *m inv* **2.** (*anthology*) antologia *f* **II.** *adj* **~ edition** antologia

omnipotence [ɑːm·'nɪ·pə·təns] *n* onnipotenza *f*

omnipotent [ɑːm·ᵛnɪpətənt] *adj* onnipotente

omnipresent [ˌɑːm·nɪ·'pre·znt] *adj form* onnipresente

omniscient [ɑːm·'nɪ·ʃnt] *adj form* onnisciente

omnivorous [ɑːm·'nɪ·və·rəs] *adj* onnivoro, -a; **to be an ~ reader** *fig* essere un avido lettore

on [ɑːn] **I.** *prep* **1.** (*place*) su; **~ the table** sul tavolo; **to hang sth ~ the wall** appendere qc al muro; **to put sth ~ sb's shoulder/finger** mettere qc sulle spalle/al dito di qu; **to be ~ the plane** essere sull'aereo; **to have sth ~ one's mind** *fig* pensare a qc **2.** (*by means of*) **to go ~ the train** andare in treno; **to go ~ foot** andare a piedi; **to keep a dog ~ a leash** tenere un cane al guinzaglio **3.** (*source of*) **to run ~ gas** andare a benzina; **to live ~ $2,000 a month** vivere con 2.000 dollari al mese **4.** MED **to be ~ drugs** (*legal*) assumere farmaci; (*illegal*) drogarsi **5.** (*spatial*) **~ the right/left** a destra/sinistra; **~ the corner** all'angolo; **~ back of sth** nella parte posteriore di qc; **a house ~ the river** una casa sul fiume **6.** (*temporal*) **~ Sunday** domenica; **~ Sundays** la domenica; **~ the evening of May the 4th** la sera del 4 maggio; **at 2:00 p.m. ~ the dot** alle due in punto **7.** (*at time of*) **to leave ~ time** partire in orario; **~ her arrival** al suo arrivo; **~ arriving there** arrivando là; **to finish ~ schedule** finire per tempo **8.** (*about*) su; **a lecture ~ Shakespeare** una conferenza su Shakespeare; **to compliment sb ~ sth** congratularsi con qu per qc; **to be there ~ business** essere là per lavoro **9.** (*through medium of*) **~ TV** alla TV; **~ video/CD** su videocassetta/CD; **to speak ~ the radio/the phone** parlare alla radio/al telefono; **to work ~ a computer** lavorare al computer; **to play sth ~ the flute** suonare qc con il flauto **10.** (*with basis in*) **~ the principle that** in base al principio che; **to do sth ~ purpose** fare qc di proposito **11.** (*in state of*) **~ sale** in vendita; **to set sth ~ fire** dare fuoco a qc; **to go ~ vacation/a trip** andare in vacanza/viaggio; **~ the whole** nel complesso **12.** (*involved in*) **to be ~ the committee** far parte della commissione; **to work ~ a project** lavorare a un progetto; **to be ~ page 10** essere a pagina 10; **two ~ each side** due per parte **13.** (*because of*) **~ account of sth/sb** a causa di qc/qu; **to depend ~ sb/sth** dipendere da qu/qc **14.** (*against*) **to turn ~ sb**

mettersi contro qu; **an attack ~ sb** un attacco a qu; **to cheat ~ sb** tradire qu **15.** (*paid by*) **to buy sth ~ credit** comprare qc a credito; **this is ~ me** *inf* offro io **II.** *adv* **1.** (*covering one's body*) **to put a hat ~** mettersi un cappello; **to have sth ~** avere qc addosso; **to try ~ sth** provarsi qc **2.** (*connected to sth*) **make sure the top's ~ properly** assicurati che sia tappato bene **3.** (*aboard*) **to get ~ a train** salire in treno; **to get ~ a horse** montare a cavallo **4.** (*not stopping*) **to keep ~ doing sth** continuare a fare qc; **to get ~ with sth** continuare a fare qc **5.** (*in forward direction*) avanti; **to move ~** andare avanti; **to urge sb ~** *fig* incoraggiare qu; **from that day ~** da quel giorno in poi; **later ~** più tardi; **and so ~** e così via **6.** (*in operation*) **to turn ~** accendere; (*tap*) aprire **7.** (*performing*) **to go ~** entrare in scena ►**~ and off** di quando in quando; **~ and ~** a lungo; **well ~ into the night** a notte inoltrata **III.** *adj* **1.** (*functioning: light*) acceso, -a; (*faucet*) aperto, -a; (*brake*) inserito, -a; **to leave the light ~** lasciare la luce accesa **2.** (*scheduled*) **what's ~ at the movies this week?** cosa danno al cinema questa settimana?; **the show will be ~ in Seattle very soon** lo spettacolo sarà in scena a Seattle molto presto; **have you got anything ~ for tomorrow?** hai programmi per domani? **3.** THEAT (*performing*) **to be ~** essere di scena **4.** (*job*) **to be ~ duty** essere di servizio; (*doctor*) essere di guardia **5.** (*good: day*) buono, -a **6.** (*acceptable*) **you're ~!** d'accordo!

once [wʌns] **I.** *adv* **1.** (*one time*) una volta; **~ a week** una volta alla settimana; **~ in a lifetime** una volta nella vita; (**every**) **~ in a while** una volta ogni tanto; **~ again** ancora una volta; **~ and for all** una volta per tutte; **just for ~** per una volta tanto; **~ more** (*one more time*) un'altra volta; (*again, as before*) ancora una volta; **~ or twice** una volta o due; **at ~** (*simultaneously*) insieme; (*immediately*) subito **2.** *liter* (*at one time past*) una volta; **~ upon a time there was ...** *liter* c'era una volta ... **II.** *conj* una volta che; **but ~ I'd arrived, ...** ma una volta arrivato ... ►**all** **at ~** tutto insieme; **at ~** subito

once-over ['wʌnts·ˌoʊ·vəʳ] *n inf* occhiata *f*; **to give sb/sth a/the ~** dare un'occhiata a qu/qc

oncoming ['ɑːn·kʌm·ɪŋ] *adj* imminente; (*traffic, vehicle*) che arriva dalla direzione opposta

one [wʌn] **I.** *n* (*number*) uno *m* ► **to land sb ~** *inf* mollarne uno a qu; (**all**) **in ~** tutto in uno; **as ~** *form* tutti insieme; **in ~** in un colpo solo **II.** *adj* **1.** *numeral* un, uno, -a; **~ hundred** cento; **it's ~ o'clock** è l'una; **~ man out of** [*o* **in**] **two** un uomo su due **2.** *indef* un, uno, -a; **we'll meet ~ day** un giorno ci incontreremo; **~ winter night** una notte d'inverno **3.** (*sole, single*) unico, -a; **her ~ and only hope** la sua unica speranza; **all files on the ~ disk** tutti i file su un unico dischetto **III.** *pron pers* **1. what can ~ do?** uno cosa fa?; **to wash ~'s**

face lavarsi la faccia **2.** (*person*) **no** ~ nessuno; **every** ~ tutti; **the little** ~**s** i piccoli; **the** ~ **who ...** quello che ...; **I for** ~ io per esempio **3.** (*particular thing or person*) **this** ~ questo; **which** ~? quale?; **the** ~ **on the table** quello sul tavolo; **the thinner** ~ il più magro

one-armed [ˌwʌn·ˈɑːrmd] *adj* con un braccio solo

one-armed bandit *n* slot machine *f inv*

one-eyed [ˌwʌn·ˈaɪd] *adj* con un occhio solo

one-handed **I.** *adv* con una sola mano **II.** *adj* con una mano sola

one-horse *adj* **1.** (*using one horse*) a un cavallo **2.** (*second-rate*) irrilevante; **a** ~ **town** un paese sconosciuto

one-legged *adj* con una gamba sola

one-liner [ˌwʌn·ˈlaɪ·nɚ] *n* battuta *f*

one-man [ˌwʌn·ˈmæn] *adj* **1.** (*consisting of one person*) di un solo uomo; **a** ~ **band** uomo *m* orchestra **2.** (*designed for one person*) singolo, -a

one-night stand [ˌwʌn·naɪt·ˈstænd] *n* **1.** *inf* (*relationship*) avventura *f* di una notte **2.** MUS, THEAT spettacolo *m* unico

one-piece (swimsuit) [ˈwʌn·piːs] *n* costume *m* intero

onerous [ˈɑːn·ɚ·əs] *adj* oneroso, -a

oneself [wʌn·ˈself] *pron reflexive* **1.** si; **to deceive** ~ illudersi; **to express** ~ esprimersi **2.** *normal* se stesso, -a; **freedom to be** ~ la libertà di essere se stessi; **not to feel** ~ non sentirsi se stessi **3.** *emphatic* da sé; **to do sth** ~ fare qc da sé **4.** (*personally*) **to see for** ~ vedere qc con i propri occhi **5.** (*alone*) da solo; **living by** ~ **can be very difficult** vivere da soli può essere difficile; **to have sth to** ~ avere qc per sé; **to keep sth for** ~ tenere qc per sé; **to speak to** ~ parlare da solo

one-sided [ˌwʌn·ˈsaɪ·dɪd] *adj* (*contest*) impari; (*decision*) di parte; (*view, account*) parziale

one-time [ˈwʌn·taɪm] *adj* **1.** di un tempo; ~ **president** ex presidente *mf* **2.** (*happening only once*) unico, -a

one-track mind [ˌwʌn·træk·ˈmaɪnd] *n* **to have a** ~ pensare soltanto a una cosa

one-upmanship [ˌwʌn·ˈʌp·mən·ʃɪp] *n inf* arte *f* di primeggiare

one-way street [ˌwʌn·weɪ·ˈstriːt] *n* strada *f* a senso unico

one-way ticket *n* biglietto *m* di sola andata

ongoing [ˈɑːn·goʊ·ɪŋ] *adj* in corso; ~ **state of affairs** situazione che perdura

onion [ˈʌn·jən] *n* cipolla *f*

online, on-line COMPUT **I.** *adj* in linea; ~ **information service** servizio *m* di informazioni in linea; ~ **shopping** acquisti *m* via Internet *pl* **II.** *adv* su Internet

onlooker [ˈɑːn·lʊ·kɚ] *n* spettatore, -trice *m, f*; **there were many** ~**s at the accident site** c'erano molti curiosi sul luogo dell'incidente

only [ˈoʊn·li] **I.** *adj* unico, -a, solo, -a; **the** ~ **plate he had** l'unico piatto che aveva; **the** ~ **way of doing sth** l'unico modo di fare qc; **I'm not the** ~ **one** non sono l'unico; **the** ~ **thing is ...** l'unica cosa è ... **II.** *adv* soltanto; **not** ~ **...** **but also** non soltanto ... ma anche; **I can** ~ **say ...** posso soltanto dire ...; **he has** ~ **two** ne ha solo due; ~ **Paul can do it** può farlo solo Paul; **I've** ~ **just eaten** ho appena mangiato **III.** *conj inf* solo che

onrush [ˈɑːn·rʌʃ] <-es> *n* **1.** (*of water*) ondata *f* **2.** (*of people*) fiumana *f*

onset [ˈɑːn·set] *n* inizio *m;* (*of winter*) arrivo *m;* (*of illness*) comparsa *f*

onshore [ˈɑːn·ʃɔːr] **I.** *adj* (*wind*) di mare **II.** *adv* a terra

onside [ˌɒn·ˈsaɪt] SPORTS **I.** *adj* **to be** ~ (*player*) non essere in fuorigioco **II.** *adv* non in fuorigioco

onside kick *n* onside kick *m inv*

onslaught [ˈɑːn·slɑːt] *n* attacco *m* violento

on-the-job training *n* formazione *f* sul posto di lavoro

onto [ˈɑːn·tuː] *prep*, **on to** *prep* **1.** (*in direction of*) su; **to put sth** ~ **the chair** mettere qc sulla sedia; **to come** ~ **a subject** arrivare a un argomento **2.** (*connected to*) **to hold** ~ **sb's arm** tenersi al braccio di qu; **to be** ~ **sb** scoprire il gioco di qu

onus [ˈoʊ·nəs] *n* onere *m*

onward [ˈɑːn·wɚd] **I.** *adj* in avanti; **the** ~ **march of time** l'inesorabile avanzare del tempo **II.** *adv* in avanti; **from today** ~ da oggi in poi

onyx [ˈɑː·nɪks] *n* GEO onice *f*

oodles [ˈuː·dlz] *npl* ~ **of money** un mucchio di soldi

oomph [ʊmf] *n inf* **1.** (*energy, vitality*) dinamismo *f* **2.** (*sex appeal*) attrattiva *f* sessuale

ooze [uːz] **I.** *vi* **1.** (*seep out*) stillare; **to** ~ **from sth** stillare da qc; **to** ~ **with sth** stillare qc; **to** ~ **away** esaurirsi **2.** *fig* (*be full of*) **to** ~ **with confidence** irradiare sicurezza **II.** *vt* stillare; **to** ~ **pus** emettere pus; **to** ~ **charisma** trasudare carisma **III.** *n* melma *f*

opacity [oʊ·ˈpæ·sə·ti] *n* **1.** (*non-transparency*) opacità *f* **2.** (*incomprehensibility*) oscurità *f*

opal [ˈoʊ·pl] *n* GEO opale *m*

opalescent [ˌoʊ·pə·ˈle·snt] *adj* opalescente

opaque [oʊ·ˈpeɪk] *adj* **1.** (*not transparent*) opaco, -a **2.** (*unintelligible*) oscuro, -a

OPEC [ˈoʊ·pek] *n abbr of* **Organization of Petroleum Exporting Countries** OPEC *f*

open [ˈoʊ·pən] **I.** *adj* **1.** aperto, -a; **wide** ~ spalancato; **to push sth** ~ aprire qc con una spinta; **to keep one's options** ~ lasciarsi aperte varie strade; **to welcome sb with** ~ **arms** accogliere qu a braccia aperte; **to have an** ~ **mind** avere una mentalità aperta **2.** (*not secret, public: scandal*) pubblico, -a; (*hostility*) dichiarato, -a; **to be an** ~ **book** *fig* essere un libro aperto; **an** ~ **secret** una cosa risaputa **3.** (*unfolded: map*) spiegato, -a **4.** (*accessible to all*) aperto, -a; (*discussion*) aperto, -a al pubblico; (*session, trial*) a porte aperte **5.** (*still* *available: job*) disponibile **II.** *n* **1.** (*outdoors, outside*) (**out**) **in the ~** all'aperto **2.** (*not secret*) **to get sth** (**out**) **in the ~** portare qc alla luce **III.** *vi* **1.** (*door, window, box*) aprirsi **2.** (*shop*) aprire **3.** (*start*) iniziare **IV.** *vt* **1.** (*door, box, shop*) aprire; **to ~ the door to sth** *fig* aprire la strada a qu; **to ~ sb's eyes** (**to sb/sth**) *fig* aprire gli occhi a qu; **to ~ fire** (**on sb**) sparare (a qu) **2.** (*reveal feelings*) **to ~ one's heart to sb** aprirsi con qu **3.** (*inaugurate*) aprire

◆**open onto** *vi* aprirsi su

◆**open up I.** *vi* **1.** (*unfold, become wider*) aprirsi **2.** (*shop*) aprire **3.** (*shoot*) aprire il fuoco **II.** *vt* aprire; (*map*) spiegare

open-air [ˌoʊ·pən·'er] *adj* all'aperto

open-ended [ˌoʊ·pn·'en·dɪd] *adj* (*question*) aperto, -a; (*contract*) a tempo indetreminato

opener ['oʊ·pən·ɚ] *n* **bottle ~** apribottiglie *m inv;* **can ~** apriscatole *m inv*

open-heart surgery [ˌoʊ·pən·hɑːrt·'sɜːr·dʒə·ri] *n* chirurgia *f* a cuore aperto

opening ['oʊ·pn·ɪŋ] *n* **1.** (*gap, hole*) apertura *f;* (*in forest*) radura *f* **2.** (*job opportunity*) posto *m* vacante **3.** (*beginning*) apertura *f;* (*of book, film*) inizio *m* **4.** (*ceremony*) inaugurazione *f;* (*new play, film*) prima *f*

opening balance *n* FIN saldo *m* iniziale

opening bid *n* offerta *f* iniziale

opening night *n* THEAT prima *f*

openly ['oʊ·pən·li] *adv* (*frankly, publicly*) apertamente

open market *n* mercato *m* aperto

open-minded [ˌoʊ·pən·'maɪn·dɪd] *adj* di mentalità aperta

open-mouthed *adj* a bocca aperta

openness ['oʊ·pən·nəs] *n* franchezza *f*

open-source *adj* open-source *inv*

open ticket *n* biglietto *m* aperto

opera ['ɑː·prə] *n* opera *f*

operable ['ɑː·pə·rə·bl] *adj* **1.** (*workable: plan*) attuabile **2.** MED operabile

opera glasses *n* binocolo *m* da teatro

opera house *n* teatro *m* lirico

operate ['ɑː·pə·reɪt] **I.** *vi* **1.** (*work, run*) funzionare **2.** (*have or produce an effect*) agire **3.** (*perform surgery*) operare; **to ~ on sb** operare qu **4.** (*do or be in business*) operare **II.** *vt* **1.** (*work*) azionare **2.** (*run, manage*) dirigere

operating ['ɑː·pə·reɪt·ɪŋ] *adj* **1.** ECON (*profit, costs*) di gestione **2.** TECH (*speed*) operativo, a **3.** MED operatorio, -a; **~ room, ~ theater** sala *f* operatoria

operation [ˌɑː·pə·'reɪ·ʃən] *n* **1.** (*way of working*) utilizzo *m;* **to be in ~** essere in funzione; **to come into ~** (*machines*) entrare in funzione **2.** *a.* MED, MIL, MATH operazione *f;* **rescue ~** operazione di soccorso **3.** (*financial transaction*) operazione *f* (finaziaria)

operational [ˌɑː·pə·'reɪ·ʃə·nl] *adj* operativo, -a

operative ['ɑː·pə·ə·tɪv] **I.** *n* **1.** (*worker*) operaio, -a *m, f* **2.** (*detective*) agente *mf* **II.** *adj* **1.** (*rules*) operativo, -a **2.** MED chirurgico, -a

operator ['ɑː·pə·reɪ·ṭɚ] *n* **1.** (*person*) operatore, -trice *m, f;* TEL centralino *m;* **machine ~** macchinista *mf;* **he's a smooth ~** *inf* è un bel furbo **2.** (*company*) impresa *f;* **a tour ~** operatore turistico

operetta [ˌɑː·pə·'re·ṭə] *n* operetta *f*

ophthalmic [ɑːf·'θæl·mɪk] *adj* (*clinic, surgeon, vein*) oftalmico, -a

ophthalmologist [ˌɑːf·θæl·'mɑː·lə·dʒɪst] *n* oculista *mf*, oftalmologo, -a *m, f*

opiate ['oʊ·pi·ɪt] *n* oppiaceo *m*

opinion [ə·'pɪn·jən] *n* opinione *f*

opinionated [ə·'pɪn·jə·neɪ·ṭɪd] *adj pej* dogmatico, -a

opinion poll *n* sondaggio *m* d'opinione

opium ['oʊ·pi·əm] *n* oppio *m*

opossum [ə·'pɑː·səm] *n* opossum *m inv*

opponent [ə·'poʊ·nənt] *n* **1.** (*of proposal*) oppositore, -trice *m, f* **2.** POL, SPORTS avversario, -a *m, f*

opportune [ˌɑː·pə·'tuːn] *adj* opportuno, -a

opportunism [ˌɑː·pə·'tuː·nɪ·zəm] *n* opportunismo *m*

opportunist [ˌɑː·pə·'tuː·nɪst] **I.** *n* opportunista *mf* **II.** *adj* opportunista

opportunity [ˌɑː·pə·'tuː·nə·ti] <-ies> *n* opportunità *f;* **~ to do** [*o* **of doing**] **sth** opportunità di fare qc; **at the earliest** (**possible**) **~** alla prima occasione

oppose [ə·'poʊz] *vt* **1.** (*be against, resist*) opporsi a **2.** (*be on other team, play against*) affrontare

opposed *adj* **to be ~ to sth** opporsi a qc

opposing *adj* (*opinion*) opposto, -a; (*team, forces*) avversario, -a

opposite ['ɑː·pə·zɪt] **I.** *n* opposto *m,* contrario *m;* **quite the ~!** tutto il contrario!
▶~**s attract** gli opposti si attraggono **II.** *adj* **1.** (*absolutely different*) opposto, -a, contrario, -a; **the ~ sex** l'altro sesso **2.** (*facing*) di fronte; **~ to/from sth** di fronte a qc; **his ~ number** il suo omologo **III.** *adv* (*facing*) di fronte; **they live ~** abitano di fronte **IV.** *prep* di fronte a; **~ to sth** di fronte a qc; **~ me** di fronte a me; **to sit ~ one another** sedersi di fronte (l'uno all'altro)

opposition [ˌɑː·pə·'zɪ·ʃən] *n* **1.** POL opposizione *f* **2.** (*contrast*) contrapposizione *f;* **in ~ to sth** in contrapposizione a qc **3.** (*opponent*) avversario, -a *m, f* **4.** ECON concorrenza *f*

oppress [ə·'pres] *vt* opprimere

oppression [ə·'pre·ʃən] *n* (*submission, feeling*) oppressione *f*

oppressive [ə·'pre·sɪv] *adj* **1.** (*harsh: regime, measures*) oppressivo, -a **2.** (*burdensome: heat*) soffocante

oppressor [ə·'pre·sɚ] *n* oppressore *m*

opt [ɑːpt] *vi* optare; **to ~ to do sth** optare di fare qc; **to ~ for sth** optare per qc

◆**opt in** *vi* **to ~** (**to sth**) scegliere di partecipare (a qc)

◆**opt out** *vi* **to ~** (**of sth**) scegliere di non partecipare (a qc)

optic ['ɑ:p·tɪk] I. *n inf* occhio *m* II. *adj* ottico, -a

optical ['ɑ:p·tɪ·kl] *adj* ottico, -a

optician [ɑ:p·'tɪ·ʃən] *n* MED optometrista *mf*

optic nerve *n* nervo *mf* ottico

optics ['ɑ:p·tɪks] *n* ottica *f*

optimal ['ɑ:p·tɪ·ml] *adj* ottimale

optimism ['ɑ:p·tə·mɪ·zəm] *n* ottimismo *m*

optimist ['ɑ:p·tə·mɪst] *n* ottimista *mf*

optimistic [ˌɑ:p·tə·'mɪs·tɪk] *adj* ottimista

optimize ['ɑ:p·tə·maɪz] *vt* ottimizzare

optimum ['ɑ:p·tə·məm] I. *n* <-ma> the ~ l'ideale II. *adj* ottimale

option ['ɑ:p·ʃən] *n* (*choice, possibility*) *a.* ECON opzione *f;* **to have no ~ but to do sth** non aver scelta se non fare qc; **call ~** opzione di acquisto

optional ['ɑ:p·ʃə·nl] *adj* facoltativo, -a; **~ accessories** optional

opulence ['ɑ:p·jə·ləns] *n* opulenza *f*

opulent ['ɑ·p·jə·lənt] *adj* opulento, -a

or [ɔ:r] *conj* o; **seven ~ eight** sette o otto; **either ... ~ ...** o... o...; **to ask whether ~ not sb is coming** chiedere se qu viene o no; **I can't read ~ write** non so né leggere né scrivere

OR *n* 1. *abbr of* **operating room** sala *f* operatoria 2. *abbr of* **Oregon** Oregon *m*

oracle ['ɔ:·rə·kl] *n* oracolo *m*

oracular [ɔ:·'ræk·ju:·lə] *adj* (*mysteriuos*) sibillino, -a

oral ['ɔ:·rəl] *adj* 1. (*tradition, exam, statement*) orale 2. (*medication*) per via orale; (*contraceptive, sex*) orale

orange ['ɔ:·rɪndʒ] I. *n* 1. (*fruit*) arancia *f;* **~ drink** aranciata *f* 2. (*color*) arancio *m* II. *adj* arancione

orangeade [ˌɔ:·rɪndʒ·'eɪd] *n* aranciata *f*

orange grove *n* aranceto *m*

orange juice *n* succo *m* d'arancia

orange peel *n* buccia *f* d'arancia

orange tree *n* arancio *m*

orangutan *n*, **orangutang** [ɔ:·'ræŋ·ə·tæn] *n* orango *m*

oration [ɔ:·'reɪ·ʃən] *n* discorso *m;* **funeral ~** orazione *f* funebre

orator ['ɔ:·rə·t̬ə] *n* oratore, -trice *m, f*

oratorical [ˌɔ:·rə·'tɔ:·rɪ·kl] *adj* oratorio, -a

oratorio [ˌɔ:·rə·'tɔ:·ri·ou] *n* MUS oratorio *m*

orb [ɔ:rb] *n liter* sfera *f*

orbit ['ɔ:r·bɪt] I. *n* ASTR orbita *f;* **to go into ~** entrare in orbita II. *vi* orbitare III. *vt* orbitare intorno a

orbital ['ɔ:r·bɪ·tl] *adj* orbitale

orchard ['ɔ:r·tʃə·d] *n* frutteto *m*

orchestra ['ɔ:r·kɪs·trə] *n* orchestra *f*

orchestral [ɔ:r·'kes·trəl] *adj* orchestrale

orchestra pit *n* fossa *f* dell'orchestra

orchestrate ['ɔ:r·kɪs·treɪt] *vt* orchestrare

orchestration [ˌɔ:r·kɪs·'treɪ·ʃən] *n* orchestrazione *f*

orchid ['ɔ:r·kɪd] *n* orchidea *f*

ordain [ɔ:r·'deɪn] *vt* 1. REL ordinare; **to ~ sb as**
(a) **priest/minister** ordinare qu sacerdote 2. (*decree, order*) **to ~ that ...** decretare che ... +*subj*

ordeal [ɔ:r·'di:l] *n* calvario *m*

order ['ɔ:r·də] I. *n* 1. (*sequence*) ordine *m;* **to put sth in ~** mettere qc in ordine; **to leave sth in ~** lasciare qc in ordine; **in alphabetical ~** in ordine alfabetico 2. (*instruction*) *a.* LAW, REL ordine *f;* **to give/receive an ~** dare/ricevere un ordine; **by ~ of sb** per ordine di qu 3. (*working condition, satisfactory arrangement*) **to keep ~** mantenere l'ordine; **a new world ~** un nuovo ordine mondiale; **the car is in perfect working ~** l'auto funziona alla perfezione; **to be out of ~** essere guasto; **are your immigration papers in ~?** ha documenti d'immigrazione in regola? 4. (*appropriate behavior*) **out of ~** inopportuno, -a 5. (*purpose*) **in ~ to** (**not**) **to do sth** allo scopo di (non) fare qc; **in ~ for, in ~ that** perché +*subj* 6. (*social class, rank, kind*) classe *f* 7. (*request to supply goods or service*) ordine *m;* **to put in an ~ for sth** ordinare qc; **made to ~** fatto su ordinazione 8. (*architectural style*) ordine *m;* **Doric ~** ordine dorico II. *vi* ordinare; **are you ready to ~?** siete pronti a ordinare? III. *vt* 1. (*command*) **to ~ sb to do sth** ordinare a qu di fare qc; **to ~ sb out** ordinare a qu di andarsene 2. (*request goods or service*) ordinare 3. (*arrange*) riordinare; **to ~ one's thoughts** chiarirsi le idee 4. (*arrange according to procedure*) organizzare

order book *n* libro *m* delle ordinazioni

order form *n* modulo *m* delle ordinazioni

orderly ['ɔ:r·də·li] <-ies> I. *n* 1. (*hospital attendant*) inserviente *mf* 2. MIL piantone *m* II. *adj* 1. (*tidy*) ordinato, -a 2. (*well-behaved*) disciplinato, -a

ordinal ['ɔ:r·də·nəl] *n*, **ordinal number** *n* ordinale *m*

ordinance ['ɔ:r·də·nənts] *n* ordinanza *f*

ordinary ['ɔ:r·də·ne·ri] I. *n* **out of the ~** fuori dal comune; **nothing out of the ~** niente di eccezionale II. *adj* ordinario, -a; **in the ~ way** ... normalmente ...

ordinary share *n* azione *f* ordinaria

ordnance ['ɔ:rd·nənts] *n* artiglieria *f*

ordure ['ɔ:r·dʒə] *n* lordura *f*

ore [ɔ:r] *n* **iron/copper ~** minerale *m* di ferro/rame

oregano [ɔ:·'re·gə·nou] *n* origano *m*

Oregon *n* Oregon *m*

organ ['ɔ:r·gən] *n* organo *m*

organ donor *n* donatore , -trice *m, f* di organi

organ grinder *n* suonatore , -trice *m, f* d'organetto

organic [ɔ:r·'gæ·nɪk] *adj* 1. (*disease, substance, part, change*) organico, -a 2. (*produce, farming method*) biologico, -a

organism ['ɔ:r·gə·nɪ·zəm] *n* organismo *m*

organist ['ɔ:r·gə·nɪst] *n* organista *mf*

organization [ˌɔ:r·gə·nɪ·'zeɪ·ʃən] *n* organizzazione *f*

organizational [ˌɔːrgəˈnɪˈzeɪˈʃəˈnəl] *adj* organizzativo, -a

organization chart *n* ECON organigramma *m*

Organization for Economic Cooperation and Development *n* Organizzazione *f* per la Cooperazione e lo Sviluppo Economico

Organization of Petroleum Exporting Countries *n* Organizzazione *f* dei Paesi Esportatori di Petrolio

organize [ˈɔːrgəˈnaɪz] I. *vt* organizzare II. *vi* organizzarsi; (*form trade union*) sindacalizzarsi

organized *adj* 1. (*systemized, arranged*) organizzato, -a 2. (*brought together in a trade union*) sindacalizzato, -a

organizer *n* 1. (*person*) organizzatore, -trice *m, f* 2. COMPUT agenda *f* elettronica

orgasm [ˈɔːrgæˈzəm] I. *n* orgasmo *m* II. *vi* raggiungere l'orgasmo

orgasmic [ɔːrˈgæsˈmɪk] *adj* orgasmico, -a

orgy [ˈɔːrˈdʒi] <-ies> *n* orgia *f*

orient [ˈɔːriˈənt] *vt* to ~ oneself orientarsi

Orient [ˈɔːriˈənt] *n* the ~ l'Oriente

oriental [ˌɔːriˈenˈtəl] *adj* orientale

orientate [ˈɔːriˈenˈteɪt] *vt* to ~ oneself orientarsi

orientation [ˌɔːriˈenˈteɪˈʃən] *n* orientamento *m*

orienteering [ˌɔːriˈenˈtɪˈrɪŋ] *n* orientamento *m*

orifice [ˈɔːrəˈfɪs] *n form* orifizio *m*

origin [ˈɔːrəˈdʒɪn] *n* origine *f*

original [əˈrɪˈdʒɪˈnəl] I. *n* originale *m* II. *adj* originale

originality [əˌrɪˈdʒɪˈnæˈləˈti] *n* originalità *f*

originally [əˈrɪˈdʒɪˈnəˈli] *adv* 1. (*initially*) originariamente 2. (*unusually*) originalmente

original sin *n* peccato *m* originale

originate [əˈrɪˈdʒɪˈneɪt] I. *vi* avere origine II. *vt* creare

ornament [ˈɔːrnəˈmənt] I. *n* ornamento *m* II. *vt* ornare

ornamental [ˌɔːrnəˈmenˈtl̩] *adj* ornamentale

ornamentation [ˌɔːrnəˈmenˈteɪˈʃən] *n form* ornamentazione *f*

ornate [ɔːrˈneɪt] *adj* 1. (*elaborately decorated*) ornato, -a 2. (*language, style*) elaborato, -a

ornithologist [ˌɔːrnəˈθɑːˈləˈdʒɪst] *n* ornitologo, -a *m, f*

ornithology [ˌɔːrnəˈθɑːˈləˈdʒi] *n* ornitologia *f*

orphan [ˈɔːrˈfn̩] I. *n* orfano, -a *m, f* II. *vt* to be ~ed rimanere orfano

orphanage [ˈɔːrfnˈɪdʒ] *n* orfanotrofio *m*

orthodontist [ˌɔːrˈθoʊˈdɑːnˈtɪst] *n* ortodontista *mf*

orthodox [ˈɔːrˈθəˈdɑːks] *adj* ortodosso, -a

orthodoxy [ˈɔːrˈθəˈdɑːksi] <-ies> *n* ortodossia *f*

orthogonal [ɔːrˈθɑːˈgəˈnl̩] *adj* MATH ortogonale

orthographic(al) [ˌɔːrˈθoʊˈgræˈfɪˈk(l)] *adj* ortografico, -a

orthography [ɔːrˈθɑːˈgrəˈfi] *n* ortografia *f*

orthopedic [ˌɔːrˈθoʊˈpiːˈdɪk] *adj* ortopedico, -a; ~ surgery chirurgia *f* ortopedica

orthopedics [ˌɔːrˈθoʊˈpiːˈdɪks] *npl* ortopedia *f*

orthopedist [ˌɔːrˈθoʊˈpiːˈdɪst] *n* ortopedico *m*

OS [ˌoʊˈes] COMPUT *abbr of* operating system SO

oscillate [ˈɑːsˈleɪt] *vi a.* PHYS oscillare; to ~ between hope and despair oscillare tra speranza e disperazione

oscillation [ˌɑːsˈleɪˈʃən] *n a.* PHYS oscillazione *f*

oscilloscope [əˈsɪˈləsˈkoʊp] *n* oscilloscopio *m*

osmosis [ɑːzˈmoʊˈsɪs] *n* osmosi *f inv*

osprey [ˈɑːsˈpri] *n* falco *m* pescatore

ossify [ˈɑːsəˈfaɪ] <-ie-> I. *vi* 1. (*turn into bone*) ossificarsi 2. *fig* (*become rigid*) fossilizzarsi II. *vt* 1. (*turn into bone*) ossificare 2. *fig* (*cause to be rigid*) fossilizzare

ostensible [ɑːˈstenˈsəˈbl̩] *adj* apparente

ostentation [ˌɑːstənˈteɪˈʃən] *n pej* ostentazione *f*

ostentatious [ˌɑːstənˈteɪˈʃəs] *adj pej* esibizionista

osteoarthritis [ˌɑːstioʊˈɑːrˈθraɪˈtɪs] *n* osteoartrite *f*

osteopath [ˈɑːstioʊˈpæθ] *n* MED osteopata *mf*

osteoporosis [ˌɑːstioʊˈpəˈroʊˈsɪs] *n* osteoporosi *f*

ostracism [ˈɑːstrəˈsɪˈzəm] *n* ostracismo *m*

ostracize [ˈɑːstrəˈsaɪz] *vt* ostracizzare

ostrich [ˈɑːstrɪtʃ] *n* struzzo *m*

OT 1. *abbr of* Old Testament A.T. 2. *abbr of* overtime straordinario *m*

other [ˈʌˈðə] I. *adj* 1. (*different*) altro, -a; some ~ way of doing sth un altro modo di fare qc 2. (*remaining*) the ~ one l'altro; the ~ three gli altri tre; any ~ questions? altre domande? 3. (*being vague*) some ~ time un'altra volta; the ~ day l'altro giorno; every ~ day un giorno sí e uno no II. *pron* 1. (*people*) the ~s gli altri; no ~ than he *form* nessuno eccetto lui 2. (*different ones*) each ~ l'un l'altro; some eat, ~s drink alcuni mangiano, altri bevono; there might be ~s ce ne potrebbero essere altri 3. *sing* (*either/or*) to choose one or the ~ scegliere l'uno o l'altro; not to have one without the ~ non aver l'uno senza l'altro 4. (*being vague*) someone or ~ qualcuno III. *adv* somehow or ~ in un modo o l'altro

otherwise [ˈʌˈðəˈwaɪz] I. *adj form* diverso, -a II. *adv* (*differently, in other ways: behave, act*) altrimenti; ~, ... altrimenti, ... III. *conj* altrimenti, se no

otter [ˈɑːˈtə] *n* lontra *f*

ouch [aʊtʃ] *interj* ahi

ought [ɑːt] *aux* dovere; you ~ to do it dovresti farlo; he ~ to be here dovrebbe essere qui; they ~ to win si meriterebbero di vincere; she ~ to have arrived by now a quest'ora dovrebbe essere arrivata

ounce [aʊns] *n* **1.** (*weight*) oncia *f* (*28,4 g*) **2.** (*of decency, common sense*) briciolo *m*

our ['aʊ·ə'] *adj pos* nostro, -a; ~ **house** la nostra casa; ~ **children** i nostri figli; ~ **uncle** nostro zio

ours ['aʊ·ə'z] *pron pos* il nostro, la nostra; **it's not their bag, it's** ~ non è la loro borsa, è la nostra; **this house is** ~ questa casa è nostra; **a book of** ~ un nostro libro; ~ **is bigger** il nostro è più grande

ourselves [aʊ·ə'selvz] *pron reflexive* **1.** ci; *emphatic* noi stessi, e; **we hurt** ~ ci siamo fatti male **2.** *after prep* noi, noi stessi, e

oust [aʊst] *vt* (*rival*) eliminare; (*president*) estromettere

out [aʊt] **I.** *vt* rivelare l'omosessualità di **II.** *adj* **1.** (*absent: person*) fuori **2.** (*released: book*) pubblicato, -a; (*news*) rilasciato, -a **3.** BOT (*flower*) in fiore **4.** (*visible*) **the sun/moon is** ~ c'è il sole/la luna **5.** (*finished*) **before the week is** ~ prima che la settimana finisca **6.** (*not functioning: fire, light*) spento, -a **7.** SPORTS (*out of bounds*) fuori (campo) **8.** (*unfashionable*) fuori moda **9.** (*not possible*) **to be** ~ fuori discussione **10.** (*in baseball*) out *inv* **III.** *adv* **1.** (*not inside*) fuori; **to go** ~ uscire; **get** ~**!** fuori!; **keep** ~**!** vietato entrare!; **to eat** ~ mangiar fuori **2.** (*remove*) **to cross** ~ **words** cancellare le parole con la penna; **to get a stain** ~ togliere una macchia; **to put** ~ **a fire** spegnere un incendio **3.** (*available*) **the best one** ~ **right now** il migliore sul mercato adesso **4.** (*away*) **to be** ~ (*person*) essere fuori; **to go** ~ **to the West Coast** trasferirsi sulla West Coast; **to be** ~ **at sea** essere in mare (aperto); **the tide is going** ~ la marea si sta abbassando **5.** (*unconscious*) **to pass** ~ perdere conoscenza; **to be** ~ **cold** essere privo di sensi ▶**to be** ~ **and** about (*on the road*) essere in giro; ~ with **it!** sputa il rospo! **IV.** *prep* **1.** (*towards outside*) ~ **of** fuori da; **to go** ~ **of the room** uscire dalla stanza; **to jump** ~ **of bed** alzarsi (dal letto) con un balzo; **to take sth** ~ **of a box** tirar fuori qc da una scatola; **to look/lean** ~ **of the window** guardare/sporgersi dalla finestra **2.** (*outside from*) ~ **of sight** non visto; ~ **of reach** non a portata di mano; **to drink** ~ **of a glass** bere da un bicchiere; **to be** ~ **of it** sentirsi escluso **3.** (*away from*) **to be** ~ **of town** essere fuori città; **to be** ~ **of the country** essere all'estero; **to get** ~ **of the rain** venir via dalla pioggia; ~ **of the way!** fate largo! **4.** (*without*) **to be** ~ **of money/work** essere senza soldi/lavoro; ~ **of breath** senza fiato; ~ **of order** guasto, -a **5.** (*not included in*) **to get** ~ **of the habit of doing sth** perdere l'abitudine di fare qc; **his dog is** ~ **of control** il suo cane è indisciplinato **6.** (*from*) **made** ~ **of wood/steel** fatto di legno/acciaio; **to copy sth** ~ **of a file** copiare qc da un file; **to get sth** ~ **of sb** ottenere qc da qu; **to read** ~ **of a novel** leggere da un romanzo; **in 3 cases** ~ **of 10** in 3 casi su 10

7. (*because of*) **to do sth** ~ **of politeness** fare qc per gentilezza

out-and-out [ˌaʊt·ənd·'aʊt] *adj* (*idiot, disaster*) vero, -a e a proprio, -a; (*liar*) matricolato, -a

outback ['aʊt·bæk] *n* **the** ~ l'outback (*entroterra australiano*)

outbid [ˌaʊt·'bɪd] *vt irr* **to** ~ **sb** (**for sth**) offrire più di qu (per qc)

outboard ['aʊt·bɔːrd] *n*, **outboard motor** *n* fuoribordo *m inv*

outbreak ['aʊt·breɪk] *n* (*of the flu*) attacco *m*; (*of war, violence*) scoppio *m*

outburst ['aʊt·bɜːrst] *n* scoppio *m*

outcast ['aʊt·kæːst] **I.** *n* emarginato, -a *m, f*; **social** ~ persona che vive ai margini della società **II.** *adj* emarginato, -a

outclass [ˌaʊt·'klæs] *vt* superare

outcome ['aʊt·kʌm] *n* (*result, consequence*) risultato *m*

outcrop ['aʊt·krɑːp] **I.** *n* affioramento *m* **II.** *vi* affiorare

outcry ['aʊt·kraɪ] <-ies> *n* protesta *f*

outdated [aʊt·'deɪ·tɪd] *adj* sorpassato, -a

outdistance [aʊt·'dɪs·təns] *vt* lasciare indietro

outdo [aʊt·'duː] *vt irr* superare; **to** ~ **sb in sth** superare qu in qc; **to** ~ **oneself** superare se stesso

outdoor [ˌaʊt·'dɔːr] *adj* all'aperto; (*clothing*) per attività all'aperto; (*plants*) da esterno

outdoors [ˌaʊt·'dɔːrz] *n* all'aperto; **the great** ~ i grandi spazi

outer ['aʊ·tə'] *adj* esterno, -a; ~ **suburbs** quartieri più periferici *mpl*

outermost ['aʊ·tə'·məst] *adj* più esterno, -a

outfield ['aʊt·fiːld] *n* (*in cricket, baseball*) parte *f* più esterna del campo

outfielder *n* outfielder *m inv*

outfit ['aʊt·fɪt] *n* **1.** (*set of clothes*) completo *m* **2.** (*team, organization*) squadra *f*

outfitter ['aʊt·fɪ·tə'] *n* **sports** ~**s** negozio *m* di articoli sportivi

outflow ['aʊt·floʊ] *n* (*of liquid*) deflusso *m*; (*of capital*) fuga *f*

outfox *vt* mostrarsi più furbo di

outgoing ['aʊt·goʊ·ɪŋ] *adj* **1.** (*sociable, extroverted*) estroverso, -a **2.** (*retiring: President*) uscente **3.** (*ship*) in partenza; ~ **call** chiamata *f* in uscita

outgrow [ˌaʊt·'groʊ] *vt irr* **1.** (*become bigger than*) cresciuta troppo per; **she's** ~**n her pants** i pantaloni le stanno ormai troppo piccoli **2.** (*habit*) diventare grande per

outgrowth ['aʊt·groʊθ] *n* **1.** BOT escrescenza *f* **2.** (*result*) risultato *m*

outhouse ['aʊt·haʊs] *n* gabinetto *m* fuori

outing ['aʊ·tɪŋ] *n* escursione *f*; **to go on an** ~ fare un'escursione

outlandish [aʊt·'læn·dɪʃ] *adj* (*clothes, idea*) stravagante

outlast [ˌaʊt·'læst] *vt* **to** ~ **sth** durare più a lungo di qc; **to** ~ **sb** sopravvivere a qu

outlaw ['aʊt·lɑː] **I.** *n* fuorilegge *mf* **II.** *vt* (*prod-*

uct, practice) dichiarare illegale; (*person*) bandire

outlay ['aʊt·leɪ] *n* esborso *m*

outlet ['aʊt·let] *n* **1.** ECON punto *m* vendita; **retail** ~ punto vendita al dettaglio **2.** (*means of expression*) valvola *f* di sfogo **3.** (*vent*) sbocco *m* **4.** ELEC presa *f* di corrente

outline ['aʊt·laɪn] **I.** *n* **1.** (*draft*) abbozzo *m* **2.** (*shape*) sagoma *f* **3.** (*general description*) schema *m* **II.** *vt* **1.** (*draw outer line of*) tracciare il contorno di **2.** (*describe, summarize*) esporre a linee generali

outlive [ˌaʊt·'lɪv] *vt* sopravvivere a

outlook ['aʊt·lʊk] *n* **1.** (*prospects*) prospettive *fpl* **2.** (*attitude*) punto *m* di vista **3.** (*view*) vista *f*

outlying ['aʊt·ˌlaɪ·ɪŋ] *adj* remoto, -a

outmaneuver [ˌaʊt·mə·'nuː·vɚ] *vt* (*person*) superare

outmoded [ˌaʊt·'moʊ·dɪd] *adj pej* antiquato, -a

outmost ['aʊt·moʊst] *adj* più remoto, -a

outnumber [ˌaʊt·'nʌm·bɚ] *vt* superare numericamnete

out-of-court settlement *n* accordo *m* extragiudiziale

out-of-date [ˌaʊt·əv·'deɪt] *adj* (*clothing*) fuori moda; (*directory*) non aggiornato, -a; (*passport*) scaduto, -a

out-of-the-way [ˌaʊt·əv·ðə·'weɪ] *adj* sperduto, -a

outpatient ['aʊt·ˌpeɪ·ʃənt] *n* paziente *mf* esterno, -a

outplay [ˌaʊt·'pleɪ] *vt* giocare meglio di

outpost ['aʊt·poʊst] *n fig* MIL. avamposto *m*

outpouring ['aʊt·ˌpɔː·rɪŋ] *n* sfogo *m;* **an ~ of anger** un'ondata *f* di rabbia

output ['aʊt·pʊt] *n* ECON produzione *f;* (*of machine*) rendimento *m*

output device *n* COMPUT dispositivo *m* di uscita

outrage ['aʊt·reɪdʒ] **I.** *n* **1.** (*atrocity*) atrocità *f;* (*terrorist act*) attentato *m* **2.** (*scandal*) scandalo *m;* **to express ~** (**at sth**) mostrare indignazione (per qc); **to feel a strong sense of ~ at sth** sentirsi oltraggiato per qc **II.** *vt* (*offend*) oltraggiare

outrageous [aʊt·'reɪ·dʒəs] *adj* **1.** (*shocking: behavior*) scandaloso, -a; (*clothing, person*) stravagante **2.** (*cruel, violent*) atroce

outré [uː·'treɪ] *adj form* bizzarro, -a

outrigger ['aʊt·rɪ·gɚ] *n* **1.** (*stabilizer*) bilanciere *m* **2.** (*boat*) proa *m inv*

outright ['aʊt·raɪt] **I.** *adj* (*disaster, defeat*) totale; (*winner*) assoluto, -a; (*hostility*) chiaro, -a **II.** *adv* **1.** (*defeat, ignore*) totalmente; (*win*) indiscutibilmente **2.** (*declare, ask*) apertamente

outrun [ˌaʊt·'rʌn] *vt irr* **to ~ sb** lasciare indietro qu

outset ['aʊt·set] *n* principio *m;* **from the ~** dall'inizio

outshine [ˌaʊt·'ʃaɪn] *vt irr* eclissare

outside [ˌaʊt·'saɪd] **I.** *adj* **1.** (*external*) esterno,

-a **2.** (*not likely*) **an ~ chance that ...** una remota possibilità che ... +*subj* **3.** (*extreme*) massimo, -a **II.** *n* **1.** (*external part or side*) esterno *m;* **judging from the ~** a giudicare da fuori **2.** (*at most*) **at the ~** al massimo **III.** *prep* **1.** (*not within*) fuori da; **to wait ~ the door** aspettare fuori dalla porta; **~ business hours** fuori dall'orario d'ufficio **2.** (*besides*) oltre a **IV.** *adv* **1.** (*outdoors*) fuori; **to go ~** uscire; **to go ~ the house** uscire di casa; **to live an hour ~ Detroit** abitare a un'ora da Detroit **2.** (*beyond*) **to be ~ the perimeter** essere fuori dal perimetro

outsider [ˌaʊt·'saɪ·dɚ] *n* **1.** (*person not from a group*) persona *f* di fuori **2.** (*in race, competition*) outsider *mf inv*

outsize [ˌaʊt·'saɪz] *adj* grande; **~ clothes** abbigliamento taglie forti

outskirts ['aʊt·skɜːrts] *npl* periferia *f;* **on the ~** in periferia

outsourcing ['aʊt·ˌsɔːr·sɪŋ] *n* outsourcing *m*

outspoken [ˌaʊt·'spoʊ·kən] *adj* diretto, -a; **to be ~** non aver peli sulla lingua

outstanding [ˌaʊt·'stæn·dɪŋ] *adj* **1.** (*excellent*) eccezionale **2.** FIN (*account*) da pagare; (*debt*) insoluto, -a **3.** (*unsolved*) in sospeso

outstay [ˌaʊt·'steɪ] *vt* **to ~ one's welcome** abusare dell'ospitalità

outstretched [ˌaʊt·'stretʃt] *adj* teso, -a

outstrip [ˌaʊt·'strɪp] *vt irr* superare

outtake *n* taglio *m*

outthink *irr vt* essere più intelligente di

outvote [ˌaʊt·'voʊt] *vt* prendere più voti di; **to be ~d** perdere le elezioni

outward ['aʊt·wɚd] **I.** *adj* **1.** (*visible, exterior, apparent*) esteriore **2.** (*voyage*) di andata **II.** *adv* verso l'esterno **III.** *n lit* esterno *m*

outwardly ['aʊt·wɚd·li] *adv* apparentemente

outwards ['aʊt·wɚdz] *adv* verso l'esterno

outweigh [ˌaʊt·'weɪ] *vt* **1.** (*weight*) pesare più di **2.** (*in importance or influence*) avere maggior peso di

outwit [ˌaʊt·'wɪt] <-tt-> *vt* prendersi gioco di

outwork ['aʊt·wɜːrk] *n* MIL struttura *f* difensiva (davanti alla fortificazione principale)

oval ['oʊ·vəl] **I.** *n* ovale *m* **II.** *adj* oval

Oval Office *n* **the ~** la Stanza ovale, *della Casa Bianca*

ovary ['oʊ·və·ri] <-ies> *n* ovaia *f*

ovation [oʊ·'veɪ·ʃən] *n* ovazione *f;* **to get an ~** essere applaudito; **a standing ~** un applauso in piedi

oven ['ʌ·vən] *n* forno *m*

ovenproof ['ʌ·vən·pruːf] *adj* da forno

oven-ready [ˌʌ·vən·'re·di] *adj* pronto, -a per il forno

ovenware *n* pentole *f* da forno *pl*

over ['oʊ·vɚ] **I.** *prep* **1.** (*above*) sopra (a), su; **the bridge ~ the freeway** il ponte sopra l'autostrada; **to fly ~ the sea** sorvolare il mare **2.** (*on*) **to hit sb ~ the head** colpire qu sulla testa; **to drive ~ sth** passare sopra qc; **to spread a cloth ~ the table** stendere un telo sul tavolo **3.** (*across*) **to go ~ the bridge** attraversare il ponte; **the house ~ the road** la casa dall'altra parte della strada; **it rained all ~ New England** ha piovuto su tutto il New England; **famous all ~ the world** famoso in tutto il mondo **4.** (*behind*) **to look ~ sb's shoulder** guardare da dietro le spalle di qu; *fig* stare addosso a qu; **~ the dune** dietro la duna **5.** (*during*) durante; **~ the winter** durante l'inverno; **~ time** col tempo; **~ a two-year period** nel corso di due anni; **to stay ~ the weekend** restare per il fine settimana **6.** (*more than*) **to speak for ~ an hour** parlare per oltre un'ora; **~ 150** oltre 150; **children ~ 14** ragazzi oltre i 14 anni; **~ and above that** oltre a questo **7.** (*through*) **I heard it ~ the radio** l'ho sentito alla radio; **to hear sth ~ the noise** sentire qc nonostante il rumore; **what came ~ him?** cosa gli è preso? *inf* **8.** (*in superiority to*) **to rule ~ the Romans** dominare i Romani; **to have command ~ sth** essere al comando di qc; **to have an advantage ~ sb** essere in vantaggio su qu **9.** (*about*) **~ sth** riguardo a qc; **to puzzle ~ a problem** scervellarsi su un problema **10.** (*for checking*) **to go ~ a text** rivedere un testo; **to watch ~ a child** badare ai bambini **11.** (*past*) **to be ~ the worst** aver passato il peggio **12.** MATH **4 ~ 12 equals a third** il 4 nel 12 ci sta 3 volte **II.** *adv* **1.** (*moving above: go, jump*) sopra; **to fly ~ the city** sorvolare la città **2.** (*at a distance*) **to move sth ~** spostare qc; **~ here** qui; **~ there** là; **~ the road** dall'altra parte della strada **3.** (*moving across*) **to come ~ here** venire qui; **to go ~ there** andare là; **he has flown ~ to Europe** è andato in Europa (in aereo); **he swam ~ to me** è venuto verso di me (a nuoto); **he went ~ to the enemy** *fig* è passato al nemico **4.** (*on a visit*) **come ~ tonight** fate un salto qui stasera **5.** (*changing hands*) **to pass/hand sth ~** passare/dare qc **6.** (*downwards*) **to fall ~** cadere; **to knock sth ~** far cadere qc **7.** (*another way up*) **to turn the page ~** voltare pagina; **to turn the pancake ~** girare la crêpe **8.** (*in exchange*) **to change ~** cambiare; **to change ~** (*from sth*) **to sth else** passare (da qc) a qualcos'altro **9.** (*completely*) **to look for sb all ~** cercare qu dappertutto; **to turn sth ~ and ~ in one's mind** continuare a rimuginare su qc; **to think sth ~** riflettere su qc **10.** (*again*) **to count them ~ again** contarli un'altra volta; **I repeated it ~ and ~** l'ho ripetuto un'infinità di volte; **to do sth all ~** rifare qc da capo **11.** (*more*) **children 14 and ~** ragazzi dai 14 anni in su **12.** RADIO, AVIAT **~** passo; **~ and out** passo e chiudo **III.** *adj* **1.** (*finished*) finito, -a; **it's all ~** è tutto passato; **the snow is ~** ha smesso di nevicare **2.** (*remaining*) rimasto, -a; **there are three left ~** ne sono rimasti tre

overabundance *n* sovrabbondanza *f*

overabundant [ˌoʊ·və·ə·'bʌn·dənt] *adj* sovrabbondante

overachiever *n persona che studia o lavora*

duramente e pretende sempre di più da se stessa

overall ['oʊ·və·rɔːl] **I.** *adj* **1.** (*general*) complessivo, -a **2.** (*above all others*) **~ winner** vincitore, -trice *m, f* assoluto, -a **II.** *adv* nel complesso **III.** *n pl* tuta *f;* **a pair of ~s** una salopette *f*

overanxious [ˌoʊ·və·'æŋ·kʃəs] *adj* molto ansioso, -a

overbearing [ˌoʊ·və·'be·rɪŋ] *adj pej* prepotente

overblown [ˌoʊ·və·'bloʊn] *adj* pomposo, -a

overboard ['oʊ·və·bɔːrd] *adv* fuori bordo; **to fall ~** cadere in mare; **man ~!** uomo in mare!; **to go ~** *inf* esagerare; **to go ~ for sth** *inf* perdere la testa per qc

overbook [ˌoʊ·və·'bʊk] *vt* prendere troppe prenotazioni per; (*flight*) prenotare in overbooking

overbooking *n* prenotazioni *m pl* in eccesso, overbooking *m*

overburden [ˌoʊ·və·'bɜːr·dən] *vt* sovraccaricare

overcapacity <-ies> *n* capacità *f* eccedente

overcast ['oʊ·və·kæst] *adj* nuvoloso, -a

overcautious [ˌoʊ·və·'kɑː·ʃəs] *adj* fin troppo cauto, -a

overcharge [ˌoʊ·və·'tʃɑːrdʒ] **I.** *vt* **to ~ sb** fare pagare troppo a qu **II.** *vi* fare prezzi troppo cari

overcoat ['oʊ·və·koʊt] *n* soprabito *m*

overcome [ˌoʊ·və·'kʌm] *irr* **I.** *vt* **1.** (*defeat*) sconfiggere **2.** (*cope with*) superare; **to ~ temptation** resistere alla tentazione **II.** *vi irr* vincere

overconfident [ˌoʊ·və·'kɑːn·fə·dənt] *adj* troppo sicuro, -a di sé

overcooked [ˌoʊ·və·'kʊkt] *adj* troppo cotto, -a; (*pasta*) scotto, -a

overcrowded [ˌoʊ·və·'kraʊ·dɪd] *adj* sovraffollato, -a

overdeveloped [ˌoʊ·və·dɪ·'vel·əpt] *adj* eccessivamente sviluppato, -a; PHOT sovrasviluppato, -a

overdo [ˌoʊ·və·'duː] *vt* **1.** (*exaggerate*) esagerare; **to ~ things** esagerare; (*work too hard*) lavorare troppo **2.** (*cook too long*) cuocere troppo

overdone [ˌoʊ·və·'dʌn] *adj* **1.** (*overexaggerated*) esagerato, -a **2.** (*overcooked*) troppo cotto, -a

overdose ['oʊ·və·doʊs] **I.** *n* overdose *f inv* **II.** *vi* **to ~ on sth** (*sleeping pills*) prendere una dose eccessiva di qc; (*heroin*) andare in overdose di qc; *fig* farsi un'overdose di qc

overdraft ['oʊ·və·dræft] *n* FIN scoperto *m;* **to have an ~** avere uno scoperto (in banca)

overdraft protection *n* FIN *automatica concessione di prestito per coprire un assegno scoperto*

overdraw [ˌoʊ·və·'drɑː] *irr* **I.** *vi* andare in scoperto **II.** *vt* **to ~ one's account** andare in scoperto

overdress [ˌoʊ·və·'dres] *vi* vestirsi troppo

elegante

overdrive ['oʊ·və·draɪv] *n fig* **to go into ~** prendere a lavorare a pieno ritmo

overdue [ˌoʊ·və·'du:] *adj* **1.**(*late*) in ritardo **2.** FIN (*payment*) arretrato, -a

overeat [ˌoʊ·və·'i:t] *irr vi* mangiare troppo

overemphasize [ˌoʊ·və·'em·fə·saɪz] *vt* enfatizzare eccessivamente

overestimate¹ [ˌoʊ·və·'es·tɪ·mɪt] *n* stima *f* eccessiva

overestimate² [ˌoʊ·və·'es·tə·meɪt] *vt* sopravvalutare

overexcited [ˌoʊ·və·ɪk·'saɪ·tɪd] *adj* sovreccitato, -a

overexert [ˌoʊ·və·ɪg·'zɜ:rt] *vt* **to ~ oneself** affaticarsi troppo

overexpose [ˌoʊ·və·ɪk·'spoʊz] *vt* PHOT sovraesporre

overexposure [ˌoʊ·və·ɪk·'spoʊ·ʒə·] *n fig* PHOT sovraesposizione *f*

overextend [ˌoʊ·və·ɪk·'stend] *vt* **to ~ oneself** assumersi troppi obblighi finanziari

overflow [ˌoʊ·və·'floʊ] **I.** *n* **1.**(*excess: of liquid*) eccesso *m* di liquido; (*of people*) eccesso *m* **2.**(*outlet*) troppopieno *m* **II.** *vi* riversarsi; (*river*) straripare

overfly [ˌoʊ·və·'flaɪ] <-ie-> *irr vt* sorvolare

overgrown [ˌoʊ·və·'groʊn] *adj* (*garden*) trascurato, -a; **to be ~ with sth** essere coperto di qc

overhang [ˌoʊ·və·'hæŋ] *irr* **I.** *n* (*cliff*) strapiombo *m;* ARCHIT aggetto *m* **II.** *vt* sovrastare

overhaul [ˌoʊ·və·'hɑ:l] **I.** *n* revisione *f* **II.** *vt* **1.**(*machine,*) fare la revisione di; (*policy, system*) revisionare **2.**(*overtake*) superare

overhead [ˌoʊ·və·'hed] **I.** *n* spese *fpl* generali **II.** *adj* **~ cable** cavo *m* aereo; **~ light** luce *f* da soffitto **III.** *adv* in alto

overhear [ˌoʊ·və·'hɪr] *irr vt* sentire per caso

overheat [ˌoʊ·və·'hi:t] *vt, vi* surriscaldare

overindulge [ˌoʊ·və·ɪn·'dʌldʒ] **I.** *vt* viziare **II.** *vi* **to ~ in sth** abusare di qc

overjoyed [ˌoʊ·və·'dʒɔɪd] *adj* contentissimo, -a

overkill ['oʊ·və·kɪl] *n fig* eccesso *m*

overland ['oʊ·və·lænd] **I.** *adj* terrestre; **by ~ mail** per posta via terra **II.** *adv* via terra

overlap¹ ['oʊ·və·læp] *n* sovrapposizione *f*

overlap² [ˌoʊ·və·'læp] <-pp-> **I.** *vi* sovrapporsi **II.** *vt* sovrapporsi

overleaf ['oʊ·və·li:f] *adv* sul retro

overload¹ ['oʊ·və·loʊd] *n* sovraccarico *m*

overload² [ˌoʊ·və·'loʊd] *vt* sovraccaricare; **to be ~ed with sth** *fig* essere sovraccarico di qc

overlook [ˌoʊ·və·'lʊk] **I.** *n* vista *f* **II.** *vt* **1.**(*look out onto*) dare su **2.**(*not notice*) non vedere; (*deliberately*) chiudere un occhio su **3.**(*forget*) dimenticare

overly ['oʊ·və·li] *adv* troppo

overmuch [ˌoʊ·və·'mʌtʃ] **I.** *adj* troppo, -a **II.** *adv* troppo

overnight [ˌoʊ·və·'naɪt] **I.** *adj* di notte; **~ bag** borsa *f* con l'occorente per una notte; **~ stay**

pernottamento *m; ~* **delivery** consegna *f* per il mattino seguente **II.** *adv* (*travel*) di notte; **to stay ~** rimanere a dormire

overpass ['oʊ·və·pæs] *n* cavalcavia *m*

overpay [ˌoʊ·və·'peɪ] *irr vt* pagare troppo

overpopulated [ˌoʊ·və·'pɑ:p·jə·leɪ·t̬ɪd] *adj* sovrappopolato, -a

overpopulation [ˌoʊ·və·ˌpɑ:p·jə·'leɪ·ʃən] *n* sovrappopolazione *f*

overpower [ˌoʊ·və·'paʊ·ə·] *vt* sopraffare

overpowering [ˌoʊ·və·'pa·ʊə·rɪŋ] *adj* (*personality*) dominante; (*attack*) schiacciante; (*taste, smell*) molto forte

overproduce [ˌoʊ·və·proʊ·'du:s] *vi, vt* produrre in eccesso

overrate [ˌoʊ·və·'reɪt] *vt* sopravvalutare

overreach [ˌoʊ·və·'ri:tʃ] *vt* **to ~ oneself** fare il passo più lungo della gamba

overreact [ˌoʊ·və·ri·'ækt] *vi* reagire in modo sproporzionato

overreaction [ˌoʊ·və·ri·'æk·ʃən] *n* reazione *f* esagerata

override [ˌoʊ·və·'raɪd] **I.** *n* override *m inv,* controllo *m* manuale **II.** *vt* **1.**(*not accept*) annulare **2.**(*interrupt*) cancellare

overriding [ˌoʊ·və·'raɪ·dɪŋ] *adj* principale

overrule [ˌoʊ·və·'ru:l] *vt* annulare; **to ~ an objection** LAW accogliere un'obiezione

overrun [ˌoʊ·və·'rʌn] **I.** *n* sforamento *m* **II.** *vt irr* **1.**(*invade*) invadere; **to be ~ with sth** essere invaso da qc **2.**(*budget*) superare **III.** *vi irr* sforare; **to ~ on costs** eccedere nei costi

overseas [ˌoʊ·və·'si:z] **I.** *adj* straniero, -a; (*trade*) estero, -a **II.** *adv* **to go/travel ~** andare/viaggiare all'estero

oversee [ˌoʊ·və·'si:] *irr vt* supervisionare

overseer ['oʊ·və·ˌsi:·ə·] *n* supervisore *m*

oversell [ˌəʊ·və·'sel] *irr vt* dare troppa enfasi a

overshadow [ˌoʊ·və·'ʃæ·doʊ] *vt* **1.**(*cast shadow over*) fare ombra su **2.**(*make insignificant*) mettere in ombra

overshoe ['oʊ·və·ʃu:] *n* soprascarpa *f*

overshoot [ˌoʊ·və·'ʃu:t] *irr vt* oltrepassare; AVIAT; **to ~ the runway** uscire di pista ▶ **to ~ the mark** passare il limite

oversight ['oʊ·və·saɪt] *n* **1.**(*omission*) svista *f; by an ~* per distrazione **2.**(*supervision*) supervisione *f*

oversimplify [ˌoʊ·və·'sɪm·plə·faɪ] <-ie-> *vt* semplificare troppo

oversize [ˌoʊ·və·'saɪz] *adj*, **oversized** *adj* **1.**(*too big*) troppo grande **2. ~ clothing** abbigliamento taglie forti

oversleep [ˌoʊ·və·'sli:p] *irr vi* non svegliarsi per tempo

overspend [ˌoʊ·və·'spend] **I.** *vi* spendere eccessivamente **II.** *vt* **to ~ one's allowance** spendere oltre il limite concesso

overstaffed [ˌoʊ·və·'stæft] *adj* con eccesso di personale

overstate [ˌoʊ·və·'steɪt] *vt* esagerare

overstay [ˌoʊ·və·'steɪ] *vt* **to ~ one's welcome** abusare della ospitalità

overstep [ˌoʊ·vəˈstep] *irr vt* oltrepassare ▸to ~ **the** <u>mark</u> passare il limite

oversupply [ˌoʊ·və·səˈplaɪ] *n* eccedenza *f*

overt [ˈoʊ·vɜːrt] *adj* aperto, -a

overtake [ˌoʊ·vəˈteɪk] *irr* I. *vt* 1. AUTO sorpassare; **events have ~n us** gli eventi ci hanno sopraffatti 2. (*in contest*) superare II. *vi* sorpassare

overtax [ˌoʊ·vəˈtæks] *vt* 1. FIN tassare eccessivamente 2. *fig* pretendere troppo da

over-the-counter [ˌoʊ·və·ðəˈkaʊn·ţə] *adj* da banco

overthrow [ˌoʊ·vəˈθroʊ] I. *n* 1. POL rovesciamento *m* 2. (*in baseball*) lancio *m* troppo lungo II. *vt irr* 1. POL rovesciare 2. (*in baseball*) **to ~ a base** lanciare oltre la base III. *vi* (*in baseball*) lanciare troppo forte

overtime [ˈoʊ·və·taɪm] *n* 1. (*work*) straordinario *m* 2. SPORTS tempo *m* supplementare

overtone [ˈoʊ·və·toʊn] *n* 1. (*implication*) tono *m* 2. MUS armonica *f* superiore

overture [ˈoʊ·və·tʃə] *n* 1. MUS ouverture *f inv* 2. (*show of friendliness*) avvicinamento *m*; **to make ~s towards sb** tentare l'approccio con qu

overturn [ˌoʊ·vəˈtɜːrn] I. *vi* capovolgersi II. *vt* rovesciare

overvalue [ˌoʊ·vəˈvæl·juː] *vt* sopravvalutare

overview [ˈoʊ·və·vjuː] *n* visione *f* generale

overweight [ˌoʊ·vəˈweɪt] *adj* sovrappeso, -a; **to be ~** (*suitcase, parcel*) pesare troppo; **to be ~ by several pounds** (*person*) essere in sovrappeso di varie libbre

overwhelm [ˌoʊ·vəˈwelm] *vt* 1. (*overcome by force*) sopraffare; **to be ~ed by sth** essere sopraffatto da qc 2. (*swamp*) inondare

overwhelming [ˌoʊ·vəˈwel·mɪŋ] *adj* travolgente; **~ grief** dolore inconsolabile; **to feel an ~ need to do sth** avere un irresistibile bisogno di fare qc

overwork [ˌoʊ·vəˈwɜːrk] I. *n* troppo lavoro *m* II. *vi* lavorare troppo III. *vt* far lavorare troppo; **to be ~ed and underpaid** lavorare troppo ed essere pagato male

overwrought [ˌoʊ·vəˈrɑːt] *adj* (*person*) teso, -a

ovulate [ˈɑː·vju·leɪt] *vi* ovulare

ovulation [ˌɑː·vjuːˈleɪ·ʃən] *n* ovulazione *f*

ovum [ˈoʊ·vəm] <ova> *n* ovulo *m*

owe [oʊ] *vt* dovere; **to ~ sb sth** [*o* **to ~ sth to sb**] dovere qc a qu

owing [ˈoʊ·ɪŋ] *adj* da pagare

owing to *prep* dovuto a

owl [aʊl] *n* gufo *m*, civetta *f*

owlish [ˈaʊ·lɪʃ] *adj* da gufo

own [oʊn] I. *adj* proprio, -a; **to see sth with one's ~ eyes** vedere qc coi propri occhi ▸to **be one's own** <u>man/person/woman</u> pensare con la propria testa; **in one's ~** <u>right</u> di per sé; **to do one's ~** <u>thing</u> fare qc a proprio modo; **in one's ~** <u>time</u> nel proprio tempo libero; **to** <u>hold</u> **one's ~** tenere duro II. *vt* possedere ▸**as if one ~ed the** <u>place</u> come se fosse

a casa propria III. *vt* **to ~ that ...** ammettere che ...

◆**own up** *vi* **to ~ to doing sth** ammettere di aver fatto qc

owner [ˈoʊ·nə] *n* proprietario, -a *m, f*

owner-occupied *adj* occupato, -a dal proprietario

owner-occupier [ˌoʊ·nə·ˈɑː·kjuː·paɪ·ə] *n* proprietario, -a e occupante *mf*

ownership [ˈoʊ·nə·ʃɪp] *n* proprietà *f*, possesso *m*; **to claim ~** rivendicare il possesso; **to be under private/public ~** essere di proprietà privata/pubblica

own goal *n* autogol *m inv*

ox [ɑːks] <-en> *n* bue *m*

ox cart *n* carro *m* di buoi

oxidation [ˌɑːk·sɪˈdeɪ·ʃən] *n* ossidazione *f*

oxide [ˈɑːk·saɪd] *n* ossido *m*

oxidize [ˈɑːk·sɪ·daɪz] I. *vi* ossidarsi II. *vt* ossidare

oxtail [ˈɑːks·teɪl] *n* coda *f* di bue

oxtail soup *n* minestra *f* di coda di bue

oxyacetylene [ˌɑːk·si·ə·ˈse·ţə·liːn] *n* ossiacetilene *m*

oxygen [ˈɑːk·sɪ·dʒən] *n* ossigeno *m*

oxygen mask *n* maschera *f* a ossigeno

oxygen tent *n* tenda *f* a ossigeno

oxymoron [ˌɑːk·sɪ·ˈmɔː·rɑːn] *n* ossimoro *m*

oyster [ˈɔɪs·tə] *n* ostrica *f*

oyster bank *n*, **oyster bed** *n* banco *m* di ostriche

oz *n*, **oz.** *n abbr of* **ounce** oncia *f* (*28,4 g*)

ozone [ˈoʊ·zoʊn] *n* ozono *m*

ozone layer *n* strato *m* di ozono

P

P, p [piː] <-'s> *n* P, p *f*; **~ as in Peter** P come Palermo ▸**to** <u>mind</u> **one's ~s and Qs** fare attenzione a quello che si dice [*o* si fa]

p *abbr of* **page** p., pag., p., pag.

pa [pɑː] *n inf* papà *m inv*

PA [ˌpiːˈeɪ] *n* 1. *abbr of* **public-address system** sistema *m* di altoparlanti 2. *abbr of* **Pennsylvania** Pennsylvania *f*

p.a. [ˌpiːˈeɪ] *abbr of* **per annum** all'anno

pace [peɪs] I. *n* 1. (*speed*) ritmo *m*; **to set the ~** SPORT fare l'andatura; **to keep ~ with sb** procedere di pari passo con qu; **to keep ~ with sth** stare al passo con qc; **to keep up/stand the ~** tenere/mantenere il ritmo 2. (*step*) passo *m*; **to quicken one's ~** allungare il passo ▸**a** <u>change</u> **of ~** qc di diverso dal solito; **to** <u>put</u> **sb through his/her ~s** mettere qu alla prova II. <pacing> *vt* 1. (*walk up and down*) camminare su e giù 2. (*measure in strides*) misurare a passi 3. SPORTS (*set a speed*) fare l'andatura per; **to ~ oneself** procedere a un ritmo regolare **III.** <pacing> *vi* to ~ **up and down** camminare avanti e indietro

pacemaker ['peɪs-ˌmeɪ·kə˞] *n* **1.** MED pacemaker *m inv* **2.** SPORTS lepre *f*

pacesetter ['peɪs-ˌse·t̬ə˞] *n* SPORTS lepre *f*

pachyderm ['pæ·kə·dɜːrm] *n* pachiderma *m*

pacific [pə·'sɪ·fɪk] *adj* pacifico, -a

Pacific [pə·'sɪ·fɪk] **I.** *n* the ~ il Pacifico; **the ~ Ocean** l'oceano Pacifico **II.** *adj* del Pacifico

pacification [ˌpæ·sə·fɪ·'keɪ·ʃən] *n* pacificazione *f*

pacifier ['pæ·sə·fa·ɪə˞] *n* **1.** (*for baby*) ciuccio *m* **2.** (*person*) pacificatore, -trice *m, f*

pacifism ['pæ·sə·fɪ·zəm] *n* pacifismo *m*

pacifist ['pæ·sə·fɪst] **I.** *n* pacifista *mf* **II.** *adj* pacifista

pacify ['pæ·sə·faɪ] <-ie-> *vt* **1.** (*establish peace*) pacificare **2.** (*calm*) calmare

pack [pæk] **I.** *n* **1.** (*bundle*) fagotto *m*; (*backpack*) zaino *m*; (*packet*) pacchetto *m*; (*of cigarettes*) pacchetto *m*; **ice** ~ borsa *f* del ghiaccio **2.** (*group*) gruppo *m*; (*of wolves*) branco *m*; (*of hounds*) muta *f*; *inf* (*of lies*) mucchio *m* **II.** *vi* (*prepare luggage*) fare le valigie **2.** *inf* to **send sb ~ing** mandare qu a farsi friggere *inf* **III.** *vt* **1.** (*fill: box, train*) riempire; **~ed with information** pieno di informazioni **2.** (*wrap*) avvolgere; (*put in packages*) impacchettare; to ~ **one's suitcase** fare la valigia **3.** (*compress*) stipare

◆**pack away** *vt* **1.** (*put back in place*) mettere via **2.** *inf* (*eat*) fare fuori

◆**pack in I.** *vt* **1.** (*put in*) mettere **2.** *inf* (*stop*) smettere; **pack it in!** smettila! **3.** (*attract audience*) richiamare **II.** *vi* entrare

◆**pack off** *vt inf* to **pack sb off** sbarazzarsi di qu

◆**pack up I.** *vt* **1.** (*put away*) mettere via **2.** *inf* (*finish*) piantare tutto **II.** *vi inf* (*stop work*) staccare

package ['pæ·kɪdʒ] **I.** *n* pacco *m*; (*of cookies*) pacchetto *m*; **software** ~ pacchetto di software **II.** *vt* **1.** (*pack*) confezionare **2.** *fig* presentare

package bomb *n* pacco *m* bomba

package deal *n* pacchetto *m* di proposte

package store *n* liquoreria *f*

packaging *n* **1.** (*wrapping*) materiale *m* di imballaggio **2.** (*action*) imballaggio *m*

packer ['pæ·kə˞] *n* imballatore, -trice *m, f*

packet ['pæ·kɪt] *n* **1.** (*parcel*) pacchetto *m*; (*of cigarettes*) pacchetto *m* di sigarette **2.** *inf* (*money*) sacco *m* di soldi **3.** COMPUT pacchetto *m*

packing *n* (*action, material*) imballaggio *m*

moving box *n* cassa *f* di imballaggio

packing routine *n* COMPUT routine *f* di compressione

pact [pækt] *n* patto *m*

pad¹ [pæd] **I.** *n* **1.** (*cushion*) cuscinetto *m*; **knee** ~ ginocchiera *f* imbottita; **mouse** ~ COMPUT tappetino *m* del mouse; **shin** ~ parastinchi *m inv*; **shoulder** ~ spallina (imbottita) *f*

2. (*of paper*) blocchetto *m* per appunti **3.** (*of animal's foot*) cuscinetto *m* (della zampa) **4.** AVIAT piattaforma *f* **5.** *sl* (*house, flat*) buco *m* **6.** (*water lily leaf*) foglia *f* di ninfea **II.** <-dd-> *vt* **1.** (*with wrapping material*) imbottire **2.** *inf* (*enflated: a bill, costs, the budget*) gonfiato

pad² [pæd] <-dd-> *vi* (*walk*) camminare con passo felpato

◆**pad out** *vt* rimpolpare; **to ~ a speech/text** rimpolpare un discorso/testo

padded *adj* imbottito, -a; ~ **cell** cella *f* di contenzione

padding *n a. fig* riempitivi *m; pl*

paddle ['pæ·dl] **I.** *n* **1.** (*type of oar*) pagaia *f* **2.** (*act of paddling*) sguazzata *f*; **to go for a ~** andare a sguazzare nell'acqua **3.** *inf* (*spank*) sculacciata *f* **II.** *vt* **1.** (*row*) mandare avanti a colpi di pagaia **2.** *inf* (*spank*) sculacciare **III.** *vi* **1.** (*row*) pagaiare **2.** (*walk, swim*) sguazzare

paddle boat *n* moscone *m* a pedali

paddle steamer *n* piroscafo *m* con ruota a pale

kiddie pool *n* piscina *f* per bambini

paddock ['pæ·dək] *n* recinto *m* per cavalli; (*at racecourse*) paddock *m inv*

paddy ['pæ·di] *n*, **paddy field** *n* risaia *f*

Paddy ['pæ·di] <-ies> *n pej, inf* irlandese *mf*

paddy wagon *n inf* vagone *m* cellulare

padlock ['pæd·lɑːk] **I.** *n* lucchetto *m* **II.** *vt* chiudere con il lucchetto

pagan ['peɪ·gən] **I.** *n* pagano, -a *m, f* **II.** *adj* pagano, -a

paganism ['peɪ·gə·nɪ·zəm] *n* paganesimo *m*

page¹ [peɪdʒ] *n a.* COMPUT (*in book, newspaper*) pagina *f*; (*sheet of paper*) foglio *m*; **front ~** prima pagina *f*

page² [peɪdʒ] **I.** *n* **1.** (*knight's attendant*) paggio *m* **2.** (*in hotel*) fattorino *m* **II.** *vt* (*over loudspeaker*) chiamare (con l'altoparlante); (*by pager*) chiamare con il cercapersone

pageant ['pæ·dʒənt] *n* (*show, ceremony*) parata *f* in costume; **beauty ~** concorso *m* di bellezza

pageantry ['pæ·dʒənt·ri] *n* spettacolo *m* sfarzoso

pageboy ['peɪdʒ·bɔɪ] *n* **1.** (*in hotel*) fattorino *m inv* **2.** (*hairstyle*) taglio *m* a caschetto

page layout *n* impaginazione *f*

page proof *n* bozza *f* impaginata

pager ['peɪ·dʒə˞] *n* cercapersone *m; inv*

page-turner *n inf* libro *m* avvincente

pagination [ˌpæ·dʒə·'neɪ·ʃən] *n* COMPUT, TYPO paginazione *f*

pagoda [pə·'goʊ·də] *n* pagoda *f*

paid [peɪd] **I.** *pt, pp* of **pay II.** *adj* pagato, -a; ~ **vacation** vacanze *fpl* pagate

paid-up *adj* (*member*) in regola con il pagamento della quota associativa

pail [peɪl] *n* secchio *m*

pain [peɪn] **I.** *n* **1.** (*physical suffering*) dolore *m*; **to be in ~** avere dolori/un dolore; **I have a ~ in my foot** mi fa male il piede **2.** *pl* (*great care*) tutto *m* il possibile; **to be at ~s to**

do sth fare tutto il possibile per fare qc; **to spare no ~ s** non tralasciare niente pur di fare qc **3.** *inf* **to be a ~ in the** backside *vulg* essere una gran rottura di scatole; *vulg;* **to be a ~ in the** neck *inf* essere una piaga; **on** [*o* under] **~ of sth** sotto pena di II. *vt* addolorare; **it ~ s me ...** mi addolora ...

pain barrier *n* soglia *f* del dolore

pained *adj* afflitto, -a; **a ~ expression** un'espressione addolorata

painful ['peɪn·fəl] *adj* **1.** (*physically*) doloroso, -a **2.** (*emotionally*) penoso, -a **3.** (*embarrassing*) spiacevole

painfully *adv* **1.** (*with pain*) dolorosamente **2.** (*shy, obvious*) terribilmente

painkiller ['peɪn·ˌkɪ·lə] *n* analgesico *m*

painless ['peɪn·ləs] *adj* **1.** (*not painful*) indolore **2.** *fig* (*easy*) facile

painstaking ['peɪnz·ˌteɪ·kɪŋ] *adj* (*research*) minuzioso, -a; (*search*) scrupoloso, -a; (*effort*) grande

paint [peɪnt] I. *n* pittura *f* II. *vi* dipingere III. *vt* **1.** (*room, picture*) dipingere; **to ~ a picture of sth** *fig* descrivere qc **2.** (*apply makeup*) **to ~ oneself** truccarsi

paintball *n* paintball *m; inv*

paint box *n* scatola *f* di colori

paintbrush <-es> *n* (*for pictures, for walls*) pennello *m*

painted ['peɪn·tɪd] *adj* dipinto, -a

painter[1] ['peɪn·tə] *n* **1.** (*artist*) pittore, -trice *m, f* **2.** (*decorator*) imbianchino *m*

painter[2] ['peɪn·tə] *n* NAUT (*rope*) barbetta *f*

painting *n* **1.** (*painted picture*) dipinto *m* **2.** (*art*) pittura *f;* **19th century French ~** la pittura francese del secolo XIX

paint roller *n* rullo (per tinteggiare) *m*

paint stripper *n* sverniciatore *m*

pair [per] I. *n* **1.** (*two matching items*) paio *m;* **a ~ of gloves/socks** un paio di guanti/calzini; **a ~ of glasses** un paio di occhiali; **a ~ of scissors** un paio di forbici; **a ~ of pants** un paio di pantaloni; **a ~ of tweezers** un paio di pinzette **2.** (*group of two people, animals*) coppia *f;* **in ~ s** a due a due II. *vi* accoppiarsi

♦**pair off** I. *vi* fare coppia II. *vt* **to pair sb off (with sb)** accoppiare qu (con qualcuno)

pairing *n* accoppiamento *m*

pajamas [pə·ˈdʒɑː·məz] *npl* pigiama *m;* **in (one's) ~** in pigiama; **a pair of ~** un pigiama

Pakistan ['pæ·kɪs·tæn] *n* Pakistan *m*

Pakistani I. *n* pakistano, -a *m, f* II. *adj* pakistano, -a

pal [pæl] *n* *inf* **1.** (*friend*) amico, -a *m, f* **2.** (*form of address*) bello, -a *m, f*

♦**pal around** *vi inf* vedersi spesso; **to ~ with sb** vedersi spesso con qu

palace ['pæ·ləs] *n* palazzo *m*

paleography [ˌpeɪ·lɪ·ˈɑː·grə·fi] *n* paleografia *f*

paleolithic [ˌpeɪ·lɪ·oʊ·ˈlɪ·θɪk] I. *adj* paleolitico, -a II. *n* **the Paleolithic** il paleolitico

paleontologist [ˌpeɪ·lɪ·ɑːn·ˈtɑː·lə·dʒɪst] *n* paleontologo, -a *m, f*

paleontology [ˌpeɪ·lɪ·ɑːn·ˈtɑː·lə·dʒi] *n* paleontologia *f*

palatable ['pæ·lə·ṭə·bl] *adj* **1.** (*food*) gustoso, -a **2.** (*suggestion*) accettabile

palate ['pæ·lət] *n* palato *m*

palatial [pə·ˈleɪ·ʃl] *adj* sontuoso, -a

palaver [pə·ˈlæ·və] *n* *inf* chiacchiere *fpl* inutili

pale[1] [peɪl] I. *adj* **1.** (*lacking color*) pallido, -a; **to look ~** essere pallido **2.** (*not dark*) chiaro, -a II. *vi* impallidire; **to ~ in comparison with sth** impallidire al confronto di qc; **to ~ into insignificance** diventare insignificante

pale[2] [peɪl] *n* (*fence post*) paletto *m* ►**to be** beyond **the ~** avere passato ogni limite

paleness ['peɪl·nɪs] *n* pallore *m*

Palestine ['pæ·ləs·taɪn] *n* Palestina *f*

Palestinian I. *n* palestinese *mf* II. *adj* palestinese

palette ['pæ·lɪt] *n* ART tavolozza *f*

palisade [ˌpæ·lə·ˈseɪd] *n* **1.** (*fence*) palizzata *f* **2.** *pl* (*cliffs*) falesia *fsing*

pall[1] [pɔːl] *vi* perdere di interesse

pall[2] [pɔːl] *n* **1.** (*cloth*) drappo *m* funebre; **a ~ of smoke** una cappa di fumo **2.** (*coffin*) feretro *m*

pallbearer ['pɔːl·ˌbe·rə] *n* portatore, -trice della bara a un funerale *m*

pallet ['pæ·lɪt] *n* **1.** (*for transporting goods*) pallet *m inv* **2.** (*bed*) tavolaccio *m*

palliative ['pæ·lɪ·ə·ṭɪv] I. *n* palliativo *m* II. *adj* palliativo, -a

pallid ['pæ·lɪd] *adj* **1.** (*very pale*) pallido, -a **2.** (*lacking energy*) scialbo, -a

pallor ['pæ·lə] *n* pallore *m*

pally ['pæ·li] <-ier, -iest> *adj inf* amico, -a; **to be ~ with sb** essere molto amico di qu

palm[1] [pɑːm] I. *n* (*of hand*) palmo *m;* **to read sb's ~** leggere la mano a qu ►**to have sb in the ~ of one's** hand avere qu in pugno; **to have sb eating out of the ~ of one's** hand avere qu in pugno II. *vt* **1.** (*hide*) nascondere nel cavo della mano **2.** (*bribe*) corrompere

palm[2] [pɑːm] *n* (*tree*) palma *f*

♦**palm off** *vt* **to palm sth off on sb** rifilare qc a qu; **to palm sb off with sth** liberarsi di qu con qc

palmist ['pɑː·mɪst] *n* chiromante *mf*

palm leaf <-leaves> *n* foglia *f* di palma

Palm Sunday *n* Domenica *f* delle Palme

palmtop *n* COMPUT palmare *m*

palpable ['pæl·pə·bl] *adj* palpabile

palpitate ['pæl·pə·teɪt] *vi* (*heart*) palpitare

palpitations [ˌpæl·pə·ˈteɪ·ʃnz] *npl* MED palpitazioni *fpl;* **to have ~** avere le palpitazioni

palsy ['pɔːl·zi] *n* MED paralisi *f inv;* **cerebral ~** paralisi cerebrale

paltry ['pɔːl·tri] <-ier, -iest> *adj* insignificante; (*wage*) miserabile

Pampas ['pæm·pəz] *n* + *sing/pl vb* pampa *f; sing*

pamper ['pæm·pə] *vt* viziare; **to ~ oneself** viziarsi

pamphlet ['pæm·flɪt] *n* (*leaflet*) opuscolo *m;*

POL pamphlet *m inv*

pan¹ [pæn] I. *n* 1. (*for cooking*) tegame *m;* **frying** ~ padella *f;* **to go down the** ~ *fig* andare a monte 2. (*of scales*) piatto *m* II. *vt* (*for gold*) lavare alla batea (per cercare l'oro)

pan² [pæn] *vi* CINE fare una panoramica

pan³ [pæn] *vt inf* stroncare; **to** ~ **a book/a film** fare a pezzi un libro/un film

♦**pan out** *vi inf* (*develop*) riuscire; **to** ~ **well** andare bene

panacea [ˌpæ·nə·'si·ə] *n* panacea *f*

panache [pə·'næʃ] *n* stile *m*

Panama ['pæ·nə·mɑː] *n* Panama *m*

Panama Canal *n* canale *m* di Panama

Panama City *n* Panama *f*

Panamanian [ˌpæ·nə·'mei·ni·ən] I. *adj* panamense II. *n* panamense *mf*

Pan-American ['pæn·ə·'me·ri·kən] *adj* panamericano, -a

pancake ['pæn·keik] *n* pancake *m inv*

pancreas ['pæŋ·kri·əs] *n* pancreas *m inv*

pancreatic [ˌpæn·kri·'æ·t̬ik] *adj* pancreatico, -a

panda ['pæn·də] *n* panda *m;* **red** ~ panda minore

pandemonium [ˌpæn·də·'mou·ni·əm] *n* (*confusion, noise*) pandemonio *m*

pander to ['pæn·də tə] *vt* assecondare

P and H [ˌpiː·ən·'eitʃ] *n abbr of* **postage and handling** spese *f* di spedizione *pl*

P and L [ˌpiː·ən·'el] *n abbr of* **profit and loss** profitti *m* e perdite *pl*

pane [pein] *n* cristal *m;* **window** ~ vetro *m* della finestra

panel ['pæ·nəl] I. *n* 1. (*wooden*) pannello *m;* (*metal*) placca *f* 2. FASHION pannello *m* 3. (*of cartoon strip*) vignetta *f* 4. (*team*) panel *m inv;* (*in exam*) commissione *f* esaminatrice 5. (*instrument board*) pannello *m* della strumentazione; **control** ~ pannello di controllo; **instrument** ~ AUTO, AVIAT quadro *m* dei comandi II. *vt* rivestire di pannelli

panel discussion *n* tavola *f* rotonda

paneling *n* pannelli *m pl* (in legno)

panelist ['pæ·nə·list] *n* (*in discussion*) ospite *mf* di una tavola rotonda; (*in quiz game*) membro *mf* di una squadra (che partecipa a un gioco)

pang [pæŋ] *n* fitta *f;* ~s **of remorse** rimorsi *mpl;* ~s **of guilt** sensi *m* di colpa *pl*

panhandle ['pæn·hæn·dl] I. *n* GEO stretta fascia di territorio di uno stato che si allunga in una direzione e ricorda la forma del manico di una padella II. *vi inf* mendicare III. *vt inf* **to** ~ **money** chiedere soldi

panhandler ['pæn·hænd·lə] *n inf* mendicante *mf*

panic ['pæ·nik] I. *n* panico *m;* **to get into a** ~ farsi prendere dal panico; **to be in a** ~ essere in preda al panico II. <-ck-> *vi* farsi prendere dal panico

panic attack *n* PSYCH attacco *m* di panico

panicky ['pæ·ni·ki] <-ier, iest> *adj* (*person*)

agitato, -a; (*feeling*) di panico

panic-stricken *adj* in preda al panico

pannier ['pæn·jə] *n* 1. (*for bicycle*) borsa (laterale) *f* 2. (*for horse*) bisaccia *f*

panorama [ˌpæ·nə·'ræ·mə] *n* panorama *m*

panoramic [ˌpæ·nə·'ræ·mik] *adj* panoramico, -a; ~ **view** vista *f* panoramica

panpipes ['pæn·paips] *npl* zampogna *f*

pansy ['pæn·zi] <-ies> *n* 1. (*flower*) viola *f* del pensiero 2. *pej, sl* (*homosexual*) frocio *m*

pant [pænt] I. *vi* (*person, dog*) ansimare; **to be** ~**ing for** [*o* **after**] **sth** morire dalla voglia di (fare) qc II. *vt* dire ansimando

pantheism ['pænt·θi·i·zəm] *n* panteismo *m*

pantheistic [ˌpənt·θi·'is·tik] *adj* panteistico, -a

pantheon ['pæt·θi·ɑːn] *n* pantheon *m inv*

panther ['pænt·θə] *n* 1. (*black leopard*) pantera *f* 2. (*puma*) puma *m inv*

panties ['pæn·t̬iz] *npl* mutandine *fpl*

pantomime ['pæn·tə·maim] *n* 1. (*gestures*) mimica *f* 2. (*mime*) pantomima *f* 3. (*performer*) mimo *m*

pantry ['pæn·tri] <-ies> *n* dispensa *f*

pants [pænts] *npl* 1. (*trousers*) pantaloni *mpl* 2. (*underpants*) mutande *fpl* ▶ **to be caught with one's** ~ **down** *inf* essere preso alla sprovvista

pantsuit *n* tailleur pantalone *m inv*

pantyhose *npl* collant *m pl*

panty liner *n* salvaslip *m inv*

pap [pæp] *n* 1. (*food*) pappa *f* 2. *inf* (*worthless entertainment*) scemenza *f*

papa ['pɑː·pə] *n* papà *m*

papacy ['pei·pə·si] *n* 1. (*office*) pontificato *m* 2. (*tenure of pope*) papato *m*

papal ['pei·pl] *adj* papale

paparazzo [pɑː·pɑː·'rɑːt·sou] <paparazzi> *n* paparazzo *m*

papaya [pə·'pa·iə] *n* papaia *f*

paper ['pei·pə] I. *n* 1. (*for writing*) carta *f;* **a sheet of** ~ un foglio di carta; **to put sth down on** ~ mettere qc per iscritto; **on** ~ sulla carta 2. (*newspaper*) giornale *m* 3. (*wallpaper*) carta da parati 4. (*official document*) documentazione *f;* ~**s** documenti *mpl* 5. (*essay*) compito *m* d'esame 6. (*academic discourse*) relazione *f;* **to give a** ~ tenere una relazione II. *vt* **to** ~ **the walls** tappezzare le pareti

♦**paper over** *vt fig* dissimulare

paperback ['pei·pə·bæk] *n* libro *m* in edizione economica; **in** ~ in brossura

paperback edition *n* edizione *f* economica

paper bag *n* sacchetto *m* di carta

paperboy *n* distributore *m* di giornali

paper chase *n* (*children's game*) finta *f* caccia alla volpe

paper clip *n* graffetta *f,* clip *f inv*

paper cup *n* bicchiere *m* di carta

paper cutter *n* taglierina *f*

paper doll *n* bambola *f* di carta

papergirl *n* distributrice *f* di giornali

paperknife <knives> *n* tagliacarte *m inv*

paper mill *n* cartiera *f*

paper money *n* carta *f* moneta
paper napkin *n* tovagliolo *m* di carta
paper profit *n* profitto *m* nominale
paper route *n* giro *m* del distributore di giornali
paper-thin *adj* sottilissimo, -a
paper tiger *n* **he's only a** ~ è una tigre di carta
paper towel *n* asciugamano *m* di carta
paper trail *n inf* serie *f* di documenti
paperweight *n* fermacarte *m inv*
paperwork *n* lavoro *m* amministrativo, scartoffie *fpl inf*
papery ['peɪ·pə·ri] *adj* sottile come la carta
papier-mâché [ˌpeɪ·pə·mə·'ʃeɪ] *n* cartapesta *f*
papist ['peɪ·pɪst] *pej* I. *n* papista *mf* II. *adj* papista
papoose [pæp·'uːs] *n* (*baby sling*) zaino *m* portabambini
pappy[1] ['pæ·pi] <-ier, -iest> *adj* 1.(*heavy*) molliccio, -a 2. *inf* (*of poor quality*) insulso, -a
pappy[2] ['pæ·pi] *n* papà *m*
paprika [pæp·'riː·kə] *n* paprica *f*
Pap smear *n* MED striscio *m* vaginale per il pap-test
Papua New Guinea [ˌpæp·ju·ə·nuː·'gɪ·ni] *n* Papua Nuova Guinea *f*
papyrus [pə·'paɪ·rəs] <-es *o* -ri> *n* papiro *m*
par [pɑːr] *n* 1.(*standard*) **to be on a** ~ **with sb** essere alla pari con qu; **below** ~ al disotto della media; **to feel below** ~ sentirsi sfasato; **to not be up to** ~ non essere all'altezza 2.(*in golf*) par *m* 3. FIN (*face value*) valore *m* nominale; **at/above/below** ~ alla/sopra/sotto la pari ▶ **to be** ~ **for the** course *inf* essere quello che ci si aspettava
par. *abbr of* **paragraph** paragrafo *m*
parable ['pæ·rə·bl] *n* parabola *f*
parabola [pə·'ræ·bə·lə] *n* parabola *f*
parabolic [ˌpæ·rə·'bɑ:·lɪk] *adj* parabolico, -a
paracetamol® [pæ·rə·'siː·tə·mɑːl] *n* paracetamolo *m*
parachute ['pæ·rə·ʃuːt] I. *n* paracadute *m inv*; ~ **pack** sacco *m* del paracadute II. *vi* lanciarsi con il paracadute III. *vt* paracadutare
parachute jump *n* salto *m* con il paracadute
parachuting *n* paracadutismo *m*
parachutist ['pæ·rə·ʃuː·t̬ɪst] *n* paracadutista *mf*
parade [pə·'reɪd] I. *n* 1.(*festive procession*) parata *f* 2.(*procession, inspection*) *a.* MIL parata *f* 3. *fig* (*series*) sfilza *f* II. *vi* 1.(*walk in procession*) *a.* MIL sfilare 2.(*show off*) **to** ~ **around** pavoneggiarsi III. *vt* 1.(*exhibit*) sfoggiare 2. *fig* (*show off*) ostentare; **to** ~ **one's knowledge/wealth/talents** fare sfoggio di cultura/ricchezze/talento
parade ground *n* MIL piazza *f* d'armi
paradigm ['pæ·rə·daɪm] *n* paradigma *m*
paradigmatic [ˌpæ·rə·dɪg·'mæ·t̬ɪk] *adj* paradigmatico, -a
paradigm shift *n* cambio *m* di paradigma
paradise ['pæ·rə·daɪs] *n* paradiso *m*
paradisiac(al) [ˌpæ·rə·'dɪ·sɪ·æ·k(l)] *adj* paradisiaco, -a

paradox ['pæ·rə·dɑːks] <-es> *n* paradosso *m*
paradoxical [ˌpæ·rə·'dɑ:k·sɪ·kəl] *adj* paradossale
paradoxically *adv* paradossalmente
paraffin ['pæ·rə·fɪn] *n*, **paraffin wax** *n* paraffina *f* liquida
kerosene heater *n* stufa *f* a cherosene
paragliding ['pæ·rə·ˌglaɪ·dɪŋ] *n* parapendio *m*
paragon ['pæ·rə·gɑːn] *n* archetipo *m*; **a** ~ **of democracy** un modello *m* di democrazia; **a** ~ **of virtue** *iron* un modello *m* di virtù
paragraph ['pæ·rə·græf] *n* 1. LING paragrafo *m* 2. PUBL (*short article*) trafiletto *m*
Paraguay ['pæ·rə·gwaɪ] *n* Paraguay *m*
Paraguayan [ˌpæ·rə·'gwa·iən] I. *adj* paraguaiano, -a II. *n* paraguaiano, -a *m, f*
parakeet ['pæ·rə·kiːt] *n* parrocchetto *m*
parallel ['pæ·rə·lel] I. *adj* 1. MAT parallelo, -a; **to run** ~ **to sth** correre parallelo a qc 2.(*similar*) simile II. *n* 1. MAT (*retta*) parallela *f* 2. GEO parallelo *m* 3. ELEC **in** ~ in parallelo 4.(*similarity*) parallelismo *f* 5. **to draw a** ~ (*make a comparison*) fare un parallelo; **to have no** ~ non avere confronto; **without** ~ senza uguali III. *vt* essere parallelo a
parallel bars *npl* SPORTS parallele *fpl*
parallel line *n* (retta) parallela *f*
paralysis [pə·'ræ·lə·sɪs] <-ses> *n* paralisi *f inv*
paralytic [ˌpæ·rə·'lɪ·t̬ɪk] I. *adj* MED paralitico, -a II. *n* paralitico, -a *m, f*
paralyze ['pæ·rə·laɪz] *vt* 1. *a. fig* paralizzare 2.(*stupefy*) inebetire; **to be** ~**d with fear** restare impietrito dalla paura
paralyzed *adj* 1.(*incapable of movement*) paralizzato, -a 2. *fig* paralizzato, -a
paramedic [ˌpæ·rə·'me·dɪk] *n* paramedico, -a *m, f*
parameter [pə·'ræ·mə·t̬ə·] *n* parametro *m*
paramilitary [ˌpæ·rə·'mɪ·lə·te·ri] I. *adj* paramilitare II. *n* **paramilitaries** truppe *f pl* paramilitari
paramount ['pæ·rə·maʊnt] *adj form* supremo, -a; **of** ~ **importance** di primaria importanza; **to be** ~ **to sth** essere essenziale per qu
paranoia [ˌpæ·rə·'nɔ·iə] *n* paranoia *f*
paranoiac [ˌpæ·rə·'nɔ·iæk] I. *adj* paranoico, -a II. *n* paranoico, -a *m, f*
paranoid ['pæ·rə·nɔid] *adj* 1. PSYCH paranoico, -a 2.(*very worried*) **to be** ~ **about sth** essere ossessionato da qc
paranoid schizophrenia *n* schizofrenia *f* paranoide
paranormal [pæ·rə·'nɔːr·məl] I. *adj* paranormale; ~ **powers** facoltà *fpl* paranormali II. *n* **the** ~ il paranormale
parapet ['pæ·rə·pɪt] *n* parapetto *m*
paraphernalia [ˌpæ·rə·fə·'neɪl·jə] *npl* armamentario *m*
paraphrase ['pæ·rə·freɪz] I. *vt* parafrasare II. *n* (*reformulation*) parafrasi *f inv*; **she gave us a quick** ~ **of what had been said** ci fece un rapido riassunto di quanto era stato detto

P

paraplegia [ˌpæ·rə·ˈpliː·dʒə] *n* paraplegia *f*
paraplegic [ˌpæ·rə·ˈpliː·dʒɪk] **I.** *adj* paraplegico, -a **II.** *n* paraplegico, -a *m, f*
parapsychology [ˌpæ·rə·saɪ·ˈkɑː·lə·dʒi] *n* parapsicologia *f*
parasite [ˈpæ·rə·saɪt] *n a. fig* parassita *mf*
parasitic [ˌpæ·rə·ˈsɪ·t̬ɪk] *adj a. fig* parassitico, -a; **~ disease** malattia *f* parassitaria
parasol [ˈpæ·rə·sɔːl] *n* parasole *m inv*
parathyroid gland [ˌpæ·rə·ˈθaɪ·ə·rɔɪd glænd] *n* paratiroide *f*
paratrooper [ˈpæ·rə·truː·pɚ] *n* parà *mf inv*
paratroops [ˈpæ·rə·truːps] *npl* reparti *m* paracadutisti *pl*
paratyphoid [ˌpæ·rə·ˈtaɪ·fɔ·ɪd] *n* MED paratifo *m*
parboil [ˈpɑːr·bɔɪl] *vt* sbollentare
parcel [ˈpɑːr·səl] **I.** *n* (*packet*) pacco *m;* (*of land*) lotto (di terreno) *m* **II.**<-l- *o* -ll-, -l- *o* -ll-> *vt* suddividere; (*land*) lottizzare
 ♦**parcel out** *vt* spartire; (*land*) distribuire
 ♦**parcel up** *vt* impacchettare
parcel bomb *n* pacco bomba *m*
parcel post *n* servizio *m* pacchi postali
parch [pɑːrtʃ] *vt* inaridire
parched *adj* **1.** (*dried-out*) secco, -a; **to be ~ with heat** essere inaridito dal caldo **2.** *fig, inf* (*very thirsty*) **to be ~** morire di sete
parchment [ˈpɑːrtʃ·mənt] *n* pergamena *f*
pardon [ˈpɑːr·dn] **I.** *vt* (*forgive*) perdonare; (*prisoner*) graziare; **to ~** (**sb**) **sth** perdonare qc (a qu); **to ~ sb for sth** perdonare qu per qc; **~ me for interrupting** chiedo scusa per l'interruzione; **if you'll ~ the expression** mi si perdoni l'espressione; (**I beg your**) **~ ?** (*requesting repetition*) come (hai [*o* ha] ha detto)?; **~ me!** (*after interrupting, burping etc.*) chiedo scusa; (*requesting to pass*) (è) permesso?; (*expressing indignation*) scusa [*o* mi scusi] [*o* scusatemi tanto!]; **~ me for breathing!** oh, scusami tanto! [*o* mi scusi] **II.** *n* grazia *f*
pardonable [ˈpɑːr·də·nə·bl] *adj* perdonabile
pare [per] *vt* **1.** (*peel: fruit*) sbucciare **2.** (*cut*) **to ~ one's nails** tagliarsi le unghie **3.** *fig* (*costs*) ridurre
 ♦**pare down** *vt* ridurre; **to pare sth down to the minimum** ridurre qc al minimo
 ♦**pare off** *vt* mondare
parent [ˈpe·rənt] *n* (*father*) padre *m;* (*mother*) madre *f; ~* **s** genitori *mpl*
parentage [ˈpe·rən·tɪdʒ] *n* famiglia *f;* **children of mixed ~** figli di coppia *f* mista
parental [pə·ˈren·təl] *adj* dei genitori
parental authority *n* patria *f* potestà
parental consent *n* consenso *m* dei genitori
parent company <-ies> *n* società *f* capogruppo
parenthesis [pə·ˈren·θə·sɪs] <-ses> *n* **1.** TYPO parentesi *f inv;* **in parentheses** tra parentesi **2.** (*remark*) inciso *m*
parenthetical [ˌpæ·rən·ˈθe·t̬ɪ·kəl] *adj* parentetico, -a; **~ remark** nota *f* esplicativa
parenthetically *adv* per inciso

parenthood [ˈpe·rənt·hʊd] *n* (*of man*) paternità *f;* (*of woman*) maternità *f*
parenting [ˈpern·t̬ɪŋ] *n* cura *m* dei figli; **~ skills** capacità *fpl* genitoriali
parentless [ˈpe·rənt·lɪs] *adj* orfano, -a
Parent Teacher Association *n*, **Parent Teacher Organization** *n* associazione *f* genitori - insegnanti
pariah [pə·ˈra·ɪə] *n* paria *mf*
paring [ˈpe·rɪŋ] *n* sbucciatura *f*
paring knife <knives> *n* coltello *m* sbucciatore
Paris [ˈpæ·rɪs] *n* Parigi *f*
parish [ˈpæ·rɪʃ] <-es> *n* **1.** REL parrocchia *f* **2.** (*in Louisiana*) distretto *m*
parish church <-es> *n* chiesa *f* parrocchiale
parish clerk *n* funzionario *m* di una chiesa parrocchiale
parishioner [pə·ˈrɪ·ʃə·nɚ] *n* parrocchiano, -a *m, f*
parish priest *n* parroco *m*
parish register *n* registro *m* parrocchiale
Parisian [pə·ˈrɪ·ʒən] **I.** *adj* parigino, -a **II.** *n* parigino, -a *m, f*
parity [ˈpæ·rɪ·t̬i] <-ies> *n* **1.** (*equality*) uguaglianza *f* **2.** FIN parità *f*
park [pɑːrk] **I.** *n* **1.** parco *m;* (*at country house*) giardini *mpl* **2.** (*stadium*) **baseball ~** campo di baseball **3.** AUTO parcheggio *m* **II.** *vt* **1.** (*leave vehicle*) parcheggiare; **to ~ a satellite** AVIAT posizionare un satellite **2.** *fig* **to ~ oneself somewhere** andarsi a mettere in qualche posto; **he ~ed himself in front of the TV** piazzarsi davanti alla TV **III.** *vi* parcheggiare
parka [ˈpɑːr·kə] *n* parka *m*
park bench *n* panchina *f* del parco
parked *adj* parcheggiato, -a
parking *n* parcheggio
parking attendant *n* custode *mf* del parcheggio
parking brake *n* freno *m* a mano
parking fine *n* multa *f* per sosta vietata
parking garage *n* posteggio *m*
parking lights *n* luci *fpl* di posizione
parking lot *n* parcheggio *m*
parking meter *n* parcometro *m*
parking offense *n* infrazione *f* al divieto di sosta
parking permit *n* permesso *m* di parcheggio
parking space *n*, **parking spot** *n* (posto di) parcheggio *m*
parking ticket *n* multa *f* per sosta vietata
Parkinson's (**disease**) [ˈpɑːr·kɪn·sənz (dɪ·ˌziːz)] *n* morbo *f* di Parkinson
Parkinson's Law *n hum* legge *f* di Parkinson
parkland [ˈpɑːrk·lænd] *n* parco *m*
parkway [ˈpɑːrk·weɪ] *n* viale *m* alberato, *spesso a doppia corsia e con ampio spartitraffico a verde*
Parl. *abbr of* **Parliament** parlamento *m*
parlance [ˈpɑːr·lənts] *n form* linguaggio *m;* **in common ~** nel linguaggio comune; **as it is known in common ~** come è noto nel lin-

guaggio popolare; **in medical** ~ nel gergo medico

parley ['pɑːr·li] I. *n* incontro *m* per parlamentare *iron* II. *vi* parlamentare

parliament ['pɑːr·lə·mənt] *n* parlamento *m*

parliamentarian [ˌpɑːr·lə·mən·'te·ri·ən] *n* (*member of parliament*) parlamentare *mf*

parliamentary [ˌpɑːr·lə·'men·tə·ri] *adj* parlamentare

parliamentary candidate *n* candidato, -a *m*, *f* al parlamento

parliamentary debate *n* dibattito *m* parlamentare

parliamentary democracy <-ies> *n* democrazia *f* parlamentare

parliamentary election *n* elezioni *fpl* parlamentari

parliamentary government *n* governo *m* parlamentare

parlor ['pɑːr·lə·] *n* 1.(*store*) **beauty** ~ salone *m* di bellezza; **ice-cream** ~ gelateria *f*; **pizza** ~ pizzeria *f* 2.(*in house*) salotto *m*

parlor car *n* RAIL carrozza *f* salone

parlor game *n* gioco *m* di società

parlormaid *n* cameriera *f*

parlous ['pɑːr·ləs] *adj* precario, -a; **to be in a ~ state** essere in uno stato precario

Parmesan (**cheese**) ['pɑːr·mə·zɑːn (tʃiːz)] *n* (formaggio) *m* parmigiano

parochial [pə·'roʊ·ki·əl] *adj* 1.REL parrocchiale 2.(*narrow-minded*) di idee ristrette

parochialism *n* campanilismo *m*

parochial school *n* scuola *f* confessionale

parodist ['pæ·rə·dɪst] *n* parodista *mf*

parody ['pæ·rə·di] I.<-ies> *n* parodia *f* II.<-ie-> *vt* fare la parodia di

parole [pə·'roʊl] I. *n* LAW libertà *f* sulla parola; **to be out on** ~ essere libero sulla parola II. *vt* **to be ~d** essere rilasciato sulla parola

paroxysm ['pæ·rək·sɪ·zəm] *n* parossismo *m*; ~ **of joy** impeto *m* di gioia; ~ **of rage** accesso *m* d'ira

parquet [pɑːr·'keɪ] *n* parquet *m*; ~ **floor** pavimento *m* a parquet

parricide ['pæ·rɪ·saɪd] *n form* 1.(*murder*) parricidio *m* 2.(*murderer*) parricida *mf*

parrot ['pæ·rət] I. *n* loro *m*, pappagallo *m* II. *vt pej* ripetere a pappagallo

parry ['pæ·ri] <-ie-> *vt* 1.(*blow*) parare 2.(*question*) eludere

parse [pɑːrs] *vt* **to ~ a sentence** analizzare sintatticamente una frase

parsimonious [ˌpɑːr·sə·'moʊ·ni·əs] *adj form* parsimonioso, -a; **to be ~ with the truth** dire mezze verità

parsimoniously *adv form* parsimoniosamente

parsimoniousness *n*, **parsimony** ['pɑːr·sə·moʊ·ni] *n form* tirchieria *f*

parsley ['pɑːrs·li] *n* prezzemolo *m*

parsnip ['pɑːrs·nɪp] *n* pastinaca *f*

parson ['pɑːr·sən] *n* parroco *m*; (*protestant*) pastore *m*

parsonage ['pɑːr·sə·nɪdʒ] *n* canonica *f*

part [pɑːrt] I. *n* 1.(*not the whole*) parte *f*; **the movie was good in ~s** certe parti del film erano buone; ~ **of the body/family** parte del corpo/della famiglia; **the easy/hard** ~ il facile/il difficile; **essential/important/integral** ~ parte essenziale/importante/integrante; **in** ~ in parte; **for the most** ~ per lo più 2.(*component*) parte *f*; **spare** ~**s** parti *fpl* di ricambio 3.(*area, region*) parte *f*; **in these ~s** *inf* da queste parti 4.(*in ratios, measure*) parte *f* 5.(*role, involvement*) parte *m*; **to want no** ~ **in sth** non volere avere niente a che fare con qc; **to do one's** ~ fare la propria parte 6.(*episode, chapter*) parte *f* 7.(*character in movie*) parte *m*; **to play the** ~ **of the King** interpretare la parte del re 8.(*in hair*) riga *f*; **a** ~ **in the middle/on the side** riga nel mezzo/su un lato 9.MUS (*score of an instrument*) parte *f* ▶ **to be** ~ **and** parcel **of sth** essere parte integrante di qc; **for my** ~ quanto a me; **to take sb's** ~ prendere le parti di qu; **on sb's** ~ da parte di qu; **it was a mistake on Julia's** ~ è stato un errore da parte di Julia II. *adv* parzialmente; **to be** ~ **African** essere in parte africano III. *vt* 1.(*detach, split*) separare; **to** ~ **sb from sb/sth** separare qu da qu/qc; **to** ~ **company** andare ciascuno per la propria strada 2.(*divide*) dividere, dividir; **to** ~ **sth in two** dividere qc in due; **to** ~ **sb's hair** fare la riga a qu IV. *vi* 1.(*separate*) separarsi; **to** ~ **from sb** separarsi da qu; *fig, inf* **to** ~ **with one's cash** tirar fuori i soldi 2.(*say goodbye*) lasciarsi 3.(*curtains*) aprire

partake [pɑːr·'teɪk] *vi irr* 1.(*participate*) **to** ~ **in sth** prendere parte a qc 2.**to** ~ **of sth** (*eat*) mangiare qc; (*drink*) bere qc

parted *adj* 1.(*slightly opened*) ~ **lips** labbra *fpl* semiaperte 2.(*unwillingly separated*) **to be** ~ **from sb** essere separato qc

partial ['pɑːr·ʃəl] *adj* 1.(*incomplete*) parziale; ~ **recovery** recupero *m* parziale 2.(*biased*) parziale 3.(*fond*) **she is** ~ **to ...** lei ha un debole per ...

partial eclipse *n* eclissi *f* parziale *inv*

partiality [ˌpɑːr·ʃi·'æ·lə·t̬i] *n* 1.(*bias*) parzialità *f* 2.(*liking*) debole *m*

partially *adv* parzialmente, in parte; ~ **cooked** parzialmente cotto

participant [pɑːr·'tɪ·sə·pənt] *n* participante *mf*; (*in contest*) concorrente *mf*

participate [pɑːr·'tɪ·sə·peɪt] *vi* partecipare; (*in contest*) concorrere

participation [pɑːr·ˌtɪ·sə·'peɪ·ʃən] *n* partecipazione *f*

participator [pɑːr·'tɪ·sə·peɪ·t̬ə·] *n* participante *mf*

participatory [pɑːr·'tɪ·sə·pə·ˌtɔː·ri] *adj* partecipativo, -a

participatory democracy <-ies> *n* democrazia *f* partecipativa

participle ['pɑːr·tɪ·sɪ·pl] *n* participio *m*

particle ['pɑːr·tɪ·kl] *n* PHYS, LING particella *f*

particle accelerator *n* acceleratore *m* di par-

P

ticelle
particleboard *n* pannello *m* truciolare
particle physics *n* fisica *f* delle particelle
particular [pəˈtɪk·jə·lə·] I. *adj* 1. (*special*) particolare, speciale; (*specific*) specifico, -a; **to be of ~ concern to sb** essere particolarmente importante per qu; **no ~ reason** nessuna ragione particolare; **in ~** in particolare; **nothing in ~** niente di speciale 2. (*fussy, meticulous*) meticoloso, -a; (*demanding*) esigente; **he is very ~ about his appearance** cura la sua immagine nei minimi particolari II. *n* particolare *m;* **the ~** i particolari *pl;* **on the general, rather than the ~** in generale anziché nei particolari
particularity [pə·tɪk·jə·ˈlæ·rɪ·ti] *n* particolarità *f inv*
particularize [pə·ˈtɪk·ju·lə·raɪz] *vt* specificare
particularly [pə·ˈtɪk·jə·lə·li] *adv* specialmente, particolarmente; **I didn't ~ want to go but I had to** non ne avevo molta voglia, ma ho dovuto andar via
parting [ˈpɑːr·tɪŋ] I. *n* 1. (*separation*) separazione *f* 2. (*saying goodbye*) addio *f* II. *adj* di addio; **~ words** parole *fpl* di commiato
parting shot *n* stoccata *f* finale (prima di andarsene)
partisan [ˈpɑː·rtɪ·zən] I. *adj* fazioso, -a, di parte; **~ spirit** spirito *m* partigiano II. *n* 1. (*supporter*) sostenitore, -trice *m, f* 2. MIL partigiano, -a *m, f*
partisanship *n* partigianeria *f*
partition [pɑː·rˈtɪ·ʃən] I. *n* 1. (*wall*) (parete) divisoria *f* 2. (*of country*) smembramento *m* 3. COMPUT segmentazione *f* II. *vt* 1. (*room*) suddividere (con tramezzi); **to ~ sth off** dividere qc con un tramezzo 2. (*country*) suddividere
partly [ˈpɑː·rt·li] *adv* parzialmente, in parte
partner [ˈpɑː·rt·nə·] I. *n* 1. COM socio, -a *m, f,* partner *mf inv* 2. (*accomplice*) **~ in crime** complice *mf* 3. (*in relationship, tennis, dancing*) compagno, -a *m, f* II. *vi* **to ~ with sb** mettersi in società con qu
partnership [ˈpɑː·rt·nə·ʃɪp] *n* 1. (*association*) associazione *f* 2. COM società *f* (in accomandita) *inv;* (*of lawyers*) studio *m;* **to go into ~ with sb** entrare in società con qu
partnership agreement *n* contratto *m* di società
part of speech *n* LING parte *f* del discorso
part-owner *n* comproprietario, -a *m, f*
part ownership *n* comproprietà *f inv*
partridge [ˈpɑː·rt·rɪdʒ] *n* pernice *f*
part song *n* canzone *f* a più voci
part-time [ˌpɑː·rtˈtaɪm] I. *adj* part time *inv;* **~ worker** lavoratore, -trice *m, f* part time II. *adv* **to work ~** lavorare part time
part-time job *n* lavoro *m* part time
part-timer *n* (*worker*) (lavoratore), (-trice) *m, f* part time; (*student*) (studente) *mf* part time
part-time staff *n* personale *m* part time
part-time student *n* (studente) *mf* part time

party [ˈpɑː·r·ti] I. *n* <-ies> 1. (*social gathering*) festa *f,* party *m inv;* **to have** [*o* **throw**] **a ~** dare una festa 2. + *sing/pl vb* POL partito *m;* **opposition/ruling ~** partito all'opposizione/al potere 3. + *sing/pl vb* (*group*) gruppo *m;* **~ of students** gruppo di studenti; **a ~ of three/eight** un gruppo di tre/otto 4. *a.* LAW parte *f;* **the guilty ~** la parte responsabile; **to be a ~ to sth** essere parte attiva in qc; **to be ~ to an arrangement** essere parte di un accordo; **to be a ~ to a crime** essere complice di un delitto 5. *inf* (*person*) tizio *m* II. <-ie-> *vi* andare alle feste
party convention *n* congresso *m* del partito
party headquarters *n* sede *f* del partito
party leader *n* segretario *m* del partito
party line *n* 1. TEL duplex *m inv* 2. POL linea *f* politica del partito; **to follow the ~** seguire la linea politica del partito
party politics *npl* interessi di partito
party pooper *n sl* guastafeste *mf inv*
parvenu [ˈpɑː·r·və·nuː] *n pej* parvenu *mf inv*
pass [pæs] I. <-es> *n* 1. (*mountain road*) passo *m,* valico *m;* **mountain ~** passo *m* di montagna 2. (*in football, soccer*) passaggio *m* 3. (*sexual advances*) **to make a ~** (**at sb**) fare delle avance (a qu) 4. (*in exam, class*) promozione *f;* **~ mark** sufficienza *f* 5. (*authorization*) permesso *m;* (*for festival, concert*) ingresso *m* 6. (*for bus, train*) abbonamento *m* 7. SCHOOL (*permit to leave class*) permesso *m* (per uscire di classe) ▶ **to come to a pretty ~** giungere a un punto critico; **things have come to a pretty ~!** ecco dove siamo arrivati! II. *vt* 1. (*go past*) passare (davanti a); (*cross*) incrociare 2. (*exceed*) oltrepassare; **to ~ a limit** passare il limite; **to ~ all expectation** andare al di là di ogni aspettativa 3. (*hand to*) **to ~ sth to sb** passare qc a qu 4. (*in football, soccer*) passare 5. (*exam, class*) passare 6. (*avoid boredom*) **to ~ the time** passare il tempo 7. POL (*officially approve*) approvare; **to ~ a bill/law** approvare un disegno di legge/una legge 8. (*utter, pronounce*) dire; **to ~ a comment** fare un commento; **to ~ the news** passare le notizie; **to ~ judgment** sentenziare; **to ~ sentence** LAW emettere una sentenza 9. MED espellere; **to ~ urine** orinare III. *vi* 1. (*move by*) passare; **we often ~ed on the stairs** ci incrociavamo spesso sulle scale; **to ~ unnoticed** passare inosservato 2. (*come to an end*) passare; **it'll soon ~** passerà presto 3. (*in football, soccer*) passare (la palla) 4. (*in exam*) essere promosso 5. (*elapse: time*) passare 6. (*not know answer*) passare; **~!** passo!
♦**pass away** *vi* (*die*) spirare
♦**pass by** I. *vi* 1. (*elapse*) passare 2. (*go past*) passare (davanti a) II. *vt* **life has passed him by,** non ha veramente vissuto, *fashion just passes her by,* la moda la lascia indifferente
♦**pass down** *vt* (*knowledge, beliefs*) trasmettere; (*clothes, possessions*) passare
♦**pass off** I. *vt* (*sell fake*) *to pass sth off as*

sth, spacciare qc per qc; (*give appearance of*); **he tried to pass himself off as an expert** ha cercato di farsi passare per esperto II. *vi* 1. (*take place successfully*) andare bene 2. (*fade away, wear off*) svanire

♦ **pass on** I. *vi* 1. (*continue moving*) andare avanti; **to ~ to a different topic** passare a un altro argomento 2. (*die*) spirare II. *vt* 1. BIO (*transmit*) trasmettere 2. (*information, advice*) passare 3. (*refer*) **to pass sb on to sb** mettere qu in contatto con qu

♦ **pass out** I. *vi* (*faint*) svenire II. *vt* (*distribute*) distribuire

♦ **pass over** *vt* non tenere conto di

♦ **pass through** *vt* attraversare

♦ **pass up** *vt* lasciarsi sfuggire

passable ['pæ·sə·bl] *adj* 1. (*unobstructed*) transitabile 2. (*average, fair*) passabile

passage ['pæ·sɪdʒ] *n* 1. (*corridor*) corridoio *m*; (*path*) passaggio *m* 2. LIT, MUS brano *m* 3. (*onward journey*) viaggio *m* 4. (*sea voyage*) traversata *f*; **bird of ~** uccello *m* di passo 5. **with the ~ of time** con il passare del tempo

passageway ['pæ·sɪdʒ·weɪ] *n* corridoio *m*

passbook ['pæs·bʊk] *n* libretto *m* di risparmio

passenger ['pæ·sən·dʒɚ] *n* passeggero, -a *m, f*

passenger list *n* elenco *m* dei passeggeri

passerby [pæ·sə·'baɪ] <passersby> *n* passante *mf*

passing I. *adj* 1. (*going past*) che passa 2. (*brief: fad, infatuation*) passeggero, -a; (*glance*) di sfuggita; (*remark*) per inciso; **~ fancy** capriccio *m* II. *n* (*death*) morte *f* ▶ **in ~** casualmente

passing grade *n*, **passing mark** *n* sufficienza *f*

passion ['pæ·ʃən] *n* (*emotion*) passione *f*; (*anger*) ira *f*; **crime of ~** delitto *m* passsionale

passionate ['pæ·ʃə·nɪt] *adj* (*emotional*) appassionato, -a; (*angry*) irascibile

passionflower ['pæ·ʃən·flaʊɚ] *n* passiflora *f*

passion fruit *n* frutto *m* della passione

passionless ['pæ·ʃən·ləs] *adj* privo di passione

Passion play *n* (dramma *m* della) passione (di Gesù)

Passion Week *n* settimana *f* di passione

passive ['pæ·sɪv] I. *n* LING passivo *m* II. *adj* passivo, -a

passiveness *n*, **passivity** [pæ·'sɪ·vɪ·ti] *n* passività *f*

passkey ['pæs·kiː] *n* (*master-key*) (chiave *f*) passe-partout

Passover ['pæs·ˌoʊ·vɚ] *n* Pasqua *f* ebraica

passport ['pæs·pɔːrt] *n* passaporto *m*; *fig*; **sb's ~ to success** la chiave *f* del successo per qu

passport control *n* controllo *m* passaporti

passport holder *n* titolare *mf* del passaporto

password ['pæs·wɜːrd] *n* INFOR password *f inv*

past [pæst] I. *n* passato *m*; **to be a thing of the ~** appartenere al passato; **sb with a ~** qu che ha un passato (oscuro); **simple ~** (tempo) passato *m* remoto; **to write in the ~** scrivere

al passato II. *adj* passato, -a; **the ~ week** la settimana scorsa; **in times ~** in altri tempi; **that's ~ history** è acqua passata III. *prep* 1. (*temporal*) dopo; **ten/quarter/half ~ two** le due e dieci/e un quarto/e mezzo; **it's ~ 2** sono le 2 passsate 2. (*spatial*) oltre 3. (*beyond*) **to be ~ thirty** aver passato la trentina; **~ belief** incredibile; **~ description** indescrivibile; **I'm ~ caring** non me ne importa più nulla; **I'm ~ that now** *iron* sono troppo vecchio per (fare) questo IV. *adv* oltre; **to go ~** passare

pasta ['pɑː·s·tə] *n* pasta *f*

past continuous *n* (tempo) passato *m* progressivo

paste [peɪst] I. *n* impasto *m*; **meat/fish ~** pasta *f* di carne/pesce; **tomato ~** concentrato *m* di pomodoro; **almond ~** pasta *f* di mandorle; **anchovy ~** pasta *f* di acciughe II. *vt* 1. *a.* COMPUT (*stick*) incollare 2. *inf* (*beat*) pestare

pasteboard ['peɪst·bɔːrd] *n* cartoncino *m*

pastel [pæs·'tel] I. *n* 1. ART (*drawing material*) pastello *m*; (*type of drawing*) disegno *m* a pastello 2. (*color*) colore *m* pastello II. *adj* pastello

paste-up ['peɪst·ʌp] *n* menabò *m inv*

pasteurization [ˌpæs·tʃə·ɪ·'zeɪ·ʃən] *n* pastorizzazione *f*

pasteurize ['pæs·tʃə·raɪz] *vt* pastorizzare

pastime ['pæs·taɪm] *n* passatempo *m*

pastor ['pæs·tɚ] *n* pastore *m*

pastoral ['pæs·tə·rəl] *adj* 1. REL pastorale 2. LIT, ART pastorale; **~ scene** scena *f* bucolica

past participle *n* participio *m* passato

past perfect *n* (tempo) trapassato *m* prossimo, (tempo) trapassato *m* remoto

pastry ['peɪs·tri] <-ies> *n* 1. (*dough*) pasta *f*; **~ brush** pennello *m* da cucina 2. (*sweet bun*) pasta *f*

pastry chef *n*, **pastry cook** *n* pasticciere, -a *m, f*

past tense *n* (tempo) *m* passato

pasture ['pæs·tʃɚ] I. *n* 1. AGR pascolo *m* 2. *fig* **new ~s** orizzonti *m pl* nuovi; **to put sb out to ~** *inf* lasciare a casa qu II. *vt* pascolare III. *vi* pascolare

pastureland *n* pascolo *m*

pasty¹ ['peɪs·ti] <-ies> *n Cornish* ~ *pasticcio di carne e verdure*

pasty² ['peɪs·ti] <-ier, -iest> *adj* (*texture*) pastoso, -a; (*complexion*) pallido, -a

pat¹ [pæt] I. <-tt-> *vt* (*touch softly*) dare colpetti affettuosi a qu; **to ~ sb on the back** *fig* congratularsi con qu II. *n* 1. (*tap*) colpetto; **to give sb a ~ on the back** *fig* congratularsi con qu *f* 2. (*of butter*) pezzetto *m*

pat² [pæt] I. *adj pej* (*answer*) preparato, -a II. *adv* **to have sth down ~** sapere qc a menadito

patch [pætʃ] I. *n* 1. (*piece of cloth*) pezza *f*; (*for mending clothes*) toppa *f* 2. (*of land*) pezzo *m* di terreno; (*of fog*) banco *m*; **~ of ice** tratto *m* ghiacciato; (*of sky*) pezzetto *m*; (*of color, damp*) macchia *f*; **vegetable ~** orto *m*; **pump-**

kin ~ pezzo di terreno coltivato a zucche *m* **3.** *inf* (*phase*) fase *f* **4.** COMPUT patch *m inv* **5.** TEL collegamento *m* telefonico temporaneo **II.** *vt* (*hole, clothes*) rattoppare

◆ **patch up** *vt* **1.** (*mend*) riparare alla meglio **2.** *fig* (*friendship*) salvare; **to patch things up** fare la pace

patchwork ['pætʃ·wɜːrk] **I.** *n* **1.** (*needlework*) patchwork *m* **2.** *fig* (*mix*) mosaico *m* **II.** *adj* patchwork *inv*; **a** ~ **quilt** una trapunta patchwork

patchy ['pæ·tʃi] <-ier, -iest> *adj* (*performance, novel*) disorganico, -a; (*weather*) variabile; (*results*) irregolare

pâté [pɑː·'teɪ] *n* pâté *m inv*

patella [pə·'te·lə] <-e> *n* ANAT patella *f*

patent ['pæ·tənt] **I.** *n* LAW brevetto *m;* **to take out a** ~ **on sth** ottenere un brevetto su qc **II.** *adj* **1.** LAW brevettato, -a **2.** (*unconcealed*) evidente **III.** *vt* LAW brevettare

patented *adj* LAW brevettato, -a

patentee [ˌpæ·tən·'tiː] *n* titolare *mf* di un brevetto

patent leather I. *n* vernice *f* **II.** *adj* (*handbag, jacket*) di vernice

patent medicine *n* specialità *f inv* farmaceutica

patent office *n* ufficio *m* brevetti

paternal [pə·'tɜːr·nəl] *adj* paterno, -a; ~ **grandfather** nonno *m* paterno; ~ **grandmother** nonna *f* paterna

paternalism [pə·'tɜːr·nə·lɪ·zəm] *n* paternalismo *m*

paternalistic [pə·ˌtɜːr·nə·'lɪs·tɪk] *adj* paternalistico, -a

paternity [pə·'tɜːr·nə·t̬i] *n* paternità *f*

paternity leave *n* congedo *m* di paternità

paternity suit *n* LAW causa *f* di riconoscimento della paternità

path [pæθ] *n* **1.** (*footway, trail*) sentiero *m;* **bike** ~ corsia *f* per ciclisti; **to clear a** ~ aprire un sentiero; **to follow a** ~ seguire un sentiero **2.** (*way*) percorso *m;* (*of bullet*) traiettoria *f;* **to cross sb's** ~ incontrare qu per caso **3.** INFOR path *m inv*

pathetic [pə·'θe·t̬ɪk] *adj* **1.** (*arousing sympathy*) penoso, -a; **a** ~ **sight** uno spettacolo pietoso **2.** (*arousing scorn*) patetico, -a; **a** ~ **performance** un'esecuzione penosa

pathfinder ['pæθ·ˌfaɪn·dɚ] *n* esploratore, -trice *m, f;* **to be a** ~ essere un pioniere

pathological [ˌpæ·θə·'lɑː·dʒɪ·kl] *adj inf* patologico, -a

pathologist [pə·'θɑː·lə·dʒɪst] *n* patologo, -a *m, f*

pathology [pə·'θɑː·lə·dʒi] *n* MED patologia *f*

pathos ['peɪ·θɑːs] *n* pathos *m inv*

pathway ['pæθ·weɪ] *n* sentiero *m*, percorso *m*

patience ['peɪ·ʃns] *n* pazienza *f;* **to have the** ~ **of a saint** avere la pazienza di un santo

patient ['peɪ·ʃnt] **I.** *adj* paziente; **to be** ~ **with sb** essere paziente con qu; **just be** ~**!** un po' di pazienza! **II.** *n* **1.** MED paziente *mf* **2.** LING paziente *m*, passivo *m*

patina ['pæ·tə·nə] *n* patina *f*

patio ['pæ·t̬ioʊ] <-s> *n* **1.** (*paved area*) terrazza; ~ **door** porta *f* che dà sulla terrazza **2.** (*courtyard*) cortile *m*

patriarch ['peɪ·tri·ɑːrk] *n* patriarca *m*

patriarchal [ˌpeɪ·tri·'ɑːr·kl] *adj* patriarcale

patriarchy ['peɪ·tri·ɑːr·ki] <-ies> *n* patriarcato *m*

patrician [pə·'trɪ·ʃən] **I.** *n* patrizio *mf* **II.** *adj* patrizio, -a

patricide ['pæ·trə·saɪd] *n* (*murderer*) parricida *mf;* (*crime*) parricidio *m*

patriot ['peɪ·tri·ət] *n* patriota *mf*

patriotic [ˌpeɪ·tri·'ɑː·t̬ɪk] *adj* patriottico, -a

patriotism ['peɪ·tri·ə·t̬ɪ·zəm] *n* patriottismo *m*

patrol [pə·'troʊl] **I.** <-ll-> *vi* pattugliare **II.** <-ll-> *vt* pattugliare **III.** *n* pattuglia *f;* **to be on** ~ essere di pattuglia

patrol car *n* auto *f* di pattuglia (della polizia)

patrol duty *n* servizio *m* di pattuglia

patrolman *n* poliziotto (di pattuglia) in divisa *m*

patrol wagon *n* (furgone) *m* cellulare

patron ['peɪ·trən] *n* **1.** (*benefactor*) patrono, -a *m, f;* (*arts*) mecenate *mf* **2.** (*customer*) cliente (abituale) *mf* **3.** REL patrono, -a *m, f*

patronage ['peɪ·trə·nɪdʒ] *n* **1.** (*support*) patrocinio *m;* ART mecenatismo *m* **2.** ECON clientela (abituale) *f*

patroness ['peɪ·trə·nɪs] *n* **1.** (*benefactor*) patronessa *f;* ART mecenate *f* **2.** REL (santa) patrona *f*

patronize ['peɪ·trə·naɪz] *vt* **1.** (*be customer*) essere cliente (abituale) di **2.** (*treat condescendingly*) trattare con condiscendenza

patronizing ['peɪ·trə·naɪ·zɪŋ] *adj* condiscendente *mf*

patter ['pæ·t̬ɚ] **I.** *n* **1.** (*tapping: of rain*) picchiettio *m;* (*of feet*) scalpiccio *m* **2.** (*talk*) parlantina *f* **II.** *vi* **1.** (*make sound*) picchiettare **2.** (*walk lightly*) zampettare; **to** ~ **about** muoversi velocemente

pattern ['pæ·t̬ɚn] **I.** *n* **1.** (*model*) modello *m* **2.** ART (*design, motif*) disegno *m;* **floral** ~ motivo *m* floreale **3.** FASHION (*paper guide*) modello *m;* ECON (*sample*) campione *m* **II.** *vt* (*emulate, follow, imitate: person*) prendere a modello, **she patterns herself on her sister,** prende a modello sua sorella; (*program, scheme*) *the course is patterned closely after the previous one,* il corso è foggiato sul modello del precedente

pattern book *n* campionario *m*

patterned *adj* stampato, -a

paunch [pɔːntʃ] *n* pancia *f*

paunchy <-ier, -iest> *adj* panciuto, -a

pauper ['pɔː·pɚ] *n* indigente *mf*

pause [pɔːz] **I.** *n* pausa *f* ▶ **to give sb** ~ **for thought** *form* dare a qu di che pensare **II.** *vi* fare una pausa

pave [peɪv] *vt* pavimentare; **to** ~ **the way for sth** *fig* preparare la strada a qc

pavement ['peɪv·mənt] *n* marciapiede *m*

pavilion [pə·'vɪl·jən] *n* padiglione *m*

paving *n* 1.(*space*) pavimentazione *f* 2.(*material*) materiale *m* (per pavimentazione)

paw [pɔ:] I. *n* zampa *f; fig, inf* (*of person*) mano *f* II. *vt* toccare con la zampa; **to ~ sb** palpeggiare qu III. *vi* **to ~ at sth** dare dei colpetti con la zampa a qc

pawn¹ [pɔ:n] *n* GAMES pedina *f;* (*in chess*) pedone *m; fig* pedina *f*

pawn² [pɔ:n] I. *vt* impegnare II. *n* **to be in ~** essere impegnato
 ◆**pawn off** *vt* **to ~ sth off on sb** sbolognare qc a qu; **to ~ sth off as sth** vendere qc spacciandolo per qc

pawnbroker ['pɔ:n‚broʊ‧kɚ] *n* titolare *mf* di agenzia di prestito su pegno

pawnbroking *n* attività *f* di prestito su pegno

pawn shop *n* agenzia *f* di prestito su pegno

pay [peɪ] I. *n* paga *f;* **to be in sb's ~** essere al soldo di qu; **to ~ through the nose** pagare un prezzo esorbitante II.<paid, paid> *vt* 1.(*redeem with money*) pagare; **to ~ cash** pagare in contanti; **to ~ one's debts** estinguere i propri debiti 2.(*be worthwhile*) convenire 3.(*give, render*) **to ~ attention** (**to sth**) prestare attenzione (a qc); **to ~ a call** (**on sb**), **to ~** (**sb**) **a call** fare una visita (a qu); **to ~ sb a compliment** fare un complimento a qu; **to ~ homage to sb** rendere omaggio a qu; **to ~ respects to sb** porgere i propri omaggi a qu III.<paid, paid> *vi* 1.(*settle, recompense*) pagare 2.(*benefit*) essere conveniente
 ◆**pay back** *vt* rimborsare; **I'll pay you back!** me la pagherai! [*o* pagherà!] [*o* pagherete!]; **to pay sb back in the same coin** ripagare qu con la stessa moneta
 ◆**pay in** *vt* versare
 ◆**pay off** I. *vt* 1.(*debt*) estinguere 2. *inf* (*bribe*) corrompere II. *vi fig* dare buoni risultati; **the waiting paid off** valeva la pena di aspettare
 ◆**pay out** I. *vt* 1.(*money*) sborsare 2. **to ~ the rope** lasciare scorrere la corda II. *vi* pagare
 ◆**pay up** *vi* pagare (quanto è dovuto)

payable ['peɪ‧ə‧bl] *adj* pagabile; **to make a check ~ to sb** emettere un assegno a favore di qu

pay agreement *n* accordo *m* salariale

pay-as-you-go *n* (*for cell phones*) servizio *m* prepagato

payback ['peɪ‧bæk] *n* 1. FIN (*equaling the sum invested*) recupero *m* dell'investimento; **we're expecting ~ within 5 years** ci aspettiamo di recuperare l'investimento entro 5 anni; **what's the ~ on this fund?** qual è il rendimento su questo investimento in titoli? 2.(*benefit from action*) ricompensa *f;* **I've helped you out and now it's time for ~** ti ho aiutato e adesso è ora di essere ricompensato

payback period *n* periodo *m* di recupero

paycheck *n* paga *f*

payday *n* giorno *m* di paga

pay deal *n* accordo *m* salariale

pay desk *n* cassa *f*

pay differential *n* differenziale *f* salariale

payee [peɪ‧'i:] *n* beneficiario, -a *m, f*

pay envelope *n* busta *f* paga

payer ['pe‧ɪɚ] *n* pagatore, -trice *m, f;* **bad ~** pagatore, -trice moroso *m*

pay freeze *n* blocco *m* salariale

pay hike *n* aumento *m* di stipendio

paying *adj* redditizio, -a

payload ['peɪ‧loʊd] *n* 1. AVIAT carico *m* utile 2. MIL carica *f* esplosiva

paymaster ['peɪ‧mæs‧tɚ] *n* pagatore, -trice *m, f*

payment ['peɪ‧mənt] *n* 1.(*sum of cash*) pagamento *m* 2.(*installment*) rata *f;* (*reward*) ricompensa *f*

pay negotiations *npl* contrattazioni *fpl* salariali

payoff ['peɪ‧ɑ:f] *n* 1.(*payment*) pagamento *m;* (*debt payment*) saldo *m* 2. *inf* (*bribe*) bustarella *f,* tangente; **to make a ~ to sb** pagare qu sottobanco 3. *inf* (*positive result*) risultato *m* positivo; (*on bet*) pagamento *m* di una vincita 4. *inf* (*climax of events*) momento *m* culminante

payout *n* FIN esborso *m*

pay-per-view *n* televisione *f* a pagamento

pay phone *n* telefono *m* pubblico

pay raise *n* aumento *m* di stipendio

payroll *n* ruolo *m* paga; **~ tax** imposta *f* sui redditi da lavoro dipendente

payslip *n* cedolino *m*

pay-TV *n* televisione *f* a pagamento

PBS [‚pi:‧bi:‧'es] *n abbr of* **Public Broadcasting System** *canale televisivo statunitense*

PC [‚pi:‧'si:] I. *n abbr of* **personal computer** PC *m* II. *adj abbr of* **politically correct** politicamente corretto, -a

p.c. *abbr of* **percent** per cento

PDT *n abbr of* **Pacific Daylight Time** ora legale della zona Pacifico

PE [‚pi:‧'i:] *abbr of* **physical education** educazione *f* fisica

pea [pi:] *n* pisello *m* ▶ **to be like two ~s in a pod** essere come due gocce d'acqua

peace [pi:s] *n* 1.(*absence of war*) pace *f* 2.(*social order*) ordine *m* pubblico; **to keep the ~** mantenere l'ordine; **to make ~** fare la pace; **to make one's ~ with sb** fare la pace con qu 3.(*tranquillity*) tranquillità *f;* **~ of mind** tranquillità; **to be at ~ with** [*o about*] **one's situation** essere contento della propria condizione; **~ and quiet** pace e tranquillità; **to be at ~** essere in pace; **to give sb no ~** non dare pace a qu; **to leave sb in ~** lasciare in pace qu 4. REL **~ be with you** la pace sia con te [*o* con voi]; (**may he**) **rest in ~** riposi in pace ▶ **to be at ~ with the** world essere in pace con il mondo; **to** hold **one's ~** stare zitto; **speak now or forever** hold **your ~** parla adesso o taci per sempre

peaceable ['pi:‧sə‧bl] *adj* pacifico, -a

P

peace activist *n* pacifista *mf*

peace agreement *n* accordo *m* di pace

peace conference *n* conferenza *f* di pace

Peace Corps *n* organizzazione statunitense di volontari per il terzo mondo

peaceful ['piːs·fəl] *adj* 1.(*calm, quiet: animal*) mansueto, -a; (*place, person*) tranquillo, -a 2.(*non-violent*) pacifico, -a

peace initiative *n* iniziativa *f* di pace

peacekeeper *n* 1.(*in family*) paciere, -a *m, f* 2.(*soldier*) soldato *m* di un contingente di pace

peacekeeping ['piːs·ˌkiː·pɪŋ] *n* mantenimento *m* della pace

peacekeeping forces *npl* forze *fpl* di pace

peace-loving *adj* amante della pace

peacemaker ['piːs·ˌmeɪ·kɚ] *n* (*between countries*) mediatore (di pace), -trice *m, f*; (*between friends*) paciere, -a *m, f*

peacemaking ['piːs·ˌmeɪ·kɪŋ] I. *n* (*between countries*) pacificazione *f*; (*between friends*) riconciliazione *f* II. *adj* (*between countries*) pacificatore, -trice; (*between friends*) conciliatore, -trice

peace march <-es> *n* marcia *f* per la pace

peace movement *n* movimento *m* pacifista

peace negotiations *npl* negoziati *mpl* di pace

peace offer *n* offerta *f* di pace

peace offering *n* pegno *m* di pace

peace pipe *n* calumet *m* della pace *inv*

peace sign *n* segno *m* di pace, *formando una V con indice e medio rivolti verso l'esterno*

peacetime I. *n* tempo *m* di pace II. *adj* del tempo di pace

peace treaty <-ies> *n* trattato *m* di pace

peach [piːtʃ] I. <-es> *n* 1.(*fruit*) pesca; ~ **orchard** pescheto *m* 2.(*tree*) pesco *m* 3. *fig, inf* (*nice person*) bellezza *f*; **a ~ of a day** una giornata incantevole II. *adj* color pesca

peach tree *n* pesco *m*

peachy ['piː·tʃi] *adj* 1.(*like peaches: smell, taste*) di pesca 2. *inf* (*fine*) **to be** (**just**) ~ andare perfettamente

peacock ['piː·kɑːk] *n* 1. ZOOL pavone *m* 2.(*vain person*) vanitoso, -a *m, f* ▸**to strut like a ~** pavoneggiarsi

pea green I. *n* verde *m* pisello II. *adj* verde pisello *inv*

peahen ['piː·hen] *n* pavonessa *f*

peak [piːk] I. *n* 1.(*mountain top*) cima *f*, vetta *f*; **beat the egg whites to stiff** [*o* **firm**] ~**s** montare gli albumi a neve 2.(*highest point, summit*) sommità *f inv*; **to be at the ~ of one's career/power** essere all'apice della carriera/del potere II. *vi* (*career*) raggiungere il punto massimo; (*athlete*) raggiungere il massimo della forma; (*skill*) raggiungere il livello più alto; (*figures, rates, production*) segnare il picco III. *adj* massimo, -a

peak capacity <-ies> *n* capacità *f* massima

peak demand *n* picco *m* della domanda

peaked *adj* (*tired or sick*) malaticcio, -a; (*pale*) pallido, -a

peak hours *npl* ore *fpl* di punta

peak level *n* livello *m* massimo

peak load *n* 1.(*full capacity*) capacità *f* massima 2. ELEC carico *m* massimo

peak period *n* periodo *m* di massima attività

peak power *n* rendimento *m* massimo

peak season *n* alta *f* stagione

peak speed *n* velocità *f* massima

peal [piːl] I. *n* 1.(*sound: of bell*) scampanio *m*; (*of thunder*) fragore *m*; **a ~ of laughter** uno scoppio *m* di risa 2.(*set*) ~ **of bells** carillon *m inv*, concerto *m* di campane II. *vi* (*thunder, thunderstorm*) rumoreggiare; (*bell*) suonare a distesa

◆**peal out** *vi* suonare a distesa; (*thunder*) echeggiare

peanut ['piː·nʌt] *n* 1.(*nut*) nocciolina *f* americana, arachide *f* 2. *inf* (*little money*) **to pay ~s** pagare pochissimo

peanut butter *n* burro *m* di arachidi

pear [per] *n* 1.(*fruit*) pera *f* 2.(*tree*) pero *m*

pearl [pɜːrl] *n* 1. perla *f*; **to wear ~s** portare una collana di perle; **a string of ~s** un filo di perle 2. *fig* (*a drop*) goccia *f*; ~ **of dew** goccia di rugiada; ~**s of sweat** goccia di sudore 3. *fig* (*a fine example*) perla *f*; **a ~ of a ...** una perla di... ▸**to cast one's ~s before the** <u>swine</u> *prov* gettare le perle ai porci *prov*

pearl barley *n* orzo *m* perlato

pearl diver *n* pescatore (-trice) *m(f)* di perle

pearl diving I. *n* pesca *f* delle perle II. *adj* di pesca delle perle

pearl onion *n* cipollina *f*

pearly ['pɜːr·li] <-ier, -iest> *adj* perlaceo, -a; (*teeth*); ~ **whites** *inf* denti; ~ **whites** denti bianchissimi; (*heaven*); **the ~ gates** *fig* le porte del paradiso

pear tree *n* pero *m*

peasant ['pe·zənt] I. *n* 1.(*poor farmer*) contadino, -a *m, f* 2. *pej, inf* (*crude person*) cafone, -a *m, f* II. *adj* contadino, -a, rurale

peasantry ['pe·zənt·ri] *n* classe *f* contadina

pea-souper ['piː·ˌsuː·pɚ] *n* Can, pej (French Canadian) canadese *mf* di lingua francese

peat [piːt] *n* torba *f*

peat bog *n* torbiera *f*

peat moss *n* sfagno *m*

pebble ['pe·bl] *n* ciottolo *m*

pebbly ['peb·li] <-ier- iest> *adj* ciottoloso, -a

pecan [pɪˈkɑːn] *n* pecan *m inv*

peccadillo [ˌpe·kəˈdɪ·loʊ] <-(oe)s> *n* peccatuccio *m*

peck [pek] I. *n* 1.(*of bird*) beccata *f* 2.(*quick kiss*) bacetto *m* II. *vt* 1.(*bird*) beccare 2.(*kiss quickly*) dare un bacetto III. *vi* 1. beccare 2.(*nag*) **to ~ at sb** assillare qu

pecker ['pe·kɚ] *n* vulg (*penis*) uccello *m*, cazzo *m*

pecking order *n* inf ordine *m* di beccata (dei polli); *fig* gerarchia *f*

peckish ['pe·kɪʃ] *adj* **to be ~** avere un (certo) languorino

pectin ['pek·tɪn] *n* pectina *f*

pectoral ['pek·tə·rəl] *adj* pettorale
peculiar [pɪ·'kju:l·jə·] *adj* **1.** (*strange*) strano, -a, insolito, -a **2.** (*belonging to*) caratteristico, -a; **to be ~ to sb/sth** essere tipico di qu/qc
peculiarity [pɪ·ˌkju:·li·'æ·rɪ·ti] <-ies> *n* **1.** (*strangeness*) stranezza *f* **2.** (*strange habit*) singolarità *f* **3.** (*idiosyncrasy*) peculiarità *f*
peculiarly [pɪ·'kju:l·jə·li] *adv* **1.** (*strangely*) stranamente **2.** (*especially*) particolarmente **3.** (*belonging to*) tipicamente
pecuniary [pɪ·'kju:·nie·ri] *adj form* **1.** (*motives*) pecuniario, -a **2.** (*problems*) finanziario, -a
pedagogic [ˌpe·də·'ga:·dʒɪk] *adj* pedagogico, -a
pedagogue ['pe·də·ga:g] *n* pedagogo, -a *m, f*
pedagogy ['pe·də·ga:·dʒi] *n* pedagogia *f*
pedal ['pe·dəl] **I.** *n* pedale *m* **II.** <-l- *o* -ll-, -l- *o* -ll-> *vt* **to ~ a bicycle** spingere una bicicletta pedalando **III.** <-l- *o* -ll-, -l- *o* -ll-> *vi* pedalare
pedal bin *n* pattumiera *f* a pedale
pedal boat *n* moscone *m* a pedali
pedant ['pe·dnt] *n pej* pedante *mf*
pedantic [pə·'dæn·tɪk] *adj pej* pedante
pedantry ['pe·dnt·ri] <-ies> *n* pedanteria *f*
peddle ['pe·dl] *vt* **1.** (*sell*) vendere (da ambulante); **to ~ drugs** spacciare droghe **2.** *pej* (*idea, lies*) spargere
peddler ['ped·lə·] *n* venditore, -trice *m, f* ambulante
pederast ['pe·də·ræst] *n* pederasta *m*
pederasty ['pe·də·ræs·ti] *n* pederastia *f*
pedestal ['pe·dɪs·təl] *n* piedistallo *m* ▶**to knock sb off their ~** fare abbassare la cresta a qu; **to put sb on a ~** mettere su sul piedistallo
pedestrian [pə·'des·tri·ən] **I.** *n* pedone *m* **II.** *adj* **1.** (*for walkers*) pedonale **2.** *form* (*uninteresting*) pedestre
pedestrianize [pə·'des·tri·ə·naɪz] *vt* pedonalizzare
pedestrian mall *n*, **pedestrian zone** *n* zona *f* pedonale
pediatric [ˌpi:·di·'æ·trɪk] *adj* pediatrico, -a
pediatrician [ˌpi:·di·ə·'trɪ·ʃən] *n* MED pediatra *mf*
pediatrics [ˌpi:·dɪ·'æ·trɪks] *n* pediatria *f*
pedicure ['pe·dɪ·kjʊr] *n* pedicure *f*
pedicurist ['pe·dɪ·kjʊ·rɪst] *n* pedicure *mf inv*
pedigree ['pe·dɪ·gri:] **I.** *n* **1.** (*genealogy: of animal*) pedigree *m inv;* (*of person*) lignaggio *f* **2.** (*background*) passato *m* **II.** *adj* (*animal*) di razza
pedometer [pɪ·'da:·mə·tə·] *n* contapassi *m inv,* pedometro *m*
pedophile ['pe·də·faɪl] *n* pedofilo *m*
pee [pi:] *sl* **I.** *n* pipì *f;* **to take a ~** *childspeak* fare (la) pipì; **to go ~** andare a fare la pipì **II.** *vi* fare pipì; **to ~ in one's pants** farsi la pipì addosso **III.** *vt* **to ~ oneself** farsi la pipì addosso
peek [pi:k] **I.** *n* occhiata *f;* **to have a ~ at sth** dare un'occhiata a qc **II.** *vi* **1.** (*look*) mirare furtivamente; **to ~ at sth** sbirciare qc **2.** (*become*

visible) spuntare
◆**peek out** *vi* spuntare (fuori); (*person*) fare capolino
peel [pi:l] **I.** *n* piel *f;* (*of fruit*) buccia *f,* pelle *f;* (*of lemon*) scorza *fpl* **II.** *vt* (*fruit, potato*) sbucciare, pelare; (*paper*) staccare; (*bark*) scortecciare **III.** *vi* (*person*) spellarsi; (*paint, layer of paper*) staccarsi; (*bark*) scortecciarsi
◆**peel off I.** *vt* (*paper*) staccare; (*paint*) scrostare; (*bark*) scortecciare; (*clothes*) togliersi **II.** *vi* **1.** (*come off: paper*) staccarsi; (*paint*) scrostarsi; (*skin*) venire via **2.** (*veer away: car, motorbike*) staccarsi (dal gruppo)
peeler ['pi:·lə·] *n* pelapatate *m inv*
peelings ['pi:·lɪŋz] *npl* (*of fruit*) bucce *fpl*
peep¹ [pi:p] **I.** *n* (*sound: of bird*) pigolio *m;* **to not say a ~** non aprire bocca **II.** *vi* pigolare
peep² [pi:p] **I.** *n* (*furtive look*) sbirciata *f;* **to have a ~ at sth** dare una rapida occhiata a qc **II.** *vi* **1.** (*look quickly*) sbirciare; **to ~ at sth** guardare qc di sfuggita; **to ~ through sth** spiare attraverso qc **2.** (*become visible*) fare capolino **III.** *vt* affacciare
◆**peep out** *vi* affacciarsi
peephole ['pi:p·hoʊl] *n* spioncino *m*
peeping Tom *n* guardone, -a *m, f*
peepshow ['pi:p·ʃoʊ] *n* peep show *inv*
peer¹ [pɪr] *vi* **to ~ at sth** scrutare qc; **to ~ into the distance** fissare lo sguardo in lontananza; **to ~ over one's glasses** osservare al disopra degli occhiali
peer² [pɪr] *n* **1.** (*equal*) pari *mf inv;* **to have no ~s** non avere uguali; LAW; **to be tried by a jury of one's ~s** essere giudicato dai propri pari **2.** (*equal*) pari *mf inv;* (*of the same age*) coetaneo, -a *m, f* **3.** (*lord*) nobile *mf*
peerage ['pɪ·rɪdʒ] *n* **1.** (*title*) **to be given a ~** ricevere un titolo nobiliare **2.** (*aristocracy*) nobiltà (britannica) *f* **3.** (*book*) almanacco *f* nobiliare
peeress ['pɪ·rɪs] <-es> *n* nobildonna (britannica) *f*
peerless ['pɪr·lɪs] *adj* senza pari, incomparabile
peeve [pi:v] *vt inf* scocciare
peeved [pi:vd] *adj inf* scocciato, -a; **to be ~ at sb for sth** essere scocciato con qu per qc
peevish ['pi:·vɪʃ] *adj* stizzoso, -a
peg [peg] **I.** *n* **1.** (*for coat*) gancio *m* dell'attaccapanni **2.** (*in furniture*) piolo *m;* (*for tent*) picchetto *m;* (*for clothes*) molletta *f;* (*on guitar*) bischero *m,* pirolo *m* ▶**to take sb down a ~ or two** ridimensionare qu; **to feel like a square ~ in a round hole** sentirsi come un pesce fuor d'acqua **II.** <-gg-> *vt* **1.** (*hold down tent*) ancorare **2.** ECON fissare; **to ~ prices** stabilizzare i prezzi **3.** (*link*) **to ~ sth to sth** agganciare qc a qc **4.** *inf* (*throw*) lanciare **5.** *fig, inf* (*guess correctly*) **to ~ sb as sth** imbroccarla nel classificare qu come qc
◆**peg away** *vi inf* darci sotto; **to ~ at sth** darci dentro a qc
◆**peg out** *vt* picchettare

peg leg *n inf* gamba *f* di legno

pejorative [pɪ·'dʒɔː·rə·ṭɪv] **I.** *adj* peggiorativo, -a, spregiativo, -a **II.** *n* peggiorativo *m*, spregiativo *m*

Pekinese [ˌpiː·kə·'niːz] **I.** *n* **1.** (*person*) pechinese *mf* **2.** (*dog*) (cane) *m* pechinese **II.** *adj* pechinese

pelican ['pe·lɪ·kən] *n* pellicano *m*

pellet ['pe·lɪt] *n* **1.** (*small ball*) pallina *f* **2.** (*animal excrement*) sterco *m inf* **3.** (*gunshot*) pallottola *f*; (*of shotgun*) pallino *m*

pellet gun *n* fucile *m* a piombini

pell-mell [ˌpel·'mel] *adv* (*hurriedly*) precipitosamente; (*confusedly*) disordinatamente

pelt[1] [pelt] *n* (*animal skin*) pelle *f*; (*fur*) pelliccia *f*

pelt[2] [pelt] **I.** *vt* (*throw*) tempestare; **to ~ sb with stones** prendere qu a sassate **II.** *vi* **1.** (*rain*) scrosciare; **to ~ with rain** piovere a dirotto **2.** (*run, hurry*) fiondarsi; **to ~ after sb** fiondarsi dietro qu **III.** *n* **1.** (*smack*) colpo *m* **2.** (*quick pace*) (gran) velocità *f*; **at full ~** di gran carriera

pelvic ['pel·vɪk] *adj* pelvico, -a

pelvis ['pel·vɪs] <-es> *n* pelvi *f inv*

pen[1] [pen] **I.** *n* (*fountain pen*) penna *f* stilografica; (*ballpoint pen*) biro *f inv*, penna *f* a sfera; **felt-tip ~** pennarello *m*; **to put ~ to paper** prendere la penna in mano ▶**the ~ is mightier than the** <u>sword</u> *prov* ne uccide più la penna che la spada *prov* **II.** <-nn-> *vt* scrivere

pen[2] [pen] **I.** *n* **1.** (*enclosure*) recinto *m*; **pig ~** porcile *m* **2.** *inf* (*jail*) **the ~** la galera **II.** *vt* **to ~ sb/sth in** chiudere qu/qc in un recinto

penal ['piː·nəl] *adj* penale

penal code *n* codice *m* penale

penal institution *n* (istituto) *m* penitenziario

penalize ['piː·nə·laɪz] *vt* penalizzare

penal offense *n* illecito *m* penale

penalty ['pe·nəl·ti] <-ies> *n* **1.** LAW pena *f*; **death ~** pena di morte; **to pay a ~ for sth** essere punito per qc **2.** (*punishment*) punizione *f* **3.** (*fine*) multa *f* **4.** SPORTS (*in soccer*) punizione *f*, (calcio di) rigore *m*

penalty area *n* SPORTS area *f* di rigore

penalty box <-es> *n* (*in ice hockey*) zona a fondo campo dove siedono i giocatori penalizzati

penalty clause *n* clausola *f* penale

penalty kick *n* SPORTS calcio *m* di rigore; **to award a ~** concedere un rigore

penance ['pe·nəns] *n* REL penitenza *f*; **to do ~ for sth** fare penitenza per qc

penchant ['pen·tʃənt] *n* propensione *f*; **to have a ~ for sth** avere una predilezione per qc

pencil ['pen·tsəl] **I.** *n* matita *f*; **colored ~** matita colorata; **a ~ of light** un fascio di luce **II.** <-l- *o* -ll-, -l- *o* -ll-> *vt* scrivere a matita, disegnare a matita

♦**pencil in** *vt* annotare (provvisoriamente)

pencil beam *n* ELEC fascio *m* filiforme

pencil box <-es> *n* astuccio *m*, portamatite *m*

inv

pencil case *n* astuccio *m*, portamatite *m inv*

pencil pusher *n sl* impiegatuccio, -a *m, f*

pencil sharpener *n* temperamatite *m inv*

pencil skirt *n* gonna *f* a tubo

pendant ['pen·dənt] **I.** *n* pendente *m* **II.** *adj* pendente

pendant lamp *n* lampadario *m*

pendent ['pen·dənt] *adj* LAW pendente

pending ['pen·dɪŋ] **I.** *adj* imminente; **~ deal** un accordo imminente; **~ law suit** una causa pendente; **patent ~** in attesa di brevetto **II.** *prep* fino a; **~ further instructions** fino a nuovo ordine

pendulous ['pen·dʒə·ləs] *adj form* pendulo, -a

pendulum ['pen·dʒə·ləm] *n* pendolo *m*

penetrate ['pe·nɪ·treɪt] *vt* **1.** (*move into or through*) penetrare; **to ~ a market** penetrare (in) un mercato **2.** (*spread through, permeate*) impregnare **3.** *fig* (*see through*) capire

penetrating *adj* (*voice, gaze, insight*) penetrante, acuto, -a; (*rain*) che infradicia; (*heat*) intenso, -a; (*cold*) penetrante

penetration [ˌpe·nɪ·'treɪ·ʃən] *n a. fig* penetrazione *f*

penguin ['peŋ·gwɪn] *n* pinguino *m*

penholder ['pen·ˌhoʊl·dəʳ] *n* portapenne *m inv*

penicillin [ˌpe·nɪ·'sɪ·lɪn] *n* penicillina *f*

peninsula [pə·'nɪn·sə·lə] *n* penisola *f*

peninsular [pə·'nɪn·sə·ləʳ] *adj* peninsulare

Peninsular War *n* **the ~** la guerra (napoleonica) di Spagna

penis ['piː·nɪs] <-nises *o* -nes> *n* pene *m*

penitence ['pe·nɪ·təns] *n* REL penitenza *f*

penitent ['pe·nɪ·tənt] REL **I.** *n* penitente *mf* **II.** *adj* pentito, -a

penitential [ˌpe·nɪ·'ten·tʃəl] *adj* penitenziale

penitentiary [ˌpe·nɪ·'ten·tʃə·ri] *n* prigione *f*, penitenziario *m*

penknife ['pen·naɪf] <-knives> *n* temperino *m*, coltellino *m*

penmanship *n* scrittura *f*, calligrafia *f*

pen name *n* pseudonimo *m*

pennant ['pe·nənt] *n* NAUT bandierina *f* (da segnalazione) *m*; SPORT gagliardetto *m*

penniless ['pe·nɪ·lɪs] *adj* squattrinato, -a; **to be ~** essere senza un soldo; **to leave sb ~** lasciare qu nella miseria

pennon ['pe·nən] *n* pennone *m*; (*on lance*) bandierina *f*

Pennsylvania [pen·sɪl·'veɪ·ni·ə] *n* Pennsylvania *f*

penny ['pe·ni] *n* centesimo *m* ▶**a ~ for your** <u>thoughts</u> a cosa stai pensando?; **to earn/cost a** <u>pretty</u> **~** guadagnare/costare mica male; **a ~ saved is a ~** <u>earned</u> *prov* soldo risparmiato soldo guadagnato *prov*; **to** <u>pinch</u> **pennies** essere tirchio

penny-pinching ['pe·ni·ˌpɪn·tʃɪŋ] **I.** *n* spilorceria *f*, tirchieria *f* **II.** *adj* tirchio, -a, spilorcio, -a

pennywhistle *n* zufolo *m*

penny-wise *adj* **to be ~ and pound-foolish** risparmiare sulle piccole spese e sperperare nelle grandi

pen pal *n* amico, -a *m, f* di penna

pension[1] ['pen·ʃən] I. *n* FIN pensione *f;* **to draw a ~** percepire una pensione II. *vt* **to ~ sb off** mettere in pensione qu

pension[2] [pãn·'sjɔ̃ʊ̃ŋ] *n* (*boarding house*) pensione *f*

pensionable ['pen·ʃə·nə·bl] *adj* pensionabile

pensioner ['pen·ʃə·nɚ] *n* pensionato, -a *m, f*

pension fund *n* fondo *m* pensioni

pension plan *n* piano *m* di pensionamento

pensive ['pent·sɪv] *adj* pensoso, -a, pensieroso, -a; **to be in a ~ mood** essere pensieroso

pentagon ['pen·tə·gɑːn] *n* pentagono *m*

> **i** Il **Pentagon** si trova a Arlington, in Virginia, nelle immediate vicinanze di Washington D.C. Viene così chiamato a causa della sua forma a cinque lati. Inaugurato il 15 gennaio 1943, ospita l' *United States Department of Defense* (Segretariato della difesa degli Stati Uniti). Quasi 30.000 persone, tra civili e militari, lavorano in questo edificio, che conta più di 28 km di corridoi.

pentameter [pen·'tæ·mə·tɚ] *n* LIT pentametro *m*

pentathlete [pen·'tæθ·liːt] *n* pentatleta *mf*

pentathlon [pen·'tæθ·lɑːn] *n* pentathlon *m*

Pentecost ['pen·tɪ·kɑːst] *n* REL Pentecoste *f*

penthouse ['pent·haʊs] *n* (*apartment*) appartamento *m* di lusso all'attico

pent-up [ˌpent·'ʌp] *adj* **1.** (*emotion*) represso, -a **2.** (*energy*) accumulato, -a

penultimate [pɪ·'nʌl·tə·mət] I. *n* **the ~** il penultimo, la penultima II. *adj* penultimo, -a

penurious [pə·'nʊ·ri·əs] *adj form* indigente, miserabile

penury ['pen·jʊ·ri] *n form* miseria *f*

peony ['piː·ə·ni] <-ies> *n* peonia *f*

people ['piː·pl] I. *n* **1.** *pl* (*plural of person*) gente *f;* **city/country ~** gente di città/di campagna; **the beautiful ~** la bella gente **2.** (*nation, ethnic group*) popolo *m;* **~'s democracy** democrazia *f* popolare; **~'s republic** repubblica *f* popolare; **the chosen ~** REL il popolo eletto **3.** *pl* (*ordinary citizens*) popolo *m;* **of/by/for the ~** del/dal/per il popolo II. *vt* **~d by** popolato di

people mover *n* (*rail vehicle*) navetta *f;* (*moving sidewalk*) tappeto *m* mobile

pep [pep] I. *n inf* energia *f;* **to be full of ~** essere pieno di energia II. <-pp-> *vt* **to ~ sb up** tirare su qu

pepper ['pe·pɚ] I. *n* **1.** (*spice*) pepe *m;* **black/ white ~** pepe nero/bianco **2.** (*vegetable*) peperone *m* II. *vt* **1.** (*add pepper*) pepare **2.** (*pelt*) **to ~ sb with bullets** crivellare qu di colpi; *fig;* **to ~ sb with questions** tempestare

qu con/di domande **3.** (*contain*) **to be ~ed with sth** (*speech, comments*) essere cosparso di qc; **to be ~ed with mistakes** esere pieno di errori

salt-and-pepper *adj* (*hair*) sale e pepe

peppercorn ['pe·pɚ·kɔːrn] *n* grano *m* di pepe

pepper mill *n* macinapepe *inv*

peppermint ['pe·pɚ·mɪnt] *n* **1.** (*mint plant*) menta *f* (piperita) **2.** (*sweet*) caramella *m* alla menta

peppermint tea *n* tè *m* di menta

peppershaker *n* pepaiola *f*

peppery ['pe·pə·ri] *adj* **1.** GASTR pepato [*o* piccante] **2.** *fig* (*irritable person*) irritabile *inv;* (*irritable thing*) irritante *inv*

pep pill *n inf* pillola *f* eccitante

pep talk *n inf* **to give sb a ~** fare un discorsetto di incoraggiamento a qu

peptic ['pep·tɪk] *adj* peptico, -a

peptic ulcer *n* ulcera *f* peptica

per [pɜːr] *prep* **1.** (*for a*) per; **$5 ~ pound/ hour** $5 (al)la libbra/(al)l'ora **2. 100 miles ~ hour** 100 miglia all'ora **3.** *form* (*as stated in*) in base a; (*as*) **~ account** come da conto; **as ~ usual** come al solito

per annum *adv* all'anno

per capita I. *adv* pro capite II. *adj* **~ consumption** consumo *m* pro capite; **~ income** reddito *m* pro capite

perceivable [pɚ·'siː·və·bl] *adj* percepibile

perceive [pɚ·'siːv] *vt* **1.** (*see*) vedere; (*sense*) percepire, notare; **to ~ that ...** notare che ... **2.** (*view, regard*) considerare; **how do the Peruvians ~ the Nicaraguans?** i peruviani come vedono i nicaraguensi? **3.** (*understand*) capire

percent [pɚ·'sent] *n* percentuale *f;* **25 ~** 25 per cento; **what ~ ...** che percentuale ...?

percentage [pɚ·'sen·tɪdʒ] *n* **1.** (*proportion*) proporzione *f;* **what ~ ...?** che percentuale ...?; **to get a ~ of sth** ricevere un tanto per cento di qc **2.** (*advantage*) vantaggio *m inf* ▶ **to play the ~s** valutare le possibilità

percentage point *n* punto *m* percentuale

perceptible [pɚ·'sep·tə·bl] *adj* percettibile

perception [pɚ·'sep·ʃən] *n* **1.** percezione *f* **2.** (*idea*) idea *f* **3.** (*insight*) intuito *m*

perceptive [pɚ·'sep·tɪv] *adj* perspicace, acuto, -a

perch[1] [pɜːrtʃ] I. <-es> *n* **1.** (*for birds*) trespolo *m* **2.** (*high location or position*) posizione *f* privilegiata ▶ **to knock sb off his ~** fare abbassare le arie a qu II. *vi* (*person, bird*) appollaiarsi

perch[2] [pɜːrtʃ] *n* (*fish*) perca *f*

percolate ['pɜːr·kə·leɪt] I. *vt* filtrare; (*coffee*) preparare II. *vi* **1.** (*filter through*) filtrare **2.** *fig* (*spread*) diffondersi

percolator ['pɜːr·kə·leɪ·tɚ] *n* caffettiera *f* a filtro

percussion [pɚ·'kʌ·ʃən] I. *n* MUS percussione *f;* **to play ~** essere percussionista II. *adj* MUS di percussione

percussionist *n* MUS percussionista *mf*
perdition [pə·'dɪ·ʃən] *n* **1.** *liter* (*hell*) perdizione *f* **2.** *fig* (*state of ruin*) rovina *f*
peregrine ['pe·rɪ·ɡrɪn] *n* peregrino, -a *m, f*
peregrine falcon *n* falco *m* pellegrino
peremptorily *adv* in tono perentorio, perentoriamente
peremptory [pə·'remp·tə·ri] *adj* **1.** (*person*) autoritario, -a; (*order, tone*) perentorio, -a, imperioso, -a **2.** LAW perentorio, -a
perennial [pə·'re·ni·əl] **I.** *n* pianta *f* perenne **II.** *adj* **1.** BOT perenne **2.** (*constant*) costante
perfect[1] ['pɜːr·fɪkt] **I.** *adj* perfetto, -a; (*calm*) totale; (*opportunity*) ideale; (*silence*) assoluto, -a; in ~ **condition** in perfette condizioni; **the ~ crime** il delitto perfetto; **a ~ gentleman** un vero signore; **to be a ~ stranger** essere un perfetto estraneo; **to have the ~ right to do sth** avere tutto il diritto di fare qc; **to be far from ~** essere (molto) lontano dalla perfezione; **to be a ~ match for sth** stare benissimo con qc; **to be a ~ match for sb** essere l'anima gemella di [*o* essere fatto su misura per] **II.** *n* LING (tempo) *m* perfetto
perfect[2] [pɜːr·'fekt] *vt* perfezionare
perfectible [pə·'fek·tə·bəl] *adj* perfettibile
perfection [pə·'fek·ʃən] *n* perfezione *f*; **to do sth to ~** fare qc alla perfezione
perfectionist *n* perfezionista *mf*
perfectly *adv* perfettamente; ~ **clear** perfettamente chiaro; ~ **happy** contentissimo; **to be ~ honest, ...** per essere del tutto sincero, ...; **to be ~ right** avere perfettamente ragione
perfidious [pə·'fɪ·di·əs] *adj* *liter* perfido, -a; ~ **attack** attacco *m* a tradimento
perforate ['pɜːr·fə·reɪt] *vt* perforare; (*ticket*) forare
perforated *adj* perforato, -a; **to have a ~ eardrum** avere un timpano perforato
perforation [ˌpɜːr·fə·'reɪ·ʃən] *n* perforazione *f*
perform [pə·'fɔːrm] **I.** *vt* **1.** THEAT, TV (*play*) rappresentare [*o* dare]; THEAT, TV (*part*) interpretare; MUS eseguire **2.** (*do, accomplish*) compiere; **to ~ one's duty/a function** svolgere un compito/una funzione; **to ~ miracles/ wonders** fare miracoli/prodigi; **to ~ a task** eseguire un compito; **to ~ a trick** fare un trucco **3.** INFOR, MED eseguire **4.** SPORTS praticare **II.** *vi* **1.** THEAT recitare; MUS esibirsi **2.** (*operate*) funzionare
performance [pə·'fɔːr·mənts] *n* **1.** (*of play*) rappresentazione *f*; (*by individual actor*) interpretazione *f*; **to give a ~ of a play** mettere in scena un'opera teatrale **2.** SPORTS prova *f*; **high/ low ~** AUTO alto/basso rendimento *m*
performance art *n* performance *f* art
performance level *n* **1.** (*degree of success*) nivel *m* de rendimiento **2.** ECON (*output*) rendimiento *m*
performance report *n* informe *m* de rendimiento
performer [pə·'fɔːr·mə] *n* **1.** THEAT artista *mf*;

star ~ estrella *f*. **2.** (*achiever*) top ~ (*at work*) empleado, -a *m, f* modelo; **bad** ~ (*at school*) mal(a)studente/studentessa *mf*; (*at work*) mal(a) lavoratore, a *m, f*
perfume ['pɜːr·fjuːm] **I.** *n* **1.** (*scented liquid*) profumo *m*; ~ **maker** profumiere, -a *m, f*; **to put on** ~ mettersi il profumo **2.** (*fragrance*) fraganza *f* **II.** *vt* profumare
perfunctory [pə·'fʌŋk·tə·ri] *adj* (*inspection*) superficiale; (*reading, mention*) frettoloso, -a; (*greeting, smile*) di circostanza; (*examination*) pro forma
pergola ['pɜːr·ɡə·lə] *n* pergola *f*
perhaps [pə·'hæps] *adv* forse
peril ['pe·rəl] *n* form pericolo *m*; **to be in** ~ essere in pericolo; **at one's** ~ a suo rischio e pericolo; **at** [*o* in] ~ **of sth** in pericolo di qc; **the ~s of sth** i pericoli di qc
perilous ['pe·rə·ləs] *adj* form pericoloso, -a
perimeter [pə·'rɪ·mə·tə] *n* perimetro *m*
perimeter fence *n* recinto *m*
period ['pɪ·ri·əd] **I.** *n* **1.** *a.* GEO periodo *m*; **in/ over a ~ of sth** nel (corso di un) periodo di qc **2.** ECON scadenza *f*; **a fixed** ~ una scadenza fissa; ~ **of grace** [*o* **grace** ~] periodo *m* di grazia **3.** SCHOOL (*lesson*) (ora di) lezione *f* **4.** (*distinct stage*) epoca *f* **5.** (*menstruation*) mestruazione *f*; **to have one's** ~ avere le mestruazioni **6.** LING punto *m* **II.** *interj* punto e basta *inf*
period furniture *n* mobili *m pl* d'epoca
periodic [ˌpɪ·ri·'ɑː·dɪk] *adj* periodico, -a
periodical [ˌpɪ·ri·'ɑː·dɪ·kl] **I.** *n* (*general*) periodico *m*; (*specific*) bollettino *m* **II.** *adj* periodico, -a
periodic table *n* tavola *f* periodica degli elementi
peripheral [pə·'rɪ·fə·rəl] **I.** *adj* **1.** (*importance, role*) secondario, -a **2.** *a.* ANAT, INFOR periferico, -a **II.** *n* INFOR periferica *f*
periphery [pə·'rɪ·fə·ri] <-ies> *n* periferia *f*; (*of society*) margine *m*
periscope ['pe·rɪs·koup] *n* periscopio *m*
perish ['pe·rɪʃ] *vi liter* (*die*) perire; (*disappear: motivation, hope*) svanire; ~ **the thought!** si spera proprio di no!
perishable ['pe·rɪ·ʃə·bl] *adj* deperibile
peritonitis [ˌpe·rɪ·tə·'naɪ·tɪs] *n* MED peritonite *f inv*
perjure ['pɜːr·dʒə] *vt* **to ~ oneself** giurare il falso
perjurer ['pɜːr·dʒə·ə] *n* spergiuro, -a *m, f*
perjury ['pɜːr·dʒə·ri] *n* falsa *f* testimonianza
perk [pɜːrk] *n inf abbr of* **perquisite 1.** (*advantage*) vantaggio *m* **2.** extra *mpl*
 ◆ **perk up I.** *vi* **1.** (*cheer up*) rallegrarsi; **to ~ at sth** rallegrarsi per qc **2.** (*improve*) riprendersi **II.** *vt* **1.** (*cheer up*) tirare su; (*make more lively*) rianimare **2.** (*raise*) **to ~ one's ears** drizzare le orecchie
perky ['pɜːr·ki] <-ier, -iest> *adj* vispo, -a
perm [pɜːrm] **I.** *n inf* (*permanent wave*) permanente *f* **II.** *vt* **to ~ one's hair, to have one's hair ~ed** farsi la permanente

permafrost ['pɜːr·mə·frɑːst] *n* permafrost *m*
permanence ['pɜːr·mə·nənts] *n*, **permanency** *n* permanenza *f*, continuità *f*
permanent ['pɜːr·mə·nənt] *adj* (*job*) fisso, -a; (*damage*) irreparabile; (*exhibition, state, position*) permanente; (*ink*) indelebile; (*relationship*) stabile; (*tooth*) permanente
permanent wave *n* permanente *f*
permanganate [pə·'mæŋ·gə·neɪt] *n* permanganato *m*
permeable ['pɜːr·mi·ə·bl] *adj* permeabile
permeate ['pɜːr·mi·eɪt] I. *vt* (*liquid, smoke, smell*) impregnare II. *vi* to ~ into/through sth penetrare in/attraverso qc
permissible [pə·'mɪ·sə·bl] *adj* (*permitted*) consentito; (*acceptable*) ammissibile
permission [pə·'mɪ·ʃən] *n* permesso *m*
permission slip *n* SCH autorizzazione *f* dei genitori
permissive [pə·'mɪ·sɪv] *adj* permissivo, -a
permissiveness *n* permissivismo *m*, permissività *f*
permit[1] ['pɜːr·mɪt] *n* work/parking ~ permesso di lavoro/di parcheggio *m;* building/fishing ~ licenza edilizia/di pesca; learner's ~ foglio *m* rosa; to hold a ~ avere un permesso
permit[2] [pə·'mɪt] <-tt-> I. *vt* permettere; I will not ~ you to go there non ti permetto di andarci; to ~ oneself sth concedersi qc II. *vi* weather ~ing se fa bel tempo, tempo permettendo; if time ~s se c'è tempo; the law ~s of no other interpretation *form* la legge non ammette altre interpretazioni
permitted [pə·'mɪ·ţɪd] *adj* permesso, -a
permutation [ˌpɜːr·mjuː·'teɪ·ʃən] *n form* MAT permutazione *f*
pernicious [pə·'nɪ·ʃəs] *adj* 1. *form* (*harmful*) pernicioso, -a 2. MED pernicioso, -a
pernicious anemia *n* anemia *f* perniciosa
peroxide [pə·'rɑːk·saɪd] I. *n* perossido *m;* hydrogen ~ acqua *f* ossigenata II. *vt* ossigenare
peroxide blonde *n* bionda *f* ossigenata
perp [pɜːrp] *n sl abbr of* **perpetrator** autore, -trice *m, f, di un delitto*
perpendicular [ˌpɜːr·pən·'dɪ·kjuː·lə·] I. *adj* perpendicolare II. *n* perpendicolare *f*
perpetrate ['pɜːr·pə·treɪt] *vt* (*crime*) perpetrare, commettere; (*error*) commettere
perpetration [ˌpɜːr·pə·'treɪ·ʃən] *n form* esecuzione *f*
perpetrator ['pɜːr·pə·treɪ·ţə·] *n* autore, -trice *m, f, di un delitto*
perpetual [pə·'pe·tʃu·əl] *adj* 1. (*lasting forever*) perpetuo, -a 2. (*repeated*) continuo, -a
perpetuate [pə·'pe·tʃu·eɪt] *vt* perpetuare
perpetuity [ˌpɜːr·pə·'tuː·ə·ţi] *n form* perpetuità *f;* in ~ a. LAW in perpetuo
perplex [pə·'pleks] *vt* sconcertare
perplexed [pə·'plekst] *adj* perplesso, -a
perplexity [pə·'plek·sə·ţi] <-ies> *n* perplessità *f*

perquisite ['pɜːr·kwɪ·zɪt] *n* extra *m inv*
persecute ['pɜːr·sɪ·kjuːt] *vt* 1. *a.* POL perseguitare 2. (*harass*) molestare
persecution [ˌpɜːr·sɪ·'kjuː·ʃən] *n* persecuzione *f;* ~ complex mania *f* di persecuzione
persecutor *n* persecutore, -trice *m, f*
perseverance [ˌpɜːr·sə·'vɪ·rəns] *n* perseveranza *f*
persevere [ˌpɜːr·sə·'vɪr] *vi* perseverare
persevering *adj* perseverante
Persia ['pɜːr·ʒə] *n* Persia *f*
Persian I. *adj* persiano, -a II. *n* 1. (*person*) persiano, -a *m, f* 2. LING persiano *m*
Persian Gulf *n* Golfo *m* Persico
persist [pə·'sɪst] *vi* 1. (*continue: cold, heat, rain*) continuare; (*habit, belief, doubts*) persistere 2. (*person*) insistere
persistence [pə·'sɪs·təns] *n* 1. (*of cold, belief*) persistenza *f* 2. (*of person*) insistenza *f*
persistent [pə·'sɪs·tənt] *adj* 1. (*cold, belief*) persistente 2. (*person*) insistente
persnickety [pə·'snɪ·kə·ţi] *adj pej* 1. (*exacting*) pignolo, -a; to be ~ about sth essere pignolo in qc 2. (*difficult*) intricato, -a
person ['pɜːr·sən] <people *o form* -s> *n* 1. (*human*) persona *f;* about [*o* on] one's ~ su di sé [*o* con sé]; as a ~ come persona; per ~ per persona 2. LING persona *f;* first/second ~ prima/seconda persona
persona [pə·'sou·nə] *n* 1. <-s *o* -nae> (*character*) personaggio *m* 2. <-s> PSYCH (*image*) personalità *f* esteriore
personable ['pɜːr·sə·nə·bl] *adj* di bell'aspetto
personage ['pɜːr·sə·nɪdʒ] *n form* personaggio *m*
personal ['pɜːr·sə·nəl] *adj* 1. (*property*) privato, -a; (*data, belongings, account*) personale 2. (*direct, done in person*) personale [*o* in persona] 3. (*private: letter*) riservato, -a; (*question*) personale; (*matter*) privato, -a, personale; (*life*) privato, -a 4. (*offensive: comment, remark*) offensivo, -a; to get ~ mettere le cose sul piano personale; it's nothing ~ non è niente di personale 5. (*bodily, physical: appearance*) personale; (*hygiene*) personale 6. (*human*) ~ quality qualità *f* umana
personal assistant *n* assistente *mf* personale
personal computer *n* personal *m* (computer) *inv*
personality [ˌpɜːr·sə·'næ·lə·ţi] *n* <-ies> 1. (*character*) personalità *f* 2. (*famous person*) personalità *f*, celebrità *f*
personally *adv* 1. (*in person*) personalmente [*o* in persona] 2. (*as offensive*) to take sth ~ offendersi per qc [*o* prendere qc sul piano personale] 3. (*refering to oneself*) personalmente; ~, I don't think it matters per conto mio non credo che abbia importanza 4. (*refering to sb's character*) personalmente; I respect him but don't like him ~ lo rispetto, ma come persona non mi piace; she's not involved with him ~ lei non ha una relazione con lui

P

personal pronoun *n* pronome *m* personale

personalty ['pɜːr·sə·nəl·ti] <-ies> *n* beni *mpl* mobili

personification [pə·ˌsɑː·nɪ·fɪ·'keɪ·ʃən] *n* personificazione *f;* **he is the ~ of kindness** è la gentilezza in persona

personify [pə·'sɑː·nɪ·faɪ] *vt* personificare

personnel [ˌpɜːr·sə·'nel] *n* **1.** *pl* (*staff, employees*) personale *m* **2.** (*department*) departamento *m* del personale

personnel department *n* ufficio *m* del personale

personnel director *n* direttore, -trice *m, f* del personale

personnel manager *n* capo, -a *m, f* del personale

perspective [pə·'spek·tɪv] *n* prospettiva *f;* **you have to keep things in ~** non si deve perdere il senso delle proporzioni; **to put a different ~ on things** vedere le cose da un altro punto di vista

perspicacious [ˌpɜːrs·pɪ·'keɪ·ʃəs] *adj form* perspicace

perspicacity [ˌpɜːrs·pɪ·'kæ·sə·ti] *n form* perspicacia *f*

perspicuity [ˌpɜːrs·pɪ·'kju·ə·ti] *n form* perspicuità *f*

perspicuous [pəs·'pɪ·kju·əs] *adj form* perspicuo, -a

perspiration [ˌpɜːrs·pə·'reɪ·ʃən] *n* traspirazione *f* [*o* perspirazione] *f* [*o* sudorazione] *f;* **beads of ~** gocce *f pl* di sudore

perspire [pəs·'pa·ɪə] *vi* sudare

persuade [pə·'sweɪd] *vt* convincere

persuasion [pə·'sweɪ·ʒən] *n* **1.** (*act*) persuasione *f* **2.** (*conviction*) convinzione *f*

persuasive [pə·'sweɪ·sɪv] *adj* (*person, manner*) persuasivo, -a; (*argument*) convincente

pert [pɜːrt] *adj* **1.** (*nose*) all'insù; **~ breasts** seni piccoli e sodi **2.** (*reply*) impertinente **3.** (*hat*) sbarazzino, -a

pertain [pə·'teɪn] *vi* **to ~ to sth** riguardare qc

pertinent ['pɜːrt·nənt] *adj* pertinente; **to be ~ to sth** riguardare qc

perturb [pə·'tɜːrb] *vt* perturbare

perturbation [ˌpɜːr·tə·'beɪ·ʃən] *n form* perturbazione *f*

Peru [pə·'ruː] *n* Perú *m*

perusal [pə·'ruː·zl] *n form* lettura *f;* **he sent a copy of the report for their ~** ha inviato copia della relazione perché la esaminassero

peruse [pə·'ruːz] *vt form* (*read*) leggere accuratamente; (*examine*) esaminare

Peruvian [pə·'ruː·vi·ən] **I.** *adj* peruviano, -a **II.** *n* peruviano, -a *m, f*

pervade [pə·'veɪd] *vt* (*attitude, idea*) pervadere; (*smell, smoke*) pervadere

pervasive [pə·'veɪ·sɪv] *adj* (*attitude, idea*) pervasivo, -a; (*influence*) onnipresente; (*smell*) penetrante

perverse [pə·'vɜːrs] *adj* **1.** (*deviant, perverted*) perverso, -a **2.** (*stubborn*) ostinato, -a

3. (*contrary*) avverso, -a

perverseness *n* **1.** (*deviancy*) perversità *f* **2.** (*stubbornness*) caparbietà *f* **3.** (*contrariness*) contraddizione *f*

perversion [pə·'vɜːr·ʒən] *n* **1.** (*sexual deviance*) perversione *f* **2.** (*corruption*) **~ of justice** parodia *f* della giustizia; **~ of the truth** distorsione *f* della verità

perversity [pə·'vɜːr·sə·ti] <-ies> *n* **1.** (*wickedness*) perversione *f* **2.** (*stubbornness*) caparbietà *f*

pervert[1] ['pɜːr·vɜːrt] *n* (*sexual deviant*) pervertito, -a *m, f*

pervert[2] [pə·'vɜːrt] *vt* alterare; (*meaning*) svisare; **to ~ the truth** distorcere la verità

perverted *adj* (*person, practice*) perverso, -a

peseta [pə·'seɪ·tə] *n* peseta *f*

peso ['peɪ·soʊ] *n* peso *m*

pessary ['pe·sə·ri] <-ies> *n* **1.** (*device*) pessario *m* **2.** (*vaginal suppository*) suppositorio *m* vaginale

pessimism ['pe·sə·mɪ·zəm] *n* pessimismo *m*

pessimist *n* pessimista *mf*

pessimistic [ˌpe·sə·'mɪs·tɪk] *adj* pessimista; **to be ~ about sth** essere pessimista su qc/ riguardo a qc

pest [pest] *n* **1.** (*destructive insect, animal*) animale *m* nocivo **2.** *inf* (*annoying person*) peste *f*

pest control *n* (*of insects*) disinfestazione *f;* (*of rats*) derattizzazione *f*

pester ['pes·tə] *vt* infastidire

pesticide ['pes·tə·saɪd] *n* pesticida *m*

pestiferous [pe·'stɪ·fə·rəs] *adj* pestifero

pestilent ['pes·tə·lənt] *adj,* **pestilential** [ˌpes·tə·'len·tʃəl] *adj* **1.** (*deadly*) pestilenziale **2.** (*troublesome*) pestifero, -a

pestle ['pe·sl] *n* pestello *m*

pet [pet] **I.** *n* **1.** (*house animal*) animale [*o* domestico] da compagnia *m* **2.** *pej* (*favorite person*) preferito, -a *m, f;* **he's the teacher's ~** è il preferito dell'insegnante **II.** *adj* **1.** (*cat, dog, snake*) domestico, -a **2.** (*favorite: project, theory*) preferito, -a **III.** <-tt-> *vi* sbaciucchiarsi **IV.** <-tt-> *vt* **1.** (*caress*) coccolare [*o* accarezzare] **2.** (*pamper*) viziare

petal ['pe·tl] *n* BOT petalo *m*

petard [pɪ·'tɑːrd] *n* **he was** <u>hoisted</u> **by his own ~** *prov* è caduto nella sua stessa trappola

peter ['piː·tə] *vi* **to ~ away** [*o* out] (*trail, track, path*) perdersi; (*conversation, flame*) languire; (*interest*) andare calando

Peter ['piː·tə] **to rob ~ to pay** <u>Paul</u> *prov* fare un debito per pagarne un altro *prov*

petite [pə·'tiːt] *adj* minuto, -a

petition [pə·'tɪ·ʃən] **I.** *n* **1.** POL petizione *f* **2.** LAW istanza *f* **II.** *vi* **1.** POL **to ~ for sth** fare una petizione per qc **2.** LAW **to ~ for divorce** presentare istanza di divorzio **III.** *vt* POL fare una petizione a

petitioner *n* **1.** POL richiedente *mf* **2.** LAW (*for divorce*) attore, -trice *m, f*

petrel ['pet·rəl] *n* procellaria *f*

petri dish ['pi:t·ri·ˌdɪʃ] *n* capsula *f* di Petri
petrifaction [ˌpet·rɪ·'fæk·ʃən] *n*, **petrification** [ˌpet·rɪ·fɪ·'keɪ·ʃən] *n* **1.** GEO pietrificazione *f* **2.** (*terror*) terrore *m*
petrified *adj* **1.** GEO pietrificato, -a **2.** (*terrified*) terrorizzato, -a
petrify ['pet·rɪ·faɪ] <-ies> **I.** *vi* GEO pietrificarsi [*o* silicizzarsi] **II.** *vt* **1.** GEO pietrificare [*o* silicizzare] **2.** (*terrify*) terrorizzare
petrochemical [ˌpet·roʊ·'ke·mɪ·kəl] **I.** *n* prodotto *m* petrolchimico **II.** *adj* petrolchimico, -a
petrodollar ['pet·roʊ·ˌdɑː·lə·] *n* petrodollaro *m*
gas can *n* tanica *f* di benzina
petroleum [pə·'troʊ·li·əm] *n* petrolio *m* (greggio), greggio *m*
pipeline *n* oleodotto *m*
gas pump *n* pompa *f* (di benzina)
gas station *n* stazione *f* di rifornimento, distributore *m* (di benzina)
pet shop *n* negozio *m* di animali domestici
petticoat ['pe·tɪ·koʊt] *n* sottoveste *f*
pettifogging ['pe·tɪ·fɑː·gɪŋ] *adj pej* (*person*) cavilloso, -a; (*paperwork*) farraginoso, -a; (*details*) insignificante
pettiness ['pe·tɪ·nəs] *n* **1.** (*small-mindedness*) meschinità *f* **2.** (*triviality, insignificance*) piccolezza *f*
petting ['pe·tɪŋ] *n* (*stroking*) carezze *fpl;* (*sexual*) petting *m*
petting zoo *n* zoo in cui si possono toccare e carezzare gli animali
petty ['pe·tɪ] <-ier, -iest> *adj* **1.** *pej* (*detail, amount*) trascurabile, insignificante; (*person, attitude*) meschino, -a **2.** LAW minore
petty cash *n* piccola *f* cassa
petty larceny *n* LAW furto *m* di cose di poco valore
petty officer *n* NAUT sottuffuciale *mf* di marina
petulant ['pe·tʃə·lənt] *adj* stizzoso, -a
petunia [pə·'tu:n·jə] *n* petunia *f*
pew [pju:] *n* banco *m* (di chiesa)
pewit ['pi:·wɪt] *n* pavoncella *f*
pewter ['pju:·tə·] *n* peltro *m*
PG *n abbr of* **parental guidance** *film per minori accompagnati*
pg. *abbr of* **page** pag. [*o* p.]
pH [ˌpi:·'eɪtʃ] pH *m*
phalanx ['feɪ·læŋks] <-es *o* phalanges> *n form* falange *f*
phallic ['fæ·lɪk] *adj* fallico, -a
phallus ['fæ·ləs] <-es *o* phalli> *n* fallo *m*
phantasmal [fæn·'tæz·məl] *adj liter* **1.** (*imaginary*) immaginario, -a **2.** (*ghost-like*) fantasmatico, -a
phantom ['fæn·təm] **I.** *n* fantasma *m* **II.** *adj* **1.** (*ghostly*) fantasmatico, -a **2.** (*imaginary*) immaginario, -a
Pharaoh ['fe·roʊ] *n* faraone *m*
pharisaic(al) [ˌfe·rɪ·'seɪ·ɪ·k(əl)] *adj* farisaico, -a
pharisee ['fe·rɪ·si:] *n* fariseo, -a *m, f*
pharmaceutic [ˌfɑː·r·mə·'su:·tɪk] *adj* farmaceutico, -a
pharmaceutical **I.** *adj* farmaceutico, -a **II.** *n pl* farmaci *mpl*
pharmaceutics *n* farmacia *f*
pharmaceutics industry *n* industria *f* farmaceutica
pharmacist ['fɑː·r·mə·sɪst] *n* farmacista *mf*
pharmacology [ˌfɑː·r·mə·'kɑː·lə·dʒi] *n* farmacologia *f*
pharmacopoeia [ˌfɑː·r·mə·'koʊ·'pi:·ə] *n* farmacopea *f*
pharmacy ['fɑː·r·mə·si] <-ies> *n* farmacia *f*
pharyngitis [ˌfæ·rɪn·'dʒaɪ·tɪs] *n* faringite *f*
pharynx ['fæ·rɪŋks] <pharynges> *n* faringe *f*
phase [feɪz] **I.** *n* (*stage*) fase *f;* **to go through a ~** attraversare una fase; **to be in ~** essere in fase; **to be out of ~** essere fuori fase **II.** *vt* **1.** (*do in stages*) realizzare per stadi **2.** (*coordinate*) sincronizzare
♦ **phase in** *vt* introdurre per gradi
♦ **phase out** *vt* (*service*) abolire per gradi; (*product*) cessare per gradi la produzione di
PhD [ˌpi:·eɪtʃ·'di:] *n abbr of* **Doctor of Philosophy 1.** (*award*) dottorato *m* di ricerca **2.** (*person*) Dott. *mf*
pheasant ['fe·zənt] <-(s)> *n* fagiano *m*
phenomena *n pl of* **phenomenon**
phenomenal *adj* (*success, achievement*) fenomenale
phenomenon [fə·'nɑː·mə·nɑːn] <phenomena *o* -s> *n* fenomeno *m*
phew [fju:] *interj inf* (*relief*) oh!; (*heat*) uffa!
vial ['va·rəl] *n* fiala *f*
philander [fɪ·'læn·də·] *vi* essere un donnaiolo
philanderer *n* donnaiolo *m*
philanthropic [ˌfɪ·læn·'θrɑː·pɪk] *adj* filantropico, -a
philanthropist [fə·'læn·θrə·pɪst] *n* filantropo, -a *m, f*
philanthropy [fə·'læn·θrə·pi] *n* filantropia *f*
philatelic [fɪ·lə·'te·lɪk] *adj* filatelico, -a
philatelist [fɪ·'læ·tə·lɪst] *n* filatelico, -a *m, f*
philately [fɪ·'læ·tə·li] *n* filatelia *f*
philharmonic [ˌfɪl·hɑː·r·'mɑː·nɪk] *adj* filarmonico, -a
Philippines ['fɪ·lə·pi:nz] *npl* **the ~** le Filippine
philistine ['fɪ·lɪs·ti:n] *pej* **I.** *n* filisteo, -a *m, f* **II.** *adj* beota
philological [ˌfɪ·lə·'lɑː·dʒɪ·kl] *adj* filologico, -a
philologist [fɪ·'lɑː·lə·dʒɪst] *n* filologo, -a *m, f*
philology [fɪ·'lɑː·lə·dʒi] *n* filologia *f*
philosopher [fɪ·'lɑː·sə·fə·] *n* filosofo, -a *m, f*
philosophic(al) [ˌfɪ·lə·'sɑː·fɪ·k(əl)] *adj* filosofico, -a
philosophize [fɪ·'lɑː·sə·faɪz] *vi* filosofare
philosophy [fɪ·'lɑː·sə·fi] *n* filosofia *f*
philter *n*, **philtre** ['fɪl·tə·] *n* filtro *m*
phlebitis [flɪ·'baɪ·tɪs] *n* MED flebite *f inv*
phlegm [flem] *n* (*substance*) muco *m;* (*calmness*) flemma *f*
phlegmatic [fleg·'mæ·tɪk] *adj* flemmatico, -a
phobia ['foʊ·bi·ə] *n* PSYCH fobia *f*
phoenix ['fi:·nɪks] *n* fenice *f*
phone [foʊn] **I.** *n* telefono *m;* **to hang up the ~** riattaccare; **to pick up the ~** alzare il

ricevitore; **by** ~ per telefono; **to be on the** ~ essere al telefono **II.** *vt* telefonare a, chiamare (al telefono) **III.** *vi* telefonare, chiamare (al telefono)

◆ **phone around** *vi* fare delle chiamate

◆ **phone back** *vt* ritelefonare a, richiamare

◆ **phone in I.** *vi* telefonare, chiamare (per telefono); **to** ~ **sick** telefonare per darsi malato **II.** *vt* telefonare a, chiamare al telefono

◆ **phone up** *vt* telefonare a, chiamare (al telefono)

phone book *n* elenco *m* telefonico

phone booth <-es> *n* cabina *f* telefonica

phone call *n* telefonata *f,* chiamata *f* (telefonica)

phone card *n* carta *f* telefonica, scheda *f* telefonica, tessera *f* telefonica

phone-in *n programma a cui radioascoltatori o telespettatori partecipano telefonicamente*

phoneme ['foʊ·niːm] *n* LING fonema *m*

phone number *n* numero *m* di telefono

phonetic [fə·'ne·t̪ɪk] *adj* fonetico, -a; **the International Phonetic Alphabet** l'alfabeto fonetico internazionale; ~ **transcription** trascrizione *f* fonetica

phonetician [ˌfoʊ·nə·'tɪ·ʃən] *n* fonetista *mf*

phonetics [fə·'ne·t̪ɪks] *n* fonetica *f*

phoney ['foʊ·ni] *adj, n s.* **phony**

phonic ['fɑː·nɪk] *adj* LING fonico, -a

phonology [fə·'nɑː·lə·dʒi] *n* fonologia *f*

phony ['foʊ·ni] **I.** <-ier, -iest> *adj inf* (*person, address, documents*) falso, -a; (*smile*) finto, -a **II.** *n* (*person*) bugiardo, -a *m, f*

phooey ['fuː·i] *interj inf* col cavolo!

phosphate ['fɑːs·feɪt] *n* fosfato *m*

phosphorescence [ˌfɑːs·fə·'re·sns] *n* fosforescenza *f*

phosphorescent [ˌfɑːs·fə·'re·sənt] *adj* fosforescente

phosphoric [fɑːs·'fɔː·rɪk] *adj,* **phosphorous** ['fɑːs·fə·rəs] *adj* fosforico, -a

phosphorus ['fɑːs·fə·rəs] *n* fosforo *m*

photo ['foʊ·t̪oʊ] <-s> *n inf abbr of* **photograph** foto *f inv*

photo album *n* album *m* di fotografie

photo call *n* opportunità *f* di essere fotografato

photocell ['foʊ·t̪oʊ·sel] *n* cellula *f* fotoelettrica, fotocellula *f*

photocopier [ˌfoʊ·t̪oʊ·'kɑː·piɚ] *n* fotocopiatrice *f*

photocopy ['foʊ·t̪oʊ·ˌkɑː·pi] **I.** <-ies> *n* fotocopia *f;* **to make a** ~ **of sth** fare una fotocopia di qc **II.** *vt* fotocopiare

photocopying store *n* fotocopisteria *f*

photoelectric [ˌfoʊ·t̪oʊ·ɪ·'lek·trɪk] *adj* fotoelettrico, -a; ~ **cell** cellula *f* fotoelettrica, fotocellula *f*

photo finish *n* SPORTS fotofinish *m inv*

photoflash *n* flash *m inv*

photogenic [ˌfoʊ·t̪oʊ·'dʒe·nɪk] *adj* fotogenico, -a

photograph ['foʊ·t̪oʊ·græf] **I.** *n* fotografia *f;* **aerial** ~ fotografia aerea; **color/black-and-**

white ~ fotografia a colori/in bianco e nero; **to take a** ~ **of sb** fare una fotografia a qu **II.** *vt* fotografare **III.** *vi* **to** ~ **well** essere fotogenico

photograph album *n* album *m* di fotografie *inv*

photographer [fə·'tɑː·grə·fɚ] *n* fotografo, -a *m, f;* **amateur** ~ fotografo(-a) dilettante; ~ **'s model** modello, -a *m, f*

photographic [ˌfoʊ·t̪ə·'græ·fɪk] *adj* fotografico, -a

photography [fə·'tɑː·grə·fi] *n* fotografia *f*

photojournalism [ˌfoʊ·t̪oʊ·'dʒɜːrn·lɪ·zəm] *n* fotogiornalismo *m*

photojournalist *n* fotogiornalista *mf*

photometer [foʊ·'tɑː·mɪ·t̪ɚ] *n* fotometro *m*

photomontage [ˌfoʊ·t̪oʊ·mɑːn·'tɑːʒ] *n* fotomontaggio *m*

photon ['foʊ·t̪ɑːn] *n* fotone *m*

photo opportunity *n* opportunità *f* di essere fotografato

photo reporter *n* fotocronista *mf,* fotoreporter *mf inv*

photosensitive [ˌfoʊ·t̪oʊ·'sen·sə·t̪ɪv] *adj* fotosensibile

photosetting ['foʊ·t̪oʊ·ˌse·t̪ɪŋ] *n* ART fotocomposizione *f*

Photostat ['foʊ·t̪oʊ·stæt] <-tt-> **I.** *n* fotocopiatrice; ~ **copy** copia fotostatica **II.** *vt* fotocopiare

photosynthesis [ˌfoʊ·t̪oʊ·'sɪn·θɪ·sɪs] *n* fotosintesi *f*

phrasal verb [ˌfreɪ·zəl·'vɜːrb] *n* LING verbo *m* frasale

phrase [freɪz] **I.** *n* frase *f;* (*idiomatic expression*) espressione *f;* **verb/noun phrase** sintagma verbal/nominal; **to have a good turn of** ~ essere molto eloquente **II.** *vt* **to** ~ **sth well/badly** esprimere bene/male qc

phrase book *n* libro *m* delle locuzioni

phraseology [ˌfreɪ·zi·'ɑː·lə·dʒi] *n* fraseologia *f*

phrenetic [frɪ·'ne·t̪ɪk] *adj s.* **frenetic**

pH factor *n* valore *m* del pH

phys ed [ˌfɪz·'ed] *n abbr of* **physical education** educazione *f* fisica

physical ['fɪ·zɪ·kəl] **I.** *adj* fisico, -a; ~ **attraction** attrazione *f* fisica; **to be in poor** ~ **condition** essere in condizioni fisiche non molto buone; **to have a** ~ **disability** avere un'invalidità fisica; ~ **exercise** esercizio *m* fisico **II.** *n* MED visita *f* medica

physical education *n* educazione *f* fisica

physically *adv* (*attractive*) fisicamente; (*dangerous*) dal punto di vista fisico

physical therapist *n* fisioterapista *mf*

physical therapy *n* fisioterapia *f*

physician [fɪ·'zɪ·ʃən] *n* medico, -a *m, f*

physicist ['fɪ·zɪ·sɪst] *n* fisico, -a *m, f;* (*student*) studente *mf* di fisica

physics ['fɪ·zɪks] **I.** *n* fisica *f* **II.** *adj* di fisica

physiognomy [ˌfɪ·zi·'ɑː·nə·mi] *n* fisionomia *f*

physiological [ˌfɪ·ziə·'lɑː·dʒɪ·kəl] *adj* fisiologico, -a

physiologist *n* fisiologo, -a *m, f;* (*student*) studente *mf* de fisiologia

physiology [ˌfɪ·zi·'ɑː·lə·dʒi] *n* fisiologia *f*

physique [fɪ·'ziːk] *n* fisico *m*

pianist ['piː·æ·nɪst] *n* pianista *mf*

piano [pi·'æ·noʊ] <-s> *n* piano(forte) *m;* **to play the** ~ suonare il piano(forte)

piazza [pɪ·'ɑːt·sə] *n* piazza *f*

picaresque [ˌpɪ·kə·'resk] *adj* LIT picaresco, -a

piccolo ['pɪ·kə·loʊ] <-s> *n* ottavino *m*

pick [pɪk] I. *vt* 1. (*select*) scegliere; **to** ~ **sth at random** scegliere qc a caso; **to** ~ **a fine time to do sth** *iron* scegliere proprio il momento giusto per fare qc; **to** ~ **one's way** stare attento a dove si mettono i piedi 2. (*harvest: fruit, vegetables*) cogliere 3. (*remove*) togliere; **to** ~ **one's nose** mettersi le dita nel naso; **to** ~ **one's teeth** stuzzicarsi i denti; **to** ~ **holes in sth** *fig* trovare difetti in qc 4. MUS (*guitar*) pizzicare [*o* suonare] 5. (*steal*) **to** ~ **a lock** scassinare una serratura; **to** ~ **sb's pocket** borseggiare qu; **to** ~ **sb's brains** *fig* chiedere lumi a qu 6. (*provoke*) **to** ~ **a fight** (**with sb**) attaccare briga (con qu) II. *vi* **to** ~ **and choose** essere selettivo III. *n* 1. (*selection*) scelta *f;* **to take one's** ~ scegliere; **to have one's** ~ avere la scelta; **the** ~ **of the bunch** il migliore del gruppo 2. (*pickax*) piccone *m;* **with** ~**s and shovels** con piccone e pala 3. (*for teeth*) stuzzicadenti *m inv*

◆**pick at** *vt insep* 1. (*toy with: food*) spilluzzicare 2. (*bone*) spolpare; (*sore, spot*) grattare 3. (*criticize*) **to** ~ **sb/sth** prendersela con qu/ qc

◆**pick off** *vt* 1. (*shoot*) abbattere (uno dopo l'altro) 2. *fig* (*take the best*) scegliersi il migliore 3. (*pull off*) separare; **to pick an apple off the tree** staccare una mela dall'albero

◆**pick on** *vt insep* 1. (*victimize*) prendersela con 2. (*select*) **to** ~ **sb for sth** scegliere qu per qc

◆**pick out** *vt* 1. (*choose*) selezionare 2. (*recognize*) riconoscere

◆**pick over** *vt* selezionare

◆**pick up** I. *vt* 1. (*lift*) tirare su, sollevare [*o* alzare]; **to** ~ **the phone** alzare il ricevitore [*o* prendere il telefono]; **to pick oneself up** rimettersi in piedi [*o* tirarsi su]; **to pick oneself up off the floor** risollevarsi; **to** ~ **the pieces** *fig* raccogliere i cocci 2. (*get*) prendere; (*conversation*) attaccare discorso; **to** ~ **a bargain** trovare un buona occasione; **to** ~ **an illness** prendersi una malattia; **to** ~ **speed** acquistare velocità; **to** ~ **the bill** [*o* **tab**] *inf* pagare il conto 3. (*collect: item*) ritirare; (*person*) (andare a) prendere; **to pick sb up** (*bus*) prendere qu 4. (*buy*) acquistare (a poco prezzo) 5. (*detect: noise*) individuare; (*signal*) captare 6. (*learn*) apprendere 7. *inf* (*sexually*) **to pick sb up** rimorchiare qu 8. *inf* (*halt*) fermare; (*arrest*) fermare; **the police picked him up for speeding** la polizia lo ha fermato per eccesso di velocità 9. *inf* (*earn*) guadagnare II. *vi* 1. (*improve*) migliorare; MED riprendersi

2. (*continue*) continuare; **to** ~ **where one left off** ricominciare da dove si è lasciato; **she picked up and left** ha preso su e se n'è andata

pickax *n*, **pickaxe** ['pɪ·kæks] *n* piccone *m*

picker *n* raccoglitore, -trice *m, f*

picket ['pɪ·kɪt] I. *n* 1. (*stake*) picchetto *f* 2. (*striker*) *a.* MIL picchetto *m* II. *vt* (*in strike*) picchettare

picket fence *n* steccato *m*

picket line *n* picchetto (di scioperanti) *m;* **to be on the** ~ far parte di un picchetto; **to cross the** ~ forzare un picchetto

picking *n* selezione *f*

pickings ['pɪ·kɪŋz] *npl* guadagni *fpl*

pickle ['pɪ·kl] I. *n* 1. (*pickled item*) sottaceto *m* 2. (*pickled cucumber*) cetriolo *m* sottaceto ▶**to be in a** (**pretty**) ~ *inf* essere in un (bel) pasticcio II. *vt* (*in vinegar*) conservare sottaceto; (*fish*) conservare in salamoia

pickled *adj* 1. (*in vinegar*) sottaceto; (*in brine*) in salamoia 2. *fig, sl* (*drunk*) sbronzo, -a; **to get** ~ sbronzarsi

picklock ['pɪk·lɑːk] *n* 1. (*thief*) scassinatore, -trice *m, f* 2. (*instrument*) grimaldello *m*

pick-me-up *n inf* tonico *m;* (*drink*) bevanda *f* stimolante

pickpocket ['pɪk·ˌpɑː·kɪt] *n* borsaiolo, -a *m, f,* borseggiatore, -trice *m, f*

pickup *n* 1. *inf* (*collection*) raccolta *f* 2. (*increase*) ripresa; **a** ~ **in sales/orders/ activity** una ripresa nelle vendite/ordinazioni/attività 3. (*pickup truck*) pick-up *m inv* 4. (*part of record player*) pick-up *m inv* 5. *sl* (*partner for sex*) conquista *f* facile

pickup point *n* punto *m* di raccolta

pickup truck *n* pick-up *m inv*

picky ['pɪ·ki] <-ier, -iest> *adj inf* difficile; **to be a** ~ **eater** essere schizzinoso nel mangiare

picnic ['pɪk·nɪk] I. *n* picnic *m inv;* **to take a** ~ fare un picnic; **to go on a** ~ andare a fare un picnic; **to be a** ~ essere piacevole; **to be no** ~ *fig* non essere [*o* una cosa da niente] una passeggiata II. <-ck-> *vi* fare un picnic

picnicker *n* partecipante *mf* a un picnic

picnic lunch *n* picnic *m*

picnic site *n* area *f* per picnic

pictogram ['pɪk·tə·græm] *n* pittogramma *m*

pictorial [pɪk·'tɔː·ri·əl] *adj* (*form, method*) pittorico, -a; (*book, brochure*) illustrato, -a

picture ['pɪk·tʃɚ] I. *n* 1. (*image*) immagine *f;* (*painting*) dipinto *m;* (*in book*) illustrazione *f;* (*drawing*) disegno *m;* **to draw a** ~ fare un disegno; **to paint a** ~ dipingere un quadro; **as pretty as a** ~ bello come una cartolina 2. (*photo*) foto(grafia) *f;* **to take a** ~ fare una foto(grafia); **satellite** ~ fotografia [*o* immagine] dal satellite 3. (*film*) film *m inv;* **to make a** ~ fare un film; (*cinema*) cinema(tografo) *m inv;* **to go to the** ~**s** andare al cinema 4. (*mental image*) immagine *f* mentale 5. *fig* (*description*) rappresentazione *f;* **to paint a** ~ **of sth** fare una descrizione di qc; **to paint a very black** ~ fare un quadro molto nero ▶**a** ~ **is**

worth a thousand <u>words</u> *prov* un'immagine vale più di mille parole; **to <u>be</u> in the ~** essere al corrente; **to <u>get</u> the ~** capire; **to <u>keep</u> sb in the ~** tenere qu al corrente; **to <u>put</u> sb in the ~** mettere qu al corrente **II.** *vt* (*imagine*) immaginare, immaginarsi; (*depict*) ritrarre; **to ~ oneself** ... immaginare sé stesso ...

picture book *n* libro *m* illustrato

picture frame *n* cornice *f*

picture gallery *n* pinacoteca *f*

moviegoer *n* cinefilo, -a *m, f*

picture library *n* fototeca *f*

picture postcard *n* cartolina *f* (illustrata)

picture puzzle *n* puzzle *m inv*

picturesque [ˌpɪk·tʃə·'resk] *adj* **1.** (*scenic*) pittoresco, -a **2.** (*language*) pittoresco, -a, colorito, -a

picture tube *n* cinescopio *m*

picture window *n* finestra *f* panoramica

piddle ['pɪ·dl] *inf* **I.** *n* pipì *f* **II.** *interj* accidenti! **III.** *vi* **1.** (*urinate*) fare la pipì **2.** (*waste time*) **to ~ around** gingillarsi

piddling ['pɪd·lɪŋ] *adj inf* insignificante; **the ~ sum of $5** la misera somma di 5 dollari

pidgin ['pɪ·dʒɪn] *n* LING pidgin *m inv*

pie [paɪ] *n* (*vegetables, meat*) pasticcio *m* (in crosta); (*fruit*) crostata *f*, torta *f* ► **it's ~ in the <u>sky</u>** resterà una pia intenzione; **(as) <u>easy</u> as ~** un gioco da ragazzi; **to eat <u>humble</u> ~** andare a Canossa, cospargersi il capo di cenere

piebald ['paɪ·bɔːld] *adj* pezzato, -a

piece [piːs] *n* **1.** (*small unit: of wood, metal, bread*) pezzo *m*; (*smaller*) pezzetto *m*; **a ~ of land** un appezzamento di terreno; **a ~ of paper** (*scrap*) un pezzo di carta; (*sheet*) un foglio; **in one ~** (tutto)intero; **in ~s** a pezzi; **to break sth to/in ~s** fare a pezzi qc; **to tear sth into ~s** stracciare qc; **(all) in one ~** (*not damaged*) incolume; **~ by ~** pezzo per pezzo; **to go (all) to ~s** (*collapse, break*) crollare **2.** (*item, one of set*) unità *f*; **~ of luggage** collo *m*; **~ of clothing** indumento *m* **3.** (*in games*) pezzo *m* **4.** (*with mass nouns*) **a ~ of advice** un consiglio; **a ~ of evidence** una prova; **a ~ of information** un'informazione; **a ~ of news** una notizia **5.** ART, MUS pezzo *m*, brano *m;* PUBL annuncio *m;* **a ~ of writing** uno scritto **6.** (*coin*) moneta *f*; **a 50 cent ~** una moneta da 50 centesimi **7.** *sl* (*gun*) **to carry a ~** avere una pistola ► **to get a ~ of the <u>action</u>** (*profits*) avere una fetta della torta; (*excitement*) passare bene; **to be a ~ of <u>cake</u>** *inf* essere facilissimo; **to want a ~ of the <u>pie</u>** volere un pezzo della torta; **to give sb a ~ of one's <u>mind</u>** *inf* dirne quattro a qu; **to <u>say</u> one's ~** dire la propria

♦ **piece together** *vt* mettere insieme; (*reconstruct*) ricostruire; **to ~ evidence** ricostruire la verità in base alle prove

piecemeal ['piːs·miːl] **I.** *adv* a pezzi e bocconi **II.** *adj* frammentario, -a

piece number *n* numero *m* di pezzi

piece price *n* prezzo *m* per unità

piece rate *n* prezzo *m* per unità

piecework ['piːs·wɜːrk] *n* lavoro *m* a cottimo; **to do ~** lavorare a cottimo

pieceworker *n* cottimista *mf*

pied [paɪd] *adj* variopinto, -a

pie-eyed [ˌpaɪ·'aɪd] *adj inf* (*drunk*) **to be ~** essere ciucco tradito

pier [pɪr] *n* **1.** (*at the water*) molo *m,* banchina *f* **2.** ARCHIT (*pillar*) piedritto *m;* (*buttress*) contrafforte *m*

pierce [pɪrs] **I.** *vt* (*perforate*) perforare; (*skin*) trafiggere; **to ~ a hole in sth** fare un buco in qc; **to have one's ears ~d** farsi fare i buchi alle orecchie **II.** *vi* (*drill*) **to ~ into sth** penetrare in qc; **to ~ through sth** attraversare qc

piercing I. *adj* **1.** (*wind*) penetrante; (*cold*) pungente **2.** (*eyes, gaze, look*) penetrante; (*question, reply, wit*) pungente; (*sarcasm*) acuto, -a **3.** (*cry*) lacerante **II.** *n* piercing *m inv*

piety ['paɪ·ə·t̬i] *n* pietà *f*

piffle ['pɪ·fl] *n inf* stupidaggini *fpl*

piffling ['pɪf·lɪŋ] *adj inf* insignificante

pig [pɪg] *n* **1.** ZOOL maiale *m*, porco *m* **2.** *inf* (*person*) maiale, -a *m, f;* **to be a ~** essere un maiale; **to be a ~ to sb** comportarsi da cafone con qu **3.** *pej, sl* (*policeman*) sbirro *m;* **the ~s** la pula, la madama ► **to buy/sell a ~ in a <u>poke</u>** comprare/vendere a scatola chiusa; **to <u>make</u> a ~ of oneself** mangiare come un porco

♦ **pig out** <-gg-> *vi inf* mangiare come un porco; **to ~ out on sth** abbuffarsi di qc

pigeon ['pɪ·dʒən] *n* **1.** (*bird*) piccione *m* **2.** *fig* (*easy prey*) merlo *m*

pigeonhole ['pɪ·dʒən·houl] **I.** *n* casella *f;* **to put sb in a ~** etichettare qu **II.** *vt* **to ~ sb/sth** classificare qu/qc; **to ~ sb as sth** etichettare qu come qc

pigeon-toed ['pɪ·dʒən·toud] *adj* **to be ~** avere il piede varo

piggery ['pɪ·gə·ri] <-ies> *n* **1.** AGR porcile *m* **2.** (*gluttony*) golosità *f*

piggish ['pɪ·gɪʃ] *adj* (*in manners*) grossolano, -a; (*greedy*) ingordo, -a

piggy ['pɪ·gi] <-ies> *n childspeak* porcellino, -a *m, f,* maialino, -a *m, f*

piggyback ['pɪ·gi·bæk] *n* **to carry sb/ride ~** portare qu/far fare un giro a cavalluccio a qu; **to give a child a ~ ride** far fare un giro a cavalluccio a un bambino

piggy bank *n* salvadanaio *m, a forma di maialino*

pigheaded [ˌpɪg·'he·dɪd] *adj* testardo, -a

pig iron *n* ghisa *f* grezza

pig Latin *n gergo infantile ottenuto con l'inversione dell'ordine dei suoni di ogni parola e con l'aggiunta alla fine del suono 'ai'. Esempio: "he likes meat" = "i:hel alkslel i:tmel"*

piglet ['pɪg·lɪt] *n* maialino *m*, porcellino *m*

pigment ['pɪg·mənt] *n* pigmento *m*

pigmentation [ˌpɪg·men·'teɪ·ʃən] *n* pigmentazione *f*

Pigmy ['pɪg·mi] **I.** <-ies> *n* **1.** (*short person*) pigmeo, -a *m, f* **2.** (*unimportant person*) pigmeo, -a *m, f* II. *adj* ZOOL nano, -a

pigskin ['pɪg·skɪn] *n* **1.** (*leather*) pelle *f* di cinghiale **2.** *inf* (*a football*) pallone *m* da football americano

pigsty ['pɪgs·taɪ] *n a. fig, pej* porcile *m*

pigswill ['pɪgs·wɪl] *n* imbratto *m; fig* schifezza *f*

pigtail ['pɪg·teɪl] *n* (*one of two braids*) treccina *f;* **to have one's hair in ~s** portare le treccine

pike¹ [paɪk] *n* (*fish*) luccio *m*

pike² [paɪk] *n* (*weapon*) picca *f*

pike³ [paɪk] *n* (*highway*) autostrada *f*

pilaster [pɪ·'læs·tə·] *n* pilastro *m*

pilchard ['pɪl·tʃə·d] *n* sardina *f*

pile [paɪl] I. *n* **1.** (*stack*) pila *f* **2.** (*heap*) mucchio *m;* **to have ~s of sth** *inf* avere un mucchio di qc; **to make a ~** *fig, inf* fare un mucchio di soldi **3.** ELEC pila *f* **4.** ARCHIT pilastro *m* **5.** (*of carpet*) pelo *m* II. *vt* (*to stack*) impilare; (*to heap*) ammucchiare; **to ~ sth high** ammucchiare una gran quantità di qc

◆**pile in** *vi* ~**!** tutti dentro!

◆**pile on** *vt* **1.** (*enter*) accalcarsi per entrare **2.** (*heap*) aggiungere; **to pile sth on sth** aggiungere qc sopra qc **3.** *inf* (*exaggerate*) **to** (**really**) **pile it on** esagerare

◆**pile up** I. *vi* **1.** (*accumulate*) accumularsi **2.** (*form a pile*) accatastarsi II. *vt* accumulare

pile driver *n* battipalo *m*

piles *npl inf* emorroidi *fpl*

pileup ['paɪl·ʌp] *n* tamponamento *m*

pilfer ['pɪl·fə·] *vt* rubacchiare

pilfering *n* piccolo *m* furto

pilgrim ['pɪl·grɪm] *n* pellegrino, -a *m, f*

pilgrimage ['pɪl·grɪ·mɪdʒ] *n* pellegrinaggio *m*

pill [pɪl] *n* **1.** pillola *f*, pastiglia *f*, compressa *f;* **the ~** (*contraception*) la pillola; **to be on the ~** prendere la pillola; **to pop ~s** impasticcarsi **2.** *inf* (*pesky person*) rompiscatole *mf inv* ▶**to be a** bitter **~ to swallow** essere duro da mandar giù; **to** sweeten [*o* sugar] **the ~** indorare la pillola

pillage ['pɪ·lɪdʒ] I. *vt* saccheggiare II. *vi* compiere un saccheggio III. *n* saccheggio *m*

pillar ['pɪ·lə·] *n* **1.** ARCHIT pilar *m*, pilastro *m*, colonna *f;* **a ~ of flame/smoke** una colonna di fiamme/fumo **2.** *fig* (*of support*) sostegno *m;* **to be a ~ of strength** essere una roccia; **a ~ of society** un pilastro della società ▶**to chase sb from ~ to** post mandare qu da Erode a Pilato

pillbox ['pɪl·ba:ks] *n* **1.** (*for tablets*) portapillole *m inv* **2.** MIL casamatta *f*

pillion ['pɪl·jən] I. *n* (*on motorcycle*) sellino *m* posteriore II. *adv* **to ride/sit ~** viaggiare/sedersi dietro

pillory ['pɪ·lə·ri] I.<-ie-> *vt* **to ~ sb/sth** mettere in ridicolo qu/qc II. *n* gogna *f*

pillow ['pɪ·loʊ] *n* **1.** (*for bed*) cuscino *m*, guanciale *m* **2.** (*cushion*) cuscino *m*

pillowcase *n*, **pillow cover** *n*, **pillowslip** *n* federa *f*

pilot ['paɪ·lət] I. *n* **1.** AVIAT pilota *mf* **2.** NAUT pilota *mf* **3.** TV episodio *m* pilota **4.** TECH (*flame*) fiammella *f* pilota II. *vt* **1.** (*plane*) pilotare **2.** (*boat*) pilotare **3.** COM (*product*) sperimentare; **to ~ a bill** pilotare una legge

pilot boat *n* pilotina *f*

pilot burner *n* **1.** (*on boiler*) fiammella *f* pilota **2.** (*flame*) fiammella *f* pilota

pilot fish *n* pesce *m* pilota

pilothouse *n* NAUT timoniera *f*

flight instructor *n* istruttore, -trice *m, f* di volo

pilotless *adj* senza pilota

pilot light *n* fiammella *f* pilota

pilot plant *n* impianto *m* pilota

pilot program *n* TV episodio *m* pilota

pilot's license *n* licenza *f* di volo

pilot study *n* studio *m* pilota

pilot survey *n* studio *m* sperimentale

pilot test *n* prova *f* pilota

pimento [pɪ·'men·toʊ] <-s> *n* peperone *m* rosso dolce

pimp [pɪmp] I. *n* protettore (di prostitute) *m*, magnaccia *m* II. *vi* fare il protettore [*o* magnaccia]

pimple ['pɪm·pl] *n* foruncolo *m*

pimply ['pɪmp·li] <-ier, -iest> *adj* pieno, -a di foruncoli

pin [pɪn] I. *n* **1.** (*needle*) spillo *m;* MIL (*on grenade*) linguetta *f* di sicurezza; **tie ~** fermacravatta *m inv* **2.** (*brooch*) spilla *f* **3.** *pl, fig* (*legs*) gambe *fpl* ▶**to have ~s and** needles avere un formicolio; **you could have heard a ~** drop non si sentiva volare una mosca II.<-nn-> *vt* **1.** (*attach using pin*) **to ~ sth on** appuntare qc con uno spillo; **to ~ back one's ears** *fig* aprire bene le orecchie **2.** (*associate with: crime*) **to ~ sth on sb** addossare la responsabilità di qc a qu

◆**pin down** *vt* **1.** (*define*) definire con precisione **2.** (*locate*) localizzare **3.** (*pressure to decide*) **to ~ sb to a particular date** impegnare qu per una certa data **4.** (*restrict movement*) immobilizzare

◆**pin together** *vt* unire; **to pin papers together** spillare insieme dei fogli

◆**pin up** *vt* (*attach using pins*) appuntare; (*on the wall*) appendere; **to ~ one's hair** tirarsi su i capelli

PIN [pɪn] *n abbr of* **personal identification number** pin *m* (*codice numerico personale*)

pinafore ['pɪ·nə·fɔːr] *n* **1.** (*apron*) grembiule *m* **2.** (*dress*) scamiciato *m*

pinafore dress *n* scamiciato *m*

pinball ['pɪn·bɔːl] *n* **to play ~** giocare a flipper

pinball machine *n* flipper *m inv*

pincers ['pɪn·sə·z] *npl* **1.** ZOOL chele *fpl* **2.** (*tool*) tenaglie *fpl*

pinch [pɪntʃ] I. *vt* **1.** (*with fingers*) pizzicare; **to ~ oneself** *fig* darsi dei pizzicotti (per accertarsi che non si sta sognando) **2.** (*be too tight*) essere troppo stretto; **the shoes ~ my feet** le scarpe mi vanno strette **3.** *inf* (*steal*) fregare *inf* II. *vi* **1.** (*with fingers*) stringere **2.** (*boots, shoes, slippers*) essere stretto III. *n* **1.** (*nip*)

P

pizzicotto *m;* **to give sb a ~** dare un pizzicotto a qu; **in a ~** se così ha da essere; **to feel the ~** sentire gli effetti negativi **2.** (*small quantity*) pizzico *m*

pinched [pɪntʃt] *adj* emaciato, -a

pincushion ['pɪn·ˌku·ʃən] *n* puntaspilli *m inv*

pine¹ [paɪn] *n* (*tree, wood*) pino *m*

pine² [paɪn] *vi* **1.** (*waste away*) **to ~** (**away**) deperire **2.** (*long for*) **to ~ for sb** sospirare per la mancanza di qu

pineal ['pɪ·ni·əl] *adj* pineale

pineal gland *n* ghiandola *f* pineale

pineapple ['paɪn·æ·pl] *n* ananas *m inv*

pinecone *n* pigna *f*

pine forest *n* foresta *f* di pini

pine grove *n* pineta *f*

pine needle *n* ago *m* di pino

pine nut *n* pinolo *m*

pine tree *n* pino *m*

ping [pɪŋ] **I.** *n* (*sound: of bell*) din(din) *m;* (*of glass, metal*) tic *m* **II.** *vi* fare din; (*click*) fare tic

pinfeather *n* spuntone *m* di penna

Ping-Pong® ['pɪŋ·ˌpɑːŋ] *n inf* ping-pong *m*

pinhead ['pɪn·hed] *n* **1.** (*part of pin*) capocchia *f* di spillo **2.** *inf* (*simpleton*) cervello *m* di gallina

pinhole *n* forellino *m* (di spillo)

pinion¹ ['pɪn·jən] *vt* **1.** (*bird*) tarpare le ali a **2.** (*hold down*) immobilizzare; **she was ~ed against the wall** era inchiodata al muro

pinion² ['pɪn·jən] *n* TECH pignone *m*

pink [pɪŋk] **I.** *n* **1.** (*color*) rosa *m* **2.** BOT garofano *m* ▶ **to be in the ~** essere in perfetta forma **II.** *adj* (di colore) rosa

pinkie ['pɪŋ·ki] *n inf* mignolo *m*

pinking shears *npl* forbici *fpl* per dentellare

pinko ['pɪŋ·koʊ] <-s *o* -es> *n pej* POL sinistroide *mf*

pink slip *n* lettera *f* di licenziamento

pinnacle ['pɪ·nə·kl] *n* **1.** ARCHIT (*tower*) pinnacolo *m* **2.** (*of mountain*) vetta *f* **3.** *fig* apice *m*

pinpoint ['pɪn·pɔɪnt] **I.** *vt* (*location, reason*) individuare (con esattezza); **to ~ the cause of sth** determinare la causa di qc **II.** *adj* preciso, -a; **~ accuracy** precisione assoluta

pinprick ['pɪn·prɪk] *n pl* puntura *f* di spillo; *fig* seccatura *f*

pinstripe ['pɪn·straɪp] **I.** *adj* gessato, -a **II.** *n* (*stripe*) righina *f;* (*suit*) abito *m* (in tessuto) gessato

pint [paɪnt] *n* pinta *f* (*0,47 l*); **a ~ of beer/ milk** una pinta di birra/latte

pintsize(d) ['paɪn·tsaɪz(d)] *adj inf* minuscolo, -a

pinup ['pɪn·ʌp] *n* **1.** (*poster*) poster *m* (*di una celebrità*) **2.** (*man*) bello *m* da calendario; (*girl*) pin-up(-girl) *f*

pioneer [ˌpaɪ·ə·'nɪr] **I.** *n* pioniere, -a *m, f; fig* pioniere, -a *m, f* **II.** *vt* essere il pioniere in qc

pioneering *adj* pionieristico, -a

pious ['pa·ɪəs] *adj* **1.** REL pio, -a **2.** *iron* pio, -a; **~ intentions** pie intenzioni; **~ fraud** bugia

pietosa

pip¹ [pɪp] *n* BOT seme *m*

pip² [pɪp] **I.** *n* (*sound*) bip *m* **II.** <-pp-> *vi* (*hatch*) rompere il guscio (dell'uovo)

pipe [paɪp] **I.** *n* **1.** TECH (*tube*) tubo *m;* (*smaller*) canna *f;* (*for gas, water*) conduttura *f,* tubatura *f* **2.** (*for smoking*) pipa *f;* **to light one's ~** accendersi la pipa; **put that in your ~ and smoke it** *fig* beccati questa! **3.** MUS (*wind instrument*) zufolo *m,* piffero *m;* (*in organ*) canna *f;* **~s** cornamusa *f,* zampogna *f* **II.** *vt* **1.** (*transport*) trasportare mediante tubazioni; **to ~ music in** diffondere musica con altoparlanti in luoghi pubblici **2.** (*speak shrilly*) pronunciare con voce acuta **III.** *vi* cinguettare; (*very loudly*) parlare a voce alta

◆**pipe down** *vi inf* (*be quiet*) abbassare la voce; (*become quieter*) calmarsi

◆**pipe up** *vi* farsi sentire

pipe cleaner *n* scovolino *m inv*

pipe dream *n* idea *f* campata in aria

pipe fitter *n* tubista *mf;* (*plumber*) idraulico, -a *m, f*

pipeline ['paɪp·laɪn] *n* (*oil*) oleodotto *m;* (*natural gas*) gasdotto *m;* (*methane*) metanodotto *m;* **to be in the ~** *fig* essere in cantiere

piper ['paɪ·pɚ] *n* suonatore, -trice di cornamusa *m* ▶ **he who pays the ~ calls the** tune *prov* chi paga comanda

piping ['paɪ·pɪŋ] *n* **1.** FASHION profilo *m* **2.** (*pipes*) tubazione *f*

piping hot *adv* bollente

pip-squeak ['pɪp·skwiːk] *n inf* nullità *f*

piquant ['piː·kənt] *adj* **1.** (*food*) saporito, -a **2.** (*intriguing*) intrigante

pique [piːk] **I.** *n* stizza *f* **II.** *vt* **1.** (*annoy*) offendere **2.** (*arouse*) **to ~ sb's curiosity/interest** stuzzicare la curiosità/l'interesse di qu

piracy ['paɪ·rə·si] *n* NAUT, COM pirateria *f;* **software ~** pirateria *f* di software

pirate ['paɪ·rət] **I.** *n* pirata *m* **II.** *adj* pirata; **~ copy** copia *f* pirata; **~ video** video *m* pirata **III.** *vt* pirateggiare

pirouette [ˌpɪ·ru·'et] **I.** *n* piroetta *f* **II.** *vi* fare piroette

Pisces ['paɪ·siːz] *n* Pesci *m*

piss [pɪs] *vulg* **I.** *n* piscio *m; vulg* piscia *f; vulg;* **to take a ~** fare una pisciata; **to have to take a ~** avere bisogno di pisciare **II.** *vi* pisciare **III.** *vt* **to ~ one's pants** pisciarsi addosso

◆**piss off** *vulg sl* **I.** *vi ~!* (*go away*) fuori dalle palle! **II.** *vt* **to piss sb off** (*make angry*) fare incazzare qu

pissed [pɪst] *adj vulg sl,* **pissed off** *adj sl* **to be ~** (*angry*) essere incazzato

pistachio [pɪ·'stæ·ʃioʊ] <-s> *n* pistacchio *m*

pistil ['pɪs·tɪl] *n* pistillo *m*

pistol ['pɪs·təl] *n* pistola *f;* **to hold a ~ to sb's head** *fig* mettere qu con le spalle al muro

pistol shot *n* colpo *m* di pistola

piston ['pɪs·tən] *n* TECH pistone *m*

piston engine *n* motore *m* a pistoni

piston ring *n* fascia *f* elastica

pit¹ [pɪt] I. *n* **1.** (*in ground*) fossa *f;* (*on metal*) scalfittura *f;* (*on face*) segno *m;* **in the ~ of one's stomach** alla bocca dello stomaco **2.** (*in a mine*) pozzo *m;* (*coal mine*) miniera *m* di carbone; (*chalk, gravel*) cava *f;* **to go down the ~** scendere in miniera; **to work in the ~s** lavorare in miniera; *fig* REL; **the ~** l'inferno **3.** **the ~s** *pl, fig, inf* il peggio che ci sia **4.** *inf* (*messy place*) casino *m* **5.** THEAT (*seating area*) platea *f;* (*orchestral area*) golfo *m* mistico **6.** **the ~s** *pl* SPORTS i box II. <-tt-> *vt* **to be ~ted** (**with sth**) avere segni (causati da qc)

pit² [pɪt] <-tt-> I. *n* (*of fruit*) nocciolo *m* II. *vt* GASTR snocciolare

pita (**bread**) ['pi:·tə] *n* pane *m* arabo

pitapat ['pɪ·ṭə·pæt] *adv, n s.* **pitterpatter**

pitch¹ [pɪtʃ] I. *n* **1.** (*in baseball: field*) campo *m;* (*in baseball: throw*) lancio *m,* tiro *m* **2.** (*in cricket*) terreno *m* (di gioco) **3.** (*movement of ship*) beccheggio *m* **4.** (*slope*) grado *m* di inclinazione; **low/steep ~** inclinazione *f* lieve/pronunciata **5.** (*volume*) volume *m;* **to be at fever ~** essere molto eccitato **6.** MUS, LING tono *m* **7.** (*spiel*) imbonimento *m;* **sales ~** parlantina *f* da imbonitore; **to make a ~** fare un discorso per convincere qu II. *vt* **1.** (*throw*) lanciare, tirare; **to ~ sb into a situation** scaraventare qu in una situazione; **to be ~ed** (**headlong**) **into despair** essere sprofondato nella disperazione **2.** SPORTS (*throw*) tirare **3.** (*fix level of sound*) **this tune is ~ed** (**too**) **high/low** questo motivo è in un tono (troppo) alto/basso **4.** (*direct at: speech, advertisement*) **to ~ sth at sb** rivolgere qc a qu **5.** (*set up*) **to ~ camp/a tent** piantare il campo/la tenda **6.** (*sell forcefully: product*) promuovere energicamente III. *vi* **1.** (*fall headlong*) cadere in avanti; (*move back and forth: boat*) beccheggiare **2.** SPORTS (*throw baseball*) lanciare **3.** (*slope*) avere una certa pendenza

◆**pitch in** *vi inf* dare una mano

◆**pitch into** *vt* **1.** (*attack verbally*) saltare addosso **2.** (*begin enthusiastically*) darci sotto

◆**pitch out** *vt* buttare fuori

pitch² [pɪtʃ] *n* (*bitumen*) pece *f*

pitch-black [ˌpɪtʃ·'blæk] *adj* (*extremely dark*) di un buio assoluto; (*very black*) nero, -a come la pece

pitched battle *n* battaglia *f* campale

pitched roof *n* tetto *m* a due spioventi

pitcher¹ ['pɪ·tʃɚ] *n* (*large jug*) anfora *f;* (*smaller*) brocca *f*

pitcher² ['pɪ·tʃɚ] *n* SPORTS (*in baseball*) lanciatore, -trice *m, f*

pitchfork ['pɪtʃ·fɔːrk] *n* forcone *m,* forca *f*

pitch pine *n* pitch-pine *m inv*

piteous ['pɪ·ṭi·əs] *adj* pietoso, -a; **a ~ sight** una scena pietosa

pitfall ['pɪt·fɔːl] *n pl* insidia *f*

pith [pɪθ] *n* **1.** BOT (*of lemon, orange*) albedo; BOT midollo *m* **2.** *fig* (*main point*) nocciolo *m;* (*substance of speech*) essenza *f*

pithead ['pɪt·ˌhed] *n* ingresso *m* di miniera, bocca *f*

pith helmet *n* casco *m* coloniale

pithy ['pɪ·θi] <-ier, -iest> *adj* (*remark, summary, phrase*) conciso, -a

pitiable ['pɪ·ṭi·ə·bl] *adj s.* **pitiful**

pitiful ['pɪ·ṭɪ·fəl] *adj* **1.** (*terrible*) pietoso, -a; **~ conditions** condizioni *fpl* pietose; **a ~ sight** una scena pietosa **2.** (*unsatisfactory*) deplorevole; **a ~ excuse** una scusa patetica

pitiless ['pɪ·ṭɪ·ləs] *adj* spietato, -a

piton ['pi:·tɑːn] *n* SPORTS chiodo *m* (da roccia)

pit stop *n* **1.** (*in racing*) pit stop *m inv* **2.** *fig* (*quick stop*) sosta *f* (durante un viaggio in auto)

pittance ['pɪ·tənts] *n* miseria; **to live on a ~** vivere con un reddito miserabile

pitter-patter ['pɪ·ṭɚ·pæ·ṭɚ] I. *adv* **to go ~** (*feet*) muoversi velocemente; (*rain*) battere forte; (*rain*) picchiettare II. *n* (*of feet*) passi *m* leggeri *pl;* (*of heart*) battito *m;* (*of rain*) picchiettio *m*

pituitary (**gland**) [pɪ·'tuː·ə·te·ri] *n* ghiandola *f* pituitaria

pity ['pɪ·ṭi] I. *n* **1.** (*compassion*) compassione *f,* pietà *f;* **in ~** per la compassione; **to feel ~ for sb** provare pietà per qu; **to take ~ on sb** impietosirsi di qu; **for ~'s sake** per pietà! **2.** (*shame*) **to be a ~** essere un peccato; **(it's a) ~ that ...** (è un) peccato che ...; **what a ~!** che peccato! II. <-ies, -ied> *vt* commiserare qu

pitying *adj* compassionevole

pivot ['pɪ·vət] I. *n* **1.** TECH perno *m* **2.** (*focal point*) fulcro *m;* **to be the ~ of sth** essere il fulcro di qc; (*person*) essere il perno di qc II. *vi* **to ~ around** ruotare; **to ~ around sth** *a. fig* girare intorno a qc; **to ~ 90 degrees** ruotare di 90 gradi; **to ~ on sth** (*depend on*) imperniarsi su qc; **the entire plan pivots on his decision** tutto il progetto dipende dalla sua decisione

pivotal ['pɪ·və·ṭəl] *adj* (*role*) cardinale; (*decision*) cruciale; (*idea, person*) fondamentale

pixel [pɪk·səl] *n* INFOR pixel *m inv*

pixie *n,* **pixy** ['pɪk·si] <-ies> *n* LIT folletto *m*

pizza ['pi:t·sə] *n* pizza *f*

placard ['plæ·kɑːrd] *n* cartello *m*

placate ['pleɪ·keɪt] *vt* **1.** (*soothe*) placare **2.** (*appease*) conciliare

placatory ['pleɪ·kə·tɔː·ri] *adj form* **1.** (*calming*) tranquillizzante **2.** (*appeasing, conciliatory*) conciliante

place [pleɪs] I. *n* **1.** (*location, area*) luogo *m;* **~ of birth** luogo di nascita; **~s of interest** luoghi di interesse; **~ of refuge** rifugio *m;* **people in high ~s** gente in alto loco; **to be in ~** essere a posto; *fig* (*organized*) essere sistemato; **if I were in your ~, ...** al tuo posto io ...; **in ~ of sb/sth** al posto di qu/qc; **to not be the ~ to do sth** non essere il luogo adatto per fare qu; **it is no ~ to bring up your children** non è un luogo adatto a crescere i tuoi figli; **it is not your ~ to say that** non sta [*o* spetta] a te dirlo **2.** *inf* (*house*) casa *f;* **at my ~** a casa mia **3.** (*building*) edificio *m* **4.** (*commercial location*) locale *m* **5.** (*position*) posizione *f;* **to lose one's ~** (*in book*) perdere il segno; **to take first/second ~** avere primaria/secondaria importanza; **in the first ~** in primo luogo; **in the second ~** in secondo luogo; **a ~ among the best directors** un posto tra i migliori direttori **6.** (*seat*) posto *m;* (*in theater*) posto *m;* **is this ~ taken?** è libero questo posto?; **to change ~s with sb** scambiare il posto con qu; **to save sb a ~** tenere il posto a/per qu; **to set a ~ at the table** mettere un posto a tavola **7.** (*in organization*) posto *f;* **she has got a ~ at the university** ha ottenuto un posto all'università **8.** MAT **decimal ~** decimale *m* **9.** *inf* (*in location*) **any ~** in qualsiasi posto; **every ~** in ogni posto; **some ~** in qualche posto; **no ~** in nessun posto ▶**a ~ in the sun** un posto al sole; **to fall into ~** andare (perfettamente) a posto; **to go ~s** *inf* (*become successful*) fare strada; **to know one's ~** sapere qual è il proprio posto; **to put sb in his/her ~** mettere a posto qu; **all over the ~** dappertutto; **to feel out of ~** sentirsi fuori posto; **a ~ for everything and everything in its ~** un posto per ogni cosa e ogni cosa al suo posto **II.** *vt* **1.** (*position, put*) sistemare, collocare; **to ~ sth somewhere** sistemare qc da qualche parte; **to ~ an advertisement in the newspaper** fare un'inserzione sul giornale; **to ~ a comma/period** mettere una virgola/un punto; **to ~ sth on the agenda** mettere qc all'ordine del giorno; **we are well ~d to see the match** siamo in una buona posizione per vedere la partita **2.** (*impose*) porre; **to ~ an embargo on sth** imporre un embargo su qc; **to ~ a limit on sth** imporre un limite a qc; **to ~ sb under arrest** arrestare qu; **to ~ sb under surveillance** mettere qu sotto sorveglianza **3.** (*ascribe*) **to ~ the blame on sb** addossare la colpa a qu; **to ~ one's hopes on sb/sth** riporre le proprie speranze in qu/qc; **to ~ importance on sb/sth** dare importanza a qu/qc; **to ~ emphasis on sth** porre l'enfasi su qc; **to ~ one's faith in sb** confidare in qu **4.** (*arrange for*) piazzare; **to ~ an order for sth** piazzare un ordine per; **to ~ a bet** piazzare [*o* fare] una scommessa; **to ~ sth at sb's disposal** mettere qc a disposizione di qu **5.** (*appoint to a position*) **to ~ sb in charge (of sth)** mettere qu a capo (di qc); **to ~ sth under the control of sb** mettere qc sotto il controllo di qu; **to ~ sb in jeopardy** mettere qu in pericolo; **to ~ sb under pressure** mettere qu sotto pressione; **to ~ sb on (the) alert** mettere in guardia qu; **to ~ sth above sth** mettere qc sopra qc; **to be ~d first/second** SPORTS classificarsi al primo/secondo posto **6.** (*employ*) trovare un posto (di lavoro) **7.** (*identify*) riconoscere; **I can't ~ him** [*o* his face] il suo viso non mi è nuovo, ma non so dove l'ho visto **III.** *vi* SPORTS classsificarsi

placebo [plə·'siː·boʊ] <-s> *n* a. *fig* contentino *m*
place card *n* segnaposto *m*
place kick *n* SPORTS calcio *m* piazzato
place mat *n* tovaglietta *f* all'americana
placement ['pleɪs·mənt] *n* collocamento *m*
place name *n* toponimo *m*
placenta [plə·'sen·tə] <-s *o* -ae> *n* MED placenta *f*
placid ['plæ·sɪd] *adj* placido, -a
plagiarism ['pleɪ·dʒə·ɪ·zəm] *n* plagio *m*
plagiarist ['pleɪ·dʒə·ɪst] *n* plagiario, -a *m, f*
plagiarize ['pleɪ·dʒə·raɪz] **I.** *vt* plagiare; **to ~ sth from sth** copiare qc da qc **II.** *vi* fare un plagio; **to ~ from sth** plagiare qc
plague [pleɪg] **I.** *n* (*epidemic*) epidemia *f;* (*infestation of insects*) invasione *f;* (*source of annoyance*) persecuzione *f;* **the ~** (*bubonic plague*) la peste; **to avoid sb like the ~** fuggire qu come la peste **II.** *vt* infastidire; **to ~ sb for sth** assillare qu per qc
plaice [pleɪs] *inv n* platessa *f*
plaid [plæd] **I.** *n* tessuto *m* (a disegno) scozzese **II.** *adj* (a disegno) scozzese; **~ skirt** gonna *f* (a disegno) scozzese
plain [pleɪn] **I.** *adj* **1.** semplice; (*one color*) di un solo colore; (*without additions*) senza additivi; **~ yogurt** yogurt *m* naturale **2.** (*uncomplicated*) semplice; **the ~ folks** la gente semplice; **~ and simple** puro e semplice **3.** (*clear, obvious*) chiaro; **it is ~ that ...** è chiaro che ...; **to be ~ enough** essere abbastanza chiaro; **to make sth ~** mettere in chiaro qc; **to make oneself ~ (to sb)** spiegarsi (con qu); **to be ~ with sb** essere franco con qu; **to be as ~ as the nose on your face** essere chiaro come la luce del sole **4.** (*mere, pure*) puro, -a; **the ~ truth** la pura verità **5.** (*not pretty*) non attraente; **a ~ girl** una ragazza bruttina **II.** *adv inf* (*downright*) semplicemente; **~ awful** proprio orribile **III.** *n* **1.** GEO pianura *f;* **the ~s** *pl* le pianure; **the great Plains** le Grandi Pianure **2.** (*knitting stitch*) d(i)ritto *m*
plainclothes LAW **I.** *n* (*of policeman*) abiti *m* borghesi *pl* **II.** *adj* (*policeman*) in borghese
plainclothesman *n* poliziotto, -a in borghese *m*
plainly ['pleɪn·li] *adv* **1.** (*simply*) semplicemente **2.** (*clearly*) chiaramente; (*obviously*) evidentemente; **to be ~ visible** essere distintamente visibile **3.** (*undeniably*) senza dubbio
plainness ['pleɪn·nəs] *n* **1.** (*unattractiveness*) mancanza *f* di attrattiva **2.** (*simplicity*) semplicità *f* **3.** (*obviousness*) chiarezza *f*
plain sailing *n fig* **to be ~** essere una passeggiata
plainspoken [ˌpleɪn·'spoʊ·kən] *adj* franco, -a
plaintiff ['pleɪn·tɪf] *n* LAW attore, -trice *m, f*
plaintive ['pleɪn·tɪv] *adj* lamentoso, -a
plait [plæt] **I.** *n* treccia *f* **II.** *vt* intrecciare **III.** *vi* fare la treccia
plan [plæn] **I.** *n* **1.** (*scheme, program*) piano *m*, progetto *m;* **to draw up a ~** elabor-

are un progetto; **to go according to** ~ procedere secondo i piani; **to change** ~**s** cambiare i programmi; **to have** ~**s** avere dei progetti; **to make** ~**s for sth** fare programmi per qc **2.** FIN, ECON (*policy*) piano *m;* **healthcare** ~ programma *m* sanitario; **savings** ~ programma *m* di risparmio **3.** (*diagram*) disegno *m;* **street** ~ pianta *f* stradale II. <-nn-> *vt* **1.** (*work out in detail*) pianificare; (*prepare*) programmare; ~**ned economy** economia *f* pianificata; **to** ~ **sth for sb** programmare qc per qu **2.** (*intend*) ripromettersi; **to** ~ **to do sth** ripromettersi di fare qc III. <-nn-> *vi* **1.** (*prepare*) fare progetti; **to** ~ **carefully** fare piani dettagliati **2.** (*reckon with*) **to** ~ **on sth** avere in programma qc; **I'm planning on going** conto di andare

plane¹ [pleɪn] I. *n* **1.** (*level surface*) piano *m;* MAT piano *m* **2.** (*level of thought*) livello *m* [*o* piano] *m* II. *vi* planare III. *adj* piano, -a; MAT piano, -a; ~ **angle** angolo *m* piatto

plane² [pleɪn] *n* (*airplane*) aereo *m;* **by** ~ in aereo

plane³ [pleɪn] I. *n* (*tool*) pialla *f* II. *vt* piallare

plane⁴ [pleɪn] *n* (*tree*) platano *m*

plane crash *n* incidente *m* aereo

planet ['plæ·nɪt] *n* pianeta *m;* ~ **Earth** il pianeta Terra; ~ **Jupiter/Venus** il pianeta Giove/Venere; **to be on a different** ~ *fig* essere su un altro pianeta

planetarium [ˌplæ·nɪ·'te·ri·əm] <-s *o* -ria> *n* planetario *m*

planetary ['plæ·nɪ·te·ri] *adj* planetario, -a; ~ **motion** movimento *m* planetario

plane tree *n* platano *m*

plank [plæŋk] *n* **1.** (*long board*) asse *m,* tavola *f;* NAUT tavola *m* di fasciame **2.** (*of policy, ideology*) principio *m*

planking *n* tavolato *m;* (*of ship*) fasciame

plankton ['plæŋk·tən] *n* plancton *m*

planner *n* pianificatore, -trice *m, f;* **city** ~ urbanista *mf*

planning *n* pianificazione *f;* **city** ~ urbanistica; **environmental** ~ progetti *mpl* ambientali; **at the** ~ **stage** in fase di programmazione

planning board *n* comitato *m* per la pianificazione

building permit *n* licenza *f* edilizia

plant [plænt] I. *n* **1.** BOT pianta *f* **2.** (*factory*) stabilimento *m,* fabbrica *f* **3.** (*machinery*) macchinari *mpl* **4.** (*misleading evidence*) **he said that the drugs were a** ~ disse che la droga era stata messa lì per incriminarlo; (*spy*) infiltrato, -a *m, f* II. *vt* **1.** AGR (*put in earth*) piantare; **to** ~ **the fields with wheat** seminare i campi a grano **2.** (*put*) piazzare; **to** ~ **oneself somewhere** *inf* piazzarsi da qualche parte; **to** ~ **one's feet on the ground** piantare i piedi per terra; **to** ~ **a bomb** mettere una bomba; **to** ~ **a secret agent** infiltrare un agente segreto **3.** *inf* (*incriminate*) **to** ~ **evidence on sb** nascondere prove false addosso a qu per incriminarlo III. *adj* vegetal; **the** ~ **kingdom** il regno vegetale; ~ **life** vita *f* vegetale

plantain ['plæn·tɪn] *n* (*fruit, tree*) banano *m*

plantation [plæn·'teɪ·ʃən] *n* piantagione *f;* (*of trees*) albereto *m*

planter ['plæn·t̬ə˞] *n* **1.** (*plantation owner*) proprietario, -a di piantagione *m* **2.** (*plant holder*) vaso *m*

plaque [plæk] *n* **1.** (*on building*) targa *f* **2.** MED placca *f*

plash [plæʃ] I. *n* (*splash*) sciaguattamento *f;* (*sound*) ciac *m* II. *vi* **to** ~ **about** (*play*) sguazzare

plasm ['plæ·zm] *n* molde *m*

plasma ['plæz·mə] *n* plasma *m*

plaster ['plæs·t̬ə˞] I. *n a.* MED gesso *m;* (*for walls*) intonaco *m* II. *vt* **1.** (*wall, ceiling*) intonacare **2.** *fig, inf* (*put all over*) ricoprire

plasterboard ['plæs·t̬ə˞·bɔːrd] *n* cartongesso *m*

plaster cast *n* **1.** MED ingessatura *f* **2.** ART calco *m* in gesso

plastered *adj inf* (*drunk*) ciucco, -a; **to get** ~ inciuccarsi

plasterer *n* intonacatore, -trice *m, f*

plaster of Paris *n* gesso *m* a presa rapida

plastic ['plæs·tɪk] I. *n* **1.** (*material*) plastica *m* **2.** ~**s** *pl* (*manufacturing sector*) industria *f* della plastica **3.** *inf* (*credit cards*) carte *fpl* di credito II. *adj* **1.** (*made from plastic*) di plastica **2.** *pej* (*artifical*) falso, artificioso **3.** ART (*malleable*) ~ **arts** arti *fpl* plastiche **4.** *fig* (*impressionable*) influenzabile

plastic bag *n* sacchetto *m* di plastica

plastic bomb *n* bomba *f* al plastico

plastic bullet *n* pallottola *f* di plastica

plastic explosive *n* esplosivo *m* (al) plastico

plasticity [plæsˈtɪ·sə·t̬i] *n* plasticità *f*

plastic money *n* moneta *f* di plastica

plastics industry *n* industria *f* della plastica

plastic surgery *n* chirurgia *f* plastica

plate [pleɪt] I. *n* **1.** (*dinner plate*) piatto *m* **2.** (*panel, sheet*) lamiera *f;* **steel** ~ lamiera di acciaio **3.** AUTO **license** ~ targa *f* **4.** TYPO lastra *f* **5.** (*layer of metal*) placcatura *f;* **gold** ~ placcatura a foglia d'oro **6.** (*picture in book*) illustrazione *f* ▶ **to have a lot on one's** ~ avere molte cose da fare II. *vt* **to** ~ **sth with gold/silver** placcare qc in oro/in argento

plateau [plæ·'toʊ] <-x *o* -s> *n* altopiano *m*

plated *adj* (*coated in metal*) placcato, -a; (*jewelry*) placcato, -a

plateful ['pleɪt·fʊl] *n* piatto *m*

plate glass *n* vetro *m* in lastre

platelet ['pleɪ·lət] *n* piastrina *f*

plate rack *n* scolapiatti *m inv*

plate warmer *n* scaldapiatti *m inv*

platform ['plæt·fɔːrm] *n* **1.** *a.* INFOR piattaforma *f* **2.** RAIL marciapiede *m;* **railroad** ~ marciapiede di stazione ferroviaria **3.** (*stage*) palco *m* **4.** (*means for expressing view*) tribuna *f* **5.** POL (*policy*) programma *m* elettorale **6.** *pl* (*shoe*) zatterone *m*

platform shoes *npl* zatteroni *mpl*

plating *n* rivestimento *m* metallico; **gold/**

silver ~ placcatura *f* in oro/in argento
platinum ['plæt·nəm] *n* platino *m*
platitude ['plæ·ʈə·tuːd] *n* luogo *m* comune
Platonic [plə·'tɑː·nɪk] *adj* platonico, -a; ~ **love** amore *m* platonico
platoon [plə·'tuːn] *n* MIL plotone *m*
platter ['plæ·ʈɚ] *n* **1.** (*large dish*) piatto *m* (di portata), vassoio *m* **2.** (*food*) piatto *m* ▶ **to give** sth **to** sb **on a** ~ servire qc a qu su un vassoio
platypus ['plæ·ʈɪ·pəs] <-es> *n* ornitorinco *m*
plausibility [ˌplɔː·zə·'bɪ·lə·ʈi] *n* plausibilità *f*
plausible ['plɔː·zə·bl] *adj* plausibile
play [pleɪ] **I.** *n* **1.** (*recreation*) gioco *m;* **to be at** ~ giocare; **to do** sth **in** ~ fare qc per scherzo [*o* per gioco]; **it's only in** ~ è solo uno scherzo **2.** SPORTS gioco *m;* **to be in/out of** ~ essere in gioco/fuori gioco **3.** SPORTS (*move*) mossa *f;* **foul** ~ (*crime*) delitto; SPORTS gioco falloso; **to make a bad/good** ~ fare una cattiva/buona mossa **4.** THEAT opera *f* teatrale; **a one-act** ~ una pièce in un atto; **radio** ~ sceneggiato *m* radiofonico **5.** (*free movement*) gioco *m;* **to allow** [*o* **give**] sth **full** ~ dare libero sfogo a qc **6.** (*interaction*) gioco *m;* **to bring** sth **into** ~ mettere qc in gioco; **to come into** ~ entrare in gioco; **the police suspect foul** ~ la polizia sospetta che si tratti di un delitto ▶ **to make a** ~ **for** sth cercare di ottenere qc **II.** *vi* **1.** *a.* SPORTS giocare; **to** ~ **for a team** giocare in una squadra; **to** ~ **fair/rough** fare un gioco pulito/sporco **2.** (*perform: of actor*) recitare; **to** ~ **to a full house** fare il tutto esaurito **3.** MUS suonare **4.** *inf* (*be received*) **to** ~/**not** ~ **well with** sb essere preso bene/male da qu **III.** *vt* **1.** (*participate in game, sport*) giocare; **to** ~ **bridge/soccer** giocare a bridge/a calcio; **to** ~ **a card** giocare una carta **2.** (*perform a role*) interpretare, fare la parte di; **to** ~ **the clown** [*o* **fool**] fare lo spiritoso **3.** MUS (*piano, guitar, saxophone*) suonare **4.** (*CD, tape, video, DVD*) mettere; **do you have to** ~ **the music so loud?** devi proprio suonare la musica così forte? **5.** (*perpetrate: joke*) fare ▶ **to** ~ **it safe** andare sul sicuro
♦ **play along** *vi* **to** ~ **with** sb stare al gioco di qu
♦ **play around** *vi* **1.** (*play*) gingillarsi **2.** (*commit adultery*) **to** ~ **with** sb avere una tresca con qu **3.** (*experiment*) **to** ~ **with ideas** prendere in considerazione varie idee **4.** (*tamper*) **to** ~ **with** sth giocherellare con qc
♦ **play at** *vt* **1.** (*pretend*) **to** ~ (**being**) sth giocare a (essere) qc **2.** (*do for amusement*) **to** ~ (**being**) sth giocare a (essere) qc; **she is playing at being a student** gioca a fare la studentessa **3.** *pej* (*do*) **what are you playing at?** cosa diavolo stai facendo?
♦ **play back** *vt* riascoltare
♦ **play down** *vt* minimizzare
♦ **play off I.** *vi* disputare lo spareggio **II.** *vt* **to play** sb **off against** sb aizzare qu contro qu
♦ **play on I.** *vt* **1.** (*exploit*) **to** ~ sb's **feelings/**

weakness giocare sui sentimenti/sulla debolezza di qu **2.** (*words*) giocare su **II.** *vi* (*keep playing*) SPORTS, GAMES continuare a giocare; MUS continuare a suonare
♦ **play out** *vt* rappresentare; **to** ~ **one's fantasies** trsformare le proprie fantasie in realtà
♦ **play through** *vt* suonare
♦ **play up I.** *vt* (*exaggerate: problem, difficulty*) ingigantire **II.** *vi* **1.** *inf* **to** ~ **to** sb (*flatter*) lisciare qu **2.** (*hurt: knee, elbow, back*) fare male
♦ **play upon** *vt* **to** ~ sb's **feelings/weakness** giocare sui sentimenti/sulla debolezza di qu
♦ **play with** *vt a. fig* (*play*) giocare con
♦ **play with** *vt* **1.** (*toy, friends*) giocare con **2.** (*manipulate nervously*) giocherellare con; **to** ~ **one's food** giocherellare con il cibo **3.** (*consider*) **to** ~ **an idea** prendere in considerazione un'idea
playable ['ple·ɪə·bl] *adj* (*pitch*) praticabile
play-act ['pleɪ·ækt] *vi* **1.** THEAT recitare **2.** *fig* fare la commedia
playback ['pleɪ·bæk] *n* (*of tape*) riproduzione *f*
playbill *n* THEAT **1.** (*poster*) locandina *f* **2.** (*program*) programma *m*
playboy ['pleɪ·bɔɪ] *n* playboy *m*
play date *n* (*for children*) giorno stabilito per riunirsi a giocare
Play-Doh® ['pleɪ·dɔː] *n* plastilina *f*
player ['ple·ɪɚ] *n* **1.** SPORTS giocatore, -trice *m, f;* **card** ~ giocatore, -trice *m, f* di carte; **soccer** ~ calciatore, -trice *m, f;* **tennis** ~ tennista *mf* **2.** MUS suonatore, -trice *m, f;* **cello** ~ violoncellista *mf;* **flute** ~ flautista *mf;* **oboe** ~ oboista *mf* **3.** THEAT attore, -trice *m, f* **4.** (*playback machine*) **cassette** ~ registratore *m* a cassette; **CD** ~ lettore *m* di CD; **record** ~ giradischi *m inv* **5.** *sl* (*important person*) protagonista *mf*
playful ['pleɪ·fəl] *adj* **1.** (*full of fun*) giocherellone, -ona; **the children were in a** ~ **mood** i bambini avevano voglia di giocare **2.** (*comment, tone*) scherzoso; **he's only being** ~ sta solo scherzando
playground ['pleɪ·graʊnd] *n* (*at school*) area *f* per la ricreazione; (*in park*) parco *m* giochi
playgroup ['pleɪ·gruːp] *n* asilo *m* nido
playhouse ['pleɪ·haʊs] *n* **1.** (*theater*) teatro *m* **2.** (*miniature house*) casetta *f* per giocare
playing card *n* carta *f* da gioco
playing field *n* campo [*o* sportivo] di gioco *m*
playmate ['pleɪ·meɪt] *n* compagno, -a *m, f* di gioco
playoff ['pleɪ·ɑːf] *n* spareggio *m;* ~ **match** partita *m* di spareggio; (*championship games*); **the** ~**s** i turni eliminatori
playpen ['pleɪ·pen] *n* box *m inv*
playroom ['pleɪ·ruːm] *n* stanza *f* dei giochi
nursery school *n* asilo *m* nido
playsuit ['pleɪ·suːt] *n* (*for baby*) tutina *f*
plaything ['pleɪ·θɪŋ] *n a. fig* giocattolo *m*

playtime ['pleɪ·taɪm] *n* SCHOOL ricreazione *f*
playwright ['pleɪ·raɪt] *n* scrittore, -trice teatrale *m*
plaza ['plɑː·zə] *n* **1.** (*open square*) piazza *f* **2.** (*shopping center*) (**shopping**) ~ centro *m* commerciale
plea [pliː] *n* **1.** (*appeal*) appello *m*, supplica *f*; **to make a** ~ **for help/mercy** implorare aiuto/clemenza **2.** LAW dichiarazione *m;* **to enter a** ~ **of guilty/not guilty** dichiararsi colpevole/non colpevole **3.** *form* (*excuse*) scusante *f*
plea-bargaining *n* LAW *patteggiamento*
plead [pliːd] <-ed *o* pled, -ed *o* pled> I. *vi* **1.** (*implore, beg*) implorare, invocare; **to** ~ **for forgiveness** implorare il perdono; **to** ~ **for justice** chiedere giustizia; **to** ~ **with sb** (**to do sth**) scongiurare qu (di fare qc) **2.** LAW **to** ~ **guilty/innocent** (**to a charge**) dichiararsi colpevole/innocente (rispetto a un'accusa) II. *vt* **1.** LAW **to** ~ **sb's case** patrocinare la causa di qu; **to** ~ **insanity** invocare l'infermità mentale **2.** (*claim as pretext*) addurre come scusante; **to** ~ **ignorance of sth** addurre come pretesto l'ignoranza **3.** (*argue for*) **to** ~ **sb's cause** difendere la causa di qu; **to** ~ **one's suit** *form* patrocinare la causa di qu
pleading ['pliː·dɪŋ] I. *n* **1.** (*entreaty, appeal*) suppliche *fpl* **2.** LAW patrocinio *m* II. *adj* (*look, tone*) implorante
pleasant ['ple·zənt] *adj* **1.** (*pleasing*) piacevole; **what a** ~ **surprise!** che bella sorpresa!; **have a** ~ **journey!** buon viaggio!; ~ **weather** bel tempo **2.** (*friendly*) carino; **to be** ~ (**to sb**) essere cortese (con qu)
pleasantry ['ple·zən·tri] <-ies> *n* **1.** (*joke*) battuta (scherzosa) *f* **2.** *pl* (*remarks*) convenevoli *mpl;* **an exchange of pleasantries** uno scambio di convenevoli
please [pliːz] I. *vt* **1.** (*make happy*) fare contento; (*give pleasure to*) fare piacere a; **to be hard to** ~ essere difficile da accontentare; **she's notoriously hard to** ~ tutti sanno quanto sia difficile da accontentare **2.** *inf* (*do as one wishes*) ~ **yourself** fai [*o* come ti pare] quello che vuoi II. *vi* **1.** (*be agreeable*) **eager to** ~ sempre disponibile **2.** (*think fit, wish*) **to do as one** ~**s** fare quello che si vuole; **you can do as you** ~ puoi fare come meglio credi; **to do whatever one** ~**s** fare tutto quello che si vuole III. *interj* per [*o* piacere] favore, fare contento; **if you** ~ *form* con il suo [*o* tuo] permesso [*o* vostro]; **more potatoes?** — (**yes**) ~ altre patate? Sí, grazie; **oh,** ~**!** (*in annoyance*) ma fammi [*o* mi faccia] il piacere! [*o* fatemi]
pleased *adj* **1.** (*satisfied, contented*) contento, -a, soddisfatto, -a; **to be** ~ **about sth** essere contento di qc; **to be** ~ **that ...** essere contento che ... +*subj;* **to be** ~ **with oneself** essere compiaciuto di sé **2.** (*happy, glad*) contento, -a, lieto, -a; **I'm** ~ **to inform you/to report that ...** sono lieto di comunicarle/informarla che ...; (**I'm very**) ~ **to meet you** (sono molto) lieto

di conoscerla, piacere! **3.** (*willing*) **to be** ~ **to do sth** essere felice di fare qc ▶ **to be as** ~ **as Punch** (**about sth**) essere contento come una Pasqua (per qc)
pleasing *adj* piacevole, gradevole; ~ **news** buone notizie *fpl*
pleasurable ['ple·ʒə·rə·bl] *adj* piacevole, gradevole; **a** ~ **sensation** una piacevole sensazione
pleasure ['ple·ʒəʳ] *n* **1.** (*feeling of enjoyment*) piacere *m;* **it was such a** ~ **to meet you** è stato un vero piacere conoscerla; **to take** ~ **in sth/in doing sth** divertirsi con qc/a fare qc; **with** ~ con piacere **2.** (*source of enjoyment*) piacere *m;* **the** ~**s and pains of camping** le gioie e i dolori del campeggio; **are you here on business or** ~**?** è qui per lavoro o per svago? **3.** *form* (*will, desire*) **what is your** ~**, Madame?** in che posso servirla, signora? *f*
pleasure principle *n* PSYCH principio *m* del piacere
pleasure trip *n* gita *m* di piacere
pleat [pliːt] *n* piega *f*
pleb [pleb] *n inf abbr of* **plebian** plebeo, -a *m, f*
plebeian [plɪ·ˈbiː·ən] I. *adj form* plebeo, -a II. *n* HIST plebeo, -a *m, f*
plebiscite ['ple·bə·saɪt] *n* plebiscito *m;* **to hold a** ~ (**on sth**) tenere un plebiscito (su qc)
pled [pled] *pt, pp of* **plead**
pledge [pledʒ] I. *n* **1.** (*solemn promise*) promessa *f* (solenne); **to fulfill a** ~ onorare un impegno, mantenere una promessa; **to make a** ~ **that ...** promettere (solennemente) che ... **2.** (*symbolic sign of promise*) **as a** ~ **of sth** in pegno di qc; **a** ~ **of good faith** una garanzia di buona fede **3.** (*promised donation*) contributo *m* promesso **4.** (*pawned item*) pegno *m* **5.** (*in fraternity*) *studente che ha compiuto un periodo di prova prima di entrare in una confraternita* II. *vt* **1.** (*promise*) promettere; **to** ~ **loyalty** promettere fedeltà; **to** ~ **to do sth** promettere di fare qc; **to** ~ **that ...** promettere che ...; **we've** ~**d ourselves to fight for justice** ci siamo ripromessi di lottare per la giustizia; **I've been** ~**d to secrecy** mi sono impegnato a mantenere il segreto **2.** (*give as security*) **to** ~ **money** dare del denaro come garanzia
plenary ['pliː·nə·ri] *adj* plenario, -a
plenary meeting *n* assemblea *f* plenaria
plenary powers *npl* pieni poteri *mpl*
plenary session *n* sessione *f* plenaria
plenipotentiary [ˌple·nə·pə·ˈten·ʃie·ri] I. <-ries> *n* ADMIN, POL plenipotenziario, -a *m, f* II. *adj* ADMIN, POL plenipotenciario, -a; ~ **power** pieni poteri *mpl*
plentiful ['plen·tɪ·fəl] *adj* abbondante; **strawberries are** ~ **in the summer** d'estate le fragole abbondano
plenty ['plen·ti] I. *n* **1.** (*abundance*) abbondanza *f;* **land of** ~ paese *m* dell'abbondanza; **food in** ~ cibo *m* in abbondanza **2.** (*a lot*) ~ **of money/time** un mucchio di soldi/tempo

II. *adv* a sufficienza; **there is ~ more** ce n'è ancora in quantità; **there's ~ more beer in the fridge** nel frigo c'è ancora birra in quantità

plenum ['pli:·nəm] *n* plenum *m*

plethora ['ple·θəʳ·ə] *n* sovrabbondanza *f;* MED, BOT pletora *f*

pleurisy ['plʊ·rə·si] *n* MED pleurite *f*

plexus ['plek·səs] <-(es)> *n* plesso *m;* **solar ~** plesso solare

pliable ['pla·ɪə·bl] *adj* **1.** (*supple*) flessibile **2.** *fig* (*easily influenced*) arrendevole

pliers ['pla·ɪəz] *npl* pinze *fpl;* **a pair of ~** una pinza

plight [plaɪt] I. *n* situazione *f* difficile; **a dreadful ~** una situazione disperata II. *vt form* **to ~ one's troth** scambiarsi una promessa di matrimonio

Plimsoll line *n*, **Plimsoll mark** *n* NAUT marca *f* di bordo libero

PLO [ˌpiː·elˈoʊ] *n abbr of* **Palestine Liberation Organization** OLP *f*

plod [plɑːd] I. *n* passo *m* lento II. <-dd-> *vi* **1.** (*walk heavily*) camminare con passo pesante; **to ~ through the mud** procedere a fatica attraverso il fango **2.** (*do without enthusiasm*) **to ~ through one's work** andare avanti a rilento con il proprio lavoro; **to ~ through a book** procedere faticosamente nella lettura di un libro

◆**plod away** *vi* **to ~ at sth** fare lenti ma costanti progressi in qc

◆**plod on** *vi* cammminare con difficoltà

plonk [plɑŋk] *n*, *vt s.* **plunk**

plop [plɑːp] I. *n* pluf *m;* **to fall with a ~** cadere facendo pluf II. <-pp-> *vi* (*fall*) **to ~ into a chair/onto the bed** sprofondare su una sedia/sul letto

plot [plɑːt] I. *n* **1.** (*conspiracy, secret plan*) complotto *m;* **to foil a ~** sventare un complotto; **to hatch a ~** architettare un complotto; **the ~ thickens** *iron* la faccenda si complica **2.** (*story line*) intreccio *m*, trama *f* **3.** (*small piece of land*) terreno *m;* **a ~ of land** un appezzamento di terra; **building ~** terreno *m* edificabile II. <-tt-> *vt* **1.** (*conspire*) tramare **2.** (*create*) **to ~ a story line** ideare una trama; **to ~ a play/novel** abbozzare un testo teatrale/un racconto **3.** (*graph, line*) tracciare; (*mark on map*) riportare; **to ~ a course** tracciare una rotta III. <-tt-> *vi* **to ~ against sb** complottare contro qu; **to ~ to do sth** programmare (segretamente) di fare qc

◆**plot out** *vt* tracciare

plotter ['plɑː·ɪ̯əʳ] *n* **1.** (*person*) cospiratore, -trice *m*, *f* **2.** INFOR plotter *m*, plotter *m inv*

plough [plaʊ] *n*, *vt*, *vi s.* **plow**

plow [plaʊ] I. *n* aratro *m* ▶ **to put one's hand to the ~** mettersi all'opera II. *vt* **1.** AGR arare **2.** (*move through*) **to ~ one's way through sth** farsi strada attraverso qc; (*work through*) portare avanti a rilento **3.** (*invest*) **to ~ money into a project** investire molto denaro in un progetto III. *vi* **1.** AGR arare **2. to ~ through**

sth (*move through*) farsi strada attraverso qc; (*work through*) portare avanti a rilento

◆**plow back** *vt* **to plow sth back** (*into sth*) reinvestire qc (in qc); **to plow profits back** reinvestire gli utili

◆**plow into** *vt insep* andare a sbattere contro

◆**plow up** *vt* (*fields, land*) dissodare

Plow [plaʊ] *n* **the ~** ASTR l'Orsa Maggiore, il Gran Carro

ploy [plɔɪ] *n* **1.** (*activity*) attività *f* **2.** (*tactics*) espediente *m*

pluck [plʌk] I. *n* **1.** (*sharp pull*) strappo *m* **2.** *inf* (*courage*) fegato *m;* **to have a lot of ~** avere un bel fegato; **it takes a lot of ~** richiede un gran coraggio II. *vt* **1.** (*remove quickly*) strappare **2.** (*remove hair, feathers*) **to ~ a chicken** spennare un pollo; **to ~ one's eyebrows** depilarsi le sopracciglia **3.** MUS pizzicare III. *vi* **to ~ at sb's sleeve** tirare qu per la manica

◆**pluck out** *vt* strappare

◆**pluck up** *vt* **to ~ one's courage** armarsi di coraggio; **to ~ the courage to do sth** trovare il coraggio di fare qc

plucky ['plʌ·ki] <-ier, -iest> *adj* di fegato

plug [plʌg] I. *n* **1.** ELEC (*connector*) spina *f;* (*socket*) presa *f* (di corrente) **2.** (*stopper*) tappo *m* **3.** *inf* (*publicity*) **to give sth a ~** reclamizzare qc **4.** (*spark plug*) candela *f* **5.** (*chunk*) **~ of tobacco** tavoletta *f* di tabacco da masticare II. <-gg-> *vt* **1.** (*connect*) collegare; ELEC collegare (alla rete) **2.** (*stop up, close*) **to ~ a hole** tappare un buco; **to ~ a leak** tamponare una perdita **3.** (*publicize*) propagandare **4.** *sl* (*shoot*) imbottire di piombo

◆**plug away** *vi* **to ~ (at sth)** perseverare (in qc)

◆**plug in** I. *vt* collegare; ELEC collegare (alla rete) II. *vi* collegare; ELEC collegare (alla rete)

◆**plug up** *vt* tappare

plug-in *n* INFOR plug-in *m*, plug-in *m*

plum [plʌm] I. *n* **1.** (*fruit*) prugna *f*, susina *f;* (*tree*) susino *m*, prugno *m* **2.** (*opportunity, reward*) premio *m* **3.** (*color*) color *m* prugna II. *adj* **1.** (*color*) color prugna **2.** (*exceptionally good*) isuperabile; **a ~ job** un lavoro fantastico

plumage ['pluː·mɪdʒ] *n* piumaggio *m*

plumb [plʌm] I. *vt* **1.** *a. fig* sondare; **to ~ the depth** sondare la profondità; **to ~ the depths** *fig* toccare il fondo (di); **to ~ the mystery of the universe** capire i misteri dell'universo **2.** (*straighten, make vertical: wall, frame, mast*) mettere a piombo II. *adv inf* **1.** (*exactly*) esattamente; **he hit me ~ on the nose** mi ha colpito in pieno sul naso **2.** (*completely*) **to be ~ wrong/right/tired/crazy** avere assolutamente torto/ragione; **to be ~ tired/crazy** essere proprio stanco/pazzo III. *n* piombo *f;* **to be out of** [*o off*] **~** non essere a piombo

plumber ['plʌ·məʳ] *n* idraulico, -a *m*, *f*

plumbing ['plʌ·mɪŋ] I. *n* idraulica *f* II. *adj* **~ fixture** impianto *m* idraulico; **~ work** impianto idraulico

plume [pluːm] **I.** *n* **1.** (*feather*) piuma *f* **2.** (*cloud: of smoke, gas*) nube *f* **II.** *vt* to ~ **oneself on sth** essere fiero di qc

plummet ['plʌ·mɪt] *vi* crollare

plummy ['plʌ·mi] <-ier, -iest> *adj* (*voice, tone*) snob

plump [plʌmp] *adj* (*person*) rotondetto, -a; (*animal*) grassoccio, -a
  ◆**plump down** *inf* **I.** *vt* mettere giù (pesantemente) **II.** *vi* lasciarsi cadere
  ◆**plump for** *vt inf* optare per
  ◆**plump up** *vt* **1.** (*pillow*) sprimacciare **2.** (*chicken*) ingrassare

plumpness ['plʌmp·nəs] *n* rotondità *f*

plum pudding *n dolce natalizio tradizionale del Regno Unito a base di farina, frutta secca e spezie*

plum tree *n* susino *m*, prugno *m*

plunder ['plʌn·dɚ] **I.** *n* **1.** (*stolen goods*) bottino *m* **2.** (*act of plundering*) saccheggio *m* **II.** *vt* **1.** (*village, city*) saccheggiare **2.** (*goods, gold, treasures*) rubare **III.** *vi* fare razzia

plunderer ['plʌn·dɚ·ɚ] *n* saccheggiatore, -trice *m, f*

plunge [plʌndʒ] **I.** *n* **1.** (*sharp decline*) crollo *m* **2.** (*dive*) tuffo *m* ▶ **to take the** ~ buttarsi; (*get married*) fare il passo e sposarsi **II.** *vi* **1.** (*fall suddenly*) precipitarsi; **to** ~ **to one's death** fare una caduta mortale **2.** (*leap, enter*) **we** ~**d into the sea** ci siamo tuffati in mare; **he** ~**d into the forest** si immerse nella foresta **3.** (*begin abruptly*) **to** ~ **into sth** gettarsi in qc **III.** *vt* immergere; **to** ~ **a knife into sth** affondare il coltello in qc; **we've** ~**d ourselves into debt** siamo sprofondati nei debiti
  ◆**plunge in** *vi* lanciarsi

plunger ['plʌn·dʒɚ] *n* (*of syringe*) stantuffo *m;* (*for drain*) sturalavandini *m inv*

plunk [plʌŋk] **I.** *n inf* (*sound*) rumore *m* sordo **II.** *vt inf* (*set down heavily*) lasciarsi andare pesantemente; **she** ~**ed the books onto the table** ha mollato i libri sul tavolo
  ◆**plunk down** *vt inf* mollare; **to plunk oneself down on a chair** lasciarsi cadere su una sedia

pluperfect ['pluː·ˌpɝ·fɪkt] *n* LING piuccheperfetto *m*

plural ['plʊ·rəl] **I.** *n* plurale *m;* **in the** ~ al plurale; **second person** ~ seconda persona plurale **II.** *adj* **1.** *a.* LING plurale **2.** (*multiple*) multiplo, -a

pluralism ['plʊ·rə·lɪ·zəm] *n* PHILOS pluralismo *m*

pluralistic [ˌplʊ·rə·'lɪs·tɪk] *adj* pluralistico, -a

plurality [plʊ·'ræ·lə·ti] <-ies> *n* **1.** (*variety*) pluralità *f;* **a** ~ **of opinions** una molteplicità di opinioni **2.** (*share of votes*) maggioranza *f* relativa; **to have a** ~ avere la maggioranza relativa

plus [plʌs] **I.** *prep* più; **5** ~ **2 equals 7** 5 più 2 fa 7 **II.** *conj* in più **III.** <-es> *n* **1.** (*mathematical symbol*) (segno) *m* più **2.** (*advantage*) punto *m* a favore **IV.** *adj* **1.** (*above zero*) positivo, -a; ~ **8** più 8; ~ **two degrees** due gradi

sopra zero **2.** (*more than*) più di; **200** ~ più di 200 **3.** (*advantageous*) **the** ~ **side** (**of sth**) il lato positivo (di qc)

plus fours *npl* pantaloni *mpl* alla zuava

plush [plʌʃ] **I.** *adj* **1.** (*luxurious*) lussuoso, -a, di lusso **2.** (*fabric, carpet*) felpato, -a **II.** <-es> *n* felpa *f*

plus sign *n* segno *m* più

Pluto ['pluː·ˌtoʊ] *n* Plutone *m*

plutocracy [pluː·'tɑː·krə·si] <-ies> *n* plutocrazia *f*

plutocrat ['pluː·tə·kræt] *n* plutocrate *mf*

plutocratic [ˌpluː·tə·'kræ·ṭɪk] *adj* plutocratico, -a

plutonium [pluː·'toʊ·ni·əm] *n* plutonio *m*

ply[1] [plaɪ] *n* **1.** (*thickness: of cloth, wood*) capa *f* **2.** (*strand of rope*) **two-**~ **rope**

ply[2] [plaɪ] <-ie-> **I.** *vt* **1.** (*utilize: needle, tool*) usare; **to** ~ **one's trade** svolgere la propria attività **2.** **to** ~ **sb with questions** assillare qu di domande; **to** ~ **sb with wine** offrire vino a qu in continuazione **3.** (*sell*) **to** ~ **drugs** spacciare droghe; **to** ~ **one's wares** vendere le proprie mercanzie **4.** (*travel: ship*) navigare su; **to** ~ **a route** fare una rotta **II.** *vi* **to** ~ **between Paris and Lyon** fare la spola tra Parigi e Lione

plywood ['plaɪ·wʊd] *n* (legno) *m* compensato

p.m. [ˌpiː·'em] *abbr of* **post meridian** dopo mezzogiorno; **one** ~ l'una di notte; **four** ~ le quattro del pomeriggio; **eight** ~ le otto di sera

PM [ˌpiː·'em] *n* **1.** *abbr of* **postmortem** autopsia *f* **2.** *abbr of* **prime minister** primo ministro *m*, prima ministra *f*

PMS [ˌpiː·em·'es] *n abbr of* **premenstrual syndrome** sindrome *f* premestruale

pneumatic [nuː·'mæ·ṭɪk] *adj* pneumatico, -a

pneumatic brakes *npl* freni *mpl* pneumatici

pneumatic tire *n* pneumatico *m*

pneumonia [nuː·'moʊn·jə] *n* polmonite *f*

PO [ˌpiː·'oʊ] *n abbr of* **Post Office** ufficio *m* postale

poach[1] [poʊtʃ] *vt* (*eggs*) cuocere in camicia; (*fish*) cuocere in bianco

poach[2] [poʊtʃ] **I.** *vt* **1.** (*hunt illegally*) cacciare di frodo; (*fish*) pescare di frodo **2.** (*take unfairly*) soffiare; **to** ~ **someone's ideas** rubare le idee a qu **II.** *vi* cacciare di frodo; (*fish*) pescare di frodo; **to** ~ **on sb's territory** *fig* sconfinare nel territorio di qu

poacher ['poʊ·tʃɚ] *n* (*hunter*) cacciatore, -trice di frodo *m;* (*fisherman*) pescatore, -trice di frodo *m*

poaching ['poʊ·tʃɪŋ] *n* (*hunting*) caccia *f* di frodo; (*fishing*) pesca *f* di frodo

POB *n abbr of* **post office box** casella *f* postale

PO Box [ˌpiː·'oʊ·bɑːks] <-es> *n abbr of* **post office box** casella *f* postale

pock [pɑːk] *n* (*scar*) buttero *m;* (*pimple*) pustola *f*

pocket ['pɑː·kɪt] **I.** *n* **1.** (*in pants, jacket*) tasca *f;* **back** ~ tasca posteriore; **breast** ~ taschino; **inside** ~ tasca interna; **to be in** ~ /

P

out of ~ essere in attivo/in passivo; **to pay for sth out of one's own** ~ pagare di tasca propria per qc **2.** (*isolated group, area*) ~ **of green** [*o* **greenery**] angolo *m* verde; **a** ~ **of resistance** una sacca di resistenza; ~ **of turbulence** AVIAT, METEO vuoto *m* d'aria **3.** (*in pool table*) buca *f* ▸ **to have sth in one's** ~ avere qc in tasca; **to have sb in one's** ~ tenere qu in pugno; **to line one's** ~**s** riempirsi le tasche di soldi **II.** *vt* **1.** (*put in pocket*) **to** ~ **sth** mettersi in tasca qc **2.** (*keep for oneself*) appropriarsi di **3.** (*in billiards*) **to** ~ **a ball** mandare una palla in buca ▸ **to** ~ **one's pride** mettersi l'orgoglio sotto i piedi **III.** *adj* ~ **dictionary** dizionario *m* tascabile; ~ **edition** edizione *f* tascabile

pocketbook ['pɑ:·kɪt·bʊk] *n* **1.** (*woman's handbag*) borsa *f* **2.** (*billfold*) portafoglio *m;* **to vote with one's** ~ votare pensando solo alle proprie tasche **3.** (*book*) (libro) *m* tascabile

pocket calculator *n* calcolatrice *f* tascabile

pocket camera *n* macchina *f* fotografica tascabile

pocketful ['pɑ:·kɪt·fʊl] *n* **a** ~ **of sth** una tascata di qc

pocket handkerchief *n* fazzoletto *m* da taschino

pocketknife <-knives> *n* temperino *m*

pocket money *n* **1.** (*for small expenses*) denaro *m* per piccole spese **2.** (*from one's parents*) paghetta *f*

pocket-sized *adj* tascabile

pockmarks *npl* butteri

pod [pɑːd] *n* **1.** BOT baccello *m* **2.** AVIAT gondola *f*

podiatrist [pə·'da·ɪə·trɪst] *n* pedicure *mf*

podium ['poʊ·diəm] <-s *o* -dia> *n* podio *m*

poem ['poʊ·əm] *n* poema *m*

poet ['poʊ·ət] *n* poeta, poetessa *m, f*

poetic [poʊ·'e·t̬ɪk] *adj* poetico, -a

poetry ['poʊ·ɪ·tri] *n a. fig* poesia *f*

pogrom [pə·'grɑːm] *n* pogrom *m inv*

poignant ['pɔɪn·jənt] *adj* toccante

poinsettia [pɔɪnt·'se·t̬iə] *n* poinsettia *f*, stella *f* di Natale

point [pɔɪnt] **I.** *n* **1.** (*sharp end*) punta *f;* **knife** ~ punta del coltello; **pencil** ~ punta della matita **2.** GEO punta *f*, promontorio *m* **3.** (*particular place*) punto *m;* **boiling/freezing** ~ punto *m* di ebollizione/congelamento; **starting** ~ punto di partenza **4.** (*particular time*) punto *m;* **to do sth up to a** ~ fare qc fino a un certo punto; **to get to the** ~ **that ...** arrivare al punto che ...; **at that** ~ a quel punto; **at this** ~ **in time** al momento **5.** (*significant idea*) questione *f;* **that's just the** ~**!** è proprio così!; **to be to the** ~ essere pertinente; **to be beside the** ~ non avere niente a che vedere; **to get to the** ~ venire al punto; **to get the** ~ (**of sth**) afferrare il concetto (di qc); **to make one's** ~ esprimere il proprio punto di vista; **to miss the** ~ non cogliere il concetto; **to see sb's** ~ capire il concetto di qu; **to take sb's** ~ essere d'accordo con qu; ~ **taken!** hai ragione

tu!; ~ **by** ~ punto per punto **6.** (*characteristic*) **sb's strong/weak** ~**s** il forte/il debole di qu **8.** (*in score, result*) punto *m;* **percentage** ~ punto *m* percentuale; **to win** (**sth**) **on** ~**s** (*in boxing*) vincere (qc) ai punti **9.** MAT **decimal** ~ virgola *f* (decimale) **10.** *a.* TYPO punto *m;* **join** ~**s A and B together** unire i punti A e B **11.** *pl* AUTO (*electrical contact*) puntina *f* ▸ **to make a** ~ **of doing sth** farsi un dovere di fare qc **II.** *vi* (*with finger*) additare; (*indicate*); **to** ~ **to sth** indicare qc; **to** ~ **to an icon** INFOR portare il puntatore su un'icona **III.** *vt* **1.** (*aim*) puntare; **to** ~ **sth at sb** puntare qc verso qu; **the man had** ~**ed a knife at him** l'uomo gli aveva puntato contro il coltello; **to** ~ **a finger at sb** *a. fig* puntare il dito contro qu **2.** (*direct, show position or direction*) guidar qc/qu; **to** ~ **sb toward sth** indicare a qu la strada verso qc ♦**point out** *vt* **1.** (*show*) indicare; **if you see her, please point her out to me** se la vedi indicamela, per piacere **2.** (*inform of*) **to point sth out to sb** far notare qc a qu; **to** ~ **that ...** far notare che ...

point-blank [,pɔɪnt·'blæŋk] **I.** *adv* **1.** (*fire*) a bruciapelo **2.** (*ask*) a bruciapelo; **to refuse** ~ rifiutare categoricamente **II.** *adj* **1.** (*very close, not far away*) **to shoot sb at** ~ **range** sparare a bruciapelo a qu **2.** (*blunt, direct*) diretto, -a

pointed ['pɔɪn·t̬ɪd] *adj* **1.** (*implement, stick*) appuntito, -a **2.** *fig* (*criticism*) pungente; (*question*) diretto, -a; (*remark*) intenzionale

pointer ['pɔɪn·t̬ɚ] *n* **1.** (*for blackboard*) bacchetta (per indicare) *f;* (*of clock*) lancetta *f;* (*of scale*) ago *m* **2.** INFOR cursore *m;* **mouse** ~ puntatore *m* **3.** (*advice, tip*) indicazione *f* **4.** (*dog*) pointer *m inv*

pointless ['pɔɪnt·ləs] *adj* inutile; **it's** ~ **arguing with him** non serve a niente discutere con lui

point of view <points of view> *n* punto *m* di vista; **from a purely practical** ~ da un punto di vista puramente pratico

point of no return *n a.* AVIAT punto *m* di non ritorno *fig; inf* punto *m* di non ritorno

poise [pɔɪz] **I.** *n* **1.** (*composure*) padronanza *f* di sé; **to lose/regain one's** ~ perdere/ritrovare la calma **2.** (*elegance*) eleganza *f* di portamento **II.** *vt* **to be** ~**d to do sth** esssere sul punto di fare qc

poised *adj* **1.** (*suspended*) sospeso, -a (in aria) **2.** (*ready*) pronto, -a **3.** (*calm*) posato, -a

poison ['pɔɪ·zən] **I.** *n* veleno *m;* **rat** ~ veleno *m* per topi; **to lace sth with** ~ avvelenare qc; **to take** ~ avvelenarsi ▸ **what's your** ~**?** *fig* cosa bevi? **II.** *vt* **1.** (*give poison to*) avvelenare **2.** (*spoil, corrupt*) corrompere; **the long dispute has** ~**ed relations between the two countries** la lunga controversia ha avvelenato i rapporti tra i due paesi; **to** ~ **sb's mind** (**against sb**) instillare in qu odio (contro qc)

poison gas *n* gas *m* tossico

poisoning *n* avvelenamento *m*

poison ivy *n* BOT edera *f* velenosa
poisonous ['pɔɪ·zə·nəs] *adj* velenoso, -a; *fig;*
~ **atmosphere** atmosfera *f* avvelenata;
~ **remark** osservazione *f* maligna
poke[1] [pouk] *n dial* (*bag*) borsa *f,* sacca *f*
poke[2] [pouk] I. *n* (*push*) spinta *m;* (*with elbow*) gomitata *f;* **to give sb a** ~ dare una gomitata a qu II. *vt* **1.** (*with finger*) dare una ditata a; (*with elbow*) dare una gomitata a; **to** ~ **a hole in sth** fare un buco in qc; **to** ~ **holes in an argument** trovare difetti in un'argomentazione; **to** ~ **one's nose into sb's business** ficcare il naso nelle faccende di qu **2.** (*emerge*) **to** ~ **one's arm through a sleeve** infilarsi una manica; **it poked its head out of the water** fece capolino dall'acqua **3. to** ~ **fun at sb/sth** mettere in ridicolo qu/qc III. *vi* **to** ~ **at sth/sb** percuotere qc/qu; **to** ~ **through** (**sth**) spuntare fuori (da qc)
◆**poke around** *vi* frugare
◆**poke out** I. *vi* **to** ~ (**of sth**) spogere fuori (da qc) II. *vt* **1.** (*stick out*) **to poke one's head out** sporgere la testa **2.** (*push out*) **to poke sth out** spingere fuori qc; **to poke sb's eye**(**s**) **out** strappare gli occhi a qu
◆**poke up** *vi* spuntare
poker[1] ['pou·kɚ] *n* (*card game*) poker *m*
poker[2] ['pou·kɚ] *n* (*fireplace tool*) attizzatoio *m*
pokey ['pou·ki] I. *n inf* (*prison*) gattabuia *f;* **he'll get three years in the** ~ gli daranno tre anni di galera II. *adj s.* **poky**
poky ['pou·ki] I.<-ier, -iest> *adj inf* **1.** (*slow*) lento, -a **2.** (*small*) angusto, -a; **a** ~ **little room** una stanzuccia II. *n s.* **pokey**
Poland ['pou·lənd] *n* Polonia *f*
polar ['pou·lə] *adj* GEO, MAT polare; ~ **opposites** poli *mpl* opposti
polar bear *n* orso polare *m*
polar circle *n* circolo *m* polare
polar front *n* METEO fronte *m* polare
polar ice cap *n* calotta *f* polare
polarity [pou·'læ·rə·ti] *n* polarità *f*
polarization [ˌpou·lə·ɪ·'zei·ʃən] *n* polarizzazione *f*
polarize ['pou·lə·raɪz] I. *vt* polarizzare; **to** ~ **sth into two groups** dividere qc in due II. *vi* polarizzarsi
polar lights *npl* aurora *f* boreale
polar region *n* regione *f* polare
polar zone *n* zona *f* polare
pole[1] [poul] *n* palo *m;* **electricity** ~ palo *m* della luce; **flag** ~ asta *f* della bandiera; **fishing** ~ canna *f* da pesca; **telegraph** ~ palo *m* del telegrafo ▶**to not touch sth with a 10-foot** ~ tenersi alla larga di qc
pole[2] [poul] *n* **1.** GEO, ELEC polo *m;* **the magnetic** ~**s** GEO i poli magnetici; **the negative/positive** ~ il polo negativo/positivo **2.** *fig* **opposite** ~**s** poli opposti; **to be** ~**s apart** essere agli antipodi; **political** ~**s** poli *mpl* (politici)
Pole[1] [poul] *n* (*person*) polacco, -a *m, f*

Pole[2] [poul] *n* GEO **the North/South** ~ il Polo Nord/Sud
poleax(**e**) ['pou·læks] I. *n* **1.** (*medieval weapon*) ascia *f* d'armi **2.** (*axe in naval warfare*) ascia *f* di abbordaggio II. *vt* (*strike powerfully*) atterrare, abbattere; **he was completely** ~**d when his wife left him** rimase come inebetito quando sua moglie lo lasciò
polemic [pə·'le·mɪk] I. *n* polemica *f* II. *adj* polemico, -a
polemical *adj* polemico, -a
pole position *n* pole *f* position *inv;* **to be in** ~ essere in pole position
polestar *n* stella *f* polare
pole vault *n* salto *m* con l'asta
pole vaulter *n* saltatore, -trice *m, f* con l'asta
police [pə·'liːs] I. *n* polizia *f;* **the secret/military** ~ la polizia segreta/militare; **the riot** ~ la squadra antisommossa; *a. fig;* **the thought/morality** ~ *a. fig,* **the fashion/thought/morality** ~, **the riot/secret/military** ~, **the fashion** ~ *unità di polizia dedicate alla prevenzione dei comportamenti antisociali;* **thought** ~ polizia del pensiero; **morality** ~ squadra del buon costume II. *vt* **to** ~ **an area** vigilare una zona
police car *n* auto *f* della polizia
police court *n tribunale competente per reati minori*
police department *n* reparto *m* di polizia
police dog *n* cane *m* poliziotto
police escort *n* scorta *f* della polizia; **under** ~ sotto scorta (della polizia)
police force *n* forza *f* pubblica
police informer *n* informatore, -trice della polizia *m*
policeman [pə·'liːs·mən] <-men> *n* poliziotto *m,* agente *m* di polizia
police officer *n* poliziotto, -a *m, f,* agente *m* di polizia
police patrol *n* pattuglia *f* della polizia
police raid *n* irruzione *f* della polizia
police record *n* **1.** (*file*) fedina *f* penale sporca **2.** (*history of convictions*) precedenti *mpl* penali; **to have a long** ~ avere molti precedenti penali
police reporter *n* cronista di fatti polizieschi
police state *n* stato *m* di polizia
police station *n* commissariato *m*
policewoman [pə·'liːs·wʊ·mən] <-women> *n* donna *f* poliziotto
policy[1] ['pɑː·lə·si] <-ies> *n* **1.** POL, ECON politica *f;* **a change in** ~ un cambiamento di politica; **domestic/economic** ~ politica interna/economica; **company** ~ politica aziendale; **to set** ~ (**on sth**) stabilire una linea di condotta (riguardo a qc) **2.** (*principle*) principio *m;* **my** ~ **is to tell the truth whenever possible** la mia regola è di dire sempre la verità se appena possibile
policy[2] ['pɑː·lə·si] <-ies> *n* FIN polizza *f;* **insurance** ~ polizza di assicurazione; **to take out a** ~ fare un'assicurazione

P

policyholder ['pɑː·lə·si·ˌhoʊl·dɚ] *n* assicurato, -a *m, f*
policy maker *n* responsabile *mf* delle politiche
policy-making *n* formulazione *f* delle politiche
policy number *n* numero *m* di polizza
policy owner *n* titolare *mf* di polizza
polio [ˌpoʊ·lioʊ] *n,* **poliomyelitis** [ˌpoʊ·lioʊ·ˌma·ɪə·'laɪ·təs] *n* MED polio *f,* poliomielite *f*
polio vaccine *n* vaccino *m* antipolio
polish ['pɑː·lɪʃ] **I.** *n* **1.** (*substance: for furniture*) cera *f;* (*for shoes, silver*) lucido *m;* (*for nails*) smalto *m* **2.** (*action*) lucidatura *f;* **to give sth a ~** dare una lucidata a qc **3.** (*sophisticated, refined style*) raffinatezza *f* **II.** *vt* **1.** (*make shine*) far risplendere; (*shoes, silver*) lucidare **2.** *fig* (*refine*) raffinare
◆**polish off** *vt* (*food*) far fuori; (*work*) sbrigare; (*opponent*) liquidare
◆**polish up** *vt* **1.** (*polish to a shine*) lucidare **2.** (*improve, brush up*) perfezionare
Polish ['poʊ·lɪʃ] **I.** *adj* polacco, -a **II.** *n* LING polacco *m*
polished *adj* **1.** (*shiny*) lucido, -a **2.** *fig* (*sophisticated*) raffinato, -a; **~ manners** modi *mpl* distinti; **a ~ performance** un'esecuzione impeccabile
polite [pə·'laɪt] *adj* **1.** (*courteous*) cortese; **~ refusal** un cortese rifiuto **2.** (*cultured*) educato, -a; (*refined*) raffinato, -a; **~ society** buona società *f* **3.** (*superficially courteous*) beneducato, -a; **to keep a ~ conversation going** mantenere una conversazione garbata
politeness *n* **1.** (*good manners*) cortesia *f* **2.** (*consideration*) premura *f*
politic ['pɑː·lə·tɪk] *adj* **1.** (*judicious, prudent*) prudente **2.** POL **the body ~** la nazione
political [pə·'lɪ·tə·kəl] *adj* politico, -a; **~ pundit** esperto, -a *m, f* di politica; **to make ~ capital (out) of sth** trarre un vantaggio politico da qc
politically correct *adj* politically correct (*che non dà adito a discriminazioni razziste o sessiste*)
politician [ˌpɑː·lə·'tɪ·ʃən] *n* politico, -a *m, f*
politicize [pe·'lɪ·tə·saɪz] *vt* politicizzare
politics *n pl* **1.** (*activities of government*) politica *f;* **to go into ~** darsi alla politica; **to talk ~** parlare di politica **2.** (*political science*) scienze *fpl* politiche **3.** (*intrigue*) **company/ office ~** rivalità interne dell'azienda/dell'ufficio; **party ~** manovre di partito; (*complex relationship*)
polka ['poʊl·kə] **I.** *n* polca *f* **II.** *vi* ballare la polca
poll [poʊl] **I.** *n* **1.** (*public survey*) sondaggio *m;* **opinion ~** sondaggio *m* d'opinione; **to conduct a ~** fare un sondaggio **2.** *pl* (*elections*) **to go to the ~s** andare alle urne **3.** (*results of a vote*) **to head the ~** ottenere la maggioranza dei voti **4.** (*number of votes cast*) voti *mpl;* **there was a heavy/light ~** c'è stata un'alta/una bassa affluenza alle urne **II.** *vt* **1.** (*record the opinion*) sondare; **half the people ~ed**

la metà degli intervistati per il sondaggio **2.** (*receive*) **to ~ votes** ottenere voti
pollard ['pɑː·lɚd] *vt* capitozzare
pollen ['pɑː·lən] *n* polline *m*
pollen count *n* indice *m* di concentrazione del polline
pollinate ['pɑː·lə·neɪt] *vt* impollinare
polling *n* votazione *f*
voter's registration (card) *n* certificato *m* elettorale
voting day *n no art* giorno *m* delle votazioni
polling place *n* seggio *m* elettorale
pollster ['poʊls·tɚ] *n* intervistatore (in sondaggi), -trice *m, f*
pollutant [pə·'luː·tənt] *n* inquinante *m,* agente *m* inquinante
pollute [pə·'luːt] *vt* **1.** (*river, atmosphere, environment*) inquinare **2.** *fig* (*corrupt*) corrompere; **to ~ sb's mind** contaminare la mente di qu
polluter [pə·'luː·tɚ] *n* inquinatore, -trice *m, f*
pollution [pə·'luː·ʃən] *n* inquinamento *m*
polo ['poʊ·loʊ] *n* SPORTS polo *m*
polo shirt *n* polo *f*
polyamide ['pɑː·li·'æ·maɪd] *n* poliammide *f*
polychrome [ˌpɑː·lɪ·'kroʊm] *adj* policromo, -a
polyclinic ['pɑː·lɪ·klɪ·nɪk] *n* policlinico *m*
polyester [ˌpɑː·li·'es·tɚ] *n* poliestere *m*
polyethylene ['pɑː·lɪ·e·θə·liːn] *n* polietilene *m,* politene *m*
polygamist [pə·'lɪ·gə·mɪst] *n* poligamo *m*
polygamous [pə·'lɪ·gə·məs] *adj* poligamo, -a
polygamy [pə·'lɪ·gə·mi] *n* poligamia *f*
polyglot ['pɑː·lɪ·glɑːt] **I.** *adj* poliglotta **II.** *n* poliglotta *mf*
polygon ['pɑː·lɪ·gɑːn] *n* poligono *m*
polygonal [pə·'lɪ·gə·nəl] *adj* poligonale
polygraph ['pɑː·lɪ·græf] *n* poligrafo *m;* (*lie detector*) macchina *f* della verità
polymeric [ˌpɑː·lɪ·'me·rɪk] *adj* polimerico, -a
polymorphous [ˌpɑː·lɪ·'mɔːr·fəs] *adj* polimorfo, -a
Polynesia [ˌpɑː·lə·'niː·ʒə] *n* Polinesia *f*
Polynesian **I.** *adj* polinesiano, -a **II.** *n* polinesiano, -a *m, f*
polyp ['pɑː·lɪp] *n* MED, ZOOL polipo *m*
polyphonic [ˌpɑː·lɪ·'fɑː·nɪk] *adj* MUS polifonico, -a
polyphony [pə·'lɪ·fə·ni] *n* MUS polifonia *f*
polystyrene [ˌpɑː·lɪ·'sta·ɪə·riːn] *n* poliestirolo *m*
polysyllabic [ˌpɑː·lɪ·sɪ·'læ·bɪk] *adj* polisillabo, -a
polysyllable [ˌpɑː·lɪ·'sɪ·lə·bəl] *n* LING polisillabo *m*
polytechnic [ˌpɑː·lɪ·'tek·nɪk] *n* istituto *m* tecnico universitario
polytheism ['pɑː·lɪ·θiː·ɪ·zəm] *n* politeismo *m*
polytheistic [ˌpɑː·lɪ·θiː·'ɪs·tɪk] *adj* politeista
polyunsaturated [ˌpɑː·li·ʌn·'sæ·tʃə·reɪ·tɪd] *adj* polinsaturo, -a
polyunsaturated fats *npl,* **polyunsaturates** [ˌpɑː·lːi·ʌn·'sæ·tʃə·rəts] *npl* grassi *mpl* polinsa-

turi

polyurethane [ˌpɑːlɪˈjʊ·rə·θeɪn] *n* poliuret-
ano *m*

polyvalent [ˌpɑːlɪˈveɪ·lənt] *adj* polivalente

pomade [poʊˈmeɪd] *n* pomata *f*

pomegranate [ˈpɑːmˈɡræ·nɪt] *n* **1.**(*fruit*) melagrana *f* **2.**(*tree*) melograno *m*

pomp [pɑːmp] *n* pompa *f;* ~ **and circumstance** gran pompa

pomposity [pɑːmˈpɑːsə·t̬i] *n* pomposità *f*

pompous [ˈpɑːm·pəs] *adj* **1.**pomposo, -a
2.(*pretentious*) sfarzoso, -a; ~ **language** linguaggio *m* ampolloso

poncho [ˈpɑːn·tʃoʊ] *n* poncho *m*

pond [pɑːnd] *n* **1.**stagno *m,* laghetto *m;*
duck ~ laghetto delle anatre; **fish** ~ laghetto
dei pesci *m* **2.**fig (*Atlantic ocean*) **the Pond**
l'Oceano Atlantico

ponder [ˈpɑːn·dɚ] I. *vt* ponderare, soppesare;
to ~ **whether/why ...** riflettere se/sul perché
... II. *vi* riflettere; **to** ~ **on sth** riflettere su qc

ponderous [ˈpɑːn·də·rəs] *adj* **1.**(*movement*)
impacciato, -a **2.**(*style*) pesante

pone [poʊn] *n dial corn* ~ pane *m* di farina di
granturco

pontiff [ˈpɑːn·t̬ɪf] *n* REL **the** ~ il pontefice

pontifical [pɑːnˈt̬ɪ·fɪ·kəl] *adj* pontificale

pontificate[1] [pɑːnˈt̬ɪ·fɪ·keɪt] *vi* pontificare

pontificate[2] [pɑːnˈt̬ɪ·fɪ·kət] *n* (*office of pontiff*) pontificato *m*

pontoon [pɑːnˈtuːn] *n* (*floating device*) pon-
tone *m*

pontoon bridge *n* ponte *m* di barche

pony [ˈpoʊ·ni] <-ies> *n* pony *m inv*

ponytail [ˈpoʊ·ni·teɪl] *n* coda *f* di cavallo

pooch [puːtʃ] *n inf* (*dog*) cane

poodle [ˈpuː·dl] *n* (cane) barbone *m,* barbon-
cino *m*

poof [puːf] *interj inf* tacchete!

pooh [puː] I. *n childspeak* pupù *f,* cacca *f;* **to
do** ~ fare la pupù II. *vi childspeak* fare la pupù
III. *interj inf* (*indicating disgust*) ~! **what a
ghastly smell!** puah, che puzzo!

pooh-pooh [ˌpuːˈpuː] *vt inf* **to** ~ **a plan/a
proposal** ridicolizzare un progetto/una proposta

pool[1] [puːl] *n* **1.**(*of water, blood*) pozza *f;* **a** ~
of oil una sacca di petrolio; **a rock** ~ una zona
di mare tra gli scogli; **a** ~ **of light** una zona di
luce **2.**(*pond*) laghetto *m;* **swimming** ~ piscina *f*

pool[2] [puːl] I. *n* **1.**(*common fund*) fondo *m*
comune **2.**(*common supply*) riserva *f;* **car** ~
parco *m* macchine; **gene** ~ pool *m* genico;
typing ~ centro *m* dattilografia **3.**SPORTS
biliardo [*o* da pool] americano *m;* **to play** [*o inf*
shoot] (**a game of**) ~ giocare a biliardo; **to be
dirty** ~ essere un gioco sporco II. *vt* (*money,
resources*) mettere in comune; (*information*)
mettere insieme

pool hall *n,* **pool room** *n* sala *f* da biliardo

pool table *n* tavolo *f* da biliardo

poop[1] [puːp] *n* NAUT poppa *f;* ~ **deck** ponte *m*

del casseretto

poop[2] [puːp] *n inf* (*information*) **to get the** ~
on sth/sb mettersi al corrente su qc/qu

poop[3] [puːp] *inf* I. *n* cacca *f;* **dog** ~ cacca di
cane II. *vi* fare la cacca

◆**poop out** *vi inf* schiantare

pooper-scooper.   [ˈpuː·pɚ·ˌskuː·pə]   *n*
paletta *f* (per la raccolta di escrementi canini)

poop sheet *n sl* foglietto *m* informativo

poor [pʊr] I. *adj* **1.**(*lacking money*) povero, -a
2.(*attendance, harvest*) scarso, -a; (*memory,
performance*) cattivo, -a; ~ **soil** terreno *m*
povero; ~ **visibility** visibilità *f* scarsa; **to be** ~
at sth non essere bravo in qc; **to be in** ~
health non stare bene di salute; **to be a** ~
loser non saper perdere; **to give a** ~ **account
of oneself** dare cattiva prova di sé; **to cut a** ~
figure (**as sth**) fare una brutta figura (come
qc); **to be a** ~ **excuse for sth** essere la brutta
copia di qc; **to have** ~ **eyesight** avere la vista
debole; **to have** ~ **hearing** non sentirci bene;
to do a ~ **job of** (**doing**) **sth** fare male qc
3.(*deserving of pity*) povero, -a; **you** ~ **thing!**
poverino! II. *n* **the** ~ i poveri

poor box <-es> *n* cassetta *f* delle elemosine

poorhouse *n* ospizio *m* dei poveri

poorly [ˈpʊr·li] I. *adv* **1.**(*resulting from poverty*) poveramente **2.**(*inadequately*) male;
~ **dressed** malvestito; **to think** ~ **of sb** avere
una cattiva opinione di qu II. *adj* **to feel** ~ sentirsi poco bene

poorness [ˈpʊr·nɪs] *n* **1.**(*inadequacy*) scarsezza *f;* **the** ~ **of his judgment** la sua carenza
di giudizio **2.**(*poverty*) povertà *f*

poor relative *n* parente *mf* povero

pop[1] [pɑːp] I. *adj* pop; ~ **culture** cultura *f* pop
II. *n* MUS pop *m*

pop[2] [pɑːp] *n inf* (*father*) papà *m*

pop[3] [pɑːp] I. *n* **1.**(*small explosive noise*)
botto *m;* **the** ~ **of a champagne cork** il botto
di una bottiglia di champagne **2.**(*soda pop*)
gassosa *f;* **orange** ~ aranciata *f* II. <-pp-> *vi*
1.(*explode*) scoppiettare; (*burst*) scoppiare; **to
let the cork** ~ fare saltare il tappo **2.**(*come,
go quickly*) **to** ~ **upstairs** fare un salto al piano
di sopra; **to** ~ **out for sth** uscire un attimo per
qc III. <-pp-> *vt* **1.**(*make burst*) fare scoppiare; **to** ~ **popcorn** fare scoppiare i chicchi di
granturco **2.**(*put quickly*) mettersi; **to** ~ **sth
on/off** mettersi/togliersi qc

◆**pop in** *vi* fare un salto; **we popped in at
my brother's on our way home** tornando a
casa siamo passati da mio fratello

◆**pop for** *vi sl* **1.**(*pay for*) pagare **2.**(*get
caught at*) **to get popped for sth** essere bec-
cato per qc

◆**pop out** *vi* saltar fuori; **to** ~ **from somewhere** schizzare fuori da non si sa dove; **to** ~
for sth fare un salto fuori a fare qc

◆**pop up** *vi* (*appear*) saltar fuori; **to** ~ **out of
nowhere** spuntare all'improvviso

pop. *n abbr of* **population** popolazione *f*

pop art *n* pop art *f*

postcard *n* cartolina *f* (postale)
postdate [ˌpoʊstˈdeɪt] *vt* **1.** (*write a later date on*) postdatare **2.** (*happen after*) essere posteriore a
postdoctoral [ˌpoʊstˈdɑːktərəl] *adj* postdottorale
poster ['poʊstər] *n* **1.** (*picture*) poster *m* **2.** (*notice*) cartellone *m*
posterior [pɑːsˈtɪrɪər] **I.** *adj form* posteriore **II.** *n fig* posteriore *m inf*
posterity [pɑːsˈterəti] *n form* posterità *f;* **to preserve sth for** ~ conservare qc per i posteri
postern ['poʊstərn] *n* postierla *f;* MIL poterna *f*
postgraduate [ˌpoʊstˈgrædʒuˌwɪt] **I.** *n* laureato, -a che segue corsi di specializzazione *m* **II.** *adj* postuniversitario, -a; ~ **studies** studi *mpl* postuniversitari
posthaste [ˌpoʊstˈheɪst] *adv form* in gran fretta
posthumous ['pɑːstʃəməs] *adj form* postumo, -a
posting ['poʊstɪŋ] *n* destinazione *f*
Post-It® *n* foglietti *mpl* adesivi
postman ['poʊstmən] <-men> *n* postino *m*
postmark ['poʊstmɑːrk] **I.** *n* timbro *m* postale **II.** *vt* timbrare; **the letter is** ~**ed Rome** la lettera ha il timbro postale di Roma
postmaster ['poʊstˌmæstər] *n* capo *m* ufficio postale; ~ **general** (*head of a national postal service*) direttore *m* generale delle poste
post meridiem *adv s.* **P.M.**
post-modern [ˌpoʊstˈmɑːdərn] *adj* postmoderno, -a
post-modernism *n* postmodernismo *m*
postmortem [ˌpoʊstˈmɔːrtəm] *n* autopsia *f;* **to carry out a** ~ fare un'autopsia
postnatal [ˌpoʊstˈneɪtəl] *adj* post partum; ~ **depression** depressione *f* post partum
Post Office *n* ufficio *m* postale; **to take sth to the** ~ portare qc all'ufficio postale
post office box *n* casella *f* postale
post-op [ˌpoʊstˈɑːp] *adj inf* MED *abbr of* **post-operative** postoperatorio, -a
post-operative [ˌpoʊstˈɑːpərəˌtɪv] *adj* MED postoperatorio, -a
postpaid [ˌpoʊstˈpeɪd] *adj* (*letter*) franco di porto
postpone [poʊstˈpoʊn] *vt* posporre
postponement *n* rinvio *m*
postscript ['poʊstˌskrɪp] *n* **1.** (*at end of letter*) poscritto *m* **2.** *fig* epilogo *m;* **as a** ~ **to sth** a conclusione di qc
postulate¹ ['pɑːstʃəˌleɪt] *vt form* **1.** (*hypothesize*) postulare **2.** (*assume*) presupporre
postulate² ['pɑːstʃəˌlɪt] *n form* postulato *m*
posture ['pɑːstʃər] **I.** *n* **1.** (*position of body*) postura *f* **2.** (*opinion*) atteggiamento *f* **II.** *vi* assumere ua posa; **to** ~ **as sth** *pej* darsi delle arie da qc
postwar [ˌpoʊstˈwɔːr] *adj* postbellico, -a; **the** ~ **years** gli anni del dopoguerra; ~ **Europe** l'Europa del dopoguerra
posy ['poʊzi] <-ies> *n* mazzolino *m* di fiori

pot¹ [pɑːt] **I.** *n* **1.** (*container*) recipiente *m* **2.** (*for cooking*) pentola *f;* ~**s and pans** batteria *f* da cucina **3.** (*of food*) vasetto *m*, barattolo *m;* (*of drink*) brocca *f;* (*for coffee*) caffettiera *f;* (*for tea*) teiera *f* **4.** (*for plants, flowers*) vaso *m* **5.** *inf* GAMES **to win the** ~ vincere il piatto **6.** (*common fund*) cassa *f* comune **7.** *inf* (*a lot*) mucchio *m;* ~**s of money** un mucchio di soldi **8.** *fig* (*beer belly*) trippa *f inf* ▸ **it's like the** ~ **calling the** kettle **black** da che pulpito viene la predica; **to go to** ~ *inf* andare in malora; (*business, plan*) andare a rotoli **II.** <-tt-> *vt* **1.** (*put in a pot: food*) mettere [*o* conservare] in vaso; **to** ~ (**up**) (*plants*) invasare **2.** (*shoot*) uccidere (un selvatico per mangiarlo) **3.** SPORTS (*ball*) mettere in buca
pot² [pɑːt] *n inf* (*marijuana*) erba *f;* **to smoke** ~ fumare erba
potash ['pɑːtæʃ] *n* potassa *f*
potassium [pəˈtæsiˌəm] *n* potassio *m*
potassium chloride *n* cloruro *m* di potassio
potassium cyanide *n* cianuro *m* di potassio
potassium permanganate *n* permanganato *m* di potassio
potato [pəˈteɪˌtoʊ] <-es> *n* patata *f;* **sweet** ~ patata *f* americana; **baked** ~ patata al forno; **mashed** ~**es** purè *m* di patate; **fried/ roast(ed)** ~**s** patate fritte/arrosto
potato beetle *n*, **potato bug** *n* dorifora *f*
potato chips *npl* patatine *fpl*
potato masher *n* schiacciapatate *m inv*
potato peeler *n* pelapatate *m inv*
potbellied *adj* panciuto, -a
potbelly ['pɑːtˈbeˌli] <-ies> *n* pancione *m*
potbelly stove *n* stufetta *f* panciuta
potboiler ['pɑːtˌbɔɪlər] *n pej: opera commerciale*
potency ['poʊtənsi] *n* potenza *f;* (*of drink, evil, temptation*) forza *f;* (*of spell*) potere *m*
potent ['poʊtnt] *adj* potente; (*drink, motive, symbol*) forte; (*remedy*) efficace; (*argument*) convincente
potentate ['poʊtnˌteɪt] *n liter* potentato *m*
potential [pəˈtenˌʃl] **I.** *adj* potenziale **II.** *n* potenziale *m;* **to have** (**a lot of**) ~ avere (grandi) potenzialità
potentiality [pəˌtenˌʃiˈæˌləˌti] *n form* potenzialità *f*
potentially [pəˈtenˌʃəli] *adv* potenzialmente
potholder ['pɑːtˌhoʊlˌdər] *n* sottopentola *m*
pothole ['pɑːtˌhoʊl] *n* **1.** (*in road*) buca *f* **2.** (*underground hole*) pozzo *m*
potion ['poʊˌʃən] *n* pozione *f*
potluck *n* **1.** (*sth left over*) **to take** ~ accontentarsi di quello che passa il convento **2.** (*potluck dinner*) pranzo in cui ogni partecipante porta un piatto da dividere con gli altri

---

i Negli Stati Uniti, il **pot luck** è una festa in occasione della quale ogni invitato porta un'insalata, un piatto principale o un dolce. Lo scopo è quello di mettere insieme in tal modo un pasto completo di tutte le portate, ma può capitare che tutti gli invitati portino la stessa cosa, ad esempio dei dolci.

potluck dinner *n pranzo in cui ogni partecipante porta un piatto da dividere con gli altri*
potpourri [ˌpoʊ·pʊ·'riː] *n miscuglio di fiori e foglie secche per profumare ambienti*
pot roast *n* arrosto *m* morto
potshot ['pɑːt·ʃɑːt] *n* colpo *m* a casaccio; **to take a ~ at sb** sparare a casaccio contro qu; *fig* (*criticize*) lanciare critiche a caso
potted ['pɑː·t̬ɪd] *adj* **1.** (*plant*) in vaso **2.** (*food*) in vasetto, in barattolo; **~ shrimps** pasta *f* di gamberetti
potter ['pɑː·t̬ɚ] *n* vasaio, -a *m, f;* **~'s wheel** tornio *m* da vasaio
pottery ['pɑː·t̬ɚ·i] *n* **1.** (*art*) ceramica *f* **2.** <-ies> (*workshop*) fabbrica *f* di ceramiche
potty ['pɑː·t̬i] <-ies> *n* (*for baby*) vasino *m;* **to go (to the) ~** *childspeak* farla nel vasino
pouch [paʊtʃ] *n* **1.** *a.* ANAT, ZOOL borsa *f* **2.** (*handbag*) borsetta *f;* (*for mail*) borsa *f;* **tobacco ~** borsa *f* per il tabacco
pouf [puːf] *n* pouf *m inv*
pouffy ['puː·fi] *adj* (*hair*) cotonato, -a
poultice ['poʊl·t̬ɪs] *n* cataplasma *m*
poultry ['poʊlt·ri] *n* **1.** (*birds*) pollame *m* **2.** (*meat*) carne *f* bianca
poultry farm *n* azienda *f* avicola, allevamento *m* di polli
poultry farming *n* avicoltura *f,* allevamento *m* di polli
pounce [paʊns] **I.** *n* (*spring*) balzo *m* **II.** *vi* **1.** (*jump*) saltare; **to ~ on sth** balzare addosso a qc; (*cat*) balzare su qc; (*bird of prey*) ghermire qc **2.** *fig* **to ~ on an opportunity** prendere l'occasione al volo
pound[1] [paʊnd] *n* **1.** (*weight*) libbra *f* (*454 g*); **by the ~** alla libbra **2.** (*currency*) sterlina *f;* **~ sterling** (lira) sterlina britannica
pound[2] [paʊnd] *n* (*for cars*) deposito *m* (auto rimosse per divieto di sosta); (*for dogs*) canile *m* municipale; (*for sheep*) recinto *m*
pound[3] [paʊnd] **I.** *vt* **1.** (*hit repeatedly*) picchiare; (*beat*) battere; (*with a hammer*) martellare; **the waves ~ed the ship** la violenza delle onde squassava la nave **2.** (*walk heavily*) camminare con passo pesante su; **I could hear him ~ing the floor upstairs** potevo sentirlo camminare a passi pesanti al piano di sopra **3.** (*crush*) macinare; (*spices*) pestare (al mortaio); (*meat*) battere; MIL martellare; **to ~ sth to rubble** ridurre qc a un cumulo di macerie **II.** *vi* **1.** (*beat*) battere; (*on a door*) picchiare; (*on a table*) dare pugni su; (*heart, pulse*) battere forte; (*music*) rimbombare; **to ~ away on a piano** strimpellare il pianoforte; **the waves ~ed against the shore** le onde si abbattevano sul; **my head is ~ing!** ho la testa che mi scoppia! **2.** (*run*) **to ~ downstairs** scendere giù di corsa **3.** *fig* **to ~ away at sth** insistere su qc
pounding *n* **1.** (*noise*) rimbombo *m;* (*of heart*) battito (forte) *m;* (*of sea*) furia *f;* (*in head*) martellio *m* **2.** (*crushing*) triturazione *f;* (*grinding*) macinatura *f* **3.** (*attack*) attacco *m; a. fig* (*beating*) paliza *f inf;* **to take a ~** *a. fig* prendere una batosta; **the film took a heavy ~** il film ha avuto molte critiche negative
pour [pɔːr] **I.** *vt* **1.** (*cause to flow*) versare; **to ~ coffee/wine** versare il caffè/il vino; **to ~ sb sth** servire qc a qu; **to ~ oneself a glass of wine** versarsi un bicchiere di vino **2.** (*give in large amounts*) riversare; (*money, resources*) investire in gran quantità; **to ~ energy into sth** mettere moltissima energia in qc; **to ~ time into sth** dedicare un mucchio di tempo a qc; **to ~ thought into sth** riflettere molto su qc **II.** *vi* **1.** (*flow in large amounts: water*) fluire; (*letters, messages*) arrivare in gran quantità; **to ~ into sth** (*sunshine*) entrare a fiotti in qc; (*people*) affluire in qc; **refugees are ~ing into the country** i rifugiati continuano a riversarsi nel paese; **to be ~ing with sweat** essere sudato fradicio **2.** *impers* **it's ~ing** piove a dirotto
◆**pour in** *vi* affluire
◆**pour out I.** *vt* **1.** (*from container*) versare **2.** (*cause to flow quickly: smoke*) emettere; (*water*) riversare; **to ~ one's thanks** ringraziare calorosamente **3.** (*tell*) **to ~ sth to sb** rivelare qc a qu **II.** *vi* (*liquid*) fuoriuscire; (*people*) uscire a frotte
pout [paʊt] **I.** *vi* fare il broncio **II.** *vt* **to ~ one's lips** sporgere le labbra **III.** *n* broncio *m*
poverty ['pɑː·vɚ·t̬i] *n* **1.** (*lack of money*) povertà *f;* **extreme ~** miseria *f* **2.** *fig* (*lack of ideas, imagination*) povertà *f*
poverty level *n* minimo *m* vital
poverty-stricken ['pɑː·vɚ·t̬i·ˌstrɪ·kən] *adj* poverissimo, -a
POW [ˌpiː·oʊ·'dʌ·bl·juː] *n abbr of* **prisoner of war** prigioniero *m* di guerra
powder ['paʊ·dɚ] **I.** *n* **1.** (*dust*) polvere *f;* **to crush** [*o* **reduce**] **sth to a ~** ridurre qc in polvere **2.** (*snow*) neve *f* farinosa **II.** *vt* **1.** (*cover with powder*) spolverizzare; **to ~ one's face** incipriarsi; **to ~ one's nose** *fig* andare alla toilette **2.** (*sprinkle*) spolverizzare **3.** *sl* (*win easily*) polverizzare
powder blue *n* celeste
powdered *adj* in polvere; **~ sugar** zucchero *m* a velo
powder keg *n fig* polveriera *f*
powder puff *n* piumino *m* per la cipria
powder room *n* toilette *f* (per signore) *inv*
powdery ['paʊ·də·ri] *adj* **1.** (*snow*) farinoso, -a; (*stone*) friabile **2.** (*surface*) polveroso, -a
power ['pa·ʊɚ] **I.** *n* **1.** (*ability to control*) potere *m;* **to be within one's ~ to do sth** rientrate nei poteri di qu **2.** (*country, organization*) potenza *f;* (*person*) potere **3.** (*right*) facoltà *f* **4.** (*ability*) capacità *f;* **sb's ~s of concentration/persuasion/observation** capacità di concentrazione/persuasione/osser-

P

vazione **5.**(*strength*) forza *f* **6.**(*electricity*) corrente *f* **7.**(*energy*) PHYS energia *f* **8.** MAT potenza *f;* **two to the ~ of five** due elevato alla quinta ▶ **more ~ to you!** complimenti, e in bocca al lupo!; **to be the ~ behind sb** essere l'eminenza grigia di qu; **the ~s that be** chi è al potere **II.** *vi* **to ~ along the track** portarsi avanti con un'azione di forza **III.** *vt* azionare

powerboat *n* imbarcazione *f* a motore

power brakes *npl* AUTO freni *mpl* servoassistiti

power cable *n* cavo *m* elettrico

power-driven *adj* elettrico, -a

powerful ['pa·ʊɚ·fəl] *adj* **1.**(*influential, mighty*) potente **2.**(*physically strong*) possente, forte **3.**(*having a great effect*) convincente **4.**(*anger, jealousy*) intenso, -a; **~ emotions** emozioni *fpl* forti **5.**(*able to perform well*) potente

powerfully ['pa·ʊɚ·fə·li] *adv* **1.**(*using great force*) con forza **2.**(*argue, speak*) in modo autorevole

powerhouse ['pa·ʊɚ·,haʊs] *n* centrale *f* elettrica; **to be a ~ of ideas** *fig* essere una fonte inesauribile di idee

powerless ['pa·ʊɚ·ləs] *adj* impotente; **to be ~ against sb** essere impotente contro qu

power line *n* linea *f* elettrica

power mower *n* tosaerba *m* a motore *inv*

power outage *n* interruzione *f* della corrente elettrica

power plant *n* centrale *f* elettrica; **nuclear ~** centrale *f* nucleare

power politics *n* politica *f* della forza

power station *n* centrale *f* elettrica

power steering *n* servosterzo *m*

power tool *n* utensile *f* a energia elettrica

powwow ['paʊ·waʊ] *n* **1.** riunione *f* (*di pellerossa*) **2.** *fig, inf* consiglio *m*

pox [pɑːks] *n* (*chickenpox*) varicella *f;* (*smallpox*) vaiolo *m;* (*syphilis*) sifilide *f*

pp. *abbr of* **pages** pp.

PR [piː·'ɑːr] *n* **1.** *abbr of* **public relations** pubbliche *fpl* relazioni **2.** POL *abbr of* **proportional representation** sistema *m* proporzionale

practicable ['præk·tɪ·kə·bl] *adj form* practicabile

practical ['præk·tɪ·kl] **I.** *adj* pratico, -a **II.** *n* prova *f* pratica

practicality [,præk·tɪ·'kæ·lə·ţi] *n* <-ies> **1.**(*feasibility*) attuabilità *f* **2.**(*practical detail*) **the practicalities of sth** gli aspetti pratici di qc

practical joke *n* scherzo *m*

practically ['præk·tɪk·li] *adv* **1.**(*almost*) praticamente **2.**(*of a practical nature*) **to be ~ based** basarsi sulla pratica; **to be ~ minded** avere senso pratico

practice ['præk·tɪs] **I.** *n* **1.**(*act of practicing*) pratica *f;* **to be out of ~** essere fuori esercizio; **~ makes perfect** si impara con la pratica **2.**(*custom, regular activity*) consuetudine *f;* **traditional religious ~s** pratiche *fpl* religiose;

standard ~ procedura *f* abituale; **to make a ~ of sth** avere qc come regola **3.**(*training session*) allenamento *m* **4.**(*of a profession*) esercizio *m* **5.**(*business, office*) studio *m* **II.** *vt* **1.**(*do, carry out*) practicare **2.**(*improve skill*) esercitarsi in/a; **to ~ the piano** fare esercizio al piano **3.**(*work in: medicine, law*) esercitare ▶ **to ~ what one preaches** mettere in pratica ciò che si predica **III.** *vi* **1.**(*improve skill*) esercitarsi; SPORTS allenarsi **2.**(*work in profession*) esercitare; **to ~ as a doctor** fare il medico

practiced ['præk·tɪst] *adj* (*experienced, skilled*) esperto, -a; **to be ~ in sth** essere competente in qc; **a ~ liar** un bugiardo patentato

practicing ['præk·tɪ·sɪŋ] *adj* (*doctor, lawyer*) praticante; (*Catholic, Jew*) praticante

practitioner [præk·'tɪ·ʃə·nɚ] *n* (*of a skill*) professionista *mf;* (*doctor*) medico, -a *m, f;* **legal ~** avvocato (professionista), -a/-essa *m, f*

pragmatic [præg·'mæ·ţɪk] *adj* pragmatico, -a

pragmatism ['præg·mə·tɪ·zəm] *n* pragmatismo *m*

prairie ['pre·ri] *n* prateria *f*

praise [preɪz] **I.** *vt* **1.**(*express approval*) lodare; **to ~ sb to the skies** [*o* to no end] portare qu alle stelle **2.**(*worship*) lodare **II.** *n* **1.**(*expression of approval*) lode *f;* **to heap ~ on sb, to shower sb with ~** coprire qu di lodi **2.**(*worship*) lode *f;* **~ be (to God)!** Dio sia lodato!

praiseworthy ['preɪz·,wɜːr·ði] *adj* lodevole

prance [præns] *vi* (*horse*) fare la rallegrata; (*person*) pavoneggiarsi

prank [præŋk] *n* scherzo *f;* **to play a ~ on sb** fare uno scherzo a qu

prate [preɪt] *vi form* cianciare

prattle ['præ·ţl] **I.** *vi* blaterare; (*child*) balbettare **II.** *n* ciance *fpl;* (*of child*) balbettio *m*

prawn [prɔːn] *n* gambero *m,* scampo *m*

prawn cocktail *n* cocktail di scampi *m*

pray [preɪ] **I.** *vi* **1.** REL pregare; **to ~ to sb** (*that*) pregare qu (che +*subj*) **2.**(*hope*) **to ~ for sth** sperare in qc **II.** *vt* supplicare; **and what, ~ tell, are you doing?** si può sapere, di grazia, cosa stai facendo?

prayer [prer] *n* **1.** REL preghiera *f;* **to say a ~** [*o* one's ~s] pregare **2.**(*action of praying*) preghiera *f* **3.** *pl* (*church service*) **morning/evening ~s** preghiere del mattino/della sera **4.** *fig* (*hope*) speranza *f;* **to not have a ~ of doing sth** *inf* non avere la benché minima speranza di fare qc

prayer book *n* libro *m* di preghiere

prayer meeting *n* incontro *m* di preghiera

prayer rug *n* tappeto *m* di preghiera

praying mantis ['preɪ·ɪŋ·'mæn·tɪs] *n* mantide *f inv* religiosa

preach [priːtʃ] **I.** *vi* predicare; **to ~ at sb** *pej* fare la predica a qu **II.** *vt* **1.** REL (*a sermon*) tenere; (*the Gospel*) predicare **2.**(*advocate*) predicare ▶ **to practice what you ~** mettere in pratica ciò che si predica

preacher ['priː·tʃɚ] *n* predicatore, -trice *m, f*

preamble [pri:'æm·bl] *n* preambolo *m*

prearrange [ˌpri:·ə·'reɪndʒ] *vt* prestabilire

precalculus [pri:'kælk·jə·ləs] *n corso di studi che precede gli studi di calcolo*

precarious [prɪ'ke·ri·əs] *adj* precario, -a

precast ['pri:·kæst] *adj* prefabbricato, -a

precaution [prɪ'kɔ:·ʃən] *n* precauzione *f*

precautionary [ˌprɪ'kɔ:·ʃə·ne·ri] *adj* precauzionale; ~ **measure** misura *f* preventiva

precede [prɪ'si:d] *vt* precedere; **to ~ the report with an introduction** iniziare il rapporto con un'introduzione

precedence ['pre·sə·dəns] *n* 1.(*priority*) precedenza *f;* **to take ~ over sb** avere la precedenza su qu 2.(*order of priority*) ordine *m* di precedenza

precedent ['pre·sə·dent] *n* precedente *m;* **to set a ~ (for sth/doing sth)** stabilire un precedente (per qc/fare qc)

preceding [prɪ'si:·dɪŋ] *adj* precedente; **the ~ day** il giorno precedente

precept ['pri:·sept] *n form* 1.(*rule*) norma *f* 2.(*principle*) principio *m*

precinct ['pri:·sɪŋkt] *n* 1.(*police district*) distretto *m* di polizia; (*police station*) stazione *f* di polizia 2.(*electoral district*) circoscrizione *f* 3.*form* (*environs*) dintorni *mpl*

precious ['pre·ʃəs] I. *adj* 1.(*of great value*) prezioso, -a; **you can keep your ~ ring!** *iron* tieniti il tuo maledetto anello! 2.(*beloved: child, pet*) amato, -a 3.(*affected*) affettato, -a; (*person*) manierato, -a II. *adv inf* 1.(*very*) **~ few** proprio pochi; **to be ~ little help** essere di scarso aiuto 2.(*valuable: stone, metal*) prezioso

precipice ['pre·sə·pɪs] *n* precipizio *m*

precipitate[1] [prɪ'sɪ·pɪ·teɪt] I. *vt* 1.*form* (*throw*) scaraventare 2.*form* (*provoke*) accelerare 3. CHEM precipitare II. *vi* METEO precipitare

precipitate[2] [prɪ'sɪ·pɪ·tɪt] I. *adj form* precipitoso, -a II. *n* precipitato *m*

precipitation [prɪ·ˌsɪ·pɪ·'teɪ·ʃən] *n* precipitazione *f*

precipitous [prɪ'sɪ·pɪ·təs] *adj* 1.(*very steep*) ripido, -a 2.(*having many precipices*) scosceso 3.(*rapid*) drastico, -a 4.*form* (*precipitate*) precipitoso, -a

précis [preɪ'si:] I. *n* compendio *m* II. *vt form* compendiare

precise [prɪ'saɪs] *adj* 1.(*moment, measurement*) esatto, -a [*o* preciso, -a] 2.(*person*) meticoloso, -a

precisely *adv* 1.(*exactly*) precisamente; **~!** certo!; **to do ~ the opposite** fare esattamente l'opposto 2.(*carefully*) con precisione

precision [prɪ'sɪ·ʒən] I. *n* 1.(*accuracy*) precisione *f* 2.(*meticulous care*) esattezza *f* II. *adj* (*tool, equipment*) di precisione

preclude [prɪ'klu:d] *vt form* precludere

precocious [prɪ'koʊ·ʃəs] *adj* precoce

precociousness *n*, **precocity** [prɪ'kɑ:·sə·ti] *n form* precocità *f*

preconceived [ˌpri:·kən·'si:vd] *adj* preconcetto, -a

preconception [ˌpri:·kən·'sep·ʃən] *n* preconcetto *m*

precondition [ˌpri:·kən·'dɪ·ʃən] *n* premessa *f* indispensabile

precook [pri:'kʊk] *vt* precuocere

precursor [prɪ'kɜ:r·sə] *n* precursore, -corritrice *m, f*

predate [pri:'deɪt] *vt* risalire a un periodo precedente a

predator ['pre·də·ţə] *n* predatore *m*

predatory ['pre·də·tɔ:·ri] *adj* predatore, -trice

predecessor ['pre·də·se·sə] *n* predecessore *m;* (*ancestor*) antenato, -a *m, f*

predestination [ˌpri:·des·tɪ·'neɪ·ʃən] *n* predestinazione *f*

predestine [ˌpri:·'des·tɪn] *vt* predestinare

predetermine [ˌpri:·dɪ·'tɜ:r·mən] *vt* predeterminare

predicament [prɪ'dɪ·kə·mənt] *n* impiccio *m*

predicate[1] ['pre·dɪ·kɪt] *n* LING predicato *m*

predicate[2] ['pre·dɪ·keɪt] *vt form* 1.(*be based on*) **to be ~d on sth** fondarsi su qc 2.(*state, assert*) asserire

predicative [prɪ'dɪ·kə·ţɪv] *adj* LING predicativo, -a

predict [prɪ'dɪkt] *vt* predire

predictable [prɪ'dɪk·tə·bl] *adj* prevedibile

prediction [prɪ'dɪk·ʃən] *n* 1.(*forecast*) pronostico *m* 2.(*act of predicting*) previsione *f*

predilection [ˌpre·də·'lek·ʃən] *n form* predilezione *f*

predispose [ˌpri:·dɪs·'poʊz] *vt* predisporre

predisposition [ˌpri:·dɪs·pə·'zɪ·ʃən] *n* 1.*form* (*tendency*) propensione *f* 2. MED predisposizione *f*

predominance [prɪ'dɑ:·mə·nəns] *n* predominanza *f*

predominant [prɪ'dɑ:·mə·nənt] *adj* predominante

predominate [prɪ'dɑ:·mə·neɪt] *vi* predominare

preemie ['pri:·mi:] *n inf* (*premature baby*) (bambino, -a) prematuro *m*

preeminence [ˌpri:·'e·mɪ·nənts] *n form* preminenza *f*

preeminent [ˌpri:·'e·mɪ·nənt] *adj form* preminente

preempt [ˌpri:·'empt] *vt* prevenire

preemption [ˌpri:·'emp·ʃən] *n* prelazione *f*

preemptive [pri:·'emp·tɪv] *adj* 1.**~ right** diritto di opzione 2.(*attack*) preventivo, -a

preen [pri:n] I. *vi* 1.(*bird*) lisciarsi (le penne) con il becco 2.*fig* (*congratulate oneself*) compiacersi II. *vt* 1.(*cat, bird*) lisciarsi 2.(*groom*) **to ~ oneself** agghindarsi; **to ~ oneself on sth** (*congratulate*) compiacersi di qc

preexisting [ˌpri:·ɪg·'zɪs·tɪŋ] *adj* preesistente

prefab ['pri:·fæb] *inf* I. *n abbr of* **prefabricated house** casa *f* prefabbricata II. *adj abbr of* **prefabricated** prefabbricato, -a

prefabricate [ˌpri:·'fæb·rɪ·keɪt] *vt* prefabbri-

care
prefabricated *adj* prefabbricato, -a
prefabricated house *n* casa *f* prefabbricata
preface ['pre·fɪs] I. *n* prefazione *f* II. *vt* premettere
prefatory ['pre·fə·tɔː·ri] *adj form* preliminare
prefect ['priː·fekt] *n* prefetto *m*
prefer [priː·'fɜːr] <-rr-> *vt* preferire
preferable ['pre·frə·bl] *adj* preferibile
preferably ['pre·frəb·li] *adv* preferibilmente
preference ['pref·rəns] *n* **1.**(*liking better*) preferenza *f* **2.**(*priority*) precedenza *f*
preferential [ˌpre·fə·'ren·ʃl] *adj* preferenziale; ECON preferenziale
preferred [priː·'fɜːrd] *adj* preferito, -a
prefigure [ˌpriː·'fɪɡ·jəʳ] *vt form* prefigurare
prefix ['priː·fɪks] <-es> *n* prefisso *m*
pregnancy ['preɡ·nən·tsi] *n* **1.**(*condition: woman*) gravidanza *f*; ZOOL gestazione *f* **2.**(*period of time*) gravidanza
pregnancy test *n* test *m* di gravidanza *inv*
pregnant ['preɡ·nənt] *adj* **1.**(*woman*) incinta; (*animal*) gravida; **to be ~ by sb** essere stata messa incinta da qu; **to become ~** (*woman*) rimanere incinta; (*animal*) rimanere gravida; **to get sb ~** mettere incinta qu **2.** *fig* (*silence, pause*) carico, -a di significato; **to be ~ with possibilities for sth** essere ricco di possibilità per qc
prehensile [priː·'hen·sɪl] *adj* prensile
prehistoric [ˌpriː·hɪ·'stɔː·rɪk] *adj* preistorico, -a
prehistory [ˌpriː·'hɪs·tə·ri] *n* preistoria *f*
prejudge [ˌpriː·'dʒʌdʒ] *vt* pregiudicare
prejudice ['pre·dʒʊ·dɪs] I. *n* **1.**(*preconceived opinion*) pregiudizio *m* **2.**(*bias*) pregiudizio *m;* LAW pregiudizio *m;* **without ~** senza pregiudizio; **without ~ to sth** LAW senza pregiudizio per qc II. *vt* **1.**(*bias*) **to ~ sb against sth** influenzare qu contro qc **2.**(*damage: sb's case, a defendant, a candidate*) pregiudicare
prejudiced ['pre·dʒʊ·dɪst] *adj* (*person*) prevenuto, -a; (*attitude, judgment, opinion*) prevenuto; **to be ~ against sb** essere prevenuto nei confronti di qu
prejudicial [ˌpre·dʒə·'dɪ·ʃəl] *adj form* **to be ~ to** nuocere a
preliminary [prɪ·'lɪ·mə·ne·ri] I. *adj* preliminare II. <-ies> *n* **1.**(*introduction*) preliminari *mpl* **2.** SPORTS (*heat*) (gara) eliminatoria *f* **3.** *form* (*preliminary exam*) esame *m* preliminare
prelims ['priː·lɪms] *npl inf* **1.**(*exams*) *abbr of* **preliminary exams** esami *mpl* preliminari **2.** SPORTS (gara) eliminatoria *f* **3.** *abbr of* **preliminary pages** pagine *fpl* introduttive
prelude ['prel·juːd] *n* preludio *m*
premarital [ˌpriː·'mæ·rɪ·ţl] *adj* prematrimoniale
premature [ˌpriː·mə·'tʃʊr] *adj* prematuro, -a
premature ejaculation *n* eiaculazione *f* precoce
premeditated [ˌpriː·'me·dɪ·teɪ·ţɪd] *adj* premeditato, -a

premeditation [ˌpriː·me·dɪ·'teɪ·ʃən] *n* premeditazione *f*
premenstrual [ˌpriː·'ment·strəl] *adj* premestruale
premenstrual syndrome *n* sindrome *f* premestruale
premier [prɪ·'mɪr] I. *n* POL primo ministro *m,* premier *mf inv* II. *adj* primo, -a
première [prɪ·'mɪr] I. *n* prima *f* II. *vt, vi* presentare per la prima volta
premise ['pre·mɪs] I. *n* **1.**(*of argument*) premessa *f;* **on** [*o* **under**] **the ~ that ...** in considerazione del fatto che ... **2.** *pl* (*land and building on it*) locali *mpl* e area di proprietà; **we are relocating to new ~** ci stiamo trasferendo in nuovi locali; **these premises are protected with surveillance cameras** la proprietà è controllata con telecamere a circuito chiuso; **no smoking on school ~** è proibito fumare in tutta la scuola; **the ice-cream is made on the ~** il gelato è di produzione propria II. *vt form* **1.**(*be based on*) fondare **2.**(*preface*) premettere
premium ['priː·mi·əm] I. *n* **1.**(*insurance payment*) premio *m* **2.**(*extra charge*) sovrapprezzo *m;* (*high price*) prezzo *m* elevato **3.**(*bonus*) premio *m* **4.**(*importance*) **to put a ~ on sth** dare molta importanza a qc; **to be at a ~** (*very valuable*) essere di primaria importanza **5.**(*gasoline*) super *f* II. *adj* di prima qualità
premium price *n* prezzo *m* maggiorato
premium quality *n* prima qualità *f*
premonition [ˌpriː·mə·'nɪ·ʃən] *n* premonizione *f;* **to have a ~ that ...** avere il presentimento che ...
prenatal [ˌpriː·'neɪ·ţl] *adj* prenatale
preoccupation [ˌpriː·ɑːk·jə·'peɪ·ʃən] *n* preoccupazione *f*
preoccupied [priː·'ɑːk·ju·paɪd] *adj* preoccupato, -a; **to be ~ with sth** essere assorto in qc
preoccupy [priː·'ɑːk·ju·paɪ] <-ie-> *vt* preoccupare
preordain [ˌpriː·ɔːr·'deɪn] *vt* predestinare
preowned [priː·'oʊnd] *adj* (*vehicle*) usato, -a; (*electronics*) di seconda mano; (*home*) che ha avuto un precedente proprietario
prep [prep] I. *adj abbr of* **preparatory** preparatorio, -a; **prep course** corso *m* propedeutico; **prep school** scuola superiore (privata); **prep work** lavoro *m* preparatorio II. *n inf abbr of* **preparation** preparazione *f*
prepackage [ˌpriː·'pæ·kɪdʒ] *vt* preconfezionare
prepaid [ˌpriː·'peɪd] *adj* prepagato, -a; **~ phone** [*o* **calling**] **card** carta *f* (telefonica) prepagata
prepaid postcard *n* cartolina *f* preaffrancata
prepaid reply card *n* cartolina *f* di risposta preaffrancata
preparation [ˌpre·pə·'reɪ·ʃən] I. *n* **1.**(*getting ready*) preparazione *f* **2.**(*substance*) preparazione *m* **3.** *pl* (*measures*) preparativi *mpl*

II. *adj* preparatorio, -a

preparatory [prɪ·'pæ·rə·tɔː·ri] *adj* preparatorio, -a

preparatory course *n* corso *m* propedeutico

preparatory school *n* scuola *f* privata (*di insegnamento secondario*)

prepare [prɪ·'per] **I.** *vt* preparare; **to ~ sb for sth** preparare qu per qc **II.** *vi* prepararsi; **to ~ for action** prepararsi all'azione

prepared [prɪ·'perd] *adj* **1.** (*ready*) pronto, -a **2.** (*willing*) pronto, -a; **to be ~ to do sth** essere disposto a fare qc **3.** (*food, speech*) preparato, -a (in anticipo)

preparedness [prɪ·'pe·rɪd·nɪs] *n* (*willingness*) disposizione *f*; MIL capacità *f* di reazione

prepay [ˌpriː·'peɪ] *vt irr* pagare in anticipo

prepayment [ˌpriː·'peɪ·mənt] *n* pagamento *m* anticipato

preponderance [prɪ·'pɑːn·də·rənts] *n form* preponderanza *f*

preponderant [prɪ·'pɑːn·də·rənt] *adj form* preponderante

preposition [ˌpre·pə·'zɪ·ʃən] *n* preposizione *f*

prepossessing [ˌpriː·pə·'ze·sɪŋ] *adj* avvenente

preposterous [prɪ·'pɑːs·tə·əs] *adj* ridicolo, -a

preppie, preppy ['pre·pi] **I.** <-ies> *n inf* ragazzo, -a *m*, *f* bene, preppy *mf inv* **II.** *adj* <preppier, preppiest> *inf* dei ragazzi bene, preppy

prepuce ['priː·pjuːs] *n* (*foreskin*) prepuzio *m*; (*clitoral foreskin*) prepuzio del(la) clitoride

prerequisite [ˌpriː·'rek·wɪ·zɪt] **I.** *adj* essenziale **II.** *n* requisito *m* indispensabile; **to be a ~ for sth** essere un requisito indispensabile per qc

prerogative [prɪ·'rɑː·gə·t̮ɪv] *n* (*right, privilege*) prerogativa *f*; **that's your ~** è una tua prerogativa; **skiing used to be the ~ of the rich** una volta lo sci era un privilegio dei ricchi

Pres. [prez] *n abbr of* **president** presidente *mf*

presage ['pre·sɪdʒ] **I.** *n liter* **1.** (*sign, omen*) presagio *m* **2.** (*intuition*) presentimento *m* **II.** *vt liter* (*warn*) preannunciare **III.** *vi liter* **to ~ well/ill** essere di buon/cattivo auspicio

Presbyterian [ˌprez·bɪ·'tɪ·ri·ən] **I.** *n* presbiteriano, -a *m*, *f* **II.** *adj* presbiteriano, -a

presbytery ['prez·bɪ·te·ri] *n* REL **1.** ARCHIT (*part of church*) presbiterio *m* **2.** (*priest's residence*) presbiterio, casa *f* parrocchiale

preschool ['priː·skuːl] **I.** *n* giardino *m* d'infanzia **II.** *adj* prescolastico, -a; (*child*) in età prescolare

prescribe [prɪ·'skraɪb] **I.** *vt* **1.** MED prescrivere; (*rest, diet*) raccomandare **2.** *form* (*order*) prescrivere; **~d by law** stabilito per legge **II.** *vi* MED scrivere una ricetta

prescribed [prɪ·'skraɪbd] *adj* prescritto, -a; **in the ~ way** nel modo stabilito; **at the ~ time** al momento stabilito

prescription [prɪ·'skrɪp·ʃən] *n* **1.** MED prescrizione (medica) *f*; ricetta (medica) *f*; (*medicine itself*) medicina *f*; **only available with a ~** solo dietro presentazione di ricetta medica; **to make out a ~** fare una ricetta; **to fill a ~** scrivere una ricetta **2.** *form* (*act of prescribing*) prescrizione *f*

prescription charge *n* ticket (sui medicinali) *m inv*

prescriptive [prɪ·'skrɪp·tɪv] *adj* (*strict*) rigoroso, -a

prescriptive grammar *n* LING grammatica *f* normativa

presence ['pre·zənts] *n* **1.** (*attendance*) presenza *f*; **military/police ~** presenza militare/della polizia; **~ of mind** presenza/prontezza di spirito; **in sb's ~** in presenza di qu; **in my ~** in mia presenza; **in the ~ of two witnesses** davanti a due testimoni; **your ~ is requested** è richiesta la sua presenza; **to feel sb's ~** avvertire la presenza di qu; **to make one's ~ felt** farsi notare **2.** (*personality*) presenza *f*

present[1] ['pre·zənt] **I.** *n* presente *m* ▶ **at ~** al presente/momento; **for the ~** per il presente/momento **II.** *adj* **1.** (*current: address, generation*) attuale; **at the ~ moment** [*o* **time**] al momento, attualmente; **the ~ year** l'anno in corso; **in the ~ case** in questo caso; **up to the ~ time** fino a ora; **the ~ writer** chi scrive **2.** (*in attendance*) presente; **to be ~ at sth** assistere a qc; **all those ~** tutti i presenti; **~ company excepted** esclusi i presenti

present[2] ['pre·zənt] *n* (*gift*) regalo *m*; **to give sb a ~** fare un regalo a qu; **I got it as a ~** me lo hanno regalato; **to make sb a ~ of sth** regalare qc a qu

present[3] [prɪ·'zent] *vt* **1.** (*give*) presentare; **to ~ one's apologies to sb** *form* presentare le proprie scuse a qu; **to ~ one's credentials** presentare le proprie credenziali; **to ~ sth (to sb)** consegnare qc (a qu); **to ~ sb with sth** donare qc a qu **2.** (*introduce*) presentare; **to ~ sb to sb** presentare qu a qu; **may I ~ my wife?** le presento mia moglie; **to ~ a bill** presentare un progetto di legge **3.** (*to an audience: play, musical, concert*) presentare; **~ing X as Julius Caesar** con X nel ruolo di Giulio Cesare; **to ~ a paper at a conference** presentare una relazione a un congresso **4.** (*confront*) **to ~ sb with sth** mettere qu davanti a qc; **to be ~ed with a complicated situation** trovarsi di fronte a una situazione complicata; **to ~ sb with a problem** creare un problema per qu **5.** (*constitute*) costituire; **to ~ a problem for sb** costituire un problema per qu; **to ~ difficulties for sb** creare difficoltà a qu **6.** (*offer*) presentare; (*view, atmosphere*) offrire **7.** (*exhibit: argument, plan, theory*) esporre; (*check, passport, ticket*) presentare; **to ~ a petition to sb** presentare una petizione a qu *form* **8.** MIL **to ~ arms** presentare le armi **9.** (*appear*) **to ~ oneself for sth** presentarsi per qc

presentable [prɪ·'zen·tə·bl] *adj* presentabile; **to make oneself ~** rendersi presentabile

presentation [ˌpre·zən·'teɪ·ʃən] *n* **1.** (*act*) presentazione *f*; (*of theory, thesis*) esposizione *f*;

(*of dissertation*) discussione *f;* **to make** [*o* give] **a** ~ fare una relazione; **on** ~ **of this voucher** dietro presentazione di questo buono **2.** (*of prize, award*) consegna *f*

presentation copy *n* copia *f* omaggio

present-day [ˌpre·zənt·deɪ] *adj* attuale; ~ **Boston** la Boston attuale

presenter [prɪˈzen·tə·] *n* presentatore, -trice *m, f*

presentiment [prɪˈzen·tɪ·mənt] *n form* presentimento *m;* **to have a** ~ **of sth** avere il presentimento di qc; **to have the** ~ **that ...** presagire che ...

presently [ˈpre·zənt·li] *adv* **1.** (*soon*) tra poco; **I'll be there** ~ sarò lì tra poco **2.** (*now*) ora

present participle *n* LING participio *m* presente

present tense *n* LING tempo *m* presente

preservation [ˌpre·zə·ˈveɪ·ʃən] *n* **1.** (*of building*) conservazione *f;* **to be in a poor/good state of** ~ essere in cattivo/buono stato (di conservazione) **2.** (*of species, custom*) tutela *f*

preservative [prɪˈzɜːr·və·tɪv] **I.** *adj* preservante **II.** *n* conservante *m;* **without artificial** ~**s** senza conservanti artificiali

preserve [prɪˈzɜːrv] **I.** *vt* **1.** (*maintain: customs, peace*) mantenere; (*dignity, sense of humor, building*) conservare; (*appearance, silence*) mantenere **2.** (*food*) conservare **3.** (*protect*) proteggere; **to** ~ **sb from sth** proteggere qu da qc; **heaven** ~ **us!** che Dio ci protegga! **II.** *n* **1.** *pl* (*jam*) confettura *f* **2.** (*reserve*) riserva *f;* **game** ~ riserva *f* di caccia; **wildlife** ~ riserva *f* naturale **3.** *fig* (*domain*) dominio *m;* **to be the** ~ **of the rich** essere dominio esclusivo dei ricchi; **to be a male** ~ essere riservato agli uomini

preserved *adj* **1.** (*maintained*) conservato, -a; **to be badly** ~ essere in cattivo stato **2.** (*food*) in conserva; ~ **food** conserve *fpl*

preshrunk [ˌpriːˈʃrʌŋk] *adj* (*fabric, jeans*) irrestringibile

preside [prɪˈzaɪd] *vi* presiedere; **to** ~ **at/over sth** presiedere qc; **to** ~ **at a table** sedere a capotavola

presidency [ˈpre·zɪ·dən·si] *n* **1.** (*office of president*) POL presidenza *f;* (*of company*) direzione *f;* (*of university*) rettorato *m* **2.** (*tenure as president*) mandato *m* (presidenziale)

president [ˈpre·zɪ·dənt] *n* POL presidente; (*of club, organization*) presidente, -essa *m, f;* (*of company*) presidente *mf;* (*of university*) rettore, -trice *m, f*

presidential [ˌpre·zɪˈden·tʃəl] *adj* presidenziale

presidential address *n* discorso *m* presidenziale

presidential candidate *n* candidato, -a *m, f* alla presidenza

presidential election *n* elezioni *fpl* presidenziali

Presidents' Day *n* festa nazionale statunitense in onore dei presidenti Lincoln e Washington il terzo lunedì di febbraio

press [pres] **I.** *vt* **1.** (*push: button, switch*) premere; (*doorbell*) suonare; (*trigger*) premere; **to** ~ **down on the lever** abbassare la leva **2.** (*squeeze*) spingere; **the crowd** ~**ed us against the locked door** la folla ci spingeva contro la porta chiusa **3.** (*flatten: grapes*) pigiare; (*flowers*) pressare; (*olives*) torchiare **4.** (*extract juice*) spremere **5.** (*iron: shirt, dress*) stirare **6.** MUS (*album, disk*) stampare **7.** (*try to force*) sollecitare; **to** ~ **sb to do sth** sollecitare qu a fare qc; **to** ~ **sb for sth** sollecitare qu per qc; **to** ~ **sb for payment** sollecitare qu al pagamento; **to** ~ **sth on sb** imporre qc a qu **8.** (*find difficult*) **to be** (**hard**) ~**ed to do sth** avere (grosse) difficoltà a fare qc **9.** (*be short of*) **to be** ~**ed for money/time** essere a corto di soldi/di tempo **10.** (*pursue*) insistere; **to** ~ **a claim/one's case** insistere su un reclamo/sulla propria tesi; **to** ~ **a point** insistere su un punto **11.** LAW **to** ~ **charges** presentare delle accuse **II.** *vi* **1.** (*push*) premere; **to** ~ **hard** spingere forte; **to** ~ **on the brakes** spingere sui freni **2.** (*crowd*) accalcarsi; **to** ~ **through the crowd** aprirsi un varco tra la folla; **to** ~ **down** (**on sth**) premere forte (su qc) **3.** (*be urgent*) incalzare; **time is** ~**ing** il tempo stringe **4.** (*put under pressure*) fare pressione; **to** ~ **for sth** insistere per ottenere qc **III.** *n* **1.** (*push*) pressione *f;* (*with hand*) pressione *m;* **at the** ~ **of a button** premendo un pulsante **2.** (*ironing*) stiratura *f;* **to give sth a** ~ dare una stirata a qc **3.** (*crush*) calca *f* **4.** (*machine*) pressa *f;* **printing** ~ macchina *f* da stampa; **to be in** ~ essere in (corso di) stampa; **to go to** ~ (*newspaper, book*) andare in stampa; **hot off the** ~ (*news*) fresco di stampa **5.** PUBL **the** ~ la stampa; **to have bad/good** ~ (*publicity*) avere recensioni negative/favorevoli **6.** (*for tennis racket*) tenditore *m* **7.** (*cupboard*) armadio *m*

♦ **press ahead** *vi s.* press on

♦ **press down on** *vt* **1.** (*force down*) schiacciare **2.** (*lean on*) appoggiarsi su

♦ **press forward** *vi s.* press on

♦ **press in** *vt* piantare

♦ **press on** *vi* continuare imperterrito

♦ **press upon** *vt* imporre

press agency *n* agenzia *f* di stampa

press box *n* tribuna *f* stampa

media magnate *n,* **media mogul** *n* magnate *mf* dei mass media

media campaign *n* campagna *f* mediatica

press card *n* tessera *f* di giornalista

newspaper clipping *n* ritaglio *m* di stampa

press conference *n* conferenza *f* stampa; **to hold a** ~ tenere una conferenza stampa

press coverage *n* copertura *f* (stampa)

press-gang [ˈpres·gæn] *vt* **to** ~ **sb into doing sth** costringere qu a fare qc

pressing I. *adj* (*issue, matter*) urgente; (*need*) impellente **II.** *n* (*of clothes*) stiratura *f;* (*of fruits*) pressatura *f;* (*of records*) stampa *f*

pressman [ˈpres·mən] *n* giornalista *mf*

press office *n* ufficio *m* stampa

press release *n* comunicato *m* stampa; **to issue a ~** rilasciare un comunicato stampa

newspaper report *n* servizio *m* giornalistico

pressure ['preˑʃə·] I. *n* 1. *a.* PHYS pressione *f;* **high/low ~** pressione alta/bassa; **to put ~ on sth** esercitare pressione su qc; **at full ~** a tutta pressione; **to be under ~** *a. fig* essere sotto pressione 2. (*influence*) **to put ~ on sb (to do sth)** fare pressione su qu (perché faccia qc); **to do sth under ~ from sb** fare qc perché messo alle strette da qu; **under the ~ of circumstances** sotto la pressione delle circostanze 3. *pl* (*stressful circumstances*) **the ~ of life/work/childhood** le difficoltà della vita/del lavoro/dell'infanzia 4. MED pressione *f;* **blood ~** pressione sanguigna II. *vt* **to ~ sb to do sth** fare pressione su qu perché faccia qc

pressure cabin *n* AVIAT cabina *f* pressurizzata

pressure cooker *n* pentola *f* a pressione

pressure gauge *n* manometro *m*

pressure group *n* POL gruppo *m* di interesse

pressurize ['preˑʃə·raɪz] *vt* 1. (*control air pressure*) pressurizzare 2. *inf* (*person, government*) fare pressione (su); **to ~ sb into doing sth** fare pressione su qu perché faccia qc

prestige [preˑ'stiːʒ] *n* prestigio *m*

prestigious [preˑ'stɪ·dʒəs] *adj* prestigioso, -a

pre-stressed concrete [ˌpriː'strest 'kɑːŋˑkriːt] *n* calcestruzzo *m* precompresso

presumably [prɪˑ'zuːˑməb·li] *adv* presumibilmente

presume [prɪˑ'zuːm] I. *vt* 1. (*suppose*) presumere, supporre; **to ~ that ...** immaginare che ...; **~d dead** si presume che sia morto; **to be ~d innocent** essere presunto innocente 2. (*dare*) **to ~ to do sth** osare fare qc II. *vi* 1. (*be presumptuous*) avere la presunzione di; **I don't wish to ~, but ...** non vorrei sembrare impertinente, ma ... 2. (*assume*) **Dr Smith, I ~?** lei è il dottor Smith, immagino ... 3. (*take advantage of*) **to ~ on sb** approfittare di qu

presumption [prɪˑ'zʌmpˑʃən] *n* 1. (*assumption*) supposizione *f;* **the ~ is that ...** si suppone che ...; **the ~ of innocence** LAW la presunzione di innocenza 2. *form* (*arrogance*) presunzione *f* 3. (*daring*) ardire *m*

presumptive [prɪˑ'zʌmpˑtɪv] *adj* presunto, -a

presumptuous [prɪˑ'zʌmpˑtʃuːˑəs] *adj* 1. (*arrogant*) presuntuoso, -a 2. (*forward*) sfacciato, -a

presuppose [ˌpriːˑsəˑ'poʊz] *vt form* presupporre

presupposition [ˌpriːˑsʌˑpəˑ'zɪˑʃən] *n* presupposizione *f;* **to be based on false ~s** basarsi su supposizioni errate

pretax [ˌpriːˑ'tæks] *adj* al lordo di imposte

pretend [prɪˑ'tend] I. *vt* 1. (*make believe*) fingere; **to ~ to be interested** fingere di essere interessato; **to ~ to be dead** fare finta di essere morto; **to ~ to be sb** farsi passare per qu; **the children ~ed that they were dinosaurs** i bambini giocavano ai dinosauri 2. (*claim*) pretender; **I don't ~ to know** non pretendo di sapere II. *vi* fingere; **he's just ~ing** sta solo facendo finta

pretended *adj* finto, -a

pretender *n* pretendente *mf;* **~ to the throne** pretendente al trono

pretense ['priːˑtents] *n* 1. (*simulation*) finta *f,* finzione *f;* **to make a ~ of sth** fare finta di qc; **to make no ~ of sth** non dissimulare qc 2. (*pretext*) pretesto *m;* **under (the) ~ of ...** con il pretesto di ...; **to do sth under false ~s** fare qc con l'inganno 3. (*claim*) pretesa *f;* **to make no ~ to objectivity/innocence** non pretendere di essere obiettivo/innocente

pretension [prɪˑ'tenˑtʃən] *n* 1. (*claim*) pretesa *f;* **to have ~s to (being/doing) sth** avere la pretesa di (essere/fare) qc 2. *s.* **pretentiousness**

pretentious [prɪˑ'tenˑtʃəs] *adj* pretenzioso, -a; (*in bad taste*) pacchiano, -a

pretentiousness *n* pretenziosità *f;* (*in bad taste*) pacchianeria *f*

preterit(e) ['preˑtə·ɪt] LING I. *n* preterito *m* II. *adj* preterito, -a *form*

preternatural [ˌpriːˑtə·'næ·tʃə·rəl] *adj form* (*exceptional*) preternaturale

pretext ['priːˑtekst] *n* pretesto *m;* **a ~ for doing sth** un pretesto per fare qc; **on the ~ that ...** con il pretesto di ...; **under the ~ of doing sth** con il pretesto di fare qc

prettify ['prɪˑtɪ·faɪ] *vt inf* (*room, street*) rendere (più) bello; (*account, report*) abbellire

pretty ['prɪˑti] I. *adj* <-ier, -iest> 1. (*beautiful: thing*) bello, -a, piacevole; (*child, woman*) bello, -a, carino, -a; **not a ~ sight** non bello a vedersi 2. *inf* (*considerable*) bello, -a; **a ~ mess** un bel casino *m* II. *adv* (*quite*) abbastanza 2. **~ much** più o meno; **to be ~ much the same** essere praticamente lo stesso; **I'm ~ nearly finished** ho quasi finito; **~ well everything** quasi tutto

pretzel ['pretˑsl] *n* biscotto *m* salato

prevail [prɪˑ'veɪl] *vi* 1. (*triumph*) prevalere; **to ~ over/against sth** avere il sopravvento su qc; **to ~ over/against sb** avere la meglio su/contro qu 2. (*predominate*) predominare; (*conditions, situation*) imporsi 3. (*convince*) **to ~ (up)on sb (to do sth)** *form* convincere qu (a fare qc)

prevailing *adj* prevalente; (*atmosphere, feelings*) dominante; **under the ~ circumstances** nelle circostanze attuali

prevalence ['preˑvə·lənts] *n* 1. (*common occurrence*) diffusione *f;* **the ~ of drugs in some neighborhoods** la grande diffusione della droga in certi quartieri 2. (*predominance*) prevalenza *m*

prevalent ['preˑvə·lənt] *adj* 1. (*common*) molto comune; (*disease, opinion*) molto diffuso, -a 2. (*present-day*) attuale 3. (*predominant*) prevalente

prevaricate [prɪˑ'væ·rɪ·keɪt] *vi form* essere evasivo; **to ~ over sth** tergiversare su qc

prevarication [prɪˑˌvæ·rɪ·'keɪ·ʃən] *n form* evasività *f inv*

prevent [prɪ·'vent] *vt* **1.** (*hamper*) impedire; **to ~ sb from doing sth** impedire a qu di fare qc; **the news ~ed his coming** la notizia gli ha impedito di venire **2.** (*avoid: confusion, panic, crime*) prevenire

preventative [prɪ·'ven·tə·t̬ɪv] *adj s.* **preventivo, -a**

prevention [prɪ·'ven·tʃən] *n* prevenzione *f;* **for the ~ of crime** per la prevenzione del crimine ▸**~ is better than** cure *prov,* **an ounce of ~ is worth a pound of** cure *prov* è meglio prevenire che curare *prov*

preventive [prɪ·'ven·t̬ɪv] *adj* preventivo, -a

preview ['pri:·vju:] I. *n* CINE, THEAT, OF EXHIBITION anteprima *f;* (*film extract*) trailer *m inv;* (*of TV program, exhibition*) anticipazione *f* II. *vt* CINE, THEAT presentare in anteprima

previous ['pri:·vi·əs] I. *adj* **1.** (*former*) precedente; **on the ~ day/week** il giorno/la settimana precedente; **no ~ experience required** non è richiesta nessuna esperienza **2.** (*prior*) previo, -a II. *adv* **~ to doing sth** prima di fare qc

previous convictions *npl* precedenti *mpl* penali

previously *adv* **1.** (*beforehand*) prima **2.** (*formerly*) precedentemente; **to have met sb ~** avere già incontrato qu

prewar [ˌpriː·'wɔːr] *adj* prebellico, -a; **in the ~ years** nell'anteguerra

prey [preɪ] *n* **1.** (*animal*) preda *f;* **bird of ~** rapace *m* **2.** (*person*) preda *f,* vittima *f;* **to be easy ~ for sb** essere una preda [*o* vittima] facile per qu; **to fall ~ to** (*animal*) cadere preda di; (*person*) essere vittima di

◆**prey on** *vt,* **prey upon** *vt* **1.** (*feed on*) nutrirsi di; **fear ~ed on me** *fig* ero in preda alla paura **2.** (*exploit*) sfruttare

price [praɪs] I. *n* **1.** COM prezzo *m; oil* **~s, the ~ of oil** il prezzo del petrolio; **to ask a high/low ~** chiedere un prezzo alto/basso; **to be the same ~** avere lo stesso prezzo; **to go up/down in ~** aumentare/diminuire di prezzo; **to name a ~** chiedere un prezzo; **what ~ are apples?** quanto costano le mele? **2.** FIN (*of stocks*) corso *m,* prezzo *m* **3.** *fig* (*disadvantage*) prezzo *m;* **the ~ one has to pay for fame** [*o* **the ~ of fame**] il prezzo della notorietà; **beyond** [*o* **without**] **~** che non ha prezzo; **to set a high ~ on sth** attribuire a qc un valore molto alto **4.** (*bribe*) **everyone has their price** ognuno ha il suo prezzo ▸**to set a ~ on sb's** head mettere una taglia su qu; **at** any **~** a qualunque costo; **not at** any **~** per niente al mondo; **to pay a** heavy **~** pagarla molto cara; **to** pay **the ~** pagarla cara; **at a ~** a caro prezzo II. *vt* **1.** (*mark with price tag*) prezzare **2.** (*fix price*) fissare il prezzo di; **to be reasonably ~d** avere un prezzo ragionevole ▸**to be ~d out of the** market avere un prezzo troppo alto per poter competere sul mercato

price bracket *n* fascia *f* di prezzo

price control *n* controllo *m* dei prezzi

price cutting *n* riduzione *f* dei prezzi

price fixing *n* fissazione *f* dei prezzi

price freeze *n* blocco *m* dei prezzi

price index *n* indice *m* dei prezzi

priceless ['praɪs·lɪs] *adj* **1.** (*invaluable*) inestimabile, prezioso, -a; **to be ~** non avere prezzo **2.** *fig* (*funny*) divertente; **that's ~!** è da crepare dal ridere! *inf*

price level *n* livello *m* dei prezzi

price list *n* listino *m* prezzi

price range *n* gamma *f* di prezzi

price raise *n* aumento *m* dei prezzi

price stability *n* stabilità *f* dei prezzi

price tag *n* **1.** (*label*) cartellino *m* del prezzo **2.** *inf* (*cost*) prezzo *m*

price war *n* guerra *f* dei prezzi

pricey ['praɪ·si] *adj* <pricier, priciest> *inf* (*object*) caro, -a, costoso, -a; (*shop*) caro, -a

pricing ['praɪ·sɪŋ] *n* determinazione *f* del prezzo; **~ policy** politica *f* di determinazione dei prezzi

prick [prɪk] I. *vt* **1.** (*jab*) pungere, bucare; **to ~ one's finger with** [*o* **on**] **a needle** pungersi il dito con un ago; **to ~ sb's conscience** far rimordere la coscienza a qu **2.** (*mark with holes*) bucare **3.** (*listen: animal*) **to ~ one's ears** drizzare le orecchie; (*person*) aguzzare le orecchie II. *vi* **1.** (*pin*) pungere **2.** (*hurt: eyes, skin*) irritare III. *n* **1.** (*act, pain*) puntura *f;* **to feel the ~ of conscience** avere rimorsi di coscienza **2.** (*mark*) buco *m* **3.** *vulg* (*penis*) cazzo *m* **4.** *vulg* (*idiot*) coglione *m vulg*

◆**prick out** *vt* (*flowers*) trapiantare

◆**prick up** *vt* **to ~ one's ears** (*animal*) drizzare le orecchie; (*person*) aguzzare le orecchie

prickle ['prɪ·kl] I. *n* **1.** (*thorn: of plant*) spina *f;* (*of animal*) aculeo *m* **2.** (*tingle*) formicolio *m;* **to feel a ~ of excitement** provare un brivido di emozione II. *vi* **1.** (*cause prickling sensation*) pizzicare **2.** (*tingle*) formicolare **3.** (*prick*) pungere III. *vt* (*prick*) pungere, pizzicare

prickly ['prɪk·li] <-ier, -iest> *adj* **1.** (*thorny: plant*) spinoso, -a; (*animal*) con aculei **2.** (*tingling*) pungente; (*beard*) ispido, -a; **~ sensation** formicolio *m* **3.** *inf* (*easily offended*) permaloso, -a

prickly heat *n* sudamina *f*

prickly pear *n* **1.** (*fruit*) fico *m* d'India **2.** (*plant*) fico *m* d'India, opunzia *f*

pride [praɪd] I. *n* **1.** (*proud feeling*) orgoglio *m;* **to feel great ~** essere molto orgoglioso; **to take ~ in sth** tenere molto a qc; **to be sb's ~ and joy** essere l'orgoglio di qu **2.** (*self-respect*) amor *m* proprio; **to hurt sb's ~** ferire l'orgoglio di qu; **to swallow one's ~** soffocare l'orgoglio; **false ~** vanità *f* **3.** (*arrogance*) superbia *f* **4.** (*group of lions*) branco *m* ▸**~ comes** [*o* **goes**] **before a** fall *prov* la superbia andò a cavallo e tornò a piedi; *prov;* **to have ~ of** place essere al posto d'onore II. *vt* **to ~**

oneself that ... andare fiero del fatto che ...
priest [priːst] *n* REL prete *m*, sacerdote *m*
priestess ['priːsˑtɪs] *n* REL sacerdotessa *f*
priesthood ['priːstˑhʊd] *n* REL **1.** (*position, office*) sacerdozio *m;* **to enter the ~** essere ordinato sacerdote **2.** (*priests in general*) clero *m*
priestly ['priːstˑli] *adj* sacerdotale
prig [prɪg] *n pej* moralista *mf*
priggish ['prɪˑgɪʃ] *adj* moralistico, -a
prim [prɪm] <-mmer, -mmest> *adj* **1.** *pej* perbenista; **~ and proper** prude e ammodo **2.** (*appearance*) ordinato, -a
primacy ['praɪˑməˑsi] *n form* supremazia *f*
prima donna [priːˑməˑ'dɑːˑnə] *n* **1.** (*opera singer*) primadonna *f* **2.** (*arrogant person*) primadonna *f*
primal ['praɪˑməl] *adj* **1.** (*primitive*) originario, -a **2.** (*most important*) primario, -a
primarily [praɪˑ'meˑrəˑli] *adv* principalmente, prima di tutto
primary ['praɪˑmeˑri] **I.** *adj* **1.** (*principal*) primario, -a; (*aim*) principale; **to be of ~ importance** essere di primaria importanza **2.** (*basic*) fondamentale; (*industry*) primario, -a; **~ meaning of a word** significato principale di una parola; **~ stress** LING accento *m* primario **II.** <-ies> *n* POL (*elezioni*) *fpl* primarie
primary color *n* colore *m* primario
primary education *n* istruzione *f* primaria
primary school *n* scuola elementare
primate ['praɪˑmeɪt] *n* **1.** ZOOL primate *m* **2.** REL primate *m*
prime [praɪm] **I.** *adj* **1.** (*main*) principale; (*objective*) primario, -a; **of ~ importance** di primaria importanza **2.** (*first-rate*) eccellente; (*beef*) di prima scelta; **of ~ quality** di prima qualità; **in ~ condition** in perfetto stato **II.** *n* **1.** (*best stage*) apogeo *m elev;* **to be in one's ~** [*o* to be in the ~ of life] esssere nel fiore degli anni; **to be past one's ~** non essere più nel fiore della giovinezza; **to be cut off in one's ~** essere stroncato nel fiore degli anni **2.** (*prime number*) numero *m* primo **III.** *vt* **1.** (*apply undercoat: ferrous metals*) applicare la vernice antiruggine a; (*walls*) applicare la pittura di fondo a; (*canvas*) mesticare **2.** (*prepare*) preparare; (*gun for exploding*) inserire la carica, *in un'arma ad avancarica;* (*bomb*) innescare; (*pump*) adescare; (*motor*) iniettare combustibile in (per l'avviamento) **3.** (*brief*) istruire; **to ~ sb for doing sth** preparare qu a fare qc; **to be well ~d for an interview** essere ben preparato per un colloquio **4.** (*make drunk*) ubriacare; **to be well ~d** avere bevuto troppo
prime cost *n* ECON costo *m* primo
prime interest rate *n* FIN tasso *m* (d'interesse) primario
prime meridian *n* GEO meridiano *m* fondamentale
prime minister *n* POL primo ministro *mf*
prime mover *n* forza *f* trainante; (*person*) pro-

motore, -trice *m, f*
prime number *n* MAT numero *m* primo
primer ['praɪˑmə] *n* **1.** (*for ferrous metals*) vernice *f* antiruggine; (*for walls*) pittura *f* di fondo; (*for canvas*) mestica *f* **2.** (*explosive*) innesco *m* **3.** (*textbook*) manuale *m;* (*for learning to read*) sillabario *m*
prime rate *n* FIN tasso *m* (di interesse) primario
prime ribs *n* FOOD costate *fpl* di prima scelta
prime time *n* RADIO, TV prima *f* serata
primeval [praɪˑ'miːˑvəl] *adj* primevo, -a primordiale, primordiale; (*forest*) primordiale
primitive ['prɪˑmɪˑtɪv] **I.** *adj a.* ART, HIST, ZOOL primitivo, -a; (*method, weapon*) rudimentale **II.** *n* ART, HIST, SOCIOL primitivo, -a *m, f*
primogeniture [ˌpraɪˑmoʊˑ'dʒeˑnɪˑtʃə] *n* primogenitura *f*
primordial [praɪˑ'mɔːrˑdiˑəl] *adj form* **1.** (*from beginning*) primordiale **2.** (*basic*) primordiale, -a
primrose ['prɪmˑroʊz] *n*, **primula** ['prɪmˑjəˑlə] *n* BOT primula *f*, primavera *f*
prince [prɪns] *n* principe *m;* **crown ~** principe ereditario; **Prince Charming** principe azzurro; **Prince of Wales** principe di Galles; **the Prince of Darkness** il principe delle tenebre
prince consort *n* principe *m* consorte
princely ['prɪnsˑli] *adj* principesco, -a; *fig* magnifico, -a; **the ~ sum** la favolosa somma
princess ['prɪntˑsɪs] *n* principessa *f*
principal ['prɪnˑtsəˑpl] **I.** *adj* principale **II.** *n* **1.** (*head of a primary school*) direttore, -trice *m, f;* (*head of a secondary school*) preside *mf* **2.** FIN capitale *m*
principality [ˌprɪnˑtsəˑ'pæˑləˑti] *n* principato *m*
principally *adv* principalmente
principle ['prɪnˑtsəˑpl] *n* principio *m;* **in ~** in linea di principio; **on ~** per principio
principle clause *n* clausola *f* principale
print [prɪnt] **I.** *n* **1.** (*handwriting*) stampatello *m;* (*type*); **bold ~** neretto *m*, grassetto *m* **2.** (*printed form*) **to rush sth into ~** pubblicare qc alla svelta; **to appear in ~** essere pubblicato; **to go out of ~** essere esaurito **3.** (*of artwork*) stampa *f;* (*engraving*) incisione *m;* PHOT copia *f*, stampa *f* **4.** (*printed pattern*) stampato *m* **5.** *pl, inf* (*fingerprints*) impronta *f* digitale **II.** *vt* **1.** (*publish*) pubblicare **2.** (*put into printed form*) stampare **3.** COMPUT (*make printout of*) stampare **4.** PHOT stampare **5.** (*mark fabric*) stampare **6.** (*write in unjoined letters*) scrivere in stampatello **III.** *vi* **1.** (*appear in printed form*) stamparsi **2.** (*write in unjoined letters*) scrivere in stampatello
printable ['prɪnˑtəˑbl] *adj* stampabile
printed circuit (board) *n* ELEC circuito *m* stampato
printed material *n*, **printed matter** *n* stampe *fpl*
printer ['prɪnˑtə] *n* **1.** INFOR stampante *f;* **inkjet/laser ~** stampante a inchiostro/laser **2.** (*person*) tipografo, -a *m, f*

P

printer driver *n* driver *m* per stampante *inv*
printing *n* 1. (*art*) stampa *f* 2. (*action*) impressione *f*
printing ink *n* inchiostro *m* per stampante
printing office *npl* tipografia *f*
printing press *n* macchina *f* da stampa
printout ['prɪnt·aʊt] *n* INFOR stampata *f*
print run *n* tiratura *f*
print shop *n* tipografia *f*
prior ['pra·ɪə] I. *adv form* (*before*) prima; ~ **to doing sth** prima di fare qc II. *adj form* 1. (*earlier*) previo, -a, precedente; **without ~ notice** senza preavviso 2. (*preferred*) più importante III. *n* REL priore *m*
prioritize [praɪ·'ɔː·rə·taɪz] *vt* dare priorità a
priority [praɪ·'ɔː·rə·ti] I. <-ies> *n* 1. (*being most important*) priorità *f*; (*in time*) precedenza *f* 2. *pl* (*order of importance*) priorità *fpl*; **to get one's priorities right** stabilire quali sono i propri obiettivi prioritari; **to set priorities** stabilire le priorità II. *adj* 1. (*of utmost importance*) prioritario, -a 2. *a.* FIN (*claim, right*) prioritario, -a
priory ['pra·ɪə·ri] *n* priorato *m*
prism ['prɪ·zəm] *n* prisma *m*
prismatic [prɪz·'mæ·t̬ɪk] *adj* prismatico, -a
prison ['prɪ·zən] *n* prigione *f*, carcere *m*; **to go to ~** andare in prigione; **to put sb in ~** mettere qu in prigione
prison camp *n* campo *m* di prigionia
prison cell *n* cella *f*
prisoner ['prɪ·zə·nɚ] *n* detenuto, -a *m*, *f*; MIL prigioniero, -a *m*, *f*; **to hold sb ~** tenere prigioniero qu; **to take sb ~** fare prigioniero qu
prisoner of war *n* prigioniero, -a *m*, *f* di guerra
prison inmate *n* detenuto, -a *m*, *f*
prison riot *n* rivolta *f* dei detenuti
prison yard *n* cortile *m* del carcere
pristine ['prɪs·tiːn] *adj form* intatto, -a
privacy ['praɪ·və·si] *n* privacy *f*; **I'd like some ~** vorrei rimanere un po' solo
private ['praɪ·vət] I. *adj* 1. (*not public*) privato, -a 2. (*confidential*) riservato, -a; **sb's ~ opinion** l'opinione personale di qu; **he's a very private person** è una persona molto riservata 3. (*intimate*) intimo, -a; ~ **parts** parti *fpl* intime II. *n* 1. *pl, inf* (*genitals*) parti *fpl* intime 2. MIL soldato *m* semplice
privateer [ˌpraɪ·və·'tɪr] *n* NAUT (*vessel*) nave *f* corsara; (*commander*) comandante *m* di nave corsara
private eye *n inf*, **private investigator** *n* investigatore , -trice privato *m*
privately ['praɪ·vət·li] *adv* 1. (*in private*) in privato; **to celebrate ~** festeggiare in privato 2. (*secretly*) in segreto 3. (*personally*) personalmente
private property *n* proprietà *f* privata
privation [praɪ·'veɪ·ʃən] *n form* privazione *f*; **to live in ~** vivere in miseria; **to suffer ~** soffrire privazioni
privatization [ˌpraɪ·və·tɪ·'zeɪ·ʃən] *n* privatizzazione *f*

privatize ['praɪ·və·taɪz] *vt* privatizzare
privet ['prɪ·vɪt] *n* ligustro *m*
privilege ['prɪ·və·lɪdʒ] I. *n* 1. (*special right*) privilegio *m* 2. (*honor*) onore *m* II. *vt* **to be ~d to do sth** avere il privilegio di fare qu
privileged *adj* 1. (*special*) privilegiato, -a 2. (*confidential*) confidenziale
privy¹ ['prɪ·vi] *adj form* **to be ~ to sth** essere a parte di qc
privy² ['prɪ·vi] *n* (*toilet*) gabinetto *m*
prize¹ [praɪz] I. *n* 1. (*in competition*) premio *m;* **to take home a ~** vincere un premio 2. (*reward*) ricompensa *f* II. *adj* 1. *inf* (*first-rate*) eccezionale 2. (*prizewinning*) premiato, -a III. *vt* apprezzare; **to ~ sth highly** tenere qc in gran conto
prize² [praɪz] *vt s.* **pry²**
prizefight ['praɪz·faɪt] *n* incontro *m* di boxe (con premio in denaro)
prizefighter *n* pugile *mf* professionista (che combatte per denaro)
prizefighting *n* pugilato *m* professionisti (con premi in denaro)
prize list *n* lista *f* dei premiati
prize money *n* SPORTS premio *m* in denaro
prizewinning ['praɪz·ˌwɪ·nɪŋ] *adj* premiato, -a
pro¹ [proʊ] *inf* I. *n abbr of* **professional** professionista *mf* II. *adj abbr of* **professional** professionistico, -a
pro² [proʊ] I. *adv* a favore II. *n inf* pro *m;* **the ~s and cons of sth** i pro e i contro di qc III. *prep* pro, a favore di IV. *adj* favorevole
proactive [ˌproʊ·'æk·tɪv] *adj* proattivo, -a
probability [ˌprɑː·bə·'bɪ·lə·ti] *n* probabilità *f*; **in all ~** con ogni probabilità
probable ['prɑː·bə·bl] *adj* 1. (*likely*) probabile 2. (*credible*) verosimile 3. LAW ~ **cause** motivo fondato
probably *adv* probabilmente
probate ['proʊ·beɪt] *n* LAW omologazione *f* di testamento
probation [proʊ·'beɪ·ʃən] *n* 1. (*at work*) periodo *m* di prova; **to be on ~** essere in prova 2. LAW libertà *f* vigilata
probationary [proʊ·'beɪ·ʃə·ne·ri] *adj* di prova; ~ **period** periodo *m* di prova
probationer [proʊ·'beɪ·ʃə·nɚ] *n* 1. LAW persona *f* in libertà vigilata 2. (*at work*) lavoratore, -trice *m*, *f* in prova
probation officer *n funzionario di polizia addetto alla sorveglianza di persone in libertà vigilata*
probe [proʊb] I. *vi* (*examine*) investigare; **to ~ into the possibilities** esaminare le possibilità; **to ~ into sb's private life** indagare sulla vita privata di qu II. *vt* 1. (*examine*) esaminare 2. MED esplorare con una sonda III. *n* 1. (*examination, investigation*) indagine *f* 2. MED, AVIAT sonda *f*
probity ['proʊ·bə·ti] *n form* probità *f*
problem ['prɑː·b·ləm] *n* problema *m*
problematic(al) [ˌprɑː·b·lə·'mæ·t̬ɪ·k(əl)] *adj* 1. (*creating difficulty*) problematico, -a

2. (*questionable, disputable*) dubbio, -a
problem child *n* bambino, -a *m*, *f* difficile
proboscis [proʊˈbɑːsɪs] *n* **1.** ZOOL proboscide *f* **2.** *fig, hum* (*person's nose*) nasone *m*
procedural [prəˈsiːdʒəˈəl] *adj* procedurale; LAW processuale
procedure [prəˈsiːdʒəˈ] *n* procedura *f*
proceed [proʊˈsiːd] *vi* **1.** (*move along*) procedere; (*continue*) andare avanti; (*continue driving*) procedere; **to ~ with sth** procedere con qc; **to ~ against sb** procedere legalmente contro qu **2.** (*come from*) **to ~ from** provenire da **3.** (*start, begin*) **to ~ with sth** mettersi a fare qc; **to ~ to do sth** mettersi a fare qc
proceedings [proʊˈsiːdɪŋz] *npl* **1.** LAW procedimento *m* **2.** *form* (*events*) sviluppi *mpl* **3.** *form* (*minutes of meeting*) atti *mpl*
proceeds [ˈproʊsiːdz] *n* ricavo *msg*
process[1] [ˈprɑːses] I. *n* processo *m;* **in the ~** allo stesso tempo; **to be in the ~ of doing sth** stare facendo qc II. *vt* **1.** *a.* TECH, COMPUT elaborare; (*raw materials, waste*) trattare **2.** PHOT sviluppare
process[2] [prəˈses] *vi form* sfilare in corteo
process chart *n* diagramma *m* del processo produttivo
process engineering *n* ingegneria *f* dei processi
processing [ˈprɑːsesɪŋ] *n* **1.** *a.* TECH, INFOR elaborazione *f;* (*of raw materials*) trasformazione *f;* (*of waste*) trattamento *m;* **data ~** elaborazione dei dati; **batch ~** lavorazione per lotti **2.** PHOT sviluppo *m*
procession [prəˈseʃən] *n* **1.** sfilata *m;* **funeral ~** corteo *m* funebre; **to go in ~** sfilare in corteo **2.** REL processione *f* **3.** *fig* fila *f*
processor [ˈprɑːsesəˈ] *n* INFOR processore *m*
pro-choice *adj* in favore dell'aborto
proclaim [proʊˈkleɪm] *vt form* proclamare; **to ~ war** dichiarare guerra
proclamation [ˌprɑːkləˈmeɪʃən] *n form* proclamazione *f;* **a ~ of war** una dichiarazione di guerra
proclivity [proʊˈklɪvəˌt̮i] *n form* propensione *f;* **sexual ~** tendenza *f* sessuale; **to have a ~ for sth** avere una propensione per qc
procrastinate [proʊˈkræstəˌneɪt] *vi* procrastinare, rimandare
procrastination [proʊˌkræstəˈneɪʃən] *n* procrastinazione *f*
procreate [ˈproʊkriˌeɪt] *vi form* procreare
procreation [ˌproʊkriˈeɪʃən] *n form* procreazione *f*
proctor [ˈprɑːktəˈ] *n* UNIV sorvegliante *mf*
procurable [proʊˈkjʊrəˌbl] *adj* reperibile
procurator [ˈprɑːkjəˌreɪˌtəˈ] *n* LAW procuratore, -trice *m*, *f*
procure [proʊˈkjʊr] *form* I. *vt* (*obtain*) ottenere; **to ~ sth for sb, to ~ sb sth** ottenere qc per qu II. *vi* LAW sfruttare la prostituzione
procurement [proʊˈkjʊrˌmənt] *n* approvvigionamento *m*
prod [prɑːd] I. *n* (*poke*) spintarella *f;* (*with*

elbow) colpetto con il gomito *m;* (*with sharp object*) pungolo *m;* **to give sb a ~** *fig* spronare qu II. <-dd-> *vt* **1.** (*poke*) spingere; (*with elbow*) dare un colpetto di gomito a; (*with sharp object*) pungolare **2.** (*encourage, urge on*) **to ~ sb** (**into doing sth**) spronare qu (a fare qc)
prodigal [ˈprɑːdɪgl] *adj form* prodigo, -a
prodigious [prəˈdɪdʒəs] *adj form* (*size, height*) colossale; (*achievement, talent*) prodigioso, -a
prodigy [ˈprɑːdəˌdʒi] *n* prodigio *m;* **child ~** bambino, -a *m*, *f* prodigio
produce[1] [prəˈduːs] I. *vt* **1.** (*create*) produrre; (*manufacture*) produrre, fabbricare **2.** (*give birth to*) dare alla luce **3.** CINE, THEAT, TV produrre; (*music, recording*) produrre **4.** (*show*) mostrare; **to ~ a knife** estrarre un coltello; **to ~ one's passport** presentare il proprio passaporto; **to ~ an alibi** fornire un alibi **5.** (*cause*) causare; **to ~ results** produrre risultati II. *vi* (*bear fruit*) produrre [*o* dare] frutti
produce[2] [ˈproʊduːs] *n* AGR prodotti *mpl* agricoli
producer [prəˈduːsəˈ] *n* produttore, -trice *m*, *f*
product [ˈprɑːdʌkt] *n* **1.** *a.* MAT prodotto *m* **2.** (*result*) risultato *m*
production [prəˈdʌkʃən] *n* **1.** (*of goods*) produzione *f;* (*output of factory*) produzione *f* **2.** CINE, THEAT, TV produzione *f* **3.** *form* (*presentazione: of ticket, passport*) presentazione *f*
production capacity *n* capacità *f* produttiva
production costs *npl* costi *mpl* di produzione
production director *n* direttore, -trice *m*, *f* di produzione
production line *n* catena *f* di montaggio
production manager *n* responsabile *mf* della produzione
production time *n* tempo *m* di produzione
production volume *n* volume *m* di produzione
productive [prəˈdʌktɪv] *adj* produttivo, -a; (*land, soil*) fertile; (*writer*) prolifico, -a
productivity [ˌproʊdəkˈtɪvəˌt̮i] *n* produttività *f*
productivity bonus *n* premio *f* di produttività
prof [prɑːf] *abbr of* **professor** prof *mf*
profane [proʊˈfeɪn] *adj* **1.** (*blasphemous*) blasfemo, -a **2.** *form* (*secular*) profano, -a
profanity [proʊˈfænəˌt̮i] *n* **1.** (*blasphemy*) bestemmia *f* **2.** (*obscene language*) oscenità *f* **3.** (*obscene word*) volgarità *f;* **to utter a ~** dire una parolaccia
profess [prəˈfes] *vt* **1.** (*declare*) professare; **to ~ little enthusiasm** dimostrare scarso entusiasmo; **to ~ oneself satisfied** (**with sth**) dichiararsi soddisfatto (di qc) **2.** (*pretend*) **to ~ to be sth** fingere di essere qc **3.** (*religion*) professare
professed [prəˈfest] *adj* **1.** (*self-acknowledged*) dichiarato, -a **2.** (*alleged*) presunto, -a
profession [prəˈfeʃən] *n* **1.** (*occupation*) pro-

fessione *f;* **the teaching** ~ la categoria *f* degli insegnanti **2.** (*declaration*) professione *f*
professional [prə·'fe·ʃə·nəl] I. *adj* **1.** (*related to profession*) professionale **2.** (*competent*) competente, da esperto, -a II. *n* professionista *mf*
professionalism [prə·'fe·ʃə·nə·lɪ·zəm] *n* **1.** (*attitude*) professionalità *f* **2.** SPORTS professionismo *m*
professionally *adv* **1.** (*by a professional*) professionalmente **2.** (*in professional manner*) da professionista
professor [prə·'fe·sə·] *n* UNIV professore, -essa *m, f*
professorial [ˌproʊ·fə·'sɔː·ri·əl] *adj* professorale
professorship [prə·'fe·sə·ʃɪp] *n* cattedra *f*
proffer ['prɑː·fə·] *vt form* offrire
proficiency [prə·'fɪ·ʃn·si] *n* competenza *f*
proficient [prə·'fɪ·ʃnt] *adj* competente
profile ['proʊ·faɪl] I. *n* **1.** (*side view*) profilo *m;* **in** ~ di profilo **2.** (*description*) profilo *m;* **user** ~ INFOR profilo *m* utente ▶ **to keep a** low ~ tenere un profilo basso II. *vt* **1.** (*describe*) descrivere **2.** (*police practice*) fermare (per controllo documenti)
profit ['prɑː·fɪt] I. *n* **1.** FIN profitto *m* **2.** (*advantage*) profitto *m* II. *vi* **1.** (*benefit*) trarre profitto; **to** ~ **by sth** trarre profitto da qc **2.** (*make a profit*) guadagnare
profitability [ˌprɑː·fɪ·ţə·'bɪ·lə·ţi] *n* redditività *f*
profitable ['prɑː·fɪ·ţə·bl] *adj* **1.** FIN redditizio, -a; **a** ~ **investment** un investimento lucrativo **2.** (*advantageous*) vantaggioso, -a
profit and loss *n* FIN conto profitti e perdite
profiteer [ˌprɑː·fɪ·'tɪr] *n pej* speculatore, -trice *m, f*
profiteering *n pej* speculazione *f*
profit-making *adj* remunerativo, -a; ~ **movie** film *m* di cassetta
profit margin *n* margine *m* di profitto
profit maximization *n* massimizzazione *f* dei profitti
profit-oriented *adj* orientato, -a a realizzare profitti
profit-related *adj* che dipende dai profitti
profit sharing *n* participazione *f* agli utili
profit taking *n* FIN presa *f* di beneficio
profligate ['prɑː·flɪ·gɪt] *adj form* sregolato, -a
profound [prə·'faʊnd] *adj* profondo, -a
profundity [prə·'fʌn·dɪ·ţi] *n form* profondità *f*
profuse [prə·'fjuːs] *adj* profuso, -a; **to be** ~ **in one's praise of sth** profondersi in elogi per qc
profusion [prə·'fjuː·ʒən] *n form* profusione *f;* **in** ~ in abbondanza
prog. *n abbr of* **program** programma *m*
progenitor [proʊ·'dʒe·nə·ţə·] *n form* progenitore, -trice *m, f*
progeny ['prɑː·dʒə·ni] *n pl, form* progenie *f*
prognosis [prɑːg·'noʊ·sɪs] *n* previsione *f;* MED prognosi *f*
prognosticate [prɑːg·'nɑːs·tɪ·keɪt] *vt form* pronosticare

program ['proʊ·græm] I. *n* programma *m* II. <-mm-> *vt* programmare
programmable ['proʊ·græ·mə·bl] *adj* programmabile
programmer *n* programmatore, -trice *m, f*
programming *n* programmazione *f*
programming language *n* linguaggio *m* di programmazione
progress[1] ['prɑː·gres] *n* progresso *m;* **to make** ~ fare progressi; **to be in** ~ essere in corso
progress[2] [proʊ·'gres] *vi* **1.** (*improve*) progredire, migliorare **2.** (*continue onward*) procedere; **to** ~ **to sth** passare a qc altro
progression [prə·'gre·ʃən] *n* **1.** (*development*) sviluppo *m;* (*of disease*) evoluzione *f* **2.** MAT (*series*) progressione *f*
progressive [prə·'gre·sɪv] I. *adj* **1.** (*by successive stages*) progressivo, -a; (*disease*) degenerativo, -a **2.** POL progressista **3.** (*modern*) moderno, -a **4.** MUS d'avanguardia; (*jazz*) progressivo, -a **5.** LING progressivo, -a II. *n* **1.** POL progressista *mf* **2.** LING (*verb form*) forma *f* progressiva
prohibit [proʊ·'hɪ·bɪt] *vt* **1.** (*forbid*) proibire; **to be** ~**ed by law** essere vietato per legge **2.** (*prevent*) impedire
prohibition [ˌproʊ·ə·'bɪ·ʃən] *n* **1.** (*ban*) proibizione *f,* divieto *m* **2.** HIST **Prohibition** proibizionismo *m*
prohibitive [proʊ·'hɪ·bə·ţɪv] *adj* proibitivo, -a
project[1] ['prɑː·dʒekt] *n* **1.** (*undertaking, plan*) progetto *m* **2.** SCHOOL, UNIV (*essay*) ricerca *f* **3.** (*social housing*) complesso *m* di case popolari
project[2] [prə·'dʒekt] I. *vt* **1.** (*forecast*) preventivare; **to be** ~ **ed to do sth** essere previsto per fare qc **2.** (*propel*) lanciare **3.** PSYCH proiettare; **to** ~ **sth onto sb** proiettare qc su qu **4.** (*promote*) dare un'immagine di; **to** ~ **one-self** presentare un'immagine di sé II. *vi* **1.** (*extend out*) sporgere **2.** (*speak loudly and clearly*) parlare chiaro e forte
projectile [prə·'dʒek·təl] *n* proiettile *m*
projection [prə·'dʒek·ʃən] *n* **1.** (*forecast*) proiezione *f* **2.** (*protrusion*) sporgenza *f;* (*of rock*) prominenza *f* **3.** PSYCH proiezione *f*
projectionist *n* proiezionista *mf*
project management *n* project management *m inv*
project manager *n* project manager *mf inv*
projector [prə·'dʒek·tə·] *n* proiettore *m*
prolapse ['proʊ·læps] *n* MED prolasso *m*
prole [proʊl] *adj, n pej, inf abbr of* **proletarian** proletario, -a *m, f;* **the** ~**s** il proletariato
proletarian [ˌproʊ·lə·'te·ri·ən] I. *adj* proletario, -a II. *n* proletario, -a *m, f*
proletariat [ˌproʊ·lə·'te·ri·ət] *n* proletariato *m*
proliferate [proʊ·'lɪ·fə·reɪt] *vi* proliferare
proliferation [proʊ·ˌlɪ·fə·'reɪ·ʃən] *n* proliferazione *f*
prolific [proʊ·'lɪ·fɪk] *adj* **1.** (*producing a lot*) prolifico, -a **2.** (*having many offspring*) pro-

lifico, -a

prolix [proʊ·'lɪks] *adj pej, form* prolisso, -a

prolog(ue) ['proʊ·lɑːg] *n* **1.** (*introduction*) prologo *m;* (*in play*) prologo *f* **2.** *fig, inf* (*preliminary event*) preludio *m;* **to be a ~ to sth** essere il preludio di qc

prolong [proʊ·'lɑːŋ] *vt* prolungare; (*agony*) prolungare

prolongation [ˌproʊ·lɑː·ŋ·'geɪ·ʃən] *n* prolungamento *m*

prom [prɑːm] *n* (*school dance*) ballo *m* scolastico

---

i Un **prom** è un ballo organizzato presso una *high school*. Il *senior prom* è un ballo nel quale si ritrovano tutti i *seniors*. Ci si va di solito con un *date* (un accompagnatore/ un'accompagnatrice) e una delle coppie partecipanti è eletta *prom queen and king*. Questa manifestazione costituisce uno dei momenti clou dell'anno scolastico. Un *junior prom* è spesso organizzato per i *juniors*.

---

promenade [ˌprɑː·mə·'neɪd] I. *n* **1.** (*seafront*) passeggiata *f* a mare **2.** *form* (*walk*) passeggiata *f* II. *vi* passeggiare

promenade deck *n* ponte *m* di passeggiata

prominence ['prɑː·mə·nəns] *n* **1.** (*conspicuousness*) rilievo *m;* **to give ~ to sth** dare risalto a qc **2.** (*importance*) importanza *f;* **to gain ~** venire alla ribalta

prominent ['prɑː·mə·nənt] *adj* **1.** (*conspicuous*) prominente; **to put sth in a ~ position** mettere qc bene in vista **2.** (*teeth, chin*) sporgente **3.** (*distinguished, well-known*) importante; (*position*) di spicco; **to be ~ in sth** avere un ruolo di rilievo in qc

promiscuity [ˌprɑː·mɪ·'skju·ə·t̬i] *n* promiscuità *f*

promiscuous [prə·'mɪs·kju·əs] *adj* promiscuo, -a

promise ['prɑː·mɪs] I. *vt* (*pledge, have potential*) promettere; **to ~ to do sth** promettere di fare qc II. *vi* (*pledge*) promettere; **I ~!** prometto! III. *n* **1.** (*pledge*) promessa *f;* **to make a ~** fare una promessa; **~s, ~s!** *iron* non ci credo neanche ...! **2.** (*potential*) promessa *f;* **a young person of ~** un(a) giovane promettente; **to show ~** essere una promessa; **to fulfill one's ~** tener fede a una promessa

promising *adj* promettente

promissory note ['prɑː·mɪ·sɔː·ri·ˌnoʊt] *n* pagherò *m inv*

promo ['proʊ·moʊ] *n inf s.* **promotion** promo *m inv*

promontory ['prɑː·mən·tɔː·ri] <-ies> *n* GEO promontorio *m*

promote [prə·'moʊt] *vt* promuovere

promoter *n* promotore, -trice *m, f*

promotion [prə·'moʊ·ʃən] *n* **1.** (*in army, company, organization*) promozione *f;* **to get a ~**

avere una promozione **2.** (*encouragement, advertising*) promozione *f;* **sales ~** promozione delle vendite

promotional material *n* materiale *m* promozionale

prompt [prɑːmpt] I. *vt* **1.** (*spur*) stimolare; **to ~ sb to do sth** spingere qu a fare qc **2.** THEAT suggerire II. *adj* (*quick*) rapido, -a; (*action*) immediato, -a; (*delivery*) pronto, -a; **to be ~** sbrigarsi III. *adv* in punto IV. *n* **1.** COMPUT prompt *m; inv* **2.** THEAT (*prompter*) suggeritore, -trice *m, f;* **to give sb a ~** suggerire a qu

prompt box <-es> *n* THEAT buca *f* del suggeritore

prompter ['prɑː·mp·t̬ɚ] *n* THEAT suggeritore, -trice *m, f*

promptitude ['prɑː·mp·tɪ·tuːd] *n form* prontezza *f*

promptly ['prɑː·mpt·li] *adv* **1.** (*quickly*) rapidamente **2.** *inf* (*immediately afterward*) prontamente

promptness ['prɑː·mpt·nɪs] *n s.* **tempestività**

promulgate ['prɑː·ml·geɪt] *vt form* **1.** (*theory, belief*) divulgare **2.** LAW promulgare

promulgation [ˌprɑː·ml·'geɪ·ʃən] *n form* **1.** (*of theory, belief*) divulgazione *f* **2.** LAW promulgazione *f*

prone [proʊn] I. *adj* **to be ~ to doing sth** essere incline a fare qc II. *adv* bocconi *inv;* **to lie ~ on the floor/table** essere steso a faccia in giù sul pavimento/tavolo

prong [prɑːŋ] *n* (*of fork*) rebbio *m*, dente *m;* (*of antler*) punta *f*

pronominal [proʊ·'nɑː·mə·nl] *adj* LING pronominale

pronoun ['proʊ·naʊn] *n* LING pronome *m*

pronounce [prə·'naʊnts] *vt* **1.** (*speak*) pronunciare **2.** (*declare*) dichiarare; (*judgment*) pronunciare; **to ~ that ...** dichiarare che ...

pronounceable *adj* pronunciabile

pronounced *adj* pronunciato, -a; (*accent*) marcato, -a

pronouncement [prə·'naʊnts·mənt] *n* dichiarazione *f;* **to make a ~** fare una dichiarazione; (*pass judgment*) pronunciare una sentenza

pronto ['prɑː·n·toʊ] *adv inf* subito

pronunciation [prə·ˌnʌn·tsɪ·'eɪ·ʃən] *n* LING pronuncia *f*

proof [pruːf] I. *n* **1.** *a.* LAW prova *f;* **~ of sth** prova di qc *f;* **the burden of ~** l'onere della prova **2.** TYPO bozza *f* **3.** MAT dimostrazione *f* **4.** (*coin*) moneta *f* fior di conio ▶ **the ~ of the pudding is in the eating** *prov* per sapere bisogna provare II. *adj* (*alcoholic strength*) proof, *numero che esprime il tenore alcolico di una bevanda* III. *vt* impermeabilizzare

proofread ['pruːf·ˌriːd] *irr* TYPO, PUBL I. *vt* correggere le bozze di II. *vi* correggere le bozze

proofreader *n* correttore, -trice *m, f* di bozze

proofreading *n* correzione *f* di bozze

prop¹ [prɑːp] I. *n* **1.** (*support*) sostegno *m* **2.** THEAT accessorio *m* di scena II. <-pp-> *vt* **1.** (*support*) sostenere; **to ~ a shelf up with a**

broom puntellare uno scaffale con la scopa **2.** (*lean*) appoggiare; **she propped up her head with her hand** (ap)poggiò la testa sulla mano **3.** *fig* sostenere; **the world bank is propping up the global markets** la banca mondiale sta sostenendo i mercati globali

prop² [prɑːp] *n inf* AVIAT *abbr of* **propeller** elica *f*

prop. *n* ECON *abbr of* **proprietor** proprietario, -a *m, f*

propaganda [ˌprɑːpəˈgændə] *n* propaganda *f*

propagandist [ˌprɑːpəˈgændɪst] I. *n* propagandista *mf* II. *adj* propagandistico, -a

propagate [ˈprɑːpəgeɪt] I. *vt* **1.** BOT propagare **2.** (*make known: lie, rumor*) diffondere II. *vi* propagarsi

propagation [ˌprɑːpəˈgeɪʃən] *n* **1.** BOT propagazione *f* **2.** (*of lies, rumors*) diffusione *f*

propane [ˈproʊpeɪn] *n* propano *m*

propel [prəˈpel] <-ll-> *vt* spingere

propellant [prəˈpelənt] *n* propellente *m*

propeller [prəˈpelə-] *n* elica *f*

propeller shaft *n* TECH albero *m* di trasmissione

propensity [prəˈpensəti] *n form* propensione *f*; **to have a ~ for sth/to do sth** avere una tendenza per qc/a fare qc

proper [ˈprɑːpə-] *adj* **1.** (*appropriate: place*) proprio, -a; (*time*) giusto, -a; (*use, method*) corretto, -a; **~ meaning** significato *m* esatto **2.** (*socially respectable*) **to be ~ to do sth** essere decoroso fare qc **3.** (*itself*) vero, -a; **it's not in Boston ~** non sta esattamente a Boston **4.** (*real*) autentico, -a; **a ~ job** un vero lavoro

proper fraction *n* MAT frazione *f* propria

properly [ˈprɑːpə-li] *adv* **1.** (*correctly*) correttamente; **~ speaking** per essere esatti; **~ dressed** vestito in modo appropriato **2.** (*behave*) come si deve **3.** (*politely*) educatamente

proper name *n,* **proper noun** *n* nome *m* proprio

propertied *adj* ECON possidente

property [ˈprɑːpə-ti] <-ies> *n* **1.** (*possession*) proprietà *f*; LAW (*house, land*) bene *m* immobile; **a man of ~** un possidente **2.** (*house*) immobile *m;* (*land*) terreno *m* **3.** (*attribute*) proprietà *m*

property developer *n* ECON imprenditore, -trice *m, f* edile

property development *n* ECON sviluppo *m* edilizio

property damage insurance *n* assicurazione *f* sui danni alla proprietà

property market *n* mercato *m* immobiliare

property owner *n* proprietario, -a *m, f*

land speculation *n* ECON speculazione *f* sui terreni

property tax *n* imposta *m* sugli immobili

prophecy [ˈprɑːfəsi] <-ies> *pl n* profezia *f*

prophesy [ˈprɑːfəsaɪ] <-ie-> I. *vt* (*predict*) predire; REL profetizzare II. *vi* profetizzare

prophet [ˈprɑːfɪt] *n* profeta, -a *m, f;* REL profeta, -essa *m, f; ~* **of doom, doomsday ~** profeta *mf* di sventure

prophetess [ˈprɑːfɪ·təs] *n* profetessa *f*

prophetic [prəˈfe·tɪk] *adj* profetico, -a

prophylactic [ˌproʊfəˈlæk·tɪk] I. *adj* MED profilattico, -a II. *n* **1.** MED (*preventive medicine*) (farmaco *m*) profilattico *m* **2.** (*condom*) preservativo *m*

prophylaxis [ˌproʊfəˈlæk·sɪs] *n* MED profilassi *f*

propinquity [proʊˈpɪŋkwəti] *n form* **1.** (*proximity*) prossimità *f* **2.** (*kinship*) parentela *f*

propitious [prəˈpɪʃəs] *adj form* propizio, -a

prop jet *n* turboelica *m inv*

prop man *n* THEAT attrezzista *m*

proponent [prəˈpoʊ·nənt] *n* sostenitore, -trice *m, f*

proportion [prəˈpɔːrʃən] *n* **1.** (*relationship*) rapporto *f;* **the ~ of A to B** il rapporto tra A e B; **to be out of ~ to sth** essere sproporzionato rispetto a qc; **to be in ~ to sth** essere in proporzione a qc; **to keep a sense of ~** mantenere un senso delle proporzioni; **to blow sth (all) out of ~** esagerare enormemente qc **2.** (*part*) parte *f* **3.** *pl* (*size*) dimensioni *fpl,* proporzioni *fpl;* **a building of gigantic ~s** un edificio di enormi proporzioni

proportional [prəˈpɔːrʃənəl] *adj* proporzionale; **inversely ~** inversamente proporzionale

proportionality [prəˌpɔːrʃəˈnæ·lə·ti] *n* proporzionalità *f*

proportional representation *n* POL sistema *m* (elettorale) proporzionale

proportionate [prəˈpɔːrʃənɪt] *adj s.* **proporzionale**

proportioned *adj* **well ~** ben proporzionato; **to be generously ~** *fig* avere una discreta mole

proposal [prəˈpoʊ·zəl] *n* **1.** (*suggestion*) proposta *f;* **to put forward a ~** avanzare [*o* fare] una proposta; **peace ~** proposta *f* di pace **2.** (*offer of marriage*) proposta *f* di matrimonio; **to make a marriage ~** fare una proposta di matrimonio

propose [prəˈpoʊz] I. *vt* **1.** (*put forward*) proporre; **to ~ a toast** proporre un brindisi **2.** (*intend*) **to ~ to do sth** ripromettersi di fare qc **3.** (*nominate*) candidare II. *vi* (*offer marriage*) **to ~ (to sb)** fare una proposta di matrimonio (a qc) ▶ **man ~s, God disposes** *prov* l'uomo propone e Dio dispone *prov*

proposer [prəˈpoʊ·zə-] *n* **1.** (*suggestor*) presentatore, -trice *m, f* di una mozione **2.** (*nominator*) proponente *mf*

proposition [ˌprɑːpəˈzɪʃən] I. *n* **1.** (*theory, argument*) affermazione *f* **2.** (*business*) proposta *f* **3.** (*suggestion*) suggerimento *m* II. *vt* fare proposte sessuali a

propound [prəˈpaʊnd] *vt form* avanzare

proprietary [prəˈpraɪ·ə·te·ri] *adj* **1.** (*owning property*) proprietario, -a **2.** ECON (*name,* *brand*) registrato, -a; (*article*) brevettato, -a

proprietor [prə·'praɪ·ə·t̬ə·] *n* proprietario, -a *m, f*

proprietorship *n* proprietà *f*

proprietress [prə·'praɪ·ə·trɪs] *n* proprietaria *f*

propriety [prə·'praɪ·ə·t̬i] <-ies> *n* 1.(*correctness*) correttezza *f* 2. *pl* (*standard of conduct*) convenzioni *fpl* sociali; **to observe the proprieties** rispettare le convenzioni sociali

prop room *n* THEAT attrezzeria *f*

propulsion [prə·'pʌl·ʃən] *n* propulsione *f*

pro rata [ˌproʊ·'reɪ·t̬ə] I. *adj* proporzionale II. *adv* proporzionalmente

prorate *vt* ripartire proporzionalmente

prorogation [ˌproʊ·roʊ·'geɪ·ʃən] *n* POL rinvio (alla prossima sessione) *m*

prorogue [proʊ·'roʊg] *vt* prorogare

prosaic [proʊ·'zeɪ·ɪk] *adj form* prosaico, -a

proscenium [proʊ·'si·ni·əm] <-s *o* proscenia> *n* THEAT proscenio *m*

proscribe [proʊ·'skraɪb] *vt* proscrivere

proscription [proʊ·'skrɪp·ʃən] *n form* proscrizione *f*

prose [proʊz] *n* prosa *f*

prosecutable [ˌprɑː·sɪ·'kju·t̬ə·bl] *adj* LAW perseguibile

prosecute ['prɑː·sɪ·kjuːt] I. *vt* 1. LAW **to ~ sb** (**for sth**) procedere legalmente contro qu (per qc); **he was prosecuted for fraud** è stato denunciato per frode 2. *form* (*pursue, follow up*) proseguire II. *vi* sporgere denuncia

prosecuting attorney *n* avvocato, -a dell'accusa *m*

prosecution [ˌprɑː·sɪ·'kju·ʃən] *n* 1. LAW (*proceedings*) procedimento *m* penale 2. LAW (*the prosecuting party*) **the ~** l'accusa; **witness for the ~** teste *mf* a carico 3. *form* (*of campaign, inquiry*) proseguimento *m*

prosecutor ['prɑː·sɪ·kjuː·t̬ə·] *n* LAW pubblico *m* ministero

proselyte ['prɑː·sə·laɪt] *n* REL proselito, -a *m, f*

proselytize ['prɑː·sə·lɪ·taɪz] *vi* fare proseliti

prosody ['prɑː·sə·di] *n* prosodia *f*

prospect ['prɑː·spekt] I. *n* 1.(*possibility*) probabilità *f;* **the ~ of sth** la probabilità di qc 2. *pl* (*chances*) prospettive *fpl* 3. ECON (*potential customer*) potenziale cliente *mf;* (*potential employee*) candidato, -a (al posto) *m* 4. *liter* (*view*) panorama *m;* **a ~ of/over sth** una vista di/su qc II. *vi* MIN fare prospezioni

prospective [prə·'spek·tɪv] *adj* possible; (*candidate, student*) potenziale; **~ parent/son-in-law** futuro genitore/genero

prospector ['prɑː·spek·t̬ə·] *n* MIN prospettore, -trice *m, f;* (*of gold*) cercatore, -trice d'oro *m*

prospectus [prə·'spek·t̬əs] *n* prospetto *m;* UNIV opuscolo *m* informativo

prosper ['prɑː·spə·] *vi* prosperare

prosperity [prɑː·'spe·rə·t̬i] *n* prosperità *f*

prosperous ['prɑː·spə·əs] *adj* prospero, -a; (*business*) fiorente

prostate (gland) ['prɑː·steɪt] *n* prostata *f*

prostitute ['prɑː·stə·tuːt] I. *n* prostituta *f* II. *vt*

a. fig **to ~ oneself** prostituirsi; **to ~ one's talents** prostituire il proprio ingegno

prostitution [ˌprɑː·stɪ·'tuː·ʃən] *n* prostituzione *f*

prostrate ['prɑː·streɪt] I. *adj a. fig* postrato, -a; **to be ~ with grief** essere affranto dal dolore II. *vt* **to ~ oneself** postrarsi

protagonist [proʊ·'tæ·gə·nɪst] *n* 1.(*main character*) protagonista *mf* 2.(*advocate*) paladino, -a *m, f;* **to be a ~ of sth** essere un sostenitore di qc

protect [prə·'tekt] *vt* proteggere; (*one's interests*) tutelare; **to ~ oneself** proteggersi

protection [prə·'tek·ʃən] *n* 1.(*defense*) protezione *f;* **to be under sb's ~** essere sotto la protezione di qu 2.(*blackmail*) pizzo *m*

protection factor *n* fattore *m* di protezione

protectionism [prə·'tek·ʃə·nɪ·zəm] *n* protezionismo *m*

protectionist *adj* protezionista

protective [prə·'tek·tɪv] *adj* 1.(*giving protection*) protettivo, -a; **~ custody** detenzione *f* protettiva (a tutela dell'interessato) 2.(*wishing to protect: instinct*) di protezione

protector [prə·'tek·t̬ə·] *n* 1.(*person*) protettore, -trice *m, f* 2.(*device*) dispositivo *m* protettivo

protectorate [prə·'tek·t̬ə·rɪt] *n* protettorato *m*

protégé(e) ['proʊ·t̬ə·ʒeɪ] *n m(f)* protetto, -a *m, f*

protein ['proʊ·tiːn] *n* proteina *f;* **~ deficiency** carenza *f* di proteine

protest¹ ['proʊ·test] *n* 1.(*complaint*) protesta *f;* **in ~** in segno di protesta; **to do sth under ~** fare qc malvolentieri 2.(*demonstration*) manifestazione *f* di protesta

protest² [proʊ·'test] I. *vi* protestare; **to ~ about/against sth** protestare per/contro qc II. *vt* 1.(*solemnly affirm*) **to ~ that ...** attestare che ...; **to ~ one's innocence** protestarsi innocente 2.(*show dissent*) contestare

Protestant ['prɑː·t̬əs·tənt] *n* protestante *mf*

Protestantism *n* protestantesimo *m*

protestation [ˌprɑː·t̬es·'teɪ·ʃən] *n pl* 1.(*strong objection*) protesta *f* 2.(*strong affirmation*) attestazione *f*

protester *n* dimostrante *mf*

protest march *n* marcia *f* di protesta

protest vote *n* voto *m* di protesta

protocol ['proʊ·t̬ə·kɔːl] *n* 1.(*ceremonial form*) protocollo *m* 2.(*minutes of meeting*) verbale *m* 3. COMPUT (*method of communication*) protocollo *m* 4.(*treaty*) protocollo *m*

proton ['proʊ·tɑːn] *n* protone *m*

protoplasm ['proʊ·t̬ə·plæ·zəm] *n* protoplasma *m*

prototype ['proʊ·t̬ə·taɪp] *n* prototipo *m*

protozoan [ˌproʊ·t̬ə·'zoʊ·ən] <-s *o* -zoa> *n* protozoo *m*

protract [proʊ·'trækt] *vt* protrarre

protracted [proʊ·'træk·tɪd] *adj* protratto, -a

protraction [proʊ·'træk·ʃən] *n* 1.(*prolonging*) prolungamento *m* 2. ANAT (*muscle action*)

estensione *f*
protractor [prou·'træk·tæ] *n* (*for measuring angles*) goniometro *m*
protrude [prou·'tru:d] *vi* sporgere
protruding *adj* prominente; (*ears*) a sventola
protrusion [prou·'tru:·ʒən] *n* MED protrusione *f*
protuberance [prou·'tu:·bə·rəns] *adj form* protuberanza *f*
protuberant [prou·'tu:·bə·rənt] *adj form* protuberante; (*eyes*) sporgente
proud [praud] *adj* 1.(*pleased*) orgoglioso, -a; **to be ~ of sth/sb** essere orgoglioso di qc/qu; **to be ~ to do sth** essere orgoglioso di fare qc; **to be ~ that ...** essere orgoglioso del fatto che ... 2.(*having self-respect*) orgoglioso, -a 3.(*arrogant*) arrogante
proudly *adv* con orgoglio
provable ['pru:·və·bl] *adj* dimostrabile
prove [pru:v] <proved, proved *o* proven> I. *vt* (*verify: theory*) dimostrare; (*innocence, loyalty*) dimostrare; **to ~ oneself** (**to be**) **sth** dimostrare (di essere) qc; **to ~ sb innocent** dimostrare l'innocenza di qu II. *vi* (*be established*) dimostrarsi; **to ~ to be sth** risultare essere qc
proven ['pru:·vən] I. *vi, vt pp of* prove II. *adj* (*verified*) provato, -a
provenance ['prɑ:·və·nənts] *n form* provenienza *f*
provender ['prɑ:·vən·dæ] *n* 1.AGR foraggio *m* 2.*fig, inf* (*sustenance*) cibarie *fpl*
proverb ['prɑ:·vɜ:rb] *n* proverbio *m;* **as the ~ goes ...** come dice il proverbio ...
proverbial [prə·'vɜ:r·bi·əl] *adj* proverbiale
provide [prə·'vaɪd] I. *vt* 1.fornire; **to ~ sb with sth** fornire qc a qu 2.*form* LAW stabilire II. *vi* 1.(*prepare*) **to ~ for sth** prevedere qc 2.(*support*) **to ~ for one's family/children** mantenere la famiglia/i figli 3.(*mandate*) prevedere
provided *conj* **~ that ...** sempre che ..., purché ... +*subj*
providence ['prɑ:·və·dənts] *n* provvidenza *f;* **divine ~** REL la divina provvidenza
providential [,prɑ:·və·'den·tʃəl] *adj form* providenziale
provider *n* 1.(*person*) fornitore, -trice *m, f* 2.INFOR (*for Internet services*) provider *m inv*
providing *conj* **~** (**that**) **...** sempre che ..., purché +*subj*
province ['prɑ:·vɪnts] *n* 1.POL, ADMIN provincia *f* 2.(*branch of a subject*) campo *m*
provincial [prə·'vɪn·tʃəl] I. *adj* 1.POL, ADMIN provinciale; **~ town** città di/della provincia 2.(*unsophisticated*) provinciale II. *n* (*sb from provinces*) provinciale *mf*
proving ground *n* terreno *m* di prova
provision [prə·'vɪ·ʒən] I. *n* 1.(*act of providing*) fornitura *f* 2.(*thing provided*) fornitura *f* 3.(*preparation*) preparativi *mpl;* **to make ~s for sth** provvedere a qc 4.LAW (*in will, contract*) disposizione *f* II. *vt* approvvigionare

provisional [prə·'vɪ·ʒə·nəl] *adj* provvisorio, -a
learner's permit *n* foglio *m* rosa
proviso [prə·'vaɪ·zou] <-s> *n* condizione *f;* **with the ~ that ...** a condizione che ... +*subj*
provocation [,prɑ:·və·'keɪ·ʃən] *n* provocazione *f*
provocative [prə·'vɑ:·kə·t̬ɪv] *adj* 1.(*sexually*) provocante 2.(*thought-provoking: idea, question*) stimolante 3.(*causing anger*) provocatorio, -a
provoke [prə·'vouk] *vt* 1.(*make angry*) provocare; **to ~ sb into doing sth** spingere qu a fare qc 2.(*discussion*) scatenare; (*interest*) suscitare; (*crisis*) provocare
provoking *adj* (*irritating*) irritante
provost ['prou·voust] *n* UNIV rettore, -trice *m, f*
prow [prau] *n* NAUT prua *f*
prowess ['prau·ɪs] *n form* abilità *f;* (*sexual*) virilità *f*
prowl [praul] I. *n inf* **to be on the ~** aggirarsi con circospezione II. *vt* aggirarsi per [*o* attorno a]; **to ~ the streets for victims** aggirarsi furtivamente per le strade in cerca di vittime III. *vi* **to ~** (**around**) aggirarsi
prowl car *n* auto *f* di pattuglia (della polizia)
prowler *n* tipo, -a sospetto *m*
proximity [prɑ:k·'sɪ·mə·t̬i] *n form* prossimità *f;* **to be in** (**close**) **~ to sth** essere nelle (immediate) vicinanze di qc
proxy ['prɑ:k·si] <-ies> *n* procura *f;* **to do sth by ~** fare qc per procura; **nominate sb as a ~ to do sth** delegare qu a fare qc per procura
prude [pru:d] *n* puritano, -a *m, f*
prudence ['pru:·dns] *n* prudenza *f*
prudent ['pru:·dnt] *adj* prudente
prudery ['pru:·də·ri] <-ies> *n* pruderie *f inv*
prudish ['pru:·dɪʃ] *adj* prude *inv*
prune[1] [pru:n] *vt* potare; **to ~** (**back**) **costs** ridurre i costi
prune[2] [pru:n] *n* (*dried plum*) prugna *f* secca
pruning *n* potatura *f*
pruning hook *n* potatoio *m*
pruning saw *n* segaccio *m*
pruning shears *npl* BOT cesoie *fpl* da giardiniere
prurience ['prʊ·ri·əns] *n pej, form* licenziosità *f*
prurient ['prʊ·ri·ənt] *adj pej, form* pruriginoso, -a
Prussia ['prʌ·ʃə] *n* HIST, POL, GEO Prussia *f*
Prussian ['prʌ·ʃən] I. *n* HIST prussiano, -a *m, f* II. *adj* prussiano, -a
pry[1] [praɪ] <pries, pried> *vi* (*be nosy*) ficcare il naso; **to ~ into sth** impicciarsi di qc; **to ~ around** ficcanasare
pry[2] [praɪ] *vt* **to ~ sth off** sollevare qc facendo leva; **to ~ sth open** aprire qc forzandolo
prying ~ eyes sguardi *mpl* indiscreti
PS [,pi:·'es] *abbr of* postscript P.S.
psalm [sɑ:m] *n* REL salmo *m*
psephology [si:·'fɑ:·lə·dʒi] *n* psefologia *f*
pseudo ['su:·dou] *adj* finto, -a
pseudointellectual I. *n* intellettualoide *mf*

II. *adj* intellettualoide

pseudonym ['suː·də·nɪm] *n* pseudonimo *m*

psittacosis [ˌsɪ·t̬ə·'koʊ·sɪs] *n* psittacosi *f inv*

PST *n abbr of* **Pacific Standard Time** ora della zona Pacifico

psych(e) up ['saɪk] *vt sl* **to psych(e) oneself up** caricarsi; **to psych(e) sb up** dare la carica a qu

psyche ['saɪ·ki] *n* psiche *f*

psychedelic [ˌsaɪ·kə·'de·lɪk] *adj* psichedelico, -a

psychiatric [ˌsaɪ·ki·'æt·rɪk] *adj* psichiatrico, -a

psychiatrist [saɪ·'kaɪ·ə·trɪst] *n* psichiatra *mf*

psychiatry [saɪ·'kaɪ·ə·tri] *n* psichiatria *f*

psychic ['saɪ·kɪk] I. *adj* 1.(*with occult powers*) paranormale 2.(*of the mind*) psichico, -a II. *n* sensitivo, -a *mf*

psycho ['saɪ·koʊ] *n sl* (*crazy person*) **to be a ~** essere fuori (di testa)

psychoanalysis [ˌsaɪ·koʊ·ə·'næ·lə·sɪs] *n* psicoanalisi *f inv*

psychoanalyst [ˌsaɪ·koʊ·'æ·nə·lɪst] *n* psicoanalista *mf*

psychoanalytic(al) [ˌsaɪ·koʊ·ˌæ·nə·'lɪvt̬ɪk(əl)] *adj* psicoanalitico, -a

psychoanalyze [ˌsaɪ·koʊ·'æ·nə·laɪz] *vt* psicoanalizzare

psychological [ˌsaɪ·kə·'lɑː·dʒɪ·kəl] *adj* psicologico, -a

psychologist [saɪ·'kɑː·lə·dʒɪst] *n* psicologo, -a *m, f*

psychology <-ies> *n* (*science, mentality*) psicologia *f*

psychopath ['saɪ·kə·pæθ] *n* psicopatico, -a *m, f*

psychopathic [ˌsaɪ·kə·'pæ·θɪk] *adj* psicopatico, -a

psychosis [saɪ·'koʊ·sɪs] <-ses> *n* psicosi *f inv*

psychosomatic [ˌsaɪ·koʊ·soʊ·'mæ·t̬ɪk] *adj* psicosomatico, -a

psychotherapist [ˌsaɪ·koʊ·'θe·rə·pɪst] *n* psicoterapeuta *mf*

psychotherapy [ˌsaɪ·koʊ·'θe·rə·pi] *n* psicoterapia *f*

psychotic [saɪ·'kɑː·t̬ɪk] I. *adj* psicotico, -a II. *n* psicotico, -a *m, f*

PT [ˌpiː·'tiː] 1. *abbr of* **physical therapy** fisioterapia *f* 2. *abbr of* **physical training** educazione *f* fisica 3. *abbr of* **part-time** part time

pt. *n* 1. *abbr of* **part** parte *f* 2. *abbr of* **pint** pinta *f* (≈ *0,473 litri*) 3. *abbr of* **point** punto *m*

PTA [ˌpiː·tiː·'eɪ] *n abbr of* **Parent Teacher Association** associazione *f* genitori - insegnanti

ptarmigan ['tɑːr·mɪ·gən] *n* pernice *f* bianca

p.t.o. *abbr of* **please turn over** vedi retro

PTO [ˌpiː·tiː·'oʊ] *n abbr of* **Parent Teacher Organisation** associazione *f* genitori - insegnanti

pub [pʌb] *n* pub *m*

pub crawl *n sl* **to go on a ~** fare il giro dei pub

puberty ['pjuː·bə·t̬i] *n* pubertà *f*

pubic ['pjuː·bɪk] *adj* pubico, -a

pubis ['pjuː·bɪs] <-es> *n* pube *m inv*

public ['pʌb·lɪk] I. *adj* 1.(*of/for the people, provided by state*) pubblico, -a 2.(*done openly*) pubblico, -a; **to go ~ with sth** rendere pubblico qc II. *n* 1.(*people collectively, audience*) pubblico *m;* **in ~** in pubblico 2.(*ordinary people*) gente *f*

public accountant *n* commercialista *mf*

public-address system *n* sistema *m* di altoparlanti

public affairs *npl* affari *mpl* pubblici

public appearance *n* apparizione *f* in pubblico

public appointment *n* incarico *m* statale

public assistance *n* assistenza *f* pubblica

publication [ˌpʌb·lɪ·'keɪ·ʃən] *n* pubblicazione *f*

public authority *n* 1.(*state authority*) ente *f* statale di controllo 2.(*department, authority*) ente *m* pubblico di controllo

public defender *n* LAW difensore, -a *m, f* d'ufficio

public domain *n* dominio *m* pubblico

public enemy *n* nemico pubblico *mf*

public expenditure *n*, **public expense** *n* ADMIN, POL, ECON spesa *f* pubblica

public funds *npl* POL, ADMIN, FIN, ECON fondi *mpl* pubblici

public health *n* MED, ADMIN salute *f* pubblica

public health service *n* servizio *m* sanitario nazionale

public holiday *n* festa *f* nazionale

public interest *n* interesse *m* pubblico

publicist ['pʌb·lɪ·sɪst] *n* pubblicista *mf*

publicity [pʌb·'lɪ·sə·t̬i] *n* 1.pubblicità *f* 2.(*attention*) **to attract ~** attrarre l'attenzione ▶**any ~ is good ~** bene o male, l'importante è che se ne parli

publicity agent *n* agente *mf* pubblicitario

publicity campaign *n* ECON campagna *f* pubblicitaria

publicity department *n* reparto *m* pubblicità

publicity material *n* materiale *m* pubblicitario

publicize ['pʌb·lɪ·saɪz] *vt* pubblicizzare

public law *n* LAW diritto *m* pubblico

public library <-ies> *n* biblioteca *f* pubblica

publicly *adv* 1.(*openly*) pubblicamente 2.**~ owned** società ad azionariato diffuso

public nuisance *n* disturbo *m* della quiete pubblica

public opinion *n* opinione *f* pubblica

public property *n* proprietà *f* pubblica

public prosecutor *n* pubblico ministero *m*

public records *npl* archivio *m* di stato *sg*

public relations *npl* pubbliche *f* relazioni *pl*

public-relations officer *n* addetto, -a *m, f* alle pubbliche relazioni

public restroom *n* toilette *f inv*

public school *n* scuola *f* pubblica

public sector *n* settore *m* pubblico

public servant *n* funzionario, -a *m, f*

public service *n* servizio pubblico

public-spirited [ˌpʌb·lɪk·'spɪ·rɪ·t̬ɪd] *adj* che dimostra senso civico

public transportation *n* trasporti *mpl* pubblici
public utility *n* impresa *f* che fornisce servizi pubblici
public works *npl* ADMIN, POL lavori *mpl* pubblici
publish ['pʌb·lɪʃ] *vt* (*book, author, result*) pubblicare; (*information*) divulgare
publisher *n* 1. (*company*) editore *m* 2. (*person*) editore, -trice *m, f*
publishing *n* editoria *f*
publishing house *n* casa *f* editrice
puck [pʌk] *n* SPORTS paleo *m*, disco *m*
pucker ['pʌ·kə] *vt* to ~ one's lips increspare le labbra
pudding ['pʊ·dɪŋ] *n* (*dessert*) dolce *m*
puddle ['pʌ·dl] *n* pozzanghera *f*
pudenda [pjuː·'den·də] *npl* form pudende *fpl*
pudgy ['pʊ·dʒi] <-ier, -iest> *adj* tracagnotto, -a
puerile ['pjuː·ə·rəl] *adj form* puerile
puerility [ˌpjuː·ə·'rɪ·lə·t̬i] *n* puerilità *f*
Puerto Rican [ˌpwer·t̬ə·'riː·kən] I. *n* portoricano, -a *m, f* II. *adj* portoricano, -a
Puerto Rico [ˌpwer·t̬ə·'riː·koʊ] *n* Puerto Rico *m*
puff [pʌf] I. *vi* 1. (*blow*) soffiare 2. (*be out of breath*) avere il fiato corto 3. to ~ on a pipe/cigar/cigarette tirare boccate di fumo dalla pipa/dal sigaro/dalla sigaretta II. *vt* 1. (*smoke*) sbuffare; (*cigarette smoke*) fumare 2. (*praise: product, book*) magnificare 3. (*say while panting*) dire ansimando III. *n* 1. *inf* (*breath*) fiato *m*; (*of wind*) folata *f*; (*of air*) soffio *m*; (*vapor*) sbuffo *m*; (*of dust, smoke*) nuvola *f* 2. (*quilt*) piumino *m* 3. (*drag, breathing-in*) tiro *m*; to take ~s on a cigarette dare un tiro a una sigaretta 4. *inf* (*speech, praise*) soffietto *m*
◆**puff out** *vt* 1. (*expand*) gonfiare 2. (*exhaust*) spompare
◆**puff up** I. *vt* gonfiarsi II. *vi* inorgoglirsi
puff adder *n* vipera *f* soffiante
puffin ['pʌ·fɪn] *n* pulcinella *m* di mare
puff pastry *n* pasta *f* sfoglia
puffy ['pʌ·fi] <-ier, -iest> *adj* gonfio, -a
pug [pʌg] *n* carlino *m*
pugilism ['pjuː·dʒɪ·lɪ·zəm] *n* pugilato *m*
pugilist ['pjuː·dʒɪ·lɪst] *n* pugile *m*
pugnacious [pʌg·'neɪ·ʃəs] *adj form* combattivo, -a
pugnacity [pʌg·'næ·sə·t̬i] *n form* combattività *f*
pug nose *n* naso *m* rincagnato
puke [pjuːk] *sl* I. *vt* vomitare II. *vi* vomitare; he makes me (want to) ~! mi fa venire da vomitare!
◆**puke up** *sl* I. *vt* to puke sth up vomitare qc II. *vi* vomitare
pukka ['pʌ·kə] *adj* 1. (*genuine*) genuino, -a 2. (*of good quality*) di prim'ordine
pull [pʊl] I. *vt* 1. (*draw*) tirare; (*trigger*) premere 2. *inf* (*take out: gun, knife*) estrarre 3. MED (*extract*) estrarre; (*tooth*) estrarre, togliere 4. SPORTS, MED (*strain: muscle*) stirarsi

5. (*attract: business, customers*) attrarre ▶ to ~ a fast one (on sb) *inf* giocare un brutto tiro (a qu) II. *vi* 1. (*exert force*) tirare 2. to ~ on a cigarette fare una tirata dalla sigaretta; to ~ on a beer bere una sorsata di birra 3. *inf* (*hope for success*) to be ~ing for sb/sth essere dalla parte di qu/qc III. *n* 1. (*act of pulling*) tirata *f*; (*stronger*) strappo *m*, strattone *m* 2. *inf* (*influence*) influenza *f* 3. (*knob, handle*) maniglia *f*; (*of a curtain*) cordone *m* 4. (*attraction*) attrazione *f*; (*power to attract*) attrattiva *m* 5. (*of cigarette*) boccata *f*; (*of drink*) sorsata *f*
◆**pull ahead** *vi* passare avanti
◆**pull apart** *vt insep* 1. (*break into pieces*) smontare 2. (*separate using force*) fare a pezzi 3. (*criticize*) demolire
◆**pull around** *vt* maltrattare
◆**pull away** I. *vi* (*vehicle*) allontanarsi II. *vt* strappare; to pull sth away from sth strappare via qc da qc
◆**pull back** I. *vi* 1. (*move out of the way*) ritirarsi 2. (*not proceed, back out*) fare marcia indietro II. *vt* trattenere
◆**pull down** *vt* 1. (*move down*) tirare giù, abbassare 2. (*demolish*) buttare giù, demolire 3. (*drag down, hold back*) to pull sb down abbattere qu 4. *inf* (*earn wages*) guadagnare
◆**pull in** I. *vi* (*vehicle*) accostare/entrare e fermarsi II. *vt* 1. (*attract*) attrarre 2. (*arrest*) arrestare
◆**pull off** I. *vt inf* (*succeed*) spuntarla; to pull it off farcela II. *vi* (*leave*) ripartire
pull out I. *vi* 1. (*move out to pass*) uscire (per sorpassare); (*drive onto road*) immettersi 2. (*leave*) partire 3. (*withdraw*) ritirarsi II. *vt* (*take out*) tirare fuori
◆**pull over** I. *vt* 1. (*cause to fall*) rovesciare 2. (*police*) fare accostare II. *vi* farsi da parte
◆**pull through** I. *vi* cavarsela II. *vt* to pull sth through superare qc
◆**pull together** I. *vt* 1. (*regain composure*) to pull oneself together controllarsi 2. (*organize, set up*) mettere su II. *vi* cooperare
◆**pull up** I. *vt* 1. (*raise*) sollevare; (*blinds*) tirare su 2. (*plant*) sradicare II. *vi* accostare e fermarsi
pull-down menu *n* INFOR menu *m* a tendina
pullet ['pʊ·lɪt] *n* pollastra *f*
pulley ['pʊ·li] <-s> *n* TECH puleggia *f*
Pullman (car) ['pʊl·mən] *n* RAIL vettura *f* salone
pullout I. *n* 1. MIL ritirata *f* 2. PUBL (*part of magazine*) inserto *m* staccabile II. *adj* estraibile
pullover ['pʊ·loʊ·və] *n* pullover *m*
pull-up *n* (*exercise*) sollevamento *m* sulle braccia alla sbarra
pulmonary ['pʌl·mə·ne·ri] *adj* polmonare
pulp [pʌlp] I. *n* 1. (*soft wet mass*) poltiglia *f*; (*for making paper*) pasta (per carta) *f*; ~ mill stabilimento *m* di produzione di pasta per carta; to beat sb to a ~ *inf* fare polpette di qu

2. (*of fruit*) polpa *f* **3.** (*literature*) pubblicazioni *f pl* dozzinali **II.** *vt* estrarre la polpa da

pulpit ['pʊl·pɪt] *n* REL pulpito *m*

pulsar ['pʌl·sɑːr] *n* pulsar *f inv*

pulsate ['pʌl·seɪt] *vi* pulsare

pulsation [pʌl·'seɪ·ʃən] *n* pulsazione *f*

pulse[1] [pʌls] **I.** *n* **1.** ANAT polso *m;* (*heartbeat*) battito *m;* **to take sb's ~** tastare il polso a qu **2.** (*single vibration*) pulsazione *f* **II.** *vi* pulsare

pulse[2] [pʌls] *n* GASTR legume *m*

pulverize ['pʌl·və·raɪz] *vt* polverizzare

puma ['puː·mə] *n* puma *m inv*

pumice ['pʌ·mis] *n* ~ (**stone**) (pietra) *f* pomice

pummel ['pʌ·ml] <-l- *o* -ll-, -l- *o* -ll-> *vt* prendere a pugni

pump [pʌmp] **I.** *n* pompa *f;* (*for fuel*) pompa (di benzina) *f* **II.** *vt* pompare

pumpernickel ['pʌm·pə·nɪ·kl] *n* pane *m* integrale di segale

pumping *n* pompaggio *m*

pumpkin ['pʌmp·kɪn] *n* zucca *f*

pun [pʌn] **I.** *n* gioco *m* di parole **II.** <-nn-> *vi* fare un gioco [*o* dei giochi] di parole

punch[1] [pʌntʃ] **I.** *vt* **1.** (*hit*) dare un pugno a; **to ~ sb out** *sl* riempire qu di botte **2.** (*push: button, key*) premere **3.** (*pierce*) forare; (*ticket*) forare; **to ~ holes in sth** fare/praticare fori in qc; **to ~ the clock** [*o* **card**] timbrare il cartellino **4.** AGR (*cattle*) pungolare **II.** *vi* **1.** (*hit*) colpire **2.** (*employee*) **to ~ in/out** timbrare (il cartellino) in entrata/in uscita **III.** <-es> *n* **1.** (*hit*) pugno *m;* (*in boxing*) pugno *m;* **to give sb a ~** dare un pugno a qu **2.** (*tool for puncturing*) punzone *m;* (*for metal, leather*) punteruolo *m;* (**hole**) ~ perforatore (da ufficio) *m;* (*ticket*) ~ punzone *m* per forare i biglietti **3.** *fig* (*strong effect*) forza *f;* **with ~** con efficacia ▸ **to beat sb to the ~** battere qu sul tempo; **to pull one's ~es** andarci leggero; **to roll with the ~es** incassare i colpi

punch[2] [pʌntʃ] *n* (*beverage*) punch *m*

punch bowl *n* (grande) coppa *f* per il punch

punch card *n* scheda *f* perforata

punch-drunk ['pʌntʃ·drʌŋk] *adj a. fig* suonato, a; **to be ~** essere rintronato, -a *inf*

punching bag *n* sacco *m*

punch line *n* battuta *f* finale (di una barzelletta)

punctilious [pʌŋk·'tɪ·li·əs] *adj form* (*attentive to detail*) meticoloso, -a; (*with correct behavior*) scrupoloso, -a

punctual ['pʌŋk·tʃu·əl] *adj* puntuale

punctuality [ˌpʌŋk·tʃu·'æ·lə·ti] *n* puntualità *f*

punctuate ['pʌŋk·tʃu·eɪt] *vt* **1.** LING punteggiare **2.** (*appear intermittently*) ricorrere a intervalli *fig;* (*interrupt*) punteggiare

punctuation [ˌpʌŋk·tʃu·'eɪ·ʃən] *n* punteggiatura *f,* interpunzione *f*

punctuation mark *n* segno *m* di interpunzione

puncture ['pʌŋk·tʃər] **I.** *vt* **1.** (*pierce*) forare; (*lung*) perforare; **to ~ a hole in sth** fare un

buco in qc **2.** *fig* (*sb's confidence, self-esteem, ego*) ferire **II.** *vi* (*tire, ball*) forarsi; (*car*) forare **III.** *n* **1.** (*in tire, ball*) foratura *f;* **to have a ~** (*driver*) forare **2.** MED (*in skin*) puntura *f*

pundit ['pʌn·dɪt] *n* commentatore, -trice *m, f*

pungent ['pʌn·dʒənt] *adj* **1.** (*sharp*) pungente; (*smell*) pungente; (*taste*) forte **2.** (*criticism*) caustico, -a

punish ['pʌ·nɪʃ] *vt* punire; **to ~ oneself** punirsi

punishable *adj liter* punibile; **~ by death** punibile con la morte

punishing I. *adj* (*difficult*) duro, -a; (*trying*) estenuante **II.** *n* **to take a ~** prendere una batosta; **this car has taken a real ~** quest'auto è ridotta proprio male

punishment ['pʌ·nɪʃ·mənt] *n* **1.** (*for criminal act*) pena *f;* **capital ~** pena *f* capitale **2.** (*for child's misbehavior*) **castigo, to inflict a ~ on sb** punire qu **3.** (*rough use*) maltrattamento *m;* **to take a lot of ~** essere molto maltrattato

punitive ['pju:·nɪ·tɪv] *adj form* punitivo, -a; **~ damages** LAW danni *mpl* punitivi; **~ expedition** MIL spedizione *f* punitiva; **~ sanctions** sanzioni *f* punitive *pl*

punk [pʌŋk] **I.** *n* **1.** (*punk rocker*) (musicista) punk *m* **2.** (*troublemaker*) teppista *mf* **II.** *adj* **1.** (*music, style*) punk **2.** (*poor quality*) scadente

punt[1] [pʌnt] SPORTS **I.** *vt* (*in football*) calciare al volo **II.** *vi* (*in football*) calciare al volo **III.** *n* (*kick*) calcio *m* di rinvio

punt[2] [pʌnt] **I.** *vt* (*in boat*) **to ~ sb** trasportare qu in barchino **II.** *vi* (*in boat*) andare in barchino **III.** *n* (*boat*) barchino *m*

punt[3] [pʌnt] *vi* GAMES puntare contro il banco

puny ['pju:·ni] <-ier, -iest> *adj* (*person*) mingherlino, -a; (*argument*) debole; (*attempt*) fiacco, -a

pup [pʌp] **I.** *n* **1.** (*baby dog*) cucciolo, -a *m, f* **2.** (*baby animal*) cucciolo, -a *m, f* **3.** (*young person*) pivello *m* **II.** <-pp-> *vi* figliare

pupa ['pju:·pə] <pupas *o* pupae> *n* BIO crisalide *f,* pupa *f*

pupate ['pju:·peɪt] *vi* BIO impuparsi, diventare pupa

pupil[1] ['pju:·pl] *n* SCHOOL alunno, -a *m, f*

pupil[2] ['pju:·pl] *n* ANAT pupilla *f*

puppet ['pʌ·pɪt] *n a. fig* marionetta *f,* burattino *m;* **hand ~** burattino *m*

puppeteer [ˌpʌ·pə·'tɪr] *n* burattinaio, -a *m, f*

puppet government *n* governo *m* fantoccio

puppet show *n* THEAT spettacolo [*o* burattini] di marionette *m*

puppet theater *n* teatro [*o* dei burattini] delle marionette *m*

puppy ['pʌ·pi] <-ies> *n* cucciolo, -a *m, f*

purchase ['pɜːr·tʃəs] **I.** *vt* **1.** (*buy*) acquistare, comprare **2.** NAUT **to ~ the anchor** salpare l'ancora **II.** *n* **1.** (*act of buying*) acquisto *m;* **to make a ~** fare un acquisto **2.** (*hold*) presa *f;* **to get a ~ on sth** aggrapparsi a qc

purchase price *n* prezzo *m* di acquisto

purchaser *n* **1.** (*buyer*) acquirente *mf,* compratore, -trice *m, f* **2.** (*at auction*) aggiudicatario, -a *m, f*

purchasing *n* acquisti *mpl*

purchasing department *n* reparto *m* acquisti

purchasing manager *n* responsabile *mf* acquisti

purchasing power *n* potere *m* di acquisto

pure [pjʊr] *adj* puro, -a; ~ **air** aria *f* pura; ~ **gold** oro *m* puro; ~ **mathematics** matematica *f* pura; ~ **and simple** puro e semplice; **to be** ~ **in heart** essere puro di cuore

purebred ['pjʊr·bred] **I.** *n* purosangue *m* **II.** *adj* di razza pura; **a** ~ **horse** un purosangue

purée [pjʊ·'reɪ] **I.** *vt* passare **II.** *n* purè *m*

purely ['pjʊr·li] *adv* **1.** (*completely*) puramente; ~ **by chance** per pura combinazione **2.** (*simply*) semplicemente; ~ **and simply** puramente e semplicemente

purgative ['pɜːr·gə·t̬ɪv] **I.** *n* purga *f*, purgante *m* **II.** *adj* MED purgante, purgativo, -a

purgatory ['pɜːr·gə·tɔː·ri] *n* **1.** REL **Purgatory** purgatorio *m;* **to be in Purgatory** essere in purgatorio **2.** *fig* (*unpleasant experience*) calvario *m*

purge [pɜːrdʒ] **I.** *vt* **1.** MED, POL purgare; POL epurare; **to** ~ **a group of extremist elements** epurare un gruppo di elementi estremisti; **to** ~ **sb from a party** espellere qu da un partito **2.** *a.* REL (*crime, sin*) espiare **II.** *n* MED, POL purga *f*

purification [ˌpjʊ·rə·fɪ·'keɪ·ʃən] *n a.* REL purificazione *f;* (*of water*) depurazione *f*

purify ['pjʊ·rə·faɪ] *vt* (*cleanse*) purificare; (*water*) depurare; ~ **a language** eliminare le parole straniere da una lingua; REL (*soul, body*) purificare; **to** ~ **oneself of sth** purificarsi da/di qc

purist ['pjʊ·rɪst] *n* purista *mf*

puritan ['pjʊ·rɪ·tən] *n a. fig* puritano, -a *m, f*

puritanical [ˌpjʊ·rɪ·'tæ·nɪ·kəl] *adj* puritano, -a

Puritanism *n* puritanesimo *m*

purity ['pjʊ·rɪ·t̬i] *n* purezza *f*

purl [pɜːrl] **I.** *n* rovescio *m* **II.** *adj* ~ **stitch** (punto) *m* (a) rovescio **III.** *vt* lavorare a rovescio; **knit one,** ~ **one** uno a diritto, uno a rovescio **IV.** *vi* lavorare a rovescio

purloin [pə·'lɔɪn] *vt form* sottrarre

purple ['pɜːr·pl] **I.** *adj* (*reddish*) paonazzo, -a, rosso violaceo; (*bluish*) viola, violetto; **to be** ~ **with rage** essere paonazzo per la rabbia **II.** *n* (*reddish*) rosso *m* violaceo; (*bluish*) viola *m*, violetto *m*

purport [pɜːr·'pɔːrt] **I.** *vt form* (*claim*) **to** ~ **to be sth** pretendere di essere qc **II.** *n* **1.** (*meaning*) significato *m* **2.** (*purpose*) scopo *m*

purpose ['pɜːr·pəs] *n* **1.** (*goal*) scopo *m;* **for the** ~ allo scopo; **I did that for a** ~ l'ho fatto per un preciso scopo; **for that very** ~ proprio per questo; **for practical** ~**s** per motivi pratici; **for humanitarian** ~**s** a scopi umanitari; **for future** ~**s** per esigenze future; **the sole** ~ **of sth** l'unico scopo di qc; **not to the** ~ non pertinente; **to have a** ~ **in life** avere un obiettivo

nella vita **2.** (*motivation*) (**strength of**) ~ fermezza *f* di proposito **3.** (*use*) utilità *f;* **to no** ~ inutilmente; **to serve a** ~ servire allo scopo; **what's the** ~ **of ...?** qual è lo scopo di ...? ▶ **on** ~ di proposito, apposta

purposeful ['pɜːr·pəs·fəl] *adj* **1.** (*determined*) deciso, -a, risoluto, -a **2.** (*meaningful*) significativo, -a **3.** (*intentional*) intenzionale

purposeless ['pɜːr·pəs·ləs] *adj* **1.** (*aimless*) senza scopo; (*utterance, violence*) gratuito, -a **2.** (*useless*) inutile **3.** (*character, person*) irresoluto, -a

purposely ['pɜːr·pəs·li] *adv* intenzionalmente, di proposito

purr [pɜːr] **I.** *vi* (*cat*) fare le fusa; (*engine*) ronzare **II.** *n* (*of cat*) fusa *fpl;* (*of engine*) ronzio *m*

purse [pɜːrs] **I.** *n* **1.** (*handbag*) borsa *f* **2.** (*wallet*) portamonete *m inv,* borsellino *m* **3.** (*funds*) **to be beyond one's** ~ essere al di sopra dei mezzi [o delle possibilità] di qu **4.** (*prize*) borsa *f* **II.** *vt* (*lips*) protendere

purser ['pɜːr·sə·] *n* NAUT commissario, -a di bordo *m*

purse strings *npl fig* **to hold the** ~ tenere i cordoni della borsa; **to loosen the** ~ allentare i cordoni della borsa

pursuance [pə·'suː·ənts] *n form* adempimento *m;* **in** ~ **of sth** (*in accordance with*) conformemente a; **in** ~ **of her duty** nell'adempimento dei suoi doveri

pursuant [pə·'suː·ənt] *adv* LAW ~ **to** conformemente a

pursue [pə·'suː] *vt* **1.** (*chase*) inseguire **2.** (*seek to find: goals*) perseguire; (*dreams*) inseguire; (*rights, peace*) impegnarsi per **3.** (*follow: plan*) seguire; **to** ~ **a matter** portare avanti una questione **4.** (*work towards*) **to** ~ **a career** dedicarsi a una professione; **to** ~ **a degree in sth** studiare per laurearsi in qc

pursuer [pə·'suː·ə·] *n* inseguitore, -trice *m, f*

pursuit [pə·'suːt] *n* **1.** (*chase*) inseguimento *m;* **police** ~ inseguimento da parte della polizia; **to be in** ~ **of sth** inseguire qc; (*knowledge, happiness*) essere alla ricerca di qc; (*hunt*) essere a caccia di qu; **to be in hot** ~ **of sb** stare alle calcagna di qu *fig* **2.** (*activity*) attività *f inv;* **outdoor** ~**s** attività del tempo libero

purulent ['pjʊ·rə·lənt] *adj* purulento, -a

purvey [pə·'veɪ] *vt* provvedere, fornire; **to** ~ **sth to sb** fornire qc a qu

purveyor [pə·'veɪ·ə·] *n* ECON fornitore, -trice *m, f*

pus [pʌs] *n* MED pus *m*

push [pʊʃ] **I.** *vt* **1.** (*shove*) spingere; **to** ~ **one's way through sth** farsi largo (a spinte) attraverso qc; **to** ~ **sth to the back of one's mind** cercare di non pensare a qc; **to** ~ **the door open** aprire la porta spingendola; **to** ~ **sb out of sth** spingere qu fuori da qc; **to** ~ **sb out of the way** togliere di mezzo qu a spintoni **2.** (*force*) **to** ~ **one's luck** sfidare la sorte; **to** ~ **sb too far** far uscire dai gangheri qu

3. (*coerce*) obbligare; **to ~ sb to do** [*o* into doing] sth costringere qu a fare qc; **to ~ one-self** chiedere troppo a sé stesso **4.** (*insist*) insistere con; **to ~ sb for sth** insistere con qu per qc **5.** (*press: button*) spingere, premere; (*the brakes, gas pedal*) premere; **to ~ the doorbell** suonare il campanello **6.** *inf* (*promote*) spingere; ECON promuovere **7. to be ~ing** 30 andare per i trenta **II.** *vi* **1.** (*force movement*) spingere **2.** (*press*) premere **3.** (*insist*) pressare; **to ~ for sth** fare pressione per (ottenere) qc **III.** <-es> *n* **1.** (*shove*) spinta *f*; (*slight push*) spintarella *f*; **to give sb a ~** *fig* dare una spinta a qu **2.** (*press*) **at the ~ of a button** premendo un pulsante **3.** (*strong action*) impulso *m*; (*will to succeed*) grinta *f* **4.** (*strong effort*) sforzo *m*; **to make a ~ for sth** fare uno sforzo per qc; **at a ~ ...** in caso di necessità ... **5.** *inf* (*publicity*) pubblicità *f*; **to make a ~** fare una campagna pubblicitaria **6.** MIL (*military attack*) avanzata *f* ▶**if/when ~ comes to** <u>shove</u> nella peggiore delle ipotesi

◆**push along** *vi inf* andare via
◆**push around** *vt inf* tiranneggiare *inf*
◆**push away** *vt* spingere via
◆**push back** *vt* (*move backwards*) spingere indietro; (*person*) respingere; (*hair*) tirare indietro
◆**push down** *vt* **1.** (*knock down*) demolire **2.** (*press down*) premere **3.** ECON (*price, interest rate*) fare diminuire
◆**push forward** **I.** *vt* **1.** (*force forward*) spingere **2.** (*promote*) promuovere **II.** *vi* **1.** (*advance*) avanzare **2.** (*continue*) to ~ (with sth) procedere (con qc)
◆**push in** **I.** *vt* **1.** (*nail*) piantare **2.** (*force in*) **to push one's way in** passare avanti (senza rispettare la fila) **II.** *vi* (*force way in*) intromettersi
◆**push off** **I.** *vi inf* levarsi dai piedi **II.** *vt* NAUT (*boat*) spingere al largo
◆**push on** **I.** *vi* **1.** (*continue despite problems*) **to ~ (with sth)** andare avanti (con qc) **2.** (*continue travelling*) **we pushed on to Baltimore** proseguimmo per Baltimore **II.** *vt* **1.** (*activate*) accelerare **2.** (*urge on*) **to push sb on to do sth** spingere qu a fare qc
◆**push out** *vt* **1.** (*force out*) **to push sb out (of sth)** buttare qu fuori (da qc) **2.** (*get rid of*) buttare fuori; **to push competitors out of the market** sbarazzarsi dei concorrenti sul mercato **3.** (*produce: roots, blossoms*) buttare **4.** NAUT (*boat*) spingere al largo
◆**push over** *vt always sep* (*thing*) rovesciare; (*person*) fare cadere
◆**push through** **I.** *vi* farsi largo attraverso **II.** *vt* **1.** (*legislation, proposal*) fare accettare **2.** (*help to succeed*) aiutare a superare
◆**push up** *vt* **1.** (*move higher*) sollevare; *fig* (*help*) raccomandare **2.** (*price, interest rate*) fare aumentare
pushbutton ['pʊʃ·ˌbʌ·tən] **I.** *adj* a tasti [*o* pulsanti] **II.** *n* pulsante *m*

push-button telephone *n* telefono [*o* a tastiera] a pulsanti *m*
pushcart ['pʊʃ·kɑːrt] *n* carretto *m* a mano
pusher *n inf* spacciatore, -trice *m, f*
pushover ['pʊʃ·oʊ·vəʳ] *n* **1.** (*easy success*) **to be a ~** essere una cosa da niente **2.** (*easily influenced*) **to be a ~** cascarci facilmente
pushpin ['pʊʃ·pɪn] *n* puntina *f* da disegno
push start I. *vi* fare partire un'auto a spinta **II.** *n* **to give sb a ~** spingere l'auto di qc per farla partire
pushup ['pʊʃ·ʌp] *n* SPORTS flessione *f* sulle braccia; **to do ~s** fare le flessioni
pushy ['pʊ·ʃi] *adj* (*insistant*) insistente; (*aggressive*) troppo intraprendente
puss [pʊs] <-es> *n* (*cat*) mici(n)o *m;* **Puss in Boots** il gatto con gli stivali
pussy ['pʊ·si] <-ies> *n* **1.** (*cat*) ~ (*cat*) micio, -a *m, f*, gatto, -a *m, f* **2.** *vulg* figa *f*
pussyfoot ['pʊ·si·fʊt] *vi inf* **to ~ around an issue** barcamenarsi su una questione
pussy willow *n* salice *m* americano
pustule ['pʌs·tʃuːl] *n* pustola *f*
put [pʊt] <-tt-, put, put> **I.** *vt* **1.** (*place*) mettere; (*in box, hole*) mettere; **~ the spoons next to the knives** mettere i cucchiai vicino ai coltelli; **to ~ sth to one's lips** portare qc alle labbra; **~ it there!** (*shake hands*) qua la mano!; **to ~ sth in the oven** mettere qc nel forno **2.** (*add*) mettere; **to ~ sugar/salt in sth** mettere lo zucchero/il sale in qc; **to ~ the date on sth** scrivere la data su qc; **to ~ sth on a list** mettere in lista qc **3.** (*direct*) **to ~ pressure on sb** fare pressione su qu; **to ~ a spell on sb** fare un incantesimo a qu; **to ~ one's heart into sth** mettere tutta l'anima in qc; **to ~ one's mind to sth** dedicare tutto sé stesso a qc; **to ~ one's trust in sb** riporre la propria fiducia in qu; **to put one's faith in sb** avere piena fiducia in qu; **to put one's hope in sb** riporre le speranze in qu **4.** (*invest*) **to ~ sth into sth** impiegare qc in qc; **to ~ energy/time into sth** dedicare le energie/il tempo a qc **5.** (*bet*) scommettere; **to ~ money on sth** scommettere soldi su qc; **to ~ sth toward sth** contribuire con qc a qc **6.** (*cause to be*) **to ~ sb in a good mood** mettere qu di buonumore; **to ~ sb in danger** mettere qu in pericolo; **to ~ oneself in sb's place** [*o* shoes] mettersi nei panni di qu; **to ~ sb in prison** mettere qu in galera; **to ~ sth into practice** mettere in pratica qc; **to ~ sb on the train** mettere qu sul treno; **to ~ sth right** correggere qc; **to ~ sb straight** fare capire bene qc a qu; **to ~ sb to bed** mettere a letto qu; **to ~ sb to death** mettere a morte qu; **to ~ sth to good use** fare buon uso di qc; **to ~ sb to shame** fare vergognare qu; **to ~ sb under oath** fare prestare giuramento a qu; **to ~ sb to expense** procurare spese a qu; **to ~ to flight** mettere in fuga; **to ~ a stop to sth** porre fine a qc; **to ~ sb to work** mettere qu al lavoro [*o* a lavorare] **7.** (*impose*) **to ~ an idea in sb's head** mettere in testa

un'idea a qu; **to ~ a tax on sth** mettere una tassa su qc **8.** (*attribute*) **to ~ a high value on sth** dare molto valore a qc; **to ~ the blame on sb** dare [*o* attribuire] la colpa a qu; **to ~ emphasis on sth** dare [*o* attribuire] grande importanza a qc **9.** (*present*) **to ~ one's point of view** esporre il proprio punto di vista; **to ~ a question** fare [*o* porre] una domanda; **to ~ sth to discussion** presentare qc per la discussione; **to ~ sth to vote** mettere ai voti qc; **to ~ a proposal before a committee** presentare una proposta alla commissione; **I ~ it to you that ...** ti faccio notare che ... **10.** (*express*) dire; **as John ~ it** come ha detto John; **to ~ one's feelings into words** esprimere a parole i propri sentimenti; **to ~ sth into Italian** tradurre qc in italiano; **to ~ sth in writing** mettere qc per (i)scritto **11.** (*judge, estimate*) **I ~ the number of visitors at 2,000** calcolo che i visitatori siano stati 2.000; **I'd ~ her at about 35** secondo me ha circa 35 anni; **to ~ sb on a level with sb** mettere qu allo stesso livello di qu **12.** SPORTS (*throw*) **to ~ the shot** lanciare il peso **II.** *vi* NAUT **to ~ to sea** salpare

♦**put about** <-tt-> *irr* **I.** *vt* NAUT fare virare di bordo **II.** *vi* NAUT virare di bordo

♦**put across** <-tt-> *irr vt* (*make understood*) comunicare; **to put sth across to sb** fare capire qc a qu; **to put oneself across well** fare buona impressione

♦**put aside** <-tt-> *irr vt* **1.** (*place to one side*) mettere da (una) parte **2.** (*save*) mettere da parte; (*time*) riservare **3.** (*give up*) **to put sth aside** accantonare **4.** (*reject*) rifiutare **5.** (*ignore: fears, differences*) mettere da parte

♦**put away** <-tt-> *irr vt* **1.** (*save*) mettere via **2.** *inf* (*eat a lot*) far fuori **3.** (*remove*) mettere via **4.** *inf* (*imprison*) **to put sb away** mettere qu dentro **5.** *sl* (*kill*) fare fuori

♦**put back** <-tt-> *irr* **I.** *vt* **1.** (*replace*) rimettere **2.** (*postpone*) posticipare **3.** SCHOOL (*not be promoted*) **to put sb back a year** fare ripetere l'anno a qu **4.** (*set earlier: watch*) mettere indietro **II.** *vi* NAUT (*return*) rientrare

♦**put by** <-tt-> *irr vt* mettere da parte

♦**put down** <-tt-> *irr vt* **1.** (*set down*) mettere giù; **to not be able to put a book down** leggere un libro tutto d'un fiato **2.** (*lower*) abbassare; **to put one's arm/feet down** abbassare il braccio/i piedi; **to put sb/sth down somewhere** lasciare giù qu/qc da qualche parte **3.** (*attribute*) **to put sth down to sb** attribuire qc a qu **4.** (*write*) scrivere; **to put sth down on paper** annotare qc **5.** (*assess*) classificare; **I put her down as 30** le dò 30 anni **6.** (*register*) **to put sb down for sth** mettere qu in lista per qc **7.** FIN (*prices*) ridurre **8.** ECON (*leave as deposit*) lasciare come deposito **9.** (*stop: rebellion, opposition*) domare **10.** *sl* (*humiliate*) umiliare **11.** (*have killed: animal*) far abbattere

♦**put forward** <-tt-> *irr vt* **1.** (*offer for discussion: subject*) proporre; (*idea, plan*)

esporre; (*suggestion*) avanzare; **to ~ a proposal** fare una proposta **2.** (*advance: event*) anticipare; **to put the clock forward** mettere avanti l'orologio

♦**put in** <-tt-> *irr* **I.** *vt* **1.** (*place inside*) mettere dentro **2.** (*add*) inserire; **to ~ a comma/a period** inserire una virgola/un punto **3.** (*say*) dire; (*remark*) fare; **to put a word in** intervenire nella conversazione; **to ~ a good word for sb** mettere una buona parola per qu **4.** AGR (*plant: vegetables, trees*) piantare; (*seeds*) seminare **5.** TECH (*install*) installare; **to ~ a shower** installare una doccia **6.** (*invest: money*) investire; (*time*) dedicare; **to ~ a lot of effort on sth** dedicare molto impegno a qc; **to ~ overtime** fare lo straordinario **7.** (*submit: claim, request*) presentare; (*candidate*) presentarsi; **to put oneself in for sth** iscriversi per qc **8.** (*make*) **to ~ an appearance** fare atto di presenza **II.** *vi* **1.** (*apply*) **to ~ for sth** fare domanda per qc **2.** NAUT (*dock*) fare scalo

♦**put into** <-tt-> *irr vt* **1.** (*place inside*) mettere dentro, inserire **2.** **to put sth into sth** (*add*) aggiungere qc a qc; CULIN mettere qc in qc; (*include*) includere qc in qc **3.** (*dress in*) **to put sb into sth** vestire qu con qc **4.** TECH (*install*) installare **5.** FIN (*deposit*) **to put money into a bank** versare denaro in banca **6.** (*invest*) **to put sth into sth** (*money*) investire in qc; (*time, effort*) metterci **7.** (*cause to be*) **to put a plan into operation** [*o inf* **action**] realizzare un piano **8.** (*institutionalize*) **to put sb into sth** mettere qu in qc; **to put sb into prison** mettere qu in prigione

♦**put off** <-tt-> *irr vt* **1.** (*turn off: lights, TV*) spegnere; (*take off: sweater, jacket*) togliersi **2.** (*delay*) rimandare; **to put sth off for a week** rinviare qc di una settimana **3.** *inf* (*make wait*) annullare un incontro con; **to put sb off with excuses** dare buca a qu con delle scuse *inf* **4.** (*repel*) disgustare; (*food, smell*) fare schifo a **5.** (*disconcert*) sconcertare **6.** (*distract*) distrarre; **to put sb off sth** distrarre qu da qc; **to put sb off the scent** despistare qu

♦**put on** <-tt-> *irr vt* **1.** (*place upon*) **to put sth on sth** mettere qc su [*o* sopra] qc **2.** (*attach*) **to put sth on sth** attaccare qc a qc **3.** (*wear: shirt, shoes*) mettersi; **to ~ make-up** truccarsi **4.** (*turn on*) accendere; **to ~ Mozart** mettere una musica di Mozart **5.** (*use*) **to ~ the brakes** frenare; **to put the handbrake on** tirare il freno a mano **6.** (*perform: film*) dare; (*show*) presentare; (*play*) mettere in scena **7.** (*provide: dish*) servire; **to ~ a party** dare una festa **8.** (*begin boiling: water, soup, potatoes*) mettere a scaldare **9.** (*assume: expression*) assumere; **to ~ a frown** fare una smorfia; **to ~ airs** darsi delle arie **10.** (*pretend*) fare finta; **to ~ a silly voice** fare una voce ridicola **11.** (*be joking with*) **to put sb on** prendere in giro qu **12.** (*gain: weight*) mettere su; **to ~ 10 years** invecchiare di 10 anni **13.** TEL **to put sb on the (tele)phone** passare il telefono a qu; **to put sb on to sb** passare qu a qu; **I'll put him on** te lo passo **14.** (*comput*) **to put sb on to sb** mettere qu in contatto con qu; **to put sb on to sth** mettere qu sulla buona strada per

♦**put out** <-tt-> *irr* I. *vt* **1.** (*take outside*) **to put the dog out** mettere fuori il cane **2.** (*extend*) estendere; **to ~ one's hand** tendere la mano **3.** (*extinguish: fire*) estinguere; **to ~ a cigarette** spegnere una sigaretta **4.** (*turn off: lights, TV*) spegnere **5.** (*eject*) buttare fuori; (*dismiss*) mandare via **6.** (*publish: newsletter, magazine*) pubblicare; (*announcement*) diramare **7.** (*spread: rumor*) fare circolare; **to put it out that ...** mettere in giro la notizia che ... **8.** (*produce industrially*) produrre **9.** (*sprout: leaves*) mettere **10.** (*contract out*) **to put sth out to subcontract** dare qc in subappalto a qu; **to put sth out to bid** dare qc in appalto **11.** (*inconvenience*) disturbare; **to put oneself out for sb** scomodarsi per qu **12.** (*offend*) **to be ~** seccarsi **13.** (*dislocate*) slogare; **to ~ one's shoulder** slogarsi una spalla **14.** NAUT varare II. *vi* NAUT salpare

♦**put over** <-tt-> *irr vt* **1.** (*place higher*) **to put sth over sth** mettere qc sopra qc **2.** (*make understood: idea, plan*) comunicare **3.** (*fool*) **to put sth over on sb** fregare qu

♦**put through** <-tt-> *irr vt* **1.** (*insert through*) **to put sth through sth** fare passare qc attraverso qc **2.** (*complete, implement*) portare a termine; (*proposal*) fare accettare; (*bill*) fare approvare **3.** (*send*) mandare; **to put sb through college** mantenere qu agli studi **4.** TEL poner; **to ~ a telephone call to Paris** passare una chiamata telefonica a Parigi; **to put a call through** passare una chiamata; **to put sb through** (**to sb**) passare qu (a qu) **5.** *inf* (*make endure*) **to put sb through sth** fare subire/fare qu a qc; **to put sb through it** fare passare un brutto quarto d'ora a qu

♦**put together** <-tt-> *irr vt* **1.** (*join*) unire; (*collection*) preparare; (*assemble*) mettere insieme; (*machine, model, radio*) montare; (*pieces*) assemblare **2.** *fig* (*connect: facts, clues*) mettere insieme **3.** (*create*) creare; (*list*) fare; (*team*) formare; (*meal*) preparare; (*dress*) fare **4.** MAT sommare

♦**put up** <-tt-> *irr* I. *vt* **1.** (*hang up*) appendere; (*notice*) attaccare **2.** (*raise*) alzare; (*one's collar*) tirarsi su; (*flag*) issare; (*umbrella*) aprire; **to put one's hair up** tirarsi su i capelli **3.** (*build*) costruire; (*tent*) montare **4.** (*increase: prices*) aumentare **5.** (*make available*) **to put sth up for sale** mettere in vendita qc; **to put sth up for auction** mettere qc all'asta **6.** (*give shelter*) sistemare; **I can put you up for a week** ti posso ospitare per una settimana **7.** (*provide: funds*) fornire; **to ~ the money for sth** mettere i soldi per qc **8.** (*show opposition*) **to ~ opposition** opporsi; **to ~ a**

struggle [*o* **fight**] opporre resistenza **9.** (*submit: candidate, proposal*) presentare II. *vi* **1.** (*sleep at*) alloggiare; **to ~ at a hotel** alloggiare in un albergo; **to ~ at sb's place for the night** essere ospite di qu per la notte **2.** (*tolerate unwillingly*) **to ~ with sb/sth** sopportare qu/qc

putative ['pju:·ţə·ţɪv] *adj form* (*reputed*) presunto, -a; (*father*) putativo, -a

putoff *n inf* rinvio *m;* **to give sb a ~** rinviare con un pretesto l'incontro con qu

put-on *n inf* finta *f;* (*joke*) scherzo *m*

put option *n* ECON put *m inv*

putrefaction [ˌpju:·trə·ˈfæk·ʃən] *n* putrefazione *f*

putrefy ['pju:·trə·faɪ] <-ie-> *vi* imputridire

putrid ['pju:·trɪd] *adj* **1.** (*decayed*) putrido, -a, putrefatto, -a; (*smell*) schifoso, -a **2.** (*very bad*) disgustoso, -a

putsch [pʊtʃ] <-es> *n* putsch *m*

putt [pʌt] SPORTS I. *vi* eseguire un putt II. *n* putt *m inv*

puttee [pʌ·ˈtiː] *n* mollettiera *f*

putter[1] ['pʌ·ţə] *n* (*golf club*) putter *m inv*

putter[2] ['pʌ·ţə] *vi* prendersela calma; **to ~ around the house** trafficare in casa

putty ['pʌ·ţi] *n* stucco (per vetri) *m* ▶**to be like ~ in sb's hands** lasciarsi facilmente manovrare da qu

putty knife <-knives> *n* spatola *f*

put-up *adj inf* **a ~ job** un imbroglio

put-upon *adj inf* sfruttato, -a

puzzle ['pʌ·zl] I. *vt* lasciare perplesso, -a II. *vi* **to ~ over sth** scervellarsi su qc III. *n* **1.** (*game*) puzzle *m inv*, rompicapo *m inv*; **jigsaw ~** puzzle *m inv*; **crossword ~** cruciverba *m inv* **2.** (*mystery*) mistero *m*, enigma *m*; **to be a ~ to sb** essere un mistero per qu; **to solve a ~** risolvere un enigma

puzzled *adj* perplesso, -a; **to be ~ about sth** essere perplesso riguardo a qc

puzzler ['pʌz·lə] *n* (*mystery*) enigma *m*

puzzling *adj* sconcertante

PVC [ˌpi:·vi:·ˈsi:] *n abbr of* **polyvinyl chloride** PVC *m*

pygmy ['pɪg·mi] I. *n* <-ies> **1.** (*short person*) pigmeo, -a *m, f* **2.** *fig* nano, -a *m, f* II. *adj* ZOOL nano, -a

pyjamas [pə·ˈdʒɑ:·məz] *npl s.* **pajamas**

pylon ['paɪ·lɑ:n] *n* ELEC traliccio *m*, pilone *m*

pyramid ['pɪ·rə·mɪd] *n* piramide *f*

pyre ['paɪə] *n* pira *f*

Pyrenees [pɪ·rə·ˈni:z] *npl* **the ~** i Pirenei

Pyrex® ['paɪ·reks] I. *n* pirex *m* II. *adj* di pirex

pyrites [ˌpaɪ·ˈraɪ·ţi:z] <-tae> *n* pirite *f*; **iron ~** pirite di ferro

pyromania [ˌpaɪ·rou·ˈmeɪ·ni·ə] *n* piromania *f*

pyrotechnic [ˌpaɪ·rou·ˈtek·nɪk] *adj* **1.** pirotecnico, -a; **~ display** spettacolo pirotecnico **2.** *fig* (*brilliant*) brillante

python ['paɪ·θɑ:n] <-(ons)> *n* pitone *m*

P

Q

Q, q [kjuː] *n* Q, q *f;* ~ **as in Queen** Q come Quarto

Q *abbr of* **Queen** regina *f*

Qatar ['kɑː·tɑːr] *n* Qatar *m*

QED [ˌkjuː·iː·'diː] *abbr of* **quod erat demonstrandum** qed

qtr. *abbr of* **quarter** quarto *m*

qty. *abbr of* **quantity** quantità

quack¹ [kwæk] **I.** *n* (*duck's sound*) qua qua *m* **II.** *vi* fare qua qua, schiamazzare

quack² [kwæk] *pej* **I.** *n* **1.** (*doctor*) scalzacane *mf inv* **2.** (*charlatan*) ciarlatano, -a *m, f* **II.** *adj* fasullo, -a

quad¹ [kwɑːd] *n inf* (*quadriceps*) quadricipite *m*

quad² [kwɑːd] *n inf* (*quadrangle*) quadrangolo *m*

quad³ [kwɑːd] *inf* **I.** *n* (*quadruple*) quadruplo *m* **II.** *adj* (*quadruple*) quadruplo, -a

quadrangle ['kwɑːd·ræŋ·gl] *n form* quadrangolo *m*

quadrangular [kwɑː·'dræŋ·gjə·lə·] *adj* quadrangolare

quadrant ['kwɑː·drənt] *n* quadrante *m*

quadraphonic [ˌkwɑː·drə·'fɑː·nɪk] *adj* MUS quadrifonico, -a

quadratic [kwɑː·'dræ·tɪk] *adj* quadratico, -a

quadrilateral [ˌkwɑː·drɪ·'læ·ṯə·rəl] **I.** *n* quadrilatero *m* **II.** *adj* quadrilatero, -a

quadripartite ['kwɑː·drɪ·'pɑː·taɪt] *adj form* quadripartito, -a

quadruped ['kwɑː·drʊ·ped] *n* quadrupede *m*

quadruple ['kwɑː·druː·pl] **I.** *vt* quadruplicare **II.** *vi* quadruplicarsi **III.** *adj* quadruplo, -a

quadruplet [kwɑː·'druː·p·lɪt] *n* (ogni) gemello, -a di un parto quadrigemino *m*

quaff [kwɑːf] *vt liter* tracannare

quagmire ['kwæg·maɪ·ə·] *n* **1.** (*area*) pantano *m* **2.** (*situation*) ginepraio *m*

quail¹ [kweɪl] <-(s)> *n* (*bird*) quaglia *f*

quail² [kweɪl] *vi* (*feel fear*) impaurirsi; **to ~ before sb/sth** sgomentarsi di fronte a qu/qc

quaint [kweɪnt] *adj* **1.** (*charming*) pittoresco, -a **2.** *pej* (*strange*) strano, -a **3.** (*pleasantly unusual*) bizzarro, -a

quaintness ['kweɪnt·nɪs] *n* carattere *m* pittoresco, aria *f* pittoresca; (*strangeness*) singolarità *f*

quake [kweɪk] **I.** *n* **1.** (*shaking*) tremore *m* **2.** *inf* (*earthquake*) terremoto *m* **II.** *vi* **1.** (*move*) sussultare **2.** (*shake*) tremare; **to ~ with fear** tremare di paura; **to ~ at the thought of sth** tremare all'idea di qc

Quaker ['kweɪ·kə·] **I.** *n* quacchero, -a *m, f;* **the ~s** i quaccheri **II.** *adj* quacchero, -a

qualification [ˌkwɑː·lɪ·fɪ·'keɪ·ʃən] *n* **1.** (*document*) titolo *m;* (*exam*) qualificazione *f;* **academic ~** titolo accademico; **what are your ~s?** che tipo di formazione hai ricevuto?

2. (*limiting criterion*) restrizione *f;* (*condition*) riserva *f;* **without ~** senza riserve

qualified ['kwɑː·lɪ·faɪd] *adj* **1.** (*trained*) abilitato, -a; (*certified*) qualificato, -a; (*by the state*) autorizzato, -a **2.** (*competent*) competente **3.** (*limited*) limitato, -a; **to be a ~ success** avere un certo successo

qualify ['kwɑː·lɪ·faɪ] <-ie-> **I.** *vi* **1.** (*meet standards*) **to ~ for sth** essere idoneo a qc; (*be eligible*) avere i requisiti per qc; (*have qualifications*) essere qualificato per qc **2.** (*complete training*) conseguire una qualifica **3.** SPORTS qualificarsi **II.** *vt* **1.** (*give credentials*) accreditare **2.** (*make eligible*) abilitare; **to ~ sb to do sth** dare il diritto a qu di fare qc **3.** (*explain and limit*) limitare; **to ~ a remark** fare precisazioni su un punto **4.** LING (*modify*) qualificare

qualifying ['kwɑː·lɪ·faɪ·ɪŋ] *adj* **1.** (*limiting*) limitato, -a **2.** SPORTS (*testing standard*) di qualificazione; **~ round** eliminatoria *f* **3.** LING (*modifying*) qualificativo, -a

qualitative ['kwɑː·lɪ·teɪ·ṯɪv] *adj* qualitativo, -a; **~ difference** differenza qualitativa

quality ['kwɑː·lə·ti] **I.** <-ies> *n* **1.** (*degree of goodness*) qualità *f inv;* **~ of life** qualità della vita **2.** (*characteristic*) qualità *f;* **artistic ~** qualità artistiche **II.** *adj* di qualità

quality control *n* controllo *m* di qualità

quality time *n* tempo *m* trascorso bene insieme

qualm [kwɑːm] *n* scrupolo *m;* **to feel/have ~s (about sth)** avere degli scrupoli (riguardo a qc); **to have no ~s about doing sth** non farsi scrupolo di fare qc; **without the slightest ~** senza la minima perplessità

quandary ['kwɑːn·də·ri] <-ies> *n* dilemma *m;* **to be in a ~** trovarsi di fronte a un dilemma

quantifiable ['kwɑːn·ṯə·faɪ·ə·bl] *adj* quantificabile

quantification [ˌkwɑːn·ṯə·fɪ·'keɪ·ʃən] *n* quantificazione *f*

quantify ['kwɑːn·ṯə·faɪ] <-ie-> *vt* quantificare

quantitative ['kwɑːn·ṯə·teɪ·ṯɪv] *adj* quantitativo, -a

quantity ['kwɑːn·ṯə·ti] **I.** <-ies> *n* **1.** (*amount*) quantità *f;* **a large/small ~ of sth** una gran/piccola quantità di qc **2.** (*large amounts*) (grandi) quantità *fpl;* **to buy in ~** comprare in gran quantità **II.** *adj* in quantità

quantity discount *n* sconto *m* quantità

quantum ['kwɑːn·ṯəm] <quanta> *n* **1.** *form* (*quantity*) quantità *f* (piccola) *inv* **2.** PHYS (*unit of radiant energy*) quanto *m*

quantum mechanics *n* + *sing vb* meccanica *f* quantistica

quarantine ['kwɔː·rən·tiːn] **I.** *n* quarentena *f;* **to be/place under ~** essere/mettere in quarantena **II.** *vt* **to ~ sb/an animal** mettere in quarantena qu/un animale

quark [kwɑːrk] *n* PHYS quark *m inv*

quarrel ['kwɔː·rəl] **I.** *n* lite *f* **II.** <-ll-> *vi* litigare; **to ~ about sth** litigare per qc

quarrelsome ['kwɔː·rəl·səm] *adj* **1.** (*belligerent*) litigioso, -a **2.** (*grumbly*) che ha sempre da ridire

quarry[1] ['kwɔː·ri] I. <-ies> *n* (*rock pit*) cava *f*
II. <-ie-> *vt* cavare

quarry[2] ['kwɔː·ri] <-ies> *n* preda *f*

quart [kwɔːrt] *n* quarto *m* di gallone

quarter ['kwɔːr·ṱə] I. *n* 1. (*one fourth*)
quarto *m;* **three ~s** tre quarti; **a ~ of the
Mexicans** un quarto dei messicani; **a ~ of a
century/an hour** un quarto di secolo/d'ora;
(a) ~ to three un quarto alle tre, le tre meno
un quarto; **(a) ~ past three** le tre e un quarto
2. (*25 cents*) 25 centesimi 3. *a.* FIN, SCHOOL trimestre *m* 4. (*neighborhood*) quartiere *m;*
(*area*) zona *f;* **at close ~s** da vicino; **in all ~s
of the earth** in tutte le parti della terra 5. *pl*
(*unspecified group or person*) ambienti *mpl;*
in certain ~s in certi ambienti; **in high ~s**
nelle alte sfere 6. (*area of compass*) quadrante *m;* **from the north/west ~** dal primo/
quarto quadrante 7. SPORTS quarto 8. (*mercy*)
quartiere *m*, clemenza *f;* **to give ~** dare quartiere; **to ask for ~** chiedere quartiere II. *vt*
1. (*cut into four*) dividere in quattro (parti); **to
~ sb** squartare qu 2. (*give housing*) alloggiare;
to be ~ed with sb essere alloggiato a casa di
qu; MIL acquartierare III. *adj* quarto; **~ hour** un
quarto d'ora

quarterback ['kwɔːr·ṱə·bæk] *n* (*US football*)
quarterback *mf inv*

quarterdeck *n* NAUT casseretto *m*

quarterfinal *n* SPORTS quarto *m* di finale

quartering *n* 1. (*dividing into fourths*) divisione *f* in quattro parti (uguali) 2. MIL (*housing*) acquartieramento *m* 3. (*emblems on
shield*) inquartatura *f*

quarterly ['kwɔːr·ṱə·li] I. *adv* trimestralmente
II. *adj* trimestral III. *n* trimestrale

quartermaster ['kwɔːr·ṱə,mæs·ṱə] *n* 1. MIL
quartiermastro *m* 2. NAUT capoguardia *mf inv*

quartertone *n* MUS quarto *m* di tono

quartet *n*, **quartette** [kwɔːr·'tet] *n* MUS quartetto *m*

quartz [kwɔːrts] I. *n* quarzo *m* II. *adj* di
quarzo; **~ crystal** cristallo di quarzo

quartz clock *n* orologio *m* al quarzo

quasar ['kweɪ·zɑːr] *n* quasar *m inv*

quash [kwɑːʃ] *vt* 1. (*supress*) reprimere;
(*rebellion*) soffocare; (*rumor*) mettere a tacere;
to ~ sb's dreams/plans distruggere i sogni/
progetti di qc 2. LAW (*annul: conviction, verdict, sentence*) annullare; (*indictment, decision*) invalidare; (*law, bill, writ*) revocare

quasi- ['kweɪ·saɪ] quasi-, quasi

quatrain ['kwɑː·treɪn] *n* LIT quartina *f*

quaver ['kweɪ·və] I. *vi* tremare II. *n* tremolio *m;* **with a ~ in one's voice** con un tremito
nella voce

quay [kiː] *n* banchina *f*

queasy ['kwiː·zi] <-ier, -iest> *adj* 1. (*nauseous*) nauseato, -a; **to have a ~ feeling** avere
la nausea 2. *fig* (*unsettled*) inquieto, -a; **with a
~ conscience** con la coscienza agitata; **to feel
~ about sth** sentirsi inquieto per qc

Quebec [kwiː·'bek] *n* Québec *m*

queen [kwiːn] I. *n* 1. (*monarch*) regina *f;* **~ of
hearts/diamonds** (*cards*) regina di cuori/
quadri 2. *pej* (*gay man*) checca *f;* **drag ~** travestito *m* II. *vt* 1. (*make queen*) **to ~ sb** incoronare qc regina 2. (*in chess*) promuovere a
regina

queen bee *n* 1. ZOOL ape *f* regina 2. *pej* primadonna *f inv*

queen dowager *n* regina *f* vedova

queenly ['kwiːn·li] <-ier, iest> *adj* regia

queen-size *adj* da una piazza e mezza

queer [kwɪr] I. <-er, -est> *adj* 1. (*strange*)
strano, -a; **to have ~ ideas** avere delle strane
idee 2. *pej, sl* (*homosexual*) invertito, -a II. *n
pej, sl* finocchio *m*

quell [kwel] *vt* (*unrest, rebellion, protest*) soffocare; (*doubts, fears, anxieties*) mettere a
tacere; **to ~ sb's anger** sedare la rabbia di qc

quench [kwentʃ] *vt* 1. (*satisfy*) appagare;
(*thirst*) fare passare, estinguere; **to ~ sb's
thirst for knowledge** *fig* soddisfare la sete di
sapere di qu 2. (*put out*) estinguere, spegnere;
to ~ a fire spegnere un incendio 3. (*supress*)
reprimere; **to ~ sb's desire** appagare il
desiderio di qu; **to ~ sb's enthusiasm** frenare
l'entusiasmo di qu

querulous ['kwer·jə·ləs] *adj* (*person*) querulo,
-a; (*voice*) lamentoso, -a

query ['kwɪ·ri] I. <-ies> *n* domanda *f;* **a ~
about sth** una domanda su qc II. <-ie-> *vt*
1. *form* (*dispute*) mettere in discussione;
(*doubt*) mettere in dubbio 2. (*ask*) chiedere; **to
~ whether ...** chiedere se ...

quesadilla *n* tortilla *f* al formaggio

quest [kwest] *n* ricerca *f;* **the ~ for the truth/
an answer** la ricerca della verità/di una risposta

question ['kwes·tʃən] I. *n* 1. (*inquiry*) domanda *f;* **frequently asked ~s** *a.* COMPUT domande più frequenti; **to put a ~ to sb** fare una
domanda a qu; **to pop the ~ to sb** fare una
proposta di matrimonio a qu 2. (*doubt*) dubbio *f;* **without ~** senza dubbio; **to be
beyond ~** essere certo [*o* fuor di dubbio]
3. (*issue*) questione *f;* **it's a ~ of life or death**
a. fig è una questione di vita o di morte; **to be
a ~ of time/money** essere una questione di
tempo/soldi; **to raise a ~** sollevare una questione; **to be out of the ~** essere fuori ques-
tione/discussione; **there's no ~ of sb doing
sth** non è neanche da pensare che qu faccia qc
4. SCHOOL, UNIV (*test problem*) domanda *f;* **to
do a ~** rispondere alla domanda II. *vt* 1. (*ask*)
domandare 2. (*interrogate*) interrogare
3. (*doubt: facts, findings*) mettere in dubbio

questionable ['kwes·tʃə·nə·bl] *adj* discutibile

questioner *n* chi fa domande

questioning I. *n* interrogatorio *m;* **to be taken
in for ~** essere convocato per essere interrogato II. *adj* inquisitore, -trice; **to have a ~
mind** avere una mente inquisitrice

question mark *n* punto *m* interrogativo; **a ~**

hangs over sth *fig* esserci un interrogativo su qc

questionnaire [ˌkwes·tʃəˈner] *n* questionario *m*

queue [kjuː] *n* COMPUT coda *f*

quibble [ˈkwɪ·bl] I. *n* 1. (*petty argument*) cavillo *m;* a ~ **over sth** un cavillo su qc 2. (*criticism*) sottigliezza *f* II. *vi* cavillare; **to ~ over sth** sottilizzare su qc

quibbler [ˈkwɪb·lə·] *n* sofista *mf*

quibbling [ˈkwɪb·lɪŋ] I. *n* sottigliezze *fpl* II. *adj* cavilloso, -a

quiche [kiːʃ] *n* quiche *f inv*

quick [kwɪk] I. <-er, -est> *adj* 1. (*fast*) rapido, -a, veloce; ~ **as lightning** (veloce) come un fulmine; **in ~ succession** uno dopo l'altro; **to be ~ to do sth** fare qc velocemente; **to have a ~ one** farsi una bevuta veloce; **to have a ~ meal** fare un pasto veloce 2. (*short*) breve; **the ~est way** la strada più breve; **to give sb a ~ call** fare una telefonatina a qu 3. (*hurried*) frettoloso, -a; **to say a ~ good-bye/hello** salutare velocemente 4. (*smart*) intelligente; ~ **thinking** agilità mentale; **to have a ~ mind** avere una mente sveglia; **to have a ~ temper** arrabbiarsi facilmente II. <-er, -est> *adv* in fretta, alla svelta; ~! presto!; **as ~ as possible** al più presto possibile; **to get rich ~** arricchirsi in fretta III. *n* carne *f* viva; **to bite/cut nails to the ~** mangiarsi/tagliarsi le unghie fino alla carne ▶ **to cut sb to the ~** pungere qualcuno sul vivo

quick-acting [ˌkwɪkˈæk·tɪŋ] *adj* a effetto rapido; **to be ~** agire rapidamente

quick-change artist *n* trasformista *mf*

quicken [ˈkwɪ·kən] I. *vt* 1. (*make faster*) accelerare; **to ~ the pace** affrettare il passo 2. (*stimulate*) stimolare II. *vi* 1. (*increase speed*) accelerare 2. (*become more active*) muoversi

quick-freeze [ˈkwɪk·friːz] *vt irr* surgelare

quickie [ˈkwɪ·ki] *n inf* 1. (*quick sex*) sveltina *f* 2. (*fast drink*) bevuta *f* veloce

quickly [ˈkwɪk·li] *adv* in fretta

quickness [ˈkwɪk·nɪs] *n* 1. (*speed*) rapidità *f;* ~ **of temper** facilità ad arrabbiarsi *m* 2. (*liveliness*) vivacità *f;* ~ **of mind** agilità *f* di mente

quicksand [ˈkwɪk·sænd] *n* sabbie *f* mobili

quicksilver *n s.* **mercury** mercurio *m*

quickstep *n* quickstep *m inv* (*musica e ballo di ritmo veloce*)

quick-tempered *adj* irascibile

quick-witted *adj* intelligente; **a ~ reply** una risposta pronta

quid pro quo [ˈkwɪd·prouˈkwou] *n form* ricompensa *f*

quiescent [kwaɪˈe·snt] *adj form* inattivo, -a

quiet [ˈkwaɪ·ət] I. *n* 1. (*silence*) silenzio *m* 2. (*lack of activity*) quiete *m;* **peace and ~** pace e tranquillità II. <-er, -est> *adj* 1. (*not loud*) silenzioso, -a; **to speak in a ~ voice** parlare a bassa voce 2. (*not talkative*) silenzioso, -a; **to keep ~** restare in silenzio 3. (*secret*)

segreto, -a; **to have a ~ word with sb** parlare con qu in privato; **to keep ~ about sth** non dire niente su qc 4. (*unostentatious*) sobrio, -a 5. (*unexciting*) tranquillo, -a

◆**quiet down** I. *vi* 1. (*quiet*) stare zitto 2. (*calm*) calmarsi II. *vt* 1. (*silence*) zittire 2. (*calm (down)*) calmare

quietly [ˈkwaɪ·ət·li] *adv* 1. (*not loudly*) silenziosamente; **to speak ~** parlare a bassa voce 2. (*speaking*) a bassa voce 3. (*peacefully*) tranquillamente

quietness [ˈkwaɪ·ət·nɪs] *n* tranquillità *f*

quietude [ˈkwaɪ·ə·tuːd] *n form* quiete *f*

quill [kwɪl] *n* 1. (*feather*) penna *f; liter* (*pen*) penna *f* d'oca 2. (*of porcupine*) aculeo *m*

quilt [kwɪlt] I. *n* trapunta *f* II. *vt* trapuntare

quince [kwɪns] *n* (*fruit*) (mela) *f* cotogna; (*tree*) cotogno *m*

quinine [ˈkwaɪ·naɪn] *n* chinino *m*

quintessence [kwɪnˈte·sns] *n* quintessenza *f*

quintessential [ˌkwɪn·teˈsen·ʃəl] *adj form* tipico, -a

quintet(te) [kwɪnˈtet] *n* quintetto *m*

quintuple [kwɪnˈtuː·pl] *form* I. *adj* quintuplo, -a II. *vt* quintuplicare III. *vi* quintuplicarsi

quintuplet [kwɪnˈtʌp·lɪt] *n* (ogni) gemello, -a di un parto quinquigemino *m*

quip [kwɪp] I. *n* battuta (di spirito) *f* II. *vi* dire scherzando

quirk [kwɜːrk] *n* 1. (*habit*) eccentricità *f* 2. (*oddity*) peculiarità *f* 3. (*sudden twist or turn*) **a ~ of fate** un capriccio del destino

quirky [ˈkwɜːr·ki] <-ier, -iest> *adj* 1. (*original*) peculiare 2. (*odd*) eccentrico, -a

quit [kwɪt] <quit *o* quitted, quit *o* quitted> I. *vi* smettere; (*resign*) dimettersi II. *vt* 1. (*job*) dimettersi da 2. (*stop*) smettere; (*smoking*) smettere di 3. COMPUT uscire da

quite [kwaɪt] *adv* 1. (*fairly*) abbastanza; ~ **a bit** un bel po'; ~ **a distance** una bella distanza; ~ **something** una cosa notevole 2. (*completely*) del tutto; ~ **wrong** proprio sbagliato; **not ~** non esattamente; **not ~ as clever/rich as ...** non così intelligente/ricco come ...

quits [kwɪts] *adj inf* pari; **I am ~** (**with him**) (io e lui) siamo pari; **to call it ~** farla finita

quittance [ˈkwɪ·tns] *n form* quietanza *f*

quiver[1] [ˈkwɪ·və·] I. *n* (*shiver*) brivido *m* II. *vi* tremare

quiver[2] [ˈkwɪ·və·] *n* faretra *f*

quixotic [kwɪkˈsɑː·t̬ɪk] *adj liter* donchisciottesco, -a

quiz [kwɪz] I. <-es> *n* quiz *m inv* II. *vt* interrogare

quizmaster [ˈkwɪz·ˌmæs·tə·] *n* conduttore, -trice *m, f* di uno spettacolo di giochi a quiz

quiz show *n* spettacolo *m* di giochi a quiz

quizzical [ˈkwɪ·zɪ·kəl] *adj* interrogativo, -a

quorum [ˈkwɔː·rəm] *n form* quorum *m inv*

quota [ˈkwou·t̬ə] *n* 1. (*fixed amount allowed*) quota *f;* **export ~** contingente *m* di esportazione 2. (*proportion*) parte *f*

quotable [ˈkwou·t̬ə·bl] *adj* citabile

quotation [kwoʊ·'teɪ·ʃən] *n* **1.** (*repeated words*) citazione *f* **2.** FIN quotazione *f*
quotation marks *npl* virgolette *fpl*
quote [kwoʊt] I. *n* **1.** *inf* (*quotation*) citazione *f* **2.** *pl* (*quotation marks*) virgolette *fpl* **3.** (*estimate*) preventivo *m* **4.** FIN quotazione *f* II. *vt* **1.** citare **2.** (*name*) nominare **3.** FIN quotare; **a ~d company** un'azienda quotata in borsa III. *vi* (*repeat exact words*) citare; **to ~ from sb** citare qu; **to ~ from memory** citare a memoria
quotidian [kwoʊ·'tɪ·diən] *adj form* quotidiano, -a
quotient ['kwoʊ·ʃənt] *n* **1.** MATH quoziente *m* **2.** (*factor*) fattore *m;* **intelligence ~** quoziente d'intelligenza
QWERTY keyboard [ˌkwɜ:r·ţi·'ki:·bɔ:rd] *n* tastiera *f* QWERTY

R

r, R [ɑ:r] r, R *f o m; ~* **as in Roger** r come Roma
R 1. CINE *abbr of* **restricted** *vietato ai minori di 17 anni* **2.** *abbr of* **Republican** repubblicano, -a
R. *abbr of* **River** f.
rabbi ['ræ·baɪ] *n* rabbino *m*
rabbit ['ræ·bɪt] I. *n* coniglio, -a *m, f* II. *vi* dar la caccia ai conigli
rabbit hole *n* tana *f* di coniglio
rabble ['ræ·bl] *n* accozzaglia *f* di persone; **the ~** la plebaglia
rabble-rouser ['ræ·bl·ˌraʊ·zɚ] *n* agitatore, -trice *m, f*
rabble-rousing *adj* demagogico, -a
rabid ['ræ·bɪd] *adj* **1.** (*fanatical*) accanito, -a **2.** (*suffering from rabies*) rabbioso, -a
rabies ['reɪ·biːz] *n* rabbia *f;* **to carry ~** avere la rabbia
raccoon [ræ·'ku:n] *n* procione *m*
race¹ [reɪs] I. *n* corsa *f;* **a ~ against time** una corsa contro il tempo; **100-meter ~** 100 metri piani; **to run a ~** partecipare ad una corsa
▶ **slow and steady wins the ~** *prov* chi va piano va sano e va lontano *prov* II. *vi* **1.** (*move quickly*) correre; SPORTS gareggiare; **to ~ through one's work** fare il lavoro di corsa **2.** (*engine*) girare a vuoto III. *vt* **1.** (*compete against*) gareggiare con; **to ~ sb home** fare una corsa fino a casa con qn **2.** (*enter for race: horse*) far correre
race² [reɪs] *n* **1.** (*ethnic grouping, species*) razza *f* **2.** (*lineage*) stirpe *f*
racecar *n* auto *f* da corsa
racecar driver *n* pilota *mf* di auto da corsa
race conflict *n* conflitto *m* razziale
racecourse ['reɪs·kɔ:rs] *n* ippodromo *m*
race hatred *n* odio *m* razziale

racehorse ['reɪs·ˌhɔ:rs] *n* cavallo *m* da corsa
race meet *n,* **race meeting** *n* concorso *m* ippico
racer ['reɪ·sɚ] *n* **1.** (*person*) corridore *m* **2.** (*bicycle*) bicicletta *f* da corsa
race relations *npl* relazioni *fpl* interrazziali
race riot *n* disordini *mpl* razziali
racetrack ['reɪs·træk] *n* ippodromo *m*
racewalking *n* SPORT marcia *f*
racial ['reɪ·ʃəl] *adj* razziale
racing I. *n* corse *fpl* II. *adj* da corsa
racing bicycle *n,* **racing bike** *n inf* bicicletta *f* da corsa
racing yacht *n* yacht *m inv* da regata
racism ['reɪ·sɪ·zəm] *n* razzismo *m*
racist ['reɪ·sɪst] I. *n* razzista *mf* II. *adj* razzista
rack [ræk] I. *n* **1.** (*framework, shelf*) ripiano *m;* **dish ~** scolapiatti *m inv;* AUTO; **luggage ~** portapacchi *m inv* **2.** (*bar for hanging things on*) sbarra *f* attaccapanni; **towel ~** portasciugamani *m inv* **3.** GASTR **~ of lamb** carré *m inv* di agnello; **~ of beef** lombata *f* di manzo **4.** (*torture instrument*) ruota *f;* **to be on the ~** *fig* essere in difficoltà II. *vt* tormentare
racket ['ræ·kɪt] *n* **1.** SPORTS racchetta *f* **2.** *inf* (*loud noise*) chiasso *m;* **to make a ~** fare un gran baccano **3.** (*scheme*) racket *m inv*
racketeer [ˌræ·kə·'tɪr] *n* malvivente *mf*
racoon [ræ·'ku:n] *n s.* **raccoon**
racy ['reɪ·si] <-ier, -iest> *adj* (*film, novel*) **1.** (*lively*) pieno, -a di ritmo **2.** (*explicit*) piccante
radar ['reɪ·dɑ:r] *n* radar *m inv*
radar screen *n* schermo *m* radar
radar trap *n* Autovelox® *m*
radial ['reɪ·di·əl] *adj* radiale; TECH a stella
radiant ['reɪ·di·ənt] *adj* raggiante
radiate ['reɪ·di·eɪt] I. *vi* irradiare II. *vt* (*emit, display*) emanare
radiation [ˌreɪ·di·'eɪ·ʃən] *n* radiazioni *fpl*
radiation sickness *n* sindrome *f* da radiazioni
radiation therapy *n* radioterapia *f*
radiator ['reɪ·di·eɪ·tɚ] *n* radiatore *m*
radiator cap *n* tappo *m* del radiatore
radical ['ræ·dɪ·kəl] I. *n* **1.** *a.* CHEM, MAT radicale *m* **2.** POL radicale *mf* II. *adj* (*change, idea*) radicale; (*measures*) drastico, -a
radicalism ['ræ·dɪ·kə·lɪ·zəm] *n* radicalismo *m*
radicchio *n* radicchio *m* rosso
radii ['reɪ·dɪ·aɪ] *n pl of* **radius**
radio ['reɪ·di·oʊ] I. *n* radio *f* II. *vt* (*information*) trasmettere via radio; (*person*) chiamare via radio
radioactive [ˌreɪ·dioʊ·'æk·tɪv] *adj* radioattivo, -a
radioactivity [ˌreɪ·dioʊ·æk·'tɪ·və·ti] *n* radioattività *f*
radio alarm (**clock**) *n* radiosveglia *f*
radio beacon *n* radiofaro *m*
radiocarbon dating [ˌreɪ·dioʊ·kɑ:r·bən·'deɪ·tɪŋ] *n* datazione *f* mediante carbonio radioattivo
radio cassette (**recorder**) *n* radioregistra-

tore *m* a cassette
radiogram ['reɪ·dioʊ·græm] *n* radiogramma *m*
radiograph ['reɪ·dioʊ·græf] *n* radiografia *f*
radiographer *n* radiologo, -a *m, f*
radiography [ˌreɪ·di·'ɑː·grə·fi] *n* radiografia *f*
radio ham *n* radioamatore, -trice *m, f*
radiologist [ˌreɪ·di·'ɑː·lə·dʒɪst] *n* radiologo, -a *m, f*
radiology [ˌreɪ·di·'ɑː·lə·dʒi] *n* radiologia *f*
radio operator *n* radiotelegrafista *mf*
radio program *n* programma *m* radio
radioscopy [ˌreɪ·di·'ɒs·kə·pi] *n* MED radioscopia *f*
radio station *n* stazione *f* radio; **pirate ~** emittente *f* pirata
radiotelephony [ˌreɪ·diəʊ·tɪ·'le·fə·ni] *n* radiotelefonia *f*
radio telescope *n* radiotelescopio *m*
radiotherapy [ˌreɪ·dioʊ·'θe·rə·pi] *n* radioterapia *f*
radio wave *n* onda *f* radio
radish ['ræ·dɪʃ] <-es> *n* ravanello *m*
radium ['reɪ·diəm] *n* radio *m*
radium treatment *n* radioterapia *f*
radius ['reɪ·diəs] <-dii> *n* raggio *m*
raffle ['ræ·fl] I. *n* lotteria *f* II. *vt* offrire come premio in una lotteria
raft¹ [ræft] I. *n* zattera *f* II. *vt* trasportare su una zattera III. *vi* andare su una zattera
raft² [ræft] *n* *inf* mucchio *m;* **a ~ of options** un mucchio di possibilità
rafter¹ ['ræf·tə] *n* ARCHIT travetto *m*
rafter² ['ræf·tə] *n* (*person*) persona che viaggia su una zattera
rafting *n* rafting *m*
rag [ræg] I. *n* 1. (*old cloth*) straccio *m* 2. *pl* (*worn-out clothes*) stracci *mpl* 3. *pej, sl* (*newspaper*) giornalaccio *m* 4. MUS ragtime *m* II. <-gg-> *vt inf* prendere in giro
ragamuffin ['ræ·gə·mʌ·fɪn] *n* bambino, -a *m, f* cencioso, -a
ragbag ['ræg·bæg] *n* miscuglio *m*
rage [reɪdʒ] I. *n* 1. (*anger*) rabbia *f;* **to be in a ~** andare su tutte le furie 2. (*fashion*) **to be all the ~** essere l'ultimo grido II. *vi* 1. (*express fury*) infuriarsi; **to ~ at sb/sth** infuriarsi con qn/qc 2. (*continue*) infuriare
ragged ['ræ·gɪd] *adj* 1. (*torn: clothes*) sbrindellato, -a 2. (*wearing worn clothes*) vestito, -a di stracci 3. (*rough*) rozzo, -a; (*hair*) ispido, -a 4. (*irregular*) irregolare; (*wound*) lacero, -a; (*rocks, clouds*) frastagliato, -a; (*performance*) discontinuo, -a ▶ **to run sb ~** sfinire qualcuno
raging ['reɪ·dʒɪŋ] *adj* (*fire*) furioso, -a; (*blizzard, gale*) violento, -a; (*sea*) infuriato, -a
ragout [ræ·'guː] *n* ragù *m*
ragtag ['ræg·tæg] *adj* (*unkempt: group, army*) raccogliticcio, -a
ragtime ['ræg·taɪm] *n* ragtime *m*
rag trade *n inf* industria *f* dell'abbigliamento
ragweed *n* erba *f* di San Giacomo
raid [reɪd] I. *n* 1. MIL incursione *f* 2. (*attack*) assalto *m* 3. (*robbery*) rapina *f* 4. (*by police*)

irruzione *f* II. *vt* 1. MIL fare un'incursione su 2. (*attack*) assaltare 3. (*by police*) fare irruzione in
rail [reɪl] I. *n* 1. (*of fence*) sbarra *f;* (*of balcony, stairs*) ringhiera *f* 2. (*railway system*) ferrovia *f;* **by ~** per ferrovia; **~ ticket** biglietto *m* ferroviario 3. (*track*) rotaia *f* II. *vt* **to ~ sth in** [*o* **off**] recintare qualcosa con sbarre
♦ **rail against** *vt* scagliarsi contro
railhead ['reɪl·hed] *n* stazione *f* terminale
railing ['reɪ·lɪŋ] *n* 1. (*post*) sbarra *f;* **iron ~** inferriata *f;* **wooden ~** steccato *m* 2. (*of stairs*) corrimano *m*
rail network *n* rete *f* ferroviaria
railroad ['reɪl·roʊd] I. *n* 1. (*system*) ferrovia *f* 2. (*track*) binario *m* II. *vt fig* **to ~ sb into doing sth** forzare qualcuno a fare qualcosa
railroad bridge *n* ponte *m* ferroviario
railroad crossing *n* passaggio *m* a livello
railroad engine *n* locomotore *m*
railroader *n* ferroviere, -a *m, f*
railroad line *n* linea *f* ferroviaria
railroad station *n* stazione *f* ferroviaria
railroad strike *n* sciopero *m* ferroviario
railway ['reɪl·weɪ] *n* ferrovia *f;* **commuter ~** ferrovia per pendolari
rain [reɪn] I. *n* pioggia *f;* **~ shower** acquazzone *m;* **the ~s** la stagione delle piogge ▶ **~ or shine** qualunque cosa accada; **to be as right as ~** *inf* essere in piena forma II. *vi* piovere III. *vt* riversare
♦ **rain out** *vt* **to be rained out** essere cancellato per la pioggia
rainbow *n* METEO arcobaleno *m*
rain cloud *n* nuvola *f* carica di pioggia
raincoat *n* impermeabile *m*
raindrop *n* goccia *f* di pioggia
rainfall *n* piovosità *f*
rain forest *n* foresta *f* tropicale
rain gauge *n* pluviometro *m*
rainproof I. *adj* impermeabile II. *vt* impermeabilizzare
rainstorm *n* temporale *m*
rainwater *n* acqua *f* piovana
rainy ['reɪ·ni] *adj* <-ier, -iest> piovoso, -a; **the ~ season** la stagione delle piogge
raise [reɪz] I. *n* (*of wages, prices*) aumento *m* II. *vt* 1. (*lift*) alzare; (*periscope, window*) tirar su; (*arm, hand, leg*) sollevare; (*flag*) issare; (*anchor*) levare; (*ship*) mettere a mare 2. (*stir up*) provocare; (*doubts*) suscitare 3. (*increase: wages, bet*) aumentare; (*awareness*) accrescere; MAT elevare; (*standards*) migliorare 4. (*promote*) promuovere 5. (*introduce: subject, problem*) sollevare 6. FIN raccogliere 7. (*build*) costruire; (*monument*) erigere 8. (*bring up*) tirar su; (*animals*) allevare; (*plants*) coltivare 9. (*end: embargo*) togliere 10. (*contact*) contattare; **to ~ the alarm** dare l'allarme ▶ **to ~ hell** [*o* **Cain**] scatenare un finimondo
raisin ['reɪ·zn] *n* uva *f* passa
rake¹ [reɪk] I. *n* (*tool*) rastrello *m* II. *vt* rastrel-

lare

rake² [reɪk] *n* (*dissolute man*) libertino, -a *m, f*
◆**rake in** *vt inf* (*money*) guadagnare; **to be raking it in** far soldi a palate
◆**rake up** *vt* **1.** (*gather*) mettere insieme **2.** *fig* (*refer to*) rivangare; (*quarrel*) provocare

rake-off ['reɪk·ɑ:f] *n inf* fetta *f*

rakish¹ ['reɪ·kɪʃ] *adj* (*jaunty*) disinvolto, -a; **worn at a ~ angle** indossato in modo disinvolto

rakish² ['reɪ·kɪʃ] *adj* (*dissolute*) dissoluto, -a

rally ['ræ·li] <-ies> **I.** *n* **1.** (*race*) rally *m inv* **2.** (*in tennis*) scambio *m* prolungato **3.** POL raduno *m* **II.** *vi* **1.** MED rimettersi; FIN essere in ripresa **2.** MIL radunarsi; **to ~ behind sb** stringersi intorno a qn **III.** *vt* **1.** MIL radunare **2.** (*support*) raccogliere a sostegno
◆**rally around I.** *vt* sostenere **II.** *vi* raccogliersi

ram [ræm] **I.** *n* **1.** (*male sheep*) ariete *m*; (*astrology*) Ariete *m* **2.** (*implement*) mazza *f*; MIL ariete *m* **II.** *vt* <-mm-> **1.** (*hit*) urtare **2.** (*push*) **to ~ sth into sth** ficcare qc in qc

RAM [ræm] *n* INFOR *abbr of* **Random Access Memory** RAM *f*

Ramadan [ˌræ·mə·ˈdɑːn] *n* Ramadàn *m*

ramble ['ræm·bl] **I.** *n* (*walk*) camminata *f*; **to go for a ~** fare una passeggiata **II.** *vi* **1.** (*person*) passeggiare; (*river*) serpeggiare; (*plant*) crescere in modo incontrollato **2.** (*in speech*) divagare

rambler ['ræm·blɚ] *n* **1.** (*walker*) escursionista *mf* **2.** BOT rosa *f* rampicante

rambling ['ræm·blɪŋ] **I.** *n* **1.** (*wandering*) **to go ~** (andare a) fare una lunga passeggiata **2.** *pl* (*speech*) divagazioni *fpl* **II.** *adj* **1.** (*estate, house*) dalla struttura disordinata **2.** (*speech*) sconnesso, -a **3.** (*rose*) rampicante

ramification [ˌræ·mɪ·fɪ·ˈkeɪ·ʃən] *n* ramificazione *f*

ramify ['ræ·mɪ·faɪ] *vi* ramificarsi

ramp [ræmp] *n* **1.** (*sloping way*) rampa *f*; AVIAT scaletta *f* **2.** AUTO (*on-ramp*) bretella *f* d'accesso; (*off-ramp*) bretella *f* d'uscita

rampage ['ræm·peɪdʒ] **I.** *n* furia *f* distruttiva; **to be on the ~** essere scatenato **II.** *vi* scatenarsi

rampant ['ræm·pənt] *adj* (*disease*) dilagante; (*growth*) incontrollato, -a; (*inflation*) galoppante

rampart ['ræm·pɑːrt] *n* bastione *m*

ramrod ['ræm·rɑːd] *n* bacchetta *f* ▶ **as stiff as a ~** dritto come un fuso

ramshackle ['ræm·ʃæ·kl] *adj* **1.** (*dilapidated*) malridotto, -a **2.** (*disorganized*) improvvisato, -a

ran [ræn] *pt of* **run**

ranch [ræntʃ] **I.** <-es> *n* ranch *m inv* **II.** *adj* di un ranch **III.** *vi* (*run a ranch*) condurre un ranch

rancher ['ræn·tʃɚ] *n* **1.** (*owner*) proprietario, -a *m, f* di un ranch **2.** (*worker*) addetto, -a *m, f* ad un ranch

rancid ['ræn·sɪd] *adj* rancido, -a

rancor ['ræŋ·kɚ] *n* rancore *m*

rancorous ['ræŋ·kə·rəs] *adj* pieno, -a di rancore

random ['ræn·dəm] **I.** *n* **at ~** a caso **II.** *adj* casuale

rang [ræŋ] *pt of* **ring²**

range [reɪndʒ] **I.** *n* **1.** (*variety*) varietà *f*; **a ~ of interests** una varietà di interessi **2.** (*scale*) gamma *f*; **the full ~ of sth** la gamma completa di qc **3.** (*extent*) fascia *f*; **price ~** categoria *f* di prezzo **4.** (*maximum capability*) portata *f*; **out of ~** fuori della portata; **within ~** entro la portata **5.** (*field*) campo *m*; **driving ~** (*in golf*) campo *m* pratica; **shooting ~** poligono *m* di tiro **6.** (*pasture*) prateria *f*; **to feel at home on the ~** sentirsi a proprio agio **7.** MUS estensione *f* **8.** GEO catena *f*; **mountain ~** catena montuosa **9.** (*for kitchen*) cucina *f* **II.** *vi* **1.** (*vary*) variare **2.** (*extend*) estendersi **3.** (*rove*) vagare **III.** *vt* ordinare; **to ~ oneself** schierarsi

range finder *n* telemetro *m*

ranger ['reɪn·dʒɚ] *n* guardaboschi *mf inv*

rangy ['reɪn·dʒi] *adj* <-ier, -iest> allampanato, -a

rank¹ [ræŋk] **I.** *n* **1.** (*status*) rango *m* **2.** MIL grado *m*; **the ~s** la truppa; **to break ~s** rompere le righe **II.** *vi* classificarsi; **to ~ as sth** collocarsi come qc; **to ~ above sb** collocarsi al di sopra di qn **III.** *vt* **1.** (*classify*) classificare **2.** (*arrange*) sistemare

rank² [ræŋk] *adj* **1.** (*smelling unpleasant*) maleodorante **2.** (*absolute*) completo, -a; (*beginner*) assoluto, -a
◆**rank among** *vi* collocarsi tra

ranking ['ræŋ·kɪŋ] *n* posizione *f* in classifica

rankle ['ræŋ·kl] *vi* far male; **to ~ with sb** far soffrire qn; **it ~s that ...** addolora che ... +*subj*

ransack ['ræn·sæk] *vt* **1.** (*search*) rovistare **2.** (*plunder*) saccheggiare

ransom ['ræn·səm] **I.** *n* riscatto *m*; **to hold sb (for) ~** sequestrare qn a scopo di riscatto; *fig* ricattare qn **II.** *vt* riscattare

rant [rænt] **I.** *n* vuota invettiva *f* **II.** *vi* sbraitare; **to ~ and rave** fare fuoco e fiamme

rap [ræp] **I.** *n* **1.** (*knock*) colpo *m* secco **2.** MUS rap *m* **II.** *vt* colpire **III.** *vi* **1.** (*talk*) chiacchierare **2.** MUS fare del rap

rapacious [rə·ˈpeɪ·ʃəs] *adj form* rapace; (*appetite*) vorace

rapacity [rə·ˈpæ·sə·ti] *n* rapacità *f*

rape¹ [reɪp] **I.** *n* **1.** (*of person*) stupro *m* **2.** (*of city*) saccheggio *m* **II.** *vt* **1.** (*person*) violentare **2.** (*city*) saccheggiare

rape² [reɪp] *n* BOT, AGR colza *f*

rapeseed oil *n* olio *m* di colza

rapid ['ræ·pɪd] *adj* (*quick*) rapido, -a

rapidity [rə·ˈpɪ·də·ti] *n* rapidità *f*

rapids ['ræ·pɪdz] *n* rapide *fpl*

rapid transit *n* ≈ trasporto *m* urbano su rotaie (*sistema urbano di ferrovie sotterranee o sopraelevate per il trasporto passeggeri*)

rapier ['reɪ·piɚ] *n* stocco *m*

R

rapist ['reɪ·pɪst] *n* violentatore, -trice *m, f*
rapport [ræ·'pɔːr] *n* rapporto *m*
rapprochement [ˌræ·prɔːʃ·'mɒŋ] *n* riavvicinamento *m*
rapt [ræpt] *adj* (*person, attention*) rapito, -a
rapture ['ræp·tʃɚ] *n* estasi *f inv*
rapturous ['ræp·tʃə·rəs] *adj* (*expression*) estasiato, -a; (*applause*) scrosciante; (*welcome*) caloroso, -a
rare[1] [rer] *adj* (*uncommon*) raro, -a; (*exceptional*) fuori del comune
rare[2] [rer] *adj* GASTR al sangue
rarebit ['rer·bɪt] *n* **Welsh ~** pane *m* tostato con formaggio fuso
rarefy ['re·rə·faɪ] *vt* 1.PHYS rarefare 2.*fig* raffinare
rarely ['rer·li] *adv* raramente
raring ['re·rɪŋ] *adj inf* **to be ~ to do sth** non veder l'ora di fare qc
rarity ['re·rə·ti] <-ies> *n* rarità *f*
rascal ['ræs·kl] *n* briccone, -a *m, f*
rash[1] [ræʃ] *n* 1.MED eruzione *f* cutanea 2.(*outbreak: of burglaries, etc*) ondata *f*
rash[2] [ræʃ] *adj* (*decision*) affrettato, -a; (*move*) impulsivo, -a
rasher ['ræ·ʃɚ] *n* fetta *f* di pancetta (*o di prosciutto*)
rashness ['ræʃ·nɪs] *n* precipitazione *f*
rasp [ræsp] I. *n* 1.(*tool*) raspa *f* 2.(*sound*) suono *m* stridente II. *vt* 1.(*file*) raspare 2.(*rub roughly*) raschiare 3.(*say roughly*) dire con voce aspra III. *vi* (*make grating sound*) stridere
raspberry ['ræz·ˌbe·ri] <-ies> *n* 1.(*fruit*) lampone *m* 2.*inf* (*sound*) pernacchia *f;* **to blow a ~ at sb** fare una pernacchia a qn 3. *sl* SPORTS (*wound*) escoriazione *f*
rasping ['ræs·pɪŋ] *adj* aspro, -a
Rastafarian [ˌrɑːs·tə·'fe·ri·ən] I. *n* rastafariano, -a *m, f* II. *adj* rastafariano, -a
rat [ræt] I. *n* 1.(*animal*) ratto *m* 2.(*person*) infame *mf* ► **I smell a ~** sentir puzza di bruciato II. *vi* (*betray*) fare la spia; **to ~ on sb** fare la spia su qn
ratable ['reɪ·tə·bl] *adj* stimabile
ratatouille *n* ratatouille *f inv*
ratchet ['ræt·ʃɪt] *n* TECH dente *m* d'arresto
♦ **ratchet up** *vt* incrementare
rate [reɪt] I. *n* 1.(*speed*) velocità *f;* **at this ~** a questo ritmo; **at one's own ~** al proprio passo 2.(*proportion*) quota *f;* **birth ~** indice *m* di natalità; **death ~** indice *m* di mortalità; **unemployment ~** tasso *m* di disoccupazione 3.(*price*) tariffa *f;* **~ of exchange** tasso *m* di cambio; **interest ~** tasso *m* di interesse ► **at any ~** ad ogni modo II. *vt* stimare; **to ~ sb/sth as sth** considerare qn/qc come qc III. *vi* **to ~ as** essere considerato come
rateable ['reɪ·tə·bl] *adj s.* **ratable**
rather ['ræ·ðɚ] I. *adv* 1.(*somewhat*) alquanto; **~ sleepy** mezzo addormentato, -a 2.(*more exactly*) meglio 3.(*on the contrary*) anzi 4.(*very*) piuttosto 5.(*in preference to*) I

would ~ stay here preferirei rimanere qui; **~ you than me!** non ti invidio! II. *interj* senz'altro
ratification [ˌræ·ţə·fɪ·'keɪ·ʃən] *n* ratifica *f*
ratify ['ræ·ţə·faɪ] *vt* ratificare
rating ['reɪ·ţɪŋ] *n* 1.(*estimation*) valutazione *f* 2. *pl* TV, RADIO indice *m* d'ascolto
ratio ['reɪ·ʃiou] *n* proporzione *f*
ration ['ræ·ʃən] I. *n* 1.(*fixed allowance*) razione *f* 2. *pl* (*total amount allowed*) razioni *fpl;* **food ~s** razioni di viveri II. *vt* razionare
rational ['ræ·ʃə·nəl] *adj* 1.(*able to reason*) razionale 2.(*sensible*) ragionevole
rationale [ˌræ·ʃə·'næl] *n* ragione *f* di fondo
rationalism ['ræ·ʃə·nə·lɪ·zəm] *n* razionalismo *m*
rationalist ['ræ·ʃə·nə·lɪst] PHILOS I. *n* razionalista *mf* II. *adj* razionalista
rationalistic [ˌræ·ʃə·nə·'lɪs·tɪk] *adj* razionalistico, -a
rationality [ˌræ·ʃə·'næ·lə·ti] *n* razionalità *f*
rationalization [ˌræ·ʃə·nə·lɪ·'zeɪ·ʃən] *n* razionalizzazione *f*
rationalize ['ræ·ʃə·nə·laɪz] *vt* razionalizzare
rationing *n* razionamento *m*
rat poison *n* veleno *m* per topi
rat race *n* **the ~** la corsa frenetica per aver successo
rattle ['ræ·ţl] I. *n* 1.(*noise*) rumore (*secco e ripetuto*); (*of carriage*) sferragliamento *m* 2.(*for baby*) sonaglino *m* II. *vi* fare rumore; (*carriage*) sferragliare III. *vt* 1.(*making noise*) far risuonare 2.(*make nervous*) innervosire; (*shock*) sconcertare
rattlesnake ['ræ·ţl·sneɪk] *n* serpente *m* a sonagli
rattling ['ræt·lɪŋ] *adj* 1.(*noisy*) rumoroso, -a 2.(*fast, brisk*) rapido, -a
ratty ['ræ·ţi] *adj* <-ier, -iest> *inf* conciato, -a male
raucous ['rɑː·kəs] *adj* (*shout*) fragoroso, -a; (*crowd*) rumoroso, -a
raunchy ['rɑːn-] <-ier, -iest> *adj* sconcio, -a
ravage ['ræ·vɪdʒ] *vt* devastare
rave [reɪv] I. *n* 1. *inf* (*enthusiastic review*) recensione *f* entusiastica 2.(*dance party*) rave *m inv* II. *adj inf* (*review*) entusiastico, -a III. *vi* essere entusiasta; **to ~ about sth/sb** essere entusiasta di qc/qn; **to ~ against sb/sth** inveire contro qn/qc
ravel ['ræ·vl] <-ll-, -l-> *vt* aggrovigliare
raven ['reɪ·vn] I. *n* corvo *m* II. *adj liter* corvino, -a
ravenous ['ræ·və·nəs] *adj* (*person, animal*) affamato, -a; (*appetite*) insaziabile
ravine [rə·'viːn] *n* burrone *m*
raving ['reɪ·vɪŋ] I. *adj* (*success*) strepitoso, -a; **a ~ madman** un pazzo da legare II. *adv* **to be ~ mad** essere pazzo da legare III. *npl* vaneggiamenti *mpl*
ravioli [ræ·vi·'ou·li] *n* ravioli *mpl*
ravish ['ræ·vɪʃ] *vt liter* 1.(*please greatly*) estasiare 2.(*rape*) violentare

ravishing *adj* incantevole

raw [rɑ:] *adj* **1.** (*uncooked*) crudo, -a **2.** (*unprocessed: sewage, data*) non trattato, -a; (*silk*) greggio, -a; ~ **material** materia prima; **to get a ~ deal** subire un trattamento ingiusto **3.** (*sore*) escoriato, -a **4.** (*inexperienced*) novizio, a **5.** (*unrestrained*) allo stato puro **6.** (*weather*) brutto, -a

raw bar *n* GASTR *banco in un bar o ristorante dove si servono frutti di mare crudi*

rawhide ['rɑ:·haɪd] *n* cuoio *m* greggio

rawness ['rɑ:·nɪs] *n* **1.** (*harshness*) crudezza *f* **2.** (*inexperience*) inesperienza *f*

ray¹ [reɪ] *n* **1.** (*of light*) raggio *m* **2.** (*trace*) barlume *m*

ray² [reɪ] *n* (*fish*) razza *f*

rayon ['reɪ·ɑ:n] *n* raion *m*

raze [reɪz] *vt* radere al suolo

razor ['reɪ·zɚ] **I.** *n* rasoio *m;* **electric ~** rasoio elettrico **II.** *vt* radere

razorbill *n* gazza *f* marina

razorblade *n* lametta *f* da barba

razor-sharp *adj* **1.** (*knife*) affilato, -a come un rasoio **2.** (*person*) acuto, -a

razor wire *n* filo *m* spinato

R & B [ˌɑr·ənd·'bi:] *abbr of* **rhythm and blues** rhythm and blues *m*

RC [ˌɑ:r·'si:] **1.** *abbr of* **Red Cross** Croce *f* Rossa **2.** *abbr of* **Roman Catholic** cattolico, -a *m*, *f* romano, -a

Rd. *abbr of* **road** v.

R & D [ˌɑr·ənd·'di:] *abbr of* **Research and Development** R&S

re¹ [ri:] *prep* con riferimento a

re² [reɪ] *n* MUS re *m*

reach [ri:tʃ] **I.** *n* **1.** (*range*) portata *m;* **to be within** (**sb's**) ~ *a. fig* essere alla portata (di qn); **to be out of** (**sb's**) ~ *a. fig* essere fuori della portata (di qn); **to have a long ~** riuscire a distendersi molto con il braccio **2.** (*of river*) tratto *m;* **the upper/lower ~es of the Amazon** il tratto superiore/ inferiore del Rio delle Amazzoni **II.** *vt* **1.** (*stretch out*) allungare **2.** (*arrive at: city, country, finish line*) raggiungere; (*land*) toccare **3.** (*attain*) conseguire; (*agreement*) giungere a; **to** ~ **80** compiere 80 anni **4.** (*extend to*) arrivare a **5.** (*communicate with*) contattare **III.** *vi* **to** ~ **for sth** allungare la mano per prendere qc

◆**reach down** *vi* **to** ~ **to** (*land*) estendersi fino a; (*clothes*) arrivare fino a

◆**reach out** *vi* allungare la mano; **to** ~ **for sth** allungare la mano verso qc

react [rɪ·'ækt] *vi* reagire; **to** ~ **to sth** *a.* MED reagire a qc; **to** ~ **against sth** avere una reazione contro qc; **to** ~ **on sth** reagire su qc

reaction [rɪ·'æk·ʃən] *n* **1.** *a.* CHEM reazione *f;* **chain** ~ reazione a catena **2.** *pl* MED reazioni *fpl*

reactionary [rɪ·'æk·ʃə·ne·ri] **I.** *adj* reazionario, -a **II.** <-ies> *n* reazionario, -a *m*, *f*

reactivate [ri:·'æk·tə·veɪt] **I.** *vt* riattivare **II.** *vi* riattivarsi

reactive [ri:·'æk·tɪv] *adj* reattivo, -a

reactor [rɪ·'æk·tɚ] *n* reattore *m*

read¹ [ri:d] **I.** *n* lettura *f* **II.** *vt* <read, read> **1.** leggere; **to** ~ **sth aloud** leggere qc ad alta voce; **to** ~ **sb a story** leggere una storia a qn **2.** (*decipher*) decifrare; **to** ~ **sb's mind** [*o* **thoughts**] leggere nei pensieri di qn; **to** ~ **sb's palm** leggere (il palmo della) la mano a qn; **to** ~ **sb like a book** leggere qn come un libro stampato; ~ **my lips!** ascolta con la massima attenzione! **3.** (*interpret*) interpretare **4.** (*inspect*) ispezionare; (*meter*) leggere **5.** (*understand*) intendere; **I don't** ~ **you** non ti seguo **III.** *vi* <read, read> (*person*) leggere; (*book, magazine*) leggersi

◆**read off** *vt* leggere ad alta voce

◆**read on** *vi* continuare a leggere

◆**read out** *vt* **1.** (*read aloud*) leggere ad alta voce **2.** INFOR (*data*) leggere

◆**read over** *vt* rileggere

◆**read through** *vt* leggere da cima a fondo

◆**read up on** *vt* raccogliere informazioni su

read² [red] *adj* letto, -a; **little/widely ~** poco/ molto letto

readability [ˌri:·də·'bɪ·lə·ti] *n* leggibilità *f*

readable ['ri:·də·bl] *adj* **1.** (*legible*) leggibile **2.** (*easy to read*) scorrevole

reader ['ri:·dɚ] *n* **1.** (*person*) lettore, -trice *m*, *f* **2.** (*book*) libro *m* di lettura **3.** TECH lettore *m* **4.** PUBL correttore, -trice *m*, *f*

readership ['ri:·dɚ·ʃɪp] *n* lettori, -trici *m*, *f pl*

readily ['re·dɪ·li] *adv* **1.** (*promptly*) di buon grado **2.** (*easily*) agevolmente; ~ **available** immediatamente disponibile

readiness ['re·dɪ·nɪs] *n* **1.** (*willingness*) disponibilità *f* **2.** (*preparedness*) preparazione *f*

reading ['ri:·dɪŋ] **I.** *n* **1.** lettura *f* **2.** (*interpretation*) interpretazione *f* **3.** TECH rilevazione *f* **II.** *adj* di lettura; **to have a ~ age of seven** leggere come un bambino di sette anni

reading glasses *npl* occhiali *mpl* da lettura

reading list *n* lista *f* di libri da leggere

reading room *n* sala *f* di lettura

readjust [ˌri:·ə·'dʒʌst] **I.** *vt a.* TECH riaggiustare **II.** *vi* (*objects*) riaggiustarsi; (*people*) riadattarsi

readjustment [ˌri:·ə·'dʒʌst·mənt] *n* TECH riassestamento *m*

read only memory *n* INFOR memoria *f* ROM

ready ['re·di] **I.** *adj* <-ier, -iest> **1.** (*prepared*) pronto, -a; **to be ~** essere pronto; **to get ~** (**for sth**) prepararsi (per qc); **to get sth ~** preparare qc **2.** (*willing*) disponibile **3.** (*available*) immediato, -a; ~ **cash** contanti *mpl;* **to be a ~ source of sth** essere una facile fonte di qc; ~ **at hand** a portata di mano **4.** (*quick, prompt*) pronto, -a; (*mind*) acuto, -a; (*tongue*) affilato, -a; **to find ~ acceptance** essere immediatamente accettato ▶ ~**, set, go!** SPORTS pronti, via! **II.** *n* **at the ~** pronto, -a; (**with**) **his pencil at the ~** (con) la matita in mano **III.** *vt* preparare

ready-made [ˌre·di·'meɪd] *adj* già pronto, -a;

(*meal*) pronto, -a; (*clothing*) confezionato, -a

ready-to-wear [ˌreˑdiˑtəˈweɪ] I. *adj* confezionato, -a II. *n* prêt-à-porter *m*

reaffirm [ˌriːˑəˈfɜːrm] *vt* riaffermare

real [riːl] I. *adj* 1.(*actual*) reale; (*threat, problem*) vero, -a; **for ~** sul serio 2.(*genuine*) autentico, -a; **the ~ thing** [*o* **deal**] l'originale; **a ~ man** *iron* un vero uomo ▶ **the ~ McCoy** *inf* l'originale autentico II. *adv inf* proprio

real estate *n* beni *mpl* immobili

realignment [ˌriːˑəˈlaɪnˑmənt] *n* riassestamento *m;* AUTO riconvergenza *f*

realism [ˈriːˑlɪˑzəm] *n* realismo *m*

realist [ˈriːˑlɪst] *n* realista *mf*

realistic [ˌriːˑəˈlɪsˑtɪk] *adj* realistico, -a

reality [rɪˈæˑləˑti] *n* realtà *f;* **to come back to ~** ritornare alla realtà; **to face ~** affrontare la realtà; **to become a ~** diventare realtà; **in (all) ~** in realtà

realizable [ˈriːˑəˈlaɪˑzəˑbl] *adj a.* FIN realizzabile

realization [ˌriːˑəˈlɪˈzeɪˑʃən] *n* 1.(*awareness*) percezione *f* 2. *a.* FIN realizzazione *f*

realize [ˈriːˑəˈlaɪz] I. *vt* 1.(*be aware of*) essere consapevole di; (*become aware of*) rendersi conto di 2.(*achieve, fulfill*) realizzare 3. FIN liquidare; (*acquire*) realizzare II. *vi* (*notice*) rendersi conto; (*be aware of*) essere cosciente

really [ˈriːˑəˈli] I. *adv* 1.(*genuinely*) veramente 2.(*actually*) realmente 3.(*very*) molto II. *interj* 1.(*surprise and interest*) davvero? 2.(*annoyance*) insomma 3.(*disbelief*) sul serio?

realm [relm] *n* 1.(*kingdom*) regno *m* 2.(*area of interest*) campo *m*

realtor [ˈriːˑəlˑtəʳ] *n* agente *mf* immobiliare

realty [ˈriːˑəlˑti] *n* beni *mpl* immobili

reanimate [riːˈæˑnɪˑmeɪt] *vt* rianimare

reap [riːp] I. *vt* raccogliere II. *vi* fare la raccolta

reaper [ˈriːˑpəʳ] *n* 1.(*person*) mietitore, -trice *m, f* 2.(*machine*) mietitrice *f*

reappear [ˌriːˑəˈpɪr] *vi* riapparire

reapply [ˌriːˑəˈplaɪ] I. *vi* **to ~ for sth** rifare domanda per qc II. *vt* (*paint*) dare un'altra mano di

reappoint [ˌriːˑəˈpɔɪnt] *vt* rinominare

reappraisal [ˌriːˑəˈpreɪˑzl] *n* FIN rivalutazione *f*

rear[1] [rɪr] I. *adj* posteriore II. *n* 1.(*back part*) retro *m inv* 2. *inf* (*buttocks*) posteriore *m* 3. MIL retroguardia *f;* **to bring up the ~** chiudere la fila

rear[2] [rɪr] I. *vt* 1.(*bring up: child*) tirar su; (*animals*) allevare 2.(*raise*) **to ~ one's head** alzare la testa II. *vi* (*horse*) impennarsi; **to ~ above sth** ergersi al di sopra di qc

rear admiral *n* MIL contrammiraglio *m*

rear guard [ˈrɪrˑgɑːrd] *n* retroguardia *f;* **to fight a ~ action** combattere una battaglia di retroguardia

rearm [ˌriːˈɑrm] I. *vi* riarmarsi II. *vt* riarmare

rearmament [riːˈɑːrˑməˑmənt] *n* riarmo *m*

rearmost [ˈrɪrˑmoʊst] *adj* ultimo, -a

rearrange [ˌriːˑəˈreɪndʒ] *vt* 1.(*system*) riorganizzare 2.(*furniture*) riordinare 3.(*meeting*) spostare la data di

rearview mirror *n* specchietto *m* retrovisore

rear-wheel drive *n* trazione *f* posteriore

reason [ˈriːzn] I. *n* 1.(*motive*) motivo *m;* **the ~ why ...** il motivo per cui...; **for no particular ~** senza un particolare motivo; **for some ~** per qualche ragione 2.(*common sense*) buon senso *m;* **within ~** entro limiti ragionevoli; **to listen to ~** dar retta al buon senso; **to be beyond all ~** essere al di fuori di qualsiasi logica; **the Age of Reason** HIST il secolo dei lumi 3.(*sanity*) ragione *f;* **to lose one's ~** perdere la ragione II. *vt* sostenere III. *vi* ragionare; **to ~ from sth** ragionare a partire da qc

reasonable [ˈriːzˑnəˑbl] *adj* 1.(*sensible*) ragionevole 2.(*fair*) discreto, -a 3.(*inexpensive*) non troppo caro, -a

reasonably [ˈriːzˑnəbˑli] *adv* 1.(*fairly*) ragionevolmente 2.(*acceptably*) abbastanza

reasoning [ˈriːzˑnɪŋ] *n* ragionamento *m*

reassemble [ˌriːˑəˈsemˑbl] I. *vt* (*machine*) rimontare; (*people*) riunire di nuovo II. *vi* tornare a riunirsi

reassess [ˌriːˑəˈses] *vt* 1.(*situation*) rivalutare 2. FIN (*taxes*) ricalcolare; (*damages*) fare una nuova stima di

reassurance [ˌriːˑəˈʃʊˑrəns] *n* 1.(*comfort*) rassicurazione *f* 2. FIN riassicurazione *f*

reassure [ˌriːˑəˈʃʊr] *vt* rassicurare

reassuring [ˌriːˑəˈʃʊˑrɪŋ] *adj* rassicurante

reawaken [ˌriːˑəˈweɪˑkən] *vt* risvegliare

rebate [ˈriːˑbeɪt] *n* 1.(*refund*) rimborso *m;* **tax ~** rimborso delle tasse 2.(*discount*) ribasso *m*

rebel[1] [ˈreˑbl] I. *n* ribelle *mf* II. *adj* ribelle

rebel[2] [rɪˈbel] <-ll-> *vi* ribellarsi

rebellion [rɪˈbelˑjən] *n* ribellione *f*

rebellious [rɪˈbelˑjəs] *adj* ribelle

rebirth [ˌriːˈbɜːrθ] *n* rinascita *f*

reboot [ˌriːˈbuːt] INFOR I. *vt* riavviare II. *vi* riavviarsi

rebound [riːˈbaʊnd] I. *vi* 1.(*bounce back: ball*) rimbalzare 2.(*recover*) riprendersi; **to quickly ~ from an injury** riprendersi rapidamente da un incidente 3.(*in basketball*) vincere un rimbalzo II. *vt* conquistare sul rimbalzo III. *n* 1.(*basketball*) rimbalzo *m* 2. contraccolpo *m;* **to marry on the ~** sposarsi per rivalsa

rebounder *n* rimbalzista *mf*

rebuff [rɪˈbʌf] I. *vt* rifiutare con modi bruschi II. *n* brusco rifiuto *m;* **to meet with a ~** dare un brusco rifiuto

rebuild [ˌriːˈbɪld] *vt irr* 1.(*build again*) ricostruire; *fig* (*economy*) riorganizzare; (*one's life*) rifarsi 2.(*restore*) rimettere in sesto 3.(*replenish: stock*) ricostituire

rebuke [rɪˈbjuːk] I. *vt* riprendere II. *n* 1.(*reproof*) rimprovero *m* 2.(*censure*) nota *f* di biasimo

rebut [rɪˈbʌt] <-tt-> *vt* rigettare

rebuttal [rɪˈbʌˑt̩l] *n* rigetto *m*

recalcitrant [rɪˈkælˑsɪˑtrənt] *adj* recalcitrante

recall [rɪˈkɔːl] I. *vt* 1.(*remember*) ricordare

2. (*call back: ambassador, troops*) richiamare **3.** ECON ritirare (dal mercato) **II.** *vi* ricordare **III.** *n* **1.** (*memory*) memoria *f* **2.** POL richiamo *m* **3.** ECON ritiro *m* (dal mercato) ▶ **to be lost beyond** ~ essere definitivamente perso

recant [rɪ·'kænt] **I.** *vt* ritrattare; **to** ~ **one's faith/belief** rinnegare la propria fede/le proprie convinzioni **II.** *vi* ritrattare

recap[1] ['riː·kæp] *abbr of* **recapitulate I.** <-pp-> *vi, vt inf* ricapitolare **II.** *n inf* ricapitolazione *f*

recap[2] [,riː·'kæp] <-pp-> *vt* AUTO ricostruire

recapitulate [,riː·kə·'pɪ·tʃə·leɪt] *vi, vt* ricapitolare

recapitulation [,riː·kə·,pɪ·tʃə·'leɪ·ʃən] *n* **1.** (*summary*) ricapitolazione *m* **2.** MUS, THEAT, CINE sintesi *f*

recapture [,riː·'kæp·tʃɚ] **I.** *vt* **1.** (*town*) riconquistare; (*fugitive*) ricatturare **2.** (*reexperience*) ricatturare; (*beauty, feeling*) recuperare **II.** *n* (*of town*) riconquista *f*

recast [,riː·'kæst] *vt* **1.** THEAT, CINE cambiare i ruoli di **2.** TECH, LIT rifondere

recede [rɪ·'siːd] *vi* **1.** (*move backward: sea*) ritirarsi; (*tide*) abbassarsi; (*fog*) svanire; **to** ~ **into the distance** perdersi in lontananza **2.** (*diminish*) diminuire; (*prices*) calare

receding chin *n* mento *m* sfuggente

receding hairline *n* stempiatura *f*

receipt [rɪ·'siːt] **I.** *n* **1.** (*document*) ricevuta *f* **2.** *pl* COM entrate *fpl* **3.** (*act of receiving*) ricevimento *m;* **payment on** ~ pagamento al ricevimento; **on** ~ **of** ... al ricevimento di ...; **to acknowledge** ~ **of** accusare ricevuta *f* di **II.** *vt* accusare ricevuta di

receipt book *n* registro *m* delle ricevute

receivable *adj* COM esigibile

receive [rɪ·'siːv] **I.** *vt* **1.** (*be given*) *a.* TEL, RADIO ricevere; (*pension, salary*) percepire **2.** (*react to: proposal, suggestion*) accogliere; **the book was well/bady** ~ **d** il libro ebbe una buona/cattiva accoglienza **3.** (*injury*) ricevere **4.** **to** ~ **sb into the Church** accogliere qn in seno alla Chiesa **5.** LAW **to** ~ **stolen goods** ricettare beni rubati **II.** *vi* SPORTS ricevere (la battuta)

received [rɪ·'siːvd] *adj* accettato, -a; ~ **wisdom** opinione *f* diffusa

receiver [rɪ·'siː·vɚ] *n* **1.** TEL, RADIO ricevitore *m* **2.** ECON **the official** ~ il curatore fallimentare **3.** SPORTS ricevitore, -trice *m, f;* (*tennis*) giocatore, -trice *m, f* alla ribattuta

recent ['riː·sənt] *adj* recente; **in** ~ **times** in tempi recenti

recently *adv* recentemente

receptacle [rɪ·'sep·tə·kl] *n* contenitore *m*

reception [rɪ·'sep·ʃən] *n* **1.** (*welcome*) accoglienza *f* **2.** (*in hotel*) reception *f inv*

reception area *n* reception *f inv*

reception desk *n* banco *m* dell'accettazione

receptionist [rɪ·'sep·ʃə·nɪst] *n* receptionist *mf*

receptive [rɪ·'sep·tɪv] *adj* ricettivo, -a

receptiveness *n*, **receptivity** [riː·,sep·'tɪ·və·

ti] *n* ricettività *f*

recess ['riː·ses] **I.** <-es> *n* **1.** POL sospensione *f* dell'attività **2.** SCHOOL intervallo *m* **3.** ARCHIT rientranza *f* **4.** *pl* (*place*) recessi *mpl* **II.** *vi* sospendere l'attività; (*meeting, session*) venire sospeso **III.** *vt* ARCHIT far rientrare

recession [rɪ·'se·ʃən] *n* **1.** (*retreat*) arretramento *m* **2.** ECON recessione *f*

recessive [rɪ·'se·sɪv] *adj* BIO recessivo, -a

recharge [,riː·'tʃɑːrdʒ] **I.** *vt* ricaricare **II.** *vi* ricaricarsi

rechargeable [,riː·'tʃɑːr·dʒə·bl] *adj* ricaricabile

recidivism [rɪ·'sɪ·də·vɪ·zəm] *n* recidività *f*

recidivist [rɪ·'sɪ·də·vɪst] *n* recidivo, -a *m, f*

recipe ['re·sə·pi] *n a. fig* ricetta *f*

recipient [rɪ·'sɪ·pi·ənt] *n* (*of letter*) destinatario, -a *m, f;* (*of transplant*) ricevente *mf;* (*of gift*) beneficiario, -a *m, f*

reciprocal [rɪ·'sɪ·prə·kl] **I.** *adj a.* LING, MAT reciproco, -a **II.** *n* MAT inverso *m*

reciprocate [rɪ·'sɪ·prə·keɪt] **I.** *vt* ricambiare **II.** *vi* **1.** ricambiare **2.** TECH alternarsi

reciprocity [,re·sɪ·'prɑː·sə·ti] *n* reciprocità *f*

recital [rɪ·'saɪ·tl] *n* **1.** MUS recital *m inv* **2.** (*description*) resoconto *m*

recitation [,re·sɪ·'teɪ·ʃən] *n* LIT recitazione *f*

recitative [,re·sɪ·tə·'tiːv] *n* MUS recitativo *m*

recite [rɪ·'saɪt] **I.** *vt* **1.** (*repeat*) recitare **2.** (*list*) enumerare **II.** *vi* recitare

reckless ['rek·ləs] *adj* sconsiderato, -a; LAW imprudente

recklessness *n* imprudenza *f*

reckon ['re·kən] **I.** *vt* **1.** (*calculate*) calcolare **2.** (*consider*) ritenere; **to** ~ (**that**) ... credere che ... +*subj;* **I** ~ **not** mi sembra di no; **what do you** ~? che ne pensi? **3.** (*judge*) stimare **II.** *vi inf* calcolare

◆**reckon with** *vt insep* far i conti con; **she is a force to be reckoned with** è una persona con cui bisogna fare i conti

◆**reckon without** *vt insep* non tenere conto di

reckoning ['re·kə·nɪŋ] *n* **1.** (*calculation*) calcolo *m;* **to be out in one's** ~ calcolare male **2.** (*settlement*) resa *f* dei conti

reclaim [rɪ·'kleɪm] *vt* **1.** (*claim back: title, rights*) reclamare **2.** (*reuse: land*) bonificare; (*material*) riciclare **3.** (*reform*) recuperare

reclamation [,re·klə·'meɪ·ʃən] *n* **1.** (*of title, rights*) rivendicazione *f* **2.** (*of land*) bonifica *f;* (*of material*) riciclaggio *m* **3.** (*reformation*) recupero *m*

recline [rɪ·'klaɪn] **I.** *vi* adagiarsi; **to** ~ **on** adagiarsi su **II.** *vt* reclinare

recliner [rɪ·'klaɪ·nɚ] *n* poltrona *f* reclinabile

reclining seat *n*, **reclining chair** *n* sedile *m* reclinabile

recluse ['re·kluːs] *n* eremita *mf*

reclusive *adj* solitario, -a

recognition [,re·kəg·'nɪ·ʃən] *n a.* INFOR riconoscimento *m;* **optical character** ~ riconoscimento ottico dei caratteri; **voice** ~ riconoscimento vocale; **in** ~ **of** in riconoscimento di

R

recognizable ['re·kəg·naɪ·zə·bl] *adj* riconoscibile

recognizance [rɪ·'kɑːg·nɪ·zns] *n* garanzia *f*

recognize ['re·kəg·naɪz] *vt* riconoscere

recognized ['re·kəg·naɪzd] *adj* riconosciuto, -a

recoil¹ [rɪ·'kɔɪl] *vi* 1.(*draw back*) tirarsi indietro; **to ~ in horror** indietreggiare inorridito; **to ~ at sth** provare raccapriccio per qc; **to ~ from doing sth** rifuggire dal fare qc 2.(*gun*) rinculare

recoil² ['riː·kɔɪl] *n* rinculo *m*

recollect [ˌre·kə·'lekt] *vi, vt* ricordare

recollection [ˌre·kə·'lek·ʃən] *n* ricordo *m;* **to have no ~ of sth** non aver memoria di qc

recommend [ˌre·kə·'mend] *vt* raccomandare; **it is not ~ed** non è consigliato

recommendable *adj* raccomandabile

recommendation [ˌre·kə·mən·'deɪ·ʃən] *n* 1.(*suggestion*) raccomandazione *f;* **on sb's ~** su raccomandazione di qn 2.(*advice*) consiglio *m*

recompense ['re·kəm·pents] I. *n* 1.(*reward*) ricompensa *f* 2.(*compensation*) risarcimento *m* II. *vt* 1.(*reward*) ricompensare 2.(*make amends*) risarcire

reconcile ['re·kən·saɪl] *vt* 1.(*person*) riconciliare; **to become ~d with sb** riconciliarsi con qn 2.(*difference, fact*) conciliare; **to be ~d to sth** accettare qc; **to become ~d to sth** rassegnarsi a qc

reconciliation [ˌre·kən·sɪ·li·'eɪ·ʃən] *n* 1.(*restoration of good relations*) riconciliazione *f* 2.(*making compatible*) conciliazione *f*

recondition [ˌriː·kən·'dɪ·ʃən] *vt* rimettere in sesto

reconnaissance [rɪ·'kɑː·nə·sənts] *n* ricognizione *f*

reconnaissance flight *n* volo *m* di ricognizione

reconnoiter, reconnoitre [ˌriː·kə·'nɔɪ·t̮ə·] I. *vt* fare una ricognizione di II. *vi* fare una ricognizione

reconsider [ˌriː·kən·'sɪ·də·] I. *vt* riconsiderare II. *vi* tornare a rifletterci su

reconstruct [ˌriː·kən·'strʌkt] *vt* 1.(*building*) ricostruire 2.(*life*) rifarsi; (*crime, event*) ricostruire

reconstruction [ˌriː·kən·'strʌk·ʃən] *n* 1.(*of building*) ricostruzione *f* 2.(*of crime, event*) ricostruzione *f*

record¹ ['re·kə·d] I. *n* 1.(*account*) resoconto *m;* (*document*) documento *m;* **medical ~** cartella *f* clinica; **to say sth off the ~** dire qc in maniera ufficiosa; **to put sth on the ~** mettere qc agli atti 2.(*sb's past*) precedenti *mpl;* **to have a good ~** avere buoni precedenti; **to have a clean ~** non avere precedenti 3. *pl* archivi *mpl* 4. MUS disco *m;* **to make a ~** incidere un disco 5. SPORTS record *m inv;* **to break a ~** battere un record 6. LAW verbale *m* 7. INFOR record *m inv* II. *adj* record; **to do sth in ~ time** fare qc a tempo di record; **to**

reach a ~ high raggiungere un massimo record

record² [rɪ·'kɔːrd] I. *vt* 1.(*store*) prendere nota di 2. *a.* INFOR registrare; MUS incidere 3. LAW mettere agli atti II. *vi* registrare

record-breaker ['re·kəd·ˌbreɪ·kə·] *n* SPORTS primatista *mf*

record-breaking *adj* da record

recorded [rɪ·'kɔːr·dɪd] *adj* registrato, -a; (*history*) documentato, -a; (*music*) inciso, -a

recorder [rɪ·'kɔːr·də·] *n* 1.(*tape recorder*) registratore *m* a cassette 2. MUS flauto *m* dolce

record holder *n* SPORTS primatista *mf*

recording *n* (*of sound*) registrazione *f*

recording session *n* sessione *f* di registrazione

recording studio *n* studio *m* di registrazione

record label *n* etichetta *f* discografica

record library *n* discoteca *f*

record player *n* giradischi *m inv*

recount¹ [rɪ·'kaʊnt] *vt* 1.(*narrate*) raccontare 2.(*count again*) contare di nuovo

recount² ['riː·kaʊnt] *n* POL nuovo conteggio *m*

recoup [rɪ·'kuːp] *vt* recuperare

recourse ['riː·kɔːrs] *n* ricorso *m;* **to have ~ to** fare ricorso a

recover [rɪ·'kʌ·və·] I. *vt a.* INFOR recuperare; **to ~ one's composure** ritrovare la calma II. *vi* 1.(*regain health*) ristabilirsi 2.(*return to normal*) riprendersi

re-cover [ˌriː·'kʌ·və·] *vt* ricoprire

recoverable [rɪ·'kʌ·və·rə·bl] *adj a.* INFOR, FIN recuperabile

recovery [rɪ·'kʌ·ə·i] <-ies> *n* 1. *a.* MED, ECON, FIELD ripresa *f;* **to be beyond ~** non essere più recuperabile 2. INFOR recupero *m*

recovery room *n* MED sala *f* postoperatoria

recovery ship *n* nave *f* di recupero

recovery vehicle *n* carro *m* attrezzi

recreate [ˌriː·kri·'eɪt] *vt* ricreare

recreation¹ [ˌriː·kri·'eɪ·ʃən] *n* (*of conditions, situation*) riproduzione *f*

recreation² [ˌre·kri·'eɪ·ʃən] *n* 1. *a.* SCHOOL ricreazione *f* 2.(*pastime*) divertimento *m*

recreational [ˌre·kri·'eɪ·ʃə·nəl] *adj* ricreativo, -a

recreational vehicle *n* camper *m inv*

recreation center *n* centro *m* ricreativo

recreation room *n* sala *f* di ricreazione

recreative ['re·kri·ˌeɪ·t̮ɪv] *adj* ricreativo, -a

recriminate [rɪ·'krɪ·mə·neɪt] *vi* recriminare

recrimination [rɪ·ˌkrɪ·mə·'neɪ·ʃən] *n pl* recriminazione *f*

recruit [rɪ·'kruːt] I. *vt* MIL reclutare; (*employee*) assumere II. *n* MIL recluta *f*

recruiting I. *n* MIL reclutamento *m;* ECON assunzione *f* II. *adj* MIL, ECON di reclutamento

recruiting office *n* MIL ufficio *m* assunzioni

recruitment I. *n* MIL reclutamento *m;* ECON assunzione *f;* (*of members*) reclutamento *m* II. *adj* di reclutamento

recruitment agency *n* agenzia *f* di collocamento

rectangle ['rek·tæŋ·gl] *n* rettangolo *m*

rectangular [rek·'tæŋ·gjə·lə·] *adj* rettangolare

rectification [ˌrek·tə·fɪ·'keɪ·ʃən] *n* rettificazione *f*

rectify ['rek·tə·faɪ] *vt* rettificare

rectilinear [ˌrek·tə·'lɪ·ni·əɚ] *adj* rettilineo, -a

rectitude ['rek·tə·tu:d] *n* rettitudine *f*

rector ['rek·təɚ] *n* **1.** REL ≈ parroco *m* **2.** SCHOOL direttore, -trice *m, f* **3.** UNIV rettore *m*

rectory ['rek·tə·ri] <-ies> *n* canonica *f*

rectum ['rek·təm] *n* ANAT retto *m*

recumbent [rɪ·'kʌm·bənt] *adj liter* adagiato, -a

recuperate [rɪ·'ku:·pə·reɪt] **I.** *vi* riprendersi **II.** *vt* recuperare

recuperation [rɪ·ˌku:·pə·'reɪ·ʃən] *n* recupero *m*

recur [rɪ·'kɜːr] *vi* ripetersi

recurrence [rɪ·'kɜː·rəns] *n* ripetizione *f*

recurrent [rɪ·'kɜː·rənt] *adj* ricorrente

recurring *adj* ricorrente

recycle [ˌriː·'saɪ·kl] *vt* riciclare

recycling **I.** *n* riciclaggio *m* **II.** *adj* di riciclaggio

recycling plant *n* impianto *m* di riciclaggio

red [red] **I.** <-dd-> *adj* rosso, -a; **to be** [*o* **go**] **~** diventare rosso **II.** *n* rosso *m;* **to be in the ~** FIN essere in rosso ▶ **to make** sb see **~** far infuriare qn; **to see ~** vedere rosso

Red Army *n* Armata *f* Rossa

red blood cell *n* globulo *m* rosso

red-blooded [ˌred·'blʌ·dɪd] *adj* focoso, -a

red cabbage *n* cavolo *m* rosso

redcap ['red·kæp] *n* (*railway porter*) portabagagli *mf inv*

Red Crescent *n* the **~** la Mezzaluna Rossa

Red Cross *n* the **~** la Croce Rossa

redcurrant *n* ribes *m*

red deer *n inv* cervo *m* rosso

redden ['re·dn] **I.** *vi* diventare rosso; (*person*) arrossire; **to ~ with embarrassment** arrossire d'imbarazzo **II.** *vt* far diventare rosso

reddish ['re·dɪʃ] *adj* rossiccio, -a

redecorate [ˌriː·'de·kə·reɪt] *vt* rifare; (*paint*) ridipingere; (*wallpaper*) ritappezzare

redecoration [ˌriː·de·kə·'reɪ·ʃən] *n* (*repainting*) rinnovo *m* della tinteggiatura; (*re-papering*) rinnovo *m* della carta da parati

redeem [rɪ·'diːm] *vt* **1.** *a.* REL (*person, soul*) redimere; (*situation*) salvare; **to ~ oneself** redimersi **2.** FIN (*policy, share*) incassare; (*pawned item*) riscattare; (*debt*) estinguere; **to ~ a mortgage** estinguere un mutuo **3.** (*fulfill: promise*) mantenere

redeemable *adj* FIN redimibile

Redeemer [rɪ·'diː·məɚ] *n* REL the **~** il Redentore

redeeming [rɪ·'diː·mɪŋ] *adj* positivo, -a; **he has no ~ qualities** non c'è nulla che lo salvi

redefine [ˌriː·dɪ·'faɪn] *vt* ridefinire

redemption [rɪ·'demp·ʃən] *n* **1.** *a.* REL redenzione *f* **2.** FIN (*of policy, share*) liquidazione *f;* (*of mortgage*) estinzione *f*

redeploy [ˌriː·dɪ·'plɔɪ] *vt* (*workers, staff*) ridistribuire; (*soldiers, troops*) cambiare la disloca-

zione di

redeployment *n* (*of workers, staff*) ridistribuzione *f;* (*of soldiers, troops*) nuova dislocazione *f*

redevelop [ˌriː·dɪ·'ve·ləp] *vt* dare nuovo sviluppo a

redevelopment [ˌriː·dɪ·'ve·ləp·mənt] *n* nuovo sviluppo *m*

redeye *n sl* volo *m* notturno

red-haired [ˌred·'he·əɚd] *adj* dai capelli rossi

red-handed [ˌred·'hæn·dɪd] *adj* **to catch** sb **~** cogliere qn in flagrante

redhead ['red·hed] *n* rosso, -a *m, f*

red-headed *adj* dai capelli rossi

red herring *n fig* falsa pista *f*

red-hot [ˌred·'hɑːt] *adj* **1.** (*extremely hot*) incandescente; **to be ~** essere incandescente **2.** (*exciting*) sensazionale **3.** (*up-to-the-minute: information*) dell'ultim'ora

redirect [ˌriː·dɪ·'rekt] *vt* rindirizzare; (*letter*) spedire al nuovo indirizzo; (*traffic*) deviare

redistribute [ˌriː·dɪ·'strɪb·juːt] *vt* ridistribuire

redistribution [ˌriː·dɪs·trɪ·'bjuː·ʃən] *n* ridistribuzione *f*

red-letter day [ˌred·'le·ţɚ·ˌdeɪ] *n* giorno *m* memorabile

red light *n* semaforo *m* rosso

red-light district *n* quartiere *m* a luci rosse

red meat *n* carne *f* rossa

redneck ['red·nek] *n abitante delle zone rurali del sud degli USA, di razza bianca e scarsa istruzione*

redness ['red·nɪs] *n* rossore *m*

redo [ˌriː·'duː] *vt irr* rifare

redolent ['re·də·lənt] *adj form* **1.** (*smelling of*) **~ of** sth fragrante di qc **2.** (*suggestive of*) **to be ~ of** sth essere evocativo di qc

redouble [rɪ·'dʌ·bl] *vt* raddoppiare; **to ~ one's efforts** raddoppiare gli sforzi

redoubtable [rɪ·'dau·ţə·bl] *adj* temibile

redound [rɪ·'daund] *vi form* **to ~ to** sb's **advantage** andare a beneficio di qn; **to ~ to** sb's **credit** accrescere il prestigio di qn

red pepper *n* peperone *m* rosso

redraft[1] [ˌriː·'dræft] *vt* scrivere una nuova versione di

redraft[2] ['riː·dræft] *n* nuova versione *f*

redress [rɪ·'dres] **I.** *vt* (*grievance*) soddisfare; (*fault*) rimediare a; (*imbalance*) raddrizzare **II.** *n* (*of grievance*) soddisfazione *f;* (*imbalance*) rettifica; **to seek ~** cercare una riparazione

Red Sea *n* the **~** il Mar Rosso

redskin *n pej* pellerossa *mf inv*

red tape *n* lungaggini *fpl* burocratiche

reduce [rɪ·'duːs] **I.** *vt* **1.** (*diminish*) ridurre **2.** MIL degradare **3.** **to ~** sb **to tears** ridurre qn in lacrime; **to ~** sth **to rubble/ashes** ridurre qc in rovine/cenere; **to be ~d to doing** sth essere ridotto a fare qc **4.** MAT (*fraction*) ridurre **II.** *vi* dimagrire

reduced [rɪ·'duːst] *adj* **1.** (*lower*) ridotto, -a **2.** (*impoverished*) **to be in ~ circumstances**

R

trovarsi in ristrettezze economiche

reduction [rɪ'dʌk·ʃən] *n* riduzione *f*

redundancy [rɪ'dʌn·dən·tsi] <-ies> *n* (*uselessness*) superfluità *f;* LING ridondanza *f*

redundant [rɪ'dʌn·dənt] *adj* (*superfluous*) superfluo, -a; LING ridondante

reduplicate [rɪ'duː·plə·keɪt] *vi* raddoppiarsi

reduplication [rɪ,duː·plə·'keɪ·ʃən] *n* raddoppio *m*

red wine *n* vino *m* rosso

redwood ['red·wʊd] *n* sequoia *f*

re-echo [,riː·'e·koʊ] I. *vt* riecheggiare II. *vi* riecheggiare

reed [riːd] *n* 1. (*plant, straw*) canna *f* 2. MUS ancia *f*

reed instrument *n* strumento *m* provvisto di ancia

re-educate [,riː·'ed·ʒʊ·keɪt] *vt* rieducare

reedy ['riː·di] *adj* 1. (*full of reeds*) pieno, -a di canne 2. MUS (*voice*) stridulo, -a

reef [riːf] I. *n* 1. (*ridge*) scogliera *f* 2. (*part of sail*) terzarolo *m* II. *vt* NAUT terzarolare

reefer ['riː·fə*] *n sl* spinello *m*

reek [riːk] I. *vi* puzzare; **to ~ of corruption** puzzare di corruzione II. *n* puzzo *m*

reel[1] [riːl] *n* (*storage or winding device*) rocchetto *m;* (*for film, rope, tape*) bobina *f*

reel[2] [riːl] I. *vi* 1. (*move unsteadily*) barcollare 2. (*recoil*) indietreggiare II. *n* reel *m* (*danza scozzese*)

re-elect [,riː·ɪ·'lekt] *vt* rieleggere

re-election [,riː·ɪ·'lek·ʃən] *n* rielezione *f*

re-employ [,riː·ɪm·'plɔɪ] *vt* reimpiegare

re-engage [,riː·ɪn·'geɪdʒ] *vt* impegnare di nuovo

re-enter [,riː·'en·tə*] I. *vt* 1. (*go in again*) rientrare in 2. INFOR immettere di nuovo II. *vi* rientrare

re-entry [,riː·'en·tri] <-ies> *n* rientro *m*

ref [ref] *n* 1. *inf abbr of* **referee** arbitro *m* 2. *abbr of* **reference** referenza *f*

refectory [rɪ·'fek·tə·ri] <-ies> *n* mensa *f*

refer [rɪ·'fɜːr] <-rr-> *vt* **to refer sth to sb** (*article*) rimettere qc a qn; **to ~ a patient to a specialist** mandare un paziente da uno specialista; **to ~ a case to sb/sth** LAW sottoporre un caso a qn/qc

♦**refer back to** *vt* rinviare a; **please ~ your notes** per favore consultate i vostri appunti

♦**refer to** *vt* 1. (*mention, allude*) riferirsi a; **to never ~ sth** non fare mai riferimento a qc; **to ~ sb as sth** riferirsi a qn come qc; **referring to your letter/phone call, ...** con riferimento alla sua lettera/telefonata, ... 2. (*concern*) riguardare; **does this information ~ me?** quest'informazione mi riguarda? 3. (*consult, turn to*) consultare; **to ~ one's notes** consultare i propri appunti; **~ page 70** vedere pagina 70; **I ~ the facts** mi rimetto ai fatti

referee [,re·fə·'riː] I. *n* 1. SPORTS arbitro *m* 2. (*in dispute*) mediatore, -trice *m, f* II. *vi, vt* arbitrare

reference ['re·fə·rənts] *n* 1. (*consultation*)

consultazione *f;* **to make ~ to sth** fare riferimento a qc 2. (*source*) fonte *f* 3. (*allusion*) riferimento *m;* **with ~ to what was said** con riferimento a quello che si è detto 4. ADMIN (*number*) numero *m* di riferimento 5. (*for job application*) referenza *f;* **to take up ~s** chiedere referenze

reference book *n* libro *m* di consultazione

reference library *n* biblioteca *f* di consultazione

reference number *n* 1. (*in document, on book*) numero *m* di riferimento 2. (*on product*) numero *m* di serie

referendum [,re·fə·'ren·dəm] <-s *o* -da> *n* referendum *m inv*

referral [rɪ·'fɜː·rəl] *n* rinvio *m*

refill[1] [,riː·'fɪl] *vt* (*fill again*) riempire di nuovo

refill[2] ['riː·fɪl] *n* (*replacement*) ricambio *m*

refine [rɪ·'faɪn] *vt* 1. (*oil, sugar*) raffinare 2. (*technique*) perfezionare

refined [rɪ·'faɪnd] *adj* 1. (*oil, sugar*) raffinato, -a 2. (*sophisticated*) sofisticato, -a 3. (*very polite*) fine

refinement [rɪ·'faɪn·mənt] *n* 1. (*improvement*) perfezionamento *m* 2. (*purification*) raffinazione *f* 3. (*good manners*) raffinatezza *f*

refinery [rɪ·'faɪ·nə·ri] <-ies> *n* raffineria *f*

refit[1] [,riː·'fɪt] <-tt-> I. *vi* essere rimesso a nuovo; NAUT essere raddobbato II. *vt* rimettere a nuovo; NAUT raddobbare

refit[2] ['riː·fɪt] *n* rimessa *f* a nuovo; NAUT raddobbo *m*

reflate [riː·'fleɪt] *vt* operare interventi reflazionistici su

reflation [,riː·'fleɪ·ʃən] *n* reflazione *f*

reflect [rɪ·'flekt] I. *vt* riflettere II. *vi* 1. (*cast back light*) riflettersi 2. (*contemplate*) riflettere 3. **to ~ badly on sth** gettare un'ombra su qc

reflecting *adj* riflettente

reflecting telescope *n* telescopio *m* riflettore

reflection [rɪ·'flek·ʃən] *n* 1. (*image*) riflesso *m* 2. (*thought*) riflessione *f;* **~s on sth** riflessioni su qc; **on ~** a pensarci bene 3. *fig* **to be a fair ~ of sth** essere uno specchio fedele di qc; **to be a poor ~ on sth** offrire un quadro impietoso di qc

reflective [rɪ·'flek·tɪv] *adj* 1. (*surface*) riflettente 2. (*thoughtful*) riflessivo, -a

reflector [rɪ·'flek·tə*] *n* (*mirror*) riflettore *m;* (*of bicycle, car*) catarifrangente *m*

reflex ['riː·fleks] <-es> I. *n* riflesso *m* II. *adj* istintivo, -a

reflex action *n* atto *m* istintivo

reflex camera *n* macchina *f* fotografica reflex

reflexive [rɪ·'flek·sɪv] I. *adj* 1. (*independent of will*) istintivo, -a 2. LING riflessivo, -a II. *n* LING riflessivo *m*

reflexology [,riː·flek·'sɑː·lə·dʒi] *n* riflessologia *f*

refloat [,riː·'floʊt] *vt* rimettere a galla

reflux [,riː·'flʌks] *n* riflusso *m*

reforest [,riː·'fɔː·rɪst] *vt* rimboscare

reform [rɪ·'fɔːrm] I. *vt* riformare II. *vi* ravvedersi III. *n* riforma *f*

re-form [ˌriː·ˈfɔːrm] I. *vt* formare di nuovo II. *vi* riformarsi

reformation [ˌre·fə·ˈmeɪ·ʃən] *n* riforma *f;* **the Reformation** la Riforma

reformatory [-ˈfɔːr·mə·tɔː·ri] <-ies> *n* riformatorio *m*

reformer *n* riformatore, -trice *m, f*

reform school *n* riformatorio *m*

refract [rɪ·ˈfrækt] *vt* PHYS rifrangere

refraction [rɪ·ˈfræk·ʃən] *n* rifrazione *f*

refractory [rɪ·ˈfræk·tə·ri] *adj* refrattario, -a

refrain[1] [rɪ·ˈfreɪn] *vi form* astenersi; **to ~ from doing sth** astenersi dal fare qc

refrain[2] [rɪ·ˈfreɪn] *n* MUS ritornello *m*

refresh [rɪ·ˈfreʃ] *vt* rinfrescare; **to ~ oneself** rinfrescarsi

refresher *n* aggiornamento *m* rapido; **~ course** corso *m* di aggiornamento

refreshing *adj* **1.** (*drink*) rinfrescante **2.** (*change, difference*) piacevole

refreshment [rɪ·ˈfreʃ·mənt] *n* rinfresco *m*

refrigerant [rɪ·ˈfrɪ·dʒə·rənt] *n* refrigerante *m*

refrigerate [rɪ·ˈfrɪ·dʒə·reɪt] *vt* refrigerare

refrigeration [rɪ·ˌfrɪ·dʒə·ˈreɪ·ʃən] *n* refrigerazione *f*

refrigerator [rɪ·ˈfrɪ·dʒə·reɪ·tə] *n* frigorifero *m*

refuel [ˌriː·ˈfjuː·əl] <-ll-, -l-> I. *vi* fare rifornimento (di carburante) II. *vt* rifornire di carburante; *fig* riaccendere

refuge [ˈre·fjuːdʒ] *n* rifugio *m;* **to take ~ in sth** rifugiarsi in qc

refugee [ˌre·fjʊ·ˈdʒiː] *n* rifugiato, -a *m, f*

refugee camp *n* campo *m* profughi

refund[1] [ˌriː·ˈfʌnd] *vt* rimborsare

refund[2] [ˈriː·fʌnd] *n* rimborso *m*

refurbish [ˌriː·ˈfɜːr·bɪʃ] *vt* rimettere a nuovo

refusal [rɪ·ˈfjuː·zl] *n* rifiuto *m*

refuse [rɪ·ˈfjuːz] I. *vi* rifiutar(si) II. *vt* (*request, gift*) rifiutare; (*permission, entry*) negare; **to ~ sb sth** negare qc a qn

refusenik [re·ˈfjuːz·nɪk] *n* POL refuznik *mf inv*

refutation [ˌre·fju·ˈteɪ·ʃən] *n* confutazione *f*

refute [rɪ·ˈfjuːt] *vt* confutare

regain [rɪ·ˈgeɪn] *vt* (*freedom, possession*) recuperare; (*consciousness*) riprendere; (*health*) riacquistare

regal [ˈriː·gl] *adj* regale

regale [rɪ·ˈgeɪl] *vt iron* intrattenere

regalia [rɪ·ˈgeɪl·iə] *n* **1.** (*clothes*) abiti *mpl* da cerimonia **2.** (*insignia*) insegne *fpl*

regard [rɪ·ˈgɑːrd] I. *vt* **1.** (*consider*) considerare; **to ~ sb highly** tenere qn in grande stima **2.** *form* (*watch*) osservare **3.** (*concerning*) **as ~s** ... riguardo a ... II. *n form* **1.** (*consideration*) considerazione *f;* **to pay no ~ to sth** non prestare attenzione a qc; **with ~ to** ... quanto a ... **2.** (*respect*) stima *f;* **to hold sb/sth in high ~** avere una grande stima di qn/qc **3.** (*point*) **in this ~** a questo riguardo **4.** *pl* (*in messages*) saluti *mpl;* **with kind ~s** cari saluti

regardful [rɪ·ˈgɑːrd·fəl] *adj* attento, -a

regarding *prep* quanto a

regardless [rɪ·ˈgɑːrd·ləs] I. *adv* nonostante tutto; **to press on ~** andare avanti senza curarsi di nulla II. *adj* incurante; **~ of** ... senza badare a ...

regatta [rɪ·ˈgɑː·ṭə] *n* regata *f*

regency [ˈriː·dʒən·si] *n* reggenza *f*

regenerate [rɪ·ˈdʒe·nə·reɪt] I. *vt* rigenerare II. *vi* rigenerarsi

regeneration [rɪ·ˌdʒe·nə·ˈreɪ·ʃən] *n* rigenerazione *f*

reggae [ˈre·geɪ] *n* reggae *m*

regime [rə·ˈʒiːm] *n* regime *m*

regimen [ˈre·dʒə·men] *n form* regime *m*

regiment [ˈre·dʒə·mənt] I. *n* **1.** MIL reggimento *m* **2.** *fig* esercito *m* II. *vt* irreggimentare

regimentation [ˌre·dʒə·mən·ˈteɪ·ʃən] *n* irreggimentazione *f*

region [ˈriː·dʒən] *n* regione *f;* **in the ~ of 30** intorno a 30

regional [ˈriː·dʒə·nl] *adj* regionale

regionalism [ˈriː·dʒə·nə·ˌlɪ·zəm] *n* regionalismo *m*

register [ˈre·dʒɪs·tə] I. *n* registro *m;* **class ~** registro di classe II. *vt* registrare; (*car*) immatricolare; (*voter*) iscrivere nelle liste elettorali; (*letter*) spedire per raccomandata; (*package*) assicurare III. *vi* **1.** *a.* UNIV (*record*) iscriversi **2.** (*be understood*) **the information didn't ~ with him** non fece caso a quelle notizie

registered [ˈre·dʒɪs·tə·d] *adj* registrato, -a; (*nurse*) diplomato, -a; (*student*) iscritto, -a; (*letter*) raccomandato, -a; (*package*) assicurato, -a

registrar [ˈre·dʒɪs·trɑːr] *n* **1.** ADMIN ufficiale *m* di stato civile **2.** UNIV responsabile *mf* della segreteria **3.** MED medico *m* specializzando

registration [ˌre·dʒɪ·ˈstreɪ·ʃən] *n* **1.** (*act*) registrazione *f;* **voter~** iscrizione dei votanti nelle liste elettorali **2.** AUTO libretto *m* di circolazione; **license and ~** patente e libretto di circolazione **3.** UNIV iscrizione *f*

registration fee *n a.* UNIV quota *f* d'iscrizione

registration number *n* numero *m* di targa

registry [ˈre·dʒɪs·tri] *n* anagrafe *f;* **bridal ~** anagrafe matrimoniale

regress [rɪ·ˈgres] *vi* regredire

regression [rɪ·ˈgre·ʃən] *n* regressione *f*

regressive [rɪ·ˈgre·sɪv] *adj* regressivo, -a

regret [rɪ·ˈgret] I. <-tt-> *vt* rammaricarsi di; **to ~ doing sth** pentirsi di aver fatto qc; **we ~ any inconvenience to passengers** siamo spiacenti per i disagi ai passeggeri II. *n* rammarico *m;* **to have ~s** avere rimpianti; **to have no ~s about sth** non avere rimpianti per qc; **much to my ~** con mio grande rammarico; **to send one's ~s** inviare le proprie scuse

regretful [rɪ·ˈgret·fəl] *adj* dispiaciuto, -a

regretfully *adv* con rammarico

regrettable [rɪ·ˈgre·ṭə·bl] *adj* deplorevole

regroup [ˌriː·ˈgruːp] I. *vt* raggruppare di nuovo II. *vi* raggrupparsi di nuovo

regular [ˈreg·jə·lə] I. *adj* **1.** (*pattern*) regolare; (*appearance, customer*) abituale; (*procedure*)

R

normale; **to have ~ meetings** fare riunioni periodiche **2.** (*gas*) normale **3.** LING regolare **4.** *inf* (*real*) vero, -a **II.** *n* **1.** (*customer*) cliente *mf* abituale **2.** MIL militare *m* di carriera

regularity [ˌreg·jʊ·'le·rə·ti] *n* regolarità *f*

regularize ['reg·jʊ·lə·raɪz] *vt* **1.** (*standardize*) standardizzare **2.** (*normalize*) regolarizzare

regularly *adv* regolarmente

regulate ['reg·jʊ·leɪt] *vt* **1.** (*supervise*) regolamentare **2.** (*adjust*) regolare

regulation [ˌreg·jʊ·'leɪ·ʃən] **I.** *n* **1.** (*rule*) regola *f;* **safety ~s** norme *fpl* di sicurezza; **in accordance with (the) ~s** in base al regolamento **2.** (*adjustment*) regolazione *f* **II.** *adj* regolamentare

regulator ['reg·jʊ·leɪ·tə] *n* regolatore *m*

regulatory ['reg·jə·leɪ·tɔː·ri] *adj* di controllo

regurgitate [riː·'gɜːr·dʒə·teɪt] *vt* **1.** (*food*) regurgitare **2.** (*ideas, facts*) ripetere meccanicamente

rehab *n inf abbr of* **rehabilitation** riabilitazione *f*

rehabilitate [ˌriː·hə·'bɪ·lə·teɪt] *vt* riabilitare

rehabilitation [ˌriː·hə·ˌbɪ·lə·'teɪ·ʃən] *n* riabilitazione *f*

rehabilitation center *n* centro *m* di riabilitazione

rehash¹ [ˌriː·'hæʃ] *vt* rimasticare

rehash² ['riː·hæʃ] *n* (*rediscussion*) rimasticamento *m*

rehearsal [rɪ·'hɜːrsl] *n* prova *f*

rehearse [rɪ·'hɜːrs] *vt, vi* provare

reign [reɪn] **I.** *vi* **1.** (*be monarch*) regnare **2.** *fig* (*be dominant*) dominare **II.** *n* **1.** (*sovereignty*) regno *m* **2.** (*rule*) dominio *m*

reimburse [ˌriː·ɪm·'bɜːrs] *vt* rimborsare

reimbursement *n* rimborso *m*

rein [reɪn] *n* redine *f* ▸ **to give free ~ to sb** dare carta bianca a qn; **to keep sb on a tight ~** tenere qn sotto stretto controllo; **to hold the ~s** tenere le redini

reincarnation [ˌriː·ɪn·kɑːr·'neɪ·ʃən] *n* reincarnazione *f*

reindeer ['re·ɪn·dɪr] *n inv* renna *f*

reinforce [ˌriː·ɪn·'fɔːrs] *vt a.* MIL rinforzare; (*argument*) rafforzare

reinforcement *n* rafforzamento *m*

reinstate [ˌriː·ɪn·'steɪt] *vt form* reintegrare

reinsure [ˌriː·ɪn·'ʃʊr] *vt* assicurare di nuovo

reintegrate [ˌriː·'ɪn·tə·greɪt] *vt* reintegrare; (*criminal*) reinserire

reintegration ['riː·ˌɪn·tə·'greɪ·ʃən] *n* reintegrazione *f;* (*of criminal*) reinserimento *m*

reintroduce [ˌriː·ɪn·trə·'duːs] *vt* reintrodurre

reissue [ˌriː·'ɪʃ·juː] **I.** *vt* fare una nuova edizione di **II.** *n* nuova edizione *f*

reiterate [riː·'ɪ·t̬ə·reɪt] *vt* reiterare

reiteration [riː·ˌɪ·t̬ə·'reɪ·ʃən] *n* reiterazione *f*

reject¹ [rɪ·'dʒekt] *vt a.* MED, TECH rigettare; (*application, request, accusation*) respingere; (*bill, motion*) impugnare; (*proposal*) scartare

reject² ['riː·dʒekt] *n* **1.** (*cast-off*) articolo *m* di scarto **2.** (*person*) persona *f* scartata

rejection [rɪ·'dʒek·ʃən] *n* rifiuto *m*

rejoice [rɪ·'dʒɔɪs] *vi* rallegrarsi; **to ~ in doing sth** essere felice di fare qc; **I ~d to see that ...** mi rallegrai nel vedere che ...

rejoicing *n* esultanza *f*

rejoin¹ [ˌriː·'dʒɔɪn] **I.** *vt* (*join again*) ricongiungersi a; (*political party*) rientrare in **II.** *vi* ricongiungersi

rejoin² [rɪ·'dʒɔɪn] *vt* (*reply*) replicare

rejoinder [rɪ·'dʒɔɪn·də] *n* replica *f*

rejuvenate [riː·'dʒuː·və·neɪt] *vt* ringiovanire

rekindle [riː·'kɪn·dl] *vt a. fig* ravvivare

relapse [rɪ·'læps] **I.** *n* MED ricaduta *f* **II.** *vi* ricadere; MED avere una ricaduta

relate [rɪ·'leɪt] **I.** *vt* **1.** (*establish connection*) mettere in relazione **2.** (*tell*) raccontare **II.** *vi* **1.** (*be connected with*) **to ~ to sb/sth** avere a che fare con qn/qc **2.** (*understand*) **to ~ to sth/sb** entrare in sintonia con qc/qn

related *adj* **1.** (*linked*) correlato, -a **2.** (*in same family*) imparentato, -a; **to be ~ to sb** essere imparentato con qn; **to be closely/distantly ~** essere parente stretto/lontano

relating to *prep* con riguardo a

relation [rɪ·'leɪ·ʃən] *n* **1.** (*link*) relazione *f;* **in ~ to** riguardo a; **to bear no ~ to sb/sth** non avere niente a che fare con qn/qc **2.** (*relative*) parente *mf* **3.** *pl* (*contact*) relazioni *fpl*

relationship [rɪ·'leɪ·ʃən·ʃɪp] *n* **1.** (*link*) relazione *f* **2.** (*family connection*) parentela *f* **3.** (*between two people*) rapporto *m;* **to be in a ~ with sb** avere una relazione *f* con qn; **business ~s** rapporti commerciali

relative ['re·lə·tɪv] **I.** *adj* relativo, -a **II.** *n* parente *mf*

relative clause *n* proposizione *f* relativa

relatively *adv* relativamente

relativity [ˌre·lə·'tɪ·və·ti] *n* relatività *f*

relaunch¹ [ˌriː·'lɔːntʃ] *vt* rilanciare

relaunch² ['riː·lɔːntʃ] *n* rilancio *m*

relax [rɪ·'læks] **I.** *vi* rilassarsi; (*restrictions, security*) allentarsi; **relax!** rilassati! **II.** *vt* rilassare; (*restrictions, security*) allentare; **to ~ one's efforts** diminuire i propri sforzi; **to ~ one's hold on sth** *a. fig* allentare la propria presa su qc

relaxation [ˌriː·læk·'seɪ·ʃən] *n* rilassamento *m*

relaxed *adj* rilassato, -a

relay ['riː·leɪ] **I.** *vt* (*information*) passare; TV ritrasmettere **II.** *n* **1.** (*group*) turno *m;* **to work in ~s** fare turni di lavoro **2.** SPORTS (*corsa f a*) staffetta *f* **3.** ELEC relè *m*

re-lay [ˌriː·'leɪ] *vt* metter giù di nuovo

release [rɪ·'liːs] **I.** *vt* **1.** (*set free*) rilasciare **2.** (*cease to hold*) allentare; PHOT far scattare **3.** (*allow to escape: gas*) liberare; (*steam*) emettere **4.** (*weaken: pressure*) alleggerire **5.** (*make public: information*) rendere noto; (*book*) pubblicare; (*film*) fare uscire; (*CD*) mettere in circolazione **II.** *n* **1.** (*of prisoner*) rilascio *m;* (*of hostage*) liberazione *f* **2.** PHOT scatto *m* **3.** (*relaxation*) allentamento *m* **4.** (*escape*) fuga *f* **5.** (*publication*) pubblicazione *f;* (*of film*) uscita *f;* (*of CD*) messa *f* in circolazione; **press** ~ comunicato *m* (di) stampa

relegate ['re·lə·geɪt] *vt* relegare

relent [rɪ·'lent] *vi* (*person*) cedere; (*wind, rain*) attenuarsi

relentless [rɪ·'lent·ləs] *adj* (*pursuit, opposition*) implacabile; (*pressure*) incessante; (*criticism*) spietato, -a

relevance ['re·lə·vənts] *n*, **relevancy** *n* pertinenza *f*

relevant ['re·lə·vənt] *adj* pertinente

reliability [rɪ·ˌla·ɪə·'bɪ·lə·ti] *n* 1. (*dependability*) affidabilità *f* 2. (*trustworthiness*) attendibilità *f*

reliable [rɪ·'la·ɪə·bl] *adj* 1. (*credible*) attendibile; (*authority*) serio, -a; (*evidence*) convincente 2. (*trustworthy*) degno, -a di fiducia

reliance [rɪ·'la·ɪəns] *n* 1. (*dependence*) dipendenza *f* 2. (*belief*) fiducia *f*

reliant [rɪ·'la·ɪənt] *adj* **to be** ~ **on sb/sth** fare affidamento su qn/qc

relic ['re·lɪk] *n a. fig* reliquia *f*

relief [rɪ·'li:f] I. *n* 1. (*relaxation*) sollievo *m;* **it's a** ~ **that** è un sollievo che +*subj;* **what a** ~! che sollievo! 2. (*aid*) soccorso *m* 3. (*replacement*) sostituzione *f* 4. MIL liberazione *f* 5. *a.* GEO rilievo *m;* **to throw sth into** ~ mettere in rilievo qc 6. **tax** ~ agevolazione *f* fiscale II. *adj* 1. di riserva; ~ **driver** secondo autista 2. GEO a rilievo

relief supplies *npl* aiuti *mpl* umanitari

relief worker *n* operatore, -trice *m, f* umanitario, -a

relieve [rɪ·'li:v] *vt* 1. (*assist*) soccorrere 2. (*alleviate: pain, suffering*) alleviare; (*feelings*) dare sfogo a; (*one's mind*) tranquillizzare 3. MIL liberare 4. (*urinate, defecate*) **to** ~ **oneself** liberarsi

relieved *adj* sollevato, -a

religion [rɪ·'lɪ·dʒən] *n* religione *f*

religious [rɪ·'lɪ·dʒəs] *adj* religioso, -a

relinquish [rɪ·'lɪŋ·kwɪʃ] *vt* (*claim, title*) rinunciare a; (*control*) cedere; **to** ~ **one's grip on sth** mollare la presa su qc

relish ['re·lɪʃ] I. *n* 1. (*enjoyment*) piacere *m;* **with** ~ con piacere 2. (*enthusiasm*) entusiasmo *m* 3. GASTR salsa *f* II. *vt* provar piacere per; **I don't** ~ ... non mi entusiasma ...

reload [ˌri:·'loʊd] I. *vt* ricaricare II. *vi* ricaricarsi

relocate [ˌri:·'loʊ·keɪt] I. *vi* trasferirsi II. *vt* trasferire

relocation [ˌri:·loʊ·'keɪ·ʃən] *n* trasferimento *m*

reluctance [rɪ·'lʌk·təns] *n* riluttanza *f;* **with** ~ con riluttanza

reluctant [rɪ·'lʌk·tənt] *adj* riluttante; **to be** ~ **to do sth** essere riluttante a fare qc

rely [rɪ·'laɪ] *vi* **to** ~ **on** [*o* **upon**] (*trust*) fare affidamento su; (*depend on*) dipendere da; **to** ~ **on** [*o* **upon**] **sb to do sth** contare su qn perché faccia qc

REM [ˌɑːrˈiːˈem] *abbr of* Rapid Eye Movement REM

remain [rɪ·'meɪn] *vi* 1. (*stay*) restare 2. (*continue*) rimanere; **to** ~ **aloof** tenersi appartato; **to** ~ **seated** rimanere seduto; **to** ~ **unsolved** rimanere irrisolto; **to** ~ **to be done** rimanere da fare; **much** ~ **s to be done** rimane molto da fare; **the fact** ~ **s that ...** resta il fatto che ...; **it** (**only**) ~ **s for me to ...** non mi rimane che ...; **it** ~ **s to be seen** (**who/what/how**) resta da vedere (chi/che cosa/come)

remainder [rɪ·'meɪn·dɚ] I. *n a.* MAT resto *m;* **the** ~ **of sb's life** il resto della vita di qn II. *vt* svendere

remaining [rɪ·'meɪ·nɪŋ] *adj* restante

remains [rɪ·'meɪnz] *npl* resti *mpl*

remake[1] [ˌri:·'meɪk] <remade> *vt* fare di nuovo

remake[2] ['ri:·meɪk] *n* remake *m inv*

remand [rɪ·'mænd] I. *vt* **to** ~ **sb to prison** [*o* **in custody**] mettere qn in carcere preventivo; **to** ~ **sb on bail** mettere qn in libertà dietro cauzione II. *n* **to be on** ~ essere in carcere preventivo

remark [rɪ·'mɑːrk] I. *vi* **to** ~ **on sth** fare osservazioni su qc II. *n* osservazione *f;* **to make** ~ **s about sb/sth** fare commenti *mpl* su qn/qc

remarkable [rɪ·'mɑːr·kə·bl] *adj* notevole; (*coincidence*) straordinario, -a; **to be** ~ **for sth** essere degno di nota per qc

remarkably *adj* notevolmente

remarry [ˌri:·'me·ri] <-ie-> *vi* risposarsi

remedial [rɪ·'mi:·diəl] *adj* (*action*) di riparazione; SCHOOL di recupero; MED terapeutico, -a

remedy ['re·mə·di] I. <-ies> *n* 1. rimedio *m;* **to be beyond** ~ essere irreparabile 2. LAW (**legal**) ~ azione *f* giudiziaria II. *vt* rimediare a; (*mistake*) correggere

remember [rɪ·'mem·bɚ] I. *vt* 1. (*recall*) ricordare; **I can't** ~ **his name** non ricordo il suo nome 2. (*commemorate*) commemorare II. *vi* ricordarsi

remembrance [rɪ·'mem·brənts] *n* 1. (*act of remembering*) ricordo *m;* **in** ~ **of** in memoria di 2. *pl* (*greetings*) saluti *mpl*

remind [rɪ·'maɪnd] *vt* ricordare; **to** ~ **sb to do sth** ricordare a qn di fare qc; **he** ~ **s me of you** mi ricorda te; **that** ~ **s me, ...** ora che mi viene in mente, ...

reminder [rɪ·'maɪn·dɚ] *n* 1. (*note*) messaggio *m* (per ricordare) 2. (*warning*) avvertimento *m;* **to give sb a gentle** ~ dare a qn un avvertimento amichevole 3. (*memento*) ricordo *m*

reminisce [ˌre·mə·'nɪs] *vi* abbandonarsi alle reminiscenze

reminiscence [ˌre·mə·'nɪ·sns] *n* reminiscenza *f*

reminiscent [ˌre·mə·'nɪ·snt] *adj* **to be** ~ **of sb/sth** far pensare a qn/qc

remiss [rɪ·'mɪs] *adj* negligente

remission [rɪ·'mɪ·ʃən] *n* remissione *f*

remit[1] [rɪ·'mɪt] <-tt-> *vt form* 1. (*send*) rimettere; (*money*) inviare 2. LAW ridurre

remit[2] ['ri:·mɪt] *n* competenza *f*

R

remittance [rɪˈmɪ·tns] *n* rimessa *f*
remix I. [ˈriː·miks] *n* <-es> MUS remix *m inv* II. [riːˈmiks] *vt* remixare
remnant [ˈrem·nənt] *n* resto *m*
remodel [ˌriːˈmɑː·dəl] <-ll-, -l-> *vt* ristrutturare
remonstrance [rɪˈmɑːnt·strənts] *n form* rimostranza *f*
remonstrate [rɪˈmɑːnt·streɪt] *vi* rimostrare
remorse [rɪˈmɔːrs] *n* rimorso *m;* **without ~** senza rimorsi
remorseful [rɪˈmɔːrs·fəl] *adj* pentito, -a
remorseless [rɪˈmɔːrs·ləs] *adj* (*merciless*) spietato, -a; (*attack*) implacabile
remote [rɪˈmoʊt] *adj* <-er, -est> (*place, possibility*) remoto, -a
remote control *n* telecomando *m*
remote-controlled *adj* telecomandato, -a
remoteness *n* lontananza *f*
remold [ˈriːˈmoʊld] I. *vt* ricostruire II. *n* pneumatico *m* ricostruito
remount [ˌriːˈmaʊnt] I. *vt* risalire su II. *vi* risalire
removable [rɪˈmuː·və·bl] *adj* 1. (*stain*) eliminabile 2. (*easy to take off*) rimovibile
removal [rɪˈmuː·vəl] *n* 1. (*of stain, problem*) rimozione *f* 2. (*extraction*) estrazione *f*
remove [rɪˈmuːv] I. *vt* 1. (*take away*) levare; (*clothes*) levarsi 2. (*get rid of*) eliminare; (*cork, dent*) togliere; (*entry, name*) cancellare; (*doubts, fears*) dissipare; (*problem*) risolvere; **to ~ one's hair** depilarsi 3. (*dismiss from job*) licenziare II. *n form* **to be at one ~ from sth** essere ad un passo da qc
remover [rɪˈmuː·və] *n* 1. (titolare *mf* di un')impresa *f* di traslochi 2. **stain ~** smacchiatore *m*
remunerate [rɪˈmjuː·nə·reɪt] *vt form* rimunerare
remuneration [rɪˌmjuː·nəˈreɪ·ʃən] *n form* rimunerazione *f*
remunerative [rɪˈmjuː·nə·reɪ·tɪv] *adj form* rimunerativo, -a
Renaissance [ˌre·nəˈsɑːns] *n* **the ~** il Rinascimento
renal [ˈriː·nl] *adj* renale
rename [ˌriːˈneɪm] *vt* dare un nuovo nome a
rend [rend] <rent *o* rended> *vt liter* lacerare
render [ˈren·də] *vt form* 1. (*make*) rendere; **to ~ sb speechless** far restare qn senza parole 2. (*perform*) rappresentare; MUS interpretare 3. (*give: thanks*) rendere; (*aid, service*) prestare; (*judgment*) emettere 4. (*translate*) tradurre 5. ARCHIT intonacare
rendering [ˈren·də·rɪŋ] *n* 1. (*performance*) rappresentazione *f;* MUS interpretazione *f* 2. (*translation*) traduzione *f*
rendezvous [ˈrɑːn·deɪ·vuː, ˈrɒn·dɪ·vuːz] I. *n inv* 1. (*meeting*) appuntamento *m* 2. (*place*) luogo *m* d'incontro II. *vi* incontrarsi (a seguito di un appuntamento)
rendition [renˈdɪ·ʃən] *n* 1. (*performance*) interpretazione *f* 2. (*translation*) versione *f*

renegade [ˈre·nə·geɪd] I. *n* rinnegato, -a *m, f* II. *adj* rinnegato, -a
renege [rɪˈnɪg] *vi form* **to ~ on sth** far marcia indietro su qc
renew [rɪˈnuː] *vt* 1. (*begin again: membership, passport*) rinnovare; (*relationship*) rinnodare; **to ~ one's efforts to do sth** rinnovare gli sforzi per fare qc 2. (*mend*) rifare
renewable [rɪˈnuː·ə·bl] *adj* rinnovabile
renewal [rɪˈnuː·əl] *n* rinnovo *m*
renewed [rɪˈnuːd] *adj* rinnovato, -a
rennet [ˈre·nɪt] *n* caglio *m*
renounce [rɪˈnaʊns] *vt* rinunciare a
renovate [ˈre·nə·veɪt] *vt* restaurare
renovation [ˌre·nəˈveɪ·ʃən] *n* restauro *m*
renown [rɪˈnaʊn] *n* rinomanza *f*
renowned [rɪˈnaʊnd] *adj* rinomato, -a
rent[1] [rent] I. *n* (*rip*) strappo *m* II. *pt, pp of* **rend**
rent[2] [rent] I. *vt* (*apartment, land*) affittare; (*car, video*) noleggiare II. *vi* essere in affitto III. *n* affitto *m;* **for ~** affittasi
rent-a-car *n* (*car*) macchina *f* a noleggio; (*agency*) autonoleggio *m*
rental [ˈren·təl] I. *n* affitto *m* II. *adj* d'affitto
rent control *n* controllo *m* degli affitti
rent-free *adj* concesso, -a senza pagamento di un affitto
renunciation [rɪˌnʌn·sɪˈeɪ·ʃən] *n* rinuncia *f*
reopen [riːˈoʊ·pən] I. *vt* riaprire II. *vi* riaprirsi
reorder [ˌriːˈɔː·də] I. *n* nuovo ordine *m* II. *vt* 1. (*reorganize*) riordinare 2. COM ordinare di nuovo
reorganize [riːˈɔːr·gə·naɪz] I. *vt* riorganizzare II. *vi* riorganizzarsi
rep [rep] *n inf* 1. *abbr of* **representative** rappresentante *mf* 2. THEAT *abbr of* **repertory** repertorio *m*
Rep. 1. *abbr of* **Republic** Rep. 2. *abbr of* **Republican** repubblicano, -a
repaint [riːˈpeɪnt] *vt* ridipingere
repair [rɪˈper] I. *vt* 1. (*machine*) riparare; (*clothes*) aggiustare 2. (*set right: damage*) riparare; (*friendship*) ristabilire II. *n* 1. (*mending*) riparazione *f;* **to be beyond ~** non poter essere più riparato; **to be under ~** essere in riparazione 2. (*state*) **to be in good/bad ~** essere in buono/cattivo stato
repairable [rɪˈpe·rə·bl] *adj* riparabile
repair kit *n* kit *m inv* per le riparazioni
repairman <-men> *n* (*for cars*) meccanico *m;* (*for television*) tecnico *m*
repairperson *n* riparatore, -trice *m, f*
repair shop *n* officina *f* di riparazioni
repaper [riːˈpeɪ·pæ] *vt* mettere una nuova carta da parati a
reparable [ˈre·pə·rə·bl] *adj* rimediabile
reparation [ˌre·pəˈreɪ·ʃən] *n* 1. (*setting right*) riparazione *f* 2. *pl* FIN indennizzo *m*
repartee [ˌre·pɑːrˈtiː] *n* scambio *m* di battute
repatriate [riːˈpeɪ·tri·eɪt] *vt* rimpatriare
repatriation [rɪˌpeɪ·triˈeɪ·ʃən] *n* rimpatrio *m*
repay [rɪˈpeɪ] <repaid> *vt* (*money*) restituire;

(*person*) rimborsare; **to ~ money to sb** rimborsare dei soldi a qn; **to ~ sb for sth** ripagare qn per qc; **to ~ a debt** ripagare un debito

repayable [rɪ·ˈpe·ɪə·bl] *adj* rimborsabile

repayment [rɪ·ˈpeɪ·mənt] *n* rimborso *m*

repeal [rɪ·ˈpiːl] I. *vt* abrogare II. *n* abrogazione *f*

repeat [rɪ·ˈpiːt] I. *vt* 1. (*say or do again*) ripetere 2. (*recite*) recitare II. *vi* (*happen again*) ripetersi; (*taste*) tornare su III. *n* 1. ripetizione *f* 2. TV replica *f*

repeated *adj* ripetuto, -a

repeatedly *adv* ripetutamente

repeating decimal *n* decimale *m* periodico

repeat offender *n* pregiudicato, -a *m, f*

repeat performance *n* storia *f* analoga

repel [rɪ·ˈpel] <-ll-> *vt* 1. (*ward off*) *a.* MIL, PHYS respingere 2. (*disgust*) ripugnare a

repellent [rɪ·ˈpe·lənt] I. *n* repellente *m* II. *adj* ripugnante

repent [rɪ·ˈpent] I. *vi form* pentirsi II. *vt* pentirsi di

repentance [rɪ·ˈpen·tənts] *n* pentimento *m*

repentant [rə·ˈpen·tənt] *adj* pentito, -a

repercussion [ˌriː·pə·ˈkʌ·ʃən] *n* ripercussione *f*

repertoire [ˈre·pə·twɑːr] *n* repertorio *m*

repertory company *n* compagnia *f* di repertorio

repertory theater *n* teatro *m* di repertorio

repetition [ˌre·pə·ˈtɪ·ʃən] *n* ripetizione *f*

repetitious [ˌre·pə·ˈtɪ·ʃəs] *adj*, **repetitive** [rɪ·ˈpe·tə·tɪv] *adj* ripetitivo, -a

replace [rɪ·ˈpleɪs] *vt* 1. (*take the place of*) rimpiazzare; (*person*) sostituire 2. (*put back*) rimettere a posto

replaceable [rɪ·ˈpleɪ·sə·bl] *adj* sostituibile

replacement [rɪ·ˈpleɪs·mənt] I. *n* 1. (*person*) sostituto, -a *m, f*; (*part*) ricambio *m* 2. MIL rimpiazzo *m* 3. (*act of substituting*) sostituzione *f* II. *adj* di ricambio

replay[1] [ˌriː·ˈpleɪ] *vt* 1. SPORTS rigiocare 2. MUS suonare di nuovo 3. TV mostrare la replica di

replay[2] [ˈriː·pleɪ] *n* 1. SPORTS ripetizione *f;* TV replica *f;* **instant ~** replay *m inv* 2. MUS replay *m inv*

replenish [rɪ·ˈple·nɪʃ] *vt* riempire di nuovo; (*supplies, stocks*) ricostituire

replete [rɪ·ˈpliːt] *adj* ricolmo, -a

replica [ˈre·plɪ·kə] *n* riproduzione *f*

replicate [ˈre·plɪ·keɪt] *vt* riprodurre

reply [rɪ·ˈplaɪ] I. <-ied> *vt* rispondere II. <-ied> *vi* 1. (*verbally*) rispondere 2. (*react*) reagire III. <-ies> *n* risposta *f*

report [rɪ·ˈpɔːrt] I. *n* 1. (*account*) resoconto *m;* PUBL articolo *m;* (*longer*) servizio *m;* **to give a ~** fare una relazione 2. (*unproven claim*) voce *f* 3. (*explosion*) esplosione *m* II. *vt* 1. (*recount*) riferire; (*discovery*) riportare; **nothing to ~** niente da riferire 2. (*denounce*) denunciare III. *vi* 1. (*make results public*) presentare un rapporto 2. (*arrive at work*) presentarsi; **to ~ sick** darsi malato

◆**report back** I. *vt* **to report sth back to sb**

riferire qc a qn II. *vi* fare rapporto

report card *n* scheda *f* di valutazione

reporter [rɪ·ˈpɔːr·t̬ə] *n* reporter *mf*

repose [rɪ·ˈpouz] I. *vi* 1. (*rest*) riposare 2. (*lie*) giacere II. *vt* 1. (*rest*) riposare 2. *fig* (*confidence*) riporre III. *n* riposo *m;* **in ~** in stato di riposo

repository [rɪ·ˈpɑ:·zɪ·tɔ:·ri] <-ies> *n* 1. (*store*) deposito *m* 2. (*person*) depositario, -a *m, f*

repossess [ˌri:·pə·ˈzes] *vt* riprendere possesso di

repossession [ˌri:·pə·ˈze·ʃən] *n* riappropriazione *f*

reprehensible [ˌre·prɪ·ˈhen·sə·bl] *adj* deprecabile

represent [ˌre·prɪ·ˈzent] *vt* 1. (*act for, depict*) rappresentare 2. (*state*) presentare

representation [ˌre·prɪ·zen·ˈteɪ·ʃən] *n* 1. (*acting for*) rappresentanza *f* 2. (*depiction*) rappresentazione *f* 3. (*statement*) dichiarazione *f*

representative [ˌre·prɪ·ˈzen·tə·tɪv] I. *adj* 1. *a.* POL rappresentativo, -a 2. (*typical*) tipico, -a II. *n* 1. *a.* COM rappresentante *mf* 2. LAW delegato, -a *m, f* 3. POL deputato, -a *m, f*

repress [rɪ·ˈpres] *vt* reprimere

repressed [rɪ·ˈprest] *adj* represso, -a

repression [rɪ·ˈpre·ʃən] *n* repressione *f*

repressive [rɪ·ˈpre·sɪv] *adj* repressivo, -a

reprieve [rɪ·ˈpri:v] I. *vt* sospendere l'esecuzione di II. *n* sospensione *f* dell'esecuzione

reprimand [ˈre·prə·mænd] I. *vt* redarguire II. *n* nota *f* di biasimo

reprint[1] [ˌri:·ˈprɪnt] *vt* ristampare

reprint[2] [ˈri:·prɪnt] *n* ristampa *f*

reprisal [rɪ·ˈpraɪ·zl] *n* rappresaglia *f;* **to take ~s** fare delle rappresaglie

reproach [rɪ·ˈproutʃ] I. *vt* rimproverare II. *n* rimprovero *m;* **beyond ~** irreprensibile; **to be a ~ to sb** essere un'accusa a qn

reproachful [rɪ·ˈproutʃ·fəl] *adj* pieno, -a di rimprovero

reprobate [ˈre·prə·beɪt] I. *n* *a.* REL reprobo, -a *m, f* II. *adj* 1. (*wicked*) malvagio, -a 2. REL da reprobo, -a

reprocess [ˌri:·ˈprɑ:·ses] *vt* ritrattare

reprocessing *n* ritrattamento *m*

reprocessing plant *n* ECOL, TECH impianto *m* di ritrattamento

reproduce [ˌri:·prə·ˈdu:s] I. *vi* riprodursi II. *vt* riprodurre

reproduction [ˌri:·prə·ˈdʌk·ʃən] *n* riproduzione *f*

reproductive [ˌri:·prə·ˈdʌk·tɪv] *adj* di riproduzione

reproof [rɪ·ˈpru:f] I. *n* rimprovero *m* II. *vt* rimproverare

reprove [rɪ·ˈpru:v] *vt* riprendere

reproving [rɪ·ˈpru:·vɪŋ] *adj* critico, -a

reptile [ˈrep·taɪl] *n* rettile *m*

reptilian [rep·ˈtɪ·li·ən] *adj* dei rettili

republic [rɪ·ˈpʌb·lɪk] *n* repubblica *f*

republican [rɪ·ˈpʌb·lɪ·kən] I. *n* repubblicano,

R

-a *m, f* II. *adj* repubblicano, -a

republication [ˌriː·ˌpʌb·lɪ·'keɪ·ʃən] *n* riedizione *f*

repudiate [rɪ·'pjuː·di·eɪt] *vt* (*person*) ripudiare; (*accusation*) negare; (*suggestion*) rigettare

repugnance [rɪ·'pʌg·nəns] *n* ripugnanza *f*

repugnant [rɪ·'pʌg·nənt] *adj* ripugnante

repulse [rɪ·'pʌls] I. *vt* 1. (*disgust*) ripugnare a 2. (*ward off*) rigettare 3. MIL respingere II. *n* resistenza (agli attacchi) *f*

repulsion [rɪ·'pʌl·ʃən] *n* repulsione *f*

repulsive [rɪ·'pʌl·sɪv] *adj* repulsivo, -a

repurchase [ˌriː·'pɜː·tʃəs] I. *vt* riacquistare II. *n* riacquisto *m*

reputable ['rep·jʊ·tə·bl] *adj* rispettabile

reputation [ˌrep·jʊ·'teɪ·ʃən] *n* reputazione *f;* **to have a good/bad ~** avere una buona/cattiva reputazione; **to know sb by ~** aver sentito parlare di qn

repute [rɪ·'pjuːt] *n* reputazione *f*

reputed [rɪ·'pjuː·tɪd] *adj* presunto, -a; **she is ~ to be rich** ha fama di essere ricca

request [rɪ·'kwest] I. *n* richiesta *f;* ADMIN domanda *f;* **on ~** su richiesta; **to make a ~ for sth** fare richiesta di qc II. *vt* richiedere

requiem ['re·kwi·əm] *n,* **requiem mass** *n* requiem *m inv*

require [rɪ·'kwa·ɪ♭] *vt* 1. (*need*) aver bisogno di 2. (*demand*) richiedere; **to ~ sb to do sth** richiedere a qn che faccia qc

requirement [rɪ·'kwa·ɪ♭·mənt] *n* requisito *m*

requisite ['re·kwɪ·zɪt] I. *adj* necessario, -a II. *n* requisito *m*

requisition [ˌre·kwɪ·'zɪ·ʃən] I. *vt* requisire II. *n* 1. (*act of requesting*) richiesta *f* formale 2. MIL requisizione *f*

reroute [ˌriː·'ruːt] *vt* deviare

rerun[1] [ˌriː·'rʌn] *vt irr* CINE, TV ridare; THEAT replicare

rerun[2] ['riː·rʌn] *n* CINE seconda visione *f;* THEAT, TV replica *f*

resale ['riː·seɪl] *n* rivendita *f*

reschedule [ˌriː·'sked·ʒuːl] *vt* riprogrammare

rescind [rɪ·'sɪnd] *vt* revocare

rescue ['res·kjuː] I. *vt* (*save*) salvare; (*hostage*) liberare II. *n* salvataggio *m;* **to come to sb's ~** venir in soccorso di qn

rescuer ['res·kjʊ·♭] *n* soccorritore, -trice *m, f*

research ['riː·sɜːrtʃ] I. *n* ricerca *f* II. *vi* fare delle ricerche III. *vt* fare delle ricerche su

researcher *n* ricercatore, -trice *m, f*

research work *n* lavoro *m* di ricerca

research worker *n* ricercatore, -trice *m, f*

resemblance [rɪ·'zem·bləns] *n* rassomiglianza *f*

resemble [rɪ·'zem·bl] *vt* rassomigliare a

resent [rɪ·'zent] *vt* **to ~ sth** provare risentimento per qc

resentful [rɪ·'zent·fəl] *adj* (*person*) risentito, -a

resentment [rɪ·'zent·mənt] *n* risentimento *m*

reservation [ˌre·zə·'veɪ·ʃən] *n* (*doubt*) riserva *f;* (*booking*) prenotazione *f;* **to have ~s**

about sth avere delle riserve su qc

reserve [rɪ·'zɜːrv] I. *n* 1. *a.* SPORTS riserva *f;* **to have sth in ~** avere qc di riserva 2. MIL **the ~** la riserva II. *vt* riservare

reserve currency *n* valuta *f* di riserva

reserved *adj* riservato, -a

reserve price *n* prezzo *m* minimo

reservist [rɪ·'zɜːr·vɪst] *n* MIL riservista *mf*

reservoir ['re·zə·vwɑːr] *n* 1. (*tank*) serbatoio *m* 2. (*lake*) bacino *m*

reset [ˌriː·'set] *vt irr* 1. (*machine*) regolare; INFOR resettare 2. (*jewel*) incastonare di nuovo

reset button *n* INFOR, ELEC tasto *m* di reset

resettle [ˌriː·'se·tl] I. *vi* trasferirsi II. *vt* (*person*) trasferire; (*area*) ripopolare

reshuffle [ˌriː·'ʃʌ·fl] I. *vt* riorganizzare II. *n* riorganizzazione *f*

reside [rɪ·'zaɪd] *vi form* risiedere

residence ['re·zɪ·dənts] *n* residenza *f*

residence permit *n* permesso *m* di residenza

resident ['re·zɪ·dənt] I. *n* residente *mf* II. *adj* residente

resident alien *n* straniero , -a *m, f* residente

residential [ˌre·zɪ·'den·ʃl] *adj* residenziale

residual [rɪ·'zɪ·dʒu·əl] *adj* residuo, -a

residue ['re·zə·duː] *n* residuo *m*

resign [rɪ·'zaɪn] I. *vi* 1. (*leave job*) *a.* POL dimettersi 2. GAME abbandonare II. *vt* (*leave: job*) *a.* POL dimettersi da; **to ~ oneself to sth** rassegnarsi a qc

resignation [ˌre·zɪg·'neɪ·ʃən] *n* 1. (*from job*) *a.* POL dimissioni *fpl* 2. (*conformity*) rassegnazione *f*

resigned [rɪ·'zaɪnd] *adj* rassegnato, -a

resilience [rɪ·'zɪl·jəns] *n* (*of material*) elasticità *f;* (*of person*) resistenza *f*

resilient [rɪ·'zɪl·jənt] *adj* (*material*) elastico, -a; (*person*) resistente

resin ['re·zɪn] *n* resina *f*

resinous ['re·zɪ·nəs] *adj* resinoso, -a

resist [rɪ·'zɪst] I. *vt* resistere a; **to ~ doing sth** resistere a fare qc II. *vi* resistere

resistance [rɪ·'zɪs·tənts] *n* resistenza *f*

resistance fighter *n* combattente *mf* della resistenza

resistant [rɪ·'zɪs·tənt] *adj* resistente

resistor [rɪ·'zɪs·tə♭] *n* resistore *m*

resolute ['re·zə·luːt] *adj* risoluto, -a

resolution [ˌre·zə·'luː·ʃən] *n a.* INFOR, PHOT, TV risoluzione *f*

resolvable [rɪ·'zɑː·l·və·bl] *adj* risolvibile

resolve [rɪ·'zɑː·lv] I. *vt* 1. (*solve*) risolvere 2. (*settle*) decidere; **to ~ that ...** decidere che ... +*subj* II. *n* determinazione *f*

resolved [rɪ·'zɑː·lvd] *adj* deciso, -a

resonance ['re·zə·nəns] *n* risonanza *f*

resonant ['re·zə·nənt] *adj* risonante

resonate ['re·zə·neɪt] *vi* risuonare

resort [rɪ·'zɔːrt] *n* 1. (*use*) ricorso *m;* **without ~ing to sth** senza ricorrere a qc; **as a last ~** come ultima risorsa *f* 2. (*for holidays*) località *f* turistica; **ski ~** stazione *f* sciistica

◆**resort to** *vt* ricorrere a; **to ~ violence** ricorrere alla violenza

resound [rɪ·'zaʊnd] *vi* risuonare

resounding *adj* 1. (*noise*) fragoroso, -a 2. (*failure, success*) clamoroso, -a

resource ['riː·sɔːrs] I. *n* 1. (*asset*) risorsa *f* 2. *pl* **natural ~s** risorse *fpl* naturali 3. (*resourcefulness*) capacità *f* d'iniziativa ▶ **to be thrown back on one's own ~s** doversela cavare con le proprie forze II. *vt* finanziare

resourceful [rɪ·'sɔːrs·fəl] *adj* pieno, -a di risorse

respect [rɪ·'spekt] I. *n* 1. (*relation, esteem*) rispetto *m;* **with all due ~** con tutto il rispetto 2. (*point*) aspetto *m;* **in all/many/some ~s** sotto tutti gli/molti/alcuni aspetti; **in every ~** sotto ogni aspetto; **in ~ of** rispetto a; **in this ~** sotto questo aspetto; **with ~ to** riguardo a 3. *pl* (*greetings*) rispetti *mpl* II. *vt* rispettare

respectable [rɪ·'spek·tə·bl] *adj* 1. (*person, performance, result*) rispettabile 2. (*behavior*) decente

respected [rɪ·'spek·təd] *adj* rispettato, -a

respectful [rɪ·'spekt·fəl] *adj* rispettoso, -a

respectfully [rɪ·'spekt·fə·li] *adv* rispettosamente

respecting [rɪ·'spek·tɪŋ] *prep* riguardo a

respective [rɪ·'spek·tɪv] *adj* rispettivo, -a

respectively *adv* rispettivamente

respiration [ˌre·spə·'reɪ·ʃən] *n* respirazione *f*

respirator ['re·spə·reɪ·t̬ə·] *n* respiratore *m*

respiratory ['re·spə·ə·tɔː·ri] *adj* respiratorio, -a

respiratory system *n* apparato *m* respiratorio

respite ['re·spɪt] *n* 1. (*pause*) pausa *f* 2. (*delay*) proroga *f*

resplendent [rɪ·'splen·dənt] *adj* splendente

respond [rɪ·'spɑːnd] *vi* 1. (*answer*) rispondere 2. (*react*) reagire

respondent [rɪ·'spɑːn·dənt] *n* 1. (*to questionnaire*) intervistato, -a *m, f* 2. LAW convenuto, -a *m, f*

response [rɪ·'spɑːns] *n* 1. (*answer*) risposta *f* 2. (*reaction*) reazione *f* 3. REL responsorio *m*

responsibility [rɪˌspɑːn·sə·'bɪ·lə·ti] *n* responsabilità *f*

responsible [rɪ·'spɑːn·sə·bl] *adj* responsabile; **to be ~ for sth/to sb** essere responsabile di qc/davanti a qn

responsive [rɪ·ˠspɑːn·sɪv] *adj* (*person*) reattivo, -a; (*mechanism*) sensibile; **to be ~ to sth** MED risponder bene a qc

rest[1] [rest] I. *vt* 1. (*cause to repose*) far riposare 2. (*support*) appoggiare 3. LAW **to ~ one's case** concludere la propria arringa II. *vi* 1. (*cease activity*) riposar(si) 2. (*remain*) rimanere 3. (*be supported*) appoggiarsi; **to ~ on sth** (*theory*) basarsi su qc 4. LAW concludere ▶ **you can ~ assured that ...** puoi star sicuro che ... III. *n* 1. (*period of repose*) riposo *m;* **to come to ~** fermarsi; **at ~** (*not moving*) in stato di riposo; (*dead*) in pace 2. MUS pausa *f* 3. (*support*) appoggio *m*

rest[2] [rest] *n* resto *m;* **the ~** (*the other people*) tutti gli altri; (*the other things*) il rimanente;

for the ~ quanto al resto

rest area *n* (*on highway*) area *f* di sosta

restate [ˌriː·'steɪt] *vt* ribadire

restaurant ['res·tə·rɑːnt] *n* ristorante *m*

restaurateur [ˌres·tə·ə·'tɜːr] *n* ristoratore, -trice *m, f*

rest cure *n* cura *f* del riposo

restful ['rest·fəl] *adj* riposante

rest home *n* casa *f* di riposo

resting place *n* luogo *m* di riposo

restitution [ˌres·tɪ·'tuː·ʃən] *n* 1. (*return*) restituzione *f* 2. LAW risarcimento *m*

restive ['res·tɪv] *adj* irrequieto, -a

restless ['rest·lɪs] *adj* 1. (*agitated*) irrequieto, -a 2. (*impatient*) impaziente 3. (*wakeful: night*) agitato, -a

restock [ˌriː·'stɑːk] I. *vt* rifornire; (*with animals*) ripopolare II. *vi* ricostituire le scorte

restoration [ˌres·tə·'reɪ·ʃən] *n* 1. (*act of restoring: of building, painting*) restauro *m;* (*of communication*) ripristino *m;* (*of peace*) ristabilimento *m* 2. (*return to owner*) restituzione *f*

restorative [rɪ·'stɔː·rə·tɪv] *adj* ristoratore, -trice

restore [rɪ·'stɔːr] *vt* 1. (*reestablish: building, painting*) restaurare; (*communication, peace*) ristabilire; **to ~ sb's sight** far recuperare la vista a qn; **to ~ sb's faith in sth** restituire la fede di qn in qc; **to ~ sb to health** far recuperare la salute a qn; **to ~ sb to power** riportare al potere qn 2. *form* (*return to owner*) restituire

restorer [rɪ·'stɔː·rə·] *n* restauratore, -trice *m, f*

restrain [rɪ·'streɪn] *vt* (*person, animal*) trattenere; (*temper, ambition*) controllare; (*trade*) ridurre; (*inflation*) frenare; **to ~ sb from doing sth** trattenere qn dal fare qc; **to ~ oneself** trattenersi

restrained [rɪ·'streɪnd] *adj* (*person*) controllato, -a; (*style*) sobrio, -a; (*criticism, policy*) moderato, -a

restraint [rɪ·'streɪnt] *n* 1. (*self-control*) autocontrollo *m;* **to exercise ~** *form* esercitare autocontrollo 2. (*restriction*) restrizione *f*

restrict [rɪ·'strɪkt] *vt* (*limit*) limitare; **to ~ oneself** limitarsi

restricted *adj* 1. (*limited*) limitato, -a; (*document*) confidenziale; (*parking*) riservato, -a; **entry is ~ to ...** entrata riservata a ... 2. (*small: space*) ristretto, -a; (*existence, horizon*) limitato, -a

restricted area *n* MIL zona *f* riservata

restriction [rɪ·'strɪk·ʃən] *n* restrizione *f;* **speed ~** limite *m* di velocità; **to impose ~s on sth** imporre restrizioni su qc

restrictive [rɪ·'strɪk·tɪv] *adj* restrittivo, -a

restring [ˌriː·'strɪŋ] *irr vt* (*instrument, tennis racket*) incordare di nuovo; (*necklace*) infilare di nuovo

rest room *n* toilette *f inv*

rest stop *n* (*on highway*) area *f* di sosta

restructure [ˌriː·'strʌk·tʃə·] *vt* ristrutturare

restructuring *n* ristrutturazione *f*

R

result [rɪ'zʌlt] I. *n a.* MAT, SPORTS, POL risultato *m;* (*of exam*) esito *m;* **to get ~s** ottenere buoni risultati; **with no ~** senza risultato; **as a ~ of** come conseguenza di; **as a ~** come risultato II. *vi* **to ~ from** derivare da; **to ~ in** portare a

resultant [rɪ'zʌl·tənt] *adj* risultante

resume [rɪ'zu:m] I. *vt* **1.** (*start again: work, journey*) riprendere **2.** *form* (*reoccupy: place*) riprendere; (*duties*) tornare a svolgere II. *vi form* riprendere

résumé ['re·zʊ·meɪ] *n* **1.** (*summary*) riassunto *m* **2.** (*for jobs*) curricolo *m*

resumption [rɪ'zʌmp·ʃən] *n* **1.** (*of journey, work*) ripresa *f* **2.** (*of power*) riassunzione *f;* (*of duties*) ripresa *f*

resurface [,ri:'sɜːr·fɪs] I. *vi* risalire alla superficie; *fig* riapparire II. *vt* ripavimentare

resurgence [rɪ'sɜːr·dʒəns] *n form* ripresa *f*

resurgent [rɪ'sɜːr·dʒənt] *adj form* risorgente

resurrect [,re·zə·'rekt] *vt a. fig* far risorgere

resurrection [,re·zə·'rek·ʃən] *n* risurrezione *f*

resuscitate [rɪ'sʌ·sə·teɪt] *vt* risuscitare

retail ['ri:·teɪl] COM I. *n* vendita *f* al dettaglio II. *vt* vendere al dettaglio III. *vi* venire venduto al dettaglio; **this product ~s at $5** questo prodotto viene venduto al pubblico a 5 dollari IV. *adv* al dettaglio

retail business *n* commercio *m* al dettaglio

retailer *n* rivenditore, -trice *m, f*

retailing *n* commercio *m* al dettaglio

retail outlet *n* COM punto *m* di vendita

retail price *n* COM prezzo *m* di vendita al pubblico

retail price index *n* ECON indice *m* dei prezzi al consumo

retail trade *n* ECON commercio *m* al dettaglio

retain [rɪ'teɪn] *vt* **1.** *form* (*keep: power, property*) mantenere; (*right, title*) conservare **2.** (*not lose: dignity*) mantenere; (*color*) conservare **3.** (*hold in place: water*) contenere **4.** (*remember*) tenere a mente **5.** (*employ*) impiegare

retainer *n* **1.** ECON onorario *m* anticipato (*per garantirsi futuri servizi*) **2.** (*servant*) domestico, -a *m, f*

retaining wall *n* muro *m* di contenimento

retake[1] [,ri:'teɪk] *vt irr* **1.** (*recapture: town*) riconquistare; (*person*) riprendere; **to ~ the lead** tornare in vantaggio **2.** SCHOOL, UNIV (*exam*) rifare **3.** CINE rigirare; PHOT rifare

retake[2] ['ri:·teɪk] *n* CINE nuovo ciak *m inv*

retaliate [rɪ'tæ·li·eɪt] *vi* reagire

retaliation [rɪ,tæ·li·'eɪ·ʃən] *n* ritorsione *f*

retaliatory [rɪ'tæ·lɪə·tɔː·ri] *adj* di rappresaglia; **~ measures** misure *fpl* di ritorsione

retard [rɪ'tɑːrd] *vt form* (*growth, development*) ritardare; **mentally ~ed person** persona *f* con sviluppo mentale ritardato

retardation [,ri:·tɑːr·'deɪ·ʃən] *n form* ritardo *m*

retarded *adj* **1.** *pej* (*mentally ill*) ritardato, -a **2.** *sl* (*very stupid*) ritardato, -a

retch [retʃ] *vi* aver voglia di vomitare

retention [rɪ'ten·ʃən] *n* **1.** *form* (*keeping: of properties, heat*) conservazione *f;* (*of rules, laws*) mantenimento *m* **2.** *form* (*memory*) memoria *f* **3.** (*of lawyer, consultant*) proseguimento *m* del rapporto

retentive [rɪ'ten·tɪv] *adj* capace di ricordare; **he's very ~** ha un'ottima memoria

rethink[1] [,ri:'θɪŋk] *vt irr* riconsiderare

rethink[2] ['ri:·θɪŋk] *n* ripensamento *m*

reticent ['re·tə·snt] *adj* reticente

retina ['ret·nə] <-s *o* -nae> *n* retina *f*

retinue ['ret·nu:] *n inv* seguito *m*

retire [rɪ'ta·ɪə‐] I. *vi* **1.** (*stop working*) andare in pensione; (*soldier, athlete*) ritirarsi **2.** *form* (*withdraw*) ritirarsi; **to ~ to the drawing room** trasferirsi nel salotto **3.** MIL ripiegare **4.** SPORTS (*from a race*) ritirarsi II. *vt* **1.** (*stop working*) mandare in pensione **2.** MIL (*soldier*) far ripiegare **3.** FIN (*bond*) ritirare

retired *adj* in pensione; (*soldier, athlete*) a riposo

retirement [rɪ'ta·ɪə‐·mənt] *n* **1.** (*act of retiring*) pensionamento *m;* (*from race*) ritiro *m* **2.** (*after working*) pensione *f;* (*of soldier, athlete*) ritiro *m;* **to be in ~** essere in pensione; **to come out of ~** fare il proprio rientro **3.** MIL ritirata *f*

retirement age *n* età *f* pensionabile

retirement pay *n*, **retirement pension** *n* pensione *f* (di anzianità)

retiring *adj* **1.** (*reserved*) riservato, -a **2.** (*worker, official*) uscente

retort [rɪ'tɔ:rt] I. *vt* replicare II. *vi* replicare III. *n* **1.** (*reply*) replica *f* **2.** CHEM storta *f*

retouch [,ri:'tʌtʃ] *vt a.* ART, PHOT ritoccare

retrace [ri:'treɪs] *vt* ripercorrere; **to ~ one's steps** ritornare sui propri passi

retract [rɪ'trækt] I. *vt* **1.** (*statement*) ritrattare; (*offer*) ritirare **2.** (*claws*) ritrarre; (*wheels*) ritirare II. *vi* **1.** (*withdraw statement, offer*) fare marcia indietro **2.** (*be withdrawn: claws*) ritrarsi; (*wheels*) rientrare

retractable [rɪ'træk·tə·bl] *adj* retrattile

retraction [rɪ'træk·ʃən] *n* (*of statement*) ritrattazione *f;* (*offer*) ritiro *m*

retrain [ri:'treɪn] I. *vt* riaddestrare II. *vi* fare un corso di riaddestramento

retread[1] [,ri:'tred] *vt* (*a tire*) ricostruire

retread[2] ['ri:·tred] *n* pneumatico *m* ricostruito

retreat [rɪ'tri:t] I. *vi a.* MIL ritirarsi II. *n* **1.** (*withdrawal, signal*) *a.* MIL ritirata *f;* **to sound the ~** suonare la ritirata **2.** (*safe place*) rifugio *m* **3.** (*seclusion*) ritiro *m;* **to go on a ~** andare in ritiro

retrench [rɪ'trentʃ] I. *vi* ridurre i costi II. *vt* (*reduce: personnel, expenses*) ridurre

retrenchment *n* **1.** (*spending cut*) riduzione *f* delle spese **2.** (*cutting down*) ridimensionamento *m*

retrial ['ri:·traɪl] *n* nuovo processo *m*

retribution [,re·trə·'bju:·ʃən] *n form* pena *f* severa; **divine ~** castigo *m* divino

retributive [rɪ'trɪb·jʊ·tɪv] *adj form* punitivo, -a

retrieval [rɪ·'triː·vl] n (finding) a. INFOR recupero m; on-line information ~ recupero di informazioni on-line

retrieve [rɪ·'triːv] I. vt 1.(get back) a. INFOR recuperare 2.(make amends for: error) riparare 3.(repair: loss) recuperare; (situation) salvare 4. SPORTS (game) salvare; (in tennis) ribattere II. vi SPORTS recuperare

retriever [rɪ·'triː·vəʳ] n cane m da riporto

retroactive [ˌre·troʊ·'æk·tɪv] adj retroattivo, -a

retrograde ['re·trə·greɪd] adj retrogrado, -a

retrospect ['re·trə·spekt] n in ~ in retrospettiva

retrospective [ˌre·trə·'spek·tɪv] I. adj 1.(looking back) retrospettivo, -a 2. LAW retroattivo, -a II. n ART retrospettiva f

return [rɪ·'tɜːrn] I. n 1.(going back) ritorno m; (home, to work, to school) rientro m; on his ~ al suo ritorno 2.(to previous situation) ritorno m; a ~ to sth un ritorno a qc 3. MED (of illness) ricaduta f 4.(giving back) restituzione f 5.(recompense) ricompensa f 6. FIN (proceeds) proventi mpl; (interest) rendimento m; ~ on capital rendimento del capitale 7. pl POL risultati mpl elettorali 8. INFOR (tasto m di) ritorno m 9.(report) rapporto m 10. FIN dichiarazione f ▶many happy ~s! cento di questi giorni!; by ~ mail a giro di posta; in ~ for sth in cambio di qc II. adj 1.(coming back: flight, journey) di ritorno 2. THEAT ~ performance ritorno m in scena III. vi 1.(come back) ritornare; (home) rientrare 2.(reappear) ricomparire IV. vt 1.(give back) restituire 2.(reciprocate) ricambiare; (compliment, favor, ball) restituire; to ~ sb's call restituire la chiamata di qn; to ~ good for evil rispondere al male con il bene 3.(send back) rimandare; ~ to sender rispedire al mittente 4. FIN (yield) rendere; (profit) dare 5. LAW (pronounce: verdict) emettere; (judgment) pronunciare 6. POL (elect) eleggere; (re-elect) rieleggere 7. ECON (income) dichiarare

returnable [rɪ·'tɜːr·nə·bl] adj (fee) rimborsabile; (bottle) a rendere

return flight n volo m di ritorno

return journey n viaggio m di ritorno

return key n INFOR (tasto m di) ritorno m

return ticket n biglietto m di (andata e) ritorno

reunification [riː·ˌjuː·nə·fɪ·'keɪ·ʃən] n riunificazione f

reunion [ˌriː·'juːn·jən] n 1.(meeting) riunione f 2.(after separation) riunificazione f

reunite [ˌriː·juː·'naɪt] I. vt 1.(bring together) rimettere insieme 2.(friends) riconciliare II. vi tornare insieme

reusable [ˌriː·'juː·zə·bl] adj riutilizzabile

reuse [ˌriː·'juːz] vt riusare

rev. [rev] n AUTO giro m

◆rev up AUTO I. vt <-vv-> far andare su di giri II. vi imballarsi

revaluation [riː·ˌvæl·jʊ·'eɪ·ʃən] n rivalutazione f

revalue [riː·'væl·juː] vt rivalutare

revamp [ˌriː·'væmp] vt inf rendere più attuale

Rev. abbr of Reverend Rev.

reveal [rɪ·'viːl] vt 1.(divulge: secret, identity) rivelare; he ~d his identity rivelò la sua identità; to ~ how/why ... rivelare come/perché ... 2.(uncover) svelare

revealing [rɪ·'viː·lɪŋ] adj rivelatore, -trice

reveille ['re·və·li] n MIL sveglia f

revel ['re·vl] <-ll-, -l-> vi far baldoria

◆revel in <-ll-, -l-> vi to ~ sth trovar gusto in qc

revelation [ˌre·və·'leɪ·ʃən] n rivelazione f; the Book of Revelations il Libro dell'Apocalisse

reveler n, reveller n festeggiante mf

revelry ['re·vəl·ri] <-ies> n festeggiamenti mpl

revenge [rɪ·'vendʒ] I. n 1.(retaliation) vendetta f; in ~ (for sth) come vendetta per qc; to take ~ vendicarsi 2. SPORTS rivincita f II. vt vendicare; to ~ oneself vendicarsi

revenue ['re·və·nuː] n 1.(income) proventi mpl 2.(of government) entrate fpl; tax ~ entrate fiscali

reverberate [rɪ·'vɜːr·bə·reɪt] vi 1.(sound) riecheggiare; (light, heat) riverberare 2. fig farsi sentire

reverberation [rɪ·ˌvɜːr·bə·'reɪ·ʃən] n 1.(of sound) eco f; (of heat, light) riverbero m 2. fig ripercussione f

revere [rɪ·'vɪr] vt riverire

reverence ['re·və·rəns] n riverenza f; to pay ~ to sth/sb rendere omaggio a qc/qn

reverend ['re·və·rənd] adj venerando, -a

Reverend ['re·və·rənd] REL I. adj the Very ~ il Reverendo (Decano); the Right ~ il Reverendo (Vescovo); the Most ~ il Reverendo (Arcivescovo) II. n (Protestant) pastore m; (Catholic) sacerdote m

reverent ['re·və·rənt] adj riverente

reverential [ˌre·və·'ren·ʃl] adj reverenziale

reverie ['re·və·ri] n liter fantasticheria f; to be (lost) in ~ perdersi in fantasticherie

reversal [rɪ·'vɜːr·sl] n 1.(change: of order) inversione f; (of policy, opinion) capovolgimento m; LAW (of decision) revoca f 2.(setback) insuccesso m

reverse [rɪ·'vɜːrs] I. vt (turn other way) invertire; (policy) cambiare radicalmente; (situation) capovolgere; (judgment) revocare; to ~ the charges TEL telefonare a carico del destinatario II. vi (order, situation) invertirsi III. n 1. the ~ il contrario; in ~ al contrario 2. AUTO (gear) retromarcia f; to go into ~ mettere la retromarcia 3.(setback) insuccesso m 4.(the back) retro m inv; (of cloth) rovescio m; (of document) dorso m IV. adj 1.(inverse) inverso, -a 2.(opposite: direction) opposto, -a

reverse gear n AUTO retromarcia f

reversible [rɪ·'vɜːr·sə·bl] adj 1.(jacket) double-face 2.(decision) revocabile

reversion [rɪ·'vɜːr·ʃən] n ritorno m

revert [rɪ·'vɜːrt] vi ritornare; to ~ to type fig ritornare alla propria vera natura

review [rɪ·'vjuː] I. vt 1.(consider) esaminare

2. (*reconsider*) riesaminare; (*salary*) adeguare **3.** (*look over: notes*) rivedere **4.** (*criticize: book, play, film*) recensire **5.** MIL (*inspect*) passare in rivista **6.** (*study again*) ripassare **II.** *n* **1.** (*examination*) esame *m;* **to come under ~** venir sottoposto ad esame; **to hold a ~** MIL fare una rassegna **2.** (*reconsideration*) riesame *m;* **to come up for ~** venir riesaminato **3.** (*summary*) riassunto *m* **4.** (*criticism: of book, play, film*) recensione *f* **5.** (*magazine*) rivista *f* **6.** THEAT rivista *f*

reviewer [rɪˈvjuː·ə·] *n* critico, -a *m, f*

revise [rɪˈvaɪz] *vt* (*alter: text, law*) rivedere; (*proofs*) correggere; (*opinion*) cambiare

revision [rɪˈvɪ·ʒən] *n* **1.** (*of text, law*) revisione *f;* (*of proofs*) correzione *f;* (*of policy*) modifica *f* **2.** (*book*) edizione *f* riveduta

revisionist [rɪˈvɪ·ʒə·nɪst] *n* revisionista *mf*

revitalize [riːˈvaɪ·tə·laɪz] *vt* rivitalizzare

revival [rɪˈvaɪ·vəl] *n* **1.** MED rianimazione *f* **2.** (*rebirth: of interest*) risveglio *m;* (*of idea, custom*) revival *m inv;* (*of economy*) ripresa *f;* (*of country*) rilancio *m* **3.** CINE, THEAT riedizione *f* **4.** REL risveglio *m*

revive [rɪˈvaɪv] **I.** *vt* **1.** MED rianimare **2.** (*resurrect: interest*) risvegliare; (*idea, custom*) far tornare in voga; (*economy*) far riprendere; (*conversation*) rianimare **3.** CINE riportare sullo schermo; THEAT rimettere in scena **II.** *vi* **1.** (*be restored to life*) ritornare in sé **2.** (*be restored: country, interest*) rifiorire; (*tradition*) ritornare in voga; (*style*) ritornare di moda; (*trade, economy*) riprendersi

revocation [ˌre·və·ˈkeɪ·ʃən] *n* **1.** (*of license*) ritiro *m* **2.** (*of law, decision*) revoca *f*

revoke [rɪˈvouk] **I.** *vt* **1.** (*cancel: decision, order*) revocare **2.** (*license*) ritirare **II.** *vi* GAMES rifiutare

revolt [rɪˈvoult] POL **I.** *vi* ribellarsi; **to ~ against sb/sth** ribellarsi contro qn/qc **II.** *vt* disgustare; **it ~s me** mi disgusta **III.** *n* **1.** (*uprising*) rivolta *f;* **to rise in ~ against sb/sth** sollevarsi contro qn/qc **2.** (*rebelliousness*) rivolta *f*

revolting [rɪˈvoul·tɪŋ] *adj* (*disgusting*) disgustoso, -a; **to look ~** avere un aspetto ripugnante

revolution [ˌre·və·ˈluː·ʃən] *n a.* POL rivoluzione *f*

revolutionary [ˌre·və·ˈluː·ʃən·ri] **I.** <-ies> *n* rivoluzionario, -a *m, f* **II.** *adj* rivoluzionario, -a

revolutionize [ˌre·və·ˈluː·ʃ·naɪz] *vt* rivoluzionare

revolve [rɪˈvɑːlv] *vi* girare; **to ~ on an axis** ruotare intorno ad un asse; **that problem was revolving in his mind** quel problema continuava a girargli in mente

♦ **revolve around** *vi a. fig* ruotare intorno

revolver [rɪˈvɑːl·və·] *n* revolver *m inv*

revolving *adj* girevole

revolving door *n* porta *f* girevole

revue [rɪˈvjuː] *n* THEAT rivista *f*

revulsion [rɪˈvʌl·ʃən] *n* repulsione *f*

reward [rɪˈwɔːrd] **I.** *n* ricompensa *f* **II.** *vt* ricompensare

rewarding *adj* gratificante

rewind [ˌriːˈwaɪnd] *irr* **I.** *vt* (*tape*) riavvolgere; (*clock, watch*) ricaricare **II.** *vi* riavvolgersi

rewire [ˌriːˈwa·ɪə·] *vt* rinnovare l'impianto elettrico di

reword [ˌriːˈwɜːrd] *vt* **1.** (*rewrite*) riscrivere **2.** (*say again*) dire con altre parole

rework [ˌriːˈwɜːk] *vt* rivedere; (*theme*) riadattare

rewound *pt of* **rewind**

rewrite[1] [ˌriːˈraɪt] *irr vt* riscrivere

rewrite[2] [ˈriːˌraɪt] *n* nuova stesura *f*

Rh *abbr of* **rhesus** Rh

rhapsody [ˈræp·sə·di] <-ies> *n* **1.** MUS rapsodia *f* **2.** (*enthusiasm*) estasi *f inv*

rhesus factor [ˈriː·səs·ˌfæk·tə·] *n* MED fattore *m* Rh

rhetoric [ˈre·tə·rɪk] *n* retorica *f*

rhetorical [rɪˈtɔː·rɪ·kl] *adj* retorico, -a

rhetorical question *n* domanda *f* retorica

rheumatic [ruːˈmæ·t̬ɪk] *adj* reumatico, -a

rheumatism [ˈruː·mə·t̬·zəm] *n* reumatismo *m*

rheumatoid arthritis [ˌruː·mə·tɔɪd·ˌɑːrˈθraɪ·t̬ɪs] *n* MED artrite *f* reumatoide

rhinestone *n* strass *inv*

rhino [ˈraɪ·nou] *n inf abbr of* **rhinoceros** rinoceronte *m*

rhinoceros [raɪˈnɑː·sə·əs] <-(es)> *n* rinoceronte *m*

rhinoplasty *n* rinoplastica *f*

rhododendron [ˌrou·də·ˈden·drən] *n* rododendro *m*

rhombus [ˈrɑːm·bəs] <-es *o* -i> *n* rombo *m*

rhubarb [ˈruː·bɑːrb] *n* rabarbaro *m*

rhyme [raɪm] **I.** *n* **1.** (*similar sound*) rima *f;* **in ~** in rima **2.** (*poem*) poesia *f* ▶ **without ~ or reason** senza alcuna logica **II.** *vi* fare rima

rhyming couplet [ˌraɪ·mɪŋ·ˈkʌp·lɪt] *n* distico *m* rimato

rhythm [ˈrɪ·ðəm] *n* ritmo *m*

rhythmic [ˈrɪð·mɪk] *adj*, **rhythmical** *adj* ritmico, -a

RI [ɑrˈaɪ] *abbr of* **Rhode Island** Rhode Island

rib [rɪb] **I.** *n* **1.** (*bone*) costola *f;* **to dig sb in the ~s** dare una gomitata nelle costole a qn **2.** NAUT costa *f* **3.** FASHION costa *f* **II.** <-bb-> *vt inf* prendere in giro

ribald [ˈrɪ·bld] *adj* scurrile

ribbon [ˈrɪ·bən] *n* (*long strip*) nastro *m;* **to be cut to ~s** essere fatto a brandelli

rib cage *n* gabbia *f* toracica

ribonucleic acid [ˌraɪ·bou·nju·ˈkleɪ·ɪk·ˈæ·sɪd] *n* acido *m* ribonucleico

rice [raɪs] **I.** *n* riso *m* **II.** *vt* (*potatoes*) passare (*con il passaverdura*)

rice field *n*, **rice paddy** *n* risaia *f*

rice growing *n* coltivazione *f* di riso

rice paper *n* carta *f* di riso

rice pudding *n* budino *m* di riso

rich [rɪtʃ] **I.** <-er, -est> *adj* **1.** (*person*) ricco, -a; (*soil*) fertile; (*furnishings*) riccamente lavorato, -a; **~ pickings** facili guadagni *mpl;* **to become ~** arricchirsi; **to be ~ in sth** abbondare di qc **2.** (*stimulating: life, history*) ricco, -a; (*experience*) stimolante **3.** (*food*) sostanzioso, -a **4.** (*intense: color*) vivido, -a; (*flavor*) intenso, -a; (*tone*) pieno, -a **II.** *n* **the ~ i** ricchi

richness *n* **1.** (*affluence*) ricchezza *f*; (*of soil*) fertilità *f* **2.** (*of food*) sostanziosità *f* **3.** (*intensity: of color*) vividezza *f*; (*of flavor*) intensità *f*

rickets ['rɪ·kɪts] *n* rachitismo *m*

rickety ['rɪ·kə·ti] *adj* (*car*) sgangherato, -a; (*steps*) traballante; (*person*) malfermo, -a sulle gambe

rickshaw ['rɪk·ʃɑː] *n* risciò *m*

ricochet ['rɪ·kə·ʃeɪ] **I.** *vi* rimbalzare **II.** *n* rimbalzo *m*

ricotta cheese *n* ricotta *f*

rid [rɪd] <rid *o* ridded, rid> *vt* **to ~ sth/sb of sth** liberare qc/qn da qc; **to ~ oneself of sth** sbarazzarsi di qc; **to be ~ of sth/sb** essere libero da qc/qn; **to get ~ of sb/sth** sbarazzarsi di qn/qc

riddance ['rɪ·dns] *n inf* **good ~!** è una liberazione!; **to bid sb good ~** dare a qn un addio definitivo

ridden ['rɪ·dn] *pp of* **ride**

riddle¹ ['rɪ·dl] *n* **1.** (*conundrum*) indovinello *m* **2.** *fig* (*mystery*) enigma *m*; **to speak in ~s** parlare per enigmi

riddle² ['rɪ·dl] *vt* crivellare; **to be ~d with mistakes** essere pieno di errori

ride [raɪd] **I.** *n* (*on horse, motorcycle, car*) giro *m*; **to give sb a ~** dare un passaggio a qn ▶ **to take sb for a ~** *inf* ingannare qn **II.** <rode, ridden> *vt* **1.** (*sit on*) **to ~ a bike** andare in bicicletta; **to ~ a horse** montare a cavallo; **can you ~ a bike?** sai andare in bicicletta?; **to ~ the waves** solcare le onde **2.** *inf* (*tease*) prendere in giro; **to ~ sb about sth** prendere in giro qn per qc **III.** <rode, ridden> *vi* **1.** (*on horse, bicyle*) **to ~ on a horse** andare a cavallo; **to ~ by bicycle** andare in bicicletta **2.** (*do well*) **to ~ high** essere sulla cresta dell'onda **3.** *inf* (*take no action*) **to let sth ~** lasciar passare qc

◆**ride down** *vt* agguantare

◆**ride out** *vt a. fig* uscire indenne da

◆**ride up** *vi* (*person*) avvicinarsi; (*dress*) salire

rider ['raɪ·dɚ] *n* **1.** (*on horse*) cavallerizzo, -a *m, f*; (*on bicycle*) ciclista *mf*; (*on motorcycle*) motociclista *mf* **2.** LAW clausola *f* aggiuntiva

ridge [rɪdʒ] *n* **1.** GEO cresta *f* **2.** METEO fronte *m* **3.** (*of roof*) colmo *m*

ridgepole ['rɪdʒ·poʊl] *n* trave *f* di colmo

ridgeway ['rɪdʒ·weɪ] *n* strada *f* lungo il crinale

ridicule ['rɪ·dɪ·kjuːl] **I.** *n* ridicolo *m*; **to be an object of ~** essere oggetto di scherno; **to hold sb/sth up to ~** ridicolizzare qn/qc **II.** *vt* ridicolizzare

ridiculous [rɪ·'dɪk·ju·ləs] *adj* ridicolo, -a

riding *n* equitazione *f*

riding breeches *n* calzoni *mpl* da equitazione

riding crop *n* frustino *m*

riding school *n* scuola *f* d'equitazione

riding whip *n s.* **riding crop**

rife [raɪf] *adj* diffuso, -a; **to be ~ with sth** essere pieno di qc

riffle ['rɪ·fl] *vt* (*cards*) mischiare; (*pages, book*) sfogliare

riffraff ['rɪf·ræf] *n* gentaglia *f*

rifle¹ ['raɪ·fl] *n* fucile *m*

rifle² ['raɪ·fl] **I.** *vt* **1.** (*plunder*) saccheggiare **2.** (*steal*) sottrarre **II.** *vt* rigare **III.** *vi* **to ~ through sth** frugare dentro qc

rifle butt *n* calcio *m* di fucile

rifleman <-men> *n* tiratore *m* (con il fucile)

rifle range *n* poligono *m* di tiro

rifle shot *n* colpo *m* di fucile

rift [rɪft] *n* **1.** (*in earth*) fenditura *f* **2.** *fig* spaccatura *f*; **to heal the ~** sanare il contrasto

rift zone *n* zona *f* accidentata

rig [rɪg] <-gg-> **I.** *vt* **1.** (*falsify*) truccare **2.** NAUT allestire **II.** *n* **1.** TECH (**oil**) ~ piattaforma *f* petrolifera **2.** (*truck*) autoarticolato *m* **3.** NAUT allestimento *m* **4.** *inf* (*clothing*) completo *m*

rigger ['rɪ·gɚ] *n* NAUT addetto, -a *m, f* all'allestimento

rigging ['rɪ·gɪŋ] *n* **1.** (*of result*) manipolazione *f*; **ballot ~** broglio *m* elettorale **2.** NAUT attrezzatura *f*

right [raɪt] **I.** *adj* **1.** (*correct*) corretto, -a; (*ethical*) giusto, -a; (*change*) adatto, -a; **it is ~ that ... è** giusto che ... +*subj*; **to be ~ (about sth)** aver ragione (riguardo a qc); **to do sth the ~ way** fare qc nel modo giusto; **to do the ~ thing** fare la cosa giusta; **to be in the ~ place at the ~ time** essere al posto giusto nel momento giusto; **to be on the ~ side of forty** non avere ancora quarant'anni **2.** (*direction*) destro, -a; **a ~ hook** SPORTS un gancio destro **3.** POL di destra **4.** (*well*) a posto; **to be not (quite) ~ in the head** *inf* non essere del tutto a posto con la testa **II.** *n* **1.** (*entitlement*) diritto *m*; **to have the ~ to do sth** avere il diritto di fare qc **2.** (*morality*) **to be in the ~** essere nel giusto **3.** (*right side*) destra *f*; SPORTS lato *m* destro **4.** POL **the Right** la destra **III.** *adv* **1.** (*correctly*) in modo giusto; **to do ~** agire bene **2.** (*straight*) direttamente; **~ away** immediatamente **3.** (*to the right*) a destra **4.** (*precisely*) esattamente; **~ here** proprio qui; **to be ~ behind sb** essere proprio dietro a qn **IV.** *vt* **1.** (*rectify*) sistemare; (*mistake*) riparare **2.** (*straighten*) raddrizzare **V.** *interj* bene

right angle *n* angolo *m* retto

right-angled ['raɪt·æŋ·gld] *adj* ad angolo retto

righteous ['raɪ·tʃəs] **I.** *adj form* **1.** (*person*) giusto, -a **2.** (*indignation*) giustificabile; (*tone*) moraleggiante **II.** *n pl* **the ~** i giusti

rightful ['raɪt·fəl] *adj* legittimo, -a

right-hand [ˌraɪt·'hænd] *adj* **on the ~ side** sulla destra

right-handed [ˌraɪt·'hæn·dɪd] *adj* che usa la (mano) destra

right-hander *n* **1.** (*person*) destrimano, -a *m, f* **2.** (*punch*) destro *m*

R

rightist ['raɪ·tɪst] POL I. *n* persona *f* di destra II. *adj* di destra

rightly *adv* 1. (*correctly*) giustamente; **if I remember** ~ se ricordo correttamente 2. (*justifiably*) a ragione; (**whether**) ~ **or wrongly** a ragione o a torto

right-minded [,raɪt·'maɪn·dɪd] *adj* dotato, -a di buon senso

right of way <-rights> *n* 1. (*over private land*) diritto *m* di passaggio 2. (*on road*) diritto *m* di precedenza

right-wing [,raɪt·'wɪŋ] *adj* POL di destra; **to be** ~ essere di destra

right-winger *n* POL persona *f* di destra

rigid ['rɪ·dʒɪd] *adj* 1. (*stiff*) rigido, -a; **to be** ~ **with fear/pain** essere paralizzato dalla paura/dal dolore 2. (*inflexible*) rigoroso, -a; (*censorship*) rigido, -a 3. (*intransigent*) intransigente

rigidity [rɪ·'dʒɪ·də·ti] *n* 1. (*hardness*) rigidità *f* 2. (*inflexibility*) rigore *m* 3. (*intransigence*) intransigenza *f*

rigmarole ['rɪg·mə·roʊl] *n* storie *fpl* interminabili

rigor ['rɪ·gɚ] *n* (*severity*) rigore *m*; (*hardship*) rigori *mpl*

rigor mortis [,rɪ·gɚ·'mɔːr·t̬ɪs] *n* MED rigor mortis *m*

rigorous ['rɪ·gɚ·rəs] *adj* rigoroso, -a

rile [raɪl] *vt inf* irritare

rim [rɪm] I. *n* 1. (*of cup, bowl*) bordo *m* 2. (*frame for eyeglasses*) montatura *f* 3. GEO orlo *m*; **the Pacific** ~ i paesi della costa del Pacifico 4. (*dirty mark*) orlo *m* II. <-mm-> *vt* 1. (*surround*) circondare 2. (*frame*) fare la montatura di

rimless ['rɪm·lɪs] *adj* (*eyeglasses*) senza montatura

rind [raɪnd] *n* (*of fruit*) buccia *f*; (*of bacon*) cotenna *f*; (*of cheese*) crosta *f*

ring¹ [rɪŋ] I. *n* 1. (*small circle*) anello *m*; (*of people*) cerchio *m*; (*around eyes*) occhiaia *f* 2. (*jewelery*) anello *m* 3. (*arena*) arena *f*; (*in boxing*) ring *m inv*; (*in circus*) pista *f* II. *vt* 1. (*surround*) circondare; **to be** ~ed **by sth** essere circondato da qc 2. (*bird*) inanellare

ring² [rɪŋ] I. *n* 1. (*metallic sound*) squillo *m* 2. (*telephone call*) colpo *m* di telefono; **to give sb a** ~ fare uno squillo *m* a qn II. <rang, rung> *vt* (*bell*) suonare; (*alarm*) far suonare III. <rang, rung> *vi* (*telephone, bell*) squillare; **to** ~ **false/true** suonare falso/vero

◆**ring in** *vt* **to** ~ **the New Year** festeggiare l'Anno Nuovo

◆**ring out** *vi* risuonare

◆**ring up** *vt* COM **to** ~ **sb up** [*o* **to** ~ **up sb**] battere il prezzo in cassa

ring binder *n* raccoglitore *m* ad anelli

ringer ['rɪŋ·ɚ] *n* **to be a dead** ~ (**for sb**) *inf* essere il ritratto sputato (di qn)

ring finger *n* anulare *m*

ringing I. *n* suono *m* II. *adj* squillante

ringleader ['rɪŋ·liː·dɚ] *n* capobanda *mf*

ringlet ['rɪŋ·lɪt] *n* ricciolo *m*

ringside ['rɪŋ·saɪd] I. *n* **to be at the** ~ essere a bordo ring II. *adj* (*seats*) di prima fila

ringtone *n* TEL suoneria *f*

ringworm ['rɪŋ·wɜːrm] *n* tigna *f*

rink [rɪŋk] *n* pista *f* di pattinaggio

rinse [rɪns] I. *vt* (*dishes, clothes*) risciacquare; (*hands*) sciacquare II. *n* 1. (*wash*) risciacquo *m*; **cold/hot** ~ risciacquo freddo/caldo *m* 2. (*hair coloring*) tintura *f*

riot ['ra·ɪət] I. *n* sommossa *f*; **a** ~ **of color** un tripudio *m* di colori; **to be a** ~ *inf* essere la fine del mondo II. *vi* creare disordini III. *adv* **to run** ~ *fig* scatenarsi; **to let one's imagination run** ~ dar libero sfogo alla propria immaginazione

rioter *n* rivoltoso, -a *m, f*

riot gear *n* equipaggiamento *m* antisommossa

rioting *n* disordini *mpl*

riotous ['ra·ɪə·t̬əs] *adj* 1. (*rebellious*) tumultuoso, -a 2. (*uproarious*) sfrenato, -a; (*party*) scatenato, -a

riot police *n* reparto *m* (di polizia) antisommossa

rip [rɪp] I. <-pp-> *vi* strapparsi II. <-pp-> *vt* strappare; **to** ~ **sth open** aprire qc (lacerando l'involucro) III. *n* strappo *m*

◆**rip down** *vt* strappar giù

◆**rip off** *vt* 1. (*remove*) strappar via 2. *inf* (*swindle*) fregare

◆**rip out** *vt* strappar via

◆**rip up** *vt* fare a pezzi

RIP [,ɑ:r·aɪ·'pi:] *abbr of* **rest in peace** RIP

ripcord ['rɪp·kɔːrd] *n* cavo *m* di spiegamento

ripe [raɪp] *adj* 1. (*fruit*) maturo, -a; **at the** ~ **old age of 80** alla bell'età di 80 anni 2. (*ready*) **the time is** ~ **for ...** è arrivato il momento di ... 3. (*language*) scurrile

ripen ['raɪ·pən] I. *vt* far maturare II. *vi* maturare

ripeness ['raɪp·nɪs] *n* grado *m* di maturazione

rip-off ['rɪp·ɑ:f] *n inf* furto *m*

ripple ['rɪ·pl] I. *n* increspatura *f*; ~ **of applause** un'ondata *f* d'applausi II. *vt* increspare III. *vi* incresparsi

rip-roaring [,rɪp·'rɔː·rɪŋ] *adj inf* sfrenato, -a; **a** ~ **success** un successo clamoroso

riptide ['rɪp·taɪd] *n* corrente *f* (sott'acqua)

rise [raɪz] I. *n* 1. (*increase*) aumento *m*; **to be on the** ~ essere in aumento; **to give** ~ **to sth** dar luogo a qc; **to get** [*o* **take**] **a** ~ **out of sb** mandare in bestia qn 2. (*incline*) salita *f* II. <rose, risen> *vi* 1. (*arise*) alzarsi 2. (*become higher: ground*) salire; (*temperature*) aumentare; (*river*) crescere 3. (*go up: smoke*) salire; (*moon, sun*) sorgere; (*building*) innalzarsi 4. (*improve socially*) progredire; (*in the ranks*) salire; **to** ~ **to fame** raggiungere la fama 5. (*be reborn*) resuscitare 6. (*rebel*) insorgere

◆**rise above** *vt insep* 1. (*be higher than*) levarsi al di sopra di 2. (*problem, opposition*) superare

◆**rise up** *vi* 1.(*arise*) alzarsi 2.(*rebel*) sollevarsi

risen ['rɪ·zn] *pp of* **rise**

riser ['raɪ·zə] *n* 1.(*person*) early ~ mattiniero, -a *m, f;* late ~ dormiglione, -a *m, f* 2.(*part of step*) alzata *f*

risible ['rɪ·zə·bl] *adj* risibile

rising ['raɪ·zɪŋ] I. *n* sollevazione *f* II. *adj* (*in number*) in aumento; (*in status*) in ascesa; (*floodwaters*) in crescita; (*sun*) nascente

risk [rɪsk] I. *n* 1.(*chance*) rischio *m;* to run the ~ of sth correre il rischio di qc 2.(*danger*) pericolo *m;* at one's own ~ a proprio rischio e pericolo; to be at ~ essere in pericolo II. *vt* rischiare; to ~ doing sth arrischiarsi a fare qc; to ~ one's life rischiare la propria vita

risk capital *n* ECON capitale *m* di rischio

risk factor *n* fattore *m* di rischio

risk-free *adj,* **riskless** *adj* privo, -a di rischi

risk liability *n* responsabilità *f* sui rischi

risky ['rɪs·ki] <-ier, -iest> *adj* rischioso, -a

risqué [rɪ'skeɪ] *adj* spinto, -a

rissole ['rɪ·soʊl] *n* crocchetta *f*

rite [raɪt] *n* rito *m;* last ~s estrema unzione *f;* ~s of passage rito di passaggio

ritual ['rɪ·tʃu·əl] I. *n* rituale *m* II. *adj* rituale

ritzy ['rɪt·si] <-ier, -iest> *adj inf* molto chic

rival ['raɪ·vl] I. *n* rivale *mf* II. *adj* rivale; a ~ brand una marca rivale III. <-ll-, -l-> *vt* poter competere con

rivalry ['raɪ·vl·ri] *n* rivalità *f*

river ['rɪ·və] *n* fiume *m*

river basin *n* bacino *m* fluviale

river bed *n* letto *m* del fiume

riverside ['rɪ·və·saɪd] *n* riva *f* del fiume

rivet ['rɪ·vɪt] I. *n* rivetto *m* II. *vt* 1.(*join*) rivettare 2.(*interest*) to be ~ed by sth essere rapito da qc

riveting ['rɪ·vɪ·tɪŋ] *adj inf* affascinante

rivulet ['rɪv·ju·lɪt] *n* 1. *liter* (*stream*) ruscello *m* 2.(*of sweat, blood*) rivolo *m*

RN [ˌɑːr'en] *n abbr of* **registered nurse** infermiere, -a *m, f* qualificato, -a

RNA [ˌɑːr·en·'eɪ] *n abbr of* **ribonucleic acid** RNA *m*

roach¹ [roʊtʃ] <roach *o* -es> *n* leucisco *m* (*pesce della famiglia della carpa*)

roach² [roʊtʃ] <-es> *n* 1. *inf* (*cockroach*) scarafaggio *m* 2. *sl* (*marijuana*) mozzicone *m* di spinello

road [roʊd] *n* 1.(*between towns*) strada *f;* (*in town*) via *f;* (*route*) percorso *m;* by ~ su strada; to be on the ~ (*fit for driving*) essere in circolazione; (*traveling by road*) essere in viaggio (*su strada*); (*performing on tour*) fare un tour 2. *fig* strada *f;* to be on the ~ to recovery essere sulla strada della ripresa ▶ all ~s lead to <u>Rome</u> *prov* tutte le strade portano a Roma *prov;* let's <u>hit</u> the ~! *inf* mettiamoci in moto!; to get sth <u>on</u> the ~ *inf* far partire qc

road accident *n* incidente *m* stradale

roadblock *n* posto *m* di blocco

road hog *n inf* pirata *m* della strada

roadhouse ['roʊd·haʊs] <-houses> *n* locale *m* lungo la strada

roadie ['roʊ·di] *n* roadie *mf inv* (*addetto al trasporto e installazione dell'attrezzatura di un gruppo musicale*)

roadkill *n* animale *m* rimasto vittima di un incidente stradale

road map *n* carta *f* stradale

road rage *n* furia *f* al volante

roadrunner *n* ZOOL corridore *m* della strada

road safety *n* sicurezza *f* stradale

roadshow ['roʊd·ʃoʊ] *n* tour *m inv*

roadside ['roʊd·saɪd] I. *n* bordo *m* della strada II. *adj* lungo la strada

road sign *n* cartello *m* stradale

road surface *n* pavimentazione *f* stradale

road-test *vt* to ~ a car testare una macchina su strada

road traffic *n* traffico *m* stradale

road transportation *n* trasporto *m* su strada

road warrior *n inf: persona continuamente in viaggio, specialmente per lavoro*

roadway ['roʊd·weɪ] *n* carreggiata *f*

roadwork ['roʊd·wɜːrk] *n* lavori *mpl* stradali

roam [roʊm] I. *vi* vagare II. *vt* vagare per

roan [roʊn] *n* roano *m*

roar [rɔːr] I. *vi* (*lion*) ruggire; (*person*) urlare; (*cannon*) rombare; to ~ with laughter scoppiare a ridere II. *vt* gridare III. *n* (*of lion*) ruggito *m;* (*of person*) urlo *m;* (*of engine*) rombo *m*

roaring I. *adj* ruggente; (*thunder*) fragoroso, -a; (*fire*) crepitante; (*success*) strepitoso, -a; (*trade*) (che va) a gonfie vele II. *adv* assolutamente

roast [roʊst] I. *vt* 1.(*food*) arrostire; (*coffee*) tostare 2.(*poke fun at*) prendere di mira qn II. *vi* (*food, person*) arrostirsi III. *n* 1.(*meat*) arrosto *m* 2.(*party*) festeggiamento *m* (*per un'occasione speciale nella vita di qn*) IV. *adj* (*meat*) arrosto *inv;* (*coffee*) tostato, -a

roaster ['roʊs·tə] *n* forno *m* per arrosti

roasting ['roʊs·tɪŋ] I. *n* 1.(*baking*) cottura *f* al forno 2. *inf* (*telling off*) to give sb a ~ dare una strigliata a qn II. *adj* per l'arrosto III. *adv* ~ hot rovente

rob [rɑːb] <-bb-> *vt* 1.(*person*) derubare; (*bank, house*) svaligiare; to ~ sb of sth derubare qn di qc 2.(*deprive*) to ~ sb of sth privare qn di qc

robber ['rɑː·bə] *n* rapinatore, -trice *m, f;* bank ~ rapinatore, -trice *m, f* di banche

robbery ['rɑː·b·ə·ri] <-ies> *n* rapina *f*

robe [roʊb] *n* (*formal*) toga *f;* (*dressing gown*) vestaglia *f*

robin ['rɑː·bɪn] *n* ZOOL pettirosso *m;* (*songbird*) tordo *m* migratore

robot ['roʊ·bɑːt] *n* (*machine*) robot *m inv;* (*person*) automa *m*

robotics [roʊ·'bɑː·tɪks] *npl* robotica *f*

robust [roʊ·'bʌst] *adj* 1.(*person, health*) robusto, -a; (*currency*) solido, -a 2.(*statement*) fermo, -a

R

robustness *n* 1. (*vitality*) vigore *m;* (*long-term strength*) solidità *f* 2. (*frankness*) fermezza *f*

rock¹ [rɑːk] *n* 1. GEO roccia *f;* (*in sea*) scoglio *m* 2. (*music*) rock *m* ▸ **to be stuck between a ~ and hard place** essere tra l'incudine e il martello; **as solid as a ~** saldo come una roccia; **to be on the ~s** andare a rotoli; **whiskey on the ~s** whisky con ghiaccio

rock² [rɑːk] I. *vt* 1. (*swing*) dondolare 2. (*shock*) scuotere II. *vi* dondolare

rock-and-roll [ˌrɑːk·ənd·ˈroʊl] *n* rock and roll *m*

rock band *n* gruppo *m* rock

rock bottom *n* fondo *m;* **to hit ~** toccare il fondo; **to be at ~** essere al livello più basso

rock climber *n* rocciatore, -trice *m, f*

rock climbing *n* alpinismo *m* su roccia

rocker [ˈrɑːkə] *n* 1. (*chair*) sedia *f* a dondolo 2. *inf* (*musician*) cantante *mf* rock; (*fan*) fan *mf inv* del rock ▸ **to be off one's ~** *inf* essere fuori di testa

rockery [ˈrɑːkə·i] <-ies> *n* giardino *m* roccioso

rocket [ˈrɑːkɪt] I. *n* 1. (*weapon*) missile *m* 2. (*vehicle for space travel, firework*) razzo *m* II. *vi* (*costs, prices*) salire alle stelle; **to ~ up** salire alle stelle

rocket launcher *n* lanciamissili *m inv*

rock face *n* parete *f* rocciosa

rock festival *n* festival *m inv* rock

rock garden *n* giardino *m* roccioso

Rockies [ˈrɑː·kiz] *n* **the ~** le Montagne Rocciose

rocking chair [ˈrɑː·kɪŋ] *n* sedia *f* a dondolo

rocking horse *n* cavallo *m* a dondolo

rock music *n* musica *f* rock

rock'n'roll *n* rock and roll *m*

rock salt *n* salgemma *m*

rock star *n* rockstar *f inv*

rocky¹ [ˈrɑː·ki] <-ier, -iest> *adj* roccioso, -a; (*ground*) pietroso, -a

rocky² [ˈrɑː·ki] <-ier, -iest> *adj* (*unstable*) traballante

Rocky Mountains *n* Montagne *fpl* Rocciose

rococo [rə·ˈkoʊ·koʊ] I. *n* rococò *m* II. *adj* rococò

rod [rɑːd] *n* (*stick*) asta *f;* (*fishing rod*) canna *f* da pesca

rode [roʊd] *pt of* **ride**

rodent [ˈroʊ·dnt] *n* roditore *m*

rodeo [ˈroʊ·dɪ·oʊ] <-s> *n* rodeo *m*

roe¹ [roʊ] *n* (*fish eggs*) uova *fpl* di pesce

roe² [roʊ] <-(s)> *n* (*deer*) capriolo *m*

roebuck [ˈroʊ·bʌk] *n* capriolo *m* maschio

roger [ˈrɑː·dʒə] *interj* RADIO ricevuto

rogue [roʊg] I. *n* 1. (*rascal*) briccone, -a *m, f* 2. (*villain*) mascalzone, -a *m, f* II. *adj* (*animal*) solitario, -a; (*trader, company*) disonesto, -a

roguery [ˈroʊ·gə·ri] <-ies> *n* (*of child*) bricconata *f;* (*of adult*) mascalzonata *f*

roguish [ˈroʊ·gɪʃ] *adj* malizioso, -a

ROI [ˌɑːr·oʊ·ˈaɪ] *n abbr of* **return on investment** rendimento *m* degli investimenti

role *n*, **rôle** [roʊl] *n a.* THEAT ruolo *m;* **to play a ~** THEAT interpretare un ruolo; *fig* svolgere un ruolo

role model *n* modello *m* da imitare

role play *n* gioco *m* di ruolo

role reversal *n* scambio *m* delle parti

roll [roʊl] I. *n* 1. (*turning over*) capriola *f* 2. (*swaying movement*) dondolio *m;* **to be on a ~** *fig* attraversare un periodo eccezionale 3. (*cylinder: of cloth, paper*) rotolo *m;* (*film*) rullino *m* 4. (*noise: of drum*) rullo *m;* (*of thunder*) rombo *m* 5. (*catalog of names*) ruolo *m;* (*for elections*) registro *m;* **to call the ~** fare l'appello 6. (*bread*) panino *m* (*rotondo*) II. *vt* 1. (*push: ball, barrel*) (far) rotolare; (*dice*) tirare; **to ~ one's eyes** alzare gli occhi al cielo 2. (*form into cylindrical shape*) **to ~ sth into sth** arrotolare qc in qc; **all ~ed into one** tutto in uno 3. (*make: cigarette*) arrotolare 4. (*flatten: grass*) spianare III. *vi* 1. (*move*) rotolare; (*with undulating motion*) ondeggiare 2. (*be in operation*) essere in funzione

♦**roll back** *vt* 1. (*cause to retreat*) far retrocedere 2. ECON ridurre 3. (*return to previous state*) cancellare

♦**roll by** *vi* (*vehicle, clouds*) avanzare; (*time, years*) passare

♦**roll down** I. *vt* (*sleeve*) srotolare; (*window*) abbassare II. *vi* rotolar giù

♦**roll in** *vi* 1. arrivare in gran quantità 2. **to be rolling in money** *inf* far soldi a palate

♦**roll off** *vi* rotolar giù

♦**roll on** *vi* continuare a rotolare; (*time*) scorrere

♦**roll out** I. *vt* 1. (*flatten*) spianare; (*pastry*) stendere 2. (*unroll*) srotolare 3. COM (*new product*) lanciare II. *vi* 1. (*wake up*) buttarsi giù (dal letto) 2. SPORTS allargarsi su un fianco

♦**roll over** *vi* 1. (*movement*) rigirarsi 2. TEL (*minutes*) accumularsi

♦**roll up** I. *vi inf* fare la propria comparsa II. *vt* arrotolare; (*sleeves*) rimboccarsi

roll bar *n* AUTO roll-bar *m inv*

roll call *n* appello *m*

roller [ˈroʊ·lə] *n* 1. TECH rullo *m* 2. (*wave*) onda *f* lunga 3. (*for hair*) bigodino *m*

roller bearing *n* TECH cuscinetto *m* a rulli

Rollerblade® I. *n* pattino *m* in linea II. *vi* andare sui pattini in linea

roller coaster *n* montagne *fpl* russe

rollerskate I. *n* pattino *m* a rotelle II. *vi* andare sui pattini a rotelle

rollicking [ˈrɑː·lɪ·kɪŋ] *adj* (*amusing*) molto vivace; (*party*) scatenato, -a

rolling *adj* rotolante; (*hills*) ondulato, -a; (*program*) graduale

rolling mill *n* laminatoio *m*

rolling pin *n* matterello *m*

rolling stock *n* AUTO materiale *m* rotabile

roll-on [ˈroʊl·ɑːn] *adj* (*deodorant*) a sfera

roly-poly [ˌroʊ·li·ˈpoʊ·li] *adj inf* paffuto, -a

ROM [rɑːm] *n* INFOR *abbr of* **Read Only Mem-**

ory ROM *f*
Roman ['roʊ·mən] **I.** *adj* romano, -a; (*alphabet*) latino, -a; (*religion*) cattolico, -a romano, -a **II.** *n* romano, -a *m, f*
Roman Catholic I. *n* cattolico, -a *m, f* romano, -a **II.** *adj* cattolico, -a romano, -a; **the ~ Church** la Chiesa cattolica romana
Roman numeral *n* numero *m* romano
romance [roʊ·'mænts] **I.** *n* **1.** (*love affair*) storia *f* d'amore **2.** (*novel*) romanzo *m* d'amore; (*film*) film *m inv* d'amore **3.** (*glamour*) fascino *m* **II.** *vi* fare racconti romanzati
Romanesque [ˌroʊ·mə·'nesk] *adj* romanico, -a
Romania [roʊ·'meɪ·niə] *n* Romania *f*
Romanian [roʊ·'meɪ·ni·ən] **I.** *adj* rumeno, -a **II.** *n* **1.** (*person*) rumeno, -a *m, f* **2.** LING rumeno *m*
romantic [roʊ·'mæn·t̬ɪk] **I.** *adj a.* LIT, ART romantico, -a **II.** *n* romantico, -a *m, f*
romanticism [roʊ·'mæn·t̬ə·sɪ·zəm] *n* romanticismo *m*
Rome [roʊm] *n* Roma *f* ▸ **~ was not built in a** <u>day</u> *prov* Roma non fu fatta in un giorno *prov;* <u>when</u> **in ~** (**do as the** <u>Romans</u>) *prov* paese che vai usanza che trovi *prov*
romp [rɑːmp] **I.** *vi* sfrenarsi; **to ~ home** sbaragliare il campo **II.** *n* divertimento *m* sfrenato
roof [ruːf] <-s> **I.** *n* (*of house, car*) tetto *m;* (*of tree*) cima *f;* (*of mouth*) palato *m* ▸ **to go** <u>through</u> **the ~** (*prices*) andare alle stelle; (*person*) andare su tutte le furie; **to** <u>hit</u> **the ~** andare su tutte le furie; **to** <u>raise</u> **the ~** *inf* fare un casino del diavolo **II.** *vt* mettere il tetto a
roofer ['ruː·fɚ] *n* operaio, -a *m, f* che lavora ai tetti
roof garden *n* giardino *m* pensile
roofing *n* materiale *m* da copertura per tetti
rooftop ['ruːf·tɑːp] *n* tetto *m*
rook [rʊk] **I.** *n* **1.** (*bird*) corvo *m* comune **2.** (*in chess*) torre *f* **II.** *vt inf* imbrogliare
rookery ['rʊ·kə·ri] *n* colonia *f* di corvi
rookie ['rʊ·ki] *n inf* novellino, -a *m, f*
room [ruːm] **I.** *n* **1.** (*in house*) stanza *f;* **~ and board** vitto e alloggio *m* **2.** (*space*) spazio *m;* **to make ~ for sb/sth** fare posto *m* a qn/per qc; **there's no more ~ for anything else** non c'è più posto *m* per nient'altro; **~ for improvement** possibilità *f* di miglioramento; **there is no ~ for doubt** non c'è possibilità *f* di dubbio **II.** *vi* **to ~ with sb** dividere la camera con qn
roomie *n inf* compagno, -a *m, f* d'alloggio
roommate ['ruːm·meɪt] *n* compagno, -a *m, f* d'alloggio
room service *n* servizio *m* in camera
room temperature *n* temperatura *f* ambiente
roomy ['ruː·mi] <-ier, -iest> *adj* spazioso, -a
roost [ruːst] **I.** *n* ramo o bastone dove si posano gli uccelli ▸ **to** <u>rule</u> **the ~** avere la bacchetta del comando **II.** *vi* (*bird*) fermarsi a riposare; *fig* trascorrere la notte
rooster ['ruː·s·tɚ] *n* gallo *m*

root [ruːt] *n* **1.** *a.* BOT, LING, MAT radice *f;* **to take ~** *a. fig* mettere radici **2.** (*source*) causa *f;* **the ~ of all evil** la fonte di tutti i mali; **the ~ of the problem is that ...** il nocciolo del problema è che ...
◆**root about** *vi*, **root around** *vi* frugare; **to ~ for sth** frugare alla ricerca di qc
◆**root out** *vt* sradicare
root beer *n* bevanda analcolica frizzante ricavata da varie radici
root canal *n* **1.** (*part of tooth*) canale *m* radicolare **2.** MED (*treatment*) devitalizzazione *f*
root cause *n* causa *f* primaria
rootless *adj* privo, -a di radici
root sign *n* MAT simbolo *m* della radice
root vegetable *n* ortaggio *m* dalla radice commestibile
rope [roʊp] **I.** *n* **1.** (*cord*) corda *f;* (*of garlic*) treccia *f;* (*of pearls*) filo *m* **2.** *pl* (*in boxing*) corde *fpl* **3.** (*for capital punishment*) corda *f* ▸ **to** <u>know</u> **the ~s** saper il fatto suo; **to** <u>learn</u> **the ~s** acquisire le basi; **to** <u>show</u> **sb the ~s** mostrare a qn come procedere; **to have sb** <u>on</u> **the ~s** mettere alle corde qn **II.** *vt* legare con una corda
◆**rope in** *vt* **to rope sb in** (**to doing sth**) vincere le resistenze di qn (a fare qc)
◆**rope off** *vt* delimitare con corde
◆**rope up** *vi* legarsi in cordata
rope ladder *n* scala *f* di corda
rosary ['roʊ·zə·ri] <-ies> *n* rosario *m*
rose¹ [roʊz] **I.** *n* **1.** (*flower*) rosa *f;* (*color*) rosa *m* **2.** (*on watering can, shower*) cipolla *f* **3.** ARCHIT rosone *m* ▸ **to come up smelling of ~s** cavarsela trionfalmente; <u>coming up</u> **~s** mettersi molto bene **II.** *adj* rosa *inv*
rose² [roʊz] *pt of* **rise**
rosebud ['roʊz·bʌd] *n* bocciolo *m* di rosa
rosebush *n* pianta *f* di rose
rose garden *n* roseto *m*
rosehip ['roʊz·hɪp] *n* rosa *f* canina
rosemary ['roʊz·me·ri] *n* rosmarino *m*
rosette [roʊ·'zet] *n* ARCHIT rosone *m;* (*badge*) coccarda *f*
rose water *n* acqua *f* di rose
rose window *n* ARCHIT rosone *m*
rosin ['rɑː·zən] *n* pece *f* greca
roster ['rɑː·s·tɚ] *n* elenco *m*
rostrum ['rɑː·s·trəm, 'rɑː·s·trə] <-s *o* rostra> *n* (*for conductor*) podio *m;* (*for public speaker*) palco *m*
rosy ['roʊ·zi] <-ier, -iest> *adj* **1.** (*rose-colored*) rosato, -a; (*cheek*) roseo, -a **2.** (*optimistic: viewpoint, future*) roseo, -a
rot [rɑːt] **I.** *n* marcio *m* **II.** <-tt-> *vi* marcire **III.** *vt* far marcire
◆**rot away I.** *vt* far marcire **II.** *vi* marcire
rotary ['roʊ·t̬·ɚ·i] *adj* rotatorio, -a; (*pump*) a rotazione
rotate ['roʊ·teɪt] **I.** *vt* **1.** (*turn around*) (far) ruotare **2.** (*alternate*) alternare; (*duties*) fare una rotazione di; AGR fare la rotazione di **II.** *vi* ruotare; **to ~ around sth** ruotare intorno a qc

R

rotation [roʊˈteɪ·ʃən] *n* **1.** *a.* ASTR, AGR rotazione *f* **2.** (*alternation*) alternanza *f*; **in ~ a** turno
rotatory [ˈroʊ·tə·tɔː·ri] *adj* rotatorio, -a
rote [roʊt] *n* **by ~** meccanicamente
rotor [ˈroʊ·t̬ə] *n* rotore *m*
rotten [ˈrɑː·tn] *adj* **1.** (*food*) marcio, -a; **to go ~** marcire **2.** *inf* (*nasty: behavior*) brutto, -a **3.** *inf* (*performance, book*) penoso, -a
rotund [roʊˈtʌnd] *adj* tondo, -a e paffuto, -a
rotunda [roʊˈtʌn·də] *n* ARCHIT rotonda *f*
rouble [ˈruː·bl] *n s.* **ruble**
rouge [ruːʒ] *n* fard *m*
rough [rʌf] **I.** *adj* **1.** (*uneven: road*) accidentato, -a; (*surface*) ruvido, -a **2.** (*poorly made: work*) rudimentale **3.** (*harsh: voice*) roco, -a **4.** (*imprecise*) approssimativo, -a; **~ work** lavoro *m* approssimativo **5.** (*unrefined: person, manner*) rude **6.** (*stormy: sea*) agitato, -a; (*weather*) burrascoso, -a **7.** (*difficult*) pesante; (*treatment*) senza tante cerimonie; **to be ~ on sb** *inf* andar giù pesante con qn **II.** *n* **1.** (*sketch*) schizzo *m* **2.** SPORTS **the ~** il rough ▶ **to take the ~ with the smooth** prendere le cose come vengono **III.** *vt* **to ~ it** *inf* arrangiarsi alla buona **IV.** *adv* **to play ~** giocar duro; **to live ~** vivere per strada
roughage [ˈrʌ·fɪdʒ] *n* fibra *f* (degli alimenti)
rough-and-ready [ˌrʌf·ənd·ˈre·di] *adj* (*primitive*) semplice ed efficace
rough-and-tumble *n* lotta *f* senza esclusione di colpi; *fig* gioco *m* scalmanato
roughen [ˈrʌ·fən] *vt* rendere ruvido
rough-hewn *adj* **1.** (*wood*) appena sgrossato, -a **2.** (*features*) grossolano, -a
roughhouse [ˈrʌf·haʊs] **I.** *vi* azzuffarsi **II.** *n inf* zuffa *f*
roughly *adv* **1.** (*approximately*) approssimativamente; **~ speaking** per così dire **2.** (*aggressively*) bruscamente
roughneck [ˈrʌf·nek] *n* **1.** *inf* (*violent man*) teppista *m* **2.** *sl* (*oil rig worker*) operaio *m* di una piattaforma petrolifera
roughness [ˈrʌf·nɪs] *n* **1.** (*of surface*) ruvidezza *f*; (*of ground*) asperità *f* **2.** (*unfairness*) inequità *f*
roughshod [ˈrʌf·ʃɑːd] *adv* **to ride ~ over sb** mettersi sotto i piedi qn
rough-spoken [ˌrʌf·ˈspoʊ·kən] *adj* non raffinato, -a nel parlare
roulette [ruːˈlet] *n* roulette *f*
round [raʊnd] **I.** <-er, -est> *adj* **1.** (*circular: object*) rotondo, -a; (*number*) tondo, -a; (*arch*) a tutto sesto **2.** (*not angular*) tondeggiante **3.** (*sonorous*) pieno, -a **II.** *n* **1.** (*circle*) cerchio *m* **2.** (*series*) serie *f*; (*of applause*) scroscio *m*; (*of shots*) raffica *f* **3.** *pl* (*route*) giro *m*; MIL ronda *f*; MED giro di visite **4.** (*routine*) routine *f inv* **5.** (*time period: of elections*) turno *m*; (*in card games*) mano *f*; SPORTS turno *m*; (*in boxing*) round *m* **6.** (*of drinks*) giro *m*; **this ~ is on me** questo giro tocca a me **7.** (*of ammunition*) colpo *m* **8.** MUS canone *m*

III. *vt* **1.** (*movement*) girare intorno a; (*corner*) girare **2.** MAT arrotondare; **to ~ an amount to the nearest dollar** arrotondare una somma al dollaro
◆**round down** *vt* MAT arrotondare per difetto
◆**round off** *vt* **1.** (*finish*) chiudere **2.** (*smooth*) smussare **3.** MAT arrotondare
◆**round out** *vt* completare; **to ~ a list** completare una lista
◆**round up** *vt* **1.** MAT arrotondare per eccesso **2.** (*gather*) mettere insieme; (*cattle*) radunare
roundabout [ˈraʊnd·ə·baʊt] *adj* indiretto, -a; **to take a ~ route** fare un giro tortuoso
rounded *adj* arrotondato, -a
roundly *adv* (*assert, deny*) energicamente; **to defeat sb ~** sconfiggere qn sonoramente
round robin *n* **1.** (*letter*) circolare *f* **2.** (*competition*) torneo *m* all'italiana (*in cui ogni partecipante incontra a turno tutti gli altri*)
round-shouldered [ˌraʊnd·ˈʃoʊl·dəd] *adj* incurvato, -a; **to be ~** avere le spalle curve
round-table discussion [ˌraʊnd·ˈteɪ·bl dɪs·ˈkʌ·ʃən] *n* tavola *f* rotonda
round-the-clock **I.** *adj* (*surveillance*) di ventiquattr'ore su ventiquattro **II.** *adv* ventiquattr'ore su ventiquattro; **to work ~** lavorare ventiquattr'ore su ventiquattro
round trip *n* viaggio *m* andata e ritorno; **~ ticket** biglietto di andata e ritorno
roundup [ˈraʊnd·ʌp] *n* **1.** AGR raduno *m* **2.** (*by police*) retata *f*
rouse [raʊz] *vt* **1.** (*awaken*) svegliare **2.** (*activate*) stimolare; **to ~ sb to do sth** stimolare qn a fare qc; **to ~ sb to action** stimolare qn all'azione
rousing [ˈraʊ·zɪŋ] *adj* (*welcome*) caloroso, -a; (*speech*) stimolante
roustabout [ˈraʊst·ə·baʊt] *n* (*laborer*) uomo *m* di fatica
rout [raʊt] **I.** *vt* **1.** (*defeat*) sbaragliare **2.** (*put to flight*) mettere in fuga **II.** *n* **1.** (*defeat*) disfatta *f* **2.** (*flight*) fuga *f* disordinata
◆**rout out** *vt* **1.** (*make come out*) tirar fuori **2.** (*find*) scovare '
route [raʊt] **I.** *n* **1.** (*way*) via *f*; (*of parade, bus*) percorso *m*; NAUT rotta *f*; (*to success*) strada *f* **2.** (*delivery path*) giro *m*; **to have a paper ~** fare la consegna dei giornali a domicilio **3.** (*road*) strada *f* **II.** *vt* **to ~ sth via St. Louis** spedire qc via St.Louis
routine [ruːˈtiːn] **I.** *n* **1.** *a.* INFOR routine *f inv*; **he went into his usual ~** *inf* ha rifatto la solita storia **2.** (*of dancer*) numero *m* **II.** *adj* **1.** (*regular*) abituale; (*inspection*) di routine; (*medical case*) molto comune **2.** (*uninspiring*) monotono, -a
routinely *adv* regolarmente
roux [ruː] *n* miscela di burro e farina usata per addensare la salsa
rove [roʊv] **I.** *vi* **to ~ over sth** vagare su qc **II.** *vt* vagare per
rover [ˈroʊ·və] *n* girovago, -a *m, f*
roving [ˈroʊ·vɪŋ] *adj* (*animal*) nomade;

(*thieves*) in continuo movimento; (*ambassador, instructor*) itinerante

row¹ [roʊ] *n* **1.**(*line*) fila *f;* **to stand in a ~** essere in fila **2.**(*succession*) successione *f;* **three times in a ~** tre volte di seguito

row² [roʊ] I. *vi* remare II. *vt* (*boat*) portare (con i remi); **to ~ sb across the lake** portare qn in barca a remi dall'altra parte del lago III. *n* giro *m* in barca a remi; **to go for a ~** andare a fare un giro in barca a remi

rowboat ['roʊ·boʊt] *n* barca *f* a remi

rowdy ['raʊ·di] <-ier, -iest> *adj* **1.**(*noisy*) rumoroso, -a **2.**(*quarrelsome*) dall'atteggiamento aggressivo

rower ['roʊɚ] *n* rematore, -trice *m, f*

rowing *n* SPORTS canottaggio *m*

rowing club *n* circolo *m* di canottaggio

royal ['rɔ·ɪəl] I. *adj* **1.**(*of monarch*) reale; **the ~ we** il pluralis maiestatis **2.***fig* regale; (*welcome*) accoglienza regale **3.** *inf*(*big*) immane; **a ~ pain in the ass** una rottura insopportabile II. *n inf* membro *m* della famiglia reale

royal flush *n* scala *f* reale

royal jelly *n* pappa *f* reale

royalty ['rɔ·ɪəl·ti] <-ies> *n* **1.**(*sovereignty*) famiglia *f* reale; **to treat sb like ~** trattare qn come un principe **2.** *pl* (*payment*) diritti *mpl* d'autore

rpm [ˌɑːrˈpiːˈem] *n abbr of* **revolutions per minute** giri/m

RR [ˌɑːrˈɑːr] *n abbr of* **Railroad** ferrovia *f*

R and R *abbr of* **rest and recreation/relaxation** *periodo di riposo dall'attività, specialmente in campo militare*

RSI [ˌɑːrˈesˈaɪ] *n abbr of* **repetitive strain injury** lesioni *fpl* da sforzo ripetuto

RSVP [ˌɑːrˈesˈviːˈpiː] *vi abbr of* **répondez s'il vous plait** RSVP

rub [rʌb] I. *n* **1.**(*act of rubbing*) strofinamento *m;* **to give sth a ~** strofinare qc **2.** *liter* (*difficulty*) difficoltà *f;* **there's the ~** questo è il punto critico II. <-bb-> *vt* strofinare; (*one's eyes*) stropicciarsi; (*one's hands*) fregarsi; **to ~ sth clean** pulire qc, *strofinandolo* III. <-bb-> *vi* strofinare

◆**rub against** *vi* **to ~ sth** strusciare contro qc; (*cat*) strofinarsi contro qc

◆**rub down** *vt* **1.**(*smooth*) levigare; (*horse*) strigliare **2.**(*dry*) strofinare (per asciugare)

◆**rub in** *vt* **1.**(*spread on skin*) applicare con una frizione **2.** *inf*(*keep reminding*) insistere a ricordare; *pej* fare una storia su

◆**rub off** I. *vi* **1.**(*become clean: stain*) andar via **2. to ~ on sb** (*affect*) trasmettersi a qn II. *vt* (*dirt*) togliere, *sfregando*

◆**rub out** *vt* **1.**(*remove: writing*) cancellare; (*dirt*) togliere **2.** *inf*(*murder*) far fuori

rubber ['rʌ·bɚ] *n* **1.**(*material*) gomma *f* **2.** *inf* (*condom*) preservativo *m* **3.**(*game*) serie di tre o cinque partite; (*in bridge*) rubber *m inv*

rubber band *n* elastico *m*

rubber boots *npl* stivali *mpl* di gomma

rubber check *n inf* assegno *m* a vuoto

rubber gloves *npl* guanti *mpl* di gomma

rubberneck ['rʌ·bɚ·nek] I. *n sl* (*tourist*) turista *mf, che si muove in gregge;* (*at accident*) curioso, -a *m, f* II. *vi sl* (*sightsee*) fare turismo; (*be nosy*) curiosare

rubbernecker *n sl* curioso, -a *m, f*

rubber plant *n* ficus *m inv*

rubber-stamp I. *vt* (*decision*) convalidare senza discussioni II. *n* (*device*) timbro *m*

rubber tree *n* albero *m* della gomma

rubbery <-ier, -iest> *adj* (*texture, food*) gommoso, -a

rubbing *n* sfregamento *m*

rubbing alcohol *n* alcol *m* denaturato

rubbish ['rʌ·bɪʃ] *n inf* stupidaggini *fpl*

rubble ['rʌ·bl] *n* macerie *fpl*

rubdown ['rʌb·daʊn] *n* frizione *f*

rubella [ruːˈbe·lə] *n* MED rosolia *f*

rubicund ['ruː·bə·kʌnd] *adj liter* rubicondo, -a

ruble ['ruː·bl] *n* rublo *m*

rubric ['ruː·brɪk] *n* **1.**(*heading*) titolo *m* **2.**(*instructions*) istruzioni *fpl* **3.** REL rubrica *f*

ruby ['ruː·bi] I. <-ies> *n* rubino *m* II. *adj* (di) color rubino

ruck [rʌk] I. *n* **1.**(*crowd*) folla *f* anonima **2.**(*fold*) piega *f* II. *vt* **to ~ up** (*clothes*) sgualcire

ruckus ['rʌ·kəs] *n inf* pandemonio *m*

rudder ['rʌ·dɚ] *n* AVIAT, NAUT timone *m*

rudderless *adj a. fig* senza timone

ruddy ['rʌ·di] <-ier, -iest> *adj* **1.** *liter* (*cheeks*) roseo, -a **2.**(*light*) rossastro, -a

rude [ruːd] *adj* **1.**(*impolite*) sgarbato, -a **2.**(*vulgar*) volgare; (*joke*) spinto, -a **3.**(*sudden*) brusco, -a; (*surprise*) brutto, -a **4.** *liter* (*unrefined*) rozzo, -a

rudimentary [ˌruː·dəˈmen·tə·ri] *adj* rudimentale

rudiments ['ruː·də·mənt] *npl* rudimenti *mpl*

rue [ruː] *vt liter* rammaricarsi di

rueful ['ruː·fəl] *adj* **1.**(*repentant*) contrito, -a **2.**(*sad*) sconsolato, -a

ruff [rʌf] *n* (*collar*) gorgiera *f;* (*of an animal*) collare *m*

ruffian ['rʌ·fi·ən] *n iron* mascalzone, -a *m, f*

ruffle ['rʌ·fl] I. *vt* **1.**(*agitate: hair, feathers*) arruffare; (*clothes*) scompigliare **2.**(*upset*) turbare II. *n* volant *m inv*

rug [rʌg] *n* (*small carpet*) tappeto *m*

rugby ['rʌg·bi] *n* rugby *m*

rugged ['rʌ·gɪd] *adj* **1.**(*uneven: cliff, mountains*) scosceso, -a; (*landscape, country*) aspro, -a; (*ground*) accidentato, -a **2.**(*tough: face*) dai tratti marcati; (*construction, vehicle*) resistente

ruin ['ruː·ɪn] I. *vt* **1.**(*bankrupt*) mandare in rovina **2.**(*destroy: city, building*) distruggere **3.**(*spoil: dress, surprise, child*) rovinare II. *n* **1.**(*bankruptcy, downfall*) rovina *f;* **drugs will be his ~** la droga sarà la sua rovina **2.** *pl* (*remains*) rovine *fpl*

ruination [ˌruː·əˈneɪ·ʃən] *n* rovina *f*

ruinous ['ruː·ə·nəs] *adj* rovinoso, -a

R

rule [ruːl] I. *n* 1. (*law*) regola *f;* (*principle*) norma *f;* ~s **and regulations** norme e regole; ~s **of the road** codice *m* della strada; **to be the** ~ essere la norma; **to break a** ~ infrangere una regola; **to play** (**it**) **by the** ~s attenersi alle regole; **it is against the** ~s è contro le regole; **as a** ~ di norma 2. (*control*) governo *m* 3. (*measuring device*) riga *f* ▶ **a** ~ **of thumb** una regola pratica; ~s **are made to be broken** le regole sono fatte per non essere rispettate II. *vt* 1. (*govern: country*) governare; (*company*) dirigere 2. (*control*) dominare 3. (*draw*) tracciare una riga; (*paper*) fare le righe a 4. LAW (*decide*) decretare III. *vi* 1. (*control*) governare; (*monarch*) regnare 2. (*predominate*) dominare 3. LAW **to** ~ **for/against sb/sth** emettere un verdetto a favore/contro qn/qc

◆**rule out** *vt* escludere
rule book *n* regolamento *m*
ruler *n* 1. (*governor*) governante *mf;* (*sovereign*) sovrano, -a *m, f* 2. (*measuring device*) riga *f*
ruling [ˈruːlɪŋ] I. *adj* 1. (*governing*) al governo; (*class*) dirigente; (*monarch*) regnante 2. (*primary*) dominante II. *n* sentenza *f;* **the final** ~ la sentenza definitiva
rum [rʌm] *n* rum *m*
Rumania [roʊˈmeɪ·niə] *n s.* **Romania**
Rumanian [roʊˈmeɪ·ni·ən] *s.* **Romanian**
rumba [ˈrʌm·bə] *n* rumba *f*
rumble [ˈrʌm·bl] I. *n* 1. (*sound*) rimbombo *m;* (*of thunder*) brontolio *m;* (*of stomach*) borbottio *m* 2. *inf* (*fight*) rissa *f* II. *vi* rimbombare; (*thunder*) rintronare; **my stomach is** ~**ing** il mio stomaco borbotta
rumbling I. *n* (*sound*) rombo *m;* (*of thunder*) brontolio *m;* **there were** ~s **of war** giravano voci di una possibile guerra II. *adj* rimbombante
ruminant [ˈruː·mə·nənt] ZOOL I. *n* ruminante *mf* II. *adj* ruminante
ruminate [ˈruː·mə·neɪt] *vi* ruminare
ruminative [ˈruː·mə·ˌneɪ·t̬ɪv] *adj form* riflessivo, -a
rummage [ˈrʌ·mɪdʒ] I. *vi* rovistare II. *n* (*search*) **to have a** ~ **around for sth** rovistare in giro alla ricerca di qc
rummage sale *n* vendita di roba usata, generalmente per beneficenza
rummy [ˈrʌ·mi] *n* GAMES gioco di carte sul genere del ramino
rumor [ˈruː·mɚ] I. *n* voce *f* II. *vt* **it is** ~**ed that ...** corre voce che ...
rump [rʌmp] *n* 1. (*back end: of horse, bird*) parte *f* posteriore 2. (*cut of beef*) quarto *m* posteriore 3. *iron* (*buttocks*) posteriore *m*
rumple [ˈrʌm·pl] *vt* spiegazzare; **to** ~ **sb's hair** scompigliare i capelli di qn
rump steak *n* bistecca *f* di scamone
run [rʌn] I. *n* 1. (*jog*) **to break into a** ~ mettersi a correre; **to go for a** ~ andare a fare una corsa 2. (*trip*) giro *m;* (*of train*) tragitto *m;* **to**

go for a ~ **in the car** andare a fare un giro in macchina 3. (*series*) serie *f;* (*of books*) tiratura *f* 4. (*demand*) corsa *f;* **a sudden** ~ **on the dollar** un'improvvisa pressione sul dollaro; **a** ~ **on the banks** una pressione sulle banche 5. (*type*) categoria *f* 6. (*direction, tendency*) corso *m;* (*of opinion*) corrente *f;* **the** ~ **of events** il corso degli avvenimenti 7. (*enclosure for animals*) recinto *m* 8. (*hole in tights*) smagliatura *f* 9. SPORTS (*in baseball, cricket*) run *m inv;* (*ski slope*) pista *f* 10. CINE programmazione *f;* THEAT permanenza *f* in cartellone 11. MUS volata *f* 12. MIL bombing ~ bombardamento *m* (aereo) ▶ **to give sb a** ~ **for their money** dar filo da torcere a qn; **to have a** (**good**) ~ **for one's money** non potersi lamentare; **in the long** ~ alla lunga; **in the short** ~ a breve termine; **on the** ~ in fuga; **to be on the** ~ essere latitante II. *vi* <ran, run> 1. (*move fast*) correre; **to** ~ **for the bus** fare una corsa per prendere l'autobus; **to** ~ **for help** correre a cercare aiuto; ~ **for your lives!** scappate se volete salvarvi! 2. (*operate*) andare; **to** ~ **smoothly** funzionare senza il minimo intoppo 3. (*go, travel*) andare; **to** ~ **off the road** uscire di strada; **to** ~ **ashore/onto the rocks** NAUT incagliarsi/finire sulle rocce 4. (*extend*) estendersi; **the road** ~s **along the coast** la strada corre lungo la costa 5. (*last*) ~ **for two hours** durare due ore; **to** ~ **and** ~ durare a lungo 6. (*be*) esistere 7. (*flow: river*) scorrere; (*make-up*) sciogliersi; (*nose*) colare 8. (*enter election*) candidarsi; **to** ~ **for election/President** candidarsi alle elezioni/alla presidenza 9. + *adj* (*be*) **to** ~ **dry** (*river*) prosciugarsi; **to** ~ **short** (*water*) scarseggiare 10. (*say*) dire III. *vt* <ran, run> 1. (*move fast*) **to** ~ **a race** fare una corsa 2. (*enter in race: candidate*) presentare in competizione; (*horse*) far correre 3. (*drive*) portare; **to** ~ **sb home** accompagnare qn a casa; **to** ~ **a truck into a tree** andare a sbattere con un camion contro un albero; **to** ~ **a ship ashore** far incagliare una nave 4. (*pass*) passare 5. (*operate*) far funzionare; (*car*) mantenere; (*computer program*) eseguire; (*engine*) far andare; **to** ~ **a washing machine** far andare una lavatrice 6. (*manage, govern*) gestire; **to** ~ **a farm** condurre una fattoria; **to** ~ **a government** guidare un governo; **to** ~ **a household** portar avanti una casa 7. (*conduct*) fare; (*experiment, test*) condurre 8. (*provide: course*) tenere 9. (*let flow*) far scorrere; (*bath*) preparare 10. (*show: article*) pubblicare; (*series*) trasmettere 11. (*smuggle*) fare un traffico illegale di 12. (*not heed: blockade*) forzare; (*red light*) passare con 13. (*incur*) esporsi a; (*risk*) correre 14. (*perform tasks*) **to** ~ **errands** fare commissioni

◆**run about** *vi* correre da una parte all'altra
◆**run across** I. *vi* attraversare di corsa II. *vt* imbattersi in
◆**run after** *vt* correr dietro a

◆**run against** *vt* POL essere in competizione con

◆**run along** *vi* andarsene

◆**run away** *vi* scappare; (*water*) scorrer via

◆**run away with** *vt* scappare con

◆**run back** *vi* tornare di corsa

◆**run down** I. *vi* (*clock*) fermarsi; (*battery*) scaricarsi II. *vt* 1. (*run over*) investire 2. (*disparage*) parlar male di 3. (*capture*) catturare

◆**run in** I. *vi* entrare di corsa II. *vt* 1. AUTO rodare 2. *inf* (*capture*) portar dentro

◆**run into** *vt* imbattersi in; AUTO andare a sbattere contro

◆**run off** I. *vi* scappare; (*water*) scorrer via II. *vt* 1. (*water*) fare scorrere 2. TYPO stampare 3. (*make quickly*) produrre velocemente; (*letter*) buttar giù

◆**run on** *vi* 1. (*continue to run*) continuare a correre 2. (*conversation*) continuare; (*words*) essere attaccato (senza intervalli)

◆**run out of** *vi* finire

◆**run over** I. *vi* (*person*) correr su; (*fluid*) traboccare II. *vt* AUTO investire

◆**run through** *vt* 1. (*station*) passare in transito 2. (*money*) scialacquare

◆**run up** I. *vi* 1. salire di corsa 2. **to ~ against difficulties** imbattersi in difficoltà II. *vt* 1. (*flag*) alzare 2. (*make quickly*) fare rapidamente 3. (*debt*) accumulare; **to ~ debts** accumulare debiti

runaround ['rʌn·ə·'raʊnd] *n* **to give sb the ~** tirar fuori dei pretesti con qn

runaway ['rʌn·ə·weɪ] I. *adj* 1. (*train, horse*) fuori controllo; (*person*) scappato, -a via 2. (*enormous: success*) strepitoso, -a II. *n* fuggiasco, -a *m, f*

rundown [,rʌn·'daʊn] I. *n* 1. (*report*) resoconto *m;* **to give sb the ~ on sth** fare a qn il resoconto di qc 2. (*reduction*) ridimensionamento *m;* (*of staff*) riduzione *f* II. *adj* 1. (*building, town*) in stato d'abbandono 2. (*person*) esaurito, -a

rune [ru:n] *n* runa *f*

rung¹ [rʌŋ] *n* 1. (*ladder*) piolo *m* 2. (*level*) gradino *m*

rung² [rʌŋ] *pp of* **ring²**

run-in ['rʌn·ɪn] *n* 1. *inf* (*argument*) scontro *m* 2. (*prelude*) vigilia *f*

runner ['rʌ·nə] *n* 1. SPORTS (*person*) corridore, -trice *m, f;* (*horse*) cavallo *m* partecipante ad una corsa 2. (*messenger*) messo *m* 3. (*smuggler*) contrabbandiere, -a *m, f;* **drug ~** trafficante *mf* di droga 4. (*rail*) guida *f;* (*on sledge*) pattino *m* 5. (*stem*) stolone *m* 6. (*long rug*) passatoia *f*

runner-up [,rʌ·nə·'ʌp] *n* classificato, -a dopo il primo *m*

running I. *n* 1. (*action of a runner*) corsa *f* 2. (*operation*) direzione *f;* (*of a machine*) funzionamento *m;* **the day-to-day ~ of the business** la conduzione giornaliera degli affari ▸ **to be in/out of the ~** avere/non avere possibilità di vincere II. *adj* 1. (*consecutive*) di

seguito 2. (*ongoing*) in corso 3. (*operating*) in funzione 4. (*flowing*) che scorre

running back *n* SPORTS running back *m inv*

runny ['rʌ·ni] <-ier, -iest> *adj* (*sauce*) piuttosto liquido, -a

run-off ['rʌn·ɒf] *n* 1. POL ballottaggio *m* 2. SPORTS spareggio *m* 3. (*rainfall*) deflusso *m*

run-of-the-mill [,rʌn·əv·ðə·'mɪl] *adj* senza niente di speciale

runt [rʌnt] *n* 1. ZOOL animale *m* più piccolo, *di una figliata* 2. *inf* (*weakling*) esserino *m* insignificante

run-through ['rʌn·θru:] *n* THEAT, MUS prova *f;* **to have a ~ of sth** provare qc

run-up ['rʌn·ʌp] *n* 1. SPORTS rincorsa *f* 2. (*prelude*) periodo *m* precedente; **the ~ to sth** il periodo immediatamente precedente (a) qc

runway ['rʌn·weɪ] *n* pista *f*

rupee ['ruː·piː] *n* rupia *f*

rupture ['rʌp·tʃə] I. *vi* rompersi II. *vt* rompere; **to ~ oneself** procurarsi un'ernia III. *n* 1. (*act of bursting*) rottura *f* 2. (*hernia*) ernia *f*

rural ['rʊ·rəl] *adj* rurale

ruse [ruːz] *n* espediente *m*

rush¹ [rʌʃ] *n* BOT giunco *m*

rush² [rʌʃ] I. *n* 1. (*hurry*) fretta *f;* **to be in a ~** aver fretta; **to leave in a ~** andar via in tutta fretta 2. (*charge*) corsa *f;* (*attack*) attacco *m;* (*surge*) flusso *m;* (*of air*) folata *f;* (*of customers*) ondata *f;* **there's been a ~ on oil** c'è stata una corsa al petrolio; **gold ~** febbre *f* dell'oro 3. (*dizziness*) vampata *f* di calore (alla testa) II. *vi* andar di fretta III. *vt* 1. (*do quickly*) fare in maniera affrettata 2. (*hurry*) mettere fretta a 3. (*attack*) attaccare

◆**rush about** *vi* correre di qua e di là

◆**rush at** *vt* avventarsi su

◆**rush into** *vt* 1. **to ~ sth** buttarsi alla cieca in qc 2. **to rush sb into doing sth** metter fretta a qn perché faccia qc

◆**rush out** I. *vi* (*leave*) uscire precipitosamente II. *vt* (*publish*) precipitarsi a pubblicare

◆**rush through** *vt* portare avanti in tutta fretta

rush hour *n* ora *f* di punta

rush order *n* ordinazione *f* urgente

rusk [rʌsk] *n* biscotto *m* (duro)

russet ['rʌ·sɪt] *liter* I. *adj* (di) color ruggine II. *n* color *m* ruggine

russet potato *n* patata *f* rossa

Russia ['rʌ·ʃə] *n* Russia *f*

Russian ['rʌ·ʃən] I. *adj* russo, -a II. *n* 1. (*person*) russo, -a *m, f* 2. (*language*) russo *m*

rust [rʌst] I. *n* 1. (*decay; substance*) ruggine *f* 2. (*color*) color *m* ruggine II. *vi* arrugginirsi III. *vt* arrugginire

rust-colored *adj* (di) color ruggine

rustic ['rʌs·tɪk] *adj* 1. (*rural*) rustico, -a 2. (*simple, plain*) senza nessuna pretesa

rustle ['rʌ·sl] I. *vi* (*leaves*) stormire; (*paper*) frusciare II. *vt* 1. (*leaves*) far stormire; (*paper*) far frusciare 2. (*steal: cattle*) rubare III. *n* (*of leaves*) (lo) stormire; (*of paper*) fruscio *m*

R

rustler ['rʌs·lə] *n* ladro, -a *m, f* di bestiame

rustproof ['rʌst·pruːf] *adj* a prova di ruggine

rusty ['rʌs·ti] <-ier, -iest> *adj a.* *fig* arrugginito, -a; **my Spanish is a bit ~** il mio spagnolo è un po' arrugginito

rut¹ [rʌt] *n* solco *m* ▶ **to be stuck in a ~** essere preso dal solito tran-tran

rut² [rʌt] *n* ZOOL calore *m*

rutabaga [ˌruː·tə·'beɪ·gə] *n* ravizzone *m*

ruthless ['ruː·θ·ləs] *adj* (*person*) spietato, -a; (*ambition*) sfrenato, -a; **to be ~ in doing sth** essere spietato nel fare qc; **to be ~ in enforcing the law** essere inflessibile nel far rispettare la legge

ruthlessness *n* spietatezza *f*

RV [ˌɑːr·'viː] *abbr of* **recreational vehicle** camper *m inv*

Rwanda [rʊ·'ɑːn·də] *n* Ruanda *f*

Rwandan I. *adj* ruandese II. *n* ruandese *mf*

rye [raɪ] *n* segale *f*

S

S [es], **s** *n* S, s; **~ as in Sam** S come Savona

s [es] *abbr of* **second** s

S [es] *n abbr of* **south** S *m*

SA 1. *abbr of* **South Africa** Sudafrica *m* 2. *abbr of* **South America** Sudamerica *m*

Sabbath ['sæ·bəθ] *n* sabato *m* ebraico

sabbatical [sə·'bæ·ṭɪ·kl] UNIV I. *n* anno *m* sabbatico II. *adj* sabbatico, -a

saber ['seɪ·bə] *n* sciabola *f*

saber rattling ['sei·bə·ˌræt·lɪŋ] *n* *pej* minaccia *f* dell'uso della forza

sable ['seɪ·bl] *n* (*fur*) zibellino *m*

sabotage ['sæ·bə·tɑːʒ] I. *vt* sabotare II. *n* sabotaggio *m*

saboteur [ˌsæ·bə·'tɜːr] *n* sabotatore, -trice *m, f*

sac [sæk] *n* BIO, ANAT sacco *m*

saccharin ['sæ·kə·rɪn] *n* saccarina *f*

saccharine ['sæ·kə·ɪn] *adj pej* sdolcinato, -a

sachet [sæ·'ʃeɪ] *n* bustina *f*

sack¹ [sæk] I. *n* 1. (*large bag*) sacco *m;* (*paper or plastic bag*) busta *f* 2. (*amount in bag*) **a ~ of potatoes** un sacco di patate 3. *sl* (*bed*) **to hit the ~** andarsene a letto *inf* 4. *inf* (*dismissal*) **to get the ~** essere licenziato; **to give sb the ~** licenziare qu II. *vt* licenziare

sack² [sæk] I. *n* (*plundering*) saccheggio *m* II. *vt* (*plunder*) saccheggiare

sackcloth ['sæk·klɑːθ] *n* iuta *f*

sackful ['sæk·fʊl] *n* sacco *m*

sacking¹ ['sæ·kɪŋ] *n* 1. (*sackcloth*) iuta *f* 2. *inf* (*dismissal*) licenziamento *m*

sacking² ['sæ·kɪŋ] *n* (*plundering*) saccheggio *m*

sacrament ['sæ·krə·mənt] *n* (*ceremony*) sacramento *m;* **the ~** (*consecrated bread and wine*) il vino e l'ostia consacrati

sacramental [ˌsæ·krə·'men·ṭl] *adj* sacramentale

sacred ['seɪ·krɪd] *adj* sacro, -a; **to be ~ to sb** essere sacro per qu; **is nothing ~ to you?** c'è qualcosa che rispetti?

sacrifice ['sæ·krə·faɪs] I. *vt a.* REL sacrificare; **to ~ one's free time** sacrificare il proprio tempo libero II. *vi* **to ~ to the gods** fare sacrifici agli dei III. *n* sacrificio *m;* **at the ~ of sth** a scapito di qc

sacrilege ['sæ·krə·lɪdʒ] *n* sacrilegio *m*

sacrilegious [ˌsæ·krə·'lɪ·dʒəs] *adj* sacrilego, -a

sacristan ['sæ·krɪs·tən] *n* sagrestano *m*

sacristy ['sæ·krɪs·ti] *n* REL sagrestia *f*

sacrosanct ['sæ·krou·sæŋkt] *adj* sacrosanto, -a

sacrum ['seɪk·rəm] <-a> *n* osso *m* sacro

SAD [ˌes·eɪ·'diː] *n abbr of* **seasonal affective disorder** Das *m,* disordine *m* affettivo stagionale

sad [sæd] <-dd-> *adj* 1. (*unhappy, deplorable, shameful*) triste; **it is ~ that ...** è un peccato che ... +*subj;* **to make sb ~** rattristare qu; **to become ~** rattristarsi; **~ to say ...** triste a dirsi ... 2. (*pathetic*) patetico, -a

sadden ['sæ·dən] *vt* rattristare; **to be deeply ~ed** essere profondamente rattristato

saddle ['sæ·dl] I. *n* 1. (*seat*) sella *f;* (*on bycicle*) sellino *m* 2. CULIN sella *f* ▶ **to be in the ~** tenere le redini II. *vt* 1. (*horse*) sellare 2. *inf* (*burden*) **to ~ sb with sth** accollare qc a qu

saddlebag ['sæ·dl·bæg] *n* bisaccia *f*

saddler ['sæd·lə] *n* sellaio, -a *m, f*

saddle sore ['sæ·dl·sɔːe] *adj* con il posteriore indolenzito; **he's ~** gli fa male il posteriore

sadism ['sæ·dɪ·zəm] *n* sadismo *m*

sadist ['sæ·dɪst] *n* sadico, -a *m, f*

sadistic [sə·'dɪs·tɪk] *adj* sadico, -a

sadly *adv* 1. (*unhappily*) tristemente 2. (*regrettably*) disgraziatamente; **to be ~ mistaken** sbagliarsi di grosso

sadness ['sæd·nəs] *n* tristezza *f*

safari [sə·'fɑː·ri] *n* safari *m;* **to go on ~** fare un safari

safari park *n* zoo *m* safari

safe [seɪf] I. *adj* 1. (*free of danger*) sicuro, -a; (*driver*) prudente; **at a ~ distance** a distanza di sicurezza; **it is not ~ to ...** è pericoloso ... +*infin;* **just to be ~** per precauzione; **have a ~ trip!** buon viaggio! 2. (*secure*) salvo, -a; **to feel ~** sentirsi al sicuro; **to keep sth in a ~ place** tener qc in un posto sicuro; **to put sth somewhere ~** mettere qc al sicuro; **to win by a ~ margin** vincere con un ampio margine 3. (*certain*) sicuro, -a; **a ~ bet** una scommessa sicura 4. (*trustworthy*) affidabile; **to be in ~ hands** essere in buone mani 5. (*not out in baseball*) salvo, -a ▶ **to be on the ~ side ...** per maggior sicurezza, ...; **it is better to be ~ than sorry** *prov* prevenire è meglio che curare *prov;* **~ and sound** sano e salvo II. *n* cassaforte *f*

safecracker *n* scassinatore, -trice *m, f*
safe-deposit box *n* cassetta *f* di sicurezza
safeguard ['seɪf·gɑːrd] I. *vt* salvaguardare II. *vi* difendersi; **to ~ against sth** salvaguardarsi da qc III. *n* salvaguardia *f;* **as a ~ against sth** come tutela contro qc
safekeeping [ˌseɪf·'kiː·pɪŋ] *n* custodia *f;* **to be in sb's ~** essere sotto la custodia di qu
safely *adv* tranquillamente; **he arrived home ~** è arrivato a casa sano e salvo; **I can ~ say ...** posso dire in tutta certezza che ...
safe sex [seɪf·'seks] *n* sesso *m* sicuro
safety ['seɪf·ti] *n* **1.** (*being safe*) sicurezza *f;* **a place of ~** un posto sicuro; **for sb's ~** per la sicurezza di qu **2.** (*on gun*) sicura *f* **3.** (*football player*) safety *minv* (*difensore di secondaria nel football americano*) ▶**there's ~ in numbers** *prov* l'unione fa la forza *prov*
safety belt *n* cintura *f* di sicurezza
safety curtain *n* THEAT sipario *m* tagliafuoco
safety glass *n* vetro *m* infrangibile
safety margin *n* margine *m* di sicurezza
safety measures *npl* misure *fpl* di sicurezza
safety net *n* **1.** rete *f* di sicurezza **2.** *fig* protezione *f*
safety pin *n* spilla *f* da balia
safety razor *n* rasoio *m* di sicurezza
safety regulations *npl* norme *fpl* di sicurezza
safety valve *n* valvola *f* di sicurezza
saffron ['sæf·rən] *n* zafferano *m*
sag [sæg] I.<-gg-> *vi* **1.** (*droop*) curvarsi **2.** (*sink*) infossarsi; (*spirit*) venir meno; (*interest*) calare II. *n* **1.** (*drooping condition*) cedimento *m* **2.** (*fall*) calo *m*
saga ['sɑː·gə] *n* saga *f*
sagacious [sə·'geɪ·ʃəs] *adj form* sagace
sagacity [sə·'gæ·sə·ti] *n form* sagacità *f*
sage[1] [seɪdʒ] *liter* I. *adj* (*wise*) saggio, -a II. *n* (*wise man*) saggio *m*
sage[2] [seɪdʒ] *n* (*herb*) salvia *f*
Sagittarius [ˌsæ·dʒə·'te·ri·əs] *n* Sagittario *m*
Sahara [sə·'he·rə] *n* **the ~** (**Desert**) il (deserto del) Sahara
said [sed] I. *pp, pt of* **say** II. *adj* detto, -a
sail [seɪl] I. *n* **1.** (*on boat*) vela *f* **2.** (*windmill blade*) pala *f* ▶**to set ~** (*for a place*) salpare (verso un luogo); **under full ~** a vele spiegate II. *vi* **1.** (*travel*) navigare; **to ~ around the world** far il giro del mondo in barca (a vela) **2.** (*start voyage*) salpare **3.** (*move smoothly*) avanzare deciso **4.** *fig* (*do easily*) **to ~ through sth** fare qc con facilità ▶**to ~ against the wind** andare controcorrente; **to ~ close to the wind** camminare sul filo del rasoio III. *vt* **1.** (*manage: boat, ship*) governare **2.** (*navigate*) attraversare; **to ~ the seas** solcare i mari
sailboard ['seɪl·bɔːrd] *n* tavola *f* da windsurf
sailboarding *n* windsurf *m*
sailboat ['seɪl·boʊt] *n* barca *f* a vela
sailing *n* **1.** NAUT navigazione *f* **2.** SPORTS vela *f* **3.** (*departure*) partenza *f*
sailing ship *n*, **sailing vessel** *n* veliero *m*
sailor ['seɪ·lə] *n* **1.** (*seaman*) marinaio, -a *m, f*

2. SPORTS velista *mf*
sailor suit *n* tenuta *f* alla marinara
saint [seɪnt, sənt] *n* santo, -a *m, f*

---

i Il **Saint Patrick's Day**, il 17 marzo, non è un giorno festivo riconosciuto negli USA, ma sin dal 1737, la comunità irlandese degli Stati Uniti festeggia il suo santo patrono in tale data. Il 17 marzo si commemora la morte di San Patrizio, missionario irlandese, che consacrò la sua vita alla conversione dell'Irlanda alla religione cristiana. La tradizione vuole che per il **Saint Patrick's Day**, si portino il colore verde e un trifoglio, simboli della primavera e dell'Irlanda. Vengono organizzate feste e sfilate in tutto il paese, delle quali la sfilata più famosa è quella che ha luogo a New York.

---

sainted *adj* santo, -a; **my ~ aunt!** *fig* benedetta zia!
saintliness *n* santità *f*
saintly ['seɪnt·li] *adj* pio, -a; (*life*) esemplare
saint's day *n* onomastico *m*
sake[1] [seɪk] *n* **1.** (*purpose*) **for the ~ of sth** per qc **2.** (*benefit*) **for the ~ of sb** per qn ▶**for Christ's ~!** *pej* per Dio!; **for goodness ~!** per l'amor di Dio!; **for old times' ~** in memoria dei vecchi tempi
sake[2] *n*, **saki** ['sɑː·ki] *n* sakè *m*
salable ['seɪ·lə·bl] *adj* vendibile
salacious [sə·'leɪ·ʃəs] *adj pej* salace
salad ['sæ·ləd] *n* insalata *f*
salad bowl *n* insalatiera *f*
salad days *npl* anni *mpl* giovanili
salad dressing *n* condimento *m* per insalata
salami [sə·'lɑː·mi] *n* salame *m*
sal ammoniac [ˌsæl·ə·'moʊn·iæk] *n* sale *m* ammoniaco
salaried ['sæ·lə·rɪd] *adj* (*employee, staff*) stipendiato, -a
salary ['sæ·lə·ri] *n* stipendio *m*
salary cap *n* limite *m* massimo di ingaggio (*per un giocatore o una squadra*)
sale [seɪl] *n* **1.** (*act of selling*) vendita *f* **2.** (*reduced prices*) svendita *f;* **the ~s** i saldi; **benefit ~** vendita *f* di beneficienza; **end-of-season ~** saldi *f* di fine stagione **3.** (*auction*) asta *f* **4.** *pl* (*department that sells*) (ufficio *m*) vendite *fpl* ▶**to put sth up for ~** mettere in vendita qc; **for ~** in vendita; **on ~** in vendita
saleable ['seɪ·lə·bl] *adj s.* **vendibile**
sales associate *n* assistente *mf* alla vendita
sales check *n* scontrino *m*
salesclerk *n* commesso, -a *m, f*
sales executive *n* direttore, -trice *m, f* vendite
sales force *n* personale *m* di vendita
salesman *n* (*in shop*) commesso *m;* (*for company*) rappresentante *m* (di commercio); **door-to-door ~** venditore, -trice a domicilio *m*
salesmanship *n* arte *f* di vendere

S

salesperson *n* venditore, -trice *m, f*
sales pitch *n* imbonimento *m*
sales rep *n inf,* **sales representative** *n* rappresentante *mf* di commercio
sales revenue *n* fatturato *m*
sales tax *n* FIN imposta *f* sulle vendite
saleswoman *n* (*in a shop*) commessa *f;* (*seller*) venditrice *f*
salient ['seɪl·jənt] *adj a. fig* saliente
saline ['seɪ·liːn] I. *adj* salino, -a; ~ **drip** flebo *f* di soluzione salina II. *n* soluzione *f* salina
saliva [sə·'laɪ·və] *n* saliva *f*
salivate ['sæ·lə·veɪt] *vi* salivare
sallow ['sæ·loʊ] *adj* <-er, -est> (*skin, complexion*) giallastro, -a
salmon ['sæ·mən] *n* salmone *m;* **smoked ~** salmone affumicato
salmonella [ˌsæl·mə·'ne·lə] *n* 1. (*bacteria*) salmonella *f* 2. (*illness*) salmonellosi *f*
salmon farm *n* allevamento *m* di salmoni
salmon ladder *n* scala *m* di monta per la risalita dei salmoni
salmon trout *n* trota *f* salmonata
salon [se·'lɑːn] *n* 1. (*beauty establishment*) **beauty ~** salone *m* di bellezza 2. (*reception room*) salone *m*
saloon [sə·'luːn] *n* bar *m*
salsify ['sæl·sə·faɪ] *n* scorzonera *f*
salt [sɔːlt] I. *n* sale *m;* **bath ~s** sali da bagno; **smelling ~s** sali (per rinvenire) ►~ **of the earth** sale della terra; **to take sth with a grain of** ~ prendere qc con le molle; **to rub ~ in a wound** rigirare il coltello nella piaga; **to be worth** one's ~ essere degno di rispetto II. *vt* salare III. *adj* salato, -a
SALT [sɔːlt] *n abbr of* **Strategic Arms Limitation Talks** SALT *mpl,* negoziati *mpl* per la limitazione delle armi strategiche
salt mine *n* miniera *f* di salgemma
saltpeter ['sɔːlt·ˌpiː·ţə] *n* salnitro *m*
saltshaker *n* saliera *f*
salt water *n* acqua *f* salata
saltwater ['sɔːlt·ˌwɑː·ţə] *adj* d'acqua salata
salty ['sɔːl·ti] *adj* (*taste*) salato, -a
salubrious [sə·'luː·bri·əs] *adj form* salubre
salutary ['sæl·jə·te·ri] *adj* salutare
salutation [ˌsæl·jə·'teɪ·ʃən] *n* saluto *m*
salute [sə·'luːt] I. *vt* 1. *a.* MIL salutare 2. *fig* (*honor*) rendere onore a II. *vi a.* MIL salutare III. *n* MIL 1. (*hand gesture*) saluto *m* 2. (*ceremonial firing of guns*) salva *f*
Salvadorian [ˌsæl·və·'dɔː·ri·ən] I. *adj* salvadoregno, -a II. *n* salvadoregno, -a *m, f*
salvage ['sæl·vɪdʒ] I. *vt* salvare II. *n* 1. (*retrieval*) salvataggio *m* 2. (*things saved*) oggetti *mpl* recuperati
salvage operation *n* operazione *f* di salvataggio
salvage vessel *n* imbarcazione *f* di salvataggio
salvation [sæl·'veɪ·ʃən] *n* salvezza *f*
Salvation Army *n* Esercito *m* della Salvezza
salve [sæv] I. *n* 1. (*ointment*) unguento *m* 2. *fig* balsamo *m* II. *vt* curare; *fig* (*conscience*)

mettere a posto
salvo ['sæl·voʊ] <-(e)s> *n* salva *f;* **to fire a ~** sparare a salve; ~ **of applause** scroscio *m* di applausi
sal volatile [ˌsæl·voʊ·'læ·ţə·li] *n* sale *m* ammoniaco
SAM [sæm] *n abbr of* **surface-to-air missile** missile *m* terra-aria
same [seɪm] I. *adj* 1. (*identical*) stesso, -a; **the ~** (**as sb/sth**) uguale (a qu/qc); **to go the ~ way** (**as sb**) andare nella stessa direzione (di qu) 2. (*not another*) stesso, -a; **the ~** lo stesso; **at the ~ time** allo stesso tempo, contemporaneamente 3. (*unvarying*) stesso, -a, medesimo, -a ► **to be one and the ~** essere lo stesso; **by the ~ token** nello stesso modo II. *pron* 1. (*nominal*) **the ~** lo stesso, la stessa; **she's much the ~** è più o meno uguale; **it's always the ~** è sempre la stessa cosa 2. (*adverbial*) **it's all the ~ to me** per me è lo stesso; **it's not the ~ as before** non è più la stessa cosa; **all the ~** in ogni caso; ~ **to you** altrettanto III. *adv* uguale; **to spell two words the ~** scrivere due parole nello stesso modo
sameness *n* 1. (*similarity*) uguaglianza *f* 2. (*monotony*) ripetitività *f*
Samoa [sə·'moʊ·ə] *n* Samoa *f*
Samoan I. *adj* samoano, -a II. *n* samoano, -a *m, f*
sample ['sæm·pl] I. *n* campione *m;* **free ~** campione gratuito; **urine ~** campione di urina II. *vt* 1. (*try*) provare 2. (*survey*) sondare
sampler ['sæm·plə] *n* 1. (*person*) campionatore, -trice *m, f* 2. (*device*) campionatore *m* 3. (*embroidery*) imparaticcio *m* 4. (*collection*) campione *m* 5. MUS campionatore *m* (musicale)
sampling ['sæmp·lɪŋ] *n* campionamento *m*
sanatorium [ˌsæ·nə·'tɔː·ri·əm] <-s *o* -ria> *n* casa *f* di cura
sanctify ['sæŋk·tɪ·faɪ] <-ie-> *vt* 1. REL santificare 2. *fig* (*legitimize*) sancire
sanctimonious [ˌsæŋk·tɪ·'moʊ·ni·əs] *adj pej* bigotto, -a
sanction ['sæŋk·ʃən] I. *n* 1. (*approval*) autorizzazione *f;* **to give one's ~ to sth** dare la propria approvazione a qc 2. LAW, POL sanzione *f* II. *vt* 1. (*authorize*) autorizzare 2. (*approve*) sanzionare 3. (*penalize*) sanzionare
sanctity ['sæŋk·tə·ti] *n* 1. REL (*holiness*) santità *f* 2. (*sacredness*) inviolabilità *f*
sanctuary ['sæŋk·tʃu·e·ri] *n* <-ies> 1. REL (*holy place*) santuario *m* 2. (*area around altar*) sagrato *m* 3. (*place of refuge*) rifugio *m;* **to seek ~ in sth** rifugiarsi in qc 4. (*area for animals*) riserva *f;* **wildlife ~** riserva naturale
sand [sænd] I. *n* sabbia *f;* **fine/coarse ~** sabbia fina/grossa; **grains of ~** granelli *mpl* di sabbia ► **the ~s of time are running out** il tempo vola II. *vt* 1. (*make smooth*) carteggiare; (*floor*) levigare 2. (*cover with sand*) spargere sabbia su
sandal ['sæn·dl] *n* sandalo *m*
sandalwood ['sæn·dl·wʊd] *n* sandalo *m*

sandbag ['sænd·bæg] I. *n* sacco *m* di sabbia II. <-gg-> *vt* proteggere con sacchi di sabbia

sandbank ['sænd·bæŋk] *n*, **sandbar** ['sænd·bɑːr] *n* banco *m* di sabbia

sandblast ['sænd·blæst] *vt* sabbiare

sandbox *n* recinto *m* con la sabbia (*dove giocano i bambini*)

sandcastle *n* castello *m* di sabbia

sand dune *n* duna *f*

sand flea *n* pulce *f* di mare

sandpaper ['sænd·peɪ·pəʳ] I. *n* carta *f* vetrata II. *vt* carteggiare

sandpiper ['sænd·ˌpaɪ·pəʳ] *n* piovanello *m*

sandstone *n* arenaria *f*

sandstorm *n* tempesta *f* di sabbia

sandwich ['sænd·wɪtʃ] I. <-es> *n* panino *m;* (*made with sliced bread*) tramezzino *m* II. *vt* **be -ed between** essere (schiacciato, -a) in mezzo a

sandwich board *n cartellone pubblicitario portato da un uomo sandwich*

sandwich man <- -men> *n* uomo *m* sandwich

sandy ['sæn·di] *adj* <-ier, -iest> sabbioso, -a; (*hair*) rossiccio, -a

sane [seɪn] *adj* 1. (*of sound mind*) sano, -a di mente 2. (*sensible*) sensato, -a

sang [sæŋ] *pt of* sing

sanguine ['sæŋ·gwɪn] *adj form* fiducioso, -a

sanitarium [ˌsæ·nɪ·ˈte·ri·əm] <-s *o* -ria> *n* sanatorio *m*

sanitary ['sæ·nɪ·te·ri] *adj* 1. (*relating to hygiene*) sanitario, -a 2. (*clean*) igienico, -a

sanitary napkin *n*, **sanitary pad** *n* assorbente *m* (igienico)

sanitation [ˌsæ·nɪ·ˈteɪ·ʃən] *n* impianti *mpl* igienici

sanity ['sæ·nə·ti] *n* 1. (*of person*) sanità *f* mentale 2. (*of decision*) buonsenso *m*

sank [sæŋk] *pt of* sink

Santa (Claus) ['sæn·t̬ə·ˌklɑːz] *n* Babbo *m* Natale

sap[1] [sæp] *n* 1. BOT linfa *f* 2. (*vitality*) **to feel the ~ rising** sentirsi rinvigorito

sap[2] [sæp] <-pp-> *vt* 1. (*weaken*) minare 2. MIL scavare le fondamenta di

sap[3] [sæp] *n inf* (*fool*) fesso, -a *m, f*

sapling ['sæp·lɪŋ] *n* albero *m* giovane

sapper ['sæ·pəʳ] *n* soldato *m* del genio

sapphire ['sæ·faɪ·əʳ] I. *n* 1. (*stone*) zaffiro *m* 2. (*color*) blu *m* zaffiro II. *adj* 1. (*necklace, ring*) di zaffiri 2. (*color*) blu zaffiro *inv*

sarcasm ['sɑːr·kæ·zəm] *n* sarcasmo *m*

sarcastic [sɑːr·ˈkæs·tɪk] *adj* sarcastico, -a

sarcophagus [sɑːr·ˈkɑː·fə-] <-es *o* -gi> *n* sarcofago *m*

sardine [sɑːr·ˈdiːn] *n* sardina *f* ▶**to be packed (in) like ~s** essere come sardine in scatola

Sardinia [sɑːr·ˈdɪn·iə] *n* Sardegna *f*

Sardinian I. *n* sardo, -a *m, f f* II. *adj* sardo, -a

sardonic [sɑːr·ˈdɑː·nɪk] *adj* sardonico, -a

sari ['sɑː·ri] *n* sari *m inv*

sartorial [sɑːr·ˈtɔː·ri·əl] *adj* ~ **elegance** eleganza nel vestire

SASE [ˌes·eɪ·es·ˈiː] *n abbr of* **self-addressed stamped envelope** *busta affrancata con il proprio indirizzo*

sash[1] [sæʃ] <-es> *n* fascia *f*

sash[2] [sæʃ] <-es> *n* ARCHIT telaio *m* di finestra a ghigliottina

sash window *n* ARCHIT finestra *f* a ghigliottina

sat [sæt] *pt, pp of* sit

SAT *n abbr of* **scholastic aptitude test** esame *m* attitudinale al termine delle scuole superiori (*utilizzato dalle università come criterio di ammissione*)

Satan ['seɪ·t̬ən] *n* Satana *m*

satanic [sə·ˈtæ·nɪk] *adj* satanico, -a

Satanism *n* satanismo *m*

satchel ['sæt·ʃəl] *n* cartella (della scuola) *f*

sate [seɪt] *vt form* saziare; **to ~ sb (with sth)** rimpinzare qc (di qc); **to be ~d (with sth)** essere sazio (di qc)

satellite ['sæ·t̬ə·laɪt] I. *n* 1. ASTR, TECH satellite *m* 2. (*country*) satellite II. *adj* TECH via satellite

satellite broadcasting *n* trasmissione *f* via satellite

satellite dish *n* antenna *f* parabolica

satellite state *n* stato *m* satellite

satellite television *n* televisione *f* via satellite

satiate ['seɪ·ʃi·eɪt] *vt* saziare

satiety [sə·ˈtaɪ·ə·ti] *n form* sazietà *f*

satin ['sæ·tn] I. *n* raso *m* II. *adj* (*finish, paper*) satinato, -a

satire ['sæ·taɪ·əʳ] *n* LIT satira *f*

satirical [sə·ˈtɪ·rɪ·kl] *adj* satirico, -a

satirist ['sæ·t̬ə·rɪst] *n* scrittore, -trice *m, f* satirico, -a

satirize ['sæ·t̬ə·raɪz] *vt* satireggiare

satisfaction [ˌsæ·t̬ɪs·ˈfæk·ʃən] *n* 1. soddisfazione *f*; **to derive ~ from sth** trarre soddisfazione da qc; **to do sth to sb's ~** soddisfare qu facendo qc; **to be a ~ (to sb)** essere una soddisfazione (per qu) 2. (*compensation*) riparazione *f*

satisfactory [ˌsæ·t̬ɪs·ˈfæk·t̬ə·ri] *adj* soddisfacente; SCHOOL sufficente

satisfy ['sæ·t̬əs·faɪ] <-ie-> *vt* 1. (*person, desire*) soddisfare 2. (*condition*) soddisfare 3. (*convince*) convincere; **to ~ sb that ...** convincere qu che ... 4. (*debt*) saldare

satisfying *adj* soddisfacente

saturate ['sæ·tʃə·reɪt] *vt* 1. (*soak*) impregnare; **to be ~d in tradition** essere imbevuto di tradizione 2. (*fill to capacity*) saturare; **to ~ the market** saturare il mercato

saturation [ˌsæ·tʃə·ˈreɪ·ʃən] *n* saturazione *f*

saturation point *n* punto *m* di saturazione; **to reach ~** arrivare al punto di saturazione

Saturday ['sæ·t̬ə·deɪ] *n* sabato *m; s.a.* **Friday**

Saturn ['sæ·t̬ən] *n* Saturno *m*

satyr ['seɪ·t̬əʳ] *n* satiro *m*

sauce [sɑːs] *n* 1. salsa *f*; **tomato ~** sugo di pomodoro 2. (*impertinence*) sfacciataggine *f*

sauceboat *n* salsiera *f*

S

saucepan ['sɑːs·pən] *n* casseruola *f*

saucer ['sɑː·sə·] *n* piattino *m*

saucily ['sɑː·sɪ·li] *adv* sfacciatamente

sauciness ['sɑː·sɪ·nəs] *n* sfacciataggine *f*

saucy ['sɑː·si] *adj* <-ier, -iest> sfacciato, -a

Saudi Arabia [ˌsaʊ·di ə·'reɪ·bi·ə] *n* Arabia *f* Saudita

Saudi Arabian [ˌsaʊ·di ə·'reɪ·bi·ən] I. *n* saudita *mf* II. *adj* saudita

sauerkraut ['saʊ·ə·kraʊt] *n* crauti *mpl*

sauna ['saʊː·nə] *n* sauna *f*

saunter ['sɑːn·t̮ə·] I. *vi* passeggiare II. *n* passeggiata *f*

sausage ['sɑː·sɪdʒ] *n* salsiccia *f;* (*cured*) salame *m*

sausage meat *n* carne *f* di salsiccia

sauté [soʊ·'teɪ] *vt* saltare

savage ['sæ·vɪdʒ] I. *adj* 1. (*fierce*) feroce 2. *inf* (*bad-tempered*) con un caratteraccio II. *n pej* selvaggio, -a *m, f* III. *vt* 1. (*attack*) attaccare selvaggiamente 2. (*criticize*) attaccare violentemente

savagely *adv* 1. (*attack*) selavaggiamente 2. (*criticize*) violentemente

savagery *n* ferocia *f*

savanna(h) [sə·'væ·nə] *n* savana *f*

save¹ [seɪv] I. *vt* 1. (*rescue*) salvare; **to ~ sb's life** salvare la vita a qu; **to ~ one's soul** salvarsi l'anima; **to ~ face** salvarsi la faccia; **to ~ one's own skin** salvarsi la pelle 2. (*keep for future use*) conservare 3. (*collect*) raccogliere 4. (*avoid wasting*) risparmiare 5. (*reserve: place*) tenere 6. (*prevent from doing*) **to save sb sth** risparmiare qc a qu; **to save sb doing sth** evitare a qu di fare qc 7. COMPUT salvare 8. SPORTS parare II. *vi* 1. (*keep for the future*) risparmiare; **to ~ for sth** risparmiare per qc 2. (*conserve*) **to ~ on sth** risparmiare qc III. *n* SPORTS parata *f*

save² [seɪv] *prep* ~ (**for**) tranne; **all ~ the youngest** tutti tranne i più giovani

saver ['seɪ·vəɾ] *n* risparmiatore, -trice *m, f*

saving ['seɪ·vɪŋ] I. *n* 1. *pl* (*money*) risparmi *mpl* 2. (*economy*) risparmio *m* 3. (*rescue*) salvataggio *m* II. *adj* **his ~ grace** l'unica cosa che lo salva III. *prep* eccetto

savings account ['seɪ·vɪŋ·zə·ˌkaʊnt] *n* conto *m* (di) deposito

savings bank *n* cassa *f* di risparmio

savior ['seɪv·jəɾ] *n* salvatore, -trice *m, f*

savor ['seɪ·vəɾ] I. *n* 1. (*taste*) gusto *m,* sapore *m* 2. (*pleasure*) gusto *m* II. *vt* gustare

savory ['seɪ·və·ri] *adj* 1. (*salty*) salato, -a 2. (*appetizing*) gustoso, -a; (*smell, taste*) appetitoso, -a 3. (*socially acceptable*) rispettabile

Savoy [sə·'vɔɪ] *n* Savoia *f*

savoy (**cabbage**) *n* verza *f*

savvy ['sæ·vi] *inf* I. *adj* <-ier, -iest> sensato, -a II. *n* buonsenso *m*

saw¹ [sɑː] *pt of* see

saw² [sɑː] I. *n* sega *f;* **power ~** sega elettrica II. <sawed, sawed *o* sawn> *vt* segare

saw³ [sɑː] *n* detto *m*

sawdust ['sɑː·dʌst] *n* segatura *f*

sawed-off shotgun *n* fucile *m* a canne mozze

sawmill ['sɑː·mɪl] *n* segheria *f*

sawn [sɑːn] *pp of* saw

Saxon [sæk·sən] I. *n* sassone *mf* II. *adj* sassone

Saxony ['sæk·sə·ni] *n* Sassonia *f*

saxophone ['sæk·sə·foʊn] *n* sassofono *m*

saxophonist ['sæk·sə·foʊ·nɪst] *n* sassofonista *mf*

say [seɪ] I. <said, said> *vt* 1. (*speak*) dire; **to ~ sth to sb's face** dire qc a qu in faccia; **~ no more!** non dire altro! 2. (*state information*) **to ~ (that)** ... dire che...; **to have something/nothing to ~ (to sb)** avere qualcosa/non aver niente da dire (a qu); **to ~ goodbye to sb** salutare qu 3. (*express*) dire 4. (*think*) dire; **people ~ that** ... si dice che...; **to ~ to oneself** dirsi 5. (*recite*) dire 6. (*indicate*) dire; **to ~ sth about sb/sth** dire qc su qu/qc; **the clock says it's 6 o'clock** l'orologio fa le sei; **the said sb/sth** ... *form* detto qu/qc ... 7. (*convey meaning*) significare 8. *inf* (*suggest*) dire 9. (*tell*) dire; **to ~ where/when** dire dove/quando; **it's not for me to ~** ... non sta a me dire ... 10. (*for instance*) (*let's*) **~** ... diciamo ... ▶**when all is said and done** in fin dei conti; **having said that,** ... detto ciò,...; **to ~ when** dire basta; **you don't ~ (so**!) sul serio?; **you said it!** *inf* a chi lo dici! II. <said, said> *vi* **I'll ~!** *inf* eccome!; **I must ~** ... devo ammettere che ...; **not to ~** ... per non dire ...; **that is to ~** ... cioè ... III. *n* parere *m;* **to have one's ~** esprimere il proprio parere; **to have a ~ in sth** aver voce in capitolo in qc IV. *interj* (*positive reaction*) ottimo!; **~, that's a great idea!** benissimo, è un'ottima idea!

saying ['seɪ·ɪŋ] *n* 1. (*proverb*) detto *m; as the ~ goes* come dice il detto 2. **it goes without ~** è ovvio

say-so ['seɪ·soʊ] *n inf* 1. (*authority*) **to have the final ~** avere l'ultima parola 2. (*approval*) approvazione *m;* **to get the ~** ottenere l'approvazione 3. (*assertion*) affermazione *f; don't just believe it on my ~* non devi crederci solo perché lo dico io

SC *n abbr of* **South Carolina** Carolina *f* del sud

scab [skæb] *n* 1. (*over wound*) crosta *f* 2. *pej, sl* (*strikebreaker*) crumiro, -a *m, f* 3. BOT, ZOOL rogna *f*

scabbard ['skæ·bəd] *n* guaina *f*

scabby ['skæ·bi] *adj* <-ier, -iest> 1. (*having scabs*) pieno, -a di croste 2. ZOOL rognoso, -a 3. *pej, sl* (*disgusting*) schifoso, -a

scabies ['skeɪ·bi:z] *n* MED scabbia *f*

scabrous ['skæb·rəs] *adj* scabroso, -a

scaffold ['skæ·fld] *n* 1. (*for execution*) forca *f* 2. (*for building*) impalcatura *f*

scaffolding ['skæ·fəl·dɪŋ] *n* implacature *fpl*

scald [skɑːld] I. *vt* 1. (*burn*) scottare 2. (*clean*) sterilizzare (con acqua bollente) 3. (*heat: milk*) scaldare II. *n* MED scottatura *f*

scalding ['skɑːl·dɪŋ] *adj* ~ (**hot**) bollente

scale¹ [skeɪl] **I.** *n* **1.**ZOOL squama *f* **2.**MED tartaro *m;* TECH calcare *m* **II.** *vt* **1.**(*remove scales*) squamare **2.** MED togliere il tartaro da; TECH togliere il calcare da

scale² [skeɪl] *n* (*weighing device*) piatto *m* (di bilancia); ~s bilancia *f* ▶ **to tip the** ~s far pendere la bilancia

scale³ [skeɪl] **I.** *n* (*range, magnitude, proportion*) *a.* MUS scala *f;* **a sliding** ~ ECON una scala mobile; **on a large/small** ~ su larga/piccola scala; **to draw sth to** ~ disegnare qc in scala **II.** *vt* **1.**(*climb*) scalare; **to** ~ **the heights** (of sth) scalare le vette (di qc) **2.**TECH, ARCHIT ridurre in scala

◆**scale down** *vt* (*demand, expectations*) ridurre

scale drawing *n* TECH, ARCHIT disegno *m* in scala

scale model *n* modello *m* in scala

scallop [ˈskɑːləp] *n* capasanta *f;* ~ (**shell**) conchiglia *f* di capasanta

scalp [skælp] **I.** *n* **1.**(*head skin*) cuoio *m* capelluto **2.**(*war trophy*) scalpo *m;* **to be out after sb's** ~ voler la testa di qu **II.** *vt* **1.** *inf* (*resell*) rivendere a prezzo maggiorato **2.**(*in war*) **to** ~ **sb** scalpare qu; *iron* rapare a zero qu

scalpel [ˈskælpəl] *n* MED bisturi *m*

scalper *SUBST UBST* bagarino, -a *m, f*

scaly [ˈskeɪli] *adj* <-ier, -iest> **1.**ZOOL squamato, -a **2.** MED (*skin*) secco, -a

scam [skæm] *n inf* raggiro *m*

scamper [ˈskæmpə] *vi* sgambettare

scampi [ˈskæmpi] *npl* scampi *mpl* all'aglio

scan [skæn] **I.**<-nn-> *vt* **1.**(*scrutinize*) scrutare **2.**(*look through quickly*) dare una scorsa a **3.**MED fare un'ecografia di **4.**LIT scandire **5.**COMPUT scannerizzare **II.**<-nn-> *vi* scandirsi **III.** *n* COMPUT scansione *f;* MED ecografia *f*

scandal [ˈskændl] *n* **1.**(*public outrage*) scandalo *m;* **to uncover** [*o* **expose**] **a** ~ far emergere uno scandalo; **to cover up a** ~ soffocare uno scandalo **2.**(*sth bad*) **what a** ~! che scandalo! **3.**(*gossip*) notizie *f* scandalistiche *pl;* **to spread** ~ divulgare notizie scandalistiche

scandalize [ˈskændəlaɪz] *vt* scandalizzare

scandalmonger [ˈskændlˌmɑːŋgə] *n pej* malalingua *f*

scandalous [ˈskændələs] *adj* **1.**(*spreading scandal*) scandaloso, -a **2.**(*disgraceful*) scandaloso, -a; **it is** ~ **that ...** è scandaloso che ... +*subj*

Scandinavia [ˌskændɪˈneɪviə] *n* Scandinavia *f*

Scandinavian I. *adj* scandinavo, -a **II.** *n* scandinavo, -a *m, f*

scanner [ˈskænə] *n* COMPUT scanner *m inv*

scanning *n* COMPUT, MED scansione *f*

scant [skænt] *adj* scarso, -a; ~ **attention** poca attenzione

scantily *adv* scarsamente; ~ **dressed** [*o* **clad**] in abiti succinti

scanty [ˈskænti] *adj* **1.**(*very small*) scarso, -a; (*clothing*) succinto, -a **2.**(*insufficient*) insuffi-

ciente

scapegoat [ˈskeɪpgoʊt] *n* capro *m* espiatorio; **to be a** ~ **for sb/sth** essere il capro espiatorio di qu/qc

scapula [ˈskæpjʊlə] <-s *o* -lae> *pl n* scapola *f*

scar [skɑːr] **I.** *n* **1.**MED (*on skin*) cicatrice *f;* **to leave a** ~ lasciare una cicatrice **2.**(*mark of damage*) segno *m* **3.**PSYCH trauma *m* **4.**GEO dirupo *m* **II.**<-rr-> *vt* lasciare una cicatrice a; **to be ~red** (**by sth**) avere una cicatrice (causata da qc); **to be ~red for life** farsi una cicatrice permanente **III.**<-rr-> *vi* **to** ~ (**over**) cicatrizzarsi

scarab [ˈskerəb] *n* scarabeo *m*

scarce [skers] *adj* scarso, -a; **to make oneself** ~ *inf* filarsela

scarcely [ˈskersli] *adv* **1.**(*barely*) appena **2.**(*certainly not*) per niente

scarcity [ˈskersəti] *n* scarsezza *f*

scare [sker] **I.** *vt* spaventare; **to** ~ **sb into/out of doing sth** spaventare qu perché faccia/non faccia qc; **to be ~d stiff** essere paralizzato dalla paura; **to** ~ **sb shitless** *vulg* far venire un colpo a qu **II.** *vi* spaventarsi; **to (not)** ~ **easily** (non) spaventarsi facilmente **III.** *n* **1.**(*fright*) spavento *m;* **to have a** ~ prendersi uno spavento; **to give sb a** ~ spaventare qu **2.**(*panic*) panico *m*

◆**scare away** *vt,* **scare off** *vt* far scappare

scarecrow [ˈskerkroʊ] *n* spaventapasseri *m inv*

scaremonger [ˈskerˌmɑːŋgə] *n pej* allarmista *mf*

scarf [skɑːrf, *pl* skɑːrvz] <-ves *o* -s> *n* (*around neck*) sciarpa *f;* (*around head*) foulard *m inv*

◆**scarf down** *vt sl* buttar giù

scarlet [ˈskɑːrlət] **I.** *n* scarlatto *m* **II.** *adj* scarlatto, -a; **to turn** ~ diventare rosso

scarlet fever *n* MED scarlattina *f*

scarp [skɑːrp] *n* scarpata *f*

scary [ˈskeri] *adj* <-ier, -iest> spaventoso, -a; ~ **movie** film *m* del terrore *inv*

scat [skæt] *interj inf* sciò

scathing [ˈskeɪðɪŋ] *adj* mordace

scatological [ˌskætəˈlɑːdʒɪkəl] *adj form* scatologico, -a

scatter [ˈskætə] **I.** *vt* sparpagliare; **to** ~ **sth with sth** disseminare qc di qc; **to** ~ **sth to the four winds** sparpagliare qc dappertutto **II.** *vi* sparpagliarsi; **to** ~ **in all directions** sparpagliarsi in tutte le direzioni

scatterbrain [ˈskætəbreɪn] *n pej* sbadato *m*

scatterbrained *adj* sbadato, -a

scattered *adj* sparso, -a

scavenge [ˈskævɪndʒ] *vi* **1.**(*search*) rovistare nei rifiuti **2.**ZOOL cercare cibo

scavenger [ˈskævɪndʒə] *n* **1.**ZOOL *animale che si nutre di carogne* **2.**(*person*) *persona che rovista nei rifiuti alla ricerca di oggetti, cibo*

scenario [səˈnerioʊ] *n* **1.**(*situation*) ipotesi *f* **2.**THEAT, LIT sceneggiatura *f*

S

scene [si:n] *n* **1.** THEAT, CINE (*unit of drama*) scena *f;* (*setting*) scenario *m;* **nude** ~ scena *f* di nudo; **behind the** ~**s** *a. fig* dietro le quinte **2.** (*locality*) luogo *m;* **the** ~ **of the crime** la scena del delitto **3.** (*view*) vista *f* **4.** (*milieu*) ambiente *m;* **the art/drugs** ~ l'ambiente dell'arte/della droga; **this is/isn't my** ~ *inf* non fa per me; **to appear on the** ~ presentarse; **to depart from the political** ~ ritirarsi dalla scena politica; **to set the** ~ **for sth** creare i presupposti per qc **5.** (*embarrassing incident*) scena *f;* **to make a** ~ fare una scenata

scenery ['si:·nə·ri] *n* **1.** (*landscape*) paesaggio *m* **2.** THEAT, CINE scenario *m;* **to blend into the** ~ passare inosservato

scenic ['si:·nɪk] *adj* **1.** THEAT scenico, -a **2.** (*of beautiful scenery*) pittoresco, -a; ~ **road** strada *f* panoramica

scent [sent] I. *n* **1.** (*aroma*) profumo *m* **2.** (*in hunting*) scia *f;* **to be on the** ~ **of sth/sb** essere sulle tracce di qc/qn; **to put** [*o* **throw**] **sb off the** ~ depistare qu **3.** (*perfume*) profumo *m* II. *vt* **1.** (*smell*) sentire **2.** (*sense, detect*) subodorare; **to** ~ **that ...** sospettare che ... **3.** (*apply perfume*) profumare

scent bottle *n* bottiglietta *f* di profumo

scentless *adj* inodore

scepter ['sep·tə·] *n* scettro *m*

sceptic ['skep·tɪk] *n* scettico, -a *m, f*

sceptical *adj* scettico, -a

scepticism ['skep·tɪ·sɪ·zəm] *n* scetticismo *m*

schedule ['ske·dʒu:l] I. *n* **1.** (*timetable*) orario *m;* **bus** ~ orario degli autobus; **flight** ~ orario dei voli; **to stick to a** ~ attenersi a quanto previsto; **everything went according to** ~ tutto è andato come previsto **2.** (*plan of work*) programma *m* **3.** FIN listino *m* II. *vt* **1.** (*plan*) programmare **2.** (*list*) fare una lista di

scheduled *adj* programmato, -a; ~ **flight** volo *m* di linea

schematic [ski·'mæ·tɪk] *adj* schematico, -a

scheme [ski:m] I. *n* **1.** (*structure*) schema *m* **2.** (*plot*) intrigo *m* II. *vi pej* tramare; **to** ~ **to do sth** tramare per fare qc

schemer ['ski:·mə·] *n* intrigante *mf*

scheming ['ski:·mɪŋ] *adj* intrigante

schism ['skɪ·zəm] *n* scisma *m*

schismatic [sɪz·'mæ·tɪk] REL I. *adj* scismatico, -a II. *n* scismatico, -a *m, f*

schist [ʃɪst] *n* GEO scisto *m*

schizophrenia [ˌskɪ·tsə·'fri:·niə] *n* schizofrenia *f*

schizophrenic [ˌskɪ·tsə·'fre·nɪk] I. *adj* schizofrenico, -a II. *n* schizofrenico, -a *m, f*

scholar ['skɑ:·lə·] *n* **1.** (*learned person*) erudito, -a *m, f* **2.** (*student*) studente *mf* **3.** (*scholarship holder*) borsista *mf*

scholarly *adj* erudito, -a

scholarship ['skɑ:·lə·ʃɪp] *n* **1.** (*learning*) erudizione *f* **2.** (*grant*) borsa *f* (di studio)

scholastic [skə·'læs·tɪk] *adj* accademico, -a

school[1] [sku:l] I. *n* **1.** (*institution*) scuola *f;* **primary** ~ scuola elementare; **secondary** ~

scuola superiore; **public** ~ scuola pubblica; **dancing** ~ scuola di ballo; **driving** ~ scuola-guida *f;* **to be in** ~ andare a scuola; **to go to** ~ andare a scuola; **to start** ~ comiciare la scuola; **to leave** ~ finire la scuola **2.** (*buildings*) scuola *f* **3.** (*classes*) classi *fpl* **4.** (*university division*) facoltà *f* **5.** (*university*) università *f* II. *vt* formare III. *adj* scolastico, -a

i Lo **school system** americano comincia con l'*elementary school*, che corrisponde alla scuola elementare italiana e al primo anno della scuola media. In alcune regioni, dopo il *sixth grade*, corrispondente alla prima media, gli alunni frequentano altri due anni di scuola, la *junior high school* (corrispondente agli ultimi due anni della scuola media inferiore). Gli alunni frequentano quindi la *high school* per tre anni. Nelle regioni nelle quali non esiste la *junior high school*, gli alunni, dopo otto anni di *elementary school*, passano direttamente alla *high school*, che inizia quindi dal *ninth grade*, l'equivalente del primo anno della scuola superiore italiana. La scuola termina dovunque con il *twelfth grade*, cioè, dopo dodici anni complessivi.

school[2] [sku:l] *n* ZOOL banco *m*

school board *n* ADMIN consiglio *m* scolastico

school bus *n* scuolabus *m inv*

school day *n* (*day*) giorno *m* di scuola

school district *n* distretto *m* scolastico

schooling *n* istruzione *f*

schoolmate *n* compagno, -a *m, f* di scuola

school nurse *n* infermiera *f* della scuola

schoolteacher *n* professore, -essa *m, f*

schoolwork *n* compiti (*da fare a scuola o a casa*)

schoolyard *n* cortile *m* della scuola

schooner ['sku:·nə·] *n* **1.** NAUT schooner *m inv* **2.** (*tall glass*) bicchiere alto da birra

sciatic [saɪ·'æ·tɪk] *adj* sciatico, -a

sciatica [saɪ·'æ·tɪ·kə] *n* MED sciatica *f*

science ['saɪ·ənts] I. *n* scienza *f;* **pure/applied** ~ scienze *fpl* pure/applicate; **the wonders of modern** ~ i prodigi della scienza moderna II. *adj* scientifico, -a

science fiction I. *n* fantascienza *f* II. *adj* fantascientifico

scientific [ˌsaɪ·ən·'tɪ·fɪk] *adj* scientifico, -a

scientist ['saɪ·ən·tɪst] *n* scienziato, -a *m, f*

sci-fi ['saɪ·faɪ] *n abbr of* **science fiction** fantascienza *f*

scintillating ['sɪn·t̬leɪ·t̬ɪŋ] *adj* brillante

scion ['saɪ·ən] *n form* **1.** (*descendant*) rampollo, -a *m, f* **2.** BOT innesto *m*

scissors ['sɪ·zɚz] *npl* forbici *fpl;* **a pair of** ~ un paio di forbici; ~ **kick** SPORTS sforbiciata *f;* **a** ~ **and paste job** un lavoro meccanico

sclerosis [sklɪ·'roʊ·sɪs] *n* MED sclerosi *f inv*
scoff [skɑ:f] *vi* (*mock*) beffarsi; **to ~ at sth/sb** ridere di qc/qu
scold [skoʊld] *vt* rimproverare
scolding ['skoʊl·dɪŋ] *n* rimprovero *m*
scone [skoʊn] *n* panino *m* dolce
scoop [sku:p] I. *n* 1. (*utensil*) mestolo *m;* **ice cream ~** cucchiaio *m* da gelato; **measuring ~** misurino *m* 2. (*amount*) cucchiaiata *f* 3. PUBL scoop *m inv* II. *vt* 1. (*shovel*) prendere (*con un cucchiaio, un misurino, ecc.*) 2. *inf* PUBL ottenere l'esclusiva di
◆**scoop up** *vt* raccogliere
scoot [sku:t] *vi inf* smammare; **to ~ over** scostarsi
scooter ['sku:·ţə] *n* 1. (*toy*) monopattino *m* 2. (*vehicle*) (*motor*) ~ motorino *m*
scope [skoʊp] *n* 1. (*range*) ambito *m* 2. (*possibilities*) possibilità *fpl;* **limited/considerable ~** campo *m* d'azione limitato/ampio
scorch [skɔ:rtʃ] I. *vt* bruciare II. *vi* bruciarsi III. *n* <-es> bruciatura *f*
scorcher *n inf* giornata *f* torrida
scorching *adj* torrido, -a; **it's ~ hot** c'è un caldo torrido
score [skɔ:r] I. *n* 1. SPORTS (*number of points*) punteggio *m;* **to keep (the) ~** tenere i punti 2. SPORTS (*goal, point*) gol *m* 3. SCHOOL voto *m* 4. (*twenty*) ventina *f;* **~s of people** moltissime persone 5. (*dispute*) conto *m* in sospeso; **to settle a ~** regolare i conti 6. MUS partitura *f* 7. (*line*) graffio *m* II. *vt* 1. (*goal*) segnare; (*point*) fare; (*triumph, victory*) riportare 2. (*cut*) incidere 3. *sl* (*buy: drugs*) procurarsi 4. MUS (*arrange*) arrangiare III. *vi* 1. SPORTS (*make a point*) fare un punto 2. *inf* (*succeed*) riuscire 3. *sl* (*make sexual conquest*) cuccare 4. *sl* (*buy drugs*) procurarsi la roba
scoreboard ['skɔ:r·bɔ:rd] *n* tabellone *m* segnapunti
scorecard *n* scheda *f* segnapunti
scorekeeper *n* segnapunti *mf inv*
scorer *n* 1. (*player: in soccer*) cannoniere, -a *m, f;* (*in basketball*) marcatore, -trice *m, f* 2. (*scorekeeper*) segnapunti *mf*
scoring *n* punteggio *m*
scorn [skɔ:rn] I. *n* disprezzo *m;* **to be the ~ of sb/sth** essere disprezzato da qu/qc; **to pour ~ on sb/sth** denigrare qu/qc II. *vt* 1. (*disdain*) disprezzare 2. (*refuse*) rifiutare con sdegno; **to ~ to do sth** sdegnare di fare qc
scornful ['skɔ:rn·fəl] *adj* sdegnoso, -a
Scorpio ['skɔ:r·pioʊ] *n* Scorpione *m*
scorpion ['skɔ:r·pi·ən] *n* scorpione *m*
Scot [skɑ:t] *n* scozzese *mf*
Scotch [skɑ:tʃ] I. *n* Scotch *m inv;* **a ~ on the rocks** un whisky con ghiaccio II. *adj* scozzese
Scotch tape® ['se·loʊ·teɪp] *n* Scotch® *m inv*
scot-free [ˌskɑ:t·'fri:] *adv* 1. (*without punishment*) impunemente; **to get away** [*o* **off**] **~** cavarsela impunemente 2. (*unharmed*) illeso, -a
Scotland ['skɑ:t·lənd] *n* la Scozia *f*

Scots [skɑ:ts] *adj s.* **Scottish**
Scotsman ['skɑ:ts·mən] <-men> *n* scozzese *m*
Scotswoman ['skɑ:ts·ˌwʊ·mən] <-women> *n* scozzese *f*
Scottish ['skɑ:·ţɪʃ] *adj* scozzese
scoundrel ['skaʊn·drəl] *n pej* mascalzone, -a *m, f*
scour [skaʊə] I. *vt* 1. (*scrub*) strofinare 2. (*search*) rastrellare; **the police are ~ing the neighborhood** la polizia sta rastrellando le vicinanze II. *n* strofinata *f;* **to give sth a ~** dare una strofinata a qc
scourer *n* paglietta *f*
scourge [skɜ:rdʒ] I. *n a. fig* flagello *m* II. *vt* 1. (*inflict suffering*) affliggere 2. (*whip*) flagellare
scouring pad *n* paglietta *f*
scout [skaʊt] I. *n* MIL esploratore, -trice *m, f;* **talent ~** talent scout *mf inv* II. *vi* **to ~ ahead** fare una ricognizione; **to ~ around for sth** perlustare una zona alla ricerca di qc
scoutmaster *n* capo *m* scout
scowl [skaʊl] I. *n* fronte *f* aggrottata II. *vi* aggrottare la fronte
scrabble ['skræ·bl] *vi* 1. (*grope*) tastare 2. (*claw for grip*) grattare
scraggly *adj* incolto, -a
scraggy ['skræ·gi] <-ier, -iest> *adj* ossuto, -a
scram [skræm] I. <-mm-> *vi inf* filare via II. *interj inf* via!
scramble ['skræm·bl] I. *vi* 1. (*move hastily*) affrettarsi 2. (*try to get first*) precipitarsi; **to ~ for sth** darsi da fare per qc 3. AVIAT (*take off quickly*) decollare velocemente II. *vt* 1. (*mix together*) mescolare; **~d eggs** uova strapazzate 2. (*encrypt*) criptare 3. AVIAT (*launch quickly*) far decollare III. *n* 1. (*rush*) premura *f;* (*chase*) corsa *f* 2. (*struggle*) lotta *f* 3. (*aircraft launch*) decollo *m* rapido
scrambler ['skræmb·lə] *n* scrambler *m inv*
scrap[1] [skræp] I. *n* 1. (*small piece*) pezzetto *m;* (*of fabric*) ritaglio *m* 2. (*small amount: of information*) frammento *m;* **not a ~ of truth** neanche un briciolo di verità 3. *pl* (*leftover food*) avanzi *mpl* 4. (*old metal*) rottame *m* II. <-pp-> *vt* 1. (*get rid of, abolish*) eliminare; (*abandon*) accantonare 2. (*use for scrap metal*) rottamare
scrap[2] [skræp] I. *n inf* (*fight*) rissa *f* II. <-pp-> *vi* (*have a fight*) azzuffarsi; (*have an argument*) bisticciare
scrapbook ['skræp·bʊk] *n* album *m* (dei ricordi)
scrap dealer *n* rottamaio, -a *m, f*
scrape [skreɪp] I. *vt* 1. (*remove layer, dirt*) raschiare 2. (*graze*) sbucciare; (*scratch*) graffiare 3. (*rub against*) strisciare contro II. *vi* 1. (*rub against*) strisciare 2. (*make unpleasant noise*) strisciare 3. (*economize*) risparmiare III. *n* 1. (*act of scraping*) raschiata *f* 2. (*graze on skin*) sbucciatura *f* 3. (*sound*) strisciamento *m* 4. *inf* (*situation*) guaio *m;* **to get into**

S

a ~ mettersi nei guai
◆ **scrape along** *vi s.* **scrape by**
◆ **scrape away** *vt* raschiare
◆ **scrape by** *vi* arrabattarsi
◆ **scrape through** I. *vt* superare a stento II. *vi* cavarsela a malapena
scraper ['skreɪ·pə] *n* (*tool*) raschietto *m*
scrapheap ['skræp·hi:p] *n* mucchio *m* di rottami; **to end up in** [*o* **on**] **the** ~ finire nel dimenticatoio
scrapie ['skreɪ·pi] *n* scrapie *f*
scrapings *npl* 1. (*leftovers*) avanzi *mpl* 2. TECH scarti *mpl*
scrap iron *n* rottame *m*
scrappy[1] ['skræ·pi] <-ier, -iest> *adj* 1. (*knowledge*) superficiale 2. (*performance, game*) irregolare
scrappy[2] ['skræ·pi] <-ier, -iest> *adj* (*ready to fight*) litigioso, -a
scratch [skrætʃ] I. *n* 1. (*cut on skin*) graffio *m* 2. (*mark*) riga *f* 3. (*act of scratching*) grattata *f* 4. (*start*) inizio *m;* **from** ~ da zero II. *vt* 1. (*cut slightly*) graffiare 2. (*mark*) rigare 3. (*relieve itch*) grattare 4. (*erase*) raschiare 5. (*exclude*) ritirare 6. *inf* (*cancel*) cancellare 7. (*write*) incidere III. *vi* 1. (*use claws: cat*) graffiare 2. (*relieve itch*) grattarsi IV. *adj* improvvisato, -a
◆ **scratch out** *vt* 1. (*with claws*) strappare; **to scratch sb's eyes out** *fig* cavare gli occhi a qu 2. (*line, word*) depennare
scratch card ['skrætʃ·kɑːrd] *n* gratta e vinci *m inv*
scratch paper *n* carta *f* da minuta
scratchy ['skræ·tʃi] <-ier, -iest> *adj* 1. (*record*) rigato, -a; (*voice*) roco, -a 2. (*irritating*) ruvido, -a
scrawl [skrɑːl] I. *vt* scarabocchiare II. *n* scarabocchio *m*
scrawny ['skrɑː·ni] <-ier, -iest> *adj* scheletrico, -a
scream [skri:m] I. *n* 1. (*cry*) grido *m;* (*shrill cry*) strillo *m;* (*shout*) urlo *m* 2. (*of animal*) grido *m* ▶ **to be a** ~ *inf* essere forte II. *vi* (*shout*) gridare; (*cry shrilly*) strillare; **to** ~ **with laughter** ridere a più non posso III. *vt* (*shout*) gridare; **to** ~ **oneself hoarse** gridare fino a perdere la voce
screech [skri:tʃ] I. *n* stridio *m* II. *vi* strillare; **to** ~ **with pain** urlare dal dolore
screech owl *n* gufo *m*
screen [skri:n] I. *n* 1. *a.* TV, CINE, COMPUT schermo *m;* **split/touch** ~ schermo diviso/tattile 2. (*framed panel*) paravento *m;* (*for protection*) schermo *m;* (*in front of fire*) grata *f;* **glass** ~ vetrata *f* 3. (*thing that conceals*) schermo *m* II. *vt* 1. (*conceal*) coprire 2. (*shield*) proteggere 3. (*examine*) esaminare 4. TV trasmettere; CINE proiettare 5. (*put through a sieve*) setacciare
◆ **screen off** *vt* separare con un paravento
screening *n* 1. (*showing: in cinema*) proiezione *f;* (*on television*) trasmissione *f* 2. (*test-*

ing) prova *f* 3. MED (*examination*) esame *m*
screenplay ['skri:n·pleɪ] *n* sceneggiatura *f*
screen saver *n* COMPUT salvaschermo *m inv*
screen shot *n* COMPUT cattura *f* schermo
screen test *n* prova *f*
screenwriter *n* sceneggiatore, -trice *m, f*
screw [skru:] I. *n* 1. (*small metal fastener*) vite *f;* **to tighten** (**up**)/**loosen a** ~ stringere/allentare una vite 2. (*turn*) giro *m* 3. (*propeller*) elica *f* 4. (*spin*) effetto *m* 5. (*twisted piece*) cartoccio *m* 6. *vulg* (*sexual intercourse*) **I had a good** ~ **last night** mi sono fatto una bella scopata ieri notte 7. *vulg* (*sexual partner*) **she's a great** ~ scopa benissimo ▶ **he's got a** ~ [*o* **a few** ~**s**] **loose** *inf* gli manca qualche rotella; **to put the** ~**s on sb** *sl* forzare la mano a qu II. *vt* 1. (*with a screw*) svitare 2. (*by twisting*) svitare 3. *sl* (*cheat*) fregare 4. *vulg* (*have sex with*) scopare con 5. *sl* ~ **you!** vaffanculo! III. *vi* 1. (*turn like a screw*) avvitarsi 2. (*become attached*) avvitarsi 3. *vulg* (*have sex*) scopare
◆ **screw around** *vi* 1. *sl* (*act stupidly*) cazzeggiare *vulg* 2. *vulg* (*be sexually promiscuous*) scopare con chi capita
◆ **screw up** I. *vt* 1. *sl* (*make a mess of*) mandare all'aria 2. *sl* (*injure*) distruggere 3. *inf* (*make anxious*) rendere nevrotico II. *vi* rovinare tutto
screwball ['skru:·bɔːl] *n* 1. *sl* (*odd person*) svitato, -a *m, f* 2. (*in baseball*) tiro *m* con effetto
screwdriver ['skru:·ˌdraɪ·vər] *n* 1. (*tool*) cacciavite *m* 2. (*drink*) cocktail *m* a base di vodka e succo d'arancia
screwed *adj* *inf* fregato, -a
screw top *n* tappo *m* a vite
screwy ['skru:·i] <-ier, iest> *adj* *inf* svitato, -a
scribble ['skrɪ·bl] I. *vt* scarabocchiare II. *vi* scarabocchiare III. *n* scarabocchi *mpl*
scrimmage ['skrɪ·mɪdʒ] *n* 1. SPORTS (*practice game*) partita *f* di allenamento 2. (*fight*) scaramuccia *f*
scrimp [skrɪmp] *vi* rispamiare il più possibile; **to** ~ **and save** tirare la cintura *fig*
script [skrɪpt] I. *n* 1. CINE, TV, THEAT copione *m*, sceneggiatura *f* 2. (*writing*) caratteri *mpl;* **Arabic** ~ caratteri arabi II. *vt* scrivere la sceneggiatura di
scriptural ['skrɪp·tʃər·əl] *adj* biblico, -a
Scripture *n,* **scripture** ['skrɪp·tʃər] *n* Sacre Scritture *fpl*
scriptwriter ['skrɪpt·ˌraɪ·t̬ər] *n* sceneggiatore, -trice *m, f*
scroll [skroʊl] I. *n* 1. (*roll*) rotolo *m* 2. ARCHIT voluta *f* II. *vi* COMPUT scorrere; **to** ~ (**to the**) **right/left** scorrere a destra/sinistra; **to** ~ **down/up** scorrere giù/su
scrooge [skru:dʒ] *n* taccagno, -a *m, f*
scrotum ['skroʊ·t̬əm] <-tums *o* -ta> *n* scroto *m*
scrounge [skraʊndʒ] I. *vt* *inf* scroccare; **to** ~ **sth off** [*o* **from**] **sb** scroccare qc a qu II. *vi* *inf* frugare in giro

scrounger ['skrəʊn·dʒɚ] *n pej, inf* scroccone, -a *m, f*
scrub[1] [skrʌb] <-bb-> **I.** *vt* **1.** (*clean*) fregare **2.** (*cancel*) annullare **II.** *vi* fregare; **to ~ at sth** fregare qc **III.** *n* **1.** (*act of scrubbing*) sfregata *f;* **to give sth a** (**good**) ~ dare una (bella) sfregata a qc **2.** *pl* (*clothing*) abiti *mpl* da sala operatoria **3.** SPORTS (*reserve player*) riserva *f* inesperta
scrub[2] [skrʌb] *n* boscaglia *f*
scrubber ['skrʌ·bɚ] *n* uomo *m* delle pulizie, donna *f* delle pulizie
scruff [skrʌf] *n* collottola *f;* **to grab sb by the ~ of the neck** prendere qu per la collottola
scruffy ['skrʌ·fi] <-ier, -iest> *adj* trasandato, -a
scrum [skrʌm] *n* SPORTS mischia *f*
scrummage ['skrʌ·mɪdʒ] *n s.* **scrum**
scrumptious ['skrʌmp·ʃəs] *adj inf* squisito, -a
scrunch [skrʌntʃ] **I.** *vi* scricchiolare **II.** *vt* schiacchiare **III.** *n* scricchiolio *m*
scruple ['skru:·pl] **I.** *n* scrupolo *m;* **to have no ~s** (**about doing sth**) non farsi scrupoli (a fare qc) **II.** *vi* farsi scrupoli
scrupulous ['skru:p·jʊ·ləs] *adj* scrupoloso, -a
scrutinize ['skru:·tə·naɪz] *vt* (*examine*) scrutare; (*votes*) scrutinare; (*text*) passare al setaccio
scrutiny ['skru:·tə·ni] *n* scrutinio *m*
scuba diving ['sku:·bə·ˌdaɪ·vɪŋ] *n* immersioni *fpl* (subacquee)
scuff [skʌf] **I.** *vt* **1.** (*roughen surface*) levigare **2.** (*drag along ground*) strascicare **II.** *n* (*mark*) segno *m* (di sfregamento)
scuffle ['skʌ·fl] **I.** *n* rissa *f* **II.** *vi* azzuffarsi
scull [skʌl] **I.** *vi* ramare **II.** *n* sandolino *m*
scullery ['skʌ·lə·ri] *n* retrocucina *m*
sculpt [skʌlpt] *vt* scolpire
sculptor ['skʌlp·tɚ] *n* scultore, -trice *m, f*
sculptural ['skʌlp·tʃə·rəl] *adj* scultorico, -a
sculpture ['skʌlp·tʃɚ] **I.** *n* scultura *f* **II.** *vt* scolpire
scum [skʌm] *n* **1.** (*foam*) schiuma *f* **2.** (*evil people*) gentaglia *f*
scumbag ['skʌm·bæg] *n pej* fetente *mf*
scupper ['skʌ·pɚ] *vt* **1.** (*ship*) affondare (deliberatamente) **2.** *inf* (*plan*) far naufragare
scurrilous ['skɜ:·rɪ·ləs] *adj pej* (*damaging*) diffamatorio, -a; (*insulting*) calunnioso, -a
scurry ['skɜ:·ri] <-ie-> *vi* correre
scurvy ['skɜ:r·vi] **I.** *n* scorbuto *m* **II.** *adj* meschino, -a; **a ~ trick** uno scherzo meschino
scuttle[1] ['skʌ·tl] *vi* (*run*) correre
scuttle away *vi,,* **scuttle off** *vi* (*run*) correr via
scuttle[2] ['skʌ·tl] *vt* **1.** (*sink*) affondare (producendo una falla) **2.** (*plan*) far naufragare
scuttle[3] ['skʌ·tl] *n* (*for coal*) cassa *f* di carbone
scythe [saɪð] **I.** *n* falce *f* **II.** *vt* (*with a scythe*) falciare; (*with swinging blow*) fendere
SD *n abbr of* **South Dakota** Dakota *m* del Sud
SDI [ˌes·di:·'aɪ] *n abbr of* **Strategic Defense Initiative** Iniziativa *f* di Difesa Strategica
SE [ˌes·'i:] *n abbr of* **southeast** SE *m*
sea [si:] *n* **1.** mare *m;* **at the bottom of the ~**

in fondo al mare; **by ~** per mare; **by the ~** sul mare; **out at ~** in mare aperto; **to put** (**out**) **to ~** prendere il mare; **the open ~, the high ~s** il mare aperto **2.** (*wide expanse*) **a ~ of people** una marea di gente ▶ **to sail the seven ~s** solcare i mari
sea anemone *n* anemone *f* di mare
seaboard ['si:·bɔ:rd] *n* litorale *m*
seaborne ['si:·bɔ:rn] *adj* trasportato, -a dal mare
sea change *n* cambiamento *m* radicale
sea dog *n* lupo *m* di mare
seafarer ['si:·ˌfe·rɚ] *n liter* marinaio, -a *m, f*
seafaring *adj liter* marinaro, -a
seafood ['si:·fu:d] *n* frutti *m* di mare *pl*
seafront ['si:·frʌnt] *n* **1.** (*promenade*) lungomare *m* **2.** (*beach*) spiaggia *f*
seagoing ['si:·ˌgoʊ·ɪŋ] *adj* d'altura
seagull ['si:·gʌl] *n* gabbiano *m*
sea horse *n* cavalluccio *m* marino
seal[1] [si:l] *n* ZOOL foca *f*
seal[2] [si:l] **I.** *n* **1.** (*wax mark, stamp*) sigillo *m;* **given under my hand and ~** da me sottoscritto e sigillato **2.** (*to prevent opening*) sigillo *m* ▶ ~ **of approval** approvazione *f* **II.** *vt* **1.** (*put a seal on*) sigillare **2.** (*prevent opening*) sigillare **3.** (*block access*) bloccare l'accesso a; (*border, port*) chiudere
◆ **seal up** *vt* sigillare
sealant ['si:·lənt] *n* vernice *f* isolante
sea legs *npl inf* piede *m* marino; **to get one's ~** acquisire il piede marino
sea level *n* livello *m* del mare
sealing wax *n* ceralacca *f*
sea lion *n* ZOOL leone *m* marino, otaria *f*
sealskin ['si:l·skɪn] *n* pelle *f* di foca
seam [si:m] **I.** *n* **1.** (*stitching*) cucitura *f;* **to come** [*o* **fall**] **apart at the ~s** scucirsi; *fig* fare acqua da tutte le parti **2.** (*junction*) giuntura *f* **3.** (*wrinkle*) ruga *f* **4.** MIN filone *m* **II.** *vt* (*sew*) cucire
seaman ['si:·mən] <-men> *n* (*sailor*) marinaio *m*
sea mile *n* miglio *m* marino
seamless *adj* **1.** (*without seam*) senza cuciture **2.** (*transition*) senza soluzione di continuità
seamstress ['si:ms·trɪs] *n* sarta *f*
seamy ['si:·mi] <-ier, -iest> *adj* sordido, -a
seance ['seɪ·ɑːnts] *n* seduta *f* spiritica
seaplane ['si:·pleɪn] *n* AVIAT idrovolante *m*
seaport *n* porto *m* di mare
sea power *n* **1.** (*naval strength*) forza *f* navale **2.** (*state*) potenza *f* navale
sear [sɪr] *vt* **1.** (*scorch*) bruciare; (*into memory*) imprimere **2.** (*wither*) seccare **3.** CULIN cuocere a fuoco vivo **4.** MED cauterizzare **5.** (*make numb*) rendere insensibile
search [sɜ:rtʃ] **I.** *n a.* COMPUT ricerca *f;* (*of building, person*) perquisizione *f;* **to go in ~ of sth** andare alla ricerca di qc **II.** *vi a.* COMPUT cercare; **to ~ for sth** cercare qc; **to ~ high and low** (**for sth**) cercare qc dovunque; **~ and replace** COMPUT trovare e sostituire **III.** *vt* **1.** *a.* COMPUT

cercare in; (*building, baggage, person*) perquisire **2.** (*examine*) scrutare; **to ~ one's memory** frugare nei propri ricordi; **to ~ one's conscience** fare un esame di coscienza ▶ **~ me!** *sl* che ne so!
♦**search out** *vt* (*people*) scovare; (*information*) scoprire
search engine *n* COMPUT motore *m* di ricerca
searcher *n* soccorritore *m*
search function *n* COMPUT funzione *f* di ricerca
searching *adj* **1.** (*penetrating*) inquisitorio, -a; (*look*) penetrante **2.** (*exhaustive*) minuzioso, -a
searchlight ['sɜ:rtʃ·laɪt] *n* riflettore *m*
search party <-ies> *n* squadra *f* di soccorso
search warrant *n* mandato *m* di perquisizione
searing *adj* **1.** (*heat*) scottante **2.** (*pain*) lancinante **3.** (*criticism*) virulento
sea salt *n* sale *m* marino
seascape ['si:·skeɪp] *n* **1.** (*picture*) marina *f* **2.** (*view*) veduta *f* sul mare
seashell ['si:·ʃel] *n* conchiglia *f* (marina)
seashore ['si:·ʃɔ:r] *n* **1.** (*beach*) spiaggia *f* **2.** (*near sea*) costa *f*
seasick ['si:·sɪk] *adj* **to get ~** avere il mal di mare
seasickness ['si:·sɪk·nɪs] *n* mal *m* di mare
seaside ['si:·saɪd] **I.** *n* **1.** (*beach*) spiaggia *f* **2.** (*coast*) costa *f* **II.** *adj* costiero, -a; **a ~ resort** una stazione balneare
season ['si:·zən] **I.** *n* **1.** (*period of year*) stagione *f* **2.** (*epoch*) epoca *f;* **the Christmas ~** le feste natalizie; **Season's Greetings** Buone Feste; **the** (**fishing/hunting**) **~** la stagione (della pesca/caccia); **the strawberry/apple ~** la stagione delle fragole/mele; **to be in ~** essere di stagione; **to be out of ~** essere fuori stagione; **high/low ~** alta/bassa stagione; **the concert/ballet/opera ~** la stagione dei concerti/della danza/lirica **3.** SPORTS stagione *f* **4.** ZOOL **to be in ~** essere in calore; **the mating ~** la stagione degli amori **II.** *vt* **1.** CULIN condire; (*add salt and pepper*) aggiungere sale e pepe **2.** (*dry out*) seccare **III.** *vi* **1.** (*dry out*) stagionare **2.** *fig* **to become ~ed to sth** abituarsi a qc
seasonable ['si:·zə·nə·bl] *adj* **1.** (*expected*) di stagione **2.** *liter* (*appropriate*) opportuno, -a
seasonal ['si:·zə·nəl] *adj* **1.** (*connected with time of year*) stagionale **2.** (*temporary*) stagionale; **~ worker** stagionale *mf* **3.** (*grown in a season: fruits, vegetables*) di stagione
seasoned *adj* **1.** (*experienced*) sperimentato, -a **2.** (*dried: wood*) stagionato, -a **3.** (*spiced*) condito, -a
seasoning ['si:·zə·nɪŋ] *n* condimento *m*
season ticket *n* abbonamento *m*
season ticket holder *n* RAIL, SPORTS, THEAT abbonato, -a *m, f*
seat [si:t] **I.** *n* **1.** (*furniture*) sedia *f;* (*on a bicycle*) sellino *m;* (*in theater*) poltrona *f;* (*in a car, bus*) posto *m;* **back ~** sedile posteriore; **is this ~ free/taken?** questo posto è libero/

occupato?; **to hold a ~ for sb** tenere il posto a qu; **to take one's ~** sedersi **2.** (*ticket*) ingresso *m;* **to book a ~** prenotare un ingresso **3.** (*part: of chair*) sedile *m;* (*of pants*) fondo *mpl* **4.** (*buttocks*) fondoschiena *m* **5.** POL seggio *m;* **to win/lose a ~** guadagnare/perdere un seggio **6.** (*center*) sede *f;* **~ of learning** *form* centro *m* universitario **7.** (*country residence*) casa *f* di campagna **8.** (*riding style*) **to have a good ~** montare bene ▶ **to fly by the ~ of one's pants** lasciarsi guidare dal proprio instinto **II.** *vt* **1.** (*place on a seat*) sedersi; **to ~ oneself** *form* accomodarsi; (*offer a seat to*) far sedere **2.** (*have enough seats for*) accogliere; **the bus ~s 20** l'autobus ha 20 posti a sedere **3.** ARCHIT, TECH poggiare
seat belt *n* cintura *f* di sicurezza; **to fasten one's ~** allacciarsi la cintura (di sicurezza)
seating *n* **1.** (*seats*) posti *mpl* **2.** (*number*) numero *m* di posti; **~ capacity** numero di posti (a sedere); **~ for two thousand** duemila posti **3.** (*arrangement*) disposizione *f* dei posti
SEATO ['si:·toʊ] *n abbr of* **Southeast Asia Treaty Organization** SEATO *f*
sea urchin *n* riccio *m* di mare
seaward ['si:·wəd] **I.** *adv* sul mare **II.** *adj* **1.** (*facing sea*) sul mare **2.** (*moving towards sea*) verso il mare
seawater ['si:·wɑ:·t̬ə] *n* acqua *f* di mare
seaway ['si:·weɪ] *n* **1.** (*channel*) canale *m* (marittimo) **2.** (*route*) rotta *f* marittima
seaweed ['si:·wi:d] *n* alghe *f* (marine) *pl*
seaworthy ['si:·ˌwɜ:r·ði] *adj* in grado di navigare
sebaceous gland [sə·'beɪ·ʃəs·ˌglænd] *n* ghiandola *f* sebacea
sec [sek] *n* **s. second** sec. *m;* **hang on just a ~** aspetta un secondo
sec *adj* secco, -a
SEC *n abbr of* **Securities and Exchange Commission** SEC *f, ente che vigila sul funzionamento del mercato dei titoli quotati negli USA*
secede [sɪ·'si:d] *vi* separarsi
secession [sɪ·'se·ʃən] *n* secessione *f;* **War of Secession** Guerra *f* di secessione
seclude [sɪ·'klu:d] *vt liter* isolare
secluded [sɪ·'klu:·dɪd] *adj* (*place*) isolato, -a; (*life*) ritirato, -a
seclusion [sɪ·'klu:·ʒən] *n* isolamento *m;* **to live in ~** vivere ritirato
second[1] ['se·kənd] **I.** *adj* **1.** (*after first*) secondo, -a; **every ~ boy/girl** un ragazzo/una ragazza su due; **every ~ year** ogni due anni; **every ~ week** una settimana sì e una no; **to be ~** arrivare secondo; **the ~ biggest town** la seconda città più grande; **to be ~ only to sb/sth** essere inferiore solo a qu/qc; **to be ~ to none** non essere secondo a nessuno **2.** (*another*) altro, -a; **to be a ~ Mozart** essere un nuovo Mozart; **to give sb a ~ chance** dare a qu un'altra possibilità; **to have ~ thoughts about sb/sth** avere dei ripensamenti su qu/

qc; **on ~ thought** dopo riflessione; **to do sth a ~ time** rifare qc un'altra volta; **to get one's ~ wind** riprendere fiato; **to have a ~ helping** servirsi di nuovo di qc **3. the ~ floor** il primo piano **II.** *n* **1.** (*second gear*) seconda *f* **2.** *pl* (*extra helping*) **may I have ~s?** posso servirmi di nuovo? **3.** COM (*imperfect item*) articolo *m* di seconda scelta **4.** (*in duel*) padrino *m* **5.** MUS seconda *f* **6.** (*seconder*) persona *f* che appoggia una mozione **III.** *adv* in secondo luogo **IV.** *vt* **1.** (*support in debate*) appoggiare **2.** *form* (*back up*) appoggiare

second² ['se·kənd] *n* (*unit of time*) secondo *m;* **per ~** al secondo; **at that very ~** in quel preciso istante; **just a ~!** un secondo!; **it won't take** (**but**) **a ~!** ci vuole un attimo!

secondary ['se·kən·de·ri] **I.** *adj* **1.** (*not main*) secondario, -a; **to be ~ to sth** essere secondario rispetto a qc **2.** (*school*) di scuola secondaria **3.** (*industry*) derivato, -a **II.** <-ies> *n* subalterno, -a *m, f*

secondary school *n* **1.** (*school*) scuola *f* secondaria **2.** (*education*) scuola *f* secondaria

second-best I. *adj* **to be ~** (*person*) venire subito dopo il migliore **II.** *n* secondo, -a *m, f* **III.** *adv* **to come off ~** (**to sb**) perdere (contro qu)

second class *n* seconda *f* (classe)

second-class I. *adj* **1.** (*in second class*) di seconda classe; **~ mail** posta *f* ordinaria **2.** *pej* (*inferior: hotel, service*) di seconda categoria; (*goods*) di seconda scelta **II.** *adv* **1.** RAIL (*in the second class*) in seconda (classe) **2.** (*by second-class mail*) tramite posta ordinaria

second cousin *n* cugino, -a *m, f* di secondo grado

second-degree burn *n* ustione *f* di secondo grado

second-guess [ˌse·kənd·ˈges] *vt* prevedere le mosse di

secondhand [ˌse·kənd·ˈhænd] **I.** *adj* (*clothing, information*) di seconda mano; (*bookstore*) di libri usati **II.** *adv* **1.** (*used*) di seconda mano **2.** (*from third party*) tramite terzi

second hand *n* (*on watch*) lancetta *f* dei secondi

second lieutenant *n* MIL sottotenente *m*

secondly *adv* in secondo luogo

second-rate [ˌse·kənd·ˈreɪt] *adj* mediocre

secrecy ['si·krə·si] *n* **1.** (*confidentiality*) segretezza *f;* **in ~** in segreto; **to swear sb to ~** far giurare a qu di mantenere il segreto **2.** (*secretiveness*) enigmaticità *f*

secret ['si·krɪt] **I.** *n* **1.** (*information*) segreto *m;* **an open ~** un segreto di Pulcinella; **to let sb in on a ~** rivelare un segreto a qu **2.** (*knack*) trucco *m;* (*of success*) segreto *m* **3.** (*mystery*) mistero *m* **II.** *adj* (*known to few*) segreto, -a; **to keep sth ~** (**from sb**) tenere qc nascosto (a qu)

secret agent *n* agente *m* segreto

secretarial [ˌse·krə·ˈte·ri·əl] *adj* (*work*) di segreteria; (*course*) per segretarie

secretary ['se·krə·te·ri] <-ies> *n* **1.** (*in office*) segretario, -a *m, f* **2.** POL ministro, -a *m, f;* **Secretary of the Treasury** ≈ ministro *m* dell'Economia e delle Finanze; **Secretary of State** segretario di Stato, ≈ ministro *m* degli Esteri

secretary-general [ˌse·krə·te·ri·ˈdʒe·nə·rəl] <secretaries-general> *n* segretario, -a *m, f* generale

secrete¹ [sɪ·ˈkriːt] *vt* (*discharge*) secernere

secrete² [sɪ·ˈkriːt] *vt form* (*hide*) occultare

secretion [sɪ·ˈkriː·ʃən] *n* (*discharge*) secrezione *f*

secretive ['siː·krə·tɪv] *adj* riservato, -a

sect [sekt] *n* setta *f*

sectarian [sek·ˈte·ri·ən] **I.** *adj* **1.** (*ideology*) settario, -a **2.** (*schooling*) settario, -a **II.** *n* membro *m* di una setta

section ['sek·ʃən] **I.** *n* **1.** (*part*) *a.* MIL, MUS, PUBL sezione *f;* (*of object*) parte *f* **2.** (*group*) settore *m* **3.** (*of area*) zona *f;* (*of city*) quartiere *m* **4.** (*of document*) paragrafo *m;* LAW articolo *m* **5.** (*of road*) tronco *m* **6.** (*cut*) sezione *f* **II.** *vt* **1.** (*cut*) sezionare **2.** (*divide*) suddividere

♦**section off** *vt* separare

sectional ['sek·ʃə·nl] *adj* **1.** (*limited to a group: interests*) di settore; (*differences*) tra fazioni **2.** (*done in section: design, view*) in sezione **3.** (*made in sections: furniture, sofa*) modulare

sector ['sek·tɚ] *n* settore *m;* **public/private ~** settore pubblico/privato

secular ['sek·jʊ·lɚ] *adj* **1.** (*non-religious*) secolare; (*education*) laico, -a; (*art*) profano, -a **2.** REL secolare **3.** (*centuries-old*) secolare

secularize ['sek·jʊ·lə·raɪz] *vt* secolarizzare

secure [sɪ·ˈkjʊr] **I.** *adj* <-rer, -est> **1.** (*safe*) sicuro, -a; **to be ~ from sth** essere protetto, -a da qc; **to make sth ~ against attack** proteggere qc da attacchi **2.** (*confident*) **to feel ~ about sth** sentirsi sicuro riguardo a qc; **to be ~ in the knowledge that ...** avere la certezza che ...; **to feel emotionally ~** essere emotivamente stabile **3.** (*guarantee*) **to be financially ~** avere la stabilità economica **4.** (*fixed*) firme; (*foundation*) solido, -a **II.** *vt* **1.** (*obtain*) ottenere **2.** (*make firm*) assicurare; *fig* assicurarsi; (*door*) chiudere saldamente; (*boat*) ormeggiare; (*position*) consolidare **3.** (*make safe*) proteggere **4.** (*put in safe place*) mettere al sicuro **5.** (*guarantee repayment*) garantire; **a ~d loan** un prestito con garanzia

securities market *n* mercato *m* dei valori

security [sɪ·ˈkjʊ·rə·ti] <-ies> *n* **1.** (*safety*) sicurezza *f;* **~ risk** rischio *m* per la sicurezza **2.** (*stability*) stabilità *f;* **~ of employment** stabilità lavorativa **3.** (*safeguard*) salvaguardia *f* **4.** (*payment guarantee*) garanzia *f;* **to stand ~ for sb** farsi garante per qu **5.** *pl* FIN titoli *mpl*

Security Council *n* Consiglio *m* di Sicurezza (dell'ONU)

security guard *n* guardia *f* giurata

sedan [sɪ·ˈdæn] *n* AUTO berlina *m*

sedan chair *n* portantina *f*

S

sedate [sɪ·'deɪt] I. *adj* (*lifestyle, person*) tranquillo, -a; (*color, style*) sobrio, -a II. *vt* MED sedare

sedation [sɪ·'deɪ·ʃən] *n* MED sedazione *f;* **under** ~ sotto sedativi

sedative ['se·də·t̬ɪv] I. *adj* sedativo, -a II. *n* sedativo *m*

sedentary ['se·dən·te·ri] *adj* sedentario, -a

sediment ['se·də·mənt] *n* sedimento *m;* (in *wine, coffee*) fondo *m*

sedimentary [ˌse·dɪ·'men·tri] *adj* sedimentario, -a

sedition [sɪ·'dɪ·ʃən] *n form* sedizione *f*

seditious [sɪ·'dɪ·ʃəs] *adj form* sedizioso, -a

seduce [sɪ·'duːs] *vt* sedurre; **to ~ sb into doing sth** indurre qu a fare qc allettandolo

seducer [sɪ·'duː·sə·] *n* seduttore, -trice *m, f*

seduction [sɪ·'dʌk·ʃən] *n* 1. (*act*) seduzione *f* 2. *pl* (*seductive quality*) attrattiva *f*

seductive [sɪ·'dʌk·tɪv] *adj* 1. (*sexy*) seducente 2. (*attractive*) attraente; (*offer*) allettante

see¹ [siː] <saw, seen> I. *vt* 1. (*perceive*) vedere; **to ~ that ...** vedere che...; **to ~ sth with one's own eyes** vedere qc con i propri occhi; **it is worth ~ing** vale la pena di vederlo 2. (*watch*) vedere; **you were ~n entering the building** ti hanno visto entrare nell'edificio 3. (*inspect*) vedere; **may I ~ your driver's license?** posso vedere la sua patente? 4. (*visit*) trovare; **to ~ a little/a lot of sb** vedere qu raramente/spesso; **~ you around!** ci vediamo!; **~ you (later)!** *inf* (*when meeting again later*) a più tardi! 5. (*have relationship*) **to be ~ing sb** uscire con qu 6. (*have meeting*) incontrare 7. (*talk to*) **I would like to ~ you about that matter** vorrei parlare con te di questa faccenda; **Mr. Brown will ~ you now** il Signor Brown la riceve adesso 8. (*accompany*) accompagnare 9. (*perceive*) rendersi conto di; (*understand*) capire; **I don't ~ what you mean** non capisco cosa vuoi dire; **to make sb ~ reason** far intendere ragione a qu; **to ~ sth in a new light** vedere qc sotto una nuova luce 10. (*envisage*) credere; **as I ~ it ...** da come la vedo io ...; **I don't ~ him doing that** non lo credo capace di farlo; **I could ~ it coming** me lo aspettavo 11. (*investigate*) **to ~ how/what/if ...** cercare di capire come/cosa/se ... 12. (*ensure*) **~ that you are ready when we come** fai in modo di essere pronto quando arriviamo II. *vi* 1. (*use eyes*) vedere; **as far as the eye can ~** fin dove arriva la vista 2. (*find out*) scoprire; **~ for yourself!** guarda tu stesso!; **let me ~** fammi vedere; **let's ~** vediamo; **we'll/I'll (have to) ~** vedremo; **you'll ~** vedrai 3. (*understand*) capire; **I ~** capisco; **you ~?** capisci?; **as far as I can ~** per quello che capisco ▶ **he can't ~ further than the end of his nose** non riesce a vedere al di là del suo naso

◆**see about** *vt inf* occuparsi di; (*consider*) riflettere su ▶ **we'll soon ~ that!** *inf* è ancora da vedere!

◆**see in** *vt* (*welcome*) fare accomodare; **to see the New Year in** festeggiare l'anno nuovo

◆**see off** *vt* salutare

◆**see out** *vt* 1. (*escort to door*) accompagnare alla porta 2. (*continue to end*) restare fino alla fine di; (*project*) portare a termine 3. (*last until end*) durare fino alla fine di; **to see the winter out** superare l'inverno

◆**see through** *vt* 1. (*not be deceived by*) non farsi abbindolare da; **~ sb** capire che tipo è qu; (*mystery*) penetrare 2. (*sustain*) **to see sb through (a difficult time)** essere d'aiuto a qu (in un momento difficile) 3. (*continue to end*) portare a termine

◆**see to** *vt* 1. (*attend to*) occuparsi di 2. (*ensure*) **to ~ it that ...** assicurarsi che ...

see² [siː] *n* REL sede *f;* **the Holy See** la Santa Sede

seed [siːd] I. *n* 1. BOT (*source, of fruit*) seme *m* 2. (*seeds*) semente *f* 3. (*beginning*) germe *m;* **to sow the ~s of doubt** insinuare dei dubbi; **to sow the ~s of discord** gettare il seme della discordia 4. ANAT seme *m* II. *vt* 1. AGR seminare; **to ~ itself** (*a plant*) spargere i semi 2. (*help start*) contribuire ad avviare; **to ~ a project with money** immettere capitale in un progetto 3. (*remove seeds*) togliere i semi da 4. SPORTS preselezionare III. *vi* far seme

seedbed *n* 1. AGR semenzaio *m* 2. *fig* focolaio *m*

seedless ['siːd·ləs] *adj* senza semi

seedling ['siːd·lɪŋ] *n* piantina *f*

seed money *n* capitale *m* iniziale (di un'impresa)

seedy ['siː·di] <-ier, -iest> *adj* 1. (*dubious*) losco, -a; (*place*) squallido, -a; (*clothing*) transandato, -a 2. (*unwell*) **to feel ~** stare poco bene

seeing I. *conj* ~ (that) visto che II. *n* vista *f;* **~ is believing** vedere per credere

seek [siːk] <sought> I. *vt* 1. (*look for*) cercare; **to ~ one's fortune** andare in cerca di fortuna 2. (*try to obtain*) cercare; (*damages*) reclamare 3. (*ask for: help, approval, job*) chiedere 4. (*attempt*) cercare di II. *vi* (*search*) cercare

◆**seek out** *vt* scovare

seeker *n* job-~ persona *f* alla ricerca di un lavoro

seem [siːm] *vi* 1. (*appear to be*) sembrare; **they ~ed to like the idea** sembrava che l'idea gli piacesse; **it ~ as if ...** sembrare che ... +*subj;* **it is not all that it ~s** non è esattamente come sembra; **things aren't always what they ~** l'apparenza inganna 2. (*appear*) **it ~s that ...** sembra che ... +*subj;* **so it ~s, so it would ~** così sembra

seeming *adj form* apparente

seemingly *adv* apparentemente

seemly ['siːm·li] <-ier, -iest> *adj* opportuno, -a

seen [siːn] *pp of* see

seep [siːp] *vi* filtrare

◆**seep away** *vi* colare via

seepage ['siː·pɪdʒ] *n* (*of water*) infiltrazione *f;*

(*of gas*) fuga *f*
seer [sɪr] *n liter* indovino, -a *m, f*
seersucker ['sɪr.ˌsʌ.kɚ] *n* tessuto di cotone a
strisce lisce e crespe alternate
seesaw ['si:.sɑ:] I. *n* 1.(*in playground*) altalena (*asse che oscilla*) 2.*fig* oscillazioni *fpl*
II. *vi* 1.(*play*) dondolarsi 2.*fig* oscillare III. *adj*
~ **motion** moto *m* oscillatorio
seethe [si:ð] *vi* 1.*fig* (*be angry*) essere furioso,
-a; **to ~ with anger** bollire di rabbia 2. *fig* (*be
busy*) essere affollato, -a; **to ~ with tourists**
brulicare di turisti
see-through ['si:.θru:] *adj* trasparente
segment[1] ['seg.mənt] *n* 1.MATH, ZOOL segmento *m;* (*of orange*) spicchio *m* 2.(*of
society*) parte *f*
segment[2] [seg.'ment] I. *vt* segmentare;
(*orange*) dividere a spicchi II. *vi* segmentarsi
segmentation [ˌseg.mən.'teɪ.ʃən] *n* segmentazione *f*
segregate ['se.grə.geɪt] *vt* (*races*) segregare;
(*girls and boys*) separare
segregation [ˌse.grə.'geɪ.ʃən] *n* segregazione *f*
seismic ['saɪz.mɪk] *adj* GEO sismico, -a
seismograph ['saɪz.mə.græf] *n* sismografo *m*
seismologist [saɪz.'mɑ:.lə.dʒɪst] *n* sismologo,
-a *m, f*
seismology [saɪz.'mɑ:.lə.dʒi] *n* sismologia *f*
seize [si:z] *vt* 1.(*grasp*) afferrare; **to ~ sb by
the arm/by the throat** afferrare qu per il
braccio/alla gola 2.(*take: opportunity*) cogliere; (*initiative, power*) prendere 3.(*overcome*) **he was ~d by fear/desire** era in
preda alla paura/al desiderio; **I was ~d with
panic** ero in preda al panico 4.(*capture: criminal*) catturare; (*fortress, town*) conquistare
5.(*confiscate: property*) confiscare; (*drugs,
weapons*) sequestrare 6.(*understand*) capire
7.(*kidnap*) sequestrare
♦ **seize on** *vt* cogliere al volo
♦ **seize up** *vi* (*stop*) bloccarsi; (*engine*) ingrip-
parsi; COMPUT piantarsi *inf*
seizure ['si:.ʒɚ] *n* 1.(*seizing*) presa *f* 2.(*taking
possession: of town*) conquista *f;* (*of drugs*)
sequestro *m;* (*of property, contraband*) confisca *f* 3.MED (*stroke*) attacco *m* 4.(*seizing up*)
blocco *m*
seldom ['sel.dəm] *adv* raramente
select [sə.'lekt] I. *vt* (*candidate, player,
information*) selezionare; (*gift, wine*) scegliere; **~ed works** scelta *f* di opere II. *adj*
1.(*high-class*) di classe privilegiata; (*club, restaurant, school, university*) esclusivo, -a;
(*product*) di prima scelta 2.(*exclusive*) **the ~
few** i pochi privilegiati
select committee *n* POL commissione *f* di
inchiesta
selection [sə.'lek.ʃən] *n* 1.(*act of choosing*)
selezione *f* 2.(*range*) scelta *f* 3.(*thing
chosen*) selezione *f;* (*person chosen*); **he was
a last-minute ~ for the team** è stato selezionato per la squadra all'ultimo minuto
selective [sə.'lek.tɪv] *adj* selettivo, -a

selectivity [ˌsə.lek.'tɪ.və.ti] *n* selettività *f*
selector [sə.'lek.tɚ] *n* 1.(*person*) selezion-
atore, -trice *m, f* 2.TECH selettore *m*
selenium [sɪ.'li:.ni.əm] *n* selenio *m*
self [self] *n* <selves> se stesso, -a; **his true ~**
la sua vera natura; **his better ~** la sua forma
migliore; **one's other ~** il proprio alter ego;
the ~ PSYCH l'io
self-abasement *n* svilimento *m* di se stesso
self-absorbed *adj* egocentrico, -a
self-addressed *adj* ~ **envelope** busta *f* con il
proprio indirizzo
self-adhesive *adj* autoadesivo, -a
self-analysis *n* autoanalisi *f inv*
self-appointed *adj pej* autonominato, -a
self-assurance *n* sicurezza *f* di sé; **to possess ~** essere sicuro, -a di sé
self-assured *adj* sicuro, -a di sé
self-centered *adj* egocentrico, -a
self-colored *adj* 1.(*natural*) della tinta naturale 2.(*one color*) in tinta unita
self-complacent *adj pej* compiaciuto, -a di sé
self-composed *adj* composto, -a; **to remain ~**
non perdere la calma
self-confessed *adj* confesso, -a; **she's a ~
coward** è un vigliacco per sua stessa ammissione
self-confidence *n* sicurezza *f* di sé; **to have ~**
essere sicuro, -a di sé
self-conscious *adj* 1.(*shy*) impacciato, -a; **to
feel ~** sentirsi a disagio 2. *pej* (*unnatural*) affettato, -a
self-contained *adj* 1.(*self-sufficient: community, village*) autosufficiente; (*apartment*) indipendente 2. *pej* (*reserved*) riservato, -a
self-control *n* autocontrollo *m*
self-critical *adj* autocritico, -a
self-criticism *n* autocritica *f*
self-deception *n* illusione *f*
self-defeating *adj* controproducente
self-defense *n* 1.(*protection*) autodifesa *f*
2.LAW legittima difesa *f*
self-denial *n* abnegazione *f*
self-destruct *vi* autodistruggersi
self-determination *n* POL autodeterminazione *f*
self-discipline *n* autodisciplina *f*
self-educated *adj* autodidatta
self-effacing *adj* schivo, -a
self-employed I. *adj* **to be ~** lavorare in proprio II. *n* **the ~** i lavoratori autonomi
self-esteem *n* autostima *f*
self-evident *adj* evidente
self-explanatory *adj* ovvio, -a
self-expression *n* espressione *f* della propria
personalità
self-fulfilling *adj* (*prediction*) che si realizza
self-governing *adj* autonomo, -a
self-government *n* autonomia *f*
self-help *n* autoaiuto *m;* ~ **group** gruppo *m* di
autoaiuto
self-importance *n pej* presunzione *f*
self-important *adj pej* presuntuoso, -a

S

self-imposed *adj* (*deadline*) autoimposto, -a; (*exile*) volontario, -a

self-indulgence *n* indulgenza *f* verso se stesso

self-indulgent *adj* indulgente verso se stesso

self-inflicted *adj* inflitto, -a a se stesso

self-interest *n* interesse *m* personale; **to be motivated by** ~ essere motivato da interesse personale

selfish ['sel·fɪʃ] *adj pej* egoista

selfishness *n pej* egoismo *m*

self-justification *n* autogiustificazione *f*

selfless ['self·ləs] *adj* altruista

self-made [,self·'meɪd] *adj* che si è fatto da solo

self-opinionated *adj pej* presuntuoso, -a

self-pity *n* autocommiserazione *f*

self-portrait *n* ART autoritratto *m*

self-possessed *adj* padrone, -a di sé

self-preservation *n* istinto *m* di autoconservazione

self-reliance *n* indipendenza *f*

self-reliant *adj* indipendente

self-respect *n* amor *m* proprio; **to lose all** ~ perdere ogni dignità

self-respecting *adj* con amor propio; **every** ~ **man ...** ogni uomo che si rispetti ...

self-righteous *adj pej* moralista; (*tone*) di superiorità morale

self-rising flour *n* farina *f* con lievito incorporato

self-sacrifice *n* abnegazione *f*

self-sacrificing *adj* altruista

self-satisfaction *n pej* soddisfazione *f* di sé

self-satisfied *adj pej* soddisfatto, -a di sé

self-seeking *adj form* egoista

self-service I. *n* self-service *m* II. *adj* ~ **store** self-service *m inv;* ~ **restaurant** self-service *m inv*

self-sufficiency *n* autosufficienza *f*

self-sufficient *adj* 1. autosufficiente 2. ECON autosufficiente; ~ **economy** autarchia *f*

self-taught *adj* autodidatta; **to be** ~ **in sth** essere un autodidatta in qc

self-willed *adj* ostinato, -a

self-winding watch *n* orologio *m* automatico

sell [sel] I. *vt* <sold, sold> 1. (*exchange for money*) vendere; **to** ~ **sth for $100** vendere qc per 100 dollari; **to** ~ **sth at half price** vendere qc a metà prezzo; **to** ~ **sth at a loss** vendere qc rimettendoci 2. *fig* (*make accepted*) far accettare; **I'm sold on your plan** il tuo piano mi ha convinto ▶ **to** ~ **oneself short** sminuirsi II. *vi* <sold, sold> 1. (*vendere: product*) essere venduto; (*company, shop*) essere in vendita; **to** ~ **at** [*o* **for**] **$5** essere venduto a 5 dollari 2. (*be accepted*) essere accettato III. *n* 1. (*activity of selling*) vendita *f* 2. *sl* (*deception*) fregatura *f*

◆ **sell off** *vt* svendere; (*shares, property*) cedere

◆ **sell out** I. *vi* 1. COM, FIN cedere la propria attività [*o* quota] 2. *fig* vendersi II. *vt* cedere

sellable *adj* vendibile

sell-by date ['sel·baɪ·,deɪt] *n* COM data *f* limite di vendita

seller *n* 1. (*person*) venditore, -trice *m, f;* ~'**s market** mercato *m* al rialzo 2. (*product*) **good/poor** ~ articolo *m* che si vende bene/male

selling point *n* attrattiva *f* per il consumatore

sellout ['sel·aʊt] *n* 1. THEAT, CINE **to be a** ~ registrare il tutto esaurito 2. *inf* (*betrayal*) tradimento *m*

selves [selvz] *n pl of* **self**

semantic [sə·'mæn·t̬ɪk] *adj* LING semantico, -a

semantics [sə·'mæn·t̬ɪks] *npl* LING semantica *f*

semaphore ['se·mə·fɔːr] I. *n* sistema *m* di segnalazione con le bandiere II. *vt* trasmettere con le bandiere di segnalazione III. *vi* fare segnali con le bandiere di segnalazione

semblance ['semb·ləns] *n form* apparenza *f*

semen ['siː·mən] *n* sperma *m*

semester [sə·'mes·tə̩] *n* UNIV semestre *m*

semi ['se·mi] *n* 1. *inf* (*truck*) semirimorchio *m* 2. *pl, inf* SPORTS semifinale *f;* **we lost in the** ~ **s** abbiamo perso alle semifinali

semiautomatic [,se·mi·ɑː·t̬ə·'mæ·t̬ɪk] *adj* semiautomatico, -a

semicircle ['se·mɪ·,sɜːr·kl] *n* MATH semicerchio *m*

semicircular [,se·mɪ·'sɜːrk·jə·lə̩] *adj* semicircolare

semicolon ['se·mɪ·,koʊ·lən] *n* punto *m* e virgola

semiconductor [,se·mɪ·kən·'dʌk·tə̩] *n* ELEC semiconduttore *m*

semiconscious [,se·mɪ·'kɑːn·tʃəs] *adj* semicosciente

semidetached [,se·mɪ·dɪ·'tætʃt] *adj* ~ **house** casa *f* bifamiliare

semifinal [,se·mɪ·'faɪ·nəl] *n* SPORTS semifinale *f*

semifinalist [,se·mɪ·'faɪ·nə·lɪst] *n* SPORTS semifinalista *mf*

seminal ['se·mə·nəl] *adj* (*important*) fondamentale

seminar ['se·mə·nɑːr] *n* UNIV seminario *m*

seminary ['se·mɪ·ne·ri] *n* REL seminario *m*

semiofficial *adj* semiufficiale

semiotics [,si·mi·'ɑː·t̬ɪks] *n* semiotica *f*

semiprecious [,semɪ'preʃəs] *adj* semiprezioso, -a

semiskilled [,se·mɪ·'skɪld] *adj* con una specializzazione di base; ~ **worker** operaio *m* specializzato

Semite ['se·maɪt] *n* semita *mf*

Semitic [sə·'mɪ·t̬ɪk] *adj* semitico, -a

semitone ['se·mɪ·toʊn] *n* MUS semitono *m*

semitrailer ['se·mɪ·,treɪ·lə̩] *n* semirimorchio *m*

semitropical [,se·mɪ·'trɑː·pɪ·kəl] *adj* subtropicale

semivowel ['se·mɪ·,vaʊ·əl] *n* LING semivocale *f*

semolina [,se·mə·'liː·nə] *n* semolino *m*

Sen. *n Am abbr of* **Senator** senatore, -trice *m, f*

senate ['se·nɪt] *n* 1. POL senato *m* 2. UNIV senato *m* accademico

senator ['se·nə·t̬ə̩] *n* POL senatore, -trice *m, f*

senatorial [ˌse·nə·ˈtɔː·ri·əl] *adj* senatoriale
send [send] *vt* <sent, sent> 1.(*message, letter, flowers, telegram*) inviare, mandare; **to ~ sth by mail** spedire qc per posta; **to ~ sb to prison** mandare qu in prigione; **to ~ one's love to sb** mandare i propri saluti a qu; **~ her my regards** falle i miei saluti; **Philip ~s his apologies** Philip si scusa; **to ~ word (to sb)** *form* informare (qu) 2.(*propel*) lanciare; **to ~ sth flying** far saltare qc in aria 3. RADIO trasmettere 4. *inf* (*cause*) **to ~ sb to sleep** far addormentare qu ▶ **to ~ sb packing** *inf* mandare qu a quel paese
 ◆ **send away** I. *vi* **to ~ for sth** richiedere (per posta) II. *vt* 1.(*dismiss*) mandare via 2.(*send to another place*) mandare
 ◆ **send back** *vt* mandare indietro
 ◆ **send for** *vt* (*person*) chiamare; (*assistance*) chiedere; (*goods*) ordinare
 ◆ **send forth** *vt* 1. *liter* (*make go*) inviare 2.(*emit*) emettere; (*smell, heat*) emanare
 ◆ **send in** *vt* 1.(*application, report*) inviare; (*reinforcements*) mandare 2.(*let in*) fare entrare
 ◆ **send off** I. *vt* (*cause to depart*) mandare; (*by mail*) spedire II. *vi* **to ~ for sth** richiedere qc (per posta)
 ◆ **send on** *vt* 1.(*send in advance*) spedire 2.(*forward: mail*) inoltrare; (*order*) trasmettere
 ◆ **send out** I. *vt* 1.(*ask to leave*) mandar fuori 2.(*send on errand*) mandare 3.(*dispatch*) mandare 4.(*emit: signal, rays*) emettere; (*smell, heat*) emanare II. *vi* **to ~ for sth** chiedere di portare qc
 ◆ **send up** *vt* 1.(*drive up: prices, temperature*) fare alzare 2. *inf* (*mock*) fare la parodia di 3. *inf* (*put in prison*) mettere dentro
sender *n* mittente *mf*; **'return to ~'** 'rispedire al mittente'
sendoff [ˈsend·ɑːf] *n* saluto *m*; **to give sb a good ~** fare una festa d'addio per qu
sendup *n*, **send-up** *n* *inf* parodia *f*
Senegal [ˌse·nɪ·ˈgɔːl] *n* il Senegal
Senegalese [ˌse·nɪ·gə·ˈliːz] I. *adj* senegalese II. *n* senegalese *mf*
senile [ˈsiː·naɪl] *adj* arteriosclerotico, -a; **to go ~** diventare arteriosclerotico
senile dementia *n* demenza *f* senile
senility [sə·ˈnɪ·lə·ti] *n* arteriosclerosi *f inv*
senior [ˈsiːn·jə] I. *adj* 1. *form* (*older*) più vecchio, -a; **James Smith, Senior** James Smith, padre 2.(*higher in rank*) superiore; **to be ~ to sb** essere a un livello più alto di qu 3.(*of earlier appointment*) più anziano, -a 4. SCHOOL superiore; (*pupil*) dell'ultimo anno II. *n* 1.(*older person*) più vecchio, -a *m, f*; **she is two years my ~** ha due anni più di me 2.(*of higher rank*) superiore *mf* 3. SCHOOL studente *mf* dell'ultimo anno
senior citizen *n* anziano, -a *m, f*
senior high school *n* scuola *f* superiore
seniority [siː·ˈnjɔː·rə·ti] *n* anzianità *f*

senior officer *n* alto, -a funzionario, -a *m, f*
senior partner *n* socio, -a *m, f* maggioritario, -a
sensation [sen·ˈseɪ·ʃən] *n* sensazione *f*; **to be a ~** essere sensazionale; **to cause a ~** fare sensazione
sensational [sen·ˈseɪ·ʃə·nəl] *adj* 1.(*fabulous*) sensazionale 2. *pej* (*newspaper, disclosure*) scandalistico, -a
sense [sents] I. *n* 1.(*faculty*) senso *m*; **~ of hearing** udito *m*; **~ of sight** vista *f*; **~ of smell** olfatto *m*; **~ of taste** gusto *m*; **~ of touch** tatto *m* 2.(*ability*) senso *m*; **to lose all ~ of time** perdere la nozione del tempo 3.(*way*) senso *m*; **in every ~** in tutti i sensi; **in a ~** in un certo senso; **in no ~** in nessun modo 4.(*sensation*) sensazione *f* 5. *pl* (*clear mental faculties*) giudizi *m*; **to come to one's ~s** (*see reason*) recuperare la ragione; (*recover consciousness*) recuperare i sensi; **to bring sb to his/her ~s** riportare qu alla ragione; **to take leave of one's ~s** uscire di senno 6.(*good judgment*) (**common**) **~** buonsenso *m*; **to have enough** [*o* **the good**] **~ to ...** avere il buon senso di ...; **to talk ~** dire cose sensate 7.(*feeling*) senso *m*; **to feel a ~ of belonging** provare un senso di appartenenza 8.(*meaning*) senso *m*; **to make ~** avere senso; **in the full ~ of the word** nel vero senso della parola; **there's no ~ in doing ...** non ha senso fare ...; **what's the ~ in doing ...?** che senso ha fare ...? 9.(*opinion*) opinione *f* (comune) II. *vt* percepire; **to ~ that ...** rendersi conto che...
senseless [ˈsents·ləs] *adj* 1.(*pointless*) senza senso 2. MED inconsciente; **to beat sb ~** picchiare qu fino a fargli perdere i sensi
sense organ *n* organo *m* sensoriale
sensibility [ˌsen·tsə·ˈbɪ·lə·ti] *n* sensibilità *f*; **to offend sb's sensibilities** urtare la sensibilità di qu
sensible [ˈsen·tsə·bl̩] *adj* 1.(*having good judgment: person, decision*) sensato, -a 2.(*suitable: clothing, shoes*) pratico, -a 3.(*noticeable*) sensibile 4. *form* (*aware*) consapevole
sensibly *adv* 1.(*wisely*) in modo sensato; (*behave*) con prudenza; (*decide*) con giudizio 2.(*dress*) con abiti pratici
sensitive [ˈsen·tsə·tɪv] *adj* 1.(*sympathetic*) sensibile; **to be ~ to sb's needs** essere sensibile alle necessità di qu 2.(*touchy*) suscettibile; **to be ~ about sth** essere suscettibile riguardo a qc 3.(*delicate: subject, moment, age*) delicato, -a 4.(*classified: documents, work*) confidenziale
sensitiveness *n*, **sensitivity** [ˌsen·tsə·ˈtɪ·və·ti] *n* 1.(*touchiness*) suscettibilità *f* 2.(*understanding*) sensibilità *f* 3.(*classified nature*) confidenzialità *f*
sensitize [ˈsen·tsə·taɪz] *vt* sensibilizzare; **to ~ sb to a problem** sensibilizzare qu a un problema
sensor [ˈsen·tsə] *n* TECH, ELEC sensore *m*
sensory [ˈsen·tsə·ri] *adj* sensoriale

S

sensual ['sen·tʃu·əl] *adj* sensuale

sensuality [ˌsen·tʃu·'æ·lə·ti] *n* sensualità *f*

sensuous ['sen·tʃu·əs] *adj* sensuale

sent [sent] *pp, pt of* **send**

sentence ['sen·təns] I. *n* 1. (*court decision*) sentenza *f;* (*punishment*) pena *f;* **jail** ~ pena detentiva; **life** ~ ergastolo *m;* **to receive a** ~ essere condannato; **to serve a** ~ scontare una pena 2. LING frase *f* II. *vt* condannare

sententious [sen·'ten·ʃəs] *adj form* sentenzioso, -a

sentient ['sen·ʃnt] *adj form* senziente

sentiment ['sen·tə·mənt] *n form* 1. (*opinion*) opinione *f;* **public/popular** ~ opinione pubblica/popolare; **to echo a** ~ farsi eco di un'opinione; **to share sb's** ~ condividere l'opinione di qu 2. (*emotion*) sentimento *m*

sentimental [ˌsen·tə·'men·təl] *adj* 1. (*emotional*) sentimentale; **to be** ~ **about sth** commuoversi per qc 2. *pej* (*mawkish*) sentimentalista

sentimentality [ˌsen·tə·men·'tæ·lə·ti] *n pej* sentimentalismo *m*

sentimentalize [ˌsen·tə·'men·tə·laɪz] *vt pej* fare il sentimentalista su, *la*

sentry ['sen·tri] *n* sentinella *f;* **to be on** ~ **duty** essere di guardia

sentry box *n* garitta *f*

separable ['se·pə·rə·bl] *adj form* separabile

separate[1] ['sep·ə·rɪt] I. *adj* separato, -a; **to remain a** ~ **entity** essere un'entità indipendente; **a** ~ **piece of paper** un pezzo di carta separato; **to go one's** ~ **ways** andare ognuno per la sua strada; **to keep sth** ~ tenere qc separato II. *n pl* abiti *mpl* da coordinare

separate[2] ['se·pə·reɪt] I. *vt* separare; **to** ~ **two people** separare due persone; **to** ~ **egg whites from yolks** separare gli albumi dai tuorli II. *vi* separarsi

separated *adj* separato, -a

separation [ˌse·pə·'reɪ·ʃən] *n* separazione *f*

separatism ['se·pə·rə·tɪ·zm] *n* separatismo *m*

separatist ['se·pə·rə·tɪst] I. *n* separatista *mf* II. *adj* separatista

separator ['se·pə·reɪ·tə] *n* separatore *m*

sepia ['si:·piə] I. *n* seppia *f* II. *adj* seppia *inv*

sepsis ['sep·sɪs] *n* sepsi *f inv*

September [sep·'tem·bə] *n* settembre *m; s.a.* **April**

septic ['sep·tɪk] *adj* settico, -a; **to go** [*o* **turn**] ~ infettarsi

septicemia [ˌsep·tə·'si:·miə] *n* setticemia *f*

septic tank *n* fossa *f* settica

septuagenarian [ˌsep·tu·ə·dʒə·'ne·ri·ən] I. *n* settuagenario, -a *m, f* II. *adj* settuagenario, -a

sepulcher *n* sepolcro *m*

sepulchral [sə·'pʌl·krəl] *adj liter* 1. (*silence*) sepolcrale 2. (*gloomy*) lugubre

sequel ['si:k·wəl] *n* 1. seguito *m;* **the** ~ **to an earlier success** il seguito di un successo precedente 2. (*follow-up*) seguito *m*

sequence ['si:k·wəns] *n* 1. (*order*) ordine *m;* (*of events*) serie *f* 2. (*part of film*) sequenza *f*

sequential [sɪ·'kwen·ʃl] *adj form* sequenziale

sequester *vt* sequestrare

sequin ['si:k·wɪn] *n* paillette *f inv*

sequoia [sɪ·'kwɔ·ɪə] *n* sequoia *f*

Serb [sɜːrb] I. *adj* serbo, -a II. *n* serbo, -a *m, f*

Serbia ['sɜːr·biə] *n* la Serbia *f*

Serbian ['sɜːr·biən] *n s.* **Serb**

Serbo-Croat [ˌsɜːr·bou·krou·'æt] *n* LING serbo-croato *m*

serenade [ˌse·rə·'neɪd] I. *vt* 1. (*sing to*) fare una serenata a 2. (*play music for*) fare una serenata a II. *n* serenata *f*

serene [sə·'ri:n] *adj* 1. (*calm*) sereno, -a; (*sea*) calmo, -a 2. (*tranquil*) tranquillo, -a

serenity [sə·'re·nə·ti] *n* 1. (*calmness*) serenità *f* 2. (*tranquility*) tranquillità *f*

serf [sɜːrf] *n* HIST servo, -a (della gleba) *m*

serfdom *n* HIST servitù *f* (della gleba)

sergeant ['sɑːr·dʒənt] *n* sergente *m;* ~ **at arms** ujier, *funzionario incaricato del mantenimento dell'ordine durante le sessioni parlamentari*

sergeant major *n* ≈ maresciallo *m* capo

serial ['sɪ·ri·əl] I. *n* seriale *m;* TV ~ sceneggiato *m* (televisivo), serial *m inv* II. *adj* 1. (*in series*) consecutivo, -a 2. (*shown in parts*) a puntate

serialize ['sɪ·ri·ə·laɪz] *vt* (*in newspaper, magazine*) pubblicare a puntate; TV, RADIO trasmettere a puntate

serial killer *n* serial killer *mf*

serial number *n* numero *m* di serie

serial port *n* COMPUT porta *f* seriale

series ['sɪ·ri:z] *n inv* 1. (*sequence*) serie *f* 2. (*succession*) serie *f;* **in** ~ ELEC in serie 3. (*set of broadcasts*) serie *f*

serious ['sɪ·ri·əs] *adj* 1. (*earnest, solemn*) serio, -a 2. (*problem, injury*) grave 3. (*not slight*) serio, -a; (*argument*) importante; **to do some** ~ **talking** parlare di cose serie 4. (*determined*) serio, -a; **to be** ~ **about sb** far sul serio con qu; **to be** ~ **about doing sth** voler fare qc sul serio 5. *inf* (*significant*) significativo, -a; ~ **money** un sacco di soldi 6. (*large: debt, amount*) considerevole

seriously *adv* 1. (*in earnest*) seriamente, sul serio; **to** ~ **expect sb to do sth** sperare davvero che qu faccia qc; **no,** ~ ... no, davvero ...; **it would be** ~ **wrong of him if ...** sarebbe un grave errore da parte sua se ... 2. (*ill, damaged*) gravemente 3. *inf* (*very*) estremamente; **she was** ~ **drunk** era completamente ubriaco

seriousness *n* 1. (*truthfulness*) serietà *f;* **in all** ~ in tutta onestà 2. (*serious nature*) gravità *f*

sermon ['sɜːr·mən] *n a. fig* predica *f;* **to deliver a** ~ fare la predica

serpent ['sɜːr·pənt] *n* serpente *m*

serpentine ['sɜːr·pən·taɪn] *adj liter* 1. (*snakelike*) serpentino, -a 2. (*twisting*) tortuoso, -a 3. (*complicated*) astruso, -a 4. (*sly*) scaltro, -a; (*explanation*) artificioso, -a

serrated ['se·reɪ·tɪd] *adj* dentellato, -a;

~ **knife** coltello *m* seghettato
serum ['sɪ·rəm] <-s *o* sera> *n* siero *m*
servant ['sɜːr·vənt] *n* domestico, -a *m, f*
serve [sɜːrv] I. *n* SPORTS servizio *m* II. *vt*
1. (*attend*) servire 2. (*provide: food, drink*)
servire; **to ~ alcohol** servire ·alcolici 3. (*be
enough for*) bastare per 4. (*work for*) prestare
servizio presso; **to ~ sb's interests** fare gli
interessi di qu 5. (*complete: sentence*) scontare; (*mandate*) portare a termine; **to ~ time
(for sth)** *inf* scontare una pena (per qc) 6. (*help
achieve*) essere utile a; **to ~ a purpose** servire
ad uno scopo; **if my memory ~s me right** se
la memoria non mi inganna 7. SPORTS servire
8. (*deliver: writ, summon*) notificare; **to ~ sb
with papers** notificare dei documenti a qu ▶ **it
~s him/her right!** gli/le sta bene! III. *vi*
1. (*put food on plates*) servire 2. (*be useful*)
servire; **to ~ as sth** servire da qc 3. (*work for*)
prestare servizio; **to ~ in the army** servire
nell'esercito 4. SPORTS servire
◆**serve out** *vt* (*sentence*) scontare (fino alla
fine); (*mandate*) portare a termine
◆**serve up** *vt* CULIN servire; *fig* offrire
server ['sɜːr·və] *n* 1. (*spoon*) cucchiaio *m* da
portata; **salad ~s** posate *fpl* da insalata
2. (*tray*) vassoio *m;* (*dish*) piatto *m* da portata
3. (*waiter*) cameriere, -a *m, f* 4. COMPUT
server *m inv* 5. SPORTS *giocatore che effettua il
servizio*
service ['sɜːr·vɪs] I. *n* 1. (*in shop, restaurant*)
servizio *m* 2. (*help, assistance*) servizio *m;*
bus/train ~ servizio di autobus/ferroviario; **to
be of ~ (to sb)** essere utile (a qu); **to operate
a ~** effettuare un servizio; **to press sth into ~**
ricorrere a qc 3. (*department*) **the Service** MIL
l'esercito; NAUT la marina; AVIAT l'aeronautica;
to be fit/unfit for ~ essere idoneo/ non idoneo al servizio militare 4. SPORTS servizio *m*
5. REL funzione *f;* **morning ~** funzione del mattino; **to hold a ~** celebrare una messa 6. TECH,
AUTO revisione *f* 7. (*set*) servizio *m;* **tea ~** servizio da tè ▶ **to be at sb's ~ iron** essere al servizio di qu; **to be in ~** essere in uso II. *vt*
1. (*car, TV*) revisionare 2. FIN **to ~ a loan**
pagare gli interessi di un prestito
serviceable ['sɜːr·vɪ·sə·bl] *adj* pratico, -a
service area *n* area *f* di servizio
service center *n* (*for repairs*) centro *m* riparazioni; (*garage*) officina *f*
service charge *n* costo *m* per il servizio
service industry *n* terziario *m*
servicemember *n* militare *m*
service road *n* strada *f* di accesso
service station *n* stazione *f* di servizio
servile ['sɜːr·vl] *adj pej* servile
servility [sɜːr·'vɪ·lə·ti] *n pej* servilismo *m*
serving ['sɜːr·vɪŋ] I. *n* (*portion*) razione *f*
II. *adj* (*employed*) in servizio attivo
serving spoon *n* cucchiaio *f* da portata
servitude ['sɜːr·və·tuːd] *n form* servitù *f*
servo ['sɜːr·voʊ] *n* (*servomechanism*) servo-
meccanismo *m;* (*servomotor*) servomotore *m*

sesame ['se·sə·mi] *n* sesamo *m* ▶ **open** ~!
apriti sesamo!
session ['se·ʃən] *n* 1. (*of Parliament*)
sessione *f;* (*of a court*) seduta *f;* **to be in ~**
essere in seduta; **a drinking ~** *inf* una sbevaz-
zata 2. SCHOOL **morning/afternoon ~** lezioni
del mattino/del pomeriggio; **fall/winter/
spring/summer ~** primo/secondo/terzo/
quarto trimestre *m*
set [set] I. *adj* 1. (*ready*) pronto, -a; **to get ~** (to
do sth) prepararsi (per fare qc) 2. (*fixed*) fisso,
-a; **to be ~ in one's ways** essere attaccato, -a
alle proprie abitudini 3. (*assigned: book, text*)
nel programma II. *n* 1. (*group: of people*)
gruppo *m;* (*of cups, cutlery*) servizio *m;* (*of
kitchen utensils*) batteria *f;* (*of stamps*) serie *f
inv;* (*of chess*) gioco *m;* (*of tools*) set *m inv;*
~ of glasses servizio di bicchieri; **~ of teeth**
dentiera *f* 2. (*collection*) raccolta *f;* **a complete ~** una raccolta completa 3. CINE set *m inv*
4. (*television*) televisore *m* 5. (*in tennis*) set *m
inv* 6. (*musical performance*) parte *f* (di un
concerto); **to play a long/short ~** suonare a
lungo/per poco III. *vt* <set, set> 1. (*place*)
collocare; **a house that is ~ on a hill** una casa
situata su una collina; **to ~ a broken
bone** comporre una frattura (ossea) 2. (*give:
example*) dare; (*task*) assegnare; (*problem*)
sottoporre 3. (*start*) **to ~ a boat afloat** varare
una barca; **to ~ sth on fire** dare fuoco a qc; **to
~ sth in motion** mettere in moto qc; **to ~ the
country on the road to economic recovery**
avviare la ripresa economica del paese; **to set a
dog on sb** scagliare un cane contro qu
4. (*adjust*) impostare; (*prepare*) preparare; **to
~ the table** apparecchiare la tavola 5. (*fix*) fissare; (*record*) stabilire; (*date, price*) stabilire;
to ~ oneself a goal fissarsi un obiettivo
6. (*arrange*) regolare 7. (*encrust*) ornare;
(*insert*) inserire; **to ~ a watch with
sapphires** incastonare degli zaffiri in un orologio 8. (*provide*) mettere; **to ~ sth to music**
mettere in musica qc IV. *vi* 1. MED comporsi
2. (*become firm: cement*) solidificarsi; (*Jell-O,
cheese*) rapprendersi 3. (*sun*) tramontare
◆**set about** *vt* cominciare; **to ~ doing sth**
cominciare a fare qc
◆**set against** *vt* 1. (*compare*) mettere a confronto; **to set the advantages against the
disadvantages** valutare i vantaggi e gli svant-
aggi 2. (*make oppose*) **to set sb against sb/
sth** mettere qu contro qu/qc
◆**set apart** *vt* 1. (*distinguish*) differenziare
2. (*reserve*) riservare
◆**set aside** *vt* 1. (*save: time*) riservare;
(*money*) mettere da parte 2. (*ignore*) lasciare
da parte; **to set one's differences aside** lasciare da parte le proprie divergenze d'opinione
3. (*overturn*) invalidare 4. (*put to side*) lasciare
da parte
◆**set back** *vt* 1. (*delay*) rimandare 2. (*place
away from*) allontare 3. *inf* (*cost*) costare a
◆**set down** *vt* 1. (*place on surface*) appog-

giare **2.** (*land*) sbarcare; (*airplane*) far atterrare **3.** (*write*) scrivere; (*record*) registrare
◆**set forth** I. *vt form s.* **set out** II. *vi liter* partire
◆**set off** I. *vi* partire; **to ~ (for a place)** mettersi in viaggio (verso un luogo) II. *vt* **1.** (*detonate*) fare esplodere; (*alarm*) azionare **2.** (*make sb do sth*) **to set sb off laughing** far ridere qu **3.** (*start*) scatenare **4.** (*enhance*) mettere in risalto
◆**set on** *vt* **to set sb/sth on sb** scagliare qu/ qc contro qu; **the man was set on by a tiger** l'uomo è stato attaccato da una tigre
◆**set out** I. *vi* **1.** *s.* **set off 2.** (*intend*) **to ~ to do sth** avere l'intenzione di fare qc II. *vt* **1.** (*display, arrange*) disporre **2.** (*explain*) presentare; **to set it out for sb** presentare qc a qu
◆**set to** *vi* **1.** (*begin working*) mettersi al lavoro **2.** (*begin fighting*) venire alle mani
◆**set up** *vt* **1.** (*prepare*) predisporre **2.** (*establish*) stabilire; (*arrange*) disporre; (*cause*) causare; (*committee, corporation*) istituire; (*dictatorship*) instaurare **3.** (*claim*) **to set oneself up as sth** pretendere di essere qc **4.** (*make healthy*) rimettere in sesto **5.** (*provide*) equipaggiare **6.** *inf* (*deceive*) incastrare
setback ['set·bæk] *n* intoppo *m;* **to experience a ~** avere un contrattempo
settee [se·'ti:] *n* divano *m*
setter ['se·ţə] *n* (*dog*) setter *m inv*
setting ['se·ţɪŋ] *n* **1.** (*of sun*) tramonto *m* **2.** (*scenery*) scenario *m;* (*surroundings*) quadro *m;* (*landscape*) paesaggio *m* **3.** TECH regolazione *f* **4.** (*frame for jewel*) montatura *f* **5.** MUS messa *f* in musica
settle ['se·ţl] I. *vi* **1.** (*take up residence*) stabilirsi **2.** (*get comfortable*) accomodarsi **3.** (*calm down*) calmarsi; (*weather*) diventare sereno; (*situation*) stabilizzarsi **4.** (*reach an agreement*) accordarsi **5.** *form* (*pay*) saldare il conto; **to ~ with sb** saldare i conti con qu **6.** (*accumulate*) accumularsi **7.** (*land*) assestarsi; (*bird*) posarsi **8.** (*sink*) assestarsi **9.** (*food*) **once your lunch has settled ...** una volta digerito il pranzo ..., essere digerito II. *vt* **1.** (*calm down: stomach*) mettere a posto **2.** (*decide*) stabilire; **it's been ~d that ...** è stato stabilito che ... **3.** (*conclude*) finalizzare; (*resolve*) risolvere; (*affairs*) sistemare; **to ~ a lawsuit** comporre una lite **4.** (*pay*) saldare **5.** (*colonize*) colonizzare ▸**that ~s it!** questione risolta!
◆**settle down** I. *vi* **1.** (*calm down*) calmarsi **2.** (*take up residence*) stabilirsi II. *vt* **to settle oneself down to sth** disporsi a fare qc
◆**settle for** *vt* accontentarsi di
◆**settle in** *vi* abituarsi
◆**settle on** *vt* **1.** (*decide on*) decidere **2.** (*agree on*) accordarsi su
◆**settle up** *vi* sistemare i conti
◆**settle upon** *vt form s.* **settle on**
settled ['se·ţld] *adj* **1.** (*established*) stabilito, -a; **to be ~ in a regular way of life** condurre

una vita stabile e regolare; **to feel ~** sentirse a proprio agio **2.** (*calm*) calmo, -a **3.** (*fixed: life*) regolare; (*idea*) radicato, -a
settlement ['se·ţl·mənt] *n* **1.** (*resolution*) soluzione *f;* (*of strike*) risoluzione *f* **2.** (*agreement*) accordo *m;* **to negotiate a ~ (with sb)** negoziare un accordo (con qu) **3.** FIN, ECON saldo *m;* **in ~ of sth** a saldo di qc **4.** (*village, town*) insediamento *m;* (*act of colonization*) colonizzazione *f* **5.** (*subsidence*) assestamento *m*
settler ['set·lə] *n* colono, -a *m, f*
set-to ['set·tu:] *n inf* bisticcio *m;* **to have a ~ (with sb)** bisticciare (con qu)
setup ['set·ʌp] *n* **1.** (*way things are arranged*) disposizione *f;* (*arrangement*) organizzazione *f* **2.** *inf* (*trick*) imbroglio *m*
seven ['se·vn] I. *adj* sette *inv* II. *n* sette *m; s.a.* **eight**
sevenfold ['se·vn·foʊld] I. *adj* settuplo, -a II. *adv* **to increase ~** aumentare sette volte
seventeen [,se·vn·'ti:n] I. *adj* diciassette *inv* II. *n* diciassette *m; s.a.* **eight**
seventeenth [,se·vn·'ti:nθ] I. *adj* diciassettesimo, -a II. *n* **1.** (*order*) diciassettesimo, -a *m, f* **2.** (*date*) diciassette *m* **3.** (*fraction, part*) diciassettesimo *m; s.a.* **eighth**
seventh ['se·vənθ] I. *adj* settimo, -a II. *n* **1.** (*order*) settimo, -a *m, f* **2.** (*date*) sette *m* **3.** (*fraction, part*) settimo *m; s.a.* **eighth**
seventieth ['se·vən·tiθ] I. *adj* settantesimo, -a II. *n* (*order*) settantesimo, -a *m, f;* (*fraction, part*) settantesimo *m; s.a.* **eighth**
seventy ['se·vən·ti] I. *adj* settanta *inv* II. *n* <-ies> settanta *m; s.a.* **eighty**
sever ['se·və] *vt* (*limb, branch*) tagliare; (*relationship*) troncare
several ['se·və·rəl] I. *adj* **1.** (*some, distinct*) diversi, -e; **~ times** diverse volte **2.** (*individual*) rispettivi, -e II. *pron* (*some*) alcuni, -e; (*different*) diversi, -e; **~ of us** alcuni di noi; **we've got ~** ne abbiamo diversi
severally *adv* **1.** (*individually*) rispettivamente **2.** (*separately*) distintamente
severance ['se·və·rənts] *n form* rottura *f*
severance pay *n* indennità *f* di fine rapporto
severe [sə·'vɪr] *adj* **1.** (*problem, illness*) grave; (*pain*) forte; **to be under ~ strain** attraversare un periodo di grande stress **2.** (*criticism, punishment, person*) severo, -a; (*rough*) duro, -a **3.** (*weather*) rigido, -a; **~ frost** gelata *f* intensa **4.** (*austere*) austero, -a
severely *adv* **1.** (*harshly*) severamente **2.** (*damaged, ill*) gravemente
severity [sə·'ve·rə·ti] *n* **1.** (*of illness, problem*) gravità *f* **2.** (*of criticism, punishment, person*) severità *f* **3.** (*austerity*) austerità *f*
sew [soʊ] <sewed, sewn *o* sewed> I. *vt* cucire; **hand ~n** cucito a mano II. *vi* cucire
◆**sew on** *vt* cucire
◆**sew up** *vt* **1.** (*repair*) rammendare **2.** MED suturare **3.** *inf* (*arrange*) sistemare; **to ~ a deal** stringere un accordo

sewage ['suːɪdʒ] *n* acque *fpl* di scarico

sewage plant *n* ECOL impianto *f* di depurazione delle acque di scarico

sewer ['suːər] *n* fogna *f*

sewerage ['suːəˑɪdʒ] *n* fogna *f*

sewing ['soʊɪŋ] I. *n* cucito *m* II. *adj* di cucito

sewing machine *n* macchina *f* da cucire

sewn [soʊn] *pp of* **sew**

sex [seks] I. <-es> *n* (*gender, intercourse*) sesso *m;* **to have ~** avere rapporti sessuali II. *vt* individuare il sesso di

sex appeal *n* sex appeal *m*

sex discrimination *n* discriminazione *f* sessuale

sex education *n* educazione *f* sessuale

sexism ['sek·sɪ·zəm] *n* sessimo *m*

sexist I. *adj* sessista II. *n* sessista *mf*

sexless ['seks·ləs] *adj* asessuato, -a

sex life *n* vita *f* sessuale

sex symbol *n* sex symbol *m*

sextant ['seks·tənt] *n* sestante *m*

sextet [seks·'tet] *n* sestetto *m*

sexual ['sek·ʃu·əl] *adj* sessuale

sexual harassment *n* molestie *f* sessuali *pl*

sexual intercourse *n* rapporti *mpl* sessuali

sexuality [sek·ʃu·'æ·lə·ti] *n* sessualità *f*

sexually *adv* sessualmente; **to be ~ abused** subire abusi sessuali

sexy ['sek·si] <-ier, -iest> *adj inf* **1.** (*physically appealing*) sexy *inv* **2.** (*exciting*) eccitante

SGML *n* COMPUT *abbr of* **Standard Generalized Markup Language** SGML *m*

Sgt. *n abbr of* **sergeant** sergente *m*

shabby ['ʃæ·bi] <-ier, -iest> *adj* **1.** (*badly maintained*) in cattivo stato **2.** (*poorly dressed*) transandato, -a **3.** (*substandard*) scadente

shack [ʃæk] *n* baracca *f*

♦ **shack up** *vi* andare a convivere

shackle ['ʃæ·kl] I. *vt* incatenare II. *n pl* catene *fpl*

shade [ʃeɪd] I. *n* **1.** (*shadow*) ombra *f;* **in the ~ of** all'ombra di **2.** (*covering*) parasole *m* **3.** *pl* (*window blind*) tapparella *f* **4.** (*variation*) sfumatura *f;* (*of color*) tonalità *f;* **pastel ~s** tonalità pastello **5.** (*small amount*) pizzico *m* **6.** *pl, inf* (*sunglasses*) occhiali *mpl* da sole **7.** *pl, inf* (*reminder*) **~s of David/1989** questo mi fa pensare a David/al 1989 II. *vt* **1.** (*cast shadow on*) fare ombra a; (*protect*) riparare (dalla luce) **2.** ART ombreggiare III. *vi* (*colors*) fondersi

shading *n* ombreggiatura *f*

shadow ['ʃæ·doʊ] I. *n* **1.** *a. fig* (*shade*) ombra *f;* **the ~s** le tenebre **2.** (*smallest trace*) pizzico *m;* **without a ~ of a doubt** senz'ombra di dubbio **to have ~s under one's eyes** avere le occhiaie; **to be a ~ of one's former self** essere l'ombra di se stesso; **to be afraid of one's own ~** avere paura della propria ombra; **to cast a ~ over sth** proiettare un'ombra su qc; **to be under sb's ~** vivere nell'ombra di qu II. *vt* **1.** ART ombreggiare

2. (*darken*) adombrare **3.** (*follow*) pedinare

shadowboxing ['ʃæ·doʊ·baːk·sɪŋ] *n* pugilato con un avversario immaginario

shadowy <-ier, -iest> *adj* **1.** (*place*) ombreggiato, -a; (*photograph*) scuro, -a **2.** (*vague*) confuso, -a **3.** (*suspicious*) enigmatico, -a

shady ['ʃeɪ·di] <-ier, -iest> *adj* **1.** (*protected from light*) ombreggiato, -a **2.** *inf* (*dubious*) losco, -a

shaft [ʃæft] I. *n* **1.** (*of tool*) manico *m;* (*of weapon, arrow*) asta *f* **2.** TECH albero *m* **3.** (*ray*) raggio *m* **4.** (*for elevator, of mine*) pozzo *m;* **well ~** pozzo **5.** (*of penis*) asta *f* ▶ **to give sb the ~** *sl* prendere qu a pesci in faccia II. *vt sl* (*treat unfairly*) fregare

shag¹ [ʃæg] *n* **1.** (*rug*) tappetino *m* (a pelo lungo) **2.** (*haircut*) zazzera *f*

shag² [ʃæg] *vt* SPORTS **to ~ balls** (in the outfield) fare il raccattapalle (in una partita di baseball)

shag³ [ʃæg] I. *n* (*dance*) ballo degli anni '30 a passi saltellati II. *vi* (*dance*) ballare lo shag

shaggy ['ʃæ·gi] <-ier, -iest> *adj* arruffato, -a; (*coat*) a pelo lungo

shah [ʃɑː] *n* scià *m*

shake [ʃeɪk] I. *n* **1.** (*wobble*) scossa *f;* (*vibration*) scossa *f;* (*quiver*) tremito *m;* **to give sth a good ~** agitare bene qc **2.** *inf* (*milk shake*) frappè *m inv* **3.** (*handshake*) stretta *f* di mano **4.** (*chance*) possibilità *f;* **I don't think you've given him a fair ~** non credo che tu gli abbia veramente dato una possibilità **5.** *inf* (*earthquake*) scossa *f* **6.** *pl* (*sudden trembling*) tremito *m;* **to get the ~s** *inf* avere fifa **7.** *inf* **in two ~s of a lamb's tail** in un baleno II. <shook, shaken> *vt* **1.** (*joggle*) agitare; (*person*) scuotere; (*house*) far tremare; **to ~ one's fist (at sb)** agitare il pugno (contro qu); **to ~ hands** stringersi la mano; **to ~ sb by the hand** stringere la mano a qu; **to ~ one's head** scuotere la testa; **to ~ one's hips** agitare i fianchi **2.** (*unsettle*) agitare **3.** (*make worried*) **to be shaken** essere scosso ▶ **~ a leg** *inf* darsi una mossa III. <shook, shaken> *vi* **1.** (*tremble*) tremare **2.** (*clasp hands*) **let's ~ on it** qua la mano!

♦ **shake down** *vt sl* **1.** (*extort money from*) spillare soldi a **2.** (*search*) persquisire

♦ **shake off** *vt* sbarazzarsi di

♦ **shake out** *vt* scuotere

♦ **shake up** *vt* **1.** (*reorganize*) ristrutturare **2.** (*upset*) scuotere **3.** (*jumble*) scuotere

shakedown ['ʃeɪk·daʊn] *n inf* **1.** (*extortion*) estorsione *f* (di soldi) **2.** (*search*) perquisizione *f*

shaken ['ʃeɪ·kn] *vi, vt pp of* **shake**

shaker ['ʃeɪ·kər] *n* (*for cocktails*) shaker *m inv;* **salt ~** saliera *f*

shakeup ['ʃeɪk·ʌp] *n* ristrutturazione *f*

shakily ['ʃeɪ·kɪ·li] *adv* **1.** (*physically weak*) con aria scossa **2.** (*in an uncertain manner*) in modo poco convincente

shaking ['ʃeɪ·kɪŋ] I. *n* tremito *m* II. *adj* tremante

shaky [ˈʃeɪ·ki] <-ier, -iest> *adj* **1.** (*jerky*) tremante; **to be ~ on one's feet** avere un passo malfermo **2.** (*wavering*) incerto, -a **3.** (*unstable*) instabile

shale [ʃeɪl] *n* scisto *m*

shall [ʃæl] *aux* **1.** (*future*) **I ~ give back the money** restituirò i soldi; **we ~ win the match** vinceremo la partita **2.** (*ought to*) **he ~ call his mother** dovrebbe chiamare sua madre; **we ~ overcome!** ce la faremo! **3.** (*expresses what is mandatory*) **that ~ be unlawful** è illegale

shallot [ʃə·ˈlɑːt] *n* erba *f* cipollina

shallow [ˈʃæ·loʊ] **I.** *adj* **1.** (*not deep*) poco profondo, -a **2.** (*only light*) debole **3.** (*superficial*) superficiale **II.** *npl* bassofondo *m*

shallowness *n* **1.** (*lack of depth*) scarsa profondità *f* **2.** (*superficiality*) superficialità *f*

sham [ʃæm] *pej* **I.** *n* **1.** (*fake*) finzione *f;* (*imposture*) impostura *f* **2.** (*impostor*) impostore, -a *m, f* **3.** (*cover*) **a pillow ~** federa *f* **II.** *adj* (*document, trial*) falso, -a; (*deal*) fraudulento, -a; (*sympathy*) fasullo, -a; (*marriage*) di facciata **III.** <-mm-> *vt* fingere **IV.** *vi* fingere

shambles [ˈʃæm·blz] *n inf* (*place, situation*) casino *m;* **to leave sth in ~** lasciare un gran casino in qc

shame [ʃeɪm] **I.** *n* **1.** (*humiliation*) vergogna *f;* **to die of ~** morire di vergogna; **to feel no ~** non vergognarsi; **to put sb to ~** far vergognare qu; **~ on you!** *a. iron* vergogna! **2.** (*discredit*) disonore *m;* **to bring ~ on sb** disonorare qu **3.** (*pity*) peccato *m;* **what a ~!** peccato!; **what a ~ that ...** che peccato che ... +*subj;* **it's a ~ to have to ...** +*infin* è un peccato dovere ... +*infin;* **it's a ~ that ...** è un peccato che ... +*subj;* **it's a crying ~** è un vero peccato **II.** *vt* **1.** (*mortify*) far vergognare **2.** (*discredit*) disonorare

shamefaced [ˈʃeɪm·ˈfeɪst] *adj* con aria vergognosa

shameful [ˈʃeɪm·fəl] *adj pej* **1.** (*causing disgrace*) vergognoso, -a **2.** (*outrageous*) vergognoso, -a; **it's ~ that ...** è una vergogna che ... +*subj*

shameless [ˈʃeɪm·lɪs] *adj pej* spudorato, -a

shammy [ˈʃæ·mi] <-ies> *n inf* panno *m* di camoscio

shampoo [ʃæm·ˈpuː] **I.** *n* shampoo *m inv* **II.** *vt* fare uno shampoo a; **~ and set** lavare e pettinare

shamrock [ˈʃæm·rɑːk] *n* trifoglio *m*

shank [ʃæŋk] *n* **1.** (*leg*) zampa *f* **2.** TECH gambo *m* ▸ **to go on ~'s pony** andare col cavallo di San Francesco

shanty [ˈʃæn·ti] <-ies> *n* (*shack*) baracca *f*

shantytown *n* baraccopoli *f inv*

shape [ʃeɪp] **I.** *n* **1.** (*form*) forma *f;* **to get out of ~** sformarsi; **to take ~** prendere forma; **in the ~ of sth** a forma di qc; **the ~ of things to come** quello che ci aspetta **2.** (*condition*) stato *m;* **in bad/good ~** in cattivo/buono

stato; **to get sth into ~** sistemare qc; **to get into ~** mettersi in forma; **to knock sth into ~** mettere a punto qc; **to knock sb into ~** portare qu a un buon livello **II.** *vt* **1.** (*form*) **to ~ sth into sth** dare a qc la forma di qc **2.** (*influence*) influenzare **3.** (*determine*) determinare

shapeless [ˈʃeɪp·ləs] *adj* **1.** (*without definite shape*) informe **2.** (*not shapely*) deforme

shapely [ˈʃeɪp·li] <-ier, -iest> *adj* benfatto, -a; **she has a rather ~ figure** è piuttosto benfatta

shard [ʃɑːrd] *n* frammento *m*

share [ʃer] **I.** *n* **1.** (*part*) parte *f;* **to take the lion's ~** fare la parte del leone **2.** (*portion*) parte *f;* **to do one's ~ of sth** fare la propria parte di qc **3.** FIN azione *f;* **stocks and ~s** titoli *mpl* **II.** *vi* **1.** (*divide*) dividere **2.** (*allow others to use*) condividere ▸ **to ~ and ~ alike** fare un po' per uno **III.** *vt* **1.** (*divide*) dividere **2.** (*allow others to use*) condividere **3.** (*have in common*) condividere; **to ~ sb's view** condividere le opinioni di qu; **to want to ~ one's life with sb** voler dividere la propria vita con qu

◆ **share out** *vt* dividere

sharecropper [ˈʃer·ˌkrɑː·pɚ] *n* mezzadro, -a *m, f*

shareholder [ˈʃer·ˌhoʊl·dɚ] *n* azionista *mf*

shareholding *n* partecipazione *f* azionaria

shareware [ˈʃer·wer] *n* COMPUT shareware *m inv*

shark [ʃɑːrk] <-(s)> *n* **1.** (*fish*) squalo *m* **2.** *pej, inf* (*person*) squalo *m*

sharp [ʃɑːrp] **I.** *adj* **1.** (*cutting*) affilato, -a; (*pointed*) aguzzo, -a **2.** (*angular: nose*) appuntito, -a; (*corner, edge, angle*) acuto, -a; (*curve*) stretta, -a **3.** (*severe*) severo, -a; (*pain*) acuto, -a; (*look*) penetrante; (*reprimand*) aspro, -a; **to have a ~ tongue** avere la lingua tagliente; **to be ~ with sb** essere secco, -a con qu **4.** (*astute*) astuto, -a; (*perceptive*) acuto, -a **5.** (*pungent*) aspro, -a; (*wine*) acido, -a; (*cheese*) forte **6.** (*sudden*) improvviso, -a; (*abrupt*) brusco, -a; (*marked*) pronunciato, -a **7.** (*penetrating*) penetrante; (*cry*) acudo, -a **8.** (*distinct*) netto, -a **9.** MUS diesis; **C ~ do diesis II.** *adv* **1.** (*exactly*) in punto; **at ten o'clock ~** alle dieci in punto **2.** (*suddenly*) di colpo; **to pull up ~** fermarsi di colpo **3.** MUS in una tonalità troppo alta **III.** *n* MUS diesis *m*

sharpen [ˈʃɑːr·pən] *vt* **1.** (*blade*) affilare; (*pencil*) fare la punta a **2.** (*intensify*) rinforzare; (*mind*) aguzzare; (*appetite*) stuzzicare

sharpener [ˈʃɑːr·pə·nɚ] *n* (*for knives*) affilatoio *m;* **pencil ~** temperamatite *m inv*

sharp-eyed [ˈʃɑːrp·ˈaɪd] *adj* dalla vista acuta

sharpness *n* **1.** (*of blade*) filo *m;* (*of pencil*) punta *f* **2.** (*of pain*) intensità *f* **3.** (*of comment*) asprezza *f* **4.** (*suddenness: of curve*) angolo *m* brusco **5.** (*intensity*) intensità *f;* (*of blow*) violenza *f* **6.** (*clarity*) nettezza *f* **7.** (*perceptiveness*) acutezza *f;* (*intelligence*) astuzia *f* **8.** (*chic*) eleganza *f*

sharpshooter [ˈʃɑːrp·ˈʃuː·ṭɚ] *n* tiratore,

-trice *m, f* scelto, -a

sharp-sighted ['ʃɑːrp·ˌsaɪ·tɪd] *adj* **1.**(*very observant*) dalla vista acuta **2.**(*alert*) attento, -a

sharp-tongued *adj* mordace

sharp-witted *adj* acuto, -a

shat [ʃæt] *pt, pp of* **shit**

shatter ['ʃæ·t̬ɚ] **I.** *vi* infrangersi **II.** *vt* **1.**(*smash*) infrangere; (*one's hopes, one's dreams*) mandare in fumo **2.**(*disturb*) disturbare; (*unity*) distruggere; **to ~ the peace** disturbare la quiete

shattering *adj* devastante

shatterproof ['ʃæ·t̬ɚ·pruːf] *adj* infrangibile

shave [ʃeɪv] **I.** *n* **to give oneself a ~** radersi ▶ **to have a close ~** cavarsela per un pelo **II.** *vi* radersi, farsi la barba **III.** *vt* **1.**(*remove body hair*) radere; (*head*) rasare **2.**(*decrease: budget*) ridurre; **he ~d three seconds off the world record** ha abbassato di tre secondi il record mondiale **3.**(*brush past*) rasentare

shaven ['ʃeɪ·vən] *adj* rasato, -a

shaver ['ʃeɪ·vɚ] *n* rasoio *m* elettrico

shaving cream *n* crema *f* da barba

shaving gel *n* gel *m* da barba *inv*

shawl [ʃɑːl] *n* scialle *m*

she [ʃiː] **I.** *pron pers* (*female person or animal*) lei; **~'s my mother** (lei) è mia madre; **~'s gone away, but ~'ll be back soon** è andata via, ma tornerà presto; **here ~ comes** eccola; **~ who ...** *form* colei che ... **II.** *n* (*person, animal*) femmina *f*; (*baby*) **it's a ~** è una femmina

sheaf [ʃiːf, ʃiːvz] <sheaves> *n* (*of wheat*) fascio *m*; (*of documents*) fascicolo *m*

shear [ʃɪr] <sheared, sheared *o* shorn> *vt* **1.**(*sheep*) tosare **2.**(*person*) rapare; **to be shorn of sth** *fig* essere privato di qc

◆**shear off** *vi* cedere

shears [ʃɪrz] *npl* (*for sheep*) forbici *fpl* da tosatura; (*for metal*) tenaglie *fpl*

sheath [ʃiːθ] *n* **1.**(*covering*) guaina *f*; (*for knife*) fodero *m* **2.**(*dress*) tubino *m*

sheathe [ʃiːð] *vt* **1.**(*knife*) inguainare **2.**(*cover*) rivestire

shebang [ʃɪ·ˈbæŋ] *n sl* **the whole ~** tutto quanto

shed¹ [ʃed] *n* capanno *m*

shed² [ʃed] <shed, shed> **I.** *vt* **1.**(*cast off*) disfarsi di; (*clothes*) spogliarsi di; (*hair, weight*) perdere; **to ~ one's skin** mutare **2.**(*blood, tears*) spargere; (*light*) emettere **II.** *vi* (*snake*) fare la muta; (*cat*) mutare il pelo

sheen [ʃiːn] *n* lucentezza *f*

sheep [ʃiːp] *n* pecora *f*; (*ram*) montone *m* ▶ **to separate the ~ from the goats** distinguere il grano dal loglio; **black ~** pecora nera

sheepdip ['ʃiːp·dɪp] *n AGR* bagno *m* antiparassitario

sheepdog ['ʃiːp·dɑːg] *n* cane *m* pastore

sheepfold ['ʃiːp·foʊld] *n* recinto *m* delle pecore

sheepish ['ʃiː·pɪʃ] *adj* imbarazzato, -a

sheepskin ['ʃiːp·skɪn] *n* pelle *f* di montone

sheer¹ [ʃɪr] **I.** *adj* **1.**(*unmitigated*) puro, -a; (*boredom, bliss, agony*) totale; **~ coincidence** pura coincidenza **2.**(*vertical*) **~ drop** parete *f* a picco **3.**(*thin*) fino, -a; (*transparent*) trasparente **II.** *adv liter* assolutamente

sheer² [ʃɪr] *vi NAUT* virare

sheet [ʃiːt] *n* **1.**(*for bed*) lenzuolo *m* **2.**(*of paper*) foglio *m* **3.**(*plate of material*) lamina *f*; (*of glass*) lastra *f* **4.**(*perforated set of stamps*) foglio *m* di francobolli **5.**(*paper with information*) foglietto *m* **6.**(*layer*) strato *m* **7.**(*broad mass*) **~ of flame** muro *m* di fiamme; **the rain was coming down in ~s** pioveva a dirotto

sheet lightning *n* bagliore *m* di lampi

sheet metal *n* lamiera *f*

sheet music *n* partiture *fpl*

sheik(h) [ʃiːk] *n* sceicco *m*

shelf [ʃelf, *pl* ʃelvz] <shelves> *n* **1.**(*for storage*) ripiano *m;* **to buy sth off the ~** comprare qc di finito; **to put sth on the ~** *fig* accantonare qc **2.** *GEO* **continental ~** piattaforma *f* continentale

shelf life *n* data *f* limite di vendita

shell [ʃel] **I.** *n* **1.**(*of nut, egg, snail, tortoise*) guscio *m;* (*of shellfish*) conchiglia *f;* (*of crab*) corazza *f* **2.** *TECH* (*of vehicle*) scocca *f;* (*of house*) armatura *f;* (*of ship*) carcassa *f* **3.**(*projectile*) proiettile *m* ▶ **to come** [*o* **bust**] **out of one's ~** uscire dal proprio guscio; **to crawl into one's ~** chiudersi nel proprio guscio **II.** *vt* **1.**(*remove shell: nut*) togliere il guscio a; (*peas*) sgusciare **2.** *MIL* bombardare **III.** *vi* bombardare

◆**shell out** *inf* **I.** *vt* sganciare **II.** *vi* sborsare un sacco di soldi; **to ~ for sth** sborsare un sacco di soldi per qc

shellac [ʃə·ˈlæk] *n* lacca *f*

shellfish ['ʃel·fɪʃ] *n* **1.** *CULIN* frutto *m* di mare **2.** *ZOOL* (*crustacean*) crostaceo *m;* (*mollusc*) mollusco *m*

shelling *n* bombardamento *m*

shell shock *n* trauma *m* da bombardamento

shell-shocked *adj* affetto, -a da trauma da bombardamento; *fig* traumatizzato, -a

shelter ['ʃel·t̬ɚ] **I.** *n* rifugio *m;* **to take ~** rifugiarsi **II.** *vt* dare asilo a **III.** *vi* rifugiarsi

sheltered *adj* **1.**(*protected against weather*) riparato, -a **2.** *pej* (*overprotected*) superprotetto, -a; **to lead a ~ life** vivere nella bambagia **3.**(*tax-protected*) protetto, -a

shelve [ʃelv] **I.** *vt* **1.**(*delay, postpone*) accantonare **2.**(*erect shelves in*) mettere in scaffali **II.** *vi* degradare

shelving *n* ripiani *mpl*

shenanigans [ʃɪ·ˈnæ·nɪ·gənz] *npl* intrighi *mpl*

shepherd ['ʃe·pɚd] **I.** *n* pastore *m* **II.** *vt* (*sheep*) guidare; (*people*) dirigere

shepherd's pie *n* pasticcio *di carne e patate*

sherbet ['ʃɜːr·bət] *n* sorbetto *m*

sheriff ['ʃe·rɪf] *n* sceriffo *m*

sherry ['ʃe·ri] <-ies> *n* sherry *m inv*

shield [ʃiːld] **I.** *n* **1.**(*armor*) scudo *m* **2.**(*pro-*

tective layer) schermo *m* (protettivo); *fig* scudo *m* 3.(*logo*) scudetto *m* 4.(*badge*) distintivo *m* (di polizia) II. *vt* proteggere

shift [ʃɪft] I. *vt* 1.(*change, rearrange*) spostare; **to ~ the blame onto sb** far ricadere la colpa su qu; **to ~ one's ground** cambiare opinione 2.(*in mechanics: gears, lanes*) cambiare II. *vi* (*change, rearrange position*) spostarsi; (*wind*) cambiare III. *n* 1.(*alteration, change*) cambiamento *m;* (*of power*) trasferimento *m* 2.(*period of work*) turno *m;* **to work in ~s** fare i turni 3.(*linguistic change*) slittamento *m*

shifting *adj* (*values*) mutevole; **~ sands** sabbie mobili

shift key *n* tasto *m* delle maiuscole

shiftless [ˈʃɪft·ləs] *adj pej* (*idle*) indolente; (*lacking purpose*) inconcludente

shift work [ˈʃɪft·wɜːrk] *n* lavoro *m* a turni

shift worker *n* turnista *mf*

shifty [ˈʃɪf·ti] <-ier, -iest> *adj* losco, -a; (*eyes*) furtivo, -a

Shiite [ˈʃiː·aɪt] I. *adj* sciita II. *n* sciita *mf*

shilling [ˈʃɪ·lɪŋ] *n* HIST scellino *m*

shimmer [ˈʃɪ·mɚ] I. *vi* luccicare II. *n* lucchichio *m*

shin [ʃɪn] *n* 1.(*leg below knee*) stinco *m* 2.(*lower leg of beef*) stinco *m*

shindig [ˈʃɪn·dɪɡ] *n inf* festa *f* chiassosa

shine [ʃaɪn] I. *n* lucentezza *f* ▶ **to take a ~ to sb** prendere qu in simpatia II. <shone *o* shined, shone *o* shined> *vi* 1.(*moon, sun, stars*) splendere; (*gold, metal*) luccicare; **the light is shining in my eyes** ho la luce negli occhi 2.(*be gifted*) essere brillante III. <shone *o* shined, shone *o* shined> *vt* 1.(*point light*) **to ~ a light at sth/sb** puntare una luce su qc/qu; **to ~ a flashlight onto sth** puntare una lampadina tascabile su qc 2.(*brighten by polishing*) far brillare

shiner [ˈʃaɪ·nɚ] *n inf* occhio *m* nero

shingle [ˈʃɪŋ·ɡl] *n* 1.(*roof tile*) scandola *f* 2.(*pebble mass alongside water*) ciottoli *mpl*

shining [ˈʃaɪ·nɪŋ] *adj* 1.(*gleaming*) splendente; (*eyes*) brillante; **she looked at him with ~ eyes** lo ha guardato con gli occhi che le brillavano 2.(*outstanding*) eccellente, -a; **a ~ example** un esempio perfetto

shin splints *npl, npl* dolori *mpl* agli stinchi

shiny [ˈʃaɪ·ni] <-ier, -iest> *adj* brillante

ship [ʃɪp] I. *n* nave *f;* **passenger ~** nave *m* passeggeri; **sailing ~** veliero *m;* **to board a ~** imbarcarsi su una nave II. *vt* <-pp-> 1.(*send by boat*) mandare via nave; **to ~ freight** mandare della merce via nave 2.(*transport*) trasportare

◆ **ship off** *vt* (*goods*) spedire; (*person*) mandare

◆ **ship out** *vi* imbarcarsi

shipboard [ˈʃɪp·bɔːrd] I. *adj* a bordo (della nave) II. *n* **on ~** a bordo

shipbuilder [ˈʃɪp·ˌbɪl·dɚ] *n* costruttore, -trice *m, f* navale

shipbuilding *n* costruzioni *f* navale

shipload [ˈʃɪp·loʊd] *n* carico *m*

shipmate *n* compagno, -a di bordo *m*

shipment [ˈʃɪp·mənt] *n* 1.(*quantity*) carico *m* 2.(*action*) spedizione *f*

shipowner *n* 1.(*person*) armatore, -trice *m, f* 2.(*company*) società *f* armatrice

shipper *n* spedizioniere, -a *m, f;* **wine ~** importatore *m* di vino

shipping [ˈʃɪ·pɪŋ] *n* 1.(*ships*) imbarcazioni *fpl* 2.(*freight dispatch*) spedizione *f*

shipping agent *n* agente marittimo

shipping lane *n* rotta *f* di navigazione

shipshape [ˈʃɪp·ʃeɪp] *adj inf* pulito, -a e ordinato, -a; **to get sth ~** tirare a lucido qc

shipway [ˈʃɪp·weɪ] *n* canale *m* (navigabile)

shipwreck I. *n* 1.(*accident*) naufragio *m* 2.(*remains of ship*) relitto *m* II. *vt* far naufragare; **to be ~ed** naufragare; *fig* rovinare

shipwright *n* maestro *m* d'ascia

shipyard *n* cantiere *m* navale

shire [ˈʃa·ɪɚ] *n* contea *f*

shire horse *n* cavallo *m* da tiro

shirk [ʃɜːrk] *pej* I. *vt* sottrarsi a II. *vi* defilarsi; **to ~ (away) from sth** sottrarsi a qc

shirker [ˈʃɜːr·kɚ] *n pej* scansafatiche *mf inv*

shirt [ʃɜːrt] *n* (*man's, woman's*) camicia *f* ▶ **to give sb the ~ off one's** back togliersi la camicia di dosso per qu; **to have the ~ off sb's** back lasciare qu in mutande; **to lose one's ~** *inf* rimanere in mutande; **keep your ~ on!** *inf* non scaldarti!

shirtsleeve [ˈʃɜːrt·sliːv] *n* manica *f* di camicia; **to be in ~s** essere in maniche di camicia

shit [ʃɪt] *inf* I. *n* 1.(*feces*) merda *f* 2. *pej* (*nonsense*) stronzate *fpl* 3.(*nothing*) una mazza; **he doesn't know ~ about computers** non capisce una mazza di computer 4.(*as intensifier*) **I don't give a ~!** me ne sbatto! ▶ **to beat the ~ out of sb** menare qu a sangue; **to frighten the ~ out of sb** far cagare adosso qu (dalla paura); **to be in deep ~** essere nella merda; **when the ~ hits the** fan quando scoppia il casino; **no ~!** ma va! II. *interj* merda III. <shit, shit> *vi* cagare IV. <shit, shit> *vt* cagare; **to ~ oneself** [*o* one's pants] *a. fig* cagarsi addosso; **to ~ bricks** [*o* a brick] cagarsi addosso

shitty [ˈʃɪ·ti] <-ier, -iest> *adj pej, inf* 1.(*unfair, unpleasant*) di merda 2.(*sick, ill*) di merda; **to feel ~** mi sento di merda

shiver [ˈʃɪ·vɚ] I. *vi* tremare; **to ~ with cold** tremare dal freddo II. *n* brivido *m;* **to feel a ~** rabbrividire; **to give sb the ~s** *inf* far rabbrividire qu

shoal¹ [ʃoʊl] *n* (*of fish*) banco *m*

shoal² [ʃoʊl] *n* 1.(*area of shallow water*) bassofondo *m* 2.(*sand bank*) banco *m* di sabbia

shock¹ [ʃɑːk] I. *n* 1.(*unpleasant surprise*) shock *m inv;* **the ~ of my life** *inf* il più grosso spavento della mia vita; **look of ~** espressione *f* scioccata; **to give sb a ~** scioccare qu 2. *inf* (*electric shock*) scarica *f* 3. MED shock *m inv;* **to die from ~** soccombere allo shock

4. (*impact: of explosion, earthquake*) scossa *f* **II.** *vt* **1.** (*appall*) scioccare **2.** (*scare*) spaventare **III.** *vi* scontrarsi

shock² [ʃɑːk] *n* (*of hair*) zazzera *f*

shock absorber [ˈʃɑːkˌəbˌsɔːrˌbər] *n* ammortizzatore *m*

shocker [ˈʃɑːkər] *n inf* (*unpleasant news*) notizia *f* tremenda; (*surprising news*) notizia *f* scioccante

shocking [ˈʃɑːkɪŋ] *adj* **1.** (*causing indignation, distress*) spaventoso, -a **2.** (*surprising*) scioccante **3.** (*offensive*) scandaloso, -a; (*crime*) orrendo, -a

shockproof [ˈʃɑːkˌpruːf] *adj* **1.** (*mechanism*) a prova d'urto **2.** (*person*) imperturbabile

shock therapy *n*, **shock treatment** *n* terapia *f* shock

shock troops *npl* truppe *fpl* d'assalto

shock wave *n* **1.** PHYS onda *f* d'urto **2.** *fig* **to send shock waves** provocare vivissime reazioni *fpl*

shod [ʃɒd] *pt, pp of* **shoe**

shoddy [ˈʃɑːdi] <-ier, -iest> *adj pej* **1.** (*goods*) scadente **2.** (*treatment*) meschino, -a

shoe [ʃuː] **I.** *n* (*for person*) scarpa *f*; (*for horse*) ferro *m*; **high-heeled** ~**s** scarpe *fpl* col tacco (alto); **athletic** ~**s** scarpe *fpl* da ginnastica ▶ **to fill sb's** ~**s** prendere il posto di qu; **if I were in your** ~**s** *inf* se fossi in te **II.** <shod, shod *o* shodden> *vt* (*person*) calzare; (*horse*) ferrare

shoehorn [ˈʃuːˌhɔːrn] *n* calzascarpe *m inv*, calzante *m*

shoelace *n* laccio *m* (di scarpa); **to tie one's** ~**s** allacciarsi le scarpe

shoemaker *n* calzolaio, -a *m, f*

shoe polish *n* lucido *m* da scarpe

shoeshine [ˈʃuːˌʃaɪn] *n* lucidatura *f* delle scarpe

shoestring [ˈʃuːˌstrɪŋ] **I.** *adj* **1.** (*long and narrow*) in listarelle sottili; ~ **potatoes** patate tagliate a listarelle sottili e fritte **2.** (*monetarily limited*) **to do sth on a** ~ **budget** fare qc con un budget ridottissimo **II.** *n* stringa *f* (delle scarpe) ▶ **to do sth on a** ~ *inf* fare qc con pochissimi soldi; **to start on a** ~ partire dal niente

shoetree *n* forma *f* (per scarpe)

shone [ʃoʊn] *pt, pp of* **shine**

shoo [ʃuː] **I.** *interj inf* sciò **II.** *vt inf* cacciare

shook [ʃʊk] *n pt of* **shake**

shoot [ʃuːt] **I.** <shot, shot> *vi* **1.** (*fire weapon*) sparare; **to** ~ **to kill** sparare per uccidere; **to** ~ **at sth/sb** sparare a qc/qu **2.** (*aim*) **to** ~ **for sth** mirare a qc **3.** SPORTS tirare **4.** CINE girare; PHOT scattare **5.** (*move rapidly*) sfrecciare; **to** ~ **to fame** avere un successo fulmineo; **to** ~ **past** (*car*) sfrecciare ▶ **to** ~ **for the moon** [*o* **the stars**] puntare al massimo **II.** <shot, shot> *vt* **1.** (*bullet*) sparare; (*missile, arrow*) lanciare **2.** (*person*) sparare a; **to** ~ **sb dead** sparare a qu a morte **3.** CINE (*film*) girare; (*a scene*) riprendere; PHOT scattare **4.** (*direct*) **to** ~ **questions at sb** mitragliare qu di domande; **to** ~ **a**

glance at sb lanciare un'occhiata a qu **5.** *inf* **to** ~ **a goal/basket** fare un gol/canestro **6.** *inf* (*drugs*) **to** ~ **heroin** farsi di eroina ▶ **to** ~ **the breeze** *sl* parlare del più e del meno; **to** ~ **darts at sb** *inf* fulminare qu con un'occhiata; **to** ~ **the works** *inf* dar fondo a tutte le proprie risorse **III.** *n* **1.** (*hunt*) partita *f* di caccia; **to go on a** ~ andare a caccia **2.** CINE ripresa *f*; PHOT serie *finv* di scatti **3.** BOT germoglio *m* **IV.** *interj* (*shit*) mannaggia

◆ **shoot ahead** *vi* balzare in alto

◆ **shoot down** *vt* (*aircraft*) abbattere; *inf* (*proposal*) fare a pezzi

◆ **shoot off** **I.** *vt* **to shoot one's mouth off** *sl* straparlare **II.** *vi* (*vehicle*) partire a tutta velocità

◆ **shoot out** *vi* schizzare fuori

◆ **shoot past** *vi* sfrecciare

◆ **shoot up** *vi* **1.** (*expand, increase rapidly*) crescere molto; (*skyscraper*) spuntare dal nulla *inf* **2.** *inf* (*inject drugs*) farsi una pera

shooting [ˈʃuːtɪŋ] **I.** *n* **1.** (*killing*) uccisione *f* **2.** (*firing of gun*) sparatoria *f* **3.** (*caccia*) **to go** ~ andare a caccia **4.** SPORTS tiro *m* **II.** *adj* (*pain*) lancinante

shooting gallery *n* tiro *m* a segno, *locale*

shooting star *n* stella *f* cadente

shootout [ˈʃuːtˌaʊt] *n* sparatoria *f*

shop [ʃɑːp] **I.** *n* **1.** (*for sale of goods*) negozio *f*; **book** ~ libreria *f* **2.** (*for manufacture*) officina *f* ▶ **to set up** ~ (**as sth**) mettersi in proprio (come qc); **to talk** ~ parlare di lavoro **II.** <-pp-> *vi* comprare

shopaholic [ˌʃɑːpəˈhɑːˌlɪk] *n inf* maniaco, -a *m, f* dello shopping

shopkeeper *n* negoziante *mf*

shopkeeping *n* commercio *m* (al dettaglio)

shoplifter [ˈʃɑːpˌlɪfˌtər] *n* taccheggiatore, -trice *m, f*

shoplifting *n* taccheggio *m*

shopper *n* persona *f* che fa acquisti

shopping [ˈʃɑːpɪŋ] *n* **1.** (*activity*) shopping *m inv*; **to go** ~ andare a fare shopping; (*food*) andare a fare la spesa **2.** (*purchases*) acquisti *mpl*; (*food*) spesa *f*

shopping bag *n* sacchetto *m* per acquisti; (*for food*) borsa *f* spesa

shopping basket *n* cestino *m* della spesa

shopping cart *n* carrello *m, di negozio, supermercato;* COMPUT carrello (acquisti) *m*

shopping center *n* centro *m* commerciale

shopping list *n* lista *f* della spesa

shopping mall *n* centro *m* commerciale

shop steward *n* rappresentante *mf* sindacale

shoptalk *n* discorsi *mpl* di lavoro

shopworn [ˈʃɑːpˌwɔːrn] *adj* **1.** (*goods*) deteriorato, -a **2.** (*cliché*) trito, -a

shore [ʃɔːr] *n* **1.** (*coast*) costa *f* **2.** (*beach*) spiaggia *f*; **on** ~ a terra **3.** *pl, lit* (*a country*) **these** ~**s** questi lidi **4.** ARCHIT puntello *m*

◆ **shore up** *vt a. fig* puntellare

shore leave *n* permesso *m* di sbarcare

shoreline *n* linea *f* di costa

shorn [ʃɔːrn] *pp of* **shear**

short [ʃɔːrt] I. *adj* 1. (*not long*) corto, -a 2. (*not tall*) basso, -a 3. (*brief*) breve; (*memory*) corto, -a 4. (*not enough*) scarso, -a; **to be short** [*o* **run**] **on time/money** aver poco tempo/pochi soldi; **to be ~ on brains** *inf* aver poco cervello; **to be ~ of breath** essere senza fiato; **to be in ~ supply** scarseggiare 5. LING (*vowel*) breve 6. (*brusque*) brusco, -a; **to be ~ with sb** essere brusco con qu II. *n* 1. CINE cortometraggio *m* 2. *inf* ELEC cortocircuito *m* III. *adv* 1. (*abruptly*) **to cut ~** interrompere di colpo; **to stop sth/sb ~** fermare qc/qu di colpo 2. (*below the standard*) **to fall ~** non essere sufficiente; **to fall ~ of sth** essere al di sotto di qc

shortage [ˈʃɔːr·tɪdʒ] *n* carenza *f*

shortbread [ˈʃɔːrt·bred] *n* biscotto *f* di pastafrolla

shortcake *n* *torta alla crema e alla frutta;* **strawberry ~** torta *f* alle fragole

shortchange [ʃɔːrt·ˈtʃeɪndʒ] *vt* dare il resto sbagliato a; *fig* truffare

short circuit *n* cortocircuito *m*

short-circuit [ʃɔːrt·ˈsɜːr·kɪt] I. *vi* andare in cortocircuito II. *vt* 1. ELEC mandare in cortocircuito 2. (*bypass*) bypassare

shortcoming [ˈʃɔːrt·kʌ·mɪŋ] *n* difetto *m*

shortcut *n* a. *fig* scorciatoia *f;* **keyboard ~** COMPUT combinazione *f* di tasti

shortcut key *n* COMPUT tasto *m* scorciatoia

shorten [ˈʃɔːr·tən] I. *vt* accorciare; (*name, title*) abbreviare II. *vi* accorciarsi

shortening [ˈʃɔːrt·nɪŋ] *n* 1. CULIN grasso *m* (da pasticceria) 2. (*reduction*) riduzione *f*

shortfall [ˈʃɔːrt·fɔːl] *n* differenza *f* (negativa); ECON deficit *m inv*

shorthand [ˈʃɔːrt·hænd] *n* stenografia *f*

short-handed [ʃɔːrt·ˈhæn·dɪd] *adj* a corto di personale; **a ~ goal** un gol segnato con la squadra non al completo

short-haul [ˈʃɔːrt·hɑːl] *adj* a breve raggio

short-list *vt* preselezionare

shortlist *n* lista *f* di candidati preselezionati

short-lived *adj* effimero, -a

shortly [ˈʃɔːrt·li] *adv* entro breve; **~ after ...** poco dopo ...

shortness [ˈʃɔːrt·nɪs] *n* 1. (*condition of being short*) scarsa lunghezza *f* 2. (*brevity*) brevità *f* 3. (*insufficiency*) carenza *f;* **~ of breath** mancanza *f* di fiato 4. (*brusqueness*) secchezza *f*

short order *n* pasto *m* rapido; (*order*) ordinazione *f* di pasto rapido

short-order *adj* **~ cook** cuoco addetto alla *preparazione di pasti rapidi*

short-range *adj* MIL a corto raggio

shorts [ʃɔːrts] *npl* 1. (*short pants*) pantaloncini *mpl;* **a pair of ~** un paio di pantaloncini 2. (*underpants*) mutande *fpl;* **boxer ~** boxer *mpl*

short shrift [ʃrɪft] *n* **to get ~ from sb** farsi liquidare in fretta da qu; **to give ~ to sb** liquidare in fretta qu; **to give ~ to sth** liquidare in fretta qc

short-sleeved *adj* a maniche corte

short-staffed *adj* a corto di personale

shortstop *n* 1. (*position*) interbase *m* 2. (*player*) interbase *m*

short story *n* racconto *m*

short-tempered *adj* irascibile

short-term *adj* a breve termine

shortwave I. *n* onda *f* corta II. *adj* (*radio*) a onde corte; (*broadcasting*) su onde corte

shot¹ [ʃɑːt] I. *n* 1. (*act of firing weapon*) sparo *m;* **to fire a ~** sparare un colpo 2. (*shotgun pellets*) pallini *mpl* 3. (*person*) tiratore, -trice *m, f;* **to be a good/poor ~** essere un buon/cattivo tiratore 4. SPORTS (*soccer, basketball*) tiro *m;* (*tennis*) colpo *m* 5. (*photograph*) foto *f;* CINE ripresa *f* 6. *inf* (*injection*) puntura *f* 7. *inf* (*try, stab*) tentativo *m;* **to have** [*o* **take**] **a ~ at sth** fare un tentativo con qc; **to give sth one's best ~** far del proprio meglio con qc 8. (*small amount of alcohol*) bicchierino *m* ▸ **a ~ in the arm** un incoraggiamento; **it was a ~ in the dark** *inf* ho [*o* hai] [*o* ha] tirato a indovinare; **not by a long ~** neanche lontanamente; **to call (all) the ~s** dettar legge *fig* II. *pp, pt of* **shoot**

shot² [ʃɑːt] *adj* 1. *inf* (*worn out*) distrutto, -a 2. (*woven*) striato, -a

shotgun [ˈʃɑːt·gʌn] *n* fucile *m*

shot put *n* SPORTS lancio *m* del peso

shot-putter *n* lanciatore, -trice *m, f* del peso

should [ʃʊd] *aux* 1. (*expression of advisability*) **to insist that sb ~ do sth** insistere perché qu faccia qc 2. (*asking for advice*) **~ I/we ...?** devo/dobbiamo ...? 3. (*expression of expectation*) **I ~ be so lucky!** *inf* magari fossi così fortunato! 4. *form* (*expressing a condition*) **I ~ like to see her** mi piacerebbe vederla 5. (*rhetorical expression*) **why ~ I/you ...?** perché dovrei/dovresti ...? 6. *form* (*would*) **we ~ like to invite you** ci piacerebbe invitarla

shoulder [ˈʃoʊl·də] I. *n* 1. ANAT spalla *f;* **~ to ~** fianco a fianco; **to glance over one's ~** guardare al di sopra delle spalle di qu; **to sling sth over one's ~** mettersi qc sulle spalle; **to be sb's ~ to cry on** offrire a qu una spalla su cui piangere; **to lift a burden off one's ~s** *fig* togliersi un peso 2. (*piece of meat*) spalla *f* 3. (*side of road*) area *f* di sosta 4. (*shoulder-like part of sth*) spalla *f* ▸ **to rub ~s with sb** frequentare qu; **to stand ~ to ~ with sb** spalleggiare qu II. *vt* 1. spingere; **to ~ one's way** farsi largo a spinte; **to ~ sb aside** spingere qu da una parte con una spallata 2. (*place on one's shoulders*) caricarsi in spalla 3. (*accept: responsibility*) sobbarcarsi

shoulder bag *n* borsa *f* a tracolla

shoulder blade *n* scapola *f*

shoulder pad *n* spallina *f*

shoulder strap *n* bretella *f*

shout [ʃaʊt] I. *n* grido *m* ▸ **to give sb a ~** *inf* fare un fischio a qu II. *vi* gridare; **to ~ at sb** gridare a qu; **to ~ for help** gridare aiuto ▸ **to give**

sb sth to ~ about dare a qu motivo di rallegrarsi **III.** *vt* gridare
♦**shout down** *vt* zittire a urla
♦**shout out** *vt* gridare
shouting *n* grida *fpl*
shouting distance *n* **within ~** a portata di voce
shouting match *n* serie *f* di grida *inv*
shove [ʃʌv] **I.** *n* spintone *m;* **to give sth a ~** dare uno spintone a qc **II.** *vt* **1.** (*push*) spingere; **to ~ one's way through** farsi largo spintonando; **to ~ sb about** [*o* **around**] *fig* mettere i piedi in testa a qu **2.** *vulg* **~ it** (**up your ass**)! ficcatelo su per il culo! **III.** *vi* spingere; **to ~ along** *inf* spostarsi
♦**shove off** *vi* **1.** *inf* (*go away*) smammare **2.** (*launch by foot*) lasciare la riva, *spingendosi via con un piede*
shovel [ˈʃʌvəl] **I.** *n* **1.** (*tool*) pala *f;* **a ~ of sth** una palata di qc **2.** (*machine*) escavatore *m* **II.** <-ll-, -l-> *vt* spalare; **to ~ food into one's mouth** abbuffarsi **III.** <-ll-, -l-> *vi* spalare
show [ʃoʊ] **I.** *n* **1.** (*expression*) dimostrazione *f;* **~ of solidarity** dimostrazione *f* di solidarietà **2.** (*exhibition*) mostra *f;* **dog ~** mostra canina; **fashion ~** sfilata *f* di moda; **slide ~** proiezione *f* di diapositive; **to be on ~** essere esposto **3.** (*play*) spettacolo *m;* TV programma *m;* THEAT rappresentazione *f;* **quiz ~** quiz *m inv* televisivo **4.** *inf* (*venture*) **who runs the ~?** chi manda avanti la baracca? ▶**~ of hands** voto *m* palese; **let's get the ~ on the road** *inf* diamoci dentro; **to put on a good ~** fare una bella figura; **the ~ must go on** *prov* lo spettacolo deve andare avanti; **to run the ~** comandare **II.** <showed, shown> *vt* **1.** (*display*) mostrare; (*slides*) proiettare; ART esporre **2.** (*express*) manifestare **3.** (*expose*) esporre **4.** (*point out, record*) indicare **5.** (*prove*) dimostrare; **to ~ sb that ...** dimostrare a qu che ... **6.** (*escort*) accompagnare; **to ~ sb to the door** accompagnare qu alla porta **7.** (*project*) proiettare; (*on television*) trasmettere **III.** *vi* <showed, shown> **1.** (*be visible*) vedersi **2.** (*exhibit: art*) essere esposto; **now showing at a cinema near you!** (*film*) attualmente in programmazione nelle sale cinematografiche **3.** *inf* (*arrive*) farsi vivo
♦**show around** *vt* far da guida a
♦**show in** *vt* far passare
♦**show off** **I.** *vt* mettere in risalto **II.** *vi* mettersi in mostra
♦**show out** *vt* accompagnare alla porta
♦**show up** **I.** *vi* **1.** *inf* (*arrive*) arrivare **2.** (*be apparent*) vedersi **II.** *vt* **1.** (*expose*) mettere in luce; **to show sb up as** (**being**) **sth** dimostrare che qu è qc **2.** (*embarrass*) mettere in imbarazzo
show biz *n inf s.* **show business** show business *m,* mondo *m* dello spettacolo
showboat *n* **1.** (*boat*) showboat *m inv* **2.** (*person*) spaccone, -a *m, f*

show business *n* show business *m inv,* mondo *m* dello spettacolo
showcase **I.** *n* teca *f* **II.** *vt* esporre
showdown [ˈʃoʊ·daʊn] *n* resa *f* dei conti
shower [ˈʃa·ʊə·] **I.** *n* **1.** (*for washing*) doccia *f* **2.** (*of rain*) acquazzone *m;* (*of sparks, insults*) pioggia *f* **3.** (*party*) **bridal ~** festa *f* in onore della futura sposa; **baby ~** festa in onore del nascituro **II.** *vi* **1.** (*take a shower*) farsi la doccia **2.** (*spray*) piovere **III.** *vt* **1.** (*spray*) spruzzare; **to ~ sb with water** spruzzare qu d'acqua **2.** (*bestow*) coprire; **to ~ compliments on sb** coprire qu di compliemnti; **to ~ sb with gifts** coprire qu di regali
shower curtain *n* tenda *f* della doccia
shower gel *n* gel *m inv* da doccia
showery [ˈʃa·ʊə·i] *adj* con frequenti rovesci
showgirl *n* showgirl *f inv*
showground *n luogo dove si tiene una fiera all'aperto*
showing *n* **1.** (*exhibition*) mostra *f* **2.** (*broadcasting*) proiezione *f* **3.** (*performance*) prestazione *f*
show jumping [ˈʃoʊ·ˌdʒʌm·pɪŋ] *n* concorso *m* ippico
showman [ˈʃoʊ·mən] *n* showman *m inv*
showmanship [ˈʃoʊ·mən·ʃɪp] *n* senso *m* dello spettacolo
shown [ʃoʊn] *pp of* **show**
showoff [ˈʃoʊ·ɑːf] *n* spaccone, -a *m, f*
showpiece [ˈʃoʊ·piːs] **I.** *n* fiore *m* all'occhiello **II.** *adj* modello
show room [ˈʃoʊ·ruːm] *n* showroom *f inv,* show room *m inv*
showy [ˈʃoʊ·i] <-ier, -iest> *adj* vistoso, -a
shrank [ʃræŋk] *vt, vi pt of* **shrink**
shrapnel [ˈʃræp·n(ə)l] *n* palletta *f* (di granata)
shred [ʃred] **I.** <-dd-> *vt* (*cut into shreds*) tagliare a striscioline; (*document*) distruggere **II.** *n* **1.** (*strip*) striciolina *f;* **to be in ~s** essere a brandelli; **to tear sth to ~s** ridurre a brandelli qc **2.** *fig* (*of hope, truth, evidence*) briciolo *m*
shredder [ˈʃre·də·] *n* distruggidocumenti *m inv*
shrew [ʃruː] *n* **1.** (*animal*) toporagno *m* **2.** *pej* (*bad-tempered woman*) megera *f*
shrewd [ʃruːd] *adj* (*person*) astuto, -a; (*comment*) acuto, -a; (*decision*) felice; (*eye*) penetrante
shriek [ʃriːk] **I.** *n* urlo *m* **II.** *vi* urlare; **to ~ with laughter** ridere a più non posso **III.** *vt* urlare
shrill [ʃrɪl] *adj* stridulo, -a
shrimp [ʃrɪmp] *n* <-(s)> **1.** ZOOL gamberetto *m* **2.** *inf* (*person*) scricciolo *m*
shrimp cocktail *n* cocktail *m* di gamberetti *inv*
shrine [ʃraɪn] *n* **1.** (*tomb*) tomba *f* **2.** (*site of worship*) santuario *m;* **a ~ for sb** un santuario dedicato a
shrink [ʃrɪŋk] **I.** *n inf* strizzacervelli *m inv* **II.** <shrank *o* shrunk, shrunk *o* shrunken> *vt* **1.** (*make smaller*) restringere **2.** (*reduce: costs*) ridurre **III.** <shrank *o* shrunk, shrunk *o* shrunken> *vi* **1.** (*become smaller: clothes*) restringersi **2.** (*become reduced*) ridursi

S

3. *liter* (*cower*) indietreggiare; **to ~ away from sb/sth** indietreggiare davanti a qu/qc **4.** (*be reluctant to*) **to ~ from sth** sottrarsi a qc; (*be reluctant to*); **to ~ from doing sth** essere restio a fare qc

shrinkage ['ʃrɪŋ·kɪdʒ] *n* **1.** (*of clothes*) restringimento *m* **2.** (*of costs*) riduzione *f*

shrink-wrap ['ʃrɪŋk·ræp] **I.** *n* pellicola *f* (termoretraibile) **II.** *vt* (*food*) avvolgere (nella pellicola)

shrivel ['ʃrɪ·vəl] <-ll-, -l-> **I.** *vi* (*fruit*) disidratare; (*plant*) appassire; (*skin, person*) raggrinzire **II.** *vt* (*fruit*) disidratare; (*skin*) raggrinzire

  ◆**shrivel up** *vi* (*fruit*) disidratarsi; (*plant*) appassire; (*person*) raggrinzire

shroud [ʃraʊd] **I.** *n* (*covering*) velo *m*; (*for burial*) lenzuolo *m* funebre; (*of dust, fog*) cappa *f* **II.** *vt* avvolgere; **to ~ sth in sth** avvolgere qc in qc; **~ed in mystery** avvolto nel mistero

Shrove Tuesday [ʃroʊv·'tu:z·deɪ] *n* martedì *m inv* grasso

shrub [ʃrʌb] *n* arbusto *m*

shrubbery ['ʃrʌ·bə·ri] *n* arbusti *mpl*

shrug [ʃrʌg] **I.** *n* alzata *f* di spalle **II.** <-gg-> *vt* **to ~ one's shoulders** alzare le spalle **III.** <-gg-> *vi* alzare le spalle

  ◆**shrug off** *vt* (*ignore*) prendere alla leggera

shrunk [ʃrʌŋk] *pp, pt of* **shrink**

shrunken ['ʃrʌŋ·kən] **I.** *pp of* **shrink II.** *adj* (*person*) rinsecchito, -a; (*profits*) ridotto, -a

shuck [ʃʌk] *vt* **1.** (*oysters*) aprire; (*corn*) scartocciare **2.** (*get rid of: clothes*) togliersi

shucks [ʃʌks] *interj inf* accidenti

shudder ['ʃʌ·dəʳ] **I.** *vi* (*person*) rabbrividire; (*ground, machine*) vibrare; **to ~ at the memory of sth** rabbrividire al ricordo di qc **II.** *n* (*of person*) fremito *m*; (*of ground, machine*) vibrazione *f*; **it sent a ~ down my spine** ho sentito un brivido lungo la spina dorsale

shuffle ['ʃʌfl] **I.** *n* **1.** (*of cards*) **to give the cards a ~** mischiare le carte **2.** (*of cabinet, management*) ristrutturazione *f* **3.** (*dragging of feet*) strascichio *m* **II.** *vt* **1.** (*papers, cards*) mischiare **2.** (*cabinet, management*) ristrutturare **3.** (*feet*) strascicare **III.** *vi* **1.** (*mix cards*) mischiare le carte **2.** (*drag feet*) strascicare i piedi

  ◆**shuffle off** *vi* andarsene strascicando i piedi

shun [ʃʌn] <-nn-> *vt* scansare

shunt [ʃʌnt] **I.** *vt* **1.** RAIL smistare **2.** *fig* **to ~ sb/sth aside** relegare qu/qc in un angolo **II.** *n* RAIL smistamento *m*

shush [ʃʊʃ] **I.** *interj* ssh **II.** *vt inf* zittire **III.** *vi inf* zittire

shut [ʃʌt] **I.** <shut, shut> *vt* chiudere; **to ~ one's ears to sth** fare orecchie da mercante per non sentire qc; **to ~ one's finger in the door** chiudersi un dito nella porta **II.** <shut, shut> *vi* **1.** (*door, window*) chiudersi **2.** (*shop, factory*) chiudere **III.** *adj* chiuso, -a; **to slam a door ~** chiudere una porta con una spinta

  ◆**shut away** *vt* rinchiudere; **to shut oneself**

away rinchiudersi

  ◆**shut down I.** *vt* **1.** (*shop, factory*) chiudere (*definitivamente*); (*airport*) paralizzare **2.** (*turn off*) sconnettere **II.** *vi* (*shop, factory*) chiudere; (*engine*) bloccarsi

  ◆**shut in** *vt* rinchiudere

  ◆**shut off** *vt* **1.** (*turn off*) spegnere **2.** (*isolate*) isolare

  ◆**shut out** *vt* **1.** (*block out*) non far passare; (*thoughts*) rimuovere **2.** (*exclude*) tagliare fuori; **to shut sb out** chiudere fuori qu **3.** SPORTS dare cappotto a

  ◆**shut up I.** *vt* **1.** (*confine*) rinchiudere **2.** *inf* (*cause to stop talking*) far tacere; **to shut sb up for good** *fig* chiudere la bocca a qu per sempre **II.** *vi inf* (*stop talking*) stare zitto, -a

shutdown ['ʃʌt·daʊn] *n* chiusura *f* (*definitiva*)

shuteye ['ʃʌt·aɪ] *n inf* sonno *m*; **to get some ~** farsi un sonnellino

shutoff I. *n* interruzione *f* **II.** *adj* (*valve*) di chiusura

shutout ['ʃʌt·aʊt] *n* cappotto *m* (*in partita*)

shutter ['ʃʌ·təʳ] *n* **1.** PHOT otturatore *m* **2.** (*of window*) persiana *f*; (*of shop*) saracinesca *f*; **to put up the ~s** aprire il negozio

shuttle ['ʃʌ·t̬l] **I.** *n* **1.** (*bus*) navetta; (*train*) treno *m* navetta; (*plane*) aereo *m* navetta; (*space*) navetta *f* spaziale **2.** (*sewing-machine bobbin*) spoletta *f* **II.** *vt* trasportare **III.** *vi* AVIAT effettuare il collegamento; (*travel regularly*) fare la spola

shuttlecock ['ʃʌ·t̬l·kɑːk] *n* volano *m*

shuttle flight *n* aereo *m* navetta

shuttle service *n* servizio *m* navetta

shy [ʃaɪ] **I.** <-er, -est> *adj* **1.** (*timid*) timido, -a **2.** (*lacking*) **we're still a few hundred dollars ~ of our goal** ci mancano ancora qualche centinaia di dollari per raggiungere il target **II.** <-ie-> *vi* (*horse*) fare uno scarto

  ◆**shy away from** *vi* **to ~ sth** sottrarsi a qc; **to ~ doing sth** evitare di fare qc

shyly *adv* timidamente

shyness *n* timidezza *f*

Siamese [ˌsa·iə·'mi:z] **I.** *n inv* **1.** (*person*) siamese *mf* **2.** (*language*) siamese *m* **II.** *adj* **1.** GEO, HIST siamese **2.** (*conjoined*) **~ twins** fratelli *mpl* siamesi, sorelle *fpl* siamesi

Siberia [saɪ·'bɪ·ri·ə] *n* Siberia *f*

sibling ['sɪb·lɪŋ] *n form* fratello *m*, sorella *f*

Sicilian [sɪ·'sɪl·jən] **I.** *adj* siciliano, -a **II.** *n* (*person*) siciliano, -a *m, f*

Sicily ['sɪ·sɪ·li] *n* Sicilia *f*

sick [sɪk] **I.** <-er, -est> *adj* **1.** (*ill*) malato, -a; **to feel ~** sentirsi male; **to get ~** ammalarsi; **to be off ~** essere in malattia; **to be ~ at heart** *liter* essere affranto, -a **2.** (*about to vomit*) **to be ~** (*nauseated*) avere la nausea; (*vomit*) vomitare; **to get ~** vomitare; **to feel ~ to one's stomach** avere il voltastomaco; **too much alcohol makes me ~** se bevo troppo alcol, vomito **3.** *inf* (*disgusted*) disgustato, -a; **to be ~ about sth** essere disgustato da qc **4.** (*angry*) furioso, -a; **to be ~ and tired of sth** averne fin sopra i capelli di qc **5.** *inf* (*cruel*) malato, -a; (*joke*) di pessimo gusto **6.** *inf* (*car*) guasto, -a **II.** *n* the ~ i malati

sickbag *n inf* sacchetto *m* per vomitare

sickbay *n* infermeria *f*

sickbed *n* letto *m* di malato

sicken ['sɪ·kən] **I.** *vi* (*become sick*) ammalarsi **II.** *vt* (*upset*) dare il voltastomaco a; **so much violence in films ~s me** tutta questa violenza nei film mi dà il voltastomaco

sickening ['sɪ·kə·nɪŋ] *adj* (*repulsive*) rivoltante, -a

sickle ['sɪ·kl] *n* falcetto *m*

sick leave ['sɪk·liːv] *n* congedo *m* per malattia; **to be on ~** essere in malattia

sickly ['sɪk·li] <-ier, -iest> *adj* **1.** (*not healthy*) malaticcio, -a **2.** (*pale*) pallido, -a **3.** (*disgusting*) rivoltante

sickness ['sɪk·nəs] *n* **1.** (*illness*) malattia *f* **2.** (*nausea*) nausea *f*

sick pay *n* indennità *f* di malattia

sickroom ['sɪk·ruːm] *n* camera *f* di malato

side [saɪd] *n* **1.** (*vertical surface*) lato *m;* **at the ~ of sth** a lato di qc; **at sb's ~** al fianco di qu; **~ by ~** fianco a fianco **2.** (*flat surface*) lato *m;* (*of page*) facciata *f* **3.** (*edge*) lato *m;* (*of river*) riva *f;* (*of road*) argine *m;* **on all ~(s)** su tutti i lati **4.** (*half*) lato *m;* **I like to sleep on the right ~ of the bed** mi piace dormire sul lato destro del letto; **in Great Britain, cars drive on the left ~ of the road** in Gran Bretagna, le auto viaggiano sul lato destro della strada **5.** (*cut of meat*) mezzena *f* **6.** (*direction*) **from all ~(s)** da ogni parte; **from ~ to ~** da parte a parte **7.** (*party in dispute*) fazione *f;* (*team*) squadra *f;* **to take ~s** prendere posizione; **to take sb's ~** stare dalla parte di qu; **to be on the ~ of sb/sth** essere dalla parte di qu/qc; **to have sth on one's ~** avere qc dalla propria parte; **on my father's ~** per parte di padre **8.** (*aspect*) aspetto *m;* (*of story*) versione *f* **9.** (*aside*) **on the ~** da parte; **to leave sth on one ~** lasciar qc da parte ▶ **the other ~ of the** <u>coin</u> il rovescio della medaglia; **to come down on one ~ of the** <u>fence</u> **or other** schierarsi da una parte o dall'altra; **to be on the** <u>right/wrong</u> **~ of the** <u>law</u> essere nei limiti/ fuori dei limiti della legalità; **to get on the** <u>right/wrong</u> **~ of sb** ingraziarsi/mettersi contro qu; **to be on the** <u>right/wrong</u> **~ of 40** dimostrare meno/più di quarant'anni; **to be on the** <u>safe</u> **~ ...** per maggior sicurezza

side arm *n* arma *f* da fianco

sideboard ['saɪd·bɔːrd] *n* buffet *m inv*

sideburns ['saɪd·bɜːrnz] *npl* basette *fpl*

sidecar ['saɪd·kɑːr] *n* sidecar *m inv*

side dish *n* contorno *m*

side effect *n* effetto *m* collaterale

sidekick *n* aiutante *mf*

sideline ['saɪd·laɪn] **I.** *n* **1.** SPORTS (*line*) linea *f* laterale; (*area*) bordo *m* (del campo); **on the ~s** *fig* da parte; **from the ~s** da fuori **2.** (*secondary activity*) lavoro *m* extra **II.** *vt* SPORTS

(*keep from playing*) lasciare fuori (dal campo di gioco)

sidelong ['saɪd·lɑːŋ] *adj* (*glance*) furtivo, -a

side road *n* strada *f* secondaria

sidesaddle ['saɪd·ˌsæ·dl] **I.** *n* sella *f* da amazzone **II.** *adv* **to ride ~** cavalcare all'amazzone

sideshow *n* attrazione *f;* **to be a ~ of sth** *fig* essere secondario rispetto a qc

sideslip *n* AVIAT scivolata *f* d'ala

sidestep ['saɪd·step] <-pp-> **I.** *vt a. fig* schivare **II.** *vi* fare un passo a lato

side street *n* strada *f* laterale

sidetrack ['saɪd·træk] **I.** *vt* distogliere **II.** *n* binario *m* morto; *fig* diversivo *m*

side view *n* profilo *m*

sidewalk ['saɪd·wɔːk] *n* marciapiede *m*

sideward ['saɪd·wəd], **sideways** ['saɪd·weɪz] **I.** *adv* **1.** (*to/from a side*) di lato; (*glance*) obliquamente; **to look ~ to the left and right** girare gli occhi a destra e a sinistra **2.** (*facing a side*) su un lato **II.** *adj* laterale; (*glance*) obliquo, -a

sidewinder ['saɪd·ˌwaɪn·də·] *n* **1.** ZOOL serpente *m* a sonagli **2.** (*punch*) sventola *f*

siding ['saɪ·dɪŋ] *n* **1.** (*wall*) rivestimento *m* isolante **2.** RAIL binario *m* morto

sidle ['saɪ·dl] *vi* **to ~ up to sb** avvicinarsi furtivamente a qu

siege [siːdʒ] *n* MIL assedio *m;* **to lay ~ to sth** assediare qc; **to be under ~** essere sotto assedio

Sierra Leone [sɪ·ˌe·rə·li·'oʊn] *n* Sierra Leone *f*

Sierra Leonean [sɪ·ˌe·rə·li·'oʊ·ni·ən] **I.** *adj* della Sierra Leone **II.** *n* abitante *mf* della Sierra Leone

sieve [sɪv] **I.** *n* (*for flour*) setaccio *m;* (*for liquid*) colino *m;* **to put sth through a ~** passare qc al setaccio ▶ **to have a memory like a ~** essere smemorato, -a **II.** *vt* (*flour*) setacciare; (*liquid*) colare

sift [sɪft] *vt* **1.** (*pass through sieve*) setacciare **2.** (*examine closely*) passare al setaccio

sigh [saɪ] **I.** *n* sospiro *m;* **to let out a ~** fare un sospiro; **to let out a ~ of relief** tirare un sospiro di sollievo **II.** *vi* sospirare; **to ~ with relief** tirare un sospiro di sollievo; **to ~ for sb** *form* sospirare per qu

sight [saɪt] **I.** *n* **1.** (*view, faculty*) vista *f;* **to be out of (one's) ~** essere nascosto alla (propria) vista; **to come into ~** apparire; **to catch ~ of sth** scorgere qc; **to hate the ~ of sth/sb** non poter vedere qc/qu; **to know sb by ~** conoscere qu di vista; **to lose ~ of sth** *a. fig* perdere qc di vista; **at first ~** a prima vista; **within ~ of sth** in un punto da cui si può vedere qc; **I can't bear the ~ of him!** non lo posso vedere!; **get out of my ~!** *inf* togliti dai piedi!; **at the ~ of ...** alla vista di ... **2.** *pl* (*attractions*) luoghi *mpl* di interesse (turistico) **3.** (*on gun*) mirino *m;* **to line up the ~s** prendere la mira; **to lower one's ~s** *fig* moderare le proprie ambizioni; **to set one's ~s on sth** *fig* mirare a qc ▶ **to be a ~ for sore** <u>eyes</u> *inf* essere un piacere per gli occhi; **out of ~**, **out of mind** *prov* lontano dagli occhi, lontano dal cuore *prov;* **~ unseen** senza aver visto; **I never buy anything ~ unseen** non compro mai niente senza prima averlo visto; **out of ~!** *inf* fantastico! II. *vt* vedere

sighted *adj* vedente

sightless *adj* cieco, -a

sightly ['saɪt·li] *adj* bello, -a a vedersi

sight-read ['saɪt·riːd] MUS I. *vi* suonare a prima vista II. *vt* suonare a prima vista

sightseeing ['saɪt·ˌsiː·ɪŋ] *n* turismo *m;* **to go ~** visitare luoghi di interesse

sightseeing tour *n* giro *m* turistico

sightseer ['saɪt·ˌsiː·ɚ] *n* turista *mf*

sign [saɪn] I. *n* 1.(*gesture*) segno *m;* **to make a ~** (**to sb**) far segno (a qu); **to make the ~ of the cross** farsi il segno della croce; **as a ~ that ...** per segnalare che ... 2.(*signpost*) cartello *m; (signboard)* cartellone *m* 3.(*symbol*) simbolo *m* 4. *a.* MAT, ASTR, MUS segno *m;* **a ~ that ...** segno che ... 5.(*trace*) traccia *f;* **they could not find any ~ of them** non sono riusciti a trovare traccia di loro; **it's a ~ of the times** è un segno dei tempi II. *vt* 1.(*write signature on*) firmare; **he ~ed himself 'Mark Taylor'** ha firmato con il nome di 'Mark Taylor' 2.(*employ under contract*) ingaggiare 3.(*gesticulate*) far segno a; **to ~ sb to do sth** far segno a qu di fare qc 4.(*say in sign language*) dire con il linguaggio dei segni III. *vi* 1.(*write signature*) firmare; **~ here, please** firmi qui, per favore; **to ~ for sth** firmare la ricevuta di qc; **to ~ with a team** essere ingaggiato da una squadra 2.(*use sign language*) comunicare con il linguaggio dei segni 3.(*gesticulate*) fare dei segni; **to ~ to sb to do sth** fare dei segni a qu perché faccia qc; **to ~ to sb that ...** far segno a qu che ... *+subj*

◆**sign away** *vt* cedere; (*rights*) rinunciare a

◆**sign in** I. *vi* registrarsi all'arrivo II. *vt* **to sign sb in** firmare per qu

◆**sign off** I. *vi inf* 1. RADIO, TV chiudere 2.(*end*) chiudere; **I think I'll ~ early today** penso che oggi staccherò presto II. *vt* approvare

◆**sign on** I. *vi* firmare un contratto; **to sign on as a soldier** arruolarsi nell'esercito; **to ~ for sth** iscriversi a qc; **he has signed on for courses in Japanese** si è iscritto a un corso di giapponese II. *vt* assumere

◆**sign out** I. *vi* firmare il registro di uscita II. *vt* **to ~ sth** firmare per ritirare qc; **you must sign all books out** deve firmare per ogni libro da portare via; **she signed out a company car** ha firmato per prendere un'auto aziendale

◆**sign over** *vt* cedere la proprietà di; **to sign property over to sb** trasferire dei beni a qu

◆**sign up** I. *vi* iscriversi II. *vt* assumere

signal ['sɪg·nəl] I. *n* 1.(*particular gesture*) segnale *m;* **to give a ~** dare un segnale; **to give sb a ~ to do sth** fare un segnale a qu perché faccia qc 2.(*indication*) segno *m;* **to be a ~ that**

... esser segno che ... 3. AUTO, RAIL, INFOR segnale *m* 4. ELEC, RADIO segnale *m* II. <-ll-, -l-> *vt* 1.(*indicate*) segnalare; **to ~ that ...** segnalare che ... 2.(*gesticulate*) fare dei segni; **he ~ed them to be quiet** gli ha fatto segno di tacere III. <-ll-, -l-> *vi* dare il segnale; **the teacher ~ed for the examination to begin** l'insegnante ha dato il segnale per l'inizio dell'esame; **he ~ed to stop** AUTO ha fatto segno di fermarsi IV. *adj form* eclatante

signally *adv* in modo eclatante

signalman ['sɪg·nəl·mən] <-men> *n* RAIL deviatore, -trice *m, f*

signatory ['sɪg·nə·tɔː·ri] *n* firmatario, -a *m, f*

signature ['sɪg·nət·ʃɚ] *n* firma *f*

signboard ['saɪn·bɔːrd] *n* cartellone *m* (pubblicitario)

signet ring ['sɪg·nɪt·ˌrɪŋ] *n* anello *m* con sigillo

significance [sɪg·'nɪ·fə·kəns] *n* 1.(*importance*) importanza *f* 2.(*meaning*) significato *m*

significant [sɪg·'nɪ·fə·kənt] *adj* 1.(*important*) importante; (*improvement, increase, difference*) significativo, -a 2.(*meaningful*) eloquente

signify ['sɪg·nə·faɪ] I. <-ie-> *vt* 1. *form* (*mean*) significare; **to ~ that ...** significare che ... 2.(*indicate*) indicare II. <-ie-> *vi form* (*matter*) avere importanza

sign language ['saɪn·ˌlæŋ·gwɪdʒ] *n* linguaggio *m* dei segni

signpost I. *n* cartello *m* (stradale); *fig* indicazione *f* II. *vt* indicare

Sikh [siːk] *n* sikh *mf inv*

silage ['saɪ·lɪdʒ] *n* AGR insilato *m*

silence ['saɪ·ləns] I. *n* silenzio *m* ► **~ is golden** *prov* il silenzio è d'oro II. *vt* (*machine, bells*) silenziare; (*person*) far tacere

silencer ['saɪ·lən·sɚ] *n* silenziatore *m*

silent ['saɪ·lənt] *adj* silenzioso, -a; LING muto, -a; **~ film** film *m* muto *inv;* **the ~ majority** la maggioranza silenziosa; **~ partner** ECON socio *m* accomandante; **to be ~ on sth** mantenere il silenzio su qc; **to fall ~** tacere

silently *adv* silenziosamente, in silenzio

silhouette [ˌsɪ·lu·'et] I. *n* sagoma *f* II. *vt* **to be ~d against sth** stagliarsi contro qc

silica ['sɪ·lɪ·kə] *n* silice *f*

silicate ['sɪ·lɪ·keɪt] *n* silicato *m*

silicon ['sɪ·lɪ·kən] *n* silicio *m*

silicon chip *n* INFOR, ELEC microchip *m inv*

silicone ['sɪ·lɪ·koʊn] *n* silicone *m*

silk [sɪlk] *n* seta *f;* **~ dress** vestito *m* di seta; **~ scarf** foulard *m* di seta *inv*

silken ['sɪl·kən] *adj* (*clothing*) di seta; (*hair*) setoso, -a; (*voice*) dolce

silk-screen printing *n* serigrafia *f*

silkworm *n* baco *m* da seta

silky ['sɪl·ki] <-ier, -iest> *adj* setoso, -a; (*fur*) morbido, -a; (*voice*) dolce

sill [sɪl] *n* (*of door*) predellino *m; (of window*) davanzale *m*

silly ['sɪ·li] <-ier, -iest> *adj* (*person, idea*) sciocco, -a; **~ season** periodo estivo in cui i *giornali riportano sopprattutto notizie frivole;* **it was ~ of her to ...** è stato sciocco da parte sua ...; **to look ~** avere l'aria ridicola; **to laugh oneself ~** stordirsi dal ridere; **to knock sb ~** *inf* stordire qu

silo ['saɪ·loʊ] *n* silo *m*

silt [sɪlt] *n* detriti *mpl*

♦**silt up** *vi* essere bloccato dai detriti

silver ['sɪl·və] I. *n* 1.(*metal*) argento *f* 2.(*coins*) monete *fpl* d'argento 3.(*cutlery*) argenteria *f*, posate *fpl* d'argento 4.(*dishes, trays*) argenteria *f*, vasellame *m* d'argento II. *adj* 1.(*made of silver*) d'argento 2.(*silver-colored*) argentato, -a

silver anniversary *n* nozze *fpl* d'argento

silver bullet *n* formula *f* magica (*soluzione a un problema*)

silver dollar *n* dollaro *m* d'argento

silverfish ['sɪl·və·ˌfɪʃ] *n* 1.(*fish*) varietà argentata del pesce rosso 2.(*insect*) pesciolino *m* d'argento, lepisma *m*

silver lining *n fig* lato *m* positivo

silver plate *n* 1.(*dishes, trays*) argenteria *f* 2.(*coating*) bagno *m* d'argento

silver-plate *vt* placcare d'argento

silver screen *n* CINE **the ~** lo schermo cinematografico

silversmith ['sɪl·və·smɪθ] *n* argentiere, -a *m, f*

silverware ['sɪl·və·wer] *n* 1.(*cutlery*) posate *fpl* 2.(*dishes, trays*) argenteria *f*

silvery <-ier, -iest> *adj* argentato, -a

simian ['sɪ·mi·ən] I. *n* scimmia *f* II. *adj* (*of monkeys, apes*) delle scimmie; (*like monkey, ape*) scimmiesco, -a

similar ['sɪ·mə·lə] *adj* simile

similarity [ˌsɪ·mə·'le·rə·ti] *n* somiglianza *m*

simile ['sɪ·mə·li] *n* LIT, LING similitudine *f*

similitude [sə·'mɪ·lə·tuːd] *n* (*quality of being similar*) somiglianza *f*

simmer ['sɪ·mə] I. *vi* 1.CULIN cuocere a fuoco lento 2.*fig* ribollire II. *vt* cuocere a fuoco lento III. *n* lenta ebollizione *f*; **to bring sth to a ~** portare qc a ebollizione; **to keep sth at a ~** far sobbollire qc

♦**simmer down** *vi inf* calmarsi

simple ['sɪm·pl] *adj* 1.(*not difficult*) semplice 2.(*not elaborate*) semplice 3.(*honest*) sincero, -a 4.(*ordinary*) semplice 5.(*foolish*) sempliciotto, -a

simple-minded [ˌsɪm·pl·'maɪn·dɪd] *adj inf* 1.(*dumb*) tonto, -a 2.(*naive*) ingenuo, -a

simpleton ['sɪm·pl·tən] *n inf* sempliciotto, -a *m, f*

simplicity [sɪm·'plɪ·sə·ti] *n* 1.(*plainness*) semplicità *f* 2.(*ease*) semplicità *f*

simplification [ˌsɪm·plə·fɪ·'keɪ·ʃən] *n* semplificazione *f*

simplify ['sɪm·plə·faɪ] *vt* semplificare

simplistic [sɪm·'plɪs·tɪk] *adj pej* semplicistico, -a

simply ['sɪm·pli] *adv* 1.(*not elaborately*) semplicemente 2.(*just*) semplicemente 3.(*absolutely*) semplicemente 4.(*naturally*) con semplicità

simulate ['sɪm·jʊ·leɪt] *vt* 1.(*resemble*) simulare 2.(*feign*) simulare

simulation [ˌsɪm·jʊ·'leɪ·ʃən] *n* (*imitation*) simulazione *f*; (*of feeling*) simulazione *f*

simulator ['sɪm·jʊ·leɪ·ţə] *n* INFOR, TECH simulatore *m*

simultaneous [ˌsaɪ·ml·'teɪn·jəs] *adj* simultaneo, -a; **~ broadcast** trasmissione *f* in diretta

sin [sɪn] I. *n* peccato *m*; **to confess a ~** confessare un peccato ▸**to be as ugly as ~** essere brutto come il peccato II. *vi* <-nn-> peccare

since [sɪns] I. *adv* 1.(*from then on*) da allora; **ever ~** da allora 2.(*ago*) **long ~** molto tempo fa; **not long ~** non molto tempo fa II. *prep* da, da quando; **how long has it been ~ the crime took place?** quanto tempo è passato da quando è avvenuto il crimine? III. *conj* 1.(*because*) siccome 2.(*from the time that*) da quando; **it's been a week now ~ I came back** è ormai passata una settimana da quando sono tornato

sincere [sɪn·'sɪr] *adj* sincero, -a

sincerely *adv* sinceramente

sincerity [sɪn·'se·rə·ti] *n* sincerità *f*; **in all ~** in tutta franchezza

sine [saɪn] *n* MATH seno *m*

sine qua non ['sɪ·neɪ·kwɑː·'noʊn] *n form* condicio *f inv* sine qua non

sinew ['sɪn·juː] *n* tendine *m*

sinewy *adj* 1.(*muscular*) nerboruto, -a 2.(*meat*) con nervi

sinful ['sɪn·fəl] *adj* (*person*) peccatore, -a; (*thought, act*) peccaminoso, -a; (*waste*) vergognoso, -a

sing [sɪŋ] <sang, sung> I. *vi* cantare; **to ~ to sb** cantare per qu II. *vt* cantare; **to ~ sb to sleep** cantare per far addormentare qu

♦**sing out** I. *vi* (*sing*) cantare forte II. *vt inf* (*call*) **to ~ sb's name** chiamare qu a voce alta

sing-along ['sɪŋ·ə·lɑːŋ] *n* incontro *m* per cantare insieme

Singapore ['sɪŋ·ə·pɔːr] *n* Singapore *f*

Singaporean ['sɪŋ·ə·pɔː·riːˌən] I. *adj* di Singapore II. *n* abitante *mf* di Singapore

singe [sɪndʒ] I. *vt* bruciacchiare; (*hair*) bruciare le punte di II. *n* piccola bruciatura *f*

singer ['sɪŋ·ə] *n* cantante *mf*

singer-songwriter *n* cantautore, -trice *m, f*

singing *n* canto *m*

singing telegram *n* telegramma *m* cantato

single ['sɪŋ·gl] I. *adj* 1.(*one only*) unico, -a; (*blow*) solo, -a; **not a ~ person/thing** nessuno/niente; **there wasn't a ~ soul** non c'era anima viva; **every ~ thing** ogni cosa; **in ~ figures** ad una cifra 2.(*unmarried*) single *inv* 3.(*bed, room*) singolo, -a 4.(*with one part*) semplice II. *n* 1.(*one-dollar bill*) banconota *f* da un dollaro 2.(*record*) single *m inv* 3.(*in baseball*) conquista *della prima base in un'unica battuta* 4.(*single room*) camera *f* singola

♦**single out** *vt* segnalare; **to single sb out**

S

for **criticism** prendere di mira qu con delle critiche

single-breasted *adj* (*suit*) con una sola fila di bottoni

single-handedly *adv* senza l'aiuto di nessuno

single-lens reflex *n* reflex *f* monobiettivo *inv*

single-minded *adj* risoluto, -a

single-mindedness *n* risolutezza *f*

single mother *n* madre *f* single

single parent *n* genitore *m* single

single-parent family <-ies> *n* famiglia *f* monoparentale

singles bar *n* bar *m* per single *inv*

single-seater *n* monoposto *f inv*

singly ['sɪŋ·glɪ] *adv* uno ad uno

singsong ['sɪŋ·sɑːŋ] I. *n* coro *m* II. *adj* **to speak in a ~ voice** parlare con voce cantilenante

singular ['sɪŋ·gjə·lə˞] I. *adj* **1.** LING singolare; **~ form** forma *f* singolare; **the third person ~** la terza persona singolare **2.** (*notable*) singolare; **of ~ beauty** di bellezza eccezionale; **a ~ lack of tact** un'incredibile mandanza di tatto II. *n* LING singolare *m;* **in the ~** al singolare

singularity [ˌsɪŋ·gjə·'le·rə·tɪ] *n form* singolarità *f*

singularly *adv form* singolarmente

Sinhalese [ˌsɪn·hə·'liːz] I. *n* **1.** (*person*) singalese *mf* **2.** (*language*) singalese *m* II. *adj* singalese

sinister ['sɪ·nɪs·tə˞] *adj* sinistro, -a

sink [sɪŋk] <sank *o* sunk, sunk> I. *n* (*in kitchen*) lavello *m;* (*in bathroom*) lavabo *m,* lavandino *m* II. *vi* **1.** (*in water*) affondare; **to ~ to the bottom** spronfondare sul fondo **2.** (*price, level*) calare **3.** (*drop down*) cadere; **to ~ to the ground** cadere al suolo; **to ~ to one's knees** cadere in ginocchio **4.** (*decline*) scendere; **to ~ in sb's estimation** scendere nella stima di qu; **to ~ into depression** sprofondare nella depressione; **to ~ into oblivion** fnire nel dimenticatoio; **to be ~ing (fast)** (*in health*) deperire rapidamente ▶ **to ~ or swim** cavarsela da solo III. *vt* **1.** (*cause to submerge*) affondare **2.** (*ruin*) rovinare **3.** MIN scavare **4.** (*invest*) investire; **to ~ money into a project** investire molti soldi in un progetto **5.** (*plant, bury: teeth*) affondare; **to ~ one's teeth into sth** affondare i denti in qc **6.** SPORTS (*in golf, snooker*) mettere in buca; (*in basketball*) mettere nel canestro; **to ~ the winning basket** segnare il punto decisivo

◆**sink back** *vi* (*lean back*) appoggiarsi

◆**sink in** *vi* **1.** (*go into surface*) penetrare **2.** (*be absorbed: liquid*) penetrare **3.** (*be understood*) essere recepito, -a

sinker ['sɪŋ·kə˞] *n* piombino *m*

sinkhole *n* foiba *f*

sinking ['sɪŋ·kɪŋ] I. *n* affondamento *m* II. *adj* **a ~ feeling** un brutto presentimento; **with a ~ heart** con il cuore in tumulto

sinner ['sɪ·nə˞] *n* peccatore, -trice *m, f*

sinuous ['sɪn·ju·əs] *adj* sinuoso, -a

sinus ['saɪ·nəs] *n* seno *m*

sinusitis [ˌsaɪ·nə·'saɪ·ṭɪs] *n* MED sinusite *f*

Sioux [suː] I. *adj* sioux II. *n* **1.** (*person*) sioux *mf* **2.** (*language*) sioux *m*

sip [sɪp] I. <-pp-> *vt* sorseggiare, bere a piccoli sorsi II. <-pp-> *vi* **to ~ at sth** sorseggiare qc III. *n* sorso *m;* **to have a ~** bere un sorso

siphon ['saɪ·fən] I. *n* sifone *m* II. *vt* togliere con un sifone

◆**siphon off** *vt* **1.** (*liquid*) togliere con un sifone **2.** (*money*) appropriarsi indebitamente di

sir [sɜːr] *n* signore *m*

siren ['saɪ·rən] *n* sirena *f*

sirloin ['sɜːr·lɔɪn] *n* lombo *m* di manzo

sirocco [sə·'rɑː·koʊ] *n* METEO scirocco *m*

sis [sɪs] *n inf abbr of* **sister** sorella *f*

sisal ['saɪ·səl] *n* **1.** (*plant*) sisal *f* **2.** (*fiber*) sisal *f*

sissy ['sɪ·si] I. <-ies> *n inf* femminuccia *f* II. <-ier, -iest> *adj inf* da femminuccia

sister ['sɪs·tə˞] *n a.* REL sorella *f;* **Sister Catherine** Suor Catherine; **~ company** consociata *f;* **~ ship** nave *f* gemella

sisterhood ['sɪs·tə˞·hʊd] *n* solidarietà *f* tra sorelle

sister-in-law ['sɪs·tə˞·ɪn·lɑː] <sisters-in-law> *n* cognata *f*

sisterly *adj* (*affection*) da sorella; **to feel ~ towards sb** considerarsi come una sorella per qu

sit [sɪt] <sat, sat> I. *vi* **1.** sedere; (*be in seated position*) essere seduto, -a; **~!** (*to dog*) cuccia! **2.** ART posare; **to ~ for one's portrait** posare per un ritratto **3.** *inf* (*babysit*) **to ~ for sb** fare la baby-sitter da qu **4.** (*perch*) posarsi; (*incubate eggs*) covare **5.** (*be placed*) essere, stare; (*rest unmoved*) stare fermo; **to ~ on the shelf** essere sul ripiano **6.** (*be in session*) riunirsi **7.** POL (*be in office*) **to ~ in Congress** sedere in Congresso **8.** (*fit*) **to ~ well/badly** cadere bene/male **9.** (*be agreeable*) **the idea doesn't ~ well with any of them** l'idea non va a genio a nessuno di loro ▶ **to be ~ting pretty** esser messo bene; **to ~ tight** (*not move*) non muoversi; (*not change opinion*) tenere duro II. *vt* mettere a sedere

sit around *vi* non far niente; **to ~ the house** starsene in casa a non far niente

◆**sit back** *vi* **1.** (*in chair*) mettersi comodo, -a **2.** (*do nothing*) starsene con le mani in mano

◆**sit down** *vi* **1.** (*take a seat*) sedersi; **to sit oneself down** sedersi **2.** (*be sitting*) essere seduto, -a

◆**sit in** *vi* **1.** (*attend*) assistere **2.** (*represent*) **to ~ for sb** sostituire qu **3.** (*hold sit-in*) fare un sit-in

◆**sit on** *vt inf* **1.** (*withold: information*) non divulgare; (*secret*) non rivelare **2.** (*suppress: idea, plan*) ostacolare

◆**sit out** *vt* **1.** (*not take part in*) non partecipare a; **to ~ a dance** non ballare **2.** (*remain until the end of*) assistere fino alla fine a

◆**sit through** *vt* assitere fino alla fine a

◆**sit up** I. *vi* 1.(*sit erect*) star seduto con la schiena dritta; ~! stai seduto composto! 2. *inf* (*pay attention*) rizzare le orecchie II. *vt* mettere seduto, -a

sitcom ['sɪt·kɑːm] *n inf* TV *abbr of* **situation comedy** sitcom *f inv*

site [saɪt] I. *n* 1.(*place*) sito *m;* (*of battle, accident*) luogo *m* 2.(*vacant land for building*) terreno *m;* **building** ~ cantiere *m* 3. GEO terreno *m;* HIST sito *m* 4. COMPUT sito *m;* **Web** ~ sito Internet II. *vt* situare

sit-in ['sɪt̬·ɪn] *n* sit-in *m inv;* **to hold a** ~ fare un sit-in

siting *n* ubicazione *f*

sitter *n* 1.(*babysitter*) baby-sitter *mf inv* 2. ART modello, -a *m, f*

sitting *n* (*session*) seduta *f;* (*for meal*) ciascuno degli orari in cui è ripartito il servizio di un pasto in un albergo quando non c'è posto per tutti i commensali

sitting duck *n inf* preda *f* facile

sitting room *n* soggiorno *m*

situate ['sɪt·ʃu·eɪt] *vt form* 1.(*locate*) situare 2.(*in context*) situare

situated ['sɪt·ʃu·eɪ·t̬ɪd] *adj* 1.(*located*) situato, -a; **to be** ~ **near the train station** essere situato vicino alla stazione (ferroviaria) 2.(*in a state*) **to be well/badly** ~ essere in una posizione favorevole/sfavorevole; **to be well** ~ **to do sth** essere in una posizione favorevole per fare qc

situation [ˌsɪt·ʃu·eɪ·ʃən] *n* 1. *a.* ECON, POL (*circumstances*) situazione *f;* **according to the** ~ date le circostanze 2.(*location*) posizione *f*

sit-up ['sɪt·ʌp] *n* **to do** ~**s** fare degli addominali

six [sɪks] I. *n* sei *m;* **in** ~ **figures** di sei cifre ► ~ **of one and half a dozen of the other** la stessa identica cosa II. *adj* sei *inv*

six-footer [ˌsɪks·'fʊ·t̬əe] *n inf:* persona alta almeno 1,83 *m*

six-pack ['sɪks·pæk] *n* 1.(*of beer, soda*) confezione *f* da sei 2. ANAT pettorali *mpl* scultorei

sixteen [ˌsɪks·'tiːn] I. *adj* sedici *inv* II. *n* sedici *m; s.a.* **eight**

sixteenth [ˌsɪks·'tiːnθ] I. *adj* sedicesimo, -a II. *n* 1.(*order*) sedicesimo, -a *m, f* 2.(*date*) sedici *m* 3.(*fraction, part*) sedicesimo *m; s.a.* **eighth**

sixth [sɪkstθ] I. *adj* sesto, -a II. *n* 1.(*order*) sesto, -a *m, f* 2.(*date*) sei *m* 3.(*fraction, part*) sesto *m; s.a.* **eighth**

sixtieth ['sɪks·ti·əθ] I. *adj* sessantesimo, -a II. *n* (*order*) sessantesimo, -a *m, f;* (*fraction, part*) sessantesimo *m; s.a.* **eighth**

sixty ['sɪks·ti] I. *adj* sessanta *inv* II. *n* <-ies> sessanta *m*

size¹ [saɪz] I. *n* 1.(*of person, thing, space*) grandezza *f;* (*of problem, operation*) ampiezza *f;* **a company of that** ~ un'azienda di quelle dimensioni; **to be the same** ~ **as ...** essere grande quanto ...; **to increase/ decrease in** ~ aumentare/diminuire di grand-

ezza; **to double in** ~ raddoppiare di volume; **of any** ~ di qualsiasi grandezza; **the** ~ **of a thumbnail** grande quanto l'unghia del pollice 2.(*of clothes*) taglia *f;* (*of shoes*) numero *m;* **collar** ~ misura *f* di collo 3.(*of bill, debt*) proporzioni *fpl* II. *vt* 1.(*sort*) classificare in base alla grandezza 2.(*make*) fare su misura; (*clothes*) mettere in ordine di taglia

◆**size up** *vt* valutare

size² [saɪz] *n* colla *f;* (*for cloth*) appretto *m*

sizable ['saɪ·zə·bl] *adj* piuttosto grande; (*sum*) considerevole

sizzle ['sɪ·zl] I. *vi* sfrigolare II. *n* sfrigolio *m*

sizzler ['sɪz·lə] *n inf* (*day*) giornata *f* torrida

skate¹ [skeɪt] I. *n* pattino *m* II. *vi* pattinare; **to** ~ **over an issue** glissare su una questione

skate² [skeɪt] *n* (*fish*) razza *f*

skateboard ['skeɪt·bɔːrd] *n* skateboard *m inv*

skateboarder *n* skater *mf inv*

skater *n* pattinatore, -trice *m, f;* **figure** ~ pattinatore, -trice *m, f* artistico, -a

skating *n* pattinaggio *m*

skating rink *n* pista *f* di pattinaggio

skedaddle [skɪ·'dæ·dl] *vi inf* svignarsela

skein [skeɪn] *n* 1.(*of wool*) matassa *f* 2.(*of geese, swans*) stormo *f*

skeleton ['ske·lə·tən] *n* 1. ANAT scheletro *m* 2.(*of boat, plane*) scheletro *m;* (*of building*) ossatura *f* 3.(*outline: of book, report*) ossatura *f* ►**to have** ~**s in one's** <u>closet</u> avere degli scheletri nell'armadio

skeleton key *n* passe-partout *m inv*

skeptic ['skep·tɪk] *n s.* **sceptic**

skeptical *adj s.* **sceptical**

skepticism ['skep·tɪ·sɪ·zəm] *n s.* **scepticism**

sketch [sketʃ] I. *n* 1. ART schizzo *m;* **to make a** ~ **of sb/sth** fare uno schizzo di qu/qc 2.(*rough draft*) abbozzo *m* 3.(*outline*) descrizione *f* sommaria 4. THEAT, TV sketch *m inv* II. *vt* 1. ART fare uno schizzo di 2.(*write draft of*) fare un abbozzo di III. *vi* ART fare degli schizzi

◆**sketch in** *vt* (*details*) aggiungere

◆**sketch out** *vt* 1. ART abbozzare 2.(*describe*) descrivere a grandi linee

sketchbook ['sketʃ·bʊk] *n* album *m* per schizzi *inv*

sketchy ['sket·ʃi] <-ier, -iest> *adj* (*vague*) impreciso, -a; (*incomplete*) incompleto, -a

skew [skjuː] *vt* (*distort*) falsare

skewbald ['skjuː·bɑːld] I. *n* cavallo *m* pezzato II. *adj* pezzato, -a

skewed [skjuːd] *adj* distorto, -a

skewer ['skjuː·əe] I. *n* spiedo *m* II. *vt* infilzare

ski [skiː] I. *n* sci *m inv;* **on** ~**s** sugli sci II. *vi* sciare; **to** ~ **down a slope** scendere da un pendio sciando

ski boot *n* scarpone *m* da sci

skid [skɪd] I. <-dd-> *vi* 1.(*on ice*) slittare; **to** ~ **to a halt** slittare fino a fermarsi; **to** ~ **off the road** slittare e finire fuori strada 2.(*slide over*) **to** ~ **along** [*o* **across**] **sth** scivolare su qc II. *n* 1.(*while driving*) slittata *f;* **to go into a** ~ fare

S

una slittata **2.** AVIAT carrello *m* di atterraggio ▶ to be **on** the **~s** *inf* andare di male in peggio

skidmark *n* AUTO segno *m* di sgommata

skid row *n sl* zona *f* malfamata; **to be on ~** essere un barbone

skier ['ski:·ə⸱] *n* sciatore, -trice *m, f*

skiff [skɪf] *n* skiff *m inv*

skiing *n* sci *m;* **~ equipment** attrezzatura *f* da sci; **~ lesson** lezione *f* di sci

ski instructor *n* maestro, -a di sci *m*

ski jump *n* **1.** (*jump*) salto *m* dal trampolino, con gli sci **2.** (*runway*) pista *f* per salto dal trampolino

ski lift *n* ski-lift *m inv*

skill [skɪl] *n* **1.** (*ability*) abilità *f;* **to involve some ~** richiedere una certa abilità **2.** (*technique*) dote *f;* **communication ~s** doti *f* di comunicazione *pl;* **to have language ~s** essere portato per le lingue *f;* **negotiating ~s** arte *f* di negoziare

skilled *adj* **1.** (*trained*) esperto, -a; (*skillful*) abile **2.** (*requiring skill*) qualificato, -a; **~ labor** manodopera *f* qualificata

skillet ['skɪ·lɪt] *n* padella *f*

skillful ['skɪl·fəl] *adj* dotato, -a

skillfully *adv* abilmente

skim [skɪm] <-mm-> I. *vt* **1.** CULIN asportare; (*milk*) scremare **2.** (*move above*) rasentare II. *vi* **to ~ over sth** passare rasente qc; **to ~ through sth** *fig* dare una scorsa a

ski mask *n* passamontagna *m inv*

skim milk *n* latte *m* scremato

skimp [skɪmp] *vi* **to ~ (on sth)** lesinare (su qc)

skimpy ['skɪm·pi] <-ier, -iest> *adj* **1.** (*clothing*) succinto, -a **2.** (*meal*) scarso, -a; (*knowledge*) superficiale

skin [skɪn] I. *n* **1.** (*of person, animal*) pelle *f;* **to be soaked to the ~** essere zuppo (d'acqua) **2.** (*of apple, potato, tomato*) buccia *f;* (*of melon*) scorza *f* **3.** TECH rivestimento *m* **4.** (*on milk*) panna *f* ▶ to be all **~** and **bone**(s) essere pelle e ossa; **it's no ~ off his/her back** *inf* non le/gli fa né caldo né freddo; **by the ~ of one's teeth** *inf* per un pelo; **to have a thick ~** avere la pelle dura; **to jump out of one's ~** *inf* prendersi un colpo; **to get under sb's ~** (*annoy*) dare sui nervi a qu II. <-nn-> *vt* **1.** (*remove skin from: animal*) spellare; **to ~ sb alive** *iron* scorticare qu vivo **2.** (*graze*) sbucciarsi

skin cancer *n* tumore *m* della pelle

skin-deep *adj* superficiale

skin diver *n persona che fa immersioni in apnea*

skin diving *n* immersione *f* in apnea

skin flick *n sl* film *m* porno *inv*

skinflint ['skɪn·flɪnt] *n* taccagno, -a *m, f*

skin graft *n* MED **1.** (*transplant*) innesto *m* cutaneo **2.** (*section*) frammento *m* di pelle

skinhead ['skɪn·hed] *n sl* skinhead *mf inv*

skinny ['skɪ·ni] I. <-ier, -iest> *adj* ossuto, -a II. *n sl* dettagli *mpl* piccanti; **to give sb the ~ on sth** raccontare a qu i dettagli piccanti di qc

skinny-dip ['skɪ·ni·dɪp] <-pp-> *vi inf* fare il bagno nudo

skintight [skɪn·'taɪt] *adj* attillato, -a

skip [skɪp] I. <-pp-> *vi* **1.** (*take light steps*) trotterellare; **to ~ from one subject to another** saltare di palo in frasca **2.** (*with rope*) saltare la corda **3.** MUS (*not play properly*) saltare II. <-pp-> *vt* **1.** (*leave out*) saltare **2.** *inf* (*not participate in*) saltare; **to ~ class** saltare le lezioni **3.** *inf* (*leave*) **to ~ town** lasciare di nascosto la città **4.** (*hop with rope*) **to ~ rope** saltare con la corda **5.** SCH **to ~ a grade** saltare una classe III. *n* saltello *m*

ski pants *npl* pantaloni *mpl* da sci

ski pass *n* ski-pass *m inv*

ski plane *n,* **skiplane** *n* velivolo *m* con i pattini

ski pole *n* racchetta *f* da sci

skipper ['skɪ·pə⸱] I. *n* NAUT padrone, -a *m, f;* (*captain*) capitano, -a *m, f; inf* (*form of address*) capo *m* II. *vt* (*ship, aircraft*) comandare su; (*team*) capitaneggiare

ski rack *n* portasci *m inv*

ski resort *n* stazione *f* sciistica

skirmish ['skɜːr·mɪʃ] I. *n* **1.** MIL scaramuccia *f* **2.** (*argument*) scaramuccia *f* II. *vi* **1.** MIL avere una scaramuccia **2.** (*argue*) avere una scaramuccia

skirt [skɜːrt] I. *n* (*garment*) gonna *f;* (*lower part of coat*) falda *f* II. *vt* **1.** (*path, road*) circondare **2.** (*avoid*) aggirare

ski slope *n* pista *f* da sci

skit [skɪt] *n* parodia *f;* **a ~ about sb/sth** una parodia di qu/qc

skittish ['skɪ·t̬ɪʃ] *adj* **1.** (*nervous: horse, person*) nervoso, -a **2.** (*fickle*) capriccioso, -a

skivvy ['skɪ·vi] <-ies> *n pl, inf* biancheria *f* intima da uomo

skulduggery [skʌl·'dʌ·gə·ri] *n s.* **skullduggery**

skulk [skʌlk] *vi* **1.** (*hide*) nascondersi **2.** (*move furtively*) aggirarsi furtivamente

skull [skʌl] *n a.* ANAT cranio *m* ▶ to be **bored** out of one's **~** *inf* essere annoiato a morte

skull and crossbones *npl* bandiera *f* con il teschio

skullcap ['skʌl·kæp] *n* (*small cap*) papalina *f;* REL kippah *m inv*

skullduggery [skʌl·'dʌ·gə·ri] *n* intrallazzi *mpl*

skunk [skʌŋk] *n* **1.** (*animal*) moffetta *f* **2.** *inf* (*person*) canaglia *f*

sky [skaɪ] <-ies> *n* cielo *m;* **the sunny skies of California** il cielo assolato della California; **under blue skies** sotto il cielo azzurro ▶ the **~'s the limit** tutto è possibile; **to praise sb to the skies** portare qu alle stelle

sky-blue [ˌskaɪ·blu:] *adj* azzurro, -a

sky blue *n* azzurro *m*

skybox [ˌskaɪ·bɑːks] *n* tribuna *f* dei vip

skydiving ['skaɪˌdaɪ·vɪŋ] *n* caduta *m* libera (*in paracadute*)

sky-high [ˌskaɪ·'haɪ] I. *adv a. fig* per aria; **to go ~** (*prices*) salire alle stelle II. *adj* (*prices*) astronomico, -a

skyjack ['skaɪ·dʒæk] *vt* (*plane*) dirottare

skylark ['skaɪ·lɑːrk] I. *n* allodola *f* II. *vi* fare baldoria

skylight ['skaɪ·laɪt] *n* lucernario *m*

skyline ['skaɪ·laɪn] *n* 1.(*city rooftops*) profilo *m* dei tetti 2.(*horizon*) orizzonte *m*

skyrocket ['skaɪ·ˌrɑː·kɪt] *vi* salire alle stelle

skyscraper ['skaɪ·skreɪ·pə·] *n* grattacielo *m*

slab [slæb] *n* 1.(*flat piece: of stone*) lastra *f;* (*of concrete*) blocco *m;* (*of wood*) tavola *f* 2.(*slice: of cake, of cheese*) pezzo *m;* (*of chocolate*) tavoletta *f* 3.(*in mortuary*) tavolo *m* di obitorio

slack [slæk] I. *adj* 1.(*loose: rope*) lento, -a; (*muscle*) flaccido, -a 2. *pej* (*lazy: student*) svogliato, -a; (*piece of work, writing style*) poco curato, -a; (*discipline*) lassista; (*in paying*) negligente 3.(*not busy*) fiacco, -a; ~ **period** periodo fiacco II. *n* 1.(*looseness*) allentamento *m;* **to take up the ~** (*of rope*) tendere la corda 2. COM periodo *m* fiacco ▸ **to cut sb some ~** *sl* non andarci giù troppo duro III. *vi* darsi meno da fare

slacken ['slæ·kən] I. *vt* 1.(*loosen*) allentare 2.(*reduce: speed, vigilance*) ridurre; (*pace*) rallentare II. *vi* 1.(*loosen*) allentarsi 2.(*diminish: demand, intensity*) diminuire

◆ **slack off** *vi*, **slacken off** I. *vi* 1.(*make less effort*) darsi meno da fare 2.(*go more slowly*) rallentare il passo 3.(*diminish: demand, intensity*) diminuire II. *vt* ridurre

slackening ['slæ·kə·nɪŋ] *n* 1.(*loosening*) allentamento *m* 2.(*of speed, intensity*) diminuzione *f*

slacker ['slæ·kə·] *n inf* scansafatiche *mf inv*

slackness ['slæk·nɪs] *n* 1.(*looseness*) assenza *f* di tensione 2.(*of discipline*) allentamento *m;* (*negligence*) negligenza *f* 3. COM inattività *f* 4.(*laziness*) svogliatezza *f*

slacks [slæks] *npl* pantaloni *mpl* (sportivi)

slain [sleɪn] I. *pp of* **slay** II. *n* the ~ i caduti

slake [sleɪk] *vt liter* palcare; **to ~ one's thirst** placare la sete

slalom ['slɑː·ləm] *n* slalom *m inv*

slam [slæm] I. <-mm-> *vt* 1.(*strike*) colpire; **to ~ the door** sbattere la porta; **to ~ a window shut** chiudere una finestra con un colpo; **to ~ the ball into the net** sparare il pallone in rete; **to ~ the phone down on sb** sbattere il telefono in faccia a qu 2. *inf* (*criticize*) fare a pezzi II. <-mm-> *vi* 1.(*close noisily*) sbattere 2.(*hit hard*) **to ~ against sth** sbattere contro qc; **to ~ into sth** sbattere contro qc III. *n* (*of door*) sbattimento *m;* **to close a book with a ~** chiudere un libro con un gesto brusco

slammer ['ʃlæ·mə·] *n inf* galera *f*

slander ['slæn·də·] I. *n* LAW diffamazione *f* II. *vt* diffamare

slanderer ['slæn·də·ə·] *n* diffamatore, -trice *m, f*

slanderous ['slæn·də·rəs] *adj* diffamatorio, -a

slang [slæŋ] I. *n* gergo *m* II. *adj* gergale

slangy <-ier, -iest> *adj inf* gergale, -a

slant [slænt] I. *vi* essere inclinato, -a II. *vt* 1.(*make diagonal*) inclinare 2.(*give bias to*) distorcere III. *n* 1.(*slope*) inclinazione *f;* **to be built on a ~** essere costruito su una pendenza 2.(*perspective*) taglio *m;* **to put a favorable ~ on sth** presentare qc in una luce favorevole

slanting *adj* (*roof*) inclinato, -a; (*eyes*) a mandorla

slap [slæp] I. *n* schiaffo *m;* **a ~ in the face** *fig* uno schiaffo morale; **the ~ of the waves** il fragore delle onde che si infrangono II. <-pp-> *vt* 1.(*hit*) schiaffeggiare 2.(*put*) **to ~ the book onto the table** sbattere il libro sul tavolo 3.(*put on quickly*) **to ~ paint onto the wall** dare una spennellata al muro 4. LAW **to ~ sb with a lawsuit** fare causa a qu III. *adv inf* in pieno; **to drive ~ into sth** sbattere in pieno contro qc; **to leave ~ in the middle of a meeting** andarsene nel bel mezzo di una riunione

◆ **slap down** *vt* 1.(*put down with slap*) sbattere 2.(*silence rudely*) mettere a tacere

slapdash ['slæp·dæʃ] *adj pej, inf* raffazzonato, -a

slapjack ['slæp·ˌdʒæk] *n* crêpe *f inv*

slapstick ['slæp·stɪk] *n* slapstick *m inv* (*effetto comico con torte in faccia, cadute clamorose, ecc.*)

slash [slæʃ] I. *vt* 1.(*cut deeply*) sfregiare; **to ~ one's wrists** tagliarsi le vene 2.(*reduce: spending, budget*) tagliare drasticamente; (*prices*) abbattere II. *n* 1.(*cut*) sfregio *m* 2.(*swinging blow*) ampio movimento *m* 3. FASHION spacco *m* 4. TYPO barra *f*

slat [slæt] *n* (*of wood, plastic*) stecca *f*

slate [sleɪt] I. *n* 1.(*for roof, writing*) tegola *f* 2. POL lista *f* dei candidati ▸ **to have a clean ~** *inf* ripartire da zero; **to wipe the ~ clean** *inf* metterci una pietra sopra II. *vt* 1.(*cover with slates*) mettere le tegole su 2.(*schedule*) programmare; POL mettere nella lista dei candidati

slather I. *vt inf* spalmare abbondantemente II. *n sl* un casino di

slaughter ['slɑː·t̬ə·] I. *vt* 1.(*kill: animal*) macellare; (*person*) massacrare 2. *inf* (*defeat*) stracciare II. *n* 1.(*killing: of animal*) macello *m;* (*of person*) massacro *m* 2. *inf* (*defeat*) sconfitta *f* clamorosa

slaughterhouse ['slɑː·t̬ə·haʊs] *n* macello *m*

Slav [slɑːv] I. *n* slavo, -a *m, f* II. *adj* slavo, -a

slave [sleɪv] I. *n* schiavo, -a *m, f* ▸ **to be a ~ to fashion** essere schiavo della moda II. *vi* lavorare come un negro

slave driver *n iron, inf* negriero, -a *m, f*

slaver ['sleɪ·və·] *n* HIST 1.(*ship*) nave *f* negriera 2.(*slave trader*) negriero, -a *m, f*

slavery ['sleɪ·və·ri] *n* schiavitù *f*

slave trade *n* HIST tratta *f* degli schiavi

Slavic ['slɑː·vɪk] I. *n* slavo, -a *m, f* II. *adj* slavo, -a

slavish ['sleɪ·vɪʃ] *adj* 1.(*servile*) servile 2.(*unoriginal*) pedissequo, -a

S

Slavonic [slə-'vɑː-nɪk] I. *n* slavo, -a *m, f* II. *adj* slavo, -a

slay [sleɪ] <slew, slain> *vt* LIT uccidere

sleaze [sliːz] *n* squallore *m;* POL corruzione *f*

sleazy ['sliː-zi] <-ier, -iest> *adj* (*area, bar, affair*) squallido, -a; (*person*) depravato, -a; POL corrotto, -a

sled [sled] I. *n* slitta *f* II. <-dd-> *vi* andare in slitta

sledge [sledʒ] *n s.* sledgehammer

sledgehammer ['sledʒ-ˌhæ-mə-] *n* mazza *f*

sleek [sliːk] *adj* (*fur, hair*) liscio, -a e lucido, -a; (*car, person*) elegante
♦ **sleek down** *vt* lisciare

sleep [sliːp] I. *n* 1. (*resting state*) sonno *m;* **to go** [*o* **get**] **to** ~ addormentarsi; **to fall into a deep** ~ cadere in un sonno profondo; **to not lose** ~ **over sth** non perdere il sonno per qc; **to put sb to** ~ far dormire qc; **to put an animal to** ~ (*kill*) far sopprimere; **go back to** ~! *iron* continua a dormire! 2. *inf* (*substance*) cispa *f;* **to rub the** ~ **from one's eyes** sfregarsi gli occhi, *per il sonno* II. <slept, slept> *vi* dormire; **to** ~ **sound(ly)** dormire profondamente; ~ **tight!** sogni d'oro! ▸ **to** ~ **on it** dormirci sopra III. *vt* **it** ~**s four** ci sono quattro posti letto
♦ **sleep around** *vi pej, inf* andare a letto un po' con tutti
♦ **sleep in** *vi* dormire fino a tardi
♦ **sleep off** *vt* **to sleep it off** farsi una dormita per smaltire la sbornia
♦ **sleep out** *vi* dormire all'addiaccio
♦ **sleep through** *vt* **to** ~ **noise** non svegliarsi per il rumore; **to** ~ **the entire trip** dormire (per) tutto il viaggio
♦ **sleep together** *vi* 1. (*have sex*) andare a letto insieme 2. (*share bed*) dormire insieme
♦ **sleep with** *vt* 1. (*have sex with*) andare a letto con 2. (*share bed with*) dormire con

sleeper ['sliː-pə-] *n* 1. (*person*) persona *f* addormentata; **to be a heavy/light** ~ avere il sonno pesante/leggero 2. RAIL (*carriage*) cuccetta *f*

sleepiness *n* sonnolenza *f*

sleeping bag *n* sacco *m* a pelo

Sleeping Beauty *n* la Bella Addormentata

sleeping car *n* vagone *m* letto

sleeping pill *n* sonnifero *m*

sleeping sickness *n* malattia *f* del sonno

sleepless ['sliː-p-ləs] *adj* insonne

sleepwalk ['sliː-p-ˌwɑːk] *vi* essere sonnambulo *m;* **he** ~**s** è sonnambulo

sleepwalker ['sliː-p-ˌwɑː-kə-] *n* sonnambulo, -a *m, f*

sleepy ['sliː-pi] <-ier, -iest> *adj* 1. (*drowsy*) sonnolento, -a 2. (*quiet: village*) sonnolento, -a

sleepyhead ['sliː-pi-hed] *n inf* dormiglione, -a *m, f*

sleet [sliːt] I. *n* neve *f* mista a pioggia II. *vi* **it is** ~**ing** cade neve mista a pioggia

sleeve [sliːv] *n* 1. (*of shirt*) manica *f;* **to roll up one's** ~**s** rimboccarsi le maniche 2. (*cover*)

custodia *f* 3. (*for record*) copertina *f* ▸ **to have sth up one's** ~ avere qc in serbo

sleeveless ['sliːv-lɪs] *adj* senza maniche

sleigh [sleɪ] *n* slitta *f*

sleight of hand [ˌslaɪt-ɑː-f-'hænd] *n* gioco *m* di prestigio

slender ['slen-də-] *adj* 1. (*person*) snello, -a; (*rod, branch*) sottile, -a 2. (*majority, resources*) scarso, -a; (*chance*) remoto, -a

slenderize ['slen-də-raɪz] *vi, vt inf* snellire

slept [slept] *pt, pp of* **sleep**

slew [sluː] *pt of* **slay**

slice [slaɪs] I. *n* 1. CULIN (*of bread, ham, meat, cake*) fetta *f;* (*of pizza*) pezzo *m;* (*of cucumber, lemon*) fettina *f* 2. (*share: of credit, profits*) parte *f* 3. (*tennis, golf*) slice *m inv* ▸ **to get a** ~ **of the pie** avere una fetta della torta; ~ **of life** scorcio *m* di vita II. *vt* 1. (*bread, cake*) tagliare a fette; (*ham, meat*) affettare; (*cucumber, lemon*) tagliare a fettine 2. SPORTS **to** ~ **the ball** (*in tennis, golf*) dare effetto alla palla ▸ **any way you** ~ **it** girala come vuoi III. *vi* **to** ~ **easily** tagliarsi facilmente
♦ **slice off** *vt* 1. (*bread, cake*) tagliare (a fette); (*ham, meat*) affettare; (*cucumber, lemon*) tagliare (a fettine) 2. (*reduce by*) ridurre di
♦ **slice up** *vt* (*bread, cake*) tagliare a fette; (*ham, meat*) affettare; (*cucumber*) tagliare a fettine

sliced *adj* (*bread, meat, cake*) a fette; (*ham*) affettato, -a; (*cucumber, lemon*) a fettine

sliced bread *n* pane *m* a cassetta ▸ **it's the best** thing **since** ~ non c'è niente di meglio

slicer *n* (*for bread*) macchina *f* per tagliare il pane a fette; (*for meat*) affettatrice *f*

slick [slɪk] I. <-er, -est> *adj* 1. (*performance*) pulito, -a 2. (*person*) abile; *pej* astuto, -a II. *n* 1. (*oil*) onda *f* nera 2. (*racing tire*) gomma *f* slick
♦ **slick back** *vt,* **slick down** *vt* (*hair*) lisciare (all'indietro)

slide [slaɪd] I. <slid, slid> *vi* 1. (*glide smoothly*) scorrere; **the door** ~**s open/shut** la porta si apre/chiude facendola scorrere; **to** ~ **back into one's old habits** ricadere nelle vecchie abitudini 2. (*slip*) scivolare II. <slid, slid> *vt* far scorrere; (*cause to slip*) far scivolare; **to** ~ **the door open/shut** aprire/chiudere la porta facendola scorrere; **to** ~ **sth across the floor** far scivolare qc sul pavimento III. *n* 1. (*act of sliding*) scorrimento *m* 2. (*incline*) scivolo *m;* **a water** ~ un acquascivolo *m* 3. (*playground structure*) scivolo *m* 4. PHOT diapositiva *f* 5. (*for microscope*) vetrino *m* 6. GEO smottamento *m* 7. FIN ribasso *m* 8. MUS coulisse *f inv*

slide projector *n* proiettore *m* di diapositive

slide rule *n* regolo *m* calcolatore

sliding *adj* (*sunroof, door*) scorrevole

sliding scale *n* scala *f* mobile

slight [slaɪt] I. <-er, -est> *adj* 1. (*small: chance, error*) piccolo, -a; (*change, headache*) leggero, -a; **not in the** ~**est** assolutamente no;

not to have the ~est (**idea**) non aver la minima idea **2.**(*slim: person*) minuto, -a **II.** *n* commento *m* sprezzante **III.** *vt* disprezzare

slightly *adv* leggeremente; **to be ~ familiar with sth** conoscere un po' qc

slim [slɪm] **I.**<slimmer, slimmest> *adj* **1.**(*slender: person*) snello, -a **2.**(*not as wide as tall: cigarette, book*) sottile **3.**(*slight: chance*) piccolo, -a **II.**<-mm-> *vi* (*become slim*) dimagrire; (*try to get thinner*) essere a dieta

◆**slim down** *vi* dimagrire

slime [slaɪm] *n* **1.**(*mud*) melma *f* **2.**(*of fish, slug*) bava *f*

slimebag *n*, **slimeball** *n sl* persona *f* viscida

slimy ['slaɪ·mi] <-ier, -iest> *adj* **1.**(*covered in slime*) viscido, -a **2.** *pej* (*person*) viscido, -a

sling [slɪŋ] <slung, slung> **I.** *n* **1.**(*bandage*) fascia *f* **2.**(*for carrying baby*) marsupio *m;* (*for carrying rifle*) bretella *f* **3.**(*for lifting*) imbracatura *f* **4.**(*weapon*) fionda *f* **II.** *vt* **1.**(*fling*) lanciare **2.**(*hang*) appendere

slingshot ['slɪŋ·ʃɑːt] *n* fionda *f*

slink [slɪŋk] <slunk> *vi* **to ~ away** [*o* **off**] svignarsela

slinky ['slɪŋ·ki] <-ier, iest> *adj* (*gait*) sinuoso, -a; (*outfit*) attillato, -a

slip [slɪp] <-pp-> **I.** *n* **1.**(*slipping*) scivolata *f* **2.**(*mistake*) errore *m; ~* **of the pen** lapsus *m* calami *inv; ~* **of the tongue** lapsus *m* (linguae) *inv* **3.** COM ricevuta *f;* **a ~ of paper** un foglietto **4.**(*women's underwear*) sottoveste *f* **5.** BOT innesto *m* **6.** NAUT (*place to dock*) posto *m* barca; (*slipway*) scalo di alaggio ▶ **to give sb the ~** sfuggire a qu **II.** *vi* **1.**(*slide*) scivolare **2.**(*move quietly*) **to ~ into a pub** infilarsi in un pub; **to ~ into/out of one's pajamas** infilarsi/togliersi il pigiama **3.**(*decline*) cadere; **to ~ into a depression** cadere in depressione **III.** *vt* **1.**(*put smoothly*) far scivolare; **to ~ sb a note** far scivolare una banconota in mano a qu; **to ~ in a comment** fare un commento; **to ~ some money to sb** dare dei soldi a qu discretamente **2.**(*escape from*) sfuggire a; **to ~ sb's attention** passare inosservato a qu; **it ~ped my mind** mi è sfuggito di mente **3.** NAUT (*anchor*) buttare

◆**slip away** *vi* **1.**(*leave unnoticed*) svignarsela; **to ~** (**from sb/sth**) scappare (da qu/qc) **2.**(*pass swiftly*) passare velocemente **3.**(*be dying*) spegnersi

◆**slip by** *vi* **1.**(*pass quickly: time*) volare **2.**(*pass unnoticed*) passare inosservato, -a

◆**slip down** *vi* lasciarsi scivolare

◆**slip in** *vi* infilarsi

◆**slip off I.** *vi* **1.**(*leave unnoticed*) svignarsela **2.**(*fall off*) cadere **II.** *vt* (*clothes*) togliersi

◆**slip on** *vt* (*clothes*) infilarsi

◆**slip out** *vi* **1.**(*leave unobtrusively*) svignarsela **2.**(*be spoken accidentally*) sfuggire; **the name slipped out** mi è sfuggito il nome

◆**slip up** *vi* sbagliarsi

slipcase ['slɪp·keɪs] *n* cofanetto *m*

slipknot ['slɪp·nɑːt] *n* nodo *m* scorsoio

slip-on ['slɪp·ɑːn] **I.** *adj* (*shoes*) senza lacci **II.** *n pl* mocassini *mpl*

slippage ['slɪ·pɪdʒ] *n* (*in value, standards*) calo *m*

slipper ['slɪ·pə-] *n* pantofola *f*

slippery ['slɪ·pə·ri] <-ier, -iest> *adj* **1.**(*not giving firm hold*) scivoloso, -a **2.**(*untrustworthy: character*) ambiguo, -a ▶ **to be a ~ customer** essere un individuo subdolo; **to be as ~ as an eel** essere sfuggente come la sabbia tra le dita; (**to be on**) **the ~ slope** essere sulla cattiva strada

slipshod ['slɪp·ʃɑːd] *adj* raffazzonato, -a

slipstream ['slɪp·striːm] *n* scia *f*

slip-up ['slɪp·ʌp] *n* disguido *m*

slipway ['slɪp·weɪ] *n* NAUT scalo *m* di alaggio

slit [slɪt] **I.**<slit, slit> *vt* tagliare; **to ~ sb's throat** tagliare la gola a qu; **to ~ one's wrists** tagliarsi le vene **II.** *n* **1.**(*narrow opening*) fenditura *f* **2.**(*tear*) strappo *m*

slither ['slɪ·ðə-] *vi* strisciare; **to ~ down the slope** scivolare su una discesa; **to ~ on the ice** pattinare sul ghiaccio

sliver ['slɪ·və-] *n* (*of lemon*) pezzetto *m* di scorza; (*of cake*) fettina *f;* (*of glass, wood*) scheggia *f*

slob [slɑːb] *n inf* zoticone, -a *m, f*

slobber ['slɑː·bə-] *vi* sbavare

slog [slɑːɡ] *inf* **I.**<-gg-> *vi* (*walk*) avanzare a fatica **II.**<-gg-> *vt* **1.**(*move*) **to ~ one's way** farsi strada a fatica **2.**(*hit*) colpire con forza **III.** *n* sfacchinata *f*

slogan ['sloʊ·ɡən] *n* slogan *m inv*

sloop [sluːp] *n* sloop *m inv*

slop [slɑːp] <-pp-> **I.** *n* **1.** *inf* (*watery food*) brodaglia *f* **2.** *pl* (*waste liquid*) acqua *f* sporca **II.** *vi inf* rovesciarsi; **to ~ about** [*o* **around**] ciondolare **III.** *vt inf* rovesciare

slope [sloʊp] **I.** *n* pendio *m;* (*up*) salita *f;* (*down*) discesa *f;* (*for skiing*) pista *f* **II.** *vi* essere in pendenza; **to ~ down** scendere; **to ~ up** salire **III.** *vt* inclinare

sloping *adj* (*roof*) pendente; (*shoulders*) cadente

sloppiness *n* trascuratezza *f*

sloppy ['slɑː·pi] <-ier, -iest> *adj* **1.**(*messy*) trasandato, -a **2.**(*slipshod: language*) poco curato, -a **3.**(*too wet: kiss*) baveso, -a

slosh [slɑːʃ] **I.** *vi* **1.**(*splash*) rovesciarsi **2.**(*water*) sciabordare **II.** *vt inf* (*liquid*) rovesciare

◆**slosh about** *vi*, **slosh around** *vi* sciabordare

sloshed *adj inf* sbronzo, -a; **to get ~** prendersi una sbronza

slot [slɑːt] **I.** *n* **1.**(*narrow opening*) fessura *f* **2.** TV spazio *m* **3.** AVIAT slot *m inv* **II.**<-tt-> *vt* **to ~ sb/sth in** infilare qc/qu

sloth [slɑːθ] *n* **1.** ZOOL bradipo *m* **2.**(*laziness*) pigrizia *f*

slothful ['slɑː·θ·fəl] *adj* pigro, -a

slot machine ['slɑːt·mə·ʃiːn] *n* slot machine *f*

S

inv

slouch [slaʊtʃ] I. *vi* 1.(*have shoulders bent*) avere le spalle curve 2.(*walk*) camminare ciondolando II. *n* posizione *f* con le spalle curve ▶ **to be no** ~ essere bravo, -a

slough[1] [slʌf] *n* 1.(*bog*) palude *f* 2. *liter* (*depressed state*) abisso *m*

slough[2] [slu:] *vt* ZOOL (*skin*) mutare

Slovak ['sloʊ·vɑ:k] I. *adj* slovacco, -a II. *n* 1.(*person*) slovacco, -a *m, f* 2. LING slovacco *m*

Slovakia [sloʊ·'vɑ:·kiə] *n* la Slovacchia

Slovakian *n s.* **Slovak**

sloven ['slʌ·vən] *n* sudicione, -a *m, f*

Slovene ['sloʊ·vi:n] I. *adj* sloveno, -a II. *n* 1.(*person*) sloveno, -a *m, f* 2. LING sloveno *m*

Slovenia [sloʊ·'vi:·niə] *n* la Slovenia

Slovenian *n s.* **Slovene**

slovenly ['slʌ·vən·li] *adj* trasandato, -a

slow [sloʊ] I. *adj* 1.(*not fast*) lento, -a; (*poison*) a effetto ritardato; **to be ~ to do sth** tardare a fare qc; **to be** (**10 minutes**) ~ essere indietro (di 10 minuti) 2.(*stupid*) ottuso, -a II. *vi* rallentare; **to ~ to a halt** fermarsi progressivamente III. *vt* frenare
◆**slow down** I. *vi* 1.(*reduce speed*) rallentare 2.(*be less active*) rallentare il ritmo II. *vt* rallentare

slowdown ['sloʊ·daʊn] *n* ECON rallentamento *m;* **economic** ~ rallentamento *m* economico

slowly *adv* lentamente; ~ **but surely** piano ma con fermezza

slow motion I. *n* rallentatore *m;* **in** ~ al rallentatore II. *adj* al rallentatore

slowness *n* 1.(*lack of speed*) lentezza *f* 2.(*stupidity*) ottusità *f*

slowpoke ['sloʊ·poʊk] *n inf* posapiano *mf inv*

slow-witted *adj* duro, -a di comprendonio

SLR *n abbr of* **single-lens reflex** reflex *f* monobiettivo *inv*

sludge [slʌdʒ] *n* melma *f*

slug[1] [slʌg] *n* ZOOL lumaca *f*

slug[2] [slʌg] I. *n inf* 1.(*bullet*) pallottola *f* 2.(*coin*) gettone *f* contraffatto 3. *inf* (*swig*) bicchierino *m* II. *vi* <-gg-> *inf* (*hit*) dare un cazzotto a; **to ~ it out** darsele di brutto

sluggish ['slʌ·gɪʃ] *adj* fiacco, -a

sluice [slu:s] I. *n* (*gate*) chiusa *f* II. *vt* annaffiare; **to ~ sth down** lavare qc con abbondante acqua

sluicegate *n* chiusa *f*

sluiceway *n* canale *m* con chiusa

slum [slʌm] *n* (*area*) bassifondi *mpl;* **to live in** ~ **conditions** vivere nella miseria

slumber ['slʌm·bə] I. *vi liter* 1.(*sleep*) dormire 2.(*be dormant*) essere inattivo, -a II. *n liter* 1.(*sleep*) sonno *m* 2.(*inactive state*) inattività *f*

slump [slʌmp] I. *n* ECON 1.(*decline*) flessione *f;* ~ **in prices** crollo *m* dei prezzi 2.(*recession*) recessione *f* II. *vi* crollare

slung [slʌŋ] *pt, pp of* **sling**

slunk [slʌŋk] *pt, pp of* **slink**

slur [slɜ:r] <-rr-> I. *vt* pronunciare a fatica; **to ~ one's words** mangiarsi le parole II. *n* 1.(*insult*) calunnia *f* 2.(*in speech*) pronuncia *f* incomprensibile

slurp [slɜ:rp] *inf* I. *vt, vi* bere rumorosamente II. *n* sorso *m* (rumoroso)

slush [slʌʃ] *n* 1.(*snow*) neve *f* sciolta 2.(*sentimentality*) sentimentalismo *m*

slush fund *n pej* fondi *mpl* neri

slushy *adj* <-ier, -iest> 1.(*snow*) sciolto, -a 2.(*sentimental*) sdolcinato, -a

slut [slʌt] *n pej* sgualdrina *f*

sly [slaɪ] *adj* 1.sornione, -a; **on the** ~ di nascosto 2.(*crafty*) scaltro, -a

slyly *adv* 1.(*secretively*) in modo sornione 2.(*craftily*) in modo scaltro

smack [smæk] I. *vt* 1.(*slap*) dare un ceffone a 2.(*hit noisily*) battere; **to ~ one's lips** far schioccare le labbra per il disappunto II. *n* 1. *inf* (*slap*) ceffone *m;* (*soft blow*) pacca *f* 2. *inf* (*kiss*) bacio *m* 3.(*loud noise*) fragore *m* III. *adv* 1.(*with a loud noise*) fragorosamente 2.(*directly*) in pieno
◆**smack of** *vi* puzzare di

smacker ['smæ·kə] *n inf* bacio *m* sonoro

small [smɔ:l] I. *adj* 1.(*not large*) piccolo, -a; (*person*) basso, -a 2.(*young*) piccolo, -a 3.(*insignificant*) piccolo, -a; **on a ~ scale** su scala ridotta; **in his/her own ~ way** nel suo piccolo 4. TYPO (*letter*) minuscolo; **with a ~ 'c'** con la 'c' minuscola ▶ **it's a ~ world** *prov* il mondo è piccolo *prov* II. *n* **the ~ of the back** le reni

small arms *npl* armi *fpl* leggere

small change *n* spiccioli *mpl*

small-claims court *n* tribunale con competenza ristretta a cause civili di piccola entità

small fry *n inf* **to be a** ~ essere di poco conto

small intestine *n* intestino *m* tenue

smallish ['smɔ:·lɪʃ] *adj* piuttosto piccolo, -a

small-minded [ˌsmɔ:l·'maɪn·dɪd] *adj pej* di idee ristrette

smallness ['smɔ:l·nɪs] *n* piccolezza *f*

smallpox ['smɔ:l·pɑ:ks] *n* vaiolo *m*

small-scale *adj* in scala ridotta

small talk *n* conversazione *f* leggera; **to make** ~ scambiare due chiacchiere

smalltime *adj* da strapazzo

smart [smɑːrt] I. *adj* 1.(*clever*) intelligente; **to make a ~ move** fare una mossa intelligente; **to be too ~ for sb** essere troppo intelligente per qu 2.(*elegant*) elegante 3.(*quick*) rapido, -a; **to do sth at a ~ pace** fare qc a ritmo sostenuto II. *vi* bruciare; **my eyes ~** mi bruciano gli occhi III. *n* bruciore *m*

smart-alec(k) [ˌsmɑːrt·'æ·lɪk] *n pej, inf* saccente *mf*

smart-ass ['smɑːrt·ɑːs] *n pej, inf* saccente *mf*

smart bomb *n* bomba *f* intelligente

smart card *n* COMPUT tessera *f* elettronica

smarten ['smɑː·tn] I. *vt* **to ~ sth up** dare una sistemata a II. *vi* **to ~ up** darsi una sistemata

smartness ['smɑːrt·nɪs] *n* 1.(*elegance*)

eleganza *f* **2.** (*intelligence*) intelligenza *f*
smash [smæʃ] **I.** *vt* **1.** (*break*) rompere, fare a pezzi; (*glass*) mandare in pezzi **2.** (*crush*) schiacciare; **to ~ a rebellion** soffocare una rivolta **3.** SPORTS (*record*) battere **II.** *vi* **1.** (*break into pieces*) rompersi, andare in pezzi **2.** (*strike against*) sbattere; **to ~ into sth** sbattere contro qc **III.** *n* **1.** (*sound*) schianto *m* **2.** (*accident*) scontro *m* **3.** SPORTS schiacciata *f*
◆**smash in** *vt* sfondare; **to smash sb's face in** *inf* spaccare la faccia a qu
◆**smash up** *vt* distruggere
smashed *adj inf* sbronzo, -a COLL..: on drugs, completamente fatto, -a; **to get ~** prendersi una sbronza
smash (**hit**) *n* successone *m*
smashup *n* scontro *m* violento
smattering [ˈsmæ·t̬ə·rɪŋ] *n* nozioni *fpl*
smear [smɪr] **I.** *vt* **1.** (*spread*) imbrattare; **to ~ sth over sth** imbrattare qc di qc; **to smear sth with sth** imbrattare qc di qc **2.** (*attack*) diffamare; **to ~ sb's good name** macchiare il nome di qu **II.** *n* **1.** (*blotch*) macchia *f* **2.** (*accusation*) diffamazione *f* **3.** MED **a pap ~** un pap test
smear campaign *n* campagna *f* diffamatoria
smear tactics *n* strategia *f* diffamatoria
smell [smel] <smelled *o* smelt, smelled *o* smelt> **I.** *vi* **1.** (*use sense of smell*) sentire gli odori **2.** (*give off odor*) odorare; **to ~ good** avere un buon odore **3.** (*have unpleasant smell*) puzzare **II.** *vt* (*person*) sentire odore di; (*animal*) annusare **III.** *n* **1.** (*sense of smelling*) odorato *m,* olfatto **2.** (*odor*) odore *m;* (*stink*) puzzo *m* **3.** (*sniff*) **to have a ~ of sth** odorare qc *f* **4.** (*trace*) odore *m*
smelling salts [ˈsme·lɪŋ·sɔːlts] *npl* MED sali *fpl* (ammoniacali)
smelly [ˈsme·li] *adj* <-ier, -iest> puzzolente
smelt[1] [smelt] *vt* MIN fondere
smelt[2] [smelt] <-(s)> *n* (*fish*) sperlano *m*
smelt[3] [smelt] *pt, pp of* **smell**
smidgen [ˈsmɪ·dʒən] *n inf* pizzico *m*
smile [smaɪl] **I.** *n* sorriso *m;* **to be all ~s** essere tutto sorrisi; **to give sb a ~** sorridere a qu **II.** *vi* sorridere; **to ~ at** [*o* **about**] **sth** sorridere per qc; **to ~ on sb/sth** sorridere a qu/qc
smiley [ˈsmaɪ·li] *n* COMPUT smiley *m inv,* faccina *f*
smiling *adj* sorridente
smirch [smɜːrtʃ] *vt liter* insozzare
smirk [smɜːrk] **I.** *vi* sogghignare **II.** *n* sogghigno *m*
smite [smaɪt] <smote, smitten> *vt liter* colpire (con forza)
smith [smɪθ] *n* fabbro, -a *m, f*
smithereens [ˌsmɪ·ðə·ˈriːnz] *npl* frammenti, frantumi, pezzetti *mpl;* **to smash sth to ~** mandare qc in mille pezzi
smithy [ˈsmɪ·θi] <-ies> *n* officina *f* del fabbro
smitten [ˈsmɪ·tən] *adj* **to be ~ with sb/sth** essere pazzo, -a di qu/qc; **to be ~ by sb** essere innamorato, -a pazzo, -a di qu; **she was ~ by**

remorse essere in preda al rimorso
smock [smɑːk] *n* camiciotto *m*
smocking *n* punto *m* smock
smog [smɑːg] *n* smog *m inv*
smoke [smoʊk] **I.** *n* **1.** (*from fire*) fumo *m* **2.** *inf* (*cigarette*) fumo *m* ▶**where there's ~, there's fire** *prov* non c'è fumo senza arrosto *prov;* **to go up in ~** andare in fumo **II.** *vt* **1.** (*cigarette, tobacco*) fumare; **to ~ a pipe** fumare la pipa **2.** CULIN fumare ▶**to ~ the peace pipe** fumare il calumet della pace; **put that in your pipe and ~ it!** prendi e porta a casa! **III.** *vi* **1.** (*produce smoke*) fumare **2.** (*smoke tobacco*) fumare
◆**smoke out** *vt* (*rats, insects*) stanare col fumo; (*a scandal*) portare allo scoperto
smoke bomb *n* bomba *f* fumogena
smoked *adj* affumicato, -a; **~ salmon** salmone *m* affumicato
smoke detector *n* rivelatore *m* di fumo
smokeless [ˈsmoʊk·ləs] *adj* senza fumo; **~ tobacco** tabacco *m* da masticare
smoker *n* fumatore, -trice *m, f;* **to be a heavy ~** essere un fumatore accanito
smoke screen *n a. fig* cortina *f* di fumo
smoke signal *n* segnale *f* di fumo
smokestack [ˈsmoʊk·stæk] *n* ciminiera *f*
smoking *n* fumo *m;* **to give up ~** smettere di fumare; **~ ban** divieto *m* di fumare
smoky [ˈsmoʊ·ki] *adj* <-ier, -iest> **1.** (*filled with smoke*) fumoso, -a **2.** (*producing smoke*) fumoso, -a; (*fire*) che fa fumo **3.** (*tasting of smoke*) affumicato, -a
smolder [ˈsmoʊl·dəʳ] *vi* **1.** (*burn slowly*) bruciare senza fiamma; (*cigarette*) consumarsi lentamente **2.** *fig* covare
smooch [smuːtʃ] **I.** *vi* (*kiss*) baciarsi **II.** *n* (*kiss*) **to have a ~** baciarsi
smooth [smuːð] **I.** *adj* **1.** (*not rough*) liscio, -a; (*surface*) regolare; (*sauce*) ben amalgamato, -a; (*sea*) calmo, -a; **as ~ as silk** liscio come la seta **2.** (*uninterrupted*) senza difficoltà; (*flight*) regolare; (*landing*) non brusco, -a **3.** (*mild: wine, whiskey*) amabile **4.** (*suave*) untuoso, -a; **to be a ~ talker** avere una bella parlantina **II.** *vt* lisciare
◆**smooth down** *vt* lisciare
◆**smooth over** *vt* (*difficulty*) appianare
smoothie *n,* **smoothy** [ˈsmuː·ði] *n inf* tipo, -a *m, f* untuoso, -a
smoothly *adv* **to go ~** andare bene
smoothness *n* **1.** (*evenness*) levigatezza *f* **2.** (*lack of difficulty*) assenza *f* di problemi **3.** (*mild taste or texture*) amabilità *f*
smooth-shaven *adj* ben rasato, -a
smote [smoʊt] *pt of* **smite**
smother [ˈsmʌ·ðəʳ] *vt* **1.** (*suffocate*) soffocare **2.** (*suppress*) reprimere **3.** (*cover*) **to be ~ed in sth** essere ricoperto di qc
smudge [smʌdʒ] **I.** *vt* **1.** (*smear*) far sbavare **2.** (*make dirty*) imbrattare; (*reputation*) macchiare **II.** *vi* sbavare **III.** *n* macchia *f*
smudgy [ˈsmʌ·dʒi] *adj* <-ier, -iest> macchi-

ato, -a

smug [smʌg] *adj* <-gg-> compiaciuto, -a; **to be ~ about sth** compiacersi di qc

smuggle ['smʌ·gl] *vt* LAW contrabbandare; **to ~ sth into** introdurre qc illegalmente in

smuggler ['smʌg·lə] *n* contrabbandiere, -a *m, f*

smuggling ['smʌg·lɪŋ] *n* contrabbando *m*

smut [smʌt] *n* 1. (*obscenity*) sconcezze *fpl* 2. (*soot*) fuliggine *f*

smutty ['smʌ·ti] *adj* <-ier, -iest> sconcio, -a; (*joke*) sporco,-a

snack [snæk] I. *n* spuntino *m;* **to have a ~** fare uno spuntino II. *vi* mangiucchiare

snack bar *n* snack bar *m inv*

snag [snæg] I. *n* 1. (*problem*) inconveniente *m;* **to hit a ~** incontrare un ostacolo 2. (*in clothing*) squarcio *m* II. <-gg-> *vt* 1. (*catch and pull*) agganciare 2. (*cause problems*) ostacolare III. <-gg-> *vi* **to ~ on sth** arenarsi su qc

snail [sneɪl] *n* chiocciola *m* ▶ **at a ~'s pace** a passo di lumaca

snail mail *n* COMPUT posta-lumaca *f* (*riferito alla posta tradizionale in opposizione all'e-mail*)

snake [sneɪk] I. *n* serpente *f* II. *vi* snodarsi

snake charmer *n* incantatore, -trice *m, f* di serpenti

snakeskin *n* pelle *f* di serpente

snap [snæp] <-pp-> I. *n* 1. (*sound*) botto *m;* (*of fingers*) schiocco *m* 2. (*fastener*) (bottone *m*) automatico *m* 3. METEO **a cold ~** un'ondata di freddo 4. FOOD **a ginger ~** un biscotto allo zenzero 5. (*photograph*) foto *f inv* 6. (*in football*) snap *m inv* II. *adj* improvviso, -a; **~ decision** decisione *f* improvvisa III. *vi* 1. (*break*) spezzarsi 2. (*move*) **to ~ back** ritornare; **to ~ shut** chiudersi di botto 3. (*make snapping sound*) fare un botto 4. (*bite*) **to ~ at sb** cercare di mordere qu 5. (*speak sharply*) dire con tono brusco; **to ~ at sb** rispondere male a qu IV. *vt* 1. (*break*) spezzare; **to ~ sth shut** chiudere qc di botto 2. (*make snapping sound*) schioccare; **to ~ a whip** schioccare una frusta; **to ~ one's fingers** schioccare le dita 3. PHOT fare una foto a 4. (*in football*) **to ~ the ball** snappare la palla

◆ **snap out** *vi* **to ~ of sth** uscire da qc; **~ of it!** tirati su!

◆ **snap up** *vt* accaparrarsi

snapdragon ['snæp·ˌdræ·gən] *n* bocca *f* di leone

snappy ['ʃnæ·pi] *adj* <-ier, -iest> 1. *inf* FASHION alla moda; **to be a ~ dresser** vestirsi alla moda 2. (*quick*) rapido, -a; **make it ~!** datti una mossa!

snapshot ['snæp·ʃɑːt] *n* foto *f inv*

snare [sner] I. *n* laccio *m* (*trappola*) II. *vt* (*catch: animal, person*) prendere al laccio

snare drum *n* tamburo *m*

snarl[1] [snɑːrl] I. *vi* ringhiare II. *n* ringhio *m*

snarl[2] [snɑːrl] *n* 1. (*tangle*) groviglio *m* 2. (*traffic jam*) ingorgo *m*

◆ **snarl up** *vi* intasarsi

snarl-up ['snɑːrl·ʌp] *n* ingorgo *m* (stradale)

snatch [snætʃ] I. *vt* 1. (*grab*) strappare; **to ~ sth (away) from sb** strappare qc a qu 2. *a. fig* (*steal*) portare via; **to ~ victory** strappare la vittoria 3. (*kidnap*) rapire II. *vi* **to ~ at sth** cercare di afferrare qc III. <-es> *n* 1. (*sudden grab*) strattone *m;* **to make a ~ at sth** cercare di afferrare qc 2. (*kidnapping*) rapimento *m* 3. *vulg* (*female genitals*) figa *f*

◆ **snatch up** *vt* afferrare

snazzy ['snæ·zi] *adj* <-ier, -iest> *inf* alla moda

sneak [sniːk] I. *vi* passare furtivamente; **to ~ in/out** sgattaiolare dentro/fuori; **to ~ away** [*o* off] svignarsela II. *vt* **to ~ a look at sth/sb** guardare qc/qu sottecchi; **to ~ sb/sth in/out** fare entrare/uscire di nascosto qu/qc III. *n* tipo , -a *m, f* subdolo, -a

sneaker ['sniː·kə] *n pl* scarpe *fpl* da ginnastica

sneaking *adj* 1. (*slight*) **a ~ suspicion** un vago sospetto 2. (*secret*) segreto, -a

sneak preview *n* CINE anteprima *f*

sneaky ['sniː·ki] *adj* <-ier, -iest> furtivo, -a

sneer [snɪr] I. *vi* assumere un'aria sprezzante; (*mock*); **to ~ at sth/sb** prendersi gioco di qc/qu II. *n* aria *f* sprezzante

sneering ['snɪ·rɪŋ] *adj* sprezzante

sneeze [sniːz] I. *vi* starnutire ▶ **that's not something** to be ~d at non è da buttar via II. *n* starnuto *m*

snicker I. *vi* ridacchiare (maliziosamente); **to ~ at sth** ridacchiare di qc II. *n* risolino *m*

snide [snaɪd] *adj pej* maligno, -a

sniff [snɪf] I. *vi* 1. (*inhale*) tirare su col naso; **to ~ at sth** annusare qc 2. (*show disdain*) **to ~ at sth** storcere il naso di fronte a qc 3. (*snoop*) **to go ~ing around for sth** mostrare interesse per qc ▶ **it's not to be ~ed at** non ci sputerei sopra II. *vt* annusare; (*cocaine, glue*) sniffare III. *n* 1. (*smell*) odore *m;* **to have a ~** annusare; **to catch a ~ of sth** sentire odore di qc 2. (*expression of disdain*) aria *f* sprezzante

◆ **sniff out** *vt* (*locate by smelling*) fiutare; (*discover*) scoprire

sniffer dog ['snɪ·fə·ˌdɑːg] *n* cane *m* antidroga

sniffle ['snɪ·fl] I. *vi* 1. (*sniff*) tirare su col naso; (*breath*) respirare rumorosamente 2. (*cry*) piagnucolare II. *npl* **to have the ~s** avere il naso che cola

snifter ['snɪf·tə] *n* 1. (*glass*) **a brandy ~** bicchiere *m* da brandy 2. *inf* (*small drink*) bicchierino *m*

snip [snɪp] I. *vt* tagliare (con le forbici) II. *n* 1. (*cut*) colpo *m* di forbici 2. (*piece of cloth*) ritaglio *m* (di stoffa)

snipe [snaɪp] *vi* 1. MIL sparare (da una postazione nascosta) 2. *fig* **to ~ at sb** sparare a zero su qu

sniper ['snaɪ·pə] *n* cecchino, -a *m, f*

snippet ['snɪ·pɪt] *n* (*small piece: of information, conversation, text*) frammento *m;* (*of cloth*) ritaglio *m* (di stoffa); (*of paper, cardboard*) pezzetto *m*

snitch [snɪtʃ] *inf* I. *vi pej* fare la spia; **to ~ on sb** fare la spia a qu II. *vt* (*steal*) fregare III. <-es> *n* **1.** (*thief*) ladruncolo, -a *m, f* **2.** (*tattletale*) spione, -a *m, f*

snivel ['snɪ·vəl] I. <-ll-, -l-> *vi* (*cry*) piagnucolare II. *n* piagnucolio *m*

snivel(l)ing I. *n* piagnucolio *m* II. *adj* piagnucolone, -a

snob [snɑːb] *n* (e)snob *mf,* snob *mf inv*

snobbery ['snɑː·bə·i] *n* snobismo *m*

snobbish ['snɑː·bɪʃ] <more, most> *adj* snob *inv*

snooker ['snʊ·kɚ] I. *vt* **1.** *inf* (*trick*) abbindolare **2.** GAMES (*block*) impallare; **to be ~ed** *fig, inf* essere bloccato II. *n* snooker *m inv*

snoop [snuːp] *pej, inf* I. *n* ficcanaso *mf* II. *vi* ficcanasare; **to ~ around** ficcare il naso dappertutto

snooty ['snuː·t̬i] <-ier, -iest> *adj* con la puzza sotto il naso

snooze [snuːz] *inf* I. *vi* (*nap*) fare una dormitina; (*nap lightly*) sonnecchiare II. *n* dormitina *f*

snooze button *n* pulsante di una sveglia che riattiva la suoneria dopo qualche minuto

snore [snɔːr] MED I. *vi* russare II. *n* il russare

snorkel ['snɔːr·kəl] SPORTS I. *n* boccaglio *m* II. <-ll-, -l-> *vi* fare snorkelling

snorkeling *n* SPORTS **to go ~** fare snorkelling

snort [snɔːrt] I. *vi* sbuffare II. *vt* **1.** *inf* (*inhale*) inalare; (*cocaine*) sniffare **2.** (*say with disapproval*) grugnire III. *n* sbuffo *m*

snot [snɑːt] *n inf* moccio *m*

snotrag ['snɑː·t·ræg] *n inf* fazzoletto *m*

snotty ['snɑː·t̬i] <-ier, -iest> *adj inf* **1.** (*full of mucus*) moccioso, -a **2.** (*rude*) presuntuoso, -a

snout [snaʊt] *n* **1.** ZOOL muso *m;* (*of pig*) grugno *m* **2.** *inf* (*of person*) proboscide *f*

snow [snoʊ] I. *n* **1.** METEO neve *f;* **a blanket of ~** un mantello di neve **2.** *inf* (*cocaine*) coca *f* II. *vi* nevicare

◆**snow in** *vt* **to be snowed in** essere bloccato, -a dalla neve

◆**snow under** *vt* **to be snowed under (with sth)** essere sommerso, -a (di qc)

snowball ['snoʊ·bɔːl] I. *n* palla *f* di neve ▶**to not have a ~'s chance in hell (of doing sth)** non avere la benché minima possibilità (di fare qc) II. *vi fig* aumentare progressivamente

snowball effect *n* effetto *m* valanga

snowbank *n* cumulo *m* di neve

snowboard *n* snowboard *m inv*

snowboarding *n* **to go ~** fare snowboard

snowbound ['snoʊ·baʊnd] *adj* bloccato, -a dalla neve

snowcapped ['snoʊ·kæpt] *adj* coperto, -a di neve

snow chain *n* AUTO catena *f* da neve

snow cone *n* cartoccio *m* di granita

snowfall *n* METEO **1.** (*amount snowed*) nevicata *f* **2.** (*snowstorm*) nevicata *f*

snowflake *n* fiocco *m* di neve

snowman *n* pupazzo *m* di neve

snowmobile *n* motoslitta *f*

snowplow *n* **1.** (*snow mover*) spazzaneve *m inv* **2.** SPORTS (*stop*) spazzaneve *m inv*

snowshoe *n* racchetta *f* (da neve)

snowstorm *n* tempesta *f* di neve

snowsuit *n* tuta *m* imbottita (per bambini)

snow tire *n* AUTO gomma *f* da neve

snow-white *adj* candido, -a

Snow White *n* **~ and the Seven Dwarfs** LIT Biancaneve e i sette nani

snowy ['snoʊ·i] *adj* **1.** METEO (*region, season*) nevoso, -a; (*street, field*) innevato, -a **2.** (*clouds*) da neve; (*pure white: hair, flowers*) candido, -a

snub [snʌb] I. <-bb-> *vt* **to ~ sb** snobbare qu II. *n* affronto *m*

snub nose *n* naso *m* all'insù

snub-nosed *adj* **1.** (*pliers*) con la punta arrotondata; (*gun*) a canna mozza **2.** (*person*) con il naso all'insù

snuff [snʌf] I. *vt* **1.** (*put out*) spegnere **2.** *inf* (*end*) soffocare II. *n* tabacco *m* da fiuto

◆**snuff out** *vt* **1.** (*candle*) spegnere **2.** *sl* (*opposition*) soffocare; (*person*) far fuori

snuffbox *n* tabacchiera *f*

snug [snʌg] *adj* **1.** (*cozy*) accogliente; (*warm*) bello, -a caldo, -a **2.** (*tight: dress*) attillato, -a

snuggle ['snʌ·gl] *vi* raggomitolarsi; **to ~ up to sb** raggomitolarsi contro qu

so [soʊ] I. *adv* **1.** (*in the same way*) così, tanto; **~ did/do I** anch'io; **~ to speak** per così dire **2.** (*like that*) così; **~ they say** così si dice; **is that ~?** davvero?; **I hope/think ~** spero/penso di sì **3.** (*to such a degree*) così (tanto); **I ~ love him** gli voglio così bene; **~ late** così tardi; **~ many books** così tanti libri; **not ~ ugly as that** non così brutto; **would you be ~ kind as to ...?** sarebbe così gentile da ...? **4.** (*in order that*) perché; **I bought the book ~ that he would read it** ho comprato il libro perché lo leggesse **5.** (*as a result*) quindi, così; **and ~ she won** quindi, ha vinto ▶**and ~ on** [*o* **forth**] e così via; **or ~** più o meno II. *conj* **1.** (*therefore*) perciò **2.** *inf* (*and afterwards*) **~ (then) he told me ...** quindi, mi ha detto ... **3.** (*summing up*) allora; **~ what?** e allora?; **~ now, ...** allora ...; **~, as I was saying ...** allora, come stavo dicendo ... III. *interj* **~ that's why!** ah, è per questo!

soak [soʊk] I. *vt* mettere a bagno; **to ~ sth in liquid** mettere qc a bagno II. *vi* (*lie in liquid*) essere a bagno III. *n* ammollo *m*

◆**soak in** *vi* penetrare

◆**soak up** *vt* **1.** (*absorb*) assorbere; (*money, resources*) mangiarsi **2.** (*take in: people*) assimilare **3.** (*bask in: sun*) fare un bagno di; (*atmosphere*) impregnarsi di

soaked *adj* zuppo, -a

soaking I. *n* ammollo *m;* **to get a good ~** inzupparsi II. *adj* **~ (wet)** bagnato, -a fradicio, -a

so-and-so ['soʊ·ən·soʊ] *n inf* (*person*) il tale, la tale; (*thing*) la tal cosa

soap [soʊp] I. *n* **1.**(*for washing*) sapone *m* **2.**TV (*soap opera*) soap opera *f inv* ▶**soft** ~ insaponata *f* II. *vt* insaponare

soapbox ['soʊp·bɑːks] *n* **1.**(*container*) portasapone *f* **2.**(*pedestal*) podio *m* ▶**to get on one's** ~ lanciarsi in una filippica

soapbox derby *n corsa di go-kart per bambini alla quale partecipano concorrenti provenienti da tutti gli Stati Uniti*

soap bubble *n* bolla *f* di sapone

soap opera *n* soap opera *f inv*

soapsuds *npl* schiuma *f* di sapone

soapy ['soʊ·pi] <-ier, -iest> *adj* **1.**(*full of lather*) insaponato, -a **2.**(*like soap*) saponoso, -a; **to taste** ~ sapere di sapone **3.**(*flattering*) mellifluo, -a

soar [sɔːr] *vi* **1.**(*rise*) salire; (*house*) torreggiare **2.**(*increase: temperature*) aumentare di colpo; (*prices*) salire alle stelle; (*awareness, hope*) crescere rapidamente **3.**(*bird, plane*) alzarsi in volo; (*glide*) planare

soaring *adj* (*increasing*) in vertiginoso aumento; (*very high*) altissimo, -a

sob [sɑːb] I. <-bb-> *vi* singhiozzare II. <-bb-> *vt* dire tra i singhiozzi III. *n* singhiozzo *m*

sober ['soʊ·bɚ] *adj* **1.**(*not drunk*) sobrio, -a **2.**(*serious: mood, atmosphere, expression*) serio, -a **3.**(*plain: attire, colors*) sobrio, -a **4.**(*straightforward: assessment*) sensato, -a ◆**sober up** I. *vi* **1.**(*become less drunk*) smaltire la sbornia **2.**(*become serious*) farsi serio, -a II. *vt* **to sober sb up** (*make less drunk*) far smaltire la sbornia a qu; (*make serious*) far diventare serio, -a qu

sobering *adj* che fa riflettere

soberness *n* **1.**(*not drunkenness*) sobrietà *f* **2.**(*seriousness*) serietà *f* **3.**(*plainness*) sobrietà *f*

sobriety [sə·'brɑ·ɪə·ti] *n form* **1.**(*not drunkenness*) sobrietà *f* **2.**(*seriousness*) serietà *f*

sobriety checkpoint *n* posto di controllo con alcoltest *m*

sobriquet ['soʊ·brɪ·keɪ] *n* epiteto *m*

sob story *n pej* storia *f* strappalacrime

so-called [ˌsoʊ·'kɑːld] *adj* cosiddetto, -a

soccer ['sɑː·kɚ] *n* calcio *m*

soccer player *n* calciatore, -trice *m, f*

sociability [ˌsoʊ·ʃə·'bɪ·lə·ti] *n* socievolezza *f*

sociable ['soʊ·ʃə·bl] *adj* socievole

social ['soʊ·ʃəl] *adj* sociale; ~ **drinker** *persona che beve solo in compagnia;* **to climb up the** ~ **ladder** progredire socialmente

socialism ['soʊ·ʃə·lɪ·zəm] *n* socialismo *m*

socialist *n* socialista *mf*

socialite ['soʊ·ʃə·laɪt] *n* persona *f* con un'intensa vita sociale

socialize ['soʊ·ʃə·laɪz] I. *vi* socializzare II. *vt* **1.**PSYCH rendere socievole **2.**POL, ECON nazionalizzare

socially *adv* socialmente

social science *n* scienze *fpl* sociali

social security *n* sussidi *mpl* di previdenza sociale

social service *n* **1.**(*community help*) servizio *m* sociale **2.** *pl* (*welfare*) servizi *mpl* sociali

social studies *n* SCHOOL studi *mpl* sociali

social work *n* assistenza *f* sociale

social worker *n* assistente *mf* sociale

societal [sə·'sɑ·ɪə·tl] *adj* societario, -a

society [sə·'sɑ·ɪə·ti] *n* **1.**(*all people*) società *f;* (**high**) ~ alta società *f;* **to be a menace to** ~ essere una minaccia per la società **2.**(*organization*) associazione *f*

sociocultural [ˌsoʊ·sioʊ·'kʌl·tʃə·rəl] *adj* socioculturale

socioeconomic [ˌsoʊ·sioʊ·e·kə·'nɑː·mɪk] *adj* socioeconomico, -a

sociolinguistics [ˌsoʊ·sioʊ·lɪŋ·'gwɪs·tɪks] *n* sociolinguistica *f*

sociological [ˌsoʊ·siə·'lɑː·dʒɪ·kəl] *adj* sociologico, -a

sociologist [ˌsoʊ·si·'ɑː·lə·dʒɪst] *n* sociologo, -a *m, f*

sociology [ˌsoʊ·si·'ɑː·lə·dʒi] *n* sociologia *f*

sociopolitical [ˌsoʊ·sioʊ·pə·'lɪ·tɪ·kəl] *adj* sociopolitico, -a

sock¹ [sɑːk] *n* calza *m;* **knee-high** ~ calza *f,* calzino *m* ▶**to knock sb's** ~**s off** *inf* far rimanere a bocca aperta

sock² [sɑːk] I. *vt inf* (*hit*) dare un cazzotto a; **to** ~ **sb in the eye** dare un cazzotto in un occhio a qu ▶ ~ **it to 'em!** fagliela vedere! II. *n inf* cazzotto *m*

socket ['sɑː·kɪt] *n* **1.**ELEC presa *f* (della corrente); **double/triple** ~ presa doppia/tripla **2.**(*of eye*) orbita *f;* (*of tooth*) alveolo *m;* (*of shoulder, hip*) cavità *f*

sod [sɑːd] *n* stronzo *m vulg*

soda ['soʊ·də] *n* **1.**(*drink*) bibita *f* gasata **2.**CHEM soda *f* **3.**(*water*) soda *f*

soda fountain *n* (*pouring device*) distributore *m* di bibite

soda water *n* soda *f*

sodden ['sɑː·dn] *adj* fradicio, -a

sodium ['soʊ·diəm] *n* sodio *m*

sodium bicarbonate *n* bicarbonato *m* di sodio

sodium carbonate *n* carbonato *m* di sodio

sodium chloride *n* cloruro *m* di sodio

sodomize ['sɑː·də·maɪz] *vt* sodomizzare

sodomy ['sɑː·də·mi] *n form* sodomia *f*

sofa ['soʊ·fə] *n* divano *m*

sofa bed *n* divano *m* letto

soft [sɑft] *adj* **1.**(*not hard: ground*) molle; (*sand, contact lenses, metal*) morbido, -a; (*pillow, sofa*) soffice; ~ **tissue** MED tessuti *mpl* molli **2.**(*smooth: cheeks, skin, landing*) morbido, -a; (*hair*) soffice; ~ **as silk** morbido come la seta **3.**(*mild*) leggero, -a **4.**(*not bright*) tenue **5.**(*quiet: voice*) soave, -a; (*music*) di sottofondo **6.**(*lenient*) indulgente; **to go** ~ **on sb** essere troppo indulgente con qu **7.**(*easy*) facile; **a** ~ **target** un bersaglio facile **8.**FIN (*currency*) debole

softball ['sɑːft·bɔːl] *n* softball *m inv* (*gioco simile al baseball che si gioca su un campo più* *piccolo*)

soft-boiled [ˌsɑːft·'bɔɪld] *adj* alla coque
soften ['sɑː·fən] I. *vi* 1. (*get soft: butter*)
ammorbidirsi; (*ground*) diventare molle
2. (*become lenient*) ammorbidirsi II. *vt*
1. (*make soft: butter, skin*) ammorbidire
2. (*voice*) addolcire 3. (*make easier to bear:
effect, blow*) attenuare; (*opinion, words*)
ammorbidire
♦**soften up** *vt* ammorbidire; MIL indebolire
softener ['sɑː·fə·nɚ] *n* 1. (*for clothes*) ammorbidente *m* 2. (*for water*) addolcitore *m*
softening I. *n* 1. (*reduction of hardness*)
ammorbidimento *m*; (*of voice*) addolci-
mento *m* 2. (*of light*) smorzamento *m* II. *adj*
mitigatore, -trice; (*agent*) ammorbidente
soft goods *npl* tessili *mpl* (per la casa)
soft-headed *adj pej* tonto, -a
soft-hearted ['sɑːft·ˌhɑːr·ʈɪd] *adj* dal cuore
tenero
softie ['sɑː·f·ti] *n inf* bonaccione, -a *m, f*
softly *adv* 1. (*not roughly*) dolcemente
2. (*quietly*) silenziosamente 3. (*to shine*) in
modo tenue
softness ['sɑːft·nɪs] *n* 1. (*not hardness*) mol-
lezza *f* 2. (*smoothness*) morbidezza *f* 3. (*of
light*) delicatezza *f*
soft-spoken *adj* dalla voce soave
software ['sɑːft·wer] *n* software *m inv*, programma *m*; **accounting** ~ programma *m* di
contabilità
software engineer *n* programmatore,
-trice *m, f*
software piracy *n* pirateria *f* informatica
softy ['sɑː·f·ti] *n inf* tenerone, -a *m, f*; *pej* smidollato, -a *m, f*
soggy ['sɑː·gi] <-ier, -iest> *adj* zuppo, -a
soil[1] [sɔɪl] *n* AGR suolo *m*; **fertile** ~ terreno *m*
fertile; **foreign** ~ terra *f* straniera
soil[2] [sɔɪl] I. *vt form* (*make dirty*) sporcare; **to** ~
sb's reputation macchiare la reputazione di
qu II. *vi* sporcare
soirée, soiree [swɑː·'reɪ] *n form* soirée *f inv*
sojourn ['soʊ·dʒɜːrn] *n* breve soggiorno *m*
sol *n* MUS sol *m*
solace ['sɑː·lɪs] I. *n* conforto *m* II. *vt* confortare
solar ['soʊ·lɚ] *adj* solare
solar battery *n* batteria *f* solare
solar cell *n* cella [*o* cellula] *f* solare
solar eclipse *n* eclissi *f inv* di sole
solar energy *n* energia *f* solare
solarium [soʊ·'le·ri·əm] <-s *o* solaria> *n*
(*place*) centro *m* abbronzatura; (*tanning bed*)
lettino *m* solare, solarium *m inv*
solar panel *n* pannello *m* solare
solar plexus *n* plesso *m* solare
solar power *n* energia *f* solare
solar radiation *n* radiazione *f* solare
solar system *n* sistema *m* solare
sold [soʊld] *pt, pp of* **sell**
solder ['sɑː·dɚ] I. *vt* saldare II. *n* saldatura *f*
soldering iron ['sɑː·dɚ·rɪŋ·ˌa·ɪɚn] *n* salda-

tore *m*

soldier ['soʊl·dʒɚ] I. *n* 1. MIL (*military person*)
soldato *m*; **old** ~ veterano *m* 2. (*non officer*)
soldato *m* II. *vi* fare il soldato
♦**soldier on** *vi* perseverare
sold-out [ˌsoʊld·'aʊt] *adj* esaurito, -a
sole[1] [soʊl] *adj* (*unique*) unico, -a; (*exclusive*)
esclusivo, -a; ~ **right** diritto *m* esclusivo
sole[2] [soʊl] *n* (*of foot*) pianta *f*; (*of shoe*)
suola *f*
sole[3] [soʊl] <-(s)> *n* (*fish*) sogliola *f*; **filet of** ~
filetto *m* di sogliola
solecism ['sɑː·lə·sɪ·zəm] *n form* 1. LING sol-
ecismo *m* 2. (*breach of good manners*) atto *f*
di maleducazione
solely ['soʊ·li] *adv* unicamente
solemn ['sɑː·ləm] *adj* (*occasion, promise*) solenne; (*person, appearance*) serio, -a
solemnity [sə·'lem·nə·ti] *n* solennità *f*
solemnize ['sɑː·ləm·naɪz] *vt form* celebrare
solennemente
solenoid ['soʊ·lə·nɔɪd] *n* ELEC solenoide *m*
solicit [sə·'lɪ·sɪt] I. *vt* 1. (*ask for*) sollecitare
2. (*offer sex*) adescare II. *vi* (*offer sex*) adescare clienti
solicitation *n* LAW istigazione *f* a deliquere
solicitous [sə·'lɪ·sɪ·təs] *adj* sollecito, -a
solicitude [sə·'lɪ·sɪ·tuːd] *n form* sollecitudine *f*
solid ['sɑː·lɪd] I. *adj* 1. (*hard*) solido, -a; (*table,
door, wall*) robusto, -a; (*meal*) sostanzioso, -a;
to be (as) ~ **as a rock** (*person*) essere una
roccia; (*relationship*) essere indistruttibile
2. (*not hollow*) massiccio, -a 3. (*true*) fondato, -a; (*evidence, facts*) certo, -a; (*argument*)
solido, -a; (*conviction*) fermo, -a; (*agreement*)
concreto, -a 4. (*uninterrupted: wall, line*)
continuo, -a; (*hour, day, week*) intero, -a 5. (*three-
dimensional*) solido, -a 6. (*good: work, picture*) eccellente II. *adv* **to be packed** ~ essere
pieno zeppo; **to be frozen** ~ essere completamente gelato III. *n* 1. (*shape*) solido *m* 2. *pl*
CULIN cibi *mpl* solidi
solidarity [ˌsɑː·lə·'de·rə·ti] *n* solidarietà *f*
solid fuel *n* combustibile *m* solido
solidify [sə·'lɪ·də·faɪ] <-ie-, -ying> I. *vi* solidificarsi; (*plans, project, idea*) concretizzarsi II. *vt*
1. (*make hard*) solidificare 2. (*reinforce*) rinforzare
solidity [sə·'lɪ·də·ti] *n* solidità *f*
solidly *adv* 1. (*robustly*) solidamente 2. (*without interruption*) ininterrottamente 3. (*in
strong manner*) al cento per cento 4. (*unanimously*) unanimemente
solid-state [ˌsɑː·lɪd·'steɪt] *adj* allo stato solido
soliloquy [sə·'lɪ·lə·kwi] *n* soliloquio *m*
solitaire ['sɑː·lə·ter] *n* solitario *m*
solitary ['sɑː·lə·te·ri] I. *adj* 1. (*alone*) solitario,
-a 2. (*isolated*) isolato, -a; (*unvisited*) appartato, -a; **to go for a** ~ **walk** andare a fare una
passeggiata da solo II. *n inf* (*isolation*) isolamento *m*
solitary confinement *n* isolamento *m*
solitude ['sɑː·lə·tuːd] *n* 1. (*loneliness*) solitu-

dine *f* **2.**(*isolation*) isolamento *m*

solo ['soʊ·loʊ] **I.** *adj* solo, -a; ~ **flight** volo *m* in solitario **II.** *adv* da solo; MUS da solo; **to go** ~ diventare solista; **to fly** ~ AVIAT volare in solitario **III.** *n* MUS assolo *m*

soloist ['soʊ·loʊ·ɪst] *n* solista *mf*

Solomon Islands ['sɑ·lə·mən·ˌaɪ·ləndz] *n* isole *fpl* Salomone

solstice ['sɑːl·stɪs] *n* solstizio *m*

soluble ['sɑːl·jə·bl] *adj* (*substance, problem*) solubile

solution [sə·'luː·ʃən] *n* soluzione *f*

solve [sɑːlv] *vt* risolvere

solvency ['sɑːl·vən·si] *n* solvenza *f*

solvent ['sɑːl·vənt] **I.** *n* solvente *m* **II.** *adj* solvente

Somali [soʊ·'mɑː·li] **I.**<-(s)> *n* **1.**(*person*) somalo, -a *m, f* **2.**(*language*) somalo *m* **II.** *adj* somalo, -a

Somalia [soʊ·'mɑː·liə] *n* la Somalia

somber ['sɑːm·bə·] *adj* (*mood*) cupo, -a; (*color*) scuro, -a

some [sʌm] **I.** *adj indef* **1.** *pl* (*several*) alcuni, -e; ~ **apples** alcune mele; ~ **people think ...** alcuni pensano che ... **2.**(*imprecise*) qualche; (at) ~ **place** in qualche posto; ~ **day** un giorno o l'altro; (at) ~ **time** una volta o l'altra; **for** ~ **time** per qualche tempo; ~ **other time** un'altra volta; ~ **time ago** qualche tempo fa; **in** ~ **way or another** in un modo o nell'altro; **to have** ~ **idea of sth** avere una qualche idea di qc **3.**(*amount*) un po' di; ~ **more tea** ancora un po' di tè; **to have** ~ **money** avere un po' di soldi; **to** ~ **extent** fino a un certo punto **II.** *pron indef* **1.** *pl* (*several*) alcuni, -e; **I would like** ~ ne vorrei alcuni; ~ **like it, others don't** ad alcuni piace, ad altri no **2.**(*part of it*) un po'; **I would like** ~ ne vorrei un po' **III.** *adv* qualche; ~ **more apples** qualche altra mela; ~ **more wine** ancora un po' di vino

somebody ['sʌm·ˌbɑː·di] *pron indef* qualcuno; ~ **else** qualcun altro; ~ **or other** qualcuno; **there is** ~ **Italian on the phone** c'è un italiano al telefono

somehow ['sʌm·haʊ] *adv* **1.**(*through unknown methods*) in qualche modo **2.**(*for an unclear reason*) per qualche ragione **3.**(*come what may*) in un modo o nell'altro

someone ['sʌm·wʌn] *pron s.* **somebody**

someplace ['sʌm·pleɪs] *adv* in qualche posto

somersault ['sʌ·mə·sɑːlt] **I.** *n* salto *m* mortale; **to do a** ~ fare un salto mortale **II.** *vi* (*person*) fare un salto mortale; (*vehicle*) cappottare

something ['sʌm·θɪŋ] **I.** *pron indef, sing* **1.**(*some object or concept*) qualcosa; ~ **else** qualcos'altro; ~ **nice** qualcosa di bello; ~ **or other** qualcosa; **one can't have** ~ **for nothing** non si ha niente per niente **2.**(*about*) ... **or** ~ *inf* ... o qualcosa del genere; **six-foot** ~ un metro e ottanta e qualcosa; **his name is David** ~ si chiama David qualcosa **II.** *n* **a little** ~ una cosetta; **a certain** ~ un certo non

so che ▸ **that is really** ~**!** mica male! **III.** *adv* ~ **around $10** intorno ai 10 dollari; ~ **over/ under $100** poco più/meno di 100 dollari

sometime ['sʌm·taɪm] **I.** *adv* qualche volta; ~ **before June** prima di giugno; ~ **soon** presto; ~ **tomorrow** domani in giornata; **I'll tell him** ~ prima o poi glielo dirò **II.** *adj form* ex

sometimes ['sʌm·taɪmz] *adv* a volte

somewhat ['sʌm·wɑːt] *adv* leggermente; **to feel** ~ **better** sentirsi leggermente meglio

somewhere ['sʌm·wer] *adv* **1.** da qualche parte; **to be/go** ~ **else** essere/andare da un'altra parte; **to get** ~ *fig* fare progressi; **the treatment is getting** ~ *fig* la cura sta facendo effetto; **or** ~ *inf* o in un posto simile; **he lives in Salt Lake City or** ~ vive a Salt Lake City o lì vicino **2.**(*roughly*) intorno a; **she is** ~ **around 40** lei è sulla quarantina; **he earns** ~ **around $40,000** guadagna intorno ai 40.000 dollari

somnambulism [sɑːm·'næm·bju·lɪ·zəm] *n* sonnambulismo *m*

somnolent ['sɑːm·nə·lənt] *adj* (*sleepy*) sonnolento, -a

son [sʌn] *n* figlio *m*

sonar ['soʊ·nɑːr] *n* sonar *m inv*

sonata [sə·'nɑː·t̬ə] *n* sonata *f*; **piano** ~ sonata per pianoforte

song [sɑːŋ] *n* **1.** MUS (*piece of music*) canzone *f* **2.**(*action of singing*) canto *m* ▸ ~ **and dance** *inf* (*untrue justification*) serie *f* di scuse; (**to go**) **for a** ~ essere regalato

songbird ['sɑːŋ·bɜːrd] *n* uccello *m* canterino

songbook *n* canzoniere *m*

songwriter *n* autore, -trice di canzoni *m*

sonic ['sɑː·nɪk] *adj* **1.**(*relating to sound*) sonoro, -a **2.**(*at the speed of sound*) sonico, -a

sonic boom *n* AVIAT bang *m* sonico *inv*

son-in-law ['sʌn·ɪn·lɑː] <sons-in-law> *n* genero *m*

sonnet ['sɑː·nɪt] *n* sonetto *m*

sonny (**boy**) ['sʌ·ni] *n inf* figliolo *m*

son of a bitch I.<sons of bitches> *n* **1.** *vulg* (*jerk*) figlio *m* di puttana **2.**(*person*) **he's a real lucky** ~ ha una fortuna sfacciata **II.** *interj vulg* porca puttana!

son of a gun I.<sons of guns> *n* canaglia *f* **II.** *interj* porca miseria!

sonorous [sə·'nɔː·rəs] *adj* sonoro, -a

soon [suːn] *adv* presto; ~ **after ...** poco dopo ...; **how** ~ **...?** quando ...?; **as** ~ **as possible** il più presto possibile; **I would just as** ~ **...** preferirei ...

sooner ['suː·nə·] *adv comp of* **soon** prima; ~ **or later** prima o poi; **no** ~ **had I put the phone down than it rang again** avevo appena messo gi il telefono quando èsquillato di nuovo; **no** ~ **said than done** detto fatto; **the** ~ **the better** prima è meglio è

soot [sʊt] *n* fuliggine *f*

soothe [suːð] *vt* **1.**(*make calm*) calmare **2.**(*reduce: pain*) alleviare

soothing *adj* **1.** (*calming*) calmante **2.** (*pain-re-lieving*) calmante

soothsayer ['suːθ‚seɪɚ] *n* indovino *m*

sooty ['sʊ‚ţi] <-ier, -iest> *adj* fuligginoso, -a

sophisticated [sə‚ˈfɪs‚tə‚keɪ‚t̬ɪd] *adj* **1.** (*refined*) sofisticato, -a **2.** (*cultured*) colto, -a **3.** (*highly developed*) raffinato, -a; (*method*) sofisticato, -a

sophistication [sə‚ˌfɪs‚tə‚ˈkeɪ‚ʃən] *n* **1.** (*refinement*) sofisticatezza *f* **2.** (*complexity: of systems, computers*) sofisticazione *f*

sophistry ['sɑː‚fɪs‚tri] *n* **piece of** ~ sofisma *m*

sophomore ['sɑː‚fə‚mɔːr] *n* studente, -essa del secondo anno (di università) *m*

soporific [ˌsɑː‚pə‚ˈrɪ‚fɪk] *adj* soporifero, -a

sopping ['sɑː‚pɪŋ] *inf* **I.** *adj* zuppo, -a **II.** *adv* ~ **wet** bagnato fradicio

soppy ['sɑː‚pi] <-ier, -iest> *adj inf* smielato, -a

soprano [sə‚ˈpræ‚noʊ] *n* **1.** (*vocal range*) soprano *m* **2.** (*singer*) soprano *mf*

sorbet ['sɔːr‚beɪ] *n* sorbetto *m*

sorcerer ['sɔːr‚sə‚rɚ] *n liter* stregone *m*

sorceress ['sɔːr‚sə‚rɪs] *n liter* strega *f*

sorcery ['sɔːr‚sə‚ri] *n liter* stregoneria *f*

sordid ['sɔːr‚dɪd] *adj* **1.** (*unclean*) sordido, -a **2.** *pej* (*base*) squallido, -a; **all the ~ details** tutti i dettagli pi scabrosi

sore [sɔːr] **I.** *adj* **1.** (*aching*) dolorante; **to be in ~ need of sth** avere un bisogno disperato di qc; **a ~ point** *fig* un tasto delicato **2.** *inf* (*offended*) risentito, -a; (*aggrieved*) afflitto, -a; ~ **loser** cattivo perdente **II.** *n* MED piaga *f*; *fig* ferita *f*; **to open an old ~** aprire una vecchia ferita

sorely ['sɔːr‚li] *adv form* estremamente; **he will be ~ missed** ci mancherà terribilmente; **to be ~ tempted to do sth** essere molto tentato di fare qc

sorority [-'rɔː‚rə‚ti] *n* UNIV associazione *f* universitaria femminile

sorrow ['sɑː‚roʊ] *n* dolore *m*; **to feel ~ over sth** essere addolorato per qc; **to my ~** *form* con mio grande dispiacere

sorrowful ['sɑː‚rə‚fəl] *adj* addolorato, -a; **with a ~ sigh** con un sospiro di dolore

sorry ['sɑː‚ri] **I.** <-ier, -iest> *adj* **1.** triste, dispiaciuto, -a; **I'm sorry** (**that**) mi dispiace (che) +*subj*; **to feel ~ for oneself** autocommiserarsi; **to feel ~ for sb** provare pena per qu **2.** (*regretful*) dispiaciuto, -a; **to be ~ about sth** essere dispiaciuto per qc; **to say ~** chiedere scusa **3.** (*said before refusing*) **I'm ~, but I don't agree** mi dispiace, ma non sono d'accordo **4.** (*wretched, pitiful*) penoso, -a; (*choice*) infelice; (*figure*) misero, -a **II.** *interj* **1.** (*expressing apology*) ~**!** scusa! [*o* scusi!] **2.** (*requesting repetition*) ~**?** prego?; ~**, but before continuing ...** chiedo scusa, ma prima di continuare ...

sort [sɔːrt] **I.** *n* **1.** (*type*) genere *m*; (*kind*) specie *f*; (*variety*) classe *f*; **flowers of all** ~**s** fiori di ogni genere; **something/nothing of the** ~ qualcosa/niente del genere **2.** COMPUT

sort *m inv,* ordinamento *m* **3.** (*expressing uncertainty*) **he was a friend of** ~**s** era una sorta di amico **4.** *inf* (*to some extent*) ~ **of** in un certo senso; **I** ~ **of feel that ...** in un certo senso, ho la sensazione che ...; **that's** ~ **of difficult to explain** é un po' difficile da spiegare **5.** (*not exactly*) ~ **of** più o meno **6.** (*person*) **to not be the** ~ **to do sth** non essere tipo da fare qc; **I know your** ~**!** so di che pasta sei fatto! ► **to be/feel out of** ~**s** essere gi di forma **II.** *vt* **1.** (*arrange*) mettere in ordine; (*separate*) separare **2.** COMPUT ordinare; **to** ~ **in ascending/descending order** ordinare in ordine crescente/decrescente **III.** *vi* **to** ~ **through sth** passare in rassegna qc

♦ **sort out** *vt* **1.** (*resolve*) sistemare; (*details*) definire **2.** (*choose*) separare **3.** (*tidy up*) sistemare

sorter *n* **1.** (*postal employee sorting mail*) smistatore, -trice *m, f* **2.** (*machine*) smistatrice *f*

sortie ['sɔːr‚tiː] *n* MIL incursione *f*

SOS [ˌes‚oʊ‚ˈes] *n* SOS *m inv*

so-so ['soʊ‚soʊ] *inf* **I.** *adj* cosí cosí **II.** *adv* cosí cosí

soufflè [suː‚ˈfleɪ] *n* soufflè *m inv,* sformato *m*

sought [sɑːt] *pt, pp of* **seek**

sought-after ['sɑːt‚ˌæf‚tɚ] *adj* ricercato, -a

soul [soʊl] *n* **1.** (*spirit*) anima *f*; **to pray for sb's** ~ pregare per l'anima di qu; **bless his/her** ~ riposi in pace **2.** (*person*) anima *f*; **there wasn't a** ~ **there** non c'era anima viva **3.** MUS soul *m inv* **4.** (*essence*) **to be the** ~ **of discretion** essere la discrezione personificata

soul food *n* piatti tradizionali afroamericani del sud degli Stati Uniti

soulful ['soʊl‚fəl] *adj* commovente

soulless ['soʊl‚ləs] *adj pej* (*person*) senz'anima; (*building*) impersonale; (*work*) meccanico, -a

soul mate *n* anima *f* gemella

soul music *n* musica *f* soul

soul-searching *n* esame *m* di coscienza; **after much** ~ dopo un'approfondita riflessione

sound¹ [saʊnd] **I.** *n* **1.** (*noise*) rumore *m*; **there wasn't a** ~ **to be heard** non si sentiva volare una mosca **2.** LING, PHYS suono *m* **3.** (*radio, TV*) volume *m*; **to turn the** ~ **down/up** abbassare/alzare il volume **4.** (*idea expressed in words*) **by the** ~ **of it** a quanto pare; **I don't like the** ~ **of that** non mi convince **II.** *vi* **1.** (*make noise*) suonare **2.** (*seem*) sembrare **III.** *vt* (*alarm*) far suonare; (*bell, car horn*) suonare; **to** ~ **the retreat** MIL suonare la ritirata

sound² [saʊnd] **I.** *adj* **1.** (*healthy*) sano, -a; (*robust*) robusto, -a; **to be of** ~ **mind** essere in possesso di tutte le facoltà mentali; **to be safe and** ~ essere sano e salvo **2.** (*good: character, health*) buono, -a; (*basis*) solido, -a **3.** (*trustworthy*) sicuro, -a; (*competent*) competente **4.** (*thorough*) approfondito, -a **5.** (*undisturbed: sleep*) profondo, -a; **to be a** ~ **sleeper** avere il sonno profondo II. *adv* **to be ~ asleep** dormire profondamente

sound³ [saʊnd] *vt* 1. NAUT sondare 2. MED auscultare

sound⁴ [saʊnd] *n* (*channel*) stretto *m;* (*inlet*) braccio *m* di mare

◆**sound off** *vi inf* **to ~ about sb/sth** pontificare su qc/qu

◆**sound out** *vt* tastare il polso a

sound barrier *n* barriera *f* del suono

sound bite *n* battuta *m* ad effetto

soundboard *n* MUS *s.* **sounding board**

sound card *n* scheda *f* audio

sound effects *n* effetti *mpl* sonori

sound engineer *n* tecnico *m* del suono

sounding board *n* MUS tavola *f* armonica

soundless ['saʊnd·ləs] *adj* silenzioso, -a

soundly *adv* 1. (*completely*) **to sleep ~** dormire profondamente 2. (*strongly*) **to thrash sb ~** dare una bella batosta a qu

soundness *n* 1. (*firmness*) fermezza *f* 2. (*good sense*) buonsenso *f*

soundproof ['saʊnd·pru:f] I. *vt* insonorizzare II. *adj* insonorizzato, -a

sound system *n* stereo *m inv*

soundtrack *n* CINE colonna *f* sonora

sound wave *n* onda *f* acustica

soup [su:p] *n* minestra *f;* (*clear*) brodo *m;* **home-made ~** minestra fatta in casa; **instant ~** minestra solubile

soup bowl *n* tazza *f* da consommè

souped-up *adj* AUTO truccato, -a

soup kitchen *n* mensa *f* dei poveri

soupspoon *n* cucchiaio *m* da minestra

sour ['sa·ʊə] I. *adj* 1. (*fruit, wine*) aspro, -a; (*milk*) cagliato, -a; **to go ~** inacidire; (*milk*) cagliarsi 2. (*character, person*) acido, -a II. *n* **whiskey ~** *cocktail di whisky, succo di limone e zucchero* III. *vt* inacidire; *fig* guastare IV. *vi* inacidirsi; (*milk*) cagliare; *fig* (*person*) inacidirsi

source [sɔ:rs] I. *n* 1. *a. fig* (*information giver*) fonte *f;* **according to government ~s** secondo fonti governative; **from a reliable ~** da fonte attendibile; **to list one's ~s** fare la bibliografia 2. (*origin*) fonte *f;* **a ~ of inspiration** una fonte di ispirazione; **~ text** testo *m* originale II. *vt* selezionare; **it isn't sourced** non se ne conosce la provenienza

sourpuss ['sa·ʊə·pʊs] *n inf* piaga *f*

souse [saʊs] *vt* (*food*) marinare

south [saʊθ] I. *n* sud *m;* **to lie 5 miles to the ~ of sth** essere 8 km a sud di qc; **to go/drive to the ~** andare verso sud; **further ~** più a sud; **in the ~ of France** nel sud della Francia II. *adj* del sud, meridionale; **~ wind** vento *m* da sud; **~ coast** costa *f* meridionale

South Africa *n* il Sudafrica

South African I. *adj* sudafricano, -a II. *n* sudafricano, -a *m, f*

South America *n* il Sudamerica

South American I. *adj* sudamericano, -a II. *n* sudamericano, -a *m, f*

southbound ['saʊθ·baʊnd] *adj* in direzione sud

South Carolina *n* la Carolina del Sud

South Dakota *n* il Dakota del Sud

southeast [,saʊθ·'i:st] I. *n* sudest *m* II. *adj* sudorientale; **Southeast Asia** il Sudest asiatico III. *adv* a sudest

southeasterly I. *adj* **in a ~ direction** verso sudest II. *n* (*wind*) vento *m* da sudest

southeastern *adj* sudorientale

southeastward(s) *adv* verso sudest

southerly ['sʌ·ðə·li] I. *adj* (*location*) meridionale; **in a ~ direction** in direzione sud; **~ wind** vento *m* da sud II. *n* vento *m* da sud

southern ['sʌ·ðən] *adj* meridionale; **the ~ part of the country** il sud del paese

southerner ['sʌ·ðə·nə] *n* meridionale *mf*

southern hemisphere *n* emisfero *m* australe

southern lights *npl* aurora *f* australe

southernmost *adj* più a sud

south-facing *adj* orientato, -a a sud

South Korea *n* Corea *f* del Sud

South Korean I. *adj* sudcoreano, -a II. *n* sudcoreano, -a *m, f*

southpaw ['saʊθ·pɑ:] *n* mancino, -a *m, f*

South Pole *n* Polo *m* Sud

southward(s) ['saʊθ·wəd(z)] *adv* verso sud

southwest [,saʊθ·'west] I. *n* sudovest *m* II. *adj* sudoccidentale III. *adv* a sudovest

southwesterly I. *adj* **in a ~ direction** verso sudovest II. *n* (*wind*) vento *m* da sudovest

southwestern *adj* sudoccidentale

southwestward(s) *adv* verso sudovest

souvenir [,su:·və·'nɪr] *n* souvenir *m inv,* ricordino *m*

sou'wester [,saʊ·'wes·tə] *n* (*hat*) *cappello di tela cerata con larga tesa che va a coprire il collo*

sovereign ['sɑ:v·rən] I. *n* sovrano, -a *m, f* II. *adj* (*self-governing*) sovrano, -a; **~ state** stato *m* sovrano

sovereignty ['sɑ:v·rən·ti] *n* sovranità *f*

soviet ['soʊ·viet] I. *n* soviet *m inv* II. *adj* sovietico, -a

Soviet Union *n* HIST Unione *f* Sovietica

sow¹ [soʊ] <sowed, sown *o* sowed> I. *vt* seminare II. *vi* seminare ▶ **as you ~, so shall you reap** si raccoglie quello che si semina

sow² [saʊ] *n* (*pig*) scrofa *f* ▶ **you can't make a silk purse out of a ~'s ear** *prov* è come voler cavare il sangue da una rapa

sown [soʊn] *pp of* **sow**

sox [sɑ:ks] *npl* calze *fpl*

soy [sɔɪ] *n* soia *f*

soybean *n* seme *m* di soia

soymilk *n* latte *m* di soia

soy sauce *n* salsa *f* di soia

spa [spɑ:] *n* 1. (*mineral spring*) fonte *f* termale 2. (*town*) città *f* termale 3. (*health center*) centro *m* (di) benessere

space [speɪs] I. *n* spazio *m;* **parking ~** posto *f* macchina; **in a short ~ of time** in un breve lasso di tempo; **leave some ~ for dessert** las-

cia un po' di posto per il dolce **II.** *vt* spaziare
◆**space out I.** *vt* distanziare **II.** *vi sl* **to look spaced out** avere l'aria stralunata
space age *n* era *f* spaziale
space bar *n* barra *f* spaziatrice
space cadet *n sl* tipo *m* fuso, tipa *f* fusa
space heater *n* stufa *f* elettrica
space probe *n* sonda *f* spaziale
spacer *n* distanziatore *m*
space-saving *adj* poco ingombrante
spaceship ['speɪs·ʃɪp] *n* astronave *f*
space shuttle *n* navetta *f* spaziale
space station *n* stazione *f* spaziale
spacing ['speɪ·sɪŋ] *n* **1.** (*arrangement*) distanziamento *m* **2.** TYPO spaziatura *f;* **double ~** spaziatura doppia
spacious ['speɪ·ʃəs] *adj* spazioso, -a
spade [speɪd] *n* **1.** (*tool*) pala *f* **2.** (*playing card*) **~s** picche *fpl;* **two of ~s** due di picche ►**to call a ~ a ~** dire pane al pane e vino al vino
spaghetti [spə·'ge·ʈi] *n* spaghetti *mpl*
spaghetti Western *n* CINE western *m inv* all'italiana
Spain [speɪn] *n* la Spagna
spam [spæm] **I.** *n* COMPUT spam *m inv* **II.** *vt* COMPUT mandare spam
Spam® [spæm] *n carne di maiale in scatola*
span[1] [spæn] *pt of* **spin**
span[2] [spæn] **I.** *n* **1.** (*of time*) lasso *m* (di tempo); (*of project*) durata *f* **2.** ARCHIT (*of bridge, arch*) luce *f* **3.** AVIAT, NAUT (*of wing, sail*) apertura *f* alare **II.**<-nn-> *vt* **1.** (*cross*) attraversare **2.** (*include*) abbracciare
spangle ['spæŋ·gl] *n* paillette *f inv*
spangled *adj* decorato con paillette; **to be ~ with sth** *fig* luccicare di qc
Spaniard ['spæn·jəd] *n* spagnolo, a *m, f*
spaniel ['spæn·jəl] *n* spaniel *m inv*
Spanish ['spæ·nɪʃ] **I.** *adj* spagnolo, -a; **~ speaker** ispanofono, -a *mf* **II.** *n* **1.** (*people*) spagnolo, -a *m, f;* **the ~** gli spagnoli **2.** LING spagnolo *m*
spank [spæŋk] *vt* sculacciare
spanking ['spæŋ·kɪŋ] **I.** *n* sculacciata *f;* **to give sb a ~** dare una sculacciata a qu **II.** *adj inf* (**brand**) **~ new** nuovo fiammante
spar[1] [spɑːr] *vi* <-rr-> **1.** (*in boxing*) allenarsi **2.** (*argue*) stuzzicarsi
spar[2] [spɑːr] *n* NAUT **~s** alberi *m pl*, boma e tangoni
spar[3] [spɑːr] *n* MIN spato *m*
spare [sper] **I.** *vt* **1.** (*save*) risparmiare; **to ~ sb sth** risparmiare qc a qu; **to ~ no effort** non risparmiarsi; **to ~ sb's feelings** non ferire i sentimenti di qu **2.** (*do without*) fare a meno di; (*time*) avere **II.** *adj* **1.** (*additional: key*) di ricambio; (*room, minute*) libero, -a **2.** (*remaining*) in più **3.** *liter* (*gaunt: build*) esile; (*meal*) frugale **III.** *n* **1.** (*part*) ricambio *m* **2.** AUTO ruota *f* di scorta **3.** (*in bowling*) spare *m inv*
spare part *n* pezzo *m* di ricambio
spareribs *n pl* costata *f* (di maiale)

spare time *n* tempo *m* libero
spare tire *n* **1.** AUTO ruota *f* di scorta **2.** *iron* pancetta *f*
sparing ['spe·rɪŋ] *adj* parco, -a; **to be ~ with one's praise** essere avaro di elogi
sparingly *adv* con moderazione
spark [spɑːrk] **I.** *n* **1.** (*from fire, electrical*) scintilla *f* **2.** (*small amount*) briciolo *m;* **not even a ~ of interest/intelligence** nemmeno un briciolo di interesse/intelligenza **II.** *vt* (*debate, protest, problems, riot*) scatenare; (*interest*) suscitare; **to ~ sb into action** incitare qu all'azione
sparkle ['spɑː·rkl] **I.** *n* luccichio *m* **II.** *vi* (*eyes, sea*) luccicare; (*fire*) scintillare
sparkler ['spɑː·rk·lə] *n* **1.** (*firework*) bengala *m inv* **2.** *inf* (*diamond*) diamante *m*
sparkling ['spɑː·rk·lɪŋ] *adj* **1.** (*light, diamond*) scintillante **2.** (*conversation, wit*) brillante
spark plug ['spɑː·rk·plʌg] *n* candela *f*
sparring match ['spɑː·rɪŋ] *n* combattimento *m* di allenamento
sparring partner *n* **1.** SPORTS sparring partner *m inv* **2.** *fig* antagonista *mf*
sparrow ['spe·roʊ] *n* passero *m*
sparrow hawk ['spe·roʊ·hɑːk] *n* sparviero *m*
sparse [spɑːrs] *adj* (*population, information*) scarso, -a; (*vegetation, beard*) rado, -a
sparsely *adv* scarsamente
Spartan *adj*, **spartan** ['spɑː·r·tən] *adj* spartano, -a
spasm ['spæ·zəm] *n* MED spasmo *m;* (*of coughing, pain, anger*) accesso *m;* **to have ~s** contrarsi con spasmi
spasmodic [spæz·'mɑː·dɪk] *adj* **1.** (*interest*) incostante; (*activity*) irregolare **2.** MED spasmodico, -a
spastic ['spæs·tɪk] *n pej* spastico, -a *m, f*
spat[1] [spæt] *pt, pp of* **spit**
spat[2] [spæt] **I.** *n inf* (*quarrel*) piccolo diverbio *m* **II.**<-tt-> *vi* (*quarrel*) avere un piccolo diverbio
spate [speɪt] *n* (*of burglaries*) serie *f;* (*of letters, inquiries*) valanga *f*
spatial ['speɪ·ʃəl] *adj* spaziale
spatter ['spæ·ʈə] **I.** *vt* schizzare; **to ~ sb with mud/water** schizzare qu di fango/d'acqua **II.** *vi* schizzare **III.** *n* schizzo *f;* **~ of rain** due gocce *fpl* di pioggia
spatula ['spæt·ʃə] *n* spatola *f*
spawn [spɑːn] **I.** *n* **1.** ZOOL uova *fpl* **2.** *pej* (*offspring*) creatura *f* **II.** *vt* generare, produrre **III.** *vi* moltiplicarsi
spay [speɪ] *vt* (*animal*) sterilizzare (*asportando le ovaie*)
speak [spiːk] <spoke, spoken> **I.** *vi* **1.** parlare; **to ~ to sb** parlare con qu; **to ~ in riddles** parlare per enigmi; **to ~ on behalf of sb** parlare a nome di qu; **so to ~** per così dire; **~ when you're spoken to** rispondi quando sei interpellato **2.** + *adv* **generally ~ing** in generale; **scientifically ~ing** dal punto di vista scientifico; **strictly ~ing** per essere precisi **II.** *vt* par-

S

lare; **to ~ dialect/a foreign language** parlare un dialetto/una lingua straniera; **to ~ one's mind** parlare con franchezza; **to ~ the truth** dire la verità; **to not ~ a word** non dire una parola

◆**speak for** *vi* 1.(*represent*) parlare a nome di; **speaking for myself ...** a mio parere, ...; **it speaks for itself** si commenta da solo; **to be old enough to ~ oneself** essere abbastanza grande per difendersi da solo 2.(*advocate, support*) dichiararsi a favore di

◆**speak out** *vi* esprimersi apertamente; **to ~ against sth** denunciare qc

◆**speak up** *vi* 1.(*state views*) parlare chiaramente; **to ~ for sth** dichiararsi a favore di qc 2.(*talk more loudly*) parlare pi forte

speaker *n* 1.(*person speaking*) parlante *mf* 2.(*orator*) oratore, -trice *m, f* 3.(*loudspeaker*) altoparlante *m*

speaking I. *n* 1.(*action*) parola *f* 2.(*public speaking*) oratoria *f* II. *adj* (*tour*) commentato, -a; **English ~** anglofono; **to be on ~ terms with sb** conoscere qu abbastanza bene; **to not be on ~ terms** non parlarsi

speaking part *n* THEAT, CINE copione *m*

spear [spɪr] I. *n* lancia *f;* (*for throwing*) giavellotto *f;* (*for fishing*) fiocina *f* II. *vt* trafiggere (con la lancia); (*with fork*) inforchettare

spearhead ['spɪr·hed] I. *vt* capeggiare II. *n fig* uomo [*o* gruppo] *m* di punta

spearmint ['spɪr·mɪnt] *n* menta *f* verde

special ['spe·ʃəl] I. *adj* (*attention, case, diet*) speciale; (*aptitude, character*) particolare; **nothing ~** *inf* niente di speciale II. *n* 1. TV special *m inv* 2. CULIN piatto *m* del giorno 3. *pl* COM offerte *fpl* speciali

special delivery *n* servizio *m* espresso

special edition *n* edizione *f* straordinaria

special effects *n* effetti *mpl* speciali

specialist ['spe·ʃə·lɪst] *n* specialista *mf*

specialization [ˌspe·ʃə·lɪ·'zeɪ·ʃən] *n* specializzazione *f*

specialize ['spe·ʃə·laɪz] I. *vi* specializzarsi; **to ~ in sth** specializzarsi in qc; **a lawyer specializing in divorce law** un avvocato specializzato in divorzi II. *vt* specializzare

specialized *adj* specializzato, -a

specially *adv* apposta; **a ~ good wine** un vino particolarmente buono

special offer *n* offerta *f* speciale

specialty ['spe·ʃəl·ti] *n* <-ies> specialità *f*

species ['spi:·ʃi:z] *n inv* specie *f inv*

specific [spə·'sɪ·fɪk] I. *adj* specifico, -a; **to be ~** essere specifico; **to be ~ to sth** essere proprio di qc II. *npl* particolari *mpl*

specifically *adv* 1.(*expressly*) specificamente; (*ask, mention*) espressamente 2.(*particularly*) precisamente

specification [ˌspe·sə·fɪ·'keɪ·ʃən] *n* specifica *f*

specify ['spe·sə·faɪ] <-ie-> *vt* specificare

specimen ['spe·sə·mən] *n* 1.(*of blood, urine*) campione *m;* (*example*) esemplare *m;* **a ~ copy** uno specimen 2. *inf*(*person*) soggetto *m*

specious ['spi:·ʃəs] *adj form* ingannevole

speck [spek] *n* puntino *m;* (*of paint*) macchiolina *f;* (*of dust*) granello *m;* **not a ~ of sth** non un pizzico di qc

speckle ['spe·kl] *n* macchiolina *f*

speckled *adj* con delle macchioline

specs [speks] *npl* 1. *inf abbr of* **spectacles** occhiali *mpl* 2. *inf abbr of* **specifications** specifiche *fpl*

spectacle ['spek·tə·kl] *n* 1.spettacolo *m;* **to make a real ~ of oneself** dare spettacolo di sè 2. *pl* (*glasses*) occhiali *mpl;* **a pair of ~** un paio di occhiali

spectacled *adj* con gli occhiali

spectacular [spek·'tæk·ju·lər] I. *adj* spettacolare II. *n* spettacolo *m* eccezionale

spectator [spek·'teɪ·t̬ər] *n* spettatore, -trice *m, f*

specter ['spek·tər] *n* spettro *m*

spectral ['spek·trəl] *adj* spettrale

spectroscope ['spek·trəu·skoup] *n* PHYS spettroscopio *m*

spectrum ['spek·trəm] <-ra *o* -s> *n* 1.PHYS spettro *m* 2.(*range*) gamma *f;* **the whole political ~** tutti i partiti politici

speculate ['spek·ju·leɪt] *vi* 1.**to ~ about sth** (*hypothesize, conjecture*) speculare su qc 2.(*buy and sell*) speculare

speculation [ˌspek·ju·'leɪ·ʃən] *n* speculazione *f,* congettura *f;* **stock-market ~** speculazione in borsa

speculative ['spek·ju·leɪ·t̬ɪv] *adj* speculativo, -a

speculator ['spek·ju·leɪ·t̬ər] *n* speculatore, -trice *m, f;* **property ~** speculatore in ambito immobiliare

sped [sped] *pt, pp of* **speed**

speech [spi:tʃ] <-es> *n* 1.(*capacity to speak*) parola *f;* **to lose/regain the power of ~** perdere/ritrovare la facoltà della parola 2.(*words*) parole *fpl* 3.(*public talk*) discorso *m;* **to make** [*o* give] **a ~** fare un discorso

speech defect *n* difetto *m* di pronuncia

speechify ['spi:·tʃə·faɪ] *vi* sproloquiare

speech impediment *n* difetto *m* di pronuncia

speechless ['spi:tʃ·ləs] *adj* senza parole; **to leave sb ~** lasciare qu senza parole

speech recognition *n* COMPUT, LING riconoscimento *m* vocale

speech therapist *n* logopedista *mf,* ortofonista *mf*

speech therapy *n* logopedia *f,* ortofonia *f*

speechwriter *n* autore, -trice di discorsi *m* (*per politici*)

speed [spi:d] I. *n* 1.(*velocity, quickness*) velocità *f;* **at a ~ of ...** ad una velocità di .. 2.(*gear*) marcia *f* 3.PHOT sensibilità *f* 4. *inf* (*amphetamine*) anfetamine *fpl* II. *vi* <sped *o* speeded, sped *o* speeded> 1.(*go fast*) andare veloce; **to ~ by** passare a tutta velocità 2.(*hasten*) accelerare 3.(*exceed speed restrictions*) superare i limiti di velocità, fare un eccesso di velocità III. *vt* <sped *o* speeded,

sped *o* speeded> accelerare; **to ~ sb on
their way** augurare buon viaggio a qu
◆**speed off** <sped *o* speeded, sped *o*
speeded> *vi* uscire a tutta velocitá
◆**speed up** <sped *o* speeded, sped *o*
speeded> I. *vi* accelerare II. *vt* (*process*)
accelerare; (*person*) mettere fretta a
speedboat ['spi:d·bʊot] *n* motoscafo *m*
speed bump *n* dosso *m* limitatore di velocità
speed dating *n* speed dating *m inv*
speed demon *n* pirata *mf* della strada
speed dial *n* tasto *m* rapido (*di un telefono*);
on ~ memorizzato, -a
speeding *n* eccesso *m* di velocità
speed limit *n* limite *m* di velocità
speedometer [spi:·'dɑː·mə·tə·] *n* tachimetro *m*
speed skater *n* pattinatore, -trice *m, f* di velocità
speed skating *n* pattinaggio *m* di velocità
speed trap *n* controllo *m* di velocità
speedway ['spi:d·weɪ] *n* 1. (*racetrack*) pista *f*
di speedway 2. (*expressway*) superstrada *f*
speedy ['spi:·di] <-ier, -iest> *adj* veloce
speleologist [ˌspi:·lɪ·'ɑː·lə·dʒɪst] *n* speleologo,
-a *m, f*
speleology [ˌspi:·lɪ·'ɑː·lə·dʒi] *n* speleologia *f*
spell¹ [spel] <spelled *o* spelt, spelled *o*
spelt> I. *vt* 1. (*form using letters*) scrivere;
how do you ~ it? come si scrive? 2. (*signify*)
significare; **this ~s trouble** questo vuol dire
problemi II. *vi* scrivere; **to ~ well** scrivere correttamente
spell² [spel] *n a. fig* incantesimo *m;* **to be
under a ~** essere vittima di un incantesimo
spell³ [spel] I. *n* 1. (*period*) breve periodo *m*
2. (*turn*) turno *m* II. *vt* dare il cambio a
◆**spell out** *vt* scandire (lettera per lettera); **to
spell sth out for sb** *fig* spiegare qc chiaramente a qu
spellbinding ['spel·baɪn·dɪŋ] *adj* avvincente
spellbound ['spel·baʊnd] *adj a. fig* stregato, -a
spellchecker *n*, **spell checker** *n* COMPUT correttore *m* ortografico
speller *n* **to be a good/poor ~** scrivere corret-
tamente/scorrettamente
spelling *n* ortografia *f;* **~ mistake** errore *m* di
ortografia
spelling bee *n* concorso *m* di ortografia
spelt [spelt] *pp, pt of* **spell**
spend [spend] <spent, spent> I. *vt*
1. (*money*) spendere 2. (*time*) trascorrere; **to
~ time** (**doing sth**) passare del tempo (a fare
qc) 3. (*use up*) finire II. *vi* spendere
spending *n* spese *fpl;* **public ~** la spesa pubblica
spending cut *n* FIN taglio *m* alle spese
spending money *n* soldi *m* per le spese personali *pl*
spending power *n* ECON potere *m* di acquisto
spending spree *n* **to go on a ~** darsi alle spese
folli
spendthrift ['spend·θrɪft] *inf* I. *adj* spendac-

cione, -a II. *n* spendaccione, -a *m, f*
spent [spent] I. *pp, pt of* **spend** II. *adj*
1. (*used*) speso, -a; **to be a ~ force** aver perso
vigore 2. *liter* (*very tired*) spossato, -a
sperm [spɜːrm] <-(s)> *n* sperma *m*
sperm count *n* numero *m* di spermatozoi
sperm donor *n* donatore *m* di sperma
spermicide ['spɜːr·mə·saɪd] *n* spermicida *m*
sperm whale ['spɜːrm·weɪl] *n* capodoglio *m*
spew [spju:] *vi, vt* vomitare
SPF *n abbr of* **sun protection factor** fattore *m*
di protezione solare
sphere [sfɪr] *n* sfera *f;* **~ of influence** sfera di
influenza
spherical ['sfɪ·rɪ·kl] *adj* sferico, -a
spice [spaɪs] I. *n* 1. CULIN spezia *f* 2. (*excitement*) piccante *m;* **the ~ of life** il sale della
vita II. *vt* speziare
spic(k)-and-span [ˌspɪk·ən·'spæn] *adj inf*
tirato, -a a lucido
spicy ['spaɪ·si] <-ier, -iest> *adj* 1. (*seasoned*)
piccante 2. (*sensational*) piccante
spider ['spaɪ·də·] *n* ragno *f*
spiderweb ['spaɪ·də··web] *n* ragnatela *f*
spidery *adj* filiforme; **~ handwriting** scrittura *f* a tratti lunghi e disordinati
spiel [ʃpi:l] *n inf* imbonimento *m*
spiffy ['spɪfi] *adj inf* fichissimo, -a
spigot ['spɪ·gət] *n* 1. (*stopper*) zaffo *m* 2. (*tap*)
rubinetto *m*
spike [spaɪk] I. *n* 1. (*pointed object*) punta *f*
2. (*on shoes*) chiodo *m* 3. *pl* (*running shoes*)
scarpe *fpl* chiodate (*da corsa*) 4. (*increase*)
picco *m* 5. SPORTS (*in volleyball*) schiacciata *f;*
(*in football*) spike *m inv* II. *vt* 1. *inf* **to ~ a
drink** correggere una bibita 2. (*injure*) ferire
con i chiodi delle scarpe 3. (*secure*) inchiodare
4. **to ~ a ball** (*in volleyball*) schiacciare (la
palla); (*in football*) fare uno spike III. *vi* avere
un picco
spiky ['spaɪ·ki] <-ier, -iest> *adj* 1. (*sharp*) spinoso, -a; (*hair*) dritto, -a 2. *inf* (*irritable*) permaloso, -a
spill [spɪl] I. *n* 1. (*act of spilling*) fuoriuscita *f;*
oil ~ fuoriuscita *f* di petrolio 2. *inf* (*fall*)
caduta *f;* **to take a ~** fare una caduta II. *vt*
<spilled *o* spilt, spilled *o* spilt> versare III. *vi*
versarsi
◆**spill over** *vi* propagarsi
spillage ['spɪ·lɪdʒ] *n* fuoriuscita *f*
spilt [spɪlt] *pp, pt of* **spill**
spin [spɪn] I. *n* 1. (*rotation*) giro *m* 2. (*drive*)
to go [*o* **take the car**] **for a ~** andare a fare un
giro (in macchina) 3. (*in washing machine*)
centrifugata *f* II. *vt* <spun, spun> 1. (*rotate*)
girare; (*clothes*) centrifugare; **to ~ a ball** dare
un effetto a una palla 2. (*make thread out of*)
filare 3. (*tell: story, tale*) raccontare III. *vi*
<spun, spun> 1. (*rotate*) girare 2. (*make
thread*) filare
◆**spin around** *vi* girare
◆**spin out** I. *vi* perdere il controllo (di un veicolo) II. *vt* perdere il controllo di

S

spina bifida [ˌspaɪ·nə·'bɪ·fɪ·də] *n* MED spina *f* bifida

spinach ['spɪ·nɪtʃ] *n* BOT spinacio *m;* CULIN spinaci *mpl*

spinal ['spaɪ·nəl] *adj* spinale

spinal column *n* spina *f* dorsale, colonna *f* vertebrale

spinal cord *n* midollo *f* spinale

spinal tap *n* puntura *f* lombare

spindle ['spɪn·dl] *n* fuso *m*

spindly <-ier, -iest> *adj* esile

spin doctor *n* POL portavoce *mf* (tendenzioso, -a)

spin-drier *n s.* **spin-dryer**

spin-dry ['spɪn·draɪ] *vt* centrifugare

spin-dryer *n* centrifuga *f* (*della lavatrice*)

spine [spaɪn] *n* 1.(*spinal column*) colonna *f* vertebrale 2.(*spike*) punta *f* 3.(*of book*) dorso *m* 4. BOT spina *f*

spine-chilling ['spaɪn·ˌtʃɪ·lɪŋ] *adj* agghiacciante

spineless ['spaɪn·ləs] *adj* (*weak*) smidollato, -a

spinner *n* 1.(*person*) filatore, -trice *m, f* 2.(*machine*) macchina *f* per filare

spinning *n* rotazione *f*

spinning top *n* trottola *f*

spinning wheel *n* filatoio *m*

spinoff *n*, **spin-off** ['spɪn·ɑːf] *n* 1.(*by-product*) prodotto *m* secondario 2.(*consequence*) effetto *m* indiretto

spinster ['spɪn·stɚ] *n* donna *f* nubile; *pej* zitella *f*

spiny ['spaɪ·ni] <-ier, -iest> *adj a. fig* spinoso, -a

spiny lobster *n* aragosta *f*

spiral ['spaɪ·rəl] I. *n* spirale *f* II. *adj* a spirale; ~ **staircase** scala *f* a chiocciola III. *vi* <-ll-, -l-> 1.(*travel in a spiral*) fare delle spirali; **to ~ downwards** cadere a spirale 2.(*increase*) essere in progressione costante; (*decrease*) essere in calo costante; **to ~ out of control** aumentare in modo incontrollato

spire ['spa·ɪɚ] *n* ARCHIT guglia *f*

spirit ['spɪ·rɪt] *n* 1.(*soul*) spirito *m* 2.(*ghost*) spirito *m* 3. *pl* (*mood*) morale *mpl;* **to be in high/low ~s** essere su/giù di morale 4.(*character*) carattere *m* 5. *pl* (*alcoholic drink*) superalcolici *mpl* 6.(*attitude or principle*) **the ~ of the age** lo spirito dell'epoca; **that's the ~!** questo è spirito giusto!
◆**spirit away** *vt* far sparire

spirited *adj* (*energetic*) energico, -a; (*discussion*) animato, -a; (*person*) coraggioso, -a

spiritless ['spɪ·rɪt·ləs] *adj pej* 1.(*downhearted*) abbattuto, -a 2.(*irresolute*) indeciso, -a

spiritual ['spɪ·rɪ·tʃu·əl] I. *adj* spirituale II. *n* MUS spiritual *m inv*

spiritualism ['spɪ·rɪ·tʃu·ə·lɪ·zəm] *n* spiritismo *m*

spit[1] [spɪt] I. *n inf* saliva *f* II. *vi* <spat, spat> 1.(*expel saliva*) sputare 2.(*crackle*) scoppiet-

tare III. *vt* sputare
◆**spit out** *vt* 1.(*expel from mouth*) sputare 2.(*say angrily*) ringhiare; **spit it out!** *inf* sputa il rospo!

spit [spɪt] *n* 1. CULIN spiedo *m* 2.(*sandbar*) banco *m* di sabbia

spite [spaɪt] I. *n* rancore *m;* **to do sth out of ~** fare qc per dispetto; **in ~ of** a dispetto di; **in ~ of everyone/everything** a dispetto di tutti e tutto; **in ~ of the fact that he is rich** nonostante (il fatto che) sia ricco II. *vt* fare un dispetto a

spiteful ['spaɪt·fəl] *adj pej* vendicativo, -a

spitting image *n* **she's the ~ of her mother** è sua madre sputata

spittle ['spɪ·tl̩] *n* sputo *m*

spittoon [spɪ·'tuːn] *n* sputacchiera *f*

splash [splæʃ] I. *n* 1.(*sound*) tonfo *m* 2.(*small drops*) schizzo *m;* **a ~ of color** una macchia colorata ► **to make a** (**big**) **~** fare (molto) scalpore II. *vt* spruzzare; **to ~ across the front page** mettere in prima pagina III. *vi* spruzzare
◆**splash down** *vi* ammarare

splashboard ['splæʃ·bɔːrd] *n* (*on vehicle*) parafango *m inv;* (*on boat, in kitchen*) paraspruzzi *m inv*

splashdown ['splæʃ·daʊn] *n* ammaraggio *m*

splat [splæt] *n inf* spash *m inv*

splatter ['splæ·tɚ] *vi, vt* schizzare

splay [spleɪ] I. *vt* divaricare II. *vi* divaricarsi

spleen [spliːn] *n* 1. ANAT milza *f* 2.(*anger*) malumore *m;* **to vent one's ~** sfogare il proprio malumore

splendid ['splen·dɪd] *adj* splendido, -a

splendiferous [splen·'dɪ·fə·rəs] *adj inf* splendido, -a

splendor ['splen·dɚ] *n* 1.(*grandness*) splendore *m* 2. *pl* (*beautiful things*) meraviglie *fpl*

splice [splaɪs] *vt* (*join*) giuntare; **to get ~d** *inf* sposarsi

splint [splɪnt] I. *n* stecca *f* II. *vt* steccare

splinter ['splɪn·tɚ] I. *n* scheggia *f* II. *vi* scheggiarsi

splinter group *n* POL gruppo *m* di dissidenti

split [splɪt] I. *n* 1.(*crack*) fessura *f* 2.(*in clothes*) spacco *m* 3.(*division*) spaccatura *f* II. *vt* <split, split> 1.(*divide*) dividere; (*atom*) disintegrare; **to ~ sth between two people** dividere qc tra due persone 2.(*crack*) fendere; **to ~ one's head open** spaccarsi la testa ► **to ~ one's sides laughing** sbellicarsi dalle risa; **to ~ hairs** spaccare il capello in quattro III. *vi* <split, split> 1.(*divide*) dividersi 2.(*form cracks*) fendersi 3. *inf* (*leave*) filarsela
◆**split off** I. *vt* separare II. *vi* separarsi
◆**split up** I. *vt* dividere II. *vi* **to ~ with sb** separarsi da qu

split infinitive *n* LING *infinito con un avverbio tra 'to' e il verbo*

split-level *adj* su più livelli

split pea *n* pisello *m* secco spezzato

split personality *n* PSYCH sdoppiamento *m*

della personalità

split screen *n* schermo *m* suddiviso

split second *n* frazione *f* di secondo

splitting headache *n inf*mal *m* di testa atroce

split-up ['splɪt·ʌp] *n* rottura *f*

splodge [splɑːdʒ] *n*, **splotch** [splɑːtʃ] *n* macchia *f*

splurge [splɜːrdʒ] *inf* I. *vi* scialacquare II. *vt* scialacquare III. *n* spesa *f* folle

splutter ['splʌ·t̬ə] I. *vi* (*person*) farfugliare; (*candle, engine*) scoppiettare II. *n* (*of person*) balbettio *m;* (*of candle, engine*) scoppiettio *m*

spoil [spɔɪl] I. *vt* <spoiled *o* spoilt, spoiled *o* spoilt> 1. (*ruin*) rovinare 2. (*child*) viziare II. *vi* <spoiled *o* spoilt, spoiled *o* spoilt> andare a male III. *n* 1. *pl* (*profits*) bottino *m* 2. (*debris*) macerie *fpl*

spoiler *n* alettone *m*

spoilsport ['spɔɪl·spɔːrt] *n inf* guastafeste *mf inv*

spoilt I. *pp, pt of* spoil II. *adj* viziato, -a

spoke[1] [spoʊk] *pt of* speak

spoke[2] [spoʊk] *n* (*of wheel*) raggio *m;* **to put a ~ in sb's wheel** *fig* mettere i bastoni tra le ruote a qu

spoken *pp of* speak

spokesman ['spoʊks·mən] *n* portavoce *m inv*

spokesperson ['spoʊks·ˌpɜːr·sən] *n* portavoce *mf inv*

spokeswoman ['spoʊks·ˌwʊ·mən] *n* portavoce *f inv*

sponge [spʌndʒ] I. *n* 1. (*animal*) spugna *f* 2. (*absorbent*) spugna *f* 3. (*person*) parassita *mf* II. *vt* passare una spugna su III. *vi inf* essere un parassita

 ◆ **sponge down** *vt* passare una spugna su

 ◆ **sponge off** *vt* 1. (*clean*) togliere con una spugna 2. *inf* vivere alle spalle di

 ◆ **sponge up** *vt* pulire con una spugna

sponge bath *n* lavaggio *m* con una spugna

sponge cake *n* pandispagna *m inv*

sponger *n pej* parassita *mf*

spongy ['spʌn·dʒi] <-ier, -iest> *adj* spugnoso, -a

sponsor ['spɑːn·tsə] I. *vt* sponsorizzare II. *n* sponsor *m inv*

sponsorship *n* patrocinio *m*

spontaneity [ˌspɑːn·tə·'ne·ɪə·t̬i] *n* spontaneità *f*

spontaneous [spɑːn·'teɪ·ni·əs] *adj* spontaneo, -a

spoof [spuːf] *n* parodia *f;* **to do a ~ on sth** fare una parodia di qc

spook [spuːk] I. *n* 1. *inf* (*ghost*) fantasma *m* 2. *sl* (*spy*) spia *mf* II. *vt* spaventare

spooky ['spuː·ki] <-ier, -iest> *adj inf* spettrale

spool [spuːl] *n* (*of thread*) rocchetto *m;* (*of film*) bobina *f*

spoon [spuːn] I. *n* 1. (*utensil*) cucchiaio *m* 2. (*amount*) cucchiaio *m* II. *vt* servire (con un cucchiaio)

spoonbill ['spuːn·bɪl] *n* spatola *f*

spoon-feed ['spuːn·fiːd] *vt* 1. (*feed*) dare da mangiare con un cucchiaio a 2. *pej* **to ~ sb** scodellare la pappa a qu

spoonful ['spuːn·fʊl] <-s *o* spoonsful> *n* cucchiaiata *f*

sporadic [spə·'ræ·dɪk] *adj* sporadico, -a

spore [spɔːr] *n* spora *f*

sport [spɔːrt] I. *n* 1. (*activity*) sport *m inv* 2. *inf* (*person*) **to be a good/poor ~** non prendersela/prendersela II. *vt* sfoggiare

sport coat *n* giacca *f* sportiva (da uomo)

sporting *adj* sportivo, -a

sports car *n* auto *f* sportiva *inv*

sportscast ['spɔːrts·kæst] *n* programma *m* sportivo

sportscaster *n* giornalista *mf* sportivo, -a

sportsman ['spɔːrts·mən] *n* sportivo, -a *m, f*

sportsmanlike ['spɔːrts·mən·laɪk] *adj* sportivo, -a

sportsmanship *n* sportività *f*

sports page *n* pagina *f* sportiva

sportswear *n* abbigliamento *m* sportivo

sportswoman ['spɔːrts·ˌwʊ·mən] *n* sportiva *f*

sportswriter *n* cronista *mf* sportivo, -a

sporty ['spɔːr·t̬i] <-ier, -iest> *adj* sportivo, -a

spot [spɑːt] I. *n* 1. (*mark*) macchia *f* 2. (*pattern*) pois *m inv* 3. (*on skin*) neo *m* 4. (*place*) posto *m;* **on the ~** (*at the very place*) sul posto; (*at once*) subito 5. (*part of TV, radio show*) spot *m inv* 6. *inf* faretto *m* ▶ **to really hit the ~** essere quello che ci vuole; **to have a soft ~ for sb** avere un debole per qu; **to put sb on the ~** mettere qu con le spalle al muro II. <-tt-> *vt* 1. (*see*) scorgere 2. (*speckle*) macchiare

spot check *n* controllo *m* casuale

spotless ['spɑːt·ləs] *adj* 1. (*very clean*) immacolato, -a 2. (*unblemished*) impeccabile

spotlight ['spɑːt·laɪt] I. *n* riflettore *m* ▶ **to be in the ~** essere sotto i riflettori II. <spotlighted *o* spotlit, spotlighted *o* spotlit> *vt* illuminare

spot market *n* FIN mercato *m* a pronti

spot price *n* prezzo *m* in contanti

spotted *adj* macchiato, -a; **a ~ dress** un vestito a pois

spotter *n* SPORTS, AVIAT osservatore, -trice *m, f*

spotty ['spɑː·t̬i] <-ier, -iest> *adj* 1. (*having blemished skin*) brufoloso, -a 2. (*inconsistent*) irregolare

spouse [spaʊs] *n form* coniuge *mf*

spout [spaʊt] I. *n* 1. (*of kettle, jar*) beccuccio *m;* (*tube*) orificio *m* 2. (*jet*) zampillo *m* II. *vt* 1. (*send out: flames*) sputare; (*water*) sprizzare 2. *pej* **to ~ sth** declamare qc; **to ~ facts and figures** sciorinare fatti e cifre III. *vi* 1. (*gush*) zampillare 2. *pej* (*speechify*) sproloquiare

sprain [spreɪn] I. *vt* distorcersi II. *n* storta *f*

sprang [spræŋ] *vi, vt pt of* spring

sprat [spræt] *n* spratto *m*

sprawl [sprɑːl] *pej* I. *vi* 1. (*spread out*) stravacarsi; **to send sb ~ing** mandare qu a gambe all'aria 2. (*town*) espandersi (in modo incontrollato) II. *n* (*of town*) espansione *f;* **urban ~**

S

agglomerato *m* urbano
sprawling *adj pej* **1.**(*town*) tentacolare **2.**(*handwriting*) disordinato, -a
spray¹ [spreɪ] **I.** *n* **1.**(*mist*) spruzzi *mpl* **2.**(*device*) nebulizzatore *m*, spray *m inv* **II.** *vt* (*cover in a spray*) spruzzare **III.** *vi* (*gush*) spruzzare
spray² [spreɪ] *n* ramoscello *m;* **a ~ of flowers** un mazzo di fiori
spray gun *n* pistola *f* a spruzzo
spread [spred] **I.** *n* **1.**(*act of spreading*) diffusione *f* **2.**(*range*) gamma *f* **3.**(*article*) **a full-page ~** articolo *m* su doppia pagina **4.** CULIN crema *f*, pasta *f* **5.**(*ranch*) ranch *m inv* **6.** *inf* (*meal*) banchetto *m* **7.** SPORTS (*number of points*) **point ~** punteggio *m* **II.**<spread, spread> *vt* **1.**(*news*) diffondere; (*disease*) trasmettere **2.**(*butter*) spalmare **3.**(*payments, work*) dilazionare **4.**(*unfold: map, blanket*) spiegare **III.**<spread, spread> *vi* (*news*) diffondersi; (*disease*) trasmettersi; (*liquid*) espandersi
spread-eagled ['spred·'iː·gld] *adj* con le braccia e le gambe divaricate
spreadsheet ['spred·ʃiːt] *n* COMPUT foglio *m* elettronico
spree [spriː] *n* **to go (out) on a drinking ~** farsi una bella bevuta; **to go on a shopping ~** darsi alle spese folli
sprig [sprɪg] *n* rametto *m*
sprightly ['spraɪt·li] <-ier, -iest> *adj* vivace
spring [sprɪŋ] **I.** *n* **1.**(*season*) primavera *f* **2.**(*jump*) balzo *m* **3.**(*metal coil*) molla *f* **4.**(*elasticity*) elasticità *f* **5.**(*source of water*) sorgente *f* **II.**<sprang, sprung> *vi* balzare; **to ~ to one's feet** balzare in piedi; **to ~ shut/open** chiudersi/aprirsi di colpo **III.**<sprang, sprung> *vt* **to ~ sth on sb** tirar fuori qc a qu all'improvviso
◆**spring back** *vi* balzare indietro
springboard ['sprɪŋ·bɔːrd] *n* trampolino *m*
spring break *n* vacanze (scolastiche) *f* di primavera *pl*
spring chicken *n* **he's no spring chicken** non è più un ragazzino
spring-clean [ˌsprɪŋ·'kliːn] *vt* pulire a fondo
spring-cleaning *n* pulizie *f* di Pasqua *pl*
spring roll *n* involtino *m* primavera
springtime ['sprɪŋ·taɪm] *n* primavera *f*
springy ['sprɪŋ·i] <-ier, -iest> *adj* elastico, -a
sprinkle ['sprɪŋ·kl] **I.** *vt* spargere **II.** *n* pizzico *f*
sprinkler ['sprɪŋ·klɚ] *n* sprinkler *m*
sprinkling ['sprɪŋ·klɪŋ] *n* **a ~ of sth** una spruzzata di qc
sprint [sprɪnt] SPORTS **I.** *vi* fare uno sprint **II.** *n* **1.**(*race*) corsa *f* **2.**(*burst of speed*) corsa *f* veloce
sprinter ['sprɪn·tɚ] *n* velocista *mf*
sprite [spraɪt] *n liter* folletto *m*
sprocket ['sprɑ·kɪt] *n*, **sprocket wheel** *n* ruota *f* dentata
sprout [spraʊt] **I.** *n* **1.**(*of plant*) germoglio *m* **2.** *pl* (*Brussels sprouts*) cavoletti *mpl* di Bru-

xelles **II.** *vi* (*begin to grow*) spuntare **III.** *vt* (*grow: leaves*) mettere
◆**sprout up** *vi* (*plant, child*) crescere rapidamente; (*buildings*) spuntare dal nulla
spruce¹ [spruːs] *n* BOT picea *f*
spruce² [spruːs] *adj* tirato, -a a lucido
◆**spruce up** *vt* **to spruce oneself up** darsi una sistemata
sprung [sprʌŋ] *pp, Am: pt of* **spring**
spry [spraɪ] *adj* arzillo, -a
spud [spʌd] *n inf* patata *f*
spun [spʌn] *pp, pt of* **spin**
spunk [spʌŋk] *n inf* fegato *m*
spunky [spʌŋki] *adj* energico, -a
spur [spɜːr] **I.**<-rr-> *vt a. fig* spronare **II.** *n* **1.**(*device*) sperone *m* **2.** GEO sperone *m* **3.**(*encouragement*) sprone *m* ▶**on the ~ of the moment** *inf* d'impulso
spurious ['spjʊ·ri·əs] *adj* falso, -a
spurn [spɜːrn] *vt form* respingere
spurt [spɜːrt] **I.** *n* **1.**(*jet*) fiotto *m* **2.**(*burst*) slancio *m;* **a growth ~** un'impennata **II.** *vi* **1.**(*gush*) uscire a fiotti **2.**(*accelerate*) scattare **III.** *vt* (*liquid*) mandare a fiotti
sputter ['spʌ·tɚ] **I.** *vi* (*person*) farfugliare; (*candle, engine*) scoppiettare **II.** *n* (*of person*) balbettio *m;* (*of candle, engine*) scoppiettio *m*
sputum ['spjuː·təm] *n* espettorato *m*
spy [spaɪ] **I.** *n* spia *f* **II.** *vi* spiare; **to ~ on sb** spiare qu **III.** *vt* scorgere
spyglass ['spaɪ·glæs] *n* cannocchiale *m*
spyhole ['spaɪ·hoʊl] *n* spioncino *m*
spy satellite *n* satellite *m* spia
spyware *n* spyware *m*
Sq. *abbr of* **square** P.za
squabble ['skwɑ·bl] **I.** *n* bisticcio *m* **II.** *vi* bisticciare
squad [skwɑːd] *n* **1.**(*group*) squadra *f;* (*of police*) squadra *f;* **anti-terrorist ~** squadra antiterrorista **2.**(*sports team*) squadra *f*
squad car *n* volante *f*
squadron ['skwɑː·drən] *n* squadrone *m*
squalid ['skwɑː·lɪd] *adj* **1.** *pej* (*dirty*) squallido, -a **2.**(*sordid*) squallido, -a
squall [skwɔːl] **I.** *n* temporale *m* **II.** *vi* strillare
squally ['skwɔː·li] *adj* burrascoso, -a
squalor ['skwɑː·lɚ] *n* miseria *f*
squander ['skwɑːn·dɚ] *vt* sprecare; (*money*) scialacquare; **to ~ an opportunity** sprecare un'opportunità; **to ~ the lead** perdere il primo posto
square [skwer] **I.** *n* **1.**(*shape*) quadrato *m* **2.**(*in town*) piazza *f* **3.**(*on chessboard*) casella *f* **4.**(*tool*) squadra *f* **5.** MATH quadrato *m* ▶**to go back to ~ one** ritrovarsi al punto di partenza **II.** *adj* **1.**(*square-shaped*) quadrato, -a; **forty-three ~ feet** quattro metri quadrati **2.**(*fair*) **a ~ deal** un affare corretto; **to give sb a ~ deal** trattare qn correttamente **3.**(*not owing anything*) pari **III.** *vt* **1.**(*make square*) quadrare **2.**(*settle*) far quadrare; **to ~ one's accounts** far quadrare i conti **3.** MATH elevare al quadrato **IV.** *vi* **to ~ with the facts** quadrare

con i fatti **V.** *adv* direttamente; **to run** [*o* **drive**] ~ **into sth** andare a sbattere in pieno contro qc ◆**square up** *vi* to ~ **with sb** sistemare i conti con qn

square bracket *n* parentesi *f* quadra

square dance *n ballo popolare di società americana*

> **i** **Square dance** è il nome attribuito a un ballo folcloristico americano. Gruppi composti da quattro coppie ballano formando un quadrato, un cerchio o due file e eseguono i movimenti annunciati da un *caller*. Il *caller* può dare le istruzioni cantando o parlando. Lo **square dancing** è spesso accompagnato da musicisti country che suonano il violino, il banjo e la chitarra.

squarely *adv* direttamente

square root *n* radice *f* quadrata

squash¹ [skwɑːʃ] *n* (*vegetable*) zucca *f*

squash² [skwɑːʃ] **I.** *n* **1.**SPORTS squash *m* **2.**(*dense pack*) **it's a** ~ si sta ammassati *m* **II.** *vt* schiacciare

squash court *n* campo *m* da squash

squash racket *n*, **squash racquet** *n* racchetta *f* da squash

squashy ['skwɑːʃi] <-ier, -iest> *adj* molle

squat [skwɑːt] **I.**<-tt-> *vi* **1.**(*crouch down*) accovacciarsi **2.**(*in property*) occupare una proprietà abusivamente **II.** *n* **1.**(*exercise*) fare piegamenti sulle gambe **2.** *sl* (*nothing*) **to not know** ~ non sapere un tubo **III.**<-tt-> *adj* (*person*) tracagnotto, -a

squatter ['skwɑː·t̬ɚ] *n* occupante *mf* abusivo, -a

squaw [skwɑː] *n* squaw *f inv, donna indiana del Nordamerica*

squawk [skwɑːk] **I.** *vi* gracchiare **II.** *n* gracchio *m*

squeak [skwiːk] **I.** *n* gridolino *m;* (*of mouse*) squittio *m;* (*of door*) cigolio *m* **II.** *vi* strillare; (*mouse*) squittire; (*door*) cigolare

squeaky ['skwiːki] <-ier, -iest> *adj* (*voice*) stridulo,-a; (*door*) cigolante

squeaky-clean [ˌskwiː·ki·'kliːn] *adj* immacolato, -a

squeal [skwiːl] **I.** *n* stridio *m* **II.** *vi* **1.**(*person, animal*) strillare; (*brakes, car*) stridere **2.** *sl* (*inform on sb*) spifferare ◆**squeal on** *vt sl* to ~ **sb** spifferare sul conto di qu

squeamish ['skwiː·mɪʃ] *adj* impressionabile; **to feel** ~ avere la nausea

squeegee ['skwiː·dʒiː] *n* spatola *f* di gomma

squeeze [skwiːz] **I.** *n* **1.**(*pressing action*) stretta *f;* **a** ~ **of orange** una spruzzata d'arancio **2.**ECON (*limit*) restrizione *f* **3.**(*pressure*) **to put the** ~ **on sb** fare pressione su qu **II.** *vt* **1.**(*press together: lemon, orange*) spremere; (*hand*) stringere; (*cloth*) strizzare; **freshly** ~**d**

orange juice spremuta *f* d'arancia **2.**(*force*) **to** ~ **sth out of sb** tirar fuori qc a qu

squeezer ['skwiː·zɚ] *n* spremiagrumi *m inv*

squelch [skweltʃ] **I.** *vi* avanzare sguazzando **II.** *vt* mettere a tacere **III.** *n* ciac *m*

squid [skwɪd] <-(s)> *n* calamaro *m*

squiggle ['skwɪ·gl] **I.** *n* scarabocchio *m* **II.** *vi* scarabocchiare

squint [skwɪnt] **I.** *vi* **1.**(*be cross-eyed*) essere strabico, -a **2.**(*look from corner of eye*) sbirciare **II.** *n* **1.**(*eye condition*) strabismo *m* **2.**(*quick look*) sbirciata *f*

squire ['skwa·ɪɚ] *n* HIST scudiero *m*

squirm [skwɜːrm] *vi* dimenarsi; **to** ~ **with embarrassment** sentirsi imbarazzato

squirrel ['skwɜː·rəl] *n* scoiattolo *m*

squirt [skwɜːrt] **I.** *vt* (*liquid*) spruzzare; **to** ~ **sb with sth** spruzzare qu di qc **II.** *vi* sprizzare **III.** *n* **1.**(*small quantity*) spruzzata *f* **2.** *pej* (*person*) mezzatacca *f*

Sr. *n abbr of* **senior** padre; **George Bush, Sr.** George Bush, padre

Sri Lanka [ˌsriː·'lɑː·ŋ·kə] *n* Sri Lanka *m*

Sri Lankan [ˌsriː·'lɑː·ŋ·kən] **I.** *adj* dello Sri Lanka **II.** *n* abitante *mf* dello Sri Lanka

SRO *abbr of* **standing room only** solo posti in piedi

SSE [ˌes·es·'dʌ·bl·juː] *abbr of* **south-southeast** SSE

SSgt. *n abbr of* **staff sergeant** Serg. Magg.

SSW [ˌes·es·'dʌ·bl·juː] *abbr of* **south-southwest** SSO

St. *n* **1.** *abbr of* **saint** S.; ~ **Thomas** S. Tommaso **2.** *abbr of* **street** via

stab [stæb] **I.**<-bb-> *vt* pugnalare; **to** ~ **sb to death** pugnalare qu a morte; **to** ~ **sb in the back** *fig* pugnalare qu alle spalle **II.**<-bb-> *vi* dare dei colpetti **III.** *n* **1.**(*blow*) pugnalata *f* **2.**(*sudden pain*) fitta *f* **3.**(*attempt*) **to take a** ~ **at** (**doing**) **sth** provare (a fare) qc

stabbing **I.** *n* accoltellamento *m* **II.** *adj* lancinante

stability [stə·'bɪ·lə·ti] *n* stabilità *f*

stabilization [ˌsteɪ·blɪ·'zeɪ·ʃən] *n* stabilizzazione *f*

stabilize ['steɪ·bə·laɪz] **I.** *vt* stabilizzare **II.** *vi* stabilizzarsi

stabilizer ['steɪ·bə·laɪ·zɚ] *n* **1.**(*on ship, bicycle*) stabilizzatore *m* **2.**CHEM stabilizzante *m*

stable¹ ['steɪ·bl] *adj* **1.**ECON stabile **2.**(*structure*) stabile **3.**MED stazionario, -a

stable² ['steɪ·bl] **I.** *n* stalla *f* **II.** *vt* tenere in una stalla

stack [stæk] **I.** *vt* **1.**(*arrange in a pile*) appilare **2.**(*fill: shelves*) riempire ▶ **the cards are** ~**ed against us** la sorte ci è avversa **II.** *n* **1.**(*pile*) pila *f* **2.** *inf* (*large amount*) mucchio *m* **3.** *pl* (*bookcase*) scaffali *mpl*

stadium ['steɪ·di·əm] <-s *o* -dia> *n* stadio *m*

staff [stæf] **I.** *n* **1.**(*employees*) personale *m;* **the editorial** ~ la redazione; **the teaching** ~ il corpo insegnante **2.**MIL Stato *m* Maggiore

S

3.(*stick*) bastone *m;* ~ **of office** bastone di comando **4.**(*flagpole*) asta *f* **5.**<staves> MUS pentagramma *m* **II.** *vt* dotare di personale
staff sergeant *n* sergente *m* maggiore
stag [stæg] *n* **1.** ZOOL cervo *m* **2.** (*unaccompanied male*) scapolo *m*
stag beetle *n* cervo *m* volante
stage [steɪdʒ] **I.** *n* **1.**(*period*) stadio *m;* **at this ~ in my life** a questo punto della mia vita; **to do sth in ~s** fare qc per gradi **2.** THEAT palcoscenico *m;* **the ~** il teatro; **to be on the ~** recitare (in teatro); **to go on the ~** darsi al teatro; **to hold the ~** catturare l'attenzione del pubblico **II.** *vt* **1.**(*produce on stage*) mettere in scena **2.**(*organize*) organizzare
stagecoach ['steɪdʒ·koʊtʃ] *n* diligenza *f*
stage door *n* ingresso *m* degli artisti
stage fright *n* panico *m* da palcoscenico
stagehand ['steɪdʒ·hænd] *n* THEAT macchinista *mf* (teatrale)
stage-manage ['steɪdʒ·ˌmæ·nɪdʒ] *vt* **1.** THEAT dirigere la messa in scena di **2.** *fig* orchestare
stage manager *n* THEAT direttore, -trice *m, f* di scena; CINE direttore, -trice *m, f* di produzione
stage name *n* nome *m* d'arte
stage whisper *n* THEAT battuta *f* sussurrata (*destinata al pubblico*)
stagflation [ˌstæg·ˈfleɪ·ʃən] *n* ECON stagflazione *f*
stagger ['stæ·gɚ] **I.** *vi* barcollare **II.** *vt* **1.**(*amaze*) sconcertare **2.**(*work, payments*) scaglionare **III.** *n* passo *m* barcollante
staggering *adj* (*amazing*) sconcertante
staging ['steɪ·dʒɪŋ] *n* THEAT messa *f* in scena
stagnant ['stæg·nənt] *adj a. fig* stagnante
stagnate ['stæg·neɪt] *vi* (ri)stagnare
stagnation [stæg·ˈneɪ·ʃən] *n* ristagno *m*
stag party *n* addio *m* al celibato
stagy ['steɪ·dʒi] *adj pej* teatrale
staid [steɪd] *adj* serioso, -a
stain [steɪn] **I.** *vt* **1.**(*mark*) macchiare **2.**(*dye*) dare il mordente a **II.** *vi* (*become marked*) macchiarsi **III.** *n* **1.**(*mark*) macchia *f;* **blood/ grease/red wine ~** macchia *f* di sangue/ grasso/vino rosso **2.**(*dye*) colorante *m*
stained *adj* (*marked*) macchiato, -a
stained glass *n* vetro *m* colorato
stained-glass window *n* vetrata *f* (decorata)
stainless ['steɪn·ləs] **I.** *adj* (*immaculate*) immacolato, -a; (*that cannot be stained*) antimacchia *inv* **II.** *n* acciaio *m* inossidabile
stainless steel *n* acciaio *m* inossidabile
stain remover *n* smacchiatore *m*
stair [ster] *n* **1.**(*rung*) gradino *m* **2.** *pl* (*set of steps*) scala *f*
staircase ['ster·keɪs] *n,* **stairway** ['ster·weɪ] *n* scala *f*
stairwell ['ster·wel] *n* vano *m* scale
stake [steɪk] **I.** *n* **1.**(*stick*) paletto *m;* **to be burnt at the ~** HIST bruciare sul rogo **2.**(*share*) partecipazione *f;* **to have a ~ in sth** avere una partecipazione in qc **3.**(*bet*) posta *f;* **to play for high ~s** giocare forte; **to be at ~** essere in

gioco **II.** *vt* **1.**(*mark with stakes*) segnare con paletti **2.**(*bet*) puntare; **to ~ one's life on sth** mettere la mano sul fuoco per qc; **to ~ a claim to sth** rivendicare qc
◆**stake out** *vt inf* piantonare
stakeholder ['steɪk·ˌhoʊl·dɚ] *n* FIN soggetto *m* portatore di interesse
stakeout *n* piantonamento *m*
stalactite [stə·ˈlæk·taɪt] *n* stalattite *f*
stalagmite ['stæ·ləg·maɪt] *n* stalagmite *f*
stale [steɪl] *adj* **1.**(*not fresh*) stantio, -a; (*bread*) raffermo, -a; (*air*) viziato, -a; (*joke*) trito, -a e ritrito, -a **2.**(*tired*) stanco, -a
stalemate ['steɪl·meɪt] *n* **1.**(*deadlock*) fase *f* di stallo **2.** GAMES stallo *m*
stalk[1] [stɔːk] *n* (*of plant*) gambo *m;* **her eyes were out on ~s** aveva gli occhi fuori dalle orbite
stalk[2] [stɔːk] **I.** *vt* (*follow*) seguire ossessivamente **II.** *vi* **to ~ off** allontanarsi offeso, -a
stalker *n* persona *che ne segue ossessivamente un'altra*
stalking-horse *n* POL candidato, -a *m, f* civetta
stall [stɔːl] **I.** *n* **1.**(*for animal*) posta *f* **2.**(*in market*) bancarella *f,* banco *m* **3.**(*compartment*) **shower ~** vano *m* doccia; **toilet ~** vano *m* gabinetto **II.** *vi* **1.**(*stop running: engine, vehicle*) bloccarsi **2.** *fig, inf* (*delay*) **to ~ for time** guadagnare tempo **III.** *vt* **1.**(*engine*) fare spegnere; (*vehicle*) fare spegnere il motore di **2.** *fig, inf* (*keep waiting*) tenere a bada
stallion ['stæl·jən] *n* stallone *m*
stalwart ['stɔːl·wɚt] *form* **I.** *adj* **1.**(*strong*) robusto, -a **2.**(*loyal*) fedele **II.** *n* sostenitore, -trice *m, f* fedele
stamen ['steɪ·men] <-s *o* -mina> *n* stame *m*
stamina ['stæ·mə·nə] *n* resistenza *f*
stammer ['stæ·mɚ] **I.** *vi* balbettare **II.** *vt* balbettare **III.** *n* balbettamento *m*
stammerer ['stæ·mɚ·ɚ] *n* balbuziente *mf*
stamp [stæmp] **I.** *n* **1.**(*postage stamp*) francobollo *m;* (*device*) timbro *m;* (*mark*) bollo *m* **2.**(*characteristic quality*) impronta *f* **3.**(*with foot*) impronta *f* di piede **II.** *vt* **1.**(*place postage stamp on*) affrancare **2.**(*impress a mark on*) timbrare **3. to ~ one's foot** pestare il piede per terra **III.** *vi* pestare i piedi
◆**stamp out** *vt* sradicare
stamp album *n* album *m* di francobolli *inv*
stamp collector *n* collezionista *mf* di francobolli
stampede [stæm·ˈpiːd] **I.** *n* (*of animals*) fuga *f* disordinata; (*of people*) ressa *f* **II.** *vi* fuggire disordinatamente **III.** *vt* **1.**(*cause to stampede*) seminare il panico tra **2.**(*force*) forzare; **to ~ sb into (doing) sth** forzare qn a (fare) qc
stamping ground *n s.* **stomping ground**
stance [stænts] *n* posizione *f*
stanch[1] *adj s.* **staunch**
stanch[2] *vt* arginare
stand [stænd] **I.** *n* **1.**(*position*) posizione *f;* **to take a ~ on (doing) sth** prendere una pos-

izione in qc/nel fare qc; **to make a ~ against sth** opporre resistenza a qc **2.** *pl* (*in stadium*) tribuna *f* **3.** (*support, frame*) supporto *m;* **music ~** leggio *m* **4.** (*market stall*) banco *m* del mercato **5.** (*for vehicles*) posteggio *m;* **taxi ~** posteggio *m* dei taxi **6.** (*witness box*) banco *m* dei testimoni; **to take the ~** salire sul banco dei testimoni **7.** (*group*) **a ~ of trees** una serie di alberi **II.** <stood, stood> *vi* **1.** (*be upright*) stare in piedi; **to ~ 6 feet tall** essere alto, -a un metro e ottanta; **to ~ still** stare fermo, -a **2.** (*be located*) trovarsi **3.** (*remain unchanged: decision*) rimanere valido, -a; (*law*) rimanere in vigore **III.** <stood, stood> *vt* **1.** (*place*) mettere dritto, -a **2.** (*bear*) sopportare; **I can't ~ her** non la sopporto **3.** LAW **to ~ trial** subire un processo
♦ **stand about** *vi,* **stand around** *vi* starsene
♦ **stand aside** *vi* **1.** (*move*) farsi da parte **2.** (*stay*) stare in disparte
♦ **stand back** *vi* **1.** (*move backwards*) indietreggiare **2.** (*be objective*) prendere le distanze
♦ **stand by I.** *vi* **1.** (*observe*) stare a guardare **2.** (*be ready to take action*) essere pronto, -a **II.** *vt* (*support*) appoggiare
♦ **stand down** *vi* rinunciare
♦ **stand for** *vt* **1.** (*represent*) rappresentare; (*mean*) stare per **2.** (*believe in*) sostenere **3.** (*tolerate*) tollerare
♦ **stand in** *vi* **to ~ for sb** sostituire qu
♦ **stand out** *vi* risaltare
♦ **stand over** *vt* stare addosso a
♦ **stand up I.** *vi* **1.** (*be upright*) alzarsi (in piedi) **2.** (*evidence, argument*) reggere; **to ~ in court** reggere in tribunale ▶ **to ~ and be counted** dichiarare apertamente le proprie opinioni **II.** *vt* **to stand sb up** tirare un bidone a qu

standalone *n,* **stand-alone** ['stæn·də·ˌloʊn] *adj* COMPUT **~ computer network** rete (telematica) *f* autonoma

standard ['stæn·dəd] **I.** *n* **1.** (*level*) livello *m;* (*quality*) livello *m* qualitativo **2.** (*norm*) norma *f* **3.** (*flag*) stendardo *m* **4.** MUS classico *m* **II.** *adj* **1.** (*normal*) normale; (*procedure*) usuale **2.** LING standard *m inv*

standard-bearer ['stæn·dəd·ˌbe·rə] *n* portabandiera *mf inv*

standardization [ˌstæn·də·dɪ·ˈzeɪ·ʃən] *n* standardizzazione *f;* TECH normalizzare

standardize ['stæn·də·daɪz] *vt* standardizzare; TECH normalizzare

standard size *n* taglia *f* normale

standby ['stænd·baɪ] **I.** *n* **1.** (*of money, food*) riserva *f* **2.** AVIAT lista *f* d'attesa; **to be on ~** essere in lista d'attesa; **they put me on ~** mi hanno messo in lista d'attesa; **to be on 24-hour ~** essere nella lista d'attesa con partenza entro 24 ore **II.** *adj* di riserva

stand-in ['stænd·ɪn] *n* sostituto, -a *m, f;* CINE controfigura *f*

standing ['stæn·dɪŋ] **I.** *n* **1.** (*status*) posizione *f* **2.** (*duration*) durata *f;* **of long ~** di

vecchia data **II.** *adj* **1.** (*upright*) verticale **2.** (*permanent*) permanente **3.** (*water*) stagnante

standing order *n* prelievo *m* automatico

standing ovation *n* standing ovation *f inv,* lungo applauso *m* in piedi

standing room *n* posti *mpl* in piedi

standing start *n* **to do sth from a ~** fare qc partendo da zero

standoffish [ˌstænd·ˈɑ·fɪʃ] *adj pej, inf* scostante

standpipe ['stænd·paɪp] *n* idrante *m*

standpoint ['stænd·pɔɪnt] *n* punto *m* di vista

standstill ['stænd·stɪl] *n* fase *f* di stallo; **to be at a ~** essere in fase di stallo

standup ['stænd·ˌʌp] *adj* **1.** (*cabaret*) **~ comedy** monologo *m* comico; **~ comedian** *comico che si esibisce in un monologo* **2.** (*upright*) **~ buffet** buffet *m* in piedi *inv* **3.** FASHION **a ~ collar** un colletto rigido **4.** *sl* (*honest*) fidato, -a

stank [stæŋk] *pt of* **stink**

stanza ['stæn·zə] *n* LIT strofa *f*

staple[1] ['steɪ·pl] **I.** *n* **1.** (*product, article*) prodotto *m* principale **2.** (*basic food*) alimento *m* base **3.** (*important component*) elemento *m* essenziale **II.** *adj* **1.** (*principal*) principale **2.** (*standard*) tipico, -a

staple[2] ['steɪ·pl] **I.** *n* (*fastener*) punto *m* (di pinzatrice) **II.** *vt* pinzare

staple gun *n* pinzatrice *f* industriale

stapler ['steɪp·lə] *n* pinzatrice *f*

star [stɑːr] **I.** *n* **1.** (*heavenly body*) stella *f* **2.** (*asterisk*) asterisco *m* **3.** (*popular person*) stella *f;* **a movie ~** una star del cinema ▶ **to thank one's lucky ~s** ringraziare la propria buona stella; **to be written in the ~s** essere scritto; **to reach for the ~s** puntare in alto; **to see ~s** vedere le stelle **II.** *vt* <-rr-> **1.** THEAT, CINE essere interpretato, -a da **2.** (*mark with asterisk*) segnalare con un asterisco

star billing [ˌstɑːr·ˈbɪ·lɪŋ] *n* **to get ~** avere il primo posto in cartellone

starboard ['stɑːr·bəd] **I.** *n* NAUT dritta *f* **II.** *adj* a dritta

starch [stɑːrtʃ] **I.** *n* **1.** (*stiffening agent*) amido *m* **2.** CULIN amido *m* **II.** *vt* inamidare

starchy ['stɑːr·tʃi] <-ier, -iest> *adj* **1.** (*food*) ricco, -a di amido **2.** *pej, inf* (*person*) impettito, -a

stardom ['stɑːr·dəm] *n* celebrità *f*

stare [ster] **I.** *vi* fissare **II.** *vt* fissare; **the answer was staring us in the face** avevamo la risposta sotto gli occhi **III.** *n* sguardo *m* fisso
♦ **stare down** *vt* fissare fino a mettere in imbarazzo

starfish ['stɑːr·fɪʃ] <-(es)> *n* stella *f* di mare

stargazer ['stɑːr·ˌgeɪ·zə] *n* (*astronomer*) astronomo, -a *m, f;* (*astrologer*) astrologo, -a *m, f*

staring ['ste·rɪŋ] *adj* fisso, -a; **~ eyes** sguardo *m* fisso

stark [stɑːrk] **I.** *adj* **1.** (*desolate*) desolato, -a; **a**

~ **landscape** un paesaggio desolato **2.** (*austere*) austero, -a **3.** (*complete*) totale; **a ~ contrast** un netto contrasto **II.** *adv* ~ **naked** completamente nudo, -a; ~ **raving mad** matto, -a da legare

starless ['stɑːr·lɪs] *adj* senza stelle

starlet ['stɑːr·lɪt] *n* stellina *f*

starlight ['stɑːr·laɪt] *n* luce *f* delle stelle

starling ['stɑːr·lɪŋ] *n* storno *m*

starlit ['stɑːr·ˌlɪt] *adj* illuminato, -a dalle stelle

starry ['stɑː·ri] <-ier, -iest> *adj* stellato, -a

starry-eyed ['stɑː·ri·ˌaɪd] *adj* sognatore, -trice

Stars and Stripes *n* the ~ la bandiera a stelle e strisce

star sign *n* segno *m* zodiacale

Star-Spangled Banner *n* (*flag*) bandiera *f* a stelle e strisce; (*anthem*) inno *m* nazionale americano

> [i] La **U.S. flag** porta diversi nomi, tra i quali quello di **The Stars and Stripes**. Il numero delle stelle corrisponde ai 50 stati che fanno parte attualmente degli Stati Uniti e le 13 righe rappresentano i 13 stati fondatori. L'espressione patriottica *Old Glory* è stata coniata dal capitano di vascello William Driver. Anche il titolo dell'inno nazionale americano, lo *Star-spangled Banner*, fa riferimento alla bandiera nazionale.

star-studded *adj* **1.** (*sky*) stellato, -a **2.** (*film*) pieno, -a di star; **a ~ cast** un cast pieno di star

start [stɑːrt] **I.** *vi* **1.** (*begin*) iniziare; **to ~ to do sth** iniziare a fare qc **2.** (*begin journey*) partire; **the bus ~s from the main square** l'autobus parte dalla piazza principale **3.** (*begin to operate: vehicle, motor*) mettersi in moto **4.** SPORTS (*play at beginning*) essere nella formazione iniziale **5.** (*begin at level*) partire; **ticket prices ~ as low as $10** il prezzo dei biglietti parte addirittura da 10 dollari **6.** (*make sudden movement*) sobbalzare; **to ~ at sth** sobbalzare per qc **II.** *vt* **1.** (*begin*) iniziare, cominciare; **we ~ work at 6:30 every morning** iniziamo a lavorare alle 6:30 ogni mattina **2.** (*set in operation*) mettere in moto **3.** COM mettere su **4.** SPORTS (*let play at beginning*) mettere nella formazione iniziale ▶**to ~ something** *inf* creare un casino **III.** *n* **1.** (*beginning*) principio *m;* **to make an early/a late ~** cominciare presto/tardi; **to make a fresh ~** ricominciare da capo; **to have a good ~ in life** avere un'infanzia felice **2.** SPORTS (*beginning place*) linea *f* di partenza; (*beginning time*) via *m;* **false ~** falsa partenza *f* **3.** (*sudden movement*) sobbalzo *m;* **to give a ~** sobbalzare; **to give sb a ~** far sobbalzare qu **4.** SPORTS (*action of playing at beginning*) presenza nella formazione iniziale; **he will be making his third ~ of the year** è la terza volta quest'anno che lo fanno giocare dall'inizio della partita

◆**start back** *vi* **1.** (*jump back suddenly*) retrocedere **2.** (*begin return journey*) cominciare il viaggio di ritorno

◆**start in on** *vt* cominciare a fare la predica a

◆**start off I.** *vi* **1.** (*begin*) iniziare **2.** (*begin journey*) partire **II.** *vt* empezar; **to start sb off** (**on sth**) aiutare qu (a iniziare qc)

◆**start out** *vi* **1.** (*begin*) cominciare; **to ~ to do sth** mettersi a fare qc **2.** (*begin journey*) partire

◆**start up I.** *vt* **1.** (*organization, business*) mettere su **2.** (*vehicle, motor*) mettere in moto **II.** *vi* **1.** (*begin running: vehicle, motor*) mettersi in moto **2.** (*open*) mettere su un'attività **3.** (*jump up*) balzare in piedi

START [stɑːrt] *abbr of* **Strategic Arms Reduction Talks** START

starter *n* **1.** AUTO motorino *m* di avviamento **2.** *inf* CULIN antipasto *m* **3.** SPORTS (*player at beginning*) giocatore, -trice *m*, *f* della formazione iniziale ▶**for ~s** *inf* per cominciare

starting line *n* linea *f* di partenza

starting point *n* punto *m* di partenza

startle ['stɑːr·tl̩] *vt* cogliere di sorpresa

startling *adj* (*surprising*) sorprendente; (*alarming*) allarmante

startup *n*, **start-up** ['stɑːrt·ʌp] *n* avviamento *m*

start-up capital *n* capitale *m* iniziale

start-up costs *n* costi *mpl* di avviamento

starvation [stɑːr·'veɪ·ʃən] *n* fame *f;* **to die of ~** morire di fame

starvation diet *n* dieta *m* drastica

starve [stɑːrv] **I.** *vi* **1.** soffrire di fame; (*die of hunger*) morire di fame; **to ~ to death** morire di fame **2.** *inf* (*be very hungry*) essere affamato, -a **II.** *vt* **1.** (*deprive: of food*) far soffrire di fame; **to ~ sb to death** far morire di fame **2.** (*deprive: of love, support*) privare

starving *adj* affamato, -a

stash [stæʃ] **I.** *vt* nascondere **II.** *n* <-es> *inf* **1.** (*hiding place*) nascondiglio *m* **2.** (*cache*) scorta *f*

state [steɪt] **I.** *n* **1.** (*condition*) stato *m;* ~ **of siege/war** stato di assedio/guerra; **solid/liquid ~** stato solido/liquido; ~ **of mind** stato d'animo **2.** (*nation*) stato *m* **3.** *pl, inf* (*USA*) **the States** gli Stati Uniti **4.** (*pomp*) **to lie in ~** essere nella camera ardente **II.** *adj* (*pertaining to a nation*) statale; ~ **secret** segreto *m* di Stato **III.** *vt* **1.** (*express*) dichiarare **2.** LAW (*specify*) stabilire

state-controlled *adj* controllato, -a dallo Stato; (*business*) statale

stated *adj* (*specified*) stabilito, -a

State Department *n* Dipartimento *m* di Stato, ≈ ministero *m* degli Affari Esteri

stateless ['steɪt·ləs] *adj* apolide

stately ['steɪt·li] *adj* solenne; ~ **home** dimora *f* sontuosa

statement ['steɪt·mənt] *n* **1.** (*declaration*) dichiarazione *f;* **to make a ~** LAW fare una dichiarazione **2.** (*from bank*) estratto *m* conto

state of the art [ˌsteɪt·əv·ðɪ·ˈɑːrt] *adj* d'avanguardia; ~ **technology** tecnologia d'avanguardia

state-owned *adj* statale

state prison *n* prigione *f* di Stato

stateroom [ˈsteɪt·ruːm] *n* **1.** (*in palace, hotel*) sala *f* di rappresentanza **2.** NAUT cabina *f* di lusso

stateside [ˈsteɪt·saɪd] *adv inf* negli Stati Uniti

statesman [ˈsteɪts·mən] <-men> *n* statista *m*

statesmanship *n* arte *m* di governare

stateswoman [ˈsteɪts·ˌwʊ·mən] <-men> *n* statista *f*

state visit *n* visita *f* ufficiale

static [ˈstæ·t̬ɪk] **I.** *adj* statico, -a; **to remain ~** rimanere invariato **II.** *n* PHYS elettricità *f* statica

static electricity *n* elettricità *f* statica

station [ˈsteɪ·ʃən] **I.** *n* **1.** RAIL stazione *f* **2.** (*place*) stazione *f;* **police ~** commissariato *m;* **gas ~** stazione *f* di servizio; **research ~** centro *m* di ricerca **3.** RADIO stazione *f;* TV canale *m* **4.** (*position*) postazione *m;* **action ~s!** MIL ai vostri posti! **II.** *vt* **1.** (*place*) collocare **2.** MIL appostare; **he's ~ed in Washington** é di stanza a Washington

stationary [ˈsteɪ·ʃə·ne·ri] *adj* (*not moving*) fermo, -a

stationery [ˈsteɪ·ʃə·ne·ri] *n* articoli *mpl* di cancelleria

station house *n* commissariato *m*

stationmaster *n* capostazione *mf*

station wagon *n* station wagon *f inv,* familiare *f*

statistical [stə·ˈtɪs·t̬ɪ·kl] *adj* statistico, -a

statistician [ˌstæ·tɪ·ˈstɪ·ʃən] *n* esperto, -a *m, f* di statistica

statistics [stə·ˈtɪs·tɪks] *n* **1.** (*science*) statistica *f* **2.** *pl* (*data*) statistiche *fpl*

statuary [ˈstæ·tʃu·e·ri] *n form* (*statues*) statue *fpl*

statue [ˈstæ·tʃuː] *n* statua *f*

Statue of Liberty *n* **the ~** la Statua della Libertà

statuesque [ˌstæ·tʃu·ˈesk] *adj form* statuario, -a

statuette [ˌstæ·tʃu·ˈet] *n* statuetta *f*

stature [ˈstæ·tʃɚ] *n* **1.** (*height*) statura *f* **2.** (*reputation*) levatura *f*

status [ˈsteɪ·t̬əs] *n* **1.** (*official position*) statuto *m* **2.** (*prestige*) prestigio *m*

status bar *n,* **status line** *n* COMPUT barra *f* di stato

status quo *n* status quo *m*

status report *n* COMPUT rapporto *m* sulla situazione

status symbol *n* status symbol *m inv*

statute [ˈstæ·tʃuːt] *n* LAW legge *f;* **by ~** conformemente alla legge

statute law *n* diritto *m* scritto

statute of limitations *n* legge *f* sulla prescrizione

statutory [ˈstæ·tʃə·tɔː·ri] *adj* legale; **~ rape** abuso *m* sessuale di minore

staunch[1] [stɔːntʃ] *adj* incondizionato; **a ~ supporter** un fervido sostenitore

staunch[2] [stɔːntʃ] *vt s.* **stanch**

stave [steɪv] *n* **1.** MUS pentagramma *m* **2.** (*piece of wood*) doga *f*

◆**stave off** <staved off, staved off> *vt* (*postpone*) rimandare; (*prevent*) evitare

staves *n* **1.** *pl of* **staff** I.6. **2.** *pl of* **stave**

stay [steɪ] **I.** *vi* **1.** (*remain present*) rimanere; **to ~ in bed** rimanere a letto **2.** (*reside temporarily*) alloggiare **3.** (*remain*) rimanere; **to ~ friends** rimanere amici **II.** *vt* **1.** (*endure*) resistere; **to ~ the course** [*o* **distance**] resistere fino alla fine **2.** (*assuage: hunger, thirst*) placare **3.** LAW (*suspend*) **to ~ an execution** sospendere un'esecuzione **III.** *n* soggiorno *m*

◆**stay away** *vi* stare lontano; **to ~ from sb/ sth** tenersi alla larga da qu/qc

◆**stay behind** *vi* fermarsi

◆**stay in** *vi* rimanere in casa

◆**stay out** *vi* stare fuori; **to ~ all night** stare fuori tutta la notte

◆**stay up** *vi* rimanere alzato, -a; **to ~ late** rimanere alzato fino a tardi

stay-at-home [ˈsteɪ·ət·hoʊm] **I.** *n* pantofolaio, -a *m, f* **II.** *adj* pantofolaio, -a

staying power *n* resistenza *f*

STD [ˌes·tiː·ˈdiː] *n* MED *abbr of* **sexually transmitted disease** MST *f*

Ste. *n abbr of* **saint** S.ta

stead [sted] *n* posto *m;* **in his/her ~** al suo posto ►**to stand sb in good ~ (for sth)** tornare utile a qu (per qc)

steadfast [ˈsted·fæst] *adj* fedele; **a ~ denial** un rifiuto categorico

steady [ˈste·di] **I.** <-ier, -iest> *adj* **1.** (*stable*) stabile; (*job, employment*) fisso, -a; (*temperature*) costante **2.** (*regular*) costante **3.** (*not wavering: hand*) saldo, -a **4.** (*calm*) calmo, -a **5.** (*regular: boyfriend*) fisso, -a **II.** *vt* **1.** (*stabilize*) stabilizzare **2.** (*make calm*) calmare **III.** *adv* **to be going ~** avere una relazione duratura **IV.** *interj* piano!

steak [steɪk] *n* **1.** (*for frying, grilling*) bistecca *f;*

(*ground beef*) carne *f* tritata, *per hamburger* **2.** (*of fish*) trancio *m*

steal [stiːl] I. <stole, stolen> *vt* rubare; **to ~ sb's heart** rubare il cuore a qu; **to ~ a glance (at sb/sth)** dare un'occhiata furtiva (a qu/qc) ▶**to ~ the show** monopolizzare l'attenzione; **to ~ someone's thunder** rovinare a qu l'effetto sorpresa II. <stole, stolen> *vi* **1.** (*take things illegally*) rubare **2.** (*move surreptitiously*) **to ~ in** entrare di soppiatto; **to ~ away** sgattaiolare via III. *n inf* affarone *m;* **to be a ~** essere un affarone

stealth [stelθ] *n* furtività *f;* **by ~** di nascosto

stealthy ['stel·θi] *adj* furtivo, -a

steam [stiːm] I. *n* (*water vapor*) vapore *m;* **full ~ ahead!** a tutto vapore!; **to run out of ~** *fig* perdere vigore ▶**to let off@ ~** scaricarsi II. *adj* a vapore III. *vi* (*produce steam*) emettere vapore IV. *vt* cuocere al vapore

◆**steam up** *vi* **1.** (*become steamy*) appannarsi **2.** *inf* **to get steamed up** (**about sth**) accalorarsi (per qc)

steam bath *n* bagno *m* turco

steamboat *n* battello *m* a vapore

steam engine *n* motore *m* a vapore

steamer ['stiː·mɚ] *n* **1.** (*boat*) battello *m* a vapore **2.** CULIN pentola *f* a pressione

steam iron *n* ferro *m* (da stiro) a vapore

steamroll *vt, vi s.* **steamroller**

steamroller¹ *n* rullo *m* compressore

steamroller² I. *vt* spianare; *fig* portare avanti a forza II. *vi* andare avanti a forza

steamship *n* nave *f* a vapore II. *adj* **~ line** compagnia *f* navale

steamy ['stiː·mi] <-ier, -iest> *adj* **1.** (*full of steam*) pieno, -a di vapore **2.** (*very humid*) umido, -a **3.** *inf* (*sexy*) spinto, -a

steed [stiːd] *n liter* destriero *m*

steel [stiːl] I. *n* (*metal*) acciaio *m;* **nerves of ~** nervi *mpl* d'acciaio II. *adj* d'acciaio III. *vt* **to ~ oneself for sth** armarsi di coraggio per qc

steel band *n complesso di percussionisti tipico dei Caraibi*

steel industry *n* industria *f* siderurgica

steel mill *n* stabilimento *f* per la laminazione dell'acciaio

steel wool *n* lana *f* d'acciaio

steelworker ['stiːl·ˌwɜːr·kɚ] *n* operaio, -a *m, f* siderurgico, -a

steelworks ['stiːl·wɜːrks] *n inv* acciaieria *f*

steely ['stiː·li] <-ier, -iest> *adj* (*determination*) ferreo, -a; (*gaze*) d'acciaio

steep¹ [stiːp] *adj* **1.** (*sharply sloping*) ripido, -a **2.** (*dramatic: increase, fall*) notevole; **~!** è un'esagerazione! **3.** (*expensive*) esorbitante

steep² [stiːp] I. *vt* **1.** (*soak*) mettere a bagno; **to ~ tea** lasciare il tè in infusione **2.** *fig* **to be ~ed in tradition/history** essere immerso nella tradizione/storia II. *vi* **to leave sth to ~** lasciare qc in ammollo

steepen ['stiː·pən] *vi* **1.** (*become steeper*) diventare ripido **2.** *inf* (*become more expensive*) salire vertiginosamente

steeple ['stiː·pl] *n* ARCHIT torre *f;* **church ~** campanile di una chiesa

steeplechase ['stiː·pl·tʃeɪs] *n* corsa *f* a ostacoli

steeplejack ['stiː·pl·dʒæk] *n persona che effettua riparazioni su torri, campanili, camini, ecc.*

steer¹ [stɪr] I. *vt* **1.** (*direct*) dirigere; (*car*) guidare **2.** (*guide*) portare II. *vi* (*person*) guidare; (*car*) guidarsi; **it steers well** non si guida bene; **to ~ clear of sth/sb** stare alla larga da qc/qu; **to ~ for sth** NAUT fare rotta su qc

steer² [stɪr] *n* (*young bull*) manzo *m;* (*castrated bull*) bue *m*

steering committee *n inv* comitato *m* direttivo

steering wheel *n* (*of car*) volante *m;* (*of ship*) timone *m*

stellar ['ste·lɚ] *adj* stellare; **a ~ performance** un'esecuzione brillante

stem [stem] I. *n* **1.** (*of plant*) stelo *m;* (*of leaf*) picciolo *m* **2.** (*part of glass*) gambo *m* **3.** LING radice *f* II. <-mm-> *vt* (*stop*) contenere III. <-mm-> *vi* **to ~ from** trarre origine da

stench [stentʃ] *n* puzzo *m*

stencil ['sten·sl] I. *n* **1.** (*cut-out pattern*) stencil *m inv* **2.** (*picture drawn*) stencil *m inv* II. *vt* decorare con stencil

stenographer [stə·'nɑː·grə·fɚ] *n* stenografo, -a *m, f*

stenography [stə·'nɑː·grə·fi] *n* stenografia *f*

step [step] I. *n* **1.** (*foot movement*) passo *m;* (*footprint*) impronta *f;* **to take a ~** fare un passo; **~ by ~** passo a passo; **to take a ~ towards sth** *fig* compiere un passo verso qc; **to be in/out of ~** andare/non andare al passo; *fig* essere/non essere in sintonia; **to watch one's ~** fare attenzione a dove si mettono i piedi **2.** (*of stair, ladder*) gradino *m* **3.** (*measure*) provvedimento *m;* **to take ~s (to do sth)** prendere provvedimenti (per fare qc) **4.** MUS **whole ~** tono *m;* **half ~** semitono *m* II. <-pp-> *vi* **1.** (*tread*) **~ in** [*o* on] sth calpestare qc **2.** (*walk*) camminare

◆**step aside** *vi* scansarsi

◆**step back** *vi* **1.** (*move back*) indietreggiare **2.** (*gain new perspective*) prendere le distanze

◆**step down** I. *vi* (*resign*) dimettersi; **to ~ from sth** rinunciare a qc II. *vt* (*reduce*) ridurre

◆**step in** *vi* intervenire

◆**step up** I. *vt* aumentare II. *vi* accollarsi il compito

stepbrother *n* fratellastro *m*

stepchild *n* figliastro, -a *m, f*

stepdaughter *n* figliastra *f*

stepfather *n* padrigno *m*

stepladder ['step·ˌlæ·dɚ] *n* scala *f* (a libretto)

stepmother ['step·ˌmʌ·ðɚ] *n* matrigna *f*

steppe [step] *n* steppa *f*

stepping stone ['ste·pɪŋ·stoʊn] *n* **1.** (*stone*) passatoio *m* **2.** *fig* trampolino *m*

stepsister ['step·ˌsɪs·tɚ] *n* sorellastra *f*

stepson ['step·sʌn] *n* figliastro *m*

stereo ['ste·ri·oʊ] I. *n* **1.** (*hi-fi system*) stereo

inv **2. in** ~ in stereo **II.** *adj* stereo *inv*
stereophonic [ˌste·ri·ə·ˈfɑː·nɪk] *adj* MUS stereofonico, -a
stereoscopic [ˌste·ri·ə·ˈskɑː·pɪk] *adj* stereo-
scopico, -a
stereotype [ˈste·ri·ə·taɪp] **I.** *n pej* stereotipo *m*
II. *vt pej* rendere stereotipato, -a
sterile [ˈste·rəl] *adj* sterile
sterility [stə·ˈrɪ·lə·ti] *n* sterilità *f*
sterilization [ˌste·rə·lɪ·ˈzeɪ·ʃən] *n* sterilizzazione *f*
sterilize [ˈste·rə·laɪz] *vt* sterilizzare
sterling [ˈstɜːr·lɪŋ] **I.** *n* **1.** (*metal*) argento [*o*
925] sterling *m* **2.** FIN lira *f* sterlina **II.** *adj* **1.** FIN
pound ~ lira sterlina **2.** (*of high standard*)
eccellente
stern[1] [stɜːrn] *adj* **1.** (*severe*) severo, -a; (*warning*) duro, -a **2.** (*strict*) severo, -a
stern[2] [stɜːrn] *n* NAUT poppa *f*
sternness [ˈstɜːrn·nɪs] *n* severità *f*
sternum [ˈstɜːr·nəm] <-s *o* -na> *n* sterno *m*
steroid [ˈste·rɔɪd] *n* steroide *m*
stethoscope [ˈste·θəs·koʊp] *n* MED stetoscopio *m*
stevedore [ˈstiː·və·dɔːr] *n* scaricatore *m* di
porto
stew [stuː] **I.** *n* stufato *m* ▶ **to be in a** ~ *inf*
essere in ansia **II.** *vt* (*meat*) stufare; (*fruit*) cuocere **III.** *vi* cuocere
steward [ˈstuː·ərd] *n* **1.** AVIAT steward *m inv*
2. (*at concert, demonstration*) addetto, -a *m, f*
al servizio d'ordine **3.** (*estate administrator*)
amministratore, -trice *m, f* **4.** (*representative*)
shop ~ rappresentante *mf* sindacale
stewardess [ˈstuː·ər·dɪs] <-es> *n* hostess *f inv*
STI *n* MED *abbr of* **sexually transmitted infection** MST *m*
stick[1] [stɪk] *n* **1.** (*of wood*) bastone *m;* (*of celery, rhubarb*) gambo *m;* (*of dynamite*) candelotto *m;* (*of deodorant, glue*) stick *m inv;* **a** ~
of chalk un gessetto **2.** *a.* SPORTS (*for hockey*)
mazza *f;* **walking** ~ bastone *m* (da passeggio)
3. MUS bacchetta *f* **4.** *inf* (*remote area*) **in the
~s in un posto sperduto ▶ **to get the wrong
end of the** ~ prendere fischi per fiaschi; **~s
and stones may break my bones, but
words can never hurt me** *prov* le parole non
hanno mai fatto male a nessuno
stick[2] [stɪk] <stuck, stuck> **I.** *vi* **1.** (*adhere*)
attaccarsi **2.** (*be unmovable: person, mechan-
ism*) bloccarsi; (*door, window*) incastrarsi
3. (*endure*) **to** ~ **in sb's mind** rimanere
impresso a qu **II.** *vt* **1.** (*affix*) attaccare **2.** *inf*
(*put*) mettere; **to** ~ **one's head out the
window** sporgere la testa dalla finestra
◆ **stick around** *vi inf* rimanere (nei paraggi)
◆ **stick at** *vt* perseverare in
◆ **stick by** *vt* **1.** (*continue to support: friend*)
restare al fianco di **2.** (*not change: opinion*)
rimanere fedele a **3.** (*comply with: rules*) attenersi a
◆ **stick in** *vt* **1.** (*knife, needle*) conficcare
2. (*put*) mettere

◆ **stick on** *vt* **1.** (*affix: stamp, label*) attaccare
2. *inf* **to be stuck on sb** essere pazzo di qu
◆ **stick out I.** *vt* allungare; **to stick one's
tongue out at sb** fare la linguaccia a qu ▶ **to
stick one's neck out** allungare il collo **II.** *vi*
1. (*protrude: nail, ears*) sporgere **2.** (*be
obvious*) essere evidente; **to** ~ **a mile** vedersi
lontano un miglio; **to** ~ **like a sore thumb**
dare nell'occhio **3.** (*endure*) **to stick it out**
tener duro
◆ **stick to** *vt* **1.** (*adhere to: rules*) attenersi a;
(*plan, idea*) portare avanti; (*promise*) mantenere; (*principles, beliefs*) rimanere fedele a
2. (*restrict oneself to*) limitarsi a
◆ **stick together I.** *vi* **1.** (*remain loyal*) rimanere solidali **2.** (*not separate*) rimanere insieme
3. (*adhere*) attaccarsi **II.** *vt* attaccare
◆ **stick up I.** *vt inf* **1.** (*rob*) assalire **2.** (*raise*)
stick 'em up! mani in alto! **II.** *vi* spuntare;
(*hair*) stare dritto, -a
◆ **stick up for** *vt* prendere le difese di
◆ **stick with** *vt* **1.** (*not give up on*) non lasciare; (*thought, idea*) portare avanti; (*memory*) rimanere fedele a **2.** (*persevere in*) andare
avanti con **3.** (*stay near*) stare vicino a
stickball *n* baseball *m* giocato per strada
sticker [ˈstɪ·kər] *n* (auto)adesivo *m*
sticker price *n* prezzo *m* di listino
sticker shock *n inf* shock *m* causato dal
prezzo *inv*
stick figure *n* omino *m* stilizzato
stick-in-the-mud *n inf* tipo, -a *m, f* serioso, -a
stickler [ˈstɪk·lər] *n* **to be a** ~ **for sth** essere fissato con qc
stick-on [ˈstɪk·ɑːn] *adj* adesivo, -a
stickpin *n*, **stick pin** [ˈstɪk·ˌpɪn] *n* spilla *f* da
cravatta
stick shift *n* leva *f* del cambio
stickup [ˈstɪk·ʌp] *n sl* assalto *m*
sticky [ˈstɪ·ki] <-ier, -iest> *adj* **1.** (*label*)
adesivo, -a; (*surface, hands*) appiccicoso, -a
2. (*weather*) afoso, -a
stiff [stɪf] **I.** *n inf* (*corpse*) cadavere *m* **II.** *adj*
1. (*rigid: paper*) rigido, -a; (*brush*) duro, -a;
(*shirt*) inamidato, -a; (*paste, dough*) consistente; **to be (as)** ~ **as a board** essere rigido
come una statua **2.** (*not supple: joints*) duro, -a
3. (*difficult to move: muscles*) indolenzito, -a;
to have a ~ **neck** avere il torcicollo **4.** (*very
formal: manner*) impettito, -a **5.** (*strong: competition*) duro, -a; (*opposition, drink, breeze*)
forte; (*resistance*) tenace; (*punishment, criticism*) severo, -a **6.** (*strenuous: climb, hike*)
duro, -a **7.** (*very expensive: price*) esorbitante
III. *adv* **to be bored** ~ annoiarsi a morte; **to
be scared** ~ essere paralizzato dalla paura
stiffen [ˈstɪ·fn] **I.** *vi* **1.** (*become tense: person*) diventare teso, -a; (*muscles*) irrigidirsi
2. (*become dense*) ispessirsi **3.** (*become
stronger: competition*) farsi pi duro, -a **II.** *vt*
1. (*make more difficult, severe: penalties*)
inasprire; (*competition*) rendere pi duro, -a
2. (*make rigid: collar, cuff*) inamidare

3. (*strengthen: morals*) rafforzare
stiff-necked ['stɪf·nekt] *adj* 1. (*stubborn*) ostinato, -a 2. (*proud*) altezzoso, -a
stifle ['staɪ·fl] I. *vt* 1. (*suffocate*) soffocare 2. (*suppress*) reprimere II. *vi* 1. (*suffocate*) soffocare 2. (*suffer lack of air*) asfissiare
stifling ['staɪf·lɪŋ] *adj* soffocante
stigma ['stɪg·mə] *n* stigma *m*
stigmatize ['stɪg·mə·taɪz] *vt* stigmatizzare
stiletto [stɪ·'le·toʊ] <-s> *n* 1. (*dagger*) stiletto *m* 2. *pl* (*shoes*) tacchi *mpl* a spillo
stiletto heel *n* tacco *m* a spillo
still¹ [stɪl] I. *adj* 1. (*calm*) tranquillo, -a 2. (*peaceful*) fermo, -a; (*waters*) calmo, -a; **to keep ~** stare fermo 3. PHOT **~ photography** fotografia *f* di scena II. *n* 1. *lit* (*peace*) quiete *f;* **the ~ of the night** la quiete notturna 2. CINE, PHOT fotogramma *m* III. *vt* 1. (*calm*) calmare 2. *liter* (*quieten*) quietare
still² [stɪl] *adv* 1. ancora; **to be ~ alive** essere ancora vivo; **to want ~ more** volere ancora di pi; **better ~** ancora meglio 2. (*nevertheless*) tuttavia
still³ [stɪl] *n* (*distillery*) distilleria *f*
stillbirth ['stɪl·bɜ:rθ] *n* nascita *f* di un bambino morto
stillborn ['stɪl·bɔ:rn] *adj* 1. (*born dead*) nato, -a morto, -a 2. (*unsuccessful*) fallito, -a sul nascere
still life *n* ART natura *f* morta
stillness *n* 1. (*tranquility*) tranquillità *f* 2. (*lack of movement*) immobilità *f* 3. (*calm*) calma *f*
stilt [stɪlt] *n pl* trampolo *m*
stilted ['stɪl·tɪd] *adj* (*manner, style*) affettato, -a
stimulant ['stɪm·jə·lənt] *n* 1. (*boost*) stimolo *m* 2. MED stimolante *m*
stimulate ['stɪm·jə·leɪt] *vt* 1. stimolare; (*economy*) incentivare 2. MED stimolare
stimulating *adj* stimolante
stimulation [,stɪm·jə·'leɪ·ʃən] *n* 1. (*boost*) stimolazione *f* 2. (*thought, reaction*) stimolo *m*
stimulus ['stɪm·jə·ləs] <-li> *n* stimolo *m*
sting [stɪŋ] I. *vt* 1. (*inject with poison*) pungere 2. (*cause pain: eyes*) far bruciare; (*criticism*) pungere sul vivo 3. (*goad*) incitare II. <stung, stung> *vi* 1. (*injure with poison: insect*) pungere 2. (*be painful: cut, eyes*) bruciare; (*criticism*) pungere sul vivo III. *n* 1. (*injury*) puntura *f* 2. (*pain*) bruciore *m;* **~ of remorse** rimorso *m* di coscienza 3. BOT pelo *m* urticante 4. (*of animal*) pungiglione *m* 5. *sl* **police operation** operazione *f* di infiltrazione; **to conduct a ~** organizzare un'operazione di infiltrazione
stinginess ['stɪn·dʒɪ·nɪs] *n* tirchieria *f*
stingray ['stɪŋ·reɪ] *n* ZOOL pastinaca *f*
stingy ['stɪn·dʒi] <-ier, -iest> *adj inf* (*person*) tirchio, -a; (*amount*) misero, -a
stink [stɪŋk] I. *n* 1. (*smell*) puzzo *m* 2. *fig* scandalo *m;* **to create a ~** creare uno scandalo II. <stank *o* stunk, stunk> *vi* 1. (*smell*) puzzare; **to ~ of money** *inf* essere pieno di soldi 2. *inf* (*be very bad*) fare schifo 3. *inf* (*be suspi-*

cious: business, situation) puzzare
stink bomb *n* bomba *f* puzzolente
stinker ['stɪŋ·kɚ] *n inf* 1. (*bad person*) fetente *mf* 2. (*unpleasant thing*) rottura *f*
stint [stɪnt] *n* periodo *m*
stipulate ['stɪp·jə·leɪt] *vt* stipulare
stipulation [,stɪp·jə·'leɪ·ʃən] *n* condizione *f;* **with the ~ that** a condizione che +*subj*
stir [stɜ:r] I. <-ring, -red> *vt* 1. (*mescolare: fire*) attizzare 2. (*move*) agitare 3. (*stimulate: imagination*) stimolare; **to ~ sb into action** spingere qu all'azione; **to ~ trouble** creare problemi II. *vi* 1. (*be able to be agitated*) mescolarsi; **these ingredients really ~ well** questi ingredienti si mescolano molto bene 2. (*move*) muoversi, agitarsi 3. (*rouse*) risvegliarsi III. *n* 1. (*agitation*) **to give sth a ~** dare una mescolata a qc 2. (*excitement*) agitazione *f;* **to cause a ~** creare scompiglio
stir-fry ['stɜ:r·fraɪ] <-ied, -ies> *vt* saltare
stirring I. *adj* commovente II. *n* (*of envy*) principio *m;* (*of interest*) primi segnali *mpl*
stirrup ['stɜ:r·əp] *n* staffa *f*
stitch [stɪtʃ] I. <-es> *n* 1. (*in knitting*) maglia *f;* (*in sewing*) punto *m;* **cross ~** punto (a) croce 2. MED punto *m* (di sutura) ▶**to leave sb in ~es** *inf* far sbellicare qu dalle risa; **a ~ in time saves nine** *prov* è meglio prevenire che curare *prov* II. *vi* cucire III. *vt* cucire
stock [stɑ:k] I. *n* 1. (*reserves*) scorta *f* 2. COM, ECON scorta *f* (di magazzino); **to have sth in ~** avere qc a magazzino; **to be out of ~** essere esaurito, -a; **to take ~** fare l'inventario; *fig* fare un bilancio 3. (*share*) FIN azione *f* 4. AGR, ZOOL bestiame *m* 5. (*line of descent*) origine *f;* ZOOL, BIO razza *f* 6. (*popularity*) popolarità *f;* **her ~ had fallen/risen** ha perso/guadagnato popolarità 7. (*belief*) **to put (no) ~ in sth** (non) dare peso a qc 8. FOOD (*broth*) brodo *m* II. *adj* (*model*) standard *inv;* (*response*) scontato, -a III. *vt* 1. (*keep in supply: goods*) avere disponibile 2. (*supply goods to: shop*) rifornire 3. (*fill: shelves*) rifornire
stockade [stɑ:'keɪd] *n* 1. (*wooden fence*) palizzata *f* 2. (*prison*) prigione *f* militare
stockbroker ['stɑ:k·,broʊ·kɚ] *n* operatore, -trice *m*, *f* di borsa
stockbroking *n* compravendita *f* di titoli azionari in borsa
stock car *n* 1. AUTO stock-car *f inv* 2. RAIL vagone *m* bestiame
stock exchange *n* borsa *f*
stockholder ['stɑ:k·,hoʊl·dɚ] *n* azionista *mf*
stocking ['stɑ:·kɪŋ] *n* calza *f*
stock market *n* mercato *m* azionario
stockpile ['stɑ:k·paɪl] I. *n* riserve *fpl;* (*of weapons, ammunition*) arsenale *m* II. *vt* accumulare
stockroom ['stɑ:k·ru:m] *n* magazzino *m*
stocktaking ['stɑ:k·teɪ·kɪŋ] *n* inventario *m*
stocky ['stɑ:·ki] <-ier, -iest> *adj* tarchiato, -a
stockyard ['stɒk·jɑ:d] *n* recinto *m* (del bestiame)

stodgy ['stɑ:·dʒi] <-ier, -iest> adj 1. (food) pesante 2. (person, book) noioso, -a
stoic ['stoʊ·ɪk] n stoico, -a m, f
stoical ['stoʊ·ɪ·k(l)] adj stoico, -a
stoicism ['stoʊ·ɪ·sɪ·zəm] n stoicismo m
stoke [stoʊk] vt (fire) attizzare; (furnace) alimentare; fig attizzare
stoker ['stoʊ·kɚ] n RAIL, NAUT fuochista mf
stole¹ [stoʊl] pt of steal
stole² [stoʊl] n stola f
stolid ['stɑ:·lɪd] adj impassibile
stomach ['stʌ·mək] I. n 1. (internal organ) stomaco m; to have an upset ~ avere lo stomaco sottosopra; to have a strong ~ non essere delicato di stomaco 2. (belly) pancia f II. vt inf (drink, food) digerire; to be hard to ~ (person, insult) essere difficile da digerire
stomachache n mal m di pancia
stomp [stɑmp] vi camminare con passo pesante
stomping ground n posto m preferito
stone [stoʊn] I. n 1. GEO pietra f; to be a ~'s throw (away) essere a un tiro di schioppo 2. MED calcolo m 3. (jewel) pietra f (preziosa) 4. (of fruit) nocciolo m ▶ a rolling ~ gathers no moss prov sasso che rotola non fa muschio prov; to cast the first ~ scagliare la prima pietra; to leave no ~ unturned non lasciare niente di intentato; to be carved [o set] in ~ essere indiscutibile II. adv 1. (like a stone) ~ hard duro, -a come la pietra 2. inf (completely) ~ crazy matto da legare III. vt 1. (throw stones at) tirare sassi contro 2. (fruit, olives) snocciolare
Stone Age n Età f della pietra
stone-broke adj inf al verde
stone-cold I. adj gelato, -a II. adv inf to knock sb out ~ far perdere i sensi a qu (colpendolo); to be ~ sober essere perfettamente sobrio
stoned adj inf fatto, -a
stone-deaf [ˌstoʊn·'def] adj sordo, -a come una campana
stonemason ['stoʊn·ˌmeɪ·sən] n scalpellino, -a m, f
stonewall ['stoʊn·'wɔ:l] fig I. vi essere evasivo, -a II. vt eludere le domande di
stonewashed adj scolorire; ~ jeans jeans mpl scoloriti
stony ['stoʊ·ni] <-ier, -iest> adj 1. (beach, ground) pietroso, -a 2. (expression) glaciale; (attitude) duro, -a
stood [stʊd] pt, pp of stand
stooge [stu:dʒ] n 1. THEAT spalla f 2. fig (puppet) tirapiedi m 3. inf (informer) spia f
stool [stu:l] n 1. (seat) sgabello m 2. pl MED feci fpl
stool pigeon n inf informatore, -trice m, f
stoop¹ [stu:p] vi chinarsi; to ~ to sth pej abbassarsi a qc; to ~ low chinarsi
stoop² [stu:p] n veranda f
stop [stɑp] I. n 1. (break in activity) pausa f; to come to a ~ fermarsi; to put a ~ to sth metter fine a qc 2. (halting place) tappa f; (bus

stop) fermata f 3. MUS registro m ▶ to pull out (all) the ~s far tutti gli sforzi possibili e immaginabili II. <- ping, -ped> vt 1. (cause to cease) fermare 2. (refuse payment: payment) sospendere; to ~ payment on a check bloccare un assegno 3. (switch off) spegnere 4. (block) tappare III. <- ping, -ped> vi 1. (cease moving) fermarsi 2. (cease an activity) to ~ doing sth smettere di fare qc 3. (pause) to ~ and think about sth fare una pausa per riflettere su qc
◆ **stop by** vi passare
◆ **stop in** vi starsene a casa
◆ **stop off** vi fare un salto
◆ **stop over** vi fermarsi
◆ **stop up** vt (block) tappare
stopcock ['stɑ:p·kɑ:k] n rubinetto m (di arresto)
stopgap ['stɑ:p·gæp] I. n tappabuchi mf II. adj di emergenza
stoplight ['stɑ:p·laɪt] n semaforo m
stopover ['stɑ:p·oʊ·vɚ] n (on journey) tappa f; AVIAT scalo m
stoppage ['stɑ:·pɪdʒ] n 1. (cessation of work) interruzione f 2. FIN, ECON trattenuta f 3. MED occlusione f
stopper ['stɑ:·pɚ] I. n 1. (plug) tappo m 2. (in baseball) stopper m inv II. vt tappare
stop sign n AUTO, LAW stop m inv
stopwatch n cronometro m
storage ['stɔ:·rɪdʒ] n 1. (of goods, possessions) immagazzinamento m; to put sth in ~ immagazzinare qc 2. COMPUT memoria f
storage battery n accumulatore m
storage device n dispositivo m di memorizzazione
store [stɔ:r] I. n 1. (shop) negozio m; department ~ grande magazzino m 2. (supply: of food) scorta f; (of wine) riserva f 3. (place for keeping supplies) magazzino m; (for weapons) arsenale m ▶ to be in ~ what is in ~ for us? cosa ci riserva il futuro? II. vt 1. (put into storage) immagazzinare 2. (keep for future use) mettere da parte 3. COMPUT (file) salvare; (data) memorizzare
store detective n sorvegliante mf (di un negozio)
storefront ['stɔ:r·frʌnt] n vetrina f
storehouse ['stɔ:r·haʊs] n magazzino m; fig miniera f
storekeeper ['stɔ:r·ˌki:·pɚ] n negoziante mf
storeroom ['stɔ:r·ru:m] n magazzino m; (for food) dispensa f
storied adj two/three-~ di tue/tre piani
stork [stɔ:rk] n cicogna f
storm [stɔ:rm] I. n 1. METEO tempesta f 2. fig (of protest) ondata f; (of criticism) pioggia f; (of applause) scroscio m; political ~ bufera f politica 3. to take sth by ~ prendere qc d'assalto; to take sb by ~ spopolare presso qu ▶ to ride out@ [o weather] the ~ uscire indenne dalla bufera II. vi 1. METEO esserci tempesta; (winds) infuriare 2. (speak angrily) tuonare

S

III. *vt* (*town, castle*) prendere d'assalto; (*house*) fare irruzione in
◆**storm into** *vi* fare irruzione in
◆**storm out** *vi* precipitarsi fuori
storm cloud *n* nube *f* temporalesca
storm door *n* controporta *f*
storm-tossed *adj* (*boat*) sballottato, -a dalla tempesta
stormy ['stɔːr·mi] <-ier, -iest> *adj* (*weather*) tempestoso, -a; (*sea, relationship*) burrascoso, -a; (*argument*) violento, -a
story[1] ['stɔːri] <-ies> *n* **1.** (*account*) storia *f*; (*fictional*) racconto *m*; **to tell a ~** raccontare una storia; **to tell stories** (*lie*) raccontare delle storie; **so the ~ goes** così si dice **2.** (*news report*) articolo *m* ▶**that's another ~** questa è(tutta) un'altra storia; **it's the same old ~** è sempre la stessa storia; **a tall ~** una storia inverosimile
story[2] ['stɔːri] *n* piano *m*
storybook ['stɔː·ri·bʊk] **I.** *n* libro *m* di racconti **II.** *adj* **a ~ romance** una storia d'amore da fiaba
story line *n* (*plot*) trama *f*
storyteller *n* narratore, -trice *m, f*
stout [staʊt] **I.** *adj* (*person*) robusto, -a; (*shoes, boots*) resistente; (*defender*) accanito, -a; (*resistance*) tenace **II.** *n* (*beer*) birra *f* scura
stouthearted [ˌstaʊt·'hɑːr·ʈɪd] *adj* (*support*) incondizionato, -a; (*defender*) accanito, -a; (*resistance*) tenace
stoutly ['staʊt·li] *adv* **1.** (*strongly*) solidamente **2.** (*firmly*) energicamente
stove [stoʊv] *n* **1.** (*range*) fornello *m* **2.** (*heater*) stufa *f*
stovepipe ['stoʊv·paɪp] *n* tubo *m* di stufa
stow [stoʊ] *vt* mettere via
◆**stow away I.** *vt* mettere via **II.** *vi* viaggiare come clandestino, -a
stowage ['stoʊ·ɪdʒ] *n* NAUT stiva *f*
stowaway ['stoʊ·ə·weɪ] *n* clandestino, -a *m, f*
straddle ['stræ·dl] *vt* (*horse*) cavalcare
straggle ['stræ·gl] *vi* **1.** (*lag behind*) essere indietro **2.** (*come in small numbers*) arrivare poco a poco; (*move in a disorganized group*) avanzare disordinatamente **3.** (*hang untidily: hair*) cadere in disordine
straggler ['stræg·lə·] *n* ritardatario, -a *m, f*
straggly ['stræg·li] <-ier, -iest> *adj* (*hair*) in disordine
straight [streɪt] **I.** *adj* **1.** (*not bent*) dritto, -a **2.** (*honest*) franco, -a; **to be ~ with sb** essere franco con qu **3.** (*plain*) semplice; (*undiluted: gin, vodka*) liscio, -a **4.** (*consecutive*) seguido, -a; **she won in ~ sets** ha vinto tutti i set **5.** THEAT (*not comic*) serio, -a **6.** (*traditional*) convenzionale **7.** *inf* (*heterosexual*) eterosessuale **II.** *adv* **1.** (*in a direct line*) dritto; **to go ~ ahead** andare dritto; **to come ~ at sb** andare dritto verso qu; **to head ~ for sth** andare direttamente verso qc **2.** (*at once*) **to get ~ to the point** andare dritto al punto **3.** *inf* (*honestly*) chiaramente; **to give it to sb** ~ parlare chiara-

mente a qu **4.** (*clearly: see, think*) con chiarezza **III.** *n* (*straight line*) rettilineo *m;* **the finishing ~** il rettilineo finale
straightaway [ˌstreɪʈ·ə·'weɪ] **I.** *adv* subito **II.** *n* SPORTS rettilineo *m*
straighten ['streɪ·tn] *vt* **1.** (*make straight*) raddrizzare; (*hair*) lisciare; (*wires*) tendere **2.** (*unbend: arm, body, leg*) tendere **3.** (*make level: hem*) uguagliare
◆**straighten out I.** *vt* **1.** (*make straight*) stirare **2.** (*make level*) uguagliare **3.** (*solve: situation, problem*) sistemare **4.** (*clarify*) chiarificare; **to straighten sb out** far rigare dritto **II.** *vi* (*road*) diventare dritto, -a
◆**straighten up I.** *vi* (*stand upright*) raddrizzarsi **II.** *vt* **1.** (*make tidy*) sistemare **2.** (*make level*) uguagliare
straightforward [ˌstreɪt·'fɔːr·wəd] *adj* **1.** (*honest*) schietto, -a **2.** (*easy*) semplice
straight-laced ['streɪt·leɪst] *adj s.* strait-laced
straight-out [ˌstreɪt·'aʊt] *adj inf* (*answer*) diretto, -a; (*refusal*) netto, -a
strain[1] [streɪn] **I.** *n* **1.** (*pressure*) pressione *f;* **to be under ~** essere sotto pressione; **to put a ~ on a relationship** mettere a dura prova una relazione **2.** PHYS sollecitazione *f* **3.** MED stiramento *m* **II.** *vi* (*try hard*) sforzarsi; **to ~ for effect** cercare l'effetto ad ogni costo **III.** *vt* **1.** (*sforzare*) **to ~ one's eyes** sforzare la vista; **to ~ one's ears** sforzarsi di sentire **2.** (*put stress on: relationship*) mettere a dura prova; (*credulity*) mettere alla prova **3.** CULIN (*coffee*) filtrare; (*vegetables*) scolare
strain[2] [streɪn] *n* **1.** (*variety: of virus*) ceppo *m;* (*of species*) razza *f* **2.** (*tendency or trait*) ~ **of eccentricity** vena *f* eccentrica; ~ **of puritanism** inclinazione *f* al puritanesimo **3.** MUS tono *m*
strained [streɪnd] *adj* (*relations*) teso, -a; (*smile*) forzato, -a
strainer *n* colino *m*
strait [streɪt] *n* **1.** GEO stretto *m;* **the Bering Strait** lo stretto di Bering **2.** (*bad situation*) **to be in dire ~s** avere serie difficoltà
straitjacket ['streɪt·ˌdʒæ·kɪt] *n* PSYCH, MED camicia *f* di forza
strait-laced ['streɪt·leɪst] *adj* benpensante
strand[1] [strænd] *n* **1.** (*thread: of wool, rope, string*) filo *m;* **a ~ of hair** una ciocca di capelli **2.** (*string: of pearls, plot*) filo *m*
strand[2] [strænd] **I.** *n liter* (*shore*) lido *m* **II.** *vt* **to be ~ed** rimanere bloccato
strange [streɪndʒ] *adj* **1.** (*peculiar*) strano, -a; **I felt ~** mi sentivo strano; **it's ~ that** è strano che +*subj;* ~**r things have happened** sono successe cose anche pi strane; ~ **to say** strano a dirsi **2.** (*unfamiliar: face*) sconosciuto, -a; (*bed*) diverso, -a dal proprio
strangely *adv* (*behave, dress*) in modo strano; ~ **enough ...** per quanto (possa sembrare) strano, ...
stranger ['streɪn·dʒə·] *n* sconosciuto, -a *m, f;* **he is no ~ to controversy** non è estraneo alla

polemica

strangle ['stræŋ·gl] *vt* (*person*) strangolare; **a ~d cry** un grido strozzato

stranglehold ['stræn·gl·hoʊld] *n* (*control*) controllo *m* totale; (*on market*) monopolio *m*; **to have sb in a ~** dominare totalmente qu

strangulation [ˌstræŋ·gjʊ·'leɪ·ʃən] *n* strangolamento *m*

strap [stræp] I. *n* (*of bag*) cinghia *f*; (*of dress*) spallina *f* II.<-pp-> *vt* legare

strapless ['stræp·lɪs] *adj* senza spalline

strapping ['stræ·pɪŋ] I. *adj inf* grande e grosso, -a II. *n* (*bandage*) benda *f*

stratagem ['stræ·ṭə·dʒəm] *n* stratagemma *m*

strategic [strə·'tiː·dʒɪk] *adj* strategico, -a

strategist ['stræ·ṭə·dʒɪst] *n* stratega *mf*

strategy ['stræ·ṭə·dʒi] <-ies> *n* strategia *f*

stratify ['stræ·ṭə·faɪ] *vt* stratificare

stratosphere ['stræ·ṭəs·fɪr] *n* stratosfera *f*; **to go into the ~** (*prices*) diventare astronomici

stratum ['streɪ·ṭəm] <-strata> *n* strato *m*

straw [strɑː] *n* **1.** (*dry stems*) paglia *f* **2.** (*for drinking*) cannuccia *f* ▶ **to be the last ~** essere la goccia che fa traboccare il vaso; **you've drawn the short ~** ti è andata male; **to clutch at ~s** aggrapparsi a un'illusione

strawberry ['strɑː·ˌbe·ri] <-ies> *n* (*fruit*) fragola *f*

straw-colored ['strɔː·kʌ·ləd] *adj* rosso fragola *inv*

straw man *n* uomo *m* di paglia

straw poll *n* sondaggio *m* d'opinione

stray [streɪ] I. *adj* **1.** (*homeless: dog, cat*) randagio, -a **2.** (*loose: hair*) sciolto, -a; (*bullet*) vagante II. *vi* (*wander*) vagare; (*become lost*) perdersi; **to ~ from** allontanarsi da; **to ~ off course** uscire dalla rotta; **they were warned not to stray beyond the border** erano stati avvertiti di non avventurarsi oltre il confine; **to ~ from the point** divagare III. *n* (*dog*) cane *m* randagio; (*cat*) gatto *m* randagio

streak [striːk] I. *n* **1.** (*stripe*) riga *f*; (*of light*) raggio *m*; **a ~ of lightning** un fulmine *m* **2.** (*tendency*) vena *f*; **an aggressive ~** una vena aggressiva; **to have a ~ of cowardice** avere una punta di vigliaccheria **3.** (*spell*) periodo *f*; **to be on a winning ~** attraversare un periodo fortunato; **a 20-game hitting ~** una serie di 20 vittorie ▶ **like a ~ of lightning** come un fulmine; **to talk a blue ~** *inf* parlare come una macchinetta II. *vt* rigare; **to be ~ed** essere rigato; **to be ~ed with sth** essere chiazzato di qc III. *vi* **1.** (*move very fast*) sfrecciare **2.** (*run naked in public*) correre nudo, -a (in un luogo pubblico)

streaker *n* persona che corre nuda in un luogo pubblico

streaky ['striː·ki] <-ier, -iest> *adj* non uniforme

stream [striːm] I. *n* **1.** (*small river*) ruscello *m* **2.** (*current*) corrente *f*; **to go against the ~** *fig* andare controcorrente **3.** (*flow: of oil, water, people*) flusso *m*; (*of insults*) sequela *f* II. *vi*

1. (*flow*) scorrere; **tears ~ed down her face** le lacrime le scorrevano sul viso **2.** (*move in numbers*) riversarsi **3.** (*shine: sunlight*) splendere **4.** (*run: nose*) colare; (*eyes*) lacrimare

streamer ['striː·mə·] *n* festone *m*

streamline ['striːm·laɪn] *vt* (*vehicle*) rendere aerodinamico, -a; (*method*) ottimizzare

streamlined *adj* (*vehicle*) aerodinamico, -a; (*method*) efficiente

street [striːt] *n* (*road*) strada *f*; **in** [*o* **on**] **the ~** per strada ▶ **to be out on the ~** essere sulla strada; **to walk the ~s** (*wander*) girare per le strade; (*be a prostitute*) battere il marciapiede

streetcar *n* tram *m inv*

street hockey *n* hockey *m* giocato per strada

streetlamp *n*, **streetlight** *n* lampione *m*

street lighting *n* illuminazione *f* stradale

street value *n* valore *m* commerciale

streetwalker *n* prostituta *f* (*che batte il marciapiede*)

streetwise ['striːt·waɪz] *adj* (*person*) scafato, -a; (*politician*) scaltro, -a

strength [streŋθ] *n* **1.** (*power*) forza *f*; (*of feeling, light*) intensità *f*; (*of alcohol*) gradazione *f*; (*of economy*) solidità *f*; (*mental firmness*) forza *f* **2.** (*number of members*) numero di effettivi *m*; **to be at full ~** essere al completo; **to be below ~** (*office*) essere sotto organico **3.** (*strong point*) punto *m* di forza; **one's ~s and weaknesses** i suoi pregi e i suoi difetti

strengthen ['streŋ·θən] I. *vt* **1.** (*make stronger: muscles, wall*) rinforzare; (*financial position*) consolidare **2.** (*increase: chances*) aumentare **3.** (*intensify: relations*) intensificare; (*links*) rafforzare II. *vi* rinforzarsi

strenuous ['stren·ju·əs] *adj* (*activity, exercise, sport*) faticoso, -a; (*supporter*) strenuo, -a; (*denial*) netto, -a

streptococcus [ˌstrep·tə·'kɑː·kəs] <-ci> *n* streptococco *m*

stress [stres] I. *n* **1.** (*mental strain*) stress *m inv* **2.** (*emphasis*) rilievo *m* **3.** LING accento *m* **4.** PHYS sollecitazione *f* II. *vt* **1.** (*emphasize*) sottolineare **2.** LING accentare

stressed *adj*, **stressed out** *adj inf* stressato, -a

stress fracture *n* frattura [*o* fatica] da stress *f*

stress-free *adj* antistress *inv*

stressful ['stres·fʊl] *adj* stressante

stress mark *n* LING accento *m*

stretch [stretʃ] I.<-es> *n* **1.** SPORTS allungamento *m* (muscolare) **2.** (*elasticity*) elasticità *f* **3.** GEO tratto *m* **4.** (*piece*) pezzo *m*; (*of road*) tratto *m*; (*of time*) periodo *m* **5.** (*stage of a race*) rettilineo *m*; **the home ~** la dirittura d'arrivo **6.** (*exertion*) **at full ~** a pieno regime; **to work at full ~** lavorare al massimo della propria capacità; **not by any ~ of the imagination** neanche per sogno II. *vi* **1.** (*become bigger*) stirarsi; (*clothes*) allargarsi **2.** (*extend muscles*) stirarsi **3.** (*in time*) **to ~ back to ...** risalire (fino) a ... **4.** (*cover an area: sea, influence*) estendersi III. *vt* **1.** (*extend: muscles*) fare esercizi di allunga-

S

mento per; **to ~ one's legs** distendere le gambe **2.** (*make go further*) **to ~ the limit** spingere oltre il limite **3.** (*demand a lot of*) **to ~ sb's patience** mettere alla prova la pazienza di qu; **my present job doesn't ~ me** il mio lavoro attuale non mi stimola; **his nerves are ~ed to the breaking point** le stanno per saltare i nervi **4.** (*go beyond*) **to ~ a point** fare un'eccezione; **now you're really ~ing it** ora stai proprio esagerando **5.** LAW oltrepassare i limiti di **IV.** *adj* elastico, -a

stretcher ['stret·ʃə] *n* barella *f*

stretcher bearer *n* barelliere, -a *m, f*

strew [struː] <strewed, strewn *o* strewed> *vt* disseminare

stricken ['strɪ·kən] *adj* **1.** (*distressed*) afflitto, -a **2.** (*wounded*) ferito, -a **3.** (*afflicted*) **to be stricken with illness** essere colpito dalla malattia; **she was stricken with remorse** era attanagliata dal rimorso **4.** (*damaged: tanker*) naufragato, -a

strict [strɪkt] *adj* (*person*) severo, -a; (*control, orders*) rigoroso, -a; (*sense*) stretto, -a; (*deadline*) improrogabile; (*neutrality*) totale; (*secrecy*) massimo, -a; (*confidence*) assoluto, -a; **to be ~ with sb** essere severo con qu

strictly ['strɪkt·li] *adv* **1.** (*exactly*) proprio; **not ~ comparable** non proprio paragonabile; **~ speaking** per essere precisi **2.** (*harshly*) rigorosamente; **~ forbidden** rigorosamente vietato

stride [straɪd] **I.** <strode> *vi* camminare a grandi passi; **to ~ ahead** avanzare a grandi passi; **to ~ across sth** attraversare qc a grandi passi **II.** *n* **1.** (*long step*) falcata *f* **2.** (*progress*) progresso *m;* **to make** (**positive**) **~s forward** fare progressi; **to make ~s towards sth** fare progressi verso qc ▶ **to get into** [*o* hit] **one's ~** trovare il giusto ritmo; **to take sth in ~** fare qc con comodo

strident ['straɪ·dnt] *adj* stridente

strife [straɪf] *n* conflitto *m;* (*verbal*) controversia *f;* **domestic ~** liti *fpl* domestiche

strike [straɪk] **I.** *n* **1.** (*military attack*) attacco *m* **2.** (*withdrawal of labor*) sciopero *m* **3.** (*discovery*) scoperta *f* **4.** (*in baseball*) strike *m* *inv* **5.** LAW reato *m* **II.** <struck, struck *o* stricken> *vt* **1.** (*collide with*) colpire; **to ~ a match** accendere un fiammifero; **to be struck by lightning** essere colpito da un fulmine; **to ~ a blow against sb** assestare un colpo a qu **2.** (*achieve*) trovare; **to ~ a balance** trovare un equilibrio; **to ~ a bargain with sb** concludere un accordo con qu **3.** (*seem*) sembrare; **it ~s me that ...** mi sembra che ... **4.** (*impress*) colpire; **to be struck by sth** essere colpito da qc **5.** (*engender*) **to ~ fear into sb** mettere paura a qu **6.** (*discover*) scoprire; (*find*) trovare; **to ~ gold** (*have financial fortune*) fare fortuna; (*win gold medal*) vincere l'oro **7.** (*adopt*) **to ~ an attitude** assumere un atteggiamento **8.** (*sound the time: clock*) battere; **the clock struck three** l'orologio ha bat-

tuto le tre **9.** (*manufacture: coin*) coniare **10.** (*delete*) depennare ▶ **to ~ a chord with sb** toccare il tasto giusto con qu; **to ~ the right note** trovare la formula giusta; **to ~ sb dumb** lasciare qu a bocca aperta; **to ~ it rich** *inf* fare fortuna **III.** <struck, struck *o* stricken> *vi* **1.** (*hit hard*) colpire; (*attack*) attaccare; **to ~ at sth** colpire qc; **to ~ at the heart of sth** colpire qc al cuore; **to ~ home** centrare il bersaglio **2.** (*withdraw labor*) scioperare; **the right to ~** il diritto allo sciopero; **to ~ for sth** scioperare per qc

◆ **strike back** *vi* reagire; **to ~ at sb** reagire agli attacchi di qu

◆ **strike down** *vt* **1.** **she was struck down by cancer** è stata stroncata dal cancro **2.** LAW invalidare

◆ **strike off** *vt* **to strike sb/sth off a list** depennare qu/qc da una lista

◆ **strike out I.** *vt* **1.** (*in baseball*) eliminare **2.** (*delete*) depennnare **II.** *vi* **1.** (*in baseball*) essere eliminato; *fig* fare fiasco **2.** (*move off*) andare in modo deciso; **to ~ on one's own** mettersi in proprio **3.** (*hit out*) colpire (a destra e a manca)

◆ **strike up** *vt* (*conversation*) intavolare; (*friendship*) stringere; (*relationship*) iniziare

strikebreaker ['straɪk·ˌbreɪ·kə] *n* crumiro, -a *m, f*

strikeout *n* strikeout *m inv*

striker ['straɪ·kə] *n* **1.** (*strike participant*) scioperante *mf* **2.** SPORTS attaccante *mf*

strike zone *n* zona *f* di strike

striking ['straɪ·kɪŋ] *adj* notevole; (*result, beauty, resemblance*) straordinario, -a; (*resemblance*) impressionante; **visually ~** che attira l'attenzione

string [strɪŋ] **I.** *n* **1.** (*twine*) *a.* MUS corda *f;* (*on puppet*) filo *m;* **to pull ~s** *fig* tenere le fila; **with no ~s attached** senza condizioni **2.** *pl* MUS (*section, players*) (strumenti *mpl* ad) arco *m* **3.** (*chain*) catena *f;* (*of pearls*) filo *m* **4.** (*sequence: of scandals*) serie *f;* (*of lies, oaths*) sfilza *f;* (*of people*) fila *f* **5.** COMPUT stringa *f* **II.** <strung, strung> *vt* appendere; (*beads*) infilare; (*instrument, tennis racket*) mettere le corde a

◆ **string along** *inf* **I.** *vi* **I'll ~ with you** ti accompagno **II.** *vt* **to string sb along** menare qc per il naso

◆ **string out** *vt* **1.** (*protract: activity*) tirare per le lunghe **2.** (*extend*) disporre

◆ **string together** *vt* mettere insieme

◆ **string up** *vt inf* impiccare

string band *n* gruppo *m* di archi

string bean *n* fagiolino *m*

stringed instrument *n* strumento *m* ad arco

stringency ['strɪn·dʒən·si] *n* **1.** (*of measure*) severità *f;* (*of test*) rigore *m* **2.** FIN ristrettezze *fpl*

stringent ['strɪn·dʒənt] *adj* **1.** (*measure*) severo, -a; (*rigorous: test*) rigoroso, -a; (*law, requirement*) rigido, -a **2.** FIN restrittivo, -a

stringy ['strɪŋ·i] *adj* (*meat*) fibroso, -a; (*person*) sottile ma robusto, -a

strip [strɪp] I. *vt* 1. (*lay bare*) togliere; **to ~ sb of sth** togliere qc a qu 2. (*unclothe*) spogliare 3. (*dismantle*) smontare II. *vi* spogliarsi III. *n* 1. striscia *f* 2. (*striptease*) striptease *m inv,* spogliarello *m* 3. (*landing area*) **landing ~** pista *f* (*d'atterraggio*)

stripe [straɪp] *n* 1. (*colored band*) riga *f* 2. (*type*) **of every ~** di ogni sorta; **governments of every ~** governi di ogni tendenza 3. MIL gallone *m*

striped *adj* a righe

strip mall *n* piccolo centro *m* commerciale (*disposti su una fila*)

strip mining *n* miniera *f* a cielo aperto

stripper ['strɪ·pɚ] *n* spogliarellista *mf*

strip-search ['strɪp·sɜːrtʃ] *vt* **to ~ sb** sottoporre qu a perquisizione corporale

strip search *n* perquisizione *f* corporale

striptease ['strɪp·tiːz] *n* striptease *m inv,* spogliarello *m*

stripy *adj* a righe

strive [straɪv] <strove, striven *o* strived> *vi* sforzarsi; **to ~ to do sth** sforzarsi di fare qc; **to ~ after sth** sforzarsi di ottenere qc; **to ~ for sth** sforzarsi di ottenere qc

strobe [stroʊb] *n inf* luce *f* psichedelica

strobe light *n* luce *f* psichedelica

stroboscope ['stroʊ·bəs·koʊp] *n* stroboscopio *m*

strode [stroʊd] *pt of* **stride**

stroke [stroʊk] I. *vt* 1. (*caress*) carezzare 2. SPORTS (*hit smoothly*) colpire II. *n* 1. (*caress*) carezza *f* 2. MED ictus *m inv;* **to suffer a ~** avere un ictus 3. (*of pencil*) tratto *m;* (*of brush*) pennellata *f* 4. (*style of hitting ball*) colpo *m;* (*billiards*) tiro *m* 5. *form* (*lash with whip*) frustata *f* 6. (*in swimming: style*) stile *m;* (*single movement*) bracciata *f* 7. (*bit*) **by a ~ of fate** per un colpo del destino; **a ~ of genius** un colpo di genio; **a ~ of luck** un colpo di fortuna 8. (*of clock*) rintocco *m*

stroll [stroʊl] I. *n* passeggiata *f;* **to go for a ~** fare una passeggiata II. *vi* passeggiare; **to ~ along the riverbank** passeggiare in riva al fiume

stroller ['stroʊ·lɚ] *n* 1. (*pushchair*) passeggino *m* 2. (*person*) persona *f* a passeggio

strong [strɑːŋ] I. *adj* 1. (*powerful*) forte; (*competition*) duro, -a; (*condemnation, measure*) severo, -a; (*protest*) energico, -a; (*reason*) valido, -a; **to produce ~ memories** suscitare vivi ricordi 2. (*capable*) bravo, -a 3. (*physically powerful*) forte; **to be as ~ as an ox** essere forte come un toro 4. (*fit*) sano, -a; (*constitution*) robusto, -a 5. (*durable: will*) forte; (*conviction*) profondo, -a; (*nerves*) saldo, -a 6. (*staunch: antipathy*) forte; (*believer*) fervente, -a; (*bond, character, emotion*) forte; (*friendship*) grande; (*objection, opponent*) duro, -a; (*supporter*) accanito, -a 7. (*tough*) resistente 8. (*very likely*) buono, -a; **~ chance**

of success buone probabilità di riuscita 9. (*marked*) forte; (*language*) volgare 10. (*bright*) brillante 11. (*having high value*) forte II. *adv inf* **to come on ~ to sb** (*show sexual interest in*) fare delle avances a qu; **to be still going ~** continuare ad andare bene

strong-arm ['strɑː·ŋɑːrm] I. *adj* (*methods*) forte II. *vt* usare le maniere forti con

strongbox ['strɑː·ŋbɑːks] *n* cassaforte *f*

stronghold ['strɑː·ŋhoʊld] *n* (*fortified place*) fortezza *f; fig* baluardo *m*

strongly *adv* 1. (*powerfully*) vigorosamente; (*advise*) vivamente; (*condemn*) fermamente; (*criticize, force*) duramente; **to smell ~ of sth** avere un forte odore di qc; **to be ~ opposed to sb/sth** essere fermamente contrario a qn/qc; **to be ~ biased against sb/sth** essere estremamente prevenuto nei confronti di qn/qc 2. (*sturdily*) solidamente

strong-minded [ˌstrɑːŋ·ˈmaɪn·dɪd] *adj* determinato, -a

strong room ['strɑː·ŋruːm] *n* camera *f* blindata

strong-willed [ˌstrɑːŋ·ˈwɪld] *adj* determinato, -a

strove [stroʊv] *pt of* **strive**

struck [strʌk] *pt, pp of* **strike**

structural ['strʌk·tʃə·rəl] *adj* strutturale

structure ['strʌk·tʃɚ] I. *n* struttura *f* II. *vt* strutturare

struggle ['strʌ·gl] I. *n* 1. (*effort*) sforzo *m;* **to be a real ~** richiedere un grande sforzo; **to give up the ~ to do sth** smettere di lottare per fare qc 2. (*skirmish*) lotta *f;* **to put up a ~** battersi II. *vi* 1. (*make an effort*) sforzarsi 2. (*fight*) lottare

strum [strʌm] <-mm-> *vt* MUS suonare (*pizzicando le corde tutte insieme*)

strung [strʌŋ] *pt, pp of* **string**

strut¹ [strʌt] I. <-tt-> *vi* **to ~ about** girare impettito II. *vt inf* **to ~ one's stuff** *iron* (*dance*) mettersi in mostra

strut² [strʌt] *n* (*in building, plane*) puntello *m*

strychnine ['strɪk·naɪn] *n* stricnina *f*

stub [stʌb] I. *n* (*of check*) matrice *f;* (*of cigarette, pencil*) mozzicone *m* II. <-bb-> *vt* **to ~ one's toe against sth** sbattere il piede contro qc

stubble ['stʌ·bl] *n* 1. (*beard growth*) barba *f* di tre giorni 2. AGR stoppia *f*

stubbly ['stʌb·li] *adj* (*bristly*) con la barba non fatta

stubborn ['stʌ·bɚn] *adj* (*person, animal*) testardo, -a; **as ~ as a mule** testardo come un mulo; (*insistence*) tenace; (*problem*) persistente; (*refusal, resistence*) ostinato, -a

stubby ['stʌ·bi] *adj* (*fingers*) grassoccio, -a; (*person*) tarchiato, -a

stucco ['stʌ·koʊ] *n* stucco *m*

stuck [stʌk] I. *pt, pp of* **stick** II. *adj* 1. (*jammed*) incastrato, -a 2. *inf* (*crazy about*) **to be ~ on sb** essere pazzo di qu

stuck-up [ˌstʌk·ˈʌp] *adj inf* pieno di sè

S

stud¹ [stʌd] *n* **1.**(*horse*) stallone *m* **2.**(*good-looking guy*) figaccione *m*

stud² [stʌd] *n* **1.**(*small metal item*) tacchetto *m;* (*decorative nail*) borchia *f* **2.**(*on shirt*) **collar** ~ bottoncino *m* **3.**(*on tire*) chiodo **4.**(*earring*) orecchino *m* (*a forma di chiodino con vite*)

student ['stu:·dənt] *n* studente *mf;* **the ~ body** il corpo studentesco

student teacher *n* professore, -essa *m, f* tirocinante

student union *n* (*organization*) associazione *f* studentesca; (*meeting place*) club *m* studentesco *inv*

studhorse *n,* **stud horse** *n* stallone *m*

studied ['stʌ·dɪd] *adj* studiato, -a; (*answer*) studiato, -a a tavolino; (*insult*) premeditato, -a

studio ['stu:·di·oʊ] <-s> *n* **1.**(*of artist*) atelier *m inv* **2.**CINE studio *m* **3.**(*apartment*) monolocale *m*

studio apartment *n* monolocale *m*

studio audience *n* pubblico *m* in studio

studious ['stu:·di·əs] *adj* studioso, -a

study ['stʌ·di] **I.** *vt* (*subject*) studiare; (*evidence*) esaminare **II.** *vi* studiare **III.**<-ies> *n* **1.**(*of subject*) studio *m;* (*of evidence*) esame *m* **2.**(*room*) studio *m*

study group *n* gruppo *m* di studio

stuff [stʌf] **I.** *n* **1.** *inf*(*things*) cose *fpl;* **to know one's** ~ sapere il fatto proprio **2.**(*belongings*) cose *fpl* **3.**(*material*) roba *f;* (*cloth*) stoffa *f;* **to be the ~ of which heroes are made** avere la stoffa dell'eroe; **the** (**very**) ~ **of sth** l'essenza di qc **II.** *vt* **1.**(*fill*) riempire; **to** ~ **sth into sth** mettere qc dentro a qc; **to** ~ **sb's head with sth** riempire la testa a qu di qc; **to** ~ **oneself** *inf*strafogarsi **2.**(*preserve: animal*) impagliare

stuffed shirt *n inf*manichino *m*

stuffing ['stʌ·fɪŋ] *n* ripieno *m* ▶ **to knock the ~ out of sb** *inf*riempire di botte

stuffy ['stʌ·fi] *adj pej* **1.**(*room, atmosphere*) soffocante **2.**(*blocked: nose*) tappato, -a **3.**(*person*) compassato, -a

stumble ['stʌm·bl] *vi* **1.**(*trip*) inciampare; **to ~ on sth** inciampare su qc **2.**(*while talking*) impappinarsi; **to ~ over sth** impappinarsi nel dire qc

stumbling block *n* ostacolo *m*

stump [stʌmp] **I.** *n* (*of plant*) ceppo *m;* (*of arm*) moncone *m;* (*of tooth*) radice *f* **II.** *vt inf* mettere in difficoltà **III.** *vi* **to ~ about** camminare con passo pesante

stumpy ['stʌm·pi] *adj inf* tozzo, -a; (*tail*) corto, -a

stun [stʌn] <-nn-> *vt* **1.**(*stupefy*) lasciare esterrefatto, -a **2.**(*render unconscious*) stordire

stung [stʌŋ] *pp, pt of*sting

stun grenade *n* MIL granata *f* stordente

stunk [stʌŋk] *pt, pp of*stink

stunned *adj* esterrefatto, -a

stunner ['stʌ·nə·] *n inf* **1.**(*surprise*) sorpresa *f* **2.**(*person*) she's a ~ è una bellezza

stunning ['stʌ·nɪŋ] *adj* **1.**(*surprising*) sbalorditivo, -a **2.**(*impressive*) stupendo, -a

stunt¹ [stʌnt] *n* **1.**(*acrobatics*) acrobazia *f* **2.**(*feat*) bravata *f;* **to pull a ~** *inf*fare una bravata **3.**(*publicity action*) trucco *m* pubblicitario; **advertising** ~ trovata *f* pubblicitaria **4.**CINE scena *f* pericolosa

stunt² [stʌnt] *vt* (*plant*) arrestare lo sviluppo di; (*growth*) arrestare

stunted *adj* rachitico, -a; **emotionally ~** ritardato, -a

stuntman ['stʌnt·mæn] *n* stuntman *m inv,* cascatore *m*

stupefaction [ˌstu:·pə·'fæk·ʃən] *n form* stupore *m*

stupefy ['stu:·pə·faɪ] <-ie-> *vt* stordire; *fig* lasciare stupefatto, -a

stupendous [stu:·'pen·dəs] *adj* stupendo, -a

stupid ['stu:·pɪd] *adj* stupido, -a

stupidity [stu:·'pɪ·də·ti] *n* stupidità *f*

stupor ['stu:·pə·] *n* stupore *m*

sturdy ['stɜ:r·di] *adj* **1.**robusto, -a **2.**(*resolute*) accanito, -a; **a ~ defender of sth** un accanito difensore di qc

sturgeon ['stɜ:r·dʒən] *n* storione *m*

stutter ['stʌ·ţə·] **I.** *vi* (*stammer*) balbettare **II.** *vt* balbettare **III.** *n* **to have a ~** balbettare

stutterer ['stʌ·ţə·ə·] *n* balbuziente *mf*

sty [staɪ] *n* (*pigsty*) porcile *m*

style [staɪl] **I.** *n* **1.** *a.* ART, ARCHIT stile *m* **2.**(*elegance*) classe *f;* **to have no ~** non avere classe; **with ~** con classe; **to do things with ~** fare le cose con classe; **to live in** (**grand**) ~ vivere in grande stile; **to travel in ~** viaggiare in grande stile **3.**(*fashion*) moda *f;* **in ~** alla moda **4.**(*type*) stile *m* **II.** *vt* **1.**(*design*) disegnare; (*hair*) pettinare **2.**(*label*) **to ~ oneself as ...** farsi chiamare ...

styling *n* acconciatura *f*

stylish ['staɪ·lɪʃ] *adj* **1.**(*fashionable*) alla moda **2.**(*elegant*) stiloso, -a

stylist ['staɪ·lɪst] *n* stilista *mf*

stylistic [staɪ·'lɪs·tɪk] *adj* stilistico, -a

stylize ['staɪ·laɪz] *vt* stilizzare

stylus ['staɪ·ləs] <-es *o* -li> *n* puntina *f*

stymie ['staɪ·mi] <-(y)ing> *vt inf*ostacolare

Styrofoam® *n* polistirolo *m*

suave [swɑːv] *adj* gentile; *pej* manieroso, -a

sub¹ [sʌb] *n* **1.** *inf abbr of*substitute sostituto, -a *m, f* **2.** *inf abbr of* submarine sottomarino *m* **3.** *inf abbr of* sandwich panino *m* imbottito

sub² [sʌb] <-bb-> *vi abbr of*substitute sostituire

subatomic [ˌsʌb·ə·'tɑ:·mɪk] *adj* PHYS subatomico, -a

subclass ['sʌb·klæs] *n* BIO sottoclasse *f*

subcommittee [ˌsʌb·kə·'mɪ·ti] *n* sottocomitato *m*

subconscious [ˌsʌb·'kɑ:n·ʃəs] **I.** *n* subconscio *m* **II.** *adj* subcosciente

subcontinent ['sʌb·ˌkɑ:nt·nənt] *n* GEO subcontinente *m;* **the ~** il subcontinente indiano

subcontract ['sʌb-ˌkɑːn·trækt] *vt* subappaltare
subcontractor [ˌsʌb·kən·'træk·təə] *n* subappaltatore, -trice *m, f*
subculture ['sʌb-ˌkʌlt·ʃəˈ] *n* sottocultura *f*
subcutaneous [ˌsʌb·kjuː·'teɪn·iəs] *adj* sottocutaneo, -a
subdivide [ˌsʌb·dɪ·'vaɪd] *vt* suddividere
subdivision [ˌsʌb·dɪ·'vɪ·ʒən] *n* 1.(*division*) suddivisione *f* 2.(*housing estate*) complesso *m* residenziale
subdue [səb·'duː] *vt* (*tame*) sottomettere; (*repress*) reprimere
subdued *adj* (*color*) tenue; (*person*) sottomesso, -a
subgroup ['sʌb·gruːp] *n* sottogruppo *m*
subheading ['sʌb-ˌhe·dɪŋ] *n* sottotitolo *m*
subject¹ ['sʌb·dʒɪkt] I. *n* 1.(*theme*) argomento *m;* **to change the ~** cambiare argomento; **to wander off the ~** uscire dal tema; **on the ~ of sb/sth** a proposito di qu/qc 2.SCHOOL, UNIV materia *f;* (*research area*) ambito *m* 3.POL suddito, -a *m, f;* (*citizen*) cittadino, -a *m, f* 4.LING soggetto *m* 5.(*in experiment*) soggetto *m* II. *adj* 1.POL (*nation*) sottomesso, -a 2.(*exposed to*) **to be ~ to sth** essere soggetto a qc; **to be ~ to colds** essere soggetto ai raffreddori; **to be ~ to many dangers** essere esposto a molti pericoli; **to be ~ to high taxes** essere soggetto ad imposte elevate; **~ to prosecution** perseguibile 3.(*contingent on*) **~ to approval** soggetto ad approvazione
subject² [səb·'dʒekt] *vt* sottomettere
subjection [səb·'dʒek·ʃən] *n* POL sottomissione *m*
subjective [səb·'dʒek·tɪv] *adj* soggettivo, -a
subject matter *n* (*of meeting, book*) tema *m;* (*of letter*) soggetto *m*
sub judice [ˌsʌb·'dʒuː·də·si] *adj* LAW sub iudice
subjugate ['sʌb·dʒə·geɪt] *vt form* 1.(*control*) soggiogare 2.(*make submissive*) subordinare; **to ~ sth to sth** subordinare qc a qc; **to ~ sb to sb** subordinare gli interessi di qu agli interessi di qu
subjugation [ˌsʌb·dʒə·'geɪ·ʃən] *n form* assoggettamento *m*
subjunctive [səb·'dʒʌŋk·tɪv] *n* LING congiuntivo *m*
sublease [ˌsʌb·'liːs] *vt* subaffittare
sublet [sʌb·'let] <sublet, sublet> *vt* subaffittare
sublimate ['sʌb·lɪ·meɪt] *vt* PSYCH sublimare
sublime [sə·'blaɪm] *adj* 1.(*glorious*) sublime 2. *iron* (*absolute*) estremo, -a; **~ ignorance** estrema ignoranza *f*
subliminal [ˌsʌb·'lɪ·mə·nl] *adj* PSYCH subliminale
submachine gun [ˌsʌb·mə·'ʃiːn·ˌgʌn] *n* mitra *m*
submarine ['sʌb·mə·riːn] I. *n* 1.NAUT, MIL sottomarino *m* 2. *inf* (*sandwich*) panino *m* imbottito II. *adj* sottomarino, -a
submenu [ˌsʌb·'men·juː] *n* COMPUT sottomenu *m*

submerge [səb·'mɜːrdʒ] I. *vt* sommergere; **to ~ oneself in sth** *fig* immergersi in qc II. *vi* immergersi
submersible [səb·'mɜːr·sə·bl] *n* sommergibile *m*
submersion [səb·'mɜːr·ʒən] *n* immersione *f*
submission [səb·'mɪ·ʃən] *n* 1.(*acquiescence*) sottomissione *f* 2.(*of proposal*) presentazione *f;* (*of document*) consegna *f*
submissive [səb·'mɪ·sɪv] *adj* sottomesso, -a
submit [səb·'mɪt] <-tt-> I. *vt* 1.(*hand in: proposal*) presentare; (*document*) consegnare 2. *form* (*propose*) proporre II. *vi* (*yield*) sottomettersi
subordinate¹ [sə·'bɔːr·də·nɪt] I. *n* subordinato, -a *m, f* II. *adj* (*secondary*) secondario, -a; (*lower in rank*) subordinato, -a
subordinate² [sə·'bɔːr·də·neɪt] *vt* subordinare
subordinate clause *n* LING proposizione *m* subordinata
subordination [sə·ˌbɔːr·də·'neɪ·ʃən] *n* subordinazione *f*
subplot ['sʌb·plɑːt] *n* intreccio *m* secondario
subpoena [sə·'piː·nə] LAW I. *vt* citare; **to ~ sb to testify** citare qu a deporre II. *n* citazione *f*
subscribe [səb·'skraɪb] I. *vi* 1.(*order*) abbonarsi 2.(*agree with*) **to ~ to sth** sottoscrivere qc II. *vt* 1.(*contribute*) sottoscrivere 2. *form* (*sign*) sottoscrivere
subscriber [səb·'skraɪ·bəˈ] *n* abbonato, -a *m, f*
subscript [sʌb·'skrɪpt] *n* TYPO pedice *m,* deponente *m*
subscription [səb·'skrɪp·ʃən] *n* abbonamento *m;* **to order a ~ to sth** abbonarsi a qc
subsection ['sʌb·ˌsek·ʃən] *n* 1.(*part*) paragrafo *f* 2.LAW sottosezione *f*
subsequent ['sʌb·sɪk·wənt] *adj* successivo; **~ to ...** in seguito a ...
subsequently *adv* successivamente; **~ to ...** in seguito a ..
subservient [səb·'sɜːr·vi·ənt] *adj* 1. *pej* (*servile*) servile 2.(*secondary*) subordinato, -a
subset ['sʌb·set] *n* MATH sottoinsieme *m*
subside [səb·'saɪd] *vi* 1.(*lessen*) diminuire 2.(*sink: water*) ritirarsi; (*ground*) sprofondare
subsidiary [səb·'sɪ·diə·ri] I. *adj* secondario, -a; ECON controllato, -a II.<-ies> *n* ECON società *f* controllata
subsidize ['sʌb·sə·daɪz] *vt* sovvenzionare
subsidy ['sʌb·sə·di] <-ies> *n* sovvenzione *f,* sussidio *m;* **unemployment ~** sussidio di disoccupazione
subsist [səb·'sɪst] *vi form* sostentarsi; **to ~ on sth** sostentarsi con qc
subsistence [səb·'sɪs·təns] *n* sussistenza *f;* **means of ~** mezzi *mpl* di sussistenza; **enough for a bare ~** appena sufficiente per vivere
substance ['sʌb·stəns] *n* 1.(*matter*) sostanza *f* 2.(*essence*) sostanza *f* 3.(*significance*) rilevanza *f;* **a film of real ~** un film denso di contenuti *f* 4.(*main point*) sostanza *f;* **the ~ of the conversation** la sostanza della conversazione; **in ~** in sostanza 5.(*possessions*) ric-

S

chezza *f;* **a man of** ~ un uomo ricco

substandard [ˌsʌb·'stæn·dɚd] *adj* scadente

substantial [səb·'stæn·ʃl] *adj* **1.** (*important*) sostanziale; **to be in** ~ **agreement** essere sostanzialmente d'accordo **2.** (*large*) sostanzioso, -a; (*sum, damage*) ingente **3.** (*sturdy*) solido, -a

substantially [səb·'stæn·ʃə·li] *adv* **1.** (*significantly*) notevolmente **2.** (*in the main*) sostanzialmente

substantiate [səb·'stæn·ʃi·eɪt] *vt* corroborare

substantive ['sʌb·stən·tɪv] **I.** *n* sostantivo *m* **II.** *adj form* rilevante

substation ['sʌb·steɪ·ʃən] *n* **1.** ELEC sottostazione *f* **2.** ADMIN ufficio *f* secondario; **police** ~ commissariato *f* di polizia (*che dipende da un altro*)

substitute ['sʌb·stə·tuːt] **I.** *vt* sostituire; **to** ~ **sb for sb** *inf* sostituire qu con qu; **to** ~ **butter with margarine** sostituire il burro con la margarina **II.** *vi* **to** ~ **for sb** sostituire qu **III.** *n* **1.** (*equivalent*) sostituto *m;* (*alternative: for milk, coffee*) alternativa *f;* **there's no** ~ **for him** non c'è nessuno come lui **2. a.** SPORTS riserva *f;* **to come on as a** ~ entrare in campo (*riferito a una riserva*) **3.** SCH (*teacher*) supplente *mf*

substitute teacher *n* supplente *mf*

substitution [ˌsʌb·stə·'tuː·ʃən] *n* sostituzione *f*

substratum ['sʌb·ˌstreɪ·ʈəm] <-ta> *n* sostrato *m*

subsume [səb·'suːm] *vt form* integrare; **to** ~ **sth under a category** inserire qc in una categoria

subtenant ['sʌb·ˌte·nənt] *n* subaffittuario, -a *m, f*

subterfuge ['sʌb·tɚ·fjuːdʒ] *n* sotterfugio *m;* **by** ~ con dei sotterfugi

subterranean [ˌsʌb·tə·'reɪ·ni·ən] *adj* sotterraneo, -a

subtext ['sʌb·tekst] *n* messaggio *m* (implicito)

subtitle ['sʌb·ˌtaɪ·ʈl] **I.** *vt* sottotitolare **II.** *n* sottotitolo *m*

subtle ['sʌ·ʈl] *adj* **1.** (*delicate*) delicato, -a **2.** (*slight: difference*) sottile **3.** (*astute: person*) perspicace; (*question, suggestion, humor*) sottile

subtlety ['sʌ·ʈl·ti] <-ies> *n* **1.** (*delicacy: of flavor, smell*) delicatezza *f* **2.** (*of person*) perspicacia *f;* (*of argument*) sottigliezza *f*

subtotal ['sʌb·ˌtoʊ·ʈl] *n* subtotale *m,* totale *m* parziale

subtract [səb·'trækt] *vt* sottrarre; **to** ~ **3 from 5** sottrarre 3 da 5

subtraction [səb·'træk·ʃən] *n* resta *f,* sottrazione *f*

subtropical [ˌsʌb·'trɑː·pɪ·kl] *adj* subtropicale

suburb ['sʌ·bɜːrb] *n* quartiere *m* fuori città; **the** ~**s** la periferia; **to live in the** ~**s** vivere fuori città

suburban [sə·'bɜːr·bən] *adj* **1.** (*area*) periferico, -a; (*train*) che collega la periferia **2.** (*lifestyle*) di provincia

suburbia [sə·'bɜːr·biə] *n* periferia *f*

subvention [səb·'ven·ʃən] *n form* sovvenzione *f*

subversion [səb·'vɜːr·ʒən] *n form* sovversione *f*

subversive [səb·'vɜːr·sɪv] *form* **I.** *adj* sovversiva, -a **II.** *n* sovversivo, -a *m, f*

subvert [sʌb·'vɜːrt] *vt* (*authority*) sovvertire; (*principle*) minare

subway ['sʌb·weɪ] *n* metropolitana *f*

sub-zero [ˌsʌb·'zɪ·roʊ] *adj* sotto zero

succeed [sək·'siːd] **I.** *vi* **1.** (*be successful*) riuscire; **to** ~ **in doing sth** riuscire a fare qc; **the plan** ~**ed** il piano è riuscito **2.** (*follow*) succedere ▸ **if at first you don't** ~**, try, try again** *prov* se non riesci la prima volta, continua a provare **II.** *vt* (*follow*) succedere a

succeeding *adj* **1.** (*next in line*) successivo, -a **2.** (*following*) successivo, -a; **in the** ~ **weeks** nelle settimane successive

success [sək·'ses] *n* (*outcome*) successo *m;* **to meet with** ~ avere successo, riuscire; **to be a big** ~ **with sb/sth** avere molto successo con qu/qc; **he was a** ~ **with my children** ha avuto molto successo con i miei figli; **to have** ~ **in doing sth** riuscire a fare qc; **to wish sb** ~ **with sth** augurare a qu di riuscire qc; **to be a great** ~ riuscire benissimo, essere un successone; **to enjoy** ~ avere successo; ~ **story** esempio *m* di successo, storia *f* di successo

successful [sək·'ses·fəl] *adj* riuscito, -a; (*business*) florido, -a; (*person, book*) di successo; (*candidate*) vincente; (*solution*) efficace; **to be** ~ (*person*) avere successo; (*business*) essere florido, -a; **commercially** ~ con un buon successo commerciale

succession [sək·'se·ʃən] *n* successione *f;* ~ **rights** diritti *mpl* di successione; **in** ~ in successione; **a** ~ **of** una serie di; **an endless** ~ **of** una serie infinita di

successive [sək·'se·sɪv] *adj* consecutivo, -a; **on** ~ **occasions** in occasioni consecutive

successor [sək·'se·sɚ] *n* successore *m*

succinct [sək·'sɪŋkt] *adj* succinto, -a

succor ['sʌ·kɚ] **I.** *n* soccorso *m;* **to give** ~ **to sb** prestare soccorso a qu **II.** *vt* soccorrere

succulent ['sʌk·jʊ·lənt] **I.** *adj* (*steak, fruit*) succulento, -a; (*plant*) grasso, -a **II.** *n* pianta *f* grassa

succumb [sə·'kʌm] *vi form* **1.** (*surrender*) soccombere; **to** ~ **to pressure/temptation** soccombere alla pressione/tentazione **2.** (*die*) soccombere; **to** ~ **to one's injuries** soccombere alle ferite

such [sʌtʃ] **I.** *adj* tale; ~ **great weather/a good book** tempo/un libro così bello; ~ **an honor** tale onore; **to earn** ~ **a lot of money** guadagnare tanti di quei soldi; **or some** ~ **remark** o un'osservazione del genere; **to buy some fruit** ~ **as apples** comprare della frutta, ad esempio delle mele **II.** *pron* ~ **is life** così va la vita; **people** ~ **as him** la gente come lui; ~ **as it is** tale quale; **as** ~ propriamente detto

such and such ['sʌtʃ·ən·sʌtʃ] *adj inf* tale; **to**

arrive at ~ a time arrivare a tale ora; **to meet sb in ~ a place** incontrare qu in tale posto

suck [sʌk] I. *vt* succhiare; (*with straw*) sorbire; (*air*) aspirare; **to ~ one's thumb** succhiarsi il dito II. *vi* 1. (*with mouth*) succhiare 2. *inf* this **~ s!** questo fa schifo! III. *n* succhiata *f*; (*with straw*) sorsata *m*
◆ **suck up to** *vt* leccare i piedi a

sucker ['sʌ·kə·] I. *n* 1. *pej* (*stupid person*) credulone, -a *m, f* 2. *sl* (*thing*) rottura *f* di palle 3. (*device*) *a.* ZOOL ventosa *f* II. *vt inf* fregare; **to ~ sb into** [*o* out of] **doing sth** fregare qu per fargli fare qc

suckle ['sʌ·kl] I. *vt* allattare II. *vi* succhiare il latte

suckling pig ['sʌk·lɪŋ·ˌpɪg] *n* maialino *m* da latte

sucrose ['su:k·roʊs] *n* saccarosio *m*

suction ['sʌk·ʃən] *n* aspirazione *f*

suction pump *n* pompa *f* aspirante

Sudan [su:·'dæn] *n* il Sudan

Sudanese [ˌsu:·də·'ni:z] I. *n* sudanese *mf* II. *adj* sudanese

sudden ['sʌ·dən] *adj* (*immediate*) improvviso, -a; (*death*) improvvisa; **to put a ~ stop to sth** dare un taglio a qc; **all of a ~** *inf* all'improvviso

suddenly *adv* improvvisamente

suds [sʌdz] *npl* 1. schiuma *f* 2. birra *f*

sue [su:] <suing> I. *vt* fare causa a; **to ~ sb for damages** fare causa a qu per danni; **to ~ sb for divorce** fare domanda di divorzio da qu II. *vi* **to ~ for peace** chiedere la pace

suede [sweɪd] *n* camoscio *m*

suet ['su:·ɪt] *n* grasso *m* (animale)

suffer ['sʌ·fə·] I. *vi* 1. (*be in distress*) soffrire; **to ~ from sth** MED soffrire di qc; **the economy is ~ing from ...** l'economia sta soffrendo di ...; **to ~ for sth** essere punito per qc 2. (*seem worse*) **to ~ in** [*o* by] **comparison** non reggere il confronto II. *vt* 1. (*undergo: defeat, setback*) subire; **to ~ the consequences** subire le consequenze; **to ~ the misfortune of ...** avere la sfortuna di ... 2. MED subire

sufferance ['sʌ·fə·rəns] *n* **I feel I'm here on ~** ho l'impressione di essere appena tollerato qui

sufferer ['sʌ·fə·ə·] *n* malato, -a *m, f*; **AIDS ~** malato di AIDS

suffering ['sʌ·fə·rɪŋ] *n* sofferenza *f*; **years of ~** anni *mpl* di sofferenza

suffice [sə·'faɪs] *vi* bastare; **~ (it) to say that ...** basti dire che ...

sufficiency [sə·'fɪ·ʃn·si] *n* quantità *f* sufficiente

sufficient [sə·'fɪ·ʃnt] *adj* sufficiente; **to have had ~** essere sazio; **to be ~ for sth** bastare per qc

suffix ['sʌ·fɪks] *n* LING suffisso *m*

suffocate ['sʌ·fə·keɪt] I. *vi* asfissiare II. *vt* 1. (*asphyxiate*) asfissiare 2. *fig* soffocare

suffocating *adj* 1. (*heat*) soffocante; (*fumes*) asfissiante 2. *fig* opprimente

suffrage ['sʌ·frɪdʒ] *n* suffragio *m*; **universal ~** suffragio universale

suffragette [ˌsʌf·rə·'dʒet] *n* POL, HIST suffragista *f*

sugar ['ʃʊ·gə·] I. *n* 1. CULIN zucchero *m* 2. *inf* (*term of affection*) tesoro *m* II. *vt* zuccherare

sugar beet *n* barbabietola *f* da zucchero

sugar cane *n* canna *f* da zucchero

sugarcoated [ˌsʊ·gə·'kəʊ·tɪd] *adj* ricoperto, -a di zucchero

sugar daddy *n* vecchio ricco che cerca di ottenere i favori di una donna giovane con regali

sugarless *adj* senza zucchero

sugary ['ʃʊ·gə·ri] *adj* 1. (*sweet*) zuccherato, -a 2. *fig, pej* (*insincere*) mellifluo, -a

suggest [səg·'dʒest] *vt* 1. (*propose*) proporre, suggerire; **to ~ (to sb) that ...** proporre a qu che ... +*subj;* **to ~ doing sth** proporre di fare qc; **an idea ~ed itself (to him)** gli venne in mente un'idea 2. (*indicate*) far credere 3. (*hint*) insinuare; **what are you trying to ~?** che cosa vuoi insinuare?

suggestible [səg·'dʒes·tə·bl] *adj pej, form* suggestionabile; **highly ~** facilmente suggestionabile

suggestion [səg·'dʒest·ʃən] *n* 1. (*proposed idea*) proposta *f*, suggerimento *m;* **to make the ~ that ...** suggerire che ... +*subj;* **to be open to new ~s** essere aperto a nuove proposte; **at Ann's ~** su proposta di Ann 2. (*very small amount*) accenno *m;* **there was a ~ of a smile on his face** aveva in viso un abbozzo di sorriso 3. (*insinuation*) insinuazione *f*

suggestion box *n* cassetta *m* dei suggerimenti

suggestive [səg·'dʒes·tɪv] *adj* 1. (*lewd*) allusivo, -a 2. (*evocative*) suggestivo, -a

suicidal [ˌsu:·ə·'saɪ·dl] *adj* suicida; **to feel ~** avere impulsi suicidi; *fig* essere molto depresso

suicide ['su:·ə·saɪd] *n* 1. (*act*) suicidio *m;* **to commit ~** suicidarsi 2. *form* (*person*) suicida *mf*

suit [su:t] I. *vt* 1. (*be convenient*) andare bene a; **to ~ sb** andare bene a qu; **that ~s me fine** mi va benissimo 2. (*be right*) addirsi; **they are well ~ed (to** [*o* for] **each other)** stanno bene insieme; **this lifestyle seems to ~ her** sembra che questo stile di vita le si addica 3. (*look attractive with*) stare bene; **this dress ~s you** questo vestito ti sta bene 4. (*choose at will*) **to ~ oneself** fare come si vuole; **~ yourself!** fai pure come vuoi! II. *n* 1. (*jacket and pants*) completo *m;* (*jacket and skirt*) tailleur *m* (gonna); **bathing** [*o* swim] **~** costume *m* (da bagno) 2. LAW azione *f* legale; **to bring** [*o* file] **a ~** intentare un'azione legale 3. GAMES seme *m;* **to follow ~** giocare lo stesso seme; *fig* seguire l'esempio

suitable ['su:·tə·bl] *adj* adatto, -a; **to be ~ for sb** essere adatto a qu; **not ~ for chidren under 14** sconsigliato ai minori di 14 anni

suitcase ['su:t·keɪs] *n* valigia *f*

suite [swi:t] *n* 1. (*set of rooms*) suite *f inv;* **bridal ~** suite nuziale 2. (*set of furniture for living room*) salotto *m* 3. MUS suite *f inv*

suitor ['su:·tə·] *n* 1. *a.* iron (*potential hus-*

band) pretendente *m* **2.** LAW attore *m*

sulfate ['sʌl·feɪt] *n* solfato *m*

sulfide ['sʌl·faɪd] *n* solfuro *m*

sulfur ['sʌl·fə·] *n* zolfo *m*

sulfur dioxide ['sʌl·fə·daɪ·'ɑ:k·saɪd] *n* anidride *f* solforosa

sulfuric [sʌl·'fjʊ·rɪk] *adj* solforico, -a

sulfuric acid *n* acido *m* solforico

sulfurous ['sʌl·fə·əs] *adj* (*solution*) solforoso, -a; (*smell*) di zolfo

sulk [sʌlk] **I.** *vi* fare il broncio **II.** *n* malumore *m;* **to be in a ~** fare il broncio, -a

sulky ['sʌl·ki] <-ier, -iest> *adj* imbronciato, -a

sullen ['sʌ·lən] *adj* **1.** *pej* (*person*) imbronciato, -a **2.** *liter* (*sky*) cupo, -a

sully ['sʌ·li] <-ied, -ied> *vt* sporcare

sultan ['sʌl·tən] *n* sultano *m*

sultana [sʌl·'tæ·nə] *n* uva *f* sultanina

sultry ['sʌl·tri] <-ier, -iest> *adj* **1.** (*weather*) afoso, -a **2.** (*sensual*) conturbante

sum [sʌm] *n* **1.** (*amount of money*) somma *f* **2.** (*total*) totale *m;* **in ~** in breve **3.** (*calculation*) calcolo *m*

summarize ['sʌ·mə·raɪz] *vt* riassumere

summary ['sʌ·mə·ri] **I.** *n* riassunto *m* **II.** *adj* (*dismissal, execution*) sommario, -a

summation [sə·'meɪ·ʃən] *n* **1.** MATH somma *f* **2.** LAW arringa *f* conclusiva

summer ['sʌ·mə·] **I.** *n* estate *f;* **a ~'s day** un giorno d'estate **II.** *adj* estivo, -a **III.** *vi* passare l'estate

summertime ['sʌ·mə·taɪm] *n* (*season*) estate *m;* **in the ~** d'estate

summer vacation *n* vacanze *fpl* estive

---

i Le **summer vacation** (vacanze estive) durano tre mesi negli Stati Uniti, da metà giugno a metà settembre. In origine, le vacanze avevano una durata tale da permettere ai ragazzi di lavorare in una fattoria o in un ranch. Intorno al '900, con l'incremento dell'immigrazione verso le città, hanno iniziato a svilupparsi i *summer camps* (centri estivi). Vi si mandavano i ragazzi cresciuti in città perché scoprissero la natura. Oggi, i ragazzi possono andarci per suonare, fare equitazione, giocare a baseball, ecc.

---

summery ['sʌ·mə·ri] *adj* estivo, -a

summing-up [ˌsʌ·mɪŋ·'ʌp] <summings-up> *n* LAW ricapitolazione *f*

summit ['sʌ·mɪt] *n* **1.** (*top of mountain*) vetta *f* **2.** *fig* (*of career, power*) apice *m* **3.** POL vertice *m,* summit *m;* **to hold a ~** organizzare un vertice; **~ conference** (conferenza *f* al) vertice *m*

summon ['sʌ·mən] *vt* (*people, meeting*) convocare; LAW citare (a comparire)

◆**summon up** *vt* (*fare appello a*) **to ~ the courage/strength to do sth** fare appello al proprio coraggio/alla propria forza per fare qc

summons ['sʌ·mənz] *npl* LAW mandato *m* di comparizione; **to issue a ~** emettere un mandato di comparizione; **to serve sb with a ~** notificare a qu mandato di comparizione

sump [sʌmp] *n* **1.** (*cesspit*) pozzo *m* nero **2.** MIN pozzo *m* di drenaggio

sumptuous ['sʌm·tʃʊ·əs] *adj* sontuoso, -a

sun [sʌn] **I.** *n* sole *m;* **the ~'s rays** i raggi del sole; **the rising ~** il sole nascente; **the setting ~** il sole che tramonta; **to sit in the ~** star seduto al sole ▶ **to call sb every name under the ~** dirne di tutti i colori a qu; **to do/try everything under the ~** fare/provare tutto il possibile **II.** <-nn-> *vt* **to ~ oneself** prendere il sole

sunbaked ['sʌn·beɪkt] *adj* arso, -a dal sole

sunbath *n* bagno *m* di sole

sunbathe ['sʌn·beɪð] *vi* prendere il sole

sunbeam ['sʌn·bi:m] *n* raggio *m* di sole

sunblock ['sʌn·blɑ:k] *n* crema *f* solare a schermo totale

sunburn ['sʌn·bɜ:rn] *n* scottatura *f* solare

sunburned *adj,* **sunburnt** *adj* scottato, -a; (*tanned*) abbronzato, -a

sundae ['sʌn·di] *n* coppa gelato con frutta, nocciole, panna, etc.

Sunday ['sʌn·dəɪ] *n* domenica *f;* **Palm/Easter ~** domenica delle Palme; *s.a.* **Friday**

Sunday best *n,* **Sunday clothes** *npl* vestito *m* della domenica

Sunday school *n* REL ≈ catechismo *m*

sundial *n* meridiana *f*

sundown *n* s. **sunset**

sun-dried *adj* seccato, -a al sole

sundry ['sʌn·dri] *adj* vari, -e; **~ items** oggetti *m* vari *pl*

sunflower ['sʌnˌflaˑʊə·] *n* girasole *m*

sunflower oil *n* olio *m* di semi di girasole

sunflower seed *n* seme *m* di girasole

sung [sʌŋ] *pp of* **sing**

sunglasses ['sʌnˌglæ·sɪs] *npl* occhiali *mpl* da sole

sunhat *n* cappello *m* da sole

sunk [sʌŋk] *pp of* **sink**

sunken ['sʌn·kən] *adj* **1.** (*ship, treasure*) sommerso, -a **2.** (*cheeks, eyes*) infossato, -a

sunlight ['sʌn·laɪt] *n* luce *f* del sole

sunlit ['sʌn·lɪt] *adj* soleggiato, -a

sunny ['sʌ·ni] <-ier, -iest> *adj* **1.** (*day*) di sole; **it's ~** c'è sole **2.** (*personality*) solare

sunny-side up *adj* all'occhio di bue

sun protection factor *n* fattore *m* di protezione solare

sunrise ['sʌn·raɪz] *n* alba *f;* **at ~** all'alba

sunrise industry *n* industria *f* in crescita

sunroof ['sʌn·ru:f] *n* tettuccio *m* apribile

sunroom *n* giardino *m* d'inverno, veranda *f* chiusa

sunscreen *n* crema *f* con filtro solare

sunset ['sʌn·set] *n* tramonto *m;* **at ~** al tramonto

sunshade ['sʌn·ʃeɪd] *n* **1.** (*umbrella*) parasole *m inv* **2.** (*awning*) tenda *f* (parasole)

sunshine ['sʌn·ʃaɪn] *n* sole *m;* **in the ~** al sole

sunspot ['sʌn·spɑːt] *n* macchia *f* solare

sunstroke *n* insolazione *f,* colpo *m* di sole; **to have ~** aver preso un'insolazione

suntan ['sʌn·tæn] *n* abbronzatura *f;* **to get a ~** abbronzarsi

suntan lotion *n* crema *f* solare

suntanned *adj* abbronzato, -a

suntan oil *n* olio *m* solare

sunup ['sʌn·ʌp] *n s.* **sunrise**

sun visor *n* AUTO aletta *f* parasole

super ['suː·pɚ] **I.** *adj inf* fantastico, -a **II.** *adv inf* super **III.** *n* **1.** *inf s.* **supervisor** supervisore, -a *m, f* **2.** AUTO (benzina *f*) super *f*

superabundant [ˌsuː·pər·ə·'bʌn·dənt] *adj* sovrabbondante

superb [sə·'pɜːrb] *adj* magnifico, -a

Super Bowl *n finale tra le due squadre vincitrici dei due campionati di football americano*

i Nel football americano professionistico, il **Super Bowl** è la finale disputata ogni anno i cui vincitori diventano i campioni della *U.S. National Football League* (il campionato nazionale di football - la NFL). Dal 1967, la finale è giocata dalle due migliori squadre della NFL la domenica del Super Bowl, il *Super Bowl Sunday,* al termine della stagione del football ed è oggi uno degli avvenimenti più seguiti sulla televisione americana.

supercharged ['suː·pə·tʃɑːrdʒd] *adj* **1.** (*engine*) (super)compresso, -a **2.** (*atmosphere*) carico, -a di tensione

supercharger ['suː·pɚ·ˌtʃɑːr·dʒɚ] *n* TECH compressore *m*

supercilious [ˌsuː·pɚ·'sɪ·li·əs] *adj pej* altezzoso, -a

superego [ˌsuː·pɚ·'iː·goʊ] *n* PSYCH Super Io *m*

superficial [ˌsuː·pɚ·'fɪ·ʃl] *adj* superficiale

superficiality [ˌsuː·pɚ·ˌfɪ·ʃɪ·'æ·lə·ti] *n* superficialità *f*

superfluous [suː·'pɜːr·flʊ·əs] *adj* superfluo, -a

superglue® ['suː·pə·gluː] *n* attaccatutto *m*

superhero ['suː·pɚ·ˌhɪ·ə·rəʊ] <-heroes> *n inf* supereroe *m*

superhighway ['suː·pɚ·'haɪ·weɪ] *n* autostrada *f* (a varie corsie); **information ~** superstrada *f* dell'informazione

superhuman [ˌsuː·pɚ·'hjuː·mən] *adj* sovrumano, -a

superimpose [ˌsuː·pɚ·ɪm·'poʊz] *vt* PHOT sovrapporre

superintend [ˌsuː·pɚ·ɪn·'tend] *vt* soprintendere a

superintendent [ˌsuː·pɚ·ɪn·'ten·dənt] *n* **1.** (*person in charge: of department, school district*) direttore, -trice *m, f;* (*of building*) custode *mf* **2.** LAW (*police officer*) soprintendente *mf*

superior [sə·'pɪ·ri·ɚ] **I.** *adj* **1.** (*better, senior*)

superiore; **to be ~** (**to sb/sth**) essere meglio (di qu/qc) **2.** (*greater in amount*) **a ~ number of sth** un numero superiore di qc **II.** *n* superiore *mf*

superiority [sə·ˌpɪ·ri·'ɔː·rə·ti] *n* superiorità *f*

superiority complex *n inf* complesso *m* di superiorità

superlative [sə·'pɜːr·lə·tɪv] **I.** *adj* **1.** (*best*) eccezionale **2.** LING superlativo, -a **II.** *n* LING superlativo *m*

superman ['suː·pɚ·mæn] *n* superuomo *m;* CINE Superman *m*

supermarket ['suː·pɚ·ˌmɑːr·kɪt] *n* supermercato *m*

supermodel ['suː·pɚ·ˌmɑː·dəl] *n* top model *f inv*

supernatural [ˌsuː·pɚ·'næt·ʃɚ·əl] **I.** *adj* soprannaturale **II.** *n* **the ~** il soprannaturale

supernumerary [ˌsuː·pɚ·'nuː·mə·re·ri] **I.** *adj form* soprannumerario, -a **II.** <-ies> *n form* impiegato, -a soprannumerario *m;* THEAT comparsa *f*

superpower ['suː·pɚ·ˌpa·ʊɚ] *n* POL superpotenza *f*

superscript ['suː·pɚ·skrɪpt] *n* TYPO apice *m*

supersede [ˌsuː·pɚ·'siːd] *vt* sostituire

supersonic [ˌsuː·pɚ·'sɑː·nɪk] *adj* AVIAT supersonico, -a

superstar ['suː·pər·stɑːr] *n* superstar *f inv*

superstition [ˌsuː·pɚ·'stɪ·ʃən] *n* superstizione *f*

superstitious [ˌsuː·pɚ·'stɪ·ʃəs] *adj* superstizioso, -a

superstore ['suː·pɚ·stɔːr] *n* ipermercato *m*

superstructure ['suː·pɚ·ˌstrʌk·tʃɚ] *n* sovrastruttura *f*

supertanker ['suː·pɚ·ˌtæŋ·kɚ] *n* superpetroliera *f*

supervise ['suː·pɚ·vaɪz] *vt* (*watch over*) supervisionare; (*thesis*) fare da relatore a

supervision [ˌsuː·pɚ·'vɪ·ʒən] *n* supervisione *f;* **under the ~ of sb** sotto la supervisione di qu

supervisor ['suː·pɚ·vaɪ·zɚ] *n* **1.** (*person in charge*) supervisore, -a *m, f* **2.** POL rappresentante del governo nell'amministrazione locale

supervisory [ˌsuː·pɚ·'vaɪ·zə·i] *adj* di supervisore

supine [suː·'paɪn] **I.** *adj* supino, -a **II.** *adv* **to lie ~** stare supino

supper ['sʌ·pɚ] *n* cena *f;* **to have ~** cenare

suppertime *n* ora *f* di cena

supplant [sə·'plænt] *vt* rimpiazzare

supple ['sʌ·pl] *adj* (*leather, skin*) elastico, -a; (*person*) agile

supplement ['sʌ·plə·mənt] **I.** *n* **1.** (*something extra*) supplemento *m* **2.** (*part of newspaper*) supplemento *m* **3.** (*of book*) supplemento *m* **II.** *vt* (*income*) arrotondare; (*diet*) integrare

supplementary [ˌsʌ·plə·'men·ṭɚi] *adj* supplementare

suppleness ['sʌ·pl·nɪs] *n* (*of leather, skin*) elasticità *f;* (*of person*) agilità *f*

supplicant ['sʌ·plə·kənt] *n* supplicante *mf*

supplication [ˌsʌ·plə·'keɪ·ʃən] *n* supplica *f*

S

supplier [sə·'pla·ɪə·] *n* fornitore, -trice *m, f*
supply [sə·'plaɪ] I. <-ie-> *vt* 1. (*fornire: electricity, food, money*) distribuire; **to be accused of ~ing drugs** essere accusato di spacciare droga 2. COM fornire II. *n* 1. (*act of providing: of electricity, water*) erogazione *f* 2. ECON offerta *f;* **~ and demand** offerta e domanda; **to be in short ~** scarseggiare
supply-side economics [sə·'plaɪ·saɪd ˌiː·kə·'nɑː·mɪks] *npl* economia *f* dell'offerta
support [sə·'pɔːrt] I. *vt* 1. (*hold up: roof, weight*) sostenere; (*weight*); **to ~ oneself on sth** appoggiarsi a qc 2. (*provide for*) mantenere; **to ~ four children** mantenere quattro figli; **to ~ oneself** mantenersi 3. (*provide with money*) finanziare 4. (*encourage*) appoggiare 5. (*show to be true*) avvalorare II. *n* 1. (*backing, help*) appoggio *m;* **to give sb moral ~** dare appoggio morale a qu 2. (*structure*) supporto *m; fig* (*person*) sostegno *m* 3. FIN finanziamento *m* 4. (*confirmation*) avvaloramento *f;* **to lend ~ to sth** avvalorare qc; **in ~ of sth** a sostegno di qc
supporter *n* 1. (*of cause, candidate*) sostenitore, -trice *m, f* 2. SPORTS (*fan*) tifoso, -a *m, f* 3. SPORTS (*protector for genitals*) conchiglia *f*
supporting *adj* (*film, role, actor*) secondario, -a
supportive [sə·'pɔːr·ṭɪv] *adj* comprensivo, -a; **to be ~ of sth/sb** appoggiare qc/qu
suppose [sə·'poʊz] *vt* 1. **to ~** (**that**) ... supporre che ...; **I don't ~ so** suppongo di no; **let's ~ that** supponiamo che +*subj* 2. (*believe, think*) ritenere 3. (*obligation*) **to be ~d to do sth** dover fare qc; **he was ~d to collect the money** doveva raccogliere i soldi; **you are not ~d to know that** non lo dovresti sapere 4. (*opinion*) **the book is ~d to be very good** pare che sia un libro molto bello; **she is ~d to be intelligent** dicono che sia intelligente
supposed *adj* (*killer*) presunto, -a; (*date*) supposto, -a
supposedly [sə·'poʊ·zɪd·li] *adv* a quanto pare
supposing *conj* **~ that** ... supponendo che ...
supposition [ˌsʌ·pə·'zɪ·ʃən] *n* supposizione *f*
suppository [sə·'pɑː·zə·tɔː·ri] <-ies> *n* supposta *f*
suppress [sə·'pres] *vt* 1. (*criticism, revolt, terrorism*) reprimere 2. (*sneeze, yawn, emotion*) reprimere; (*evidence, information*) occultare 3. MED inibire
suppression [sə·'pre·ʃən] *n* 1. (*of criticism, revolt*) repressione *f* 2. (*of anger, emotion*) repressione *f;* (*of evidence*) occultazione *f* 3. MED inibizione *f* 4. PSYCH (*of memories*) rimozione *f*
supremacy [sə·'pre·mə·si] *n* supremazia *f*
supreme [sə·'priːm] I. *adj* 1. (*authority*) supremo, -a; (*commander*) in capo; **Supreme Court** Corte *f* Suprema 2. (*achievement, sacrifice*) estremo, -a; **to show ~ courage** mostrare estremo coraggio II. *adv* **to reign ~** regnare incontestato

surcharge ['sɜːr·tʃɑːrdʒ] I. *n* supplemento *m* II. *vt* far pagare un supplemento a
sure [ʃʊr] I. *adj* 1. (*certain*) sicuro, -a; **to be ~ of sth** essere sicuro di qc; **to be ~** (**that**) ... essere sicuro che ... +*subj;* **to make ~** (**that**) ... assicurarsi che.. +*subj;* **to not be ~ if ...** non essere sicuro che ... +*subj;* **she is ~ to come** verrà di sicuro; **are you ~ you won't come?** sei sicuro di non venire?; **I'm not ~ why/how** non so bene perchè come; **~ thing!** certo!; **for ~** con certezza 2. (*confident*) **to be ~ of oneself** essere sicuro di sì II. *adv* certo; **~ I will!** *inf* certo (che sì); **~ enough** come volevasi dimostrare ▸ **as ~ as I'm standing here** come è vero che mi chiamo ...
sure-footed [ˌʃʊr·fʊː·ṭɪd] *adj* 1. (*when walking, climbing*) dal passo sicuro 2. (*confident*) sicuro, -a di sè
surely ['ʃʊr·li] *adv* 1. (*certainly*) indubbiamente 2. (*to show astonishment*) davvero; **~ you don't expect me to believe that?** non ti aspetti davvero che io ci creda 3. (*yes, certainly*) certo!
surety ['ʃʊ·rə·ti] <-ies> *n* LAW 1. (*person*) garante *mf;* **to stand ~** (**for sb**) farsi garante (di qu) 2. (*guarantee*) garanzia *f*
surf [sɜːrf] I. *n* onde *fpl* II. *vi* SPORTS fare surf III. *vt* COMPUT **to ~ the Internet** navigare su Internet
surface ['sɜːr·fɪs] I. *n* superficie *f;* **on the ~** *fig* in apparenza; **to scratch the ~ of sth** trattare qc superficialmente II. *vi* venire a galla III. *vt* (*road, wall*) rivestire; (*with asphalt*) asfaltare
surface mail *n* **by ~** (*land*) per via terrestra; (*sea*) per via marittima
surface tension *n* PHYS tensione *f* superficiale
surface-to-air missile *n* MIL missile *m* terraaria
surfboard ['sɜːrf·bɔːrd] *n* tavola *f* da surf
surfeit ['sɜːr·fɪt] *n form* eccesso *m*
surfer ['sɜːr·fə·] *n* 1. surfista *mf* 2. COMPUT internauta *mf*
surfing ['sɜːr·fɪŋ] *n* surf *m inv*
surge [sɜːrdʒ] I. *vi* 1. (*move forward*) riversarsi; (*waves*) sollevarsi 2. (*increase*) avere un picco II. *n* (*of waves*) ondata *f;* (*of anger*) accesso *m;* (*of indignation*) ondata *f;* (*of prices, support*) impennata *f;* **power ~** sovratensione *f*
surgeon ['sɜːr·dʒən] *n* chirurgo *m*
surgery ['sɜːr·dʒə·ri] *n* chirurgia *f;* **to perform ~** praticare un intervento (chirurgico); **to undergo ~** subire un intervento (chirurgico)
surgical ['sɜːr·dʒɪ·kl] *adj* (*procedure*) chirurgico, -a; (*collar, gloves*) da chirurgo
Surinam(e) [ˌsʊ·rɪ·'nɑːm] *n* il Suriname *m*
Surinamese [ˌsʊ·rə·næ·'miːz] I. *adj* del Suriname II. *n* abitante *mf* del Suriname
surly ['sɜːr·li] <-ier, -iest> *adj* scontroso, -a
surmise [sə·'maɪz] *vt form* supporre
surmount [sə·'maʊnt] *vt* 1. (*overcome*) sormontare 2. *form* (*be on top of*) sormontare
surname ['sɜːr·neɪm] *n* cognome *m*

surpass [səˈpæs] *vt* sorpassare; **to ~ oneself** superare se stesso

surplus [ˈsɜːrˌpləs] I. *n a.* FIN (*of product*) eccedenza *f* II. *adj* in eccedenza

surprise [səˈpraɪz] I. *n* sorpresa *f;* **in a ~** con sorpresa; **to sb's ~** con sorpresa di qu II. *vt* sorprendere; **it ~d her that ...** l'ha sorpresa (il fatto) che ... +*subj;* **to ~ sb doing sth** sorprendere qu nell'atto di fare qc

surprised *adj* sorpreso, -a

surprising *adj* sorprendente

surprisingly *adv* sorprendentemente

surreal [səˈriːˌəl] *adj* surreale

surrealism [səˈriːˌəˌlɪˌzəm] *n* ART surrealismo *m*

surrealist [səˈriːˌəˌlɪst] ART I. *n* surrealista *mf* II. *adj* surrealista

surrender [səˈrenˌdər] I. *vi* arrendersi; **to ~ to sb** arrendersi a qu II. *vt form* consegnare III. *n* 1. (*giving up*) resa *f* 2. *form* (*of document*) consegna *f*

surreptitious [ˌsɜːrəpˈtɪˌʃəs] *adj* furtivo, -a

surrogacy [ˈsʌˌrəˌgəˌsi] *n* maternità *f* sostitutiva

surrogate [ˈsɜːˌrəˌgɪt] I. *adj* (*substitute*) sostitutivo, -a II. *n* sostituto, -a *m, f*

surrogate mother *n* madre *f* surrogata

surround [səˈraʊnd] I. *vt* circondare II. *n* (*frame*) bordo *m*

surrounding *adj* cirocstante

surroundings *npl* dintorni *mpl*

surtax [ˈsɜːrˌtæks] *n* FIN, POL sovrattassa *f*

surveillance [səˈveɪˌləns] *n* sorveglianza *f;* **to be under ~** essere sotto sorveglianza

survey[1] [səˈveɪ] *vt* 1. (*poll*) fare un sondaggio su 2. GEO fare dei rilevamenti di 3. (*research*) indagare 4. (*look at carefully*) ispezionare

survey[2] [ˈsəˌveɪ] *n* 1. (*poll*) sondaggio *m* 2. GEO rilevamento *m* 3. (*report*) indagine *f* 4. (*examination*) perizia *f*

surveyor [səˈveˌɪə] *n* GEO topografo, -a *m, f*

survival [səˈvaɪˌvl] *n* 1. sopravvivenza *f* 2. (*relic*) vestigio *m* ▶ **the ~ of the fittest** la legge del più forte

survive [səˈvaɪv] I. *vi* (*stay alive: person*) sopravvivere; (*book*) conservarsi; **to ~ on sth** *inf* vivere di qc II. *vt* sopravvivere a; **to ~ an accident** sopravvivere a un incidente

surviving *adj* sopravvivente

survivor [səˈvaɪˌvə] *n* sopravvivente *mf*

susceptible [səˈsepˌtəˌbl] *adj* sensibile; MED propenso, -a

suspect[1] [səˈspekt] *vt* 1. (*think likely*) sospettare; **to ~ sth** sospettare qc 2. (*consider guilty*) sospettare di; **to ~ sb's motives** avere dei dubbi sulle motivazioni di qu

suspect[2] [ˈsʌˌspekt] I. *n* sospetto, -a *m, f* II. *adj* sospetto, -a

suspend [səˈspend] *vt* 1. (*stop temporarily*) sospendere; **to ~ one's judgement** riservarsi di giudicare; **a 6 month sentence ~ed for two years** una condanna a 6 mesi con condizionale di due anni 2. SCHOOL, UNIV sospendere

3. (*hang*) sospendere

suspender [səˈspenˌdə] *n pl* reggicalze *m inv*

suspense [səˈspens] *n* 1. (*uncertainty*) incertezza *f;* **to keep sb in ~** tenere qu in sospeso 2. CINE suspense *m*

suspension [səˈspenˌtʃən] *n* 1. (*stop*) sospensione *f* 2. SCHOOL, UNIV sospensione *f*

suspension bridge *n* ponte *m* sospeso

suspicion [səˈspɪˌʃən] *n* 1. (*belief*) sospetto *m;* **to arrest sb on ~ of sth** arrestare qu come sospetto per qc; **to be above ~** essere al di sopra di ogni sospetto 2. (*mistrust*) sospetto *m* 3. (*small amount*) accenno *m*

suspicious [səˈspɪˌʃəs] *adj* 1. (*arousing suspicion*) sospetto, -a 2. (*lacking trust*) sospettoso, -a

sustain [səˈsteɪn] *vt* 1. (*maintain*) mantenere 2. (*withstand*) sopportare 3. (*uphold: conviction*) avvalorare; (*objection*) accogliere

sustainable [səˈsteɪˌnəˌbl] *adj* sostenibile

sustained [səˈsteɪnd] *adj* sostenuto, -a; (*applause*) prolungato, -a

sustenance [ˈsʌsˌtənəns] *n* sostentamento *m;* **to give sb ~** nutrire qu

suture [ˈsuːˌtʃə] MED I. *n* (*stitch*) sutura *f;* (*thread*) filo *m* per suture II. *vt* suturare

svelte [svelt] *adj* snello, -a

SW [ˌesˈdʌˌblˌjuː] *abbr of* **southwest** SO

swab [swɑːb] I. *n* 1. MED (*pad*) tampone *m;* (*for examination*) tampone *m* 2. NAUT redazza *f* II.<-bb-> *vt* 1. MED pulire (con un tampone) 2. (*wash*) lavare (con una redazza)

swagger [ˈswæˌgə] I. *n* arroganza *f* II. *vi* pavoneggiarsi

swallow[1] [ˈswɑːˌloʊ] I. *vt* ingoiare *inf* II. *vi* deglutire III. *n* sorso *m*

◆ **swallow down** *vt* tranguggiare

◆ **swallow up** *vt* (*absorb*) mangiare

swallow [ˈswɑːˌloʊ] *n* ZOOL rondine *f* ▶ **one ~ doesn't make a summer** *prov* una rondine non fa primavera *prov*

swam [swæm] *vi pt of* **swim**

swamp [swɑːmp] I. *n* acquitrino *m* II. *vt* (*flood*) inondare; **to ~ sb (with sth)** inondare qu di qc; **to be ~ed with sth** essere inondato di qc

swamp fever *n* MED malaria *f*

swampland [ˈswɑːmpˌlænd] *n* terreno *m* acquitrinoso

swampy [ˈswɑːmˌpi] <-ier, -iest> *adj* acquitrinoso, -a

swan [swɑːn] *n* cigno *m*

swan dive *n* tuffo *m* ad angelo

swank [swæŋk] I. *adj* 1. (*grand*) sciccoso, -a 2. (*pretentious*) pretenzioso, -a II. *n* sciccheria *f*

swanky [ˈswæŋˌki] *adj* sciccoso, -a

swan song *n* canto *m* del cigno

swap [swɑːp] I.<-pp-> *vt* scambiare; **to ~ sth (for sth)** scambiare qc (con qc); **to ~ sth with sb** scambiare qc con qu II.<-pp-> *vi* scambiare III. *n* scambio *m*

swarm [swɔːrm] I. *vi* 1. ZOOL, BIO (*bees*) scia-

mare **2.**(*move in large group*) accalcarsi **3.**(*be full*) **to be ~ing with sth** brulicare di qc **II.** *n* **1.**(*of bees*) sciame *m* **2.** *fig* (*of people*) sciame *m*
swarthy ['swɔːr·ði] <-ier, -iest> *adj* scuro, -a
swashbuckling ['swɑːʃ·ˌbʌk·lɪŋ] *adj* di cappa e spada
swastika ['swɑːs·tɪ·kə] *n* svastica *f*
swat [swɑːt] <-tt-> *vt* (*insect*) schiacciare
swatch [swɑːtʃ] *n* (*sample*) campione *m;* (*sample book*) campionario *m*
swath *n* **1.**(*long strip*) striscia *f* **2.**(*space*) andana *f* ▶ **to cut a ~ across** [*o* **through**] **sth** aprirsi un varco in mezzo a qc
swathe [sweɪð] **I.** *vt* (*wrap around*) avvolgere; (*with bandages*) bendare **II.** *n* benda *f*
sway [sweɪ] **I.** *vi* oscillare **II.** *vt* **1.**(*move from side to side*) far oscillare **2.**(*persuade*) persuadere **III.** *n* **1.**(*influence*) influenza *f;* **under the ~ of sb/sth** sotto l'influsso di qu/qc **2.** *form* (*control*) controllo *m;* **to hold ~ over sth/sb** esercitare un controllo su qc/qu
Swazi ['swɑː·zi] **I.** *adj* swazi *inv* **II.** *n* swazi *mf*
Swaziland ['swɑː·zi·lænd] *n* Swaziland *m*
swear [swer] <swore, sworn> **I.** *vi* **1.**(*take oath*) giurare; **to ~ on the Bible** giurare sulla Bibbia; **I couldn't ~ to it** *inf* non ci giurerei **2.**(*curse*) imprecare **II.** *vt* giurare; **to ~ blind allegiance to sb/sth** giurare fedeltà incondizionata a qu/qc; **to ~ sb to secrecy** far giurare a qu di mantenere il silenzio
◆**swear by** *vt* **to ~ sth** avere una fiducia cieca in qc
◆**swear in** *vt* LAW **to ~ sb** far prestare giuramento a qu
◆**swear off** *vt* **to ~ sth** giurare di smettere con qc
swearing *n* parolacce *mpl*
swearword ['swer·wɜːrd] *n* parolaccia *f*
sweat [swet] **I.** *n* **1.**(*perspiration*) sudore *m;* **to break into a ~** cominciare a sudare **2.**(*effort*) faticaccia *f;* **no ~** *inf* non c'è problema **3.** *pl inf* (*sweatsuit*) tuta *f* (da ginnastica) **II.** *vi* (*perspire*) sudare; **to ~ with sth** sudare per qc **III.** *vt* sudare; **to ~ bullets** *inf* sudare freddo
◆**sweat out** *vt* **1.** *inf* (*endure*) **to sweat it out** tener duro **2.** *sl* (*await*) **to sweat it out** stare col fiato sospeso
sweatband *n* (*for head*) fascia *f* tergisudore; (*for wrists*) polsino *m*
sweater ['swe·t̬ɚ] *n* golf *m inv*
sweatshirt ['swet·ʃɜːrt] *n* felpa *f*
sweatshop ['swet·ʃɑːp] *n pej: fabbrica che sfrutta la manodopera*
sweatsuit *n,* **sweat suit** *n* tuta (da ginnastica)
sweaty ['swe·t̬i] <-ier, -iest> *adj* sudato, -a
Swede [swiːd] *n* svedese *mf*
Sweden ['swiː·dn] *n* GEO la Svezia *f*
Swedish ['swiː·dɪʃ] **I.** *adj* svedese, -a **II.** *n* **1.**(*person*) svedese *mf* **2.** LING svedese *m*
sweep [swiːp] <swept, swept> **I.** *n* **1.**(*cleaning action*) spazzata *f;* **to give sth a ~** dare una

spazzata a qc **2.**(*movement*) **with a ~ of her arm** con un movimento ampio del braccio **3.**(*search*) **to make a ~ of an area** rastrellare una zona **4.** SPORTS (*series of wins*) **a three-game ~** tre vittorie consecutive **5.**(*chimney cleaner*) **chimney ~** spazzacamino *m* ▶ **to make a clean ~** fare piazza pulita **II.** *vt* **1.**(*clean with broom: floor*) spazzare; (*chimney*) pulire **2.**(*remove*) spazzare (via) **3.**(*search*) rastrellare **4.**(*win*) riportare una vittoria schiacciante in; **to ~ a series** riportare una serie di vittorie schiacciante ▶ **to ~ sb off his/her feet** fare innamorare perdutamente qu **III.** *vi* **1.**(*clean with broom*) spazzare **2.**(*move*) **to ~ into power** riportare una vittoria schiacciante alle elezioni; **to ~ into a room** piombare in una stanza **3.**(*follow path*) **the road ~s around the lake** la strada si snoda intorno al lago **4.**(*extend*) espandersi
◆**sweep aside** *vt* **1.**(*cause to move*) spostare **2.**(*dismiss*) ignorare
◆**sweep away** *vt* (*remove*) spazzare via
◆**sweep out** *vt* portare via
◆**sweep up** *vt* **1.** spazzare **2.**(*gather*) tirare su
sweeper *n* **1.**(*device*) scopa *f* **2.**(*person*) spazzino, -a *m, f*
sweeping **I.** *adj* **1.**(*broad: gesture*) ampio, -a **2.**(*overwhelming: victory*) schiacciante **II.** *npl* spazzatura *f;* **the ~s of society** i rifiuti della società
sweepstakes ['swiː·p·steɪk] *n scommessa in cui tutte le puntate vanno al vincitore*
sweet [swiːt] **I.**<-er, -est> *adj* **1.**(*like sugar*) dolce **2.**(*pleasant*) dolce; **to go one's own ~ way** andare dritto per la propria strada **3.**(*cute*) adorabile **4.**(*kind: gentile*) dolce; **to be ~ on sb** essere innamorato di qu **II.** *n pl* (*candy*) caramella *f*
sweet-and-sour [ˌswiːt·ən·ˌsaˈʊɚ] *adj* in agrodolce
sweetbread ['swiːt·bred] *n pl* CULIN animella *f*
sweet corn ['swiːt·kɔːrn] *n* mais *m* dolce *inv*
sweeten ['swiː·t̬ən] *vt* addolcire; **to ~ sb up** conciliarsi qu
sweetener *n* **1.** CULIN dolcificante *f* **2.** *inf* (*incentive*) incentivo *m*
sweetheart ['swiːt·hɑːrt] *n* **1.**(*kind person*) tesoro *m* **2.**(*term of endearment*) tesoro *m* **3.**(*boyfriend, girlfriend*) moroso, -a *m, f*
sweetie *n inf* tesoro *m*
sweetness *n* dolcezza *m;* **to be all ~ and light** *fig* essere tutto zucchero e miele
sweet pea *n* pisello *m* odoroso
sweet potato *n* patata *f* dolce [*o* americana]
sweet-talk *vt* imbonire
sweet tooth *n* **to have a ~** essere goloso, -a (di dolci)
swell [swel] <swelled, swelled *o* swollen> **I.** *vi* **1.**(*get bigger*) gonfiarsi **2.**(*get louder: sound*) aumentare di volume **3.**(*increase*) aumentare **II.** *vt* **1.**(*in size*) accrescere **2.**(*in number*) ingrossare **III.** *n* (*of sea*) ondata *f; a*

heavy ~ una grossa ondata **IV.** <-er, -est> *adj inf* fantastico, -a

swelling *n* gonfiore *m*

swelter ['swel·tə·] *vi* morire di caldo

sweltering *adj* (*heat, temperatures*) torrido, -a

swept [swept] *vt, vi pt of* **sweep**

swerve [swɜːrv] **I.** *vi* **1.** (*car*) fare uno scarto; (*person*) sterzare bruscamente **2.** (*not uphold*) **to ~ from** sth deviare da qc **II.** *n* (*of car*) scarto *m*; (*of person*) sterzata *f* (brusca)

swift[1] [swɪft] *adj* rapido, -a

swift[2] [swɪft] *n* ZOOL rondone *m*

swiftly *adv* rapidamente

swiftness *n* rapidità *f*

swig [swɪg] **I.** <-gg-> *vt inf* tracannare **II.** *n inf* sorsata *m*; **to take a ~** bere un sorso

swill [swɪl] **I.** *n* **1.** (*pig feed*) pastone *m* per maiali; *fig, iron* bevuta *f* **2.** (*garbage*) resti *mpl* **II.** *vt* **1.** (*swirl: liquid*) remover **2.** (*drink*) trac- annare **3.** (*rinse*) sciacquare

◆**swill down** *vt inf* **to swill sth down** tracan- nare qc

swim [swɪm] **I.** <swam, swum> *vi* **1. a.** *fig* (*in water*) nuotare; **the french fries were ~ming in grease** le patatine erano grassissime **2.** (*whirl*) **her head was ~ming** le girava la testa **3.** (*be full of water*) essere inondato, -a; **to ~ with tears** essere in un mare di lacrime **II.** <swam, swum> *vt* **1.** (*cross*) attraversare a nuoto **2.** (*do*) **to ~ a few strokes** fare qualche bracciata **III.** *n* nuotata *f*; **I'm going to take a ~** vado a farmi una nuotata

swimmer ['swɪ·mə·] *n* nuotatore, -trice *m, f*

swimming *n* nuoto *m*

swimmingly *adv inf* **to go ~** filare liscio come l'olio

swimming pool *n* piscina *f*

swimming trunks *npl* calzoncini *m* da bagno *pl*

swimsuit ['swɪm·suːt] *n* costume *m* da bagno

swindle ['swɪn·dl] **I.** *vt* portare via (con la truffa) **II.** *n* truffa *f*

swindler ['swɪnd·lə·] *n pej* truffatore, -trice *m, f*

swine [swaɪn] *n* **1.** *liter* (*pig*) porco *m* **2.** <-(s)> *pej, inf* (*mean person*) porco, -a *m, f*

swing [swɪŋ] **I.** *n* **1.** (*movement*) oscillazione *f* **2.** (*punch*) pugno *m*; **to take a ~ at sb** (cer- care di) dare un pugno a qu **3.** (*hanging seat*) altalena *f* **4.** (*sharp change*) cambiamento *m* brusco; **a mood ~** uno sbalzo di umore; POL mutamento *m* di tendenza **5.** (*quick trip*) viag- gio *m* **6.** MUS swing *m* ▶ **to get** (**back**) **into the ~ of things** *inf* riprendere la mano **II.** <swung, swung> *vi* **1.** (*move back and forth*) oscillare, dondolare; (*move circularly*) ruotare **2.** (*hit*) **~ at sb** (cercare di) dare un pugno a qu **3.** (*on hanging seat*) dondolarsi **4.** (*alter*) cambiare; **to ~ between two things** oscillare tra due cose **5.** (*be exciting*) essere movimentato, -a **III.** <swung, swung> *vt* **1.** (*move back and forth*) far dondolare **2.** *inf* (*influence*) influen- zare

◆**swing around** *vi* girarsi di scatto

swing bridge *n* ponte *m* girevole

swing shift *n* turno *m* serale

swipe [swaɪp] **I.** *vt* **1.** *inf* (*steal*) fregare **2.** (*pass: card*) passare **3.** (*graze: car*) strus- ciare contro **II.** *n* (*blow*) colpo *m*; *fig* (*criti- cism*) critica *f*; **to take a ~ at sb** (*hit*) (cercare di) colpire qu; (*criticize*) criticare qu

swirl [swɜːrl] **I.** *vi* volteggiare **II.** *vt* far volteg- giare **III.** *n* turbine *m*

swish [swɪʃ] **I.** *vi* (*cane*) sibilare; (*dress*) frus- ciare; (*water*) gorgogliare **II.** *vt* (*cane*) fare sibi- lare **III.** *n* (*of cane*) sibilo *m*; (*of dress*) fus- cio *m*

Swiss [swɪs] **I.** *adj* svizzero, -a; **~ German**/ **French** svizzero tedesco/francese **II.** *n* sviz- zero, -a *m, f*

Swiss ball *n* palla *f* da ginnastica

switch [swɪtʃ] **I.** <-es> *n* **1.** ELEC interruttore *m* **2.** (*substitution*) sostituzione *f* **3.** (*change*) cambio *m* **4.** RAIL (*device*) scambio *m* **II.** *vi* cambiare; **to ~ with sb** fare cambio con qu; **to ~ from sth to sth** passare da qc a qc **III.** *vt* scambiare; **to ~ sth for sth** scambiare qc con qc

◆**switch off I.** *vt* (*machine, engine*) speg- nere; (*water, electricity*) chiudere **II.** *vi* **1.** (*machine, engine*) spegnersi **2.** (*lose atten- tion*) sconnettersi

◆**switch on I.** *vt* (*machine, engine*) accen- dere; **to ~ the charm** diventare tutto, -a sorrisi **II.** *vi* accendersi

◆**switch over** *vi* migrare; **to ~ to another channel** cambiare canale

◆**switch around** *vt* scambiare

switchback ['swɪtʃ·bæk] *n* strada *f* a zigzag

switchblade ['swɪtʃ·bleɪd] *n* coltello *m* a ser- ramanico

switchboard ['swɪtʃ·bɔːrd] *n* **1.** ELEC commu- tatore *m* **2.** TEL centralino *m*

switchboard operator *n* centralinista *mf*

switchman <-men> *n* deviatore *m*

switchyard *n* stazione *f* di smistamento

Switzerland ['swɪt·sə·lənd] *n* la Svizzera *f*

swivel ['swɪ·vəl] **I.** *n* piattaforma *f* girevole **II.** <-ll-, -l-> *vt* girare

swivel chair *n* sedia *f* girevole

swizzle stick *n* bastoncino *m* (per mescolare i cocktail)

swollen ['swoʊ·lən] **I.** *pp of* **swell II.** *adj* gon- fio, -a

swoon [swuːn] **I.** *vi* **1.** (*be in state of ecstasy*) andare in delirio; **to ~ over sb** andare in deli- rio per qu **2.** *liter* (*faint*) svenire **II.** *n liter* svenimento *m*

swoop [swuːp] **I.** *n* **1.** (*dive*) discesa *f* in pic- chiata **2.** *inf* (*surprise attack*) irruzione *f* ▶ **in one fell ~** in una volta **II.** *vi* **1.** (*dive*) piom- bare; *fig* tuffarsi **2.** *inf* (*make sudden attack*) tuffarsi; (*police*) fare irruzione

sword [sɔːrd] *n* spada *f*; **to draw a ~** sguainare una spada ▶ **to cross ~s with sb** incrociare le spade con qu

swordfish <-(es)> *n* pesce *m* spada
swordplay *n* arte *f* della scherma; **verbal ~** abilità *m* dialettica
swordsman ['sɔːrdz·mən] <-men> *n* **1.** HIST spadaccino *m* **2.** (*fencer*) schermidore *m*
swordsmanship *n* abilità *f* nel maneggiare la spada
swore [swɔːr] *pt of* **swear**
sworn [swɔːrn] **I.** *pp of* **swear II.** *adj* giurato, -a
swum [swʌm] *pp of* **swim**
swung [swʌŋ] *pt, pp of* **swing**
sycamore ['sɪ·kə·mɔːr] *n* platano *m* (americano)
sycophant ['sɪ·kə·fənt] *n pej* ruffiano, -a *m, f*
syllable ['sɪ·lə·bl] *n* sillaba *f;* **stressed/unstressed ~** sillaba tonica/atona; **not a ~** *fig* nemmeno una sillaba
syllabus ['sɪ·lə·bəs] <-es, *form:* syllabi> *n* (*in general*) piano *m* di studi; (*for specific subject*) programma *m*
symbiosis [ˌsɪm·bɪ·'oʊ·sɪs] *n* simbiosi *f*
symbiotic [ˌsɪm·bɪ·'ɑː·t̬ɪk] *adj* BIO simbiotico, -a
symbol ['sɪm·bl] *n* simbolo *m*
symbolic(al) [sɪm·'bɑː·lɪ·k(l)] *adj* simbolico, -a
symbolism ['sɪm·bə·lɪ·zəm] *n* simbolismo *m*
symbolize ['sɪm·bə·laɪz] *vt* simboleggiare
symmetrical [sɪ·'me·trɪ·kl] *adj* simmetrico, -a
symmetry ['sɪ·mə·tri] *n* simmetria *f*
sympathetic [ˌsɪm·pə·'θe·t̬ɪk] *adj* **1.** (*understanding*) comprensivo, -a; (*sympathizing*) compassionevole; **to lend a ~ ear to sb** essere disposto ad ascoltare qu **2.** POL favorevole; **to be ~ towards sb/sth** appoggiare qu/qc
sympathize ['sɪm·pə·θaɪz] *vi* **1.** (*understand*) capire; (*feel compassion for*) provare compassione **2.** (*agree*) essere d'accordo; **to ~ with sth** simpatizzare per qc
sympathizer *n* simpatizzante *mf*
sympathy ['sɪm·pə·θi] *n* **1.** (*compassion*) compassione *f;* (*understanding*) comprensione *f;* **you have my deepest ~** le faccio le mie più sincere condoglianze **2.** (*solidarity*) solidarietà *f*
symphonic [sɪm·'fɑː·nɪk] *adj* sinfonico, -a
symphony ['sɪm·fə·ni] *n* **1.** (*piece of music*) sinfonia *f* **2.** (*orchestra*) orchestra *f* sinfonica
symphony orchestra *n* orchestra *f* sinfonica
symposium [sɪm·'poʊ·zi·əm] <-s *o* -sia> *n form* simposio *m*
symptom ['sɪmp·təm] *n* sintomo *m*
symptomatic [ˌsɪmp·tə·'mæ·t̬ɪk] *adj* sintomatico, -a
synagogue ['sɪ·nə·gɑːg] *n* sinagoga *f*
synchronize ['sɪŋ·krə·naɪz] **I.** *vt* sincronizzare **II.** *vi* sincronizzarsi
synchronous ['sɪŋ·krə·nəs] *adj* sincrono, -a
syndicate[1] ['sɪn·də·kɪt] *n* **1.** ECON consorzio *m* **2.** PUBL agenzia *f* di stampa
syndicate[2] ['sɪn·də·keɪt] *vt* **1.** ECON raggruppare in un consorzio **2.** PUBL vendere

syndication [ˌsɪn·də·'keɪ·ʃən] *n* **1.** ECON raggruppamento *f* in un consorzio **2.** PUBL vendita *f*
syndrome ['sɪn·droʊm] *n* sindrome *m;* **acquired immune deficiency ~** sindrome da immunodeficienza acquisita
synergy ['sɪ·nə·dʒi] *n* sinergia *f*
synod ['sɪ·nəd] *n* sinodo *m*
synonym ['sɪ·nə·nɪm] *n* sinonimo *m*
synonymous [sɪ·'nɒ·nɪ·məs] *adj* sinonimo, -a
synopsis [sɪ·'næp·sɪs] <-es> *n* sinopsi *f inv*
syntactic(al) [sɪn·'tæk·tɪ·k(əl)] *adj* sintattico, -a
syntax ['sɪn·tæks] *n* sintassi *f inv*
synthesis ['sɪnt·θə·sɪs] <-es> *n* sintesi *f inv*
synthesize ['sɪn·θə·saɪz] *vt* sintetizzare
synthesizer *n* sintetizzatore *m*
synthetic [sɪn·'θe·t̬ɪk] *adj* **1.** (*man-made*) sintetico, -a **2.** *pej* (*fake*) artificiale
syphilis ['sɪf·lɪs] *n* sifilide *f*
syphon ['saɪ·fn] *n* sifone *m*
Syria ['sɪ·ri·ə] *n* la Siria *f*
Syrian ['sɪ·ri·ən] **I.** *adj* siriano, -a **II.** *n* siriano, -a *m, f*
syringe [sə·'rɪndʒ] **I.** *n* siringa *f* **II.** *vt* **to ~ sb's ears** riumovere il cerume dalle orecchie di qu iniettando acqua calda con una siringa
syrup ['sɪ·rəp] *n* **1.** CULIN sciroppo *m* **2.** MED sciroppo *m;* **cough ~** sciroppo per la tosse
syrupy ['sɪ·rə·pi] *adj pej* sciropposo, -a
system ['sɪs·təm] *n* **1.** (*set*) sistema *m;* **music ~** impianto *m* musicale **2.** (*method of organization*) *a.* POL sistema *m* **3.** (*order*) metodo *m* (di classificazione) ▸ **to get something out of one's ~** *inf* scaricarsi
systematic [ˌsɪs·tə·'mæ·t̬ɪk] *adj* sistematico, -a
systematize ['sɪs·tə·mə·taɪz] *vt* sistematizzare
system check *n* verifica *f* del sistema
system crash <-es> *n* blocco *m* del sistema
system disk *n* disco *m* (di) sistema
system error *n* errore *m* di sistema
system registry *n* registro *m* di sistema
systems analysis *n* analisi *m* dei sistemi
systems analyst *n* analista *mf* di sistemi
system software *n* software *m* di sistema *inv*

T

T, t [tiː] *n* T, t *f o m;* **~ for Tommy** T come Torino
t *abbr of* **tonne** t
TA *n abbr of* **teaching assistant** ≈ assistente universitario
tab [tæb] *n* **1.** (*flap*) linguetta *f;* (*on file*) linguetta *f;* **write-protect ~** INFOR linguetta di protezione **2.** (*label*) etichetta *f* **3.** *inf* (*bill*) conto *m;* **to put sth on the ~** mettere qc sul conto **4.** (*ringpull*) linguetta *f* metallica **5.** MED

a ~ **of acid** una pasticca di LSD ▶ **to** keep **~s on sth/sb** tenere d'occhio qc/qn

tabby ['tæ·bi] I. *adj* tigrato, -a II. *n* gatto *m* tigrato

tab key *n* tabulatore *m*

table ['teɪ·bl] I. *n* **1.** tavolo *m;* (*for meals*) tavola *f;* **to clear/set the ~** sparecchiare/apparecchiare (la tavola) **2.** MAT tabellina *f;* **multiplication ~** tavola *f* pitagorica **3.** (*list*) lista *f;* **~ of contents** indice *m* ▶ **the ~s have** turned son cambiate le carte in tavola II. *vt* (*postpone discussion of*) posporre

tablecloth ['teɪ·bl·klɑ:θ] *n* tovaglia *f*

tableland *n* altopiano *m*

table linen *n* biancheria *f* da tavola

table manners *npl* buone maniere *fpl* a tavola

table mat *n* sottopentola *m inv*

tablespoon *n* **1.** (*spoon*) cucchiaio *m* **2.** (*amount*) cucchiaiata *f*

tablet ['tæb·lɪt] *n* **1.** (*pill*) compressa *f* **2.** (*of stone*) lapide *f*

table tennis *n* ping-pong® *m inv*

tableware *n form* servizio *m* da tavola

table wine *n* vino *m* da tavola

tabloid ['tæb·lɔɪd] *n* tabloid *m inv;* **the ~ press** la stampa scandalistica

taboo, tabu [tə·'bu:] I. *n* tabú *m inv* II. *adj* tabú *inv*

tabular ['tæb·jʊ·lə] *adj form* tabulare

tabulate ['tæb·jʊ·leɪt] *vt* disporre in tabella; INFOR tabulare

tabulator ['tæb·jʊ·leɪ·tə] *n form* tabulatore *m*

tacit ['tæ·sɪt] *adj* tacito, -a

taciturn ['tæ·sə·tɜːrn] *adj* taciturno, -a

tack [tæk] I. *n* **1.** (*short nail*) bulletta *f* **2.** (*riding gear*) finimenti *mpl* **3.** NAUT rotta *f* **4.** (*approach*) approccio *m;* **to try a different ~** tentare un approccio diverso II. *vt* **1.** (*nail down*) imbullettare **2.** (*sew loosely*) imbastire III. *vi* NAUT virare

tackle ['tæ·kl] I. *vt* **1.** (*in soccer*) contrastare; (*in rugby, US football*) placcare **2.** (*deal with: issue, problem*) affrontare; (*job*) intraprendere II. *n* **1.** (*in soccer*) contrasto *m;* (*in rugby, US football*) placcaggio *m* **2.** (*equipment*) attrezzatura *f* **3.** NAUT paranco *m*

tacky ['tæ·ki] <-ier, -iest> *adj* **1.** (*sticky*) appiccicoso, -a **2.** *inf* (*showy*) pacchiano, -a; (*shoddy*) scadente

tact [tækt] *n* tatto *m*

tactful ['tækt·fəl] *adj* discreto, -a

tactic ['tæk·tɪk] *n* ~(**s**) tattica *f*

tactical ['tæk·tɪ·kl] *adj* tattico, -a

tactician [tæk·'tɪ·ʃən] *n* stratega *mf*

tactile ['tæk·tl] *adj form* tattile

tactless ['tæk·ləs] *adj* privo, -a di tatto

tactlessness *n* mancanza *f* di tatto

tad [tæd] *n* **a ~** un pochino

tadpole ['tæd·poʊl] *n* girino *m*

taffeta ['tæ·fɪ·tə] *n* taffettà *m*

tag [tæg] I. *n* **1.** *a.* INFOR (*label*) etichetta *f;* (*metal*) targhetta *f* **2.** (*game*) **to play ~** giocare ad acchiapparella **3.** LING **question ~** breve domanda in fondo a una frase II. <-gg-> *vt* (*label*) etichettare; **to ~ sth onto sth** aggiungere qc a qc

◆**tag along** *vi inf* seguire; **to ~ with sb** aggregarsi a qn

tail [teɪl] I. *n* **1.** ANAT, AVIAT coda *f* **2.** *pl, inf* (*tail coat*) frac *m inv* **3.** *pl* (*side of coin*) croce *f* **4.** *inf* (*person*) pedinatore, -trice *m, f* **5.** *inf* (*bottom*) didietro *m inv* ▶ **to** chase **one's ~** girare a vuoto *fig;* **to** turn **~ and run** darsela a gambe II. *vt* pedinare

◆**tail away** *vi* andar diminuendo; (*get worse*) andar peggiorando

◆**tail off** *vi* diminuire; (*sound*) smorzarsi

tail end *n* finale *m*

tailgate I. *n* (*of car*) portellone *m* posteriore; (*of truck*) sponda *f* ribaltabile II. *vt* tallonare

tailless *adj* senza coda

taillight *n* AUTO fanalino *m* di coda

tailor ['teɪ·lə] I. *n* sarto *m* II. *vt* **1.** (*clothes*) confezionare **2.** (*adapt*) adattare

tailor-made [,teɪ·lə·'meɪd] *adj* **1.** (*custom-made*) su misura **2.** (*perfect*) perfetto, -a

tailpiece ['teɪl·pi:s] *n* **1.** (*part added*) estensione *f* **2.** AVIAT coda *f* **3.** TYPO vignetta *f*

tailpipe *n* tubo *m* di scappamento

tailspin *n* avvitamento *m;* **to go into a ~** scendere in avvitamento

tail wind *n* vento *m* di coda

taint [teɪnt] I. *vt* (*food*) guastare; (*reputation*) macchiare II. *n* macchia *f*

Taiwan [,taɪ·'wɑːn] *n* Taiwan *m*

Taiwanese [,taɪ·wə·'niːz] I. *adj* taiwanese II. *n* taiwanese *mf*

Tajikistan [tɑː·'dʒiː·kɪ·,stɑːn] *n* Tagikistan *m*

take [teɪk] I. *n* **1.** (*receipts*) incassi *mpl* **2.** PHOT, CINE ripresa *f* ▶ **to be** on **the ~** *inf* prendere tangenti II. <took, taken> *vt* **1.** (*accept*) accettare; (*advice*) seguire; (*criticism*) accettare; (*responsibility*) assumere; **to ~ sth seriously** prendere qc sul serio; **to ~ one's time** prendersela comoda; **to ~ sth as it comes** prendere qc come viene **2.** (*hold*) prendere **3.** (*eat: medicine, drugs*) prendere; **I'll ~ some soup** prendo un po' di minestra **4.** (*use*) richiedere **5.** (*receive*) ricevere **6.** (*capture: prisoners*) prendere; (*city*) conquistare; (*power*) assumere **7.** (*assume*) **to ~ office** assumere una carica **8.** (*bring*) portare **9.** (*require*) volerci; **this shirt ~s a lot of ironing** ci vuole molto per stirare questa camicia **10.** (*do*) REL celebrare; UNIV fare **11.** (*have: decision*) prendere; (*bath, walk, holiday*) fare; (*ticket*) comprare; (*census*) censire; **to ~ a rest** riposarsi **12.** (*feel, assume*) **to ~ (an) interest in sb/sth** interessarsi a qn/qc; **to ~ offence** offendersi; **to ~ pity on sb/sth** aver pietà di qn/qc; **to ~ the view that ...** essere del parere che ... **13.** (*make money*) incassare **14.** (*photograph*) fotografare **15.** (*use for travel: bus, train*) prendere **16.** (*regard as*) **to ~ sb for sth** prendere qn per qc ▶ **~ it or** leave **it** prendere o lasciare; **what do you ~ me** for? per chi mi prendi?;

~ it <u>from</u> me credimi; I ~ <u>it</u> that ... suppongo che ...; ~ <u>that!</u> beccati questa! III.<took, taken> *vi* fare effetto; (*plant, dye*) prendere
◆**take aback** *vt* (*suprise*) sorprendere; (*shock*) sconcertare
◆**take after** *vt* prendere da
◆**take along** *vt* (*take*) prendere (con sé); (*bring*) portare (con sé)
◆**take apart** I. *vt* 1.(*disassemble*) smontare 2.(*analyze*) analizzare 3.(*destroy*) demolire II. *vi* smontarsi
◆**take away** I. *vt* 1.(*remove*) togliere 2.(*go away with*) portar via 3.(*lessen*) sminuire 4.(*subtract from*) sottrarre II. *vi* to ~ from the importance/worth of sth diminuire l'importanza/il valore di qc
◆**take back** *vt* 1.(*return*) riportare 2.(*accept back*) riprendere; (*employee*) riassumere; (*spouse*) riconciliarsi con 3.(*repossess*) riprendere 4.(*retract*) ritirare 5.(*carry to past time*) evocare 6.(*remind*) ricordare
◆**take down** *vt* 1.(*remove*) togliere; (*from high place*) abbassare 2.(*disassemble*) smontare 3.(*write down*) prendere nota di 4. *inf* (*diminish the pride of*) to take sb down fare abbassare la cresta a qn; (*humble*) umiliare qn
◆**take in** *vt* 1.(*bring inside*) fare entrare; (*admit*) ammettere 2.(*hold*) to take sb in one's arms prendere qn in braccio; to take sth in hand *fig* prendere in mano qc 3.(*accommodate*) accogliere; (*for rent*) ospitare 4.(*bring to police*) arrestare 5.(*deceive*) ingannare; to be taken in (by sb/sth) essere imbrogliato (da qn/qc) 6.(*go to see*) andare a vedere 7.(*understand*) comprendere; to take sth in at a glance capire qc in un batter d'occhio 8.(*include*) includere 9.FASHION restringere
◆**take off** I. *vt* 1.(*remove from*) togliere; to take sb off a list cancellare qn da una lista 2.(*clothes*) togliersi 3.(*bring away*) portare via 4.(*subtract*) scontare 5.(*stop showing*) ritirare II. *vi* 1.AVIAT decollare 2. *inf*(*leave*) filar via; *inf* (*flee*) darsela a gambe 3.(*have success*) decollare
◆**take on** I. *vt* 1.(*agree to try*) accettare 2.(*acquire*) adottare 3.(*hire*) assumere 4.(*fight*) battersi contro 5.(*stop for loading: passengers*) prendere a bordo; (*fuel*) rifornirsi di; (*goods*) caricare II. *vi* prendersela
◆**take out** *vt* 1.(*remove*) togliere; (*extract*) estrarre; (*withdraw*) ritirare 2.(*bring outside*) portar via; (*garbage*) buttare 3.(*for walk*) portar fuori 4. *inf*(*kill*) far fuori; (*destroy*) distruggere 5.(*arrange to get: license*) ottenere 6.(*borrow*) prendere in prestito 7.(*vent anger*) to take sth out on sb sfogare qc su qn 8. *inf*(*tire*) to take it out of sb sfinire qn *fig*
◆**take over** I. *vt* 1.(*buy out*) rilevare 2.(*seize control*) assumere il controllo di 3.(*assume*) assumere 4.(*possess*) prendere possesso di; to be taken over by one's work essere schiavo del lavoro 5.(*start using*) cominciare a usare

II. *vi* prendere possesso
◆**take to** *vt* 1.(*start to like*) prendere in simpatia 2.(*begin as a habit*) to ~ doing sth cominciare a fare qc; to ~ drink/drugs cominciare a bere/drogarsi 3.(*go to*) dirigersi verso; to ~ the streets (in protest) scendere in piazza (per protestare); to ~ one's bed mettersi a letto
◆**take up** I. *vt* 1.(*bring up*) sollevare 2. to ~ arms (against sth) prendere le armi (contro qn) 3.(*start doing*) cominciare; (*piano*) cominciare a studiare; (*fishing*) darsi a 4.(*discuss*) trattare 5.(*accept*) accettare 6.(*adopt*) adottare 7.(*continue doing*) proseguire 8.(*join in*) partecipare a 9.(*occupy*) occupare 10.(*pull up*) alzare 11.(*shorten*) accorciare 12.(*patronize*) patrocinare 13.(*absorb*) assorbire II. *vi* to ~ with sb fare amicizia con qn; to ~ with sth familiarizzarsi con qc
take-home pay ['teɪk·hoʊm·ˌpeɪ] *n* retribuzione *f* netta
taken *vi, vt pp of* take
takeoff ['teɪk·ɑːf] *n* AVIAT decollo *m*
takeout ['teɪk·aʊt] *n* cibo *m* da asporto
takeover ['teɪk·ˌoʊ·vɚ] *n* POL presa *f* di potere; ECON acquisizione *f* di controllo
takeover bid *n* offerta *f* pubblica di acquisto
taker ['teɪ·kɚ] *n* the suggestion had no ~s la proposta non è stata accettata
take-up ['teɪk·ʌp] *n* (*of scheme, suggestion*) accettazione *f*
taking ['teɪ·kɪŋ] I. *n* 1.(*capture*) presa *f*; it's yours for the ~ puoi prenderlo, se vuoi 2. *pl* (*receipts*) incassi *mpl* II. *adj* attraente
talc [tælk] *n*, **talcum** (**powder**) ['tæl·kəm·(ˌpaʊ·dəʊ)] *n* 1.CHEM talco *m* 2.MED borotalco® *m*
tale [teɪl] *n* 1.(*story*) storia *f*; LIT racconto *m* 2.(*lie*) frottola *f*; dead men tell no ~s i morti non parlano ► to <u>tell</u> ~s fare la spia
talent ['tæ·lənt] *n* (*ability*) talento *m*
talented *adj* dotato, -a di talento
talisman ['tæ·lɪz·mən] *n* talismano *m*
talk [tɔːk] I. *n* 1.(*conversation*) conversazione *f* 2.(*lecture*) conferenza *f* 3.(*things said*) chiacchiere *fpl*; big ~ spacconata *f* 4. *pl* (*formal discussions*) trattative *fpl* ► to be the ~ of the <u>town</u> essere sulla bocca di tutti; to be <u>all</u> ~ (and no action) parlare tanto (e non passare mai ai fatti) II. *vi* (*speak*) parlare; to ~ about sb behind their back parlar male di qn alle sue spalle; to give sb something to ~ about dare a qn di che parlare ► to ~ <u>dirty</u> dire oscenità; <u>look</u> who's ~ing *inf* senti chi parla!; you're a fine <u>one</u> to ~ *inf* parli proprio tu! III. *vt* 1.(*utter*) dire 2.(*discuss*) parlare di
◆**talk around** I. *vt* to talk sb around convincere qn II. *vi* (*avoid*) to ~ sth girare intorno a qc
◆**talk back** *vi* replicare
◆**talk down** I. *vt* (*speak louder than*) sovrastare con la voce II. *vi pej* to ~ to sb parlare a qn con condiscendenza

◆**talk out** *vt* 1.(*discuss*) discutere 2.(*convince not to*) **to talk sb out of doing sth** dissuadere qn dal fare qc

◆**talk over** *vt* **to talk sth over (with sb)** parlare di qc (con qn)

◆**talk through** *vt* 1.(*discuss*) discutere 2.(*explain*) spiegare

talkative ['tɔː·kə·ʈɪv] *adj* loquace

talker *n* parlatore, -trice *m, f*

talking I. *adj* parlante II. *n* **you do the ~** parla tu; **"no ~"** "silenzio"

talking-to ['tɔː·kɪŋ·tuː] *n* ramanzina *f;* **to give sb a ~** fare la ramanzina a qn

talk show *n* talk-show *m inv*

tall [tɔːl] *adj* alto, -a; **to grow ~(er)** crescere

tallow ['tæ·loʊ] *n* sego *m*

tally[1] ['tæ·li] <-ie-> *vi* concordare; **to ~ with sth** coincidere con qc

tally[2] ['tæ·li] <-ies> I. *n* conto *m;* **to keep a ~ (of sth)** tenere il conto (di qc) II. *vt* tenere il conto di

◆**tally up** *vt* calcolare

talon ['tæ·lən] *n* artiglio *m*

tamarind ['tæ·mə·rɪnd] *n* tamarindo *m*

tamarisk ['tæ·mə·rɪsk] *n* tamerice *f*

tambour ['tæm·bʊr] *n* tamburo *m*

tambourine [ˌtæm·bə·'riːn] *n* tamburello *m*

tame [teɪm] I. *adj* 1.(*domesticated*) addomesticato, -a; (*not savage*) mansueto, -a 2.(*unexciting*) noioso, -a II. *vt* (*feelings*) dominare; (*animal*) addomesticare

tamer ['teɪ·mə] *n* domatore, -trice *m, f*

tamper ['tæm·pə] *vi* intromettersi

◆**tamper with** *vt* manomettere; (*document*) falsificare; (*witness*) corrompere; (*lock*) forzare

tamperproof ['tæm·pə·pruːf] *adj,* **tamper-resistant** *adj* a prova di scasso

tampon ['tæm·pɑːn] *n* MED tampone *m;* (*for absorbing menstrual blood*) assorbente *m* interno

tan[1] [tæn] I. <-nn-> *vi* abbronzarsi II. <-nn-> *vt* 1.(*make brown*) abbronzare; **to be ~ned** essere abbronzato 2.(*leather*) conciare ▶**to ~ sb's** **hide** *inf* conciare qn per le feste III. *n* abbronzatura *f;* **to get a ~** abbronzarsi IV. *adj* marrone chiaro *inv*

tan[2] MAT *abbr of* **tangent** tan

tandem ['tæn·dəm] I. *n* tandem *m inv;* **to work in ~** lavorare in tandem II. *adv* in tandem

tang [tæŋ] *n* odore *m* penetrante

tangent ['tæn·dʒənt] *n* tangente *f;* **to go off on a ~** partire per la tangente

tangential [tæn·'dʒen·ʃl] *adj* tangenziale

tangerine [ˌtæn·dʒə·'riːn] *n* tangerino *m*

tangible ['tæn·dʒə·bl] *adj* tangibile; **~ asset** bene *m* materiale

Tangier [tæn·'dʒɪr] *n* Tangeri *f*

tangle ['tæŋ·gl] I. *n* 1.(*in hair*) nodo *m;* (*string*) groviglio *m* 2. *fig* (*confusion*) confusione *f* II. *vt* ingarbugliare III. *vi* ingarbugliarsi

◆**tangle with** *vi* (*quarrel*) azzuffarsi con qn

tango ['tæŋ·goʊ] I. *n* tango *m* ▶**it takes two to ~** *prov* la responsabilità sta da entrambe le parti II. *vi* ballare il tango

tangy ['tæ·ŋi] <-ier, -iest> *adj* forte

tank [tæŋk] *n* 1.(*container*) serbatoio *m* 2.(*aquarium*) acquario *m* 3. MIL carro *m* armato

tanked up *adj* **to be ~** essere sbronzo

tankard ['tæŋ·kəd] *n* boccale *m*

tanker ['tæŋ·kə] *n* 1.(*truck*) autocisterna *f* 2.(*ship*) nave *f* cisterna; **oil ~** petroliera *f* 3.(*aircraft*) aereo *m* cisterna

tanned [tænd] *adj* abbronzato, -a

tanner ['tæ·nə] *n* conciatore, -trice *m, f*

tannery ['tæ·nə·ri] *n* conceria *f*

tannic acid [ˌtæ·nɪk·'æ·sɪd] *n* acido *m* tannico

tannin ['tæ·nɪn] *n* tannino *m*

tanning ['tæ·nɪŋ] *n* 1.(*of leather*) conciatura *f* 2. *inf* (*beating*) legnata *f*

tantalize ['tæn·ʈə·laɪz] *vt* 1.(*torment*) stuzzicare 2.(*tempt*) tentare

tantalizing *adj* stuzzicante; (*smile*) seducente

tantamount ['tæn·ʈə·maʊnt] *adj* equivalente; **to be ~ to sth** equivalere a qc

tantrum ['tæn·trəm] *n* capriccio *m;* **to have [o throw] a ~** fare i capricci

Tanzania [ˌtæn·zə·'niː·ə] *n* Tanzania *f*

Tanzanian [ˌtæn·zə·'niː·ən] I. *adj* tanzaniano, -a II. *n* tanzaniano, -a *m, f*

tap[1] [tæp] I. *n* 1.(*for water*) rubinetto *m;* **beer on ~** birra *f* alla spina; **to turn the ~ on/off** aprire/chiudere il rubinetto; **on ~** *fig* a portata di mano 2. TEL microscopia *f* telefonica II. <-pp-> *vt* 1. TEL (*conversation*) intercettare; (*phone*) mettere sotto controllo 2.(*make use of*) utilizzare; (*sources*) sfruttare 3.(*let out*) spillare

tap[2] [tæp] I. *n* 1.(*light knock*) colpetto *m* 2.(*tap dancing*) tip tap *m inv* II. <-pp-> *vt* dare un colpetto a; **to ~ one's fingers on the table** tamburellare con le dita sul tavolo III. <-pp-> *vi* dare un colpetto

tap dance ['tæp·dænts] *n* tip tap *m inv*

tape [teɪp] I. *n* 1.(*adhesive strip*) nastro *m* adesivo; MED cerotto *m;* **masking ~** nastro adesivo di carta; **Scotch ~®** scotch® *m inv* 2.(*measure*) metro *m* a nastro 3. SPORTS nastro d'arrivo 4.(*cassette*) cassetta *m;* **to get sth on ~** registrare qc II. *vt* 1.(*fasten with tape*) sigillare con nastro adesivo 2.(*record*) registrare

tape cassette *n* audiocassetta *f*

tape deck *n* piastra *f* di registrazione

tape measure *n* metro *m* a nastro

taper ['teɪ·pə] I. *n* (*slim candle*) candela *f* II. *vt* assottigliare III. *vi* assottigliarsi

◆**taper off** *vi* diminuire

tape-record *vt* registrare

tape recorder *n* registratore *m*

tape recording *n* registrazione *f*

tapestry ['tæ·pəs·tri] *n* 1.(*art form*) tappezzeria *f* 2.(*object*) arazzo *m* 3. *fig* mosaico *m*

T

tapeworm ['teɪp·wɜːrm] *n* tenia *f,* verme *m* solitario

tapioca [ˌtæ·pɪ·'oʊ·kə] *n* tapioca *f*

tapir ['teɪ·pɚ] *n* tapiro *m*

tappet ['tæ·pət] *n* punteria *f*

taproom ['tæp·ruːm] *n* bar *m inv*

tap water *n* acqua *f* del rubinetto

tar [tɑːr] I. *n* catrame *m* II. <-rr-> *vt* incatramare; **to ~ and feather sb** coprire qn di pece e piume

tarantula [tə·'ræn·tʃə·lə] *n* tarantola *f*

tardy ['tɑːr·di] <-ier, -iest> *adj liter* tardivo, -a; *pej* (*sluggish*) lento, -a

tare [ter] *n* ECON tara *f*

target ['tɑːr·gɪt] I. *n* 1. (*mark aimed at*) bersaglio *m;* **to hit the ~** colpire il bersaglio 2. ECON obiettivo *m;* **to be on ~** essere in linea con gli obiettivi II. *vt* mirare a; **to ~ sth on sth** (*missile*) puntare qc su qc; (*campaign*) rivolgere qc a qc

target date *n* termine *m* ultimo

target language *n* LING lingua *f* d'arrivo; INFOR linguaggio *m* macchina

target practice *n* esercitazioni *fpl* di tiro al bersaglio

target price *n* prezzo *m* indicativo

targeted ['tɑːr·gɪ·ʈɪd] *adj* scelto, -a come obiettivo

tariff ['te·rɪf] *n* (*customs duty*) tariffa *f* doganale

tariff barrier *n* ECON barriera *f* doganale

tarmac® ['tɑːr·mæk], **tarmacadam**® *n* 1. (*paving material*) macadam *m* all'asfalto *inv* 2. AVIAT pista *f*

tarn [tɑːrn] *n* laghetto *m* di montagna

tarnish ['tɑːr·nɪʃ] I. *vi* ossidarsi II. *vt* ossidare; (*reputation*) macchiare III. *n* macchia *f*

tarpaulin [tɑːr·'pɑː·lɪn] *n* telo *m* impermeabile

tarragon ['te·rə·gɑːn] *n* dragoncello *m*

tarsus ['tɑːr·səs] *n* ANAT tarso *m*

tart¹ [tɑːrt] *adj* 1. (*sharp*) aspro, -a; (*acid*) acido, -a 2. (*caustic*) caustico, -a

tart² [tɑːrt] *n* GASTR torta *f*

tartan ['tɑːr·tn] *n* 1. (*cloth*) tessuto *f* scozzese 2. (*design*) scozzese *m*

Tartar ['tɑːr·ʈɚ] *n* (*bad-tempered person*) persona *f* intrattabile

tartar ['tɑːr·ʈɚ] *n* MED, CHEM tartaro *m*

tartar(e) sauce *n* salsa *f* tartara

tartaric [tɑːr·'tæ·rɪk] *n* acido *m* tartarico

task [tæsk] I. *n* compito *m;* **to take sb to ~** richiamare qn all'ordine II. *vt* assegnare un compito a; **to be ~ed with sth** essere incaricato di qc

task force *n* MIL task force *f inv;* (*team*) equipe *f inv*

taskmaster *n* aguzzino, -a *m, f;* **to be a hard ~** essere un vero tiranno

Tasmania [tæz·'meɪ·niə] *n* Tasmania *f*

Tasmanian [tæz·'meɪ·ni·ən] I. *adj* tasmaniano, -a II. *n* tasmaniano, -a *m, f*

tassel ['tæ·sl] *n* nappa *f*

taste [teɪst] I. *n* 1. sapore *m;* **sense of ~**

senso *m* del gusto 2. (*small portion*) assaggio *m;* **to have a ~ of sth** assaggiare qc 3. (*liking*) gusto *m;* **to lose the ~ for sth** perdere il gusto di qc; **to have different ~s** avere gusti diversi; **to get a ~ for sth** prendere gusto a qc 4. (*experience*) assaggio *m* ▶ **to leave a bad ~** (**in one's mouth**) lasciare l'amaro in bocca II. *vt* 1. (*food, drink*) assaggiare 2. (*experience*) assaporare; (*luxury*) provare III. *vi* sapere di; **to ~ bitter/sweet** avere un sapore amaro/dolce; **to ~ of** [*o* like] sth sapere di qc

taste bud ['teɪst·bʌd] *n* papilla *f* gustativa

tasteful ['teɪst·fəl] *adj* di buon gusto

tasteless ['teɪs·tləs] *adj* 1. (*without flavor*) insapore 2. (*clothes, remark*) di cattivo gusto

taster ['teɪs·tɚ] *n* (*person*) assaggiatore, -trice *m, f*

tasty ['teɪs·ti] *adj* (*tasting good*) saporito, -a

tattered ['tæ·ʈɚd] *adj* (*clothes*) a brandelli; (*person*) malridotto, -a; (*reputation*) distrutto, -a

tatters ['tæ·ʈɚz] *npl* brandelli *mpl;* **to be in ~** esser ridotto a brandelli

tattle ['tæ·ʈl] *n* pettegolezzo *m*

tattler ['tæt·lɚ] *n* petegolo, -a *m, f*

tattoo [tæ·'tuː] I. *n* 1. MIL parata *f* militare 2. (*marking on skin*) tatuaggio *m* II. *vt* tatuare

tatty ['tæ·ʈi] <-ier, -iest> *adj pej* malridotto, -a

taught [tɑːt] *pt, pp of* teach

taunt [tɑːnt] I. *vt* beffarsi di II. *n* scherno *m*

Taurus ['tɔː·rəs] *n* Toro *m*

taut [tɑːt] *adj* teso, -a

tautological [ˌtɑː·ʈə·'lɑː·dʒɪ·kəl] *adj*, **tautologous** [tɑː·'tɑː·lə·gəs] *adj* tautologico, -a

tautology [tɑː·'tɑː·lə·dʒi] <-ies> *n* tautologia *f*

tavern ['tæ·vɚn] *n* taverna *f*

tawdry ['tɑː·dri] <-ier, -iest> *adj pej* (*vulgar*) volgare; (*pompous*) pacchiano, -a

tawny ['tɑː·ni] <-ier, -iest> *adj* fulvo, -a

tawny owl *n* allocco *m*

tax [tæks] I. <-es> *n* 1. FIN imposta *f,* tassa *f;* **hidden ~es** tasse nascoste; **to collect ~es** riscuotere le imposte; **to increase ~es** aumentare le imposte; **to put a ~ on sth** mettere una tassa su qc; **free of ~** esentasse 2. *fig* (*burden*) carico *m;* **to be a ~ on sb** essere un onere per qn II. *vt* 1. FIN tassare 2. (*accuse*) accusare 3. *fig* (*need effort*) mettere a dura prova

taxable ['tæk·sə·bl] *adj* imponibile

tax allowance *n* detrazione *f* fiscale

taxation [tæk·'seɪ·ʃən] *n* (*taxes*) imposte *fpl;* (*system*) tassazione *f*

tax avoidance *n* elusione *f* fiscale

tax base *n* base *f* imponibile

tax bracket *n* scaglione *f* d'imposta

tax collector *n* esattore, -trice delle imposte *m*

tax consultant *n* consulente *mf* fiscale

tax-deductible *adj* deducibile

tax dodger *n,* **tax evader** *n* evasore *m* fiscale

tax evasion *n* evasione *f* fiscale

tax exemption *n* esenzione *f* fiscale

tax-free *adj* esente da imposte

tax haven *n* paradiso *m* fiscale

taxi ['tæk·si] I. *n* taxi *m inv* II. *vi* andare in taxi; AVIAT rullare

taxidermist ['tæk·sɪˌdɜːr·mɪst] *n* tassidermista *mf*

taxidermy ['tæk·sɪˌdɜːr·mi] *n* tassidermia *f*

taxi driver *n* taxista *mf*, tassista *mf*

taximeter ['tæk·sɪˌmiː·t̬ə] *n* tassametro *m*

taxing *adj* difficile

taxiplane *n* aerotaxi *m inv*

taxi stand *n* posteggio *m* di taxi

taxman ['tæks·mæn] *n* esattore, -trice delle imposte *m;* **the ~** il fisco

taxonomy [tæk·'saː·nə·mi] *n* tassonomia *f*

taxpayer ['tæks·ˌpe·ɪə] *n* contribuente *mf*

tax rebate *n* rimborso *m* fiscale

tax relief *n* detrazione *f* fiscale

tax return *n* dichiarazione *f* dei redditi

tax revenues *n* entrate *fpl* fiscali

tax system *n* sistema *m* tributario

tax year *n* anno *m* fiscale

TB [ˌtiː·'biː] *n abbr of* **tuberculosis** tbc *f inv*

T-bar ['tiː·baːr] *n*, **T-bar lift** *n* ≈ skilift

tbs(p) *abbr of* **tablespoonful**

tea [tiː] *n* (*plant, drink*) tè *m inv;* **a cup of ~** una tazza di tè; **strong/weak ~** tè forte/leggero; **camomile ~** camomilla *f* ▸ **not for all the ~ in China** per niente al mondo

tea bag *n* bustina *f* di tè

tea break *n* pausa *f* per il tè

tea caddy *n* barattolo *m* per il tè

teacake ['tiː·keɪk] *n* pasticcino *m* da tè

teach [tiːtʃ] <taught, taught> I. *vt* insegnare; **to ~ oneself sth** imparare qc per proprio conto; **to ~ sb a lesson** *fig* dare una lezione a qn II. *vi* insegnare

teacher ['tiː·tʃə] *n* insegnante *mf*

teacher training *n* formazione *f* degli insegnanti

tea chest *n* cassa *f* da tè

teaching I. *n* 1. (*profession*) insegnamento *m* 2. *pl* (*doctrine*) insegnamenti *mpl* II. *adj* didattico, -a

teaching staff *n* corpo *m* docente

teacup *n* tazza *f* da tè

teahouse *n* sala *f* da tè

teak [tiːk] *n* tek *m*

tea leaves *npl* foglie *fpl* di tè

team [tiːm] I. *n* (*group*) equipe *f inv;* (*of oxen, horses*) tiro *m;* (*of dogs*) muta *f* II. *adj* d'equipe III. *vt* mettere insieme; (*match*) combinare

◆**team up** *vi* raggrupparsi; **to ~ with** fare squadra con

team captain *n* capitano *m* della squadra

team effort *n* sforzo *m* congiunto

teammate *n* compagno, -a di squadra *m*

team play *n* gioco *m* di squadra

team spirit *n* spirito *m* di squadra

teamwork *n* lavoro *m* d'equipe

teapot ['tiː·paːt] *n* teiera *f*

tear¹ [tɪr] I. *n* lacrima *f;* **to bring ~s to sb's eyes** far venire le lacrime agli occhi a qn; **to burst into ~s** scoppiare a piangere; **to have**

~s in one's eyes avere le lacrime agli occhi; **to not shed** (**any**) **~s** non versare una (sola) lacrima II. *vi* lacrimare

tear² [ter] I. *n* strappo *m* II. <tore, torn> *vt* 1. (*rip*) strappare; (*ruin*) rompere; **to ~ a hole in sth** fare un buco in qc; **to be torn between two possibilities** essere combattuto tra due possibilità 2. (*strain: muscle*) strappare III. <tore, torn> *vi* 1. (*rip*) strapparsi 2. (*rush wildly*) lanciarsi; **to ~ down the stairs** precipitarsi giù per le scale

◆**tear apart** *vt* distruggere; *fig* dividere

◆**tear at** *vt* tirare violentemente

◆**tear away** I. *vi* andar via di corsa II. *vt* 1. (*make depart*) **to tear sb away** (**from sth/sb**) strappare qn (da qc); **to tear oneself away** (**from sth/sb**) staccarsi (da qc/qn) 2. (*pull*) strappare

◆**tear down** *vt* demolire

◆**tear into** *vt* (*verbally*) criticare duramente; (*physically*) scagliarsi su

◆**tear off** I. *vt* (*remove*) strappare; **to ~ one's clothes** strapparsi i vestiti di dosso II. *vi* (*leave quickly*) scappar via

◆**tear out** *vt* strappare; **to tear one's hair out over sth** *fig* strapparsi i capelli per qc

◆**tear up** *vt* strappare; *fig* (*agreement*) annullare

teardrop ['tɪr·draːp] *n* lacrima *f*

tearful ['tɪr·fəl] *adj* lacrimevole

tear gas *n* gas *m inv* lacrimogeno

tearjerker *n inf* (*film*) film *m inv* strappalacrime; (*song*) canzone *f* strappalacrime

tearoom *n* sala *f* da tè

tease [tiːz] I. *vt* 1. (*make fun of*) prendere in giro; **to ~ sb about sth** prendere in giro qn per qc 2. (*provoke*) stuzzicare; (*sexually*) provocare (*senza intenzione di soddisfare il desiderio suscitato*) 3. TECH cardare II. *n* burlone, -a *m, f;* (*sexually*) provocatore, -trice *m, f*

teaser ['tiː·zə] *n* rompicapo *m*

tea service *n*, **tea set** *n* servizio *m* da tè

teashop *n* sala *f* da tè

teaspoon *n* 1. (*spoon*) cucchiaino *m* 2. (*amount*) cucchiaino *m*

teaspoonful ['tiː·spuːn·fʊl] *n* cucchiaino *m*

tea strainer ['tiːˌstreɪ·nə] *n* colino *m* per il tè

teat [tiːt] *n* (*nipple: of animal*) capezzolo *m;* (*of bottle*) tettarella *f*

teatime ['tiː·taɪm] *n* ora *f* del tè

tea towel *n* strofinaccio *m*

tea tray *n* vassoio *m* da tè

tea wagon *n s.* **tea trolley**

technical ['tek·nɪ·kəl] *adj* tecnico, -a; **~ term** termine *m* tecnico

technical college *n* HIST istituto *m* tecnico

technicality [ˌtek·nə·'kæ·lə·t̬i] <-ies> *n* 1. (*detail*) dettaglio *m* tecnico; **to be acquitted on a ~** essere assolto grazie a un cavillo legale 2. (*technical matter*) aspetto *m* tecnico

technical school *n* scuola *f* tecnica

technician [tek·'nɪ·ʃən] *n* tecnico, -a *m, f*

T

technique [tek·'niːk] *n* tecnica *f*

technological [ˌtek·nə·'laː·dʒɪ·kl] *adj* tecnologico, -a

technology [tek·'naː·lə·dʒi] *n* tecnologia *f*

technophile [ˌtek·nəʊ·'faɪl] *n* tecnofilo, -a *m, f*

technophobe [ˌtek·nə·'foʊb] *n* tecnofobo, -a *m, f*

tectonics [tek·'taː·nɪks] *n* tettonica *f*

teddy¹ ['te·di] *n* (*underwear*) pagliaccetto *m*

teddy² ['te·di] <-ies> *n*, **teddy bear** *n* orsacchiotto (*m* di peluche)

tedious ['tiː·di·əs] *adj* noioso, -a

tediousness *n* noia *f*

tedium ['tiː·di·əm] *n* tedio *m*

tee [tiː] *n* SPORTS tee *m inv*

◆**tee off** I. *vi* 1. SPORTS dare il colpo di inizio 2. *inf* (*start*) iniziare *fig* II. *vt inf* **to tee sb off** fare imbestialire qn

teem [tiːm] *vi* pullulare; **to ~ with sth** brulicare di qc; **the city was ~ing with tourists** la città brulicava di turisti

teeming *adj* brulicante

teen [tiːn] *n* adolescente *mf*

teenage(d) ['tiːn·eɪdʒ(d)] *adj* adolescente

teenager ['tiː·neɪ·dʒɚ] *n* adolescente *mf*

teens [tiːnz] *npl* adolescenza *f*; **to be in one's ~** essere adolescente

teensy ['tiːn·zi] *adj*, **teensy-weensy** *adj*, **teeny** ['tiː·ni] *adj* piccolissimo, -a

teenybopper ['tiː·ni·ˌbaː·pɚ] *n inf*: *ragazzina adolescente fanatica delle ultime tendenze della musica pop, del cinema, della moda*

teeny-weeny [ˌtiː·ni·'wiː·ni] *adj inf s.* **teensy**

tee shirt ['tiː·ʃɜːrt] *n* maglietta *f*

teeter ['tiː·t̬ɚ] *vi* **to ~ (around)** barcollare; **to ~ on the brink of sth** essere sull'orlo di qc

teeth [tiːθ] *pl of* **tooth**

teethe [tiːð] *vi* mettere i denti

teething troubles *n fig* difficoltà *fpl* iniziali

teetotal [ˌtiː·'toʊ·t̬əl] *adj* astemio, -a

teetotaler [ˌtiː·'toʊ·t̬ə·lɚ] *n* astemio, -a *m, f*

tel. *abbr of* **telephone** tel.

telecast ['te·lɪ·kæst] *n* trasmissione *f* televisiva

telecommunications ['te·lɪ·kə·ˌmjuː·nɪ·'keɪ·ʃnz] *npl* telecomunicazioni *fpl*

telecommuting ['te·lɪ·kə·ˌmjuː·t̬ɪŋ] *n* INFOR telelavoro *m*

teleconference ['te·lɪ·ˌkaːn·fə·rəns] *n* teleconferenza *f*

Telecopier® ['te·lɪ·kɒ·pɪə] *n* fotocopiatrice *f*

telecopy ['te·lɪ·ka·pi] *n* fotocopia *f*

telefax® ['te·lɪ·fæks] *n* (tele)fax *m inv*

telegenic [ˌte·lə·'dʒe·nɪk] *adj* telegenico, -a

telegram ['te·lɪ·græm] *n* telegramma *m*

telegraph ['te·lɪ·græf] I. *n* telegrafo *m* II. *vt* telegrafare; **to ~ sb** mandare un telegramma a qn III. *adj* telegrafico, -a

telegraphese [ˌte·lɪ·græ·'fiːz] *n* stile *m* telegrafico

telegraphic [ˌte·lə·'græ·fɪk] *adj* telegrafico, -a

telegraph pole *n* palo *m* del telegrafo

telegraphy [tə·'le·grə·fi] *n* telegrafia *f*

telepathic [ˌte·lə·'pæ·θɪk] *adj* telepatico, -a; **to be ~** esser telepatico

telepathy [tə·'le·pə·θi] *n* telepatia *f*

telephone ['te·lə·foʊn] I. *n* telefono *m*; **mobile ~** (telefono *m*) cellulare *m* II. *vt* telefonare a III. *vi* telefonare; **to ~ long-distance** fare una chiamata interurbana IV. *adj* telefonico, -a; (*booking*) per telefono

telephone book *n* elenco *m* telefonico

telephone booth *n* cabina *f* telefonica

telephone call *n* telefonata *f*; **to make a ~** fare una telefonata

telephone connection *n* collegamento *m* telefonico

telephone conversation *n* conversazione *f* telefonica

telephone directory *n* elenco *m* telefonico

telephone exchange *n* centralino *m* telefonico

telephone information service *n form* servizio *m* informazioni telefoniche

telephone message *n form* messaggio *m* telefonico

telephone number *n* numero *m* di telefono

telephone operator *n* operatore, -trice telefonico, -a *m*

telephone rates *n* tariffa *f* telefonica

telephony [tə·'le·fə·ni] *n* telefonia *f*; **digital mobile ~** telefonia mobile digitale

telephoto lens ['te·lə·foʊ·t̬oʊ·'lens] *n* teleobiettivo *m*

teleprinter ['te·lə·ˌprɪn·t̬ɚ] *n* telescrivente *f*

teleprocessing ['te·lɪ·prəʊ·ˌse·sɪŋ] *n* INFOR elaborazione *f* dati a distanza

TelePrompter® ['te·lə·ˌpraːmp·t̬ɚ] *n* teleprompter *m inv*

telesales ['te·lɪ·seɪls] *n* vendita *f* per telefono

telescope ['te·ləs·koʊp] I. *n* telescopio *m* II. *vi* ripiegarsi

telescopic [ˌte·lə·'skaː·pɪk] *adj* 1. (*vision, sight*) telescopico, -a 2. (*folding*) pieghevole

teleshopping ['te·lə·ˌʃaː·pɪŋ] *n* televendita *f*

Teletype® *n*, **Teletype®** ['te·lə·taɪp] *n* telescrivente *f*

teletypewriter [ˌte·lɪ·'taɪp·raɪ·t̬ɚ] *n* telescrivente *f*

televangelist [ˌte·lɪ·'væn·dʒə·lɪst] *n* telepredicatore, -trice *m, f*

televiewer ['te·lə·ˌvjuː·ɚ] *n* telespettatore, -trice *m, f*

televise ['te·lə·vaɪz] *vt* trasmettere per televisione; **to ~ sth live** trasmettere qc in diretta

television ['te·lə·vɪ·ʒən] *n* televisione *f*; (*television set*) televisore *m*; **to watch ~** guardare la televisione; **to turn the ~ on/off** accendere/spegnere il televisore

television announcer *n* annunciatore, -trice televisivo *m*

television camera *n* telecamera *f*

television program *n* programma *m* televisivo

television set *n* televisore *m*

television studio *n* studio *m* televisivo

teleworking ['te·lɪ·ˌwɜːr·kɪŋ] *n* telelavoro *m*

telex ['te·leks] I. *n* <-es> telex *m inv* II. *adj* via telex III. *vt* mandare via telex; **to ~ sb sth** comunicare qc via telex a qn

tell [tel] I.<told, told> *vt* 1.(*say*) dire; **to ~ sb of sth** informare qn di qc; **to ~ sb whether ...** dire a qn se ...; **I told you so** te l'avevo detto, io 2.(*narrate*) raccontare; **~ me another (one)** *inf* sparane un'altra 3.(*command*) ordinare; **to ~ sb to do sth** dire a qn di fare qc; **do as you're told** *inf* fa come ti si dice 4.(*make out*) riconoscere 5.(*distinguish*) distinguere; **to ~ sth from sth** distinguere qc da qc 6.(*know*) sapere; **there is no ~ing** non si sa 7.(*count*) contare; (*add up*) sommare; **all told** in tutto ▶**to ~ it like it is** *inf* parlare chiaro; **that would be ~ing** non posso dirtelo; **you're ~ing me!** *inf* lo dici a me! II.<told, told> *vi* 1.parlare; **to ~ of sth/sb** parlare di qc/qn 2.(*know*) sapere; **you never can ~** non si sa mai; **how can I ~?** come faccio a saperlo?; **who can ~?** chi può dirlo? 3.(*have an effect*) farsi sentire

◆**tell apart** *vt* distinguere

◆**tell off** *vt* rimproverare; **to tell sb off for sth** rimproverare [*o* sgridare] qn per qc

◆**tell on** *vt* **to ~ sb** denunciare qn

teller ['te·lə·] *n* 1.(*bank employee*) cassiere, -a *m, f* 2.(*vote counter*) scrutatore, -trice *m, f*

telling ['te·lɪŋ] I. *adj* 1.(*revealing*) rivelatore, -trice 2.(*significant*) efficace II. *n* racconto *m*

telling-off [,te·lɪŋ·'ɑːf] <tellings-off> *n* ramanzina *f*; **to give sb a ~ for (doing) sth** fare una ramanzina a qn per (aver fatto) qc

telltale ['tel·teɪl] I. *n pej* spione, -a *m, f* II. *adj* rivelatore, -trice

temerity [tə·'me·rə·ţi] *n form* temerarietà *f*; **to have the ~ to do sth** avere l'audacia di fare qc

temp [temp] I. *vi* fare un lavoro temporaneo II. *n* lavoratore, -trice temporaneo, -a *m*

temp. *abbr of* **temperature** temperatura

temper ['tem·pə·] I. *n* (*temperament*) temperamento *m*; (*mood*) umore *m*; (*tendency to become angry*) caratteraccio *m*; **good ~** buon umore; **bad ~** cattivo umore; **to keep one's ~** mantenere la calma; **to lose one's ~** perdere le staffe; **~s were getting short** l'atmosfera si stava surriscaldando II. *vt* 1.(*mitigate*) mitigare; **to ~ one's criticism** attenuare le critiche 2.(*make hard*) temprare

temperament ['tem·prə·mənt] *n* (*character*) temperamento *m*; (*moodiness*) umore *m* variabile; **a fit of ~** un accesso d'ira

temperamental [,tem·prə·'men·ţl] *adj* 1.(*relating to mood*) caratteriale 2.(*unpredictable*) capriccioso, -a

temperance ['tem·pə·rəns] *n form* (*moderation*) moderazione *f*; (*abstinence*) astinenza *f*

temperate ['tem·pə·rət] *adj* (*moderate*) moderato, -a; (*climate*) temperato, -a

temperature ['tem·pə·ə·tʃə·] *n* temperatura *f*; MED febbre *f*; **to run a ~** avere la febbre

tempest ['tem·pɪst] *n liter* tempesta *f*

tempestuous [tem·'pes·tʃu·əs] *adj* tempestoso, -a

template ['tem·plɪt] *n* modello *m*

temple[1] ['tem·pl] *n* REL tempio *m*

temple[2] ['tem·pl] *n* ANAT tempia *f*

tempo ['tem·poʊ] <-s *o* -pi> *n* 1.MUS tempo *m* 2.(*pace*) ritmo *m*

temporal ['tem·pə·rəl] *adj form* temporale

temporarily ['tem·pə·re·rə·li] *adv* temporaneamente

temporary ['tem·pə·re·ri] *adj* (*improvement, relief*) temporaneo, -a; (*staff, accommodation*) provvisorio, -a; (*relief*) temporaneo, -a

temporize ['tem·pə·raɪz] *vi* temporeggiare

tempt [tempt] *vt* 1.tentare; **to ~ sb into doing sth** invogliare qn a fare qc 2.(*persuade*) convincere; **to ~ sb into doing sth** incitare qn a fare qc

temptation [temp·'teɪ·ʃən] *n* 1.(*attraction*) tentazione *f*; **to resist ~ (to do sth)** resistere alla tentazione (di fare qc); **to succumb to ~** cedere alla tentazione 2.(*tempting thing*) tentazione *f*

tempting ['temp·tɪŋ] *adj* attraente; (*offer*) allettante

temptress ['temp·trɪs] <-es> *n* tentatrice *f*

ten [ten] I. *adj* dieci II. *n* dieci *m;* **~ to one he comes** dieci a uno che viene; **~s of thousands** decine *fpl* di migliaia; *s.a.* **eight**

tenable ['te·nə·bl] *adj* sostenibile

tenacious [tə·'neɪ·ʃəs] *adj* (*belief*) fermo, -a; (*person*) tenace

tenacity [tə·'næ·sə·ţi] *n* tenacia *f*

tenancy ['te·nən·si] <-ies> *n* 1.(*status*) condizione *f* di affittuario 2.(*right*) affitto *m*

tenant ['te·nənt] *n* (*of land*) affittuario, -a *m, f;* (*of house*) inquilino, -a *m, f*

tenant farmer *n* (*of land*) mezzadro, -a *m, f*

tench [ten(t)ʃ] *n* tinca *f*

tend[1] [tend] *vi* 1.(*have tendency*) **to ~ to do sth** tendere a fare qc; **I ~ to disagree** non sono del tutto d'accordo 2.(*usually do*) tendere a

tend[2] [tend] *vt* (*look after*) ocuparsi di; (*a person*) badare a

◆**tend to** *vt* (*look after*) occuparsi di

tendency ['ten·dən·si] <-ies> *n* tendenza *f*

tendentious [ten·'den·ʃəs] *adj* tendenzioso, -a

tender[1] ['ten·də·] *adj* 1.(*not tough*) tenero, -a 2.(*easily damaged*) delicato, -a 3.*liter* (*youthful: age*) tenero, -a 4.(*painful*) dolorante; (*part of the body*) sensibile; (*subject*) delicato, -a 5.(*affectionate*) tenero, -a; **to have a ~ heart** avere il cuore tenero

tender[2] ['ten·də·] I. *n* COM offerta *f*; **to put in a ~** fare un'offerta; **to put sth out for ~** dare qc in appalto II. *vt* (*offer*) offrire; (*apology*) presentare III. *vi* **to ~ for sth** fare un'offerta per qc

tender[3] ['ten·də·] *n* RAIL tender *m inv;* NAUT nave *f* appoggio

tenderfoot ['ten·də·fʊt] <-s *o* -feet> *n* principiante *mf*

tenderhearted ['ten·də·,hɑːr·ţɪd] *adj* sensibile; **to be ~** essere di buon cuore

T

tenderize ['tɛn·də·raɪz] *vt* intenerire
tenderizer *n* batticarne *m inv*
tenderloin ['tɛn·də·lɔɪn] *n* filetto *m*
tenderly *adv* teneramente
tenderness ['tɛn·də·nɪs] *n* 1.(*softness*) tenerezza *f* 2.(*affection*) tenerezza *f* 3.(*sensitivity*) sensibilità *f*
tendon ['tɛn·dən] *n* tendine *m*
tendril ['tɛn·drəl] *n* viticcio *m*
tenement ['tɛ·nə·mənt] *n* casa *f* popolare
Tenerife [ˌtɛ·nə·'riːf] *n* Tenerife *f*
tenet ['tɛ·nɪt] *n* principio *m*
tenfold ['tɛn·foʊld] I. *adj* decuplo, -a II. *adv* dieci volte
tennis ['tɛ·nɪs] *n* tennis *m inv*
tennis ball *n* palla *f* da tennis
tennis court *n* campo *m* da tennis
tennis elbow *n* gomito *m* del tennista
tennis player *n* tennista *mf*
tennis racket *n* racchetta *f* da tennis
tenon ['tɛ·nən] *n* tenone *m*
tenor ['tɛ·nə] I. *n* 1. *a.* MUS tenore *m* 2.(*character*) tono *m;* (*of events*) corso *m* II. *adj* MUS (*voice*) tenorile; (*instrument*) tenore
tenpin bowling [ˌtɛn·pɪn·'boʊ·lɪŋ] *n* bowling *m inv*
tense[1] [tɛnts] *n* LING tempo *m*
tense[2] [tɛnts] I. *adj* (*wire, person, atmosphere*) teso, -a II. *vt* tendere III. *vi* entrare in tensione
◆**tense up** *vi* entrare in tensione
tension ['tɛn·tʃən] *n* tensione *f*
tent [tɛnt] *n* (*for camping*) tenda *f;* (*in circus*) tendone *m*
tentacle ['tɛn·tə·kl] *n* tentacolo *m*
tentative ['tɛn·tə·tɪv] *adj* 1.(*person*) esitante 2.(*decision*) provvisorio, -a
tentatively *adv* 1.(*suggest*) con esitazione 2.(*decide*) provvisoriamente
tenterhooks ['tɛn·tə·hʊks] *npl* to be on ~ stare sulle spine; to keep sb on ~ tenere qn sulle spine
tenth [tɛnθ] I. *adj* decimo, -a II. *n* 1.(*order*) decimo, -a *m, f* 2.(*date*) dieci *m* 3.(*fraction*) decimo *m;* (*part*) decima parte *f; s.a.* **eighth**
tent peg *n* picchetto *m* (da tenda)
tent pole *n* paletto *m* (da tenda)
tenuous ['tɛn·ju·əs] *adj* tenue; (*connection*) sottile; (*argument*) debole
tenure ['tɛn·jə] *n* 1.(*possession*) possesso *m* 2.(*period of holding sth*) periodo *m* di titolarità
tepee ['tiː·piː] *n* tepee *m inv*
tepid ['tɛ·pɪd] *adj* tiepido, -a
term [tɜːrm] I. *n* 1.(*label, word*) termine *m;* ~ of abuse insulto *m;* ~ of endearment termine *m* affettuoso; in glowing ~s con grande ammirazione; in no uncertain ~s senza mezzi termini; in simple ~s in parole semplici 2. *pl* (*conditions*) condizioni *fpl;* to offer easy ~s offrire facilitazioni di pagamento 3.(*limit*) limite *m;* COM termine *m;* ~ of delivery termine di consegna; ~ of notice termine di pre-

avviso 4.(*period*) periodo *m;* (*duration*) durata *f;* (*of contract*) validità *f;* (*of office*) mandato *m;* prison ~ periodo *m* di detenzione; in the short/long ~ a breve/lunga scadenza 5.(*category*) termini *mpl;* to think in ~s of sth pensare in termini di qc 6. UNIV, SCHOOL trimestre *m* 7. *pl* rapporti *mpl;* to be on good/bad ~s with sb essere in buoni/cattivi rapporti con qn II. *vt* definire
terminal ['tɜːr·mɪ·nl] I. *adj* terminale; (*extreme*) estremo, -a; (*boredom*) mortale II. *n* 1. RAIL, AVIAT terminal *m inv* 2. INFOR terminale *m* 3. ELEC terminale *m*
terminate ['tɜːr·mɪ·neɪt] *form* I. *vt* (*finish*) porre fine a; (*contract*) rescindere; (*pregnancy*) interrompere II. *vi* terminare
termination [ˌtɜːr·mɪ·'neɪ·ʃən] *n* (*ending*) fine *f;* (*of contract*) rescissione *f;* (*of pregnancy*) interruzione *f*
terminological [ˌtɜːr·mɪ·nə·'laː·dʒɪ·kl] *adj* terminologico, -a
terminology [ˌtɜːr·mɪ·'naː·lə·dʒi] *n* terminologia *f*
terminus ['tɜːr·mɪ·nəs] <-es *o* -i> *n* (*station*) terminal *m inv;* (*bus stop*) capolinea *m inv*
termite ['tɜːr·maɪt] *n* termite *f*
tern [tɜːrn] *n* sterna *f*
terrace ['tɛ·rəs] I. *n* 1. *a.* AGR terrazza *f* 2. SPORT gradinata *f* 3.(*houses*) case *fpl* a schiera II. *vt* terrazzare III. *adj* a terrazze
terraced house *n* casa *f* a schiera
terrain [tɛ·'reɪn] *n* terreno *m*
terrapin ['tɛ·rə·pɪn] <-(s)> *n* tartaruga *f* d'acqua dolce
terrestrial [tə·'rɛs·tri·əl] *adj form* terrestre
terrible ['tɛ·rə·bl] *adj* 1.(*shocking*) terribile 2.(*very bad*) pessimo, -a 3. *inf* (*as intensifier*) terribile
terribly ['tɛ·rəb·li] *adv* 1.(*very badly*) malissimo 2.(*very*) terribilmente
terrier ['tɛ·ri·ə] *n* terrier *m inv*
terrific [tə·'rɪ·fɪk] *adj* 1.(*terrifying*) spaventoso, -a 2.(*excellent*) fantastico, -a 3. *as intensifier* (*very great*) enorme
terrified *adj* terrorizzato, -a
terrify ['tɛ·rə·faɪ] <-ie-> *vt* terrorizzare
terrifying *adj* terrificante
territorial [ˌtɛ·rə·'tɔː·ri·əl] I. *n* MIL territoriale *m* II. *adj* territoriale
territory ['tɛ·rə·tɔː·ri] <-ies> *n* 1.(*area of land*) territorio *m;* forbidden ~ zona *f* proibita 2.(*activity*) terreno *m*
terror ['tɛ·rə] *n* terrore *m;* to have a ~ of sth aver il terrore di qc; to strike ~ incutere il terrore; to be in ~ of one's life temere per la propria vita; a ~ of a child *inf* una peste
terrorism ['tɛ·rə·rɪ·zəm] *n* terrorismo *m*
terrorist ['tɛ·rə·rɪst] I. *n* terrorista *mf* II. *adj* terroristico, -a
terrorize ['tɛ·rə·raɪz] *vt* terrorizzare
terror-stricken ['tɛ·rə·ˌstrɪ·kən] *adj*, **terror-struck** ['tɛ·rə·strʌk] *adj* terrorizzato, -a
terry cloth [ˌtɛ·ri·'klaː·θ] *n* tessuto *m* in spugna

terse [tɜːrs] *adj* laconico, -a
tertiary ['tɜːr·ʃie·ri] I. *adj form* terziario, -a
II. <-ies> *n* the Tertiary GEO il Terziario
tessellated ['te·sə·ler·ţid] *adj* tessellato, -a
test [test] I. *n* 1. SCHOOL, UNIV esame *m;* **to pass a ~** superare un esame; **to fail a ~** essere bocciato a un esame; **driving ~** esame di guida 2. MED esame *m;* **blood ~** analisi *f* del sangue *pl;* **pregnancy ~** test *minv* di gravidanza 3. (*trial*) **to be a ~ of endurance** essere una prova di resistenza; **to put sth to the ~** mettere qn alla prova II. *vt* 1. (*examine*) esaminare 2. MED analizzare; (*hearing, sight*) fare un esame di; **to ~ sb for sth** fare delle analisi a qn per qc 3. (*measure*) provare 4. (*try to prove*) mettere alla prova 5. (*try with senses*) provare
testament ['tes·tə·mənt] *n* 1. *form* (*will*) testamento *m;* **last will and ~** ultime volontà *fpl* 2. *form* (*evidence*) testimonianza *f* 3. REL the Old/New Testament il Vecchio/Nuovo Testamento
test ban *n* bando *m* dei test nucleari
test bench *n* banco *m* di prova
test card *n* immagine *f* di prova
test case *n* caso *m* giuridico che costituisce un precedente
test drive *n* giro *m* di prova
tester ['tes·tə] *n* 1. (*person*) collaudatore, -trice *m, f* 2. (*sample*) campione *m* di prova
test flight *n* volo *m* di prova
testicle ['tes·tɪ·kl] *n* testicolo *m*
testify ['tes·tɪ·faɪ] <-ie-> I. *vi* 1. (*give evidence*) testimoniare 2. *form* (*prove*) **to ~ to sth** dimostrare qc II. *vt* 1. (*bear witness to*) dimostrare 2. (*declare under oath*) testimoniare; **to ~ that ...** dichiarare che ...
testimonial [ˌtes·tɪ·ˈmoʊn·iəl] *n form* 1. (*character reference*) referenze *fpl* 2. (*tribute*) tributo *m*
testimony ['tes·tɪ·moʊ·ni] <-ies> *n* testimonianza *f;* **to give ~** testimoniare
testing I. *n* sperimentazione *f* II. *adj* difficile; **~ times** tempi *mpl* duri
testing ground *n* terreno *m* di prova
test piece *n* MUS pezzo *m* di prova
test pilot *n* pilota *m* collaudatore
test stage *n* stadio *m* di prova
test tube *n* provetta *f*
test-tube baby *n* bambino *m* in provetta
testy ['tes·ti] <-ier, -iest> *adj* irritabile
tetanus ['te·tə·nəs] *n* tetano *m;* **~ injection** antitetanica *f*
tetchy ['te·tʃi] <-ier, -iest> *adj* irritabile
tether ['te·ðə] I. *n* pastoia *f* ▶ **to be at the end of one's ~** essere al limite II. *vt* legare; **to be ~ed to sth** *fig* essere bloccato a qc
Teutonic [tuːˈtɑː·nɪk] *adj* teutonico, -a
Texan ['tek·sən] I. *n* texano, -a *m, f* II. *adj* texano, -a
Texas ['tek·səs] *n* Texas *m*
text [tekst] *n* testo *m*
textbook ['tekst·bʊk] I. *n* libro *m* di testo II. *adj* da manuale

text editor *n* INFOR text-editor *m inv*
textile ['teks·taɪl] I. *n pl* tessili *mpl* II. *adj* tessile
textile mill *n* stabilimento *m* tessile
text processing *n* INFOR elaborazione *f* di testi
textual ['teks·tʃu·əl] *adj* testuale
texture ['teks·tʃə] *n* consistenza *f*
Thai [taɪ] I. *adj* tailandese II. *n* 1. (*person*) tailandese *mf* 2. LING tailandese *m*
Thailand ['taɪ·lənd] *n* Tailandia *m*
thalidomide [θəˈlɪ·dəʊ·maɪd] *n* talidomide *m*
than [ðən, ðæn] *conj* di; **you are taller ~ she (is)** sei più alto di lei; **more ~ 60** più di 60; **more ~ once** più di una volta; **nothing else ~ ...** nient'altro che ...; **no other ~ you** nessun altro che te; **no sooner had she told him, ~ ...** non aveva ancora finito di dirglielo che ...
thank [θæŋk] *vt* ringraziare; **to ~ sb (for sth)** ringraziare qn (per qc); **~ you** grazie; **~ you very much!** grazie mille!; **no, ~ you** no, grazie
thankful ['θæŋk·fəl] *adj* 1. (*pleased*) contento, -a; **to be ~ that ...** esser lieto che ... +*subj* 2. (*grateful*) grato, -a
thankfully *adv* fortunatamente
thankless ['θæŋk·ləs] *adj* ingrato, -a
thanks [θæŋks] *npl* ringraziamenti *mpl;* **~ very much** grazie mille; **~ to** grazie a; **in ~ for ...** come ringraziamento per ...; **no ~ to him** certo non per merito suo
thanksgiving [ˌθæŋks·ˈgɪ·vɪŋ] *n* ringraziamento *m*
Thanksgiving Day *n* giorno *m* del Ringraziamento
that [ðæt, ðət] I. *adj dem* <those> quel, quello, -a; **~ table** quel tavolo; **~ book** quel libro II. *pron* 1. *rel* che; **the woman ~ told me ...** la donna che me l'ha raccontato ...; **all ~ I have** tutto quello che ho 2. *dem* quel, quello, -a; **what is ~?** che cos'è?; **who is ~?** chi è? .; **like ~** così; **after ~** dopo quello; **~ 's it!** è tutto! III. *adv* così; **it was ~ hot** faceva molto caldo IV. *conj* 1. che; **I told you ~ I couldn't come** te l'avevo detto che non potevo venire; **~ I should live to see this!** se solo potessi vederlo! 2. (*in order that*) affinché +*subj*
thatch [θætʃ] I. *n* 1. (*roof*) tetto *m* di paglia 2. (*hair*) zazzera *f* II. *vt* coprire con un tetto di paglia
thatched roof *n* tetto *m* di paglia
thaw [θɑː] I. *n* 1. (*weather*) disgelo *m* 2. (*in relations*) distensione *f* II. *vi* 1. (*weather*) sgelare; (*food*) scongelarsi 2. (*relations*) distendersi III. *vt* sciogliere
the [ðə, *stressed, before vowel* ðiː] I. *def art* il, lo, l' *m*, la, l' *f*, i, gli *mpl*, le *fpl;* **from ~ garden** dal giardino; **at ~ hotel** in albergo; **at ~ door** alla porta; **to ~ garden** in giardino; **in ~ winter** in inverno II. *adv* (*in comparison*) **~ more one tries, ~ less one succeeds** quanto più ci si prova, tanto meno ci si riesce; **~ sooner ~ better** prima è, meglio è
theater ['θiː·ə·ţə] *n* 1. THEAT (*place, art*)

teatro *m* **2.** CINE cinema *m inv* **3.** UNIV auditorium *m inv* **4.** *fig* (*scene*) teatro *m*

theater company *n* compagnia *f* teatrale

theater critic *n* critico *m* teatrale

theatergoer *n* habitué *mfinv* del teatro

theatrical [θɪ·'æ·trɪ·kl] *adj* teatrale; **don't be so ~ about it** non essere così melodrammatico a riguardo

thee [ðiː] *pron pers* HIST te; **with ~** con te

theft [θeft] *n* furto *m;* **petty ~** piccoli furti

their [ðer] *adj pos* il loro *m,* la loro *f,* i loro *mpl,* le loro *fpl;* **~ house** la loro casa; **~ children** i loro figli

theirs [ðerz] *pron pos* il loro *m,* la loro *f,* i loro *mpl,* le loro *fpl;* **this house is ~** questa casa è loro; **they aren't our bags, they are ~** non sono le nostre borse, sono le loro; **a book of ~** uno dei loro libri

theism ['θiː·ɪ·zəm] *n* teismo *m*

them [ðem, ðəm] *pron pers pl* **1.** (*they*) loro; **older than ~** più vecchio di loro; **if I were ~** se fossi in loro **2.** *direct object* li, le; *indirect object* loro, gli; *fam;* **look at ~** guardali; **I saw ~** li ho visti; **he gave ~ the pencil** ha dato loro la matita; *fam* gli ha dato la matita **3.** *after prep* loro; **it's for/from ~** è per/da parte loro

thematic [θiː·'mæ·t̬ɪk] *adj* tematico, -a

theme [θiːm] *n a.* MUS tema *m;* **on the ~ of** sul tema di

theme music *n* tema *m* musicale

theme park *n* parco *m* tematico

theme song *n,* **theme tune** *n* tema *m* musicale

themselves [ðəm·'selvz] *pron* **1.** *subject* essi stessi, esse stesse **2.** *object, reflexive* si; **the children behaved ~** i bambini si sono comportati bene **3.** *after prep* se stessi, se stesse; **by ~** da soli

then [ðen] **I.** *adj form* d'allora; **the ~ chairman** l'allora presidente **II.** *adv* **1.** (*at aforementioned time*) allora; **before ~** prima di allora; **from ~ on**(**ward**) da allora in poi; **since ~** da allora; **until ~** fino ad allora; (**every**) **now and ~** ogni tanto **2.** (*after that*) poi; **what ~?** e poi? **3.** (*additionally*) inoltre; **but ~** (**again**) ma d'altronde **4.** (*as a result*) dunque; **~ he must be there** allora dev'essere lì **5.** (*that being the case*) allora **6.** (*agreement*) **all right ~** allora va bene

thence [ðens] *adv form* da lì

thenceforth [ˌðens·'fɔːrθ] *adv form,* **thenceforward** [ˌðens·'fɔːr·wəd] *adv form* da allora

theocracy [θɪ·'ɑː·krə·si] <-ies> *n* teocrazia *f*

theodolite [θɪ·'ɑː·də·laɪt] *n* teodolite *m*

theologian [ˌθiː·ə·'loʊ·dʒən] *n* teologo, -a *m, f*

theological [ˌθiː·ə·'lɑː·dʒɪ·kl] *adj* teologico, -a

theology [θɪ·'ɑː·lə·dʒi] <-ies> *n* teologia *f*

theorem ['θiː·ə·əm] *n* MAT teorema *m;* **Pythagoras's ~** il teorema di Pitagora

theoretical [ˌθiː·ə·'re·t̬ɪ·kəl] *adj* teorico, -a

theoretically *adv* teoricamente

theorist ['θiː·ə·ɪst] *n* teorico, -a *m, f*

theorize ['θiː·ə·raɪz] *vi* teorizzare

theory ['θiː·ə·ri] <-ies> *n* teoria *f;* **in ~** in teoria

therapeutic(**al**) [ˌθe·rə·'pjuː·t̬ɪ·k(əl)] *adj* terapeutico, -a

therapeutics [ˌθe·rə·'pjuː·t̬ɪks] *n* terapeutica *f*

therapist ['θe·rə·pɪst] *n* terapeuta *mf*

therapy ['θe·rə·pi] <-ies> *n* terapia *f*

there [ðer] **I.** *adv* **1.** lì [*o* là]; **here and ~** qua e là; **~ is/are** c'è/ci sono; **~ will be** ci sarà/saranno; **~ you are!** eccoti qua!; **~'s the train** ecco il treno; **~ is no one** non c'è nessuno; **~ and then** subito **II.** *interj* ecco!; **~, take this** prendi questo; **~, that's enough!** insomma, basta adesso!

thereabouts ['ðer·ə·baʊts] *adv* (*approximately*) all'incirca; (*near*) nei dintorni

thereafter [ðer·'æf·t̬ə] *adv* successivamente

thereby [ðer·'baɪ] *adv form* pertanto ▸ **~ hangs a** <u>tale</u> *iron* è una storia lunga

therefore ['ðer·fɔːr] *adv* perciò; **to decide ~ to do sth** decidere, di conseguenza, di fare qc

therein [ðer·'ɪn] *adv form* ivi; *fig* in ciò

thereof [ðer·'ɑːv] *adv form* di ciò

thereupon [ˌðer·ə·'pɑːn] *adv* a quel punto

therm [θɜːrm] *n* termia *f*

thermal ['θɜːr·məl] **I.** *n* **1.** (*air current*) corrente *f* ascensionale **2.** *pl* (*underwear*) biancheria *f* termica **II.** *adj* PHYS, INFOR termico, -a; (*water*) termale

thermal underwear *n* biancheria *f* termica

thermodynamic [ˌθɜːr·moʊ·daɪ·'næ·mɪk] *adj* termodinamico, -a

thermoelectric [ˌθɜːr·moʊ·ɪ·'lek·trɪk] *adj* termoelettrico, -a

thermometer [θə·'mɑː·mə·t̬ə] *n* termometro *m*

thermonuclear [ˌθɜːr·moʊ·'nuː·k·lɪə] *adj* termonucleare

Thermos® (**bottle**) ['θɜːr·məs·(ˌbɑː·t̬l)] *n,* **Thermos**® **flask** *n* thermos® *m inv*

thermostat ['θɜːr·mə·stæt] *n* termostato *m*

thermostatic [ˌθɜːr·mə·'stæt] *adj* termostatico, -a

thesaurus [θɪ·'sɔː·rəs] <-es *o* -ri> *n* dizionario *m* dei sinonimi

these [ðiːz] *pl of* **this**

thesis ['θiː·sɪs] <-ses> *n* tesi *f inv*

they [ðeɪ] *pron pers* **1.** (*3rd person pl*) loro; **~ are my parents/sisters** (loro) sono i miei genitori/le mie sorelle **2.** (*people in general*) **~ say that ...** dicono che ...

they'll [ðeɪl] = **they will** *s.* **will**

they're [ðer] = **they are** *s.* **be**

they've [ðeɪv] = **they have** *s.* **have**

thick [θɪk] **I.** *adj* **1.** (*not thin: wall*) spesso, -a; (*coat*) pesante **2.** (*dense: hair*) folto, -a; (*forest*) fitto, -a; (*liquid*) denso, -a **3.** (*extreme: darkness*) fitto, -a; (*accent*) marcato, -a **4.** (*stupid*) tonto, -a; **to be a bit ~** essere un po' tonto; **to be as ~ as two short planks** *inf* essere duro di comprendonio **5.** (*very friendly*) **to be ~ with sb** esser molto amico di qn ▸ **through ~ and** <u>thin</u> nella buona e nella cattiva sorte **II.** *n inf* to be in the ~ of sth esser nel pieno di qc

thicken ['θɪ·kən] **I.** *vt* ispessire **II.** *vi* ispessirsi

thickener *n*, **thickening** *n* addensante *m*

thicket ['θɪ·kɪt] *n* boscaglia *f*

thickheaded ['θɪk·ˌhe·dɪd] *adj* ottuso, -a

thickness ['θɪk·nɪs] *n* **1.** (*size*) spessore *m* **2.** (*of hair*) foltezza *f;* (*of sauce*) consistenza *f*

thickset ['θɪk·set] *adj* tozzo, -a

thick-skinned ['θɪk·skɪnd] *adj* insensibile; **he is** ~ tutto gli scivola addosso

thief [θiːf, *s* 'θiːvz] <thieves> *n* ladro, -a *m, f*

thieve [θiːv] *vi, vt liter* rubare

thieving ['θiː·vɪŋ] **I.** *n liter* furto *m* **II.** *adj* ladro, -a

thigh [θaɪ] *n* coscia *f*

thighbone *n* femore *m*

thimble ['θɪm·bl] *n* ditale *m*

thin [θɪn] <-nn-> **I.** *adj* **1.** (*not thick: clothes*) leggero, -a; (*person*) delicato, -a; (*very slim*) magro, -a **2.** (*soup, sauce*) liquido, -a; (*wine*) annacquato, -a **3.** (*sparse: hair*) rado, -a; **to be ~ on top** esser un po' pelato **4.** (*voice*) sottile; (*excuse*) debole **II.** <-nn-> *vt* (*dilute*) diluire

◆**thin down I.** *vi* assottigliarsi **II.** *vt* diluire

◆**thin out I.** *vt* diradare; (*plants*) sfoltire **II.** *vi* ridursi

thine [ðaɪn] *pron pos* HIST (il) tuo *m*, (la) tua *f*, (i) tuoi *mpl*, (le) tue *fpl*

thing [θɪŋ] *n* **1.** (*object, action*) cosa *f;* **the good/best/main** ~ la cosa buona/migliore/ principale; **one** ~ **after another** una cosa dopo l'altra; **to be a** ~ **of the past** esser una cosa passata; **the last** ~ **she wants to do is ...** l'ultima cosa che vuol fare è ... **2.** (*matter*) **to know a** ~ **or two** saperla lunga; **above all** ~**s** più di tutto; **another** ~ un'altra cosa; **and another** ~, **...** e inoltre, ...; **if it's not one** ~, **it's another** se non è una cosa è l'altra **3.** (*social behavior*) **it's the done** ~ è la cosa da farsi **4.** (*fashion*) **the latest** ~ **in shoes** l'ultima moda in fatto di scarpe **5.** *fam* (*the important point*) **the real** ~ la cosa autentica; **the very** ~ quello che ci vuole **6.** *pl* (*possessions*) cose *fpl;* **all his** ~**s** tutta la sua roba **7.** *pl* (*the situation*) **as** ~**s stand, the way** ~**s are** così come stanno le cose **8.** *inf* (*term of affection*) **the poor** ~! povero!; (*children, animals*) poverino!; **you lucky** ~! fortunato mortale!; **lazy** ~! pigrone!; **stupid** ~! imbecille! ▶**to be all** ~**s to all men** cercare di accontentare tutti; **it's just one of those** ~**s** son cose che capitano; **he won but it was a close** ~ ha vinto per un pelo; **all** ~**s being equal** a parità di condizioni; **first** ~**s first** prima le cose più importanti; **to not know the first** ~ **about sth** non intendersi minimamente di qc; **to be onto a good** ~ *inf* aver trovato la pacchia; **to do one's own** ~ far quello che si vuole; **to have a** ~ **about sth** *inf* avere un debole per qc; **to be hearing** ~**s** sentire voci immaginarie; **to make a** (**big**) ~ **out of sth** fare un putiferio per qc

thingamabob ['θɪŋ·ə·məˌbɑːb] *n*, **thinga-majig** ['θɪŋ·ə·məˌdʒɪg] *n*, **thingy** ['θɪ·ŋi] *n* (*object*) cosa *f;* (*person*) coso, -a *m, f*

think [θɪŋk] <thought, thought> **I.** *n* to have a ~ **about sth** pensarci su **II.** *vt* **1.** (*believe*) pensare, credere; **who would have thought it!** chi l'avrebbe pensato! **2.** (*consider*) considerare; **to** ~ **sb** (**to be**) **sth** considerare qn (come) qc; **to** ~ **nothing of sb** non avere una grande opinione di qn; ~ **nothing of it!** non dirlo neppure! **III.** *vi* pensare; **to** ~ **aloud** pensare ad alta voce; **to** ~ **for oneself** pensare con la propria testa; **to** ~ **to oneself** pensare tra sé e sé; **to** ~ **of doing sth** pensare di fare qc; **to** ~ **about/of sb/sth** pensare a qn/qc

◆**think ahead** *vi* pensare con anticipo

◆**think back** *vi* to ~ **to sth** ripensare a qc; **to** ~ **over sth** ritornare con la memoria a qc

◆**think of** *vi* pensare di

◆**think out** *vt* **1.** (*consider*) considerare bene **2.** (*plan*) escogitare

◆**think over** *vt* riflettere su

◆**think through** *vt* riflettere attentamente su

◆**think up** *vt* inventare

thinker *n* pensatore, -trice *m, f*

thinking I. *n* **1.** (*thought process*) pensiero *m* **2.** (*reasoning*) riflessione *f* **3.** (*opinion*) opinione *f* **II.** *adj* intelligente

think tank *n* gruppo *m* di esperti

thinner *n* diluente *m*

thinness *n* magrezza *f*

thin-skinned ['θɪn·skɪnd] *adj* sensibile

third [θɜːrd] **I.** *adj* terzo, -a **II.** *n* **1.** (*order*) terzo, -a *m, f* **2.** (*date*) tre *m* **3.** (*fraction*) terzo *m* **4.** MUS, AUTO terza *f; s.a.* **eighth**

third degree *n* to give sb the ~ fare il terzo grado a qn

third-degree burns *npl* ustioni *fpl* di terzo grado

thirdly *adv* in terzo luogo

third party *n* terzo *m*

third-party insurance *n*, **third-party liability** *n* assicurazione *f* contro terzi

third person *n* LING terza persona *f*

third-rate *adj* scadente

Third World *n* the ~ il Terzo Mondo

thirst [θɜːrst] *n* sete *f;* **to die of** ~ morire di sete; **to quench one's** ~ dissetarsi; ~ **for power** sete di potere

thirsty ['θɜːrs·ti] <-ier, -iest> *adj* assetato, -a; **to be** ~ aver sete; **to be** ~ **for sth** *fig* aver sete di qc

thirteen [θɜːr·'tiːn] **I.** *adj* tredici **II.** *n* tredici *m; s.a.* **eight**

thirteenth [θɜːr·'tiːnθ] **I.** *adj* tredicesimo, -a **II.** *n* **1.** (*order*) tredicesimo, -a *m, f* **2.** (*date*) tredici *m* **3.** (*fraction*) tredicesimo *m;* (*part*) tredicesima parte *f; s.a.* **eighth**

thirtieth ['θɜːr·tɪ·əθ] **I.** *adj* trentesimo, -a **II.** *n* **1.** (*order*) trentesimo, -a *m, f* **2.** (*date*) trenta *m* **3.** (*fraction*) trentesimo *m;* (*part*) trentesima parte *f; s.a.* **eighth**

thirty ['θɜːr·ti] <-ies> **I.** *adj* trenta **II.** *n*

T

trenta *m; s.a.* **eighty**

this [ðɪs] I.<these> *adj det* questo, -a; ~ **car** quest'automobile; ~ **house** questa casa; ~ **one** questo; ~ **day** oggi; ~ **morning/evening** stamattina/stasera; ~ **time** questa volta; ~ **time last month** esattamente un mese fa; **these days** di questi tempi II.<these> *pron dem* questo *m*, questa *f*; **what is** ~**?** che cos'è?; **who is** ~**?** chi è?; ~ **and that** questo e quello; ~ **is Anna (speaking)** (*on the phone*) sono Anna III. *adv* così; ~ **late** così tardi; ~ **much** tanto così; ~ **big** così grande

thistle ['θɪ·sl] *n* cardo *m*

tho [ðoʊ] *conj s.* **though**

thong [θɑːŋ] *n* **1.** (*strip of leather*) correggia *f* **2.** (*G-string*) perizoma *m* **3.** *pl* (*sandal*) infradito *m inv*

thorax ['θɔː·ræks] <-es *o* -aces> *n* torace *m*

thorn [θɔːrn] *n* spina *f* ▶**that's a** ~ **in my flesh** è la mia spina nel fianco

thorny ['θɔːr·ni] <-ier, -iest> *adj* spinoso, -a

thorough ['θɜː·roʊ] *adj* **1.** (*complete*) assoluto, -a **2.** (*detailed*) esauriente **3.** (*careful*) minuzioso, -a

thoroughbred ['θɜː·roʊ·bred] I. *n* purosangue *mf inv* II. *adj* purosangue *inv*

thoroughfare ['θɜː·roʊ·fer] *n form* via *f* principale

thoroughgoing [ˌθɜː·roʊ·'goʊ·ɪŋ] *adj form* **1.** (*conscientious: analysis*) rigoroso, -a **2.** (*complete: reform*) radicale

thoroughly *adv* **1.** (*in detail*) a fondo **2.** (*completely*) completamente

thoroughness *n* meticolosità *f*

those [ðoʊz] *pl of* **that**

thou[1] [ðaʊ] *pron pers, liter* tu

thou[2] [θaʊ] *abbr of* **thousand** mille *m*

though [ðoʊ] I. *conj* nonostante +*subj;* **as** ~ come se +*subj;* **even** ~ anche se; **even** ~ **it's cold** nonostante faccia freddo II. *adv* comunque; **he did do it,** ~ comunque, lui l'ha fatto

thought [θɑːt] *n* **1.** (*process*) pensiero *m;* **on second** ~ ripensandoci bene; **without** ~ senza pensare; **after much** ~ dopo aver riflettuto a lungo; **to be deep in** ~ esser immerso nei propri pensieri; **lost in** ~ assorto nei propri pensieri **2.** (*idea, opinion*) idea *f;* **that's a** ~ è una buona idea ▶**a penny for your** ~**s** *prov* a cosa pensi?

thoughtful ['θɑːt·fəl] *adj* **1.** (*pensive*) pensieroso, -a **2.** (*careful*) ponderato, -a **3.** (*considerate*) premuroso, -a

thoughtless ['θɑːt·ləs] *adj* (*not thinking enough*) irriflessivo, -a; (*tactless*) poco delicato, -a; (*careless*) avventato, -a

thought-out [ˌθɑːt·'aʊt] *adj* pianificato, -a

thought-provoking *adj* che fa pensare

thousand ['θaʊ·znd] I. *adj* mille II. *n* mille *m*

thousandth ['θaʊ·zntθ] I. *n* millesimo *m* II. *adj* **1.** (*being one of a thousand*) millesimo, -a **2.** (*in a series*) **the** ~ il numero mille

thrash [θræʃ] *vt* **1.** (*beat*) picchiare **2.** *inf* (*defeat*) battere

◆**thrash out** *vt inf* (*problem*) risolvere; (*agreement*) arrivare a

thrashing *n* botte *fpl*

thread [θred] I. *n* **1.** (*for sewing*) filo *m* **2.** (*of screw*) filettatura *f* ▶**to hang by a** ~ essere appeso a un filo II. *vt* (*needle*) infilare; **to** ~ **sth through sth** passare qc attraverso qc; **to** ~ **sth onto sth** infilare qc in qc

threadbare ['θred·ber] *adj* **1.** (*worn*) logoro, -a **2.** (*argument, excuse*) trito, -a

threat [θret] *n* minaccia *f*

threaten ['θre·tən] I. *vt* minacciare; **to** ~ **to do sth** minacciare di fare qc II. *vi* fare minacce

threatening *adj* minaccioso, -a

three [θriː] I. *adj* tre II. *n* tre *m; s.a.* **eight**

three-cornered [ˌθriː·'kɔːr·nəd] *adj* triangolare; ~ **hat** tricorno *m*

three-D *adj inf abbr of* **three-dimensional** tridimensionale

three-dimensional *adj* tridimensionale

threefold ['θriː·foʊld] I. *adj* triplice II. *adv* tre volte tanto

three-part *adj* di tre parti

three-piece [ˌθriː·'piːs] *adj* in tre pezzi

three-piece suit *n* abito *m* in tre pezzi

three-ply ['θriː·plaɪ] *adj* (*wood*) a tre strati; (*wool*) a tre capi

three-quarter (length) *adj* tre quarti

threesome ['θriː·səm] *n* trio *m*

three-wheeler [θrɪ·'wiː·lə] *n* veicolo *m* a tre ruote

thresh [θreʃ] *vt* trebbiare

threshing machine ['θre·ʃɪŋ mə·'ʃiːn] *n* trebbiatrice *f*

threshold ['θreʃ·hoʊld] *n a. fig* soglia *f;* **pain** ~ soglia del dolore; **tax** ~ minimo *m* imponibile

threw [θruː] *pt of* **throw**

thrice [θraɪs] *adv* tre volte

thrift [θrɪft] *n* parsimonia *f*

thrifty ['θrɪf·ti] <-ier, -iest> *adj* parsimonioso, -a

thrill [θrɪl] I. *n* brivido *m* II. *vt* entusiasmare III. *vi* entusiasmarsi

thriller ['θrɪ·lə] *n* thriller *m inv*

thrilling ['θrɪ·lɪŋ] *adj* entusiasmante

thrive [θraɪv] <thrived *o* throve, thrived *o* thriven> *vi* (*person, plant*) crescere molto; (*business*) prosperare

thriving *adj* prospero, -a

throat [θroʊt] *n* ANAT gola *f;* **sore** ~ mal *m* di gola; **to grab sb by the** ~ prendere qn per la gola ▶**to stick in sb's** ~ (*proposal*) non andare giù a qn; (*words*) fermarsi in gola a qn; **to be at each other's** ~**s** esser come cani e gatti

throaty ['θroʊ·ti] <-ier, -iest> *adj* (*voice*) roco, -a; (*laugh*) gutturale

throb [θrɑːb] I. *n* (*of engine*) vibrazione *f;* (*of heart*) palpitazione *f* II.<-bb-> *vi* (*engine*) vibrare; (*heart*) palpitare

throes [θroʊz] *npl* angustia *f;* (*of death*) agonia *f;* **to be in the** ~ **of sth** essere nel bel mezzo di qc

thrombosis [θrɑːmˈboʊ·sɪs] <-es> n trombosi f inv

throne [θroʊn] n trono m

throng [θrɑːŋ] I. n moltitudine f II. vt affollare; **to be ~ed** essere affollato III. vi affollarsi; **to ~ to do sth** accorrere in massa a fare qc

throttle [ˈθrɑːˌt̬l] I. n acceleratore m; **to open the ~** accelerare; **at full ~** a manetta inf II. <-ll-> vt strangolare
♦**throttle back** vi rallentare

through [θruː] I. prep 1. (spatial) attraverso, per; **to go right ~ sth** attraversare qc; **to go ~ the door** entrare dalla porta; **to walk ~ a room** attraversare una stanza; **to walk ~ a village** camminare per un paese 2. (temporal) durante; **all ~ my life** per tutta la mia vita; **to be ~ sth** aver terminato qc 3. (until) da; **open Monday ~ Friday** aperto da lunedì a venerdì 4. (by means of) per mezzo di II. adv 1. (of place) da parte a parte; **I read the book ~** ho letto il libro da cima a fondo; **to go ~ to sth** andar dritto a qc 2. (of time) **all day ~** per tutto il giorno; **halfway ~** a metà 3. TEL **to put sb ~ to sb** passare qn a qn 4. (completely) completamente; **to think sth ~** riflettere bene su qc ▸~ **and** ~ da capo a piedi III. adj 1. (finished) finito, -a; **we are ~** abbiamo finito 2. (direct) diretto, -a 3. SCHOOL **to get ~** passare

through flight n volo m diretto

throughout [θruːˈaʊt] I. prep 1. (spatial) in tutto, -a; **~ the town** per tutta la città 2. (temporal) durante tutto, -a; **~ his stay** per tutta la sua permanenza II. adv 1. (spatial) dappertutto 2. (temporal) tutto il tempo

throughput [ˈθruːˌpʊt] n volume m di produzione; INFOR volume m di trasferimento dati

through traffic n traffico m di transito

through train n treno m diretto

throughway [ˈθruːˌweɪ] n autostrada f a pagamento

throve [θroʊv] pt of **thrive**

throw [θroʊ] I. n 1. (act of throwing) lancio m 2. SPORTS lancio m, tiro m 3. inf (chance) chance f inv; **his last ~** la sua ultima chance II. <threw, thrown> vi lanciare III. <threw, thrown> vt 1. (propel) tirare; (ball, javelin) lanciare; **to ~ oneself into sb's arms** buttarsi tra le braccia di qn; **to ~ oneself at sb** gettarsi su qn 2. (cause to fall: rider) disarcionare; (opponent) atterrare 3. (dedicate) **to ~ oneself into sth** buttarsi in qc 4. (direct: glance) lanciare; (remark) fare; (kiss) mandare 5. inf (confuse) sconcertare 6. TECH tornire 7. (turn on) accendere; **to ~ the switch** schiacciare l'interruttore 8. (have) **to ~ a tantrum** fare una scenata 9. (give) **to ~ a party** dare una festa
♦**throw away** vt 1. (discard) buttare 2. (waste) buttar via; **to throw money away on sth** buttar via i soldi in qc; **to throw oneself away** buttarsi via 3. (speak casually) buttare là
♦**throw back** vt 1. (return) rilanciare

2. (open: curtains) tirare; (blanket) buttare indietro 3. (remind unkindly) rinfacciare; **to throw sth back in sb's face** rinfacciare qc a qn; (retort angrily) replicare
♦**throw down** vt 1. (throw from above) buttare giù 2. (deposit forcefully) deporre; (weapons) gettare 3. (drink quickly) trangugiare
♦**throw in** I. vt 1. (put into) buttar dentro 2. (include) aggiungere; (comment) buttare lì II. vi (propel) lanciare
♦**throw off** vt 1. (remove) togliere 2. (escape from) depistare 3. (rid oneself of) disfarsi di 4. (write quickly) improvvisare
♦**throw on** vt 1. (clothes) infilare 2. (pounce upon) **to throw oneself on sb** gettarsi su qn
♦**throw out** vt 1. (eject: person) buttar fuori; (thing) buttar via; (case) respingere; (suggestion) rifiutare 2. (emit: heat, light) emettere
♦**throw over** vt (lover) piantare
♦**throw together** vt 1. inf (make quickly) mettere insieme qc 2. (cause to meet) fare incontrare
♦**throw up** I. vt 1. (project upwards) lanciare in aria 2. (bring to light) rivelare 3. (build quickly) tirar su alla svelta 4. inf (give up) mollare 5. inf (vomit) vomitare II. vi inf vomitare

throwaway [ˈθroʊ·ə·ˌweɪ] adj usa e getta inv; **~ razor** rasoio m usa e getta; **~ remark** commento m buttato là

throwback [ˈθroʊ·ˌbæk] n ritorno m; BIO atavismo m

thrower n lanciatore, -trice m, f

throw-in [ˈθroʊ·ˌɪn] n (in soccer) rimessa m in gioco; (in baseball) lancio m

throwing n lancio m

thrown pp of **throw**

thru [θruː] prep, adj s. **through**

thrum [θrʌm] I. <-mm-> vt (guitar) strimpellare II. vi (engine) vibrare III. n (of engine) vibrazione f

thrush[1] [θrʌʃ] n tordo m

thrush[2] [θrʌʃ] n MED mughetto m

thrust [θrʌst] I. <-, -> vi 1. (shove) spingere; **to ~ at sb with sth** assestare un colpo a qn con qc 2. (force one's way) farsi largo II. <-, -> vt (push) spingere; (insert) ficcare; **to ~ one's hands into one's pockets** ficcarsi le mani in tasca III. n 1. (shove) spinta f; **sword ~** stoccata f 2. (impetus) spinta f; **the main ~ of an argument** l'idea centrale di una discussione 3. TECH (propulsion) spinta f

thrusting [ˈθrʌs·tɪŋ] adj arrivista

thruway [ˈθruː·ˌweɪ] n autostrada f

thud [θʌd] I. <-dd-> vi colpire con un tonfo; **to ~ on the table with one's fist** colpire il tavolo con un pugno II. n tonfo m

thug [θʌg] n teppista mf

thumb [θʌm] I. n pollice m ▸ **to be all fingers and ~s, to be all ~s** essere impacciato, nei movimenti delle dita; **to stand out like a sore ~** esser un pugno in un occhio; **to be under sb's ~** esser dominato da qn II. vt

1. (*hitchhike*) **to ~ a lift** fare l'autostop **2.** (*soil with the thumbs*) sciupare **3.** (*glance through: book*) sfogliare

thumb index *n* indice *m* a rubrica

thumbnail ['θʌm·neɪl] *n* unghia *f* del pollice

thumbnail sketch *n* breve descrizione *f*

thumbscrew ['θʌms·kruː] *n* serrapollici *m inv*

thumbtack *n* puntina *f* da disegno

thump [θʌmp] **I.** *vt* colpire; **to ~ sth down** abbattere qc **II.** *vi* **1.** (*heart*) battere forte **2.** (*beat*) **to ~ on sth** battere su qc **III.** *n* **1.** (*blow*) colpo *m;* **to give sb a ~** dare un pugno a qn **2.** (*noise*) tonfo *m*

thumping *adj inf* tremendo; **I've got a ~ head-ache** ho un mal di testa pazzesco

thunder ['θʌn·də] **I.** *n* **1.** METEO tuono *m;* **a clap of ~** un tuono **2.** (*sound*) rombo *m* ▶ **to steal** sb's **~** battere qn sul tempo **II.** *vi* tuon-are; (*shout*) urlare **III.** *vt* tuonare

thunderbolt ['θʌn·də·boʊlt] *n* **1.** METEO ful-mine *m* **2.** *fig* fulmine a ciel sereno ▶ **to drop a ~ on sb** lasciare qn di stucco

thunderclap *n* tuono *m*

thundercloud *n pl* nuvolone *m*

thundering ['θʌn·də·rɪŋ] **I.** *n* rombo *m* **II.** *adj inf* (*very noisy*) assordante; *fig* (*very great*) tre-mendo

thunderous ['θʌn·də·rəs] *adj* fragoroso, -a

thunderstorm ['θʌn·də·stɔːrm] *n* tem-porale *m*

thunderstruck ['θʌn·də·strʌk] *adj form* stu-pefatto, -a

thundery ['θʌn·də·ri] *adj* <-ier, -iest> tempo-ralesco, -a

Thursday ['θɜːrz·deɪ] *n* giovedì *m inv;* **Maundy ~** giovedì santo; *s.a.* **Friday**

thus [ðʌs] *adv form* **1.** (*therefore*) pertanto **2.** (*like this*) così; **~ far** fino ad ora

thwart [θwɔːrt] *vt* frustrare; (*plan*) ostacolare

thy [ðaɪ] *pron pos, liter* il tuo, la tua, i tuoi, le tue

thyme [taɪm] *n* timo *m*

thyroid ['θaɪ·rɔɪd] *adj* tiroide *f*

tiara [tɪ·'e·rə] *n* diadema *f*

tibia ['tɪ·biə] <-iae> *n* tibia *f*

tic [tɪk] *n* tic *m inv*

tick¹ [tɪk] *n* zecca *f*

tick² [tɪk] **I.** *n* **1.** (*sound*) tic-tac *m inv* **2.** (*mark*) segno *m* di spunta **II.** *vi* fare tic-tac; **I don't know what makes her ~** non capisco il suo modo di ragionare **III.** *vt* spuntare

◆ **tick off** *vt* **1.** (*mark off*) spuntare **2.** *inf* (*exas-perate*) esasperare

◆ **tick over** *vi* **1.** TECH andare al minimo **2.** *fig* tirare avanti

ticker ['tɪ·kə] *n* **1.** TEL telescrivente *f* **2.** (*watch*) orologio *m* **3.** *inf* (*heart*) cuore *m*

ticker tape *n* nastro *m* di telescrivente

ticker-tape parade *n* sfilata *f* trionfale

ticket ['tɪ·kɪt] *n* **1.** biglietto *m;* (*for library*) tes-sera *f;* **return ~** biglietto *m* di andata e ritorno **2.** (*price, information tag*) etichetta *f* **3.** AUTO multa *f* **4.** POL rosa *f* di candidati ▶ **just the ~** proprio quello che ci vuole

ticket agency *n* agenzia *f* per la vendita di big-lietti

ticket collector *n* bigliettaio, -a *m, f*

ticket counter *n* sportello *m* di vendita di big-lietti

ticket holder *n* persona *f* munita di biglietto

ticket machine *n* biglietteria *f* automatica

ticket office *n* biglietteria *f*

ticking¹ ['tɪ·kɪŋ] *n* (*sound*) ticchettio *m*

ticking² ['tɪ·kɪŋ] *n* (*textile*) tela *m* da materassi

tickle ['tɪ·kl] **I.** *vi* fare il solletico; (*clothes*) piz-zicare **II.** *vt* **1.** fare il solletico a **2.** (*amuse*) divertire ▶ **to be ~d pink** esser incantato **III.** *n* solletico *m;* (*tingling*) pizzicore *m*

ticklish ['tɪk·lɪʃ] *adj* che soffre il solletico; (*deli-cate*) delicato, -a

tidal ['taɪ·dəl] *adj* della marea

tidal wave *n* tsunami *m inv*

tidbit ['tɪd·bɪt] *n s.* **titbit**

tiddly ['tɪd·li] *adj* <-ier, -iest> *inf* (*slightly drunk*) alticcio, -a

tiddlywink ['tɪd·lɪ·wɪŋk] *n* pulci *fpl;* **~s** gioco *m* delle pulci

tide [taɪd] *n* **1.** (*of sea*) marea *f;* **high ~** alta marea; **low ~** bassa marea **2.** (*of opinion*) cor-rente *f;* **to go against the ~** andare controcor-rente; **to swim with the ~** seguire la corrente

◆ **tide over** *vt always sep* **to tide sb over** aiu-tare qn a tirare avanti

tideland ['taɪd·lænd] *n* bassofondo *m*

tidemark *n* (*mark left by high tide*) linea *f* di marea

tidiness ['taɪ·dɪ·nɪs] *n* ordine *m*

tidy ['taɪ·di] **I.** *adj* <-ier, -iest> **1.** (*orderly*) ordinato, -a; **to have a ~ mind** essere metodico **2.** *inf* (*considerable*) considerevole **II.** *vt* mettere in ordine

tie [taɪ] **I.** *n* **1.** (*necktie*) cravatta *f* **2.** (*cord*) lac-cio *m* **3.** *pl* (*bond*) legame *mpl;* (*diplomatic*) relazioni *fpl* **4.** (*equal ranking*) pareggio *m* **II.** *vi* **1.** (*fasten*) legare **2.** SPORTS pareg-giare **III.** *vt* **1.** (*fasten*) legare; (*knot*) fare **2.** (*restrict*) limitare; **to be ~d by/to sth** essere costretto da/a qc

◆ **tie back** *vt* fissare

◆ **tie down** *vt* legare; **to tie sb down to sth** *inf* vincolare qn a qc

◆ **tie in I.** *vt* collegare **II.** *vi* coincidere

◆ **tie up** *vt* **1.** (*bind*) legare; (*hair*) raccogliere; **to ~ some loose ends** *fig* ultimare i dettagli **2.** (*delay*) bloccare **3.** (*be busy*) **to be tied up** essere occupato **4.** FIN, ECON (*capital*) immobi-lizzare; **to be tied up in sth** essere impegnato in qc

tiebreak ['taɪ·breɪk] *n*, **tiebreaker** *n* tie-break *m inv*

tie clip *n* fermacravatta *m*

tie-in ['taɪ·ɪn] *n* **1.** (*agreement*) accordo *m* **2.** (*connection*) legame *m*

tie-on *adj* che si lega

tiepin ['taɪ·pɪn] *n* spilla *f* da cravatta

tier [tɪr] *n* (*row*) fila *f;* (*level*) gradinata *f;* (*in a* *hierarchy*) livello *m*

tie-up ['taɪ·ʌp] *n* legame *m*

tiff [tɪf] *n inf* scaramuccia *f;* **to have a ~** avere un battibecco

tiger ['taɪ·gə] *n* tigre *f* ▶ **to have a ~ by the** <u>tail</u> prendere il toro per le corna

tight [taɪt] **I.** *adj* **1.** (*screw, knot*) stretto, -a; (*clothing*) aderente **2.** (*rope*) teso, -a; (*skin*) tirato, -a **3.** (*condition, discipline*) rigoroso, -a; (*budget*) limitato, -a; (*situation*) difficile; (*schedule*) rigido, -a; **to keep a ~ hold on sth** tenere qc sotto stretto controllo; **to be ~ for money/time** essere a corto di soldi/tempo **4.** (*bend*) stretto, -a **5.** (*hard-fought*) combattuto, -a **6.** *inf* (*drunk*) sbronzo, -a **II.** *adv* forte; **to close sth ~** chiudere bene qc; **sleep ~!** dormi bene!

tighten ['taɪ·ten] **I.** *vt* **1.** (*make tight*) stringere; (*rope*) tendere **2.** (*restrictions*) intensificare **II.** *vi* stringersi; (*restrictions*) intensificarsi

tightfisted [ˌtaɪt·'fɪs·tɪd] *adj inf* tirchio, -a

tight-fitting *adj* attillato, -a

tightlipped [ˌtaɪt·'lɪpt] *adj* riservato, -a; **to be ~ about sth** tener la bocca chiusa a proposito di qc

tightness *n* **1.** (*of clothing*) strettezza *f* **2.** (*of discipline*) rigore *m;* (*of budget*) limitatezza *f;* (*of schedule*) rigidità *f* **3.** PSYCH tensione *f*

tightrope ['taɪ·troʊp] *n* fune *f;* **to walk a ~** *a. fig* stare sul filo del rasoio

tightrope walker *n* funambolo, -a *m, f*

tights [taɪts] *npl* **1.** (*leggings*) collant *m inv* **2.** (*for dancing*) calzamaglia *f*

tightwad ['taɪt·wɑːd] *n inf* taccagno, -a *m, f*

tigress ['taɪ·grɪs] *n* tigre (*f* femmina)

tike [taɪk] *n s.* **tyke**

tile [taɪl] **I.** *n* (*for roof*) tegola *f;* (*for walls, floors*) piastrella *f* **II.** *vt* (*roof*) rivestire di tegole; (*wall, floor*) piastrellare

tiler ['taɪ·lə] *n* piastrellista *mf*

till¹ [tɪl] **I.** *prep* fino a **II.** *conj* finché

till² [tɪl] *n* cassa *f* ▶ **he was caught with his** <u>hand</u> **in the ~** l'han colto con le mani nel sacco

till³ [tɪl] *vt* coltivare

tiller ['tɪ·lə] *n* barra *f* del timone; **at the ~** al timone

tilt [tɪlt] **I.** *n* inclinazione *f* ▶ (**at**) <u>full</u> **~** a tutta velocità **II.** *vt* inclinare; **to ~ sth back** inclinare qc indietro **III.** *vi* inclinarsi; **to ~ back** inclinarsi indietro; **to ~ over** rovesciarsi

timber ['tɪm·bə] *n* **1.** (*wood*) legname *m* **2.** (*beam*) trave *f* **3.** (*trees*) alberi *m* da legname *pl;* **~!** attenzione, cade!

timbered *adj* in legno

timberline ['tɪm·bə·laɪn] *n* limite *m* forestale

time [taɪm] **I.** *n* **1.** tempo *m;* **to kill ~** ammazzare il tempo; **to make ~** trovare il tempo; **to spend ~** passare il tempo; (**how**) **~ flies** il tempo vola; **~ passes** il tempo stringe; **as ~ goes by** col passare del tempo; **in the course of ~** nel corso del tempo; **to be a matter of ~** essere questione di tempo; (**only**) **~ can tell**

solo il tempo lo dirà; **of all ~** di tutti i tempi; **in ~** col tempo; **over ~** col tempo **2.** (*period*) tempo *m;* **access ~** INFOR tempo di accesso; **extra ~** SPORTS tempo supplementare; **free ~** tempo libero; **after a ~** dopo un certo tempo; **all the ~** continuamente; **a long ~ ago** molto tempo fa; **some ~ ago** un po' di tempo fa; **for the ~ being** per il momento; **given ~** col tempo; **to have a good ~** divertirsi; **to have all the ~ in the world** avere tutto il tempo che si vuole; **to run out of ~**, **to be (all) out of ~** *inf* essere fuori tempo; **to save ~** guadagnare tempo; **to waste ~** perdere tempo; **most of the ~** la maggior parte del tempo; **in one week's ~** in una settimana; **for a short/long period of ~** per un breve/lungo periodo di tempo; **there's no ~ to lose** non c'è tempo da perdere; **can I have ~ off to go to the dentist?** posso prendere un permesso per andare dal dentista?; **to take one's ~ in doing sth** prendersela comoda a fare qc; **it takes a long/short ~** ci vuole molto/poco tempo; **to give sb a hard ~** *inf* rendere la vita difficile a qn; **I don't have a lot of ~ for him** non mi sta molto a genio **3.** (*clock*) ora *f;* **arrival/departure ~** ora di arrivo/partenza; **bus/train ~s** orario *m* degli autobus/dei treni; **to have the ~** sapere [*o* avere] l'ora **4.** (*moment*) momento *m;* **the best ~ of day** il momento migliore della giornata; **this ~ tomorrow** domani a quest'ora; **at all ~s** sempre; **at a different ~** in un altro momento; **each ~** ogni volta; **the right ~** il momento giusto **5.** (*specific point in time*) ora *f;* **at any ~** a qualsiasi ora; **at any given ~**, **at (any) one ~** in un dato momento; **the last/next ~** l'ultima/la prossima volta; **at other ~s** in altri momenti; **at the present ~** attualmente; **it is about ~ that ...** è ora che ... +*subj;* **~ and (~) again** molto spesso; **ahead of ~** in anticipo; **to know the ~ ...** sapere al momento; **to remember the ~ ...** ricordare quando ... **6.** (*occasion*) volta *f;* **three ~ champion** tre volte campione; **lots of ~s** molte volte; **for the hundredth ~** per la centesima volta; **from ~ to ~** di quando in quando **7.** (*right moment*) ora *f;* **breakfast ~** ora di colazione; **it's high ~ that ...** è ora che ... +*subj;* **ahead of ~** in anticipo; **to do sth dead on ~** far qc esattamente a tempo; **the ~ comes** viene il momento **8.** (*epoch*) epoca *f;* **at one ~** un tempo; **from** [*o since*] **~ immemorial** da tempo immemorabile; **to be behind the ~s** non essere al passo coi tempi; **in ~s gone by** in epoche passate; **to keep up with the ~s** tenersi al passo coi tempi **9.** SPORTS tempo *m;* **record ~** tempo da record **10.** MUS tempo *m* **11.** ECON ore *fpl* di lavoro; **to work full/part ~** lavorare a tempo pieno/parziale; **to be on short ~** avere un orario ridotto ▶ **~ is of the** <u>essence</u> non c'è tempo da perdere; **to have ~ on one's** <u>hands</u> aver tempo libero; **~ is a great** <u>healer</u> *prov* il tempo guarisce le ferite; **~ is** <u>money</u> *prov* il tempo è denaro;

prov; **there's a ~ and a** place **(for every-thing)** *prov* ogni cosa a suo tempo; **a week is a long ~ in** politics *prov* tutto può succedere in politica; **there's no ~ like the** present *prov* non rimandare a domani quel che puoi fare oggi *prov;* ~ **and** tide **wait for no man** *prov* chi ha tempo non aspetti tempo; *prov;* ~ **heals all** wounds *prov* il tempo guarisce le ferite; **in** less **than no ~** in men che non si dica; **to** buy **~** prender tempo; **~s are** changing i tempi cambiano; **to** do **~** *inf* essere in prigione; **~** moves **on** la vita continua II. *vt* 1. SPORTS cronometrare 2. (*choose best moment for*) scegliere il momento adatto per III. *adj* SPORTS **~ trial** prova *f* a cronometro

time and motion study *n* COM studio *m* dei tempi e dei movimenti

time bomb *n* bomba *f* ad orologeria

timecard *n* cartellino (*m* di presenza)

time clock *n* orologio *m* marcatempo

time-consuming ['taɪm·kən·ˌsuː·mɪŋ] *adj* che richiede molto tempo

time difference *n* differenza *f* oraria

timekeeper *n* 1. (*device*) cronometro *m* 2. (*person*) cronometrista *mf;* **to be a poor ~** non essere una persona puntuale

time lag *n* lasso *m* di tempo

time-lapse photography *n* ripresa *f* temporizzata

timeless ['taɪm·ləs] *adj* senza tempo

time limit *n* limite *m* di tempo

time lock *n* serratura *f* a tempo

timely ['taɪm·li] *adj* <-ier, -iest> opportuno, -a; **in a ~ fashion** tempestivamente

time-out [ˌtaɪm·'aʊt] *n* 1. SPORTS time out *m inv* 2. (*rest*) pausa *f*

timer ['taɪ·mɚ] *n* timer *m inv;* GASTR contaminuti *m inv*

timesaving ['taɪm·ˌseɪ·vɪŋ] *adj* salvatempo *inv*

timescale ['taɪm·skeɪl] *n* lasso *m* di tempo

time-share *n* multiproprietà *f inv*

time-sharing *n* 1. (*on holiday*) multiproprietà *f inv* 2. INFOR time-sharing *m inv*

time sheet *n* cartellino (*m* di presenza)

timetable I. *n* (*for bus, train*) orario *m;* (*for project, events*) programma *m* II. *vt* programmare

timeworn ['taɪm·wɔːrn] *adj* logoro, -a; (*trite*) trito, -a; (*excuse*) banale

time zone *n* fuso *m* orario

timid ['tɪ·mɪd] *adj* <-er, -est> timido, -a

timidity [tɪ·'mɪ·də· t̬i] *n* timidezza *f*

timing ['taɪ·mɪŋ] *n* 1. cronometraggio *m;* **that was perfect ~** ha scelto il momento opportuno 2. (*rhythm*) tempismo *m*

timpani ['tɪm·pə·ni] *npl* MUS timpani *mpl*

tin [tɪn] I. *n* 1. (*metal*) stagno *m;* (*tinplate*) latta *f* 2. (*container*) barattolo *m* 3. (*for baking*) teglia *f* II. *vt* inscatolare

tin can *n* lattina *f*

tincture ['tɪŋk·tʃɚ] *n* tintura *f*

tinder ['tɪn·dɚ] *n* esca *f*

tinfoil *n* stagnola *f*

ting [tɪŋ] *n* tintinnio *m*

tinge [tɪndʒ] I. *n* 1. (*of color*) sfumatura *f* 2. (*of emotion*) nota *f* II. *vt* 1. (*dye*) tingere 2. *fig* sfumare

tingle ['tɪŋ·gl] I. *vi* formicolare II. *n* formicolio *m*

tin god *n pej, inf* eroe *m* di cartone

tin hat *n* elmetto *m* di protezione

tinhorn *n inf* presuntuoso, -a *m, f*

tinker ['tɪŋ·kɚ] I. *n* 1. HIST stagnino, -a ambulante *m* 2. zingaro, -a *m, f* II. *vi* **to ~ with sth** cercare di riparare qc

tinkle ['tɪŋ·kl] I. *vi* tintinnare II. *vt* far tintinnare III. *n* tintinnio *m;* **to give sb a ~** *inf* dare un colpo di telefono a qn

tinny ['tɪ·ni] *adj* <-ier, -iest> (*sound, taste*) metallico, -a

tin-pot ['tɪn·pɑːt] *adj pej, inf* da poco

tinsel ['tɪn·sl] *n* decorazioni *f* natalizie *pl*

tint [tɪnt] I. *n* (*color*) sfumatura *f;* (*for hair*) tinta *f* II. *vt* tingere

tiny ['taɪ·ni] *adj* <-ier, -iest> minuscolo, -a

tip[1] [tɪp] I. <-pp-> *vt* rovesciare II. *n* punta *f;* **from ~ to toe** dalla testa ai piedi; **the southern ~ of Florida** la punta estrema a sud della Florida; **it's on the ~ of my tongue** ce l'ho sulla punta della lingua

tip[2] [tɪp] I. <-pp-> *vt* (*incline*) inclinare; **to ~ the balance against/in favor of sb** far pendere la bilancia contro/a favore di qn II. *vi* inclinarsi

tip[3] [tɪp] I. *n* 1. (*for service*) mancia *f;* **10 per cent ~** una mancia del 10 per cento 2. (*hint*) suggerimento *m;* **to give sb a ~** dare una dritta a qn; **to take a ~ from sb** seguire il consiglio di qn II. <-pp-> *vt* (*give money*) dare una mancia a III. <-pp-> *vi* lasciare la mancia

◆**tip off** *vt* informare

◆**tip over** I. *vt* capovolgere II. *vi* capovolgersi

◆**tip up** I. *vt* ribaltare II. *vi* ribaltarsi

tip-off ['tɪp·ɑːf] *n inf* soffiata *f*

tipple ['tɪ·pl] I. *vi* (*drink*) bere II. *vt* bere III. *n inf* bicchierino *m;* **favorite ~ drink** *m inv* preferito

tipster ['tɪp·stɚ] *n* SPORTS *chi fornisce pronostici alle corse di cavalli*

tipsy ['tɪp·si] *adj* <-ier, -iest> alticcio, -a

tiptoe ['tɪp·toʊ] I. *n* **on ~(s)** in punta di piedi II. *vi* camminare in punta di piedi

tiptop ['tɪp·tɑːp] *adj inf* eccellente

tip-up seat ['tɪp·ʌp·'siːt] *n* sedile *m* reclinabile

tirade ['taɪ·reɪd] *n* filippica *f*

tire[1] ['ta·ɪɚ] *n* pneumatico *m;* **spare ~** ruota *f* di scorta

tire[2] ['ta·ɪɚ] I. *vt* stancare II. *vi* stancarsi

tire gauge *n* manometro *m* per pneumatici

tire pressure *n* pressione *f* delle gomme

tired ['ta·ɪɚd] *adj* <-er, -est> (*person*) stanco, -a; (*excuse*) debole; **to be sick and ~ of sth** esser stufo di qc; **the same ~ old faces** le solite facce

tiredness *n* stanchezza *f*

tireless ['ta·ɪɚ·ləs] *adj* instancabile

tiresome ['ta·ɪɚ·səm] *adj* fastidioso, -a; (*per-*

son) noioso, -a

tiring ['taɪ·rɪŋ] *adj* stancante

'tis [tɪz] = **it is** *s*. be

tissue ['tɪ·ʃu:] *n* **1.** (*paper*) carta *f* velina **2.** (*handkerchief*) fazzoletto *m* di carta **3.** ANAT, BIO tessuto *m*

tit[1] [tɪt] *n* cincia *f;* **blue ~** cinciarella *f;* **coal ~** cincia *f* mora

tit[2] [tɪt] *n vulg* tetta *f*

titanic [taɪ·'tæ·nɪk] *adj* titanico, -a

titanium [taɪ·'teɪ·ni·əm] *n* titanio *m*

titbit ['tɪt·bɪt] *n* **1.** (*delicacy*) bocconcino *m* **2.** (*piece: of information*) notizia *f* ghiotta; (*of gossip*) pettegolezzo *m*

titillate ['tɪ·tə·leɪt] *vt* titillare

titillation [ˌtɪ·tə·'leɪ·ʃən] *n* titillamento *m*

titivate ['tɪ·tə·veɪt] *vt* agghindare; **to ~ one-self** agghindarsi

title ['taɪ·t̬l] **I.** *n* **1.** (*name*) titolo *m* **2.** (*championship*) titolo *m* **3.** LAW diritto *m* **II.** *vt* intitolare

title deed *n* titolo *m* di proprietà

titleholder *n* detentore, -trice del titolo *m*

title page *n* frontespizio *m*

title role *n* ruolo *m* principale

title track *n* brano *m* che dà nome all'album

titter ['tɪ·tə·] **I.** *vi* ridacchiare nervosamente **II.** *n* risatina *f* nervosa

tittle-tattle ['tɪ·t̬l·ˌtæ·t̬l] *n inf* pettegolezzi *mpl*

tizz [tɪz] *n*, **tizzy** ['tɪ·zi] *n inf* agitazione *f;* **to be in a ~** essere molto agitato

TNT [ˌti:·en·'ti:] *n abbr of* **trinitrotoluene** TNT *m*

to [tu:] **I.** *prep* **1.** (*in direction of*) a; **to go ~ Mexico/Brasil** andare in Messico/Brasile; **to go ~ Los Angeles/New York** andare a Los Angeles/New York; **to go ~ town** andare in città; **to go ~ the dentist('s)** andare dal dentista; **to go ~ the cinema/theater** andare al cinema/a teatro; **to go ~ bed** andare a letto; **to go ~ the south** andare al sud; **~ the left/right** a sinistra/destra; **to fall ~ the ground** cadere a terra; **the path ~ the lake** il sentiero che porta al lago **2.** (*before*) **a quarter ~ five** le cinque meno un quarto **3.** (*until*) fino a; **to count up ~ 10** contare fino a un 10; **~ this day** fino ad oggi; **frightened ~ death** spaventato a morte; **done ~ perfection** fatto alla perfezione; **~ some extent** fino ad un certo punto **4.** *with indirect object* **to talk ~ sb** parlare con qn; **to show sth ~ sb** mostrare qc a qn; **I said ~ myself ...** mi sono detto ...; **this belongs ~ me** questo appartiene a me **5.** (*towards*) con; **to be kind/rude ~ sb** essere gentile/sgarbato con qn **6.** (*against*) contro; **elbow ~ elbow** gomito a gomito; **close ~ sth** vicino a qc; **to clasp sb ~ one's bosom** stringersi qn al petto; **to fix sth ~ the wall** fissare qc al muro; **5 added ~ 10 equals 15** 5 più 10 fa 15 **7.** (*in comparison*) a; **3** (**goals**) **~ 1** 3 (gol) a 1; **superior ~ sth/sb** superiore a qc/qn **8.** (*from opinion of*) **to sound strange ~ sb** suonar strano a qn; **it doesn't make any sense ~ me**

non ha senso per me; **what's it ~ them?** *inf* che cosa gliene importa a loro?; **~ all appearances** all' apparenza **9.** (*proportion*) **one liter ~ one person** un litro a persona; **by a majority of 5 ~ 1** con una maggioranza di 5 a 1; **the odds are 3 ~ 1** le probabilità sono 3 a 1 **10.** (*causing*) **much ~ my surprise** con mia grande sorpresa **11.** (*by*) da; **known ~ sb** conosciuto da qn **12.** (*matching*) di; **the top ~ this jar** il coperchio di questo barattolo **13.** (*of*) di; **the secretary ~ the boss** la segretaria del capo **14.** (*for purpose of*) per ▶ **that's all there is ~ it** questo è tutto **II.** *infinitive particle* **1.** (*infinitive: not translated*) **~ do/walk/put** fare/camminare/mettere **2.** (*in command*) **I told him ~ eat** gli ho detto di mangiare **3.** (*after interrogative words*) **I know what ~ do** so cosa fare; **she didn't know how ~ say it** non sapeva come dirlo **4.** (*wishes*) **he wants ~ listen** vuole ascoltare; **she wants ~ go** vuole andarsene **5.** (*purpose*) **he comes ~ see me** viene a trovarmi; **to phone ~ ask sth** telefonare per chiedere qc **6.** (*attitude*) **she seems ~ enjoy it** sembra che si diverta; **~ be honest ...** sinceramente... **7.** (*future intention*) **the work ~ be done** il lavoro da fare; **sth ~ buy** qc da comprare **8.** (*in consecutive acts*) per; **I came back ~ find she had left Madrid** quando son tornato ho scoperto che lei se n'era andata via da Madrid **9.** (*introducing a complement*) **he wants me ~ tell him a story** vuole che gli racconti una storia; **to be too tired ~ do sth** esser troppo stanco per fare qc **10.** (*in general statements*) **it is easy ~ do it** è facile farlo **11.** (*in ellipsis*) **he doesn't want ~ eat, but I want ~** lui non vuole mangiare, ma io sì **III.** *adv* **to push the door ~** chiudere la porta

toad [toʊd] *n* **1.** (*animal*) rospo *m* **2.** (*person*) rospo, -a *m, f*

toadstool ['toʊd·stu:l] *n* fungo *m* velenoso

toady ['toʊ·di] *n.* <-ies> *n* leccapiedi *mf* **II.** *vi* leccare i piedi

to and fro *adv* avanti e indietro

toast [toʊst] **I.** *n* **1.** (*bread*) pane *m* tostato; **a piece of ~** una fetta di pane tostato **2.** (*drink*) brindisi *m inv* **II.** *vt* **1.** (*cook*) tostare **2.** (*drink*) brindare a **III.** *vi* tostarsi

toaster *n* tostapane *m*

toastmaster ['toʊst·ˌmæs·tə·] *n* maestro di cerimonie

tobacco [tə·'bæ·koʊ] *n* tabacco *m*

tobacconist [tə·'bæ·kə·nɪst] *n* tabaccaio, -a *m, f*

to-be [tə·'bi:] *adj* futuro, -a

toboggan [tə·'bɑ·gən] **I.** *n* toboga *m inv* **II.** *vi* andare in toboga

toboggan run *n*, **toboggan slide** *n* pista *f* di toboga

toby (**jug**) ['toʊ·bi·(dʒʌg)] *n* caraffa *f* (*a forma di uomo*)

today [tə·'deɪ] **I.** *adv* **1.** (*this day*) oggi **2.** (*nowadays*) al giorno d'oggi **II.** *n* **1.** (*this day*)

T

oggi *m* **2.** (*nowadays*) oggi *m*

toddle ['tɑːdl] *vi* **1.** (*walk*) camminare senza fretta; (*child*) fare i primi passi **2.** *inf* (*go*) **to ~** (**off**) incamminarsi senza fretta

toddler ['tɑːdˑlə] *n* bambino, -a ai primi passi *m*

toddy ['tɑːdi] <-ies> *n* (**hot**) ~ grog *m inv*

to-do [tə·'duː] *n inf* putiferio *m*

toe [toʊ] I. *n* **1.** ANAT dito *m* del piede; **on one's ~s** sulle punte **2.** (*of sock, shoe*) punta *f* ▶ **to keep sb on their ~s** tenere qn in stato di allerta; **to step on sb's ~s** pestare i piedi a qn *fig* II. *vt* **to ~ the line** mettersi in linea

toecap *n* rinforzo *m*

toehold *n* **1.** (*when climbing*) appiglio *m* **2.** *fig* punto *m* d'appoggio

toenail *n* unghia *f* del piede

toffee ['tɑːfi] *n* caramella *f* mou

together [tə·'ge·ðə] I. *adv* **1.** (*jointly*) insieme; **all ~** tutti insieme; **~ with sb/sth** insieme a qn/qc; **to live ~** vivere insieme; **to get ~** riunirsi; **to get it ~** *inf* organizzarsi **2.** (*at the same time*) insieme, allo stesso tempo II. *adj inf* equilibrato, -a

togetherness *n* senso *m* di intimità

toggle ['tɑːgl] I. *n* **1.** INFOR tasto *m* bistabile **2.** TECH cavicchio *m* II. *vt* premere

toggle switch *n* interruttore *m* a levetta

Togo ['toʊ·goʊ] *n* Togo *m*

Togolese [ˌtoʊ·goʊ·'liːs] I. *adj* togolese II. *n* togolese *mf*

toil [tɔɪl] I. *n* lavoro *m* faticoso II. *vi* **1.** (*work hard*) faticare **2.** (*move*) muoversi con difficoltà

toilet ['tɔɪ·lɪt] *n* **1.** (*room*) gabinetto *m* **2.** (*appliance*) gabinetto *m* **3.** *form* (*process*) toilette *f inv*

toilet paper *n* carta *f* igienica

toiletries ['tɔɪ·lɪ·triz] *npl* articoli *mpl* da toilette

toiletries bag *n* pochette *f inv*

toilet roll *n* rotolo *m* di carta igienica

toilet soap *n* saponetta *f*

toilet water *n* acqua *f* di colonia

token ['toʊ·kən] I. *n* **1.** (*sign*) segno *m;* **by the same ~** per la stessa ragione; **in ~ of** *form* in segno di **2.** (*for machines*) gettone *m* II. *adj* (*symbolic*) simbolico, -a

told [toʊld] *pt, pp of* **tell**

tolerable ['tɑː·lə·bl] *adj* tollerabile

tolerably ['tɑːl·əəb·li] *adv form* abbastanza

tolerance ['tɑː·lə·əns] *n* tolleranza *f*

tolerant ['tɑː·lə·ənt] *adj* tollerante

tolerate ['tɑː·lə·reɪt] *vt* **1.** (*accept*) *a.* MED sopportare **2.** (*endure*) tollerare

toleration [ˌtɑː·lə·'reɪ·ʃən] *n* tolleranza *f*

toll[1] [toʊl] *n* **1.** AUTO pedaggio *m* **2.** TEL tariffa *m* **3.** (*damage*) numero *m* delle vittime

toll[2] [toʊl] I. *vt* suonare a morto; **to ~ the knell** *fig* suonare la campana a morto II. *vi* suonare

toll bridge *n* ponte *m* a pedaggio

toll call *n* interurbana *f*

toll-free *adv* gratis

tollhouse *n* HIST casello *m* per il pagamento del pedaggio

toll road *n* strada *f* a pedaggio

tom [tɑːm] *n* (*cat*) gatto *m* (maschio)

tomato [tə·'meɪ·toʊ] <-es> *n* pomodoro *m*

tomato ketchup *n* ketchup *m inv*

tomb [tuːm] *n* tomba *f*

tomboy ['tɑːm·bɔɪ] *n* maschiaccio *m*

tombstone ['tuːm·stoʊn] *n* pietra *f* tombale

tomcat ['tɑːm·kæt] *n* gatto (*m* maschio)

tome [toʊm] *n* tomo *m*

tomfoolery [ˌtɑːm·'fuː·lə·i] *n* stupidaggini *fpl*

tommy gun ['tɑ·mi·gʌn] *n* mitra *m inv*

tomograph ['tɒ·mə·grɑːf] *n* MED tomografo *m*

tomography [toʊ·'mɑː·grə·fi] *n* MED tomografia *f*

tomorrow [tə·'mɑː·roʊ] I. *adv* domani; **the day after ~** dopodomani; **all** (**day**) ~ tutto il giorno di domani; **a week from ~** una settimana a partire da domani; **~ morning/evening** domani mattina/sera; **see you ~!** a domani! II. *n* domani *m* ▶ **~ is another day** *prov* domani è un altro giorno; **never put off until ~ what you can do today** *prov* non rimandare a domani quel che puoi fare oggi *prov;* **who knows what ~ will bring?** chissà cosa ci riserva il futuro?

tom-tom ['tɑːm·tɑːm] *n* tam-tam *m inv*

ton [tʌn] *n* tonnellata *f;* **~s of** *inf* un sacco di

tone [toʊn] I. *n* **1.** (*sound*) tono *m;* (*of instrument*) tonalità *f;* (*of voice*) timbro *m* **2.** (*style*) tono *m* **3.** (*of color*) tonalità *f* **4.** (*condition*) tono *m* II. *vt* (*muscles, skin*) tonificare

♦**tone down** *vt* moderare

♦**tone in** *vi* armonizzare

♦**tone up** *vt* tonificare

tone control *n* tasto *m* regolatore del suono

tone-deaf [toʊn·'def] *adj* che non ha orecchio musicale

toneless ['toʊn·ləs] *adj* monotono, -a

tone poem *n* poema *m* sinfonico

toner ['toʊ·nə] *n* **1.** (*for skin*) tonico *m* **2.** (*for printer*) toner *m*

Tonga ['tɑː·ŋə] *n* Tonga *m*

Tongan I. *adj* tonganese II. *n* **1.** (*person*) tonganese *mf* **2.** LING tonganese *m*

tongs [tɑːŋz] *npl* molle *fpl*

tongue [tʌŋ] I. *n* **1.** ANAT lingua *f;* **to bite one's ~** mordersi la lingua; **to find one's ~** ritrovare la parola; **to hold one's ~** tenere a freno la lingua; **to stick one's ~ out** (**at sb**) fare la linguaccia (a qn); **to get one's ~ around a word** riuscire a pronunciare una parola **2.** (*language*) lingua *f* **3.** (*expressive style*) espressione *f;* **to have a sharp ~** aver una lingua tagliente ▶ **to say sth ~ in cheek** dir qc in tono ironico; **to give sb the rough side of one's ~** *inf;* **to speak with a forked ~** aver la lingua biforcuta; **have you lost your ~?** hai perso la lingua?; **to set ~s wagging** dare di che parlare II. *vt* MUS staccare

tongue-tied ['tʌŋ·taɪd] *adj fig* **to be ~** ammutolire

tongue twister *n* scioglilingua *m inv*

tonic[1] ['tɑː·nɪk] *n* (*stimulant*) tonico *m*

tonic[2] ['tɑː·nɪk] *n* MUS tonica *f*

tonic[3] ['tɑː·nɪk] *n*, **tonic water** *n* acqua *f* tonica

tonight [tə·'naɪt] *adv* (*evening*) stasera; (*night*) stanotte

tonnage ['tʌ·nɪdʒ] *n* tonnellaggio *m*

tonne [tʌn] *n* tonnellata *f*

tonsil ['tɑːn·sl] *n* MED tonsilla *f*

tonsillitis [ˌtɑːn·sə·'laɪ·t̬ɪs] *n* tonsillite *f*

too [tuː] *adv* 1. (*overly*) troppo; **that's ~ much!** questo è troppo! 2. (*very*) molto 3. (*also*) anche; **me ~!** *inf* anch'io! 4. (*moveover*) troppo 5. *inf* (*for emphasis*) pure

took [tʊk] *vt, vi pt of* **take**

tool [tuːl] I. *n* 1. (*implement*) attrezzo *m* 2. (*instrument*) strumento *m* II. *vt* (*shape with a tool*) lavorare con attrezzi

tool bag *n* borsa *f* degli attrezzi

toolbar *n* INFOR barra *f* degli strumenti

toolbox *n*, **tool chest** *n* cassetta *f* porta attrezzi

toolkit *n* kit *m inv* degli attrezzi

toolmaker *n* fabbricante *mf* di attrezzi

toolshed *n* capanno *m* degli attrezzi

toot [tuːt] I. *n* colpo *m* di clacson; **to give a ~** suonare il clacson II. *vt* (*sound*) suonare III. *vi* suonare il clacson

tooth [tuːθ] <teeth> *n* 1. ANAT (*of person, animal*) dente *m;* **to bare one's teeth** mostrare i denti; **he's cutting a ~** sta mettendo un dente 2. (*of comb, saw*) dente *m* ▶ **to set sb's teeth on edge** far venire i brividi a qn; **to fight ~ and nail** (**to do sth**) lottare con le unghie e con i denti (per fare qc); **to be long in the ~** essere avanti con gli anni; **to have a sweet ~** esser goloso; **to cut one's teeth on sth** farsi le ossa con qc; **to get one's teeth into sth** buttarsi in qc; **to give sth teeth** dar forza a qc; **to grit one's teeth** stringere i denti; **to lie through one's teeth** mentire spudoratamente; **in the ~ of sth** (*straight into*) contro; (*despite*) a dispetto di qc

toothache ['tuːθ·eɪk] *n* mal *m* di denti

toothbrush ['tuːθ·brʌʃ] *n* spazzolino *m* da denti

toothed *adj* dentato, -a

toothpaste ['tuːθ·peɪst] *n* dentifricio *m*

toothpick *n* stuzzicadenti *m inv*

toothsome ['tuːθ·səm] *adj* saporito, -a

toothy ['tuː·θi] <-ier, -iest> *adj* **to give a ~ smile** sorridere mostrando tutti i denti

tootle ['tuː·t̬l] *vi inf* **to ~ along** andare senza fretta

toots [tʊts] *n inf* dolcezza *f*

top[1] [tɑːp] *n* (*spinning top*) trottola *f*

top[2] [tɑːp] I. *n* 1. (*highest part*) cima *f;* **to get on ~ of sth** *a. fig* avere qc sotto controllo; **from ~ to bottom** da cima a fondo; **from ~ to toe** dalla testa ai piedi; **to feel on ~ of the world** sentirsi al settimo cielo 2. (*surface*)

superficie *f;* **on ~ of** sopra a 3. highest rank, apice *m;* **to be at the ~** essere al vertice; **to be at the ~ of the class** essere il primo della classe; **to go to the ~** arrivare in cima 4. (*clothing*) top *m inv* 5. (*end: of street*) fine *f;* (*of list*) cima *f;* **at the ~ of the table** a capotavola 6. (*lid: of bottle*) tappo *m* ▶ **at the ~ of one's voice** a squarciagola; **to go over the ~** esagerare II. *adj* 1. (*highest, upper*) più alto, -a; (*floor*) ultimo, -a; (*layer*) superiore; (*drawer, botton*) primo, -a 2. (*best*) di prim'ordine 3. (*most successful*) migliore 4. (*most important*) principale 5. (*maximum*) massimo, -a III. <-pp-> *vt* 1. (*be at top of*) essere in testa a 2. (*provide topping*) ricoprire 3. (*surpass*) superare

◆**top off** *vt* 1. GASTR ricoprire 2. (*conclude*) coronare

◆**top up** *vt* 1. (*fill up again*) rabboccare; **can I top you up?** *inf* posso riempirti il bicchiere? 2. (*add to*) integrare

topaz ['toʊ·pæz] *n* topazio *m*

topcoat ['tɑːp·koʊt] *n* soprabito *m*

top copy *n* originale *m*

top dog *n inf* 1. (*boss*) capo, -a *m, f* 2. (*victor*) vincitore, -trice *m, f*

top-drawer *adj* d'alta classe

top executive *n* alto dirigente *m*

topflight *adj* di prim'ordine

top hat *n* cappello *m* a cilindro

top-heavy *adj* instabile

topic ['tɑː·pɪk] *n* tema *m*

topical ['tɑː·pɪ·kl] *adj* attuale

topicality [ˌtɑː·pɪ·'kæ·lə·t̬i] *n* attualità *f*

topless ['tɑː·plɪs] I. *adj* (*person*) in topless; (*clothes*) senza parte di sopra II. *adv* **to go ~** mettersi in topless

top-level ['tɑː·pˌle·vəl] *adj* 1. (*of highest rank*) d'alto livello 2. (*of highest importance*) di prima categoria

top loader *n* lavatrice *f* con carico dall'alto

top management *n* top management *m*

topmost ['tɑː·pˌmoʊst] *adj* più alto, -a

top-notch [ˌtɑː·pˈnɑːtʃ] *adj inf* di prim'ordine

topographer [tə·'pɑː·grə·fɚ] *n* topografo, -a *m, f*

topographical [ˌtɑː·pə·'græ·fɪ·kl] *adj* topografico, -a

topography [tə·'pɑː·grə·fi] *n* topografia *f*

topping ['tɑː·pɪŋ] *n* GASTR guarnizione *f*

topple ['tɑː·pl] I. *vt a.* POL rovesciare II. *vi* **to ~ (down)** cadere

◆**topple over** *vi* cadere

top price *n* prezzo *m* massimo

top priority *n* priorità *f* assoluta

top quality *n* prima qualità *f*

top-ranking *adj* d'alto rango; (*university*) di prim'ordine

topsail *n* vela *f* di gabbia

top salary *n* salario *m* massimo

top-secret *adj* top secret *inv*

top-selling *adj* in testa alle vendite

topsoil *n* strato *m* superiore del terreno

T

top speed *n* massima velocità *f*
topspin *n* SPORTS effetto *m* topspin
topsy-turvy [ˌtɑːpˈsɪˈtɜːrvi] *inf* I. *adj* disordinato, -a II. *adv* sottosopra
torch [tɔːrtʃ] <-es> *n* 1. (*burning stick*) fiaccola *f;* **to carry a ~ for sb** essere segretamente innamorato di qn; **to put sth to the ~** dar fuoco a qc 2. (*blowlamp*) lampada *f* per saldare
torchlight [ˈtɔːrtʃˈlaɪt] *n* (*electric*) luce *f* di torcia elettrica; (*burning*) luce di fiaccola
torchlight procession *n* fiaccolata *f*
tore [tɔːr] *vi, vt pt of* **tear**
torment [ˈtɔːrˈment] I. *n* 1. (*suffering*) tormento *m;* **to be in ~** soffrire molto; **to go through ~s** patire le pene dell'inferno 2. (*physical pain*) supplizio *m* 3. (*torture*) tortura *f* 4. (*annoying thing*) supplizio *m* II. *vt* tormentare
tormentor [tɔːrˈmenˈt̬ər] *n* tormentatore, -trice *m, f*
torn [tɔːrn] *vi, vt pp of* **tear**
tornado [tɔːrˈneɪˈdoʊ] *n* <-(e)s> tornado *m inv*
torpedo [tɔːrˈpiːˈdoʊ] MIL, NAUT I. <-es> *n* siluro *m* II. *vt* silurare
torpid [ˈtɔːrˈpɪd] *adj form* apatico, -a
torpor [ˈtɔːrˈpər] *n form* apatia *f*
torque [tɔːrk] *n* PHYS forza *f* di torsione
torrent [ˈtɔːˈrənt] *n* 1. (*large amount of water*) torrente *m;* **to rain in ~s** piovere a dirotto 2. (*of complaints, abuse*) valanga *f*
torrential [tɔːˈrenˈʃl] *adj* torrenziale
torsion [ˈtɔːrˈʃən] *n* TECH, MED torsione *f*
torso [ˈtɔːrˈsoʊ] *n* torso *m*
tortoise [ˈtɔːrˈtəs] *n* tartaruga *f*
tortoiseshell [ˈtɔːrˈtəsˈʃel] *n* guscio *m* di tartaruga
tortuous [ˈtɔːrˈtʃuˈəs] *adj* (*complicated, indirect*) tortuoso, -a; (*reasoning*) contorto, -a
torture [ˈtɔːrˈtʃər] I. *n* 1. (*cruelty*) tortura *f* 2. (*suffering*) supplizio *m* II. *vt* 1. (*cause suffering to*) torturare 2. (*disturb*) tormentare; **to ~ oneself with sth** torturarsi con qc
torturer [ˈtɔːrˈtʃəˈ-ər] *n* torturatore, -trice *m, f*
toss [tɑːs] I. *n* 1. (*throw*) lancio *m;* (*of head*) scrollata *f* 2. (*throwing of a coin*) lancio *m;* **to win/lose the ~** vincere/perdere a testa o croce II. *vt* 1. (*throw*) lanciare; (*pancake*) rigirare; **to ~ a coin** fare a testa o croce 2. (*shake: head*) scrollare III. *vi* **to ~ for sth** giocarsi qc a testa o croce ▶ **to ~ and <u>turn</u>** girarsi e rigirarsi nel letto
◆**toss about** *vt,* **toss around** *vt* 1. (*move roughly*) sballottare; (*head, hair*) scuotere 2. (*consider*) considerare
◆**toss away** *vt* gettar via
◆**toss off** *vt* 1. *inf* (*do quickly*) fare rapidamente *sl;* (*write*) scrivere rapidamente 2. (*drink quickly*) bere d'un fiato
◆**toss out** *vt* gettar via
◆**toss up** *vi* **to ~ for sth** giocarsi qc a testa o croce
toss-up [ˈtɑːsˈʌp] *n* **it's a ~ between ...** è una

scelta tra ...
tot [tɑːt] *n* 1. *inf* (*child*) bimbo, -a *m, f* 2. (*alcohol*) dito *m*
◆**tot up** I. *vt inf* sommare II. *vi* **to ~ to** (**an amount**) ammontare a (una quantità)
total [ˈtoʊˈtl] I. *n* (*sum, cost*) totale *m* II. *adj* 1. (*entire: sum, cost*) totale 2. (*absolute*) totale, assoluto, -a; **a ~ failure** un fallimento totale III. *vt* 1. (*count*) sommare 2. (*amount to*) ammontare a
totalitarian [toʊˌtæˈləˈteˈriˈən] *adj* POL totalitario, -a
totalitarianism *n* POL totalitarismo *m*
totality [toʊˈtæˈləti] *n* totalità *f;* **in its ~** in totale
totally [ˈtoʊˈtəˈli] *adv* totalmente
tote¹ [toʊt] *n* SPORTS totalizzatore *m*
tote² [toʊt] *vt inf* trascinare
tote bag *n* sporta *f*
totem (**pole**) [ˈtoʊˈtəm (ˌpoʊl)] *n* totem *m inv*
totter [ˈtɑːˈt̬ər] *vi* barcollare
tottery [ˈtɑːˈt̬əˈri] *adj* barcollante
toucan [ˈtuːˈkæn] *n* tucano *m*
touch [tʌtʃ] <-es> I. *n* 1. (*sensation*) tatto *m* 2. (*act of touching*) tocco *m* 3. (*communication*) **to be/get/keep in ~** (**with sb/sth**) essere/mettersi/restare in contatto (con qn/qc); **to be out of ~ with sb** non essere più in contatto con qn; **to lose ~ with sb** perdere i contatti con qn 4. (*skill*) tocco *m;* **to lose one's ~** perdere la mano 5. (*small amount*) pizzico *m;* (*of bitterness, irony*) punta *f;* **a ~ of genius** una punta di genialità 6. (*detail*) tocco; **the human ~** il calore umano ▶ **to be a <u>soft</u> ~** *inf* essere un credulone II. *vt* 1. (*feel*) toccare; **to ~ the brake** frenare 2. (*brush against*) sfiorare 3. (*reach*) raggiungere 4. (*eat, drink*) toccare; **he didn't ~ any food** non ha toccato cibo 5. (*move emotionally*) commuovere 6. (*equal*) **there's no painter to ~ him** non c'è pittore che lo possa uguagliare III. *vi* toccarsi; **for a moment our hands ~ed** per un attimo le nostre mani si sono toccate
◆**touch at** *vi* NAUT fare scalo a
◆**touch down** *vi* AVIAT atterrare
◆**touch in** *vt* ART ritoccare
◆**touch off** *vt* provocare; (*protest*) scatenare
◆**touch on** *vt* toccare
◆**touch up** *vt* (*improve*) rifinire; PHOT ritoccare
◆**touch upon** *vt* toccare
touch-and-go *adj* **to be ~ whether ...** essere incerto se ...
touchdown [ˈtʌtʃˈdaʊn] *n* 1. AVIAT atterraggio *m* 2. SPORTS (*American football*) touchdown *m inv;* (*rugby*) meta *f*
touched [tʌtʃt] *adj* 1. (*moved*) conmosso, -a 2. *inf* (*crazy*) toccato, -a
touchiness [ˈtʌˈtʃɪˈnəs] *n inf* 1. (*of person*) suscettibilità *f* 2. (*of issue*) delicatezza *f*
touching [ˈtʌtˈʃɪn] *adj* commovente
touch-sensitive *adj* INFOR sensibile al tatto
touchstone [ˈtʌtʃˈstoʊn] *n* pietra *f* di paragone

touch-type ['tʌtʃ·taɪp] *vi scrivere a macchina senza guardare i tasti*

touchy ['tʌt·ʃi] <-ier, -iest> *adj* 1.(*person*) suscettibile; **she's very ~ about her work** è molto suscettibile quando si tratta del suo lavoro 2.(*issue*) delicato, -a

tough [tʌf] I.*adj* 1.(*fabric, substance*) resistente; (*meat, skin*) duro, -a; **to be ~ as old boots** (*meat*) essere duro come una suola di scarpa 2.(*hardy: person*) forte 3.(*strict*) severo, -a; (*negotiator*) inflessibile; **to be ~ on sb** essere severo con qn 4.(*difficult*) arduo, -a; (*exam, question*) difficile 5.(*violent*) violento, -a 6.*inf*(*unlucky*) **~ luck** sfortuna nera II. *n inf* teppista *mf*
◆**tough out** *vt* **to tough it out** (*endure*) sopportare; (*face up to*) affrontare

toughen ['tʌ·fən] I.*vt* temprare II. *vi* temprarsi

toughness *n* 1.(*strength*) resistenza *f* 2.(*hardness: of meat*) durezza *f* 3.(*difficulty*) difficoltà *f*

toupée [tuː·'peɪ] *n* parrucchino *m*

tour [tʊr] I.*n* 1.(*journey*) giro *m;* **guided ~** visita *f* guidata; **sightseeing ~** visita *f* dei luoghi di maggiore interesse 2.(*of factory*) visita *f* 3.MUS tournée *f inv;* **to be/go on ~** essere/andare in tournée II.*vt* 1.(*travel around*) girare 2.(*visit professionally*) visitare 3.(*perform*) fare una tournée in III.*vi* viaggiare

touring company *n* compagnia *f* teatrale itinerante

tourism ['tʊ·rɪ·zəm] *n* turismo *m*

tourist ['tʊ·rɪst] *n* (*traveler*) turista *mf*

tourist agency *n* agenzia *f* turistica

tourist bureau *n* ufficio *f* turistico

tourist class *n* classe *f* turistica

tourist guide *n* 1.(*book*) guida *f* turistica 2.(*person*) guida *f*

tourist industry *n* turismo *m*

tourist information office *n* ufficio *m* informazioni turistiche

tourist season *n* stagione *f* turistica

tourist ticket *n* biglietto *m* turistico

tourist visa *n* visto *m* turistico

tournament ['tɜːr·nə·mənt] *n* SPORTS torneo *m*

tour operator *n* operatore, -trice turistico *m*

tousle ['taʊ·zl] *vt* spettinare

tousled ['taʊ·zlt] *adj* spettinato, -a

tout [taʊt] I.*n* bagarino, -a *m, f* II.*vt* (*try to sell*) cercare di vendere III.*vi* **to ~ for customers** procacciare clienti

tow [toʊ] I.*n* rimorchio *m;* **to give sth/sb a ~** rimorchiare qc/qn; **to have sb in ~** *fig* avere qn al seguito II.*vt* rimorchiare; **to ~ a vehicle** trainare un veicolo

toward(s) [tɔːrd(z)] *prep* 1.(*in direction of*) verso; (*of time*) verso 2.(*for*) per 3.(*in respect of*) nei confronti di; **to feel sth ~ sb** provare qc per qn

tow bar *n* barra *f* di rimorchio

towboat *n* NAUT rimorchiatore *m*

towel ['ta·ʊəl] I. *n* asciugamano *m* ▶**to throw**

in the ~ gettare la spugna II. *vt* <-ll-> **to ~ sth dry** asciugare qc (*con un asciugamano*)

towel(l)ing *n* (tessuto *m* di) spugna *f*

towel rack *n* portasciugamani *m inv*

tower ['ta·ʊəʳ] *n* torre *f* ▶**a ~ of strength** un pilastro
◆**tower above** *vi*, **tower over** *vi* **to ~ sth/sb** torreggiare su qn/qc

towering *adj* 1.(*very high*) torreggiante 2.(*very large*) immenso, -a; (*temper*) violento, -a

town [taʊn] *n* (*large*) città *f;* (*small*) cittadina *f;* **the ~** il centro ▶**to go out on the ~** uscire a far baldoria; **to paint the ~ red** far baldoria

town center *n* centro *m*

town clerk *n* segretario, -a comunale *m*

town council *n* consiglio *m* comunale

town councilor *n* consigliere *m* comunale

town hall *n* POL municipio *m*

townhouse *n* 1.(*residence in town*) casa *f* di città 2.(*part of terrace*) casa *f* a schiera

town planning *n* urbanistica *f*

townscape ['taʊn·skeɪp] *n* paesaggio *m* urbano

townsfolk ['taʊnz·foʊk] *npl* cittadinanza *f*

township ['taʊn·ʃɪp] *n* 1.municipio *m* 2.(*in South Africa*) township, *area abitata da gente di colore inv*

townspeople ['taʊnz·ˌpiː·pl] *npl* cittadini *mpl*

tow truck *n* carro *m* attrezzi

toxemia *n*, **toxemia** [taːk·'siː·mɪə] *n* tossiemia *f*

toxic ['taːk·sɪk] *adj* tossico, -a

toxicology [ˌtaːk·sɪ·'kaː·lə·dʒi] *n* tossicologia *f*

toxic waste *n* residui *mpl* tossici

toxin ['taːk·sɪn] *n* tossina *f*

toy [tɔɪ] *n* giocattolo *m;* **cuddly ~** peluche *m inv*
◆**toy with** *vt* giocherellare con; **to ~ an idea** accarezzare l'idea; **to ~ sb's affections** giocare con i sentimenti di qn

toy car *n* automobilina *f*

toy dog *n* cane *m* di piccola taglia

toyshop *n* negozio *m* di giocattoli

trace¹ [treɪs] *n* (*for horse*) tirella *f;* **to kick over the ~s** ribellarsi

trace² [treɪs] I.*n* 1.(*sign*) traccia *f;* **to leave a ~ of sth** lasciar traccia di qc; **to disappear without a ~** sparire senza lasciar traccia 2.(*slight amount*) pizzico *m;* **~s of a drug/poison** tracce di droga/veleno; **without any ~ of sarcasm/humor** senza una punta di sarcasmo/umorismo II.*vt* 1.(*locate*) rintracciare; **to ~ sb to somewhere** rintracciare qn in qualche posto; **it can be ~d back to the Middle Ages** risale al Medioevo 2.(*draw outline of*) tracciare; (*with tracing paper*) ricalcare

traceable ['treɪ·sə·bl] *adj* rintracciabile; **an easily ~ reference** una fonte facilmente reperibile

trace element *n* oligoelemento *m*

tracer ['treɪ·səʳ] *n* MIL proiettile *m* tracciante

T

tracery ['treɪ·sə·ri] *n* traforo *m*
trachea ['treɪ·kɪə] <-s *o* -chae> *n* trachea *f*
tracing *n* ricalco *m*
tracing paper *n* carta *f* da lucido
track [træk] I. *n* 1. (*path*) sentiero *m* 2. (*rails*) binari *mpl* 3. (*in station*) binario *m* 4. (*mark*) traccia *f;* (*of animal*) orma *f;* (*of bullet*) traiettoria *f;* **to cover one's ~s** nascondere le proprie tracce; **to leave ~s** lasciare tracce; **to be on the ~ of sb** essere sulle tracce di qn 5. (*path*) pista *f;* **to be on the right/wrong ~** *a. fig* essere sulla strada giusta/sbagliata 6. (*logical course*) corso *m;* **the ~ of an argument** il filo di un discorso; **to get off the ~** uscire dal tema; **to be on ~ (to do sth)** essere sulla buona strada (per fare qc) 7. (*career path*) indirizzo *m;* **to change ~** cambiare strada 8. SPORTS pista *f* 9. (*song*) brano *m* ▶ **to live on the wrong** <u>side</u> **of the ~s** *inf* vivere nei quartieri poveri; **to** <u>keep</u> **~ (of sth/sb)** tenersi informato su qc/qn; **to** <u>lose</u> **~ (of sth/sb)** perdere di vista (qc/qn); **to** <u>make</u> **~s** *inf* levare le tende; **to** <u>stop</u> **sb (dead) in his ~s** fermarsi di colpo; **to** <u>throw</u> **sb off the ~** mettere qn fuori strada II. *vt* 1. (*pursue*) seguire le tracce di; **to ~ sth/sb** seguire qc/qn 2. (*trace*) seguire la traiettoria di III. *vi* CINE fare una carrellata
◆ **track down** *vt* rintracciare
track and field *n* atletica *f* leggera
trackball *n* INFOR trackball *f inv*
track event *n* SPORTS gara *f* di atletica leggera
tracking station ['træ·kɪŋ·'steɪ·ʃən] *n* AVIAT, TECH osservatorio *m* spaziale
track record *n* curriculum *m*
track shoe *n* scarpetta *f* chiodata
tracksuit *n* tuta (*f* da ginnastica)
tract[1] [trækt] *n* (*leaflet*) opuscolo *m*
tract[2] [trækt] *n* 1. (*of land*) estensione *f* 2. ANAT, MED apparato *m;* **digestive/respiratory ~** apparato digestivo/respiratorio
tractable ['træk·tə·bl] *adj* (*person, animal*) docile; (*problem*) risolvibile
traction ['træk·ʃən] *n* 1. (*grip*) aderenza *f* 2. MED trazione *f*
traction engine *n* trattrice *f*
tractor ['træk·tə·] *n* trattore *m*
trade [treɪd] I. *n* 1. (*buying and selling*) commercio *m;* **~ in sth** commercio di qc 2. (*business activity*) attività *f* economica 3. (*type of business*) industria *f;* **building ~** (settore *m* dell') edilizia *f;* **fur ~** industria delle pellicce 4. (*profession*) mestiere *m;* **to learn a ~** imparare un mestiere; **to be a baker by ~** essere panettiere di professione 5. (*swap*) scambio *m* II. *vi* commerciare; **to ~ with sb** intrattenere scambi commerciali con qn; **to ~ in sth** commerciare in qc III. *vt* 1. (*swap, exchange*) scambiare; **to ~ sth for sth** scambiare qc per qc 2. (*sell*) vendere
◆ **trade in** *vt* dare in permuta
◆ **trade on** *vt* approfittare di
trade agreement *n* accordo *m* commerciale
trade association *n* associazione *f* commer-

ciale
trade balance *n* bilancia *f* commerciale
trade barrier *n* barriera *f* commerciale
trade cycle *n* ciclo *m* economico
trade directory *n* guida *f* commerciale
trade discount *n* sconto *m* commerciale
trade fair *n* COM fiera *f* commerciale
trade gap *n* deficit *minv* della bilancia commerciale
trade-in ['treɪd·ɪn] *n* COM permuta *f*
trade-in value *n* valore *m* di permuta
trade journal *n* rivista *f* commerciale
trademark *n* 1. COM marchio *m* di fabbrica; **registered ~** marchio registrato 2. *fig* marchio *m* distintivo
trade name *n* (*of a firm*) nome *m* commerciale; (*trademark*) marchio *m*
tradeoff ['treɪd·ɑːf] *n* 1. (*exchange*) intercambio *m;* **to make a ~ between things** fare uno scambio tra cose 2. *fig* (*inconvenience*) compromesso *m*
trade policy *n* politica *f* commerciale
trade press *n* stampa *f* specializzata, *nel settore commerciale*
trader ['treɪ·də·] *n* commerciante *mf*
trade register *n* registro *m* commerciale
trade route *n* rotta *f* commerciale
trade secret *n* segreto *m* professionale
tradesman ['treɪdz·mən] <-men> *n* negoziante *mf*
tradespeople ['treɪdz·ˌpiː·pl] *npl* commercianti *mpl*
trade surplus *n* avanzo *m* commerciale
trade union *n* sindacato *m*
trade unionism *n* sindacalismo *m*
trade unionist *n* sindacalista *mf*
trade war *n* guerra *f* commerciale
trade wind *n* aliseo *m*
trading ['treɪ·dɪŋ] *n* commercio *m;* **insider ~** uso *m* di informazioni riservate
trading area *n* area *f* commerciale
trading license *n* licenza *f* commerciale
trading volume *n* volume *m* degli scambi
tradition [trə·'dɪ·ʃən] *n* tradizione *f;* **by ~** per tradizione; **to be in the ~ of sb/sth** essere nella tradizione di qn/qc
traditional [trə·'dɪ·ʃə·nəl] *adj* tradizionale
traditionalism [trə·'dɪ·ʃə·nə·lɪ·zəm] *n* tradizionalismo *m*
traditionalist [trə·'dɪ·ʃə·nə·lɪst] *n* tradizionalista *mf*
traffic ['træ·fɪk] I. *n* 1. (*vehicles*) traffico *m;* **heavy ~** traffico intenso; **air/rail ~** traffico aereo/ferroviario; **commercial ~** traffico commerciale; **passenger ~** traffico di passeggeri; **to get stuck in ~** rimanere bloccato nel traffico 2. (*movement: of goods, passengers*) trasporto *m;* **drug ~** traffico di droga 3. *form* (*dealings*) **to have ~ with sb** intrattenere scambi commerciali con qn II. <trafficked, trafficked> *vi pej* **to ~ in sth** trafficare in qc
traffic accident *n* incidente *m* di traffico
traffic circle *n* rotatoria *f*

traffic island *n* isola *f* spartitraffico *inv*

traffic jam *n* ingorgo *m*

trafficker ['træ·fɪ·kə] *n pej* trafficante *mf;* **drug/arms ~** trafficante di armi/droga

traffic light *n* semaforo *m*

traffic regulation *n* norme *fpl* di circolazione

traffic sign *n* cartello *m* stradale

tragedy ['træ·dʒə·di] <-ies> *n* tragedia *f*

tragic ['træ·dʒɪk] *adj* tragico, -a

tragicomedy [ˌtræ·dʒɪ·'kɑː·mə·di] <-ies> *n* tragicommedia *f*

trail [treɪl] I. *n* 1. (*path*) sentiero *m* 2. (*track*) traccia *f;* (*of airplane*) scia *f;* **a ~ of destruction** una scia di distruzione; **to be on the ~ of sth/sb** essere sulle tracce di qc/qn; **to be hot on the ~ of sb** essere alle calcagna di qn; **to follow a ~** (*in hunting*) seguire una traccia II. *vt* 1. (*follow*) seguire le tracce di; **to ~ an animal** seguire le orme di un animale 2. (*drag*) trascinare 3. (*be losing to*) **to ~ sb/sth** essere in svantaggio rispetto a qn/qc III. *vi* 1. (*drag*) **to ~ (somewhere)** trascinarsi (in qualche posto) 2. SPORTS essere in svantaggio; **to ~ by 6 points** essere in svantaggio di 6 punti; **to ~ behind sth/sb** trascinarsi dietro qc/qn

◆**trail along** I. *vi* trascinarsi II. *vt* trascinare

◆**trail away** *vi* andare sfumando

◆**trail behind** *vi* trascinarsi dietro

◆**trail off** *vi* andare sfumando

trailblazer ['treɪlˌbleɪ·zə] *n* pioniere, -a *m, f*

trailer *n* 1. (*wheeled container*) rimorchio *m* 2. (*mobile home*) roulotte *f inv* 3. CINE trailer *m inv*

trailer park *n* campeggio *m* per roulotte

train [treɪn] I. *n* 1. (*railway*) treno *m;* **to travel by ~** viaggiare in treno 2. (*series*) serie *f;* **~ of thought** filo *m* dei pensieri; **to put sth in ~** mettere qc in moto 3. (*retinue*) seguito *m* 4. (*procession: of animals, things*) fila *f* 5. (*of dress*) strascico *m* II. *vi* allenarsi; **to ~ to be sth** studiare per diventare qc III. *vt* formare; (*animal*) ammaestrare; SPORT allenare; **to ~ sb in the use of sth** addestrare qn nell'uso di qc; **to ~ sb for sth** preparare qn per qc

train accident *n* incidente *m* ferroviario

train connection *n* coincidenza *f*

train driver *n* macchinista *mf*

trained ['treɪnd] *adj* 1. (*educated*) preparato, -a; (*animal*) ammaestrato, -a; **to be ~ in sth** essere preparato in qc 2. (*expert*) qualificato, -a

trainee [treɪ·'niː] *n* apprendista *mf*

trainer *n* (*person*) allenatore, -trice *m, f*

training *n* 1. (*education*) formazione *f;* **~ on-the-job** formazione *f* sul posto di lavoro 2. SPORTS allenamento *m;* **to be in ~ for sth** allenarsi per qc; **to be good ~ for sth** essere un buon allenamento per qc

training camp *n* SPORTS campo *m* di allenamento

training course *n* corso *m* di formazione

training program *n* programma *m* di allenamento

train schedule *n* orario *m* dei treni

train service *n* servizio *m* ferroviario

traipse [treɪps] *vi pej* gironzolare; **to ~ around the shops** girare per negozi

trait [treɪt] *n* tratto *m*

traitor ['treɪ·t̬ə] *n* traditore, -trice *m, f;* **to turn ~** tradire

traitorous ['treɪ·t̬ə·əs] *adj pej, form* traditore, -trice

trajectory [trə·'dʒek·tə·i] *n* 1. PHYS traiettoria *f* 2. *fig* (*path*) direzione *f;* **to be on a downward/an upward ~** essere in discesa/ascesa

tram [træm] *n* tram *m inv;* **to go by ~** andare in tram

tramline ['træm·laɪn] *n* 1. (*track*) rotaia *f* del tram; (*route*) linea *f* tranviaria 2. *pl* (*in tennis*) linee *fpl* laterali

trammel ['træ·ml] *liter* I. *n pl* restrizioni *fpl* II. *vt* <-ll-> ostacolare

tramp [træmp] I. *vi* 1. (*walk heavily*) camminare con passo pesante 2. (*go on foot*) girovagare II. *vt* calpestare; (*town, miles*) percorrere *inf* III. *n* 1. (*sound*) rumore *m* di passi 2. (*walk*) camminata *f;* **to go for a ~** andare a fare una camminata 3. (*down-and-out*) vagabondo, -a *m, f* 4. *pej* (*woman*) sgualdrina *f*

trample ['træm·pl] I. *vt* pestare; **to ~ sb's foot** pestare un piede a qn; **to be ~d to death** morire calpestato; **to ~ sth underfoot** calpestare qc II. *vi* **to ~ on sth** calpestare qc

trampoline ['træm·pə·liːn] *n* trampolino *m*

tramway ['træm·weɪ] *n* 1. (*rails*) rotaie *fpl* del tram 2. (*system*) tranvia *f*

trance [træns] *n* trance *f inv;* **to be in a ~** essere in trance

tranquil ['træŋ·kwɪl] *adj* tranquillo, -a

tranquility [træŋ·'kwɪ·lə·t̬i] *n* tranquillità *f*

tranquilize ['træŋ·kwɪ·laɪz] *vt* MED calmare con tranquillante

tranquilizer *n* tranquillante *m;* **to be on ~s** prendere tranquillanti

transact [træn·'zækt] *vt* trattare; **to ~ business** trattare affari

transaction [træn·'zæk·ʃən] *n* COM transazione *f;* **business ~** operazione *f* commerciale

transalpine [træn·'zæl·paɪn] *adj* transalpino, -a

transatlantic *adj,* **trans-Atlantic** [ˌtrænts·æt·'læn·t̬ɪk] *adj* transatlantico, -a

transceiver [træn·'siː·və] *n* ricetrasmittente *f*

transcend [træn·'send] *vt* 1. (*go beyond*) trascendere; **to ~ barriers/limitations** superare barriere/limiti 2. (*surpass*) superare

transcendent [træn·'sen·dənt] *adj* trascendente; (*superior*) supremo, -a

transcendental [ˌtrænt·sen·'den·t̬əl] *adj* trascendentale

transcontinental [ˌtrænts·ˌkɑːn·tə·'nen·t̬əl] *adj* transcontinentale

transcribe [træn·'skraɪb] *vt* trascrivere

transcript ['trænts·krɪpt] *n* trascrizione *f*

transcription [træn·'skrɪp·ʃən] *n* trascrizione *f*

transducer [trænts·'duː·sə] *n* ELEC trasduttore *m*

transept ['trænt·sept] *n* ARCHIT transetto *m*

transfer[1] [træns·'fɜːr] I. <-rr-> *vt* 1. (*move*) trasferire 2. (*reassign: power*) passare 3. COM (*shop*) cedere 4. SPORTS (*sell*) cedere II. <-rr-> *vi* 1. (*move*) trasferirsi 2. (*change train, plane*) cambiare

transfer[2] ['trænts·fɜːr] *n* 1. (*process of moving*) trasferimento *m;* ~ **of information** trasmissione *f* di informazioni 2. (*reassignment*) passaggio *m* 3. COM (*of a shop*) cessione *f* 4. SPORTS cessione *f* 5. (*ticket*) biglietto *m* cumulativo 6. (*picture*) decalcomania *f*

transferable [træns·'fɜː·rə·bl] *adj* trasferibile

transference ['trænts·fɜː·rəns] *n form* 1. (*process of moving*) trasferimento *m* 2. PSYCH transfert *m inv*

transfigure [trænts·'fɪg·jɚ] *vt* trasfigurare

transfix [trænts·'fɪks] *vt form* trafiggere; **to be ~ed by sb/sth** essere completamente paralizzato da qn/qc

transform [trænts·'fɔːrm] *vt* trasformare

transformation [ˌtrænts·fɚ·'meɪ·ʃən] *n* trasformazione *f*

transformer *n* ELEC trasformatore *m*

transfuse [trænts·'fjuːz] *vt* MED fare una trasfusione di

transfusion [trænts·'fjuː·ʒən] *n* trasfusione *f;* **blood ~** trasfusione di sangue; **to give sb a ~** fare una trasfusione di sangue a qn

transgress [trænts·'gres] *form* I. *vt* trasgredire; **to ~ a law** violare una legge II. *vi* commettere una violazione

transgression [trænts·'gre·ʃən] *n form* trasgressione *f*

transgressor *n* trasgressore, -ditrice *m, f;* REL peccatore, -trice *m, f*

transient ['trænt·ʃənt] *form* I. *adj* (*fashion, joy*) passeggero, -a; (*population*) di passaggio II. *n* persona *f* di passaggio

transistor [træn·'zɪs·tɚ] *n* ELEC transistor *m inv*

transistorize [træn·'zɪs·tə·raɪz] *vt* transistorizzare

transit ['træn·tsɪt] *n* transito *m;* **in ~** in viaggio

transit business *n* commercio *m* di transito

transition [træn·'zɪ·ʃən] *n* transizione *f*

transitional [træn·'zɪ·ʃə·nəl] *adj* (*period*) transitorio, -a; (*government*) di transizione

transitive ['træn·tsə·tɪv] *adj* LING transitivo, -a

transit lounge *n* sala *f* transiti

transitory ['træn·tsə·tɔː·ri] *adj* passeggero, -a

transit passenger *n* passeggero, -a *m, f* in transito

transit visa *n* visto *m* di transito

translatable *adj* traducibile

translate [træns·'leɪt] I. *vt* 1. LING tradurre; **to ~ sth from English into Spanish** tradurre qc dall'inglese allo spagnolo 2. (*adapt*) adattare; **to ~ a play for the cinema** adattare un'opera teatrale per il cinema 3. (*transform*) **to ~ a plan into action** mettere in atto un piano II. *vi* LING tradurre; **to ~ from English into Spanish** tradurre dall'inglese allo spagnolo

translation [træns·'leɪ·ʃən] *n* traduzione *f*

translator *n* traduttore, -trice *m, f*

transliterate [træns·'lɪ·ţə·reɪt] *vt* traslitterare

transliteration [træns·ˌlɪ·ţə·'reɪ·ʃən] *n* LING traslitterazione *f*

translucent [træns·'luː·sənt] *adj*, **translucid** *adj* traslucido, -a

transmigration [ˌtrænts·maɪ·'greɪ·ʃən] *n* trasmigrazione *f*

transmissible [træns·'mɪ·sə·bl] *adj* trasmissibile

transmission [træns·'mɪ·ʃən] *n* trasmissione *f;* **data ~** INFOR trasmissione di dati

transmission speed *n* INFOR velocità *f* di trasmissione

transmit [træns·'mɪt] <-tt-> *vt* trasmettere

transmitter *n* 1. (*apparatus*) trasmettitore *m* 2. (*station*) emittente *f*

transmitting station *n* emittente *f*

transmogrify [træns·'mɑː·grə·faɪ] *vt* trasformare completamente

transmutation [ˌtrænts·mjuː·'teɪ·ʃən] *n form* tramutazione *f*

transmute [ˌtrænts·'mjuːt] *form* I. *vt* tramutare; **to ~ sth into sth** tramutare qc in qc II. *vi* **to ~ into sth** tramutarsi in qc

transoceanic [ˌtrænts·oʊ·ʃi·'æ·nɪk] *adj* transoceanico, -a

transom ['træn·tsəm] *n* 1. (*horizontal bar*) traversa *f* 2. (*window*) lunetta *f*

transparency [træns·'pe·rən·tsi] *n* <-ies> trasparenza *f*

transparent [træns·'pe·rənt] *adj* trasparente

transpiration [ˌtrænts·pɪ·'reɪ·ʃən] *n* traspirazione *f*

transpire [træn·'spa·ɪɚ] *vi* 1. (*happen*) succedere; **it ~d that ...** è successo che ... 2. (*come to be known*) trapelare 3. (*emit water vapor*) traspirare

transplant[1] [træns·'plænt] *vt* 1. MED, BOT trapiantare 2. (*relocate*) trasferire

transplant[2] ['trænts·plænt] *n* trapianto *m*

transplantation [ˌtrænts·plæn·'teɪ·ʃən] *n* trapianto *m*

transport[1] [træns·'pɔːrt] *vt* 1. (*people, goods*) trasportare 2. *liter* (*fill with emotion*) **to be ~ed with joy/grief** essere sopraffatto dalla gioia/dal dolore

transport[2] ['trænts·pɔːrt] *n* 1. (*means of conveyance*) trasporto *m;* **public ~** mezzi *mpl* pubblici; **~ costs** spese *fpl* di trasporto 2. (*plane*) aereo *m* da trasporto; (*ship*) nave *f* da trasporto 3. *form* (*strong emotion*) slancio *m;* **to be in ~s of joy** essere sopraffatto dalla gioia

transportable *adj* trasportabile

transportation [ˌtrænts·pɚ·'teɪ·ʃən] *n* 1. (*of people, goods*) trasporto *m* 2. (*of a convict*) deportazione *f*

transporter [træns·'pɔːr·ţɚ] *n* transporter *m inv*

transpose [træns·'poʊz] *vt* 1. (*reverse position of*) trasporre 2. (*change location*) spostare

3. MUS, MAT trasportare

transsexual [træn·'sek·ʃu·əl] **I.** *n* transessuale *mf* **II.** *adj* transessuale

transverse ['trænts·vɜːs] *adj* trasversale

transvestite ['trænts·'ves·taɪt] *n* travestito, -a *m, f*

trap [træp] **I.** *n* **1.** (*device*) trappola *f;* **to set a ~** tendere una trappola **2.** (*dangerous situation*) tranello *m;* (*ambush*) imboscata *f;* **to fall into a ~** cadere in un'imboscata **3.** *inf* (*mouth*) becco *m;* **to shut one's ~** chiudere il becco; **to keep one's ~ shut** tenere il becco chiuso **4.** (*curve in pipe*) sifone *m* **5.** HIST (*carriage*) calesse *m* **6.** (*for clay pigeons*) lanciapiattello *m inv* **II.** *vt* <-pp-> intrappolare; **to feel ~ped** sentirsi in trappola

trapdoor ['træp·dɔːr] *n* botola *f*

trapeze [træ·'piːz] *n* trapezio *m*

trapezoid ['træ·pɪ·zɔɪd] *n* MAT trapezio *m*

trapper ['træ·pər] *n* persona *fm* che piazza le trappole; **fur ~** cacciatore, -trice *m, f* di pelli

trappings ['træ·pɪŋz] *npl* simboli *mpl;* **the ~ of power** i simboli del potere

Trappist ['træ·pɪst] **I.** *adj* trappista **II.** *n* trappista *m*

trapshooting *n* tiro *m* al piattello

trash [træʃ] **I.** *n* **1.** (*rubbish*) spazzatura *f;* **to take the ~ out** buttare la spazzatura **2.** *inf* (*people*) gentaglia *f;* (*book, film*) schifezza *f* **3.** *inf* (*nonsense*) stupidaggini *fpl;* **to talk ~** dire stupidaggini **II.** *vt inf* **1.** (*wreck*) distruggere **2.** (*criticize*) stroncare

trash can ['træʃ·kæn] *n* bidone *m* della spazzatura

trashy ['træ·ʃi] *adj inf* di pessima qualità

trauma ['trɑː·mə] *n* PSYCH, MED trauma *m*

traumatic [trɑː·'mæ·tɪk] *adj* traumatico, -a

traumatize ['trɔː·mə·taɪz] *vt* traumatizzare; **to be ~d by sth** essere traumatizzato da qc

travel ['træ·vəl] **I.** *vi* **1.** (*make journey*) viaggiare; **to ~ by air/car/train** viaggiare in aereo/macchina/treno; **to ~ first-class** viaggiare in prima classe; **to ~ light** viaggiare leggero **2.** (*light, sound*) propagarsi **3.** (*be away*) essere in viaggio **4.** *inf* (*go fast*) andare a manetta **II.** *vt* viaggiare per; **to ~ a country/ the world** viaggiare per un paese/per il mondo; **to ~ the length and breadth of a country** viaggiare in lungo e in largo per un paese **III.** *npl* viaggi *mpl*

travel agency *n* agenzia *f* di viaggi

travel agent *n* agente *mf* di viaggi

travel bureau *n* agenzia *f* di viaggi

travel card *n* abbonamento *m*

traveled *adj* che ha viaggiato

traveler ['træ·və·lər] *n* viaggiatore, -trice *m, f;* **commercial ~** commesso *m* viaggiatore

traveler's check *n* traveller's cheque *m inv*

travel expenses *n* spese *fpl* di viaggio

travel guide *n* (*person*) guida *f* turistica; (*book*) guida *f* turistica

traveling *n* (il) viaggiare *m*

travel insurance *n* assicurazione *f* di viaggio

traveling allowance *n* indennità *f* di viaggio

traveling circus *n* circo *m* itinerante

traveling exhibition *n* mostra *f* itinerante

traveling salesman *n* commesso *m* viaggiatore

travelog ['træ·və·lɑːg] *n* TV documentario *m* di interesse turistico; CINE film *m* su un viaggio *inv*

travel sickness *n* (*in car*) mal *m* d'auto; (*in plane*) mal *m* d'aria; (*in boat*) mal *m* di mare

traverse ['træ·vərs] *vt* (*cross*) attraversare

travesty ['træ·vɪs·ti] <-ies> *n pej* farsa *f*

trawl [trɑːl] **I.** *vi* **1.** (*fish*) pescare con rete a strascico **2.** (*search*) **to ~ through sth** setacciare qc **II.** *vt* (*fish: sea*) setacciare con rete a strascico **III.** *n* **1.** (*net*) rete *f* a strascico **2.** (*search*) ricerca *f* accurata

trawler ['trɑː·lər] *n* peschereccio *m, per pesca a strascico*

tray [treɪ] *n* vassoio *m*

treacherous ['tre·tʃə·rəs] *adj* **1.** (*disloyal*) infido, -a **2.** (*dangerous: road, weather*) pericoloso, -a

treachery ['tre·tʃə·ri] *n* tradimento *m*

treacly ['triː·k·li] *adj* **1.** (*thick and sticky*) appiccicoso, -a **2.** (*sentimental*) mellifluo, -a

tread [tred] **I.** <trod, trodden or trod> *vi* procedere; **to ~ on** [*o* in] **sth** pestare qc **II.** *vt* calpestare; **to ~ one's weary way** andare coi piedi di piombo **III.** *n* **1.** (*manner of walking*) passo *m;* **a heavy ~** un passo pesante **2.** (*step*) gradino *m* **3.** AUTO battistrada *m inv*

treadle ['tre·dl] *n* pedale *m*

treadmill ['tred·mɪl] *n* **1.** (*exercise machine*) tapis roulant *m inv* **2.** *fig* routine *f inv*

treason ['triː·zn] *n* tradimento *m;* **high ~** *form* alto tradimento

treasonable ['triː·zə·nə·bl] *adj,* **treasonous** ['triː·zə·nəs] *adj* proditorio, -a

treasure ['tre·ʒər] **I.** *n* **1.** (*precious items*) tesoro *m* **2.** (*highly valued thing, person*) tesoro *m;* **my assistant is a ~** la mia assistente è un tesoro **II.** *vt* tenere molto a; **to ~ the memories of sb** custodire come un tesoro il ricordo di qn

treasure house *n* stanza *f* del tesoro

treasure hunt *n* caccia *f* al tesoro

treasurer ['tre·ʒə·rər] *n* tesoriere, -a *m, f*

treasure trove *n* tesoro *m* trovato

treasury ['tre·ʒə·ri] <-ies> *n* tesoreria *f;* **the Treasury** il Tesoro

Treasury bill *n* buono *m* ordinario del Tesoro

Treasury bond *n* buono *m* del Tesoro a lungo termine

Treasury note *n* buono *m* del Tesoro a medio termine

Treasury Secretary *n* ≈ Ministro *m* del Tesoro

treat [triːt] **I.** *vt* **1.** (*deal with, handle*) trattare; MED curare; **to ~ sth/sb badly** trattar male qc/qn; **to ~ sth/sb as if ...** trattare qc/qn come se ... +*subj* **2.** (*process*) trattare; **to ~ a substance with acid** trattare una sostanza con acido **3.** (*discuss*) trattare **4.** (*pay for*) offrire; **to ~ sb to an ice cream** offrire un gelato

T

a qn **II.** *vi* to ~ **with sb** trattare con qn **III.** *n* **1.** (*pleasurable event*) piacevole sorpresa *m;* (*present*) regalo *m;* **it's my** ~ offro io **2.** (*pleasure*) piacere *m;* **it was a real** ~ è stato un vero piacere

treatise ['triː·ţɪs] *n* trattato *m*

treatment ['triːt·mənt] *n* **1.** trattamento *m;* **to get rough** ~ **from sb** essere maltrattato da qn; **special** ~ trattamento speciale **2.** MED cura *f;* **to respond to** ~ rispondere al trattamento

treaty ['triː·ţi] <-ies> *n* trattato *m;* **peace** ~ trattato di pace

treble ['tre·bl] **I.** *adj* **1.** (*three times greater*) triplo, -a **2.** MUS di soprano **II.** *n* MUS soprano *m* **III.** *vt* triplicare **IV.** *vi* triplicarsi

treble clef *n* chiave *f* di sol

tree [triː] *n* albero *m;* **to climb a** ~ salire su un albero; **the Tree of Knowledge** l'albero della conoscenza ▸**you can't see the** forest **for the** ~**s** non cogliere il quadro d'insieme, *sperdendosi nei dettagli;* **to bark up the** wrong ~ *inf* prendere lucciole per lanterne; **to** grow **on** ~**s** piovere giù dal cielo; **money doesn't grow on** ~**s** i soldi non piovon giù dal cielo

tree frog *n* raganella *f*

tree house *n* capanna *f* sull'albero

treeless *adj* brullo, -a

tree line *n* limite *m* della vegetazione

tree-lined ['triː·laɪnd] *adj* alberato, -a; **a** ~ **street** una strada alberata

tree surgeon *n* addetto, -a alla potatura delle piante *m*

treetop *n* cima *f* dell'albero; **in the** ~**s** in cima agli alberi

tree trunk *n* tronco *m* dell'albero

trefoil ['triː·fɔɪl] *n* trifoglio *m*

trek [trek] **I.** <-kk-> *vi* camminare **II.** *n* **1.** (*walk*) (lunga) camminata *f* **2.** (*migration*) migrazione *f*

trekking ['tre·kɪŋ] *n* trekking *m inv;* **to go** ~ fare trekking

trellis ['tre·lɪs] <-es> *n* (*for plants*) graticcio *m*

tremble ['trem·bl] *vi* tremare; **to** ~ **with cold** tremare di freddo; **to** ~ **like a leaf** tremare come una foglia

tremendous [trɪ·'men·dəs] *adj* **1.** (*enormous*) enorme, tremendo, -a; (*crowd, scope*) immenso, -a; (*help*) inestimabile; (*success*) strepitoso, -a **2.** *inf* (*extremely good*) staordinario, -a

tremolo ['tre·mə·loʊ] *n* MUS tremolo *m*

tremor ['tre·mɚ] *n* **1.** (*shake*) tremito *m;* (*earthquake*) scossa *f* **2.** (*of fear, excitement*) brivido *m*

tremulous ['trem·jʊ·ləs] *adj* tremulo, -a

trench [trentʃ] <-es> *n* fosso *m;* MIL trincea *f*

trenchant ['tren·tʃənt] *adj* pungente

trench coat *n* FASHION trench *m inv*

trench warfare *n* guerra *f* di trincea

trend [trend] **I.** *n* **1.** (*tendency*) tendenza *f;* **downward/upward** ~ tendenza al ribasso/al rialzo; **a** ~ **toward(s)** ... una tendenza verso ... **2.** (*fashion*) moda *f;* **the latest** ~ l'ultima

moda; **to set a new** ~ lanciare una nuova moda **II.** *vi* tendere; **to** ~ **to sth** tendere a qc

trendsetter ['trend·ˌse·ţɚ] *n* persona *f* che fa tendenza

trendy ['tren·di] **I.** <-ier, -iest> *adj* trendy *inv* **II.** <-ies> *n* persona *f* alla moda

trepidation [ˌtre·pɪ·'deɪ·ʃən] *n* trepidazione *f;* **to do sth with** ~ far qc con apprensione

trespass ['tres·pəs] *vi* **1.** LAW sconfinare **2.** REL peccare

trespasser ['tres·pæ·sɚ] *n* intruso, -a *m, f*

trestle ['tre·sl] *n* cavalletto *m*

trestle table *n* tavolo *m* su cavalletti

triad ['traɪ·æd] *n* triade *f*

trial ['traɪ·əl] *n* **1.** LAW processo *m;* ~ **by jury** processo *m* con giuria; **to stand** ~ esser processato; **to be on** ~ **for one's life** essere sotto processo per reato capitale **2.** (*test*) prova *f;* **clinical** ~**s** test *mpl* clinici; ~ **of strength** prova di forza; **to give sb a** ~ concedere un periodo di prova; **to have sth on** ~ avere qc in prova **3.** (*source of problems*) difficoltà *f;* ~**s and tribulations** tribolazioni *fpl* **4.** (*competition*) selezione *f*

trial flight *n* volo *m* di prova

trial period *n* periodo *m* di prova

trial separation *n* separazione *f* di prova

triangle ['traɪ·æŋ·gl] *n* triangolo *m*

triangular [traɪ·'æŋ·gjʊ·lɚ] *adj* triangolare

tribal ['traɪ·bl] *adj* tribale

tribalism ['traɪ·blɪ·zəm] *n* tribalismo *m*

tribe [traɪb] *n* tribù *f inv;* **the twelve** ~**s of Israel** HIST le dodici tribù di Israele

tribesman ['traɪbz·mən] <-men> *n* membro *m* di una tribù

tribulation [ˌtrɪb·jə·'leɪ·ʃən] *n form* tribolazione *f*

tribunal [traɪ·'bjuː·nl] *n* tribunale *m;* (*investigative body*) commissione *f* di inchiesta

tribune¹ ['trɪb·juːn] *n* HIST tribuno *m*

tribune² ['trɪb·juːn] *n* ARCHIT tribuna *f*

tributary ['trɪb·jə·te·ri] **I.** <-ies> *n* **1.** (*river*) affluente *m* **2.** HIST (*person*) persona *f* che versa un tributo; (*state*) stato *m* tributario **II.** *adj form* **1.** (*river*) affluente **2.** HIST (*state*) tributario, -a

tribute ['trɪb·juːt] *n* **1.** (*token of respect*) omaggio *m;* **to pay** ~ **sb/sth** rendere omaggio a qn/qc; **floral** ~ *form* omaggio floreale **2.** (*sign of sth positive*) **to be a** ~ **to sth/sb** fare onore a qc/qn **3.** HIST (*money paid to a superior power*) tributo *m*

trice [traɪs] *n inf* **in a** ~ in un battibaleno

trick [trɪk] **I.** *n* **1.** (*ruse*) scherzo *m;* **a dirty** ~ *inf* un brutto scherzo; **to play a** ~ **on sb** fare uno scherzo a qn; **to be up to one's (old)** ~**s again** essere tornato alle vecchie abitudini **2.** (*of magician*) trucco *m* **3.** (*technique*) trucco *m* **4.** (*illusion*) illusione *f;* **a** ~ **of the light** un'illusione ottica; **his eyes are playing** ~**s on him** gli occhi gli stanno giocando brutti scherzi ▸**to try every** ~ **in the** book tentarle tutte; **the** ~**s of the** trade i trucchi del mestiere; **that'll** <u>do</u> **the** ~ questo funzionerà di sicuro; **to not** <u>miss</u> **a** ~ non sbagliare un colpo II. *adj* 1.(*deceptive*) **a** ~ **question** una domanda a tranello 2. *inf* (*weak*) sifolino, -a III. *vt* (*deceive*) ingannare; (*swindle*) imbrogliare

trickery ['trɪ·kə·ri] *n* frode *f;* **to resort to** ~ ricorrere all'inganno

trickle ['trɪ·kl] I. *vi* 1.(*flow slowly*) scorrere lentamente; (*in drops*) gocciolare 2. *fig* (*people*) **to** ~ **in**/**out** entrare/uscire alla spicciolata; **to** ~ **out** (*information*) trapelare II. *n* 1.(*of liquid*) rivolo *m;* (*drops*) goccia *f* 2.(*of people, information*) flusso *m*
♦**trickle away** *vi* consumarsi poco a poco

trickster ['trɪk·stɚ] *n pej* imbroglione, -a *m, f*

tricksy ['trɪk·si] *adj* (*playful*) scherzoso, -a

tricky ['trɪ·ki] <-ier, -iest> *adj* 1.(*crafty*) astuto, -a 2.(*difficult*) complicato, -a; (*situation*) delicato, -a; **to be** ~ **to do** essere difficile da fare

tricycle ['traɪ·sɪ·kl] *n* triciclo *m*

trident ['traɪ·dnt] *n* tridente *m*

tried [traɪd] I. *vi, vt pt, pp of* **try** II. *adj* provato, -a; ~ **and tested** sperimentato

triennial [traɪ·'en·iəl] *adj* triennale

trier ['tra·ɪɚ] *n inf* persona *f* che si sforza molto

trifle ['traɪ·fəl] *n* 1.(*insignificant thing*) bazzecola *f* 2.(*small amount*) inezia *f;* **a** ~ leggermente 3.(*dessert*) ≈ zuppa *f* inglese
♦**trifle away** *vt* sprecare; **to trifle one's time away** perdere tempo
♦**trifle with** *vt* scherzare con; **to** ~ **sb's affections** giocare con i sentimenti di qn

trifling *adj* insignificante

trig. *abbr of* **trigonometry** trigonometria *f*

trigger ['trɪ·gɚ] I. *n* 1.(*of gun*) grilletto *m;* **to pull the** ~ premere il grilletto 2. *fig* avvio *m* II. *vt* 1.(*reaction*) provocare; (*revolt*) scatenare 2.(*start*) innescare; **to** ~ **an alarm** far scattare un allarme

trigger-happy ['trɪ·gɚ·ˌhæpi] *adj* dal grilletto facile

trigonometry [ˌtrɪ·gə·'nɑː·mə·tri] *n* MAT trigonometria *f*

trike [traɪk] *n inf abbr of* **tricycle** triciclo *m*

trilateral [traɪ·'læ·t̬ə·əl] *adj* 1.(*involving three parties*) trilaterale 2. MAT trilatero, -a

trilingual [ˌtraɪ·'lɪŋ·gwəl] *adj* trilingue

trill [trɪl] I. *n* 1.(*birdsong*) trillo *m* 2.(*quavering note*) trillo *m* II. *vi* 1.(*bird*) trillare 2.(*speak*) parlare in modo affettato III. *vt* **to** ~ **one's r's** arrotare la r

trillion ['trɪl·jən] *n* trilione *m*

trilogy ['trɪ·lə·dʒi] <-ies> *n* trilogia *f*

trim [trɪm] I. *n* 1.(*state*) (buono) stato *m;* **to be in** ~ (**for sth**) essere in forma (per qc); **to be in fighting** ~ essere in assetto di guerra 2.(*hair*) spuntatina *f;* **to give sb a** ~ spuntare i capelli a qn; **to give sth a** ~ dare una spuntatina a qc 3.(*decorative edge*) bordo *m* II. *adj* 1.(*attractively thin, compact*) snello, -a 2.(*neat*) ordinato, -a; (*lawn*) curato, -a III. <-mm-> *vt* 1.(*cut*) spuntare; **to** ~ **one's**

beard regolare la barba 2.(*reduce*) ridurre
♦**trim down** *vt* tagliare
♦**trim off** *vt* tagliare via

trimming *n* 1.(*decoration*) decorazione *f* 2. *pl* GASTR guarnizioni *fpl*

Trinidad ['trɪ·nɪ·dæd] *n* Trinidad *f;* ~ **and Tobago** Trinidad e Tobago

Trinidadian ['trɪ·nɪ·dæ·diən] I. *adj* di Trinidad II. *n* abitante *mf* di Trinidad

Trinity ['trɪ·nə·ti] *n* Trinità *f;* **the** (**Holy**) ~ la (Santissima) Trinità

trinket ['trɪŋ·kɪt] *n* ninnolo *m*

trio ['triː·oʊ] *n a.* MUS trio *m;* **string** ~ trio di archi

trip [trɪp] I. *n* 1.(*journey*) viaggio *m;* (*shorter*) gita *f;* **business** ~ viaggio d'affari; **to go on a** ~ fare un viaggio 2. *inf* (*effect of drugs*) trip *m inv* 3.(*fall*) inciampata *f* II. <-pp-> *vi* 1.(*stumble*) inciampare; **to** ~ **on sth** inciampare in qc 2.(*move lightly*) camminare con passo leggero III. <-pp-> *vt* 1.(*cause to stumble*) **to** ~ **sb** (**up**) far inciampare qn 2.(*switch on*) accendere
♦**trip over** *vi* inciampare
♦**trip up** I. *vi* 1.(*stumble*) inciampare 2.(*verbally*) impappinarsi II. *vt* 1.(*cause to stumble*) far inciampare 2.(*cause to fail*) far impappinare

tripartite [ˌtraɪ·'pɑːr·taɪt] *adj* tripartitico, -a

tripe [traɪp] *n* 1. GASTR trippa *f* 2. *pej, inf* (*nonsense, rubbish*) fesseria *f;* **to talk** ~ dire fesserie

triple ['trɪ·pl] I. *adj* triplo, -a II. *vt* triplicare III. *vi* triplicarsi

triple jump *n* triplo salto *m*

triplet ['trɪp·lɪt] *n* 1.(*baby*) **to have** ~**s** avere tre gemelli 2. MUS terzina *f*

triplicate ['trɪp·lɪ·kɪt] *adj* **in** ~ in triplice copia

tripod ['traɪ·pɑːd] *n* tripode *m*

tripping ['trɪ·pɪŋ] *adj* leggero, -a

trisect [traɪ·'sekt] *vt* tripartire

trite [traɪt] *adj* trito, -a

triumph ['tra·ɪʌmf] I. *n* 1.(*success*) trionfo *m;* **a** ~ **over sth**/**sb** un trionfo su qn/qc; **to do sth in** ~ far qc trionfalmente; **to hail sth as a** ~ accogliere qc trionfalmente 2.(*supreme example*) trionfo *m;* **a** ~ **of engineering**/**medicine** un trionfo dell'ingegneria/della medicina II. *vi* 1.(*achieve success*) trionfare; **to** ~ **over sth**/**sb** trionfare su qc/qn 2.(*exult excessively*) mostrarsi trionfante

triumphal [traɪ·'ʌm·fəl] *adj* trionfale

triumphant [traɪ·'ʌm·fnt] *adj* 1.(*victorious*) trionfante; (*return*) trionfale; **to emerge** ~ **from sth** uscire vittorioso da qc 2.(*successful*) vittorioso, -a

trivia ['trɪ·viə] *npl* banalità *fpl*

trivial ['trɪ·viəl] *adj* 1.(*unimportant*) irrilevante; (*dispute, matter*) futile 2.(*insignificant*) insignificante

triviality [ˌtrɪ·vi·'æ·lə·ti] *n* <-ies> 1.(*unimportance*) irrilevanza *f* 2.(*unimportant thing*) futilità *f*

T

trivialize ['trɪ·vɪ·ə·laɪz] *vt* sminuire

trod [trɑːd] *pt, pp of* **tread**

trodden ['trɑː·dn] *pp of* **tread**

troglodyte ['trɑːg·lə·daɪt] *n* troglodita *mf*

Trojan ['troʊ·dʒən] **I.** *n* troiano, -a *m, f* ►to **work** like a ~ lavorare come un mulo **II.** *adj* troiano, -a; **the ~ Horse/War** il cavallo/la guerra di Troia

trolley ['trɑː·li] *n* (*trolley car*) tram *m inv*

trolley bus ['trɑː·li·bʌs] *n* filobus *m inv*

trolley car *n* tram *m inv*

trollop ['trɑː·ləp] *n pej, inf* sgualdrina *f*

trombone [trɑːm·'boʊn] *n* trombone *m*

trombonist [trɑːm·'boʊ·nɪst] *n* trombonista *mf*

troop [truːp] **I.** *n* **1.** *pl* MIL truppe *fpl;* **cavalry ~** squadrone *m* di cavalleria **2.** (*of people*) frotta *f* **II.** *vi* **to ~ in/out** entrare/uscire a frotte

troop carrier *n* mezzo *m* corazzato per il trasporto delle truppe

trooper ['truː·pɚ] *n* **1.** MIL soldato *m* di cavalleria **2.** (*state police officer*) poliziotto, -a *m, f;* **state ~** poliziotto di uno stato ►to **swear** like **a ~** bestemmiare come uno scaricatore di porto

trophy ['troʊ·fi] *n* <-ies> trofeo *m*

tropic ['trɑː·pɪk] *n* (*latitude*) tropico *m;* **the ~ s** i tropici; **tropic of Cancer/Capricorn** tropico del Cancro/Capricorno

tropical ['trɑː·pɪ·kl] *adj* tropicale

troposphere ['trəʊ·pəs·fɪ·əɚ] *n* troposfera *f*

trot [trɑːt] **I.** *n* **1.** (*of horse*) trotto *m* **2.** *pl, inf* (*diarrhea*) **to have the ~s** aver la cagarella ►**on** the ~ di fila **II.** *vi* **1.** (*horse*) trottare; (*person*) trotterellare **2.** (*run at moderate pace*) camminare a passo veloce **3.** (*go busily*) trottare **III.** <-tt-> *vt* (*horse*) mettere al trotto

♦**trot along** *vi*, **trot off** *vi* affrettarsi

♦**trot out** *vt* (*excuse, explanation*) ritirar fuori; **to ~ arguments** ritirare in ballo gli stessi argomenti

trotter ['trɑː·tɚ] *n* **1.** CULIN zampetto *m* di maiale **2.** SPORT cavallo *m* da trotto

trouble ['trʌ·bl] **I.** *n* **1.** (*difficulty*) difficoltà *f,* guaio *m;* **to have ~** avere difficoltà; **to ask for ~** cercare guai; *inf;* **to spell ~** significare guai; **to store up ~** peggiorare il problema; **to be in/get into ~** essere/mettersi nei guai; **to be in serious ~** essere in un bel guaio; **to be in ~ with sb** avere delle grane con qn; **to land sb in ~** mettere qn nei guai; **to stay out of ~** tenersi fuori dai guai **2.** *pl* (*series of difficulties*) problemi *mpl;* **to be the least of sb's ~s** essere il minore dei mali di qn **3.** (*inconvenience*) disturbo *m;* **to go to the ~ of doing sth** prendersi il disturbo di fare qc; **to go to a lot of ~ for sb** darsi molta pena per qn; **to put sb to the ~ of doing sth** dare a qn il disturbo di fare qc; **to be (not) worth the ~ (of doing sth)** (non) valere la pena (di fare qc) **4.** (*physical ailment*) disturbo *m;* **stomach ~** disturbi gastrici **5.** (*malfunction*) guasto *m;* **engine ~** guasto al motore **6.** (*strife*) scontri *mpl;* **to stir**

up ~ creare dei conflitti **II.** *vt* **1.** *form* (*cause inconvenience*) disturbare; **to ~ sb for sth** disturbare qn per qc; **to ~ sb to do sth** dare a qn il disturbo di fare qc **2.** (*make an effort*) **to ~ oneself about sth** darsi pena per qc **3.** (*cause worry*) preoccupare; (*cause pain*) affliggere; **to be ~d by sth** essere preoccupato per qc **III.** *vi* incomodarsi; **to ~ to do sth** darsi pena per fare qc

troubled *adj* **1.** (*period*) turbolento, -a; (*water*) agitato, -a **2.** (*worried*) preoccupato, -a

trouble-free [ˌtrʌ·bl·'friː] *adj* senza problemi

troublemaker ['trʌ·bl·ˌmeɪ·kɚ] *n* agitatore, -trice *m, f*

troubleshooting ['trʌ·bl·ˌʃuː·tɪŋ] *n* individuazione *f* e riparazione di un guasto

troublesome ['trʌ·bl·səm] *adj* problematico, -a

trouble spot *n* zona *f* calda

trough [trɑːf] *n* **1.** (*for drinking*) abbeveratoio *m;* (*for feeding*) mangiatoia *f;* **to feed at the public ~** *fig* appropriarsi indebitamente dei fondi pubblici **2.** (*low point*) valore *m* minimo **3.** METEO saccatura *f*

troupe [truːp] *n* THEAT troupe *f inv*

trouper ['truː·pɚ] *n* artista *mf* veterano, -a

trouser clip *n* molletta *f* per pantaloni, *per andare in bicicletta*

trouser leg *n* gamba (*f* dei pantaloni)

trousers ['traʊ·zɚz] *n pl* pantaloni *mpl;* **a pair of ~** un paio di pantaloni ►to **wear** the ~ portare i pantaloni

trousseau ['truː·soʊ] *n* corredo *m* da sposa

trout [traʊt] *n* <-(s)> (*fish*) trota *f*

trowel ['traʊ·əl] *n* (*for building*) cazzuola *f;* (*for gardening*) paletta *f*

Troy [trɔɪ] *n* HIST Troia *f*

troy ounce *n* oncia *f* troy

truancy ['truː·ən·si] *n* assenze *f* ingiustificate (da scuola) *pl*

truant ['truː·ənt] **I.** *n* persona *f* che marina la scuola; **to play ~** marinare la scuola **II.** *vi* marinare la scuola

truce [truːs] *n* tregua *f;* **to call a ~** dichiarare una tregua

truck[1] [trʌk] **I.** *n* (*lorry*) camion *m;* **pickup ~** pickup *m inv* **II.** *vt* trasportare (su camion)

truck[2] [trʌk] *n inf* (*dealings*) **to have no ~ with sb/sth** non aver niente a che vedere con qn/qc

truck driver *n* camionista *mf*

trucker *n* camionista *mf*

truck farming *n* ortofrutticoltura *f*

trucking *n* autotrasporto *m*

trucking company *n* impresa *f* di trasporti

truculence ['trʌk·jʊ·ləns] *n* truculenza *f*

truculent ['trʌk·jʊ·lənt] *adj* truculento, -a

trudge [trʌdʒ] **I.** *vi* trascinarsi a fatica **II.** *vt* percorrere faticosamente **III.** *n* camminata *f* faticosa

true [truː] **I.** *adj* **1.** (*not false*) vero, -a; **to be ~ (that ...)** esser vero (che ...); **to hold sth to be ~** ritenere che qc sia vero; **to ring ~** suo-

nare vero **2.** (*genuine, real*) vero, -a; **~ love**
vero amore *m;* **the ~ faith** la vera fede; **sb's ~
self** la vera personalità di qn; **to come ~** avverarsi; **in the ~ sense of the word** nel vero
senso della parola **3.** (*faithful, loyal*) fedele; **to
be/remain ~ to sth/sb** essere/restare fedele
a qc/qn; **to be ~ to one's word** tener fede alla
parola data; **to be ~ to oneself** rimanere
fedele a se stesso **4.** (*accurate*) esatto, -a **II.** *adv*
1. (*truly*) sinceramente **2.** (*accurately*) esattamente; **to aim ~** mirare bene **III.** *n* **to be out
of ~** essere fuori centro
◆**true up** *vt* centrare
true-blue [ˌtruː·'bluː] *adj inf* leale
trueborn ['truː·bɔːrn] *adj form* autentico, -a
true-hearted ['truː·ˌhɑːr·tɪd] *adj form* fedele
true-life [ˌtruː·'laɪf] *adj* realistico, -a; (*story*)
basato, -a su fatti realmente accaduti
truelove ['truː·lʌv] *n liter* amato, -a *m, f*
truffle ['trʌ·fl] *n* tartufo *m*
truism ['truː·ɪ·zəm] *n* (*obviously true*) verità *f*
ovvia; (*cliché*) luogo *m* comune
truly ['truː·li] *adv* **1.** (*accurately*) veramente
2. (*sincerely*) sinceramente **3.** (*as intensifier*)
realmente ▸**yours ~** (*at end of letter*) distinti
saluti; (*the speaker*) il sottoscritto *form*
trump [trʌmp] **I.** *n* (*in cards*) atout *m inv* **II.** *vt*
1. (*in cards*) tagliare **2.** (*surpass*) battere
◆**trump up** *vt* inventare; **to ~ an accusation**
montare un'accusa
trumpet ['trʌm·pət] **I.** *n* tromba *f* ▸**to blow
one's own ~** *inf* tessere le proprie lodi **II.** *vi*
(*elephant*) barrire **III.** *vt* (*news, success*)
strombazzare
trumpeter ['trʌm·pə·t̬ɚ] *n* trombettista *mf*
truncate [trʌŋ·'keɪt] *vt* troncare
truncheon ['trʌn·tʃən] *n* manganello *m*
trundle ['trʌn·dl] **I.** *vi* rotolare **II.** *vt* far rotolare
trunk [trʌŋk] *n* **1.** ANAT, BOT tronco *m* **2.** (*of
elephant*) proboscide *f* **3.** (*for storage*)
baule *m* **4.** (*of car*) portabagagli *m inv* **5.** *pl*
costume *m* da bagno (da uomo); **a pair of
swimming ~s** un costume da bagno (da
uomo)
trunk road *n* strada *f* principale
truss [trʌs] **I.** *n* **1.** (*bundle*) fascio *m* **2.** MED
cinto *m* erniario **II.** *vt* legare
◆**truss up** *vt* legare
trust [trʌst] **I.** *n* **1.** (*belief*) fiducia *f;* **to gain
sb's ~** guadagnarsi la fiducia di qn; **to place
one's ~ in sb/sth** riporre la propria fiducia in
qn/qc; **to take sth on ~** accettare qc sulla
fiducia; **to betray sb's ~** tradire la fiducia di qn
2. (*responsibility*) responsabilità *f;* **a position
of ~** un incarico di fiducia **3.** FIN, COM trust *m
inv;* **investment ~** fondo *m* comune di investimento **4.** LAW **to hold sth in ~** tenere qc in
fedecommesso **5.** (*association*) associazione *f*
II. *vt* **1.** (*place trust in*) fidarsi di; **to ~ sb to do
sth** fidarsi che qn farà qc **2.** (*rely on*) fare affidamento su; **to ~ sb with sth** affidare qc a qn
3. (*hope*) **to ~ that ...** sperare che ... *+subj*
III. *vi* fidarsi; **to ~ in sth/sb** fidarsi di qc/qn

trusted ['trʌs·tɪd] *adj* (*friend, servant*) fidato,
-a; (*method, remedy*) affidabile
trustee [trʌs·'tiː] *n* amministratore, -trice fiduciario, -a *m;* **board of ~s** consiglio *m* d'amministrazione
trustful ['trʌst·fəl] *adj* fiducioso, -a
trust fund *n* FIN fondo *m* fiduciario
trusting *adj* fiducioso, -a
trustworthiness ['trʌst·ˌwɜːr·ðɪ·nɪs] *n* (*of person*) affidabilità *f;* (*of data*) attendibilità *f*
trustworthy ['trʌst·ˌwɜːr·ði] *adj* (*person*) affidabile; (*data*) attendibile
trusty ['trʌs·ti] <-ier, -iest> *adj* fedele
truth [truːθ] *n* verità *f;* **a grain of ~** un pizzico
di verità; **in ~** in verità; **the ~ about sth/sb** la
verità su qc/qn; **to tell the ~** dire la verità; **to
tell the ~, ...** a dire la verità ...
truthful ['truːθ·fəl] *adj* **1.** (*honest*) sincero, -a;
to be ~ with sb esser sincero con qn **2.** (*accurate*) veritiero, -a
truthfulness *n* **1.** (*sincerity*) sincerità *f*
2. (*accuracy*) veridicità *f*
try [traɪ] **I.** *n* **1.** (*attempt*) tentativo *m;* **to give
sth a ~** tentare qc **2.** (*in rugby*) meta *f*
II. <-ie-> *vi* provare; **to ~ and do sth** *inf* cercare di fare qc **III.** <-ie-> *vt* **1.** (*attempt*) provare; **to ~ one's best** mettercela tutta; **to ~
one's luck** tentare la sorte **2.** (*test*) provare
3. (*sample*) assaggiare **4.** (*annoy*) stancare; **his
demands would ~ the patience of a saint** le
sue richieste metterebbero alla prova anche la
pazienza di un santo **5.** LAW processare
◆**try for** *vt insep* mirare a ottenere
◆**try on** *vt* (*put on*) provare; **to try sth on for
size** misurarsi qc
◆**try out** *vt* provare; **to try sth out on sb** far
provare qc a qn
trying *adj* (*exasperating*) esasperante; (*difficult*) difficile
tryout ['traɪ·aʊt] *n* prova *f*
tsar [zɑːr] *n* zar *m inv*
tsarina [zɑː·'riː·nə] *n* zarina *f*
tsarist ['zɑː·rɪst] **I.** *adj* zarista **II.** *n* zarista *mf*
tsetse fly ['tse·tsi·ˌflaɪ] *n* mosca *f* tse-tse
T-shirt ['tiː·ʃɜːrt] *n* maglietta *f*
tsp *abbr of* **teaspoon** (*amount*) cucchiaino *m*
T-square ['tiː·skwer] *n* TECH squadra *f* a T
tub [tʌb] *n* **1.** (*container*) tinozza *f* **2.** (*bathtub*) vasca *f* **3.** (*carton*) vaschetta *f;* **a ~ of ice
cream** una vaschetta di gelato
tuba ['tjuː·bə] *n* tuba *f*
tubby ['tʌ·bi] <-ier, -iest> *adj inf* tracagnotto, -a
tube [tuːb] *n* **1.** (*hollow cylinder*) tubo *m*
2. ANAT tuba *f;* **Fallopian ~** tube di Falloppio
3. *inf* TV tele *f* ▸**to go down the ~s** andare in
malora
tuber ['tuː·bɚ] *n* tubero *m*
tubercular [tuː·'bɜːr·kjə·lɚ] *adj* MED tubercolare
tuberculosis [tuː·ˌbɜːr·kjə·'loʊ] *n* tubercolosi *f
inv*
tuberculous [tuː·'bɜːr·kjʊ·ləs] *adj* tubercolare

T

tub-thumper ['tʌb-ˌθʌm-pə] *n pej, inf* oratore da quattro soldi, -trice *m, f*

tuck [tʌk] **I.** *n* (*fold*) piega *f* **II.** *vt* (*fold*) piegare
◆**tuck away I.** *vt* (*hide*) mettere al sicuro; **to be tucked away** essere in un posto al sicuro **II.** *vi* mangiare voracemente
◆**tuck in** *vt* **1.** (*push into position*) infilare; **to tuck one's shirt in** infilarsi la camicia nei pantaloni **2.** (*settle in bed*) rimboccare le coperte a

tucker ['tʌ-kə] *vt inf* consumare

Tuesday ['tu:z-dəɪ] *n* martedì *m inv;* **Shrove ~** martedì grasso; *s.a.* **Friday**

tuft [tʌft] *n* ciuffo *m*

tug [tʌg] **I.** *n* **1.** (*pull*) strattone *m;* **to give sth a ~** dare uno strattone a qc **2.** NAUT rimorchiatore *m* **II.** <-gg-> *vt* **1.** (*pull*) tirare **2.** NAUT rimorchiare

tuition [tju:-'ɪ-ʃən] *n* **1.** (*fee*) tasse *f* scolastiche *pl* **2.** (*teaching*) lezioni *fpl*

tuition fees *n* tasse *f* scolastiche *pl*

tulip ['tu:-lɪp] *n* tulipano *m*

tumble ['tʌm-bl] **I.** *n* caduta *f;* **to take a ~** cadere **II.** *vi* **1.** (*fall*) cadere **2.** *fig* (*decline*) crollare
◆**tumble down** *vi* crollare
◆**tumble over** *vi* ruzzolare

tumbledown ['tʌm-bl-ˌdaʊn] *adj* in rovina

tumble drier *n,* **tumble dryer** *n* asciugabiancheria *f inv*

tumbler ['tʌmb-lə] *n* bicchiere *m* (da bibita)

tumbleweed ['tʌ-bl-wi:d] *n* pianta che cresce in zone aride e rotola quando trasportata dal vento

tumescent [tu:-'me-snt] *adj* tumescente

tummy ['tʌ-mi] <-ies> *n childspeak* pancia *f*

tummy ache *n childspeak* mal *m* di pancia

tumor ['tu:-mə] *n* tumore *m;* **brain/malignant ~** tumore cerebrale/maligno

tumult ['tu:-mʌlt] *n* tumulto *m*

tumultuous [tu:-'mʌl-tʃu:-əs] *adj* (*uproariously noisy*) tumultuoso, -a

tun [tʌn] *n* (*large vat*) botte *f;* (*in brewery*) barile *m*

tuna ['tu:-nə] *n* <-(s)> tonno *m*

tundra ['tʌn-drə] *n* tundra *f*

tune [tu:n] **I.** *n* **1.** MUS melodia *f;* **a catchy ~** una melodia orecchiabile **2. to be in/out of ~** (*person*) essere intonato/stonato; (*instrument*) essere accordato/scordato; **to be in/out of ~ with sth** *fig* essere in/fuori sintonia con qc ► **to change one's ~** cambiare parere; **to sing another ~** cambiare musica; **to the ~ of** $100 per la bellezza di 100 dollari **II.** *vt* **1.** MUS accordare **2.** AUTO mettere a punto
◆**tune in I.** *vi* **1.** RADIO, TV sintonizzarsi su **2.** *fig, inf* entrare in sintonia **II.** *vt* RADIO, TV sintonizzare
◆**tune up** *vt* AUTO mettere a punto

tuneful ['tju:n-fəl] *adj* MUS armonioso, -a

tuneless ['tju:n-ləs] *adj* MUS disarmonico, -a

tuner *n* **1.** MUS (*person*) accordatore, -trice *m, f* **2.** (*radio*) sintonizzatore *m*

tune-up ['tju:n-ʌp] *n* **1.** MUS accordatura *m* **2.** AUTO messa *f* a punto

tungsten ['tʌŋs-tən] *n* tungsteno *m*

tunic ['tu:-nɪk] *n* FASHION casacca *f;* HIST tunica *f*

tuning *n* **1.** MUS accordatura *f* **2.** RADIO sintonizzazione *f* **3.** AUTO messa *f* a punto

tuning fork *n* MUS diapason *m inv*

Tunisia [tu:-'ni:-ʒə] *n* Tunisia *f*

Tunisian [tu:-'ni:-ʒən] **I.** *n* tunisino, -a *m, f* **II.** *adj* tunisino, -a

tunnel ['tʌ-nl] **I.** *n* **1.** ARCHIT tunnel *m inv* **2.** MIN galleria *f* **II.** *vi* scavare una galleria **III.** *vt* scavare una galleria in; **to ~ one's way out** scappare scavandosi una galleria

turban ['tɜ:r-bən] *n* turbante *m*

turbid ['tɜ:r-bɪd] *adj* (*water*) torbido, -a

turbine ['tɜ:r-bɪn] *n* turbina *f*

turbocharged ['tɜ:r-boʊ-tʃa:rdʒd] *adj* ELEC, TECH turbocompresso, -a

turbocharger ['tɜ:r-boʊ-tʃa:r-dʒə] *n* ELEC, TECH turbocompressore *m*

turbo engine *n* motore *m* turbo *inv*

turbojet *n* turboreattore *m*

turbot ['tɜ:r-bət] *n* <-(s)> rombo *m*

turbulence ['tɜ:r-bju-ləns] *n* turbolenza *f*

turbulent ['tɜ:r-bju-lənt] *adj* turbolento, -a

turd [tɜ:rd] *n vulg* **1.** (*excrement*) stronzo *m* **2.** (*person*) stronzo, -a *m, f*

tureen [tʊ-'ri:n] *n* zuppiera *f*

turf [tɜ:rf] <-s *o* -ves> *n* **1.** BOT tappeto *m* erboso; **a** (*piece of*) **~** una zolla erbosa; **the ~** (*horse racing*) corse *fpl* ippiche **2.** (*territory*) territorio *m*

turgid ['tɜ:r-dʒɪd] *adj form* **1.** *pej* (*style*) ampolloso, -a **2.** (*swollen*) turgido, -a

Turk [tɜ:rk] *n* turco, -a *m, f*

turkey ['tɜ:r-ki] *n* **1.** ZOOL tacchino *m* **2.** *inf* THEAT fiasco *m* **3.** *inf* (*stupid person*) sciocco, -a *m, f* ► **to talk ~** *inf* parlare chiaro

Turkey ['tɜ:r-ki] *n* Turchia *f*

Turkish ['tɜ:r-kɪʃ] **I.** *adj* turco, -a **II.** *n* **1.** (*person*) turco, -a *m, f* **2.** LING turco *m*

turmoil ['tɜ:r-mɔɪl] *n* **1.** (*state of chaos*) scompiglio *m inv;* **to be thrown into ~** esser gettato nello scompiglio **2.** (*of mind*) subbuglio *m;* **to be in a ~** essere in subbuglio

turn [tɜ:rn] **I.** *vi* **1.** (*rotate*) girare; **to ~ on sth** girare su qc **2.** (*switch direction*) voltare; (*tide*) cambiare; (*car*) svoltare; **to ~ around** voltarsi; **to ~ right/left** girare a destra/sinistra **3.** (*change*) trasformarsi in; (*for worse*) diventare; **to ~ traitor** rivelarsi un traditore; **he ~ed gray** (*overnight*) gli son venuti i capelli bianchi (da un giorno all'altro) **4.** (*change color: leaves*) cambiare colore **5.** (*feel nauseous: stomach*) rivoltarsi **6.** (*spoil: cream, milk*) inacidire **II.** *vt* **1.** (*rotate*) (far) girare; (*key*) girare; (*screw on*) avvitare; (*unscrew*) svitare **2.** (*switch direction*) voltare; **to ~ one's head** voltare la testa; **to ~ a page** voltare pagina; **to ~ the coat inside out** rivoltare il cappotto **3.** (*attain a particular age*) compiere **4.** (*pass a particular hour*) **it has ~ed three o'clock** sono le tre **5.** (*cause to feel nauseated*) **it ~ed**

my stomach mi ha fatto rivoltare lo stomaco
▶ **to ~ sth** upside **down** capovolgere qc III. *n*
1. (*change in direction*) svolta *f;* **to make a ~
to the right** svoltare a destra; **to take a ~ for
the worse/better** cambiare in peggio/meglio
2. (*changing point*) svolta *f;* **the ~ of the century** l'inizio del secolo 3. (*period of duty*)
turno *m;* **to be sb's ~ to do sth** toccare a qn
fare qc; **it's your ~** tocca a te; **to do sth in ~**
fare qc a turno; **to miss a ~** saltare un turno;
to speak out of ~ parlare a sproposito
4. (*rotation, twist*) giro *m* 5. (*service*)
favore *m;* **to do sb a good ~** fare un favore a
qn; **one good ~ deserves another** *prov* ogni
favore va contraccambiato *prov*
◆**turn against** *vt* mettersi contro
◆**turn away** I. *vi* allontanare; **to ~ from sb/
sth** allontanarsi da qn/qc II. *vt* 1. (*refuse
entry*) non fare entrare 2. (*deny help*) mandar
via
◆**turn back** I. *vi* (*return to starting point*) tornare indietro II. *vt* 1. (*send back*) far ritornare
2. (*fold towards itself: bedcover, corner of
paper*) ripiegare
◆**turn down** *vt* 1. (*reject*) respingere
2. (*reduce volume*) abbassare 3. (*fold*) ripiegare
◆**turn in** I. *vt* (*hand over*) consegnare II. *vi inf*
(*go to bed*) andare a letto
◆**turn into** *vt* trasformarsi in
◆**turn off** I. *vt* 1. ELEC, TECH spegnere; (*gas,
faucet*) chiudere 2. *inf* (*be unappealing*) disgustare II. *vi* (*leave path*) svoltare
◆**turn on** *vt* 1. ELEC, TECH accendere; (*gas, faucet*) aprire 2. (*excite*) eccitare; (*attract*) attirare 3. (*show, demonstrate*) mettere in mostra; **to ~ the charm** sfoderare tutto il proprio
fascino 4. (*attack*) aggredire
◆**turn out** I. *vi* 1. (*end up, work out*) finire
2. (*be revealed*) rivelarsi; **it turned out to be
true** si è rivelato essere vero II. *vt* 1. (*light*)
spegnere 2. (*kick out*) cacciare; **to turn sb out
on the street** buttare qn in mezzo alla strada
3. (*empty*) vuotare
◆**turn over** I. *vi* (*start, operate: engine*)
accendere II. *vt* 1. (*change the side*) girare
2. (*criminal*) consegnare 3. (*control*) affidare;
(*possession*) cedere 4. (*facts*) meditare; **to ~
an idea** riflettere a lungo su un'idea 5. COM, FIN
fatturare 6. *inf* (*search*) mettere sottosopra
frugando
◆**turn around** I. *vi* girarsi II. *vt* 1. (*move*)
girare 2. (*change*) cambiare; (*reform*) riformare
◆**turn to** *vt* 1. (*face*) dedicarsi a 2. (*request
aid*) **to ~ sb** (**for sth**) rivolgersi a qn (per qc)
◆**turn up** I. *vi* 1. (*arrive*) arrivare 2. (*become
available*) saltar fuori 3. (*point upwards*) girare
insù II. *vt* 1. (*volume*) alzare 2. (*shorten*)
accorciare 3. (*point upwards*) girare insù
4. (*find*) trovare
turnabout ['tɜːrn·ə·ˌbaʊt] *n*, **turnaround**
['tɜːrn·ə·ˌaʊnd] *n* 1. (*change*) cambia-

mento *m* radicale 2. (*improvement*) svolta *f*
positiva
turnaround time *n* AVIAT, NAUT tempo *m* di rotazione; (*of project*) tempo di sviluppo
turncoat ['tɜːrn·koʊt] *n* voltagabbana *mf inv*
turner ['tɜːr·nɚ] *n inf* tornitore, -trice *m, f*
turning ['tɜːr·nɪŋ] *n* 1. (*road*) traversa *f* 2. (*act
of changing direction*) svolta *f*
turning point *n* svolta *f* decisiva; **a ~ in one's
career** una svolta decisiva nella sua carriera
turnip ['tɜːr·nɪp] *n* rapa *f*
turnkey operation [ˌtɜːrn·ki: ˌɑː·pə·'reɪ·ʃən] *n*
operazione *f* chiavi in mano
turnoff ['tɜːrn·ɑːf] *n* 1. AUTO uscita *f* 2. *inf*
(*something unappealing*) **to be a real ~** far
passare ogni voglia
turnout ['tɜːrn·aʊt] *n* 1. (*attendance*)
numero *m* di partecipanti 2. POL affluenza *f*
3. ECON produzione *f*
turnover ['tɜːrn·ˌoʊ·vɚ] *n* 1. COM, FIN volume *m* d'affari; (*sales*) fatturato *m* 2. (*in staff*)
rotazione *f* 3. GASTR *focaccia ripiena di frutta*
turnpike ['tɜːrn·paɪk] *n* AUTO autostrada *f* a
pagamento
turnstile ['tɜːrn·staɪl] *n* SPORTS cancelletto *m*
girevole
turntable ['tɜːrn·ˌteɪ·bl] *n* 1. MUS (*record
player*) giradischi *m inv* 2. RAIL piattaforma *f*
girevole
turpentine ['tɜːr·pən·taɪn] *n* trementina *f*
turpitude ['tɜːr·pɪ·tu:d] *n form* turpitudine *f;*
moral ~ depravazione *f*
turquoise ['tɜːrk·wɔɪz] *n* 1. (*stone*) turchese *m* 2. (*color*) turchese *m*
turret ['tɜːr·rɪt] *n* 1. (*tower*) torretta *f* 2. (*of
tank, ship*) torretta *f*
turtle ['tɜːr·t̬l] <-(s)> *n* tartaruga *f* d'acqua
turtledove ['tɜːr·t̬l·dʌv] *n* tortora *f*
turtleneck ['tɜːr·t̬l·nek] *n* dolcevita *m inv*
tusk [tʌsk] *n* zanna *f*
tussle ['tʌ·sl] I. *vi* azzuffarsi II. *n* (*physical
struggle*) zuffa *f;* (*quarrel*) lite *f*
tussock ['tʌ·sək] *n* ciuffo *m* d'erba
tut [tʌt] *interj* ~ ~! no, no, così non si fa!
tutelage ['tu:·t̬·lɪdʒ] *n* tutela *f*
tutor ['tu:·tɚ] I. *n* SCHOOL, UNIV (*private
teacher*) tutor, *professore di riferimento per
uno o più studenti inv;* (*at home*) insegnante *mf* privato, -a II. *vt* SCHOOL, UNIV **to ~ sb**
(**in sth**) dare lezioni individuali a qn (di qc)
tutorial [tu:·'tɔː·ri·əl] *n* COMPUT tutorial *m inv*
tuxedo [tʌk·'si:·doʊ] *n* smoking *m inv*
TV [ˌti:·'vi:] *n abbr of* **television** TV *f inv*
twaddle ['twɑː·dl] *n inf* fesserie *fpl;* **to talk ~**
dire fesserie
twang [twæŋ] I. *n* 1. MUS suono *m* vibrante
2. LING accento *m* nasale II. *vt* far vibrare;
(*strings*) pizzicare; **to ~ someone's nerves**
urtare i nervi di qn III. *vi* vibrare
tweak [twi:k] I. *vt* pizzicare II. *n* pizzicotto *m*
tweed [twi:d] *n* 1. (*textile*) tweed *m inv* 2. *pl*
(*suit*) completo *m* in tweed
tweedy ['twi:·di] *adj* <-ier, -iest> *fig* da genti-

T

luomo di campagna

tweet [twi:t] I. *n* cinguettio *m* II. *vi* cinguettare

tweeter ['twi:·ţə·] *n* tweeter *m inv*

tweezers ['twi:·zə·z] *npl* (**a pair of**) ~ (un paio di) pinzette *fpl*

twelfth [twelfθ] I. *adj* dodicesimo, -a II. *n* 1. (*order*) dodicesimo, -a *m, f* 2. (*date*) dodici *m* 3. (*fraction*) dodicesimo *m;* (*part*) dodicesima parte *f; s.a.* **eighth**

twelve [twelv] I. *adj* dodici II. *n* dodici *m; s.a.* **eight**

twentieth ['twen·ţı·əθ] I. *adj* ventesimo, -a II. *n* 1. (*order*) ventesimo, -a *m, f* 2. (*date*) venti *m* 3. (*fraction*) ventesimo *m;* (*part*) ventesima parte *f; s.a.* **eighth**

twenty ['twen·ţi] <-ies> I. *adj* venti II. *n* venti *m; s.a.* **eighty**

twerp [twɜ:rp] *n inf* idiota *mf*

twice [twaɪs] *adv* due volte

twiddle ['twɪ·dl] I. *vt a.* TECH, ELEC (far) girare ►to ~ **one's thumbs** girare i pollici II. *vi* to ~ **with sth** giocherellare con qc III. *n* giro *m*

twig [twɪg] I. *n* ramoscello *m* II. *vi inf* rendersi conto

twilight ['twaɪ·laɪt] *n* crepuscolo *m*

twin [twɪn] I. *n* gemello, -a *m, f;* **identical** ~**s** gemelli identici II. *adj* gemello, -a III. *vt* <-nn-> gemellare IV. *vi* <-nn-> gemellarsi

twin beds *npl* letti *m* gemelli *pl*

twin brother *n* fratello *m* gemello

twine [twaɪn] I. *vt* 1. (*wind up*) attorcigliare 2. (*encircle*) cingere II. *n* spago *m*

twinge [twɪndʒ] *n* 1. MED fitta *f* 2. *fig* punta *f;* a ~ **of conscience** un rimorso di coscienza

twinkle ['twɪŋ·kl] I. *vi* (*eyes*) brillare; (*star, diamond*) scintillare II. *n* (*of stars, jewels, light*) scintillio *m;* (*of eyes*) luccichio *m* ►**to be just a** ~ **in sb's father's eye** non essere ancora nato; **to do sth in a** ~ far qc in un batter d'occhio

twinkling ['twɪŋk·lɪŋ] I. *adj* (*eyes*) brillante; (*star, diamond*) scintillante II. *n* **in the** ~ **of an eye** in un batter d'occhio

twinning ['twɪ·nɪŋ] *n* gemellaggio *m*

twin room *n* camera *f* a due letti

twin sister *n* sorella *f* gemella

twirl [twɜ:rl] I. *vi* girare; **to** ~ **around sth** girare intorno a qc II. *vt* (*whirl*) far girare; (*moustache*) arricciare III. *n* piroetta *f*

twist [twɪst] I. *vt* 1. (*turn*) girare 2. (*wind around*) attorcigliare; **to** ~ **sth around sth** avvolgere qc intorno a qc 3. MED slogarsi 4. (*distort: truth*) distorcere ►**to** ~ **sb's arm** forzare la mano a qn; **to** ~ **sb round one's little finger** far fare a qn ciò che si vuole II. *vi* 1. (*squirm around*) (ri)girarsi 2. (*curve: path, road*) curvare; **to** ~ **and turn** serpeggiare 3. (*dance*) ballare il twist III. *n* 1. (*turn*) torsione *f;* **to give sth a** ~ far girare qc 2. (*unexpected change*) svolta *f* 3. (*curl: of hair*) ciocca *f;* (*of lemon*) fettina *f;* (*of paper*) cartoccio *m;* (*of coil*) giro *m* 4. (*dance*) twist *m*

◆**twist off** *vt* svitare

twisted ['twɪs·tɪd] *adj* 1. (*cable*) attorcigliato, -a; (*metal*) contorto, -a; (*ankle*) slogato, -a 2. (*perverted*) perverso, -a; (*logic, humor*) contorto, -a

twister ['twɪs·tə·] *n* 1. METEO tornado *m inv* 2. *inf* (*swindler*) truffatore, -trice *m, f*

twisty ['twɪs·ti] *adj* <-ier, -iest> *inf* (*road*) serpeggiante

twit [twɪt] *n inf* sciocco, -a *m, f*

twitch [twɪtʃ] I. *vi* ANAT, MED muoversi a scatti; (*face*) contrarsi II. *vt* 1. ANAT, MED contrarre 2. (*pull*) tirare III. *n* <-es> 1. ANAT, MED contrazione *f* muscolare *inv;* **to have a** (**nervous**) ~ avere un tic *inv* (nervoso) 2. (*pull*) tiratina *f*

twitter ['twɪ·ţə·] I. *vi* 1. ZOOL cinguettare 2. (*talk*) parlottare II. *n* cinguettio *m*

two [tu:] I. *adj* dos II. *n* due *m* ►**that makes** ~ **of us** *inf* così siamo in due; **to put** ~ **and** ~ **together** *inf* fare due più due; *s.a.* **eight**

two-bit [tu:·'bɪt] *adj inf* da due soldi

two-dimensional [ˌtu:·dɪ·'men·tʃə·nəl] *adj* 1. bidimensionale 2. *fig* superficiale

two-door *adj* AUTO a due porte

two-edged *adj* a doppio taglio

two-faced *adj pej* falso, -a

twofold ['tu:·foʊld] I. *adv* doppiamente II. *adj* doppio, -a

two-part *adj* in due parti

two-party system *n* sistema *m* bipartitico

two-phase *adj* ELEC bifase

two-piece *n* 1. (*suit*) completo *m* a due pezzi 2. (*bikini*) bikini *m inv*

two-seater AUTO I. *n* biposto *m inv* II. *adj* biposto *inv*

twosome ['tu:·səm] *n* (*duo*) duo *m inv;* (*couple*) coppia *f*

two-stroke AUTO I. *n* motore *m* a due tempi II. *adj* a due tempi

two-tiered *adj* a due livelli

two-time *vt inf* mettere le corna a

two-way ['tu:·'weɪ] *adj* (*tunnel, bridge*) a doppio senso; (*process*) reciproco, -a; (*conversation*) bilaterale; (*switch*) bipolare

two-way radio *n* radio *f inv* ricetrasmittente

tycoon [taɪ·'ku:n] *n* FIN magnate *mf*

tyke [taɪk] *n* 1. (*child*) monello, -a *m, f* 2. (*dog*) cane *m* randagio

tympanum ['tɪm·pə·nəm] *n* timpano *m*

type [taɪp] I. *n* 1. (*sort, kind: style, print, language*) genere *m;* (*of machine*) modello *m* 2. (*class: animal, person*) genere *m;* (*skin*) tipo 3. *inf* (*person*) tipo, -a *m, f;* **he's not her** ~ non è il suo tipo 4. TYPO carattere *m* II. *vt* 1. (*write with machine*) scrivere a macchina; (*on computer*) scrivere al computer 2. (*categorize*) classificare III. *vi* scrivere a macchina; (*on computer*) scrivere al computer

◆**type out** *vt* scrivere a macchina; (*on computer*) scrivere al computer

◆**type up** *vt* riscrivere a macchina; (*on computer*) riscrivere al computer

typecast ['taɪp·kæst] <typecast, typecast> *vt* incasellare

typeface ['taɪp·feɪs] *n* carattere (*m* di stampa)
typescript ['taɪp·skrɪpt] *n* dattiloscritto *m*
typesetter *n* 1. (*machine*) compositrice *f* 2. (*person*) compositore, -trice *m, f*
typesetting ['taɪp·ˌse·t̬ɪŋ] *n* composizione *f*
typewrite ['taɪp·raɪt] *irr vt* scrivere a macchina
typewriter ['taɪp·ˌraɪ·t̬ɚ] *n* macchina *f* da scrivere
typewriter ribbon *n* nastro *m* dattilografico
typewritten *adj* dattilografato, -a
typhoid ['taɪ·fɔɪd] *n*, **typhoid fever** *n* febbre *f* tifoidea
typhoon [taɪ·'fuːn] *n* METEO tifone *m*
typhus ['taɪ·fəs] *n* tifo *m*
typical ['tɪ·pɪ·kəl] *adj* tipico, -a; (*symptom*) caratteristico, -a; **to be ~ of sb to do sth** esser tipico di qn (il) fare qc
typically *adv* tipicamente
typify ['tɪ·pɪ·faɪ] <-ie-> *vt* simboleggiare
typing ['taɪ·pɪŋ] *n* dattilografia *f*
typist ['taɪ·pɪst] *n* dattilografo, -a *m, f*
typographer [taɪ·'pɑː·grə·fɚ] *n* tipografo, -a *m, f*
typographic(al) [ˌtaɪ·pə·'græ·fɪ·k(əl)] *adj* tipografico, -a
typographic(al) error *n* errore *m* di battitura
typography [taɪ·'pɑː·grə·fi] *n* tipografia *f*
tyrannical [tɪ·'ræ·nɪ·kəl] *adj pej* tirannico, -a
tyrannize ['tɪ·rə·naɪz] *vt* tiranneggiare
tyranny ['tɪ·rə·ni] *n* tirannia *f*
tyrant ['taɪ·rənt] *n* tiranno, -a *m, f*
tzar [zɑːr] *n* zar *m inv*
tzetze fly ['tet·si·ˌflaɪ] *n* mosca *f* tse-tse

U

U, u [juː] *n* U, u *f;* **~ as in Unicorn** U come Udine
U[1] *abbr of* **uranium** U
U[2] *inf abbr of* **university** U
UAE [ˌjuː·eɪ·'iː] *npl abbr of* **United Arab Emirates** EAU *mpl*
ubiquitous [juː·'bɪk·wə·t̬əs] *adj* onnipresente
ubiquity [juː·'bɪk·wə·t̬i] *n* ubiquità *f,* onnipresenza *f*
U-boat ['juː·boʊt] *n* sommergibile *m*
udder ['ʌ·dɚ] *n* mammella *f*
UFO [ˌjuː·ef·'oʊ] *n abbr of* **unidentified flying object** UFO *m inv*
Uganda [juː·'gæn·də] *n* Uganda *m*
Ugandan I. *adj* ugandese II. *n* ugandese *mf*
ugh [ɜːh] *interj inf* puah
ugliness ['ʌg·lɪ·nɪs] *n* bruttezza *f*
ugly ['ʌg·li] <-ier, iest> *adj* 1. (*not attractive*) brutto, -a; **to be ~ as sin** essere brutto come la fame 2. (*threatening*) minaccioso, -a; **to turn ~** degenerare 3. (*morally repulsive*) infame; **~ rumors** (vili) calunnie *fpl*

ugly duckling brutto anatroccolo *m*
UHF [ˌjuː·eɪtʃ·'ef] *n abbr of* **ultrahigh frequency** UHF *fpl*
UK [ˌjuː·'keɪ] *n abbr of* **United Kingdom** RU *m,* UK *f*
ukelele [ˌjuː·kəl·'eɪ·li] *n* ukelele *m inv*
Ukraine [juː·'kreɪn] *n* Ucraina *f*
Ukrainian I. *adj* ucraino, -a II. *n* 1. (*person*) ucraino, -a *m, f* 2. LING ucraino *m*
ulcer ['ʌl·sɚ] *n* 1. MED ulcera *f* 2. *fig* piaga *f*
ulcerate ['ʌl·sə·reɪt] *vi* ulcerarsi
ulcerous ['ʌl·sə·rəs] *adj* ulceroso, -a
ulna ['ʌl·nə] <ulnae *o* s> *n* ulna *f*
ulterior [ʌl·'tɪ·ri·ɚ] *adj* **~ motive** secondo fine *m*
ultimate ['ʌl·tə·mɪt] I. *adj* 1. (*highest degree of*) massimo, -a; (*honor, sacrifice, accolade*) supremo, -a 2. (*final*) finale; (*cost, consequences, effect*) definitivo, -a 3. (*fundamental*) fondamentale II. *n* (*the best*) **the ~ in** il non plus ultra (di)
ultimately ['ʌl·tə·mɪt·li] *adv* in definitiva
ultimatum [ˌʌl·tə·'meɪ·t̬əm] <ultimata *o* -tums> *n* ultimatum *m inv*
ultimo ['ʌl·tɪ·moʊ] *adv* ECON, COM ultimo scorso
ultrahigh frequency [ˌʌl·trə·ˌhaɪ·'fri·kwən·tsi] *n* frequenza *f* ultraelevata
ultramarine [ˌʌl·trə·mə·'riːn] I. *adj* ultramarino II. *n* blu *m* oltremare *inv*
ultramodern [ˌʌlt·rə·'mɑː·dɚn] *adj* ultramoderno, -a
ultrashort wave [ˌʌl·trə·ˌʃɔːrt·'weɪv] *n* onda *f* ultracorta
ultrasonic [ˌʌl·trə·'sɑː·nɪk] *adj* ultrasonico, -a
ultrasound ['ʌl·trə·saʊnd] *n* ultrasuono *m*
ultraviolet [ˌʌl·trə·'vaɪ·ə·lɪt] *adj* ultravioletto, -a
Ulysses [juː·'lɪ·siːz] *n* Ulisse *m*
umber ['ʌm·bɚ] I. *adj* terra d'ombra II. *n* terra d'ombra *m*
umbilical [ʌm·'bɪ·lɪ·kl] *adj* ombelicale
umbilical cord *n* cordone *m* ombelicale
umbrage ['ʌm·brɪdʒ] *n form* **to take ~ at sth** adombrarsi per qc
umbrella [ʌm·'bre·lə] *n* 1. ombrello *m;* **beach ~** ombrellone *m* 2. MIL ombrello *m* aereo; **under the ~ of sth** sotto la protezione di qc
umbrella organization *n* POL, ADMIN organizzazione *f* ombrello
umpire ['ʌm·paɪ·ɚ] SPORTS I. *n* arbitro *mf* II. *vt* arbitrare III. *vi* arbitrare
umpteen ['ʌmp·tiːn] *adj inf* innumerevole; **to do sth ~ times** fare qc milioni di volte
umpteenth ['ʌmp·tiːnθ] *adj* ennesimo, -a
UN [ˌjuː·'en] *n abbr of* **United Nations** ONU *f*
unabashed [ˌʌn·ə·'bæʃt] *adj* (*romantic*) incorreggibile; (*communist*) incallito; **~ by sth** per nulla impressionato da qc
unabated [ˌʌn·ə·'beɪ·t̬ɪd] *adj* (*winds, storm*) incessante; (*fighting, rioting*) costante; (*energy, enthusiasm*) inesauribile
unable [ʌn·'eɪ·bl] *adj* incapace; **to be ~ to do sth** non poter fare qc

unabridged [ˌʌn·ə·ˈbrɪdʒd] *adj* LIT, PUBL integrale

unacceptable [ˌʌn·ək·ˈsep·tə·bl] *adj* **1.**(*not good enough*) inaccettabile **2.**(*intolerable*) inammissibile

unaccompanied [ˌʌn·ə·ˈkʌm·pə·nid] *adj* **1.**(*without companion*) non accompagnato, -a **2.**MUS senza accompagnamento

unaccountable [ˌʌn·ə·ˈkaʊn·tə·bl] *adj* **1.**(*not responsible*) irresponsabile **2.**(*inexplicable*) inspiegabile

unaccounted-for [ˌʌn·ə·ˈkaʊn·tɪd·fɔːr] *adj* **to be ~** mancare

unaccustomed [ˌʌn·ə·ˈkʌs·təmd] *adj* insolito, -a; **to be ~ to doing sth** non essere abituato, -a a fare qc

unacknowledged [ˌʌn·ək·ˈnɑː·lɪdʒd] *adj* (*greeting*) ignorato, -a; (*author, scientist*) non riconosciuto, -a

unaddressed [ˌʌn·ə·ˈdrest] *adj* senza indirizzo

unadorned [ˌʌn·ə·ˈdɔːrnd] *adj* disadorno -a; **the ~ truth** la verità nuda e cruda

unadulterated [ˌʌn·ə·ˈdʌl·tə·reɪ·tɪd] *adj* puro, -a; (*alcohol, wine*) non sofisticato, -a; **~ nonsense** sciocchezze *f* belle e buone *pl*

unadventurous [ˌʌn·əd·ˈven·tʃə·rəs] *adj* poco avventuroso, -a

unaffected [ˌʌn·ə·ˈfek·tɪd] *adj* **1.**(*not changed*) **to be ~ by sth** non essere toccato, -a da qc **2.**(*not influenced*) spontaneo, -a **3.**(*down to earth*) non affettato, -a; (*manner, speech*) naturale

unafraid [ˌʌn·ə·ˈfreɪd] *adj* senza paura; **to be ~ of sb/sth** non aver paura di qu/qc

unaided [ˌʌn·ˈeɪ·dɪd] *adj* senza aiuto; **to do sth ~** fare qc senza l'aiuto di nessuno

unalloyed [ˌʌn·ə·ˈlɔɪd] *adj liter* puro, -a

unaltered [ʌn·ˈɔːl·tə·d] *adj* inalterato, -a

unambiguous [ˌʌn·æm·ˈbɪg·juː·əs] *adj* inequivocabile

un-American [ˌʌn·ə·ˈme·rɪ·kən] *adj* antiamericano, -a

unanimity [ˌjuː·ne·ˈnɪ·mə·ti] *n form* unanimità *f*

unanimous [juː·ˈnæ·nə·məs] *adj* unanime

unannounced [ˌʌn·ə·ˈnaʊnst] I. *adj* inatteso, -a II. *adv* senza preavviso

unanswerable [ˌʌn·ˈæn·sə·rə·bl] *adj* **1.**(*without an answer*) a cui è impossibile rispondere **2.** *form* (*irrefutable*) irrefutabile

unanswered [ˌʌn·ˈæn·sə·d] *adj* senza risposta

unappealing *adj* poco attraente

unappetizing [ˌʌn·ˈæ·pə·taɪ·zɪŋ] *adj* poco appetitoso, -a

unapproachable [ˌʌn·ə·ˈproʊ·tʃə·bl] *adj* **1.**(*person*) inavvicinabile **2.**(*building*) inaccessibile

unarmed [ˌʌn·ˈɑːrmd] *adj* disarmato, -a

unashamed [ˌʌn·ə·ˈʃeɪmd] *adj* sfrontato, -a; **to be ~ of sth** non vergognarsi di qc

unasked [ˌʌn·ˈæskt] *adj* **1.**(*not questioned*) non richiesto, -a **2.**(*spontaneous*) spontaneo, -a

unassignable [ˌʌn·ə·ˈsaɪ·nə·bl] *adj* LAW non trasferibile

unassuming [ˌʌn·ə·ˈsuː·mɪŋ] *adj* modesto, -a

unattached [ˌʌn·ə·ˈtætʃt] *adj* **1.**(*not connected*) staccato, -a **2.**(*independent*) indipendente **3.**(*unmarried*) single

unattainable [ˌʌn·ə·ˈteɪ·nə·bl] *adj* irrealizzabile

unattended [ˌʌn·ə·ˈten·dɪd] *adj* **1.**(*alone*) senza sorveglianza **2.**(*unmanned*) incustodito, -a **3.**(*not taken care of*) ignorato, -a

unattractive [ˌʌn·ə·ˈtræk·tɪv] *adj* poco attraente

unauthorized [ˌʌn·ˈɑː·θə·raɪzd] *adj* non autorizzato, -a

unavailable [ˌʌn·ə·ˈveɪ·lə·bl] *adj* non disponibile

unavailing [ˌʌn·ə·ˈveɪ·lɪŋ] *adj form* (*denial*) inutile; (*effort, attempt*) vano, -a

unavoidable [ˌʌn·ə·ˈvɔɪ·də·bl] *adj* inevitabile

unaware [ˌʌn·ə·ˈwer] *adj* **to be ~ of sth** essere ignaro, -a di qc

unawares [ˌʌn·ə·ˈwerz] *adv* **to catch sb ~** cogliere qu alla sprovvista

unbalanced [ˌʌn·ˈbæ·lənst] *adj* **1.**(*uneven: report*) di parte **2.**(*mental state*) precario, -a; **a mentally unbalanced individual,** uno squilibrato

unbearable [ˌʌn·ˈbe·rə·bl] *adj* insopportabile

unbeatable [ˌʌn·ˈbiː·tə·bl] *adj* (*record, team*) imbattibile; (*army*) invincibile; (*value, quality*) insuperabile

unbeaten [ˌʌn·ˈbiː·tn] *adj* imbattuto, -a

unbecoming [ˌʌn·bɪ·ˈkʌ·mɪŋ] *adj* **1.**(*dress, suit*) che non dona **2.**(*attitude, manner*) indecoroso, -a

unbeknown(st) [ˌʌn·bɪ·ˈnoʊn] *adv form* **~ to her** a sua insaputa

unbelievable [ˌʌn·bɪ·ˈliː·və·bl] *adj* incredibile

unbeliever [ˌʌn·bɪ·ˈliː·və] *n* REL non credente *mf*

unbelieving [ˌʌn·bɪ·ˈliː·vɪŋ] *adj* incredulo, -a

unbend [ˌʌn·ˈbend] I. *vt* raddrizzare II. *vi irr* **1.**(*straighten out*) raddrizzarsi **2.**(*relax*) distendersi

unbending *adj* inflessibile

unbiased [ˌʌn·ˈbaɪ·əst] *adj* imparziale

unbidden [ˌʌn·ˈbɪ·dən] *liter* I. *adv* spontaneamente II. *adj* spontaneo, -a

unbind [ˌʌn·ˈbaɪnd] *irr vt* slegare

unbleached [ˌʌn·ˈbliːtʃt] *adj* non sbiancato, -a; **~ flour** farina *f* non sbiancata

unblinking [ˌʌn·ˈblɪn·kɪŋ] *adj* **1.**(*without blinking*) impassibile **2.**(*without doubt*) risoluto, -a

unblushing [ˌʌn·ˈblʌ·ʃɪŋ] *adj* sfrontato, -a

unbolt [ˌʌn·ˈboʊlt] *vt* togliere il chiavistello a

unborn [ˌʌn·ˈbɔːrn] *adj* **1.**(*not yet born*) non ancora nato, -a **2.** *lit* (*future*) futuro, -a

unbosom [ˌʌn·ˈbʊ·zəm] *vt form* **1.**(*reveal*) confidare **2.**(*confide in*) **to ~ oneself to sb** confidarsi con qu

unbounded [ˌʌn·ˈbaʊn·dɪd] *adj* immenso, -a

unbowed [ʌn·'baʊd] *adj* 1.(*erect*) non chino, -a 2.(*not submitting*) non sottomesso, -a

unbreakable [ʌn·'breɪ·kə·bl] *adj* infrangibile

unbribable [ʌn·'braɪ·bə·bl] *adj* incorruttibile

unbridled [ʌn·'braɪ·dld] *adj* sfrenato, -a

unbroken [ʌn·'broʊ·kən] *adj* 1.(*not broken*) **an ~ promise** una promessa mantenuta 2.(*uncrushed*) intatto, -a 3.(*continuous, without a break*) ininterrotto, -a 4.(*unsurpassed*) imbattuto, -a 5.(*not tamed*) non addomesticato, -a

unbuckle [ʌn·'bʌ·kl] *vt* slacciare (la fibbia di); **to ~ a seatbelt** slacciare la cintura di sicurezza

unburden [ʌn·'bɜːr·dən] *vt* **to ~ oneself (of sth)** sfogarsi (di qc); **to ~ oneself (to sb)** sfogarsi (con qu); **to ~ one's sorrows** confidare le proprie pene

unbusinesslike [ʌn·'bɪz·nɪs·laɪk] *adj* poco professionale

unbutton [ʌn·'bʌ·tən] **I.** *vt* sbottonare **II.** *vi* sbottonarsi

uncalled-for [ʌn·'kɔːld·fɔːr] *adj* fuori luogo; **an ~ remark** un commento fuori luogo

uncanny [ʌn·'kæ·ni] *adj* <-ier, -iest> sorprendente

uncared-for [ʌn·'kerd·fɔːr] *adj* trascurato, -a

unceasing [ʌn·'siː·sɪŋ] *adj form* incessante

unceremonious [ʌn·ˌse·rɪ·'moʊ·ni·əs] *adj* 1.(*abrupt*) precipitoso, -a 2.(*informal*) senza cerimonie

unceremoniously *adv* 1.(*abruptly*) precipitosamente 2.(*informally*) senza cerimonie

uncertain [ʌn·'sɜːr·tən] *adj* 1.(*unsure*) insicuro, -a; **to be ~ about sth** non essere sicuro di qc; **it's ~ whether/when ...** non si sa se/quando...; **in no ~ terms** chiaramente 2.(*unpredictable, chancy*) incerto, -a; **an ~ future** un futuro incerto 3.(*volatile*) instabile

uncertainty [ʌn·'sɜːr·tən·ti] <-ies> *n* incertezza *f*

unchallenged [ʌn·'tʃæ·lɪndʒd] *adj* incontestato, -a; **to go ~** non essere contestato

unchanged [ʌn·'tʃeɪndʒd] *adj* (*prices, rates*) invariato, -a; (*tradition*) immutato, -a

uncharacteristic [ʌn·ˌke·rɪk·tə·'rɪs·tɪk] *adj* poco caratteristico, -a; **to be ~ of sb** essere insolito, -a per qu

uncharitable [ʌn·'tʃe·rə·tə·bl] *adj* 1.(*unkind*) crudele; **to be ~ (of sb) to do sth** essere crudele (da parte di qu) fare qc 2.(*ungenerous*) poco caritatevole

unchecked [ʌn·'tʃekt] *adj* 1.(*unrestrained*) incontrollato, -a 2.(*not examined or verified*) non accertato, -a

unchristian [ʌn·'krɪs·tʃən] *adj* poco cristiano, -a

uncivil [ʌn·'sɪ·vl] *adj form* incivile; **to be ~ to sb** essere scortese con qu

unclad [ʌn·'klæd] *adj form* nudo, -a

unclaimed [ʌn·'kleɪmd] *adj* non reclamato, -a

unclassified [ʌn·'klæ·sɪ·faɪd] *adj* non classificato, -a

uncle ['ʌŋ·kl] *n* zio *m* ▶ **to say ~** *childspeak*

arrendersi

unclean [ʌn·'kliːn] *adj* 1.(*unhygienic*) sporco, -a 2.(*impure*) impuro, -a

unclear [ʌn·'klɪr] *adj* 1.(*not obvious*) poco chiaro, -a; **it's ~ what/whether ...** non è chiaro che cosa/se... 2.(*not certain*) **to be ~ about sth** non essere sicuro, -a di qc

uncluttered [ʌn·'klʌ·tə·d] *adj* sgombro, -a

uncollected [ʌn·kə·'lek·tɪd] *adj* 1.(*garbage*) non ritirato, -a 2.(*taxes*) non riscosso, -a 3.(*thoughts*) non raccolto, -a

uncolored [ʌn·'kʌ·lə·d] *adj* incolore

uncomfortable [ʌn·'kʌmp·fə·tə·bl] *adj* 1.(*not comfortable*) scomodo, -a 2.(*embarrased*) a disagio; **an ~ silence** un silenzio imbarazzato

uncommitted [ʌn·kə·'mɪ·tɪd] *adj* non schierato, -a

uncommon [ʌn·'kɑː·mən] *adj* 1.(*rare*) raro, -a; **to be not ~ for sb** capitare non di rado a qu; **it is not ~ for this to happen** una cosa che capita non di rado 2.*form* (*exceptional*) eccezionale

uncommonly *adv* 1.(*unusually*) raramente 2.*form* (*extremely*) estremamente

uncommunicative [ʌn·kə·'mjuː·nɪ·kə·tɪv] *adj* poco comunicativo, -a; **to be ~ about sth/sb** essere riservato su qc/qu

uncompromising [ʌn·'kɑːm·prə·maɪ·zɪŋ] *adj* intransigente; **to take an ~ stand** assumere una posizione intransigente

unconcerned [ʌn·kən·'sɜːrnd] *adj* 1.(*not worried*) noncurante; **to be ~ about sth/sb** non curarsi di qc/qu 2.(*indifferent*) indifferente; **to be ~ with sth** essere indifferente a qc

unconditional [ʌn·kən·'dɪ·ʃə·nl] *adj* senza condizioni; **~ love** amore *m* senza condizioni

unconfirmed [ʌn·kən·'fɜːrmd] *adj* non confermato, -a

uncongenial [ʌn·kən·'dʒiː·ni·əl] *adj* 1.(*unfriendly*) antipatico, -a 2.(*not pleasant*) sfavorevole; **~ conditions** condizioni *fpl* sfavorevoli

unconnected [ʌn·kə·'nek·tɪd] *adj* scollegato, -a; **to be ~ to sth** non essere collegato a qc

unconscionable [ʌn·'kɑːn·tʃə·nə·bl] *adj form* eccessivo, -a

unconscious [ʌn·'kɑːn·tʃəs] **I.** *adj* 1.(*not conscious*) svenuto, -a; **to knock sb ~** far perdere i sensi a qu; **~ state** stato *m* d'inconscienza 2.PSYCH inconscio, -a 3.(*unaware*) non intenzionale; **to be ~ of sth** *form* non essere cosciente di qc **II.** *n* PSYCH **the ~** l'inconscio *m*

unconsciously *adv* inconsciamente

unconsciousness *n* 1.(*loss of consciousness*) incoscienza *f* 2.*form* (*unawareness*) inconsapevolezza *f*

unconsidered [ʌn·kən·'sɪ·də·d] *adj form* sconsiderato, -a

unconstitutional [ʌn·ˌkɑːnt·stə·'tuː·ʃə·nəl] *adj* incostituzionale

unconsummated [ʌn·'kɑːnt·sə·meɪ·tɪd] *adj* non consumato, -a

U

uncontested [ˌʌn·kən·'tes·tɪd] *adj* **1.** (*unquestioned*) incontestato, -a **2.** LAW non conteso, -a; **an ~ divorce** divorzio *m* consensuale

uncontrollable [ˌʌn·kən·'trou·lə·bl] *adj* **1.** (*irresistible*) incontrollabile **2.** (*frenzied*) sfrenato, -a; **an ~ child** un bambino indisciplinato

uncontrolled [ˌʌn·kən·'trould] *adj* incontrollato, -a

uncontroversial [ˌʌn·kɒn·trə·'vɜː·ʃl] *adj* indiscutibile

unconvinced [ˌʌn·kən·'vɪnst] *adj* **to be ~ of sth** non essere convinto, -a di qc

unconvincing [ˌʌn·kən·'vɪn·sɪŋ] *adj* **1.** (*not persuasive*) poco convincente **2.** (*not credible*) poco credibile

uncooked [ˌʌn·'kʊkt] *adj* crudo, -a

uncooperative [ˌʌn·koʊ·'ɑ:p·ə·ə·tɪv] *adj* poco collaborativo, -a

uncork [ˌʌn·'kɔːrk] *vt* **1.** (*extract cork from bottle*) stappare **2.** *inf* (*let out sth repressed*) **to ~ one's anger** sfogare la propria rabbia

uncorroborated [ˌʌn·kə·'rɑː·bə·reɪ·tɪd] *adj* non corroborato, -a

uncountable noun [ˌʌn·'kaun·tə·bl naun] *n* LING sostantivo *m* non numerabile

uncouple [ˌʌn·'kʌ·pl] *vt* **to ~ sth (from sth)** sganciare qc (da qc)

uncouth [ˌʌn·'kuːθ] *adj* rozzo, -a

uncover [ˌʌn·'kʌ·və] *vt* **1.** (*expose: wound*) scoprire **2.** (*discover*) svelare; **to ~ a secret** scoprire un segreto; **to ~ the truth** far venire a galla la verità

uncritical [ˌʌn·'krɪ·tɪ·kl] *adj* poco critico, -a; **to be ~ of sth/sb** non essere critico nei confronti di qc/qu

uncrowned [ˌʌn·'kraund] *adj* (*champion*) non ufficiale

uncut [ˌʌn·'kʌt] *adj* **1.** (*diamond*) non tagliato, -a **2.** (*film*) in versione integrale

undated [ˌʌn·'deɪ·tɪd] *adj* senza data

undaunted [ˌʌn·'dɑːn·tɪd] *adj* imperterrito, -a; **to be ~ by sth** non farsi scoraggiare da qc

undeceive [ˌʌn·dɪ·'siːv] *vt liter* **to ~ sb (of sth)** disilludere qu (su qc)

undecided [ˌʌn·dɪ·'saɪ·dɪd] *adj* indeciso, -a; **an ~ voter** un elettore indeciso; **to be ~ about sth** essere indeciso su qc; **to be ~ as to what to do** essere indeciso sul da farsi

undeclared [ˌʌn·dɪ·'klerd] *adj* non dichiarato, -a

undefined [ˌʌn·dɪ·'faɪnd] *adj* **1.** (*not defined*) indefinito, -a **2.** (*lacking clarity*) vago, -a

undeliverable [ˌʌn·dɪ·'lɪv·rə·bl] *adj* non recapitabile

undelivered [ˌʌn·dɪ·'lɪ·vəd] *adj* non recapitato, -a

undemanding [ˌʌn·dɪ·'mɑːn·dɪŋ] *adj* **1.** (*requiring little effort*) poco faticoso, -a **2.** (*easy-going: person*) poco esigente

undemocratic [ˌʌn·de·mə·'kræ·tɪk] *adj* antidemocratico, -a

undemonstrative [ˌʌn·dɪ·'mɑːns·trə·tɪv] *adj* *form* riservato, -a

undeniable [ˌʌn·dɪ·'naɪ·ə·bl] *adj* innegabile; **~ evidence** prova *f* irrefutabile

undeniably *adv* innegabilmente

under ['ʌn·də] I. *prep* **1.** (*below*) sotto; **~ the bed** sotto il letto; **~ there** là sotto **2.** (*supporting*) sotto; **to break ~ the weight of sth** rompersi sotto il peso di qc **3.** (*less than*) **to cost ~ 10 dollars** costare meno di 10 dollari; **those ~ the age of 30** quelli sotto i 30 anni **4.** (*governed by*) **~ Napoleon** sotto Napoleone; **those born ~ the star sign Pisces** i nati sotto il segno dei Pesci **5.** (*in state of*) **~ the circumstances** date le circostanze; **~ repair** in riparazione **6.** (*in category of*) **listed ~ fiction** catalogato come narrativa **7.** (*according to*) **~ the treaty** in base al trattato II. *adv* **1.** (*fewer*) meno **2.** (*below*) **to crawl/go ~** strisciare/andare sotto **3.** *inf* (*unconscious*) **to go ~** svenire

underachiever [ˌʌn·də·ə·'tʃiː·vər] *n* chi non rende come dovrebbe

underage [ˌʌn·də·'eɪdʒ] *adj* minorenne

underbid [ˌʌn·də·'bɪd] *irr vt* **to ~ sb/sth** fare un'offerta più bassa di qu/qc

undercapitalized [ˌʌn·də·'kæ·pɪ·tə·laɪzd] *adj* sottocapitalizzato, -a

undercarriage ['ʌn·də·ke·rɪdʒ] *n* AVIAT carrello *m* d'atterraggio

undercharge [ˌʌn·də·'tʃɑːrdʒ] I. *vt* **to ~ sb** far pagare meno del dovuto a qu II. *vi* far pagare meno del dovuto; **to ~ for sth** far pagare qc meno del dovuto

underclothes ['ʌn·də·klouðz] *npl*, **underclothing** ['ʌn·də·ˌklou·ðɪŋ] *n* biancheria *f* intima

undercoat ['ʌn·də·kout] *n* mano *f* di fondo

undercover [ˌʌn·də·'kʌ·və] I. *adj* segreto, -a; **~ agent** agente *mf* sotto copertura II. *adv* sotto copertura, in incognito

undercurrent ['ʌn·də·kɜː·rənt] *n* **1.** (*undertow*) corrente *f* sottomarina **2.** (*underlying influence*) vena *f* nascosta

undercut [ˌʌn·də·'kʌt] *irr vt* **1.** (*charge less than competitors*) vendere a un prezzo inferiore rispetto a **2.** (*undermine*) indebolire

underdeveloped [ˌʌn·də·dɪ·'ve·ləpt] *adj* **1.** (*below its economic potential*) sottosviluppato, -a; **an ~ country** un Paese sottosviluppato **2.** PHOT sviluppato, -a insufficientemente **3.** (*insufficiently mature*) immaturo, -a

underdog ['ʌn·də·dɑːg] *n* debole *mf*; **to side with the ~** stare dalla parte dei perdenti

underdone [ˌʌn·də·'dʌn] *adj* (*cooked less than necessary*) poco cotto, -a

underemployed [ˌʌn·də·ɪm·'plɔɪd] *adj* **1.** (*having too little work*) sottocupato, -a **2.** (*insufficiently used*) sottoutilizzato, -a

underequipped [ˌʌn·dər·ɪ·'kwɪpt] *adj* mal equipaggiato, -a

underestimate [ˌʌn·də·'es·tə·meɪt] I. *vt* **to ~ sth/sb** sottovalutare qc/qu II. *n* sottovalutazione *f*

underexpose [ˌʌn·dəˈɪkˈspoʊz] *vt* PHOT sottoesporre

underexposure [ˌʌn·dəˈɪkˈspoʊ·ʒəˈ] *n* PHOT sottoesposizione *f*

underfed [ˌʌn·dəˈˈfed] *n* malnutrito, -a *m, f*

underfloor heating [ˌʌn·dəˈˈflɔːrˈhiːˈ̱ɪŋ] *n* riscaldamento *f* a pavimento

underfoot [ˌʌn·dəˈˈfʊt] *adv* (*below one's feet*) sotto i piedi; **to trample sb/sth ~** *a. fig* calpestare qu/qc

underfund [ˌʌn·dəˈˈfʌnd] *vt* sottofinanziare

underfunding [ˌʌn·dəˈˈfʌn·dɪŋ] *n* sottofinanziamento *m*

undergarment [ˈʌn·dəˈˈɡɑːr·mənt] *n form* indumento *m* intimo

undergo [ˌʌn·dəˈˈgoʊ] *irr vt* subire; **to ~ a change** subire modifiche; **to ~ surgery** subire un intervento chirurgico

undergraduate [ˌʌn·dəˈˈgræ·dʒu·ət] *n* universitario, -a *m, f*

underground [ˈʌn·dəˈˈgraʊnd] I. *adj* 1. (*below earth surface*) sotterraneo, -a 2. (*clandestinely anti-government*) clandestino, -a; ~ **movement** organizzazione *f* clandestina II. *adv* 1. (*below earth surface*) sottoterra 2. **to go ~** entrare in clandestinità; **to drive sb ~** spingere qu alla clandestinità III. *n* **the ~** POL la resistenza

undergrowth [ˈʌn·dəˈˈgroʊθ] *n* sottobosco *m*

underhand [ˌʌn·dəˈˈhænd], **underhanded** I. *adj* 1. (*secret*) subdolo, -a 2. SPORTS (*with arm below shoulder*) basso, -a II. *adv* 1. (*secretly*) subdolamente 2. SPORTS (*below shoulder*) basso

underinsure [ˌʌn·dəˈɪnˈʃʊr] *vt* sottoassicurare

underlay [ˌʌn·dəˈˈleɪ] *vt pt of* **underlie**

underlie [ˌʌn·dəˈˈlaɪ] *irr vt* **to ~ sth** stare alla base di qc

underline [ˌʌn·dəˈˈlaɪn] *vt a. fig* sottolineare

underling [ˈʌn·dəˈˈlɪŋ] *n pej* subalterno, -a *m, f*

underlying [ˌʌn·dəˈˈlaɪ·ɪŋ] *adj* di fondo; **the ~ reason for sth** il motivo di fondo di qc

undermanned [ˌʌn·dəˈˈmænd] *adj* sotto organico

undermanning [ˌʌn·dəˈˈmæ·nɪŋ] *n* mancanza *f* di organico

undermine [ˌʌn·dəˈˈmaɪn] *vt* 1. (*damage, sap, weaken*) minare; **to ~ a currency** indebolire una moneta 2. (*tunnel under*) scavare

undermost [ˈʌn·dəˈˈmoʊst] *adj* **the ~ ...** il più basso...

underneath [ˌʌn·dəˈˈniːθ] I. *prep* sotto II. *adv* sotto III. *n* **the ~** la parte inferiore IV. *adj* di sotto

undernourished [ˌʌn·dəˈˈnɜːˈrɪʃt] *adj* denutrito, -a

underpaid [ˌʌn·dəˈˈpeɪd] *adj* sottopagato, -a

underpants [ˈʌn·dəˈˈpænts] *npl* mutande *fpl*

underpass [ˈʌn·dəˈˈpæs] <-es> *n* sottopassaggio *m*

underpay [ˌʌn·dəˈˈpeɪ] *irr vt* sottopagare

underperform [ˈʌn·dəˈˈpər·fɔːrm] *vi* rendere meno del previsto

underplay [ˌʌn·dəˈˈpleɪ] *vt* 1. (*play down*) minimizzare; **to ~ the importance of sth** minimizzare l'importanza di qc 2. (*act with restraint: role*) recitare sotto le righe

underpopulated [ˌʌn·dəˈˈpɑːp·jə·leɪ·tɪd] *adj* scarsamente popolato, -a

underprivileged [ˌʌn·dəˈˈprɪ·və·lɪdʒd] I. *adj* svantaggiato, -a II. *n* **the ~** *pl* i meno fortunati

underrate [ˌʌn·dəˈˈreɪt] *vt* sottovalutare

underrepresented [ˌʌn·dəˈˈre·prɪˈzen·̱ɪd] *adj* insufficientemente rappresentato, -a

underscore [ˌʌn·dəˈˈskɔːr] *vt* sottolineare

undersea *adj* sottomarino, -a

undersecretary *n* sottosegretario *m*

undersell [ˌʌn·dəˈˈsel] *irr vt* 1. (*offer goods cheaper*) vendere a prezzi inferiori; **to ~ the competition** vendere a prezzi inferiori alla concorrenza 2. (*undervalue*) non valorizzare a sufficienza; **to ~ oneself** non sapersi valorizzare

undershirt [ˈʌn·dəˈˈʃɜːrt] *n* (*with short sleeves*) maglietta *f* intima; (*without sleeves*) canottiera *f*

underside [ˈʌn·dəˈˈsaɪd] *n* parte *f* inferiore

undersigned [ˈʌn·dəˈˈsaɪnd] *n form* sottoscritto, -a *m, f*

undersize *adj*, **undersized** [ˈʌn·dəˈˈsaɪzd] *adj* troppo piccolo, -a

underskirt [ˈʌn·dəˈˈskɜːrt] *n* sottogonna *f*

understaffed [ˌʌn·dəˈˈstæft] *adj* sotto organico

understand [ˌʌn·dəˈˈstænd] *irr* I. *vt* 1. (*perceive meaning, sympathize with*) capire; **to make oneself understood** farsi capire; **to not ~ a word** non capire una parola; **to ~ that/why/how ...** capire che/perché/come...; **to ~ sb's doing sth** capire che qu faccia qc; **she doesn't ~ me** non mi capisce 2. *form* (*be informed*) **to ~ that ...** sapere che...; **to ~ from sb that ...** sapere da qu che... 3. (*believe*) credere; **as I ~ it** se ho capito bene; **it is understood that ...** è inteso che... II. *vi* capire; **to ~ about sth** capirne di qc

understandable [ˌʌn·dəˈˈstæn·də·bl] *adj* comprensibile; **to be ~ that ...** essere comprensibile che...

understanding I. *n* 1. (*comprehension, rapport*) comprensione *f*; **to not have any ~ of sth** non capire niente di qc; **his ~ of the agreement** la sua interpretazione dell'accordo 2. (*entente, agreement*) intesa *f*; **to come to an ~** venire ad un'intesa; **a tacit ~** una tacita intesa 3. (*condition*) condizione *f*; **to do sth on the ~ that ...** fare qc a condizione che... *f* II. *adj* comprensivo, -a

understate [ˌʌn·dəˈˈsteɪt] *vt* minimizzare

understated *adj* di un'eleganza discreta

understatement [ˌʌn·dəˈˈsteɪt·mənt] *n* understatement *m inv*

understocked [ˌʌn·dəˈˈstɑːkt] *adj* poco fornito, -a

understood [ˌʌn·dəˈˈstʊd] *vt, vi pt, pp of* **understand**

understudy [ˈʌn·dəˈˌstʌ·di] THEAT I. <-ies> *n*

U

sostituto, -a *m, f;* **to be the ~ for sb** sostituire qu **II.** <-ie-> *vt* studiare la parte di

undertake [ˌʌn·də·'teɪk] *irr vt* **1.** (*set about, take on*) intraprendere; **to ~ a journey** intraprendere un viaggio **2.** *form* (*commit oneself to*) **to ~ to do sth** impegnarsi a fare qc; **to ~ (that)** ... garantire (che)...

undertaker ['ʌn·də·ˌteɪ·kə] *n* impresario, -a *m, f* di pompe funebri

undertaking [ˌʌn·də·'teɪ·kɪŋ] *n* **1.** (*professional project*) impresa *f;* **noble ~** nobile impresa **2.** *form* (*pledge*) promessa *f;* **an ~ to do sth** la promessa di fare qc

under-the-counter [ˌʌn·də·ðə·'kaʊn·tə] **I.** *adj* illlegale **II.** *adv* illegalmente

undertone ['ʌn·də·toʊn] *n* **1.** (*low voice*) voce *f* sommessa; **to say sth in an ~** dire qc con voce sommessa **2.** (*undercurrent*) sfumatura *f*

underused [ˌʌn·də·'juːzd] *adj,* **underutilized** [ˌʌn·də·'juː·tə·laɪzd] *adj* sottoutilizzato, -a

undervalue [ˌʌn·də·'væl·juː] *vt* sottovalutare

underwater [ˌʌn·də·'wɑː·tə] **I.** *adj* subacqueo, -a **II.** *adv* sott'acqua

underwear ['ʌn·də·wer] *n* biancheria *f* intima

underweight [ˌʌn·də·'weɪt] *adj* sottopeso *inv*

underworked *adj* poco usato, -a

underworld ['ʌn·də·wɜːrld] *n* **1.** (*criminal milieu*) malavita *f* **2.** ART, LIT (*afterworld*) **the Underworld** gli Inferi

underwrite ['ʌn·də·raɪt] *irr vt* **1.** (*sign*) firmare; **to ~ a contract** firmare un contratto **2.** FIN, ECON (*guarantee share issues*) sottoscrivere **3.** (*provide insurance for*) assicurare

underwriter ['ʌn·də·ˌraɪ·tə] *n* **1.** FIN, ECON sottoscrittore, -trice *m, f* **2.** (*in insurance*) assicuratore, -trice *m, f*

undesirable [ˌʌn·dɪ·'zaɪ·rə·bl] **I.** *adj* indesiderato, -a; **an ~ character** un tipo poco raccomandabile **II.** *n* persona *f* indesiderata

undetected [ˌʌn·dɪ·'tek·tɪd] *adj* non scoperto, -a; **to go ~** passare inosservato, -a

undeveloped [ˌʌn·dɪ·'ve·ləpt] *adj* non sfruttato, -a

undid [ʌn·'dɪd] *vt, vi pt of* **undo**

undies ['ʌn·dɪz] *npl inf* mutandine *fpl*

undisclosed [ˌʌn·dɪs·'kloʊzd] *adj* **an ~ amount** una cifra non precisata; **an ~ location** una località segreta; **an ~ source** una fonte anonima

undiscovered [ˌʌn·dɪs·'kʌ·vəd] *adj* inesplorato, -a; **to go ~** non essere scoperto, -a

undisputed [ˌʌn·dɪs·'pjuː·tɪd] *adj* incontestato, -a

undistinguished [ˌʌn·dɪs·'tɪŋ·gwɪʃt] *adj* mediocre

undisturbed [ˌʌn·dɪs·'tɜːrbd] *adj* indisturbato, -a

undivided [ˌʌn·dɪ·'vaɪ·dɪd] *adj* **1.** (*not split*) unito, -a **2.** (*intense*) intenso, -a; **sb's ~ attention** tutta l'attenzione di qu

undo [ʌn·'duː] *irr vt* **1.** (*unfasten*) slacciare; **to ~ a zipper** aprire una cerniera **2.** (*cancel*) dis-

fare; **to ~ the damage** riparare il danno **3.** (*cause ruin*) rovinare; **to ~ sb's good name** rovinare la reputazione a qu ▶ **what's** <u>done</u> **cannot be undone** *prov* cosa fatta capo ha *prov*

undoing *n form* rovina *f*

undone [ʌn·'dʌn] **I.** *vt pp of* **undo II.** *adj* **1.** (*not fastened*) slacciato, -a; **to come ~** slacciarsi **2.** (*uncompleted*) da fare; **to leave sth ~** non fare qc

undoubted [ʌn·'daʊ·tɪd] *adj* indubbio, -a

undoubtedly *adv* indubbiamente

undreamed-of [ʌn·'driːmd·ˌɑːv] *adj,* **undreamt-of** [ʌn·'dremt·ˌɑːv] *adj* inimmaginabile

undress [ʌn·'dres] **I.** *vt* spogliare; **to ~ sb with one's eyes** *fig* spogliare qu con gli occhi **II.** *vi* spogliarsi **III.** *n* **to be in a state of ~** essere in déshabillé

undressed *adj* svestito, -a; **to get ~** spogliarsi

undue [ʌn·'duː] *adj form* eccessivo, -a

undulate ['ʌn·dʒə·leɪt] *vi form* ondeggiare

undulating *adj form* **1.** (*moving like a wave*) ondeggiante **2.** (*shaped like waves*) ondulato, -a

unduly [ʌn·'duː·li] *adv* eccessivamente

undying [ˌʌn·'daɪ·ɪŋ] *adj liter* imperituro, -a; **~ love** amore *m* eterno

unearned [ˌʌn·'ɜːrnd] *adj* **1.** (*undeserved*) immeritato, -a **2.** (*not worked for*) **~ income** reddito *m* non derivante da lavoro

unearth [ʌn·'ɜːrθ] *vt* **1.** (*dig up*) dissotterrare **2.** (*discover*) scoprire; **to ~ the truth** far venire a galla la verità

unearthly [ʌn·'ɜːrθ·li] *adj* **1.** (*unsettling*) sinistro, -a **2.** *inf* (*inconvenient*) inopportuno, -a; **at an ~ hour** a un'ora inopportuna

unease [ʌn·'iːz] *n* disagio *m;* **with growing ~** con crescente inquietudine

uneasiness *n* inquietudine *f*

uneasy [ʌn·'iː·zi] *adj* <-ier, -iest> **1.** (*anxious*) preoccupato, -a; **to be/feel ~ about sth/sb** essere preoccupato per qc/qu **2.** (*awkward: person*) a disagio; **an ~ relationship** un rapporto difficile; **an ~ silence** un silenzio imbarazzato **3.** (*restless: sleep*) agitato, -a

uneconomic [ʌn·ˌe·kə·'nɑː·mɪk] *adj* antieconomico, -a

uneducated [ʌn·'ed·ʒʊ·keɪ·tɪd] **I.** *adj* illetterato, -a **II.** *n* **the ~** gli analfabeti

unemotional [ˌʌn·ɪ·'moʊ·ʃə·nəl] *adj* **1.** (*not feeling emotions*) distaccato, -a **2.** (*not revealing emotions*) razionale

unemployable [ˌʌn·ɪm·'plɔː·ɪə·bl] *adj* incapace di conservare un lavoro

unemployed [ˌʌn·ɪm·'plɔɪd] **I.** *n pl* **the ~** i disoccupati **II.** *adj* disoccupato, -a

unemployment [ˌʌn·ɪm·'plɔɪ·mənt] *n* disoccupazione *f*

unemployment benefit *n* indennità *f* di disoccupazione

unending [ʌn·'en·dɪŋ] *adj* interminabile

unenlightened [ˌʌn·ɪn·'laɪ·tənd] *adj* **1.** (*ignor-*

ant) ignorante **2.** *a. iron* (*not informed*) disinformato, -a

unenviable [ʌn·'en·vi·ə·bl] *adj* non invidiabile

unequal [ʌn·'iːk·wəl] *adj* **1.** *form* (*different*) disuguale; **a triangle with ~ sides** un triangolo con i lati disuguali *m* **2.** (*ill-matched*) non equilibrato, -a **3.** (*unable*) **to be ~ to sth** non essere all'altezza di qc; **to be ~ to a task** non essere all'altezza di un compito

unequaled *adj*, **unequalled** *adj* senza pari

unequivocal [ʌn·ɪ·'kwɪ·və·kəl] *adj* inequivocabile; **an ~ success** un successo inequivocabile; **to be ~ in sth** essere esplicito su qc

unerring [ʌn·'ɜː·rɪŋ] *adj* infallibile

UNESCO *n*, **Unesco** [juː·'nes·koʊ] *n abbr of* **United Nations Educational, Scientific, and Cultural Organization** UNESCO *f*

unethical [ʌn·'e·θɪ·kəl] *adj* poco etico, -a

uneven [ʌn·'iː·vən] *adj* **1.** (*surface, margins*) irregolare **2.** (*color*) poco uniforme **3.** (*contest*) impari **4.** (*performance*) discontinuo, -a **5.** (*in gymnastics*) **~ bars** parallele *f* asimmetriche *pl*

uneventful [ʌn·ɪ·'vent·fəl] *adj* tranquillo, -a; **an ~ week** una settimana senza scossoni

unexceptionable [ʌn·ɪk·'sep·ʃə·nə·bl] *adj form* ineccepibile

unexceptional [ʌn·ɪk·'sep·ʃə·nəl] *adj* ordinario, -a

unexciting *adj* **1.** (*novel*) poco emozionante **2.** (*life*) monotono, -a

unexpected [ʌn·ɪks·'pek·tɪd] I. *adj* inaspettato, -a II. *n* **the ~** gli imprevisti *mpl*

unexplained [ʌn·ɪks·'pleɪnd] *adj* inspiegato, -a

unexploded [ʌn·ɪks·'pləʊ·dɪd] *adj* inesploso, -a; **~ ordinance** ordigni *m* inesplosi *pl*

unexploited *adj* poco sfruttato, -a

unexpressed *adj* inespresso, -a

unexpressive [ʌn·ɪks·'pre·sɪv] *adj* inespressivo, -a

unfailing [ʌn·'feɪ·lɪŋ] *adj* **1.** (*always present when needed*) costante **2.** (*not running out*) inesauribile

unfair [ʌn·'fer] *adj* ingiusto, -a; **~ competition** concorrenza *f* sleale; **~ dismissal** licenziamento *m* senza giusta causa

unfaithful [ʌn·'feɪθ·fʊl] *adj* **1.** (*adulterous*) infedele **2.** (*disloyal*) sleale **3.** *form* (*not accurate*) poco fedele

unfaltering [ʌn·'fɑːl·tə·rɪŋ] *adj* **1.** (*without hesitation*) risoluto, -a; **with ~ steps** con passo fermo **2.** (*unshakeable*) incrollabile

unfamiliar [ʌn·fə·'mɪl·jə] *adj* sconosciuto, -a; **to be ~ with sth** avere poca dimestichezza con qc

unfashionable [ʌn·'fæ·ʃə·nə·bl] *adj* fuori moda

unfasten [ʌn·'fæ·sn] I. *vt* slacciare II. *vi* slacciarsi

unfathomable [ʌn·'fæ·ðə·mə·bl] *adj* **1.** *a. fig* (*too deep to measure*) insondabile **2.** (*inexplicable*) impenetrabile

unfavorable [ʌn·'feɪ·və·rə·bl] *adj* sfavorevole

unfeeling [ʌn·'fiː·lɪŋ] *adj* insensibile

unfeigned [ʌn·'feɪnd] *adj* sincero, -a

unfettered [ʌn·'fe·tə·d] *adj* senza restrizioni

unfilled *adj* vuoto, -a

unfinished [ʌn·'fɪ·nɪʃt] *adj* **1.** (*furniture*) al grezzo **2.** (*symphony*) incompiuto, -a **3.** (*business*) in sospeso

unfit [ʌn·'fɪt] I. *adj* **1.** (*unhealthy*) fuori forma **2.** (*unsuitable*) inadatto, -a; **to be ~ for sth** essere inadatto a qc; **to be ~ for human habitation** essere inabitabile; **to be ~ for work/ military duty** essere inabile al lavoro/al servizio militare **3.** (*incompetent*) incapace; **to be ~ to do sth** essere incapace di fare qc; **to be ~ to run the country** essere incapace di governare II. *vt* <-tt-> *form* rendere inadatto, -a

unflagging [ʌn·'flæ·gɪŋ] *adj* instancabile

unflappable [ʌn·'flæ·pə·bl] *adj inf* imperturbabile

unflinching [ʌn·'flɪn·tʃɪŋ] *adj* (*person*) intrepido, -a; (*support, honesty*) che non viene a mancare

unfold [ʌn·'foʊld] I. *vt* **1.** (*open out sth folded*) aprire, spiegare; **to ~ one's arms** aprire le braccia **2.** *form* (*make known*) **to ~ one's ideas/plans** esporre le proprie idee/i propri progetti II. *vi* **1.** (*develop, evolve*) svolgersi **2.** (*become unfolded*) schiudersi

unforeseeable [ʌn·fɔːr·'siː·ə·bl] *adj* imprevedibile

unforeseen [ʌn·fɔːr·'siːn] *adj* imprevisto, -a

unforgettable [ʌn·fə·'ge·tə·bl] *adj* indimenticabile

unforgivable [ʌn·fə·'gɪ·və·bl] *adj* imperdonabile

unfortunate [ʌn·'fɔːrtʃ·nət] I. *adj* **1.** (*luckless*) sfortunato, -a; **it's ~ that ...** purtroppo... +*subj* **2.** *form* (*regrettable*) deplorevole **3.** (*inopportune*) infelice II. *n* sventurato, -a *m, f*

unfortunately *adv* sfortunatamente, purtroppo

unfounded [ʌn·'faʊn·dɪd] *adj* infondato, -a

unfrequented [ʌn·'friːk·wen·tɪd] *adj* poco frequentato, -a

unfriendly [ʌn·'frend·li] *adj* <-ier, -iest> **1.** (*unsociable*) antipatico, -a **2.** *fig* (*hard to use*) complicato, -a **3.** (*inhospitable*) ostile

unfulfilled [ʌn·fʊl·'fɪld] *adj* **1.** (*not carried out*) non realizzato, -a **2.** (*unsatisfied*) insoddisfatto, -a **3.** (*frustrated*) frustrato, -a

unfurl [ʌn·'fɜːrl] I. *vt* spiegare; **to ~ an umbrella** aprire un ombrello; **to ~ a sail** spiegare una vela; **to ~ a flag** srotolare una bandiera II. *vi* spiegarsi

unfurnished [ʌn·'fɜːr·nɪʃt] *adj* non ammobiliato, -a

ungainly [ʌn·'geɪn·li] *adj* <-ier, -iest> goffo, -a

ungodly [ʌn·'gɑːd·li] *adj* <-ier, -iest> **1.** *inf* (*unreasonable*) **at an ~ hour** a un'ora impossibile **2.** (*impious*) empio, -a

ungovernable [ʌn·'gʌ·və·nə·bl] *adj* ingovernabile

ungraceful [ʌn·'greɪs·fəl] *adj* sgraziato, -a

U

ungracious [ˌʌnˈgreɪ·ʃəs] *adj form* sgarbato, -a
ungrateful [ʌnˈgreɪt·fəl] *adj* ingrato, -a
ungrudging [ʌnˈgrʌ·dʒɪŋ] *adj* generoso, -a
ungrudgingly *adv* volentieri
unguarded [ʌnˈgɑː·r·dɪd] *adj* 1.(*not defended or watched*) indifeso, -a 2.(*careless*) imprudente; **in an ~ moment** in un momento di distrazione
unhallowed [ʌnˈhæ·loʊd] *adj* 1.(*not consecrated*) profano, -a 2.(*unholy*) sacrilego, -a
unhappy [ʌnˈhæ·pi] *adj* <-ier, -iest> 1.(*sad*) infelice 2.(*displeased*) scontento, -a 3.(*inappropriate*) sfortunato, -a
unharmed [ʌnˈhɑːrmd] *adj* illeso, -a
UNHCR [ˌjuː·en·eɪtʃ·siːˈɑːɹ] *n abbr of* United Nations High Commission for Refugees ACNUR *m*
unhealthy [ʌnˈhel·θi] *adj* <-ier, -iest> 1.(*sick*) malaticcio, -a 2.(*unwholesome*) dannoso, -a; **an ~ diet** un'alimentazione scorretta 3.*inf* (*dangerous*) pericoloso, -a 4.PSYCH (*morbid*) morboso, -a
unheard [ʌnˈhɜːrd] *adj* inascoltato, -a
unheard-of [ʌnˈhɜːrd·ˌɑːv] *adj* 1.(*unknown*) sconosciuto, -a 2.(*unparalleled*) inaudito, -a
unhelpful [ʌnˈhelp·fʊl] *adj* di scarso aiuto
unhinge [ʌnˈhɪndʒ] *vt* 1.(*take off hinges*) scardinare 2.(*make crazy*) sconvolgere
unholy [ʌnˈhoʊ·li] <-ier, -iest> *adj* 1.(*wicked*) malvagio, -a 2.REL (*profane*) profano, -a 3.(*outrageous*) tremendo, -a; **to get up at some ~ hour** alzarsi a un'ora assurda
unhook [ʌnˈhʊk] *vt* 1.(*remove hooks*) sganciare 2.(*unfasten*) slacciare
unhoped-for [ʌnˈhoʊpt·ˌfɔːr] *adj* insperato, -a
unhurt [ʌnˈhɜːrt] *adj* incolume
UNICEF *n*, Unicef [ˈjuː·nɪ·sef] *n abbr of* United Nations International Children's Emergency Fund UNICEF *m o f*
unicorn [ˈjuː·nɪ·kɔːrn] *n* unicorno *m*
unidentified [ˌʌn·aɪˈden·tə·faɪd] *n* non identificato, -a
unification [ˌjuː·nɪ·fɪˈkeɪ·ʃən] *n* unificazione *f*
uniform [ˈjuː·nə·fɔːrm] I. *n* uniforme *f*, divisa *f* II. *adj* uniforme
uniformity [ˌjuː·nəˈfɔːr·mə·ti] *n* uniformità *f*
unify [ˈjuː·nə·faɪ] *vt* unificare
unilateral [ˌjuː·nəˈlæ·t̬ərəl] *adj* unilaterale
unimaginable [ˌʌn·ɪˈmædʒ·nə·bl] *adj* inimmaginabile
unimpeachable [ˌʌn·ɪmˈpiː·tʃə·bl] *adj form* irreprensibile; **an ~ source** una fonte attendibile
unimportant [ˌʌn·ɪmˈpɔːr·tənt] *adj* senza importanza
uninformed [ˌʌn·ɪnˈfɔːrmd] *adj* disinformato, -a
uninhabitable [ˌʌn·ɪnˈhæ·bɪ·tə·bl] *adj* inabitabile
uninhabited [ˌʌn·ɪnˈhæ·bɪ·tɪd] *adj* 1.(*not lived in*) disabitato, -a 2.(*deserted*) deserto, -a
uninhibited [ˌʌn·ɪnˈhɪ·bɪ·tɪd] *adj* disinibito, -a
uninjured [ˌʌn·ɪnˈdʒɚd] *adj* illeso, -a

uninsured [ˌʌn·ɪnˈʃʊrd] *adj* non assicurato, -a
unintelligent [ˌʌn·ɪnˈte·lɪ·dʒənt] *adj* poco intelligente
unintelligible [ˌʌn·ɪnˈte·lɪ·dʒə·bl] *adj* 1.(*not comprehensible*) incomprensibile 2.(*unreadable*) inintelligibile
unintentional [ˌʌn·ɪnˈten·tʃə·nəl] *adj* involontario, -a
unintentionally *adv* involontariamente
uninterested [ʌnˈɪn·trəs·tɪd] *adj* indifferente; **to be ~ in sth** non essere interessato a qc
uninteresting *adj* poco interessante
uninterrupted [ʌnˌɪn·tərˈʌp·tɪd] *adj* ininterrotto, -a
union [ˈjuːn·jən] *n* 1.(*act of becoming united*) unione *f* 2.(*instance of becoming united*) associazione *f* 3.+ *sing/pl vb* (*organization representing employees*) sindacato *m;* **the ~ demands** le rivendicazioni sindacali 4. *form* (*marriage*) unione *f*
unionist [ˈjuːn·jə·nɪst] *n* sindacalista *mf*
unionize [ˈjuːn·jə·naɪz] I. *vt* sindacalizzare II. *vi* sindacalizzarsi
Union Jack *n* (*British national flag*) bandiera *del Regno Unito*
unique [juːˈniːk] *adj* unico, -a; **a ~ characteristic** una caratteristica esclusiva
uniqueness *n* unicità *f*
unisex [ˈjuː·nə·seks] *adj* unisex *inv*
unison [ˈjuː·nə·sən] *n* **in ~** all'unisono
unit [ˈjuː·nɪt] *n* 1. *a.* COMPUT, COM unità *f;* **central processing ~** unità centrale di elaborazione, processore *m;* **~ of currency** unità monetaria 2.+ *sing/pl vb* (*organized group of people*) reparto *m* 3.(*element of furniture*) elemento (componibile) *m*
unit cost *n* COM costo *m* unitario
unite [juːˈnaɪt] I. *vt* (*join together*) unire; (*bring together*) unificare II. *vi* unirsi
united *adj* unito, -a
United Arab Emirates *npl* **the ~** gli Emirati Arabi Uniti
United Kingdom *n* **the ~** il Regno Unito
United Nations *n* **the ~** le Nazioni Unite
United States *n* + *sing vb* Stati *mpl* Uniti; **the ~ of America** gli Stati Uniti d'America

---

i La **U.S. flag** porta diversi nomi, tra i quali quello di **The Stars and Stripes**. Il numero delle stelle corrisponde ai 50 stati che fanno parte attualmente degli Stati Uniti e le 13 righe rappresentano i 13 stati fondatori. L'espressione patriottica *Old Glory* è stata coniata dal capitano di vascello William Driver. Anche il titolo dell'inno nazionale americano, lo *Star-spangled Banner*, fa riferimento alla bandiera nazionale.

---

unit price *n* COM prezzo *m* unitario
unity [ˈjuː·nə·ti] *n* 1.(*oneness*) unità *f* 2.(*harmony, consensus*) armonia *f*

Univ. *abbr of* **university** Univ.

universal [ˌjuːnəˈvɜːrsəl] I. *adj* universale II. *n* universale *m*

universe [ˈjuːnəvɜːrs] *n* the ~ l'universo

university [ˌjuːnəˈvɜːrsəti] <-ies> *n* università *f*; **a ~ campus** un campus universitario

unjust [ʌnˈdʒʌst] *adj* ingiusto, -a

unjustifiable [ʌnˌdʒʌstɪˈfaɪəbl] *adj* ingiustificabile

unjustified [ʌnˈdʒʌstɪfaɪd] *adj* ingiustificato, -a

unjustly *adv* 1. (*in an unjust manner*) immeritatamente 2. (*wrongfully*) ingiustamente

unkempt [ʌnˈkempt] *adj* (*garden*) trascurato, -a; (*appearance*) trasandato, -a; (*hair*) spettinato, -a

unkind [ʌnˈkaɪnd] *adj* 1. (*not kind*) scortese; **to be ~ to sb** trattare male qu 2. (*not gentle*) **to be ~ to hair/skin** danneggiare i capelli/la pelle

unkindly *adv* male; **to take sth ~** prendere male qc

unknowing [ʌnˈnoʊɪŋ] *adj* inconsapevole

unknown [ʌnˈnoʊn] I. *adj* sconosciuto, -a; **~ to me ...** a mia insaputa... II. *n* 1. (*thing*) **the ~** l'ignoto; MATH l'incognita 2. (*person*) sconosciuto, -a *m, f*

unlawful [ʌnˈlɔːfəl] *adj* illegal; (*possession, association*) illecito, -a

unleaded [ʌnˈledɪd] *adj* senza piombo

unleash [ʌnˈliːʃ] *vt* (*dog*) sguinzagliare; *fig* (*passions*) scatenare

unleavened [ʌnˈlevənd] *adj* (*bread*) non lievitato, -a

unless [ənˈles] *conj* se non, a meno che + *subj*; **I'll have it ~ you want it** lo prendo io, a meno che lo voglia tu; **don't stop taking the medicine ~ your doctor says so** non interrompere la cura se non te lo ordina il medico; **~ I'm mistaken** se non sbaglio

unlike [ʌnˈlaɪk] I. *adj* diverso, -a II. *prep* 1. (*in contrast to*) a differenza di; **~ you, I'm not a great dancer** a differenza di te, io non sono un grande ballerino 2. (*different from*) diverso, -a da; **he's so ~ his father** è così diverso dal padre 3. (*not characteristic of*) **it's ~ him** (*to be so quiet*) non è da lui (essere così silenzioso)

unlikely [ʌnˈlaɪkli] <-ier, -iest> *adj* 1. (*improbable*) poco probabile; **it's ~ that ...** è difficile che... 2. (*unconvincing*) inverosimile

unlimited [ʌnˈlɪmɪtɪd] *adj* 1. (*not limited*) illimitato, -a 2. (*very great*) sconfinato, -a

unlisted [ʌnˈlɪstɪd] *adj* 1. (*not in the phone book*) fuori elenco 2. FIN (*stock market*) non quotato, -a

unload [ʌnˈloʊd] I. *vt* 1. (*remove*) scaricare 2. (*express*) sfogare; **to ~ one's worries on sb** sfogare le proprie preoccupazioni su qu II. *vi* scaricare

unlock [ʌnˈlɑːk] *vt* 1. (*release a lock*) aprire 2. (*solve*) risolvere

unlocked *adj* non chiuso, -a a chiave

unlucky [ʌnˈlʌki] *adj* 1. (*unfortunate*) sfortunato, -a; **to be ~ enough to get a cold** avere la sfortuna di prendersi un raffreddore 2. *form* (*bringing bad luck*) **to be ~** portare sfortuna

unmanageable [ʌnˈmænɪdʒəbəl] *adj* 1. (*unwieldy*) poco maneggevole 2. (*incontrollable*) difficile da gestire

unmanned *adj* AVIAT, TECH senza equipaggio

unmarked [ʌnˈmɑːrkt] *adj* (*grave*) anonimo, -a; (*cards, bills*) non segnato, -a; **an ~ police car** un'auto civetta

unmarried [ʌnˈmerɪd] *adj* non sposato, -a; **~ mother** ragazza *f* madre

unmask [ʌnˈmæsk] *vt a. fig* smascherare

unmatched [ʌnˈmætʃt] *adj* 1. (*unequaled*) ineguagliato, -a 2. (*extremely great*) senza pari

unmentionable [ʌnˈmentʃənəbl] *adj* innominabile

unmentioned [ʌnˈmentʃənd] *adj* **to go ~** passare sotto silenzio

unmindful [ʌnˈmaɪndfəl] *adj* **to be ~ of sth** essere incurante di qc

unmistakable [ʌnmɪsˈteɪkəbl] *adj* inconfondibile

unmitigated [ʌnˈmɪtəɡeɪtɪd] *adj* assoluto, -a

unmoved [ʌnˈmuːvd] *adj* impassibile

unnamed [ʌnˈneɪmd] *adj* anonimo, -a

unnatural [ʌnˈnætʃərəl] *adj* 1. (*contrary to nature*) innaturale; (*affected*) affettato, -a 2. (*not normal*) anormale

unnecessarily [ʌnˈnesəˈserəli] *adv* inutilmente

unnecessary [ʌnˈnesəseri] *adj* 1. (*not necessary*) non necessario, -a 2. (*uncalled for*) inutile

unnerve [ʌnˈnɜːrv] *vt* mettere a disagio

unnerving *adj* inquietante

unnoticed [ʌnˈnoʊtɪst] *adj* **to go ~** passare inosservato, -a

unnumbered [ʌnˈnʌmbərd] *adj* 1. (*not marked with a number*) senza numero 2. *form* (*too many to be counted*) innumerevole

UNO [ˈjuːnoʊ] *n abbr of* **United Nations Organization** ONU *f*

unobtainable [ʌnəbˈteɪnəbl] *adj* introvabile

unobtrusive [ʌnəbˈtruːsɪv] *adj* discreto, -a

unoccupied [ʌnˈɑːkjəpaɪd] *adj* 1. (*uninhabited*) disabitato, -a 2. MIL non occupato, -a 3. (*not being used*) libero, -a

unofficial [ʌnəˈfɪʃəl] *adj* ufficioso, -a

unorganized [ʌnˈɔːrɡənaɪzd] *adj* disorganizzato, -a

unorthodox [ʌnˈɔːrθədɑːks] *adj* poco ortodosso, -a

unpack [ʌnˈpæk] I. *vt* (*bag, suitcase*) disfare; (*car*) scaricare II. *vi* disfare i bagagli

unpaid [ʌnˈpeɪd] *adj* 1. (*not remunerated*) non remunerato, -a 2. (*not paid*) non pagato, -a

unpalatable [ʌnˈpælətəbl] *adj a. fig* sgardevole

unparalleled [ʌnˈperəleld] *adj form* senza

U

precedenti

unperturbed [ˌʌn·pə·ˈtɜːrbd] *adj* imperterrito, -a; **to be ~ by sth** restare imperturbabile davanti a qc

unplanned [ʌn·ˈplænd] *adj* imprevisto, -a

unpleasant [ʌn·ˈple·zənt] *adj* **1.**(*not pleasing*) sgradevole **2.**(*unfriendly*) antipatico, -a

unpleasantness *n* **1.**(*quality of being unpleasant*) sgradevolezza *f* **2.**(*unfriendly feelings*) antipatia *f*

unplug [ʌn·ˈplʊg] <-gg-> *vt* **1.**(*electric plug, appliance*) staccare (la spina di) **2.**(*sink*) sturare

unpolished [ʌn·ˈpɑː·lɪʃt] *adj* (*shoes*) non lucidato, -a; (*gemstones*) grezzo, -a

unpolluted [ˌʌnpəˈluː·tɪd] *adj* non inquinato, -a

unpopular [ʌn·ˈpɑː·p·jə·lɚ] *adj* impopolare

unpopularity [ʌn·ˌpɑː·p·jə·ˈle·rə·ti] *n* impopolarità *f*

unpractical [ʌn·ˈpræk·tɪ·kəl] *adj* poco pratico, -a

unpracticed [ʌn·ˈpræk·tɪst] *adj form* inesperto, -a; **to be ~ in sth** non aver pratica di qc

unprecedented [ʌn·ˈpre·sə·den·tɪd] *adj* senza precedenti

unpredictable [ˌʌn·prɪ·ˈdɪk·tə·bl] *adj* imprevedibile

unprejudiced [ʌn·ˈpre·dʒə·dɪst] *adj* imparziale

unpremeditated [ˌʌn·priː·ˈme·dɪ·teɪ·tɪd] *adj* non premeditato, -a

unpretentious [ˌʌn·prɪ·ˈten·tʃəs] *adj* senza pretese

unprincipled [ʌn·ˈprɪn·tsə·pld] *adj* senza scrupoli

unproductive [ˌʌn·prə·ˈdʌk·tɪv] *adj* improduttivo, -a

unprofessional [ˌʌn·prə·ˈfe·ʃə·nəl] *adj* poco professionale

unprofitable [ʌn·ˈprɑː·fɪ·tə·bl] *adj* **1.**(*not making a profit*) non redditizio, -a **2.**(*unproductive*) infruttuoso, -a

unprompted [ʌn·ˈprɑː·mp·tɪd] *adj* spontaneo, -a

unprovided for [ˌʌn·prə·ˈvaɪ·dɪd·ˌfɔːr] *adj* senza mezzi di sussistenza

unprovoked [ˌʌn·prə·ˈvoʊkt] *adj* non provocato, -a

unpublished [ˌʌn·ˈpʌb·lɪʃt] *adj* inedito, -a

unqualified [ʌn·ˈkwɑː·lə·faɪd] *adj* **1.**(*without qualifications*) non qualificato, -a **2.**(*unlimited, unreserved*) senza riserve

unquestionable [ʌn·ˈkwes·tʃə·nə·bl] *adj* incontestabile

unquestionably *adv* indubitabilmente

unquestioning [ʌn·ˈkwes·tʃə·nɪŋ] *adj* cieco, -a

unquoted *adj* FIN non quotato, -a

unravel [ʌn·ˈræ·vəl] <-ll-, -l-> I. *vt* **1.**(*unknit, undo*) disfare **2.**(*solve*) risolvere II. *vi* disfarsi

unreadable [ʌn·ˈriː·də·bl] *adj* illeggibile

unreal [ʌn·ˈriːl] *adj* **1.**(*not real*) irreale **2.** *inf* (*astonishingly good*) incredibile

unrealistic [ʌn·ˌrɪ·ə·ˈlɪs·tɪk] *adj* **1.**(*not realistic*) non realistico, -a **2.**(*not convincingly real*) inverosimile

unrealized *adj* irrealizzato, -a

unreasonable [ʌn·ˈriː·zə·nə·bl] *adj* **1.**(*not showing reason*) irragionevole **2.**(*unfair*) eccessivo, -a

unrecognized [ʌn·ˈre·kəg·naɪzd] *adj* non riconosciuto, -a

unredeemed [ˌʌn·rɪ·ˈdiːmd] *adj* (*property, deposits*) non reclamato, -a; REL irredento, -a

unrefined [ˌʌn·rɪ·ˈfaɪnd] *adj* **1.**(*not refined*) non raffinato, -a **2.**(*not socially polished*) grossolano, -a

unregistered [ʌn·ˈre·dʒɪs·tɚd] *adj* non registrato, -a

unrelated [ˌʌn·rɪ·ˈleɪ·tɪd] *adj* **1.**(*not connected*) senza nesso **2.**(*by kinship*) non imparentato, -a

unrelenting [ˌʌn·rɪ·ˈlen·t̬ɪŋ] *adj* **1.**(*not yielding*) implacabile **2.**(*incessant, not easing: pain, pressure, rain*) incessante **3.** *form* (*unmerciful*) spietato, -a

unreliable [ˌʌn·rɪ·ˈlaɪ·ə·bl] *adj* inaffidabile

unrelieved [ˌʌn·rɪ·ˈliːvd] *adj* totale

unremarkable [ˌʌn·rɪ·ˈmɑːr·kə·bl] *adj* mediocre

unremitting [ˌʌn·rɪ·ˈmɪ·t̬ɪŋ] *adj form* incessante; **to be ~ in sth** essere infaticabile in qc

unrepeatable [ˌʌn·rɪ·ˈpiː·t̬ə·bl] *adj* irripetibile

unrepentant [ˌʌn·rɪ·ˈpen·tənt] *adj* impenitente

unrequited [ˌʌn·rɪ·ˈkwaɪ·tɪd] *adj* non corrisposto, -a

unreserved [ˌʌn·rɪ·ˈzɜːrvd] *adj* **1.**(*not having been reserved*) non riservato, -a **2.**(*absolute*) senza riserve **3.**(*not aloof*) franco, -a

unresolved [ˌʌn·rɪ·ˈzɑːlvd] *adj* irrisolto, -a

unrest [ʌn·ˈrest] *n* disordini *mpl*

unrestrained [ˌʌn·rɪ·ˈstreɪnd] *adj* sfrenato, -a

unrestricted [ˌʌn·rɪ·ˈstrɪk·tɪd] *adj* illimitato, -a

unripe [ʌn·ˈraɪp] *adj* non maturo

unrivaled *adj*, **unrivalled** [ʌn·ˈraɪ·vəld] *adj* senza pari

unroll [ʌn·ˈroʊl] I. *vt* srotolare II. *vi* srotolarsi

unruffled [ʌn·ˈrʌ·fld] *adj* **1.**(*not nervous*) imperturbato, -a **2.**(*not ruffled up*) non increspato, -a

unruly [ʌn·ˈruː·li] <-ier, -iest> *adj* **1.**(*disorderly: crowd, children*) turbolento, -a **2.**(*difficult to control: hair*) ribelle

unsaddle [ʌn·ˈsæ·dl] *vt* **1.**(*remove a saddle*) dissellare **2.**(*unseat*) disarcionare

unsafe [ʌn·ˈseɪf] *adj* pericoloso, -a

unsaid [ʌn·ˈsed] I. *vt pt, pp of* **unsay** II. *adj form* taciuto, -a; **to leave sth ~** passare qc sotto silenzio; **some things are better left ~** certe cose è meglio non dirle

unsatisfactory [ʌn·ˌsæ·t̬ɪs·ˈfæk·tə·ri] *adj* **1.**(*not satisfactory*) poco soddisfacente **2.** SCHOOL insufficiente

unsatisfied [ʌn·ˈsæ·t̬ɪs·faɪd] *adj* **1.**(*not content*) insoddisfatto, -a **2.**(*not convinced*) poco convinto, -a; **sth leaves sb ~** qc non convince qu **3.** (*not sated*) non appagato, -a

unsavory [ʌn·'seɪ·və·ri] *adj* **1.** (*unpleasant to the taste, smell*) sgradevole **2.** (*disgusting*) ripugnante **3.** (*socially offensive*) scandaloso, -a

unsay [ʌn·'seɪ] *irr vt* ritrattare ▸ **what's said cannot be unsaid** *prov* quel che è detto è detto *prov*

unscathed [ʌn·'skeɪðd] *adj* illeso, -a

unscheduled [ʌn·'sked·ʒʊld] *adj* non previsto, -a

unscientific *adj* poco scientifico, -a

unscramble *vt* ricomporre

unscrew [ʌn·'skruː] **I.** *vt* svitare **II.** *vi* svitarsi

unscripted [ʌn·'skrɪp·tɪd] *adj* improvvisato, -a

unscrupulous [ʌn·'skruːp·jə·ləs] *adj* senza scrupoli

unseal [ʌn·'siːl] *vt* aprire

unseat [ʌn·'siːt] *vt* **1.** (*remove from power*) spodestare **2.** (*throw*) disarcionare

unsecured [ˌʌn·sɪ·'kjʊrd] *adj* **1.** FIN non garantito, -a **2.** (*unfastened*) non assicurato, -a

unseemly [ʌn·'siːm·li] *adj form* indecoroso, -a

unseen [ʌn·'siːn] *adj* non visto, -a; **sight ~** a scatola chiusa

unselfish [ʌn·'sel·fɪʃ] *adj* generoso, -a

unserviceable [ʌn·'sɜːr·vɪ·sə·bl] *adj* inservibile

unsettle [ʌn·'se·t̬l] *vt* **1.** (*make nervous*) scombussolare **2.** (*make unstable*) destabilizzare

unsettled [ˌʌn·'se·t̬ld] *adj* **1.** (*changeable*) instabile **2.** (*troubled*) inquieto, -a **3.** (*unresolved*) non risolto, -a

unsettling *adj* inquietante

unshakable [ʌn·'ʃeɪ·kə·bl] *adj* irremovibile

unshaved *adj*, **unshaven** [ʌn·'ʃeɪ·vən] *adj* non rasato, -a

unshrinkable [ʌn·'ʃrɪŋ·kə·bl] *adj* irrestringibile

unshrinking [ʌn·'ʃrɪŋ·kɪŋ] *adj fig* impavido, -a

unsightly [ʌn·'saɪt·li] <-ier, -iest> *adj* brutto, -a

unsigned [ʌn·'saɪnd] *adj* non firmato, -a

unskilled [ʌn·'skɪld] *adj* non specializzato, -a

unsociable [ʌn·'soʊ·ʃə·bl] *adj* poco socievole

unsocial [ʌn·'soʊ·ʃəl] *adj* asociale

unsold [ʌn·'soʊld] *adj* invenduto, -a

unsolicited [ˌʌn·sə·'lɪ·sɪ·tɪd] *adj* non richiesto, -a

unsolved [ʌn·'sɑːlvd] *adj* irrisolto, -a

unsophisticated [ˌʌn·sə·'fɪs·tə·keɪ·t̬ɪd] *adj* **1.** (*person*) semplice **2.** (*machine*) rudimentale

unsound [ʌn·'saʊnd] *adj* **1.** (*weak, unstable*) insicuro, -a **2.** (*unreliable*) inaffidabile **3.** (*not financially stable*) poco sicuro, -a **4.** (*not valid*) infondato, -a *f* **5.** (*unhealthy*) **of ~ mind** infermo di mente

unsparing [ʌn·'spe·rɪŋ] *adj* **1.** (*merciless*) spietato, -a **2.** *form* (*lavish*) prodigo, -a; **to be ~ in one's efforts** non risparmiare gli sforzi

unspeakable [ʌn·'spiː·kə·bl] *adj* indicibile;

~ atrocities atrocità *fpl* inqualificabili

unspecified [ʌn·'spe·sɪ·faɪd] *adj* imprecisato, -a

unspoiled [ʌn·'spɔɪld] *adj* incontaminato, -a

unspoken [ʌn·'spoʊ·kən] *adj* tacito, -a

unstable [ʌn·'steɪ·bl] *adj* instabile

unsteady [ʌn·'ste·di] *adj* (*chair, market*) instabile; (*hand, voice*) tremante

unstressed [ʌn·'strest] *adj* LING atono, -a

unstuck [ʌn·'stʌk] *adj* **to come** [*o* **become**] **~** (*be no longer stuck*) staccarsi; *inf* (*fail*) fallire

unsubscribe *vi* disdire l'iscrizione [*o* l'abbonamento]

unsubstantial [ˌʌn·səb·'stæn·tʃəl] *adj* insignificante

unsubstantiated [ˌʌn·səb·'stæn·tʃi·eɪ·t̬ɪd] *adj* infondato, -a

unsuccessful [ˌʌn·sək·'ses·fəl] *adj* (*attempt*) non riuscito, -a; (*candidate, applicant*) non selezionato, -a; **to be ~ in sth** non riuscire in qc; **to be ~ in doing sth** non riuscire a fare qc

unsuitable [ʌn·'suː·tə·bl] *adj* inadatto, -a; **~ moment** momento *m* inopportuno; **to be ~ for sth** non essere adatto, -a a qc

unsuited [ʌn·'suː·t̬ɪd] *adj* **to be ~ to** [*o* **for**] **sth** non essere fatto per qc; **to be ~ to each other** non essere fatti l'uno per l'altro

unsullied [ʌn·'sʌ·lɪd] *adj form* intatto, -a

unsung [ʌn·'sʌŋ] *adj* **the ~ hero** l'eroe misconosciuto

unsure [ʌn·'ʃʊr] *adj* incerto, -a; **to be ~ about sth** essere incerto su qc; **to be ~ of oneself** essere insicuro, -a

unsuspecting [ˌʌn·səs·'pek·tɪŋ] *adj* ignaro, -a

unsustainable [ˌʌn·səs·'teɪ·nə·bl] *adj* insostenibile

unswerving [ˌʌn·'swɜːr·vɪŋ] *adj* incrollabile

unsympathetic [ˌʌn·sɪm·pə·'θe·t̬ɪk] *adj* poco comprensivo, -a

untangle [ʌn·'tæŋ·gl] *vt* sbrogliare

untapped [ˌʌn·'tæpt] *adj* non sfruttato, -a

untaxed [ˌʌn·'tækst] *adj* (*goods*) esente da imposta; (*income, revenue*) non imponibile

untenable [ˌʌn·'te·nə·bl] *adj* insostenibile

untested [ʌn·'tes·tɪd] *adj* non testato, -a

unthinkable [ʌn·'θɪŋ·kə·bl] **I.** *adj* impensabile **II.** *n* **the ~** l'inconcepibile *m*

unthinking [ʌn·'θɪŋ·kɪŋ] *adj* sconsiderato, -a

unthought-of [ʌn·'θɑːt·ɑːv] *adj* inimmaginabile

untidy [ʌn·'taɪ·di] <-ier, -iest> *adj* disordinato, -a

untie [ˌʌn·'taɪ] <-y-> *vt* (*knot*) sciogliere; (*boat, hands, shoelaces*) slegare

until [ən·'tɪl] **I.** *prep* fino a; **~ now** finora; **~ then** fino ad allora; **we danced ~ dawn** abbiamo ballato fino all'alba; **she won't be able to leave ~ Friday** non potrà partire prima di venerdì **II.** *conj* finché non; **~ he comes** finché non arriva lui; **he can't leave ~ his work is finished** non può andare via finché non ha finito il lavoro

untimely [ʌn·'taɪm·li] *adj* **1.** (*premature*) pre-

maturo, -a; **sb's ~ death** la scomparsa prematura di qu **2.**(*inopportune*) inopportuno, -a
unto ['ʌn·tuː] *prep* HIST *s.* **to**
untold [ˌʌn·'toʊld] *adj* **1.**(*beyond enumeration*) incalcolabile; **~ damage** danni *mpl* incalcolabili **2.**(*beyond description*) indicibile; **~ suffering** sofferenze *fpl* indicibili **3.**(*not told*) mai rivelato, -a
untouched [ˌʌn·'tʌtʃt] *adj* **1.**(*not affected*) non toccato, -a; **to leave sth ~** lasciare qc intatto; **~ by tourism** non contaminato dal turismo **2.**(*not eaten*) **I left my meal ~** non ho toccato cibo **3.**(*not emotionally moved*) insensibile
untoward [ˌʌn·'tɔːrd] *adj form* **1.**(*unpropitious*) imprevisto, -a **2.**(*adverse*) deplorevole; **an ~ incident** un episodio increscioso **3.**(*improper*) disdicevole
untrained [ʌn·'treɪnd] *adj* (*troops*) non addestrato, -a; (*voice*) non esercitato, -a; **to the ~ eye** ad un occhio inesperto
untransferable [ˌʌn·trænts·'fɜː·rə·bl] *adj* LAW non trasferibile
untreated [ʌn·'triː·t̬ɪd] *adj* **1.**(*sewage, wood*) non trattato, -a **2.**(*illness*) non curato, -a
untried [ʌn·'traɪd] *adj* **1.**(*not tested*) non testato, -a **2.** LAW non processato, -a
untroubled [ʌn·'trʌ·bld] *adj* tranquillo, -a; **they seemed ~ about her decision** non sembravano turbati dalla sua decisione
untrue [ʌn·'truː] *adj* **1.**(*not true*) falso, -a **2.**(*not faithful*) **to be ~ to sb** tradire qn; **I'll never be ~** non ti tradirò mai
untrustworthy [ʌn·'trʌst·ˌwɜːr·ði] *adj* inaffidabile
untruth [ʌn·'truːθ] *n* falsità
untruthful [ʌn·'truː·θ·fəl] *adj* **1.**(*not truthful*) falso, -a **2.**(*mendacious*) menzognero, -a
unturned [ˌʌn·'tɜːrnd] *adj* (*soil*) non rivoltato, -a
untutored [ʌn·'tuː·t̬ɚd] *adj form* non istruito, -a
unused [ʌn·'juːzd] *adj* **1.**(*not in use*) non usato, -a **2.**(*never having been used*) nuovo, -a
unused to [ʌn·'juːst tʊ] *adj* **to be ~ sth** non essere abituato, -a a qc
unusual [ʌn·'juː·ʒu·əl] *adj* insolito, -a; **to be ~ for sb** essere insolito per qu; **it's ~ for her to complain** non è da lei lamentarsi
unutterable [ʌn·'ʌ·t̬ə·rə·bl] *adj form* indicibile
unvarnished [ʌn·'vɑːr·nɪʃt] *adj* non verniciato, -a; **the ~ truth** *fig* la verità nuda e cruda
unveil [ʌn·'veɪl] **I.** *vt fig* **1.**(*expose*) **~ oneself** togliersi il velo **2.**(*memorial, plans*) rivelare **II.** *vi* togliersi il velo
unversed [ˌʌn·'vɜːrst] *adj* **to be ~ in sth** essere poco versato, -a in qc
unwanted [ʌn·'wɑːn·t̬ɪd] *adj* indesiderato, -a
unwarranted [ʌn·'wɔː·rən·t̬ɪd] *adj* ingiustificato, -a
unwavering [ʌn·'weɪ·və·rɪŋ] *adj* incrollabile; **to be ~ in one's support for sb** appoggiare incondizionatamente qu

unwed [ʌn·'wed] *adj form* non sposato, -a
unwelcome [ʌn·'wel·kəm] *adj* non gradito, -a
unwell [ʌn·'wel] *adj* indisposto, -a; **to feel ~** non sentirsi bene
unwieldy [ʌn·'wiːl·di] *adj* **1.**(*cumbersome*) ingombrante **2.**(*difficult to manage*) poco maneggevole
unwilling [ʌn·'wɪ·lɪŋ] *adj* riluttante
unwillingly *adv* malvolentieri
unwind [ʌn·'waɪnd] *irr* **I.** *vt* srotolare **II.** *vi* **1.**(*unroll*) srotolarsi **2.** *fig* (*relax*) rilassarsi
unwise [ʌn·'waɪz] *adj* imprudente
unwitting [ʌn·'wɪ·t̬ɪŋ] *adj* **1.**(*unaware*) inconsapevole **2.**(*unintentional*) non intenzionale
unwittingly *adv* **1.**(*without realizing*) inconsapevolmente **2.**(*unintentionally*) senza volere
unwonted [ʌn·'wɔːn·t̬ɪd] *adj form* inconsueto, -a
unworkable [ʌn·'wɜːr·kə·bl] *adj* inattuabile
unworldly [ʌn·'wɜːrld·li] *adj* **1.**(*spiritual*) ultraterreno, -a **2.**(*naive*) ingenuo, -a **3.**(*unearthly*) non mondano, -a
unworthy [ʌn·'wɜːr·ði] <-ier, -iest> *adj* **1.**(*not worthy*) non degno, -a; **to be ~ of interest** non essere degno di interesse **2.**(*discreditable, contemptible*) indegno, -a
unwrap [ʌn·'ræp] <-pp-> *vt* **1.**(*remove wrapping*) scartare, aprire **2.** *fig* (*open, reveal*) portare alla luce
unwritten [ʌn·'rɪ·tən] *adj* **1.**(*not official*) tacito, -a **2.**(*not written down*) non scritto, -a
unyielding [ʌn·'jiː·l·dɪŋ] *adj* **1.**(*stubborn, obstinate*) inflessibile **2.**(*physically hard, firm*) rigido, -a
unzip [ʌn·'zɪp] <-pp-> *vt* **1.**(*suitcase*) aprire (la cerniera di) **2.** COMPUT (*file*) decomprimere
up [ʌp] **I.** *adv* **1.**(*movement*) su, in alto; **~ here/there** quassù/lassù; **to look ~** guardare in alto; **to stand/get ~** stare in piedi/alzarsi; **to go ~** salire; **to throw sth ~** gettare qc in aria; **to jump ~** saltare in piedi; (**stand**) **~!** in piedi!; **on the way ~** in salita **2.**(*to another point*) **~ in Seattle** su a Seattle; **to go ~ to Maine** andare su nel Maine **3.**(*position*) **to be ~ all night** stare alzato, -a tutta la notte; **to jump ~ on sth** saltare sopra qc; **with one's head ~** a testa alta **4.**(*limit*) **time's ~** il tempo è scaduto; **when 5 hours were ~** allo scadere delle 5 ore; **from the age of 18 ~** a partire dai 18 anni; **to have it ~ to one's ears** (with sb/sth) *fig* averne fin sopra i capelli (di qu/qc) **5.** SPORTS (*ahead*) **to be 7 points ~** essere in vantaggio di 7 punti **6.** COMPUT, TECH in funzione ▸ **~ and down** su e giù; **to walk ~ and down** camminare su e giù; **what's ~?** come va?; **what's ~ with him?** cos'ha? **II.** *prep* **1.**(*at top of*) in cima a; **to climb ~ a tree** arrampicarsi in cima a un albero **2.**(*higher*) **to go ~ the stairs** salire le scale; **to row ~ the river** risalire il fiume; **to go ~ and down sth** andare su e giù per qc **3.**(*along*) **to go ~ the street** percorrere la strada **III.** *n* **~s and**

downs alti e bassi *mpl;* **to be on the ~ and ~** *inf* andare di bene in meglio **IV.** <-pp-> *vi inf* **to ~ and do sth** +*infin* prendere e fare qc +*infin* **V.** <-pp-> *vt* alzare **VI.** *adj* **1.** (*position: tent*) montato, -a; (*flag*) issato, -a; (*curtains, picture*) appeso, -a; (*hand, blinds*) alzato, -a; (*person*) in piedi **2.** (*healthy*) **to be ~ and about** [*o around*] essere di nuovo in piedi **3.** (*ready*) **to be ~ for doing sth** starci a fare qc; **~ for sale/discussion/trial** in vendita/in discussione/in giudizio

♦**up against** *vt* **to be ~ sth/sb** trovarsi di fronte qc/qu

♦**up to** *vt* **1.** (*capable of*) **to feel ~ sth** sentirsi di fare qc **2.** (*limit*) fino a; **~ here** fino a qui; **~ now** fino ad ora; **~ $100** fino a 100 dollari **3.** (*responsibility of*) **it's ~ you** sta a te decidere; **it's ~ me to decide** sta a me decidere

up-and-coming ['ʌp·ən·'kʌ·mɪŋ] *adj* promettente

upbeat ['ʌp·biːt] **I.** *n* MUS tempo *m* in levare **II.** *adj inf* ottimistico, -a; **to be ~ about sth** essere ottimista riguardo a qc

upbringing ['ʌp·brɪŋ·ɪŋ] *n* educazione *f;* **to have a good ~** avere avuto una buona educazione

upcoming ['ʌp·ˌkʌ·mɪŋ] *adj* imminente

upcountry ['ʌp·kʌn·tri] **I.** *adv* verso l'interno **II.** *adj* dell'interno **III.** *n* interno *m*

update[1] [ʌp·'deɪt] *vt* (*bring up to date*) mettere al corrente; COMPUT aggiornare

update[2] ['ʌp·deɪt] *n* aggiornamento *m;* **to give sb an ~ (on sth)** aggiornare qu (su qc)

updating *n* aggiornamento *m*

updraft ['ʌp·drɑːft] *n* corrente *f* ascendente

upend [ʌp·'end] *vt* capovolgere

up front, up-front ['ʌp·frʌnt] *adj inf* **1.** (*open, frank*) franco, -a, essere franco riguardo a qc **2.** (*advance*) **~ payment** pagamento *m* immediato

upgrade ['ʌp·greɪd] **I.** *vt* **1.** (*improve*) migliorare; (*hardware*) sostituire con un modello più potente; (*software*) sostituire con una versione superiore **2.** AVIAT (*move to better class*) **they ~ed him to first class** gli hanno dato un upgrade in prima classe **II.** *vi* **1.** COMPUT, TECH, COM (*improve quality*) passare a un modello [*o* una versione] superiore **2.** AVIAT (*move to better class*) fare un upgrade alla classe superiore **III.** *n* upgrade *m inv*

upgradable *adj* COMPUT espandibilie

upgrading *n* upgrade *m inv*

upheaval [ʌp·'hiː·vəl] *n* **1.** (*condition of violent change*) sconvolgimento *m* **2.** (*instance of violent change*) cataclisma *m* **3.** GEO (*violent upward push*) sollevamento *m; ~* **of the earth's crust** sollevamento *m* della crosta terrestre

uphill [ʌp·'hɪl] **I.** *adv* (*in an ascending direction*) in salita; **to run/walk ~** correre/camminare in salita **II.** *adj* **1.** (*sloping upward*) in salita **2.** (*difficult*) arduo, -a; **an ~ struggle** un'ardua battaglia

uphold [ʌp·'hoʊld] *irr vt* **1.** (*support, maintain*) difendere; **to ~ the law** difendere la legge **2.** LAW (*confermare*) **to ~ a verdict** confermare un verdetto

upholster [ʌp·'hoʊls·tɚ] *vt* **to ~ sth (in sth)** tappezzare qc (di qc)

upholsterer *n* tappezziere, -a *m, f*

upholstery *n* (*covering for furniture*) tappezzeria *m;* **leather ~** rivestimento *m* in pelle

UPI *n* *abbr of* **United Press International** UPI *f*

upkeep ['ʌp·kiːp] *n* **1.** (*maintenance*) manutenzione *m* **2.** (*cost*) costi *mpl* di manutenzione

upland ['ʌp·lənd] **I.** *adj* montuoso, -a **II.** *n* **the ~s** gli altipiani

uplift[1] [ʌp·'lɪft] *vt* **1.** (*raise up*) elevare **2.** (*inspire*) risollevare; **to ~ sb's heart** risollevare il morale di qu

uplift[2] ['ʌp·lɪft] *n* **1.** GEO sollevamento *m* **2.** (*spiritual/mental*) **to provide moral ~** risollevare il morale

uplifting [ʌp·'lɪf·tɪŋ] *adj* positivo, -a

upload ['ʌp·loʊd] *vt* COMPUT caricare sul server

upmarket ['ʌp·ˌmɑːr·kɪt] **I.** *adj* esclusivo, -a **II.** *adv* **to go ~** orientarsi a una clientela più esclusiva

upon [ə·'pɑːn] *prep form* **1.** (*on top of*) su **2.** (*at time of*) **~ her arrival** al suo arrivo **3.** (*long ago*) **once ~ a time** c'era una volta

upper ['ʌ·pɚ] **I.** *adj* **1.** (*further up*) superiore; **~ management** i dirigenti **2.** GEO (*northern*) **the ~ Northeast** le estreme regioni nordorientali **II.** *n* **1.** (*of shoe*) tomaia *f* **2.** *inf* (*drug*) stimolante *m*

uppercase *n* TYPO maiuscolo *m*

upper class <-es> *n* alta società *f*

upper-class *adj* dell'alta società; **in ~ circles** nell'alta società

uppercut *n* SPORTS uppercut *m inv*

upper deck *n* (*of ship*) ponte *m* superiore; (*of bus*) piano *m* superiore; (*of stadium*) gradinata *f* superiore

uppermost *adj* più alto, -a; **to be ~ in one's mind** essere al primo posto nei pensieri di qu

uppish ['ʌ·pɪʃ] *adj,* **uppity** ['ʌ·pə·ti] *adj inf* presuntuoso, -a

upright ['ʌp·raɪt] **I.** *adj* **1.** (*post, rod*) verticale **2.** (*upstanding*) retto, -a; (*citizen*) onesto, -a **II.** *adv* verticalmente; **to stand ~** stare in posizione eretta; **to sit bolt ~** rizzarsi a sedere **III.** *n* **1.** (*upright piano*) pianoforte *m* verticale **2.** TECH montante *m* **3.** SPORTS palo *m*

uprising ['ʌp·raɪ·zɪŋ] *n* sommossa *f;* **to crush an ~** reprimere una sommossa

uproar ['ʌp·rɔːr] *n* scalpore *m;* **to cause an ~** provocare scalpore

uproarious [ʌp·'rɔː·riəs] *adj* **1.** (*noisy: debate*) tumultuoso, -a **2.** (*amusing: joke*) spassosissimo, -a

uproot [ʌp·'ruːt] *vt a. fig* sradicare

upset[1] [ʌp·'set] **I.** *vt irr* **1.** (*unsettle*) turbare; (*distress*) scovolgere; **to ~ oneself** prendersela **2.** (*throw into disorder*) disturbare **3.** (*boat*) capovolgere; (*table*) rovesciare **4.** (*cause pain*) **onions ~ him/his stomach** le cipolle gli scombussolano lo stomaco **II.** *adj* **1.** (*disquieted*) turbato, -a; (*distressed*) sconvolto, -a; **to get ~ about sth** prendersela per qc; **to be ~** (**that**) ... essere offeso, -a (perché)...; **don't be ~** non ti offendere **2.** (*nauseated*) **to have an ~ stomach** avere lo stomaco sottosopra **3.** (*overturned*) capovolto, -a

upset² ['ʌp·set] *n* **1.** (*great surprise*) sorpresa *f* **2.** (*illness*) **stomach ~** disturbi *m* dí stomaco *pl* **3.** (*confusion, problems*) scompiglio *m*

upset price *n* COM prezzo *m* minimo

upsetting *adj* sconvolgente

upshot ['ʌp·ʃɑːt] *n* risultato *m;* **the ~** (**of it all**) **is that ...** il risultato è che...

upside down [ʌp·saɪd 'daʊn] **I.** *adj* **1.** (*reversed in vertical axis*) sottosopra; **to be ~** (*pictures*) essere alla rovescia **2.** (*confused*) sottosopra; **the house was ~** la casa era sottosopra **II.** *adv* alla rovescia; **to turn sth ~** capovolgere qc

upstage¹ ['ʌp·steɪdʒ] **I.** *adj* THEAT del fondo del palco **II.** *adv* sul fondo del palco; **to go ~** andare verso il fondo del palco

upstage² [ʌp·'steɪdʒ] *vt* rubare la scena a

upstairs [ʌp·'sterz] **I.** *adj* **the ~ rooms** le stanze al piano di sopra; **the ~ windows** le finestre del piano di sopra **II.** *adv* di sopra; **to go ~** andare di sopra; **the people who live ~** i vicini del piano di sopra **III.** *n* (**the**) **~** il piano di sopra

upstanding [ʌp·'stæn·dɪŋ] *adj* form retto, -a

upstart ['ʌp·stɑːrt] *n* parvenu *m inv*

upstate ['ʌp·steɪt] **I.** *adj* **in ~ New York** nel nord dello Stato di New York **II.** *adv* al nord

upstream [ʌp·'striːm] **I.** *adj* della parte alta di un corso d'acqua; **~ pollution** contaminazione *f* della parte alta di un corso d'acqua **II.** *adv* controcorrente; **to swim ~** nuotare controcorrente

upsurge ['ʌp·sɜːrdʒ] *n* impennata *f;* **an ~ in sth** un'impennata di qc

upswing ['ʌp·swɪŋ] *n* ripresa *m;* **an ~ in sth** una ripresa di qc; **to be on the ~** essere in ripresa

uptake ['ʌp·teɪk] *n* **1.** (*level of absorption*) assorbimento *m* **2.** (*vent*) condotto *m* di aerazione ▸ **to be quick on the ~** *inf* capire al volo; **to be slow on the ~** *inf* essere duro di comprendonio

uptight [ʌp·'taɪt] *adj* inf teso, -a

up-to-date [ʌp·tə·'deɪt] *adj* (*technology*) moderno, -a; (*fashion*) attuale; (*timetable*) aggiornato, -a; **to bring sb ~** aggiornare qu

up-to-the-minute ['ʌp·tə·ðə·'mɪ·nɪt] *adj* (*fashion*) del momento; (*news*) dell'ultimo minuto

uptown ['ʌp·taʊn] **I.** *adj* **in ~ Manhattan** i quartieri alti di Manhattan; **an ~ shop** un negozio dei quartieri alti **II.** *adv* verso i quartieri alti

uptrend ['ʌp·trend] *n* tendenza *f* al rialzo; **an ~ in sth** una tendenza al rialzo in qc

upturn ['ʌp·tɜːrn] *n* ripresa *f;* **an ~ in the economy** una ripresa dell'economia

upturned [ˌʌp·'tɜːrnd] *adj* capovolto, -a; **~ nose** naso *m* all'insù

upward ['ʌp·wəd] **I.** *adj* verso l'alto; **~ movement** movimento *m* verso l'alto; **~ trend** tendenza *f* al rialzo **II.** *adv* **1.** (*toward higher level*) verso l'alto **2.** (*toward a later age*) in su; **from adolescence ~** dall'adolescenza in poi **3.** (*going higher in number*) in rialzo

upwards *adv* in su; **and ~** e più

uranium [jʊə·'reɪ·ni·əm] *n* uranio *m*

Uranus ['jʊ·rə·nəs] *n* Urano *m*

urban ['ɜːr·bən] *adj* urbano, -a; **~ sprawl** sviluppo *m* urbanistico incontrollato; **~ decay** degrado *m* urbano

urbane [ɜːr·'beɪn] *adj* civile

urbanity [ɜːr·'bæ·nə·ti] *n* cortesia *f*

urbanization [ˌɜːr·bə·nɪ·'zeɪ·ʃən] *n* urbanizzazione *f*

urbanize ['ɜːr·bə·naɪz] *vt* urbanizzare

urchin ['ɜːr·tʃɪn] *n* iron monello, -a *m, f;* **street ~** monello di strada

urethra [jʊ·'riː·θrə] <-s *o* -e> *n* uretra *f*

urge [ɜːrdʒ] **I.** *n* impulso *m;* **an ~ to do sth** l'impulso di fare qc; **to feel an irresistible ~ to do sth** sentire il desiderio irresistibile di fare qc; **sexual ~** desiderio *m* sessuale **II.** *vt* **1.** (*strongly encourage*) esortare; **to ~ sb to do sth** esortare qu a fare qc **2.** (*recommend*) raccomandre; **to ~ caution upon sb** raccomandare prudenza a qu

◆ **urge on** *vt* **to urge sb on** (**to do sth**) incitare qu (a fare qc)

◆ **urge upon** *vt form* **to ~ sb to do sth** spronare qu a fare qc

urgency ['ɜːr·dʒən·si] *n* **1.** (*top priority, imperativeness*) urgenza *f;* **to be a matter of great ~** essere una questione della massima urgenza **2.** (*insistence, clamorousness*) insistenza *f*

urgent ['ɜːr·dʒənt] *adj* **1.** (*imperative, crucial*) urgente; **to be in ~ need of sth** avere un bisogno urgente di qc **2.** *form* (*insistent, pleading*) insistente

urgently *adv* **1.** (*immediately*) urgentemente **2.** (*earnestly*) insistentemente

urinal ['jʊ·rə·nəl] *n* orinale *m*

urinary ['jʊ·rə·ne·ri] *adj* urinario, -a; **~ diseases** malattie *fpl* (delle vie) urinarie; **~ incontinence** incontinenza *f* (urinaria)

urinate ['jʊ·rə·neɪt] *vi* urinare

urine ['jʊ·rɪn] *n* urina *f*

URL *n* COMPUT *abbr of* **universal resource locator** URL *m*

urn [ɜːrn] *n* **1.** urna *f* **2.** (*for tea*) dispenser *m inv*

Uruguay ['jʊ·rəg·weɪ] *n* Uruguay *m*

Uruguayan [jʊ·rə·'gweɪ·ən] **I.** *adj* uruguaiano, -a **II.** *n* uruguaiano, -a *m, f*

us [əs, *stressed:* ʌs] *pron pers* ci; *after prep* noi; it's ~ siamo noi; **older than** ~ più vecchi di noi; **look at** ~ guardaci; **he saw** ~ ci ha visto; **he gave the pencil to** ~ ha dato la matita a noi; **it's for** ~ è per noi; **it's from** ~ è da parte nostra

US *n*, **U.S.** *n abbr of* United States USA *mpl*

USA [ˌjuːˌesˈeɪ] *n* 1. *abbr of* United States of America USA *mpl* 2. *abbr of* United States Army *esercito statunitense*

USAF [ˌjuːˌesˌeɪˈef] *n abbr of* United States Air Force *aeronautica militare statunitense*

usage [ˈjuːzɪdʒ] *n* 1.(*how sth is used*) impiego *m;* in **common**/**general** ~ d'uso comune 2.(*amount used*) consumo *m* 3. LING uso *m;* in **common**/**general** ~ d'uso comune

use¹ [juːs] *n* 1.(*practical application*) uso *m* 2.(*possibility of applying*) impiego *m;* **in** ~ in uso; **to be of** ~ **to sb** essere utile a qu; **a ban on the** ~ **of sth** il divieto di usare qc; **to make** ~ **of sth** utilizzare qc; **to put sth to good** ~ fare buon uso qc; **to be out of** ~ essere fuori servizio [o uso]; **to come into** ~ entrare in uso; **to go out of** ~ cadere in disuso 3.(*purpose*) **to be no** ~ non servire a niente; **there's no** ~ **doing sth** non serve a niente fare qc; **it's no** ~ è inutile; **what's the** ~ **of doing sth?** a che serve fare qc? 4.(*consumption*) consumo *m*

use² [juːz] I. *vt* 1.(*make use of*) usare; **to** ~ **sth to do sth** usare qc per fare qc; **to** ~ **drugs** fare uso di droghe; **I could** ~ **some help** *inf* mi servirebbe una mano; ~ **discretion** sii discreto; ~ **your head** usa il cervello 2.(*consume*) consumare; **to** ~ **energy** consumare energia 3.(*manipulate*) usare; (*exploit*) sfruttare 4. *form* (*treat in stated way*) **to** ~ **sb badly**/**well** trattare male/bene qu II. *vi* **he** ~**d to be**/**do** ... era/faceva...; **she** ~**d not to enjoy horror films** i film dell'orrore non le piacevano; **didn't you** ~ **to work in banking?** non lavoravi in banca?

♦ **use up** *vt* consumare

used [juːzd] *adj* usato, -a

used to [juːst tʊ] *adj* (*familiar with*) abituato, -a; **to be** ~ **sth** essere abituato a qc; **to become** ~ **sth** abituarsi a qc; **to be** ~ **the cold**/**heat** essere abituato al freddo/al caldo; **to be** ~ **doing sth** avere l'abitudine di fare qc

useful [ˈjuːsfəl] *adj* 1.(*convenient*) utile; **to be** ~ (**for sth**) essere utile (per qc); **a** ~ **experience** un'esperienza utile; **to do sth** ~ fare qc di utile 2.(*competent*) **to be** ~ **with sth** *inf* saperci fare in qc

usefulness *n* utilità *f*

useless [ˈjuːsləs] *adj* 1.(*in vain*) inutile; **it's** ~ **doing sth** è inutile fare qc; **to be** ~ **to do sth** non servire a niente fare qc 2.(*unusable*) inutilizzabile 3. *inf* (*incompetent*) incapace

user *n* utente *mf;* **drug** ~ tossicodipendente *mf*

user-friendly *adj* COMPUT facile da usare

user interface *n* COMPUT interfaccia *f* utente

username *n* COMPUT nome *m* utente

usher [ˈʌʃə] I. *n* (*in a courtroom*) usciere *m;*

(*in a theater*) maschera *f* II. *vt* **to** ~ **sb into the office** far accomodare qu in ufficio; **to** ~ **sb out** accompagnare qu alla porta

USMA *n abbr of* United States Military Academy *accademia militare statunitense*

USMC *n abbr of* United States Marine Corps *corpo dei marines statunitense*

USN *n abbr of* United States Navy *marina militare statunitense*

USNA *n abbr of* United States Naval Academy *accademia navale statunitense*

USO *n abbr of* United Service Organizations *fondazione di sostegno alle truppe statunitensi*

USPS [ˌjuːˌesˈpiːˌes] *n abbr of* United States Postal Service *poste statunitensi*

USS [ˌjuːˌesˈes] *n* 1. *abbr of* United States Ship *nave da guerra statunitense* 2. *abbr of* United States Senate *senato degli Stati Uniti*

usual [ˈjuːʒʊəl] I. *adj* solito, -a; (**the**) ~ **problems** i soliti problemi; **in its** ~ **place** al solito posto; **as** ~ come al solito; **to be** ~ **for sb** essere d'abitudine per qu II. *n* **the** ~ *inf* (*regular drink*/*food*) il solito

usually *adv* normalmente

usufruct [ˈjuːsˌzʊˈfrʌkt] *n form* LAW usufrutto *m*

usurer [ˈjuːʒəˌrə] *n* LAW usuraio, -a *m, f*

usurious [juːˈʒʊriˌəs] *adj form* LAW usuraio, -a

usurp [juːˈsɜːrp] *vt* usurpare

usurper [juːˈsɜːrˌpə] *n* usurpatore, -trice *m, f*

usury [ˈjuːʒəˌi] *n* LAW usura *f*

UT *n abbr of* Utah UT

Utah *n* Utah *m*

utensil [juːˈtensl] *n* utensile *m;* **kitchen** ~ **s** utensili *mpl* di cucina

uterine [ˈjuːtəˌɪn] *adj* uterino, -a

uterus [ˈjuːtəˌəs] <-ri *o* -es> *n* utero *m*

utilitarian [juːˌtɪləˈteˌriˌən] *adj* utilitario, -a

utility [juːˈtɪləˌti] <-ies> *n* 1. *form* (*usefulness*) utilità *f* 2.(*public service*) impresa *f* di servizi pubblici 3. COMPUT utility *f inv*

utilization [ˌjuːˌtəˌlɪˈzeɪˌʃən] *n* utilizzazione *f*

utilize [ˈjuːˌtəˌlaɪz] *vt* utilizzare

utmost [ˈʌtˌmoʊst] I. *adj* massimo, -a; **of the** ~ **brilliance** intelligentissimo, -a; **with the** ~ **caution** con la massima cautela; **a matter of** ~ **importance** una faccenda della massima importanza II. *n* **to try one's** ~ fare tutto il possibile; **to the** ~ al massimo; **to live life to the** ~ vivere la vita al massimo

utopia [juːˈtoʊˌpiˌə] *n* utopia *f*

utopian *adj* utopico, -a

utter¹ [ˈʌˌtə] *adj* completo, -a; **in** ~ **despair** nella più totale disperazione; ~ **nonsense** tutte sciocchezze; **an** ~ **fool** un perfetto idiota

utter² [ˈʌˌtə] *vt* proferire; **without** ~**ing a word** senza proferire parola

utterance [ˈʌˌtəˌrənts] *n* 1.(*speech act*) enunciato *m* 2.(*style of delivery*) espressione *f;* **to give** ~ **to sth** esprimere qc

utterly *adv* completamente; **to be** ~ **convinced that ...** essere completamente convinto che...; ~ **irresistible** assolutamente irre-

sistibile
uttermost ['ʌ·tə·moʊst] *adj, n s.* **utmost**
U-turn ['juː·tɜːrn] *n* (*on road*) inversione *f* a U; (*in policy*) dietrofront *m inv*
UV [juː·'viː] *abbr of* **ultraviolet** UV
uvula ['juː·vjə·lə] *n* ugola *f*
Uzbek ['ʊz·bək] I. *adj* uzbeko, -a II. *n* uzbeko, -a *m, f*
Uzbekistan [ʌz·ˌbe·kɪ·'stæn] *n* Uzbekistan *m*

V

V, v [viː] *n* V, v *f;* ~ **as in Victor** V come Venezia
V 1. *abbr of* **volt** V **2.** *abbr of* **volume** vol.
VA *n abbr of* **Virginia** VA
vac [væk] I. *n inf* **1.** *abbr of* **vacuum cleaner** aspirapolvere *m;* **to give sth a quick** ~ dare una passata di aspirapolvere a qc **2.** *abbr of* **vacuum** vuoto *m* II. <-cc-> *vi abbr of* **vacuum clean** passare l'aspirapolvere
vacancy ['veɪ·kən·tsi] <-ies> *n* **1.** (*room*) camera *f* libera; '~' 'camere *fpl* libere'; **'no ~'** 'completo' **2.** (*employment opportunity*) posto (di lavoro) vacante *m;* **to fill a** ~ coprire un posto (di lavoro) vacante; **to have a** ~ offrire un posto di lavoro **3.** (*lack of expression*) vacuità *f*
vacant ['veɪ·kənt] *adj* **1.** (*empty*) libero, -a; ~ **lot** terreno *m* libero; **to leave sth** ~ (*building, apartment*) lasciare qc libero; '~' 'libero' **2.** (*position*) vacante; **to become** ~ diventare disponibile; **to fill a** ~ **position** coprire un posto vacante **3.** (*expressionless*) assente
vacate ['veɪ·keɪt] *vt form* (*house, seat*) lasciare libero, -a; (*position, post*) lasciare vacante
vacation [veɪ·'keɪ·ʃən] I. *n* vacanza *f*, ferie *fpl;* **to take a** ~ prendersi una vacanza; **on** ~ in ferie; **paid** ~ ferie pagate II. *vi* andare in vacanza
vacationer *n* vacanziere, -a *m, f*
vaccinate ['væ·ksə·neɪt] *vt* MED vaccinare; **to be ~d against measles** essere vaccinato contro il morbillo
vaccination [ˌvæ·ksə·'neɪ·ʃən] *n* MED vaccinazione *f;* **a** ~ **against measles** la vaccinazione contro il morbillo; **oral** ~ vaccinazione orale
vaccine [væk·'siːn] *n* MED vaccino *m*
vacillate ['væ·sə·leɪt] *vi* tentennare; **to** ~ **between ... and ...** oscillare tra ... e ...; **to** ~ **between hope and despair** oscillare tra speranza e disperazione
vacillation [ˌvæ·səl·'eɪ·ʃən] *n* tentennamento *m*
vacuous ['væk·juəs] *adj* vacuo, -a; **a** ~ **remark** un'osservazione insulsa
vacuum ['væk·juːm] I. *n* **1.** PHYS (*area without gas, air*) vuoto *m* **2.** (*absence of direction*) **to**

fill/leave a ~ colmare/lasciare un vuoto **3.** (*isolated from influences, people*) **in a** ~ in isolamento **4.** (*vacuum cleaner*) aspirapolvere *m* II. *vt* passare l'aspirapolvere in; **to** ~ **sth up** pulire qc con l'aspirapolvere
vacuum cleaner *n* aspirapolvere *m*
vacuum-packaged *adj,* **vacuum-packed** [ˌvæk·ju·əm·'pækt] *adj* sottovuoto
vagabond ['væ·gə·bɑːnd] I. *n* vagabondo, -a *m, f* II. *adj* vagabondo, -a
vagary ['veɪ·gə·ri] <-ies> *n* capriccio *m;* **the vagaries of fashion/of the weather** i capricci della moda/del tempo
vagina [və·'dʒaɪ·nə] *n* vagina *f*
vagrancy ['veɪ·grən·si] *n* vagabondaggio *m*
vagrant ['veɪ·grənt] I. *n* vagabondo, -a *m, f* II. *adj* vagabondo, -a
vague [veɪg] *adj* **1.** (*imprecise*) vago, -a; **I haven't the** ~ **st idea** non ho la minima idea **2.** (*absent-minded*) distratto, -a
vagueness *n* **1.** (*imprecision*) vaghezza *f* **2.** (*absent-mindedness*) distrazione *f*
vain [veɪn] *adj* **1.** (*conceited, self-admiring*) vanitoso, -a **2.** (*fruitless*) vano, -a; **it is** ~ **to ...** +*infin* è inutile ... +*infin* **3. in** ~ invano; **it was all in** ~ è stato inutile
vainglorious [ˌveɪn·'glɔː·ri·əs] *adj form* vanaglorioso, -a
vale *n,* **Vale** [veɪl] *n liter* (*valley*) valle *m;* **this** ~ **of tears** *fig* questa valle di lacrime
valediction [ˌvæ·lə·'dɪk·ʃən] *n form* **1.** (*farewell*) addio *m* **2.** (*speech given when taking leave*) discorso *m* di commiato
valedictorian *n* studente che pronuncia il discorso di commiato ai diplomandi
valedictory [ˌvæ·lə·'dɪk·tə·ri] *adj* di commiato; ~ **address** discorso *m* di commiato
valence ['veɪ·lənts], **valency** ['veɪləntsi] <-ies> *n* valenza *f*
valentine ['væ·lən·taɪn] *n* **1.** (*card*) biglietto che ci si scambia per la festa degli innamorati **2.** (*sweetheart*) innamorato, -a *m, f*
Valentine's Day *n* festa *f* degli innamorati, San Valentino *m*
valerian [və·'lɪ·ri·ən] *n* valeriana *f*
valet ['væ·lɪt] *n* **1.** (*professional car parker*) parcheggiatore *m* **2.** (*in a hotel*) boy *m inv* **3.** HIST valletto *m*
valet parking *n* servizio *m* parcheggiatore
valiant ['væl·jənt] *adj* coraggioso, -a
valid ['væ·lɪd] *adj* **1.** (*worthwhile, weighty*) valido, -a; **no longer** ~ scaduto, -a **2.** (*well-founded*) legittimo, -a
validate ['væ·lə·deɪt] *vt* convalidare
validity [və·'lɪ·də·ti] *n* (*legal force*) validità *f*
valley ['væ·li] *n* valle *f*
valor ['væ·lə] *n form* valore *m*, coraggio *m*
valuable ['væl·ju·ə·bl] I. *adj* prezioso, -a; **this ring is very** ~ quest'anello è preziosissimo II. *n pl* oggetti *mpl* di valore
valuation [ˌvæl·ju·'eɪ·ʃən] *n* **1.** (*estimation of financial value*) valutazione *f* **2.** (*estimated value*) valore *m*

valuator *n* FIN valutatore, -trice *m, f*

value ['væl·ju:] I. *n* 1. *a.* MATH, MUS (*worth, significance*) valore *m;* ~ **judgment** giudizio *m* di valore; **to be of** ~ **to sb** essere importante per qu; **to be of little** ~ essere di scarso valore; **to place a high** ~ **on sth** dare molta importanza a qc; **to be good** ~ (**for one's money**) avere un buon prezzo; **to be of great** ~ avere molta importanza; **to increase** (**in**) ~ aumentare di valore; **to lose** (**in**) ~ perdere valore; **market** ~ valore di mercato 2. *pl* (*moral ethics, standards*) valori *mpl;* **set of** ~ **s** scala *f* di valori II. *vt* 1. (*think to be significant*) apprezzare; **to** ~ **sb as a friend** tenere all'amicizia di qu 2. (*estimate financial worth*) valutare; **to** ~ **sth at sth** valutare qc a qc

valued *adj form* stimato, -a; ~ **customer** stimato cliente

valueless ['væl·ju:·ləs] *adj* privo, -a di valore

valve [vælv] *n* valvola *f*

vamp¹ [væmp] I. *n* 1. (*of a shoe*) tomaia *f* 2. MUS accompagnamento *m* improvvisato II. *vt* 1. (*shoe*) mettere la tomaia a 2. MUS improvvisare un accompagnamento per III. *vi* MUS improvvisare un accompagnamento

vamp² [væmp] *n* vamp *f inv*

vampire ['væm·paɪ·ə·] *n* vampiro *m*

vampire bat *n* pipistrello *m* vampiro

van¹ [væn] *n* furgone *m;* **delivery** ~ furgone delle consegne; **moving** ~ furgone per traslochi

van² [væn] *n inf abbr of* **vanguard** avanguardia *f*

vandal ['væn·dəl] *n* vandalo *m*

vandalism ['væn·də·lɪ·zəm] *n* vandalismo *m*

vandalize ['væn·də·laɪz] *vt* vandalizzare

vane [veɪn] *n* 1. (*weathercock*) segnavento *m* 2. (*of windmill*) pala *f* 3. (*of propeller*) paletta *f*

vanguard ['væn·gɑːrd] *n* avanguardia *f*

vanilla [və·'nɪ·lə] *n* vaniglia *f*

vanish ['væ·nɪʃ] *vi* **to** ~ (**from sth**) scomparire (da qc); **to** ~ **into thin air** *fig* svanire

vanishing point *n* punto *m* di fuga

vanity ['væ·nə·ti] <-ies> *n* 1. (*self-satisfaction*) vanità *f* 2. (*dressing table*) tavolo *m* da toeletta 3. (*bathroom cabinet*) mobile *m* portalavabo

vanity bag *n*, **vanity case** *n* necessaire *m inv,* beauty case *m inv*

vanity plate *n* targa *f* personalizzata

vanquish ['væŋ·kwɪʃ] *vt* sconfiggere

vantage ['væn·t̬ɪdʒ] *n* vantaggio *m*

vantage point *n* posizione *f* vantaggiosa

Vanuatu [væn·'wɑː·tu:] *n* Vanuatu *m*

vapid ['væ·pɪd] *adj* insulso, -a

vapor ['veɪ·pə·] *n* vapore *m;* **water** ~ vapore acqueo

vaporization [ˌveɪ·pə·rɪ·'zeɪ·ʃən] *n* vaporizzazione *f*

vaporize ['veɪ·pə·raɪz] I. *vt* vaporizzare II. *vi* vaporizzarsi

vaporizer *n* vaporizzatore *m*

vapor pressure *n* pressione *f* del vapore

vapor trail *n* AVIAT scia *f*

variability [ˌve·ri·ə·'bɪ·lə·ti] *n* variabilità *f*

variable ['ve·riə·bl] I. *n* MATH variabile *f* II. *adj* variabile

variance ['ve·ri·ənts] *n* 1. (*disagreement, difference*) divergenza *f;* **at** ~ **in** contraddizione; **to be at** ~ **with sth** divergere da qc 2. (*variation*) variazione *f* 3. (*in statistics*) varianza *f*

variant ['ve·ri·ənt] I. *n* variante *f* II. *adj* 1. (*different*) diverso, -a; ~ **spelling** variante *f* ortografica 2. (*tending to change*) variabile

variation [ˌve·ri·'eɪ·ʃən] *n* 1. *a.* BIO, MUS variazione *f;* **a** ~ **on sth** una variazione di qc; **variations on a theme** variazioni sul tema 2. (*difference*) differenza *f;* **wide** ~ **s in sth** grandi differenze in qc

varicose ['ve·rə·koʊs] *adj* MED varicoso, -a; ~ **veins** varici *fpl*

varied ['ve·rɪd] *adj* 1. (*altered, diverse*) vario, -a 2. (*having different colors*) variegato, -a

variegated ['ve·ri·ə·geɪ·t̬ɪd] *adj* variegato, -a

variety [və·'raɪ·ə·ti] <-ies> *n* 1. (*diversity*) varietà *f;* **to lend** ~ **to sth** variare qc 2. (*assortment*) assortimento *m;* **for a** ~ **of reasons** per vari motivi; **a** ~ **of snacks** un vasto assortimento di stuzzichini 3. (*sort, category*) varietà *f;* **a new** ~ **of tulip** una nuova varietà di tulipano 4. THEAT varietà *m* ► ~ **is the** spice **of life** *prov* il mondo è bello perché è vario *prov*

variety show *n* spettacolo *m* di varietà

various ['ve·riəs] *adj* 1. (*numerous*) vari, -e; **for** ~ **reasons** per vari motivi 2. (*diverse*) diversi, -e

varmint ['vɑːr·mɪnt] *n* 1. ZOOL animali *m* nocivi *pl* 2. (*person*) peste *f*

varnish ['vɑːr·nɪʃ] I. *n* vernice *f* II. *vt* verniciare

varsity ['vɑːr·sə·ti] <-ies> *n* squadra *f* del college

vary ['ve·ri] <-ie-> I. *vi* 1. (*change, be different*) variare; **opinions** ~ ci sono opinioni diverse; **entry requirements** ~ **between schools** i criteri di ammissione variano da una scuola all'altra 2. (*diverge*) differire; **to** ~ **from sth** differire da qc II. *vt* (*change, diversify*) variare

varying *adj* vario, -a

vascular ['væs·kjə·lə·] *adj* vascolare

vase [veɪs] *n* vaso *m*

vassal ['væ·səl] *n* HIST vassallo *m*

vast [væst] *adj* 1. (*great in area*) vasto, -a; **a** ~ **country** un Paese vasto 2. (*great in number*) enorme; **the** ~ **majority** la stragrande maggioranza 3. (*great in degree*) considerevole; **his** ~ **knowledge of ...** la sua vasta conoscenza di ...; **a** ~ **amount of money** un'ingente somma di denaro

vastly *adv* (*very*) enormemente; ~ **superior** infinitamente superiore

vastness *n* immensità *f*

vat [væt] *n* tino *m*

Vatican ['væ·t̬ɪ·kən] I. *n* **the** ~ il Vaticano

V

II. *adj* vaticano, -a
Vatican City *n* Città *f* del Vaticano
vaudeville ['vɑ:d·vɪl] *n* vaudeville *m inv*
vault[1] [vɑːlt] *n* **1.** ARCHIT (*arched structure*) volta *f;* (*under churches*) cripta *f;* (*at cemeteries*) tomba *f;* **family ~** tomba di famiglia **2.** (*in a bank*) caveau *m inv*
vault[2] [vɑːlt] **I.** *n* salto *m* **II.** *vi, vt* saltare
vaulted *adj* ARCHIT a volta
vaulting I. *n* ARCHIT costruzione *f* a volta **II.** *adj* (*exaggerated*) sfrenato, -a
vaulting horse *n* (*in gymnastics*) cavallo (con maniglie) *m*
vaunt [vɑːnt] *vt* vantare
VC [ˌviː·'siː] *n abbr of* **Vietcong** Vietcong *mf inv*
VCR [ˌviː·siː·'ɑːr] *n abbr of* **videocassette recorder** VCR *m*
VD [ˌviː·'diː] *n* MED *abbr of* **venereal disease** malattia *f* venerea
V-E Day [ˌviː·'iː] *abbr of* **Victory in Europe Day** V-E Day (*8 maggio, giorno della vittoria in Europa; la resa della Germania agli Alleati segna la fine della II guerra mondiale*)
veal [viːl] *n* (carne *f* di) vitello *m*
veal cutlet *n* fettina *f* di vitello
vector ['vek·tə] **I.** *n* MATH, BIO, MED vettore *m* **II.** *adj* MATH vettoriale
veer [vɪr] **I.** *vi* **1.** (*alter course: airplane*) virare; (*wind, road*) cambiare direzione; **the truck veered off the road** il camion è uscito di strada **2.** (*alter attitude, goal*) cambiare; **to ~ from/towards sth** deviare da/verso qc **II.** *n* deviazione *f*
veg [vedʒ] *vi inf* rilassarsi
vegan ['viː·gən] *n* vegetaliano, -a *m, f*
vegetable ['vedʒ·tə·bl] *n* **1.** (*plant*) vegetale *m* **2.** (*edible plant*) verdura *f;* (**green**) ~ verdura *f* a foglia; **~ soup** minestra *f* di verdura; **root ~** tubero *m;* **seasonal ~** verdura di stagione
vegetable butter *n*, **vegetable fat** *n* margarina *f*
vegetable garden *n* orto *m*
vegetable kingdom *n* regno *m* vegetale
vegetable oil *n* olio *m* vegetale
vegetarian [ˌve·dʒə·'te·riən] **I.** *n* vegetariano, -a *m, f* **II.** *adj* vegetariano, -a
vegetate ['ve·dʒə·teɪt] *vi a. fig* vegetare
vegetation [ˌve·dʒə·'teɪ·ʃən] *n* vegetazione *f*
veggie *n*, **vegie** *n inf* vegetariano, -a *m, f*
veggieburger *n* hamburger *m* vegetariano *inv*
vehemence ['viː·ə·məns] *n* veemenza *f*
vehement ['viː·ə·mənt] *adj* veemente
vehicle ['viː·ə·kl] *n* **1.** (*for transporting*) veicolo *m;* **motor ~** veicolo a motore, automezzo *m* **2.** (*channel, means of expression*) mezzo *m;* **to be a ~ for sth** essere un mezzo di qc
vehicular [viː·'hɪk·jə·lə] *adj form* stradale; **~ traffic** circolazione *f* stradale; **~ manslaughter** omicidio *m* colposo stradale
veil [veɪl] **I.** *n* velo *m;* **bridal ~** velo da sposa; **a ~ of secrecy** un alone di mistero; **under the ~ of sth** *fig* con il pretesto di qc; **to draw a ~**

over sth *fig* stendere un velo pietoso su qc **II.** *vt* velare; (*disguise*) dissimulare; **to ~ one's face** velarsi il viso; **to be ~ed in secrecy** essere avvolto dal mistero; **the mist ~ed the mountains** *fig, liter* la nebbia avvolgeva i monti
veiled *adj* **1.** (*wearing a veil*) velato, -a **2.** (*indirect, concealed*) velato, -a; **thinly ~** a malapena dissimulato
vein [veɪn] *n* **1.** ANAT, GEO vena *f;* BOT nervatura *f;* **a quartz ~** una vena di quarzo; **a ~ of madness** *fig* una vena di pazzia **2.** (*style*) tono *m;* **to talk in a more serious ~** parlare in tono più serio; **in** (**a**) **similar ~** sullo stesso filone; **in the ~ of sth** sul filone di qc
veined *adj* **1.** (*stone*) venato, -a **2.** (*leaf*) nervato, -a
velar ['viː·lə] **I.** *adj* LING velare **II.** *n* LING velare *f*
Velcro® ['vel·kroʊ] *n* Velcro® *m*
veld *n*, **veldt** [velt] *n* veld *m inv* (*savana tipica del Sudafrica*)
velocity [və·'lɑː·sə·ti] <-ies> *n form* velocità *f;* **at the ~ of** a una velocità di; **sound/light ~** velocità del suono/della luce
velvet ['vel·vɪt] **I.** *n* velluto *m* **II.** *adj* **1.** (*made of velvet*) di velluto **2.** *fig* (*smooth*) vellutato, -a
velveteen [ˌvel·vɪ·'tiːn] *n* vellutino *n*
velvety ['vel·və·ti] *adj fig* vellutato, -a
venal ['viː·nəl] *adj* **1.** (*corrupt*) corrotto, -a **2.** (*that can be purchased*) venale
venality [vɪ·'næ·lə·ti] *n* **1.** (*corruptibility*) venalità *f* **2.** (*corruption*) corruzione *f*
vend [vend] *vt* vendere
vendetta [ven·'de·tə] *n* vendetta *f*
vending machine *n* distributore *m* automatico
vendor ['ven·də] *n* venditore, -trice *m, f*
veneer [və·'nɪr] **I.** *n* **1.** impiallacciatura *f* **2.** *fig* parvenza *f* **II.** *vt* impiallacciare
venerable ['ve·nə·rə·bl] *adj* (*person, tradition*) venerabile; **~ ruins** rovine *fpl* millenarie
venerate ['ve·nə·reɪt] *vt* venerare
veneration [ˌve·nə·'reɪ·ʃen] *n* venerazione *f;* **to hold sb in ~** venerare qu
venereal [və·'nɪ·ri·əl] *adj* MED venereo, -a; **~ disease** malattia *f* venerea
venetian blind [və·ˌniː·ʃən·'blaɪnd] *n* veneziana *f*
Venezuela [ˌve·nə·'zweɪ·lə] *n* Venezuela *m*
Venezuelan I. *adj* venezuelano, -a **II.** *n* venezuelano, -a *m, f*
vengeance ['ven·dʒənts] *n* vendetta *f;* **to take ~ (up)on sb** vendicarsi di qu; **with a ~** a più non posso
venial ['viː·ni·əl] *adj form* veniale
venial sin *n* peccato *m* veniale
venison ['ve·nɪ·sən] *n* (carne *f* di) cervo *m*
venom ['ve·nəm] *n* veleno *m; fig* cattiveria *f*
venomous ['ve·nə·məs] *adj* velenoso, -a; (*malicious*) cattivo, -a
venous ['viː·nəs] *adj* venoso, -a
vent[1] [vent] **I.** *n* **1.** (*outlet for gas*) sfiato *m;* **air ~** presa *f* d'aria **2.** GEO camino *m* **3.** (*release*

of feelings) **to give ~ to sth** sfogare qc; **to give ~ to one's feelings** sfogarsi **II.** *vt* sfogare; **to ~ one's anger on sb** sfogare la propria rabbia su qu

vent² [vent] *n* FASHION spacco *m*

ventilate ['ven·tə·leɪt] *vt* **1.** (*oxygenate a space*) arieggiare; **artificially ~d** MED in respirazione assistita **2.** (*give utterance to, verbalize*) esprimere

ventilation [ˌven·tə·'leɪ·ʃən] *n* aerazione *f*

ventilation duct *n* condotto *m* di aerazione

ventilator ['ven·tə·leɪ·tə˞] *n* **1.** (*device*) ventilatore *m* **2.** MED respiratore *m*

ventricle ['ven·trɪ·kl] *n* ventricolo *m*

ventriloquist [ven·'trɪ·lək·wɪst] *n* ventriloquo, -a *m, f*

venture ['ven·tʃə˞] **I.** *n* **1.** (*endeavor*) impresa *f* **2.** COM iniziativa *f* imprenditoriale; **joint ~** joint venture *f inv* **II.** *vt* **1.** (*dare*) **to ~ to do sth** azzardarsi a fare qc; **may I ~ a suggestion?** posso azzardare un suggerimento? **2.** (*dare to express: an opinion*) azzardare **3.** (*put at risk, endanger*) rischiare; **to ~ sth (on sth)** mettere a rischio qc (per qc) ▸ **nothing ~d, nothing gained** *prov* chi non risica non rosica *prov* **III.** *vi* avventurarsi

◆**venture out** *vi* avventurarsi fuori

venture capital *n* FIN capitale *m* di rischio

venturesome ['ven·tʃə˞·səm] *adj form* **1.** (*adventurous*) avventuroso, -a **2.** (*risky, not safe*) rischioso, -a

venue ['ven·juː] *n* sede *f* (dell'evento)

Venus ['viː·nəs] *n* **1.** ASTRON Venere *m* **2.** (*in mythology*) Venere *f*

veracious [və·'reɪ·ʃəs] *adj form* **1.** (*honest*) sincero, -a **2.** (*accurate and precise*) veridico, -a

veracity [və·'ræ·sə·ti] *n* **1.** (*truthfulness*) sincerità *f* **2.** (*accuracy*) veridicità *f*

veranda *n*, **verandah** [və·'ræn·də] *n* veranda *f*

verb [vɜːrb] *n* verbo *m;* **intransitive/transitive ~** verbo intransitivo/transitivo

verbal ['vɜːr·bəl] *adj* **1.** (*oral, unwritten*) verbale; **~ agreement** accordo *m* verbale **2.** (*word for word: translation*) letterale

verbalize ['vɜːr·bə·laɪz] *vt* verbalizzare

verbally *adv* verbalmente

verbatim [və˞·'beɪ·tɪm] **I.** *adj* letterale **II.** *adv* letteralmente

verbiage ['vɜːr·bɪdʒ] *n* verbalismo *m*

verbose [və˞·'boʊs] *adj* verboso, -a; (*speech*) prolisso, -a

verbosity [və˞·'bɑː·sə·ti] *n* verbosità *f*

verdant ['vɜːr·dənt] *adj liter* verdeggiante

verdict ['vɜːr·dɪkt] *n* **1.** LAW verdetto *m;* **~ of guilty/not guilty** verdetto di colpevolezza/innocenza; **to bring in** [*o* **to return**] **a ~** emettere il verdetto **2.** (*opinion*) parere *m;* **to give a ~ on sth/sb** dire la propria su qc/qu; **what is your ~?** che cosa ne pensi?

verdigris ['vɜːr·dɪ·griːs] *n* verderame *m*

verge [vɜːrdʒ] *n* **1.** (*physical edge, margin*)

margine *m* **2.** *fig* (*brink*) orlo *m;* **to be on the ~ of ...** essere sull'orlo di ...; **to be on the ~ of despair** essere sull'orlo della disperazione; **to be on the ~ of doing sth** essere sul punto di fare qc; **to be on the ~ of tears** essere sul punto di piangere

◆**verge on** *vt* rasentare; **to ~ the ridiculous** rasentare il ridicolo; **she is verging on fifty** è sulla cinquantina

verger ['vɜːr·dʒə˞] *n* sagrestano *m*

verifiable ['ve·rə·faɪ·ə·bl] *adj* verificabile

verification [ˌve·rə·fɪ·'keɪ·ʃən] *n* **1.** (*checking*) verifica *f* **2.** (*confirmation*) riscontro *m*

verify ['ve·rə·faɪ] <-ie-> *vt* **1.** (*corroborate*) corroborare **2.** (*authenticate*) verificare

verisimilitude [ˌve·rə·sə·'mɪ·lə·tuːd] *n* verosimiglianza *f*

veritable ['ve·rə·tə·bl] *adj* autentico, -a

vermicelli [ˌvɜːr·mə·'tʃe·li] *n* vermicelli *mpl*

vermicide ['vɜːr·mə·saɪd] *n* vermicida *m*

vermiform ['vɜːr·mə·fɔːrm] *adj* vermiforme

vermilion [və˞·'mɪl·jən], **vermillion I.** *n* vermiglio *m* **II.** *adj* vermiglio *inv*

vermin ['vɜːr·mɪn] *n* **1.** *pl* (*animals*) animali *mpl* nocivi **2.** *pej* (*people*) parassiti *mpl*

verminous *adj* (*disease*) causato, -a da animali nocivi

Vermont *n* Vermont *m*

vermouth [və˞·'muːθ] *n* vermut *m inv*

vernacular [və˞·'næk·jə·lə˞] *n* vernacolo *m*

vernal equinox [ˌvɜːr·nəl·'iː·kwɪ·nɑːks] <-es> *n* equinozio *m* di primavera

versatile ['vɜːr·sə·təl] *adj* versatile

versatility [ˌvɜːr·sə·'tɪ·lə·ti] *n* versatilità *f*

verse [vɜːrs] *n* **1.** LIT verso *m* **2.** MUS strofa *f* **3.** REL versetto *m*

versed *adj* **to be** (**well**) **~ in sth** essere (molto) versato, -a in qc

versify ['vɜːr·sə·faɪ] <-ie-> **I.** *vi* verseggiare **II.** *vt* mettere in versi

version ['vɜːr·ʒən] *n* versione *f*

verso ['vɜːr·soʊ] *n form* verso *m*

versus ['vɜːr·səs] *prep* **1.** (*in comparison*) in contrapposizione a **2.** SPORTS, LAW contro

vertebra ['vɜːr·tə·brə] <-ae> *n* vertebra *f*

vertebral ['vɜːr·tə·brəl] *adj* vertebrale

vertebrate ['vɜːr·tə·brɪt] **I.** *n* vertebrato *m* **II.** *adj* vertebrato, -a

vertex ['vɜːr·teks] <-es *o* -tices> *n* vertice *m*

vertical ['vɜːr·tə·kəl] *adj* verticale; **~ drop** parete *f* verticale

vertiginous [və˞·'tɪ·dʒə·nəs] *adj form* vertiginoso, -a

vertigo ['vɜːr·tə·goʊ] *n* vertigini *fpl*

verve [vɜːrv] *n* verve *f inv;* **with ~** con verve

very ['ve·ri] **I.** *adv* **1.** (*extremely*) molto; **~ much** moltissimo; **not ~ much** non molto; **to feel ~ much at home** sentirsi come a casa; **I am ~, ~ sorry** sono dispiaciutissimo **2.** (*expression of emphasis*) **the ~ best** il migliore; **the ~ first** il primissimo; **at the ~ most** al massimo; **at the ~ least** come minimo; **the ~ next day** proprio il giorno dopo; **the ~**

V

same proprio lo stesso ▶ ~ **well** molto bene; **it's all ~ fine ...**, **but ...** va benissimo ..., però ... **II.** *adj* **at the ~ bottom** proprio in fondo; **the ~ fact** il fatto stesso; **the ~ man we need** proprio l'uomo che fa per noi

Very light *n* bengala *m inv*

Very pistol *n* pistola *f* lanciarazzi

vespers ['ves·pə·z] *npl* REL (*evensong*) vespro *m*

vessel ['ve·səl] *n* **1.** (*any kind of boat*) imbarcazione *f* **2.** (*container*) recipiente *m* **3.** ANAT, BOT vaso *m*

vest¹ [vest] *n* panciotto *m;* **bullet-proof ~** giubbotto *m* antiproiettile

vest² [vest] *vt* **to ~ sb with sth** investire qu di qc; **to ~ sth in sb** conferire qc a qu; **to ~ one's hopes in sb/sth** riporre le proprie speranze in qu/qc; **~ed interests** interessi *mpl* acquisiti

vestibule ['ves·tə·bju:l] *n* vestibolo *m*

vestige ['ves·tɪdʒ] *n form* vestigio *m;* **a ~ of hope** un barlume *m* di speranza; **the last ~s of sth** le ultime vestigia di qc

vestments ['vest·mənts] *npl* paramenti *m* sacri *pl*

vestry ['ves·tri] <-ies> *n* sagrestia *f*

vet¹ [vet] *inf* **I.** *n* (*animal doctor*) veterinario, -a *m, f* **II.** *vt* <-tt-> **1.** (*examine carefully*) esaminare **2.** (*screen*) passare al vaglio

vet² [vet] *n a. fig, inf* MIL veterano, -a *m, f*

vetch [vetʃ] <-es> *n* veccia *f*

veteran ['ve·ţə·ən] **I.** *n* **1.** MIL reduce *mf* **2.** *fig* veterano, -a *m, f* **II.** *adj* **1.** MIL dei reduci **2.** *fig* veterano, -a

Veterans Day *n* giornata *f* dei reduci e dei caduti

> **i** Il **Veterans Day**, l'11 novembre, fu originariamente istituito in memoria dell'armistizio del 1918 tra la Germania e gli Stati Uniti d'America. Oggi, con questo giorno festivo si vuole rendere onore a tutti i veterani delle guerre americane.

veterinarian [ˌve·tə·rɪ·'ne·ri·ən] *n* veterinario, -a *m, f*

veterinary ['ve·tə·rɪ·ne·ri] *adj* veterinario, -a; **~ surgeon** medico *m* veterinario

veto ['vi:·ţoʊ] **I.** *n* <-es> veto *m;* **to have a ~ over sth** avere il diritto di veto su qc **II.** *vt* <vetoed> **1.** (*exercise a veto against*) opporre il veto a **2.** (*forbid*) proibire

vex [veks] *vt* **1.** (*cause trouble for*) irritare **2.** (*upset*) affliggere

vexation [vek·'seɪ·ʃən] *n* irritazione *f;* **to be a ~ to sb** essere un cruccio per qu

vexatious [vek·'seɪ·ʃəs] *adj* irritante

VHF [ˌvi:·eɪtʃ·'ef] *abbr of* **very high frequency** VHF

VI *n abbr of* **Virgin Islands** Isole *fpl* Vergini

via ['vaɪ·ə] *prep* per; **~ Denver** passando per Denver; **~ airmail** (per) via aerea

viability [ˌvaɪ·ə·'bɪ·lə·ti] *n* attuabilità *f*

viable ['vaɪ·ə·bl] *adj* attuabile

viaduct ['vaɪ·ə·dʌkt] *n* viadotto *m*

vibe [vaɪb] *n sl* atmosfera *f;* **good/bad ~s** buone/cattive vibrazioni

vibrant ['vaɪ·brənt] *adj* **1.** (*lively*) vivace **2.** (*resonant*) vibrante

vibrate ['vaɪ·breɪt] **I.** *vi* **1.** (*shake*) vibrare; **to ~ with anger** fremere per l'ira **2.** (*resonate*) risuonare **II.** *vt* fare vibrare

vibration [vaɪ·'breɪ·ʃən] *n* vibrazione *f*

vibrator ['vaɪ·breɪ·ţə] *n* TECH vibromassaggiatore *m; (for sexual stimulation)* vibratore *m*

vicar ['vɪ·kə] *n* REL pastore *m*

vicarage ['vɪ·kə·rɪdʒ] *n* canonica *f*

vicarious [vɪ·'ke·ri·əs] *adj* (*thrill*) indiretto, -a; (*authority*) delegato, -a

vice [vaɪs] *n* vizio *m;* **the ~ squad** la buoncostume *f inv*

vice chairman [ˌvaɪs·'tʃer·mən] <-men> *n* vicepresidente *m*

vice chancellor *n* UNIV vicerettore *m*

vice president *n* vicepresidente *m*

vice versa [ˌvaɪ·sə·'vɜːr·sə] *adv* viceversa

vicinity [və·'sɪ·nə·ti] <-ies> *n* vicinanze *fpl;* **in the ~ of ...** nelle vicinanze di ...

vicious ['vɪ·ʃəs] *adj* **1.** (*malicious*) malvagio, -a; (*gossip*) maligno, -a **2.** (*cruel, violent: attack*) brutale **3.** (*able to cause pain: dog*) cattivo, -a **4.** (*extremely powerful: wind*) violento, -a

vicious circle *n* circolo *m* vizioso

vicissitudes [vɪ·'sɪ·sə·tu:dz] *n form pl* vicissitudini *fpl;* **the ~s of life** le alterne vicende della vita

victim ['vɪk·tɪm] *n* vittima *f;* **to be the ~ of sth** essere vittima di qc ▶ **to fall ~ to sb/sth** cadere vittima di qu/qc

victimize ['vɪk·tə·maɪz] *vt* perseguitare; **to be ~d by the media** essere perseguitato dalla stampa

victor ['vɪk·tə] *n* vincitore, -trice *m, f*

Victorian [vɪk·'tɔː·ri·ən] **I.** *adj* vittoriano, -a **II.** *n* vittoriano, -a *m, f*

victorious [vɪk·'tɔː·ri·əs] *adj* vittorioso, -a; **~ team** squadra *f* vincitrice; **to emerge ~** risultare vittorioso

victory ['vɪk·tə·ri] <-ies> *n* vittoria *f;* **to clinch a ~ (over sb)** riportare una victoria (su qu); **to win a ~ (in sth)** conseguire una vittoria (in qc)

victuals ['vɪ·təlz] *n pl, a. iron* vettovaglie *fpl*

videlicet [vɪ·'de·lə·sɪt] *adv form* vale a dire

video ['vɪ·di·oʊ] **I.** *n* **1.** video *m inv;* **to come out on ~** uscire in video **2.** (*tape*) videocassetta *f;* **blank ~** videocassetta vergine **II.** *vt* registrare

video camera *n* videocamera *f*

videocassette *n* videocassetta *f*

videoconference *n* videoconferenza *f*

video game *n* videogioco *m*

videophone *n* videotelefono *m*

video recorder *n* videoregistratore *m*

video surveillance *n* videosorveglianza *f*

videotape **I.** *n* videocassetta *f* **II.** *vt* registrare

vie [vaɪ] <vying> *vi* **to ~ (with sb) for sth**

competere (con qu) per qc
Vienna [vi·'e·nə] *n* Vienna *f*
Viennese [ˌviː·ə·'niːz] I. *n inv* viennese *mf*
II. *adj* viennese
Vietcong [ˌviː·et·'kɑːŋ] *n inv* Vietcong *m inv*
Vietnam [ˌviː·et·'nɑːm] *n* Vietnam *m*
Vietnamese [vi·ˌet·nə·'miːz] I. *adj* vietnamita
II. *n* 1.(*person*) vietnamita *mf* 2. LING vietnamita *m*
view [vjuː] I. *n* 1.(*opinion*) parere *m,* opinione *f;* **point of** ~ punto *m* di vista; **exchange of** ~s scambio *m* di opinioni; **conflicting** ~s pareri *mpl* contrastanti; **to express a** ~ esprimere un parere; **to hold strong** ~s **about sth** credere fermamente in qc; **to share a** ~ condividere un'opinione; **in her** ~ ... a suo modo di vedere ... 2.(*sight*) vista *f;* **panoramic** ~ vista panoramica; **to block sb's** ~ impedire la visuale a qu; **to come into** ~ apparire; **to disappear from** ~ sparire; **to keep sb/sth in** ~ non perdere di vista qu/qc 3.(*picture*) veduta *f* ▶ **to take a <u>dim</u>** ~ **of sth** non vedere di buon occhio qc; **to <u>have</u> sth in** ~ avere in mente qc; **<u>in</u>** ~ **of sth** considerato qc; **in** ~ **of what you've said** ... considerato quello che hai detto ...; **to be <u>on</u>** ~ essere in mostra; **to be on** ~ **to the public** essere esposto al pubblico; **<u>with</u> a** ~ **to doing sth** con l'intenzione di fare qc; **<u>with</u> this in** ~ a questo scopo II. *vt* 1.(*consider*) considerare; **to** ~ **sth from a different angle** considerare qc da un altro punto di vista; **to** ~ **sth with suspicion** guardare qc con sospetto 2.(*watch*) guardare 3.(*take a look at*) vedere
viewer *n* 1.(*person*) spettatore, -trice *m, f* 2.(*device*) visore *m* 3. COMPUT visualizzatore *m*
viewfinder ['vjuː·ˌfaɪn·dər] *n* mirino *m*
viewing *n* **private** ~ (*of exhibition*) vernissage *m inv;* (*of film*) proiezione *f* privata
viewpoint ['vjuː·pɔɪnt] *n* 1.(*point of view*) punto *m* di vista 2.(*vista point*) belvedere *m inv*
vigil ['vɪ·dʒəl] *n* veglia *f;* **to keep** ~ vegliare; **to hold a** ~ organizzare una veglia (di protesta)
vigilance ['vɪ·dʒɪ·ləns] *n* vigilanza *f;* **to relax** ~ abbassare la guardia
vigilant ['vɪ·dʒɪ·lənt] *adj* vigile
vignette [vɪ·'njet] *n* vignetta *f*
vigor ['vɪ·gər] *n* vigore *m*
vigorous ['vɪ·gə·rəs] *adj* 1.(*energetic*) energico, -a 2.(*healthy*) vigoroso, -a
vile [vaɪl] *adj* 1.(*disgusting, shameful*) ignobile 2. *inf* (*very bad*) schifoso, -a; ~ **mood** pessimo umore; **to be** ~ **to sb** comportarsi malissimo nei confronti di qu; **to smell** ~ puzzare
vilify ['vɪ·lə·faɪ] <-ie-> *vt form* diffamare
village ['vɪ·lɪdʒ] I. *n* 1.(*small settlement*) paese *m* 2. + *pl/sing vb* (*populace*) paese *m* II. *adj* del paese
village idiot *n* scemo *m* del villaggio
villager ['vɪ·lə·dʒər] *n* paesano, -a *m, f*
villain ['vɪ·lən] *n* 1.(*evil person*) mascal-

zone *m;* **small-time** ~ delinquente *mf* di mezza tacca 2.(*in book, film*) cattivo *m;* **to cast sb as a** ~ affidare a qu il ruolo del cattivo ▶ **the** ~ **of the <u>piece</u>** *inf* il cattivo della situazione
villainous [vɪ·lə·nəs] *adj* infame
villainy ['vɪ·lə·ni] *n* scelleratezza *f*
vim [vɪm] *n* energia *f*
VIN *n abbr of* **vehicle identification number** numero *m* (identificativo) di telaio
vinaigrette [ˌvɪ·nə·'gret] *n* vinaigrette *f inv*
vindicate ['vɪn·də·keɪt] *vt* 1.(*justify*) giustificare 2.(*support*) dare ragione a 3.(*clear of blame, suspicion*) scagionare
vindication [ˌvɪn·də·'keɪ·ʃən] *n* 1.(*justification*) giustificazione *f* 2.(*act of clearing blame*) scagionamento *m*
vindictive [vɪn·'dɪk·tɪv] *adj* vendicativo, -a
vine [vaɪn] *n* 1.(*grape plant*) vite *f* 2.(*climbing type*) rampicante *m*
vinegar ['vɪ·nə·gər] *n* aceto *m*
vineyard ['vɪn·jərd] *n* vigneto *m,* vigna *f*
vintage ['vɪn·ˌtɪdʒ] I. *n* (*harvest*) vendemmia *f;* (*year*) annata *f* II. *adj* 1. COMPUT d'annata 2.(*classic*) classico, -a; ~ **music of the sixties** classici *mpl* della musica anni Sessanta 3. AUTO d'epoca
vintner ['vɪnt·nər] *n* vinaio, -a *m, f*
vinyl ['vaɪ·nəl] I. *n* vinile *m* II. *adj* di vinile
viola¹ [vi·'oʊ·lə] *n* MUS viola *f*
viola² ['viː·ə·lə] *n* BOT viola *f*
violate ['vaɪ·ə·leɪt] *vt* 1.(*law*) violare; **to** ~ **a cease-fire agreement** violare un cessate il fuoco 2.(*tomb*) profanare; **to** ~ **sb's privacy** violare la privacy di qu
violation [ˌvaɪ·ə·'leɪ·ʃən] *n* violazione *f;* **traffic** ~ violazione del codice stradale
violence ['vaɪ·ə·ləns] *n* violenza *f*
violent ['vaɪ·ə·lənt] *adj* violento, -a
violet ['vaɪ·ə·lɪt] I. *n* 1. BOT violetta *f* 2.(*color*) violetto *m* II. *adj* violetto, -a
violin [ˌvaɪ·ə·'lɪn] *n* MUS violino *m*
violinist [vaɪ·ə·'lɪ·nɪst] *n* MUS violinista *mf*
violoncellist [ˌviː·ə·lɑːn·'tʃe·lɪst] *n* MUS violoncellista *mf*
violoncello [ˌviː·ə·lɑːn·'tʃe·loʊ] *n* violoncello *m*
VIP [ˌviː·aɪ·'piː] *s.* **very important person** VIP
viper ['vaɪ·pər] *n a. fig* vipera *f*
virgin ['vɜːr·dʒɪn] *n* vergine *f;* **the Blessed Virgin** la Beata Vergine
virginal ['vɜːr·dʒɪ·nəl] *n* verginale
virgin forest *n* foresta *f* vergine
Virginia [və·'dʒɪ·njə] *n* Virginia *f*
Virgin Islands *n* Isole *fpl* Vergini
virginity [və·'dʒɪ·nə·ti] *n* verginità *f;* **to lose one's** ~ perdere la verginità
Virgo ['vɜːr·goʊ] *n* Vergine *f*
virile ['vɪ·rəl] *adj* virile
virility [və·'rɪ·lə·ti] *n* 1.(*sexual vigor*) virilità *f* 2.(*forcefulness*) forza *f*
virology [vaɪ·'rɑː·lə·dʒi] *n* virologia *f*
virtual ['vɜːr·tʃu·əl] *adj* virtuale; **to be a** ~

V

unknown essere praticamente sconosciuto; **a ~ certainty** praticamente una certezza

virtually *adv* praticamente

virtual reality *n* realtà *f* virtuale

virtue ['vɜːr·tʃuː] *n* **1.**(*good moral quality*) virtù *f* **2.**(*advantage, benefit*) vantaggio *m* ▶**to make a ~ of necessity** fare di necessità virtù; **by ~ of** *form* in virtù di

virtuosity [ˌvɜːr·tʃuˈɑː·sə·ti] *n form* virtuosismo *m*

virtuoso [ˌvɜːr·tʃuˈoʊ·soʊ] <-s *o* -osi> I. *n* virtuoso, -a *m, f* II. *adj* virtuosistico, -a

virtuous ['vɜːr·tʃu·əs] *adj* virtuoso, -a

virulence ['vɪr·jə·lənts] *n* virulenza *f*

virulent ['vɪr·jə·lənt] *adj* **1.** MED virulento, -a **2.** *form* (*hateful and fierce*) violento, -a

virus ['vaɪ·ə·rəs] <-es> *n* COMPUT, MED virus *m inv*

visa ['viː·zə] I. *n* visto *m* II. *adj* del visto

vis-à-vis [ˌviː·zəˈviː] *prep* riguardo a; (*compared to*) in confronto a

viscera ['vɪ·sə·rə] *npl* viscere *fpl*

viscose ['vɪs·koʊs] *n* viscosa *f*

viscosity [vɪˈskɑː·sə·ti] *n* viscosità *f*

viscount ['vaɪ·kaʊnt] *n* visconte *m*

viscountess ['vaɪ·kaʊn·tɪs] *n* viscontessa *f*

viscous ['vɪs·kəs] *adj* viscoso, -a

vise [vaɪs] *n* morsa *f*

visibility [ˌvɪ·zəˈbɪ·lə·ti] *n* visibilità *f;* **poor ~** scarsa visibilità

visible ['vɪ·zə·bl] *adj* visibile; **to be barely ~** essere appena visibile

vision ['vɪ·ʒən] *n* **1.**(*sight*) vista *f;* **blurred ~** vista offuscata **2.** *a.* REL (*mental image*) visione *f* **3.** *fig* (*beautiful sight*) apparizione *f*

visionary ['vɪ·ʒə·ne·ri] I. *n* visionario, -a *m, f* II. *adj* visionario, -a

visit ['vɪ·zɪt] I. *n* visita *f;* **to have a ~ from sb** ricevere una visita da qu; **to pay a ~ to sb** andare a trovare qu II. *vt* visitare III. *vi* fare una visita

visitation [ˌvɪ·zəˈteɪ·ʃən] *n* **1.**(*act of visiting*) visita *f* **2.** *iron* (*official visit*) visita *f* ufficiale **3.**(*parent's right*) diritto *m* di visita **4.** REL apparizione *f*

visiting hours *npl* orario *m* delle visite

visiting professor *n* visiting professor *m inv*

visitor ['vɪ·zɪ·tə˞] *n* visitatore, -trice *m, f;* **we've got ~s** abbiamo visite; **~s' book** registro *m* dei visitatori

visor ['vaɪ·zə˞] *n* visiera *f*

vista ['vɪs·tə] *n* **1.**(*splendid view*) vista *f* **2.** *fig* prospettiva *f;* **to open up a ~** aprire una prospettiva

visual ['vɪ·ʒuəl] *adj* visivo, -a; **~ memory** memoria *f* visiva; **~ aid** supporto *m* visivo

visualize ['vɪ·ʒu·ə·laɪz] *vt* immaginare

vital ['vaɪ·təl] *adj* vitale; **~ ingredient** ingrediente *m* essenziale; **~ organs** organi *mpl* vitali; **~ part** parte *f* cruciale; **~ statistics** statistiche *fpl* demografiche; **it is ~ to do ...** è essenziale fare ...

vitality [vaɪˈtæ·lə·ti] *n* vitalità *f*

vitalize ['vaɪ·tə·laɪz] *vt* rivitalizzare

vitamin ['vaɪ·tə·mɪn] *n* vitamina *f*

vitamin deficiency *n* avitaminosi *f inv*

vitreous ['vɪ·tri·əs] *adj* **1.**(*china, enamel*) vetrificato, -a; (*rock*) vetroso, -a **2.** ANAT vitreo, -a

vitrify ['vɪ·trə·faɪ] <-ie-> I. *vt* vetrificare II. *vi* vetrificarsi

vitriol ['vɪ·tri·əl] *n* vetriolo *m*

vitriolic [ˌvɪ·triˈɑː·lɪk] *adj* al vetriolo

vituperate [vaɪˈtuː·pə·reɪt] *form* I. *vt* ingiuriare II. *vi* ingiuriare

vituperation [vaɪˌtuː·pəˈreɪ·ʃən] *n form* vituperio *m*

vivacious [vɪˈveɪ·ʃəs] *adj* vivace

vivacity [vɪˈvæ·sə·ti] *n* vivacità *f*

vivarium [vaɪˈve·ri·əm] <-s *o* vivaria> *n* vivaio *m*

viva voce [ˌvaɪ·vəˈvoʊ·siː] I. *n* esame *m* orale II. *adj* orale III. *adv* a voce

vivid ['vɪ·vɪd] *adj* vivido, -a; **~ imagination** fervida immaginazione

viviparous [vaɪˈvɪ·pə·rəs] *adj* viviparo, -a

vivisect ['vɪ·və·sekt] *vt* vivisezionare

vivisection [ˌvɪ·vəˈsek·ʃən] *n* vivisezione *f*

vixen ['vɪk·sən] *n* **1.** ZOOL volpe *f* femmina **2.** *pej* (*woman*) arpia *f*

viz. [vɪz] *adv abbr of* **videlicet** (**namely**) vale a dire

V-J Day *abbr of* **Victory over Japan Day** V-J Day (*15 agosto, giorno della vittoria in Giappone; la resa del Giappone durante la II guerra mondiale*)

vocabulary [voʊˈkæb·jə·le·ri] *n* vocabolario *m;* **limited ~** vocabolario limitato; **to widen one's ~** ampliare il proprio vocabolario; **the word 'politeness' isn't in his ~** *iron* la parola 'cortesia' non fa parte del suo vocabolario

vocal ['voʊ·kəl] I. *adj* **1.**(*of the voice*) vocal; **~ music** musica *f* vocale **2.**(*outspoken*) veemente; **a ~ minority** una minoranza che si fa sentire; **to be ~** (**about sth**) non aver peli sulla lingua (a proposito di qc) II. *n* voce *f;* **lead ~** voce solista; **to be on ~s** cantare

vocal cords *n pl* corde *fpl* vocali

vocalist ['voʊ·kə·lɪst] *n* cantante *mf*

vocalize ['voʊ·kə·laɪz] I. *vi* fare vocalizzi II. *vt* vocalizzare

vocation [voʊˈkeɪ·ʃən] *n* vocazione *f;* **to miss one's ~** sbagliare mestiere

vocational [voʊˈkeɪ·ʃə·nəl] *adj* professionale; **~ counseling** orientamento *m* professionale; **~ training** formazione *f* professionale

vociferate [voʊˈsɪ·fə·reɪt] I. *vi* urlare II. *vt* urlare

vociferation [voʊˌsɪ·fəˈreɪ·ʃən] *n form* clamore *m*

vociferous [voʊˈsɪ·fə·rəs] *adj* veemente

vogue [voʊg] *n* voga *f* ▶**in ~** in voga; **to be back in ~** essere di nuovo in voga; **no longer in ~** non più in voga

voice [vɔɪs] I. *n* voce *f;* **in a loud ~** a voce alta;

to raise/lower one's ~ alzare/abbassare la voce; **to lose one's** ~ perdere la voce; **to listen to the** ~ **of reason** acoltare la voce della ragione; **to make one's** ~ **heard** farsi sentire; **with one** ~ all'unisono; **to give** ~ **to sth** esprimere qc; **the** ~ **within sb** la voce della coscienza (di qu) **II.** *vt* esprimere

voice box <-es> *n inf* laringe *f*

voiced *adj* sonoro, -a

voiceless ['vɔɪs·ləs] *adj* **1.** LING sordo, -a **2.** *liter* muto, -a

voice-over *n* TV, CINE voce *f* fuoricampo

void [vɔɪd] **I.** *n a. fig* vuoto *m;* **to fill the** ~ colmare il vuoto **II.** *adj* nullo, -a; ~ **contract** contratto nullo; **to be** ~ **of sth** mancare di qc **III.** *vt* annullare

vol. *abbr of* **volume** vol.

volatile ['va·lə·təl] *adj* **1.** CHEM, COMPUT volatile **2.** (*situation*) instabile; (*person*) volubile

volcanic [va·l·'kæ·nɪk] *adj* vulcanico, -a

volcano [va·l·'keɪ·noʊ] <-(e)s> *n* vulcano *m*

vole [voʊl] *n* arvicola *f* dei campi

volition [voʊ·'lɪ·ʃən] *n form* volontà *f;* **to do sth** (**out**) **of one's own** ~ fare qc di spontanea volontà

volley ['va·li] **I.** *n* **1.** (*salvo*) salva *f* **2.** (*onslaught*) raffica *f;* **a** ~ **of enquiries/insults** una raffica di domande/insulti **3.** SPORTS volée *f inv* **II.** *vi* SPORTS fare una volée **III.** *vt* **to** ~ **a ball** colpire la palla

volleyball ['va·li·bɔːl] *n* pallavolo *f*

volt [voʊlt] *n* volt *m inv*

voltage ['voʊl·t̬ɪdʒ] *n* tensione *f,* voltaggio *m*

voltage detector *n* ELEC rivelatore *m* di tensione

voltage drop *n* ELEC caduta *f* di tensione

volte-face [ˌva·lt·'faːs] *n* voltafaccia *m inv*

voluble ['va·l·jə·bl] *adj form* loquace

volume ['va·l·juːm] *n* (*all senses*) volume *m;* ~ **of sales** COM volume delle vendite; **to turn the** ~ **up/down** alzare/abbassare il volume ▶ **to speak** ~**s for sth** dirla lunga su qc

volume control, volume regulator *n* (controllo *m* del) volume

volume discount *n* sconto *m* a volume

voluminous [və·'luː·mə·nəs] *adj form* **1.** (*extensive*) dettagliato, -a **2.** (*very large*) voluminoso, -a

voluntary ['va·lən·te·ri] *adj* volontario, -a

volunteer [ˌva·lən·'tɪr] **I.** *n* volontario, -a *m, f* **II.** *vt* **to** ~ **oneself for sth** offrirsi volontario per qc; **to** ~ **information** dare informazioni spontaneamente **III.** *vi* offrirsi volontario **IV.** *adj* volontario, -a

voluptuous [və·'lʌp·tʃu·əs] *adj* **1.** (*sexually appealing*) sensuale **2.** (*epicurean*) voluttuoso, -a

volute [və·'luːt] *n* ARCHIT voluta *f*

vomit ['va·mɪt] **I.** *vi* vomitare; **it makes me want to** ~ *a. fig* mi fa vomitare **II.** *vt* vomitare **III.** *n* vomito *m*

voodoo ['vuː·duː] *n* vudù *m inv*

voracious [vɔː·'reɪ·ʃəs] *adj* vorace

voracity [vɔː·'ræ·sə·ti] *n* voracità *f*

vortex ['vɔːr·teks] <-es *o* vortices> *n* vortice *m;* ~ **of emotion** turbine *m* di emozioni

vote [voʊt] **I.** *vi* **1.** (*elect*) votare; **to** ~ **for/against sb/sth** votare per/contro qu/qc **2.** (*formally decide*) **to** ~ **on sth** mettere qc ai voti **II.** *vt* **1.** (*elect*) eleggere (per votazione) **2.** (*propose*) **to** ~ **that ...** proporre che ... +*subj* **3.** (*declare*) considerare **III.** *n* **1.** (*formally made choice*) voto *m* **2.** (*election*) votazione *f;* **to put sth to the** ~ mettere qc ai voti **3.** (*right to elect*) **to have the** ~ avere diritto di voto

◆ **vote down** *vt* respingere (per votazione)

◆ **vote in** *vt* eleggere (per votazione)

◆ **vote on** *vt* approvare (per votazione)

◆ **vote out** *vt* **to vote sb out** (**of sth**) non rieleggere qu (a qc)

voter *n* votante *mf*

voting I. *adj* di voto **II.** *n* votazione *f,* voto *m*

voting booth <-es> *n* cabina *f* elettorale

voting machine *n* macchina *f* contavoti

vouch [vaʊtʃ] **I.** *vi* **to** ~ **for sth/sb** rispondere di qc/qu **II.** *vt* **to** ~ **that ...** garantire che ...

voucher ['vaʊ·tʃɚ] *n* **1.** (*coupon*) buono *m,* coupon *m inv* **2.** (*receipt*) tagliando *m*

vouchsafe [ˌvaʊtʃ·'seɪf] *vt form* **to** ~ (**sb**) **sth** concedere qc (a qu); **to** ~ **to do sth** assicurare di fare qc

vow [vaʊ] **I.** *vt* giurare; **to** ~ **chastity** fare voto di castità **II.** *n* **to take the** ~**s** prendere i voti

vowel ['vaʊ·əl] *n* vocale *f*

voyage ['vɔɪ·ɪdʒ] **I.** *n* viaggio (per mare) *m* **II.** *vi* viaggiare; **to** ~ **to distant lands** viaggiare verso terre lontane

voyager ['vɔɪ·ɪd·ʒɚ] *n* viaggiatore, -trice *m, f*

voyeur [vɔɪ·'jɜːr] *n* guardone, -a *m, f,* voyeur *mf inv*

VT *n abbr of* **Vermont** VT

VTOL ['viː·tɑːl] AVIAT *abbr of* **vertical take-off and landing** VTOL

vulcanite ['vʌl·kə·naɪt] *n* gomma *f* vulcanizzata

vulcanization [ˌvʌl·kə·naɪ·'zeɪ·ʃən] *n* vulcanizzazione *f*

vulcanize ['vʌl·kə·naɪz] *vt* vulcanizzare

vulgar ['vʌl·gɚ] *adj* volgare

vulgarity [vʌl·'ge·rə·ti] *n* volgarità *f*

vulgarize ['vʌl·gə·raɪz] *vt* volgarizzare

vulnerable ['vʌl·nɚ·ə·bl] *adj* vulnerabile

vulture ['vʌl·tʃɚ] *n a. fig* avvoltoio *m*

vulva ['vʌl·və] <-s *o* -e> *n* vulva *f*

vying ['vaɪ·ɪŋ] *pres p of* **vie**

V

W

W, w ['dʌbl·juː] *n* W, w *f;* **~ as in William** W come Washington
W *n* **1.** *abbr of* **watt** W **2.** *abbr of* **west** O
WA *n abbr of* **Washington** Washington *f*
wack *adj sl* penoso, -a
wacko ['wæ·koʊ] *n sl* tipo *m* strambo
wacky ['wæ·ki] <-ier, -iest> *adj sl* strambo, -a
wad [wɑːd] *n* (*of banknotes*) mazzetta *f;* (*of cotton*) batuffolo *m;* (*of chewing tobacco*) cicca *f;* (*of forms*) plico *m*
wadding ['wɑː·dɪŋ] *n* materiale *m* per imbottitura
waddle ['wɑː·dl] **I.** *vi* camminare dondolando **II.** *n* andatura *f* dondolante
wade [weɪd] **I.** *vi* avanzare a fatica nell'acqua; **to ~ across** guadare; **to ~ into sth** addentrarsi in qc; **to ~ into sb** prendersela con qu; **to ~ through a book** leggere un libro con difficoltà **II.** *vt* guadare
wader ['weɪ·də] *n* **1.** (*bird*) trampoliere *m* **2.** *pl* (*boots*) stivali *mpl* da pescatore
wafer ['weɪ·fə] *n* **1.** (*biscuit*) cialda *f* **2.** REL ostia *f*
wafer-thin [ˌweɪ·fə·'θɪn] *adj* sottile come un'ostia
waffle¹ ['wɑː·fl] *n* GASTR cialda *f*
waffle² ['wɑː·fl] *inf* **I.** *vi* (*to talk*) **to ~ (on)** blaterare **II.** *n* sproloquio *m*
waffle iron *n* stampo *m* per cialde
waft [wɑːft] *liter* **I.** *vi* (*scent, sound*) diffondersi; **a delicious smell ~ed in from the kitchen** un bel profumino arrivò dalla cucina **II.** *vt* portare
wag¹ [wæg] **I.** <-gg-> *vt* agitare; **the dog ~ged its tail** il cane scodinzolò; **to ~ one's finger at sb/sth** minacciare qu con il dito **II.** <-gg-> *vi* agitarsi **III.** *n* scodinzolamento *m*
wag² [wæg] *n inf* burlone, -a *m, f*
wage [weɪdʒ] **I.** *vt* (*war*) fare; **to ~ war against sth/sb** fare la guerra contro qc/qu; **to ~ a campaign for/against sth** intraprendere una campaña a favore di/contro qc **II.** *n* salario *m;* **living ~** salario sufficiente per vivere; **minimum ~** minimo *m* salariale; **real ~s** salario effettivo; **to earn a ~** percepire un salario; **to get a good ~** essere pagato bene
wage earner *n* salariato, -a *m, f*
wage freeze *n* blocco *m* dei salari
wage increase *n* aumento *m* salariale
wager ['weɪ·dʒə] **I.** *n* scommessa *f;* **to place a ~** fare una scommessa **II.** *vt* scommettere; **to ~ one's reputation/life** giocarsi la reputazione/vita
wage scale *n* scala *f* dei salari
wageworker *n* salariato, -a *m, f*
waggish ['wæ·gɪʃ] *adj inf* burlone, -a
waggle ['wæ·gl] **I.** *vt* muovere **II.** *vi* muoversi
waggly ['wæg·li] <-ier, -iest> *adj* traballante
wagon ['wæ·gən] *n* **1.** (*horse-drawn*) carro *m*

2. (*truck*) camion *m inv* ▶ **to be on the ~** *inf* non bere alcol; **to fall off the ~** *inf* riprendere a bere; **to go on the ~** *inf* smettere di bere
waif [weɪf] *n liter* **1.** (*child*) trovatello, -a *m, f* **2.** (*animal*) animale *m* abbandonato
wail [weɪl] **I.** *vi* gemere; (*wind, siren*) ululare **II.** *vt* gemere **III.** *n* gemito *m*
wailing *n* gemiti *mpl*
Wailing Wall *n* Muro *m* del Pianto
waist [weɪst] *n* vita *f*
waistband ['weɪst·bænd] *n* cintura *f*
waist-deep [ˌweɪst·'diːp] *adj* fino alla cintura
waistline ['weɪst·laɪn] *n* girovita *m inv;* **to watch one's ~** stare attento alla linea
wait [weɪt] **I.** *vi* aspettare; **to ~ for sth/sb** aspettare qc/qu; **to keep sb ~ing** far aspettare qu; **he cannot ~ to see her** non vede l'ora di vederla; **~ and see** aspetta e vedrai; (**just**) **you ~!** stai a vedere! **II.** *vt* aspettare; **to ~ one's turn** aspettare il proprio turno **III.** *n* attesa *f;* **to lie in ~** essere in agguato
◆ **wait about** *vi*, **wait around** *vi* **to ~ for sth** stare in attesa di qc
◆ **wait behind** *vi* trattenersi
◆ **wait on** *vt* **1.** (*serve*) servire **2.** *form* (*expect*) **to ~ sth** aspettare qc
◆ **wait up** *vi* **to ~ for sb** aspettare qu alzato
waiter ['weɪ·tə] *n* cameriere *m*
waiting *n* **the ~** l'attesa
waiting game *n* **to play the ~** temporeggiare
waiting list *n* lista *f* d'attesa
waiting room *n* sala *f* d'attesa
waitress ['weɪ·trɪs] *n* cameriera *f*
waive [weɪv] *vt form* (*right*) rinunciare a; (*rule*) non applicare; (*charge*) eliminare
waiver ['weɪ·və] *n* deroga *f*
wake¹ [weɪk] *n* NAUT scia *f;* **in the ~ of sth** in seguito a qc
wake² [weɪk] *n* veglia *f* funebre
wake³ [weɪk] <woke *o* waked, woken *o* waked> **I.** *vi* svegliarsi **II.** *vt* svegliare
◆ **wake up** **I.** *vi* svegliarsi **II.** *vt* svegliare
wakeful ['weɪk·fəl] *adj form* **1.** (*sleepless*) sveglio, -a; **~ night** notte *f* in bianco **2.** (*vigilant, alert*) attento, -a; **to feel ~** sentirsi lucido
waken ['weɪ·kən] *vt form* svegliare
Wales ['weɪlz] *n* Galles *m;* **North/South ~** Galles del Nord/Sud; **New South ~** Nuovo Galles del Sud
walk [wɑːk] **I.** *n* **1.** (*stroll*) passeggiata *f;* **to take a ~** fare una passeggiata; **to take sb out for a ~** portare qu a fare una passeggiata; **it's a five minute ~** sono cinque minuti a piedi; **to do sth in a ~** fare qc; **they won in a ~** hanno vinto senza problemi **2.** (*gait*) andatura *f* **3.** (*walking pace*) passo *m* ▶ **~ of life** people from all (**different**) **~s of life** gente di ogni tipo **II.** *vt* **1.** (*go on foot*) camminare per; (*distance*) percorrere a piedi **2.** (*accompany*) **to ~ sb home** accompagnare qu a casa **3.** (*take for a walk*) **to ~ the dog** portare a spasso il cane **III.** *vi* (*go on foot*) andare a piedi, camminare; (*stroll*) passeg-

giare ▶**to ~ on air** camminare a un metro da terra

> **i** È a Hollywood, la capitale mondiale del cinema, che si trova il celebre **Walk of Fame**, marciapiede sul quale numerose celebrità del mondo dello spettacolo sono immortalate con una stella.

◆**walk about** *vi*, **walk around** *vi* andare a spasso
◆**walk away** *vi form* andarsene; **to ~ from sb** lasciare qu; **to ~ from sth** abbandonare qc; **to ~ from an accident without a scratch** uscire illeso da un incidente
◆**walk back** *vi* tornare a piedi
◆**walk in** *vi* entrare
◆**walk in on** *vt* **to ~ sb** (**doing sth**) entrare e sorprendere qu (a fare qc)
◆**walk off** I. *vt* **to ~ the meal** smaltire un pasto facendo una passeggiata II. *vi* andarsene
◆**walk on** *vi* continuare a camminare
◆**walk out** *vi* **1.**(*leave*) andarsene **2.**(*go on strike*) scioperare
◆**walk out on** *vt inf* **to ~ sb** piantare qu
◆**walk over** *vt* (*rights*) calpestare; **to walk (all) over sb** mettere i piedi in testa a qu
◆**walk through** *vt insep* (*part*) aiutare con
◆**walk up** I. *vi* **1.**(*go up*) salire **2.**(*approach*) **to ~ to sb** avvicinarsi a qu II. *vt* **to ~ sth** salire qc

walkaway ['wɑː·kə·weɪ] *n* passeggiata *f;* **to win in a ~** vincere senza problemi
walker ['wɑː·kɚ] *n* **1.**(*stroller*) persona che ama passeggiare *f* **2.** SPORTS podista *mf* **3.**(*sb whose hobby is walking*) escursionista *mf*
walkie-talkie [ˌwɑː·ki·'tɑː·ki] *n* walkie-talkie *m inv*
walk-in ['wɑː·k·ɪn] *adj* **1.**(*big*) **~ closet** cabina *f* armadio **2.**(*on street*) **~ apartment** *con ingresso sulla strada*
walking I. *n* passeggio *m;* SPORTS marcia *f;* **to do a lot of ~** camminare molto II. *adj* **1.** it is within **~ distance** ci si può andare a piedi **2.**(*human*) ambulante; **to be a ~ encyclopedia** essere una enciclopedia ambulante
walking papers *npl inf* **to give sb his/her ~** dare a qu il benservito
walking stick *n* bastone (*m* da passeggio)
walking wounded *npl* feriti *mpl* in grado di camminare
Walkman® ['wɑː·k·mən] <-s> *n* walkman® *m inv*
walk-on ['wɑː·k·ɑːn] I. *adj* **~ part** THEAT, CINE ruolo *m* di figurante II. *n* THEAT, CINE figurante *m*
walkout ['wɑː·k·aʊt] *n* abbandono *m;* (*strike*) sciopero *m;* **to stage a ~** andarsene in segno di protesta
walkover ['wɑː·k·ˌoʊ·vɚ] *n inf* **it was a ~** è

stata una passeggiata
walkthrough ['wɑː·k·ˌθruː] *n* collaudo *m*
walkway ['wɑː·k·weɪ] *n* passerella *f*
wall [wɔːl] I. *n* muro *m;* (*in the interior*) *a.* ANAT parete *f;* (*enclosing town*) muraglia *f;* **the city ~s** le mura della città; **the Great Wall of China** la Grande Muraglia cinese; **artery ~** parete arteriosa; **a ~ of silence** un muro di silenzio; **a ~ of water** un muro d'acqua ▶**to have one's back to** [*o* **up against**] **the ~** trovarsi con le spalle al muro; **to drive sb up the ~** *inf* far infuriare qu; **to hit a brick ~** trovarsi davanti un muro; **to be off the wall** *sl* essere strambo; **the writing** [*o* **handwriting**] **is on the ~** ci sono segnali d'allarme II. *vt* (*garden*) recintare con un muro; (*town*) cintare di mura
◆**wall in** *vt* **1.**(*garden*) recintare con un muro; (*town*) cintare di mura **2.***fig* circondare
◆**wall off** *vt* separare con un muro; **to wall oneself off** *fig* chiudersi in se stesso
◆**wall up** *vt* murare
wall chart *n* cartellone *m*
wallet ['wɑː·lɪt] *n* portafoglio *m*
wallflower ['wɔːl·ˌflɑ·ʊɚ] *n* **1.** BOT violacciocca *f* **2.** *fig* **to be a ~** fare da tappezzeria
wall hanging *n* arazzo *m*
Walloon [wɑː·'luːn] I. *adj* vallone, -a II. *n* **1.**(*person*) vallone, -a *m, f* **2.** LING vallone *m*
wallop ['wɑː·ləp] I. *vt inf* **1.**(*hit hard*) dare un colpo a **2.**(*defeat*) stracciare II. *n inf* (*hit*) colpo *m;* **to give sb a ~** menare qu
walloping I. *adj inf* **1.**(*very big*) enorme **2.**(*very good*) stupendo, -a II. *n inf* **to give sb a ~** menare qu
wallow ['wɑː·loʊ] I. *n* rotolamento *m* II. *vi* **1.**(*lie in earth*) rotolarsi **2.**(*remain in negative state*) **to ~ in self-pity** autocommiserarsi **3.**(*revel*) crogiolarsi; **to ~ in wealth** nuotare nell'oro
wallpaper ['wɔːl·ˌpeɪ·pɚ] I. *n* carta *f* da parati; **a roll of ~** un rotolo di carta da parati; **to hang ~** mettere la carta da parati II. *vt* metere la carta da parati in/su
Wall Street *n* **1.**(*street*) Wall Street *f* **2.** *fig* mondo *m* della Borsa (americana)
wall-to-wall ['wɔːl·tə·'wɔːl] *adj* **~ carpeting** moquette *f*
walnut ['wɔːl·nʌt] *n* **1.**(*nut*) noce *f* **2.**(*tree*) noce *m*
walrus ['wɔːl·rəs] <walruses *o* walrus> *n* tricheco *m*
waltz [wɔːlts] <-es> I. *n* valzer *m inv* II. *vi* **1.**(*dance*) ballare il valzer **2.** *inf* (*walk confidently*) camminare disinvoltamente III. *vt* **to ~ sb** far ballare il valzer a qu
◆**waltz about** *vi*, **waltz around** *vi* fare un giro di valzer
◆**waltz in** *vi inf* entrare come se niene fosse
◆**waltz off** *vi inf* **to ~ with sth** fregare qc
◆**waltz out** *vi inf* uscire come se niente fosse

W

wan [wɑːn] <-nn> *adj liter* smunto, -a

wand [wɑːnd] *n* (*conjuror's stick*) bacchetta *f* magica; **to wave one's magic** ~ agitare la bacchetta magica

wander ['wɑːn·dɚ] I. *vt* vagare per; **to ~ the streets** vagare per le strade II. *vi* (*roam*) vagare; (*stroll*) gironzolare; **to let one's thoughts** ~ lasciare libera l'immaginazione III. *n inf* giro *m;* **to go for a ~ around the city** fare un giro per la città

wanderer ['wɑːn·dɚ·ɚ] *n* girovago, -a *m, f; pej* vagabondo, -a *m, f*

wandering ['wɑːn·dɚ·rɪŋ] *adj* 1. (*nomadic*) errante; (*salesman*) ambulante; ~ **tribe** tribù nomade 2. (*not concentrating*) distratto, -a

wanderings ['wɑːn·dɚ·rɪŋz] *n* giri *mpl; pej* vagabondaggi *mpl*

wane [weɪn] I. *vi* calare; **to wax and** ~ avere alti e bassi II. *n* calo *m;* **to be on the** ~ essere in calo

wangle ['wæŋ·gl] *vt inf* rimediare; **to** ~ **one's way into sth** riuscire a farsi strada in qc

want [wɑːnt] I. *vt* 1. (*wish*) volere; **to** ~ **to do sth** voler fare qc; **to** ~ **sb to do sth** volere che qu faccia qc; **to** ~ **sth done** volere che qc sia fatto; **you're** ~**ed on the phone** ti vogliono al telefono; **I was** ~**ing to leave** volevo andarmene 2. (*need*) aver bisogno di; **he is** ~**ed by the police** è ricercato dalla polizia; '~**ed**' 'cercasi' II. *n* 1. (*need*) bisogno *m;* **to be in** ~ **of sth** aver bisogno di qc 2. (*lack*) mancanza *f;* **for** ~ **of sth** per mancanza di qc; **to live in** ~ *form* vivere nel bisogno

◆**want in** *vi* 1. (*want to take part*) **do you** ~? vuoi partecipare? 2. (*want to enter*) voler entrare

◆**want out** *vi* 1. (*not want to take part*) **to** ~ (**of sth**) non voler partecipare (a qc) 2. (*want to exit*) voler uscire

wanting *adj* **to be** ~ **in sth** mancare di qc; **there is sth** ~ manca qc

wanton ['wɑːn·tən] *adj* 1. (*extreme*) sfrenato, -a 2. (*mindless*) gratuito, -a; ~ **destruction** distruzione senza senso; ~ **disregard** totale sconsideratezza; ~ **waste** spreco vano 3. (*licentious*) lascivo, -a 4. (*capricious*) capriccioso, -a; (*playful*) burlesco, -a

WAP TEL, INFOR *abbr of* **wireless application protocol** WAP

wapiti ['wɑː·pə·ti] *n inv* wapiti *m*

war [wɔːr] *n* guerra *f;* **civil** ~ guerra civil; **the Great War** la Prima Guerra Mondiale; **the Second World War** la Seconda Guerra Mondiale; **a holy** ~ una guerra santa; **the horrors of** ~ gli orrori della guerra; **in time of** ~ in tempo di guerra; **to be at** ~ essere in guerra; **to declare** ~ **on sb** *a.fig* dichiarare guerra a qu; **to go to** ~ entrare in guerra; **to make** ~ **on sb** fare la guerra a qu

war baby *n* bambino, -a della guerra *m*

warble ['wɔːr·bl] *vi* (*bird*) cinguettare; (*lark*) gorgheggiare; *iron* (*person*) fare gorgheggi

warbler ['wɔːr·bl·ɚ] *n* silvia *f*

war bond *n* obbligazione *f* di guerra

war correspondent *n* inviato, -a di guerra *m*

war crime *n* crimine *m* di guerra

war criminal *n* criminale *mf* di guerra

war cry *n* grido *m* di guerra

ward [wɔːrd] *n* 1. (*wardship*) tutela *f;* **in** ~ sotto tutela 2. (*person*) pupillo, -a *m, f* 3. (*in a hospital*) reparto *m;* (*room*) corsia *f;* **geriatric/psychiatric** ~ reparto di geriatria/psichiatria; **maternity** ~ reparto maternità

◆**ward off** *vt* evitare

warden ['wɔːr·dn] *n* guardiano, -a *m, f;* (*of a prison*) direttore *m;* **game** ~ guardacaccia *m inv*

wardrobe ['wɔːrd·roʊb] *n* 1. (*closet*) armadio *m* 2. (*clothes*) guardaroba *m*

wardrobe trunk *n* baule *m*

wardship ['wɔːrd·ʃɪp] *n* tutela *f*

warehouse ['we·rə·haʊs] *n* deposito *m*

wares [werz] *npl inf* merci *fpl*

warfare ['wɔːr·fer] *n* guerra *f*

war game *n* war game *m inv*

warhead ['wɔːr·hed] *n* (*of rocket*) testata *f*

warily ['we·rɪ·li] *adv* in maniera guardinga

warlike ['wɔːr·laɪk] *adj* 1. (*of war*) bellico, -a 2. (*belligerent*) bellicoso, -a

warlord ['wɔːr·lɔːrd] *n* capo *m* militare

warm [wɔːrm] I. *adj* 1. caldo, -a; (*not too hot*) tiepido, -a; **nice and** ~ bello caldo; **to be** ~ (*person*) avere caldo; (*thing*) essere caldo; (*weather*) fare caldo 2. (*affectionate*) affettuoso, -a; ~ **welcome** accoglienza calorosa; **to be** ~ essere affettuoso 3. (*fresh*) fresco, -a; ~ **tracks** tracce fresche ▶**you're getting** ~ fuochino! II. *n* **the** ~ il calore III. *vt* riscaldare; **to** ~ **one's feet** riscaldarsi i piedi; **to** ~ **the soup** riscaldare la minestra; **to** ~ **sb's heart** confortare qu

◆**warm up** I. *vi* riscaldarsi II. *vt* riscaldare

warm-blooded [ˌwɔːrm·'blʌ·dɪd] *adj* a sangue caldo

warm front *n* fronte *m* caldo

warm-hearted [ˌwɔːrm·'hɑːr·ţɪd] *adj* premuroso, -a; (*affectionate*) affettuoso, -a

warmly *adv* 1. (*of heat*) **wrap yourself up** ~! copriti bene! 2. (*enthusiasm*) calorosamente; **she shook my hand** ~ mi ha stretto calorosamente la mano

warmth [wɔːrmθ] *n* (*heat, affection*) calore *m*

warm-up, warmup ['wɔːm·ʌp] *n* SPORTS riscaldamento *m*

warn [wɔːrn] *vt* 1. (*make aware*) avvisare, avvertire; **to** ~ **sb not to do sth** avvertire qu di non fare qc; **to** ~ **sb of sth** (*danger*) mettere in guardia qu da qc 2. LAW dare la diffida a

◆**warn off** *vt* **to warn sb off doing sth** sconsigliare a qu di fare qc

warning ['wɔːr·nɪŋ] I. *n* avviso *m,* avvertimento *m;* **a word of** ~ un avvertimento; **to give sb a** ~ avvertire qu; **to issue a** ~ (**about sth**) emettere un avviso (per qc); **without** ~ senza preavviso; ~! attenzione! II. *adj* di avvertimento

warning shot *n* colpo *m* d'avvertimento; **to fire a ~** sparare un colpo d'avvertimento

warp [wɔːrp] **I.** *vi* distorcersi; (*wood*) imbarcarsi **II.** *vt* **1.** (*wood*) fare imbarcare, deformare **2.** (*mind*) distorcere; **to ~ sb's judgment** distorcere il giudizio di qu **III.** *n* deformazione *f*

war paint ['wɔːr·peɪnt] *n* pittura *f* di guerra

warpath ['wɔːr·pæθ] *n* **to be on the ~** *a.fig, inf* essere sul sentiero di guerra

warped *adj* deformato, -a; (*mind*) perverso, -a; **to have a ~ way of looking at things** vedere le cose in modo contorto

warrant ['wɔːr··rənt] **I.** *n* **1.** LAW mandato *m;* **arrest ~** mandato d'arresto; **search ~** mandato di perquisizione; **to execute a ~** eseguire un mandato **2.** (*justification*) giustificazione *f* **3.** COM garanzia *f* **II.** *vt* **1.** (*promise*) garantire **2.** (*justify*) giustificare

warrantee [ˌwɔːr··rən·'tiː] *n* beneficiario, -a *m, f* di una garanzia

warrant officer *n* maresciallo *m*

warrantor ['wɔːr··rən·tɔːr] *n* garante *mf*

warranty ['wɔːr··rən·ti] <-ies> *n* garanzia *f*

warren ['wɔːr··rən] *n* **1.** ZOOL tane *fpl* **2.** *fig* labirinto *m*

warring *adj* in guerra; **~ factions** fazioni belligeranti

warrior ['wɔːr·jɚ] *n* guerriero, -a *m, f*

Warsaw ['wɔːr·saː] *n* Varsavia *f*

Warsaw Pact *n*, **Warsaw Treaty** *n* HIST Patto *m* di Varsavia

warship ['wɔːr·ʃɪp] *n* nave *f* da guerra

wart [wɔːrt] *n* verruca *f;* **~s and all** *inf* (*description, portrait*) con pregi e difetti

wart hog ['wɔːrt·haːg] *n* facocero *m*

wartime ['wɔːr·taɪm] *n* tempo *m* di guerra; **in ~** in tempo di guerra

war-torn ['wɔːr·tɔːn] *adj* martoriato, -a dalla guerra

war-weary ['wɔːr·ˌwɪ·ri] *adj* stanco, -a della guerra

wary ['we·ri] <-ier, -iest> *adj* (*not trusting*) diffidente; (*watchful*) guardingo, -a; **to be ~ of sth/sb** diffidare di qc/qu

war zone ['wɔːr·zoʊn] *n* zona *f* di guerra

was [waːz] *pt of* be

wash [waːʃ] **I.** *vt* **1.** (*clean*) lavare; **to ~ one's hair/hands** lavarsi i capelli/le mani **2.** (*waves*) bagnare **3.** (*river, sea*) trascinare; **to ~ sb overboard** gettare qu a mare **II.** *vi* **1.** (*person, cloth*) lavarsi; **that excuse won't ~ with me** *inf* questa scusa con me non attacca **2.** (*do the laundry*) fare il bucato **3.** (*sea*) sciabordare **III.** *n* **1.** (*cleaning with water*) lavata *m;* **to have a ~** lavarsi **2.** (*clothes for cleaning*) **the ~** i panni da lavare; **to be in the ~** essere a lavare **3.** *liter* (*sound of water*) sciabordio *m* **4.** NAUT scia *f;* AVIAT turbolenza *f* **5.** (*painting*) mano *f* **6.** (*even situation*) bilanciamento *m* ▸ **to come out in the ~** *prov* venire a galla

◆**wash away** *vt* **1.** (*clean*) lavare via **2.** (*carry elsewhere*) portare via

◆**wash down** *vt* **1.** (*clean*) lavare **2.** (*carry elsewhere*) portare via **3.** *fig* (*drink*) **to ~ sth with sth** mandare giù qc con qc

◆**wash out** **I.** *vi* andare via **II.** *vt* **1.** (*clean*) lavare via; (*remove*) togliere **2.** *fig* **our party was washed out** la festa fu annullata a causa della pioggia

◆**wash over** *vt* **1.** (*flow over*) spazzare **2.** (*have no effect on*) non intaccare

◆**wash up** **I.** *vt* **1.** (*bring via water*) **the sea washed it up** trasportare **2.** (*clean*) lavare **II.** *vi* (*wash*) lavarsi (le mani e il viso)

washable *adj* lavabile

wash-and-wear *adj* lava e metti

washbasin *n* (*basin*) lavandino *m;* (*bowl*) bacinella *f*

washboard *n* asse *f* da lavare

washbowl *n s.* **washbasin**

washcloth *n* panno *m* per lavarsi la faccia

washed-out [ˌwaːʃt·'aʊt] *adj* **1.** (*faded*) scolorito, -a; **~ jeans** jeans scoloriti; (*pale*) smunto, -a **2.** (*tired*) esausto, -a

washer ['waː·ʃɚ] *n* **1.** (*washing machine*) lavatrice *f* **2.** (*plastic ring*) guarnizione *f*

washing ['waː·ʃɪŋ] *n* **1.** (*clothes for cleaning*) panni *mpl* da lavare **2.** (*act*) lavaggio *m;* **to do the ~** fare il bucato

washing machine *n* lavatrice *f*

Washington [ˌwaː·ʃɪŋ·tən] *n* Washington *f*

Washington D.C. *n* Washington D.C.

Washington's Birthday *inf* fiasco *m;* **a complete ~** un totale fiasco

> **i** **Washington's Birthday** è un giorno festivo riconosciuto negli USA. Nonostante George Washington sia in realtà nato il 22 febbraio 1732, da qualche anno a questa parte è consuetudine festeggiare il suo compleanno il terzo lunedì di febbraio, così da prolungare il fine settimana.

wasn't [·waː·znt] = **was not** *s.* be

wasp [waːsp] *n* vespa *f*

WASP [waːsp] *n pej, inf abbr of* **White Anglo-Saxon Protestant** cittadino americano bianco, di origine anglosassone e protestante

waste [weɪst] **I.** *n* **1.** (*misuse*) spreco *m;* **it's a ~ of energy/money** è energia sprecata/denaro sprecato; **it's a ~ of time** è una perdita di tempo; **to lay ~ to the land** devastare la terra; **to go to ~** andare sprecato; **what a ~!** che spreco! **2.** (*unwanted matter*) rifiuti *mpl;* **household/industrial ~** rifiuti domestici/industriali; **nuclear/toxic ~** scorie *fpl* radioattive/tossiche; **to recycle ~** riciclare i rifiuti **II.** *vt* sprecare; (*time*) perdere; **to ~ one's breath** *fig* sprecare il fiato; **to ~ no time in doing sth** non perdere tempo a fare qc; **to not ~ words** non fare tanti giri di parole **III.** *vi* consumarsi ▸ **~ not, want not** *prov* il risparmio è il miglior guadagno *prov* **IV.** *adj* (*bin*) dei rifiuti; (*material*) di scarto; (*land*) incolto, -a

W

◆**waste away** *vi* consumarsi
wastebasket ['weɪst·bæs·kət] *n* cestino *m* per la carta straccia
wasteful ['weɪst·fəl] *adj* (*method*) dispendioso, -a; **to be ~ with electricity** sprecare corrente
waste heat *n* energia *f* residuale
wasteland *n* terreno *m* abbandonato
waste management *n* trattamento *m* dei rifiuti
wastepaper *n* carta *f* straccia; (*recyclable*) carta *f* riciclabile
wastepaper basket *n* cestino *m* della carta straccia
waste pipe *n* tubatura *f* di scarico
waste product *n* materiale *m* di scarto
waster *n* **1.**(*person*) sprecone, -a *m, f;* **a money ~** uno spendaccione **2.**(*good-for-nothing*) fannullone, -a *m, f*
wastewater *n* acque *fpl* di scolo
wasting ['weɪs·tɪŋ] *adj* (*disease*) debilitante
wastrel ['weɪs·trəl] *n* **1.**(*wasteful person*) sprecone, -a *m, f* **2.**(*good-for-nothing*) fannullone, -a *m, f*
watch [wɑːtʃ] I. *n* **1.**(*clock*) orologio *m* **2.**(*act of observation*) sorveglianza *f;* **to keep a close ~ on sb/sth** sorvegliare bene qu/qc; **to be on the ~ for sb/sth** stare in guardia da qc/qu; **to put a ~ on sb/sth** mettere qu sotto sorveglianza; **to be under ~** essere sotto sorveglianza **3.**(*group of guards*) guardia *f;* HIST ronda *f* **4.**(*period of duty*) guardia *f;* **to keep** [*o* **be on**] **~** essere di guardia **5.**(*alert*) METEO **a tornado/hurricane ~** una veglia del tornado/dell'uragano II. *vt* **1.**(*observe*) guardare; **to ~ the clock** guardare l'orologio; **to ~ a film** vedere un film; **to ~ TV** guardare la televisione; **to ~ the world go by** guardare la gente che passa; **to ~ sb/sth do sth** guardare qu/qc fare qc; **to ~ how sb does sth** guardare come qu fa qc **2.**(*keep vigil*) sorvegliare; **to ~ the kids** tenere d'occhio i bambini **3.**(*mind*) stare attento a; **to ~ every penny (one spends)** spendere oculatamente; **to ~ one's weight** tenere la linea sotto controllo; **~ it!** attento!; **to ~ it (with sb)** stare attento (con qu); **~ yourself** stare attento III. *vi* guardare; **to ~ as sb/sth does sth** guardare mentre qu/qc fa qc
◆**watch out** *vi* stare attento; **~!** attento!
watchband ['wɑːtʃ·bænd] *n* cinturino *m* da orologio
watchdog ['wɑːtʃ·dɑːg] *n* **1.**(*dog*) cane *m* da guardia **2.**(*keeper of standards*) supervisore *m;* (*official organization*) organismo *m* di controllo
watcher ['wɑːt·ʃɚ] *n* osservatore, -trice *m, f*
watchful ['wɑːtʃ·fəl] *adj* vigile; **to keep a ~ eye on sb/sth** tenere d'occhio qu/qc; **under the ~ eye of sb** sotto lo sguardo vigile di qu
watchmaker ['wɑːtʃ·meɪ·kɚ] *n* orologiaio, -a *m, f*
watchman ['wɑːtʃ·mən] <-men> *n* guardiano *m;* **night ~** guardiano *m* notturno

watchtower ['wɑːtʃ·ta·ʊɚ] *n* torre *f* di vedetta
watchword ['wɑːtʃ·wɜːrd] *n* **1.**(*symbol*) motto *m* **2.**(*password*) parola *f* d'ordine
water ['wɑː·t̬ɚ] I. *n* **1.**(*liquid*) acqua *f;* **bottled ~** acqua in bottiglia; **a bottle of ~** una bottiglia d'acqua; **a drink/a glass of ~** un po'/un bicchier d'acqua; **hot and cold running ~** acqua corrente calda e fredda **2.**(*area of water*) **the ~s of the Mississippi** le acque del Mississippi; **coastal ~s** acque costiere; **territorial ~s** acque territoriali; **unchartered ~s** *fig* territorio *m* sconosciuto; **by ~** via mare **3.** MED **~ on the brain** idrocefalia *f;* **~ on the knee** versamento *m* al ginocchio ▶**to be ~ under the** **bridge** essere acqua passata; **it's like ~ off a duck's back** è fiato sprecato; **to spend money like ~** avere le mani bucate; **to pour cold ~ on sth** scoraggiare qc; **to be in deep ~** essere nei guai; **still ~s run deep** *prov* essere più profondo di quel che sembri; **to get into hot ~** finir in cattive acque; **to hold ~** (*explanation*) filare; **to muddy the ~s** intorpidire le acque II. *vt* (*plants*) annaffiare; (*livestock*) abbeverare III. *vi* **1.**(*produce tears*) lacrimare **2.**(*salivate*) secernere saliva; **it makes my mouth ~** mi fa venire l'acquolina in bocca
waterborne ['wɑː·t̬ɚ·bɔːrn] *adj* via mare; **a ~ disease** una malattia trasmessa attraverso l'acqua; **~ attack** attacco dal mare
water bottle *n* borsa *m* dell'acqua calda; (*for soldiers, travelers*) borraccia *f*
water cannon *n* *inv* cannone *m* ad acqua
watercolor I. *n* acquarello *m* II. *adj* ad acquarello
water-cooled ['wɑː·t̬ɚ·kuːld] *adj* raffreddato, -a a acqua
watercraft *n* *liter* imbarcazione *f*
watercress *n* crescione *m*
waterfall *n* cascata *f*
waterfowl *n* *inv* uccello *m* acquatico
waterfront *n* (*harbor*) porto *m*
water heater *n* scaldaacqua *m* *inv*
water hose *n* tubo *m* (di gomma) dell'acqua
watering can ['wɑː·t̬ɚ·ɪŋ·kæn] *n* annaffiatoio *m*
watering hole *n* pozza (*f* d'acqua)
watering place *n* abbeveratoio *m*
waterless ['wɑː·t̬ɚ·ləs] *adj* arido, -a
water level *n* livello *m* dell'acqua
water lily <-ies> *n* ninfea *f*
water line *n* linea *f* di galleggiamento
waterlogged ['wɑː·t̬ɚ·lɑːgd] *adj* (*pitch*) fradicio, -a
Waterloo ['wɑː·t̬ɚ·'luː] *n* **to meet one's ~** subire una pesante sconfitta dopo una serie di vittorie
water main *n* tubatura *m* principale dell'acqua
waterman <-men> *n* barcaiolo *m*
watermark *n* **1.**(*river or tide level*) livello *f* della marea **2.**(*on paper*) filigrana *f*
watermelon *n* anguria *f*
water meter *n* contatore *m* dell'acqua

water pipe *n* **1.** (*for transporting water*) tubo *m* dell'acqua **2.** (*hookah*) pipa *f* ad acqua

water pistol *n* pistola *f* ad acqua

water pollution *n* inquinamento *f* delle acque

water polo *n* waterpolo *m*, pallanuoto *f*

water pressure *n* pressione *f* dell'acqua

waterproof ['wɑː·tə·pruːf] **I.** *adj* impermeabile **II.** *vt* impermeabilizzare

water-repellent *adj* idrorepellente

water-resistant *adj* resistente all'acqua

watershed ['wɑː·tə·ʃed] *n* **1.** (*high ground*) spartiacque *m* **2.** *fig* (*great change*) punto *m* di svolta; **to mark a ~** segnare una svolta

waterside *n* riva *f*

water-ski ['wɑː·tə·skiː] **I.** *vi* fare sci d'acqua; **to go ~ing** fare sci d'acqua **II.** <-s> *n* sci *m* d'acqua

water-skiing *n* sci *m* d'acqua

water softener *n* (*substance*) dolcificante *m* per acqua; (*device*) dolcificatore *m*

water-soluble *adj* idrosolubile

waterspout *n* METEO tromba *f* marina

water supply *n* fornitura *m* d'acqua

water table *n* falda *f* freatica

water tank *n* cisterna (*f* dell'acqua)

watertight ['wɑː·tə·taɪt] *adj* **1.** (*not allowing water in/out*) ermetico, -a **2.** *fig* (*not allowing doubt*) incontestabile; **a ~ alibi** un alibi di ferro

water tower *n* cisterna *f* (dell'acqua) sopraelevata

water vapor *n* vapore *m* acqueo

waterway *n* canale *m*

water wings *npl* braccioli *mpl;* **to wear ~** avere i braccioli

waterworks *n pl* (*where public water is stored*) riserva *f* idrica ▶ **to turn on the ~** mettersi a piangere

watery ['wɑː·tə·ri] <-ier, -iest> *adj* **1.** (*bland*) acquoso, -a; **a ~ soup** una minestra troppo liquida **2.** (*weak in color*) slavato, -a; (*weak in strength*) debole; **a ~ sun** un sole pallido

watt [wɑːt] *n* ELEC watt *m inv*

wattage ['wɑː·tɪdʒ] *n* ELEC wattaggio *m*

wave [weɪv] **I.** *n* **1.** (*of water*) onda *f;* (*on surface, of hair*) ondulazione *f;* **to be on the crest of the ~** *fig* essere sulla cresta dell'onda **2.** PHYS onda *f* **3.** (*hand movement*) **to give sb a ~** salutare qu con la mano ▶ **to make ~s** creare problemi **II.** *vi* **1.** (*make hand movement*) **to ~ at** [*o* **to**] **sb** salutare qu con la mano **2.** (*move from side to side*) ondeggiare **III.** *vt* **1.** (*signal*) **to ~ goodbye** fare ciao con la mano; **to ~ sb away** salutare qu con la mano **2.** (*move from side to side*) agitare **3.** (*hair*) arricciare; **to ~ one's hair** arricciarsi i capelli

◆**wave down** *vt* **to wave sb/sth down** fare cenno a qu/qc di fermarsi

◆**wave on** *vt* **to wave sb/sth on** fare cenno a qu/qc di proseguire

◆**wave through** *vt* fare cenno di passare

waveband *n* RADIO banda *f* de frequenza

wavelength *n* lunghezza *f* d'onda; **to be on**

the same ~ *fig* essere sulla stessa lunghezza d'onda

waver ['weɪ·və‑] *vi* **1.** (*lose determination*) vacillare **2.** (*be unable to decide*) esitare; **to ~ between ... and ...** essere indeciso tra ... e ...; **to ~ over sth** essere titubante riguardo a qc **3.** (*lose strength*) indebolirsi

waverer ['weɪ·və‑·ə‑] *n* indeciso, -a *m, f*

wavering *adj* vacillante; (*between two options*) indeciso, -a

wavy ['weɪ·vi] <-ier, -iest> *adj* ondulato, -a

wax[1] [wæks] **I.** *n* **1.** cera *f;* **candle ~** cera *f* di candela **2.** (*inside ear*) cerume *m* **II.** *vt* **1.** (*polish: floor*) passare la cera su; (*shoes, furniture*) lucidare **2.** (*remove hair from*) fare la ceretta

wax[2] [wæks] *vi liter* **1.** (*moon*) crecere; **to ~ and wane** crecere e decrescere; *fig* avere alti e bassi **2.** (*become*) **to ~ poetic/lyrical** diventare poetico

wax paper *n* carta *f* cerata

waxy ['wæk·si] <-ier, -iest> *adj* **1.** (*oily, shiny*) lucido, -a **2.** (*apparently of wax*) ceroso, -a

way [weɪ] **I.** *n* **1.** (*route*) strada *f,* via *f;* **to be (well) on the ~ to doing sth** *fig* essere sulla via di fare qc; **to be on the ~** essere sulla strada; **to be out of the ~** essere in un posto remoto; **to be under ~** essere in corso; **on the ~ to sth** sulla strada di qc; **to elbow one's ~ somewhere** farsi strada a gomitate verso qualche posto; **to find one's ~ around sth** orientarsi in qc; *fig* trovare il modo di evitare qc; **to find one's ~ into/out of sth** trovare il modo di entrare in/uscire da qc; **to find one's ~ through sth** trovare la strada attraverso qc; **to go out of one's ~ to do sth** *fig* darsi veramente daffare per fare qc; **to go one's own ~** *fig* andarsene per la propria strada; **(to go) by ~ of sth** (andare) via qc; **to know one's ~ around sth** orientarsi bene in qc; **to lead the ~** fare strada; **to lose one's ~** perdersi; **to make one's ~** farsi strada; **to make one's ~ through the crowd** farsi strada nella folla; **to pay one's ~** *fig* pagare tutto da sé; **to see the error of one's ~s** rendersi conto dei propri errori; **to work one's ~ up the ladder** *fig* farsi strada da sé **2.** (*road*) strada *f;* (*small one*) sentiero *m;* **Way** (*name of road*) Via *f* **3.** (*facing direction*) direzione *f;* **the right/wrong ~ around** perbene/al rovescio; **to show the ~ forward** indicare la strada **4.** (*distance*) **all the ~** (*the whole distance*) tutta la strada; (*completely*) completamente; **to be a long ~ off** essere molto lontano; **to have a (long) ~ to go** avere molta strada da fare; **to have come a long ~** *fig* aver fatto molta strada; **to go a long ~** *fig* andare lontano **5.** (*fashion*) maniera *f;* **in many ~s** per molti versi; **in some ~s** in un certo verso; **there are no two ~s about it** non ci sono alternative; **the ~ to do sth** il modo per fare qc; **by ~ of** a mo'di **6.** (*manner*) modo *m;* (*customs*) usanze *fpl;* **sb's ~ of life** lo stile di vita di qu; **to my ~**

of thinking a mio modo di vedere; **she wouldn't have it any other** ~ non le andrebbe bene in nessun altro modo; **in a big** ~ alla grande; **either** ~ in entrambi i casi; **no** ~! *inf* (*definitely no!*) neanche per sogno!; **to get one's own** ~ ottenere quello che uno vuole; **in a** ~ in un certo senso **7.** (*free space*) passaggio *m;* **to be in sb's** ~ bloccare il passaggio a qu; **to stand in sb's** ~ essere d'ostacolo a qu; **in the** ~ nel mezzo; **to get out of sb's/ sth's** ~ lasciare passare qu/qc; **to give** ~ dare la precedenza; *fig* cedere il passo; **to give** ~ **to sth** cedere il passo a qc; **to make** ~ (**for sb/ sth**) fare posto (a qu/qc) **8.** (*condition*) stato *m;* **to be in a bad** ~ essere messo male; **to be in a terrible** ~ essere in pessime condizioni; **to be in the family** ~ *inf* essere incinta ▶ **to go the** ~ **of all** flesh soccombere all'inevitabilità della morte; **the** ~ **to a man's** heart **is through his stomach** *prov* prendere qu per la gola *prov;* **to want** things **both** ~**s** volere la botte piena e la moglie ubriaca *prov;* **to rub sb the** wrong ~ prendere qu per il verso sbagliato; **by the** ~ a proposito **II.** *adv* **1.** *inf* decisamente; **to be** ~ **past sb's bedtime** è ben passata l'ora di andare a letto **2.** *sl* (*very*) veramente; **that's** ~ **cool!** grande!

waybill ['weɪ·bɪl] *n* bolla *f* di accompagnamento

waylay ['weɪ·leɪ] <waylaid, waylaid> *vt* tendere un agguato a

way-out [ˌweɪ·'aʊt] *adj sl* (*very modern*) ultramoderno, -a; (*unusual or amazing*) straordinario, -a

ways and means *npl* **the** ~ **of doing/to do sth** i modi per fare qc

wayside ['weɪ·saɪd] **I.** *n* ciglio *f* della strada; **to fall by the** ~ *fig* non arrivare in fondo **II.** *adj* lungo la strada; ~ **inn** motel *m inv*

wayward ['weɪ·wəd] *adj* difficile

we [wiː] *pron pers* noi; ~**'re on our way to Philadelphia, but** ~**'ll be back tomorrow** stiamo andando a Filadelfia ma torniamo domani; **as** ~ **say** come diciamo noi

weak [wiːk] *adj* debole; (*coffee, tea*) leggero, -a; **to be** ~ **with hunger/thirst** essere debilitato dalla fame/la sete; **she went** ~ **at the knees** le tremavano le ginocchia; **the** ~ **link/ spot** *fig* il punto debole *f;* **to be** ~ (**at sth**) essere debole (in qc)

weaken ['wiː·kən] **I.** *vi* (*become less strong*) indebolirsi; (*diminish*) diminuire **II.** *vt* (*make less strong*) indebolire; (*diminish*) diminuire

weakling ['wiːk·lɪŋ] *n* persona *f* gracile

weakly ['wiːk·li] *adv* **1.** (*without strength*) debolmente **2.** (*unconvincingly*) senza convinzione

weak-minded [ˌwiːk·'maɪn·dɪd] *adj* **1.** (*lacking determination*) indeciso, -a; (*weak-willed*) poco determinato, -a **2.** *pej* (*stupid*) tonto, -a

weakness ['wiːk·nɪs] <-es> *n* **1.** (*lack of strength*) debolezza *f* **2.** (*area of vulnerability*) punto *m* debole; (*flaw*) difetto *m* **3.** (*fond-*

ness) **to have a** ~ **for sth** avere un debole per qc

weal [wiːl] *n* segno *m* di frustata

wealth [welθ] *n* **1.** (*money*) ricchezza *f;* (*fortune*) fortuna *f* **2.** (*large amount*) abbondanza *f*

wealthy ['wel·θi] **I.** <-ier, -iest> *adj* ricco, -a **II.** *n* **the** ~ i ricchi

wean [wiːn] *vt* (*animal, baby*) svezzare; **to** ~ **sb** (**off sth**) *fig* far perdere a qu l'abitudine (di qc)

weapon ['we·pən] *n* arma *f*

weaponry ['we·pən·ri] *n* armamento *m*

wear [wer] <wore, worn> **I.** *vt* **1.** (*have on body: clothes, jewelry*) portare, indossare; **to** ~ **one's hair loose/tied back** portare i capelli sciolti/raccolti **2.** (*deteriorate*) logorare **II.** *vi* (*spoil: clothes, machine parts*) logorarsi; **to** ~ **thin** *fig* cominciare a essere un po' vecchio **III.** *n* **1.** (*clothing*) abbigliamento *f;* **casual/ sports** ~ abbigliamento casual/sportivo **2.** (*amount of use*) consumo *m;* **to be the worse for** ~ (*person*) essere ubriaco; (*thing*) essere rovinato

♦ **wear away I.** *vt* consumare **II.** *vi* consumarsi

♦ **wear down** *vt* **1.** (*reduce*) diminuire; *fig* (*tire*) sfinire **2.** (*make weak and useless*) logorare

♦ **wear off** *vi* sparire

♦ **wear on** *vi* (*time*) passare lentamente

♦ **wear out I.** *vi* logorarsi **II.** *vt* logorare; (*patience*) far perdere

wearable ['we·rə·bl] *adj* portabile

wear and tear *n* logoramento *m;* **to take some/a lot of** ~ essere parecchio/molto resistente

wearing ['we·rɪŋ] *adj* stancante

wearisome ['wɪ·rɪ·səm] *adj form* (*causing boredom*) noioso, -a; (*causing tiredness*) stancante

weary ['wɪ·ri] **I.** <-ier, -iest> *adj* **1.** (*very tired*) sfinito, -a **2.** (*tiring*) stancante **3.** (*bored*) annoiato, -a; (*unenthusiastic*) poco entusiasta; **to be** ~ **of sth** essere stufo di qc; **a** ~ **joke** una barzelletta trita e ritrita **II.** *vt* (*make tired*) **to** ~ **sb with sth** stancare qu con qc; (*make bored*) annoiare qu con qc **III.** *vi* (*become tired*) stancarsi; (*become bored*) annoiarsi

weasel ['wiː·zl] *n* donnola *f*

weather ['we·ðə] **I.** *n* tempo *m;* (*climate*) clima *m;* ~ **permitting** tempo permettendo ▶ **to make** heavy ~ **of sth** complicare qc; **to be** under **the** ~ non sentirsi bene **II.** *vi* trasformarsi **III.** *vt* **1.** (*wear*) consumare **2.** (*endure*) superare; **to** ~ **the storm** *fig* superare la crisi

weather-beaten ['we·ðəˌbiː·tən] *adj* consumato, -a dalle intemperie; ~ **face** volto *m* segnato dalle intemperie

weather-bound *adj* bloccato, -a dal maltempo

weather bureau <-s *o* -x> *n* servizio *m* meteorologico

weather chart *n* carta *f* meteorologica

weather forecast *n* previsioni *fpl* del tempo

weathering ['we·ðə·rɪŋ] *n* azione *f* degli agenti atmosferici

weatherman ['we·ðə·mæn] *n* persona *f* che presenta le previsioni del tempo

weatherproof ['we·ðə·pru:f] *adj* resistente alle intemperie

weathervane *n* banderuola *f*

weave [wi:v] I.<wove *o* weaved, woven *o* weaved> *vt* **1.** (*produce cloth*) tessere; **to ~ wool into fabric** confezionare un tessuto di lana **2.** (*intertwine things*) intrecciare; *fig* intessere **3.** (*move back and forth*) **to ~ one's way through sth** infiltrarsi in qc II.<wove *o* weaved, woven *o* weaved> *vi* **1.** (*produce cloth*) tessere **2.** (*move by twisting and turning*) zigzagare III. *n* trama *f*; **striped ~** tessitura *f* a righe; **loose/tight ~** trama rada/fitta

weaver ['wi:·və] *n* tessitore, -trice *m, f*; **basket ~** canestraio *m*

web¹ [web] *n* **1.** (*woven net*) tela *f*; **spider('s) ~** tela *f* del ragno; **to spin a ~** tessere una tela **2.** *fig* (*complex network*) groviglio *m*; **a ~ of intrigue/lies** un groviglio di intrighi/menzogne **3.** *fig* (*trap*) trappola *f* **4.** (*connective tissue*) membrana *f*

web² [web] I. *n* INFOR web *m*; **on the ~** in rete II. *adj inv* INFOR Internet

web browser *n* INFOR browser *m inv*

webcam *n* webcam *f inv*

web-footed ['web·ˌfʊ·ţɪd] *adj* palmipede

weblog *n* weblog *m inv*

webmaster *n* INFOR webmaster *m inv*

webpage *n* INFOR pagina *f* web

Web site *n* INFOR sito *m* web; **to visit a ~** visitare un sito web

web server *n* INFOR server web *m inv*

webzine *n* INFOR rivista *f* web

wed [wed] <wedded *o* wed, wedded *o* wed> *form* I. *vt* **1.** (*marry*) **to ~ sb** sposare qu, sposarsi con qu **2.** *fig* (*join closely*) unire; **to ~ sth and sth** unire qc a qc II. *vi* sposarsi

we'd [wi:d] **1.** = we had *s.* have **2.** = we would *s.* would

wedded ['we·dɪd] *adj* **1.** (*married*) sposato, -a; **lawfully ~ wife** *form* legittima sposa **2.** (*united*) **to be ~ to sth** essere unito a qc; **to be ~ to a habit** avere un'abitudine; **to be ~ to an opinion** essere ancorato a un'idea

wedding ['we·dɪŋ] *n* matrimonio *m*

wedding anniversary <-ies> *n* anniversario *m* di matrimonio

wedding cake *n* torta *f* nuziale

wedding day *n* giorno *m* del matrimonio

wedding dress *n* vestito *m* da sposa

wedding night *n* prima notte *f* di nozze

wedding present *n* regalo *m* di nozze

wedding ring *n* fede *f* nuziale

wedge [wedʒ] I. *n* **1.** (*tapered block*) cuneo *m*; (*for door*) zeppa *f* **2.** *fig* (*triangular piece*) fetta *f*; **a ~ of cake/pie** una fetta di torta II. *vt* **to ~ the door open** tenere aperta la porta con una zeppa; **to be ~d between sth** essere incastrato tra qc

wedlock ['wed·lɑ:k] *n* matrimonio *m*; **out of ~** fuori dal matrimonio; **sex out of ~** rapporti *mpl* sessuali extraconiugali; **to be born in/out of ~** essere figlio legittimo/illegittimo

Wednesday ['wenz·deɪ] *n* mercoledì *m inv*; **Ash ~** mercoledì delle Ceneri; *s.a.* **Friday**

wee [wi:] *adj* **1.** (*tiny*) piccolino, -a; **a ~ bit** un pochino **2.** (*early*) **in the ~ hours of Sunday morning** nelle prime ore di domenica

weed [wi:d] I. *n* **1.** (*plant*) erbaccia *f* **2.** *inf* (*marijuana*) erba *f* II. *vt* diserbare III. *vi* togliere le erbacce

◆ **weed out** *vt* eliminare

weedkiller ['wi:d·kɪ·lə] *n* diserbante *m*

weedy ['wi:·di] *adj* <-ier, iest> **1.** (*full of weeds*) pieno, -a di erbacce **2.** *pej* (*very thin*) gracile; (*underdeveloped*) scarno, -a

week [wi:k] *n* **1.** (*seven days*) settimana *f*; **it'll be ~s before ...** passeranno settimane prima che... +*subj*; **a few ~s ago** qualche settimana fa; **last ~** la settimana scorsa; **once a ~** una volta alla settimana; **during the ~** durante la settimana; **~ after ~** settimana dopo settimana; **~ by ~** di settimana in settimana **2.** (*work period, working days*) settimana *f* lavorativa; **a forty hour ~** una settimana lavorativa di quaranta ore

weekday ['wi:k·deɪ] *n* giorno *m* infrasettimanale; **on ~s** nei giorni feriali

weekend ['wi:k·end] *n* fine settimana *m inv*; **on the ~** nel/il fine settimana; **over the ~** nel/per il fine settimana

weekender ['wi:k·ˌen·də] *n persona che viene solo nel fine settimana*

weekly ['wi:k·li] I. *adj* settimanale; **~ magazine** (rivista *f*) settimanale *m* II. *adv* settimanalmente; **to meet/publish ~** ritrovarsi/pubblicare una volta alla settimana III. *n* <-ies> settimanale *m*

weenie *n* **1.** *inf* (*a hot dog*) hotdog *m inv* **2.** *sl* (*penis*) pisello *m*

weeny ['wi:·ni] *adj*, **weensy** *adj* <-ier, -iest> *inf* piccolino, -a; **a ~ bit** un pochino

weep [wi:p] I. *vi* <wept, wept> **1.** (*cry*) piangere; **to ~ like a baby** piangere come un bambino; **to ~ with joy/rage** piangere di gioia/rabbia; **to ~ inconsolably** piangere inconsolabilmente **2.** (*secrete liquid*) suppurare II. *vt* <wept, wept> (*tears*) piangere; **to ~ tears of joy/rage** (**over sb/sth**) piangere di gioia/rabbia (per qu/qc) III. *n* pianto *m*; **to have a** (**good**) **~** farsi un bel pianto

weeping I. *adj* piangente II. *n* pianto *m*

weeping willow *n* salice *m* piangente

wee-wee I. *n childspeak, inf* pipì *f*; **to have to go ~** dover fare la pipì II. *vi childspeak, inf* fare la pipì

weigh [weɪ] I. *vi* pesare II. *vt* **1.** (*measure weight*) pesare; **to ~ oneself** pesarsi **2.** (*consider carefully*) soppesare; **to ~ one's words** misurare le parole; **to ~ sth against sth** met-

W

tere sulla bilancia qc e qc; **to ~ one's options** considerare le proprie opzioni **3.** NAUT (*pull up*) **to ~ anchor** levare l'ancora

◆**weigh down** *vt* **1.** (*cause to bend*) piegare sotto il peso **2.** *fig* (*depress*) opprimere; **to weigh sb down with sth** opprimere qu con qc

◆**weigh in** *vi* **1.** (*be weighed*) pesarsi; **to ~ at 176 pounds** pesare 80 chili **2.** *inf* (*enter into, take part*) intervenire; **to ~ (to sth) with sth** intervenire (in qc) con qc; **to ~ to a discussion with one's opinion** intervenire in una discussione dicendo la propria opinione

weigh-in ['weɪ·ɪn] *n* pesatura *f*

weight [weɪt] **I.** *n* **1.** (*amount weighed*) peso *m;* **a decrease/an increase in ~** un calo/aumento di peso; **to lift a heavy ~** sollevare qualcosa di molto pesante; **to put on ~** ingrassare **2.** (*metal specific weight*) peso *m;* **to lift ~s** sollevare pesi **3.** (*value, importance*) peso *m;* **to attach ~ to sth** dare peso a qc; **to carry ~** avere peso ▶ **to take the ~ off one's feet** mettersi a sedere; **to be a ~ off sb's mind** essere un sollievo per qu; **it's a great ~ off my mind** mi sono tolto un gran peso; **to pull one's (own) ~** *inf* fare la propria parte **II.** *vt* tenere fermo; **to ~ sth with stones** tenere fermo qc con delle pietre

◆**weight down** *vt* **1.** (*overload*) sovraccaricare **2.** *a.fig* (*make heavy*) appesantire

weightless ['weɪt·ləs] *adj* (*conditions*) in assenza di gravità

weightlessness *n* assenza *f* di gravità

weightlifter *n* pesista *mf*

weightlifting ['weɪt·lɪf·tɪŋ] *n* sollevamento *m* pesi; **to do ~** fare il sollevamento pesi

weighty ['weɪ·t̬i] *adj* <-ier, -iest> **1.** (*heavy*) pesante **2.** (*important*) importante; **~ matters** questioni *fpl* importanti

weir [wɪr] *n* diga *f*

weird [wɪrd] *adj* strano, -a; **how ~** che strano!; **~ and wonderful** straordinario

weirdie ['wɪr·di] *n*, **weirdo** ['wɪr·doʊ] *n inf* tipo *m* strano

welcome ['wel·kəm] **I.** *vt* **1.** (*greet kindly*) dare il benvenuto a; **to ~ sb warmly** accogliere calorosamente **2.** (*support*) accogliere in modo favorevole **II.** *n* **1.** (*friendly reception*) benvenuto *m;* **to give sb a warm ~** accogliere calorosamente qu **2.** (*period of being wanted*) **to wear out one's ~** abusare dell'ospitalità **3.** (*expression of approval*) approvazione *f;* **to give sth a cautious ~** accogliere qc con qualche riserva **III.** *adj* gradito, -a; **a ~ guest** un ospite gradito; **to be ~** essere benvenuto; **a ~ break** una pausa gradita ▶ **you are ~** prego; **to be ~ to do sth** *inf* poter fare qc; **you are ~ to use it** è a sua disposizione **IV.** *interj* benvenuto!; **~ aboard** NAUT benvenuti a bordo

welcoming *adj* accogliente; **~ arms** braccia aperte; **a ~ smile** un sorriso cordiale

weld [weld] **I.** *vt* **1.** (*join metal*) saldare; **to ~ sth (together)** saldare qc **2.** (*unite*) unire; **to ~**

players into a team unire i giocatori di una squadra **II.** *n* saldadura *f*

welder *n* saldatore, -trice *m, f*

welding *n* saldatura *f*

welfare ['wel·fer] *n* **1.** (*health, happiness*) benessere *m* **2.** (*state aid*) previdenza *f* sociale; **social ~** assistenza *f* sociale; **to be on ~** vivere grazie a sussidi statali

welfare state *n* stato *m* assistenziale

welfare work *n* servizio *m* di assistenza sociale

welfare worker *n* assistente *mf* sociale

we'll [wiːl] = **we will** *s.* **will**

well[1] [wel] **I.** *adj* <better, best> bene; **to feel ~** sentirsi bien; **to get ~** rimettersi; **to look ~** avere un bell'aspetto **II.** <better, best> *adv* **1.** (*in a satisfactory manner*) bene; **~ enough** abbastanza bene; **~ done!** bravo!; **to do sth as ~ as ...** fare qc bene quanto ...; **~ put** ben detto; (**time/money**) **~ spent** (tempo/denaro) ben speso **2.** (*thoroughly, fully, extensively*) bene; **~ enough** abbastanza bene; **pretty ~** parecchio bene; **to know sb pretty ~** conoscere qu bene; **~ and truly** completamente; **it costs ~ over...** costa ben più di... **3.** (*very, completely*) molto; **to be ~ pleased with sth** essere molto soddisfatto di qc **4.** (*fairly, reasonably*) **he couldn't very ~ refuse their kind offer** non poteva rifiutare la loro generosa offerta; **you may ~ think it was his fault** si potrebbe anche pensare che sia stata colpa sua; **he might ~ be the best person to ask** potrebbe essere la persona più adatta a cui chiedere; **you might (just) as ~ tell her the truth** tanto varrebbe che tu le dicessi verità ▶ **all ~ and good** molto bene; **that's all very ~, but ...** va benissimo, ma...; **as ~** (*also*) anche; **as ~ as** così come; **just as ~** meglio così; **to be in ~ with sb** *inf* trovarsi bene con qu **III.** *interj* (*exclamation*) bene; **~, ~** ¡bene, bene!; **very ~!** benissimo!

well[2] [wel] **I.** *n* (*hole for water etc.*) pozzo *m;* **water ~** sorgente *f* d'acqua; **to drill a ~** scavare un pozzo **II.** *vi* (*flow*) sgorgare; **to ~ up in sth** affiorare in qc; **to ~ (up) out of sth** (*water*) sgorgare da qc

◆**well up** *vi a. fig* (*rise*) affiorare

well-advised [ˌwel·əd·ˈvaɪzd] *adj form* **he would be ~ to stay at home** farebbe bene a rimanere a casa

well-appointed [ˌwel·ə·ˈpɔɪn·t̬ɪd] *adj form* ben arredato, -a

well-balanced [ˌwel·ˈbæ·ləntst] *adj* equilibrato, -a; **~ diet** dieta bilanciata

well-behaved [ˌwel·bɪ·ˈheɪvd] *adj* (*child*) beneducato, -a; (*dog*) ben addestrato, -a

well-being ['wel·ˌbiː·ɪŋ] *n* benessere *m;* **a feeling of ~** una sensazione di benessere

well-bred [ˌwel·ˈbred] *adj* (*well brought up*) beneducato, -a; (*classy, refined*) raffinato, -a

well-chosen [ˌwel·ˈtʃoʊ·zən] *adj* scelto, -a con cura

well-connected [ˌwel·kə·ˈnek·tɪd] *adj* **to be ~** avere molti contatti; **a ~ family** una famiglia

influente
well-deserved [‚wel·dɪ·'sɜːvd] *adj* meritato, -a
well-developed [‚wel·dɪ·'ve·ləpt] *adj* sviluppato, -a; **a ~ sense of humor** un acuto senso dell'umorismo
well-disposed [‚wel·dɪs·'poʊzd] *adj* bendisposto, -a; **to be ~ towards sth** essere favorevole a qc; **to feel ~ towards sb** essere bendisposto verso qu
well-done [‚wel·'dʌn] *adj* 1. (*task*) benfatto, -a 2. (*meat*) ben cotto, -a
well-dressed [‚wel·'drest] *adj* benvestito, -a
well-educated [‚wel·'ed·ʒʊ·keɪ·t̬ɪd] *adj* colto, -a
well-fed [‚wel·'fed] *adj* (*full of food*) ben nutrito, -a
well-founded [‚wel·'faʊn·dɪd] *adj* fondato, -a; **~ suspicions** sospetti fondati
well-heeled [‚wel·'hiːld] I. *adj inf* ricco, -a II. *npl* **the ~** i ricchi
well-informed [‚wel·ɪn·'fɔːrmd] *adj* beninformato, -a; **to be ~ about sb/sth** essere beninformato su qu/qc; **to be ~ on a particular topic** conoscere a fondo un tema specifico
well-intentioned [‚wel·ɪn·'ten·tʃənd] *adj* benintenzionato, -a
well-kept [‚wel·'kept] *adj* curato, -a; (*secret*) ben mantenuto, -a
well-knit [‚wel·'nɪt] *adj* (*body*) robusto, -a; *fig* (*scheme, idea*) logico, -a; (*family*) molto affiatato, -a; **a ~ plot/story** una trama/storia ben costruita
well-known [‚wel·'noʊn] *adj* noto, -a; **to be ~ for sth** essere noto per qc; **it is ~ that ...** è risaputo che...
well-mannered [‚wel·'mæ·nə·d] *adj* educato, -a; **a ~ child** un bambino educato
well-meaning [‚wel·'miː·nɪŋ] *adj* benintenzionato, -a; **~ comments** commenti *mpl* fatti in buona fede
well-meant [‚wel·'ment] *adj* benintenzionato, -a
well-nigh ['wel·naɪ] *adv* quasi; **to be ~ impossible** essere pressoché impossibile
well-off [‚wel·'ɑːf] I. *adj* 1. (*wealthy*) benestante 2. (*having a lot*) **to be ~ for sth** essere ricco, -a di qc; **the city is ~ for parks** la città è ricca di parchi; **to not know when one is ~** non saper quanto si è fortunati II. *npl* **the ~** i ricchi
well-oiled [‚wel·'ɔɪld] *adj* 1. (*functioning smoothly*) efficiente 2. *inf* (*inebriated, drunk*) sbronzo, -a
well-organized [‚wel·'ɔːr·gə·naɪzd] *adj* ben organizzato, -a
well-paid [‚wel·'peɪd] *adj* ben retribuito, -a
well-placed [‚wel·'pleɪst] *adj* situato, -a bene
well-proportioned [‚wel·prə·'pɔːr·ʃənd] *adj* ben proporzionato, -a
well-read [‚wel·'red] *adj* 1. (*knowledgeable*) colto, -a 2. (*read frequently*) molto letto, -a
well-spoken [‚wel·'spoʊ·kən] *adj* cortese e istruito, -a

well-thought-of [‚wel·'θɑː·t̬·ə·v] *adj* (*person*) stimato, -a; (*school*) prestigioso, -a
well-timed [‚wel·'taɪmd] *adj* opportuno, -a
well-to-do [‚wel·tə·'duː] *inf* I. *adj* agiato, -a II. *n* **the ~** le persone agiate
well-turned [‚wel·'tɜːrnd] *adj* 1. (*gracefully shaped*) elegante 2. (*cleverly expressed: phrase*) ben costruito, -a
well-wisher ['wel·ˌwɪ·ʃə·] *n* simpatizzante *mf*
well-worn [‚wel·'wɔːrn] *adj* 1. (*damaged by wear*) consumato, -a 2. *fig* (*over-used*) trito, -a e ritrito, -a
Welsh [welʃ] I. *adj* gallese II. *n* 1. (*person*) gallese *mf* 2. LING gallese *m*
Welshman ['welʃ·mən] <-men> *n* gallese *m*
Welshwoman ['welʃ·ˌwʊ·mən] <-women> *n* gallese *f*
welt [welt] *n* 1. (*from blow*) rosso, -a *f* 2. (*in shoe*) tramezza *f*
welterweight ['wel·tə·weɪt] *n* welter *m inv*
went [went] *pt of* **go**
wept [wept] *pt, pp of* **weep**
were [wɜːr] *pt of* **be**
we're [wɪr] = **we are** *s.* **be**
weren't [wɜːrnt] = **were not** *s.* **be**
west [west] I. *n* 1. (*cardinal point*) ovest *m*; **in the ~ of Mexico** nel Messico occidentale; **to lie 5 miles to the ~ of ...** trovarsi 8 km a ovest di...; **to go/drive to the ~** dirigersi a ovest 2. (*part of the world*) **the West** l'Occidente 3. (*part of the US*) **the Far West** il Far West; **the Wild West** il selvaggio west II. *adj* occidentale; **~ wind** vento *m* da ovest; **~ coast** costa *f* occidentale; **West African** dell'Africa occidentale; **West Berlin** Berlino ovest; **West Indies** Antille *fpl* III. *adv* a ovest; **further ~** più a ovest ▶ **to go ~** (*thing*) perdersi; (*person*) finire all'altro mondo
westbound ['west·baʊnd] *adj* in direzione ovest
West End I. *n* **the ~** il West End di Londra II. *adj* **the ~ theaters** i teatri del West End
westerly ['wes·tə·li] *adj* occidentale; **~ winds** venti *mpl* da ovest
western ['wes·tə·n] I. *adj* occidentale; **the ~ part of the country** la parte occidentale del paese II. *n* CINE western *m inv*
westerner *n* 1. (*person from the west*) occidentale *mf* 2. (*person from the western US*) nordamericano, -a *m*, *f* dell'ovest
westernize ['wes·tə·naɪz] *vt* occidentalizzare
Western Samoa *n* Samoa *f* Occidentale
West Germany *n* HIST Germania *f* Ovest
Westminster Abbey [‚west·mɪnts·tə·'æ·bi] *n* Abbazia *f* di Westminster
West Virginia *n* Virginia *f* Occidentale
westward(s) ['west·wə·d(z)] *adj* (verso) ovest
wet [wet] I. *adj* <-tt-> 1. (*soaked*) bagnato, -a; **to get ~** bagnarsi; **to get sth ~** bagnare qc; **~ through** bagnato fradicio 2. (*not yet dried*) umido, -a; **~ paint** pittura fresca 3. (*rainy*) piovoso, -a; **~ weather** tempo piovoso ▶ **to be ~ behind the ears** avere la bocca che sa ancora

W

di latte; **to be all** ~ *sl* sbagliarsi di grosso II. <wet, wet> *vt* **1.** (*make damp*) inumidire **2.** (*urinate on*) **to ~ oneself/one's pants** farsi la pipì addosso; **to ~ the bed** fare la pipì a letto III. *n* **1. the ~** (*rain*) la pioggia **2.** *inf* POL antiproibizionista *mf*

wet nurse I. *n* HIST balia *f* II. *vt* fare da balia a

wetsuit *n* muta *f* da sub

we've [wiːv] = **we have** *s.* **have**

whack [hwæk] I. *vt* colpire II. *n* (*blow*) colpo *m;* **to give sth** (**a good**) ~ colpire qc ▶ **to be out of** ~ essere sfasciato; **to have a ~ at sth** *inf* tentare qc

whacking *n* botte *fpl;* **to give sb a** (**real**) ~ dare a qu un sacco di botte; **to take a** (**real**) ~ prendere un sacco di botte

whale [hweɪl] *n* balena *f;* **a beached ~** una balena spiaggiata ▶ **to have a ~ of a time** divertirsi un mondo; **a ~ of a ...** un(a) enorme...; **a ~ of a difference** una bella differenza

whaling *n* caccia *f* alle balene

wham [hwæm] *interj inf* **1.** (*sound-effect for blow*) bang **2.** (*describes action*) zac

wharf [hwɔːrf] <-ves> *n* molo *m;* **price ex ~** prezzo *m* franco molo

what [hwʌt] I. *adj interrog* che, quale; **~ kind of book?** che tipo di libro?; **~ time is it?** che ore sono?; **~ men is he talking about?** di quale uomo parla?; **~ an idiot!** che idiota!; **~ a fool I am!** che stupido che sono! II. *pron* **1.** *interrog* (che) cosa; **~ can I do?** cosa posso fare?; **~ does it matter?** cosa importa?; **~ 's on for tonight?** cosa c'è in programma stasera?; **~ 's up?** cosa c'è?; **~ for?** a che scopo?; **~ is he like?** com'è?; **~ 's his name?** come si chiama?; **~ 's it called?** come si chiama?; **~ about Paul?** e Paul?; **~ about a walk?** vi va una passeggiata?; **~ if it snows?** *inf* e se nevica? **2.** *rel* ciò/quello che; **~ I like is ~** he says/is talking about quello che mi piace è quello che dice/ciò di cui parla; **~ is more** per di più III. *interj* **~!?** cosa!?; **so ~?** e allora?; **is he coming, or ~?** viene o no?

whatever [hwʌt·'e·və·] I. *pron* **1.** (*anything*) qualunque cosa; **~ happens, happens** succeda quel che succeda **2.** (*any of them*) qualunque; **~ you pick is fine** qualunque tu scelga va bene II. *adj* **1.** (*being what it may be*) qualunque; **~ the reason** qualunque sia il motivo **2.** (*of any kind*) **there is no doubt ~** non c'è alcun dubbio

whatnot ['hwʌt·nɑːt] *n* **and ~** *inf* e roba del genere

whatsoever [ˌhwʌt·sou·'e·və·] *adv* **to have no interest ~ in sth** non avere interesse alcuno in qc; **nothing ~** niente di niente

wheat [hwiːt] *n* grano *m* ▶ **to separate the ~ from the** chaff separare il grano dal loglio

wheat belt *n* zona *f* coltivata a grano

wheat germ *n* germe *m* di grano

wheel [hwiːl] I. *n* **1.** (*of vehicle*) ruota *f;* **front/rear ~** ruota anteriore/posteriore; **big ~**

ruota *f;* **to be on ~s** avere le ruote **2.** TECH tornio *m;* **spinning ~** filatoio *m* a mano **3.** AUTO volante *m;* **to be at the ~** essere al volante; **to take the ~** mettersi al volante; **to get behind the ~** mettersi al volante **4.** *pl, inf* (*vehicle, car*) mezzo *m* **5.** NAUT timone *m* ▶ **to be hell on ~s** *inf* essere un pericolo al volante II. *vt* spingere III. *vi* volteggiare ▶ **to ~ and** deal *inf* intrallazzare

◆**wheel around** *vi* voltarsi di scatto

wheelbarrow ['hwiːl·ˌbe·rou] *n* carriola *f*

wheelchair *n* sedia *f* a rotelle

wheeler-dealer [ˌhwiː·lə·'diː·lə·] *n pej, inf* intrallazzone, -a *m, f*

wheelhouse ['hwiːl·haus] *n* timoniera *f*

wheeze [hwiːz] I. <-zing> *vi* sibilare (respirando) II. *n* (*of breath*) sibilo *m*

wheezy *adj* <-ier, -iest> ansante

whelp [hwelp] I. *n* cucciolo *m* II. *vt* partorire

when [hwen] I. *adv* quando; **since ~?** da quando?; **I'll tell him ~ to go** gli dirò io quando andare II. *conj* **1.** (*at which time*) quando; **at the moment ~ he arrived** nel momento in cui è arrivato **2.** (*during the time that*) **~ singing that song** quando cantava quella canzone **3.** (*every time that*) **~ it snows** quando nevica **4.** (*although*) **he buys it ~ he could** (**just as easily**) **borrow it** lo compra quando potrebbe prenderlo in prestito **5.** (*considering that*) se; **how can I listen ~ I can't hear?** come faccio ad ascoltare se non riesco a sentire?

whence [hwents] *adv form* dove; (*interrogative*) da dove?

whenever [hwen·'e·və·] I. *conj* **1.** (*every time that*) quando; **~ I can** ogni volta che posso **2.** (*at any time that*) **he can come ~ he likes** può venire quando vuole II. *adv* **~ did I say that?** quando mai l'ho detto?; **I can do it tomorrow or ~** posso farlo domani o un giorno di questi

where [hweə·] *adv* **1.** *interrog* dove; **~ does he come from?** da dove viene?; **~ does he live?** dove abita?; **~ is he going** (**to**)? dove va? **2.** *rel* dove; **I'll tell him ~ to go** gli dirò io dove andare; **the box ~ he puts his things** la scatola dove mette le sue cose; **this is ~ my horse was found** qui è dove hanno trovato il mio cavallo; **Minnesota, ~ Paul comes from, is ...** il Minnesota, da dove viene Paul, è...

whereabouts ['hwer·ə·bauts] I. *n* + *sing/pl vb* posizione *f;* **do you know the ~ of my book?** *form* sa dov'è il mio libro? II. *adv inf* dove; **~ in San Francisco do you live?** in che zona di San Francisco abiti?

whereas [hwer·'æz] *conj* **1.** (*while*) mentre **2.** LAW considerato che

whereby [hwer·'baɪ] *conj form* tramite cui

wherein [hwer·'ɪn] *conj form* dove

wheresoever [ˌhwer·sou·e·və·] *adv, conj form s.* **wherever**

whereupon ['hwer·ə·ˌpɑːn] *conj form* al che

wherever [ˌhwerˈeˑvəˈ] I. *conj* dovunque; ~ I am/I go dovunque sia/vada; ~ there is sth dovunque ci sia qc; ~ he likes dovunque voglia II. *adv* ~ did she find that? dove mai l'ha trovato?; ... or ~ ...o da qualche altro posto

wherewithal [ˈhwerˑwɪðˑɔːl] *n liter* mezzi *mpl;* to lack the ~ (to do sth) non avere i mezzi (per fare qc)

whet [hwet] <-tt-> *vt* 1.(*sharpen*) affilare 2.*fig*(*increase, stimulate*) stimulare; to ~ sb's appetite (for sth) stuzzicare il desiderio di qu (di qc)

whether [ˈhweˑðəˈ] *conj* 1.(*if*) se; to tell/ask ~ it's true (or not) dire/chiedere se è vero (o no); she doesn't know ~ to buy it or not non sa se comprarlo o no; I doubt ~ he'll come dubito che venga 2.(*all the same*) ~ rich or poor... che siano ricchi o poveri...; ~ I go by bus or bike ... che vada in autobus o in bicicletta...

whetstone [ˈhwetˑstoʊn] *n* cote *f*

whew [fjuː] *interj inf* fiu

whey [hweɪ] *n* siero *m*

which [hwɪtʃ] I. *adj interrog* quale; ~ one/ ones? quale/quali? II. *pron* 1.*interrog* quale; ~ is his? qual è il suo? 2.*rel* che; the book ~ I read/of ~ I'm speaking il libro che ho letto/ di cui sto parlando; he said he was there, ~ I believed ha detto che c'era, cosa che credo

whichever [hwɪtʃˈeˑvəˈ] I. *pron* qualunque; you can choose ~ you like scegli quello che ti pare II. *adj* qualunque; you can take ~ book you like puoi prendere qualunque libro tu voglia

whiff [hwɪf] *n* 1.(*quick smell*) ondata *f;* to catch a ~ of sth sentire odore di qc 2.*fig* (*slight trace*) pizzico *m;* a ~ of corruption un minimo sospetto di corruzione

while [hwaɪl] I. *n* a short ~ un pochino; quite a ~ un bel po'; after a ~ dopo un po'; for a ~ per un po'; once in a ~ una volta (ogni) tanto II. *conj* 1.(*during which time*) mentre; I did it ~ he was sleeping l'ho fatto mentre dormiva; ~ I'm alive finché sono vivo 2.(*although*) benché; ~ I like it, I won't buy it nonostante mi piaccia, non lo compro; ~ I know it's true ... benché pensi sia vero...
◆**while away** *vt* passare; to ~ the time far passare il tempo

whim [hwɪm] *n* capriccio *m;* to do sth on a ~ fare qc per capriccio; as the ~ takes him quando gli gira

whimper [ˈhwɪmˑpəˈ] I. *vi* gemere; (*child*) piagnucolare; (*dog*) guaire II. *n* gemito *m;* (*of dog*) guaito *m;* to give a ~ emettere un gemito

whimsical [ˈhwɪmˑzɪˑkəl] *adj* 1.(*odd*) bizzarro, -a 2.(*capricious*) capriccioso, -a

whimsicality [ˌhwɪmˑzɪˈkæˑləˑti] *n* 1.(*odd character*) stravaganza *f* 2.(*caprice*) capriccio *m*

whimsy [ˈhwɪmˑzi] <-ies> *n pej* 1.(*odd fancifulness*) stravaganza *f* 2.(*odd, fanciful thing or work*) fantasia *f* 3.(*whim*) capriccio *m*

whine [hwaɪn] I.<-ning> *vi* 1.(*complaining noise, cry*) gemito 2.(*engine*) fischiare II. *n* (*of a person*) gemito *m;* (*of an animal*) guaito *m;* (*of an engine*) fischio *m*

whinny [ˈhwɪˑni] I.<-ied, -ing> *vi* nitrire II. *n* <-ies> nitrito *m*

whip [hwɪp] I. *n* 1.(*lash*) frusta *f;* to crack a ~ far schioccare la frusta 2.(*person*) *persona encargada de la disciplina de partido;* chief ~ capogruppo *mf* II.<-pp-> *vt* 1.(*strike with whip*) frustare 2.(*strike*) sferzare 3.*fig, inf* (*battere*) to ~ sb at [*o* in] sth battere qu a/in qc 4.GASTR montare III.<-pp-> *vi* 1.(*strike*) sbattere 2.(*move fast*) sfrecciare; to ~ around the corner (*car*) svoltare a tutta velocità
◆**whip back** *vi* (*bounce back*) tornare indietro di scatto
◆**whip off** *vt* (*one's clothes*) togliersi in fretta; (*tablecloth*) togliere di scatto
◆**whip on** *vt* 1.(*urge on*) incitare 2.(*put on quickly*) mettersi in fretta
◆**whip out** *vt* tirare fuori
◆**whip up** *vt* 1.(*encourage*) stimolare 2.*inf* (*prepare quickly*) preparare rapidamente 3.GASTR to ~ eggs sbattere le uova

whipcord [ˈhwɪpˑkɔːrd] *n* whipcord *m*

whip hand *n* to hold the ~ avere una posizione di forza

whiplash *n* <-es> 1.(*whip part*) sverzino *m* 2.(*blow from whip*) frustata *m* 3.(*injury*) colpo *m* di frusta

whipped cream *n* panna *f* montata

whippersnapper [ˈhwɪˑpəˈˌsnæˑpəˈ] *n iron* sbruffoncello, -a *m, f*

whippet [ˈhwɪˑpɪt] *n* cane simile al levriero

whipping I. *n* 1.(*punishment, physical beating*) fustigazione *f;* to be given a (good) ~ essere preso a frustate 2.(*gusting*) the ~ of the wind lo sferzare del vento II. *adj* (*gusty*) sferzante; a ~ wind un vento sferzante

whipping boy [ˈhwɪˑpɪŋˑbɔɪ] *n* capro *m* espiatorio

whipping cream *n* panna *f* da montare

whirl [hwɜːrl] I. *vi* turbinare; my head ~s *fig* mi gira la testa II. *vt* far girare; to ~ sb around far volteggiare qu III. *n* turbinio *m;* a ~ of dust un turbine di polvere ▸ to give sth a ~ provare qc

whirligig [ˈhwɜːrˑlɪˑɡɪɡ] *n* 1.(*toy*) trottola *f* 2.*fig* turbine *m*

whirlpool [ˈhwɜːrlˑpuːl] *n* mulinello *m*

whirlwind *n* turbine *m;* a ~ romance una turbinosa storia d'amore

whirlybird [ˈhwɜːrˑlɪˑbɜːrd] *n inf* (*helicopter*) elicottero *m*

whirr [hwɜːr] I. *vi* ronzare II. *n* ronzio *m;* (*of bird's wings*) frullio *m*

whisk [hwɪsk] I. *vt* 1.GASTR battere 2.(*take quickly*) portare rapidamente; to ~ sb off somewhere portare rapidamente qu da qualche parte 3.(*with sweeping movement: tail*) agitare II. *n* 1.(*kitchen tool*) frusta *f;* electric ~ frullino *m* elettrico 2.(*sweeping*

W

motion) colpo *m*

whisker [ˈhwɪs·kəˑ] *n* **1.** ~**s** (*facial hair*) pelo *m* della barba **2.** *pl* (*of animal*) baffi *mpl* ▶ **by a** ~ per un pelo; **within a** ~ **of sth/doing sth** a un passo da qc/dal fare qc

whiskey *n*, **whisky** [ˈhwɪs·ki] *n* <-ies> whisky *m inv*

whisper [ˈhwɪs·pəˑ] **I.** *vi* sussurrare **II.** *vt* **1.** (*speak softly*) sussurrare; **to** ~ **sth in sb's ear** sussurrare qc all'orecchio di qu **2.** *fig* (*gossip, speak privately*) mormorare; **it is** ~**ed that ...** si mormora che... **III.** *n* **1.** (*soft sound or speech*) mormorio *m;* **to lower one's voice to a** ~ abbassare la voce e parlare sussurrando; **to speak in a** ~ sussurrare **2.** *fig* (*rumor*) voce *f* **3.** *fig, liter* (*soft rustle*) susurrio *m;* **the** ~ **of the leaves** il fruscio delle foglie

whispering *n* **1.** (*talking very softly*) susurro *m* **2.** *fig* (*gossiping*) voci *fpl*

whispering campaign *n* campagna *f* diffamatoria

whist [hwɪst] *n* whist *m;* **a game of** ~ una partita a whist

whistle [ˈhwɪ·sl] **I.** <-ling> *vi* fischiare; **to** ~ **at sb/sth** fischiare a qu/qc; **to** ~ **in admiration** fare fischi di approvazione **II.** <-ling> *vt* fischiettare **III.** *n* **1.** (*blowing sound*) fischio *m;* **the** ~ **of the wind** il fischiare del vento **2.** (*musical device*) fischio *m;* **referee's** ~ fischio *m* dell'arbitro; **to blow a** ~ fischiare ▶ **to** <u>blow</u> **the** ~ **on sb** denunciare qu; **to** <u>wet</u> **one's** ~ bagnarsi la bocca

white [hwaɪt] **I.** *adj* bianco, -a; ~ **sauce** besciamella *f;* ~ **wedding** matrimonio *m* tradizionale; **to turn** [*o* go] ~ **with fear** sbiancare dalla paura ▶ **to fly into a** ~ <u>rage</u> andare su tutte le furie **II.** *n* **1.** (*color*) bianco *m;* **the** ~ **of an egg** il bianco dell'uovo; **the** ~ **of sb's eyes** il bianco degli occhi di qu **2.** (*person*) bianco, -a *m, f*

white-collar [ˌhwaɪt·ˈkɑː·ləˑ] *adj* ~ **worker** impiegato, -a *m, f*

white elephant *n* cattedrale *f* nel deserto

white flag *n* bandiera *f* bianca; **to fly** [*o* raise] **a** ~ alzare una bandiera bianca

white goods *npl* **1.** (*major household appliances*) elettrodomestici *mpl* **2.** (*household linen*) biancheria *f* per la casa

Whitehall [ˈhwaɪt·hɔːl] *n* **1.** (*offices of Britain's government*) strada londinese in cui hanno sede vari ministeri **2.** *fig* (*government of Britain*) governo britannico

white heat *n* **1.** (*of metal*) calor *m* bianco **2.** *fig* (*passion*) fervore *m*

White House *n* **the** ~ la Casa Bianca

white lie *n* piccola bugia *f*

white man <-men> *n* uomo *m* bianco

white meat *n* carne *f* bianca

whiten [ˈhwaɪ·tən] **I.** *vt* (*wall*) imbiancare; (*teeth*) sbiancare **II.** *vi* diventare bianco, -a

whitener [ˈhwaɪt·nəˑ] *n* sbiancante *m*

whiteness *n* bianchezza *f*

whiteout *n* **1.** (*dense blizzard*) bufera *f* di neve **2.** TYPO bianchetto *m*

white sale *n* fiera *f* del bianco

white-tie I. *adj* ~ **dinner** cena *f* di gala **II.** *n* papillon *m* bianco *inv*

whitewash [ˈhwaɪt·wɑːʃ] **I.** <-es> *n* **1.** (*for whitening walls*) calce *m* **2.** (*coverup*) copertura *m* **3.** *inf* (*overwhelming victory*) vittoria *f* schiacciante **II.** *vt* **1.** (*cover in white solution*) imbiancare **2.** (*conceal negative side of*) coprire **3.** *inf* SPORTS (*defeat completely*) schiacciare

white-water rafting [ˌhwaɪt·wɑ·təˑ·ˈræf·tɪŋ] *n* rafting *m* in acque bianche

white wine *n* vino *m* bianco

whither [ˈhwɪ·ðəˑ] *adv form* dove

whiting¹ [ˈhwaɪ·tɪŋ] *n* (*fish*) merlano *m*

whiting² [ˈhwaɪ·tɪŋ] *n* (*white substance*) sbiancante *c*

Whitmonday [ˌhwɪt·ˈmʌn·deɪ] *n* Lunedì *m inv* di Pentecoste

Whitsun [ˈhwɪt·sən] **I.** *n* Pentecoste *f;* **at** ~ per la Pentecoste **II.** *adj* di Pentecoste

Whitsunday [ˌhwɪt·ˈsʌn·deɪ] *n* Pentecoste *f*

Whitsuntide [ˈhwɪt·sən·taɪd] *n s.* **Whitsun**

whittle [ˈhwɪ·t̩l] <-ling> *vt* tagliuzzare

◆ **whittle away at** *vt* **1.** (*take little bits off*) tagliuzzare **2.** *fig* (*decrease*) ridurre gradualmente

◆ **whittle down** *vt* ridurre gradualmente

whiz [hwɪz] **I.** *n* **1.** *inf* (*brilliant person*) genio *m* **2.** (*noise*) ronzio *m* **3.** *sl* (*act of urinating*) **to take a** ~ pisciare **II.** *vi* **1.** (*move fast*) sfrecciare; **to** ~ **along** *inf* sfrecciare; **to** ~ **by** *inf* passare sfrecciando **2.** *sl* (*urinate*) pisciare

whiz kid *n inf* genietto *m*

whizz [hwɪz] *n, vi s.* **whiz**

who [huː] *pron* **1.** *interrog* chi; ~ **broke the window?** chi ha rotto la finestra?; ~ **were they?** chi erano? **2.** *rel* che; **they have a daughter** ~ **works in Alaska** hanno una figlia che lavora in Alaska; **the people ~ work here** la gente che lavora qui; **all those ~ know her** tutti quelli che la conoscono; **it was your sister ~ did it** l'ha fatto tua sorella

WHO [ˌdʌ·bl·juː·ˌeɪtʃ·'oʊ] *n abbr of* **World Health Organization** OMS *f*

whoa [hwoʊ] *interj* **1.** (*command to stop a horse*) ferma **2.** *fig, inf* (*to stop something*) calma

whodunit *n*, **whodunnit** [ˌhuː·'dʌ·nɪt] *n inf* giallo *m*

whoever [huː·'e·vɚ] *pron* **1.** *rel* (*who*) chiunque; **~ said that doesn't know me** chiunque l'abbia detto non mi conosce **2.** *interrog, inf* (*angry*) chi (diavolo); **~ said that?** chi diavolo l'ha detto?

whole [hoʊl] **I.** *adj* **1.** (*entire*) tutto, -a; **the ~ world** tutto il mondo **2.** (*in one piece, intact*) intero, -a **3.** *inf* (*big*) **a ~ lot of people** un sacco di gente; **to be a ~ lot faster** essere molto più veloce **II.** *n* **1.** (*a complete thing*) tutto *m*; **as a ~** (*concept*) nella sua interezza; **on the ~** nel complesso **2.** (*entirety*) totalità *f*; **the ~ of Los Angeles** tutta Los Angeles; **the ~ of next week** tutta la settimana prossima **III.** *adv* completamente; **~ new** completamente nuevo

whole food *n* **1.** (*unprocessed food*) alimenti *mpl* integrali **2.** *pl* (*unprocessed food products*) alimenti *mpl* integrali

wholegrain ['hoʊl·greɪn] *adj* integrale; **~ bread** pane *m* integrale; **~ food products** alimenti *mpl* integrali

wholehearted [ˌhoʊl·'hɑːr·tɪd] *adj* entusiasta; (*completely sincere*) profondamente sincero, -a; **~ thanks** ringraziamenti *m* sinceri

wholesale ['hoʊl·seɪl] **I.** *n* vendita *f* all'ingrosso **II.** *adj* **1.** all'ingrosso; **~ business** magazzino *m* all'ingrosso; **~ prices** prezzi *mpl* all'ingrosso; **~ supplier** grossista *mf* **2.** (*on a large scale*) su grande scala; **~ reform** riforma *f* su grande scala **III.** *adv* **1.** COM all'ingrosso **2.** (*in bulk*) in massa

wholesaler ['hoʊl·seɪ·lɚ] *n* grossista *mf*; **furniture ~** grossista di mobili

wholesome ['hoʊl·səm] *adj* sano, -a; **the ~ outdoor life** la vita sana all'aria aperta; (*good*) **~ fun** sano divertimento *f*; (*good*) **~ food** alimenti *plm* sani (e genuini)

whole-wheat *adj* di grano integrale

who'll [huːl] = **who will** *s.* **will**

wholly ['hoʊ·li] *adv* totalmente; **to be ~ aware of sth** essere del tutto consapevole di qc; **~ different** completamente differente

whom [huːm] *pron* **1.** *interrog* chi; **~ did he see?** chi ha visto?; **to ~ did he talk?** con chi ha parlato? **2.** *rel* che; *after prep* il/la quale, i/le quali; **those ~ I love** coloro che amo; **I met a man with ~ I used to work** ho incontrato un signore con il quale lavoravo

whoop [huːp] **I.** *vi* gridare **II.** *vt* **to ~ it up** fare baldoria **III.** *n* grido *m;* **a ~ of triumph** grido *m* di vittoria; **to give a loud ~** gridare forte

whoopee ['hwuː·pi] **I.** *interj* urrà **II.** *n* giubilo *m;* **to make ~** *sl* (*have sex*) fare sesso; (*celebrate*) fare baldoria

whooping cough ['huː·pɪŋ·kɑːf] *n* pertosse *f*

whoops [hwʊps] *interj inf* oplà

whop [hwɑːp] *inf* **I.** <-pp-> *vt* **1.** (*strike*) colpire **2.** (*in competition*) battere **II.** *n* botta *f*

whopper ['hwɑː·pɚ] *n iron* **1.** (*huge thing*) cosa *m* gigante; **a ~ of a fish** un pescione **2.** (*lie*) balla *f;* **to tell a ~** raccontare una balla

whopping ['hwɑː·pɪŋ] *adj inf* enorme; **a ~ lie** una balla enorme

whore [hɔːr] *n pej* puttana *f*

whorl [hwɜːrl] *n liter* spirale *f*

who's [huːz] **1.** = **who is** *s.* **is 2.** = **who has** *s.* **has**

whose [huːz] **I.** *adj* **1.** *interrog* di chi; **~ book is this?** di chi è questo libro?; **~ son is he?** di chi è figlio? **2.** *rel* il/la cui; **the girl ~ brother I saw** la ragazza di cui ho visto il fratello **II.** *pron pos* di chi; **~ is this pen?** di chi è questa penna?; **I know ~ this is** questo so di chi è

why [hwaɪ] **I.** *adv* perché; **~ didn't you tell me about that?** perché non me ne hai parlato?; **that's ~ I didn't tell you** ecco perché non ti ho detto niente; **I want to know ~ you came late** voglio sapere perché sei arrivato tardi; **~ not?** perché no?; **~'s that?** perché? **II.** *n* perché *m inv;* **the ~s and** **wherefores** of **sth** il perché e il percome di qc **III.** *interj* come mai?

WI *n abbr of* **Wisconsin** Wisconsin

wick [wɪk] *n* stoppino *m*

wicked ['wɪ·kɪd] **I.** *adj* **1.** (*evil*) malvagio, -a **2.** (*playfully malicious*) malizioso, -a; **a ~ grin** un sorriso malandrino **3.** (*likely to cause pain*) temibile **4.** *inf* (*great fun*) grande **II.** *n* **the ~** i malvagi

wicker ['wɪ·kɚ] *n* vimine *m*

wickerwork *n* **1.** (*material*) vimine *m* **2.** (*art*) articolo *m* in vimine

wicket ['wɪ·kɪt] *n* **1.** (*cricket target*) wicket *m inv* **2.** (*ground*) campo *m;* **to be in a sticky ~** essere nei casini

wicketkeeper ['wɪ·kɪt·ˌkiː·pɚ] *n* difensore *m* del wicket

wide [waɪd] **I.** *adj* **1.** (*broad*) ampio, -a; (*as a measurement*) largo, -a; **it is 3 feet ~** largo 1 m; **the** (*great*) **~ world** il mondo (intero); **to search** (**for sb/sth**) **the ~ world over** cercare (qu/qc) in tutto il mondo **2.** (*very open*) spalancato, -a; **eyes ~ with fear/surprise** occhi *mpl* sbarrati per la paura/sorpresa **3.** (*varied*) vasto, -a; **a ~ range** una vasta gamma; **to have ~ experience in sth** avere vasta esperienza in qc **4.** (*extensive*) ampio, -a; **~ support** grosso appoggio *m;* **~ of the mark** mancare il bersaglio **II.** *adv* **to be ~ apart** essere lontanissimi (l'uno dall'altro); **to open ~** aprire bene; **~ open** spalancato

wide-angle [ˌwaɪd·'æŋ·gl] *adj* (*lente*) grandangolare

W

wide-awake [ˌwaɪd·ə·'weɪk] *adj* completamente sveglio, -a

wide-eyed ['waɪd·aɪd] *adj fig* innocente

widely *adv* 1.(*broadly, extensively*) ampiamente; **to gesture** ~ fare grandi gesti; **to smile** ~ **at sb** fare un gran sorriso a qu; ~ **accepted** comunemente accettato; ~ **admired** molto ammirato 2.(*to a large degree*) notevolmente; ~ **differing aims** obiettivi *mpl* notevolmente diversi

widen ['waɪ·dən] I. *vt* ampliare II. *vi* allargarsi

wide-open ['waɪd·ˌoʊ·pən] *adj* 1.(*undecided*) aperto, -a 2.(*vulnerable, exposed*) esposto, -a; **to be** ~ **to comments** essere esposto ai commenti

widespread ['waɪd·spred] *adj a.fig* diffuso, -a; **there is** ~ **speculation that …** gira voce che…

widow ['wɪ·doʊ] I. *n* vedova *f;* **to be left a** ~ rimanere vedova II. *vt* **to** ~ **sb** lasciare vedovo qu [*o* lasciare vedova qu]; **to be ~ed** rimanere vedovo [*o* rimanere vedova]

widowed *adj* vedovo, -a

widower ['wɪ·do·ʊɚ] *n* vedovo *m;* **to be left a** ~ rimanere vedovo

widowhood ['wɪ·doʊ·hʊd] *n* vedovanza *f*

widow's peak *n* attaccatura *f* dei capelli a forma di V

width [wɪdθ] *n* 1.ampiezza *f,* larghezza *f;* (*of wallpaper, cloth*) altezza *f;* **to be 4 inches in** ~ essere largo 10 cm; (*wallpaper, cloth*) essere alto 10 cm 2.(*of pool*) vasca *f;* **to swim two ~s** fare due vasche (a nuoto)

wield [wiːld] *vt* 1.(*weapon, tool*) impugnare 2.(*power*) esercitare

wife [waɪf] <wives> *n* moglie *f;* **my** ~ mia moglie

wifely ['waɪf·li] *adj* di moglie

wig [wɪg] *n* parrucca *f*

wiggle ['wɪ·gl] I. *vt* muovere II. *vi* agitarsi III. *n* movimento *m*

wigwam ['wɪg·wɑːm] *n* wigwam *m*

wild [waɪld] I. *adj* 1.(*animal, man, landscape*) selvaggio, -a; (*flower, cat*) selvatico, -a 2.(*undisciplined*) scatenato, -a 3.(*not sensible, extreme*) assurdo, -a 4.(*not accurate*) azzardato, -a 5.(*stormy*) burrascoso, -a; (*wind*) furioso, -a 6. *inf* (*angry*) furioso, -a; **to drive sb** ~ mandare qu su tutte le furie; **to go** ~ andare su tutte le furie 7. *inf* (*very enthusiastic*) entusiasta 8.(*untidy: hair*) arruffato, -a 9.GAMES, INFOR (*substitutable*) jolly 10. *inf* (*wonderful*) fantastico, -a II. *adv* allo stato selvatico ▸**to run** ~ (*child*) crecere come un selvaggio; (*horse*) vivere allo stato brado; **to let one's imagination run** ~ lasciare libera la fantasia III. *n* 1.**the** ~ (*natural environment*) in **the** ~ allo stato libero 2. *pl* **the ~s** le terre vergini; (out) **in the ~s** in capo al mondo *inf*

wild card *n* 1. *a.* INFOR carattere *m* jolly 2.SPORTS wild card *f inv*

wildcat I. *n* 1.ZOOL (*wild cat*) gatto *m* selvatico 2.*fig* (*fierce woman*) tigre *f* II. *adj* 1.(*very*

risky) azzardato, -a 2.(*unofficial: strike*) selvaggio, -a 3.(*exploratory: drilling, well*) esplorativo, -a

wilderness ['wɪl·dɚ·nəs] *n* 1.(*desert tract*) distesa *f* desolata 2.(*unspoiled land*) terra *f* vergine 3.*fig* (*uncultivated garden*) giungla *f iron*

wildfire ['waɪld·ˌfa·ɪɚ] *n* incendio *m* in zona campestre ▸**to spread like** ~ diffondersi rapidamente

wildfowl ['waɪld·faʊl] *inv n* uccelli *mpl* selvatici

wild goose <- geese> *n* oca *f* selvatica

wild-goose chase *n* impresa *f* vana; (*hopeless search*) ricerca *f* vana

wildlife *n* fauna *f* e flora

wildly *adv* 1.(*in an uncontrolled way*) sfrenatamente; **to gesticulate** ~ fare un sacco di gesti; **to behave** ~ comportarsi come un selvaggio; **to beat** ~ battere all'impazzata 2.(*haphazardly*) a casaccio 3. *inf* (*very*) molto; ~ **exaggerated** ingigantito, -a; ~ **expensive** carissimo; ~ **improbable** veramente improbabile

wildness *n* 1.(*natural state*) stato *m* selvaggio 2.(*uncontrolled behavior*) sfrenatezza *f* 3.(*haphazardness*) insensatezza *f*

wiles [waɪlz] *npl* astuzie *fpl;* **to use all one's** ~ ricorrere a ogni astuzia

wilful ['wɪl·fəl] *adj s.* willful

wiliness ['waɪ·lɪ·nəs] *n* astuzia *f*

will¹ [wɪl] <would, would> I. *aux* 1.(*to form future tense*) **they'll be delighted** saranno felicissimi; **I'll be with you in a minute** dammi solo un momento; **I expect they'll come by car** suppongo che vengano in auto; **I'll answer the telephone** rispondo io al telefono; **she** ~ **have received the letter by now** avrà già ricevuto la lettera 2.(*with tag question*) **you won't forget to tell him,** ~ **you?** non dimenticarti di dirglielo!; **they** ~ **accept this credit card in the pizzeria, won't they?** questa carta di credito l'accetteranno in pizzeria, no? 3.(*to express immediate future*) **we'll be off now** ora ce ne andiamo; **I'll be going then** allora me ne vado; **there's someone at the door — I'll go** hanno suonato il campanello — vado io 4.(*to express an intention*) **sb** ~ **do that** qu lo farà; **I'll not be spoken to like that!** non permetto che mi si parli così! 5.(*in requests and instructions*) ~ **you let me speak!?** mi fai parlare!; **just pass me that knife,** ~ **you?** mi passi il coltello?; **give me a hand,** ~ **you?** mi dai una mano? 6.(*in polite requests*) ~ **you sit down?** prego, si sieda; ~ **you be having a slice of cake?** vuole un pezzo di torta? 7.(*used to express willingness*) **who'll mail this letter for me? — I** ~ chi m'imbuca questa lettera? — lo faccio io; ~ **you do that for me? — of course I** ~ puoi farmelo? — certamente 8.(*used to express a fact*) **eat it now, it won't keep** mangialo ora, se no va a male; **the car won't run without gasoline** la macchina non funziona senza benzina **9.** (*to express persistence*) **he ~ keep doing that** continuerà a farlo; **they ~ keep sending me those brochures** non smetteranno di mandarmi quei dépliant; **the door won't open** la porta non si apre **10.** (*to express likelihood*) **they'll be tired** saranno stanchi; **as you ~ all probably know already...** come tutti probabilmente sapranno... **II.** *vi form* volere; **as you ~** come vuole

will² [wɪl] **I.** *n* **1.** (*faculty*) volontà *f;* (*desire*) voglia *f;* **the ~ of the people** la volontà del popolo; **to have the ~ to do sth** voler fare qc; **to lose the ~ to live** perdere la volontà di vivere; **at ~** a volontà/piacere **2.** (*testament*) testamento *m* ▶ **where there's a ~, there's a way** *prov* volere è potere *prov;* **with the best ~ in the world** con tutta la buona volontà del mondo; **to have a ~ of one's own** essere caparbio **II.** *vt* **1.** (*try to cause by will-power*) volere; **to ~ sb to do sth** esortare qu a fare qc **2.** *form* (*ordain*) volere; **God ~ed it and it was so** Dio lo ha voluto e così è stato **3.** (*bequeath*) lasciare per testamento

willful ['wɪl·fəl] *adj* **1.** (*deliberate*) deliberato, -a; (*murder*) premeditato, -a **2.** (*self-willed*) volitivo, -a; (*obstinate*) ostinato, -a

willies ['wɪ·liz] *npl sl* **to have the ~** avere i brividi; **to give sb the ~** far venire i brividi a qu

willing ['wɪ·lɪŋ] *adj* **1.** (*not opposed*) (ben) disposto, -a; **to be ~ to do sth** essere disposto a fare qc; **to lend a ~ hand** dare una mano; **God ~** se Dio vuole **2.** (*compliant*) volenteroso, -a

willingness *n* disponibilità *f;* **to show a ~ to do sth** mostrarsi disposto a fare qc; **lack of ~** mancanza *f* di entusiasmo

will-o'-the-wisp [ˌwɪl·ə·ðə·'wɪsp] *n* **1.** (*ghostly light*) fuoco *m* fatuo **2.** *fig* (*elusive thing*) chimera *f*

willow ['wɪ·loʊ] *n* salice *m*

willowy ['wɪ·loʊ·i] *adj* slanciato, -a

willpower ['wɪl·ˌpa·ʊɚ] *n* forza *f* di volontà

willy-nilly [ˌwɪ·li·'nɪ·li] *adv* **1.** (*like it or not*) volente o nolente **2.** (*in disorder*) a casaccio

wilt [wɪlt] *vi* **1.** (*droop: plants*) appassire **2.** (*feel weak: person*) indebolirsi; (*lose confidence*) scoraggiarsi

wily ['waɪ·li] <-ier, -iest> *adj* astuto, -a

wimp [wɪmp] *n inf* imbranato *mf*

win [wɪn] **I.** *n* vittoria *f* **II.** <won, won> *vt* **1.** (*be victorious in*) vincere; **to ~ first prize** vincere il primo premio **2.** (*obtain*) ottenere; (*recognition, popularity*) guadagnarsi; **to ~ a reputation as a writer** affermarsi come scrittore; **to ~ sb's heart** conquistare la simpatia di qu ▶ **to ~ the day** averla vinta; **you can't ~ them all** non si può vincere sempre; **you ~ some, you lose some** a volte si vince, a volte si perde **III.** <won, won> *vi* vincere; **to ~ easily** vincere con facilità ▶ **to ~ hands down** vincere con facilità; **you (just) can't ~ with him/her** per lui/lei non è mai abbastanza;

you ~! come vuoi!

◆**win back** *vt* riconquistare

◆**win over** *vt* **to win sb over to sth** (*persuade to change mind*) convincere qu di qc; (*persuade to transfer allegiance*) guadagnarsi l'appoggio di qu per qc

wince [wɪns] **I.** *vi* trasalire **II.** *n* smorfia *f* (di dolore); **to give a ~** fare una smorfia

winch [wɪntʃ] **I.** <-es> *n* argano *m* **II.** *vt* tirare su con l'argano

wind¹ [wɪnd] **I.** *n* **1.** (*current of air*) vento *m;* **a breath of ~** un po' di vento; **gust of ~** raffica *f* di vento **2.** (*breath*) fiato *m;* **to get** [*o* **catch**] **one's ~** riprendere fiato; **to have the ~ knocked out of sb** far rimanere qu senza fiato **3.** MED aria *f;* **to break ~** passare aria ▶ **to take the ~ out of sb's sails** scoraggiare qu; **he who sows the ~ shall reap the whirlwind** *prov* chi semina vento raccoglie tempesta *prov;* **to sail close to the ~** navigare di bolina; **to get ~ of sth** fiutare qc; **to go** [*o* **run**] **like the ~** andare come il vento; **there's sth in the ~** c'è qc nell'aria **II.** *vt* mozzare il fiato a

wind² [waɪnd] <wound, wound> **I.** *vt* **1.** (*coil*) arrotolare, aggomitolare; (*wool*); **to ~ sth around sth** arrotolare qc intorno a qc **2.** (*wrap*) avvolgere **3.** (*turn: handle*) girare; (*clock, watch*) caricare **4.** (*film*) far avvolgere **II.** *vi* serpeggiare

◆**wind down I.** *vt* **1.** (*gradually reduce*) ridurre progressivamente; (*business*) cessare progressivamente **2.** (*relax*) rilassare **II.** *vi* **1.** (*become less active*) rallentare; (*business*) cessare progressivamente **2.** (*relax after stress*) rilassarsi

◆**wind up I.** *vt* **1.** (*finish*) finire; (*debate, meeting, speech*) concludere **2.** *inf* (*make tense*) innervosire **II.** *vi inf* (*end up*) **to ~ in prison** finire in carcere

windbag ['wɪnd·bæg] *n inf* ciarlatano, -a *m, f*

windbreaker ['wɪnd·breɪk] *n* giacca *f* a vento

winder ['waɪn·dɚ] *n* **1.** (*on watch*) remontoir *m inv* **2.** (*on toy*) manovella *f*

windfall ['wɪnd·fɔːl] *n* **1.** *fig* (*money*) guadagno *f* imprevisto **2.** (*fruit*) frutta *f* caduta

wind farm *n* ECOL centrale *f* eolica

winding ['waɪn·dɪŋ] *adj* sinuoso, -a

wind instrument *n* strumento *m* a fiato

windjammer *n* NAUT veliero *m*

windlass *n* argano *m*

windmill *n* **1.** (*wind-powered mill*) mulino *m* a vento **2.** (*toy*) girandola *f*

window ['wɪn·doʊ] *n* **1.** (*in building, in envelope*) A.INFOR finestra *f;* **~ ledge** davanzale *m;* **a ~ on the world** *fig* una finestra sul mondo, ventana *f;* **pop-up ~** finestra popup **2.** (*of shop*) vetrina *f* **3.** (*of vehicle*) finestrino *m;* **rear ~** finestrino di dietro **4.** *fig* (*time period*) buco *m;* **a ~ of opportunity** una opportunità ▶ **to go out (of) the ~** *inf* (*plan*) sfumare

window box <-es> *n* vaso *m* da davanzale

window-dressing *n* **1.** (*in shop*) allesti-

mento *m* vetrine **2.** *fig* facciata *f*
window envelope *n* busta *f* con finestra
window-shopping *n* **to go** ~ guardare le vetrine
windowsill *n* davanzale *m*
windpipe ['wɪnd·paɪp] *n* trachea *f*
windshield ['wɪnd·ʃiːld] *n* parabrezza *m inv*
windshield wiper *n* tergicristalli *m inv*
windsock *n* manica *f* a vento
windsurfer ['wɪnd·sɜːr·fə·] *n* surfista *mf*
windsurfing ['wɪnd·sɜːr·fɪŋ] *n* windsurf *m*
windswept ['wɪnd·swept] *adj* **1.** (*exposed to wind*) spazzato, -a da vento **2.** (*looking wind-blown*) spettinato, -a
wind tunnel *n* TECH tunnel *m* aerodinamico
windward ['wɪnd·wə·d] NAUT **I.** *adj* sopravento **II.** *n* sopravento *m;* (**to**) ~ sopravento
windy¹ ['wɪn·di] <-ier, -iest> *adj* ventoso, -a
windy² ['wɪn·di] <-ier, -iest> *adj* sinuoso, -a
wine [waɪn] **I.** *n* vino *m* **II.** *vt* **to** ~ **and dine sb** far bere e mangiare qu molto bene
wine cooler *n* **1.** (*drink*) bevanda a base di vino e succo di frutta **2.** (*container*) refrigeratore *m* da tavolo
wineglass <-es> *n* bicchiere *f* da vino
winegrower *n*, **winegrower** *n* viticoltore, -trice *m, f*
wine list *n* carta *f* dei vini
wine merchant *n* **1.** (*seller of wines*) commerciante *mf* di vini, vinaio *m* **2.** (*shop*) enoteca *f,* vinaio *m*
winepress ['waɪn·pres] <-es> *n* pigiatrice *f*
winery ['waɪ·nə·ri] <-ies> *n* azienda *f* vinicola
winetasting *n* **1.** (*activity*) enodegustazione *f* **2.** (*event*) enodegustazione *f*
wing [wɪŋ] **I.** *n* **1.** ZOOL, AVIAT, ARCHIT, POL ala *f;* **to take** ~ *liter* prendere il volo; **the west** ~ **of the house** l'ala ovest della casa; **left/right** ~ ala sinistra/destra **2.** SPORTS (*side of field*) fascia *f;* (*player*) ala *f* **3.** *pl* THEAT quinte *fpl;* **to be waiting in the** ~**s** *fig* aspettare il momento opportuno **4.** *pl* MIL (*pilot's badge*) gradi *mpl* ▶ **to spread one's** ~**s** prendere il volo; **to stretch one's** ~**s** spiegare le ali; **to take sb under one's** ~ prendere qu sotto le proprie ali **II.** *vt* **1.** (*wound: bird*) ferire all'ala; (*person*) ferire superficialmente **2.** (*fly*) volare ▶ ~ **it** *inf* improvvisare **III.** *vi* volare
wing chair *n* poltrona *f* con ampio poggiatesta
wing commander *n* tenente *m* colonnello
winged [wɪŋd] *adj* alato, -a
winger ['wɪŋ·ə·] *n* SPORTS ala *f;* **left/right** ~ ala sinistra/destra
wing nut *n* TECH galletto *m*
wingspan ['wɪŋ·spæn] *n*, **wingspread** ['wɪŋ·spred] *n* apertura *f* alare
wink [wɪŋk] **I.** *n* occhiolino *m;* **to give sb a** ~ fare l'occhiolino a qu ▶ **to have forty** ~**s** *inf* fare un sonnellino; **to not sleep a** ~ non chiudere occhio; **in a** ~ in un batter d'occhio **II.** *vi* **1.** (*close one eye*) fare l'occhiolino; **to** ~ **at sb** fare l'occhiolino a qu **2.** (*flash: a light*) lampeggiare

winner ['wɪ·nə·] *n* **1.** (*person*) vincitore, -trice *m, f* **2.** *inf* SPORTS **the game** ~ punto *m* vincente (della partita) **3.** *inf* (*success*) successone *m;* **they are on to a** ~ **with this latest product** con quest'ultimo prodotto faranno un successone
winning ['wɪ·nɪŋ] **I.** *adj* **1.** (*that wins*) vincente **2.** (*charming*) accattivante **II.** *n* **1.** (*act of achieving victory*) vincita *f* **2.** *pl* (*money*) vincite *fpl*
winnow ['wɪ·noʊ] *vt* **1.** (*grain*) ventilare **2.** (*select*) distinguere; **to** ~ **the list down to 8** ridurre la lista a 8
winsome ['wɪn·səm] *adj liter* accattivante
winter ['wɪn·ţə·] **I.** *n* inverno *m* **II.** *vi* svernare
winter coat *n* cappotto *m* pesante; (*of animal*) pelliccia *f*
winter solstice *n* solstizio *m* d'inverno
winter sports *npl* sport *mpl* invernali
wintertime *n* inverno *m;* **in** (**the**) ~ d'inverno
wint(e)ry ['wɪnt·ri] *adj* **1.** (*typical of winter*) invernale **2.** *fig* (*cold, unfriendly*) freddo, -a
wipe [waɪp] **I.** *n* **1.** (*act of wiping*) pulita *f;* **to give sth a** ~ dare una pulita a qc, pulire qc **2.** (*tissue*) salvietta *f* **II.** *vt* **1.** (*remove dirt*) pulire; (*one's nose*) asciugarsi; **to** ~ **sth dry** asciugare qc con un panno **2.** (*erase material from: disk, a tape*) cancellare **III.** *vi* pulire
◆ **wipe down** *vt* passare uno straccio su
◆ **wipe off** *vt* **1.** (*remove by wiping*) eliminare (con uno straccio) **2.** (*erase: data, program*) cancellare **3.** ECON azzerare ▶ **to wipe the smile off sb's face** far passare a qu la voglia di ridere
◆ **wipe out I.** *vt* **1.** (*destroy: population*) sterminare; (*village*) distruggere completamente; (*sb's profits*) annientare **2.** (*cancel: debt*) estinguere **3.** *inf* (*tire out*) sfinire **4.** *inf* (*economically*) rovinare **5.** *sl* (*murder*) eliminare **II.** *vi inf* (*driving, skiing*) perdere il controllo
◆ **wipe up I.** *vt* pulire **II.** *vi* asciugare
wire ['waɪ·ə·] **I.** *n* **1.** (*metal thread*) filo *m* di ferro **2.** ELEC cavo *m* **3.** (*telegram*) telegramma *m* **4.** (*hidden microphone*) microspia *f* **5.** (*prison camp fence*) filo *m* spinato ▶ **to get one's** ~**s crossed** *inf* fraintendere; **to get in under the** ~ *inf* arrivare all'ultimo minuto; **to go** (**down**) **to the** ~ **the elections will go** (**down**) **to the** ~ *inf* si vedrà solo all'ultimo come andranno le elezioni **II.** *vt* **1.** (*fasten with wire*) attaccare col filo di ferro; **to** ~ **sth to the door** attaccare qc alla porta col filo di ferro **2.** ELEC collegare; **to be** ~**d for cable TV** avere l'attacco per la televisione via cavo **3.** (*fit with concealed microphone*) mettere una microspia a/in; **to be** ~**d** (*person*) avere indosso una microspia **4.** (*send telegram to*) **to** ~ **sb** inviare un telegramma a qu; **to** ~ **sb money** inviare denaro a qu con trasferimento telegrafico/telematico
wirehaired terrier [ˌwa·ɪə··herd·'te·ri·ə·] *n* terrier *m* a pelo ruvido *inv*
wireless ['wa·ɪə··ləs] *adj* wireless

wiretapping ['waɪəˌtæˌpɪŋ] *n* intercettazione *f* telefonica

wire transfer *n* trasferimento *f* telegrafico/telematico

wiring ['waɪəˌɪŋ] *n* ELEC impianto *m* elettrico

wiry ['waɪəˌi] <-ier, -iest> *adj* **1.** (*course: hair*) ispido, -a **2.** (*lean and strong: build, person*) asciutto, -a

Wisconsin *n* Wisconsin *m*

wisdom ['wɪzˌdəm] *n* **1.** (*state of being wise*) saggezza *f;* **with the ~ of hindsight** con il senno di poi **2.** (*sensibleness*) buon senso *m*

wisdom tooth <- teeth> *n* dente *m* del giudizio

wise [waɪz] *adj* **1.** (*having knowledge and sagacity, showing sagacity*) saggio, -a; **the Three Wise Men** i Re Magi; **it's easy to be ~ after the fact** è facile dirlo a posteriori **2.** (*sensible*) sensato, -a **3.** *inf* (*aware*) **to be ~ to sb** capire che tipo è qu; **to be ~ to sth** sapere come qc funziona; **to get ~ to sth** capire come qc funziona; **to get ~ to sb's game** capire il gioco di qu; **to be none the ~r** saperne quanto prima **4.** *inf* (*cheeky*) sfrontato, -a; **to get ~ with sb** essere sfrontato con qu
◆ **wise up** I. *vi* **to ~ to sth** svegliarsi e capire qc II. *vt* **to wise sb up about sth** far capire qc a qu

wiseacre ['waɪˌzeɪˌkəˈ] *n* saccente *mf*

wisecrack ['waɪzˌkræk] I. *n* battuta *f;* **to make a ~ about sth** fare una battuta su qc II. *vi* fare battute

wise guy *n inf* saputello, -a *m, f*

wish [wɪʃ] I. <-es> *n* **1.** (*desire*) desiderio *m;* **against my ~es** contro la mia volontà; **to have no ~ to do sth** non aver alcuna voglia di fare qc; **to make a ~** esprimere un desiderio **2.** *pl* (*friendly greetings*) auguri *mpl;* **give him my best ~es** fagli gli auguri da parte mia; (**with**) **best ~es** (*at end of letter*) cordiali saluti II. *vt* **1.** (*feel a desire*) desiderare, volere; **I ~ he hadn't come** vorrei che non fosse venuto; **I ~ you'd told me** (*expressing annoyance*) me lo potevi dire **2.** *form* (*want*) **to ~ to do sth** voler fare qc; **I ~ to be alone** desidero stare da solo **3.** (*hope*) **to ~ sb luck** augurare buona fortuna a qu; **to ~ sb happy birthday** fare a qu gli auguri di compleanno; **to ~ sb good night** dare la buonanotte a qu III. *vi* **1.** (*want*) desiderare, volere; **as you ~** come vuoi; **if you ~** come vuoi; **to ~ for sth** desiderare qc **2.** (*make a wish*) **to ~ for sth** chiedere qc; **everything one could ~ for** tutto ciò che si potrebbe desiderare

wishbone ['wɪʃˌboʊn] *n* forcella *f*

wishful thinking *n* illusione *f*

wishy-washy ['wɪˌʃiˌwɑːˌʃi] *adj pej* **1.** (*indeterminate and insipid*) insulso, -a **2.** (*weak and watery: coffee, drink, soup*) acquoso, -a; (*food*) insipido, -a

wisp [wɪsp] *n* (*of hair*) ciocca *f;* (*of straw*) filo *m;* (*of smoke*) voluta *f;* (*of clouds*) bioccolo *m;* **a little ~ of a boy** un ragazzino minuto

wispy ['wɪsˌpi] <-ier, -iest> *adj* (*hair*) a ciuffetti; (*person*) minuto, -a; (*clouds*) a bioccoli

wisteria [wɪˈstɪˌriˌə] *n* glicine *m*

wistful ['wɪstˌfəl] *adj* (*melancholy,*) malinconico, -a; (*nostalgic*) nostalgico, -a

wit [wɪt] I. *n* **1.** (*clever humor*) arguzia *f;* **to have a dry ~** essere pungente **2.** (*practical intelligence*) intelligenza *f;* **to be at one's ~ s' end** stare per uscire di cervello; **to gather one's ~s** chiarirsi le idee; **to frighten sb out of his/her ~s** spaventare a morte qu; **to have/keep one's ~s about one** mantenersi calmo/mantenere la calma **3.** (*witty person*) persona *f* arguta II. *vi form* **to ~** vale a dire

witch [wɪtʃ] <-es> *n* **1.** (*woman with magic powers*) strega *f* **2.** *pej, inf* (*ugly or unpleasant woman*) arpia *f*

witchcraft ['wɪtʃˌkræft] *n* stregoneria *f*

witch doctor *n* stregone *m*

witch-hunt *n,* **witch hunt** ['wɪtʃˌhʌnt] *n pej* caccia *f* alle streghe

witching hour ['wɪtʃˌɪŋˌaʊr] *n liter* mezzanotte *f*

with [wɪð, wɪθ] *prep* **1.** (*accompanied by*) con; **together ~ sb** insieme a qu **2.** (*by means of*) con; **to take sth ~ one's fingers/both hands** prendere qc con le dita/con ambo le mani; **to replace sth ~ something else** sostituire qc con qualcos'altro **3.** (*having*) **the man ~ the umbrella** l'uomo con l'ombrello; **~ no hesitation at all** senza alcuna esitazione **4.** (*on one's person*) **he took it ~ him** lo prese con sé **5.** (*manner*) **~ all speed** a gran velocità; **~ one's whole heart** di tutto cuore **6.** (*in addition to*) **and ~ that he went out** e così dicendo se ne andò **7.** (*despite*) **~ all his faults** con tutti i suoi torti **8.** (*caused by*) **to cry ~ rage** piangere di rabbia; **to turn red ~ anger** diventare rosso di rabbia **9.** (*full of*) **black ~ flies** nero di mosche; **to fill up ~ fuel** fare il pieno di benzina **10.** (*opposing*) **a war ~ Italy** una guerra con l'Italia; **to be angry ~ sb** essere arrabbiato con qu **11.** (*supporting*) **to be ~ sb/sth** essere dalla parte di qu/qc; **popular ~ young people** popolare tra i giovani **12.** (*concerning*) **to be pleased ~ sth** essere soddisfatto di qc; **what's up** [*o* **what's the matter**] **~ him?** cosa gli è successo? **13.** (*understanding*) **I'm not ~ you** *inf* non ti seguo; **to be ~ it** *inf* essere in gamba; **to get ~ it** darsi una mossa ▶ **away ~ him!** basta con lui!

withdraw [wɪðˈdrɑː] *irr* I. *vt* **1.** (*take out, take back*) ritirare; (*money*) prelevare **2.** (*cancel*) cancellare; (*motion, action*) annullare; (*charge*) revocare II. *vi* **1.** *form a.* MIL, SPORTS (*leave*) ritirarsi; **to ~ from public life** allontanarsi dalla scena pubblica **2.** *fig* (*become quiet and unsociable*) chiudersi in se stesso; (*into silence*) chiudersi

withdrawal [wɪðˈdrɑːˌəl] *n* **1.** *a.* MIL ritiro *m;* **to make a ~** FIN effettuare un prelievo **2.** LAW

W

ritrattazione *f;* (*of consent, support*) revoca *f* **3.** (*sports*) abbandono *m* **4.** (*distancing from others*) estraneamento *m* **5.** MED astinenza *f;* ~ **symptoms** crisi *f* d'astinenza *inv*

wither ['wɪ·ðə·] I. *vi* **1.** (*plants*) appassire **2.** *fig* (*lose vitality*) perdere vitalità ▶ **to** ~ **on the** vine sparire poco a poco II. *vt* **1.** (*plant*) far appassire **2.** *fig* (*strength*) ridurre

withering ['wɪ·ðə·rɪŋ] *adj* **1.** (*fierce and destructive*) distruttivo, -a **2.** (*contemptuous: criticism*) caustico, -a

withhold [wɪð·'hoʊld] *irr vt* **1.** (*not give name*) non rendere noto, -a; (*one's support*) negare; (*evidence*) occultare; **to** ~ **sth from sb** nascondere qc a qu **2.** (*not pay: benefits, rent*) non pagare

within [wɪð·'ɪn] I. *prep* **1.** *form* (*inside of*) all'interno di, in; ~ **the country/town** nel paese/nella città **2.** (*in limit of*) **to be** ~ **sight/hearing** essere visibile/udibile; ~ **easy reach** a portata di mano **3.** (*in less than*) entro; ~ **one hour** entro un'ora; ~ **3 days** nello spazio di tre giorni; ~ **5 miles of the town** a meno di 8 km dalla città **4.** (*in accordance to*) in conformità con; ~ **the law** nei termini di legge II. *adv* dentro; **from** ~ da dentro

without [wɪð·'aʊt] I. *prep* senza; ~ **warning** senza preavviso; **to be** ~ **relatives** non avere parenti; **to do** ~ **sth** fare a meno di qc II. *adv liter* fuori; **from** ~ da fuori

withstand [wɪð·'stænd] *irr vt* resistere; (*heat, pressure*) sopportare

witness ['wɪt·nəs] I. *n* **1.** *a.* LAW testimone *mf;* ~ **for the defense** testimone a discarico; **according to** ~**es** a quanto dicono i testimoni; **to be** (a) ~ **to sth** essere testimone di/a qc **2.** *form* (*testimony*) testimonianza *f;* **to bear** ~ **to sth** deporre su qc II. *vt* **1.** (*see, be there during*) essere testimone di; **to** ~ **sb doing sth** vedere qu che fa qc **2.** (*attest authenticity of*) sottoscrivere

witness stand *n* banco *m* dei testimoni

witty ['wɪ·t̬i] <-ier, -iest> *adj* arguto, -a

wizard ['wɪ·zə·d] *n* **1.** (*magician*) mago, -a *m, f* **2.** (*expert*) genio *m;* **to be a** ~ **at sth** essere un genio di/in qc

wizardry ['wɪ·zə·dri] *n* magia *f*

wizened ['wɪ·znd] *adj* avvizzito, -a

wk. *n abbr of* **week** sett.

WNBA *n abbr of* **Women's National Basketball Association** Associazione *f* Nazionale Femminile di Pallacanestro

WNW *abbr of* **west-northwest** ONO

w/o *prep abbr of* **without** senza

wobble ['wɑː·bl] I. *vi* **1.** (*move unsteadily*) traballare; (*jelly, fat*) tremolare **2.** (*tremble: voice*) tremolare **3.** *fig* (*fluctuate: prices, shares*) fluttuare II. *vt* far traballare; (*camera*) muovere III. *n* **1.** (*wobbling movement*) traballio *m* **2.** (*quavering sound*) tremolio *m* **3.** ECON fluttuazione *f*

wobbly ['wɑː·b·li] <-ier, -iest> *adj* **1.** (*unsteady*) traballante; (*line*) a zigzag

2. (*wavering: a note, a voice*) tremolante

woe [woʊ] *n* **1.** *liter* (*unhappiness*) pena *f;* **a tale of** ~ tragedia *f* **2.** *pl, form* (*misfortunes*) disgrazie *fpl;* **to pour out one's** ~**s** raccontare le proprie disgrazie ▶ ~ **betide you!** peste ti colga!; **woe is** me! ahimè!

woebegone ['woʊ·bɪ·gɑːn] *adj liter* angustiato, -a

woeful ['woʊ·fəl] *adj* **1.** (*deplorable*) penoso, -a **2.** *liter* (*sad*) afflitto, -a

wok [wɑːk] *n* wok *m inv*

woke [woʊk] *vt, vi pt of* **wake**

woken ['woʊ·kən] *vt, vi pp of* **wake**

wolf [wʊlf] I. <wolves> *n* **1.** (*animal*) lupo *m* **2.** *inf* (*seducer*) dongiovanni *m inv* ▶ **to keep the** ~ **from the** door sbarcare il lunario; **a** ~ **in** sheep's clothing un lupo in veste d'agnello; **to** cry ~ gridare al lupo; **to** throw **sb to the wolves** dare qu in pasto ai leoni II. *vt inf* ingollare

wolfhound *n* cane *m* lupo

wolf whistle *n* fischio *m* di ammirazione

woman ['wʊ·mən] <women> *n* **1.** (*female human*) donna *f;* **the other** ~ l'altra; ~ **candidate** candidata *f;* ~ **president** presidente *m* donna; **women's libber** femminista *f* **2.** *inf* (*man's female partner*) donna *f*

womanhood ['wʊ·mən·hʊd] *n* **1.** (*female adulthood*) l'essere *m* donna; **to reach** ~ diventare donna **2.** (*women as a group*) donne *fpl*

womanish ['wʊ·mə·nɪʃ] *adj pej* effeminato, -a

womanize ['wʊ·mə·naɪz] *vi inf* andare a donne

womanizer *n* donnaiolo *m*

womankind ['wʊ·mən·kaɪnd] *n form* sesso *m* femminile; **all** ~ tutte le donne

womanly ['wʊ·mən·li] *adj* **1.** (*not manly*) femminile **2.** (*not girlish*) di donna

womb [wuːm] *n* utero *m;* **in the** ~ nel grembo materno

women's center *n* consultorio *m*

women's lib *n inf abbr of* **women's liberation** liberazione *f* della donna

women's shelter *n* casa *f* di accoglienza e ospitalità per donne

won [wʌn] *vt, vi pt, pp of* **win**

wonder ['wʌn·də·] I. *vt* (*ask oneself, feel surprise*) chiedersi; **it makes you** ~ ti fa pensare; **I** ~ **why he said that** mi chiedo perché l'abbia detto II. *vi* **1.** (*ask oneself*) **to** ~ **about sth** chiedersi qc; **to** ~ **about doing sth** chiedersi se fare qc **2.** (*feel surprise*) meravigliarsi; **to** ~ **at sth/sb** meravigliarsi di qc/qu; **I don't** ~ non mi meraviglio III. *n* **1.** (*marvel*) meraviglia *f;* **to do** [*o* **work**] ~**s** fare miracoli; **the** ~**s of modern technology** i miracoli della tecnologia moderna; **it's a** ~ **(that)** ... è un miracolo (che)...; ~**s** (**will**) **never cease!** *iron* non si finisce mai di meravigliarsi! **2.** (*feeling*) meraviglia *f,* stupore *m;* **in** ~ con meraviglia; **to listen in** ~ ascoltare stupefatto

wonder boy *n iron, inf* ragazzo *m* prodigio

wonder drug *n* rimedio *m* miracoloso

wonderful ['wʌn·də·fəl] *adj* meraviglioso, -a
wonderland ['wʌn·də·lænd] *n* paese *m* delle
meraviglie
wonderment *n* meraviglia *f*
wont [wɔːnt] I. *adj form* abituato, -a; **to be ~ to
do sth** essere abituato a fare qc II. *n form* abitudine *f*; **as is her ~** come sua abitudine
won't [woʊnt] = **will not** *s.* **will**
woo [wuː] *vt* 1. (*try to attract*) attirare
2. (*court*) corteggiare
wood [wʊd] *n* 1. (*material*) legno *m*; (*for a
fire*) legna *f* 2. *pl* (*group of trees*) bosco *m*
3. SPORTS (*golf*) legno *m* ▶ (to) **touch** [*o* **knock
on**] ~ toccare ferro; **to be out of the ~s** *inf*
essere salvo
wood alcohol *n* metanolo *m*
woodcraft *n* 1. (*outdoor skills*) conoscenza *f*
dei boschi 2. (*artistic skill*) arte *f* del lavorare il
legno
woodcut *n* ART xilografia *f*
woodcutter *n* boscaiolo *m*
wooded ['wʊ·dɪd] *adj* boscoso, -a
wooden ['wʊ·dn] *adj* 1. (*made of wood*) di
legno; ~ **leg** gamba *f* di legno 2. (*awkward*)
legnoso, -a; (*smile*) inespressivo, -a
woodland ['wʊd·lənd] I. *n* bosco *m* II. *adj*
boschivo, -a
woodpecker *n* picchio *m*
woodpile *n* catasta *f* di legna
wood pulp *n* TECH pasta *f* di legno
woodshed ['wʊd·ʃed] I. *n* legnaia *f* II. <-dd->
vi sl suonare uno strumento musicale
woodwind ['wʊd·wɪnd] MUS I. *n* legni *mpl*
II. *adj* a fiato
woodwork ['wʊd·wɜːrk] *n* (*wooden parts of
building*) strutture *fpl* in legno di un edificio
▶ to **come out of the** ~ *sl* uscire allo scoperto
woodworking *n* lavorazione *f* del legno
woodworm *n inv* 1. (*larva that attacks wood*)
tarlo *m* 2. (*damage*) tarlatura *f*
woody ['wʊ·di] I. <-ier, -iest> *adj* 1. (*tough
like wood: plant, stem, tissue*) legnoso, -a
2. (*like wood: flavor*) di legno 3. (*wooded*)
boscoso, -a II. *n vulg* erezione *f*
woof [wuːf] I. *n* (*dog*) latrato *m*; **to give a
loud ~** latrare II. *vi* latrare; **to ~ at sb** urlare a
qu
woofer ['wuː·fə·] *n* woofer *m inv*
wool [wʊl] *n* lana *f*
woolen *adj*, **woollen** ['wʊ·lən] *adj* di lana
woolly *n*, **wooly** ['wʊ·li] <-ier, -iest> *adj*
1. (*made of wool*) di lana 2. (*wool-like*) lanoso,
-a 3. (*vague*) confuso, -a
woozy ['wuː·zi] <-ier, -iest> *adj inf* rintontito, -a
word [wɜːrd] I. *n* 1. (*unit of language*) parola *f*;
a ~ of Hebrew origin una parola di origine
ebraica; **to be a man/woman of few ~s**
essere un uomo/una donna di poche parole; **to
not breathe a ~ of sth** non dire una parola di
qc; **to be too ridiculous for ~s** essere veramente ridicolo; **in other ~s** in altre parole;
~ **for** ~ parola per parola 2. (*news*) notizie *fpl*;

(*message*) messaggio *m*; **to get ~ of sth** sentire di qc; **to have ~ from sb** avere notizie da
qu; **to have ~ that ...** sapere che... 3. (*order*)
ordine *m*; **a ~ of advice** un consiglio; **a ~ of
warning/caution** un avvertimento; **to say
the ~** dare l'ordine; **just say the ~** devi soltanto chiederlo 4. (*promise*) parola *f* (d'onore);
to be a man/woman of one's ~ essere un
uomo/una donna di parola; **to keep one's ~**
mantenere la parola; **take my ~ for it!**
credimi! 5. (*statement of facts*) spiegazione *f*
6. *pl* MUS (*lyrics*) parole *f*, testo *m* 7. REL the
Word of God la parola di Dio ▶ **to have a
quick ~ with sb** parlare in privato con qu; **by
~ of mouth** a voce; **to put ~s in(to) sb's
mouth** attribuire a qu qc che non ha detto; **to
take the ~s (right) out of sb's mouth** togliere la parola di bocca a qu; **to not have a
good ~ to say about sb/sth** non aver niente
di buono da dire su qu/qc; **to put in a good ~
for sb** mettere una buona parola per qu; ~**s
fail me!** non ho parole!; **from the ~ go** fin
dal'inizio; **mark my ~s!** ricordati di quanto ho
detto!; **to mince one's ~s** misurare le parole;
to not mince one's ~s non avere peli sulla
lingua; **my ~!** per bacco! II. *vt* esprimere
wording *n* 1. (*words used*) parole *fpl* 2. (*style*)
stile *m*
wordless ['wɜːrd·ləs] *adj* muto, -a
word order *n* LING ordine *m* delle parole
wordplay ['wɜːrd·pleɪ] *n* gioco *m* di parole
word processing *n* INFOR videoscrittura *f*
word processor *n* INFOR programma *m* di
videoscrittura
word wrap *n* INFOR a capo *m* automatico
wordy ['wɜːr·di] <-ier, iest> *adj pej* prolisso, -a
wore [wɔːr] *vt, vi pt of* **wear**
work [wɜːrk] I. *n* 1. (*useful activity, employment, place of employment*) PHYS lavoro *m*; **to
be hard ~ (doing sth)** essere dura (fare qc); **to
set sb to ~** mettere a lavorare qu; **good ~!**
bravo!; **to be out of ~** essere disoccupato
2. (*product*) *a.* ART, MUS opera *f*; **reference ~**
opera *f* di consultazione 3. *pl* + *sing/pl vb* (*factory*) fabbrica *f*; **steel ~s** acciaieria *f* 4. *pl* TECH
(*of a clock*) meccanismo *m* ▶ **to have one's ~
cut out to do sth** non essere facile per qu fare
qc; **to make short ~ of sb** sbrigarsela in fretta
con qu; **to make short ~ of sth** fare fuori qc
rapidamente; **to get to ~ on sb/sth** *inf* lavorarsi qu/qc; **the ~s** *inf* tutto quanto; **give me a
pizza with the ~s** voglio una pizza con tutto;
to give sb the ~s *sl* pestare qu II. *vi* 1. (*do
job,*) lavorare; **to ~ abroad** lavorare all'estero;
to ~ as a teacher fare l'insegnante 2. (*be
busy*) essere occupato; **to get ~ing** mettersi al
lavoro; **to ~ hard** lavorare sodo; **to ~ to do sth**
impegnarsi a fare qc 3. TECH (*be successful*)
funzionare; **to get sth to ~** far funzionare qc
4. MED fare effetto 5. (*have an effect*) **to ~
against sb/sth** agire contro qu/qc; **to ~
against/for a candidate** risultare a sfavore/a
favore di un candidato; **to ~ both ways** essere

W

un'arma a doppio taglio **6.**(*move*) **to ~ (some-where)** spostarsi (da qualche parte) **7.**+ *adj* (*become*) **to ~ free** liberarsi; **to ~ loose** allentarsi **8.** *liter* (*change expression: sb's face*) contrarsi ▶ **to ~ like a** charm funzionare a meraviglia; **to ~ like a** dog, **to ~ like a** slave lavorare come un mulo; **to ~** around **to** sth prepararsi a poco a poco per qc **III.** *vt* **1.**(*make sb work*) **to ~ sb hard** far lavorare molto qu; **to ~ oneself to death** ammazzarsi di lavoro; **to ~ a forty-hour week** avere una settimana lavorativa di quaranta ore **2.** TECH (*operate*) far funzionare; **to be ~ed by sth** essere azionato da qc **3.**(*move back and forward*) muovere; **to ~ sth free** liberare qc; **to ~ sth loose** allentare qc; **to ~ one's way along sth** farsi strada lungo qc **4.**(*bring about*) produrre; (*a miracle*) fare; **to ~ it** [*o* things] **so that ...** fare in modo che ... +*subj* **5.**(*shape*) modellare; (*bronze, iron*) lavorare **6.** FASHION (*embroider*) ricamare **7.** MIN sfruttare; AGR lavorare **8.**(*pay for by working*) **to ~ one's way through college** mantenersi all'università lavorando

◆**work away** *vi* lavorare senza sosta

◆**work in** *vt* **1.**(*mix in*) amalgamare; (*on one's skin*) far penetrare **2.**(*include*) inserire; (*fit in*) trovare posto a

◆**work off I.** *vt* **1.**(*counter effects of: one's anger, frustration*) sfogare; (*stress*) alleviare **2.**(*pay by working*) pagare lavorando **II.** *vi* TECH separarsi

◆**work on** *vt* (*a car, project*) lavorare a; (*accent, fitness, skills*) lavorare per migliorare; (*assumption, hypothesis*) esaminare; (*person*) lavorarsi

◆**work out I.** *vt* **1.**(*solve*) risolvere; **to work things out** sistemare le cose **2.**(*calculate*) calcolare **3.**(*develop*) elaborare; (*a settlement, solution*) trovare; (*decide*) decidere **4.**(*understand*) capire **5.**(*complete*) completare; (*one's contract*) lavorare fino alla fine del **6.** **to be worked out** (*lode, mine, quarry*) essere sfruttato **II.** *vi* **1.**(*give a result: a calculation, sum*) ammontare a; (*cheaper, more expensive*) risultare **2.**(*be resolved*) risolversi **3.**(*be successful*) funzionare; **to ~ for the best** finire bene **4.**(*do exercise*) allenarsi

◆**work over** *vt inf* pestare

◆**work up** *vt* **1.**(*generate: courage, energy, enthusiasm*) trovare **2.**(*arouse strong feelings*) stimolare; **to work oneself up** agitarsi; **to ~ into a frenzy** mettersi in grande agitazione; **to work sb up into a rage** far arrabbiare qu **3.**(*develop*) sviluppare; (*idea, plan, sketch*) elaborare; **to work one's way up through the company** fare carriera all'interno dell'azienda

workable ['wɜːr·kə·bl] *adj* **1.**(*feasible*) fattibile; (*compromise, plan*) realizzabile **2.**(*able to be manipulated: land, metal*) lavorabile

workaday ['wɜːr·kə·deɪ] *adj* di tutti i giorni

workbench <-es> *n* banco *m* (di lavoro)

workbook *n* quaderno *m* degli esercizi

workday *n* (*weekday*) giorno *m* lavorativo; (*time*) giornata *f* di lavoro

worker ['wɜːr·kə] *n* lavoratore, -trice *m, f*; (*in factory*) operaio, -a *m, f*

work force *n* + *sing/pl vb* popolazione *f* attiva

workhorse *n* cavallo *m* da lavoro

working I. *adj* **1.**(*employed*) che lavora; (*population*) attivo, -a **2.**(*pertaining to work*) lavorativo, -a; (*clothes*) da lavoro **3.**(*functioning*) funzionante **4.**(*used as basis: theory, hypothesis*) di base; **to have a ~ knowledge of sth** avere conoscenze di base di qc **II.** *n* **1.**(*activity*) funzionamento *m* **2.**(*employment*) lavoro *m*

working class ['wɜːr·kɪŋ·ˌklæs] <-es> *n* **the ~** la classe operaia

working-class *adj* operaio, -a; (*background*) umile

workload ['wɜːrk·loʊd] *n* (carico *m* di) lavoro *m;* **to have a heavy/light/unbearable ~** avere molto/poco/troppo lavoro

workman ['wɜːrk·mən] <-men> *n* operaio *m*

workmanlike ['wɜːrk·mən·laɪk] *adj* **1.**(*showing skill: performance, job*) qualificato, -a **2.**(*technically sufficient: performance*) accurato, -a

workmanship ['wɜːrk·mən·ˌʃɪp] *n* **1.**(*skill in working*) destrezza *f* **2.**(*work executed*) lavoro *m* **3.**(*quality of work*) esecuzione *f;* **shoddy ~** lavoro malfatto; **of fine ~** di eccellente fattura

work of art *n* opera *f* d'arte

workout ['wɜːrk·aʊt] *n* SPORTS allenamento *m*

work permit *n* permesso *m* di lavoro

workplace *n* COM posto *m* di lavoro; **safety in the ~** sicurezza *f* sul lavoro

work-sharing ['wɜːrk·ˌʃe·rɪŋ] *n* ripartizione *f* del lavoro

worksheet ['wɜːrk·ˌʃiːt] *n* foglio *m* di lavorazione

workshop ['wɜːrk·ʃɑːp] *n* **1.**(*repair place*) laboratorio *m* **2.**(*meeting for learning*) seminario *m;* **drama ~** laboratorio teatrale

workspace ['wɜːrk·speɪs] *n* INFOR spazio *f* di lavoro

workstation *n* INFOR stazione *f* di lavoro

work-study program *n* SCHOOL, UNIV, COM programma *m* di lavoro-studio

worktable ['wɜːrk·ˌteɪ·bl] *n* tavolo *m* di lavoro

workweek ['wɜːrk·wiːk] *n* settimana *f* lavorativa

world [wɜːrld] *n* **1.** GEO mondo *m;* **the ~'s population** la popolazione mondiale; **a ~ authority** una autorità mondiale; **the ~ champion** il campione del mondo; **the best/worst in the ~** il migliore/peggiore del mondo; **the tallest man in the ~** l'uomo più alto del mondo; **the (whole) ~ over** in tutto il mondo; **to see the ~** girare il mondo; **to travel all over the ~** viaggiare in tutto il mondo **2.**(*defined group*) **the ~ of dogs/horses** il mondo dei cani/cavalli; **the ani-**

mal ~ il mondo animale; **the Christian/Muslim** ~ il mondo cristiano/musulmano; **the New/Old/Third** ~ il Nuovo/Vecchio/Terzo Mondo ▸ **there's a ~ of <u>difference</u> between** ... c'è un'enorme differenza tra...; **to have the ~ at one's <u>feet</u>** avere il mondo ai propri piedi; **the ~ at <u>large</u>** un po' tutto il mondo; **the ~ is his/her <u>oyster</u>** ha il mondo ai suoi piedi; **to feel on <u>top</u> of the ~** essere al settimo cielo; **that's the <u>way</u> of the ~** c'est la vie!; **to be for <u>all</u> the ~ like** ... essere tale e quale a...; **to be ~s <u>apart</u>** essere come la notte e il giorno; **to have the <u>best</u> of both ~s** avere il meglio di ambedue le cose; **to be <u>dead</u> to the ~** dormire profondamente; **to be <u>out</u> of this ~** *inf* essere fantastico; **it's a <u>small</u> ~!** il mondo è piccolo!; **I wouldn't <u>do</u> that for (all) the (money in the)** ~ non lo farei per tutto l'oro del mondo; **to <u>move up</u> in the ~** *inf* prosperare; **to <u>move down</u> in the ~** *inf* decadere; **to <u>live</u> in a ~ of one's own** vivere in un mondo tutto suo; **to <u>mean</u> (all) the ~ to sb** essere tutto per qu; **to <u>think</u> the ~ of sb/sth** avere grande ammirazione per qu/qc; **<u>what</u>/who/how in the ~** ...? cosa/chi/come diavolo...?
World Bank *n* the ~ la Banca Mondiale
world-class *adj* a livello mondiale
World Cup *n* SPORTS **the** ~ i Mondiali; **the ~ Finals** la finale di Coppa del Mondo
world-famous ['wɜːrld‑ˌfeɪ‑məs] *adj* di fama mondiale
world language *n* lingua *f* universale
worldly ['wɜːrld‑li] *adj* **1.** (*of physical, practical matters*) materiale; **~ goods** beni materiali **2.** (*having experience*) mondano, ‑a; (*manner*) sofisticato, ‑a; **~ wise** (*person*) esperto, ‑a
world power *n* potenza *f* mondiale
world record *n* SPORTS record *m* mondiale *inv*
World Series *n* World Series *f inv*

> **ⅰ** Le **World Series** sono le finali del campionato professionistico di baseball negli Stati Uniti e consistono in una serie di sette *play-offs* (partite di finale) tra la squadra vincitrice dell'*American League* (campionato americano) e la vincitrice della *National League* (campionato nazionale). I vincitori diventano *World Champions*, cioè campioni del mondo, in quanto campioni della *Major League Baseball* negli Stati Uniti e in Canada, che è il campionato di più alto livello mondiale. Queste finalissime hanno luogo ogni anno dal 1903 nel mese di ottobre e sono seguite da un altissimo numero di appassionati di baseball negli Stati Uniti e in Canada.

World's Fair *n* fiera *f* mondiale
world-shaking *adj*, **world-shattering** *adj* **a ~ piece of news** una notizia sconvolgente

world war *n* HIST guerra *f* mondiale
world-weary ['wɜːrld‑ˌwɪ‑ri] *adj* stanco, ‑a; **to be** [*o* feel] ~ esere stanco della vita
worldwide ['wɜːrld‑ˌwaɪd] **I.** *adj* mondiale **II.** *adv* in tutto il mondo
World Wide Web *n* INFOR Rete *f*
worm [wɜːrm] **I.** *n* **1.** verme *m;* (*insect larva*) bruco *m;* **earth ~** lombrico *m* **2.** (*computer virus*) virus *m inv* **II.** *vt* **1.** (*treat for worms*) dare un vermifugo a **2.** (*squeeze slowly through*) **to ~ one's way through people** farsi strada tra la gente; **to ~ oneself under sth** infilarsi sotto qc **3.** (*gain trust dishonestly*) **to ~ oneself into someone's trust** conquistarsi astutamente la fiducia di qu **4.** (*obtain dishonestly*) **to ~ a secret out of sb** estorcere un secreto a qu **III.** *vi* **to ~ through the crowd** farsi strada tra la folla
worm-eaten ['wɜːrm‑ˌiː‑tən] *adj* (*beam, table, wood*) tarlato, ‑a; (*fruit*) bacato, ‑a; (*cloth*) tarmato, ‑a
wormhole ['wɜːrm‑hoʊl] *n* buco *m* (di verme/tarlo); **the cupboard was full of ~s** l'armadio era tutto tarlato
wormy ['wɜːr‑mi] <‑ier, ‑iest> *adj* (*full of worms: fruit*) bacato, ‑a; (*wood*) tarlato, ‑a
worn [wɔːrn] **I.** *vt, vi pp of* **wear II.** *adj* **1.** (*shabby, deteriorated*) logoro, ‑a **2.** (*exhausted: person*) sfinito, ‑a **3.** (*overused: expression, news, story*) vecchio, ‑a
worn-out [ˌwɔːrn‑'aʊt] *adj* **1.** (*exhausted: person, animal*) sfinito, ‑a **2.** (*used up: clothing*) logoro, ‑a; (*wheel bearings*) consumato, ‑a
worried *adj* preoccupato, ‑a; **to be ~ about** [*o* by] sth essere preoccupato per qc; **I am ~ that he may be angry** ho paura che sia arrabbiato; **to be ~ sick about sb/sth** essere preoccupatissimo per qu/qc; **with a ~ expression** con aria preoccupata
worrisome ['wɜːr‑ri‑səm] *adj form* preoccupante
worry ['wɜːr‑ri] **I.** <‑ies> *n* **1.** (*anxiety, concern*) preoccupazione *f;* **to be a cause of ~ to sb** preoccupare qu; **to have a ~ (about sth)** preoccuparsi (per/di qc); **do you really have no ~s about the future?** il futuro non ti preoccupa affatto? **2.** (*trouble*) problema *m;* **financial worries** problemi *mpl* economici; **it is a great ~ to me** mi preoccupa molto **II.** *vt* <‑ie‑, ‑ing> **1.** (*preoccupy, concern*) preoccupare; **she is worried that she might not be able to find another job** ha paura di non riuscire a trovare un altro impiego **2.** (*bother*) seccare **3.** (*pursue and scare*) **to ~ an animal** correre dietro a un animale **4.** (*shake around*) **to ~ sth** scuotere qc; **the dog worries the bone** il cane gioca con l'osso **III.** <‑ie‑, ‑ing> *vi* (*be preoccupied, concerned*) **to ~ (about sth)** preoccuparsi (di/per qc); **don't ~!** stai tranquillo!; **not to ~!** *inf* non fa niente!
worrying *adj* preoccupante
worse [wɜːrs] **I.** *adj comp of* **bad** peggiore; **to be ~ than** ... essere peggiore di...; **to be**

even/much ~ essere anche/molto peggiore; **he was none the** ~ **for it** no gli è successo niente; **from bad to** ~ di male in peggio; **to get** ~ **and** ~ andare sempre peggio; **it could have been** ~ poteva andare peggio; **to make matters** ~ ... a peggiorare le cose...; **so much the** ~ **for her!** tanto peggio per lei!; ~ **luck** *inf* sfortunatamente; **to get** ~ peggiorare; **if he gets any** ~ ... se peggiora ancora... II. *n* **the** ~ il peggio; **to change for the** ~ peggiorare; **to have seen** ~ aver visto di peggio; **I don't think any the** ~ **of her** la mia opinione su di lei non è peggiorata; ~ **was to follow** il peggio doveva ancora venire III. *adv comp of* **badly** peggio; **to do sth** ~ **than** ... fare qc peggio di/che...; **he did** ~ **than he was expecting in the exams** gli esami gli sono andati peggio di quanto si aspettasse; **to be** ~ **(off)** stare peggio

worsen ['wɜːr·sən] *vi, vt* peggiorare

worship ['wɜːr·ʃɪp] I. *vt* <-pp-, -p-> 1. *a.* REL adorare; **to** ~ **money/sex** essere ossessionato dai soldi/dal sesso 2. *(feel great admiration for)* idolatrare ▶ **to** ~ **the ground sb walks on** baciare la terra su cui qu cammina II. *vi* <-pp-, -p-> REL pregare III. *n* 1. *(adoration)* adorazione *f*, venerazione *f* 2. *a.* REL culto *m;* *(religious service)* funzione *f*

worshipper *n* REL fedele *mf;* **hundreds of** ~**s attended the ceremony** centinaia di fedeli hanno assistito alla ceremonia; **devil** ~ seguace *mf* di setta satanica

worst [wɜːrst] I. *adj superl of* **bad the** ~ il/la peggiore; **the** ~ **soup I've ever eaten** la peggior minestra che abbia mai mangiato; **the** ~ **mistake** l'errore più grave II. *adv superl of* **badly** peggio; **to be** ~ **hit/affected by sth** essere il più gravemente colpito da qc III. *n* *(most terrible one, time, thing)* **the** ~ il peggio; **the** ~ **of it is that** ... il peggio è che...; **the** ~ **is over now** il peggio ora è passato; **at** ~ nel peggiore dei casi; **she's at her** ~ **in the morning** la mattina non è al meglio; **this problem has shown him at his** ~ questo problema ha tirato fuori il suo lato peggiore; **to fear the** ~ temere il peggio; ~ **of all** il peggio ▶ **if (the)** ~ **comes to (the)** ~ alla peggio; **to get the** ~ **of it** *(suffer the worst)* soffrire di più

worsted ['wʊs·tɪd] *n* *(fabric)* pettinato *m* di lana

worth [wɜːrθ] I. *n* 1. *(excellence, importance, monetary value: of a person)* valore *m;* **to prove one's** ~ dimostrare quanto si vale; **to be of great/little** ~ **to sb** avere grande/poco valore per qu; **4 thousand dollars** ~ **of gift items** regali per un valore di quattromila dollari; **to get one's money's** ~ **from sth** sfruttare al meglio qc; **a month's/three hour's** ~ **of work** un mese/tre ore di lavoro 2. *(wealth)* fortuna *f* II. *adj* 1. *a.* COM, FIN, ECON **to be** ~ ... valere...; **it is** ~ **about $200 000** è stato valutato circa 200 000 dollari; **it's** ~ **a lot to me** ha un grande valore per me; **to be** ~ **millions** *inf* essere milionario 2. *(significant enough, use-*

ful) **to be** ~ ... meritare...; **to be** ~ **a mention** meritare di essere ricordato; **it's not** ~ **arguing about!** non vale la pena discuterne!; **it is** ~ **seeing** va visto; **it's** ~ **remembering that** ... si ricorda che...; **it is (well)** ~ **a visit/listen** merita una visita/di essere ascoltato; **it's** ~ **a try** vale la pena provare ▶ **to be** ~ **sb's while (doing sth)** valere la pena (che qu faccia qc); **to make sth** ~ **sb's while** ricompensare qu per qc; **if a thing is** ~ **doing,** **it's** ~ **doing well** *prov* se vale la pena fare qualcosa tanto vale farla bene; **to do sth** **for** **all one's** ~ fare qc con tutte le proprie forze; **for what it's** ~ *inf* se serve a qc; **to be (well)** ~ **it** valerne la pena

worthless ['wɜːθ·ləs] *adj* 1. *(of no monetary value)* di nessun valore 2. *(of no significance, use)* inutile

worthwhile [ˌwɜːθ·'hwaɪl] *adj* 1. *(profitable, beneficial)* che vale la pena; **it's not** ~ **making such an effort** non vale la pena impegnarsi tanto; **it isn't financially** ~ **for me** non vale economicamente la pena per me 2. *(useful)* utile

worthy ['wɜːr·ði] I. <-ier, -iest> *adj* 1. *form* *(admirable)* encomiabile; *(principle, cause)* nobile 2. *(appropriate for, to)* degno, -a; **to be** ~ **of sth** meritare qc; **to be** ~ **of attention** meritare attenzione II. <-ies> *n iron* *(import-* *ant person)* personalità *f inv;* **the local worthies** le personalità del posto

would [wʊd] *aux pt of* **will** 1. *(future in the past)* **he said he** ~ **do it later on** disse che lo avrebbe fatto dopo 2. *(future seeing past in the past)* **we thought they** ~ **have done it before** pensammo che lo avrebbero fatto prima 3. *(intention in the past)* **he said he** ~ **always love her** disse che l'avrebbe sempre amata 4. *(shows possibility)* **I'd go myself, but I'm too busy** ci andrei io, ma sono troppo impegnato; **it** ~ **have been very boring to do that** sarebbe stato molto noioso farlo 5. *(condi-* *tional)* **what** ~ **you do if you lost your job?** cosa faresti se tu rimanessi senza lavoro?; **I** ~ **have done it if you had asked** lo avrei fatto se tu l'avessi chiesto 6. *(polite request)* **if you** ~ **just wait a moment, I'll see if I can find her** se aspetta un attimo, vado a cercarla; ~ **you phone him, please?** mi farebbe la cortesia di chiamarlo?; ~ **you mind saying that again?** le dispiacerebbe ripetere?; ~ **you like** ...? vuole...?; ~ **you like me to come with you?** vuoi che ti accompagni? 7. *(regularity in past)* **they** ~ **help each other with their homework** si aiutavano a fare i compiti 8. *(stresses as being typical)* **of course the bus** ~ **be late when I'm in a hurry** come sempre l'autobus è in ritardo quando ho fretta; **he** ~ **say that, wouldn't he?** c'era da aspettarselo che lo dicesse, no? 9. *(courteous opinion)* **I** ~ **imagine that** ... suppongo che...; **I** ~**n't have thought that** ... non avrei mai pensato che... 10. *(probably)* **the guy on the phone had an Australian accent — that** ~

be Tom, **I expect** il ragazzo al telefono aveva l'accento australiano — doveva essere Tom 11.(*shows preference*) **I ~ rather have water** preferisco l'acqua; **I ~ rather die than do that** preferirei morire piuttosto di fare una cosa simile 12.(*offering polite advice*) **I ~n't worry, if I were you** al tuo posto non mi starei a preoccupare 13.(*asking motives*) **why ~ anyone want to do something like that?** per quale motivo uno farebbe una cosa del genere? 14.(*shows a wish*) **ah, ~ I were richer and younger!** ah, se fossi più ricco e più giovane!; **~ that he were here!** ah se solo fosse qui lui!

would-be ['wʊd·bi:] *adj* 1.(*wishing to be*) aspirante; **a ~ politician** un aspirante politico 2.(*pretending to be*) sedicente

wouldn't ['wʊ·dənt] = **would not** *s.* **would**

wound[1] [waʊnd] *vi, vt pt, pp of* **wind**[2]

wound[2] [wu:nd] **I.** *n* ferita *f;* **a gunshot/war ~** una ferita dda arma da fuoco/di guerra; **a leg ~** una ferita alla gamba **II.** *vt a. fig* ferire

wounded I. *adj a. fig* ferito, -a **II.** *npl* **the ~** i feriti

wove [woʊv] *vt, vi pt of* **weave**

woven ['woʊ·vən] **I.** *vt, vi pp of* **weave II.** *adj* (*made by weaving*) tessuto, -a

wow [waʊ] *inf* **I.** *interj* (*demonstrates surprise, excitement*) caspita! **II.** *n* (*hit, popular item*) successone *m;* **to be a ~ with the public** incontrare il favore del pubblico; **I had a ~ of a time** mi sono divertito un mondo **III.** *vt* (*delight*) **to ~ sb** far impazzire qu

wpm, w.p.m. *abbr of* **words per minute** ppm

wraith [reɪθ] *n liter* spettro *m*

wrangle ['ræŋ·gl] **I.** <-ling> *vi* 1.(*argue, debate angrily*) accapigliarsi; **to ~ (with sb) about sth** discutere (con qu) per qc 2.(*round up cattle*) radunare il bestiame **II.** *vt* (*round up: horses, cattle*) radunare **III.** *n* (*intricate argument*) lite *f;* **a ~ about sth** una lite per qc

wrap [ræp] **I.** *n* 1.(*robe-like covering*) accappatoio *m* 2.(*shawl*) scialle *m* 3.(*protective covering material*) involucro *m;* **foil ~** carta *f* d'alluminio ▶ **to keep sth under ~s** tenere qc segreto; **to take the ~s off (of) sth** svelare qc **II.** *vt* <-pp-> **to ~ sth (up) (in a blanket)** avvolgere qc (con una coperta); **~ the glasses in plenty of paper** avvolgi bene i bicchieri con la carta; **to ~ sth around sth/sb** avvolgere qc/qu con qc; **he ~ped a scarf around his neck** si avvolse una sciarpa al collo; **to ~ one's fingers around sth** stringere qc tra le dita; **to ~ one's arms around sb** abbracciare qu; **a matter ~ped in secrecy** una questione avvolta nel mistero

◆**wrap up I.** *vt* <-pp-> 1.(*completely cover*) avvolgere; **to wrap oneself/sb up (against the cold)** (*dress warmly*) coprirsi (per proteggersi dal freddo) 2. *inf* (*finish well*) portare a buon fine; (*deal*) concludere; (*problem*) mettere fine a; **that wraps it up for today** questo è tutto per oggi **II.** *vi* 1.(*dress warmly*)

coprirsi; **to ~ well/warm** coprirsi bene 2.(*be absorbed in*) **to be wrapped up in sth** essere assorto in qc; **to be wrapped up in one's work** essere completamente preso dal proprio lavoro 3.(*finish*) terminare

wraparound ['ræp·ə·ˌraʊnd] *adj* (*skirt, dress*) a portafoglio; (*sunglasses*) avvolgente

wrapper ['ræ·pɚ] *n* 1.(*packaging*) involucro *m;* (*for a book*) sovraccoperta *f* 2.(*robe-like covering*) accappatoio *m*

wrapping paper *n* (*plain*) carta *f* da pacchi; (*for presents*) carta *f* da regalo

wrath [ræθ] *n liter* (*fury, anger*) ira *f*

wrathful ['ræθ·fəl] *adj liter* irato, -a

wreak [ri:k] <-ed, -ed wrought, wrought> *vt form* 1.(*forcefully cause*) causare; **to ~ damage/havoc (on sth)** devastare (qc) 2.(*anger*) **to ~ vengeance on sb** vendicarsi di qu

wreath [ri:θ] <wreaths> *pl n* (*of flowers, greenery*) ghirlanda *f;* (*of smoke*) spirale *f*

wreathe [ri:ð] *vt liter* 1.(*gather around*) **to be ~d in sth** essere avvolto di qc; **~d in clouds** avvolto dalle nuvole; **to be ~d in melancholy** essere molto malinconico; **to be ~d in smiles** essere tutto un sorriso 2.(*crown as with a wreath*) coronare 3.(*intertwine*) intrecciare

wreck [rek] **I.** *vt* 1.(*damage, demolish*) distruggere; (*ship*) far naufragare 2.(*hopes, plan*) rovinare; **to ~ sb's life** distruggere la vita di qu **II.** *n* 1. NAUT naufragio *m;* AUTO distruzione *f* 2.(*ship*) relitto *m;* **~ of a car/a plane** una carcassa d'auto/d'aereo; **an old ~** un rottame 3. *inf* (*any derelict thing*) resti *mpl;* (*mess*) caos *m;* **to feel like a complete ~** sentirsi a pezzi; **to be a nervous ~** avere i nervi a pezzi

wreckage ['re·kɪdʒ] *n* (*of ship, car, plane*) resti *mpl;* (*of building*) rovine *fpl*, macerie *fpl*

wrecker ['re·kɚ] *n* 1.(*tow truck*) carro *m* attrezzi 2.(*worker who demolishes houses*) demolitore *m;* (*worker who demolishes cars*) sfasciacarrozze *m inv* 3.(*person who causes shipwrecks*) persona che provoca di proposito il naufragio di una nave per poi saccheggiarla 4.(*hooligan*) teppista *fm*

wren [ren] *n* scricciolo *m*

wrench [rentʃ] **I.** *vt* 1. *a.fig* (*jerk and twist out*) strappare; **to ~ sth from sb** strappare qc a qu; **to ~ oneself away** liberarsi con uno strattone; **to ~ sb/sth from sb/sth** strappare qu/qc a qu/qc 2.(*injure*) **to ~ one's ankle** slogarsi una caviglia; **to ~ one's shoulder** lussarsi una spalla **II.** *n* 1. TECH (*spanner*) chiave *f* 2.(*twisting jerk*) strattone *m;* **to give sb a ~** dare uno strattone a qu 3.(*injury*) distorsione *f;* **to give one's ankle a ~** slogarsi una caviglia 4.(*pain caused by a departure*) strazio *m* (*causato da una separazione*)*;* **what a ~, seeing you board the plane!** che strazio, vederti salire sull'aereo!

wrestle ['re·sl] SPORTS **I.** <-ling> *vt a. fig a.* SPORTS lottare con; **to ~ sb** lottare con qu [*o* contro]; **to ~ sb to the ground** atterrare qu **II.** <-ling> *vi* lottare; **to ~ professionally** lot-

tare a livello agonistico **III.** *n* lotta *f*
wrestler *n* lottatore, -trice *m, f*
wrestling *n* SPORTS lotta *f;* **freestyle ~** lotta libera
wrestling bout *n,* **wrestling match** *n* SPORTS combattimento *m* di lotta
wretch [retʃ] <-es> *n* **1.** (*unfortunate person*) disgraziato, -a *m, f;* **a poor ~** un povero diavolo **2.** (*mean person*) spilorcio, -a *m, f;* (*mischievous person*) mascalzone, -a *m, f*
wretched ['ret·ʃɪd] *adj* **1.** (*miserable, pitiable: life, person*) disgraziato, -a; **to be in a ~ state** essere in condizioni pietose; (*house*) squallido, -a **2.** (*despicable*) spregevole **3.** (*very bad, awful: weather*) da cani; **to feel ~** stare da cani **4.** (*expressing annoyance*) **my ~ car's broken down again!** questa macchina del cavolo si è guastata un'altra volta!
wriggle ['rɪ·gl] **I.** <-ling> *vi* **1.** (*squirm around*) contorcersi **2.** (*move forward by twisting*) serpeggiare; **to ~ through sth** attraversare qc serpeggiando; **to ~ out of sth** *fig, inf* tirarsi fuori da qc **II.** <-ling> *vt* (*jiggle back and forth*) dimenare; (*body, hand, toes*) muovere; **to ~ one's way along** avanzare serpeggiando; **to ~ oneself into sth** infilarsi in qc (dimenandosi); **to ~** (*one's way*) **out of sth** sgusciare fuori da qc **III.** *n* dimenamento *m;* **with a ~, she managed to crawl through the gap** dimenandosi, riuscì a passare attraverso il buco
wring [rɪŋ] <wrung, wrung> *vt* **1.** (*twist forcibly, twist to squeeze out*) torcere; **to ~ one's hands** torcersi le mani; **to ~ sb's neck** *inf* torcere il collo a qu; **to ~ water out of a shirt** strizzare una camicia **2.** (*extract forcibly*) **to ~ the truth out of sb** tirar fuori la verità a qu **3.** (*cause pain to*) **to ~ sb's heart** stringere il cuore a qu
wringer ['rɪŋ·ɚ] *n* strizzatoio *m* ▶ **to put sb through the ~** *inf* mettere qu sotto torchio
wrinkle ['rɪŋ·kl] **I.** *n* (*fold, crease*) ruga *f* ▶ **to iron the ~s out** appianare le difficoltà **II.** <-ling> *vi* (*form folds, creases*) sgualcirsi; (*apple, fruit*) avvizzire **III.** <-ling> *vt* (*make have folds, creases*) sgualcire ▶ **to ~ one's brow** corrugare la fronte
wrinkled *adj,* **wrinkly** ['rɪŋk·li] *adj* (*clothes*) sgualcito, -a; (*face, skin*) rugoso, -a; (*apple, fruit*) avvizzito, -a
wrist [rɪst] *n* **1.** ANAT polso *m;* **to slash one's ~s** tagliarsi le vene **2.** (*of a garment*) polsino *m*
wristband ['rɪst·bænd] *n* **1.** (*end of sleeve, sweatband*) polsino *m* **2.** (*strap*) cinturino *m*
wristlet *n* polsino *m*
wristwatch <-es> *n* orologio *m* da polso
writ [rɪt] *n* mandato *m;* **~ of summons** mandato *f* di comparizione; **to issue a ~ against sb** emanare un mandato contro qu; **to serve a ~ on sb** presentare un mandato a qu
write [raɪt] <wrote, written, writing> **I.** *vt* **1.** scrivere; **to ~ sth in capital letters** scrivere qc in stampatello; **to ~ a book/a thesis** scrivere un libro/una tesi; **he wrote me a poem**

mi ha scritto una poesia; **to ~ sb** scrivere a qu; **to ~ sb a check** fare un assegno a qu **2.** MUS comporre; **to ~ a song** scrivere una canzone **3.** INFOR (*save*) salvare; **to ~ sth to a disk** salvare qc su un dischetto ▶ **to be nothing to ~ home about** non essere niente di straordinario **II.** *vi* **1.** scrivere; **to ~ clearly/legibly** scrivere in modo chiaro/leggibile; **to ~ to sb** scrivere a qu; **to ~ about sth** scrivere di/su qc; **to ~ for a newspaper** scrivere per un giornale **2.** INFOR (*save*) **to ~ to sth** salvare su qc
◆**write away** *vi* **to ~ for sth** (*brochures, information*) scrivere per chiedere qc
◆**write back** *vt* **to write** (**sb/sth**) **back** rispondere (a qu/qc) **II.** *vi* rispondere
◆**write down** *vt* scrivere, appuntare
◆**write in** **I.** *vi* (*send a letter to*) scrivere **II.** *vt* **1.** (*insert*) scrivere; **to write sth in a space** scrivere qc in uno spazio; **just write your name in — you can fill the rest of the form in later** scriva solo il suo nome — potrà riempire il resto del modulo dopo **2.** LAW (*put in: clause*) inserire **3.** TV, CINE (*character*) inserire
◆**write off** **I.** *vi* (*send away to ask for*) **to ~ for** (*brochures, information*) mandare a chiedere per iscritto **II.** *vt* **1.** (*give up doing*) abbandonare **2.** (*abandon as no good*) **to write sth/sb off as useless** scartare qc/qu in quanto inutile **3.** FIN (*debt*) cancellare
◆**write out** *vt* **1.** (*put into writing*) scrivere **2.** (*copy*) ricopiare **3.** (*fill in*) riempire; **to write a check out to sb** fare un assegno a qu **4.** (*remove from*) eliminare; **to write sb out of a will** diseredare qu
◆**write up** *vt* mettere per iscritto; (*article, report, thesis*) redigere; **to ~ a concert** recensire un concerto
write-in ['raɪt·ɪn] *adj* POL **a ~ candidate** un candidato fuori lista
write-off ['raɪt·ɒf] *n* **1.** FIN (*cancellation*) cancellazione *f* di un debito **2.** (*sth reduced in value*) **the camera was a complete ~** la macchina fotografica ha subito una notevole svalutazione
write-protected ['raɪt·prə·'tek·təd] *adj* INFOR protetto, -a da sovrascrittura
writer ['raɪ·tɚ] *n* **1.** (*person*) scrittore, -trice *m, f;* **~ of children's books** autore, -trice *m, f* di libri per bambini **2.** INFOR **CD-ROM/DVD ~** masterizzatore *m* CD-ROM/DVD
write-up ['raɪt·ʌp] *n* ART, THEAT, MUS recensione *f*
writhe [raɪð] <writhing> *vi* **1.** (*squirm and twist around*) contorcersi; **to ~** (**around**) **in pain** contorcersi dal dolore **2.** (*be uncomfortable: with embarrassment*) sentirsi a disagio; **to make sb ~** mettere a disagio qu
writing ['raɪ·tɪŋ] *n* **1.** (*handwriting*) calligrafia *f;* **in ~** per iscritto; **to put sth in ~** mettere qc per iscritto; **there was some ~ in the margin of the page** c'era qualcosa scritto nel margine della pagina **2.** *a.* LIT la scrittura; **she likes ~** le piace scrivere **3.** LIT, THEAT (*process*)

redazione *f;* **creative** ~ scrittura *f* creativa **4.** LIT, THEAT (*written work*) opera *f;* **women's** ~ letteratura *f* femminile **5.** LIT (*style*) stile *m* ▶ **the** ~ **is on the** wall ci sono chiari segnali
writing desk *n* scrivania *f*
writing pad *n* blocco *m*
writing paper *n* carta *f* da lettere
written I. *vt, vi pp of* **write** II. *adj* (*recorded in writing*) scritto, -a ▶ **to have** guilt ~ **all over one's face** avere scritto in faccia che si è colpevoli; **the** ~ word la lingua scritta
wrong [rɑːŋ] I. *adj* **1.** (*not right: answer*) sbagliato, -a, errato, -a; **to be** ~ **about sth/sb** sbagliarsi su qc/qu; **he is** ~ **in thinking that ...** si sbaglia se pensa che...; **to be in the** ~ **place** essere nel posto sbagliato; **to be plainly** ~ sbagliarsi di grosso; **to get the** ~ **number** sbagliare numero; **sorry, you've got the** ~ **number!** guardi, ha sbagliato numero; **to go the** ~ **direction** sbagliare direzione; **to prove sb** ~ dimostrare che qu si sbaglia **2.** (*not appropriate*) inopportuno, -a; **to do/say the** ~ **thing** fare una gaffe; **she's the** ~ **person for the job** non è la persona adatta per questo lavoro; **this is the** ~ **time to ...** non è il momento opportuno per...; **the** ~ **side of town** una zona malfamata della città; **she got in with the** ~ **crowd** cominciò a frequentare cattive compagnie **3.** (*bad*) **is there anything** ~**?** cosa c'è che non va?; **what's** ~ **with you today?** cosa ti succede oggi?; **there's nothing** ~ **with your stomach** non ha niente allo stomaco; **something's** ~ **with the television** la televisione non funziona bene **4.** LAW, REL **it is** ~ **to do that** non si deve farlo; **it was** ~ **of him** (**to do that**) ha fatto male (a farlo); **what's** ~ **with that?** cosa c'è di sbagliato in questo? ▶ **to fall into the** ~ hands cadere in cattive mani; **to go down the** ~ way (*food, drink*) andare di traverso II. *adv* **1.** (*incorrectly*) erroneamente; **to do sth** ~ far male qc; **to get sth** ~ sbagliare qc; **to get it** ~ capire male; **you got it** ~ — **it's Maria who's coming, not Marina** hai capito male — viene Maria, non Marina; **don't get me** ~ non mi fraintendere; **to go** ~ sbagliarsi; (*stop working*) guastarsi; (*fail*) andare male; **after 300 feet turn to the left, you can't go** ~ dopo 100 m giri a sinistra, non si può sbagliare **2.** (*in a morally reprehensible way*) **to do sth** ~ fare qc di male III. *n* **1.** *a.* LAW, REL male *m;* (**to know**) **right from** ~ saper distinguere il bene dal male; **to put sb in the** ~ dare torto a qu; **to do sb no** ~ non fare nienete di male a qu **2.** (*unjust action*) ingiustizia *f;* **to do sb** (**a**) ~ (**in doing sth**) commettere un'ingiustizia verso qu (facendo qc); **to right a** ~ rimediare a un'ingiustizia; **to suffer a** ~ subire un'ingiustizia ▶ **to** do ~ agire male; **he can** do **no** ~ non fa mai niente di male; **to be in the** ~ (*not right, mistaken*) avere torto; (*do something bad*) agire male IV. *vt form* **to** ~ **sb** (*treat unjustly*) fare un torto a qu; (*judge*

unjustly) giudicare male qu
wrongdoer [ˈrɑːŋˌduːɚ] *n* malfattore, -trice *m, f*
wrongdoing *n* disonestà *f;* **to accuse sb of** ~ accusare qu di azioni illecite
wrongful *adj* **1.** (*unfair*) ingiusto, -a **2.** LAW (*unlawful: arrest*) illegale; (*dismissal*) senza giusta causa
wrong-headed *adj pej* (*person*) irragionevole; (*concept, idea, plan*) insensato, -a
wrongly *adv* mal; (*spell*) incorrettamente; (*believe, state*) erroneamente; (*accuse, convict*) ingiustamente
wrote [rovt] *vi, vt pt of* **write**
wrought [rɑːt] I. *vt pt, pp of* **work** III. **4.**, **5.**, **wreak** II. *adj form* (*crafted*) lavorato, -a; (*metal*) battuto, -a
wrought iron *n* ferro *m* battuto
wrought-up [rɔːtˈʌp] *adj* nervoso, -a; **to be/ get** ~ (**about sth**) essere nervoso/innervosirsi (per qc)
wrung [rʌŋ] *vt pt, pp of* **wring**
wry [raɪ] <wrier, wriest *o* wryer, wryest> *adj* **1.** (*dry and ironic: comments, humor*) caustico, -a; **a** ~ **smile** un sorriso beffardo **2.** (*showing dislike*) **to make a** ~ **face** arricciare il naso
WSW *abbr of* **west-southwest** OSO
wt. *n abbr of* **weight** peso *m*
WV *n abbr of* **West Virginia** Virginia *f* Ovest
WWI *n abbr of* **World War I** Prima Guerra *f* Mondiale
WWII *n abbr of* **World War II** Seconda Guerra *f* Mondiale
WWW *n abbr of* **World Wide Web** INFOR WWW *m*
WY *n abbr of* **Wyoming** Wyoming *m*
Wyoming *n* Wyoming *m*

X

X, x [eks] I. *n* **1.** X, x *f;* ~ **as in X-ray** X come Xeres **2.** MAT (*unknown number*) x *f* **3.** (*used in place of name*) Mr./Mrs./Ms. ~ il Sig./la Sig.ra. X **4.** (*symbol for kiss*) un bacio; **all my love, Katy** ~~~ baci, Katy **5.** (*cross symbol*) croce *f;* ~ **marks the spot** il punto è contrassegnato da una croce II. *vt* (*delete*) **to** ~ (**out**) **sth** cancellare qc
X-chromosome [ˈeksˌkrovməˌsovm] *n* cromosoma *m* X
xenophobia [ˌzeˑnəˈfovˑbiə] *n* xenofobia *f*
xenophobic [ˌzeˑnəˈfovˑbɪk] *adj* xenofobo, -a
Xerox®, xerox [ˈzɪˑrɑːks] I. *n* (*photocopy*) fotocopia *f* II. *vt* (*photocopy*) fotocopiare; **a** ~**ed copy of the document** una fotocopia del documento
XL *adj abbr of* **extra large** XL
Xmas [ˈkrɪsˑməs] *n abbr of* **Christmas**

Natale *m*

X-rated ['eks·ˌreɪ·tɪd] *adj* an ~ film un film vietato ai minori

X-ray ['eks·reɪ] I. *n* 1. (*photo*) radiografia *f*; ~ s raggi *mpl* X 2. (*hospital department*) radiologia *f* II. *vt* radiografare, fare una radiografia di qc/a qu

xylophone ['zaɪ·lə·foʊn] *n* MUS xilofono *m*

Y

Y, y [waɪ] *n* 1. Y, y *f*; ~ as in Yankee Y come yacht 2. MAT (*unknown quantity*) y *f*

yacht [jɑːt] I. *n* (*for pleasure, racing*) yacht *m inv*; ~ club yacht club *m inv*; ~ race regata *f* II. *vi* 1. (*sail in a yacht*) navigare su uno yacht 2. (*race in a yacht*) partecipare a una regata

yachting *n* 1. (*sailing in yachts*) navigazione *f* da diporto 2. (*racing in yachts*) vela *f*; to go ~ fare vela

yachtsman ['jɑːts·mən] <-men> *n* (*yacht owner*) padrone *m* di uno yacht; (*yacht sailor*) velista *m*

yack, yak [jæk] I. *n sl* chiacchiere *fpl* II. *vi sl* chiacchierare

yam [jæm] *n* 1. (*plant, vegetable*) igname *m* 2. (*sweet potato*) patata *f* dolce

yank [jæŋk] I. *vt inf* to ~ sth tirare qc II. *vi inf* to ~ (on sth) tirare (qc); she ~ ed at his hair gli tirò i capelli III. *n inf* to give sth a (good) ~ tirare (forte) qc

◆ **yank out** *vt* (*remove forcefully*) staccare; to ~ a tooth strappare un dente

Yank [jæŋk] *n*, **Yankee** ['jæŋ·ki] *n pej, inf* yanquee *mf inv*

yap [jæp] I. <-pp-> *vi* 1. (*bark*) abbaiare 2. *inf* (*talk continuously*) blaterare II. *n* 1. (*bark*) latrato *m* 2. *pej, inf* (*foolish talk*) ciarle *fpl*

yard[1] [jɑːrd] *n* 1. (*3 feet*) iarda *f* (*0'91 m*); square ~ iarda quadra; it's about a hundred ~ s down the road è a un centinaio di metri da qui 2. NAUT pennone *m*

yard[2] [jɑːrd] *n* 1. (*enclosed paved area: of a house, school, prison*) cortile *m* 2. (*land next to house*) pratino *m* 3. (*work area*) cantiere *m*; shipbuilding ~ cantiere *m* navale 4. (*outside area used for storage*) deposito *m*; wood ~ deposito *m* di legna 5. (*enclosure for livestock*) recinto *m*

yardstick ['jɑːrd·stɪk] *n* 1. (*measuring tool*) stecca *f* lunga una iarda 2. (*standard*) criterio *m*

yarn [jɑːrn] I. *n* 1. (*thread*) filato *m* 2. *inf* (*story*) storia *f*; to spin a ~ raccontare una frottola II. *vi inf* raccontare frottole

yaw [jɑː] AVIAT, NAUT, TECH I. *vi* (*move sideways: car*) sbandare II. *n* (*sideways movement: of a car*) sbandamento *m*; (*of a boat*)

yawl [jɑːl] *n* iolla *f*

yawn [jɑːn] I. *vi* 1. (*show tiredness*) sbadigliare 2. *fig, liter* (*open wide*) aprirsi II. *n* 1. (*sign of tiredness*) sbadiglio *m* 2. *inf* (*boring thing*) barba *f*; it was a ~ è stata una barba

yawning *adj* 1. (*bored: audience*) annoiato, -a 2. (*wide and deep: chasm, crater*) enorme; there's a ~ gap between ... and ... c'è un abisso tra... e...

Y-chromosome ['waɪ·ˌkrəʊ·mə·səʊm] *n* cromosoma *m* Y

yd. *abbr of* **yard**(s) iarda *f*

yea [jeɪ] I. *adv* HIST (*yes*) sì II. *n* sì *m inv*, voto *m* a favore; the ~ s and the nays i voti a favore e quelli contrari

yeah [jeə] *adv inf* (*yes*) sì; oh ~! *iron* (*indicating disbelief*) eh sì!; ~, ~, we've heard that one before sì, sì, questa l'ho già sentita!

year [jɪr] *n* 1. (*twelve months*) anno *m*; ~ of birth anno di nascita; ~ in, ~ out per anni; fiscal ~ FIN anno contabile; leap ~ anno bisestile; all (the) ~ round (durante) tutto l'anno; every other ~ ogni due anni; happy new ~! buon anno!; last/next ~ l'anno scorso/ prossimo; $5000 a ~ 5000 dollari all'anno; the ~ when ... l'anno in cui...; this ~ quest'anno; I'm eight ~ s old ho otto anni; ~ s ago anni fa; I haven't seen her for ~ s è tantissimo che non la vedo; it's taken me ~ s to ... mi ci sono voluti anni a...; it's been ~ s since we had a summer as good as this one erano anni che non faceva un'estate così bella; it'll be ~ s before... passeranno anni prima che/di...; over the ~ s nel corso degli anni 2. SCHOOL, UNIV anno *m*; the academic ~ l'anno accademico; she was in my ~ at college faceva il mio stesso anno all'università ▶ to put ~ s on sb invecchiare qu; to take ~ s off (of) sb ringiovanire qu

yearbook ['jɪr·bʊk] *n* annuario *m*

yearling ['jɪr·lɪŋ] I. *adj* (*colt, calf, goat*) di un anno II. *n* (*colt*) puledrino *m* di un anno; (*yearold calf, goat, sheep*) bestia *f* di un anno

yearlong ['jɪr·lɑːŋ] *adj* di un anno

yearly I. *adj* (*happening every year*) annuale II. *adv* (*every year*) annualmente; to take place ~ aver luogo annualmente; twice ~ due volte l'anno

yearn [jɜːrn] *vi* (*long*) to ~ to do sth desiderare fare qc; to ~ after sth anelare a qc; to ~ for sth/sb desiderare ardentemente qc/qu

yearning *n* desiderio *m*; ~ for sth desiderio di qc; to have a ~ to do sth avere una gran voglia di fare qc

yeast [jiːst] *n* lievito *m*

yeasty <-ier, -iest> *adj* di lievito

yell [jel] I. *n* 1. (*loud shout*) urlo *m*; to give a ~ cacciare un urlo; a ~ of laughter una risata sonora 2. (*chant*) grido d'incitamento II. *vi* (*shout loudly*) urlare; to ~ at sb (to do sth) urlare a qu (di fare qc); to ~ for sb chiamare qu a gran voce; to ~ for help gridare aiuto III. *vt* (*shout loudly*) urlare

yellow ['je·loʊ] I. *adj* 1.(*color*) giallo, -a; golden ~ giallo dorato; to turn [*o* go] ~ ingiallire 2. *pej, inf* (*cowardly*) vigliacco, -a II. *n* giallo *m;* ~ of an egg tuorlo *m* d'uovo III. *vi, vt* ingiallire

yellow-belly ['je·loʊ·ˌbe·li] <-ies> *n pej, inf* coniglio *m*

yellow fever *n* MED febbre *f* gialla

yellowish ['je·loʊ·ɪʃ] *adj* giallognolo, -a

yellowness ['je·loʊ·nəs] *n* giallezza *f*

Yellow Pages® *npl* the ~ le Pagine Gialle®

yellowy *adj* giallognolo, -a

yelp [jelp] I. *vi* (*cry: a dog*) guaire; (*a person*) gemere; to ~ with pain gemere di dolore II. *n* (*cry: of animal*) guaito *m;* (*of person*) gemito *m*

Yemen ['je·mən] *n* Yemen *m*

Yemeni ['je·mə·ni] I. *adj* yemenita II. *n* yemenita *mf*

yen[1] [jen] *inv n* FIN yen *m inv*

yen[2] [jen] *n inf* (*strong desire*) voglia *f;* (to have) a ~ for sth/sb (avere) voglia di qc/qu; (to have) a ~ to do sth (aver) voglia di fare qc

yeoman ['joʊ·mən] <-men> *n* 1.(*sailor in the Navy*) sottoufficiale di marina con mansioni amministrative 2.(*freeholder*) contadino che lavora un piccolo appezzamento di sua proprietà ▸ to do ~('s) service prestare onorato servizio

yep [jep] *adv inf* (*yes*) sì

yes [jes] I. *adv* 1.(*affirmative answer*) sì; ~, sir/ma'am sì, signore/signora; ~, please sì, grazie; to answer ~ to sth rispondere (di) sì a qc; I'm not a very good cook — ~ you are non sono un bravo cuoco — sì che lo sei; ~ indeed certo che sì; ~, of course! sì, certo! 2.(*as question*) ~? TEL sì?; Johnny? — yes? — can I have a word? Johnny — sì? — posso parlarti? 3.(*indicating doubt*) oh ~? davvero? II. <yeses> *n* (*statement in favor*) sì *m inv*

yes man ['jes·mæn] <-men> *n pej* persona servile

yesterday ['jes·tə·deɪ] I. *adv* ieri; ~ morning ieri mattina; the day before ~ l'altroieri II. *n* ieri *m*

yet [jet] I. *adv* 1.(*up to a particular time*) ancora; it's too early ~ to ... è ancora troppo presto per...; not ~ non ancora; she hasn't told him ~ non glielo ha ancora detto; as ~ finora; the issue is as ~ undecided la questione resta ancora da definire; her best/worst film ~ il suo migliore/peggiore film fino ad ora; have you finished ~? hai finito?; isn't supper ready ~? non è ancora pronta la cena?; can you see the lighthouse ~? si vede già il faro?; the best is ~ to come il meglio deve ancora venire; there's a great deal of work ~ to be done c'è ancora molto lavoro da fare 2.(*in addition*) ~ again un'altra volta; ~ more food ancora più roba da mangiare 3. + *comp* (*even*) ~ bigger/more beautiful ancora più grande/bello 4.(*despite that*) eppure 5.(*in spite of everything*) nonostante

tutto; you'll do it ~ lo finirai; we're not giving up, we'll get there ~ non ci arrendiamo, prima o poi ce la faremo II. *conj* tuttavia

yew [ju:] *n* (*tree and wood*) tasso *m*

YHA *n abbr of* Youth Hostel Association Associazione *f* Alberghi della Gioventù

Yiddish ['jɪ·dɪʃ] I. *adj* yiddish 5*nv* II. *n* yiddish *m*

yield [ji:ld] I. *n* 1.(*amount produced*) produzione *f;* AGR raccolto *m* 2. COM, FIN (*profits*) rendimento *m;* (*interest*) interesse *m;* fixed/variable ~ rendita *f* fissa/variabile II. *vt* 1.(*provide: results, information*) dare 2. AGR (*produce*) produrre 3. COM, FIN (*profit, interest*) fruttare; to ~ 8% interest dare un interesse dell'8% 4.(*give up*) to ~ ground cedere terreno; to ~ responsibility delegare responsabilità; to ~ sth to the enemy cedere qc al nemico III. *vi* 1. AGR, COM, FIN essere produttivo 2.(*give way*) to ~ to sth/sb cedere davanti a qc/qu; to ~ to temptation cedere alla tentazione 3.(*surrender*) arrendersi 4.(*give priority*) to ~ to sth/sb dare la precedenza a qc/qu 5. AUTO dare la precedenza

yielding *adj* 1.(*pliable: a material, a substance*) flessibile; (*soft*) molle 2. *fig* (*compliant*) accomodante

yippee ['jɪ·piː] *interj inf* urrà

YMCA [ˌwaɪ·em·si·'eɪ] *abbr of* Young Men's Christian Association Associazione Cristiana dei Giovani

yodel, yodle ['joʊ·dəl] MUS I. <-ll-, -l-> *vi* (*sing*) cantare alla tirolese II. *vt* (*sing*) cantare alla tirolese III. *n* (*yodeled song*) canzone *f* tirolese

yoga ['joʊ·gə] *n* yoga *m*

yoghourt *n*, **yoghurt** ['joʊ·gət] *n s.* yogurt

yogi ['joʊ·gi] *n* yogi *mf inv*

yogurt ['joʊ·gət] *n* yogurt *m inv*

yoke [joʊk] I. *n* 1. *a. fig* AGR giogo *m;* to throw off the ~ liberarsi dal giogo 2. FASHION sprone *m* II. *vt* 1. AGR (*fit with yoke*) aggiogare; to ~ an animal (to sth) aggiogare un animale (a qc) 2. *fig* (*combine*) to ~ two things together legare due cose insieme

yokel ['joʊ·kl] *n iron, pej* (*country person*) zoticone, -a *m, f*

yolk [joʊk] *n* tuorlo *m*

Yom Kippur [ˌjɑ:m·kɪ·'poʊ·əɚ] *n* Yom Kippur *m*

yonder ['jɑ:n·dɚ] *dial* I. *adv* (*over there*) là II. *adj* (*situated over there*) quello, -a; *pl:* quelli, -e

yore [jɔːr] *n liter* in (the) days of ~ un tempo

you [juː] *pron pers* 1. 2*nd pers sing* tu; *pl:* voi; I see ~ ti/vi vedo; do ~ see me? mi vedi/vedete?; I love ~ ti/vi amo; it is for ~ è per te/voi; older than ~ più grande di te/voi; if I were ~ se fossi in te/voi; ~'re my brother sei mio fratello 2.(*2nd person sing, polite form*) lei; ~ have a car ha una macchina; ~'re going to Toronto va a Toronto

you'd [juːd] = you would *s.* would

you'll [juːl] = you will *s.* will

young [jʌŋ] **I.** *adj* **1.** *a.* GEO (*not old*) giovane; ~ **children** bambini *mpl* piccoli; **a** ~ **man** un ragazzo; ~ **people/persons** i giovani; **sb's** ~**er brother/son** il fratello/figlio minore di qu; **the** ~**er generation** la nuova generazione; **the night is still** ~ la notte è giovane **2.** (*junior*) **old Mr. Brown and** ~ **Mr. Brown** il Sig. Brown padre e il Sig. Brown figlio **3.** (*young-seeming: appearance, clothes*) giovanile; **to be** ~ **at heart** essere giovane di spirito; **she is** ~ **for her age** porta bene i suoi anni; **to be** ~ **looking** avere un aspetto giovanile **4.** (*pertaining to youth: love*) giovanile; **in my** ~ (**er**) **days** quando ero giovane ▶**you're only** ~ **once!** si vive una volta sola! **II.** *n pl* **1.** (*young people*) **the** ~ i giovani **2.** ZOOL (*offspring*) piccoli *mpl;* **with** ~ gravida

youngster ['jʌŋks·tə'] *n* giovane *mf*

your [jʊr] *adj pos* **1.** *2nd pers sing* tuo, -a; *pl:* vostro, -a **2.** (*2nd pers sing: polite form*) suo, -a

you're [jʊr] = **you are** *s.* be

yours [jʊrz] *pron pos* **1.** *sing:* (il) tuo, (la) tua, (i) tuoi, (le) tue; *pl:* (il) vostro, (la) vostra, (i) vostri, (le) vostre; **this glass is** ~ questo bicchiere è il tuo/vostro **2.** *polite form* (il) suo, (la) sua, (i) suoi, (le) sue; ~ **truly** cordiali saluti

yourself [jʊr·'self] *pron reflexive* **1.** *sing:* ti; *emphatic:* tu (stesso, a); *after prep:* te (stesso, a) **2.** *polite form:* si; *emphatic:* lei (stesso, a); *after prep:* sé, lei stesso, a

yourselves *pron reflexive* vi; *emphatic, after prep:* voi (stessi, -e)

youth [juːθ] *n* **1.** (*period when young*) gioventù *f,* giovinezza *f;* **during her** (**early**) ~ quando era (molto) giovane; **he is a friend from my** ~ è un amico di gioventù **2.** (*young man*) giovane *m* **3.** (*young people*) giovani *mpl;* **the** ~ i giovani; ~ **culture** cultura *f* giovanile

youth center *n,* **youth club** *n* centro *m* giovanile

youthful ['juːθ·fəl] *adj* **1.** (*young-looking*) giovanile; ~ **appearance** aspetto *m* giovanile **2.** (*typical of the young*) dei giovani **3.** (*young*) giovane

youth hostel *n* albergo *m* della gioventù

you've [juːv] = **you have** *s.* have

yowl [jaʊl] **I.** *vi* (*howl: dog*) guaire; (*cat*) miagolare; (*person*) gemere **II.** *n* (*howl: of a dog*) guaito *m;* (*of a cat*) miagolio *m;* (*of a person*) gemito *m*

yo-yo ['joʊ·joʊ] *n* (*toy*) yo-yo *m inv*

yr. *abbr of* **year** a.

yuan [ˌjuː·'æn] *n* FIN yuan *m inv*

yucky ['jʌ·ki] *adj inf* schifoso, -a

Yugoslav ['juː·goʊs·laːv] *adj, n s.* **Yugoslavian**

Yugoslavia ['juː·goʊ·'slaː·viə] *n* HIST Jugoslavia *f*

Yugoslavian I. *adj* jugoslavo, -a **II.** *n* jugoslavo, -a *m, f*

yukky ['jʌ·ki] <-ier, -iest> *adj s.* **yucky**

Yukon Territory ['juː·kaːn 'te·rə·tɔː·ri] *n* (Territorio *m* dello) Yukon, m

yule log ['juːl·ˌlaːg] *n* **1.** (*log*) ceppo que si brucia nel camino per Natale **2.** A.GASTR tronchetto *m* di Natale

Yuletide ['juːl·taɪd] *n liter* Natale *m*

yummy ['jʌ·mi] *adj* buonissimo, -a

yuppie ['jʌ·pi] *n* yuppy *mf inv*

YWCA *abbr of* **Young Women's Christian Association** *Associazione Cristiana delle Giovani*

Z

Z, z [ziː] *n* Z, z *f;* ~ **as in Zebra** Z come Zara ▶**to catch some** ~**'s** *inf* dormire un po'

Zaire [zaɪ·'ɪr] *n* Zaire *m*

Zairean [zaɪ·'ɪə·riən] **I.** *adj* zairese **II.** *n* zairese *mf*

Zambia ['zæm·biə] *n* Zambia *f*

Zambian ['zæm·biən] **I.** *adj* zambiano, -a **II.** *n* zambiano, -a *m, f*

zany ['zeɪ·ni] <-ier, -iest> *adj inf* bislacco, -a

zap [zæp] **I.** <-pp-> *vt* **1.** *inf* (*destroy*) distruggere **2.** *inf* (*send fast*) inviare rapidamente **3.** *inf* FOOD (*microwave*) sbattere nel microonde **II.** <-pp-> *vi inf* **1.** TV **to** ~ **through the channels** fare zapping **2.** (*move fast*) **to** ~ **somewhere** fiondarsi in un posto **III.** *interj inf* zac

zapping ['zæ·pɪŋ] *n inf* zapping *m*

zeal [ziːl] *n* zelo *m;* **religious** ~ fervore *m* religioso

zealot ['ze·lət] *n* fanatico, -a *m, f*

zealous ['ze·ləs] *adj* fervente; **to be** ~ **in sth/ in doing sth** essere zelante in qc/nel fare qc

zebra ['ziː·b·rə] *n* zebra *f*

zenith ['ziː·nɪθ] <-es> *n* **1.** ASTR (*highest point*) zenit *m* **2.** (*most successful point*) apice *m;* **to be at the** ~ **of sth** essere all'apice di qc

zero ['zɪ·roʊ] **I.** <-s *o* -es> *n* zero *m;* **below** ~ METEO sottozero; **to be a** ~ non valere una cicca **II.** *adj* zero *inv;* ~ **growth** natalità *f* zero; ~ **hour** ora *f* zero; ~ **visibility** visibilità *f* nulla; **my chances are** ~ ho zero possibilità **III.** *vt* (*return to zero: device*) azzerare ◆**zero in on** *vi* **1.** (*aim precisely*) mirare a **2.** (*focus on*) **to** ~ **sth** concentrarsi su qc

zero tolerance *n* policy of ~ tolleranza *f* zero

zest [zest] *n* **1.** (*enthusiastic energy*) entusiasmo *m;* **to do sth with** ~ fare qc con entusiasmo; ~ **for life** gioia *f* di vivere **2.** (*charm, interest*) sapore *m;* **the story lacks** ~ la storia non ha pepe **3.** (*rind*) scorza *f;* **lemon/ orange** ~ scorza di limone/arancia; **grated lemon** ~ scorza di limone grattugiata

zigzag ['zɪg·zæg] **I.** *n* (*crooked line*) zigzag *m inv* **II.** *adj* (*crooked*) a zigzag **III.** <-gg-> *vi* zigzagare

Zimbabwe [zɪm·'bɑːb·weɪ] *n* Zimbabwe *m*

Zimbabwean [zɪm·'bɑːb·wi·ən] **I.** *adj* zimbabwiano, -a **II.** *n* zimbabwiano, -a *m, f*

zinc [zɪŋk] *n* zinco *m*

zip [zɪp] **I.** *n* **1.** (*ZIP code*) CAP *m inv* **2.** (*whistle*) sibilo *m* **3.** *inf* (*vigor*) brio *m* **4.** *sl* (*nothing*) zero *m;* I know ~ about that ne so zero **II.** <-pp-> *vt* to ~ a bag/a dress chiudere la lampo di una borsa/un vestito; to ~ sth open aprire la lampo di qc; to ~ sth shut chiudere la lampo di qc; to ~ sth up chiudere la lampo di qc; will you ~ me up? mi chiudi la lampo? **III.** <-pp-> *vi* to ~ in/past entrare/passare di corsa; the days ~ped by i giorni sono volati

ZIP code *n* codice *m* di avviamento postale

zipper ['zɪ·pɚ] *n* lampo *f,* cerniera *f*

zippy ['zɪ·pi] <-ier, -iest> *adj inf* (*fast: car*) veloce; (*energetic*) vivace

zither ['zɪ·ðɚ] *n* zither *m inv*

zloty ['zlɔː·t̬i] *n* zloty *m inv*

zodiac ['zoʊ·di·æk] *n* zodiaco *m*

zombie ['zɑːm·bi] *n* zombi *mf inv*

zonal ['zoʊ·nəl] *adj* di zona; a ~ division una divisione in zone

zone [zoʊn] **I.** *n* zona *f;* **nuclear-free** ~ zona denuclearizzata; **time** ~ fuso *m* orario; **frigid/temperate/torrid** ~ METEO zona polare/temperata/torrida **II.** *vt* **1.** (*divide*) suddividere in zone **2.** ADMIN, LAW (*designate*) to ~ **an area for residential use** designare una zona residenziale

zoning *n* ADMIN, LAW zonizzazione *f*

zoo [zuː] *n* zoo *m inv*

zoological [ˌzoʊ·ə·'lɑː·dʒɪ·kəl] *adj* zoologico, -a; ~ **garden** giardino *m* zoologico

zoologist [zoʊ·'ɑː·lə·dʒɪst] *n* zoologo, -a *m, f*

zoology [zoʊ·'ɑː·lə·dʒi] *n* zoologia *f*

zoom [zuːm] **I.** *n* **1.** PHOT zoom *m inv* **2.** AVIAT impennata *f* **3.** (*buzz*) frastuono *m* **II.** *vt* **1.** AVIAT (*plane*) impennare **2.** PHOT zumare **III.** *vi* **1.** *inf* (*move very fast*) sfrecciare; to ~ **away** sfrecciare via; to ~ **past** passare sfrecciando **2.** (*plane*) impennarsi; (*costs, sales*) subire un'impennata

♦**zoom in** *vi* PHOT fare uno zoom; to ~ **on** sth/sb fare uno zoom di qc/qu

♦**zoom out** *vi* PHOT fare uno zoom all'indietro

zoom lens *n* zoom *m inv*

zucchini [zuː·'kiː·ni] <-(s)> *n inv* zucchino *m*

Z

Short Grammar of the Italian Language
Minigrammatica della lingua italiana

Articles

In Italian nouns and adjectives are accompanied by the article. The gender of the article and whether it is singular or plural is dependent on the noun.

1. Definite Article

masculine		sing	pl
before a *consonant*		**il** treno	**i** treni
before *s* + *consonant, gn, ps, x, z, i* or *y* + *vowel*		**lo** sciopero	**gli** scioperi
		lo zio	**gli** zii
		lo yoghurt	**gli** yoghurt
before a *vowel*		**l'**anno	**gli** anni
feminine			
before a *consonant*		**la** strada	**le** strade
before a *vowel*		**l'**ora	**le** ore

- Before an adjective the article varies according to the first letter of the adjective:

l'ultimo treno – gli ultimi treni

2. Combination of prepositions and the definite article

	il	lo	l'	la	i	gli	le
a	al	allo	all'	alla	ai	agli	alle
da	dal	dallo	dall'	dalla	dai	dagli	dalle
di	del	dello	dell'	della	dei	degli	delle
in	nel	nello	nell'	nella	nei	negli	nelle
su	sul	sullo	sull'	sulla	sui	sugli	sulle

- In Italian when the above prepositions precede a definite article they are *always* combined.

3. Indefinite article and the partitive

masculine	sing		pl
	countable	uncountable	countable
before a *consonant*	un treno a train	del sale (some) salt	dei treni (some) trains
before *s* + *consonant, gn, ps, x, z, i* or *j* + vowel	uno sciopero a strike	dello zucchero (some) sugar	degli scioperi (some) strikes
before a *vowel*	un anno a year	dell'aceto (some) vinegar	degli anni (some) years
feminine			
before a *consonant*	una casa a house	della frutta (some) fruit	delle case (some) houses
before a *vowel*	un'ora an hour	dell'acqua (some) water	delle ore (some) hours

- The indefinite article (un, una, un') is used only in the **singular** with **countable nouns**. **Uncountable nouns** in the **singular** and **countable nouns** in the **plural** take the partitive (di + definite article). The singular and plural partitive forms indicate an unspecified quantity of something.

Compro del pane.	I buy (some) bread.
Ho incontrato degli amici in centro.	I met (some) friends in town.
Vuoi del vino?	Do you want (some) wine?

- In the plural the partitive can sometimes be deleted.

Ho ancora dubbi.	I still have some doubts.
Non ci sono treni per Milano.	There are no trains going to Milan.

- **Nessun, nessuno** (no, none, nobody) follow the same formation as un, uno, una, etc.

Nouns

Gender of nouns

Italian nouns have two genders (masculine and feminine):

masculine *m*	il treno lo studente	the train the student
feminine *f*	la strada la lezione	the street the lesson

- Nouns ending in -o are mostly masculine: *il libro, l'albero, il castello, lo zaino.*
Nouns ending in -a are feminine: *la banca, la panchina, la luna.*
- Nouns ending in -e may be either masculine or feminine: *il giornale, la regione.*

Plurals of nouns

The plural (pl) of a noun differs from the singular (sing) according to the following rules:

1. General rule for the plural of nouns:

	sing	pl
m	il tren**o**	i tren**i**
m, f	il mar**e** la torr**e**	i mar**i** le torr**i**
f	la strad**a**	le strad**e**

- Nouns ending in -o and -e have a plural form ending in -i.
Nouns ending in -a have a plural form ending in -e.

There are some exceptions:

2. Nouns ending in *-co, -ca, -go, -ga*

sing		pl	
	il bu̲co		i bu̲chi
	la bo̲cca		le bo̲cche
	il la̲go		i la̲ghi
	il colle̲ga		i colle̲ghi
	la botte̲ga		le botte̲ghe

- As a rule, when the stress falls on the penultimate syllable, the plural of these nouns is formed by adding an *h* after the final -*c* or -*g* and then adding the usual plural ending.

Exception: *l'amico – gli amici*

- When the stress falls on the second syllable of the word the plural is -*ci* or -*gi*.

sing	il medico	pl	i medici
	l'asparago		gli asparagi

Exceptions: *lo stomaco – gli stomachi*
l'obbligo – gli obblighi

- Nouns ending in -logo generally change to -logi if they refer to people and to -loghi if they refer to objects.

sing	il biologo	pl	i biologi
	il catalogo		i cataloghi

3. Nouns ending in *-io*

sing	il pendio	pl	i pendii
	lo zio		gli zii

- When the stress is on the final -i in the plural this becomes -ii.

sing	l'inizio	pl	gli inizi
	l'esempio		gli esempi

- When the stress is **not** on the final -i the plural is simply -i:

4. Nouns ending in *-cio, -gio* and *-glio*

sing	il negozio	pl	i negozi
	il bacio		i baci
	il figlio		i figli

- When the stress is **not** on the final -i in nouns ending in -cio, -gio and -glio then the plural is simply -i.

5. Feminine nouns ending in *-cia, -gia*

sing	l'arancia	pl	le arance
	la goccia		le gocce
	la spiaggia		le spiagge
	la camicia		le camicie
	la valigia		le valigie
	la figlia		le figlie

- When a feminine noun ending in -cia or -gia has a consonant before the -c or the -g, the plural is -ce or -ge. When the -c or -g is preceded by a vowel the plural is normally -cie or -gie.

6. Masculine nouns ending in *-a*

sing	il problema	pl	i problemi
	il geometra		i geometri

- Masculine nouns ending in -**a** form the plural with -**i**

7. Nouns which do not change in the plural

sing		pl	
	la città		le città
	il film		i film
	il cinema		i cinema
	la foto		le foto
	la crisi		le crisi
	la serie		le serie
	il re		i re

- Nouns do not change in the plural when:
  - they end in an accented vowel: *il caffè – i caffè*
  - they end in a consonant: *lo sport – gli sport.* These are often words adopted from other languages.
  - they are generally used in an abbreviated form in Italian: *la fotografia – la foto – le foto*
  - they consist of only one syllable and end in a vowel: *il re – i re*
  - they end in –i or –ie: *il brindisi – i brindisi, la specie – le specie* (*Exception: la moglie – le mogli*)

8. Nouns with more than one form in the plural

sing		pl		
	il braccio		i bracci	the arms (of a river) ...
			le braccia	the arms (of a human being) ...
	il labbro		i labbri	the lips (of a wound) ...
			le labbra	the lips (of a human being) ...
	il muro		i muri	the walls (of a house) ...
			le mura	the walls (of a city) ...

9. Compound nouns

sing		pl	
	l'arcobaleno		gli arcobaleni
	il francobollo		i francobolli
	il grattacielo		i grattacieli
	il capostazione		i capistazione
	la cassaforte		le casseforti

- In general compound nouns form their plural like ordinary nouns. However, in some cases the plural occurs at the end of the first part of the noun (*capistazione*) or at the end of both parts of the word (*casseforti*).

10. Irregular plurals of nouns

sing			pl	
	la mano	the hand		le mani
	l'uovo *m*	the egg		le uova *f*
	l'uomo	the man		gli uomini

→ You will find all irregular plural forms in the relevant entry of the dictionary.
Example: uomo <uomini>

Adjectives

Gender and declension of adjectives

sing		pl	
m	f	m	f
caldo	calda	caldi	calde
mite	miti		

- Adjectives vary in gender and number dependent on the noun which accompanies them.
- Adjectives ending in -**co**, -**go**, -**io** follow the same rules in the plural as nouns with the same endings.

Position of the Adjective

In Italian the adjective normally comes after the noun. The following adjectives may go before nouns:

bello, bravo, buono, caro, cattivo, giovane, grande, piccolo, santo, strano, vecchio.

- **Bello, buono, grande** and **santo** have special forms when they occur before a noun:
- **bello** before nouns follows the declension of the definite article: **bel, bell', bello, bella, bei, begli, belle**.
- **buono** in the singular before masculine nouns follows the declension of the indefinite article: **buon**. Before *s + consonant, gn, ps, x, z:* it becomes **buono**.
- **santo** shortens to **san** before masculine singular nouns beginning with a consonant
- before masculine and feminine singular nouns beginning with a vowel **santo** often becomes **sant'**.

Comparison of Adjectives

positive	una macchina veloce	a fast car
comparative	una macchina più veloce	a faster car
relative superlative	la macchina più veloce del mondo	the fastest car in the world
absolute superlative	una macchina velocissima	a very fast car

- The comparative is formed by adding **più** before the adjective: *più piccolo – smaller*
- The relative superlative is formed by adding the definite article to the comparative form: *il più piccolo – the smaller*
- The absolute superlative is formed by adding the ending **–issimo/a** etc. to the adjective: *una casa piccolissima: a very small house.*
- Some adjectives have special forms of the absolute superlative:

celebre	celeberrimo
integro	integerrimo
misero	miserrimo

Generally the absolute superlative of these adjectives is not used. Instead a combination with adverbs is favored:

celebre	molto celebre
integro	perfettamente integro

- **buono, cattivo, grande** and **piccolo** – in addition to their regular forms (*più buono – il più buono – buonissimo*) – irregular comparative forms also exist and are frequently used:

buono	migliore	il migliore	ottimo
cattivo	peggiore	il peggiore	pessimo
grande	maggiore	il maggiore	massimo
piccolo	minore	il minore	minimo

- Note that in Italian the relative superlative is often followed by the preposition **di**: *è più alta di me: she's taller than me.*

Demonstrative adjectives

questo this, this one	m	sing	pl
	before a *consonant*	questo treno	questi treni
	before a *vowel*	quest'anno	questi anni
	f		
	before a *consonant*	questa casa	queste case
	before a *vowel*	quest'ora	queste ore

- **questo** designates things, people or situations close to the speaker.

quello that, that one	m	sing	pl
	before a *consonant*	quel treno	quei treni
	before *s + consonant,* *gn, ps, x, z,* *i* or *y + vowel*	quello zio	quegli zii
	before a *vowel*	quell'anno	quegli anni
	F		
	before a *consonant*	quella casa	quelle case
	before a *vowel*	quell'ora	quelle ore

- **quello** designates things, people or situations distant from the speaker.

Possessive adjectives

These are formed by the relevant definite article (reflecting the gender and number of the thing owned) and the relevant possessive adjective:

Person/owner		Gender and number of the noun possessed			
		m		f	
		sing	pl	sing	pl
sing	1.pers	il mio my	i miei	la mia	le mie
	2.pers	il tuo your	i tuoi	la tua	le tue
	3.pers	il suo his, her, your (polite)	i suoi	la sua	le sue
pl	1.pers	il nostro our	i nostri	la nostra	le nostre
	2.pers	il vostro your (also polite)	i vostri	la vostra	le vostre
	3.pers	il loro their	i loro	la loro	le loro

Examples:
il mio libro: my book
la sua casa: his/her house
il nostro cane: our dog
i vostri gatti: your cats
i loro giornali: their newspapers

- In the singular polite form (lei) the third person singular possessive adjective is used (il suo, la sua, etc). *Questo è il suo libro? – Is this your book?*

In the plural the second person plural is most commonly used: *Dove sono i vostri ospiti? – Where are your guests?*

Before terms for relations such as

- *madre, padre, sorella, fratello, nonna, nonno, zia, zio, nipote, etc.* there is no definite article in the singular: *mia madre* **(not la mia madre), nostro zio (not il nostro zio)**. However the definite article is required for relations in the plural (*i suoi fratelli*), with a more precise description (*la tua nonna di Torino*) and with *loro* (*la loro sorella: their sister*).
- the possessive adjective normally comes before the noun, but in some fixed expressions it comes after the noun (and there is no article): *a casa mia (at, to my house), per colpa sua (because of him/her)*.
- the possessive adjective is left out
  - before terms for parts of the body and
  - in general before nouns if it is completely clear to whom they belong:

Alice ha perso il figlio in guerra.	Alice lost her son in the war.
Mi sono lavato il viso.	I washed my face.
Pietro si è spazzolato i cappelli.	Peter brushed his hair.

Pronouns

1. Personal pronouns

As in English, personal pronouns in Italian can be emphatic or nonemphatic:

<u>Gli</u> ho dato il libro.	*(nonemphatic)*	I gave him the book.
Ho dato il libro <u>a lui</u>.	*(emphatic)*	I gave the book to him.

Nonemphatic personal pronouns

	sing					Pl				
	1st pers	2nd pers	3rd pers			1st pers	2nd pers	3rd pers		
			m	f	rfl			m	f	rfl
Direct object (who?)	mi	ti	lo	la	si	ci	Vi	li	le	si
Indirect object (whom?)			gli	le				loro/gli		

Emphatic personal pronouns

	sing					pl				
	1st pers	2nd pers	3rd pers			1st pers	2nd pers	3rd pers		
			m	f	rfl			m	f	rfl
Subject (who?)	io	tu	lui esso	lei essa		noi	voi	loro essi	loro esse	
Direct object (who?)	me	te	lui	lei	sé	noi	voi	loro	loro	sé
Indirect object (whom?)	a me	a te	a lui a esso	a lei a essa	a sé	a noi	a voi	a loro a essi	a loro a esse	a sé

- the pronoun for the singular **polite** you form is the third person feminine: **la, le, lei, a lei**; in the plural **vi, voi, a voi** are used.

- Generally speaking **subject pronouns** are not obligatory in Italian. They are used when you wish to emphasize a point:

Amo la musica.	I love music.
Io amo la musica e lui il teatro.	I love music and he loves the theater.

- Object pronouns generally occur in the nonemphatic form. An emphatic personal pronoun is used to emphasize the person concerned:

– <u>Ti</u> è piaciuta la festa?	Did you like the party?
– <u>A me</u> no, e <u>a te</u>?	I didn't like it – did you?
– Neanche <u>a me</u>.	I didn't like it either.

- the nonemphatic personal pronoun comes before the verb:

Ti vedo	I see you.
Mi dai il libro?	Can you give me the book?

- but **follows** the – infinitive,
  gerund,
  participle
  and certain forms of the imperative.

Bisogna farlo.	One has to do it.
Fatemi un piacere!	Do me a favor!
Leggiamolo adesso!	Let's read it now!
Mangiandolo adesso …	By eating it now ….

Loro always comes **after** the verb: *Scrive loro tutti i giorni – He writes to them every day.*
- the emphatic object forms of personal pronouns come after the verb:

Amo solo te.	I love only you.

- the emphatic forms **lui, lei, loro** are used for persons and animals, **esso, essa, essi** for animals, things or situations.
- **lo** can be used both for persons and for animals, things and situations.

Lo so.	I know (that).

- **lo** and **la** before vowels can be substituted by **l'**:

L'avete visto?	Did you see him?
L'ho salutata.	I said hello to her.

The pronouns *ci* and *ne*

ci	Ci puoi contare. You can count on it. Ci andiamo ogni domenica. We go there every Sunday.
ne	Abbiamo visto i tuoi risultati e ne siamo fieri. We've seen your results and we're proud of them. Vuole delle patate? Sì, ne prendo un chilo. Would you like some potatoes? Yes, I'll take a kilo.
	La nave si allontana dalla costa. → La nave se ne allontana. The ship moves away from the coast. → The ship moves away from it.

- **ci** can have the function of an adverb of place (*ci vado domani = vado lì domani*) or of a demonstrative pronouns (*ci penserò domani = penserò a questo domani*)
- **ne** can have the function of an adverb of place (*me ne vado = vado via da lì*), of a demonstrative pronoun *(ne voglio un po' = voglio un po' di questo)* or of a personal pronoun (*Roberta? Ne ho sentito parlare = Ho sentito parlare di lei*).

Combined forms of the nonemphatic personal pronouns

	Lo	la	li	le	ne
mi	me lo	me la	me li	me le	me ne
ti	te lo	te la	te li	te le	te ne
gli le	Glielo	gliela	glieli	gliele	gliene
ci	ce lo	ce la	ce li	ce le	ce ne
vi	ve lo	ve la	ve li	ve le	ve ne
si	se lo	se la	se li	se le	se ne

- If there are two nonemphatic pronouns the indirect object pronoun goes before the direct.

Te lo presto volentieri.	I'll lend it (to) you willingly.

- **loro** comes after the verb and thus does not combine as above.

2. Indefinite pronouns

Indefinite pronouns can relate to persons or things:

	person		thing	
	m	f	m	f
one	uno	una	uno	una
somebody/someone	qualcuno	qualcuna		
something			qualche cosa/qualcosa	
no/nobody	nessuno	nessuna		
nothing			niente/nulla	

- *Examples:*

Qualcuno di voi parla inglese?	Do any of you speak English?
Nessuno è perfetto.	Nobody is perfect.
Non prendo niente, grazie.	Thank you, I don't want anything.

3. Demonstrative pronouns

	sing			pl	
	m	f	neutral	m	f
this (one)	questo	questa	questo/ciò	questi	queste
that (one)	quello	quella	quello/ciò	quelli	quelle

- In comparisons **questo** is used first, then **quello**:

Questa (camicia) è bella, ma quella è più elegante.	This (shirt) is nice, but that that (one) is more elegant.

- **Quello** can also be used as a substitute for a noun mentioned earlier:

I miei genitori e quelli del mio ragazzo non si conoscono ancora.	My parents and those of my boyfriend haven't met yet.

- **Questo** and **quello** are also used to describe situations or things in general:

Non volevo dire questo.	I did not mean that.
Pensi sempre e solo a quello.	You always think of one thing only.

4. Relative pronouns

	sing		pl	
	m	f	m	f
as a subject/direct object	che			
after prepositions	cui			
in every position	il quale	la quale	i quali	le quali

- *Examples*:

Le donne che vengono …	The women who come …
Le donne che vedo …	The women I see …
La donna di cui parliamo …	The woman we are talking about …
Le donne le quali si sono presentate …	The women who turned up …

- the relative pronoun **cui** may occur after the definite article **il/la cui, i/le cui.** *Pietro, il cui ristorante è qui vicino…: Peter, whose restaurant is nearby…*

5. Possessive pronouns

- the possessive pronoun **il mio, la mia,** etc. has the same form as the possessive adjective **il mio, la mia, etc.** throughout.

Adjective:	La tua casa è molto grande,	Your house is very big.
Pronoun:	La nostra è più piccola.	Ours is smaller.

- however, unlike the possessive adjectives, the article is always used with nouns denoting members of the family:

Adjective:	È quello tuo fratello?	Is that your brother?
Pronoun:	No, il mio è quel ragazzo lì in fondo.	No, my brother is that boy over there.

- When *essere* + possessive pronouns are used to denote possession, then the article can be deleted: **mio, tuo, suo,** etc.

Di chi sono questi libri? – Sono miei.	Who do these books belong to? They are mine.

6. Interrogative pronouns

The interrogative pronoun can refer to a person, a thing, a situation or a quantity.

Person	Thing/situation	Quantity			
		sing		pl	
		m	f	m	f
chi?	(che) cosa?	quanto?	quanta?	quanti?	quante?

Examples:

Chi è venuto?	Who has come?	A chi scrivi?	Who are you writing to?
(Che) cosa vuoi?	What do you want?	A (che) cosa pensi?	What are you thinking of?
Quante persone sono?	How many people are there?	Quanto costa?	How much does it cost?

	sing	pl
	mf	**mf**
which?	che	
	quale	quali

- the interrogative pronouns **quale** and **che** are used to ask about a specific person, thing or situation:

Che libri leggi?	Which books do you read?
Quali intenzioni hai?	What are your intentions?

Verbs

1. Regular verbs

- In Italian there are three types of regular verbs: verbs ending in -**are** (amare), in -**ere** (vendere) and in –**ire** (partire and capire).

Indicative

Present tense

Present tense		-are	-ere	-ire	
		amare	vendere	partire	capire
		to love	to sell	to leave	to understand
sing	1st pers	amo	vendo	parto	capisco
	2nd pers	ami	vendi	parti	capisci
	3rd pers	ama	vende	parte	capisce
pl	1st pers	amiamo	vendiamo	partiamo	capiamo
	2nd pers	amate	vendete	partite	capite
	3rd pers	amano	vendono	partono	capiscono

- the **polite** form is the third person singular (**ama, vende, parte, capisce**) if only one person is addressed and the second person plural if more than one person is addressed (**amate, vendete, partite, capite**).
- Some verbs ending in -**ire** in the present tense have special forms with –**isc** (see **capire** above). For example, *preferire* (to prefer) and *finire* (to finish) are conjugated like *capire*.

→ Verbs ending in -ire which take an –isc in the present tense are clearly marked in the dictionary where the first person present tense is always given: preferire <preferisco>.

- With verbs ending in -**care** and -**gare** an **h** is added before the letter -**i** (-**ch**- and -**gh**-)

  mancare   manco, manchi, manca, manchiamo …
  pagare   pago, paghi, paga, paghiamo …

This is to ensure that the pronunciation remains the same throughout the conjugation of the verb.

- With verbs ending in -**cere** and -**gere** the pronunciation of -**c**- and -**g** varies according to the final vowel of the ending.
  vincere [-tʃ-] vinco [-k-], vinci [-tʃ-], …
  conoscere [-ʃ-] conosco [-sk-], conosci [-ʃ-]
  leggere [-dʒ-] leggo [-g-], leggi [-dʒ-]
- Verbs ending in -**iare** with an accented **i** in the first person of the present (io inv<u>i</u>o) keep the **i** even if it is followed by another **i** for the second person singular (tu invii).

If the **i** of the first singular person of the present is not accented (st<u>u</u>dio) there is no second **i** for the second person singular (tu studi).

- Verbs ending in -**ciare** and -**giare** do **not** require the addition of a second **i** before the second person singular -**i** ending.
  cominciare   comincio, comin*ci*, comincia
  mangiare   mangio, man*gi*, mangia

Indicative

Other tenses

Imperfect				
sing	1st pers	amavo	vendevo	partivo
	2nd pers	amavi	vendevi	partivi
	3rd pers	amava	vendeva	partiva
pl	1st pers	amavamo	vendevamo	partivamo
	2nd pers	amavate	vendevate	partivate
	3rd pers	am<u>a</u>vano	vend<u>e</u>vano	part<u>i</u>vano

Past Historic				
sing	1st pers	am<u>ai</u>	vend<u>ei</u>/vend<u>etti</u>	part<u>ii</u>
	2nd pers	amasti	vendesti	partisti
	3rd pers	amò	vendé/vend<u>ette</u>	partì
pl	1st pers	amammo	vendemmo	partimmo
	2nd pers	amaste	vendeste	partiste
	3rd pers	am<u>a</u>rono	vend<u>e</u>rono	part<u>i</u>rono

Future				
sing	1st pers	amerò	venderò	partirò
	2nd pers	amer<u>ai</u>	vender<u>ai</u>	partir<u>ai</u>
	3rd pers	amerà	venderà	partirà
pl	1st pers	ameremo	venderemo	partiremo
	2nd pers	amerete	venderete	partirete
	3rd pers	ameranno	venderanno	partiranno

- Verbs such as cominciare and mangiare, whose infinitive ends in -**ciare** and -**giare**, form the future by deleting the -*i: comincerò, mangerò,* etc.
- Verbs such as mancare and pagare, whose infinitive ends in -**care** and -**gare** form the future by adding an -*h: pagherò, mancherai,* etc.

Present perfect tense

sing	1st pers	Ho		sono	
	2nd pers	Hai		sei	partito/partita
	3rd pers	Ha		è	
			amato/venduto/capito		
pl	1st pers	abbiamo		siamo	
	2nd pers	avete		siete	partiti/partite
	3rd pers	hanno		sono	

Past perfect

sing	1st pers	avevo amato/venduto/capito	ero partito/partita

Future perfect

sing	1st pers	avrò amato/venduto/capito	sarò partito/partita
	...	...	...

- The present perfect, the past perfect and the future perfect are formed:
  - for transitive verbs (those which take an object):
    by the auxiliary *avere* + *the past participle of the verb*
    (ho amato Giovanni, ha venduto la casa ...).
  - for intransitive verbs (those which don't take an object), verbs of motion or verbs which
    denote the change of a state/condition, reflexive verbs and the verb *essere* itself:
    by the auxiliary *essere* + *the past participle of the verb*
    (sono partita; la situazione è cambiata; si sono lavati; sono stata al cinema)

Subjunctive

Present tense

sing	1st pers	che io	ami	venda	parta	capisca
	2nd pers	che tu	ami	venda	parta	capisca
	3rd pers	che lui	ami	venda	parta	capisca
pl	1st pers	che noi	amiamo	vendiamo	partiamo	capiamo
	2nd pers	che voi	amiate	vendiate	partiate	capiate
	3rd pers	che loro	amino	vendano	partano	capiscano

Imperfect subjunctive

sing	1st pers	che io	amassi	vendessi	partissi
	2nd pers	che tu	amassi	vendessi	partissi
	3rd pers	che lui	amasse	vendesse	partisse
pl	1st pers	che noi	amassimo	vendessimo	partissimo
	2nd pers	che voi	amaste	vendeste	partiste
	3rd pers	che loro	amassero	vendessero	partissero

Present perfect subjunctive

sing	1st pers	abbia	sia	
	2nd pers	abbia	sia	partito/partita
	3rd pers	abbia	sia	
		amato/venduto/capito		
pl	1st pers	abbiamo	siamo	
	2nd pers	abbiate	siate	partiti/partite
	3rd pers	abbiano	siano	

Past perfect subjunctive

sing	1st pers	avessi amato/venduto/capito	fossi partito/partita
	…	…	…

Conditional

Present

sing	1st pers	amer**ei**	vender**ei**	part**irei**
	2nd pers	amer**esti**	vender**esti**	part**iresti**
	3rd pers	amer**ebbe**	vender**ebbe**	part**irebbe**
pl	1st pers	amer**emmo**	vender**emmo**	part**iremmo**
	2nd pers	amer**este**	vender**este**	part**ireste**
	3rd pers	amer**ebbero**	vender**ebbero**	part**irebbero**

Past Conditional

sing	1st pers	avrei	sarei	
	2nd pers	avresti	saresti	partito/partita
	3rd pers	avrebbe	sarebbe	
		amato/venduto/capito		
pl	1st pers	avremmo	saremmo	
	2nd pers	avreste	sareste	partiti/partite
	3rd pers	avrebbero	sarebbero	

Imperative of regular verbs

sing	2nd pers	ama!	vendi!	parti!	capisci!
	3rd pers	ami!	venda!	parta!	capisca!
pl	1st pers	amiamo!	vendiamo!	partiamo!	capiamo!
	2nd pers	amate!	vendete!	partite!	capite!
	3rd pers	amino!	vendano!	partano!	capiscano!

- The **negative** of the imperative is formed by adding **non** in front of the imperative form, **except** for the second person singular, when **non** is added to the infinitive form: *non vendere! non venda! non vendiamo! non vendete! non vendano!*
- Pronouns follow the affirmative imperative except for the third persons singular and plural: *vendila! la venda! vendiamola! vendetela! la vendano!*

- In the negative imperative the pronoun can go before or after the verb: *non venderla!* or *non la vendere!*

But in the third persons singular and plural the pronoun always comes before the verb: *non la venda! non la vendano!*

Passive

The passive voice is formed with the required tense of *essere* and the past participle of the main verb:

È venduto/venduto	it is sold
era venduto/venduta	it was sold
...	

Sometimes v*enire* can be used instead of *essere*:

sono/vengo informato	I am informed
sono/vengo aiutato	I am helped

but only the forms *sono stato aiutato, sono stato informato* are possible.

Infinitive, participle and gerund

Infinitive		amare	vendere	partire
Participle	Present	amante	vendente	partente
	Past	amato	venduto	partito
Gerund		amando	vendendo	partendo

2. Irregular verbs

→ In the dictionary irregular verbs are clearly marked. The *first person singular* of the *present tense* and the *past historic* are given, and these are followed by the past participle.

Example: **fare** <faccio, feci, fatto>.

Note that in the *past historic* irregular verbs are often only irregular in the **first and third person singular** and the **third person plural**:

vedere   **vidi**, vedesti, **vide**, vedemmo, vedeste, **videro**.

There is an appendix of irregular Italian verbs in the dictionary which should be consulted in all cases.

3. Auxiliaries

avere

Indicative					
		Present	Imperfect	Past Historic	Future
sing	1st pers	ho	avevo	ebbi	avrò
	2nd pers	hai	avevi	avesti	avrai
	3rd pers	ha	aveva	ebbe	avrà
pl	1st pers	abbiamo	avevamo	avemmo	avremo
	2nd pers	avete	avevate	aveste	avrete
	3rd pers	hanno	avevano	ebbero	avranno
		Present Perfect	Past Perfect		Future Perfect
sing	1st pers	ho avuto	avevo avuto		avrò avuto
	...	...	...		...

		Subjunctive		Conditional	Imperative
		Present	Imperfect		
sing	1st pers	abbia	avessi	avrei	
	2nd pers	abbia	avessi	avresti	abbi!
	3rd pers	abbia	avesse	avrebbe	abbia!
pl	1st pers	abbiamo	avessimo	avremmo	abbiamo!
	2nd pers	abbiate	aveste	avreste	abbiate!
	3rd pers	abbiano	avessero	avrebbero	abbiano!

Infinitive	Participle		Gerund
	Present	Past	
avere	avente	avuto	avendo

essere

Indicative					
		Present	Imperfect	Past Historic	Future
sing	1st pers	sono	ero	fui	sarò
	2nd pers	sei	eri	fosti	sarai
	3rd pers	è	era	fu	sarà
pl	1st pers	siamo	eravamo	fummo	saremo
	2nd pers	siete	eravate	foste	sarete
	3rd pers	sono	erano	furono	saranno
		Present Perfect	Past Perfect		Future Perfect
sing	1st pers	sono stato/stata	ero stato/stata		sarò stato/stata
	...	....	...		...

		Subjunctive		Conditional	Imperative
		Present	Imperfect		
sing	1st pers	sia	fossi	sarei	
	2nd pers	sia	fossi	saresti	sii!
	3rd pers	sia	fosse	sarebbe	sia!
pl	1st pers	siamo	fossimo	saremmo	siamo!
	2nd pers	siate	foste	sareste	siate!
	3rd pers	siano	fossero	sarebbero	siano!

Infinitive	Past Participle	Gerund
essere	stato	essendo

Adverbs

Adverbs do not change according to gender or number. They can refer to a verb, another adverb or an adjective.

Examples:

Verb:	Va' <u>piano</u>. Arrivo <u>subito</u>.	Drive slowly. I'll be with you in a second.
Adverb:	Ci vediamo molto <u>spesso</u>.	We see each other very often.
Adjective:	Il libro è <u>abbastanza</u> interessante.	The book is quite interesting.

- In Italian there are adverbs of time, adverbs of place, adverbs of manner and adverbs of quantity.

Adverbs of time:	Vengo <u>domani</u>. <u>Ieri</u> ho visto la partita.	I'll come tomorrow. I watched the football game yesterday.
Adverbs of place:	L'ufficio postale è lì <u>in fondo</u> a destra.	The post office is over there on the right.
Adverbs of manner:	Sto <u>male</u>. Aggiungere <u>lentamente</u> il latte caldo.	I don't feel well. Add the hot milk slowly.
Adverbs of quantity:	Non bere <u>molto</u>, devi guidare!	Don't drink much, you have to drive!

- In Italian some adverbs have their own unique form (*oggi* today, *qui* here, *forse* perhaps) but most can be derived from an adjective by adding the ending **-mente**:

Adjective	ending in **-o/-a**	ending in **-e**	ending in **-le, -re**
	perfetto/-a	Veloce	facile
Adverb	perfettamente	velocemente	facilmente

- Exceptions: **leggermente, violentemente** (from *leggero/-a, violento/-a*)
  bene (from *buono/-a*).
- Like adjectives, many adverbs have a comparative and superlative form:

Positive	facilmente	Tardi
Comparative	più facilmente	più tardi
Superlative	facilissimamente	tardissimo

- The comparative is formed by placing **più** in front of the adverb.
- The superlative is formed by adding **-issimamente** to the end of the original adjective.

  Exceptions: **bene   meglio   benissimo   ottimamente**
  male   peggio   malissimo   pessimamente
  molto   più   moltissimo
  poco   meno   pochissimo

Verbi italiani

Italian verbs

Qui sotto sono riportate le coniugazioni dei principali tempi di alcuni verbi, che servono come modello nella coniugazione degli altri verbi regolari.

Listed below are the conjugations of the main tenses of selected verbs which illustrate how other regular verbs are conjugated.

cantare

1ª coniugazione (verbi in -are)

presente	imperfetto	futuro semplice	passato remoto
(io) canto	(io) cantavo	(io) canterò	(io) cantai
(tu) canti	(tu) cantavi	(tu) canterai	(tu) cantasti
(lui/lei) canta	(lui/lei) cantava	(lui/lei) canterà	(lui/lei) cantò
(noi) cantiamo	(noi) cantavamo	(noi) canteremo	(noi) cantammo
(voi) cantate	(voi) cantavate	(voi) canterete	(voi) cantaste
(loro) cantano	(loro) cantavano	(loro) canteranno	(loro) cantarono

condizionale presente	congiuntivo presente	congiuntivo imperfetto
(io) canterei	che (io) canti	che (io) cantassi
(tu) canteresti	che (tu) canti	che (tu) cantassi
(lui/lei) canterebbe	che (lui/lei) canti	che (lui/lei) cantasse
(noi) canteremmo	che (noi) cantiamo	che (noi) cantassimo
(voi) cantereste	che (voi) cantiate	che (voi) cantaste
(loro) canterebbero	che (loro) cantino	che (loro) cantassero

participio passato	imperativo	gerundio
cantato(a/i/e)	canta (tu)	cantando
	canti (lei)	
	cantiamo (noi)	
	cantate (voi)	
	cantino (loro)	

mancare

1ª coniugazione (verbi in -care e -gare)

presente	imperfetto	futuro semplice	passato remoto
(io) manco	(io) mancavo	(io) mancherò	(io) mancai
(tu) manchi	(tu) mancavi	(tu) mancherai	(tu) mancasti
(lui/lei) manca	(lui/lei) mancava	(lui/lei) mancherà	(lui/lei) mancò
(noi) manchiamo	(noi) mancavamo	(noi) mancheremo	(noi) mancammo
(voi) mancate	(voi) mancavate	(voi) mancherete	(voi) mancaste
(loro) mancano	(loro) mancavano	(loro) mancheranno	(loro) mancarono

condizionale presente	congiuntivo presente	congiuntivo imperfetto
(io) mancherei	che (io) manchi	che (io) mancassi
(tu) mancheresti	che (tu) manchi	che (tu) mancassi
(lui/lei) mancherebbe	che (lui/lei) manchi	che (lui/lei) mancasse
(noi) mancheremmo	che (noi) manchiamo	che (noi) mancassimo
(voi) manchereste	che (voi) manchiate	che (voi) mancaste
(loro) mancherebbero	che (loro) manchino	che (loro) mancassero

participio passato	imperativo	gerundio
mancato(a/i/e)	manca (tu) manchi (lei) manchiamo (noi) mancate (voi) manchino (loro)	mancando

bagnare

1ª coniugazione (verbi in -gnare)

presente	imperfetto	futuro semplice	passato remoto
(io) bagno	(io) bagnavo	(io) bagnerò	(io) bagnai
(tu) bagni	(tu) bagnavi	(tu) bagnerai	(tu) bagnasti
(lui/lei) bagna	(lui/lei) bagnava	(lui/lei) bagnerà	(lui/lei) bagnò
(noi) bagniamo	(noi) bagnavamo	(noi) bagneremo	(noi) bagnammo
(voi) bagnate	(voi) bagnavate	(voi) bagnerete	(voi) bagnaste
(loro) bagnano	(loro) bagnavano	(loro) bagneranno	(loro) bagnarono

condizionale presente	congiuntivo presente	congiuntivo imperfetto
(io) bagnerei	che (io) bagni	che (io) bagnassi
(tu) bagneresti	che (tu) bagni	che (tu) bagnassi
(lui/lei) bagnerebbe	che (lui/lei) bagni	che (lui/lei) bagnasse
(noi) bagneremmo	che (noi) bagniamo	che (noi) bagnassimo
(voi) bagnereste	che (voi) bagniate	che (voi) bagnaste
(loro) bagnerebbero	che (loro) bagnino	che (loro) bagnassero

participio passato	imperativo	gerundio
bagnato(a/i/e)	bagna (tu) bagni (lei) bagniamo (noi) bagnate (voi) bagnino (loro)	bagnando

mangiare

1ª coniugazione (verbi in -ciare e -giare)

presente	imperfetto	futuro semplice	passato remoto
(io) mangio	(io) mangiavo	(io) mangerò	(io) mangiai
(tu) mangi	(tu) mangiavi	(tu) mangerai	(tu) mangiasti
(lui/lei) mangia	(lui/lei) mangiava	(lui/lei) mangerà	(lui/lei) mangiò
(noi) mangiamo	(noi) mangiavamo	(noi) mangeremo	(noi) mangiammo
(voi) mangiate	(voi) mangiavate	(voi) mangerete	(voi) mangiaste
(loro) mangiano	(loro) mangiavano	(loro) mangeranno	(loro) mangiarono

condizionale presente	congiuntivo presente	congiuntivo imperfetto
(io) mangerei	che (io) mangi	che (io) mangiassi
(tu) mangeresti	che (tu) mangi	che (tu) mangiassi
(lui/lei) mangerebbe	che (lui/lei) mangi	che (lui/lei) mangiasse
(noi) mangeremmo	che (noi) mangiamo	che (noi) mangiassimo
(voi) mangereste	che (voi) mangiate	che (voi) mangiaste
(loro) mangerebbero	che (loro) mangino	che (loro) mangiassero

participio passato	imperativo	gerundio
mangiato(a/i/e)	mangia (tu) mangi (lei) mangiamo (noi) mangiate (voi) mangino (loro)	mangiando

inviare

1ª coniugazione (verbi in -iare con -i- tonica al presente indicativo)

presente	imperfetto	futuro semplice	passato remoto
(io) invio (tu) invii (lui/lei) invia (noi) inviamo (voi) inviate (loro) inviano	(io) inviavo (tu) inviavi (lui/lei) inviava (noi) inviavamo (voi) inviavate (loro) inviavano	(io) invierò (tu) invierai (lui/lei) invierà (noi) invieremo (voi) invierete (loro) invieranno	(io) inviai (tu) inviasti (lui/lei) inviò (noi) inviammo (voi) inviaste (loro) inviarono

condizionale presente	congiuntivo presente	congiuntivo imperfetto
(io) invierei (tu) invieresti (lui/lei) invierebbe (noi) invieremmo (voi) inviereste (loro) invierebbero	che (io) invii che (tu) invii che (lui/lei) invii che (noi) inviamo che (voi) inviate che (loro) inviino	che (io) inviassi che (tu) inviassi che (lui/lei) inviasse che (noi) inviassimo che (voi) inviaste che (loro) inviassero

participio passato	imperativo presente	gerundio
inviato(a/i/e)	invia (tu) invii (lei) inviamo (noi) inviate (voi) iniino (loro)	inviando

studiare

1ª coniugazione (altri verbi in -iare)

presente	imperfetto	futuro semplice	passato remoto
(io) studio (tu) studi (lui/lei) studia (noi) studiamo (voi) studiate (loro) studiano	(io) studiavo (tu) studiavi (lui/lei) studiava (noi) studiavamo (voi) studiavate (loro) studiavano	(io) studierò (tu) studierai (lui/lei) studierà (noi) studieremo (voi) studierete (loro) studieranno	(io) studiai (tu) studiasti (lui/lei) studiò (noi) studiammo (voi) studiaste (loro) studiarono

condizionale presente	congiuntivo presente	congiuntivo imperfetto
(io) studierei (tu) studieresti (lui/lei) studierebbe (noi) studieremmo (voi) studiereste (loro) studierebbero	che (io) studi che (tu) studi che (lui/lei) studi che (noi) studiamo che (voi) studiate che (loro) studino	che (io) studiassi che (tu) studiassi che (lui/lei) studiasse che (noi) studiassimo che (voi) studiaste che (loro) studiassero

participio passato	imperativo presente	gerundio
studiato(a/i/e)	studia (tu) studi (lei) studiamo (noi) studiate (voi) studino (loro)	studiando

temere

2ª coniugazione (verbi in -ere)

presente	imperfetto	futuro semplice	passato remoto
(io) temo (tu) temi (lui/lei) teme (noi) temiamo (voi) temete (loro) temono	(io) temevo (tu) temevi (lui/lei) temeva (noi) temevamo (voi) temevate (loro) temevano	(io) temerò (tu) temerai (lui/lei) temerà (noi) temeremo (voi) temerete (loro) temeranno	(io) temei o temetti (tu) temesti (lui/lei) temé o temette (noi) tememmo (voi) temeste (loro) temerono o temettero

condizionale presente	congiuntivo presente	congiuntivo imperfetto
(io) temerei (tu) temeresti (lui/lei) temerebbe (noi) temeremmo (voi) temereste (loro) temerebbero	che (io) tema che (tu) tema che (lui/lei) tema che (noi) temiamo che (voi) temiate che (loro) temano	che (io) temessi che (tu) temessi che (lui/lei) temesse che (noi) temessimo che (voi) temeste che (loro) temessero

participio passato	imperativo	gerundio
temuto(a/i/e)	temi (tu) tema (lei) temiamo (noi) temete (voi) temano (loro)	temendo

vincere

2ª coniugazione (verbi in -cere e -gere)

presente	imperfetto	futuro semplice	passato remoto
(io) vinco (tu) vinci (lui/lei) vince (noi) vinciamo (voi) vincete (loro) vincono	(io) vincevo (tu) vincevi (lui/lei) vinceva (noi) vincevamo (voi) vincevate (loro) vincevano	(io) vincerò (tu) vincerai (lui/lei) vincerà (noi) vinceremo (voi) vincerete (loro) vinceranno	(io) vinsi (tu) vincesti (lui/lei) vinse (noi) vincemmo (voi) vinceste (loro) vinsero

condizionale presente	congiuntivo presente	congiuntivo imperfetto
(io) vincerei (tu) vinceresti (lui/lei) vincerebbe (noi) vinceremmo (voi) vincereste (loro) vincerebbero	che (io) vinca che (tu) vinca che (lui/lei) vinca che (noi) vinciamo che (voi) vinciate che (loro) vincano	che (io) vincessi che (tu) vincessi che (lui/lei) vincesse che (noi) vincessimo che (voi) vinceste che (loro) vincessero

participio passato	imperativo	gerundio
vinto(a/i/e)	vinci (tu) vinca (lei) vinciamo (noi) vincete (voi) vincano (loro)	vincendo

muovere

2ª coniugazione (verbi in -ere con dittongo mobile)

presente	imperfetto	futuro semplice	passato remoto
(io) muovo	(io) muovevo	(io) muoverò	(io) mossi
(tu) muovi	(tu) muovevi	(tu) muoverai	(tu) muovesti
(lui/lei) muove	(lui/lei) muoveva	(lui/lei) muoverà	(lui/lei) mosse
(noi) muoviamo	(noi) muovevamo	(noi) muoveremo	(noi) muovemmo
(voi) muovete	(voi) muovevate	(voi) muoverete	(voi) muoveste
(loro) muovono	(loro) muovevano	(loro) muoveranno	(loro) mossero

condizionale presente	congiuntivo presente	congiuntivo imperfetto
(io) muoverei	che (io) muova	che (io) muovessi
(tu) muoveresti	che (tu) muova	che (tu) muovessi
(lui/lei) muoverebbe	che (lui/lei) muova	che (lui/lei) muovesse
(noi) muoveremmo	che (noi) muoviamo	che (noi) muovessimo
(voi) muovereste	che (voi) muoviate	che (voi) muoveste
(loro) muoverebbero	che (loro) muovano	che (loro) muovessero

participio passato	imperativo	gerundio
mosso(a/i/e)	muovi (tu) muova (lei) muoviamo (noi) muovete (voi) muovano (loro)	muovendo

spegnere

2ª coniugazione (verbi in -gnere)

presente	imperfetto	futuro semplice	passato remoto
(io) spengo	(io) spegnevo	(io) spegnerò	(io) spensi
(tu) spegni	(tu) spegnevi	(tu) spegnerai	(tu) spegnesti
(lui/lei) spegne	(lui/lei) spegneva	(lui/lei) spegnerà	(lui/lei) spense
(noi) spegniamo	(noi) spegnevamo	(noi) spegneremo	(noi) spegnemmo
(voi) spegnete	(voi) spegnevate	(voi) spegnerete	(voi) spegneste
(loro) spengono	(loro) spegnevano	(loro) spegneranno	(loro) spensero

condizionale presente	congiuntivo presente	congiuntivo imperfetto
(io) spegnerei	che (io) spenga	che (io) spegnessi
(tu) spegneresti	che (tu) spenga	che (tu) spegnessi
(lui/lei) spegnerebbe	che (lui/lei) spenga	che (lui/lei) spegnesse
(noi) spegneremmo	che (noi) spegniamo	che (noi) spegnessimo
(voi) spegnereste	che (voi) spegniate	che (voi) spegneste
(loro) spegnerebbero	che (loro) spengano	che (loro) spegnessero

participio passato	imperativo	gerundio
spento(a/i/e)	spegni (tu) spenga (lei) spegniamo (noi) spegnete (voi) spengano (loro)	spegnendo

sedere

2ª coniugazione (verbi in -ere con alternanza di -ie- ed -e- nella radice)

presente	imperfetto	futuro semplice	passato remoto
(io) siedo	(io) sedevo	(io) sederò *o* siederò	(io) sedei o sedetti
(tu) siedi	(tu) sedevi	(tu) sederai *o* siederai	(tu) sedesti
(lui/lei) siede	(lui/lei) sedeva	(lui/lei) sederà *o* siederà	(lui/lei) sedé *o* sedette
(noi) sediamo	(noi) sedevamo	(noi) sederemo *o* siederemo	(noi) sedemmo
(voi) sedete	(voi) sedevate	(voi) sederete *o* siederete	(voi) sedeste
(loro) siedono	(loro) sedevano	(loro) sederanno *o* siederanno	(loro) sederono *o* sedettero

condizionale presente	congiuntivo presente	congiuntivo imperfetto
(io) sederei *o* siederei	che (io) sieda	che (io) sedessi
(tu) sederesti *o* siederesti	che (tu) sieda	che (tu) sedessi
(lui/lei) sederebbe *o* siederebbe	che (lui/lei) sieda	che (lui/lei) sedesse
(noi) sederemmo *o* siederemmo	che (noi) sediamo	che (noi) sedessimo
(voi) sedereste *o* siedereste	che (voi) sediate	che (voi) sedeste
(loro) sederebbero *o* siederebbero	che (loro) siedano	che (loro) sedessero

participio passato	imperativo	gerundio
seduto(a/i/e)	siedi (tu) sieda (lei) sediamo (noi) sedete (voi) siedano (loro)	sedendo

partire

3ª coniugazione (verbi in -ire)

presente	imperfetto	futuro semplice	passato remoto
(io) parto	(io) partivo	(io) partirò	(io) partii
(tu) parti	(tu) partivi	(tu) partirai	(tu) partisti
(lui/lei) parte	(lui/lei) partiva	(lui/lei) partirà	(lui/lei) partì
(noi) partiamo	(noi) partivamo	(noi) partiremo	(noi) partimmo
(voi) partite	(voi) partivate	(voi) partirete	(voi) partiste
(loro) partono	(loro) partivano	(loro) partiranno	(loro) partirono

condizionale presente	congiuntivo presente	congiuntivo imperfetto
(io) partirei	che (io) parta	che (io) partissi
(tu) partiresti	che (tu) parta	che (tu) partissi
(lui/lei) partirebbe	che (lui/lei) parta	che (lui/lei) partisse
(noi) partiremmo	che (noi) partiamo	che (noi) partissimo
(voi) partireste	che (voi) partiate	che (voi) partiste
(loro) partirebbero	che (loro) partano	che (loro) partissero

participio passato	imperativo	gerundio
partito(a/i/e)	parti (tu) parta (lei) partiamo (noi) partite (voi) partano (loro)	partendo

finire

3ª coniugazione (verbi in -ire con l'aggiunta del suffisso -isc- per alcuni tempi)

presente	imperfetto	futuro semplice	passato remoto
(io) finisco	(io) finivo	(io) finirò	(io) finii
(tu) finisci	(tu) finivi	(tu) finirai	(tu) finisti
(lui/lei) finisce	(lui/lei) finiva	(lui/lei) finirà	(lui/lei) finì
(noi) finiamo	(noi) finivamo	(noi) finiremo	(noi) finimmo
(voi) finite	(voi) finivate	(voi) finirete	(voi) finiste
(loro) finiscono	(loro) finivano	(loro) finiranno	(loro) finirono

condizionale presente	congiuntivo presente	congiuntivo imperfetto
(io) finirei	che (io) finisca	che (io) finissi
(tu) finiresti	che (tu) finisca	che (tu) finissi
(lui/lei) finirebbe	che (lui/lei) finisca	che (lui/lei) finisse
(noi) finiremmo	che (noi) finiamo	che (noi) finissimo
(voi) finireste	che (voi) finiate	che (voi) finiste
(loro) finirebbero	che (loro) finiscano	che (loro) finissero

participio passato	imperativo	gerundio
finito(a/i/e)	finisci (tu) finisca (lei) finiamo (noi) finite (voi) finiscano (loro)	finendo

Verbi irregolari italiani
Italian Irregular Verbs

Infinito	Presente	Imperfetto	Futuro	Passato remoto	Cong. presente	Cong. imperfetto	Gerundio	Part. passato	Imperativo
accendere	(io) accendo ...	(io) accendevo ...	(io) accenderò ...	(io) accesi (tu) accendesti (lui/lei) accese (noi) accendemmo (voi) accendeste (loro) accesero	che (io) accenda ...	che (io) accendessi ...	accendendo	acceso(a/i/e)	accendi ...
accludere	(io) accludo ...	(io) accludevo ...	(io) accluderò ...	(io) acclusi (tu) accludesti (lui/lei) accluse (noi) accludemmo (voi) accludeste (loro) acclusero	che (io) accluda ...	che (io) accludessi ...	accludendo	accluso(a/i/e)	accludi ...
accorgersi	(io) mi accorgo ...	(io) mi accorgevo ...	(io) mi accorgerò ...	(io) mi accorsi (tu) ti accorgesti (lui/lei) si accorse (noi) ci accorgemmo (voi) vi accorgeste (loro) si accorsero	che (io) mi accorga	che (io) mi accorgessi ...	accorgendosi accortosi(a/i/e)		accorgiti ...
addurre – *vedi* **condurre**									
affliggere	(io) affliggo ...	(io) affliggevo ...	(io) affliggerò ...	(io) afflissi (tu) affliggesti (lui/lei) afflisse (noi) affliggemmo (voi) affliggeste (loro) afflissero	che (io) affligga ...	che (io) affliggessi ...	affliggendo	afflitto(a/i/e)	affliggi ...

Infinito	Presente	Imperfetto	Futuro	Passato remoto	Cong. presente	Cong. imperfetto	Gerundio	Part. passato	Imperativo
alludere	(io) alludo, ...	(io) alludevo, ...	(io) alluderò, ...	(io) allusi, (tu) alludesti, (lui/lei) alluse, (noi) alludemmo, (voi) alludeste, (loro) allusero	che (io) alluda, ...	che (io) alludessi, ...	alludendo	alluso(a/i/e)	alludi, ...
andare	(io) vado, (tu) vai, (lui/lei) va, (noi) andiamo, (voi) andate, (loro) vanno	(io) andavo, (tu) andavi, (lui/lei) andava, (noi) andavamo, (voi) andavate, (loro) andavano	(io) andrò, (tu) andrai, (lui/lei) andrà, (noi) andremo, (voi) andrete, (loro) andranno	(io) andai, (tu) andasti, (lui/lei) andò, (noi) andammo, (voi) andaste, (loro) andarono	che (io) vada, che (tu) vada, che (lui/lei) vada, che (noi) andiamo, che (voi) andiate, che (loro) vadano	che (io) andassi, che (tu) andassi, che (lui/lei) andasse, che (noi) andassimo, che (voi) andaste, che (loro) andassero	andando	andato(a/i/e)	vai, vada, andiamo, andate, vadano
annettere	(io) annetto, ...	(io) annettevo, ...	(io) annetterò, ...	(io) annettei o annessi, (tu) annettesti, (lui/lei) annetté o annesse, (noi) annettemmo, (voi) annetteste, (loro) annetterono o annessero	che (io) annetta, ...	che (io) annettessi, ...	annettendo	annesso(a/i/e)	annetti, ...
apparire	(io) appaio, (tu) appari, (lui/lei) appare, (noi) appariamo, (voi) apparite, (loro) appaiono	(io) apparivo, ...	(io) apparirò, ...	(io) apparvi, (tu) apparisti, (lui/lei) apparve, (noi) apparimmo, (voi) appariste, (loro) apparvero	che (io) appaia, che (tu) appaia, che (lui/lei) appaia, che (noi) appaiamo, che (voi) appaiate, che (loro) appaiano	che (io) apparissi, ...	apparendo	apparso(a/i/e)	appari, appaia, appaiamo, apparite, appaiano

Infinito	Presente	Imperfetto	Futuro	Passato remoto	Cong. presente	Cong. imperfetto	Gerundio	Part. passato	Imperativo
appendere	(io) appendo ...	(io) appendevo ...	(io) appenderò ...	(io) appesi (tu) appendesti (lui/lei) appese (noi) appendemmo (voi) appendeste (loro) appesero	che (io) appenda ...	che (io) appendessi ...	appendendo	appeso(a/i/e)	appendi ...
aprire	(io) apro ...	(io) aprivo ...	(io) aprirò ...	(io) aprii (tu) apristi (lui/lei) aprì (noi) aprimmo (voi) apriste (loro) aprirono	che (io) apra ...	che (io) aprissi ...	aprendo	aperto(a/i/e)	apri ...
ardere	(io) ardo ...	(io) ardevo ...	(io) arderò ...	(io) arsi (tu) ardesti (lui/lei) arse (noi) ardemmo (voi) ardeste (loro) arsero	che (io) arda ...	che (io) ardessi ...	ardendo	arso(a/i/e)	ardi ...
assistere – *participio passato* assistito(a/i/e)									
assolvere	(io) assolvo ...	(io) assolvevo ...	(io) assolverò ...	(io) assolsi (tu) assolvesti (lui/lei) assolse (noi) assolvemmo (voi) assolveste (loro) assolsero	che (io) assolva ...	che (io) assolvessi ...	assolvendo	assolto(a/i/e)	assolvi ...
assumere	(io) assumo ...	(io) assumevo ...	(io) assumerò ...	(io) assunsi (tu) assumesti (lui/lei) assunse (noi) assumemmo (voi) assumeste (loro) assunsero	che (io) assuma ...	che (io) assumessi ...	assumendo	assunto(a/i/e)	assumi ...

Infinito	Presente	Imperfetto	Futuro	Passato remoto	Cong. presente	Cong. imperfetto	Gerundio	Part. passato	Imperativo
avere	(io) ho	(io) avevo	(io) avrò	(io) ebbi	che (io) abbia	che (io) avessi	avendo	avuto/a/i/e	—
	(tu) hai	(tu) avevi	(tu) avrai	(tu) avesti	che (tu) abbia	che (tu) avessi			abbi
	(lui/lei) ha	(lui/lei) aveva	(lui/lei) avrà	(lui/lei) ebbe	che (lui/lei) abbia	che (lui/lei) avesse			abbia
	(noi) abbiamo	(noi) avevamo	(noi) avremo	(noi) avemmo	che (noi) abbiamo	che (noi) avessimo			abbiamo
	(voi) avete	(voi) avevate	(voi) avrete	(voi) aveste	che (voi) abbiate	che (voi) aveste			abbiate
	(loro) hanno	(loro) avevano	(loro) avranno	(loro) ebbero	che (loro) abbiano	che (loro) avessero			abbiano
bere	(io) bevo	(io) bevevo	(io) berrò	(io) bevvi o bevetti	che (io) beva	che (io) bevessi	bevendo	bevuto(a/i/e)	—
	(tu) bevi	(tu) bevevi	(tu) berrai	(tu) bevesti	che (tu) beva	che (tu) bevessi			bevi
	(lui/lei) beve	(lui/lei) beveva	(lui/lei) berrà	(lui/lei) bevve o bevette	che (lui/lei) beva	che (lui/lei) bevesse			beva
	(noi) beviamo	(noi) bevevamo	(noi) berremo	(noi) bevemmo	che (noi) beviamo	che (noi) bevessimo			beviamo
	(voi) bevete	(voi) bevevate	(voi) berrete	(voi) beveste	che (voi) beviate	che (voi) beveste			bevete
	(loro) bevono	(loro) bevevano	(loro) berranno	(loro) bevvero o bevettero	che (loro) bevano	che (loro) bevessero			bevano
cadere	(io) cado	(io) cadevo	(io) cadrò	(io) caddi	che (io) cada	che (io) cadessi	cadendo	caduto(a/i/e)	—
	...	...	...	(tu) cadesti	...	...			cadi
				(lui/lei) cadde					...
				(noi) cademmo					
				(voi) cadeste					
				(loro) caddero					
chiedere	(io) chiedo	(io) chiedevo	(io) chiederò	(io) chiesi	che (io) chieda	che (io) chiedessi	chiedendo	chiesto(a/i/e)	—
	...	...	...	(tu) chiedesti	...	...			chiedi
				(lui/lei) chiese					...
				(noi) chiedemmo					
				(voi) chiedeste					
				(loro) chiesero					

Infinito	Presente	Imperfetto	Futuro	Passato remoto	Cong. presente	Cong. imperfetto	Gerundio	Part. passato	Imperativo
chiudere	(io) chiudo ...	(io) chiudevo ...	(io) chiuderò ...	(io) chiusi (tu) chiudesti (lui/lei) chiuse (noi) chiudemmo (voi) chiudeste (loro) chiusero	che (io) chiuda ...	che (io) chiudessi ...	chiudendo	chiuso(a/i/e)	chiudi ...
cingere	(io) cingo ...	(io) cingevo ...	(io) cingerò ...	(io) cinsi (tu) cingesti (lui/lei) cinse (noi) cingemmo (voi) cingeste (loro) cinsero	che (io) cinga ...	che (io) cingessi ...	cingendo	cinto(a/i/e)	cingi ...
cogliere	(io) colgo (tu) cogli (lui/lei) coglie (noi) cogliamo (voi) cogliete (loro) colgono	(io) coglievo ...	(io) coglierò ...	(io) colsi (tu) cogliesti (lui/lei) colse (noi) cogliemmo (voi) coglieste (loro) colsero	che (io) colga che (tu) colga che (lui/lei) colga che (noi) cogliamo che (voi) cogliate che (loro) colgano	che (io) cogliessi ...	cogliendo	colto(a/i/e)	cogli colga cogliamo cogliete colgano

comparire – *vedi* **apparire**

Infinito	Presente	Imperfetto	Futuro	Passato remoto	Cong. presente	Cong. imperfetto	Gerundio	Part. passato	Imperativo
comprimere	(io) comprimo ...	(io) comprimevo ...	(io) comprimerò ...	(io) compressi (tu) comprimesti (lui/lei) compresse (noi) comprimemmo (voi) comprimeste (loro) compressero	che (io) comprima ...	che (io) comprimessi ...	comprimendo	compresso(a/i/e)	comprimi ...

Infinito	Presente	Imperfetto	Futuro	Passato remoto	Cong. presente	Cong. imperfetto	Gerundio	Part. passato	Imperativo
concedere	(io) concedo	(io) concedevo	(io) concederò	(io) concessi	che (io) conceda	che (io) concedessi	concedendo	concesso(a/i/e)	
	...	...	...	(tu) concedesti	...	...			concedi
				(lui/lei) concesse					...
				(noi) concedemmo					
				(voi) concedeste					
				(loro) concessero					

concludere – *vedi* **accludere**

Infinito	Presente	Imperfetto	Futuro	Passato remoto	Cong. presente	Cong. imperfetto	Gerundio	Part. passato	Imperativo
condurre	(io) conduco	(io) conducevo	(io) condurrò	(io) condussi	che (io) conduca	che (io) conducessi	conducendo	condotto(a/i/e)	
	(tu) conduci	...	...	(tu) conducesti	che (tu) conduca	...			conduci
	(lui/lei) conduce			(lui/lei) condusse	che (lui/lei) conduca				conduca
	(noi) conduciamo			(noi) conducemmo	che (noi) conduciamo				conduciamo
	(voi) conducete			(voi) conduceste	che (voi) conduciate				conducete
	(loro) conducono			(loro) condussero	che (loro) conducano				conducano

connettere – *participio passato* connesso(a/i/e)

Infinito	Presente	Imperfetto	Futuro	Passato remoto	Cong. presente	Cong. imperfetto	Gerundio	Part. passato	Imperativo
conoscere	(io) conosco	(io) conoscevo	(io) conoscerò	(io) conobbi	che (io) conosca	che (io) conoscessi	conoscendo	conosciuto(a/i/e)	
	...	...	...	(tu) conoscesti	...	...			conosci
				(lui/lei) conobbe					...
				(noi) conoscemmo					
				(voi) conosceste					
				(loro) conobbero					

consistere – *participio passato* consistito(a/i/e)

coprire – *vedi* **aprire**

correggere – *vedi* **leggere**

Infinito	Presente	Imperfetto	Futuro	Passato remoto	Cong. presente	Cong. imperfetto	Gerundio	Part. passato	Imperativo
correre	(io) corro ...	(io) correvo ...	(io) correrò ...	(io) corsi (tu) corresti (lui/lei) corse (noi) corremmo (voi) correste (loro) corsero	che (io) corra ...	che (io) corressi ...	correndo	corso(a/i/e)	corri ...
crescere	(io) cresco ...	(io) crescevo ...	(io) crescerò ...	(io) crebbi (tu) crescesti (lui/lei) crebbe (noi) crescemmo (voi) cresceste (loro) crebbero	che (io) cresca ...	che (io) crescessi ...	crescendo	cresciuto(a/i/e)	cresci ...
cuocere	(io) cuocio (tu) cuoci (lui/lei) cuoce (noi) c(u)ociamo (voi) c(u)ocete (loro) cuociono	(io) c(u)ocevo (tu) c(u)ocevi (lui/lei) c(u)oceva (noi) c(u)ocevamo (voi) c(u)ocevate (loro) c(u)ocevano	(io) cuocerò (tu) cuocerai (lui/lei) cuocerà (noi) cuoceremo (voi) cuocerete (loro) cuoceranno	(io) cossi (tu) c(u)ocesti (lui/lei) cosse (noi) c(u)ocemmo (voi) c(u)oceste (loro) cossero	che (io) cuocia che (tu) cuocia che (lui/lei) cuocia che (noi) cuociamo che (voi) cuociate che (loro) cuociano	che (io) c(u)ocessi che (tu) c(u)ocessi che (lui/lei) c(u)ocesse che (noi) c(u)ocessimo che (voi) c(u)oceste che (loro) c(u)ocessero	c(u)ocendo	cotto(a/i/e)	cuoci cuocia c(u)ociamo c(u)ocete cuociano
dare	(io) do (tu) dai (lui/lei) dà (noi) diamo (voi) date (loro) danno	(io) davo ...	(io) darò ...	(io) diedi o detti (tu) desti (lui/lei) diede o dette (noi) demmo (voi) deste (loro) diedero o dettero	che (io) dia che (tu) dia che (lui/lei) dia che (noi) diamo che (voi) diate che (loro) diano	che (io) dessi ...	dando	dato(a/i/e)	da' o dai dia diamo date diano

Infinito	Presente	Imperfetto	Futuro	Passato remoto	Cong. presente	Cong. imperfetto	Gerundio	Part. passato	Imperativo
decidere	(io) decido	(io) decidevo	(io) deciderò	(io) decisi	che (io) decida	che (io) decidessi	decidendo	deciso(a/i/e)	
	...	...	...	(tu) decidesti		...			decidi
				(lui/lei) decise					...
				(noi) decidemmo					
				(voi) decideste					
				(loro) decisero					

dedurre – *vedi* **condurre**

devolvere – *participio passato* devoluto(a/i/e)

Infinito	Presente	Imperfetto	Futuro	Passato remoto	Cong. presente	Cong. imperfetto	Gerundio	Part. passato	Imperativo
difendere	(io) difendo	(io) difendevo	(io) difenderò	(io) difesi	che (io) difenda	che (io) difendessi	difendendo	difeso(a/i/e)	
	...	...	...	(tu) difendesti	...	...			difendi
				(lui/lei) difese					...
				(noi) difendemmo					
				(voi) difendeste					
				(loro) difesero					

deludere – *vedi* **alludere**

deprimere – *vedi* **comprimere**

Infinito	Presente	Imperfetto	Futuro	Passato remoto	Cong. presente	Cong. imperfetto	Gerundio	Part. passato	Imperativo
dipingere	(io) dipingo	(io) dipingevo	(io) dipingerò	(io) dipinsi	che (io) dipinga	che (io) dipingessi	dipingendo	dipinto(a/i/e)	
	...	...	...	(tu) dipingesti	...	...			dipingi
				(lui/lei) dipinse					...
				(noi) dipingemmo					
				(voi) dipingeste					
				(loro) dipinsero					

dipendere – *vedi* **appendere**

Infinito	Presente	Imperfetto	Futuro	Passato remoto	Cong. presente	Cong. imperfetto	Gerundio	Part. passato	Imperativo
dire	(io) dico	(io) dicevo	(io) dirò	(io) dissi	che (io) dica	che (io) dicessi	dicendo	detto(a/i/e)	
	(tu) dici	(tu) dicevi	(tu) dirai	(tu) dicesti	che (tu) dica	che (tu) dicessi			di' *o* dici
	(lui/lei) dice	(lui/lei) diceva	(lui/lei) dirà	(lui/lei) disse	che (lui/lei) dica	che (lui/lei) dicesse			dica
	(noi) diciamo	(noi) dicevamo	(noi) diremo	(noi) dicemmo	che (noi) diciamo	che (noi) dicessimo			diciamo
	(voi) dite	(voi) dicevate	(voi) direte	(voi) diceste	che (voi) diciate	che (voi) diceste			dite
	(loro) dicono	(loro) dicevano	(loro) diranno	(loro) dissero	che (loro) dicano	che (loro) dicessero			dicano

Infinito	Presente	Imperfetto	Futuro	Passato remoto	Cong. presente	Cong. imperfetto	Gerundio	Part. passato	Imperativo
dirigere	(io) dirigo ...	(io) dirigevo ...	(io) dirigerò ...	(io) diressi (tu) dirigesti (lui/lei) diresse (noi) dirigemmo (voi) dirigeste (loro) diressero	che (io) diriga ...	che (io) dirigessi ...	dirigendo	diretto(a/i/e)	dirigi ...
discutere	(io) discuto ...	(io) discutevo ...	(io) discuterò ...	(io) discussi (tu) discutesti (lui/lei) discusse (noi) discutemmo (voi) discuteste (loro) discussero	che (io) discuta ...	che (io) discutessi ...	discutendo	discusso(a/i/e)	discuti ...

dissolvere – *vedi* **assolvere**

dissuadere – *vedi* **persuadere**

Infinito	Presente	Imperfetto	Futuro	Passato remoto	Cong. presente	Cong. imperfetto	Gerundio	Part. passato	Imperativo
distinguere	(io) distinguo ...	(io) distinguevo ...	(io) distinguerò ...	(io) distinsi (tu) distinguesti (lui/lei) distinse (noi) distinguemmo (voi) distingueste (loro) distinsero	che (io) distingua ...	che (io) distinguessi ...	distinguendo	distinto(a/i/e)	distingui ...
dividere	(io) divido ...	(io) dividevo ...	(io) dividerò ...	(io) divisi (tu) dividesti (lui/lei) divise (noi) dividemmo (voi) divideste (loro) divisero	che (io) divida ...	che (io) dividessi ...	dividendo	diviso(a/i/e)	dividi ...

Infinito	Presente	Imperfetto	Futuro	Passato remoto	Cong. presente	Cong. imperfetto	Gerundio	Part. passato	Imperativo
dolere	(io) dolgo (tu) duoli (lui/lei) duole (noi) do(g)liamo (voi) dolete (loro) dolgono	(io) dolevo ...	(io) dorrò (tu) dorrai (lui/lei) dorrà (noi) dorremo (voi) dorrete (loro) dorranno	(io) dolsi (tu) dolesti (lui/lei) dolse (noi) dolemmo (voi) doleste (loro) dolsero	che (io) dolga che (tu) dolga che (lui/lei) dolga che (noi) doliamo che (voi) do(g)liate che (loro) dolgano	che (io) dolessi ...	dolendo	doluto(a/i/e)	duoli dolga do(g)liamo dolete
dovere	(io) devo o debbo (tu) devi (lui/lei) deve (noi) dobbiamo (voi) dovete (loro) devono o debbono	(io) dovevo ...	(io) dovrò (tu) dovrai (lui/lei) dovrà (noi) dovremo (voi) dovrete (loro) dovranno	(io) dovei o dovetti (tu) dovesti (lui/lei) dovette (noi) dovemmo (voi) doveste (loro) dovettero	che (io) deva o debba che (tu) debba che (lui/lei) debba che (noi) dobbiamo che (voi) dobbiate che (loro) debbano	che (io) dovessi ...	dovendo	dovuto(a/i/e)	(manca)
eccellere	(io) eccello ...	(io) eccellevo ...	(io) eccellerò ...	(io) eccelsi (tu) eccellesti (lui/lei) eccelse (noi) eccellemmo (voi) eccelleste (loro) eccelsero	che (io) eccella ...	che (io) eccellessi ...	eccellendo	eccelso(a/i/e)	eccelli ...
elidere	(io) elido ...	(io) elidevo ...	(io) eliderò ...	(io) elisi (tu) elidesti (lui/lei) elise (noi) elidemmo (voi) elideste (loro) elisero	che (io) elida ...	che (io) elidessi ...	elidendo	eliso(a/i/e)	elidi ...

Infinito	Presente	Imperfetto	Futuro	Passato remoto	Cong. presente	Cong. imperfetto	Gerundio	Part. passato	Imperativo
emergere	(io) emergo ...	(io) emergevo ...	(io) emergerò ...	(io) emersi (tu) emergesti (lui/lei) emerse (noi) emergemmo (voi) emergeste (loro) emersero	che (io) emerga ...	che (io) emergessi ...	emergendo	emerso(a/i/e)	emergi ...

erigere – *vedi* dirigere

escludere – *vedi* accludere

esistere – *participio passato* esistito(a/i/e)

Infinito	Presente	Imperfetto	Futuro	Passato remoto	Cong. presente	Cong. imperfetto	Gerundio	Part. passato	Imperativo
espellere	(io) espello ...	(io) espellevo ...	(io) espellerò ...	(io) espulsi (tu) espellesti (lui/lei) espulse (noi) espellemmo (voi) espelleste (loro) espulsero	che (io) espella ...	che (io) espellessi ...	espellendo	espulso(a/i/e)	espelli ...
esplodere	(io) esplodo ...	(io) esplodevo ...	(io) esploderò ...	(io) esplosi (tu) esplodesti (lui/lei) esplose (noi) esplodemmo (voi) esplodeste (loro) esplosero	che (io) esploda ...	che (io) esplodessi ...	esplodendo	esploso(a/i/e)	esplodi ...

esprimere – *vedi* comprimere

Infinito	Presente	Imperfetto	Futuro	Passato remoto	Cong. presente	Cong. imperfetto	Gerundio	Part. passato	Imperativo
essere	(io) sono (tu) sei (lui/lei) è (noi) siamo (voi) siete (loro) sono	(io) ero (tu) eri (lui/lei) era (noi) eravamo (voi) eravate (loro) erano	(io) sarò (tu) sarai (lui/lei) sarà (noi) saremo (voi) sarete (loro) saranno	(io) fui (tu) fosti (lui/lei) fu (noi) fummo (voi) foste (loro) furono	che (io) sia che (tu) sia che (lui/lei) sia che (noi) siamo che (voi) siate che (loro) siano	che (tu) fossi che (tu) fossi che (lui/lei) fosse che (noi) fossimo che (voi) foste che (loro) fossero	essendo	stato(a/i/e)	sii sia siamo siate siano

estinguere – *vedi* distinguere

Infinito	Presente	Imperfetto	Futuro	Passato remoto	Cong. presente	Cong. imperfetto	Gerundio	Part. passato	Imperativo
evadere	(io) evado	(io) evadevo	(io) evaderò	(io) evasi	che (io) evada	che (io) evadessi	evadendo	evaso(a/i/e)	
	...	...	...	(tu) evadesti	...	...			evadi
				(lui/lei) evase					...
				(noi) evademmo					
				(voi) evadeste					
				(loro) evasero					

evolvere – *participio passato* evoluto(a/i/e)

Infinito	Presente	Imperfetto	Futuro	Passato remoto	Cong. presente	Cong. imperfetto	Gerundio	Part. passato	Imperativo
fare	(io) faccio	(io) facevo	(io) farò	(io) feci	che (io) faccia	che (io) facessi	facendo	fatto(a/i/e)	
	(tu) fai	(tu) facevi	(tu) farai	(tu) facesti	che (tu) faccia	che (tu) facessi			fa' o fai
	(lui/lei) fa	(lui/lei) faceva	(lui/lei) farà	(lui/lei) fece	che (lui/lei) faccia	che (lui/lei) facesse			faccia
	(noi) facciamo	(noi) facevamo	(noi) faremo	(noi) facemmo	che (noi) facciamo	che (noi) facessimo			facciamo
	(voi) fate	(voi) facevate	(voi) farete	(voi) faceste	che (voi) facciate	che (voi) faceste			fate
	(loro) fanno	(loro) facevano	(loro) faranno	(loro) fecero	che (loro) facciano	che (loro) facessero			facciano
fingere	(io) fingo	(io) fingevo	(io) fingerò	(io) finsi	che (io) finga	che (io) fingessi	fingendo	finto(a/i/e)	
	...	...	...	(tu) fingesti	...	...			fingi
				(lui/lei) finse					...
				(noi) fingemmo					
				(voi) fingeste					
				(loro) finsero					

flettere – *participio passato* flesso(a/i/e)

Infinito	Presente	Imperfetto	Futuro	Passato remoto	Cong. presente	Cong. imperfetto	Gerundio	Part. passato	Imperativo
fondere	(io) fondo	(io) fondevo	(io) fonderò	(io) fusi	che (io) fonda	che (io) fondessi	fondendo	fuso(a/i/e)	
	...	...	...	(tu) fondesti	...	...			fondi
				(lui/lei) fuse					...
				(noi) fondemmo					
				(voi) fondeste					
				(loro) fusero					

Infinito	Presente	Imperfetto	Futuro	Passato remoto	Cong. presente	Cong. imperfetto	Gerundio	Part. passato	Imperativo
frangere	(io) frango ...	(io) frangevo ...	(io) frangerò ...	(io) fransi (tu) frangesti (lui/lei) franse (noi) frangemmo (voi) frangeste (loro) fransero	che (io) franga ...	che (io) frangessi ...	frangendo	franto(a/i/e)	frangi ...
friggere	(io) friggo ...	(io) friggevo ...	(io) friggerò ...	(io) frissi (tu) friggesti (lui/lei) frisse (noi) friggemmo (voi) friggeste (loro) frissero	che (io) frigga ...	che (io) friggessi ...	friggendo	fritto(a/i/e)	friggi ...

fungere – *vedi* fingere

giacere – *vedi* piacere

giungere – *vedi* fingere

Infinito	Presente	Imperfetto	Futuro	Passato remoto	Cong. presente	Cong. imperfetto	Gerundio	Part. passato	Imperativo
godere	(io) godo ...	(io) godevo ...	(io) godrò (tu) godrai (lui/lei) godrà (noi) godremo (voi) godrete (loro) godranno	(io) godei *o* godetti (tu) godesti (lui/lei) godette (noi) godemmo (voi) godeste (loro) godettero	che (io) goda ...	che (io) godessi ...	godendo	goduto(a/i/e)	godi ...

immergere – *vedi* emergere

imprimere – *vedi* comprimere

incidere – *vedi* decidere

includere – *vedi* accludere

incutere – *vedi* discutere

indurre – *vedi* condurre

infliggere – *vedi* affliggere

insistere – *participio passato* insistito(a/i/e)

introdurre – *vedi* condurre

invadere – *vedi* evadere

Infinito	Presente	Imperfetto	Futuro	Passato remoto	Cong. presente	Cong. imperfetto	Gerundio	Part. passato	Imperativo
ledere	(io) ledo ...	(io) ledevo ...	(io) lederò ...	(io) lesi (tu) ledesti (lui/lei) lese (noi) ledemmo (voi) ledeste (loro) lesero	che (io) leda ...	che (io) ledessi ...	ledendo	leso(a/i/e)	ledi ...

Infinito	Presente	Imperfetto	Futuro	Passato remoto	Cong. presente	Cong. imperfetto	Gerundio	Part. passato	Imperativo
leggere	(io) leggo ...	(io) leggevo ...	(io) leggerò ...	(io) lessi	che (io) legga	che (io) leggessi	leggendo	letto(a/i/e)	
				(tu) leggesti	...	...			leggi
				(lui/lei) lesse					...
				(noi) leggemmo					
				(voi) leggeste					
				(loro) lessero					
mettere	(io) metto	(io) mettevo	(io) metterò	(io) misi	che (io) metta	che (io) mettessi	mettendo	messo(a/i/e)	
	...	...	...	(tu) mettesti	...	...			metti
				(lui/lei) mise					...
				(noi) mettemmo					
				(voi) metteste					
				(loro) misero					
mordere	(io) mordo	(io) mordevo	(io) morderò	(io) morsi	che (io) morda	che (io) mordessi	mordendo	morso(a/i/e)	
	...	...	...	(tu) mordesti	...	...			mordi
				(lui/lei) morse					...
				(noi) mordemmo					
				(voi) mordeste					
				(loro) morsero					
morire	(io) muoio	(io) morivo	(io) mor(i)rò	(io) morii	che (io) muoia	che (io) morissi	morendo	morto(a/i/e)	
	(tu) muori	(tu) morivi	(tu) mor(i)rai	(tu) moristi	che (tu) muoia	che (tu) morissi			muori
	(lui/lei) muore	(lui/lei) moriva	(lui/lei) mor(i)rà	(lui/lei) morì	che (lui/lei) muoia	che (lui/lei) morisse			muoia
	(noi) moriamo	(noi) morivamo	(noi) mor(i)remo	(noi) morimmo	che (noi) moriamo	che (noi) morissimo			moriamo
	(voi) morite	(voi) morivate	(voi) mor(i)rete	(voi) moriste	che (voi) moriate	che (voi) moriste			morite
	(loro) muoiono	(loro) morivano	(loro) mor(i)ranno	(loro) morirono	che (loro) muoiano	che (loro) morissero			muoiano

mungere – *vedi* **fingere**

Infinito	Presente	Imperfetto	Futuro	Passato remoto	Cong. presente	Cong. imperfetto	Gerundio	Part. passato	Imperativo
nascere	(io) nasco ...	(io) nascevo ...	(io) nascerò ...	(io) nacqui (tu) nascesti (lui/lei) nacque (noi) nascemmo (voi) nasceste (loro) nacquero	che (io) nasca ...	che (io) nascessi ...	nascendo	nato(a/i/e)	nasci ...
nascondere	(io) nascondo ...	(io) nascondevo ...	(io) nasconderò ...	(io) nascosi (tu) nascondesti (lui/lei) nascose (noi) nascondemmo (voi) nascondeste (loro) nascosero	che (io) nasconda ...	che (io) nascondessi ...	nascondendo	nascosto(a/i/e)	nascondi ...
nuocere	(io) n(u)occio (tu) nuoci (lui/lei) nuoce (noi) n(u)ociamo (voi) n(u)ocete (loro) n(u)occiono	(io) n(u)ocevo (tu) n(u)ocevi (lui/lei) n(u)oceva (noi) n(u)ocevamo (voi) n(u)ocevate (loro) n(u)ovecano	(io) n(u)ocerò (tu) n(u)ocerai (lui/lei) n(u)ocerà (noi) n(u)oceremo (voi) n(u)ocerete (loro) n(u)oceranno (loro) nocquero	(io) nocqui (tu) n(u)ocesti (lui/lei) nocque (noi) n(u)ocemmo (voi) n(u)oceste che (loro) n(u)occiano che (loro) n(u)ocessero	che (io) n(u)occia che (tu) n(u)occia che (lui/lei) n(u)occia che (lui/lei) n(u)ocesse che (noi) n(u)ociamo che (voi) n(u)ociate	che (io) n(u)ocessi che (tu) n(u)ocessi che (noi) n(u)ocessimo che (voi) n(u)oceste	n(u)ocendo	n(u)ociuto(a/i/e) n(u)occiano	nuoci n(u)occia n(u)ociamo n(u)ocete

offendere – *vedi* **difendere**

	Presente	Imperfetto	Futuro	Passato remoto	Cong. presente	Cong. imperfetto	Gerundio	Part. passato	Imperativo
offrire	(io) offro ...	(io) offrivo ...	(io) offrirò ...	(io) offrii (tu) offristi (lui/lei) offrì (noi) offrimmo (voi) offriste (loro) offrirono	che (io) offra ...	che (io) offrissi ...	offrendo	offerto(a/i/e)	offri ...

opprimere – *vedi* **comprimere**

Infinito	Presente	Imperfetto	Futuro	Passato remoto	Cong. presente	Cong. imperfetto	Gerundio	Part. passato	Imperativo
parere	(io) paio	(io) parevo	(io) parrò	(io) parvi	che (io) paia	che (io) paressi	parendo	parso(a/i/e)	parvi
	(tu) pari	...	(tu) parrai	(tu) paresti	che (tu) paia	che (tu) paressi			*(manca)*
	[lui/lei] pare		[lui/lei] parrà	[lui/lei] parve	che [lui/lei] paia	che [lui/lei] paresse			
	(noi) pariamo		(noi) parremo	(noi) paremmo	che (noi) paiamo	che (noi) paressimo			
	(voi) parete		(voi) parrete	(voi) pareste	che (voi) paiate	che (voi) pareste			
	(loro) paiono		(loro) parranno	(loro) parvero	che (loro) paiano	che (loro) paressero			

percuotere – *vedi* **scuotere**

Infinito	Presente	Imperfetto	Futuro	Passato remoto	Cong. presente	Cong. imperfetto	Gerundio	Part. passato	Imperativo
perdere	(io) perdo	(io) perdevo	(io) perderò	(io) persi *o* perdetti	che (io) perda	che (io) perdessi	perdendo	perso(a/i/e) *o*	perdi
	...	...	...	(tu) perdesti	...	...		perduto(a/i/e)	...
				[lui/lei] perse *o* perdette					
				(noi) perdemmo					
				(voi) perdeste					
				(loro) persero *o* perdettero					
persuadere	(io) persuado	(io) persuadevo	(io) persuaderò	(io) persuasi	che (io) persuada	che (io) persuadessi	persuadendo	persuaso(a/i/e)	persuadi
	...	...	...	(tu) persuadesti	...	...			...
				[lui/lei] persuase					
				(noi) persuademmo					
				(voi) persuadeste					
				(loro) persuasero					
piacere	(io) piaccio	(io) piacevo	(io) piacerò	(io) piacqui	che (io) piaccia	che (io) piacessi	piacendo	piaciuto(a/i/e)	piaci
	(tu) piaci	...	...	(tu) piacesti	che (tu) piaccia	...			piaccia
	[lui/lei] piace			[lui/lei] piacque	che [lui/lei] piaccia				piacciamo
	(noi) pia(c)ciamo			(noi) piacemmo	che (noi) piacciamo				piacete
	(voi) piacete			(voi) piaceste	che (voi) piacciate				piacciano
	(loro) piacciono			(loro) piacquero	che (loro) piacciano				

Infinito	Presente	Imperfetto	Futuro	Passato remoto	Cong. presente	Cong. imperfetto	Gerundio	Part. passato	Imperativo
piangere	(io) piango	(io) piangevo	(io) piangerò	(io) piansi	che (io) pianga	che (io) piangessi	piangendo	pianto(a/i/e)	
	...	...	...	(tu) piangesti	...	...			piangi
				(lui/lei) pianse					...
				(noi) piangemmo					
				(voi) piangeste					
				(loro) piansero					

piovere – *passato remoto* piovve

Infinito	Presente	Imperfetto	Futuro	Passato remoto	Cong. presente	Cong. imperfetto	Gerundio	Part. passato	Imperativo
porgere	(io) porgo	(io) porgevo	(io) porgerò	(io) porsi	che (io) porga	che (io) porgessi	porgendo	porto(a/i/e)	
	...	...	...	(tu) porgesti	...	...			porgi
				(lui/lei) porse					...
				(noi) porgemmo					
				(voi) porgeste					
				(loro) porsero					

Infinito	Presente	Imperfetto	Futuro	Passato remoto	Cong. presente	Cong. imperfetto	Gerundio	Part. passato	Imperativo
porre	(io) pongo	(io) ponevo	(io) porrò	(io) posi	che (io) ponga	che (io) ponessi	ponendo	posto(a/i/e)	
	(tu) poni	(tu) ponevi	(tu) porrai	(tu) ponesti	che (tu) ponga	che (tu) ponessi			poni
	(lui/lei) pone	(lui/lei) poneva	(lui/lei) porrà	(lui/lei) pose	che (lui/lei) ponga	che (lui/lei) ponesse			ponga
	(noi) poniamo	(noi) ponevamo	(noi) porremo	(noi) ponemmo	che (noi) poniamo	che (noi) ponessimo			poniamo
	(voi) ponete	(voi) ponevate	(voi) porrete	(voi) poneste	che (voi) poniate	che (voi) poneste			ponete
	(loro) pongono	(loro) ponevano	(loro) porranno	(loro) posero	che (loro) pongano	che (loro) ponessero			pongano

possedere – *vedi sedere (verbi modello)*

Infinito	Presente	Imperfetto	Futuro	Passato remoto	Cong. presente	Cong. imperfetto	Gerundio	Part. passato	Imperativo
potere	(io) posso	(io) potevo	(io) potrò	(io) potei	che (io) possa	che (io) potessi	potendo	potuto(a/i/e)	*(manca)*
	(tu) puoi	...	(tu) potrai	(tu) potesti	che (tu) possa	...			
	(lui/lei) può		(lui/lei) potrà	(lui/lei) poté	che (lui/lei) possa				
	(noi) possiamo		(noi) potremo	(noi) potemmo	che (noi) possiamo				
	(voi) potete		(voi) potrete	(voi) poteste	che (voi) possiate				
	(loro) possono		(loro) potranno	(loro) poterono	che (loro) possano				

Infinito	Presente	Imperfetto	Futuro	Passato remoto	Cong. presente	Cong. imperfetto	Gerundio	Part. passato	Imperativo
prendere	(io) prendo ...	(io) prendevo ...	(io) prenderò ...	(io) presi (tu) prendesti (lui/lei) prese (noi) prendemmo (voi) prendeste (loro) presero	che (io) prenda ...	che (io) prendessi ...	prendendo	preso(a/i/e)	prendi ...

presumere – *vedi* assumere

radere	(io) rado ...	(io) radevo ...	(io) raderò ...	(io) rasi (tu) radesti (lui/lei) rase (noi) rademmo (voi) radeste (loro) rasero	che (io) rada ...	che (io) radessi ...	radendo	raso(a/i/e)	radi ...

produrre – *vedi* condurre
proteggere – *vedi* leggere
pungere – *vedi* fingere

recidere – *vedi* decidere

redigere	(io) redigo ...	(io) redigevo ...	(io) redigerò ...	(io) redassi (tu) redigesti (lui/lei) redasse (noi) redigemmo (voi) redigeste (loro) redassero	che (io) rediga ...	che (io) redigessi ...	redigendo	redatto(a/i/e)	redigi ...
redimere	(io) redimo ...	(io) redimevo ...	(io) redimerò ...	(io) redensi (tu) redimesti (lui/lei) redense (noi) redimemmo (voi) redimeste (loro) redensero	che (io) redima ...	che (io) redimessi ...	redimendo	redento(a/i/e)	redimi ...

reggere – *vedi* leggere
rendere – *vedi* prendere
reprimere – *vedi* comprimere
resistere – *participio passato* resistito(a/i/e)

Infinito	Presente	Imperfetto	Futuro	Passato remoto	Cong. presente	Cong. imperfetto	Gerundio	Part. passato	Imperativo
ridere	(io) rido	(io) ridevo	(io) riderò	(io) risi	che (io) rida	che (io) ridessi	ridendo	riso(a/i/e)	ridi
	...	...	...	(tu) ridesti	...	...			...
				(lui/lei) rise					
				(noi) ridemmo					
				(voi) rideste					
				(loro) risero					

ridurre – *vedi* condurre

riflettere – *participio passato* riflesso(a/i/e) *o* riflettuto(a/i/e)

Infinito	Presente	Imperfetto	Futuro	Passato remoto	Cong. presente	Cong. imperfetto	Gerundio	Part. passato	Imperativo
rimanere	(io) rimango	(io) rimanevo	(io) rimarrò	(io) rimasi	che (io) rimanga	che (io) rimanessi	rimanendo	rimasto(a/i/e)	
	(tu) rimani	...	(tu) rimarrai	(tu) rimanesti	che (tu) rimanga	...			rimani
	(lui/lei) rimane		(lui/lei) rimarrà	(lui/lei) rimase	che (lui/lei) rimanga				rimanga
	(noi) rimaniamo		(noi) rimarremo	(noi) rimanemmo	che (noi) rimaniamo				rimaniamo
	(voi) rimanete		(voi) rimarrete	(voi) rimaneste	che (voi) rimaniate				rimanete
	(loro) rimangono		(loro) rimarranno	(loro) rimasero	che (loro) rimangano				rimangano

risolvere – *vedi* assolvere

Infinito	Presente	Imperfetto	Futuro	Passato remoto	Cong. presente	Cong. imperfetto	Gerundio	Part. passato	Imperativo
rispondere	(io) rispondo	(io) rispondevo	(io) risponderò	(io) risposi	che (io) risponda	che (io) rispondessi	rispondendo	risposto(a/i/e)	
	...	...	...	(tu) rispondesti	...	...			rispondi
				(lui/lei) rispose					...
				(noi) rispondemmo					
				(voi) rispondeste					
				(loro) risposero					

Infinito	Presente	Imperfetto	Futuro	Passato remoto	Cong. presente	Cong. imperfetto	Gerundio	Part. passato	Imperativo
rodere	(io) rodo	(io) rodevo	(io) roderò	(io) rosi	che (io) roda	che (io) rodessi	rodendo	roso(a/i/e)	
	...	...	...	(tu) rodesti	...	...			rodi
				(lui/lei) rose					...
				(noi) rodemmo					
				(voi) rodeste					
				(loro) rosero					

Infinito	Presente	Imperfetto	Futuro	Passato remoto	Cong. presente	Cong. imperfetto	Gerundio	Part. passato	Imperativo
rompere	(io) rompo ...	(io) rompevo ...	(io) romperò ...	(io) ruppi (tu) rompesti (lui/lei) ruppe (noi) rompemmo (voi) rompeste (loro) ruppero	che (io) rompa ...	che (io) rompessi ...	rompendo	rotto(a/i/e)	rompi
salire	(io) salgo (tu) sali (lui/lei) sale (noi) saliamo (voi) salite (loro) salgono	(io) salivo ...	(io) salirò ...	(io) salii (tu) salisti (lui/lei) salì (noi) salimmo (voi) saliste (loro) salirono	che (io) salga che (tu) salga che (lui/lei) salga che (noi) saliamo che (voi) saliate che (loro) salgano	che (io) salissi ...	salendo	salito(a/i/e)	
sapere	(io) so (tu) sai (lui/lei) sa (noi) sappiamo (voi) sapete (loro) sanno	(io) sapevo ...	(io) saprò (tu) saprai (lui/lei) saprà (noi) sapremo (voi) saprete (loro) sapranno	(io) seppi (tu) sapesti (lui/lei) seppe (noi) sapemmo (voi) sapeste (loro) seppero	che (io) sappia che (tu) sappia che (lui/lei) sappia che (noi) sappiamo che (voi) sappiate che (loro) sappiano	che (io) sapessi ...	sapendo	saputo(a/i/e)	
scegliere	(io) scelgo (tu) scegli (lui/lei) sceglie (noi) scegliamo (voi) scegliete (loro) scelgono	(io) sceglievo ...	(io) sceglierò ...	(io) scelsi (tu) scegliesti (lui/lei) scelse (noi) scegliemmo (voi) sceglieste (loro) scelsero	che (io) scelga che (tu) scelga che (lui/lei) scelga che (noi) scegliamo che (voi) scegliate che (loro) scelgano	che (io) scegliessi ...	scegliendo	scelto(a/i/e)	scegli scelga scegliamo scegliete scelgano

Infinito	Presente	Imperfetto	Futuro	Passato remoto	Cong. presente	Cong. imperfetto	Gerundio	Part. passato	Imperativo
scendere	(io) scendo ...	(io) scendevo ...	(io) scenderò ...	(io) scesi (tu) scendesti (lui/lei) scese (noi) scendemmo (voi) scendeste (loro) scesero	che (io) scenda ...	che (io) scendessi	scendendo	sceso(a/i/e)	scendi ...
scindere	(io) scindo ...	(io) scindevo ...	(io) scinderò ...	(io) scissi (tu) scindesti (lui/lei) scisse (noi) scindemmo (voi) scindeste (loro) scissero	che (io) scirda ...	che (io) scindessi	scindendo	scisso(a/i/e)	scindi ...

sciogliere – *vedi* **cogliere**

scorgere – *vedi* **sorgere**

Infinito	Presente	Imperfetto	Futuro	Passato remoto	Cong. presente	Cong. imperfetto	Gerundio	Part. passato	Imperativo
scrivere	(io) scrivo ...	(io) scrivevo ...	(io) scriverò ...	(io) scrissi (tu) scrivesti (lui/lei) scrisse (noi) scrivemmo (voi) scriveste (loro) scrissero	che (io) scriva ...	che (io) scrivessi ...	scrivendo	scritto(a/i/e)	scrivi ...
scuotere	(io) scuoto ...	(io) scuotevo ...	(io) scuoterò ...	(io) scossi (tu) sc(u)otesti (lui/lei) scosse (noi) sc(u)otemmo (voi) sc(u)oteste (loro) scossero	che (io) scuota ...	che (io) scuotessi ...	scuotendo	scosso(a/i/e)	scuoti ...

sedurre – *vedi* **condurre**

soffrire – *vedi* **offrire**

Infinito	Presente	Imperfetto	Futuro	Passato remoto	Cong. presente	Cong. imperfetto	Gerundio	Part. passato	Imperativo
solere	(io) soglio, (tu) suoli, (lui/lei) suole, (noi) sogliamo, (voi) solete, (loro) sogliono	(io) solevo, ...	*(manca)*	*(manca)*	che (io) soglia, che (tu) soglia, che (lui/lei) soglia, che (noi) sogliamo, che (voi) sogliate, che (loro) sogliano	che (io) solessi, ...	solendo	solito(a/i/e)	*(manca)*

sommergere – *vedi* emergere

sopprimere – *vedi* comprimere

Infinito	Presente	Imperfetto	Futuro	Passato remoto	Cong. presente	Cong. imperfetto	Gerundio	Part. passato	Imperativo
sorgere	(io) sorgo, ...	(io) sorgevo, ...	(io) sorgerò, ...	(io) sorsi, (tu) sorgesti, (lui/lei) sorse, (noi) sorgemmo, (voi) sorgeste, (loro) sorsero	che (io) sorga, ...	che (io) sorgessi, ...	sorgendo	sorto(a/i/e)	sorgi, ...

sospendere – *vedi* appendere

Infinito	Presente	Imperfetto	Futuro	Passato remoto	Cong. presente	Cong. imperfetto	Gerundio	Part. passato	Imperativo
spargere	(io) spargo, ...	(io) spargevo, ...	(io) spargerò, ...	(io) sparsi, (tu) spargesti, (lui/lei) sparse, (noi) spargemmo, (voi) spargeste, (loro) sparsero	che (io) sparga, ...	che (io) spargessi, ...	spargendo	sparso(a/i/e)	spargi, ...

spendere – *vedi* appendere

spingere – *vedi* fingere

Infinito	Presente	Imperfetto	Futuro	Passato remoto	Cong. presente	Cong. imperfetto	Gerundio	Part. passato	Imperativo
stare	(io) sto, (tu) stai, (lui/lei) sta, (noi) stiamo, (voi) state, (loro) stanno	(io) stavo, ...	(io) starò, ...	(io) stetti, (tu) stesti, (lui/lei) stette, (noi) stemmo, (voi) steste, (loro) stettero	che (io) stia, che (tu) stia, che (lui/lei) stia, che (noi) stiamo, che (voi) stiate, che (loro) stiano	che (io) stessi, che (tu) stessi, che (lui/lei) stesse, che (noi) stessimo, che (voi) steste, che (loro) stessero	stando	stato(a/i/e)	stai *o* sta', stia, stiamo, state, stiano

Infinito	Presente	Imperfetto	Futuro	Passato remoto	Cong. presente	Cong. imperfetto	Gerundio	Part. passato	Imperativo
stringere	(io) stringo	(io) stringevo	(io) stringerò	(io) strinsi	che (io) stringa	che (io) stringessi	stringendo	stretto(a/i/e)	
	...	...	...	(tu) stringesti	...	...			stringi
				(lui/lei) strinse					
				(noi) stringemmo					...
				(voi) stringeste					
				(loro) strinsero					

struggere – *vedi* **leggere**

succedere – *vedi* **concedere**

Infinito	Presente	Imperfetto	Futuro	Passato remoto	Cong. presente	Cong. imperfetto	Gerundio	Part. passato	Imperativo
tacere	(io) taccio	(io) tacevo	(io) tacerò	(io) tacqui	che (io) taccia	che (io) tacessi	tacendo	taciuto(a/i/e)	
	...	...	...	(tu) tacesti	...	...			taci
				(lui/lei) tacque					
				(noi) tacemmo					...
				(voi) taceste					
				(loro) tacquero					

tendere – *vedi* **prendere**

Infinito	Presente	Imperfetto	Futuro	Passato remoto	Cong. presente	Cong. imperfetto	Gerundio	Part. passato	Imperativo
tenere	(io) tengo	(io) tenevo	(io) terrò	(io) tenni	che (io) tenga	che (io) tenessi	tenendo	tenuto(a/i/e)	
	(tu) tieni	(tu) tenevi	(tu) terrai	(tu) tenesti	che (tu) tenga	che (tu) tenessi			tieni
	(lui/lei) tiene	(lui/lei) teneva	(lui/lei) terrà	(lui/lei) tenne	che (lui/lei) tenga	che (lui/lei) tenesse			tenga
	(noi) teniamo	(noi) tenevamo	(noi) terremo	(noi) tenemmo	che (noi) teniamo	che (noi) tenessimo			teniamo
	(voi) tenete	(voi) tenevate	(voi) terrete	(voi) teneste	che (voi) teniate	che (voi) teneste			tenete
	(loro) tengono	(loro) tenevano	(loro) terranno	(loro) tennero	che (loro) tengano	che (loro) tenessero			tengano

tingere – *vedi* **fingere**

togliere – *vedi* **cogliere**

Infinito	Presente	Imperfetto	Futuro	Passato remoto	Cong. presente	Cong. imperfetto	Gerundio	Part. passato	Imperativo
torcere	(io) torco	(io) torcevo	(io) torcerò	(io) torsi	che (io) torca	che (io) torcessi	torcendo	torto(a/i/e)	
	...	...	...	(tu) torcesti	...	...			torci
				(lui/lei) torse					
				(noi) torcemmo					...
				(voi) torceste					
				(loro) torsero					

tradurre – *vedi* **condurre**

Infinito	Presente	Imperfetto	Futuro	Passato remoto	Cong. presente	Cong. imperfetto	Gerundio	Part. passato	Imperativo
trarre	(io) traggo (tu) trai (lui/lei) trae (noi) traiamo (voi) traete (loro) traggono	(io) traevo (tu) traevi (lui/lei) traeva (noi) traevamo (voi) traevate (loro) traevano	(io) trarrò (tu) trarrai (lui/lei) trarrà (noi) trarremo (voi) trarrete (loro) trarranno	(io) trassi (tu) traesti (lui/lei) trasse (noi) traemmo (voi) traeste (loro) trassero	che (io) tragga che (tu) tragga che (lui/lei) tragga che (noi) traiamo che (voi) traiate che (loro) traggano	che (io) traessi che (tu) traessi che (lui/lei) traesse che (noi) traessimo che (voi) traeste che (loro) traessero	traendo	tratto(a/i/e)	trai tragga traiamo traete traggano
uccidere – *vedi* decidere									
udire	(io) odo (tu) odi (lui/lei) ode (noi) udiamo (voi) udite (loro) odono	(io) udivo ...	(io) ud(i)rò (tu) ud(i)rai (lui/lei) ud(i)rà (noi) ud(i)remo (voi) ud(i)rete (loro) ud(i)ranno	(io) udii (tu) udisti (lui/lei) udì (noi) udimmo (voi) udiste (loro) udirono	che (io) oda che (tu) oda che (lui/lei) oda che (noi) udiamo che (voi) udiate che (loro) odano	che (io) udissi ...	udendo	udito(a/i/e)	odi oda udiamo udite odano
ungere – *vedi* fingere									
uscire	(io) esco (tu) esci (lui/lei) esce (noi) usciamo (voi) uscite (loro) escono	(io) uscivo ...	(io) uscirò ...	(io) uscii ...	che (io) esca che (tu) esca che (lui/lei) esca che (noi) usciamo che (voi) usciate che (loro) escano	che (io) uscissi che (tu) uscissi che (lui/lei) uscisse che (noi) uscissimo che (voi) usciste che (loro) uscissero	uscendo	uscito(a/i/e)	esci esca usciamo uscite escano
valere	(io) valgo (tu) vali (lui/lei) vale (noi) valiamo (voi) valete (loro) valgono	(io) valevo (tu) valevi (lui/lei) valeva (noi) valevamo (voi) valevate (loro) valevano	(io) varrò (tu) varrai (lui/lei) varrà (noi) varremo (voi) varrete (loro) varranno	(io) valsi (tu) valesti (lui/lei) valse (noi) valemmo (voi) valeste (loro) valsero	che (io) valga che (tu) valga che (lui/lei) valga che (noi) valiamo che (voi) valiate che (loro) valgano	che (io) valessi ...	valendo	valso(a/i/e)	vali valga valiamo valete valgano

Infinito	Presente	Imperfetto	Futuro	Passato remoto	Cong. presente	Cong. imperfetto	Gerundio	Part. passato	Imperativo
vedere	(io) vedo ...	(io) vedevo ...	(io) vedrò (tu) vedrai (lui/lei) vedrà (noi) vedremo (voi) vedrete (loro) vedranno	(io) vidi (tu) vedesti (lui/lei) vide (noi) vedemmo (voi) vedeste (loro) videro	che (io) veda ...	che (io) vedessi ...	vedendo	visto(a/i/e) o veduto(a/i/e)	vedi ...
venire	(io) vengo (tu) vieni (lui/lei) viene (noi) veniamo (voi) venite (loro) vengono	(io) venivo ...	(io) verrò (tu) verrai (lui/lei) verrà (noi) verremo (voi) verrete (loro) verranno	(io) venni (tu) venisti (lui/lei) venne (noi) venimmo (voi) veniste (loro) vennero	che (io) venga che (tu) venga che (lui/lei) venga che (noi) veniamo che (voi) veniate che (loro) vengano	che (io) venissi ...	venendo	venuto(a/i/e)	vieni venga veniamo venite vengano
vivere	(io) vivo ...	(io) vivevo ...	(io) vivrò ...	(io) vissi (tu) vivesti (lui/lei) visse (noi) vivemmo (voi) viveste (loro) vissero	che (io) viva ...	che (io) vivessi ...	vivendo	vissuto(a/i/e)	vivi ...
volere	(io) voglio (tu) vuoi (lui/lei) vuole (noi) vogliamo (voi) volete (loro) vogliono	(io) volevo (tu) volevi (lui/lei) voleva (noi) volevamo (voi) volevate (loro) volevano	(io) vorrò (tu) vorrai (lui/lei) vorrà (noi) vorremo (voi) vorrete (loro) vorranno	(io) volli (tu) volesti (lui/lei) volle (noi) volemmo (voi) voleste (loro) vollero	che (io) voglia che (tu) voglia che (lui/lei) voglia che (noi) vogliamo che (voi) vogliate che (loro) vogliano	che (io) volessi che (tu) volessi che (lui/lei) volesse che (noi) volessimo che (voi) voleste che (loro) volessero	volendo	voluto(a/i/e)	*(manca)*

Infinito	Presente	Imperfetto	Futuro	Passato remoto	Cong. presente	Cong. imperfetto	Gerundio	Part. passato	Imperativo
volgere	(io) volgo	(io) volgevo	(io) volgerò	(io) volsi	che (io) volga	che (io) volgessi	volgendo	volto(a/i/e)	
	...	...	...	(tu) volgesti	...	...			volgi
				(lui/lei) volse					...
				(noi) volgemmo					
				(voi) volgeste					
				(loro) volsero					

Minigrammatica della lingua inglese
Short Grammar of the English Language

Il sostantivo

In inglese si può riconoscere il **genere** di un sostantivo non tramite il suo articolo, che è invariabile, ma tramite il pronome che può sostituirlo:

a/the boy	**he**	lui
a/the girl	**she**	lei
a/the book	**it**	esso

I nomi delle imbarcazioni sono in genere femminili.

Spesso anche paesi e aeroplani possono essere personificati utilizzando un pronome femminile.

Per parlare di bambini piccoli e di animali si usa normalmente **it**, a meno che non se ne conosca il sesso:

A dog came into the garden and I chased **it** out.	È entrato un cane in giardino e io l'ho cacciato fuori.
I called my **dog, Rex,** and he came running.	Ho chiamato il mio cane, Rex, e lui è arrivato di corsa.
I made a funny face at **the baby** and **it** smiled at me.	Ho fatto una faccia buffa al bambino e lui mi ha sorriso.
We have **a** new **baby** – **she's** called Karen.	Abbiamo un'altra bambina: si chiama Karen.

A volte i nomi di animali hanno la stessa forma al singolare e al plurale:

a bison – two **bison**	un bisonte – due bisonti
a sheep – two **sheep**	una pecora – due pecore

Per formare il **plurale** in genere si aggiunge una **-s** alle fine della parola:

day**s**	giorni
dog**s**	cani
boy**s**	ragazzi
book**s**	libri
hat**s**	cappelli

Anche le parole che finiscono per **-ce**, **-ge**, **-se**, e **-ze**, formano il plurale con una **-s** finale:

pie**ces**	pezzi
si**zes**	taglie

Le parole che finiscono con le consonanti **-s**, **-ss**, **-sh**, **-ch**, **-x**, **-z**, al plurale prendono la desinenza **-es**:

bo**xes**	scatole
bo**sses**	capi

La **y** in fine di parola preceduta da una consonante si trasforma in **-ies** al plurale:

lad**y**	lad**ies**	signore
bod**y**	bod**ies**	corpi

I sostantivi che finiscono in -**o** preceduta da una consonante prendono molto spesso la desinenza -**es** al plurale:

tomat**oes**	pomodori
her**oes**	eroi

Alcune parole che finiscono in -**f** o in -**fe** al plurale prendono la desinenza -**ves**:

Singolare	Plurale	
half	hal**ves**	metà *pl*
kni**fe**	kni**ves**	coltelli
leaf	lea**ves**	foglie
wi**fe**	wi**ves**	mogli

Altre parole subiscono una modifica della vocale o delle vocali:

Singolare	Plurale	
f**oo**t	f**ee**t	piedi
m**a**n	m**e**n	uomini
wom**a**n	wom**e**n	donne

Nella parte inglese-italiano del dizionario sono indicate le forme irregolari del plurale diverse da quelle in -**ves**, -**oes** o -**os**.

Il complemento di specificazione

Il complemento di specificazione che esprime un'idea di appartenenza o di possesso può essere espresso con *of* (usato di norma per le cose) o con '**s** (usato in genere per le persone e per gli oggetti personificati). Questa costruzione si chiama genitivo sassone.

- Con *of:*

the name **of** the hotel	il nome dell'albergo
the leg **of** the table	la gamba del tavolo

- Per la costruzione con il genitivo sassone, il possessore va posto prima della cosa posseduta e, se il sostantivo è al **singolare,** alla cosa posseduta vanno aggiunti un **apostrofo** e una **s**:

my sister**'s** room	la camera di mia sorella

se il sostantivo è al **plurale** va aggiunto solamente un **apostrofo**:

my sisters**'** room	la camera delle mie sorelle

Alcune parole come **shop**, **church**, **cathedral** in genere non compaiono dopo il genitivo sassone:

at the butcher**'s**	*invece di:* at the butcher's shop	in macelleria
St. Paul**'s**	*invece di:* St. Paul's Cathedral	la cattedrale di St. Paul

L'aggettivo

L'aggettivo fornisce informazioni sul sostantivo a cui si riferisce, qualificandolo o determinandolo (per esempio: a *sunny* day, *financial* problems), dando informazioni sul colore (a *blue* shirt) o sottolineandone una qualità (an *utter* flop).

La forma dell'aggettivo non varia di genere e numero:

a **nice** postman	un postino simpatico
three **nice** postmen	tre postini simpatici
a **good** song	una bella canzone
two **good** songs	due belle canzoni

L'aggettivo dimostrativo precede il sostantivo. Per i sostantivi indicanti qualcosa di vicino nello spazio o nel tempo, in inglese si utilizzano *this* e *these*.

this hat	**this** pen	questo cappello	questa penna
these pants	**these** girls	questi pantaloni	queste ragazze

Per i sostantivi indicanti qualcosa di più lontano nel tempo o nello spazio, in inglese si utilizzano *that* e *those*.

that man	**that** party	quell'uomo	quella festa
those children	**those** windows	quei bambini	quelle finestre

L'aggettivo possessivo indica il possesso o la relazione tra il sostantivo e la persona cui si riferisce.

my	friend	il mio amico
your	friend	il tuo amico
his, her	friend	il suo amico
its	attractions	le sue attrattive
our	friend	il nostro amico
your	friend	il vostro amico
their	friend	il loro amico

La comparazione (forme regolari)

Per formare il comparativo e il supersativo regolari degli aggettivi monosillabici, basta aggiungere -**er** al comparativo e -**est** al superlativo:

great	great**er** (than)	the great**est**
grande	più grande (di)	il più grande

- Gli aggettivi che finiscono in -**e** perdono la **e** finale: fine, fin**er**, fin**est**.
- La -**y** in fine di parola degli aggettivi bisillabici si trasforma in -**ier** e -**iest**: happy, happ**ier**, happ**iest**.
- Le consonanti **d**, **g** e **t** in fine di parola vengono raddoppiate nella costruzione del comparativo e del superlativo con -**er** e -**est** quando seguono **a**, **e**, **i** od **o** breve e accentata: big, big**ger**, big**gest**.

La comparazione degli altri aggettivi con due o più sillabe si forma usando ***more*** (più) al comparativo e ***most*** (il più) al superlativo.

difficult	**more** difficult (than)	the **most** difficult
difficile	più difficile (di)	il più difficile

La comparazione (forme irregolari)

good	better	the best
buono	migliore	il migliore

bad	worse	the worst
cattivo	peggiore	il peggiore

much/many	more	the most
molto	più	il più

Nella parte inglese-italiano del dizionario sono indicate le forme irregolari degli aggettivi.

L'avverbio

In genere gli avverbi si formano aggiungendo -**ly** agli aggettivi.

slow	slow**ly**	He speaks slowly.	Parla lentamente.
quick	quick**ly**	He runs quickly.	Corre veloce.

- *well* rappresenta un caso particolare. È l'avverbio che corrisponde all'aggettivo *good* (buono):

He speaks English **well**.	Parla bene l'inglese.

- alcuni avverbi non finiscono in -**ly**:

You're doing **fine**.	Stai andando bene.
You've arrived too **late**.	Sei arrivato troppo tardi.
See you **soon**!	A presto!
She ran **fast**.	Correva veloce.

La comparazione degli avverbi che finiscono in -**ly** si forma usando *more* e *most*:

more slowly	**most** slowly
più lentamente	il più lentamente

Agli avverbi che non finiscono in -**ly** vanno aggiunti -**er** ed -**est**:

fast	fast**er**	fast**est**
rapidamente	più rapidamente	il più rapidamente

Il verbo

Il presente

Infinito:		to knock	to call	to go	to wash	to study
		Colpire	chiamare	andare	lavare	studiare
I	(io)	knock	call	go	wash	study
you	(tu)	knock	call	go	wash	study
he she it	(lui) (lei) (esso, essa)	knocks	calls	goes	washes	studies
we	(noi)	knock	call	go	wash	study
you	(voi)	knock	call	go	wash	study
they	(loro)	knock	call	go	wash	study

Solo la forma della terza persona singolare cambia. In genere la terza persona singolare del presente si forma aggiungendo una -s all'infinito del verbo *(to stop – he stops)*. I verbi che finiscono con le consonanti -**ss**, -**sh**, -**ch**, o -**x** alla terza persona prendono la desinenza -**es** *(to pass – he passes)*, mentre quelli che finiscono in -**y** preceduta da una consonante prendono la desinenza -**ies** *(to carry – he carries)*.

Il presente si usa per esprimere:

– fatti:

The earth **goes** around the sun.	La terra gira attorno al sole.

– abitudini:

I **brush** my teeth after breakfast.	Mi lavo denti dopo colazione.

– intenzioni in un futuro prossimo:

We **leave** for London next Friday.	Partiamo per Londra venerdì prossimo.

Il passato e il participio passato

Per costruire le forme del passato si aggiunge -**ed** all'infinito del verbo senza il **to**.

Infinito:	to open	to arrive	to stop	to carry
	aprire	arrivare	fermare	portare
I, you, he, she, it, we, you, they	opened	arrived	stopped	carried

- I verbi che finiscono in -**e** perdono la **e** finale: agr**ee**d, arriv**ed**.
- La -**y** in fine di parola si trasforma in -**ied**: tr**y**, tr**ied**
- Le consonanti **b**, **d**, **g**, **m**, **n**, **p**, **s**, **t** in fine di parola raddoppiano se sono precedute da una vocale breve accentata.
- Nell'inglese britannico in genere tutte le consonanti dei verbi plurisillabici raddoppiano: trave**l**, trave**ll**ed.
- Il participio passato ha la stessa forma del passato:

open**ed**	arriv**ed**	stopp**ed**	carr**ied**
aperto	arrivato	fermato	portato

Le forme dei **verbi irregolari** sono state raccolte in un elenco separato.

Il passato si usa:

* per descrivere azioni finite passate, avvenute in un momento o in un periodo preciso:

They **arrived** yesterday.	Sono arrivati ieri.
We **moved** last year.	Abbiamo cambiato casa l'anno scorso.
Who **invented** the telephone?	Chi ha inventato il telefono?

* nei racconti:

Then he **planted** the magic beans.	Poi piantò i fagioli magici.

I verbi ausiliari

Il presente e il participio presente

Infinito:	to be	to have	to do
	essere	avere	fare
I	am	have	do
you	are	have	do
he, she, it	is	has	does
we	are	have	do
you	are	have	do
they	are	have	do
Participio presente:	being	having	doing

Il verbo **be** è usato come ausiliare per formare i tempi continui, come il "present continuous": *I am reading; are you listening?*

Il verbo **have** è usato come ausiliare per formare i tempi perfetti, come il "present perfect": *she has already gone; have you read the paper?*

Il verbo **do** è usato come ausiliare per la forma negativa e interrogativa del presente e del passato: *I don't speak Chinese; did you watch TV yesterday?*

Nell'inglese parlato si utilizzano spesso delle **forme contratte**:

am	→	'm	**I'm**
are	→	're	**you're**
is	→	's	**he's**
have	→	've	**I've**
has	→	's	**he's**

Negazione		Forma contratta
are not	→	**aren't**
is not	→	**isn't**
have not	→	**haven't**
has not	→	**hasn't**
do not	→	**don't**
does not	→	**doesn't**

Il passato e il participio passato

Infinito:	to be	to have	to do
	essere	avere	fare
I	was	had	did
you	were	had	did
he, she, it	was	had	did
we	were	had	did
you	were	had	did
they	were	had	did
Participio presente:	been	had	done
Forma contratta:		'd	
Negazione:	wasn't	hadn't	didn't
	weren't		

Il "present perfect"

A differenza del passato prossimo italiano per cui si possono usare avere o essere, a seconda del verbo, il "present perfect" si forma sempre con *have* (avere) + participio passato.

I **have** had	ho avuto
I **have** been	sono stato
I **have** done	ho fatto
I **have** called	ho chiamato
I **have** arrived	sono arrivato
I **have** gone	sono andato

Questo tempo verbale è usato:
- per dare spiegazioni:

I can't pay – I**'ve lost** my wallet.	Non posso pagare: ho perso il portafoglio.

- per esprimere una conseguenza:

Jack **has arrived**, so we can begin.	Jack è arrivato, si può cominciare.

- con alcuni avverbi come **already, just, never**:

I**'ve already** collected the mail.	Ho già ritirato la posta.

- per fatti iniziati nel passato che continuano ancora nel presente:

I**'ve known** him since Christmas.	Lo conosco da Natale.

1192

Il "past perfect"

Il piuccheperfetto si costruisce sempre con **had** (avere) + participio passato.

I **had** had	avevo avuto
I **had** been	ero stato
I **had** done	avevo fatto
I **had** called	avevo chiamato
I **had** arrived	ero arrivato
I **had** gone	ero partito

Questo tempo verbale è usato per descrivere fatti che si sono svolti prima di un momento preciso nel passato:

When I arrived at the bus stop the bus **had** already **gone**.

Quando sono arrivato alla fermata, l'autobus era già partito.

I hurt myself in the accident because I **hadn't fastened** my seat belt.

Mi sono fatta male nell'incidente perché non avevo allacciato la cintura di sicurezza.

Gli ausiliari modali

I verbi ausiliari modali inglesi non possono essere usati da soli, e sono sempre accompagnati da un altro verbo (all'infinito e senza il **to**).

I, you, he, she, it, we, you, they	can	may	shall	will	must
Negazione:	cannot	must not	shall not	will not	must not
Forma contratta:	can't	mustn't	shan't	won't	mustn't

Questi verbi hanno la stessa forma per tutte le persone: non prendono la **-s** alla terza persona singolare.

Passato	Parafrasi	
could	to be able (to)	potere, essere in grado (di)
might	to be allowed (to)	potere, avere il diritto (di), avere il permesso (di)
would	to want, to wish (to)	volere, suggerire
should	to be obliged (to)	essere obbligato (a)

Negazione:	could not	might not	would not	should not
Forma contratta:	couldn't	mightn't	wouldn't	shouldn't

- Le forme passate di questi verbi, che si traducono spesso con il condizionale in italiano, sono spesso usate per fare una richiesta:

Could you give me ...?	Potresti darmi ...?
Would you ..., please.	Potreste per favore...
Would you like ...?	Vi piacerebbe/Vorreste ...?

Uso dei verbi ausiliari modali:

- *can* si usa:
- per esprimere capacità

Can you **ride** a horse? – No, I can't.	Sai cavalcare? – No.

- per chiedere un favore o un'autorizzazione

Can you **help** me, please?	Potresti aiutarmi per favore?
Can I **borrow** your bike? – Yes, of course you can.	Puoi prestarmi la bici? – Certo.

- per i suggerimenti

Can you **ask** your mother for the money?	Non potresti chiedere i soldi a tua madre?
Can't you **find out** on the Internet?	Non potresti cercare in Internet?

- *could* si usa:
- per formare il passato di *can*

I asked if he **could ride** a horse, but he said he **couldn't**.	Gli ho chiesto se sapesse andare a cavallo ma lui mi ha detto di no.
I **couldn't believe** it.	Non riuscivo a crederci.

- per le proposte

We **could go** for a swim this afternoon.	Potremmo andare a fare una nuotata questo pomeriggio.

- per le richieste

Please **could** I **open** a window?	Potrei aprire una finestra?
Could we **take** a break?	Potremmo fare una pausa?

- per esprimere condizioni

We **could fly** if we had wings.	Potremmo volare se avessimo le ali.

- *would* si usa
- per formare il passato di *will*

He promised he **would come** early.	Ha promesso che sarebbe arrivato presto.
I asked him to lend me his bike, but he **wouldn't**.	Gli ho chiesto di prestarmi la bici, ma mi ha detto di no.

- per chiedere gentilmente qualcosa

Please **would** you **move** your car?	Potrebbe per favore spostare la macchina?

- assieme a *like*, per esprimere suggerimenti o fare proposte

Would you **like** something to eat?	Vuoi qualcosa da mangiare?
I bet you **would like** to see the movie.	Sono sicuro che ti piacerebbe vedere il film.

– per esprimere condizioni

I **would buy** a new car if I had any money.	Comprerei una macchina nuova se avessi soldi.

- *should* si usa per esprimere:
– un comportamento da tenersi

You **shouldn't tell** lies, **should** you?	Non dovresti dire bugie, lo sai vero?

– idea del dovere

Kids **should have** supportive teachers and parents.	I bambini dovrebbero avere insegnanti e genitori che li sostengano.

– proposte e consigli

Shouldn't we **book** tickets?	Non pensi che dovremmo prenotare i biglietti?
You really **should check out** this new CD.	Dovresti veramente ascoltare questo nuovo CD.

– probabilità

The program **should work** OK.	Il programma dovrebbe funzionare bene.

- *may* si usa per esprimere:
– possibilità, eventualità

Bring a swimsuit – we **may go** swimming.	Porta un costume da bagno, che potremmo andare a nuotare.

– richiesta di favori o autorizzazioni

May I **use** your cell phone? – Yes, of course you **may**.	Potrei usare il tuo cellulare? – Sì, certo.
You **may not take** calculators into the exam.	Non si può usare calcolatrici durante l'esame.

- *might* si usa:
– per esprimere possibilità, eventualità

Take an umbrella – it **might** rain.	Prendi l'ombrello: potrebbe piovere.

– per formare il passato di *may*

We thought we **might go** swimming.	Pensammo che avremmo pututo andare a nuotare.

- *must* si usa per esprimere:
– proibizioni o ordini

You **mustn't move forward** till the light goes green.	Non devi partire finché il semaforo è verde.
The doctor told her that she **must lose** weight.	Il medico le ha detto che deve dimagrire.

– decisioni sgradevoli

I **must** get up early tomorrow.	Devo alzarmi presto domani mattina.

– necessità

We **must try** to be fair.	Dobbiamo cercare di essere giusti.

– proposte e inviti

You **must** read this book!	Devi assolutamente leggere questo libro!
You **must** come round one evening.	Devi passare da me una di queste sere.

– supposizioni o certezze

They **must have arrived** by now.	Ormai dovrebbero essere arrivati.
It **must be** nice to live in the country.	Dev'essere bello vivere in campagna.

- *need not* si usa per sottolineare che non è necessario fare qualcosa:

We **needn't get up** yet – it's only 6 o'clock.	Non dobbiamo ancora alzarci: sono appena le 6.

Il futuro e il condizionale

Il futuro si forma in genere con *will*, e il condizionale con *would* per tutte le persone. *Shall* è usato per la prima persona solo quando si vuole esprimere la forte volontà di chi parla, mentre **should** esprime sempre l'idea di qualcosa che si deve fare. Nell'inglese parlato si adopera quasi sempre la forma contratta.

Futuro		Condizionale	
I **will** go	andrò	I **would** go	andrei
you **will** go	andrai	you **would** go	andresti
he, she, it **will** go	andrà	he, she, it **would** go	andrebbe
we **will** go	andremo	we **would** go	andremmo
you **will** go	andrete	you **would** go	andreste
they **will** go	andranno	they **would** go	andrebbero
Forma contratta:	I'**ll** go, you'**ll** go, he'**ll** go, etc.		
	I'**d** go, you'**d** go, he'**d** go, etc.		

shall e *will* sono usati per esprimere:
- intenzioni

Ok, we **shall** (or we'**ll**) see you tomorrow.	Ok, ci vediamo domani.

- promesse

I **will remember** to buy milk.	Mi ricorderò di comprare il latte.

- suggerimenti, proposte

Shall we **tell** him or **shan't** we?	Dobbiamo dirglielo o no?

- conseguenze

You'll **be** late if you don't hurry.	Se non ti affretti farai tardi.

- decisioni

No, I **won't go** mountain climbing.	No, non andrò a fare scalate in montagna.

- previsioni

You'll **love** Scotland.	Ti piacerà moltissimo la Scozia.

- rifiuto

He **won't** eat his dinner.	Non vuole mangiare la cena.
The car **won't** start.	La macchina non parte.

- per sottolineare qualcosa

You will water the flowers, **won't** you?	Bagnerai i fiori, vero?

La forma interrogativa e negativa con do

Per formare la forma interrogativa e negativa dei verbi si usa il verbo ausiliare *do*, e per la forma negativa anche l'avverbio *not*.

Do you speak German?	Parli tedesco?
Does he know?	Lo sa?
Did you call her?	L'hai chiamata?

I **do not** (**don't**) speak German.	Non parlo tedesco.
He **does not** (**doesn't**) know.	Non lo sa.
I **did not** (**didn't**) call her.	Non l'ho chiamata.

Didn't he come?	Non è venuto?
Didn't she call you?	Non ti ha chiamato?

- *do* <u>non va usato</u> nelle frasi interrogative il cui soggetto è un pronome interrogativo:

Who wrote the letter?	Chi ha scritto la lettera?
Which of these trains goes to London?	Quale di questi treni va a Londra?

- e <u>non va usato</u> con gli ausiliari:

am, are, is, was, were, can, could, may, might, must, shall, should, will, would

La forma progressiva

La forma progressiva si forma con l'ausiliare *be* e il participio presente (in -**ing**). Serve a descrivere, al presente, al passato o al futuro, azioni durante il loro svolgimento, e azioni che durano ancora nel tempo o non sono ancora concluse.

I **am** work**ing**.	Lavoro./Sto lavorando.
I **was** work**ing**.	Lavoravo./Stavo lavorando.
I **will** be work**ing**.	Lavorerò./Starò lavorando.
It **is** rain**ing**.	Piove./Sta piovendo.

- I verbi che finiscono in -**e** perdono la *e* finale: arrive, arriv**ing**.
- La terminazione dei verbi in -**ie** si trasforma in **y**: lie, l**ying**.
- Anche in questo caso, come avviene per la formazione del passato, la consonante finale di molti verbi raddoppia: sto**p**, sto**pping**; trave**l**, trave**lling**.
- La forma *be going to* è utilizzata per esprimere un'azione che si svolgerà in un futuro prossimo o che si prevede certa al momento in cui si parla.

I **am going to** go to London next week.	Andrò a Londra la prossima settimana.
I **am going to** buy a new dress.	Mi comprerò un vestito nuovo.

Il gerundio

Il gerundio (verbo + -**ing**) è la forma sostantivata dell'infinito.

Smoking is dangerous.	Fumare è pericoloso.

Il passivo

La forma passiva si forma con l'ausiliare *be* e il participio passato.

The doctor examines Peter.	**Peter is examined** (by the doctor).
Il dottore visita Peter.	**Peter è visitato (dal dottore).**

Somebody stole my bike.	**My bike was stolen.**
Qualcuno mi ha rubato la bici.	La bici mi è stata rubata.

I pronomi personali

Soggetto		Oggetto	
I	io	**me**	me, mi
you	tu	**you**	te, ti
he	lui	**him**	lui, lo, gli
she	lei	**her**	lei, la, le
it	esso/essa	**it**	esso/essa, lo/la
we	noi	**us**	noi
you	voi	**you**	voi
they	loro	**them**	loro, li/le

- I pronomi personali soggetto sono <u>sempre</u> espressi in inglese:

She's very tall.	È molto alta.
I'm tired.	Sono stanco.
They're on holiday.	Sono in vacanza.

- A differenza dell'italiano, in inglese i pronomi oggetto diretti e indiretti hanno la stessa forma. Ecco alcuni esempi:

You should give it to **me**.	Devi darlo a me.
Could you give **me** your pen?	Mi daresti la tua penna?
Come with **me**.	Vieni con me.
I'll see **her** tomorrow.	La vedrò domani.
I gave **her** a pencil.	Le ho dato una matita.
I can't live without **her**.	Non posso vivere senza di lei.
He loves **them** very much.	Li ama molto.
I told **them** I wouldn't come.	Ho detto loro che non sarei venuto.

- Quando si vuole enfatizzare il pronome, va usato **_to_** (oggetto indiretto):

I gave the book **to him**.	Ho dato <u>a lui</u> il libro.
invece di: I gave him the book.	Gli ho dato il libro.

Aggettivi·e pronomi possessivi

La forma degli aggettivi e pronomi possessivi è la stessa al singolare e al plurale. In inglese pronomi e aggettivi possessivi non sono mai preceduti dall'articolo.

L'aggettivo possessivo (accompagna un sostantivo)

my	book	il mio libro	**my**	books	i miei libri
your	book	il tuo libro	**your**	books	i tuoi libri
his	book	il suo libro	**his**	books	i suoi libri
her	book	il suo libro	**her**	books	i suoi libri
its	book	il suo libro	**its**	books	i suoi libri
our	car	la nostra macchina	**our**	cars	le nostre macchine
your	car	la vostra macchina	**your**	cars	le vostre macchine
their	car	la loro macchina	**their**	cars	le loro macchine

Il pronome possessivo (usato da solo)

mine	il mio, la mia, i miei, le mie
yours	il tuo, la tua, i tuoi, le tue
his	il suo, la sua, i suoi, le sue
hers	il suo, la sua, i suoi, le sue
ours	il nostro, la nostra, i nostri, le nostre
yours	il vostro, la vostra, i vostri, le vostre
theirs	il loro, la loro, i loro, le loro

It's not my book. It's **yours**.	Non è il mio libro. È il tuo.

Gli aggettivi e i pronomi dimostrativi

La forma degli aggettivi e pronomi dimostrativi varia in funzione del numero. Questi aggettivi e pronomi esprimono la vicinanza o la lontananza (nello spazio o nel tempo).

L'aggettivo dimostrativo (accompagna un sostantivo)

Singolare:	this	questo, questa	**Plurale:**	these	questi, queste
	that	quello, quella		those	quelli, quelle

Do you prefer **this** book or **that** book?
Preferisci questo libro o quello?

These pictures are nicer than **those** pictures.
Questi quadri sono più belli di quei quadri.

Il pronome dimostrativo (usato da solo)

Singolare:	this	questo, questa	**Plurale:**	these	questi, queste
	that	quello, quella		those	quelli, quelle

This is an English book and **that** is a German book.
Questo è un libro in inglese e quello un libro in tedesco.

These are wild flowers and **those** are garden flowers.
Questi sono fiori di campo e quelli sono fiori coltivati.

I pronomi riflessivi

myself	mi	ourselves	ci
yourself	ti	yourselves	vi
himself	si	themselves	si
herself	si		
itself	si		

I enjoy **myself**.	Mi diverto.
You enjoy **yourself**.	Ti diverti.
He enjoys **himself**.	Si diverte.
She enjoys **herself**.	Si diverte.
We enjoy **ourselves**.	Ci divertiamo.
You enjoy **yourselves**.	Vi divertite.
They enjoy **themselves**.	Si divertono.

I pronomi relativi

	Persone	Cose	Persone e cose
Soggetto (Chi? Cosa?)	who	which	that
Complemento di specificazione (Di chi? Di che cosa?)	whose	of which	
Oggetto indiretto (A chi? A che cosa?)	to whom	to which	
Oggetto diretto (Chi? Che cosa?)	whom/who	which	that

Il pronome relativo ha la stessa forma al singolare e al plurale.

• Quando *that* è complemento oggetto, può essere omesso:

This is the strangest book (**that**) I've ever read.	Questo è il libro più strano che abbia mai letto.

I pronomi e gli aggettivi interrogativi

Il pronome interrogativo (usato da solo)

who?	chi?	**Who** are you?	Chi sei?
whose?	di chi?	**Whose** car is this?	Di chi è questa macchina?
whom?/**who?**	chi?	**Who**(m) did you see?	Chi hai visto?
what?	che cosa?, cosa?	**What** is that?	Cos'è quello?
which?	che?, quale?, quali?	**Which** is the quickest way?	Quale è la strada più breve?

who/*whose*/*whom* servono a porre domande in relazione a persone, *what* in relazione a cose e *which* in relazione a persone e cose (all'interno di un insieme).

• Nelle frasi interrogative le preposizioni vanno poste alla fine della frase.

Where do you come **from**?	Da dove?
What are you looking **for**?	Cosa?
What do you want this **for**?	Per che motivo?
What are you laughing **at**?	Di cosa?
Who are you speaking **to**?	Con chi?

- Oggi, sia all'orale che allo scritto, si utilizza quasi esclusivamente *who* piuttosto di *whom* per il complemento oggetto diretto e indiretto. *Who* non va mai posto subito dopo una preposizione. In questi casi la preposizione si mette spesso alla fine della frase:

The man (**who**) he sold his car to... *invece di:* The man <u>to</u> **whom** he sold his car...	L'uomo a cui ha venduto la macchina...
Who did you buy the flowers for? *invece di:* <u>For</u> **whom** did you buy the flowers?	Per chi hai comprato i fiori?

L'aggettivo interrogativo (accompagna un sostantivo)

What book?	Quale libro?
What English songs?	Quali canzoni inglesi?
Which book?	Quale libro? *(tra più libri)*

I pronomi indefiniti: some e any

1. some/somebody/someone/something

some e i suoi composti sono usati:
- nelle frasi affermative

I'd like **some** strawberry jam.	Vorrei della marmellata di fragole.
Give me **some** stamps, please.	Mi dia qualche francobollo, per favore.
Somebody/Someone has stolen my wallet.	Qualcuno mi ha rubato il portafoglio.
I'd like **something** to drink.	Vorrei bere qualcosa.

- nelle frasi interrogative per le quali ci si aspetta una risposta positiva.

May I have **some** more tea, please? – Yes, of course.	Potrei avere ancora un po' di tè, per favore? – Certo.

2. any/anybody/anyone/anything

any e i suoi composti sono usati:
- nelle frasi negative

I haven't **any** friends in London.	Non ho amici a Londra.

- nelle frasi interrogative per le quali la risposta è incerta

Is there **anybody/anyone** who speaks Italian?	C'è nessuno che parla italiano qui?
Do you have **any** stamps?	Avete francobolli di qualche tipo?
Can I do **anything** for you?	Posso fare niente per te?

- nelle frasi che esprimono una condizione

If I had **any** stamps I would mail the letter.	Se avessi francobolli spedirei la lettera.

I pronomi indefiniti **somebody/someone**, **anybody/anyone**, **nobody/no one** e **everybody/everyone** sono singolari, ma si possono usare anche per il plurale.

Phone **everybody** and tell **them** about the change of the plan	Telefona a tutti e dì loro che c'è stato un cambiamento di programma.

Verbi irregolari inglesi
English Irregular Verbs

Infinitive	Past	Past Participle	Infinitive	Past	Past Participle
abide	abided	abided	creep	crept	crept
arise	arose	arisen	cut	cut	cut
awake	awaked, awoke	awaked, awoken	deal	dealt	dealt
			dig	dug	dug
be	was *(I/he/she/it)*, were *(you/we/they)*	been	dive	dived, dove	dived
			do	did	done
			draw	drew	drawn
bear	bore	borne	dream	dreamed, dreamt	dreamed, dreamt
beat	beat	beaten	drink	drank	drunk
become	became	become	drive	drove	driven
beget	begot	begotten	dwell	dwelt, dwelled	dwelt, dwelled
begin	began	begun			
behold	beheld	beheld	eat	ate	eaten
bend	bent	bent	fall	fell	fallen
beseech	besought, beseeched	besought, beseeched	feed	fed	fed
beset	beset	beset	feel	felt	felt
bet	bet	bet	fight	fought	fought
bid	bid, bad, *say* bade	bid, *say* bidden	find	found	found
			flee	fled	fled
bind	bound	bound	fling	flung	flung
bite	bit	bitten	fly	flew	flown
bleed	bled	bled	forbid	forbade, forbad	forbidden
blow	blew	blown			
break	broke	broken	forget	forgot	forgotten
breed	bred	bred	forsake	forsook	forsaken
bring	brought	brought	freeze	froze	frozen
build	built	built	get	got	gotten, got
burn	burned, burnt	burned, burnt	gild	gilded, gilt	gilded, gilt
burst	burst	burst	gird	girded, girt	girded, girt
buy	bought	bought	give	gave	given
can	could	-	go	went	gone
cast	cast	cast	grind	ground	ground
catch	caught	caught	grow	grew	grown
choose	chose	chosen	hang	hung, LAW hanged	hung, LAW hanged
cleave *(cut)*	cleft, cleaved, clove	cleft, cleaved, cloven	have	had	had
cling	clung	clung	hear	heard	heard
come	came	come	heave	heaved, NAUT hove	heaved, NAUT hove
cost	cost, *vt* costed	cost, *vt* costed			

Infinitive	Past	Past Participle	Infinitive	Past	Past Participle
hew	hewed	hewn, hewed	sew	sewed	sewn, sewed
hide	hid	hidden	shake	shook	shaken
hit	hit	hit	shave	shaved	shaved, shaven
hold	held	held	shear	sheared	sheared, shorn
hurt	hurt	hurt	shed	shed	shed
keep	kept	kept	shine	shone	shone
kneel	knelt, kneeled	knelt, kneeled	shit	shit, shitted	shat
know	knew	known	shoe	shod	shod
lade	laded	laden	shoot	shot	shot
lay	laid	laid	show	showed	shown, showed
lead	led	led	shrink	shrank	shrunk
leap	leaped, leapt	leaped, leapt	shut	shut	shut
learn	learned, learnt	learned, learnt	sing	sang	sung
leave	left	left	sink	sank	sunk
lend	lent	lent	sit	sat	sat
let	let	let	sleep	slept	slept
lie	lay	lain	slide	slid	slid
light	lighted, lit	lighted, lit	sling	slung	slung
lose	lost	lost	slink	slunk	slunk
make	made	made	slit	slit	slit
may	might	-	smell	smelled, smelt	smelled, smelt
mean	meant	meant	smite	smote	smitten
meet	met	met	sow	sowed	sown, sowed
mistake	mistook	mistaken	speak	spoke	spoken
mow	mowed	mown, mowed	speed	sped, speeded	sped, speeded
pay	paid	paid	spell	spelled, spelt	spelled, spelt
put	put	put	spend	spent	spent
quit	quit, quitted	quit, quitted	spill	spilled, spilt	spilled, spilt
read [rid]	read [red]	read [red]	spin	spun	spun
rend	rent, rended	rent, rended	spit	spat	spat
rid	rid	rid	split	split	split
ride	rode	ridden	spoil	spoiled, spoilt	spoiled, spoilt
ring	rang	rung	spread	spread	spread
rise	rose	risen	spring	sprang, sprung	sprung
run	ran	run	stand	stood	stood
saw	sawed	sawed, sawn	steal	stole	stolen
say	said	said	stick	stuck	stuck
see	saw	seen	sting	stung	stung
seek	sought	sought	stink	stank, stunk	stunk
sell	sold	sold	strew	strewed	strewn, strewed
send	sent	sent	stride	strode	stridden
set	set	set	strike	struck	struck

Infinitive	Past	Past Participle	Infinitive	Past	Past Participle
string	strung	strung	throw	threw	thrown
strive	strove	striven, strived	thrust	thrust	thrust
swear	swore	sworn	tread	trod	trodden, trod
sweep	swept	swept	wake	waked, woke	waked, woken
swell	swelled	swollen, swelled	wear	wore	worn
swim	swam	swum	weave	wove	woven
swing	swung	swung	weep	wept	wept
take	took	taken	win	won	won
teach	taught	taught	wind	wound	wound
tear	tore	torn	wring	wrung	wrung
tell	told	told	write	wrote	written
think	thought	thought			
thrive	thrived, throve	thrived, thriven			

Prefixes and suffixes: Italian-English
Prefissi e suffissi: italiano-inglese

Prefix	English Equivalents	Meanings and Uses	Examples	English Equivalents
a-[1]	a-	lack of, absence	apolitico	apolitical
a-[2]	a-	1. towards direction 2. formation of verbs from nouns	accorrere accasare	run up to marry off
acro-	acro-	high, height	Acropoli	Acropolis
ad-	ad-	variant of a-	adattare	adapt
aero-	aero-, air-	relating to air, air travel	aeroporto	airport
afro-	Afro-	African	Afro-caribico	Afro-Caribbean
agora-	agora-	relating to crowded or open spaces	agorafobia	agoraphobia
agri-	agri-	relating to fields	agricoltura	agriculture
agro-	c	variant of agri-	agronomia	agronomy
allo-	allo-	different from	allopatia	allopathy
ambi-	ambi-	both	ambivalente	ambivalent
an-	an-	variant of a-	anarchia	anarchy
ana-[1]	ana-	lack of, absence	anabattista	Anabaptist
ana-[2]	ana-	back	anagramma	anagram
andro-	andro-	man	androgino	androgynous
anfi-	amphi-	around	anfiteatro	amphitheater
anglo-	Anglo-	English	angloamericano	Anglo-American
ant(i)-	ant(i)-	1. opposition in location 2. opposition in action	antartico antigelo	Antarctic antifreeze
anti-, ante-	ante-, pre-	preceding something else	antidiluviano anticamera antecedente	antediluvian antechamber previous
antropo-	anthropo-	relating to human beings	antropologia	anthropology
acqua-	aqua-	water	acquarello	watercolor
archeo-	arch(a)e-	old; ancient	archeologia	archeology
arci-, archi-	arch-	superior; chief	arcivescovo archi-mandrita	archbishop archimandrite
arci-		very, much	arcinoto	very well known
astro-	astro-	relating to stars or outer space	astronauta	astronaut
audio-	audio-	relating to sounds or hearing	audiovisivo	audiovisual
auri-	auri-	gold	aurifero	auriferous
austro-	Austro-	Austrian	austrungarico	Austro-Hungarian
auto-[1]	auto-, self	oneself	autodifesa autobiografia	self-defense autobiography
auto-[2]	auto-	vehicle	autobus	bus
avan-	fore-, avant-	ahead, before	avambraccio avan-guardia	forearm avant-garde

Prefix	English Equivalents	Meanings and Uses	Examples	English Equivalents
avi-	avi-	1. birds 2. planes	avicoltore aviazione	bird breeder aviation
avio-	avi-	relating to planes	aviotrasporto	air transport
baro-	baro-	pressure	barometro	barometer
bi-	bi-	two or twice	bicentenario	bicentennial
biblio-	biblio-	book	biblioteca	library
bio-	bio-	relating to life	biografia biologia	biography biology
bis-	great-	used with relatives	bisavolo	great-grandfather
caco-	caco-	bad	cacofonia	cacophony
capo-		head	capostazione	station master
cardio-	cardio-	heart	cardiologo	cardiologist
cento-	centi-	hundred	centopiedi centometrista	centipede hundred meters runner
chiro-	chiro-	hand	chiropratico	chiropractor
ciber-	cyber-	computer-controlled	ciberspazio	cyberspace
ciclo-	cyclo-	1. circle 2. cycle	ciclone cicloturismo	cyclone cycling holidays
circon-, circum-	circum-	around	circonferenza circumnavigare	circumference circumnavigate
cis-	cis-	on this side of	cispadano	cispadane
co-	co-	variant of con-	coautore coabitare	co-author cohabit
con-	con-	with; together	connazionale congresso	compatriot congress
contra-	contra-	see contro-	contraddizione	contradiction
contro-	counter-	1. opposite 2. verification 3. reciprocity	controtendenza controanalisi controbilanciare	countertrend further test counterbalance
cosmo-	cosmo-	world, universe	cosmonauta	cosmonaut
crio-	cryo-	cold	crioterapia	cryotherapy
cripto-	crypto-	hidden	criptare	encrypt
critto-	crypto-	variant of cripto-	crittografia	cryptography
crom(o)-	chrom(o)-	color	cromatico	chromatic
cron(o)-	chron(o)-	time	cronologia	chronology
de-	de-	1. distance, separation 2. removal 3. lower 4. intensifier	deviare decalcificare degradare designare	deviate decalcify debase designate
deca-	deca-	multiplied by ten	decametro	decameter
deci-	deci-	divided by ten	decimetro	decimeter
demo-[1]	demo-	people	democrazia	democracy
demo-[2]	demo-	democracy	democristiano	Christian Democrat
derma-	derma-	skin	dermatologo	dermatologist

Prefix	English Equivalents	Meanings and Uses	Examples	English Equivalents
di-[1]	di-	two	disillabico	disyllabic
di-[2]	de-	downwards	discendere	descend
dia-	dia-	across	diapositiva diacronico	slide (film) diachronic
dis-[1]	dis-	1. not 2. separation	disattento disabile disgiungere	inattentive disabled separate
dis-[2]	dys-	alteration, anomaly	disfunzione	dysfunction
dopo-	after-	after	doposole dopolavoro	aftersun recreational activities
e-[1]	e-	outside; toward the outside	emettere	emit
e-[2]	e-	transformation	edulcorare	sweeten
eco-	eco-	environment	ecologia	ecology
ego-	ego-	I	egocentrico	egocentric
elettro-	electro-	electrical	elettrostatico	electrostatic
eli-	heli-	helicopter	eliporto	heliport
emato-	hemo-	blood; variant of emo-	ematopatia	hemopathy
emi-	hemi-	half	emisfero	hemisphere
emo-	hemo-	blood	emofilia	hemophilia
endo-	endo-	into; toward the inside	endocrinologia	endocrinology
eno-	(o)eno-	wine	enologo	(o)enologist
entomo-	entomo-	insect	entomologia	entomology
epi-	epi-	on; in	epigrafe	epigraph
equi-	equi-	1. equality 2. horse	equivalente equitazione	equivalent (horse) riding
es-	ex-	1. outside; toward the outside 2. removal	esportare esfoliare esautorare	export exfoliate deprive of power
esa-	hexa-	six	esagono	hexagon
eso-	ex-	outside	esodo	exodus
etero-	hetero-	different	eterosessuale	heterosexual
etno-	ethno-	people, race	etnologia	ethnology
etto-	hecto-	hundred	ettogrammo	hectogram
eu-	eu-	well	eucalipto	eucalyptus
euro-	Euro-	European	europarlamento	European Parliament
ex-	ex-	former	ex-ministro	ex-minister
extra-	extra-	1. outside 2. more than; better than	extraparlamentare extravergine	extra-parliamentary extra virgin
fanta-		fantasy	fantascienza	science fiction
fil(o)-[1]	phil(o)-, pro-	liking	filocinese filantropia	pro-Chinese philanthropy
fil(o)-[2]		cable	filodiffusione	cable radio
fisio-	physio-	body	fisionomia	physiognomy

Prefix	English Equivalents	Meanings and Uses	Examples	English Equivalents
fleb(o)-	phleb(o)-	vein	flebite	phlebitis
fono-	phono-	relating to voice or sound	fonologia	phonology
foto-	photo-	photography	fotocopia	photocopy
franco-	Franco-	French	francofono	Francophone
gastr(o)-	gastr(o)-	relating to the stomach or abdomen	gastrico	gastric
giga-	giga-	billion	gigawatt	gigawatt
gineco-	gyneco-	relating to the female anatomy	ginecologo	gynecologist
giro-	gyro-	circle	giroscopio	gyroscope
geo-	geo-	relating to the Earth	geografia	geography
glotto-	glotto-	language	glottologia	glottology
graf(o)-	graph(o)-	writing	grafologia	graphology
guard(i)a-		keeper	guardalinee guardiacaccia	linesman gamekeeper
idro-	hydro-	water	idrofobo	hydrophobic
il-	il-	1. negation 2. formation of verbs; variant of in- before l	illeggibile illuminare	illegible illuminate
im-	im-	1. negation 2. variant of in- before b, m, p	impreciso impaccare	imprecise pack
in-[1]	in-	negation	infedele	unfaithful
in-[2]	in-	1. start of a condition 2. in; into	infiammare insaccare	inflame put into a sack
indo-	Indo-	Indian	indoeuropeo	Indo-European
infra-	infra-	1. below 2. between	infrarosso infradito	infrared thong
inter-	inter-	between	interazione	interaction
intra-	intra-	in; inside	intramuscolare	intramuscular
intro-	intro-	in; into	introdurre	introduce
ir-	ir-, in-	negation; variant of in- before r	irresistibile	irresistible
iper-	hyper-	above normal; excessive	ipermercato ipersensibile	hypermarket hypersensitive
ipno-	hypno-	sleep	ipnotizzare	hypnotize
ipo-	hypo-	below normal; insufficient	ipocalorico ipotensione	low-calorie hypotension
ippo-		horse	ippodromo	racecourse
iso-	iso-	equivalence	isoscele	isosceles
ispano-	Hispano-; Spanish-	Spanish	ispanoamericano	Hispano-American
istero-	hystero-	uterus	isterectomia	hysterectomy
isto-	histo-	relating to organic tissues	istologia	histology
italo-	Italo-	Italian	italoamericano	Italo-American

Prefix	English Equivalents	Meanings and Uses	Examples	English Equivalents
kilo-	kilo-	one thousand	kilogrammo	kilogram
kinesi-	kine(si)-	movement	kinesiterapia	physical therapy
latto-	lacto-	milk	lattosio	lactose
lipo-	lipo-	fat	liposuzione	liposuction
lito-	litho-	stone	litografia	lithograph
logo-		language	logopedista	speech therapist
ludo-		play	ludoteca	toy library
macro-	macro-	big	macroeconomico	macroeconomic
mal-	mal-, mis-, ill-	bad; badly	malavoglia male-ducato	ill-will ill-mannered
mani-	mani-	hand	manicure	manicure
maxi-	maxi-	very large; very long	maxischermo	maxiscreen
mega-	mega-	1. very large; huge 2. one million	megalite megahertz	megalith megahertz
megalo-	megalo-	very large; huge	megalopoli	megalopolis
meta-	meta-	1. change, trans-formation 2. after 3. beyond	metamorfosi metatarso metalinguaggio	metamorphosis metatarsal metalanguage
metr(o)-	metr(o)-	1. measurement 2. mother	metronomo metropoli	metronome metropolis
micro-	micro-	small	microrganismo	micro-organism
milli-	milli-	one thousandth	milligrammo	milligram
mini-	mini-	small	minibus	minibus
mis-	mis-	1. negation 2. pejorative	misconoscere misfatto	disregard misdeed
mono-	mon(o)-	single; only	monogamia	monogamy
morfo-	morph(o)-	relating to shape or form	morfologia	morphology
moto-	moto(r)-	relating to an engine or motor	motoscafo	motorboat
multi-	multi-	several; many	multiculturale	multicultural
narco-[1]	narco-	sleep	narcosi	narcosis
narco-[2]	narco-	drug	narcotraffico	drug trafficking
necro-	necro-	relating to death	necropoli	necropolis
nefr(o)-	nephr(o)-	kidney	nefrite	nephritis
neo-	neo-	new	neocolonialismo	neocolonialism
neuro-	neur(o)-	relating to nerves	neurologia	neurology
nevr-	neur(o)-	variant of neuro-	nevralgico	neuralgic
non-	non-	negation	non-aggressione	nonaggression
olo-	holo-	whole	olocausto	holocaust
omeo-	homeo-	similar	omeopatia	homeopathy
omo-	homo-	similar; same	omogeneo	homogenous
onni-	omni-	all	onnivoro	omnivorous
ornito-	ornitho-	bird	ornitologia	ornithology

Prefix	English Equivalents	Meanings and Uses	Examples	English Equivalents
oro-	or(e)o-	mountain	orografia	orography
orto-	ortho-	1. correct 2. straight	ortografia ortodonzia	orthography orthodontics
osteo-	osteo-	bone	osteoporosi	osteoporosis
ott(o)-	oct(o)-	eight	ottagono	octagon
ov(i)-	ov-	egg	ovaio	ovary
paleo-	paleo-	old; ancient	paleontologia	paleontology
pan-	pan-	all	panteismo	pantheism
para-	para-	1. similar 2. beside 3. protecting against	paramilitare paramedico paracadute	paramilitary paramedical parachute
pato-	patho-	illness	patologia	pathology
ped(i)-	ped(i)-	relating to feet	pedicure	podiatrist
pedo-	ped(o)-	child	pedofilia	pedophilia
penta-	penta-	five	pentagono	pentagon
per-	per-	across	permeabile	permeable
peri-	peri-	around	perimetro	perimeter
piro-	pyro-	fire	piromane	pyromaniac
pluri-	multi-, poly-	more than one	pluricellulare	multicellular
pneum(o)-	pneum(o)-	lung	pneumologo	lung specialist
podo-	pod(o)-	relating to feet; see ped-	podologo	podiatrist
poli-	poly-	many; much	poliedro	polyhedron
porno-	porn-	pornographic	pornostar	porn star
pos(t)-	post-	after	poscritto postdatare	postscript postdate
pre-	pre-, fore-	before	precedere prevedere	precede foresee
pro-	pro-	1. instead of 2. used with relatives 3. forward	prorettore prozia prologo	pro-rector great-aunt prologue
proto-	prot(o)-	first	prototipo	prototype
pseudo-	pseudo-	false	pseudonimo	pseudonym
psico-	psycho-	mind	psicoterapeuta	psychotherapist
quadr-	quadr-	four	quadrangolare	quadrangular
quint-	quint-	five	quintuplo	quintuplets
radi(o)-[1]	rad(io)-	rays	radiatore	radiator
radi(o)-[2]	rad(io)-	radium	radioattivo	radioactive
radi(o)-[3]	rad(io)-	radio	radiofonico	radio
re-	re-	1. again 2. change of direction	reiterare respingere	reiterate reject
retro-	retro-	back; backward	retroattivo	retroactive
rett(o)-	rect(i)-	straight	rettificare	rectify

Prefix	English Equivalents	Meanings and Uses	Examples	English Equivalents
ri-	re-	1. again 2. change of direction 3. used with verbs to add emphasis	riformulare rigettare ricercare	reformulate reject refined
rin(o)-	rhin(o)-	nose	rinite	rhinitis
s-	dis-	1. negation 2. movement away from 3. formation of verbs from other verbs	sfiorire svantaggio sfuggire sbiancare	wither disadvantage flee whiten
sclero-	sclero-	hardening	sclerosi	sclerosis
semi-	semi-	half	semiconduttore	semiconductor
seri-	seri-	silk	serigrafia	serigraphy
servo-	servo-	help	servosterzo servofreno	power steering servo brake
sidero-		iron	siderurgico	iron and steel
si(n)-	sy(n)-, syl-, sym-	together	sincronizzare	synchronize
sino-	Sino-	China	sinologo	Sinologist
sism(o)-	seism(o)-	earthquake	sismografo	seismograph
socio-	socio-	society	sociologia	sociology
sol(i)-	sol(i)-, solo-	alone	solitario	solitary
sopra-	over-	1. on; over 2. in addition 3. too much	sopracciglia soprascarpe soprannome sopravvalutare	eyebrow overshoe nickname overestimate
sor-		over; variant of sopra-	sorvolare	fly over
sotto-	sub-	1. below 2. lack of 3. with verbs	sottosuolo sottoalimentare sottointendere	subsoil undernourished imply
sovra-	over-	variant of sopra-	sovrascrivere sovrapproduzione	overwrite overproduction
speleo-	speleo-	cave	speleologia	speleology
stereo-	stereo-	solid	stereofonico	stereophonic
stra-	over-	1. too much 2. beyond normal	strafare straordinario	overdo extraordinary
strato-	strato-	layer	stratosfera	stratosphere
sub-	sub-	1. below; to a lower level 2. dependence	suburbano subordinare	suburban subordinate
super-	super-	1. above 2. the highest level	supervisione supersonico	supervision supersonic
sur-	sur-, over-, out-	1. higher; above 2. a higher degree or extent	surriscaldato sur-reale surclassare	overheated surreal outclass
tachi-	tach(e)-, tach(y)-	speed	tachimetro	speedometer
tecn(o)-	techn(o)	technical	tecnologia	technology

Prefix	English Equivalents	Meanings and Uses	Examples	English Equivalents
tele-[1]	tel(e)-	far	telecomando	remote control
tele-[2]	tel(e)-	TV	telefilm	TV movie
teo-	theo-	God	teocrazia	theocracy
term(o)-	therm(o)-	heat	termocoperta	electric blanket
tetr(a)-	tetr(a)-	four	tetraplegico	tetraplegic
tipo-	typo-	imprint, character	tipografia	typography
topo-	topo-	place	toponimo	place name
tra-	trans-	1. change, trans-formation 2. beyond; across	tradurre transitare trasparire	translate pass through show through
trans-	trans-	beyond; across; variant of tra-	transalpino transizione	transalpine transition
tre-	tri-	variant of tri-	treppiede	tripod
tri-	tri-	three	triangolo	triangle
tropo-	trop(o)-	turning	troposfera	troposphere
ultra-	ultra-	extreme or excessive	ultramoderno	ultramodern
uni-	uni-	alone; one	uniforme	uniform
vice-	vice-	in place of	vicepresidente	vice-president
video-	video-	TV	videocassetta	videocassette
xeno-	xeno-	foreign	xenofobia	xenophobia
xilo-	xylo-	wood	xilofono	xylophone
zoo-	zoo-	relating to animals	zoologia	zoology

Suffix	English Equivalents	Resulting gramm. category	Meanings and Uses	Examples	English Equivalents
-a		n. – adj.	regular formation of feminine of nouns and adjectives	bambina	girl
-abile	-able	adj.	formation of adjectives with meaning of possibility/ability from verbs	affidabile	reliable
-abilità	-ability	n.	formation of nouns from adjectives in –abile	affidabilità	reliability
-acchione		n. – adj.	augmentative, diminutive, pejorative	furbacchione	crafty (fellow)
-acchiotto/ -acchiotta		n. – adj.	diminutive	orsacchiotto	teddy bear
-accio/ -accia		n.	1. pejorative; augmentative 2. formation of nouns from verbs	odoraccio coltellaccio strofinaccio	nasty smell big knife cloth
-accione/ -acciona		n. – adj.	augmentative, pejorative	pasticcione	bungler *n.*, bungling *adj.*
-aceo/ -acea	-aceous	adj.	similar in quality or form	rosaceo	rosaceous
-aggine		n.	negative condition or quality	infingardaggine	laziness
-aggio	-ing	n.	action, result of an action	canottaggio lavaggio	canoeing washing
-aglio/ -aglia		n.	instrument derogatory	ventaglio tenaglia ferraglia marmaglia	fan pliers scrap (iron) (bunch of) kids
-aio/-aia[1]	-ery, -ary	n.	1. place with plants/ crops 2. place for particular purpose	granaio colombaia	granary dovecote
-aio/-aia[2]	-or	n.	profession	marinaio	sailor
-aiolo/ -aiola		n.	profession	pizzaiolo	pizza chef
-ale	-al, -y	adj.	1. relating to something 2. belonging to something	invernale aggettivale	winter, wintry adjectival
-algia	-algia	n.	pain	nevralgia	neuralgia
-ame		n.	collective noun	legname	timber
-ando[1]		n.	relating to something which is to happen	cresimando	confirmand
-ando[2]		v.	formation of gerund	mangiando	eating
-andro		n.	man	scafandro	diving suit
-aneo/ -anea	-aneous	adj.	relating to something	cutaneo	cutaneous
-ano/-ana	-an	adj. – n.	origin, language	cubano romano isolano	Cuban Roman islander

Suffix	English Equivalents	Resulting gramm. category	Meanings and Uses	Examples	English Equivalents
-ante	-ant, -er	adj. – n.	present participle	commerciante amante	trader lover
-anza	-ance, -ence	n.	1. state 2. action, result of an action 3. quality	lontananza concordanza arroganza	distance concordance arrogance
-arca	-arch	n.	governing person	monarca	monarch
-archia	-archy	n.	government	monarchia	monarchy
-ardo/ -arda		adj. – n.	pejorative	beffardo bugiardo	mocking lying *adj.*, liar *n.*
-are[1]		v.	infinitive, 1st conjugation	amare	love
-are[2]		adj.	1. relating to something 2. quality	polmonare salutare	pulmonary healthy
-ariato	-ariat	n.	Function	segretariato	secretariat
-ario/-aria		adj. – n.	1. containing or enclosing something 2. relating to something	questionario universitario	questionnaire university
-astro/ -astra	-ish	adj. – n.	1. pejorative 2. approximate	giovinastro bluastro	hoodlum bluish
-atario/ -ataria		adj. – n.	performer of an action	Locatario	tenant
-ata		n.	formation of nouns from nouns or verbs; see also -ato/-ata	nevicata	snowfall
-ate		adj. – n.	origin	ravennate	from Ravenna
-ato		n.	1. condition, profession 2. function 3. office	artigianato volontariato papato	artisans voluntary service papacy
-ato/-ata	-ed	adj.	past participle of verbs in -are	amato	loved
-azzo		n.	pejorative	andazzo	latest trend
-cardia	-cardia	n.	heart	tachicardia	tachycardia
-cefalo/ -cefala	-cephalus	n. – adj.	head	idrocefalo	hydrocephalus
-centrico/ -centrica	-centric	adj.	having its center in	egocentrico	egocentric
-cida	-cide, -cidal	n. – adj.	killer	omicida fratricida	murderer *n*, homicidal *adj.* fratricide *n.*, fratricidal *adj.*
-cidio	-cide	n.	act of killing	omicidio fratricidio	murder fratricide
-cinesi	-cinesia, -kinesia	n.	movement	ipercinesi	hyperkinesis
-cita	-cyte	n.	cell	leucocita	leukocyte
-colo/ -cola	-culum	adj.- n.	1. relating to something 2. small	agricolo cubicolo	agricultural cubiculum

Suffix	English Equiva-lents	Resulting gramm. category	Meanings and Uses	Examples	English Equivalents
-coltore/ -coltrice		n.	who cultivates	agricoltore	farmer
-coltura	-culture	n.	cultivation	viticoltura	viticulture
-comio		n.	hospital	manicomio	mental hospital
-cosmo	-cosm	n.	universe	microcosmo	microcosm
-crate	-crat	n.	person who has power	burocrate	bureaucrat
-crazia	-cracy	n.	1. power 2. governing class	partitocrazia aristocrazia	party power aristocracy
-cromia	-chromy	n.	color	policromia	polychromy
-cromo/ -croma	-chrome	adj	color	policromo	polychrome
-crono/ -crona	-cronous	adj.	time	sincrono	synchronous
-derma	-derm, -dermis	n.	skin	pachiderma epidermico	pachyderm epi-dermic
-dimensio-nale	-dimen-sional	adj.	bidimensional	bidimen-sionale	two-dimensional
-dino/-dina	-dyne	adj.	force, intensity	anodino	anodyne
-dipen-dente	-aholic	adj.- n.	dependence on some-thing	videodipen-dente lavoro-dipendente	video addict(ed) workaholic
-dotto		n.	course	viadotto	viaduct
-dromo	-drome	n.	place for races	ippodromo	racecourse
-efico/ -efica	-ficial	adj.	which does, creates	benefico	beneficial
-ellare		v.	diminutive and repeti-tive movement	saltellare	skip
-ellino/ -ellina		n.	small	sorellina ombrellino	little sister parasol
-ello/-ella		n.	small	campanello	bell
-emia	-emia	n.	relating to blood	setticemia	septicemia
-endo[1]		n.	relating to something which is to happen	addendo	addend
-endo[2]		v.	formation of gerund	credendo	believing
-enne	year(s)-old	n. – adj.	years of age	quindicenne	fifteen-year-old *adj.*, fifteen year old *n.*
-ennio		n.	period	decennio	decade
-ente	-ent	n. – adj.	1. performing an action 2. quality	presidente fluorescente	president fluorescent
-enza	-ance, -ence	n.	1. action, result of an action 2. quality	presidenza esigenza	presidency need
-eo/-ea		adj.	similar in quality or form	vitreo	glass
-ere		v.	infinitive, 2nd conju-gation	vedere credere	see believe

Suffix	English Equivalents	Resulting gramm. category	Meanings and Uses	Examples	English Equivalents
-eria	-ing, -er's	n.	1. quality 2. action, result of an action 3. shop	tirchieria pirateria gioielleria	stinginess piracy jeweler's shop
-esco/-esca	-ish, -ean	adj.	1. having appearance of 2. relating to	moresco dantesco	Moorish Dantean
-ese[1]		adj. – n.	1. origin 2. language	genovese francese	Genoese French
-ese[2]		n.	pejorative	burocratese	officialese
-esimo/-esima	-th	adj. – n.	in numerals	millesimo	thousandth
-essa	-ess	n.	female	principessa leonessa	princess lioness
-eta, -eto		n.	cultivated place	pineta frutteto	pine forest orchard
-ettare		v.	diminutive and repetitive	zampettare	trot
-ettino/-ettina		n.	diminutive	berrettino	small beret
-etto/-etta		n. – adj.	1. formation of nouns and adjectives from verbs 2. diminutive	fischietto giardinetto piccoletto	whistle small garden tiny
-evole		adj.	formation of adjectives from nouns and verbs	consapevole	aware
-ezza	-ness	n.	abstract nouns	amarezza	bitterness
-fagia	-phagia	n.	eating	aerofagia	aerophagia
-fago/-faga	-phageous	adj. n.	eating	antropofago	anthropophagous
-fare	-fy	v.	action	liquefare	liquefy
-fero/-fera	-ferous	n.- adj	1. containing 2. producing	conifera frigorifero	coniferous refrigerating *adj.*, refrigerator *n.*
-ficare	-fy	v.	action	amplificare prolificare	amplify proliferate
-ficio		n.	place of production	panificio	bakery
-fico/-fica	-fic	adj.	doing	malefico calorifico	evil calorific
-filia	-philia	n.	love of	pedofilia	pedophilia
-filo/-fila	-phile	adj. – n.	who loves	cinefilo	cinema buff
-fobia	-phobia	n.	aversion to	claustrofobia	claustrophobia
-fobo/-foba	-phobic, -phobe	adj. – n.	with aversion to	idrofobo	hydrophobic *adj.*, hydrophobe *n.*
-fonia	-phony	n.	sound	stereofonia	stereophony
-fonico/-fonica	-phonic	adj.	relating to sound	sinfonico	symphonic

Suffix	English Equiva-lents	Resulting gramm. category	Meanings and Uses	Examples	English Equivalents
-fono/-fona	– phone	adj. – n.	speaking	anglofono	Anglophone
-forico/-forica	-phoric(al)	adj.	formation of adjectives from nouns	metaforico	metaphoric(al)
-forme	-form, -shaped	adj.	having the shape of	cruciforme	cross-shaped
-foro	-phore	n.	bearing	semaforo	semaphore
-frenia	-phrenia	n.	mind	schizofrenia	schizophrenia
-frenico/-frenica	-phrenic	adj. – n.	relating to the mind	schizofrenico	schizophrenic
-fugo/-fuga	-repellant	adj. – n.	repellant	insettifugo	insect-repellant
-gamia	-gamy	n.	marriage	poligamia	polygamy
-gamo/-gama	-gamous	adj. – n.	relating to marriage	poligamo	polygamous
-genico/-genica	-genic	adj.	which can be repro-duced	fotogenico, transgenico	photogenic gen-etically modified
-geno/-gena	-genic	adj. – n.	giving origin to	patogeno	pathogenic
-gino/-gina	-gynous, -gyne	adj. – n.	woman	androgino	androgynous *adj.*, androgyne *n.*
-gione		n.	action, result of an action	impiccagione	hanging
-gnosi	-gnosis	n.	knowledge	prognosi	prognosis
-gnostico/-gnostica	-gnostic	adj. n.	formation of nouns and adjectives	agnostico	agnostic
-gono	-gon	n.	angle	pentagono	pentagon
-grado/-grada		adj. – n.	walking	plantigrado	plantigrade
-grafia	-graphy	n.	1. writing 2. science or art of	ortografia oceanografia	orthography oceanography
-grafico/-grafica	-gra phic(al)	adj.	formation of adjectives from nouns in -grafia and -grafo	ortografico	orthographic(al)
-grafo/-grafa	-grapher	n.	who writes	biografo	biographer
-grafo	-graph	n.	instrument which writes	sismografo	seismograph
-gramma	-gram	n.	writing	telegramma	telegram
-grammo	-gram	n.	weight	chilogrammo	kilogram
-ia[1]		n	quality	cortesia astuzia	courtesy astute-ness
-ia[2]		n	1. abstract nouns 2. place	fobia birreria	phobia pub
-iale	-ial	adj.	see -ale	industriale	industrial
-iano/-iana	-ial	adj. – n.	formation of adjectives and nouns from proper nouns	parmigiano	Parmesan

Suffix	English Equivalents	Resulting gramm. category	Meanings and Uses	Examples	English Equivalents
-iasi	-iasis	n.	illness, condition	elefantiasi	elephantiasis
-iatra	-trist, -trician	n.	doctor	pediatra	pediatrician
-iatria	-iatrics, -iatry	n.	treatment	geriatria	geriatrics
-iatrico/ -iatrica	-iatrico	adj.	formation of adjectives from nouns in -iatria	psichiatrico	psychiatric
-ibile	-able, -ible	adj.	possibility, ability	prevedibile	foreseeable
-icare		v.	formation of verbs from adjectives and nouns	nevicare	snow
-iccio/ -iccia		adj.	approximate	bianchiccio	whiteish
-icello/ -icella	-icle	n.	diminutive	orticello particella	little orchard particle
-iciattolo/ -iciattola		n.	diminutive, pejorative	fiumiciattolo	little river
-icino/ -icina		n.	diminutive	posticino	tiny place
-ico/-ica	-ic, -ical	adj.	relating to something	poetico matematico	poetic(al) mathematical
-ide	-id	n.	member of a zoological family	aracnide	arachnid
-iere/-iera		n.	1. profession 2. formation of nouns from nouns	giardiniere pattumiera candeliere	gardener trash can candlestick
-ificare	-ify	v.	see –ficare	codificare semplificare	codify simplify
-ile		adj.	formation of adjectives from verbs and nouns	febbrile	feverish
-ina		n.	1. formation of feminine 2. diminutive 3. place 4. numeral	gallina manina cantina dozzina	hen tiny hand cellar dozen
-ino		n. – adj.	1. family of animals 2. diminutive 3. tool 4. profession 5. formation of adjectives and nouns from nouns 6. origin	suino codino accendino arrotino marino triestino	pig ponytail, small tail lighter knife-grinder sailor from Trieste
-io		n.	intensity, repetition	vocio	clamor
-ire		v.	infinitive, 3rd conjugation	finire	finish
-ismo	-ism	n.	1. state; the fact of being 2. doctrine 3. linguistic expression	snobismo capitalismo anglicismo	snobbery capitalism Anglicism
-issimo/ -issima		adj.	very high degree or great extent, superlative	rarissimo	extremely rare

Suffix	English Equivalents	Resulting gramm. category	Meanings and Uses	Examples	English Equivalents
-ista	-ist, -er	n. – adj.	1. profession, activity 2. formation of nouns and adjectives from nouns in -ismo	linguista dentista comunista	linguist dentist Communist
-istico/ -tica	-istic	adj.	formation of adjectives from nouns in -ismo	autistico	Autistic
-ita	-ite, -itis	adj. – n.	origin	moscovita	Muscovite
-ità	-ity, -acy	n.	1. quality, state 2. collective quality	intimità maturità natalità	intimacy maturity birthrate
-ite	-ite, -itis	n.	illness of	bronchite	bronchitis
-ito[1]		n.	cry of animals	barrito	trumpeting
-ito[2]	-ed	v.	past participle of verbs in -ire	stupito	amazed
-itudine	-itude, -ness	n.	quality, state	abitudine	habit
-ivo	-ive	adj. – n.	1. doing something 2. quality	esplosivo sportivo	explosive sports
-izia	-ness	n.	characteristic, condition	sporcizia	dirt(iness)
-izzare		v.	transformation	privatizzare	privatize
-latra	-latrous, -later/ress	adj. – n.	formation of adjectives and nouns from nouns in -latria	idolatra	idolatrous *adj.*, idolater/ress *n.*
-latria	-latry	n.	cult	idolatria	idolatry
-logia	-logy	n.	science	antropologia	anthropology
-logo/-loga	-logist	adj. – n.	scientist, doctor	dermatologo	dermatologist
-mane	-addict(e-d)	adj. – n.	obsessed	eroinomane	heroin addict
-mania	-mania	n.	obsession	megalomania	megalomania
-mante		n.	diviner	cartomante	card reader
-mente	-ly	adv	formation of adverbs of manner	lentamente	slowly
-mento	-ment	n.	action, result of an action	allineamento	alignment
-metria	-metry	n.	formation of nouns from nouns in -metro	geometria	geometry
-metrico/ -metrica	-metric(al)	adj.	formation of adjectives from nouns in -metro	chilometrico	kilometric
-metro	-meter	n.	measure	cronometro	chronometer
-morfo/ -morfa	-mor-phous	adj.	shape, aspect	polimorfo	polymorphous
-nomia	-nomy	n.	science	astronomia	astronomy
-nomo	-nomer	n.	expert in	astronomo	astronomer
-occio/ -occia		adj	diminutive	grassoccio	plump

Suffix	English Equivalents	Resulting gramm. category	Meanings and Uses	Examples	English Equivalents
-oide	-oid	adj. – n.	1. similar to 2. relating to something 3. pejorative	asteroide reumatoide anarcoide	asteroid rheumatoid anarchic, anarchist
-olo/-ola		adj. – n.	1. diminutive 2. origin	porticciolo spagnolo	little harbor Spanish
-oma	-oma	n.	1. tumor 2. illness	melanoma ematoma	melanoma hematoma
-one/-ona		adj. – n.	1. formation of adjectives and nouns from verbs 2. augmentative	chiacchie-rone pancione pigrona	talkative adj., chatterbox n. paunch very lazy (woman)
-onimia	-onymy	n.	formation of nouns from adjectives in -omico	sinonimia	synonymy
-onimico/-onimica	-oni mic(al)	adj.	formation of adjectives from nouns in -onimo	sinonimico	synonimic
-onimo/-onima	-onym	n.	relating to a noun	sinonimo	synonym
-opia	-opia	n.	relative to the eye	miopia	myopia
-osi	-osis	n.	1. state, condition 2. illness	ipnosi tubercolosi	hypnosis tuberculosis
-oso/-osa	-ous	adj	full of; having	misterioso voluminoso	mysterious voluminous
-otto/-otta		adj. – n.	diminutive	grassotto isolotto	a bit fat small island
-paro/-para	-para	n.	giving origin	primipara	primipara
-pata	-path	n.	doctor	omeopata	homeopath
-patia	-pathy	n.	illness	epatopatia	hepatopathy
-patico/-patica	-pathic	adj	formation of adjectives from nouns in -patia	omeopatico	homeopathic
-pede	-ped	adj. – n.	foot	bipede	biped
-poli	-polis	n.	1. city 2. corruption, scandal	metropoli tangentopoli	metropolis bribes scandal
-ragia	-rrhage	n.	abnormal flux	emorragia	hemorrhage
-scopia	-scopy	n.	examination, observation	gastroscopia	gastroscopy
-scopico/-scopica	-scopic(al)	adj.	formation of adjectives from nouns in -scopio and -scopia	microscopico	microscopic(al)
-scopio	-scope	n.	instrument for observation	microscopio stetoscopio	microscope stethoscope
-sore		n.	see -tore	professore	professor
-statico/-statica	-static	adj.	without movement	elettrostatico	electrostatic
-stato	-stat	n.	instrument which maintains constant state	termostato	thermostat
-teca		n.	collection, custody	biblioteca	library

Suffix	English Equiva-lents	Resulting gramm. category	Meanings and Uses	Examples	English Equivalents
-terapia	-therapy	n.	therapy	massoterapia	massage therapy
-tipo	-type	n.	model	prototipo	prototype
-tomia	-tomy	n.	cut	isterectomia	hysterectomy
-tore/-trice	-ator	adj. – n.	1. performer of an action 2. device, machine	creatore ventilatore perforatrice	creator fan card punch
-tura	-ing	n.	formation of nouns from verbs	abbotton-atura	buttoning
-uccio		n.	diminutive	tettuccio	canopy
-ucolo		n.	pejorative	avvocatucolo	hack lawyer
-uto/-uta[1]		adj.	full of	barbuto	bearded
-uto/-uta[2]		v.	past participle of verbs in -ere	cresciuto	grown
-ubile	-able, -ible	adj.	1. possibility, ability 2. variant of -abile	volubile	changeable
-voro/ -vora	-vore -vorous	n. adj.	eating	carnivoro	carnivore *n.*, carnivorous *adj.*
-zione	-ation	n.	1. action 2. effect, result	creazione combina-zione	creation combination

Prefissi e suffissi: inglese-italiano
Prefixes and suffixes: English-Italian

Prefisso	Equivalenti italiani	Significati e usi	Esempi	Equivalenti italiani
a-[1]		di	anew	di nuovo
a-[2]		a	ashore	a riva, verso riva
a-[3]	a-	variante di ab-	aversion	avversione
a-[4]	a-	variante di ad-	aspect	aspetto
a-[5]	a-	variante di an-	asexual	asessuato
ab-	ab-	allontanamento	abdicate	abdicare
ac-	ac-	variante di ad-	acquire	acquisire
acro-	acro-	altezza	acrobat	acrobata
ad-	ad-	verso, in direzione di	adsorb	assorbire
af-	af-	variante di ad-	affable	affabile
Afro-	afro-	dell'Africa	Afro-Caribbean	afro-caraibico
after-	dopo-	in seguito	aftermath	conseguenze
ag-	ag-	variante di ad-	aggravate	aggravare
agora-	agora-	folla o grande spazio	agoraphobia	agorafobia
agri-	agri-, agro-	agricoltura	agribusiness agricultural	agroalimentare agricolo
all-		1. intero 2. completamente	all-night all-around	tutta la notte tutto; completo
alti-	alti-	alto, altezza	altimeter	altimetro
ambi-	ambi-	1. entrambi 2. attorno	ambidextrous ambient	ambidestro ambientale
amphi-	anfi-	1. due lati 2. attorno	amphibian amphitheater	anfibio anfiteatro
an-[1]	an-	variante di ad-	annotate	annotare
an-[2]	an-	senza	anarchy	anarchia
andro-	andro-	maschile	androgynous	androgino
Anglo-	anglo-	inglese	Anglophile	anglofilo
ante-	ante-, anti-	prima	antecedent	antecedente
anthropo-	antropo-	essere umano	anthropology	antropologia
anti-	anti-	1. contrario a 2. negazione 3. opposizione 4. che contrasta	antiabortion antisocial antithesis antifreeze	contro l'aborto antisociale antitesi antigelo
ap-	ap-	variante di ad-	appear	apparire
aqua-	acqua-	acqua	aquaplaning	aquaplaning
aqui-	acqui-	variante di aqua-	aquifer	acquifero
ar-	ar-	variante di ad-	arrogant	arrogante
arch-	archi-	1. autorità superiore 2. grado estremo	archbishop archenemy	arcivescovo principale nemico
as-	as-	variante di ad-	assail	assalire

Prefisso	Equivalenti italiani	Significati e usi	Esempi	Equivalenti italiani
astro-	astro-	relativo agli astri, allo spazio	astronaut astronomy	astronauta astronomia
at-	at-	variante di ad-	attorney	avvocato
audio-	audio-	relativo al suono, all'ascolto	audiology	audiologia
auto-	auto-	(di) se stesso	autobiography	autobiografia
avi-	avi-	1. relativo agli uccelli 2. relativo agli aerei	aviary aviation	voliera aviazione
be-		1. far diventare 2. togliere	befriend behead	farsi amico decapitare
bene-	bene-	bene	beneficial	benefico
bi-	bi-	1. due volte 2. due	bimonthly bilingual	bimensile bilingue
biblio-	biblio-	relativo ai libri	bibliophile	bibliofilo
bin-	bin-	per due	binary	binario
bio-	bio-	vita	biography	biografia
brevi-	brevi-	corto	brevity	brevità
cardio-	cardio-	cuore	cardiogram	cardiogramma
centi-	cento- centi-	1. cento 2. centesimo	centipede centimeter	centopiedi centimetro
chiro-	chiro-	mano	chiropractor	chiropratico
chrom(o)-	crom(o)-	colore	chromatic	cromatico
chron(o)-	cron(o)-	tempo	chronology	cronologia
circum-	circon-, circum-	attorno	circumference circumnavigate	circonferenza circumnavigare
co-	co-	con, insieme	coalesce	coalizzarsi
col-	col-	variante di co-	collaborate	collaborare
com-	com-	variante di co-	combat	combattere
con-	con-	variante di co-	concave	concavo
contra-	contra-	contro	contradict contraception	contraddire contraccezione
cor-	cor-	variante di co-	correct	corretto
cosmo-	cosmo-	1. relativo allo spazio 2. relativo al mondo	cosmonaut cosmopolitan	cosmonauta cosmopolita
counter-	contro-	1. opposizione 2. parallelo 3. duplicato	counteract counterbalance counterfeit	contrastare compensare contraffare
cross-	cruci-	croce	crossfire	fuoco incrociato
crypto-	critto-	nascosto	cryptic cryptographer	criptico crittografo
custom-		speciale, particolare	custom-built	fatto su ordinazione
cyber-	ciber-	informatico	cyberspace	ciberspazio
de-	de-	1. separazione 2. negazione 3. degrado	deforest decriminalize decrepit	deforestare depenalizzare decrepito
deca-	deca-	dieci	decade	decennio

Prefisso	Equivalenti italiani	Significati e usi	Esempi	Equivalenti italiani
deci-	deci-	decimo	decibel	decibel
demi-	semi-	metà	demigod	semidio
derma-	derma-	pelle	dermatology	dermatologia
di(a)-	di(a)-	1. attraverso 2. completamente	diagonal diatribe	diagonale diatriba
di-[1]	di-	doppio, due	dilemma	dilemma
di-[2]	di-	variante di dis-	digress	fare una digressione
dif-	dis-	variante di dis-	differentiate	differenziare
dis-	dis-, s-	1. negazione 2. separazione, allontanamento 3. completamente	disadvantage disappear disgruntle	inconveniente sparire scontentare
down-		giù, basso	downhill	in discesa
duo-	duo-	due	duodenum	duodeno
dyna-	dina-	forza	dynamic	dinamico
dys-	dis-	male	dysfunctional	che funziona male
e-[1]	e-	elettronico	e-mail e-commerce	e-mail commercio elettronico
e-[2]	e-	variante di ex-[1]	eviscerate	sviscerare
eco-	eco-	ambiente, natura	ecology	ecologia
ef-	e-	variante di ex-[2]	effusion	effusione
electro-	elettro-	elettricità	electromagnet	elettromagnete
em-[1]		variante di en-[1]	emboss	goffrare
em-[2]	em-	variante di en-[2]	embryo	embrione
en-[1]	in-	1. mettere dentro 2. passaggio da uno stato ad un altro	encode enact	codificare mettere in atto
en-[2]	en-	in, all'interno di	energy	energia
entomo-	entomo-	insetto	entomology	entomologia
ep-	ep-	variante di epi-	epoch	epoca
eph-	ef-	variante di epi-	ephemeral	effimero
epi-	epi-	1. su, sopra 2. accanto 3. prima 4. dopo	epicenter epidemic epidermis epilogue	epicentro epidemia epidermide epilogo
equi-	equi-	uguaglianza	equinox	equinozio
eso-	eso-	nascosto, segreto	esoteric	esoterico
ethno-	etno-	popolo, razza	ethnology	etnologia
eu-	eu-	bene, buono	eulogy	eulogia
Euro	euro-	europeo	eurocrat	eurocrate
ever-	sempre-	sempre	evergreen	sempreverde
ex-[1]	ex-	precedente	ex-girlfriend	ex-ragazza
ex-[2]	s-	fuori da	excavate	scavare
exo-	eso-	fuori, all'esterno	exodus	esodo

Prefisso	Equivalenti italiani	Significati e usi	Esempi	Equivalenti italiani
extra-	extra-, stra-	fuori da	extraordinary	straordinario
extro-	estro-	variante di extra-	extrovert	estroverso
fore-	pre- avan-	1. prima 2. davanti	forecast forearm	previsione avambraccio
Franco-	franco-	francese	francophone	francofono
fresh-		nuovo, recente	freshman	matricola
gastr(o)-	gastr(o)-	relativo all'addome	gastroscopy	gastroscopia
gen-	gene-	nascita	genealogy gender	genealogia genere
geno-	geno-	popolo, razza	genocide	genocidio
geo-	geo-	relativo alla terra	geography	geografia
giga-	giga-	miliardo	gigabyte	gigabyte
grand-		della generazione precedente	grandmother grandfather	nonna nonno
graph(o)-	graf(o)-	scrittura	graphology	grafologia
great-	pro-	della generazione precedente	great-nephew	pronipote (di zii)
gyneco-	gineco-	femminile	gynecologist	ginecologo
gyr-	giro-	cerchio, giro	gyroscope	giroscopio
hecto-	etto-	cento	hectare	ettaro
heli-	eli-	relativo ad elicotteri	heliport	eliporto
hema-	emo-	sangue	hemophilia	emofilia
hemi-	emi-	metà	hemisphere	emisfero
hepta-	etta-	sette	heptagon	ettagono
hetero-	etero-	diverso	heterosexual	eterosessuale
hexa-	esa-	sei	hexagon	esagono
histo-	isto-	relativo a tessuti organici	histology	istologia
holo-	olo-	intero, completo	holocaust	olocausto
homeo-	omeo-	simile	homeopathy	omeopatia
homo-	omo-	simile, uguale	homograph	omografo
hydro-	idro-	acqua	hydrophobia	idrofobia
hyper-	iper-	molto grande; eccessivo	hyperbole	iperbole
hypno-	ipno-	sonno	hypnotherapy hypnosis	terapia del sonno ipnosi
hypo-	ipo-	1. sotto 2. sotto la norma	hypodermic hypothermia	ipodermico ipotermia
hyster(o)-	ister(o)-	utero	hysterectomy	isterectomia
il-[1]	il-	variante di in-[1]	illuminate	illuminare
il-[2]	il-	variante di in-[2]	illiterate	illetterato
im-[1]	im-	variante di in-[1]	impregnate	impregnare
im-[2]	im-	variante di in-[2]	immobile	immobile
in-[1]	in-	dentro	introduce	introdurre
in-[2]	in-	negazione	inapt	inadatto

Prefisso	Equivalenti italiani	Significati e usi	Esempi	Equivalenti italiani
Indo-	indo-	indiano	Indonesia	Indonesia
infra-	infra-	sotto	infrastructure	infrastruttura
inter-	inter-	tra	international	internazionale
intra-	intra-	dentro, all'interno	intravenous	intravenoso
intro-	intro-	verso l'interno	introvert	introverso
ir-[1]	ir-	variante di in-[1]	irrupt	irrompere
ir-[2]	in-	variante di in-[2]	irregular	irregolare
iso-	iso-	uguaglianza	isotope	isotopo
kilo-	chilo-	mille	kilometer	chilometro
lacto-	latto-	latte	lactose	lattosio
litho-	lito-	pietra	lithography	litografia
macro-	macro-	grande	macroeconomic	macroeconomico
magn(i)-	magni-	grande, eccessivo	magnificent	magnifico
mal-	mal(e)-	male	malice	malizia
mani-	mani-	mano	manicure	manicure
mega-	mega-	molto grande	megaphone	megafono
meta-	meta-	1. cambiamento 2. dopo 3. relativo a un ordine superiore in astratto	metamorphosis metacarpal metaphysics metaphor	metamorfosi metacarpo metafisica metafora
metro-	metro-	misura	metronome	metronomo
micro-	micro-	molto piccolo	microorganism	microrganismo
mid-	mezza-, mezzo-	metà, mezzo	midnight midday	mezzanotte mezzogiorno
milli-	milli-	1. mille 2. millesimo	millipede millibar	millepiedi millibar
mini-	mini-	piccolo	miniskirt	minigonna
mis-	mis-	errore; male	miscalculate	calcolare male
mono-	mono-	unico	monopoly	monopolio
morph(o)-	morf(o)-	forma	morphology	morfologia
multi-	multi-	molteplice	multilingual	multilingue
must-		obbligatorietà	must-see	da non perdere
near-		prossimità	nearsighted	miope
neo-	neo-	nuovo	neoconservative	neoconservatore
nephr(o)-	nefr(o)-	rene	nephritis	nefrite
neur(o)-	neur(o)- nevr(o)-	nervo	neurophychiatrist neurosis	neuropsichiatra nevrosi
new-		nuovo, recente	new-found	nuovo, appena scoperto
non-	non-	negazione	nonaggression	non-aggressione
octa-	ott(a)-	otto	octagon octave	ottagono ottavo
octo-	ott-	otto	octogenarian octopus	ottuagenario polipo

Prefisso	Equivalenti italiani	Significati e usi	Esempi	Equivalenti italiani
omni-	onni-	tutto	omnipotent	onnipotente
ornitho-	ornito-	uccello	ornithology	ornitologia
ortho-	orto-	1. corretto 2. diritto	orthography orthodontist	ortografia ortodontista
osteo-	osteo-	osso	osteoporosis	osteoporosi
out-	fuori-	al di fuori	outlaw	fuorilegge
ov-	ov(i)-	uovo	ovary	ovaia
over-	sovra-	1. troppo; eccessivo 2. sopra	overact overwrite	esagerare sovrascrivere
pale(o)-	pale(o)-	antico	paleontology	paleontologia
pan-	pan-	tutto	pantheon	pantheon
para-	para-	1. accanto a 2. simile, analogo a	paragraph paramilitary	paragrafo paramilitare
patho-	pato-	malattia	pathology	patologia
patri-	patri-	1. padre 2. paese natale	patriarchy patriotism	patriarcato patriottismo
ped(i)-	ped(i)-	piede	pedicure	pedicure
ped(o)-	ped(o)-	bambino	pediatrics	pediatria
penta-	penta-	cinque	pentagon pentathlon	pentagono pentathlon
per-	per-	1. attraverso 2. molto; completamente	perennial perfect	perenne perfetto
peri-	peri-	attorno	periphery	periferia
phil(o)-	fil(o)-	amore per; affinità con	philanthropy philharmonic	filantropia filarmonico
phleb(o)-	fleb(o)-	vena	phlebitis	flebite
phon(o)-	fon(o)-	suono	phonology	fonologia
photo-	foto-	luce	photosensitive	fotosensibile
physio-	fisio-	corpo	physiognomy	fisionomia
plur-	plur(i)-	molteplice	pluralistic	pluralista
pneum-	pneuma-	aria	pneumatic	pneumatico
pneumo-	pneumo-	respirazione; polmoni	pneumonia	polmonite
poly-	poli-	molteplice	polytheism	politeismo
post-	dopo-	dopo	postwar	del dopoguerra
pre-	pre-	prima	prewar	prima della guerra
preter-	preter-	al di là di	preternatural	preternaturale
pro-	pro-	per, a favore di	proactive	proattivo
prot(o)-	prot(o)-	primo	prototype	prototipo
pseud(o)-	pseud(o)-	falso	pseudonym	pseudonimo
psych(o)-	psic(o)-	psiche	psychosis	psicosi
pyro-	piro-	fuoco	pyrotechnic	pirotecnico
quadri-, quadru-	quadr(i)-	quattro	quadrilateral quadruped	quadrilatero quadrupede

Prefisso	Equivalenti italiani	Significati e usi	Esempi	Equivalenti italiani
quasi-	para-	quasi	quasi-governmental	paragovernativo
radio-	radio-	1. tramite onde radio 2. radioattivo	radiotelegraphy radiotherapy	radiotelegrafia radioterapia
re-	re-, ri-	ripetizione	rearrange	risistemare
rect(i)-	rett(i)-	diritto	rectify	rettificare
rent-a-		locazione	rent-a-car	noleggio autovetture
retro-	retro-	in dietro	retroactive	retroattivo
rhino-	rino-	naso	rhinoplasty	rinoplastica
sclero-	sclero-	duro	sclerosis	sclerosi
seism(o)-	sism(o)-	terremoto	seismograph	sismografo
self-	auto-	autonomo, solo	self-help	autoaiuto
semi-	semi-	a metà, mezzo	semifinal	semifinale
septi-	sett-	sette	septimole	settima
sex-	sest-	sei	sextet	sestetto
short-		breve, corto; mancante	shortfall	deficit
soli-	soli-	solo	soliloquy solitaire	soliloquio solitario
step-		relativo a legame familiare in seguito a nuovo matrimonio	stepmother	matrigna
stereo-	stereo-	solido	stereophonic	stereofonico
strato-	strato-	strato	stratosphere	stratosfera
sub-	sub-, sotto-	sotto	submarine subtropical	sottomarino subtropicale
suc-	soc-	variante di sub-	succumb	soccombere
suf-	suf-	variante di sub-	suffix	suffisso
sup-	sop-	variante di sub-	suppress	sopprimere
super-	sovra-, sopra-	sopra	superimpose supervision	sovrapporre supervisione
sur-		variante di sub-	surreptitious	furtivo
sus-		variante di sub-	susceptible	suscettibile
syl-		variante di syn-	syllable	sillaba
sym-		variante di syn-	symbiosis	simbiosi
syn-	sin-	contemporaneità	synergy	sinergia
tele-	tele-	a distanza	television	televisione
tetra-	tetra-	quattro	tetrahedron	tetraedro
theo-	teo-	relativo alla divinità	theology	teologia
therm(o)-	term(o)-	calore, caldo	thermostat	termostato
top(o)-	top(o)-	luogo	topical	topico
trans-	trans-	al di là di, attraverso	transaction	transazione
tri-	tri-	tra	triangle	triangolo
tropo-	tropo-	cambio di senso	troposphere	troposfera
typo-	tipo-	impronta, carattere	typography	tipografia

Prefisso	Equivalenti italiani	Significati e usi	Esempi	Equivalenti italiani
ultra-	ultra-	oltre; di grado estremo	ultrasound	ultrasuono
un-	dis-, de-	1. negazione 2. inversione	unlike unzip undo	differente dezippare disfare
under-	sott(o)-	sotto	underscore	sottolineare
uni-	uni-	uno (solo)	unilateral	unilaterale
up-		verso l'alto	uptown upgrade	in centro aggiornamento
vermi-	vermi-	relativo ai vermi	vermicide	vermicida
vice-	vice-	che sostituisce	vice-chairman	vicepresidente
with-		1. contro 2. indietro	withstand withdraw	resistere ritirare
xeno-	xeno-	straniero	xenophobia	xenofobia
xylo-	xilo-	legno	xylophone	xilofono
zoo-	zoo-	animale	zoology	zoologia

Suffisso	Equivalenti italiani	Significati e usi	Esempi	Equivalenti italiani
-a	-a	1. formazione del femminile di sostantivi greci e latini 2. formazione del femminile	curricula Roberta	programmi Roberta
-ability	-abilità	formazione di sostantivi da aggettivi in -able o -ible	reliability, stability	affidabilità, stabilità
-able, -ble, -ible	-abile, -ibile	formazione aggettivi indicanti possibilità	reliable, acceptable, edible	affidabile, accettabile, commestibile
-ably	-mente	formazione di avverbi indicanti modo, maniera	reliably, remarkably	affidabilmente, considerevolmente
-ac	-aco/-aca	avente le caratteristiche di; variante di -ic	maniac, cardiac, aphrodisiac	maniaco, cardiaco, afrodisiaco
-aceous	-aceo/-acea	formazione di aggettivi con il senso di avente le caratteristiche di	sebaceous, herbaceous	sebaceo, erboso
-acious	-ace	variante di -aceous	efficacious, loquacious	efficace, loquace
-acity	-cità	formazione di sostantivi indicanti qualità, caratteristica	capacity, sagacity	capacità, sagacia
-acy	-ezza, -zia	formazione di sostantivi indicanti qualità	accuracy, intimacy	esattezza, intimità
-ade	-ata	formazione di sostantivi	lemonade, barricade, crusade	limonata, barricata, crociata
-age	-aggio, -tura, -io	formazione di sostantivi indicanti: 1. azione, risultato di un'azione 2. stato 3. luogo	blockage, coverage, dosage, drainage, espionage marriage, shortage orphanage	ostruzione, copertura, dosaggio, drenaggio, spionaggio matrimonio, mancanza orfanotrofio
-agog, -agogue	-agogo/-agoga	leader	pedagogue, demagogue	pedagogo, demagogo
-aholic, -oholic	-olico/-olica -dipendente	dipendente da	alcoholic, workaholic, chocoholic	alcolista, lavoro-dipendente, cioccolato-dipendente
-aire	-ario/-aria	persona o cosa avente una certa qualità	millionaire, questionnaire	milionario, questionario
-al	-ale	formazione di aggettivi astratti nel senso di relativo a	causal, functional, cultural, national, racial	causale, funzionale, culturale, nazionale, razziale
-algia, -algy	-algia	dolore	nostalgia, neuralgia	nostalgia, nevralgia
-ally	-mente	formazione di avverbi	theoretically, occasionally, officially	teoricamente, occasionalmente, ufficialmente

Suffisso	Equivalenti italiani	Significati e usi	Esempi	Equivalenti italiani
-an, -ian	-ano/-ana, -ese -co/-ca	1. nativo di 2. che si occupa di, relativo a	American, Canadian optician, politician, geriatrician	americano, canadese ottico, politico, geriatra
-ana		raccolta	Americana	cultura e storia americana
-ance, -ancy, -ence, -ency	-anza, -enza	formazione di aggettivi e sostantivi con il senso di: 1. azione 2. processo	intolerance, ignorance, importance, infancy, assistance, resistance	intolleranza, ignoranza, importanza infanzia, assistenza, resistenza
-ant	-ante	agente	informant, inhabitant, accountant, disinfectant	informatore, abitante, contabile, disinfettante
-ar	-are	1. variante di -al 2. agente	jocular, linear beggar, liar	giocoso, lineare, mendicante, bugiardo
-arch	-arca	dirigente	monarch	monarca
-archy	-archia	governo	monarchy	monarchia
-arian	-ario/-aria	formazione di aggettivi riferiti a persone per indicare: 1. età 2. dottrina, credo 3. segno zodiacale	octogenarian totalitarian, vegetarian Aquarian	ottuagenario totalitario, vegetariano dell'Acquario
-armed		che ha un certo numero di braccia	one-armed	con un braccio
-arium	-ario	luogo in cui si può osservare	aquarium, planetarium	acquario, planetario
-ary, -ery		1. azione 2. luogo di un'azione 3. qualità	burglary bakery bravery	furto con scasso panetteria coraggio
-ast	-asta	persona con determinate caratteristiche	enthusiast, gymnast	entusiasta, ginnasta
-ate		formazione di verbi nel senso di provocare, fare	habituate, hallucinate, humiliate	abituare, avere allucinazioni, umiliare
-athon		1. gara simile a maratona 2. attività che dura molto tempo	walkathon talkathon	marcia discussione fiume
-atic	-ico/-ica, -atico/-atica	stato, relazione	problematic, rheumatic, schematic, symptomatic	problematico, reumatico, schematico, sintomatico
-ation	-zione	variante di –ion	celebration	celebrazione
-atious		formazione di aggettivi dai sostantivi in -ation	flirtatious, ostentatious	galante, ostentato
-backed		appoggiato da	US-backed	appoggiato dagli Stati Uniti
-based		1. la cui sede si trova a 2. a base di	community-based, US-based wine-based punch	a livello comunitario, con sede negli Stati Uniti punch a base di vino

Suffisso	Equivalenti italiani	Significati e usi	Esempi	Equivalenti italiani
-bedroom		che ha un certo numero di stanze	a three-bedroom house	una casa con tre camere da letto
-behaved		descrive comportamento	well-/badly-behaved	che si comporta bene/male
-bodied		relativo al fisico	strong-bodied, weak-bodied	dal fisico forte, dal fisico fragile
-born		relativo a nascita	newborn, American-born	appena nato, nato in America
-borne		portato da	airborne	portato dall'aria
-bound		1. formazione di avverbi indicanti moto verso una direzione	westbound, inbound, outbound	diretto ad ovest, in entrata, in uscita
		2. costretto	housebound, wheelchair-bound	chiuso in casa costretto su una sedia a rotelle
		3. formazione di aggettivi indicanti il materiale di rilegatura	leather-bound	rilegato in pelle
-brained		indica le capacità intellettuali di una persona	bird-brained, scatterbrained	che ha un cervello di gallina, sbadato
-burger		indica panino simile ad hamburger	veggieburger	hamburger vegetariano
-centric	-centrico/ -centrica	che ha il suo centro in	geocentric, egocentric	geocentrico, egocentrico
-chrome	-cromo/ -croma	colore	monochrome	monocromo
-cian		indica persona che ha delle competenze	electrician, magician, mathematician	elettricista, mago, matematico
-cidal	-cida	formazione di aggettivi dai sostantivi in -cide	homicidal	omicida
-cide	-cidio -cida	1. atto di uccidere 2. chi uccide	homicide, fratricide fratricide	omicidio, fratricidio fratricida
-cle	-colo/-cola	variante di -cule	particle, cuticle	particella, cuticola
-conscious		che fa attenzione a	fashion-conscious, health-conscious	che segue la moda, attento alla propria salute
-corn		corno	unicorn	unicorno
-cosm	-cosmo	relativo al cosmo, allo spazio	microcosm	microcosmo
-cracy	-crazia	1. governo, autorità 2. classe dirigente	democracy, meritocracy aristocracy	democrazia, meritocrazia aristocrazia
-crat	-crate	membro di entità politica	democrat, aristocrat, bureaucrat	democratico, aristocratico, burocrate
-cule, -cle	-colo/-cola	molto piccolo	miniscule, molecule, particle	minuscolo, molecola, particella

Suffisso	Equivalenti italiani	Significati e usi	Esempi	Equivalenti italiani
-cy	-anza, -enza	1. stato 2. funzione 3. qualità	pregnancy presidency proficiency, secrecy	gravidanza presidenza competenze, segretezza
-cyte	-cita	cellula	leukocyte	leucocita
-derm, -dermis	-derma	pelle	pachyderm, epidermis	pachiderma, epidermide
-dimen- sio- nal	-dimensionale	riferito al numero di dimensioni	two-dimensional, three-dimensional	bidimensionale, tridimensionale
-dom		1. stato 2. dominio	boredom kingdom	noia regno
-driven		1. che funziona con 2. stimolato, spinto da	menu-driven export-driven	attivabile tramite menu basato sulle esportazioni
-drome	-dromo	luogo dove si svolgono corse	velodrome	velodromo
-dyne	-dino	forza, intensità	anodyne	anodino
-ean	-ano/-ana, -ino/-ina	nativo di, relativo a	Belizean, Andean	belizano, andino
-ectomy	-ectomia	operazione, taglio	appendectomy	appendicectomia
-ed	-to	1. formazione del participio passato dei verbi 2. formazione di aggettivi indicanti qualità 3. possesso	talked midpriced moneyed, bearded	parlato, detto di prezzo medio agiato, barbuto
-ee		1. destinatario di un'azione 2. condizione	devotee, employee refugee	appassionato, impiegato profugo
-eer		1. agente 2. formazione di verbi	auctioneer electioneer	banditore fare propaganda elettorale
-ella		malattia	rubella, salmonella	rosolia, salmonellosi
-eme	-ema	unità	morpheme, lexeme, phoneme	morfema, lessema, fonema
-emia	-emia	relativo al sangue	leukemia, anemia	leucemia, anemia
-en		1. che è fatto di 2. formazione di verbi nel senso di rendere	woolen toughen, soften	di lana indurire, ammorbidire
-enabled		1. avente una certa tecnologia 2. funzionante grazie a	WAP-enabled voice-enabled	WAP con riconoscimento vocale
-ence, -ency	-enza	formazione di sostantivi da aggettivi in -ent	turbulence, vehemence, clemency	turbolenza, veemenza, clemenza
-enne		formazione del femminile	comedienne	attrice comica

Suffisso	Equivalenti italiani	Significati e usi	Esempi	Equivalenti italiani
-ent	-ento -ente	1. sostantivi astratti 2. sostantivi indicanti un agente 3. aggettivi indicanti un'azione o uno stato	alignment, agreement, nourishment opponent absorbent, obedient	allineamento, accordo, nutrimento avversario assorbente, obbediente
-eous	-oso/-osa	formazione di aggettivi da sostantivi	courageous, courteous, advantageous	coraggioso, cortese, vantaggioso
-er	-iere/-iera	1. agente: professioni e azioni 2. origine 3. comparativo di aggettivi monosillabici	baker, teacher, driver foreigner, New Yorker clearer	panettiere, professore, autista straniero, newyorkese più chiaro
-ern			northern, southern	del nord, del sud
-ery, -ry	-ria	1. gruppo di cose 2. attività 3. luogo dove si fa qualcosa 4. stato, condizione	jewelry, pottery chemistry, industry, cookery bakery slavery	gioielli, ceramiche chimica, industria, cucina panetteria schiavitù
-es		1. formazione del plurale di sostantivi 2. formazione della 3ª persona singolare dei verbi	churches goes	chiese (lui) va
-escence	-escenza	formazione di sostantivi dai verbi in -esce	convalescence	convalescenza
-escent	-escente	formazione di sostantivi ed aggettivi dai verbi in -esce	convalescent	convalescente
-ese	-ese	origine, lingua	Japanese, officialese	giapponese, burocratese
-esque	-esco/-esca	relativo ad aspetto, stile	picturesque, picaresque	pittoresco, picaresco
-ess	-essa	formazione del femminile di alcuni sostantivi	princess	principessa
-est		formazione del superlativo di aggettivi monosillabici	softest	il più morbido
-et	-etto/-etta	formazione di alcuni diminutivi	wristlet, cutlet, anklet	braccialetto, cotoletta, calzino
-eth		formazione dei numerali ordinali	thirtieth	trentesimo
-etic	-ico/-ica	formazione di aggettivi da verbi e altri sostantivi	sympathetic, apathetic, apologetic	compassionevole, apatico, di scusa
-ette	-etta	1. formazione di diminutivi 2. imitazione 3. formazione del femminile	kitchenette, launderette, statuette leatherette usherette	angolo cottura, lavanderia, statuetta similpelle maschera
-eur	-tore	professione	masseur, restaurateur, entrepreneur	massaggiatore, restauratore, imprenditore

Suffisso	Equivalenti italiani	Significati e usi	Esempi	Equivalenti italiani
-euse	-trice	femminile di -eur	masseuse	massaggiatrice
-ey		variante di -y	New-Agey	che segue la new-age
-ferous	-fero/-fera	che contiene; che produce	coniferous, pestiferous	conifera, pestifero
-fest		occasione speciale	music fest	festa della musica
-fic	-fico/-fica	che provoca una reazione	soporific	soporifero
-fication	-ficazione	formazione di sostantivi da verbi in -fy	specification	specificazione
-filled		pieno di	fun-filled, smoke-filled	molto divertente, pieno di fumo
-flavored		avente gusto di	lemon-flavored	al gusto di limone
-fold		un certo numero di volte	threefold, fourfold	triplice, quadruplice
-footed		relativo a piede, piedi	bare-footed, four-footed	a piedi nudi, quadrupede
-footer		relativo alla lunghezza in piedi	a fifty-footer	che misura 50 piedi
-form	-forme	avente la forma di	cruciform	cruciforme
-free		privo di, senza	interest-free, lead-free, trouble-free	senza interessi, senza piombo, senza problemi
-friendly		1. che non danneggia	environmentally-friendly	ecologico
		2. adatto a	family-friendly	per famiglie
-fugal	-fugo/-fuga	formazione di aggettivi da sostantivi in -fuge	centrifugal	centrifugo
-fuge	-fugo/-fuga	verso l'esterno	subterfuge, centrifuge	sotterfugio, centrifuga
-ful		1. pieno di 2. caratteristica 3. quantità contenuta in un determinato oggetto	doubtful, spiteful watchful cupful, spoonful, mouthful	dubbioso, maligno attento tazza, cucchiaio, boccone
-fy	-ficare	fare	fortify, intensify	fortificare, intensificare
-gamous	-gamo/-gama	formazione di aggettivi indicanti unione	monogamous	monogamo
-gamy	-gamia	formazione di sostantivi indicanti unione	monogamy	monogamia
-genic	-genico/-genica -geno/-gena	1. che conviene a 2. che provoca, genera	photogenic, telegenic hallucinogenic, allergenic	fotogenico, telegenico allucinogeno, allergico
-gnosis	-gnosi	conoscenza	prognosis, diagnosis	prognosi, diagnosi
-gnostic	-gnostico/-gnostica	formazione di aggettivi da sostantivi in -gnosis	diagnostic	diagnostico
-goer		che frequenta un certo luogo	movie-goer	chi va spesso al cinema
-gon	-gono	angolo	hexagon	esagono

Suffisso	Equivalenti italiani	Significati e usi	Esempi	Equivalenti italiani
-grade	-grado/-grada	che cambia	retrograde	retrogrado
-grader		indica persona di un certo livello scolastico	second-grader	scolaro di seconda
-gram	-gramma -grammo	1. scrittura 2. pesi	diagram kilogram	diagramma chilogrammo
-graph	-grafo	relativo a scrittura	autograph, cardiograph	autografo, cardiografo
-graphy	-grafia	1. scienza, arte di 2. scrittura	oceanography, lexicography stenography, orthography	oceanografia lessicografia stenografia, ortografia
-gynous	-gino	relativo a una donna	androgynous	androgino
-haired		relativo ai capelli	long-haired, dark-haired	dai capelli lunghi, dai capelli scuri
-hater		chi odia	woman-hater	chi odia le donne
-head		1. relativo alla testa 2. indica stupidità 3. parte alta di	redhead knucklehead hammerhead, letterhead	rosso cretino testa del martello, intestazione
-hearted		formazione di aggettivi indicanti caratteristiche	wholehearted, broken-hearted	completo, che ha il cuore infranto
-hood		stato o condizione gruppo di persone	falsehood, fatherhood, childhood brotherhood	falsità, paternità, infanzia confraternita
-hungry		che desidera fortemente qualcosa	power-hungry	avido di potere
-hunter		chi cerca qualcosa	job-hunter, house-hunter	chi cerca attivamente un lavoro, chi cerca una casa
-ia		1. paesi e regioni 2. formazione del plurale di parole di origine latina	Australia, Andalusia bacteria	Australia, Andalusia batteri
-oholic		variante di -aholic	alcoholic	alcolista
-ial	-iale	formazione di aggettivi nel senso di relativo a	ministerial, industrial, managerial	ministeriale, industriale, manageriale
-ian	-iano/-iana	variante di -an	Canadian, Italian	canadese, italiano
-iana		variante di -ana	Canadiana	cultura e storia del Canada
-iasis	-iasi	malattia	elephantiasis, amebiasis	elefantiasi, amebiasi
-iatrics, -iatry	-iatria	specializzazione medica	geriatrics, psychiatry	geriatria, psichiatria
-ibility	-ibilità	variante di -ability	compatibility	compatibilità
-ible	-ibile	variante di -able	edible	commestibile
-ibly	-mente	variante di -ably	audibly	rumorosamente

Suffisso	Equivalenti italiani	Significati e usi	Esempi	Equivalenti italiani
-ic, -ical	-ico/-ica	1. che assomiglia a 2. relativo a	acidic, heroic poetic, mathematic	acido, eroico poetico, matematico
-ically	-camente	formazione di avverbi dagli aggettivi in -ic, -ical	alphabetically, heroically	alfabeticamente, eroi-camente
-ice	-izia	stato, condizione	cowardice, service, justice	codardia, servizio, giustizia
-ics	-ica	formazione di sostantivi indicanti un settore di attività	ceramics, classics, cybernetics, econ-omics	ceramica, classici, cibernetica, econ-omia
-id	-ide	membro di una famiglia zoologica	arachnid	aracnide
-ie		variante colloquiale di -y (diminutivo)	birdie	uccellino
-ier	-iere/-iera	1. formazione di sostantivi indicanti professione 2. formazione del comparativo degli aggettivi in -y	cashier happier	cassiere più felice
-ify	-ficare	formazione di verbi indic-anti attività da aggettivi	clarify, glorify	chiarire, celebrare
-ile	-ile	1. relativo a 2. indica qualità	infantile mobile	infantile mobile
-ility	-ilità	formazione di aggettivi indicanti capacità di essere o fare qualcosa	versatility, visibility	versatilità, visibilità
-in	-ina	sostanze chimiche	vitamin, gelatin, lanolin, toxin	vitamina, gelatina, lanolina, tossina
-ina	-ina	formazione del femmi-nile	tsarina, ballerina	zarina, ballerina
-induced		causato, indotto	self-induced, work-induced	autoinflitto, dovuto al lavoro
-ine	-ino/-ina	1. di particolare natura 2. formazione di sostantivi astratti 3. originario di, relativo a 4. sostanze chimiche	crystalline medicine Argentine caffeine	cristallino medicina argentino caffeina
-ing	-ando, -endo -ante, -ente	1. formazione del gerundio 2. formazione del participio presente	playing playing children	giocando bambini che giocano
-ious	-oso/-osa	formazione di aggettivi indicanti una caratteristica	capricious, cautious	capriccioso, prudente
-ish		1. natura 2. origine, lingua 3. che assomiglia a 4. abbastanza	childish British, English piggish, nightmarish newish	infantile britannico, inglese goloso, da incubo abbastanza nuovo

Suffisso	Equivalenti italiani	Significati e usi	Esempi	Equivalenti italiani
-ism	-ismo	1. formazione di sostantivi indicanti un sistema, una dottrina 2. qualità, caratteristica 3. fenomeno, condizione	totalitarianism cynicism tourism	totalitarismo cinismo turismo
-ist	-ista	1. professione 2. chi fa qualcosa	artist, dentist plagiarist, tourist	artista, dentista plagiatore, turista
-istic	-istico/-istica	formazione di aggettivi dai sostantivi in –ist	realistic	realistico
-istics	-istica	scienza, disciplina	linguistics, statistics, logistics	linguistica, statistica, logistica
-ite	-ita	1. nativo di 2. che crede in	Israelite Shiite, socialite	israelita sciita, socialista
-itis	-ite	infezione	conjunctivitis, cystitis	congiuntivite, cistite
-itive	-ivo/-iva	che ha tendenza a, che causa	inquisitive, repetitive	inquisitorio, ripetitivo
-ity	-ità	stato, qualità	absurdity, captivity, clarity, complexity	assurdità, cattività, chiarezza, complessità
-ive	-ivo/-iva	che ha tendenza a, che causa	appreciative, digestive	riconoscente, digestivo
-ization	-izzazione	formazione di sostantivi dai verbi in –ize	familiarization, centralization	familiarizzazione, centralizzazione
-ize	-izzare	compiere un'azione	familiarize, centralize, categorize, computerize	familiarizzare, centralizzare, classificare, informatizzare
-ject		gettare	eject, inject, reject	espellere, iniettare, rigettare
-kin		diminutivo	bumpkin, manikin, napkin	zoticone, manichino, tovagliolo
-land		formazione di nomi di paesi, regioni, zone	Switzerland, Newfoundland, swampland	Svizzera, Terranova, palude
-legged		indica numero di gambe	eight-legged	che ha otto zampe
-length		indica lunghezza	knee-length, shoulder-length	che arriva al ginocchio, che arriva alle spalle
-lepsy	-lessia	attacco	epilepsy, narcolepsy	epilessia, narcolessia
-less		senza	effortless, careless, homeless	facile, negligente, senzatetto
-let	-etto/-etta	diminutivo	leaflet, piglet, rivulet	foglietto, maialino, ruscelletto
-like		che è come, che assomiglia a	sportsmanlike, businesslike, childlike	sportivo, serio, infantile
-ling		1. diminutivo 2. esprime sdegno	duckling, fledgling underling	anatroccolo, uccellino subordinato

Suffisso	Equivalenti italiani	Significati e usi	Esempi	Equivalenti italiani
-lite	-lite	1. indica un minerale 2. variante di -it, indicante condizione	cryolite cellulite	criolite cellulite
-lith	-lito	pietra	monolith	monolito
-lithic	-litico/-litica	periodo dell'archeologia	Paleolithic	paleolitico
-load		indica il carico di un mezzo di trasporto	busload, truckload	(carico di) autobus, camionata
-log, -logue	-logo	relativo a parole	monologue, epilogue	monologo, epilogo
-logic, -logy	-logia	studio di	anthropology, dermatology	antropologia, dermatologia
-ly	-mente	1. formazione di avverbi di modo 2. formazione di aggettivi e avverbi indicanti intervalli di tempo	madly, carelessly weekly, monthly	follemente, negligentemente settimanale, mensile
-maker		persona o macchina che fa qualcosa	dressmaker, watchmaker, coffeemaker	sarto, orologiaio, caffettiera
-man		1. indica un uomo che ha certe caratteristiche, che esercita un'attività o una professione particolare 2. indica il numero di persone di un gruppo	linesman, madman, mailman a four-man team	giudice di linea, pazzo, postino una squadra di quattro persone
-mania	-mania	indica ossessione	pyromania, megalomania, kleptomania	piromania, megalomania, cleptomania
-mannered		indica comportamento	ill-mannered, mild-mannered	maleducato, gentile
-manship		indica competenze	swordsmanship, workmanship	abilità con la spada, abilità (tecnica)
-ment	-mento	formazione di sostantivi indicanti: 1. stato 2. risultato	contentment, excitement alignment	soddisfazione, eccitazione allineamento
-meter	-metro	misura	chronometer, speedometer	cronometro, tachimetro
-minded		indica stato d'animo	narrow-minded, strong-minded	di mentalità ristretta, deciso
-morphous	-morfo/-morfa	indica forma, aspetto	amorphous, polymorphous	amorfo, polimorfo
-most		formazione del superlativo	outermost, rearmost, southernmost	il più esterno, il più arretrato, il più meridionale
-motive		movimento, propulsione	automotive, locomotive	veicolo a motore, locomotiva
-mouthed		indica modo di parlare	loud-mouthed, foul-mouthed	che parla ad alta voce, sboccato

Suffisso	Equivalenti italiani	Significati e usi	Esempi	Equivalenti italiani
-natured		indica l'indole	good-natured	di buon carattere
-ness, -iness		stato o qualità	hopelessness, carelessness, bitterness, sleepiness	disperazione, disattenzione, amarezza, sonnolenza
-nik		indica persona associata a credenza, qualità	beatnik, peacenik	beatnik, pacifista
-nomy	-nomia	1. norma, struttura di 2. studio di	taxonomy, economy astronomy	tassonomia, economia astronomia
-o		formazione di parole indicanti persone con certe abitudini o caratteristiche	wino, weirdo, dumbo	beone, strambo, tonto
-ock		diminutivo	bullock, hillock	torello, collinetta
-oholic	-olico/-olica	dipendente da	alcoholic	alcolista
-oid	-oide	che assomiglia a	spheroid	sferoide
-ology	-logia	studio di	biology, geology	biologia, geologia
-oma	-oma	tumore	carcinoma, melanoma	carcinoma, melanoma
-onym	-onimo	relativo a un nome	synonym, pseudonym	sinonimo, pseudonimo
-onymous	-onimico/-onimica	formazione di aggettivi dai sostantivi in -onym	synonymous	sinonimico
-onymy	-onimia	formazione di sostantivi dagli aggettivi in -onymous	synonymy	sinonimia
-opia	-opia	relativo all'occhio	myopia	miopia
-or	-tore/-trice	agente	actor, exhibitor, agitator, processor	attore, espositore, agitatore, processore
-orial	-oriale	formazione di aggettivi dai sostantivi in -or, -ory	senatorial, dictatorial	senatoriale, dittatoriale
-oriented		indica scopo	profit-oriented	orientato al profitto
-orium	-orio	luogo	crematorium, emporium, sanatorium	crematorio, emporio, sanatorio
-ory	-orio/-oria	relativo a, avente una certa natura	circulatory, transitory, contradictory	circolatorio, transitorio, contraddittorio
-ose	-oso/-osa	pieno di, caratterizzato da	verbose	verboso
-osis	-osi	1. malattia 2. processo	psychosis, neurosis hypnosis, narcosis	psicosi, nevrosi ipnosi, narcosi
-ous	-oso/-osa	1. pieno di 2. che ha una certa caratteristica	mysterious, nervous, voluminous, cancerous	misterioso, nervoso, voluminoso, canceroso
-owned		indica possesso	family-owned, state-owned	di famiglia, dello stato

Suffisso	Equivalenti italiani	Significati e usi	Esempi	Equivalenti italiani
-packed		pieno di	action-packed	animato
-path	-pata -patico/-patica	1. indica persona che pratica un tipo di cura 2. indica persona con una malattia particolare	homeopath, naturopath psychopath	omeopata, naturopata psicopatico
-pathic	-patico/-patica	formazione di aggettivi dai sostantivi in -pathy	homeopathic, telepathic	omeopatico, telepatico
-pathy	-patia	1. sentimento 2. relativo a cura medica	empathy, telepathy, sympathy homeopathy	empatia, telepatia, compassione omeopatia
-ped	-pede	che ha un certo numero di piedi, zampe	biped, quadruped	bipede, quadrupede
-pepsia	-pepsia	relativo alla digestione	dyspepsia	dispepsia
-person		formazione di parole che indicano una persona avente una professione, una carica, senza specificare il genere	spokesperson, chairperson	portavoce, presidente
-phile	-filo/-fila	che ama qualcosa	technophile, bibliophile, anglophile	che ama la tecnica, bibliofilo, anglofilo
-phobe	-fobo/-foba	indica persona che odia	technophobe, Anglophobe	che detesta la tecnica, anglofobo
-phobia	-fobia	odio per	claustrophobia, xenophobia, hydrophobia,	claustrofobia, xenofobia, idrofobia
-phobic	-fobico/-fobica	formazione di aggettivi dai sostantivi in -phobia	xenophobic, claustrophobic	xenofobo, claustrofobico
-phone	-fono	1. strumento, apparecchio che produce o si serve del suono 2. parlante una lingua	saxophone, megaphone, microphone, telephone Anglophone, Francophone	sassofono, megafono, microfono, telefono anglofono, francofono
-phony	-fonia	suono	cacophony, euphony	cacofonia, eufonia
-plane	-plano	aeroplano	seaplane, biplane	idrovolante, biplano
-plex	-plex	composto da un certo numero di unità	duplex, multiplex	duplex, multiplex
-pod		piede	tripod	treppiede
-polis		città	metropolis	metropoli
-powered		relativo all'alimentazione di una macchina	battery-powered, nuclear-powered	a batterie, (alimentato con energia) nucleare
-proof		che resiste a	ovenproof, rust-proof, shatterproof, soundproof, bomb-proof, bulletproof	che può andare in forno, antiruggine, infrangibile, insonorizzato, a prova di bomba, antiproiettile
-prone		che è soggetto a	accident-prone	soggetto a incidenti
-red		condizione	hatred, sacred	odio, sacro

Suffisso	Equivalenti italiani	Significati e usi	Esempi	Equivalenti italiani
-ria	-ria	1. nomi di malattie e nomi scientifici 2. nomi di luoghi, paesi	diphtheria, malaria, wisteria Bulgaria	difterite, malaria, glicine Bulgaria
-rrhage	-ragia	flusso anormale di	hemorrhage	emorragia
-ridden		1. pieno di 2. confinato a	guilt-ridden bedridden	pieno di sensi di colpa costretto a letto
-ry		variante di -ery	chemistry	chimica
-scape		indica un certo tipo di paesaggio	landscape, seascape, townscape,	paesaggio, paesaggio marino, paesaggio urbano
-scope	-scopio	strumento che consente di vedere, esaminare	microscope, stethoscope, stroboscope, hygroscope	microscopio, stetoscopio, stroboscopio, igroscopio
-scopy	-scopia	esame con uno strumento	gastroscopy	gastroscopia
-sect		taglio	dissect	sezionare
-ship		1. stato 2. funzione 3. competenze	friendship championship, dictatorship horsemanship, marksmanship	amicizia campionato, dittatura equitazione, abilità nel tiro
-sion	-sione	1. azione 2. risultato 3. condizione	emission, inclusion emulsion, explosion tension	emissione, inclusione emulsione, esplosione tensione
-some		1. incline a 2. gruppo di (usato assieme ad un numero)	quarrelsome, tiresome twosome, foursome	litigioso, faticoso un paio, un gruppo di quattro
-speak		indica la lingua, il gergo di un gruppo di persone	doublespeak, netspeak	linguaggio doppio, linguaggio di Internet
-sphere	-sfero	sfera	hemisphere	emisfero
-ster		persona con determinate caratteristiche o che agisce in un determinato modo	youngster, mobster, pollster, trickster	giovane, gangster, sondaggista, imbroglione
-stress		formazione del femminile	seamstress	sarta
-sy		formazione di aggettivi e sostantivi con connotazione negativa	tipsy, whimsy, artsy	brillo, capriccioso, che ostenta interessi culturali
-teen		1. formazione di numeri da 13 a 19 2. somigliante a	nineteen velveteen	diciannove simile a velluto
-th		1. stato, azione 2. numerali ordinali	youth, death, growth, thirteenth	gioventù, morte, crescita, tredicesimo
-tion	-zione	1. risultato 2. stato	inflation, reflection, infection, inhibition	inflazione, riflesso, infezione, inibizione

Suffisso	Equivalenti italiani	Significati e usi	Esempi	Equivalenti italiani
-tious	-oso/-osa	formazione di aggettivi dai sostantivi in -tion	ambitious, cautious	ambizioso, prudente
-tomy	-tomia	operazione, taglio	appendectomy	appendicectomia
-tor	-tore/ -trice	agente	arbitrator, collaborator, calculator	arbitro, collaboratore, calcolatrice
-tory	-torio/-toria	formazione di aggettivi indicanti stato o qualità	anticipatory, accusatory	anticipatore, accusatorio
-tude	-itudine	stato	gratitude, solitude	gratitudine, solitudine
-ty		1. qualità, stato 2. formazione delle decine dei numeri	royalty, safety, seventy	regalità, sicurezza, settanta
-ule	-ulo	diminutivo	granule	granulo
-ulent	-lento	che ha molto	fraudulent	fraudolento
-ulous	-oso/-osa	adatto a, che tende ad essere	miraculous, nebulous	miracoloso, nebuloso
-ure		1. risultato 2. condizione	mixture, exposure moisture, pleasure	misto, esposizione umidità, piacere
-ville		1. luogo 2. luogo, cosa o condizione avente determinate qualità	Jacksonville hicksville	Jacksonville luogo dimenticato da Dio
-vore	-voro/-vora	che mangia qualcosa	carnivore, herbivore	carnivoro, erbivoro
-vorous	-voro/-vora	formazione di aggettivi dai sostantivi in -vore	carnivorous, herbivorous, omnivorous	carnivoro, erbivoro, onnivoro
-ward(s)		in direzione di	backward(s), inwards, outwards, upwards	indietro, verso l'interno, verso l'esterno, verso l'alto
-ways		direzione	lengthways	per lungo
-wide		indica totalità	worldwide, nationwide	in tutto il mondo, in tutto il paese
-wise		formazione di avverbi indicanti direzione	clockwise	in senso orario
-woman		equivalente femminile di -man	chairwoman	presidentessa
-worthy		1. che merita qualcosa 2. appropriato a	trustworthy, newsworthy roadworthy	degno di fiducia, interessante in grado di viaggiare
-y, -ey	-tà	1. formazione di sostantivi indicanti stato o azione 2. diminutivo 3. formazione di aggettivi nel significato di pieno di, che ha la tendenza a essere	captivity puppy bumpy, faulty, bubbly, creamy, clingy	cattività cucciolo accidentato, difettoso, frizzante, cremoso, aderente
-yer		variante di -er	lawyer	avvocato

Falsi amici

False friends

Ecco un elenco dei principali significati che possono essere confusi per la somiglianza dei termini nelle due lingue. Per informazioni più complete sulle traduzioni si consiglia al lettore di cercare le parole nel dizionario. I falsi amici sono elencati in ordine alfabetico in base all'ortografia italiana.

This list gives the main meanings of the words which are most likely to cause confusion in Italian and English. Readers should consult the main section of the dictionary for more complete translations. False friends are arranged in alphabetical order by the Italian words.

Meaning of the Italian word:	Falsi amici False friends		Significato del termine inglese:
	italiano Italian	English inglese	
1. mishap 2. stroke, fit	accidente	accident	1. incidente (d'auto) 2. puro caso
1. repair 2. settlement	accomodamento	accommodation	sistemazione, alloggio
1. to repair 2. to arrange 3. to settle	accomodare	to accommodate	1. ospitare 2. contenere 3. soddisfare 4. adattarsi a
addition	addizione	addiction	dipendenza
1. food 2. JUR (pl) alimony	alimento	ailment	disturbo
1. old 2. senior	anziano	ancient	antico
bee	ape	ape	scimmia
1. subject, matter 2. argument (reasoning)	argomento	argument	1. lite, litigio 2. discussione, dibattito 3. argomentazione, argomento
teetotal	astemio	abstemious	morigerato, moderato
1. present 2. topical	attuale	actual	reale, effettivo
presently	attualmente	actually	1. veramente 2. in realtà
1. remainder 2. (pl) leftovers 3. ECON surplus	avanzo	advance	1. avanzata 2. progresso, sviluppo 3. anticipo (di denaro)
1. shack 2. hovel	baracca	barracks	caserma
bartender	barista	barrister	avvocato
sanctimonious	bigotto	bigot	fazioso, fanatico
1. baby 2. little boy, child	bimbo	bimbo	bambolona, pollastra
1. (lock-up) garage 2. pit	box	box	1. scatola 2. cassa 3. casella 4. SPORT area di rigore 5. THEATRE palco

Meaning of the Italian word:	Falsi amici False friends		Significato del termine inglese:
	italiano Italian	English inglese	
1. good 2. clever, skilful 3. honest	bravo	brave	coraggioso
1. bully 2. tough guy	bullo	bull	toro
1. warm 2. hot	caldo	cold	freddo
1. room 2. chamber	camera	camera	macchina fotografica
cellar	cantina	canteen	1. mensa 2. borraccia 3. servizio (di posate)
1. randomness 2. chance happening	casualità	casualty	1. vittima 2. pronto soccorso
1. comfort 2. convenience	comodità	commodity	merce
extortion	concussione	concussion	commozione cerebrale
sugared almonds	confetti	confetti	coriandoli
to conspire	congiurare	to conjure	far comparire
1. solid 2. substantial	consistente	consistent	coerente
context	contesto	contest	1. SPORT gara 2. lotta
1. horn 2. antler	corno	corn	1. grano 2. granturco, mais 3. callo
to give	dare	to dare	1. osare 2. sfidare
to disappoint	deludere	to delude	illudere
disappointment	delusione	delusion	illusione
tooth	dente	dent	ammaccatura
mistrustful	diffidente	diffident	timido, riservato
to ask	domandare	to demand	1. esigere, pretendere 2. richiedere
well-mannered	educato	educated	istruito
1. real 2. permanent	effettivo	effective	1. efficace 2. in vigore 3. effettivo, reale
emergency	emergenza	emergence	il verificarsi
summer	estate	estate	1. proprietà 2. patrimonio, beni
possible	eventuale	eventual	finale, ultimo
1. in case 2. if possible	eventualmente	eventually	1. alla fine 2. finalmente
1. factory 2. manufacture	fabbrica	fabric	1. tessuto 2. struttura

Meaning of the Italian word:	Falsi amici False friends		Significato del termine inglese:
	italiano Italian	English inglese	
annoying	fastidioso	fastidious	1. pignolo 2. schizzinoso
TV series	fiction	fiction	1. narrativa 2. finzione
1. signature 2. famous name	firma	firm	ditta, impresa
1. thick 2. heavy 3. dense	fitto	fit	1. in forma 2. adatto, giusto
1. supplying 2. supply	fornitura	furniture	mobili
1. fresh 2. recent 3. wet	fresco	fresco	affresco
1. brilliant, ingenious 2. talented	geniale	genial	gioviale, cordiale
1. kind 2. gentle	gentile	genteel	1. distinto 2. affettato
gratuitousness	gratuità	gratuity	mancia
1. taste 2. liking 3. flavor 4. pleasure	gusto	gust	1. folata 2. scoppio
1. accident, crash 2. (diplomatic) incident	incidente	incident	1. avvenimento, fatto 2. incidente (diplomatico)
1. flimsy 2. groundless	inconsistente	inconsistent	1. incoerente 2. discontinuo
1. flimsiness 2. groundlessness	inconsistenza	inconsistency	1. incoerenza 2. discontinuità
insult	ingiuria	injury	ferita
to insult	ingiuriare	to injure	ferire
1. to order 2. to summon	intimare	to intimate	lasciar intendere
envious	invidioso	invidious	1. antipatico, poco invidiabile 2. ingiusto
reading	lettura	lecture	1. lezione 2. conferenza 3. predica, ramanzina
1. bookstore 2. bookcase	libreria	library	biblioteca
moody	lunatico	lunatic	matto, pazzo
1. filthy 2. corrupt	lurido	lurid	1. sconvolgente, spaventoso 2. scandaloso 3. sgargiante
lustful	lussurioso	luxurious	lussuoso

Meaning of the Italian word:	Falsi amici / False friends		Significato del termine inglese:
	italiano / Italian	English / inglese	
1. warehouse 2. department store	magazzino	magazine	1. rivista 2. caricatore
1. task 2. office	mansione	mansion	casa signorile
sea	mare	mare	cavalla
1. soft 2. smooth	morbido	morbid	morboso
ship	nave	nave	navata centrale
boring	noioso	noisy	rumoroso
1. piece of new 2. piece of information	notizia	notice	1. avviso 2. preavviso 3. annuncio 4. attenzione
short story	novella	novel	romanzo
1. eventuality 2. need	occorrenza	occurrence	1. evento, avvenimento 2. il verificarsi
1. to need 2. to take (time)	occorrere	to occur	1. avvenire 2. verificarsi 3. venire in mente
oyster	ostrica	ostrich	struzzo
1. spade 2. signal paddle 3. slice	paletta	palette	tavolozza
1. comparison 2. example	paragone	paragon	modello
relative	parente	parent	genitore
driving license	patente	patent	brevetto
floor	pavimento	pavement	marciapiedi
condom	preservativo	preservative	conservante
1. sting 2. injection 3. MED puncture	puntura	puncture	foratura
1. ray 2. MATH radius	raggio	rage	1. rabbia, collera 2. scatto d'ira 3. mania, moda
to slow down	rallentare	to relent	cedere
1. to stay 2. to be left over 3. to become 4. MATH to leave	restare	to rest	1. riposare 2. stare 3. appoggiare
to take (in)	ricoverare	to recover	1. recuperare 2. riottenere, avere indietro 3. riprendersi 4. ristabilirsi

Meaning of the Italian word:	Falsi amici False friends		Significato del termine inglese:
	italiano Italian	English inglese	
1. admission (to hospital) 2. shelter 3. home	ricovero	recovery	1. recupero 2. guarigione 3. ripresa 4. rimborso, risarcimento
important	rilevante	relevant	1. pertinente 2. corrispondente, in questione
1. to pour 2. to pour again	riversare	to reverse	1. invertire 2. rivoltare, rovesciare 3. fare marcia indietro
1. stuff 2. cloth 3. goods *pl* 4. thing	roba	robe	accappatoio
to break	rompere	to romp	1. giocare rumorosamente 2. fare senza difficoltà
1. broken 2. torn 3. tired	rotto	rotten	1. marcio 2. andato a male 3. brutto, pessimo 4. corrotto
noise	rumore	rumor	pettegolezzo
salt	sale	sale	vendita saldi, svendita
pupil	scolaro	scholar	studioso
purpose	scopo	scope	1. possibilità 2. ambito 3. portata
1. liking 2. likeableness	simpatia	sympathy	1. compassione 2. comprensione 3. appoggio; condivisione
nice	simpatico	sympathetic	1. compassionevole 2. comprensivo 3. favorevole
internship	stage	stage	1. stadio, fase 2. palcoscenico 3. teatro 4. scena
1. to stay 2. to be 3. to go 4. to live	stare	to stare	fissare
heel	tallone	talon	artiglio
1. stage 2. stop 3. stopping place 4. SPORT lap	tappa	tap	rubinetto
1. key 2. button 3. touch	tasto	taste	gusto

Meaning of the Italian word:	Falsi amici False friends		Significato del termine inglese:
	italiano Italian	English inglese	
terrifying	terrificante	terrific	1. fantastico, stupendo 2. enorme, grande
vulgar	triviale	trivial	insignificante, di poco conto
unofficial	ufficioso	officious	invadente
recently	ultimamente	ultimately	in fin dei conti, in definitiva
1. to knock 2. to bump into 3. to crash 4. to irritate 5. to conflict	urtare	to hurt	1. ferire 2. far male
vacation	vacanza	vacancy	1. posto (di lavoro) vacante 2. stanza libera
to avenge	vendicare	to vindicate	confermare (la fondatezza di)
1. fickle 2. changeable	volubile	voluble	loquace

I numeri

Numerals

I numerali cardinali

Cardinal numbers

zero	0	zero
uno, una	1	one
due	2	two
tre	3	three
quattro	4	four
cinque	5	five
sei	6	six
sette	7	seven
otto	8	eight
nove	9	nine
dieci	10	ten
undici	11	eleven
dodici	12	twelve
tredici	13	thirteen
quattordici	14	fourteen
quindici	15	fifteen
sedici	16	sixteen
diciassette	17	seventeen
diciotto	18	eighteen
diciannove	19	nineteen
venti	20	twenty
ventuno	21	twenty-one
ventidue	22	twenty-two
ventitré	23	twenty-three
ventiquattro	24	twenty-four
venticinque	25	twenty-five
trenta	30	thirty
trentuno	31	thirty-one
trentadue	32	thirty-two
trentatré	33	thirty-three
quaranta	40	forty
quarantuno	41	forty-one
quarantadue	42	forty-two
cinquanta	50	fifty
cinquantuno	51	fifty-one
cinquantadue	52	fifty-two
sessanta	60	sixty
sessantuno	61	sixty-one
sessantadue	62	sixty-two
settanta	70	seventy

settantuno	71	seventy-one
settantadue	72	seventy-two
settantacinque	75	seventy-five
settantanove	79	seventy-nine
ottanta	80	eighty
ottantuno	81	eighty-one
ottantadue	82	eighty-two
ottantacinque	85	eighty-five
novanta	90	ninety
novantuno	91	ninety-one
novantadue	92	ninety-two
novantanove	99	ninety-nine
cento	100	one hundred
centouno	101	one hundred and one
centodue	102	one hundred and two
centodieci	110	one hundred and ten
centoventi	120	one hundred and twenty
centonovantanove	199	one hundred and ninety-nine
duecento	200	two hundred
duecentouno	201	two hundred and one
duecentoventidue	222	two hundred and twenty-two
trecento	300	three hundred
quattrocento	400	four hundred
cinquecento	500	five hundred
seicento	600	six hundred
settecento	700	seven hundred
ottocento	800	eight hundred
novecento	900	nine hundred
mille	1 000	one thousand
milleuno	1 001	one thousand and one
milledue	1 010	one thousand and ten
millecento	1 100	one thousand one hundred
duemila	2 000	two thousand
diecimila	10 000	ten thousand
centomila	100 000	one hundred thousand
un milione	1 000 000	one million
due milioni	2 000 000	two million
due milioni e cinquecentomila	2 500 000	two million, five hundred thousand
un miliardo	1 000 000 000	one billion
mille miliardi	1 000 000 000 000	one thousand billion

A differenza dell'italiano in inglese in genere si usa una virgola per indicate le migliaia: 1,000, 2,500,00 ecc.

Unlike in English, in Italian the fullstop is used when writing numbers from a thousand upwards – 1.000, 2.500.000 etc.

I numerali ordinali

Ordinal numbers

primo, a	$1°$, 1^a	1st	first
secondo, a	$2°$, 2^a	2nd	second
terzo	$3°$	3rd	third
quarto	$4°$	4th	fourth
quinto	$5°$	5th	fifth
sesto	$6°$	6th	sixth
settimo	$7°$	7th	seventh
ottavo	$8°$	8th	eighth
nono	$9°$	9th	ninth
decimo	$10°$	10th	tenth
undicesimo	$11°$	11th	eleventh
dodicesimo	$12°$	12th	twelfth
tredicesimo	$13°$	13th	thirteenth
quattordicesimo	$14°$	14th	fourteenth
quindicesimo	$15°$	15th	fifteenth
sedicesimo	$16°$	16th	sixteenth
diciassettesimo	$17°$	17th	seventeenth
diciottesimo	$18°$	18th	eighteenth
diciannovesimo	$19°$	19th	nineteenth
ventesimo	$20°$	20th	twentieth
ventunesimo	$21°$	21st	twenty-first
ventiduesimo	$22°$	22nd	twenty-second
ventitreesimo	$23°$	23rd	twenty-third
trentesimo	$30°$	30th	thirtieth
trentunesimo	$31°$	31st	thirty-first
trentaduesimo	$32°$	32nd	thirty-second
quarantesimo	$40°$	40th	fortieth
cinquantesimo	$50°$	50th	fiftieth
sessantesimo	$60°$	60th	sixtieth
settantesimo	$70°$	70th	seventieth
settantunesimo	$71°$	71st	seventy-first
settantaduesimo	$72°$	72nd	seventy-second
settantanovesimo	$79°$	79th	seventy-ninth
ottantesimo	$80°$	80th	eightieth
ottantunesimo	$81°$	81st	eighty-first
ottantaduesimo	$82°$	82nd	eighty-second
novantesimo	$90°$	90th	ninetieth
novantunesimo	$91°$	91st	ninety-first
novantanovesimo	$99°$	99th	ninety-ninth
centesimo	$100°$	100th	(one) hundredth
centunesimo	$101°$	101st	(one) hundred and first
centodecimo	$110°$	110th	(one) hundred and tenth

centonovantacinquesimo	195º	195th	(one) hundred and ninety-ninth
duecentesimo	200º	200th	two hundredth
trecentesimo	300º	300th	three hundredth
cinquecentesimo	500º	500th	five hundredth
millesimo	1000º	1 000th	one thousandth
duemillesimo	2000º	2 000th	two thousandth
milionesimo	1000000º	1 000 000th	one millionth
diecimilionesimo	10000000º	10 000 000th	ten millionth

Le frazioni   Fractional numbers

un mezzo	$^1/_2$	a half
un terzo	$^1/_3$	a third
un quarto	$^1/_4$	a quarter
un quinto	$^1/_5$	a fifth
un decimo	$^1/_{10}$	a tenth
un centesimo	$^1/_{100}$	a hundredth
un millesimo	$^1/_{1000}$	a thousandth
un milionesimo	$^1/_{1\,000\,000}$	a millionth
due terzi	$^2/_3$	two thirds
tre quarti	$^3/_4$	three quarters
due quinti	$^2/_5$	two fifths
tre decimi	$3/_{10}$	three tenths
uno e mezzo	$1\,^1/_2$	one and a half
due e mezzo	$2\,^1/_2$	two and a half
cinque e tre ottavi	$5\,^3/_8$	five and three eighths
uno virgola uno	1,1	one point one

In inglese per i numeri decimali viene usato il punto invece della virgola.
In Italian the comma is used instead of the full stop in decimal numbers.

Pesi, misure e temperature

Sistema decimale

Weights, measures and temperatures

Decimal system

giga-	1 000 000 000	G	giga-
mega-	1 000 000	M	mega-
miria-	10 000	ma	myria-
chilo, kilo-	1 000	k	kilo-
etto-	100	h	hecto-
deca-	10	da	deca-
deci-	0,1	d	deci-
centi-	0,01	c	centi-
milli-	0,001	m	milli-
decimilli-	0,000 1	dm	decimilli-
centomilli-	0,000 01	cm	centimilli-
micro-	0,000 001	μ	micro-

Tavola di conversione

Negli Stati Uniti viene ancora utilizzato il sistema imperiale di misura, e in Gran Bretagna il vecchio sistema rimane ancora un punto di riferimento per molte persone anche se è stato ufficialmente adottato il sistema metrico decimale. Lo stesso vale per la scala Fahrenheit delle temperature. Nella tabella sono state elencate solamente le misure imperiali oggi ancora in uso. Moltiplicando una misura metrica per il fattore di conversione indicato in **grassetto** si ottiene la misura imperiale corrispondente; per ottenere la misura metrica basterà invece dividere la misura imperiale per il fattore di conversione.

Conversion tables

Only U.S. Customary units still in common use are given here. To convert a metric measurement to U.S. Customary measures, multiply by the conversion factor in **bold**. Likewise dividing a U.S. Customary measurement by the same factor will give the metric equivalent. Note that the decimal comma is used throughout rather than the decimal point.

Unità metriche
Metric measurement

Medidas de longitud

Unità imperiali
U.S. Customary Measures

Length measure

miglio marino	1 852 m	–	nautical mile			
chilometro	1 000 m	km	kilometer	**0,62**	mile (=1760 yards)	m, mi
ettometro	100 m	hm	hectometer			
decametro	10 m	dam	decameter			
metro	1 m	m	meter	**1,09** **3,28**	yard (= 3 feet) foot (= 12 inches)	yd ft
decimetro	0,1 m	dm	decimeter			
centimetro	0,01 m	cm	centimeter	**0,39**	inch	in
millimetro	0,001 m	mm	millimeter			
micron	0,000 001 m	μ	micron			
millimicron	0,000 000 001 m	mμ	millimicron			
Angstrœm	0,000 000 000 1 m	Å	angstrom			

Superfici   Surface measure

chilometro quadrato	$1\,000\,000\ m^2$	km^2	square kilometer	**0,386**	square mile (= 640 acres)	sq. m., sq. mi.
ettometro quadrato, ettaro	$10\,000\ m^2$	hm^2 ha	square hecto-meter hectare	**2,47**	acre (= 4840 square yards)	a.
decametro quadrato ara	$100\ m^2$	dam^2 a	square deca-meter are			
metro quadrato	$1\ m^2$	m^2	square meter	**1.196** **10,76**	square yard (9 square feet) square feet (= 144 square inches)	sq. yd sq. ft
decimetro quadrato	$0,01\ m^2$	dm^2	square deci-meter			
centimetro quadrato	$0,000\,1\ m^2$	cm^2	square cen-timeter	**0,155**	square inch	sq. in.
millimetro quadrato	$0,000\,001\ m^2$	mm^2	square milli-meter			

Volumi e capacità   Volume and capacity

chilometro cubo	$1\,000\,000\,000\ m^3$	km^3	cubic kilometer			
metro cubo stero	$1\ m^3$	m^3 st	cubic meter stere	**1,308** **35,32**	cubic yard (= 27 cubic feet) cubic foot (= 1728 cubic inches)	cu. yd cu. ft
ettolitro	$0,1\ m^3$	hl	hectoliter			
decalitro	$0,01\ m^3$	dal	decaliter			
decimetro cubo litro	$0,001\ m^3$	dm^3 l	cubic decimeter liter	**0,26** **2,1**	gallon pint	gal. Pt
decilitro	$0,000\,1\ m^3$	dl	deciliter			
centilitro	$0,000\,01\ m^3$	cl	centiliter	**0,352** **0,338**	fluid ounce	fl. Oz
centimetro cubo	$0,000\,001\ m^3$	cm^3	cubic centimeter	**0,061**	cubic inch	cu. in.
millilitro	$0,000\,001\ m^3$	ml	milliliter			
millimetro cubo	$0,000\,000\,001\ m^3$	mm^3	cubic millimeter			

Pesi   ## Weight

tonnellata	1 000 kg	t	tonne	**1,1**	[short] ton (= 2000 pounds)	t.
quintale	100 kg	q	quintal			
chilogrammo	1 000 g	kg	kilogram	**2,2**	pound (= 16 ounces)	lb
ettogrammo	100 g	hg	hectogram			
decegrammo	10 g	dag	decagram			
grammo	1 g	g	gram	**0,035**	ounce	oz
carato	0,2 g	–	carat			
decigrammo	0,1 g	dg	decigram			
centigrammo	0,01 g	cg	centigram			
milligrammo	0,001 g	mg	milligram			
microgrammo	0,000001 g	μg, g	microgram			

Temperature

Per convertire una temperatura espressa in gradi Fahrenheit in una temperatura in gradi Celsius bisogna detrarre 32 e moltiplicare per 5/9. Per convertire invece una temperatura da gradi Celsius a gradi Fahrenheit, bisogna moltiplicare per 9/5 e aggiungere 32.

Temperatures

To convert a temperature in degrees Fahrenheit to Celsius, deduct 32 and multiply by 5/9. To convert Celsius to Fahrenheit, multiply by 9/5 and add 32.

Geographical names: English-Italian
Nomi geografici: inglese-italiano

Countries, Derivatives, Capitals, Currencies –
Paesi, Derivati, Capitali, Unità monetarie

Countries are arranged in alphabetical order by their English names.
I paesi sono elencati in ordine alfabetico in base all'ortografia inglese.

Country Paese	Derivate Derivato	Capital Capitale	Currency Unità monetaria
Afghanistan L'Afghanistan *m*	Afghan afg(h)ano(a)	Kabul Kabul	afghani afgani
Albania L'Albania *f*	Albanian albanese	Tiranë Tirana	lek lek
Algeria L'Algeria *f*	Algerian algerino(a)	Algiers Algeri	Algerian dinar dinaro algerino
Andorra Andorra *f*	Andorran andorrano(a)	Andorra la Vella Andorra la Vella	euro (formerly French franc and peseta) euro (in passato: franco francese e peseta spagnola)
Angola L'Angola *m*	Angolan angolano(a)	Luanda Luanda	new kwanza nuovo kwanza
Antigua and Barbuda Antigua e Barbuda *f*	Antiguan, Barbudan	St. John's St John's	East Caribbean dollar dollaro dei Caraibi dell'Est
Argentina L'Argentina *f*	Argentine, argentinian argentino(a)	Buenos Aires Buenos Aires	Argentine peso peso argentino
Armenia L'Armenia *f*	Armenian armeno(a)	Yerevan Jerevan	dram dram
Australia L'Australia *f*	Australian australiano(a)	Canberra Canberra	Australian dollar dollaro australiano
Austria L'Austria *f*	Austrian austriaco(a)	Vienna Vienna	euro (formerly schilling) euro (in passato: scellino)
Azerbaijan L'Azerbaijan *m*	Azerbaijani azerbaigiano(a)	Baku Baku	manat manat
Bahamas Le Bahamas	Bahamian	Nassau Nassau	Bahamian dollar dollaro delle Bahamas
Bahrain Il Bahrain	Bahraini	Al Manama Manama	Bahrainian dinar dinaro del Bahrain
Bangladesh Il Bangladesh	Bangladeshi bangladese	Dhaka Dhaka	taka taka
Barbados Le Barbados	Barbadian	Bridgetown Bridgetown	Barbadian dollar dollaro delle Barbados
Belarus La Bielorussia	Belarusian bielorusso(a)	Minsk Minsk	Belarusian ruble rublo bielorusso
Belgium Il Belgio	Belgian belga	Brussels Bruxelles	euro (formerly Belgian franc) euro (in passato: franco belga)

Country Paese	Derivate Derivato	Capital Capitale	Currency Unità monetaria
Belize Il Belize	Belizean	Belmopan Belmopan	Belizean dollar dollaro del Belize
Benin Il Benin	Beninese	Porto Novo Porto-Novo	CFA franc franco CFA
Bhutan Il Bhutan	Bhutanese bhutanese	Thimphu Thimphu	ngultrum ngultrum
Bolivia La Bolivia	Bolivian boliviano(a)	Sucre Sucre	Boliviano boliviano
Bosnia-Herzegovina La Bosnia-Erzegovina	Bosnian bosniaco(a)	Sarajevo Sarajevo	Convertible Mark marco convertibile
Botswana Il Botswana	Botswanan	Gaborone Gaborone	pula pula
Brazil Il Brasile	Brazilian brasiliano(a)	Brasilia Brasilia	real real
Brunei Il Brunei	Bruneian	Bandar Seri Begawan Bandar Seri Begawan	Brunei dollar dollaro del Brunei
Bulgaria La Bulgaria	Bulgarian bulgaro(a)	Sofia Sofia	lev lev bulgaro
Burkina Faso Il Burkina Faso	Burkinese	Ouagadougou Ouagadougou	CFA franc franco CFA
Burma/Myanmar La Birmania/Myanmar	Burmese birmano(a)	Rangoon/Yangon Rangoon	kyat kyat
Burundi Il Burundi	Burundian burundese	Bujumbura Bujumbura	Burundi franc franco di Burundi
Cambodia La Cambogia	Cambodian cambogiano(a)	Phnom Penh Phnom Penh	riel riel
Cameroon Il Camerun	Cameroonian camerunese	Yaoundé Yaoundé	CFA franc franco CFA
Canada Il Canada	Canadian canadese	Ottawa Ottawa	Canadian dollar dollaro canadese
Cape Verde Capo Verde *m*	Cape Verdean capoverdiano(a)	Praia Praia	Cape Verde escudo scudo di Capo Verde
Central African Republic La Repubblica centafricana	Central African centrafricano(a)	Bangui Bangui	CFA franc franco CFA
Chad Il Ciad	Chadian	N'Djamena N'Djamena	CFA franc franco CFA
Chile Il Cile	Chilean cileno(a)	Santiago de Chile Santiago	Chilean peso peso cileno
China La Cina	Chinese cinese	Beijing/Peking Pechino	yuan yuan
Colombia La Colombia	Colombian colombiano(a)	Bogota Bogotá	Colombian peso peso colombiano
Comoros Le Comore	Comoran	Moroni Moroni	Comoran franc franco delle Comore
Congo (Democratic Republic of the Congo) (La Repubblica Demo- cratica del) Congo	Congolese congolese	Kinshasa Kinshasa	Congolese franc franco congolese

Country / Paese	Derivate / Derivato	Capital / Capitale	Currency / Unità monetaria
Congo (Republic of the Congo) (La Repubblica del) Congo	Congolese congolese	Brazzaville Brazzaville	CFA franc franco CFA
Cook Islands Le isole Cook	Cook Islander	Avarua Avarua	New Zealand dollar dollaro neozelandese
Costa Rica La Costa Rica	Costa Rican costaricano(a)	San José San José	Costa Rican colón colón costaricano
Croatia La Croazia	Croatian croato(a)	Zagreb Zagrabia	kuna kuna
Cuba Cuba *f*	Cuban cubano(a)	Havana L'Avana	Cuban peso peso cubano
Cyprus Cipro *f*	Cypriot cipriota	Nicosia Nicosia	Cypriot pound sterlina cipriota
Czech Republic La Repubblica ceca	Czech ceco(a)	Prague Praga	Czech koruna corona slovacca
Denmark La Danimarca	Danish danese	Copenhagen Copenhagen	Danish krone corona danese
Djibouti Il Gibuti	Djiboutian	Djibouti Gibuti	Djiboutian franc franco del Gibuti
Dominica La Dominica	Dominican dominicano(a)	Roseau Roseau	East Caribbean dollar dollaro dei Caraibi dell'Est
Dominican Republic La Repubblica dominicana	Dominican dominicano(a)	Santo Domingo Santo Domingo	Dominican peso peso dominicano
Ecuador L'Ecuador *m*	Ecuadorian ecuadoregno(a), equadoriano(a)	Quito Quito	US dollar dollaro americano
Egypt L'Egitto *m*	Egyptian egiziano(a)	Cairo Il Cairo	Egyptian pound sterlina egiziana
El Salvador Il Salvador	Salvadoran salvadoregno(a)	San Salvador San Salvador	US dollar dollaro americano
England (UK) L'Inghilterra *f*	English inglese	London Londra	pound sterling lira sterlina
Equatorial Guinea La Guinea Equatoriale	Equatorial Guinean	Malab Malabo	CFA franc franco CFA
Eritrea L'Eritrea *f*	Eritrean eritreo(a)	Asmara Asmara	nafka nakfa
Estonia L'Estonia *f*	Estonian estone	Tallinn Tallinn	Estonian kroon corona estone
Ethiopia L'Etiopia *f*	Ethiopian etiope	Addis Abeba Addis Abeba	birr birr
Fiji Le Figi	Fijian	Suva Suva	Fijian dollar dollaro delle Figi
Finland La Finlandia	Finnish finlandese	Helsinki Helsinki	euro (formerly Finnish markka) euro (in passato: marco finlandese)

Country Paese	Derivate Derivato	Capital Capitale	Currency Unità monetaria
France La Francia	French francese	Paris Parigi	euro (formerly French franc) euro (in passato: franco francese)
Gabon Il Gabon	Gabonese gabonese	Libreville Libreville	CFA franc franco CFA
Gambia Il Gambia	Gambian	Banjul Banjul	dalasi dalasi
Georgia La Georgia	Georgian georgiano(a)	Tbilisi/Tiflis Tbilisi	lari lari
Germany La Germania	German tedesco(a)	Berlin Berlino	euro (formerly deutsch-mark) euro (in passato: marco tedesco)
Ghana Il Ghana	Ghanaian ghanese	Accra Accra	cedi cedi
Great Britain La Gran Bretagna	British britannico(a)	London Londra	pound sterling lira sterlina
Greece La Grecia	Greek greco(a)	Athens Atene	euro (formerly drachma) euro (in passato: dracma)
Grenada Grenada *f*	Grenadian	St. George's St George's	East Caribbean dollar dollaro dei Caraibi dell'Est
Guatemala Il Guatemala	Guatemalan guatemalteco(a), guate-maltegno(a)	Guatemala Città del Guatemala	quetzal quetzal
Guinea La Guinea	Guinean guineano(a)	Conakry Conakry	Guinean franc franco guineano
Guinea-Bissau La Guinea-Bissau		Bissau Bissau	CFA franc franco CFA
Guyana La Guyana	Guyanese	Georgetown Georgetown	Guyanese dollar dollaro della Guyana
Haiti Haiti *f*	Haitian haitiano(a)	Port-au-Prince Port-au-Prince	gourde gourde
Honduras L'Honduras *m*	Honduran honduregno(a), honduriano(a)	Tegucigalpa Tegucigalpa	lempira lempira
Hungary L'Ungheria *f*	Hungarian ungherese	Budapest Budapest	forint fiorino ungherese
Iceland L'Islanda *f*	Icelandic islandese	Reykjavik Reykjavík	Icelandic krona corona islandese
India L'India *f*	Indian indiano(a)	New Delhi Nuova Delhi	rupee rupia indiana
Indonesia L'Indonesia *f*	Indonesian indonesiano(a)	Jakarta Giacarta	rupiah rupia indonesiana
Iran L'Iran *m*	Iranian iraniano(a)	Tehran Teheran	rial rial iraniano

Country Paese	Derivate Derivato	Capital Capitale	Currency Unità monetaria
Iraq L'Irak *m*	Iraqi iracheno(a)	Baghdad Baghdad	Iraqi dinar dinaro iracheno
Ireland L'Irlanda *f*	Irish irlandese	Dublin Dublino	euro (formerly Irish pound) euro (in passato: sterlina irlandese)
Israel Israele *f*	Israeli israeliano(a)	Jerusalem Gerusalemme	new shekel nuovo shekel
Italy L'Italia *f*	Italian italiano(a)	Rome Roma	euro (formerly lira) euro (in passato: lira italiana)
Ivory Coast/Côte d'Ivoire La Costa d'Avorio	Ivoirian ivoriano(a)	Yamoussoukro Yamoussoukro	CFA franc franco CFA
Jamaica La Giamaica	Jamaican giamaicano(a)	Kingston Kingston	Jamaican dollar dollaro giamaicano
Japan Il Giappone	Japanese giapponese	Tokyo Tokyo	yen yen
Jordan La Giordania	Jordanian giordano(a)	Amman Amman	Jordanian dinar dinaro giordano
Kazakhstan Il Kazakistan	Kazakh kazako(a)	Astana Astana	tenge tenge
Kenya Il Kenia	Kenyan keniano(a), keniota	Nairobi Nairobi	Kenyan shilling scellino keniano
Kiribati Il Kiribati		South Tawara Tarawa-Sud	Australian dollar dollaro australiano
Kuwait Il Kuwait	Kuwaiti kuwaitiano(a)	Kuwait City Madinat-al-Kuwait	Kuwaiti dinar dinaro kuwaitano
Kyrgyzstan Il Kirghizstan	Kyrgyz chirghiso(a), kirghiso(a)	Bishkek Bishkek	Kyrgystani som som chirghiso
Laos Il Laos	Laotian laotiano(a)	Vientiane Vientiane	kip kip
Latvia La Lettonia	Latvian lettone	Riga Riga	Lats lat lettone
Lebanon Il Libano	Lebanese libanese	Beirut Beirut	Lebanese pound sterlina libanese
Lesotho Il Lesoto	Sotho	Maseru Maseru	loti loti
Liberia La Liberia	Liberian liberiano(a)	Monrovia Monrovia	Liberian dollar dollaro liberiano
Libya La Libia	Libyan libico(a)	Tripoli Tripoli	Libyan dinar dinaro libico
Liechtenstein Il Liechtenstein	Liechtensteiner	Vaduz Vaduz	Swiss franc franco svizzero
Lithuania La Lituania	Lithuanian lituano(a)	Vilnius Vilnius	litas lita lituana
Luxemburg Il Lussemburgo	Luxemburg lussemburghese	Luxemburg Lussemburgo	euro (formerly Luxemburg franc) euro (in passato: franco lussemburghese)

Country Paese	Derivate Derivato	Capital Capitale	Currency Unità monetaria
Macedonia (Former Yugoslav Republic of Macedonia) La Macedonia	Macedonian macedone	Skopje Skopje	Macedonian denar dinaro macedone
Madagascar Il Madagascar	Madagascan malgascio(a)	Antananarivo Antananarivo	Madagascan franc franco malgascio
Malawi Il Malawi	Malawian	Lilongwe Lilongwe	Malawian kwacha kwacha
Malaysia La Malaysia	Malaysian malese	Kuala Lumpur Kuala Lumpur	Malaysian ringgit ringgit malese
Maldives Le Maldive	Maldivian	Malé Malé	rufiyaa rufiyaa
Mali Il Mali	Malian	Bamako Bamako	CFA franc franco CFA
Malta Malta *f*	Maltese maltese	Valletta Valetta	Maltese lira lira maltese
Marshall Islands Le isole Marshall	Marshall Islander	Majuro Majuro	US dollar dollaro americano
Mauritania La Mauritania	Mauritanian mauritano(a)	Nouakchott Nouakchott	ouguiya ouguiya
Mauritius Mauritius *f*	Mauritian	Port Louis Port Louis	Mauritian rupee rupia di Mauritius
Mexico Il Messico	Mexican messicano(a)	Mexico City Città del Messico	Mexican peso peso messicano
Micronesia (Federated States of Micronesia) La Micronesia	Micronesian micronesiano	Palikir Palikir	US dollar dollaro americano
Moldavia La Moldavia	Moldavian moldavo(a)	Chişinău Chisinau	Moldavian leu leu moldavo
Monaco Il Principato di Monaco	Monegasque monegasco(a)	Monaco-Ville Monaco	euro (formerly French franc) euro (in passato: franco francese)
Mongolia La Mongolia	Mongolian mongolo(a)	Ulaanbaatar Ulan-Bator	tugrik tugrik
Montenegro Il Montenegro	Montenegran montenegrino(a)	Podgorica Podgorica	euro euro
Morocco Il Marocco	Moroccan marocchino(a)	Rabat Rabat	dirham dirham marocchino
Mozambique Il Mozambico	Mozambican mozambicano(a)	Maputo Maputo	metical metical
Myanmar/Burma Il Myanmar/La Birmania	Burmese birmano(a)	Rangoon/Yangon Rangoon	kyat kyat
Namibia La Namibia	Namibian namibiano(a)	Windhoek Windhoek	Namibian dollar dollaro namibiano
Nauru Il Nauru	Nauruan	Yaren Yaren	Australian dollar dollaro australiano
Nepal Il Nepal	Nepalese nepalese	Kathmandu Kathmandu	Nepalese rupee rupia nepalese

Country Paese	Derivate Derivato	Capital Capitale	Currency Unità monetaria
Netherlands L'Olanda *f*	Dutch olandese	Amsterdam Amsterdam	euro (formerly gulden) euro (in passato: fiorino olandese)
New Zealand La Nuova Zelanda	New Zealander neozelandese	Wellington Wellington	New Zealand dollar dollaro neozelandese
Nicaragua Il Nicaragua	Nicaraguan nicaraguense, nicaraguegno(a)	Managua Managua	córdoba córdoba
Niger Il Niger	Nigerois nigerino(a)	Niamey Niamey	CFA franc franco CFA
Nigeria La Nigeria	Nigerian nigeriano(a)	Abuja Abuja	naira naira
North Korea La Corea del Nord	North Korean nordcoreano(a)	Pyongyang Pyongyang	won won
Northern Ireland (UK) L'Irlanda *f* del Nord	Northern Irish nordirlandese	Belfast Belfast	pound sterling lira sterlina
Norway La Norvegia	Norwegian norvegese	Oslo Oslo	Norwegian krone corona norvegese
Oman L'Oman *m*	Omani	Muscat Muscat	Omani rial rial dell'Oman
Pakistan Il Pakistan	Pakistani pachistano(a)	Islamabad Islamabad	Pakistani rupee rupia pachistana
Palau Le Palau	Palauan	Koror Koror	US dollar dollaro americano
Panama Panama *m*	Panamanian panamense	Panama City Panamá	balboa balboa
Papua New Guinea La Papua-Nuova-Guinea	Papuan	Port Moresby Port Moresby	kina kina
Paraguay Il Paraguay	Paraguayan paraguaiano(a)	Asunción Asunción	guaraní guarani
Peru Il Perù	Peruvian peruviano(a)	Lima Lima	nuevo sol nuovo sol
Philippines Le Filippine	Philippine, Filipino filippino(a)	Manila Manila	Philippines peso peso filippino
Poland La Polonia	Polish polacco(a)	Warsaw Varsavia	zloty zloty
Portugal Il Portogallo	Portuguese portoghese	Lisbon Lisbona	euro (formerly escudo) euro (in passato: scudo)
Puerto Rico (USA) Il Porto Rico (USA)	Puerto Rican portoricano(a)	San Juan San Juan	US dollar dollaro americano
Qatar Il Qatar	Qatari	Doha Doha	Qatari riyal riyal del Qatar
Romania La Romania	Romanian romeno(a), rumeno(a)	Bucharest Bucarest	leu leu rumeno
Russia (Russian Federation) La Russia	Russian russo(a)	Moscow Mosca	ruble rublo russo
Rwanda Il Ruanda	Rwandan ruandese	Kigali Kigali	Rwandan franc franco ruandese

Country Paese	Derivate Derivato	Capital Capitale	Currency Unità monetaria
Samoa Samoa *f*	Samoan	Apia Apia	tala tala
San Marino San Marino *m*	San Marinese	San Marino San Marino	euro (formerly lira) euro (in passato: lira italiana)
Sao Tomé and Príncipe São Tomé e Principe *f*	Soa Tomean	São Tomé São Tomé	dobra dobra
Saudi Arabia L'Arabia Saudita *f*	Saudi Arabian saudita	Riyadh Riyād	Saudi riyal riyal saudita
Scotland (GB) La Scozia (GB)	Scottish scozzese	Edinburgh Edimburgo	pound sterling lira sterlina
Senegal Il Senegal	Senegalese senegalese	Dakar Dakar	CFA franc franco CFA
Serbia La Serbia	Serbian serbo(a)	Belgrade Belgrado	Serbian dinar dinaro serbo
Seychelles Le Seychelles	Seychellois	Victoria Victoria	Seychelles rupee rupia delle Seychelles
Sierra Leone La Sierra Leone	Sierra Leonean	Freetown Freetown	leone leone
Singapore Singapore *f*	Singaporean singaporiano(a)	Singapore Singapore	Singapore dollar dollaro singaporiano
Slovakia/Slovak Republic La Repubblica Slovacca/La Slovacchia	Slovak slovacco(a)	Bratislava Bratislava	Slovak koruna corona slovacca
Slovenia La Slovenia	Slovene, Slovenian sloveno(a)	Ljubljana Lubiana	tolar tallero
Solomon Islands Le Isole Salomone	Solomon Islander	Honiara Honiara	Salomon dollar dollaro delle Salomone
Somalia La Somalia	Somali somalo(a)	Mogadishu Mogadiscio	Somalian shilling scellino somalo
South Africa Il Sudafrica	South African sudafricano(a)	Pretoria Pretoria	rand rand
South Korea La Corea del Sud	South Korean sudcoreano(a)	Seoul Seul	won won sudcoreano
Spain La Spagna	Spanish spagnolo(a)	Madrid Madrid	euro (formerly peseta) euro (in passato: peseta)
Sri Lanka Lo Sri Lanka	Sri Lankan singalese	Colombo Colombo	Sri Lankan rupee rupia dello Sri Lanka
St. Kitts and Nevis Saint Kitts e Nevis *m*		Basseterre Basseterre	East Caribbean dollar dollaro dei Caraibi dell'Est
St. Lucia Santa Lucia *f*	St. Lucian	Castries Castries	East Caribbean dollar dollaro dei Caraibi dell'Est
St. Vincent and the Grenadines Saint Vincent e Grenadine *m*	Saint Vincentian	Kingstown Kingstown	East Caribbean dollar dollaro dei Caraibi dell'Est

Country Paese	Derivate Derivato	Capital Capitale	Currency Unità monetaria
Sudan Il Sudan	Sudanese sudanese	Khartoum al-Khartūm	Sudanese pound sterlina sudanese
Suriname Il Suriname	Surinamese	Paramaribo Paramaribo	Surinamese gulden fiorino del Suriname
Swaziland Lo Swaziland *m*	Swazi	Mbabane Mbabane	lilangeni lilangeni
Sweden La Svezia	Swedish svedese	Stockholm Stoccolma	Swedish krone corona svedese
Switzerland La Svizzera	Swiss svizzero(a)	Berne Berna	Swiss franc franco svizzero
Syria La Siria	Syrian siriano(a)	Damaskus Damasco	Syrian pound sterlina siriana
Taiwan Taiwan *m*	Taiwanese	Taipei Taipei	Taiwanese dollar dollaro di Taiwan
Tajikistan Il Tagikistan	Tajik tagicco(a)	Dushanbe Dushanbe	ruble rublo tagicco
Tanzania La Tanzania	Tanzanian tanzaniano(a)	Dodoma Dodoma	Tanzanian shilling scellino tanzaniano
Thailand La Tailandia	Thai thailandese, tailandese	Bangkok Bangkok	baht baht
Togo Togo *m*	Togolese togolese	Lomé Lomé	CFA franc franco CFA
Tonga Tonga *m*	Tongan	Nuku'alofa Nuku'alofa	pa'anga pa'anga
Trinidad and Tobago Trinidad e Tobago *m*	Trinidadian, Tobagan	Port of Spain Port of Spain	Trinidad and Tobago dollar dollaro di Trinidad e Tobago
Tunisia La Tunisia	Tunesian tunisino(a)	Tunis Tunisi	Tunesian dinar dinaro tunisino
Turkey La Turchia	Turkish turco(a)	Ankara Ankara	Turkish lira nuova lira turca
Turkmenistan Il Turkmenistan	Turkmen turkmeno(a)	Ashgabat Ashgabat	manat manat
Tuvalu Il Tuvalu	Tuvaluan	Funafuti Funafuti	Australian dollar dollaro australiano
Uganda L'Uganda *f*	Ugandan ugandese	Kampala Kampala	Ugandan shilling scellino ugandese
Ukraine L'Ucraina *f*	Ukrainian ucraino(a)	Kiev Kiev	hryvnia hrivna
United Arab Emirates Gli Emirati Arabi Uniti		Abu Dhabi Abu Dhabi	dirham dirham
United Kingdom Il Regno Unito	UK/British britannico(a)	London Londra	pound sterling lira sterlina
United States of America Gli Stati Uniti d'America	American americano(a)	Washington D. C. Washington	US dollar dollaro americano
Uruguay L'Uruguay *m*	Uruguayan uruguaiano(a)	Montevideo Montevideo	Uruguayan peso peso uruguaiano

Country Paese	Derivate Derivato	Capital Capitale	Currency Unità monetaria
USA Gli USA	American americano(a)	Washington D. C. Washington	US dollar dollaro americano
Uzbekistan L'Uzbekistan *m*	Uzbek usbeco(a)	Tashkent Tachkent	Uzbek sum soum
Vanuatu Il Vanuatu		Port Vila Port Vila	vatu vatu
Vatican City Il Vaticano *m*	Vatican vaticano(a)		euro (formerly lira) euro (in passato: lira italiana)
Venezuela Il Venezuela	Venezuelan venezuelano(a)	Caracas Caracas	bolivar bolívar
Vietnam Il Vietnam	Vietnamese vietnamita	Hanoi Hanoi	dong dong
Wales (GB) Il Galles	Welsh gallese	Cardiff Cardiff	pound sterling lira sterlina
Yemen Lo Yemen	Yemeni yemenita	Sanaa San'a'	Yemeni rial rial yemenita
Yugoslavia *see* Serbia and Montenegro La Iugoslavia	Yugoslavian iugoslavo(a)	Belgrade Belgrado	Yugoslavian dinar dinaro iugoslavo
Zambia Lo Zambia	Zambian zambiano(a)	Lusaka Lusaka	kwacha kwacha
Zimbabwe Lo Zimbabwe	Zimbabwean	Harare Harare	Zimbabwean dollar dollaro dello Zimbabwe

* CFA franc = Franco della Comunità Finanziaria Africana

Continents, Islands, Oceans, Seas, Lakes, Rivers, Gulfs, and Mountains – Continenti, Isole, Oceani, Mari, Laghi, Fiumi, Golfi e Monti

Continents
Continenti

Africa *L'Africa f*	Eurasia *L'Eurasia f*
America *L'America f*	Europe *L'Europa f*
Antarctica *L'Antartide m*	Oceania *L'Oceania*
Asia *L'Asia f*	South America *L'America f del Sud*
Central America *L'America f centrale*	

Islands
Isole

Aleutian Islands *Le (isole) Aleutine*	Celebes *Le Celebes*
Antigua *Antigua f*	Channel Islands *Le isole del Canale*
Antilles *Le Antille*	Comoros *Le Comore*
Aruba *Aruba f*	Corfu *Corfù f*
Australia *L'Australia f*	Corsica *La Corsica*
Azores *Le Azzorre*	Crete *Creta f*
Baffin Island *Baffin f*	Curaçao *Curaçao f*
Balearic Islands *Le (isole) Baleari*	Easter Island *L'isola di Pasqua*
Bali *Bali f*	Falkland Islands *Le (isole) Falkland*
Bermuda *Le Bermude*	Faroe Islands *Le (isole) Faroe*
Borneo *Il Borneo*	Galapagos Islands *Le Galapagos*
Burano *Burano f*	Greater Antilles *Le Antille Maggiori*
Canary Islands *Le (isole) Canarie*	Greenland *La Groenlandia*
Cape Verde Islands *Le isole di Capo Verde*	Guadalcanal *Guadalcanal f*
Capri *Capri f*	Guadeloupe *La Guadalupa*
Caroline Islands *Le (isole) Caroline*	Guam *Guam f*

Hebrides *Le Ebridi*	Minorca *Minorca f*
Hispaniola *Hispaniola f*	Murano *Murano f*
Hokkaido *Hokkaido f*	Okinawa *Okinawa f*
Honshu *Honshu f*	Orkney Islands *Le (isole) Orcadi*
Iceland *L'Islanda f*	Prince Edward Island *L'isola del Principe Edoardo*
Isle of Elba *L'(isola d')Elba f*	Réunion *L'isola Riunione f*
Isle of Ischia *Ischia f*	Rhodes *Rodi f*
Isle of Man *L'isola di Man*	Ryukyu Islands *Le isole Ryukyu*
Iwo Jima *Iwo Jima f*	Sakhalin *Sakhalin f*
Java *Giava f*	Sardinia *La Sardegna*
Kyushu *Kyushu f*	Shetland Islands *Le (isole) Shetland*
Leeward Islands *Le isole Sottovento*	Shikoku *Shikoku f*
Lesser Antilles *Le Antille Minori*	Sicily *La Sicilia*
Leyte *Leyte f*	Solomon Islands *Le (isole) Salomone*
Long Island *Long Island f*	Sumatra *Sumatra f*
Luzon *Luzon f*	Tahiti *Tahiti f*
Madagascar *Il Madagascar*	Tasmania *La Tasmania*
Madeira Islands *Madera f*	Tierra del Fuego *La Terra del Fuoco*
Majorca *Maiorca f*	Timor *Timor f*
Maldive Islands *Le Maldive*	Vancouver Island *L'isola di Vancouver*
Mariana Islands *Le isole Mariana*	Victoria Island *L'isola Victoria*
Marquesas Islands *Le (isole) Marchesi*	Virgin Islands *Le isole Vergini*
Marshall Islands *Le (isole) Marshall*	Windward Islands *Le isole Sopravvento*
Martinique *La Martinica*	Zanzibar *Zanzibar f*
Mindanao *Mindanao f*	

Oceans
Oceani

Antarctic Ocean *Il Mar Glaciale Antartico*	Indian Ocean *L'Oceano m Indiano*
Arctic Ocean *Il Mar Glaciale Artico*	Pacific Ocean *L'Oceano m Pacifico*
Atlantic Ocean *L'Oceano m Atlantico*	

Seas
Mari

Adriatic Sea *Il Mare Adriatico*	Ligurian Sea *Il Mar Ligure*
Aegean Sea *Il Mare Egeo*	Mediterranean Sea *Il Mar Mediterraneo*
Aral Sea *Il Mar di Aral*	North Sea *Il Mare del Nord*
Baltic Sea *Il Mar Baltico*	Red Sea *Il Mar Rosso*
Bering Sea *Il Mare di Bering*	Sargasso Sea *Il Mar dei Sargassi*
Black Sea *Il Mar Nero*	Sea of Azov *Il Mar di Azov*
Caribbean Sea *Il Mar dei Caraibi*	Sea of Japan *Il Mare del Giappone*
Caspian Sea *Il Mar Caspio*	Sea of Okhotsk *Il Mare d'Okhotsk*
Dead Sea *Il Mar Morto*	South China Sea *Il Mare della Cina meridionale*
East China Sea *Il Mare della Cina orientale*	Tyrrhenian Sea *Il Mar Tirreno*
Ionian Sea *Il Mar Ionio*	White Sea *Il Mare Bianco*
Irish Sea *Il Mar d'Irlanda*	Yellow Sea *Il Mare Giallo*

Lakes
Laghi

Albert (Nyanza) *Il lago Alberto*	Great Bear *Il Grande Lago degli Orsi*
Baikal *Il lago Bajkal*	Great Lakes *I Grandi Laghi*
Chad *Il lago Ciad*	Great Slave *Il Grande Lago degli Schiavi*
Como Lake *Il lago di Como*	Huron *Il lago Huron*
Erie *Il lago Erie*	Ladoga *Il lago Ladoga*
Garda Lake *Il lago di Garda*	Lago Maggore *Il Lago Maggiore*

Lake Nyasa/Lake Malawi *Il lago Niassa/Il lago Malawi*	Superior *Il lago Superiore*
Michigan *Il lago Michigan*	Tanganyika *Il lago Tanganica*
Onega *Il lago Onega*	Titicaca *Il lago Titicaca*
Ontario *Il lago Ontario*	Victoria *Il lago Vittoria*

Rivers
Fiumi

Amazon *Il Rio delle Amazzoni*	Mekong *Il Mekong*
Amur *L'Amur m*	Mississippi *Il Mississippi*
Columbia *Il Colombia*	Missouri *Il Missouri*
Congo *Il Congo*	Niger *Il Niger*
Danube *Il Danubio*	Nile *Il Nilo*
Delaware *Il Delaware*	Ob *L'Ob m*
Dnieper *La Dniepr*	Oder *L'Oder m*
Don *Il Don*	Ohio *L'Ohio m*
Elbe *L'Elba f*	Orinoco *L'Orinoco m*
Euphrates *L'Eufrate m*	Paraná *Il Paraná*
Ganges *Il Gange*	Po *Il Po*
Huang Ho/Yellow River *Lo Huang He/Il Fiume Giallo*	Potomac *Il Potomac*
Hudson *L'Hudson m*	Rhine *Il Reno*
Indus *L'Indo m*	Rhône *Il Rodano*
Irrawaddy *L'Irrawaddy m*	Rio Grande *Il Rio Grande*
Irtysh *L'Irtys m*	Seine *La Senna*
Jordan *Il Giordano*	St. Lawrence *Il San Lorenzo*
Lena *La Lena*	Susquehanna *Il Susquehanna*
Loire *La Loira*	Thames *Il Tamigi*
Mackenzie *Il Mackenzie*	Tiber *Il Tevere*

Tigris *Il Tigri*	Yangtze *Lo Yangtze*
Ural *L'Ural m*	Yellow *Il Fiume Giallo*
Vistula *La Vistola*	Yukon *Lo Yukon*
Volga *Il Volga*	Zambezi *Lo Zambesi*
Volta *Il Volta*	

Gulfs, Bays, Straits, Canals
Golfi, Baie, Stretti, Canali

Gulf of Aden *Il golfo di Aden*	Hudson Bay *La baia di Hudson*
Bay of Bengal *Il golfo del Bengala*	Strait of Magellan *Lo stretto di Magellano*
Bering Strait *Lo stretto di Bering*	Strait of Messina *Lo Stretto di Messina*
Bay of Biscay *Il golfo di Biscaglia*	Gulf of Mexico *Il golfo del Messico*
Bosporus *Il Bosforo*	Panama Canal *Il Canale di Panama*
Gulf of California *Il golfo della California*	Persian Gulf *Il golfo Persico*
English Channel *La Manica, il Canale della Manica*	Gulf of St. Lawrence *Il golfo di San Lorenzo*
Straits of Florida *Lo stretto di Florida*	Suez Canal *Il canale di Suez*
Strait of Gibraltar *Lo stretto di Gibilterra*	

Mountain Ranges
Catene Montuose

Adirondack Mountains *I monti Adirondack*	Caucasus *Il Caucaso*
Allegheny Mountains *I monti Allegheny*	Dolomites *Le Dolomiti*
Alps *Le Alpi*	Himalayas/Himalaya Mountains *L'Himalaya m/La catena dell'Himalaya*
Andes *Le Ande*	Pyrenees *I Pirenei*
Appalachian Mountains *Gli Appalachi*	Rocky Mountains *Le Montagne Rocciose*
Appenines *Gli Appenini*	Sierra Nevada *La Sierra Nevada*
Balkans *I Balcani*	Ural Mountains *Gli Urali*
Catskill Mountains *I monti Catskill*	

Mountain Peaks
Cime

Aconcagua (Andes) *L'Aconcagua m (Ande)*	Matterhorn *Il Cervino*
Elbrus *L'Elbrus m*	McKinley *Il Monte McKinley*
Etna *L'Etna m*	Mont Blanc *Il Monte Bianco*
Everest *L'Everest m*	Monte Rosa *Il Monte Rosa*
Fujiyama *Il Fujiyama*	Orizaba *Il Picco di Orizaba*
Kilimanjaro *Il Kilimangiaro*	Vesuvius *Il Vesuvio*
Logan *Il Monte Logan*	

Nomi Geografici: italiano-inglese
Geographical Names: Italian-English

Paesi, Derivati, Capitali, Unità monetarie
Countries, Derivatives, Capitals, Currencies

I paesi sono elencati in ordine alfabetico in base all'ortografia italiana.
Countries are arranged in alphabetical order by their Italian names.

Paese Country	Derivato Derivato	Capitale Capital	Unità monetaria Currency
L'Afghanistan *m* Afghanistan	afg(h)ano(a) Afghan	Kabul Kabul	afghani afghani
L'Albania *f* Albania	albanese Albanian	Tirana Tiranë	lek lek
L'Algeria *f* Algeria	algerino(a) Algerian	Algeri Algiers	dinaro algerino Algerian dinar
L'Andorra *f* Andorra	andorrano(a) Andorran	Andorra la Vella Andorra la Vella	euro (in passato: franco francese e peseta spagnola) euro (formerly French franc and peseta)
L'Angola *m* Angola	angolano(a) Angolan	Luanda Luanda	nuovo kwanza new kwanza
L'Antigua e Barbuda *f* Antigua and Barbuda	Antiguan, Barbudan	St John's St. John's	dollaro dei Caraibi dell'Est East Caribbean dollar
L'Arabia Saudita *f* Saudi Arabia	saudita Saudi Arabian	Riyad Riyadh	riyal saudita Saudi riyal
L'Argentina *f* Argentina	argentino(a) Argentine, Argentinian	Buenos Aires Buenos Aires	peso argentino Argentine peso
L'Armenia *f* Armenia	armeno(a) Armenian	Jerevan Yerevan	dram dram
L'Australia *f* Australia	australiano(a) Australian	Canberra Canberra	dollaro australiano Australian dollar
L'Austria *f* Austria	austriaco(a) Austrian	Vienna Vienna	euro (in passato: scellino) euro (formerly schilling)
L'Azerbaijan *m* Azerbaijan	azerbaigiano(a) Azerbaijani	Baku Baku	manat manat
Le Bahamas Bahamas	Bahamian	Nassau Nassau	dollaro delle Bahamas Bahamian dollar
Il Bahrain Bahrain	Bahraini	Manama Al Manama	dinaro di Bahrain Bahrainian dinar
Il Bangladesh Bangladesh	bangladese Bangladeshi	Dhaka Dhaka	taka taka
Le Barbados Barbados	Barbadian	Bridgetown Bridgetown	dollaro delle Barbados Barbadian dollar
Il Belgio Belgium	belga Belgian	Bruxelles Brussels	euro (in passato: franco belga) euro (formerly Belgian franc)

Paese Country	Derivato Derivato	Capitale Capital	Unità monetaria Currency
Il Belize Belize	Belizean	Belmopan Belmopan	dollaro di Belize Belizean dollar
Il Benin Benin	Beninese	Porto Novo Porto Novo	franco CFA CFA franc
Il Bhutan Bhutan	bhutanese Bhutanese	Thimphu Thimphu	ngultrum ngultrum
La Bielorussia Belarus	bielorusso(a) Belarusian	Minsk Minsk	rublo bielorusso Belarusian ruble
La Birmania/Myanmar Burma/Myanmar	birmano(a) Burmese	Rangoon Rangoon/Yangon	kyat kyat
La Bolivia Bolivia	boliviano(a) Bolivian	Sucre Sucre	boliviano Boliviano
La Bosnia-Erzegovina Bosnia-Herzegovina	bosniaco(a) Bosnian	Sarajevo Sarajevo	marco convertibile Convertible Mark
Il Botswana Botswana	Botswanan	Gaborone Gaborone	pula pula
Il Brasile Brazil	brasiliano(a) Brazilian	Brasilia Brasilia	real real
Il Brunei Brunei	Bruneian	Bandar Seri Begawan Bandar Seri Begawan	dollaro del Brunei Brunei dollar
La Bulgaria Bulgaria	bulgaro(a) Bulgarian	Sofia Sofia	lev bulgaro lev
Il Burkina Faso Burkina Faso	Burkinese	Ouagadougou Ouagadougou	franco CFA CFA franc
Il Burundi Burundi	burundese Burundian	Bujumbura Bujumbura	franco di Burundi Burundi franc
La Cambogia Cambodia	cambogiano(a) Cambodian	Phnom Penh Phnom Penh	riel riel
Il Camerun Cameroon	camerunese Cameroonian	Yaoundé Yaoundé	franco CFA CFA franc
Il Canada Canada	canadese Canadian	Ottawa Ottawa	dollaro canadese Canadian dollar
Capo Verde *m* Cape Verde	capoverdiano(a) Cape Verdean	Praia Praia	scudo di Capo Verde Cape Verde escudo
Il Ciad Chad	Chadian	N'Djamena N'Djamena	franco CFA CFA franc
Il Cile Chile	cileno(a) Chilean	Santiago Santiago de Chile	peso cileno Chilean peso
La Cina China	cinese Chinese	Pechino Beijing/Peking	yuan yuan
Cipro *f* Cyprus	cipriota Cypriot	Nicosia Nicosia	sterlina cipriota Cypriot pound
La Colombia Colombia	colombiano(a) Colombian	Bogota Bogotá	peso colombiano Colombian peso
Le Comore Comoros	Comoran	Moroni Moroni	franco delle Comore Comoran franc

Paese Country	Derivato Derivato	Capitale Capital	Unità monetaria Currency
Il Congo (La Repubblica del Congo) Congo (Republic of the Congo)	congolese Congolese	Brazzaville Brazzaville	franco CFA CFA franc
Il Congo (La Repubblica Democratica del Congo) Congo (Democratic Republic of the Congo)	congolese Congolese	Kinshasa Kinshasa	franco congolese Congolese franc
Le (isole/ Cook Cook Islands	Cook Islander	Avarua Avarua	dollaro neozelandese New Zealand dollar
La Corea del Nord North Korea	nordcoreano(a) North Korean	Pyongyang Pyongyang	won won
La Corea del Sud South Korea	sudcoreano(a) South Korean	Seoul Seoul	won won
La Costa d'Avorio Ivory Coast/Côte d'Ivoire	ivoriano(a) Ivoirian	Yamoussoukro Yamoussoukro	franco CFA CFA franc
La Costa Rica Costa Rica	costaricano(a) Costa Rican	San José San José	colón costaricano Costa Rican colón
La Croazia Croatia	croato(a) Croatian	Zagrabia Zagreb	kuna kuna
Cuba *f* Cuba	cubano(a) Cuban	L'Avana Havana	peso cubano Cuban peso
La Danimarca Denmark	danese Danish	Copenhagen Copenhagen	corona danese Danish krone
La Dominica Dominica	dominicano(a) Dominican	Roseau Roseau	dollaro dei Caraibi dell'Est East Caribbean dollar
L'Ecuador *m* Ecuador	ecuadoregno(a), ecuadoriano(a) Ecuadorian	Quito Quito	dollaro americano US dollar
L'Egitto *m* Egypt	egiziano(a) Egyptian	Il Cairo Cairo	sterlina egiziana Egyptian pound
Gli Emirati Arabi Uniti United Arab Emirates		Abu Dhabi Abu Dhabi	dirham dirham
L'Eritrea *f* Eritrea	eritreo(a) Eritrean	Asmara Asmara	nakfa nafka
L'Estonia *f* Estonia	estone Estonian	Tallinn Tallinn	corona estone Estonian kroon
L'Etiopia *f* Ethiopia	etiope Ethiopian	Addis Abeba Addis Abeba	birr etiope birr
Le Figi Fiji	Fijian	Suva Suva	dollaro delle Figi Fijian dollar
Le Filipine Philippines	filippino(a) Philippine, Filipino	Manila Manila	peso filippino Philippines peso
La Finlandia Finland	finlandese Finnish	Helsinki Helsinki	euro (in passato: marco finlandese) euro (formerly Finnish markka)

Paese Country	Derivato Derivato	Capitale Capital	Unità monetaria Currency
La Francia France	francese French	Parigi Paris	euro (in passato: franco francese) euro (formerly French franc)
Il Gabon Gabon	gabonese Gabonese	Libreville Libreville	franco CFA CFA franc
Il Galles Wales (GB)	gallese Welsh	Cardiff Cardiff	lira sterlina pound sterling
Il Gambia Gambia	Gambian	Banjul Banjul	dalasi dalasi
La Georgia Georgia	georgiano(a) Georgian	Tbilissi Tbilisi/Tiflis	lari lari
La Germania Germany	tedesco(a) German	Berlino Berlin	euro (in passato: marco tedesco) euro (formerly deutsch-mark)
Il Ghana Ghana	ghanese Ghanaian	Accra Accra	cedi cedi
La Giamaica Jamaica	giamaicano(a) Jamaican	Kingston Kingston	dollaro giamaicano Jamaican dollar
Il Giappone Japan	giapponese Japanese	Tokyo Tokyo	yen yen
Gibuti Djibouti	Djiboutian	Gibuti Djibouti	franco di Gibuti Djiboutian franc
La Giordania Jordan	giordano(a) Jordanian	Amman Amman	dinaro giordano Jordanian dinar
La Gran Bretagna Great Britain	britannico(a) British	Londra London	lira sterlina pound sterling
La Grecia Greece	greco(a) Greek	Atene Athens	euro (in passato: dracma) euro (formerly drachma)
Grenada f Grenada	Grenadian	St George's St. George's	dollaro dei Caraibi dell'Est East Caribbean dollar
Il Guatemala Guatemala	guatemalteco(a), guatemaltegno(a) Guatemalan	Città del Guatemala Guatemala	quetzal quetzal
La Guinea Guinea	guineano(a) Guinean	Conakry Conakry	franco guineano Guinean franc
La Guinea-Bissau Guinea-Bissau		Bissau Bissau	franco CFA CFA franc
La Guinea Equatoriale Equatorial Guinea	Equatorial Guinean	Malabo Malab	franco CFA CFA franc
La Guyana Guyana	Guyanese	Georgetown Georgetown	dollaro della Guyana Guyanese dollar
Haiti f Haiti	haitiano(a) Haitian	Port-au-Prince Port-au-Prince	gourde gourde

Paese Country	Derivato Derivato	Capitale Capital	Unità monetaria Currency
L'Honduras *m* Honduras	honduregno(a), hondu- riano(a) Honduran	Tegucigalpa Tegucigalpa	lempira lempira
L'India *f* India	indiano(a) Indian	Nuova Delhi New Delhi	rupia indiana rupee
L'Indonesia *f* Indonesia	indonesiano(a) Indonesian	Jakarta Jakarta	rupia indonesiana rupiah
L'Inghilterra *f* England (UK)	inglese English	Londra London	lira sterlina pound sterling
L'Irak *m* Iraq	iracheno(a) Iraqi	Baghdad Baghdad	dinaro iracheno Iraqi dinar
L'Iran *m* Iran	iraniano(a) Iranian	Teheran Tehran	rial iraniano rial
L'Irlanda *f* Ireland	irlandese Irish	Dublino Dublin	euro (in passato: ster- lina irlandese) euro (formerly Irish pound)
L'Irlanda *f* del Nord Northern Ireland (UK)	nordirlandese Northern Irish	Belfast Belfast	lira sterlina pound sterling
L'Islanda *f* Iceland	islandese Icelandic	Reykjavík Reykjavik	coronna islandese Icelandic krona
Israele *f* Israel	israeliano(a) Israeli	Gerusalemme Jerusalem	shekel new shekel
L'Italia *f* Italy	italiano(a) Italian	Roma Rome	euro (in passato: lira italiana) euro (formerly lira)
La Iugoslavia (*vedi* La Serbia e il Montenegro) Yugoslavia	iugoslavo(a) Yugoslavian	Belgrado Belgrade	dinaro iugoslavo Yugoslavian dinar
Il Kazakistan Kazakhstan	kazako(a) Kazakh	Astana Astana	tenge tenge
Il Kenia Kenya	keniano(a), keniota Kenyan	Nairobi Nairobi	scellino keniano Kenyan shilling
Il Kirghizstan Kyrgyzstan	chirghiso(a), kirghiso(a) Kyrgyz	Bichkek Bishkek	som chirghiso Kyrgystani som
Kiribati *m* Kiribati		Tarawa-Sud South Tawara	dollaro australiano Australian dollar
Il Kuwait Kuwait	kuwaitiano(a) Kuwaiti	Madinat-al-Kuwait Kuwait City	dinaro kuwaitiano Kuwaiti dinar
Il Laos Laos	laotiano(a) Laotian	Vientiane Vientiane	kip kip
Il Lesotho Lesotho	Sotho	Maseru Maseru	loti loti
La Lettonia Latvia	lettone Latvian	Riga Riga	lats lats
Il Libano Lebanon	libanese Lebanese	Beirut Beirut	sterlina libanese Lebanese pound
La Liberia Liberia	liberiano(a) Liberian	Monrovia Monrovia	dollaro liberiano Liberian dollar

Paese Country	Derivato Derivato	Capitale Capital	Unità monetaria Currency
La Libia Libya	libico(a) Libyan	Tripoli Tripoli	dinaro libico Libyan dinar
Il Liechtenstein Liechtenstein	Liechtensteiner	Vaduz Vaduz	franco svizzero Swiss franc
La Lituania Lithuania	lituano(a) Lithuanian	Vilnius Vilnius	lita lituana litas
Il Lussemburgo Luxemburg	lussemburghese Luxembourg	Lussemburgo Luxemburg	euro (in passato: franco lussemburghese) euro (formerly Luxembourg franc)
La Macedonia Macedonia (Former Yugoslav Republic of Macedonia)	macedone Macedonian	Skopje Skopje	dinaro macedone Macedonian denar
Il Madagascar Madagascar	malgascio(a) Madagascan	Antananarivo Antananarivo	franco malgascio Madagascan franc
La Malaysia Malaysia	malaysiano(a), malese Malaysian	Kuala Lumpur Kuala Lumpur	ringgit malese Malaysian ringgit
Il Malawi Malawi	Malawian	Lilongwe Lilongwe	kwacha Malawian kwacha
Le Maldive Maldives	Maldivian	Malé Malé	rufiyaa rufiyaa
Il Mali Mali	Malian	Bamako Bamako	franco CFA CFA franc
Malta *f* Malta	maltese Maltese	Valetta Valletta	lira maltese Maltese lira
Il Marocco Morocco	marocchino(a) Moroccan	Rabat Rabat	dirham marocchino dirham
Le isole Marshall Marshall Islands	Marshall Islander	Majuro Majuro	dollaro americano US dollar
Mauritius *f* Mauritius	mauritiano(a) Mauritian	Port Louis Port Louis	rupia di Mauritius Mauritian rupee
La Mauritania Mauritania	mauritano(a) Mauritanian	Nouakchott Nouakchott	ouguiya ouguiya
Il Messico Mexico	messicano(a) Mexican	Mexico Mexico City	peso messicano Mexican peso
La Micronesia Micronesia (Federated States of Micronesia)	micronesiano Micronesian	Palikir Palikir	dollaro americano US dollar
La Moldavia Moldavia	moldavo(a) Moldavian	Chisinau Chişinău	leu moldavo Moldavian leu
La Mongolia Mongolia	mongolo(a) Mongolian	Ulan-Bator Ulaanbaatar	tugrik tugrik
Il Montenegro Montenegro	montenegrino(a) Montenegran	Podgorica Podgorica	euro euro
Il Mozambico Mozambique	mozambicano(a) Mozambican	Maputo Maputo	metical metical
Myanmar/La Birmania Myanmar/Burma	birmano(a) Burmese	Rangoon Rangoon/Yangon	kyat kyat

Paese Country	Derivato Derivato	Capitale Capital	Unità monetaria Currency
La Namibia Namibia	namibiano(a) Namibian	Windhoek Windhoek	dollaro namibiano Namibian dollar
Nauru *m* Nauru	Nauruan	Yaren Yaren	dollaro australiano Australian dollar
Il Nepal Nepal	nepalese Nepalese	Kathmandu Kathmandu	rupia nepalese Nepalese rupee
Il Nicaragua Nicaragua	nicaraguense, nicara- guegno(a) Nicaraguan	Managua Managua	córdoba córdoba
Il Niger Niger	nigerino(a) Nigerois	Niamey Niamey	franco CFA CFA franc
La Nigeria Nigeria	nigeriano(a) Nigerian	Abuja Abuja	naira naira
La Norvegia Norway	norvegese Norwegian	Oslo Oslo	corona norvegese Norwegian krone
La Nuova Zelanda New Zealand	neozelandese New Zealander	Wellington Wellington	dollaro neozelandese New Zealand dollar
L'Olanda *f* Netherlands	olandese Dutch	Amsterdam Amsterdam	euro (in passato: fiorino olandese) euro (formerly gulden)
L'Oman *m* Oman	Omani	Muscat Muscat	rial dell'Oman Omani rial
Il Pakistan Pakistan	pachistano(a) Pakistani	Islamabad Islamabad	rupia pachistana Pakistani rupee
Le Palau Palau	Palauan	Koror Koror	dollaro americano US dollar
Panama *m* Panama	Panamanian	Panamá Panama City	balboa balboa
La Papua-Nuova- Guinea Papua New Guinea	Papuan	Port Moresby Port Moresby	kina kina
Il Paraguay Paraguay	paraguaiano(a) Paraguayan	Asunción Asunción	guarani guaraní
Il Perù Peru	peruviano(a) Peruvian	Lima Lima	nuovo sol nuevo sol
La Polonia Poland	polacco(a) Polish	Varsavia Warsaw	zloty zloty
Il Porto Rico (USA) Puerto Rico (USA)	portoricano(a) Puerto Rican	San Juan San Juan	dollaro americano US dollar
Il Portogallo Portugal	portoghese Portuguese	Lisbona Lisbon	euro (in passato: scudo) euro (formerly escudo)
Il Principato di Monaco Monaco	monegasco(a) Monegasque	Monaco Monaco-Ville	euro (in passato franco francese) euro (formerly French franc)
Il Qatar Qatar	Qatari	Doha Doha	riyal del Qatar Qatari riyal
Il Regno Unito United Kingdom	britannico UK/British	Londra London	lira sterlina pound sterling

Paese Country	Derivato Derivato	Capitale Capital	Unità monetaria Currency
La Repubblica ceca Czech Republic	ceco(a) Czech	Praga Prague	corona slovacca Czech koruna
La Repubblica centafri- cana Central African Repub- lic	centrafricano(a) Central African	Bangui Bangui	franco CFA CFA franc
La Repubblica Domini- cana Dominican Republic	dominicano(a) Dominican	Santo Domingo Santo Domingo	peso dominicano Dominican peso
La Romania Romania	romeno(a), rumeno(a) Romanian	Bucarest Bucharest	leu rumeno leu
Il Ruanda Rwanda	ruandese Rwandan	Kigali Kigali	franco ruandese Rwandan franc
La Russia Russia (Russian Feder- ation)	russo(a) Russian	Mosca Moscow	rublo russo ruble
Saint Kitts e Nevis *m* St. Kitts and Nevis		Basseterre Basseterre	dollaro dei Caraibi dell'Est East Caribbean dollar
Saint Vincent e Grena- dine *m* St. Vincent and the Grenadines	Saint Vincentian	Kingstown Kingstown	dollaro dei Caraibi dell'Est East Caribbean dollar
Le (isole) Salomone Solomon Islands	Solomon Islander	Honiara Honiara	dollaro delle Salomone Salomon dollar
Il Salvador El Salvador	salvadoregno(a) Salvadoran	San Salvador San Salvador	dollaro americano US dollar
Samoa *f* Samoa	Samoan	Apia Apia	tala tala
San Marino *m* San Marino	San Marinese	San Marino San Marino	euro (in passato: lira italiana) euro (formerly lira)
Santa Lucia *f* St. Lucia	St. Lucian	Castries Castries	dollaro dei Caraibi dell'Est East Caribbean dollar
Sao Tomé e Principe *f* Sao Tomé and Príncipe	Sao Tomean	Sao Tomé Sao Tomé	dobra dobra
Il Senegal Senegal	senegalese Senegalese	Dakar Dakar	franco CFA CFA franc
La Serbia Serbia	serbo(a) Serbian	Belgrado Belgrade	dinaro serbo Serbian dinar
Le Seychelles Seychelles	Seychellois	Victoria Victoria	rupia delle Seychelles Seychelles rupee
La Sierra Leone Sierra Leone	Sierra Leonean	Freetown Freetown	leone leone
Singapore *f* Singapore	singaporiano(a) Singaporean	Singapore Singapore	dollaro singaporiano Singapore dollar
La Siria Syria	siriano(a) Syrian	Damasco Damaskus	sterlina siriana Syrian pound

Paese Country	Derivato Derivato	Capitale Capital	Unità monetaria Currency
La Slovacchia/La Repubblica Slovacca Slovakia/Slovak Republic	slovacco(a) Slovak	Bratislava Bratislava	corona slovacca Slovak koruna
La Slovenia Slovenia	sloveno(a) Slovene, Slovenian	Lubiana Ljubljana	tallero tolar
La Somalia Somalia	somalo(a) Somali	Mogadiscio Mogadishu	scellino somalo Somalian shilling
La Spagna Spain	spagnolo(a) Spanish	Madrid Madrid	euro (in passato: peseta) euro (formerly peseta)
Lo Sri Lanka Sri Lanka	singalese Sri Lankan	Colombo Colombo	rupia dello Sri Lanka Sri Lankan rupee
Gli Stati Uniti d'America United States of America	americano(a) American	Washington Washington D. C.	dollaro americano US dollar
Il Sudafrica South Africa	sudafricano(a) South African	Pretoria Pretoria	rand rand
Il Sudan Sudan	sudanese Sudanese	al-Khartūm Khartoum	sterlina sudanese Sudanese pound
Il Suriname Suriname	Surinamese	Paramaribo Paramaribo	fiorino del Suriname Surinamese gulden
La Svezia Sweden	svedese Swedish	Stoccolma Stockholm	corona svedese Swedish krone
La Svizzera Switzerland	svizzero(a) Swiss	Berna Berne	franco svizzero Swiss franc
Lo Swaziland Swaziland	Swazi	Mbabane Mbabane	lilangeni lilangeni
Il Tagikistan Tajikistan	tagicco(a) Tajik	Dushanbe Dushanbe	rublo tagicco ruble
La Tailandia Thailand	thailandese, tailandese Thai	Bangkok Bangkok	baht baht
Taiwan *m* Taiwan	Taiwanese	Taipei Taipei	dollaro del Taiwan Taiwanese dollar
La Tanzania Tanzania	tanzaniano(a) Tanzanian	Dodoma Dodoma Dar es-Salam	scellino tanzaniano Tanzanian shilling
Il Togo Togo	togolese Togolese	Lomé Lomé	franco CFA CFA franc
Tonga *m* Tonga	Tongan	Nuku'alofa Nuku'alofa	pa'anga pa'anga
Trinidad e Tobago *m* Trinidad and Tobago	Trinidadian, Tobagan	Port of Spain Port of Spain	dollaro di Trinidad e Tobago Trinidad and Tobago dollar
La Tunisia Tunisia	tunisino(a) Tunesian	Tunisi Tunis	dinaro tunisino Tunesian dinar
La Turchia Turkey	turco(a) Turkish	Ankara Ankara	nuova lira turca Turkish lira

Paese Country	Derivato Derivato	Capitale Capital	Unità monetaria Currency
Il Turkmenistan Turkmenistan	turkmeno(a) Turkmen	Ashgabat Ashgabat	manat manat
Il Tuvalu Tuvalu	Tuvaluan	Funafuti Funafuti	dollaro australiano Australian dollar
L'Ucraina f Ukraine	ucraino(a) Ukrainian	Kiev Kiev	hrivna hryvnia
L'Uganda f Uganda	ugandese Ugandan	Kampala Kampala	scellino ugandese Ugandan shilling
L'Ungheria f Hungary	ungherese Hungarian	Budapest Budapest	fiorino ungherese forint
L'Uruguay m Uruguay	uruguaiano(a) Uruguayan	Montevideo Montevideo	peso uruguaiano Uruguayan peso
Gli USA USA	americano(a) American	Washington Washington D. C.	dollaro americano US dollar
L'Uzbekistan m Uzbekistan	usbeco Uzbek	Tachkent Tashkent	soum Uzbek sum
Il Vanuatu Vanuatu		Port Vila Port Vila	vatu vatu
Il Vaticano Vatican City	vaticano(a) Vatican		euro (in passato: lira italiana) euro (formerly lira)
Il Venezuela Venezuela	venezuelano(a) Venezuelan	Caracas Caracas	bolívar bolívar
Il Vietnam Vietnam	vietnamita Vietnamese	Hanoi Hanoi	dong dong
Lo Yemen Yemen	yemenita Yemeni	San'a' Sanaa	rial yemenita Yemeni rial
Lo Zambia Zambia	zambiano(a) Zambian	Lusaka Lusaka	kwacha kwacha
Lo Zimbabwe Zimbabwe	Zimbabwean	Harare Harare	dollaro dello Zimbabwe Zimbabwean dollar

* CFA franc = Franco della **C**omunità **F**inanziaria **A**fricana

Continenti, Isole, Oceani, Mari, Laghi, Fiumi, Golfi e Monti –
Continents, Islands, Oceans, Seas, Lakes, Rivers, Gulfs, and Mountains

Continenti
Continents

L'Africa *f* *Africa*	L'Antartide *m* *Antarctica*
L'America *f* *America*	L'Asia *f* *Asia*
L'America *f* centrale *Central America*	L'Eurasia *f* *Eurasia*
L'America *f* del Nord *North America*	L'Europa *f* *Europe*
L'America *f* del Sud *South America*	L'Oceania *Oceania*

Isole
Islands

Le (isole) Aleutine *Aleutian Islands*	Capri *f* *Capri*
Antigua *f* *Antigua*	Le isole Caroline *Caroline Islands*
Le Antille *Antilles*	Le Celebes *Celebes*
Le Antille Maggiori *Greater Antilles*	Le Comore *Comoros*
Le Antille Minori *Lesser Antilles*	Corfù *f* *Corfu*
Aruba *f* *Aruba*	La Cosica *Corsica*
L'Australia *f* *Australia*	Creta *f* *Crete*
Le (isole) Azzorre *Azores*	Curaçao *f* *Curaçao*
Baffin *f* *Baffin Island*	Le (isole) Ebridi *Hebrides*
Le (isole) Baleari *Balearic Islands*	L'(isola d')Elba *f* *Isle of Elba*
Bali *f* *Bali*	Le (isole) Falkland *Falkland Islands*
Le Bermude *Bermuda*	Le (isole) Faroe *Faroe Islands*
Il Borneo *Borneo*	Le (isole) Galapagos *Galapagos Islands*
Burano *f* *Burano*	La Groenlandia *Greenland*
Le (isole) Canarie *Canary Islands*	Guadalcanal *f* *Guadalcanal*
Le isole di Capo Verde *Cape Verde Islands*	La Guadalupa *Guadeloupe*

Guam *f* *Guam*	Minorca *f* *Minorca*
Ischia *f* *Isle of Ischia*	Murano *f* *Murano*
Hispaniola *f* *Hispaniola*	Okinawa *f* *Okinawa*
Hokkaido *f* *Hokkaido*	Le (isole) Orcadi *Orkney Islands*
Honshu *f* *Honshu*	L'isola di Pasqua *Easter Island*
Le Indie occidentali *West Indies*	L'isola del Principe Edoardo *Prince Edward Island*
Le Indie orientali *East Indies*	L'isola Riunione *Réunion*
L'Islanda *f* *Iceland*	Rodi *f* *Rhodes*
Le Isole del Canale *Channel Islands*	Le (isole) Salomone *Solomon Islands*
Iwo Jima *f* *Iwo Jima*	La Sardegna *Sardina*
Java *f* *Java*	Le (isole) Shetland *Shetland Islands*
Kyushu *f* *Kyushu*	Shikoku *f* *Shikoku*
Leyte *f* *Leyte*	La Sicilia *Sicily*
Long Island *f* *Long Island*	Le isole Sopravvento *Windward Islands*
Luzon *f* *Luzon*	Le isole Sottovento *Leeward Islands*
Il Madagascar *Madagascar*	Sumatra *f* *Sumatra*
Madera *f* *Madeira Islands*	Tahiti *f* *Tahiti*
Maiorca *f* *Majorca*	La Tasmania *Tasmania*
Le (isole) Maldive *Maldive Islands*	La Terra del Fuoco *Tierra del Fuego*
L'isola di Man *Isle of Man*	Timor *f* *Timor*
Le isole Mariana *Mariana Islands*	L'isola di Vancouver *Vancouver Island*
Le (isole) Marchesi *Marquesas Islands*	Le (isole) Vergini *Virgin Islands*
Le (isole) Marshall *Marshall Islands*	L'isola Victoria *Victoria Island*
La Martinica *Martinique*	Zanzibar *f* *Zanzibar*
Mindanao *f* *Mindanao*	

Oceani
Oceans

L'Oceano Atlantico *Atlantic Ocean*	L'Oceano Indiano *Indian Ocean*
Il Mar Glaciale Antartico *Antarctic Ocean*	L'Oceano Pacifico *Pacific Ocean*
Il Mar Glaciale Artico *Arctic Ocean*	

Seas
Mari

Il Mare Adriatico *Adriatic Sea*	Il Mare d'Irlanda *Irish Sea*
Il Mar d'Aral *Aral Sea*	Il Mare Giallo *Yellow Sea*
Il Mare di Azov *Sea of Azov*	Il Mare del Giappone *Sea of Japan*
Il Mar Baltico *Baltic Sea*	Il Mar Ligure *Ligurian Sea*
Il Mare di Bering *Bering Sea*	Il Mar Meditteraneo *Mediterranean Sea*
Il Mare Bianco *White Sea*	Il Mar Morto *Dead Sea*
Il Mar dei Caraibi *Caribbean Sea*	Il Mar Nero *Black Sea*
Il mar Caspio *Caspian Sea*	Il Mare del Nord *North Sea*
Il Mare della Cina meridionale *South China Sea*	Il Mare d'Okhotsk *Sea of Okhotsk*
Il Mare del Cina orientale *East China Sea*	Il Mar Rosso *Red Sea*
Il Mare Egeo *Aegean Sea*	Il Mar dei Sargassi *Sargasso Sea*
Il Mar Ionio *Ionio Sea*	Il Mar Tirreno *Tyrrhenian Sea*

Laghi
Lakes

Il lago Alberto *Albert (Nyanza)*	Il Grande Lago degli Schiavi *Great Slave*
Il lago Bajkal *Baikal*	Il Grande Lago degli Orsi *Great Bear*
Il lago Ciad *Chad*	I Grandi Laghi *Great Lakes*
Il lago di Como *Como Lake*	Il lago Huron *Huron*
Il lago Erie *Erie*	Il lago Ladoga *Ladoga*
Il lago di Garda *Garda Lake*	Il lago Maggiore *Maggiore Lake*

Il lago Michigan *Michigan*	Il lago Tanganica *Tanganyika*
Il lago Onega *Onega*	Il lago Titicaca *Titicaca*
Il lago Ontario *Ontario*	Il lago Vittoria *Victoria*
Il lago Superiore *Superior*	

Fiumi
Rivers

L'Amur *m* *Amur*	La Lena *Lena*
La Colombia *Columbia*	La Loira *Loire*
Il Congo *Congo*	Il Mackenzie *Mackenzie*
Il Danubio *Danube*	Il Mekong *Mekong*
Il Delaware *Delaware*	Il Mississippi *Mississippi*
La Dniepr *Dnieper*	Il Missouri *Missouri*
La Dniestr *Dniester*	Il Niger *Niger*
Il Don *Don*	Il Nilo *Nile*
L'Elba *f* *Elbe*	L'Ob *m* *Ob*
L'Eufrate *m* *Euphrates*	L'Oder *m* *Oder*
Il Gange *Ganges*	L'Ohio *m* *Ohio*
Lo Huang He/Il Fiume Giallo *Huang Ho/Yellow River*	L'Orinoco *m* *Orinoco*
L'Hudson *m* *Hudson*	Il Paraná *Paraná*
Lo Yenisei *Yenisei*	Il Po *Po*
L'Indo *m* *Indus*	Il Potomac *Potomac*
L'Irrawaddy *m* *Irrawaddy*	Il Reno *Rhine*
L'Irtys *m* *Irtysh*	Il Rio delle Amazzoni *Amazon*
Il Fiume Giallo *Yellow*	Il Rio Grande *Rio Grande*
Il Giordano *Jordan*	Il Rodano *Rhône*

Il San Lorenzo *St. Lawrence*	Il Volga *Volga*
La Senna *Seine*	Il Volta *Volta*
Il Susquehanna *Susquehanna*	Il Tevere *Tiber*
Il Tamigi *Thames*	Lo Yangtze *Yangtze*
Il Tigri *Tigris*	Lo Yukon *Yukon*
L'Ural *m* *Ural*	Lo Zambesi *Zambezi*
La Vistola *Vistula*	

Golfi, Baie, Stretti, Canali
Gulfs, Bays, Straits, Canals

Il golfo di Aden *Gulf of Aden*	Lo stretto di Magellano *Strait of Magellan*
Il golfo del Bengala *Bay of Bengal*	La Manica, il Canale della Manica *English Channel*
Lo stretto di Bering *Bering Strait*	Il golfo del Messico *Gulf of Mexico*
Il golfo di Biscaglia *Bay of Biscay*	Lo Stretto di Messina *Stretto di Messina*
Il Bosforo *Bosporus*	Il canale di Panama *Panama Canal*
Il golfo della California *Gulf of California*	Il golfo Persico *Persian Gulf*
Lo stretto di Florida *Straits of Florida*	Il golfo di San Lorenzo *Gulf of St. Lawrence*
Lo stretto di Gibilterra *Strait of Gibraltar*	Il canale di Suez *Suez Canal*
La baia di Hudson *Hudson Bay*	

Catene Montuose
Mountain Ranges

I monti Adirondack *Adirondack Mountains*	I Balcani *Balkans*
I monti Allegheny *Allegheny Mountains*	I Carpazi *Carpathian Mountains*
Le Alpi *Alps*	I monti Catskill *Catskill Mountains*
Le Ande *Andes*	Il Caucaso *Caucasus*
Gli Appalachi *Appalachian Mountains*	Le Dolomiti *Dolomites*
Gli Appennini *Appenines*	l'Himalaya *m*/La catena dell'Himalaya *Himalayas/Himalaya Mountains*

I Pirenei *Pyrenees*	La Sierra Nevada *Sierra Nevada*
Le Montagne Rocciose *Rocky Mountains*	Gli Urali *Ural Mountains*

Cime
Mountain Peaks

L'Aconcagua *m* (Ande) *Aconcagua (Andes)*	Il Kilimangiaro *Kilimanjaro*
Il Monte Bianco *Mont Blanc*	Il Monte Logan *Logan*
Il Cervino *Matterhorn*	Il Monte McKinley *McKinley*
L'Elbrus *m* *Elbrus*	Il Pico de Orizaba *Orizaba*
L'Etna *m* *Etna*	Il Popocatepetl *Popocatepetl*
L'Everest *m* *Everest*	Il Monte Rosa *Monte Rosa*
Il Fujiyama *Fujiyama*	Il Vesuvio *Vesuvius*

L'Italia
Italy

Regione *Region*	Capoluogo di regione *Regional capital*
L'Abruzzo *Abruzzo*	L'Aquila *Aquila*
La Basilicata *Basilicata*	Potenza
La Calabria *Calabria*	Catanzaro
La Campania *Campania*	Napoli *Naples*
L'Emilia-Romagna *Emilia-Romagna*	Bologna
Il Friuli-Venezia Giulia *Friuli-Venezia Giulia*	Trieste
La Liguria *Liguria*	Genova *Genoa*
La Lombardia *Lombardy*	Milano *Milan*
Le Marche *The Marche*	Ancona
Il Molise *Molise*	Campobasso
Il Piemonte *Piedmont*	Torino *Turin*
La Puglia *Puglia*	Bari
Il Lazio *Lazio*	**Roma** ***Rome***
La Sardegna *Sardinia*	Cagliari
La Sicilia *Sicily*	Palermo
La Toscana *Tuscany*	Firenze *Florence*
Il Trentino-Alto Adige *Trentino-Alto Adige*	Trento
L'Umbria *Umbria*	Perugia
La Valle d'Aosta *Valle d'Aosta*	Aosta
Il Veneto *Veneto*	Venezia *Venice*

Canada
Il Canada

Capital (Capitale): Ottawa

Province *Provincia*	Abbreviation *Abbreviazione*	Capital *Capitale*
Alberta	Alta., AB	Edmonton
British Columbia *La Columbia britannica*	B.C., BC	Victoria
Manitoba *Il Manitoba*	Man., MB	Winnipeg
New Brunswick *Il New Brunswick*	N.B., NB	Fredericton
Newfoundland *Terranova (m)*	Nfld., NF	Saint John's
Nova Scotia *La Nuova Scozia*	N.S:, NS	Halifax
Ontario *L'Ontario (m)*	Ont., ON	Toronto
Prince Edward Island *L'isola del principe Edoardo*	P.E.I., PE	Charlottetown
Quebec *Il Quebec*	Que. or PQ, QC	Quebec
Saskatchewan *Il Saskatchewan*	Sask, SK	Regina

Territory *Territorio*	Abbreviation *Abbreviazione*	Capital *Capitale*
Northwest Territories *I Territori del Nordovest*	N.W.T., NT	Yellowknife
Nunavut Territory (*since 1st April 1999*)	NU	Iqaluit
Yukon Territory *Il Territorio dello Yukon*	Y.T., YT	Whitehorse

The United States of America – federal states, abbreviations, nicknames, inhabitants and capital cities
Gli Stati Uniti d'America – Stati federali, abbreviazioni, soprannomi, nomi degli abitanti e capitali

Capital (capitale): Washington, D.C.

Federal state *Stato federale*	Abbreviation *Abbreviazione*	Nickname *Soprannome*	Inhabitant *Abitante*	Capital *Capitale*
Alabama *L'Alabama (m)*	Ala., AL	Yellow Hammer State Heart of Dixie	Alabamian	Montgomery
Alaska *L'Alaska (f)*	Alas., AK	The Last Frontier	Alaskan	Juneau
Arizona *L'Arizona (f)*	Ariz., AZ	Grand Canyon State	Arizonan	Phoenix
Arkansas *L'Arkansas (m)*	Ark., AR	Land of Opportunity	Arkansan	Little Rock
California *La California*	Calif., CA	Golden State	Californian *californiano(a)*	Sacramento
Colorado *Il Colorado*	Colo., CO	Centennial State	Colorad(o)an	Denver
Connecticut *Il Connecticut*	Conn., CT	Constitution State Nutmeg State	Nutmegger; (Connecticut) Yankee	Hartford
Delaware *Il Delaware*	Del., DE	First State Diamond State	Delawarean	Dover
Florida *La Florida*	Fla., FL	Sunshine State	Floridian	Tallahassee
Georgia *La Georgia*	Ga., GA	Empire State of the South Peach State	Georgian *georgiano(a)*	Atlanta
Hawaii *Le Hawaii*	HI	Aloha State Paradise of the Pacific	Hawaiian *hawaiano(a)*	Honolulu
Idaho *L'Idaho (m)*	Id., ID	Gem State	Idahoan	Boise
Illinois *L'Illinois (m)*	Ill., IL	Prairie State	Illinoisan	Springfield
Indiana *L'Indiana (f)*	Ind., IN	Hoosier State	Indianan, Hoosier	Indianapolis
Iowa *L'Iowa (m)*	Ia., IA	Hawkeye State	Iowan	Des Moines
Kansas *Il Kansas*	Kans., KS	Sunflower State	Kansan	Topeka
Kentucky *Il Kentucky*	Ky., KY	Bluegrass State	Kentuckian	Frankfort *Francfort*
Louisiana *La Louisiana*	La., LA	Pelican State	Louisianan	Baton Rouge
Maine *Il Maine*	Me., ME	Pine Tree State	Mainer	Augusta
Maryland *Il Maryland*	Md., MD	Old Line State	Marylander	Annapolis

Federal state *Stato federale*	Abbreviation *Abbreviazione*	Nickname *Soprannome*	Inhabitant *Abitante*	Capital *Capitale*
Massachusetts *Il Massachusetts*	Mass., MA	Bay State	New Englander, Bay Stater	Boston
Michigan *Il Michigan*	Mich., MI	Wolverine State Lake State	Michiganian	Lansing
Minnesota *Il Minnesota*	Minn., MN	Gopher State North Star State	Minnesotan	Saint Paul
Mississippi *Il Mississippi*	Miss., MS	Magnolia State	Mississippian	Jackson
Missouri *Il Missouri*	Mo., MO	Show Me State	Missourian	Jefferson City
Montana *Il Montana*	Mont., MT	Treasure State Big Sky Country	Montanan	Helena
Nebraska *Il Nebraska*	Nebr., NE	Corn Husker State	Nebraskan	Lincoln
Nevada *Il Nevada*	Nev., NV	Sagebrush State Silver State	Nevadan	Carson City
New Hampshire *Il New Hampshire*	N.H., NH	Granite State	New Hampshirite	Concord
New Jersey *Il New Jersey*	N.J., NJ	Garden State	New Jerseyite, New Jersian	Trenton
New Mexico *Il Nuovo Messico*	N.M., NM	Land of Enchantment	New Mexican	Santa Fe
New York *Lo stato di New York*	N.Y., NY	Empire State	New Yorker *newyorkese*	Albany
North Carolina *La Carolina del Nord*	N.C., NC	Tarheel State Old North State	North Carolinian	Raleigh
North Dakota *Il Nord Dakota*	N.D., ND	Sioux State Peace Garden State Flickertail State	North Dakotan	Bismarck
Ohio *L'Ohio (m)*	O., OH	Buckeye State	Ohioan	Columbus
Oklahoma *L'Oklahoma (m)*	Okla., OK	Sooner State	Oklahoman	Oklahoma City
Oregon *L'Oregon (m)*	Ore., OR	Beaver State	Oregonian	Salem
Pennsylvania *La Pennsylvania*	Pa., PA	Keystone State	Pennsylvanian	Harrisburg
Rhode Island *Rhode Island (f)*	R.I., RI	Ocean State Little Rhody	Rhode Islander	Providence
South Carolina *La Carolina del Sud*	S.C., SC	Palmetto State	South Carolinian	Columbia
South Dakota *Il Sud Dakota*	S.D., SD	Coyote State Sunshine State	South Dakotan	Pierre
Tennessee *Il Tennessee*	Tenn., TN	Volunteer State	Tennessean	Nashville
Texas *Il Texas*	Tex., TX	Lone Star State	Texan *texano(a)*	Austin

Federal state *Stato federale*	Abbreviation *Abbreviazione*	Nickname *Soprannome*	Inhabitant *Abitante*	Capital *Capitale*
Utah *L'Utah (m)*	Ut., UT	Beehive State Mormon State	Utahan	Salt Lake City
Vermont *Il Vermont*	Vt., VT	Green Mountain State	Vermonter	Montpelier
Virginia *La Virginia*	Va., VA	Old Dominion Mother of Presidents Mother of States	Virginian	Richmond
Washington *Lo stato di Washington*	Wash., WA	Evergreen State	Washingtonian	Olympia
West Virginia *La Virginia Occidentale*	W.V., WV	Mountain State	West Virginian	Charleston
Wisconsin *Il Wisconsin*	Wis., WI	Badger State	Wisconsinite	Madison
Wyoming *Il Wyoming*	Wyo., WY	Equality State	Wyomingite	Cheyenne

Territories and Districts
Territori e distretti

Territory or District *Territorio o distretto*	Abbreviation *Abbreviazione*
American Samoa *Samoa americane*	AS
District of Columbia *Distretto della Colombia*	DC
Guam *Guam*	GU
Northern Mariana Islands *Isole Mariane del Nord*	MP
Puerto Rico *Portorico*	PR
United States Virgin Islands *Isole Vergini americane*	VI

Nicknames of some of the cities in the US
Soprannomi di alcune città americane

City *Città*	Nickname *Soprannome*
Chicago, Ill	The Windy City
Denver	The Mile-High City
Detroit	Motor City
New York	The Big Apple, Gotham
Los Angeles	The City of the Angels, The Big Orange
Minneapolis and St. Paul, Wis.	Twin Cities
New Orleans	The Big Easy
Philadelphia	The City of Brotherly Love

Notes

FREE E-DICTIONARY DOWNLOADING INSTRUCTIONS

1. To download your FREE e-dictionary visit:

   www.barronsbooks.com/download303

2. Please have the printed book in front of you. You will be asked two
   security questions. For example, "What is the headword on page 242?"

3. Follow the prompts.

This electronic dictionary can be installed and used on any PC or laptop
with Windows or Mac operating systems. It is not compatible with PDAs
or Smartphones.

SYSTEM REQUIREMENTS

Windows® PC:
Windows XP and above
22MB hard drive space

MAC® PC:
Mac OS 10.5 and above
22MB hard drive space

Simboli e abbreviazioni

fraseologia	▶	phraseology
contrazione	=	contraction
corrisponde a	≈	equivalent to
cambio d'interlocutore	–	change of speaker
marchio depositato	®	trademark
phrasal verb	◆	phrasal verb
Anche	a.	also
abbreviazione	abbr	abbreviation
acronimo	acro	acronym
aggettivo	adj	adjective
amministrazione	ADMIN	administration
avverbio	adv	adverb
aeronautica, aviazione	AERO	aeronautics, aviation
aggettivo	agg	adjective
agricoltura	AGR	agriculture
amministrazione	AMM	administration
anatomia	ANAT	anatomy
architettura	ARCHIT	architecture
arte	ART	art
articolo determinativo	art det	definite article
articolo indeterminativo	art indet	indefinite article
astronomia, astrologia	ASTR	astronomy, astrology
astronomia	ASTRON	astronomy
attributivo	attr	attributive
ausiliare	aus	auxiliary verb
automobile, mezzi di trasporto	AUTO	automobile, means of transportation
ausiliare	aux	auxiliary verb
aviazione, aeronautica	AVIAT	aviation, aeronautics
avverbio	avv	adverb
biologia	BIO	biology
botanica	BOT	botany
inglese canadese	Can	Canadian English
chimica	CHEM, CHIM	chemistry
cinema	CINE	cinema
commercio	COM	commerce
comparativo	comp	comparative
informatica	COMPUT	computing
congiunzione	cong, conj	conjunction
cucina, culinaria	CULIN	culinary, art of cooking
articolo determinativo	def art	definite article
dialettale	dial	Dialect/dialectical
dimostrativo	dim	demonstrative
ecologia	ECOL	ecology

Symbols and abbreviations

economia, industria	ECON	economics, industry
elettricità, elettronica	ELEC, ELETT	electricity, electronics
Unione Europea	eu	European Union
femminile	f	feminine
moda, cucito	FASHION	fashion, sewing
ferrovia	FERR	railways
figurato	fig	figurative
filosofia	FILOS	philosophy
finanza, borsa, tassazione	FIN	finance, banking, taxation
fiorentino	fior	Florentine
fisica	FIS	physics
linguaggio formale	form	formal language
fotografia	FOTO	photography
femminile plurale	fpl	feminine plural
gastronomia	GASTR	gastronomy
generalmente	gener	generally
geografia, geologia	GEO	geography, geology
geografia	GEOG	geography
geologia	GEOL	geology
giurisprudenza	GIUR	law
storia, storico	HIST	history, historical
imperfetto	imp	imperfect
imperativo	imper	imperative
impersonale	impers	impersonal
indicativo	ind	indicative
articolo indeterminativo	indef art	indefinite article
pronome indefinito	indef pron	indefinite pronoun
linguaggio familiare	inf	informal language
infinito	infin	infinitive
non separabile	insep	inseparable
interiezione	inter, interj	interjection
interrogativo	interrog	interrogative
invariabile	inv	invariable
ironico	iron	ironic
irregolare	irr	irregular
giornalismo	JOURN	journalism
giurisprudenza	LAW	law
letteratura, poesia	LETT	literature, poetry
letterario	letter	literary language
linguistica, grammatica	LING	linguistics, grammar
letteratura, poesia	LIT	literature, poetry
letterario	liter	literary language
locuzione	loc	phrase
lombardo	lomb	Lombard
maschile	m	masculine
marina	MAR	nautical, naval